AF344561

This
Holy Bible
is presented to

____

by

____

on

____

Let the word of Christ dwell in you richly.
Colossians 3:16

THE
HOLY BIBLE

THOMAS NELSON

Since 1798

www.ThomasNelsonBibles.com

NET Bible, Large Print Thinline Reference Edition

Copyright © 2025 by Thomas Nelson, a division of HarperCollins Christian Publishing, Inc.

Published in Nashville, TN, by Thomas Nelson Publishers, a registered trademark of HarperCollins Christian Publishing, Inc.

The NET Bible, New English Translation

Copyright © 1996, 2019 by Biblical Studies Press, L.L.C.

NET Bible® is a registered trademark.

Library of Congress Control Number: 2025935943

Published by Thomas Nelson, 501 Nelson Place, Nashville, TN 37214, USA. Thomas Nelson is a registered trademark of HarperCollins Chrisitan Publishing, Inc.

The text of the New English Translation® (NET Bible®) may be quoted or reprinted without prior written permission with the following qualifications: (1) up to and including 500 verses may be quoted in printed form as long as the verses quoted amount to less than 50% of a complete book of the Bible and make up less than 25% of the total work in which they are quoted; (2) all NET Bible quotations must conform accurately to the NET Bible text.

Any use of the NET Bible text must include a proper acknowledgment as follows:

The Scriptures quoted are from the NET Bible® http://netbible.com copyright © 1996, 2019 used with permission from Biblical Studies Press, L.L.C. All rights reserved.

For noncommercial requests, visit https://netbible.com/copyright.

For quotation requests not covered by the above guidelines, write to Thomas Nelson, Attention: Bible Rights and Permissions, P.O. Box 141000, Nashville, TN 37214–1000.

For free access to the NET Bible, the complete set of more than 60,000 translators' notes, and Bible study resources, visit:

https://www.bible.org
https://www.netbible.org
https://www.netbible.com

Without limiting the exclusive rights of any author, contributor or the publisher of this publication, any unauthorized use of this publication to train generative artificial intelligence (AI) technologies is expressly prohibited. HarperCollins also exercise their rights under Article 4(3) of the Digital Single Market Directive 2019/790 and expressly reserve this publication from the text and data mining exception.

HarperCollins Publishers, Macken House, 39/40 Mayor Street Upper, Dublin 1, D01 C9W8, Ireland (https://www.harpercollins.com).

Printed in India

25   26   27   28   29   30   31   32   33   34   /BPI/   10   9   8   7   6   5   4   3   2   1

Contents

Alphabetical List of Bible Books

About the NET Bible

"You have been born anew … through the
living and enduring word of God."
1 Peter 1:23

In 1995, a multidenominational team of more than twenty-five of the world's foremost biblical scholars gathered around the shared vision of creating an English Bible translation of the original biblical languages that could overcome old challenges and boldly open the door for new possibilities. The translators completed the first edition of the New English Translation (NET) in 2001 and incorporated revisions based on scholarly and user feedback in 2003 and 2005. In 2019, a major update reached its final stages. The NET's unique translation process has yielded a beautiful, faithful English Bible for the worldwide church today.

Transparent and Accountable

Bible translation usually happens behind closed doors—few outside the translation committee see the complex decisions underlying the words that appear in their English Bibles. Fewer still have the opportunity to review and speak into the translators' decisions.

Throughout the NET's translation process, every working draft was made publicly available on the Internet. Bible scholars, ministers, and laypersons from around the world logged millions of review sessions. No other translation is so openly accountable to the worldwide church or has been so thoroughly vetted.

And yet, the ultimate accountability was to the biblical text itself. The NET Bible is neither crowdsourced nor a "translation by consensus." Rather, the NET translators filtered every question and suggestion through the very best insights from biblical linguistics, textual criticism, and their unswerving commitment to following the text wherever it leads. Thus, the NET remains supremely accurate and trustworthy, while also benefiting from extensive review by those who would be reading, studying, and teaching from its pages.

The uniquely transparent and accountable translation process of the NET has been crystalized in the most extensive set of Bible translators' notes ever created. Around 60,000 notes highlight every major decision, outline alternative views, and explain difficult or nontraditional renderings. These notes are freely available at netbible.org and in print in the *NET Bible, Full Notes Edition.*

Ministry First

One more reason to love the NET: modern Bible translations are typically copyrighted, posing a challenge for ministries hoping to quote more than a few passages in their Bible study resources, curriculum, or other programming. But the NET is for everyone, with "ministry first" copyright innovations that encourage ministries to quote and share the life-changing message of Scripture as freely as possible. In fact, one of the major motivations behind the creation of the NET was the desire to ensure that ministries had unfettered access to a top-quality modern Bible translation, without needing to embark on a complicated process of securing permissions. Visit netbible.com/copyright to learn more.

THE HEBREW TEXT BEHIND THE OLD TESTAMENT

The starting point for the Hebrew text[1] translated to produce the NET Bible Old Testament was the standard edition known as *Biblia Hebraica Stuttgartensia* (BHS), which represents the text of the Leningrad Codex B19A (L), still the oldest dated manuscript of the complete Hebrew Bible. Thus, the Hebrew text on

[1] This includes the brief portions of the OT written in Aramaic.

which the present translation of the OT is based does not represent a critical, or reconstructed, text in the same way the standard critical editions of the Greek NT do. It is generally recognized that the Hebrew text represented by the Leningrad Codex occasionally needs to be corrected based on other Hebrew manuscripts, early versions, and the biblical manuscripts found among the Dead Sea Scrolls. In the case of the OT, such decisions were left up to the individual translators who prepared the initial drafts for consideration by the OT Editorial Committee. The textual decisions made by the translators were then reviewed by the editors and a textual consultant, and in some cases were revised. Conjectural emendation was employed only where necessary to make sense of the Hebrew text to be able to translate it.

How Are the Verses in the Old Testament Arranged?

Some of the divisions found in copies of the Hebrew Bible were already established by the end of the Masoretic era (ca. AD 900). While it is generally understood that the division of the OT text into verses goes back to the early centuries of the Christian era, the standard verse division which has continued in use up to the present was fixed by the Ben Asher family around AD 900.

In the places where the Hebrew versification differs from that of the English Bible, the NET Bible follows standard English practice. Unlike the Hebrew text, which treats the superscriptions to individual psalms as the first verse, the NET Bible follows most English Bibles in leaving the superscriptions unnumbered, and they are set in a different style to distinguish them from the text of the psalm proper.

THE GREEK TEXT BEHIND THE NEW TESTAMENT

As for the Greek text used in the NET Bible New Testament, an eclectic text was followed, differing in several hundred places from the standard critical text as represented by the Nestle-Aland 28th edition (these differences are indicated by a double dagger [‡] preceding the translator note). The translators who prepared the initial drafts of individual NT books made preliminary decisions regarding textual variants, and these were then checked and discussed by editors and a textual consultant. For passages that lack adequate textual authority (i.e., those that are almost certainly not part of the autographs), the words were included in the translation in double square brackets.

How Is the New Testament Text Arranged?

Divisions in the NT text like chapters, paragraphs, and verses were added later in the process of handing the text down from one generation to the next.[2] Verse divisions were added to the NT, for example, in 1551. They are not part of the original documents and in many cases give the appearance of being rather arbitrary. Still, they have become accepted over time and are useful to students of the Bible as "aids to navigation" when reading through or referring to the text. The text of the NET Bible itself has been arranged in paragraphs determined by the translators and editors. In almost all cases, the verse divisions follow standard English practice.

PRINCIPLES OF TRANSLATION

Form of Translation

This translation, like every other to some degree, ends up somewhere between the two extremes of formal equivalence (word-for-word) and dynamic equivalence (thought-for-thought). The goal has been to translate the text faithfully to how the original audience would have received and understood it.

A Gender Accurate Translation approach,

---

[2] Divisions of material in the NT (somewhat analogous to chapter divisions) date back to codex Vaticanus (B) in the fourth century AD. The present chapter divisions in the English Bible are attributed to Stephen Langton, Archbishop of Canterbury, around AD 1205. The first edition of the NT to be divided into verses was the fourth edition of Robertus Stephanus published in 1551. One of the first translations to be divided into paragraphs (as opposed to the individual verses of the King James Version) was the American Standard Version (1901).

which simply means translating terms without respect to gender when the intended meaning or application is broad and not gender-specific, was followed. This approach is to be distinguished from a Gender Neutral Translation approach, which attempts, on an ideological basis, to remove "objectionable" elements like patriarchalism or even male metaphors for God himself. No such radical approach has been followed with the NET Bible.

In terms of using the NT to translate the OT, the translators and editors for the NET Bible have generally chosen to concentrate solely on the native context of the older passages for a variety of reasons. It is beneficial to the Bible reader to have the progress of revelation accurately represented in the translation of particular texts. This helps the reader see how God has worked through the centuries, and it helps the reader to stand more accurately in the place of the original recipients of the text. Both are very instructive and inspirational, and they help the reader to connect with the text in a more fulfilling way.

In addition:

- In vocabulary and grammatical forms, every attempt has been made to reflect the different styles of the authors of the Bible. Paul's letters should not sound like John's or Peter's or that of Hebrews in the English translation where possible.
- The level of English style is formal (not, however, technical), except in passages where somewhat more informal style would be more in keeping with the content. In general, the use of contractions has been avoided, except in quoted speech.
- The language of average adults had priority. The translation attempts to use good literary style but is not overly formal or embellished.
- The translation is intended to be understandable to non-Christians as well as Christians, so liturgical language or Christian "jargon" has been avoided.
- Archaisms have also been avoided (e.g., "letter" was used instead of "epistle" in the NT). This includes the absolute avoidance of "thou" and "thee," because there were no distinctions in the original Hebrew or Greek between pronouns used to address people and those used to address deity. On a related note, pronouns that refer to Deity are not capitalized for this same reason.
- Long, complicated sentences in the original languages have been broken up into shorter sentences more acceptable in contemporary English. However, an attempt has been made to maintain the connections present in the original languages wherever possible.
- Idiomatic expressions and figurative language in the original languages have been changed when they make no sense to a typical modern English reader or are likely to lead to misunderstanding by a typical modern English reader.
- Nouns have been used for pronouns where the English pronoun would be obscure or ambiguous to a modern reader.
- Questions expecting a negative answer have been phrased to indicate this to the English reader.
- Clearly redundant expressions such as "answered and said" have been avoided unless they have special rhetorical force in context.
- Introductory expressions like "verily, verily" have been translated idiomatically, the single *amen* as "I tell you the truth" and the double *amen* (peculiar to John's Gospel) as "I tell you the solemn truth."
- Introductory particles like the Greek *idou* ("behold") have been translated to fit the context (sometimes "listen," "pay attention," "look," or occasionally left untranslated).
- Use of quotation marks (which did not exist in the original Hebrew and Greek manuscripts) conforms to contemporary American English usage.
- The basic unit of translation is the paragraph. Poetry is set out as poetry.
- Greek historical presents have been translated by English simple past tenses because English has no corresponding use of the present tense.
- In places where passive constructions create ambiguity, obscurity, or awkwardness in contemporary English, either the agent has been specified from context or the construction has been changed to active voice in the English translation.
- Ellipses have been filled out according to current English requirements (e.g., 1 John 2:19).
- Proper names have been standardized in accordance with accepted English usage.

How Is the Divine Name Translated in the Old Testament?

The translation of the Divine Name represents special problems for all English Bibles. The most difficult issue is the handling of the so-called tetragrammaton, the four consonants which represent the name of God in the OT. This was rendered traditionally as "Jehovah" in the King James Version, but it is generally recognized that this represents a combination of the consonants of the tetragrammaton, YHWH, and the vowels from a completely different Hebrew word, *'adonai*, "master," which were substituted by the Masoretes so that pronunciation of the Divine Name could be avoided: Whenever YHWH appeared in the text, the presence of the vowels from the word *'adonai* signaled to the reader that the word *'adonai* was to be pronounced instead.

Today most OT scholars agree that the vocalization of the Divine Name would originally have been something like *Yahweh*, and this has become the generally accepted rendering. The Executive Steering Committee of the NET Bible spent considerable time discussing whether to employ *Yahweh* in the translation. Several OT editors and translators favored its use, reasoning that because of its use in the lyrics of contemporary Christian songs and its appearance in Bible study materials, the

name *Yahweh* had gained more general acceptance. Despite this, the Committee eventually decided to follow the usage of most English translations and render the Divine Name as "Lord" in small caps. Thus the frequent combination *Yahweh 'elohim* is rendered as "Lord God."

Other combinations like *Yahweh Tséva'ot*, traditionally rendered "Lord of hosts," has been translated either as "the Lord who rules over all" or "the Lord who commands armies," depending on the context.

Additional Features of the Translation and Notes

The paragraph-style Bible text allows you to follow along with the text's logical flow, while in-text subject headings provide additional clarity about the events and ideas in the text.

The many books of Scripture form a unified whole that points to Christ and the gospel message. The NET helps readers see the links between various parts of Scripture by using footnotes and typographic design to indicate every place in the NT that refers to a passage from the OT. Whenever the NT directly quotes from the OT, the words are displayed with **semi-bold italic type**. In other cases, the NT writers allude to an OT passage without quoting it verbatim; these cases are indicated with *italics*.

THE TRANSLATION NOTES IN THIS BIBLE

The translator notes in this NET Bible are a collection of the most important text-critical (TC) and translator's notes (TN) found in the *NET Bible, Full Notes Edition*. Several types of translation notes are provided in this NET Bible:

The Creation of the World

1 In the ᵃbeginning ᵇGod created①the heavens and the earth. ²Now the earth was ᵃwithout shape ᵇand empty, and darkness was over the surface of the watery deep, but the Spirit of God was moving over the surface of the water. ³ᵃGod said, "ᵇLet there be ᶜlight." And there was light! ⁴God saw that the light was good,¹ so

---

A superior number after a word or phrase in the Scripture text indicates a translator note is provided.

The bold numbers in the cross-references/translator notes field indicates the verse to which an entry applies.

1:1 Ps 102:25; Isa 40:21; [John 1:1–3; Heb 1:10] ᵇGen 2:4; [Ps 8:3; 89:11; 90:2]; Isa 44:24; Acts 17:24; Rom 1:20; [Heb 1:2; 11:3]; Rev 4:11 ¹This Heb. verb always describes the divine activity of fashioning something new, fresh, and perfect; it does not necessarily describe creation out of nothing. **1:2** ᵃJer 4:23 ᵇ[Gen 6:3]; Job 26:13; Ps 33:6; 104:30; Isa 40:13–14 **1:3** ᵃPs 33:6, 9 ᵇ2 Cor 4:6 ᶜ[Heb 11:3] **1:4** ¹The Heb. word signifies whatever enhances, promotes, produces, or is conducive for life. **1:5** ᵃJob 37:18; Ps 19:2; 33:6; 74:16; 104:20; 136:5; Jer 10:12 **1:6** ᵃJob 37:18; Jer 10:12; 2 Pet 3:5 **1:7** ᵃJob 38:8–11;

There are six types of translator notes:

A **literal translation**, introduced by "lit.," provides the most precise English equivalent of the text, presenting the original word order, idioms, and so on. Here, "and purified with it" is the most precise English equivalent of the Hebrew.

> ### The Offerings for the People
>
> [15]Then [a]he presented the people's offering. He took the sin-offering male goat which was for the people, slaughtered it, and performed a purification rite with it[1] like the first one. [16]He then presented the burnt offering, and did it [a]according to the standard regulation. [17]Next he presented the grain offering, filled his hand with some

8:33 [a] Exod 29:30, 35; Lev 10:7; Ezek 43:25–26   8:34 [a] [Heb 7:16]   8:35 [a] Num 1:53; 3:7; 9:19; Deut 11:1; 1 Kgs 2:3; Ezek 48:11   9:1 [a] Ezek 43:27   9:2 [a] Exod 29:21; Lev 4:1–12   9:3 [a] Lev 4:23, 28; Ezra 6:17; 10:19   9:4 [a] Lev 2:4   [b] Exod 29:43; Lev 9:6, 23   9:7 [a] Lev 4:3; 1 Sam 3:14; [Heb 5:3–5; 7:27]   [b] Lev 4:16, 20; Heb 5:1   9:10 [a] Exod 23:18; Lev 8:16   9:11 [a] Lev 4:11–12; 8:17   9:13 [a] Lev 8:20   9:14 [a] Lev 8:21   9:15 [a] [Isa 53:10; Heb 2:17; 5:3]   [1] Lit. *and purified* [with] *it.*   9:16 [a] Lev 1:1–13   9:17 [a] Exod 29:38–39   9:18 [a] Lev 3:1–11   9:20 [a] Lev 3:5, 16   9:21 [a] Exod 29:24, 26, 27; Lev 7:30–34

An **alternative translation**, introduced by "or," provides a translation that may appear in other Bibles or indicates that the translation team could have used in the NET Bible. Here, "he ceased" could have been translated as "he rested."

> there was morning, the sixth day.
>
> **2** The heavens and the earth were completed with [a]everything that was in them. [2]By the seventh day God finished the work that he had been doing, [a]and he ceased[1] on the seventh day all the work that he had been doing. [3]God [a]blessed the seventh day and made it holy because on it he ceased all the work that he had been doing in creation.

them with fruitfulness; the capacity to reproduce.   1:29 [a] Gen 9:3; Ps 104:14–15   1:30 [a] Ps 145:15   [b] Job 38:41   1:31 [a] [Ps 104:24; 1 Tim 4:4]   2:1 [a] Ps 33:6   2:2 [a] Exod 20:9–11; 31:17; Heb 4:4, 10   [1] Or *he rested.*   2:3 [a] [Isa 58:13]   2:4 [a] Gen 1:1; Ps 90:1–2   2:5 [a] Gen 1:11–12   [b] Gen 7:4; Job 5:10; 38:26–28   [c] Gen 3:23   2:7 [a] Gen 3:19, 23; Ps 103:14   [b] Job 33:4   [c] Gen 7:22   [d] 1 Cor 15:45   2:8 [a] Isa 51:3   [b] Gen 3:23–24   [c] Gen 4:16   2:9 [a] Ezek 31:8   [b] [Gen 3:22; Rev 2:7; 22:2, 14]   [c] [Deut 1:39]   2:10 [1] Or *was flowing.*   2:11 [a] Gen 25:18   2:12 [a] Num 11:7   [1] Heb. *good.*   2:14 [a] Dan 10:4

A **traditional translation**, introduced by "trad.," provides an alternate translation for how the text has appeared in other English Bibles. Here, "companion" can also be rendered as "helper."

> [18]The LORD God [a]said, "It is not good for the man to be alone. I will make a companion[1] for him who corresponds to him." [19]The LORD God formed [a]out of the ground every living animal of the field and every bird of the air. He [b]brought them to the man to see what he would name them, and whatever the man called each living creature, that was its name. [20]So the man named all the

2:17 [a] Gen 3:1, 3, 11, 17   [b] Gen 3:3, 19; [Rom 6:23]   [c] Rom 5:12; 1 Cor 15:21–22   2:18 [a] 1 Cor 11:8–9; 1 Tim 2:13   [1] Trad. *helper;* does not suggest a subordinate role.   2:19 [a] Gen 1:20, 24   [b] Ps 8:6   2:21 [a] Gen 15:12; 1 Sam 26:12   [1] Trad. *rib.*   2:22 [a] Gen 3:20; 1 Tim 2:13   [b] Heb 13:4   2:23 [a] Gen 29:14; Eph 5:28–30   [b] 1 Cor 11:8–9   2:24 [a] Matt 19:5; Eph 5:31   [b] Mark 10:6–8; 1 Cor 6:16   [1] Trad. *cleaves* [to]; an inseparable joining.   2:25 [a] Gen 3:7, 10   [b] Isa 47:3   3:1 [a] 1 Chr 21:1; [Rev 12:9; 20:2, 10]   [b] 2 Cor 11:3   [1] Or *clever, cunning* (negative), *prudent* (positive).   3:2 [a] Gen 2:16–17   3:3 [a] Exod 19:12–13; Rev 22:14   3:4 [a] John

[10] Now a river flows[1] from Eden to water the orchard, and from there it divides into four headstreams. [11] The name of [a] the first is Pishon; it runs through the entire land of Havilah, where there is gold. [12] (The gold of that land is pure[1] [a] pearls and lapis lazuli are also there.) [13] The name of the second river is Gihon; it runs through the entire land of Cush. [14] The name of the third river is

A **language note,** introduced by "Aram.," "Heb.," or "Grk," provides further nuances of terms or phrases. Here, the Hebrew word translated as "pure" could also carry a meaning of "good."

them with fruitfulness; the capacity to reproduce.   1:29 [a] Gen 9:3; Ps 104:14–15   1:30 [a] Ps 145:15   [b] Job 38:41   1:31 [a] [Ps 104:24; 1 Tim 4:4]   2:1 [a] Ps 33:6   2:2 [a] Exod 20:9–11; 31:17; Heb 4:4, 10   [1] Or *he rested.*   2:3 [a] [Isa 58:13]   2:4 [a] Gen 1:1; Ps 90:1–2   2:5 [a] Gen 1:11–12   [b] Gen 7:4; Job 5:10; 38:26–28   [c] Gen 3:23   2:7 [a] Gen 3:19, 23; Ps 103:14   [b] Job 33:4   [c] Gen 7:22   [d] 1 Cor 15:45   2:8 [a] Isa 51:3   [b] Gen 3:23–24   [c] Gen 4:16   2:9 [a] Ezek 31:8   [b] [Gen 3:22; Rev 2:7; 22:2, 14]   [c] [Deut 1:39]   2:10 [1] Or *was flowing.*   2:11 [a] Gen 25:18   2:12 [a] Num 11:7   [1] Heb. *good.*   2:14 [a] Dan 10:4

birds, domestic animals, wild animals, all the creatures that swarm over the earth, [a] and all humankind. [22] Everything on dry land that had the breath[1] of life in its nostrils died. [23] So the LORD destroyed every living thing that was on the surface of the ground, including people, animals, creatures that creep along the ground, and birds of the sky. They were wiped off the earth.

A **textual note,** introduced by a manuscript name or abbreviation, points out significant textual variants concerning the text found in the verse. Here, the Masoretic Text (MT) reads "breath of the breath/spirit of life."

Ezek 26:19   [c] Gen 8:2; Ps 78:23   7:12 [a] Gen 7:4, 17; 1 Sam 12:18   7:14 [a] Gen 6:19   [b] Gen 1:21   7:15 [a] Gen 6:19–20; 7:9   7:16 [a] Gen 7:2–3   7:17 [a] Gen 7:4, 12; 8:6   7:18 [a] Ps 104:26   [1] Heb. *and the waters were great and multiplied exceedingly.*   7:21 [a] Gen 6:7, 13, 17; 7:4   7:22 [1] MT *breath of the breath/spirit of life.*   7:23 [a] Matt 24:38–39; Luke 17:26–27; Heb 11:7; 1 Pet 3:20; 2 Pet 2:5   7:24 [a] Gen 8:3–4   8:1 [a] Gen 19:29; Exod 2:24; 1 Sam 1:19; Ps 105:42; 106:4   [b] Exod 14:21; 15:10; Job 12:15; Ps 29:10; Isa 44:27; Nah 1:4   8:2 [a] Gen 7:11   [b] Deut 11:17   [c] Gen 7:4, 12; Job 38:37

[21] Isaac prayed to the LORD on behalf of his wife because she was childless. The LORD answered his prayer, [a] and his wife Rebekah became pregnant. [22] But the children struggled[1] inside her, and she said, "Why is this happening to me?" [a] So she asked the LORD, [23] and the LORD said to her,

"[a] Two nations are in your womb,

An **explanatory note** provides information on language or translation nuances that a reader might find helpful. Here, "struggle" is explained as being "an out of the ordinary violent struggle."

35:29; 49:29, 33   25:9 [a] Gen 23:9, 17; 49:30   25:10 [a] Gen 23:3–16   [b] Gen 49:31   25:11 [a] Gen 16:14   25:12 [a] Gen 11:10, 27; 16:15   25:13 [a] 1 Chr 1:29–31   25:16 [a] Gen 17:20   25:17 [a] Gen 25:8; 49:33   25:18 [a] Gen 20:1; 1 Sam 15:7   25:19 [a] Gen 36:1, 9   [b] Matt 1:2   25:20 [a] Gen 22:23; 24:15, 29, 67   [b] Gen 24:29   25:21 [a] 1 Sam 1:17; 1 Chr 5:20; 2 Chr 33:13; Ezra 8:23; Ps 127:3   25:22 [a] 1 Sam 1:15; 9:9; 10:22   [1] An out of the ordinary violent struggle.   25:23 [a] Gen 17:4–6, 16; 24:60; Num 20:14; Deut 2:4–8   [b] 2 Sam 8:14   [c] Gen 27:29, 40; Mal 1:2–3; Rom 9:12   25:24 [1] Heb. *look!*

In addition, notes are provided to indicate where the OT is quoted or alluded to in the NT. The OT reference for a quotation is simply provided; an OT reference in square braces denotes an allusion to the OT.

the Lord through the prophet would be fulfilled: [23]"[a]*Look! The virgin will conceive and give birth to a son, and they will name him Emmanuel,*"①which means "*God with us.*"[2] [24]When Joseph awoke from sleep he did what the angel of the Lord told him. He took his wife, [25]but did not have marital relations with [a]her until she gave birth to a son, whom he named Jesus.

1:20 [a] Luke 1:35   [1] Grk. *behold, an angel.*   1:21 [a] [Isa 7:14; 9:6–7]; Luke 1:31; 2:21   [b] Luke 2:11; John 1:29; [Acts 4:12; 5:31; 13:23, 38; Rom 5:18–19; Col 1:20–23]   1:23 [a] Isa 7:14   (①Isa 7:14)   [2] Isa 8:8, 10 LXX   1:25 [a] Exod 13:2; Luke 2:7, 21   2:1 [a] Mic 5:2; Luke 2:4–7   [b] Gen 25:6; 1 Kgs 4:30   2:2 [a] Luke 2:11   [b] [Num 24:17; Isa 60:3]   2:4 [a] 2 Chr 36:14   [b] 2 Chr 34:13   [c] Mal 2:7   [1] Or *and scribes of the people.*   [2] Or *Messiah*; both "Christ" (Grk.) and "Messiah" (Heb., Aram.) mean "one who has been anointed."   2:6 [a] Mic 5:2; John 7:42   [b] Gen 49:10; [Rev 2:27]   [1] Mic 5:2   2:7 [a] Num 24:17   2:11 [a] Ps 72:10; Isa 60:6   2:12 [a] [Job 33:15–16]; Matt 1:20

Some important but more detailed issues cannot be addressed in these translation notes. In these instances, the note directs the reader to the *NET Bible, Full Notes Edition*, which provides a more detailed discussion.

NET BIBLE ABBREVIATIONS

Aram.	Aramaic		**masc.**	masculine
cf.	Compare		**MSS**	manuscripts
DSS	Dead Sea Scrolls, OT manuscripts from about 300 BC to AD 100		**MT**	Masoretic Text, the Hebrew OT that serves as the basis for most English translations
esp.	especially			
fem.	feminine		**Orig.**	Origen
Grk.	Greek		**pl.**	plural
Heb.	Hebrew		**Qe.**	*Qere*, the oral portion of the *kethib-qere* notation in the Masoretic OT text
incl.	including			
Ket.	*Kethib*, the written portion of the *kethib-qere* notation in the Masoretic OT text		**Qum.**	Qumran, OT and extrabiblical writings found near the Dead Sea
lit.	literally		**ref.**	referent
Luc.	Lucian, a revision of the Greek Septuagint from about AD 250 to 300		**sev.**	several
			sig.	significant
LXX	Septuagint, the Greek OT originally translated from about 285 BC to AD 100		**sing.**	singular
			Smr.	Samaritan Pentateuch, OT manuscripts dating from about AD 800 to 1500
maj.	majority			

Sym.	Symmachus, a revision of the Greek Septuagint from about AD 150 to 200	var.	variation
Syr.	Syriac, a literal translation of the OT from about AD 100 to 200	Vg.	Vulgate, a Latin translation of the Bible made from about AD 390 to 405
Tg.	Targum, OT manuscripts written in Aramaic dating from about AD 100 to 500	wss	witnesses, includes church fathers, lectionaries, and other extrabiblical writings
Thd.	Theodotion, a revision of the Greek Septuagint from about AD 150 to 200	‡	notes where the NT translation differs from the standard critical text as represented by the Nestle-Aland 28th edition
trad.	traditionally		

The NET Bible Translation Team

FIRST EDITION TRANSLATORS, EDITORS, AND CONSULTANTS

Old Testament Translators and Editors

PENTATEUCH

Richard E. Averbeck, PhD
  Dropsie College
Robert B. Chisholm, ThD
  Dallas Theological Seminary
Dorian Coover-Cox, PhD
  Dallas Theological Seminary

Eugene H. Merrill, PhD
  Columbia University
Allen P. Ross, PhD
  Cambridge University

HISTORICAL BOOKS

Robert B. Chisholm, ThD
  Dallas Theological Seminary
Dorian Coover-Cox, PhD
  Dallas Theological Seminary

Gordon H. Johnston, ThD
  Dallas Theological Seminary
Richard A. Taylor, PhD
  Catholic University of America

WISDOM BOOKS

Robert B. Chisholm, ThD
  Dallas Theological Seminary
Gordon H. Johnston, ThD
  Dallas Theological Seminary

Allen P. Ross, PhD
  Cambridge University
Steven H. Sanchez, PhD
  Dallas Theological Seminary

MAJOR AND MINOR PROPHETS

William D. Barrick, ThD
  Grace Theological Seminary
M. Daniel Carroll R., PhD
  University of Sheffield
Robert B. Chisholm, ThD
  Dallas Theological Seminary
Dorian Coover-Cox, PhD
  Dallas Theological Seminary
Donald R. Glenn, MA
  Brandeis University
Michael A. Grisanti, PhD
  Dallas Theological Seminary

W. Hall Harris III, PhD
  University of Sheffield
Gordon H. Johnston, ThD
  Dallas Theological Seminary
Eugene H. Merrill, PhD
  Columbia University
Steven H. Sanchez, PhD
  Dallas Theological Seminary
Brian L. Webster, PhD
  Hebrew Union College—Jewish
  Institute of Religion

New Testament Translators and Editors

GOSPELS AND ACTS

Darrell L. Bock, PhD
  University of Aberdeen
Michael H. Burer, PhD
  Dallas Theological Seminary
W. Hall Harris III, PhD
  University of Sheffield

Gregory J. Herrick, PhD
  Dallas Theological Seminary
David K. Lowery, PhD
  University of Aberdeen

PAULINE LETTERS

John D. Grassmick, PhD
  University of Glasgow
W. Hall Harris III, PhD
  University of Sheffield
Gregory J. Herrick, PhD
  Dallas Theological Seminary

Harold W. Hoehner, PhD
  Cambridge University
David K. Lowery, PhD
  University of Aberdeen
Jay E. Smith, PhD
  Trinity Evangelical Divinity School

GENERAL LETTERS AND REVELATION

Buist M. Fanning III, DPhil
  Oxford University
W. Hall Harris III, PhD
  University of Sheffield
Gregory J. Herrick, PhD
  Dallas Theological Seminary

David K. Lowery, PhD
  University of Aberdeen
Daniel B. Wallace, PhD
  Dallas Theological Seminary

Translation Consultants

Wayne Leman, MA
  University of Kansas

James Routt, PhD
  Cambridge University

English Style Consultant

W. Hall Harris III, PhD
  University of Sheffield

NET Bible Executive Steering Committee

W. Hall Harris III, PhD, *Project Director
  and Managing Editor*
Michael H. Burer, PhD, *Editor and
  Assistant Project Director*
Robert B. Chisholm, ThD, *Senior OT
  Editor*

Daniel B. Wallace, PhD, *Senior NT Editor*
Buist M. Fanning, PhD, *NT Editor*
Donald R. Glenn, MA, *OT Editor*
Gordon H. Johnston, ThD, *OT Editor*
Steven H. Sanchez, PhD, *OT Editor*
Richard A. Taylor, PhD, *OT Editor*

Project Management and Production

J. Hampton Keathley IV, ThM,
  Technical Director

Todd Lingren, MA, *Director of
  Publication*

Second Edition Translators, Editors, and Consultants

W. Hall Harris III, PhD, *Project Director
  and Managing Editor*
James Davis, PhD, *Managing Editor*
Brian Webster, PhD, *OT Editor*
Harold Holmyard, PhD, *OT Consultant*

Technical Staff
Brian Seagraves
Frank Walton
J. Hampton Keathley IV, ThM

A Brief Guide to Translating the Bible

The goal of a Bible translator is to communicate God's Word to readers as faithfully and accurately as possible. Achieving this goal, however, is neither straightforward nor simple, as the number of English Bible translations affirms.

Before Bible translators can consider how to translate three ancient complex languages into modern English, they must first determine what exactly is being translated. The scriptures were written from about 1450 BC to about AD 100 and none of these original writings (often called *autographs*) have survived, mostly because of the biodegradable papyrus and leather used for ancient writing. Thus the modern church has only copies of copies of the original writings of the Old Testament (OT) and the New Testament (NT), and these copies (called *manuscripts*) at times do not seem to agree. The first key challenge to translating the Bible is determining what the original text of the Bible should be.

Tangential to this challenge is how to translate the Bible originally written in Hebrew, Aramaic, and Greek into modern English. Each language has a different grammar, structure, and vocabulary. Ancient Hebrew, for example, was written without vowels, leading to uncertainty over what was meant at times, while Greek allows for a word order that often differs from the typical English subject-verb-object arrangement.

CHALLENGE 1: IDENTIFYING THE WORDS OF SCRIPTURE

Determining the original writings of Scripture based on the existing manuscript evidence is called *textual criticism* or *lower criticism* (*higher criticism* is the study of the history and message of the scripture text itself). The work of copying the OT and NT manuscripts was done by trained professional monks and scribes, notably the Masoretes, who copied the OT in Hebrew from AD 500 to AD 1000. These copyists learned techniques to write carefully and with consistency (e.g., in lettering style, spacing, and layout). Despite the copyists' extreme vigilance, though, some variations appear between the existing manuscripts. To understand how textual criticism works, it is first important to understand the available manuscript evidence and why these differences between the manuscripts are present.

Old Testament Manuscripts
The OT was written in mostly Hebrew with some Aramaic, but OT manuscripts also exist in Greek, Syriac, Latin, and other languages. Still, most major English versions base their translation of the OT on the Hebrew text rather than the others.

Between the various manuscripts, it is estimated that about 90 percent of the text is in agreement, and most of the variants are quite minor (e.g., pronunciation and spelling differences). Few variants affect the meaning of the text.

The Hebrew Manuscripts
The Dead Sea Scrolls: In 1947, shepherds discovered several scrolls in a cave in an area known as Qumran near the Dead Sea, eight miles south of Jericho. Scrolls were then found in ten other nearby caves. The thousands of scrolls found turned out to be a mixture of OT texts and nonbiblical documents dating from 300 BC–AD 100. These scrolls immediately moved OT textual scholarship back nearly a thousand years. Fragments of all the OT books except Esther were found.

Just as important as the dating of the Dead Sea Scrolls is their striking agreement with the Hebrew Masoretic Text, supporting the accuracy of the latter, which is the basis of most modern English translations of the OT. Furthermore, the Dead Sea Scrolls help scholars understand variant readings, with about 95 percent of the

Dead Sea Scrolls reflecting the Masoretic Text and the other 5 percent reflecting the Samaritan Pentateuch and the Septuagint.

The Masoretic Text: The Masoretic Text is the Hebrew text of the OT that was normative within Judaism. These manuscripts are primarily from about AD 700 to AD 1000; however, over 3,000 additional manuscripts come from the twelfth century and later. The Masoretic Text is the most important witness to the OT and is the basis of most English translations, but it is not the *default* text.

The copyists, or Masoretes, provided four key elements in their work: (1) **Vocalizations.** Hebrew was written without vowels, and these vowel markings were placed above, below, or superimposed upon the consonantal text to guide how words should be pronounced. (2) **Accents.** These written symbols marked the stressed syllables and were used to know how to chant the text musically. (3) **Masorah.** These specialized marginal notes were placed on pages and after books and sections to provide technical information about the text, such as spelling differentiations (including how often and where they occur), the number of words in a book, the middle word and letter of a book, and other data that was used to test the accuracy of the copies made. Another important note is the *kethib-qere* ("written-read"). These notes show where a difference in meaning occurs between what is written and its supplied vocalization. While the consonants would not be changed, feasible alternative vowels were provided. (4) **Other Elements.** Verse and textual divisions were noted, heavy dots were placed over doubtful letters and words, blank spaces were used to signify omissions, and other notations were made.

The Samaritan Pentateuch: The Samaritans were estranged relatives of the Jews who had remained in the Holy Land during the Assyrian exile. They lived between Galilee to the north and Judea to the south in Jesus' day. The Samaritans and Jews differed in some matters of theology, most notably the location of worship and the extent of Scripture. The Samaritans considered Mount Gerizim to be the holiest site, not Jerusalem, and they held only to the Pentateuch. As such, they made copies of the first five books of the OT, which became known as the Samaritan Pentateuch.

Today, we have about 150 manuscripts of this unvocalized text dating from about AD 800 to AD 1500 that includes some additions, rearrangements, and alterations to the text that reflect the Samaritan theology. Despite these modifications, which are few and later in date, the Samaritan Pentateuch is quite valuable in textual criticism as it preserves some older variant readings of the text.

The Aramaic Targums
After the Babylonian exile, Aramaic became the common language of the region, and knowledge of the Hebrew language began to fade. In time, many Jews were unable to understand the Hebrew OT text when it was read aloud. Thus the Aramaic Targums were used for oral reading; the Hebrew text would be read first, followed by the Aramaic.

While the targums are believed to align closely with the Hebrew over 85 percent of the time, those who completed the translation were prone to interpret the OT according to the theology and practices of rabbinic Judaism of their day and included additions, updates, and harmonizations in places. The targums are divided into two categories, based on where they were used: Palestinian (ca. AD 150–300) and Babylonian (ca. AD 100–500). Targums exist for all the OT books except Ezra and Daniel, perhaps because portions of these books were already in Aramaic.

Because of the targums' interpretive nature, they are challenging to use in textual criticism, but even so, they do not present any significant variation from the Masoretic Text.

The Greek Septuagint
The Septuagint was created in Egypt and is one of the earliest known translations of the OT. The name comes from the Latin word for "seventy," based on the claim that seventy (or perhaps seventy-two) translators completed the work. The Pentateuch was completed between 285 and 246 BC, and the rest of the OT manuscripts were completed from about 250 BC to about AD 100. The original translation was then revised several times, most likely to bring it into greater harmony with the early Hebrew texts of the time. Aquila (ca. AD 150) was a hyper literal revision followed by

revisions of decreasing literalness: Theodotion (ca. AD 150–200), Symmachus (ca. AD 150–200), and Lucian (ca. AD 250–300). The Septuagint provides more significant deviations from the Masoretic Text than all the other OT witnesses combined.

The Syriac Peshitta

Syriac is a language similar to Aramaic that was used in southeastern Turkey. The name *Peshitta*, which means "Simple," is a literal translation from the Hebrew made between about AD 100 and AD 200 without additional content. It is not the only Syriac translation. The Peshitta is similar to the Masoretic Text, but it contains more variants than the Aramaic Targums and the Latin Vulgate, and it provides different vocalizations.

The Latin Vulgate

As the Roman Empire expanded throughout the Mediterranean world, Latin slowly replaced Greek as the common language of the day. As such, Latin translations of the OT, mostly based on the Greek Septuagint, began to emerge around the second century AD.

In time, the Western church recognized the need for a single, authoritative Latin translation. Jerome believed that such a translation should base the OT on the Hebrew rather than the Greek, so he settled in Bethlehem, learned Hebrew, and interviewed Jewish teachers. He completed his translation from AD 390 to AD 405, which included the NT, and it became known as the Vulgate, which means "Common One." Because of Jerome's approach, the Vulgate is quite similar to the Masoretic Text; still, it does reflect Jerome's translation philosophy and theological bent, especially in making christological connections clear. Even so, for textual criticism, the Vulgate does not provide many noteworthy variants.

New Testament Manuscripts

Dating from between about AD 40 and AD 100, the NT was written almost entirely in Greek with a handful of words recorded in Aramaic. Copies were almost immediately made in Greek and spread out as the church expanded. From about AD 200 to AD 400, manuscripts were produced on papyrus, a paperlike material made from Egyptian plants. From about AD 300 to AD 1000, parchment made of animal skins was used, and the writing was in all capital letters. These manuscripts were referred to as *majuscules* or *uncials*. No spaces were placed between words and no punctuation was used. Then, from about AD 800 on, *miniscule script*, a different writing style that resembled lowercase cursive was used, preserving space. Most of the surviving manuscripts are in this latter style.

Starting in the second century AD, along with the Greek, translations were also made in Latin, Syriac, Coptic, and other languages as the church grew. In time, however, geographical centers of scholarship sharing key manuscript characteristics formed. Rome, Alexandria, and Constantinople became three of the most prominent of these centers. The manuscripts from these cities were similar enough to be recognized as the three core "families" of texts today: Byzantine (Constantinople), Alexandrian, and Western (Rome).

The Greek Byzantine Tradition

Prompted by Emperor Constantine's Edict of Milan in AD 313, Constantinople (Istanbul in modern Turkey), the capital of the Byzantine Empire, became one of the primary places for biblical scholarship until about AD 700. Eventually, the primary seat of biblical authority shifted to Rome, but Constantinople remained important and became the center of the Eastern Orthodox Church. Scholars continued to make copies of the NT in Greek here, and of the roughly 5,800 Greek manuscripts today, about 4,000 come from this area. Most of these manuscripts, however, are from the ninth century or later. The Byzantine manuscript family is known for smoother, easier readings of the text. The Textus Receptus and Majority Text, which will be discussed in the pages ahead, are both based on these Byzantine manuscripts.

The Greek Alexandrian Tradition

Alexandria (in northern Egypt) was perhaps best known for its impressive library and top-notch scholarship. It is not surprising, then, that this city would become one of the important centers of copying the Christian scriptures. Manuscripts were produced in Greek, and some of our earliest existing manuscripts, dating back to the second century AD, were produced here. The

Alexandrian manuscript family is known for its shorter, more difficult readings. Despite there being a much smaller quantity of existing manuscripts, of the three text families many modern scholars consider this one the most important.

The Latin Western Tradition

Beginning in the second century AD, Latin became the language of the church. Thus, in the west, most copies of Scripture were made in Latin, resulting in around ten thousand Latin manuscripts. While Jerome's Vulgate was used as the base text for many of these NT manuscripts, it changed over time, leading to divergent readings. In 1592, Pope Clement VII declared a revision, known as the Clementine Version, as the official Latin Bible of the church. The Western manuscript family is known for more harmonistic readings, and because of that (and because the Latin must be translated backward into Greek for NT work), its use in textual criticism is more limited. Yet, it is often helpful when the textual issue concerns the inclusion or omission of an entire verse or phrase.

The Three Key NT Texts

As the Masoretic Text is the basis for modern translations of the OT, three key texts serve as the basis for modern translations of the NT: the Textus Receptus, the Majority Text, and the Critical Text.

The Textus Receptus: In AD 1500, no Greek NT was in print. About this time, Erasmus, a student of Greek manuscripts, set out to publish a Greek NT text based on a handful of manuscripts at his disposal in Basel, Switzerland. The manuscripts that Erasmus used dated from between the tenth and fifteenth centuries AD, and all were of the Byzantine tradition. Because he used a manuscript of Revelation that lacked the last six verses, he translated these verses from the Latin Vulgate back into Greek.

Erasmus's NT was printed in 1516. He almost immediately began work on a second edition, which was published in 1519, and a third edition was published in 1522. Soon after, others began making their own editions of Erasmus's text. In 1522, Martin Luther used Erasmus's work to translate the NT into German, and in 1525, William Tyndale used it for his English translation. Over the next hundred years, several other Greek NTs were printed, each using Erasmus's text but with added footnotes to show variant readings found in manuscripts beyond the ones originally used. In 1624, the Elzevir brothers published an edition with a preface that called it the *Textus Receptus*, Latin for "Received Text," meaning it was the accepted, approved, or standard version. This is how it became known, and it was the accepted Greek NT text for 300 years.

The Majority Text: Unlike the *Textus Receptus* that used a limited number of Byzantine manuscripts, the Majority Text was developed in the twentieth century and uses roughly 4,000 Byzantine manuscripts to determine the reading of the NT that is based on what is used in the majority of existing manuscripts. Because of this, the Majority Text and the *Textus Receptus* differ in about 2,000 places, although this still leaves them in agreement roughly 99 percent of the time.

The Critical Text: In the nineteenth century AD, archaeologists began discovering Greek NT manuscripts along with other extrabiblical manuscripts that used the same Greek as the NT. These extrabiblical finds helped show how words were used in the culture of the day, which was especially helpful for understanding words that occur rarely in the NT. In 1881, two scholars, B. F. Westcott and F. J. A. Hort, published *The New Testament in the Original Greek* that considered these newly discovered manuscripts and relied mostly on the Alexandrian and western texts. It later became known as the Critical Text. The Critical Text differs from the *Textus Receptus* in some significant ways. At times, entire passages appear in one but not both, such as Mark 16:9–20, John 7:53–8:11, and Acts 8:37. In addition, words or groups of words are found in one or the other, such as in Matthew 6:4 and 6:6, 1 Corinthians 6:20 and 11:24, and 1 John 3:1. At still other times, words may differ between these two texts, such as in 1 Timothy 3:16 and Revelation 22:14.

The two most common modern Greek New Testaments based on the Critical Text are the Nestle-Aland New Testament and the United Bible Societies New Testament. They differ in only minor ways, such as in punctuation and paragraph breaks. Most modern English Bibles use the Critical Text as the basis for the NT.

Manuscript Differences

Before considering the textual criticism principles used to decide what best represents the original text of Scripture, scholars must consider the question of *why* differences between manuscripts exist. There are two basic reasons for textual variants: (1) accidental mistakes and (2) intentional changes.

Accidental Mistakes

Although those who copied Scripture understood the weighty nature of their work and employed meticulous methods to ensure accuracy, they were human after all, and humans make mistakes. These mistakes could happen for three primary reasons: (1) errors in hearing, (2) errors in reading, or (3) errors in writing.

Errors in Hearing: One way the text was transmitted was by one person reading the text aloud to several scribes who sat at desks and wrote what they heard. This could lead to mistakes made by a scribe mishearing what was said, which was especially likely for words that sound similar.

Errors in Reading: Another common way of transmitting the text was by a single scribe reading from one manuscript, remembering what he read, and then writing it anew. Some common reading errors include confusing two similar letters (especially if the source document was smeared or tattered), identifying the wrong word division (especially when words were written close together to preserve space, such as in the NT), assigning the wrong Hebrew vowels, returning to the wrong place in the original document because of similar word endings (called *homoioteleuton*), and returning to the wrong place in the original document because of similar word beginnings (called *homoioarkton*). For example, the last two items in the prior sentence are quite similar. It would be easy to repeat a phrase or skip a phrase because of that.

Errors in Writing: Some of the common mistakes scribes made include writing a letter or word once that should have been written twice (called *haplography*), writing a letter or word twice that should have been written once (called *dittography*), and transposing two letters.

Intentional Changes

While the scribes who copied the scriptures were quite faithful to producing exact copies, at times they made intentional changes. They might change a text to reconcile what they perceived to be contradictions or mistakes. They might add or align content from one parallel text to another (e.g., within the Gospels or when comparing portions of Samuel, Kings, Chronicles, Psalms, and Isaiah with each other), believing it was mistakenly omitted. They might correct what they thought was a mistake made by a prior scribe who produced the manuscript from which they were working. They might see the need to clarify something, such as turning a vague pronoun into a proper name. Or they might change an OT quote in the NT to better align with the OT text. These "corrections" were not made from a failure to honor the text; they were made because the scribes believed they were restoring the text to what it should have been.

In addition, the OT was intentionally changed at times to allow for what are called *emendations*—changing the vowels when those existing do not seem to make sense, changing the text to use euphemisms for indelicate or potentially offensive content, changing the names of pagan deities, or combining two or more variant readings into one.

Principles of Textual Criticism

Most manuscript variants are rather minor differences, such as a reading of "Jesus" versus another of "Jesus Christ." None of the variants pose a significant concern for developing Christian doctrines. But the goal of the Bible translator is to produce a Bible as accurate as possible—thus textual criticism developed. In textual criticism, a translator collects the manuscript evidence surrounding what is being translated and then uses this evidence, and at times other sources, to determine the reading that is best supported. In doing so, translators appeal to two primary types of evidence: (1) external considerations and (2) internal considerations.

External Considerations

The external considerations used in textual criticism concern the manuscript itself, not necessarily the wording of the variants. Three key areas are evaluated: (1) the age of the manuscripts, (2) the quantity of manuscripts, and (3) the geographical distribution of the manuscripts.

The Age of the Manuscripts: In general, the reading of an older manuscript is preferred over a more recent one. This is not absolute, however. At times, a much more recent manuscript will be preferred, even strongly, over an ancient one. There are several ways to date a manuscript. First, the material of the manuscript is considered. A papyrus manuscript is generally going to be older than a parchment manuscript. Second, the style of writing is evaluated. Is an OT text written in an older Hebrew script called *paleo-Hebrew* or a newer one called *square-script Hebrew*? Are vowel points provided? Is a NT text written in an earlier or later majuscule script? Is the text plain, or is it accompanied by ornate flourishes denoting a later dating? Also, at times, parchments were erased and dated material was written over the scripture text, which allows an estimate to be made of when the erased scripture was produced.

The Quantity of Manuscripts: In general, readings that are found more often in manuscripts are preferred over those occurring less often. This preference goes hand in hand with the last test of geographical distribution.

The Geographical Distribution of Manuscripts: In general, a reading from manuscripts that can be found in more than one location is preferred even over a reading that might be older and that appears in a greater number of manuscripts. The reason is that, if an error was introduced in one region, it would likely have been copied repeatedly. Still, if the same reading can be found in more than one place, that increases the confidence that they each drew from the same correct source.

Internal Considerations
In addition to weighing the age, quantity, and geographic distribution of the manuscripts, textual criticism involves analyzing the variants themselves with the goal of determining the logic of why they exist. This considers possible transcription errors as well as intentional changes the scribes may have made. The length of the reading, the difficulty of the reading, the author's style, and the literary and theological context of the reading are all considered.

The Length of the Reading: Shorter readings are preferred over longer ones because scribes would be more prone to add rather than remove content.

The Difficulty of the Reading: More difficult readings are preferred over easier ones because scribes would be more prone to smooth a rougher reading rather than make a smoother reading more complex. In addition, less harmonious readings in parallel passages are preferred over more harmonious ones for the same reason.

The Style of the Reading: Words or phrases that align more with those used elsewhere in a book of Scripture are preferred over unique ones.

The Context of the Reading: Readings that align more closely with the literary and theological context of the period when a text was originally written are preferred over those that do not.

Other Textual Criticism Aids
In addition to the manuscript evidence, translators often consult other materials in the process of textual criticism. About 2,000 lectionaries, teaching guides that contain portions of the Scriptures, have been found, all dating from the tenth century AD or later. In addition, the writings of the church fathers, who quoted almost the entire NT, are often considered. While these resources are indeed helpful, especially to determine what a reading was in a certain period of history and in a certain location, they are given far less weight than manuscripts. It is not as easy to determine whether a statement is a direct quote or an allusion or paraphrase, and scribes copying these works would have felt far greater license to adapt them as needed.

CHALLENGE 2: TRANSLATING THE WORDS OF SCRIPTURE

In mathematics, we can determine equivalent fractions by multiplying the numerator and denominator by the same number, thus ½ is the same as ²⁄₄. When it comes to the work of translation, however, there is no such one-to-one formula to follow. Words can have shades of meaning; idioms untethered from their culture of origin are often unclear; and some words or concepts might have multiple meanings or no meaning at

all in another language. Translating the Hebrew, Aramaic, and Greek into English must therefore be framed by three related contexts: (1) linguistic context, namely, whether words or thoughts are to be translated, (2) cultural context, namely, whether to retain gender specific language or adapt it, and (3) theological context, namely, whether to allow the NT to inform the translation of the OT.

Translating Word for Word or Thought for Thought

If you have researched English versions of the Bible, you have probably encountered a *translation spectrum*—a simple chart with the far left representing a word-for-word translation approach that produces the most wooden-but-precise English translations and the far right representing a thought-for-thought translation approach that produces the loosest-but-easiest-to-read English translations and paraphrases. In the former, more technically called *formal equivalence*, each word of the original language is represented by a word in the receptor (target) language, and the word and clause order is kept as nearly identical to that of the original language as possible. In the latter, called *dynamic equivalence* or *functional equivalence*, the goal is to render the original language text in the closest natural equivalent in the receptor language in both meaning and style.

Some translators intentionally lean toward one end of the spectrum or the other, embracing the strengths and weaknesses of their chosen approach. Most try to strike a balance between the extremes, weighing accuracy against readability—striving to reflect the grammar of the underlying biblical languages while still achieving acceptable English style. But this spectrum is more complicated than it appears. No translation can ever achieve complete formal equivalence. Even a translation that sometimes reflects Hebrew and Greek word order at the expense of English style must resort to paraphrase in some places. Furthermore, translating between two languages is not often a one-to-one exchange. It is not as if there is one and only exact word in the receptor language for each word of the original language. And it is not as if each word in the original language has only one clear use and meaning. Just as English words have

shades of meanings, so do the Hebrew, Aramaic, and Greek words of Scripture.

Making translating even more difficult is the structural differences between languages, such as different word order, different verb tenses, gendered definite and indefinite articles, and so forth, meaning even a direct word-for-word ordering of sentences often is not possible. Beyond this, idioms and cultural references often require some level of translation beyond moving their words and grammar into English. But just as complete formal equivalence is not possible, neither is complete dynamic equivalence.

Translating Original, Accurate, or Neutral Gender

A significant issue in Bible translation that is increasing in attention concerns how to translate gendered terms into modern English. In the patriarchal cultures of ancient Hebrew and Greek, words like *man* and *brothers* could include both men and women. And in the past, these words were understood similarly in English-speaking cultures. *Man* could be understood to represent mankind, humanity, or all people, male and female alike, and *brothers* could be read as any believers, male or female. Recently, however, these terms have become more commonly understood as male specific.

The question has thus become how these words are to be accurately translated for a modern, English-speaking audience. There are three approaches for doing so. The first could be considered Gender Original Translation, in which the gender of the Hebrew, Aramaic, or Greek is retained no matter the context. At the other extreme would be what can be called Gender Neutral Translation, in which all or nearly all gendered language is neutralized, no matter its context. In between these two approaches is the third, what can be called Gender Accurate Translation, in which the context of the gendered language is considered and modified when appropriate.

For example, in Revelation 16:21, we read "gigantic hailstones, weighing about 100 pounds each, fell from heaven on [Grk. *anthrōpos*]," with this final Greek word meaning "men." A Gender Original Translation would place "men" here, while a Gender Accurate Translation would consider how translating the phrase as "men" could give

the impression that the hail only hit males, which surely was not the case. Thus, it would place "people" here, as would a Gender Neutral Translation.

Another example is where Hebrews 2:6 alludes to Psalm 8 in saying, "What is man that you think of him or the son of man that you care for him?" While a Gender Neutral Translation would modify "man" to something like "people" and "son of man" to "humans" and a Gender Original Translation would retain "man" and "son of man," a Gender Accurate Translation would have to consider the context to make a decision. Because "son of man" points to Jesus, that would likely stay intact. The question would then be how to translate "man," which surely means all humanity. Translating it as "people," however, loses the connective thread of the sentence. In this case, while "people" might be more accurate in terms of what is meant, "men" might be preserved for style.

Translating the OT Based on the NT

The Bible was not written at one time, but rather in stages over roughly 1,600 years. Besides changes in language and culture over this span, one other change must be considered when it comes to translating the Bible: progressive revelation. Simply put, progressive revelation recognizes that God has revealed himself—his nature as well as his word, plans, and purposes—over time. God did not reveal everything about himself and what he was doing in the world all at once; instead, he graciously revealed more and more as time went on. Later revelation thus serves to complement and supplement what had come before it.

The question becomes whether progressive revelation should inform Bible translation, especially at times when the NT informs what was written in the OT. Does the translator translate the older passage with a view to the clarification that the later passage provides, or does the translator concentrate solely on the native context of the older passage?

Isaiah 7:14 perhaps represents this challenge the best: "For this reason the Lord himself will give you a confirming sign. Look, this [Heb. *almah*] is about to conceive and will give birth to a son. You, [Heb. *almah*], will name him Immanuel." At question is how to translate the Hebrew term *almah*, which can mean either "virgin" or "young woman." Because Matthew 1:23 quotes this verse and supplies "virgin," some translators may see cause to use this term in Isaiah as well. The questions, though, are these: Did Isaiah write this understanding it to be a messianic prophecy? How would his original audience have understood what he wrote? And because the historical and literary context of the verse expect Isaiah to be speaking of a woman present in that day, would two virgin births—that of this woman and Mary in the NT—be expected?

Thus, a case can be made that Isaiah should be translated as "young woman," because that is how the original audience would have understood the prophet, and that doing so does not undermine the virgin birth of Jesus. Rather, just because the Jews of Isaiah's day might not have recognized the virgin birth of the Messiah, it does not mean that detail was not revealed later in God's unfolding plan of redemption.

CONCLUSION

The challenges to translating the Bible into English are indeed considerable, but they are far from insurmountable. Thankfully, we have a rich history of scholars who have been faithful to study manuscripts, research ancient Near Eastern languages and history, and develop standards for textual criticism and translation methods. As such, we are able to hold God's Word in our hands, faithfully and accurately translated into English and understandable and trustworthy for our reading and studying.

THE
OLD TESTAMENT

GENESIS

The first part of Genesis focuses on the beginning and spread of sin in the world and culminates in the devastating flood in the days of Noah. The second part of the book focuses on God's dealings with one man, Abraham, through whom God promises to bring salvation and blessing to the world. Abraham and his descendants learn first-hand that it is always safe to trust the Lord in times of famine and feasting, blessing and bondage. From Abraham God's promises begin to come to fruition in a great nation possessing a great land. *Genesis* is a Greek word meaning "origin," "source," "generation," or "beginning." The original Hebrew title *Bereshith* means "In the Beginning." The literary structure of Genesis is clear and is built around eleven separate units: (1) Introduction to the Genealogies (1:1–2:3); (2) Heaven and Earth (2:4–4:26); (3) Adam (5:1–6:8); (4) Noah (6:9–9:29); (5) Sons of Noah (10:1–11:9); (6) Shem (11:10–26); (7) Terah (11:27–25:11); (8) Ishmael (25:12–18); (9) Isaac (25:19–35:29); (10) Esau (36:1–37:1); (11) Jacob (37:2–50:26).

The Creation of the World

1 In the [a]beginning [b]God created[1] the heavens and the earth.

[2]Now the earth was [a]without shape [b]and empty, and darkness was over the surface of the watery deep, but the Spirit of God was moving over the surface of the water. [3][a]God said, "[b]Let there be [c]light." And there was light! [4]God saw that the light was good,[1] so God separated the light from the darkness. [5]God called the light "day" and the [a]darkness "night." There was evening, and there was morning, marking the first day.

[6]God said, "[a]Let there be an expanse in the midst of the waters and let it separate water from water." [7]So God made the expanse [a]and separated the water under the expanse from the water [b]above it. It was so. [8]God called the expanse "sky." There was evening, and there was morning, a second day.

[9]God said, "[a]Let the water under the sky be gathered to one place and [b]let dry ground appear." It was so. [10]God called the dry ground "land" and the gathered waters he called "seas." God saw that it was good. [11]God said, "Let the land produce vegetation: plants yielding seeds and trees on the land bearing fruit with seed [a]in [b]it, according to their kinds." It was so. [12]The land produced vegetation—plants yielding seeds according to their kinds, and trees bearing fruit with seed in it according to their kinds. God saw that it was good. [13]There was evening, and there was morning, a third day.

[14]God said, "Let there be [a]lights in the expanse of the sky to separate the day from the night, and let them be signs to indicate [b]seasons and days and years, [15]and let them serve as lights in the expanse of the sky to give light on the earth." It was so. [16]God made two [a]great lights—the greater light to rule over the day and the [b]lesser light to rule over [c]the night. He made the stars also. [17]God placed the lights in the expanse of the [a]sky to shine on the earth, [18]to [a]preside over the day and the night, and to separate the light from the darkness. God saw that

1:1 [a]Ps 102:25; Isa 40:21; [John 1:1–3; Heb 1:10]   [b]Gen 2:4; [Ps 8:3; 89:11; 90:2]; Isa 44:24; Acts 17:24; Rom 1:20; [Heb 1:2; 11:3]; Rev 4:11   [1]This Heb. verb always describes the divine activity of fashioning something new, fresh, and perfect; it does not necessarily describe creation out of nothing.   1:2 [a]Jer 4:23   [b][Gen 6:3]; Job 26:13; Ps 33:6; 104:30; Isa 40:13–14   1:3 [a]Ps 33:6, 9   [b]2 Cor 4:6   [c][Heb 11:3]   1:4 [1]The Heb. word signifies whatever enhances, promotes, produces, or is conducive for life.   1:5 [a]Job 37:18; Ps 19:2; 33:6; 74:16; 104:20; 136:5; Jer 10:12   1:6 [a]Job 37:18; Jer 10:12; 2 Pet 3:5   1:7 [a]Job 38:8–11; Prov 8:27–29   [b]Ps 148:4   1:9 [a]Job 26:10; Ps 104:6–9; Prov 8:29; Jer 5:22; 2 Pet 3:5   [b]Ps 24:1–2; 33:7; 95:5   1:11 [a]Ps 65:9–13; 104:14; Heb 6:7   [b]2 Sam 16:1; Luke 6:44   1:14 [a]Deut 4:19; Ps 74:16; 136:5–9   [b]Ps 104:19   1:16 [a]Ps 136:8   [b]Deut 17:3; Ps 8:3   [c]Deut 4:19; Job 38:7; Isa 40:26   1:17 [a]Gen 15:5; Jer 33:20, 25   1:18 [a]Jer 31:35

it was good. [19]There was evening, and there was morning, a fourth day.

[20]God said, "Let the water swarm with swarms of living creatures and let birds fly above the earth across the expanse of the sky." [21a]God created the great sea creatures and every living and moving thing with which the water swarmed, according to their kinds, and every winged bird according to its kind. God saw that it was good. [22]God blessed them and said, "[a]Be fruitful and multiply and fill the water in the seas, and let the birds multiply on the earth." [23]There was evening, and there was morning, a fifth day.

[24]God said, "Let the land produce living creatures according to their kinds: cattle, creeping things, and wild animals, each according to its kind." It was so. [25]God made the wild animals according to their kinds, the cattle according to their kinds, and all the creatures that creep along the ground according to their kinds. God saw that it was good.

[26]Then God said, "[a]Let us make humankind in our image, after our likeness, [b]so they may rule over the fish of the sea and the birds of the air, over the cattle, and over all the earth,[1] and over all the creatures that move on the earth."

[27] God created [a]humankind in his own image,
in the image of God he created them,
[b]male and female he created them.

[28]God blessed[1] them and said to them, "[a]Be fruitful and multiply! Fill the earth and [b]subdue it! Rule over the fish of the sea and the birds of the air and every creature that moves on the ground." [29]Then God said, "I now give you every seed-bearing plant on the face of the entire earth and every tree that has fruit with seed in it. [a]They will be yours for food. [30]And to all the animals of the earth, and to [a]every [b]bird of the air, and to all the creatures that move on the ground—everything that has living breath in it—I give every green plant for food." It was so. [31a]God saw all that he had made—and

it was very good! There was evening, and there was morning, the sixth day.

2 The heavens and the earth were completed with [a]everything that was in them. [2]By the seventh day God finished the work that he had been doing, [a]and he ceased[1] on the seventh day all the work that he had been doing. [3]God [a]blessed the seventh day and made it holy because on it he ceased all the work that he had been doing in creation.

The Creation of Man and Woman

[4a]This is the account of the heavens and the earth when they were created—when the LORD God made the earth and heavens. [5]Now no [a]shrub of the field had yet grown on the earth, and no plant of the field had yet sprouted, for the LORD God had not [b]caused it [c]to rain on the earth, and there was no man to cultivate the ground. [6]Springs would well up from the earth and water the whole surface of the ground. [7]The LORD God formed the man from the [a]soil of the ground and [b]breathed into his [c]nostrils the breath of life, and the [d]man became a living being. [8]The LORD God [a]planted an orchard in the [b]east, in [c]Eden; and there he placed the man he had formed. [9]The LORD God made all kinds [a]of trees grow from [b]the soil, every tree that was pleasing to look at and good for food. (Now the tree of life and the tree of the knowledge of good and [c]evil were in the middle of the orchard.)

[10]Now a river flows[1] from Eden to water the orchard, and from there it divides into four headstreams. [11]The name of [a]the first is Pishon; it runs through the entire land of Havilah, where there is gold. [12](The gold of that land is pure;[1] [a]pearls and lapis lazuli are also there.) [13]The name of the second river is Gihon; it runs through the entire land of Cush. [14]The name of the third river is [a]Tigris; it runs along the east side of Assyria. The fourth river is the Euphrates.

[15]The LORD God took the man and placed him in the orchard in Eden to care for it and to maintain it. [16]Then the LORD God commanded the man, "You may freely eat fruit from every tree of the orchard, [17]but

1:21 [a]Ps 104:25–28 **1:22** [a]Gen 8:17 **1:26** [a]Gen 9:6; Ps 100:3; Eccl 7:29; [Eph 4:24]; Jas 3:9 [b]Gen 9:2; Ps 8:6–8 [1]Syr. *wild animals.* **1:27** [a]Gen 5:2; 1 Cor 11:7 [b]Matt 19:4; [Mark 10:6–8] **1:28** [a]Gen 9:1, 7; Lev 26:9 [b]1 Cor 9:27 [1]Or *God endowed them with fruitfulness; the capacity to reproduce.* **1:29** [a]Gen 9:3; Ps 104:14–15 **1:30** [a]Ps 145:15 [b]Job 38:41 **1:31** [a][Ps 104:24; 1 Tim 4:4] **2:1** [a]Ps 33:6 **2:2** [a]Exod 20:9–11; 31:17; Heb 4:4, 10 [1]Or *he rested.* **2:3** [a][Isa 58:13] **2:4** [a]Gen 1:1; Ps 90:1–2 **2:5** [a]Gen 1:11–12 [b]Gen 7:4; Job 5:10; 38:26–28 [c]Gen 3:23 **2:7** [a]Gen 3:19, 23; Ps 103:14 [b]Job 33:4 [c]Gen 7:22 [d]1 Cor 15:45 **2:8** [a]Isa 51:3 [b]Gen 3:23–24 [c]Gen 4:16 **2:9** [a]Ezek 31:8 [b][Gen 3:22; Rev 2:7; 22:2, 14] [c][Deut 1:39] **2:10** [1]Or *was flowing.* **2:11** [a]Gen 25:18 **2:12** [a]Num 11:7 [1]Heb. *good.* **2:14** [a]Dan 10:4

[a]you must not eat from the tree of the knowledge of good and evil, for when [b]you eat from it you will surely [c]die." [18]The LORD God [a]said, "It is not good for the man to be alone. I will make a companion[1] for him who corresponds to him." [19]The LORD God formed [a]out of the ground every living animal of the field and every bird of the air. He [b]brought them to the man to see what he would name them, and whatever the man called each living creature, that was its name. [20]So the man named all the animals, the birds of the air, and the living creatures of the field, but for Adam no companion who corresponded to him was found. [21]So the LORD God caused the man to fall into a [a]deep sleep, and while he was asleep, he took part of the man's side[1] and closed up the place with flesh. [22]Then the LORD God made [a]a woman from the part he had taken out of the man, and he [b]brought her to the man. [23]Then the man said,

"This one at last is [a]bone of my bones
  and flesh of my flesh;
this one will be called 'woman,'
  for she was [b]taken out of man."

[24]That is [a]why a man leaves his father and mother and unites with[1] his wife, and they [b]become one family. [25]The man [a]and his wife were both naked, but they were not [b]ashamed.

The Temptation and the Fall

3 Now [a]the serpent was [b]shrewder[1] than any of the wild animals that the LORD God had made. He said to the woman, "Is it really true that God said, 'You must not eat from any tree of the orchard'?" [2]The woman said to the serpent, "We may eat of the [a]fruit from the trees of the orchard; [3]but concerning the fruit of the tree that is in the middle of the orchard God said, 'You must not eat from it, and you must not [a]touch it, or else you will die.'" [4]The serpent said to [a]the woman, "Surely you will not die,

[5]for God knows that when you eat from it your eyes will open and you will be like God, knowing good and evil." [6]When the woman [a]saw that the tree produced fruit that was good for food, was attractive to the eye, [b]and was desirable for making one wise, she took some of its fruit and ate it. She also gave some of it to her husband who was with her, and he ate it. [7]Then the eyes of both of them opened, [a]and they knew they were naked; so they sewed fig leaves together and made coverings for themselves.

The Judgment Oracles of God at the Fall

[8]Then [a]the man and his wife heard the sound of the LORD God moving about[1] in the orchard at the breezy time of the day, and they [b]hid from the LORD God among the trees of the orchard. [9]But the LORD God called to the man and said to him, "Where are you?" [10]The man replied, "I heard you moving about in the orchard, [a]and I was afraid because I was naked, so I hid." [11]And the LORD God said, "Who told you that you were naked? Did you eat from the tree that I commanded you not to eat from?" [12]The man said, "[a]The woman whom you gave me, she gave me some fruit from the tree and I ate it." [13]So [a]the LORD God said to the woman, "What is this you have done?" And the woman replied, "The serpent tricked me, and I ate."

[14]The LORD God said to the serpent,

"Because [a]you have done this,
  cursed are you above all the cattle
  and all the living creatures of the field!
On your belly you will crawl
  and dust you will eat all the days of
  your life.
[15] And I will put hostility between [a]you
  and the woman
  and between your offspring and [b]her
  offspring;
  [c]he will strike your head,
  and you will strike his heel."

2:17 [a] Gen 3:1, 3, 11, 17 [b] Gen 3:3, 19; [Rom 6:23] [c] Rom 5:12; 1 Cor 15:21–22 **2:18** [a] 1 Cor 11:8–9; 1 Tim 2:13 [1] Trad. *helper*; does not suggest a subordinate role. **2:19** [a] Gen 1:20, 24 [b] Ps 8:6 **2:21** [a] Gen 15:12; 1 Sam 26:12 [1] Trad. *rib.* **2:22** [a] Gen 3:20; 1 Tim 2:13 [b] Heb 13:4 **2:23** [a] Gen 29:14; Eph 5:28–30 [b] 1 Cor 11:8–9 **2:24** [a] Matt 19:5; Eph 5:31 [b] Mark 10:6–8; 1 Cor 6:16 [1] Trad. *cleaves* [to]; an inseparable joining. **2:25** [a] Gen 3:7, 10 [b] Isa 47:3 **3:1** [a] 1 Chr 21:1; [Rev 12:9; 20:2, 10] [b] 2 Cor 11:3 [1] Or *clever, cunning* (negative), *prudent* (positive). **3:2** [a] Gen 2:16–17 **3:3** [a] Exod 19:12–13; Rev 22:14 **3:4** [a] John 8:44; [2 Cor 11:3; 1 Tim 2:14] **3:6** [a] 1 John 2:16 [b] 1 Tim 2:14 **3:7** [a] Gen 2:25 **3:8** [a] Job 38:1 [b] Job 31:33; Jer 23:24 [1] Or *walking about*; assumes a theophany, the presence of the Lord God in a human form. **3:10** [a] Gen 2:25; Exod 3:6; Deut 9:19; 1 John 3:20 **3:12** [a] [Prov 28:13] **3:13** [a] Gen 3:4; 2 Cor 11:3; 1 Tim 2:14 **3:14** [a] Deut 28:15–20; Isa 65:25; Mic 7:17 **3:15** [a] John 8:44; Acts 13:10; 1 John 3:8 [b] Isa 7:14; Luke 1:31, 34, 35; Gal 4:4 [c] Rom 16:20; [Rev 12:7, 17]

[16]To the woman he said,

> "[a]I will greatly increase [b]your labor
>   pains;
> with pain you will give birth to
>   children.
> You will want to control your
>   husband,[1]
> but he will [c]dominate you."

[17]But to Adam he said,

> "[a]Because you obeyed your wife
> and ate from the tree [b]about which I
>   commanded you,
> 'You must not eat from it,'
> the ground is [c]cursed because
>   of you;
> [d]in painful toil you will eat of it all
>   the days of your life.
> [18] It will produce thorns and thistles
>   for [a]you,
> but you will eat the grain of
>   the field.
> [19] [a]By the sweat of your brow you
>   will eat food
> until you return to the ground,
> [b]for out of it you were taken;
> for you are dust, and [c]to dust you
>   will return."

[20]The man named his wife [a]Eve, because she was the mother of all the living.[1] [21]The LORD God made garments from skin for Adam and his wife, and clothed them. [22]And the LORD God said, "Now that the man has become like one of us, knowing good and evil, he must not be allowed to stretch out his hand and take also from the tree of life and eat, and live forever." [23]So the LORD God expelled him from the orchard in Eden [a]to cultivate the ground from which he had been taken. [24]When [a]he drove the man out, he placed on the eastern side of the orchard in Eden angelic [b]sentries who used the flame of [c]a whirling sword to guard the way to the tree of [d]life.

The Story of Cain and Abel

4 Now the man was intimate with his wife Eve, and she became pregnant and gave birth to Cain. Then she said, "I have created[1] a man just as the LORD did!" [2]Then she gave birth to his brother [a]Abel. Abel took care of the flocks, while Cain cultivated the ground.

[3]At the designated time Cain brought some [a]of the fruit of the ground for an offering[1] to the LORD. [4]But Abel brought some of [a]the firstborn of his flock—even [b]the fattest of them. And the LORD was [c]pleased with Abel and his offering, [5]but with Cain and his offering he was not pleased. So Cain became very angry, and his expression was downcast. [6]Then the LORD said to Cain, "Why are you angry, and why is your expression downcast? [7]Is it not true that if you do what is right, you will be fine? But if you do not do what is right, sin is crouching at the door. It desires to dominate you, but you must subdue it."

[8]Cain said to his brother Abel, "Let's go out to the field."[1] While they were in the field, Cain attacked his brother Abel and [a]killed him.

[9]Then the LORD [a]said to Cain, "Where is your brother Abel?" And he replied, "I don't know! Am I [b]my brother's guardian?" [10]But the LORD said, "What have you done? The voice of your brother's blood is crying [a]out to me from the ground! [11]So now [a]you are banished from the ground, which has opened its mouth to receive your brother's blood from your hand. [12]When you try to cultivate the ground it will no longer yield its best for you. You will be a homeless wanderer on the earth."

[13]Then Cain said to the LORD, "My punishment is too great to endure! [14]Look, you are [a]driving me off the land today, and I must [b]hide from your presence. I will be a homeless wanderer on the earth; [c]whoever finds me will kill me!" [15]But the LORD said to him, "All right then,[1] if anyone kills Cain, Cain will be avenged seven [a]times as much." Then the LORD put a special [b]mark on Cain

3:16 [a]Isa 13:8; John 16:21   [b]Gen 4:7   [c]1 Cor 11:3; Eph 5:22; 1 Tim 2:12, 15   [1]Heb. *and toward your husband* [will be] *your desire.*
3:17 [a]1 Sam 15:23   [b]Gen 2:17   [c]Gen 5:29; Rom 8:20–22; Heb 6:8   [d]Job 5:7; 14:1; Eccl 2:23   3:18 [a]Ps 104:14   3:19 [a]2 Thess
3:10   [b]Gen 2:7; 5:5   [c]Job 21:26; Eccl 3:20   3:20 [a]2 Cor 11:3; 1 Tim 2:13   [1]A word play between *Eve* (Heb. *khavvah*) and
living (Heb. *khay*).   3:23 [a]Gen 4:2; 9:20   3:24 [a]Ezek 31:3, 11   [b]Exod 25:18–22; Ps 104:4; Ezek 10:1–20; Heb 1:7
[c]Gen 2:8   [d]Gen 2:9; [Rev 22:2]   4:1 [1]A word play between *I have created* (Heb. *qaniti*) and *Cain* (Heb. *qayin*).
4:2 [a]Luke 11:50–51   4:3 [a]Num 18:12   [1]Heb. *tribute, gift, offering.*   4:4 [a]Num 18:17   [b]Lev 3:16   [c]Heb 11:4
4:8 [a]Matt 23:35; Luke 11:51; [1 John 3:12–15]; Jude 11   [1]MT omits *Let's go out to the field.*   4:9 [a]John 8:44
[b]1 Cor 8:11–13   4:10 [a]Num 35:33; Deut 21:1–9; Heb 12:24; Rev 6:9–10   4:11 [a]Gen 3:14; Deut 11:28;
28:15–20; Gal 3:10   4:14 [a]Ps 51:11   [b]Deut 31:18; Isa 1:15   [c]Gen 9:6; Num 35:19, 21, 27   4:15 [a]Gen
4:24; Ps 79:12   [b]Gen 9:6; Ezek 9:4, 6   [1]Heb. *in that case then I will do this.*

so that no one who found him would strike him down. [16] So Cain [a]went out from the [b]presence of the LORD and lived in the land of Nod, east of Eden.

The Beginning of Civilization

[17] Cain was intimate with[1] his wife, [a]and she became pregnant and gave birth to Enoch. Cain was building a city, and he named the city after his son Enoch. [18] To Enoch was born Irad, and Irad was the father of Mehujael. Mehujael was the father of Methushael, and Methushael was the father of Lamech.

[19] Lamech took[a] two wives for himself; the name of the first was Adah, and the name of the second was Zillah. [20] Adah gave birth to Jabal; he was the first of those who live in tents and keep livestock. [21] The name of his brother was Jubal; he was the first of all who play the harp and the flute. [22] Now Zillah also gave birth to Tubal-Cain, who heated metal and shaped all kinds of tools made of bronze and iron. The sister of Tubal-Cain was Naamah.

[23] Lamech said to his wives,

"Adah and Zillah, listen to me!
You wives of Lamech, hear my words!
I have killed a man for wounding me,
a young man for hurting me.
[24] [a]If Cain is to be avenged seven times
as much,
then Lamech seventy-seven times!"

[25] And Adam was intimate with his wife again, and she gave birth to a son. She [a]named him Seth, saying, "God has given me another child in place of Abel because Cain killed him." [26] And a son was also born [a]to Seth, whom he named Enosh. At that time people began [b]to worship the LORD.

From Adam to Noah

5 This is the record of the family [a]line of Adam.
When God created humankind, [b]he made them[1] in the likeness of God. [2] He created them [a]male and female; when they were created, he [b]blessed them and named them "humankind."

[3] When Adam had lived 130 years he fathered a son [a]in his own likeness, according to his image, and he [b]named him Seth. [4] The length of time Adam lived after [a]he became the father of Seth was 800 years; during this time he had other sons [b]and daughters. [5] The entire lifetime of Adam was 930 years, [a]and then he died.

[6] When Seth had lived 105 years, he became the father of [a]Enosh. [7] Seth lived 807 years after he became the father of Enosh, and he had other sons and daughters. [8] The entire lifetime of Seth was 912 years, and then he died.

[9] When Enosh had lived 90 years, he became the father of Kenan. [10] Enosh lived 815 years after he became the father of Kenan, and he had other sons and daughters. [11] The entire lifetime of Enosh was 905 years, and then he died.

[12] When Kenan had lived 70 years, he became the father of Mahalalel. [13] Kenan lived 840 years after he became the father of Mahalalel, and he had other sons and daughters. [14] The entire lifetime of Kenan was 910 years, and then he died.

[15] When Mahalalel had lived 65 years, he became the father of Jared. [16] Mahalalel lived 830 years after he became the father of Jared, and he had other sons and daughters. [17] The entire lifetime of Mahalalel was 895 years, and then he died.

[18] When Jared had lived 162 years, he became the father of [a]Enoch. [19] Jared lived 800 years after he became the father of Enoch, and he had other sons and daughters. [20] The entire lifetime of Jared was 962 years, and then he died.

[21] When Enoch had lived 65 years, he became the father of Methuselah. [22] After he became the father of Methuselah, Enoch [a]walked with God for 300 years, and he had other sons and daughters. [23] The entire lifetime of Enoch was 365 years. [24a] Enoch walked with God, and then he disappeared because God [b]took him away.

[25] When Methuselah had lived 187 years,

4:16 [a] 2 Kgs 13:23; 24:20; Jer 23:39; 52:3 [b] Jonah 1:3 4:17 [a] Ps 49:11 [1] Heb. *knew*; a euphemism for sexual relations. 4:19 [a] Gen 2:24; 16:3; 1 Tim 3:2 4:24 [a] Gen 4:15 4:25 [a] Gen 5:3 4:26 [a] Gen 5:6 [b] Gen 12:8; 26:25; 1 Kgs 18:24; Ps 116:17; Joel 2:32; Zeph 3:9; 1 Cor 1:2 5:1 [a] Gen 2:4; 6:9; 1 Chr 1:1; Matt 1:1 [b] Gen 1:26; 9:6; [Eph 4:24; Col 3:10] [1] Heb. *him*; the next verse makes it clear that this Heb. word is collective, referring to humankind. 5:2 [a] Gen 1:27; Deut 4:32; Matt 19:4; Mark 10:6 [b] Gen 1:28; 9:1 5:3 [a] 1 Cor 15:48–49 [b] Gen 4:25 5:4 [a] 1 Chr 1:1–4; Luke 3:36–38 [b] Gen 1:28; 4:25 5:5 [a] Gen 2:17; 3:19; 6:17; [Heb 9:27] 5:6 [a] Gen 4:26 5:18 [a] Jude 14, 15 5:22 [a] Gen 6:9; 17:1; 24:40; 48:15; 2 Kgs 20:3; Ps 16:8; [Mic 6:8]; Mal 2:6; 1 Thess 2:12; [Heb 11:39] 5:24 [a] 2 Kgs 2:11; Jude 14 [b] 2 Kgs 2:10; Ps 49:15; 73:24; Heb 11:5

he became the father of Lamech. [26]Methuselah lived 782 years after he became the father of Lamech, and he had other sons and daughters. [27]The entire lifetime of Methuselah was 969 years, and then he died.

[28]When Lamech had lived 182 years, he had a son. [29]He named him [a]Noah, saying, "This one will bring us comfort from our labor and from the painful toil of our hands because of the ground [b]that the LORD has cursed." [30]Lamech lived 595 years after he became the father of Noah, and he had other sons and daughters. [31]The entire lifetime of Lamech was 777 years, and then he died.

[32]After Noah was 500 years old, he became the father of [a]Shem, Ham, [b]and Japheth.

God's Grief over Humankind's Wickedness

6 [a]When humankind began to multiply on the face of the earth, and daughters were born to them, [2]the sons of God saw that the daughters of humankind were beautiful. Thus they [a]took wives for themselves from any they chose. [3]So the LORD said, "[a]My Spirit will not [b]remain in[1] humankind indefinitely, since they are mortal. They will remain [c]for 120 more years."[2]

[4]The Nephilim[1] were on the earth in those [a]days (and also after this) when the sons of God would sleep with the daughters of humankind, who gave birth to their children. They were the mighty heroes of old, the famous men.

[5]But the LORD saw that the wickedness of humankind had become great on the earth. Every [a]inclination of the thoughts of their minds was only evil all the time. [6]The LORD regretted that [a]he had made humankind on [b]the earth, and he was [c]highly offended. [7]So the LORD said, "I will [a]wipe humankind, whom I have created, from the face of the earth—everything from humankind to animals, including creatures that move on the ground and birds of the air, for I regret that I have made them."

[8]But Noah [a]found favor in the sight of the LORD.

The Judgment of the Flood

[9]This is the account of [a]Noah.

Noah was a godly man; he was blameless among his contemporaries. He [b]walked with God. [10]Noah had three sons: [a]Shem, Ham, and Japheth.

[11]The earth was ruined in the [a]sight of God; the earth was [b]filled with violence.[1] [12]God [a]saw the earth, and indeed it was ruined, for [b]all living creatures on the earth were sinful. [13]So God said to Noah, "I have decided that all living creatures must die, for [a]the earth is filled with violence because of [b]them. Now [c]I am about to destroy them and the earth. [14]Make for yourself an ark of cypress wood. Make rooms in the ark, and cover it with pitch inside and out. [15]This is how you should make it: The ark is to be 450 feet long, 75 feet wide, and 45 feet high. [16]Make a roof for the ark and finish it, leaving 18 inches from the top. Put a door in the side of the ark, and make lower, middle, and upper decks. [17a]I am about to bring [b]floodwaters on the earth to destroy from under the sky all the living creatures that have the breath of life in them. Everything that is on the earth will [c]die, [18]but I will confirm my [a]covenant with [b]you. You will enter the ark—you, your sons, your wife, and your sons' wives with you. [19]You must bring into the ark [a]two of every kind of living creature from all flesh, male and female, to keep them alive with you. [20]Of the birds after their kinds, and of the cattle after their kinds, and of every creeping thing of the ground after its kind, two of every kind [a]will come to you so you can keep them alive. [21]And you must take for yourself every kind of food that is eaten, and gather it together. It will be food for you and for them."

[22a]And Noah did all that [b]God commanded him—he did indeed.

5:29 [a]Luke 3:36; Heb 11:7; 1 Pet 3:20 [b]Gen 3:17–19; 4:11 **5:32** [a]Gen 6:10; 7:13 [b]Gen 10:21 **6:1** [a]Gen 1:28 **6:2** [a]Deut 7:3–4 **6:3** [a]Gen 41:38; [Gal 5:16–17]; 1 Pet 3:19–20 [b]2 Thess 2:7 [c]Ps 78:39 [1]Or *strive, contend with*. [2]Heb. *his days will be 120 years*. **6:4** [a]Num 13:32–33; Luke 17:27 [1]The Heb. word is simply transliterated because its meaning is uncertain. **6:5** [a]Gen 8:21; Ps 14:1–3; Prov 6:18; Matt 15:19; Rom 1:28–32 **6:6** [a]Gen 6:7; 1 Sam 15:11, 29; 2 Sam 24:16; Jer 18:7–10; Zech 8:14 [b]Ps 78:40; Isa 63:10; Eph 4:30 [c]Mark 3:5 **6:7** [a]Gen 7:4, 23; Deut 28:63; 29:20; Ps 7:11 **6:8** [a]Gen 19:19; Exod 33:12, 17; Luke 1:30; Acts 7:46 **6:9** [a]Gen 7:1; Ezek 14:14, 20; Heb 11:7; 2 Pet 2:5 [b]Gen 5:22, 24; 2 Kgs 23:3 **6:10** [a]Gen 5:32; 7:13 **6:11** [a]Deut 31:29; Judg 2:19; Rom 2:13 [b]Ezek 8:17 [1]The Heb. word can refer to a range of crimes, including unjust treatment (Gen 16:5; Amos 3:10), injurious legal testimony (Deut 19:16), deadly assault (Gen 49:5), murder (Judg 9:24), and rape (Jer 13:22). **6:12** [a]Ps 14:2; 53:2–3 [b]Ps 14:1–3; Isa 28:8 **6:13** [a]Isa 34:1–4; Jer 51:13; Ezek 7:2–3; Amos 8:2; 1 Pet 4:7 [b]Gen 6:17 [c]2 Pet 2:4–10 **6:17** [a]Gen 7:4, 21–23; 2 Pet 2:5 [b]2 Pet 3:6 [c]Luke 16:22 **6:18** [a]Gen 8:20–9:17; 17:7 [b]Gen 7:1, 7, 13; 1 Pet 3:20; 2 Pet 2:5 **6:19** [a]Gen 7:2, 8, 9, 14–16 **6:20** [a]Gen 7:9, 15 **6:22** [a]Gen 7:5; 12:4–5; Heb 11:7 [b][1 John 5:3]

7 The [a]LORD said to Noah, "[b]Come into the ark, [c]you and all your household, for I consider you godly among this generation. [2]You must take with you seven pairs of every kind of [a]clean animal, the male and its mate, [b]two of every kind of unclean animal, the male and its mate, [3]and also seven pairs of every kind of bird in the sky, male and female, to preserve their offspring on the face of the entire earth. [4]For in [a]seven days I will cause it to rain on the earth for [b]40 days and 40 nights, and I will wipe from the face of the ground every living thing that I have made."

[5]And Noah did all that the LORD [a]commanded him.

[6]Noah was [a]600 years old when the floodwaters engulfed the earth. [7]Noah entered the ark along with his [a]sons, his wife, and his sons' wives because of the floodwaters. [8]Pairs of clean animals, of unclean animals, of birds, and of everything that creeps along the ground, [9]male and female, came into the ark to Noah, just as God had commanded him. [10]And after seven days the floodwaters engulfed the earth.

[11]In the six hundredth year of Noah's life, in the second month, on the seventeenth day of the month—on [a]that day all [b]the fountains of the great deep burst open and the [c]floodgates of the heavens were opened. [12]And the rain fell on the earth 40 days [a]and 40 nights.

[13]On that very day Noah entered the ark, accompanied by his sons Shem, Ham, and Japheth, along with his wife and his sons' three wives. [14a]They entered, along with every living creature after its kind, every animal after its kind, every creeping thing that creeps on the earth after its kind, and every bird after its kind, everything with [b]wings. [15]Pairs of all creatures that have the breath of life [a]came into the ark to Noah. [16]Those that entered were male and female, just [a]as God commanded him. Then the LORD shut him in.

[17]The flood [a]engulfed the earth for 40 days.

As the waters increased, they lifted the ark and raised it above the earth. [18]The waters completely overwhelmed[1] the earth, [a]and the ark floated on the surface of the waters. [19]The waters completely inundated the earth so that even all the high mountains under the entire sky were covered. [20]The waters rose more than 20 feet above the mountains. [21]And all living things that moved on the earth died, including the birds, domestic animals, wild animals, all the creatures that swarm over the earth, [a]and all humankind. [22]Everything on dry land that had the breath[1] of life in its nostrils died. [23]So the LORD destroyed every living thing that was on the surface of the ground, including people, animals, creatures that creep along the ground, and birds of the sky. They were wiped off the earth. Only [a]Noah and those who were with him in the ark survived. [24a]The waters prevailed over the earth for 150 days.

8 But God [a]remembered Noah [b]and all the wild animals and domestic animals that were with him in the ark. God caused a wind to blow over the earth and the waters receded. [2]The fountains of [a]the deep and the floodgates of heaven were [b]closed, and [c]the rain stopped falling from the sky. [3]The waters kept receding steadily from the earth, so that they had gone down by the end [a]of the 150 days. [4]On the seventeenth day of the seventh month, the ark came to rest on one of the mountains of Ararat.[1] [5]The waters kept on receding until the tenth month. On the first day of the tenth month, the tops of the mountains became visible.

[6]At [a]the end of 40 days, Noah opened the window he had made in the ark [7]and sent out a raven; it kept flying back and forth until the waters had dried up on the earth.

[8]Then Noah sent out a dove to see if the waters had receded from the surface of the ground. [9]The dove could not find a resting place for its feet because water still covered the surface of the entire earth, and so it

7:1 [a] Matt 11:28   [b] Matt 24:38; Luke 17:26; Heb 11:7; 1 Pet 3:20; 2 Pet 2:5   [c] Gen 6:9; Ps 33:18; Prov 10:9; 2 Pet 2:9   7:2 [a] Lev 11; Deut 14:3–20   [b] Lev 10:10; Ezek 44:23   7:4 [a] Gen 7:10; Exod 7:25   [b] Gen 7:12, 17   7:5 [a] Gen 6:22   7:6 [a] Gen 5:4, 32   7:7 [a] Gen 6:18; 7:1, 13; Matt 24:38; Luke 17:27   7:11 [a] Matt 24:39; Luke 17:27; 2 Pet 2:5; 3:6   [b] Gen 8:2; Prov 8:28; Isa 51:10; Ezek 26:19   [c] Gen 8:2; Ps 78:23   7:12 [a] Gen 7:4, 17; 1 Sam 12:18   7:14 [a] Gen 6:19   [b] Gen 1:21   7:15 [a] Gen 6:19–20; 7:9   7:16 [a] Gen 7:2–3   7:17 [a] Gen 7:4, 12; 8:6   7:18 [a] Ps 104:26   [1] Heb. *and the waters were great and multiplied exceedingly.*   7:21 [a] Gen 6:7, 13, 17; 7:4   7:22 [1] MT *breath of the breath/spirit of life.*   7:23 [a] Matt 24:38–39; Luke 17:26–27; Heb 11:7; 1 Pet 3:20; 2 Pet 2:5   7:24 [a] Gen 8:3–4   8:1 [a] Gen 19:29; Exod 2:24; 1 Sam 1:19; Ps 105:42; 106:4   [b] Exod 14:21; 15:10; Job 12:15; Ps 29:10; Isa 44:27; Nah 1:4   8:2 [a] Gen 7:11   [b] Deut 11:17   [c] Gen 7:4, 12; Job 38:37   8:3 [a] Gen 7:24   8:4 [1] Heb. *on the mountains of Ararat.*   8:6 [a] Gen 6:16

returned to Noah in the ark. He stretched out his hand, took the dove, and brought it back into the ark. [10]He waited seven more days and then sent out the dove again from the ark. [11]When the dove returned to him in the evening, there was a freshly plucked olive leaf in its beak! Noah knew that the waters had receded from the earth. [12]He waited another seven days and sent the dove out again, but it did not return to him this time.

[13]In Noah's six hundred and first year, in the first day of the first month, the waters had dried up from the earth, and Noah removed the covering from the ark and saw that the surface of the ground was dry. [14]And by the twenty-seventh day of the second month the earth was dry.

[15]Then God spoke to Noah and said, [16]"Come out of the ark, [a]you, your wife, your sons, and your sons' wives with you. [17]Bring out with you all the living creatures that are with you. Bring out every living thing, including the birds, animals, and every creeping thing that creeps on the earth. Let them increase and [a]be fruitful and multiply on the earth!"

[18]Noah went out along with his sons, his wife, and his sons' wives. [19]Every living creature, every creeping thing, every bird, and everything that moves on the earth went out of the ark in their groups.

[20]Noah built an [a]altar to the Lord. He then took some of every kind [b]of clean animal and clean bird and offered [c]burnt offerings on the altar. [21]And the Lord smelled the soothing [a]aroma and said to himself, "I will never again [b]curse the ground because of humankind, even though the [c]inclination of their minds is evil from childhood on. I will [d]never again destroy everything that lives, as I have just done.

[22] "While the earth continues to [a]exist,
    planting time[1] and harvest,
    cold and heat,
    summer and winter,
    and [b]day and night will not cease."

God's Covenant with Humankind through Noah

9 Then God blessed Noah and his sons and said to them, "[a]Be fruitful and multiply and fill the earth. [2]Every living creature of the earth [a]and every bird of the sky will be terrified of you. Everything that creeps on the ground and all the fish of the sea are under your authority.[1] [3]You may eat [a]any moving thing that lives. As I gave you the [b]green plants, I now give you everything.

[4]"[a]But you must not eat meat with its life (that is, its blood) in it. [5]For your lifeblood I will surely exact punishment, [a]from every living creature I will exact punishment. [b]From each person I will exact punishment for the life of the individual since the [c]man was his relative.[1]

[6] "Whoever [a]sheds human blood,
    by other humans[1]
    must his blood be shed;
    [b]for in God's image
    God has made humankind.

[7]"But as for you, [a]be fruitful and multiply; increase abundantly on the earth and multiply on it."

[8]God said to Noah and his sons, [9]"Look. I now confirm [a]my covenant with you and your descendants after you [10]and with every living creature that is with you, including the birds, the domestic animals, [a]and every living creature of the earth with you, all those that came out of the ark with you—every living creature of the earth. [11]I [a]confirm my covenant with you: Never again will all living things be wiped out by the waters of a flood; never again will a flood destroy the earth."

[12]And God said, "[a]This is the guarantee of the covenant I am making with you and every living creature with you, a covenant for all subsequent[1] generations: [13]I will place [a]my rainbow in the clouds, and it will become a guarantee of the covenant between

8:16 [a]Gen 7:13   8:17 [a]Gen 1:22, 28; 9:1, 7   8:20 [a]Gen 12:7; Exod 29:18, 25   [b]Gen 7:2; Lev 11   [c]Gen 22:2; Exod 10:25   8:21 [a]Exod 29:18, 25; Lev 1:9; Ezek 20:41; 2 Cor 2:15; Eph 5:2   [b]Gen 3:17; 6:7, 13, 17; Isa 54:9   [c]Gen 6:5; 11:6; Job 14:4; Ps 51:5; Jer 17:9; Rom 1:21; 3:23; Eph 2:1–3   [d]Gen 9:11, 15   8:22 [a]Isa 54:9   [b]Ps 74:16; Jer 33:20, 25   [1]Heb. seed.   9:1 [a]Gen 1:28–29; 8:17; 9:7, 19; 10:32   9:2 [a]Gen 1:26, 28; Ps 8:6   [1]Heb. into your hand are given; signifies power or authority.   9:3 [a]Deut 12:15; 14:3, 9, 11; Acts 10:12–13   [b]Gen 1:29   9:4 [a]Lev 7:26; 17:10–16; 19:26; Deut 12:16, 23; 15:23; 1 Sam 14:33–34; Acts 15:20, 29   9:5 [a]Exod 21:28   [b]Gen 4:9–10; Ps 9:12   [c]Acts 17:26   [1]Heb. from the hand of a man, his brother.   9:6 [a]Exod 21:12–14; Lev 24:17; Num 35:33; Matt 26:52   [b]Gen 1:26–27   [1]Heb. by man; a generic term for other human beings.   9:7 [a]Gen 9:1, 19   9:9 [a]Isa 54:9   9:10 [a]Ps 145:9   9:11 [a]Gen 8:21; Isa 54:9   9:12 [a]Gen 9:13, 17; 17:11   [1]Heb. ever, forever, lasting, perpetual.   9:13 [a]Ezek 1:28; Rev 4:3

me and the earth. [14]Whenever I bring clouds over the earth and the rainbow appears in the clouds, [15]then [a]I will remember my covenant with you and with all living creatures of all kinds. Never again will the waters become a flood and destroy all living things. [16]When [a]the rainbow is in the clouds, I will notice it and remember the perpetual covenant between God and all living creatures of all kinds that are on the earth." [17]So God said to Noah, "This is the guarantee of the covenant that I am confirming between me and all living things that are on the earth."

The Curse on Canaan

[18]The sons of Noah who came out of the ark were Shem, Ham, [a]and Japheth. (Now Ham was the father of Canaan.) [19]These were [a]the three sons of Noah, [b]and from them the whole earth was populated.

[20]Noah, [a]a man of the soil, began to plant a vineyard. [21]When he drank some of the wine, he got drunk [a]and uncovered himself inside his tent. [22]Ham, the father of Canaan, saw his father's nakedness[1] and told his two brothers who were outside. [23a]Shem and Japheth took the garment and placed it on their shoulders. Then they walked in backwards and covered up their father's nakedness. Their faces were turned the other way so they did not see their father's nakedness. [24]When Noah awoke from his drunken stupor he learned what his youngest son had done to him. [25]So he said,

> "[a]Cursed be Canaan!
> The [b]lowest of slaves[1]
> he will be to his brothers."

[26]He also said,

> "Worthy of [a]praise is the LORD, the
> God of Shem!
> May Canaan be the slave of Shem!
> [27] May God [a]enlarge Japheth's territory
> [b]and numbers!

> May he live in the tents of Shem
> and may Canaan be the slave of
> Japheth!"

[28]After the flood Noah lived 350 years. [29]The entire lifetime of Noah was 950 years, and then he died.

The Table of Nations

10 This is the account of Noah's sons: Shem, Ham, [a]and Japheth. Sons were born to them after the flood.

[2a]The sons of Japheth were Gomer, Magog, Madai, Javan, Tubal, Meshech, and Tiras. [3]The sons of Gomer were Ashkenaz, Riphath, and Togarmah. [4]The sons of Javan were Elishah, Tarshish, the Kittim, and the Dodanim. [5]From [a]these the coastlands of the nations were separated into their lands, every one according to its language, according to their families, by their nations.

[6a]The sons of Ham were Cush, Mizraim, Put, and Canaan. [7]The sons of Cush were Seba, Havilah, Sabtah, Raamah, and Sabteca. The sons of Raamah were Sheba and Dedan.

[8]Cush was the father of [a]Nimrod; he began to be a valiant warrior on the earth. [9]He was a mighty [a]hunter [b]before the LORD. (That is why it is said, "Like Nimrod, a mighty hunter before the LORD.") [10a]The primary regions of his kingdom were [b]Babel, Erech, Akkad, and Calneh in the land of Shinar. [11]From that land he went [a]to Assyria, where he built Nineveh, Rehoboth Ir, Calah, [12]and Resen, which is between Nineveh and the great city Calah.

[13]Mizraim was the father of the Ludites, Anamites, Lehabites, Naphtuhites, [14]Pathrusites, Casluhites ([a]from whom the Philistines came), and Caphtorites.

[15]Canaan was the father of Sidon his firstborn, [a]Heth,[1] [16a]the Jebusites, Amorites, Girgashites, [17]Hivites, Arkites, Sinites, [18]Arvadites, Zemarites, and Hamathites. Eventually the families of the Canaanites were scattered [19]and the borders of Canaan

---

9:15 [a]Lev 26:42, 45; Deut 7:9; Ezek 16:60   **9:16** [a]Gen 17:13, 19; 2 Sam 23:5; Isa 55:3; Jer 32:40; Heb 13:20   **9:18** [a]Gen 9:25–27; 10:6   **9:19** [a]Gen 5:32   [b]Gen 9:1, 7; 10:32; 1 Chr 1:4   **9:20** [a]Gen 3:19, 23; 4:2; Prov 12:11; Jer 31:24   **9:21** [a]Prov 20:1; Eph 5:18   **9:22** [1]Or *had sexual relations with*; understanding that Ham committed a homosexual act with his drunken father, but v. 23 clearly indicates it is to be understood as visual observation.   **9:23** [a]Exod 20:12; Gal 6:1   **9:25** [a]Deut 27:16; Josh 9:23, 27   [b]Josh 9:23; 1 Kgs 9:20–21   [1]Heb. *a servant of servants*.   **9:26** [a]Gen 14:20; 24:27; Ps 144:15; Heb 11:16   **9:27** [a]Gen 10:2–5; 39:3; Isa 66:19   [b]Luke 3:36; John 1:14; Eph 2:13–14; 3:6   **10:1** [a]Gen 9:1, 7, 19   **10:2** [a]1 Chr 1:5–7   **10:5** [a]Gen 11:8; Ps 72:10; Jer 2:10; 25:22   **10:6** [a]1 Chr 1:8–16   **10:8** [a]Mic 5:6   **10:9** [a]Jer 16:16; Mic 7:2   [b]Gen 21:20   **10:10** [a]Mic 5:6   [b]Gen 11:9   **10:11** [a]Gen 25:18; 2 Kgs 19:36; Mic 5:6   **10:14** [a]1 Chr 1:12   **10:15** [a]Gen 23:3   [1]Some see a reference to Hittites here.   **10:16** [a]Gen 14:7; 15:19–21; Deut 7:1; Neh 9:8

extended from Sidon all the way to Gerar as far as Gaza, [a]and all the way to Sodom, Gomorrah, Admah, and Zeboyim, as far as Lasha. [20]These are the sons of Ham, according to their families, according to their languages, by their lands, and by their nations.

[21]And sons were also born to Shem (the older brother of Japheth), the father of all the sons of Eber.

[22]The [a]sons of Shem were Elam, Asshur, [b]Arphaxad, Lud, and Aram. [23]The sons of Aram were Uz, Hul, Gether, and Mash.[1] [24]Arphaxad was the father of [a]Shelah,[1] and Shelah was the father of Eber. [25]Two sons were born [a]to Eber: One was named Peleg because in his days the earth was divided, and his brother's name was Joktan. [26]Joktan was the father of Almodad, Sheleph, Hazarmaveth, Jerah, [27]Hadoram, Uzal, Diklah, [28]Obal, Abimael, Sheba, [29]Ophir, Havilah, and Jobab. All these were sons of Joktan. [30]Their dwelling place was from Mesha all the way to Sephar in the eastern hills. [31]These are the sons of Shem according to their families, according to their languages, by their lands, and according to their nations.

[32]These are [a]the families of the sons of Noah, according to their genealogies, by their nations, [b]and from these the nations spread over the earth after the flood.

The Dispersion of the Nations at Babel

11 The whole earth had a common language and a common vocabulary. [2]When the people moved eastward, they found a plain in Shinar and settled there. [3]Then they said to one another, "Come, let's make bricks and bake them thoroughly." (They had brick instead of stone and tar instead of mortar.) [4]Then they said, "Come, let's build ourselves a city and a tower with its top in the heavens so that we may make a [a]name for ourselves. Otherwise we will [b]be scattered across the face of the entire earth."

[5a]But the LORD came down to see the city and the tower that the people had started building. [6]And [a]the LORD said, "If as [b]one people all sharing a common language they have begun to do this, then nothing they [c]plan to do will be beyond them. [7]Come, [a]let's go down and [b]confuse their language so they won't be able to understand each other."

[8]So [a]the LORD scattered them from there [b]across the face of the entire earth, and they stopped building the city. [9]That is why its name was called Babel—[a]because there the LORD confused the language of the entire world, and from there the LORD scattered them across the face of the entire earth.

The Genealogy of Shem

[10]This [a]is the account of Shem.

Shem was 100 years old when he became the father of Arphaxad, two years after the flood. [11]And after becoming the father of Arphaxad, Shem lived 500 years and had other sons and daughters.

[12]When Arphaxad had lived 35 years, he became the father of Shelah. [13]And after he became the father of Shelah, Arphaxad lived 403 years and had other sons and daughters.[1]

[14]When Shelah had lived 30 years, he became the father of Eber. [15]And after he became the father of Eber, Shelah lived 403 years and had other sons and daughters.

[16]When [a]Eber had lived 34 years, he became the father of [b]Peleg. [17]And after he became the father of Peleg, Eber lived 430 years and had other sons and daughters.

[18]When Peleg had lived 30 years, he became the father of Reu. [19]And after he became the father of Reu, Peleg lived 209 years and had other sons and daughters.

[20]When Reu had lived 32 years, he became the father of [a]Serug. [21]And after he became the father of Serug, Reu lived 207 years and had other sons and daughters.

[22]When Serug had lived 30 years, he became the father of Nahor. [23]And after he became the father of Nahor, Serug lived 200 years and had other sons and daughters.

[24]When Nahor had lived 29 years, he

10:19 [a] Gen 13:12, 14, 15, 17; 15:18–21; Num 34:2–12   10:22 [a] Gen 11:10–26; 1 Chr 1:17–28   [b] Gen 10:24; 11:10; Luke 3:36   10:23 [1] LXX *Meshech*.   10:24 [a] Gen 11:12; Luke 3:35   [1] LXX *Arphaxad fathered Cainan, and Cainan fathered Sala* [= Shelah].   10:25 [a] 1 Chr 1:19   10:32 [a] Gen 10:1   [b] Gen 9:19; 11:8   11:4 [a] Gen 6:4; 2 Sam 8:13   [b] Deut 4:27   11:5 [a] Gen 18:21; Exod 3:8; 19:11, 18, 20   11:6 [a] Gen 9:19; Acts 17:26   [b] Gen 11:1   [c] Deut 31:21; Ps 2:1   11:7 [a] Gen 1:26   [b] Gen 42:23; Exod 4:11; Deut 28:49; Isa 33:19; Jer 5:15   11:8 [a] Gen 11:4; Deut 32:8; Ps 92:9; [Luke 1:51]   [b] Gen 10:25, 32   11:9 [a] 1 Cor 14:23   11:10 [a] Gen 10:22–25; 1 Chr 1:17   11:13 [1] LXX *And* [= when] *Arphaxad had lived 35 years,* [and] *he fathered* [= became the father of] *Cainan. And after he fathered* [= became the father of] *Cainan, Arphaxad lived 430 years and fathered* [= had] [other] *sons and daughters, and* [then] *he died. And* [= when] *Cainan had lived 130 years,* [and] *he fathered* [= became the father of] *Sala* [= Shelah]. *And after he fathered* [= became the father of] *Sala* [= Shelah], *Cainan lived 330 years and fathered* [= had] [other] *sons and daughters, and* [then] *he died.*   11:16 [a] 1 Chr 1:19   [b] Luke 3:35   11:20 [a] Luke 3:35

became the father of ªTerah. ²⁵And after he became the father of Terah, Nahor lived 119 years and had other sons and daughters. ²⁶When Terah had lived 70 years, he became the father ªof Abram, Nahor, and Haran.

The Record of Terah

²⁷This is the account of Terah.

Terah became the father of ªAbram, Nahor, and Haran. And Haran became the father of Lot. ²⁸Haran died in the land of his birth, in Ur of the Chaldeans, while his father Terah was still alive. ²⁹And Abram and Nahor took wives for themselves. The name of Abram's wife was ªSarai. And the name of Nahor's wife was ^bMilcah; she was the daughter of Haran, who was the father of both Milcah and Iscah. ³⁰But ªSarai was barren; she had no children.

³¹Terah ªtook his son Abram, his grandson Lot (the son of Haran), and his daughter-in-law Sarai, his son Abram's wife, and with them he set out from ^bUr of ^cthe Chaldeans to go to Canaan. When they came to Haran, they settled there. ³²The lifetime of Terah was 205 years, and he died in Haran.

The Obedience of Abram

12 Now the ªLORD said to Abram,¹

"Go ^bout from your country, your
relatives, and your father's
household
to the land that I will show you.
² Then ªI ^bwill make you into ^ca great
nation, and I will bless you,
and I will make your name great,¹
so that you will exemplify divine
blessing.
³ I ªwill bless those who bless ^byou,
but the one who treats you lightly I
must curse,
so that all the families of the earth
may receive ^cblessing¹ through
you."

⁴So Abram left, just as the LORD had told him to do, and Lot went with him. (Now Abram was 75 years old when he departed from Haran.) ⁵And Abram took his wife Sarai, his nephew Lot, and all ªthe possessions they had accumulated and the people they had acquired ^bin Haran, and they left for the land of Canaan. They entered the land of Canaan.

⁶Abram ªtraveled through the land ^bas far as the oak tree of Moreh at Shechem. (At that time the Canaanites were in the ^cland.) ⁷ªThe LORD appeared ^bto Abram and said, "To your descendants I will give this land." So Abram built an ^caltar there to the LORD, who had appeared to him.

⁸Then he moved from there to the hill country east of Bethel and pitched his tent, with Bethel on the west and Ai on the east. There he built an altar to the LORD and ªworshiped the LORD.¹ ⁹Abram ªcontinually journeyed by stages down to the Negev.

The Promised Blessing Jeopardized

¹⁰There ªwas a famine in the land, so Abram ^bwent down to Egypt to stay for a while¹ because the famine was ^csevere. ¹¹As he ªapproached Egypt, he said to his wife Sarai, "Look, I know that you are a beautiful woman. ¹²When the Egyptians see you they ªwill say, 'This is his wife.' Then they will kill me but will keep you alive. ¹³ªSo tell them you are my ^bsister so that it may go well for me because of you and my life will be spared on account of you."

¹⁴When Abram entered Egypt, the Egyptians saw that the woman was very beautiful. ¹⁵When Pharaoh's officials saw her, they praised her to Pharaoh. So Abram's wife was taken into the household of Pharaoh, ¹⁶and he did ªtreat Abram well on account of her. Abram received sheep and cattle, male donkeys, male servants, female servants, female donkeys, and camels.

¹⁷But the LORD ªstruck Pharaoh and his household with severe diseases because

11:24 ªGen 11:31; Josh 24:2; Luke 3:34　**11:26** ªJosh 24:2; 1 Chr 1:26　**11:27** ªGen 11:31; 17:5　**11:29** ªGen 17:15; 20:12　^bGen 22:20, 23; 24:15　**11:30** ªGen 16:1–2; Luke 1:36　**11:31** ªGen 12:1　^bGen 15:7; Neh 9:7; Acts 7:4　^cGen 10:19　**12:1** ªGen 15:7; Acts 7:2–3; [Heb 11:8]　^bGen 13:9　¹The Heb. verb indicates purpose or consequence, i.e., *that I may* or *then I will*. **12:2** ª[Gen 17:4–6]; 18:18; 46:3; Deut 26:5; 1 Kgs 3:8　^bGen 22:17; 24:35　^cGen 28:4; Zech 8:13; Gal 3:14　¹Or *I will make you famous.* **12:3** ªGen 24:35; 27:29; Exod 23:22; Num 24:9　^bGen 18:18; 22:18; 26:4; 28:14; Ps 72:17; Matt 1:1; Luke 3:34; Acts 3:25; [Gal 3:8]　^cIsa 41:27　¹Heb. *they may consider themselves blessed through you, they may find/receive blessing through you.* **12:5** ªGen 14:14　^bGen 11:31　**12:6** ªHeb 11:9　^bDeut 11:30; Judg 7:1　^cGen 10:18–19　**12:7** ªGen 17:1; 18:1　^bGen 13:15; 15:18; 17:8; Deut 34:4; Ps 105:9–12; Acts 7:5; Gal 3:16　^cGen 13:4, 18; 22:9　**12:8** ªGen 4:26; 13:4; 21:33　¹Heb. *he called in the name of the LORD.* **12:9** ªGen 13:1, 3; 20:1; 24:62　**12:10** ªGen 26:1　^bPs 105:13　^cGen 43:1　¹Trad. *to sojourn.* **12:11** ªGen 12:14; 26:7; 29:17　**12:12** ªGen 20:11; 26:7　**12:13** ªGen 20:1–18; 26:6–11　^bGen 20:12　**12:16** ªGen 20:14　**12:17** ªGen 20:18; 1 Chr 16:21; [Ps 105:14]

of Sarai, Abram's wife. [18] So Pharaoh summoned Abram and said, "[a]What is this you have done to me? Why didn't you tell me that she was your wife? [19] Why did you say, 'She is my sister,' so that I took her to be my wife? Now, here is your wife. Take her and go!" [20] Pharaoh gave his men orders about Abram, and [a]so they expelled him, along with his wife and all his possessions.

Abram's Solution to the Strife

13 So Abram went up from Egypt into the Negev. He took his wife and all his possessions with him, as well as [a]Lot. [2] (Now [a]Abram was very wealthy in livestock, silver, and gold.)

[3] And he journeyed [a]from place to place from the Negev as far as Bethel. He returned to the place where he had pitched his tent at the beginning, between Bethel and Ai. [4] This was the [a]place where he had first built the altar, and there Abram [b]worshiped the LORD.

[5] Now Lot, who was traveling with Abram, also had flocks, herds, and tents. [6] But [a]the land could not support them while they were living side by side. Because their possessions were so great, they were not able to live alongside one another. [7] So there were [a]quarrels[1] between Abram's herdsmen and Lot's herdsmen. (Now [b]the Canaanites and the Perizzites were living in the land at that time.)

[8] Abram said to Lot, "[a]Let there be no quarreling between me and you, and between my herdsmen and your herdsmen, for we are close relatives. [9a] Is not the whole land before you? [b]Separate yourself now from me. [c]If you go to the left, then I'll go to the right, but if you go to the right, then I'll go to the left."

[10] Lot looked up and saw [a]the whole region of the Jordan. He noticed that all of it was well watered (this was before the LORD [b]obliterated Sodom and Gomorrah) [c]like the garden of the LORD, like the land of Egypt, all the way to [d]Zoar. [11] Lot chose for himself the whole region of the Jordan and traveled toward the east.

So the relatives separated from each other. [12] Abram [a]settled in the land of Canaan, but Lot settled among the cities of the Jordan plain and [b]pitched his tents next to Sodom. [13] (Now the people of Sodom [a]were extremely wicked [b]rebels against the LORD.)[1]

[14] After Lot [a]had departed, the LORD said to Abram, "Look from the place where you stand to the [b]north, south, east, and west. [15] I [a]will give all the land that [b]you see to you and your descendants forever. [16] And [a]I will make your descendants like the dust of the earth, so that if anyone is able to count the dust of the earth, then your descendants also can be counted. [17] Get up and walk[1] throughout the land, for I will give it to you."

[18a] So Abram moved his tents and went to [b]live by the oaks[1] of Mamre in Hebron, and he built an [c]altar to the LORD there.

The Blessing of Victory for God's People

14 At that time Amraphel king [a]of Shinar, Arioch king of Ellasar, Kedorlaomer king of [b]Elam, and Tidal king of nations [2] went to war against Bera king of Sodom, Birsha king of Gomorrah, Shinab king of [a]Admah, Shemeber king of Zeboyim, and the king of Bela (that is, [b]Zoar). [3] These last five kings joined forces[1] in the Valley of Siddim ([a]that is, the Salt Sea). [4] For twelve years [a]they had served Kedorlaomer, but in the thirteenth year they rebelled. [5] In [a]the fourteenth year, Kedorlaomer and [b]the kings who were his allies came and defeated [c]the Rephaites in Ashteroth Karnaim, the Zuzites in Ham, the Emites in Shaveh Kiriathaim, [6a] and the Horites in their hill country of Seir, as far as El Paran, which is near the desert. [7] Then they attacked En Mishpat (that is, Kadesh) [a]again, and they conquered all the territory of the Amalekites, as well as the Amorites who were living in Hazezon Tamar.

[8] Then the king of Sodom, the king of Gomorrah, the king of Admah, the king of

12:18 [a] Gen 20:9–10; 26:10   **12:20** [a] [Prov 21:1]   **13:1** [a] Gen 12:4; 14:12, 16   **13:2** [a] Gen 24:35; 26:14; Ps 112:3; Prov 10:22   **13:3** [a] Gen 12:8–9   **13:4** [a] Gen 12:7–8; 21:33   [b] Ps 116:17   **13:6** [a] Gen 36:7   **13:7** [a] Gen 26:20   [b] Gen 12:6; 15:20–21   [1] Heb. *strife, conflict, quarreling*; later *legal controversy, dispute.*   **13:8** [a] 1 Cor 6:7; [Phil 2:14–15]   **13:9** [a] Gen 20:15; 34:10   [b] Gen 13:11, 14   [c] [Rom 12:18]   **13:10** [a] Gen 19:17–29; Deut 34:3   [b] Gen 19:24   [c] Gen 2:8, 10; Isa 51:3   [d] Gen 14:2, 8; 19:22; Deut 34:3   **13:12** [a] Gen 19:24–25, 29   [b] Gen 14:12; 19:1   **13:13** [a] Gen 18:20–21; Ezek 16:49; 2 Pet 2:7–8   [b] Gen 6:11; 39:9; Num 32:23   [1] Heb. *wicked and sinners against the LORD exceedingly.*   **13:14** [a] Gen 13:11   [b] Gen 28:14   **13:15** [a] Gen 12:7; 13:17; 15:7, 18; 17:8; Deut 34:4; Acts 7:5   [b] 2 Chr 20:7; Ps 37:22   **13:16** [a] Gen 22:17; Exod 32:13; Num 23:10   **13:17** [1] Heb. *to walk about.*   **13:18** [a] Gen 26:17   [b] Gen 14:13   [c] Gen 8:20; 22:8–9   [1] Or *terebinths.*   **14:1** [a] Gen 10:10; 11:2   [b] Isa 11:11; 21:2; Dan 8:2   **14:2** [a] Gen 10:19; Deut 29:23   [b] Gen 13:10; 19:22   **14:3** [a] Num 34:12; Deut 3:17; Josh 3:16   [1] Heb. *to join together, to unite, to be allied.*   **14:4** [a] Gen 9:26   **14:5** [a] Gen 15:20   [b] Deut 2:20   [c] Num 32:37; Deut 2:10   **14:6** [a] Gen 36:20; Deut 2:12, 22   **14:7** [a] 2 Chr 20:2

Zeboyim, and the king of Bela (that is, Zoar) went out and prepared for battle. In the Valley of Siddim they met [9]Kedorlaomer king of Elam, Tidal king of nations, Amraphel king of Shinar, and Arioch king of Ellasar. Four kings fought against five. [10]Now the Valley of Siddim was full of [a]tar pits. When the kings of Sodom and Gomorrah fled, they fell [b]into them, but some survivors fled to the hills. [11]The four victorious kings took [a]all the possessions and food of Sodom and Gomorrah and left. [12]They also took Abram's [a]nephew Lot and his possessions when they left, for Lot was living in Sodom.

[13]A fugitive came and told Abram the [a]Hebrew. Now Abram was living by [b]the oaks[1] of Mamre the Amorite, the brother of Eshcol [c]and Aner. (All these were allied by treaty with Abram.) [14]When Abram heard that his nephew had been taken captive, [a]he mobilized [b]his 318 trained men who had been [c]born in his household, and he pursued the invaders [d]as far as Dan. [15]Then, during the night, Abram divided his forces against them and [a]defeated them. He chased them as far as Hobah, which is north of Damascus. [16]He retrieved all the stolen property. He also [a]brought back his nephew Lot and his possessions, as well as the women and the rest of the people.

[17a]After Abram returned from defeating Kedorlaomer and the kings who were with him, the king of Sodom [b]went out to meet Abram in the Valley of Shaveh (known as the [c]King's Valley). [18a]Melchizedek king of Salem brought out [b]bread and wine. (Now [c]he was the priest of the Most High [d]God.) [19]He [a]blessed Abram, saying,

"Blessed be Abram by the Most High
  God,
  [b]Creator of heaven and earth.
[20] Worthy of [a]praise is the Most High
  God,
  who delivered your enemies into
  your hand."

Abram [b]gave Melchizedek a tenth of everything.

[21]Then the king of Sodom said to Abram, "Give me the people and take the possessions for yourself." [22]But Abram [a]replied to [b]the king of Sodom, "I raise my hand[1] to the Lord, the Most High God, Creator of heaven and earth, and vow [23]that [a]I will take nothing[1] belonging to you, not even a thread or the strap of a sandal. That way you can never say, 'It is I who made Abram rich.' [24]I will take nothing except compensation for what the young men have eaten. As for the share of the men who went with me—Aner, Eshcol, and Mamre—let them take their share."

The Cutting of the Covenant

15 After these [a]things the Lord's message came to Abram in a vision: "Fear not, Abram! I am your [b]shield and the one who will reward you in great [c]abundance."[1]

[2a]But Abram said, "O Sovereign Lord, what will you give me since [b]I continue to be childless, and my heir is Eliezer of Damascus?" [3]Abram added, "Since you have not given me a descendant, then look, [a]one born in my house will be my heir!"

[4]But look, the Lord's message came to him: "This man [a]will not be your heir, but instead[1] a son who comes from your own body will be your heir." [5]The Lord took him outside and said, "Gaze into the sky and [a]count the [b]stars—if you are able to count them!" Then he said to him, "[c]So will your [d]descendants be."

[6]Abram [a]believed the Lord, and the Lord [b]credited it[1] as righteousness to him.

[7]The Lord said to him, "I am the Lord who [a]brought you out from [b]Ur of the Chaldeans [c]to give you this land to possess." [8]But Abram said, "O Sovereign Lord, by [a]what can I know that I am to possess it?" [9]The Lord said to him, "Take for me a heifer, a goat, and a ram, each three years old, along with a dove and a young pigeon."

14:10 [a]Gen 11:3 [b]Gen 19:17, 30 14:11 [a]Gen 14:16, 21 14:12 [a]Gen 11:27; 12:5 14:13 [a]Gen 39:14; 40:15 [b]Gen 13:18 [c]Gen 14:24; 21:27, 32 [1]Or *terebinths.* 14:14 [a]Gen 19:29 [b]Gen 13:8; 14:12 [c]Gen 12:5; 15:3; 17:27; Eccl 2:7 [d]Deut 34:1; Judg 18:29; 1 Kgs 15:20 14:15 [a]Isa 41:2–3 14:16 [a]Gen 31:18; 1 Sam 30:8, 18, 19 14:17 [a]Heb 7:1 [b]1 Sam 18:6 [c]2 Sam 18:18 14:18 [a]Ps 110:4; Heb 7:1–10 [b]Gen 18:5; Exod 29:40; Ps 104:15 [c]Ps 110:4; Heb 5:6 [d]Acts 16:17 14:19 [a]Ruth 3:10 [b]Gen 14:22; Matt 11:25 14:20 [a]Gen 24:27 [b]Gen 28:22; Heb 7:4 14:22 [a]Gen 14:2, 8, 10 [b]Gen 14:19 [1]Heb. *Here and now I raise my hand.* 14:23 [a]2 Kgs 5:16; Esth 9:15–16 [1]Heb. [May the Lord deal with me] *if I take.* 15:1 [a]Gen 15:4; 46:2; 1 Sam 15:10; Dan 10:1 [b]Deut 33:29; Ps 3:3; 84:11; 91:4 [c]Num 18:20; Ps 58:11; Prov 11:18 [1]Smr. *I will make* [your reward very] *great.* 15:2 [a]Gen 17:18 [b]Acts 7:5 15:3 [a]Gen 14:14 15:4 [a]2 Sam 7:12; Gal 4:28 [1]A very strong adversative. 15:5 [a]Gen 22:17; 26:4; Deut 1:10; Ps 147:4 [b]Jer 33:22 [c]Exod 32:13; Rom 4:18; Heb 11:12 [d]Gen 17:19 15:6 [a]Gen 21:1; Rom 4:3, 9, 22; Gal 3:6; Jas 2:23 [b]Ps 32:2; 106:31 [1]Heb. *and he imputed it*; refers to Abram's act of faith. 15:7 [a]Gen 12:1 [b]Gen 11:28, 31 [c]Gen 13:15, 17; Ps 105:42, 44 15:8 [a]Gen 24:13–14; Judg 6:36–40; 1 Sam 14:9–10; Luke 1:18

[10] So Abram took all these for him and then [a] cut [b] them in two and placed each half opposite the other, but he did not cut the birds in half. [11] When birds of prey came down on the carcasses, Abram drove them away. [12] When the sun went down, [a] Abram fell sound asleep, and great terror overwhelmed him. [13] Then the LORD said to Abram, "Know for certain [a] that your descendants will be strangers in a foreign country. [b] They will be enslaved and oppressed for 400 years. [14] But [a] I will execute judgment on [b] the nation that they will serve. Afterward they will come out with many possessions. [15] But as for [a] you, you will go [b] to [c] your ancestors in peace and be buried at a good old age. [16] In the fourth generation your descendants will return here, for the [a] sin [b] of the Amorites has not yet reached its limit."

[17] When the sun had gone down and it was dark, a smoking firepot with a flaming torch [a] passed between the animal parts. [18] That day the LORD [a] made a covenant with Abram: "[b] To your descendants I give this land, from the river of Egypt to the great river, the Euphrates River— [19] the land of the Kenites, Kenizzites, Kadmonites, [20] Hittites, Perizzites, Rephaites, [21] Amorites, Canaanites, Girgashites, and Jebusites."

The Birth of Ishmael

16 Now Sarai, Abram's wife, [a] had not given birth to [b] any children, but she had an Egyptian servant[1] named [c] Hagar. [2] [a] So Sarai said to Abram, "Since the LORD [b] has prevented me from having children, please [c] sleep with my servant. Perhaps I can have a family by her." Abram [d] did what Sarai told him.

[3] So after Abram [a] had lived in Canaan for ten years, Sarai, Abram's wife, gave Hagar, her Egyptian servant, to her husband to be his wife. [4] He slept with Hagar, and she became pregnant. Once Hagar realized she was pregnant, she [a] despised Sarai.[1] [5] Then Sarai said to Abram, "You have brought this wrong on me! I gave my servant into your embrace, but when she realized that she was pregnant, she despised me. May [a] the LORD judge between you and me!"

[6] Abram said to Sarai, "Since your servant is under your authority, do to her whatever you think best." Then Sarai treated Hagar harshly, [a] so [b] she ran away from Sarai.

[7] The [a] angel of the LORD found Hagar near a spring of water in the wilderness—the spring that is along the road to [b] Shur. [8] He said, "Hagar, servant of Sarai, where have you come from, and where are you going?" She replied, "I'm running away from my mistress, Sarai."

[9] Then the angel of the LORD said to her, "Return to your mistress and [a] submit to her authority. [10] I [a] will greatly multiply your descendants," the angel of the LORD added, "so that they will be too numerous to count." [11] Then the angel of the LORD said to her,

> "You are now pregnant
>   [a] and are about to give birth to a son.
>   You are to name him Ishmael,
>   for the LORD has heard your painful
>   groans.
> [12] He will be a wild donkey of a man.
>   [a] He will be hostile to everyone,
>   [b] and everyone will be hostile to him.
>   He will live away from his brothers."

[13] So Hagar named the LORD [a] who spoke to her, "You are the God who sees me," for she said, "Here I have seen one who sees me!" [14] That is why the well was called Beer Lahai [a] Roi. (It is located [b] between Kadesh and Bered.)

[15] So [a] Hagar gave birth to Abram's son, whom Abram named Ishmael. [16] (Now Abram was eighty-six years old when Hagar gave birth to Ishmael.)

The Sign of the Covenant

17 When Abram was ninety-nine years old, the LORD [a] appeared to [b] him and said, "I am the Sovereign God.[1] [c] Walk before me and be [d] blameless. [2] Then I will confirm

15:10 [a] Gen 15:17; Jer 34:18   [b] Lev 1:17   **15:12** [a] Gen 2:21; 28:11; Job 33:15   **15:13** [a] Exod 1:11; Acts 7:6   [b] Exod 12:40   **15:14** [a] Exod 6:6   [b] Exod 12:36   **15:15** [a] Job 5:26   [b] Gen 25:8; 47:30   [c] Gen 25:8   **15:16** [a] Gen 15:13; Exod 12:41   [b] Gen 48:22; Lev 18:24–28; 1 Kgs 21:26   **15:17** [a] Jer 34:18–19   **15:18** [a] Gen 24:7   [b] Gen 12:7; 17:8; Exod 23:31; Num 34:3; Deut 11:24; Josh 1:4; 21:43; Acts 7:5   **16:1** [a] Gen 11:30; 15:2–3   [b] Gen 12:16; 21:9   [c] Gal 4:24   [1] A menial female servant (also vv. 2, 3, 5–6, 8).   **16:2** [a] Gen 30:3   [b] Gen 20:18   [c] Gen 30:3, 9   [d] Gen 3:17   **16:3** [a] Gen 12:4–5   **16:4** [a] 1 Sam 1:6–7; [Prov 30:21, 23]   [1] Heb. *to despise, to treat lightly, to treat with contempt*; in Hagar's opinion, Sarai had been demoted.   **16:5** [a] Gen 31:53; Exod 5:21   **16:6** [a] 1 Pet 3:7   [b] Gen 16:9; Exod 2:15   **16:7** [a] Gen 21:17–18; 22:11, 15; 31:11   [b] Exod 15:22   **16:9** [a] [Titus 2:9]   **16:10** [a] Gen 17:20   **16:11** [a] Luke 1:13, 31   **16:12** [a] Gen 21:20; Job 24:5; 39:5–8   [b] Gen 25:18   **16:13** [a] Gen 31:42   **16:14** [a] Gen 24:62   [b] Gen 14:7; Num 13:26   **16:15** [a] Gal 4:22   **17:1** [a] Gen 12:7; 18:1   [b] Gen 28:3; 35:11; Exod 6:3; Job 42:2   [c] 2 Kgs 20:3   [d] Gen 6:9; Deut 18:13   [1] Or *God Almighty*; Heb. *El Shaddai*; Jerome translated it *omnipotens* ("all powerful") in the Vg.

my [a]covenant between me and you, and [b]I will give you a multitude of descendants."

[3]Abram bowed down with his face to the ground,[1] and God said to him, [4]"As for me, this is my [a]covenant with you: You will be the father of a multitude of nations. [5]No longer will [a]your name be Abram. Instead, your name will be Abraham because I will make you the father of a multitude of nations. [6]I will make you extremely[1] fruitful. I will make [a]nations of you, and [b]kings will descend from you. [7]I will [a]confirm my covenant as a perpetual covenant between me and you. It will extend [b]to [c]your descendants after you throughout their generations. I will be your God and the God of your descendants after you. [8]I [a]will give the whole land of Canaan—the land where you are now [b]residing[1]—to you and your descendants after you as a permanent [c]possession. I will be their God."

[9]Then God said to Abraham, "As for [a]you, you must keep the covenantal requirement I am imposing on you and your descendants after you throughout their generations. [10]This is my requirement that you and your descendants after you must keep: [a]Every male among you must be circumcised. [11]You must circumcise the flesh of your foreskins. This will be [a]a reminder of the covenant between me and you. [12]Throughout your generations every male among you who is eight days old must be circumcised, whether born in your house or bought with money from any foreigner who is not one of your descendants. [13]They must indeed be circumcised, whether born in your house or bought with money. The sign of my covenant will be visible in your flesh as a permanent reminder. [14]Any uncircumcised male who has not been circumcised in the flesh of his foreskin will be cut off from his people—he has failed to carry out my requirement."

[15]Then God said to Abraham, "As for your wife, you must no longer call her Sarai; Sarah will be her name. [16]I will bless her [a]and will give you a son through her. I will bless her and she will become a mother [b]of nations. [c]Kings of countries will come from her!"

[17]Then Abraham bowed down with his face to the ground [a]and laughed as he said to himself, "Can a son be born to a man who is a hundred years old? Can Sarah bear a child at the age of ninety?" [18]Abraham [a]said to God, "O that Ishmael might live before you!"

[19]God said, "No, [a]Sarah your wife is going to bear you a son, and you will name him Isaac.[1] I will confirm my [b]covenant with him as a perpetual covenant for his descendants after him. [20]As for Ishmael, [a]I have heard you. I will indeed bless him, make him fruitful, and give him a multitude of descendants.[1] He will become the father of [b]twelve princes; I will make him into [c]a great nation. [21]But I will establish my [a]covenant with Isaac, [b]whom Sarah will bear to you at this [c]set time next year." [22]When he finished speaking with Abraham, God went up from him.

[23]Abraham took his son Ishmael and every male in his household (whether born in his house or bought with money) and circumcised them on that very same day, just as God had told him to do. [24]Now Abraham was ninety-nine years old when he was circumcised; [25]his son Ishmael was thirteen years old when he was circumcised. [26]Abraham and his son Ishmael were circumcised on the very same day. [27][a]All the men of his household, whether born in his household or bought with money from a foreigner, were circumcised with him.

Three Special Visitors

18 The LORD appeared to Abraham by the [a]oaks of Mamre while he was sitting at the entrance to his tent during the hottest time of the day. [2][a]Abraham looked up [b]and saw three men standing across from him. When he saw them he ran from the entrance of the tent to meet them and bowed low to the ground.

[3]He said, "My lord,[1] if I have found favor in your sight, do not pass by and leave your

17:2 [a]Gen 15:18; Exod 6:4; [Gal 3:19] [b]Gen 12:2; 13:16; 15:5; 18:18 17:3 [1]Heb. *And Abram fell on his face*; a posture of humility and reverence. 17:4 [a][Rom 4:11–12, 16] 17:5 [a]Neh 9:7 17:6 [a]Gen 17:16; 35:11 [b]Matt 1:6 [1]Heb. *exceedingly, exceedingly*; an emphatic Heb. construction. 17:7 [a][Gal 3:17] [b]Gen 26:24; 28:13; Lev 11:45; 26:12, 45; Heb 11:16 [c]Rom 9:8; Gal 3:16 17:8 [a]Gen 12:7; 13:15, 17; Acts 7:5 [b]Gen 23:4; 28:4 [c]Exod 6:7; 29:45; Lev 26:12; Deut 29:13; Rev 21:7 [1]Heb. *to sojourn, to reside temporarily.* 17:9 [a]Exod 19:5 17:10 [a]John 7:22; Acts 7:8 17:11 [a]Exod 12:13, 48; [Rom 4:11] 17:16 [a]Gen 18:10 [b]Gen 35:11; Gal 4:31; 1 Pet 3:6 [c]Gen 17:6; 36:31; 1 Sam 8:22 17:17 [a]Gen 17:3; 18:12; 21:6 17:18 [a]Gen 18:23 17:19 [a]Gen 18:10; 21:2; [Gal 4:28] [b]Gen 22:16; Matt 1:2; Luke 3:34 [1]Heb. *he laughs*, or perhaps *may he laugh.* 17:20 [a]Gen 16:10 [b]Gen 25:12–16 [c]Gen 21:13, 18 [1]Heb. *And I will multiply him exceedingly, exceedingly*; an emphatic Heb. construction. 17:21 [a]Gen 26:2–5 [b]Gen 21:2 [c]Gen 18:14 17:27 [a]Gen 18:19 18:1 [a]Gen 13:18; 14:13 18:2 [a]Gen 18:16, 22; 32:24; Josh 5:13; Judg 13:6–11; Heb 13:2 [b]Gen 19:1; 1 Pet 4:9 18:3 [1]MT *Master*; reserved for God.

servant. [4]Let [a]a little water be brought so that you may all wash your feet and rest under the tree. [5]And let me get a [a]bit of food[1] so that [b]you may refresh yourselves since you have passed by your servant's home. After that you may be on your way." "All right," they replied, "you may do [c]as you say."

[6]So Abraham hurried into the tent and said to Sarah, "Quick! Take three measures of fine flour, knead it, and make bread." [7]Then Abraham ran to the herd and chose a fine, tender calf, and gave it to a servant, who quickly prepared it. [8]Abraham [a]then took some curds and milk, along with the calf that had been prepared, and placed the food before them. They ate while he was standing near them under a tree.

[9]Then they asked him, "Where is Sarah your wife?" He replied, "There, [a]in the tent." [10]One of them said, "[a]I will surely return[1] to you when the season comes round again, and your wife [b]Sarah will have a son!" (Now Sarah was listening at the entrance to the tent, not far behind him. [11a]Abraham and Sarah were old and advancing in years; Sarah [b]had long since passed menopause.) [12]So Sarah [a]laughed to herself, thinking, "[b]After I am worn out will I have pleasure, especially when my [c]husband is old too?"

[13]The LORD said to Abraham, "Why did Sarah laugh and say, 'Will I really have a child when I am old?' [14]Is anything impossible for the LORD? [a]I will return to you when the season comes round again and Sarah will have [b]a son." [15]Then Sarah lied, saying, "I did not laugh," because she was afraid. But the LORD said, "No! You did laugh."

Abraham Pleads for Sodom

[16]When the men got up [a]to leave, they looked out over Sodom. (Now Abraham was walking with them to see them on their way.) [17]Then the LORD said, "Should I hide from Abraham what I am about to do? [18]After all, Abraham will surely become a great and powerful nation, and all the nations on the earth may receive [a]blessing through him. [19]I have chosen him so [a]that he may command his children and his household after him to keep the way of the LORD by doing what is right and just. Then the LORD will give to Abraham what he promised him."

[20]So [a]the LORD said, "The outcry against Sodom and Gomorrah is so great and their [b]sin so blatant [21]that [a]I must go down and see [b]if they are as wicked as the outcry suggests. If not, I want to know."

[22]The two men turned [a]and headed toward Sodom, but Abraham was still standing before the LORD.[1] [23]Abraham approached and said, "Will you really sweep [a]away the [b]godly along with the wicked? [24]What if there are 50 godly people in the city? Will you really wipe it out and not spare the place for the sake of the 50 godly people who are in it? [25]Far be it from you to do such [a]a thing—to kill the godly with the wicked, treating the godly and the wicked alike! Far be it from you! Will not the judge of the [b]whole earth do what is right?"

[26]So the LORD replied, "[a]If I find in the city of Sodom 50 godly people, I will spare the whole place for their sake."

[27]Then Abraham asked, "Since I have undertaken to speak to the Lord (although I am [a]but dust and ashes), [28]what if there are five less than the 50 godly people? Will you destroy the whole city because five are lacking?" He replied, "I will not destroy it if I find 45 there."

[29]Abraham spoke to him again, "What if 40 are found there?" He replied, "I will not do it for the sake of the 40."

[30]Then Abraham said, "May the Lord not be angry so that I may speak! What if 30 are found there?" He replied, "I will not do it if I find 30 there."

[31]Abraham said, "Since I have undertaken to speak to the Lord, what if only 20 are found there?" He replied, "I will not destroy it for the sake of the 20."

[32]Finally Abraham said, "May the Lord not be angry so that I may speak just once more.

18:4 [a]Gen 19:2; 24:32; 43:24　**18:5** [a]Judg 6:18–19; 13:15–16　[b]Judg 19:5; Ps 104:15　[c]Gen 19:8; 33:10　[1]Heb. *a piece of bread.*
18:8 [a]Gen 19:3　**18:9** [a]Gen 24:67　**18:10** [a]2 Kgs 4:16　[b]Gen 17:19, 21; 21:2; Rom 9:9　[1]An emphatic Heb. construction.
18:11 [a]Gen 17:17; Luke 1:18; Rom 4:19; Heb 11:11–12, 19　[b]Gen 31:35　**18:12** [a]Gen 17:17　[b]Luke 1:18　[c]1 Pet 3:6　**18:14** [a]Num 11:23; Jer 32:17; Zech 8:6; Matt 3:9; 19:26; Luke 1:37; Rom 4:21　[b]Gen 17:21; 18:10; 2 Kgs 4:16　**18:16** [a]Acts 15:3; Rom 15:24
18:18 [a][Gen 12:3; 22:18]; Matt 1:1; Luke 3:34; [Acts 3:25–26; Gal 3:8]　**18:19** [a][Deut 4:9–10; 6:6–7]　**18:20** [a]Gen 4:10; 19:13; Ezek 16:49–50　[b]Gen 13:13　**18:21** [a]Gen 11:5; Exod 3:8; Ps 14:2　[b]Deut 8:2; 13:3; Josh 22:22; Luke 16:15; 2 Cor 11:11
18:22 [a]Gen 18:16; 19:1　[1]Heb. scribal tradition *but the LORD remained standing before Abraham.*　**18:23** [a]Job 9:22
[b]Gen 20:4　**18:25** [a]Job 8:20; Isa 3:10–11　[b]Deut 1:16–17; 32:4; Job 8:3, 20; 34:17; Ps 58:11; 94:2; Isa 3:10–11; Rom 3:5–6　**18:26** [a]Jer 5:1; Ezek 22:30　**18:27** [a][Gen 3:19]; Job 4:19; 30:19; 42:6; [1 Cor 15:47–48]

What if 10 are found there?" He replied, "I will not destroy it for the sake of the 10."

[33]The LORD went on his way when he had finished speaking to Abraham. Then Abraham returned home.

The Destruction of Sodom and Gomorrah

19 The two angels came to Sodom in [a]the evening while [b]Lot was sitting in the city's gateway. When Lot saw them, he got up to meet them and bowed down with his face toward the ground.

[2]He said, "Here, my lords, please turn [a]aside to your servant's house. Stay the night and [b]wash your feet. Then you can be on your way early in the morning." "[c]No," they replied, "we'll spend the night in the town square."

[3]But [a]he urged[1] them persistently, so they turned aside with him and entered his house. He prepared [b]a feast for them, including bread baked without yeast, and they ate. [4]Before they could lie down to sleep, all the men—both young and old, from every part of the city of Sodom—surrounded the house.[1] [5][a]They shouted to Lot, "Where are the men who came to you tonight? [b]Bring them out to us so we can take carnal knowledge of[1] them!"

[6][a]Lot went outside to them, shutting the door behind him. [7]He said, "No, my brothers! Don't act so wickedly! [8][a]Look, I have two daughters who have never been intimate with a man. Let me bring them out to you, and you can do to them whatever you please. Only don't do anything to these men, [b]for they have come under the protection of my roof."

[9]"Out of our way!" they cried, "This man [a]came to live here as [b]a foreigner, and now he dares to judge us! We'll do more harm to you than to them!" They kept pressing in on Lot until they were close enough to break down the door.

[10]So the men inside reached out and pulled Lot back into the house as they shut the door. [11]Then they [a]struck the men who were at the door of the house, from the youngest to the oldest, with blindness. The men outside wore themselves out trying to find the door. [12]Then the two visitors said to Lot, "Who else do you have here? Do you have any sons-in-law, sons, daughters, or other relatives in the city? Get them out of this place [13]because we are about to destroy it. The [a]outcry against this place is so great before [b]the LORD that he has sent us to destroy it."

[14]Then Lot went out and spoke to his sons-in-law [a]who were going to marry his daughters. He said, "Quick, [b]get out of this place because the LORD is about to destroy the city!" [c]But his sons-in-law thought he was ridiculing them.[1]

[15]At dawn the angels hurried Lot along, saying, "Get [a]going! Take your wife and your two daughters who are here, or else you will be destroyed when the city is judged!" [16]When Lot hesitated, the men grabbed his hand and the hands of his wife and two daughters because the [a]LORD had compassion on them. They led them away [b]and placed them outside the city. [17]When they had brought them outside, they said, "Run for your lives! Don't look[1] behind you or stop anywhere in the valley! [a]Escape [b]to the mountains or you will be destroyed!"

[18]But Lot said to them, "[a]No, please, Lord! [19]Your servant has found favor with you, and you have shown me great kindness by sparing my life. But I am not able to escape to the mountains because this disaster will overtake[1] me and I'll die. [20]Look, this town over here is close enough to escape to, and it's just a little one. Let me go there. It's just a little place, isn't it? Then I'll survive."

[21]"Very well," he [a]replied, "I will grant this request too and will not overthrow the town you mentioned. [22]Run there [a]quickly, for I cannot do anything until you arrive [b]there." (This incident explains why the town was called Zoar.)

[23]The sun had just risen over the land as

19:1[a]Gen 18:2, 16, 22   [b]Gen 18:1–5   19:2[a]Gen 24:31; [Heb 13:2]   [b]Gen 18:4; 24:32   [c]Luke 24:28   19:3[a]Gen 18:6–8; Exod 23:15; Num 9:11; 28:17   [b]Exod 12:8   [1]Heb. *to press, to insist*; ironically foreshadows the hostile actions of the men of the city.   19:4[1]Heb. *and the men of the city, the men of Sodom, surrounded the house, from the young to the old, all the people from the end* [of the city].   19:5[a]Isa 3:9   [b]Judg 19:22   [1]Heb. *know*; a euphemism for sexual relations. Elsewhere, "be intimate with" is used, but not here because of the perverse overtones of force in this context.   19:6[a]Judg 19:23   19:8[a]Judg 19:24   [b]Gen 18:5   19:9[a]2 Pet 2:7–8   [b]Exod 2:14   19:11[a]Gen 20:17–18   19:13[a]Gen 18:20   [b]Lev 26:30–33; Deut 4:26; 28:45; 1 Chr 21:15   19:14[a]Matt 1:18   [b]Num 16:21, 24, 26, 45; Rev 18:4   [c]Exod 9:21; Jer 43:1–2; Luke 17:28; 24:11   [1]Heb. *and he was like one taunting in the eyes of his sons-in-law.*   19:15[a]Ps 37:2; Rev 18:4   19:16[a]Exod 34:7; Ps 32:10; 33:18–19; Luke 18:13   [b]Ps 34:22   19:17[a]1 Kgs 19:3; Jer 48:6   [b]Gen 14:10   [1]Heb. *an intense gaze*; not a passing glance.   19:18[a]Acts 10:14   19:19[1]Heb. *to stick to, to cleave, to join.*   19:21[a]Job 42:8–9; Ps 145:19   19:22[a]Exod 32:10; Deut 9:14   [b]Gen 13:10; 14:2

Lot reached Zoar. [24] Then the LORD rained down [a]sulfur and [b]fire on Sodom and Gomorrah. It was sent down from the sky by the LORD. [25] So he overthrew those cities and all that region, including all the inhabitants of the cities and the vegetation that grew from the ground. [26] But Lot's wife looked [a]back longingly and was turned into a pillar of salt.

[27] Abraham got up early in [a]the morning and went to the place where he had stood before the LORD. [28] He looked out toward Sodom and Gomorrah and all [a]the land of that region. As he did so, he saw the smoke rising up from the land like smoke from a furnace.

[29] So when God destroyed the cities of the region, God [a]honored[1] Abraham's request. He removed Lot from the midst of the destruction when he destroyed the cities Lot had lived in.

[30] Lot went up from Zoar with his two daughters and [a]settled in the mountains because he was afraid to live in Zoar. So he lived in a cave with his two daughters. [31] Later the older daughter said [a]to the younger, "Our father is old, and there is no man in the country to sleep with us,[1] the way everyone does. [32] Come, let's make our father drunk with wine so we can go to bed with him and preserve our family line through our father."

[33] So that night they made their father drunk with wine, and the older daughter came in and went to bed with[1] her father. But he was not aware of when she lay down with him or when she got up. [34] So in the morning the older daughter said to the younger, "Since I went to bed with my father last night, let's make him drunk again tonight. Then you go in and go to bed with him so we can preserve our family line through our father." [35] So they made their father drunk that night as well, and the younger one came and went to bed with him. But he was not aware of when she lay down with him or when she got up.

[36] In this way both of Lot's daughters became pregnant by their father. [37] The older daughter gave birth to a son and named him Moab. [a]He is the ancestor of the Moabites of today. [38] The younger daughter also gave birth to a son and named him Ben Ammi. [a]He is the ancestor of the Ammonites of today.

Abraham and Abimelech

20 Abraham journeyed from [a]there to the Negev region and settled between [b]Kadesh and Shur. While he lived as a temporary [c]resident in Gerar, [2] Abraham said about his wife Sarah, "[a]She is my sister." So Abimelech, king of Gerar, sent for Sarah and [b]took her.

[3] But [a]God appeared to Abimelech [b]in a dream at night and said to him, "[c]You are as good as dead because of the woman you have taken, for she is someone else's wife."

[4] Now Abimelech had not gone near her. He said, "Lord, would you really slaughter an innocent nation?[1] [5] Did Abraham not say to me, 'She is my sister'? And she herself said, 'He is my brother.' [a]I have done this with a clear conscience and with innocent hands!"

[6] Then [a]in the dream God replied to him, "Yes, I know that you have done this with a clear conscience. That is why I have kept you from sinning against me and [b]why I did not allow you to touch her. [7] But now give back the man's wife. Indeed he is a prophet and he will pray [a]for you; thus you will live. But if you don't give her back, [b]know that you will surely die[1] along with all who belong to you."

[8] Early in the morning Abimelech summoned all his servants. When he told them about all these things, they were terrified. [9] Abimelech summoned Abraham and said to him, "What have you done to us? What sin did I commit against you [a]that would cause you to bring such great guilt on me and my kingdom? You have done things to me [b]that should not be done!" [10] Then Abimelech asked Abraham, "What prompted you to do this thing?"

19:24 [a]Deut 29:23; Ps 11:6; Isa 13:19; Jer 20:16; 23:14; 49:18; 50:40; Ezek 16:49–50; Hos 11:8; Amos 4:11; Zeph 2:9; Matt 10:15; Mark 6:11; Luke 17:29; Rom 9:29; 2 Pet 2:6; Jude 7; Rev 11:8 [b]Lev 10:2 **19:26** [a]Gen 19:17; Luke 17:32 **19:27** [a]Gen 18:22 **19:28** [a]Rev 9:2; 18:9 **19:29** [a]Gen 8:1; 18:23; Deut 7:8; 9:5, 27 [1]Heb. *remembered.* **19:30** [a]Gen 19:17, 19 **19:31** [a]Gen 16:2, 4; 38:8–9; Deut 25:5 [1]Heb. *to come over us according to the manner of the whole world*; a euphemism for sexual relations. **19:33** [1]Heb. *came and lied down with*; a euphemism for sexual relations. **19:37** [a]Num 25:1; Deut 2:9 **19:38** [a]Num 21:24; Deut 2:19 **20:1** [a]Gen 18:1 [b]Gen 12:9; 16:7, 14 [c]Gen 26:1, 6 **20:2** [a]Gen 12:11–13; 26:7 [b]Gen 12:15 **20:3** [a]Ps 105:14 [b]Job 33:15 [c]Gen 20:7 **20:4** [1]Or perhaps *Would you really kill someone who is innocent?* **20:5** [a]1 Kgs 9:4; 2 Kgs 20:3; Ps 7:8; 26:6 **20:6** [a]Gen 31:7; 35:5; Exod 34:24; 1 Sam 25:26, 34 [b]Gen 39:9; 2 Sam 12:13 **20:7** [a]1 Sam 7:5; 2 Kgs 5:11; Job 42:8; Jas 5:14–15 [b]Gen 2:17 [1]An emphatic Heb. construction. **20:9** [a]Gen 26:10; 39:9; Exod 32:21; Josh 7:25 [b]Gen 34:7

[11]Abraham replied, "Because I thought, 'Surely no one fears God in this place. [a]They will kill me because of my wife.' [12]What's more, [a]she is indeed my sister, my father's daughter, but not my mother's daughter. She became my wife. [13]When [a]God made me wander from my father's house, I told her, 'This is what you can do to show your loyalty to me: Every place we go, [b]say about me, "He is my brother."'"

[14]So Abimelech [a]gave sheep, cattle, and male and female servants to Abraham. He also gave his wife Sarah back to him. [15]Then Abimelech said, "Look, [a]my land is before you; live wherever you please." [16]To Sarah he said, "[a]Look, I have given 1,000 pieces of silver to your 'brother.' This is [b]compensation for you so that you will stand vindicated before all who are with you."[1]

[17]Abraham [a]prayed to God, and God [b]healed Abimelech, as well as his wife and female slaves so that they were able to have children. [18]For the LORD [a]had caused infertility to strike every woman in the household of Abimelech because he took Sarah, Abraham's wife.

The Birth of Isaac

21 The LORD [a]visited Sarah just [b]as he had said he would and did for Sarah what he had promised. [2]So Sarah became [a]pregnant and bore Abraham [b]a son in his old age at the appointed time that God had told him. [3]Abraham named his son—whom Sarah bore to him—[a]Isaac. [4]When his son Isaac was eight days old, Abraham [a]circumcised him just [b]as God had commanded him to do. [5](Now [a]Abraham was one hundred years old when his son Isaac was born to him.)

[6]Sarah said, "[a]God has made me laugh.[1] Everyone who hears about this [b]will laugh with me." [7]She went on to say, "Who would have said to Abraham that Sarah would nurse children? Yet I have given birth to a son [a]for him in his old age!"

[8]The child grew and was weaned. Abraham prepared a great feast on the day that Isaac was weaned. [9]But Sarah noticed [a]the son of Hagar the Egyptian—the son whom Hagar had borne to Abraham—[b]mocking.[1] [10]So she said to Abraham, "Banish that slave woman and her son, for the son of that slave woman will not be an heir along with my son Isaac!"

[11]Sarah's demand displeased Abraham greatly [a]because Ishmael was his son. [12]But God said to Abraham, "Do not be upset about the boy or your slave wife. Do all that Sarah is [a]telling you because through Isaac your descendants will be counted. [13]But I will [a]also make the son of the slave wife into a great nation,[1] for he is your descendant too."

[14]Early in the morning Abraham took some food and a skin of water and gave them to Hagar. He put them on her shoulders, gave her the child, and [a]sent her away. So she went wandering aimlessly through the wilderness[1] of Beer Sheba. [15]When the water in the skin was gone, she shoved the child under one of the shrubs. [16]Then she went and sat down by herself across from him at quite a distance, about a bowshot, away; for she thought, "I refuse to watch the child die." So she sat across from him and wept uncontrollably.

[17]But [a]God heard the boy's voice. The [b]angel of God called to Hagar from heaven and asked her, "What is the matter, Hagar? Don't be afraid, for God has heard the boy's voice right where he is crying. [18]Get up! Help the boy up and hold [a]him by the hand, for I will make him into a great nation." [19]Then [a]God enabled Hagar to see a well of water. She went over and filled the skin with water, and then gave the boy a drink.

[20]God [a]was with the boy as he grew. He lived in the wilderness [b]and became an archer. [21]He lived in the wilderness of Paran. His mother [a]found a wife for him from the land of Egypt.

[22]At that time [a]Abimelech and Phicol, the

20:11 [a]Gen 42:18; Neh 5:15; Ps 36:1; Prov 16:6   **20:12** [a]Gen 11:29   **20:13** [a]Gen 12:1–9, 11; [Heb 11:8]   [b]Gen 12:13; 20:5   **20:14** [a]Gen 12:16   **20:15** [a]Gen 13:9; 34:10; 47:6   **20:16** [a]Gen 26:11   [b]Mal 2:9   [1]Heb. *Look, it is for you a covering of the eyes, for all who are with you, and with all, and you are set right.*   **20:17** [a]Num 12:13; 21:7; Job 42:9; [Jas 5:16]   [b]Gen 21:2   **20:18** [a]Gen 12:17   **21:1** [a]1 Sam 2:21   [b]Gen 17:16, 19, 21; 18:10, 14; [Gal 4:23, 28]   **21:2** [a]Acts 7:8; Gal 4:22; Heb 11:11–12   [b]Gen 17:21; 18:10, 14; Gal 4:4   **21:3** [a]Gen 17:19, 21   **21:4** [a]Acts 7:8   [b]Gen 17:10, 12; Lev 12:3   **21:5** [a]Gen 17:1, 17   **21:6** [a]Gen 18:13; Ps 126:2; Isa 54:1   [b]Luke 1:58   [1]Heb. *Laughter God has made for me*; a word play based on *Isaac* being based on "to laugh."   **21:7** [a]Gen 18:11–12   **21:9** [a]Gen 16:1, 4, 15   [b][Gal 4:29]   [1]A word play using the same root as the name "Isaac."   **21:11** [a]Gen 17:18   **21:12** [a]Matt 1:2; Luke 3:34; [Rom 9:7–8]; Heb 11:18   **21:13** [a]Gen 16:10; 17:20; 21:18; 25:12–18   [1]MT omits *great.*   **21:14** [a]John 8:35   [1]Or *desert*; an arid wasteland with sparse vegetation.   **21:17** [a]Exod 3:7; Deut 26:7; Ps 6:8   [b]Gen 22:11   **21:18** [a]Gen 16:10; 21:13; 25:12–16   **21:19** [a]Gen 3:7; Num 22:31; 2 Kgs 6:17; Luke 24:31   **21:20** [a]Gen 28:15; 39:2–3, 21   [b]Gen 16:12   **21:21** [a]Gen 24:4   **21:22** [a]Gen 20:2, 14; 26:26

commander of his army, said to Abraham, "[b]God is with you in all that you do. [23]Now [a]swear to me right here in God's name that you will not deceive me, my children, or my descendants. Show me, and the land[1] where you are staying,[2] the same loyalty that I have shown you."

[24]Abraham said, "I swear to do this." [25]But Abraham lodged [a]a complaint against Abimelech concerning a well that Abimelech's servants had seized. [26]"I do not know who has done this thing," Abimelech replied. "Moreover, you did not tell me. I did not hear about it until today."

[27]Abraham took some sheep and cattle and gave them to Abimelech. The two of them [a]made a treaty. [28]Then Abraham set seven ewe lambs apart from the flock by themselves. [29]Abimelech asked Abraham, "[a]What is the meaning of these seven ewe lambs that you have set apart?" [30]He replied, "You must take these seven ewe lambs from my hand as legal proof that I dug this well." [31]That is why he [a]named that place Beer Sheba, because the two of them swore an oath there.

[32]So they made a treaty at Beer Sheba; then Abimelech and Phicol, the commander of his army, returned to the land of the Philistines. [33]Abraham planted a tamarisk tree in Beer Sheba. [a]There [b]he worshiped the LORD, the eternal God. [34]So Abraham stayed in the land of the Philistines for quite some time.

The Sacrifice of Isaac

22 Some time after these things [a]God tested Abraham. He said to him, "Abraham!" "Here I am!" Abraham replied. [2]God said, "Take [a]your son—your only son, whom you [b]love, Isaac—and go [c]to the land of Moriah! Offer him up there as a [d]burnt offering on one of the mountains which I will indicate to you."

[3]Early in the morning Abraham got up and saddled his donkey. He took two of his young servants with him, along with his son Isaac. When he had cut the wood for the burnt offering, he started out for the place God had spoken to him about.

[4]On the third day Abraham caught sight of the place in the distance. [5]So he said to his servants, "You two stay[1] here with the donkey while the boy and I go up there. We will worship and then return to you."

[6]Abraham took the wood for the burnt offering and [a]put it on his son Isaac. Then he took the fire and the knife in his hand, and the two of them walked on together. [7]Isaac said to his father Abraham, "My father?" "What is it, my son?" he replied. "Here is the fire and the wood," Isaac said, "but where is the lamb for the burnt offering?" [8]"God will provide for himself the [a]lamb for the [b]burnt offering, my son," Abraham replied. The two of them continued on together.

[9]When they came to the place God had told him about, Abraham built the altar there and arranged the wood on it. Next he tied up his son Isaac and [a]placed him on the altar on top of the wood. [10]Then Abraham reached out his hand, took the knife, and prepared to slaughter his son. [11]But the [a]angel of the LORD called to him from heaven, "Abraham! Abraham!" "Here I am!" he answered. [12]"Do not harm the boy!" the angel said. "[a]Do not do anything to him, for [b]now I know that you fear God because you did not [c]withhold your son, your only son, from me."

[13]Abraham looked up and saw behind him[1] a ram caught in the bushes by its horns. So he went over and got the ram and offered it up as a burnt offering instead of his son. [14]And Abraham called the name of that place "The LORD provides." It is said to this day, "In the mountain of the LORD provision will be made."

[15]The angel of the LORD called to Abraham a second time from heaven [16]and said, "I solemnly swear [a]by my own name, decrees the LORD, that because you have done this and have not withheld your son, your only son, [17]I will indeed [a]bless you, and I will greatly multiply your descendants[1] so that

21:22 [b]Gen 26:28; Isa 8:10   **21:23** [a]Josh 2:12; 1 Sam 24:21   [1]I.e., the people in the land.   [2]Heb. *to stay, to live, to sojourn.*
21:25 [a]Gen 26:15, 18, 20–22   **21:27** [a]Gen 26:31; 31:44; 1 Sam 18:3   **21:29** [a]Gen 33:8   **21:31** [a]Gen 21:14; 26:33   **21:33** [a]Gen 4:26; 12:8; 13:4; 26:25   [b]Gen 35:11; Exod 15:18; Deut 32:40; 33:27; Ps 90:2; 93:2; Isa 40:28; Jer 10:10; Hab 1:12; Heb 13:8
22:1 [a]Deut 8:2, 16; 1 Cor 10:13; Heb 11:17; [Jas 1:12–14; 1 Pet 1:7]   **22:2** [a]Gen 22:12, 16; John 3:16; Heb 11:17; 1 John 4:9   [b]John 5:20   [c]2 Chr 3:1   [d]Gen 8:20; 31:54   **22:5** [1]Masc. pl.; i.e., the two young servants who accompanied Abraham and Isaac.   **22:6** [a]John 19:17   **22:8** [a]John 1:29, 36   [b]Exod 12:3–6   **22:9** [a][Heb 11:17–19; Jas 2:21]   **22:11** [a]Gen 16:7–11; 21:17–18; 31:11   **22:12** [a]1 Sam 15:22   [b]Gen 26:5; Jas 2:21–22   [c]Gen 22:2, 16; John 3:16   **22:13** [1]Sev. wss *one.*
22:16 [a]Ps 105:9; Luke 1:73; [Heb 6:13–14]   **22:17** [a]Gen 17:16; 26:3, 24   [1]Heb. *seed* (for planting), *offspring* (occasionally of animals, but usually of people), *descendants.*

they will be [b]as countless as the stars in the sky or the grains of [c]sand on the seashore. [d]Your descendants will take possession of the strongholds of their enemies. [18][a]Because you have obeyed me, all the nations of the earth will pronounce [b]blessings on one another using the name of your descendants."

[19]Then Abraham returned to his servants, and they set out together for Beer [a]Sheba where Abraham stayed.

[20]After these things Abraham was told, "[a]Milcah also has borne children to your brother Nahor—[21][a]Uz the firstborn, his brother Buz, Kemuel (the father [b]of Aram), [22]Kesed, Hazo, Pildash, Jidlaph, and Bethuel." [23](Now [a]Bethuel became the father of Rebekah.) These were the eight sons Milcah bore to Abraham's brother Nahor. [24]His concubine, whose name was Reumah, also bore him children—Tebah, Gaham, Tahash, and Maacah.

The Death of Sarah

23 Sarah lived 127 years. [2]Then she died in Kiriath [a]Arba (that is, [b]Hebron) in the land of Canaan. Abraham went to mourn for Sarah and to weep for her.

[3]Then Abraham got up from mourning his dead wife and said to the sons of [a]Heth, [4]"I am a [a]foreign resident, a temporary settler,[1] among you. [b]Grant me ownership of a burial site among you so that I may bury my dead."

[5]The sons of Heth answered Abraham, [6]"Listen, sir, you [a]are a mighty prince[1] among us! You may bury your dead in the choicest of our tombs. None of us will refuse you his tomb to prevent you from burying your dead."

[7]Abraham got up and bowed down to the local people, the sons of Heth. [8]Then he said to them, "If you agree that I may bury my dead, then hear me out. Ask Ephron the son of Zohar [9]if he will sell me the cave of [a]Machpelah that belongs to him; it is at the end of his field. Let him sell it to me publicly for the full price, so that I may own it as a burial site."

[10](Now Ephron was sitting among the sons of Heth.) Ephron the Hittite replied to Abraham in the hearing of the sons of Heth—before all who [a]entered the gate of his city—[11]"[a]No, my lord! Hear me out. I sell you both the field and the cave that is in it. In the presence of my people I sell it to you. Bury your dead."

[12]Abraham bowed before the local people [13]and said to Ephron in their hearing, "Hear me, if you will. I pay to you the price of the field. Take it from me so that I may bury my dead there."

[14]Ephron answered Abraham, saying to him, [15]"Hear me, my lord. The land is worth 400 [a]pieces of silver, but what is that between me and you? So bury your dead."

[16]So Abraham agreed to Ephron's price and weighed [a]out for him the price that Ephron had quoted in the hearing of the sons of Heth—400 pieces of silver, according to the standard measurement at the time.

[17]So Abraham secured Ephron's field in Machpelah, next to Mamre, including [a]the field, the cave that was in it, and all the trees that were in the field and all around its border, [18]as his property in the presence of the sons of Heth before all who entered the gate of Ephron's city.

[19]After this Abraham buried his wife Sarah in the cave in the field of Machpelah next to Mamre (that is, Hebron) in the land of Canaan. [20]So Abraham secured the field and the cave that was in it as a burial site from the sons of Heth.

The Wife for Isaac

24 Now Abraham [a]was old, well advanced in years, and the LORD [b]had blessed him in everything. [2]Abraham said [a]to his servant, the senior one[1] in his household who was in [b]charge of everything he had, "[c]Put your hand under my thigh [3]so that I may make you solemnly [a]promise by the LORD, the God of heaven and the God of the earth: [b]You must not acquire a wife for my son from the daughters of the

22:17 [b]Gen 15:5; 26:4; Deut 1:10; Jer 33:22; Heb 11:12   [c]Gen 13:16; 32:12; 1 Kgs 4:20   [d]Gen 24:60   **22:18** [a]Gen 18:19; 22:3, 10; 26:5   [b]Gen 12:3; 18:18; 26:4; Matt 1:1; Luke 3:34; [Acts 3:25–26]; Gal 3:8–9, 16, 18   **22:19** [a]Gen 21:31   **22:20** [a]Gen 11:29; 24:15   **22:21** [a]Job 1:1   [b]Job 32:2   **22:23** [a]Gen 24:15   **23:2** [a]Gen 35:27; Josh 14:15; 15:13; 21:11   [b]Gen 13:18; 23:19   **23:3** [a]Gen 10:15; 15:20; 2 Kgs 7:6   **23:4** [a][Gen 17:8]; Lev 25:23; 1 Chr 29:15; Ps 39:12; 105:12; 119:19; [Heb 11:9, 13]   [b]Acts 7:5, 16   [1]Heb. *a resident foreigner and an immigrant.*   **23:6** [a]Gen 13:2; 14:14; 24:35   [1]Heb. *prince of God.*   **23:9** [a]Gen 25:9   **23:10** [a]Gen 23:18; 34:20, 24; Ruth 4:1, 4, 11   **23:11** [a]2 Sam 24:21–24   **23:15** [a]Exod 30:13; Ezek 45:12   **23:16** [a]2 Sam 14:26; Jer 32:9–10; Zech 11:12   **23:17** [a]Gen 25:9; 49:29–32; 50:13; Acts 7:16   **24:1** [a]Gen 18:11; 21:5   [b]Gen 12:2; 13:2; 24:35; Ps 112:3; Prov 10:22; [Gal 3:9]   **24:2** [a]Gen 15:2   [b]Gen 24:10; 39:4–6   [c]Gen 47:29; 1 Chr 29:24   [1]I.e., the servant who is oldest in age or senior in authority (or both).   **24:3** [a]Gen 14:19, 22   [b]Gen 26:35; 28:2; Exod 34:16; Deut 7:3; 2 Cor 6:14–17

Canaanites, among whom I am living. 4aYou must go instead bto my country and to my relatives to find a wife for my son Isaac."

5The servant asked him, "What if the woman is not willing to come back with me to this land? Must I then1 take your son back to the land from which you came?"

6"Be careful never to take my son back there!" Abraham told him. 7"The LORD, the God of heaven, who atook me from my father's house and the land of my relatives, promised me with a solemn oath, 'bTo your descendants I will give this land.' cHe will send his angel before you so that you may find a wife for my son from there. 8But if the woman is not willing to come back with ayou, you will be free from this oath of mine. But you must not take my son back there!" 9So the servant placed his hand under the thigh of his master Abraham and gave his solemn promise he would carry out his wishes.

10Then athe servant took ten of his master's camels and departed with all kinds of gifts from his master at his disposal. He journeyed to the region of Aram Naharaim and the city of Nahor. 11He made the camels kneel down by the well outside the city. It was evening, the time awhen the women would go out to draw water. 12He aprayed, "O LORD, God of my master Abraham, guide me today. Be faithful to my master Abraham. 13Here aI am, standing by bthe spring, and the daughters of the people who live in the town are coming out to draw water. 14I will say to a young woman, 'Please lower your jar so I may drink.' May the one you have chosen for your servant Isaac reply, 'Drink, and I'll give your camels water too.' In this way I will know that you have been faithful to my master."

15Before he had finished praying, there came aRebekah1 with her water jug on her shoulder. She was the daughter of Bethuel son of bMilcah (Milcah was the wife of Abraham's brother Nahor). 16Now the young woman awas very beautiful. She was a virgin; no man had ever been physically intimate with her.1 She went down to the spring, filled her jug, and came back up. 17Abraham's servant ran to meet her and said, "Please give me a sip of water from your jug." 18"aDrink, my lord," she replied, and quickly lowering her jug to her hands, she gave him a drink. 19When she had done so, she said, "I'll draw water for your camels too, until they have drunk as much as they want." 20She quickly emptied her jug into the watering trough and ran back to the well to draw more water until she had drawn enough for all his camels. 21Silently athe man watched her with interest to determine if the LORD had made his journey successful or not.

22After the camels had finished drinking, the man took out a gold anose ring weighing a beka and two gold wrist bracelets weighing ten shekels and gave them to her. 23"Whose daughter are you?" he asked. "Tell me, is there room in your father's house for us to spend the night?"

24She asaid to him, "I am the daughter of Bethuel the son of Milcah, whom Milcah bore to Nahor. 25We have plenty of straw and feed," she added, "and room for you to spend the night."

26The man abowed his head and worshiped the LORD, 27saying, "aPraised be the LORD, the God of my master Abraham, who has not abandoned bhis faithful love for my master! The LORD has led cme to the house of my master's relatives!"

28The young woman ran and told her mother's household all about these things. 29(Now Rebekah had a brother named aLaban.) Laban rushed out to meet the man at the spring. 30When he saw the bracelets on his sister's wrists and the nose ring and heard his sister Rebekah say, "This is what the man said to me," he went out to meet the man. There he was, standing1 by the camels near the spring. 31Laban said ato him, "Come, you who are blessed by the LORD! Why are you standing out here when I have prepared the house and a place for the camels?"

24:4 aGen 28:2   bGen 12:1; Heb 11:15   24:5 1An emphatic Heb. construction.   24:7 aGen 12:1; 24:3   bGen 12:7; 13:15; 15:18; 17:8; Exod 32:13; Deut 1:8; 34:4; Acts 7:5   cGen 16:7; 21:17; 22:11; Exod 23:20, 23; 33:2; Heb 1:4, 14   24:8 aJosh 2:17–20   24:10 aGen 11:31–32; 22:20; 27:43; 29:5   24:11 aExod 2:16; 1 Sam 9:11   24:12 aGen 24:27, 42, 48; 26:24; 32:9; Exod 3:6, 15   24:13 aGen 24:43   bExod 2:16   24:15 aGen 24:45; 25:20   bGen 22:20, 23   1Heb. Look, Rebekah was coming out!   24:16 aGen 12:11; 26:7; 29:17   1Heb. And the young woman was very good of appearance, a virgin, and a man had not known her; "to know" is a euphemism for sexual relations.   24:18 aGen 24:14, 46; [1 Pet 3:8–9]   24:21 aGen 24:12–14, 27, 52   24:22 aGen 24:47; Exod 32:2–3; Isa 3:19–21   24:24 aGen 22:23; 24:15   24:26 aGen 24:48, 52; Exod 4:31   24:27 aGen 24:12, 42, 48; Exod 18:10; Ruth 4:14; 1 Sam 25:32, 39; 2 Sam 18:28; Luke 1:68   bGen 32:10; Ps 98:3   cGen 24:21, 48   24:29 aGen 29:5, 13   24:30 1Heb. and look, he was standing.   24:31 aGen 26:29; Judg 17:2; Ruth 3:10; Ps 115:15

[32]So Abraham's servant went to the house and unloaded the camels. Straw and feed were [a]given to the camels, and water was provided so that he and the men who were with him could [b]wash their feet. [33]When food was served, he [a]said, "I will not eat until I have said what I want to say." "Tell us," Laban said.[1]

[34]"I am the servant of Abraham," he began. [35]"The LORD [a]has richly blessed my master and he has become very wealthy.[1] The LORD has given him sheep and cattle, silver and gold, male and female servants, and camels and donkeys. [36]My master's wife Sarah [a]bore a son [b]to him when she was old, and my master has given him everything he owns. [37]My master [a]made me swear an oath. He said, 'You must not acquire a wife for my son from the daughters of the Canaanites, among whom I am living, [38a]but you must go to the family of my father and to my relatives to find a wife for my son.' [39a]But I said to my master, 'What if the woman does not want to go with me?' [40a]He answered, 'The LORD, [b]before whom I have walked, will send his angel with you. He will make your journey a success and you will find a wife for my son from among my relatives, from my father's family. [41]You will be free from [a]your oath if you go to my relatives and they will not give her to you. Then you will be free from your oath.' [42]When I came [a]to the spring today, I prayed, 'O LORD, God of my master Abraham, if you have decided to make my journey successful, may events unfold as follows: [43a]Here I am, standing by the spring. When the young woman goes out to draw water, I'll say, "Please give me a little water to drink from your jug." [44]Then she will reply to me, "Drink, and I'll draw water for your camels too." May that woman be the one whom the LORD has chosen for my master's son.'

[45]"[a]Before I finished [b]praying in my heart, along came Rebekah [1]with her water jug on her shoulder! She went down to the spring and drew water. So I said to her, 'Please give me a drink.' [46]She quickly lowered her jug from her shoulder and said, 'Drink, and I'll give your camels water too.' So I drank, and she also gave the camels water. [47]Then I asked her, 'Whose daughter are you?' She replied, 'The daughter of Bethuel the son of Nahor, whom Milcah bore to Nahor.' I put the ring in her nose and the bracelets on her wrists. [48]Then I bowed down [a]and worshiped the LORD. I praised the LORD, the God of my master Abraham, who had led me on the right path to [b]find the granddaughter[1] of my master's brother for his son. [49]Now, if you will [a]show faithful love to my master, tell me. But if not, tell me as well, so that I may go on my way."

[50]Then Laban and Bethuel replied, "This is [a]the LORD's doing. Our wishes are of no [b]concern.[1] [51]Rebekah stands [a]here before you. Take her and go so that she may become the wife of your master's son, just as the LORD has decided."

[52]When Abraham's servant [a]heard their words, he bowed down to the ground before the LORD. [53]Then he brought out gold, silver [a]jewelry, and clothing and gave them to Rebekah. He also gave valuable gifts to her brother and to her mother. [54]After this, he and the men who were with him ate a meal and stayed there overnight.

When they got up in the morning, he said, "Let me leave now so I can return to my master." [55]But Rebekah's brother and her mother replied, "Let the girl stay with us a few more days, perhaps ten. Then she can go." [56]But he said to them, "Don't detain me—the LORD has granted me success on my journey. Let me leave now so I may return to my master." [57]Then they said, "We'll call the girl and find out what she wants to do." [58]So they called Rebekah and asked her, "Do you want to go with this man?" She replied, "I want to go." [59]So they sent their sister Rebekah on her way, accompanied by her female attendant, with Abraham's servant [a]and his men. [60]They blessed Rebekah with [a]these words:

"Our sister, may you become the
   mother of [b]thousands of ten
   thousands!

24:32 [a]Gen 43:24; Judg 19:21   [b]Gen 19:2; John 13:5, 13–15   **24:33** [a]Job 23:12; John 4:34; Eph 6:5–7   [1]Some wss *and they said.* **24:35** [a]Gen 13:2; 24:1   [1]Heb. *become great.*   **24:36** [a]Gen 21:1–7   [b]Gen 21:10; 25:5   **24:37** [a]Gen 24:2–4   **24:38** [a]Gen 24:4   **24:39** [a]Gen 24:5   **24:40** [a]Gen 24:7   [b]Gen 5:22, 24; 17:1; 1 Kgs 8:23   **24:41** [a]Gen 24:8   **24:42** [a]Gen 24:12   **24:43** [a]Gen 24:13   **24:45** [a]Gen 24:15   [b]1 Sam 1:13   [1]Heb. *Look, Rebekah was coming out.*   **24:48** [a]Gen 24:26, 52   [b]Gen 22:23; 24:27; Ps 32:8; 48:14; Isa 48:17   [1]Heb. *daughter.*   **24:49** [a]Gen 47:29; Josh 2:14   **24:50** [a]Ps 118:23; Matt 21:42; Mark 12:11   [b]Gen 31:24, 29   [1]Heb. *We are not able to speak to you bad or good;* i.e., they could not say one way or the other, for they viewed it as God's will.   **24:51** [a]Gen 20:15   **24:52** [a]Gen 24:26, 48   **24:53** [a]Gen 24:10, 22; Exod 3:22; 11:2; 12:35   **24:59** [a]Gen 35:8   **24:60** [a]Gen 17:16   [b]Gen 22:17; 28:14

May your descendants possess the
strongholds of their enemies."

⁶¹ Then Rebekah and her female servants
mounted the camels and rode away with
the man. So Abraham's servant took Rebekah and left.

⁶² Now Isaac came from Beer Lahai ᵃRoi,
for he was living in the Negev. ⁶³ He went out
ᵃto relax in the field in the early evening.
Then he looked up and saw that there were
camels approaching. ⁶⁴ Rebekah looked up
and saw Isaac. ᵃShe got down from her
camel ⁶⁵ and asked Abraham's servant, "Who
is that man walking in the field toward us?"
"That is my master," the servant replied. So
she took her veil and covered herself.

⁶⁶ The servant told Isaac everything that
had happened. ⁶⁷ Then Isaac brought Rebekah into his mother Sarah's tent. He
ᵃtook her ᵇas his wife and loved her. So Isaac
was comforted after his mother's death.

The Death of Abraham

25 Abraham had taken another wife,
named ᵃKeturah. ² She bore him
Zimran, Jokshan, Medan, Midian, Ishbak,
and Shuah. ³ Jokshan became the father
of Sheba and Dedan. The descendants of
Dedan were the Asshurites, Letushites,
and Leummites. ⁴ The sons of Midian were
Ephah, Epher, Hanoch, Abida, and Eldaah.
All these were descendants of Keturah.

⁵ Everything he owned ᵃAbraham left to
his son Isaac. ⁶ But while he was still alive,
Abraham gave gifts to the sons of his concubines and ᵃsent ᵇthem off to the east, away
from his son Isaac.

⁷ Abraham lived a total of¹ 175 years. ⁸ Then
Abraham breathed his last and ᵃdied at ᵇa
good old age, an old man who had lived a
full life. He joined his ancestors. ⁹ His sons
Isaac and Ishmael buried him in the cave
of ᵃMachpelah near Mamre, in the field of
Ephron the son of Zohar, the Hittite. ¹⁰ This
was ᵃthe field Abraham had purchased from
ᵇthe sons of Heth. There Abraham was buried with his wife Sarah. ¹¹ After Abraham's

death, God blessed his son Isaac. Isaac lived
near Beer Lahai ᵃRoi.

The Sons of Ishmael

¹² This is the ᵃaccount of Abraham's son
Ishmael, whom Hagar the Egyptian, Sarah's
servant, bore to Abraham.

¹³ These are ᵃthe names of Ishmael's
sons, by their names according to their
records: Nebaioth (Ishmael's firstborn),
Kedar, Adbeel, Mibsam, ¹⁴ Mishma, Dumah,
Massa, ¹⁵ Hadad, Tema, Jetur, Naphish, and
Kedemah. ¹⁶ These are the sons of Ishmael,
and these are their names by their settlements and their camps—ᵃtwelve princes
according to their clans.

¹⁷ Ishmael lived a total of 137 years. ᵃHe
breathed his last and died; then he joined
his ancestors. ¹⁸ His descendants settled
from Havilah to Shur, which runs next to
Egypt all ᵃthe way to Asshur. They settled
away from all their relatives.

Jacob and Esau

¹⁹ This is the ᵃaccount of Isaac, the son of
ᵇAbraham.

Abraham became the father of Isaac.
²⁰ When Isaac was forty years old, ᵃhe married Rebekah, ᵇthe daughter of Bethuel the
Aramean from Paddan Aram and sister of
Laban the Aramean.

²¹ Isaac prayed to the LORD on behalf of
his wife because she was childless. The
LORD answered his prayer, ᵃand his wife Rebekah became pregnant. ²² But the children
struggled¹ inside her, and she said, "Why is
this happening to me?" ᵃSo she asked the
LORD, ²³ and the LORD said to her,

"ᵃTwo nations are in your womb,
 and two peoples will be separated
  from within you.
One people will be stronger than
  ᵇthe other,
 ᶜand the older will serve the younger."

²⁴ When the time came for Rebekah to
give birth, there were¹ twins in her womb.

24:62 ᵃGen 16:14; 25:11   **24:63** ᵃJosh 1:8; Ps 1:2; 77:12; 119:15, 27, 48; 143:5; 145:5   **24:64** ᵃJosh 15:18   **24:67** ᵃGen 25:20; 29:20; Prov 18:22   ᵇGen 23:1–2; 38:12   **25:1** ᵃ1 Chr 1:32–33   **25:5** ᵃGen 24:35–36   **25:6** ᵃGen 21:14   ᵇJudg 6:3   **25:7** ¹Heb. *and these are the days of the years of the lifetime of Abraham that he lived.*   **25:8** ᵃGen 15:15; 47:8–9   ᵇGen 25:17; 35:29; 49:29, 33   **25:9** ᵃGen 23:9, 17; 49:30   **25:10** ᵃGen 23:3–16   ᵇGen 49:31   **25:11** ᵃGen 16:14   **25:12** ᵃGen 11:10, 27; 16:15   **25:13** ᵃ1 Chr 1:29–31   **25:16** ᵃGen 17:20   **25:17** ᵃGen 25:8; 49:33   **25:18** ᵃGen 20:1; 1 Sam 15:7   **25:19** ᵃGen 36:1, 9   ᵇMatt 1:2   **25:20** ᵃGen 22:23; 24:15, 29, 67   ᵇGen 24:29   **25:21** ᵃ1 Sam 1:17; 1 Chr 5:20; 2 Chr 33:13; Ezra 8:23; Ps 127:3   **25:22** ᵃ1 Sam 1:15; 9:9; 10:22   ¹An out of the ordinary violent struggle.   **25:23** ᵃGen 17:4–6, 16; 24:60; Num 20:14; Deut 2:4–8   ᵇ2 Sam 8:14   ᶜGen 27:29, 40; Mal 1:2–3; Rom 9:12   **25:24** ¹Heb. *look!*

[25] The first came out reddish all over, [a]like a hairy garment, so they named him Esau. [26] When [a]his brother came out with [b]his hand clutching Esau's heel, they named him Jacob. Isaac was sixty years old when they were born.

[27] When the boys grew up, [a]Esau [b]became a skilled hunter, a man of the open fields, but Jacob was an even-tempered man, [c]living in tents. [28] Isaac loved Esau because he had a taste [a]for fresh game,[1] [b]but Rebekah loved Jacob.

[29] Now Jacob cooked some stew, and when Esau came in from the open fields, he was famished. [30] So Esau said to Jacob, "Feed[1] me some of the red stuff—yes, this red stuff— because I'm starving!" (That is why he was also called Edom.)

[31] But Jacob replied, "First sell me your birthright." [32] "Look," said Esau, "I'm about to die! [a]What use is the birthright to me?" [33] But Jacob said, "Swear an oath to me now." So Esau swore an oath to him and [a]sold his birthright to Jacob.

[34] Then Jacob gave Esau some bread and lentil stew; Esau ate and drank, [a]then got up and went out. So Esau [b]despised his birthright.

Isaac and Abimelech

26 There was a famine in [a]the land, subsequent to the earlier famine that occurred in the days of Abraham. Isaac went to [b]Abimelech king of the Philistines at Gerar. [2] The Lord appeared to Isaac and said, "[a]Do not go down to Egypt; settle down in [b]the land that I will point out to you. [3] [a]Stay[1] [b]in this land. Then I will be with you and will [c]bless you, for [d]I will give all [e]these lands to you and to your descendants, and I will fulfill the solemn promise I made to your father Abraham. [4] I [a]will multiply your descendants so they will be as numerous as the stars in the sky, [b]and I will give them all these lands. All the nations of the earth will pronounce blessings on one another using the name of your descendants. [5] All this will come to pass [a]because Abraham obeyed me and kept my charge, my commandments, my statutes, and my laws." [6] So Isaac settled in Gerar.

[7] When [a]the men of that place asked him about his wife, [b]he replied, "She is my sister." He was afraid to say, "She is my wife," for he thought to himself, "The men of this place will kill me to get Rebekah because she is very [c]beautiful."

[8] After Isaac had been there a long time, Abimelech king of the Philistines happened to look out a window and observed[1] Isaac caressing[2] his wife Rebekah. [9] So Abimelech summoned Isaac and said, "She is really your wife! Why did you say, 'She is my sister'?" Isaac replied, "Because I thought someone might kill me to get her."

[10] Then Abimelech exclaimed, "What in the world have [a]you done to us? One of the men[1] nearly took your wife to bed,[2] and you would have brought guilt on us!" [11] So Abimelech commanded all the people, "Whoever [a]touches[1] this man or his wife will surely be put to death."

[12] When [a]Isaac planted in that land, he reaped in the same year a hundred times what he had sown, because the Lord [b]blessed him. [13] The man became wealthy. His influence continued to grow until he became very prominent. [14] He had so many sheep and cattle and such a great household of servants that the Philistines became jealous [a]of him. [15] So the Philistines took dirt and filled up all the wells that his father's servants had dug back in the days of his father Abraham.

[16] Then Abimelech said to Isaac, "Leave us and go elsewhere, for [a]you have become much more powerful than we are." [17] So Isaac left there and settled in the Gerar Valley. [18] Isaac reopened [a]the wells that had been dug back in the days of his father Abraham, for the Philistines had stopped them up after Abraham died. Isaac gave these wells the same names his father had given them.

25:25 [a]Gen 27:11, 16, 23   25:26 [a]Hos 12:3   [b]Gen 27:36   25:27 [a]Gen 27:3, 5   [b]Job 1:1, 8   [c]Heb 11:9   25:28 [a]Gen 27:4, 19, 25, 31   [b]Gen 27:6–10   [1]Heb. *the taste of game was in his mouth.*   25:30 [1]Used in later Heb. for feeding animals; it may depict Esau in a negative light, comparing him to a hungry animal.   25:32 [a]Matt 16:26; Mark 8:36–37   25:33 [a]Heb 12:16   25:34 [a]Eccl 8:15; Isa 22:13; 1 Cor 15:32   [b]Heb 12:16–17   26:1 [a]Gen 12:10   [b]Gen 20:1–2   26:2 [a]Gen 12:7; 17:1; 18:1; 35:9   [b]Gen 12:1   26:3 [a]Gen 20:1; Ps 39:12; Heb 11:9   [b]Gen 28:13, 15   [c]Gen 12:2   [d]Gen 12:7; 13:15; 15:18   [e]Gen 22:16; Ps 105:9   [1]Heb. *to live temporarily without ownership of land.*   26:4 [a]Gen 15:5; 22:17; Exod 32:13   [b]Gen 12:3; 22:18; Gal 3:8   26:5 [a]Gen 22:16, 18   26:7 [a]Gen 12:13; 20:2, 12, 13   [b]Prov 29:25   [c]Gen 12:11; 24:16; 29:17   26:8 [1]Heb. *window and saw, and look, Isaac.*   [2]Or *fondling.*   26:10 [a]Gen 20:9   [1]LXX *one of my kin.*   [2]Heb. *almost lied down with;* going to bed to sleep or can be a euphemism for sexual relations.   26:11 [a]Ps 105:15   [1]Heb. *strikes;* with a nuance of "to harm in any way."   26:12 [a]Matt 13:8, 23; Mark 4:8   [b]Gen 24:1; 25:8, 11; 26:3; Job 42:12; Prov 10:22   26:14 [a]Gen 37:11; Eccl 4:4   26:16 [a]Exod 1:9   26:18 [a]Gen 21:31

[19] When Isaac's servants dug in the valley and discovered a well with fresh flowing[1] water there, [20] the herdsmen of Gerar [a]quarreled with Isaac's herdsmen, saying, "The water belongs to us!" So Isaac named the well Esek because they argued with him about it. [21] His servants dug another well, but they quarreled over it too, so Isaac named it Sitnah. [22] Then he moved away from there and dug another well. They did not quarrel over it, so Isaac named it Rehoboth, saying, "For now the Lord has made room for us, and we will prosper in the land."

[23] From there Isaac went up to Beer Sheba. [24] The Lord [a]appeared to [b]him that night and said, "I am the God of your father Abraham. [c]Do not be [d]afraid, for I am with you. I will bless you and multiply your descendants for the sake of my servant Abraham." [25] Then Isaac [a]built an altar there and [b]worshiped the Lord. He pitched his tent there, and his servants dug a well.

[26] Now Abimelech had come to him from Gerar along with Ahuzzah his friend [a]and Phicol the commander of his army. [27] Isaac asked them, "Why have you come to me? You hate me and [a]sent me away from you." [28] They replied, "We could plainly see that the Lord [a]is with you. So we decided there should be a pact between us—between us and you. Allow us to make a treaty with you [29] so that [a]you will not do us any harm, just as we have not harmed you, but have always treated you well before sending you away in peace. Now you are blessed by the Lord."[1]

[30] [a]So Isaac held a feast for them and they celebrated. [31] Early in the morning the men made a [a]treaty with each other. Isaac sent them off; they separated on good terms.

[32] That day Isaac's servants came and told him about the well they had dug. "We've found water," they reported. [33] So he named it Shibah; that is [a]why the name of the city has been Beer Sheba to this day.

[34] When Esau was forty years old, [a]he married Judith the daughter of Beeri the Hittite, as well as Basemath the daughter of Elon the Hittite. [35] They caused Isaac and Rebekah great anxiety.

Jacob Cheats Esau out of the Blessing

27 When Isaac was [a]old and [b]his eyes were so weak that he was almost blind, he called his older son Esau and said to him, "My son!" "Here I am!" Esau replied. [2] Isaac said, "Since I am so old, I could die at any time. [3] [a]Therefore, take your weapons—your quiver and your bow—and go out into the open fields and hunt down some wild game for me. [4] Then prepare for me some tasty food, the kind I love, and bring it to me. Then I will eat it so that I [a]may bless you before I die."

[5] Now Rebekah had been listening while Isaac spoke to his son Esau. When Esau went out to the open fields to hunt down some wild game and bring it back,[1] [6] Rebekah said to her son Jacob, "Look, I overheard your father tell your brother Esau, [7] 'Bring me some wild game and prepare for me some tasty food. Then I will eat it and bless you in the presence of the Lord before I die.' [8] Now then, my son, do [a]exactly what I tell you! [9] Go to the flock and get me two of the best young goats. I'll prepare them in [a]a tasty way for your father, just the way he loves them. [10] Then you will take it to your father. Thus he will eat it and bless you before he dies."

[11] "But [a]Esau my brother is a hairy man," Jacob protested to his mother Rebekah, "and I have smooth skin! [12] My father may [a]touch me! Then he'll think I'm mocking him [b]and I'll bring a curse on myself instead of a blessing." [13] So his mother told him, "Any curse against you will fall on me, my son! Just obey me! Go and get them for me!"

[14] So he went and got the goats and brought them to his mother. She [a]prepared some tasty food, just the way his father loved it. [15] Then Rebekah took her older son Esau's best [a]clothes, which she had with her in the house, and put them on her younger son Jacob. [16] She put the skins of the young goats on his hands and the smooth part of his neck. [17] Then she handed the tasty food and the bread she had made to her son Jacob.

[18] He went to his father and said, "My father!" Isaac replied, "Here I am. Which are

26:19 [1] Heb. *living*; a well that is supplied by subterranean streams.   26:20 [a] Gen 21:25   26:24 [a] Gen 26:2   [b] Gen 17:7–8; 24:12; Exod 3:6; Acts 7:32   [c] Gen 15:1   [d] Gen 26:3–4   26:25 [a] Gen 12:7–8; 13:4, 18; 22:9; 33:20   [b] Gen 21:33; Ps 116:17   26:26 [a] Gen 21:22   26:27 [a] Gen 26:16   26:28 [a] Gen 21:22–23   26:29 [a] Gen 24:31; Ps 115:15   [1] Or *may you be blessed*.   26:30 [a] Gen 19:3   26:31 [a] Gen 21:31   26:33 [a] Gen 21:31; 28:10   26:34 [a] Gen 28:8; 36:2   27:1 [a] Gen 35:28   [b] Gen 48:10; 1 Sam 3:2   27:3 [a] Gen 25:27–28   27:4 [a] Gen 27:19, 25, 27, 31; 48:9, 15, 16; 49:28; Deut 33:1; Heb 11:20   27:5 [1] LXX adds *to his father*.   27:8 [a] Gen 27:13, 43   27:9 [a] Gen 27:4   27:11 [a] Gen 25:25   27:12 [a] Gen 27:21–22   [b] Gen 9:25; Deut 27:18   27:14 [a] Prov 23:3; Luke 21:34   27:15 [a] Gen 27:27

you, my son?" [19]Jacob said to his father, "I am Esau, your firstborn. I've done as you told me. Now sit up and eat some of my wild game so [a]that you can bless me."[1] [20]But Isaac asked his son, "How in the world did you find it so quickly, my son?" "Because the LORD your God brought it to me," he replied. [21]Then Isaac said to Jacob, "Come closer so I can touch you, my son, and know for certain if you really are my son Esau." [22]So Jacob went over to his father Isaac, who felt him and said, "The voice is Jacob's, but the hands are Esau's." [23]He did not recognize him because [a]his hands were hairy, like his brother Esau's hands. So Isaac blessed Jacob. [24]Then he asked, "Are you really my son Esau?" "I am," Jacob replied. [25]Isaac said, "Bring some of the wild game for me to eat, my son. Then I will bless you." So Jacob brought it to him, and he ate it. He also brought him wine, and Isaac drank. [26]Then his father Isaac said to him, "Come here and kiss me, my son." [27]So Jacob went over and [a]kissed him. When Isaac caught [b]the scent of his clothing, he blessed him, saying,

"Yes, my son smells
   like the scent of an open field
   which the LORD has blessed.
[28] May [a]God give you
   [b]the dew of [c]the sky
   and the richness of the earth,
   and [d]plenty of grain and new wine.
[29] [a]May peoples serve you
   and nations bow down to you.
   You will be[1] lord[2] over your brothers,
   and the sons of your mother will bow
      down to you.
   May those who [b]curse you be cursed,
   and those who bless you be blessed."

[30]Isaac had just finished blessing Jacob, and Jacob had scarcely left[1] his father's presence, when his brother Esau returned from the hunt. [31]He also prepared some tasty food and brought it to his father. Esau said to him, "My father, get up and [a]eat some of your son's wild game. Then you can bless me." [32]His father Isaac asked, "Who are you?" "I am your firstborn son," he replied, "Esau!" [33]Isaac began to shake violently [a]and asked, "Then who else hunted game and brought it to me? I ate all of it just before you arrived, and I blessed him. He will indeed be blessed!"

[34]When Esau [a]heard his father's words, he wailed loudly and bitterly. He said to his father, "Bless me too, my father!" [35]But Isaac replied, "Your brother came in here deceitfully and took away your blessing." [36]Esau exclaimed, "Jacob [a]is the right name for him![1] He has tripped me up two times! He took away my birthright, and now, look, he has taken away my blessing!" Then he asked, "Have you not kept back a blessing for me?"

[37]Isaac replied to Esau, "Look! [a]I have made him lord over you. I have made all his relatives his servants and provided him with [b]grain and new wine. What is left that I can do for you, my son?" [38]Esau said to his father, "Do you have only that one blessing, my father? Bless me too!" Then Esau wept loudly.

[39]So his father Isaac said to him,

"See here, [a]your home will be by the
      richness of the earth,
   and by the dew of the sky above.
[40] You will live by [a]your sword
   but you will serve your brother.
   When you grow restless,
   you will tear off his yoke
      from your neck."

[41]So Esau [a]hated[1] Jacob because of [b]the blessing his father had given to his brother. Esau said privately, "[c]The time of mourning for my father is near; then I will kill my brother Jacob!"

[42]When Rebekah heard what her older son Esau had said, she quickly summoned her younger son Jacob and told him, "Look, your brother Esau is planning to get [a]revenge by killing you. [43]Now then, my son, do what [a]I say. Run away immediately to my brother Laban in Haran. [44]Live with him for a [a]little while until your brother's rage subsides. [45]Stay there until your brother's

27:19 [a] Gen 27:4   [1] Heb. *so that your soul may bless me.*   27:23 [a] Gen 27:16   27:27 [a] Gen 29:13   [b] Song 4:11; Hos 14:6   27:28 [a] Heb 11:20   [b] Gen 27:39; Deut 33:13, 28; 2 Sam 1:21; Ps 133:3; Prov 3:20; Mic 5:7; Zech 8:12   [c] Gen 45:18; Num 18:12   [d] Deut 7:13; 33:28   27:29 [a] Gen 9:25; 25:23; Isa 45:14; 49:7; 60:12, 14   [b] Gen 12:2–3; Zeph 2:8–9   [1] Heb. *and be.*   [2] Heb. *lord, mighty one.*   27:30 [1] An emphatic Heb. construction.   27:31 [a] Gen 27:4   27:33 [a] Gen 25:23; 28:3–4; Num 23:20; Rom 11:29   27:34 [a] [Heb 12:17]   27:36 [a] Gen 25:26, 32–34   [1] Heb. *Is he not rightly named Jacob?*   27:37 [a] 2 Sam 8:14   [b] Gen 27:28–29   27:39 [a] Gen 27:28; Heb 11:20   27:40 [a] Gen 25:23; 27:29; 2 Sam 8:14; [Obad 18–20]   27:41 [a] Gen 26:27; 32:3–11; 37:4–5, 8   [b] Gen 50:2–4, 10   [c] Obad 10   [1] Or *bore a grudge against.*   27:42 [a] Ps 64:5   27:43 [a] Gen 11:31; 25:20; 28:2, 5   27:44 [a] Gen 31:41

anger against you subsides and he forgets what you did to him. Then I'll send someone to bring you back from there.[1] Why should I lose both of you in one day?"

[46]Then Rebekah [a]said to Isaac, "[b]I am deeply depressed[1] because of the daughters of Heth. If Jacob were to marry one of these daughters of Heth who live in this land, I would want to die!"

28 So Isaac called for Jacob and [a]blessed him. Then he commanded him, "[b]You must not marry a Canaanite woman! [2]Leave [a]immediately for Paddan [b]Aram! Go to the house of [c]Bethuel, your mother's father, and find yourself a wife there, among the daughters of [d]Laban, your mother's brother. [3]May the Sovereign [a]God bless you! May he make you [b]fruitful and give you a multitude of descendants! Then you will become a large nation. [4]May [a]he give you and your descendants the [b]blessing he gave to Abraham so that you may possess the land God gave to Abraham, the land where you have been living as a temporary resident." [5]So Isaac sent Jacob on his way, and he went to Paddan Aram, to Laban son of Bethuel the Aramean and brother of Rebekah, the mother of Jacob and Esau.

[6]Esau saw that Isaac had blessed Jacob and sent him off to Paddan Aram to find a wife there. As he blessed him, Isaac commanded him, "You must not marry a Canaanite woman." [7]Jacob obeyed his father and mother and left for Paddan Aram. [8]Then Esau realized [a]that the Canaanite women were displeasing to his father Isaac. [9]So Esau went to Ishmael and [a]married [b]Mahalath, [c]the sister of Nebaioth and daughter of Abraham's son Ishmael, along with the wives he already had.

Jacob's Dream at Bethel

[10]Meanwhile Jacob left Beer Sheba and set out for [a]Haran. [11]He reached a certain place where he decided to camp because the sun had gone down. He took one of the stones and placed it near his head.[1] Then he fell asleep in that place [12]and had a [a]dream. [b]He saw a stairway erected on the earth with its top reaching to the heavens. The angels of God were going up and coming down it [13]and the LORD stood at its top. He said, "I am the LORD, the God of your [a]grandfather Abraham and the God of your father [b]Isaac.[1] I will give you and your descendants [c]the ground you are lying on. [14]Your [a]descendants will be like the dust of the earth, and you will spread out [b]to the west, east, north, and south. And so all the families of the earth may receive [c]blessings through you and through your descendants. [15]I am [a]with you! I will [b]protect you wherever you go and will [c]bring you back to [d]this land. I will not leave you [e]until I have done what I promised you!"

[16]Then Jacob woke up and thought, "Surely the LORD [a]is in this place, but I did not realize it!" [17]He was afraid and said, "What an awesome place this is! This is nothing else than the house of God! This is the gate of heaven!"

[18]Early in the morning Jacob took the stone he had placed near his head and [a]set it up as [b]a sacred stone. Then he poured oil on top of it. [19]He called [a]that place Bethel,[1] although the former name of the town was Luz. [20a]Then Jacob made a vow, saying, "If [b]God is with me and protects me on this journey I am taking and gives me [c]food to eat and clothing to wear, [21]and [a]I return safely to my father's home, [b]then the LORD will become my God. [22]Then this stone that I have set up as [a]a sacred stone will be the house of God, [b]and I will surely[1] give you back a tenth of everything you give me."

The Marriages of Jacob

29 So Jacob moved on [a]and came to the land of the eastern people. [2]He saw in the field a [a]well with three flocks

27:45[1] Heb. *and I will send and I will take you from there.*   **27:46**[a] Gen 26:34–35; 28:8   [b] Gen 24:3   [1] Heb. *loathe my life.*   **28:1**[a] Gen 27:33   [b] Gen 24:3   **28:2**[a] Hos 12:12   [b] Gen 25:20   [c] Gen 22:23   [d] Gen 24:29; 27:43; 29:5   **28:3**[a] Gen 17:16; 35:11; 48:3   [b] Gen 26:4, 24   **28:4**[a] Gen 12:2–3; 22:17; Gal 3:8   [b] Gen 17:8; 23:4; 36:7; 1 Chr 29:15; Ps 39:12   **28:8**[a] Gen 24:3; 26:34–35; 27:46   **28:9**[a] Gen 26:34–35   [b] Gen 36:2–3   [c] Gen 25:13   **28:10**[a] Gen 12:4–5; 27:43; 29:4; 2 Kgs 19:12; Acts 7:2   **28:11**[1] Heb. *and he put* [it at] *the place of his head.*   **28:12**[a] Gen 31:10; 41:1; Num 12:6   [b] John 1:51; Heb 1:4, 14   **28:13**[a] Gen 35:1; 48:3; Amos 7:7   [b] Gen 26:24   [c] Gen 13:15, 17; 26:3; 35:12   [1] Heb. *the God of your father Abraham and the God of Isaac;* the Heb. word for "father" can typically be used in a broader sense than the English word.   **28:14**[a] Gen 13:16; 22:17   [b] Gen 13:14–15; Deut 12:20   [c] Gen 12:3; 18:18; 22:18; 26:4; Matt 1:2; Luke 3:34; Gal 3:8   **28:15**[a] Gen 26:3, 24; 31:3   [b] Gen 48:16; Num 6:24; Ps 121:5, 7, 8   [c] Gen 35:6; 48:21; Deut 30:3   [d] Lev 26:44; Deut 7:9; 31:6, 8; Josh 1:5; 1 Kgs 8:57; Heb 13:5   [e] Num 23:19   **28:16**[a] Exod 3:5; Josh 5:15; Ps 139:7–12   **28:18**[a] Gen 31:13, 45   [b] Lev 8:10–12   **28:19**[a] Judg 1:23, 26   [1] *Bethel* means "house of God."   **28:20**[a] Gen 31:13; Judg 11:30; 2 Sam 15:8   [b] Gen 28:15   [c] 1 Tim 6:8   **28:21**[a] Judg 11:31; 2 Sam 19:24, 30   [b] Deut 26:17; 2 Sam 15:8   **28:22**[a] Gen 35:7, 14   [b] Gen 14:20; [Lev 27:30]; Deut 14:22   [1] An emphatic Heb. construction.   **29:1**[a] Gen 25:6; Num 23:7; Judg 6:3, 33; Hos 12:12   **29:2**[a] Gen 24:10–11; Exod 2:15–16

of sheep lying beside it, because the flocks were watered from that well. Now a large stone covered the mouth of the well. [3]When all the flocks were gathered there, the shepherds would roll the stone off the mouth of the well and water the sheep. Then they would put the stone back in its place over the well's mouth.

[4]Jacob asked them, "My brothers, where are you from?" They replied, "We're from [a]Haran." [5]So he said to them, "Do you know [a]Laban, the grandson of Nahor?" "We know him," they said. [6]"Is he well?" Jacob asked. They replied, "He [a]is well. Now look, here comes [b]his daughter Rachel with the sheep." [7]Then Jacob said, "Since it is still the middle of the day, it is not time for the flocks to be gathered. You should water the sheep and then go and let them graze some more."[1] [8]"We can't," they said, "until all the flocks are gathered and the stone is rolled off the mouth of the well. Then we water the sheep."

[9]While he was still speaking with them, [a]Rachel arrived with her father's sheep, for she was tending them. [10]When Jacob saw Rachel, the daughter of his uncle Laban, and the sheep of his uncle Laban, he went over and [a]rolled the stone off the mouth of the well and watered the sheep of his uncle Laban. [11]Then Jacob [a]kissed Rachel and began to weep loudly. [12]When Jacob explained to Rachel that [a]he was a relative of her father and the [b]son of Rebekah, she ran and told her father. [13]When Laban [a]heard this news about Jacob, his sister's son, he rushed out to meet him. He embraced him and kissed him and brought him to his house. Jacob told Laban how he was related to him.[1] [14]Then Laban said to him, "You are [a]indeed my own flesh and blood." So Jacob stayed with him for a month.

[15]Then Laban said to Jacob, "Should you work for me for nothing because you are my relative?[1] Tell me [a]what your wages should be." [16](Now Laban had two daughters; the older one was named Leah, and the younger one Rachel. [17]Leah's eyes were tender,[1] but Rachel had a lovely figure and [a]beautiful appearance.) [18]Since Jacob had fallen [a]in love with Rachel, he said, "I'll serve you seven years in exchange for your younger daughter Rachel." [19]Laban replied, "I'd rather give her to you than to another man. Stay with me." [20]So Jacob [a]worked for seven years to acquire Rachel. But they seemed like only a few days to him because his love for her was so great.

[21]Finally Jacob said to Laban, "Give me my wife, for my time of service is up. And I want to sleep with her."[1] [22]So Laban invited all the people of that place and [a]prepared a feast. [23]In the evening he brought his daughter Leah to Jacob, and he slept with her. [24](Laban gave his female servant [a]Zilpah to his daughter Leah to be her servant.)

[25]In the morning Jacob discovered it was Leah![1] So Jacob said to Laban, "What in the world have you done to me? Didn't I work for you in exchange for Rachel? Why have you [a]tricked me?" [26]"It is not our custom here," Laban replied, "to give the younger daughter in marriage before the firstborn. [27][a]Complete my older daughter's bridal week. Then we will give you the younger one too, in exchange for seven more years of work."

[28]Jacob did as Laban said. When Jacob completed Leah's bridal week, Laban gave him his daughter Rachel to be his wife. [29](Laban gave his female servant [a]Bilhah to his daughter Rachel to be her servant.) [30]Jacob slept with Rachel as well. He also [a]loved Rachel more than Leah. Then he worked for Laban for seven more years.

The Family of Jacob

[31]When the LORD [a]saw that Leah was unloved,[1] he [b]enabled her to become pregnant while Rachel remained childless. [32]So Leah became pregnant and gave birth to a son. She named him Reuben, for she said,

29:4 [a]Gen 11:31; 28:10   29:5 [a]Gen 24:24, 29; 28:2   29:6 [a]Gen 43:27   [b]Gen 24:11; Exod 2:16–17   29:7 [1]Heb. *water the sheep and go and pasture* [them]; the nuance is probably one of advice.   29:9 [a]Exod 2:16   29:10 [a]Exod 2:17   29:11 [a]Gen 33:4; 45:14–15   29:12 [a]Gen 13:8; 14:14, 16; 28:5   [b]Gen 24:28   29:13 [a]Gen 24:29–31; Luke 15:20   [1]Heb. *and he told to Laban all these things.*   29:14 [a]Gen 2:23; 37:27; Judg 9:2; 2 Sam 5:1; 19:12–13   29:15 [a]Gen 30:28; 31:41   [1]Heb. *my brother;* used in a loose sense as Jacob was Laban's nephew.   29:17 [a]Gen 12:11, 14; 26:7   [1]Or *delicate;* perhaps she had appealing eyes, or they were plain, not having the brightness normally expected.   29:18 [a]Gen 31:41; 2 Sam 3:14; Hos 12:12   29:20 [a]Gen 30:26; Hos 12:12   29:21 [1]Heb. *I want to approach;* a euphemism for sexual relations.   29:22 [a]Judg 14:10; John 2:1–2   29:24 [a]Gen 30:9–10   29:25 [a]Gen 27:35; 31:7; 1 Sam 28:12   [1]Heb. *and it happened in the morning that look, it was Leah.*   29:27 [a]Gen 31:41; Judg 14:2   29:29 [a]Gen 30:3–5   29:30 [a]Gen 29:17–20; Deut 21:15–17   29:31 [a]Ps 127:3   [b]Gen 30:1   [1]Heb. *hated;* a rhetorical device of overstatement emphasizing that Rachel, as Jacob's true love and the primary object of his affections, had an advantage over Leah.

"The LORD has looked with [a]pity on my oppressed condition. Surely my husband will love me now." [33]She became pregnant again and had another son. She said, "Because the LORD heard that I was unloved, he gave me this one too." So she named him Simeon. [34]She became pregnant again and had another son. She said, "Now this time my husband will show me affection, because I have given birth to three sons for him." That is why he was named Levi. [35]She became pregnant again and had another son. She said, "This time I will praise the LORD." That is why she named him [a]Judah. Then she stopped having children.

30 When Rachel saw that [a]she could not give Jacob children, she became [b]jealous of her sister. She said to Jacob, "Give me children [c]or I'll die!" [2]Jacob [a]became furious with Rachel and exclaimed, "Am I in the place of God, who has kept you from having children?" [3]She replied, "Here is [a]my servant Bilhah! Sleep with[1] her so that she can bear children for me[2] [b]and I can have [c]a family through her."

[4]So Rachel gave him her servant Bilhah [a]as a wife, and Jacob slept with her. [5]Bilhah became pregnant and gave Jacob a son. [6]Then Rachel said, "God has [a]vindicated me. He has responded to my prayer[1] and given me a son." That is why she named him Dan.

[7]Bilhah, Rachel's servant, became pregnant again and gave Jacob another son. [8]Then Rachel said, "I have fought a desperate struggle with my sister, but I have won." So she named him Naphtali.

[9]When Leah saw that she had stopped having children, she [a]gave her servant Zilpah to Jacob as a wife. [10]Soon Leah's servant Zilpah gave Jacob a son. [11]Leah said, "How fortunate!" So she named him Gad.

[12]Then Leah's servant Zilpah gave Jacob another son. [13]Leah said, "How happy [a]I am,[1] for women will call me happy!" So she named him Asher.

[14]At the time of the wheat harvest Reuben went out and found some mandrake plants in a field and brought them to his mother Leah. Rachel said to Leah, "[a]Give me some of your son's mandrakes." [15]But Leah replied, "Wasn't it enough that you've taken away my husband? Would you take away my son's mandrakes too?" "All right," Rachel said, "he may go to bed with you tonight in exchange for your son's mandrakes." [16]When Jacob came in from the fields that evening, Leah went out to meet him and said, "You must sleep[1] with me because I have paid for your services with my son's mandrakes." So he went to bed with her that night. [17]God paid attention to Leah; she became pregnant and gave Jacob a son for the fifth time. [18]Then Leah said, "God has granted me a reward because I gave my servant to my husband as a wife." So she named him Issachar.

[19]Leah became pregnant again and gave Jacob a son for the sixth time. [20]Then Leah said, "God has given me a good gift. Now my husband will honor me because I have given him six sons." So she named him Zebulun.

[21]After that she gave birth to a [a]daughter and named her Dinah.

[22]Then God took note [a]of[1] Rachel. He paid attention to her and [b]enabled her to become pregnant. [23]She became pregnant and gave birth to a son. Then she said, "God has taken away [a]my shame." [24]She named him Joseph, saying, "May [a]the LORD give me yet another son."

The Flocks of Jacob

[25]After Rachel had given birth to Joseph, Jacob said to Laban, "[a]Send me on [b]my way so that I can go home to my own country. [26]Let me take my wives and my children whom I have acquired by working [a]for you. Then I'll depart, because you know how hard I've worked for you."

[27]But Laban [a]said to him, "If I have found favor in your sight, please stay here, for I have learned by divination that the LORD has blessed me on account of you." [28]He added, "Just [a]name your wages—I'll pay whatever you want."

29:32 [a]Gen 16:11; 31:42; Exod 3:7; 4:31; Deut 26:7; Ps 25:18   **29:35** [a]Gen 49:8; Matt 1:2   **30:1** [a]Gen 16:1–2; 29:31   [b]Gen 37:11   [c]1 Sam 1:5–6; [Job 5:2]   **30:2** [a]Gen 16:2; 1 Sam 1:5   **30:3** [a]Gen 16:2   [b]Gen 50:23; Job 3:12   [c]Gen 16:2–3   [1]Heb. *came to, approached*; a euphemism for sexual relations.   [2]Heb. *upon my knees*; an idiom for Bilhah being simply a surrogate mother.   **30:4** [a]Gen 16:3–4   **30:6** [a]Gen 18:25; Ps 35:24; 43:1; Lam 3:59   [1]Heb. *and also he has heard my voice.*   **30:9** [a]Gen 30:4   **30:13** [a]Prov 31:28; Luke 1:48   [1]Heb. *with my happiness.*   **30:14** [a]Gen 25:30   **30:16** [1]Heb. *must come to me*; can be a euphemism for sexual relations.   **30:21** [a]Gen 34:1   **30:22** [a]Gen 19:29; 1 Sam 1:19–20   [b]Gen 29:31   [1]Heb. *remembered.*   **30:23** [a]1 Sam 1:6; Isa 4:1; Luke 1:25   **30:24** [a]Gen 35:16–18   **30:25** [a]Gen 24:54, 56   [b]Gen 18:33   **30:26** [a]Gen 29:18–20, 27, 30; Hos 12:12   **30:27** [a]Gen 26:24; 39:3; Isa 61:9   **30:28** [a]Gen 29:15; 31:7, 41

²⁹"You know how I have worked for ᵃyou," Jacob replied, "and how well your livestock have fared under my care. ³⁰Indeed, you had little before I arrived, but now your possessions have increased many times over. The LORD has blessed you wherever I worked. But now, how long must it be before I ᵃdo something for my own family too?"

³¹So Laban asked, "What should I give you?" "You don't need to give me a thing," Jacob replied, "but if you agree to this one condition, I will continue to care for your flocks and protect them: ³²Let me walk among all your flocks today and remove from them every speckled or spotted sheep, every dark-colored lamb,¹ and ᵃthe spotted or speckled goats. These animals will be my wages. ³³My ᵃintegrity will testify for me later on. When you come to verify that I've taken only the wages we agreed on, if I have in my possession any goat that is not speckled or spotted or any sheep that is not dark-colored, it will be considered stolen."

³⁴"Agreed!" said Laban, "It will be as you say."

³⁵So that day Laban removed the male goats that were ᵃstreaked or spotted, all the female goats that were speckled or spotted (all that had any white on them), and all the dark-colored lambs, and put them in the care of his sons. ³⁶Then he separated them from Jacob by a three-day journey, while Jacob was taking care of the rest of Laban's flocks.

³⁷But ᵃJacob took fresh-cut branches from poplar, almond, and plane trees. He made white streaks by peeling them, making the white inner wood in the branches visible. ³⁸Then he set up the peeled branches in all the watering troughs where the flocks came to drink. He set up the branches in front of the flocks when they were in heat and came to drink. ³⁹When the sheep mated¹ in front of the branches, they gave birth to young that were streaked or speckled or spotted. ⁴⁰Jacob removed these lambs, but he made the rest of the flock face the streaked and completely dark-colored animals in Laban's flock. So he made separate flocks for himself and did not mix them

with Laban's flocks. ⁴¹When the stronger females were in heat, Jacob would set up the branches in the troughs in front of the flock, so they would mate near the branches. ⁴²But if the animals were weaker, he did not set the branches there. So the weaker animals ended up belonging to Laban and the stronger animals to Jacob. ⁴³In this way Jacob ᵃbecame extremely prosperous. He owned large flocks, male and female servants, camels, and donkeys.

Jacob's Flight from Laban

31 Jacob heard that Laban's sons were complaining, "Jacob has taken everything that belonged to our father! He has gotten ᵃrich at our father's expense!" ²When Jacob saw the look on Laban's ᵃface, he could tell his attitude toward him had changed.

³The LORD said to Jacob, "ᵃReturn to the land of your fathers¹ and to your relatives. I will ᵇbe with you." ⁴So Jacob sent a message for Rachel and Leah to come to the field where his flocks were. ⁵There he ᵃsaid to them, "I can tell that your father's attitude toward me ᵇhas changed, but the God of my father has been with me. ⁶ᵃYou know that I've worked for your father as hard as I could, ⁷but your father has humiliated¹ me and ᵃchanged my wages ᵇten times. But God has not permitted him to do me any harm. ⁸If ᵃhe said, 'The speckled animals will be your wage,' then the entire flock gave birth to speckled offspring. But if he said, 'The streaked animals will be your wage,' then the entire flock gave birth to streaked offspring. ⁹In this way God has snatched away your father's livestock and given them to me.

¹⁰"Once during breeding season I saw in a dream that the male goats mating with the flock were streaked, speckled, and spotted. ¹¹In ᵃthe dream the angel of God said to me, 'Jacob!' 'Here I am!' I replied. ¹²Then he ᵃsaid, 'Observe that all the male goats mating with the flock are streaked, speckled, or spotted, for I have observed all that Laban has done to you. ¹³I am the God of Bethel,

30:29 ᵃGen 31:6, 38–40; Matt 24:45; Titus 2:10   **30:30** ᵃ[1 Tim 5:8]   **30:32** ᵃGen 31:8   ¹Or *every black lamb*; Heb. *and every dark sheep among the lambs.*   **30:33** ᵃPs 37:6   **30:35** ᵃGen 31:9–12   **30:37** ᵃGen 31:9–12   **30:39** ¹Heb. *to be in heat, to mate, to conceive, to become pregnant.*   **30:43** ᵃGen 12:16; 30:30   **31:1** ᵃPs 49:16   **31:2** ᵃGen 4:5   **31:3** ᵃGen 28:15, 20, 21; 32:9   ᵇGen 46:4   ¹Or perhaps *ancestors.*   **31:5** ᵃGen 31:2–3   ᵇGen 21:22; 28:13, 15; 31:29, 42, 53; Isa 41:10; Heb 13:5   **31:6** ᵃGen 30:29; 31:38–41   **31:7** ᵃGen 29:25; 31:41   ᵇNum 14:22; Neh 4:12; Job 19:3; Zech 8:23   ¹Heb. *to make a fool of*; deceiving someone so that their public reputation suffers.   **31:8** ᵃGen 30:32   **31:11** ᵃGen 16:7–11; 22:11, 15; 31:13; 48:16   **31:12** ᵃGen 31:42; Exod 3:7; Ps 139:3; Eccl 5:8

[a]where you anointed the sacred stone and made a vow to me. Now leave this land [b]immediately and return to your native land.'"

[14]Then Rachel and Leah replied to him, "Do we still have any portion or inheritance in our father's house? [15]Hasn't [a]he treated us like foreigners? He not only sold us, but completely wasted the money paid for us![1] [16]Surely all the wealth that God snatched away from our father belongs to us and to our children. So now do everything God has told you."

[17]So Jacob immediately put his children and his wives on the camels. [18]He took away[1] all the livestock he had acquired in Paddan Aram and all his moveable property that he had accumulated. Then he set out toward the land of [a]Canaan to return to his father Isaac.

[19]While Laban had gone to shear his sheep, Rachel stole the [a]household idols[1] that belonged to her father. [20]Jacob also deceived[1] Laban the Aramean by not telling him that he was leaving. [21]He left with all he owned. He quickly crossed the Euphrates River and headed [a]for the hill country of Gilead.

[22]Three days later Laban discovered Jacob had left. [23]So he took [a]his relatives with him and pursued Jacob for seven days. He caught up with him in the hill country of Gilead. [24]But God came to Laban the Aramean in [a]a dream at night and warned him, "Be careful that you [b]neither bless nor curse Jacob."

[25]Laban overtook Jacob, and when Jacob pitched his tent in the hill country of Gilead, Laban and his relatives set up camp there too.[1] [26]"What have you done?" Laban demanded of Jacob. "You've deceived me and [a]carried away my daughters as if they were captives of war! [27]Why did you run away secretly and deceive me? Why didn't you tell me so I could send you off with a celebration complete with singing, tambourines, and harps? [28]You didn't even allow me [a]to kiss my daughters and my grandchildren goodbye. [b]You have acted foolishly! [29]I have the power to do you harm, but the [a]God of your father told me [b]last night, 'Be careful that you neither bless nor curse Jacob.'[1] [30]Now I understand that you have gone away because you longed desperately for your father's house. Yet why did you [a]steal my gods?"

[31]"I left secretly because I was [a]afraid!" Jacob replied to Laban. "I thought you might take your daughters away from me by force. [32]Whoever has taken your gods will be put to death! In the presence of our relatives identify whatever is yours and take it." (Now Jacob did not know that Rachel had stolen them.)

[33]So Laban entered Jacob's tent, and Leah's tent, and the tent of the two female servants, but he did not find the idols. Then he left Leah's tent and entered Rachel's. [34](Now Rachel had taken the idols and put them inside her camel's saddle and sat on them.) Laban searched the whole tent, but did not find them. [35]Rachel said to her father, "Don't be angry, my lord. I cannot stand [a]up in your presence because I am having my period."[1] So he searched thoroughly, but did not find the idols.

[36]Jacob became angry and argued with Laban. "What did I do wrong?" he demanded of Laban. "What sin of mine prompted you to chase after me in hot pursuit? [37]When you searched through all my goods, did you find anything that belonged to you? Set it here before my relatives and yours, and let them settle the dispute between the two of us!

[38]"I have been with you for the past 20 years. Your ewes and female goats have not miscarried, nor have I eaten rams from your flocks. [39]Animals torn by wild beasts I never brought to you; I always absorbed the loss myself. You always made me pay for every missing animal, whether it was taken by day or [a]at night. [40]I was consumed by scorching heat during the day and by piercing cold at night, and I went without sleep. [41]This was

31:13 [a]Gen 28:16–22; 35:1, 6, 15   [b]Gen 31:3; 32:9   31:15 [a]Gen 29:15, 20, 23, 27; Neh 5:8   [1]Heb. *our money.*   31:18 [a]Gen 17:8; 33:18; 35:27   [1]Heb. *drove away.*   31:19 [a]Gen 31:30, 34; 35:2; Judg 17:5; 1 Sam 19:13; Hos 3:4   [1]Or *household gods; items that guaranteed the right of inheritance, or that were viewed as protective deities.*   31:20 [1]Heb. *stole the heart of.* 31:21 [a]Gen 46:28; 2 Kgs 12:17; Luke 9:51, 53   31:23 [a]Gen 13:8   31:24 [a]Gen 20:3; 31:29; 46:2–4; Job 33:15; Matt 1:20   [b]Gen 24:50; 31:7, 29   31:25 [1]Heb. *and Jacob pitched his tent in the hill country, and Laban pitched with his brothers in the hill country of Gilead.*   31:26 [a]1 Sam 30:2   31:28 [a]Gen 31:55; Ruth 1:9, 14; 1 Kgs 19:20; Acts 20:37   [b]1 Sam 13:13   31:29 [a]Gen 28:13; 31:5, 24, 42, 53   [b]Gen 31:24   [1]Heb. *from speaking with Jacob from good to evil.*   31:30 [a]Gen 31:19; Josh 24:2; Judg 17:5; 18:24   31:31 [a]Gen 26:7; 32:7, 11   31:35 [a]Exod 20:12; Lev 19:32   [1]Heb. *the way of women is to me;* an idiom for a woman's menstrual period.   31:39 [a]Exod 22:10

my lot for 20 years in your house: I worked like a [a]slave for [b]you—14 years for your two daughters and 6 years for your flocks—but you changed my wages 10 times! [42][a]If [b]the [c]God of my father—the God of Abraham, the one whom Isaac fears—had not been with me, you would certainly have sent me away empty-handed! But God saw how I was oppressed and how hard I worked, and he [d]rebuked you last night."

[43]Laban replied to Jacob, "These women are my daughters, these children are my grandchildren, and these flocks are my flocks. All that you see belongs to me. But how can I harm these daughters of mine today or the children to whom they have given birth? [44]So now, come, [a]let's make a formal agreement, [b]you and I, and it will be proof that we have made peace."

[45]So Jacob [a]took a stone and set it up as a memorial pillar. [46]Then he said to his relatives, "Gather stones." So they brought stones and put them in a pile. They ate there by the pile of stones. [47]Laban called it Jegar Sahadutha, but Jacob called it Galeed. [48]Laban said, "[a]This pile of stones is a witness of our agreement today." That is why it was called Galeed. [49]It was also called [a]Mizpah because he said, "May the LORD watch between us when we are out of sight of one another. [50]If you mistreat my daughters or if you take wives besides my daughters, although no one else is with us, realize that God is witness to your actions."

[51]"Here is this pile of stones and this pillar I have set up between me and you," Laban said to Jacob. [52]"This pile of stones and the pillar are reminders that I will not pass beyond this pile to come to harm you and that you will not pass beyond this pile and this pillar to come to harm me. [53]May the God of Abraham and the god of Nahor, the gods of their father, [a]judge between us." Jacob took an [b]oath by [c]the God whom his father Isaac feared. [54]Then Jacob offered a sacrifice on the mountain and invited his relatives to eat the meal. They ate the meal and spent the night on the mountain.

[55]Early in the morning Laban [a]kissed his grandchildren and his daughters goodbye and [b]blessed them. Then Laban left and [c]returned home.

Jacob Wrestles at Peniel

32 So Jacob went on his way and [a]the angels of God met him. [2]When Jacob saw them, he exclaimed, "This is the [a]camp of God!" So he named that place Mahanaim.

[3]Jacob sent messengers on ahead to his brother Esau [a]in [b]the land of Seir, the region of Edom. [4]He [a]commanded them, "This is what you must say to my lord Esau: 'This is what your servant Jacob says: I have been staying with Laban until now. [5]I have oxen, donkeys, sheep, and male and female servants. [a]I have sent [b]this message to inform my lord, so that I may find favor in your sight.'"

[6]The messengers returned to Jacob and said, "We went to your [a]brother Esau. He is coming to meet you and has 400 men with him." [7]Jacob [a]was very afraid and upset. So he divided the people who were with him into two camps, as well as the flocks, herds, and camels. [8]"If Esau attacks one camp," he thought, "then the other camp will be able to escape."[1]

[9][a]Then [b]Jacob prayed, "[c]O God of my father Abraham, God of my father Isaac, O LORD, you said to me, 'Return to your land and to your relatives and I will make you prosper.' [10]I am not worthy of all the faithful [a]love you have shown your servant. With only [b]my walking stick I crossed the Jordan, but now I have become two camps. [11]Rescue me, [a]I pray, from [b]the hand[1] of my brother Esau, for I am afraid he will come and attack me, as well as the mothers with their children. [12]But [a]you said, 'I will certainly make you prosper and will make your descendants like the [b]sand on the seashore, too numerous to count.'"

[13]Jacob [a]stayed there that night. Then he sent as a gift to his brother Esau [14]200 female goats and 20 male goats, 200 ewes and 20 rams, [15]30 female camels with their

31:41 [a]Gen 29:20, 27–30 [b]Gen 31:7   31:42 [a]Gen 31:5, 29, 53; Ps 124:1–2 [b]Gen 31:53; Isa 8:13 [c]Gen 29:32; Exod 3:7 [d]Gen 31:24, 29; 1 Chr 12:17   31:44 [a]Gen 21:27, 32; 26:28 [b]Josh 24:27   31:45 [a]Gen 28:18; 35:14; Josh 24:26–27   31:48 [a]Josh 24:27   31:49 [a]Judg 10:17; 11:29; 1 Sam 7:5–6   31:53 [a]Gen 16:5 [b]Gen 21:23 [c]Gen 31:42   31:55 [a]Gen 29:11, 13; 31:28, 43 [b]Gen 28:1 [c]Gen 18:33; 30:25; Num 24:25   32:1 [a]Num 22:31; 2 Kgs 6:16–17; [Ps 34:7; 91:1; Heb 1:14]   32:2 [a]Josh 5:14; Ps 103:21; 148:2; Luke 2:13   32:3 [a]Gen 14:6; 33:14, 16 [b]Gen 25:30; 36:6–9; Deut 2:5; Josh 24:4   32:4 [a]Prov 15:1   32:5 [a]Gen 30:43 [b]Gen 33:8, 15   32:6 [a]Gen 33:1   32:7 [a]Gen 32:11; 35:3   32:8 [1]Heb. *the surviving camp will be for escape.*   32:9 [a][Ps 50:15] [b]Gen 28:13; 31:42 [c]Gen 31:3, 13   32:10 [a]Gen 24:27 [b]Job 8:7   32:11 [a]Ps 59:1–2 [b]Hos 10:14 [1]I.e., power.   32:12 [a]Gen 28:13–15 [b]Gen 22:17   32:13 [a]Gen 43:11

young, 40 cows and 10 bulls, and 20 female donkeys and 10 male donkeys. [16]He entrusted them to his servants, who divided them into herds. He told his servants, "Pass over before me, and keep some distance between one herd and the next." [17]He instructed the servant leading the first herd, "When my brother Esau meets you and asks, 'To whom do you belong? Where are you going? Whose herds are you driving?' [18]then you must say, 'They belong to your servant Jacob. They have been sent as a gift to my lord Esau. In fact Jacob himself is behind us.'"

[19]He also gave these instructions to the second and third servants, as well as all those who were following the herds, saying, "You must say the same thing to Esau when you meet him. [20]You must also say, 'In fact your servant Jacob is behind us.'" Jacob thought,[1] "I will first [a]appease him by sending a gift ahead of me. After that I will meet him. Perhaps he will accept me."[2] [21]So the gifts were sent on ahead of him while he spent that night in the camp.

[22]During the night Jacob quickly took his two wives, his two female servants, [a]and his eleven sons and crossed the ford of the Jabbok. [23]He took them and sent them across the stream along with all his possessions. [24]So [a]Jacob was left alone. Then a man wrestled with him until daybreak. [25]When [a]the man saw that he could not defeat Jacob, he struck[1] the socket of his hip so the socket of Jacob's hip was dislocated while he wrestled with him.

[26]Then [a]the man [b]said, "Let me go, for the dawn is breaking." "I will not let you go," Jacob replied, "unless you bless me." [27]The man asked him, "What is your name?" He answered, "Jacob." [28]"No longer will [a]your name be Jacob," the man told him, "but Israel, because you have [b]fought [c]with God and with men and have prevailed."

[29]Then Jacob asked, "Please tell me your name." "[a]Why do you ask my name?" the man replied. Then he [b]blessed[1] Jacob there. [30]So Jacob named the place [a]Peniel, explaining, "Certainly I have seen God face to face and have survived."

[31]The sun rose over him as he crossed over Penuel, but he was limping because of his hip. [32]That is why to this day the Israelites do not eat the sinew which is attached to the socket of the hip, because he struck the socket of Jacob's hip near the attached sinew.

Jacob Meets Esau

33 Jacob looked up and saw that [a]Esau was coming[1] along with 400 men. So he divided the children among Leah, Rachel, and the two female servants. [2]He put the servants and their children in front, with Leah and her children behind them, and Rachel and Joseph behind them. [3]But Jacob himself went on ahead of them, and he [a]bowed toward the ground seven times as he approached his brother. [4a]But Esau ran to meet him, embraced him, hugged his neck, [b]and kissed him. Then they both wept. [5]When Esau looked up and saw the women and the children, he asked, "[a]Who are these people with you?" Jacob replied, "The children whom God has graciously given[1] your servant." [6]The female servants came forward with their children and bowed down. [7]Then Leah came forward with her children and they bowed down. Finally Joseph and Rachel came forward and bowed down.

[8]Esau then asked, "What did you intend by sending [a]all these herds [b]to meet me?" Jacob replied, "To find favor in your sight, my lord." [9]But Esau said, "I have plenty, my brother. Keep what belongs to you." [10]"No, please take them," Jacob said. "If I [a]have found favor in your sight, accept my gift from my hand. Now that I have seen your face and you have accepted me, it is as if I have seen the face of God. [11]Please take [a]my present that was brought to you, for God has been [b]generous to me and I have all I need." When Jacob urged him, he took it.

[12]Then Esau said, "Let's be on our way! I will go in front of you." [13]But Jacob said to him, "My lord knows that the children are young, and that I have to look after the sheep and cattle that are nursing their young. If they are driven too hard for even

32:20 [a][Prov 21:14] [1]Heb. *for he said.* [2]Heb. *Perhaps he will lift up my face.*   32:22 [a]Num 21:24; Deut 3:16; Josh 12:2   32:24 [a]Josh 5:13–15; Hos 12:2–4   32:25 [a]Matt 26:41; 2 Cor 12:7 [1]Or *injured;* trad. *touched.*   32:26 [a]Luke 24:28 [b]Hos 12:4   32:28 [a]Gen 35:10; 1 Kgs 18:31; 2 Kgs 17:34 [b]Hos 12:3–4 [c]Gen 25:31; 27:33   32:29 [a]Judg 13:17–18 [b]Gen 35:9 [1]I.e., endowed Jacob with success, including meeting Esau.   32:30 [a]Gen 16:13; Exod 24:10–11; 33:20; Num 12:8; Deut 5:24; Judg 6:22; Isa 6:5; [Matt 5:8; 1 Cor 13:12]   33:1 [a]Gen 32:6 [1]Or *and look, Esau was coming.*   33:3 [a]Gen 18:2; 42:6   33:4 [a]Gen 32:28 [b]Gen 45:14–15   33:5 [a]Gen 48:9; [Ps 127:3]; Isa 8:18 [1]Heb. *to be gracious, to show favor.*   33:8 [a]Gen 32:13–16 [b]Gen 32:5   33:10 [a]Gen 43:3; 2 Sam 3:13; 14:24, 28, 32   33:11 [a]Judg 1:15; 1 Sam 25:27; 30:26 [b]Gen 30:43; Exod 33:19

a single day, all the animals will die. [14]Let my lord go on ahead of his servant. [a]I will travel more slowly, at the pace of the herds and the children, until I come to my lord at Seir."

[15]So Esau said, "[a]Let me leave some of my men with you."[1] "Why do that?" Jacob replied. "My lord has already been kind enough to me."

[16]So that same day Esau made his way back to Seir. [17]But Jacob traveled to [a]Sukkoth where he built himself a house and made shelters for his livestock. That is why the place was called[1] Sukkoth.

[18]After [a]he left Paddan Aram, Jacob came safely to the city of [b]Shechem in the land of Canaan, and he camped near the city. [19]Then [a]he purchased the portion of the field where he had pitched his tent; he bought it from the sons of Hamor, Shechem's father, for 100 pieces of money. [20]There he set up an altar and called it "The God of [a]Israel is God."

Dinah and the Shechemites

34 Now [a]Dinah, Leah's daughter whom she bore to Jacob, went to meet the young women of the land. [2]When Shechem son of Hamor the Hivite, who ruled that area, saw her, he [a]grabbed her, forced himself on her, and sexually assaulted her.[1] [3]Then he became very attached to Dinah, Jacob's daughter. He fell in love with the young woman and spoke romantically to her.[1] [4]Shechem [a]said to his father Hamor, "Acquire this young girl as my wife." [5]When Jacob heard that Shechem had violated his daughter Dinah, his sons were with the livestock in the field. So Jacob remained silent until they came in.

[6]Then Shechem's father Hamor went to speak with Jacob about Dinah. [7]Now Jacob's sons [a]had come in from the field when they [b]heard the news. They were offended[1] and very angry because Shechem had disgraced Israel by sexually assaulting[2] Jacob's daughter, a crime that should not be committed.

[8]But Hamor made this appeal to them: "My son Shechem is in love with your daughter.[1] Please give her to him as his wife. [9]Intermarry with us. Let us marry your daughters, and take our daughters as wives for yourselves. [10]You may live among us, and the land will be open to you. Live in it, travel freely in it, and acquire property in it."

[11]Then Shechem said to Dinah's father and brothers, "Let me find favor in your sight, and whatever you require of me I'll give. [12]You can make the bride [a]price and the gift I must bring very expensive, and I'll give whatever you ask of me. Just give me the young woman as my wife!"

[13]Jacob's sons answered Shechem and his father Hamor [a]deceitfully when they spoke because Shechem had violated their sister Dinah. [14]They said to them, "We cannot give our sister to a man who is not [a]circumcised, for it would be [b]a disgrace[1] to us. [15]We will give you our consent on this one condition: You must become like us by circumcising all your males. [16]Then we will give you our daughters to marry, and we will take your daughters as wives for ourselves, and we will live among you and become one people. [17]But if you do not agree to our terms by being circumcised, then we will take our sister and depart."

[18]Their offer pleased Hamor and his son Shechem. [19]The young man did not delay in doing what they asked because he wanted Jacob's daughter Dinah badly. (Now he was [a]more important than anyone in his father's household.) [20]So Hamor and his son Shechem went to the [a]gate of their city and spoke to the men of their city, [21]"These men are at peace with us. So let them live in the land and travel freely in it, for the land is wide enough for them. We will take their daughters for wives, and we will give them our daughters to marry. [22]Only on this one condition will these men consent to live with us and become one people: They demand that every male among us be circumcised just as they are circumcised. [23]If we

33:14 [a]Gen 32:3; 36:8   33:15 [a]Gen 34:11; 47:25; Ruth 2:13   [1]A polite offer of help.   33:17 [a]Josh 13:27; Judg 8:5; Ps 60:6   [1]Heb. *why he called.*   33:18 [a]John 3:23   [b]Gen 12:6; 35:4; Josh 24:1; Judg 9:1; Ps 60:6   33:19 [a]Josh 24:32; John 4:5   33:20 [a]Gen 35:7   34:1 [a]Gen 30:21   34:2 [a]Gen 20:2   [1]Heb. *to defile, to mistreat, to violate, to rape, to shame, to afflict.*   34:3 [1]Or *he reassured the young woman;* Heb. *and he spoke to the heart of the young woman.*   34:4 [a]Judg 14:2   34:7 [a]Deut 22:20–30; Josh 7:15; Judg 20:6   [b]Deut 23:17; 2 Sam 13:12   [1]Heb. *to be injured; to experience emotional pain, to be depressed emotionally, to be worried; to be embarrassed, to be insulted, to be offended.*   [2]Heb. *by lying with the daughter of Jacob;* a euphemism for sexual relations, or in this case, sexual assault.   34:8 [1]Heb. *Shechem my son, his soul is attached to your daughter.*   34:12 [a]Exod 22:16–17; Deut 22:29   34:13 [a]Gen 31:7; Exod 8:29   34:14 [a]Exod 12:48   [b]Josh 5:2–9   [1]Heb. *ridicule, taunt, reproach.*   34:19 [a]1 Chr 4:9   34:20 [a]Gen 19:1; 23:10; Ruth 4:1, 11; 2 Sam 15:2

do so, won't their livestock, their property, and all their animals become ours? So let's consent to their demand, so they will live among us."

²⁴All the men who assembled at the city gate agreed with Hamor and his son Shechem. Every male who assembled at the city gate was circumcised. ²⁵In three days, when they were still in pain, two of Jacob's sons, ªSimeon and Levi, Dinah's brothers, each took his sword and went to the unsuspecting city¹ and slaughtered every male. ²⁶They ªkilled Hamor and his son Shechem with the sword, took Dinah from Shechem's house, and left. ²⁷Jacob's sons killed them and looted the city because their sister had been violated. ²⁸They took their flocks, herds, and donkeys, as well as everything in the city and in the surrounding fields. ²⁹They captured as plunder all their wealth, all their little ones, and their wives, including everything in the houses.

³⁰Then Jacob said to Simeon and Levi, "ªYou have brought ruin ᵇon¹ me ᶜby making me ᵈa foul odor among the inhabitants of the land—among the Canaanites and the Perizzites. I am few in number; they will join forces against me and attack me, and both I and my family will be destroyed!" ³¹But Simeon and Levi replied, "Should he treat our sister like a common prostitute?"

The Return to Bethel

35 Then God said to Jacob, "Go up at once to ªBethel and live there. Make an altar there to God, ᵇwho appeared to you ᶜwhen you fled from your brother Esau." ²So Jacob told his ªhousehold and all who were with him, "Get rid of ᵇthe foreign gods you have among you. ᶜPurify yourselves and change your clothes. ³Let us go up at once to Bethel. Then I will make an altar there to God, ªwho responded to me in my time of distress ᵇand has been with me wherever I went."

⁴So they gave Jacob all the foreign gods that were in their possession and the ªrings that were in ᵇtheir ears.¹ Jacob buried them under the oak near Shechem ⁵and ªthey started on their journey. The surrounding cities were afraid of God, and they did not pursue the sons of Jacob.

⁶Jacob and all those who were with him arrived at ªLuz (that is, Bethel) in the land of Canaan. ⁷He ªbuilt an altar ᵇthere and named the place El Bethel because there God had revealed himself to him when he was fleeing from his brother. ⁸(ªDeborah, Rebekah's nurse, died and was buried under the oak below Bethel; thus it was named Oak of Weeping.)¹

⁹ªGod appeared to Jacob again after he returned from Paddan Aram and ᵇblessed him. ¹⁰God said to him, "ªYour name is Jacob, ᵇbut your name will no longer be called Jacob; Israel will be your name." So God named him Israel. ¹¹Then God ªsaid to him, "I am the Sovereign God. ᵇBe fruitful ᶜand multiply! A nation—even a company of nations—will descend from you; kings will be among your descendants! ¹²The ªland I gave to Abraham and Isaac I will give to you. To your descendants I will also give this land." ¹³Then God ªwent up from the place where he spoke with him. ¹⁴So Jacob ªset up a sacred stone pillar in the place where God spoke with him. He poured out a drink offering on it, and then he poured oil on it. ¹⁵Jacob named the place where God spoke with him ªBethel.¹

¹⁶They traveled on from Bethel, and when Ephrath was still some distance away, Rachel went into labor¹—and her labor was hard. ¹⁷When her labor was at its hardest, the midwife said to her, "Don't be afraid, for ªyou are having another son." ¹⁸With her dying breath, she named him Ben Oni. But his father called him Benjamin instead. ¹⁹So ªRachel died and was buried on the way to ᵇEphrath (that is, Bethlehem). ²⁰Jacob set up a marker over her grave; it is the Marker of Rachel's Grave ªto this day.

34:25 ª Gen 29:33–34; 42:24; 49:5–7 ¹ Heb. *and they came upon the city,* [which was] *secure; the city was caught unprepared and at peace, not expecting an attack.* **34:26** ª Gen 49:5–6 **34:30** ª Gen 49:6 ᵇ Josh 7:25 ᶜ Exod 5:21; 1 Sam 13:4; 2 Sam 10:6 ᵈ Gen 46:26–27; Deut 4:27; 1 Chr 16:19; Ps 105:12 ¹ Trad. *troubled me.* **35:1** ª Gen 28:19; 31:13 ᵇ Gen 28:13 ᶜ Gen 27:43 **35:2** ª Gen 18:19; Josh 24:15 ᵇ Gen 31:19, 30, 34; Josh 24:2, 14, 23 ᶜ Exod 19:10, 14; Lev 13:6 **35:3** ª Gen 32:7, 24; Ps 107:6 ᵇ Gen 28:15, 20; 31:3, 42 **35:4** ª Hos 2:13 ᵇ Josh 24:26; Judg 9:6 ¹ Or *the rings that were in the ears of the idols.* **35:5** ª Exod 15:16; 23:27; [Deut 2:25; 11:25]; Josh 2:9; 1 Sam 14:15 **35:6** ª Gen 28:19, 22; 48:3 **35:7** ª Gen 33:20; 35:3; Eccl 5:4 ᵇ Gen 28:13 **35:8** ª Gen 24:59 ¹ Or *Allon Bacuth.* **35:9** ª Josh 5:13; Dan 10:5 ᵇ Gen 32:29; Hos 12:4 **35:10** ª Gen 17:5 ᵇ Gen 32:28 **35:11** ª Gen 17:1; 28:3; 48:3–4; Exod 6:3 ᵇ Gen 9:1, 7 ᶜ Gen 17:5–6, 16; 28:3; 48:4 **35:12** ª Gen 12:7; 13:15; 26:3–4; 28:13; 48:4; Exod 32:13 **35:13** ª Gen 17:22; 18:33 **35:14** ª Gen 28:18–19; 31:45 **35:15** ª Gen 28:19 ¹ *Bethel* means "house of God." **35:16** ¹ Heb. *she gave birth.* **35:17** ª Gen 30:24; 1 Sam 4:20 **35:19** ª Gen 48:7 ᵇ Ruth 1:2; 4:11; Mic 5:2; Matt 2:6 **35:20** ª 1 Sam 10:2

[21]Then Israel traveled on and pitched his tent beyond Migdal Eder. [22]While Israel was living in that land, Reuben went to [a]bed with[1] Bilhah, his father's concubine, and Israel heard about it.

Jacob had twelve sons:

[23] The sons of Leah were [a]Reuben, Jacob's firstborn, as well as Simeon, Levi, Judah, Issachar, and Zebulun.
[24] The sons of Rachel were Joseph and Benjamin.
[25] The sons of Bilhah, Rachel's servant, were Dan and Naphtali.
[26] The sons of Zilpah, Leah's servant, were Gad and Asher.

These were the sons of Jacob who were born to him in Paddan Aram.

[27]So Jacob came back to his father Isaac in [a]Mamre, to Kiriath [b]Arba (that is, Hebron), where Abraham and Isaac had stayed.[1] [28]Isaac lived to be 180 years old. [29]Then Isaac breathed his last and joined his ancestors. He died an old man who had lived [a]a full life. [b]His sons Esau and Jacob buried him.

The Descendants of Esau

36 What follows is the account of Esau (also known as Edom).

[2a]Esau took his wives from the Canaanites: Adah the daughter of Elon the [b]Hittite, and [c]Oholibamah the daughter of Anah and granddaughter of Zibeon the Hivite, [3]in addition to [a]Basemath the daughter of Ishmael and sister of Nebaioth.

[4a]Adah bore Eliphaz to Esau, Basemath bore Reuel, [5]and Oholibamah bore Jeush, Jalam, and Korah. These were the sons of Esau who were born to him in the land of Canaan.

[6]Esau took his wives, his sons, his daughters, all the people in his household, his livestock, his animals, and all his possessions that he had acquired in the land of Canaan, and he went to a land some distance away from Jacob his brother [7a]because [b]they had too many possessions to be able to stay together, and the land where they had settled was not able to support them because of their livestock. [8]So [a]Esau (also known as Edom) lived in the hill [b]country of Seir.[1]

[9]This is the account of Esau, the father of the Edomites, in the hill country of Seir.

[10]These were the names of Esau's sons: [a]Eliphaz, the son of Esau's wife Adah, and Reuel, the son of Esau's wife Basemath.

[11]These were the sons of Eliphaz: Teman, Omar, Zepho, Gatam, and Kenaz.

[12]Timna, a concubine of Esau's son Eliphaz, bore [a]Amalek to Eliphaz. These were the sons of Esau's wife Adah.

[13]These were the sons of Reuel: Nahath, Zerah, Shammah, and Mizzah. These were the sons of Esau's wife Basemath.

[14]These were the sons of Esau's wife Oholibamah the daughter of Anah and granddaughter of Zibeon: She bore Jeush, Jalam, and Korah to Esau.

[15]These were the chiefs among the descendants of Esau, the sons of Eliphaz, Esau's firstborn: chief Teman, chief Omar, chief Zepho, chief Kenaz, [16]chief Korah,[1] chief Gatam, chief Amalek. These were the chiefs descended from Eliphaz in the land of Edom; these were the sons of Adah.

[17]These were the sons of Esau's son Reuel: chief Nahath, chief Zerah, chief Shammah, chief Mizzah. These were the chiefs descended from Reuel in the land of Edom; these were the sons of Esau's wife Basemath.

[18]These were the sons of Esau's wife Oholibamah: chief Jeush, chief Jalam, chief Korah. These were the chiefs descended from Esau's wife Oholibamah, the daughter of Anah.

[19]These were the sons of Esau (also known as Edom), and these were their chiefs.

[20]These were [a]the sons of Seir [b]the Horite, who were living in the land: Lotan, Shobal, Zibeon, Anah, [21]Dishon, Ezer, and Dishan. These were the chiefs of the Horites, the descendants of Seir in the land of Edom.

[22]The sons of Lotan were Hori and Homam;[1] Lotan's sister was Timna.

[23]These were the sons of Shobal: Alvan, Manahath, Ebal, Shepho, and Onam.

[24]These were [a]the sons of Zibeon: Aiah

35:22 [a]Gen 49:4; 1 Chr 5:1 [1]Heb. *lay down with*; going to bed to sleep or can be a euphemism for sexual relations. **35:23** [a]Gen 29:31–35; 30:18–20; 46:8; Exod 1:1–4 **35:27** [a]Gen 13:18; 18:1; 23:19 [b]Josh 14:15 [1]Trad. *to sojourn.* **35:29** [a]Gen 15:15; 25:8; 49:33 [b]Gen 25:9; 49:31 **36:2** [a]Gen 26:34; 28:9 [b]2 Kgs 7:6 [c]Gen 36:25 **36:3** [a]Gen 28:9 **36:4** [a]1 Chr 1:35 **36:7** [a]Gen 13:6, 11 [b]Gen 17:8; 28:4; Heb 11:9 **36:8** [a]Gen 36:1, 19 [b]Gen 32:3; Deut 2:5; Josh 24:4 [1]Trad. *Mount Seir.* **36:10** [a]1 Chr 1:35 **36:12** [a]Exod 17:8–16; Num 24:20; Deut 25:17–19; 1 Sam 15:2–3 **36:16** [1]Smr. omits *Korah* (see v. 11; 1 Chr 1:36). **36:20** [a]1 Chr 1:38–42 [b]Gen 14:6; Deut 2:12, 22 **36:22** [1]Heb. *Hemam.* **36:24** [a]Lev 19:19

and Anah (who discovered the hot springs in the wilderness as he pastured the donkeys of his father Zibeon).

[25]These were the children of Anah: Dishon and Oholibamah, the daughter of Anah.

[26]These were the sons of Dishon: Hemdan, Eshban, Ithran, and Keran.

[27]These were the sons of Ezer: Bilhan, Zaavan, and Akan.

[28]These were the sons of Dishan: [a]Uz and Aran.

[29]These were the chiefs of the Horites: chief Lotan, chief Shobal, chief Zibeon, chief Anah, [30]chief Dishon, chief Ezer, chief Dishan. These were the chiefs of the Horites, according to their chief lists in the land of Seir.

[31][a]These were the kings who reigned in the land of Edom before any king ruled over the Israelites:

[32]Bela the son of Beor reigned in Edom; the name of his city was Dinhabah.

[33]When Bela died, Jobab the son of Zerah from Bozrah reigned in his place.

[34]When Jobab died, Husham from the land of the Temanites reigned in his place.

[35]When Husham died, Hadad the son of Bedad, who defeated the Midianites in the land of Moab, reigned in his place; the name of his city was Avith.

[36]When Hadad died, Samlah from Masrekah reigned in his place.

[37]When Samlah died, Shaul from [a]Rehoboth on the River[1] reigned in his place.

[38]When Shaul died, Baal Hanan the son of Achbor reigned in his place.

[39]When Baal Hanan the son of Achbor died, Hadad[1] reigned in his place; the name of his city was Pau. His wife's name was Mehetabel, the daughter of Matred, the daughter of Me-Zahab.

[40]These were the names of the chiefs of Esau, according to their families, according to their places, by their names: chief Timna, chief Alvah, chief Jetheth, [41]chief Oholibamah, chief Elah, chief Pinon, [42]chief Kenaz, chief Teman, chief Mibzar, [43]chief Magdiel, chief Iram. These were the chiefs of Edom, according to their settlements in the land they possessed. This was Esau, the father of the Edomites.

Joseph's Dreams

37 But Jacob lived in the land [a]where his father had stayed, in the land of Canaan.

[2]This is the [a]account of Jacob.

Joseph, his seventeen-year-old son, was taking care of the flocks with his brothers. Now he was a youngster working with the sons of Bilhah and Zilpah, his father's wives. Joseph brought back a bad report about them to their father.

[3]Now Israel loved Joseph more than all his sons because [a]he was a son born to him late in life, and he [b]made a special tunic for him. [4]When Joseph's brothers saw that their father loved him more than any of them, they [a]hated Joseph and were not able to speak to him kindly.

[5]Joseph had a dream, and when he told his brothers about it they hated him even more. [6]He said to them, "Listen to this dream I had: [7]There we were, binding sheaves of grain in [a]the middle of the field. Suddenly my sheaf rose up and stood upright and your sheaves surrounded my sheaf and bowed down to it!" [8]Then his brothers asked him, "Do you really think you will rule over us or have dominion over us?" They hated him even more because of his dream and because of what he said.

[9]Then [a]he had another dream, and told it to his brothers. "Look," he said. "I had another dream. The sun, the moon, and eleven stars were bowing down to me." [10]When he told his father and his brothers, his father rebuked him, saying, "What is this dream that [a]you had? Will I, your mother, and your brothers really come and bow down to you?"[1] [11]His brothers were jealous of him, but [a]his father kept in [b]mind what Joseph said.

[12]When his brothers had gone to graze their father's flocks near [a]Shechem, [13]Israel said to Joseph, "Your brothers are grazing the flocks near Shechem. Come, I will send you to them." "I'm ready," Joseph replied. [14]So Jacob said to him, "Go now and check on the welfare of your brothers and of the flocks, and bring me word." So Jacob sent him from the valley of [a]Hebron.

36:28 [a] Job 1:1   **36:31** [a] Gen 17:6, 16; 35:11; 1 Chr 1:43   **36:37** [a] Gen 10:11   [1] Perhaps the Euphrates River.   **36:39** [1] Maj. MT MSS *Hadar.*   **37:1** [a] Gen 17:8; 23:4; 28:4; 36:7; Heb 11:9   **37:2** [a] Gen 35:25–26; 1 Sam 2:22–24   **37:3** [a] Gen 44:20   [b] Gen 37:23, 32; Judg 5:30; 1 Sam 2:19   **37:4** [a] Gen 27:41; 49:23; 1 Sam 17:28; John 15:18–20   **37:7** [a] Gen 42:6, 9; 43:26; 44:14   **37:9** [a] Gen 46:29; 47:25   **37:10** [a] Gen 27:29   [1] Heb. *Coming, will we come, I and your mother and your brothers, to bow down to you to the ground?*; an emphatic Heb. construction.   **37:11** [a] Matt 27:17–18; Acts 7:9   [b] Dan 7:28; Luke 2:19, 51   **37:12** [a] Gen 33:18–20   **37:14** [a] Gen 13:18; 23:2, 19; 35:27; Josh 14:14–15; Judg 1:10

[15]When Joseph reached Shechem, a man found him wandering in the field, so the man asked him, "What are you looking for?" [16]He replied, "I'm looking for my brothers. [a]Please tell me where they are grazing their flocks." [17]The man said, "They left this area, for I heard them say, 'Let's go to Dothan.'" So Joseph went after his brothers and found them at [a]Dothan.

[18]Now Joseph's brothers saw him from a distance, and before [a]he reached them, they plotted to kill him. [19]They said to one another, "Here comes this master of dreams! [20a]Come now, let's kill him, throw him into one of the cisterns, and then say that a wild animal ate him. Then we'll see how his dreams turn out!"

[21]When [a]Reuben heard this, he rescued Joseph from their hands, saying, "Let's not take his life!" [22]Reuben continued, "Don't shed blood! Throw him into this cistern that is here in the wilderness, but don't lay a hand on him." (Reuben said this so he could rescue Joseph from them and take him back to his father.)

[23]When Joseph reached his brothers, they [a]stripped him of his tunic, the special tunic that he wore. [24]Then they took him and threw him into the cistern. (Now the cistern was empty; there was no water in it.)

[25]When they sat down to eat their food, they looked up [a]and saw[1] a caravan of [b]Ishmaelites coming from Gilead. Their camels were carrying spices, [c]balm, and myrrh down to Egypt. [26]Then Judah said to his brothers, "What profit is there if we kill our brother and [a]cover up his blood? [27]Come, [a]let's sell him to the Ishmaelites, but let's not lay a hand on him, for after all, he is [b]our brother, [c]our own flesh." His brothers agreed. [28]So when the [a]Midianite merchants passed by, Joseph's brothers pulled him out of the cistern [b]and sold him to the Ishmaelites for [c]20 pieces of silver. The Ishmaelites then took Joseph to Egypt.

[29]Later Reuben returned to the cistern to find that Joseph was not in it! He [a]tore his clothes, [30]returned to [a]his brothers, and said, "The boy isn't there! And I, where can I go?" [31]So they took [a]Joseph's tunic, killed a young goat, and dipped the tunic in the blood. [32]Then they brought the special tunic to their father and said, "We found this. Determine now whether it is your son's tunic or not."

[33]He recognized it and exclaimed, "It is my son's tunic! A [a]wild animal has eaten him! Joseph has surely been torn to pieces!" [34]Then Jacob [a]tore his clothes, put on sackcloth, and [b]mourned for his son many days. [35]All his sons and daughters [a]stood by [b]him to console him, but he refused to be consoled. "No," he said, "I will go to the grave mourning my son."[1] So Joseph's father wept for him.

[36]Now in Egypt [a]the Midianites[1] sold Joseph to Potiphar, one of Pharaoh's officials, the captain of the guard.

Judah and Tamar

38 At that time Judah left his brothers and [a]stayed with an Adullamite man named Hirah. [2]There Judah [a]saw the daughter of a Canaanite man named [b]Shua. Judah acquired her as a wife[1] and slept with her. [3]She became pregnant and had a son. Judah named[1] him [a]Er. [4]She became pregnant again and had another son, whom she named [a]Onan. [5]Then she had yet another son, whom she named [a]Shelah. She gave birth to him in Kezib.

[6]Judah [a]acquired a wife for Er his firstborn; her name was [b]Tamar. [7]But [a]Er, Judah's firstborn, was evil in the LORD's sight, so the LORD killed him.

[8]Then Judah said to Onan, "Sleep with [a]your brother's wife and fulfill the duty of a brother-in-law to her so that you may raise up a descendant for your brother." [9]But Onan knew that the child would not be considered [a]his.[1] So whenever he slept with his brother's wife, he wasted his emission

37:16 [a] Song 1:7   37:17 [a] 2 Kgs 6:13   37:18 [a] 1 Sam 19:1; Ps 31:13; 37:12, 32; Matt 21:38; 26:3–4; 27:1; Mark 14:1; John 11:53; Acts 23:12   37:20 [a] Gen 37:22; Prov 1:11   37:21 [a] Gen 42:22   37:23 [a] Matt 27:28   37:25 [a] Prov 30:20   [b] Gen 16:11–12; 37:28, 36; 39:1   [c] Jer 8:22   [1] Heb. *and they saw and look.*   37:26 [a] Gen 37:20   37:27 [a] 1 Sam 18:17   [b] Gen 42:21   [c] Gen 29:14   37:28 [a] Gen 37:25; Judg 6:1–3; 8:22, 24   [b] Gen 45:4–5; Ps 105:17; Acts 7:9   [c] Matt 27:9   37:29 [a] Gen 37:34; 44:13; Job 1:20   [1] Heb. *and look, Joseph was not in the cistern.*   37:30 [a] Gen 42:13, 36   37:31 [a] Gen 37:3, 23   37:33 [a] Gen 37:20   37:34 [a] Gen 37:29; 2 Sam 3:31   [b] Gen 50:10   37:35 [a] 2 Sam 12:17   [b] Gen 25:8; 35:29; 42:38; 44:29, 31   [1] Heb. *and he said, "Indeed I will go down to my son mourning to Sheol.";* Sheol was viewed as the place where departed spirits went after death.   37:36 [a] Gen 39:1   [1] MT *Medanites.*   38:1 [a] 2 Kgs 4:8   38:2 [a] Gen 34:2   [b] 1 Chr 2:3   [1] Heb. *and he took her,* an idiom for getting a wife.   38:3 [a] Gen 46:12; Num 26:19   [1] Some mss *she called.*   38:4 [a] Gen 46:12; Num 26:19   38:5 [a] Num 26:20   38:6 [a] Gen 21:21   [b] Ruth 4:12   38:7 [a] Gen 46:12; Num 26:19   38:8 [a] Deut 25:5–6; Matt 22:24   38:9 [a] Deut 25:6   [1] Heb. *would not be his;* i.e., legally.

on the ground so as not to give his brother a descendant. [10]What he did was evil in the LORD's sight, so the LORD killed [a]him too.

[11]Then Judah said to his daughter-in-law Tamar, "[a]Live as a widow [b]in your father's house until Shelah my son grows up." For he thought, "I don't want him to die like his brothers." So Tamar went and lived in her father's house.

[12]After some time Judah's wife, the daughter of Shua, died. After Judah [a]was consoled, he left for Timnah to visit his sheepshearers, along with his friend Hirah the Adullamite. [13]Tamar was [a]told, "Look, your father-in-law is going up to Timnah to shear his sheep." [14]So she removed her widow's clothes and covered herself with a veil. She wrapped herself and [a]sat [b]at the entrance to Enaim which is on the way to Timnah. (She did this because she saw that she had not been given to Shelah as a wife, even though he had now grown up.)

[15]When Judah saw her, he thought she was a prostitute because she had covered her face. [16]He turned aside to her along the road and said, "Come, please, I want to sleep with you."[1] (He did not realize it was his daughter-in-law.) She asked, "What will you give me so that you may sleep with me?" [17]He [a]replied, "[b]I'll send you a young goat from the flock." She asked, "Will you give me a pledge until you send it?" [18]He said, "What pledge should I give [a]you?" She replied, "Your seal, your cord, and the staff that's in your hand." So he gave them to her, then slept with her, and she became pregnant by him. [19]She left immediately, removed her veil, and put on her widow's clothes.

[20]Then Judah had his friend Hirah the Adullamite take a young goat to get back from the woman the items he had given in pledge, but Hirah could not find her. [21]He asked the men who were there, "Where is the cult prostitute who was at Enaim by the road?" But they replied, "There has been no cult prostitute here." [22]So he returned to Judah and said, "I couldn't find her. Moreover, the men of the place said, 'There has been no cult prostitute here.'" [23]Judah said, "Let her keep the things for herself. Otherwise we will appear to be dishonest. I did indeed send this young goat, but you couldn't find her."

[24]After three months Judah was told, "Your daughter-in-law Tamar has turned to prostitution,[1] and as [a]a result she has become pregnant." Judah said, "Bring her out [b]and let her be burned!" [25]While they were bringing her out, she sent word to her father-in-law: "I am pregnant by the man to whom these belong." Then she said, "[a]Identify the one to whom the seal, cord, and staff belong." [26]Judah [a]recognized them and said, "[b]She [c]is more upright than I am, because I [d]wouldn't give her to Shelah my son." He was not physically intimate with her again.[1]

[27]When it was time for her to give birth, there were twins in her womb. [28]While she was giving birth, one child put out his hand, and the midwife took a scarlet thread and tied it on his hand, saying, "This one came out first." [29]But then he drew back his hand, and his brother came out before him. She said, "How you have broken out of the womb!" So he was named [a]Perez. [30]Afterward his brother came out—the one who had the scarlet thread on his hand—and he was named [a]Zerah.

Joseph and Potiphar's Wife

39 Now Joseph had been brought [a]down to Egypt. An Egyptian named [b]Potiphar, an official of Pharaoh and the captain of the guard, [c]purchased him from the Ishmaelites who had brought him there. [2]The LORD was with Joseph. [a]He was successful[1] and lived in the household of his Egyptian master. [3]His master observed that the LORD was with him and that the LORD [a]made everything he was doing successful. [4]So Joseph [a]found favor in his sight and became his personal attendant. Potiphar [b]appointed Joseph overseer of his household and put him in charge of everything he owned. [5]From [a]the time Potiphar appointed him over his

38:10 [a]Gen 46:12; Num 26:19   38:11 [a]Ruth 1:12–13   [b]Lev 22:13   38:12 [a]2 Sam 13:39   38:13 [a]Josh 15:10, 57; Judg 14:1   38:14 [a]Prov 7:12   [b]Gen 38:11, 26   38:16 [1]Heb. *I want to approach*; a euphemism for sexual relations.   38:17 [a]Judg 15:1; Ezek 16:33   [b]Gen 38:20   38:18 [a]Gen 38:25; 41:42   38:24 [a]Judg 19:2   [b]Lev 20:14; 21:9; Deut 22:21   [1]Or *has been sexually promiscuous.*   38:25 [a]Gen 37:32; 38:18   38:26 [a]Gen 37:33   [b]1 Sam 24:17   [c]Gen 38:14   [d]Job 34:31–32   [1]Heb. *and he did not repeat to know her, he did not know her again*; a euphemism for sexual relations.   38:29 [a]Gen 46:12; Num 26:20; Ruth 4:12; 1 Chr 2:4; Matt 1:3   38:30 [a]Gen 46:12; 1 Chr 2:4; Matt 1:3   39:1 [a]Gen 12:10; 43:15   [b]Gen 37:36; Ps 105:17   [c]Gen 37:28; 45:4   39:2 [a]Gen 26:24, 28; 28:15; 35:3; 39:3, 21, 23; 1 Sam 16:18; 18:14, 28; Acts 7:9   [1]Heb. *and he was a prosperous man.*   39:3 [a]Ps 1:3   39:4 [a]Gen 18:3; 19:19; 39:21   [b]Gen 24:2, 10; 39:8, 22; 41:40   39:5 [a]Gen 18:26; 30:27; 2 Sam 6:11

household and over all that he owned, the LORD blessed the Egyptian's household for Joseph's sake. The blessing of the LORD was on everything that he had, both in his house and in his fields. [6] So Potiphar left everything he had in Joseph's care; he gave no thought to anything except the food he ate.

Now Joseph [a] was well built and good-looking.[1] [7] Soon after these things, his master's wife took notice of Joseph and said, "Come to [a] bed with me." [8] But he refused, saying to his master's wife, "Look, my master does not give any thought to his household with me here, and everything that he owns he has put into my care. [9] There is no one greater in this household than I am. He has withheld nothing from me except you because you are his wife. So [a] how could I do such a great evil and [b] sin against God?" [10] Even though she continued to speak to Joseph day after day, he [a] did not respond to her invitation to go to bed with her.

[11] One day he went into the house to do his work when none of the household servants were there in the house. [12] She [a] grabbed him by his outer garment, saying, "Come to bed with me!" But he left his outer garment in her hand and ran outside. [13] When she saw that he had left his outer garment in her hand and had run outside, [14] she called for her household servants and said to them, "See, my husband brought in a [a] Hebrew man to us to humiliate us.[1] He tried to go to bed with me, but I screamed loudly. [15] When he heard me raise my voice and scream, he left his outer garment beside me and ran outside."

[16] So she laid his outer garment beside her until his master came home. [17] This is what she [a] said to him: "That Hebrew slave you brought to us tried to humiliate me, [18] but when I raised my voice and screamed, he left his outer garment and ran outside."

[19] When his master heard his wife say, "This is the way your slave treated me," [a] he became furious. [20] Joseph's master took him and [a] threw him into the [b] prison, the place where the king's prisoners were confined. So he was there in the prison.

[21] But the LORD was with Joseph and showed him kindness. He [a] granted him favor in the sight of the prison warden. [22] The warden [a] put all the prisoners under Joseph's care. He was in charge of whatever they were doing.[1] [23] The warden did not concern himself with anything that was in Joseph's care because [a] the LORD was with him and whatever he was doing the LORD was making successful.

The Cupbearer and the Baker

40 After these things happened, the cupbearer to the king of Egypt and the royal baker offended their master, the king of Egypt. [2] Pharaoh was [a] enraged with his two officials,[1] the cupbearer and the baker, [3] so he [a] imprisoned them in the house of the captain of the guard in the same facility where Joseph was confined. [4] The captain of the guard appointed Joseph to be their attendant, and he served them.

They spent some time in custody. [5] Both of them, the cupbearer and the baker of the king of Egypt, who were confined in the prison, [a] had a dream the same night. Each man's dream had its own meaning. [6] When Joseph came to them in the morning, he saw that they were looking depressed. [7] So he asked Pharaoh's officials, who were with him in custody in his master's house, "[a] Why do you look so sad today?" [8] They told him, "[a] We both had dreams, but there is no one to interpret them." Joseph responded, "[b] Don't interpretations belong to God? Tell them to me."

[9] So the chief cupbearer told his dream to Joseph: "In my dream, there was a vine in front of me. [10] On the vine there were three branches. As it budded, its blossoms opened and its clusters ripened into grapes. [11] Now Pharaoh's cup was in my hand, so I took the grapes, squeezed them into his cup, and put the cup in Pharaoh's hand."

[12] "This [a] is its meaning," Joseph said to him. "The three branches represent three days. [13] In three more days Pharaoh will reinstate you[1] and restore you to your office.

39:6 [a] Gen 29:17; 1 Sam 16:12   [1] Heb. *handsome of form and handsome of appearance.*   **39:7** [a] 2 Sam 13:11   **39:9** [a] Lev 20:10; Prov 6:29, 32   [b] Gen 20:6; 42:18; 2 Sam 12:13; Ps 51:4   **39:10** [a] Prov 1:10   **39:12** [a] Prov 7:13   **39:14** [a] Gen 14:13; 41:12   [1] Heb. *to make fun of us.*   **39:17** [a] Exod 23:1; Ps 120:3; Prov 26:28   **39:19** [a] Prov 6:34–35   **39:20** [a] Ps 105:18; [1 Pet 2:19]   [b] Gen 40:3, 15; 41:14   **39:21** [a] Gen 39:2; Exod 3:21; Ps 105:19; [Prov 16:7]; Dan 1:9; Acts 7:9–10   **39:22** [a] Gen 39:4; 40:3–4   [1] Heb. *all which they were doing there, he was doing.*   **39:23** [a] Gen 39:2–3   **40:2** [a] Prov 16:14   [1] Heb. *eunuch.*   **40:3** [a] Gen 39:1, 20, 23; 41:10   **40:5** [a] Gen 37:5; 41:1   **40:7** [a] Neh 2:2   **40:8** [a] Gen 41:15   [b] [Gen 41:16; Dan 2:11, 20–22, 27, 28, 47]   **40:12** [a] Gen 40:18; 41:12, 25; Judg 7:14; Dan 2:36; 4:18–19   **40:13** [1] Heb. *Pharaoh will lift up your head;* an idiom usually of restoring dignity, office, or power.

You will put Pharaoh's cup in his hand, just as you did before when you were cupbearer. [14]But [a]remember me when it goes well for you, and show me kindness. Make mention of me to Pharaoh and bring me out of this prison, [15]for I really was kidnapped[1] from the [a]land of the Hebrews and I have done nothing wrong here for which they should put me in a dungeon."

[16]When the chief baker saw that the interpretation of the first dream was favorable, he said to Joseph, "I also appeared in my dream and there were three baskets of white bread on my head. [17]In the top basket there were baked goods of every kind for Pharaoh, but the birds were eating them from the basket that was on my head."

[18]Joseph replied, "[a]This is its meaning: The three baskets represent three days. [19a]In three more days Pharaoh will decapitate you and [b]impale you on a pole. Then the birds will eat your flesh from you."

[20]On the third day it was Pharaoh's [a]birthday, so he [b]gave a feast for all his servants. He "[c]lifted up" the head of the chief cupbearer and the head of the chief baker in the midst of his servants. [21]He [a]restored [b]the chief cupbearer to his former position so that he placed the cup in Pharaoh's hand, [22]but the chief baker he [a]impaled, just as Joseph had predicted. [23]But the chief cupbearer did not remember Joseph—he [a]forgot him.

Joseph's Rise to Power

41 At the end of two full years [a]Pharaoh had a dream. As he was standing by the Nile, [2]seven fine-looking, fat cows were coming up out of the Nile, and they grazed in the reeds. [3]Then seven bad-looking, thin cows were coming up after them from the Nile, and they stood beside the other cows at the edge of the river.[1] [4]The bad-looking, thin cows ate the seven fine-looking, fat cows. Then Pharaoh woke up.

[5]Then he fell asleep again and had a second dream: There were seven heads of grain growing on one stalk, healthy and good. [6]Then seven heads of grain, thin and burned by the [a]east wind, were sprouting up after them. [7]The thin heads swallowed up the seven healthy and full heads. Then Pharaoh woke up and realized it was a dream.

[8]In [a]the morning he was troubled, so he called for all the diviner-priests of Egypt and all its [b]wise men. Pharaoh told them his dreams, but no one could interpret them for him. [9]Then the [a]chief cupbearer said to Pharaoh, "Today I recall my failures. [10]Pharaoh was [a]enraged with his servants, [b]and he put me in prison in the house of the captain of the guards—me and the chief baker. [11a]We each had a dream one night; each of us had a dream with its own meaning. [12]Now a young man, a [a]Hebrew, a [b]servant of the captain of the guards, was with us there. We told him our dreams, and he [c]interpreted the meaning of each of our respective dreams for us. [13]It happened just [a]as he had said to us—Pharaoh restored me to my office, but he impaled the baker."

[14]Then Pharaoh summoned Joseph. So they brought him quickly out of [a]the dungeon; he shaved himself, [b]changed his clothes, and came before Pharaoh. [15]Pharaoh said to Joseph, "I had a dream, and there is no one who can interpret it. [a]But I have heard about you, that you can interpret dreams." [16]Joseph replied to Pharaoh, "[a]It is not within my power, but [b]God will speak concerning the welfare of Pharaoh."

[17]Then Pharaoh said to Joseph, "[a]In my dream I was standing[1] by the edge of the Nile. [18]Then seven fat and fine-looking cows were coming up out of the Nile, and they grazed in the reeds. [19]Then seven other cows came up after them; they were scrawny, very bad looking, and lean. I had never seen such bad-looking cows as these in all the land of Egypt! [20]The lean, bad-looking cows ate up the seven fat cows. [21]When they had eaten them, no one would have known that they had done so, for they were just as bad looking as before. Then I woke up. [22]I also saw in my dream seven heads of grain

40:14 [a]1 Sam 25:31; Luke 23:42   **40:15** [a]Gen 39:20   [1]Heb. *to steal.*   **40:18** [a]Gen 40:12   **40:19** [a]Gen 40:13   [b]Deut 21:22   **40:20** [a]Matt 14:6–10   [b]Mark 6:21   [c]Gen 40:13, 19; 2 Kgs 25:27; Jer 52:31; Matt 25:19   **40:21** [a]Gen 40:13   [b]Neh 2:1   **40:22** [a]Gen 40:19; Deut 21:23; Esth 7:10   **40:23** [a]Job 19:14; Ps 31:12; Eccl 9:15–16; Isa 49:15; Amos 6:6   **41:1** [a]Gen 40:5; Judg 7:13   **41:3** [1]Heb. *the Nile.*   **41:6** [a]Exod 10:13; Ezek 17:10   **41:8** [a]Exod 7:11, 22; Isa 29:14; Dan 1:20; 2:2; 4:7   [b]Matt 2:1   **41:9** [a]Gen 40:1, 14, 23   **41:10** [a]Gen 40:2–3   [b]Gen 39:20   **41:11** [a]Gen 40:5; Judg 7:15   **41:12** [a]Gen 39:14; 43:32   [b]Gen 37:36   [c]Gen 40:12   **41:13** [a]Gen 40:21–22   **41:14** [a]Ps 105:20   [b]2 Kgs 25:27–29   **41:15** [a]Gen 41:8, 12; Dan 5:16   **41:16** [a]Dan 2:30; Acts 3:12; [2 Cor 3:5]   [b]Gen 40:8; 41:25, 28, 32; Deut 29:29; Dan 2:22, 28, 47   **41:17** [a]Gen 41:1   [1]Heb. *In my dream look, I was standing.*

growing on one stalk, full and good. [23]Then seven heads of grain, withered and thin and burned with the east wind, were sprouting up after them. [24]The [a]thin heads of grain swallowed up the seven good heads of grain. So I told all this to the diviner-priests, but no one could tell me its meaning."

[25]Then Joseph said to Pharaoh, "Both dreams of Pharaoh have the same meaning. [a]God has revealed to Pharaoh what he is about to do. [26]The seven good cows represent seven years, and the seven good heads of grain represent seven years. Both dreams have the same meaning. [27]The [a]seven lean, bad-looking cows that came up after them represent seven years, as do the seven empty heads of grain burned with the east wind. They represent seven years of famine. [28]This [a]is just what I told Pharaoh: God has shown Pharaoh what he is about to do. [29][a]Seven years of great abundance are coming throughout the whole land of Egypt. [30]But seven years of famine will [a]occur after them, and all the abundance [b]will be forgotten in the land of Egypt. The famine will devastate[1] the land. [31]The previous abundance of the land will not be remembered because of the famine that follows, for the famine will be very severe. [32]The dream was repeated to Pharaoh because the [a]matter has been decreed by God, and God will make it happen soon.

[33]"So now Pharaoh should look for a wise and discerning man and give him authority over all the land of Egypt. [34]Pharaoh should do this—he should appoint officials throughout the land [a]to collect one-fifth of the produce of the land of Egypt during the seven years of abundance. [35]They should gather all the excess food during these good years that are coming. By Pharaoh's authority they should store up grain so the cities will have food, and they should preserve it. [36]This food should be held in storage for the land in preparation for the seven years of famine that will occur throughout the land of Egypt. In this way the land will survive the famine."

[37]This advice made sense to Pharaoh and all his officials. [38]So Pharaoh asked his officials, "Can we [a]find a man like Joseph, one in whom the Spirit of God is present?" [39]So Pharaoh said to Joseph, "Because God has enabled you to know all this, there is no one as wise and discerning as you are! [40]You will oversee my household, and all my people will submit to [a]your commands. Only I, the king, will be greater than you.

[41]"See here," Pharaoh said to Joseph, "I [a]place[1] you in authority over all the land of Egypt." [42]Then Pharaoh [a]took his signet ring from his own hand and put it on Joseph's. He [b]clothed him with fine linen[1] clothes [c]and put a gold chain around his neck. [43]Pharaoh had him ride in the [a]chariot used by his [b]second-in-command, and they cried out before him, "Kneel down!" So he placed him [c]over all the land of Egypt. [44]Pharaoh also said to Joseph, "I am Pharaoh, but without your permission no one will move his hand or his foot in all the land of Egypt." [45]Pharaoh gave Joseph the name Zaphenath-Paneah. He also gave him [a]Asenath daughter of Potiphera, priest of On, to be his wife. So Joseph took charge of all the land of Egypt.

[46]Now Joseph was 30 years old when he began [a]serving Pharaoh king of Egypt. Joseph was commissioned by Pharaoh and was in charge of all the land of Egypt. [47]During the seven years of abundance the land produced large, bountiful harvests. [48]Joseph collected all the excess food in the land of Egypt during the seven years and stored it in the cities. In every city he put the food gathered from the fields around it. [49]Joseph stored up [a]a vast amount of grain, like the sand of the sea, until he stopped measuring it because it was impossible to measure.

[50][a]Two sons were born to Joseph before the famine came. Asenath daughter of Potiphera, priest of On, was their mother. [51]Joseph named the firstborn Manasseh, saying, "Certainly God has made me forget all my trouble and all my [a]father's house." [52]He named the second child Ephraim, saying,

41:24 [a]Gen 41:8; Exod 7:11; Isa 8:19; Dan 4:7   **41:25** [a]Gen 41:28, 32; Dan 2:28–29, 45; Rev 4:1   **41:27** [a]2 Kgs 8:1   **41:28** [a][Gen 41:25, 32; Dan 2:28]   **41:29** [a]Gen 41:47   **41:30** [a]Gen 41:54, 56   [b]Gen 47:13; Ps 105:16   [1]Heb. *to finish, to destroy, to bring an end to.*   **41:32** [a]Gen 41:25, 28; Num 23:19; Isa 46:10–11   **41:34** [a][Prov 6:6–8]   **41:38** [a]Num 27:18; [Job 32:8; Prov 2:6]; Dan 4:8–9, 18; 5:11, 14; 6:3   **41:40** [a]Ps 105:21; Acts 7:10   **41:41** [a]Gen 42:6; Ps 105:21; Dan 6:3; Acts 7:10   [1]Or *I will have placed, I will place*; Heb. *I hereby place you.*   **41:42** [a]Esth 3:10   [b]Esth 8:2, 15   [c]Dan 5:7, 16, 29   [1]From an Egyptian loanword that describes the fine linen robes Egyptian royalty wore.   **41:43** [a]Gen 46:29   [b]Esth 6:9   [c]Gen 42:6   **41:45** [a]Gen 46:20   **41:46** [a]1 Sam 16:21; 1 Kgs 12:6, 8; Dan 1:19   **41:49** [a]Gen 22:17; Judg 7:12; 1 Sam 13:5   **41:50** [a]Gen 46:20; 48:5   **41:51** [a]Ps 45:10

"Certainly God has made me [a]fruitful in the land of my suffering."

[53]The seven years of abundance in the land of Egypt came to an end. [54]Then the seven years of famine began, just as Joseph had predicted. There was famine in all the other [a]lands, but throughout the land of Egypt there [b]was food. [55]When all the land of Egypt experienced the famine, the people cried out to Pharaoh for food. Pharaoh said to all the people of Egypt,[1] "Go to Joseph and do [a]whatever he tells you."

[56]While the famine was over all the earth, Joseph opened the storehouses[1] and sold [a]grain to the Egyptians. The famine was severe throughout the land of Egypt. [57a]People from every country[1] came to Joseph in Egypt to buy [b]grain because the famine was severe throughout the earth.

Joseph's Brothers in Egypt

42 When [a]Jacob heard there was grain in Egypt, he said to his sons, "Why are you looking at each other?" [2]He then said, "Look, I hear that there is grain in Egypt. Go down there and buy grain for us so that we may [a]live and not die."

[3]So ten of Joseph's brothers went down to buy grain from Egypt. [4]But Jacob did not send Joseph's brother Benjamin with his brothers, for he said, "What [a]if some accident[1] happens to him?" [5]So Israel's sons came to buy [a]grain among the other travelers, for the famine was severe in the land of Canaan.

[6]Now Joseph was the ruler [a]of the country, the one who sold grain to all the people of the country. Joseph's brothers came and [b]bowed down before him with their faces to the ground. [7]When Joseph [a]saw his brothers, he recognized them, but he pretended to be a stranger to them and spoke to them harshly. He asked, "Where do you come from?" They answered, "From the land of Canaan, to buy grain for food."

[8]Joseph recognized his brothers, but they did not recognize him. [9]Then Joseph [a]remembered the dreams he had dreamed about them, and he said to them, "You are spies; you have come to see if our land is vulnerable!"

[10]But they exclaimed, "No, my lord! Your servants have come to buy grain for food! [11]We are all the sons of one man; we are honest men! Your servants are not spies."

[12]"No," he insisted, "but you have come to see if our land is vulnerable." [13]They replied, "Your servants are from a family of twelve brothers. We are the sons of one man in the land of Canaan. The youngest [a]is with our father at this time, and one is no longer alive."

[14]But Joseph told them, "It is just as I said to you: You are spies! [15]You will be tested in this way: As surely as Pharaoh lives, you will not depart from this place unless your youngest brother comes here. [16]One of you must go and get your brother, while the rest of you remain in prison. In this way your words may be tested to see if you are telling the truth. If not, then, as surely as Pharaoh lives, you are spies!" [17]He imprisoned them all for [a]three days. [18]On the third day Joseph said to them, "Do as I say and you will live, [a]for I fear God. [19]If you are honest men, leave one of your brothers confined here in prison while the rest of you go and take grain back for your hungry families. [20]But you must [a]bring your youngest brother to me. Then your words will be verified and you will not die." They did as he said.

[21]They said to one another, "Surely [a]we're[b] being punished[1] because of our brother, because we saw how distressed he was when he cried to us for mercy, but we refused to listen. That is why this distress has come on us!" [22]Reuben said to them, "[a]Didn't I say to you, 'Don't sin against the boy,' but you wouldn't listen? So now we must [b]pay for shedding his blood!" [23](Now they did not know that Joseph could understand them, for he was speaking through an interpreter.) [24]He turned away from them and [a]wept. When he turned around and spoke to them again, he had [b]Simeon taken from them and tied up before their eyes.

41:52 [a]Gen 17:6; 28:3; 49:22   **41:54** [a]Ps 105:16; Acts 7:11   [b]Gen 41:30   **41:55** [a]John 2:5   [1]Heb. *to all Egypt.*   **41:56** [a]Gen 42:6   [1]MT *he opened all that was in* [among] *them.*   **41:57** [a]Ezek 29:12   [b]Gen 27:28, 37; 42:3   [1]Heb. *all the earth.*   **42:1** [a]Acts 7:12   **42:2** [a]Gen 43:8; Ps 33:18–19; Isa 38:1   **42:4** [a]Gen 42:38   [1]Heb. *accident, harm.*   **42:5** [a]Gen 12:10; 26:1; 41:57; Acts 7:11   **42:6** [a]Gen 41:41, 55   [b]Gen 37:7–10; 41:43; Isa 60:14   **42:7** [a]Gen 45:1–2   **42:9** [a]Gen 37:5–9   **42:13** [a]Gen 37:30; 42:32; 44:20; Lam 5:7   **42:17** [a]Gen 40:4, 7, 12   **42:18** [a]Gen 22:12; 39:9; Exod 1:17; Lev 25:43; Neh 5:15; Prov 1:7; 9:10   **42:20** [a]Gen 42:34; 43:5; 44:23   **42:21** [a]Gen 37:26–28; 44:16; 45:3; Job 36:8–9; Hos 5:15   [b]Prov 21:13; Matt 7:2   [1]Or *we are guilty.*   **42:22** [a]Gen 37:21–22, 29   [b]Gen 9:5–6; 1 Kgs 2:32; 2 Chr 24:22; Ps 9:12; Luke 11:50–51   **42:24** [a]Gen 43:30; 45:14–15   [b]Gen 34:25, 30; 43:14, 23

[25] Then Joseph [a]gave orders to fill their bags with grain, to [b]return each man's money to his sack, and to give them provisions for the journey. His [c]orders were carried out. [26] So they loaded their grain on their donkeys and left.

[27] When [a]one of them opened his sack to get feed for his donkey at their resting place, he saw his money in the mouth of his sack.[1] [28] He said to his brothers, "My money was returned! Here it is in my sack!" They were dismayed; they turned trembling to one another and said, "What in the world has God done to us?"

[29] They returned to their father Jacob in the land of Canaan and told him all the things that had happened to them, saying, [30] "The man, the lord of the land, [a]spoke harshly to us and treated us as if we were spying on the land. [31] But we said to him, 'We are honest men; we are not spies! [32] We are from a family of twelve brothers; we are the sons of one father. One is no longer alive, and the youngest is with our father at this time in the land of Canaan.'

[33] "Then the man, the lord of the land, said to us, 'This is how I will find out if you are honest men. Leave one of your brothers with me, and take grain for your hungry households and go. [34] But bring your [a]youngest brother back to me so I will know that you are honest men and not spies. Then I will give your brother back to you and you may move about [b]freely in the land.'"

[35] When they were emptying their sacks, there was [a]each man's bag of money in his sack! When they and their father saw the bags of money, they were afraid. [36] Their father Jacob said to them, "You are [a]making me childless! Joseph is gone. Simeon is gone. And now you want to take [b]Benjamin! Everything is against me."

[37] Then Reuben said to his father, "You may put my two sons to death if I do not bring him back to you. Put him in my care and I will bring him back to you." [38] But Jacob replied, "My son will not go down there with you, for [a]his brother is dead and he alone is left. [b]If an accident happens to him

on the journey you have to make, then you will [c]bring down my gray hair in sorrow to the grave."[1]

The Second Journey to Egypt

43 Now the famine was [a]severe in the land. [2] When they finished eating the grain they had brought from Egypt, their father said to them, "[a]Return, buy us a little more food."

[3] But Judah said to him, "The man solemnly warned[1] us, 'You will not see my face[2] unless your [a]brother is with you.' [4] If you send our brother with us, we'll go down and buy food for you. [5] But if you will not send him, we won't go down there because the man said to us, 'You will not see my face unless your brother is with you.'"

[6] Israel said, "Why did you bring this trouble on me by telling the man you had one more brother?"

[7] They replied, "The man questioned us thoroughly about ourselves and our family, saying, 'Is your father still alive? Do you have another brother?' So we answered him in this way. How could we possibly know that he would say, 'Bring your brother down'?"

[8] Then Judah said to his father Israel, "Send the boy with me and we will go immediately. Then we will [a]live and not die—we and you and our little ones. [9] I myself pledge security for him; you may hold me liable. [a]If I do not bring him back to you and place him here before you, I will bear the blame before you all my life. [10] But if we had not delayed, we could have traveled there and back twice by now!"

[11] Then their father Israel said to them, "If it must be so, then do this: Take some of the best products of the land in your bags, and take [a]a gift down to the man—a little [b]balm and a little honey, spices and myrrh, pistachios and almonds. [12] Take double the money with you; you must take back the money [a]that was returned in the mouths of your sacks—perhaps it was an oversight. [13] Take your brother too, and go right away to the man. [14] May the [a]Sovereign God [b]grant you mercy before the man so that he may

42:25 [a] Gen 44:1   [b] Gen 43:12   [c] [Matt 5:44; Rom 12:17, 20, 21; 1 Pet 3:9]   **42:27** [a] Gen 43:21–22   [1] Heb. *and look, it* [was] *in the mouth of his sack.*   **42:30** [a] Gen 42:7   **42:34** [a] Gen 42:20; 43:3, 5   [b] Gen 34:10   **42:35** [a] Gen 43:12, 15, 21   **42:36** [a] Gen 43:14   [b] Gen 35:18; [Rom 8:28, 31]   **42:38** [a] Gen 37:22; 42:13; 44:20, 28   [b] Gen 42:4; 44:29   [c] Gen 37:35; 44:31   [1] Heb. *to Sheol*; the dwelling place of the dead.   **43:1** [a] Gen 41:54, 57; 42:5; 45:6, 11   **43:2** [a] Gen 42:2; 44:25   **43:3** [a] Gen 42:20; 43:5; 44:23   [1] Heb. *to witness, to testify.*   [2] An idiom meaning "have an audience with me."   **43:8** [a] Gen 42:2; 47:19   **43:9** [a] Gen 42:37; 44:32; Phlm 18, 19   **43:11** [a] Gen 32:20; 33:10; 43:25–26; [Prov 18:16]   [b] Gen 37:25; Jer 8:22; Ezek 27:17   **43:12** [a] Gen 42:25, 35; 43:21–22   **43:14** [a] Gen 17:1; 28:3; 35:11; 48:3   [b] Gen 39:21; Ps 106:46

release your other brother and Benjamin! As for me, [c]if I lose my children I lose them."

[15]So the men took these gifts, and they took double the money with them, along with Benjamin. Then they hurried [a]down to Egypt and stood before Joseph. [16]When Joseph saw Benjamin with them, he said to the servant who was over his household, "Bring the men to the house. Slaughter an animal and prepare it, for the men will eat with me at noon." [17]The man did just as Joseph said; he brought the men into Joseph's house.

[18]But the men were [a]afraid when they were brought to Joseph's house. They said, "We are being brought in because of the money that was returned in our sacks last time. He wants to capture us, make us slaves, and take our donkeys!" [19]So they approached the man who was in charge of Joseph's household and spoke to him at the entrance to the house. [20]They said, "My lord, [a]we did indeed come down the first time to buy food. [21]But when we came to the place where we spent the night, we opened our sacks and each of us found his money—the full amount—in the mouth of his sack. So we have returned [a]it. [22]We have brought additional money with us to buy food. We do not know who put the money in our sacks!"

[23]"Everything is fine," the man in charge of Joseph's household told them. "Don't be afraid. Your God and the God of your father has given you treasure in your sacks. I had your money." Then he brought [a]Simeon out to them.

[24]The servant in charge brought the men into Joseph's house. He [a]gave them water, and they washed their feet. Then he gave food to their donkeys. [25]They got their gifts ready for Joseph's arrival at noon, for they had heard that they were to have a meal there.

[26]When Joseph came home, they presented him with the gifts they had brought inside, and they bowed [a]down to the ground before him. [27]He asked them how they were doing. Then he said, "Is your aging father well, the one you spoke about? Is he still alive?" [28]"Your servant our father is well," they replied. "He is still alive." They bowed down in humility.

[29]When Joseph looked up and saw [a]his brother Benjamin, his mother's son, he said, "Is this your youngest brother, whom you told me about?" Then he said, "May God be gracious to you, my son." [30]Joseph hurried out, for he was overcome by affection for [a]his brother and was at the point of tears. So he went to his room and [b]wept there.

[31]Then he washed his face and came out. With composure he said, "Set out the [a]food." [32]They set a place for him, a separate place for his brothers, and another for the Egyptians who were eating with him. (The Egyptians are not able to eat with [a]Hebrews, for the [b]Egyptians think it is disgusting[1] to do so.) [33]They sat before him, arranged by order of birth, [a]beginning with the firstborn and ending with the youngest. The men looked at each other in astonishment. [34]He gave them portions of the food set before him, but the portion for Benjamin was [a]five times greater than the portions for any of the others. They drank with Joseph until they all became drunk.

The Final Test

44 He instructed the servant who was over his household, "[a]Fill the sacks of the men with as much food as they can carry and put each man's money in the mouth of his sack. [2]Then put my cup—the silver cup—in the mouth of the youngest one's sack, along with the money for his grain." He did as Joseph instructed.

[3]When morning came, the men and their donkeys were sent off. [4]They had not gone very far from the city when Joseph said to the servant who was over his household, "Pursue the men at once! When you overtake them, say to them, 'Why have you [a]repaid good with evil? [5]Doesn't my master drink from this cup and use it for divination? You have done wrong!'"

[6]When the man overtook them, he spoke these words to them. [7]They answered him, "Why does my lord say such things? Far be it from your servants to do such a thing! [8]Look, [a]the money that we found in the mouths of our sacks we brought back to you from the land of Canaan. Why then would we steal silver or gold from your master's

43:14 [c]Gen 42:36; Esth 4:16   43:15 [a]Gen 39:1; 46:3, 6   43:18 [a]Gen 42:28   43:20 [a]Gen 42:3, 10   43:21 [a]Gen 42:27, 35   43:23 [a]Gen 42:24   43:24 [a]Gen 18:4; 19:2; 24:32   43:26 [a]Gen 37:7, 10; 42:6; 44:14   43:29 [a]Gen 35:17–18   43:30 [a]1 Kgs 3:26   [b]Gen 42:24; 45:2, 14, 15; 46:29   43:31 [a]Gen 43:25   43:32 [a]Gen 41:12; Exod 1:15   [b]Gen 46:34; Exod 8:26   [1]Or disgraceful; Heb. abomination.   43:33 [a]Gen 27:36; 42:7; Deut 21:16–17   43:34 [a]Gen 35:24; 45:22   44:1 [a]Gen 42:25   44:4 [a]1 Sam 25:21   44:8 [a]Gen 43:21

house? ⁹If one of us has it, he will die, and the rest of us will become my lord's slaves!"

¹⁰He replied, "You have suggested your own punishment! The one who has it will become my slave, but the rest of you will go free."¹ ¹¹So each man quickly lowered his sack to the ground and opened it. ¹²Then the man searched. He began with the oldest and finished with the youngest. The cup was found in Benjamin's sack! ¹³They all ᵃtore their clothes! Then each man loaded his donkey, and they returned to the city.

¹⁴So Judah and his brothers came back to Joseph's house. He was still there, and they ᵃthrew themselves to the ground before him. ¹⁵Joseph said to them, "What did you think you were doing? Don't you know that a man like me can find out things like this by divination?"

¹⁶Judah replied, "What can we say to my lord? What can we speak? How can we clear ourselves? God has exposed the sin of your servants! We are now my lord's slaves, we and the one in whose possession the cup was ᵃfound."

¹⁷But Joseph said, "ᵃFar be it from me to do this! The man in whose hand the cup was found will become my slave, but the rest of you may go back¹ to your father in peace."

¹⁸Then Judah approached him and said, "My lord, please allow your servant to speak a word with you. Please ᵃdo not get angry with your servant, for you are just like Pharaoh. ¹⁹My lord asked his servants, 'Do you have a father or a brother?' ²⁰We ᵃsaid to my lord, 'We have an aged father, and there is a young boy who was born when our father was old.¹ The boy's brother is ᵇdead. He is the only ᶜone of his mother's sons left, and his ᵈfather loves him.'

²¹"Then you told your servants, 'ᵃBring him down to me so I can see him.' ²²We said to my lord, 'The boy cannot leave his father. If he leaves his father, his father will die.' ²³But you said to your servants, 'If your youngest brother does ᵃnot come down with you, you will not see my face again.' ²⁴When we returned to your servant my father, we told him the words of my lord.

²⁵"Then ᵃour father said, 'Go back and buy us a little food.' ²⁶But we replied, 'We cannot go down there. If our youngest brother is with us, then we will go, for we won't be permitted to see the man's face if our youngest brother is not with us.'

²⁷"Then your servant ᵃmy father said to us, 'You know that my wife gave me two sons. ²⁸The first disappeared and I said, "He has surely been ᵃtorn to pieces." I have not seen him since. ²⁹If you ᵃtake this one from me too and an accident happens to him, then you will bring down my gray hair in tragedy to the grave.'¹

³⁰"So now, when ᵃI return to your servant my father, and the boy is not with us—his very life is bound up in his son's life. ³¹When he sees the boy is not with us, he will die, and your servants will bring down the gray hair of your servant our father in sorrow to the grave. ³²Indeed, your servant pledged security for the boy with my father, saying, 'ᵃIf I do not bring him back to you, then I will bear the blame before my father all my life.'

³³"So now, please ᵃlet your servant remain as my lord's slave instead of the boy. As for the boy, let him go back with his brothers. ³⁴For how can I go back to my father if the boy is not with me? I couldn't bear to see my father's pain."

The Reconciliation of the Brothers

45 Joseph was no longer able to control himself before all his attendants, so he cried out, "Make everyone go out from my presence!" No one remained with Joseph when he made himself known to his brothers. ²He ᵃwept loudly;¹ the Egyptians heard it and Pharaoh's household heard about it.

³Joseph ᵃsaid to his brothers, "I am Joseph! Is my father still alive?" His brothers could not answer him because they were dumbfounded before him. ⁴Joseph said to his brothers, "Come closer to me," so they came near. Then he said, "I am Joseph your brother, ᵃwhom you sold into Egypt. ⁵Now, do not be upset and do not be angry with yourselves because you sold me here, ᵃfor God sent me ahead of you to preserve life!

44:10 ¹Heb. *acquitted.* **44:13** ᵃGen 37:29, 34; Num 14:6; 2 Sam 1:11 **44:14** ᵃGen 37:7, 10 **44:16** ᵃ[Num 32:23] **44:17** ᵃProv 17:15 ¹Heb. *up*; i.e., up to Canaan. **44:18** ᵃGen 18:30, 32; Exod 32:22 **44:20** ᵃGen 37:3; 43:8; 44:30 ᵇGen 42:38 ᶜGen 46:19 ᵈGen 42:4 ¹Heb. *and a small boy of old age.* **44:21** ᵃGen 42:15, 20 **44:23** ᵃGen 43:3, 5 **44:25** ᵃGen 43:2 **44:27** ᵃGen 30:22–24; 35:16–18; 46:19 **44:28** ᵃGen 37:31–35 **44:29** ᵃGen 42:36, 38; 44:31 ¹Heb. *to Sheol*; the dwelling place of the dead. **44:30** ᵃ[1 Sam 18:1; 25:29] **44:32** ᵃGen 43:9 **44:33** ᵃExod 32:32 **45:2** ᵃGen 43:30; 46:29 ¹Heb. *and he gave his voice in weeping.* **45:3** ᵃGen 43:27; Acts 7:13 **45:4** ᵃGen 37:28; 39:1; Ps 105:17 **45:5** ᵃGen 45:7–8; 50:20; Ps 105:16–17

[6]For these past two years there has been [a]famine in the land and for five more years there will be neither plowing nor harvesting. [7]God [a]sent me ahead of you to preserve you on the earth and to save your lives by a great deliverance. [8]So now, it is not you who sent me here, but [a]God. He [b]has made me an adviser to Pharaoh, lord over all his household, and [c]ruler over all the land of Egypt. [9]Now go up to my father quickly and tell him, 'This is what your son Joseph says: "God has made me lord of all Egypt. Come down to me; do not delay! [10]You will live in the land of Goshen, and [a]you will be near me—you, your children, your grandchildren, your flocks, your herds, and everything you have. [11]I will [a]provide you with food there because there will be five more years of famine. Otherwise you would become poor—you, your household, and everyone who belongs to you."' [12]You and [a]my brother Benjamin can certainly see with your own eyes that I really am the one who speaks to you. [13]So tell my father about all my honor [a]in Egypt and about everything you have seen. But bring my father down here quickly!"

[14]Then he threw himself on the neck of his brother Benjamin and wept, and Benjamin wept on his neck. [15]He [a]kissed all his brothers and wept over them. After this his brothers talked with him.

[16]Now it was reported in the household of Pharaoh, "Joseph's brothers have arrived." It pleased Pharaoh and his servants. [17]Pharaoh said to Joseph, "Say to your brothers, 'Do this: Load your animals and go to the land of Canaan! [18]Get your [a]father and your households and come to me! Then I will give you the best land in Egypt and you will eat the best of the land.' [19]You are also commanded to say, 'Do this: Take for yourselves wagons from the land of Egypt for your little ones and for your wives. Bring your father and come. [20]Don't worry about your belongings, for the best of all the land of Egypt will be yours.'"

[21]So the sons of Israel did as he said. Joseph gave them [a]wagons as Pharaoh had instructed, and he gave them provisions for the journey. [22]He gave [a]sets of clothes to each one of them, but to Benjamin he gave 300 pieces of silver and [b]five sets of clothes. [23]To his father he sent the following: ten donkeys loaded with the best products of Egypt and ten female donkeys loaded with grain, food, and provisions for his father's journey. [24]Then he sent his brothers on their way and they left. He said to them, "As you travel don't be overcome with fear."[1]

[25]So they went up from Egypt and came to their father Jacob in the land of Canaan. [26]They told him, "Joseph is still alive [a]and he is ruler over all the land of Egypt!" Jacob was stunned, for he did not believe them. [27]But when they related to him everything Joseph had said to them, and when he saw the wagons that Joseph had sent to transport him, their father Jacob's spirit revived. [28]Then Israel said, "Enough! My son Joseph is still alive! I will go and see him before I die."

The Family of Jacob Goes to Egypt

46 So Israel began his journey, taking with him all that he had. When he came to Beer [a]Sheba he offered sacrifices [b]to the God of his father Isaac. [2]God spoke to Israel [a]in a vision during the night and said, "Jacob, Jacob!" He replied, "Here I am!" [3]He said, "I am God, [a]the God of your father. Do not be afraid to go down to Egypt, for I will [b]make you into a great nation there. [4]I [a]will go down with you to Egypt and [b]I myself will certainly bring you back from there.[1] [c]Joseph will close your eyes."

[5]Then [a]Jacob started out from Beer Sheba, and the sons of Israel carried their father Jacob, their little children, and their wives in the wagons that Pharaoh had sent along to transport him. [6a]Jacob and all his descendants took their livestock and the possessions they had acquired in the land of Canaan, and they went to Egypt. [7]He brought with him to Egypt his sons and grandsons, his daughters and granddaughters—all his descendants.

[8]These are [a]the names of the sons of Israel who went to Egypt—Jacob and his sons: [b]Reuben, the firstborn of Jacob.

45:6 [a]Gen 43:1; 47:4, 13   45:7 [a]Gen 45:5; 50:20   45:8 [a][Rom 8:28] [b]Judg 17:10; Isa 22:21 [c]Gen 41:43; 42:6   45:10 [a]Gen 46:28, 34; 47:1, 6; Exod 9:26   45:11 [a]Gen 47:12   45:12 [a]Gen 42:23   45:13 [a]Gen 46:6–28; Acts 7:14   45:15 [a]Gen 48:10   45:18 [a]Gen 27:28; 47:6; Deut 32:9–14   45:21 [a]Gen 45:19; 46:5   45:22 [a]2 Kgs 5:5 [b]Gen 43:34   45:24 [1]Heb. *do not be stirred up in the way.*   45:26 [a]Job 29:24; Ps 126:1; Luke 24:11, 41   46:1 [a]Gen 21:31, 33; 26:32–33; 28:10 [b]Gen 26:24–25; 28:13; 31:42; 32:9   46:2 [a]Gen 15:1; 22:11; 31:11; Num 12:6; Job 33:14–15   46:3 [a]Gen 17:1; 28:13 [b]Gen 12:2; Exod 1:9; 12:37; Deut 26:5   46:4 [a]Gen 28:15; 31:3; 48:21; Exod 3:12 [b]Gen 15:16; 50:12, 24, 25; Exod 3:8 [c]Gen 50:1 [1]Heb. *and I, I will bring you up, also bringing up.*   46:5 [a]Gen 47:9; Acts 7:15   46:6 [a]Deut 26:5; Josh 24:4; Ps 105:23; Isa 52:4; Acts 7:15   46:8 [a]Exod 1:1–4 [b]Num 26:4–5; 1 Chr 2:1

9 The [a]sons of Reuben: Hanoch, Pallu, Hezron, and Carmi.

10 The sons of Simeon: Jemuel, Jamin, Ohad, Jakin, Zohar, and Shaul ([a]the son of a Canaanite woman).

11 The sons of [a]Levi: Gershon, Kohath, and Merari.

12 The sons of [a]Judah: [b]Er, Onan, Shelah, Perez, and Zerah (but Er and Onan died in [c]the land of Canaan).
The sons of Perez were Hezron and Hamul.

13 The sons of Issachar: Tola, Puah,[1] Jashub,[2] and Shimron.

14 The [a]sons of Zebulun: Sered, Elon, and Jahleel.

15 These were the [a]sons of Leah, whom she bore to Jacob in Paddan Aram, along with Dinah his daughter. His sons and daughters numbered thirty-three in all.

16 The sons of Gad: Zephon,[1] Haggi, Shuni, Ezbon, Eri, Arodi, and Areli.

17 The sons of Asher: Imnah, Ishvah, Ishvi, Beriah, and Serah [a]their sister.
The sons of Beriah were Heber and Malkiel.

18 These were [a]the sons of Zilpah, [b]whom Laban gave to Leah his daughter. She bore these to Jacob, sixteen in all.

19 The [a]sons of Rachel the wife of [b]Jacob: Joseph and Benjamin.

20 Manasseh [a]and Ephraim were born to Joseph in the land of Egypt. Asenath daughter of Potiphera, priest of On, bore them to him.

21 [a]The sons of Benjamin: Bela, Beker, Ashbel, Gera, Naaman, [b]Ehi, Rosh, [c]Muppim, Huppim and Ard.

22 These were the sons of Rachel who were born to Jacob, fourteen in all.

23 The son of Dan: Hushim.

24 [a]The sons of Naphtali: Jahziel, Guni, Jezer, and Shillem.

25 These were [a]the sons of Bilhah, [b]whom Laban gave to Rachel his daughter. She bore these to Jacob, seven in all.

26 [a]All the direct descendants of Jacob who went to Egypt with him were sixty-six in number. (This number does not include the wives of Jacob's sons.) 27Counting the two sons of Joseph who were born to him in Egypt, [a]all the people of the household of Jacob who were in Egypt numbered seventy.

28Jacob sent Judah before him [a]to Joseph [b]to accompany him to Goshen. So they came to the land of Goshen. 29Joseph harnessed his [a]chariot and went up to meet his father Israel in Goshen. When he met him, he [b]hugged his neck and wept on his neck for quite some time.

30Israel said to Joseph, "[a]Now let me die since I have seen your face and know that you are still alive." 31Then Joseph [a]said to his brothers and his father's household, "I will go up and tell Pharaoh, 'My brothers and my father's household who were in the land of Canaan have come to me. 32The men are [a]shepherds; they take care of livestock. They have brought their flocks and their herds and all that they have.' 33Pharaoh will summon you and say, '[a]What is your occupation?' 34Tell him, 'Your servants have taken care of cattle [a]from our youth until now, both we [b]and our fathers,' so that you may live in the land of Goshen, for everyone who takes care of sheep is disgusting[1] to the Egyptians."

Joseph's Wise Administration

47 Joseph [a]went and told Pharaoh, "My [b]father, my brothers, their flocks and herds, and all that they own have arrived from the land of Canaan. They are now in the land of Goshen." 2He took five of his brothers and [a]introduced them to Pharaoh.

3Pharaoh said to Joseph's brothers, "[a]What is [b]your occupation?" They said to Pharaoh, "Your servants take care of flocks, just as our ancestors did." 4Then they said to Pharaoh, "[a]We have come to live as temporary residents in the land. There is no

46:9 [a]Exod 6:14   46:10 [a]Exod 6:15; Num 26:12   46:11 [a]Exod 6:16–17; 1 Chr 6:1, 16   46:12 [a]Num 26:19–20; 1 Chr 2:3; 4:21   [b]Gen 38:3, 7, 10   [c]Gen 38:29   46:13 [1]MT *Puvah*.   [2]MT *Job*.   46:14 [a]Num 26:26   46:15 [a]Gen 35:23; 49:31   46:16 [1]MT *Ziphion*.   46:17 [a]Num 26:44–47; 1 Chr 7:30   46:18 [a]Gen 30:10; 37:2   [b]Gen 29:24   46:19 [a]Gen 35:24   [b]Gen 44:27   46:20 [a]Gen 41:45, 50–52; 48:1   46:21 [a]1 Chr 7:6; 8:1   [b]Num 26:38   [c]Num 26:39; 1 Chr 7:12   46:24 [a]Num 26:48   46:25 [a]Gen 30:5, 7   [b]Gen 29:29   46:26 [a]Exod 1:5   46:27 [a]Exod 1:5; Deut 10:22; Acts 7:14   46:28 [a]Gen 31:21   [b]Gen 47:1   46:29 [a]Gen 41:43   [b]Gen 45:14–15   46:30 [a]Luke 2:29–30   46:31 [a]Gen 47:1   46:32 [a]Gen 47:3   46:33 [a]Gen 47:2–3   46:34 [a]Gen 30:35; 34:5; 37:17   [b]Gen 43:32; Exod 8:26   [1]Heb. *is an abomination*.   47:1 [a]Gen 46:31   [b]Gen 45:10; 46:28; 50:8   47:2 [a]Acts 7:13   47:3 [a]Gen 46:33; Jonah 1:8   [b]Gen 46:32, 34; Exod 2:17, 19   47:4 [a]Gen 15:13; Deut 26:5; Ps 105:23

pasture [b]for your servants' flocks because the famine is severe in the land of Canaan. So now, please let your servants [c]live in the land of Goshen."

[5]Pharaoh said to Joseph, "Your father and your brothers have come to you. [6]The land of Egypt is before you; settle your [a]father and your brothers [b]in the best region of the land. They may live in the land of Goshen. If you know of any highly capable men among them, put them in charge of my livestock."

[7]Then Joseph brought in his father Jacob and presented him before Pharaoh. Jacob [a]blessed Pharaoh. [8]Pharaoh said to Jacob, "How long have you lived?" [9]Jacob said to Pharaoh, "All [a]the years of my travels are 130. All the years of my life have been [b]few and painful;[1][c]the years of my travels are not as long as those of my ancestors." [10]Then Jacob [a]blessed Pharaoh and went out from his presence.

[11]So Joseph settled his father and his brothers. He gave them territory in the land of Egypt, in the best region of the land, the land of [a]Rameses, just [b]as Pharaoh had commanded. [12]Joseph also provided food for [a]his father, his brothers, and all his father's household, according to the number of their little children.

[13]But there was no food in all the land because the famine was very severe; the land of Egypt and the land of Canaan wasted away because of the famine. [14]Joseph collected all the money that could be found in the [a]land of Egypt and in the land of Canaan as payment for the grain they were buying. Then Joseph brought the money into Pharaoh's palace. [15]When the money from the lands of Egypt and Canaan was used up, all the Egyptians[1] came to Joseph and said, "Give us food! [a]Why should we die before your very eyes because our money has run out?"

[16]Then Joseph said, "If your money is gone, bring your livestock, and I will give you food in exchange for your livestock." [17]So they brought their livestock to Joseph, and Joseph gave them food in exchange for their horses, the livestock of their flocks and herds, and their donkeys. He got them through that year by giving them food in exchange for all their livestock.

[18]When that year was over, they came to him the next year and said to him, "We cannot hide from our lord that the money is used up and the livestock and the animals belong to our lord. Nothing remains before our lord except our bodies and our land. [19]Why should we die before your very eyes, both we and our land? Buy us and our land in exchange for food, and we, with our land, will become Pharaoh's slaves. Give us seed that we may [a]live and not die. Then the land will not become desolate."

[20]So Joseph [a]bought all the land of Egypt for Pharaoh. Each of the Egyptians sold his field, for the famine was severe. So the land became Pharaoh's. [21]Joseph made all the people slaves[1] from one end of Egypt's border to the other end of it. [22][a]But he did not purchase the land of the [b]priests because the priests had an allotment from Pharaoh and they ate from their allotment that Pharaoh gave them. That is why they did not sell their land.

[23]Joseph said to the people, "Since I have bought you and your land today for Pharaoh, here is seed for you. Cultivate the land. [24]When the crop comes in, give one-fifth of it to Pharaoh. The remaining four-fifths will be yours for seed for the fields and for you to eat, including those in your households and your little children." [25]They replied, "You have saved [a]our lives! You are showing us favor,[1] and we will be Pharaoh's slaves."

[26]So Joseph made it a statute, which is in effect to this day throughout the land of Egypt: One-fifth belongs to Pharaoh. [a]Only the land of the priests did not become Pharaoh's.

[27]Israel [a]settled in the land of Egypt, in the land of Goshen, and they owned land there. They were [b]fruitful and increased rapidly in number.

[28]Jacob lived in the land of Egypt 17 years; the years of Jacob's life were 147 in all. [29]The time for Israel to die approached, so he called for his son Joseph and said to him, "If now

47:4[b] Gen 43:1; Acts 7:11   [c] Gen 46:34   47:6 [a] Gen 20:15; 45:10, 18; 47:11   [b] Gen 47:4   47:7 [a] Gen 47:10; 48:15, 20; 2 Sam 14:22; 1 Kgs 8:66; Heb 7:7   47:9 [a] Ps 39:12; [Heb 11:9, 13]   [b] [Job 14:1]   [c] Gen 5:5; 11:10–11; 25:7-8; 35:28   [1] Heb. evil.   47:10 [a] Gen 47:7   47:11 [a] Exod 1:11; 12:37   [b] Gen 47:6, 27   47:12 [a] Gen 45:11; 50:21   47:14 [a] Gen 41:56; 42:6   47:15 [a] Gen 47:19   [1] Heb. all Egypt.   47:19 [a] Gen 43:8   47:20 [a] Jer 32:43   47:21 [1] MT and the people he removed to the cities.   47:22 [a] Lev 25:34; Ezra 7:24   [b] Gen 41:45   47:25 [a] Gen 33:15   [1] Or may we find favor in the eyes of my lord; Heb. we find favor in the eyes of my lord.   47:26 [a] Gen 47:22   47:27 [a] Gen 47:11   [b] Gen 17:6; 26:4; 35:11; 46:3; Exod 1:7; Deut 26:5; Acts 7:17

I have found favor in your sight, [a]put your hand under my thigh and[b]show me kindness and faithfulness. [c]Do not bury me in Egypt, [30]but when I rest[1] with my fathers, carry me out of Egypt and [a]bury me in their burial place." Joseph said, "I will do as you say."

[31]Jacob said, "Swear to me that you will do so." So Joseph gave him his word. Then [a]Israel bowed down at the head of his bed.[1]

Manasseh and Ephraim

48 After these things Joseph was told, "Your father is weakening." So he took his two sons [a]Manasseh and Ephraim with him. [2]When Jacob was told, "Your son Joseph has just come to you," Israel regained strength and sat up on his bed. [3]Jacob said to Joseph, "The [a]Sovereign God appeared to me at [b]Luz in the land of Canaan and blessed me. [4]He said to me, 'I am going to [a]make you fruitful[1] and will multiply you. I will make you into a group of nations, and I will [b]give this land to your descendants [c]as an everlasting possession.'

[5]"Now, as for your [a]two sons, who were born to you in the land of Egypt before I came to you in Egypt, they will be mine. Ephraim and Manasseh will be mine just as Reuben and Simeon are. [6]Any children that you father after them will be yours; they will be listed under the names of their brothers in their inheritance. [7]But as for me, when I was returning from Paddan, [a]Rachel died—to my sorrow—in the land of Canaan. It happened along the way, some distance from Ephrath. So I buried her there on the way to Ephrath" (that is, Bethlehem).

[8]When Israel saw Joseph's sons, he asked, "Who are these?" [9]Joseph [a]said to his father, "They are the sons God has given me in this place." His father said, "Bring them to me so I may bless them." [10]Now Israel's eyes were failing because of his age; [a]he was not able to see well. So Joseph brought his sons near to him, and his father [b]kissed them and embraced them. [11]Israel [a]said to Joseph, "I never expected to see you again, but now God has allowed me to see your children too."

[12]So Joseph moved them from Israel's knees and bowed down with his face to the ground. [13]Joseph positioned them; he put Ephraim on his right hand across from Israel's left hand, and Manasseh on his left hand across from Israel's right hand. Then Joseph brought them closer to his father. [14]Israel stretched out his right hand and [a]placed it on Ephraim's head, although he was the younger. Crossing his hands, he put his left hand on Manasseh's head, for Manasseh was the [b]firstborn. [15]Then [a]he blessed Joseph and said,

"May the God [b]before whom my
  fathers
  Abraham and Isaac walked—
  the God who has been my shepherd[1]
  all my life long to this day,
[16] the angel [a]who has protected me[1]
  from all harm—
  bless these boys.
  May [b]my name be named in them,
  and the name of my fathers Abraham
  and Isaac.
  May they [c]grow into a multitude on
  the earth."

[17]When Joseph saw that his father [a]placed his right hand on Ephraim's head, it displeased him. So he took his father's hand to move it from Ephraim's head to Manasseh's head. [18]Joseph said to his father, "Not so, my father, for this is the firstborn. Put your right hand on his head." [19]But [a]his father refused and said, "[b]I know, my son, I know. He too will become a nation and he too will become great. In spite of this, his younger brother will be even greater and his descendants will become a multitude of nations." [20]So he blessed them that day, saying,

"[a]By you will Israel bless, saying,
  'May God make you like Ephraim and
  Manasseh.'"
Thus he put Ephraim before
  Manasseh.

47:29 [a] Gen 24:2–4 [b] Gen 24:49; Josh 2:14 [c] Gen 50:25 **47:30** [a] Gen 49:29; 50:5–13; Heb 11:21 [1] Heb. *lie down*; i.e., die. **47:31** [a] Gen 48:2; 1 Kgs 1:47; Heb 11:21 [1] LXX *staff, rod.* **48:1** [a] Gen 41:51, 56; 46:20; 50:23; Josh 14:4 **48:3** [a] Gen 43:14; 49:25 [b] Gen 28:13, 19; 35:6, 9 **48:4** [a] Gen 46:3 [b] Gen 35:12; Exod 6:8 [c] Gen 17:8 [1] Heb. *Look, I am making you fruitful.* **48:5** [a] Gen 41:50; 46:20; 48:8; Josh 13:7; 14:4 **48:7** [a] Gen 35:9, 16, 19, 20 **48:9** [a] Gen 27:4; 47:15 **48:10** [a] Gen 27:1; 1 Sam 3:2 [b] Gen 27:27; 45:15; 50:1 **48:11** [a] Gen 45:26 **48:14** [a] Matt 19:15; Mark 10:16 [b] Gen 41:51–52; Josh 17:1 **48:15** [a] Gen 47:7, 10; 49:24; [Heb 11:21] [b] Gen 17:1; 24:40; 2 Kgs 20:3 [1] Heb. *shepherded me.* **48:16** [a] Gen 22:11, 15–18; 28:13–15; 31:11; [Ps 34:22; 121:7] [b] Amos 9:12; Acts 15:17 [c] Num 26:34, 37 [1] Heb. *deliver, protect, avenge.* **48:17** [a] Gen 48:14 **48:19** [a] Gen 48:14 [b] Num 1:33, 35; Deut 33:17 **48:20** [a] Ruth 4:11–12

²¹Then Israel said to Joseph, "I am about to die, but ^aGod will be with you and will bring you back to the land of your fathers. ²²As one who ^ais above your brothers, I give to you the mountain slope, which I took from the Amorites with my sword and my bow."

The Blessing of Jacob

49 Jacob called for his sons and said, "Gather together so I can ^atell you what will happen to you ^bin future days.

² "Assemble and listen, you sons of
   Jacob;
  listen to Israel, your father.
³ Reuben, you are ^amy firstborn,
  my might and the beginning of my
   strength,
  outstanding in dignity, outstanding
   in power.
⁴ You are destructive¹ like water and
   will not excel,
  for you got on your father's bed,
  then you defiled it—he got on my
   couch!
⁵ Simeon and Levi are brothers,
  weapons of violence are their knives!¹
⁶ ^aO my soul, do not come ^binto their
   council,
  do not be united to their assembly,
   my heart,
  ^cfor in their anger they have killed
   men,
  and for pleasure they have
   hamstrung oxen.
⁷ Cursed be ^atheir anger, for it was
   fierce,
  and their fury, for it was cruel.
  I will divide them in Jacob,
  and scatter them in Israel!
⁸ ^aJudah, ^byour brothers will praise
   ^cyou.
  Your hand will be on the neck of your
   enemies,
  your father's sons will bow down
   before you.

⁹ You ^aare a lion's cub, Judah,
  from ^bthe prey, my son, you have
   gone up.
  He crouches and lies down like a lion;
  like a lioness—who will rouse him?
¹⁰ The scepter will not depart from
   Judah,
  nor ^athe ruler's ^bstaff from between
   his feet,
  ^cuntil he comes to whom it belongs;¹
  the nations will obey him.
¹¹ Binding his foal to the vine,
  and his colt to the choicest vine,
  he will wash his garments in wine,
  his robes in the blood of grapes.
¹² His eyes will be red from wine,
  and his teeth white from milk.
¹³ ^aZebulun will live¹ by the haven of
   the sea
  and become ^ba haven for ships;
  his border will extend to Sidon.
¹⁴ ^aIssachar is a strong-boned donkey
  lying down between two saddlebags.
¹⁵ When he sees a good resting place,
  and the pleasant land,
  he will bend ^ahis shoulder to the
   burden
  and become a slave laborer.
¹⁶ ^aDan will judge his people
  as one of the tribes of Israel.
¹⁷ May ^aDan be a snake beside the road,
  a viper by the path,
  that bites the heels of the horse
  so that its rider falls backward.
¹⁸ I ^await for your deliverance, O LORD.
¹⁹ ^aGad will be raided by marauding
   bands,
  but he will attack them at their
   heels.
²⁰ Asher's food will be rich,¹
  and ^ahe will provide delicacies to
   royalty.
²¹ ^aNaphtali is a free running doe,
  he speaks delightful words.
²² Joseph is a fruitful bough,
  a fruitful bough near a spring
  whose branches climb over the wall.

48:21 ^aGen 28:15; 46:4; 50:24   **48:22** ^aGen 14:7; Josh 24:32; John 4:5   **49:1** ^aDeut 33:1, 6–25; [Amos 3:7]   ^bNum 24:14; [Deut 4:30]; Isa 2:2; 39:6; Jer 23:20; Heb 1:2   **49:3** ^aGen 29:32   **49:4** ¹Heb. *frothy, boiling, turbulent.*   **49:5** ¹Or *habitations, merchandise, counsels, swords, wedding feasts.*   **49:6** ^aPs 64:2; Prov 1:15–16   ^bPs 26:9; Eph 5:11   ^cGen 34:26   **49:7** ^aNum 18:24; Josh 19:1, 9; 21:1–42; 1 Chr 4:24–27   **49:8** ^aDeut 33:7; Rev 5:5   ^bPs 18:40   ^cGen 27:29; 1 Chr 5:2   **49:9** ^aDeut 33:22; Ezek 19:5–7; Mic 5:8; [Rev 5:5]   ^bNum 23:24; 24:9   **49:10** ^aNum 24:17; Jer 30:21; Matt 1:3; 2:6; Luke 3:33; Rev 5:5   ^bPs 60:7   ^cIsa 11:1; [Matt 21:9]   ¹Or *Shiloh, until the* [or *his*] *ruler comes, until tribute is brought to him.*   **49:13** ^aDeut 33:18–19; Josh 19:10–11   ^bGen 10:19; Josh 11:8   ¹Heb. *to settle.*   **49:14** ¹1 Chr 12:32   **49:15** ^a1 Sam 10:9   **49:16** ^aGen 30:6; Deut 33:22; Judg 18:26–27   **49:17** ^aJudg 18:27   **49:18** ^aExod 15:2; Ps 25:5; 40:1–3; 119:166, 174; Isa 25:9; Mic 7:7   **49:19** ^aGen 30:11; Deut 33:20; 1 Chr 5:18   **49:20** ^aDeut 33:24; Josh 19:24–31   ¹I.e., abundant in quantity and quality.   **49:21** ^aDeut 33:23

23 The archers will attack him,
   they will shoot at him and oppose
   him.
24 But his [a]bow will remain steady,
   and his hands will be skillful;
   because of [b]the hands of the
   Powerful One of Jacob,
   because of the Shepherd, the Rock of
   [c]Israel,
25 [a]because of the God of your father,
   who will help you,
   because of the Sovereign God,
   who will bless you
   with blessings from the sky above,
   blessings from the deep that lies
   below,
   [b]and blessings of the breasts and
   womb.
26 The blessings of your father are
   greater
   than [a]the blessings of the eternal
   mountains
   or the desirable things of the age-old
   hills.
   They will be on the head of Joseph
   and on the brow of the prince of his
   brothers.
27 Benjamin is a [a]ravenous wolf;
   in the morning devouring the prey,
   [b]and in the evening dividing the
   plunder."

28 These are the twelve tribes of Israel. This is what their father said to them when he blessed them. He gave each of them an appropriate blessing.

29 Then he instructed them,[1] "I [a]am about to go to my people. [b]Bury me with my fathers [c]in the cave in the field of Ephron the Hittite. 30 It is the cave in the field of Machpelah, near Mamre in the land of Canaan, [a]which Abraham bought for a burial plot from Ephron the Hittite. 31 There they buried Abraham and his wife Sarah; [a]there they buried Isaac and his wife Rebekah; and [b]there I buried Leah. 32 The field and the cave in it were acquired from the sons of Heth."

33 When Jacob finished giving these instructions to his sons, he pulled his feet up onto the bed, breathed his last breath, and went to his people.

The Burials of Jacob and Joseph

50 Then Joseph [a]hugged his father's face. He [b]wept over him and kissed him. 2 Joseph instructed the physicians in his service to [a]embalm his father, so the physicians embalmed Israel. 3 They took 40 days, for that is the full time needed for embalming. The Egyptians mourned [a]for him 70 days.

4 When [a]the days of mourning had passed, Joseph said to Pharaoh's royal court, "If I have found favor in your sight, please say to Pharaoh, 5 'My father made me swear an oath. He said, "I am about to die. Bury me in [a]my tomb that [b]I dug for myself there in the land of Canaan." Now let me go and bury my father; then I will return.'" 6 So Pharaoh said, "Go and bury your father, just as he made you swear to do."

7 So Joseph went up to bury his father; all Pharaoh's officials went with him—the senior courtiers of his household, all the senior officials of the land of Egypt, 8 all Joseph's household, his brothers, and his father's household. But they left their little children and their flocks and herds in the land of Goshen. 9 Chariots and horsemen also went up with him, so it was a very large entourage.

10 When they came to the threshing floor of Atad on the other side of the Jordan, they [a]mourned [b]there with very great and bitter sorrow. There Joseph observed a seven-day period of mourning for his father. 11 When the Canaanites who lived in the land saw them mourning at the threshing floor of Atad, they said, "This is a very sad occasion for the Egyptians." That is why its name was called Abel Mizraim, which is beyond the Jordan.

12 So the sons of Jacob did for him just as he had instructed them. 13 His sons carried him to the land of Canaan and buried him in the cave of the field of Machpelah, near Mamre. [a]This is the field Abraham [b]purchased as a burial plot from Ephron the Hittite. 14 After

49:24 [a]Job 29:20; Ps 37:15 [b]Ps 132:2, 5; Isa 1:24; 49:26 [c][Ps 23:1; 80:1] 49:25 [a]Gen 28:13; 32:9; 35:3; 43:23; 50:17 [b]Gen 17:1; 35:11 49:26 [a]Deut 33:16 49:27 [a]Judg 20:21, 25 [b]Num 23:24; Esth 8:11; Ezek 39:10; Zech 14:1 49:29 [a]Gen 15:15; 25:8; 35:29 [b]Gen 47:30; 2 Sam 19:37 [c]Gen 23:16–20; 50:13 [1]The Heb. text adds *and he said to them.* 49:30 [a]Gen 23:3–20 49:31 [a]Gen 23:19–20; 25:9 [b]Gen 35:29; 50:13 50:1 [a]Gen 46:4, 29 [b]2 Kgs 13:14 50:2 [a]Gen 50:26; 2 Chr 16:14; Matt 26:12; Mark 16:1; Luke 24:1; John 19:39–40 50:3 [a]Gen 37:34; Num 20:29; Deut 34:8 50:4 [a]Esth 4:2 50:5 [a]Gen 47:29–31 [b]2 Chr 16:14; Isa 22:16; Matt 27:60 50:10 [a]Acts 8:2 [b]1 Sam 31:13; Job 2:13 50:13 [a]Gen 49:29–31; Acts 7:16 [b]Gen 23:16–20

he buried his father, Joseph returned to Egypt, along with his brothers and all who had accompanied him to bury his father.

[15] When Joseph's brothers saw that their father was dead, [a] they said, "What if Joseph bears a grudge and wants to repay us in full for all the harm we did to him?" [16] So they sent word to Joseph, saying, "Your father gave these instructions before he died: [17] 'Tell Joseph this: Please [a] forgive [b] the sin of your brothers and the wrong they did when they treated you so badly.' Now please forgive the sin of the servants of the God of your father." When this message was reported to him, Joseph wept. [18] Then his brothers also came and threw themselves down before him; they said, "Here we are; we are your slaves." [19] But Joseph answered them, "[a] Don't be afraid. Am I in the place of God? [20] As for you, you meant to harm me, [a] but [b] God intended it for a good purpose, so he could preserve the lives of many people, as you can see this day. [21] So now, don't be [a] afraid. I will provide for you and your little children." Then he consoled them and spoke kindly to them.

[22] Joseph lived in Egypt, along with his father's family. Joseph lived 110 years. [23] Joseph saw the descendants of Ephraim [a] to [b] the third generation. He also saw the children of Makir the son of Manasseh; they [c] were given special inheritance rights by Joseph.

[24] Then Joseph said to his brothers, "I am about to die. But [a] God will surely come to you[1] and lead you up from this land to the land he swore on oath to give to Abraham, Isaac, and Jacob." [25a] Joseph made the sons of Israel swear an oath. He said, "God will surely come to [b] you. Then you must carry my [c] bones up from this place." [26] So Joseph died at the age of 110. After they embalmed him, his body was placed in a coffin in Egypt.

50:15 [a] [Job 15:21]   50:17 [a] [Prov 28:13]   [b] Gen 49:25   50:19 [a] Gen 45:5   50:20 [a] Gen 45:5, 7; Ps 56:5   [b] [Acts 3:13–15]   50:21 [a] [Matt 5:44]   50:23 [a] Gen 48:1; Job 42:16   [b] Num 26:29; 32:39   [c] Gen 30:3   50:24 [a] Gen 15:14; 46:4; 48:21; Exod 3:16–17; Josh 3:17; Heb 11:22   [1] Heb. to visit; to intervene for blessing or cursing.   50:25 [a] Gen 47:29–30; Exod 13:19; Josh 24:32; Acts 7:15–16; Heb 11:22   [b] Gen 17:8; 28:13; 35:12; Deut 1:8; 30:1–8   [c] Exod 13:19

EXODUS

Exodus is the record of Israel's birth as a nation. Within the protective womb of Egypt, the Jewish family of seventy rapidly multiplies. At the right time, an infant nation numbering around two million people is brought into the world where it is divinely protected, fed, and nurtured. The Hebrew title, *We'elleh Shemoth*, "These Are the Names," comes from the first phrase in 1:1. The Greek title is *Exodus*, a word meaning "exit," "departure," or "going out." The Septuagint uses this word to describe the book by its key event (see 19:1, "went out from"). In Luke 9:31 and in 2 Peter 1:15, the word "departure" speaks of physical death (Jesus' and Peter's). This embodies Exodus's theme of redemption because redemption is accomplished only through death. The Latin title is *Liber Exodus*, "Book of Departure," taken from the Greek title.

Blessing during Bondage in Egypt

1 [a]These are the names of the sons of Israel[1] who entered Egypt—each man with his household entered with Jacob: [2]Reuben, Simeon, Levi, and Judah, [3]Issachar, Zebulun, and Benjamin, [4]Dan and Naphtali, Gad and Asher. [5]All the people[1] who were directly descended from Jacob numbered [a]70. But Joseph was already in Egypt, [6]and in time [a]Joseph and his brothers and all that generation died. [7][a]The Israelites, however, were fruitful, increased greatly, multiplied, and became extremely strong, so that the land was filled with them.

[8]Then a new king, [a]who did not know about Joseph, came to power over Egypt. [9]He said to his people, "Look at the Israelite people, more numerous and [a]stronger than we are! [10][a]Come, let's [b]deal wisely[1] with them. Otherwise they will continue to multiply, and if a war breaks out, they will ally themselves with our enemies and fight against us and leave the country."

[11]So they put foremen[1] over the Israelites [a]to oppress them with hard [b]labor. As a result they built Pithom and Rameses as [c]store cities for Pharaoh. [12]But the more the Egyptians oppressed them, the more they multiplied and spread. As a result the Egyptians loathed the Israelites, [13]and they made the Israelites [a]serve rigorously. [14]They [a]made their lives bitter by hard service with mortar and bricks and by all [b]kinds of service in the fields. Every kind of service the Israelites were required to give was rigorous.

[15]The king of Egypt said to the [a]Hebrew midwives, one of whom was named Shiphrah and the other Puah, [16]"When you assist the Hebrew women in childbirth, observe at the delivery: If it is a [a]son, kill him, but if it is a daughter, she may live." [17]But the midwives [a]feared God and did not do what the king of Egypt had told them; they let the boys live.

[18]Then the king of Egypt summoned the midwives and said to them, "Why have you done this and let the boys live?" [19]The midwives said to Pharaoh, "Because [a]the Hebrew women are not like the Egyptian women—for the Hebrew women are vigorous; they give birth before the midwife gets to them!" [20]So God treated [a]the midwives well, and the people multiplied and became

1:1 [a] Gen 46:8–27; Exod 6:14–16 [1] Often refers to the entire nation (*Israelites*), but here refers primarily to the sons of the patriarch Israel, who are named. 1:5 [a] Gen 46:26–27; [Deut 10:22] [1] Heb. *soul*; but refers to the whole person. 1:6 [a] Gen 50:26; Acts 7:15 1:7 [a] Gen 12:2; 28:3; 35:11; 46:3; 47:27; 48:4; Num 22:3; Deut 1:10–11; 26:5; Ps 105:24; Acts 7:17 1:8 [a] Acts 7:18–19 1:9 [a] Gen 26:16 1:10 [a] Ps 83:3–4 [b] Ps 105:25; [Prov 16:25]; Acts 7:19 [1] I.e., acting shrewdly or making a skillful decision. 1:11 [a] Gen 15:13; Exod 3:7; 5:6 [b] Exod 1:14; 2:11; 5:4–9; 6:6 [c] 1 Kgs 9:19; 2 Chr 8:4 [1] Heb. *princes of work*. 1:13 [a] Gen 15:13; Exod 5:7–19 1:14 [a] Exod 2:23; 6:9; Num 20:15; [Acts 7:19, 34] [b] Ps 81:6 1:15 [a] Exod 2:6 1:16 [a] Matt 2:16; Acts 7:19 1:17 [a] Exod 1:21; Prov 16:6 1:19 [a] Josh 2:4; 2 Sam 17:19–20 1:20 [a] Gen 15:1; Ruth 2:12; [Prov 11:18]; Eccl 8:12; [Isa 3:10]; Heb 6:10

very strong. [21]And because the midwives feared God, he made households for them.

[22]Then Pharaoh commanded [a]all his people, "All sons that are born you must throw into the river, but all daughters you may let live."

The Birth of the Deliverer

2 A [a]man from the household of Levi married a woman who was a descendant of Levi. [2]The woman became pregnant and gave birth to a son. [a]When she saw that he was a healthy child, she hid him for three months. [3]But when she was no longer able to hide him, she took a [a]papyrus basket for him and sealed it with [b]bitumen and [c]pitch. She put the child in it and set it among the reeds along the edge of the Nile. [4]His sister stationed herself at [a]a distance to find out what would happen to him.

[5]Then the [a]daughter of Pharaoh came down to wash herself by the Nile, while her attendants were walking alongside the river, and she saw the basket among the reeds. She sent one of her attendants,[1] took it, [6]opened it, and saw the child—a boy, crying!—and she felt compassion for him and said, "This is one of the Hebrews' children."

[7]Then his sister said to Pharaoh's daughter, "Shall I go and get a nursing woman for you from the Hebrews, so that she may nurse the child for you?" [8]Pharaoh's daughter said to her, "Yes, do so." So the young girl went and got the child's mother. [9]Pharaoh's daughter said to her, "Take this child and nurse him for me, and I will pay your wages." So the woman took the child and nursed him.

[10]When the child grew older[1] she brought him to Pharaoh's daughter, and [a]he became her son. She named him Moses, saying, "Because I drew him from the water."

The Presumption of the Deliverer

[11]In those days, [a]when Moses had grown up, he went out to his people and observed their hard labor, and he saw an Egyptian man attacking[1] a Hebrew man, one of his own people. [12]He looked this way and that and saw that no one was there, and then he [a]attacked the Egyptian and concealed the body in the sand. [13]When [a]he went out the next day, there [b]were two Hebrew men fighting. So he said to the one who was in the wrong, "Why are you attacking your fellow Hebrew?"

[14]The man replied, "[a]Who made you a ruler and a judge over us? Are you planning to kill me like you killed that Egyptian?" Then Moses was [b]afraid, thinking,[1] "Surely what I did[2] has become known." [15]When Pharaoh heard about this event, he sought to kill [a]Moses. So Moses fled from Pharaoh and settled in the land of [b]Midian, [c]and he settled by a certain well.

[16a]Now [b]a priest of Midian had seven daughters, and they came and began to draw water and fill the [c]troughs in order to water their father's flock. [17]When some [a]shepherds came and [b]drove them away, Moses came up and defended them and then [c]watered their flock. [18]So when they came home to their father [a]Reuel, [b]he asked, "Why have you come home so early today?" [19]They said, "An Egyptian man rescued us from the shepherds, and he actually drew water for us and watered the flock!" [20]He said to his daughters, "So where is he? Why in the world did you leave the man? Call him, so that he may [a]eat a meal[1] with us."

[21]Moses agreed to stay with the man, and he gave his daughter [a]Zipporah to Moses in marriage. [22]When she bore a son, Moses named him [a]Gershom, for he [b]said, "I have become a resident foreigner in a foreign land."

The Call of the Deliverer

[23]During that long period of time the [a]king of Egypt died, and the Israelites [b]groaned because of [c]the slave labor. They cried out, and their desperate cry because of their slave labor went up to God. [24]God [a]heard their groaning; God [b]remembered

1:22 [a]Acts 7:19   **2:1** [a]Exod 6:16–20; Num 26:59; 1 Chr 23:14   **2:2** [a]Acts 7:20; Heb 11:23   **2:3** [a]Isa 18:2   [b]Gen 14:10   [c]Gen 6:14; Isa 34:9   **2:4** [a]Exod 15:20; Num 26:59   **2:5** [a]Exod 7:15; Acts 7:21   [1]Heb. *female slave.*   **2:10** [a]Acts 7:21   [1]Heb. *and he became great.*   **2:11** [a]Acts 7:23–24; Heb 11:24–26   [1]Heb. *strike, smite, beat, attack.*   **2:12** [a]Acts 7:24–25   **2:13** [a]Acts 7:26–28   [b]Prov 25:8   **2:14** [a]Gen 19:9; Acts 7:27–28   [b]Judg 6:27; Heb 11:27   [1]Heb. *and he said.*   [2]Heb. *the word* [thing, matter, incident].   **2:15** [a]Acts 7:29; Heb 11:27   [b]Exod 3:1   [c]Gen 24:11; 29:2; Exod 15:27   **2:16** [a]Exod 3:1; 4:18; 18:12   [b]Gen 24:11, 13, 19; 29:6–10; 1 Sam 9:11   [c]Gen 30:38   **2:17** [a]Gen 47:3; 1 Sam 25:7   [b]Gen 26:19–21   [c]Gen 29:3, 10   **2:18** [a]Num 10:29   [b]Exod 3:1; 4:18   **2:20** [a]Gen 31:54; 43:25   [1]Heb. *bread;* i.e., food.   **2:21** [a]Exod 4:25; 18:2   **2:22** [a]Exod 4:20; 18:3–4   [b]Gen 23:4; Lev 25:23; Acts 7:29; Heb 11:13–14   **2:23** [a]Acts 7:34   [b]Deut 26:7   [c]Exod 3:7, 9; Jas 5:4   **2:24** [a]Exod 6:5; Acts 7:34   [b]Gen 15:13; 22:16–18; 26:2–5; 28:13–15; Ps 105:8, 42

his ᶜcovenant with Abraham, with Isaac, and with Jacob. ²⁵God ᵃsaw the Israelites, and God ᵇunderstood.

3 Now Moses was shepherding the flock of his father-in-law ᵃJethro, ᵇthe priest of Midian, and he led the flock to the far side of the desert and came to the mountain of God, to ᶜHoreb. ²The angel of ᵃthe Lᴏʀᴅ appeared[1] to him in a flame of fire from within a bush. He looked, and the bush was ablaze with fire, but it was not being consumed! ³So Moses thought, "I will turn aside to see this ᵃamazing[1] sight. Why does the bush not burn up?" ⁴When the Lᴏʀᴅ saw that he had turned aside ᵃto look, God called to him from within the bush and said, "Moses, Moses!" And Moses said, "Here I am." ⁵God said, "Do not approach any closer! ᵃTake your sandals off your feet, for the place where you are standing is holy ground." ⁶He added, "ᵃI am ᵇthe God of your father, the God of Abraham, the God of Isaac, and the God of Jacob." Then Moses hid his face, because he was afraid to look at God.

⁷The Lᴏʀᴅ ᵃsaid, "I have surely seen the affliction of my people who are in Egypt. I have heard their cry ᵇbecause of their taskmasters, ᶜfor I know their sorrows. ⁸I have come down to ᵃdeliver them from the hand of the Egyptians and ᵇto bring them up from that land to a land that is both good and spacious, to a land ᶜflowing with milk and honey, to ᵈthe region of the Canaanites, Hittites, Amorites, Perizzites, Hivites, and Jebusites. ⁹And now indeed ᵃthe cry of the Israelites has come to me, and I have also seen how ᵇseverely the Egyptians oppress them. ¹⁰So now ᵃgo, and I will send you to Pharaoh to bring my people, the Israelites, out of Egypt."

¹¹Moses said to God, "ᵃWho am I that I should go to Pharaoh, or that I should bring the Israelites out of Egypt?" ¹²He ᵃreplied,[1] "Surely I will be with you, and this will be the ᵇsign to you that I have sent you: When you bring the people out of Egypt, you and they will serve God at this mountain."

¹³Moses said to God, "If I go to the Israelites and tell them, 'The God of your fathers has sent me to you,' and they ask me, 'What is his name?'—what should I say to them?"

¹⁴God ᵃsaid to Moses, "I AM that I AM."[1] And he said, "You must say this to the Israelites, 'I AM has sent me to you.'" ¹⁵God also said to Moses, "You must say this to the Israelites, 'The Lᴏʀᴅ—the God of your fathers, the God of Abraham, the God of Isaac, and the God of Jacob—has sent me to you. This is ᵃmy name forever, and this is my memorial from generation to generation.'

¹⁶"Go and bring ᵃtogether the elders of ᵇIsrael and tell them, 'The Lᴏʀᴅ, the God of your fathers, appeared to me—the God of Abraham, Isaac, and Jacob—saying, "I have attended carefully to you and to what has been done to you in Egypt, ¹⁷and ᵃI have promised that I will bring you up out of the affliction of Egypt to the land of the Canaanites, Hittites, Amorites, Perizzites, Hivites, and Jebusites, to a land flowing with milk and honey."'

¹⁸"The elders will listen to you, and then you and ᵃthe elders of Israel must go to the king of Egypt and tell him, 'The Lᴏʀᴅ, the God of the Hebrews, has ᵇmet with us. So now, let us go three days' journey into the wilderness, so that we may sacrifice to the Lᴏʀᴅ our God.' ¹⁹But ᵃI know that the king of Egypt will not let you go, not even under force. ²⁰So I will extend my hand and strike Egypt with ᵃall my wonders[1] that I will do among them, and ᵇafter that he will release you.

²¹"I ᵃwill grant this people favor with the Egyptians, so that when you depart you will not leave empty-handed. ²²ᵃEvery woman will ask her neighbor and the one who happens to be staying in her house for

2:24 ᶜGen 12:1–3; 15:14; 17:1–14   **2:25** ᵃExod 4:31; Luke 1:25; Acts 7:34   ᵇExod 3:7   **3:1** ᵃExod 4:18   ᵇExod 2:16   ᶜExod 17:6; 1 Kgs 19:8   **3:2** ᵃDeut 33:16; Mark 12:26; Luke 20:37; Acts 7:30   ¹I.e., God allows himself to be seen, or presents himself. **3:3** ᵃActs 7:31   ¹Heb. *great.*   **3:4** ᵃExod 4:5; Deut 33:16   **3:5** ᵃJosh 5:15; Acts 7:33   **3:6** ᵃGen 28:13; Exod 3:16; 4:5; [Matt 22:32; Mark 12:26–27; Luke 20:37–38]; Acts 7:32   ᵇ1 Kgs 19:13   **3:7** ᵃExod 2:23–25; Neh 9:9; Ps 106:44   ᵇExod 1:11   ᶜGen 18:21; Exod 2:25   **3:8** ᵃExod 6:6–8; 12:51   ᵇNum 13:27; Deut 1:25; 8:7–9; Josh 3:17   ᶜExod 3:17; 13:5; Jer 11:5; Ezek 20:6   ᵈGen 15:19–21; Josh 24:11   **3:9** ᵃExod 2:23   ᵇExod 1:11, 13, 14   **3:10** ᵃGen 15:13–14; Exod 12:40–41; [Mic 6:4]; Acts 7:6–7   **3:11** ᵃExod 4:10; 6:12; 1 Sam 18:18   **3:12** ᵃGen 31:3; Exod 4:12, 15; 33:14–16; Deut 31:23; Josh 1:5; Isa 43:2; Rom 8:31   ᵇExod 4:8; 19:3   ¹Heb. *And he said.*   **3:14** ᵃ[Exod 6:3; John 8:24, 28, 58; Heb 13:8; Rev 1:8; 4:8]   ¹Or *I will be*; the Heb. verb is first-person sing., but when people refer to him as "Yahweh" (third-person sing.), they say "he is."   **3:15** ᵃPs 30:4; 97:12; 102:12; 135:13; [Hos 12:5]   **3:16** ᵃExod 4:29   ᵇGen 50:24; Exod 2:25; 4:31; Ps 33:18; Luke 1:68   **3:17** ᵃGen 15:13–21; 46:4; 50:24–25   **3:18** ᵃExod 4:31   ᵇNum 23:3–4, 15, 16   **3:19** ᵃExod 5:2   **3:20** ᵃDeut 6:22; Neh 9:10; Ps 105:27; 135:9; Jer 32:20; Acts 7:36   ᵇExod 11:1; 12:31–37   ¹Heb. *that which is extraordinary, surpassing, amazing, difficult to comprehend.*   **3:21** ᵃExod 11:3; 12:36; 1 Kgs 8:50; Ps 105:37; 106:46; [Prov 16:7]   **3:22** ᵃExod 11:2

[b]items of silver and gold and for clothing. [c]You will put these articles on your sons and daughters—thus you will plunder Egypt!"

The Source of Sufficiency

4 Moses answered again, "And if they do not believe me or pay attention to me, but say, 'The LORD has not appeared to you'?" [2]The LORD said to him, "What is that in your hand?" He said, "A staff." [3]The LORD said, "Throw it to the ground." So he threw it to the ground, and it became a snake, and Moses ran from it. [4]But the LORD said to Moses, "Put out your hand and grab it by the tail"—so he put out his hand and caught it, and it became a staff in his hand—[5]"that they may [a]believe that the [b]LORD, the God of their fathers, the God of Abraham, the God of Isaac, and the God of Jacob, has appeared to you."

[6]The LORD also said to him, "Put your hand into your robe."[1] So he put his hand into his robe, and when he brought it out—there was his hand, leprous [a]like snow! [7]He said, "Put your hand back into your robe." So he put his hand back into his robe, and when he brought [a]it out from his robe—there it was, restored like the rest of his skin! [8]"If they do not believe you or pay attention to the [a]former sign, then they may believe the latter sign. [9]And if [a]they do not believe even these two signs or listen to you, then take some water from the Nile and pour it out on the dry ground. The water you take out of the Nile will become blood on the dry ground."

[10]Then Moses [a]said to the LORD, "O my Lord,[1] I am not an eloquent man, neither in the past nor since you have spoken to your servant, for I am slow of speech and slow of tongue."[2]

[11]The LORD said to him, "[a]Who gave a mouth to man, or who makes a person mute or deaf or seeing or blind? Is it not I, the LORD? [12]So now go, and [a]I will be with your mouth and will teach you what you must say."

[13]But Moses said, "O my Lord, [a]please send anyone else whom you wish to send!" [14]Then [a]the LORD became angry with Moses, and he said, "What about your [b]brother Aaron [c]the Levite? I know that he can speak very well. Moreover, he is coming to meet you, and when he sees you he will be glad in his heart. [15]"So [a]you are to speak to him and [b]put the words [c]in his mouth. And as for me, I will be with your mouth and with his mouth, and I will teach you both what you must do. [16]He[1] will speak for [a]you to the people, and it will be as if he were your mouth and as if you were his God. [17]You will also take in your hand this staff, with which you will do the signs."

The Return of Moses

[18]So Moses went back to his father-in-law [a]Jethro and said to him, "Let me [b]go, so that I may return to my relatives in Egypt and see if they are still alive." Jethro said to Moses, "Go in peace." [19]The LORD said to Moses in [a]Midian, "Go back to [b]Egypt, because all the men who were [c]seeking your life are dead." [20]Then Moses [a]took his wife and sons and put [b]them on a donkey and headed back to the land of Egypt, and Moses took the staff of God in his hand. [21]The LORD said to Moses, "When you go back to Egypt, see that you do before Pharaoh all the [a]wonders [b]I have put under your control. But I will harden[1] his heart and he will not let the people go. [22]You must [a]say to Pharaoh, 'This is what the LORD has said, "[b]Israel is [c]my son, my firstborn, [23]and [a]I said to you, 'Let my son go that he may serve me,' but since you have refused to let him go, I will surely kill your son, your firstborn!"'"

[24]Now on the way, at a place [a]where they stopped for the night, the LORD [b]met Moses and sought to [c]kill him. [25]But [a]Zipporah

3:22[b]Exod 33:6 [c]Job 27:17; Prov 13:22; [Ezek 39:10] **4:5**[a]Exod 4:31; 19:9 [b]Gen 28:13; 48:15; Exod 3:6, 15 **4:6**[a]Num 12:10; 2 Kgs 5:27 [1]Or *bosom.* **4:7**[a]Num 12:13–15; Deut 32:39 **4:8**[a]Exod 7:6–13 **4:9**[a]Exod 7:19–20 **4:10**[a]Exod 3:11; 4:1; 6:12; Jer 1:6 [1]Heb. *adonay*, a term of respect and deference such as *lord, master,* or *sir.* [2]Heb. *heavy of mouth and heavy of tongue.* **4:11**[a]Ps 94:9; 146:8; Matt 11:5; Luke 1:20, 64 **4:12**[a]Exod 4:15–16; Deut 18:18; Isa 50:4; Jer 1:9; [Matt 10:19; Mark 13:11; Luke 12:11–12; 21:14–15] **4:13**[a]Jonah 1:3 **4:14**[a]Num 11:1, 33 [b]Num 26:59 [c]Exod 4:27; 1 Sam 10:2–3, 5 **4:15**[a]Exod 4:12, 30; 7:1–2 [b]Num 23:5, 12; Deut 18:18; 2 Sam 14:3, 19; Isa 51:16; 59:21; Jer 1:9 [c]Deut 5:31 **4:16**[a]Exod 7:1–2 [1]An emphatic Heb. construction. **4:18**[a]Exod 2:21; 3:1; 4:18 [b]Gen 43:23; Judg 18:6 **4:19**[a]Exod 3:1; 18:1 [b]Gen 46:3, 6 [c]Exod 2:15, 23; Matt 2:20 **4:20**[a]Exod 18:2–5; Acts 7:29 [b]Exod 4:17; 17:9; Num 20:8–9, 11 **4:21**[a]Exod 3:20; 11:9–10 [b]Exod 7:3, 13; 9:12, 35; 10:1, 20, 27; 14:4, 8; Deut 2:30; Josh 11:20; 1 Sam 6:6; Isa 63:17; John 12:40; Rom 9:18 [1]Heb. *strengthen*; in the sense of making stubborn or obstinate. **4:22**[a]Exod 5:1 [b]Isa 63:16; 64:8; Hos 11:1; [Rom 9:4; 2 Cor 6:16, 18] [c]Jer 31:9; [Jas 1:18] **4:23**[a]Exod 11:5; 12:29; Ps 105:36; 135:8; 136:10 **4:24**[a]Gen 42:27 [b]Exod 3:18; 5:3; Num 22:22 [c]Gen 17:14 **4:25**[a]Exod 2:21; 18:2

took [b]a flint knife, cut off the foreskin of her son and touched it to Moses' feet,[1] and said, "Surely you are a bridegroom of blood to me." [26]So the LORD let him alone. (At that time she said, "A bridegroom of blood," referring to the circumcision.)

[27]The LORD said [a]to Aaron, "Go to [b]the wilderness to meet Moses." So he went and met him at the mountain of God and greeted him with a kiss. [28]Moses [a]told Aaron all the words of the LORD who had sent him and all the [b]signs that he had commanded him. [29]Then Moses and Aaron [a]went and brought together all the Israelite elders. [30]Aaron spoke all the words that the LORD had spoken to Moses [a]and did the signs in the sight of the people, [31]and the people [a]believed. When they heard[1] that the LORD had attended [b]to[2] the Israelites and that he [c]had seen their affliction, [d]they bowed down close to the ground.[3]

Opposition to the Plan of God

5 Afterward Moses [a]and Aaron went to Pharaoh and said, "This is what the LORD, the God of Israel, has said, 'Release my people so that they may hold a pilgrim feast to me in the wilderness.'" [2]But Pharaoh said, "[a]Who is the LORD[1] that I should obey him by releasing Israel? I do [b]not know the LORD, and I will not release Israel!" [3]And [a]they said, "The God of the Hebrews has [b]met with us. Let us go a three-day journey into the wilderness so that we may sacrifice to the LORD our God, so that he does not strike us with [c]plague or the sword." [4]The king of Egypt said to them, "Moses and Aaron, why do you cause the people to refrain from their work? Return to your [a]labor!" [5]Pharaoh was thinking, "The people of the land are now [a]many, and you are giving them rest from their labor."

[6]That same day Pharaoh commanded the slave [a]masters and foremen who were over the people: [7]"You must no longer give straw to the people for making [a]bricks as before. Let them go and collect straw for themselves. [8]But you must require of them the same quota of bricks that they were making before. Do not reduce it, for they are slackers. That is why they are crying, 'Let us go sacrifice to our God.' [9]Make the work harder for the men so they will keep at it and pay no attention to lying words!"

[10]So the slave masters of the people and their foremen went to the Israelites and said, "Thus says Pharaoh: 'I am not giving you straw. [11]You[1] go get straw for yourselves wherever you can find it, because there will be no reduction at all in your workload.'" [12]So the people spread out through all the land of Egypt to collect stubble for straw. [13]The slave masters were pressuring them, saying, "Complete your work for each day, just like when there was straw!" [14]The Israelite [a]foremen whom Pharaoh's slave masters had set over them were [b]beaten and were asked, "Why did you not complete your requirement for brickmaking as in the past— both yesterday and today?"

[15]The Israelite foremen went and cried out to Pharaoh, "Why are you treating your servants this way? [16]No straw is given to your servants, but we are told, 'Make bricks!' Your servants are even being beaten, but the fault[1] is with your people."

[17]But Pharaoh replied, "You are slackers! Slackers! That is why you are saying, 'Let us go sacrifice to the LORD.' [18]So now, get back to work! You will not be given straw, but you must still produce your quota of bricks!" [19]The Israelite foremen saw that they were in trouble when they were told, "You must not reduce the daily quota of your bricks." [20]When they went out from Pharaoh, they encountered Moses and Aaron standing there to meet them, [21]and they said to them, "May the LORD look on you [a]and judge, because you have made us stink in the opinion of Pharaoh and his servants, so that you have given them an excuse to kill us!"

The Assurance of Deliverance

[22]Moses returned to the LORD, and said, "Lord, why have you caused trouble for this people?[1] Why did you ever send me? [23]From the time I went to speak to Pharaoh in your name, he has caused trouble for this people, and you have certainly not rescued them!"

4:25 [b] Gen 17:14; Josh 5:2–3   [1] Heb. *to his feet.*   **4:27** [a] Exod 4:14   [b] Exod 3:1; 18:5; 24:13   **4:28** [a] Exod 4:15–16   [b] Exod 4:8–9   **4:29** [a] Exod 3:16; 12:21   **4:30** [a] Exod 4:15–16   **4:31** [a] Exod 3:18; 4:8–9; 19:9   [b] Gen 50:24; Exod 3:16   [c] Exod 2:25; 3:7   [d] Gen 24:26; Exod 12:27; 1 Chr 29:20   [1] LXX *and they rejoiced.*   [2] Or *intervened for*; trad. *visited.*   [3] Or *worshiped.*   **5:1** [a] Exod 3:18; 7:16; 10:9   **5:2** [a] 2 Kgs 18:35; 2 Chr 32:14; Job 21:15   [b] Exod 3:19; 7:14   [1] Heb. *Yahweh.*   **5:3** [a] Exod 3:18; 7:16   [b] Exod 4:24; Num 23:3   [c] Exod 9:15   **5:4** [a] Exod 1:11; 2:11; 6:6   **5:5** [a] Exod 1:7, 9   **5:6** [a] Exod 1:11; 3:7; 5:10, 13, 14   **5:7** [a] Exod 1:14   **5:11** [1] An emphatic Heb. construction.   **5:14** [a] Exod 5:6   [b] Isa 10:24   **5:16** [1] Heb. *to err, sin, miss the mark, way, or goal.*   **5:21** [a] Exod 6:9; 14:11; 15:24; 16:2   **5:22** [1] Heb. *to cause evil*; i.e., pain, calamity, trouble, or affliction, and not always sin.

6 Then the LORD said to Moses, "Now you will see what [a]I will do to Pharaoh, for compelled by my strong hand[1] [b]he will release them, and by my strong hand he will drive them out of his land."

[2]God spoke to Moses and said to him, "I am the LORD. [3]I appeared to Abraham, to [a]Isaac, and to Jacob as [b]God Almighty, but by my name 'the [c]LORD' I was not known to them. [4]I also [a]established my covenant with them [b]to give them the land of Canaan, where they were [c]living as resident foreigners.[1] [5]I have also heard the [a]groaning of the Israelites, whom the Egyptians are enslaving, and I have remembered my covenant. [6]Therefore, tell the [a]Israelites, [b]I am the LORD. I will bring you out from your enslavement to the Egyptians, I will [c]rescue you from the hard labor they impose, and I will redeem you with an outstretched arm and with great judgments. [7]I will [a]take you to myself for a people, and [b]I will be your God. Then you will know that I am the LORD your God, who brought you out [c]from your enslavement to the Egyptians. [8]I will bring you to the land I [a]swore to give to Abraham, to Isaac, and to Jacob—and I will give it to you as a possession. I am the LORD.'"

[9]Moses told this to the Israelites, [a]but they did not listen to him because of their [b]discouragement[1] and hard labor. [10]Then the LORD said to Moses, [11]"Go, tell Pharaoh king of Egypt that he must release the Israelites from his land." [12]But Moses [a]replied to the LORD, "If the Israelites did not listen to me, then how will Pharaoh listen to me, since I speak with difficulty?"[1]

[13]The LORD spoke to Moses and Aaron and [a]gave them a charge for the Israelites and Pharaoh king of Egypt to bring the Israelites out of the land of Egypt.

The Ancestry of Moses and Aaron

[14]These were [a]the heads of their fathers' households:

The sons of Reuben, the firstborn son of Israel, were Hanoch and Pallu, Hezron and Carmi. These were the clans of Reuben.

[15]The sons of Simeon were Jemuel, Jamin, Ohad, Jakin, Zohar, [a]and Shaul, the son of a Canaanite woman. These were the clans of Simeon.

[16]Now [a]these were the names of the sons of Levi, according to their records: Gershon, Kohath, and Merari. (The length of Levi's life was 137 years.)

[17]The sons of Gershon, by [a]their families, were Libni and Shimei.

[18]The sons of Kohath were Amram, Izhar, Hebron, and Uzziel. ([a]The length of Kohath's life was 133 years.)

[19]The sons of Merari were Mahli and Mushi. [a]These were the clans of Levi, according to their records.

[20][a]Amram married his father's sister [b]Jochebed, and she bore him [c]Aaron and Moses. (The length of Amram's life was 137 years.)

[21][a]The sons of Izhar were Korah, Nepheg, and Zikri.

[22]The sons of Uzziel were Mishael, Elzaphan, and Sithri.

[23]Aaron married Elisheba, the daughter of [a]Amminadab and sister of Nahshon, and she bore him [b]Nadab and Abihu, [c]Eleazar and Ithamar.

[24]The sons of Korah were Assir, Elkanah, and Abiasaph. [a]These were the Korahite clans.

[25]Now Eleazar son of Aaron married one of the daughters of Putiel and [a]she bore him Phinehas.

These were the heads of the fathers' households of Levi according to their clans.

[26]It was the same Aaron and Moses to whom the LORD said, "Bring the Israelites out of the land of Egypt by their [a]regiments." [27]They were the men who were speaking [a]to Pharaoh king of Egypt, in order to bring the Israelites out of Egypt. It was the same Moses and Aaron.

6:1 [a]Exod 3:19 [b]Exod 12:31, 33, 39 [1]Heb. with a strong hand. 15:3; Ps 68:4; 83:18; Isa 52:6; Jer 16:21; Ezek 37:6, 13; John 8:58 25:23 [c]Gen 28:4 [1]Heb. the land of their sojournings. 6:5 [a]Exod 2:24; [Job 34:28]; Acts 7:34 6:6 [a]Exod 13:3, 14; 20:2; Deut 6:12 [b]Exod 3:17; 7:4; 12:51; 16:6; 18:1; Deut 26:8; Ps 136:11 [c]Exod 15:13; Deut 7:8; 1 Chr 17:21; Neh 1:10 6:7 [a]Exod 19:5; Deut 4:20; 7:6; 2 Sam 7:24 [b]Gen 17:7; Exod 29:45–46; Lev 26:12–13, 45; Deut 29:13; Rev 21:7 [c]Exod 5:4-5 6:8 [a]Gen 15:18; 26:3; Num 14:30; Neh 9:15; Ezek 20:5–6 6:9 [a]Exod 5:21 [b]Exod 2:23; Num 21:4 [1]Heb. because of the shortness of spirit. 6:12 [a]Exod 4:10; 6:30; Jer 1:6 [1]Heb. and [since] I am of uncircumcised lips; i.e., unacceptable, unprepared, foreign, and of no use to God. 6:13 [a]Num 27:19, 23; Deut 31:14 6:14 [a]Gen 46:9; Num 26:5–11; 1 Chr 5:3 6:15 [a]Gen 46:10; Num 26:12–14; 1 Chr 4:24 6:16 [a]Gen 46:11; Num 3:17; 1 Chr 6:16–30 6:17 [a]1 Chr 6:17 6:18 [a]1 Chr 6:2, 18 6:19 [a]1 Chr 6:19; 23:21 6:20 [a]Exod 2:1–2; Num 3:19 [b]Num 26:59 [c]Num 26:59 6:21 [a]Num 16:1; 1 Chr 6:37–38 6:23 [a]Ruth 4:19–20; 1 Chr 2:10; Matt 1:4 [b]Lev 10:1; Num 3:2; 26:60 [c]Exod 28:1 6:24 [a]Num 26:11 6:25 [a]Num 25:7, 11; Josh 24:33 6:26 [a]Exod 7:4; 12:17, 51; Num 33:1 6:27 [a]Exod 6:13; 32:7; 33:1; Ps 77:20
6:3 [a]Gen 17:1; 35:9; 48:3 [b]Gen 28:3; 35:11 [c]Exod 3:14–15; 6:4 [a]Gen 12:7; 15:18; 17:4, 7, 8; 26:3; 28:4, 13 [b]Gen 47:9; Lev

The Authentication of the Word

[28] When the LORD spoke to Moses in the land of Egypt, [29] he [a]said to him, "I am the LORD. Tell Pharaoh king of Egypt all that I am telling you." [30] But Moses [a]said before the LORD, "Since I speak with difficulty, why should Pharaoh listen to me?"

7 So the LORD said to Moses, "See, I have made [a]you like God to Pharaoh, and your brother Aaron will be your prophet. [2] You are to speak everything I command you, and your brother Aaron is to tell Pharaoh that he must release the Israelites from his land. [3] But [a]I will harden Pharaoh's heart, and although I will [b]multiply my [c]signs and my wonders in the land of Egypt, [4][a]Pharaoh will not listen to you. I will reach into Egypt and bring out my regiments, my people the Israelites, from the land of Egypt with great acts of judgment. [5] Then the Egyptians will know that I am the LORD when I [a]extend my hand over Egypt and [b]bring the Israelites out from among them."

[6] And Moses and Aaron [a]did so; they did just as the LORD commanded them. [7] Now Moses was [a]eighty years old and [b]Aaron was eighty-three years old when they spoke to Pharaoh.

[8] The LORD said to Moses and Aaron, [9] "When Pharaoh says to you, '[a]Do a miracle,' and you say to Aaron, '[b]Take your staff and throw it down before Pharaoh,' it will become a snake." [10] When Moses and Aaron went to Pharaoh, they did so, just [a]as the LORD had commanded them—Aaron threw down his staff before Pharaoh and his servants, and it [b]became a snake. [11] Then Pharaoh also [a]summoned wise men and sorcerers, and [b]the magicians of Egypt by their secret arts [c]did the same thing. [12] Each man threw down his staff, and the staffs became snakes. But Aaron's staff swallowed up their staffs. [13] Yet Pharaoh's heart became hard, and he did not listen to them, just as the LORD had predicted.

Plague One: Water to Blood

[14] The LORD said to Moses, "[a]Pharaoh's heart is hard; he refuses to release the people. [15] Go to Pharaoh in the morning when he goes out to the [a]water. Position yourself to meet him by [b]the edge of the Nile, and take in your hand the staff that was turned into a snake. [16] Tell him, '[a]The LORD, the God of the Hebrews, has sent me to you to say, "Release my people, [b]that they may serve me in the wilderness!" But until now you have not listened. [17] This is what the LORD has said: "By this [a]you will know that I am [b]the LORD: I am going [c]to strike the water of the Nile with the staff that is in my hand, and it will be turned into blood. [18] Fish in the Nile will die, the Nile will stink, and the Egyptians will be [a]unable to drink water from the Nile."'"

[19] Then the LORD said to Moses, "Tell Aaron, 'Take your staff and stretch [a]out your hand over Egypt's waters—over their rivers, over their canals, over their ponds, and over all their reservoirs—so that it becomes blood.' There will be blood everywhere in the land of Egypt, even in wooden and stone containers." [20] Moses and Aaron did so, just as the LORD had commanded. He raised[1] the staff and struck the [a]water that was in the Nile right before the eyes of Pharaoh and his servants, and all the water that was in the Nile was turned to blood. [21] When the fish that were in the Nile died, the Nile began to stink, so that the Egyptians [a]could not drink water from the Nile. There was blood everywhere in the land of Egypt! [22] But [a]the magicians of Egypt did the same by their secret arts, and [b]so Pharaoh's heart remained hard,[1] and he refused to listen to Moses and Aaron—just [c]as the LORD had predicted. [23] And Pharaoh turned and went into his house. He did not pay any attention to this. [24] All the Egyptians dug around the Nile for water to drink, because they could not drink the water of the Nile.

Plague Two: Frogs

[25] Seven full days passed after the LORD **8** struck the Nile. [1] Then the LORD said to Moses, "Go to Pharaoh and tell him, 'This is what the LORD has said: "Release my

6:29 [a]Exod 6:11; 7:2 **6:30** [a]Exod 4:10; 6:12; Jer 1:6 **7:1** [a]Exod 4:15–16 **7:3** [a]Exod 4:21; 9:12 [b]Exod 11:9; Acts 7:36 [c]Exod 4:7; Deut 4:34 **7:4** [a]Exod 3:19–20; 10:1; 11:9 **7:5** [a]Exod 9:15 [b]Exod 3:20; 6:6; 12:51 **7:6** [a]Exod 7:2 **7:7** [a]Deut 29:5; 31:2; 34:7; Acts 7:23, 30 [b]Num 33:39 **7:9** [a]Exod 10:1; Isa 7:11; John 2:18; 6:30 [b]Exod 4:2–3, 17 **7:10** [a]Exod 7:9 [b]Exod 4:3 **7:11** [a]Gen 41:8 [b]Dan 2:2; 2 Tim 3:8 [c]Exod 7:22; 8:7, 18; 2 Tim 3:9; Rev 13:13–14 **7:14** [a]Exod 8:15; 10:1, 20, 27 **7:15** [a]Exod 2:5; 8:20 [b]Exod 4:2–3; 7:10 **7:16** [a]Exod 3:13, 18; 4:22 [b]Exod 3:12, 18; 4:23; 5:1, 3; 8:1 **7:17** [a]Exod 5:2; 7:5; 10:2; Ps 9:16; Ezek 25:17 [b]Exod 4:9; 7:20 [c]Rev 11:6; 16:4, 6 **7:18** [a]Exod 7:24 **7:19** [a]Exod 8:5–6, 16; 9:22; 10:12, 21; 14:21, 26 **7:20** [a]Ps 78:44; 105:29–30 [1]Probably Aaron who was instructed to do so in v. 19. **7:21** [a]Exod 7:18 **7:22** [a]Exod 7:11 [b]Exod 8:7 [c]Exod 3:19; 7:3 [1]Heb. *and the heart of Pharaoh became hard.*

people in order [a]that they may serve me! [2]But if you [a]refuse to release them, then I am going to plague all your territory with [b]frogs.[1] [3]The Nile will swarm with frogs, and they will come up and go into your house, in your [a]bedroom, and on your bed, and into the houses of your servants and your people, and into your ovens and your kneading troughs. [4]Frogs will come up against you, your people, and all your servants.'"'

[5]The LORD spoke to Moses, "Tell Aaron, 'Extend your hand with your staff over the rivers, over the canals, and over the ponds, and bring the frogs up over the land of Egypt.'" [6]So Aaron extended his hand over [a]the waters of Egypt, and frogs came up and covered the land of Egypt.

[7]The magicians did the same with their secret arts [a]and brought up frogs on the land of Egypt too.

[8]Then Pharaoh summoned Moses and Aaron and said, "[a]Pray to the LORD that he may take the frogs away from me and my people, and I will [b]release the people that they may sacrifice to the LORD." [9]Moses said to Pharaoh, "You may have the honor over me—when shall I pray for you, your servants, and your people, for the frogs to be removed from you and your houses, so that they will be left only in the Nile?" [10]He said, "Tomorrow." And Moses said, "It will be as you say, so that you may know that [a]there is no one like the LORD our God. [11]The frogs will depart from you, your houses, your servants, and your people; they will be left only in the Nile."

[12]Then Moses and Aaron went out from Pharaoh, and Moses [a]cried[1] to the LORD because of the frogs that he had brought on Pharaoh. [13]The LORD did as Moses asked— the frogs died in the houses, the villages, and the fields. [14]The Egyptians piled them in countless heaps,[1] and the land stank. [15]But when Pharaoh saw that there was [a]relief, [b]he hardened his heart and did not listen to them, just as the LORD had predicted.

Plague Three: Gnats

[16]The LORD said to Moses, "Tell Aaron, 'Extend your staff and strike the dust of the ground, and it will become gnats[1] throughout all the land of Egypt.'" [17]They did so; Aaron extended his hand [a]with his staff, he struck the dust of the ground, and it became gnats on people and on animals. All the dust of the ground became gnats throughout all the land of Egypt. [18]When [a]the magicians attempted to bring forth gnats by their secret arts, they [b]could not. So there were gnats on people and on animals. [19]The magicians said to Pharaoh, "It is [a]the finger of God!" But Pharaoh's [b]heart remained hard, and he did not listen to them, just as the LORD had predicted.

Plague Four: Flies

[20]The LORD said to Moses, "Get up early in the morning and position yourself before Pharaoh as he goes out to the water, and tell him, 'This [a]is what the LORD has said, "Release my people that they may serve me! [21]If you do not release my people, then I am going to send swarms of flies on you and on your servants and on your people and in your houses. The houses of the Egyptians will be full of flies, and even the ground they stand on. [22]But on that day [a]I will mark off the land of [b]Goshen, where my people are staying, so that no swarms of flies will be there, that you may [c]know that I am the LORD in the midst of this [d]land. [23]I will put a division between my people and your people. This [a]sign will take place tomorrow."'" [24]The LORD did so; a [a]thick swarm of flies came into Pharaoh's house and into the houses of his servants, and throughout the whole land of Egypt the land was ruined[1,2] because of the swarms of flies.

[25]Then Pharaoh summoned Moses and Aaron and said, "Go, sacrifice to your God within the land." [26]But Moses said, "That would not be [a]the right thing to do, for the sacrifices we make to the LORD our God would be an abomination to the Egyptians.

8:1 [a]Exod 3:12, 18; 4:23; 5:1, 3   8:2 [a]Exod 7:14; 9:2   [b]Rev 16:13   [1]Heb. *plague all your border with frogs.*   8:3 [a]Ps 105:30   8:6 [a]Ps 78:45; 105:30   8:7 [a]Exod 7:11, 22   8:8 [a]Exod 8:28; 9:28; 10:17; Num 21:7; 1 Kgs 13:6   [b]Exod 10:8, 24   8:10 [a]Exod 9:14; 15:11; Deut 4:35, 39; 33:26; 2 Sam 7:22; 1 Chr 17:20; Ps 86:8; Isa 46:9; [Jer 10:6–7]   8:12 [a]Exod 8:30; 9:33; 10:18; 32:11; [Jas 5:16–18]   [1]I.e., a prayer in which a person cries out of trouble or danger.   8:14 [1]*heaps* is repeated; an emphatic Heb. construction.   8:15 [a]Eccl 8:11   [b]Exod 7:14, 22; 9:34; 1 Sam 6:6   8:16 [1]Heb. *lice, gnats, ticks, flies, fleas,* or *mosquitoes.*   8:17 [a]Ps 105:31   8:18 [a]Exod 7:11–12; 8:7   [b]Dan 5:8; 2 Tim 3:8–9   8:19 [a]Exod 7:5; 10:7; 1 Sam 6:3, 9; Ps 8:3; Luke 11:20   [b]Exod 8:15   8:20 [a]Exod 7:15; 9:13   8:22 [a]Exod 9:4, 6, 26; 10:23; 11:6–7; 12:13   [b]Gen 50:8   [c]Exod 7:5, 17; 10:2; 14:4   [d]Exod 9:29   8:23 [a]Exod 4:8   8:24 [a]Ps 78:45; 105:31   [1]LXX, Smr., Syr. *and the land was ruined.*   [2]Heb. *utter devastation.*   8:26 [a]Gen 43:32; 46:34; [Deut 7:25–26; 12:31]

If we make sacrifices that are an abomination to the Egyptians right before their eyes, will they not stone us? [27] We must go on a [a]three-day journey[1] into [b]the wilderness and sacrifice to the LORD our God, just as he is telling us."

[28] Pharaoh said, "I will release you so that you may sacrifice to the LORD your God in the wilderness. Only you must not go very far. Do [a]pray for me."

[29] Moses said, "I am going to go out from you and pray to the LORD, and the swarms of flies will go away from Pharaoh, from his servants, and from his people tomorrow. Only do not let Pharaoh [a]deal falsely again by not releasing the people to sacrifice to the LORD." [30] So Moses went out from Pharaoh and [a]prayed to the LORD, [31] and the LORD did as Moses asked—he removed the swarms of flies from Pharaoh, from his servants, and from his people. Not one remained! [32] But Pharaoh [a]hardened his heart this time also and did not release the people.

Plague Five: Disease

9 Then the LORD said to Moses, "[a]Go to Pharaoh and tell him, 'This is what the LORD, the God of the Hebrews, has said, "Release my people that they may [b]serve me! [2] For if you [a]refuse to release them and continue holding them, [3] then the [a]hand of the LORD will surely bring a very terrible plague[1] on your livestock in the field, on the horses, the donkeys, the camels, the herds, and the flocks. [4] But [a]the LORD will distinguish between the livestock of Israel and the livestock of Egypt, and nothing[1] will die of all that the Israelites have."'"

[5] The LORD set an appointed time, saying, "Tomorrow the LORD will do this in the land." [6] And the LORD did this on the next day; [a]all the livestock of the Egyptians died, but of the Israelites' livestock not one died. [7] Pharaoh sent representatives to investigate, and indeed, not even one of the livestock of Israel had died. But Pharaoh's [a]heart remained hard, and he did not release the people.

Plague Six: Boils

[8] Then the LORD said to Moses and Aaron, "Take handfuls of soot from a furnace, and have Moses throw it into the air while Pharaoh is watching. [9] It will become fine dust over the whole land of Egypt and will cause [a]boils to break out and fester[1] on both people and animals in all the land of Egypt." [10] So they took soot from a furnace and stood before Pharaoh, Moses threw it into the air, and it caused festering [a]boils to break out on both people and animals.

[11] The [a]magicians could not stand before Moses because of the [b]boils, for boils were on the magicians and on all the Egyptians. [12] But the LORD hardened Pharaoh's heart, and he [a]did not listen to them, just [b]as the LORD had predicted to Moses.

Plague Seven: Hail

[13] The LORD said to Moses, "Get up early in the morning, stand before Pharaoh, and tell him, 'This [a]is what the LORD, the God of the Hebrews, has said: "Release my people so that they may [b]serve me! [14] For this time I will send all my plagues on your very self and on your servants and your people, so [a]that you may know that there is no one like me in all the earth. [15] For by now I could have [a]stretched out my hand and struck you and your people with [b]plague, and you would have been destroyed from the earth. [16] But for [a]this purpose I have caused you to stand: to [b]show you my strength, and so that my [c]name may be declared in all the earth. [17] You are still exalting yourself against my people by not releasing them. [18] I am going to cause very severe hail to rain down about this time tomorrow, such hail as has never occurred in Egypt from the day it was founded until now. [19] So now, send instructions to gather your livestock and all your possessions in the fields to a safe place. Every person or animal caught in the field and not brought into the house—the hail will come down on them, and they will die!"'"

8:27 [a] Exod 3:18; 5:3   [b] Exod 3:12   [1] This phrase is placed first in the sentence to stress the distance required.   8:28 [a] Exod 8:8, 15, 29, 32; 9:28; 1 Kgs 13:6   8:29 [a] Exod 8:8, 15   8:30 [a] Exod 8:12   8:32 [a] Exod 4:21; 8:8, 15; Ps 52:2   9:1 [a] Exod 4:23; 8:1   [b] Exod 7:16   9:2 [a] Exod 8:2   9:3 [a] Exod 7:4; 1 Sam 5:6; Ps 39:10; Acts 13:11   [1] Or pestilence.   9:4 [a] Exod 8:22   [1] There is a wordplay in vv. 3–4; a "plague" (Heb. dever) will fall on Egypt's cattle, but "nothing" (Heb. davar) belonging to Israel would die.   9:6 [a] Exod 9:19–20, 25; Ps 78:48, 50   9:7 [a] Exod 7:14; 8:32   9:9 [a] Deut 28:27; Rev 16:2   [1] Heb. boils.   9:10 [a] Deut 28:27   9:11 [a] [Exod 8:18–19; 2 Tim 3:9]   [b] Deut 28:27; Job 2:7; Rev 16:1–2   9:12 [a] Exod 7:13   [b] Exod 4:21   9:13 [a] Exod 8:20   [b] Exod 9:1   9:14 [a] Exod 8:10; Deut 3:24; 2 Sam 7:22; 1 Chr 17:20; Ps 86:8; Isa 45:5–8; 46:9; Jer 10:6–7   9:15 [a] Exod 3:20; 7:5   [b] Exod 5:3   9:16 [a] Exod 14:17; Prov 16:4; [Rom 9:17–18; 1 Pet 2:8–9]   [b] Exod 7:4–5; 10:1; 11:9; 14:17   [c] 1 Kgs 8:43

[20]Those of Pharaoh's servants who [a]feared the LORD's message hurried to bring their [b]servants and livestock into the houses, [21]but those who did not take the LORD's message seriously left their servants and their cattle in the field.

[22]Then the LORD said to Moses, "Extend your hand toward the sky that there may be [a]hail in all the land of Egypt, on people and on animals, and on everything that grows in the field in the land of Egypt." [23]When Moses extended his staff toward [a]the sky, the LORD[1] sent thunder and hail, and fire fell to the earth; so the LORD caused hail to rain down on the land of Egypt. [24]Hail fell and fire mingled with the hail; the hail was so severe that there had not been any like it in all the land of Egypt since it had become a nation. [25]The [a]hail struck everything in the open fields, both people and animals, throughout all the land of Egypt. The hail struck everything that grows in the field, and it broke all the trees of the field to pieces. [26a]Only in the land of Goshen, where the Israelites lived, was there no hail.

[27]So Pharaoh sent and [a]summoned Moses and Aaron and [b]said to [c]them, "I have sinned this time! The LORD is righteous, and I and my people are guilty. [28a]Pray to the LORD, for the mighty thunderings and hail are too much! I will [b]release you and you will stay no longer."

[29]Moses said to him, "When I leave the city I will [a]spread my hands to the LORD, the thunder will cease, and there will be no more hail, so that you may know that the [b]earth belongs to the LORD. [30]But as for you[1] and your servants, [a]I know that you do not yet fear the LORD God."

[31](Now the flax and the barley were struck by the hail, [a]for the barley had ripened and the flax was in bud. [32]But the wheat and the spelt were not struck, for they are later crops.)

[33]So Moses left Pharaoh, went out of the city, and [a]spread out his hands to the LORD, and the thunder and the hail ceased, and the rain stopped pouring on the earth. [34]When Pharaoh saw that the rain and hail and thunder ceased, he sinned again: both he and his servants hardened their hearts. [35]So Pharaoh's heart remained hard, and [a]he did not release the Israelites, as the LORD had predicted through Moses.

Plague Eight: Locusts

10 The LORD said to Moses, "Go to Pharaoh, [a]for I have hardened his heart and the heart of his servants, in order to display these signs of mine before him, [2]and in order that in the hearing of [a]your son and your grandson you may tell[1] how I made fools of the Egyptians and about my signs that I displayed among them, so that you may [b]know that I am the LORD."

[3]So Moses and Aaron came to Pharaoh and told him, "This is what the LORD, the God of the Hebrews, has said: 'How long do you refuse to [a]humble yourself before me? Release my people so that they may [b]serve me! [4]But if you refuse to release my people, I am going to bring [a]locusts into your territory tomorrow. [5]They will cover [a]the surface of the earth, so that you will be unable to see the ground. They will eat the remainder of what escaped—what is left over for you—from the hail, and they will eat every tree that grows for you from the field. [6]They will [a]fill your houses, the houses of your servants, and all the houses of Egypt, such as neither your fathers nor your grandfathers have seen since they have been[1] in the land until this day!'" Then Moses turned and went out from Pharaoh.

[7]Pharaoh's [a]servants [b]said to him, "How long will this man be a menace to us? Release the people so that they may serve the LORD their God. Do you not know that Egypt is destroyed?"

[8]So Moses and Aaron were brought back to Pharaoh, and he said to them, "Go, serve the LORD your God. Exactly who is going

9:20 [a]Exod 1:17; 14:31; [Prov 13:13]   9:20 [b]Exod 8:19; 10:7   9:22 [a]Rev 16:21   9:23 [a]Gen 19:24; Josh 10:11; Ps 18:13; 78:47; 105:32; 148:8; Isa 30:30; Ezek 38:22; Rev 8:7   [1]An emphatic Heb. construction.   9:25 [a]Exod 9:19; Ps 78:47–48; 105:32–33   9:26 [a]Exod 8:22–23; 9:4, 6; 10:23; 11:7; 12:13; Isa 32:18–19   9:27 [a]Exod 8:8   [b]Exod 9:34; 10:16–17   [c]2 Chr 12:6; Ps 129:4; 145:17; Lam 1:18   9:28 [a]Exod 8:8, 28; 10:17; Acts 8:24   [b]Exod 8:25; 10:8, 24   9:29 [a]1 Kgs 8:22, 38; Ps 143:6; Isa 1:15   [b]Exod 8:22; 19:5; 20:11; Ps 24:1; 1 Cor 10:26, 28   9:30 [a]Exod 8:29; [Isa 26:10]   [1]A Heb. construction of strong contrast.   9:31 [a]Ruth 1:22; 2:23   9:33 [a]Exod 8:12; 9:29   9:35 [a]Exod 4:21   10:1 [a]Exod 4:21; 7:14; 9:12; 10:27; 11:10; 14:4; Josh 11:20; John 12:40; Rom 9:18   10:2 [a]Exod 12:26; 13:8, 14; Deut 4:9; 6:7; 11:19; Ps 44:1; 78:5; Joel 1:3   [b]Exod 7:5, 17; 8:22   [1]Heb. [that] *you may declare in the ears of.*   10:3 [a][1 Kgs 21:29; 2 Chr 34:27]; Job 42:6; [Jas 4:10; 1 Pet 5:6]   [b]Exod 4:23; 8:1; 9:1   10:4 [a]Prov 30:27; Rev 9:3   10:5 [a]Exod 9:32; Joel 1:4; 2:25   10:6 [a]Exod 8:3, 21   [1]Lit. *from the day of their being.*   10:7 [a]Exod 7:5; 8:19; 9:20; 12:33   [b]Exod 23:33; Josh 23:13; 1 Sam 18:21; Eccl 7:26; 1 Cor 7:35

with you?"[1] [9] Moses said, "[a]We will go with our young and our old, with our sons and our daughters, and with our sheep and our cattle we will go, because we are to hold a pilgrim feast for the LORD."

[10] He said to them, "The LORD will need to be with you if I release you and your dependents! Watch out! Trouble is right in front of you. [11] No! Go, you men only, and serve the LORD, for that is what you want." Then Moses and Aaron were [a]driven out of Pharaoh's presence.

[12] The LORD said to Moses, "Extend your hand over the land of Egypt for the locusts, that they may come up over the land of Egypt and [a]eat everything that grows in the ground, everything that the hail has left." [13] So Moses extended his staff over the land of Egypt, and then the LORD[1] brought an east wind on the land all that day and all night. The morning came, and the east wind had brought up the locusts! [14] The locusts went up over all [a]the land of Egypt and settled down in all the territory of Egypt. It was very severe;[1] there had been no locusts like them [b]before, nor will there be such ever again. [15] They [a]covered the surface of all the ground so that the ground became dark with them, and they [b]ate all the vegetation of the ground and all the fruit of the trees that the hail had left. Nothing green remained on the trees or on anything that grew in the fields throughout the whole land of Egypt.

[16] Then Pharaoh [a]quickly summoned Moses and Aaron and said, "I have sinned against the LORD your God and against you! [17] So now, forgive my sin this time only, and [a]pray to the LORD your God that he would only take this death away from me." [18] Moses [a]went out from Pharaoh and prayed to the LORD, [19]and the LORD turned a very strong west wind,[1] and it picked up the locusts and blew them [a]into the Red Sea.[2] Not one locust remained in all the territory of Egypt. [20] But the LORD [a]hardened Pharaoh's heart, and he did not release the Israelites.

Plague Nine: Darkness

[21] The LORD said to Moses, "Extend your hand toward heaven so that there may be darkness over the land of Egypt, a darkness so thick it can be felt."

[22] So Moses extended his hand toward heaven, and there was [a]absolute darkness throughout the land of Egypt for [b]three days. [23] No one could see another person, and no one could rise from his place for three days. [a]But the Israelites had light in the places where they lived.

[24] Then Pharaoh summoned Moses and [a]said, "Go, serve the LORD—only your flocks and herds will be detained. Even your families may go with you."

[25] But Moses said, "Will you also provide us with sacrifices and burnt offerings that we may present them to the LORD our God? [26] Our [a]livestock must also go with us! Not a hoof is to be left behind! For we must take these animals to serve the LORD our God. Until we arrive there, we do not know what we must use to serve the LORD."

[27] But the LORD [a]hardened Pharaoh's heart, and he was not willing to release them. [28] Pharaoh said to him, "Go from me! Watch out for yourself! Do not appear before me again, for when you see my face you will die!" [29] Moses [a]said, "As you wish! I will not see your face again."

Plague Ten: Death

11 The LORD said to Moses, "I will bring one more plague on Pharaoh and on Egypt; [a]after that [b]he will release you from this place. When he releases you, he will drive you out completely[1] from this place. [2] Instruct the people that each man and each woman is to request from his or her neighbor [a]items of silver and gold."

[3] ([a]Now the LORD granted the people favor with the Egyptians. Moreover, the man [b]Moses was very great in the land of Egypt, respected by Pharaoh's servants and by the Egyptian people.)

[4] Moses said, "This is what the LORD has said: '[a]About midnight I will go throughout

10:8 [1] Lit. *who and who are the ones going?*; a question intending for Pharaoh to control who went. 10:9 [a] Exod 5:1; 7:16 10:11 [a] Exod 10:28 10:12 [a] Exod 10:5, 15 10:13 [1] An emphatic Heb. construction. 10:14 [a] Deut 28:38; Ps 78:46; 105:34 [b] Joel 1:4, 7; 2:1–11; Rev 9:3 [1] Heb. *it was very heavy.* 10:15 [a] Exod 10:5 [b] Ps 105:35 10:16 [a] Exod 9:27 10:17 [a] Exod 8:8, 28; 9:28; 1 Kgs 13:6 10:18 [a] Exod 8:30 10:19 [a] Joel 2:20 [1] Or perhaps *sea wind*; a wind off the Mediterranean. [2] The Heb. name *Yam Suf* is sometimes translated as *Reed Sea* or *Sea of Reeds.* 10:20 [a] Exod 4:21; 10:1; 11:10 10:22 [a] Ps 105:28; Rev 16:10 [b] Exod 3:18 10:23 [a] Exod 8:22–23 10:24 [a] Exod 8:8, 25; 10:8 10:26 [a] Exod 10:9 10:27 [a] Exod 4:21; 10:1, 20; 14:4, 8 10:29 [a] Exod 11:8; Heb 11:27 11:1 [a] Exod 12:31, 33, 39 [b] Exod 6:1; 12:39 [1] An emphatic Heb. construction. 11:2 [a] Exod 3:22; 12:35–36 11:3 [a] Exod 3:21; 12:36; Ps 106:46 [b] Deut 34:10–12; 2 Sam 7:9; Esth 9:4 11:4 [a] Exod 12:12, 23, 29

Egypt, ⁵and ᵃall the firstborn in the land of Egypt will die, from the firstborn son of Pharaoh who sits on his throne, to the firstborn son of the slave girl who is at her hand mill, and all the firstborn of the cattle. ⁶There will be a great cry throughout ᵃthe whole land of Egypt, ᵇsuch as there has never been, nor ever will be again. ⁷ᵃBut against any of the Israelites not even ᵇa dog will bark against either people or animals, so that you may know that the LORD distinguishes between Egypt and Israel.' ⁸ᵃAll these your servants will come down to me and bow down to me, saying, 'Go, you and all ᵇthe people who follow you,' and after that I will go out." Then Moses went out from Pharaoh in great anger.

⁹The LORD said to Moses, "ᵃPharaoh will not listen to you, so that ᵇmy wonders may be multiplied in the land of Egypt."

¹⁰So Moses ᵃand Aaron did all these wonders before Pharaoh, but the LORD hardened Pharaoh's heart, and he did not release the Israelites from his land.

The Institution of the Passover

12 The LORD said to Moses and Aaron in the land of Egypt, ²"This month ᵃis to be your beginning of months; it will be your first month of the year. ³Tell the whole community of Israel, 'On the ᵃtenth day of this month they each must take a lamb for themselves according to their families—a lamb for each household. ⁴If any household is too small for a lamb, the man and his next-door neighbor are to take a lamb according to the number of people—you will make your count for the lamb according to how much each one can eat. ⁵Your lamb must be perfect,¹ a male, one year old; you may take ᵃit from the sheep or from the goats. ⁶You must care for it until the ᵃfourteenth day of this month, and then the whole community of Israel will kill it around sundown. ⁷They will take some of the blood and put it on the two side posts and top of the doorframe of the houses where they will eat it. ⁸They will eat the meat the same ᵃnight; they will eat it ᵇroasted over the fire with bread made without yeast and with bitter herbs. ⁹Do not eat it raw or boiled in water, but ᵃroast it over the fire with its head, its legs, and its entrails. ¹⁰You must leave nothing until morning, but ᵃyou must burn with fire whatever remains of it until morning. ¹¹This is how you are to eat ᵃit—dressed to travel, your sandals on your feet, and your staff in your hand. You are to eat it in haste. It is the LORD's Passover.

¹²"'I ᵃwill pass through the land of Egypt ᵇin the same ᶜnight, and I will attack¹ all the firstborn in the land of Egypt, both of humans and of animals, and on all the gods of Egypt I will execute judgment. I am the LORD. ¹³The blood will be a sign for you on the houses where you are, so that when I see the blood I will pass over you, and this plague will not fall on you to destroy you when I attack the land of Egypt.

¹⁴"'This ᵃday will become a memorial for you, and you will celebrate it as a ᵇfestival to the LORD—you will celebrate it perpetually as a lasting ordinance. ¹⁵For ᵃseven days you must eat bread made without yeast. Surely on the first day you must put away yeast from your houses because anyone who eats bread made with yeast from the first day to the seventh day will be cut off from Israel.

¹⁶"'On the first ᵃday there will be a holy convocation, and on the seventh day there will be a holy convocation for you. You must do no work of any kind on them, only what every person will eat—that alone may be prepared for you. ¹⁷So you will keep the Feast of Unleavened Bread, because ᵃon this very day I ᵇbrought your regiments¹ out from the land of Egypt, and so you must keep this day perpetually as a lasting ordinance. ¹⁸In the first month, from the fourteenth day of the month, ᵃin the evening, you will eat bread made without yeast until the twenty-first day of the month in the evening. ¹⁹For ᵃseven days yeast must not be found in your houses, for whoever eats what

11:5 ᵃExod 4:23; 12:12, 29; Ps 78:51; 105:36; 135:8; 136:10; Amos 4:10   **11:6** ᵃExod 12:30; Amos 5:17   ᵇExod 10:14   **11:7** ᵃExod 8:22   ᵇJosh 10:21   **11:8** ᵃExod 12:31–33   ᵇExod 10:29; Heb 11:27   **11:9** ᵃExod 3:19; 7:4; 10:1   ᵇExod 7:3; 9:16   **11:10** ᵃExod 7:3; 9:12; 10:1, 20, 27; Josh 11:20; Isa 63:17; John 12:40; Rom 2:5   **12:2** ᵃExod 13:4; 23:15; 34:18; Deut 16:1   **12:3** ᵃJosh 4:19   **12:5** ᵃLev 22:18–21; 23:12; Mal 1:8, 14; [Heb 9:14; 1 Pet 1:19]   ¹Heb. *perfect, whole, complete*; having no physical defects.   **12:6** ᵃExod 12:14, 17; Lev 23:5; Num 9:1–3, 11; 28:16; Deut 16:1, 4, 6   **12:8** ᵃExod 34:25; Num 9:12   ᵇDeut 16:7   **12:9** ᵃDeut 16:7   **12:10** ᵃExod 16:19; 23:18; 34:25   **12:11** ᵃExod 12:13, 21, 27, 43   **12:12** ᵃExod 11:4–5   ᵇNum 33:4   ᶜExod 6:2   ¹Heb. *to strike, smite, attack.*   **12:14** ᵃExod 13:9   ᵇLev 23:4–5; 2 Kgs 23:21   **12:15** ᵃExod 13:6–7; 23:15; 34:18; Lev 23:6; Num 28:17; Deut 16:3, 8   **12:16** ᵃLev 23:2, 7, 8; Num 28:18, 25   **12:17** ᵃExod 12:14; 13:3, 10   ᵇNum 33:1   ¹Heb. *armies, divisions.*   **12:18** ᵃExod 12:2; Lev 23:5–8; Num 28:16–25   **12:19** ᵃExod 12:15; 23:15; 34:18

is made with yeast—that person[1] will be cut off from the community of Israel, whether a resident foreigner[2] or one born in the land. [20]You will not eat anything made with yeast; in all the places where you live you must eat bread made without yeast.'"

[21]Then [a]Moses summoned all the [b]elders of Israel, and told them, "Go and select for yourselves a lamb or young goat for your families, and kill the Passover animals. [22]Take [a]a branch of hyssop, dip it in the blood that is in the basin, and [b]apply to the top of the doorframe and the two side posts some of the blood that is in the basin. Not one of you is to go out[1] the door of his house until morning. [23a]For the LORD will pass through to strike Egypt, and when he sees the [b]blood on the top of the doorframe and the two side posts, then the LORD will pass over the door, and he will [c]not permit [d]the destroyer to enter your houses to strike you. [24]You must [a]observe this event as an ordinance for you and for your children forever. [25]When you enter the land that the LORD will give to you, [a]just as he said, you must observe this ceremony. [26a]When your children ask you, 'What does this ceremony mean to you?'—[27]then you will say, '[a]It is the sacrifice of the LORD's Passover, when he passed over the houses of the Israelites in Egypt, when he struck[1] Egypt and delivered our households.'" The people [b]bowed down low to the ground, [28]and the Israelites went away and [a]did exactly as the LORD had commanded Moses and Aaron.

The Deliverance from Egypt

[29]It happened at midnight—the LORD attacked all the firstborn in the [a]land of Egypt, from [b]the firstborn of Pharaoh who sat on his throne to the firstborn of the captive who was in the prison, and all the firstborn of the [c]cattle. [30]Pharaoh got up[1] in the night, along with all his servants and all Egypt, and there was a great cry in Egypt,

for there was no house in which there was not someone dead. [31]Pharaoh [a]summoned Moses and Aaron in the night and said, "Get up, get out from among my people, [b]both you and the Israelites! Go, serve the LORD as you have [c]requested! [32]Also, take your flocks and your herds, just as you have requested, and leave. But bless me [a]also."

[33a]The Egyptians were [b]urging[1] the people on, in order to send them out of the land quickly, for they were saying, "We are all dead!" [34]So the people took their dough before the yeast was added, with their kneading troughs bound up in their clothing on their shoulders. [35]Now the Israelites had done as Moses told them—they had requested from the Egyptians silver and gold [a]items and clothing. [36]The LORD gave the people favor in the sight of the Egyptians, [a]and [b]they gave them whatever they wanted, and so they plundered Egypt.

[37a]The Israelites journeyed from [b]Rameses to Sukkoth. There were about [c]600,000 men on foot, plus their dependents. [38]A [a]mixed multitude[1] also went up with them, and flocks and herds—a very large number of [b]cattle. [39]They baked cakes of bread without yeast using [a]the dough they had brought from Egypt, for it was made without yeast. Because they were thrust out of Egypt and were not able to delay, they could not prepare food for themselves either.

[40]Now the length of time the Israelites lived in Egypt was [a]430 years. [41]At the end of the 430 years, on the very day, [a]all the regiments of the LORD went out of the land of Egypt. [42]It [a]was a night of vigil for the LORD to bring them out from the land of Egypt, and so on this night all Israel is to keep the vigil to the LORD for generations to come.

Participation in the Passover

[43]The LORD said to Moses and Aaron, "This is [a]the ordinance of the Passover. No foreigner may share in eating it. [44]But

12:19 [1] Heb. *soul; but refers to the whole person.* [2] Or *alien, stranger.*   **12:21** [a] [Heb 11:28]   [b] Exod 3:16   **12:22** [a] Heb 11:28   [b] Exod 12:7   [1] Heb. *and you, you shall not go out, a man from the door of his house;* an emphatic Heb. construction.   **12:23** [a] Exod 11:4; 12:12–13   [b] Exod 24:8   [c] Ezek 9:6; Rev 7:3; 9:4   [d] 1 Cor 10:10; Heb 11:28   **12:24** [a] Exod 12:14, 17; 13:5, 10   **12:25** [a] Exod 3:8, 17   **12:26** [a] Exod 10:2; 13:8, 14, 15; Deut 32:7; Josh 4:6; Ps 78:6   **12:27** [a] Exod 12:11   [b] Exod 4:31   [1] Heb. *to strike, smite, plague.*   **12:28** [a] [Heb 11:28]   **12:29** [a] Exod 11:4–5   [b] Num 8:17; 33:4; Ps 135:8; 136:10   [c] Exod 9:6   **12:30** [1] Heb. *arose.*   **12:31** [a] Exod 10:28–29   [b] Exod 8:25; 11:1   [c] Exod 10:9   **12:32** [a] Exod 10:9, 26   **12:33** [a] Exod 10:7   [b] Exod 11:8; Ps 105:38   [1] I.e., being resolved or insistent in this—they were not going to change.   **12:35** [a] Exod 3:21–22; 11:2–3; Ps 105:37   **12:36** [a] Exod 3:21   [b] Gen 15:14   **12:37** [a] Num 33:3, 5   [b] Gen 47:11; Exod 1:11; Num 33:3–4   [c] Gen 12:2; Exod 38:26; Num 1:46; 2:32; 11:21; 26:51   **12:38** [a] Num 11:4   [b] Exod 17:3; Num 20:19; 32:1; Deut 3:19   [1] I.e., folks who joined the Israelites, people who were impressed by the defeat of Egypt, who came to faith, or who just wanted to escape Egypt (maybe slaves or descendants of the Hyksos).   **12:39** [a] Exod 6:1; 11:1; 12:31–33   **12:40** [a] Gen 15:13, 16; Acts 7:6; Gal 3:17   **12:41** [a] Exod 3:8, 10; 6:6; 7:4   **12:42** [a] Exod 13:10; 34:18; Deut 16:1, 6   **12:43** [a] Exod 12:11; Num 9:14

everyone's servant who is bought for money, after you have [a]circumcised him, may eat it. [45]A foreigner [a]and a hired worker must not eat it. [46]It must be eaten in one house; you must not bring any of the meat outside the house, and you must not break a bone of it. [47]The [a]whole community of Israel must observe it.

[48]"When a resident foreigner lives with you and wants to observe the Passover to the LORD, all his males must be circumcised, and then [a]he may approach and observe it, and he will be like one who is born in the land—but no uncircumcised person may eat of it. [49]The [a]same law will apply to the person who is native-born and to the resident foreigner who lives among you."

[50]So all the Israelites did exactly as the LORD commanded Moses and Aaron. [51]And on this very day the LORD brought the Israelites out of the [a]land of Egypt by their regiments.

The Law of the Firstborn

13 The LORD spoke to Moses, [2]"Set [a]apart to me every firstborn male— the first offspring of every womb among the Israelites, whether human or animal; it is mine."

[3]Moses said to the people, "[a]Remember this day on which you came out from Egypt, from the place where you were enslaved, for the LORD brought you out of there with a mighty hand—and [b]no bread made with yeast may be eaten. [4]On this day, in the [a]month of Abib, you are going out.

[5]"When the LORD [a]brings you to the [b]land of the Canaanites, Hittites, Amorites, Hivites, and Jebusites, which he [c]swore to your fathers to give you, [d]a land flowing with milk and honey, then you will keep this ceremony in this month. [6]For [a]seven days you must eat bread made without yeast, and on the seventh day there is to be a festival to the LORD. [7]Bread made without yeast must be eaten for seven days; [a]no bread made with yeast shall be seen among you, and you must have no yeast among you within any of your borders.

[8]"You are to [a]tell your son on that day, 'It is because of what the LORD did for me when I came out of Egypt.' [9]It will be [a]a sign for you on your hand and a memorial on your forehead, so that the law of the LORD may be in your mouth, for with a mighty hand the LORD brought you out of Egypt. [10]So [a]you must keep this ordinance at its appointed time from year to year.

[11]"When the LORD [a]brings you into the land of the [b]Canaanites, as he swore to you and to your fathers, and gives it to you, [12]then you must give over to the LORD the first offspring of every womb. Every firstling of [a]a beast that you have—the males will be the LORD's. [13]Every firstling of a donkey you must redeem with a lamb, and if you do not redeem it, then you must break its neck. [a]Every firstborn of [b]your sons you must redeem.

[14]"In the future, when your [a]son asks you 'What is this?' you are to tell him, 'With a mighty hand the LORD brought us out from Egypt, from the land of slavery. [15]When Pharaoh stubbornly refused to release us, [a]the LORD killed all the firstborn in the land of Egypt, from the firstborn of people to the firstborn of animals. That is why I am sacrificing to the LORD the first male offspring of every womb, but all my firstborn sons I redeem.' [16]It will be for [a]a sign on your hand and for frontlets[1] on your forehead, for with a mighty hand the LORD brought us out of Egypt."

The Leading of God

[17]When Pharaoh released the people, God did not lead them by the way to the land of the Philistines, although that was nearby, for God said, "Lest the people [a]change their minds[1] and [b]return to Egypt when they experience war." [18]So God brought the people around by the way of the wilderness to the Red Sea, and the Israelites went up from the land of Egypt prepared for battle.[1]

12:44 [a]Gen 17:12–13; Lev 22:11   12:45 [a]Lev 22:10   12:47 [a]Exod 12:6; Num 9:13–14   12:48 [a]Num 9:14   12:49 [a]Lev 24:22; Num 15:15–16; [Gal 3:28]   12:51 [a]Exod 12:41; 20:2   13:2 [a]Exod 13:12–13, 15; 22:29; Lev 27:26; Num 3:13; 8:16; 18:15; Deut 15:19; Luke 2:23   13:3 [a]Exod 12:42; Deut 16:3 [b]Exod 12:8, 19   13:4 [a]Exod 12:2; 23:15; 34:18; Deut 16:1   13:5 [a]Exod 3:8, 17; Josh 24:11 [b]Gen 17:8; Deut 30:5 [c]Exod 6:8 [d]Exod 12:25–26   13:6 [a]Exod 12:15–20   13:7 [a]Exod 12:19   13:8 [a]Exod 10:2; 12:26; 13:14; Ps 44:1   13:9 [a]Exod 12:14; 13:16; 31:13; Deut 6:8; 11:18; Matt 23:5   13:10 [a]Exod 12:14, 24   13:11 [a]Exod 13:5 [b]Num 21:3   13:12 [a]Exod 13:1–2; 22:29; 34:19; Lev 27:26; Num 18:15; Ezek 44:30; Luke 2:23   13:13 [a]Exod 34:20; Num 18:15 [b]Num 3:46–47; 18:15–16   13:14 [a]Exod 10:2; 12:26–27; 13:8; Deut 6:20; Josh 4:6, 21   13:15 [a]Exod 12:29   13:16 [a]Exod 13:9; Deut 6:8   [1]I.e., a sign or an object placed on the forehead.   13:17 [a]Exod 14:11; Num 14:1–4 [b]Deut 17:16   [1]Or *repent, relent.*   13:18 [1]An emphatic Heb. construction.

[19]Moses took the [a]bones of [b]Joseph with him, for Joseph had made the Israelites solemnly swear, "[c]God will surely attend to you, and you will carry my bones up from this place with you."

[20a]They journeyed from [b]Sukkoth and camped in Etham, on the edge of the desert. [21]Now [a]the LORD was going before them by day in a pillar of cloud to lead them in the way, and by night in a pillar of fire to give them light, so that they could travel day or night. [22]He did not remove the pillar of cloud by day nor the pillar of fire by night from before the people.

The Victory at the Red Sea

14 The LORD spoke to Moses, [2]"Tell the Israelites [a]that they must turn and camp before Pi [b]Hahiroth, between [c]Migdol and the sea; you are to camp by the sea before Baal Zephon opposite it. [3]Pharaoh will think regarding [a]the Israelites, 'They are wandering around confused in the land—the desert has closed in on them.' [4]I [a]will harden Pharaoh's heart, and he [b]will chase after them. I will gain honor because of Pharaoh and because of all his army, and the Egyptians will know [c]that I am the LORD." So this is what they did.

[5]When it was reported to [a]the king of Egypt that the people had fled, the heart of Pharaoh and his servants was turned against the people, and the king and his servants said, "What in the world have we done?[1] For we have released the people of Israel[2] from serving us!" [6]Then he prepared his chariots and took his army with him. [7]He took [a]600 select chariots, and all the rest of the chariots of Egypt, and officers on all of them.

[8]But the LORD [a]hardened [b]the heart of Pharaoh king of Egypt, and he chased after the Israelites. Now the Israelites were going out defiantly. [9]The [a]Egyptians chased after them, and all the horses and chariots of Pharaoh and his horsemen and his army overtook them camping by the sea,

beside Pi Hahiroth, before Baal Zephon. [10]When Pharaoh got closer, the Israelites looked up, and there were the Egyptians marching after them, and they were terrified. The Israelites [a]cried out to the LORD, [11]and they said to Moses, "Is it because there are no graves in Egypt that you have taken us away to die in [a]the desert? What in the world have you done to us by bringing us out of Egypt? [12]Isn't [a]this what we told you in Egypt, 'Leave us alone so that we can serve the Egyptians, because it is better for us to serve the Egyptians than to die in the desert!'"

[13]Moses said to the people, "[a]Do not fear! [b]Stand firm and see the [c]salvation of the LORD that he will provide for you today; for the Egyptians [a]that you [d]see today you will never, ever see again. [14a]The LORD will fight for you, and you can be still."

[15]The LORD said to Moses, "Why do you cry out to me? Tell the Israelites to move on. [16]And as for you, [a]lift up your staff and extend your hand toward the sea and divide it, so that the Israelites may go through the middle of the sea on dry ground. [17]And as for me, I am going to [a]harden the hearts of the Egyptians so that they will come after them, that [b]I may be honored because of Pharaoh and his army and his chariots and his horsemen. [18]And the Egyptians will know that I am the LORD when I have gained my honor because of Pharaoh, his chariots, and his horsemen."

[19]The angel of God, [a]who was going before the camp of Israel, moved and went behind them, and the pillar of cloud moved from before them and stood behind them. [20]It came between the Egyptian camp and the Israelite camp; it was a dark cloud and it lit up the night so that one camp did not come near the other the whole night.[1] [21]Moses stretched out his hand toward the sea, and the LORD drove the sea apart by a strong east wind all that night, and he [a]made the sea into dry land, and the water was [b]divided. [22]So [a]the [b]Israelites went through the

13:19 [a]Gen 50:24–25; Josh 24:32   [b]Exod 1:6; Deut 33:13–17   [c]Exod 4:31   **13:20** [a]Num 33:6–8   [b]Exod 12:37   **13:21** [a]Exod 14:19, 24; 33:9–10; Num 9:15; 14:14; Deut 1:33; Neh 9:12; Ps 78:14; 99:7; 105:39; [Isa 4:5]; 1 Cor 10:1   **14:2** [a]Exod 13:18   [b]Num 33:7   [c]Jer 44:1   **14:3** [a]Ps 71:11   **14:4** [a]Exod 4:21; 7:3; 14:17   [b]Exod 9:16; 14:17–18, 23; Rom 9:17, 22, 23   [c]Exod 7:5; 14:25   **14:5** [a]Ps 105:25   [1]Lit. *What is this we have done?*   [2]Heb. *released Israel.*   **14:7** [a]Exod 15:4   **14:8** [a]Exod 14:4   [b]Exod 6:1; 13:9; Num 33:3; Acts 13:17   **14:9** [a]Exod 15:9; Josh 24:6   **14:10** [a]Josh 24:7; Neh 9:9; Ps 34:17; 107:6   **14:11** [a]Exod 5:21; 15:24; 16:2; 17:3; Num 14:2–3; 20:3; Ps 106:7–8   **14:12** [a]Exod 5:21; 6:9   **14:13** [a]Gen 15:1; 46:3; Exod 20:20; 2 Chr 20:15, 17; Isa 41:10, 13, 14   [b]Ps 46:10–11   [c]Exod 14:30; 15:2   [d]Deut 28:68   **14:14** [a]Exod 14:25; 15:3; Deut 1:30; 3:22; Josh 10:14, 42; 23:2; 2 Chr 20:29; Neh 4:20; Isa 31:4   **14:16** [a]Exod 4:17, 20; 7:19; 14:21, 26; 17:5–6, 9; Num 20:8–9, 11; Isa 10:26   **14:17** [a]Exod 14:8   [b]Exod 14:4   **14:19** [a]Exod 13:21–22; [Isa 63:9]   **14:20** [1]LXX *and there was darkness and blackness and the night passed.*   **14:21** [a]Ps 66:6; 106:9; 136:13–14   [b]Exod 15:8; Josh 3:16; 4:23; Neh 9:11; Ps 74:13; 78:13; 114:3, 5; Isa 63:12–13   **14:22** [a]Exod 15:19; Josh 3:17; 4:22; Neh 9:11; Ps 66:6; 78:13; Isa 63:13; 1 Cor 10:1; Heb 11:29   [b]Exod 14:29; 15:8; Hab 3:10

middle of the sea on dry ground, the water forming a wall for them on their right and on their left.

[23] The Egyptians chased them and followed them into the middle of the sea—all the horses of Pharaoh, his chariots, and his horsemen. [24] In the morning [a]watch[1] [b]the LORD looked down on the Egyptian army through the pillar of fire and cloud, and he threw the Egyptian army into a panic. [25] He jammed the wheels of their chariots so that they had difficulty driving, and the Egyptians said, "Let's flee from Israel, for the LORD [a]fights for them against Egypt!"

[26] The LORD said to Moses, "Extend your hand toward the sea, so that the waters may flow back on the Egyptians, on their chariots, and on their horsemen!" [27] So Moses extended his hand toward the sea, and the sea [a]returned to its normal state when the sun began to rise. Now the Egyptians were fleeing before it, but the LORD [b]overthrew[1] the Egyptians in the middle of the sea. [28] The water returned and covered [a]the chariots and the horsemen and all the army of Pharaoh that was coming after the Israelites into the sea—not so much as one of them survived! [29] But [a]the Israelites walked on dry ground in the middle of the sea, the water forming a wall for them on their right and on their left. [30] So the LORD [a]saved Israel on that day from the power[1] of the Egyptians, and Israel [b]saw the Egyptians dead on the shore of the sea. [31] When Israel saw the great power[1] that the LORD had exercised over the Egyptians, they feared the LORD, and they [a]believed in the LORD and in his servant Moses.

The Song of Triumph

15 Then [a]Moses and the Israelites sang this song to the LORD. They said,

"I will [b]sing to the LORD, for he has triumphed gloriously,
the horse and its rider he has thrown into the sea.

[2] The LORD is my strength and my [a]song,
and he has become my [b]salvation.
This is my God, and I will praise him,
my [c]father's God, and [d]I will exalt him.

[3] The LORD is a [a]warrior—
the LORD is his [b]name.[1]

[4] The chariots of [a]Pharaoh and [b]his army he has thrown into the sea,
and his chosen officers were drowned in the Red Sea.

[5] The depths have covered them;
[a]they went down to the bottom like a stone.

[6] Your [a]right hand, O LORD, was majestic in power;
your right hand, O LORD, shattered the enemy.

[7] In the abundance of your [a]majesty [b]you have overthrown
those who rise up against you.
You sent forth your wrath;
it [c]consumed them [d]like stubble.

[8] By [a]the blast of your nostrils the waters were piled up,
the flowing water stood upright like a heap,
and the deep waters were solidified in the heart of the sea.

[9] The enemy said, 'I will chase, I will overtake,
I will divide [a]the spoil;
my desire[1] will be satisfied on them.
[b]I will draw my sword, my hand will destroy them.'

[10] But you blew with your breath, and the sea covered them.
They sank like lead in the mighty waters.

[11] [a]Who is like you, O LORD, among the gods?
Who is like you—[b]majestic in holiness, fearful in [c]praises,
[d]working wonders?

[12] You stretched out your right hand,
the earth swallowed them.

13 By ᵃyour loyal love you will lead
    the people whom you have
    redeemed;
    you will guide them by your
    strength to your holy dwelling
    place.
14 The ᵃnations will hear and tremble;
    ᵇanguish will seize the inhabitants of
    Philistia.
15 ᵃThen the chiefs of Edom will be
    terrified,
    trembling will seize ᵇthe leaders of
    Moab,
    and ᶜthe inhabitants of Canaan will
    shake.
16 ᵃFear and dread will fall on them;
    by the greatness of your arm they
    will be ᵇas still as stone
    until your people pass by, O LORD,
    until the people ᶜwhom you have
    bought pass by.
17 You will bring them in and ᵃplant
    them in the ᵇmountain of your
    inheritance,
    in the place you made for your
    residence, O LORD,
    the ᶜsanctuary, O Lord, that your
    hands have established.
18 The LORD will reign forever and ever!
19 For the ᵃhorses of Pharaoh came
    with his chariots and his footmen
    into ᵇthe sea,
    and the LORD brought back the
    waters of the sea on them,
    but the Israelites walked on dry land
    in the middle of the sea."

20 Miriam ᵃthe prophetess, ᵇthe sister
of Aaron, ᶜtook a hand drum in her hand,
and all the women went out after her ᵈwith
hand drums and with dances. 21Miriam sang
in ᵃresponse to them,

    "ᵇSing to the LORD, for he has
    triumphed gloriously;
    the horse and its rider he has thrown
    into the sea."

The Bitter Water

22Then Moses led Israel to journey away
from the Red Sea. They went out to the wilderness of ᵃShur, walked for three days into
the wilderness, and found no ᵇwater. 23Then
they came to ᵃMarah, but they were not
able to drink the waters of Marah, because
they were bitter. (That is why its name was
Marah.)

24So the people ᵃmurmured¹ against
Moses, saying, "What can we drink?" 25He
cried out to the LORD, and the LORD
showed him a tree. ᵃWhen Moses threw it
into the water, the water became safe to
drink. There the LORD ᵇmade for ᶜthem
a binding ordinance, and there he tested
them. 26He said, "ᵃIf you will diligently
obey the LORD your God, and do what is
right in his sight, and pay attention to his
commandments, and keep all his statutes,
then all the ᵇdiseases that I brought on the
Egyptians I will not bring on you, for I, the
LORD, am your healer."

27Then they came to Elim, where there
were twelve wells of water and seventy
palm trees, and they camped there by ᵃthe
water.

The Provision of Manna

16 When they ᵃjourneyed from Elim, the
entire company of Israelites came
to the wilderness of Sin, which is between
Elim and ᵇSinai, on the fifteenth day of the
second month after their exodus from the
land of Egypt. 2The entire company of Israelites ᵃmurmured against Moses and Aaron
in the wilderness. 3The Israelites said to
them, "If ᵃonly we had died by the hand of
the LORD in the land of Egypt, ᵇwhen we
sat by the pots of meat, when we ate bread
to the full, for you have brought us out into
this wilderness to kill this whole assembly
with hunger!"

4Then the LORD said to Moses, "I am
going to rain ᵃbread from heaven for you,
and the people will go out and gather the
amount for each day, so that I may ᵇtest

15:13 ᵃ Exod 15:17; Deut 12:5; Ps 78:54   **15:14** ᵃ Josh 2:9   ᵇ Ps 48:6   **15:15** ᵃ Gen 36:15, 40   ᵇ Deut 2:4   ᶜ Num 22:3–4   **15:16** ᵃ Exod 23:27; Deut 2:25; Josh 2:9   ᵇ 1 Sam 25:37   ᶜ Exod 15:13; Ps 74:2; Isa 43:1; Jer 31:11; [Titus 2:14]; 2 Pet 2:1   **15:17** ᵃ Ps 44:2; 80:8, 15   ᵇ Ps 2:6; 78:54, 68   ᶜ Ps 68:16; 76:2; 132:13–14   **15:19** ᵃ Exod 14:23   ᵇ Exod 14:28   **15:20** ᵃ Judg 4:4   ᵇ Exod 2:4; Num 26:59; 1 Chr 6:3; Mic 6:4   ᶜ 1 Sam 18:6; 1 Chr 15:16; Ps 68:25; 81:2; 149:3; Jer 31:4   ᵈ Judg 11:34; 21:21; 2 Sam 6:16; Ps 30:11; 150:4   **15:21** ᵃ 1 Sam 18:7   ᵇ Exod 15:1   **15:22** ᵃ Gen 16:7; 20:1; 25:18; Num 33:8   ᵇ Exod 17:1; Num 20:2   **15:23** ᵃ Num 33:8; Ruth 1:20   **15:24** ᵃ Exod 14:11; 16:2; Ps 106:13   ¹ Or *to grumble, to complain.*   **15:25** ᵃ 2 Kgs 2:21   ᵇ Josh 24:25   ᶜ Exod 16:4; Deut 8:2, 16; Judg 2:22; 3:1, 4; Ps 66:10   **15:26** ᵃ Exod 19:5–6; Deut 7:12, 15   ᵇ Deut 28:27, 58, 60   **15:27** ᵃ Num 33:9   **16:1** ᵃ Num 33:10–11; Ezek 30:15   ᵇ Exod 12:6, 51; 19:1   **16:2** ᵃ Exod 14:11; 15:24; Ps 106:25; 1 Cor 10:10   **16:3** ᵃ Exod 17:3; Num 14:2–3; 20:3; Lam 4:9   ᵇ Num 11:4–5   **16:4** ᵃ Neh 9:15; Ps 78:23–25; 105:40; [John 6:31–35]; 1 Cor 10:3   ᵇ Exod 15:25; Deut 8:2, 16

them. Will they [c]walk in my law or not? [5]On the sixth day they will prepare what they bring in, and [a]it will be twice as much as they gather every other day."

[6]Moses and Aaron said to all the Israelites, "In the evening you will know [a]that the LORD has brought you out of the land of Egypt, [7]and in [a]the morning you will see the glory of the LORD, because he has [b]heard your murmurings against the LORD. As for us, [c]what are we,[1] that you should murmur against us?"

[8]Moses said, "You will know this when the LORD gives you meat to eat [a]in the evening and bread in the morning to satisfy you, because the LORD has heard your murmurings that you are murmuring against him. As for us, what are we?[1] Your murmurings are not against us, but against the LORD."

[9]Then Moses said to Aaron, "Tell the whole community of the Israelites, '[a]Come[1] before the LORD, because he has heard your murmurings.'"

[10]As Aaron spoke to the whole community of the Israelites and they looked toward the wilderness, there the glory of the LORD [a]appeared in the cloud, [11]and the LORD spoke to Moses, [12]"I have heard the [a]murmurings of the Israelites. Tell them, '[b]During the [c]evening you will eat meat, and in the morning you will be satisfied with bread, so that you may know that I am the LORD your God.'"

[13]In the evening the [a]quail came up and covered [b]the camp, and in the morning a layer of dew was all around the camp. [14]When the [a]layer of dew had evaporated, there on the surface of the wilderness was a thin flaky [b]substance, thin like frost on the earth. [15]When the Israelites saw it, they said to one another, "What [a]is it?" because they did not know what it was. Moses said to them, "It is the bread that the LORD has given you for food.

[16]"This is what the LORD has commanded: 'Each person is to gather from it [a]what he can eat, an [b]omer per person according to the number of your people; each one will pick it up for whoever lives in his tent.'" [17]The Israelites did so, and they gathered—some more, some less. [18]When [a]they measured with an omer, the one who gathered much had nothing left over, and the one who gathered little lacked nothing; each one had gathered what he could eat.

[19]Moses said to them, "No one is to [a]keep any of it until morning." [20]But they did not listen to Moses; some kept part of it until morning, and it was full of worms and began to stink, and Moses was angry with them. [21]So they gathered it each morning,[1] each person according to what he could eat, and when the sun got hot, it would melt. [22]And on the sixth day they gathered twice as much food, two omers per person; and all the leaders of the community came and told Moses. [23]He [a]said to them, "This is what the LORD has said: 'Tomorrow is a time of cessation from work, a holy Sabbath to the LORD. Whatever you want to bake, bake today; whatever you want to boil, boil today; whatever is left put aside for yourselves to be kept until morning.'"

[24]So they put it aside until the morning, just as Moses had commanded, and it did not [a]stink, nor were there any worms in it. [25]Moses said, "Eat it today, for today is a Sabbath to the LORD; today you will not find it in the area. [26a]Six days you will gather it, but on the seventh day, the Sabbath, there will not be any."

[27]On the seventh day some of the people went out to gather it, but they found nothing. [28]So the LORD said to Moses, "How long [a]do you refuse[1] to obey my commandments and my instructions? [29]See, because the LORD has given you the Sabbath, that is why he is giving you food for two days on the sixth day. Each of you stay where you are; let no one go out of his place on the seventh day." [30]So the people rested on the seventh day.

[31]The house of Israel called [a]its name "manna." It was like coriander seed and was white, and it tasted like wafers with honey.

16:4 [c]Judg 2:22   **16:5** [a]Exod 16:22, 29; Lev 25:21   **16:6** [a]Exod 6:7   **16:7** [a]Exod 16:10, 12; Isa 35:2; 40:5; John 11:4, 40   [b]Num 14:27; 17:5   [c]Num 16:11   [1]An emphatic Heb. construction.   **16:8** [a]1 Sam 8:7; Luke 10:16; [Rom 13:2]; 1 Thess 4:8   [1]An emphatic Heb. construction.   **16:9** [a]Num 16:16   [1]Heb. *approach, draw near*; used of drawing near for religious purposes.   **16:10** [a]Exod 13:21; 16:7; Num 16:19; 1 Kgs 8:10   **16:12** [a]Exod 16:8; Num 14:27   [b]Exod 16:6   [c]Exod 16:7; 1 Kgs 20:28; Joel 3:17   **16:13** [a]Num 11:31; Ps 78:27–29; 105:40   [b]Num 11:9   **16:14** [a]Exod 16:31; Num 11:7–8; Deut 8:3; Neh 9:15; Ps 78:24; 105:40   [b]Ps 147:16   **16:15** [a]Exod 16:4; Neh 9:15; Ps 78:24; [John 6:31, 49, 58]; 1 Cor 10:3   **16:16** [a]Exod 12:4   [b]Exod 16:32, 36   **16:18** [a]2 Cor 8:15   **16:19** [a]Exod 12:10; 16:23; 23:18   **16:21** [1]Heb. *morning by morning*.   **16:23** [a]Gen 2:3; Exod 20:8–11; 23:12; 31:15; 35:2; Lev 23:3; Neh 9:13–14   **16:24** [a]Exod 16:20   **16:26** [a]Exod 20:9–10   **16:28** [a]2 Kgs 17:14; Ps 78:10; 106:13   [1]The verb is pl., addressing the nation.   **16:31** [a]Num 11:7–9; Deut 8:3, 16

[32]Moses said, "This is what the LORD has commanded: 'Fill an omer with it to be kept for generations to come, so that they may see the food I fed you in the wilderness when I brought you out from the land of Egypt.'" [33]Moses said to Aaron, "[a]Take a jar and put in it an omer full of manna, and place it before the LORD to be kept for generations to come." [34]Just as the LORD commanded Moses, so Aaron placed it [a]before the ark of the testimony for safekeeping. [35]Now the Israelites [a]ate manna [b]40 years, [c]until they came to a land that was inhabited; they ate manna until they came to the border of the land of Canaan. [36](Now an omer is one-tenth of an ephah.)[1]

Water at Massah and Meribah

17 The whole community of the Israelites traveled on their journey from the wilderness of [a]Sin according to the LORD's instruction, and they pitched camp in Rephidim. Now there was no water for the people to [b]drink. [2]So [a]the people contended[1] with Moses, and they said, "Give us water to drink!" Moses said to them, "Why do you contend with me? Why do you [b]test the LORD?" [3]But the people were very thirsty there for water, and they [a]murmured against Moses and said, "Why in the world did you bring us up from Egypt—to kill us and our children and our [b]cattle with thirst?"

[4]Then Moses cried [a]out to the LORD, "What will I do with this people?—a little more and they will [b]stone me!" [5]The LORD said to Moses, "Go [a]over before the people; take with [b]you some of the elders of Israel and take in your hand your staff with which you struck the Nile and go. [6]I will [a]be standing before you there on the rock in Horeb, and you will strike the rock, and water will come out of it so that the people may drink." And Moses did so in plain view of the elders of Israel.

[7]He called the name of the place [a]Massah and Meribah, because of the contending of the Israelites and because of their testing the LORD, saying, "Is the LORD among us or not?"

Victory over the Amalekites

[8a]Amalek came and attacked Israel in Rephidim. [9]So Moses said to Joshua, "Choose some of our men and go out, fight against Amalek. Tomorrow I will stand on top of [a]the hill with the staff of God in my hand." [10]So Joshua fought against Amalek just as Moses had instructed him, and Moses and Aaron and Hur went up to the top of the hill. [11]Whenever Moses would raise his hands, then Israel prevailed, but whenever [a]he would rest his hands, then Amalek prevailed. [12]When the hands of Moses became heavy, they took a stone and put it under him, and Aaron and Hur held up his hands, one on one side and one on the other, and so his hands were steady[1] until the sun went down. [13]So Joshua destroyed Amalek and his army with the sword.

[14]The LORD said to Moses, "[a]Write [b]this as a memorial in the book, and rehearse it in Joshua's hearing; for I will surely wipe out the remembrance of Amalek from under heaven." [15]Moses built an altar, and he called it "The LORD is my Banner," [16]for he said, "For a hand was lifted up to the throne of the LORD—that the LORD will have war with Amalek from generation to generation."

The Advice of Jethro

18 [a]Jethro, the priest of Midian, Moses' father-in-law, heard about all that [b]God had done for Moses and for his people Israel, that the LORD had brought Israel out of Egypt.

[2]Jethro, Moses' father-in-law, took Moses' wife [a]Zipporah after he had sent her back, [3]and her [a]two sons, one of whom was named Gershom[1] (for Moses had [b]said, "I have been a foreigner[2] in a foreign land") [4]and the other Eliezer (for Moses had said, "The God of my father has been my [a]help[1] and delivered me from the sword of Pharaoh").

16:33 [a]Heb 9:4; Rev 2:17   **16:34** [a]Exod 25:16, 21; 27:21; 40:20; Num 17:10   **16:35** [a]Deut 8:3, 16   [b]Num 33:38; John 6:31, 49   [c]Josh 5:12; Neh 9:20–21   **16:36** [1]*omer* and *ephah* are transliterated Heb. words.   **17:1** [a]Num 33:11–15   [b]Exod 15:22; Num 20:2   **17:2** [a]Exod 14:11; Num 20:2–3, 13   [b][Deut 6:16]; Ps 78:18, 41; [Matt 4:7]; 1 Cor 10:9   [1]Heb. *strive, quarrel, be in contention.*   **17:3** [a]Exod 16:2–3   [b]Exod 12:38   **17:4** [a]Exod 14:15   [b]John 8:59; 10:31   **17:5** [a]Ezek 2:6   [b]Num 20:8   **17:6** [a]Num 20:10–11; Deut 8:15; Neh 9:15; Ps 78:15; 105:41; 114:8; [1 Cor 10:4]   **17:7** [a]Num 20:13, 24; 27:14; Ps 81:7   **17:8** [a]Gen 36:12; Num 24:20; Deut 25:17–19; 1 Sam 15:2   **17:9** [a]Exod 4:20   **17:11** [a][Jas 5:16]   **17:12** [1]Heb. *firm, steady, reliable, dependable.*   **17:14** [a]Exod 24:4; 34:27; Num 33:2   [b]Deut 25:19; 1 Sam 15:3; 2 Sam 1:1; 1 Chr 4:43   **18:1** [a]Exod 2:16, 18; 3:1   [b][Ps 106:2, 8]   **18:2** [a]Exod 2:21; 4:20–26   **18:3** [a]Exod 2:20; 4:20; Acts 7:29   [b]Exod 2:22   [1]*Gershom* means "foreign [resident] there" or "outcast."   [2]There is a wordplay here; *foreigner* (Heb. *Ger*) sounds like *Gershom.*   **18:4** [a]Gen 49:25   [1]*Eliezer* means "my God is a help."

[5] Jethro, Moses' [a]father-in-law, together with Moses' sons and his wife, came to Moses in the wilderness where he was camping by the mountain of God. [6] He said to Moses, "I, your father-in-law Jethro, am coming to you, along with your wife and her two sons with her." [7] Moses [a]went out to meet his father-in-law and bowed down and [b]kissed him; they each asked about the other's welfare, and then they went into the tent. [8] Moses told his father-in-law all that the LORD had done to Pharaoh and to Egypt for Israel's sake, and all the hardship that had come on them along the way, and how the LORD had [a]delivered them.

[9] Jethro rejoiced because of all the [a]good that the LORD had done for Israel, whom he had delivered from the hand of Egypt. [10] Jethro said, "[a]Blessed be the LORD who has delivered you from the hand of Egypt, and from the hand of Pharaoh, who has delivered the people from the Egyptians' control! [11] Now I know that the LORD is [a]greater than all the gods, [b]for in the thing in which they dealt [c]proudly against them he has destroyed them." [12] Then Jethro, Moses' father-in-law, brought a burnt [a]offering and sacrifices for God, and Aaron and all the elders of Israel came [b]to eat food[1] with the father-in-law of Moses before God.

[13] On the next day Moses [a]sat to judge the people, and the people stood around Moses from morning until evening. [14] When Moses' father-in-law saw all that he was doing for the people, he said, "What is this that you are doing for the people? Why are you sitting by yourself, and all the people stand around you from morning until evening?"

[15] Moses said to his [a]father-in-law, "Because the people come to me to inquire of God. [16] When they [a]have a dispute, it comes to me and I decide between a man and his neighbor, and I make known the decrees of God and his laws."

[17] Moses' father-in-law said to him, "What you are doing is not good! [18] You will surely wear out, both [a]you and these people who are with you, for this is too heavy a burden for you; you are not able to do it by yourself. [19] Now listen to me, I will give you advice, and may God be with you. You be a [a]representative for the people to God, and you [b]bring their disputes to God; [20] [a]warn [b]them of the statutes and the laws, and make known to them the way in which they must walk and the work they must do. [21] But you choose[1] from the people [a]capable men, [b]God-fearing men, [c]men of truth, those who [d]hate bribes, and put them over the people as rulers of thousands, rulers of hundreds, rulers of fifties, and rulers of tens. [22] They will judge [a]the people under normal circumstances, and every difficult case [b]they will bring to you, but every small case they themselves will judge, so that you may make it easier for yourself, and they will bear the burden with you. [23] If you do this thing, and God so commands you, then you will be able to endure, and all these people will be able to go [a]home satisfied."

[24] Moses listened to his father-in-law and did everything he had said. [25] [a]Moses chose capable men from all Israel, and he made them heads over the people, rulers of thousands, rulers of hundreds, rulers of fifties, and rulers of tens. [26] They judged the people under normal circumstances; the [a]difficult cases they would bring to Moses, but every small case they would judge themselves.

[27] Then Moses sent his [a]father-in-law on his way, and so Jethro went to his own land.

Israel at Sinai

19 In [a]the third month after the Israelites went out from the land of Egypt, on the very day, they came to the desert of Sinai. [2] After they journeyed from [a]Rephidim, [b]they came to the desert of Sinai, and they camped in the desert; Israel camped there in front of the mountain.

[3] [a]Moses went up to God, and the LORD [b]called to him from the mountain, "Thus you will tell the house of Jacob, and declare to the people of Israel: [4] 'You [a]yourselves

18:5 [a] Exod 3:1, 12; 4:27; 24:13   **18:7** [a] Gen 18:2   [b] Gen 29:13; Exod 4:27   **18:8** [a] Exod 15:6, 16; Ps 81:7   **18:9** [a] [Isa 63:7–14]   **18:10** [a] Gen 14:20; 2 Sam 18:28; 1 Kgs 8:56; Ps 68:19–20   **18:11** [a] Exod 12:12; 15:11; 2 Chr 2:5; Ps 95:3; 97:9; 135:5   [b] Exod 1:10, 16, 22; 5:2, 7   [c] Luke 1:51   **18:12** [a] Exod 24:5   [b] Gen 31:54; Deut 12:7   [1] I.e., the sacrifice and all the foods offered with it.   **18:13** [a] Deut 33:4–5; Matt 23:2   **18:15** [a] Lev 24:12; Num 9:6, 8; 27:5; Deut 17:8–13   **18:16** [a] Exod 24:14; Deut 19:17   **18:18** [a] Num 11:14, 17; Deut 1:12   **18:19** [a] Exod 4:16; 20:19   [b] Num 9:8; 27:5   **18:20** [a] Deut 5:1   [b] Deut 1:18   **18:21** [a] Exod 18:24–25; Deut 1:13, 15; 2 Chr 19:5–10; Ps 15:1–5; Acts 6:3   [b] Gen 42:18; 2 Sam 23:3   [c] Ezek 18:8   [d] Deut 16:19   [1] Heb. *and you will see from all*; an emphatic Heb. construction.   **18:22** [a] Lev 24:11; Deut 1:17   [b] Num 11:17   **18:23** [a] Exod 16:29   **18:25** [a] Exod 18:21; Deut 1:15   **18:26** [a] Job 29:16   **18:27** [a] Num 10:29–30   **19:1** [a] Num 33:15   **19:2** [a] Exod 17:1   [b] Exod 3:1, 12; 18:5   **19:3** [a] Acts 7:38   [b] Exod 3:4   **19:4** [a] Deut 29:2

have seen what [b]I did to Egypt and how I lifted you on eagles' wings and brought you to myself. [5][a]And now, if you will diligently listen to me and [b]keep my covenant, then [c]you will be my special possession out of all the nations, for all the earth is [d]mine, [6]and you will be to me a [a]kingdom of priests and a [b]holy nation.' These are the words that you will speak to the Israelites."

[7]So Moses came and summoned the [a]elders of Israel. He set before them all these words that the LORD had commanded him, [8]and [a]all the people answered together, "All that the LORD has commanded we will do!" So Moses brought the words of the people back to the LORD.

[9]The LORD said to Moses, "[a]I am going to come to you in [b]a dense cloud, so that the people may hear when I speak with you and so that they will always believe in you." And Moses told the words of the people to the LORD.

[10]The LORD said to Moses, "Go to the people and [a]sanctify them today and tomorrow, and make them wash their clothes [11]and be ready for the third day, for on the third day the LORD will come down on Mount Sinai in the sight of all the people. [12]You must set boundaries for the people all around, saying, 'Take heed to yourselves not to go up on the mountain nor touch its edge. [a]Whoever touches the mountain will surely be put to death! [13]No hand will touch him—but he will surely be stoned or shot through, whether a beast or a human being; he must not live.' When the ram's horn sounds a long blast they may go up on the mountain."

[14]Then Moses went down from the mountain to the people and sanctified the people, and they washed their clothes. [15]He said to the people, "Be ready for the third day. [a]Do not approach your wives for marital relations."[1]

[16]On the third day in the morning there was [a]thunder and lightning and a dense cloud on the mountain, and the sound of a very loud horn; all the people who were in the camp [b]trembled. [17][a]Moses brought the people out of the camp to meet God, and they took their place at the foot of the mountain. [18]Now [a]Mount Sinai was completely covered [b]with smoke because the LORD had descended on [c]it in fire, and its smoke went up like the smoke of a great furnace, and the [d]whole mountain shook violently. [19]When the sound of the horn grew louder and louder, [a]Moses was speaking and [b]God was answering him with a voice.

[20]The LORD came down on Mount Sinai, on the top of the mountain, and the LORD summoned Moses to the top of the mountain, and Moses went up. [21]The LORD said [a]to Moses, "Go down and solemnly warn the people, lest they force their way through to the LORD to look, and many of them perish. [22]Let the [a]priests also, who approach the LORD, [b]sanctify themselves, lest the LORD [c]break through against them."

[23]Moses said to the LORD, "The people are not able to come up to Mount Sinai, because you solemnly warned us,[1] '[a]Set boundaries for the mountain and set it apart.'" [24]The LORD said to him, "Go, get down, and then come up, and Aaron with you, but do not let the priests and the people force their way through to come up to the LORD, lest he break through against them." [25]So Moses went down to the people and spoke to them.

The Decalogue

20 God spoke [a]all these words: [2]"[a]I, the LORD, am your God, who brought you[1] from the land of Egypt, from the house of slavery.

[3]"[a]You shall have no other gods before me.

[4]"You shall not make for [a]yourself a carved image[1] or any likeness of anything that is in heaven above or that is on the earth beneath or that is in the water below.

19:4 [b]Deut 32:11; Isa 63:9; Rev 12:14   **19:5** [a]Exod 15:26; 23:22   [b]Deut 5:2; Ps 78:10   [c]Deut 4:20; 7:6; 14:2; 26:18; 1 Kgs 8:53; Ps 135:4; Titus 2:14; 1 Pet 2:9   [d]Exod 9:29; Deut 10:14; Job 41:11; Ps 50:12; 1 Cor 10:26   **19:6** [a]Deut 33:2–4; [1 Pet 2:5, 9; Rev 1:6; 5:10]   [b]Deut 7:6; 14:21; 26:19; Isa 62:12; [1 Cor 3:17]   **19:7** [a]Exod 4:29–30   **19:8** [a]Exod 4:31; 24:3, 7; Deut 5:27; 26:17   **19:9** [a]Exod 19:16; 20:21; 24:15; Deut 4:11; Ps 99:7; Matt 17:5   [b]Deut 4:12, 36; John 12:29–30   **19:10** [a]Lev 11:44–45; [Heb 10:22]   **19:12** [a]Exod 34:3; Heb 12:20   **19:15** [a][1 Cor 7:5]   [1]Heb. *do not approach a woman*; a euphemism for sexual relations.   **19:16** [a]Heb 12:18–19   [b]Heb 12:21   **19:17** [a]Deut 4:10   **19:18** [a]Deut 4:11; Judg 5:5; Ps 104:32; 144:5   [b]Exod 3:2; 24:17; Deut 5:4; 2 Chr 7:1–3; Heb 12:18   [c]Gen 15:17; 19:28; Rev 15:8   [d]Ps 68:8; 1 Kgs 19:12; Jer 4:24; [Heb 12:26]   **19:19** [a]Heb 12:21   [b]Neh 9:13; Ps 81:7   **19:21** [a]1 Sam 6:19   **19:22** [a]Exod 19:24; 24:5   [b]Lev 10:3; 21:6–8   [c]2 Sam 6:7–8   **19:23** [a]Exod 19:12   [1]Heb. *because you—you solemnly warned us*; an emphatic Heb. construction.   **20:1** [a]Deut 5:22   **20:2** [a]Hos 13:4   [1]The Heb. verb is sing.; God addresses all his people, but he addresses them individually for their obedience.   **20:3** [a]Deut 6:14; 2 Kgs 17:35; Jer 25:6; 35:15   **20:4** [a]Lev 19:4; 26:1; Deut 4:15–19; 27:15   [1]I.e., an image carved out of wood or stone.

⁵You shall not bow down to them or serve them, for I, the LORD, ᵃyour God, am a jealous God, responding ᵇto the transgression of fathers by dealing with children to the third and fourth generations of those who reject me, ⁶and ᵃshowing covenant faithfulness to a thousand generations of those who love me and keep my commandments.

⁷"You shall not take the name of the LORD ᵃyour God in vain,¹ for the LORD ᵇwill not hold guiltless anyone who takes his name in vain.

⁸ᵃRemember the Sabbath¹ day to set it apart as holy. ⁹For ᵃsix days you may labor and do all your work, ¹⁰but the ᵃseventh day is a Sabbath to the LORD your God; on it you shall not do any work, you, ᵇor your son, or your daughter, or your male servant, or your female servant, or your cattle, or the resident foreigner who is in your gates. ¹¹For ᵃin six days the LORD made the heavens and the earth and the sea and all that is in them, and he rested on the seventh day; therefore the LORD blessed the Sabbath day and set it apart as holy.

¹²ᵃHonor¹ your father and your mother, that you may live a ᵇlong time in the land the LORD your God is giving to you.

¹³ᵃYou shall not murder.¹

¹⁴ᵃYou shall not commit ᵇadultery.

¹⁵ᵃYou shall not steal.

¹⁶"You shall not give false testimony against ᵃyour neighbor.

¹⁷"You shall not covet ᵃyour neighbor's house. ᵇYou shall not covet your neighbor's wife, nor his male servant, nor his female servant, nor his ox, nor his donkey, nor anything that belongs to your neighbor."

¹⁸ᵃAll the people were ᵇseeing the thundering and the lightning, and heard the sound of the horn, and saw the mountain ᶜsmoking—and when the people saw it they trembled with fear and kept their distance. ¹⁹They said to Moses, "ᵃYou speak to us and we will listen, but do not ᵇlet God speak with us, lest we die." ²⁰Moses said to the people, "ᵃDo not fear, ᵇfor God has come to test you,¹ ᶜthat the fear of him may be before you so that you do not sin." ²¹The people kept ᵃtheir distance, but Moses drew near the thick darkness where God was.

The Altar

²²The LORD said to Moses, "Thus you will tell the Israelites: 'You yourselves have seen that I have spoken with you ᵃfrom heaven. ²³You must not make gods of silver alongside me, nor make gods of gold for yourselves.

²⁴"You must make for me an altar made of ᵃearth, and ᵇyou will sacrifice on it your burnt offerings and your peace offerings, your sheep and your cattle. In every ᶜplace where I cause my name to be honored I will come to you and I will ᵈbless you. ²⁵If you make me an altar of stone, you must not build it of stones shaped with tools, for ᵃif you ᵇuse your tool on it you have defiled it. ²⁶And you must not go up by steps to my altar, so that your ᵃnakedness is not exposed.'

The Ordinances

21 "These are the ordinances that you will ᵃset before them:

Hebrew Servants

²ᵃIf you buy a Hebrew servant, he is to serve you for six years, but in the seventh year he will go out free without paying anything. ³If he came in by himself he will go out by himself; if he had a wife when he came in, then his wife will go out with him. ⁴If his master gave him a wife, and she bore sons or daughters, the wife and the children will belong to her master, and he will go out by himself. ⁵ᵃBut if the servant should

---

20:5 ᵃIsa 44:15, 19   ᵇNum 14:18, 33; Deut 5:9–10; 1 Kgs 21:29; Ps 79:8; Jer 32:18   **20:6** ᵃDeut 7:9; Rom 11:28   **20:7** ᵃLev 19:12; Deut 6:13; 10:20; [Matt 5:33–37]   ᵇMic 6:11   ¹I.e., perjury, pagan incantations, or idle talk.   **20:8** ᵃExod 23:12; 31:13–16; Lev 26:2; Deut 5:12   ¹*Sabbath* is clearly connected to the Heb. verb "to cease, desist, rest."   **20:9** ᵃExod 34:21; 35:2–3; Lev 23:3; Deut 5:13; Luke 13:14   **20:10** ᵃGen 2:2–3   ᵇNeh 13:16–19   **20:11** ᵃGen 2:2–3; Exod 31:17   **20:12** ᵃLev 19:3; Deut 27:16; Matt 15:4; 19:19; Mark 7:10; 10:19; Luke 18:20; Eph 6:2   ᵇDeut 5:16, 33; 6:2; 11:8–9   ¹I.e., give them the weight of authority that they deserve.   **20:13** ᵃ[Matt 5:21–22]; 19:18; Mark 10:19; Luke 18:20; Rom 13:9; [1 John 3:15]   ¹I.e., the premeditated or accidental taking of the life of another human being; any unauthorized killing.   **20:14** ᵃMatt 5:27; Mark 10:19; Luke 18:20; Rom 13:9; Jas 2:11   ᵇLev 20:10; Deut 5:18   **20:15** ᵃExod 21:16; Lev 19:11, 13; Matt 19:18; Rom 13:9   **20:16** ᵃExod 23:1, 7; Deut 5:20; Matt 19:18   **20:17** ᵃ[Luke 12:15]; Rom 7:7; 13:9; [Eph 5:3, 5]; Heb 13:5   ᵇ2 Sam 11:2; [Matt 5:28]   **20:18** ᵃHeb 12:18–19   ᵇRev 1:10, 12   ᶜExod 19:16, 18   **20:19** ᵃGal 3:19; Heb 12:19   ᵇDeut 5:5, 23–27   **20:20** ᵃExod 14:13; [Isa 41:10, 13]   ᵇExod 15:25; [Deut 13:3]   ᶜDeut 4:10; 6:24; Prov 3:7; 16:6; Isa 8:13   ¹Heb. *to try, test, prove.*   **20:21** ᵃExod 19:16; Deut 5:22   **20:22** ᵃDeut 4:36; 5:24, 26; Neh 9:13   **20:24** ᵃExod 20:25; 27:1–8   ᵇExod 24:5; Lev 1:2   ᶜDeut 12:5; 16:6, 11; 1 Kgs 9:3; 2 Chr 6:6   ᵈGen 12:2   **20:25** ᵃDeut 27:5   ᵇJosh 8:30–31   **20:26** ᵃExod 28:42–43   **21:1** ᵃExod 24:3–4; Deut 4:14; 6:1   **21:2** ᵃLev 25:39–43; Deut 15:12–18; Jer 34:14   **21:5** ᵃDeut 15:16–17

declare, 'I love my master, my wife, and my children; I will not go out free,' [6]then his master must bring him to the [a]judges,[1] and he will bring him to the door or the doorpost, and his master will pierce his ear with an awl, and he shall serve him forever.

[7]"If a man [a]sells his daughter as a female servant,[1] she will not go out as the male servants do. [8]If she does not please her master, who has designated her for himself, then he must let her be redeemed. He has no right to sell her to a foreign nation, because he has dealt deceitfully with her. [9]If he designated her for his son, then he will deal with her according to the customary rights of daughters. [10]If he takes another wife, he must not diminish the first one's food,[1] her clothing, or her marital rights. [11]If he does not provide her with these three things, then she will go out free, without paying money.

Personal Injuries

[12]"Whoever strikes someone so that [a]he dies[1] must surely be put to death. [13]But [a]if he does not do it with premeditation, but it [b]happens by [c]accident, then I will appoint for you a place where he may flee. [14]But if a man willfully [a]attacks his neighbor to kill him cunningly,[1] [b]you will take him even from my altar that he may die.

[15]"Whoever strikes his father or his mother must surely be put to death.

[16]"[a]Whoever kidnaps someone and [b]sells him, or is [c]caught still holding him, must surely be put to death.

[17]"Whoever treats his [a]father or his mother disgracefully must surely be put to death.

[18]"If men fight, and one strikes his neighbor with a stone or with his fist and he does not die, but must remain in bed, [19]and then if he gets up and walks about outside on his staff, then the one who struck him is innocent, except he must pay for the injured person's loss of time and see to [a]it that he is fully healed.

[20]"If a man strikes his male servant or his female servant with a staff so that he or she dies as a result of the blow, he will surely be punished.[1] [21]However, if the injured servant survives one or two days, the owner will not be punished, for he has suffered the [a]loss.

[22]"If men fight and hit a pregnant woman and her child is born prematurely,[1] but there is no serious injury, the one who hit her will surely be punished in accordance with what the woman's husband demands of him, and he will [a]pay what the court decides.[2] [23]But if there is serious injury, then you will give a life for a life, [24][a]eye for eye, tooth for tooth, hand for hand, foot for foot, [25]burn for burn, wound for wound, bruise for bruise.

[26]"If a man strikes the eye of his male servant or his female servant so that he destroys it, he will let the servant go free as compensation for the eye. [27]If he knocks out the tooth of his male servant or his female servant, he will let the servant go free as compensation for the tooth.

Laws about Animals

[28]"If an ox[1] gores a man or a woman so that [a]either dies, then the ox must surely be stoned and its flesh must not be eaten, but the owner of the ox will be acquitted. [29]But if the ox had the habit of goring, and its owner was warned but he did not take the necessary precautions, and then it killed a man or a woman, the ox must be stoned and the man must be put to death. [30]If a ransom is set for him, then he must pay the redemption for his life according [a]to whatever amount was set for him. [31]If the ox gores a son or a daughter, the owner will be dealt with according to this rule. [32]If the ox gores a male servant or a female servant, the owner must pay [a]thirty shekels of silver, and the [b]ox must be stoned.

[33]"If a man opens a pit or if a man digs a pit and does not cover it and an ox or a donkey falls into it, [34]the owner of the pit must repay the loss. He must give money to its owner, and the dead animal will become

his. [35]If the ox of one man injures the ox of his neighbor so that it dies, then they will sell the live ox and divide its proceeds, and they will also divide the dead ox.[1] [36]Or if it is known that the ox had the habit of goring, and its owner did not take the necessary precautions, he must surely pay ox for ox, and the dead animal will become his.

Laws about Property

22 "If a man steals an ox or a sheep and kills it or sells it, he must pay [a]back five head of cattle for the ox, and four sheep for the one sheep.

[2]"If a thief is caught breaking [a]in and is struck so that he dies, there will be [b]no blood guilt for him. [3]If the sun has risen on him, then there is blood guilt for him. A thief must surely make full restitution; if he has nothing, then he will be [a]sold for his theft. [4]If the stolen item should in fact be [a]found alive in his possession, whether it be an ox or a donkey or a sheep, he must pay [b]back double.

[5]"If a man grazes his livestock in a field or a vineyard and he lets the livestock loose and they graze in the field of another man, he must make restitution from the best of his own field and the best of his own vineyard.

[6]"If a fire breaks out and spreads to thorn bushes, so that stacked grain or standing grain or the whole field is consumed, the one who started the fire must surely make restitution.

[7]"If a man [a]gives his neighbor money or articles[1] for safekeeping[2] and it is stolen from the man's house, [b]if the thief is caught, he must repay double. [8]If the thief is not caught, then the owner of the house will be brought before the [a]judges to see whether he has laid his hand on his neighbor's goods. [9]In all [a]cases of illegal possessions, whether for an ox, a donkey, a sheep, a garment, or any kind of lost item, about which someone says 'This belongs to me,' the matter of the two of them will come before the judges, and the one whom the judges declare guilty must repay double to his neighbor. [10]If a man gives his neighbor a donkey or an ox or a sheep or any beast to keep, and it dies or is injured or is carried away[1] without anyone seeing it, [11]then there will be an [a]oath to the LORD between the two of them, that he has not laid his hand on his neighbor's goods, and its owner will accept this, and he will not have to pay. [12]But [a]if it was stolen from him, he will pay its owner. [13]If it is [a]torn in pieces, then he will bring it for evidence, and he will not have to pay for what was torn.

[14]"If a man borrows an animal[1] from his neighbor and it is hurt or dies when its owner was not with it, the man who borrowed it will surely pay. [15]If its owner was with it, he will not have to pay; if it was hired, what was paid for the hire covers it.

Moral and Ceremonial Laws

[16]"If a man seduces a virgin[1] who is not engaged and goes to bed[2] with her, he must surely pay the marriage price for her to be his [a]wife. [17]If her father refuses to give her to him, he must pay money for the bride [a]price of virgins.

[18]"[a]You must not allow a sorceress to live.

[19]"[a]Whoever has sexual relations[1] with a beast must surely be put to death.

[20]"Whoever sacrifices to a god [a]other than the LORD alone must be utterly destroyed.

[21]"You must not wrong a resident foreigner nor oppress him, for [a]you were foreigners in the land of Egypt.

[22]"[a]You must not afflict[1] any widow or orphan. [23]If you afflict them in any way and they [a]cry to me, I will surely [b]hear their cry, [24]and my [a]anger will burn and I will kill [b]you with the sword, and your wives will be widows and your children will be fatherless.

21:35 [1]Heb. *divide the dead.* **22:1** [a]2 Sam 12:6; Prov 6:31; Luke 19:8 **22:2** [a]Job 24:16; Matt 6:19; 24:43; 1 Pet 4:15 [b]Num 35:27 **22:3** [a]Exod 21:2; Matt 18:25 **22:4** [a]Exod 21:16 [b]Prov 6:31 **22:7** [a]Lev 6:1–7 [b]Exod 22:4 [1]I.e., household goods and articles, anything from jewels and ornaments to weapons or pottery. [2]Heb. *to keep.* **22:8** [a]Exod 21:6, 22; 22:28; Deut 17:8–9; 19:17 **22:9** [a]Deut 25:1; 2 Chr 19:10 **22:10** [1]Heb. *to take captive.* **22:11** [a]Heb 6:16 **22:12** [a]Gen 31:39 **22:13** [a]Gen 31:39 **22:14** [1]Heb. *if a man asks* [an animal] *from his neighbor; animal* is supplied. **22:16** [a]Deut 22:28–29 [1]I.e., an unmarried young woman or an engaged young woman who is presumed to be a virgin. [2]Heb. *lied down with;* can imply going to bed to sleep or can be a euphemism for sexual relations. **22:17** [a]Gen 34:12; 1 Sam 18:25 **22:18** [a]Lev 19:31; 20:6, 27; Deut 18:10–11; 1 Sam 28:3–10; Jer 27:9–10 **22:19** [a]Lev 18:23; 20:15–16; Deut 27:21 [1]Heb. *lies down with;* can imply going to bed to sleep or can be a euphemism for sexual relations. **22:20** [a]Exod 32:8; 34:15; Lev 17:7; Num 25:2; Deut 17:2–3, 5; 1 Kgs 18:40; 2 Kgs 10:25 **22:21** [a]Exod 23:9; Deut 10:19; Zech 7:10 **22:22** [a]Deut 24:17–18; Prov 23:10–11; Jer 7:6–7; [Jas 1:27] [1]Heb. *afflict, oppress, humiliate, rape.* **22:23** [a][Luke 18:7] [b]Deut 10:17–18; Ps 18:6 **22:24** [a]Ps 69:24 [b]Ps 109:9

25"ªIf you lend money to any of my people who are needy among you, do not be like a moneylender to him; do not charge him ᵇinterest. 26ªIf you do take the garment of your neighbor in pledge, you must return it to him by the time the sun goes down, 27for it is his only covering—it is his garment for his body. What else can he sleep in? And when he cries out to me, I will hear, for I am ªgracious.

28"ªYou must not blaspheme God[1] or curse the ᵇruler of your people.

29"Do not hold back offerings from your granaries or your vats. You must give me ªthe firstborn of your sons. 30You must also do ªthis for your oxen and for your sheep; ᵇseven days they may remain with their mothers, but give them to me on the eighth day.

31"You will be ªholy people to me; ᵇyou must not eat any meat torn by animals in the field. You must throw it to the dogs.

Justice

23 "You must not give ªa false report. Do not make common cause with the wicked to be a ᵇmalicious[1] witness.

2"You must not follow a crowd in doing evil things; in a lawsuit ªyou must ᵇnot offer testimony that agrees with a crowd so as to pervert justice, 3and you must not show partiality to a poor ªman in his lawsuit.

4"ªIf you encounter your enemy's ox or donkey wandering off, you must by all means return it to him. 5ªIf you see the donkey of someone who hates you fallen under its load, you must not ignore him, but be sure to help[1] him with it.

6"You must not turn away justice for ªyour poor people in their lawsuits. 7ªKeep your distance from a false charge—ᵇdo not ᶜkill the innocent and the righteous, for I will not justify the wicked.

8"You must not accept a bribe, for a bribe blinds those who see and subverts the words of the righteous.

9"You must not oppress a resident foreigner, since ªyou know the life of a foreigner, for you were foreigners in the land of Egypt.

Sabbaths and Feasts

10"For ªsix years you are to sow your land and gather in its produce. 11But in the seventh year you must let it lie fallow and leave it alone so that the poor of your people may eat, and what they leave any animal in the field may eat; you must do likewise with your vineyard and your olive grove. 12For ªsix days you are to do your work, but on the seventh day you must cease, in order that your ox and your donkey may rest and that your female servant's son and the resident foreigner may refresh themselves.[1]

13"Pay attention to do everything I have told you, and do not even mention the names of other gods—do not let them ªbe heard on your lips.

14"ªThree times in the year you must make a pilgrim feast to me. 15You are to observe the Feast of Unleavened Bread; seven days ªyou must eat bread made without yeast, as I commanded you, at the appointed time of the month of Abib, for at that time you came out of Egypt. ᵇNo one may appear before me empty-handed.

16"You are also to observe the Feast of Harvest, the firstfruits of your labors that you have sown in the field, ªand ᵇthe Feast of Ingathering at the end of the year when you have gathered in your harvest out of the field. 17At ªthree times in the year all your males will appear before the Sovereign LORD.

18"ªYou must not offer the blood of my sacrifice with bread containing ᵇyeast; the fat of my festal sacrifice must not remain until morning. 19The first of ªthe firstfruits of ᵇyour soil you must bring to the house of the LORD your God.

"You must not cook a young goat in its mother's milk.

22:25 ªLev 25:35-37   ᵇDeut 23:19-20; Neh 5:1-13; Ps 15:5; Ezek 18:8   **22:26** ªDeut 24:6, 10-13; Job 24:3; Prov 20:16; Amos 2:8   **22:27** ªExod 34:6-7   **22:28** ªEccl 10:20   ᵇActs 23:5   [1]Heb. *gods, God*; it could refer to human judges.   **22:29** ªExod 23:16, 19; Deut 26:2-11; Prov 3:9   **22:30** ªDeut 15:19   ᵇLev 22:27   **22:31** ªExod 19:6; Lev 11:44; 19:2   ᵇLev 7:24; 17:15; Ezek 4:14   **23:1** ªExod 20:16; Lev 19:11; Deut 5:20; Ps 101:5; [Prov 10:18]   ᵇDeut 19:16-21; Ps 35:11; [Prov 19:5]; Acts 6:11   [1]Heb. *violence*; i.e., social injustices done usually to the poor and needy.   **23:2** ªGen 7:1   ᵇLev 19:15   **23:3** ªExod 23:6; Lev 19:15; Deut 1:17; 16:19   **23:4** ª[Rom 12:20]   **23:5** ªDeut 22:4   [1]An emphatic Heb. construction.   **23:6** ªEccl 5:8   **23:7** ªExod 20:16; Ps 119:29; Eph 4:25   ᵇMatt 27:4   ᶜExod 34:7; Deut 25:1; Rom 1:18   **23:9** ªExod 22:21; Lev 19:33; Deut 24:17; 27:19   **23:10** ªLev 25:1-7   **23:12** ªLuke 13:14   [1]Or *soul, life.*   **23:13** ªDeut 4:9, 23; 1 Tim 4:16   **23:14** ªExod 23:17; 34:22-24; Deut 16:16   **23:15** ªExod 12:14-20; Lev 23:6-8; Num 28:16-25   ᵇExod 22:29; 34:20   **23:16** ªExod 34:22; Lev 23:10; Num 28:26   ᵇDeut 16:13   **23:17** ªExod 23:14; 34:23; Deut 16:16   **23:18** ªExod 34:25; Lev 2:11   ᵇExod 12:10; Lev 7:15; Deut 16:4   **23:19** ªExod 22:29; 34:26; Deut 26:2, 10; Neh 10:35; Prov 3:9   ᵇDeut 14:21

The Angel of the Presence

[20] "I am [a]going to send an angel before you to protect you as you journey and to bring you into the place that I have prepared. [21]Take heed because of him, and obey his voice; [a]do [b]not rebel against him, for he will not pardon your transgressions, for [c]my Name is in him. [22]But [a]if you diligently obey him and do all that I command, then I will be an enemy to your enemies, and I will be an adversary to your adversaries. [23]For my angel will go [a]before you and [b]bring you to the Amorites, the Hittites, the Perizzites, the Canaanites, the Hivites, and the Jebusites, and I will destroy them completely.

[24]"You must not [a]bow down to their gods; you must not serve them [b]or do according to their practices. Instead you must completely overthrow them and smash their standing stones to pieces. [25]You must [a]serve [b]the LORD your God, and he [c]will bless your bread and your water, and I will remove sickness from your midst. [26a]No woman will miscarry her young or be barren in your land. I will [b]fulfill the number of your days.

[27]"I will send [a]my terror before you, and I will alarm all the people whom you encounter; I will make all your enemies turn their backs to you. [28]I [a]will send hornets before you that will drive out the Hivite, the Canaanite, and the Hittite before you. [29]I [a]will not drive them out before you in one year, lest the land become desolate and the wild animals multiply against you. [30]Little by little I will drive them out before you, until you become fruitful and inherit the land. [31]I [a]will set your boundaries from the Red Sea to the Sea of the Philistines, and from the desert to the River,[1] for I will [b]deliver the inhabitants of the land into your hand, and you will drive them out before you.

[32]"[a]You must make no covenant with them or with their gods. [33]They must not live in your land, lest they make you sin against me, for if you serve their gods, [a]it will surely be a snare to you."

The Lord Ratifies the Covenant

24 But to Moses the LORD said, "Come up to the LORD, you and Aaron, [a]Nadab [b]and Abihu, and seventy of the elders of Israel, and worship from a distance. [2]Moses alone may come near the LORD, but the others must not come near, nor may the people go up with him."

[3]Moses came and told the people [a]all the LORD's words and all the decisions. All the people answered together,[1] "We are willing to do all the words that the LORD has said," [4]and Moses wrote [a]down all the words of the LORD. Early in the morning he built an altar at the foot of the mountain and arranged twelve standing [b]stones—according to the twelve tribes of Israel. [5]He sent young Israelite men, and they offered [a]burnt offerings and sacrificed young bulls for peace offerings to the LORD. [6]Moses [a]took half of the blood and put it in bowls, and half of the blood he splashed on the altar. [7]He [a]took the Book of the Covenant and read it aloud to the people, and they said, "We are willing to do and obey all that the LORD has spoken." [8]So Moses took [a]the blood and splashed it on the people and said, "This is the blood of the covenant that the LORD has made with you in accordance with all these words."

[9]Moses and Aaron, Nadab and Abihu, and the seventy elders of Israel went up, [10]and they [a]saw the God of Israel. Under his feet there was something like a pavement made of [b]sapphire, clear like the sky [c]itself.[1] [11]But he [a]did not lay a hand on [b]the leaders of the Israelites, so they saw God,[1] and they [c]ate and they drank.

[12]The LORD said to Moses, "[a]Come up to me on the mountain and remain there, and I will give you the stone [b]tablets with the law and the commandments that I have written, so that you may teach them." [13]So Moses set out with Joshua [a]his attendant, and Moses went up the mountain of God. [14]He told the elders, "Wait for us in this

23:20 [a]Exod 3:2; 13:15; 14:19; Josh 5:14   **23:21** [a]Num 14:11; Deut 9:7; Ps 78:40, 56 [b]Deut 18:19; 1 John 5:16 [c]Isa 9:6; Jer 23:6   **23:22** [a]Gen 12:3; Num 24:9; Deut 30:7; Jer 30:20   **23:23** [a]Exod 23:20 [b]Josh 24:8, 11   **23:24** [a]Exod 20:5; 23:13, 33 [b]Deut 12:30–31   **23:25** [a]Deut 6:13; [Matt 4:10] [b]Deut 28:5 [c]Exod 15:26; Deut 7:15   **23:26** [a]Deut 7:14; 28:4; Mal 3:11 [b]1 Chr 23:1   **23:27** [a]Gen 35:5; Exod 15:16; Deut 2:25; Josh 2:9   **23:28** [a]Deut 7:20; Josh 24:12   **23:29** [a]Deut 7:22   **23:31** [a]Gen 15:18; Deut 1:7–8; 11:24; 1 Kgs 4:21, 24 [b]Josh 21:44 [1]Usually refers to the Euphrates.   **23:32** [a]Exod 34:12, 15; Deut 7:2   **23:33** [a]Exod 34:12; Deut 12:30; Josh 23:13; Judg 2:3; 1 Sam 18:21; Ps 106:36   **24:1** [a]Exod 6:23; 28:1; Lev 10:1–2 [b]Exod 1:5; Num 11:16   **24:3** [a]Exod 19:8; 24:7; Deut 5:27; [Gal 3:19] [1]Heb. one voice.   **24:4** [a]Exod 17:14; 34:27; Deut 31:9 [b]Gen 28:18   **24:5** [a]Exod 18:12; 20:24   **24:6** [a]Exod 29:16, 20; Heb 9:18   **24:7** [a]Exod 24:4; Heb 9:19   **24:8** [a]Zech 9:11; [Matt 26:28; Mark 14:24; Luke 22:20; 1 Cor 11:25; Heb 9:19–20; 13:20; 1 Pet 1:2]   **24:10** [a]Exod 24:11; Num 12:8; Isa 6:5; [John 1:18; 6:46]; 1 John 4:12 [b]Ezek 1:26; Rev 4:3 [c]Matt 17:2 [1]Heb. and like the body of heaven for clearness.   **24:11** [a]Exod 19:21 [b]Gen 32:30; Judg 13:22 [c]1 Cor 10:18 [1]Heb. to see, perceive, see a vision.   **24:12** [a]Exod 24:2, 15 [b]Exod 31:18; 32:15; Deut 5:22   **24:13** [a]Exod 32:17

place until we return to you. Here are Aaron and ᵃHur with you. Whoever has any matters of dispute can approach them."

¹⁵Moses went up the ᵃmountain, and the cloud covered the mountain. ¹⁶The glory of ᵃthe LORD resided on Mount Sinai, and the cloud covered it for six days. On the seventh day he called to Moses from within the cloud. ¹⁷Now the ᵃappearance of the glory of the LORD was like a devouring fire on the top of the mountain in plain view of the people. ¹⁸ᵃMoses went into the cloud when he went up the mountain, and Moses was on the mountain 40 days and 40 nights.

The Materials for the Tabernacle

25 The LORD spoke to Moses, ²"Tell the Israelites to take an offering[1] for me; ᵃfrom every person motivated by a willing heart you are to receive my offering. ³This is the offering you are to accept from them: gold, silver, bronze, ⁴blue, purple, scarlet, fine linen, goats' hair, ⁵ram skins dyed red, fine leather,[1] acacia wood, ⁶ᵃoil for the light, ᵇspices for the anointing oil and for fragrant incense, ⁷onyx stones, and other gems to be set in the ᵃephod and in the breastpiece. ⁸Let them make for me a ᵃsanctuary, so that ᵇI may live among them. ⁹According to all that I am showing you[1]—the pattern of the tabernacle and the pattern of all its furnishings—you[2] must make it exactly so.

The Ark of the Testimony

¹⁰"They are to make ᵃan ark of acacia wood—its length is to be 45 inches, its width 27 inches, and its height 27 inches. ¹¹You are to overlay it with pure ᵃgold—both inside and outside you must overlay it, and you are to make a surrounding border of gold over it. ¹²You are to cast four gold rings for it and put them on its four feet, with two rings on one side and two rings on the other side. ¹³You are to make poles of acacia wood, overlay them with gold, ¹⁴and put the poles into the rings at the sides of the ark in order to carry the ark with them. ¹⁵The poles must

remain in ᵃthe rings of the ark; they must not be removed from it. ¹⁶You are to put into ᵃthe ark the testimony that I will give to you.

¹⁷"ᵃYou are to make an atonement lid of pure gold; its length is to be 45 inches, and its width is to be 27 inches. ¹⁸You are to make two cherubim of gold; you are to make them of hammered metal on the two ends of the atonement lid. ¹⁹Make one cherub on one end and one cherub on the other end; from the atonement lid you are to make the cherubim on the two ends. ²⁰The cherubim are to be spreading ᵃtheir wings upward, overshadowing the atonement lid with their wings, and the cherubim are to face each other, looking toward the atonement lid. ²¹You are to put the atonement lid on top of the ark, and in the ark ᵃyou are to put the testimony ᵇI am giving you. ²²I will meet with you ᵃthere, and from above the atonement lid, from ᵇbetween the two cherubim that are over the ark of the testimony, I will speak with you about all that I will command you for the Israelites.

The Table for the Bread of the Presence

²³"ᵃYou are to make a table of acacia wood; its length is to be 36 inches, its width 18 inches, and its height 27 inches. ²⁴You are to overlay it with pure gold, and you are to make a surrounding border of gold for it. ²⁵You are to make a surrounding frame for it about three inches broad, and you are to make a surrounding border of gold for its frame. ²⁶You are to make four rings of gold for it and attach the rings at the four corners where its four legs are. ²⁷The rings are to be close to the frame to provide places for the poles to carry the table. ²⁸You are to make the poles of acacia wood and overlay them with gold, so that the table may be carried with them. ²⁹You are to make ᵃits plates, its ladles, its pitchers, and its bowls, to be used in pouring out offerings; you are to make them of pure gold. ³⁰You are to set the ᵃBread of the Presence on the table before me continually.

24:14 ᵃExod 17:10, 12   **24:15** ᵃExod 19:9; Matt 17:5   **24:16** ᵃExod 16:10; 33:18; Num 14:10   **24:17** ᵃExod 3:2; Deut 4:26, 36; 9:3; Heb 12:18, 29   **24:18** ᵃExod 34:28; Deut 9:9; 10:10   **25:2** ᵃExod 35:4–9, 21; 1 Chr 29:3, 5, 9; Ezra 2:68; Neh 11:2; [2 Cor 8:11–13; 9:7]   ¹Trad. *heave-offering.*   **25:5** ¹Perhaps the skins of a sea animal like a dolphin or porpoise.   **25:6** ᵃExod 27:20   ᵇExod 30:23   **25:7** ᵃExod 28:4, 6–14   **25:8** ᵃExod 36:1, 3, 4; Lev 4:6; 10:4; 21:12; Heb 9:1–2   ᵇExod 29:45; 1 Kgs 6:13; [2 Cor 6:16; Heb 3:6; Rev 2:13]   **25:9** ¹The pronoun is sing.   ²The pronoun is pl.   **25:10** ᵃExod 37:1–9; Deut 10:3; Heb 9:4   **25:11** ᵃExod 37:2; Heb 9:4   **25:15** ᵃNum 4:6; 1 Kgs 8:8   **25:16** ᵃExod 16:34; 31:18; Deut 10:2; 31:26; 1 Kgs 8:9; Heb 9:4   **25:17** ᵃExod 37:6; Heb 9:5   **25:20** ᵃ1 Kgs 8:7; 1 Chr 28:18; Heb 9:5   **25:21** ᵃExod 26:34; 40:20   ᵇExod 25:16   **25:22** ᵃExod 29:42–43; 30:6, 36; Lev 16:2; Num 17:4   ᵇNum 7:89; 1 Sam 4:4; 2 Sam 6:2; 2 Kgs 19:15; Ps 80:1; Isa 37:16   **25:23** ᵃExod 37:10–16; 1 Kgs 7:48; 2 Chr 4:8; Heb 9:2   **25:29** ᵃExod 37:16; Num 4:7   **25:30** ᵃExod 39:36; 40:23; Lev 24:5–9

The Lampstand

[31] "[a]You are to make a lampstand of pure gold. The lampstand is to be made of hammered metal; its base and its shaft, its cups, its buds, and its blossoms are to be from the same piece. [32] Six branches are to extend from the sides of the lampstand, three branches of the lampstand from one side of it and three branches of the lampstand from the other side of it. [33a] Three cups shaped like almond flowers with buds and blossoms are to be on one branch, and three cups shaped like almond flowers with buds and blossoms are to be on the next branch, and the same for the six branches extending from the lampstand. [34] On the lampstand there are to be four cups shaped like [a]almond flowers with buds and blossoms, [35] with a bud under the first two branches from it, and a bud under the next two branches from it, and a bud under the third two branches from it, according to the six branches that extend from the lampstand. [36] Their buds and their branches will be one piece, all of it one hammered piece of pure gold.

[37] "You are to make its seven lamps and then set its lamps up on it, so that it will give light to [a]the area in front of it. [38] Its trimmers and its trays are to be of pure gold. [39] About 75 pounds of pure gold is to be used for it and for all these utensils. [40] Now be [a]sure to make them according to the pattern you were shown on the mountain.

The Tabernacle

26 "The tabernacle itself [a]you are to make with ten curtains of fine twisted linen and blue and purple and scarlet; you are to make them with cherubim that are the work of an artistic designer. [2] The length of each curtain is to be 42 feet, and the width of each curtain is to be 6 feet—the same size for each of the curtains. [3] Five curtains are to be joined, one to another, and the other five curtains are to be joined, one to another. [4] You are to make loops of blue material along the edge of the end curtain in one set, and in the same way you are to make loops in the outer edge of the end curtain in the second set. [5] You are to make 50 loops on the one curtain, and you are to make 50 loops on the end curtain which is on the second set, so that the loops are opposite one to another. [6] You are to make 50 gold clasps and join the curtains together with the clasps, so that the tabernacle is a unit.

[7] "You are to make curtains of goats' hair for a tent over the tabernacle; [a]you are to make 11 curtains. [8] The length of each curtain is to be 45 feet, and the width of each curtain is to be 6 feet—the same size for the 11 curtains. [9] You are to join five curtains by themselves and six curtains by themselves. You are to double over the sixth curtain at the front of the tent. [10] You are to make 50 loops along the edge of the end curtain in one set and 50 loops along the edge of the curtain that joins the second set. [11] You are to make 50 bronze clasps and put the clasps into the loops and join the tent together so that it is a unit. [12] Now the part that remains of the curtains of the tent—the half curtain that remains will hang over at the back of the tabernacle. [13] The foot and a half on the one side and the foot and a half on the other side of what remains in the length of the curtains of the tent will hang over the sides of the tabernacle, on one side and the other side, to cover it.

[14] "[a]You are to make a covering for the tent out of ram skins dyed red and over that a covering of fine leather.

[15] "You are to [a]make the frames[1] for the tabernacle out of acacia wood as uprights. [16] Each frame is to be 15 feet long, and each frame is to be 27 inches wide, [17] with two projections per frame parallel one to another. You are to make all the frames of the tabernacle in this way. [18] So you are to make the frames for the tabernacle: 20 frames for the south side, [19] and you are to make 40 silver bases to go under the 20 frames—two bases under the first frame for its two projections, and likewise two bases under the next frame for its two projections; [20] and for the second side of the tabernacle, the north side, 20 frames, [21] and their 40 silver bases, two bases under the first frame, and two bases under the next frame. [22] And for the back of the tabernacle on the west you will make six frames. [23] You are to make two frames for the corners of the tabernacle on

25:31 [a] Exod 37:17–24; 1 Kgs 7:49; Zech 4:2; Heb 9:2; Rev 1:12; 27:21; 30:8; Lev 24:3–4; 2 Chr 13:11 25:40 [a] Exod 25:9; 26:30; 36:8–19 26:7 [a] Exod 36:14 26:14 [a] Exod 35:7, 23; 36:19 25:33 [a] Exod 37:19 25:34 [a] Exod 37:20–22 25:37 [a] Exod Num 8:4; 1 Chr 28:11, 19; Acts 7:44; [Heb 8:5] 26:1 [a] Exod 26:15 [a] Exod 36:20–34 1 Or boards, planks, beams.

the back. [24]At the two corners they must be doubled at the lower end and finished together at the top in one ring. So it will be for both. [25]So there are to be eight frames and their silver bases, sixteen bases, two bases under the first frame, and two bases under the next frame.

[26]"You are to make bars of acacia wood, five for the frames on one side of the tabernacle, [27]and five bars for the frames on the second side of the tabernacle, and five bars for the frames on the back of the tabernacle on the west. [28]The [a]middle bar in the center of the frames will reach from end to end. [29]You are to overlay the frames with gold and make their rings of gold to provide places for the bars, and you are to overlay the bars with gold. [30]You are to set up the tabernacle [a]according to the plan[1] that you were shown on the mountain.

[31]"[a]You are to make a special curtain of blue, purple, and scarlet yarn and fine twisted linen; it is to be made with cherubim, the work of an artistic designer. [32]You are to hang it with gold hooks on four posts of acacia wood overlaid with gold, set in four silver bases. [33]You are to hang this curtain under [a]the clasps and bring [b]the ark of the testimony in there behind the curtain. The curtain will make a division for you between the Holy Place and the Most Holy Place.[1] [34a]You are to put the atonement lid on the ark of the testimony in the Most Holy Place. [35]You are to put the table outside the curtain and the lampstand on the south side of the tabernacle, opposite the table, and [a]you are to place [b]the table on the north side.

[36]"[a]You are to make a hanging for the entrance of the tent of blue, purple, and scarlet yarn and fine twisted linen, the work of an embroiderer.[1] [37]You are to make for the hanging [a]five posts of acacia wood and overlay them with gold, and their hooks will be gold, and you are to cast five bronze bases for them.

The Altar

27 "You are to make the altar of acacia wood, 7½ feet long, [a]and 7½ feet wide; the altar is to be square, and its height is to be 4½ feet. [2]You are to make its four horns on its four corners; its horns will be part of it, and you are to overlay it with bronze. [3]You are to make its pots for the ashes, its shovels, its tossing bowls, its meat hooks, and its fire pans—you are to make all its utensils of bronze. [4]You are to make a grating for it, a network of bronze, and you are to make on the network four bronze rings on its four corners. [5]You are to put it under the ledge of the altar below, so that the network will come halfway up the altar. [6]You are to make poles for the altar, poles of acacia wood, and you are to overlay them with bronze. [7]The poles are to be put into the rings so that the poles will be on two sides of the altar when carrying it. [8]You are to make the altar hollow, out of boards. Just [a]as it was shown you on the mountain, so they must make it.

The Courtyard

[9]"[a]You are to make the courtyard of the tabernacle. For the south side there are to be hangings for the courtyard of fine twisted linen, 150 feet long for one side, [10]with 20 posts and their 20 bronze bases, with the hooks of the posts and their bands of silver. [11]Likewise for its length on the north side, there are to be hangings for 150 feet, with 20 posts and their 20 bronze bases, with silver hooks and bands on the posts. [12]The width of the court on the west side is to be 75 feet with hangings, with their 10 posts and their 10 bases. [13]The width of the court on the east side, toward the sunrise, is to be 75 feet. [14]The hangings on one side[1] of the gate are to be 22½ feet long, with their three posts and their three bases. [15]On the second side there are to be hangings 22½ feet long, with their three posts and their three bases. [16]For the gate of the courtyard there is to be a curtain of 30 feet, of blue, purple, and scarlet yarn and fine twisted linen, the work of an embroiderer, with four posts and their four bases. [17]All the posts around the courtyard are to have silver bands; their [a]hooks are to be silver, and their bases bronze. [18]The length of the courtyard is to be 150 feet and the width

26:28 [a] Exod 36:33   **26:30** [a] Exod 25:9, 40; 27:8; 39:32; Num 8:4; Acts 7:44; [Heb 8:2, 5]   [1] Heb. *judgment, decision*.
26:31 [a] Exod 27:21; 36:35–38; Lev 16:2; 2 Chr 3:14; Matt 27:51; Heb 9:3; 10:20   **26:33** [a] Exod 25:10–16; 40:21   [b] Lev 16:2; Heb 9:2–3   [1] Or *the holy of holies*.   **26:34** [a] Exod 25:17–22; 40:20; Heb 9:5   **26:35** [a] Exod 40:22; Heb 9:2   [b] Exod 40:24   **26:36** [a] Exod 36:37   [1] I.e., someone who made cloth with colors.   **26:37** [a] Exod 36:38
27:1 [a] Exod 38:1; Ezek 43:13   **27:8** [a] Exod 25:40; 26:30; Acts 7:44; [Heb 8:5]   **27:9** [a] Exod 38:9–20
27:14 [1] Heb. *shoulder; of the gate* is supplied.   **27:17** [a] Exod 38:19

75 feet,[1] and the height of the fine twisted linen hangings is to be 7½ feet, with their bronze bases. [19]All the utensils of the tabernacle used in all its service, all its tent pegs, and all the tent pegs of the courtyard are to be made of bronze.

Offering the Oil

[20]"You are to command the Israelites that they bring to [a]you pure oil of pressed olives for the light, so that the lamps will burn regularly. [21]In the tent of meeting [a]outside the curtain that is before the testimony, [b]Aaron and his sons are to arrange [c]it from evening to morning before the LORD. This is to be a lasting ordinance among the Israelites for generations to come.

The Clothing of the Priests

28 "And you, bring near to you your brother [a]Aaron and his sons with him from among the Israelites, so that they may minister [b]as my priests—Aaron, [c]Nadab and Abihu, [d]Eleazar and Ithamar, Aaron's sons. [2]You must make holy garments for [a]your brother Aaron, for glory and for beauty. [3]You are to speak to all [a]who are specially skilled,[1] whom I have filled with the spirit of wisdom, so that they may make Aaron's garments to set him apart to minister as my priest. [4]Now these [a]are the garments that they are to make: [b]a [c]breastpiece, [d]an ephod, [e]a robe, a fitted tunic, a turban, and a sash. They are to make holy garments for your brother Aaron and for his sons, that they may minister as my priests. [5]The artisans are to use the gold, blue, purple, scarlet, and fine linen.

[6]"They are to make the ephod of gold, blue, purple, scarlet, [a]and fine twisted linen, the work of an artistic designer. [7]It is to have two shoulder pieces attached to two of its corners, so it can be joined together. [8]The artistically woven waistband of the ephod that is on it is to be like it, of one piece with the ephod, of gold, blue, purple, scarlet, and fine twisted linen.

[9]"You are to take two onyx [a]stones and engrave on them the names of the sons of Israel, [10]six of their names on one stone, and the six remaining names on the second stone, according to the order of their [a]birth. [11]You are to engrave the two stones with the names of the sons of Israel with the work of an [a]engraver in stone, like the engravings of a seal; you are to have them set in gold filigree settings. [12]You are to put the two stones on the shoulders of the ephod, stones of memorial for the sons of Israel, and [a]Aaron will bear their names before the LORD on his two shoulders for [b]a memorial. [13]You are to make filigree settings of gold [14]and two braided chains of pure gold, like a cord, and attach the chains to the settings.

[15]"You are to make a breastpiece for use in making decisions,[1] the work of an artistic designer; [a]you are to make it in the same fashion as the ephod; you are to make it of gold, blue, purple, scarlet, and fine twisted linen. [16]It is to be square when doubled, nine inches long and nine inches wide. [17]You are to set in it [a]a setting for stones, four rows of stones, a row with a ruby, a topaz, and a beryl—the first row; [18]and the second row, a turquoise, a sapphire, and an emerald; [19]and the third row, a jacinth, an agate, and an amethyst; [20]and the fourth row, a chrysolite, an onyx, and a jasper. They are to be enclosed in gold in their filigree settings. [21]The stones are to be for the names of the sons of Israel, twelve, according to the number of their names. Each name according to the twelve tribes is to be like the engravings of a seal.

[22]"You are to make for the breastpiece braided chains like cords of pure gold, [23]and you are to make for the breastpiece two gold rings and attach the two rings to the upper two ends of the breastpiece. [24]You are to attach the two gold chains to the two rings at the ends of the breastpiece; [25]the other two ends of the two chains you will attach to the two settings and then attach them to the shoulder pieces of the ephod at the front of it. [26]You are to make two rings of gold and put them on the other two ends of the breastpiece, on its edge that is on the inner side of the ephod. [27]You are

27:18 [1]Heb. *and the width 50* [cubits] *with 50.*   **27:20** [a]Exod 35:8, 28; Lev 24:1–4   **27:21** [a]Exod 26:31, 33   [b]Exod 30:8; 1 Sam 3:3; 2 Chr 13:11   [c]Exod 28:43; 29:9; Lev 3:17; 16:34; Num 18:23; 19:21; 1 Sam 30:25   **28:1** [a]Num 3:10; 18:7   [b]Ps 99:6; Heb 5:4   [c]Exod 24:1, 9; Lev 10:1   [d]Exod 6:23; Lev 10:6, 16   **28:2** [a]Exod 29:5, 29; 31:10; 39:1–31; Lev 8:7–9, 30   **28:3** [a]Exod 31:3; 35:30–31; Isa 11:2; Eph 1:17   [1]Heb. *wise of heart.*   **28:4** [a]Exod 28:15   [b]Exod 28:6   [c]Exod 28:31   [d]Exod 28:39   [e]Lev 8:7   **28:6** [a]Exod 39:2–7; Lev 8:7   **28:9** [a]Exod 35:27   **28:10** [a]Gen 29:31–30:24; 35:16–18   **28:11** [a]Exod 35:35   **28:12** [a]Exod 28:29–30; 39:6–7   [b]Lev 24:7; Num 31:54; Josh 4:7; Zech 6:14; 1 Cor 11:24   **28:15** [a]Exod 39:8–21   [1]Heb. *a breastpiece of decision.*   **28:17** [a]Exod 39:10

to make two more gold rings and attach them to the bottom of the two shoulder pieces on the front of the ephod, close to the juncture above the waistband of the ephod. [28]They are to tie the breastpiece by its rings to the rings of the ephod by blue cord, so that it may be above the waistband of the ephod, and so that the breastpiece will not be loose from the ephod. [29]Aaron will [a]bear the names of the sons of Israel in the breastpiece of decision over his heart when he goes into the Holy Place, for a memorial before the LORD continually.

[30]"You are to put the Urim and the Thummim into the breastpiece of decision; and they are to be over Aaron's heart when he goes in before the LORD. Aaron is to bear the decisions[1] of the Israelites over his heart before the LORD continually.

[31]"[a]You are to make the robe of the ephod completely blue. [32]There is to be an opening in its top in the center of it, with an edge all around the opening, the work of a weaver, like the opening of a collar, so that it cannot be torn. [33]You are to make pomegranates of blue, purple, and scarlet all around its hem and bells of gold between them all around. [34]The pattern is to be a gold bell and a pomegranate, a gold bell and a pomegranate, all around the hem of the robe. [35]The robe is to be on Aaron as he ministers, and his sound will be heard when he enters the Holy Place before the LORD and when he leaves, so that he does not die.

[36]"[a]You are to make a plate[1] of pure gold and engrave on it the way a seal is engraved: 'Holiness to the LORD.' [37]You are to attach to it a blue cord so that it will be on the turban; it is to be on the front of the turban. [38]It will be on Aaron's forehead, and Aaron will [a]bear the iniquity of the holy things, which the Israelites are to sanctify by all their holy gifts; it will always be on his forehead, for their [b]acceptance before the LORD. [39]You are to weave the tunic of fine linen and make the turban of fine linen, and make the sash the work of an embroiderer.

[40]"For Aaron's sons you are to make tunics, sashes, and headbands [a]for glory and for [b]beauty.

[41]"You are to clothe them—your brother Aaron and his sons with him—and [a]anoint them and ordain them and set them apart as holy, so that they may minister as my priests. [42]Make [a]for them linen undergarments to cover their naked bodies; they must cover from the waist to the thighs. [43]These must be on Aaron and his sons when [a]they enter the tent of meeting, or when they approach the altar to minister in the Holy Place, so that they bear no [b]iniquity and die. It is to be a perpetual ordinance for him and for his descendants[1] after him.

The Consecration of Aaron and His Sons

29 "Now this is what you are to do for them to consecrate them so that they may minister as my priests. [a]Take a young bull and two rams without blemish; [2]and bread made without [a]yeast, and perforated cakes without yeast mixed with oil, and wafers without yeast spread with oil—you are to make them using fine wheat flour. [3]You are to put them in one basket and present them in the basket, along with the bull and the two rams.

[4]"You are to present Aaron [a]and his sons at the entrance of the tent of meeting. You are to wash them with water [5]and take [a]the garments and [b]clothe Aaron with the tunic, the robe of the ephod, the ephod, and the breastpiece; you are to fasten the ephod on him by using the skillfully woven waistband. [6][a]You are to put the turban on his head and put the holy diadem on the turban. [7]You are to take the anointing [a]oil and pour it on his head and anoint him. [8]You are to present his sons and clothe them with tunics [9]and wrap [a]the sashes around Aaron and his sons[1] and put headbands on them, and so the ministry of priesthood will belong to them by a perpetual ordinance. Thus you are to [b]consecrate Aaron and his sons.

[10]"You are to present the bull at the front of the tent of meeting, and [a]Aaron and his

28:29 [a]Exod 28:12   **28:30** [1]Or judgment.   **28:31** [a]Exod 39:22–26   **28:36** [a]Exod 39:30–31; Lev 8:9; Zech 14:20   [1]Heb. a shining thing.   **28:38** [a]Exod 28:43; Lev 10:17; 22:9, 16; Num 18:1; [Isa 53:11]; Ezek 4:4–6; [John 1:29; Heb 9:28; 1 Pet 2:24] [b]Lev 1:4; 22:27; 23:11; Isa 56:7   **28:40** [a]Exod 28:4; 39:27–29, 41; Ezek 44:17–18   [b]Exod 28:2   **28:41** [a]Exod 29:7–9; 30:30; 40:15; Lev 10:7   **28:42** [a]Exod 39:28; Lev 6:10; 16:4; Ezek 44:18   **28:43** [a]Exod 20:26   [b]Exod 27:21; Lev 17:7   [1]Heb. seed.   **29:1** [a]Lev 8; [Heb 7:26–28]   **29:2** [a]Lev 2:4; 6:19–23   **29:4** [a]Exod 40:12; Lev 8:6; [Heb 10:22]   **29:5** [a]Exod 28:2; Lev 8:7 [b]Exod 28:8   **29:6** [a]Exod 28:36–37; Lev 8:9   **29:7** [a]Exod 25:6; 30:25–31; Lev 8:12; 10:7; 21:10; Num 35:25; Ps 133:2   **29:9** [a]Exod 40:15; Num 3:10; 18:7; 25:13; Deut 18:5   [b]Exod 28:41; Lev 8   [1]LXX omits Aaron and his sons.   **29:10** [a]Lev 1:4; 8:14

sons are to put their hands on the head of the bull. [11]You are to kill the bull before the LORD at the entrance to the tent of meeting [12]and take some of [a]the blood of the bull and put it on the horns of the altar with your finger; all the rest of the blood you are to pour [b]out at the base of the altar. [13]You are to take all the fat that covers the entrails, and the lobe that is above the liver, and the two kidneys and the fat that is on them, and burn them[1] on the altar. [14]But [a]the meat of the bull, its skin, and its dung you are to burn up outside the camp. It is the purification offering.

[15]"[a]You are to take one ram, and Aaron and his sons are to [b]lay their hands on the ram's head, [16]and you are to kill the ram and take its blood and [a]splash it all around on the altar. [17]Then you are to cut the ram into pieces and wash the entrails and its legs and put them on its pieces and on its head [18]and [a]burn[1] the whole ram on the altar. It is a burnt offering to the LORD, a soothing aroma; it is an offering made by fire to the LORD.

[19]"[a]You are to take the second ram, and Aaron and his sons are to lay their hands on the ram's head, [20]and you are to kill the ram and take some of its blood and put it on the tip of the right ear of Aaron, on the tip of the right ear of his sons, on the thumb of their right hand, and on the big toe of their right foot, and then splash the blood all around on the altar. [21]You are to take some of [a]the blood that is on [b]the altar and some of the anointing oil and sprinkle it on Aaron, on his garments, on his sons, and on his sons' garments with him, so that he may be holy, he and his garments along with his sons and his sons' garments.

[22]"You are to take from the ram the fat, the fat tail, the fat that covers the entrails, the lobe of the liver, the two kidneys and the fat that is on them, and the right thigh—for it is the ram for consecration—[23]and [a]one round flat cake of bread, one perforated cake of oiled bread, and one wafer from the basket of bread made without yeast that is before the LORD. [24]You are

to put all these in Aaron's hands and in his sons' hands, and you are to [a]wave them as a wave offering before the LORD. [25]Then [a]you are to take them from their hands and burn[1] them on the altar for a burnt offering, for a soothing aroma before the LORD. It is an offering made by fire to the LORD. [26]You are to take [a]the breast of the ram of Aaron's consecration; you are to wave it as a wave offering before the LORD, and it is to be your share. [27]You are to sanctify [a]the breast of the wave offering and the thigh of the contribution, which were waved and lifted up as a contribution from the ram of consecration, from what belongs to Aaron and to his sons. [28]It is to belong to Aaron and to his sons from the Israelites, [a]by a perpetual ordinance, for [b]it is a contribution. It is to be a contribution from the Israelites from their peace offerings, their contribution to the LORD.

[29]"The [a]holy garments that belong [b]to Aaron are to belong to his sons after him, so that they may be anointed in them and consecrated in them. [30][a]The priest who succeeds him from his sons, when he first comes to the tent of meeting to minister in the Holy Place, is to wear them for [b]seven days.

[31]"You are to take the ram of the consecration and [a]cook its meat in a holy place. [32]Aaron and his sons are to eat the meat of the ram and the [a]bread that was in the basket at the entrance of the tent of meeting. [33]They are to eat those things by which atonement was made to consecrate and to set them apart, but no one else may eat them, for [a]they are holy. [34]If any of the meat from the consecration offerings[1] or any of the bread is left over until morning, then [a]you are to burn up what is left over. It must not be eaten, because it is holy.

[35]"Thus you are to do for Aaron and for his sons according to all that I have commanded you; you are to consecrate them for [a]seven days. [36]Every day you are to prepare [a]a bull for a purification offering for atonement. [b]You are to purify the altar by making atonement for it, and you are to anoint it

29:12 [a] Lev 8:15   [b] Exod 27:2; 30:2; Lev 4:7   **29:13** [1] Heb. *turn* [them] *into sweet smoke.*   **29:14** [a] Lev 4:11–12, 21; Heb 13:11
29:15 [a] Lev 8:18   [b] Lev 1:4–9   **29:16** [a] Exod 24:6; Lev 1:5, 11   **29:18** [a] Exod 20:24   [1] Heb. *turn to sweet smoke.*   **29:19** [a] Lev
8:22   **29:21** [a] Exod 30:25, 31; Lev 8:30   [b] Exod 28:41; 29:1; [Heb 9:22]   **29:23** [a] Lev 8:26   **29:24** [a] Lev 7:30; 10:14
29:25 [a] Lev 8:28   [1] Heb. *turn to sweet smoke.*   **29:26** [a] Lev 7:31, 34; 8:29   **29:27** [a] Lev 7:31, 34; Num 18:11, 18; Deut 18:3
29:28 [a] Lev 10:15   [b] Lev 3:11; 7:34   **29:29** [a] Exod 28:2   [b] Exod 28:41; 30:30; Num 18:8   **29:30** [a] Num 20:28   [b] Lev 8:35
29:31 [a] Lev 8:31   **29:32** [a] Matt 12:4   **29:33** [a] Lev 10:14–15, 17   **29:34** [a] Exod 12:10; 23:18; 34:25; Lev 7:18; 8:32
[1] Or *ordination offerings*; Heb. *fillings.*   **29:35** [a] Lev 8:33–35   **29:36** [a] Heb 10:11   [b] Exod 30:26–29; 40:10–11

to set it apart as holy. [37]For seven days you are to make atonement for the altar and set it apart as holy. Then the altar will be most holy.[1] Anything that touches the altar will be holy.

[38]"Now this is what you are to prepare on the altar every day continually: [a]two lambs [b]a year old. [39]The first lamb you are to prepare [a]in the morning, and the second lamb you are to prepare around sundown.[1] [40]With the first lamb offer a tenth of an ephah of fine flour mixed with a fourth of a hin[1] of oil from pressed olives, and a fourth of a hin of wine as a drink offering. [41]The second lamb you are to [a]offer around sundown; you are to prepare for it the same meal offering as for the morning and the same drink offering, for a soothing aroma, an offering made by fire to the LORD.

[42]"This will be [a]a regular burnt offering throughout your generations at the entrance of the tent of meeting before the LORD, [b]where I will meet with you to speak to you there. [43]There I will meet with the Israelites, and it will be set apart as holy by my glory.

[44]"So I will set apart as [a]holy the tent of meeting and the altar, and I will set apart as holy Aaron and his sons that they may minister as priests to me. [45]I [a]will reside[1] among the Israelites, and I will [b]be their God, [46]and they [a]will know that I am the LORD their God, who [b]brought them out from the land of Egypt, so that I may reside among them. I am the LORD their God.

The Altar of Incense

30 "You are to make [a]an altar for burning incense; you are to make it of acacia wood. [2]Its length is to be 18 inches and its width 18 inches; it will be square. Its height is to be 36 inches, with its horns of one piece with it. [3]You are to overlay it with pure gold—its top, its four walls, and its horns—and make a surrounding border of gold for it. [4]You are to make two gold rings for it under its border, on its two flanks; you are to make them on its two sides. The rings will be places for poles to carry it with. [5]You are to make the poles of acacia wood and overlay them with gold.

[6]"You are to put it in front of the [a]curtain that is before the ark of the testimony (before the atonement lid that is over the testimony), where I will meet you. [7]Aaron is to burn [a]sweet incense on it morning by morning; [b]when he attends to the lamps he is to burn incense. [8]When Aaron sets up the lamps around sundown he is to burn incense on it; it is to be a regular incense offering before the LORD throughout your generations. [9]You must not offer [a]strange incense on it, nor burnt offering, nor meal offering, and you must not pour out a drink offering on it. [10a]Aaron is to make atonement on its horns once in the year with some of the blood of the sin offering for atonement; once in the year he is to make atonement on it throughout your generations. It is most holy to the LORD."

The Ransom Money

[11]The LORD spoke to Moses, [12]"When you take a census of the Israelites according to their number, then each man is to pay a ransom for his life to the LORD [a]when you number them, so [b]that there will be no [c]plague among them when you number them. [13]Everyone who crosses over to those who are numbered [a]is to [b]pay this: a half shekel according to [c]the shekel of the sanctuary (a shekel weighs 20 gerahs). The half shekel is to be an offering to the LORD. [14]Everyone who crosses over to those numbered, from twenty years old and up, is to pay an offering to the LORD. [15]The [a]rich are not to pay more and the poor are not to pay less than the half shekel when giving the offering of the LORD, to make atonement for your lives. [16]You are to receive the atonement money from the Israelites and give it for the service of the tent of meeting. It will be [a]a [b]memorial for the Israelites before the LORD, to make atonement for your lives."

29:37 [1]Or *holy of holies.* **29:38** [a]Num 28:3–31; 29:6–38; 1 Chr 16:40; Ezra 3:3 [b]Dan 12:11 **29:39** [a]Ezek 46:13–15 [1]Heb. *between the two evenings, between the two settings;* Tg. *between the two suns.* **29:40** [1]*Hin* is a transliterated Heb. word. **29:41** [a]1 Kgs 18:29, 36; 2 Kgs 16:15; Ezra 9:4–5; Ps 141:2 **29:42** [a]Exod 30:8 [b]Exod 25:22; 33:7, 9; Num 17:4 **29:44** [a]Lev 21:15 **29:45** [a]Exod 25:8; Lev 26:12; Num 5:3; Deut 12:11; Zech 2:10; [John 14:17, 23; Rev 21:3] [b]Gen 17:8; Lev 11:45 [1]This verb's root (Heb. *shakan*) is related to the dwelling place, or sanctuary, itself and to "the Shekinah glory." **29:46** [a]Exod 16:12; 20:2; Deut 4:35 [b]Lev 11:45 **30:1** [a]Exod 37:25–29 **30:6** [a]Exod 26:31–35 **30:7** [a]Exod 30:34; 1 Sam 2:28; 1 Chr 23:13; Luke 1:9 [b]Exod 27:20–21 **30:9** [a]Lev 10:1 **30:10** [a]Lev 16:3–34 **30:12** [a]Exod 38:25–26; Num 1:2; 26:2; 2 Sam 24:2 [b]Num 31:50; [Matt 20:28; 1 Pet 1:18–19] [c]2 Sam 24:15 **30:13** [a]Matt 17:24 [b]Lev 27:25; Num 3:47; Ezek 45:12 [c]Exod 38:26 **30:15** [a]Job 34:19; Prov 22:2; [Eph 6:9] **30:16** [a]Exod 38:25–31 [b]Num 16:40

The Bronze Laver

[17] The LORD spoke to Moses, [18] "You are also to make a large bronze basin with a bronze stand for washing. [a] You are to [b] put it between the tent of meeting and the altar and put water in it, [19] and Aaron and his sons must wash their hands and their feet from it. [20] When they enter the tent of meeting, they must wash with water so that they do not die. Also, when they approach the altar to minister by burning incense as an offering made by fire to the LORD, [21] they must wash their hands and their feet so that they do not die. And this will be a perpetual ordinance for them and for their descendants[1] throughout their generations."

Oil and Incense

[22] The LORD spoke to Moses, [23] "Take [a] choice spices: 12½ pounds[1] of free-flowing [b] myrrh, half that—about 6¼ pounds—of sweet-smelling cinnamon, 6¼ pounds of sweet-smelling [c] cane, [24] and 12½ pounds of [a] cassia, all weighed according to the sanctuary shekel, and four [b] quarts[1] of olive oil. [25] You [a] are to make this into a sacred anointing oil, a perfumed compound, the work of a perfumer. It will be sacred anointing oil.

[26] "With [a] it you are to anoint the tent of meeting, the ark of the testimony, [27] the table and all its utensils, the lampstand and its utensils, the altar of incense, [28] the altar for the burnt offering and all its utensils, and the laver and its base. [29] So you are to sanctify them, and they will be most holy;[1] anything that touches them will be holy.

[30] "You are to anoint Aaron [a] and his sons and sanctify them so that they may minister as my priests. [31] And you are to tell the Israelites: 'This is to be my sacred anointing oil throughout your generations. [32] It must not be applied to people's bodies, and you must not make any like [a] it with the same recipe. It is holy, and it must be holy to you. [33] Whoever makes perfume like it and [a] whoever puts any of it on someone not [b] a priest will be cut off from his people.'"

[34] The LORD said to Moses, "[a] Take spices, gum resin, onycha, galbanum, and pure frankincense of equal amounts [35] and make it into an incense, [a] a perfume, the work of a perfumer. It is to be finely ground,[1] and pure and sacred. [36] You are to beat some of it very fine and put some of it before the ark of the testimony in the tent of meeting [a] where [b] I will meet with you; it is to be most holy to you. [37] And the incense that [a] you are to make, you must not make for yourselves using the same recipe; it is to be most holy to you, belonging to the LORD. [38] [a] Whoever makes anything like it, to use as perfume, will be cut off from his people."

Willing Artisans

31 The LORD spoke to Moses, [2] "[a] See, I have chosen Bezalel [b] son of Uri, the son of Hur, of the tribe of Judah, [3] and I have [a] filled him with the Spirit of God in skill, in understanding, in knowledge, and in all kinds of craftsmanship, [4] to make artistic designs for work with gold, with silver, and with bronze, [5] and with cutting and setting stone, and with cutting wood, to work in all kinds of craftsmanship. [6] Moreover, I have also given him [a] Oholiab son of Ahisamach, of the tribe of Dan, and I have given ability to all the specially [b] skilled, that they may make everything I have commanded you: [7] the tent of meeting, [a] the ark of [b] the testimony, [c] the atonement lid that is on it, all the furnishings of the tent, [8] the table with its utensils, [a] the pure lampstand with all its utensils, [b] the altar of incense, [9] the altar for [a] the burnt offering with all its utensils, [b] the large basin with its base, [10] the woven garments, [a] the holy garments for Aaron the priest and the garments for his sons, to minister as priests, [11] the anointing oil, [a] and [b] sweet incense for the Holy Place. They will make all these things just as I have commanded you."

Sabbath Observance

[12] The LORD said to Moses, [13] "Tell the Israelites, '[a] Surely you must keep my Sabbaths,

30:18 [a] Exod 38:8; 1 Kgs 7:38   [b] Exod 40:30   30:21 [1] Heb. for his seed.   30:23 [a] Song 4:14; Ezek 27:22   [b] Ps 45:8; Prov 7:17   [c] Song 4:14; Jer 6:20   [1] Or 500 shekels.   30:24 [a] Ps 45:8   [b] Exod 29:40   [1] Or a hin.   30:25 [a] Exod 37:29; 40:9; Lev 8:10; Num 35:25; Ps 89:20; 133:2   30:26 [a] Exod 40:9; Lev 8:10; Num 7:1   30:29 [1] Or holy of holies.   30:30 [a] Exod 29:7; Lev 8:12   30:32 [a] Exod 30:25, 37   30:33 [a] Exod 30:38   [b] Gen 17:14; Exod 12:15; Lev 7:20–21   30:34 [a] Exod 25:6; 37:29   30:35 [a] Exod 30:25   [1] Heb. salted.   30:36 [a] Exod 29:42; Lev 16:2   [b] [Exod 29:37; 30:32]; Lev 2:3   30:37 [a] Exod 30:32   30:38 [a] Exod 30:33   31:2 [a] Exod 35:30—36:1   [b] 1 Chr 2:20   31:3 [a] Exod 28:3; 35:31; 1 Kgs 7:14; Eph 1:17   31:6 [a] Exod 35:34   [b] Exod 28:3; 35:10, 35; 36:1   31:7 [a] Exod 36:8   [b] Exod 37:1–5   [c] Exod 37:6–9   31:8 [a] Exod 37:10–16   [b] Exod 37:17–24; Lev 24:4   31:9 [a] Exod 38:1–7   [b] Exod 38:8   31:10 [a] Exod 39:1, 41   31:11 [a] Exod 30:23–33   [b] Exod 30:34–38   31:13 [a] Exod 31:17; Lev 19:3, 30; 26:2; Ezek 20:12, 20

for it is a sign between me and you through-out your generations, that you may know that I am the LORD who [b]sanctifies you. [14]So [a]you must keep the Sabbath, for it is holy for you. Everyone [b]who defiles it must sure-ly be put to death; indeed, if anyone does any work on it, then that person will be cut off from among his people. [15a]Six days work may be done, but on the [b]seventh day is a Sabbath of complete rest, holy to the LORD; anyone who does work on the Sabbath day must surely be put to death. [16]The Israelites must keep the Sabbath by observing the Sabbath throughout their generations as a perpetual covenant. [17]It is [a]a sign between me and the Israelites forever; for [b]in six days the LORD made the heavens and the earth, and on the seventh day he rested and was refreshed.'"

[18]He gave Moses [a]two tablets of testimo-ny when he had finished speaking with him on Mount Sinai, tablets of stone written by the finger of God.

The Sin of the Golden Calf

32 When the people saw that Moses [a]delayed[1] in coming down from [b]the mountain, they gathered around Aaron and said to him, "Get [c]up, make us gods that will [d]go before us. As for this fellow Moses, the man who [e]brought us up from the land of Egypt, we do not know what has become of him!"

[2]So Aaron said to them, "Break off the [a]gold earrings that are on the ears of your wives, your sons, and your daughters, and bring them to me." [3]So all the people broke off the gold earrings that were on their ears and brought them to Aaron. [4]He accept-ed the gold from them, fashioned it with [a]an engraving tool, and made a molten calf. Then they said, "These are your gods,[1] [b]O Israel, who brought you up out of Egypt."

[5]When Aaron saw this, he built an altar before it, and Aaron made a [a]proclamation and said, "Tomorrow will be a feast to the

LORD." [6]So they got up early on the next day and offered up burnt offerings and brought peace offerings, and the people [a]sat down to eat and drink, and they rose up to play.

[7]The LORD spoke to Moses, "[a]Go quickly, descend, because your people, whom you brought up from the land of Egypt, [b]have acted corruptly. [8]They have [a]quickly turned aside from the way that [b]I commanded them—they have made for themselves a molten calf and have bowed down to it and sacrificed to it and said, 'These are your gods, O Israel, which brought you up from the land of Egypt.'"

[9]Then the LORD [a]said to Moses, "I have seen this people. Look what a stiff-necked people they are! [10]So now, leave me alone so that [a]my anger can burn [b]against them and I can destroy them, and I will make from you a great nation."

[11]But Moses sought [a]the favor of the LORD his God and said, "O LORD, why does your anger burn against your people, whom you have brought out from the land of Egypt with great power and with a mighty hand? [12a]Why should the Egyptians say, 'For evil[1] he led them out to kill them in the moun-tains and to destroy them from the face of the earth'? Turn from your burning anger, and [b]relent of this evil against your peo-ple. [13]Remember Abraham, Isaac, and Israel your servants, to whom you [a]swore by your-self and told them, '[b]I will multiply your descendants[1] like the stars of heaven, and all this land that I have spoken about I will give to your descendants,[2] and they will in-herit it forever.'" [14]Then the LORD [a]relented over the evil that he had said he would do to his people.

[15a]Moses turned and went down from the mountain with the two tablets of the testi-mony in his hands. The tablets were written on both sides—they were written on the front and on the back. [16]Now the [a]tablets were the work of God, and the writing was the writing of God, engraved on the tablets.

31:13 [b]Lev 20:8   **31:14** [a]Exod 20:8; Deut 5:12   [b]Exod 31:15; 35:2; Num 15:32–36; John 7:23   **31:15** [a]Exod 20:9–11; Lev 23:3; Deut 5:12–14   [b]Gen 2:2; Exod 16:23; 20:8; 35:2   **31:17** [a]Exod 31:13; Ezek 20:12   [b]Gen 1:31; 2:2–3; Exod 20:11   **31:18** [a][Exod 24:12; 32:15–16; Deut 4:13; 5:22; 2 Cor 3:3]   **32:1** [a]Exod 24:18; Deut 9:9–12   [b]Exod 17:1–3   [c]Acts 7:40   [d]Exod 13:21   [e]Exod 32:8   [1]Heb. *caused shame*; i.e., disappointment.   **32:2** [a]Exod 11:2; 35:22; Judg 8:24–27   **32:4** [a]Exod 20:3–4, 23; Deut 9:16; Judg 17:3–4; 1 Kgs 12:28; Neh 9:18; Ps 106:19; Acts 7:41   [b]Exod 29:45–46   [1]Or perhaps *This is your god.*   **32:5** [a]Lev 23:2, 4, 21, 37; 2 Kgs 10:20; 2 Chr 30:5   **32:6** [a]Exod 32:17–19; Num 25:2; 1 Cor 10:7   **32:7** [a]Deut 9:8–21; Dan 9:14   [b]Gen 6:11–12   **32:8** [a]Exod 20:3–4, 23; Deut 32:17   [b]1 Kgs 12:28   **32:9** [a]Exod 33:3, 5; 34:9; Deut 9:6; 2 Chr 30:8; Isa 48:4; [Acts 7:51]   **32:10** [a]Exod 22:24   [b]Num 14:12   **32:11** [a]Deut 9:18, 26–29   **32:12** [a]Num 14:13–19; Deut 9:28; Josh 7:9   [b]Exod 32:14   [1]I.e., that which hinders, interrupts, causes pain to, or destroys life.   **32:13** [a]Gen 22:16–18; [Heb 6:13]   [b]Gen 12:7; 13:15; 15:7, 18; 22:17; 26:4; 35:11–12; Exod 13:5, 11; 33:1   [1]Heb. *your seed.*   [2]Heb. *seed.*   **32:14** [a]2 Sam 24:16   **32:15** [a]Deut 9:15   **32:16** [a]Exod 31:18

[17] When Joshua heard the noise of the people as they shouted, he said to Moses, "It is the sound of war in the camp!" [18] Moses said, "It is not the sound of those who shout for victory, nor is it the sound of those who cry because they are overcome, but the sound of singing I hear."

[19] When [a] he approached the camp and saw the calf and the dancing, Moses became extremely angry. He threw the tablets from his hands and broke them to pieces at the bottom of the mountain. [20] He took [a] the calf they had made and burned it in the fire, ground it to powder, poured it out on the water, and made the Israelites drink it.

[21] Moses said to Aaron, "[a] What did this people do to you, that you have brought on them so great a sin?" [22] Aaron said, "Do not let [a] your anger burn hot, my lord; you know these people, that they tend to evil. [23] They said to me, 'Make us gods that will go before us, for as for this fellow Moses, the man who brought us up out of the land of Egypt, we do not know what has happened to him.' [24] So I said to them, 'Whoever has gold, break it off.' So they gave it to me, and I threw it into the fire, and this calf came out."

[25] Moses saw that the people were running [a] wild,[1] for Aaron [b] had let them get completely out of control, causing derision from their enemies. [26] So Moses stood at the entrance of the camp and said, "Whoever is for the LORD, come to me." All the Levites gathered around him, [27] and he said to them, "This is what the LORD, the God of Israel, has said 'Each man fasten his sword on his side, and go back and forth from entrance to entrance throughout the camp, and each one kill his brother, his friend, and his neighbor.'"

[28] The Levites did what Moses ordered, and that day about 3,000 men of the people died. [29] Moses said, "You have been consecrated today for [a] the LORD, for each of you was against his son or against his brother, so he has given a blessing to you today."

[30] The next day Moses said to the people, "[a] You have committed a very serious sin, but now I will go up to the LORD—[b] perhaps I can [c] make atonement on behalf of your sin."

[31] So Moses [a] returned to the LORD and said, "Alas, this people has committed a very serious sin, and they have [b] made for themselves gods of gold. [32] But now, if you will forgive their sin..., but if not, [a] wipe me [b] out[1] from your book that you have written." [33] The LORD said to Moses, "[a] Whoever has sinned against me—that person I will wipe [b] out of my book. [34] So now go, lead the people to the place I have [a] spoken to you about. [b] See, my angel will go before you. But on the day that [c] I [d] punish, I will indeed punish them for their sin."

[35] And the LORD sent [a] a plague on the people because they had made the calf— the one Aaron made.

33

The LORD said to Moses, "Go up from here, you [a] and the people whom you brought up out of the land of Egypt, [b] to the land I promised on oath to Abraham, to Isaac, and to Jacob, saying, 'I will give it to your descendants.'[1] [2] I will send [a] an angel before you, [b] and I will drive out the Canaanite, the Amorite, the Hittite, the Perizzite, the Hivite, and the Jebusite. [3] Go up [a] to a land [b] flowing with milk and honey. But I will not go up among you, for you are a [c] stiff-necked people, and I might destroy you on the way."

[4] When [a] the people heard this troubling word they mourned; no one put on his ornaments. [5] For the LORD had said to Moses, "Tell the Israelites, 'You are a stiff-necked people. If I went up among you for a moment, I might destroy you. Now take off your ornaments that I may [a] know what I should do to you.'" [6] So the Israelites stripped off their ornaments by Mount Horeb.

The Presence of the Lord

[7] Moses took the tent and pitched it outside the camp, at a good distance from the camp, and he [a] called it the tent of meeting. Anyone [b] seeking the LORD would go out to the tent of meeting that was outside the camp.

32:19 [a] Deut 9:16–17   32:20 [a] Num 5:17, 24; Deut 9:21   32:21 [a] Gen 26:10   32:22 [a] Exod 14:11; Deut 9:24   32:25 [a] Exod 33:4–5 [b] 2 Chr 28:19 [1] Or *let loose, lack restraint.*   32:29 [a] Exod 28:41; 1 Sam 15:18, 22; Prov 21:3; Zech 13:3   32:30 [a] 1 Sam 12:20, 23 [b] 2 Sam 16:12 [c] Num 25:13   32:31 [a] Deut 9:18 [b] Exod 20:23   32:32 [a] Ps 69:28; Isa 4:3; Mal 3:16; Rom 9:3 [b] Dan 12:1; Phil 4:3; Rev 3:5; 21:27 [1] Trad. *blot.*   32:33 [a] Lev 23:30; [Ezek 18:4; 33:2, 14, 15] [b] Exod 17:14; Deut 29:20; Ps 9:5; Rev 3:5; 21:27   32:34 [a] Exod 3:17 [b] Exod 23:20; Josh 5:14 [c] Deut 32:35; Rom 2:5–6 [d] Ps 89:32   32:35 [a] Neh 9:18   33:1 [a] Exod 32:1, 7, 13; Josh 3:17 [b] Gen 12:7 [1] Heb. *seed.*   33:2 [a] Exod 32:34; Josh 5:14 [b] Exod 23:27–31; Josh 24:11   33:3 [a] Exod 3:8 [b] Num 16:21, 45 [c] Exod 32:9; 33:5   33:4 [a] Num 14:1, 39   33:5 [a] [Ps 139:23]   33:7 [a] Exod 29:42–43 [b] Deut 4:29

[8]And when Moses went out to the tent, all the people would get up and stand [a]at the entrance to their tents and watch Moses until he entered the tent. [9]And whenever Moses entered the tent, the pillar of cloud would descend and stand at the entrance of the tent, and the LORD would [a]speak with Moses. [10]When all the people would see the pillar of cloud standing at the entrance of the tent, all the people, each one at the entrance of his own tent, would rise and [a]worship. [11]The LORD would speak to Moses face to face, [a]the way a person speaks to a friend. Then Moses would return to the camp, but [b]his servant, Joshua son of Nun, a young man, did not leave the tent.

[12]Moses said to the LORD, "See, [a]you have been [b]saying to me, 'Bring this people up,' but you have not let me know whom you will send with me. But you said, 'I know you by name, and also you have found favor in my sight.' [13]Now [a]if I have found favor in your sight, [b]show me[1] [c]your way, that I may know you, that I may continue to find favor in your sight. And see that this nation is your people."

[14]And the LORD said, "[a]My presence will go with you, and I will give you [b]rest."

[15]And Moses said to him, "[a]If your presence does not go[1] with us, do not take us up from here. [16]For how will it be known then that I have found favor in your sight, I and your people? Is it not by your going with us, so that we will be distinguished, I and your people, from [a]all the people who are on the face of the earth?"

[17]The LORD [a]said to Moses, "I will do this thing also that you have requested, for you have found favor in my sight, and I know you by name."

[18]And Moses said, "Show me [a]your glory."

[19]And the LORD said, "I will make all my [a]goodness pass before your face, and [b]I will proclaim the LORD by name before you; I will be [c]gracious to whom I will be gracious; I will show mercy to whom I will show mercy." [20]But he added, "You [a]cannot see my face, for no one can see me and live." [21]The LORD said, "Here is a place by me; you will station yourself on a rock. [22]When my glory passes by, [a]I will put you in a cleft in the rock and will [b]cover you with my hand while I pass by. [23]Then I will take away my hand, and you will see my back, but my face must [a]not be seen."

The New Tablets of the Covenant

34 The LORD said to Moses, "Cut [a]out two tablets of stone [b]like the first, and I will write on the tablets the words that were on the first tablets, which you smashed. [2]Be prepared in the morning, and go up in the morning to Mount Sinai, and [a]station yourself for me there on the top of the mountain. [3]No one is to [a]come up with you; do not let anyone be seen anywhere on the mountain; not even the flocks or the herds may graze in front of that mountain." [4]So Moses cut out two tablets of stone like the first; early in the morning he went up to Mount Sinai, just as the LORD had commanded him, and he took in his hand the two tablets of stone.

[5]The LORD descended in the [a]cloud and stood with him there and [b]proclaimed the LORD by name. [6]The LORD passed by before him and proclaimed: "The LORD, the LORD, the compassionate and gracious [a]God, slow to anger, and abounding in loyal [b]love and [c]faithfulness, [7a]keeping loyal love for thousands, [b]forgiving iniquity and transgression and sin. But he [c]by no means leaves the guilty unpunished, responding to the transgression of fathers by dealing with children and children's children, to the third and fourth generation."

[8]Moses quickly [a]bowed to the ground and worshiped [9]and said, "If now I have found favor in your sight, O Lord, [a]let my Lord go among us, for we are a [b]stiff-necked people; pardon [c]our iniquity and our sin, and take us for your inheritance."

[10]He [a]said, "See, I am going to make a covenant before all your people. I will [b]do

33:8 [a] Num 16:27   **33:9** [a] Exod 25:22; 31:18; Ps 99:7   **33:10** [a] Exod 4:31   **33:11** [a] Num 12:8; Deut 34:10   [b] Exod 24:13   **33:12** [a] Exod 3:10; 32:34   [b] Exod 33:17; John 10:14–15; 2 Tim 2:19   **33:13** [a] Exod 34:9   [b] Ps 25:4; 27:11; 86:11; 119:33   [c] Exod 3:7, 10; 5:1; 32:12, 14; Deut 9:26, 29   [1] Heb. *show me, reveal to me, teach or inform me.*   **33:14** [a] Exod 3:12; Deut 4:37; Isa 63:9   [b] Deut 12:10; 25:19; Josh 21:44; 22:4   **33:15** [a] Exod 33:3   [1] I.e., a continual going of the presence.   **33:16** [a] Exod 34:10; Deut 4:7, 34   **33:17** [a] [Jas 5:16]   **33:18** [a] Exod 24:16–17; [1 Tim 6:16]   **33:19** [a] Exod 34:6–7   [b] [Rom 9:15–16, 18]   [c] [Rom 4:4, 16]   **33:20** [a] [Gen 32:30]   **33:22** [a] Song 2:14; Isa 2:21   [b] Ps 91:1, 4; Isa 49:2; 51:16   **33:23** [a] Exod 33:20; [John 1:18]   **34:1** [a] [Exod 24:12; 31:18; 32:15–16, 19; Deut 4:13]   [b] Deut 10:2, 4   **34:2** [a] Exod 19:11, 18, 20   **34:3** [a] Exod 19:12–13; 24:9–11   **34:5** [a] Exod 19:9   [b] Exod 33:19   **34:6** [a] Num 14:18; Deut 4:31; Neh 9:17; Joel 2:13   [b] Rom 2:4   [c] Ps 108:4   **34:7** [a] Exod 20:6   [b] Ps 103:3–4; Dan 9:9; Eph 4:32; 1 John 1:9   [c] Josh 24:19; Job 10:14; Mic 6:11; Nah 1:3   **34:8** [a] Exod 4:31   **34:9** [a] Exod 33:12–16   [b] Exod 33:3   [c] Ps 33:12; 94:14   **34:10** [a] Exod 34:27–28; Deut 5:2   [b] Deut 4:32; Ps 77:14

wonders such as have not been done in all the earth, nor in c any nation. All the people among whom you live will see the work of the LORD, for it is a fearful thing that I am doing with you.

11 "a Obey what b I am commanding you this day. I am going to drive out before you the Amorite, the Canaanite, the Hittite, the Perizzite, the Hivite, and the Jebusite. 12 Be careful not to make a a covenant with the inhabitants of the land where you are going, lest it become a snare among you. 13 Rather you must a destroy their altars, smash their images, and b cut down their Asherah poles.1 14 For you must a not worship any other god, for the LORD, whose b name is c Jealous, is a jealous God. 15 Be careful not to make a a covenant with the inhabitants of the land, for when they prostitute themselves1 to their gods and sacrifice to their gods, and someone b invites you, you will c eat from his sacrifice; 16 and you then take a his daughters for your sons, and when his daughters prostitute themselves to their gods, they will make your sons prostitute themselves to their gods as well. 17 You must not make a yourselves molten gods.

18 "You must keep the Feast of a Unleavened Bread. For seven days you must eat bread made without yeast, as I commanded you; do this at the appointed time of the b month Abib, for in the month Abib you came out of Egypt.

19 "Every firstborn of the womb belongs to me, even a every firstborn of your cattle that is a male, whether ox or sheep. 20 Now a the firstling of a donkey you may redeem with a lamb, but if you do not redeem it, then break its neck. You must redeem all the firstborn of your sons.

"No one will appear before me b empty-handed.

21 "On a six days you may labor, but on the seventh day you must rest; even at the time of plowing and of harvest you are to rest.

22 "You must observe the Feast of Weeks— the firstfruits of the harvest of wheat—and the Feast of Ingathering at the end of the year. 23 At a three times in the year all your men must appear before the Sovereign LORD, the God of Israel. 24 For I will drive out the nations before you and enlarge your borders; no one will covet your land when you go up to appear before the LORD your God three times in the year.

25 "You must not offer the blood of my sacrifice with yeast; the sacrifice from the Feast of Passover must not remain until the following morning.

26 "The first of a the firstfruits of your soil you must bring to the house of the LORD your God.

"You must not cook a young goat in its mother's milk."

27 The LORD said to Moses, "Write down a these words, for in accordance with these words I have made a covenant with you and with Israel." 28 a So b he was there with the LORD 40 days and 40 nights; he did not eat bread, and he did not drink water. He wrote on the tablets the words of the covenant, the Ten Commandments.1

The Radiant Face of Moses

29 Now when Moses came down from Mount Sinai with the a two tablets of b the testimony in his hand—when he came down from the mountain, Moses did not know that the skin of his face shone1 while he talked with him. 30 When Aaron and all the Israelites saw Moses, the skin of his face shone,1 and they were afraid to approach him. 31 But Moses called to them, so Aaron and all the leaders of the community came back to him, and Moses spoke to them. 32 After this all the Israelites approached, a and he commanded them all that the LORD had spoken to him on Mount Sinai. 33 When Moses finished a speaking with them, he would put a veil on his face. 34 But a when Moses went in before the LORD to speak with him, he would remove the veil until he came out. Then he would come out and tell the Israelites what he had

34:10 c Ps 145:6   34:11 a Deut 6:25   b Exod 23:20–33; 33:2; Josh 11:23   34:12 a Exod 23:32–33   34:13 a Exod 23:24; Deut 12:3   b Deut 16:21; Judg 6:25–26; 2 Kgs 18:4; 2 Chr 34:3–4   1 Or images of Asherah.   34:14 a [Exod 20:3–5]   b [Isa 9:6; 57:15]   c [Exod 20:5; Deut 4:24]   34:15 a Judg 2:17   b Num 25:1–2; Deut 32:37–38   c 1 Cor 8:4, 7, 10   1 Heb. to play the prostitute, to commit whoredom; to be a harlot.   34:16 a Gen 28:1; Deut 7:3; Josh 23:12–13; 1 Kgs 11:2; Ezra 9:2; Neh 13:25   34:17 a Exod 20:4, 23; 32:8; Lev 19:4; Deut 5:8   34:18 a Exod 12:15–16   b Exod 12:2; 13:4   34:19 a Exod 13:2; 22:29   34:20 a Exod 13:13   b Exod 22:29; 23:15; Deut 16:16   34:21 a Exod 20:9; 23:12; 31:15; 35:2; Lev 23:3; Deut 5:13   34:23 a Exod 23:14–17   34:26 a Exod 23:19; Deut 26:2   34:27 a Exod 17:14; 24:4; Deut 31:9   34:28 a Exod 24:18   b Exod 34:1, 4; Deut 4:31; 10:2, 4   1 Heb. the ten words.   34:29 a Exod 32:15   b Matt 17:2; 2 Cor 3:7   1 In the sense of a ray of light.   34:30 1 A surprising or sudden action.   34:32 a Exod 24:3   34:33 a [2 Cor 3:13–14]   34:34 a [2 Cor 3:13–16]

been commanded. [35]When the Israelites would see the face of Moses, that the skin of Moses' face shone, Moses would put the veil on his face again, until he went in to speak with the LORD.

Sabbath Regulations

35 Moses assembled [a]the whole community of the Israelites and said to them, "These are the things that the LORD has commanded you to do. [2]In [a]six days work may be done, but on the seventh day there must be a holy day for you, a Sabbath of complete rest to the LORD. Anyone who does work on it will be put to [b]death. [3]You must not kindle a fire in any of [a]your homes on the Sabbath day."

Willing Workers

[4]Moses spoke to the whole community of the Israelites, "[a]This is the word that the LORD has commanded: [5]Take an offering for the LORD. Let [a]everyone who has a willing heart bring an offering to the LORD: [b]gold, silver, bronze; [6a]blue, purple, and scarlet yarn; fine linen; goats' [b]hair; [7]ram skins dyed red; fine leather; acacia wood; [8]olive oil for the light; spices for the anointing oil [a]and for the fragrant incense; [9]onyx stones, and other gems for mounting on the ephod and the breastpiece. [10]Every skilled person among you is to come and make [a]all that the LORD has commanded: [11a]the tabernacle with its tent, its covering, its clasps, its frames, its crossbars, its posts, and its bases; [12]the ark, with its poles, [a]the atonement lid, and the special curtain that conceals it; [13]the [a]table with its poles [b]and all its vessels, and the Bread of the Presence; [14]the lampstand for [a]the light and its accessories, its lamps, and oil for the light; [15]and [a]the altar of incense with its poles, [b]the anointing oil, and [c]the fragrant incense; the hanging for the door at the entrance of the tabernacle; [16]the altar for [a]the burnt offering with its bronze grating that is on it, its poles, and all its utensils; the large basin and its pedestal; [17]the hangings of [a]the courtyard, its posts and its bases, and the curtain for the gateway to the courtyard; [18]tent pegs for the tabernacle and tent pegs for the courtyard and their ropes; [19]the woven garments for serving in [a]the Holy Place, the holy garments for Aaron the priest, and the garments for his sons to minister as priests.'"

[20]So the whole community of the Israelites went out from the presence of Moses. [21]Everyone [a]whose heart stirred him to action and everyone whose spirit was willing came and [b]brought the offering for the LORD for the work of the tent of meeting, for all its service, and for the holy garments.[1] [22]They came, men and women alike, all who had willing hearts. They brought brooches, [a]earrings, rings and ornaments, all kinds of gold [b]jewelry, and everyone came who waved a wave offering of gold to the LORD. [23]Everyone who had blue, purple, or scarlet yarn, fine linen, goats' hair, ram skins dyed red, or fine leather brought them. [24]Everyone making an offering of silver or bronze brought it as an offering to the LORD, and everyone who had acacia wood for any work of the service brought it. [25]Every woman who was [a]skilled[1]spun with her hands and brought what she had spun, blue, purple, or scarlet yarn, or fine linen, [26]and all the women whose heart stirred them to action and who were skilled spun goats' hair.

[27]The leaders brought onyx stones and [a]other gems to be mounted for the ephod and the breastpiece, [28]and [a]spices and olive oil for the light, for the anointing oil, and for the fragrant incense.

[29]The Israelites brought a [a]freewill offering to the LORD, every man and woman whose heart was willing to bring materials for all the work that the LORD through Moses had commanded them to do.

[30]Moses said to [a]the Israelites, "See, the LORD has chosen Bezalel son of Uri, the son of Hur, of the tribe of Judah. [31]He has filled him with the Spirit of God—with skill, with understanding, with knowledge, and in all kinds of work— [32]to design artistic designs, to work in gold, in silver, and in bronze,

35:1 [a]Exod 34:32   **35:2** [a]Exod 20:9–10; Lev 23:3; Deut 5:13   [b]Num 15:32–36   **35:3** [a]Exod 12:16; 16:23   **35:4** [a]Exod 25:1–2   **35:5** [a]Exod 25:2; 1 Chr 29:14; Mark 12:41–44; 2 Cor 8:10–12; 9:7   [b]Exod 38:24   **35:6** [a]Exod 36:8   [b]Exod 36:14   **35:8** [a]Exod 25:6; 30:23–25   **35:10** [a]Exod 31:2–6; 36:1–2   **35:11** [a]Exod 26:1–2; 36:14   **35:12** [a]Exod 25:10–22   **35:13** [a]Exod 25:23   [b]Exod 25:30; Lev 24:5–6   **35:14** [a]Exod 25:31   **35:15** [a]Exod 30:1   [b]Exod 30:25   [c]Exod 30:34–38   **35:16** [a]Exod 27:1–8   **35:17** [a]Exod 27:9–18   **35:19** [a]Exod 31:10; 39:1, 41   **35:21** [a]Exod 25:2; 35:5, 22, 26, 29; 36:2   [b]Exod 35:24   [1]Lit. *the garments of holiness.*   **35:22** [a]Exod 32:2–3   [b]Exod 11:2; Ezra 2:68   **35:25** [a]Exod 28:3; 31:6; 36:1   [1]Heb. *wisdom of heart.*   **35:27** [a]1 Chr 29:6;   **35:28** [a]Exod 30:23   **35:29** [a]Exod 35:5, 21; 36:3; 1 Chr 29:9   **35:30** [a]Exod 31:1–6

[33] and in cutting stones for their setting, and in cutting wood, to do work in every artistic craft. [34] And he has put it in his heart to teach, he and [a]Oholiab son of Ahisamach, of the tribe of Dan. [35] He has [a]filled them with skill[1] to do all kinds of work as craftsmen, as designers, as embroiderers in blue, purple, and scarlet yarn and in fine linen, and as weavers. They are craftsmen in all the work and artistic designers.

36 [1] So Bezalel and Oholiab and every [a]skilled person in whom the LORD has put skill and ability to know how to do all the work for the service of the [b]sanctuary are to do the work according to all that the LORD has commanded."

[2] Moses summoned Bezalel and Oholiab and every skilled person in whom the LORD had put skill—everyone [a]whose heart stirred him to volunteer to do the work. [3] They received from Moses all the [a]offerings the Israelites [b]had brought to do the work for the service of the sanctuary, and they still continued to bring him a freewill offering each morning. [4] So all the skilled people who were doing all the work on the sanctuary came from the work they were doing [5] and told Moses, "[a]The people are bringing much more than is needed for the completion of the work which the LORD commanded us to do!"

[6] Moses instructed them to take his message throughout the camp, saying, "Let no man or woman do anymore work for the offering for the sanctuary." So the people were restrained from bringing any more. [7] Now the materials were more [a]than enough for them to do all the work.

The Building of the Tabernacle

[8] All [a]the skilled among those who were doing the work made the tabernacle with ten curtains of fine twisted linen and blue and purple and scarlet yarn; they were made with cherubim that were the work of an artistic designer. [9] The length of one curtain was 42 feet, and the width of one curtain was 6 feet—the same size for each of the curtains. [10] He joined[1] five of the curtains to one another, and the other five curtains he joined to one another. [11] He made loops of blue material along the edge of the end curtain in the first set; he did the same along the edge of the end curtain in the second set. [12] He made [a]50 loops on the first curtain, and he made 50 loops on the end curtain that was in the second set, with the loops opposite one another. [13] He made 50 gold clasps and joined the curtains together to one another with the clasps, so that the tabernacle was a unit.

[14] He made curtains of goats' hair for a tent over [a]the tabernacle; he made 11 curtains. [15] The length of one curtain was 45 feet, and the width of one curtain was 6 feet—one size for all 11 curtains. [16] He joined five curtains by themselves and six curtains by themselves. [17] He made 50 loops along the edge of the end curtain in the first set and 50 loops along the edge of the curtain that joined the second set. [18] He made 50 bronze clasps to join the tent together so that it might be a unit. [19] He made a covering for [a]the tent out of ram skins dyed red and over that a covering of fine leather.

[20] He made [a]the frames[1] for the tabernacle of acacia wood as uprights. [21] The length of each frame was 15 feet, the width of each frame was 2¼ feet, [22] with two projections per frame parallel one to another. He made all the frames of the tabernacle in this way. [23] So he made frames for the tabernacle: 20 frames for the south side. [24] He made 40 silver bases under the 20 frames—two bases under the first frame for its two projections, and likewise two bases under the next frame for its two projections, [25] and for the second side of the tabernacle, the north side, he made 20 frames [26] and their 40 silver bases, two bases under the first frame and two bases under the next frame. [27] And for the back of the tabernacle on the west he made six frames. [28] He made two frames for the corners of the tabernacle on the back. [29] At the two corners they were doubled at the lower end and finished together at the top in one ring. So he did for both. [30] So there were eight frames and their silver bases, 16 bases, two bases under each frame.

[31] He made [a]bars of acacia wood, five for the frames on one side of the tabernacle [32] and five bars for the frames on the second side of the tabernacle, and five bars for the

---

35:34 [a] Exod 31:6   **35:35** [a] Exod 31:3, 6; 35:31; 1 Kgs 7:14; 2 Chr 2:14; Isa 28:26   [1] Heb. *wisdom of heart.*   **36:1** [a] Exod 28:3; 31:6; 35:10, 35   [b] Exod 25:8   **36:2** [a] Exod 35:21, 26; 1 Chr 29:5, 9, 17   **36:3** [a] Exod 35:5   [b] Exod 35:27   **36:5** [a] 2 Chr 24:14; 31:6–10; [2 Cor 8:2–3]   **36:7** [a] 1 Kgs 8:64   **36:8** [a] Exod 26:1–14   **36:10** [1] Or *they joined.*   **36:12** [a] Exod 26:5   **36:14** [a] Exod 26:7   **36:19** [a] Exod 26:14   **36:20** [a] Exod 26:15–29   [1] Or *boards, planks, beams.*   **36:31** [a] Exod 26:26–29

frames of the tabernacle for the back side on the west. [33]He made the middle bar to reach from end to end in the center of the frames. [34]He overlaid the frames with gold and made their rings of gold to provide places for the bars, and he overlaid the bars with gold.

[35]He [a]made the special curtain of blue, purple, and scarlet yarn and fine twisted linen; he made it with cherubim, the work of an artistic designer. [36]He made for it four posts of acacia wood and overlaid them with gold, with gold hooks, and he cast for them four silver bases.

[37]He made a [a]hanging for the entrance of the tent of blue, purple, and scarlet yarn and fine twisted linen, the work of an embroiderer, [38]and its five posts and their hooks. He overlaid their tops[1] and their bands with gold, but their five bases were bronze.

The Making of the Ark

37 [a]Bezalel made [b]the ark of acacia wood; its length was 45 inches, its width 27 inches, and its height 27 inches. [2]He overlaid it with pure gold, inside and out, and he made a surrounding border of gold for it. [3]He cast four gold rings for it that he put on its four feet, with two rings on one side and two rings on the other side. [4]He made poles of acacia wood, overlaid them with gold, [5]and put the poles into the rings on the sides of the ark in order to carry the ark.

[6]He made an atonement lid of pure gold; its length was 45 inches, and its width was 27 inches. [7]He made two cherubim of gold; he made them of hammered metal on the two ends of the atonement lid, [8]one cherub on one end and one cherub on the other end. He made the cherubim from the atonement lid on its two ends. [9]The cherubim were spreading their wings upward, overshadowing the atonement lid with their wings. The cherubim faced each other, looking toward the atonement lid.

The Making of the Table

[10]Bezalel made [a]the table of acacia wood; its length was 36 inches, its width 18 inches, and its height 27 inches. [11]He overlaid it with pure gold, and he made a surrounding border of gold for it. [12]He made a surrounding frame for it about three inches wide, and he made a surrounding border of gold for its frame. [13]He cast four gold rings for it and attached the rings at the four corners where its four legs were. [14]The rings were close to the frame to provide places for the poles to carry the table. [15]He made the poles of acacia wood and overlaid them with gold, to carry the table. [16]He made the vessels which were on the table out of pure gold, its [a]plates, its ladles, its pitchers, and its bowls, to be used in pouring out offerings.

The Making of the Lampstand

[17]Bezalel made the [a]lampstand of pure gold. He made the lampstand of hammered metal; its base and its shaft, its cups, its buds, and its blossoms were from the same piece. [18]Six branches were extending from its sides, three branches of the lampstand from one side of it, and three branches of the lampstand from the other side of it. [19]Three cups shaped like almond flowers with buds and blossoms were on the first branch, and three cups shaped like almond flowers with buds and blossoms were on the next[1] branch, and the same for the six branches that were extending from the lampstand. [20]On the lampstand there were four cups shaped like almond flowers with buds and blossoms, [21]with a bud under the first two branches from it, and a bud under the next two branches from it, and a bud under the third two branches from it; according to the six branches that extended from it. [22]Their buds and their branches were of one piece; all of it was one hammered piece of pure gold. [23]He made its seven lamps, its [a]trimmers, and its trays of pure gold. [24]He made the lampstand and all its accessories with seventy-five pounds of pure gold.

The Making of the Altar of Incense

[25]Bezalel made [a]the incense altar of acacia wood. Its length was 18 inches and its width 18 inches—a square—and its height was 36 inches. Its horns were of one piece with it.[1] [26]He overlaid it with pure gold—its top, its four walls, and its horns—and he

---

36:35 [a]Exod 26:31–37   **36:37** [a]Exod 26:36   **36:38** [1]Or *their capitals*; Heb. *their heads*.   **37:1** [a]Exod 35:30; 36:1   [b]Exod 25:10–20   **37:10** [a]Exod 25:23–29   **37:16** [a]Exod 25:29   **37:17** [a]Exod 25:31–39   **37:19** [1]Heb. *the one branch*.   **37:23** [a]Num 4:9   **37:25** [a]Exod 30:1–5   [1]Heb. *from it were its horns*.

made a surrounding border of gold for it. 27He also made two gold rings for it under its border, on its two sides, on opposite sides, as places for poles to carry it with. 28He amade the poles of acacia wood and overlaid them with gold.

29He made athe sacred anointing oil and the pure fragrant incense, the work of a perfumer.

The Making of the Altar for the Burnt Offering

38 Bezalel made athe altar for the burnt offering of acacia wood 7½ feet long and 7½ feet wide—it was square—and its height was 4½ feet. 2He made its horns on its four corners; its horns were part of it, and he overlaid it with bronze. 3He made all the utensils of the altar—the pots, the shovels, the tossing bowls, the meat hooks, and the fire pans—he made all its utensils of bronze. 4He made a grating for the altar, a network of bronze under its ledge, halfway up from the bottom. 5He cast four rings for the four corners of the bronze grating, to provide places for the poles. 6He made the poles of acacia wood and overlaid them with bronze. 7He put the poles into the rings on the sides of the altar, with which to carry it. He made the altar hollow, out of boards.

8He made athe large basin of bronze and its pedestal of bronze from the mirrors of the women who served at the entrance of the tent of meeting.

The Construction of the Courtyard

9Bezalel made athe courtyard. For the south side the hangings of the courtyard were of fine twisted linen, 150 feet long, 10with their 20 posts and their 20 bronze bases, with the hooks of the posts and their bands of silver. 11For the north side the hangings were 150 feet, with their 20 posts and their 20 bronze bases, with the hooks of the posts and their bands of silver. 12For the west side there were hangings 75 feet long, with their 10 posts and their 10 bases, with the hooks of the posts and their bands of silver. 13For the east side, toward the sunrise, it was 75 feet wide,1 14with hangings on one side of the gate that were 22½ feet long, with their three posts and their three bases, 15and for the second side of the gate of the courtyard, just like the other, the hangings were 22½ feet long, with their three posts and their three bases. 16All the hangings around the courtyard were of fine twisted linen. 17The bases for the posts were bronze. The hooks of the posts and their bands were silver, their tops were overlaid with silver, and all the posts of the courtyard had silver bands. 18The curtain for the gate of the courtyard was of blue, purple, and scarlet yarn and fine twisted linen, the work of an embroiderer. It was 30 feet long and, like the hangings in the courtyard, it was 7½ feet high, 19with four posts and their four bronze bases. Their hooks and their bands were silver, and their tops were overlaid with silver. 20All the tent apegs of the tabernacle and of the courtyard all around were bronze.

The Materials of the Construction

21This is athe inventory1 of the tabernacle, the tabernacle of the testimony, which was counted bby the order of Moses, being the work of the Levites under the direction of cIthamar, son of Aaron the priest. 22Now aBezalel son of Uri, the son of Hur, of the tribe of Judah, made everything that the LORD had commanded Moses; 23and with him was aOholiab son of Ahisamach, of the tribe of Dan, an artisan, a designer, and an embroiderer in blue, purple, and scarlet yarn and fine linen.

24All the gold that was used for the work, in all the work of the sanctuary (namely, the gold of the wave aoffering) was 29 talents and 730 shekels, according to bthe sanctuary shekel.

25The silver of those who were anumbered of the community was 100 talents and 1,775 shekels, according to the sanctuary shekel, 26one abeka per person, that is, a half shekel, according to the sanctuary shekel, for everyone who crossed over to those numbered, from twenty years old or older, b603,550 in all. 27The 100 talents of silver were used for casting athe bases of the sanctuary and the bases of the special curtain—100 bases for 100 talents, one talent

37:28 aExod 30:5   **37:29** aExod 30:23–25   **38:1** aExod 27:1–8   **38:8** aExod 30:18   **38:9** aExod 27:9–19   **38:13** 1Heb. 75 feet.   **38:20** aExod 27:19   **38:21** aNum 1:50, 53; 9:15; 10:11; 17:7–8; 2 Chr 24:6; Acts 7:44   bNum 4:28, 33   cExod 28:1; Lev 10:6, 16   1Lit. visitations of; with the idea of numbering or appointing.   **38:22** aExod 31:2, 6; 1 Chr 2:18–20   **38:23** aExod 31:6; 36:1   **38:24** aExod 35:5, 22   bExod 30:13, 24; Lev 5:15; 27:3, 25; Num 3:47; 18:16   **38:25** aExod 30:11–16; Num 1:2   **38:26** aExod 30:13, 15   bExod 12:37; Num 1:46; 26:51   **38:27** aExod 26:19, 21, 25, 32

per base. [28]From the remaining 1,775 shekels he [a]made hooks for the posts, overlaid their tops, and made bands for them.

[29]The bronze of the wave offering was seventy talents and 2,400 shekels. [30]With it he made the bases for the door of the tent of meeting, the bronze altar, the bronze grating for it, and all the utensils of the altar, [31]the bases for the courtyard all around, the bases for the gate of the courtyard, all the tent pegs of the tabernacle, and all the tent pegs of the courtyard all around.

The Making of the Priestly Garments

39 From the [a]blue, purple, and scarlet yarn they made woven [b]garments for serving in the sanctuary; they made holy garments that were for Aaron, just [c]as the LORD had commanded Moses.

The Ephod

[2]He made [a]the [b]ephod of gold, blue, purple, scarlet yarn, and fine twisted linen. [3]They hammered the gold into thin sheets and cut it into narrow strips to weave them into the blue, purple, and scarlet yarn, and into the fine linen, the work of an artistic designer. [4]They made shoulder pieces for it, attached to two of its corners, so it could be joined together. [5]The artistically woven waistband of the ephod that was on it was like it, of one piece with it, of gold, blue, purple, and scarlet yarn and fine twisted linen, just as the LORD had commanded Moses.

[6]They set the onyx stones in gold filigree settings, engraved as with the engravings of [a]a seal with the names of the sons of Israel. [7]He put them on the shoulder pieces of the ephod as stones of [a]memorial for the Israelites, just as the LORD had commanded Moses.

The Breastpiece of Decision

[8]He made the breastpiece, the work of [a]an artistic designer, in the same fashion as the ephod, of gold, blue, purple, and scarlet yarn, and fine twisted linen. [9]It was square—they made the breastpiece doubled, nine inches long and nine inches wide when doubled. [10]They set on it four rows of stones: [a]a row with a ruby, a topaz, and a beryl—the first row; [11]and the second row, a turquoise, a sapphire, and an emerald; [12]and the third row, a jacinth, an agate, and an amethyst; [13]and the fourth row, a chrysolite, an onyx, and a jasper. They were enclosed in gold filigree settings. [14]The stones were for the names of the sons of Israel, [a]twelve, corresponding to the number of their names. Each name corresponding to one of the twelve tribes was like the engravings of a seal.

[15]They made for the breastpiece braided chains like cords of pure gold, [16]and they made two gold filigree settings and two gold rings, and they attached the two rings to the upper two ends of the breastpiece. [17]They attached the two gold chains to the two rings at the ends of the breastpiece; [18]the other two ends of the two chains they attached to the two settings, and they attached them to the shoulder pieces of the ephod at the front of it. [19]They made two rings of gold and put them on the other two ends of the breastpiece on its edge, which is on the inner side of the ephod. [20]They made two more gold rings and attached them to the bottom of the two shoulder pieces on the front of the ephod, close to the juncture above the waistband of the ephod. [21]They tied the breastpiece by its rings to the rings of the ephod by blue cord, so that it was above the waistband of the ephod, so that the breastpiece would not be loose from the ephod, just as the LORD had commanded Moses.

The Other Garments

[22]He made [a]the [b]robe of the ephod completely blue, the work of a weaver. [23]There was an opening in the center of the robe, like the opening of a collar, with an edge all around the opening so that it could not be torn. [24]They made pomegranates of blue, purple, and scarlet yarn and twisted linen[1] around the hem of the robe. [25]They made [a]bells of pure gold and attached the bells between the pomegranates around the hem of the robe between the pomegranates. [26]There was a bell and a pomegranate, a bell and a pomegranate, all around the hem of the robe, to be used in ministering, just as the LORD had commanded Moses.

[27]They made tunics of fine linen—[a]the

38:28 [a]Exod 27:17   **39:1** [a]Exod 25:4; 35:23   [b]Exod 31:10; 35:19   [c]Exod 28:4   **39:2** [a]Exod 28:6–14   [b]Lev 8:7   **39:6** [a]Exod 28:9–11   **39:7** [a]Exod 28:12, 29; Josh 4:7   **39:8** [a]Exod 28:15–30   **39:10** [a]Exod 28:17   **39:14** [a]Rev 21:12   **39:22** [a]Exod 28:31–35   [b]Exod 29:5; Lev 8:7   **39:24** [1]Heb. *twined, twisted.*   **39:25** [a]Exod 28:33   **39:27** [a]Exod 28:39–40

work of a weaver, for Aaron and for his sons—[28] and the [a]turban of fine linen, the headbands of fine linen, and the undergarments of fine twisted linen. [29] The sash was of fine twisted linen [a] and blue, purple, and scarlet yarn, the work of an embroiderer, just as the LORD had commanded Moses. [30] They made a plate, [a]the holy diadem, of pure gold and wrote on it an inscription, as on the engravings of a seal, "[b]Holiness to the LORD." [31] They attached to it a blue cord to attach it to the turban above, just as the LORD had commanded Moses.

Moses Inspects the Tabernacle

[32] So all the work of the tabernacle, the tent of meeting, was [a]completed, and the Israelites did [b]according to all that the LORD had commanded Moses—they did it exactly so. [33] They brought the tabernacle to Moses, the tent and all its furnishings, clasps, frames, bars, posts, and bases; [34] and the coverings of ram skins dyed red, the covering of fine leather, and the protecting curtain; [35] the ark of the testimony and its poles, and the atonement lid; [36] the table, all its utensils, and the [a]Bread of the Presence; [37] the pure[1] lampstand, its lamps, with the lamps set in order, and all its accessories, and oil for the light; [38] and the gold altar, and the anointing oil, and the fragrant incense; and the curtain for the entrance to the tent; [39] the bronze altar and its bronze grating, its poles, and all its utensils; the large basin with its pedestal; [40] the hangings of the courtyard, its posts and its bases, and the curtain for the gateway of the courtyard, its ropes and its tent pegs, and all the furnishings[1] for the service of the tabernacle, for the tent of meeting; [41] the woven garments for serving in the sanctuary, the holy garments for Aaron the priest, and the garments for his sons to minister as priests.

[42] The Israelites [a]did all the work according to all that the LORD had commanded Moses. [43] Moses inspected all the work, and they had done it just as the LORD had commanded—they had done it exactly—and Moses [a]blessed them.

Setting up the Sanctuary

40 Then the LORD [a]spoke to Moses: [2] "On the first day of the [a]first month you are to set up [b]the tabernacle, the tent of meeting. [3] [a]You are to place the ark of the testimony in it and shield the ark with the special curtain. [4] [a]You are to bring in the table and set [b]out the things that belong on it; then you are to bring in the [c]lampstand and set up its lamps. [5] [a]You are to put[1] the gold altar for incense in front of the ark of the testimony and put the curtain at the entrance to the tabernacle. [6] You are to put the [a]altar for the burnt offering in front of the entrance to the tabernacle, the tent of meeting. [7] You are to put the large basin between the tent of meeting and the altar and put water in it. [8] You are to set up the courtyard around it and put the curtain at the gate of the courtyard. [9] And take the anointing oil, and [a]anoint the tabernacle and all that is in it, and sanctify it and all its furnishings, and it will be holy. [10] Then you are to [a]anoint [b]the altar for the burnt offering with all its utensils; you are to sanctify the altar, and it will be the most holy altar. [11] You must also anoint the large basin and its pedestal, and you are to sanctify it.

[12] "You are to bring Aaron and his sons to [a]the entrance of the tent of meeting and wash them with water. [13] Then you are to clothe Aaron with the holy [a]garments [b]and anoint him and sanctify him so that he may minister as my priest. [14] You are to bring his sons and clothe them with tunics [15] and [a]anoint them just as you anointed their father, so that they may minister as my priests; their anointing will make them a priesthood that will continue throughout their generations." [16] This is what Moses did, according to all the LORD had commanded him—so he did.

[17] So the [a]tabernacle was set up on the first day of the first month, in the second year. [18] When Moses set up the tabernacle and put its bases in place, he set up its frames, attached its bars, and set up its posts. [19] Then he spread the tent over the

39:28 [a] Exod 28:4, 39; Lev 8:9; Ezek 44:18   **39:29** [a] Exod 28:39   **39:30** [a] Exod 28:36–37   [b] Zech 14:20   **39:32** [a] Exod 40:17   [b] Exod 25:40; 39:42–43   **39:36** [a] Exod 25:23–30   **39:37** [1] Possibly meaning *pure gold lampstand.*   **39:40** [1] Heb. *utensils, vessels.*   **39:42** [a] Exod 35:10   **39:43** [a] Lev 9:22–23; Num 6:23–26; Josh 22:6; 2 Sam 6:18; 1 Kgs 8:14; 2 Chr 30:27   **40:1** [a] Exod 25:1–31:18   **40:2** [a] Exod 12:2; 13:4   [b] Exod 26:1, 30; 40:17   **40:3** [a] Exod 26:33; 40:21; Lev 16:2; Num 4:5   **40:4** [a] Exod 26:35; 40:22   [b] Exod 25:30; 40:23   [c] Exod 40:24–25   **40:5** [a] Exod 40:26   [1] Heb. *give.*   **40:6** [a] Exod 39:39   **40:9** [a] Exod 30:26; Lev 8:10   **40:10** [a] Exod 30:26–30   [b] Exod 29:36–37   **40:12** [a] Exod 29:4–9; Lev 8:1–13   **40:13** [a] Exod 29:5; 39:1, 41   [b] [Exod 28:41]; Lev 8:12   **40:15** [a] Exod 29:9; Num 25:13   **40:17** [a] Exod 40:2; Num 7:1

tabernacle and put the covering of the tent over it, as the LORD had commanded him.[1] [20]He took [a]the testimony and put it in the ark, attached the poles to the ark, and then put the atonement lid on the ark. [21]And he brought the ark into the tabernacle, [a]hung the protecting curtain, and shielded the ark of the testimony from view, just as the LORD had commanded him.

[22]And Moses put [a]the table in the tent of meeting, on the north side of the tabernacle, outside the curtain. [23]And he set the bread in order on it before the LORD, just as the LORD had [a]commanded him.

[24]And [a]he put the lampstand in the tent of meeting opposite the table, on the south side of the tabernacle. [25]Then [a]he set up the lamps before the LORD, just as the LORD had commanded him.

[26]And [a]he put the gold altar in the tent of meeting in front of the curtain, [27]and he burned fragrant incense on it, just as the LORD had [a]commanded him.

[28]Then Moses put [a]the curtain at the entrance to the tabernacle. [29]He also put the altar for the burnt offering by the entrance to the tabernacle, the tent of meeting, [a]and [b]offered on it the burnt offering and the meal offering, just as the LORD had commanded him.

[30]Then [a]he put the large basin between the tent of meeting and the altar and put water in it for washing. [31]Moses and Aaron and his sons would [a]wash their hands and their feet from it. [32]Whenever they entered the tent of meeting, and whenever they approached the altar, they would [a]wash, just as the LORD had commanded Moses.

[33]And he set up the courtyard around the tabernacle [a]and the altar, and put the curtain at the gate of the courtyard. So Moses [b]finished the work.

[34]Then [a]the [b]cloud covered the tent of meeting, and the [c]glory of the LORD filled the tabernacle. [35]Moses [a]was not able to enter the tent of meeting because the cloud settled on it and the glory of the LORD filled the tabernacle. [36]But [a]when the cloud was lifted up from the tabernacle, the Israelites would set out on all their journeys; [37]but [a]if the cloud was not lifted up, then they would not journey farther until the day it was lifted up. [38]For [a]the cloud of the LORD was on the tabernacle by day, but fire would be on it at night, in plain view of all the house of Israel throughout all their journeys.

40:19[1]Heb. *Moses.*　**40:20**[a]Exod 25:16; Deut 10:5; 1 Kgs 8:9; 2 Chr 5:10; Heb 9:4　**40:21**[a]Exod 26:33　**40:22**[a]Exod 26:35　**40:23**[a]Exod 40:4; Lev 24:5-6　**40:24**[a]Exod 26:35　**40:25**[a]Exod 25:37; 30:7-8; 40:4; Lev 24:3-4　**40:26**[a]Exod 30:1, 6; 40:5　**40:27**[a]Exod 30:7　**40:28**[a]Exod 26:36; 40:5　**40:29**[a]Exod 40:6　[b]Exod 29:38-42　**40:30**[a]Exod 30:18; 40:7　**40:31**[a]Exod 30:19-20; John 13:8　**40:32**[a]Exod 30:19　**40:33**[a]Exod 27:9-18; 40:8　[b][Heb 3:2-5]　**40:34**[a]Exod 29:43; Lev 16:2; Num 9:15; 2 Chr 5:13; Isa 6:4　[b]1 Kgs 8:10-11　[c]Lev 9:6, 23　**40:35**[a][Lev 16:2]; 1 Kgs 8:11; 2 Chr 5:13-14　**40:36**[a]Exod 13:21-22; Num 9:17; Neh 9:19　**40:37**[a]Num 9:19-22　**40:38**[a]Exod 13:21; Num 9:15; Ps 78:14; Isa 4:5

LEVITICUS

Leviticus is God's guidebook for his newly redeemed people to show them how to worship, serve, and obey a holy God. Fellowship with God through sacrifice and obedience shows the awesome holiness of the God of Israel. Indeed, "You must be holy because I, the LORD your God, am holy" (19:2). In Exodus, Israel was redeemed and established as a kingdom of priests and a holy nation. Leviticus shows how God's people are to fulfill their priestly calling. The Hebrew title is *Wayyiqra,* "And He Called." The Talmud refers to Leviticus as the "Law of the Priests" and the "Law of the Offerings." The Greek title appearing in the Septuagint is *Leuitikon,* "That Which Pertains to the Levites." From this word, the Latin Vulgate derived its name *Leviticus,* which was adopted as the English title. This title is slightly misleading because the book does not deal with the Levites as a whole but more with the priests, a segment of the Levites.

Introduction to the Sacrificial Regulations

1 Then the LORD [a]called to Moses and spoke to him [b]from the Meeting Tent: [2]"Speak to the Israelites and tell them, '[a]When someone[1] among you presents an offering[2] to the LORD, you must present your offering from the domesticated animals, either from the herd or from the flock.

Burnt-Offering Regulations: Animal from the Herd

[3]"'If his offering is a burnt offering from the herd, he must present [a]it as a flawless male; he must present it at the entrance of the Meeting Tent for its acceptance before the LORD. [4]He must lay his hand on [a]the head of the burnt offering, and it will be [b]accepted for him [c]to make atonement[1] on his behalf. [5]Then the one presenting the offering must slaughter the [a]bull before the LORD, [b]and the sons of Aaron, the priests, must present the blood [c]and splash[1] the blood against the sides of the altar, which is at the entrance of the Meeting Tent. [6]Next, the one presenting the offering must [a]skin the burnt offering and cut it into parts, [7]and the sons of Aaron, the priests,[1] must put [a]fire on the altar and arrange wood on the fire. [8]Then the sons of Aaron, the priests, must arrange the parts with the head and the suet[1] on the wood that is in the fire on the altar. [9]Finally, the one presenting the offering must wash its entrails and its legs in water, and the priest must offer all of it up in smoke on the altar—it is a burnt offering, a gift of a [a]soothing aroma to the LORD.

Animal from the Flock

[10]"'If his offering is from the flock for a burnt offering—from the sheep or the goats—he must present a flawless male, [11]and must slaughter it on [a]the north side of the altar before the LORD, and the sons of Aaron, the priests, will splash its blood against the altar's sides. [12]Next, the one presenting the offering must cut it into parts, with its head and its suet, and the priest must arrange them on the wood that is in the fire on the altar. [13]Then the one presenting the [a]offering must wash the entrails and the legs in water, and the priest must

1:1 [a] Exod 19:3; 25:22; Num 7:89   [b] Exod 40:34   **1:2** [a] Lev 22:18–19   [1] Heb. *a man, human being;* in this case any male or female, because women could bring such offerings.   [2] Or *offers an offering.*   **1:3** [a] Exod 12:5; Lev 22:20–24; Deut 15:21; Eph 5:27; Heb 9:14; 1 Pet 1:19   **1:4** [a] Exod 29:10, 15, 19; Lev 3:2, 8, 13; 4:15   [b] [Rom 12:1]; Phil 4:18   [c] Lev 4:20, 26, 31; 2 Chr 29:23–24   [1] Heb. *to wipe* [something off (or on)]; the English word derives from a combination of "at" plus Middle English "one[ment]," referring primarily to reconciliation or reparation that is made in order to accomplish reconciliation.   **1:5** [a] Mic 6:6   [b] 2 Chr 35:11   [c] Lev 1:11; 3:2, 8, 13; [Heb 12:24; 1 Pet 1:2]   [1] Or *sprinkle.*   **1:6** [a] Lev 7:8   **1:7** [a] Lev 6:8–13; Mal 1:10   [1] Some wss *priests.*   **1:8** [1] Some wss *and the head and the suet.*   **1:9** [a] Gen 8:21; [Ezek 20:28, 41; 2 Cor 2:15]   **1:11** [a] Exod 24:6; 40:22; Lev 1:5; Ezek 8:5   **1:13** [a] Num 15:4–7; 28:12–14

present all of it and offer it up in smoke on the altar—it is a burnt offering, a gift of a soothing aroma to the LORD.

Offering of Birds

[14]"If his offering to the LORD is a burnt offering of birds, he must present his offering from the [a]turtledoves or from the young pigeons. [15]The priest must present it at the altar, pinch off[1] its head and offer the head up in smoke on the altar, and its blood must be drained out against the side of the altar. [16]Then the priest must remove its entrails by cutting off its tail feathers, and throw them to the east [a]side of the altar into the place of fatty ashes, [17]and tear it open by its wings without dividing it into two parts. Finally, the priest must offer it up in smoke on the altar on the wood which is in the fire—it is [a]a burnt offering, a gift of a soothing aroma to the LORD.

Grain-Offering Regulations: Offering of Raw Flour

2 ["]"When [a]a person presents a grain offering to the LORD, his offering must consist of choice wheat flour,[1] and he must pour olive oil on it and put [b]frankincense on it. [2]Then he must bring [a]it to the sons of Aaron, the priests, and the priest must scoop out from there a handful of its choice wheat flour and some of its olive oil in addition to all of its frankincense, and the priest must offer its memorial portion up in smoke on the altar—it is a gift of a soothing aroma to the LORD. [3]The remainder of [a]the grain offering belongs to Aaron and to his [b]sons—[c]it is most holy from the gifts of the LORD.

Processed Grain Offerings

[4]"When you present an offering of grain baked in an oven, it must be made of choice wheat flour baked into unleavened loaves mixed with olive oil or unleavened wafers [a]smeared[1] with olive oil. [5]If your offering is a grain offering made on the griddle, it must be choice wheat flour mixed with olive oil, unleavened. [6]Crumble it in pieces and pour olive oil on it—it is a grain offering. [7]If your offering is a grain offering made in a pan, it must be made of choice wheat flour deep fried in olive oil.

[8]"You must bring the grain offering that must be made from these to the LORD. Present it to the priest,[1] and he will bring it to the altar. [9]Then the priest must [a]take up from the grain [b]offering its memorial portion and offer it up in smoke on the altar—it is a gift of a soothing aroma to the LORD. [10]The remainder of the grain offering belongs to Aaron and to his sons—it is most holy from the gifts of the LORD.

Additional Grain-Offering Regulations

[11]"No grain offering which you present to the LORD can be made with [a]yeast, for you must not offer up in smoke any yeast or honey as a gift to the LORD.[1] [12]You can present them to the LORD [a]as an offering of firstfruit, but they must not go up to the altar for a soothing aroma. [13]Moreover, [a]you must season every one of your grain offerings with salt; you must not allow [b]the salt of the covenant of your God to be missing from your grain offering—on every one of your grain offerings you must present salt.

[14]"If [a]you present a grain offering of first ripe grain to the LORD, you must present your grain offering of first ripe grain as soft kernels roasted in fire—crushed bits of fresh grain. [15]And [a]you must put olive oil on it and set frankincense on it—it is a grain offering. [16]Then [a]the priest must offer its memorial portion up in smoke—some of its crushed bits, some of its olive oil, in addition to all of its frankincense—it is a gift to the LORD.

Peace-Offering Regulations: Animal from the Herd

3 ["]"Now if his offering is a peace-offering [a]sacrifice, if he presents an offering from the herd, he must present before the LORD a flawless male or a female. [2]He must lay his hand on [a]the head of his offering and slaughter it at the entrance of the Meeting

---

1:14 [a] Gen 15:9; Lev 5:7, 11; 12:8; Luke 2:24   1:15 [1] I.e., a twisting action, breaking the bird's neck and severing its vertebrae, as well as pinching or nipping the skin to sever the head from the body.   1:16 [a] Lev 6:10   1:17 [a] Gen 15:10; Lev 5:8
2:1 [a] Lev 6:14; 9:17; Num 15:4   [b] Lev 5:11   [1] Or *fine flour*.   2:2 [a] Lev 2:9; 5:12; 6:15; 24:7; Acts 10:4   2:3 [a] Lev 7:9   [b] Lev 6:6; 10:12-13   [c] Exod 29:37; Num 18:9   2:4 [a] Exod 29:2   [1] This Heb. word is translated as *anointed* elsewhere.   2:8 [a] LXX, Qum. *he must bring the grain offering.*   2:9 [a] Lev 2:2, 16; 5:12; 6:15   [b] Exod 29:18   2:11 [a] Exod 23:18; 34:25; Lev 6:16-17; [Matt 16:12; Mark 8:15; Luke 12:1; 1 Cor 5:8; Gal 5:9]   [1] Some wss *present.*   2:12 [a] Exod 22:29; 34:22; Lev 23:10-11, 17, 18   2:13 [a] [Mark 9:49-50; Col 4:6]   [b] Num 18:19; 2 Chr 13:5   2:14 [a] Lev 23:10, 14   2:15 [a] Lev 2:1   2:16 [a] Lev 2:2
3:1 [a] Lev 7:11, 29   3:2 [a] Exod 29:10-11, 16, 20; Lev 1:4-5; 16:21

Tent, and the sons of Aaron, the priests, must [b]splash the blood against the altar's sides. [3]Then [a]the one presenting the offering must present a gift to the LORD from the peace-offering sacrifice: He must remove the fat that covers the entrails and all the fat that surrounds the entrails, [4]the two kidneys with the fat on their sinews, and the protruding lobe on the liver (which he is to remove along with the kidneys). [5]Then the sons of Aaron must offer it up in smoke on the altar atop the burnt offering that is on the wood in the fire as [a]a gift [b]of a [c]soothing aroma to the LORD.

Animal from the Flock

[6]"If his offering for a peace-offering sacrifice to [a]the LORD is from the flock, he must present a flawless male or female. [7]If he presents a [a]sheep as his offering, he must [b]present it [c]before the LORD. [8]He must lay his hand on the head of his offering and slaughter it before the Meeting Tent, and the sons of Aaron must splash its blood against the altar's sides. [9]Then he must present a gift to the LORD from the peace-offering sacrifice: He must remove all the fatty tail up to the end of the spine, the fat covering the entrails, and all the fat on the entrails, [10]the two kidneys with the fat on their sinews, and the protruding lobe on the liver (which he is to remove along with the kidneys). [11]Then the priest must offer it up in smoke on the altar as a [a]food gift to the LORD.

[12]"If his [a]offering is a goat, [b]he must present it before the LORD, [13]lay his hand on its head, and slaughter it before the Meeting Tent, and the sons of Aaron must splash its blood against the altar's sides. [14]Then he must present from it his offering as a gift to the LORD: the fat which covers the entrails and all the fat on the entrails, [15]the two kidneys with the fat on their sinews, and the protruding lobe on the liver (which he is to remove along with the kidneys). [16]Then the priest must offer them up in smoke on the altar as [a]a food gift for a soothing aroma— all the fat belongs to the LORD. [17]This is a [a]perpetual statute throughout your generations[1] in all the places where you live: You must never eat any fat or any [b]blood.'"

Sin-Offering Regulations

4 Then the LORD spoke to Moses: [2]"Tell the Israelites, 'When a person sins by straying unintentionally from any of the LORD's commandments which must not be violated, and violates any[1] one of them—

For the Priest

[3]"[a]If the high priest sins so [b]that the people are guilty on account of the [c]sin he has committed, he must present a flawless young bull to the LORD for a sin offering. [4]He must bring the bull [a]to the entrance of the Meeting Tent before the LORD, lay his hand on the head of the bull, and slaughter the bull before the LORD. [5]Then that high priest must take some of the blood of the bull and bring it to the Meeting Tent. [6]The priest must dip his finger in the blood and sprinkle[1] some of it seven times before the LORD toward the front of the special [a]curtain[2] of the sanctuary. [7]The priest must [a]put some of [b]the blood on the horns of the altar of fragrant incense that is before the LORD in the Meeting Tent, and all the rest of the bull's blood he must pour out at the base of the altar of burnt offering that is at the entrance of the Meeting Tent.

[8]"Then he must take up all the fat from the sin-offering bull: the fat covering the entrails[1] and all the fat surrounding the entrails, [9]the two kidneys with the fat on their sinews, and the protruding lobe on the liver (which he is to remove along with the kidneys) [10]—just [a]as it is taken from the ox of the peace-offering sacrifice—and the priest must offer them up in smoke on the altar of burnt offering. [11][a]But the hide of the bull, all its flesh along with its head and its legs, its entrails, and its dung—[12]all the rest of the bull—he must bring [a]outside the camp to a ceremonially clean place,[1] to the fatty-ash pile, and he must [b]burn it on a wood fire; it must be burned on the fatty-ash pile.

3:2 [b] Lev 1:5   **3:3** [a] Exod 29:13, 22; Lev 1:8; 3:16; 4:8–9   **3:5** [a] Exod 29:13; Lev 6:12; 7:28–34   [b] Num 28:3–10   [c] Num 15:8–10   **3:6** [a] Lev 3:1; 22:20–24   **3:7** [a] Num 15:4–5   [b] 1 Kgs 8:62   [c] Lev 17:8–9   **3:11** [a] Lev 21:6, 8, 17, 21; 22:25; Num 28:2; [Ezek 44:7; Mal 1:7, 12]   **3:12** [a] Num 15:6–11   [b] Lev 3:1, 7   **3:16** [a] Lev 7:23–25; 1 Sam 2:15; 2 Chr 7:7   **3:17** [a] Lev 6:18; 7:36; 17:7; 23:14   [b] Gen 9:4; Lev 7:23, 26; 17:10, 14; 1 Sam 14:33   [1] Heb. *for your generations.*   **4:2** [1] An emphatic Heb. construction.   **4:3** [a] Exod 40:15; Lev 8:12   [b] Lev 3:11; 9:2   [c] Lev 9:7   **4:4** [a] Lev 1:3–4; 4:15; Num 8:12   **4:6** [a] Exod 40:21, 26   [1] This Heb. verb is different from the one translated as "splash" in 1:5.   [2] Or *veil.*   **4:7** [a] Lev 4:18, 25, 30, 34; 8:15; 9:9; 16:18   [b] Exod 40:5–6; Lev 5:9   **4:8** [1] MT *which covers on the entrails.*   **4:10** [a] Lev 3:3–5   **4:11** [a] Exod 29:14; Lev 9:11; Num 19:5   **4:12** [a] Lev 4:21; 6:10–11; 16:27   [b] [Heb 13:11–12]   [1] Heb. *a clean place.*

For the Whole Congregation

[13]"'If the whole congregation of Israel strays unintentionally [a]and the matter is not noticed by the assembly, and they violate one of the LORD's commandments, which must not be violated, so they become guilty, [14]the assembly must present a young bull for a sin offering when the sin they have committed becomes known. They must bring it before the Meeting Tent, [15]the elders of the congregation must lay their hands on the head of the bull before the LORD, and someone must slaughter[1] the bull before the LORD. [16]Then [a]the high priest must bring some of the blood of the bull to the Meeting Tent, [17]and that priest must dip his finger in the blood and sprinkle[1] some of the blood seven times[2] before the LORD toward the front of the curtain. [18]He must put some of the blood on the horns of the altar which is before the LORD in the Meeting Tent, and all the rest of the blood he must pour out at the base of the altar of burnt offering that is at the entrance of the Meeting Tent.

[19]"'Then the priest must take all its fat and offer the fat up in smoke on the altar. [20]He must do [a]with the rest of the bull just as he did with the bull of the sin offering; this is what he must do with it. [b]So the priest will make atonement on their behalf, and they will be forgiven. [21]He must bring the rest of the bull outside the camp and burn it just as he burned the first bull—it is the sin offering of the assembly.

For the Leader

[22]"'Whenever a leader, by straying unintentionally, sins and [a]violates one of the commandments of the LORD his God which must not be violated, and he pleads guilty, [23]or his sin that he committed is made known to him, he must bring a flawless male goat as his offering. [24]He must lay his hand on [a]the head of the male goat and slaughter it in the place where the burnt offering is slaughtered before the LORD—it is a sin offering. [25]Then [a]the priest must take some of the blood of the sin offering with his finger and put it on the horns of the altar of burnt offering, and he must pour out the rest of its blood at the base of the altar of burnt offering. [26]Then [a]the priest must offer all of its fat up in smoke on the altar like the fat of the peace-offering sacrifice. [b]So the priest will make atonement on his behalf for[1] his sin, and he will be forgiven.

For the Common Person

[27]"'[a]If an ordinary individual sins by straying unintentionally when he violates one of the LORD's commandments which must not be violated, and he pleads guilty, [28]or his sin that he committed is made known to him, he must bring a flawless female goat as his offering for the sin that he committed. [29]He must lay his [a]hand on the head of the sin offering and slaughter[1] the sin offering in the place where the burnt offering is slaughtered. [30]Then the priest must take some of its blood with his finger and put it on the horns of the altar of burnt offering, and he must pour out all the rest of its blood at the base of the altar. [31]Then [a]he must remove all of its fat (just [b]as fat was removed from the peace-offering sacrifice), and the priest must offer it up in smoke on the altar for a [c]soothing aroma to the LORD. [d]So the priest will make atonement on his behalf, and he will be forgiven.

[32]"'But if [a]he brings a sheep as his offering, for a sin offering, he must bring a flawless female. [33]He must [a]lay his hand on the head of the sin offering and slaughter it for a sin offering in the place where the burnt offering is slaughtered. [34]Then the priest must take some of the blood of the sin offering with his finger and put it on the horns of the altar of burnt offering, and he must pour out all the rest of its blood at the base of the altar. [35]Then the one who brought the offering must remove all its fat (just as the fat of the sheep is removed from the peace-offering sacrifice), and the priest must offer them up [a]in smoke on the altar on top of the other gifts for the LORD. [b]So the priest will make atonement on his behalf for his sin that he has committed, and he will be forgiven.

4:13 [a]Lev 5:2–4, 17   **4:15** [1]Heb. *and he shall slaughter;* perhaps one of the elders referred to at the beginning of the verse, or the officiating priest (cf. v. 21).   **4:16** [a]Lev 4:5; [Heb 9:12–14]   **4:17** [1]This Heb. verb is different from the one translated as "splash" in 1:5.   [2]MT *and the priest shall dip his finger from the blood and sprinkle seven times.*   **4:20** [a]Lev 4:3   [b]Lev 1:4; Num 15:25   **4:22** [a]Lev 4:2, 13, 27   **4:24** [a]Lev 4:4; [Isa 53:6]   **4:25** [a]Lev 4:7, 18, 30, 34   **4:26** [a]Lev 3:3–5   [b]Lev 4:20; Num 15:28   [1]Heb. *from.*   **4:27** [a]Lev 4:2; Num 15:27   **4:29** [a]Lev 1:4; 4:4, 24   [1]LXX *they slaughter.*   **4:31** [a]Lev 3:14   [b]Lev 3:3–4   [c]Gen 8:21; Exod 29:18; Lev 1:9, 13; 2:2, 9, 12   [d]Lev 4:26   **4:32** [a]Lev 4:28   **4:33** [a]Lev 1:4; Num 8:12   **4:35** [a]Lev 3:5   [b]Lev 4:26, 31

Additional Sin-Offering Regulations

5 ["When a person sins in that he [a]hears a public curse against one who fails to testify and he is a witness (he either saw or knew what had happened) and he does not make it known, then he will [b]bear his punishment for iniquity. [2]Or when there is[1] a person who touches anything ceremonially unclean, whether the carcass of an unclean wild animal, or the carcass of an unclean domesticated animal, or the carcass of an unclean creeping thing, even [a]if he did not realize it,[2] he has become unclean and is [b]guilty; [3]or when he touches [a]human uncleanness with regard to anything by which he can become unclean, even if he did not realize it, but he has later come to know it and is guilty; [4]or when a person swears an oath, speaking thoughtlessly with his lips, whether [a]to do evil or [b]to do good, with regard to anything which the individual might speak thoughtlessly in an oath, even if he did not realize it, but he has later come to know it and is guilty with regard to one of these oaths—[5]when an individual becomes guilty with regard to one of these things he must [a]confess how he has sinned, [6]and he must bring his penalty for guilt to the LORD for his sin that he has committed—a female from the flock, whether a female sheep or a female goat, for a sin offering. So the priest will make atonement on his behalf for his sin.

[7]"[a]If he cannot afford an animal from the flock,[1] he must bring his penalty for guilt for his sin that he has committed, two [b]turtledoves or two young pigeons, to the LORD, one for a sin offering and one for a burnt offering. [8]He must bring them to the priest and present first the one that is for a sin offering. The priest must pinch its head at the nape of its neck, but must not sever the head from the body. [9]Then he must sprinkle[1] some of the blood of the sin offering on the wall of the altar, and the [a]remainder of the blood must be squeezed out at the base of the altar—it is a sin offering. [10]The second bird he must make a burnt offering according to the standard regulation. So the priest will make atonement on behalf of this person for his sin which he has committed, and he will [a]be forgiven.

[11]"'If he [a]cannot afford two turtledoves or two young pigeons, [b]he must bring as his offering for his sin which he has committed a tenth of an ephah of choice wheat flour for a sin offering. He must not place olive oil on it, and he must not put frankincense on it, because it is a sin offering. [12]He must bring it to the priest, and the priest must scoop out from it [a]a handful as its memorial portion and offer it up [b]in smoke on the altar on top of the other gifts of the LORD—it is a sin offering. [13]So [a]the priest will make atonement on his behalf for his sin which [b]he has committed by doing one of these things, and he will be forgiven. The remainder of the offering will belong to the priest like the grain offering.'"

Guilt-Offering Regulations: Known Trespass

[14]Then the LORD spoke to Moses: [15]"[a]When a person commits a trespass and sins by straying unintentionally from [b]the regulations about [c]the LORD's holy things, then he must bring his penalty for guilt to the LORD, a flawless ram from the flock, convertible into silver shekels according to the standard of the sanctuary shekel, for a guilt offering. [16]And whatever holy thing he violated he must restore [a]and must add one-fifth to it and give it to the priest. [b]So the priest will make atonement on his behalf with the guilt-offering ram, and he will be forgiven.

Unknown Trespass

[17]"If a person sins and violates any of the LORD's commandments that must not be violated ([a]although he did not know it at the time, but later realizes he is [b]guilty), then he will bear his punishment for iniquity[1] [18]and must bring [a]a flawless ram from the flock, convertible into silver shekels, for a guilt offering to the priest. So the

---

5:1 [a] Prov 29:24; [Jer 23:10] [b] Lev 5:17; 7:18; 17:16; 19:8; 20:17; Num 9:13 **5:2** [a] Lev 11:24, 28, 31, 39; Num 19:11–16; Deut 14:8 [b] Lev 5:17 [1] MT *who.* [2] Heb. *and it is hidden from him.* **5:3** [a] Lev 5:12–13, 15 **5:4** [a] 1 Sam 25:22; Acts 23:12 [b] [Matt 5:33–37]; Mark 6:23; [Jas 5:12] **5:5** [a] Lev 16:21; 26:40; Num 5:7; Ezra 10:11–12; Ps 32:5; Prov 28:13 **5:7** [a] Lev 12:6, 8; 14:21 [b] Lev 1:14 [1] Or *lamb, sheep.* **5:9** [a] Lev 4:7, 18, 30, 34 [1] This Heb. verb is different from the one translated as "splash" in 1:5. **5:10** [a] Lev 1:14–17 **5:11** [a] Lev 14:21–32 [b] Lev 2:1–2; 6:15; Num 5:15 **5:12** [a] Lev 2:2 [b] Lev 4:35 **5:13** [a] Lev 4:26 [b] Lev 2:3; 6:17, 26 **5:15** [a] Lev 4:2; 22:14; Num 5:5–8 [b] Ezra 10:19 [c] Exod 30:13; Lev 27:25 **5:16** [a] Lev 6:5; 22:14; 27:13, 15, 27, 31; Num 5:7 [b] Lev 4:26 **5:17** [a] Lev 4:2, 13, 22, 27 [b] Lev 5:1–2 [1] Heb. *and he did not know, and he shall be guilty and he shall bear his iniquity.* **5:18** [a] Lev 5:15

priest will make atonement on his behalf for his error that he committed (although he himself had not known it), and he will be forgiven. [19]It is a guilt offering; [a]he was surely guilty before the LORD."

Trespass by Deception and False Oath

6 Then the LORD spoke to Moses: [2]"When a person sins and [a]commits a trespass against the LORD by [b]deceiving his fellow citizen in regard to something held in trust, or [c]a pledge, or something stolen, or by [d]extorting something from his fellow citizen, [3]or [a]has found something lost and denies it and [b]swears falsely concerning any one of the things that someone might do to sin—[4]when it happens that he sins and he is found guilty, then he must return [a]whatever he had stolen, or whatever he had extorted, or the thing that he had held in trust, or the lost thing that he had found, [5]or anything about which he swears falsely. He must [a]restore it in full and add one-fifth to it; he must give it to its owner when he is found guilty.[1] [6]Then he must bring his guilt offering to the LORD, [a]a flawless ram from the flock, convertible into silver shekels, for a guilt offering to the priest. [7][a]So the priest will make atonement on his behalf before the LORD and he will be forgiven for whatever he has done to become guilty."

Sacrificial Instructions for the Priests: The Burnt Offering

[8]Then the LORD spoke to Moses: [9]"Command Aaron and his sons, 'This is the [a]law of the burnt offering. The burnt offering is to remain on the hearth on the altar all night until morning, and the fire of the altar must be kept burning on it. [10]Then the priest must put on his linen robe [a]and must put linen leggings[1] over his bare flesh, and he must take up the fatty ashes of the burnt offering that the fire consumed on the altar, and he must place them [b]beside the altar. [11]Then [a]he must take off his clothes and put on other clothes, and he must bring the fatty ashes outside the camp [b]to a ceremonially clean place, [12]but [a]the fire which is on the altar must be kept burning on it. It must not be extinguished. So the priest must kindle wood on it morning by morning, and he must arrange the burnt offering on it and offer the fat of the peace offering up in smoke on it. [13]A continual fire must be kept burning on the [a]altar. It must not be extinguished.

The Grain Offering of the Common Person

[14]"'This is the law of the grain offering. The sons of Aaron are to present it before the LORD in front of the altar, [15]and the priest must take up with his hand some of the choice wheat flour of the grain offering and some of its olive oil, and all of the frankincense that is on the grain offering, and he must offer its memorial portion up in smoke on the altar as a soothing aroma to the LORD. [16]Aaron and his sons are to eat what is left over from it. It must be eaten unleavened in a holy place; they are to eat it in the courtyard of the Meeting Tent. [17]It must not be baked with yeast.[1] I have given it [a]as their portion from my gifts. It is most holy, like the sin offering and the guilt offering. [18]Every male among the sons of Aaron may eat it. It is [a]a perpetual allotted portion throughout your generations from the gifts of the LORD. Anyone who touches these gifts[1] must be holy.'"

The Grain Offering of the Priests

[19]Then the LORD spoke to Moses: [20]"This [a]is the offering of Aaron and his sons which they must present to the LORD on the day when he is anointed: a tenth of an [b]ephah of choice wheat flour as a continual grain offering, half of it in the morning and half of it in the evening. [21]It must be made with olive oil on a [a]griddle, and you must bring it well soaked, so you must present a grain offering of broken pieces[1] as a soothing aroma to the LORD. [22]The high priest [a]who succeeds him from among his sons must do [b]it. It is a perpetual statute; it must be offered up in smoke as a whole offering to the LORD. [23]Every grain offering of a priest must be a whole offering; it must not be eaten."

5:19 [a]Ezra 10:2   **6:2** [a]Num 5:6   [b]Lev 19:11; Acts 5:4; Col 3:9   [c]Exod 22:7, 10   [d]Prov 24:28   **6:3** [a]Exod 23:4; Deut 22:1–4   [b]Exod 22:11; Lev 19:12; Jer 7:9; Zech 5:4   **6:4** [a]Lev 24:18, 21   **6:5** [a]Lev 5:16; Num 5:7–8; 2 Sam 12:6   [1]Heb. *to whom it is to him he shall give it in the day of his being guilty.*   **6:6** [a]Lev 1:3; 5:15   **6:7** [a]Lev 4:26   **6:9** [a]Exod 29:38–42; Num 28:3–10   **6:10** [a]Exod 28:39–43; Lev 16:4; Ezek 44:17–18   [b]Lev 1:16   [1]The exact nature of this article of the priest's clothing is difficult to determine.   **6:11** [a]Ezek 44:19   [b]Lev 4:12   **6:12** [a]Lev 3:3, 5, 9, 14   **6:13** [a]Lev 1:7   **6:17** [a]Lev 7:7   [1]Heb. *be baked leavened.*   **6:18** [a]Lev 6:29; 7:6; Num 18:10; 1 Cor 9:13   [1]Heb. *touches them.*   **6:20** [a]Exod 29:2   [b]Exod 16:36   **6:21** [a]Lev 2:5; 7:9   [1]Or perhaps baked pieces.   **6:22** [a]Lev 4:3   [b]Exod 29:25

The Sin Offering

[24]Then the LORD spoke to Moses: [25]"Tell Aaron and his sons, 'This is the law of the [a]sin offering. In the place where the burnt offering is slaughtered the sin offering must be slaughtered before the LORD. It is most holy. [26]The priest who offers it for sin is to eat it. It must be eaten in a holy place, in [a]the courtyard of the Meeting Tent. [27]Anyone who touches its meat must be holy, and whoever spatters some of its blood [a]on a garment must wash[1] whatever he spatters it on in a holy place. [28]Any clay vessel it is boiled in must be broken, and if it was boiled in [a]a bronze vessel, then that vessel must be rubbed out and rinsed in water. [29]Any male among the priests may eat it. It is most holy. [30a]But any sin offering from which some of its blood is brought into the Meeting Tent to make atonement in the sanctuary must not be [b]eaten. It must be burned [c]up in the fire.[1]

The Guilt Offering

7 [a]"This is the law of the guilt offering. It is most holy. [2]In the place where they slaughter the burnt offering they must slaughter the guilt offering, and the officiating priest must splash the blood against the altar's sides. [3]Then the one making the offering must present all its fat: the fatty tail, the fat covering the entrails, [4]the two kidneys and the fat on their sinews, and the protruding lobe on the liver (which he must remove along with the kidneys). [5]Then the priest must offer them up in smoke on the altar as a gift to the LORD. It is a guilt offering. [6a]Any male among the priests may eat [b]it. It must be eaten in a holy place. It is most holy. [7]The law is [a]the same for the sin offering and the guilt offering; it belongs to the priest who makes atonement with it.

Priestly Portions of Burnt and Grain Offerings

[8]"As for the priest who presents someone's burnt offering, the hide of that burnt offering which he presented belongs to him. [9]Every grain offering which is baked in the oven or made in the pan or on the griddle belongs to the priest who presented it. [10]Every grain offering, whether mixed with olive oil or dry, belongs to all the sons of Aaron, each one alike.

The Peace Offering

[11]"This [a]is the law of the peace-offering sacrifice which he is to present to the LORD. [12]If he presents it on account of thanksgiving, along with the thank-offering sacrifice he must present unleavened loaves mixed with olive oil, unleavened wafers [a]smeared with olive oil, and well-soaked, ring-shaped loaves made of choice wheat flour mixed with olive oil. [13]He must present this grain offering in addition to ring-shaped loaves of [a]leavened bread which regularly accompany the sacrifice of his thanksgiving peace offering. [14]He must present one of each kind of grain offering as a contribution offering to the LORD; [a]it belongs to the priest who splashes the blood of the peace offering. [15]The meat of his thanksgiving peace offering must be eaten on [a]the day of his offering; he must not set any of it aside until morning.

[16]"If his offering is a votive or freewill [a]sacrifice, it may be eaten on the day he presents his sacrifice, and also the leftovers from it may be eaten on the next day, [17]but the leftovers from the meat of the sacrifice must be burned up in the fire[1] on the third day. [18]If some of the meat of his peace-offering sacrifice is ever eaten on the third day, it will not be accepted; it will not be [a]accounted to the one who presented it since it is [b]spoiled, and the person who eats from it will bear his punishment for iniquity. [19]The meat which touches anything ceremonially unclean must not be eaten; it must be burned up in the fire. As for ceremonially clean meat, everyone who is ceremonially clean may eat the meat. [20]The person who eats meat from the peace-offering sacrifice which belongs to the [a]LORD [b]while that person's uncleanness persists will be cut off from his people. [21]When a person touches anything unclean (whether [a]human uncleanness, or an [b]unclean animal, or

6:25 [a] Lev 1:1, 3, 5, 11   **6:26** [a] [Lev 10:17–18]; Num 18:9–10; [Ezek 44:28–29]   **6:27** [a] Exod 29:37; Num 4:15; Hag 2:11–13   [1] Some wss [the garment] *must be washed.*   **6:28** [a] Lev 11:33; 15:12   **6:30** [a] Lev 4:7, 11, 12, 18, 21; 10:18; 16:27; [Heb 13:11–12]   [b] Lev 6:16, 23, 26   [c] Lev 16:27   [1] Heb. *burned with fire.*   **7:1** [a] Lev 5:14—6:7   **7:6** [a] Lev 6:16–18, 29; Num 18:9   [b] Lev 2:3   **7:7** [a] Lev 6:24–30; 14:13   **7:11** [a] Lev 3:1; 22:18, 21; Ezek 45:15   **7:12** [a] Lev 2:4; Num 6:15   **7:13** [a] Lev 2:12; 23:17–18; Amos 4:5   **7:14** [a] Num 18:8, 11, 19   **7:15** [a] Lev 22:29–30   **7:16** [a] Lev 19:5–8   **7:17** [1] Heb. *burned with fire.*   **7:18** [a] Num 18:27   [b] Lev 11:10–11, 41; 19:7; [Prov 15:8]   **7:20** [a] [Heb 2:17]   [b] Lev 5:3; 15:3; 22:3–7; Num 19:13; [1 Cor 11:28]   **7:21** [a] Lev 5:2–3, 5   [b] Lev 11:24, 28

an unclean detestable ᶜcreature) and eats some of the meat of the peace-offering sacrifice which belongs to the LORD, that person will be cut off from his people.'"

Sacrificial Instructions for the Common People: Fat and Blood

[22]Then the LORD spoke to Moses: [23]"Tell the Israelites, 'ᵃYou must not eat any fat of an ox, sheep, or goat. [24]Moreover, the fat of an animal that has died of natural causes[1] and the fat of an animal torn by beasts may be used for any other purpose, but you must certainly never eat it. [25]If anyone eats fat from the animal from which he presents a gift to the LORD, that person will be cut off from his people. [26]And you must not eat any blood of the birds ᵃor of the domesticated land animals in any of the places where you live. [27]Any person who eats any blood—that person will be cut off from his people.'"

Priestly Portions of Peace Offerings

[28]Then the LORD spoke to Moses: [29]"Tell ᵃthe Israelites, 'The one who presents his peace-offering sacrifice to the LORD must bring part of his offering to the LORD as his sacrifice. [30]With ᵃhis own hands he must bring the LORD's gifts. He must bring the fat with the ᵇbreast to wave the breast as a wave offering before the LORD, [31]ᵃand the priest must offer the fat up in smoke on the altar, but the ᵇbreast will belong to Aaron and his sons. [32]The right thigh you must give as ᵃa contribution offering to the priest from your peace-offering sacrifice. [33]The one from Aaron's sons who presents the blood of the peace offering and fat will have the right thigh as his share, [34]for ᵃthe breast of the wave offering and the thigh of the contribution offering I have taken from the Israelites out of their peace-offering sacrifices and have given them to Aaron the priest and to his sons from the people of Israel as a perpetual allotted portion.'"

[35]This is the allotment of Aaron and the allotment of his sons from the LORD's gifts on the day Moses presented them to serve as priests to the LORD. [36]This is what the LORD commanded to give to them from the Israelites ᵃon the day Moses anointed them[1]—a perpetual allotted portion throughout their generations.

Summary of Sacrificial Regulations in Leviticus 6:8–7:36

[37]This is the law for the burnt ᵃoffering, ᵇthe grain offering, ᶜthe sin offering, ᵈthe guilt offering, ᵉthe ordination offering, and ᶠthe peace-offering sacrifice, [38]which the LORD commanded Moses on Mount Sinai on the day he commanded the Israelites ᵃto present their offerings to the LORD in the desert of Sinai.

Ordination of the Priests

8 Then the LORD spoke to Moses: [2]"ᵃTake Aaron and his sons with him, and ᵇthe garments, ᶜthe anointing oil, the sin-offering ᵈbull, the two ᵉrams, and the basket of unleavened bread, [3]and assemble the whole congregation at the entrance of the Meeting Tent." [4]So Moses did just as the LORD commanded him, and the congregation assembled at the entrance of the Meeting Tent. [5]Then Moses said to the congregation: "This is what the LORD has commanded to be done."

Clothing Aaron

[6]So Moses brought Aaron and his sons forward and ᵃwashed them with water. [7]Then he ᵃput the tunic on Aaron, wrapped the sash around him,[1] and clothed him with the robe. Next he put the ephod on him and placed on him the decorated band of the ephod, and fastened the ephod closely to him with the band. [8]He then set the breastpiece on him and ᵃput the Urim and Thummim into the breastpiece. [9]Finally, he set the turban[1] on his head ᵃand attached the gold plate, the holy diadem, to the front of the turban just as the LORD had commanded Moses.

7:21 ᶜEzek 4:14   7:23 ᵃLev 3:17; 17:10–15; Deut 14:21; Ezek 4:14; 44:31   7:24 [1]Heb. *carcass*; i.e., an animal that has died on its own.   7:26 ᵃGen 9:4; Lev 3:17; 17:10–16; 19:26; Deut 12:23; 1 Sam 14:33; Ezek 33:25; Acts 15:20, 29   7:29 ᵃLev 3:1; 22:21; Ezek 45:15   7:30 ᵃLev 3:3–4, 9, 14   ᵇExod 29:24, 27; Lev 8:27; 9:21; Num 6:20   7:31 ᵃLev 3:5, 11, 16   ᵇNum 18:11; Deut 18:3   7:32 ᵃExod 29:27; Lev 7:34; 9:21; Num 6:20   7:34 ᵃExod 29:28; Lev 10:14–15; Num 18:18–19; Deut 18:3   7:36 ᵃExod 40:13–15; Lev 8:12, 30   [1]Heb. *which the LORD commanded to give to them in the day he anointed them from the children of Israel.*   7:37 ᵃLev 6:9   ᵇLev 6:14   ᶜLev 6:25   ᵈLev 7:1   ᵉExod 29:1; Lev 6:20   ᶠLev 7:11   7:38 ᵃLev 1:1–2; Deut 4:5   8:2 ᵃExod 29:1–3   ᵇExod 28:2, 4   ᶜExod 30:24–25   ᵈExod 29:10   ᵉExod 29:15, 19   8:6 ᵃExod 30:20; Heb 10:22   8:7 ᵃExod 39:1–31   [1]Heb. *girded him with the sash.*   8:8 ᵃExod 28:30; Num 27:21; Deut 33:8; 1 Sam 28:6; Ezra 2:63; Neh 7:65   8:9 ᵃExod 28:36–37; 29:6   [1]Perhaps a turban-like headband wound around the forehead area.

Anointing the Tabernacle and Aaron, and Clothing Aaron's Sons

[10]Then Moses took the anointing oil and anointed the tabernacle and everything in it, and [a]so consecrated them. [11]Next he sprinkled some of it on the altar seven times and so anointed the altar, all its vessels, and the washbasin and its stand to consecrate them. [12]He then [a]poured some of the anointing oil on the head of Aaron and anointed him to consecrate him. [13]Moses also brought forward Aaron's sons, clothed them with tunics, wrapped sashes around them,[1] and wrapped headbands on them just as [a]the LORD had commanded Moses.

Consecration Offerings

[14]Then he brought near the sin-offering bull, [a]and Aaron and his sons [b]laid their hands on the head of the sin-offering bull, [15]and [a]he slaughtered it. Moses then took the blood and put it all around on the horns of the altar with his finger and purified the altar,[1] and he poured out the rest of the blood at the base of the altar and so consecrated it to make atonement on it. [16]Then [a]he took all the fat on the entrails, the protruding lobe of the liver, and the two kidneys and their fat, and Moses offered it all up in smoke on the altar, [17]but the rest of the bull—its hide, its flesh, and its dung—he completely burned up outside the camp just as the LORD [a]had commanded Moses.

[18]Then [a]he presented the burnt-offering ram, and Aaron and his sons laid their hands on the head of the ram, [19]and he slaughtered it. Moses then splashed the blood against the altar's sides. [20]Then he[1] cut the ram into parts, and Moses [a]offered the head, the parts, and the suet up in smoke, [21]but the entrails and the legs he [a]washed with water,[1] and Moses offered the whole ram up in smoke on the altar—it was a burnt offering for a soothing aroma, a gift to the LORD, just as the LORD had commanded Moses.

[22]Then [a]he presented the second ram, the ram of ordination, and Aaron and his sons laid their hands on the head of the ram, [23]and he slaughtered [a]it.[1] Moses then took some of its blood and put it on Aaron's right earlobe, on the thumb of his right hand, and on the big toe of his right foot. [24]Next he brought Aaron's sons forward, and Moses put some of the [a]blood on their right earlobes, on their right thumbs, and on the big toes of their right feet, and Moses splashed the rest of the blood against the altar's sides.

[25]Then [a]he took the fat (the fatty tail, all the fat on the entrails, the protruding lobe of the liver, and the two kidneys and their fat) and the right thigh, [26]and from the basket of unleavened bread that was before the LORD he took one unleavened loaf, one loaf of bread mixed with olive oil, [a]and one wafer, and placed them on the fat parts and on the right thigh. [27]He then put all of them on the palms of Aaron and his sons, who waved[1] them as a wave [a]offering before the LORD. [28]Moses [a]then took them from their palms and offered them up in smoke on the altar on top of the burnt offering—they were an ordination offering for a soothing aroma; it was a gift to the LORD. [29]Finally, [a]Moses took the [b]breast and waved it as a wave offering before the LORD from the ram of ordination. It was Moses' [c]share just as the LORD had commanded Moses.

Anointing Aaron, His Sons, and Their Garments

[30]Then [a]Moses took some of the anointing oil and some of the blood which was on the altar and sprinkled it on Aaron and his garments, and on his sons and his sons' garments. So he consecrated Aaron, his garments, and his sons and his sons' garments. [31]Then Moses said to Aaron and his sons, "[a]Boil the meat at the entrance of the Meeting Tent, and there you are to eat it and the bread which is in the ordination-offering basket, just as I have commanded, saying, 'Aaron and his sons are to eat it,' [32]but the remainder of the meat and the bread you must burn with fire. [33]And you must not

8:10 [a]Exod 30:26–29; 40:10–11; Lev 8:2   8:12 [a]Exod 29:7; 30:30; Lev 21:10, 12; Ps 133:2   8:13 [a]Exod 29:8–9   [1]MT *sash*.   8:14 [a]Exod 29:10; Ps 66:15; Ezek 43:19   [b]Lev 4:4   8:15 [a]Exod 29:12, 36; Lev 4:7; Ezek 43:20, 26; [Heb 9:22]   [1]The Heb. verb means "to de-sin"; the main purpose of the sin offering was to purify the tabernacle and its furniture from impurity.   8:16 [a]Exod 29:13; Lev 4:8   8:17 [a]Exod 29:14; Lev 4:11–12   8:18 [a]Exod 29:15   8:20 [a]Lev 1:8   [1]Probably done by Aaron.   8:21 [a]Exod 29:18   [1]Probably done by Aaron.   8:22 [a]Exod 29:19, 31; Lev 8:2   8:23 [a]Exod 29:20–21; Lev 14:14   [1]Probably done by Aaron.   8:24 [a][Heb 9:13–14, 18–23]   8:25 [a]Exod 29:22   8:26 [a]Exod 29:23   8:27 [a]Exod 29:24; Lev 7:30, 34   [1]Heb. *and he waved.*   8:28 [a]Exod 29:25   8:29 [a]Ps 99:6   [b]Exod 29:27   [c]Exod 29:26   8:30 [a]Exod 29:21; 30:30; Num 3:3   8:31 [a]Exod 29:31–32   8:32 [a]Exod 29:34

go out from the entrance of the Meeting Tent for [a]seven days, until the day when your days of ordination are completed, because you must be ordained over a seven-day period. [34]What [a]has been done on this day the LORD has commanded to be done to make atonement for you. [35]You must reside at the entrance of the Meeting Tent day and night for seven days and [a]keep the charge of the LORD so that you will not die, for this is what I have been commanded." [36]So Aaron and his sons did all the things the LORD had commanded through Moses.

Inauguration of Tabernacle Worship

9 On the [a]eighth day Moses summoned Aaron and his sons and the elders of Israel, [2]and said to Aaron, "Take for yourself a [a]bull calf for a sin offering and a ram for a burnt offering, both flawless, and present them before the LORD. [3]Then tell the Israelites: '[a]Take a male goat for a sin offering and a calf and a lamb, both a year old and flawless, for a burnt offering, [4]and [a]an ox and a ram for peace offerings to sacrifice before the LORD, and a grain offering mixed with olive oil, for [b]today the LORD is going to appear to you.'" [5]So they took what Moses had commanded to the front of the Meeting Tent, and the whole congregation presented them and stood before the LORD. [6]Then Moses said, "This is what the LORD has commanded you to do so that the glory of the LORD may appear to you." [7]Moses then said to Aaron, "Approach the altar and [a]make your sin offering and your burnt offering, and make atonement on behalf of yourself and on behalf of the people; and also [b]make the people's offering and make atonement on behalf of them just as the LORD has commanded."

The Sin Offering for the Priests

[8]So Aaron approached the altar and slaughtered the sin-offering calf which was for himself. [9]Then Aaron's sons presented the blood to him, and he dipped his finger in the blood and put it on the horns of the altar, and the rest of the blood he poured out at the base of the altar. [10a]The fat and the kidneys and the protruding lobe of the liver from the sin offering he offered up in smoke on the altar just as the LORD had commanded Moses, [11]but [a]the flesh and the hide he completely burned up outside the camp.

The Burnt Offering for the Priests

[12]He then slaughtered the burnt offering, and his sons handed the blood to him, and he splashed it against the altar's sides. [13]The burnt offering itself they handed to him by its parts, including [a]the head, and he offered them up in smoke on the altar, [14]and he washed the entrails [a]and the legs and offered them up in smoke on top of the burnt offering on the altar.

The Offerings for the People

[15]Then [a]he presented the people's offering. He took the sin-offering male goat which was for the people, slaughtered it, and performed a purification rite with it[1] like the first one. [16]He then presented the burnt offering, and did it [a]according to the standard regulation. [17]Next he presented the grain offering, filled his hand with some of it, and offered it up in smoke on the altar in addition [a]to the morning burnt offering. [18]Then he slaughtered the ox and the ram—the peace-offering [a]sacrifices which were for the people—and Aaron's sons handed the blood to him, and he splashed it against the altar's sides. [19]As for the fat parts from the ox and from the ram (the fatty tail, the fat covering the entrails, the kidneys, and the protruding lobe of the liver), [20]they set those on [a]the breasts, and he offered the fat parts up in smoke on the altar. [21]Finally Aaron waved the [a]breasts and the right thigh as a wave offering before the LORD just as Moses had commanded. [22]Then Aaron lifted up his hands toward the people and [a]blessed them and descended from making the sin offering, the burnt offering, and the peace offering. [23]Moses and Aaron then entered into the Meeting Tent. When they came out, they blessed the people, and the glory of the LORD appeared to all the people. [24]Then [a]fire went

8:33 [a]Exod 29:30, 35; Lev 10:7; Ezek 43:25–26   8:34 [a][Heb 7:16]   8:35 [a]Num 1:53; 3:7; 9:19; Deut 11:1; 1 Kgs 2:3; Ezek 48:11   9:1 [a]Ezek 43:27   9:2 [a]Exod 29:21; Lev 4:1–12   9:3 [a]Lev 4:23, 28; Ezra 6:17; 10:19   9:4 [a]Lev 2:4   [b]Exod 29:43; Lev 9:6, 23   9:7 [a]Lev 4:3; 1 Sam 3:14; [Heb 5:3–5; 7:27]   [b]Lev 4:16, 20; Heb 5:1   9:10 [a]Exod 23:18; Lev 8:16   9:11 [a]Lev 4:11–12; 8:17   9:13 [a]Lev 8:20   9:14 [a]Lev 8:21   9:15 [a][Isa 53:10; Heb 2:17; 5:3]   [1]Lit. and purified [with] it.   9:16 [a]Lev 1:1–13   9:17 [a]Exod 29:38–39   9:18 [a]Lev 3:1–11   9:20 [a]Lev 3:5, 16   9:21 [a]Exod 29:24, 26, 27; Lev 7:30–34   9:22 [a]Num 6:22–26; Deut 21:5; Luke 24:50   9:24 [a]Gen 4:4; Judg 6:21; 2 Chr 7:1; Ps 20:3

out from the presence of the LORD and consumed the burnt offering and the fat parts on the altar, and all the people saw it, so they shouted [b]loudly and fell down with their [c]faces to the ground.

Nadab and Abihu

10 Then Aaron's sons, [a]Nadab and Abihu, [b]each took his fire pan and put fire in it, set incense on it, and present-ed [c]strange fire before the LORD, which he had not commanded them to do. [2]So [a]fire went out from the presence of the LORD and consumed them so that they died before the LORD. [3]Moses then said to Aaron, "This is what the LORD spoke: 'Among the ones close to me I will show myself holy,[1] and in the presence of all the people I will be honored.'" So Aaron kept silent. [4]Moses then called to Mishael and Elzaphan, the sons of Uzziel, Aaron's uncle, and said to them, "Come near, [a]carry your brothers from the front of the sanctuary to a place outside the camp." [5]So they came near and carried them away in their tunics to a place outside the camp just as Moses had spoken. [6]Then Moses said to Aaron and to Eleazar and Ithamar his other two sons, "Do not dishevel the hair of your heads[1] and do not tear your garments, so that you do not die and so that [a]wrath does not come on the whole congregation. Your brothers, all the house of Israel, are to mourn the burning that the LORD has caused, [7]but [a]you must not go out from the entrance of the Meeting Tent lest you die, [b]for the LORD's anointing oil is on you." So they acted according to the word of Moses.

Perpetual Statutes the Lord Spoke to Aaron

[8]Then the LORD spoke to Aaron, [9]"Do not drink wine or strong drink, you and your sons with you, when you enter into the Meeting Tent, so that you [a]do not die. This is a perpetual statute throughout your generations, [10]as well as to [a]distinguish between the holy and the common, and between the unclean and the clean, [11a]and to teach the Israelites all the statutes that the LORD has spoken to them through Moses."

Perpetual Statutes Moses Spoke to Aaron

[12]Then Moses spoke to Aaron and to Eleazar and Ithamar, his remaining sons, "[a]Take the grain offering which remains from the gifts of the LORD and eat it unleavened beside the altar, [b]for it is most holy. [13]You must eat it in a [a]holy place because it is your allotted portion and the allotted portion of your [b]sons from the gifts of the LORD, for this is what I have been commanded. [14]Also, [a]the breast of the wave offering and the thigh of the contribution offering you must eat in a ceremonially clean place, you and your sons and [b]daughters with you, for the foods have been given as your allotted [c]portion and the allotted portion of your sons from the peace-offering sacrifices of the Israelites. [15]The thigh of [a]the contribution offering and the breast of the wave offering they must bring in addition to the gifts of the fat parts to wave them as a wave offering before the LORD, and it will belong to you and your sons with you for a perpetual statute just as the LORD has commanded."

The Problem with the Inaugural Sin Offering

[16]Later Moses sought diligently for [a]the sin-offering male goat, but it had actually been burnt. So he became angry at Eleazar and Ithamar, Aaron's remaining sons, saying, [17]"[a]Why did you not eat [b]the sin offering in the sanctuary? For it is most holy, and he gave it to you to bear the iniquity of the congregation, to make atonement on their behalf before the LORD. [18]See here! [a]Its blood [b]was not brought into the Holy Place within! You should certainly have eaten it in the sanctuary just as I commanded!" [19]But Aaron spoke to Moses, "See here! Just today they presented their sin offering and their burnt offering before the LORD, and such things as these have happened to me! If [a]I

9:24 [b]Ezra 3:11   [c]1 Kgs 18:38–39   10:1 [a]Exod 24:1, 9; Num 3:2–4; 1 Chr 24:2   [b]Lev 16:12   [c]Exod 30:9; 1 Sam 2:17   10:2 [a]Gen 19:24; Num 11:1; 16:35; Rev 20:9   10:3 [1]Or perhaps *be treated as holy.*   10:4 [a]Acts 5:6, 10   10:6 [a]Num 1:53; 16:22, 46; 18:5; Josh 7:1; 22:18, 20; 2 Sam 24:1   [1]Or *do not take off your headgear;* Heb. *do not let free your heads.*   10:7 [a]Lev 8:33; 21:12   [b]Lev 8:30   10:9 [a]Gen 9:21; [Prov 20:1; 31:5]; Isa 28:7; Ezek 44:21; Hos 4:11; Luke 1:15; [Eph 5:18]; 1 Tim 3:3; Titus 1:7   10:10 [a]Lev 11:47; 20:25; Ezek 22:26; 44:23   10:11 [a]Deut 24:8; Neh 8:2, 8; Jer 18:18; Mal 2:7   10:12 [a]Num 18:9   [b]Lev 21:22   10:13 [a]Num 18:10   [b]Lev 2:3; 6:16   10:14 [a]Exod 29:24, 26, 27; Lev 7:30–34; Num 18:11   [b]Lev 22:13   [c]Num 18:10   10:15 [a]Lev 7:29–30, 34   10:16 [a]Lev 9:3, 15   10:17 [a]Lev 6:24–30   [b]Exod 28:38; Lev 22:16; Num 18:1   10:18 [a]Lev 6:30   [b]Lev 6:26, 30   10:19 [a]Lev 9:8, 12

had eaten a sin offering today, [b]would the LORD have been pleased?" [20]When Moses heard this explanation, he was satisfied.

Clean and Unclean Land Creatures

11 The LORD spoke to Moses and Aaron, saying to them, [2]"Tell [a]the Israelites: 'This is the kind of creature you may eat from among all the animals that are on the land. [3]You may eat any among the animals that has a divided hoof (the hooves are completely split in two) and that also chews the cud. [4]However, you must [a]not eat these from among those that chew the cud and have divided hooves: The camel is unclean to you because it chews the cud even though its hoof is not divided. [5]The rock badger is unclean to you because it chews the cud even though its hoof is not divided. [6]The hare is unclean to you because it chews the cud even though its hoof is not divided. [7]The pig [a]is unclean to you because its hoof is divided (the hoof is completely split in two), even though it does not chew the cud. [8]You must not eat from their meat, and you must not touch their carcasses; [a]they are unclean to you.

Clean and Unclean Water Creatures

[9]"'These you can eat from all creatures that are in [a]the water: Any creatures in the water that have both fins and scales, whether in the seas or in the streams, you may eat. [10]But any creatures that do not have both fins and scales, whether in the seas or in the streams, from all the swarming things of the water and from all the living creatures that are in the water, are [a]detestable to you. [11]Since they are detestable to you, you must not eat their meat, and their carcass you must detest. [12]Any creature in the water that does not have both fins and scales is detestable to you.

Clean and Unclean Birds

[13]"'[a]These you are to detest from among the birds—they must not be eaten, because they are detestable: the griffon vulture, the bearded vulture, the black vulture, [14]the kite, the buzzard of any kind, [15]every kind of crow, [16]the eagle owl, the short-eared owl, the long-eared owl, the hawk of any kind, [17]the little owl, the cormorant, the screech owl, [18]the white owl, the scops owl, the osprey, [19]the stork, the heron of any kind, the hoopoe, and the bat.

Clean and Unclean Insects

[20]"'Every winged swarming thing that walks on all fours is detestable to you. [21]However, this you may eat from all the winged swarming things that walk on all fours, which have jointed legs to hop with on the land. [22]These you may eat from [a]them: the locust of any kind, the bald locust of any kind, the cricket of any kind, the grasshopper of any kind. [23]But any other winged swarming thing that has four legs is detestable to you.

Carcass Uncleanness

[24]"'By these you defile yourselves—anyone who touches their carcass will be unclean until the evening, [25]and anyone who carries their carcass must wash his clothes and will be unclean until the evening.

Inedible Land Quadrupeds

[26]"'All animals that divide the hoof, but it is not completely split in two, and do not chew the cud are unclean to you; anyone who touches them becomes unclean. [27]All that walk on their paws among all the creatures that walk on all fours are unclean to you. Anyone who touches their carcass will be unclean until the evening, [28]and the one who carries their carcass must wash his clothes and be unclean until the evening; they are unclean to you.

Creatures That Swarm on the Land

[29]"'Now this is what is unclean to you among [a]the swarming things that swarm on the land: the rat, the mouse, the large lizard of any kind, [30]the Mediterranean gecko, the spotted lizard, the wall gecko, the skink, and the chameleon. [31]These are the ones that are unclean to you among all the swarming things. Anyone who [a]touches these creatures when they die will be unclean until evening. [32]Also, anything they fall on when they die will become unclean—any wood

10:19[b] [Isa 1:11–15]; Jer 6:20; 14:12; Hos 9:4; [Mal 1:10, 13; 3:1–4] 11:2 [a] Deut 14:4; Ezek 4:14; Dan 1:8; [Matt 15:11]; Acts 10:12, 14; [Rom 14:14; Heb 9:10; 13:9] 11:4 [a] Acts 10:14 11:7 [a] Isa 65:4; 66:3, 17; Mark 5:1–17 11:8 [a] Isa 52:11; [Mark 7:2, 15, 18]; Acts 10:14–15; 15:29 11:9 [a] Deut 14:9 11:10 [a] Lev 7:18, 21; Deut 14:3 11:13 [a] Deut 14:12–19; Isa 66:17 11:22 [a] Matt 3:4; Mark 1:6 11:29 [a] Isa 66:17 11:31 [a] Hag 2:13

vessel or garment or article of leather or sackcloth. Any such vessel [a]with which work is done must be immersed in water and will be unclean until the evening. Then it will become clean. [33]As for any [a]clay vessel they fall into, everything in it will become unclean, and [b]you must break it. [34]Any food that may be eaten which becomes soaked with water will become unclean. Anything drinkable in any such vessel will become unclean. [35]Anything their carcass may fall on will become unclean. An oven or small stove must be smashed to pieces; they are unclean, and they will stay unclean to you. [36]However, a spring or a cistern which collects water will be clean, but one who touches the creature's carcass will be unclean. [37]Now, if such a carcass falls on any sowing seed which is to be sown, it is clean, [38]but if water is put on the seed and such a carcass falls on it, it is unclean to you.

Edible Land Animals

[39]"'Now if an animal that you may eat dies, whoever touches its carcass will be [a]unclean until the evening. [40]One who eats from its carcass must wash his [a]clothes and be unclean until the evening, and whoever carries its carcass must wash his clothes and be unclean until the evening. [41]Every swarming thing that swarms on the land is detestable; it must not be eaten. [42]You must not eat anything that crawls on its belly or anything that walks on all fours or on any number of legs of all the swarming things that swarm on the land, because they are detestable. [43]Do not make [a]yourselves detestable by any of the swarming things. You must not defile yourselves by them and become unclean by them, [44]for I am the LORD your [a]God, and [b]you are to sanctify yourselves and be holy because I am holy. You must not defile yourselves by any of the swarming things that creep on the ground, [45a]for I am the LORD who brought [b]you up from the land of Egypt to be your God, and you are to be holy because I am holy. [46]This is the law of the land animals, the birds, all

the living creatures that move in the water, and all the creatures that swarm on the land, [47a]to distinguish between the unclean and the clean, between the living creatures that may be eaten and the living creatures that must not be eaten.'"

Purification of a Woman after Childbirth

12 The LORD spoke to Moses: [2]"Tell the Israelites, 'When a [a]woman produces offspring[1] and bears a male child, [b]she will be unclean seven days, [c]as she is unclean during the days of her menstruation. [3]On the [a]eighth day the flesh of his foreskin[1] must be circumcised. [4]Then she will remain thirty-three days in blood purity. She must not touch anything holy, and she must not enter the sanctuary until the days of her purification are fulfilled. [5]If she bears a female child, she will be impure fourteen days as during her menstrual flow, and she will remain sixty-six days in blood purity. [6]"'When the days of her purification are completed for a son or for a daughter, she must bring a one-year-old [b]lamb for a burnt offering and a young pigeon or turtledove for a [c]sin offering to the entrance of the Meeting Tent, to the priest. [7]The priest is to present it before the LORD and make atonement on her behalf, and she will be clean from her flow of blood. This is the law of the one who bears a child, for the male or the female child. [8]If she cannot afford [a]a sheep, then she must take two turtledoves or two young pigeons, one for a burnt offering and one for a sin offering, and the priest is to make atonement on her behalf, and she will be clean.'"

Infections on the Skin

13 The LORD spoke to Moses and Aaron: [2]"When someone [a]has a swelling or a scab or a bright spot on [b]the skin of his body that may become a diseased infection, he must be brought to Aaron the priest or one of his sons, the priests.[1] [3]The priest must then examine the infection on the skin of

11:32 [a]Lev 15:12   **11:33** [a]Lev 6:28   [b]Lev 15:12; Ps 2:9; Jer 48:38; [2 Tim 2:21]; Rev 2:27   **11:39** [a]Hag 2:11–13   **11:40** [a]Exod 22:31; Lev 17:15; 22:8; Deut 14:21; Ezek 4:14; 44:31   **11:43** [a]Lev 20:25   **11:44** [a]Exod 6:7; Lev 22:33; 25:38; 26:45   [b]Exod 19:6; Lev 19:2; 20:7, 26; [Amos 3:3]; Matt 5:48; 1 Thess 4:7; 1 Pet 1:15–16; [Rev 22:11, 14]   **11:45** [a]Exod 6:7; 20:2; Lev 22:33; 25:38; 26:45; Ps 105:43–45; Hos 11:1   [b]Lev 11:44   **11:47** [a]Lev 10:10; Ezek 44:23; Mal 3:18   **12:2** [a]Lev 15:19; [Job 14:4; Ps 51:5]   [b]Exod 22:30; Lev 8:33; 13:4; Luke 2:22   [c]Lev 18:19   [1]Heb. *produces seed*; i.e., the whole process of childbearing, from conception to birth.   **12:3** [a]Gen 17:12; Luke 1:59; 2:21; John 7:22–23; Gal 5:3   [1]Or perhaps *the foreskin of his member.*   **12:6** [a]Luke 2:22   [b][John 1:29; 1 Pet 1:18–19]   [c]Lev 5:7   **12:8** [a]Lev 5:7; Luke 2:22–24   **13:2** [a]Deut 28:27; Isa 3:17   [b]Deut 17:8–9; 24:8; Mal 2:7; Luke 17:14   [1]Or *it shall be reported to Aaron the priest.*

the body, and if the hair in the infection has turned white and the infection appears to be deeper than the skin of the body, then it is a diseased infection, so when the priest examines it, he must pronounce the person unclean.

A Bright Spot on the Skin

[4]"If it is a white bright spot on the skin of his body, but it does not appear to be deeper than the skin, and the hair has not turned white, then the priest is to quarantine the person with the infection for [a]seven days. [5]The priest must then examine it on the seventh day, and if, as far as he can see, the infection has stayed the same and has not spread on the skin, then the priest is to quarantine the person for another seven days. [6]The priest must then examine it again on the seventh day, and if the infection has faded and has not spread on the skin, then the priest is to pronounce the person clean. It is [a]a scab, so he must wash his clothes and be clean. [7]If, however, the scab is spreading further on the skin after he has shown himself to the priest for his purification, then he must show himself to the priest a second time. [8]The priest must then examine it, and if the scab has spread on the skin, then the priest is to pronounce the person unclean. It is a disease.

A Swelling on the Skin

[9]"When someone has a diseased infection, he must be brought to the priest. [10]The priest will then examine it, [a]and if a white swelling is on the skin, it has turned the hair white, and there is raw flesh in the swelling, [11]it is a chronic disease on the skin of his body, so the priest is to pronounce him unclean. The priest must not merely quarantine him, for he is unclean. [12]If, however, the disease breaks out on the skin so that the disease covers all the skin of the person with the infection from his head to his feet, as far as the priest can see, [13]the priest must then examine it,[1] and if the disease covers his whole body, he is to pronounce the person with the infection clean. He has turned all [a]white, so he is clean. [14]But whenever raw flesh appears in it, he will be unclean, [15]so the priest is to examine the raw flesh and pronounce him unclean—it is diseased. [16]If, however, the raw flesh once again turns white, then he must come to the priest. [17]The priest will then examine it, and if the infection has turned white, the priest is to pronounce the person with the infection clean—he is clean.

A Boil on the Skin

[18]"When someone's body has a [a]boil on its skin[1] and it heals, [19]and in the place of the boil there is a white swelling or a reddish white bright spot, he must show himself to the priest.[1] [20]The priest will then examine it, and if it appears to be deeper than the skin and its hair has turned white, then the priest is to pronounce the person unclean. It is a diseased infection that has broken out in the boil. [21]If, however, the priest examines it, and there is no white hair in it, it is not deeper than the skin, and it has faded, then the priest is to quarantine him for seven days. [22]If it is spreading farther on the skin, then the priest is to pronounce him unclean. It is an infection. [23]But if the bright spot stays in its place and has not spread, it is the scar of the boil, so the priest is to pronounce him clean.

A Burn on the Skin

[24]"When a body has a [a]burn on its skin and the raw area of the burn becomes a reddish white or white bright spot, [25]the priest must examine it, and if the hair has turned white in the bright spot and it appears to be deeper than the skin, it is a disease that has broken out in the burn. The priest is to pronounce the person unclean. It is a diseased infection. [26]If, however, the priest examines it and there is no white hair in the bright spot, it is not deeper than the skin, and it has faded, then the priest is to quarantine him for seven days. [27]The priest must then examine it on the seventh day, and if it is spreading further on the skin, then the priest is to pronounce him unclean. It is a diseased infection. [28]But if the bright spot stays in its place, has not spread on the skin, and it has faded, then it is the swelling of the burn, so the priest is to pronounce him clean, because it is the scar of the burn.

13:4 [a] Lev 14:8   **13:6** [a] Lev 11:25; 14:8; [John 13:8, 10]   **13:10** [a] Num 12:10, 12; 2 Kgs 5:27; 2 Chr 26:19–20   **13:13** [a] Exod 4:6
[1] Heb. *and the priest shall see*; probably the infection.   **13:18** [a] Exod 9:9; 15:26   [1] Smr. omits *its skin*.
13:19 [1] Or *it shall be shown to* [or *be seen by*] *the priest*.   **13:24** [a] Isa 3:24

Scall on the Head or in the Beard

[29]"When a man or a woman has an infection on the head or in the beard, [30]the priest is to examine the infection, and if it appears to be deeper than the skin and the hair in it is reddish yellow and thin, then the priest is to pronounce the person unclean. It is scall,[1] a disease of the head or the beard. [31]But if the priest examines the scall infection and it does not appear to be deeper than the skin, and there is no black hair in it, then the priest is to quarantine the person with the scall infection for seven days. [32]The priest must then examine the infection on the seventh day, and if the scall has not spread, there is no reddish yellow hair in it, and the scall does not appear to be deeper than the skin, [33]then the individual is to shave himself,[1] but he must not shave the area affected by the scall, and the priest is to quarantine the person with the scall for another seven days. [34]The priest must then examine the scall on the seventh day, and if the scall has not spread on the skin and it does not appear to be deeper than the skin, then the priest is to pronounce him clean. So he is to wash his clothes and be clean. [35]If, however, the scall spreads further on the skin after his purification, [36]then the priest is to examine it, and if the scall has spread on the skin, the priest is not to search further for reddish yellow hair. The person[1] is unclean. [37]If, as far as the priest can see, the scall has stayed the same and black hair has sprouted in it, the scall has been healed; the person is clean. So the priest is to pronounce him clean.

Bright White Spots on the Skin

[38]"When a man or a woman has bright spots—white bright spots—on the skin of their body, [39]the priest is to examine them,[1] and if the bright spots on the skin of their body are faded white, it is a harmless rash that has broken out on the skin. The person is clean.[2]

Baldness on the Head

[40]"When a man's head is bare so that he is balding in back, he is clean. [41]If his head is bare on the forehead so that he is balding in front, he is clean. [42]But if there is a reddish white infection in the back or [a]front bald area, it is a disease breaking out in his back or front bald area. [43]The priest is to examine it,[1] and if the swelling of the infection is reddish white in the back or the front bald area like the appearance of a disease on the skin of the body, [44]he is a diseased man. He is unclean. The priest must surely pronounce him unclean because of his infection on his [a]head.

The Life of the Person with Skin Disease

[45]"As for the diseased person who has the infection, his clothes must be torn, the hair of his head must be [a]unbound, he must [b]cover his mustache,[1] and he must call out 'Unclean! [c]Unclean!' [46]The whole time he has the infection he will be continually unclean. He must live in isolation, and his place of residence must be [a]outside the camp.

Infections in Garments, Cloth, or Leather

[47]"When a garment has a diseased infection in it, whether a wool or linen garment, [48]or in the warp or woof of the linen or the wool, or in leather or anything made of leather, [49]if the infection in the garment or leather or warp or woof or any article of leather is yellowish green or reddish, it is a diseased infection, and it must be shown to the priest. [50]The priest is to examine and then quarantine the article with the infection for seven days. [51]He must then examine the infection on the seventh day. If the infection has spread in the garment, or in the warp, or in the woof, or in the leather—whatever the article into which the leather was made—the infection is [a]a malignant disease. It is unclean. [52]He must burn the garment or the warp or the woof, whether wool or linen, or any article of leather which has the infection in it. Because it is a malignant disease it must be burned up in the fire. [53]But if the priest examines it and

---

13:30 [1]Related to the Heb. verb *to tear, to tear out, to tear apart*; perhaps derived from the scratching and/or the tearing out of the hair or the scales of the skin in response to the itching sensation caused by the disease.   13:33 [1]Or perhaps *he shall be shaven.*   13:36 [1]Heb. *he.*   13:39 [1]Heb. *and the priest shall see.*   [2]Heb. *he*; but the regulation applies to a man or a woman.   13:42 [a]2 Chr 26:19   13:43 [1]Heb. *and the priest shall see him/it.*   13:44 [a]Isa 1:5   13:45 [a]Lev 10:6; 21:10   [b]Ezek 24:17, 22; Mic 3:7   [c]Isa 6:5; 64:6; Lam 4:15; Luke 5:8   [1]Heb. *and his head shall be unbound, and he shall cover on* [his] *mustache*; ways of expressing shame, grief, or distress.   13:46 [a]Num 5:1–4; 12:14; 2 Kgs 7:3; 15:5; 2 Chr 26:21; Ps 38:11; Luke 17:12   13:51 [a]Lev 14:44

the infection has not spread in the garment or in the warp or in the woof or in any article of leather, [54] the priest is to command that they wash whatever has the infection and quarantine it for another seven days. [55] The priest must then examine it after the infection has been washed out, and if the infection has not changed its appearance even though the infection has not spread, it is unclean. You must burn it up in the fire. It is a fungus, whether on the back side or front side of the article.[1] [56] But if the priest has examined it and the infection has faded after it has been washed, he is to tear it out of the garment or the leather or the warp or the woof. [57] Then if it still appears again in the garment or the warp or the woof, or in any article of leather, it is an outbreak. Whatever has the infection in it you must burn up in the fire. [58] But the garment or the warp or the woof or any article of leather which you wash and infection disappears from it is to be washed a second time, and it will be clean."

Summary of Infection Regulations

[59] This is the law of the diseased infection in the garment of wool or linen, or the warp or woof, or any article of leather, for pronouncing it clean or unclean.

Purification of Diseased Skin Infections

14 The LORD spoke to Moses: [2] "This is the law of the diseased person on the day of his purification, when he is brought to the priest.[1] [3] The priest is to go outside the camp and examine the infection. If the infection of the diseased person has been healed, [4] then the priest will command that two live clean birds, a piece of [a]cedar wood, a scrap of [b]crimson fabric,[1] and some twigs of [c]hyssop be taken up for the one being cleansed. [5] The priest will then command that one bird be slaughtered into a clay vessel over fresh water. [6] Then he is to take the live bird along with the piece of cedar wood, the scrap of crimson fabric, and the twigs of hyssop, and he is to dip them and

the live bird in the blood of the bird slaughtered over the fresh water, [7] and [a]sprinkle it [b]seven times on the one being cleansed from the disease, pronounce him clean, and send the live bird away over the open countryside.

The Seven Days of Purification

[8] "The one being cleansed must then wash his clothes, shave off [a]all his hair, and [b]bathe in water, and so be clean. Then afterward he may enter the camp, but he must live outside his tent seven days. [9] When the [a]seventh day comes, he must shave all his hair—his head, his beard, his eyebrows, all his hair—and he must wash his clothes, bathe his body in water, and so be clean.

The Eighth-Day Atonement Rituals

[10] "On [a]the eighth [b]day he[1] must take two flawless male lambs, one flawless yearling female lamb, three-tenths of an ephah of choice wheat flour as a grain offering mixed with olive oil, and one log of olive oil,[2] [11] and the priest who pronounces him clean will have the man who is being cleansed stand along with these offerings before the LORD at the entrance of the Meeting Tent. [12] "The priest is to take one male lamb and [a]present it for a guilt offering along with the log of olive oil and [b]present them as a wave offering before the LORD.[1] [13] He must then slaughter the male lamb [a]in the place where the sin offering and the burnt offering are slaughtered,[1] in the sanctuary, because, like the sin offering, the guilt offering belongs to the priest; [b]it is most holy. [14] Then the priest is to take some of the blood of the guilt offering and put it [a]on the right earlobe of the one being cleansed, on the thumb of his right hand, and on the big toe of his right foot. [15] The priest will then take some of the log of olive oil and pour it into his own left hand. [16] Then the priest is to dip his right forefinger into the olive oil that is in his left hand, and [a]sprinkle some of the olive oil with his finger seven times before the LORD. [17] The priest will then put

13:55 [1] I.e., the inside versus the outside, or the back versus the front.   **14:2** [1] Or *when it is reported to the priest.*
14:4 [a] Lev 14:6, 49, 51, 52; Num 19:6; Heb 9:19   [b] Exod 25:4   [c] Exod 12:22; Ps 51:7   [1] Lit. *crimson of worm*; the source for a crimson dye.   **14:7** [a] Num 19:18–19; [Heb 9:13, 21; 12:24]   [b] 2 Kgs 5:10, 14; Ps 51:2   **14:8** [a] Lev 11:25; 13:6; Num 8:7   [b] Lev 11:25; [Eph 5:26; Heb 10:22; Rev 1:5–6]   **14:9** [a] Num 19:19   **14:10** [a] Matt 8:4; Mark 1:44; Luke 5:14   [b] Lev 2:1; Num 15:4   [1] Probably the formerly diseased person.   [2] About ⅙ liter, ⅓ pint, or ⅔ cup.   **14:12** [a] Lev 5:6, 18; 6:6; 14:19   [b] Exod 29:22–24, 26   [1] Or *elevate them* [as] *an elevation offering before the LORD, present them* [as] *a presentation offering before the LORD;* Heb. *wave them* [as] *a wave offering before the LORD.*   **14:13** [a] Exod 29:11; Lev 1:5, 11; 4:4, 24   [b] Lev 2:3; 7:6; 21:22   [1] Probably by the priest.   **14:14** [a] Exod 29:20; Lev 8:23–24   **14:16** [a] Lev 4:6

some of the rest of the olive oil that is in his hand on the right earlobe of the one being cleansed, on the thumb of his right hand, and on the big toe of his right foot, on the blood of the guilt offering, [18]and the remainder of the olive oil that is in his hand the priest is to put on the head of the one being cleansed. [a]So the priest is to make atonement for him before the LORD.

[19]"The priest must [a]then perform the sin offering and make atonement for the one being cleansed from his impurity. After that he[1] is to slaughter the burnt offering, [20]and the priest is to offer the burnt offering and the grain offering on the altar. So the priest is to make atonement for him and he will be [a]clean.

The Eighth-Day Atonement Rituals for the Poor Person

[21]"If the person is poor and does not have sufficient means, he must take one male lamb as a guilt offering for a wave offering to make atonement for himself, one-tenth of an ephah of choice wheat flour mixed with olive oil for a grain offering, a log of olive oil, [22]and two turtledoves or two young pigeons, which are within his means. One will be [a]a sin offering and the other a burnt offering.

[23]"On [a]the eighth day he must bring them for his purification to the priest at the entrance of the Meeting Tent before the LORD, [24]and the priest is to take the male lamb of the guilt offering [a]and the log of olive oil and wave them[1] as a wave offering before the LORD. [25]Then he is to slaughter the male lamb of the guilt offering, [a]and the priest is to take some of the blood of the guilt offering and put it on the right earlobe of the one being cleansed, on the thumb of his right hand, and on the big toe of his right foot. [26]The priest will then pour some of the olive oil into his own left hand, [27]and sprinkle some of the olive oil that is in his left hand with his right forefinger seven times before the LORD. [28]Then the priest is to put some of the olive oil that is in his hand on the right earlobe of the one being cleansed, on the thumb of his right hand, and on the big toe of his right foot, on the place of the blood of the guilt offering, [29]and the remainder of the olive oil that is in the hand of the priest he is to put on the head of the one being cleansed to make atonement for him before the LORD.

[30]"He will [a]then make one of the turtledoves or young pigeons, which are within his means,[1] [31]a sin offering and the other a burnt offering along with the grain offering. So the priest is to make atonement for the one being cleansed before the LORD. [32]This is [a]the law of the one in whom there is a diseased infection, who does not have sufficient means for his purification."

Purification of Disease-Infected Houses

[33]The Lord spoke to Moses and Aaron: [34]"[a]When you enter the land of Canaan [b]which I am about to give to you for a possession, and I put a diseased infection in a house in the land you are to possess, [35]then whoever owns the house must come and declare to the priest, '[a]Something like an infection is visible to me in the house.' [36]Then the priest will command that the house be cleared before the priest enters to examine the infection so that everything in the house does not become unclean, and afterward the priest will enter to examine the house. [37]He is to examine the infection, and if the infection in the walls of the house consists of yellowish green or reddish eruptions,[1] and it appears to be deeper than the surface of the wall,[2] [38]then the priest is to go out of the house to the doorway of the house and quarantine the house for seven days. [39]The priest must return on the seventh day and examine it, and if the infection has spread in the walls of the house, [40]then the priest is to command that the stones that had the infection in them be pulled and thrown outside the city into an unclean place. [41]Then they shall scrape[1] the house all around on the inside, and the plaster which they have scraped off[2] must be dumped outside the city into an unclean place. [42]They are then to take other stones and replace those stones, and he is to take other plaster and replaster the house.

14:18 [a] Lev 4:26; 5:6; Num 15:28; [Heb 2:17]   14:19 [a] Lev 5:1, 6; 12:7; [2 Cor 5:21]   [1] Probably the offerer.   14:20 [a] Lev 14:8–9   14:22 [a] Lev 12:8; 15:14–15   14:23 [a] Lev 14:10–11   14:24 [a] Lev 14:12   [1] Heb. *and the priest shall wave them.*   14:25 [a] Lev 14:14, 17   14:30 [a] Lev 14:22; 15:14–15   [1] Heb. *from which his hand reaches.*   14:32 [a] Lev 14:10   14:34 [a] Gen 12:7; 13:17; 17:8; Num 32:22; Deut 7:1; 32:49   [b] [Prov 3:33]   14:35 [a] [Ps 91:9–10; Prov 3:33; Zech 5:4]   14:37 [1] Or *depressions, streaks.*   [2] I.e., a coating of plaster made of limestone and sand.   14:41 [1] MT *he shall scrape/he shall have* [it] *scraped.*   [2] MT possibly *they caused to be cut off.*

[43]"If the infection returns and breaks out in the house after he has pulled out the stones, scraped the house, and it is re-plastered, [44]the priest is to come [a]and examine it, and if the infection has spread in the house, it is a malignant disease in the house. It is unclean. [45]He must tear down the house, its stones, its wood, and all the plaster of the house, and take all of it outside the city to an unclean place. [46]Anyone who enters the house all the days the priest has quarantined it will be unclean [a]until evening. [47]Anyone who lies down in the house must [a]wash his clothes. Anyone who eats in the house must wash his clothes.

[48]"If, however, the priest enters and examines it, and the infection has not spread in the house after the house has been re-plastered, then the priest is to pronounce the house clean because the infection has been healed. [49]Then [a]he is to take two birds, a piece of cedar wood, a scrap of crimson fabric, and some twigs of hyssop to purify the house, [50]and he is to slaughter one bird into a clay vessel over fresh water. [51]He must then take the piece of cedar wood, the twigs of hyssop, the scrap of crimson fabric, and the live bird, and dip them in the blood of the slaughtered bird and in the fresh water, and sprinkle the house seven times. [52]So he is to purify the house with the blood of the bird, the fresh water, the live bird, the piece of cedar wood, the twigs of hyssop, and the scrap of crimson fabric, [53]and he is to send the live bird away outside the city into the open countryside. So he is to [a]make atonement for the house, and it will be clean.

Summary of Purification Regulations for Infections

[54]"This is the law for all [a]diseased infections, for scall, [55]for the [a]diseased garment, for the house, [56]for the swelling, [a]for the scab, and for the bright spot, [57]to [a]teach when something is unclean and when it is clean. This is the law for dealing with infectious disease."

Male Bodily Discharges

15 The LORD spoke to Moses and Aaron: [2]"Speak to the Israelites and tell them, '[a]When any man has a discharge from his body,[1] his discharge is unclean. [3]Now this is his uncleanness in regard to his discharge—whether his body secretes his discharge or blocks his discharge, he is unclean. All the days that his body has a discharge or his body blocks his discharge,[1] this is his uncleanness.

[4]"'Any bed the man with a discharge lies on will be unclean, and any furniture he sits on will be unclean. [5]Anyone who [a]touches his bed must [b]wash his clothes, [c]bathe in water, and be unclean until evening. [6]The one who sits on the furniture the man with a [a]discharge sits on must wash his clothes, bathe in water, and be unclean until evening. [7]The one who touches the body[1] of the man with a discharge must wash his clothes, bathe in water, and be unclean until evening. [8]If the man with a discharge [a]spits on a person who is ceremonially clean, that person must wash his clothes, bathe in water, and be unclean until evening. [9]Any means of riding that the man with a discharge rides on will be unclean. [10]Anyone who touches anything that was under him will be unclean until evening, and the one who carries those items must wash his clothes, bathe in water, and be unclean until evening. [11]Anyone whom the man with the discharge touches without having rinsed his hands in water must wash his clothes, bathe in water, and be unclean until evening. [12]A clay vessel which the man with the discharge touches must be broken, and any wooden [a]utensil must be rinsed in water.

Purity Regulations for Male Bodily Discharges

[13]"'When [a]the man with the discharge becomes clean from his discharge, he is to count off for himself seven days for his purification, and he must wash his clothes, bathe in fresh water, and be clean. [14]Then on

14:44 [a]Lev 13:51; [Zech 5:4]   **14:46** [a]Lev 11:24; 15:5   **14:47** [a]Lev 14:8   **14:49** [a]Lev 14:4   **14:53** [a]Lev 14:20   **14:54** [a]Lev 13:30; 26:21   **14:55** [a]Lev 13:47–52   **14:56** [a]Lev 13:2   **14:57** [a]Lev 11:47; 20:25; Deut 24:8; Ezek 44:23   **15:2** [a]Lev 22:4; Num 5:2; 2 Sam 3:29   [1]Heb. *when there is a discharge from his flesh*; a euphemism for the male and female genital members or areas of the body.   **15:3** [1]Smr. adds *he is unclean; all the days that his body has a discharge or his body blocks his discharge*; LXX adds *all the days of the flow of his body, by which his body is affected by the flow*.   **15:5** [a]Lev 5:2; 14:46   [b]Lev 14:8, 47   [c]Lev 11:25; 17:15   **15:6** [a]Lev 15:10; Deut 23:10   **15:7** [1]Heb. *And the one who touches in the flesh*; probably refers literally to any part of the body, not the genitals specifically.   **15:8** [a]Num 12:14   **15:12** [a]Lev 6:28; 11:32–33   **15:13** [a]Lev 14:8; 15:28; Num 19:11–12

the eighth day he is to take for himself [a]two turtledoves or two young pigeons, and he is to present himself[1] before the LORD at the entrance of the Meeting Tent and give them to the priest, [15]and [a]the priest is to make one of them a sin offering and the other a burnt offering. [b]So the priest is to make atonement for him before the LORD for his discharge.

[16]"[a]When a man has a seminal emission, he must bathe his whole body in water and be unclean until evening, [17]and he must wash in water any clothing or leather that has semen on it, and it will be unclean until evening. [18]As for a woman whom a man goes to [a]bed with, then has a seminal emission, they must bathe in water and be unclean until evening.

Female Bodily Discharges

[19]"[a]When a woman has a discharge and her discharge is blood from her body,[1] she is to be in her menstruation seven days, and anyone who touches her will be unclean until evening. [20]Anything she lies on during her menstruation will be unclean, and anything she sits on will be unclean. [21]Anyone who touches her bed must wash his clothes, bathe in water, and be unclean until evening. [22]Anyone who touches any furniture she sits on must wash his clothes, bathe in water, and be unclean until evening. [23]If there is something on the bed or on the furniture she sits on, when he touches it,[1] he will be unclean until evening, [24]and [a]if a man actually goes to bed[1] with her so that her menstrual impurity touches him, then he will be unclean seven days, and any bed he lies on will be unclean.

[25]"When [a]a woman's discharge of blood flows many days not at the time of her menstruation, or if it flows beyond the time of her menstruation, all the days of her discharge of impurity will be like the days of her menstruation—she is unclean. [26]Any bed she lies on all the days of her discharge will be to her like the bed of her menstruation, any furniture she sits on will be unclean like the impurity of her menstruation, [27]and anyone who touches them will be unclean, and he must wash his clothes, bathe in water, and be unclean until evening.

Purity Regulations for Female Bodily Discharges

[28]"If she becomes clean from her discharge, then she is to count off for herself seven days, and afterward she will be clean. [29]Then on the eighth day she must take for herself two turtledoves or two young pigeons, and she must bring them to the priest at the entrance of the Meeting Tent, [30]and the priest is to make one a sin offering and the other a [a]burnt offering. So the priest is to make atonement for her before the LORD from her discharge of impurity.

Summary of Purification Regulations for Bodily Discharges

[31]"Thus you are to [a]set the Israelites apart from their impurity so that they do not die in their impurity by [b]defiling my tabernacle which is in their midst. [32]This [a]is the law for the one with [b]a discharge: for the one who has a seminal emission and becomes unclean by it, [33]for the one who is sick in her menstruation, for the one with [a]a discharge, whether male [b]or female, [c]and for a man who goes to bed[1] with an unclean woman.'"

The Day of Atonement

16 The LORD spoke to Moses after [a]the death of Aaron's two sons when they approached the presence of the LORD and died, [2]and the LORD said to Moses: "Tell Aaron your brother that he must [a]not enter at any [b]time into the Holy Place inside the special curtain in front of the atonement lid[1] that is on the ark so that he may not die, for I will appear in the cloud over the atonement lid.

Day of Atonement Offerings

[3]"In this way Aaron is to [a]enter into the sanctuary—[b]with a young bull for a sin

15:14 [a] Lev 14:22–23, 30, 31 [1] MT *to come*; LXX *to bring.*   15:15 [a] Lev 14:30–31 [b] Lev 14:19, 31   15:16 [a] Lev 22:4; Deut 23:10–11   15:18 [a] [Exod 19:15; 1 Sam 21:4; 1 Cor 6:18]   15:19 [a] Lev 12:2 [1] Heb. *blood shall be her discharge in her flesh*; a euphemism for the female genitals.   15:23 [1] This phrase could go with the preceding line or be an introduction to what follows.   15:24 [a] Lev 18:19; 20:18 [1] Heb. *actually lies down with*; a euphemism for sexual relations.   15:25 [a] Matt 9:20; Mark 5:25; Luke 8:43   15:30 [a] Lev 5:7   15:31 [a] Lev 11:47; 14:57; 22:2; Deut 24:8; Ezek 44:23; [Heb 12:15] [b] Lev 20:3; Num 5:3; 19:13, 20; Ezek 5:11; 23:38; 36:17   15:32 [a] Lev 15:2 [b] Lev 15:16   15:33 [a] Lev 15:19 [b] Lev 15:25 [c] Lev 15:24 [1] Heb. *who lies down with*; a euphemism for sexual relations.   16:1 [a] Lev 10:1–2; 2 Sam 6:6–8   16:2 [a] Exod 30:10; Lev 16:34; 23:27; [Heb 6:19; 9:7–8, 12; 10:19] [b] Exod 25:21–22; 40:34; 1 Kgs 8:10–12 [1] Trad. *mercy seat*; Heb. *to the faces of the atonement lid.*   16:3 [a] Lev 4:1–12; 16:6; [Heb 9:7, 12, 24, 25] [b] Lev 4:3

offering and a ram for a burnt offering. [4]He must put on a [a]holy linen tunic, linen leggings are to cover his body,[1] and [b]he is to wrap himself with a linen sash and wrap his head with a linen turban. They are holy garments, so he must bathe his body in water and put them on. [5]He must also take two male goats from [a]the congregation of the Israelites for a sin offering and one ram for a burnt offering. [6]Then Aaron is to present the sin-offering bull which is for himself and is to [a]make atonement on behalf of himself and his household. [7]Next he must take the two goats and stand them before the LORD at the entrance of the Meeting Tent, [8]and Aaron is to cast lots over the two goats, one lot for the LORD and one lot for Azazel.[1] [9]Aaron must then present the goat which has been designated by lot for the LORD, and he is to make it a sin offering, [10]but the goat which has been designated by lot for Azazel is to be stood alive before the LORD to make [a]atonement on it by sending it away into the desert to Azazel.[1]

The Sin-Offering Sacrificial Procedures

[11]"Aaron is to present the sin-offering bull which is for [a]himself, and he is to make atonement on behalf of himself and his household. He is to slaughter the sin-offering bull which is for himself, [12]and [a]take a censer full of coals of fire from the altar before the LORD and a full double handful of finely ground [b]fragrant incense, and bring them inside the curtain. [13]He must then put the incense on the fire before the LORD, [a]and the cloud of incense will cover the atonement lid which is above the ark of the testimony, so that he will not [b]die. [14]Then [a]he is to take some of the blood of the bull and [b]sprinkle it with his finger on the eastern face of the atonement lid, and in front of the atonement lid he is to sprinkle some of the blood seven times with his finger.

[15]"Aaron must [a]then slaughter the sin-offering goat which is for the people. He is to bring its blood [b]inside the curtain, and he is to do with its blood just as he did to the blood of the bull: He is to sprinkle it on the atonement lid and in front of the atonement lid. [16]So he is to [a]make atonement for the Holy Place from the impurities of the Israelites and from their transgressions with regard to all their sins, and thus he is to do for the Meeting Tent which resides with them in the midst of their impurities. [17]Nobody is to be in the Meeting Tent when he enters to make atonement in the Holy Place until he goes out, and he has made atonement on his behalf, on behalf of his household, and on behalf of the whole assembly of Israel.

[18]"Then Aaron is to go out to the altar which is before the LORD and make atonement for [a]it. He is to take some of the blood of the bull and some of the blood of the goat, and put it all around on the horns of the altar. [19]Then he is to sprinkle on it some of the blood with his finger seven times, and cleanse and [a]consecrate it from the impurities of the Israelites.

The Live Goat Ritual Procedures

[20]"When Aaron has finished purifying the Holy Place, the Meeting Tent, and the altar, he is to present the live goat. [21]Aaron is to lay his two hands on the head of the live goat and [a]confess over it all the iniquities of the Israelites and all their transgressions in regard to all their sins, and thus he is to [b]put them on the head of the goat and send it away into the desert by the hand of a man standing ready.[1] [22]The goat is to [a]bear on itself all their iniquities into an inaccessible land,[1] so he is to [b]send the goat away into the desert.

The Concluding Rituals

[23]"Aaron must then enter the Meeting Tent and take off the linen garments which he had put on when he entered the sanctuary, and leave them there. [24]Then he must bathe his body in water in the Holy Place, put on his clothes, and go out and make

16:4 [a] Exod 28:39, 42, 43; Lev 6:10; Ezek 44:17–18 [b] Exod 30:20; Lev 8:6–7 [1] Heb. *shall be on his flesh*; a euphemism for the genitals.   16:5 [a] Lev 4:14; Num 29:11; 2 Chr 29:21; Ezra 6:17; Ezek 45:22–23   16:6 [a] Lev 9:7; [Heb 5:3; 7:27–28; 9:7]   16:8 [1] Perhaps a combination of "goat" (Heb. *ez*) and "to go away" (Heb. *azal*), meaning the "goat that departs" or "scapegoat"; the name of the wilderness area to which the goat was dispatched; or the proper name of a particular demon (perhaps even the devil) associated with the wilderness desert regions (without intention of appeasing that demon).   16:10 [a] [Isa 53:5–6; Rom 3:25; Heb 7:27; 9:23–24; 1 John 2:2] [1] See the note on v. 8.   16:11 [a] [Heb 7:27; 9:7]   16:12 [a] Lev 10:1; Num 16:7, 18; Isa 6:6–7; Rev 8:5 [b] Exod 30:34–38   16:13 [a] Exod 30:7–8; Num 16:7, 18, 46 [b] Exod 28:43; Lev 22:9; Num 4:15, 20   16:14 [a] Lev 4:5; [Heb 9:25; 10:4] [b] Lev 4:6, 17   16:15 [a] [Heb 2:17] [b] [Heb 6:19; 7:27; 9:3, 7, 12]   16:16 [a] Exod 29:36; 30:10; Ezek 45:18; [Heb 9:22–24]   16:18 [a] Exod 29:36   16:19 [a] Lev 16:14; Ezek 43:20   16:21 [a] Lev 5:5; 26:40 [b] [Isa 53:6] [1] Or *appointed*; i.e., designated for the task.   16:22 [a] Lev 8:14; [Isa 53:6, 11, 12; John 1:29; Heb 9:28; 1 Pet 2:24] [b] Lev 14:7 [1] Or *infertile land*.

his burnt offering and the people's burnt offering. So he is to make atonement on behalf of himself and the people.

[25]"Then [a]he is to offer up the fat of the sin offering in smoke on the altar, [26]and the one who sent the goat away to Azazel[1] must wash his clothes, bathe his body in water, [a]and afterward he may reenter the camp. [27]The bull of [a]the sin offering and the goat of the sin offering, whose blood was brought to make atonement in the Holy Place, must be brought outside the camp and their hide, their flesh, and their dung must be burned up,[1] [28]and the one who burns them must wash his clothes and bathe his body in water, and afterward he may reenter the camp.

Review of the Day of Atonement

[29]"This is to be a perpetual statute for you. [a]In the seventh month, on the tenth day of the month, you must humble yourselves and do no work of any kind, both the native citizen and the resident foreigner who lives in your midst, [30]for on this day atonement is to be made for you to [a]cleanse you from all your sins; you must be clean before the LORD. [31]It is to be a Sabbath of complete rest for you, and you must humble yourselves. [a]It is a perpetual statute.

[32]"The priest who is anointed [a]and [b]ordained to act as high priest in place of his father is to make atonement. He is to put on the linen garments, the holy garments, [33]and he is to purify the Most Holy Place,[1] he is to purify the Meeting Tent and the altar, and he is to make atonement for the priests and for all the people of the assembly. [34]This [a]is to be a perpetual statute for you to make atonement for the Israelites for all their sins [b]once a year." So he did just as the LORD had commanded Moses.

The Slaughter of Animals

17 The LORD spoke to Moses, [2]"Speak to Aaron, his sons, and all the Israelites, and tell them, 'This is the word that the LORD has commanded, [3]"Blood guilt will be accounted to any man from the house of Israel who [a]slaughters an ox or a lamb or a goat inside the camp or outside the camp, [4]but has not brought it to the entrance of the Meeting Tent to present it as[1] an offering to the LORD before the tabernacle of the LORD. He has shed blood, so that man will be cut off from the midst of his people. [5]This is so that the Israelites will bring their sacrifices that they are sacrificing in the open field to the LORD at the entrance of the Meeting Tent— to the priest—and sacrifice them there as peace-offering sacrifices to the LORD. [6]The priest [a]is to splash the blood on the altar of the LORD at the entrance of the Meeting Tent, and [b]offer the fat up in smoke for a soothing aroma to the LORD. [7]So the people must no longer offer[1] their sacrifices [a]to the goat demons, acting like prostitutes by going after them. This is to be [b]a perpetual statute for them throughout their generations.'"

[8]"You are to say to them: 'Any man from the house of Israel or from the resident foreigners [a]who live in their[1] midst, who offers a burnt offering or a sacrifice [9]but does not [a]bring it to the entrance of the Meeting Tent to offer it to the LORD—that person will be cut off from his people.

Prohibition against Eating Blood

[10]"'Any man from the house of Israel or from the resident foreigners who live in their[1] midst who eats any blood, I will set my face against that person who eats the blood, [a]and [b]I will cut him off from the midst of his people, [11]for the [a]life of every living thing[1] is in the blood. So I myself have assigned it [b]to you on the altar to make atonement for your lives, for the blood makes atonement by means of the life. [12]Therefore, I have said to the Israelites: No person among you is to eat blood, and no resident foreigner who lives among you is to eat blood.

[13]"'Any man from the Israelites[1] or from the resident foreigners who live in their[2] midst who [a]hunts a wild animal or a bird that may be eaten must [b]pour out its blood

16:25 [a] Lev 1:8; 4:10   **16:26** [a] Lev 15:5   [1] See the note on v. 8.   **16:27** [a] Lev 4:12, 21; 6:30; Heb 13:11   [1] Heb. *they shall burn with fire.*   **16:29** [a] Exod 30:10; Lev 23:27–32; Num 29:7   **16:30** [a] Ps 51:2; Jer 33:8; [Eph 5:26; Heb 9:13–14; 1 John 1:7, 9]   **16:31** [a] Lev 23:27, 32; Ezra 8:21; Isa 58:3, 5; Dan 10:12   **16:32** [a] Lev 4:3, 5, 16; 21:10   [b] Exod 29:29–30; Num 20:26, 28   **16:33** [1] Heb. *the sanctuary of the holy place.*   **16:34** [a] Lev 23:31; Num 29:7   [b] Exod 30:10; [Heb 9:7, 25, 28]   **17:3** [a] Deut 12:5, 15, 21   **17:4** [1] Smr. adds *it.*   **17:6** [a] Lev 3:2   [b] Exod 29:13, 18; Num 18:17   **17:7** [a] Exod 22:20; 32:8; 34:15; Deut 32:17; 2 Chr 11:15; Ps 106:37; 1 Cor 10:20   [b] Exod 34:15; Deut 31:16; Ezek 23:8   [1] Heb. *sacrifice.*   **17:8** [a] Lev 1:2–3; 18:26   [1] LXX, Syr., Vg. *your* (pl.).   **17:9** [a] Lev 14:23   **17:10** [a] Gen 9:4; Lev 3:17; 7:26–27; Deut 12:16, 23–25; 15:23; 1 Sam 14:33   [b] Lev 20:3, 5, 6   [1] LXX, Syr., Vg. *your* (pl.).   **17:11** [a] Gen 9:4; Lev 17:14   [b] [Matt 26:28; Rom 3:25; Eph 1:7; Col 1:14, 20; 1 Pet 1:2; 1 John 1:7]   [1] Heb. *the life of the flesh.*   **17:13** [a] Lev 7:26   [b] Deut 12:16, 24   [1] Some wss *from the house of Israel.*   [2] Some wss *your* (pl.).

and [c]cover it with soil, [14][a]for the life of all flesh is its blood. So I have said to the Israelites: You must not eat the blood of any living thing because the life of every living thing is its blood—all who eat it will be cut off.

Regulations for Eating Carcasses

[15]"'Any person who eats [a]an animal that has died of natural causes[1] or an animal torn by beasts, [b]whether a native citizen or a resident foreigner, must wash his clothes, [c]bathe in water, and be unclean until evening; then he will be clean. [16]But if [a]he does not wash his clothes and does not bathe his body, he will bear his punishment for his iniquity.'"

Exhortation to Obedience and Life

18 The LORD spoke to Moses: [2]"Speak to the [a]Israelites and tell them, 'I am the LORD your God! [3]You must not do as they do [a]in the land of Egypt where you have been living, and you must not do as they do [b]in the land of Canaan into which I am about to bring you; you must not walk in their statutes. [4]You must observe my regulations, and [a]you must be sure to walk in my statutes. I am the LORD your God. [5]So you must keep my statutes and my regulations; anyone who does so will live by keeping them. I am the LORD.

Laws of Sexual Relations

[6]"'No man is to approach any close relative[1] to have sexual relations with her.[2] I am the LORD. [7]You must not expose your father's nakedness by having sexual relations with your mother. She is your mother; you must not have sexual relations with her. [8]You must not have sexual relations with your [a]father's wife; she is your father's nakedness. [9]You must not have sexual relations with your sister, [a]whether she is your father's daughter or your mother's daughter, whether she is born in the same household or born outside it; you must not have sexual

relations with either of them. [10]You must not expose the nakedness of your son's daughter or your daughter's daughter by having sexual relations with them, because they are your own nakedness. [11]You must not have sexual relations with the daughter of your father's wife born of your father; she is your sister. You must not have sexual relations with her. [12]You must not have sexual relations with [a]your father's sister; she is your father's flesh. [13]You must not have sexual relations with your mother's sister, because she is your mother's flesh. [14]You must not expose the nakedness of [a]your father's brother; you must not approach his wife to have marital relations with her. She is your aunt. [15]You must not have sexual relations with your daughter-in-law; she is your son's wife. You must not have sexual relations with her. [16]You must not have sexual relations with your brother's wife; she is your brother's nakedness. [17]You must not have sexual relations with both a woman and her [a]daughter; you must not take as wife either her son's daughter or her daughter's daughter to have sexual relations with them. They are closely related to her[1]—it is lewdness.[2] [18]You must not take [a]a woman in marriage and then marry her sister as a rival wife[1] while she is still alive, to have sexual relations with her.

[19]"'You must not approach [a]a woman in her menstrual impurity to have sexual relations with her. [20][a]You must not have sexual relations with the wife of your fellow [b]citizen to become unclean with her. [21]You must not give any of your children [a]as an [b]offering to [c]Molech, so that you do not profane the name of your God. I am the LORD! [22]You must not [a]have sexual relations with a male as one has sexual relations with a woman; it is a detestable act.[1] [23]You must not have sexual relations with any [a]animal to become defiled with it, and a woman must not stand before an animal to have sexual relations with it; it is a perversion.

Warning against the Abominations of the Nations

[24]"'Do not defile yourselves with any of these things, for the nations that I am about to drive out before you have been defiled with all these things. [25]Therefore the land has become unclean, and I have brought the punishment for its iniquity upon it, so that the land has vomited out its inhabitants. [26]You yourselves must obey my statutes and my regulations and must not do any of these abominations, both the native citizen and the resident foreigner in your midst, [27]for the people who were in the land before you have done all these abominations, and the land has become unclean. [28]So do not make the land vomit you out because you defile it just as it has vomited out the nations[1] that were before you. [29]For if anyone does any of these abominations, that person who does them will be cut off from the midst of the people. [30]You must obey my charge not to practice any of the abominable statutes that have been done before you, so that you do not defile yourselves by them. I am the LORD your God.'"

Religious and Social Regulations

19 The LORD spoke to Moses: [2]"Speak to the whole congregation of the Israelites and tell them, 'You must be holy because I, the LORD your God, am holy. [3]Each of you must respect his mother and his father, and you must keep my Sabbaths. I am the LORD your God. [4]Do not turn to idols, and you must not make for yourselves gods of cast metal. I am the LORD your God.

Eating the Peace Offering

[5]"When you sacrifice a peace-offering sacrifice to the LORD, you must sacrifice it so that it is accepted for you. [6]It must be eaten on the day of your sacrifice and on the following day, but what is left over until the third day must be burned up.[1] [7]If, however, it is eaten on the third day, it is spoiled; it will not be accepted, [8]and the one who eats it will bear his punishment for iniquity because he has profaned what is holy to the LORD. That person will be cut off from his people.

Leaving the Gleanings

[9]"When you gather in the harvest of your land, you must not completely harvest the corner of your field, and you must not gather up the gleanings of your harvest. [10]You must not pick your vineyard bare, and you must not gather up the fallen grapes of your vineyard. You must leave them for the poor and the resident foreigner. I am the LORD your God.

Dealing Honestly

[11]"You must not steal, you must not tell lies, and you must not deal falsely with your fellow citizen. [12]You must not swear falsely in my name, so that you do not profane the name of your God. I am the LORD. [13]You must not oppress your neighbor or commit robbery against your neighbor. You must not withhold the wages of the hired laborer overnight until morning. [14]You must not curse a deaf person or put a stumbling block in front of a blind person. You must fear your God; I am the LORD.

Justice, Love, and Propriety

[15]"You[1] must not deal unjustly in judgment: You must neither show partiality to the poor nor honor the rich. You must judge your fellow citizen fairly. [16]You must not go about as a slanderer among your people.[1] You must not stand idly by when your neighbor's life is at stake. I am the LORD. [17]You must not hate your brother in your heart. You must surely reprove your fellow citizen so that you do not incur sin on account of him.[1] [18]You must not take vengeance or bear a grudge against[1] any of your people, but you must love your neighbor as yourself. I am the LORD. [19]You must keep my statutes. You must not allow two different kinds of your animals to breed

18:24 a Matt 15:18–20; 1 Cor 3:17   b Lev 18:3; 20:23; Deut 18:12   **18:25** a Num 35:33–34; Ezek 36:17   b Isa 26:21; Jer 5:9   c Lev 18:28; 20:22   **18:26** a Lev 18:5, 30   **18:28** a Jer 9:19   1 MT *nation.*   **18:30** a Lev 18:3; 22:9   b Lev 18:2   **19:2** a Exod 19:6; Lev 11:44; 20:7, 26; [Eph 1:4]; 1 Pet 1:16   **19:3** a Exod 20:12; Deut 5:16; Matt 15:4; Eph 6:2   b Exod 16:23; 20:8; 31:13   **19:4** a Exod 20:4; Ps 96:5; 115:4–7; 1 Cor 10:14; [Col 3:5]   **19:5** a Lev 7:16   **19:6** 1 Heb. *shall be burned with fire.*   **19:9** a Lev 23:22; Deut 24:19–22   **19:11** a Exod 20:15–16   **19:12** a Exod 20:7; Deut 5:11; [Matt 5:33–37]; Jas 5:12]   **19:13** a Exod 22:7–15, 21–27; Mark 10:19   b Deut 24:15; Mal 3:5; Jas 5:4   **19:14** a Deut 27:18   **19:15** a Deut 16:19   1 Smr. *you* (sing.).   **19:16** a Prov 11:13; 18:8; 20:19   b Exod 23:7; Deut 27:25; 1 Kgs 21:7–19   1 Or perhaps *not to go about as a spy.*   **19:17** a [1 John 2:9, 11; 3:15]   b Matt 18:15; [Luke 17:3]; Eph 5:11   1 Heb. *and you will not lift up on him sin.*   **19:18** a [Deut 32:35; 1 Sam 24:12; Rom 12:19; Heb 10:30]   b Matt 5:43; 19:19; Mark 12:31; Luke 10:27; [Rom 13:9; Gal 5:14]; Jas 2:8   1 Heb. *and you shall not retain* [anger?].

together, you must not sow your field with two different kinds of seed, and you must not wear a garment made of two different kinds of material.

Lying with a Slave Woman

20 "When a man goes to bed with a woman for intercourse, although she is a slave woman [a]designated for another man and she has not yet been ransomed, or freedom has not been granted to her, there will be an obligation to pay compensation. They must not be put to death, because she was not free. [21]He must bring his guilt offering to the LORD at the entrance of the Meeting Tent, a guilt-offering ram, [22]and the priest is to make atonement for him with the ram of the guilt offering before the LORD for his sin that he has committed, and he will be forgiven of his sin that he has committed.

The Produce of Fruit Trees

[23]"When you enter the land and plant any fruit tree, you must consider its fruit to be forbidden. Three years it will be forbidden to you; it must not be eaten. [24]In the fourth year all its fruit will be holy, praise offerings to the LORD. [25]Then in the fifth year you may eat its fruit to add its produce to your harvest. I am the LORD your God.

Blood, Hair, Body, and Prostitution

[26]"You must not eat anything with the blood still in it. You must not practice either divination or soothsaying. [27]You must not round off the corners of the hair on your head or ruin the corners of your beard.[1] [28]You must not [a]slash your body for a dead person or incise a tattoo on yourself. I am the LORD. [29]Do not profane your daughter by making her a prostitute,[1] so that the land [a]does not practice prostitution and become full of lewdness.

Sabbaths, Purity, Honor, Respect, and Honesty

[30]"You must keep my Sabbaths and [a]fear my sanctuary. I am the LORD. [31]Do not turn to [a]the spirits of the dead and do not seek familiar spirits to become unclean by them.

I am the LORD your God. [32][a]You must stand up in the presence of the aged, honor the presence of an elder, and [b]fear your God. I am the LORD. [33]When a resident foreigner lives with you in your land, you must not oppress him. [34]The resident foreigner who lives with you must be to you as a native citizen among you; so you must love [a]the foreigner as [b]yourself, because you were foreigners in the land of Egypt. I am the LORD your God. [35]You must not do injustice in the regulation of measures, whether of length, weight, or volume. [36]You must have [a]honest balances, honest weights, an honest ephah, and an honest hin. I am the LORD your God who brought you out from the land of Egypt. [37]You must be sure to obey all my statutes and regulations. I am [a]the LORD.'"

Prohibitions against Illegitimate Family Worship

20 The LORD spoke to Moses: [2]"You are to say to the Israelites, 'Any man from the Israelites (or any of the resident foreigners who live [a]in Israel) [b]who gives any of his children to Molech must be put to death; the people of the land must [c]pelt him with stones. [3]I myself [a]will set my face against that man and cut him off from the midst of his people, because he has given some of his children to Molech and thereby defiled my sanctuary and profaned my holy name. [4]If, however, the people of the land shut their eyes to that man when he gives some of his children to Molech so that they do not put him to death, [5]I myself will set my face against that man and his clan. I will cut off from the midst of the people both him and all who follow after him in spiritual prostitution, committing prostitution by worshiping Molech.[1]

Prohibition against Spiritists and Mediums

[6]"The person who turns to [a]the spirits of the dead and familiar spirits to commit prostitution by going after them, I will set my face against that person and cut him off from the midst of his people.

19:20 [a]Deut 22:23–27   19:27 [1]Heb. *you ... your* (sing.); Some wss *you ... your* (pl.).   19:28 [a]1 Kgs 18:28; Jer 16:6   19:29 [a]Lev 21:9; Deut 22:21; 23:17–18   [1]Heb. *to make her practice harlotry*; perhaps religious or temple prostitution.   19:30 [a]Lev 26:2; Eccl 5:1   19:31 [a]Lev 20:6, 27; Deut 18:11; 1 Sam 28:3; Isa 8:19   19:32 [a]Prov 23:22; Lam 5:12; 1 Tim 5:1   [b]Lev 19:14   19:34 [a]Exod 12:48   [b]Deut 10:19   19:36 [a]Deut 25:13–15; Prov 20:10   19:37 [a]Lev 18:4–5; Deut 4:5–6; 5:1; 6:25   20:2 [a]Lev 18:2   [b]Lev 18:21; 2 Kgs 23:10; 2 Chr 33:6; Jer 7:31   [c]Deut 17:2–5   20:3 [a]Lev 17:10   20:5 [1]Heb. *to commit harlotry after Molech.*   20:6 [a]Lev 19:31; 1 Sam 28:7–25

Exhortation to Holiness and Obedience

7 "'You must [a]sanctify yourselves and be holy, because I am the LORD your God. 8 You must be sure to obey [a]my statutes. [b]I am the LORD who sanctifies you.

Family Life and Sexual Prohibitions

9 "'If anyone curses his father or mother, he must be put to death. He has cursed his father or mother; his blood guilt is [a]on himself. 10 If a man commits adultery with his neighbor's wife,[1] both [a]the adulterer and the adulteress must be put to death. 11 If a man goes to bed with[1] his [a]father's wife, he has exposed his father's nakedness. Both of them must be put to death; their blood guilt is on themselves. 12 If a man goes to bed with his [a]daughter-in-law, both of them must be put to death. They have committed perversion; their blood guilt is on themselves. 13 [a]If a man goes to bed with a male as one goes to bed with a woman, the two of them have committed an abomination. They must be put to death; their blood guilt is on themselves. 14 If a man has marital relations with both a woman and her [a]mother,[1] it is lewdness. Both he and they must be burned to death, so there is no lewdness in your midst. 15 If a man has sexual relations with any [a]animal, he must be put to death, and you must kill the animal. 16 If a woman approaches any animal to copulate with it, you must kill the woman, and the animal must be put to death; their blood guilt is on themselves.

17 "'If a man has marital relations with[1] his [a]sister, whether the daughter of his father or of his mother, so that he sees her nakedness and she sees his nakedness, it is a disgrace. They must be cut off in the sight of the children of their people. He has exposed his sister's nakedness; he will bear his punishment for iniquity. 18 [a]If a man goes to bed with a menstruating woman and uncovers her nakedness, he has laid bare her fountain of blood, and she has exposed the fountain of her blood, so both of them must be cut off from the midst of their people. 19 You must not expose the nakedness of your [a]mother's sister or your [b]father's sister, for such a person has exposed his own close relative. They must bear their punishment for iniquity. 20 If a man goes to bed with his aunt, he has exposed his [a]uncle's nakedness; they must bear responsibility for their sin, they will die childless. 21 If a man has marital relations with his [a]brother's wife, it is indecency. He has exposed his brother's nakedness; they will be childless.

Exhortation to Holiness and Obedience

22 "'You must be sure to obey all my [a]statutes and regulations, so that the land to which I am about to bring you to take up residence does not vomit you out. 23 You must not walk in the statutes of the nations[1] which I am about to drive out before you, because they have done all these things [a]and I am filled with disgust against them. 24 So [a]I have said to you: You yourselves will possess their land and I myself will give it to you for a possession, a land flowing with milk and honey. I am the LORD your God [b]who has set you apart from the other peoples.[1] 25 Therefore [a]you must distinguish between the clean animal [b]and the unclean, and between the unclean bird and the clean, and you must not make yourselves detestable by means of an animal or bird or anything that creeps on the ground—creatures I have distinguished for you as unclean.[1] 26 You must be holy to me because I, the LORD, am holy, and I have set you apart from the other peoples to be mine.

Prohibition against Spiritists and Mediums

27 "'A [a]man or woman who[1] has in them a spirit of the dead or a familiar spirit must be put to death. They must pelt them with stones;[2] their blood guilt is on themselves.'"

20:7 [a]Lev 19:2; Heb 12:14   20:8 [a]Lev 19:19, 37   [b]Exod 31:13; Deut 14:2; Ezek 37:28   20:9 [a]Exod 21:17; Deut 27:16; Prov 20:20; Matt 15:4   20:10 [a]Exod 20:14; Lev 18:20; Deut 5:18; 22:22; John 8:4–5   [1]MT duplicates *a man who commits adultery with the wife of.*   20:11 [a]Lev 18:7–8; Deut 27:20   [1]Heb. *lies down with*; a euphemism for sexual relations. 20:12 [a]Lev 18:15   20:13 [a]Lev 18:22; Deut 23:17; Judg 19:22   20:14 [a]Lev 18:17   [1]Heb. *takes a woman and her mother*; either in marriage or a euphemism for sexual relations.   20:15 [a]Lev 18:23; Deut 27:21   20:17 [a]Lev 18:9; Deut 27:22   [1]Heb. *to take*; either in marriage or a euphemism for sexual relations.   20:18 [a]Lev 15:24; 18:19   20:19 [a]Lev 18:13   [b]Lev 18:12   20:20 [a]Lev 18:14   20:21 [a]Lev 18:16; Matt 14:3–4   20:22 [a]Lev 18:26; 19:37   20:23 [a]Lev 18:3, 24   [1]MT *nation.*   20:24 [a]Exod 3:17; 6:8; 13:5; 33:1–3   [b]Exod 19:5; 33:16; Lev 20:26; Deut 7:6; 14:2; 1 Kgs 8:53   [1]LXX *all the peoples.*   20:25 [a]Lev 10:10; 11:1–47; Deut 14:3–21   [b]Lev 11:43   [1]MT *to defile.*   20:27 [a]Lev 19:31; 1 Sam 28:9   [1]MT *for/because/that.*   [2]LXX, Smr. *you [pl.] shall pelt them.*

Rules for the Priests

21 The LORD said to Moses, "Say to the priests, the sons of Aaron—say to them: 'For a dead person[1] [a]no priest is to defile himself among his people,[2] [2]except for his close relative who is near to him—his mother, his father, his son, his daughter, his brother, [3]and his virgin sister who is near to him, who has no husband—he may defile himself for her. [4]He must not defile himself as a husband among his people so as to profane himself. [5]Priests must not have a bald spot shaved on their head, [a]they must not shave the corner of their beard, and they must not cut slashes in their body.

[6]"'They must be [a]holy to their God, and they must not profane the name of their God, because they are the ones who present the LORD's gifts, the [b]food of their God. [c]Therefore they must be holy. [7]They must not take a wife defiled by prostitution, nor are [a]they to take a wife [b]divorced from her husband, for the priest is holy to his God. [8]You must [a]sanctify him because he presents the food of your God. He must be holy to you because I, the LORD who [b]sanctifies you all, am holy. [9]If a daughter of a priest profanes herself by engaging in prostitution, she is profaning her father. She must be [a]burned to death.

Rules for the High Priest

[10]"'The high priest—who is greater than his brothers, and on whose head the anointing oil is [a]poured, and who has been ordained to wear the priestly garments—must neither [b]dishevel the hair of his head nor tear his garments. [11]He must not go where there is any dead person;[1] he must not defile himself even for his father or for his mother. [12a]He must not go out from the sanctuary and must not profane the sanctuary of his God, because the [b]dedication of the anointing oil of his God is on him. I am the LORD. [13]He must take a wife who is a virgin. [14]He must not marry a widow, a divorced woman, or one profaned by prostitution; he may only take a virgin from his people[1] as a wife, [15]so that he does not profane his children among his people,[1] for I am the LORD who sanctifies him.'"

Rules for the Priesthood

[16]The LORD spoke to Moses: [17]"Tell Aaron, 'No man from your descendants throughout their generations who has a physical flaw[1] is to approach to present the food of his God. [18]Certainly no man who has a physical [a]flaw is [b]to approach: a blind man, or one who is lame, or one with a slit nose,[1] or who has a limb too long, [19]or a man who has had a broken leg or arm, [20]or a hunchback, or a dwarf, or one with a spot in his eye, or a festering eruption, or a feverish rash,[1] or a crushed testicle. [21]No man from the descendants of Aaron the priest who has a physical flaw may step forward to present the LORD's gifts; he has a physical flaw, so he must not step forward to present the food of his God. [22]He may eat both the most holy and the holy food of his God, [23]but he must not go near the special [a]curtain or step forward to [b]the altar because he has a physical flaw. Thus he must not profane my holy places, for I am the LORD who sanctifies them.'"

[24]So Moses spoke these things to Aaron, his sons, and all the Israelites.

Regulations for the Eating of Priestly Stipends

22 The LORD spoke to Moses: [2]"Tell Aaron and his sons that they must deal [a]respectfully with the holy offerings of the Israelites, which they consecrate to me, so that they [b]do not profane my holy name. [c]I am the LORD. [3]Say to them, 'Throughout your generations, if any man from all your descendants approaches the holy offerings, which the Israelites consecrate to the LORD, [a]while he is impure, that person must be cut off from before me. I am the LORD. [4]No man from the descendants of Aaron who is [a]diseased or [b]has a discharge may eat the holy offerings [c]until he becomes clean. The one [d]who touches [e]anything made unclean by contact with a dead person, or with a man who has a seminal emission, [5]or with a [a]man who touches [b]a swarming thing by which he becomes unclean, or who touches a person by which he becomes unclean, whatever that person's impurity—[6]the person who

21:1 [a]Lev 19:28; Ezek 44:25 [1]Heb. *soul, person, life.* [2]MT *peoples.* 21:5 [a]Lev 19:27; Deut 14:1; Ezek 44:20 21:6 [a]Exod 22:31 [b]Lev 3:11 [c]Isa 52:11 21:7 [a]Ezek 44:22 [b]Deut 24:1-2 21:8 [a]Lev 11:44-45 [b]Lev 8:12, 30 21:9 [a]Deut 22:21 21:10 [a]Lev 8:12 [b]Lev 10:6-7 21:11 [1]MT *persons.* 21:12 [a]Lev 10:7 [b]Exod 29:6-7 21:14 [1]MT *peoples.* 21:15 [1]MT *peoples.* 21:17 [1]Heb. *who in him is a flaw.* 21:18 [a]Lev 22:19-25 [b]Lev 22:23 [1]Perhaps a number of facial defects. 21:20 [1]The exact meaning and medical reference of these terms is unknown. 21:23 [a]Lev 16:2 [b]Lev 21:12 22:2 [a]Num 6:3 [b]Lev 18:21 [c]Exod 28:38; Lev 16:19; 25:10; Num 18:32; Deut 15:19 22:3 [a]Lev 7:20-21; Num 19:13 22:4 [a]Num 5:2 [b]Lev 15:2 [c]Lev 14:2; 15:13 [d]Lev 11:24-28, 39, 40; Num 19:11 [e]Lev 15:16-17 22:5 [a]Lev 11:23-28 [b]Lev 15:7, 19

touches any of these will be unclean until evening and must not eat from the holy offerings unless he has [a]bathed his body in water. [7]When the sun goes down he will be clean, and afterward he may eat from the holy offerings, because they are his food. [8][a]He must not eat an animal that has died of natural causes[1] or an animal torn by beasts and thus become unclean by it. I am the LORD. [9]They must keep [a]my charge so that they do not incur sin on account of it and therefore die because they profane it. I am the LORD who sanctifies them.

[10]"No lay person may eat anything holy. Neither a priest's lodger [a]nor a hired laborer may eat anything holy, [11]but if a priest [a]buys a person with his own money, that person may eat the holy offerings, and those born in the priest's own house may eat his food. [12]If a priest's daughter marries a lay person, she may not eat the holy contribution offerings, [13]but if a priest's daughter is a widow or divorced, and she has no children so that she returns to live in her father's house as in her youth, she may eat from her father's food, but no lay person may eat it.

[14]"If a man eats a holy offering by mistake, he must add one-fifth to it and give the holy offering to the priest. [15]They[1] must not profane the holy [a]offerings which the Israelites contribute to the LORD, [16]and so cause them to incur a penalty for guilt when they eat their holy offerings, for I am the LORD who sanctifies them.'"

Regulations for Offering Votive and Freewill Offerings

[17]The LORD spoke to Moses: [18]"Speak to Aaron, his sons, and all the Israelites and tell them, 'When [a]any man from the house of Israel or from the resident foreigners in Israel presents his offering for any of the votive or freewill offerings, which they present to the LORD as a burnt offering, [19]if it is to be acceptable for [a]your benefit, it must be a flawless male from the cattle, sheep, or goats. [20]You must not present anything that has [a]a flaw, because it will not be acceptable for your benefit. [21]If a [a]man presents a peace-offering sacrifice [b]to the LORD for a special votive offering[1] or for a freewill offering from the herd or the flock, it must be flawless to be acceptable; it must have no flaw.

[22]"'[a]You must not present to the LORD something blind, or with [b]a broken bone, or mutilated, or with a running sore, or with a festering eruption, or with a feverish rash. You must not give any of these as a gift on the altar to the LORD. [23]As for an ox or a sheep with a limb [a]too long or stunted, you may present it as a freewill offering, but it will not be acceptable for a votive offering. [24]You must not present to the LORD something with testicles that are bruised, crushed, torn, or cut off; you must not do this in your land. [25]Even [a]from a foreigner you must not present [b]the food of your God from such animals as these, for they are [c]ruined and flawed; they will not be acceptable for your benefit.'"

[26]The LORD spoke to Moses: [27]"[a]When an ox, lamb, or goat is born, it must be under the care of its mother seven days, but from the eighth day onward it will be acceptable as an offering gift to the LORD. [28]You must not slaughter [a]an ox or a sheep and its young on the same day. [29]When you [a]sacrifice a thanksgiving offering to the LORD, you must sacrifice it so that it is acceptable for your benefit. [30]On that very day it must be eaten; you must not leave any part of it over until morning. I am the LORD.

[31]"You must be sure to do my commandments. I am [a]the LORD. [32][a]You must not profane my holy name, and [b]I will be sanctified in the midst of the Israelites. I am the LORD who [c]sanctifies you, [33]the one [a]who brought you out from the land of Egypt to be your God. I am the LORD."

Regulations for Israel's Appointed Times

23 The LORD spoke to Moses: [2]"Speak to the Israelites and tell them, 'These are the LORD's appointed times which you must proclaim as [a]holy assemblies—my appointed times.

22:6 [a]Lev 15:5   **22:8** [a]Exod 22:31; Lev 7:24; 11:39–40; 17:15; Ezek 44:31   [1]Heb. *carcass*; i.e., an animal that has died on its own.   **22:9** [a]Lev 18:30   **22:10** [a]Exod 29:33; Lev 22:13; Num 3:10   **22:11** [a]Exod 12:44   **22:15** [a]Num 18:32   [1]Probably the priests.   **22:18** [a]Lev 1:2–3, 10   **22:19** [a]Lev 1:3; Deut 15:21   **22:20** [a]Deut 15:21; 17:1; Mal 1:8, 14; [Eph 5:27; Heb 9:14; 1 Pet 1:19]   **22:21** [a]Lev 3:1, 6   [b]Num 15:3, 8; Ps 61:8; 65:1; Eccl 5:4–5   [1]Or perhaps *for making a vow.*   **22:22** [a]Lev 22:20; Mal 1:8   [b]Lev 1:9, 13; 3:3, 5   **22:23** [a]Lev 21:18   **22:25** [a]Num 15:15–16   [b]Lev 21:6, 17   [c]Mal 1:14   **22:27** [a]Exod 22:30   **22:28** [a]Deut 22:6–7   **22:29** [a]Lev 7:12; Ps 107:22; 116:17; Amos 4:5   **22:31** [a]Lev 19:37; Num 15:40; Deut 4:40   **22:32** [a]Lev 18:21   [b]Lev 10:3; Matt 6:9; Luke 11:2   [c]Lev 20:8   **22:33** [a]Lev 19:36–37; Num 15:40; Deut 4:40   **23:2** [a]Exod 12:16

The Weekly Sabbath

3 "'a Six days work may be done, but on the seventh day there must be a Sabbath of complete rest, a holy assembly. You must not do any work; it is a Sabbath to the Lord in all the places where you live.

The Passover and Feast of Unleavened Bread

4 "'These are a the Lord's appointed times, holy assemblies, which you must proclaim at their appointed time. 5 In the first a month, on the fourteenth day of the month, at twilight, is a Passover offering to the Lord. 6 Then on the fifteenth day of the same month will be the Feast of Unleavened Bread to the Lord; seven days you must eat unleavened bread. 7a On the first day there will be a holy assembly for you; you must not do any regular work. 8 You must present a gift to the Lord for seven days, and the seventh day is a holy assembly; you must not do any regular work.'"

The Presentation of Firstfruits

9 The Lord spoke to Moses: 10 "Speak to the Israelites and tell them, 'a When you enter b the land that I am about to give to you and you gather in its harvest, then you must bring the sheaf of the first portion of your harvest to the priest, 11 and he must a wave the sheaf before the Lord to be accepted for your benefit—on the day after the Sabbath the priest is to wave it. 12 On the day you wave the sheaf you must also offer a flawless yearling lamb for a burnt offering to the Lord, 13 along with its grain offering, two-tenths of an ephah of choice wheat flour mixed with olive oil, as a gift to the Lord, a soothing aroma, and its drink offering, one-fourth of a hin of wine.1 14 You must not eat bread, roasted grain, or fresh grain until this very day, until you bring the offering to your God. This is a perpetual statute throughout your generations in all the places where you live.

The Feast of Weeks

15 "'You must count for yourselves seven weeks from the day after the Sabbath, from the day you bring the wave-offering sheaf; they must be complete weeks. 16 You must count a 50 b days—until the day after the seventh Sabbath—and then you must present a new grain offering to the Lord. 17 From a the places where you live you must bring two loaves of1 bread for a wave offering; they must be made from two-tenths of an ephah of fine wheat flour, baked with yeast, as firstfruits to the Lord. 18 Along with the loaves of bread, you must also present seven flawless yearling lambs, one young bull, and two rams.1 They are to be a burnt offering to the Lord along with their grain offering and drink offerings, a gift of a soothing aroma to the Lord. 19 You must also offer a one male goat for b a sin offering and two yearling lambs for a peace-offering sacrifice, 20 and a the priest is to wave them—the two lambs—along with the bread of the firstfruits, as a wave offering before the Lord; they will be holy to the Lord for the priest.

21 "'On this very day you must proclaim an assembly; it is to be a holy assembly for you. You must not do any regular work. This is a perpetual statute in all the places where you live throughout your generations. 22a When you gather in the harvest of your land, you must not completely harvest the corner of your field, and you must not gather up the gleanings of your harvest. You must leave them for the poor and the resident foreigner. I am the Lord your God.'"

The Feast of Horn Blasts

23 The Lord spoke to Moses: 24 "Tell the Israelites, 'In the a seventh month, on the first b day of the month, you must have a complete rest, a memorial announced by loud horn blasts, a holy assembly. 25 You must not do any regular work, but you must present a gift to the Lord.'"

The Day of Atonement

26 The Lord spoke to Moses: 27 "The tenth day of this seventh month is the Day of Atonement. It is to be a a holy assembly for you, and you must humble yourselves and present a gift to the Lord. 28 You must not do any work on this particular day, because

23:3 a Exod 20:9; 23:12; 31:15; Lev 19:3; Deut 5:13–14; Luke 13:14   23:4 a Exod 23:14–16; Lev 23:2, 37   23:5 a Exod 12:1–28; Num 9:1–5; 28:16–25; Deut 16:1–8; Josh 5:10   23:7 a Exod 12:16; Num 28:18, 25   23:10 a Exod 23:19; 34:26   b [Rom 11:16]; Jas 1:18; Rev 14:4   23:11 a Exod 29:24   23:13 1 Heb. wine, one-fourth of the hin; about 1 quart (1 liter).   23:16 a Acts 2:1   b Num 28:26   23:17 a Exod 23:16, 19; Num 15:17–21   1 MT omits loaves.   23:18 1 LXX, Smr. add flawless.   23:19 a Lev 4:23, 28; Num 28:30; [2 Cor 5:21]   b Lev 3:1   23:20 a Lev 14:13; Num 18:12; Deut 18:4   23:22 a Lev 19:9–10; Deut 24:19–22; Ruth 2:2, 15   23:24 a Num 29:1   b Lev 25:9   23:27 a Lev 16:1–34; 25:9; Num 29:7

it is a day of [a]atonement to make atonement for yourselves before the LORD your God. [29]Indeed, any person who does not behave with [a]humility on this particular day will be cut off from his people. [30]As for any person who does any work on this particular day, I will exterminate [a]that person from the midst of his people—[31]you must not do any work! This is a perpetual statute throughout your generations in all the places where you live. [32]It is a Sabbath of complete rest for you, and you must humble yourselves on the ninth day of the month in the evening, from evening until evening you must observe your Sabbath."

The Feast of Temporary Shelters

[33]The LORD spoke to Moses: [34]"Tell [a]the Israelites, 'On the fifteenth day of this seventh month is the Feast of Shelters[1] for seven days to the LORD. [35]On the first day is a holy assembly; you must do no regular work. [36]For seven days you must present a gift to the LORD. [a]On the eighth day there is to be [b]a holy assembly for you, and you must present a gift to the LORD. It is a solemn assembly day;[1] you must not do any regular work.

[37]"'These are [a]the appointed times of the LORD that you must proclaim as holy assemblies to present a gift to the LORD—burnt offering, grain offering, sacrifice, and drink offerings, each day according to its regulation, [38a]besides the Sabbaths of the LORD and all your gifts, votive offerings, and freewill offerings which you must give to the LORD.

[39]"'On the fifteenth day of the seventh month, when you gather [a]in the produce of the land, you must celebrate a pilgrim festival of the LORD for seven days. On the first day is a complete rest and on the eighth day is complete rest. [40]On the first day [a]you must take for yourselves branches from majestic trees—palm branches, branches of leafy trees, [b]and willows of the brook—and you must rejoice before the LORD your God for seven days. [41]You must celebrate it as a pilgrim festival to the LORD for seven days in the year. This is a perpetual statute throughout [a]your generations; you must celebrate it in the seventh month. [42a]You must live in temporary shelters for seven days; every native citizen in Israel must live in shelters, [43]so [a]that your future generations may [b]know that [c]I made the Israelites live in shelters when I brought them out from the land of Egypt. I am the LORD your God.'"

[44]So Moses [a]spoke to the Israelites about the appointed times of the LORD.

Regulations for the Lampstand and the Table of Bread

24 The LORD spoke to Moses: [2]"[a]Command the Israelites to bring to you pure oil of beaten olives for the light, to make a lamp burn continually. [3]Outside the special curtain of the congregation in the Meeting Tent, Aaron[1] must arrange it from evening until morning before the LORD continually. This is a perpetual statute throughout your generations. [4]On [a]the ceremonially pure lampstand he must arrange the lamps before the LORD continually.

[5]"You must take choice wheat flour and bake twelve [a]loaves; there must be two-tenths of an ephah of flour in each loaf, [6]and you must set them in two rows, six in a row, [a]on the ceremonially pure table before the LORD. [7]You must put pure frankincense on each row, and it will become a memorial [a]portion for the bread, a gift to the LORD. [8a]Each Sabbath day Aaron must arrange it before the LORD continually; this portion is from the Israelites as a perpetual covenant. [9]It will belong to Aaron and his sons, and they must eat [a]it in [b]a holy place because it is most holy to him, a perpetually-allotted portion from the gifts of the LORD."

A Case of Blaspheming the Name

[10]Now an Israelite woman's son whose father was an Egyptian went out among the Israelites, and the Israelite woman's son and an Israelite man had a fight in the

---

23:28 [a]Lev 16:34   **23:29** [a]Isa 22:12; Jer 31:9; Ezek 7:16   **23:30** [a]Lev 20:3–6   **23:34** [a]Exod 23:16; Num 29:12; Deut 16:13–16; Ezra 3:4; Neh 8:14; Zech 14:16–19; John 7:2   [1]Or *booths*; trad. *tabernacles*.   **23:36** [a]Num 29:35–38; Neh 8:18; John 7:37   [b]Deut 16:8; 2 Chr 7:8   [1]I.e., a closing special assembly day of the festival.   **23:37** [a]Lev 23:2, 4   **23:38** [a]Num 29:39   **23:39** [a]Exod 23:16; Deut 16:13   **23:40** [a]Neh 8:15   [b]Deut 12:7; 16:14–15   **23:41** [a]Num 29:12; Neh 8:18   **23:42** [a][Isa 4:6]   **23:43** [a]Exod 13:14; Deut 31:13; Ps 78:5   [b]Exod 10:2   [c]Lev 22:33   **23:44** [a]Lev 23:2   **24:2** [a]Exod 27:20–21   **24:3** [1]Some wss add *and his sons*.   **24:4** [a]Exod 25:31; 31:8; 37:17   **24:5** [a]Exod 25:30; 39:36; 40:23   **24:6** [a]Exod 25:23–24; 1 Kgs 7:48; 2 Chr 4:19; 13:11; Heb 9:2   **24:7** [a]Lev 2:2, 9, 16   **24:8** [a]Num 4:7; 1 Chr 9:32; 2 Chr 2:4; Matt 12:4–5   **24:9** [a]1 Sam 21:6; Matt 12:4; Mark 2:26; Luke 6:4   [b]Exod 29:33; Lev 8:31

camp. [11]The Israelite woman's son [a]misused the Name and [b]cursed, so they [c]brought him to Moses. (Now his mother's name was Shelomith, daughter of Dibri, of the tribe of Dan.) [12]So they placed him in custody until they were able to make [a]a clear legal decision for themselves based on words from the mouth of the LORD.

[13]Then the LORD spoke to Moses: [14]"Bring the one who cursed outside the camp, and all who heard him are to [a]lay their hands on his head, and the whole congregation is to stone him to death. [15]Moreover, you are to tell the Israelites, 'If any man curses his God, he will bear responsibility for his sin, [16]and one who [a]misuses the name of the LORD must surely be put to death. The whole congregation must surely stone him, whether he is a resident foreigner or a native citizen; when he misuses the Name he must be put to death.

[17]"'If a [a]man beats any person to death, he must be put to death. [18]One [a]who beats an animal to death must make restitution for it, life for life. [19]If a man inflicts an injury on his fellow citizen, just as [a]he has done it must be done to him—[20][a]fracture for fracture, [b]eye for eye, tooth for tooth—just as he inflicts an injury on another person that same injury must be inflicted on him. [21]One who beats an animal to death must make restitution for it, but one who beats a person to death must be put to death. [22]There will be one regulation for you, [a]whether a resident foreigner or a native citizen, for I am the LORD your God.'"

[23]Then Moses spoke to the Israelites and they brought the one who cursed outside the camp and stoned him with stones. So the Israelites did just as the LORD had commanded Moses.

Regulations for the Sabbatical Year

25 The LORD spoke to Moses at Mount [a]Sinai: [2]"Speak to the Israelites and tell them, 'When you enter the land that I am giving you, the land must [a]observe a Sabbath to the LORD. [3]Six years you may sow your field, and six years you may prune your vineyard and gather the produce, [4]but in the [a]seventh year the land must have a Sabbath of complete [b]rest—a Sabbath to the LORD. You must not sow your field or prune your vineyard. [5]You must not gather in the aftergrowth of your harvest, and you must not pick the grapes of your unpruned vines;[1] the land must have [a]a year of complete rest. [6]You may have the Sabbath produce of the land to eat—you, your male servant, your female servant, your hired worker, the resident foreigner who stays with you, [7]your cattle, and the wild animals that are in your land—all its produce will be for you to eat.

Regulations for the Jubilee Year of Release

[8]"'You must count off seven weeks of years, seven times seven years, and the days of the seven weeks of years will amount to 49 years. [9]You must sound loud horn blasts—in the seventh [a]month, on the tenth day of the month, on the Day of Atonement—you must sound the horn in your entire land. [10]So you must consecrate the fiftieth year, and you must [a]proclaim [b]a release in the land for all its inhabitants. That year will be your Jubilee; each one of you must return to his property, and each one of you must return to his clan. [11]That fiftieth year will be [a]your Jubilee; you must not sow the land, harvest its aftergrowth, or pick the grapes of its unpruned vines. [12]Because that year is a Jubilee, it will be holy to [a]you—you may eat its produce from the field.

Release of Landed Property

[13]"'[a]In this Year of Jubilee you must each return to your property. [14]If you make a sale to your fellow citizen or buy from your fellow citizen, no one is to [a]wrong his brother. [15]You may buy it from your fellow citizen [a]according to the number of years since the last Jubilee; he may sell it to you according to the years of produce that are left. [16]The more years there are, the more you may make its purchase price, and the fewer years there are, the less you must make its purchase price, because he is only selling to you

24:11 [a]Exod 22:28   [b]Job 1:5, 11, 22; Isa 8:21   [c]Exod 18:22, 26   24:12 [a]Num 27:5   24:14 [a]Deut 13:9; 17:7   24:16 [a]Exod 20:7; 1 Kgs 21:10, 13; [Matt 12:31; Mark 3:28–29]   24:17 [a]Gen 9:6; Exod 21:12; Num 35:30–31; Deut 19:11–12; 27:24   24:18 [a]Lev 24:21   24:19 [a]Exod 21:24   24:20 [a]Exod 21:23; Deut 19:21   [b][Matt 5:38–39]   24:22 [a]Exod 12:49; Lev 19:33–37; Num 9:14; 15:15–16, 29   25:1 [a]Lev 26:46   25:2 [a]Lev 26:34–35   25:4 [a]Deut 15:1; Neh 10:31   [b][Heb 4:9]   25:5 [a]2 Kgs 19:29   [1]Heb. consecrated, devoted, forbidden; the same term (Heb. nazir) is used for the consecration of the Nazirite (Num 6:2, 18, etc.).   25:9 [a]Lev 23:24, 27   25:10 [a]Isa 61:2; 63:4; Jer 34:8, 15, 17; [Luke 4:19]   [b]Lev 25:13, 28, 54; Num 36:4   25:11 [a]Lev 25:5   25:12 [a]Lev 25:6–7   25:13 [a]Lev 25:10; 27:24; Num 36:4   25:14 [a]Lev 19:13   25:15 [a]Lev 27:18, 23

a number of years of produce. [17]No one is to oppress his fellow citizen, but [a]you must fear your God, because I am the LORD your God. [18]You must obey my statutes and my regulations; you must be sure to keep them [a]so that you may live securely in the [b]land.

[19]"The land will give its fruit, and [a]you may eat until you are satisfied, and you may live securely in the land. [20]If you say, "[a]What will [b]we eat in the seventh year if we do not sow and gather our produce?" [21]I will [a]command my blessing for you in the [b]sixth year so that it may yield the produce for three years, [22]and you may sow the eighth year [a]and eat from that sixth year's produce—old [b]produce. Until you bring in the ninth year's produce, you may eat old produce. [23]The land must not be sold without reclaim because [a]the land belongs to me, for you are foreign [b]residents, temporary settlers, with me. [24]In all your landed property you must provide for the right of redemption of the land.

[25]"[a]If your brother becomes impoverished and sells some of [b]his property, his near redeemer is to come to you and redeem what his brother sold. [26]If a man has no redeemer, but he prospers and gains enough for its redemption, [27]he is to calculate the value of the years it was sold, refund the balance to the man to whom he had sold it, and return to his property. [28]If he has not prospered enough to refund [a]a balance to him, then what he sold will belong to the one who bought it until the Jubilee year, but it must revert in the Jubilee and the original owner may return to his property.

Release of Houses

[29]"If a man sells a residential house in a walled city, its right of redemption must extend until one full year from its sale; its right of redemption must extend to a full calendar year. [30]If it is not redeemed before the full calendar year is ended, the house in the walled city will belong without reclaim to the one who bought it throughout his generations; it will not revert in the Jubilee. [31]The houses of villages, however, which have no wall surrounding them must be considered as the field of the land; they will have the right of redemption and must revert in the Jubilee. [32]As for [a]the cities of the Levites, the houses in the cities which they possess, the Levites must have a perpetual right of redemption. [33]Whatever someone among the Levites might redeem—the sale of a house which is his property in a city—must revert in the Jubilee, because the houses of the cities of the Levites are their property in the midst of the Israelites. [34]Moreover, [a]the open field areas of their cities must not be [b]sold, because that is their perpetual possession.

Debt and Slave Regulations

[35]"If your brother[1] becomes impoverished and is indebted to you, you must [a]support him; he must live with you like a foreign resident.[2] [36]Do not [a]take interest or profit from him,[1] but you must [b]fear your God, and your brother must live with you. [37]You must not lend him your money at interest, and you must not sell him food for profit. [38]I am the LORD your God who brought you out from the land of Egypt to [a]give you the land of Canaan—to be your God.

[39]"If your brother becomes impoverished with regard to you so that he sells himself to you, you must not subject him to slave service. [40]He must be with you as a hired worker, as a resident foreigner; he must serve with you until the Year of Jubilee, [41]but then he may go free, he and his children [a]with him, and may return to his family and to the property of his ancestors. [42]Since the Israelites are [a]my servants whom I brought out from the land of Egypt, they must not be sold in a slave sale. [43]You must not rule over them harshly, but [a]you must fear your God.

[44]"As for your male and female slaves who may belong to you—you may buy male and female slaves from the nations all around you. [45]Also, you may buy slaves from [a]the children of the foreigners who reside with you and from their families that are with you, whom they have fathered in your land;

25:17 [a] Lev 25:14; Prov 14:31; 22:22; Jer 7:5–6; 1 Thess 4:6   25:18 [a] Lev 19:37   [b] Lev 26:5; Deut 12:10; Ps 4:8; Jer 23:6   25:19 [a] Lev 26:5; Ezek 34:25   25:20 [a] Matt 6:25, 31   [b] Lev 25:4–5   25:21 [a] Deut 28:8   [b] Exod 16:29   25:22 [a] 2 Kgs 19:29   [b] Lev 26:10; Josh 5:11   25:23 [a] Exod 19:5; 2 Chr 7:20   [b] Gen 23:4; Exod 6:4; 1 Chr 29:15; Ps 39:12; Heb 11:13; 1 Pet 2:11   25:25 [a] Ruth 2:20; 4:4, 6   [b] Num 5:8; Ruth 3:2, 9, 12; [Job 19:25]; Jer 32:7–8   25:28 [a] Lev 25:10, 13   25:32 [a] Num 35:1–8; Josh 21:2   25:34 [a] Num 35:2–5   [b] Acts 4:36–37   25:35 [a] Deut 15:7–11; 24:14–15; Luke 6:35; 1 John 3:17   [1] Perhaps any relatives beyond a sibling or any fellow Israelite.   [2] Heb. a foreigner and resident.   25:36 [a] Exod 22:25; Deut 23:19–20   [b] Neh 5:9   [1] Perhaps a percentage of money and a percentage of produce.   25:38 [a] Lev 11:45; 22:32–33   25:41 [a] Exod 21:3   25:42 [a] Lev 25:55; [Rom 6:22; 1 Cor 7:22–23]   25:43 [a] Eph 6:9; Col 4:1   25:45 [a] [Isa 56:3, 6, 7]

they may become your property. ⁴⁶You may give them as an inheritance to ᵃyour children after you to possess as property. You may enslave them perpetually. However, as for your brothers the Israelites, no man may rule over his brother harshly.

⁴⁷"'If a resident foreigner who is with you prospers and your brother becomes impoverished with regard to him so that he sells himself to a resident foreigner who is with you or to a member of a foreigner's family, ⁴⁸after he has sold himself he retains a right of redemption. One of his brothers may redeem him, ⁴⁹or his uncle or his cousin may redeem him, or any one of the rest of his blood relatives—his family—may redeem him, or if¹ he prospers, he may redeem himself. ⁵⁰He must calculate with the one who bought him the number of years from the year he sold himself to him until the Jubilee year, and the cost of his sale must correspond to the number of years, ᵃaccording to the rate of wages a hired worker would have earned while with him. ⁵¹If there are still many years, in keeping with them, he must refund most of the cost of his purchase for his redemption, ⁵²but if only a few years remain until the Jubilee, he must calculate for himself in keeping with the remaining years and refund it for his redemption. ⁵³He must be with the one who bought him like a yearly hired worker. The one who bought him must not rule over him harshly in your sight. ⁵⁴If, however, he is not redeemed in these ways, he must go free in the Jubilee year, he and his children with him, ⁵⁵because the Israelites are my own servants; they are my servants whom I brought out from the land of Egypt. I am the LORD your God.

Exhortation to Obedience

26 "'You must ᵃnot make for yourselves idols, so you must not set up for yourselves a carved image or a pillar, and you must not place a sculpted stone in your land to bow down before it, for I am the LORD your God. ²ᵃYou must keep my Sabbaths and reverence my sanctuary. I am the LORD.

The Benefits of Obedience

³"'ᵃIf you walk in my statutes and are sure to obey my commandments, ⁴I will give you your rains in their time so that ᵃthe land will give its yield and ᵇthe trees of the field will produce their fruit. ⁵Threshing season will extend for ᵃyou until the season for harvesting grapes, and the season for harvesting grapes will extend until sowing season, so you will eat your bread until you are satisfied, and you will ᵇlive securely in your land. ⁶I ᵃwill grant peace in the land so that ᵇyou will lie down to sleep without anyone terrifying you. I will remove ᶜharmful animals from ᵈthe land, and no sword of war will pass through your land. ⁷You will pursue your enemies, and they will fall before you by the sword. ⁸ᵃFive of you will pursue a hundred, and a hundred of you will pursue ten thousand, and your enemies will fall before you by the sword. ⁹I will turn to you, ᵃmake you fruitful, multiply you, and maintain my ᵇcovenant with you. ¹⁰You will still be eating stored produce from the previous ᵃyear and will have to clean out what is stored from the previous year to make room for new.

¹¹"'I ᵃwill put my tabernacle in your midst, and I will not abhor you. ¹²I ᵃwill walk among you, and I will be your God, and you will be my people. ¹³I am the LORD your God who brought you out from the land of Egypt, from being their slaves, and I broke the bars of your ᵃyoke and caused you to walk upright.

The Consequences of Disobedience

¹⁴"'If, however, you do not obey me and keep all these commandments—¹⁵if you reject my statutes and abhor my regulations so that you do not keep all my commandments and you break my covenant—¹⁶I for my part will do this to you: ᵃI will inflict horror on you, consumption and fever, which ᵇdiminish eyesight and drain away the vitality of life.¹ You will sow your seed in vain ᶜbecause ᵈyour enemies will eat it. ¹⁷I will set ᵃmy face against ᵇyou. You will be struck down before your enemies; ᶜthose who hate you will rule over you, and you will ᵈflee when there is no one pursuing you.

25:46 ᵃ Isa 14:2   25:49 ¹ MT omits *if*.   25:50 ᵃ Job 7:1; Isa 16:14   26:1 ᵃ Exod 20:4–5; Deut 4:15–18; 5:8   26:2 ᵃ Lev 19:30   26:3 ᵃ Deut 28:1–14   26:4 ᵃ Isa 30:23   ᵇ Ps 67:6   26:5 ᵃ Deut 11:15; Joel 2:19, 26; Amos 9:13   ᵇ Lev 25:18–19; Ezek 34:25   26:6 ᵃ Isa 45:7   ᵇ Job 11:19; Ps 4:8; Zeph 3:13   ᶜ 2 Kgs 17:25; Hos 2:18   ᵈ Ezek 14:17   26:8 ᵃ Deut 32:30; Judg 7:7–12   26:9 ᵃ Gen 17:6–7; Ps 107:38   ᵇ Gen 17:1–7   26:10 ᵃ Lev 25:22   26:11 ᵃ Exod 25:8; 29:45–46; Josh 22:19; Ps 76:2; Ezek 37:26; Rev 21:3   26:12 ᵃ Deut 23:14; [2 Cor 6:16]   26:13 ᵃ Gen 27:40   26:16 ᵃ Deut 28:22   ᵇ 1 Sam 2:33   ᶜ Ezek 24:23; 33:10   ᵈ Judg 6:3–6; Job 31:8; Mic 6:15   ¹ Heb. *soul*; either physical or psychological effects.   26:17 ᵃ Ps 34:16   ᵇ Deut 28:25; 1 Sam 4:10; 31:1   ᶜ Ps 106:41   ᵈ Prov 28:1

[18]"'If, in spite of all these things, you do not obey me, I will discipline you [a]seven times more on account of your sins. [19]I will [a]break your strong pride and make your sky like iron and your land like bronze. [20]Your [a]strength will be used up in vain; your [b]land will not give its yield, and the trees of the land will not produce their fruit.

[21]"'If you walk in hostility against me and are not willing to obey me, I will increase your affliction seven times according to your sins. [22]I [a]will send the wild animals against [b]you, and they will bereave you of your children, annihilate your cattle, and diminish your population so that your roads will become deserted.

[23]"'If in spite of these things you do not allow yourselves to be disciplined and you walk in hostility against me, [24a]then I myself will also walk in hostility against you and strike you seven times on account of your sins. [25]I [a]will [b]bring on you an avenging sword, a covenant vengeance. Although you will gather together into your cities, I will send pestilence among you, and you will be given into enemy hands. [26a]When I break off your supply of bread, ten women will bake your bread in one oven; they will ration your bread by weight, [b]and you will eat and not be satisfied.

[27]"'If in spite of this you do not obey me but walk in hostility against me, [28]I will walk in hostile rage against you, and I myself will also discipline you seven times on account of your sins. [29]You will eat the flesh of [a]your sons and the flesh of your daughters. [30]I [a]will destroy your high places and cut down your incense altars, and I will stack your dead bodies on top of the lifeless bodies of your idols.[1] I will abhor you. [31]I will lay your [a]cities waste and make your sanctuaries desolate, and [b]I will refuse to [c]smell your soothing aromas. [32]I myself [a]will make the land desolate, and your enemies who live in it will be appalled. [33]I [a]will scatter you among the nations and unsheathe the sword after you, so your land will become desolate and your cities will become a waste.

[34]"'Then [a]the land will make up for its Sabbaths all the days it lies desolate while you are in the land of your enemies; then the land will rest and make up its Sabbaths. [35]All the days of the desolation it will have the rest it did not have on your [a]Sabbaths when you lived on it.

[36]"'As for the ones who remain among you, I will bring [a]despair into their hearts in the lands of their enemies. The sound of a blowing leaf will pursue them, and they will flee as one who flees the sword and will fall down even though there is no pursuer. [37a]They will stumble over each other as those who flee before a sword, though there is no pursuer, and there will be no one to take a stand for [b]you before your enemies. [38]You will [a]perish among the nations; the land of your enemies will consume you.

Restoration through Confession and Repentance

[39]"'As for the ones who remain among you, they will rot away because of their iniquity in the lands of your enemies, and they will also rot away because of their [a]ancestors' iniquities which are with them. [40]However, when they confess their iniquity and their ancestors' iniquities which they committed by trespassing against me, by which they also walked in hostility against me [41](and I myself will walk in hostility against them and bring them into the land of their enemies), and then their [a]uncircumcised hearts become [b]humbled and they make up [c]for their iniquities, [42]I will [a]remember my covenant with Jacob and also my covenant with Isaac and also my covenant with Abraham,[1] and I will [b]remember the land. [43]The land will be abandoned by [a]them in order that it may make up for its Sabbaths while it is made desolate without them, and they will make up for their iniquity because they have [b]rejected my regulations and have abhorred my statutes. [44]In

26:18 [a]1 Sam 2:5   26:19 [a]Isa 25:11   26:20 [a]Ps 127:1; Isa 17:10–11; 49:4; Jer 12:13   [b]Gen 4:12; Deut 11:17   26:22 [a]Deut 32:24; Ezek 14:21   [b]Judg 5:6; 2 Chr 15:5; Zech 7:14   26:24 [a]Lev 26:28, 41; Ps 18:26   26:25 [a]Ezek 5:17   [b]Num 16:49; Deut 28:21; 2 Sam 24:15   26:26 [a]Ps 105:16; Isa 3:1; Ezek 4:16–17; 5:16   [b]Mic 6:14; Hag 1:6   26:29 [a]Deut 28:53; 2 Kgs 6:28–29   26:30 [a]1 Kgs 13:2; 2 Chr 34:3; Isa 27:9; Ezek 6:3–6, 13   [1]Heb. *your corpses . . . the corpses of your idols.*   26:31 [a]2 Kgs 25:4, 10   [b]2 Chr 36:19; Ps 74:7   [c]Isa 1:11–15   26:32 [a]Jer 9:11; 18:16   26:33 [a]Deut 4:27; Ps 44:11; Ezek 12:15; 20:23; 22:15; Zech 7:14   26:34 [a]Lev 26:43; 2 Chr 36:21   26:35 [a]Lev 25:2   26:36 [a]Isa 30:17; Lam 1:3, 6; 4:19; Ezek 21:7, 12, 15   26:37 [a]Judg 7:22; 1 Sam 14:15–16; Isa 10:4   [b]Josh 7:12–13; Judg 2:14   26:38 [a]Deut 4:26   26:39 [a]Exod 34:7   26:41 [a]Acts 7:51; Rom 2:29   [b]2 Chr 12:6–7, 12; 1 Pet 5:5–6   [c]Ps 39:9; 51:3–4; Dan 9:7   26:42 [a]Exod 2:24; 6:5; Ps 106:45; Ezek 16:60   [b]Ps 136:23   [1]Heb. *my covenant with Abraham I will remember.*   26:43 [a]Lev 26:34–35   [b]Lev 26:15

[a]spite of this, however, when they are in the land of their enemies, I will not reject them and abhor them to make a complete end of them, to break my covenant with them, for I am the LORD their God. [45]I will remember [a]for them the covenant with their ancestors [b]whom [c]I brought out from the land of Egypt in the sight of the nations to be their God. I am the LORD.'"

Summary Colophon

[46]These are [a]the statutes, [b]regulations, and instructions which the LORD established between himself and the Israelites at Mount Sinai through Moses.

Redemption of Persons Given as Votive Offerings

27 The LORD spoke to Moses: [2]"Speak to the Israelites and tell them, '[a]When a man makes a special votive offering based on the conversion value of a person to the LORD, [3]the conversion value of the male from twenty years old up to sixty years old is 50 shekels by the standard of the sanctuary shekel. [4]If the person is a female, the conversion value is 30 shekels. [5]If the person is from five years old up to twenty years old, the conversion value of the male is 20 shekels, and for the female 10 shekels. [6]If the person is one month old up to five years old, the conversion value of the male is five shekels of silver, and for the female the conversion value is three shekels of silver. [7]If the person is from sixty years old and older, if he is a male, the conversion value is 15 shekels, and for the female 10 shekels. [8]If the person making the votive offering is too poor to pay the conversion value, he must stand the person before the priest, and the priest will establish his conversion value; according to what the man who made the votive offering can afford, the priest will establish his conversion value.

Redemption of Animals Given as Votive Offerings

[9]"If what is vowed is a kind of animal from which an offering may be presented to the LORD, anything which he gives to the LORD from this kind of animal will be holy. [10]He must not replace or exchange it, good for bad or bad for good, and if he does indeed exchange one animal for another animal, then both the original animal and its substitute will be [a]holy. [11]If what is vowed is an unclean animal from which an offering must not be presented to the LORD, then he must stand the animal before the priest, [12]and the priest will establish its conversion value, whether good or bad. According to the conversion value assessed by the priest, thus it will be. [13a]If, however, the person who made the vow redeems the animal, he must add one-fifth to its conversion value.

Redemption of Houses Given as Votive Offerings

[14]"If a man consecrates his house as holy to the LORD, the priest will establish its conversion value, whether good or bad. Just as the priest establishes its conversion value, thus it will stand.[1] [15]If the one who consecrates it redeems his house, he must add to it one-fifth of its conversion value in silver, and it will belong to him.

Redemption of Fields Given as Votive Offerings

[16]"If a man consecrates to the LORD some of his own landed property, the conversion value must be calculated in accordance with the amount of seed needed to sow it, a homer of barley seed being priced at 50 shekels of silver. [17]If he consecrates his field in the Jubilee year, the conversion value will stand, [18]but if he consecrates his field after the Jubilee, the priest will [a]calculate the price for him according to the years that are left until the next Jubilee year, and it will be deducted from the conversion value. [19]If, however, the one who consecrated the field redeems it, he must add to it one-fifth of the conversion price, and it will belong to him. [20]If he does not redeem the field, but sells the field to someone else, he may never redeem it. [21]When it reverts in the Jubilee, the field will be holy to the LORD like a permanently [a]dedicated field; it will become [b]the priest's property.

[22]"If he consecrates to the LORD a field he has purchased, which [a]is not part of his

---

26:44 [a]Deut 4:31; 2 Kgs 13:23; Jer 30:11; [Rom 11:1–36]   26:45 [a][Rom 11:28]   [b]Lev 22:33; 25:38   [c]Ps 98:2; Ezek 20:9, 14, 22   26:46 [a]Lev 27:34; Deut 6:1; 12:1; [John 1:17]   [b]Lev 25:1   27:2 [a]Lev 7:16; Num 6:2; Deut 23:21–23; Judg 11:30–31, 39   27:10 [a]Lev 27:33   27:13 [a]Lev 6:5; 22:14; 27:15, 19   27:14 [1]Perhaps meaning it shall be legally valid.   27:18 [a]Lev 25:15–16, 28   27:21 [a]Lev 27:28   [b]Num 18:14; Ezek 44:29   27:22 [a]Lev 25:10, 25

own landed property, [23]the priest will calculate for him the amount of its conversion value until the Jubilee year, and he must pay the conversion value on that Jubilee day as something that is holy to the LORD. [24a]In the Jubilee year the field will return to the one from whom he bought it, the one to whom it belongs as landed property. [25]Every conversion value must be calculated by the standard of the sanctuary shekel; [a]20 gerahs to the shekel.

Redemption of the Firstborn

[26]"Surely no man may consecrate a [a]firstborn that already belongs to the LORD as a firstborn among the animals; whether it is an ox or a sheep, it belongs to the LORD. [27]If, however, it is among the unclean animals, he may ransom it according to its conversion value and must add one-fifth to it, but if it is not redeemed, it must be sold according to its conversion value.

Things Permanently Dedicated to the Lord

[28]"Surely anything that a man permanently dedicates to [a]the LORD from all that belongs to him, whether from people, animals, or his landed property, must be neither sold nor redeemed; anything permanently dedicated is most holy to the LORD. [29]Any human being who is permanently dedicated to the LORD must [a]not be ransomed; such a person must be put to death.

Redemption of the Tithe

[30]"Any tithe of the land, from the grain of the land or from the fruit of the trees, belongs to the LORD; it is holy to the LORD. [31]If a man redeems part of his tithe, however, he must add [a]one-fifth to it. [32]All the tithe of herds or flocks, everything which [a]passes under the rod, the tenth one will be holy to the LORD. [33]The owner must not examine the animals to distinguish between good and bad, and he must not exchange it. If, however, he does exchange it, both the original animal and its substitute will be holy and must not be redeemed.'"

Final Colophon

[34]These are [a]the commandments which the LORD commanded Moses to tell the Israelites at Mount [b]Sinai.

27:24 [a] Lev 25:10–13, 28   27:25 [a] Exod 30:13; Lev 27:3; Num 3:47; 18:16; Ezek 45:12   27:26 [a] Exod 13:2, 12; 22:30   27:28 [a] Lev 27:21; Num 18:14; Josh 6:17–19   27:29 [a] Num 21:2   27:31 [a] Lev 27:13   27:32 [a] Jer 33:13; Ezek 20:37; Mic 7:14   27:34 [a] Lev 26:46; Deut 4:5; Mal 4:4   [b] Exod 19:1–6, 25; [Heb 12:18–29]

NUMBERS

Numbers takes its name from the two numberings of the Israelites—the first at Mount Sinai and the second on the plains of Moab. Most of the book, however, describes the Israelites' experiences as they wandered in the wilderness. The lesson of Numbers is clear: while it may be necessary to pass through wilderness experiences, one does not have to live there. For Israel an eleven-day journey became a forty-year agony. The title of Numbers comes from the first word in the Hebrew text, *Wayyedabber,* "And He Said." Jewish writings, however, usually refer to it by the fifth Hebrew word in 1:1, *Bemidbar,* "In the Wilderness," which more nearly indicates the content of the book. The Greek title in the Septuagint is *Arithmoi,* "Numbers." The Latin Vulgate followed this title and translated it *Liber Numeri,* "Book of Numbers." These titles are based on two people groups: the generation of Exodus (Num 1) and the generation that grew up in the wilderness and conquered Canaan (Num 26). Numbers has also been called the Book of the Journeyings, the Book of the Murmurings, and the Fourth Book of Moses.

Organizing the Census of the Israelites

1 Now the LORD spoke to Moses [a]in the tent of [b]meeting in the desert of Sinai on the [c]first day of the second month of the second year after the Israelites departed from the land of Egypt. He said: [2]"[a]Take a census[1] of the entire[2] Israelite community by their clans and families, counting the name of every [b]individual male. [3]You and Aaron are to number[1] all in Israel who can serve in the army, those who are [a]twenty years old or older, by their divisions. [4]And to help you there is to be a man from each tribe, each man the head of his family. [5]Now these are the names of the men who are to help[1] you:

from Reuben, Elizur son of Shedeur;
[6] from Simeon, Shelumiel son of Zurishaddai;
[7] from Judah, Nahshon son of Amminadab;
[8] from Issachar, Nethanel son of Zuar;
[9] from Zebulun, Eliab son of Helon;
[10] from the sons of Joseph:
from Ephraim, Elishama son of Ammihud;

from Manasseh, Gamaliel son of Pedahzur;
[11] from Benjamin, Abidan son of Gideoni;
[12] from Dan, Ahiezer son of Ammishaddai;
[13] from Asher, Pagiel son of Ocran;
[14] from Gad, Eliasaph son of [a]Deuel;[1]
[15] from Naphtali, Ahira son of Enan."

The Census of the Tribes

[16]These were [a]the ones [b]chosen from the community, leaders of their ancestral tribes. They were the [c]heads of the thousands of Israel.

[17]So Moses and Aaron took these men who had been mentioned specifically [a]by name, [18]and they assembled the entire community together on the first day of the second month.[1] Then the people recorded their [a]ancestry by their clans and families, and the men who were twenty years old or older were listed by name individually, [19]just as the LORD had commanded Moses. And so he numbered them in the desert of Sinai.

1:1 [a] Exod 19:1; Num 10:11–12   [b] Exod 25:22   [c] Exod 40:2, 17; Num 9:1; 10:11   1:2 [a] Exod 30:12; Num 26:2, 63, 64; 2 Sam 24:2; 1 Chr 21:2   [b] Exod 30:12–13; 38:26   [1] Lit. *lift up the head[s].*   [2] Smr. omits *entire.*   1:3 [a] Exod 30:14; 38:26   [1] Heb. *to visit, appoint, muster, number.*   1:5 [1] Lit. *who will stand with you.*   1:14 [a] Num 7:42   [1] LXX, Syr. *Reuel.*   1:16 [a] Exod 18:21; Num 7:2; 1 Chr 27:16–22   [b] Num 16:2   [c] Exod 18:21, 25; Jer 5:5; Mic 3:1, 9; 5:2   1:17 [a] Isa 43:1   1:18 [a] Ezra 2:59; Heb 7:3   [1] LXX adds *of the second year.*

[20]And they were as follows:

The [a]descendants of Reuben, the firstborn son of Israel: According to the records of their clans and families, all the males twenty years old or older who could serve in the army were listed by name individually. [21]Those of them who were numbered from the tribe of Reuben were 46,500.

[22]From the [a]descendants of Simeon: According to the records of their clans and families, all the males numbered of them[1] twenty years old or older who could serve in the army were listed by name individually. [23]Those of them who were numbered from the tribe of Simeon were 59,300.

[24][1]From the [a]descendants of Gad: According to the records of their clans and families, all the males twenty years old or older who could serve in the army were listed by name. [25]Those of them who were numbered from the tribe of Gad were 45,650.

[26]From the [a]descendants of Judah: According to the records of their clans and families, all the males twenty years old or older who could serve in the army were listed by name. [27]Those of them who were numbered from the tribe of Judah were 74,600.

[28]From the [a]descendants of Issachar: According to the records of their clans and families, all the males twenty years old or older who could serve in the army were listed by name. [29]Those of them who were numbered from the tribe of Issachar were 54,400.

[30]From the [a]descendants of Zebulun: According to the records of their clans and families, all the males twenty years old or older who could serve in the army were listed by name. [31]Those of them who were numbered from the tribe of Zebulun were 57,400.

[32]From the [a]sons of Joseph:

From the descendants of Ephraim: According to the records of their clans and families, all the males twenty years old or older who could serve in the army were listed by name. [33]Those of them who were numbered from the tribe of Ephraim were 40,500. [34]From the [a]descendants of Manasseh: According to the records of their clans and families, all the males twenty years old or older who could serve in the army were listed by name. [35]Those of them who were numbered from the tribe of Manasseh were 32,200.

[36]From the [a]descendants of Benjamin: According to the records of their clans and families, all the males twenty years old or older who could serve in the army were listed by name. [37]Those of them who were numbered from the tribe of Benjamin were 35,400.

[38]From the [a]descendants of Dan: According to the records of their clans and families, all the males twenty years old or older who could serve in the army were listed by name. [39]Those of them who were numbered from the tribe of Dan were 62,700.

[40]From the [a]descendants of Asher: According to the records of their clans and families, all the males twenty years old or older who could serve in the army were listed by name. [41]Those of them who were numbered from the tribe of Asher were 41,500.

[42]From the descendants of Naphtali: According to the records of their clans and families, all the males twenty years old or older who could serve in the army were listed by name. [43]Those of them who were numbered from the tribe of Naphtali were 53,400.

[44]These were [a]the men whom Moses and Aaron numbered along with the twelve leaders of Israel, each of whom was from his own family. [45]All the Israelites who were twenty years old or older, who could serve in Israel's army, were numbered according to their families. [46]And all those numbered totaled [a]603,550.

The Exemption of the Levites

[47]But [a]the Levites, according to the tribe of their fathers, were not numbered among them. [48]The LORD had said to Moses, [49]"[a]Only the tribe of Levi you must not number or count with the other Israelites. [50][a]But appoint[1] the Levites over the tabernacle of the testimony, over all its furnishings [b]and over everything in it.

1:20 [a]Num 2:10–11; 26:5–11; 32:6, 15, 21, 29   1:22 [a]Num 2:12–13; 26:12–14   [1]Some wss omit *those that were numbered of them.*   1:24 [a]Gen 30:11; Num 26:15–18; Josh 4:12; Jer 49:1   [1]LXX places vv. 24–35 after v. 37.   1:26 [a]Gen 29:35; Num 26:19–22; 2 Sam 24:9; Ps 78:68; Matt 1:2   1:28 [a]Num 2:5–6   1:30 [a]Num 2:7–8; 26:26–27   1:32 [a]Gen 48:1–22; Num 26:28–37; Deut 33:13–17; Jer 7:15; Obad 19   1:34 [a]Num 2:20–21; 26:28–34   1:36 [a]Gen 49:27; Num 26:38–41; 2 Chr 17:17; Rev 7:8   1:38 [a]Gen 30:6; 46:23; Num 2:25–26; 26:42–43   1:40 [a]Num 2:27–28; 26:44–47   1:44 [a]Num 26:64   1:46 [a]Exod 12:37; 38:26; Num 2:32; 26:51, 63; Heb 11:12; Rev 7:4–8   1:47 [a]Num 2:33; 3:14–22; 26:57–62; 1 Chr 6:1–47; 21:6   1:49 [a]Num 2:33; 26:62   1:50 [a]Exod 38:21; Num 3:7–8; 4:15, 25–27, 33   [b]Num 3:23, 29, 35, 38   [1]Heb. *number, appoint.*

They must carry the tabernacle and all its furnishings; and they[2] must attend to it and camp around it. [51]Whenever the tabernacle is to move, the Levites must take it down, [a]and whenever the tabernacle is to be reassembled, the Levites must set it [b]up. Any unauthorized person who approaches it must be killed.

[52]"The Israelites will camp according to their divisions, each [a]man in his camp, and each man by his standard. [53a]But the Levites must camp around the tabernacle of the testimony, so that the LORD's [b]anger[1,2] will not fall on the Israelite community. The Levites are responsible [c]for the care of the tabernacle of the testimony."

[54]The Israelites did according to all that the LORD commanded Moses[1]—that is what they did.

The Arrangement of the Tribes

2 The LORD spoke to Moses and to Aaron: [2]"Every [a]one of the Israelites must camp under his standard with the emblems of his family; they must camp at [b]some distance around the tent of meeting.

The Tribes on the East

[3]"Now those who will be camping on the [a]east, toward the sunrise, are the divisions of the camp of Judah under their standard. The leader of the people of Judah is [b]Nahshon son of Amminadab. [4]Those numbered in his division are 74,600. [5]Those who will be camping next to them are the tribe of Issachar. The leader of the people of Issachar is Nethanel son of Zuar. [6]Those numbered in his division are 54,400. [7]Next will be the tribe of Zebulun. The leader of the people of Zebulun is Eliab son of Helon. [8]Those numbered in his division are 57,400. [9]All those numbered of [a]the camp of Judah, according to their divisions, are 186,400. They will travel at the front.

The Tribes on the South

[10]"On the [a]south will be the divisions of the camp of Reuben under their standard. The leader of the people of Reuben is Elizur son of Shedeur. [11]Those numbered in his division are 46,500. [12]Those who will be camping next to them are the tribe of Simeon. The leader of the people of Simeon is Shelumiel son of Zurishaddai. [13]Those numbered in his division are 59,300. [14]Next will be the tribe of Gad. The leader of the people of Gad is Eliasaph son of Deuel.[1] [15]Those numbered in his division are 45,650. [16]All those numbered of [a]the camp of Reuben, according to their divisions, are 151,450. They will travel second.

The Tribe in the Center

[17]"Then the tent of meeting with the camp of the Levites will travel in the middle of the camps. They will travel in the same order as they camped, each in his own place under his [a]standard.

The Tribes on the West

[18]"On the west will be the divisions of the camp of Ephraim under their standard. The leader of the people of Ephraim is Elishama son of Ammihud. [19]Those numbered in his division are 40,500. [20]Next to them will be the tribe of Manasseh. The leader of the people of Manasseh is Gamaliel son of Pedahzur. [21]Those numbered in his division are 32,200. [22]Next will be the tribe of Benjamin. The leader of the people of Benjamin is Abidan son of Gideoni. [23]Those numbered in his division are 35,400. [24]All those numbered of [a]the camp of Ephraim, according to their divisions, are 108,100. They will travel third.

The Tribes on the North

[25]"On the north will be the divisions of the camp of Dan, under their standards. The leader of the people of Dan is Ahiezer son of Ammishaddai. [26]Those numbered in his division are 62,700. [27]Those who will be camping next to them are the tribe of Asher. The leader of the people of Asher is Pagiel son of Ocran. [28]Those numbered in his division are 41,500. [29]Next will be the tribe of Naphtali. The leader of the people of Naphtali is Ahira son of Enan. [30]Those numbered in his division are 53,400. [31]All those numbered of [a]the camp of Dan are 157,600. They will travel last, under their standards."

1:50 [2]An emphatic Heb. construction.   1:51 [a]Num 4:5–15; 10:17, 21   [b]Num 10:21   1:52 [a]Num 2:2, 34; 24:2   1:53 [a]Num 1:50   [b]Lev 10:6; Num 8:19; 16:46; 18:5; 1 Sam 6:19   [c]Num 8:24; 18:2–4; 1 Chr 23:32   [1]LXX sin.   [2]Heb. so that there be no wrath on.   1:54 [1]LXX adds and Aaron.   2:2 [a]Num 1:52; 24:2   [b]Josh 3:4   2:3 [a]Num 10:5   [b]Num 1:7; 7:12; 10:14; Ruth 4:20; 1 Chr 2:10; Matt 1:4; Luke 3:32–33   2:9 [a]Num 10:14   2:10 [a]Num 10:6   2:14 [1]MT Reuel.   2:16 [a]Num 10:18   2:17 [a]Num 10:17, 21   2:24 [a]Num 10:22   2:31 [a]Num 10:25

Summary

[32]These are the Israelites, numbered according to their families. [a]All those numbered in the camps, by their divisions, are 603,550. [33]But [a]the Levites were not numbered among the other Israelites, as the LORD commanded Moses.

[34]So the Israelites [a]did according to all that the LORD commanded Moses; that is the way they camped under their standards, and that is the way they traveled, each with his clan and family.

The Sons of Aaron

3 Now these are the [a]records[1] of Aaron and Moses when the LORD spoke with Moses on Mount Sinai. [2]These are the names of the sons of Aaron: Nadab the [a]firstborn, [b]Abihu, Eleazar, and Ithamar. [3]These are [a]the names of the sons of Aaron, the anointed priests, whom he consecrated[1] to minister as priests.

[4a]Nadab and Abihu died before the LORD[1] when they offered strange[2] fire[3] before the LORD in the desert of Sinai, and they had no children. So Eleazar and Ithamar ministered as priests in the presence of Aaron their father.

The Assignment of the Levites

[5]The LORD spoke to Moses: [6]"[a]Bring the tribe of Levi near, and present them before Aaron the priest, that they may serve him. [7]They are responsible for his needs and [a]the needs of the whole community before the tent of meeting, by attending to the service of the tabernacle. [8]And they are responsible for all the furnishings of the tent of meeting, and for the needs of the Israelites, as they serve in the tabernacle. [9]You are to assign the Levites to Aaron and his sons; they will be assigned exclusively to him out of all the Israelites. [10]So you are to appoint Aaron [a]and his sons, and they will be responsible for their priesthood,[1] [b]but the unauthorized person who comes near must be put to death."

[11]Then the LORD spoke to Moses: [12]"Look, [a]I myself have taken the Levites from among the Israelites instead of every firstborn who opens the womb among the Israelites. So the Levites belong to me, [13]because [a]all the firstborn are mine. When I destroyed all the firstborn in the land of Egypt, I set apart for myself all the firstborn in Israel, both man and beast. They [b]belong to me. I am the LORD."

The Numbering of the Levites

[14]Then the LORD spoke to Moses in the desert of Sinai: [15]"Number the Levites by their clans and their families; [a]every male from a month old and upward you are to number." [16]So Moses numbered them according to the word of the LORD, just as he had been commanded.

The Summary of Families

[17]These were [a]the sons of Levi by their names: Gershon, Kohath, and Merari. [18]These are the names of the sons of [a]Gershon by their families: [b]Libni and Shimei. [19]The sons of [a]Kohath by their families were: [b]Amram, Izhar, Hebron, and Uzziel. [20]The sons of Merari by their families were Mahli [a]and Mushi. These are the families of the Levites by their clans.

The Numbering of the Gershonites

[21]From Gershon came the family of the Libnites and the family of the Shimeites; these were the families of the Gershonites. [22]Those of them who were numbered, counting every male from a month old and upward, were 7,500. [23]The families of [a]the Gershonites were to camp behind the tabernacle toward the west. [24]Now the leader of the clan of the Gershonites was Eliasaph son of Lael.

[25]And [a]the responsibilities of [b]the Gershonites in [c]the tent of meeting included the tabernacle, the tent with [d]its covering, [e]the curtain at the entrance of the tent of meeting, [26]the hangings of [a]the courtyard,

---

2:32 [a]Exod 38:26; Num 1:46; 11:21   **2:33** [a]Num 1:47; 26:57–62   **2:34** [a]Num 1:54   **3:1** [a]Exod 6:16–27   [1]Trad. *Now these are the generations.*   **3:2** [a]Exod 6:23   [b]Lev 10:1–2; Num 26:60–61; 1 Chr 24:2   **3:3** [a]Exod 28:41; Lev 8   [1]Lit. *he filled their hand*; in the ordination service, Moses placed some of the meat from the sacrifice in the hand of the ordinand.   **3:4** [a]Lev 10:1–2; Num 26:61; 1 Chr 24:2   [1]Some mss omit the initial clause.   [2]Or *prohibited*.   [3]I.e., perhaps using coals from a place other than the burnt offering altar, using the wrong kind of incense, or entering the holy of holies at an inappropriate time.   **3:6** [a]Num 8:6–22; 18:1–7; Deut 10:8; 33:8–11   **3:7** [a]Num 1:50; 8:11, 15, 24, 26   **3:10** [a]Exod 29:9; Num 18:7   [b]Num 1:51; 3:38; 16:40   [1]LXX adds *and all things pertaining to the altar and within the veil.*   **3:12** [a]Num 3:41; 8:16; 18:6   **3:13** [a]Exod 13:2; Lev 27:26; Num 8:16–17; Neh 10:36; Luke 2:23   [b]Exod 13:12, 15; Num 8:17   **3:15** [a]Num 3:39; 26:62   **3:17** [a]Gen 46:11; Exod 6:16–22; Num 26:57; 1 Chr 6:1, 16; 23:6   **3:18** [a]Num 4:38–41   [b]Exod 6:17   **3:19** [a]Num 4:34–37   [b]Exod 6:18   **3:20** [a]Exod 6:19; Num 4:42–45   **3:23** [a]Num 1:53   **3:25** [a]Num 4:24–26   [b]Exod 25:9   [c]Exod 26:1   [d]Exod 26:7, 14   [e]Exod 26:36   **3:26** [a]Exod 27:9, 12, 14, 15

[b]the curtain at [c]the entrance to the courtyard that surrounded the tabernacle and the altar, and their ropes, plus all the service connected with these things.

The Numbering of the Kohathites

[27a]From Kohath came the family of the Amramites, the family of the Izharites, the family of the Hebronites, and the family of the Uzzielites; these were the families of the Kohathites. [28]Counting every male from a month old and upward, there were 8,600. They were responsible for the care of the sanctuary. [29]The families of [a]the Kohathites were to camp on the south side of the tabernacle. [30]Now the leader of the clan of the families of the Kohathites was Elizaphan son of [a]Uzziel.

[31]Their responsibilities included [a]the ark, [b]the table, [c]the lampstand, [d]the altars, and [e]the utensils of [f]the sanctuary with which they ministered, the curtain, and all their service. [32]Now the head of all the Levitical leaders was Eleazar son of Aaron the priest. He was appointed over those who were responsible for the sanctuary.

The Numbering of Merari

[33]From Merari came the family of the Mahlites and the family of the Mushites; these were the families of Merari. [34]Those of them who were numbered, counting every male from a month old and upward, were 6,200. [35]Now [a]the leader of the clan of the families of Merari was Zuriel son of Abihail. These were to camp on the north side of the tabernacle.

[36]The appointed responsibilities of [a]the Merarites included the frames of the tabernacle, its crossbars, its posts, its sockets, its utensils, plus all the service connected with these things, [37]and the pillars of the courtyard all around, with their sockets, their pegs, and their ropes.

[38a]But those who were to camp in front of the tabernacle on the east, in front of the tent of meeting, were Moses, Aaron,[1] and his sons. They were responsible [b]for the needs of the sanctuary and for the needs of the Israelites, but the unauthorized person who approached was [c]to be put to death. [39]All who were numbered of the Levites, whom Moses and Aaron numbered by the word of the LORD, according to their families, every male from [a]a month old and upward, were 22,000.

The Substitution for the Firstborn

[40]Then the LORD said to Moses, "[a]Number all the firstborn males of the Israelites from a month old and upward, and take the number of their names. [41]And take the Levites for me—I am the LORD—instead of all the firstborn males among the Israelites, [a]and the livestock of the Levites instead of all the firstborn of the livestock of the Israelites." [42]So Moses numbered all the firstborn males among the Israelites, as the LORD had commanded him. [43]And all the firstborn males, by the number of the names from a month old and upward, totaled 22,273.

[44]Then the LORD spoke to Moses: [45]"[a]Take the Levites instead of all the firstborn males among the Israelites, and the livestock of the Levites instead of their livestock. And the Levites will be mine. I am the LORD. [46]And for [a]the redemption of the 273 firstborn males of the Israelites [b]who exceed the number of the Levites, [47]collect [a]five shekels for each one [b]individually; you are to collect this amount in [c]the currency of the sanctuary shekel (this shekel is 20 gerahs). [48]And give the money for the redemption of the excess number of them to Aaron and his sons."

[49]So Moses took the redemption money from those who were in excess of those redeemed by the Levites. [50]From the firstborn males of the Israelites he collected the [a]money, 1,365 shekels, according to the sanctuary shekel. [51]Moses [a]gave the redemption money to Aaron and his sons, according to the word of the LORD, as the LORD had commanded Moses.

The Service of the Kohathites

4 Then the LORD spoke to Moses and Aaron: [2]"Take a census of the [a]Kohathites from among the Levites, by their families and by their clans, [3a]from thirty

---

3:26 [b]Exod 27:16   [c]Exod 35:18   **3:27** [a]1 Chr 26:23   **3:29** [a]Exod 6:18; Num 1:53   **3:30** [a]Lev 10:4   **3:31** [a]Num 4:15   [b]Exod 25:10   [c]Exod 25:23   [d]Exod 25:31   [e]Exod 27:1; 30:1   [f]Exod 26:31–33   **3:35** [a]Num 1:53; 2:25   **3:36** [a]Num 4:31–32   **3:38** [a]Num 1:53   [b]Num 18:5   [c]Num 3:7–8   [1]Some Heb. mss, Smr. omit *Aaron*.   **3:39** [a]Num 3:43; 4:48; 26:62   **3:40** [a]Num 3:15   **3:41** [a]Num 3:12, 45   **3:45** [a]Num 3:12, 41   **3:46** [a]Exod 13:13, 15; 18:15–16   [b]Num 3:39, 43   **3:47** [a]Lev 27:6; Num 18:16   [b]Num 1:2, 18, 20   [c]Exod 30:13   **3:50** [a]Num 3:46–47   **3:51** [a]Num 3:48   **4:2** [a]Num 3:27–32   **4:3** [a]Num 4:23, 30, 35; 8:24; 1 Chr 23:3, 24, 27; Ezra 3:8

years old and upward to fifty years old, all who enter the company[1] to do the work in the tent of meeting. [4]This [a]is [b]the service of the Kohathites in the tent of meeting, relating to the most holy things. [5]When it is time for [a]the camp to journey, Aaron and his sons must come and take down the screening curtain and cover the [b]ark of the testimony with it. [6]Then they must put over it a covering of fine leather[1] and spread over that a cloth entirely of [a]blue, and then they must insert [b]its poles.

[7]"On the [a]table of the presence they must spread a blue cloth, and put on it the dishes, the pans, the bowls, and the pitchers for pouring, and the [b]Bread of the Presence must be on it continually. [8]They must spread over them a scarlet cloth, and cover the same with a covering of fine leather; and they must insert its poles.

[9]"They must take a blue cloth and cover the [a]lampstand of the light, [b]with its lamps, its wick-trimmers, its trays, and all its oil vessels, with which they service it. [10]Then they must put it with all its utensils in a covering of fine leather, and put it on a carrying beam.

[11]"They must spread a blue cloth on [a]the gold altar, and cover it with a covering of fine leather; and they must insert its poles. [12]Then they must take all the [a]utensils of the service, with which they serve in the sanctuary, put them in a blue cloth, cover them with a covering of fine leather, and put them on a carrying beam. [13]Also, they must take away the ashes from the altar[1] and spread a purple cloth over it. [14]Then they must place on it all its implements with which they serve there—the trays, the meat forks, the shovels, the basins, and all the utensils of the altar—and they must spread on it a covering of fine leather, and then insert its poles.[1]

[15]"When Aaron and his sons have finished covering [a]the sanctuary and all the furnishings of the sanctuary, when the camp is ready to journey, then the Kohathites will come to carry them; [b]but they must not touch any holy thing, or they will die. [c]These are the responsibilities of the Kohathites with the tent of meeting.

[16]"The appointed responsibility of Eleazar son of Aaron [a]the priest is for the oil for the light, and the [b]spiced incense, and [c]the daily grain offering, and the [d]anointing oil; he also has the appointed responsibility over all the tabernacle with all that is in it, over the sanctuary and over all its furnishings."

[17]Then the LORD spoke to Moses and Aaron: [18]"Do not allow the tribe of the families of the Kohathites to be cut off from among the Levites; [19]but in order that [a]they will live[1] and not die when they approach the most holy things, do this for them: Aaron and his sons will go in and appoint each man to his service and his responsibility. [20a]But the Kohathites are not to go in to watch while the holy things are being covered, or they will die."

The Service of the Gershonites

[21]Then the LORD spoke to Moses: [22]"Also take a census of the [a]Gershonites also, by their clans and by their families. [23]You must number them [a]from thirty years old and upward to fifty years old, all who enter the company to do the work of the tent of meeting. [24]This is the [a]service of the families of Gershonites, as they serve and carry it. [25]They must carry [a]the [b]curtains for the tabernacle and the tent of meeting with its covering, the covering of fine leather that is over it, the curtains for the entrance of the tent of meeting, [26]the hangings for the courtyard, the curtain for the entrance of the gate of the court,[1] which is around the tabernacle and the altar, and their ropes, along with all the furnishings for their service and everything that is made for them. So they are to serve.

[27]"All the service of the Gershonites, whether carrying loads or for any of their work, will be at the direction of Aaron and his sons. You will assign them all their tasks as their responsibility. [28]This is the service of the families of the Gershonites

4:3[1]Lit. *host, army.*   **4:4**[a]Num 4:15   [b]Num 4:19   **4:5**[a]Exod 26:31; Heb 9:3   [b]Exod 25:10, 16   **4:6**[a]Exod 39:1   [b]Exod 25:13; 1 Kgs 8:7–8   [1]Perhaps the skins of a sea animal like a dolphin or porpoise.   **4:7**[a]Exod 25:23, 29, 30   [b]Lev 24:5–9   **4:9**[a]Exod 25:31   [b]Exod 25:37–38   **4:11**[a]Exod 30:1–5   **4:12**[a]Exod 25:9; 1 Chr 9:29   **4:13**[1]LXX *and he must place the cover upon the altar.*   **4:14**[1]LXX, Smr. add text on the purple cloth for the laver and its base, and a further covering of skin.   **4:15**[a]Num 7:9; 10:21; Deut 31:9; Josh 4:10; 2 Sam 6:13; 1 Chr 15:2, 15   [b]2 Sam 6:6–7; 1 Chr 13:9–10   [c]Num 3:31   **4:16**[a]Exod 25:6; Lev 24:2   [b]Exod 30:34   [c]Exod 29:38   [d]Exod 30:23–25   **4:19**[a]Num 4:4   [1]Heb. *Do this…and they will live.*   **4:20**[a]Exod 19:21; 1 Sam 6:19   **4:22**[a]Num 3:22   **4:23**[a]Num 4:3; 1 Chr 23:3, 24, 27   **4:24**[a]Num 7:7   **4:25**[a]Num 3:25–26   [b]Exod 36:8   **4:26**[1]LXX omits this clause.

concerning the tent of meeting. Their responsibilities will be [a]under the authority of Ithamar son of Aaron the priest.

The Service of the Merarites

[29]"As for the sons of [a]Merari, you are to number them by their families and by their clans. [30]You must number them [a]from thirty years old and upward to fifty years old, all who enter the company to do the work of the tent of meeting. [31]This [a]is [b]what [c]they are responsible to carry as their entire service in the tent of meeting: the frames of the tabernacle, its crossbars, its posts, its sockets, [32]and the posts of the surrounding courtyard with their sockets, tent pegs, and ropes, along with all their furnishings and everything for their service. You are to [a]assign by name the items that each man is responsible to carry. [33]This is the service of the families of the Merarites, their entire service concerning the tent of meeting, under the authority of Ithamar son of Aaron the priest."

Summary

[34]So Moses [a]and Aaron and the leaders of the community numbered the Kohathites by their families and by clans, [35]from thirty [a]years old and upward to fifty years old, everyone who entered the company for the work in the tent of meeting; [36]and those of them numbered by their families were 2,750. [37]These were those numbered from the families of the Kohathites, everyone who served in the tent of meeting, whom Moses and Aaron numbered according to the word of the LORD by the authority of Moses.

[38]Those numbered from the Gershonites, by their families and by their clans, [39]from thirty years old and upward to fifty years old, everyone who entered the company for the work in the tent of meeting—[40]those of them numbered by their families, by their clans, were 2,630. [41]These were those numbered from [a]the families of the Gershonites, everyone who served in the tent of meeting, whom Moses and Aaron numbered according to the word of the LORD.

[42]Those numbered from the families of the Merarites, by their families, by their clans, [43]from thirty years old and upward to fifty years old, everyone who entered the company for the work in the tent of meeting—[44]those of them numbered by their families were 3,200. [45]These are those numbered from the families of the Merarites, whom Moses and Aaron numbered [a]according to the word of the LORD by the authority of Moses.

[46]All who were [a]numbered of the Levites, whom Moses, Aaron, and the leaders of Israel numbered by their families and by their clans, [47a]from thirty years old and upward to fifty years old, everyone who entered to do the work of service and the work of carrying relating to the tent of meeting—[48]those of them numbered were 8,580. [49]According to the word of the LORD they were numbered, by the authority of Moses, [a]each according to his service and according to what he [b]was to carry. Thus were they numbered by him, as the LORD had commanded Moses.

Separation of the Unclean

5 Then the LORD spoke to Moses: [2]"Command the Israelites to expel from the camp every [a]leper, everyone who has a [b]discharge, and whoever becomes [c]defiled by a corpse.[1] [3]You must expel both men and women; you must put them outside the camp, so that they will not defile their camps, among which [a]I live." [4]So the Israelites did so, and expelled them outside the camp. As the LORD had spoken to Moses, so the Israelites did.

Restitution for Sin

[5]Then the LORD spoke to Moses: [6]"Tell the Israelites, '[a]When a man or a woman commits any sin that people commit, thereby breaking faith[1] with the LORD, and that person is found guilty, [7]then [a]he must confess his [b]sin that he has committed and must make full reparation,[1] add one-fifth to it, and give it to whomever he wronged. [8]But if [a]the individual has no close relative to whom reparation can be made for the wrong, the reparation for the wrong must be paid to the LORD for the priest, in

4:28 [a]Num 4:33   4:29 [a]Num 3:33-37   4:30 [a]Num 4:3; 8:24-26   4:31 [a]Num 3:36-37   [b]Num 7:8   [c]Exod 26:15   4:32 [a]Exod 25:9; 38:21   4:34 [a]Num 4:2   4:35 [a]Num 4:47   4:41 [a]Num 4:22   4:45 [a]Num 4:29   4:46 [a]Num 3:39; 26:57-62; 1 Chr 23:3-23   4:47 [a]Num 4:3, 23, 30   4:49 [a]Num 4:15, 24, 31   [b]Num 4:1, 21   5:2 [a]Lev 13:3, 8, 46; Num 12:10, 14, 15   [b]Lev 15:2   [c]Lev 21:1; Num 9:6, 10; 19:11, 13; 31:19   [1]Heb. [whole] *life;* i.e., the soul in the body, the person.   5:3 [a]Lev 26:11-12; Num 35:34; [2 Cor 6:16]   5:6 [a]Lev 5:14-6:7   [1]Heb. *to deal treacherously, do an act of treachery.*   5:7 [a]Lev 5:5; 26:40-41; Josh 7:19; Ps 32:5; 1 John 1:9   [b]Lev 6:4-5   [1]Trad. *guilt offering.*   5:8 [a]Lev 5:15; 6:6-7; 7:7

addition to the ram of atonement by which atonement is made for him. [9]Every [a]offering of all the Israelites' holy things that they bring to the priest will be [b]his. [10]Every man's holy things will be [a]his; whatever any man gives the priest will be his.'"

The Jealousy Ordeal

[11]The LORD spoke to Moses: [12]"Speak to the Israelites and tell them, 'If any man's wife goes astray and behaves unfaithfully toward him, [13]and a man goes to [a]bed with her for sexual relations without her husband knowing it, and it is undetected that she has defiled herself since there was no witness against her, nor was she [b]caught in the act—[14]and if jealous feelings[1] come over him and he becomes suspicious [a]of his wife when she is defiled, or if jealous feelings come over him and he becomes suspicious of his wife, when she is not defiled—[15]then the man must [a]bring his wife to the priest, and he must [b]bring the offering required for her, one-tenth of an ephah of barley meal; he must not pour olive oil on it or put frankincense on it because it is a grain offering of suspicion,[1] a grain offering for remembering, for bringing iniquity to remembrance.

[16]"Then the priest will bring her near and have her stand before the LORD. [17]The priest will then take holy water in a pottery jar, and take some of the dust that is on the floor of the tabernacle, and put it into the water. [18]Then the priest will have the woman stand before the [a]LORD, and he will uncover the woman's head and put the grain offering for remembering in her hands, which is the grain offering of suspicion. The priest will hold in his hand the bitter water that brings a curse. [19]Then the priest will put the woman under oath and say to her, "If no other man has gone to bed[1] with you, and if you have not gone astray and become defiled while under your husband's authority, may you be free from this bitter water that brings a curse. [20]But if you[1] have gone astray while under your husband's authority, and if you have defiled yourself and some man other than your husband has had sexual relations with you—"[2] [21](then the priest will [a]put [b]the woman under the oath of the curse and will say to her) "the LORD make you an attested curse among your people if the LORD makes your thigh fall away and your abdomen swell, [22]and this water that causes the curse will [a]go into your stomach and make your abdomen swell and your thigh rot." [b]Then the woman must say, "Amen, amen."[1]

[23]"Then the priest will write these curses on a scroll and then scrape them off into the bitter water. [24]He will make the woman drink the bitter water that brings a curse, and the water that brings a curse will enter her to produce bitterness. [25]The priest will take [a]the grain offering of suspicion from the woman's hand, [b]wave the grain offering before the LORD, and bring it to the altar. [26]Then the priest will take [a]a handful of the grain offering as its memorial portion, burn it on the altar, and afterward make the woman drink the water. [27]When he has made her drink the water, then if she has defiled herself and behaved unfaithfully toward her husband, the water that brings a [a]curse [b]will enter her to produce bitterness—her abdomen will swell, her thigh will fall away, and the woman will become a curse among her people. [28]But if the woman has not defiled herself, and is clean, then she will be free of ill effects and will be able to bear children.

[29]"This is the law for cases of jealousy, when a wife, while under her husband's authority, [a]goes astray and defiles herself, [30]or when jealous feelings come over a man and he becomes suspicious of his wife; then he must have the woman stand before the LORD, and the priest will carry out all this law upon her. [31]Then the man will be free from iniquity, but that woman will bear the consequences of her iniquity.'"

The Nazirite Vow

6 Then the LORD spoke to Moses: [2]"Speak [a]to the Israelites, and tell them, 'When someone—either a man or a woman—takes

5:9 [a]Exod 29:28; Lev 6:17–18, 26; 7:6–14   [b]Lev 7:32–34; 10:14–15   5:10 [a]Lev 10:13   5:13 [a]Lev 18:20; 20:10   [b]John 8:4   5:14 [a]Prov 6:34; Song 8:6   [1]Heb. *spirit of jealousy*; i.e., an attitude, mood, or feeling.   5:15 [a]Lev 5:11   [b]1 Kgs 17:18; Ezek 29:16; Heb 10:3   [1]Or *jealousy*.   5:18 [a]Heb 13:4   5:19 [1]Heb. *has lain down with*; a euphemism for sexual relations. 5:20 [1]Heb. *But you, if you have*; an emphatic Heb. construction.   [2]A figure of speech of a sudden silence (an aposiopesis) is used; the reader is left to conclude what the sentence would have said.   5:21 [a]Josh 6:26; 1 Sam 14:24; Neh 10:29   [b]Jer 29:22   5:22 [a]Ps 109:18   [b]Deut 27:15–26   [1]Carries the idea of "so be it" or "truly."   5:25 [a]Lev 8:27   [b]Lev 2:2, 9   5:26 [a]Lev 2:2, 9   5:27 [a]Deut 28:37; Isa 65:15; Jer 24:9; 29:18, 22; 42:18   [b]Num 5:21   5:29 [a]Num 5:19   6:2 [a]Lev 27:2; Judg 13:5; [Lam 4:7; Amos 2:11–12]; Acts 21:23; Rom 1:1

a special vow, to take a vow as a Nazirite,[1] to separate himself to the Lord, [3]he must separate[1] himself from wine and strong drink; [a]he must drink neither vinegar made from wine nor vinegar made from strong drink, nor may he drink any juice of grapes, nor eat fresh grapes or raisins. [4]All the days of his separation he must not eat anything that is produced by the grapevine, from seed to skin.

[5]"'All the days of the vow of his separation no [a]razor may be used on his head until the time is fulfilled for which he separated himself to the Lord. He will be holy, and he must let the locks of hair on his head grow long.

[6]"'All [a]the days that he separates himself to the Lord he must not contact a dead body.[7] He must not defile himself even for his [a]father or his mother or his brother or his sister if they die, because the separation for his God is on his head. [8a]All the days of his separation he must be holy to the Lord.

Contingencies for Defilement

[9]"'If anyone dies very suddenly beside him and he defiles his consecrated head, then he must [a]shave his head on the day of his purification—on the seventh day he must shave it. [10]On the eighth day he is to bring two turtledoves or two young [a]pigeons to the priest, to the entrance to the tent of meeting. [11]Then the priest will offer one for a purification offering[1] and the other as a burnt offering, and make atonement for him, because of his transgression in regard to the corpse. So he must reconsecrate his head on that day. [12]He must rededicate to the Lord the days of his separation and bring [a]a male lamb in its first year as a reparation offering, but the former days will not be counted because his separation was defiled.

Fulfilling the Vows

[13]"'Now this is the law of the Nazirite: [a]When the days of his separation are fulfilled, he must be brought to the entrance of the tent of meeting, [14]and he must present his offering to the Lord: one male

lamb in its first year without blemish for [a]a burnt offering, one ewe lamb in its first year without blemish for [b]a purification offering, one ram without blemish for a peace offering, [15]and a basket of bread made without yeast, [a]cakes of fine flour mixed with olive oil, wafers made without yeast and [b]smeared with olive oil, and their grain offering and their [c]drink offerings.

[16]"'Then the priest must present all these before the Lord and offer his purification offering and his burnt offering. [17]Then he must offer the ram as a peace offering to the Lord along with the basket of bread made without yeast; the priest must also offer his grain offering and his drink offering.

[18]"'Then [a]the Nazirite must shave his consecrated head at the entrance to the tent of meeting and must take the hair from his consecrated head and put it on the fire where the peace offering is burning. [19]And the priest must take the [a]boiled shoulder of the ram, one cake made without [b]yeast from the basket, and one wafer made without yeast, and [c]put them on the hands of the Nazirite after he has shaved his consecrated head; [20]then [a]the priest must wave them as a wave offering before the Lord; it is a holy portion for the priest, together with the breast of the wave offering and the thigh of the raised offering. After this the Nazirite may drink wine.

[21]"'This is the law of the Nazirite who vows to the Lord his offering according to his separation, as well as whatever else he can provide. Thus he must fulfill his vow that he makes, according to the law of his separation.'"

The Priestly Benediction

[22]The Lord spoke to Moses: [23]"Tell Aaron and his sons, 'This is the way you are to bless the Israelites. Say to them:

[24] "'"The Lord [a]bless you and [b]protect you;
[25] The Lord [a]make his face to shine upon you,
     and [b]be gracious to you;

6:2 [1]From the verb (Heb. *nazar*) *to consecrate oneself*; those who take an oath for a time or for a lifetime to be committed to the Lord and show signs of separation from the world.   6:3 [a]Lev 10:9; Amos 2:12; Luke 1:15 [1]The verb (Heb. *nazar*) is the root of "Nazirite" (v. 2).   6:5 [a]Judg 13:5; 16:17; 1 Sam 1:11   6:6 [a]Lev 21:1–3, 11; Num 19:11–22 [1]Heb. *dead person.*   6:7 [a]Lev 21:1–2, 11; Num 9:6   6:8 [a][2 Cor 6:17–18]   6:9 [a]Lev 14:8–9; Acts 18:18; 21:24   6:10 [a]Lev 5:7; 14:22; 15:14, 29   6:11 [1]Trad. *sin offering.*   6:12 [a]Lev 5:6   6:13 [a]Acts 21:26   6:14 [a]Lev 4:2, 27, 32 [b]Lev 3:6   6:15 [a]Lev 2:4 [b]Exod 29:2 [c]Num 15:5, 7, 10   6:18 [a]Num 6:9; Acts 21:23–24   6:19 [a]1 Sam 2:15 [b]Exod 29:23–24 [c]Lev 7:30   6:20 [a]Exod 29:27–28   6:24 [a]Deut 28:3–6 [b]Ps 121:7; John 7:11   6:25 [a]Ps 31:16; 67:1; 80:3, 7, 19; 119:135; Dan 9:17 [b]Gen 43:29; Exod 33:19; Mal 1:9

26 aThe LORD lift up his countenance
upon you
and bgive you peace."'"

27"aSo they bwill put my name on the Israelites, and I will bless them."

The Leader's Offerings

7 When Moses had completed asetting up the tabernacle, he banointed it and consecrated it and all its furnishings, and he anointed and consecrated the altar and all its utensils. 2Then athe leaders of Israel, the heads of their clans, made an offering. They were the leaders of the tribes; they were the ones who had been supervising the numbering. 3They brought their offerings before the LORD, six covered carts and twelve oxen—one cart for every two of the leaders, and an ox for each one; and they presented them in front of the tabernacle.

The Distribution of the Gifts

4Then the LORD spoke to Moses: 5"Receive these gifts from them, that they may be used in doing the work of the tent of meeting; and you must give them to the Levites, to every man as his service requires."

6So Moses accepted the carts and the oxen and gave them to the Levites. 7He gave two carts and four oxen to athe Gershonites, as their service required; 8and he gave four carts aand eight oxen to the Merarites, as their service required, under the authority of Ithamar son of Aaron the priest. 9But to athe Kohathites he gave none, because the service of the holy things, bwhich they carried on their shoulders, was their responsibility.

The Time of Presentation

10The leaders offered gifts for athe dedication of the altar when it was anointed. And the leaders presented1 their offering before the altar. 11For the LORD said to Moses, "They must present their offering, one leader for each day, for the dedication of the altar."

The Tribal Offerings

12The one who presented his offering on the first day was aNahshon son of Amminadab, from the tribe of Judah. 13His offering was one silver platter weighing 130 shekels, and one silver sprinkling bowl weighing 70 shekels, both according to athe sanctuary shekel, each of them full of fine flour mixed with olive oil as ba grain offering; 14one gold pan weighing 10 shekels, full of aincense; 15aone young bull, one ram, and one male lamb bin its first year, for a burnt offering; 16one male goat for a purification offering; 17and for athe sacrifice of peace offerings: two bulls, five rams, five male goats, and five male lambs in their first year. This was the offering of Nahshon son of Amminadab.

18On the second day Nethanel son of Zuar, leader of Issachar, presented an offering. 19He offered for his offering one silver platter weighing 130 shekels and one silver sprinkling bowl weighing 70 shekels, both according to the sanctuary shekel, each of them full of fine flour mixed with olive oil as a grain offering; 20one gold pan weighing 10 shekels, full of incense; 21one young bull, one ram, and one male lamb in its first year, for a burnt offering; 22one male goat for a purification offering; 23and for the sacrifice of peace offerings: two bulls, five rams, five male goats, and five male lambs in their first year. This was the offering of Nethanel son of Zuar.

24On the third day Eliab son of Helon, leader of the Zebulunites, presented an offering. 25His offering was one silver platter weighing 130 shekels and one silver sprinkling bowl weighing 70 shekels, both according to the sanctuary shekel, each of them full of fine flour mixed with olive oil as a grain offering; 26one gold pan weighing 10 shekels, full of incense; 27one young bull, one ram, and one male lamb in its first year, for a burnt offering; 28one male goat for a purification offering; 29and for the sacrifice of peace offerings: two bulls, five rams, five male goats, and five male lambs in their first year. This was the offering of Eliab son of Helon.

30On the fourth day aElizur son of Shedeur, leader of the Reubenites, presented an offering. 31His offering was one silver platter weighing 130 shekels and one silver sprinkling bowl weighing 70 shekels,

6:26 aPs 4:6; 89:15 bLev 26:6; Isa 26:3, 12; John 14:27; Phil 4:7 6:27 aDeut 28:10; 2 Sam 7:23; 2 Chr 7:14; Isa 43:7; Dan 9:18–19 bExod 20:24; Num 23:20; Ps 5:12; 67:7; 115:12–13; Eph 1:3 7:1 aExod 40:17–33 bLev 8:10–11 7:2 aNum 1:4 7:7 aNum 4:24–28 7:8 aNum 4:29–33 7:9 aNum 4:15 bNum 4:6–14 7:10 aNum 7:1; Deut 20:5; 1 Kgs 8:63; 2 Chr 7:5, 9; Ezra 6:16; Neh 12:27 1Heb. offered. 7:12 aNum 2:3 7:13 aExod 30:13 bLev 2:1 7:14 aExod 30:34–35 7:15 aLev 1:2 bExod 12:5 7:17 aLev 3:1 7:30 aNum 1:5; 2:10

both according to the sanctuary shekel, each of them full of fine flour mixed with olive oil as a grain offering; [32]one gold pan weighing 10 shekels, full of incense; [33]one young bull, one ram, and one male lamb in its first year, for a burnt offering; [34]one male goat for a purification offering; [35]and for the sacrifice of peace offerings: two bulls, five rams, five male goats, and five lambs in their first year. This was the offering of Elizur son of Shedeur.

[36]On the fifth day [a]Shelumiel son of Zurishaddai, leader of the Simeonites, presented an offering. [37]His offering was one silver platter weighing 130 shekels and one silver sprinkling bowl weighing 70 shekels, both according to the sanctuary shekel, each of them full of fine flour mixed with olive oil as a grain offering; [38]one gold pan weighing 10 shekels, full of incense; [39]one young bull, one ram, and one male lamb in its first year, for a burnt offering; [40]one male goat for a purification offering; [41]and for the sacrifice of peace offerings: two bulls, five rams, five male goats, and five lambs in their first year. This was the offering of Shelumiel son of Zurishaddai.

[42]On the sixth day [a]Eliasaph son of Deuel, leader of the Gadites, presented an offering. [43]His offering was one silver platter weighing 130 shekels and one silver sprinkling bowl weighing 70 shekels, both according to the sanctuary shekel, each of them full of fine flour mixed with olive oil as a grain offering; [44]one gold pan weighing 10 shekels, full of incense; [45]one young bull, one [a]ram, and one male lamb in its first year, for a burnt offering; [46]one male goat for a purification offering; [47]and for the sacrifice of peace offerings: two bulls, five rams, five male goats, and five lambs in their first year. This was the offering of Eliasaph son of Deuel.

[48]On the seventh day [a]Elishama son of Ammihud, leader of the Ephraimites, presented an offering. [49]His offering was one silver platter weighing 130 shekels and one silver sprinkling bowl weighing 70 shekels, both according to the sanctuary shekel, each of them full of fine flour mixed with olive oil as a grain offering; [50]one gold pan weighing 10 shekels, full of incense; [51]one young bull, one ram, and one male lamb in its first year, for a burnt offering; [52]one male goat for a purification offering; [53]and for the sacrifice of peace offerings: two bulls, five rams, five male goats, and five lambs in their first year. This was the offering of Elishama son of Ammihud.

[54]On the eighth day [a]Gamaliel son of Pedahzur, leader of the Manassehites, presented an offering. [55]His offering was one silver platter weighing 130 shekels and one silver sprinkling bowl weighing 70 shekels, both according to the sanctuary shekel, each of them full of fine flour mixed with olive oil as a grain offering; [56]one gold pan weighing 10 shekels, full of incense; [57]one young bull, one ram, and one male lamb in its first year, for a burnt offering; [58]one male goat for a purification offering; [59]and for the sacrifice of peace offerings: two bulls, five rams, five male goats, and five lambs in their first year. This was the offering of Gamaliel son of Pedahzur.

[60]On the ninth day [a]Abidan son of Gideoni, leader of the Benjaminites, presented an offering. [61]His offering was one silver platter weighing 130 shekels and one silver sprinkling bowl weighing 70 shekels, both according to the sanctuary shekel, each of them full of fine flour mixed with olive oil as a grain offering; [62]one gold pan weighing 10 shekels, full of incense; [63]one young bull, one ram, and one male lamb in its first year, for a burnt offering; [64]one male goat for a purification offering; [65]and for the sacrifice of peace offerings: two bulls, five rams, five male goats, and five lambs in their first year. This was the offering of Abidan son of Gideoni.

[66]On the tenth day [a]Ahiezer son of Ammishaddai, leader of the Danites, presented an offering. [67]His offering was one silver platter weighing 130 shekels and one silver sprinkling bowl weighing 70 shekels, both according to the sanctuary shekel, each of them full of fine flour mixed with olive oil as a grain offering; [68]one gold pan weighing 10 shekels, full of incense; [69]one young bull, one ram, and one male lamb in its first year, for a burnt offering; [70]one male goat for a purification offering; [71]and for the sacrifice of peace offerings: two bulls, five rams, five male goats, and five lambs in their first year. This was the offering of Ahiezer son of Ammishaddai.

7:36 [a]Num 1:6; 2:12; 7:41   7:42 [a]Num 1:14; 2:14; 10:20   7:45 [a]Ps 40:6   7:48 [a]Num 1:10; 2:18; 1 Chr 7:26   7:54 [a]Num 1:10; 2:20   7:60 [a]Num 1:11; 2:22   7:66 [a]Num 1:12; 2:25

[72]On the eleventh day [a]Pagiel son of Ocran, leader of the Asherites, presented an offering. [73]His offering was one silver platter weighing 130 shekels and one silver sprinkling bowl weighing 70 shekels, both according to the sanctuary shekel, each of them full of fine flour mixed with olive oil as a grain offering; [74]one gold pan weighing 10 shekels, full of incense; [75]one young bull, one ram, and one male lamb in its first year, for a burnt offering; [76]one male goat for a purification offering; [77]and for the sacrifice of peace offerings: two bulls, five rams, five male goats, and five lambs in their first year. This was the offering of Pagiel son of Ocran.

[78]On the twelfth day [a]Ahira son of Enan, leader of the Naphtalites, presented an offering. [79]His offering was one silver platter weighing 130 shekels and one silver sprinkling bowl weighing 70 shekels, both according to the sanctuary shekel, each of them full of fine flour mixed with olive oil as a grain offering; [80]one gold pan weighing 10 shekels, full of incense; [81]one young bull, one ram, and one male lamb in its first year, for a burnt offering; [82]one male goat for a purification offering; [83]and for the sacrifice of peace offerings: two bulls, five rams, five male goats, and five lambs in their first year. This was the offering of Ahira son of Enan.

Summary

[84]This was [a]the dedication for the altar from the leaders of Israel, when it was anointed: twelve silver platters, twelve silver sprinkling bowls, and twelve gold pans. [85]Each silver platter weighed 130 shekels, and each silver sprinkling bowl weighed 70 shekels. All the silver of the vessels weighed 2,400 shekels, according to the sanctuary shekel. [86]The twelve gold pans full of incense weighed 10 shekels each, according to the sanctuary shekel; all the gold of the pans weighed 120 shekels. [87]All the animals for the burnt offering were 12 young bulls, 12 rams, 12 male lambs in their first year, with their grain offering, and 12 male goats for a purification offering. [88]All the animals for the sacrifice for the peace offering were 24 young bulls, 60 rams, 60 male goats, and 60 lambs in their first year. These were the dedication offerings for the altar after it was [a]anointed.

[89]Now when Moses went [a]into [b]the tent of meeting to speak with the LORD,[1] he heard the voice speaking to him from above the atonement lid that was on the ark of the testimony, from [c]between the two cherubim. Thus he spoke to him.

Lighting the Lamps

8 The LORD spoke to Moses: [2]"Speak to Aaron and tell him, 'When you set [a]up the [b]lamps, the seven lamps are to give light in front of the lampstand.'"

[3]And Aaron did so; he set up the lamps to face toward the front of the lampstand, as the LORD commanded Moses. [4][a]This is how the lampstand was made: It was beaten work [b]in gold; from its shaft to its flowers it was beaten work. According to the pattern that the LORD had shown Moses, so he made the lampstand.

The Separation of the Levites

[5]Then the LORD spoke to Moses: [6]"Take the Levites from among the Israelites and purify them. [7]And do this[1] to them to purify them: Sprinkle [a]water of purification on them; then have them shave all their body and wash their clothes, and so purify themselves. [8]Then they are to take a young bull with [a]its grain offering of fine flour mixed with olive oil; and you are to take a second young bull for a purification offering. [9]You are to bring the Levites before the tent of meeting [a]and assemble the entire community of the Israelites. [10]Then you are to bring the Levites before the LORD, and the Israelites are to lay their hands on the Levites; [11]and Aaron is to offer the Levites before the LORD as [a]a wave offering from the Israelites, that they may do the work of the LORD. [12]When [a]the Levites lay their hands on the heads of the bulls, offer the one for a purification offering and the other for a whole burnt offering to the LORD, to make atonement for the Levites. [13]You are to have the Levites stand before Aaron[1] and his sons, and then offer them as a wave offering to the LORD. [14]And so you

7:72 [a]Num 1:13; 2:27   7:78 [a]Num 1:15; 2:29   7:84 [a]Num 7:10   7:88 [a]Num 7:1, 10   7:89 [a][Exod 33:9, 11]; Num 12:8   [b]Exod 25:21–22   [c]Ps 80:1; 99:1   [1]MT *with him*; LXX adds *Lord* after *voice.*   8:2 [a]Lev 24:2–4   [b]Exod 25:37; 40:25   8:4 [a]Exod 25:31   [b]Exod 25:40; Acts 7:44   8:7 [a]Num 19:9, 13, 17, 20; Ps 51:2, 7; [Heb 9:13–14]   [1]Lit. *and thus you shall do.*   8:8 [a]Lev 2:1; Num 15:8–10   8:9 [a]Exod 29:4; 40:12   8:11 [a]Num 18:6   8:12 [a]Exod 29:10   8:13 [1]LXX *before the LORD and before Aaron.*

are to [a]separate the Levites from among the Israelites, and the Levites will be [b]mine. [15]"After this, the Levites will go in[1] to do the work of the tent of meeting. So you must cleanse them and [a]offer them like a wave offering.[2] [16]For they are [a]entirely given to me from among the Israelites. [b]I have taken them for myself instead of all who open the womb, the firstborn sons of all the Israelites. [17]For all the firstborn males among the Israelites are mine, both humans and animals; when I destroyed all the firstborn in the land of Egypt I set them apart [a]for myself. [18]So I have taken the Levites instead of all the firstborn sons among the Israelites. [19]I have [a]given the Levites as [b]a gift to Aaron and his sons from among the Israelites, to do the work for the Israelites in the tent of meeting, and to make atonement for the Israelites, so there will be no plague among the Israelites when the Israelites come near the sanctuary."

[20]So Moses and Aaron and the entire community of the Israelites did this with the Levites. According to all that the LORD commanded Moses concerning the Levites, this is what the Israelites did with them. [21]The Levites purified themselves [a]and washed their clothing; then Aaron presented them like a wave offering before the LORD, and Aaron made atonement for them to purify them. [22a]After this, the Levites went in to do their work in the tent of meeting before Aaron and before his sons. [b]As the LORD had commanded Moses concerning the Levites, so they did.

The Work of the Levites

[23]Then the LORD spoke to Moses: [24]"This is what pertains to the Levites: At the age of twenty-five years and upward one may begin to join the company in the work of the tent of meeting, [25]and at the age of fifty years they must retire from performing the work and may no longer work. [26]They may assist their colleagues in the tent of meeting [a]to attend to needs, but they must do no work. This is the way you must establish the Levites regarding their duties."

Passover Regulations

9 The LORD spoke to Moses in the desert of Sinai, in the first month of the second year after they had come out of the land of Egypt: [2]"The Israelites are to observe[1] [a]the Passover at its appointed [b]time.[2] [3]In the fourteenth day of this month, at twilight,[1] you are to observe it at its appointed time; you must keep it in accordance with all its statutes and all its customs." [4]So Moses instructed the Israelites to observe the Passover. [5]And [a]they observed the Passover[1] on the fourteenth day of the first month at twilight in the desert of Sinai; in accordance with all that the LORD had commanded Moses, so the Israelites did.

[6]It happened that some men who were ceremonially [a]defiled by the dead body of [b]a man[1] could not keep the Passover on that day, so they came before Moses and before Aaron on that day. [7]And those men said to Moses, "We are ceremonially defiled by the dead body of a man; why are we kept back from offering the LORD's offering at its appointed time among the Israelites?" [8]So Moses [a]said to them, "Remain here and I will hear what the LORD will command concerning you."

[9]The LORD spoke to Moses: [10]"Tell the Israelites, 'If any of you or of your posterity become ceremonially defiled by touching a dead body, or are on a journey far away, then he may observe the Passover to the LORD. [11]They may observe it on [a]the fourteenth day of the second month at twilight; they are to [b]eat it with bread made without yeast and with bitter herbs. [12]They must not leave any of it until morning, nor break any of its bones; [a]they must observe it [b]in accordance with every statute of the Passover.

[13]"But the man who is ceremonially clean, and was not on [a]a journey, and fails[1] to keep the Passover, that person must be cut off from his people. Because he [b]did not bring the LORD's offering at its appointed time, that man must [c]bear his sin. [14]If a resident foreigner lives among [a]you and wants to keep the Passover to the LORD, he must do

8:14 [a]Num 16:9   [b]Num 3:12, 45; 16:9   8:15 [a]Num 8:11, 13   [1]Or *may go in.*   [2]LXX adds *before the LORD.*   8:16 [a]Num 3:9   [b]Exod 13:2; Num 3:12, 45   8:17 [a]Exod 12:2, 12, 13, 15; Num 3:13; Luke 2:23   8:19 [a]Num 3:9   [b]Num 1:53; 16:46; 18:5; 2 Chr 26:16   8:21 [a]Num 8:7   8:22 [a]Num 8:15   [b]Num 8:5   8:26 [a]Num 1:53   9:2 [a]Exod 12:1–16; Lev 23:5; Num 28:16; Deut 16:1–2   [b]2 Chr 30:1–15; Luke 22:7; [1 Cor 5:7–8]   [1]Heb. *to do, to make.*   [2]LXX, Smr. *times.*   9:3 [1]Heb. *between the evenings.*   9:5 [a]Josh 5:10   [1]LXX omits the first clause and *at twilight.*   9:6 [a]Num 5:2; 19:11–22; John 18:28   [b]Exod 18:15, 19, 26; Num 27:2   [1]Or *a human corpse.*   9:8 [a]Exod 18:22; Num 27:5   9:11 [a]2 Chr 30:2, 15   [b]Exod 12:8   9:12 [a]Exod 12:10   [b]Exod 12:43   9:13 [a]Gen 17:14; Exod 12:15, 47   [b]Num 9:7   [c]Num 5:31   [1]Heb. *to cease, to leave off, to fail;* i.e., he made the decision to leave it undone.   9:14 [a]Exod 12:49; Lev 24:22; Num 15:15–16, 29

so according to the statute of the Passover, and according to its custom. You must have the same statute for the resident foreigner and for the one who was born in the land.'"

The Lord Leads the Israelites by the Cloud

[15]On the day that the tabernacle was set up, the cloud covered the tabernacle—the tent of the [a]testimony—and from evening until morning there was a fiery appearance [b]over the tabernacle. [16]This is the way it used to be continually: The cloud would cover it by day,[1] and there was a fiery appearance by night. [17]Whenever the cloud [a]was taken up from the tabernacle, then after that the Israelites would begin their journey; and in whatever place the cloud settled, there the Israelites would make camp. [18]At the commandment of the LORD the Israelites would begin their journey, and at the commandment of the LORD they would make camp; as long [a]as the cloud remained settled over the tabernacle they would camp. [19]When the cloud remained over the tabernacle many days, then the Israelites [a]obeyed the instructions of the LORD and did not journey.

[20]When the cloud remained over the tabernacle a number of days, they remained camped according to the LORD's commandment, and according to the LORD's commandment they would journey. [21]And when the cloud remained only from evening until morning, when the cloud was taken up the following morning, then they traveled on. Whether by day or by night, when the cloud was taken up they traveled. [22]Whether it was for two days, or a month, or a year that the cloud prolonged its stay over the tabernacle, the Israelites remained camped without traveling; but when it was taken up, they traveled on. [23]At the commandment of the LORD they camped, and at the commandment of the LORD they traveled on; they [a]kept the instructions of the LORD according to the commandment of the LORD, by the authority of Moses.

The Blowing of Trumpets

10 The LORD spoke to Moses: [2]"Make two trumpets of silver; you are to make them from a single hammered piece. You will use them for [a]assembling the community and for directing the traveling of the camps. [3]When [a]they blow them both, all the community must come to you to the entrance of the tent of meeting.

[4]"But if they blow with one trumpet, then the leaders, the [a]heads of the thousands of Israel, must come to you. [5]When you blow an [a]alarm,[1] [b]then the camps that are located on the east side must begin to travel. [6]And when you blow an alarm the [a]second time, then the camps that are located on the south side must begin to travel.[1] An alarm must be sounded for their journeys. [7]But when [a]you assemble the community, you must blow the trumpets, but you must not [b]sound an alarm. [8]The sons of Aaron, [a]the priests, must blow the trumpets, and they will be to you for an eternal ordinance throughout your generations. [9a]If you go to war in your land against an adversary who [b]opposes[1] you, then you must sound an alarm with the trumpets, and you will be [c]remembered before the LORD your God, and you will be saved from your enemies.

[10]"Also, [a]in the time when you rejoice, such [b]as[1] on your appointed festivals or at the beginnings of your months, you must blow with your trumpets over your burnt offerings and over the sacrifices of your peace offerings, so that they may become a memorial for you before your God: I am the LORD your God."

The Journey from Sinai to Kadesh

[11]On the twentieth day of the second month, in the second year, the cloud [a]was taken up from the tabernacle of the testimony.[1] [12]So the Israelites set out on their journeys from the desert[1] of Sinai; and the cloud settled in the [a]wilderness of Paran.

Judah Begins the Journey

[13]This was the first time they set out on their journey [a]according to the

9:15 [a]Exod 40:33–34; Neh 9:12, 19; Ps 78:14   [b]Isa 4:5   9:16 [1]MT omits *by day*.   9:17 [a]Exod 40:36–38; Num 10:11–12, 33, 34; Ps 80:1   9:18 [a]1 Cor 10:1   9:19 [a]Num 1:53; 3:8   9:23 [a]Num 9:19   10:2 [a]Isa 1:13   10:3 [a]Jer 4:5; Joel 2:15   10:4 [a]Exod 18:21; Num 1:16; 7:2   10:5 [a]Joel 2:1   [b]Num 2:3   [1]Heb. *to give a blast on the trumpet, give a shout.*   10:6 [a]Num 2:10   [1]LXX adds departures of the northerly and westerly tribes.   10:7 [a]Num 10:3   [b]Joel 2:1   10:8 [a]Num 31:6; Josh 6:4; 1 Chr 15:24; 2 Chr 13:12   10:9 [a]Num 31:6; Josh 6:5; 2 Chr 13:14   [b]Judg 2:18; 4:3; 6:9; 10:8, 12   [c]Gen 8:1; Ps 106:4   [1]Heb. *to hem in, oppress, harass.*   10:10 [a]Lev 23:24; Num 29:1; 1 Chr 15:24; 2 Chr 5:12; Ps 81:3   [b]Lev 23:24; Num 10:9   [1]Or perhaps *especially.*   10:11 [a]Num 9:17   [1]Smr. adds a portion of Deut 1:6–8.   10:12 [a]Gen 21:21; Num 12:16; Deut 1:1   [1]I.e., a dry region that receives less than twelve inches of rain per year.   10:13 [a]Num 10:5–6

commandment of the LORD, by the authority of Moses.

[14] The standard of the camp of the Judahites [a] set out first according to their companies, and over his company was [b] Nahshon son of Amminadab.

[15] Over the company of the tribe of Issacharites was Nathanel son of Zuar, [16] and over the company of the tribe of the Zebulunites was Eliab son of Helon. [17] Then [a] the tabernacle was dismantled, and the sons of Gershon and the sons of Merari set out, [b] carrying the tabernacle.

Journey Arrangements for the Tribes

[18] The standard of [a] the camp of Reuben set out according to their companies; over his company was Elizur son of Shedeur. [19] Over the company of the tribe of the Simeonites was Shelumiel son of Zurishaddai, [20] and over the company of the tribe of the Gadites was Eliasaph son of Deuel. [21] And the Kohathites set out, carrying the articles for the sanctuary; the tabernacle was to be set up before they arrived. [22] And [a] the standard of the camp of the Ephraimites set out according to their companies; over his company was Elishama son of Ammihud. [23] Over the company of the tribe of the Manassehites was Gamaliel son of Pedahzur, [24] and over the company of the tribe of Benjaminites was Abidan son of Gideoni.

[25] The standard of [a] the camp of the Danites set out, which was the rear guard of all the camps by their companies; over his company was Ahiezer son of Ammishaddai. [26] Over the company of the tribe of the Asherites was Pagiel son of Ocran, [27] and over the company of the tribe of the Naphtalites was Ahira son of Enan. [28a] These were the traveling arrangements of the Israelites according to their companies when they traveled.

The Appeal to Hobab

[29] Moses said to [a] Hobab son of [b] Reuel, the [c] Midianite, Moses' father-in-law, "[d] We are journeying to [e] the place about which the LORD said, 'I will give it to you.' Come with us and we will treat you well, for the LORD has promised good things for Israel."
[30] But Hobab said to him, "I will not go, but I will go instead to my own land and to my kindred." [31] Moses said, "Do not leave us, because you know places for us to camp in the wilderness, and you could be our [a] guide.[1] [32] And if you come with us, it is certain that [a] whatever good things the LORD will favor us with, we will share with you as well."

[33] So [a] they [b] traveled from the mountain of the LORD three days' journey; and the ark of the covenant of the LORD was traveling before them during the three days' journey, to find a resting place for them. [34] And [a] the cloud of the LORD was over them by day, when they traveled from the camp. [35] And when the ark traveled, Moses would say, "[a] Rise up, O LORD! May your enemies be scattered, and may those who hate you flee before you!" [36] And when it came to rest he would say, "Return, O LORD, to the many thousands of Israel!"

The Israelites Complain

11 When the people complained, it displeased[1] the LORD. [a] When the LORD heard it, his anger burned,[2] and so the [b] fire of the LORD burned among them and consumed some of the outer parts of the camp. [2] When the people [a] cried to Moses, he [b] prayed to the LORD, and the fire died out. [3] So he called the name of that place Taberah because there the fire of the LORD burned among them.

Complaints about Food

[4] Now the [a] mixed multitude[1] [b] who were among them craved more desirable foods, and so the Israelites wept again and said, "If only we had meat to eat![2] [5] We remember the fish [a] we used to eat freely in Egypt, the cucumbers, the melons, the leeks, the onions, and the garlic. [6] But now we are dried up, and there is nothing at all before us except this manna!" [7] (Now [a] the manna was like coriander seed, and its color like the color of bdellium. [8] And the people went about and gathered [a] it, and ground it with

10:14 [a] Num 2:3–9 [b] Num 1:7   10:17 [a] Num 1:51 [b] Num 4:21–32; 7:7–9   10:18 [a] Num 2:10–16   10:22 [a] Num 2:18–24   10:25 [a] Num 2:25–31; Josh 6:9   10:28 [a] Num 2:34   10:29 [a] Judg 4:11 [b] Exod 2:18; 3:1; 18:12 [c] Gen 12:7; Exod 6:4–8 [d] Judg 1:16 [e] Gen 32:12; Exod 3:8   10:31 [a] Job 29:15 [1] Heb. *you will be for us for eyes.*   10:32 [a] Exod 18:9; Lev 19:34; Judg 1:16   10:33 [a] Exod 3:1; Deut 1:6 [b] Deut 1:33; Josh 3:3–6; Ezek 20:6   10:34 [a] Exod 13:21; Neh 9:12, 19   10:35 [a] Ps 68:1–2; 132:8; Isa 17:12–14   11:1 [a] Num 14:2; 16:11; 17:5; Deut 9:22 [b] Lev 10:2; 2 Kgs 1:12 [1] Heb. *it was evil in the ears of the LORD.* [2] Heb. *to be hot, to burn, to be kindled;* an emphatic Heb. construction.   11:2 [a] Num 12:11, 13; 21:7 [b] [Jas 5:16]   11:4 [a] Exod 12:38 [b] [Ps 78:18] [1] Or *rabble;* perhaps *riff-raff.* [2] Heb. *Who will give us flesh to eat?*   11:5 [a] Exod 16:3   11:7 [a] Exod 16:14, 31   11:8 [a] Exod 16:31

mills or pounded it in mortars; they baked it in pans and made cakes of it. It tasted like fresh olive oil. [9] And [a]when the dew came down on the camp in the night, the manna fell with it.)

Moses' Complaint to the Lord

[10] Moses heard [a]the people weeping throughout their families, everyone at the door of his tent; and when the anger of the LORD was kindled greatly, Moses was also displeased. [11][a]And Moses said to the LORD, "Why have you afflicted your servant? Why have I not found favor in your sight, that you lay the burden of this entire people on me? [12]Did I conceive this entire people? Did I give birth to them, that you should say to me, '[a]Carry them in your arms, as a foster [b]father[1] bears a nursing child,' to the land that you [c]swore to their fathers? [13]From [a]where shall I get meat to give to this entire people, for they cry to me, 'Give us meat, that we may eat!' [14]I am not able to bear [a]this entire people alone, because it is too heavy for me! [15]But if you are going to deal with me like this, then kill me immediately. If I have found favor in your sight then [a]do not let me see my trouble."[1]

The Response of God

[16]The LORD said to Moses, "Gather to me [a]seventy men of the elders of Israel, whom you know are elders of the people and [b]officials over them, and bring them to the tent of meeting; let them take their position there with you. [17]Then [a]I will come down and speak with you there, and I will take part of the Spirit that is on you, and will put it on them, and they will bear some of the burden of the people with you, so that you do not bear it all by yourself.

[18]"And say to the people, 'Sanctify yourselves for tomorrow, and you will eat meat, for you have wept [a]in the hearing of the LORD, saying, "Who will give us meat to eat, for life was good for us in Egypt?" Therefore the LORD will give you meat, and you will eat. [19]You will eat, not just one day, nor two days, nor five days, nor ten days, nor twenty days, [20][a]but a whole month, until it comes out your nostrils and makes you sick, because you have [b]despised the LORD who is among you and have wept before him, saying, "[c]Why did we ever come out of Egypt?"'"

[21]Moses said, "[a]The people around me are 600,000 on foot;[1] but you say, 'I will give them meat,[2] that they may eat for a whole month.' [22]Would they have enough if the flocks and herds were slaughtered for them? If [a]all the fish of the sea were caught for them, would they have enough?" [23]And the LORD said to Moses, "Is the LORD's hand shortened? Now you will see whether my word to you will come true or not!"

[24]So Moses went out and told the people the words of the LORD. He then [a]gathered seventy men of the elders of the people and had them stand around the tabernacle. [25]And the LORD came down in the cloud and spoke to them, and [a]he took some of [b]the Spirit that was on Moses and put it on the seventy elders. When the Spirit rested on them, they prophesied, but did not do so again.[1]

Eldad and Medad

[26]But two men remained in the camp; one's name was Eldad, and the other's name was Medad. And the Spirit rested on them. (Now they were among those in the registration, but [a]had not gone to the tabernacle.) So they prophesied in the camp. [27]And a young man ran and told Moses, "Eldad and Medad are prophesying in the camp!" [28]Joshua son of Nun, the servant of Moses, one of his choice young men, said, "My lord Moses, [a]stop them!" [29]Moses said to him, "Are you jealous for me? I [a]wish that all the LORD's people were prophets, that the LORD would put his Spirit on them!" [30]Then Moses returned to the camp along with the elders of Israel.

Provision of Quail

[31]Now a [a]wind went out from the LORD and brought quail from the sea, and let them fall near the camp, about a day's

11:9 [a] Exod 16:13–14   11:10 [a] Ps 78:21   11:11 [a] Exod 5:22; Deut 1:12   11:12 [a] Isa 40:11   [b] Isa 49:23; 1 Thess 2:7   [c] Gen 26:3   [1] Or nurse.   11:13 [a] Matt 15:33; Mark 8:4   11:14 [a] Exod 18:18; Deut 1:12   11:15 [a] Rev 3:17   [1] Or my own ruin.   11:16 [a] Exod 18:25; 24:1, 9   [b] Deut 16:18   11:17 [a] 1 Sam 10:6; 2 Kgs 2:15; [Joel 2:28]   11:18 [a] Exod 16:7   11:20 [a] Ps 78:29; 106:15   [b] 1 Sam 10:19   [c] Num 21:5   11:21 [a] Gen 12:2; Exod 12:37; Num 1:46; 2:32   [1] The Heb. sentence begins 600,000 . . .; an emphatic Heb. construction.   [2] Heb. Meat I will give them.   11:22 [a] 2 Kgs 7:2   11:24 [a] Num 11:16   11:25 [a] 2 Kgs 2:15   [b] 1 Sam 10:5–6, 10; Joel 2:28; Acts 2:17–18; 1 Cor 14:1   [1] Some wss they did not cease prophesying.   11:26 [a] Jer 36:5   11:28 [a] [Mark 9:38–40; Luke 9:49]   11:29 [a] 1 Cor 14:5   11:31 [a] Exod 16:13; Ps 78:26–28; 105:40

journey on this side, and about a day's journey on the other side, all around the camp, and about three feet high on the surface of the ground. [32]And the people stayed up all that day, all that night, and all the next day, and gathered the quail. The one who gathered the least gathered ten [a]homers, and they spread them out for themselves all around the camp. [33]But while the [a]meat was still between their teeth, before they chewed it, the anger of the LORD burned against the people, and the LORD struck the people with a very great plague.

[34]So the name of that place was called Kibroth Hattaavah, because there they buried the people that craved different food. [35]The people traveled [a]from Kibroth Hattaavah to Hazeroth, and they stayed at Hazeroth.

Miriam and Aaron Oppose Moses

12 Then [a]Miriam and Aaron spoke [b]against Moses because of [c]the Cushite woman he had married (for he had married an Ethiopian woman). [2]They said, "Has the LORD spoken only through [a]Moses? [b]Has he not also spoken through us?" And the LORD [c]heard it.

[3](Now the man Moses was very humble,[1] more so than any man on the face of the earth.)

The Response of the Lord

[4]The LORD spoke [a]immediately to Moses, Aaron, and Miriam: "The three of you come to the tent of meeting." So the three of them went. [5]And [a]the LORD came down in a pillar of cloud and stood at the entrance of the tent; he then called Aaron and Miriam, and they both came forward. [6]The LORD said, "Hear now my words: If there is a prophet among you, [a]I the LORD will make myself known to him [b]in a vision; I will speak with him in a dream. [7]My servant Moses is not like this; he is faithful in all [a]my house. [8]With him I will speak [a]face to face,[1] [b]openly and not in riddles, and [c]he will see the form of the LORD. Why then

[d]were you not afraid to speak against my servant Moses?" [9]The anger of the LORD burned against them, and he departed. [10]After the cloud had departed from above the tent, there was Miriam, [a]leprous like snow. Then Aaron turned toward Miriam, and realized that she was leprous.

The Intercession of Moses

[11]So Aaron said to Moses, "[a]O my lord, please do not hold this sin against us, in which we have acted foolishly and have sinned! [12]Do not let her be like a baby born dead, whose flesh is half consumed when it comes out of its mother's womb!"

[13]Then Moses cried to the LORD, "[a]Heal her now, O God." [14]The LORD said to Moses, "If her father had only [a]spit in her face, would she not have been disgraced for seven days? [b]Shut her out from the camp seven days, and afterward she can be brought back in again."

[15a]So Miriam was shut outside of the camp for seven days, and the people did not journey on until Miriam was brought back in. [16]After that the people moved from [a]Hazeroth and camped in the wilderness of Paran.

Spies Sent out

13 The LORD spoke to Moses: [2]"Send out men to investigate the land of Canaan, which I am giving to the Israelites. You are to [a]send one man from each ancestral tribe, each one a leader among them." [3]So Moses sent them [a]from the wilderness of Paran at the command of the LORD. All of them were leaders of the Israelites.

[4]Now these were their names: from the tribe of Reuben, Shammua son of Zaccur; [5]from the tribe of Simeon, Shaphat son of Hori; [6a]from the tribe of Judah, [b]Caleb son of Jephunneh; [7]from the tribe of Issachar, Igal son of Joseph; [8]from the tribe of Ephraim, Hoshea son of Nun; [9]from the tribe of Benjamin, Palti son of Raphu; [10]from the tribe of Zebulun, Gaddiel son of

---

11:32 [a]Exod 16:36; Ezek 45:11　**11:33** [a]Ps 78:29–31; 106:15　**11:35** [a]Num 33:17　**12:1** [a]Exod 15:20–21; Num 20:1　[b]Num 11:1　[c]Exod 2:21　**12:2** [a]Num 16:3　[b]Exod 15:20; Mic 6:4　[c]Gen 29:33; Num 11:1; 2 Kgs 19:4; Isa 37:4; Ezek 35:12–13　**12:3** [1]Or *more tolerant, long suffering.*　**12:4** [a][Ps 76:9]　**12:5** [a]Exod 19:9; 34:5; Num 11:25; 16:19　**12:6** [a]Gen 46:2; 1 Sam 3:15; Job 33:15; Ezek 1:1; Dan 8:2; Luke 1:11; Acts 10:11, 17; 22:17–18　[b]Gen 31:10; 1 Kgs 3:5, 15; Matt 1:20　**12:7** [a]Josh 1:1; Ps 105:26　**12:8** [a]Exod 33:11; Deut 34:10; Hos 12:13　[b][1 Cor 13:12]　[c]Exod 33:19–23　[d]2 Pet 2:10; Jude 8　[1]Lit. *mouth to mouth I will speak with him; beyond the idea of friendship, almost to that of a king's confidant.*　**12:10** [a]Exod 4:6; 2 Kgs 5:27; 15:5; 2 Chr 26:19–20　**12:11** [a]2 Sam 19:19; 24:10　**12:13** [a]Ps 103:3　**12:14** [a]Deut 25:9; Job 30:10; Isa 50:6　[b]Lev 13:46; Num 5:1–4　**12:15** [a]Deut 24:9; 2 Chr 26:20–21　**12:16** [a]Num 11:35; 33:17–18　**13:2** [a]Num 32:8; Deut 1:22; 9:23　**13:3** [a]Num 12:16; 32:8; Deut 1:19; 9:23　**13:6** [a]Num 34:19　[b]Num 14:6, 30; Josh 14:6–7; Judg 1:12; 1 Chr 4:15

Sodi; [11]from the tribe of Joseph, namely, the tribe of Manasseh, Gaddi son of Susi; [12]from the tribe of Dan, Ammiel son of Gemalli; [13]from the tribe of Asher, Sethur son of Michael; [14]from the tribe of Naphtali, Nahbi son of Vopshi; [15]from the tribe of Gad, Geuel son of Maki. [16]These are the names of the men whom Moses sent to investigate the land. And Moses gave [a]Hoshea son of Nun the name Joshua.

The Spies' Instructions

[17]When Moses sent [a]them to investigate the land of Canaan, he told them, "Go up through the Negev, and then go up into the hill country [18]and see what the land is like, and whether the people who live in it are strong or weak, few or many, [19]and whether the land they live in is good or bad, and whether the cities they inhabit are like camps or fortified cities, [20]and whether the land is rich or poor, and whether or not there are forests in it. And [a]be brave,[1] and bring back some of the fruit of the land." Now it was the time of year for the first ripe grapes.

The Spies' Activities

[21]So they went up and investigated the land [a]from the wilderness of Zin to [b]Rehob, at Lebo [c]Hamath. [22]When they went up through the Negev, they[1] came to [a]Hebron where Ahiman, Sheshai, and Talmai, descendants of [b]Anak, were living. (Now Hebron had been built seven years before Zoan in Egypt.) [23]When they came to [a]the valley of Eshcol, they cut down from there a branch with one cluster of grapes, and they carried it on a staff between two men, as well as some of the pomegranates and the figs. [24]That place was called the Eshcol Valley,[1] because of the cluster of grapes that the Israelites cut from there. [25]They returned from investigating the land after 40 days.

The Spies' Reports

[26]They came back to Moses and Aaron and to the whole community of the Israelites in the wilderness of Paran at [a]Kadesh. They reported to the whole community and showed the fruit of the land. [27]They told Moses, "We went to the land where you sent us. It is indeed flowing with [a]milk [b]and honey, and this is its fruit. [28]But the [a]inhabitants are strong, and the cities are fortified and very large. Moreover we saw the descendants of [b]Anak there. [29]The Amalekites live in [a]the land of the Negev; the Hittites, Jebusites, and Amorites live in the hill country; and the Canaanites live by the sea and along the banks of the Jordan."

[30]Then [a]Caleb silenced the people before Moses, saying, "Let us go up and occupy it, for we are well able to conquer it."[1] [31][a]But the men who had gone up with him said, "We are not able to go up against these people, because they are stronger than we are!" [32]Then they [a]presented the Israelites with [b]a discouraging report of the land they had investigated, saying, "The land that we passed through to investigate is a land that devours its inhabitants. All the people we saw there are of great stature. [33]We even saw [a]the Nephilim[1] there (the descendants of Anak came from the Nephilim), and we seemed [b]like grasshoppers both to ourselves and to them."

The Israelites Respond in Unbelief

14 Then all the community raised a loud cry, and the people [a]wept that night. [2]And all the Israelites murmured against Moses [a]and Aaron, and the whole congregation said to them, "If only we had died in the land of Egypt, or if only we had perished in this wilderness! [3]Why has the LORD brought us into this land only to be killed by the sword, that our wives and our [a]children should become plunder? Wouldn't it be better for us to return to Egypt?" [4]So they said to one another, "[a]Let's appoint[1] a leader and [b]return to Egypt."

[5]Then Moses and Aaron fell down with their faces to the ground before the whole assembled community of the Israelites.

13:16 [a]Exod 17:9; Deut 32:44   13:17 [a]Judg 1:9   13:20 [a]Deut 31:6–7, 23   [1]Heb. *strengthen yourselves, be courageous, be determined.*   13:21 [a]Num 20:1; 27:14; 33:36; Josh 15:1   [b]Josh 19:28   [c]Num 34:8; Josh 13:5   13:22 [a]Josh 15:13–14; Judg 1:10   [b]Josh 11:21–22   [1]MT sing.   13:23 [a]Gen 14:13; Num 13:24; 32:9; Deut 1:24–25   13:24 [1]Or *Wadi Eshcol*; a river bed, ravine, or valley through which torrents of rain would rush in the rainy season; at other times it might be completely dry.   13:26 [a]Num 20:1, 16; 32:8; 33:36; Deut 1:19; Josh 14:6   13:27 [a]Exod 3:8, 17; 13:5; 33:3   [b]Deut 1:25   13:28 [a]Deut 1:28; 9:1–2   [b]Josh 11:21–22   13:29 [a]Exod 17:8; Judg 6:3   13:30 [a]Num 14:6, 24   [1]Heb. *we are fully able.*   13:31 [a]Num 32:9; Deut 1:28; 9:1–3; Josh 14:8   13:32 [a]Num 14:36–37; Ps 106:24   [b]Amos 2:9   13:33 [a]Deut 1:28; 9:2; Josh 11:21   [b]Isa 40:22   [1]LXX *giants* and omits *(the descendants of Anak came from the Nephilim).*   14:1 [a]Num 11:4; Deut 1:45   14:2 [a]Exod 16:2; 17:3; Num 16:41; Ps 106:25; 1 Cor 10:10   14:3 [a]Num 14:31; Deut 1:39   14:4 [a]Neh 9:17   [b]Deut 17:16; Acts 7:39   [1]Heb. *give, make, choose, designate.*

[6]And Joshua son of Nun and Caleb son of Jephunneh, two of those who had investigated the land, tore their garments. [7]They said to [a]the whole community of the Israelites, "The land we passed through to investigate is an exceedingly good land. [8]If the LORD [a]delights in us, then he will bring us into this [b]land and give it to us—a land that is flowing with milk and honey. [9]Only [a]do not rebel against [b]the LORD, [c]and do not fear the people of the land, for they are bread for us. Their protection has turned aside from them, but the LORD is with us. Do not fear them!"

[10a]However, [b]the whole community threatened to stone them. But the glory of the LORD appeared to all the Israelites at the tent[1] of meeting.

The Punishment from God

[11]The LORD said to Moses, "How long will this people [a]despise me, and how long will they not [b]believe in me, in spite of the signs that I have done among them? [12]I will strike them with the pestilence,[1] and I will disinherit them—I will [a]make you into a nation that is greater and mightier than they!"

[13a]Moses said to [b]the LORD, "When the Egyptians hear it—for you brought up this people by your power from among them—[14]then they will tell it to the inhabitants of this land. They have [a]heard that you, LORD, are among this people, that you, LORD, are seen face to face, that your cloud stands over them, and that you go before them by day in a pillar of cloud and in a pillar of fire by night. [15]If you kill this entire people at once, then the nations that have heard of your fame will say, [16]'Because the LORD was not [a]able to bring this people into the land that he swore to them, he killed them in the wilderness.' [17]So now, let the power of my Lord be great, just as you have said, [18]'The LORD is slow to anger and abounding in loyal love,[1] forgiving iniquity and transgression, but by no means clearing [a]the guilty, [b]visiting the iniquity of the fathers on the children until the third and fourth generations.' [19]Please [a]forgive the iniquity of this people [b]according to your great loyal love, just [c]as you have forgiven this people from Egypt even until now."

[20]Then the LORD said, "[a]I have forgiven them as you asked. [21]But truly, as I live, [a]all the earth will be filled with the glory of the LORD. [22a]For all [b]the people have seen my glory and my signs that I did in Egypt and in the wilderness, and yet have tempted[1] me now these ten times,[2] and have not obeyed me—[23]they will by no means [a]see the land that I promised on oath to their fathers, nor will any of them who despised me see it—[24]Only my servant [a]Caleb, because he had [b]a different spirit and has followed me fully—I will bring him into the land where he had gone, and his descendants will possess it. [25](Now the Amalekites and the Canaanites were living in the valleys.) Tomorrow, turn and journey into the wilderness by the way of the Red Sea."

[26]The LORD spoke to Moses and Aaron: [27]"[a]How long must [b]I bear[1] with this evil congregation that murmurs against me? I have heard the complaints of the Israelites that they murmured against me. [28]Say to them, '[a]As I live, says the LORD, I will surely do to you just what you have spoken in my hearing. [29]Your dead bodies will [a]fall in this wilderness—all those of you who were numbered, according to your full number, from twenty years old and upward, who have murmured against me. [30]You will by no means enter into the land where I swore to settle you. The only [a]exceptions are Caleb son of Jephunneh and Joshua son of Nun. [31a]But I will bring in [b]your little ones, whom you said would become victims of war, and they will enjoy the land that you have despised. [32]But as for [a]you, your dead bodies will fall in this wilderness, [33]and your

14:7 [a]Num 13:27; Deut 1:25   14:8 [a]Deut 10:15; 2 Sam 15:25–26; 1 Kgs 10:9; Ps 147:11   [b]Exod 3:8; Num 13:27   14:9 [a]Deut 1:26; 9:7, 23, 24; 1 Sam 15:23   [b]Num 24:8   [c]Gen 48:21; Exod 33:16; Deut 20:1, 3, 4; 31:6–8; Josh 1:5; Judg 1:22; 2 Chr 13:12; Ps 46:7, 11; Zech 8:23; Matt 28:20; Heb 13:5   14:10 [a]Exod 17:4   [b]Exod 16:10; Lev 9:23   [1]Some wss in the cloud over the tent.   14:11 [a]Ps 95:8; Heb 3:8   [b]Deut 9:23; [John 12:37]   14:12 [a]Exod 32:10   [1]LXX death.   14:13 [a]Ps 106:23   [b]Exod 32:12; Deut 9:26–28; 32:27   14:14 [a]Deut 2:25   14:16 [a]Deut 9:28   14:18 [a]Exod 34:6–7; Deut 5:10; 7:9; Ps 103:8; 145:8; Jonah 4:2   [b]Exod 20:5; Deut 5:9   [1]Or faithful love.   14:19 [a]Exod 32:32; 34:9   [b]Ps 51:1; 106:45   [c]Ps 78:38   14:20 [a]2 Sam 12:13; Mic 7:18–20; [1 John 5:14–16]   14:21 [a]Ps 72:19; Isa 6:3; 66:18–19; Hab 2:14   14:22 [a]Deut 1:35; 1 Cor 10:5; Heb 3:17   [b]Gen 31:7   [1]Heb. to test, to tempt, to prove.   [2]A round figure, emphasizing the complete testing.   14:23 [a]Num 26:65; 32:11; Heb 3:18   14:24 [a]Josh 14:6, 8, 9   [b]Num 32:12   14:27 [a]Exod 16:28   [b]Exod 16:12   [1]A figure of speech of a sudden silence (an aposiopesis) is used; the verb is not present, lit. how long . . . this evil community, indicating an intensity of emotion.   14:28 [a]Deut 1:35; 2:14–15; Heb 3:16–19   14:29 [a]Num 1:45–46; 26:64; Josh 5:6   14:30 [a]Num 26:65; 32:12; Deut 1:36–38; Josh 14:6–15   14:31 [a]Num 14:3; Deut 1:39   [b]Ps 106:24   14:32 [a]Num 26:64–65; 32:13; 1 Cor 10:5

children will wander in the wilderness [a]40 years and [b]suffer for your unfaithfulness,[1] until your dead bodies lie finished in the wilderness. [34]According to the number of the days you have investigated this land, 40 days—one day for [a]a year—you will suffer for your iniquities, [b]40 years, [c]and you will know what it means to thwart me. [35]I, the LORD, have [a]said, "[b]I will surely do so to all this evil congregation that has gathered together against me. In this wilderness they will be finished, and there they will die!'"

[36]The men whom Moses sent to investigate the land, who returned and made the whole community murmur against him by producing an evil report about the land, [37]those men who produced the evil report about the land, [a]died by the plague before the LORD. [38a]But Joshua son of Nun and Caleb son of Jephunneh, who were among the men who went to investigate the land, lived. [39]When Moses told these things to all the Israelites, the people mourned greatly.

[40]And early in the morning they went up to the crest of the hill country, saying, "[a]Here we are, and we will go up to the place that the LORD commanded, for we have sinned." [41]But Moses said, "Why are you now transgressing the commandment of the LORD? It will not succeed! [42a]Do not go up, for the LORD is not among you, and you will be defeated before your enemies. [43]For the Amalekites and the Canaanites are there before you, and you will fall by the sword. [a]Because you have turned away from the LORD, the LORD will not be with you."

[44a]But they dared to go up to the crest of the hill, although neither the ark of the covenant of the LORD nor Moses departed from the camp. [45]So the Amalekites and the Canaanites who lived in that hill country swooped down and attacked them as far as [a]Hormah.[1]

Sacrificial Rulings

15 The LORD spoke to Moses: [2]"[a]Speak to the Israelites and tell them, 'When you enter the land where you are to live, which I am giving you, [3]and you [a]make an offering by fire [b]to the LORD from the herd or from the flock (whether a burnt [c]offering or a sacrifice for discharging a vow or as a freewill offering or in your solemn feasts) to create a [d]pleasing aroma to the LORD, [4]then [a]the one who presents his offering to the LORD must bring [b]a grain offering of one-tenth of an ephah of finely ground flour mixed [c]with one-fourth of a hin of olive oil. [5]You must also prepare one-fourth of [a]a hin of wine for a drink offering with the burnt offering or the sacrifice for each [b]lamb. [6]Or [a]for a ram, you must prepare as a grain offering two-tenths of an ephah of finely ground flour mixed with one-third of a hin of olive oil, [7]and for a drink offering you must offer one-third of a hin of wine as a pleasing aroma to the LORD. [8]And when you prepare [a]a young bull as a burnt offering or a sacrifice for discharging a vow or as a peace offering to the LORD, [9]then a grain offering of three-tenths of an ephah of finely ground flour mixed [a]with half a hin of olive oil must be presented with the young bull, [10]and you must present as the drink offering half a hin of wine with the fire offering as a pleasing aroma to the LORD. [11a]This is what is to be done for each ox, or each ram, or each of the male lambs or the goats. [12]You must do so for each one according to the number that you prepare.

[13]"'Every native-born person must do these things in this way to present an offering made by fire as a pleasing aroma to the LORD. [14]If a resident foreigner is living[1] with you—or whoever is among you in future generations—and prepares an offering made by fire as a pleasing aroma to the LORD, he must do it the same way you are to do it. [15a]One statute must apply to you who belong to the congregation and to the resident foreigner who is living among you, as a permanent statute for your future generations. You and the resident foreigner will be alike before the LORD. [16]One law and one custom must apply to you and to the resident foreigner who lives alongside you.'"

14:33 [a]Deut 2:14 [b]Ezek 23:35 [1]Heb. *you shall bear your whoredoms.* 14:34 [a]Num 13:25 [b]Ps 95:10; Ezek 4:6 [c]1 Kgs 8:56; [Heb 4:1] 14:35 [a]Num 23:19 [b]1 Cor 10:5 14:37 [a]Num 16:49; [1 Cor 10:10]; Heb 3:17–18 14:38 [a]Josh 14:6, 10 14:40 [a]Deut 1:41–44 14:42 [a]Deut 1:42; 31:17 14:43 [a]2 Chr 15:2 14:44 [a]Deut 1:43 14:45 [a]Num 21:3 [1]*Hormah* means "destruction"; it is from the word that means "ban, devote" for either destruction or temple use. 15:2 [a]Lev 23:10; Num 15:18; Deut 7:1 15:3 [a]Lev 1:2–3 [b]Lev 7:16; 22:18, 21 [c]Lev 23:2, 8, 12, 38; Num 28:18–19, 27; Deut 16:10 [d]Gen 8:21; Exod 29:18; Lev 1:9 15:4 [a]Lev 2:1; 6:14 [b]Exod 29:40; Lev 23:13 [c]Lev 14:10; Num 28:5 15:5 [a]Num 28:7, 14 [b]Lev 1:10; 3:6; Num 15:11; 28:4–5 15:6 [a]Num 28:12, 14 15:8 [a]Lev 7:11 15:9 [a]Num 28:12, 14 15:11 [a]Num 28 15:14 [1]Trad. *to sojourn.* 15:15 [a]Exod 12:49; Num 9:14; 15:29

Rules for Firstfruits

[17]The LORD spoke to Moses: [18]"[a]Speak to the Israelites and tell them, 'When you enter the land to which I am bringing you [19]and you eat some of [a]the food of the land, you must offer up a raised offering to the LORD. [20]You must offer up a cake of the first of [a]your finely ground flour [b]as a raised offering; as you offer the raised offering of the threshing floor, so you must offer it up. [21]You must give to the LORD some of the first of your finely ground flour as a raised offering in your future generations.

Rules for Unintentional Offenses

[22]"[a]If you sin unintentionally and do not observe all these commandments that the LORD has spoken to Moses—[23]all that the LORD has commanded you by the authority of Moses, from the day that the LORD commanded Moses and continuing through your future generations—[24]then [a]if anything is done unintentionally[1] [b]without the knowledge of the community, the whole community must prepare [c]one young bull for a burnt offering—for a pleasing aroma to the LORD—along with its grain offering and its customary drink offering, and one male goat for a purification offering. [25a]And the priest is to make atonement for the whole community of the Israelites, and they will be forgiven, because it was unintentional and they have brought their offering, an offering made by fire to the LORD, and their purification offering before the LORD, for their unintentional offense. [26]And the whole community of the Israelites and the resident foreigner who lives among them will be forgiven, since all the people were involved in the unintentional offense.

[27]"If any person sins unintentionally, then he must bring a yearling female goat for a [a]purification offering. [28]And the priest must make atonement for the [a]person who sins unintentionally—when he sins unintentionally before the LORD—to make atonement for him, and he will be forgiven. [29a]You must have one law for the person who sins unintentionally, both for the native-born among the Israelites and for the resident foreigner who lives among them.

Deliberate Sin

[30]"[a]But the person who acts defiantly,[1] whether native-born or a resident foreigner, insults the LORD. That person must be cut off from among his people. [31]Because he has [a]despised the LORD's message and has broken his commandment, that person must be completely cut off. His iniquity will be on him.'"

[32]When [a]the Israelites were in the wilderness they found a man gathering wood on the Sabbath day. [33]Those who found him gathering wood brought him to Moses and Aaron and to the whole community. [34]They put him in custody, because there was no clear instruction about what should be done to him. [35]Then [a]the LORD said to Moses, "The man must surely be put to death; the whole community must [b]stone him with stones outside the camp." [36]So the whole community took him outside the camp and stoned him to death, just as the LORD commanded Moses.

Rules for Tassels

[37]The LORD spoke to Moses: [38]"Speak to [a]the Israelites and tell them to make tassels for themselves on the corners of their garments throughout their generations, and put a blue thread on the tassel of the corners. [39]You must have this tassel so that you may look at it and [a]remember all the commandments of the LORD and obey them and so that you do not [b]follow after your own heart and your own eyes that lead you to unfaithfulness. [40]Thus you will remember and obey all my commandments and be [a]holy to your God. [41]I am the LORD your God, who brought you out of the land of Egypt to be your God. I am the LORD your God."

The Rebellion of Korah

16 Now [a]Korah son of Izhar, the son of Kohath, the son of Levi, and [b]Dathan and Abiram, the sons of Eliab, and On son

15:18 [a]Num 15:2; Deut 26:1   15:19 [a]Josh 5:11–12   15:20 [a]Exod 34:26; Lev 23:10, 14, 17; Deut 26:2, 10; Prov 3:9–10   [b]Lev 2:14; 23:10, 16   15:22 [a]Lev 4:2   15:24 [a]Lev 4:13   [b]Num 15:8–10   [c]Lev 4:23   [1]Probably any transgressions done in ignorance of the law that involved a violation of tabernacle procedure or priestly protocol, or a social misdemeanor.   15:25 [a]Lev 4:20; [Heb 2:17]   15:27 [a]Lev 4:27–31   15:28 [a]Lev 4:35   15:29 [a]Num 15:15   15:30 [a]Num 14:40–44; Deut 1:43; 17:12; Ps 19:13; Heb 10:26   [1]Heb. *with a high hand.*   15:31 [a]2 Sam 12:9; Prov 13:13   15:32 [a]Exod 31:14–15; 35:2–3   15:35 [a]Exod 31:14–15   [b]Lev 24:14; Deut 21:21; 1 Kgs 21:13; Acts 7:58   15:38 [a]Deut 22:12; Matt 23:5   15:39 [a]Ps 103:18   [b]Ps 73:27; 106:39; Jas 4:4   15:40 [a][Lev 11:44–45; Rom 12:1; Col 1:22; 1 Pet 1:15–16]   16:1 [a]Exod 6:21   [b]Num 26:9; Deut 11:6

of Peleth, who were Reubenites,[1] took men [2]and rebelled against Moses, along with some of the Israelites, 250 leaders of the community, [a]chosen from the assembly, famous men. [3]And [a]they assembled against Moses [b]and Aaron, saying to them, "You take too much upon yourselves,[1] seeing that the whole community is holy, every one of them, and the LORD is among them. Why then do you exalt yourselves above the community of the LORD?"

[4]When Moses heard it he fell [a]down with his face to the ground. [5]Then he said to Korah and to all [a]his company, "In the morning the LORD will make known who are his, and who is [b]holy. He will cause that person to approach him; the person he has chosen he will cause to approach him. [6]Do this, Korah, you and all your company: Take censers, [7]put fire in them, and set incense on them before the LORD tomorrow, and the man whom the LORD chooses will be holy. You take too much upon yourselves, you sons of Levi!" [8]Moses said to Korah, "Listen now, you sons of Levi! [9]Does it seem too [a]small a thing to you that the God of Israel has [b]separated you from the community of Israel to bring you near to himself, to perform the service of the tabernacle of the LORD, and to stand before the community to minister to them? [10]He has brought you near and all your brothers, the sons of Levi, with you. Do you now seek the priesthood also? [11]Therefore you [a]and all your company have assembled together against the LORD! And Aaron—what is he that you murmur against him?" [12]Then Moses summoned Dathan and Abiram, the sons of Eliab, but they said, "We will not come up. [13]Is it [a]a small thing that you have brought us up out of the land that flows with milk and honey, to kill us in the wilderness? Now do you want to make yourself a prince over us? [14]Moreover, [a]you [b]have not brought us into a land that flows with milk and honey, nor given us an inheritance of fields and vineyards. Do you think you can blind[1] these men? We will not come up."

[15]Moses was very angry, and he said to the LORD, "Have no respect for their offering! I have not taken so much as one [a]donkey from them, nor have [b]I harmed any one of them!" [16]Then Moses said to Korah, "You and all your company present yourselves [a]before the LORD—you and they, and Aaron—tomorrow. [17]And each of you take his censer, put incense in it, and then each of you present his censer before the LORD: 250 censers, along with you, and Aaron—each of you with his censer." [18]So everyone took his censer, put fire in it, and set incense on it, and stood at the entrance of the tent of meeting, with Moses and Aaron. [19]When Korah assembled [a]the whole community against them at the entrance of the tent of meeting, then the glory of the LORD appeared to the whole community.

The Judgment on the Rebels

[20]The LORD spoke to Moses and Aaron: [21]"[a]Separate yourselves from among this community, that I may [b]consume them in an instant." [22]Then they [a]threw [b]themselves down with their faces to the ground and said, "O God, the God of the spirits of all people, will you be angry with the whole [c]community when only one man sins?"

[23]So the LORD spoke to Moses: [24]"Tell the community: 'Get away from around the homes of Korah, Dathan, and Abiram.'" [25]Then Moses got up and went to Dathan and Abiram; and the elders of Israel went after him. [26]And he said to the community, "Move [a]away from the tents of these wicked[1] men, and do not touch anything they have, lest you be destroyed because of all their sins." [27]So they got away from the homes of Korah, Dathan, and Abiram on every side, and Dathan and Abiram came out and stationed themselves in the entrances of their tents with their wives, their children, and their [a]toddlers. [28]Then Moses said, "This is how you will know that the LORD has sent me to do all these works, for I have not done them [a]of my own will. [29]If these men die a natural death, or if they [a]share the fate of

16:1 [1]LXX, Smr. *the son of Reuben.*   16:2 [a]Num 1:16; 26:9   16:3 [a]Num 12:2; 14:2; Ps 106:16   [b]Exod 29:45   [1]Or *You have assumed far too much authority.*   16:4 [a]Num 14:5; 20:6   16:5 [a][2 Tim 2:19]   [b]Lev 21:6–8, 12   16:9 [a]1 Sam 18:23; Isa 7:13   [b]Num 3:41, 45; 8:13–16; Deut 10:8   16:11 [a]Exod 16:7–8   16:13 [a]Exod 16:3; Num 11:4–6   16:14 [a]Num 14:1–4   [b]Exod 3:8; Lev 20:24   [1]Heb. *Will you bore out the eyes of these men?*; i.e., "Will you continue to mislead them?"   16:15 [a]Gen 4:4–5   [b]1 Sam 12:3; Acts 20:33   16:16 [a]1 Sam 12:3, 7   16:19 [a]Exod 16:7, 10; Lev 9:6, 23; Num 14:10   16:21 [a]Gen 19:17; Jer 51:6   [b]Exod 32:10; 33:5   16:22 [a]Num 14:5   [b]Num 27:16; Job 12:10; Eccl 12:7; Heb 12:9   [c]Gen 18:23–32; 20:4   16:26 [a]Gen 19:12, 14, 15, 17   [1]With the sense of being a guilty criminal.   16:27 [a]Exod 20:5; Num 26:11   16:28 [a]Num 24:13; John 5:30   16:29 [a]Exod 20:5; Job 35:15; Isa 10:3

all men, then the LORD has not sent me. [30]But if the LORD does something entirely new,[1] [a]and the earth opens its mouth and swallows them up along with all that they have, and they [b]go down alive to the grave,[2] then you will know that these men have despised the LORD!"

[31][a]When he had finished speaking all these words, the ground that was under them split open, [32]and the earth opened its mouth and [a]swallowed them, along with their households, and all Korah's men, and all their goods. [33]They and all that they had went down alive into the pit, and the earth closed over them. So they perished from among the community. [34]All the Israelites who were around them fled at their cry, for they said, "What if the earth swallows us too?" [35]Then [a]a fire went out from the LORD and devoured the 250 men who offered incense.

The Atonement for the Rebellion

[36]The LORD spoke to Moses: [37]"Tell Eleazar son of Aaron [a]the priest to pick up the censers out of the flame, for they are holy, and then scatter the coals of fire at a distance. [38]As for [a]the censers of these men who sinned at the cost of their lives, they must be made into hammered sheets for covering the altar, because they presented them before the LORD [b]and sanctified them. They will become a sign to the Israelites." [39]So Eleazar the priest took the bronze censers presented by those who had been burned up, and they were hammered out as a covering for the altar. [40]It was [a]a memorial for the Israelites, that no outsider who is not a descendant of Aaron should approach to burn incense before the LORD, that he might not become like Korah and his company—just as the LORD had spoken by the authority of Moses. [41]But on the next day the whole community of Israelites murmured against Moses and Aaron, saying, "You have killed the LORD's people!" [42]When [a]the community assembled against Moses and Aaron, they turned toward the tent of meeting—and[1] the cloud covered it, and the

glory of the LORD appeared. [43]Then Moses and Aaron stood before the tent of meeting. [44]The LORD spoke to Moses: [45]"Get away from this community, so that I can consume them in an instant!" But they threw themselves down with their faces to the ground. [46]Then Moses said to Aaron, "Take the censer, put burning coals from the altar in it, place incense on it, and go quickly into the assembly and make atonement [a]for them, for wrath has gone out from the LORD—the plague has begun!" [47]So Aaron did as Moses commanded and ran into the middle of the assembly, where the plague was just beginning among the people. So he placed incense on the coals and made atonement for the people. [48]He stood between [a]the dead and the living, and the plague was stopped. [49]Now 14,700 people died in the plague, in addition to those who died in the event with Korah. [50]Then Aaron returned to Moses at the entrance of the tent of meeting, and the plague was stopped.

The Budding of Aaron's Staff

17 The LORD spoke to Moses: [2]"Speak to the Israelites, and receive from them a staff from each tribe, one from every tribal leader, twelve staffs; you must write each man's name on his staff. [3]You must write Aaron's name on the staff of Levi; for one staff is for the head of every tribe. [4]You must place [a]them in the tent of meeting before the ark of the covenant [b]where I meet with you. [5]And the staff of the man [a]whom [b]I choose will blossom; so I will rid myself of the complaints of the Israelites, which they murmur against you."

[6]So Moses spoke to the Israelites, and each of their leaders gave him a staff, one for each leader, according to their tribes—twelve staffs; the staff of Aaron was among their staffs. [7]Then Moses placed [a]the staffs before the LORD in the tent of the testimony.

[8]On the next day Moses went into the tent of the testimony—and the [a]staff of Aaron for the house of Levi had sprouted,

---

16:30 [a] Job 31:3; Isa 28:21   [b] [Ps 55:15]   [1] Heb. *create.*   [2] Heb. *Sheol*; the grave, the realm of the departed (wicked) spirits, also known as Hell, death in general, or a place of extreme danger (one that will lead to the grave if God does not intervene).   16:31 [a] Num 26:10; Ps 106:17   16:32 [a] Num 26:11; 1 Chr 6:22, 37   16:35 [a] Lev 10:2; Num 11:1–3; 26:10; Ps 106:18   16:37 [a] Lev 27:28   16:38 [a] Prov 20:2; Hab 2:10   [b] Num 17:10; Ezek 14:8   16:40 [a] Num 3:10; 2 Chr 26:18   16:42 [a] Exod 40:34   [1] Heb. *and behold.*   16:46 [a] Lev 10:6; Num 18:5   16:48 [a] Num 25:8; Ps 106:30   17:4 [a] Exod 25:16   [b] Exod 25:22; 29:42–43; 30:36; Num 17:7   17:5 [a] Num 16:5   [b] Num 16:11   17:7 [a] Exod 38:21; Num 1:50–51; 9:15; 18:2; Acts 7:44   17:8 [a] [Ezek 17:24]; Heb 9:4

and brought forth buds, and produced blossoms, and yielded almonds! [9]So Moses brought out all the staffs from before the LORD to all the Israelites. They looked at them, and each man took his staff.

The Memorial

[10]The LORD said to Moses, "Bring [a]Aaron's staff back before the testimony to be preserved for [b]a sign to the rebels, so [c]that you may bring their murmurings to an end before me, that they will not die." [11]So Moses did as the LORD commanded him—this is what he did.

[12]The Israelites said to Moses, "We are bound to die! We perish, we all perish! [13]Anyone [a]who even comes close to the tabernacle of the LORD will die! Are we all to die?"

Responsibilities of the Priests

18 The LORD said to Aaron, "[a]You and your sons and your tribe with you must [b]bear the iniquity of the sanctuary, and you and your sons with you must bear the iniquity of your priesthood.

[2]"Bring with you your brothers, the [a]tribe of Levi, the tribe of your father, so that they may [b]join with you and minister to you while you and your sons with you are before the tent of the testimony. [3]They must be responsible to care for you and to care for the entire tabernacle. However, they must not come near the furnishings of the sanctuary and the altar, or both they and you will die. [4]They must join with you, and they will be responsible for the care of the tent of meeting, for all the service of the tent, [a]but no unauthorized person[1] may approach you. [5]You will be responsible for [a]the care of the sanctuary and the care of the altar, so [b]that there will be no more wrath on the Israelites. [6]I myself have [a]chosen your brothers [b]the Levites from among the Israelites. They are given to you as a gift from the LORD, to perform the duties of the tent of meeting. [7]But [a]you and your sons with you are responsible for your priestly duties, for everything at the altar and [b]within the curtain. And you must serve. I give you the priesthood as a [c]gift for service, but the unauthorized person who approaches must be put to death."

The Portion of the Priests

[8]The LORD spoke to Aaron, "See, [a]I have given you the responsibility for my raised offerings; I have given all the holy things of the Israelites to you [b]as your priestly portion and to your sons as a perpetual ordinance. [9]Of all the most holy offerings reserved from the fire this will be yours: Every offering of theirs, whether from every [a]grain offering or from every purification offering or from every reparation offering which they bring to me, will be most holy for you and for your sons. [10]You are to eat it as a most holy [a]offering; every male may eat it. It will be holy to you.

[11]"And this is yours: [a]the raised offering of their gift, along with all the wave offerings of the Israelites. I have given them to you and to your sons and daughters with you as a perpetual ordinance. [b]Everyone who is ceremonially clean in your household may eat of it.

[12]"[a]All the best of the olive oil and all [b]the best of the wine and of the wheat, the firstfruits of these things that they give to the LORD, I have given to you. [13]And whatever first ripe fruit in their land they bring to the LORD will be yours; everyone who is ceremonially clean in your household may eat of it.

[14]"[a]Everything devoted in Israel will be yours. [15]The firstborn of every womb which [a]they present to [b]the LORD, whether human or animal, will be yours. Nevertheless, the firstborn sons you must redeem, and the firstborn males of unclean animals you must redeem. [16]And those that must be redeemed you are to redeem when they are [a]a month old, according to your estimation, for five shekels of silver according to the sanctuary shekel (which is [b]20 gerahs). [17a]But [b]you must not redeem the firstborn of a cow or a sheep or a goat; they are holy. You must splash their blood on the altar and burn their fat for an offering made by fire for a pleasing aroma to the LORD. [18]And their meat will be yours, just as the breast and

17:10 [a]Heb 9:4 [b]Num 16:38; Deut 9:7, 24 [c]Num 17:5   17:13 [a]Num 1:51, 53; 18:4, 7   18:1 [a]Num 17:13 [b]Exod 28:38; Lev 10:17; 22:16   18:2 [a]Gen 29:34; Num 1:47 [b]Num 3:5–10   18:4 [a]Num 3:10 [1]Heb. *stranger, alien.*   18:5 [a]Exod 27:21; 30:7; Lev 24:3 [b]Num 8:19; 16:46   18:6 [a]Num 3:12, 45 [b]Num 3:9   18:7 [a]Num 3:10; 18:5 [b]Heb 9:3, 6 [c]Matt 10:8; 1 Pet 5:2–3   18:8 [a]Lev 6:16, 18; 7:28–34; Num 5:9 [b]Exod 29:29; 40:13, 15   18:9 [a]Lev 2:2–3; 10:12–13   18:10 [a]Lev 6:16, 26   18:11 [a]Exod 29:27–28; Deut 18:3–5 [b]Lev 22:1–16   18:12 [a]Exod 23:19; Neh 10:35–36 [b]Exod 22:29; Lev 23:20   18:14 [a]Lev 27:1–33   18:15 [a]Exod 13:2 [b]Exod 13:12–15; Num 3:46; Luke 2:22–24   18:16 [a]Lev 27:6 [b]Exod 30:13   18:17 [a]Deut 15:19 [b]Lev 3:2, 5

the right hip of the raised [a]offering is yours. [19]All the raised offerings of the holy things that the [a]Israelites offer to the LORD, I have given to you, and to your sons and daughters with you, as a perpetual ordinance. It is a covenant of salt forever before the LORD for you and for your descendants with you."

Duties of the Levites

[20]The LORD spoke to Aaron, "You will have [a]no [b]inheritance in their land, nor will you have any portion of property among them—I am your portion and your inheritance among the Israelites. [21]See, [a]I have given [b]the Levites all the tithes in Israel for an inheritance, for their service that they perform—the service of the tent of meeting. [22]No [a]longer may the Israelites approach the tent of meeting, or else they will bear their sin and die. [23]But the Levites must perform the service of the tent of meeting, and they must bear their iniquity. It will be a perpetual ordinance throughout your generations that among the Israelites the Levites have no inheritance.[1] [24]But I have given to the Levites for an inheritance the tithes of the Israelites that are offered to the LORD as a raised offering. That is why I said to them that among the Israelites they are to have no inheritance."

Instructions for the Levites

[25]The LORD spoke to Moses: [26]"You [a]are to speak to the Levites, and you must tell them, 'When you receive from the Israelites the tithe that I have given you from them as your inheritance, then you are to offer up from it as a raised offering to the LORD a tenth of the tithe. [27]And your raised offering will be credited to you as though it were grain from the [a]threshing floor or as new wine from the winepress. [28]Thus you are to offer up a raised offering to the LORD of all your tithes that you receive from the Israelites; and you must give the LORD's raised offering from it to Aaron the priest. [29]From all your gifts you must offer up every raised offering due the LORD, from all the best of it, and the holiest part of it.'

[30]"Therefore you will say to them, 'When you offer up the best of it, then it will be credited to the Levites as the product of the threshing floor and as the product of the winepress. [31]And [a]you may eat it in any place, you and your household, because it is your wages for your service in the tent of meeting. [32]And you will [a]bear no sin concerning it when you offer up the best of it. And you must not [b]profane the holy things of the Israelites, or else you will die.'"

The Red Heifer Ritual

19 The LORD spoke to Moses and Aaron: [2]"This is the ordinance of the law that the LORD has commanded: 'Instruct the Israelites to bring you a red[1] heifer without blemish, which has no [a]defect [b]and has never carried a yoke. [3]You must give it to Eleazar the priest so that he can take it [a]outside the camp, and it must be slaughtered before him. [4]Eleazar the priest is to take some of its blood with his finger, and [a]sprinkle some of the blood seven times in the direction of the front of the tent of meeting. [5]Then the heifer must be burned in his sight—[a]its skin, its flesh, its blood, and its offal is to be burned. [6]And the priest must take [a]cedar wood, [b]hyssop, and scarlet wool and throw them into the midst of the fire where the heifer is burning. [7]Then [a]the priest must wash his clothes and bathe himself in water, and afterward he may come into the camp, but the priest will be ceremonially unclean until evening. [8]The one who burns it must wash his clothes in water and bathe himself in water. He will be ceremonially unclean until evening.

[9]"Then a man who is ceremonially clean must [a]gather up the ashes of the red heifer and put them in a ceremonially clean place outside the camp. They must be kept [b]for the community of the Israelites for use in the water of purification[1]—it is a purification for sin. [10]The one who gathers the ashes of the heifer must wash his clothes and be ceremonially unclean until evening. This will be a permanent ordinance both for the Israelites and the resident foreigner who lives among them.

18:18 [a]Exod 29:26–28; Lev 7:31–36   **18:19** [a]Lev 2:13; 2 Chr 13:5; [Mark 9:49–50]   **18:20** [a]Deut 10:8–9; 12:12; 14:27–29; 18:1–2; Josh 13:14, 33   [b]Ps 16:5; Ezek 44:28   **18:21** [a]Lev 27:30–33; Deut 14:22–29; Neh 10:37; 12:44; Mal 3:8–10; [Heb 7:4–10]   [b]Num 3:7–8   **18:22** [a]Num 1:51   **18:23** [1]Heb. *will not inherit an inheritance.*   **18:26** [a]Neh 10:38   **18:27** [a]Num 15:20; [2 Cor 8:12]   **18:31** [a][Matt 10:10; Luke 10:7]; 1 Cor 9:13; [1 Tim 5:18]   **18:32** [a]Lev 19:8; 22:16; Ezek 22:26   [b]Lev 22:2, 15   **19:2** [a]Lev 22:20–25   [b]Deut 21:3; 1 Sam 6:7   [1]A tanned red-brown color.   **19:3** [a]Lev 4:12, 21; Num 19:9; Heb 13:11   **19:4** [a]Lev 4:6; Heb 9:13   **19:5** [a]Exod 29:14; Lev 4:11–12; 9:11   **19:6** [a]Lev 14:4, 6, 49   [b]Exod 12:22; 1 Kgs 4:33   **19:7** [a]Lev 11:25; 15:5; 16:26, 28   **19:9** [a][Heb 9:13–14]   [b]Num 19:13, 20, 21   [1]Heb. *for waters of impurity.*

Purification from Uncleanness

[11] "'Whoever [a]touches the corpse of any person will be ceremonially unclean seven days. [12]He must purify himself with water on [a]the third day and on the seventh day, and so will be clean. But if he does not purify himself on the third day and the seventh day, then he will not be clean. [13]Anyone who touches the corpse of any dead person and [a]does not purify himself [b]defiles [c]the tabernacle of the LORD. And that person must be cut off from Israel, because the water of purification was not sprinkled on him. He will be unclean; [d]his uncleanness remains on him.

[14]"'This is the law: When a man dies in a tent, anyone who comes into the tent and all who are in the tent will be ceremonially unclean seven days. [15]And every [a]open container that has no covering fastened on it is unclean. [16]And [a]whoever touches the body of someone killed with a sword in the open fields, or the body of someone who died of natural causes,[1] or a human bone, or a grave, will be unclean seven days.

[17]"'For a ceremonially unclean person you must take some of the [a]ashes of the heifer burnt for purification from sin and pour fresh running[1] water over them in a vessel. [18]Then a ceremonially clean person must take [a]hyssop, dip it in the water, and sprinkle it on the tent, on all its furnishings, and on the people who were there, or on the one who touched a bone, or one who was killed, or one who died, or a grave. [19]And the clean person must sprinkle the unclean on the third day [a]and on the seventh day; and on the seventh day he must purify him, and then he must wash his clothes, and bathe in water, and he will be clean in the evening. [20]But the man who is [a]unclean and does not purify himself, that person must be cut off from among the community, because he has polluted the sanctuary of the LORD; the water of purification was not sprinkled on him, so he is unclean.

[21]"'So this will be a perpetual ordinance for them: The one who sprinkles the water of purification must wash his clothes, and the one who touches the water of purification will be unclean until evening. [22]And [a]whatever [b]the unclean person touches will be unclean, and the person who touches it will be unclean until evening.'"

The Israelites Complain Again

20 Then [a]the entire community of Israel entered the wilderness of Zin in the first month, and the people stayed in [b]Kadesh. [c]Miriam died and was buried there.

[2]And there was [a]no water for the community, and [b]so they gathered themselves together against Moses and Aaron. [3]The people [a]contended[1] with Moses, saying, "If only we had died [b]when our brothers died before the LORD! [4a]Why have you brought up the LORD's community into this wilderness? So that we and our cattle should die here? [5]Why have you brought us up from Egypt only to bring us to this dreadful place? It is no place for grain, or figs, or vines, or pomegranates; nor is there any water to drink!"

Moses Responds

[6]So Moses and Aaron went from [a]the presence of [b]the assembly to the entrance to the tent of meeting. They then threw themselves down with their faces to the ground, and the glory of the LORD appeared to them. [7]Then the LORD spoke to Moses: [8]"[a]Take the staff and assemble the community, [b]you and Aaron your brother, and then speak to the rock before their eyes. It will pour forth its water, and you will bring water out of the rock for them, and so you will give the community and their beasts water to drink."

[9]So Moses took the staff [a]from before the LORD, just as he commanded him. [10]Then Moses and Aaron gathered the community together in front of the rock, and he said to them, "[a]Listen, you rebels, must we bring water out of this rock for you?" [11]Then Moses raised his [a]hand, and struck the rock twice with his staff. And water came out abundantly. So the community drank, and their beasts drank too.

19:11 [a] Lev 21:1, 11; Num 5:2; 6:6; 9:6, 10; 31:19; Lam 4:14; Hag 2:13   **19:12** [a] Num 19:19; 31:19   **19:13** [a] Lev 22:3–7   [b] Lev 15:31   [c] Num 8:7; 19:9   [d] Lev 7:20; 22:3   **19:15** [a] Lev 11:32; Num 31:20   **19:16** [a] Num 19:11; 31:19   [1] Heb. *a dead body.*   **19:17** [a] Num 19:9   [1] Heb. *living water,* i.e., water that flows.   **19:18** [a] Ps 51:7   **19:19** [a] Lev 14:9   **19:20** [a] Num 19:13   **19:22** [a] Hag 2:11–13   [b] Lev 15:5   **20:1** [a] Num 13:21; 33:36   [b] Num 13:26   [c] Exod 15:20; Num 26:59   **20:2** [a] Exod 17:1   [b] Num 16:19, 42   **20:3** [a] Exod 17:2; Num 14:2   [b] Num 11:1, 33; 14:37; 16:31–35, 49   [1] Heb. *legal complaint, lawsuit, quarrel, strife.*   **20:4** [a] Exod 17:3   **20:6** [a] Num 14:5; 16:4, 22, 45   [b] Num 14:10   **20:8** [a] Exod 4:17, 20; 17:5–6   [b] Neh 9:15; Ps 78:15–16; 105:41; Isa 43:20; 48:21; [1 Cor 10:4]   **20:9** [a] Num 17:10   **20:10** [a] Ps 106:33   **20:11** [a] Exod 17:6; Deut 8:15; Ps 78:16; Isa 48:21; [1 Cor 10:4]

The Lord's Judgment

[12]Then the LORD spoke to Moses and Aaron, "Because [a]you did not trust me enough to [b]show me as holy before the Israelites, therefore you will not bring this community into the land I have given them."

[13]These are the waters of Meribah, because the Israelites contended with the LORD, and [a]his holiness was maintained among them.

Rejection by the Edomites

[14a]Moses sent messengers from Kadesh to the king of [b]Edom: "[c]Thus says your brother Israel: 'You know all the hardships we have experienced, [15a]how our ancestors went down into Egypt, [b]and we lived in Egypt [c]a long time, and the Egyptians treated us and our ancestors badly. [16]So [a]when we cried to the LORD, he heard our voice and [b]sent a messenger, and has brought us up out of Egypt. Now we are here in Kadesh, a town on the edge of your country. [17]Please [a]let us pass through your country. We will not pass through the fields or through the vineyards, nor will we drink water from any well. We will go by the King's Highway; we will not turn to the right or the left until we have passed through your region.'"

[18]But [a]Edom said to him, "You will not pass through me, or I will come out against you with the sword." [19]Then [a]the Israelites said to him, "We will go along the highway, and if we or our cattle drink any of your water, we will pay for it. We will only pass through on our feet, without doing anything else."

[20]But he said, "[a]You may not pass through." Then Edom came out against them with a large and powerful force. [21]So Edom [a]refused to give Israel passage through his border; therefore Israel turned [b]away from him.

Aaron's Death

[22]So the entire company of Israelites traveled from [a]Kadesh [b]and came to Mount Hor. [23]And the LORD spoke to Moses and Aaron at Mount Hor, by the border of the land of Edom. He said: [24]"Aaron will be [a]gathered to his ancestors, for he will not enter into the land I have given to the Israelites because both of you rebelled against my word at the waters of Meribah. [25a]Take Aaron and Eleazar his son, and bring them up on Mount Hor. [26]Remove Aaron's priestly garments and put them on Eleazar his son, and Aaron will be gathered to his ancestors and will die there."

[27]So Moses did as the LORD commanded; and they went up Mount Hor in the sight of the whole community. [28]And [a]Moses removed Aaron's garments and put them on his son Eleazar. So [b]Aaron died there on the top of the mountain. And Moses and Eleazar came down from the mountain. [29]When all the community saw that Aaron was dead, the whole house of Israel mourned for Aaron [a]thirty days.

Victory at Hormah

21 When the Canaanite [a]king of Arad who lived in the Negev[1] heard that Israel was approaching along the road to Atharim, he fought against Israel and took some of them prisoner.

[2a]So [b]Israel made a vow to the LORD and said, "If you will indeed deliver this people into our hand, then we will utterly destroy their cities." [3]The LORD listened to the voice of Israel and delivered up the Canaanites,[1] and they utterly destroyed them and their cities. So the name of the place was called Hormah.

Fiery Serpents

[4]Then they traveled from Mount Hor by the road to the Red Sea,[1] to [a]go around the land of Edom, but the people became impatient along the way. [5]And the people [a]spoke against God and against Moses, "Why have you brought us up from Egypt to die in the wilderness, for there is no bread or water, and we detest this worthless[1] food."

[6]So [a]the LORD sent [b]venomous snakes among the people, and they bit the people;

20:12 [a]Num 20:28; 27:14; Deut 1:37; 3:26–27; 34:5   [b]Lev 10:3; Ezek 20:41; 36:23; 1 Pet 3:15   20:13 [a]Deut 33:8; Ps 106:32   20:14 [a]Judg 11:16–17   [b]Gen 36:31–39   [c]Deut 2:4; Obad 10–12   20:15 [a]Gen 46:6; Acts 7:15   [b]Exod 12:40   [c]Exod 1:11; Deut 26:6; Acts 7:19   20:16 [a]Exod 2:23; 3:7   [b]Exod 3:2; 14:19   20:17 [a]Num 21:22   20:18 [a]Num 24:18; Ps 137:7; Ezek 25:12–13; Obad 10–15   20:19 [a]Deut 2:6, 28   20:20 [a]Judg 11:17   20:21 [a]Deut 2:27, 30   [b]Deut 2:8; Judg 11:18   20:22 [a]Num 33:37   [b]Num 21:4   20:24 [a]Gen 25:8; Deut 32:50   20:25 [a]Num 33:38; Deut 32:50   20:28 [a]Exod 29:29–30; Deut 10:6   [b]Num 33:38   20:29 [a]Gen 50:3, 10; Deut 34:8   21:1 [a]Num 33:40; Josh 12:14; Judg 1:16   [1]Or the south.   21:2 [a]Gen 28:20; Judg 11:30   [b]Deut 2:34   21:3 [1]Some wss add into his hand.   21:4 [a]Judg 11:18   [1]I.e., gulfs on either side of the Sinai peninsula.   21:5 [a]Num 20:4–5   [1]Heb. good for nothing, worthless, miserable.   21:6 [a]1 Cor 10:9   [b]Deut 8:15

many people of Israel died. [7]Then [a]the people came to Moses and said, "We have [b]sinned, for we have spoken against the LORD and against you. [c]Pray to the LORD that he would take away the snakes from us." So Moses prayed for the people.

[8]The LORD said to Moses, "[a]Make a poisonous snake and set it on a pole. When anyone who is bitten looks[1] at it, he will live." [9]So [a]Moses made a bronze snake and put it on a pole, so that if a snake had bitten someone, when he looked at the bronze snake he lived.

The Approach to Moab

[10]The Israelites traveled on and [a]camped in Oboth. [11]Then they traveled on from Oboth and camped at Iye Abarim, in the wilderness that is before Moab on the eastern side. [12][a]From there they moved on and camped in the valley of Zered. [13]From [a]there they moved on and camped on the other side of the Arnon, in the wilderness that extends from the regions of the Amorites, for Arnon is the border of Moab, between Moab and the Amorites. [14]This is why it is said in the Book of the Wars of the LORD,

> "Waheb in Suphah[1] and the wadis,
> the Arnon [15]and the slope of the
> valleys
> that extends to the dwelling of [a]Ar,
> and falls off at the border of Moab."

[16]And from there they traveled [a]to Beer; that is the well where the LORD spoke to Moses, "Gather the people and I will give them water." [17][a]Then Israel sang this song:

> "Spring up, O well, sing to it!
> [18] The well which the princes dug,
> which the leaders of the people
> opened
> with their [a]scepters and their staffs."

And from the wilderness they traveled to Mattanah; [19]and from Mattanah to Nahaliel; and from Nahaliel to Bamoth; [20]and from Bamoth to the valley that is in the country of Moab, near the top of Pisgah, which [a]overlooks the wastelands.[1]

The Victory over Sihon and Og

[21]Then [a]Israel sent messengers to King Sihon of the Amorites, saying,[1] [22]"[a]Let us pass through your land;[1] we will not turn aside into the fields or into the vineyards, nor will we drink water from any well, but we will go along the King's Highway until we pass your borders." [23][a]But Sihon did not permit Israel to pass through his border; he gathered all his forces together [b]and went out against Israel into the wilderness. When he came to Jahaz, he fought against Israel. [24]But the [a]Israelites defeated him in battle and took possession of his land from the Arnon to the Jabbok, as far as the Ammonites, for the border of the Ammonites was strongly defended. [25]So Israel took all these cities; and Israel [a]settled in all the cities of the Amorites, in Heshbon, and in all its villages. [26]For Heshbon was the city of King Sihon of the Amorites. Now he had fought against the former king of Moab and had taken all his land from his control, as far as the Arnon. [27]That is why those who speak in proverbs say,

> "Come to Heshbon, let it be built.
> Let the city of Sihon be established!
> [28] For [a]fire went out from Heshbon,
> a flame from the city of Sihon.
> It has consumed [b]Ar of Moab
> and the lords of the high [c]places of
> Arnon.
> [29] Woe to you, [a]Moab.
> You are ruined, O people of
> [b]Chemosh!
> He has made his [c]sons fugitives,
> and his [d]daughters the prisoners of
> King Sihon of the Amorites.
> [30] We have overpowered them;[1]
> Heshbon [a]has perished as far as
> Dibon.

21:7 [a] Num 11:2; Ps 78:34; Isa 26:16; Hos 5:15   [b] Lev 26:40   [c] Exod 8:8; 1 Sam 12:19; 1 Kgs 13:6; Acts 8:24   21:8 [a] [John 3:14–15]   [1] Heb. and it shall be anyone who is bitten when he looks at it he shall live.   21:9 [a] 2 Kgs 18:4; John 3:14–15   21:10 [a] Num 33:43–44   21:12 [a] Deut 2:13   21:13 [a] Num 22:36; Judg 11:18   21:14 [1] Smr. Waheb on the Sea of Reeds; LXX he has set Zoob on fire and the torrents of Arnon.   21:15 [a] Num 21:28; Deut 2:9, 18, 29   21:16 [a] Judg 9:21   21:17 [a] Exod 15:1   21:18 [a] Isa 33:22   21:20 [a] Num 23:28   [1] Or perhaps Jeshimon; a name.   21:21 [a] Num 32:33; Deut 2:26–37; Judg 11:19   [1] LXX, Smr. words of peace.   21:22 [a] Num 20:16–17   [1] Smr. by the King's way I will go. I will not turn aside to the right or the left.   21:23 [a] Deut 29:7   [b] Deut 2:32; Judg 11:20   21:24 [a] Deut 2:33; Josh 12:1; Neh 9:22; Ps 135:10; 136:19; Amos 2:9   21:25 [a] Amos 2:10   21:28 [a] Jer 48:45–46   [b] Deut 2:9, 18; Isa 15:1   [c] Num 22:41; 33:52   21:29 [a] Jer 48:46   [b] Judg 11:24; 1 Kgs 11:33; 2 Kgs 23:13   [c] Isa 15:2, 5   [d] Isa 16:2   21:30 [a] Num 32:3, 34; Jer 48:18, 22   [1] MT we shot at them; LXX their posterity perished.

We have shattered them as far as
  Nophah,
  which reaches to [b]Medeba."

[31]So the Israelites lived in the land of the
Amorites. [32]Moses sent spies to reconnoiter
[a]Jazer, and they captured its villages and
dispossessed the Amorites who were there.
[33]Then they turned [a]and went up by the
road to [b]Bashan. And King Og of Bashan and
all his forces marched out against them to
do [c]battle at Edrei. [34]And the LORD said to
Moses, "[a]Do not fear him, for I have delivered him and all his people and his land
into [b]your hand. You will do to him what
you did to King Sihon of the Amorites, who
lived in Heshbon." [35]So they defeated Og,
his [a]sons, and all his people, until there
were no survivors, and they possessed his
land.

Balaam Refuses to Curse Israel

22 The Israelites traveled on and
camped in [a]the rift valley plains[1]
of Moab on the side of the Jordan River
across from Jericho. [2a]Balak son of Zippor
saw all that the Israelites had done to the
Amorites. [3]And the [a]Moabites were greatly
afraid of the people, because they were so
numerous. The Moabites were sick with
fear because of the Israelites.

[4]So [a]the Moabites said to the elders
of Midian, "Now this mass of people will
lick up everything around us, as the bull
devours the grass of the field." Now Balak
son of Zippor was king of the Moabites
at this time. [5]And [a]he sent messengers to
Balaam son of Beor at [b]Pethor, which is by
the Euphrates River in the land of Amaw,
to summon him, saying, "Look, a nation
has come out of Egypt. They cover the face
of the earth, and they are settling next to
me. [6]So now, please come and curse this
nation [a]for me, for they are too powerful
for me. Perhaps I will prevail so that we may
conquer them and drive them out of the
land. For I know that whoever you bless is
blessed, and whoever you [b]curse is cursed."

[7]So [a]the elders of Moab and the elders of
Midian departed with the fee for divination
in their hands. They came to Balaam and
reported to him the words of Balak. [8]He
replied to them, "[a]Stay[1] here tonight, and
I will bring back to you whatever word the
LORD may speak to me." So the princes of
Moab stayed with Balaam. [9a]And God came
to Balaam and said, "Who are these men
with you?" [10]Balaam said to God, "Balak son
of Zippor, king of Moab, has sent a message
to me, saying, [11]'Look, a nation has come out
of Egypt, and it covers the face of the earth.
Come now and put a curse on them for me;
perhaps I will be able to defeat them and
drive them out.'" [12]But God said to Balaam,
"You must not go with them; you must not
curse [a]the people, for they are blessed."
[13]So Balaam got up in the morning, and
said to the princes of Balak, "Go to your
land,[1] for the LORD has refused to permit
me to go with you." [14]So the princes of Moab
departed and went back to Balak and said,
"Balaam refused to come with us."

Balaam Accompanies the Moabite Princes

[15]Balak again sent princes, more numerous and more distinguished than the first.
[16]And they came to Balaam and said to him,
"Thus says Balak son of Zippor: 'Please do
not let anything hinder you from coming
to me. [17]For I will [a]honor you greatly, and
whatever you tell me I will do. So come, put
a curse on this nation [b]for me.'"
[18]Balaam [a]replied to the servants of Balak,
"Even if Balak would give me his palace full
of silver and gold, I could not transgress the
commandment of the LORD my God to do
less or more. [19]Now therefore, please [a]stay
the night here also, that I may know what
more the LORD might say to me." [20]God
came to Balaam that night, [a]and said to him,
"If the men have come to call you, get up
and go with them, [b]but the word that I will
say to you, that you must do." [21]So Balaam
got up in the morning, saddled his donkey,
and went with the princes of Moab.

21:30 [b]Isa 15:2   21:32 [a]Num 32:1, 3, 35; Jer 48:32   21:33 [a]Deut 29:7   [b]Deut 3:1   [c]Josh 13:12   21:34 [a]Deut 3:2   [b]Num 21:24;
Ps 135:10; 136:20   21:35 [a]Deut 3:3–4; 29:7; Josh 13:12   22:1 [a]Num 33:48–49   [1]The rift valley extends from Mount Hermon
to the Gulf of Aqaba; this is just north of the Dead Sea.   22:2 [a]Josh 24:9; Judg 11:25; Mic 6:5; Rev 2:14   22:3 [a]Exod 15:15
22:4 [a]Num 25:15–18; 31:1–3; Josh 13:21   22:5 [a]Num 31:8, 16; Deut 23:4; Josh 13:22; 24:9; Neh 13:1–2; Mic 6:5; 2 Pet 2:15; Jude
11; Rev 2:14   [b]Deut 23:4   22:6 [a]Num 22:17; 23:7–8   [b]Num 22:12; 24:9   22:7 [a]1 Sam 9:7–8   22:8 [a]Num 22:19   [1]Heb. to
lodge, spend the night.   22:9 [a]Gen 20:3   22:12 [a]Num 23:20; [Rom 11:28]   22:13 [1]LXX adds to your lord.
22:17 [a]Num 24:11   [b]Num 22:6   22:18 [a]1 Kgs 22:14; 2 Chr 18:13   22:19 [a]Num 22:8
22:20 [a]Num 22:9   [b]Num 22:35; 23:5, 12, 16, 26; 24:13

God Opposes Balaam

[22] Then God's anger was kindled because he went, [a]and the angel of the LORD stood in the road to oppose[1] him. Now he was riding on his donkey and his two servants were with him. [23] And [a]the donkey saw the angel of the LORD standing in the road with his sword drawn in his hand, so the donkey turned aside from the road and went into the field. But Balaam beat the donkey, to make her turn back to the road.

[24] Then the angel of the LORD stood in a path among the vineyards, where there was a wall on either side. [25] And when the donkey saw the angel of the LORD, she pressed herself into the wall, and crushed Balaam's foot against the wall. So he beat her again.

[26] Then the angel of the LORD went farther, and stood in a narrow place, where there was no way to turn either to the right or to the left. [27] When the donkey saw the angel of the LORD, she crouched down under Balaam. Then Balaam was angry, and he beat his donkey with a staff.

[28] Then the LORD [a]opened the mouth of the donkey, and she said to Balaam, "What have I done to you that you have beaten me these three times?" [29] And Balaam said to the donkey, "You have made me look stupid; I wish there were a sword in my hand, [a]for I would kill you right now." [30a]The donkey said to Balaam, "Am I not your donkey that you have ridden ever since I was yours until this day? Have I ever attempted to treat you this way?" And he said, "No." [31] Then the LORD [a]opened Balaam's eyes, and he saw the angel of the LORD standing in the way with his sword drawn in his hand; so he bowed his head and threw himself down with his face to the ground.[1] [32] The angel of the LORD said to him, "Why have you beaten your donkey these three times? Look, I came out to oppose you because what you are doing is [a]perverse before me. [33] The donkey saw me and turned from me these three times. If she had not turned from me, I would have killed you but saved her alive." [34] Balaam [a]said to the angel of the LORD, "I have sinned, for I did not know that you stood against me in the road. So now, if it is evil in your sight, I will go back home." [35] But the angel of the LORD said to Balaam, "Go with the men, [a]but you may only speak the word that I will speak to you."[1] So Balaam went with the princes of Balak.

Balaam Meets Balak

[36] When Balak [a]heard that Balaam was coming, he went out to meet him at a city of Moab that was on the border of the Arnon at the boundary of his territory. [37] Balak said [a]to Balaam, "Did I not send again and again to you to summon you? Why did you not come to me? Am I not able to honor you?" [38] Balaam said to Balak, "Look, I have come to you. Now, am I able to speak just anything? I must speak only [a]the word that God puts in my mouth." [39] So Balaam went with Balak, and they came to Kiriath Huzoth. [40] And Balak sacrificed bulls and sheep, and sent some to Balaam, and to the princes who were with him. [41] Then on the next morning Balak took Balaam, and brought him up to Bamoth Baal. From there he saw the extent of the nation.

Balaam Blesses Israel

23 Balaam said to Balak, "[a]Build me seven altars here, and prepare for me here seven bulls and seven rams." [2] So Balak did just as Balaam had said. Balak and Balaam then [a]offered on each altar a bull and a ram. [3] Balaam said to Balak, "[a]Station yourself[1] by your burnt offering, and I will go off; perhaps the LORD will come [b]to meet me, and whatever he reveals to me I will tell you." Then he went to a deserted height.

[4] Then God met Balaam, who said to him, "I have prepared seven altars, [a]and I have offered on each altar a bull and a ram." [5] Then the LORD [a]put a message in Balaam's mouth and said, "Return to Balak, and speak what I tell you."

[6] So he returned to him, and he was still standing by his burnt offering, he and all the princes of Moab. [7] Then Balaam uttered his oracle, saying,

> "Balak, the king of Moab, brought me
>   from Aram,
>   out of the mountains of the east,
>   saying,

‘[a]Come, pronounce a curse on Jacob
   for me;
come, [b]denounce Israel.’
8 [a]How[1] can I curse one whom God has
   not cursed,
or how can I denounce one whom
   the LORD has not denounced?
9 For from the top of the rocks I see
   them;
from the hills I [a]watch them.
Indeed, a nation that lives alone,
and it will [b]not be reckoned among
   the nations.
10 Who[1] can count [a]the dust of Jacob,
or number the fourth part of Israel?
Let me die the death of the upright,
and let the end of my life be like
   theirs.”

Balaam Relocates

[11]Then Balak [a]said to Balaam, "What have you done to me? I brought you to curse my enemies, but on the contrary you have only blessed them!" [12]Balaam replied, "[a]Must I not be careful to speak what the LORD has put in my mouth?" [13]Balak said to him, "Please come with me to another place from which you can observe them. You will see only a part of them, but you will not see all of them. Curse them for me from there."

[14]So Balak brought Balaam[1] to the field of Zophim, to the top of Pisgah, where he built seven altars [a]and offered a bull and a ram on each altar. [15]And Balaam said to Balak, "Station yourself here by your burnt offering, while I meet the LORD there." [16]Then the LORD met Balaam and [a]put a message in his mouth and said, "Return to Balak, and speak what I tell you." [17]When Balaam came to him, he was still standing by his burnt offering, along with the princes of Moab. And Balak said to him, "What has the LORD spoken?"

Balaam Prophesies Again

[18]Balaam uttered his oracle, and said,

"[a]Rise up, Balak, and hear;
   Listen to me, son of Zippor:
19 [a]God is not a man, that he should lie,

nor a human being, that he should
   change his mind.
Has he [b]said, and will he not do it?
Or has he spoken, and will he not
   make it happen?
20 Indeed, I have received a command
   to bless;
[a]he has blessed, and I cannot reverse it.
21 He has not looked on iniquity in
   Jacob,
nor has [a]he seen trouble[1] in Israel.
The LORD their God is with them;
his acclamation as king is among
   them.
22 [a]God brought them out of Egypt.
They have, as it were, the [b]strength of
   a wild bull.
23 For there is no spell against Jacob,
nor is there any divination against
   Israel.
[a]At this time it must be said of Jacob
and of Israel, 'Look at what God has
   done!'
24 Indeed, the people will rise up [a]like a
   lioness,
and like a lion raises himself up;
they will not lie down until they eat
   their prey,
and drink the blood of the slain."

Balaam Relocates yet Again

[25]Balak said to Balaam, "Neither curse them at all nor bless them at all!" [26]But Balaam replied to Balak, "Did I not tell you, '[a]All that the LORD speaks, I must do'?"

[27]Balak said to Balaam, "Come, please; I will take you to another place. Perhaps it will please God to let you curse them for me from there." [28]So Balak took Balaam to the top of Peor, that [a]looks toward the wastelands.[1] [29]Then Balaam said to Balak, "Build seven altars here for me, and prepare seven bulls and seven rams." [30]So Balak did as Balaam had said, and offered a bull and a ram on each altar.

Balaam Prophesies yet Again

24 When Balaam saw that it pleased [a]the LORD to bless Israel, he did not go as at the other times to seek for omens,[1]

23:7 [a]Num 22:6, 11, 17   [b]1 Sam 17:10   **23:8** [a]Num 22:12   [1]A rhetorical question.   **23:9** [a]Deut 32:8; 33:28; Josh 11:23   [b]Exod 33:16; Ezra 9:2; [Eph 2:14]   **23:10** [a]Ps 116:15   [1]A rhetorical question.   **23:11** [a]Num 22:11   **23:12** [a]Num 22:38   **23:14** [a]Num 23:1–2   [1]Heb. *he brought him.*   **23:16** [a]Num 22:35; 23:5   **23:18** [a]Judg 3:20   **23:19** [a]1 Sam 15:29; Mal 3:6; Jas 1:17   [b]Num 11:23; 1 Kgs 8:56   **23:20** [a]Gen 12:2; 22:17; Num 22:12   **23:21** [a]Ps 32:2; [Rom 4:7–8]   [1]Heb. *wrong, misery, trouble, disaster.*   **23:22** [a]Num 24:8   [b]Deut 33:17; Job 39:10   **23:23** [a]Ps 31:19; 44:1   **23:24** [a]Gen 49:9   **23:26** [a]Num 22:38   **23:28** [a]Num 21:20   [1]Or perhaps *Jeshimon*; a name.   **24:1** [a]Num 23:3, 15   [1]Or possibly *auguries.*

but he set his face toward the wilderness. [2]When Balaam lifted up his eyes, he saw Israel [a]camped tribe by tribe; and [b]the Spirit of God came upon him. [3]Then [a]he uttered this oracle:

> "The oracle of Balaam son of Beor,
> the oracle of the man whose eyes are
> open,
> [4] the oracle of the one who hears the
> words of God,
> who sees a vision from the Almighty,
> although [a]falling flat on the ground[1]
> with eyes open:
> [5] 'How beautiful are your tents, O Jacob,
> and your dwelling places, O Israel!
> [6] They are [a]like valleys stretched forth,
> like gardens by the river's side,
> like aloes that the LORD has [b]planted,
> and like cedar trees beside the
> waters.
> [7] He will pour the water out of his
> buckets,[1]
> and their descendants will be like
> abundant water;
> their [a]king will be greater than [b]Agag,
> and their [c]kingdom will be exalted.
> [8] [a]God brought them out of Egypt.
> They have, as it were, the strength of
> a young bull;
> they will [b]devour hostile people,
> and will [c]break their bones,
> and will [d]pierce them through with
> arrows.
> [9] They crouch and lie down like a lion,
> and as a lioness, who can stir him?
> Blessed is [a]the one who [b]blesses you,
> and cursed is the one who curses
> you!'"

[10]Then Balak became very angry at Balaam, and he [a]struck [b]his hands together. Balak said to Balaam, "I called you to curse my enemies, and look, you have done nothing but bless them these three times! [11]So now, go back where you came from! [a]I said that I would greatly honor you, but now the LORD has stood in the way of your honor."

[12]Balaam said to Balak, "Did I not also tell your messengers whom you sent to me, [13]'If Balak would give me his palace full of silver and gold, I cannot go beyond the commandment of the LORD to do either good or evil of my own will, but whatever the LORD tells me I must speak'? [14]And now, [a]I am about to go back to my own people. Come now, and I will advise you as to what this people will do to your people in [b]future days."

Balaam Prophesies a Fourth Time

[15]Then he uttered this oracle:

> "The oracle of Balaam son of Beor,
> the oracle of the man whose eyes are
> open,
> [16] the oracle of the one who hears the
> words of God,
> and who knows the knowledge of the
> Most High,
> who sees a vision from the Almighty,
> although falling flat on the ground
> with eyes open:
> [17] 'I see [a]him, but not now;
> I behold him, but not close [b]at [c]hand.
> A star will march forth out of Jacob,
> and a scepter will rise out of Israel.
> He will crush the skulls[1] of Moab,
> and the heads[2] of all the sons of
> Sheth.
> [18] [a]Edom will be a possession,
> Seir, his enemy, will also be a
> possession;
> but Israel will act valiantly.
> [19] [a]A ruler will be established from
> Jacob;
> he will destroy the remains of the
> city.'"[1]

Balaam's Final Prophecies

[20]Then Balaam looked on Amalek and delivered this oracle:

> "Amalek was the first of the nations,
> but his end will be that he will perish."

[21]Then he looked on the Kenites and uttered this oracle:

> "Your dwelling place seems strong,
> and your nest is set on a rocky cliff.

24:2 [a]Num 2:2, 34 [b]Num 11:25; 1 Sam 10:10; 19:20, 23; 2 Chr 15:1   **24:3** [a]Num 23:7, 18   **24:4** [a]Ezek 1:28 [1]*flat on the ground is supplied.*   **24:6** [a]Ps 1:3; Jer 17:8 [b]Ps 104:16   **24:7** [a]Jer 51:13; Rev 17:1, 15 [b]1 Sam 15:8–9 [c]2 Sam 5:12; 1 Chr 14:2 [1]LXX *a man shall come out of his seed.*   **24:8** [a]Num 23:22 [b]Num 14:9; 23:24 [c]Ps 2:9; Jer 50:17 [d]Ps 45:5   **24:9** [a]Gen 49:9; Num 23:24 [b]Gen 12:3; 27:29   **24:10** [a]Ezek 21:14, 17 [b]Num 23:11; Neh 13:2   **24:11** [a]Num 22:17, 37   **24:14** [a][Mic 6:5] [b]Gen 49:1; Deut 4:30; Dan 2:28   **24:17** [a]Rev 1:7; Matt 1:2; Luke 3:34 [b]Matt 2:2 [c]Gen 49:10 [1]Lit. *corners.* [2]MT *shatter, devastate.*   **24:18** [a]2 Sam 8:14   **24:19** [a]Gen 49:10; Amos 9:11–12 [1]Or perhaps *Ir,* a name.

²² Nevertheless the Kenite will be consumed.¹

How long will Asshur take you away captive?"

²³Then he uttered this oracle:

"O, who will survive when God does this!

²⁴ Ships will come from the coast of ᵃKittim,

and will afflict Asshur,¹ and will afflict ᵇEber,

and he will also perish forever."

²⁵Balaam got up and departed and ᵃreturned to his home, and Balak also went his way.

Israel's Sin with the Moabite Women

25 When Israel lived in Shittim, the ᵃpeople began to commit sexual immorality with the daughters of Moab. ²These women invited ᵃthe people to ᵇthe sacrifices of their gods; then the people ate and ᶜbowed down to their gods. ³When Israel joined ᵃthemselves to Baal Peor, the anger of the LORD flared up against Israel.

God's Punishment

⁴The LORD said to Moses, "ᵃArrest all the leaders of the people, and hang them up before the LORD in broad daylight, so ᵇthat the fierce anger of the LORD may be turned away from Israel." ⁵So Moses said to ᵃthe judges of Israel, "Each of you must execute those of his men who were joined to Baal Peor."

⁶Just then one of the Israelites came and brought to his brothers a Midianite woman in the plain view of Moses and of the ᵃwhole community of the Israelites, while they were weeping at the entrance of the tent of meeting. ⁷When Phinehas son of Eleazar, the son of Aaron the priest, saw it, ᵃhe got up from among ᵇthe assembly, took a javelin in his hand, ⁸and went after ᵃthe Israelite man into the tent and thrust through the Israelite man and into the woman's abdomen. So the plague was ᵇstopped from the Israelites. ⁹Those that died in the plague were 24,000.

The Aftermath

¹⁰The LORD spoke to Moses: ¹¹"ᵃPhinehas son of Eleazar, the son of Aaron the priest, has turned ᵇmy anger away from the Israelites, when he manifested such zeal¹ for my sake among them, so that I did not consume the Israelites in my zeal.² ¹²Therefore, announce: 'I am going to give to him my ᵃcovenant of peace. ¹³So it will be to him and ᵃhis ᵇdescendants after him a covenant of a permanent priesthood, because he has been ᶜzealous for his God, and has ᵈmade atonement for the Israelites.'"

¹⁴Now the name of the Israelite who was stabbed—the one who was stabbed with the Midianite woman—was Zimri son of Salu, a leader of a clan of the Simeonites. ¹⁵The name of the Midianite woman who was killed was Cozbi daughter of ᵃZur. He was a leader over the people of a clan of Midian.

¹⁶Then the LORD spoke to Moses: ¹⁷"Bring ᵃtrouble to the Midianites, and destroy them, ¹⁸because they bring trouble to you by their ᵃtreachery with which they have deceived you in the matter of Peor, and in the matter of Cozbi, the daughter of a prince of Midian, their sister, who was killed on the day of the plague that happened as a result of Peor."

A Second Census Required

26 After the ᵃplague the LORD said to Moses and to Eleazar son of Aaron the priest, ²"ᵃTake a census of the whole community of Israelites, ᵇfrom twenty years old and upward, by their clans, everyone who can serve in the army of Israel." ³So Moses and Eleazar the priest spoke with them ᵃin the rift valley plains¹ of Moab, along the Jordan River across from Jericho. They said, ⁴"Number the people from

24:22 ¹Heb. *Nevertheless Cain will be wasted.* **24:24** ᵃGen 10:4; Ezek 27:6; Dan 11:30 ᵇGen 10:21, 25 ¹Or perhaps Assyria. **24:25** ᵃNum 22:5; 31:8 **25:1** ᵃRev 2:14 **25:2** ᵃJosh 22:17; Hos 9:10 ᵇExod 34:15; Deut 32:38; 1 Cor 10:20 ᶜExod 20:5 **25:3** ᵃPs 106:28–29 **25:4** ᵃDeut 4:3 ᵇNum 25:11; Deut 13:17 **25:5** ᵃExod 18:21 **25:6** ᵃJoel 2:17 **25:7** ᵃPs 106:30 ᵇExod 6:25 **25:8** ᵃPs 106:30 ᵇNum 16:46–48 **25:11** ᵃPs 106:30 ᵇ[Exod 20:5]; Deut 32:16, 21; 1 Kgs 14:22; Ps 78:58; Ezek 16:38 ¹Heb. *he was zealous with my zeal*; an emphatic Heb. construction. ²Or *jealousy.* **25:12** ᵃIsa 54:10; Ezek 34:25; 37:26; Mal 2:5 **25:13** ᵃ1 Chr 6:4–15 ᵇExod 40:15 ᶜActs 22:3; Rom 10:2 ᵈ[Heb 2:17] **25:15** ᵃNum 31:8; Josh 13:21 **25:17** ᵃNum 31:1–3 **25:18** ᵃNum 31:16; Rev 2:14 **26:1** ᵃNum 25:9 **26:2** ᵃExod 30:12; 38:25–26; Num 1:2; 14:29 ᵇNum 1:3 **26:3** ᵃNum 22:1; 31:12; 33:48; 35:1 ¹The rift valley extends from Mount Hermon to the Gulf of Aqaba; this is just north of the Dead Sea.

twenty years old and upward, just as the LORD [a]commanded Moses and the Israelites who went out from the land of Egypt."

Reuben

[5][a]Reuben was the firstborn of Israel. The Reubenites: from Hanoch, the family of the Hanochites; from Pallu, the family of the Palluites; [6]from Hezron, the family of the Hezronites; from Carmi, the family of the Carmites. [7]These were the families of the Reubenites; and those numbered of them were 43,730. [8]Pallu's descendant[1] was Eliab. [9]Eliab's descendants were Nemuel, Dathan, and Abiram. It was Dathan and Abiram who as leaders of the community rebelled against Moses and Aaron with the followers of Korah when they rebelled against the LORD. [10]The earth opened its mouth [a]and swallowed them [b]and Korah at the time that company died, when the fire consumed 250 men. So they became a warning. [11]But [a]the descendants of Korah did not die.

Simeon

[12]The Simeonites by their families: from Nemuel, the family of the Nemuelites; from Jamin, the family of the Jaminites; from Jakin, the family of the Jakinites; [13]from Zerah, the family of the Zerahites; and from Shaul, the family of the Shaulites. [14]These were the families of the Simeonites, 22,200.

Gad

[15]The Gadites by their families: from Zephon, the family of the Zephonites; from Haggi, the family of the Haggites; from Shuni, the family of the Shunites; [16]from Ozni, the family of the Oznites; from Eri,[1] the family of the Erites; [17]from Arod,[1] the family of the Arodites; and from Areli, the family of the Arelites. [18]These were the families of the Gadites according to those numbered of them, 40,500.

Judah

[19]The descendants of Judah were Er and Onan, but Er and Onan died in [a]the land of Canaan. [20]And [a]the Judahites by their families were: from Shelah, the family of the Shelahites; from Perez, the family of the Perezites; and from Zerah, the family of the Zerahites. [21]And the Perezites were: from Hezron, the family of the Hezronites; from Hamul,[1] the family of the Hamulites. [22]These were the families of Judah according to those numbered of them, 76,500.

Issachar

[23]The Issacharites by their families: from Tola, the family of the Tolaites; from Puah, the family of the Puites; [24]from Jashub, the family of the Jashubites; and from Shimron, the family of the Shimronites. [25]These were the families of Issachar, according to those numbered of them, 64,300.

Zebulun

[26]The Zebulunites by [a]their families: from Sered, the family of the Sardites; from Elon, the family of the Elonites; from Jahleel, the family of the Jahleelites. [27]These were the families of the Zebulunites, according to those numbered of them, 60,500.

Manasseh

[28]The descendants of Joseph by [a]their families: Manasseh and Ephraim. [29]The [a]Manassehites: from [b]Machir, the family of the Machirites (now Machir became the father of Gilead); from Gilead, the family of the Gileadites. [30]These were the Gileadites: from Iezer, the family of the Iezerites; from Helek, the family of the Helekites; [31]from Asriel, the family of the Asrielites; from Shechem, the family of the Shechemites; [32]from Shemida, the family of the Shemidaites; from Hepher, the family of the Hepherites. [33]Now [a]Zelophehad son of Hepher had no sons, but only daughters; and the names of the daughters of Zelophehad were Mahlah, Noah, Hoglah, Milcah, and Tirzah. [34]These were the families of Manasseh; those numbered of them were 52,700.

Ephraim

[35]These are the Ephraimites by their families: from Shuthelah, the family of the Shuthelahites; from Beker, the family of the Bekerites; from Tahan, the family of the Tahanites. [36]Now these were the

---

26:4 [a] Num 1:1   26:5 [a] Gen 46:8; Exod 6:14; 1 Chr 5:1–3   26:8 [1] MT *and the sons of Pallu.*   26:10 [a] Num 16:32–35
[b] Num 16:38–40; 1 Cor 10:6; 2 Pet 2:6   26:11 [a] Exod 6:24; 1 Chr 6:22–23   26:16 [1] LXX, Smr. *Ad[d]i.*   26:17 [1] LXX *Arodi.*
26:19 [a] Gen 38:2; 46:12   26:20 [a] 1 Chr 2:3   26:21 [1] LXX, Smr. *Hamuel.*   26:26 [a] Gen 46:14   26:28 [a] Gen 46:20;
Deut 33:16   26:29 [a] Josh 17:1   [b] 1 Chr 7:14–15   26:33 [a] Num 27:1; 36:11

Shuthelahites: from Eran, the family of the Eranites. [37]These were the families of the Ephraimites, according to those numbered of them, 32,500. These were the descendants of Joseph by their families.

Benjamin

[38]The Benjaminites by [a]their families: from Bela, the family of the Belaites; from Ashbel, the family of the Ashbelites; from [b]Ahiram, the family of the Ahiramites; [39]from [a]Shupham,[1] the family of the Shuphamites; from Hupham, the family of the Huphamites. [40]The descendants [a]of Bela were Ard[1] and Naaman. From Ard,[2] the family of the Ardites; from Naaman, the family of the Naamanites. [41]These are the Benjaminites, according to their families, and according to those numbered of them, 45,600.

Dan

[42]These are the Danites by their families: from Shuham, the family of the Shuhamites. These were the families of Dan, according to their families. [43]All the families of the Shuhamites according to those numbered of them were 64,400.

Asher

[44]The Asherites by [a]their families: from Imnah, the family of the Imnahites; from Ishvi, the family of the Ishvites; from Beriah, the family of the Beriahites. [45]From the Beriahites: from Heber, the family of the Heberites; from Malkiel, the family of the Malkielites. [46]Now the name of the daughter of Asher was Serah. [47]These are the families of the Asherites, according to those numbered of them, 53,400.

Naphtali

[48]The Naphtalites by [a]their families: from Jahzeel, the family of the Jahzeelites; from Guni, the family of the Gunites; [49]from Jezer, the family of the Jezerites; from [a]Shillem, the family of the Shillemites. [50]These were the families of Naphtali according to their families; and those numbered of them were 45,400.

Total Number and Division of the Land

[51]These were those numbered of [a]the Israelites, 601,730.

[52]Then the LORD spoke to Moses: [53]"[a]To these the land must be [b]divided as an inheritance according to the number of the names. [54]To a larger group you will give a larger inheritance, and [a]to a smaller group you will give a smaller inheritance. To each one its inheritance must be given according to the number of people in it.[1] [55]The land must be [a]divided by lot; and they will inherit in accordance with the names of their ancestral tribes. [56]Their inheritance must be apportioned by lot among the larger and smaller groups."

[57][a]And these are the Levites who were numbered according to their families: from Gershon, the family of the Gershonites; of Kohath, the family of the Kohathites; from Merari, the family of the Merarites. [58]These are the families of the Levites: the family of the Libnites, the family of the Hebronites, the family of the Mahlites, the family of the Mushites, the family of the Korahites. Kohath became the father of Amram. [59]Now the name of Amram's wife was [a]Jochebed, daughter of Levi, who was born to Levi in Egypt. And to Amram she bore Aaron, Moses, and Miriam their sister. [60]And [a]to Aaron were born Nadab and Abihu, Eleazar and Ithamar. [61]But [a]Nadab and Abihu died when they offered strange fire before the LORD. [62]Those of the Levites who were numbered were 23,000, all males from a month old and upward, for they were not numbered among the Israelites; [a]no inheritance was given to them among the Israelites.

[63]These are those who were numbered by Moses and Eleazar the priest, who numbered the Israelites [a]in the rift valley plains of Moab along the Jordan River opposite Jericho. [64][a]But there was not a man among these who had been among those numbered by Moses and Aaron the priest when they numbered the Israelites in the [b]desert of Sinai. [65]For the LORD had said of them, "They will surely die in the wilderness." And there was not left [a]a single man of them, [b]except Caleb son of Jephunneh and Joshua son of Nun.

26:38 [a]Gen 46:21; 1 Chr 7:6 [b]Gen 46:21; 1 Chr 8:1–2   26:39 [a]1 Chr 7:12 [1]MT *Shephupham*.   26:40 [a]1 Chr 8:3 [1]LXX *Adar*. [2]Heb. omits *From Ard*.   26:44 [a]Gen 46:17; 1 Chr 7:30   26:48 [a]Gen 46:24; 1 Chr 7:13   26:49 [a]1 Chr 7:13   26:51 [a]Exod 12:37; 38:26; Num 1:46; 11:21   26:53 [a]Josh 11:23; 14:1 [b]Num 33:54   26:54 [a]Num 33:54 [1]Heb. *according to those that were numbered of him.*   26:55 [a]Num 33:54; 34:13; Josh 11:23; 14:2   26:57 [a]Gen 46:11; Exod 6:16–19; Num 3:15; 1 Chr 6:1, 16   26:59 [a]Exod 2:1–2; 6:20   26:60 [a]Num 3:2   26:61 [a]Lev 10:1–2; Num 3:3–4; 1 Chr 24:2   26:62 [a]Num 3:39   26:63 [a]Num 26:3   26:64 [a]Num 14:29–35; Deut 2:14–16; Heb 3:17 [b]Num 1:1–46   26:65 [a]Num 14:26–35; [1 Cor 10:5–6] [b]Num 14:30

Special Inheritance Laws

27 Then the daughters of [a]Zelophehad son of Hepher, the son of Gilead, the son of Machir, the son of Manasseh of the families of Manasseh, the son of Joseph came forward. Now these are the names of his daughters: Mahlah, Noah, Hoglah, Milcah, and Tirzah. [2]And they stood before Moses and Eleazar the priest and the leaders of the whole assembly at the entrance to the tent of meeting and said, [3]"Our father [a]died [b]in the wilderness, although he was not part of the company of those that gathered themselves together against the LORD in the company of Korah, but he died for his own sin,[1] and he had no sons. [4]Why should the name of our father be [a]lost from among his family because he had no son? [b]Give us a possession among the relatives of our father."

[5]So Moses [a]brought their case before the LORD. [6]The LORD said to Moses: [7]"The daughters of Zelophehad have a valid claim. [a]You must indeed give them possession of an inheritance among their father's relatives, and you must transfer the inheritance of their father to them. [8]And you must tell the Israelites, 'If a man dies and has no son, then you must transfer his inheritance to his daughter; [9]and if he has no daughter, then you are to give his inheritance to his brothers; [10]and if he has no brothers, then you are to give his inheritance to his father's brothers; [11]and if his [a]father has no brothers, then you are to give his inheritance to his relative nearest to him from his family, and he will possess it. This will be for the Israelites a legal requirement,[1] as the LORD commanded Moses.'"

Leadership Change

[12]Then the LORD said to Moses, "[a]Go up this mountain of the Abarim range,[1] and see the land I have given to the Israelites. [13]When you have seen it, you will be gathered to your ancestors, as Aaron your brother was gathered to his ancestors. [14]For in the wilderness of Zin when the community rebelled against me, you[1] [a]rebelled against my command to show me as holy before their eyes over the [b]water—the water of Meribah in Kadesh in the wilderness of Zin."

[15]Then Moses spoke to the LORD: [16]"Let [a]the LORD, the God of the spirits of all humankind, appoint a man over the community, [17]who will go out before them, and [a]who will come in before them, and who will lead them out, and who will bring them in, so that the community of the LORD may not be [b]like sheep that have no shepherd."

[18]The LORD replied to Moses, "Take Joshua son of Nun, a man [a]in whom is the Spirit, and [b]lay your hand on him; [19]set him before Eleazar the priest and before the whole community, and [a]commission[1] him publicly. [20]Then [a]you must delegate some of your authority[1] to him, so that the whole community of the Israelites will be obedient. [21]And [a]he will stand before Eleazar the priest, who will seek counsel for him before the LORD [b]by the decision of the Urim. [c]At his command they will go out, and at his command they will come in, he and all the Israelites with him, the whole community."

[22]So Moses did as the LORD commanded him; he took Joshua and set him before Eleazar the priest and before the whole community. [23]He laid his [a]hands on him and commissioned him, just as the LORD commanded, by the authority of Moses.

Daily Offerings

28 The LORD spoke to Moses: [2]"Command the Israelites: 'With regard to [a]my offering, be sure to offer my food for my offering made by fire, as a pleasing aroma to me at its appointed time.' [3]You will say to them, '[a]This is the offering made by fire that you must offer to the LORD: two unblemished lambs one year old each day for a continual burnt offering. [4]The first lamb you must offer in the morning, and the second lamb you must offer in the late afternoon,[1] [5]with [a]one-tenth of an ephah of finely ground flour as [b]a grain offering mixed with

27:1 [a]Num 26:33; 36:1, 11; Josh 17:3   27:3 [a]Num 14:35; 26:64–65   [b]Num 16:1–2   [1]Heb. *but in/on account of his own sins he died*; an emphatic Heb. construction.   27:4 [a]Deut 25:6   [b]Josh 17:4   27:5 [a]Exod 18:13–26   27:7 [a]Num 36:2; Josh 17:4   27:11 [a]Num 35:29   [1]Heb. *a statute of judgment.*   27:12 [a]Num 33:47; Deut 3:23–27; 32:48–52; 34:1–4   [1]LXX adds *which is Mount Nebo.*   27:14 [a]Num 20:12, 24; Deut 1:37; 32:51; Ps 106:32–33   [b]Exod 17:7   [1]Masc. pl.   27:16 [a]Num 16:22; Heb 12:9   27:17 [a]Deut 31:2; 1 Sam 8:20; 18:13; 2 Chr 1:10   [b]1 Kgs 22:17; Zech 10:2; Matt 9:36; Mark 6:34   27:18 [a]Gen 41:38; Judg 3:10; 1 Sam 16:13, 18   [b]Deut 34:9   27:19 [a]Deut 3:28; 31:3, 7, 8, 23   [1]Lit. *to command.*   27:20 [a]Num 11:17   [1]Some wss *glory.*   27:21 [a]Judg 20:18, 23, 26; 1 Sam 23:9; 30:7   [b]Exod 28:30; 1 Sam 28:6   [c]Josh 9:14; 1 Sam 22:10   27:23 [a]Deut 3:28; 31:7–8   28:2 [a]Lev 3:11; 21:6, 8; [Mal 1:7, 12]   28:3 [a]Exod 29:38–42   28:4 [1]Heb. *between the evenings.*   28:5 [a]Exod 16:36; Num 15:4   [b]Lev 2:1

one-quarter of a hin of pressed olive oil. [6]It is [a]a continual burnt offering that was instituted on Mount Sinai as a pleasing aroma, an offering made by fire to the LORD.

[7]"And its [a]drink offering must be one-quarter of a hin for each lamb. You must pour out the strong drink as a drink offering to the LORD in the Holy Place. [8]And the second lamb you must offer in the late afternoon; just as you offered the grain offering and drink offering in the morning, you must offer it as an offering made by fire, as a pleasing aroma to the LORD.

Weekly Offerings

[9]"On the Sabbath day, you must offer two unblemished lambs a year old, and two-tenths of an ephah of finely ground flour as a grain offering, mixed with olive oil, along with its drink offering. [10]This is [a]the burnt offering for every Sabbath, besides the continual burnt offering and its drink offering.

Monthly Offerings

[11]"On the first day of each month you must offer as [a]a burnt offering to the LORD two young bulls, one ram, and seven unblemished lambs a year old, [12]with [a]three-tenths of an ephah of finely ground flour mixed with olive oil as a grain offering for each bull, and two-tenths of an ephah of finely ground flour mixed with olive oil as a grain offering for the ram, [13]and one-tenth of an ephah of finely ground flour mixed with olive oil as a grain offering for each lamb, as a burnt offering for a pleasing aroma, an offering made by fire to the LORD. [14]For their drink offerings, include half a hin of wine with each bull, one-third of a hin for the ram, and one-fourth of a hin for each lamb. This is the burnt offering for each month throughout the months of the year. [15]And [a]one male goat must be offered to the LORD as a purification offering, in addition to the continual burnt offering and its drink offering.

The Passover

[16]"On the fourteenth day of the first [a]month is the LORD's Passover. [17a]And on the fifteenth day of this month is the festival. For seven days bread made without yeast must be eaten. [18]And on the [a]first day there is to be a holy assembly; you must do no ordinary work on it.

[19]"But you must offer to the LORD an offering made by fire, a burnt offering of two young bulls, one ram, and seven lambs one year old; they must all [a]be unblemished. [20]And their grain offering is to be of finely ground flour mixed with olive oil. For each bull you must offer three-tenths of an ephah, and two-tenths for the ram. [21]For each of the seven lambs you are to offer one-tenth of an ephah, [22]as well as [a]one goat for a purification offering, to make atonement for you. [23]You must offer these in addition to the burnt offering in the morning that is for a continual burnt offering. [24]In this manner you must offer daily throughout the seven days the food of the sacrifice made by fire as a sweet aroma to the LORD. It is to be offered in addition to the continual burnt offering and its drink offering. [25]On the seventh day you are to have a holy assembly, you must do no regular work.

Firstfruits

[26]"Also, [a]on the day of the firstfruits, when you bring a new grain offering to the LORD during your Feast of Weeks, you are to have a holy assembly. You must do no ordinary work. [27]But you must offer as the burnt offering, as a sweet aroma to the LORD, [a]two young bulls, one ram, seven lambs one year old, [28]with their grain offering of finely ground flour mixed with olive oil: three-tenths of an ephah for each bull, two-tenths for the one ram, [29]with one-tenth for each of the seven lambs, [30]as well as one male goat to make an atonement for you. [31]You are to offer them with their drink offerings in addition to the continual burnt offering and its grain offering—they must [a]be unblemished.

Blowing Trumpets

29 "On the first day of the seventh month, you are to hold a holy assembly. You must not do your ordinary work, for [a]it is a day of blowing trumpets for you. [2]You must offer a burnt offering as a sweet aroma to the LORD: one young bull, one ram, and seven lambs one year old without blemish.

28:6 [a]Exod 29:42; Amos 5:25 28:7 [a]Exod 29:42 28:10 [a]Ezek 46:4 28:11 [a]Num 10:10; 1 Sam 20:5; 1 Chr 23:31; 2 Chr 2:4; Ezra 3:5; Neh 10:33; Isa 1:13–14; Ezek 45:17; 46:6–7; Hos 2:11; Col 2:16 28:12 [a]Num 15:4–12 28:15 [a]Num 15:24; 28:3, 22 28:16 [a]Exod 12:1–20; Lev 23:5–8; Num 9:2–5; Deut 16:1–8; Ezek 45:21 28:17 [a]Lev 23:6 28:18 [a]Exod 12:16; Lev 23:7 28:19 [a]Lev 22:20; Num 28:31; 29:8; Deut 15:21 28:22 [a]Num 28:15 28:26 [a]Exod 23:16; 34:22; Lev 23:10–21; Deut 16:9–12; Acts 2:1 28:27 [a]Lev 23:18–19 28:31 [a]Num 28:3, 19 29:1 [a]Exod 23:16; 34:22; Lev 23:23–25

³“‘Their grain offering is to be of finely ground flour mixed with olive oil, three-tenths of an ephah for the bull, two-tenths of an ephah for the ram, ⁴and one-tenth for each of the seven lambs, ⁵with one male goat for a purification offering to make an atonement for you; ⁶this is in addition to ᵃthe monthly burnt offering and its grain offering, and ᵇthe daily burnt offering with its grain offering and their drink offerings as prescribed, as ᶜa sweet aroma, a sacrifice made by fire to the LORD.

The Day of Atonement

⁷“‘On the tenth day of this seventh ᵃmonth you are to have a holy assembly. You must ᵇhumble yourselves; you must not do any work on it. ⁸But you must offer a burnt offering as a pleasing aroma to the LORD, one young bull, one ram, and seven lambs one year old, all of them without blemish. ⁹Their grain offerings must be of finely ground flour mixed with olive oil, three-tenths of an ephah for the bull, two-tenths for the ram, ¹⁰and one-tenth for each of the seven lambs, ¹¹along with one male goat for a purification offering, in addition to ᵃthe purification offering for atonement and the continual burnt offering with its grain offering and their drink offerings.

The Feast of Temporary Shelters

¹²“‘On the fifteenth day of the seventh ᵃmonth you are to have a holy assembly; you must do no ordinary work, and you must keep a festival to the LORD for seven days. ¹³You must offer a burnt offering, an offering made by fire as a pleasing aroma to the LORD: thirteen ᵃyoung bulls, two rams, and fourteen lambs each one year old, all of them without blemish. ¹⁴Their grain offerings must be of finely ground flour mixed with olive oil, three-tenths of an ephah for each of the thirteen bulls, two-tenths of an ephah for each of the two rams, ¹⁵and one-tenth for each of the fourteen lambs, ¹⁶along with one male goat for a purification offering, in addition to the continual burnt offering with its grain offering and its drink offering.

¹⁷“‘On the ᵃsecond day you must offer twelve young bulls, two rams, fourteen lambs one year old, all without blemish, ¹⁸and their grain offerings and their drink offerings for the bulls, for the rams, and for the lambs, ᵃaccording to their number as prescribed, ¹⁹along with one male goat for a purification offering, in addition to the continual burnt offering with its grain offering and their drink offerings.

²⁰“‘On the third day you must offer eleven bulls, two rams, fourteen lambs one year old, all without blemish, ²¹and their grain offerings and their drink offerings for the bulls, for the rams, and for the lambs, ᵃaccording to their number as prescribed, ²²along with one male goat for a purification offering, in addition to the continual burnt offering with its grain offering and its drink offering.

²³“‘On the fourth day you must offer ten bulls, two rams, and fourteen lambs one year old, all without blemish, ²⁴and their grain offerings and their drink offerings for the bulls, for the rams, and for the lambs, according to their number as prescribed, ²⁵along with one male goat for a purification offering, in addition to the continual burnt offering with its grain offering and its drink offering.

²⁶“‘On the fifth day you must offer nine bulls, two rams, and fourteen lambs one year old, all without blemish, ²⁷and their grain offerings and their drink offerings for the bulls, for the rams, and for the lambs, according to their number as prescribed, ²⁸along with one male goat for a purification offering, in addition to the continual burnt offering with its grain offering and its drink offering.

²⁹“‘On the sixth day you must offer eight bulls, two rams, and fourteen lambs one year old, all without blemish, ³⁰and their grain offering and their drink offerings for the bulls, for the rams, and for the lambs, according to their number as prescribed, ³¹along with one male goat for a purification offering, in addition to the continual burnt offering with its grain offering and its drink offering.

³²“‘On the seventh day you must offer seven bulls, two rams, and fourteen lambs one year old, all without blemish, ³³and their grain offerings and their drink offerings for the bulls, for the rams, and for the lambs,

29:6 ᵃNum 28:11–15   ᵇNum 28:3   ᶜNum 15:11–12   29:7 ᵃLev 16:29–34; 23:26–32   ᵇPs 35:13; Isa 58:5   29:11 ᵃLev 16:3, 5
29:12 ᵃLev 23:33–35; Deut 16:13–15; Ezek 45:25   29:13 ᵃEzra 3:4   29:17 ᵃLev 23:36
29:18 ᵃNum 15:12; 28:7, 14; 29:3–4, 9, 10   29:21 ᵃNum 29:18

according to their number as prescribed, [34] along with one male goat for a purification offering, in addition to the continual burnt offering with its grain offering and its drink offering.

[35] "On the eighth day you are to have [a] a holy assembly; you must do no ordinary work on it. [36] But you must offer a burnt offering, an offering made by fire, as a pleasing aroma to the LORD, one bull, one ram, seven lambs one year old, all of them without blemish, [37] and with their grain offerings and their drink offerings for the bull, for the ram, and for the lambs, according to their number as prescribed, [38] along with one male goat for a purification offering, in addition to the continual burnt offering with its grain offering and its drink offering.

[39] "These things you must present to the LORD at your [a] appointed times, in addition to your vows and your freewill offerings, as your burnt offerings, your grain offerings, your drink offerings, and your peace offerings.'" [40] So Moses told the Israelites everything, just as the LORD had commanded him.

Vows Made by Men

30 Moses told [a] the leaders of the tribes concerning the Israelites, "This is what the LORD has commanded: [2a] If a man makes a vow to the LORD or [b] takes an oath of binding obligation on himself,[1] he must not break his word, but must [c] do whatever he has promised.

Vows Made by Single Women

[3] "If a young woman who is still living in her father's house makes a vow to the LORD or places herself under an obligation, [4] and her father hears of her vow or the obligation to which she has pledged herself, and her father remains silent about her, then all her vows will stand,[1] and every obligation to which she has pledged herself will stand. [5] But if her father overrules her when he hears about it, then none of her vows or her obligations that she has pledged for herself will stand. And the LORD will release[1] her from it, because her father overruled her.

Vows Made by Married Women

[6] "And if she marries a husband while under a vow, or she uttered anything impulsively by which she has pledged herself, [7] and her husband hears about it but remains silent about her when he hears about it, then her vows will stand and her obligations that she has pledged for herself will stand. [8] But if when her husband hears it he [a] overrules her, then he will nullify the vow she has taken, and whatever she uttered impulsively that she has pledged for herself. And the LORD will release her from it.

Vows Made by Other Women

[9] "But every vow of a widow or of a divorced woman which she has pledged for herself will remain intact. [10] If she made the vow in her husband's house or put herself under obligation with an oath, [11] and her husband heard about it, but remained silent about her, and did not overrule her, then all her vows will stand, and every obligation which she pledged for herself will stand. [12] But if her husband clearly nullifies them when he hears them, then whatever she says by way of vows or obligations will not stand. Her husband has made them void, and the LORD will release her from them.

[13] "Any vow or sworn obligation that would bring affliction to her, her husband can confirm or nullify. [14] But if her husband remains completely silent about her from day to day, he thus confirms all her vows or all her obligations which she is under; he confirms them because he remained silent about her when he heard them. [15] But if he should nullify them after he has heard them, then he will bear her iniquity."

[16] These are the statutes that the LORD commanded Moses, relating to a man and his wife, and a father and his young daughter who is still living in her father's house.

The Midianite War

31 The LORD spoke to Moses: [2a] "Exact vengeance for the Israelites from the Midianites—after that you will [b] be gathered to your people."

29:35 [a] Lev 23:36   29:39 [a] Lev 23:1–44; 1 Chr 23:31; 2 Chr 31:3; Ezra 3:5; Neh 10:33; Isa 1:14   30:1 [a] Num 1:4, 16; 7:2   30:2 [a] Lev 27:2; Deut 23:21–23; Judg 11:30–31, 35; Eccl 5:4   [b] Lev 5:4; Matt 14:9; Acts 23:14   [c] Job 22:27; Ps 22:25; 50:14; 66:13–14; Nah 1:15   [1] I.e., the person abstains from something that is otherwise permissible, such as fasting or abstaining from marital sex, but it might also involve some goal to be achieved and the abstaining from distractions until the vow is fulfilled.   30:4 [1] I.e., what she vows is established as a genuine oath with the father's approval (or acquiescence).   30:5 [1] Or *forgive.*   30:8 [a] [Gen 3:16]   31:2 [a] Num 25:17   [b] Num 27:12–13

[3]So Moses spoke to the people: "Arm[1] men from among you for the war, to attack the Midianites and to execute the LORD's vengeance on [a]Midian. [4]You must send to the battle 1,000 men from every tribe throughout all the tribes of Israel." [5]So 1,000 from every tribe, 12,000 armed for battle in all, were provided out of the thousands of Israel.

Campaign against the Midianites

[6]So Moses sent [a]them to the war, 1,000 from every tribe, with Phinehas son of Eleazar the priest, who was in charge of the holy articles and the signal trumpets. [7]They fought against [a]the Midianites, as the LORD commanded Moses, and they killed every [b]male. [8]They killed the kings of Midian in addition to those slain—[a]Evi, Rekem, [b]Zur, Hur, and Reba—five Midianite kings. They also killed [c]Balaam son of Beor with the sword. [9]The Israelites took the women of Midian captive along with their little ones, and took all their herds, all their flocks, and all their goods as plunder. [10]They burned all their towns where they lived and all their encampments. [11]They took all [a]the plunder and all the spoils, both people and animals. [12]They brought the captives and the spoils and the plunder to Moses, to Eleazar the priest, and to the Israelite community, to the camp on the rift valley plains of Moab, along the Jordan River across from Jericho.[1] [13]Moses, Eleazar the priest, and all the leaders of the community went out to meet them outside the camp.

The Death of the Midianite Women

[14]But Moses was furious with the officers of the army, the commanders over thousands and commanders over hundreds, who had come from service in the war. [15]Moses said to them, "Have you [a]allowed all the women to live? [16]Look, these [a]people through the [b]counsel of Balaam caused [c]the Israelites to act treacherously against the LORD in the matter of Peor—which resulted in the plague among the community of the LORD! [17]Now therefore [a]kill every boy, and kill every woman who has been intimate with a man in bed. [18]But all the young women who have not experienced a man's bed[1] will be yours.

Purification after Battle

[19]"Any of you who has killed anyone or touched any of the dead, [a]remain outside the camp for seven days; purify yourselves and your captives on the third day, and on the seventh day. [20]You must purify each garment and everything that is made of skin, everything made of goats' hair, and everything made of wood."

[21]Then Eleazar the priest said to the men of war who had gone into the battle, "This is the ordinance of the law that the LORD commanded Moses: [22]'Only the gold, the silver, the bronze, the iron, the tin, and the lead, [23]everything that may stand the fire, you are to pass through the fire, and [a]it will be ceremonially clean, but it must still be purified with the water of purification. Anything that cannot withstand the fire you must pass through the water. [24]You must wash your clothes on the seventh day, [a]and you will be ceremonially clean, and afterward you may enter the camp.'"

The Distribution of Spoils

[25]Then the LORD spoke to Moses: [26]"You and Eleazar the priest, and all the family leaders of the community, take the sum of the plunder that was captured, both people and animals. [27a]Divide the plunder into two parts, one for those who took part in the war—who went out to battle—and the other for all the community.

[28]"You must exact a tribute for the LORD from the fighting men who went out to battle: [a]one life out of 500, from the people, the cattle, and from the donkeys and the sheep. [29]You are to take it from their half share and [a]give it to Eleazar the priest for a raised offering to the LORD. [30]From the Israelites' half share you are to take [a]one portion out of 50 of the people, the cattle, the donkeys, and the sheep—from every kind of animal—and you are to give them to the Levites, [b]who are responsible for the care of the LORD's tabernacle."

31:3 [a]Josh 13:21 [1]Heb. *arm yourselves.* 31:6 [a]Num 10:9 31:7 [a]Deut 20:13; Judg 21:11; 1 Sam 27:9; 1 Kgs 11:15–16 [b]Gen 34:25 31:8 [a]Josh 13:21 [b]Num 25:15 [c]Num 31:16; Josh 13:22 31:11 [a]Deut 20:14 31:12 [1]Heb. *the Jordan of Jericho.* 31:15 [a]Deut 20:14 31:16 [a]Num 25:2 [b]Num 24:14; 2 Pet 2:15; Rev 2:14 [c]Num 25:9 31:17 [a]Deut 7:2; 20:16–18; Judg 21:11 31:18 [1]Heb. *who have not known a man's bed*; a euphemism for sexual relations. 31:19 [a]Num 5:2 31:23 [a]Num 19:9, 17 31:24 [a]Lev 11:25 31:27 [a]Josh 22:8; 1 Sam 30:24 31:28 [a]Num 31:30, 47 31:29 [a]Deut 18:1–5 31:30 [a]Num 31:42–47 [b]Num 3:7–8, 25, 31, 36; 18:3–4

[31] So Moses and Eleazar the priest did as the LORD commanded Moses. [32] The spoil that remained of the plunder that the fighting men had gathered was 675,000 sheep, [33] 72,000 cattle, [34] 61,000 donkeys, [35] and 32,000 young women who had not experienced a man's bed.[1]

[36] The half portion of those who went to war numbered 337,500 sheep; [37] the LORD's tribute from the sheep was 675. [38] The cattle numbered 36,000; the LORD's tribute was 72. [39] The donkeys were 30,500, of which the LORD's tribute was 61. [40] The people were 16,000, of which the LORD's tribute was 32 people.

[41] So Moses gave the tribute, which [a] was the LORD's raised offering, to Eleazar the priest, as the LORD commanded Moses.

[42] From the Israelites' half share that Moses had separated from the fighting men, [43] there were 337,500 sheep from the portion belonging to the community, [44] 36,000 cattle, [45] 30,500 donkeys, [46] and 16,000 people.

[47] From the Israelites' share Moses took one of every 50 people and animals and gave them to the Levites who were responsible for the care of the LORD's tabernacle, just as the LORD commanded Moses.

[48] Then the officers who were over the thousands of the army, the commanders over thousands and the commanders over hundreds, approached Moses [49] and said to him, "Your servants have taken a count of the men who were in the battle, who were under our authority, and not one is missing. [50] So we have brought as an offering for the LORD what each man found: gold ornaments, armlets, bracelets, signet rings, earrings, and necklaces, [a] to make atonement for ourselves before the LORD." [51] Moses and Eleazar the priest took the gold from them, all of it in the form of ornaments. [52] All the gold of the offering they offered up to the LORD from the commanders of thousands and the commanders of hundreds weighed 16,750 shekels. [53] [a] Each soldier had taken plunder for himself. [54] So Moses and Eleazar the priest received the gold from the commanders of thousands and commanders of hundreds and brought it into the tent of meeting [a] as a memorial for the Israelites before the LORD.

The Petition of the Reubenites and Gadites

32 Now the Reubenites and the Gadites possessed a very large number of cattle. When they saw that the lands of [a] Jazer and [b] Gilead were ideal for cattle, [2] the Gadites and the Reubenites came and addressed Moses, Eleazar the priest, and the leaders of the community. They said, [3] "Ataroth, Dibon, Jazer, [a] Nimrah, [b] Heshbon, Elealeh, [c] Sebam,[1] Nebo, and [d] Beon, [4] the land that the LORD subdued before the community of Israel, is ideal for cattle, and your servants have cattle." [5] So they said, "If we have found favor in your sight, let this land be given to your servants for our inheritance. Do not have us cross the Jordan River."

Moses' Response

[6] Moses said to the Gadites and the Reubenites, "Must your brothers go to war while you remain here? [7] Why do you [a] frustrate the intent of the Israelites to cross over into the land that the LORD has given them? [8] Your fathers did the same thing [a] when I sent them from Kadesh Barnea [b] to see the land. [9] When they went up to the Eshcol Valley and saw the land, they frustrated the intent of the Israelites so that they did not enter the land that the LORD had given them. [10] [a] So the anger of the LORD was kindled that day, and he swore, [11] "Because they have not followed me wholeheartedly, not one of the men twenty years old and upward[1] who came [a] from Egypt will see [b] the land that I swore to give to Abraham, Isaac, and Jacob, [12] except Caleb son of Jephunneh the Kenizzite, and Joshua son of Nun, [a] for they followed the LORD wholeheartedly.' [13] So the LORD's anger was kindled against the Israelites, and he made them [a] wander in the wilderness for 40 years, until [b] all that generation that had done wickedly before the LORD was finished. [14] Now look, you are standing in your fathers' place, a brood of

31:35 [1] Heb. *who have not known a man's bed*; a euphemism for sexual relations.   31:41 [a] Num 5:9–10; 18:8, 19
31:50 [a] Exod 30:12–16   31:53 [a] Num 31:32; Deut 20:14   31:54 [a] Exod 30:16   32:1 [a] Num 21:32; Josh 13:25; 2 Sam 24:5
[b] Deut 3:13   32:3 [a] Num 32:36   [b] Josh 13:17, 26   [c] Num 32:38   [d] Num 32:38   [1] LXX, Smr. *Sibmah*.   32:7 [a] Num 13:27—14:4
32:8 [a] Num 13:3, 26   [b] Deut 1:19–25   32:10 [a] Num 14:11; Deut 1:34–36   32:11 [a] Num 14:28–29; 26:63–65; Deut 1:35   [b] Num
14:24, 30   [1] LXX adds *those knowing bad and good.*   32:12 [a] Num 14:6–9, 24, 30; Deut 1:36; Josh 14:8–9
32:13 [a] Num 14:33–35   [b] Num 26:64–65

sinners, to increase still further the [a]fierce wrath of the LORD against the Israelites. [15]For if you [a]turn away from following him, he will once again abandon them in the wilderness, and you will be the reason for their destruction."

The Offer of the Reubenites and Gadites

[16]Then they came very close to him and said, "We will build sheep folds here for our flocks and cities for our families, [17]but [a]we will maintain ourselves in armed readiness and go before the Israelites until whenever we have brought them to their place. Our descendants will be living in fortified towns as a protection against the inhabitants of the land. [18a]We will not return to our homes until every Israelite has his inheritance. [19]For we will not accept any inheritance on the other side of the Jordan River and beyond, [a]because our inheritance has come to us on this eastern side of the Jordan."

[20]Then [a]Moses replied, "If you will do this thing, and if you will arm yourselves for battle before the LORD, [21]and if all your armed men cross the Jordan before the LORD until he drives out his enemies from his presence [22]and [a]the land is subdued before the LORD, then afterward [b]you may return and be free of your obligation to the LORD and to Israel. [c]This land will then be your possession in the LORD's sight.

[23]"But if [a]you do not do this, then look, you will have sinned against the LORD. And know that your sin will find you out. [24]So [a]build cities for your descendants and pens for your sheep, but do what you have said you would do."

[25]So the Gadites and the Reubenites replied to Moses, "Your servants will do as our lord commands. [26]Our children, [a]our wives, our flocks, and all our livestock will be there in the cities of Gilead, [27a]but your servants will cross over, every man armed for war, to do battle in the LORD's presence, just as our lord says."

[28]So Moses gave orders about them to Eleazar the priest, to Joshua son of Nun, and to the heads of the families of the Israelite tribes. [29]Moses said to them: "If the Gadites and the Reubenites cross the Jordan with you, each one equipped for battle in the LORD's presence, and you conquer the land, then you must allot them the territory of Gilead as their possession. [30]But if they do not cross over with you armed, they must receive possessions among you in Canaan." [31]Then the Gadites and the Reubenites answered, "Your servants will do what the LORD has spoken. [32]We will cross armed in the LORD's presence into the land of Canaan, and then the possession of our inheritance that we inherit will be ours on this side of the Jordan River."

Land Assignment

[33]So [a]Moses gave to [b]the Gadites, the Reubenites, and to half the tribe of Manasseh son of Joseph the realm of King Sihon of the Amorites, and the realm of King Og of Bashan, the entire land with its cities and the territory surrounding them. [34]The Gadites rebuilt [a]Dibon, Ataroth, [b]Aroer, [35]Atroth Shophan, [a]Jazer, Jogbehah, [36]Beth [a]Nimrah, and Beth Haran as [b]fortified cities, and constructed pens for their flocks. [37]The Reubenites rebuilt [a]Heshbon, Elealeh, Kiriathaim, [38a]Nebo, Baal [b]Meon (with a change of name), and Sibmah. They renamed [c]the cities they built.

[39]The descendants of [a]Machir son of Manasseh went to Gilead, took it, and dispossessed the Amorites who were in it. [40]So Moses [a]gave Gilead to Machir, son of Manasseh, and he lived there. [41]Now [a]Jair son of Manasseh went and captured their small towns and named them Havvoth [b]Jair. [42]Then Nobah went and captured Kenath and its villages and called it Nobah after his own name.

Wanderings from Egypt to Sinai

33 These are the journeys of the Israelites, who went out of the land of Egypt by their divisions under the [a]authority of Moses and Aaron. [2]Moses recorded their departures according to their journeys, by

32:14 [a] Num 11:1; Deut 1:34   32:15 [a] Deut 30:17–18; Josh 22:16–18; 2 Chr 7:19; 15:2   32:17 [a] Josh 4:12–13   32:18 [a] Josh 22:1–4   32:19 [a] Josh 12:1; 13:8   32:20 [a] Deut 3:18; Josh 1:14   32:22 [a] Deut 3:20; Josh 11:23   [b] Josh 22:4   [c] Deut 3:12, 15, 16, 18; Josh 1:15; 13:8, 32; 22:4, 9   32:23 [a] Gen 4:7; 44:16; Josh 7:1–26; Isa 59:12; [Gal 6:7]   32:24 [a] Num 32:16   32:26 [a] Josh 1:14   32:27 [a] Josh 4:12   32:33 [a] Deut 3:8–17; 29:8; Josh 12:1–6; 13:8–31; 22:4   [b] Num 21:24, 33, 35   32:34 [a] Num 33:45–46   [b] Deut 2:36   32:35 [a] Num 32:1, 3   32:36 [a] Num 32:3   [b] Num 32:24   32:37 [a] Num 21:27   32:38 [a] Isa 46:1   [b] Ezek 25:9   [c] Exod 23:13; Josh 23:7   32:39 [a] Gen 50:23; Num 27:1; 36:1   32:40 [a] Deut 3:12–13, 15; Josh 13:31   32:41 [a] Deut 3:14; Josh 13:30   [b] Judg 10:4; 1 Kgs 4:13   33:1 [a] Ps 77:20

the commandment of the LORD; now these are their journeys according to their departures. [3]They [a]departed from Rameses in [b]the first month, on the fifteenth day of the first month; on the day after the Passover the Israelites went out defiantly[1] in plain sight of all the Egyptians. [4]Now the Egyptians were burying all their firstborn, [a]whom the LORD had killed [b]among them; the LORD also executed judgments on their gods.

[5][a]The Israelites traveled from Rameses and camped in Sukkoth.

[6]They traveled from [a]Sukkoth, and camped in Etham, which is on the edge of the desert. [7]They traveled from Etham, and turned again to Pi Hahiroth, which is before Baal Zephon; and [a]they camped before Migdal. [8]They traveled from Pi Hahiroth, and [a]passed through the middle of the sea into the wilderness, and went three days' journey in the wilderness of Etham, and camped in Marah. [9]They traveled from Marah and [a]came to Elim; in Elim there are twelve fountains of water and seventy palm trees, so they camped there.

[10]They traveled from Elim, and camped by the Red Sea. [11]They traveled from the Red Sea and camped in the [a]wilderness of Sin. [12]They traveled from the wilderness of Sin and camped in Dophkah. [13]And they traveled from Dophkah, and camped in Alush.

[14]They traveled from Alush and camped at [a]Rephidim, where there was no water for the people to drink. [15]They traveled from Rephidim and camped in the [a]desert of Sinai.

Wanderings in the Wilderness

[16]They traveled from the desert of Sinai and camped [a]at Kibroth Hattaavah. [17]They traveled from Kibroth Hattaavah and [a]camped at Hazeroth. [18]They traveled from Hazeroth and camped in [a]Rithmah. [19]They traveled from Rithmah and camped at Rimmon Perez. [20]They traveled from Rimmon Perez and camped in Libnah. [21]They traveled from Libnah and camped at Rissah. [22]They traveled from Rissah and camped in Kehelathah. [23]They traveled from Kehelathah and camped at Mount Shepher. [24]They

traveled from Mount Shepher and camped in Haradah. [25]They traveled from Haradah and camped in Makheloth. [26]They traveled from Makheloth and camped at Tahath. [27]They traveled from Tahath and camped at Terah. [28]They traveled from Terah and camped in Mithcah. [29]They traveled from Mithcah and camped in Hashmonah. [30]They traveled from Hashmonah and [a]camped in Moseroth. [31]They traveled from Moseroth and camped in Bene Jaakan. [32]They traveled from Bene [a]Jaakan and [b]camped at Hor Haggidgad. [33]They traveled from Hor Haggidgad and camped in Jotbathah. [34]They traveled from Jotbathah and camped in Abronah. [35]They traveled from Abronah [a]and camped at Ezion Geber. [36]They traveled from Ezion Geber and camped in the [a]wilderness of Zin, that is, Kadesh.

Wanderings from Kadesh to Moab

[37]They traveled from [a]Kadesh and camped at Mount Hor at the edge of the land of Edom. [38][a]Aaron the priest ascended Mount Hor at the command of the LORD, and he died there in the fortieth year after the Israelites had come out of the land of Egypt on the first day of the fifth month. [39]Now Aaron was 123 years old when he died on Mount Hor. [40]The king of Arad, [a]the Canaanite king who lived in the south of the land of Canaan, heard about the approach of the Israelites.

[41]They traveled from Mount Hor and camped in Zalmonah. [42]They traveled from Zalmonah and camped in Punon. [43]They traveled from Punon and [a]camped in Oboth. [44]They traveled from Oboth and camped in Iye Abarim, on [a]the border of Moab. [45]They traveled from Iim and camped in Dibon Gad. [46]They traveled from Dibon Gad and camped in Almon [a]Diblathaim. [47]They traveled from Almon Diblathaim [a]and camped in the mountains of Abarim before Nebo. [48]They traveled from the mountains of Abarim and [a]camped in the rift valley plains by Moab along the Jordan River across from Jericho. [49]They camped by the Jordan, from Beth Jeshimoth as far as Abel [a]Shittim in the rift valley plains of Moab.

33:3 [a]Exod 12:37 [b]Exod 12:2; 13:4 [1]Heb. *with a high hand*; i.e., arrogant sin and pride; the defiant fist, as it were. 33:4 [a]Exod 12:29 [b][Exod 12:12; 18:11]; Isa 19:1   33:5 [a]Exod 12:37   33:6 [a]Exod 13:20   33:7 [a]Exod 14:1–2, 9   33:8 [a]Exod 14:22; 15:22–23   33:9 [a]Exod 15:27   33:11 [a]Exod 16:1   33:14 [a]Exod 17:1; 19:2   33:15 [a]Exod 16:1; 19:1–2   33:16 [a]Num 11:34   33:17 [a]Num 11:35   33:18 [a]Num 12:16   33:30 [a]Deut 10:6   33:32 [a]Deut 10:6 [b]Deut 10:7   33:35 [a]Deut 2:8; 1 Kgs 9:26; 22:48   33:36 [a]Num 20:1; 27:14   33:37 [a]Num 20:22–23; 21:4   33:38 [a]Num 20:25, 28; Deut 10:6; 32:50   33:40 [a]Num 21:1   33:43 [a]Num 21:10   33:44 [a]Num 21:11   33:46 [a]Jer 48:22; Ezek 6:14   33:47 [a]Num 21:20; Deut 32:49   33:48 [a]Num 22:1; 31:12; 35:1   33:49 [a]Num 25:1; Josh 2:1

At the Border of Canaan

[50] The LORD spoke to Moses in the rift valley plains of Moab along the Jordan, across from Jericho. He said: [51] "Speak to the Israelites and tell them, [a]When you have crossed the Jordan into the land of Canaan, [52] you must drive out all [a] the inhabitants of the land before you. Destroy all their carved images, all their molten images,[1] and demolish their high places. [53] You must dispossess the inhabitants of the land and live in it, for I have given you the land to [a]possess it. [54] You must divide the land by lot for an inheritance among [a] your families. To a larger group you must give a larger inheritance, and to a smaller group you must give a smaller inheritance. Everyone's inheritance must be in the place where his lot falls. You must inherit according to your ancestral tribes. [55] But if you do not drive out the inhabitants of the land before you, then those whom you allow to remain will be [a]irritants in your eyes and thorns in your side, and will cause you trouble in the land where you will be living. [56] And what I intended to do to them I will do to you.'"

The Southern Border of the Land

34 Then the LORD spoke to Moses: [2]"Give [a]these instructions to the Israelites, and tell them: 'When you enter Canaan, the land that has been assigned to you as an inheritance, the land of Canaan with its borders,[3] your southern border[1] will extend from the wilderness of Zin along the Edomite border, and [a]your [b]southern border will run eastward to the extremity of the Salt Sea, [4] and [a] then the border will turn from the south to the Scorpion Ascent, continue to Zin, and then its direction will be from the south to Kadesh [b]Barnea. Then it will go to Hazar [c]Addar and pass over to Azmon. [5] There the border will turn from Azmon [a]to the Stream of Egypt, and then its direction is to the sea.

The Western Border of the Land

[6] "'And for a [a]western border[1] you will have the Great Sea. This will be your western border.

The Northern Border of the Land

[7] "'And this will be your northern border: From the Great Sea you will draw a line to [a]Mount Hor; [8] from Mount Hor you will draw a line [a]to Lebo Hamath, and the direction of the border will be to [b]Zedad. [9] The border will continue to Ziphron, and its direction will be to Hazar [a]Enan. This will be your northern border.

The Eastern Border of the Land

[10] "'For your eastern border you will draw a line from Hazar Enan to Shepham. [11] The border will run down from Shepham [a]to Riblah, on the east side [b]of Ain, and the border will descend and reach the eastern side of the Sea of Kinnereth. [12] Then [a]the border will continue down the Jordan River and its direction will be to the Salt Sea. This will be your land by its borders that surround it.'"

[13] Then Moses commanded the Israelites: "[a]This is the land that you will inherit by lot, which the LORD has commanded to be given to the nine-and-a-half tribes, [14a] because the tribe of the Reubenites by their families, the tribe of the Gadites by their families, and the half-tribe of Manasseh have received their inheritance. [15] The two-and-a-half tribes have received their inheritance on this side of the Jordan, east of Jericho, toward the sunrise."

Appointed Officials

[16] The LORD said to Moses: [17]"These are the names of the men who are to allocate the land to you as an inheritance:[1] [a]Eleazar the priest and Joshua son of Nun. [18] You must take one [a]leader from every tribe to assist in allocating the land as an inheritance.[1] [19] These are the names of the men: from the tribe of Judah, Caleb son of Jephunneh; [20] from the tribe of the Simeonites, Shemuel son of Ammihud; [21] from the tribe of Benjamin, Elidad son of Kislon; [22] and from the tribe of the Danites, a leader, Bukki son of Jogli. [23] From the Josephites, Hanniel son of Ephod, a leader from the tribe of Manasseh; [24] from the tribe of the Ephraimites, a leader,

33:51 [a] Deut 7:1–2; 9:1; Josh 3:17   33:52 [a] Exod 23:24, 33; 34:13; Deut 7:2, 5; 12:3; Judg 2:2; Ps 106:34–36   [1] The Heb. text repeats *you will destroy*.   33:53 [a] Deut 11:31; Josh 21:43   33:54 [a] Num 26:53–56   33:55 [a] Josh 23:13; Judg 2:3   34:2 [a] Gen 17:8; Deut 1:7–8; Ps 78:54–55; 105:11   34:3 [a] Josh 15:1–3; Ezek 47:13, 19   [b] Gen 14:3; Josh 15:2   [1] I.e., the corner or extremity of the Negev, the South.   34:4 [a] Josh 15:3   [b] Num 13:26; 32:8   [c] Josh 15:3–4   34:5 [a] Gen 15:18; Josh 15:4, 47; 1 Kgs 8:65; Isa 27:12   34:6 [a] Exod 23:31; Josh 15:12; Ezek 47:20   [1] Heb. *sea*; the sea is west of Israel.   34:7 [a] Num 33:37   34:8 [a] Num 13:21; Josh 13:5; 2 Kgs 14:25   [b] Ezek 47:15   34:9 [a] Ezek 47:17   34:11 [a] 2 Kgs 23:33; Jer 39:5–6   [b] Deut 3:17; Josh 11:2; 12:3; 13:27; 19:35; Matt 14:34; Luke 5:1   34:12 [a] Num 34:3   34:13 [a] Gen 15:18; Num 26:52–56; Deut 11:24; Josh 14:1–5   34:14 [a] Num 32:33   34:17 [a] Josh 14:1–2; 19:51   [1] Heb. *divide*.   34:18 [a] Num 1:4, 16   [1] Heb. *to divide, apportion*.

Kemuel son of Shiphtan; [25] from the tribe of the Zebulunites, a leader, Elizaphan son of Parnach; [26] from the tribe of the Issacharites, a leader, Paltiel son of Azzan; [27] from the tribe of the Asherites, a leader, Ahihud son of Shelomi; [28] and from the tribe of the Naphtalites, a leader, Pedahel son of Ammihud." [29] These are the ones whom the LORD commanded to divide up the inheritance among the Israelites in the land of Canaan.

The Levitical Cities

35 Then [a] the LORD spoke to Moses in the rift valley plains of Moab along the Jordan near Jericho. He said: [2] "[a] Instruct the Israelites to give the Levites towns to live in from the inheritance the Israelites will possess. You must also give the Levites grazing [b] land around the towns. [3] Thus they will have towns in which to live, and their grazing lands will be for their cattle, for their possessions, and for all their animals. [4] The grazing lands around the towns that you will give to the Levites must extend to a distance of 500 yards[1] from the town wall.

[5] "You must measure from outside the wall of the town on the east 1,000 yards,[1] and on the south side 1,000 yards, and on the west side 1,000 yards, and on the north side 1,000 yards, with the town in the middle. This territory must belong to them as grazing land for the towns. [6] Now from these towns that you will give to the Levites you must select [a] six towns of refuge to which a person who has killed someone may flee. And you must give them 42 other towns. [7] "So the total of the towns you will give the Levites is [a] 48. You must give these together with their grazing lands. [8] The towns you will give must be [a] from the possession of the Israelites. [b] From the larger tribes you must give more; and from the smaller tribes fewer. Each must contribute some of its own towns to the Levites in proportion to the inheritance allocated to each."

The Cities of Refuge

[9] Then the LORD spoke to Moses: [10] "Speak to the Israelites and tell them, [a] When you cross over the Jordan River into the land of Canaan, [11] you must then designate some towns as towns of refuge for [a] you, to which a person who has killed someone unintentionally may flee. [12] And [a] they must stand as your towns of refuge from the avenger in order that the killer may not die until he has stood trial before the community. [13] These towns that you must give shall be your [a] six towns for refuge.

[14] "You must give three towns on this side of the Jordan, and [a] you must give three towns in the land of Canaan; they must be towns of refuge. [15] These six towns will be places of refuge [a] for the Israelites, and for the resident foreigner, and for the settler among them, so that anyone who kills any person accidentally may flee there.

[16] "[a] But if he hits someone with an iron tool so that he dies, he is a murderer. The murderer must surely be put to death. [17] If he strikes him by throwing a stone large enough that he could die, and he dies, he is a murderer. The murderer must surely be put to death. [18] Or if he strikes him with a wooden hand weapon so that he could die, and he dies, he is a murderer. The murderer must surely be put to death. [19] The avenger[1] of blood himself must kill [a] the murderer; when he meets him, he must kill him.

[20] "But [a] if he strikes him out of hatred or throws something at him intentionally so that he dies, [21] or with enmity he strikes him with his hand and he dies, the one who struck him must surely be put to death, for he is a murderer. The avenger of blood must kill the murderer when he meets him.

[22] "But if he strikes him suddenly, [a] without enmity, or throws anything at him unintentionally, [23] or with any stone large enough that a man could die, without seeing him, and throws it at him, and he dies, even though he was not his enemy nor sought his harm, [24] then [a] the community must judge between the slayer and the avenger of blood according to these decisions. [25] The community must deliver [a] the slayer out of the hand of the avenger of blood, and the community must restore him to the town of refuge to

35:1 [a] Num 33:50   **35:2** [a] Josh 14:3–4; 21:2–3; Ezek 45:1; 48:10–20   [b] Lev 25:32–34   **35:4** [1] Heb. *1,000 cubits.*   **35:5** [1] Heb. *2,000 cubits.*   **35:6** [a] Deut 4:41; Josh 20:2, 7, 8; 21:3, 13   **35:7** [a] Josh 21:41   **35:8** [a] Josh 21:3   [b] Num 26:54; 33:54   **35:10** [a] Deut 19:2; Josh 20:1–9   **35:11** [a] Exod 21:13; Num 35:22–25; Deut 19:1–13   **35:12** [a] Deut 19:6; Josh 20:3, 5, 6   **35:13** [a] Num 35:6   **35:14** [a] Deut 4:41; Josh 20:8   **35:15** [a] Num 15:16   **35:16** [a] Exod 21:12, 14; Lev 24:17; Deut 19:11–12   **35:19** [a] Num 35:21, 24, 27; Deut 19:6, 12   [1] I.e., the one who protects the family by seeking vengeance for a crime; the same Heb. word is used for levirate marriages and other related customs.   **35:20** [a] Gen 4:8; 2 Sam 3:27; 20:10; 1 Kgs 2:31–32   **35:22** [a] Exod 21:13   **35:24** [a] Num 35:12; Josh 20:6   **35:25** [a] Josh 20:6

which he fled, and he must live there until the death of the high priest, [b]who was anointed with the consecrated oil. [26]But if the slayer at any time goes outside the boundary of the town to which he had fled, [27]and the avenger of blood finds him outside the borders of the town of refuge, and the avenger of blood kills the slayer, he will not be guilty of blood, [28]because the slayer should have stayed in his town of refuge until the death of the high priest. But after the death of the high priest, the slayer may return to the land of his possessions. [29]So these things must be [a]a statutory ordinance for you throughout your generations, in all the places where you live.

[30]"Whoever kills any person, the murderer must be put to death by the [a]testimony of witnesses, but one witness cannot testify against any person to cause him to be put to death. [31]Moreover, you must not accept a ransom for the life of a murderer who is guilty of death; he must surely be put to death. [32]And you must not accept a ransom for anyone who has fled to a town of refuge, to allow him to return home and live on his own land before the death of the high priest.

[33]"You must not pollute the land where you live, for blood [a]defiles the land, and the land cannot be cleansed of the blood that is shed there, except [b]by the blood of the person who shed it. [34]Therefore [a]do not [b]defile the land that you will inhabit, in which I live, for I the LORD live among the Israelites.'"

Women and Land Inheritance

36 Then the heads of the family groups of the [a]Gileadites, the descendant of Machir, the descendant of Manasseh, who were from the Josephite families, approached and [b]spoke before Moses and the leaders who were the heads of the Israelite families. [2]They said, "[a]The LORD commanded [b]my lord to give the land as an inheritance by lot to the Israelites; and my lord was commanded by the LORD to give the inheritance of our brother Zelophehad to his daughters. [3]Now if they should be married to one of the men from another Israelite tribe, their inheritance would be [a]taken from the inheritance of our fathers and added to the inheritance of the tribe into which they marry. As a result, it will be taken from the lot of our inheritance. [4]And when [a]the Jubilee of the Israelites is to take place, their inheritance will be added to the inheritance of the tribe into which they marry. So their inheritance will be taken away from the inheritance of our ancestral tribe."

Moses' Decision

[5]Then Moses gave [a]a ruling to the Israelites by the word of the LORD: "What the tribe of the Josephites is saying is right. [6]This is what the LORD has commanded for Zelophehad's daughters: 'Let them marry whomever they think best, only they must marry within the family of their father's tribe. [7]In this way the inheritance of the Israelites will not be transferred from tribe to tribe. But every one of the Israelites must [a]retain the ancestral heritage. [8]And [a]every daughter who possesses an inheritance from any of the tribes of the Israelites must become the wife of a man from any family in her father's tribe, so that every Israelite may retain the inheritance of his fathers. [9]No inheritance may pass from tribe to tribe. But every one of the tribes of the Israelites must retain its inheritance.'"

[10]As the LORD had commanded Moses, so the daughters of Zelophehad did. [11a]For the daughters of Zelophehad—Mahlah, Tirzah, Hoglah, Milcah, and Noah—were married to the sons of their uncles. [12]They were married into the families of the Manassehites, the descendants of Joseph, and their inheritance remained in the tribe of their father's family.

[13]These are the commandments and the decisions that the LORD commanded the Israelites through the authority of Moses, [a]in the rift valley plains by Moab along the Jordan River opposite Jericho.

35:25 [b]Exod 29:7; Lev 4:3; 21:10   35:29 [a]Num 27:11   35:30 [a]Deut 17:6; 19:15; Matt 18:16; John 7:51; 8:17–18; 2 Cor 13:1; Heb 10:28   35:33 [a]Deut 21:7–8; Ps 106:38   [b]Gen 9:6   35:34 [a]Lev 18:24–25; Deut 21:23   [b]Exod 29:45–46   36:1 [a]Num 26:29   [b]Num 27:1–11   36:2 [a]Num 26:55; 33:54; Josh 17:4   [b]Num 27:1, 5–7   36:3 [a]Num 27:4   36:4 [a]Lev 25:10   36:5 [a]Num 27:7   36:7 [a]1 Kgs 21:3   36:8 [a]1 Chr 23:22   36:11 [a]Num 26:33; 27:1   36:13 [a]Num 26:3; 33:50

DEUTERONOMY

Deuteronomy, Moses' upper-desert discourse, consists of a series of farewell messages by Israel's 120-year-old leader. He addresses these talks to the new generation destined to possess the land of promise—those who have survived the forty years of wilderness wandering. Like Leviticus, Deuteronomy contains a vast amount of legal detail, but its emphasis is on the laymen rather than the priests. Moses reminds the new generation of Israelites of the importance of obedience if they are to learn from the sad example of their parents. The Hebrew title of Deuteronomy is *Haddebharim,* "The Words," taken from the opening phrase in 1:1, "This is what Moses said." The parting words of Moses to the new generation are given in oral and written form so that they will endure to all generations. Deuteronomy has been called "five-fifths of the law" since it completes the five books of Moses. The Jewish people have also called it *Mishneh Hattorah,* "Repetition of the Law," which is translated in the Septuagint as *To Deuteronomion Touto,* "This Second Law." Deuteronomy, however, is not a second law but an adaptation and expansion of much of the original law given on Mount Sinai. The English title comes from the Greek title *Deuteronomion,* "Second Law." Deuteronomy has also been appropriately called the Book of Remembrance.

The Covenant Setting

1 This is what Moses said to all of Israel in the Transjordanian[1] wilderness, the arid rift valley opposite Suph, between Paran and Tophel, Laban, Hazeroth, and Di Zahab. [2] Now it is ordinarily an eleven-day journey from Horeb [a] to Kadesh Barnea by way of Mount Seir. [3] However, it was not until the first day of the eleventh month of the fortieth year that Moses addressed the Israelites just as the LORD had [a] instructed him to do. [4] This took place [a] after the defeat of [b] King Sihon of the Amorites, whose capital was in Heshbon, and King Og of Bashan, whose capital was in Ashtaroth, specifically in Edrei. [5] So it was in the Transjordan, in Moab, that Moses began to deliver these words:[1]

Events at Horeb

[6] The LORD our God spoke to us at Horeb and said, "You have stayed [a] in the area of this mountain long [b] enough. [7] Head out and resume your journey. Enter the Amorite hill country, and all its neighboring areas, including the rift valley, the hill country, the foothills,[1] the Negev, and the coastal plain—all of Canaan and Lebanon as far as the Great River, that is, the Euphrates. [8] Look! I have already given the land to you. Go, occupy the territory that I, the LORD, promised to give to your ancestors [a] Abraham, Isaac, and Jacob, and to their descendants." [9] I also [a] said to you at that time, "I am no longer able to sustain you by myself. [10] The LORD your God has increased your population to the point that you are now as numerous as the very stars of the sky. [11] Indeed, [a] may the LORD, the God of your ancestors, make you [b] a thousand times more numerous than you are now, blessing you just as he said he would! [12] But [a] how can I alone bear up under the burden of your hardship and strife? [13] Select wise and

1:1[1] Heb. *on the other side of the Jordan;* a name appropriate from any geographical vantage point.   1:2[a] Num 13:26; 32:8; Deut 9:23   1:3[a] Num 33:38   1:4[a] Num 21:23–24, 33–35; Deut 2:26–35; Josh 13:10; Neh 9:22   [b] Josh 13:12   1:5[1] Heb. *this instruction;* i.e., the Book of Deuteronomy, not the Pentateuch as a whole.   1:6[a] Exod 3:1, 12   [b] Exod 19:1–2   1:7[1] Or *western foothills, Judean foothills, lowland, Shephelah;* the region between the Mediterranean coastal plain and the hill country.   1:8[a] Gen 12:7; 15:5; 22:17; 26:3; 28:13; Exod 33:1; Num 14:23; 32:11   1:9[a] Exod 18:18, 24; Num 11:14, 24   1:11[a] 2 Sam 24:3   [b] Gen 15:5   1:12[a] 1 Kgs 3:8–9

practical men, those known among your tribes, whom I may appoint as your leaders." [14]You replied to me that what I had said to you was good. [15]So I chose[1] as your tribal leaders wise and well-known men, placing [a]them over you as administrators of groups of thousands, hundreds, fifties, and tens, and also as other tribal officials. [16]I furthermore admonished your judges at that time that they should pay attention to issues among your fellow citizens[1] and [a]judge fairly, whether between one person and a [b]native Israelite[2] or a resident foreigner. [17][a]They must not discriminate in judgment, but hear [b]the lowly and the great alike. Nor should they be intimidated by human beings, for judgment belongs to God. If the matter being adjudicated is too difficult for them, they should [c]bring it before me for a hearing.

Instructions at Kadesh Barnea

[18]So I instructed you at that time regarding everything you should do. [19]Then we left Horeb [a]and passed through all that immense, forbidding wilderness that you saw on the way to the Amorite hill country as the LORD our God had commanded us to do, finally arriving at Kadesh Barnea. [20]Then I said to you, "You have come to the Amorite hill country, which the LORD our God is about to give us. [21]Look, he[1] has placed the land in front of you! Go up, take possession of it, just as the LORD, the God of your ancestors, said to [a]do. Do not be afraid or discouraged!" [22]So all of you approached me and said, "Let's send some men ahead of us to scout out the land and bring us back word as to how we should attack it and what the cities are like there." [23]I thought [a]this was a good idea, so I sent twelve men from among you, one from each tribe. [24]They left [a]and went up to the hill country, coming to the Eshcol Valley,[1] which they scouted out. [25]Then they took some of the produce of the land and carried it back down to us. They also brought a report to us, saying,

"The land that the LORD our God is about to give us is [a]good."

Disobedience at Kadesh Barnea

[26]You were not willing to go up, however, but instead rebelled against [a]the LORD your God. [27]You [a]complained among yourselves privately and said, "Because the LORD [b]hates us he brought us from Egypt to deliver us over to the Amorites so they could destroy us! [28]What is going to happen to us? Our [a]brothers have drained away our courage by describing people who are more numerous and taller than we are, and great cities whose defenses appear to be as high as heaven itself! Moreover, they said they saw [b]Anakites there." [29]So I responded to you, "Do not be terrified of them! [30]The LORD your God is about to go ahead of you; [a]he will fight for you, just as you saw him do in Egypt [31]and in the wilderness, where you saw him carrying you along like a [a]man carries his son. This he did everywhere you went until you came to this very place." [32]However, through all this [a]you did not have confidence in the LORD your God, [33][a]who would go before you on the way [b]to find places for you to camp, appearing in a fire at night and in a cloud by day to show you the way you ought to go.

Judgment at Kadesh Barnea

[34]When the LORD heard you, he became angry [a]and made this vow: [35]"[a]Not a single person of this evil generation will see the good land that I promised to give to your ancestors! [36]The [a]exception is Caleb son of Jephunneh; [b]he will see it and I will give him and his descendants the territory on which he has walked, because he has wholeheartedly followed me." [37]As for me, [a]the LORD was also angry with me on your account. He said, "You also will not be able to go there. [38]However, [a]Joshua son of Nun, your assistant, will go. [b]Encourage him, because he will enable Israel to inherit the land. [39][a]Also, [b]your infants, who you thought would die

1:15 [a]Exod 18:25 [1]Or *selected*; Heb. *took*.   1:16 [a]Deut 16:18; John 7:24 [b]Lev 24:22 [1]Heb. *brothers*. [2]Heb. *between a man and his brother*.   1:17 [a]Lev 19:15; Deut 10:17; 16:19; 24:17; 1 Sam 16:7; Prov 24:23–26; Acts 10:34; Jas 2:1, 9 [b]2 Chr 19:6 [c]Exod 18:22, 26   1:19 [a]Num 10:12; Deut 2:7; 8:15; 32:10; Jer 2:6   1:21 [a]Josh 1:6, 9 [1]Heb. *the LORD your God*.   1:23 [a]Num 13:2–3   1:24 [a]Num 13:21–25 [1]Or *the Wadi Eshcol*.   1:25 [a]Num 13:27   1:26 [a]Num 14:1–4; Ps 106:24   1:27 [a]Ps 106:25 [b]Deut 9:28   1:28 [a]Num 13:28, 31–33; Deut 9:1–2 [b]Num 13:28   1:30 [a]Exod 14:14; Deut 3:22; 20:4; Neh 4:20   1:31[a]Deut 32:10–12; Isa 46:3–4; 63:9; Hos 11:3   1:32 [a]Num 14:11; 20:12; Ps 106:24; Heb 3:9–10, 16–19; 4:1–2; Jude 5   1:33 [a]Exod 13:21; Num 9:15–23; Neh 9:12; Ps 78:14 [b]Num 10:33; Ezek 20:6   1:34 [a]Deut 2:14–15   1:35 [a]Num 14:22–23; Ps 95:10–11   1:36 [a]Num 14:24; [Josh 14:9] [b]Num 32:11–12   1:37 [a]Num 20:12; 27:14; Deut 3:26; 4:21; 34:4; Ps 106:32   1:38 [a]Num 14:30 [b]Num 27:18–19; Deut 31:7, 23; Josh 11:23   1:39 [a]Num 14:31 [b]Num 14:3

on the way, and your children, who as yet do not know good from bad, will go there; I will give them the land and they will possess it. 40aBut as for you, turn back and head for the wilderness by the way to the Red Sea."1

Unsuccessful Conquest of Canaan

41Then you responded to me and admitted, "aWe have sinned against the LORD. We will now go up and fight as the LORD our God has told us to do." So you each put on your battle gear and prepared to go up to the hill country. 42But the LORD told me: "Tell them this: 'aDo not go up and fight, because I will not be with you and you will be defeated by your enemies.'" 43I spoke to you, but you did not listen. Instead you arebelled against the LORD and brecklessly went up to the hill country. 44The Amorite inhabitants of that area confronted you and achased you like a swarm of bees, striking you down from Seir as far as Hormah. 45Then you came back and wept before the LORD, but he paid no attention to you whatsoever. 46aTherefore, you remained at Kadesh for a long time—indeed, for the full time.

The Journey from Kadesh Barnea to Moab

2 Then we turned and set aout toward the wilderness on the way to the Red Sea1 just bas the LORD told me to do, detouring around Mount Seir for a long time. 2At this point the LORD said to me, 3"You have circled around this mountain along enough; now turn north. 4Instruct these people as follows: 'aYou are about to cross the border of byour relatives1 the descendants of Esau, who inhabit Seir. They will be afraid of you, so watch yourselves carefully. 5Do not abe hostile toward them, because I am not giving you any of their land, not even a footprint, for I have given Mount Seir as an inheritance for Esau. 6You may purchase food to eat and water to drink from them. 7All along athe way I, the LORD your God, have blessed your every effort. I have been attentive to your travels through this great

wilderness. These 40 years I have been with you; you have lacked nothing.'"

8So we turned away from our relatives the descendants of Esau, the inhabitants of Seir, turning from the route of the rift valley which comes up from aElat and Ezion Geber, and btraveling the way of the wilderness of Moab. 9Then the LORD said to me, "Do not harass Moab and provoke them to war, for I will not give you any of their land as your territory. This is because I have given aAr to bthe descendants of Lot as their possession. 10(The Emites used to live athere, a people as powerful, numerous, and tall as bthe Anakites. 11These people, as well as the Anakites, are also considered Rephaites; the Moabites call them Emites. 12Previously athe Horites lived in Seir, but the descendants of Esau dispossessed and destroyed them and settled in their place, just as Israel did to the land it came to possess, the land the LORD gave them.) 13Now, get up and cross athe Wadi Zered." So we did so. 14Now the length of time it took for us to go afrom Kadesh Barnea to the crossing of Wadi Zered was thirty-eight years, time for all the military men of that generation to die, bjust as the LORD had vowed to them. 15Indeed, it was the very hand of the LORD that eliminated them from within1 the camp until they were all gone.

Instructions Concerning Ammon

16So it was that after all the military men had been eliminated from the community, 17the LORD said to me, 18"Today you are going to cross the border of Moab, that is, of Ar. 19But when you come close to athe Ammonites, do not harass or provoke them because I am not giving you any of the Ammonites' land as your possession; I have already given it to Lot's descendants as their possession."

20(That also is considered to be a land of the Rephaites. The Rephaites lived there originally; the Ammonites call them aZamzummites. 21They aare a people as powerful, numerous, and tall as the Anakites. But the LORD destroyed the Rephaites in advance of

1:40 a Num 14:25   1Heb. the Reed Sea; Trad. "Red" based on the LXX.   1:41 a Num 14:40   1:42 a Num 14:41–43
1:43 a Num 14:44   b Deut 17:12–13   1:44 a Num 14:45; Ps 118:12   1:46 a Num 13:25; 20:1, 22; Deut 2:7, 14   2:1 a Deut
1:40   b Num 14:25   1Heb. the Reed Sea; Trad. "Red" based on the LXX.   2:3 a Deut 2:7, 14   2:4 a Num 20:14–21   b Deut
23:7   1Heb. brothers.   2:5 a Gen 36:8; Josh 24:4   2:7 a Deut 8:2–4; [Matt 6:8, 32]   2:8 a Judg 11:18; 1 Kgs 9:26   b Num 21:4
2:9 a Num 21:15, 28; Deut 2:18, 29   b Gen 19:36–38   2:10 a Gen 14:5   b Num 13:22, 33; Deut 9:2   2:12 a Gen 14:6; 36:20; Deut
2:22   2:13 a Num 21:12   2:14 a Num 13:26   b Num 14:35; Ezek 20:15   2:15 1Heb. from the middle of.
2:19 a Gen 19:38; Num 21:24   2:20 a Gen 14:5   2:21 a Deut 2:10

the Ammonites, so they dispossessed them and settled down in their place. [22] This is exactly what he did for the descendants of Esau [a] who lived in Seir when [b] he destroyed the Horites before them so that they could dispossess them and settle in their area to this very day. [23] As for [a] the Avvites who lived in settlements as far west as Gaza, Caphtorites who came from Crete[1] destroyed [b] them and settled down in their place.)

[24] "Get up, make your way [a] across Wadi Arnon. Look, I have already delivered over to you [b] Sihon the Amorite, king of Heshbon, and his land. Go ahead—take it! Engage him in war! [25] This very day [a] I will begin to fill all the people of the earth with dread and to terrify them when they hear about you. They will [b] shiver and shake in anticipation of your approach."

Defeat of Sihon, King of Heshbon

[26] Then I [a] sent messengers from the Kedemoth wilderness to King Sihon of Heshbon [b] with an offer of peace: [27] "[a] Let us pass through your land; we will keep strictly to the roadway. We will not turn aside to the right or the left. [28] Sell us food for cash so that we can eat and sell us water to drink. Just allow us to go through [a] on foot, [29] just as the descendants of Esau who live at Seir and the Moabites who live in Ar did for us, until we cross the Jordan to the land the LORD our God is giving [a] us." [30] [a] But King Sihon of Heshbon was unwilling to allow us to pass near him because [b] the LORD our[1] God had made him [c] obstinate and stubborn so that he might deliver him over to you this very day. [31] The LORD said to me, "Look! I have already begun to [a] give over Sihon and his land to you. Start right now to take his land as your possession." [32] [a] When Sihon and all his troops emerged to encounter us in battle at Jahaz, [33] the LORD our God delivered him over to us and [a] we struck him down, along with his sons and everyone else. [34] At that time we seized all his cities and put every one of them under divine judgment,

including even the women and children; we left no survivors. [35] We kept only the livestock and plunder from the cities for ourselves. [36] [a] From Aroer, which is at [b] the edge of Wadi Arnon (it is [c] the city in the wadi), all the way to Gilead there was not a town able to resist us—the LORD our God gave them all to us. [37] However, you did not approach the land of the Ammonites, the Wadi [a] Jabbok, the cities of the hill country, or any place else forbidden by the LORD our God.

Defeat of Og, King of Bashan

3 Next we set out on the route to Bashan, but King [a] Og of Bashan and his whole army came out to meet us in [b] battle at Edrei. [2] The LORD, however, said to me, "Don't be afraid of him because I have already given him, his whole army, and his land to you. You will do to him exactly what you did to King [a] Sihon of the Amorites who lived in Heshbon." [3] So the LORD our God did indeed give over to us King Og of Bashan and his whole army, and we struck them down until not a single survivor was left. [4] We captured [a] all his cities at that time—there was not a town we did not take from them—sixty cities, all the region of Argob, the dominion of Og in Bashan. [5] All of these cities were fortified by high walls, gates, and locking bars; in addition there were a great many open villages. [6] We put all [a] of these under divine judgment just as we had done to King Sihon of Heshbon—every occupied city, including women and children. [7] But all the livestock and plunder from the cities we kept for ourselves. [8] So at that time we took the [a] land of the two Amorite kings in the Transjordan from Wadi Arnon to Mount [b] Hermon [9] (the Sidonians call [a] Hermon Sirion and the Amorites call it Senir), [10] all the cities of the plateau, [a] all of Gilead and Bashan as far as Salecah and Edrei, cities of the kingdom of Og in Bashan. [11] [a] Only King Og of Bashan was left of [b] the remaining Rephaites. (It is noteworthy that his sarcophagus[1] was made of iron. Does it not, indeed, still remain in

2:22 [a] Gen 36:8; Deut 2:5 [b] Gen 14:6; 36:20–30   2:23 [a] Josh 13:3 [b] Gen 10:14; 1 Chr 1:12; Jer 47:4; Amos 9:7 [1] Heb. *Caphtor.*
2:24 [a] Num 21:13–14; Judg 11:18 [b] Deut 1:4   2:25 [a] Exod 23:27; Deut 11:25; Josh 2:9 [b] Exod 15:14–16   2:26 [a] Num 21:21–32;
Deut 1:4; Judg 11:19–21 [b] Deut 20:10   2:27 [a] Num 21:21–22; Judg 11:19   2:28 [a] Num 20:19   2:29 [a] Num 20:18; Deut 23:3–4;
Judg 11:17   2:30 [a] Num 21:23 [b] Josh 11:20 [c] Exod 4:21 [1] MT *your.*   2:31 [a] Deut 1:3, 8   2:32 [a] Num 21:23   2:33 [a] Num 21:24
2:36 [a] Deut 3:12; 4:48; Josh 13:9 [b] Josh 13:9, 16 [c] Ps 44:3   2:37 [a] Gen 32:22; Num 21:24; Deut 3:16   3:1 [a] Num 21:33–35;
Deut 29:7 [b] Deut 1:4   3:2 [a] Num 21:34; Josh 13:21   3:4 [a] Deut 3:13–14   3:6 [a] Deut 2:24, 34, 35   3:8 [a] Num 32:33; Josh 12:6;
13:8–12 [b] Deut 4:48; 1 Chr 5:23   3:9 [a] 1 Chr 5:23   3:10 [a] Deut 4:49   3:11 [a] Amos 2:9 [b] Gen 14:5; Deut 2:11, 20 [1] Trad. *bed*;
likely a basaltic (volcanic) stone sarcophagus of suitable size to contain the coffin of the giant Rephaite king. Its
iron-like color and texture caused it to be described as an iron container.

ᶜRabbath of the Ammonites? It is 13½ feet[2] long and 6 feet[3] wide according to standard measure.)[4]

Distribution of the Transjordanian Allotments

[12]This is the ᵃland we brought under our control at that time: The territory extending ᵇfrom Aroer by the Wadi Arnon and half the Gilead hill country with ᶜits cities I gave to the Reubenites and Gadites. [13]The rest of Gilead and all of Bashan, ᵃthe kingdom of Og, I gave to half the tribe of Manasseh. (All the region of Argob, that is, all Bashan, is called the land of Rephaim. [14]ᵃJair, son of Manasseh, took all the Argob region as far as the border with the Geshurites and Maacathites—namely Bashan—and ᵇcalled it by his name, Havvoth Jair, which it retains to this very day.) [15]I gave ᵃGilead to Machir. [16]To the Reubenites ᵃand Gadites I allocated ᵇthe territory extending from Gilead as far as Wadi Arnon (the exact middle of the wadi was a boundary) all the way to the Wadi Jabbok, the Ammonite border. [17]The rift valley and the Jordan River were also ᵃa border, from ᵇthe Sea of Kinnereth to the sea of the rift valley (that is, the Salt Sea), beneath the slopes of Pisgah to the east.

Instructions to the Transjordanian Tribes

[18]At that time I instructed you as follows: "The LORD your God has given you this land for your possession. You warriors are to cross over equipped for battle before your fellow Israelites. [19]But your wives, children, and livestock (of which I know you have many) may remain in the cities I have given you. [20]You must fight until the LORD ᵃgives your countrymen victory as he did you and they take possession of the land that the LORD your God is giving them on the other side of the Jordan River. Then each of you may ᵇreturn to his own territory that I have given you." [21]I also commanded Joshua at the same ᵃtime, "You have seen everything the LORD your God did to these two kings; he will do the same to all the kingdoms where you are going. [22]Do not be afraid of ᵃthem, for the LORD your God will personally fight for you."

Denial to Moses of the Promised Land

[23]Moreover, at that ᵃtime I pleaded with the LORD, [24]"O, Sovereign LORD, ᵃyou have begun to show me your greatness and strength. (ᵇWhat god in heaven or earth can rival your works and mighty deeds?) [25]Let me please cross over to see ᵃthe good land on the other side of the Jordan River—this good hill country and the Lebanon!" [26]But the LORD ᵃwas angry at me because of you and would not listen to me. Instead, he said to me, "Enough of that! Do not speak to me anymore about this matter. [27]Go up to the top of Pisgah and take a ᵃgood look to the west, north, south, and east, for you will not be allowed to cross the Jordan. [28]Commission Joshua, ᵃand encourage and strengthen him, because he will lead these people over and will enable them to inherit the land you will see." [29]So we settled down in ᵃthe valley opposite Beth Peor.

The Privileges of the Covenant

4 Now, Israel, pay attention to ᵃthe statutes and ordinances[1] I am about to teach you, so that you might live and go on to enter and take possession of the land that the LORD, the God of your ancestors, is giving you. [2]Do not add a thing to what I command ᵃyou nor subtract from it, so that you may keep the commandments of the LORD your God that I am delivering to you. [3]You have witnessed what the LORD did at Baal ᵃPeor,[1] how he eradicated from your midst everyone who followed Baal Peor. [4]But you who remained faithful to the LORD your God are still alive to this very day, every one of you. [5]Look! I have taught you statutes and ordinances just as the LORD my God told me to do, so that you might carry them out in the land you are about to enter and

3:11ᶜ2 Sam 12:26; Jer 49:2; Ezek 21:20 [2]Heb. 9 cubits. [3]Heb. 4 cubits. [4]Heb. by the cubit of man. 3:12ᵃNum 32:33; Josh 12:6; 13:8–12 ᵇDeut 2:36; Josh 12:2 ᶜNum 34:14 3:13ᵃJosh 13:29–31; 17:1 3:14ᵃ1 Chr 2:22 ᵇNum 32:41 3:15ᵃNum 32:39–40 3:16ᵃ2 Sam 24:5 ᵇNum 21:24; Deut 2:37; Josh 12:2 3:17ᵃNum 34:11–12; Deut 4:49; Josh 12:3 ᵇGen 14:3; Josh 3:16 3:20ᵃDeut 12:9–10 ᵇJosh 22:4 3:21ᵃ[Num 27:22–23]; Josh 11:23 3:22ᵃExod 14:14; Deut 1:30; 20:4; Neh 4:20 3:23ᵃ[2 Cor 12:8–9] 3:24ᵃDeut 5:24; 11:2 ᵇExod 8:10; 15:11; 2 Sam 7:22; Ps 71:19; 86:8 3:25ᵃExod 3:8; Deut 4:22 3:26ᵃNum 20:12; 27:14; Deut 1:37; 31:2; 32:51–52; 34:4 3:27ᵃNum 23:14; 27:12 3:28ᵃNum 27:18, 23; Deut 31:3, 7, 8, 23 3:29ᵃDeut 4:46; 34:6 4:1ᵃLev 19:37; 20:8; 22:31; Deut 5:1; 8:1; Ezek 20:11; [Rom 10:5] [1]These technical Heb. terms occur repeatedly throughout Deuteronomy to describe the covenant stipulations to which Israel had been called to subscribe. They are virtually synonymous and are used interchangeably. 4:2ᵃDeut 12:32; [Josh 1:7]; Prov 30:6; [Rev 22:18–19] 4:3ᵃNum 25:1–9; Josh 22:17; Ps 106:28 [1]LXX, Syr. to Baal Peor.

possess. [6]So be sure to do them, because this will testify of [a]your wise understanding to the people who will learn of all these statutes and say, "Indeed, this great nation is a very wise people." [7]In fact, [a]what other great nation has a [b]god so near to them like the LORD our God whenever we call on him? [8]And what other great nation has statutes and ordinances as just as this whole law that I am about to share with you today?

Reminder of the Horeb Covenant

[9]Again, however, [a]pay very careful attention, lest you [b]forget the things you have seen and disregard them for the rest of your life; instead [c]teach them to your children and grandchildren. [10]You stood before [a]the LORD your God at Horeb and he said to me, "Assemble the people before me so that I can tell them my commands. Then they will learn to revere me all the days they live in the land, and they will instruct their children." [11]You approached and stood at the foot of the mountain, a mountain ablaze to the sky above it and yet dark with a thick cloud. [12]Then the LORD spoke to you from the middle of the fire; you heard speech but you could not see anything—only [a]a voice was heard. [13a]And [b]he revealed to you [c]the covenant he has commanded you to keep, the Ten Commandments,[1] writing them on two stone tablets. [14]Moreover, at that same time [a]the LORD commanded me to teach you statutes and ordinances for you to keep in the land that you are about to enter and possess.

The Nature of Israel's God

[15a]Be very careful, then, because you saw no [b]form at the time the LORD spoke to you at Horeb from the middle of the fire. [16a]I say this so you will not corrupt yourselves by [b]making an image in [c]the form of any kind of figure. This includes the likeness of a human male or female, [17]any kind of land animal, any bird that flies in the sky, [18]anything that crawls on the ground, or any fish in the deep waters under the earth. [19]When you look [a]up to the sky and see the sun, moon, and stars—[b]the whole heavenly creation—you must not be seduced to [c]worship and serve them, for the LORD your God has assigned them to all the people of the world. [20]You, however, the LORD has selected and [a]brought from Egypt, that iron-smelting furnace, to be [b]his special people as you are today. [21]But [a]the LORD became angry [b]with me because of you and vowed that I would never cross the Jordan nor enter the good land that he is about to give you. [22]So [a]I must [b]die here in this land; I will not cross the Jordan. But you are going over and will possess [c]that good land. [23]Be on guard so that you do not forget the covenant of the LORD your God that he has made with you, [a]and that you do not make an image of any kind, just as he has forbidden you. [24]For [a]the LORD your God is [b]a consuming fire; he is a jealous God.

Threat and Blessing following Covenant Disobedience

[25]After you have produced children and grandchildren and have been in the land a long time, if you become corrupt and make an image of any kind and [a]do other evil things before the LORD your God that enrage him, [26]I [a]invoke heaven and earth as witnesses against you today that you will surely and swiftly be removed from the very land you are about to cross the Jordan to possess. You will not last long there because you will surely be annihilated. [27]Then the LORD [a]will scatter you among the peoples and there will be very few of you among the nations where the LORD will drive you. [28]There you will worship gods made by human hands—wood and stone that can neither see, hear, eat, nor smell. [29a]But if you seek the LORD your God from there, you will find him, if, indeed, you seek him with all your heart and soul. [30]In your distress when all these things happen to you in [a]future days, if you [b]return to the LORD your God and obey him [31](for he is a merciful God), he will not let you down or [a]destroy you, for

4:6 [a] Deut 30:19–20; 32:46–47; Job 28:28; Ps 19:7; 111:10; Prov 1:7; [2 Tim 3:15]   4:7 [a] [Deut 4:32–34; 2 Sam 7:23]   [b] [Ps 46:1; Isa 55:6]   4:9 [a] Prov 4:23   [b] Deut 29:2–8   [c] Gen 18:19; Deut 4:10; 6:7, 20–25; Ps 78:5–6; Prov 22:6; Eph 6:4   4:10 [a] Exod 19:9, 16, 17   4:12 [a] Deut 5:4, 22   4:13 [a] Deut 9:9, 11   [b] Exod 34:28; Deut 10:4   [c] Exod 24:12   [1] Heb. the ten words.   4:14 [a] Exod 21:1   4:15 [a] Josh 23:11   [b] Isa 40:18   4:16 [a] Exod 32:7; Deut 9:12; 31:29   [b] Exod 20:4–5   [c] Rom 1:23   4:19 [a] Deut 17:3; Job 31:26–28   [b] 2 Kgs 21:3   [c] [Rom 1:25]   4:20 [a] 1 Kgs 8:51; Jer 11:4   [b] Deut 7:6; 27:9; [Titus 2:14]   4:21 [a] Num 20:12; Deut 1:37; 3:26   [b] Num 27:13–14   4:22 [a] 2 Pet 1:13–15   [b] Deut 3:27   [c] Deut 3:25   4:23 [a] Exod 20:4–5; Deut 4:16   4:24 [a] Exod 24:17; Deut 9:3; Isa 33:14; Heb 12:29   [b] Exod 20:5; 34:14   4:25 [a] 2 Kgs 17:17   4:26 [a] Deut 30:18–19; 2 Chr 36:14–20; Isa 1:2; Mic 6:2   4:27 [a] Lev 26:33; Deut 28:62; Neh 1:8   4:29 [a] [Lev 26:39–45; Deut 30:1–3; 2 Chr 15:4; Neh 1:9]   4:30 [a] Gen 49:1; Deut 31:29; Jer 23:20; Hos 3:5   [b] Joel 2:12; Heb 1:2   4:31 [a] Lev 26:44; Jer 30:11

he cannot forget the covenant with your ancestors that he confirmed by oath to them.

The Uniqueness of Israel's God

[32]Indeed, [a]ask about the distant past, starting [b]from the day God created humankind[1] on the earth, and ask from one end of heaven to the other, whether there has ever been such a great thing as this, or even a rumor of it. [33a]Have a people ever heard the voice of God speaking from the middle of fire, as you yourselves have, and lived to tell about it? [34]Or has God ever before tried to deliver a nation from the middle of another nation, accompanied [a]by judgments, signs, wonders, war, strength, power, [b]and other very terrifying things like the Lord your God did for you in Egypt before your very eyes? [35]You have been taught that [a]the Lord alone is God—there is no other besides him. [36a]From heaven he spoke to you in order to teach you, and on earth he showed you his great fire from which you also heard his words. [37]Moreover, because [a]he loved[1] your ancestors, [b]he chose their[2] descendants who followed them and personally brought you out of Egypt with his great power [38a]to dispossess nations greater and stronger than you and brought you here this day to give you their land as your property. [39]Today realize and carefully consider that [a]the Lord is God in heaven above and on earth below—there is no other! [40]Keep his statutes and commandments that I am setting forth today so that it may go well with [a]you and your descendants and that you may enjoy longevity in the land that the Lord your God is about to give you as a permanent possession.

The Narrative Concerning Cities of Refuge

[41]Then Moses selected three cities in the Transjordan, toward the east. [42]Anyone who accidentally killed someone without hating him [a]at the time of the accident could flee to one of those cities and be safe. [43]These cities are [a]Bezer, in the wilderness plateau, for the Reubenites; Ramoth in Gilead for the Gadites; and Golan in Bashan for the Manassehites.

The Setting and Introduction of the Covenant

[44]This is the law that Moses set before the Israelites. [45]These are the stipulations, statutes, and ordinances that Moses spoke to the Israelites after he had brought them out of Egypt, [46]in the Transjordan, [a]in the valley opposite Beth Peor, in the land of King Sihon of the Amorites, who lived in Heshbon. (It is he whom Moses and the Israelites [b]attacked after they came out of Egypt. [47]They possessed his land and that [a]of King Og of Bashan—both of whom were Amorite kings in the Transjordan, to the east. [48]Their territory extended[1] [a]from Aroer at the edge of the Arnon valley as far as Mount Siyon—that is, [b]Hermon—[49]including all the rift valley of the Transjordan in the east to the sea of the rift valley, beneath the [a]slopes of Pisgah.)

The Opening Exhortation

5 Then Moses called all the people of Israel together and said to them: "Listen, Israel, to the statutes and ordinances that I am about to deliver to you today; learn them and be careful to keep them! [2a]The Lord our God made a covenant with us at Horeb. [3]He [a]did not make this covenant with our ancestors but with us, we who are here today, all of us living now. [4]The Lord spoke face to face with you at [a]the mountain, from the middle of the fire. [5](I was [a]standing between the Lord and [b]you at that time to reveal the Lord's message to you, because you were afraid of the fire and would not go up the mountain.) He said:

The Ten Commandments

[6a]I am the Lord your God—he who brought you from the land of Egypt, from the place of slavery.

[7a]You must not have any other gods besides me.

4:32 [a] Deut 32:7; Job 8:8 [b] Deut 28:64; Matt 24:31 [1] The Heb. *adam* may refer either to "Adam" or, more likely, to "man" in the sense of the human race.   4:33 [a] Exod 20:22; 24:11; Deut 5:24–26   4:34 [a] Deut 7:19 [b] Exod 6:6   4:35 [a] Exod 8:10; 9:14; [Deut 4:39; 32:12, 39; 1 Sam 2:2; Isa 43:10–12; 44:6–8; 45:5–7]; Mark 12:32   4:36 [a] Exod 19:9, 19; 20:18, 22; Deut 4:33; Neh 9:13; Heb 12:19, 25   4:37 [a] Deut 7:7–8; 10:15; 33:3 [b] Exod 13:3, 9, 14 [1] Not primarily emotional affection but commitment or devotion. [2] MT *his*.   4:38 [a] Deut 7:1   4:39 [a] Deut 4:35; Josh 2:11   4:40 [a] Lev 22:31; Deut 5:16; 32:46–47   4:42 [a] Deut 19:4   4:43 [a] Josh 20:8   4:46 [a] Deut 3:29 [b] Num 21:24; Deut 1:4   4:47 [a] Num 21:33–35   4:48 [a] Deut 2:36; 3:12 [b] Deut 3:9; Ps 133:3 [1] *their territory extended* is supplied; in the Heb. text, vv. 47–49 are one sentence.   4:49 [a] Deut 3:17   5:2 [a] Exod 19:5; Deut 4:23; Mal 4:4   5:3 [a] Jer 31:32; Matt 13:17; Heb 8:9   5:4 [a] Exod 19:9   5:5 [a] Exod 20:21; Gal 3:19 [b] Exod 19:16   5:6 [a] Exod 20:2–17; Lev 26:1; Deut 6:4; Ps 81:10   5:7 [a] Exod 20:2–3; 23:13; Hos 13:4

[8]"You must not make for [a]yourself an image of anything in heaven above, on earth below, or in the waters beneath. [9]You must not worship or serve them, for I, the LORD your God, am a jealous God. I punish the sons, grandsons, and great-grandsons for the sin of the fathers who reject[1] me, [10a]but I show covenant faithfulness[1] to the thousands who choose me and keep my commandments.

[11]"You must not make use of the name of the LORD [a]your God for worthless purposes,[1] for the LORD will not exonerate anyone who abuses his name that way.

[12]"Be [a]careful to observe the Sabbath day just as the LORD your God has commanded you. [13]You are to work and do all your tasks in [a]six days, [14]but the seventh day is the [a]Sabbath of the LORD your God. On that day you must not do any work, you, your son, your daughter, your male slave, your female slave, your ox, your donkey, any other animal, or the resident foreigner who lives with you, so that your male and female slaves, like yourself, may have rest. [15]Recall that you were slaves in the [a]land of Egypt and that the LORD your God brought you out of there [b]by strength and power. That is why the LORD your God has commanded you to observe the Sabbath day.

[16]"[a]Honor your father and your mother just as the LORD your God has commanded you to do, so [b]that [c]your days may be extended and that it may go well with you in the land that he is about to give you.

[17]"[a]You must not murder.[1]

[18]"[a]You must not commit adultery.

[19]"[a]You must not steal.

[20]"[a]You must not offer false testimony against another. [21]You must not desire[1] another man's wife, nor should [a]you crave his house, his field, his male and female servants, his ox, his donkey, or anything else he owns."

The Narrative of the Sinai Revelation and Israel's Response

[22]The LORD said [a]these things to your entire assembly at the mountain from the middle of the fire, the cloud, and the darkness with a loud voice, and that was all he said. Then he inscribed the words on two stone tablets and gave them to me. [23a]Then, when you heard the voice from the midst of the darkness while the mountain was ablaze, all your tribal leaders and elders approached me. [24]You said, "The LORD our God has shown us his great glory, and [a]we have heard him speak from the middle of the fire. It is now clear to us that God can speak to human beings and they can keep on living. [25]But now, why should we die, because this intense fire will consume us? [a]If we keep hearing the voice of the LORD our God we will die! [26a]Who is there from the entire human race who has heard the voice of the living God speaking from the middle of the fire as we have, and has lived? [27]You go near so that you can hear everything the LORD our God is saying and then you can [a]tell us whatever he says to you; then we will pay attention and do it." [28]When [a]the LORD heard you speaking to me, he said to me, "I have heard what these people have said to you—they have spoken well. [29a]If only it would really be their desire to fear me and obey all my commandments in the [b]future, so [c]that it may go well with them and their descendants forever. [30]Go and tell them, 'Return to your tents!' [31]But as for you, remain here with me so I can declare to you all the [a]commandments, statutes, and ordinances that you are to teach them, so that they can carry them out in the land I am about to give them." [32]Be careful, therefore, to do exactly what the LORD [a]your God has commanded you; do not turn right or left! [33]Walk just [a]as he has [b]commanded you so

---

5:8 [a]Exod 20:4   5:9 [1]Heb. *who hate*; in a covenant context, "to love" means "to choose, obey" while "to hate" means "to reject, disobey."   5:10 [a]Num 14:18; Deut 7:9; Jer 32:18; Dan 9:4   [1]This theologically rich term (Heb. *khesed*) describes God's loyalty to those who keep covenant with him.   5:11 [a]Exod 20:7; Lev 19:12; Deut 6:13; 10:20; Matt 5:33   [1]Heb. *take up the name of the LORD your God to emptiness*; i.e., not using the divine name for unholy, mundane purposes, that is, for meaningless and empty ends. In ancient Israel, this would include using the Lord's name as a witness in vows one did not intend to keep.   5:12 [a]Exod 20:8; Ezek 20:12; Mark 2:27   5:13 [a]Exod 23:12; 35:2   5:14 [a][Gen 2:2]; Exod 16:29; [Heb 4:4]   5:15 [a]Deut 15:15   [b]Deut 4:34, 37   5:16 [a]Exod 20:12; Lev 19:3; Matt 15:4; Eph 6:2–3; Col 3:20   [b]Deut 6:2   [c]Deut 4:40   5:17 [a]Exod 20:13; Matt 5:21   [1]Trad. *kill*; generic for homicide but, in the OT, both killing in war and capital punishment were permitted and even commanded (13:5, 9; 20:13, 16–17).   5:18 [a]Exod 20:14; Mark 10:19; Luke 18:20; [Rom 13:9]; Jas 2:11   5:19 [a]Exod 20:15; Lev 19:11; [Rom 13:9]   5:20 [a]Exod 20:16; 23:1; Matt 19:18   5:21 [a]Exod 20:17; [Rom 7:7; 13:9]   [1]The Heb. verb has sexual overtones ("lust" or the like).   5:22 [a]Exod 24:12; 31:18; Deut 4:13   5:23 [a]Exod 20:18–19   5:24 [a]Exod 19:19   5:25 [a]Exod 20:18–19; Deut 18:16   5:26 [a]Deut 4:33   5:27 [a]Exod 20:19; Heb 12:19   5:28 [a]Deut 18:17   5:29 [a]Deut 32:29; Ps 81:13; Isa 48:18   [b]Deut 11:1   [c]Deut 4:40   5:31 [a][Gal 3:19]   5:32 [a]Deut 17:20; 28:14; Josh 1:7; 23:6; Prov 4:27   5:33 [a]Deut 10:12; Ps 119:3; Jer 7:23; Luke 1:6   [b]Deut 4:40; Eph 6:3

that you may live, that it may go well with you, and that you may live long in the land you are going to possess.

Exhortation to Keep the Covenant Principles

6 Now [a]these are the commandments, statutes, and ordinances that the LORD your God instructed me to teach you so that you may carry them out in the land where you are headed [2]and [a]that you may so revere the LORD your God that you will keep all his statutes [b]and commandments that I am giving you—you, your children, and your grandchildren—all your lives, to prolong your days. [3]Pay attention, Israel, and be careful to do this so that it may go well with you and that you may [a]increase greatly in number—[b]as the LORD, the God of your [c]ancestors, said to you, you will have a land flowing with milk and honey.

The Essence of the Covenant Principles

[4a]Hear, O Israel: The LORD is our God, the LORD is one! [5]You must love[1] the LORD [a]your God [b]with your whole mind,[2] your whole being, and all your strength.

Exhortation to Teach the Covenant Principles

[6]These words I am commanding you today must be kept in mind, [7]and [a]you must teach them to your children and speak of them as you sit in your house, as you walk along the road, as you lie down, and as you get up. [8]You should tie them as a reminder on [a]your forearm and fasten them as symbols on your forehead. [9]Inscribe them on the doorframes of [a]your houses and gates.

Exhortation to Worship the Lord Exclusively

[10]Then when the LORD your God brings you to the land he promised your ancestors Abraham, Isaac, and Jacob to give you—a land with large, fine cities you did not build, [11]houses filled with choice things you did not accumulate, hewn-out cisterns you did not dig, and vineyards and olive groves you did not plant—and you eat your fill, [12]be careful not to forget the [a]LORD who brought you out of Egypt, that place of slavery. [13]You must [a]revere the LORD your God, serve him, and take oaths using only his name. [14]You must not go after [a]other gods, those of the surrounding peoples, [15]for [a]the LORD your God, who is present [b]among you, is a jealous God—his anger will erupt against you and remove you from the land.

Exhortation to Obey the Lord Exclusively

[16]You must not put the LORD [a]your God to the test [b]as you did at Massah. [17]Keep his commandments very [a]carefully, as well as the stipulations and statutes he commanded you to observe. [18]Do whatever is proper and good before the LORD so that it may go well with you and that you may enter and occupy the good land that he promised your ancestors, [19a]and that you may drive out all your enemies just as the LORD said.

Exhortation to Remember the Past

[20a]When your children ask you later on, "What are the stipulations, statutes, and ordinances that the LORD our God commanded you?" [21]you must say to them, "We were Pharaoh's slaves in Egypt, but the LORD brought us out of Egypt in a powerful way. [22]And he brought signs and great, devastating wonders on Egypt, on Pharaoh, and on his whole family before our very eyes. [23]He delivered us from there so that he could give us the land he had promised our ancestors. [24]The LORD commanded us [a]to obey all these statutes and to revere him so that it may always go well [b]for us and [c]he may preserve us, as he has to this day. [25]We will be innocent if we carefully keep all these commandments before the LORD our God, just as he demands."

The Dispossession of Nonvassals

7 When the LORD your God brings you to the land that you are going to [a]occupy and forces out many [b]nations before

6:1 [a]Deut 12:1   6:2 [a]Exod 20:20; Deut 10:12–13; [Ps 111:10; 128:1; Eccl 12:13]   [b]Deut 4:40   6:3 [a]Deut 7:13   [b]Gen 22:17   [c]Exod 3:8, 17   6:4 [a]Deut 4:35; Mark 12:29; John 17:3; [1 Cor 8:4, 6]   6:5 [a]Matt 22:37; Mark 12:30; Luke 10:27   [b]2 Kgs 23:25   [1]Not primarily emotional affection but commitment or devotion.   [2]Heb. *heart*; in OT physiology, the heart was considered the seat of the mind or intellect, so one could think with one's heart.   6:7 [a]Deut 4:9; 11:19; [Eph 6:4]   6:8 [a]Exod 12:14; 13:9, 16; Deut 11:18; Prov 3:3; 6:21; 7:3   6:9 [a]Deut 11:20; Isa 57:8   6:12 [a]Deut 8:11–18   6:13 [a]Deut 13:4; Matt 4:10; Luke 4:8   6:14 [a]Deut 13:7   6:15 [a]Exod 20:5; Deut 4:24   [b]Exod 33:3   6:16 [a]Matt 4:7; Luke 4:12   [b][1 Cor 10:9]   6:17 [a]Deut 11:22; Ps 119:4   6:19 [a]Num 33:52–53   6:20 [a]Exod 13:8, 14   6:24 [a]Deut 6:2   [b]Deut 10:12–13; Job 35:7–8; Jer 32:39   [c]Deut 4:1   7:1 [a]Deut 6:10   [b]Gen 15:19–21

you—Hittites, Girgashites, Amorites, Canaanites, Perizzites, Hivites, and Jebusites, seven nations more numerous and powerful than you—²and ᵃhe delivers them over to ᵇyou and you attack them, you must utterly annihilateᵃ them. Make no treaty with them and show them no mercy! ³You must not intermarry with them. Do not give your daughters to their sons ᵃor take their daughters for your sons, ⁴for they will turn your ᵃsons away from me to worship other gods. Then the anger of the LORD will erupt against you and he will quickly destroy you. ⁵Instead, this is what you must do to them: You must tear ᵃdown their altars, shatter their sacred pillars, cut down their sacred Asherah poles, and burn up their idols. ⁶For you are a people holy to ᵃthe LORD your God. He has chosen you to be his people, prized[1] above all others on the face of the earth.

The Basis of Israel's Election

⁷It is not because you were more numerous than all the other peoples that the LORD ᵃfavored and chose you—for in fact you were ᵇthe least numerous of all peoples. ⁸Rather it is ᵃbecause of his love for you and his faithfulness to ᵇthe promise ᶜhe solemnly vowed to your ancestors that the LORD brought you out with great power, redeeming you from the place of slavery, from the power of Pharaoh king of Egypt. ⁹So realize that ᵃthe LORD your God is the true God, the faithful God ᵇwho keeps covenant faithfully with those who love him and keep his commandments, to a thousand generations, ¹⁰but who pays back those who hate him as they deserve and destroys them. He will not ᵃignore those who hate him but will repay them as they deserve! ¹¹So keep the commandments, statutes, and ordinances that I today am commanding you to do.

Promises of Good for Covenant Obedience

¹²If you obey these ordinances and are careful to do them, the LORD your God will faithfully keep covenant with you as he promised your ancestors. ¹³He will ᵃlove and bless you, and make you numerous. ᵇHe will bless you with many children, with the produce of your soil, your grain, your new wine, your olive oil, the offspring of your oxen, and the young of your flocks in the land that he promised your ancestors to give you. ¹⁴You will be blessed beyond all peoples; there will be no ᵃbarrenness among you or your livestock. ¹⁵The LORD will protect you from all sickness, and you will not experience any of the ᵃterrible diseases that you knew in Egypt; instead he will inflict them on all those who hate you.

Exhortation to Destroy Canaanite Paganism

¹⁶You must destroy all the people whom the LORD your God is about to deliver over to you; you must not pity them or worship their gods, for that will ᵃbe a snare to you. ¹⁷If you think, "These nations are more numerous than I—how can I dispossess them?" ¹⁸you must not fear them. You must ᵃcarefully recall what the LORD your God did to Pharaoh and all Egypt, ¹⁹the great judgments you saw, ᵃthe signs and wonders, the strength and power by which he brought you out—thus the LORD your God will do to all the people you fear. ²⁰ᵃFurthermore, the LORD your God will release hornets[1] among them until the very last ones who hide from you perish. ²¹You must not tremble in their presence, for the LORD your God, who is present among you, is a great and awesome God. ²²He, the God who leads you, will expel the nations ᵃlittle by little. You will not be allowed to destroy them all at once lest the wild animals overrun you. ²³The LORD your God will give them over to you; he will throw them into a great panic until they are destroyed. ²⁴He will hand over ᵃtheir kings to you, and you will erase their very names from memory. ᵇNobody will be able to resist you until you destroy them. ²⁵You must burn the images of their gods, but do not ᵃcovet the silver and gold that covers them so much that you take it for yourself and thus become ensnared by it; for it is

---

7:2 ᵃ Num 31:17; Deut 20:16–18   ᵇ Exod 23:32–33; Josh 2:14   7:3 ᵃ Exod 34:15–16; Josh 23:12; 1 Kgs 11:2; Ezra 9:2   7:4 ᵃ Deut 6:15   7:5 ᵃ Exod 23:24; 34:13; Deut 12:3   7:6 ᵃ Exod 19:5–6; Amos 3:2; 1 Pet 2:9   [1] Or *treasured.*   7:7 ᵃ Deut 4:37   ᵇ Deut 10:22   7:8 ᵃ Deut 10:15   ᵇ Luke 1:55, 72, 73   ᶜ Exod 13:3, 14   7:9 ᵃ 1 Cor 1:9; 2 Thess 3:3; 2 Tim 2:13   ᵇ Exod 20:6; Deut 5:10; Neh 1:5; Dan 9:4   7:10 ᵃ [2 Pet 3:9–10]   7:13 ᵃ Ps 146:8; Prov 15:9; John 14:21   ᵇ Deut 28:4   7:14 ᵃ Exod 23:26   7:15 ᵃ Exod 9:14; 15:26; Deut 28:27, 60   7:16 ᵃ Exod 23:33; Judg 8:27; Ps 106:36   7:18 ᵃ Ps 105:5   7:19 ᵃ Deut 4:34; 29:3   7:20 ᵃ Exod 23:28; Josh 24:12   [1] Or possibly *discouragement, leprosy.*   7:22 ᵃ Exod 23:29–30   7:24 ᵃ Josh 10:24, 42; 12:1–24   ᵇ Josh 23:9   7:25 ᵃ Prov 23:6

abhorrent[1] to the LORD your God. [26]You must not bring any abhorrent thing into your house and thereby become an object of divine wrath along with it. You must absolutely detest and abhor it, [a]for it is an object of divine wrath.

The Lord's Provision in the Desert

8 You must keep carefully all these commandments I am giving [a]you today so that you may live, increase in [b]number, and go in and occupy the land that the LORD promised to your ancestors. [2]Remember the whole way by which he has [a]brought you these 40 years through the wilderness so that he might, by humbling you, [b]test you [c]to see if you have it within you to keep his commandments or not. [3]So he humbled you by making you hungry and then [a]feeding you with unfamiliar manna. He did this to teach you that humankind[1] [b]cannot live by bread alone, but also by everything that comes from the LORD's mouth. [4]Your clothing did not wear out nor did [a]your feet swell all these 40 years. [5]Be keenly aware that just as a parent disciplines his child, so the LORD [a]your God disciplines you. [6]So you must keep his commandments, live according [a]to his standards, and revere him. [7]For the LORD your God is bringing you to [a]a good land, a land of brooks, springs, and fountains flowing forth in valleys and hills, [8]a land of wheat, barley, vines, fig trees, and pomegranates, of olive trees and honey, [9]a land where you may eat food[1] in plenty and find no lack of anything, a land whose stones are iron and from whose hills you can mine copper. [10]You will eat your fill and then praise the LORD your God because of the good land [a]he has given you.

Exhortation to Remember That Blessing Comes from God

[11]Be sure you do not forget the LORD your God by not keeping his commandments, ordinances, and statutes that I am giving you today. [12a]When you eat your fill, when you build and occupy good houses, [13]when your cattle and flocks increase, when you have plenty of silver and gold, and when you have abundance of everything, [14a]be sure you do not feel self-important and [b]forget the LORD your God who brought you from the land of Egypt, the place of slavery, [15]and who [a]brought you through the great, fearful wilderness of venomous serpents[1] and scorpions, an arid place with no water. He made water flow from a [b]flint rock and [16]fed you in the wilderness with [a]manna (which your [b]ancestors had never before known) so that he might by humbling you test you and eventually bring good to you. [17]Be careful not to say, "My own ability and skill have gotten me this wealth." [18]You must remember the LORD your God, [a]for he is the one who gives ability to get wealth; if you do this he will confirm his covenant [b]that he made by oath to your ancestors,[1] even as he has to this day. [19]Now [a]if you forget the LORD your God at all and follow other gods, worshiping and prostrating yourselves before them, I testify to you today that you will surely be annihilated. [20]Just like the nations the LORD is about to destroy from your sight, [a]so he will do to you because you would not obey him.

Theological Justification of the Conquest

9 Listen, Israel: Today you are about to cross the Jordan so you can dispossess the nations there, people greater and stronger than you who live in large cities with extremely high fortifications. [2]They include the [a]Anakites, a numerous and tall people whom you know about and of whom it is said, "Who is able to resist the Anakites?" [3]Understand today that the LORD your God who [a]goes before you is a [b]devouring fire; [c]he will defeat and subdue them before you. You will dispossess and destroy them quickly just as he has told you. [4a]Do not think to yourself after the LORD your God has driven them out before you, "[b]Because of my own righteousness

7:25 [1] Heb. *abhorrent, detestable*; i.e., anything detestable to the Lord because of its innate evil or inconsistency with his nature and character.   7:26 [a] Deut 13:17   8:1 [a] Deut 4:1; 6:24   [b] Deut 30:16   8:2 [a] Deut 1:3; 2:7; 29:5; Ps 136:16; Amos 2:10   [b] Exod 16:4   [c] [John 2:25]   8:3 [a] Exod 16:12, 14, 35   [b] Matt 4:4; Luke 4:4   [1] Heb. *the man*; used in a generic sense, referring to the whole human race.   8:4 [a] Deut 29:5; Neh 9:21   8:5 [a] 2 Sam 7:14; Ps 89:30–33; Prov 3:11–12; Heb 12:5–11; Rev 3:19   8:6 [a] [Deut 5:33]   8:7 [a] Deut 11:9–12; Jer 2:7   8:9 [1] Or *bread.*   8:10 [a] Deut 6:11–12   8:12 [a] Deut 28:47; Prov 30:9; Hos 13:6   8:14 [a] 1 Cor 4:7   [b] Deut 8:11; Ps 106:21   8:15 [a] Isa 63:12–14   [b] Num 21:6   [1] Heb. *flaming serpents.*   8:16 [a] Exod 16:15   [b] Jer 24:5–6; [Heb 12:11]   8:18 [a] Prov 10:22; Hos 2:8   [b] Deut 7:8, 12   [1] Smr., Luc. add *Abraham, Isaac, and Jacob.*   8:19 [a] Deut 4:26; 30:18   8:20 [a] [Dan 9:11–12]   9:2 [a] Num 13:22, 28, 33; Josh 11:21–22   9:3 [a] Deut 1:33; 31:3; Josh 3:11; 5:14; John 10:4   [b] Deut 4:24; Heb 12:29   [c] Deut 7:24   9:4 [a] Deut 8:17; [Rom 11:6, 20; 1 Cor 4:4, 7]   [b] Gen 15:16; Lev 18:3, 24–30; Deut 12:31; 18:9–14

the Lord has brought me here to possess this land." It is because of the wickedness of these nations that the Lord is driving them out ahead of you. [5a]It is not because of your righteousness, or even your inner uprightness, that you have come here to possess their land. Instead, because of the wickedness of these nations, the Lord your God is driving them out ahead of you in order to confirm the [b]promise he made on oath to your ancestors, to Abraham, Isaac, and Jacob. [6]Understand, therefore, that it is not because of your righteousness that the Lord your God is about to give you this good land as a possession, for you are a stubborn people!

The History of Israel's Stubbornness

[7]Remember—don't ever forget[1]—how you [a]provoked the Lord your God in the wilderness; [b]from the time you left the land of Egypt until you came to this place you were constantly rebelling against him. [8]At Horeb you provoked him and he was angry enough with you to destroy you. [9a]When I went up the mountain to receive the stone tablets, the tablets of the covenant that the Lord made with you, I remained there [b]40 days and nights, eating and drinking nothing. [10]The Lord gave me [a]the two stone tablets, written by the very [b]finger of God, and on them was everything he said to you at the mountain from the midst of the fire at the time of that assembly. [11]Now at the end of the 40 days and nights the Lord presented me with the two stone tablets, the tablets of the covenant. [12]And he said to me, "Get [a]up, go down at once from here because your people whom you brought out of Egypt have sinned! They have [b]quickly turned from the way I commanded them and have made for themselves a cast metal image."[1] [13]Moreover, [a]he said to me, "I have taken note of these people; [b]they are a stubborn lot! [14a]Stand aside [b]and I will destroy them, obliterating their very name from memory, and I will make you into a stronger and more numerous nation than they are." [15a]So I turned and went down [b]the

mountain while it was blazing with fire; the two tablets of the covenant were in my hands. [16]When [a]I looked, you had indeed sinned against the Lord your God and had cast for yourselves a metal calf; you had quickly turned aside from the way he had commanded you! [17]I grabbed the two tablets, threw them down, and [a]shattered them before your very eyes. [18]Then I again [a]fell down before the Lord for 40 days and nights; I ate and drank nothing because of all the sin you had committed, doing such evil before the Lord as to enrage him. [19a]For I was terrified at the Lord's intense anger that threatened to destroy you. [b]But he listened to me this time as well. [20]The Lord was also angry enough at Aaron to kill him, but at that time I prayed for him too. [21]As for your sinful thing that you had made, the calf, I took it, melted it down, ground it up until it was as fine as dust, and [a]tossed the dust into the stream that flows down the mountain. [22]Moreover, you continued to provoke the Lord at [a]Taberah, [b]Massah, and Kibroth [c]Hattaavah. [23]And [a]when he sent [b]you from Kadesh Barnea and told you, "Go up and possess the land I have given you," you rebelled against the Lord your God and would neither believe nor obey him. [24]You have been rebelling against him from the very first day I knew [a]you!

Moses' Plea on behalf of God's Reputation

[25a]I lay flat on the ground before the Lord for 40 days and nights, for he had said he would destroy you. [26]I prayed to him: [a]O, Sovereign Lord, do not destroy your people, your valued property that you have powerfully redeemed, whom you brought out of Egypt by your strength. [27]Remember your servants Abraham, Isaac, and Jacob; ignore the stubbornness, wickedness, and sin of these people. [28]Otherwise the people of the land[1] from which you brought us will say, "The Lord was unable to bring them to the land he promised them, and because of his hatred for them he has brought them out to kill them in the wilderness." [29]They are your people,

9:5 [a] [Titus 3:5] [b] Gen 50:24   9:7 [a] Num 14:22 [b] Exod 14:11 [1] An emphatic Heb. construction.   9:9 [a] Exod 24:12, 15; Deut 5:2–22 [b] Exod 24:18   9:10 [a] Exod 31:18; Deut 4:13 [b] Exod 19:17   9:12 [a] Exod 32:7–8 [b] Deut 31:29 [1] Heb. *a casting*; some wss add *calf/a molten calf.*   9:13 [a] Exod 32:9 [b] Deut 9:6   9:14 [a] Exod 32:10 [b] Num 14:12   9:15 [a] Exod 32:15–19 [b] Exod 19:18   9:16 [a] Exod 32:19   9:17 [a] Exod 32:19   9:18 [a] Exod 34:28; Ps 106:23   9:19 [a] Exod 32:10–11; Heb 12:21 [b] Exod 32:14   9:21 [a] Exod 32:20   9:22 [a] Num 11:1, 3 [b] Exod 17:7 [c] Num 11:4, 34   9:23 [a] Num 13:3 [b] Ps 106:24–25   9:24 [a] Deut 9:7; 31:27   9:25 [a] Deut 9:18   9:26 [a] Deut 32:9   9:28 [1] MT omits *the people.*

your valued property, whom you brought out with great strength and power.

The Opportunity to Begin Again

10 At that same time the LORD said to me, "Carve out for yourself two stone tablets like the first ones and come up the mountain to me; also make for yourself a wooden [a]ark.[1] [2]I will write on the tablets the same words that were on the first tablets [a]you broke, and you must put them into the ark." [3]So I made an ark of acacia wood and carved out two stone tablets just like the first ones. Then I went up the mountain with the two tablets in my hands. [4]The LORD then wrote on the tablets the same words, the Ten Commandments,[1] [a]which he had spoken to you at the mountain from the middle of the fire at the time of that assembly, and he gave them to me. [5]Then I turned, [a]went down the mountain, and [b]placed the tablets into the ark I had made—they are still there, just as the LORD [c]commanded me.

Conclusion of the Historical Résumé

[6]During those days the Israelites traveled from Beeroth Bene Jaakan to Moserah. There Aaron [a]died and was buried, and his son Eleazar became priest in his place. [7]From there they traveled to Gudgodah, and [a]from Gudgodah to Jotbathah, a place of flowing streams. [8]At that time [a]the LORD set apart the tribe of Levi [b]to carry the ark of the LORD's covenant, [c]to stand before the LORD [d]to serve him, and to formulate blessings in his name, as they do to this very day. [9]Therefore Levi has no allotment [a]or inheritance among his brothers; the LORD is his inheritance just as the LORD your God told him. [10]As for me, [a]I stayed at [b]the mountain as I did the first time, 40 days and nights. The LORD listened to me that time as well and decided not to destroy you. [11]Then [a]he said to me, "Get up, set out leading the people so they may go and possess the land I promised to give to their ancestors."

An Exhortation to Love Both God and People

[12]Now, Israel, [a]what does the LORD your God require of you except to revere him, to obey all his commandments, to [b]love him, to serve him with all your mind and being, [13]and to keep the LORD's commandments and statutes that I am giving you today [a]for your own good? [14]The heavens—indeed the highest heavens—belong to the [a]LORD your God, as does the earth and everything in it. [15]However, only to your ancestors did he show his loving favor,[1] and he chose you, their descendants, from all peoples—as is apparent today. [16]Therefore, cleanse[1] your [a]hearts and stop being so stubborn! [17]For the LORD your [a]God is God of gods and Lord of [b]lords, the great, [c]mighty, and awesome God who is [d]unbiased and takes no bribe, [18]who justly treats [a]the orphan and widow, and who loves resident foreigners, giving them food and clothing. [19]So you must love the resident foreigner because you were foreigners in the land of Egypt. [20]Revere the LORD [a]your God, serve him, be loyal to him, and take oaths only in his name. [21]He is the one you should praise; he is your God, the one who has done these great and awesome things for you that you have seen. [22]When your ancestors went down to Egypt, they numbered only seventy, but now the LORD your God has made you as numerous as the stars of the sky.

Reiteration of the Call to Obedience

11 You must love the LORD your God and do what he requires; keep his statutes, ordinances, and commandments at all times. [2]Bear in mind today that I am not speaking to your children who have not personally experienced the judgments of the LORD your God, which revealed his greatness, strength, and power. [3]They did not see the awesome deeds he performed in the midst of Egypt against Pharaoh king of Egypt and his whole land, [4]or what he did to the army of Egypt, including their

10:1 [a] Exod 25:10 [1] Or *chest*; later known as the ark of the covenant. 10:2 [a] Exod 25:16, 21 10:4 [a] Exod 20:1; 34:28 [1] Heb. *ten words*. 10:5 [a] Exod 34:29 [b] Exod 40:20 [c] 1 Kgs 8:9 10:6 [a] Num 20:25–28; 33:38 10:7 [a] Num 33:32–34 10:8 [a] Num 3:6 [b] Num 4:5, 15; 10:21 [c] Deut 18:5 [d] Num 6:23 10:9 [a] Num 18:20, 24; Deut 18:1–2; Ezek 44:28 10:10 [a] Exod 34:28; Deut 9:18 [b] Exod 32:14 10:11 [a] Exod 33:1 10:12 [a] Mic 6:8 [b] Deut 6:5; Matt 22:37; 1 Tim 1:5 10:13 [a] Deut 6:24 10:14 [a] [Neh 9:6; Ps 68:33; 115:16] 10:15 [1] Heb. *take delight to love*. 10:16 [a] Lev 26:41; Deut 30:6; Jer 4:4; Rom 2:28–29 [1] Heb. *circumcise the foreskin of*; as physical circumcision signified total covenant obedience (Gen 17:9–14), so spiritual circumcision (cleansing of the heart) signified, more internally, a commitment to be pliable and obedient to the will of God. 10:17 [a] Deut 4:35, 39; Isa 44:8; 46:9; Dan 2:47; 1 Cor 8:5–6 [b] Rev 19:16 [c] Deut 7:21 [d] Acts 10:34 10:18 [a] Exod 22:22–24; Ps 68:5; 146:9 10:20 [a] Matt 4:10

horses and chariots, when he made the waters of the Red Sea[1] overwhelm them while they were pursuing you and he annihilated them. [5]They did not see what he did to you in the wilderness before you reached this place, [6]or [a]what he did to Dathan and Abiram, sons of Eliab the Reubenite, when the earth opened its mouth in the middle of the Israelite camp and swallowed them, their families, their tents, and all the property they brought with them. [7]I am speaking to you because you are the ones who [a]saw with your own eyes all the great deeds of the LORD.

The Abundance of the Land of Promise

[8]Now pay attention to all the commandments I am giving you today, so that you may [a]be strong enough to enter and possess the land where you are headed, [9]and [a]that you [b]may enjoy long life in the land the LORD promised to give to your ancestors and their descendants, a land flowing with milk and honey. [10]For the land where you are headed is not like the land of Egypt from which you came, a land where you planted seed and which you irrigated by hand[1] like a vegetable garden. [11a]Instead, the land you are crossing the Jordan to occupy is one of hills and valleys, a land that drinks in water from the rains, [12]a land [a]the LORD your God looks after. He is constantly attentive to it from the beginning to the end of the year. [13]Now, if you pay close attention to my commandments that I am giving you today and love the LORD your God and serve him with all your mind and being, [14]then he [a]promises, "I will send rain for your land in its season, [b]the autumn and the spring rains, so that you may gather in your grain, new wine, and olive oil. [15]I will provide pasture for your livestock [a]and you will [b]eat your fill."

Exhortation to Instruction and Obedience

[16]Make sure you do not turn away to [a]serve and worship other gods! [17]Then [a]the anger of the LORD will erupt against [b]you, and he will close up the sky so that it does not rain. The land will not yield its produce, and you will soon be removed from the good land that the LORD is about to give you. [18]Fix these words of mine into [a]your mind and [b]being, [c]tie them as a reminder on your hands, and let them be symbols on your forehead. [19]Teach them to [a]your children and speak of them as you sit in your house, as you walk along the road, as you lie down, and as you get up. [20]Inscribe them on the doorframes of your houses [a]and on your gates [21]so that [a]your days and those of your descendants may be extended in [b]the land that the LORD promised to give to your ancestors, like the days of heaven itself. [22]For if [a]you carefully observe all of these commandments I am giving you[1] and love the LORD your God, live according [b]to his standards, and remain loyal to him, [23]then he will [a]drive out all these nations ahead of you, and you will [b]dispossess nations greater and stronger than you. [24a]Every place you set your foot[1] will be yours; your border will extend [b]from the desert to Lebanon and from the River (that is, the Euphrates) as far as the Mediterranean Sea. [25]Nobody will be able to [a]resist you; the LORD your God will spread the [b]fear and terror of you over the whole land on which you walk, just as he promised you.

Anticipation of a Blessing and Cursing Ceremony

[26]Take [a]note—I am setting before you today a blessing and a curse: [27]the blessing if you take to heart [a]the commandments of the LORD your God that I am giving you today, [28]and the [a]curse if you pay no attention to his commandments and turn from the way I am setting before you today to pursue other gods you have not known. [29]When the LORD your God brings you into the land you are to possess, you must pronounce the [a]blessing on Mount Gerizim and the [b]curse on Mount Ebal. [30]Are they not across the

---

11:4 [1] Heb. *the Reed Sea*; Trad. "Red" based on the LXX.   11:6 [a] Num 16:1–35; Ps 106:16–18   11:7 [a] Deut 10:21; 29:2   11:8 [a] Deut 31:6–7, 23; Josh 1:6–7   11:9 [a] Deut 4:40; 5:16, 33; 6:2; Prov 10:27   [b] Exod 3:8   11:10 [1] Heb. *with your foot*; water sometimes had to be pumped into fields and gardens by foot power.   11:11 [a] Deut 8:7   11:12 [a] 1 Kgs 9:3   11:14 [a] Lev 26:4; Deut 28:12   [b] Joel 2:23; Jas 5:7   11:15 [a] Ps 104:14   [b] Deut 6:11; Joel 2:19   11:16 [a] Deut 8:19   11:17 [a] Deut 6:15; 9:19   [b] Deut 4:26; 2 Chr 36:14–20   11:18 [a] Deut 6:6–9   [b] Ps 119:2, 34   [c] Deut 6:8   11:19 [a] Deut 4:9–10; 6:7; Prov 22:6   11:20 [a] Deut 6:9   11:21 [a] Deut 4:40   [b] Ps 72:5; 89:29; Prov 3:2; 4:10; 9:11   11:22 [a] Deut 11:1   [b] Deut 10:20   [1] Heb. *commanding you to do it.*   11:23 [a] Deut 4:38   [b] Deut 9:1   11:24 [a] Josh 1:3; 14:9   [b] Gen 15:18; Exod 23:31; Deut 1:7–8   [1] Heb. *the sole of your foot walks*; symbolizing conquest and dominion.   11:25 [a] Deut 7:24   [b] Exod 23:27; Deut 2:25; Josh 2:9–11   11:26 [a] Deut 30:1, 15, 19   11:27 [a] Deut 28:1–14   11:28 [a] Deut 28:15–68   11:29 [a] Deut 27:12–13; Josh 8:33   [b] Deut 27:13–26

Jordan River, toward the west, in the land of the Canaanites who live in the rift valley opposite Gilgal [a]near the oak[1] of Moreh? [31]For you are about to cross the Jordan to possess the land the LORD your God is giving you, and you will possess and inhabit it. [32]Be certain to keep all the statutes and ordinances that I am presenting to you today.

The Central Sanctuary

12 These [a]are the statutes and ordinances you must be careful to obey as long as you live in the land the LORD, the God of your ancestors, has given you to possess. [2]You must by all means destroy all the places where the nations [a]you are about to dispossess worship their gods—[b]on the high mountains and hills and under every leafy tree. [3]You must tear down their altars, shatter their sacred pillars, burn up their sacred Asherah poles, and cut down the images of their gods; [a]you must eliminate their very memory from that place. [4]You must not [a]worship the LORD your God the way they worship. [5]But you must seek only the [a]place he chooses from all your tribes to establish his name as his place of residence, and you must go there. [6]And [a]there you must take your burnt offerings, your sacrifices, your tithes, the personal offerings you have prepared, your votive offerings, your freewill offerings, and the [b]firstborn of your herds and flocks. [7]Both you and your families[1] must feast [a]there before the LORD [b]your God and rejoice in all the output of your labor with which he has blessed you. [8]You must not do as we are doing here today, with [a]everyone doing what seems best to him, [9]for you have not yet come to the final [a]stop and inheritance the LORD your God is giving you. [10]When you do go across the Jordan River and settle in the land he is granting you as an inheritance and you find [a]relief from all the enemies who surround you, you will live in safety. [11]Then you must come to the place the LORD your God chooses for his name to reside, bringing everything I am commanding you—your burnt offerings, sacrifices, tithes, the personal offerings you have prepared, and all your choice votive offerings that you devote to him. [12]You shall rejoice in the presence of the LORD [a]your God, along with your sons, daughters, male and female servants, and the [b]Levites in your villages (since they have no allotment or inheritance with you). [13]Make sure you do not offer burnt offerings in any place you wish, [14]for you may do so only in the place the LORD chooses in one of your tribal areas—there you may do everything I am commanding you.

Regulations for Eating Sacrificial and Non-Sacrificial Foods

[15]On the other hand, [a]you may slaughter and eat meat as you please when [b]the LORD your God blesses you in all your villages. Both the ritually pure and impure may eat it, whether it is a gazelle or an ibex. [16]However, you must not eat blood—pour it out [a]on the ground like water. [17]You will not be allowed to eat in your villages your tithe of grain, new wine, olive oil, the firstborn of your herd and flock, any votive offerings you have vowed, or your freewill and personal offerings. [18]Only in the presence of the LORD your God may you eat these, in the place he chooses. This applies to you, your son, your daughter, your male and female servants, and the Levites in your villages. In that place you will rejoice before the LORD your God in all the output of your labor. [19]Be careful not to overlook the Levites as long as you live in the land.

The Sanctity of Blood

[20]When the LORD your God [a]extends your borders as he said he would do and you say, "I want to eat meat just as I please," you may do so as you wish. [21]If the place he chooses to locate his name is too far for [a]you, you may slaughter any of your herd and flock he has given you just as I have stipulated; you may eat them in your villages just as you wish. [22]As you eat the gazelle or ibex, so you may eat these; the ritually impure and pure alike may eat them. [23]However, by no means eat the blood, [a]for the blood is life itself—you must not eat the life with the meat. [24]You must not eat it! You must pour it out on the ground like water. [25]You must not eat it so [a]that it may go well with you

11:30 [a] Gen 12:6   [1] MT *oaks.*   **12:1** [a] Deut 6:1   **12:2** [a] Exod 34:13   [b] 2 Kgs 16:4; 17:10–11   **12:3** [a] Num 33:52; Deut 7:5; Judg 2:2   **12:4** [a] Deut 12:31   **12:5** [a] Exod 20:24   **12:6** [a] Lev 17:3–4   [b] Deut 14:23   **12:7** [a] Deut 14:26   [b] Deut 12:12, 18   [1] Heb. *and your houses.*   **12:8** [a] Judg 17:6; 21:25   **12:9** [a] Deut 3:20; 25:19; Ps 95:11   **12:10** [a] Josh 11:23   **12:12** [a] Deut 12:18; 26:11   [b] Deut 10:9; 14:29   **12:15** [a] Deut 12:21   [b] Deut 12:22   **12:16** [a] Gen 9:4; Lev 7:26; 17:10–12; 1 Sam 14:33; Acts 15:20, 29   **12:20** [a] Gen 15:18; Exod 34:24; Deut 11:24; 19:8   **12:21** [a] Deut 14:24   **12:23** [a] Gen 9:4; Lev 17:10–14; Deut 12:16   **12:25** [a] Deut 4:40; 6:18; Isa 3:10

and your children after you; you will be doing what is right in the LORD's sight.[1] 26But the [a]holy things and votive offerings that belong to you, you must pick up and take to the place the LORD will choose.[1] 27You must offer [a]your burnt offerings, both meat and blood, on the altar of the LORD your God; the blood of your other sacrifices you must pour out on his altar while you eat the meat. 28Pay careful attention to all these things I am commanding you so [a]that it may always go well with you and your children after you when you do what is good and right in the sight of the LORD your God.

The Abomination of Pagan Gods

29When [a]the LORD your God eliminates the nations from the place where you are headed and you dispossess them, you will settle down in their land. 30After they have been destroyed from your presence, be careful not to be ensnared like they are; do not pursue their gods and say, "How do these nations serve their gods? I will do the same." 31You must not worship the LORD [a]your God [b]the way they do! For everything that is abhorrent to him, everything he hates, they have done when worshiping their gods. They even burn up their sons and daughters before their gods!

Idolatry and False Prophets

32You must be careful to do everything I am commanding [a]you. Do not add to it or subtract from it! 13 1Suppose a prophet or one who [a]foretells by dreams should appear among you [b]and show you a sign or wonder, 2and [a]the sign or wonder should come to pass concerning what he said to you, namely, "Let us follow other gods"—gods whom you have not previously known—"and let us serve them." 3You must not [a]listen to the words of that prophet or dreamer, for the LORD your God will be testing you to see if you love him[1] with all your mind and being. 4You must follow the LORD your God and revere only him; and you must observe his commandments, obey him, serve him, and remain loyal to him. 5As for [a]that prophet or dreamer, he must be executed because he encouraged rebellion against the LORD your God who brought you from the land of Egypt, redeeming you from that place of slavery, and because he has tried to entice you from the way the LORD your God has commanded you to go. In this way you must purge evil from among you.

False Prophets in the Family

6Suppose your own full brother, your son, your daughter, your beloved [a]wife, or your closest friend should seduce you secretly and encourage you to go and serve [b]other gods that neither you nor your ancestors have previously known, 7the gods of the surrounding people (whether near you or far from you, from one end of the earth to the other). 8You must [a]not give in to him or even listen to him; do not feel sympathy for him or spare him or cover up for him. 9Instead, you must kill him without fail! Your own hand must be the first to [a]strike him, and then the hands of the whole community. 10You must stone him to death because he tried to entice you away from the LORD your God, who delivered you from the land of Egypt, that place of slavery. 11Thus all Israel will hear and be [a]afraid; no longer will they continue to do evil like this among you.

Punishment of Community Idolatry

12[a]Suppose you should hear in one of your cities, which the LORD your God is giving you as a place to live, that 13some evil people[1] have departed from among you to entice the inhabitants of their cities,[2] saying, "Let's go and serve other gods" (whom you have not known before). 14You must investigate thoroughly and inquire carefully. If it is indeed true that such a disgraceful thing is being done among you,[1] 15you must by all means slaughter the inhabitants of that city with the sword; annihilate[1] with the sword everyone in it, as well as the livestock. 16You must gather all of its plunder into the middle of the plaza and [a]burn the

12:25 [1]Heb. *in the eyes of the LORD*; LXX *the LORD your God.* 12:26 [a]Num 5:9–10; 18:19 [1]LXX adds *to place his name there.* 12:27 [a]Lev 1:5, 9, 13, 17 12:28 [a]Deut 12:25 12:29 [a]Exod 23:23; Deut 19:1; Josh 23:4 12:31 [a]Lev 18:3, 26, 30; 20:1–2 [b]Deut 18:10; Ps 106:37; Jer 32:35 12:32 [a]Deut 4:2; 13:18; Josh 1:7; Prov 30:6; Rev 22:18–19 13:1 [a]Num 12:6; Jer 23:28; Zech 10:2 [b]Matt 24:24; Mark 13:22; 2 Thess 2:9 13:2 [a]Deut 18:22 13:3 [a]Exod 20:20; Deut 8:2, 16 [1]Heb. *the LORD your God.* 13:5 [a]Deut 18:20; Jer 14:15 13:6 [a]Deut 17:2 [b]Gen 16:5 13:8 [a]Deut 7:16; Prov 1:10 13:9 [a]Lev 24:14; Deut 17:7 13:11 [a]Deut 17:13 13:12 [a]Judg 20:1–48 13:13 [1]Heb. *men, sons of Belial*; this Heb. term has the idea of worthlessness, without morals or scruples. [2]LXX, Tg. *your.* 13:14 [1]Thd. adds *in Israel.* 13:15 [1]Or *put under divine judgment*; refers to placing persons or things under God's judgment, usually to the extent of their complete destruction.

city [b]and all its plunder as a whole burnt offering to the LORD your God. It will be an abandoned ruin[1] forever—it must never be rebuilt again. [17][a]You must not take for yourself anything that has been placed under judgment. Then the LORD will [b]relent from his intense anger, show you compassion, have mercy on you, and multiply you as he promised your ancestors. [18]Thus you must obey the LORD your God, keeping all his commandments that I am giving you [a]today and doing what is right[1] before him.

The Holy and the Profane

14 You are children of [a]the LORD [b]your God. Do not cut yourselves or shave your forehead bald for the sake of the dead. [2][a]For you are a people holy to the LORD your God. He has chosen you to be his people, prized[1] above all others on the face of the earth.

[3][a]You must not eat any forbidden thing.[1] [4]These are [a]the animals you may eat: the ox, the sheep, the goat, [5]the ibex, the gazelle, the deer, the wild goat, the antelope,[1] the wild oryx, and the mountain sheep.[2] [6]You may eat any animal that has hooves divided into two parts and that chews the cud. [7]However, you may not eat the following animals among those that chew the cud or those that have divided hooves: the camel, the hare, and the rock badger. (Although they chew the cud, they do not have divided hooves and are therefore ritually impure to you.) [8]Also, the pig is ritually impure to you; though it has divided hooves,[1] it does not chew the cud. You may not eat their meat [a]or even touch their remains.

[9][a]These you may eat from among water creatures: anything with fins and scales you may eat, [10]but whatever does not have fins and scales you may not eat; it is ritually impure to you.

[11]All ritually clean birds[1] you may eat. [12][a]These are the ones you may not eat: the eagle, the vulture, the black vulture, [13]the kite, the black kite, the dayyah after its species,

[14]every raven after its species, [15]the ostrich, the owl, the seagull, the falcon after its species, [16]the little owl, the long-eared owl, the white owl, [17]the jackdaw, the carrion vulture, the cormorant, [18]the stork, the heron after its species, the hoopoe, and the bat.

[19]And any swarming winged thing is impure to you—[a]they may not be eaten.[1] [20]You may eat any winged creature that is clean. [21]You may not eat any corpse, though [a]you may give it to the resident [b]foreigner who is living in [c]your villages and he may eat it, or you may sell it to a foreigner. You are a people holy to the LORD your God. Do not boil a young goat in its mother's milk.

The Offering of Tithes

[22]You must be certain to tithe all the produce of [a]your seed that comes from the field year after year. [23]In the presence of the LORD your God, in the place he chooses to locate his name, you must eat from the tithe of your grain, your new wine,[1] your olive oil, [a]and [b]the firstborn of your herds and flocks, so that you may learn to revere the LORD your God always. [24]When he blesses you, [a]if the place where he chooses to locate his name is distant, [25]you may convert the tithe into money, secure the money, and travel to the place the LORD your God chooses for himself. [26]Then you may spend the money however you wish for cattle, sheep, wine, beer, or whatever you desire. You and your household may eat there in the presence of the LORD your God and [a]enjoy it. [27]As for the [a]Levites in your villages, you must not ignore them, for they have no allotment or inheritance along with you. [28]At the end of every three years you must bring all the tithe of your produce, in [a]that very year, and you must store [b]it up in your villages. [29]Then the Levites (because they have no allotment or inheritance with you), the resident foreigners, the orphans, and the widows of your villages may come and eat their fill so that the LORD your God may bless you in all the work you do.

13:16 [a] Josh 6:24 [b] Josh 8:28; Isa 17:1; 25:2; Jer 49:2 [1] Heb. *mound*; a built-up mound of dirt or debris. **13:17** [a] Josh 6:18 [b] Josh 7:26 **13:18** [a] Deut 12:25, 28, 32 [1] LXX, Smr. add *and good.* **14:1** [a] [Rom 8:16; Gal 3:26] [b] Lev 19:28; 21:1–5 **14:2** [a] Lev 20:26; Deut 7:6; [Rom 12:1] [1] Or *treasured.* **14:3** [a] Ezek 4:14 [1] Heb. *abhorrent, detestable*; i.e., anything detestable to the Lord because of its innate evil or inconsistency with his nature and character. **14:4** [a] Lev 11:2–45 **14:5** [1] Likely a variety of antelope. [2] Or possibly *wild sheep.* **14:8** [a] Lev 11:26–27 [1] MT omits *has divided hooves.* **14:9** [a] Lev 11:9 **14:11** [1] Heb. *bird, winged creature*; it appears to include bats, while insects are put in their own list next. **14:12** [a] Lev 11:13 **14:19** [a] Lev 11:23 [1] LXX, Smr. *you shall not eat from them.* **14:21** [a] Lev 17:15; 22:8; Ezek 4:14; 44:31 [b] Deut 14:2 [c] Exod 23:19; 34:26 **14:22** [a] Lev 27:30; Deut 12:6, 17; Neh 10:37 **14:23** [a] Deut 12:5–7 [b] Deut 15:19–20 [1] I.e., wine in the early stages of fermentation. **14:24** [a] Deut 12:5, 21 **14:26** [a] Deut 12:7 **14:27** [a] Deut 12:12 **14:28** [a] Deut 26:12; Amos 4:4 [b] Num 18:21–24

The Year of Debt Release

15 At the end of [a]every seven years you must declare a cancellation of debts. [2]This is the nature of the cancellation: Every creditor must remit what he has loaned to another person; he must not force payment from his fellow Israelite, for it is to be recognized as "the LORD's cancellation of debts." [3]You may exact payment from a foreigner, but whatever your fellow Israelite owes you, you must remit. [4]However, there should not be any poor among you, for the LORD[1] will surely [a]bless you in the land that he is giving you as an inheritance, [5]if you carefully obey him by keeping all these commandments that I am giving you today. [6]For the LORD [a]your God will bless you just as he has promised; you will lend to many nations but will not borrow from any, and you will rule over many nations but they will not rule over you.

The Spirit of Liberality

[7]If a fellow Israelite from one of [a]your villages in the land that the LORD your God is giving you should be poor, you must not harden your heart or be insensitive to his impoverished condition. [8]Instead, [a]you must be sure to open your hand to him and generously lend him whatever he needs.[1] [9]Be careful lest you entertain the wicked thought that the seventh year, the year of cancellation of debts, has almost arrived, and your [a]attitude be wrong toward your [b]impoverished fellow [c]Israelite and you do not lend him anything; he will cry out to the LORD against you, and you will be regarded as having sinned. [10]You must by all means lend to him and not be upset by doing it,[1] for because of this the LORD [a]your God will bless you in all your work and in everything you attempt. [11]There will never cease to be some poor people in [a]the land; therefore, I am commanding you to make sure you open your hand to your fellow Israelites who are needy and poor in your land.

Release of Debt Slaves

[12a]If your fellow Hebrew—whether male or female[1]—is [b]sold to you and serves you for six years, then in the seventh year you must let that servant go free. [13]If you set them free, you must not send them away empty-handed. [14]You must supply them generously from your flock, your threshing floor, and your winepress—as the LORD your God has [a]blessed you, you must give to them. [15]Remember that [a]you were a slave in the land of Egypt and the LORD your God redeemed you; therefore, I am commanding you to do this thing today. [16]However, [a]if the servant says to you, "I do not want to leave you," because he loves you and your household, since he is well off with you, [17]you shall take an awl and pierce a hole through his ear to the door. Then he will become your servant permanently (this applies to your female servant as well). [18]You should not consider it difficult to let him go free, for he will [a]have served you for six years, twice the time of a hired worker; the LORD your God will bless you in everything you do.

Giving God the Best

[19a]You must set apart for the LORD your God every firstborn male born to your herds and flocks. You must not work the firstborn of your bulls or shear the firstborn of your flocks. [20]You and [a]your household must eat them annually before the LORD your God in the place he chooses. [21a]If one of them has any kind of blemish—lameness, blindness, or anything else—you may not offer it as a sacrifice to the LORD your God. [22]You may eat it in your villages, [a]whether you are ritually impure or clean,[1] just as you would eat a gazelle or an ibex. [23]However, you must not eat its blood; you must pour it out on the ground like water.

The Passover

16 Observe the [a]month Abib and keep the Passover to the LORD your God, for [b]in that month he brought you out of Egypt by night. [2]You must sacrifice [a]the Passover animal (from the flock or the herd) to the LORD your God in the [b]place where he chooses to locate his name. [3]You must

15:1 [a]Exod 21:2; 23:10–11; Lev 25:4; Jer 34:14 **15:4** [a]Deut 7:13 [1]Many MSS add *your God.* **15:6** [a]Deut 28:12, 44 **15:7** [a]Exod 23:6; Lev 25:35–37; Deut 24:12–14; [1 John 3:17] **15:8** [a]Matt 5:42; Gal 2:10 [1]Heb. *whatever his need that he needs for himself.* **15:9** [a]Deut 28:54, 56 [b]Exod 22:23; Deut 24:15; Job 34:28; Ps 12:5; Jas 5:4 [c][Matt 25:41–42] **15:10** [a]2 Cor 9:5, 7 [1]Heb. *your heart must not be grieved in giving to him;* LXX, Orig. add *you shall surely lend to him sufficient for his need.* **15:11** [a]Matt 26:11; Mark 14:7; John 12:8 **15:12** [a]Exod 21:2–6; Jer 34:14 [b]Lev 25:39–46 [1]Heb. *your brother, a Hebrew* (masc.) *or Hebrew* (fem.). **15:14** [a]Prov 10:22 **15:15** [a]Deut 5:15 **15:16** [a]Exod 21:5–6 **15:18** [a]Isa 16:14 **15:19** [a]Exod 13:2, 12 **15:20** [a]Lev 7:15–18; Deut 12:5; 14:23 **15:21** [a]Lev 22:19–25; Deut 17:1 **15:22** [a]Deut 12:15–16, 22 [1]LXX adds *among you.* **16:1** [a]Exod 12:2 [b]Exod 13:4 **16:2** [a]Num 28:19 [b]Deut 12:5, 26; 15:20

not eat any yeast with it; for [a]seven days you must eat bread made without yeast, as symbolic of affliction, for you came out of Egypt hurriedly. You must do this so you will [b]remember for the rest of your lives the day you came out of the land of Egypt. [4]There must not be [a]a scrap of yeast within your land for seven days, nor can any of the meat you sacrifice on the evening of the first day remain until the next [b]morning. [5]You may not sacrifice the Passover in just any of your villages that the LORD your God is giving you, [6]but you must sacrifice it[1] in the evening in[2] the place where he chooses to [a]locate his name, at sunset, the time of day you came out of Egypt. [7]You must cook and eat it [a]in the place the LORD your God chooses; you may return the next morning to your tents. [8]You must eat bread made without yeast for six days. The seventh day you are to hold an assembly for the LORD your God; you must not do any work [a]on that day.

The Feast of Weeks

[9]You must count seven weeks; you must begin to count them from the time you begin to harvest the standing grain. [10]Then you are to celebrate the [a]Feast of Weeks before the LORD your God with the voluntary offering that you will bring, in proportion to how he [b]has blessed you. [11]You shall rejoice before him—[a]you, your son, your daughter, your male and female slaves, the Levites in your villages, the resident foreigners, the orphans, and the widows among you—in the place where the LORD chooses to locate his name. [12]Furthermore, remember that you were [a]a slave in Egypt, and so be careful to observe these statutes.

The Feast of Temporary Shelters

[13a]You must celebrate the Feast of Shelters[1] for seven days, at the time of the grain and grape harvest. [14]You are to rejoice in [a]your festival, you, your son, your daughter, your male and female slaves, the Levites, the resident foreigners, the orphans, and the widows who are in your villages. [15]You are to celebrate the festival [a]seven days before the LORD your God in the place he chooses, for he will bless you in all your productivity and in whatever you do; so you will indeed rejoice! [16a]Three times a year all your males must appear before [b]the LORD your God in the place he chooses for the Feast of Unleavened Bread, the Feast of Weeks, and the Feast of Shelters; and they must not appear before him empty-handed. [17]Every one of you must give as you are able, [a]according to the blessing of the LORD your God that he has given you.

Provision for Justice

[18]You must appoint [a]judges and civil servants for each tribe in all your villages that the LORD your God is giving you, and they must judge the people fairly. [19a]You must not pervert justice [b]or show favor. Do not take a bribe, for bribes blind the eyes of the wise and distort the words of the righteous. [20]You must pursue justice alone so that you may [a]live and inherit the land the LORD your God is giving you.

Examples of Legal Cases

[21]You must not plant any kind of tree as a sacred Asherah pole near the altar of the LORD [a]your God which you build for yourself. [22]You must not erect a sacred pillar, a thing the LORD [a]your God detests.

17 You must not sacrifice to him [a]a bull or sheep that has a blemish or any other defect, because that is considered offensive[1] to the LORD your God. [2a]Suppose a man or woman is discovered among you [b]in one of your villages that the LORD your God is giving you who sins before the LORD your God and breaks his covenant [3]by serving [a]other gods and worshiping them—the sun,[1] moon, or any other heavenly bodies that [b]I have not permitted you to worship. [4]When it is reported to you [a]and you hear about it, you must investigate carefully. If it is indeed true that such a disgraceful thing[1] is being done in Israel, [5]you must bring [a]to your city

16:3 [a] Num 29:12 [b] Exod 13:3; Deut 4:9   16:4 [a] Exod 13:7 [b] Num 9:12   16:6 [a] Exod 12:7–10 [1] Heb. *the Passover.* [2] MT *unto the place.*   16:7 [a] 2 Kgs 23:23   16:8 [a] Exod 12:16; 13:6; Lev 23:8, 36   16:10 [a] Exod 34:22; Lev 23:15–16; Num 28:26 [b] 1 Cor 16:2   16:11 [a] Deut 16:14   16:12 [a] Deut 15:15   16:13 [a] Exod 23:16 [1] Or *Feast of Huts;* trad. *Feast of Tabernacles.*   16:14 [a] Neh 8:9   16:15 [a] Lev 23:39–41   16:16 [a] Exod 23:14–17; 34:22–24 [b] Exod 23:15   16:17 [a] Lev 14:30–31; Deut 16:10   16:18 [a] Exod 23:1–8; Deut 1:16–17; John 7:24   16:19 [a] Exod 23:2, 6 [b] Exod 23:8   16:20 [a] Ezek 18:5–9   16:21 [a] Exod 34:13   16:22 [a] Lev 26:1   17:1 [a] Deut 15:21; Mal 1:8, 13 [1] Heb. *an abomination;* persons, things, or practices offensive to ritual or moral order.   17:2 [a] Deut 13:6 [b] Josh 7:11   17:3 [a] Deut 4:19 [b] Jer 7:22 [1] Thd., Luc. *or to the sun.*   17:4 [a] Deut 13:12, 14 [1] Heb. *an abomination;* persons, things, or practices offensive to ritual or moral order.   17:5 [a] Deut 13:6–18

gates that man or woman who has done this wicked thing—that very man or woman—and you must stone that person to death. [6]At the testimony of two or three [a]witnesses the person must be executed. They cannot be put to death on the testimony of only one witness. [7]The witnesses must be first to begin the execution, and then all the people are to join in afterward. In this way [a]you will purge the evil from among you.

Appeal to a Higher Court

[8]If a matter is too [a]difficult for you to judge—bloodshed, legal claim, or assault—matters of controversy in your villages—you must leave there and go up to the [b]place the LORD your God chooses. [9]You will go [a]to [b]the Levitical priests and the judge in office in those days and seek a solution; they will render a verdict. [10]You must then do as they have determined at that place the LORD chooses. Be careful to do just as you are taught. [11]You must do what you are instructed, and the verdict they pronounce to you, without fail. Do not deviate right or left from what they tell you. [12]The person who pays no attention to [a]the priest currently serving the LORD your God there, or to the judge—that person must die, so that you may purge evil from Israel. [13]Then all the people will hear [a]and be afraid, and not be so presumptuous again.

Provision for Kingship

[14]When you come to the land the LORD your God [a]is giving you and take it over and live in it and then say, "I will select a king like all the nations surrounding me," [15]you must select without fail a king [a]whom the LORD your God chooses. [b]From among your fellow citizens[1] you must appoint a king—you may not designate a foreigner who is not one of your fellow Israelites. [16]Moreover, he must not accumulate [a]horses for himself or allow the people [b]to return to Egypt to do so, for [c]the LORD has said [d]you must never again return that way. [17]Furthermore, he must not

marry many wives lest his affections turn aside, and he must not accumulate much silver and [a]gold. [18]When he sits on his royal throne he must make a copy of this law[1] on a scroll[2] [a]given to him by the Levitical priests. [19]It must be [a]with him constantly, and he must read it as long as he lives, so that he may learn to revere the LORD his God and observe all the words of this law and these statutes and carry them out. [20]Then he will not exalt himself above his fellow citizens or turn from the commandments to the right or left, and he and his descendants will enjoy many years ruling over his kingdom[1] in Israel.

Provision for Priests and Levites

18 The Levitical priests—indeed, the entire tribe of Levi—will have no allotment or [a]inheritance with Israel; they may eat the burnt offerings of the LORD and of his inheritance. [2]They will have no inheritance in the midst of their fellow Israelites; the LORD alone is their inheritance, just as he had told them. [3]This shall be the priests' fair [a]allotment from the people who offer sacrifices, whether bull or sheep—they must give to the priest the shoulder, the jowls, and the stomach. [4]You must give [a]them the best of your grain, new wine, and olive oil, as well as the best of your wool when you shear your flocks. [5]For [a]the LORD your God has chosen them and their sons from all your tribes [b]to stand[1] and serve in his name permanently. [6]Suppose a Levite comes by his own free will from one of your villages, from any part of Israel where he is [a]living, [b]to the place the LORD chooses [7]and serves in the name of the LORD his God like his fellow Levites who stand there before the LORD. [8]He must eat the [a]same share they do, despite any profits he may gain from the sale of his family's inheritance.[1]

Prohibited Occult Practices

[9]When [a]you enter the land the LORD your God is giving you, you must not learn

17:6 [a]Num 35:30; Deut 19:15; Matt 18:16; John 8:17; 2 Cor 13:1; 1 Tim 5:19; Heb 10:28   17:7 [a]Deut 13:5; 19:19; 1 Cor 5:13   17:8 [a]Deut 1:17; 2 Chr 19:10   [b]Deut 12:5; 16:2   17:9 [a]Deut 19:17–19   [b]Ezek 44:24   17:12 [a]Num 15:30; Deut 1:43   17:13 [a]Deut 13:11   17:14 [a]1 Sam 8:5, 19, 20; 10:19   17:15 [a]1 Sam 9:15–16; 10:24; 16:12–13; 1 Chr 22:8–10; Hos 8:4   [b]Jer 30:21   [1]Heb. your brothers.   17:16 [a]1 Kgs 4:26; 10:26–29; Ps 20:7   [b]Isa 31:1; Ezek 17:15   [c]Exod 13:17–18; Hos 11:5   [d]Deut 28:68   17:17 [a]1 Kgs 10:14   17:18 [a]Deut 31:24–26   [1]Or instruction.   [2]Or book; Heb. writing, document.   17:19 [a]Ps 119:97–98   17:20 [1]Heb. upon his kingship.   18:1 [a]Deut 10:9; 1 Cor 9:13   18:3 [a]Lev 7:32–34; Num 18:11–12; 1 Sam 2:13–16, 29   18:4 [a]Exod 22:29   18:5 [a]Exod 28:1   [b]Deut 10:8   [1]Some wss add before the LORD your God.   18:6 [a]Num 35:2   [b]Deut 12:5; 14:23   18:8 [a]Lev 27:30–33; Num 18:21–24; 2 Chr 31:4; Neh 12:44   [1]Presumably this would not refer to a land inheritance, because that was forbidden to the descendants of Levi (v. 1). More likely it referred to some family possessions or other private property, or even support sent by relatives.   18:9 [a]Lev 18:26–27, 30; Deut 12:29–30; 20:16–18

the abhorrent practices of those nations. [10]There must never be found among you anyone who [a]sacrifices his son [b]or daughter in the fire,[1] anyone who practices divination,[2] an omen reader,[3] a soothsayer,[4] a sorcerer,[5] [11]one who casts spells,[1] one who conjures up spirits,[2] a practitioner of the occult,[3] [a]or a necromancer.[4] [12]Whoever does these things is abhorrent to the LORD, and because [a]of these detestable things[1] the LORD your God is about to drive them out from before you. [13]You must be blameless before the LORD your God. [14]Those nations that you are about to dispossess listen to omen readers and diviners, but the LORD your God has not given you permission to do such things.

[15a]The LORD your God will raise up for you a prophet like me from among you—from your fellow Israelites; you must listen to him. [16]This accords with what happened at Horeb [a]in the day of the assembly. You asked the LORD your God: "Please do not make us hear the voice of the LORD our God anymore or see this great fire anymore lest we die." [17]The LORD then said to me, "[a]What they have said is good. [18]I [a]will raise up a prophet like you for them from among their fellow Israelites. [b]I will put my words in his mouth [c]and he will speak to them whatever I command. [19a]I will personally hold responsible anyone who then pays no attention to the words that prophet speaks in my name.

[20]"But if any prophet presumes to speak anything in my name that I have not authorized him to speak, or speaks in [a]the name of other gods, that prophet must die. [21]Now if you say to yourselves, 'How can we tell that a message is not from the LORD?'—[22a]whenever a prophet speaks in my name and the prediction is not fulfilled, then [b]I have not spoken it; the prophet has [c]presumed to speak it, so you need not fear him."

Laws Concerning Manslaughter

19 When the LORD your God destroys the nations whose land he is about to give you and you dispossess them and settle in their cities and houses, [2]you must set apart for [a]yourselves three cities in the middle of your land that the LORD your God is giving you as a possession. [3]You shall build a roadway and divide into thirds the whole extent of your land that the LORD your God is providing as your inheritance; anyone who kills another person should flee to the closest of these cities. [4]Now [a]this is the law pertaining to one who flees there in order to live, if he has accidentally killed another without hating him at the time of the accident. [5]Suppose he goes with someone else to the forest to cut wood and when he raises the ax to cut the tree, the ax head flies loose from the handle and strikes his fellow worker so hard that he dies. The person responsible may then flee to one of these cities to save himself. [6a]Otherwise the blood avenger will chase after the killer in the heat of his anger, eventually overtake him, and kill him, though this is not a capital case since he did not hate him at the time of the accident. [7]Therefore, I am commanding you to set apart for yourselves three cities. [8]If the LORD your God [a]enlarges [b]your borders as he promised your ancestors and gives you all the land he pledged to them, [9]and [a]then you are careful to observe all these commandments[1] I am giving you today (namely, to love the LORD your God and to always walk in his ways), then you must add three more cities to these three. [10a]You must not shed innocent blood in your land that the LORD your God is giving you as an inheritance, for that would make you guilty. [11]However, suppose a person hates someone else and stalks him, attacks him, kills him, and then flees to one of these cities. [12]The

18:10 [a] Lev 18:21; Deut 12:31   [b] Exod 22:18; Lev 19:26, 31; 20:6, 27; Isa 8:19   [1] Heb. *who passes his son or his daughter through the fire*; a euphemism for human sacrifice.   [2] Heb. *a diviner of divination*; a means to determine the future or the outcome of events by observation of various omens and signs.   [3] Heb. *one who causes to appear*; a practitioner thought to be able to conjure up spirits or apparitions.   [4] Heb. *a seeker of omens*; a subset of divination, one illustrated by the use of a "divining cup" in the story of Joseph (Gen 44:5).   [5] Heb. *a doer of sorcery*; having to do with magic or the casting of spells to manipulate the gods or the powers of nature.   **18:11** [a] Lev 20:27   [1] Heb. *a binder of binding*; immobilizing someone or something by using magical words.   [2] Heb. *asker of a* [dead] *spirit*; a form of necromancy.   [3] Heb. *a knowing* [or *familiar*] [spirit]; one who is expert in mantic arts.   [4] Heb. *a seeker of the dead*; much the same as "one who conjures up spirits."   **18:12** [a] Lev 18:24; Deut 9:4   [1] Heb. *these abhorrent things*; an emphatic Heb. construction.   **18:15** [a] Matt 21:11; Luke 1:76; 2:25–34; 7:16; 24:19; Acts 3:22   **18:16** [a] Deut 5:23–27   **18:17** [a] Deut 5:28   **18:18** [a] Deut 34:10; John 1:45; Acts 3:22   [b] Num 23:5; Isa 49:2; 51:16; John 17:8   [c] [John 4:25; 8:28]   **18:19** [a] Acts 3:23; [Heb 12:25]   **18:20** [a] Deut 13:5; Jer 14:14–15; Zech 13:2–5   **18:22** [a] Jer 28:9   [b] Deut 13:2   [c] Deut 18:20   **19:2** [a] Exod 21:13; Num 35:10–15; Deut 4:41; Josh 20:2   **19:4** [a] Num 35:9–34; Deut 4:42   **19:6** [a] Num 35:12   **19:8** [a] Deut 12:20   [b] Gen 15:18–21   **19:9** [a] Josh 20:7–9   [1] Heb. *all this commandment*; the entire covenant agreement of the Book of Deuteronomy as encapsulated in the *Shema* (6:4–5).   **19:10** [a] Num 35:33; Deut 21:1–9

elders of his own city must send for him and remove him from there to deliver him over to the blood avenger[1] to die. [13] You must not pity him, but purge from Israel the guilt of shedding innocent blood, so that it may go well with [a] you.

Laws Concerning Witnesses

[14] You must not encroach on [a] your neighbor's property, which will have been defined in the inheritance you will obtain in the land the LORD your God is giving you.

[15] A [a] single witness may not testify against another person for any trespass or sin that he commits. A matter may be legally established only on the testimony of two or three witnesses. [16] If a false witness [a] testifies against another person and accuses him of a crime, [17] then both parties to the controversy must stand [a] before the LORD, that is, before the priests and judges who will be in office in those days. [18] The judges will thoroughly investigate the matter, and if the witness should prove to be false and to have given false testimony against the accused, [19] you must do to him what [a] he had intended to do to the accused. In this way [b] you will purge[1] the evil from among you. [20] The rest of the people will hear [a] and become afraid to keep doing such evil among you. [21a] You must not show pity; the principle will be a [b] life for a life, an eye for an eye, a tooth for a tooth, a hand for a hand, and a foot for a foot.

Laws Concerning War with Distant Enemies

20 When you go to war against your enemies and see [a] chariotry and troops who outnumber you, do not be [b] afraid of them, for the LORD your God, who brought you up out of the land of Egypt, is [c] with you. [2] As you move forward for battle, the priest will approach and say to the soldiers, [3] "Listen, Israel! Today you are moving forward to do battle with your enemies. Do not be fainthearted. Do not fear and tremble or be terrified because of them, [4] for the LORD

your God goes with you [a] to fight on your behalf against your enemies to give you victory." [5] Moreover, the officers are to say to the troops, "Who among you has built a new house and not [a] dedicated[1] it? He may go home, lest he die in battle and someone else dedicate it. [6] Or who among you has planted a vineyard and not benefited from it? He may go home, lest he die in battle and someone else benefit from it. [7] Or who among you has become engaged to [a] a woman but has not married her? He may go home, lest he die in battle and someone else marry her." [8] In addition, the officers are to say to the troops, "Who among you is afraid and fainthearted? He may go home so that he will not make his fellow soldier's heart as fearful as his own." [9] Then, when the officers have finished speaking,[1] they must appoint unit commanders to lead the troops.

[10] When you approach a city to wage war against it, offer it terms of peace. [11] If it accepts your terms and submits to you, all the people found in it will become your slaves.[1] [12] If it does not accept terms of peace but makes war with you, then you are to lay siege to it. [13] The LORD [a] your God will deliver it over to you, and you must kill every single male by the sword. [14] However, [a] the women, little children, cattle, and anything else in the city—all its plunder—[b] you may take for yourselves as spoil. You may take from your enemies the plunder that the LORD your God has given you. [15] This is how you are to deal with all those cities located far from you, those that do not belong to these nearby nations.

Laws Concerning War with Canaanite Nations

[16] As for the cities [a] of these peoples that the LORD your God is going to give you as an inheritance, you must not allow a single living thing to survive. [17] Instead you must utterly annihilate them—the Hittites, Amorites, Canaanites, Perizzites, Hivites, and Jebusites[1]—just as the LORD your God

19:12 [1] Heb. *avenger of blood*; ordinarily a member of the victim's family who, after due process of law, was invited to initiate the process of execution (cf. 35:16–28).   **19:13** [a] Deut 13:8   **19:14** [a] Deut 27:17; Job 24:2; Prov 22:28; Hos 5:10   **19:15** [a] Num 35:30; Deut 17:6; Matt 18:16; John 8:17; 2 Cor 13:1; 1 Tim 5:19; Heb 10:28   **19:16** [a] Exod 23:1; Ps 27:12; 35:11   **19:17** [a] Deut 17:8–11; 21:5   **19:19** [a] Prov 19:5; Dan 6:24   [b] Deut 13:5; 17:7; 21:21; 22:21   [1] Heb. *you will burn out.*   **19:20** [a] Deut 17:13; 21:21   **19:21** [a] Deut 19:13   [b] Exod 21:23–24; Lev 24:20; Matt 5:38–39   **20:1** [a] Ps 20:7; Isa 31:1   [b] Deut 7:18   [c] Num 23:21; Deut 5:6; 31:6, 8; 2 Chr 13:12; 32:7–8; Ps 23:4; Isa 41:10   **20:4** [a] Deut 1:30; 3:22; Josh 23:10   **20:5** [a] Neh 12:27   [1] Perhaps with a religious connotation.   **20:7** [a] Deut 24:5   **20:9** [1] The Heb. text includes *to the people.*   **20:11** [1] Heb. *become as a vassal and will serve you.*   **20:13** [a] Num 31:7   **20:14** [a] Josh 8:2   [b] 1 Sam 14:30   **20:16** [a] Exod 23:31–33; Num 21:2–3; Deut 7:1–5; Josh 11:14   **20:17** [1] LXX adds *Girgashites.*

has commanded you, [18]so that [a]they cannot teach you all the abhorrent ways they worship their gods, causing you to [b]sin against the LORD your God. [19]If you besiege a city for a long time while attempting to capture it, you must not chop down its trees, for you may eat fruit from them and should not cut them down. A tree in the field is not human that you should besiege it! [20]However, you may chop down any tree you know is not suitable for food, and you may use it to build siege works against the city that is making war with you until that city falls.

Laws Concerning Unsolved Murders

21 If a homicide victim should be found lying in a field in the land the LORD your God is giving you, and no one knows who killed him, [2]your elders and judges must go out and measure how far it is to the cities in the vicinity of the corpse. [3]Then the elders of the city nearest to the corpse must take from the herd a heifer that has not been worked—that has never pulled with the [a]yoke—[4]and bring the heifer down to a wadi with flowing water, to a valley that is neither plowed nor sown. There at the wadi they are to break the heifer's neck. [5]Then [a]the Levitical priests will approach (for the LORD your God has chosen them to serve him and to pronounce blessings in his name, and to decide every judicial verdict), [6]and [a]all the elders of that city nearest the corpse must wash their hands over the heifer whose neck was broken in the valley.[1] [7]Then they must proclaim, "Our hands have not spilled this blood, nor have we witnessed the crime.[1] [8]Do not blame your people Israel whom you redeemed, O LORD, [a]and do not hold them accountable for the bloodshed of an innocent person." Then atonement will be made for the bloodshed. [9]In this manner [a]you will purge the guilt of innocent blood from among you, for you must do what is right before the LORD.

Laws Concerning Female Captives

[10]When you go out to do battle with your enemies and the LORD your God allows you to prevail and you take prisoners, [11]if you should see among them an attractive woman whom you wish to take as a [a]wife, [12]you may bring her back to your house. She must [a]shave her head, trim her nails, [13]discard the clothing she was wearing when captured, and stay in your house, [a]lamenting for her father and mother for a full month. After that you may sleep with her[1] and become her husband and she your wife. [14]If you are not pleased with her, then you must let her go where she pleases. You cannot in any case sell her; you must not take advantage of her, since you have already [a]humiliated her.

Laws Concerning Children

[15]Suppose [a]a man has two wives, one whom he loves more than the other, and they both bear him sons, with the firstborn being the child of the less-loved wife. [16]In the day he divides his inheritance he must not appoint as firstborn the [a]son of the favorite wife in place of the other wife's son who is actually the firstborn. [17]Rather, he must acknowledge the son of the less-loved wife as firstborn and give him the double portion of all he has, for that son [a]is [b]the beginning of his father's procreative power[1]—to him should go the right of the firstborn.

[18]If a person has a stubborn, rebellious son who pays no attention to his father or mother, and they discipline him to no avail, [19]his father and mother must seize him and bring him to the elders at the gate of his city. [20]They must declare to the elders[1] of his city, "Our son is stubborn and rebellious and pays no attention to what we say—he is a glutton and drunkard." [21]Then all the men of his city must stone him to death. In this way you will purge wickedness from among you, [a]and all Israel[1] will hear about it and be afraid.

Disposition of a Criminal's Remains

[22]If a person commits a sin punishable [a]by death and is executed, and you hang the corpse on a tree, [23]his body must not remain all night on the tree; instead you must make certain you bury him that same

20:18 [a]Exod 34:12–16; Deut 7:4; 12:30; 18:9 [b]Exod 23:33; 2 Kgs 21:3–15; Ps 106:34–41   21:3 [a]Num 19:2   21:5 [a]Deut 10:8; 1 Chr 23:13   21:6 [a]Ps 19:12; 26:6; Matt 27:24 [1]Heb. *wadi*; a seasonal watercourse through a valley.   21:7 [1]Heb. *seen*; *the crime* is supplied.   21:8 [a]Deut 19:10, 13; Jonah 1:14   21:9 [a]Deut 19:13   21:11 [a]Num 31:18   21:12 [a]Lev 14:8–9; Num 6:9   21:13 [a]Ps 45:10 [1]Heb. *to come*; a euphemism for sexual relations.   21:14 [a]Gen 34:2; Deut 22:29; Judg 19:24   21:15 [a]Gen 29:33   21:16 [a]1 Chr 5:2; 26:10   21:17 [a]Gen 49:3 [b]Gen 25:31, 33 [1]Heb. *his generative power.*   21:20 [1]LXX, Smr. add *to the men.*   21:21 [a]Deut 13:11 [1]Some LXX traditions *those who remain.*   21:22 [a]Deut 22:26; Matt 26:66; Mark 14:64; Acts 23:29

day, for the one who [a]is left exposed[1] on a tree is cursed by God. [b]You must not defile your land that [c]the LORD your God is giving you as an inheritance.

Laws Concerning Preservation of Life

22 When you see your neighbor's ox or sheep going astray, do not ignore it; you must return it without fail to your neighbor. [2]If the owner does not live near you or you do not know who the owner is, then you must corral the animal at your house and let it stay with you until the owner looks for it; then you must return it to him. [3]You shall do the same to his donkey, his clothes, or anything else your neighbor has lost and you have found; you must not refuse to get involved. [4]When [a]you see your neighbor's donkey or ox fallen along the road, do not ignore it; instead, you must be sure to help him get the animal on its feet again.

[5]A woman must not wear men's clothing, nor should a man dress up in women's clothing, for anyone who does this is offensive[1] to the LORD your God.

[6]If [a]you happen to notice a bird's nest along the road, whether in a tree or on the ground, and there are chicks or eggs with the mother bird sitting on them, you must not take the mother that is with her young. [7]You must be sure to let the mother go, but you may take the young for yourself. Do this so [a]that it may go well with you and you may have a long life.

[8]If you build a new house, you must construct a guardrail around your roof to avoid being culpable in the event someone should fall from it.

Illustrations of the Principle of Purity

[9]You must not plant [a]your vineyard with two kinds of seed; otherwise the entire yield, both of the seed you plant and the produce of the vineyard, will be defiled. [10a]You must not plow with an ox and a donkey harnessed together. [11a]You must not wear clothing made with wool and linen meshed together. [12]You shall make yourselves [a]tassels for the four corners of the clothing you wear.

Purity in the Marriage Relationship

[13]Suppose a man marries a woman, sleeps with her, and then [a]rejects her, [14]accusing her of impropriety and defaming her reputation by saying, "I married this woman but when I approached her for marital relations I discovered she was not a virgin!" [15]Then the father and mother of the young woman must produce the evidence of virginity for the elders of the city at the gate. [16]The young woman's father must say to the elders, "I gave my daughter to this man and he has rejected her. [17]Moreover, he has raised accusations of impropriety by saying, 'I discovered your daughter was not a virgin,' but this is the evidence of my daughter's virginity!" The cloth must then be spread out before the city's elders. [18]The elders of that city must then seize the man and punish him. [19]They will fine him 100 shekels of silver and give them to the young woman's father, for the man who made the accusation ruined the reputation of an Israelite virgin. She will then become his wife, and he may never divorce her as long as he lives.

[20]But if the accusation is true and the young woman was not a virgin, [21]the men of her city must bring the young woman to the door of her father's house and [a]stone her to death, for she has [b]done a disgraceful thing[1] in Israel by behaving like a prostitute while living in her father's house. In this way you will purge the evil from among you.

[22a]If a man is discovered in bed with a married woman, both the man lying in bed with the woman and the woman herself must die; in this way you will purge the evil from Israel.

[23]If a virgin is [a]engaged to a man and another man meets her in the city and goes to bed with her, [24]you must bring the two of them to the gate of that city and stone them to death, the young woman because she did not cry out though in the city and the man because he [a]violated his neighbor's fiancée; in this way you will purge evil from among you. [25]But if the man came across the engaged woman in the field and overpowered her and raped her, then only the

rapist must die. [26]You must not do anything to the young woman—she has done nothing deserving of death. This case is the same as when someone attacks another person and murders him, [27]for the man met her in the field and the engaged woman cried out, but there was no one to rescue her.

[28a]Suppose a man comes across a virgin who is not engaged and takes hold of her and sleeps with her and they are discovered. [29]The man who has slept with her must pay her father [a]50 shekels of silver and she must become his wife. [b]Because he has humiliated her, he may never divorce her as long as he lives.

[30]A [a]man may not marry his father's former wife and in this way [b]dishonor his father.

Purity in Public Worship

23 A man with crushed or severed genitals may [a]not enter the assembly of the LORD. [2]A person of illegitimate birth may not enter the assembly of the LORD; to the tenth generation no one related to him may do so.

[3]No Ammonite or Moabite may enter the assembly of the LORD; to the tenth generation none of their [a]descendants shall ever do so, [4a]for they did not meet you with food and water on the way as you came from Egypt, and furthermore, they hired Balaam son of Beor of Pethor in Aram Naharaim to curse you. [5]But the LORD your God refused to listen to Balaam and changed the curse to a blessing, for the LORD your God [a]loves[1] you. [6a]You must not seek peace and prosperity for them through all the ages to come. [7]You must not hate an Edomite, [a]for he is [b]your relative; you must not hate an Egyptian, for you lived as a foreigner in his land. [8]Children of the third generation born to them may enter the assembly of the LORD.

Purity in Personal Hygiene

[9]When you go out as an army against your enemies, guard yourselves against anything impure. [10a]If there is someone among you who is impure because of some nocturnal emission,[1] he must leave the camp; he may not reenter it immediately. [11]When evening arrives [a]he must wash himself with water, and then at sunset he may reenter the camp.

[12]You are to have a place outside the camp to serve as a latrine. [13]You must have a spade among your other equipment, and when you relieve yourself[1] outside you must dig a hole with the spade and then turn and cover your excrement. [14]For the LORD your God walks [a]about in the middle of your camp to deliver you and defeat your enemies for you. Therefore your camp should be holy, so that he does not see anything indecent[1] among you and turn away from you.

Purity in the Treatment of the Unprivileged

[15]You must not return an escaped slave to his master when he has run away to [a]you. [16]Indeed, he may live among [a]you in any place he chooses, in whichever of your villages he prefers; you must not oppress him.

Cultic Prostitution Banned

[17]There must never be a sacred prostitute among the young women [a]of Israel nor a sacred male [b]prostitute among the young men of Israel. [18]You must never bring the pay of a female prostitute or the wage of a male prostitute[1] into the temple of the LORD your God in fulfillment of any vow, for both of these are abhorrent to the LORD your God.

Respect for Others' Property

[19]You must not charge interest on a loan to [a]your fellow Israelite, whether on money, food, or anything else that has been loaned with interest. [20]You may lend with interest [a]to [b]a foreigner, but not to your fellow Israelite; if you keep this command the LORD your God will bless you in all you undertake in the land you are about to enter to possess. [21]When you make a vow to the LORD

22:28 a Exod 22:16–17   **22:29** a Exod 22:16–17   b Deut 22:24   **22:30** a Lev 18:8; 20:11; Deut 27:20; 1 Cor 5:1   b Ruth 3:9; Ezek 16:8   **23:1** a Lev 21:20; 22:24   **23:3** a Neh 13:1–2   **23:4** a Deut 2:27–30   **23:5** a Deut 4:37   1 I.e., God's elective grace toward Israel.   **23:6** a Ezra 9:12   **23:7** a Gen 25:24–26; Deut 2:4, 8; Amos 1:11; Obad 10, 12   b Exod 22:21; 23:9; Lev 19:34; Deut 10:19   **23:10** a Lev 15:16   1 Heb. *nocturnal happening*; a euphemism for some kind of bodily emission such as excrement or semen.   **23:11** a Lev 15:5   **23:13** 1 Heb. *sit*; a euphemism.   **23:14** a Lev 26:12; Deut 7:21   1 Heb. *nakedness of a thing*; specifically sexual organs and, by extension, to any function associated with them.   **23:15** a 1 Sam 30:15   **23:16** a Exod 22:21; Prov 22:22   **23:17** a Lev 19:29; Deut 22:21   b Gen 19:5; 2 Kgs 23:7   **23:18** 1 Heb. *of a dog*; a common Heb. term for a noncultic male prostitute.   **23:19** a Exod 22:25; Lev 25:35–37; Neh 5:2–7; Ps 15:5   **23:20** a Deut 15:3   b Deut 15:10

your God you must not delay in fulfilling it, for otherwise [a]he will surely hold you accountable as a sinner. [22]If you refrain from making a vow, it will not be sinful. [23]Whatever you vow, you must be careful to do what you have promised, such as what you have vowed to the LORD your God as [a]a freewill offering. [24]When you enter the vineyard of your neighbor you may eat as many grapes as you please, but you must not take away any in a container. [25]When [a]you go into the ripe grain fields of your neighbor you may pluck off the kernels with your hand, but you must not use a sickle on your neighbor's ripe grain.

24 If a [a]man marries a woman and she does not please him because he has found something indecent in her, then he may draw up a divorce [b]document, give it to her, and evict her from his house. [2]When she has left him she may go and become someone else's wife. [3]If the second husband rejects her and then divorces her, gives her the papers, and evicts her from his house, or if the second husband who married her dies, [4]her first husband who divorced her is not permitted to remarry her after she has become ritually impure, for that is offensive to [a]the LORD. You must not bring guilt on the land that the LORD your God is giving you as an inheritance.

[5]When a man is newly married, [a]he need not go into the army nor be obligated [b]in any way; he must be free to stay at home for a full year and bring joy to[1] the wife he has married.

[6]One must not take either lower or upper millstones as security on a loan, for that is like taking a life itself as security.

[7]If a man is [a]found kidnapping [b]a person from among his fellow Israelites, and regards him as mere property and sells him, that kidnapper must die. In this way you will purge the evil from among you.

Respect for Human Dignity

[8]Be careful during [a]an outbreak of leprosy to follow precisely all that the Levitical priests instruct you; as I have commanded them, so you should do. [9][a]Remember what the LORD your God did [b]to Miriam along the way after you left Egypt.

[10]When you [a]make any kind of loan to your neighbor, you may not go into his house to claim what he is offering as security. [11]You must stand outside and the person to whom you are making the loan will bring out to you what he is offering as security. [12]If the person is poor you may not use what he gives you as security for a covering. [13]You must by all means return to him at sunset the item he gave [a]you as security so that he may sleep in his outer garment and [b]bless you for [c]it; it will be considered a just deed by the LORD your God.

[14]You must not [a]oppress a lowly and poor servant, whether one from among your fellow Israelites or from the resident foreigners who are living in your land and villages. [15]You must pay his wage that very day before the sun sets, for he is poor and his life depends on it. Otherwise he will cry out to the LORD against [a]you, and you will be guilty of sin.

[16][a]Fathers must not be put to death for what their children do, nor children for what their fathers do; each must be put to death for his own sin.

[17][a]You must not pervert justice due a resident foreigner [b]or an orphan, or take a widow's garment as security for a loan. [18]Remember that [a]you were slaves in Egypt and that the LORD your God redeemed you from there; therefore I am commanding you to do all this. [19][a]Whenever you reap your harvest in your field and leave some unraked grain there, you must not return to get it; it should go to the resident foreigner, orphan, and widow so that the LORD your God may [b]bless all the work you do. [20]When you beat your olive tree you must not repeat the procedure; the remaining olives belong to the resident foreigner, orphan, and widow. [21]When you gather the grapes of your vineyard you must not do so a second time; they should go to the resident foreigner, orphan, and widow. [22]Remember that you were slaves in the land of Egypt; therefore, I am commanding you to do all this.

23:21[a]Num 30:1–2; Job 22:27; Ps 61:8; Eccl 5:4–5; Matt 5:33 **23:23**[a]Num 30:2; Ps 66:13–14 **23:25**[a]Matt 12:1; Mark 2:23; Luke 6:1 **24:1**[a][Matt 5:31; 19:7; Mark 10:4] [b][Jer 3:8] **24:4**[a][Jer 3:1] **24:5**[a]Deut 20:7 [b]Prov 5:18 [1]Some wss *enjoy*. **24:7**[a]Exod 21:16 [b]Deut 19:19 **24:8**[a]Lev 13:2; 14:2 **24:9**[a][1 Cor 10:6] [b]Num 12:10 **24:10**[a]Matt 5:42 **24:13**[a]Exod 22:26; Ezek 18:7 [b]Job 29:11; 2 Tim 1:18 [c]Deut 6:25; Ps 106:31; Dan 4:27 **24:14**[a]Lev 19:13; Deut 15:7–18; [Prov 14:31]; Amos 4:1; [Mal 3:5; 1 Tim 5:18] **24:15**[a]Lev 19:13; Jer 22:13 **24:16**[a]2 Kgs 14:6; 2 Chr 25:4; Jer 31:29–30; Ezek 18:20 **24:17**[a]Exod 23:6 [b]Exod 22:26 **24:18**[a]Deut 24:22 **24:19**[a]Lev 19:9–10 [b]Deut 15:10; Ps 41:1; Prov 19:17

25 If ᵃcontroversy arises between people, they should go to court for judgment. When the judges hear the case, they shall ᵇexonerate the innocent but condemn the guilty. ²Then, if the guilty person is sentenced ᵃto ᵇa beating, the judge shall force him to lie down and be beaten in his presence with the number of blows his wicked behavior deserves. ³The judge may sentence him to ᵃ40 blows, but no more. If he is struck with more than these, you might view your fellow Israelite with contempt.

⁴You must not muzzle ᵃyour ox when it is treading grain.

Respect for the Sanctity of Others

⁵If brothers live together and one of them dies without having a son, the dead man's ᵃwife must not remarry someone outside the family. Instead, her late husband's brother must go to her, marry her, and perform the duty of a brother-in-law. ⁶Then the first son she bears ᵃwill continue the name of the dead brother, thus preventing ᵇhis name from being blotted out of Israel. ⁷But if the man does not want to marry his brother's widow, then she must go to the elders at the town ᵃgate and say, "My husband's brother refuses to preserve his brother's name in Israel; he is unwilling to perform the duty of a brother-in-law to me!" ⁸Then the elders of ᵃhis city must summon him and speak to him. If he persists, saying, "I don't want to marry her," ⁹then his sister-in-law must approach him in view of the elders, ᵃremove his sandal from his foot, and spit in his face. She will then respond, "Thus may it be done to any man who does not maintain his brother's family line!" ¹⁰His family name will be referred to in Israel as "the family of the one whose sandal was removed."

¹¹If two men get into a hand-to-hand fight, and the wife of one of them gets involved to help her husband against his attacker, and she reaches out her hand and grabs his private parts,¹ ¹²then ᵃyou must cut off her hand—do not pity her.

¹³You must not have in ᵃyour bag different stone weights, a heavy and a light one. ¹⁴You must not have in your house different measuring containers,¹ a large and a small one. ¹⁵You must have an accurate and correct stone weight and an accurate and correct measuring container, so ᵃthat your life may be extended in the land the LORD your God is about to give you. ¹⁶For anyone who acts dishonestly in these ways is abhorrent to the LORD your God.

Treatment of the Amalekites

¹⁷ᵃRemember what the Amalekites did to you on your way from Egypt, ¹⁸how they met you along the way and cut off all your stragglers in the rear of the march when you were exhausted and tired; they were unafraid of God. ¹⁹So ᵃwhen the LORD your God gives you relief from all the enemies who surround you in the land he is giving you as an inheritance, you must wipe out the memory of the Amalekites from under heaven—do not forget!

Presentation of the Firstfruits

26 When you enter the land that the LORD your God is giving you as an inheritance, and you occupy it and live in it, ²you must take the first of all the ground's produce you harvest from the land the LORD your God is giving you, place it in ᵃa basket, and ᵇgo to the place where he chooses to locate his name. ³You must go to the priest in office at that time and say to him, "I declare today to the LORD your¹ God that I have come into the land that the LORD² promised to our ancestors to give us." ⁴The priest will then take the basket from you and set it before the altar of the LORD your God. ⁵Then you must ᵃaffirm before the LORD your God, "ᵇA wandering Aramean was my ancestor, and ᶜhe went down to Egypt and lived there as a foreigner with a household ᵈfew in number, but there he became a ᵉgreat, powerful, and numerous people. ⁶But the ᵃEgyptians mistreated and oppressed us, forcing us to do burdensome labor. ⁷So we cried out to ᵃthe LORD, the God of our ancestors, and he heard us

25:1 ᵃDeut 17:8–13; 19:17; Ezek 44:24   ᵇProv 17:15   25:2 ᵃProv 19:29; Luke 12:48   ᵇMatt 10:17   25:3 ᵃ2 Cor 11:24   25:4 ᵃ[Prov 12:10; 1 Cor 9:9; 1 Tim 5:18]   25:5 ᵃMatt 22:24; Mark 12:19; Luke 20:28   25:6 ᵃGen 38:9   ᵇRuth 4:5, 10   25:7 ᵃRuth 4:1–2   25:8 ᵃRuth 4:6   25:9 ᵃRuth 4:7–8   25:11 ¹Heb. *shameful parts.*   25:12 ᵃDeut 7:2; 19:13   25:13 ᵃLev 19:35–37; Prov 11:1; 20:23; Ezek 45:10; Mic 6:11   25:14 ¹Heb. *an ephah and an ephah.*   25:15 ᵃExod 20:12   25:17 ᵃExod 17:8–16; 1 Sam 15:1–3   25:19 ᵃ1 Sam 15:3   26:2 ᵃExod 22:29; 23:16, 19; Num 18:13; Deut 16:10; Prov 3:9   ᵇDeut 12:5   26:3 ¹Some LXX MSS *my God.*   ²Syr. adds *your God.*   26:5 ᵃGen 25:20; Hos 12:12   ᵇGen 43:1–2; 45:7, 11   ᶜGen 46:1, 6; Acts 7:15   ᵈGen 46:27; Deut 10:22   ᵉDeut 1:10   26:6 ᵃExod 1:8–11, 14   26:7 ᵃExod 2:23–25; 3:9; 4:31

and saw our humiliation, toil, and oppression. [8]Therefore [a]the LORD brought us out of Egypt [b]with tremendous strength and power, as well as with great awe-inspiring signs and wonders. [9]Then he brought us to this [a]place and gave us this land, a land flowing with milk and honey. [10]So now, look! I have brought the first of the ground's produce that you, LORD, have given me." Then you must set it down before the LORD your God and worship before him. [11]You will celebrate all the good things that the LORD [a]your God has given you and your family, along with the Levites and the resident foreigners among you.

Presentation of the Third-Year Tithe

[12]When you finish [a]tithing all[1] your income in [b]the third year (the year of tithing), you must give it to the Levites, the resident foreigners, the orphans, and the widows so that they may eat to their satisfaction in your villages. [13]Then you shall say before the LORD your God, "I have removed the sacred offering from my house and given it to the Levites, the resident foreigners, the orphans, and the widows just as you have commanded me. I have not violated [a]or forgotten your commandments. [14]I have not eaten [a]anything when I was in mourning, or removed any of it while ceremonially unclean, or offered any of it to the dead; I have obeyed you and have done everything you have commanded me. [15a]Look down from your holy dwelling [b]place in heaven and bless your people Israel and the land you have given us, just as you promised our ancestors—a land flowing with milk and honey."

Narrative Interlude

[16]Today the LORD your God is commanding you to keep these statutes and ordinances, something you must do with all your heart and soul. [17]Today you have [a]declared the LORD to be your God, and that you will walk in his ways, keep his statutes, commandments, and ordinances, and [b]obey him. [18]And today [a]the LORD has declared you to be his special people (as he already promised you) so you may keep all his commandments. [19]Then he will [a]elevate you [b]above all the nations he has made and you will receive praise, fame, and honor. You will be a people holy to the LORD your God, as he has said.

The Assembly at Shechem

27 Then Moses and the elders of Israel commanded the people: "Pay attention to all the commandments I am giving you today. [2]When [a]you cross the Jordan River to the land the LORD your God is giving you, you must erect great stones and cover them with plaster. [3]Then you must inscribe on them [a]all the words of this law when you cross over, so that you may enter the land the LORD your God is giving you, a land flowing with milk and honey just as the LORD, the God of your ancestors, said to you. [4]So when you cross the Jordan you must erect [a]on Mount Ebal[1] these stones about which I am commanding you today, and you must cover them with plaster. [5]Then [a]you must build an altar there to the LORD your God, an altar of stones—do not use an iron tool on them. [6]You must build the altar of the LORD your God with whole stones and offer burnt offerings on it to the LORD your God. [7]Also you must offer fellowship offerings and eat them there, [a]rejoicing before the LORD your God. [8]You must [a]inscribe on the stones all the words of this law, making them clear."

[9]Then Moses and the Levitical priests spoke to all Israel: "Be quiet and pay attention, Israel. Today you have become the people of the LORD your God. [10]You must obey him and keep his commandments and statutes that I am giving you today." [11]Moreover, Moses commanded the people that day: [12]"The following tribes must stand to bless the people [a]on Mount Gerizim when you cross the Jordan: Simeon, Levi, Judah, Issachar, Joseph, and Benjamin. [13]And [a]these other tribes must stand for the curse on Mount Ebal: Reuben, Gad, Asher, Zebulun, Dan, and Naphtali.

26:8 [a] Exod 12:37, 51; 13:3, 14, 16; Deut 5:15 [b] Deut 4:34; 34:11–12 **26:9** [a] Exod 3:8, 17 **26:11** [a] Deut 12:7; 16:11; Eccl 3:12–13; 5:18–20 **26:12** [a] Lev 27:30; Num 18:24 [b] Deut 14:28–29 [1] The Heb. text includes *the tithes of.* **26:13** [a] Ps 119:141, 153, 176 **26:14** [a] Lev 7:20; Jer 16:7; Hos 9:4 **26:15** [a] Ps 80:14; Isa 63:15; Zech 2:13 [b] Exod 3:8 **26:17** [a] Exod 20:19 [b] Deut 15:5 **26:18** [a] Exod 6:7; 19:5; Deut 7:6; 14:2; 28:9; [Titus 2:14; 1 Pet 2:9] **26:19** [a] Deut 4:7–8; 28:1 [b] Exod 19:6; Deut 7:6; 28:9; Isa 62:12; [1 Pet 2:9] **27:2** [a] Josh 8:32 **27:3** [a] Exod 3:8 **27:4** [a] Deut 11:29; Josh 8:30–31 [1] Smr. *Mount Gerizim.* **27:5** [a] Exod 20:25; Josh 8:31 **27:7** [a] Deut 26:11 **27:8** [a] Josh 8:32 **27:12** [a] Deut 11:29; Josh 8:33; Judg 9:7 **27:13** [a] Deut 11:29; Josh 8:33

The Covenant Curses

[14]"The Levites will call out to every Israelite with a loud voice: [15]'[a]Cursed is the one who makes [b]a carved or metal image—something abhorrent to the LORD, the work of the craftsman—and sets it up in a secret place.' Then all the people will say, 'Amen!' [16]'[a]Cursed is the one who disrespects his father and mother.' Then all the people will say, 'Amen!' [17]'[a]Cursed is the one who moves his neighbor's boundary marker.' Then all the people will say, 'Amen!' [18]'[a]Cursed is the one who misleads a blind person on the road.' Then all the people will say, 'Amen!' [19]'[a]Cursed is the one who perverts justice for the resident foreigner, the orphan, and the widow.' Then all the people will say, 'Amen!' [20]'[a]Cursed is the one who goes to bed with his father's former wife, for he dishonors his father.' Then all the people will say, 'Amen!' [21]'[a]Cursed is the one who commits bestiality.' Then all the people will say, 'Amen!' [22]'[a]Cursed is the one who goes to bed with his sister, the daughter of either his father or mother.' Then all the people will say, 'Amen!' [23]'[a]Cursed is the one who goes to bed with his mother-in-law.' Then all the people will say, 'Amen!' [24]'[a]Cursed is the one who kills his neighbor in private.' Then all the people will say, 'Amen!' [25]'[a]Cursed is the one who takes a bribe to kill an innocent person.' Then all the people will say, 'Amen!' [26]'[a]Cursed is the one who refuses to keep the words of this law.' Then all the people will say, 'Amen!'

The Covenant Blessings

28 "If you indeed obey the LORD your God and are careful to observe all his commandments [a]I am giving you today, the LORD your God [b]will elevate you above all the nations of the earth. [2]All these blessings will come to you in [a]abundance if you obey the LORD your God: [3]You will be [a]blessed [b]in the city and blessed in the field. [4]Your children will be blessed, as well as [a]the produce of your soil, the offspring of your livestock, the calves of your herds, and the lambs of your flocks. [5]Your basket and your mixing bowl will be blessed. [6]You will be [a]blessed when you come in and blessed when you go out. [7]The LORD [a]will cause your enemies who attack you to be struck down before you; they will attack you from one direction but flee from you in seven different directions. [8]The LORD will [a]decree blessing for you with respect to your barns and in everything you [b]do—yes, he will bless you in the land he is giving you. [9]The LORD will designate you as his holy people just as [a]he promised you, if you keep his commandments and obey him. [10]Then all the peoples of the earth will see that you belong [a]to the LORD,[1] and they will [b]respect you. [11]The LORD will greatly multiply your children, [a]the offspring of your livestock, and the produce of your soil in the land that he promised your ancestors he would give you. [12]The LORD will open for you his good treasure house, the heavens, [a]to give you rain for the land in its season and [b]to bless all [c]you do; you will lend to many nations but you will not borrow from any. [13]The LORD will make [a]you the head and not the tail, and you will always end up at the top and not at the bottom, if you obey his commandments that I am urging you today to be careful to do. [14][a]But you must not turn away from all the commandments I am giving you today, to either the right or left, nor pursue other gods and worship them.

Curses as Reversal of Blessings

[15]"But [a]if you ignore the LORD your God and are not careful to keep all his commandments and statutes I am giving you today, then all these curses will come upon you in full force: [16]You will be cursed in the city and cursed in the field. [17]Your basket and your mixing bowl will be cursed. [18]Your children will be cursed, as well as the produce of your soil, the calves of your herds, and the lambs of your flocks. [19]You will be cursed when you come in and cursed when you go out.

27:15 [a]Exod 20:4, 23; 34:17; Lev 19:4; 26:1; Deut 4:16, 23; Isa 44:9; Hos 13:2 [b]Num 5:22; Jer 11:5; 1 Cor 14:16 **27:16** [a]Exod 20:12; Lev 19:3; 20:9; Deut 5:16; 21:18–21; Ezek 22:7 **27:17** [a]Deut 19:14; Prov 22:28 **27:18** [a]Lev 19:14 **27:19** [a]Exod 22:21–22; 23:9; Lev 19:33; Deut 10:18; 24:17 **27:20** [a]Lev 18:8; 20:11; Deut 22:30; 1 Cor 5:1 **27:21** [a]Exod 22:19; Lev 18:23; 20:15–16 **27:22** [a]Lev 18:9 **27:23** [a]Lev 18:17; 20:14 **27:24** [a]Exod 20:13; 21:12; Lev 24:17; Num 35:30–31 **27:25** [a]Exod 23:7; Ps 15:5; Ezek 22:12 **27:26** [a]Ps 119:21; Jer 11:3; Gal 3:10 **28:1** [a]Exod 15:26; Lev 26:3–13; Deut 7:12–26; 11:13 [b]Deut 26:19; 1 Chr 14:2 **28:2** [a]Deut 28:15 **28:3** [a]Ps 128:1, 4 [b]Gen 39:5 **28:4** [a]Gen 22:17 **28:6** [a]Ps 121:8 **28:7** [a]Lev 26:7–8 **28:8** [a]Lev 25:21 [b]Deut 15:10 **28:9** [a]Exod 19:5–6 **28:10** [a]Num 6:27; 2 Chr 7:14; Isa 63:19; Dan 9:18–19 [b]Deut 11:25 [1]Heb. *the name of the Lord is called over you*; an idiom indicating ownership. **28:11** [a]Deut 30:9 **28:12** [a]Lev 26:4; Deut 11:14 [b]Deut 14:29 [c]Deut 15:6 **28:13** [a][Isa 9:14–15] **28:14** [a]Deut 5:32; Josh 1:7 **28:15** [a]Lev 26:14–39; Josh 23:15; Dan 9:10–14; Mal 2:2

Curses by Disease and Drought

20 "The LORD will send on you a [a]curse, [b]confusing you and [c]opposing you in everything you undertake until you are destroyed and quickly perish because of the evil of your deeds, in that you have forsaken me.[1] 21 The LORD will plague you with deadly diseases until he has completely removed you from the land you are about to possess. 22[a] He will afflict you with weakness, fever, inflammation, infection, sword, [b]blight, and mildew; these will attack you until you perish. 23 The sky above [a]your heads will be bronze and the earth beneath you iron. 24 The LORD will make the rain of your land powder and dust; it will come down on you from the sky until you are destroyed.

Curses by Defeat and Deportation

25 "The LORD will allow you to be struck down before your enemies; you will attack [a]them from one direction but flee from them in seven directions and will become an object of terror to all the kingdoms of the earth. 26[a] Your carcasses will be food for every bird of the sky and wild animal of the earth, and there will be no one to chase them off. 27 The LORD will afflict you with [a]the boils of Egypt and with [b]tumors, eczema, and scabies, all of which cannot be healed. 28 The LORD will also subject you to madness, blindness, and [a]confusion of mind. 29 You will [a]feel your way along at noon like the blind person does in darkness and you will not succeed in anything you do; you will be constantly oppressed and continually robbed, with no one to save you. 30 You will be engaged to a woman, and another man will rape[1] her. [a]You will build a house but not live in it. [b]You will plant a vineyard but not even begin to use it. 31 Your ox will be slaughtered before your very eyes, but you will not eat of it. Your donkey will be stolen from you as you watch and will not be returned to you. Your flock of sheep will be given to your enemies, and there will be no one to save you. 32 Your sons and daughters will be given to [a]another people while you look on in [b]vain all day, and you will be powerless to do anything about [c]it. 33 As for

[a]the produce of your land and all your labor, a people you do not know will consume it, and you will be nothing but oppressed and crushed for the rest of your lives. 34 You will go insane from seeing all this. 35 The LORD will afflict you in your knees and on your legs with painful, incurable boils—from the soles of your feet to the top of your head. 36 The LORD will [a]force you and your king[1] whom you will appoint over you to go away to a people whom you and your ancestors have not known, and you will serve other gods of wood and stone [b]there. 37 You will become [a]an occasion of horror, [b]a proverb, and an object of ridicule to all the peoples to whom the LORD will drive you.

The Curse of Reversed Status

38 "[a]You will take much seed to [b]the field but gather little harvest, because locusts will consume it. 39 You will plant vineyards and cultivate them, but you will not drink [a]wine or gather in grapes, because worms will eat them. 40 You will have olive trees throughout your territory, but you will not anoint yourself with olive oil, because the olives will drop off the trees while still unripe. 41 You will bear sons and daughters but not keep them, because [a]they will be taken into captivity. 42 Whirring locusts will take over every tree and all the produce of your soil. 43 The resident foreigners who reside among you will become higher and higher over you, and you will become lower and lower. 44 They will lend to you, but you will not lend to them; they will become the head, and you will become the tail!

45 "All these curses will fall on you, pursuing and overtaking you until you are destroyed, because you would not obey the LORD your God by keeping his commandments and statutes that he has given you. 46 These curses will be a perpetual sign and wonder with reference to [a]you and your descendants.

The Curse of Military Siege

47 "[a]Because you have not served the LORD your God joyfully and wholeheartedly with the abundance of everything you have,

28:20 [a] Mal 2:2 [b] Isa 65:14 [c] Ps 80:16; Isa 30:17 [1] LXX *Lord* (Luc.) or *him*. 28:22 [a] Lev 26:16 [b] Amos 4:9 28:23 [a] Lev 26:19 28:25 [a] Deut 32:30 28:26 [a] 1 Sam 17:44; Ps 79:2 28:27 [a] Exod 15:26 [b] 1 Sam 5:6 28:28 [a] Jer 4:9 28:29 [a] Job 5:14 28:30 [a] 2 Sam 12:11; Job 31:10; Jer 8:10 [b] Amos 5:11; Zeph 1:13 [1] Some wss *lie with*. 28:32 [a] 2 Chr 29:9 [b] Ps 119:82 [c] Neh 5:5 28:33 [a] Lev 26:16; Jer 5:15, 17 28:36 [a] 2 Kgs 17:4, 6; 24:12, 14; 25:7, 11; 2 Chr 36:1–21; Jer 39:1–9 [b] Deut 4:28; Jer 16:13 [1] LXX *kings*. 28:37 [a] 1 Kgs 9:7–8; Jer 24:9; 25:9 [b] Ps 44:14 28:38 [a] Mic 6:15; Hag 1:6 [b] Exod 10:4; Joel 1:4 28:39 [a] Zeph 1:13 28:41 [a] Lam 1:5 28:46 [a] Num 26:10; Isa 8:18; Ezek 14:8 28:47 [a] Deut 12:7; Neh 9:35-37

[48]instead in [a]hunger, thirst, nakedness, and poverty you [b]will serve your enemies whom the LORD will send against you. They will place an iron yoke on your neck until they have destroyed you. [49]The LORD will raise up a distant nation against you, one from [a]the other side of the earth [b]as the eagle flies,[1] a nation whose language you will not understand, [50]a nation of stern appearance that will have no regard for the elderly or pity for the young. [51]They will devour the offspring of your livestock and the produce of your soil until you are destroyed. They will not leave you with any grain, new wine, olive oil, calves of your herds, or lambs of your flocks until they have destroyed you. [52]They will [a]besiege all of your villages until all of your high and fortified walls collapse— those in which you put your confidence throughout the land. They will besiege all your villages throughout the land the LORD your God has given you. [53]You will then eat [a]your own offspring, the flesh of the sons and daughters the LORD your God has given you, because of the severity of the siege by which your enemies will constrict you. [54]The man among you who is by nature tender and sensitive [a]will turn against his [b]brother, his beloved wife, and his remaining children. [55]He will withhold from all of them his children's flesh that he is eating (since there is nothing else left), because of the severity of the siege by which your enemy will constrict you in your villages. [56]Likewise, the most[1] tender and delicate of your women, who would never think of putting even the sole of her foot on the ground because of her daintiness, will turn against her beloved husband, her sons and daughters, [57]and will secretly eat her afterbirth and her newborn children (since she has nothing else), because of the severity of the siege by which your enemy will constrict you in your villages.

The Curse of Covenant Termination

[58]"If you refuse to obey all the words of [a]this law, the things written in this scroll, and refuse to fear this glorious and awesome name, the LORD your God, [59]then the LORD will [a]increase your punishments and those of your descendants—great and long-lasting afflictions and severe, enduring illnesses. [60]He will infect you with all [a]the diseases of Egypt that you dreaded, and they will persistently afflict you. [61]Moreover, the LORD will bring upon you every kind of sickness and plague not mentioned in this scroll of commandments,[1] until you have perished. [62]There will be very few of you left, though at one time you were [a]as numerous as the stars in the sky, because you will have disobeyed the LORD your God. [63]This is what will happen: Just as the LORD [a]delighted to do good for you and make you numerous, so he [b]will also take delight in destroying and decimating you. You will be [c]uprooted from the land you are about to possess. [64]The LORD [a]will scatter you among all nations, from one end of [b]the earth to the other. There you will worship other gods that neither you nor your ancestors have known, gods of wood and stone. [65]Among those nations you will have no rest, nor will there be [a]a place of peaceful rest for the soles of your feet, for there the LORD will give you an anxious heart, failing eyesight, and a spirit of [b]despair. [66]Your life will hang in doubt before you; you will be terrified by night and day and will have no certainty of surviving from one day to the next. [67]In the [a]morning you will say, 'If only it were evening!' And in the evening you will say, 'I wish it were morning!' [b]because of the things you will fear and the things you will see. [68]Then the LORD [a]will make [b]you return to Egypt by ship, over a route I said to you that you would never see again. There you will sell yourselves to your enemies as male and female slaves, but no one will buy you."

Narrative Interlude

29 These are the words of the [a]covenant that the LORD commanded Moses to make with the people of Israel in the land of Moab, in addition to the covenant he had made with them at Horeb.

28:48 [a]Lam 4:4–6 [b]Jer 28:13–14 28:49 [a]Isa 5:26–30; 7:18–20; Jer 5:15 [b]Jer 48:40; 49:22; Lam 4:19; Hos 8:1 [1]Or *like an eagle swoops down.* 28:52 [a]2 Kgs 25:1–2, 4 28:53 [a]Lev 26:29; 2 Kgs 6:28–29; Jer 19:9; Lam 2:20; 4:10 28:54 [a]Deut 15:9 [b]Deut 13:6 28:56 [1]LXX adds *very.* 28:58 [a]Exod 6:3 28:59 [a]Dan 9:12 28:60 [a]Deut 7:15 28:61 [1]Either the whole Pentateuch or, more likely, the Book of Deuteronomy or even only this curse section. 28:62 [a]Deut 10:22; Neh 9:23 28:63 [a]Deut 30:9; Jer 32:41 [b]Prov 1:26; [Isa 1:24] [c]Jer 12:14; 45:4 28:64 [a]Lev 26:33; Deut 4:27–28; Neh 1:8; Jer 16:13; Amos 9:9 [b]Deut 28:36 28:65 [a]Lam 1:3; Amos 9:4 [b]Lev 26:16 28:67 [a]Job 7:4 [b]Deut 28:34 28:68 [a]Jer 43:7; Hos 8:13 [b]Deut 17:16 29:1 [a]Lev 26:46; Deut 5:2–3

The Exodus, Wandering, and Conquest Reviewed

[2] Moses proclaimed to all Israel as follows: "[a] You have seen all that the LORD did in the land of Egypt to Pharaoh, all his servants, and his land. [3] Your eyes have seen [a] the great judgments,[1] those signs and mighty wonders. [4] But to this very day [a] the LORD has not given you an understanding mind, perceptive eyes, or discerning ears! [5] I have led you through the wilderness for 40 years. Your clothing has not worn out nor have your [a] sandals deteriorated. [6] You have eaten no bread and drunk no wine or beer—all so that [a] you might know that I[1] am the LORD your God! [7] When you came to this place King [a] Sihon of Heshbon and King Og of Bashan came out to make war and we defeated them. [8] Then we took their land and [a] gave it as an inheritance to Reuben, Gad, and half the tribe of Manasseh.

The Present Covenant Setting

[9] "Therefore, [a] keep the terms of this covenant and obey them so that you may be [b] successful in everything you do. [10] You are standing today, all of you, before the LORD your God—the heads of your tribes,[1] your elders, your officials, every Israelite man, [11] your infants, your wives, and [a] the resident foreigners living in your encampment, those who chop wood and those who carry water—[12] so that you may enter by oath [a] into the covenant the LORD your God is making with you today. [13] Today he will [a] affirm that you are his people and that he is your God, [b] just as he promised you and as he swore by oath to your ancestors Abraham, Isaac, and Jacob. [14] It is [a] not with you alone that I am making this covenant by oath, [15] but with whoever stands with us here today before the LORD our God [a] as well as those not with us here today.

The Results of Disobedience

[16] "(For you know how we lived in the land of Egypt and how we crossed through the nations as we traveled. [17] You have seen their detestable things[1] and idols of wood, stone, silver, and gold.) [18] Beware that the heart of no man, woman, clan, or tribe among you turns away from the LORD our God today to pursue [a] and serve the gods of those nations; beware that there is among you no root producing [b] poisonous and bitter fruit. [19] When such a person hears the words of this oath he secretly blesses himself and says, 'I will have peace though I continue to walk with a [a] stubborn spirit.' This will destroy the watered ground with the parched. [20] The LORD will be unwilling to forgive him, and his intense anger will rage against that man; all [a] the curses written in this scroll will fall upon him, and [b] the LORD will obliterate [c] his name from memory. [21] The LORD will single him out for judgment from all the tribes of Israel according to all the curses of the covenant written in this scroll of the [a] law. [22] The generation to come—your descendants who will rise up after you, as well as the foreigner who will come from distant places—will [a] see the afflictions of that land and the illnesses that the LORD has brought on it. [23] The whole land will be covered with brimstone, [a] salt, and burning debris; it will not be planted nor will it sprout or produce grass. It will resemble the destruction of Sodom and Gomorrah, Admah and Zeboyim, which the LORD destroyed in his intense anger. [24] Then all the nations will ask, '[a] Why has the LORD done all this to this land? What is this fierce, heated display of anger all about?' [25] Then people will say, 'Because they abandoned the covenant of the LORD, the God of their ancestors, which he made with them when he brought them out of the land of Egypt. [26] They went and served other gods and worshiped them, gods they did not know and that he did not permit them to worship. [27] That is why the LORD's anger erupted against this land, bringing on it all the curses written in this scroll. [28] So the LORD has [a] uprooted them from their land in anger, wrath, and great rage and has deported them to another land, as is clear today.' [29] The secret things belong to the

29:2 [a] Exod 19:4; Deut 11:7   29:3 [a] Deut 4:34; 7:19   [1] Heb. *testings*; a reference to the plagues.   29:4 [a] [Isa 6:9–10; Ezek 12:2]; Matt 13:14; [Acts 28:26–27]; Rom 11:8; [Eph 4:18]   29:5 [a] Deut 1:3; 8:2   29:6 [a] Exod 16:12; Deut 8:3   [1] LXX *he is.*   29:7 [a] Num 21:23–24; Deut 2:26—3:3   29:8 [a] Num 32:33; Deut 3:12–13   29:9 [a] Deut 4:6; 1 Kgs 2:3   [b] Josh 1:7   29:10 [1] Heb. *your heads, your tribes;* Syr. *heads of your tribes/your heads, your judges.*   29:11 [a] Josh 9:21, 23, 27   29:12 [a] Neh 10:29   29:13 [a] Deut 28:9   [b] Exod 6:7   29:14 [a] [Jer 31:31; Heb 8:7–8]   29:15 [a] Acts 2:39   29:17 [1] I.e., anything out of keeping with the nature and character of the Lord and therefore to be avoided by Israel.   29:18 [a] Heb 12:15   [b] Deut 32:32; Acts 8:23   29:19 [a] Jer 3:17; 7:24   29:20 [a] Ezek 14:7   [b] Ps 74:1   [c] Ps 79:5; Ezek 23:25   29:21 [a] Deut 30:10   29:22 [a] Jer 19:8; 49:17; 50:13   29:23 [a] Jer 17:6; Zeph 2:9   29:24 [a] 1 Kgs 9:8; Jer 22:8   29:28 [a] 1 Kgs 14:15; 2 Chr 7:20; Ps 52:5; Prov 2:22

LORD our God, but those that are revealed belong to us and our descendants forever, so that we might obey all the words of this law.

The Results of Covenant Reaffirmation

30 "[a]When you have experienced [b]all these things, both the blessings and the [c]curses I have set before [d]you, you will reflect upon them in all the nations where the LORD your God has banished you. [2]Then if you and your descendants [a]turn to the LORD your God and obey him with your whole mind and being just as I am commanding you today, [3][a]the LORD your God will reverse your captivity and have pity on you. He will turn and [b]gather you from all the peoples among whom he[1] has scattered you. [4]Even [a]if your exiles are in the most distant land, from there the LORD your God will gather you and bring you back. [5]Then he will bring you to the land your ancestors possessed and you also will possess it; he will do better for you and multiply you more than he did your ancestors. [6]The LORD your God will also cleanse your heart, and [a]the hearts of your descendants so that you may love him with all your mind and being and so that you may live. [7]Then the LORD your God will put all these [a]curses on your enemies, on those who hate you and persecute you. [8]You will [a]return and obey the LORD, keeping all his commandments I am giving you today. [9]The LORD your God will make [a]the labor of your hands[1] abundantly successful and multiply your children, the offspring of your cattle, and the produce of your soil. For the LORD will once more [b]rejoice over you to make you prosperous just as he rejoiced over your ancestors, [10]if you obey the LORD your God and keep his commandments and statutes that are written in this scroll of the law. But you must turn to him with your whole mind and being.

Exhortation to Covenant Obedience

[11]"This commandment [a]I am giving you today is not too difficult for you, nor is it too remote. [12]It is not in heaven, as though one must say, 'Who will go up to heaven to get [a]it for us and proclaim it to us so we may obey it?' [13]And it is not across the sea, as though one must say, 'Who will cross over to the other side of the sea and get it for us and proclaim it to us so we may obey it?' [14]For the [a]thing is very near you—it is in your mouth and in your mind so that you can do it.

[15]"Look! [a]I have set before you today life and prosperity on the one hand, and death and disaster on the other. [16]What[1] I am commanding you today is to love the LORD your God, to walk in his ways, and to obey his commandments, his statutes, and his ordinances. Then you will live and become numerous and the LORD your God will bless you in the land that you are about to possess. [17]However, if you[1] turn aside and do not obey, but are lured away to worship and serve other gods, [18]I declare to you [a]this very day that you will certainly perish! You will not extend your time in the land you are crossing the Jordan to possess. [19]Today [a]I [b]invoke heaven and earth as witnesses against you that I have set life and death, blessing and curse, before you. Therefore choose life so that you and your descendants may live! [20]I also call on you to love the LORD your God, to obey him and be loyal to him, for he gives you [a]life and enables you to live continually in the land the LORD promised to give to your ancestors Abraham, Isaac, and Jacob."

Succession of Moses by Joshua

31 Then Moses went[1] and spoke these words to all Israel. [2]He said to them, "Today I [a]am 120 years old. I am no longer able to get about, and the LORD has said to me, '[b]You will not cross the Jordan.' [3]As for the LORD your God, he is about to cross over before you; he will destroy these nations before you, and you will dispossess them. As for [a]Joshua, he is about to cross before you just [b]as the LORD has said. [4]The LORD will do to them just what he did to Sihon [a]and Og, the Amorite kings, and to their land, which he destroyed. [5]The LORD will deliver [a]them over to you, and you will do to them

30:1 [a]Lev 26:40 [b]Deut 28:2 [c]Deut 28:15–45 [d]Deut 4:29–30   30:2 [a]Deut 4:29–30; Neh 1:9; Isa 55:7; Lam 3:40; Joel 2:12   30:3 [a]Ps 106:45; Jer 29:14; Lam 3:22, 32 [b]Ps 147:2; Jer 32:37; Ezek 34:13 [1]Heb. *the LORD your God.*   30:4 [a]Deut 28:64; Neh 1:9; Isa 62:11   30:6 [a]Deut 10:16; Jer 32:39; Ezek 11:19   30:7 [a]Isa 54:15–17; Jer 30:16, 20   30:8 [a]Zeph 3:20   30:9 [a]Deut 28:11 [b]Deut 28:63; Jer 32:41 [1]MT *hand.*   30:11 [a]Isa 45:19   30:12 [a]Prov 30:4; Rom 10:6–8   30:14 [a]Rom 10:8   30:15 [a]Deut 30:1, 19   30:16 [1]Sev. LXX MSS add *if you obey the commandments of the LORD your God.*   30:17 [1]Heb. *your heart.*   30:18 [a]Deut 4:26; 8:19   30:19 [a]Deut 4:26 [b]Deut 30:15   30:20 [a]Ps 27:1; [John 11:25; 14:6; Col 3:4]   31:1 [1]LXX, Qum. *he finished.*   31:2 [a]Exod 7:7; Deut 34:7 [b]Num 20:12   31:3 [a]Num 27:18 [b]Num 27:21   31:4 [a]Deut 3:21   31:5 [a]Deut 7:2; 20:10–20

according to the whole commandment I have given you. [6] Be strong and courageous! Do not fear or tremble [a]before them, for the LORD your God is the one who is going with you. He will not fail you or [b]abandon you!" [7]Then Moses called out to Joshua in the presence of all Israel, "[a]Be strong and courageous, for you will accompany these people to the land that the LORD promised to give their ancestors, and you will enable them to inherit it. [8]The LORD is indeed going before you—[a]he will be with you; [b]he will not fail you or abandon you. Do not be afraid or discouraged!"

The Deposit of the Covenant Text

[9]Then Moses wrote down this law [a]and gave it to the Levitical priests, [b]who carry the ark of the LORD's covenant, and to all Israel's elders. [10]He commanded them: "At the end of seven [a]years, [b]at the appointed time of the cancellation of debts,[1] at the Feast of Shelters,[2] [11]when all Israel comes to [a]appear before the LORD your God in the [b]place he chooses, [c]you must read this law before them within their hearing. [12]Gather [a]the people—men, women, and children, as well as the resident foreigners in your villages—so they may hear and thus learn about and fear the LORD your God and carefully obey all the words of this law. [13]Then their children, [a]who have not known this law, will also hear about and learn to fear the LORD your God for as long as you live in the land you are crossing the Jordan to possess."

The Commissioning of Joshua

[14]Then the LORD [a]said to Moses, "The day of your death is near. Summon Joshua and present yourselves in the tent[1] of meeting so that I can commission him." So Moses and Joshua presented themselves in the tent of meeting. [15]The LORD appeared in [a]the tent in a pillar of cloud that stood above the door of the tent. [16]Then the LORD said to Moses, "You are about to die, and then these people will [a]begin to prostitute themselves with the foreign gods of the land into which they are going. They will [b]reject me and [c]break my covenant that I have made with them. [17]At that time my anger will [a]erupt [b]against them, and I will abandon them and [c]hide my face from them until they are devoured. Many disasters and distresses will overcome them so that they will say at that time, '[d]Have [e]not these disasters overcome us because our God is not among us?' [18]But [a]I will certainly hide myself at that time because of all the wickedness they will have done by turning to other gods. [19]Now write down for yourselves the following song [a]and teach it to the Israelites. Put it into their very mouths so that this song may serve as my witness against the Israelites! [20]For after I have brought them to the [a]land I promised to their ancestors—one flowing with milk and honey—and they eat their fill and become fat, [b]then they will turn to other gods and worship them; they will reject me and break my covenant. [21]Then [a]when many [b]disasters and distresses overcome them this song will testify against them, for their descendants will not forget it. I know the intentions they have in mind today, even before I bring them to the land I have promised." [22]So on that day Moses wrote down this song and taught it to the Israelites, [23]and [a]the LORD commissioned Joshua son of Nun, "[b]Be strong and courageous, for you will take the Israelites to the land I have promised them, and I will be with you."[1]

Anticipation of Disobedience

[24]When Moses finished writing on a scroll the words of this law in their entirety, [25]he commanded the Levites who carried the ark of the LORD's covenant, [26]"Take this scroll of the law [a]and place it beside the ark of the covenant of the LORD your God. It will remain there [b]as a witness against you, [27][a]for I know about your rebellion and [b]stubbornness. Indeed, even while I have been living among you to this very day, you have rebelled against the LORD; you will be even more rebellious after my death! [28]Gather to me all your tribal elders [a]and

31:6 [a] Josh 10:25; 1 Chr 22:13 [b] Deut 1:29   31:7 [a] Num 27:19; Deut 31:23; Josh 1:6   31:8 [a] Exod 13:21 [b] Deut 31:6; Josh 1:5; 1 Chr 28:20; Heb 13:5   31:9 [a] Deut 17:18; 31:25–26 [b] Num 4:5–6, 15; Deut 10:8; 31:25–26; Josh 3:3   31:10 [a] Deut 15:1–2 [b] Lev 23:34; Deut 16:13 [1] Heb. *to release, relinquish.* [2] Or *Feast of Huts;* trad. *Feast of Tabernacles.*   31:11 [a] Deut 16:16 [b] Deut 12:5 [c] Josh 8:34; 2 Kgs 23:2   31:12 [a] Deut 4:10   31:13 [a] Deut 11:2   31:14 [a] Num 27:19; Deut 3:28 [1] LXX *by the door of the tent.*   31:15 [a] Exod 33:9   31:16 [a] Deut 29:22 [b] Deut 32:15 [c] Judg 2:20   31:17 [a] Judg 2:14; 6:13 [b] 2 Chr 15:2 [c] Deut 32:20 [d] Judg 6:13 [e] Num 14:42   31:18 [a] Deut 31:17; [Isa 1:15–16]   31:19 [a] Deut 31:22, 26   31:20 [a] Deut 32:15–17 [b] Deut 31:16   31:21 [a] Deut 31:17 [b] Hos 5:3   31:23 [a] Num 27:23; Deut 31:14 [b] Deut 31:7 [1] LXX *as the LORD promised them, and he will be with you.*   31:26 [a] 2 Kgs 22:8 [b] Deut 31:19   31:27 [a] Deut 9:7, 24 [b] Exod 32:9; Deut 9:6, 13   31:28 [a] Deut 30:19

officials so I can speak to them directly about these things and call the heavens and the earth to witness against them. ²⁹For I know that after I die you will totally corrupt yourselves and turn away from the path I have commanded you to walk. ªDisaster will confront you ᵇin future days because you will act wickedly before the LORD, inciting him to anger because of your actions."

³⁰Then Moses recited the words of this song from start to finish in the hearing of the whole assembly of Israel:

Invocation of Witnesses

32 Listen, O heavens, and I will speak; ªhear, O ᵇearth, the words of my mouth.

2 My teaching will drop like the rain, ªmy sayings will drip like the dew, ᵇas rain drops upon the grass, and showers upon new growth.

3 For I will proclaim the ªname¹ of the LORD; you must ᵇacknowledge the greatness of our God.

4 As for ªthe Rock,¹ ᵇhis work is perfect, for ᶜall his ways are just. He is a reliable God who is never unjust, he is fair and upright.

5 His people have been unfaithful¹ to him; ªthey have not acted like his children—this is their sin. They are a ᵇperverse and deceitful generation.

6 Is this how you ªrepay the LORD, ᵇyou foolish, unwise people? Is he not your father, your ᶜCreator? He has ᵈmade you and established you.

7 ªRemember the ancient days; bear in mind the years of past generations. ᵇAsk your father and he will inform you, your elders, and they will tell you.

8 When the Most High¹ gave the nations their inheritance, when he divided ªup humankind, he set the boundaries of the peoples, according to the number of the heavenly assembly.²

9 For ªthe LORD's allotment is his people, Jacob is his special possession.¹

10 The LORD found him ªin a desolate land,¹ in an empty wasteland where animals howl. He continually guarded him and taught him; he continually ᵇprotected him like the pupil of his eye.

11 ªLike an eagle that stirs up its nest, that hovers over its young, so the LORD spread out his wings and took him, he lifted him up on his pinions.

12 The LORD alone was guiding him, no foreign god was with him.

13 He enabled him to travel over ªthe high terrain of the land, and he ate of the produce of the fields. He provided honey for him from the cliffs, and olive oil from the hardest of rocks,

14 butter from the herd and milk from the flock, along ªwith the fat of lambs, rams and goats of Bashan, along with the best of the kernels of wheat; and from the ᵇjuice of grapes you drank wine.

Israel's Rebellion

15 But Jeshurun became fat and kicked; ªyou¹ got fat, thick, and stuffed! Then he ᵇdeserted the God who ᶜmade him, and treated the ᵈRock who saved him with contempt.

31:29 ª Deut 28:15 ᵇ Gen 49:1; Deut 4:30   32:1 ª Deut 4:26; Ps 50:4; Isa 1:2 ᵇ Jer 6:19   32:2 ª Isa 55:10–11 ᵇ Ps 72:6   32:3 ª Deut 28:58 ᵇ 1 Chr 29:11 ¹ Smr., Tg. *in the name.*   32:4 ª Deut 32:15, 18, 30; Ps 18:2 ᵇ 2 Sam 22:31 ᶜ Deut 7:9; Isa 65:16; Jer 10:10 ¹ LXX *God.*   32:5 ª Deut 4:25; 31:29 ᵇ Phil 2:15 ¹ Heb. *have acted corruptly.*   32:6 ª Ps 116:12 ᵇ Exod 4:22; Deut 1:31; Isa 63:16 ᶜ Ps 74:2 ᵈ Deut 32:15   32:7 ª Ps 44:1 ᵇ Exod 12:26; 13:14; Ps 78:5–8   32:8 ª Acts 17:26 ¹ An abbreviated form of the divine name *El Elyon,* frequently translated as "God Most High." ² Heb. *the sons of Israel*; LXX *angels of God.*   32:9 ª Exod 19:5 ¹ Heb. *the portion of his inheritance*; LXX, Smr. add *Israel.*   32:10 ª Jer 2:6; Hos 13:5 ᵇ Ps 17:8; Prov 7:2; Zech 2:8 ¹ Heb. *a land of wilderness*; a dry region which is characterized as receiving less than twelve inches of rain per year.   32:11 ª Isa 31:5   32:13 ª Isa 58:14   32:14 ª Ps 81:16 ᵇ Gen 49:11   32:15 ª Deut 31:20 ᵇ Isa 1:4 ᶜ Isa 51:13 ᵈ Ps 95:1 ¹ LXX *he.*

16 They made him jealous with other
gods,[1]
ᵃthey enraged him with abhorrent
idols.
17 They sacrificed to demons, not God,
to gods ᵃthey had not known;
to new gods who had recently come
along,
gods your ancestors had not known
about.
18 You forgot the Rock who fathered
you,
and put out ᵃof ᵇmind the God who
gave you birth.

A Word of Judgment

19 But the LORD took note ᵃand
despised them
because his sons and daughters
enraged him.
20 He said, "I will reject them.
I will see what will happen to
them;
for they are a perverse generation,
ᵃchildren who show no loyalty.
21 They have made me jealous with
false gods,
enraging me with their worthless
gods;
so I will make them jealous with a
people ᵃthey do not ᵇrecognize,
with a nation slow to learn I will
enrage them.
22 For ᵃa fire has been kindled by my
anger,
and it burns to lowest Sheol;
it consumes the earth and its
produce,
and ignites the foundations of the
mountains.
23 I will ᵃincrease ᵇtheir disasters;
I will use up my arrows on them.
24 They will be starved by famine,
eaten by plague, and bitterly stung;
I will send the ᵃteeth of wild animals
against them,
along with the poison of creatures
that crawl in the dust.
25 The sword will make people childless
outside,
and terror will do so inside;

they will destroy both the young
man and the virgin,
the infant and the gray-haired man.

The Weakness of Other Gods

26 "I ᵃsaid, 'I want to cut them in pieces.[1]
I want to make people forget they
ever existed.
27 But I fear the reaction of their
enemies,
for their adversaries would
misunderstand
and say, "ᵃOur power is great,
and the LORD has not done all this!"'
28 They are a nation devoid of wisdom,
and there is no understanding
among them.
29 ᵃI wish that they were wise and could
understand this,
and that they could comprehend
what will happen to them."
30 How can one man chase ᵃa thousand
of them,
and two pursue ten thousand,
unless their Rock had delivered them
up—
and the LORD had handed them over?
31 For our enemies' rock is not like our
Rock,
as ᵃeven our enemies concede.
32 For ᵃtheir vine is from the stock of
Sodom,
and from the fields of Gomorrah.
Their grapes contain venom;
their clusters of grapes are bitter.
33 Their wine is snakes' poison,
ᵃthe deadly ᵇvenom of cobras.
34 "Is this not stored up with me?" says
the LORD,
"Is it not sealed up in my
storehouses?
35 I will get ᵃrevenge and pay them back
at the time their foot slips;
ᵇfor the day of their disaster is near,
and the impending judgment is
rushing upon them!"
36 The LORD will judge his people,
and will change his plans concerning
his servants;
when he sees that their power has
disappeared,

32:16 ᵃPs 78:58; 1 Cor 10:22   [1]Heb. *with strange* (things).   32:17 ᵃRev 9:20   32:18 ᵃIsa 17:10   ᵇJer 2:32   32:19 ᵃJudg 2:14   32:20 ᵃMatt 17:17   32:21 ᵃPs 78:58   ᵇRom 10:19   32:22 ᵃNum 16:33–35; Ps 18:7–8; Lam 4:11   32:23 ᵃExod 32:12; Deut 29:21, 24   ᵇPs 7:12–13   32:24 ᵃLev 26:22   32:26 ᵃEzek 20:23   [1]LXX *I said I would scatter them*.   32:27 ᵃIsa 10:12–15   32:29 ᵃPs 81:13; [Luke 19:42]   32:30 ᵃJudg 2:14; Ps 44:12   32:31 ᵃ[1 Sam 4:7–8; Jer 40:2–3]   32:32 ᵃIsa 1:8–10   32:33 ᵃPs 58:4   ᵇRom 3:13   32:35 ᵃPs 94:1; Rom 12:19; Heb 10:30   ᵇ2 Pet 2:3

and that no one is left, whether
   confined ^aor set free.
37 He will say, "^aWhere are their gods,
   the rock in whom they sought
     security,
38 who ate the best of their sacrifices,
   and drank the wine of their drink
     offerings?
   Let them rise and help you;
   let them be your refuge!

The Vindication of the Lord

39 "See now that ^aI, indeed I, am ^bhe!"
   says the LORD,
   "and there ^cis no other god
     besides me.
   I kill and give life,
   I smash and I heal,
   and none can resist my power.
40 For I raise up my hand to heaven,
   and say, 'As surely as I live forever,
41 I will sharpen my lightning-like
     sword,
   and my hand will grasp hold of the
     weapon of judgment;
   ^aI will execute vengeance on my foes,
   and repay those who hate me!'
42 I will make my arrows drunk with
     blood,
   and my sword will devour flesh—
   the blood of the slaughtered and
     captured,
   the chief of the enemy's leaders.'"
43 Cry ^aout, O nations, with his people,
   for he will ^bavenge his servants' blood;
   he ^cwill take vengeance against his
     enemies,
   and make atonement for his land
     and people.

Narrative Interlude

44 Then Moses went with Joshua[1] son of Nun and recited all the words of this song to the people. 45 When Moses finished reciting all these words to all Israel 46 he said to them, "^aKeep in mind all the words I am solemnly proclaiming to you today; you must command your ^bchildren to observe carefully all the words of this law. 47 For this is no idle word for you—it is your ^alife! By this word you will live a long time in the land you are about to cross the Jordan to possess."

Instructions about Moses' Death

48 Then the LORD said to Moses that same day, 49 "^aGo up to this Abarim hill country, to Mount Nebo (which is in the land of Moab opposite Jericho), and look at the land of Canaan that I am giving to the Israelites as a possession. 50 You will die on the mountain that you ascend and join your deceased ancestors, just as ^aAaron your brother died on Mount Hor and joined his deceased ancestors, 51 for both of ^ayou rebelled against me among the Israelites at the waters of Meribah Kadesh in the wilderness of Zin when you ^bdid not show me proper respect among the Israelites. 52 ^aYou will see the land before you, but you will not enter the land that I am giving to the Israelites."

Introduction to the Blessing of Moses

33 This is ^athe blessing Moses ^bthe man of God pronounced upon the Israelites before his death. 2 He said:

A Historical Review

   "^aThe LORD came from Sinai
   and revealed himself to Israel[1] from
     ^bSeir.
   He appeared in splendor from
     ^cMount Paran,
   and came forth with ^dten thousand
     holy ones.
   With his right hand he gave a fiery
     law to them.
3 Surely ^ahe loves the people;[1]
   ^ball your holy ones[2] are in your
     power.
   And they ^csit[3] at your feet,
   each ^dreceiving your words.
4 ^aMoses delivered to us ^ba law,[1]
   an inheritance for the assembly of
     Jacob.

32:36 ^a Ps 135:14; Heb 10:30   32:37 ^a Judg 10:14; Jer 2:28   32:39 ^a Isa 41:4; 43:10 ^b Deut 32:12; Isa 45:5 ^c 1 Sam 2:6; Ps 68:20   32:41 ^a Isa 1:24; 66:16; Jer 50:28–32 [1] In a covenant context, "to hate" means "to reject, disobey."   32:43 ^a Rom 15:10 ^b 2 Kgs 9:7; Rev 6:10; 19:2 ^c Ps 65:3; 79:9; 85:1   32:44 [1] Heb. *Hoshea*; another name for the same individual.   32:46 ^a Ezek 40:4; 44:5 ^b Deut 11:19   32:47 ^a Deut 8:3; 30:15–20   32:49 ^a Num 27:12–14; Deut 3:27   32:50 ^a Num 20:25, 28; 33:38   32:51 ^a Num 20:11–13 ^b Lev 10:3   32:52 ^a Num 27:12; Deut 34:1–5   33:1 ^a Gen 49:28 ^b Ps 90   33:2 ^a Exod 19:18, 20; Ps 68:8, 17; Hab 3:3 ^b Deut 2:1, 4 ^c Num 10:12 ^d Dan 7:10; Acts 7:53; Rev 5:11 [1] Heb. *to him*; LXX *to us.*   33:3 ^a Ps 47:4; Hos 11:1 ^b 1 Sam 2:9 ^c [Luke 10:39] ^d Prov 2:1 [1] Heb. *peoples.* [2] Heb. *his holy ones*; Luc., Orig. *the holy ones*; Thd., Vg. *his hands.* [3] The Heb. term is otherwise unknown.   33:4 ^a Deut 4:2; John 1:17; 7:19 ^b Ps 119:111 [1] Understood more broadly as instruction.

5 The LORD was [a]king over [b]Jeshurun,
  when the leaders of the people
    assembled,
  the tribes of Israel together.

Blessing on Reuben

6 "May [a]Reuben live and not die,
  and may his people multiply."

Blessing on Judah

7 And this is the blessing to [a]Judah. He
    [b]said,
  "Listen, O LORD, to Judah's voice,
  and bring him to his people.
  May his power be great,
  and may you help him against his
    foes."

Blessing on Levi

8 Of [a]Levi he said:
  "Your Thummim and Urim belong to
    your godly one,
  whose authority you challenged at
    Massah,
  and with [b]whom you argued at the
    waters of Meribah.
9 [a]He said to his father and mother, 'I
    have not [b]seen him,'
  and he did not acknowledge his own
    brothers
  [c]or know his own children,
  for [d]they kept your word,
  and guarded your covenant.
10 They will teach Jacob your ordinances
  and Israel your law;
  [a]they will offer incense as [b]a pleasant
    odor,
  and a whole offering on your altar.
11 Bless, O LORD, his goods,
  and be pleased [a]with his efforts;
  undercut the legs of any who attack
    him,
  and of those who hate him, so that
    they cannot stand."

Blessing on Benjamin

12 Of Benjamin he said:
  "The beloved of the LORD will live
    safely by him;
  he protects him all the time,
  and the LORD places him on his chest."

Blessing on Joseph

13 Of Joseph he said:
  "May the LORD [a]bless his land
  with the harvest produced by the sky,
    by the [b]dew,
  and by the depths crouching
    beneath;
14 with the harvest produced by the
    daylight
  and by the moonlight;
15 with [a]the best [b]of the ancient
    mountains
  and the harvest produced by the
    age-old hills;
16 with the harvest of the earth and its
    fullness
  and the pleasure of [a]him who resided
    in the burning bush.
  May blessing rest [b]on Joseph's head,
  and on the top of the head of the one
    set apart from his brothers.
17 May the [a]firstborn of his bull bring
    him honor,
  and may his [b]horns be those of a
    wild ox;
  with [c]them may [d]he gore all peoples,
  all the far reaches of the earth.
  They are the ten thousands of
    Ephraim,
  and they are the thousands of
    Manasseh."

Blessing on Zebulun and Issachar

18 Of Zebulun he said:
  "[a]Rejoice, Zebulun, when you go
    outside,
  and Issachar, when you are in your
    tents.
19 They will [a]summon peoples to [b]the
    mountain,
  there they will sacrifice proper
    sacrifices;
  for they will enjoy the abundance of
    the seas,
  and the hidden treasures of the
    shores."

Blessing on Gad

20 Of Gad he said:
  "Blessed be the one who [a]enlarges
    Gad.

33:5 [a] Exod 15:18   [b] Deut 32:15   33:6 [a] Gen 49:3–4   33:7 [a] Gen 49:8–12   [b] Ps 146:5   33:8 [a] Gen 49:5   [b] Num 20:2–13; Deut 6:2–3, 16; Ps 81:7   33:9 [a] [Num 25:5–8; Matt 10:37; 19:29]   [b] [Gen 29:32]   [c] Exod 32:26–28   [d] Mal 2:5–6   33:10 [a] Lev 10:11; Deut 31:9–13; Mal 2:7   [b] Lev 1:9; Ps 51:19   33:11 [a] 2 Sam 24:23; Ezek 20:40   33:13 [a] Gen 49:22–26   [b] Gen 27:28   33:15 [a] Gen 49:26   [b] Hab 3:6   33:16 [a] Exod 3:2–4; Acts 7:30–35   [b] Gen 49:26   33:17 [a] 1 Chr 5:1   [b] Num 23:22   [c] 1 Kgs 22:11; Ps 44:5   [d] Gen 48:19   33:18 [a] Gen 49:13–15   33:19 [a] Exod 15:17; Ps 2:6; Isa 2:3   [b] Ps 4:5; 51:19   33:20 [a] 1 Chr 12:8

Like a lioness he will dwell;
he will tear at an arm—indeed, a
scalp.
21 He has selected ᵃthe best part for
himself,
for ᵇthe portion of the ruler is set
aside there;
he came with the leaders of the
people,
he obeyed the righteous laws of the
LORD
and his ordinances with Israel."

Blessing on Dan

22 Of Dan ᵃhe said:
"Dan is a lion's cub;
he will leap forth from Bashan."

Blessing on Naphtali

23 Of Naphtali he said:
"O Naphtali, ᵃoverflowing with favor,
and full of the LORD's blessing,
ᵇpossess the west and south."

Blessing on Asher

24 Of ᵃAsher he said:
"Asher is blessed with children;
may he be favored by his brothers,
and may he ᵇdip his foot in olive oil.
25 The bars of your gates will be made
of ᵃiron and bronze,
and may you have lifelong strength."

General Praise and Blessing

26 "There is ᵃno one like God,
O ᵇJeshurun,
ᶜwho rides through the sky to help
you,
on the clouds in majesty.
27 The everlasting God is a ᵃrefuge,
and underneath you are his eternal
arms;
ᵇhe has driven out enemies before
you,
and has said, 'Destroy!'
28 ᵃIsrael lives in safety,
the fountain of Jacob is quite ᵇsecure,
in a land of grain and new wine;
indeed, its ᶜheavens rain down dew.

29 You have ᵃjoy, Israel! ᵇWho is like
you?
You are a people delivered by ᶜthe
LORD,
ᵈyour protective shield
and your exalted sword.
May your enemies cringe before you;
may you trample on their backs."

The Death of Moses

34 Then Moses ascended from the rift
valley plains of Moab ᵃto Mount
Nebo, to the summit of Pisgah, which is opposite Jericho. The LORD showed him the
whole land—Gilead to Dan, 2and all of Naphtali, the land of Ephraim and Manasseh, all
the land of Judah as far as the distant sea,
3the Negev, and ᵃthe plain of the Valley of
Jericho, the city of date palm trees, as far
as Zoar. 4Then the LORD said to him, "ᵃThis
ᵇis the land I promised to Abraham, Isaac,
and Jacob when I said, 'I will give it to your
descendants.'1 I have let you see it, but you
will not cross over there."

5ᵃSo Moses, the servant of the LORD, died
there in the land of Moab as the LORD had
said. 6He1 buried him in the valley in the
land of Moab near Beth Peor, but ᵃno one
knows his exact burial place to this very day.
7ᵃMoses was 120 years old when he died, but
ᵇhis eye was not dull nor had his vitality departed. 8The Israelites mourned for Moses
in the rift valley plains of Moab for ᵃthirty
days; then the days of mourning for Moses
ended.

An Epitaph for Moses

9Now Joshua son of Nun was full of the
ᵃspirit of wisdom, for ᵇMoses had placed his
hands on him; and the Israelites listened to
him and did just what the LORD had commanded Moses. 10No prophet ever again
arose in Israel like Moses, ᵃwho knew the
LORD face to face. 11He did all ᵃthe signs and
wonders the LORD had sent him to do in the
land of Egypt, to Pharaoh, all his servants,
and the whole land, 12and he displayed great
power and awesome might in view of all
Israel.

33:21ᵃNum 32:16–17 ᵇJosh 4:12 **33:22**ᵃGen 49:16–17; Josh 19:47 **33:23**ᵃGen 49:21 ᵇJosh 19:32 **33:24**ᵃGen 49:20 ᵇJob 29:6 **33:25**ᵃDeut 8:9 **33:26**ᵃExod 15:11; Deut 4:35; Ps 86:8; Jer 10:6 ᵇDeut 32:15 ᶜDeut 10:14; Ps 68:3, 33, 34; 104:3 **33:27**ᵃ[Ps 90:1; 91:2, 9] ᵇDeut 9:3–5 **33:28**ᵃDeut 33:12; Jer 23:6; 33:16 ᵇNum 23:9 ᶜGen 27:28 **33:29**ᵃPs 144:15 ᵇDeut 4:32–34; 2 Sam 7:23 ᶜGen 15:1; Ps 115:9 ᵈNum 33:52 **34:1**ᵃNum 27:12; Deut 32:49 **34:3**ᵃ2 Chr 28:15 **34:4**ᵃGen 12:7 ᵇDeut 3:27 1Heb. *seed.* **34:5**ᵃNum 20:12; Deut 32:50; Josh 1:1–2 **34:6**ᵃJude 9 1Smr., some LXX MSS *they.* **34:7**ᵃDeut 31:2 ᵇGen 27:1; 48:10 **34:8**ᵃGen 50:3, 10 **34:9**ᵃIsa 11:2 ᵇNum 27:18, 23 **34:10**ᵃExod 33:11; Num 12:8; Deut 5:4 **34:11**ᵃDeut 7:19

JOSHUA

Joshua, the first of the twelve historical books (Joshua through Esther), forges a link between the Pentateuch and the remainder of Israel's history. Through three major military campaigns involving more than thirty enemy armies, the people of Israel learn a crucial lesson under Joshua's capable leadership: victory comes through faith in God and obedience to his word rather than through military might or numerical superiority. The title of this book is appropriately named after its central figure, Joshua. His original name is *Hoshea*, "Salvation" (Num 13:8), but Moses evidently changes it to *Joshua*, "Yahweh Is Salvation" (Num 13:16). He is also called *Yeshua*, a shortened form of *Yehoshua*. This is the Hebrew equivalent of the Greek name *Iesous* (Jesus). Thus the Greek title given to the book in the Septuagint is *Iesous Naus*, "Joshua the Son of Nun." The Latin title is *Liber Josue*, the "Book of Joshua." His name is symbolic of the fact that although he is the leader of the Israelite nation during the conquest, the Lord is the Conqueror.

The Lord Commissions Joshua

1 After Moses the LORD's servant died, the LORD said to Joshua son of Nun, Moses' [a] assistant: 2 "[a] Moses my servant is dead. Get ready! Cross the Jordan River. Lead these people into the land that I am ready to hand over to them.[1] 3 I am handing over to you [a] every place you set foot, as I promised Moses.[1] 4 Your territory will extend [a] from the desert in the south to Lebanon in the north. It will extend all the way to the great River Euphrates in the east (including all Syria) and all the way to the Mediterranean Sea in the west. 5 No one will be able to resist you[1] all the days of your life. As I was with Moses, so I will be with you. I will [a] not abandon you or leave you alone. 6 [a] Be strong and brave! You must lead these people in the conquest of this land that I solemnly promised their ancestors I would hand over to them. 7 Make sure you are very strong and brave! Carefully obey all the law my servant Moses charged you to keep. [a] Do not swerve from it to the right or to the left, so that you may be successful in all you do. 8 This law scroll must not leave your lips. You must memorize it day and night so you can carefully obey all that [a] is written in it. Then [b] you will prosper and be successful. 9 [a] I repeat, be strong and brave! [b] Don't be afraid and don't panic, for I, the LORD your God, am with you in all you do."

Joshua Prepares for the Invasion

10 Joshua instructed the leaders of the people: 11 "Go through the camp and command the people, 'Prepare your supplies, for [a] within three days you will cross the Jordan River and begin the conquest of the land the LORD your God is ready to hand over to you.'"

12 Joshua told the Reubenites, the Gadites, and the half-tribe of Manasseh: 13 "Remember what Moses [a] the LORD's servant commanded you. The LORD your God is giving you a place to settle and is handing this land over to you.[1] 14 Your wives, children, and cattle may stay in the land that Moses assigned to you east of the Jordan River. But all of you warriors must cross over armed for battle ahead of your brothers. You must help them 15 until [a] the LORD gives your brothers a place like yours to settle and they conquer the land the LORD your God is ready to hand over to them. Then you may go back

1:1 [a] Exod 24:13; Num 13:16; 14:6, 29, 30, 37, 38; Deut 1:38; Acts 7:45   1:2 [a] Num 12:7; Deut 34:5   [1] MT adds *to the children of Israel.*   1:3 [a] Deut 11:24; Josh 11:23   [1] "You" and "your" in vv. 3–4 are pl.   1:4 [a] Gen 15:18; Exod 23:31; Num 34:3–12   1:5 [a] Deut 7:24   [1] "You" and "your" are sing.   1:6 [a] Deut 31:7, 23   1:7 [a] Deut 5:32   1:8 [a] Deut 17:18–19; 31:24, 26; Josh 8:34   [b] Deut 29:9; Ps 1:1–3   1:9 [a] Deut 31:7   [b] Ps 27:1   1:11 [a] Deut 9:1; Josh 3:17   1:13 [a] Num 32:20–28   [1] Heb. *is providing rest for you and is giving to you this land.*   1:15 [a] Josh 22:1–4

to your allotted land and occupy the land Moses the LORD's servant assigned you east of the Jordan."

[16]They told Joshua, "We will do everything you say. We will go wherever you send us. [17]Just as we [a]obeyed Moses, so we will obey you. But may the LORD your God be with you as he was with Moses. [18]Any man who rebels against what you say and does not obey all your commands will be executed. But be strong and brave!"

Joshua Sends Spies into the Land

2 Joshua son of Nun sent two spies out [a]from Shittim secretly and instructed them: "Find out what you can about the land, especially Jericho." They stopped [b]at the house of a prostitute named [c]Rahab and spent the night there. [2]The king of Jericho received this report: "Note well! [a]Israelite men have come here tonight to spy on the land." [3]So the king of Jericho sent this order to Rahab: "Turn over the men who came to you[1]—the ones who came to your house—for they have come to spy on the whole land!" [4]But [a]the woman hid the two men and replied, "Yes, these men were clients of mine,[1] but I didn't know where they came from. [5]When it was time to shut the city gate for the night, the men left. I don't know where they were heading. Chase after them quickly, for you have time to catch them!" [6](Now [a]she had taken them up to the roof and had hidden them in the stalks of flax she had spread out on the roof.) [7]Meanwhile, the king's men tried to find them on the road to the Jordan River near the fords. The city gate was shut as soon as they set out in pursuit of them.

[8]Now before the spies went to sleep, Rahab went up to the roof. [9]She [a]said to [b]the men, "I know the LORD is handing this land over to you. We [c]are absolutely terrified of you, and all who live in the land are cringing before you. [10]For we heard how the LORD [a]dried up the water of the Red Sea before you when you left Egypt and how you annihilated the two Amorite kings, Sihon and Og, on the other side of the Jordan. [11]When

we [a]heard the news, we lost [b]our courage, and no one could even [c]breathe for fear of you. For the LORD your God is God in heaven above and on earth below! [12]So now, [a]promise me this with an oath sworn in the LORD's name. Because I have shown allegiance to you, show allegiance to [b]my family. [c]Give me a solemn pledge [13]that you will spare the [a]lives of my father, mother, brothers, sisters, and all who belong to them, and will rescue us from death." [14]The men said to her, "If you[1] die, may [a]we die too! If you do not report what we've been up to, then we will show unswerving allegiance to you when the LORD hands the land over to us."

[15]Then Rahab [a]let them down by a rope[1] through the window. (Her house was built as part of the city wall; she lived in the wall.)[2] [16]She told them, "Head to the hill country, so the ones chasing you don't find you. Hide from them there for three days, long enough for those chasing you to return. Then you can be on your way." [17]The men said to her, "We are not [a]bound by this oath you made us swear unless the following conditions are met: [18][a]When we invade the [b]land,[1] tie this red rope in the window through which you let us down, and gather together in your house your father, mother, brothers, and all who live in your father's house. [19]Anyone who leaves your house will be responsible for [a]his own death—we are innocent in that case! But if anyone with you in the house is harmed, we will be responsible. [20]If you should report what we've been up to, we are not bound by this oath you made us swear." [21]She said, "I agree to these conditions." She sent them on their way and then tied the red rope in the window. [22]They went to the hill country and stayed there for three days, long enough for those chasing them to return. Their pursuers looked all along the way but did not find them. [23]Then the two men returned—they came down from the hills, crossed the river, came to Joshua son of Nun, and reported to him all they had discovered. [24]They told Joshua, "Surely [a]the LORD is handing over all the land to us! All who live in the land are cringing before us!"

1:17 [a]1 Sam 20:13; 1 Kgs 1:37   2:1 [a]Num 25:1; Josh 3:1   [b]Heb 11:31; Jas 2:25   [c]Matt 1:5   2:2 [a]Josh 2:22   2:3 [1]An idiom that probably has sexual connotations.   2:4 [a]2 Sam 17:19–20   [1]Heb. the men came to me.   2:6 [a]Exod 1:17; 2 Sam 17:19   2:9 [a]Deut 1:8   [b]Gen 35:5; Exod 23:27; Deut 2:25; 11:25; Josh 9:9–10   [c]Exod 15:15; Josh 5:1   2:10 [a]Exod 14:21; Josh 4:23   2:11 [a]Exod 15:14–15   [b]Josh 5:1; 7:5; Ps 22:14; Isa 13:7   [c]Deut 4:39   2:12 [a]1 Sam 20:14–15, 17   [b]1 Tim 5:8   [c]Exod 12:13; Josh 2:18   2:13 [a]Josh 6:23–25   2:14 [a]Gen 47:29; Judg 1:24; [Matt 5:7]   [1]Pl., indicating Rahab's entire family.   2:15 [a]Acts 9:25   [1]LXX omits by a rope.   [2]LXX omits this parenthetical sentence.   2:17 [a]Exod 20:7   2:18 [a]Josh 2:12   [b]Josh 6:23   [1]Heb. Look! We are about to enter the land.   2:19 [a]1 Kgs 2:32; Matt 27:25   2:24 [a]Exod 23:31; Josh 6:2; 21:44

Israel Crosses the Jordan

3 Bright and early the next morning Joshua and the Israelites left Shittim and came to the Jordan. They camped there before crossing the river. [2a] After three days the leaders went through the camp [3] and commanded the people: "[a] When you see the ark of the covenant of the LORD your God being carried by the Levitical priests, you must leave here [b] and walk behind it. [4a] But stay about 3,000 feet behind it. Keep your distance so you can see which way you should go, for you have not traveled this way before." [5] Joshua told the people, "Ritually [a] consecrate yourselves, for tomorrow the LORD will perform miraculous deeds among you." [6] Joshua told the priests, "Pick up the ark of the covenant and pass on ahead of the people." So they picked up the ark of the covenant and went ahead of the people.

[7] The LORD told Joshua, "This very day I will begin to [a] honor you before all Israel, so they will know that I am with you just [b] as I was with Moses. [8] Instruct [a] the priests carrying the ark of the covenant, 'When [b] you reach the bank of the Jordan River, wade into the water.'"

[9] Joshua told the Israelites, "Come here and listen to the words of the LORD your God!" [10] Joshua continued, "This is how you will know [a] the living God is among you and that he will truly [b] drive out before you the [c] Canaanites, Hittites, Hivites, Perizzites, Girgashites, Amorites, and Jebusites. [11] Look! [a] The ark of the covenant of the Lord[1] of the whole earth is ready to enter the Jordan ahead of you. [12] Now [a] select for yourselves 12 men from the tribes of Israel, one per tribe. [13] When [a] the feet of the priests carrying the ark of the LORD, the Lord of the whole earth, touch[1] the water of the Jordan, the water coming downstream toward you will stop flowing and pile up."

[14] So when the people left their tents to cross the Jordan, the priests carrying the [a] ark of the covenant went ahead of them. [15] When [a] the ones carrying the ark reached the [b] Jordan, and the feet of the priests carrying the ark touched the surface of the water—(the Jordan is at flood stage all [c] during harvest time)—[16] the water coming downstream toward them stopped flowing. It piled up far upstream at Adam (the city near [a] Zarethan); there was no water at all flowing [b] to [c] the sea of the rift valley (the Salt Sea). The people crossed the river opposite Jericho. [17] The priests carrying the ark of the covenant of the LORD stood firmly on dry ground in the middle of the Jordan. All Israel crossed over on dry ground until the entire nation was on the other side.

Israel Commemorates the Crossing

4 When the entire nation [a] was on the other side, the LORD told Joshua, [2] "[a] Select for yourselves 12 men from the people, one per tribe. [3] Instruct [a] them, 'Pick up 12 stones from [b] the middle of the Jordan, from the very place where the priests stand firmly, and carry them over with you and put them in the place where you camp tonight.'"

[4] Joshua summoned the 12 men he had appointed from the Israelites, one per tribe. [5] Joshua told them, "Go in front of the ark of the LORD your God to the middle of the Jordan. Each of you is to put a stone on his shoulder, according to the number of the Israelite tribes. [6] The stones will be [a] a reminder to you.[1] [b] When your children ask someday, 'Why are these stones important to you?'[7] tell [a] them how the [b] water of the Jordan stopped flowing before the ark of the covenant of the LORD. When it crossed the Jordan, the water of the Jordan stopped flowing. These stones will be a lasting memorial for the Israelites."

[8] The Israelites did just as Joshua commanded. They picked up 12 stones, according to the number of the Israelite tribes, from the middle of the Jordan as the LORD had instructed Joshua. They carried them over with them to the camp and put them there. [9] Joshua also set up 12 stones in the middle of the Jordan in the very place where the priests carrying the ark of the covenant stood. They remain there to this very day. [10] Now the priests carrying the ark of the

3:2 [a] Josh 1:10–11   **3:3** [a] Num 10:33   [b] Deut 31:9, 25   **3:4** [a] Exod 19:12   **3:5** [a] Exod 19:10, 14, 15; Lev 20:7; Num 11:18; Josh 7:13; 1 Sam 16:5; Job 1:5; Joel 2:16   **3:7** [a] Josh 4:14; 1 Chr 29:25; 2 Chr 1:1   [b] Josh 1:5, 9   **3:8** [a] Josh 3:3   [b] Josh 3:17   **3:10** [a] Deut 5:26; Josh 11:23; 1 Sam 17:26; 2 Kgs 19:4; Hos 1:10; Matt 16:16; 1 Thess 1:9   [b] Exod 33:2; Deut 7:1; 18:12; Ps 44:2   [c] Acts 13:19   **3:11** [a] Josh 3:13; Job 41:11; Ps 24:1; Mic 4:13; Zech 4:14; 6:5   [1] Or *Ruler, Master.*   **3:12** [a] Josh 4:2, 4   **3:13** [a] Josh 3:11   [1] Or *rest in.*   **3:14** [a] Ps 132:8; Acts 7:44–45   **3:15** [a] Josh 3:13   [b] 1 Chr 12:15; Jer 12:5; 49:19   [c] Josh 4:18; 5:10, 12   **3:16** [a] 1 Kgs 4:12; 7:46   [b] Deut 3:17   [c] Gen 14:3; Num 34:3   **4:1** [a] Deut 27:2; Josh 3:17   **4:2** [a] Josh 3:12   **4:3** [a] Josh 3:13   [b] Josh 4:19–20   **4:6** [a] Deut 27:2; Ps 103:2   [b] Exod 12:26; 13:14; Deut 6:20   [1] Heb. *in order that this might be a sign among you.*   **4:7** [a] Josh 3:13, 16   [b] Exod 12:14; Num 16:40

covenant were standing in the middle of the Jordan until everything the LORD had commanded Joshua to tell the people was accomplished, in accordance with all that Moses had commanded Joshua. The people went across quickly, [11] and when all the people had finished crossing, the [a] ark of the LORD and the priests crossed as the people looked on.[1] [12] The Reubenites, [a] the Gadites, and the half-tribe of Manasseh crossed over armed for battle ahead of the Israelites, just as Moses had instructed them. [13] About 40,000 battle-ready troops marched past the LORD to fight on the rift valley plains of Jericho. [14] That day the LORD brought honor [a] to Joshua before all Israel. They respected him all his life, just as they had respected Moses.

[15] The LORD told Joshua, [16] "Instruct [a] the priests carrying the ark of the covenantal laws[1] to come up from the Jordan." [17] So Joshua instructed the priests, "Come up from the Jordan!" [18] The priests carrying the ark of the covenant of the LORD came up from the middle of the Jordan, [a] and as soon as they set foot on dry land, the water of the Jordan flowed again and returned to flood stage.

[19] The people went up from the Jordan on the tenth day of the first month and camped [a] in Gilgal on the eastern border of Jericho. [20] Now Joshua set up in Gilgal the 12 stones they had taken from the Jordan. [21] He told the Israelites, "[a] When your children someday ask their fathers, 'What do these stones represent?' [22] explain to your children, '[a] Israel crossed the Jordan River on [b] dry ground.' [23] For the LORD your God dried up the water of the Jordan before you while you crossed over. It was just like when the LORD your God dried up the Red Sea before us while we crossed it. [24] [a] He has done this so all the nations of the earth might recognize the [b] LORD's power and so you might always [c] obey[1] the LORD your God."

5 When all the Amorite kings on the west side of the Jordan and all the Canaanite kings along the seacoast [a] heard how the LORD had dried up the water of the Jordan before the Israelites while they[1] crossed, they lost their courage [b] and could not even breathe for fear of the Israelites.

A New Generation Is Circumcised

[2] At that time the LORD told Joshua, "Make [a] flint knives and circumcise the Israelites once again." [3] So Joshua made flint knives and circumcised the Israelites at the Hill of the Foreskins.[1] [4] This is why Joshua had to circumcise them: [a] All the men old enough to fight when they left Egypt died on the journey through the wilderness after they left Egypt. [5] Now all the men who left were circumcised, but all the sons born on the journey through the wilderness after they left Egypt were uncircumcised. [6] Indeed, for [a] 40 years [b] the [c] Israelites traveled through the wilderness until all the men old enough to fight when they left Egypt, the ones who had disobeyed the LORD, died off. For the LORD had sworn a solemn oath to them that he would not let them see the land he had sworn by oath to their ancestors to give them, a land rich in milk and honey. [7] He replaced them with [a] their sons, whom Joshua circumcised. They were uncircumcised; their fathers had not circumcised them along the way. [8] When all the men had been circumcised, they stayed there in the camp until they had healed. [9] The LORD said to Joshua, "Today I have taken away [a] the disgrace of Egypt from you." So that place is called [b] Gilgal even to this day.

[10] So the Israelites camped in Gilgal and celebrated the Passover in the evening of the fourteenth day of the [a] month in the rift valley plains of Jericho. [11] They ate some of the produce of the land the day after the Passover, including unleavened bread and roasted grain. [12] The manna stopped appearing [a] the day they ate[1] some of the produce of the land; the Israelites never ate manna again. They ate from the produce of the land of Canaan that year.

Israel Conquers Jericho

[13] When [a] Joshua was near Jericho, he looked up and saw a man standing in front

4:11 [a] Josh 3:11; 6:11   [1] Heb. *in the presence of the people.*   4:12 [a] Num 32:17, 20, 27, 28; Josh 1:14   4:14 [a] Josh 3:7; 1 Chr 29:25   4:16 [a] Exod 25:16, 22   [1] Trad. *the ark of the testimony.*   4:18 [a] Josh 3:15; 1 Chr 12:15   4:19 [a] Josh 5:9   4:21 [a] Josh 4:6   4:22 [a] Exod 12:26–27; 13:8–14; Deut 26:5–9   [b] Josh 3:17   4:24 [a] 1 Kgs 8:42; 2 Kgs 19:19; Ps 106:8   [b] Exod 15:16; 1 Chr 29:12; Ps 89:13   [c] Exod 14:31; Deut 6:2; Ps 76:7; Jer 10:7   [1] Heb. *fear.*   5:1 [a] Exod 15:14–15   [b] Josh 2:10–11; 9:9; 1 Kgs 10:5   [1] Ket. *we crossed.*   5:2 [a] Exod 4:25   5:3 [1] Or *Gibeath Haaraloth.*   5:4 [a] Num 14:29; 26:64–65; Deut 2:14–16   5:6 [a] Num 14:33; Deut 1:3; 29:5   [b] Num 14:23, 29–35; 26:23–65; Heb 3:11   [c] Exod 3:8   5:7 [a] Num 14:31; Deut 1:39   5:9 [a] Gen 34:14   [b] Josh 4:19   5:10 [a] Exod 12:6; Num 9:5   5:12 [a] Exod 16:35   [1] Heb. *the day after, when they ate.*   5:13 [a] Gen 18:1–2; 32:24, 30; Exod 23:23; Num 22:31; Zech 1:8; Acts 1:10

of him holding a drawn sword. Joshua approached him and asked him, "Are you on our side or allied [b]with our enemies?" [14]He answered,[1] "Truly I am the commander of the LORD's army. Now I have arrived!" Joshua [a]bowed down with his face to the ground and asked, "What does my master want to say to his servant?" [15]The commander of the LORD's army answered Joshua, "Remove your sandals from your feet because the place where you stand is holy." Joshua did so.

6 Now [a]Jericho was shut tightly because of the Israelites. No one was allowed to leave or enter. [2]The LORD told Joshua, "See, [a]I am about to defeat Jericho for you,[1] along with its [b]king and its warriors. [3]Have all the warriors march around the city one time; do this for six days. [4]Have seven priests carry seven rams' [a]horns in front of the ark. On the seventh day march around the city [b]seven times, while [c]the priests blow the horns. [5]When you hear the signal from the rams' horns, have the whole army give a loud battle cry. Then the city wall will collapse, and the warriors should charge straight ahead."

[6]So Joshua son of Nun summoned the priests and instructed them, "Pick up the ark of the covenant, and seven priests must carry seven rams' horns in front of the ark of the LORD." [7]And he told the army, "Move ahead and march around the city, with armed troops going ahead of the ark of the LORD."

[8]When Joshua gave the army its orders, the seven priests carrying the seven rams' horns before the LORD moved ahead and blew the horns as the ark of the covenant of the LORD followed behind. [9]Armed troops marched ahead of the priests blowing the horns, while the rear guard followed along behind the ark blowing rams' horns. [10]Now Joshua had instructed the army, "Do not give a battle cry or raise your voices; say nothing until the day I tell you, 'Give the battle cry.' Then give the battle cry!" [11]So Joshua made sure [a]they marched the ark of the LORD around the city one time. Then they went back to the camp and spent the night there.

[12]Bright [a]and early the next morning Joshua had the priests pick up the ark of the LORD. [13]The seven priests carrying the seven rams' horns before the ark of the LORD marched along blowing their horns. Armed troops marched ahead of them, while the rear guard followed along behind the ark of the LORD blowing rams' horns. [14]They marched around the city one time on the second day, then returned to the camp. They did this six days in all.

[15]On the seventh day they were up at the crack of dawn and marched around the city as before—only this time they marched around it seven times. [16]The seventh time around, the priests blew the rams' horns, and Joshua told the army, "Give the battle cry, for the LORD is handing the city over to you![1] [17]The city and all that is in it must be set [a]apart for the LORD; only [b]Rahab the prostitute and all who are with her in her house will live, because [c]she hid the spies we sent. [18]But be careful when you are setting apart the riches for God. If you take any of it, then you will make the Israelite camp subject to annihilation [a]and cause a disaster. [19]All the silver and gold, as well as bronze and iron items, belong to the LORD. They must go into the LORD's treasury."

[20]The rams' horns sounded,[1] and when [a]the army heard the signal, they gave a loud battle cry. The wall collapsed, and the warriors charged straight ahead into the city and captured it. [21]They annihilated with the sword everything that breathed in the city,[1] including men and women, young and old, as well as cattle, sheep, and donkeys. [22]Joshua told the two men who had spied on the land, "Enter the prostitute's house and bring out the woman and all who belong to her [a]as you promised her." [23]So the young spies went and brought out Rahab, [a]her father, mother, brothers, and all who belonged to her. They brought out her whole family and took them to a place outside the Israelite camp. [24]But they burned the city and all that was in it, except for the silver, gold, and bronze and iron items they put in the treasury of the LORD's house. [25]Yet Joshua spared Rahab the prostitute, her father's family, and all who belonged to her. [a]She lives in Israel to this very day because she

5:13 [b]Num 22:23; 1 Chr 21:16   5:14 [a]Exod 34:8   [1]MT *He said, "No, neither.*   6:1 [a]Josh 2:1   6:2 [a]Josh 2:9, 24; 8:1   [b]Deut 7:24   [1]Heb. *I have given into your hand Jericho.*   6:4 [a]Lev 25:9; Judg 7:16, 22   [b]1 Kgs 18:43; 2 Kgs 4:35; 5:10   [c]Num 10:8   6:11 [a]Josh 4:11   6:12 [a]Deut 31:25   6:16 [1]Heb. *for the LORD has given to you the city.*   6:17 [a]Deut 13:17; Josh 7:1   [b]Josh 2:1; Matt 1:5   [c]Josh 2:4, 6   6:18 [a]Josh 7:1, 12, 25; 1 Kgs 18:17–18; [Jonah 1:12]   6:20 [a]Heb 11:30   [1]MT *And the people shouted and they blew the rams' horns.*   6:21 [1]Heb. *all which was in the city.*   6:22 [a]Josh 2:12–19; Heb 11:31   6:23 [a]Josh 2:13   6:25 [a][Matt 1:5]

hid the messengers Joshua sent to spy on Jericho. [26]At that time Joshua made this solemn declaration: "The man who attempts to rebuild this city of Jericho[1] will stand [a]condemned before the LORD. He will lose his firstborn son when he lays its foundations and his youngest son when he erects its gates!" [27]The LORD was with Joshua, and he became famous throughout the land.

Achan Sins and Is Punished

7 But the Israelites disobeyed the [a]command about the city's [b]riches. [c]Achan son of Carmi, son of Zabdi, son of Zerah, from the tribe of Judah, stole some of the riches. The LORD was furious with the Israelites.

[2]Joshua sent men from Jericho to Ai (which is located near Beth Aven, east of Bethel) and instructed them, "Go up and spy on the land." So the men went up and spied on Ai. [3]They returned and reported to Joshua, "Don't send the whole army. About two or three thousand men are adequate to defeat Ai. Don't tire out the whole army, for Ai is small."

[4]So about 3,000 men went up, [a]but they fled from the men of Ai. [5]The men of Ai killed about thirty-six of [a]them and chased them from in front of the city gate all the way to the fissures and defeated them on the steep slope. The people's[1] courage melted away like water.

[6]Joshua [a]tore his clothes; he and the leaders of Israel lay face down on the ground before the ark of the LORD until evening and [b]threw dirt on their heads. [7]Joshua prayed, "O, Sovereign LORD! [a]Why did you bring these people across the Jordan to hand us over to the Amorites so they could destroy us? If only we had been satisfied to live on the other side of the Jordan! [8]O Lord, what can I say now that Israel has retreated before its enemies? [9]When the Canaanites and all who live in the land hear about this, they will turn against us and destroy the very memory of us[1] from the earth. [a]What will you do to protect your great reputation?"[2]

[10]The LORD responded to Joshua, "Get up! Why are you lying there face down? [11]Israel has sinned; they have violated my covenantal commandment! They have taken some of the riches; they have stolen them and [a]deceitfully put them among their own possessions. [12a]The Israelites are unable to stand before their enemies; [b]they retreat because they have become subject to annihilation.[1] I will no longer be with you, unless you destroy what has contaminated you.[2] [13]Get up! Ritually [a]consecrate the people and tell them this: 'Ritually [b]consecrate yourselves for tomorrow because this is what the LORD God of Israel has said, "You are contaminated, O Israel! You will not be able to stand before your enemies until you remove what is contaminating you." [14]In [a]the morning you must approach in tribal order. The tribe the LORD selects must approach by clans. The clan the LORD selects must approach by families. The family the LORD selects must approach man by man. [15]The one caught with [a]the riches must be burned up along with all who belong to him because he [b]violated the LORD's covenant and did such [c]a disgraceful thing in Israel.'"

[16]Bright and early the next morning Joshua made Israel approach in tribal order, and the tribe of Judah was selected. [17]He then made the clans of Judah approach, and the clan of the Zerahites was selected. He made the clan of the Zerahites approach, and Zabdi was selected. [18]He then made Zabdi's family approach man by man and Achan son of Carmi, son of Zabdi, son of Zerah, from the tribe of Judah, [a]was selected. [19]So Joshua said to Achan, "My son, [a]honor the LORD God of Israel [b]and give him praise! [c]Tell me what you did; don't hide anything from me." [20]Achan told Joshua, "[a]It is true. I have sinned against the LORD God of Israel in this way: [21]I saw among the goods we seized a nice robe from Babylon, 200 silver pieces, and a bar of gold weighing 50 shekels. I wanted them, so I took them. They are hidden in the ground right in the middle of my tent, with the silver underneath."

6:26 [a]1 Kgs 16:34   [1]LXX omits *Jericho*.   **7:1** [a]Josh 7:20–21   [b]Josh 6:17–19   [c]Josh 22:20   **7:4** [a]Lev 26:17; Deut 28:25   **7:5** [a]Lev 26:36; Josh 2:9, 11   [1]Or *army's*.   **7:6** [a]Gen 37:29, 34   [b]1 Sam 4:12   **7:7** [a]Exod 17:3; Num 21:5   **7:9** [a]Exod 32:12; Num 14:13   [1]Heb. *and cut off our name*.   [2]Heb. *What will you do for your great name?*   **7:11** [a]Acts 5:1–2   **7:12** [a]Judg 2:14   [b]Deut 7:26; [Hag 2:13–14]   [1]Heb. *they turn* [the] *back before their enemies because they are set apart* [for destruction by the Lord].   [2]Heb. *what is set apart* [for destruction by the Lord] *from your midst*.   **7:13** [a]Exod 19:10   [b]Josh 3:5   **7:14** [a][Prov 16:33]   **7:15** [a]1 Sam 14:38–39   [b]Josh 7:11   [c]Gen 34:7; Judg 20:6   **7:18** [a]1 Sam 14:42   **7:19** [a]1 Sam 6:5; Jer 13:16; John 9:24   [b]Num 5:6–7; 2 Chr 30:22; Ezra 10:10–11; Ps 32:5; Prov 28:13; Jer 3:12–13; Dan 9:4   [c]1 Sam 14:43   **7:20** [a]Num 22:34; 1 Sam 15:24

[22] Joshua sent messengers who ran to the tent. The things were hidden right in his tent, with the silver underneath. [23] They took it all from the middle of the tent, brought it to Joshua and all the Israelites, and placed it before the LORD. [24] Then Joshua and [a] all Israel took Achan, son of Zerah, along with [b] the silver, the robe, the bar of gold, his sons, daughters, oxen, donkeys, sheep, tent, and all that belonged to him and brought them up to the Valley of Disaster. [25] Joshua said, "[a] Why have you brought disaster on us? The LORD will bring disaster on you today!" All Israel stoned him to death. (They [b] also stoned and burned the others.)[1] [26] Then they [a] erected over him a large pile of stones (it remains to this very day[1]), and [b] the LORD's anger subsided. So that place is called [c] the Valley of Disaster to this very day.

Israel Conquers Ai

8 The LORD told Joshua, "[a] Don't be [b] afraid and don't panic! Take the whole army with you and march against Ai! See, I am handing over to you the king of Ai, along with his people, city, and land. [2] Do to Ai and its king what you did to [a] Jericho and [b] its king, except you may plunder its goods and cattle. Set an ambush behind the city."

[3] Joshua and the whole army marched against Ai. Joshua selected 30,000 brave warriors and sent them out at night. [4] He ordered them, "Look, set an ambush behind the city. Don't go very far from the city; all of [a] you be ready! [5] I and all the troops who are with me will approach the city. When they come out to fight us like before, [a] we will retreat from them. [6] They will attack us until we have lured them from the city, for they will say, 'They are retreating from us like before.' We will retreat from them. [7] Then you rise up from your hiding place and seize the city. The LORD your God will hand it over to you. [8] When you capture the city, set it on fire in keeping with the LORD's message. [a] See, I have given you orders." [9] Joshua sent them away and they went to their hiding place west of Ai, between Bethel and Ai. Joshua spent that night with the army.

[10] Bright and early the next morning Joshua gathered the army, and he and the leaders of Israel marched at the head of it to Ai. [11] All the troops that were with him marched up [a] and drew near the city. They camped north of Ai on the other side of the valley. [12] He took 5,000 men and set an ambush west of the city between Bethel and Ai. [13] The army was in position—the main army north of the city and the rear guard west of the city. That night Joshua went into the middle of the valley.

[14] When the king of Ai and all his people saw Israel, they rushed to get up early. Then the king and the men of the city went out to meet Israel in battle, at the meeting place near the rift valley. But he [a] did not realize an ambush was waiting for him behind the city. [15] Joshua and all Israel pretended to be defeated by them, and they retreated along the way to the wilderness. [16] All the reinforcements[1] in Ai[2] were ordered to chase them; they chased Joshua and were lured away from the city. [17] No men were left in Ai or Bethel;[1] they all went out after Israel. They left the city wide open and chased Israel.

[18] The LORD told Joshua, "Hold out toward Ai the curved sword[1] in your hand, for I am handing the city over to you." So Joshua held out toward Ai the curved sword in his hand. [19] When he held out his hand, the men waiting in ambush rose up quickly from their place and attacked. They entered the city, captured it, and immediately set it on fire. [20] When the men of Ai turned around, they saw the smoke from the city ascending into the sky and were so shocked they were unable to flee in any direction. In the meantime the men who were retreating to the wilderness turned against their pursuers. [21] When Joshua and all Israel saw that the men in ambush had captured the city and that the city was going up in smoke, they turned around and struck down the men of Ai. [22] At the same time the men who had taken the city came out to fight, and the men of Ai were trapped in the middle. The Israelites struck them down, [a] leaving no survivors or refugees. [23] But they captured the king of Ai alive and brought him to Joshua.

[24]When Israel had finished killing all the men[1] of Ai who had chased them toward the wilderness (they all fell by the sword),[2] all Israel returned to Ai and put the sword to it. [25]So 12,000 men and women died that day, including all the men of Ai. [26]Joshua kept holding out his curved sword until Israel had annihilated all who lived in Ai. [27a]But Israel did plunder the cattle and the goods of the city, in keeping with the [b]LORD's orders to Joshua. [28]Joshua burned [a]Ai and made it a permanently uninhabited mound (it remains that way to this very day). [29]He hung the king of Ai on [a]a tree, leaving him exposed until evening. At sunset Joshua ordered that his corpse be taken down from the tree. They threw it down at the entrance of the city gate [b]and [c]erected over it a large pile of stones (it remains to this very day).

Covenant Renewal

[30]Then Joshua built an altar for the LORD God of Israel on Mount Ebal, [31]just as Moses the LORD's [a]servant had commanded [b]the Israelites. As described in the law scroll of Moses, it was made with uncut stones untouched by an iron tool. On it they offered burnt sacrifices to the LORD and sacrificed tokens of peace. [32]There, in [a]the presence of the Israelites, Joshua inscribed on the stones a duplicate of the law written by Moses. [33]All the people, rulers, leaders, and judges were standing on either side of the ark, in front of the Levitical priests [a]who carried [b]the ark of the covenant of the LORD. Both resident foreigners and native Israelites were there. Half the people stood in front of Mount Gerizim and the other half in front of Mount Ebal, [c]as Moses the LORD's servant had previously instructed them to do for the formal blessing ceremony. [34]Then Joshua read aloud all [a]the words of [b]the law, including the blessings and the curses, just as they are written in the law [c]scroll. [35]Joshua read aloud every [a]commandment Moses had given before the whole assembly of Israel, including the women, children, and resident foreigners who lived among them.

The Gibeonites Deceive Israel

9 When the news reached [a]all [b]the kings on [c]the west side of the Jordan—in the hill country, the foothills, and all along the Mediterranean coast as far as Lebanon (including the Hittites, Amorites, Canaanites, Perizzites, Hivites, and Jebusites)—[2]they [a]formed an alliance to fight against Joshua and Israel.

[3]When the residents of [a]Gibeon [b]heard what Joshua did to Jericho and Ai, [4]they did something clever. They collected some provisions[1] and put worn-out sacks on their donkeys, along with worn-out wineskins that were ripped and patched. [5]They had worn-out, patched sandals on their feet and dressed in worn-out clothes. All their bread was dry and hard. [6]They came [a]to Joshua at the camp in Gilgal and said to him and the men of Israel, "We have come from a distant land. Make a treaty with us." [7]The men of Israel said to the [a]Hivites, "Perhaps you live near us.[1] So [b]how can we make a treaty with you?" [8]But they said to Joshua, "[a]We are willing to be your subjects." So Joshua said to them, "Who are you and where do you come from?" [9]They told him, "Your subjects have come [a]from a very distant land because of the reputation of the LORD your God, for we have [b]heard the news about all he did in Egypt [10]and [a]all he did to the two Amorite kings on the other side of the Jordan—King Sihon of Heshbon and King Og of Bashan in Ashtaroth. [11]Our leaders and all who live in our land told us, 'Take provisions for your journey and go meet them. Tell them, "We are willing to be your subjects. Make a treaty with us."' [12]This bread of ours was warm when we packed it in our homes the day we started out to meet you, but now it is dry and hard. [13]These wineskins we filled were brand new, but look how they have ripped. Our clothes and sandals have worn out because it has been a very long journey." [14]The men examined some of their provisions,

[a]but they failed to ask the LORD's advice. [15]Joshua [a]made a peace treaty with them and agreed to let them live. The leaders of the community sealed it with an oath.

[16]Three days after they made the treaty with them, the Israelites found out they were from the local area and lived nearby. [17]So the Israelites set out and on the third day arrived at their cities—[a]Gibeon, Kephirah, Beeroth, and Kiriath Jearim. [18]The Israelites did not attack them [a]because the leaders of the community had sworn an oath to them in the name of the LORD God of Israel. The whole community criticized the leaders, [19]but all the leaders told the whole community, "We swore an oath to them in the name of the LORD God of Israel! So now we can't hurt them. [20]We must let them live so we can escape the [a]curse attached to the oath we swore to them." [21]The leaders then added,[1] "Let them live." So they became [a]woodcutters and water carriers for the whole community, as the leaders had [b]decided.

[22]Joshua summoned the Gibeonites and said to them, "Why did you trick us by saying, '[a]We live far away from [b]you,' when you really live nearby?[1] [23]Now you are [a]condemned to perpetual servitude as woodcutters and water carriers for the house of my God." [24]They said to Joshua, "It was carefully reported to your subjects how the LORD your God [a]commanded Moses his servant to assign you the whole land and to destroy all who live in the land from before you. Because of you [b]we were terrified we would lose our lives, so we did this thing. [25]So now we are [a]in your power. Do to us what you think is good and appropriate." [26]Joshua did as they said; he kept the Israelites from killing them[1] [27]and that day made them [a]woodcutters and water carriers for the community and for the altar of the LORD at the [b]divinely chosen site. (They continue in that capacity to this very day.)

Israel Defeats an Amorite Coalition

10 Adoni-Zedek, king of Jerusalem, [a]heard how Joshua captured [b]Ai and annihilated it and its king [c]as he did Jericho and its king. He also heard [d]how the people of Gibeon made peace with Israel and lived among them. [2]All Jerusalem was [a]terrified because Gibeon was a large city, like one of the royal cities. It was larger than Ai, and all its men were warriors. [3]So King Adoni-Zedek of Jerusalem sent this message to King Hoham of Hebron, King Piram of Jarmuth, King Japhia of Lachish, and King Debir of Eglon: [4]"Come to my aid so we can attack Gibeon, for [a]it has made peace with Joshua and the Israelites." [5]So the five [a]Amorite kings (the kings of Jerusalem, Hebron, Jarmuth, Lachish, and Eglon) and all their troops gathered [b]together and advanced. They deployed their troops and fought against Gibeon.

[6]The men of Gibeon sent this message to Joshua [a]at the camp in Gilgal, "Do not abandon your subjects! Come up here quickly and rescue us! Help us! For all the Amorite kings living in the hill country are attacking us." [7]So Joshua and his [a]whole army, including the bravest warriors, marched up from Gilgal. [8]The LORD told Joshua, "[a]Don't be afraid of them, for I am handing them over to you. [b]Not one of them can [c]resist you." [9]Joshua attacked them by surprise after marching all night from Gilgal. [10]The LORD [a]routed[1] them before Israel. Israel[2] thoroughly defeated them at Gibeon. They chased them up the road [b]to the pass of Beth Horon and struck them down all the way to [c]Azekah and Makkedah. [11]As they fled from Israel on the slope leading down from Beth Horon, the LORD threw down on them large hailstones from the sky, all the way to Azekah. They died—in fact, more died from the hailstones than the Israelites killed with the sword.

[12]The day the LORD delivered the Amorites over to the Israelites, Joshua prayed to the LORD before Israel:

"O [a]sun, stand still over Gibeon;
    O moon, over the Valley of [b]Aijalon!"

[13]The sun stood still and the moon stood motionless while the nation took

9:14[a] Num 27:21; Isa 30:1 **9:15**[a] 2 Sam 21:2 **9:17**[a] Josh 18:25 **9:18**[a] Ps 15:4 **9:20**[a] 2 Sam 21:1–2, 6; Ezek 17:13, 15 **9:21**[a] Deut 29:11 [b] Josh 9:15 [1] LXX omits *The leaders then added.* **9:22**[a] Josh 9:6, 9 [b] Josh 9:16 [1] Heb. *live in our midst?* **9:23**[a] Gen 9:25 **9:24**[a] Exod 23:31–33; Deut 7:1–2 [b] Exod 15:14 **9:25**[a] Gen 16:6 **9:26**[1] Heb. *And he did to them so and he rescued them from the hand of the sons of Israel and they did not kill them.* **9:27**[a] Josh 9:21, 23 [b] Deut 12:5 **10:1**[a] Josh 9:1 [b] Josh 8:22, 26, 28 [c] Josh 6:21 [d] Josh 9:15 **10:2**[a] Exod 15:14–16; Deut 11:25; 1 Chr 14:17 **10:4**[a] Josh 9:15; 10:1 **10:5**[a] Num 13:29 [b] Josh 9:2 **10:6**[a] Josh 5:10; 9:6 **10:7**[a] Josh 8:1 **10:8**[a] Josh 11:6; Judg 4:14 [b] Josh 1:5, 9 [c] Josh 21:44 **10:10**[a] Judg 4:15; 1 Sam 7:10, 12; Isa 28:21 [b] Josh 16:3, 5 [c] Josh 15:35 [1] Or *caused to panic.* [2] Heb. *he.* **10:12**[a] Isa 28:21; Hab 3:11 [b] Judg 12:12

vengeance on its enemies. The event ᵃis recorded in the Scroll of the Upright One. The sun stood motionless in the middle of the sky and did not set for about a full day. ¹⁴There has ᵃnot been a day like it before or since. ᵇThe LORD listened to a human being, for the LORD fought for Israel! ¹⁵Then Joshua and all Israel returned to ᵃthe camp at Gilgal.

¹⁶The five Amorite kings ran away and hid in the cave at Makkedah. ¹⁷Joshua was told, "The five kings have been found hiding in the cave at Makkedah." ¹⁸Joshua said, "Roll large stones over the mouth of the cave and post guards in front of it. ¹⁹But don't you delay! Chase your enemies and catch them. Don't allow them to retreat to their cities, for the LORD your God is handing them over to you." ²⁰Joshua and the Israelites almost totally wiped them out, but some survivors did escape to the fortified cities. ²¹Then the whole army safely returned to Joshua at the camp in Makkedah. ᵃNo one¹ dared threaten the Israelites. ²²Joshua said, "Open the cave's mouth and bring the five kings out of the cave to me." ²³They did as ordered; they brought the five kings out of the cave to him—the kings of Jerusalem, Hebron, Jarmuth, Lachish, and Eglon. ²⁴When they brought the kings out to Joshua, he summoned all the men of Israel and said to the commanders of the troops who accompanied him, "Come here and ᵃput your feet on the necks of these kings." So they came up and put their feet on their necks. ²⁵Then Joshua said to them, "Don't be afraid and don't panic! Be strong and brave, for the LORD will ᵃdo the same thing to all your enemies you fight." ²⁶Then Joshua executed them and hung them on five trees. They ᵃwere left hanging on the trees until evening. ²⁷At sunset Joshua ordered his men ᵃto take them down from the trees. They threw them into the cave where they had hidden and piled large stones over the mouth of the cave. (They remain to this very day.)

Joshua Launches a Southern Campaign

²⁸That day Joshua captured Makkedah and put the sword to it and its king. He ᵃannihilated everyone who lived in it; he left no survivors. He did to its king what he had done to the king of Jericho.

²⁹Joshua and all Israel marched from Makkedah to ᵃLibnah and fought against it. ³⁰The LORD handed it and its king over to Israel, and Israel put the sword to all who lived there; they left no survivors. They did to its king what they had done to the king of Jericho.

³¹Joshua and all Israel marched from Libnah to Lachish. He deployed his troops and fought against it. ³²The LORD handed Lachish over to Israel, and they captured it on the second day. They put the sword to all who lived there, just as they had done to Libnah. ³³Then King Horam of Gezer came up to help Lachish, but Joshua struck him down, as well as his army, until no survivors remained.

³⁴Joshua and all Israel marched from Lachish to Eglon. They deployed troops and fought against it. ³⁵That day they captured it and put the sword to all who lived there. That day they annihilated it just as they had done to Lachish.

³⁶Joshua and all Israel marched up from Eglon to ᵃHebron and fought against it. ³⁷They captured it and put the sword to its king, all its surrounding cities, and all who lived in it; they left no survivors. As they had done at Eglon, they annihilated it and all who lived there.

³⁸Joshua and all Israel turned to ᵃDebir and fought against it. ³⁹They captured it, its king, and all its surrounding cities and put the sword to them. They annihilated everyone who lived there; they left no survivors. They did to Debir and its king what they had done to Libnah and its king and to Hebron.

⁴⁰Joshua defeated the whole land, including the hill ᵃcountry, the Negev, the foothills, the slopes, and ᵇall their kings. He left no survivors. He annihilated everything that breathed, just as the LORD God of Israel had commanded. ⁴¹Joshua conquered the area between Kadesh ᵃBarnea and ᵇGaza ᶜand the whole region of Goshen, all the way to Gibeon. ⁴²Joshua captured in one campaign all these kings and their lands,

10:13 ᵃ2 Sam 1:18   10:14 ᵃIsa 38:7–8   ᵇExod 14:14; Deut 1:30; 20:4; Josh 10:42; 23:3   10:15 ᵃJosh 10:43   10:21 ᵃExod 11:7   ¹MT *to man.*   10:24 ᵃPs 107:40; Isa 26:5–6; Mal 4:3   10:25 ᵃDeut 31:6–8; Josh 1:9   10:26 ᵃJosh 8:29; 2 Sam 21:9   10:27 ᵃDeut 21:22–23; Josh 8:29   10:28 ᵃDeut 7:2, 16   10:29 ᵃJosh 15:42; 21:13; 2 Kgs 8:22; 19:8   10:36 ᵃNum 13:22; Josh 14:13–15; 15:13; Judg 1:10, 20; 2 Sam 5:1, 3, 5, 13; 2 Chr 11:10   10:38 ᵃJosh 15:15; Judg 1:11; 1 Chr 6:58   10:40 ᵃDeut 1:7   ᵇDeut 7:24   10:41 ᵃNum 13:26; Deut 9:23   ᵇGen 10:19; Josh 11:22   ᶜJosh 11:16; 15:51

for the Lord God of Israel fought for Israel. ⁴³Then Joshua and all Israel returned to the camp at Gilgal.

Israel Defeats a Northern Coalition

11 When King Jabin of Hazor heard the news about Israel's victories, he organized a ᵃcoalition, including¹ King Jobab ᵇof Madon, the king of Shimron, the king of Acshaph, ²and the northern kings who ruled in the hill country, in the rift valley south of ᵃKinnereth, in the foothills, and on the heights ᵇof Dor to the west. ³Canaanites came from the east and west; ᵃAmorites, Hittites, Perizzites, ᵇand Jebusites from the hill country; and Hivites from below ᶜHermon ᵈin the area of Mizpah. ⁴These kings came out with their armies; they were ᵃas numerous as the sand on the seashore and had a large number of horses and chariots. ⁵All these kings gathered and joined forces at the Waters of Merom to fight Israel.

⁶The Lord told Joshua, "ᵃDon't be afraid of them, for about this time tomorrow I will cause all of them to lie dead before Israel. You must ᵇhamstring their horses and burn their chariots." ⁷Joshua and his whole army caught them by surprise at the Waters of Merom and attacked them. ⁸The Lord handed them over to Israel, and they struck them down and chased them all the way to Greater ᵃSidon, Misrephoth ᵇMaim, and the Mizpah Valley to the east. They struck them down until no survivors remained. ⁹Joshua did to them as the Lord had commanded him; he hamstrung their horses and burned their chariots.

¹⁰At that time Joshua turned, captured Hazor, and struck down its king with the sword, for Hazor was at that time the leader of all these kingdoms. ¹¹They annihilated everyone who lived there with the sword—no one who ᵃbreathed remained—and burned Hazor.

¹²Joshua captured all these royal cities and all their kings and annihilated them with the sword, ᵃas Moses the Lord's servant had commanded. ¹³But Israel did not burn any of the cities located on mounds except for Hazor; it was the only one Joshua burned. ¹⁴The Israelites plundered all the ᵃgoods of these cities and the cattle, but they totally destroyed all the people and allowed no one who breathed to live. ¹⁵ᵃMoses the Lord's servant passed on the Lord's commands to Joshua, and Joshua did as he was told. He did not ignore any of the commands the Lord had given Moses.

A Summary of Israel's Victories

¹⁶Joshua conquered ᵃthe whole land, including the hill country, ᵇall the Negev, all the land of Goshen, the foothills, the rift valley, the hill country of Israel and its foothills, ¹⁷ᵃfrom Mount Halak up to Seir, as far as Baal Gad in the Lebanon Valley below Mount Hermon. He captured ᵇall their kings and executed them. ¹⁸Joshua campaigned against these kings for quite some time. ¹⁹No city made peace with ᵃthe Israelites (except the Hivites living in Gibeon); they had to conquer all of them, ²⁰for the Lord determined to make them obstinate so they would attack Israel. He wanted Israel to annihilate them ᵃwithout mercy, ᵇas he had instructed Moses.

²¹At that time Joshua attacked and eliminated ᵃthe Anakites from the hill country—from Hebron, Debir, Anab, and all the hill country of Judah and Israel. Joshua annihilated them and their cities. ²²No Anakites were left ᵃin Israelite territory, though some remained in Gaza, Gath, ᵇand Ashdod. ²³Joshua conquered the whole land, just as the Lord had promised Moses,¹ and he assigned Israel their tribal portions.² Then the land was ᵃfree of war.

12 Now these are the kings of the land whom the Israelites defeated and drove ᵃfrom their land on the east side of the Jordan, from the Arnon Valley ᵇto Mount Hermon, including all the eastern rift valley:

²King ᵃSihon of the Amorites who lived in Heshbon and ruled from Aroer (on the

11:1 ᵃJosh 10:3 ᵇJosh 19:15 ¹Heb. *he sent to.* 11:2 ᵃNum 34:11 ᵇJosh 17:11; Judg 1:27; 1 Kgs 4:11 11:3 ᵃJosh 9:1 ᵇDeut 7:1; Judg 3:3, 5; 1 Kgs 9:20 ᶜJosh 11:17; 13:5, 11 ᵈGen 31:49 11:4 ᵃGen 22:17; 32:12; Judg 7:12; 1 Sam 13:5 11:6 ᵃJosh 10:8 ᵇ2 Sam 8:4 11:8 ᵃGen 49:13 ᵇJosh 13:6 11:11 ᵃJosh 10:40 11:12 ᵃNum 33:50–56; Deut 7:2; 20:16 11:14 ᵃDeut 20:14–18 11:15 ᵃDeut 31:7–8 11:16 ᵃJosh 12:8 ᵇJosh 10:40–41 11:17 ᵃJosh 12:7 ᵇDeut 7:24 11:19 ᵃJosh 9:3–7 11:20 ᵃDeut 2:30 ᵇJosh 20:16–17 11:21 ᵃNum 13:22, 33; Deut 1:28; 9:2; Josh 15:13–14 11:22 ᵃ1 Sam 17:4 ᵇJosh 15:46; 1 Sam 5:1; Isa 20:1 11:23 ᵃDeut 12:9–10; 25:19; [Heb 4:8] ¹Or *just as the Lord had instructed Moses.* ²Heb. *and Joshua gave it for an inheritance to Israel according to their allotted portions by their tribes.* 12:1 ᵃNum 21:24 ᵇDeut 3:8 12:2 ᵃNum 21:24; Deut 2:24–27

edge of the Arnon Valley)—including the city in the middle of the valley[1] and half of Gilead—all the way to the Jabbok Valley bordering Ammonite territory. [3]His kingdom included [a]the eastern rift valley from [b]the Sea of Kinnereth to [c]the sea of the rift valley (the Salt Sea), including the route to Beth Jeshimoth and the area southward below the slopes of Pisgah.

[4]The territory of King [a]Og of Bashan, one of [b]the few remaining Rephaites, [c]who lived in Ashtaroth and Edrei [5]and ruled over [a]Mount Hermon, Salecah, all [b]Bashan to the border of the Geshurites and Maacathites, and half of Gilead as far as the border of King Sihon of Heshbon.

[6a]Moses the LORD's servant and the Israelites defeated them, and Moses the LORD's servant assigned their land to Reuben, Gad, and the half-tribe of Manasseh.

[7]These are the kings of the land whom Joshua and the Israelites defeated on the west side of the Jordan, from Baal Gad in the Lebanon Valley to Mount Halak up to [a]Seir. Joshua [b]assigned this territory to the Israelite tribes, [8a]including [b]the hill country, the foothills, the rift valley, the slopes, the wilderness, and the Negev—the land of the Hittites, Amorites, Canaanites, Perizzites, Hivites, and Jebusites:

[9] the king of Jericho (one),
     [a]the king of Ai—located near
        [b]Bethel—(one),
[10] the king of Jerusalem (one),
     [a]the king of Hebron (one),
[11] the king of Jarmuth (one),
     the king of Lachish (one),
[12] the king of Eglon (one),
     [a]the king of Gezer (one),
[13] the king of Debir (one),
     [a]the king of Geder (one),
[14] the king of Hormah (one),
     the king of Arad (one),
[15] the king of Libnah (one),
     [a]the king of Adullam (one),
[16] the king of Makkedah (one),
     [a]the king of [b]Bethel (one),
[17] the king of Tappuah (one),
     [a]the king of Hepher (one),
[18] the king of Aphek (one),
     the king of Lasharon (one),
[19] the king of Madon (one),
     [a]the king of Hazor (one),
[20] the king of Shimron [a]Meron (one),
     the king of Acshaph (one),
[21] the king of Taanach (one),
     the king of Megiddo (one),
[22] the king of Kedesh (one),
     [a]the king of Jokneam near Carmel
        (one),
[23] the king of Dor—near [a]Naphath
        Dor—(one),
     [b]the king of Goyim—near
        Gilgal—(one),
[24] the king of Tirzah (one),

a [a]total of thirty-one kings.

The Lord Speaks to Joshua

13 When Joshua [a]was very old, the LORD told him, "You are very old, and a great deal of land remains to be conquered. [2]This [a]is the land that remains: [b]all the territory of the Philistines and all the Geshurites, [3a]from the Shihor River east of Egypt northward to the territory of Ekron (it is regarded as Canaanite territory), including the area belonging to the [b]five Philistine lords who ruled in Gaza, Ashdod, Ashkelon, Gath, and Ekron, as well as Avvite land [4]to the south; all the Canaanite territory, from Arah[1] in the region of Sidon to Aphek, [a]as far as Amorite territory; [5]the territory of Byblos[1] and all Lebanon to [a]the east, [b]from Baal Gad below Mount Hermon to Lebo Hamath. [6]I will drive out before [a]the [b]Israelites all who live in the hill country from Lebanon to Misrephoth Maim, all the Sidonians; you be sure to parcel it out to Israel as [c]I instructed you. [7]Now, divide up this land among the nine tribes and the half-tribe of Manasseh."

Tribal Lands East of the Jordan

[8]The other half of Manasseh, Reuben, and Gad received their allotted tribal lands on

12:2 [1]MT omits *including the city in.* 12:3 [a]Deut 3:17 [b]Josh 13:20 [c]Deut 3:17; 4:49 12:4 [a]Num 21:33; Deut 3:4, 10 [b]Deut 3:11; Josh 13:12 [c]Deut 1:4 12:5 [a]Deut 3:8 [b]Deut 3:14; 1 Sam 27:8 12:6 [a]Num 32:29–33; Deut 3:12; Josh 13:8 12:7 [a]Gen 14:6; 32:3; Deut 2:1, 4 [b]Josh 11:23 12:8 [a]Josh 10:40; 11:16 [b]Exod 3:8; 23:23; Josh 9:1 12:9 [a]Josh 6:2 [b]Josh 8:29 12:10 [a]Josh 10:23 12:12 [a]Josh 10:33 12:13 [a]Josh 10:38–39 12:15 [a]Josh 10:29–30 12:16 [a]Josh 10:28 [b]Josh 8:17; Judg 1:22 12:17 [a]1 Kgs 4:10 12:19 [a]Josh 11:10 12:20 [a]Josh 11:1; 19:15 12:22 [a]Josh 19:37; 20:7; 21:32 12:23 [a]Josh 11:2 [b]Gen 14:1–2; Isa 9:1 12:24 [a]Deut 7:24 13:1 [a]Josh 14:10; 23:1–2 13:2 [a]Judg 3:1–3 [b]Joel 3:4 13:3 [a]1 Chr 13:5; Jer 2:18 [b]Judg 3:3 13:4 [a]Josh 12:18; 19:30; 1 Sam 4:1; 1 Kgs 20:26, 30 [1]MT *and a cave, and Mearah.* 13:5 [a]1 Kgs 5:18; Ezek 27:9 [b]Josh 12:7 [1]Heb. *and the land of the Gebalites.* 13:6 [a]Josh 11:8 [b]Josh 23:13; Judg 2:21, 23 [c]Josh 14:1–2

the east [a]side of the Jordan, just as Moses, the LORD's servant, had assigned them. [9]Their territory started from Aroer (on the edge of the Arnon Valley), included the city in the middle of the valley, the whole plain of Medeba as far as Dibon, [10]and [a]all the cities of King Sihon of the Amorites who ruled in Heshbon, and ended at the Ammonite border. [11]Their territory also included [a]Gilead, Geshurite and Maacathite territory, all Mount Hermon, and all Bashan to Salecah—[12]the whole kingdom of Og in Bashan, who ruled in Ashtaroth and Edrei. ([a]He was one of the few remaining Rephaites.) Moses defeated them and took their lands. [13]But the Israelites [a]did not conquer the Geshurites and Maacathites; Geshur and Maacah live among Israel to this very day. [14a]However, Moses did not [b]assign land as an inheritance to the Levites; their inheritance is the sacrificial offerings[1] made to the LORD God of Israel, as he instructed[2] them.

[15]Moses assigned [a]land to the tribe of Reuben by its clans. [16]Their territory started at Aroer (on the edge of the Arnon Valley) [a]and included the city in the middle of the valley, the whole plain of Medeba, [17a]Heshbon and all its surrounding cities on the plain, including Dibon, Bamoth Baal, Beth Baal Meon, [18a]Jahaz, Kedemoth, Mephaath, [19a]Kiriathaim, [b]Sibmah, Zereth Shahar on the hill in the valley, [20]Beth Peor, [a]the slopes of Pisgah, and Beth Jeshimoth. [21]It encompassed [a]all the cities of the plain and the whole realm of King Sihon of the Amorites [b]who ruled in Heshbon. Moses defeated him and the Midianite leaders Evi, Rekem, Zur, Hur, and Reba (they were subjects of Sihon and lived in his territory).[1] [22]The Israelites killed [a]Balaam son of Beor, the omen reader, along with the others.[1] [23]The border of the tribe of Reuben was the Jordan. The land allotted to the tribe of Reuben by its clans included these cities and their towns.

[24a]Moses assigned land to the tribe of Gad by its clans. [25]Their territory included Jazer, all [a]the cities of Gilead, [b]and half the Ammonite territory as far as Aroer near [c]Rabbah. [26]Their territory ran from Heshbon to Ramath Mizpah and Betonim, and from Mahanaim to the territory of Debir. [27]It included the valley of Beth [a]Haram,[1] Beth Nimrah, [b]Sukkoth, and Zaphon, and the rest [c]of the realm of King Sihon of Heshbon, the area east of the Jordan to the end of the Sea of Kinnereth. [28]The land allotted to the tribe of Gad by its clans included these cities and their towns.

[29a]Moses assigned land to the half-tribe of Manasseh by its clans. [30]Their territory started at Mahanaim and encompassed [a]all Bashan, the whole realm of King Og of Bashan, including all 60 cities in Havvoth Jair in Bashan. [31]Half of Gilead, [a]Ashtaroth, and Edrei, cities in the kingdom of Og in Bashan, were assigned to the [b]descendants of Makir son of Manasseh, to half the descendants of Makir by their clans.

[32]These are the land assignments made by Moses in the rift valley plains of Moab east of the Jordan River opposite Jericho. [33a]However, Moses did not [b]assign land as an inheritance to the Levites; their inheritance is the LORD God of Israel, as he instructed them.

Judah's Tribal Lands

14 The following is a record of the territory assigned to the Israelites in the land of Canaan by Eleazar the priest, Joshua son of Nun, and the Israelite tribal leaders. [2]The land assignments to the nine-and-a-half tribes were made [a]by drawing lots, as the LORD had instructed Moses. [3a]Now Moses had assigned land[1] to the two-and-a-half tribes east of the Jordan, but he assigned no land[2] to the Levites. [4]The descendants of Joseph were considered as two tribes, Manasseh and Ephraim. [a]The Levites were allotted no territory, though they were assigned [b]cities in which to live, along with the grazing areas for their cattle

13:8 [a] Josh 12:1–6   **13:10** [a] Num 21:24–25   **13:11** [a] Num 32:1; Josh 12:5   **13:12** [a] Deut 3:11; Josh 12:4   **13:13** [a] Josh 13:11   **13:14** [a] Num 18:20, 23, 24; Deut 18:1; Josh 14:3–4   [b] Josh 13:33   [1] Or *offerings made by fire.*   [2] Or *promised*; Heb. *spoke.*   **13:15** [a] Num 34:14; Josh 13:15–23   **13:16** [a] Num 21:28   **13:17** [a] Num 21:28, 30   **13:18** [a] Num 21:23; Judg 11:20; Isa 15:4; Jer 48:34   **13:19** [a] Num 32:37; Jer 48:1, 23; Ezek 25:9   [b] Num 32:38   **13:20** [a] Deut 3:17; Josh 12:3   **13:21** [a] Deut 3:10   [b] Num 21:24   [1] Heb. *princes of Sihon, inhabitants of the land.*   **13:22** [a] Num 22:5; 31:8   [1] Heb. *Balaam son of Beor, the omen-reader, the Israelites killed with the sword, along with their slain ones.*   **13:24** [a] Num 34:14; 1 Chr 5:11   **13:25** [a] Num 32:1, 35   [b] Judg 11:13, 15   [c] Deut 3:11; 2 Sam 11:1; 12:26   **13:27** [a] Num 32:36   [b] Gen 33:17; 1 Kgs 7:46   [c] Num 34:11; Deut 3:17   [1] Or *it included in the valley, Beth Haram.*   **13:29** [a] Num 34:14; 1 Chr 5:23   **13:30** [a] Num 32:41; 1 Chr 2:23   **13:31** [a] Josh 9:10; 12:4; 13:12; 1 Chr 6:71   [b] Num 32:39–40; Josh 17:1   **13:33** [a] Deut 18:1; Josh 13:14; 18:7   [b] Num 18:20; Deut 10:9; 18:1–2   **14:2** [a] Num 26:55; 33:54; 34:13; Ps 16:5   **14:3** [a] Num 32:33; Josh 13:8, 32, 33   [1] Or *assigned an inheritance.*   [2] Or *no inheritance.*   **14:4** [a] Gen 41:51; 46:20; 48:1, 5; Num 26:28; 2 Chr 30:1   [b] Num 35:2–8; Josh 21:1–42

and possessions. [5]The Israelites followed the [a]LORD's instructions to Moses and divided up the land.

[6]The men of Judah approached Joshua in Gilgal, and Caleb son of Jephunneh the [a]Kenizzite said to him, "You know what [b]the LORD said about [c]you and me to Moses, the man of God, at Kadesh Barnea. [7]I was forty years old when Moses, the LORD's servant, [a]sent me from Kadesh Barnea to spy on the land and I brought back to him an honest report.[1] [8a]My countrymen who accompanied me frightened the people, but I remained [b]loyal to the LORD my God. [9]That day Moses made this solemn promise: '[a]Surely the land on which you walked will belong to you and your descendants permanently, for you remained loyal to the LORD your God.' [10]So now, look, the LORD has [a]preserved my life, just [b]as he promised, these past forty-five years since the LORD spoke these words to Moses, while Israel traveled through the wilderness. See here, I am today eighty-five years old! [11]Today I am still [a]as strong as when Moses sent me out. I can fight and go about my daily activities with the same energy I had then. [12]Now, assign me this hill country that [a]the LORD promised me at that time! No doubt you heard then that the [b]Anakites [c]live there in large, fortified cities. But assuming the LORD is with me, I will conquer them, as the LORD promised." [13]Joshua asked God to [a]empower Caleb son of Jephunneh [b]and assigned him Hebron.[1] [14]So [a]Hebron remains the assigned land of Caleb son of Jephunneh the Kenizzite to this very day because he [b]remained loyal to the LORD God of Israel. [15](Hebron used to be called Kiriath Arba. Arba was a famous Anakite.) [a]Then [b]the land was free of war.

15

The land allotted to [a]the tribe of Judah by its clans reached to the border of Edom, to the [b]wilderness of Zin in the Negev far to the south. [2]Their [a]southern border started at the southern tip of the Salt Sea, [3]extended south of [a]the Scorpion Ascent,[1] crossed to Zin, went up from the south to Kadesh Barnea, crossed to Hezron, went up to Addar, and turned toward Karka. [4]It then crossed [a]to Azmon, extended to the Stream of Egypt,[1] and ended at the Mediterranean Sea. This was their southern border.

[5]The eastern [a]border was the Salt Sea to the mouth of the Jordan River.

The northern border started north of the Salt Sea at the mouth of the Jordan, [6]went up to Beth [a]Hoglah, crossed north of Beth Arabah, and went up [b]to the Stone of Bohan son of Reuben. [7]It then went up to [a]Debir from [b]the Valley of Achor, turning northward to Gilgal (which is opposite the Pass of Adummim south of the valley), crossed to the waters of En Shemesh, and extended to En [c]Rogel. [8]It then went up the Valley of Ben Hinnom to the slope of the [a]Jebusites on the south (that is, Jerusalem), going up to the top [b]of the hill opposite the Valley of Ben Hinnom to the west, which is at the end of the Valley of the Rephaites to the north. [9]It [a]then went from the [b]top of the hill to the spring of the waters of Nephtoah, extended to the cities of Mount Ephron, and went to Baalah (that is, Kiriath [c]Jearim). [10]It then turned from Baalah westward to Mount Seir, crossed to the slope of Mount Jearim on the north (that is Kesalon), descended to Beth Shemesh, and crossed to [a]Timnah. [11]It then extended to the slope of [a]Ekron to the north, went toward Shikkeron, crossed to Mount Baalah, extended to Jabneel, and ended at the sea.

[12]The western border was [a]the Mediterranean Sea. These were the borders of the tribe of Judah and its clans.

[13a]Caleb son of Jephunneh was assigned Kiriath Arba (that is Hebron) within the tribe of [b]Judah, according to the LORD's instructions to Joshua. ([c]Arba was the father of Anak.) [14]Caleb drove out from [a]there three Anakites—[b]Sheshai, Ahiman, and Talmai, descendants of Anak. [15]From [a]there he attacked the people of Debir. (Debir used to be called Kiriath Sepher.) [16]Caleb said, "To

14:5 [a]Num 35:2; Josh 21:2   14:6 [a]Num 32:11–12   [b]Num 14:24, 30   [c]Num 13:26   14:7 [a]Num 13:6, 17; 14:6   [1]Heb. and I brought back to him a word just as [was] in my heart.   14:8 [a]Num 13:31–32; Deut 1:28   [b]Num 14:24; Deut 1:36   14:9 [a]Num 14:23–24   14:10 [a]Num 14:24, 30, 38   [b]Josh 5:6; Neh 9:21   14:11 [a]Deut 34:7   14:12 [a]Num 13:28, 33   [b]Rom 8:31   [c]Josh 15:14; Judg 1:20   14:13 [a]Josh 22:6   [b]Josh 10:37; 15:13   [1]Heb. Joshua blessed him and gave Hebron to Caleb son of Jephunneh as an inheritance.   14:14 [a]Josh 21:12   [b]Josh 14:8–9   14:15 [a]Gen 23:2; Josh 15:13   [b]Josh 11:23   15:1 [a]Num 34:3   [b]Num 33:36   15:2 [a]Num 34:3–4   15:3 [a]Num 34:4   [1]Or the Ascent of Akrabbim.   15:4 [a]Num 34:5   [1]Or the Wadi of Egypt; trad. the Brook of Egypt.   15:5 [a]Josh 18:15–19   15:6 [a]Josh 18:19, 21   [b]Josh 18:17   15:7 [a]Josh 13:26   [b]Josh 7:26   [c]2 Sam 17:17; 1 Kgs 1:9   15:8 [a]Josh 15:63; 18:28; Judg 1:21; 19:10   [b]Josh 18:16   15:9 [a]Josh 18:15   [b]1 Chr 13:6   [c]Judg 18:12   15:10 [a]Gen 38:13; Judg 14:1   15:11 [a]Josh 19:43   15:12 [a]Num 34:6–7; Josh 15:47   15:13 [a]Josh 14:13   [b]Num 13:6   [c]Josh 14:15   15:14 [a]Judg 1:10, 20   [b]Num 13:22   15:15 [a]Josh 10:38; Judg 1:11

the man who attacks [a]and captures Kiriath Sepher I will give my daughter Achsah as a wife." [17]When [a]Othniel [b]son of Kenaz, Caleb's brother, captured it, Caleb gave [c]Achsah his daughter to him as a wife.

[18]One [a]time Achsah came and charmed her father so that [b]she could ask him for some land. When she got down from her donkey, Caleb said to her, "What would you like?" [19]She answered, "Please give me a special [a]present.[1] Since you have given me land in the Negev, now give me springs of water." So he gave her both the upper and lower springs.

[20]This is the land assigned to the tribe of Judah by its clans: [21]These cities were located at the southern extremity of Judah's tribal land near the border of Edom: Kabzeel, [a]Eder, Jagur, [22]Kinah, Dimonah, Adadah, [23]Kedesh, Hazor, Ithnan, [24a]Ziph, Telem, Bealoth, [25]Hazor Hadattah, Kerioth Hezron (that is, Hazor), [26]Amam, Shema, Moladah, [27]Hazar Gaddah, Heshbon, Beth Pelet, [28]Hazar Shual, Beer [a]Sheba, Biziothiah, [29]Baalah, Iim, Ezem, [30]Eltolad, Kesil, [a]Hormah, [31a]Ziklag, Madmannah, Sansannah, [32]Lebaoth, Shilhim, Ain, and [a]Rimmon—a total of 29 cities and their towns.

[33]These cities were in the foothills: [a]Eshtaol, Zorah, Ashnah, [34]Zanoah, En Gannim, Tappuah, Enam, [35]Jarmuth, [a]Adullam, Socoh, Azekah, [36]Shaaraim, Adithaim, and Gederah (or Gederothaim)—a total of 14 cities and their towns.

[37]Zenan, Hadashah, Migdal Gad, [38]Dilean, Mizpah, [a]Joktheel, [39a]Lachish, Bozkath, [b]Eglon, [40]Cabbon, Lahmas, Kitlish, [41]Gederoth, Beth Dagon, Naamah, and Makkedah—a total of 16 cities and their towns.

[42a]Libnah, Ether, Ashan, [43]Iphtah, Ashnah, Nezib, [44]Keilah, Achzib, and Mareshah—a total of nine cities and their towns.

[45]Ekron and its surrounding towns and settlements; [46]from Ekron westward, all those in the vicinity of [a]Ashdod and their towns; [47]Ashdod with its surrounding towns and settlements, and Gaza with its surrounding towns and settlements, as far as [a]the Stream of Egypt[1] and [b]the border at the Mediterranean Sea.

[48]These cities were in the hill country: Shamir, Jattir, Socoh, [49]Dannah, Kiriath Sannah (that is, Debir), [50]Anab, Eshtemoh, Anim, [51a]Goshen, Holon, and Giloh—a total of eleven cities and their towns.

[52]Arab, Dumah,[1] Eshan, [53]Janim, Beth Tappuah, Aphekah, [54]Humtah, Kiriath [a]Arba (that is, Hebron), and Zior—a total of nine cities and their towns.

[55a]Maon, Carmel, Ziph, Juttah, [56]Jezreel, Jokdeam, Zanoah, [57]Kain, Gibeah, and Timnah—a total of 10 cities and their towns.

[58]Halhul, Beth Zur, Gedor, [59]Maarath, Beth Anoth, and Eltekon—a total of six cities and their towns.

[60]Kiriath [a]Baal (that is, Kiriath Jearim) and Rabbah—a total of two cities and their towns.

[61]These cities were in the wilderness: Beth Arabah, Middin, Secacah, [62]Nibshan, the City of Salt, and En [a]Gedi—a total of six cities and their towns.

[63]The men of Judah were unable to conquer [a]the Jebusites living in Jerusalem. The Jebusites live with the people of Judah in Jerusalem to this very day.

Joseph's Tribal Lands

16 The land allotted to Joseph's descendants extended from the Jordan at Jericho to the waters of Jericho to the east, through the [a]desert and on up from Jericho into the hill country of Bethel. [2]The southern border extended from [a]Bethel to Luz, and crossed to Arkite territory at Ataroth. [3]It then descended westward to Japhletite territory, [a]as far as the territory of lower Beth Horon and [b]Gezer, and ended at the sea.

[4a]Joseph's descendants, Manasseh and Ephraim, were assigned their land. [5]The territory of [a]the tribe of Ephraim by its clans included the following: The border of their assigned land to the east was Ataroth [b]Addar [c]as far as upper Beth Horon. [6]It then extended on to the sea, with [a]Micmethath on the north. It turned eastward to Taanath

15:16 [a] Judg 1:12 **15:17** [a] Judg 1:13; 3:9. [b] Num 32:12; Josh 14:6 [c] Judg 1:12 **15:18** [a] Judg 1:14 [b] Gen 24:64; 1 Sam 25:23 **15:19** [a] Gen 33:11 [1] Or *blessing*. **15:21** [a] Gen 35:21 **15:24** [a] 1 Sam 23:14 **15:28** [a] Gen 21:31; Josh 19:2 **15:30** [a] Josh 19:4 **15:31** [a] Josh 19:5; 1 Sam 27:6; 30:1 **15:32** [a] Judg 20:45, 47 **15:33** [a] Judg 13:25; 16:31 **15:35** [a] 1 Sam 22:1 **15:38** [a] 2 Kgs 14:7 **15:39** [a] 2 Kgs 14:19 [b] Josh 10:3 **15:42** [a] Josh 21:13 **15:46** [a] Josh 11:22 **15:47** [a] Josh 15:4 [b] Num 34:6 [1] Or the *Wadi of Egypt*; trad. the *Brook of Egypt*. **15:51** [a] Josh 10:41; 11:16 **15:52** [1] Some MSS, LXX *Rumah*. **15:54** [a] Josh 14:15 **15:55** [a] 1 Sam 23:24–25 **15:60** [a] Josh 18:14; 1 Sam 7:1–2 **15:62** [a] 1 Sam 23:29; Ezek 47:10 **15:63** [a] Judg 1:8, 21; 2 Sam 5:6; 1 Chr 11:4 **16:1** [a] Josh 8:15; 18:12 **16:2** [a] Josh 18:13; Judg 1:26 **16:3** [a] Josh 18:13; 1 Kgs 9:17; 2 Chr 8:5 [b] Josh 21:21; 1 Kgs 9:15; 1 Chr 7:28 **16:4** [a] Josh 17:14 **16:5** [a] Judg 1:29; 1 Chr 7:28–29 [b] Josh 18:13 [c] 2 Chr 8:5 **16:6** [a] Josh 17:7

Shiloh and crossed it on the east to Janoah. [7] It then descended from Janoah to Ataroth and Naarah, touched Jericho, and extended to the Jordan River. [8] From [a] Tappuah it went westward to the [b] Valley of Kanah and ended at the sea. This is the land assigned to the tribe of Ephraim by its clans. [9] Also included were [a] the cities set apart for the tribe of Ephraim within Manasseh's territory, along with their towns.

[10] The Ephraimites did not conquer the Canaanites living in Gezer. The Canaanites live among the Ephraimites to this very day [a] and do hard labor as their servants.

17 The tribe of Manasseh, Joseph's [a] firstborn son, was also allotted land. The descendants of [b] Makir, Manasseh's firstborn and the father of [c] Gilead, received land, for they were warriors. They were assigned Gilead and Bashan. [2] The rest of Manasseh's descendants were also assigned land by [a] their clans, including [b] the descendants of Abiezer, Helek, Asriel, Shechem, Hepher, and Shemida. [c] These are the male descendants of Manasseh son of Joseph by their clans.

[3] Now [a] Zelophehad son of Hepher, son of Gilead, son of Makir, son of Manasseh, had no sons, only daughters. These are the names of his daughters: Mahlah, Noah, Hoglah, Milcah, and Tirzah. [4] They went before [a] Eleazar [b] the priest, Joshua son of Nun, and the leaders and said, "The LORD told Moses to assign us land among our relatives." So Joshua assigned them land among their uncles, as the LORD had commanded. [5a] Manasseh was allotted 10 shares of land, in addition to the land of Gilead and Bashan east of the Jordan, [6] for the daughters of Manasseh were assigned land among his sons. The land of Gilead belonged to the rest of the descendants of Manasseh.

[7] The border of Manasseh went from Asher to [a] Micmethath, which is near Shechem. It then went south toward those who live by En Tappuah.[1] [8] (The land of [a] Tappuah belonged to Manasseh, but Tappuah, located on the border of Manasseh, belonged to the tribe of Ephraim.) [9] The border then descended southward to [a] the Valley of Kanah. Ephraim was assigned cities there among the cities of Manasseh, but the border of Manasseh was north of the valley and ended at the sea. [10] Ephraim's territory was to the south, and Manasseh's to the north. The sea was Manasseh's western border, and their territory touched Asher on the north and Issachar on the east. [11] Within Issachar's and Asher's territories [a] Manasseh was assigned Beth [b] Shean, Ibleam, the residents of Dor, the residents of Endor, the residents of Taanach, the residents of Megiddo, the three of Napheth,[1] and the towns surrounding all these cities. [12] But [a] the men of Manasseh were unable to conquer these cities; the Canaanites managed to remain in those areas. [13] Whenever the Israelites were strong militarily, they [a] forced the Canaanites to do hard labor, but they never totally conquered them.

[14a] The descendants of Joseph said to Joshua, "Why have you assigned us only one tribal [b] allotment? [c] After all, we have many people, for until now the LORD has enabled us to increase in number." [15] Joshua replied to them, "Since you have so many people, go up into the forest and clear out a place to live in the land of the Perizzites and Rephaites, if the hill country of Ephraim is too small for you." [16] The descendants of Joseph said, "The whole hill country is inadequate for us, and the Canaanites living down in the valley in Beth Shean and its surrounding towns and in the Valley of Jezreel have [a] chariots with iron-rimmed wheels." [17] Joshua said to the family of Joseph—to both Ephraim and Manasseh: "You have many people and great military strength. You will not have just one tribal allotment. [18] The whole hill country will be yours; [a] though it is a forest, you can clear it, and it will be entirely yours. You can conquer the Canaanites, though they have chariots with iron-rimmed wheels and are strong."

The Tribes Meet at Shiloh

18 The entire Israelite community assembled [a] at Shiloh and there they [b] set up the tent of meeting. Though they had subdued the land,[1] [2] seven Israelite

16:8 [a] Josh 17:8   [b] Josh 17:9   16:9 [a] Josh 17:9   16:10 [a] Josh 15:63; 17:12–13; Judg 1:29; 1 Kgs 9:16   17:1 [a] Gen 41:51; 46:20; 48:18   [b] Gen 50:23; Judg 5:14   [c] Deut 3:15   17:2 [a] Num 26:29–33   [b] Num 26:31   [c] Num 26:32   17:3 [a] Num 26:33; 27:1; 36:2   17:4 [a] Josh 14:1   [b] Num 27:2–11   17:5 [a] Josh 22:7   17:7 [a] Josh 16:6   [1] Or *the spring of Tappuah*.   17:8 [a] Josh 16:8   17:9 [a] Josh 16:9   17:11 [a] 1 Chr 7:29   [b] Judg 1:27; 1 Sam 31:10; 1 Kgs 4:12   [1] Or *the third [is] Napheth*; or *Napheth-dor*.   17:12 [a] Judg 1:19, 27, 28   17:13 [a] Josh 16:10   17:14 [a] Josh 16:4   [b] Gen 48:22   [c] Gen 48:19; Num 26:34, 37   17:16 [a] Josh 17:18; Judg 1:19; 4:3   17:18 [a] Deut 20:1   18:1 [a] Josh 19:51; 21:2; 22:9; Jer 7:12   [b] Judg 18:31; 1 Sam 1:3, 24; 4:3–4   [1] Heb. *and the land was subdued before them.*

tribes had not been assigned their allotted land. [3]So Joshua said to the Israelites: "[a]How long do you intend to put off occupying the land the LORD God of your ancestors has given you? [4]Pick three men from each tribe. I will send them out to walk through the land and make a map of it for me. [5]Divide it into seven regions. [a]Judah will stay in its territory in the south and the [b]family of Joseph in its territory in the north. [6]But as for you, map out the land into seven regions and bring it to me. I will draw lots for you here before the LORD our God. [7][a]But the Levites will not have [b]an allotted portion among you, for their inheritance is to serve the LORD.[1] Gad, Reuben, and the half-tribe of Manasseh have already received their allotted land east of the Jordan, which Moses the LORD's servant assigned them."

[8]When the men started out, Joshua told those going to map out the land, "Go, walk [a]through the land, map it out, and return to me. Then I will draw lots for you before the LORD here in Shiloh." [9]The men journeyed through the land and mapped it and its cities out into seven regions on a scroll. Then they came to Joshua at the camp in Shiloh. [10]Joshua drew [a]lots for them in Shiloh before the LORD and [b]divided the land among the Israelites according to their allotted portions.

Benjamin's Tribal Lands

[11][a]The first lot belonged to the tribe of Benjamin by its clans. Their allotted territory was between Judah and Joseph. [12]Their northern border started at [a]the Jordan, went up to the slope of Jericho on the north, ascended westward to the hill country, and extended to the wilderness of Beth Aven. [13]It then crossed from there to Luz, to the slope [a]of Luz to the south (that is, Bethel), and descended to Ataroth Addar located on the hill that is south of lower Beth Horon. [14]It then turned on the west side southward from the hill near Beth Horon on the south and extended to Kiriath [a]Baal (that is, Kiriath Jearim), a city belonging to the tribe of Judah. This is the western border. [15]The [a]southern side started on the edge of Kiriath Jearim and extended westward to the spring of the waters of Nephtoah. [16]The border [a]then descended to the edge of the hill country near the Valley of Ben Hinnom located in the Valley of the Rephaites to the north. It descended through the Valley of Hinnom to the slope of the Jebusites to the south and then down to En [b]Rogel. [17]It went northward, extending to En Shemesh and Geliloth opposite [a]the Pass of Adummim, and descended to the Stone of Bohan son of Reuben. [18]It crossed to the slope in front of the rift valley to the north and descended into the rift valley. [19]It then crossed to the slope of Beth Hoglah to the north and ended at the northern tip of the [a]Salt Sea at the mouth of the Jordan River. This was the southern border. [20]The Jordan River bordered it on the east. These were the borders of the land assigned to the tribe of Benjamin by its clans.

[21]These cities belonged to the tribe of Benjamin by its clans: Jericho, Beth Hoglah, Emek Keziz, [22]Beth Arabah, Zemaraim, Bethel, [23]Avvim, Parah, Ophrah, [24]Kephar Ammoni, Ophni, and Geba—a total of 12 cities and their towns.

[25][a]Gibeon, [b]Ramah, Beeroth, [26]Mizpah, Kephirah, Mozah, [27]Rekem, Irpeel, Taralah, [28]Zelah, Haeleph, the [a]Jebusite city (that is, Jerusalem), Gibeah, and Kiriath—a total of 14 cities and their towns. This was the land assigned to the tribe of Benjamin by its clans.

Simeon's Tribal Lands

19 The [a]second lot belonged to the tribe of Simeon by its clans.[1] Their assigned [b]land was in the middle of Judah's assigned land. [2][a]Their assigned land included Beer Sheba,[1] Moladah, [3]Hazar Shual, Balah, Ezem, [4]Eltolad, Bethul, Hormah, [5]Ziklag, Beth Marcaboth, Hazar Susah, [6]Beth Lebaoth, and Sharuhen—a total of 13 cities and their towns, [7]Ain, Rimmon, Ether, and Ashan—a total of four cities and their towns, [8]as well as all the towns around these cities as far as Baalath Beer ([a]Ramah of the Negev). This was the land assigned to the tribe of Simeon by its clans. [9]Simeon's assigned land was taken from Judah's allotted portion, [a]for Judah's territory was too large for them; so Simeon was assigned land within Judah.

18:3 [a]Judg 18:9   **18:5** [a]Josh 15:1   [b]Josh 16:1–17:18   **18:7** [a]Num 18:7, 20; Josh 13:33   [b]Josh 13:8   [1]Or *the priesthood of the* LORD.   **18:8** [a]Gen 13:17   **18:10** [a]Acts 13:19   [b]Num 34:16–29; Josh 19:51   **18:11** [a]Judg 1:21   **18:12** [a]Josh 16:1   **18:13** [a]Josh 16:3   **18:14** [a]Josh 15:9   **18:15** [a]Josh 15:9   **18:16** [a]Josh 15:8   [b]Josh 15:7   **18:17** [a]Josh 15:6   **18:19** [a]Josh 15:2, 5   **18:25** [a]Josh 11:19; 21:17; 1 Kgs 3:4–5   [b]Jer 31:15   **18:28** [a]Josh 15:8, 63   **19:1** [a]Judg 1:3   [b]Josh 19:9   [1]Heb. *to Simeon, to the tribe of Simeon.*   **19:2** [a]1 Chr 4:28   [1]MT adds *and Sheba*; LXX *Shema.*   **19:8** [a]1 Sam 30:27   **19:9** [a]Josh 19:1

Zebulun's Tribal Lands

[10] The third lot belonged to the tribe of Zebulun by its clans. The border of their territory[1] extended to Sarid. [11] Their border went up westward to Maralah and touched Dabbesheth and [a] the valley [b] near Jokneam. [12] From Sarid it turned eastward to the territory of Kisloth Tabor, extended to [a] Daberath, and went up to Japhia. [13] From there it crossed eastward to [a] Gath Hepher and Eth Kazin, and extended to Rimmon, turning toward Neah. [14] It then turned on the north to Hannathon and ended at the Valley of Iphtah El. [15] Their territory included Kattah, Nahalal, Shimron, Idalah, and Bethlehem; in all they had 12 cities and their towns. [16] This was the land assigned to the tribe of Zebulun by its clans, including these cities and their towns.

Issachar's Tribal Lands

[17] The fourth lot belonged to the tribe of Issachar by its clans. [18] Their assigned land included Jezreel, Kesulloth, Shunem, [19] Hapharaim, Shion, Anaharath, [20] Rabbith, Kishion, Ebez, [21] Remeth, En Gannim, En Haddah and Beth Pazzez. [22] Their border touched Tabor, Shahazumah, and Beth [a] Shemesh, and ended at the Jordan. They had 16 cities and their towns. [23] This was the land assigned to the tribe of Issachar by its clans, including these cities and their towns.

Asher's Tribal Lands

[24] The fifth lot belonged to [a] the tribe of Asher by its clans. [25] Their territory included Helkath, Hali, Beten, Acshaph, [26] Alammelech, Amad, and Mishal. Their border touched Carmel to the west and Shihor Libnath. [27] It turned eastward toward Beth Dagon, touched Zebulun and the Valley of Iphtah El to the north, as well as Beth Emek and Neiel, and extended to [a] Cabul on the north [28] and on to Ebron,[1] Rehob, Hammon, and Kanah, [a] as far as Greater Sidon. [29] It then turned toward Ramah as far as the fortified city of Tyre, turned to Hosah, and ended at the sea near Hebel, [a] Achzib, [30] Umah, Aphek, and Rehob. In all they had 22 cities and their towns. [31] This was the land assigned to the tribe of Asher by its clans, including these cities and their towns.

Naphtali's Tribal Lands

[32] The sixth lot belonged to [a] the tribe of Naphtali by its clans. [33] Their border started at Heleph and the oak of Zaanannim, went to Adami Nekeb, Jabneel and on to Lakkum, and ended at the Jordan River. [34] It turned westward to Aznoth Tabor, extended [a] from there to Hukok, touched Zebulun on the south, Asher on the west, and the Jordan[1] on the east. [35] The fortified cities included Ziddim, Zer, Hammath, Rakkath, Kinnereth, [36] Adamah, Ramah, Hazor, [37] [a] Kedesh, Edrei, En Hazor, [38] Yiron, Migdal El, Horem, Beth Anath, and Beth Shemesh. In all they had 19 cities and their towns. [39] This was the land assigned to the tribe of Naphtali by its clans, including these cities and their towns.

Dan's Tribal Lands

[40] The seventh lot belonged to [a] the tribe of Dan by its clans. [41] Their assigned land included Zorah, [a] Eshtaol, Ir Shemesh, [42] [a] Shaalabbin, [b] Aijalon, Ithlah, [43] Elon, Timnah, [a] Ekron, [44] Eltekeh, Gibbethon, Baalath, [45] Jehud, Bene Berak, Gath Rimmon, [46] the waters of Jarkon, and Rakkon, including the territory in front of Joppa. [47] (The Danites failed to conquer their [a] territory,[1] so they went up and fought with Leshem and captured it. They put the sword to it, took possession of it, and lived in it. They renamed it [b] Dan after their ancestor.) [48] This was the land assigned to the tribe of Dan by its clans, including these cities and their towns.

Joshua Receives Land

[49] When they finished dividing the land into its regions, the Israelites gave Joshua son of Nun some land.[1] [50] As the LORD had instructed, they gave him the city he requested—Timnath [a] Serah in the Ephraimite hill country. He built up the city and lived in it.

[51] These are [a] the land assignments that Eleazar the priest, Joshua son of Nun, and

19:10 [1] Or *inheritance*.   19:11 [a] Gen 49:13   [b] Josh 12:22   19:12 [a] 1 Chr 6:72   19:13 [a] 2 Kgs 14:25   19:22 [a] Josh 15:10; Judg 1:33   19:24 [a] Judg 1:31–32   19:27 [a] 1 Kgs 9:13   19:28 [a] Gen 10:19; Josh 11:8; Judg 1:31; Acts 27:3   [1] Some MSS *Abdon*.   19:29 [a] Judg 1:31   19:32 [a] Josh 19:32–39; Judg 1:33   19:34 [a] Deut 33:23   [1] MT *Judah, the Jordan*.   19:37 [a] Josh 20:7   19:40 [a] Josh 19:40–48; Judg 1:34–36   19:41 [a] Josh 15:33   19:42 [a] Judg 1:35; 1 Kgs 4:9   [b] Josh 10:12; 21:24   19:43 [a] Josh 15:11; Judg 1:18   19:47 [a] Judg 18   [b] Judg 18:29   [1] Heb. *the territory of the sons of Dan went out from them*.   19:49 [1] Heb. *an inheritance in their midst*.   19:50 [a] 1 Chr 7:24   19:51 [a] Num 34:17; Josh 14:1

the Israelite tribal leaders made by [b]drawing lots in Shiloh before the LORD at the entrance of the tent of meeting. So they finished dividing up the land.

Israel Designates Cities of Refuge

20 The LORD instructed Joshua: [2]"Have the Israelites [a]select[1] the cities of refuge that I told you about through Moses. [3]Anyone who accidentally kills someone can escape there; these cities will be a place of asylum from the avenger of blood. [4]The one who committed manslaughter should escape to one of these cities, stand at the entrance of the city gate, and present his case to the leaders of that city. They should then bring him into the city, give him a place to stay, and let him live there. [5]When [a]the avenger of blood comes after him, they must not hand over to him the one who committed manslaughter, for he accidentally killed his fellow man without premeditation.[1] [6]He must remain in that city [a]until his case is decided by the assembly, and the high priest dies. Then the one who committed manslaughter may return home to the city from which he escaped."

[7]So they selected [a]Kedesh in Galilee in the hill country of Naphtali, [b]Shechem in the hill country of Ephraim, and Kiriath [c]Arba (that is, Hebron) in [d]the hill country of Judah. [8]Beyond the Jordan east of Jericho they selected [a]Bezer in the wilderness on the plain belonging to the tribe of Reuben, [b]Ramoth in Gilead belonging to the tribe of Gad, and [c]Golan in Bashan belonging to the tribe of Manasseh. [9]These were [a]the cities of refuge appointed for all the Israelites and for resident foreigners living among them. Anyone who accidentally killed someone could escape there and not be executed by the avenger of blood, at least [b]until his case was reviewed by the assembly.

Levitical Cities

21 The tribal leaders of the [a]Levites went before [b]Eleazar the priest and Joshua son of Nun and the Israelite tribal leaders [2]in [a]Shiloh in [b]the land of Canaan and said, "The LORD told Moses to assign us cities in which to live along with the grazing areas for our cattle." [3]So the Israelites assigned these cities and their grazing areas to the Levites from their own holdings, as the LORD had instructed.

[4]The first lot belonged to [a]the Kohathite clans. The Levites who were descendants of Aaron the priest were allotted 13 cities from the tribes of Judah, Simeon, and Benjamin. [5]The rest of Kohath's descendants were allotted 10 cities from [a]the clans of the tribe of Ephraim, and from the tribe of Dan and the half-tribe of Manasseh. [6]Gershon's descendants were allotted 13 cities from [a]the clans of the tribe of Issachar, and from the tribes of Asher and Naphtali and the half-tribe of Manasseh in Bashan. [7]Merari's descendants by [a]their clans were allotted 12 cities from the tribes of Reuben, Gad, and Zebulun. [8]So the Israelites assigned to the Levites by lot these cities [a]and their grazing [b]areas, as the LORD had instructed Moses.

[9]They assigned from the tribes of Judah and Simeon the cities listed below. [10](They were assigned to the Kohathite clans of the Levites who were descendants of Aaron, for the first lot fell to them.) [11a]They assigned them Kiriath Arba (Arba was the father of [b]Anak), that is, Hebron, in the hill country of Judah, along with its surrounding grazing areas. [12](Now [a]the city's fields and surrounding towns they had assigned to Caleb son of Jephunneh as his property.) [13]So [a]to the descendants of Aaron the priest they assigned [b]Hebron (a city of refuge for one who committed manslaughter), [c]Libnah, [14a]Jattir, [b]Eshtemoa, [15a]Holon, [b]Debir, [16a]Ain, [b]Juttah, and Beth [c]Shemesh, along with the grazing areas of each—a total of nine cities taken from these two tribes. [17]From the tribe of Benjamin they assigned [a]Gibeon, [b]Geba, [18]Anathoth, and [a]Almon, along with the grazing areas of each—a total of four cities. [19]The priests descended from Aaron received 13 cities and their grazing areas.

[20a]The rest of the Kohathite clans of the

19:51 [b]Josh 18:1, 10 **20:2** [a]Exod 21:13; Num 35:6–34; Deut 19:2, 9 [1]Heb. *Say to the sons of Israel, 'Set aside for yourselves.'* **20:5** [a]Num 35:12 [1]Heb. *for without knowledge he killed his neighbor, and he was not hating him prior to that.* **20:6** [a]Num 35:12, 24, 25 **20:7** [a]Josh 21:32; 1 Chr 6:76 [b]Josh 21:21; 2 Chr 10:1 [c]Josh 14:15; 21:11, 13 [d]Luke 1:39 **20:8** [a]Deut 4:43; Josh 21:36; 1 Chr 6:78 [b]Josh 21:38; 1 Kgs 22:3 [c]Josh 21:27 **20:9** [a]Num 35:15 [b]Josh 20:6 **21:1** [a]Num 35:1–8 [b]Num 34:16–29; Josh 14:1; 17:4 **21:2** [a]Josh 18:1 [b]Num 35:2 **21:4** [a]Josh 21:8, 19 **21:5** [a]Josh 21:20 **21:6** [a]Josh 21:27 **21:7** [a]Josh 21:34 **21:8** [a]Josh 21:3 [b]Num 35:2 **21:11** [a]Josh 20:7; 1 Chr 6:55 [b]Josh 14:15; 15:13–14 **21:12** [a]Josh 14:14; 1 Chr 6:56 **21:13** [a]1 Chr 6:57 [b]Josh 15:54; 20:2, 7 [c]Josh 15:42; 2 Kgs 8:22 **21:14** [a]Josh 15:48 [b]Josh 15:50 **21:15** [a]1 Chr 6:58 [b]Josh 15:49 **21:16** [a]1 Chr 6:59 [b]Josh 15:55 [c]Josh 15:10 **21:17** [a]Josh 18:25 [b]Josh 18:24 **21:18** [a]1 Chr 6:60 **21:20** [a]1 Chr 6:66

Levites were allotted cities from the tribe of Ephraim. [21]They assigned them [a]Shechem (a city of refuge for one who committed manslaughter) in the hill country of Ephraim, [b]Gezer, [22]Kibzaim, and Beth Horon, along with the grazing areas of each—a total of four cities. [23]From the tribe of Dan they assigned Eltekeh, Gibbethon, [24a]Aijalon, and Gath Rimmon, along with the grazing areas of each—a total of four cities. [25]From the half-tribe of Manasseh they assigned Taanach and Gath Rimmon, along with the grazing areas of each—a total of two cities. [26]The rest of the Kohathite clans received 10 cities and their grazing areas.

[27]They assigned to the Gershonite clans of the Levites the following cities: from the half-tribe of Manasseh: Golan in Bashan ([a]a city of refuge for one who committed manslaughter) and Beeshtarah, along with the grazing areas of each—[b]a total of two cities; [28]from the tribe of Issachar: Kishon, Daberath, [29]Jarmuth, and En Gannim, along with the grazing areas of each—a total of four cities; [30]from the tribe of Asher: Mishal, Abdon, [31]Helkath, and Rehob, along with the grazing areas of each—a total of four cities; [32]from the tribe of Naphtali: [a]Kedesh in Galilee (a city of refuge for one who committed manslaughter), Hammoth Dor, and Kartan, along with the grazing areas of each—a total of three cities. [33]The Gershonite clans received 13 cities and their grazing areas.

[34a]They assigned to the Merarite clans (the remaining Levites) the following cities: from the tribe of Zebulun: Jokneam, Kartah, [35]Dimnah, and Nahalal, along with the grazing areas of each—a total of four cities; [36][1]from the tribe of Reuben: [a]Bezer, Jahaz, [37]Kedemoth, and Mephaath, along with the grazing areas of each—a total of four cities; [38]from the tribe of Gad: [a]Ramoth in Gilead (a city of refuge for one who committed manslaughter), Mahanaim, [39]Heshbon, and Jazer, along with the grazing areas of each—a total of four cities. [40]The Merarite clans (the remaining Levites) were allotted 12 cities.

[41]The Levites received within the land owned by the Israelites[1] 48 cities in [a]all and their grazing areas. [42]Each of these cities had grazing areas around it; they were alike in this regard.

[43]So the LORD gave Israel [a]all the land he had solemnly promised [b]to their ancestors, and they conquered it and lived in it. [44a]The LORD [b]made them secure,[1] in fulfillment of all he had solemnly promised their ancestors. None of their enemies could resist them. The LORD handed all their enemies over to them. [45a]Not one of the LORD's faithful promises to the family of Israel[1] was left unfulfilled; every one was realized.

Joshua Sends Home the Eastern Tribes

22 Then Joshua summoned the Reubenites, the Gadites, and the half-tribe of Manasseh [2]and told them: "You have carried out [a]all the instructions of Moses the LORD's servant, [b]and you have obeyed all I have told you. [3]You have not abandoned your fellow Israelites this entire time, right up to this very day. You have completed the task given you by the LORD your God.[1] [4]Now the LORD your God has [a]made your fellow Israelites secure,[1] just as he promised them. So now you may turn around and go to your homes in your own land that Moses the LORD's servant assigned to you east of the Jordan. [5]But carefully obey the commands and instructions Moses the LORD's servant gave you. Love[1] the LORD your God, follow all his instructions, obey his commands, be loyal [a]to him,[2] and serve him with all your heart and being!"

[6]Joshua [a]rewarded them and sent them on their way; they returned to their homes. [7](Now to one half-tribe of Manasseh, Moses had assigned land in Bashan; and to the other half Joshua had assigned land on the west side of the Jordan with their fellow Israelites.) When Joshua sent them home, he rewarded them, [8]saying, "Take home great wealth, a lot of cattle, silver, gold, bronze, iron, and a lot of clothing. Divide

21:21 [a]Josh 20:7 [b]Judg 1:29 **21:24** [a]Josh 10:12 **21:27** [a]Josh 21:6; 1 Chr 6:71 [b]Josh 20:8 **21:32** [a]Josh 20:7 **21:34** [a]Josh 21:7; 1 Chr 6:77–81 **21:36** [a]Deut 4:43; Josh 20:8 [1]Some sig. MSS omit vv. 36–37. **21:38** [a]Josh 20:8 **21:41** [a]Num 35:7 [1]Heb. *in the midst of the possession of the sons of Israel.* **21:43** [a]Gen 12:7; 26:3–4; 28:4, 13, 14 [b]Num 33:53; Josh 1:11 **21:44** [a]Deut 7:23–24; Josh 11:23; 22:4 [b]Josh 1:13, 15; 11:23 [1]Heb. *gave them rest all around.* **21:45** [a][Num 23:19]; Josh 23:14; 1 Kgs 8:56 [1]Heb. *the house of Israel.* **22:2** [a]Num 32:20–22; Deut 3:18 [b]Josh 1:12–18 **22:3** [1]Heb. *you have kept the charge of the command of the LORD your God.* **22:4** [a]Josh 21:44 [1]Heb. *has given rest to your brothers.* **22:5** [a]Deut 10:12; 11:13, 22 [1]Heb. *But be very careful to do the commandment and the law which Moses, the LORD's servant, commanded you, to love.* [2]Heb. *hug him.* **22:6** [a]Gen 47:7; Exod 39:43; Josh 14:13; 2 Sam 6:18; Luke 24:50 **22:8** [a]Num 31:27; 1 Sam 30:24

[a]up the goods captured from your enemies with your brothers." [9]So [a]the Reubenites, the Gadites, and the half-tribe of Manasseh left the Israelites in Shiloh in the land of Canaan and headed home to their own land in Gilead, which they acquired by the LORD's command through Moses.

Civil War Is Averted

[10]The Reubenites, the Gadites, and the half-tribe of Manasseh came to Geliloth near the Jordan in the land of Canaan and built there, near the Jordan, an impressive altar. [11]The Israelites [a]received this report: "Look, the Reubenites, the Gadites, and the half-tribe of Manasseh have built an altar at the entrance to the land of Canaan, at Geliloth near the Jordan on the Israelite side." [12]When [a]the Israelites heard this, the entire Israelite community assembled at Shiloh to launch an attack against them.

[13]The Israelites [a]sent [b]Phinehas son of Eleazar, the priest, to the land of Gilead to the Reubenites, the Gadites, and the half-tribe of Manasseh. [14]He was accompanied by 10 leaders, one from [a]each of the Israelite tribes, each one a family leader among the Israelite clans. [15]They went to the land of Gilead to the Reubenites, the Gadites, and the half-tribe of Manasseh, and said to them: [16]"The entire community of the LORD says, 'Why have you disobeyed the God of Israel by turning back today from following the LORD? You built an altar for yourselves and have rebelled today against the LORD. [17]The sin we committed at Peor was bad enough. To this very day we have not purified ourselves; it even brought a plague on the community [a]of the LORD. [18]Now today you dare to turn back from following [a]the LORD! You are rebelling today against the LORD; tomorrow he may break out in anger against the entire community of Israel. [19]But if your own land is impure, cross over to the LORD's own land, [a]where the LORD himself lives,[1] and settle down among us. But don't rebel against the LORD or us[2] by building for yourselves an altar other than the altar of the LORD our God. [20a]When Achan son of Zerah disobeyed the command about the city's riches, the entire Israelite community was judged, though only one man had sinned. He most certainly died for his sin!'"[1]

[21]The Reubenites, the Gadites, and the half-tribe of Manasseh answered the leaders of the Israelite clans: [22]"El, God, the LORD! [a]El, God, the LORD! He [b]knows the truth! Israel must also know! If we have rebelled or disobeyed the LORD, don't spare us today! [23]If we have built an altar for ourselves to turn back from following the LORD by making burnt sacrifices and grain offerings on it, or by offering tokens of peace on it, the LORD himself will [a]punish us. [24]We swear we have done this because we were worried that in the future your descendants would say to our descendants, 'What relationship do you have with the LORD God of Israel? [25]The LORD made the Jordan a boundary between us and you Reubenites and Gadites. You have no right to worship the LORD.'[1] In this way your descendants might cause our descendants to stop obeying the LORD. [26]So we decided to build this altar, not for burnt offerings and sacrifices, [27]but [a]as a reminder to us and you and our descendants who follow us, that we will [b]honor the LORD in his very presence with burnt offerings, sacrifices, and tokens of peace. Then in the future your descendants will not be able to say to our descendants, 'You have no right to worship the LORD.' [28]We said, 'If in the future they say such a thing to us or to our descendants, we will reply, "See the model of the LORD's altar that our ancestors made, not for burnt offerings or sacrifices, but as a reminder to us and you."' [29]Far be it from us [a]to rebel against the LORD by turning back today from following after the LORD by building an altar for burnt offerings, sacrifices, and tokens of peace aside from the altar of the LORD our God located in front of his dwelling place!"

[30]When Phinehas the priest and the community leaders and Israel's clan leaders who accompanied him heard the defense of the Reubenites, the Gadites, and the Manassehites, they were satisfied. [31]Phinehas son of Eleazar, the priest, said to the Reubenites,

22:9 [a]Num 32:1, 26, 29   22:11 [a]Deut 13:12–18; Judg 20:12–13   22:12 [a]Josh 18:1; Judg 20:1   22:13 [a]Deut 13:14; Judg 20:12   [b]Exod 6:25; Num 25:7, 11–13   22:14 [a]Num 1:4   22:17 [a]Num 25:1–9; Deut 4:3   22:18 [a]Num 16:22   22:19 [a]Josh 18:1   [1]Heb. *where the dwelling place of the LORD resides.*   [2]Heb. *and us to you rebel.*   22:20 [a]Josh 7:1–26   [1]Lit. *and he [was] one man, he did not die for his sin.*   22:22 [a]Deut 4:35; 10:17; Isa 44:8; 45:5; 46:9; [1 Cor 8:5–6]   [b][Job 10:7; 23:10; Jer 12:3; 2 Cor 11:11, 31]   22:23 [a]Deut 18:19; 1 Sam 20:16   22:25 [1]Heb. *You have no portion in the LORD.*   22:27 [a]Gen 31:48; Josh 22:34; 24:27   [b]Deut 12:5, 14   22:29 [a]Deut 12:13–14

the Gadites, and the Manassehites, "Today we know that the LORD is [a]among us because you have not disobeyed the LORD in this. Now you have rescued the Israelites from the LORD's judgment."

[32] Phinehas son of Eleazar, the priest, and the leaders left the Reubenites and Gadites in the land of Gilead and reported back to the Israelites in the land of Canaan. [33] The Israelites were satisfied with their report and gave thanks [a]to God. They said nothing more about launching an attack to destroy the land in which the Reubenites and Gadites lived. [34] The Reubenites and Gadites named the altar, "Surely it is a Reminder to us that the LORD is God."

Joshua Challenges Israel to Be Faithful

23 A long time passed after the LORD made Israel secure from all their enemies, and Joshua [a]was very old. [2] So Joshua [a]summoned all Israel, including the elders, rulers, judges, and leaders, and told them: "I am very old. [3] You saw everything the [a]LORD your God did to all these nations on your behalf, for the [b]LORD your God fights for you. [4] See, [a]I have parceled out to your tribes these remaining nations, from the Jordan to the Mediterranean Sea in the west, including all the nations I defeated. [5] The LORD your God [a]will drive them out from before you and remove them, so you can occupy their land [b]as the LORD your God promised you. [6] Be very strong! Carefully obey[1] all that is written in [a]the law scroll of Moses so you won't swerve from it to the right or the left, [7] or [a]associate with these nations that remain near you. You must not invoke or [b]make solemn [c]declarations by the names of their gods![1] You must not [d]worship or bow down to them! [8] But you must be loyal to[1] the LORD your God, as you have been to this very day.

[9] "The LORD drove out from [a]before you great and mighty nations; no one has been able to resist you to this very day. [10][a]One of you makes [b]a thousand run away, for the LORD your God fights for you, as he promised you he would. [11] Watch yourselves carefully! Love [a]the LORD your God![1] [12] But if you ever turn away and [a]make alliances with[1] these nations that remain near you, and intermarry with them and establish friendly relations with them, [13] know for certain that [a]the LORD your God will no longer drive out these nations from before you. They will trap and ensnare you; they will be a whip that tears your sides and thorns that blind your eyes until you disappear from this good land the LORD your God gave you.

[14] "Look, today [a]I am about to die. You know with all your heart and being that [b]not even one of all the faithful promises the LORD your God made to you is left unfulfilled; every one was realized—not one promise is unfulfilled! [15] But in [a]the same way that [b]every faithful promise the LORD your God made to you has been realized, it is just as certain that if you disobey, then the LORD will bring on you every judgment until he destroys you from this good land that the LORD your God gave you. [16] If you violate the covenantal laws of the LORD your God which he commanded you to keep, and you follow, worship, and bow down to other gods, then the [a]LORD will be very angry with you and you will disappear quickly from the good land that he gave to you."

Israel Renews Its Commitment to the Lord

24 Joshua assembled all the Israelite tribes at [a]Shechem. He [b]summoned Israel's elders, rulers, judges, and leaders, and they [c]appeared before God. [2] Joshua told all the people, "This is what the LORD God of Israel has said: 'In the distant past [a]your ancestors lived beyond [b]the Euphrates River,[1] including Terah the father of Abraham and Nahor. They worshiped other gods, [3] but I took your father Abraham from beyond [a]the Euphrates and brought him into the entire land of Canaan. I made his descendants numerous; I [b]gave him Isaac, [4] and to

22:31 [a] Exod 25:8; Lev 26:11–12; 2 Chr 15:2; Zech 8:23   22:33 [a] 1 Chr 29:20; Neh 8:6; Dan 2:19; Luke 2:28   23:1 [a] Josh 13:1; 24:29   23:2 [a] Deut 31:28   23:3 [a] Ps 44:3   [b] Exod 14:14; Deut 1:30; Josh 10:14, 42   23:4 [a] Josh 13:2, 6; 18:10   23:5 [a] Exod 23:30; 33:2   [b] Num 33:53   23:6 [a] Josh 1:7   [1] Heb. *Be strong so you can be careful to do.*   23:7 [a] Exod 23:33; Deut 7:2–3; [Prov 4:14; Eph 5:11]   [b] Exod 23:13; Ps 16:4; Jer 5:7; Hos 2:17   [c] Deut 6:13; 10:20   [d] Exod 20:5   [1] Heb. *and in the name of their gods you must not invoke and you must not make solemn declarations.*   23:8 [1] Heb. *hug.*   23:9 [a] Deut 7:24; 11:23; Josh 1:5   23:10 [a] Lev 26:8; Deut 28:7; Isa 30:17   [b] Exod 14:14   23:11 [a] Josh 22:5   [1] Heb. *Watch carefully yourselves so as to love the LORD your God.*   23:12 [a] Deut 7:3–4; Ezra 9:2; Neh 13:25   [1] Heb. *and hug.*   23:13 [a] Judg 2:3   23:14 [a] 1 Kgs 2:2   [b] Josh 21:45; [Luke 21:33]   23:15 [a] Deut 28:63   [b] Lev 26:14–39; Deut 28:15–68   23:16 [a] Deut 4:24–28   24:1 [a] Gen 35:4   [b] Josh 23:2   [c] 1 Sam 10:19   24:2 [a] Gen 11:7–32   [b] Josh 24:14   [1] Heb. *the river.*   24:3 [a] Gen 12:1; Acts 7:2–3   [b] Gen 21:1–8; [Ps 127:3]

Isaac I gave [a]Jacob and [b]Esau. To Esau I assigned Mount Seir, while Jacob and his sons went down to Egypt. [5][a]I sent Moses and Aaron, and [b]I struck Egypt down when I intervened in their land. Then I brought you out. [6]When I [a]brought your fathers out of Egypt, you arrived at the sea. The Egyptians chased your fathers with chariots and horsemen to the Red Sea. [7]Your fathers cried out for help to the LORD; he made the area between you and the Egyptians [a]dark, and then he drowned them in the sea. [b]You witnessed with your very own eyes [c]what I did in Egypt. You lived in the wilderness for a long time. [8]Then I brought you to the [a]land of the Amorites who lived east of the Jordan. They fought with you, but I handed them over to you; you conquered their land, and I destroyed them from before you. [9][a]Balak son of Zippor, king of Moab, launched an attack against Israel. He [b]summoned Balaam son of Beor to call down judgment on[1] you. [10][a]I refused to respond to Balaam; [b]he kept prophesying good things about[1] you, and I rescued you from his power. [11]You crossed the Jordan and came to Jericho. The leaders[1] of Jericho, as well as the Amorites, Perizzites, Canaanites, Hittites, Girgashites, Hivites, and Jebusites, fought against [a]you, but I handed [b]them over to you. [12]I sent terror[1] ahead of you to [a]drive out before you the two Amorite kings. I gave you the victory; it was [b]not by your swords or bows. [13]I gave you a land in which you had not worked hard; you took up residence in [a]cities you did not build, and you are eating the produce of vineyards and olive groves you did not plant.'

[14]"[a]Now obey[1] the LORD and worship him with [b]integrity and loyalty. [c]Put aside the gods your ancestors worshiped beyond the Euphrates and [d]in Egypt, and worship the LORD. [15]If you have no desire to worship the LORD, then [a]choose today whom you will worship, [b]whether it be [c]the gods whom your ancestors worshiped beyond

the Euphrates or the gods of the Amorites in whose land you are living. [d]But I and my family will worship the LORD."

[16]The people responded, "Far be it from us to abandon the LORD so we can worship other gods! [17]For the LORD our God took us and our fathers out of slavery in the land of Egypt and performed these awesome miracles before our very eyes. He continually protected us as we traveled and when we passed through nations. [18]The LORD drove out from before us all the nations, including the Amorites who lived in the land. So [a]we too will worship the LORD, for he is our God!"

[19]Joshua warned the people, "[a]You will not keep worshiping[1] the LORD, for he is a [b]holy God. He is [c]a jealous God who will not forgive your rebellion or your sins. [20][a]If you abandon [b]the LORD and worship foreign gods, he will turn against you; he will bring disaster on you and destroy you, though he once treated you well."

[21]The people said to Joshua, "No! We really will[1] worship the LORD." [22]Joshua said to the people, "Do [a]you agree to be witnesses against yourselves that you have chosen to worship the LORD?"[1] They replied, "We are witnesses!" [23]Joshua said, "Now [a]put aside the foreign gods that are among you and [b]submit to the LORD God of Israel."

[24]The people [a]said to Joshua, "We will worship the LORD our God and obey him."

[25]That day Joshua drew [a]up an agreement for the people, and he established rules and regulations for them [b]in Shechem. [26]Joshua [a]wrote these words in the [b]Law Scroll of God. He then took a large stone and [c]set it up there [d]under the oak tree near the LORD's sanctuary. [27]Joshua [a]said to all the people, "Look, this stone will be a [b]witness against us, for it has heard everything the LORD said to us. It will be a witness against you if[1] you deny your God." [28]When [a]Joshua dismissed the people, they went to their allotted portions of land.

24:4 [a]Gen 25:24-26 [b]Gen 36:8; Deut 2:5   24:5 [a]Exod 3:10 [b]Exod 7-10   24:6 [a]Exod 12:37, 51; 14:2-31   24:7 [a]Exod 14:20 [b]Deut 4:34 [c]Josh 5:6   24:8 [a]Num 21:21-35   24:9 [a]Judg 11:25 [b]Num 22:2-14 [1]Or to curse.   24:10 [a]Deut 23:5 [b]Num 23:11, 20; 24:10 [1]Heb. blessing.   24:11 [a]Josh 3:14, 17 [b]Josh 6:1; 10:1 [1]Or perhaps citizens.   24:12 [a]Exod 23:28; Deut 7:20 [b]Ps 44:3 [1]Trad. the hornet.   24:13 [a]Deut 6:10-11   24:14 [a]Deut 10:12-13; 1 Sam 12:24 [b]2 Cor 1:12 [c]Josh 24:2, 23; Ezek 20:18 [d]Ezek 20:7-8 [1]Heb. fear.   24:15 [a]Ruth 1:15; 1 Kgs 18:21 [b]Josh 24:2; Ezek 20:39 [c]Exod 23:24, 32 [d]Gen 18:19; Ps 101:2; [1 Tim 3:4-5]   24:18 [a]Ps 116:16   24:19 [a]Matt 6:24 [b]Lev 11:44-45; 1 Sam 6:20 [c]Exod 20:5 [1]Heb. you are not able to serve.   24:20 [a]1 Chr 28:9; Ezra 8:22; Isa 1:28; 63:10; 65:11-12; Jer 17:13 [b]Deut 4:24-26; Josh 23:15   24:21 [1]Or No, for we will.   24:22 [a]Ps 119:173 [1]Heb. You are witnesses against yourselves that you have chosen for yourselves the LORD to serve him.   24:23 [a]Gen 35:2; Josh 24:14; Judg 10:15-16; 1 Sam 7:3 [b]1 Kgs 8:57-58; Ps 119:36; 141:4   24:24 [a]Exod 19:8; 24:3, 7; Deut 5:24-27   24:25 [a]Exod 15:25 [b]Josh 24:1   24:26 [a]Deut 31:24 [b]Judg 9:6 [c]Gen 28:18 [d]Gen 35:4   24:27 [a]Gen 31:48 [b]Deut 32:1 [1]Or lest, so that you might not.   24:28 [a]Judg 2:6-7

An Era Ends

[29a]After all this Joshua son of Nun, the LORD's servant, died at the age of 110. [30]They buried him in his allotted territory in Timnath [a]Serah in the hill country of Ephraim, north of Mount Gaash. [31a]Israel worshiped the LORD throughout Joshua's lifetime and as long as the elderly men who outlived him remained alive. These men had experienced [b]firsthand everything the LORD had done for Israel.

[32]The bones of Joseph, which [a]the Israelites had brought up from Egypt, were buried at Shechem in the part of the field that Jacob bought from the sons of Hamor, the father of Shechem, for 100 pieces of money. So it became the inheritance of the tribe of Joseph.

[33a]Eleazar son of Aaron died, and they buried him in Gibeah in the hill country of Ephraim, where his son [b]Phinehas had been assigned land.

24:29 [a] Judg 2:8   24:30 [a] Josh 19:50; Judg 2:9   24:31 [a] Judg 2:7   [b] Deut 11:2   24:32 [a] Gen 50:25; Exod 13:19; Heb 11:22
24:33 [a] Exod 28:1; Num 20:28; Josh 14:1   [b] Exod 6:25

JUDGES

The Book of Judges stands in stark contrast to Joshua. In Joshua an obedient people conquered the land through trust in the power of God. In Judges, however, a disobedient and idolatrous people are defeated time and time again because of their rebellion against God. In seven distinct cycles of sin to salvation, Judges shows how the Israelites have set aside God's law and instead "each man did what he considered to be right" (21:25). The recurring result of abandoning God's law is corruption from within and oppression from without. During the nearly four centuries spanned by this book, God raises up military champions to throw off the yoke of bondage and to restore the nation to pure worship. But all too soon the sin cycle begins again as the nation's spiritual temperature grows steadily colder. The Hebrew title is *Shophetim*, meaning "Judges," "Rulers," "Deliverers," or "Saviors." *Shophet* carries not only the idea of maintaining justice and settling disputes, but it is also used to mean "liberating" and "delivering." First the judges deliver the people; then they rule and administer justice. The Septuagint used the Greek equivalent of this word, *Kritai* ("Judges"). The Latin Vulgate called it *Liber Judicum*, the "Book of Judges." This book could also appropriately be titled the Book of Failure.

Judah Takes the Lead

1 After Joshua [a]died, the Israelites [b]asked the LORD, "Who should lead the invasion against the [c]Canaanites and launch the attack?" [2]The LORD said, "The men of [a]Judah should take the lead. Be sure of this! I am handing the land over to them." [3]The men of Judah said to their relatives, the men of [a]Simeon, "[b]Invade our allotted land with us and help us attack the Canaanites. Then we will go with you into your allotted land." So the men of Simeon went with them.

[4]The men of Judah attacked, and the LORD handed the Canaanites and Perizzites over to them. They killed 10,000 men at [a]Bezek. [5]They met Adoni-Bezek at Bezek and fought him. They defeated the Canaanites and Perizzites. [6]When Adoni-Bezek ran away, they chased him and captured him. Then they cut off his thumbs and big toes. [7]Adoni-Bezek said, "Seventy kings, with thumbs and big toes cut off, used to lick up[1] food scraps under my table. God [a]has repaid me for what I did to them." They brought him to Jerusalem, where he died. [8]The men of Judah attacked Jerusalem and captured it. [a]They put the sword to it and set the city on fire.

[9]Later the men of Judah went down to attack the Canaanites living in the hill country, the Negev, [a]and the foothills. [10]The men of Judah attacked the Canaanites living in [a]Hebron. (Hebron used to be called Kiriath [b]Arba.) They killed Sheshai, Ahiman, and Talmai. [11a]From there they attacked the people of Debir. (Debir used to be called Kiriath Sepher.) [12]Caleb said, "To [a]the man who attacks and captures Kiriath Sepher I will give my daughter Achsah as a wife." [13]When Othniel son of Kenaz, [a]Caleb's younger brother, captured it, Caleb gave him his daughter Achsah as a wife.

[14a]One time Achsah came and charmed her father so she could ask him for some land. When she got down from her donkey, Caleb said to her, "What would you like?"

1:1 [a] Josh 24:29   [b] Num 27:21; Judg 20:18   [c] Josh 17:12–13   1:2 [a] Gen 49:8–9; Rev 5:5   1:3 [a] Josh 19:1   [b] Judg 1:17
1:4 [a] 1 Sam 11:8   1:7 [a] Lev 24:19; 1 Sam 15:33; [Jas 2:13]   [1] Heb. *to gather, to pick up, to glean.*   1:8 [a] Josh 15:63; Judg 1:21   1:9 [a] Josh 10:36; 11:21; 15:13   1:10 [a] Josh 15:13–19   [b] Josh 14:15   1:11 [a] Josh 15:15
1:12 [a] Josh 15:16–17   1:13 [a] Judg 3:9   1:14 [a] Josh 15:18–19

[15] She answered, "Please [a]give me a special present.[1] Since you have given me land in the Negev, now give me springs of water." So Caleb gave her both the upper and lower springs.[2]

[16a] Now the descendants of the Kenite, Moses' father-in-law, went up with the people of Judah [b]from the city of date palm trees to [c]Arad in the wilderness of Judah,[1] located in the Negev. They went [d]and lived with the people of Judah.

[17] The men of Judah went with their brothers the men of Simeon [a]and defeated the Canaanites living in Zephath. They wiped out Zephath. So people now call the city [b]Hormah. [18] The men of Judah captured [a]Gaza, Ashkelon, Ekron, and the territory surrounding each of these cities.

[19] The LORD was with the men of Judah. They conquered the hill country, but they could not conquer the people living in the coastal plain because they had [a]chariots with iron-rimmed wheels. [20a] Caleb received Hebron, just as Moses had promised. He drove out the [b]three Anakites. [21a] The men of Benjamin, however, did not conquer the Jebusites living in Jerusalem. The Jebusites live with the people of Benjamin in Jerusalem to this very day.

Partial Success

[22] When the men of Joseph attacked Bethel, the LORD was with them. [23] When the men of Joseph spied out Bethel (it used to be called [a]Luz), [24] the spies spotted a man leaving the city. They said to him, "If you show us a secret entrance into the city, [a]we will reward you." [25] He showed them a secret entrance into the city, and they put the city to the sword. But they let the man and his extended family leave safely. [26] He moved to Hittite country and built a city. He named it Luz, and it has kept that name to this very day.

[27a] The men of Manasseh did not conquer Beth Shean, [b]Taanach, or their surrounding towns. Nor did they conquer the people living in [c]Dor, Ibleam, Megiddo, or their surrounding towns. The Canaanites managed to remain in those areas. [28] Whenever Israel was strong militarily, they forced the Canaanites to do hard labor, but they never totally conquered them.

[29] The men of Ephraim did [a]not conquer the Canaanites living in Gezer. The Canaanites lived among them in Gezer.

[30] The men of [a]Zebulun did not conquer the people living in Kitron and Nahalol. The Canaanites lived among them and were forced to do hard labor.

[31] The men of Asher did [a]not conquer the people living in Acco or Sidon, nor did they conquer Ahlab, Achzib, Helbah, Aphek, or Rehob. [32] The people of Asher [a]live among the Canaanites residing in the land because they did not conquer them.

[33] The men of Naphtali did [a]not conquer the people living in Beth Shemesh or Beth Anath. They live among the Canaanites residing in the land. The Canaanites living in Beth Shemesh and Beth Anath were forced to do hard labor for them.

[34] The Amorites forced the people of Dan to live in the hill country. They did not allow them to live in the coastal plain. [35] The Amorites managed to [a]remain in Har Heres, Aijalon, and Shaalbim. Whenever the tribe of Joseph was strong militarily, the Amorites were forced to do hard labor. [36] The border of Amorite territory ran [a]from the Scorpion Ascent to Sela and on up.

Confrontation and Repentance at Bokim

2 The angel of the LORD went up from [a]Gilgal to Bokim. He said, "I brought you up from Egypt and [b]led you [c]into the land I had solemnly promised to give to your ancestors. I said, 'I will never break my covenant with you, [2] but [a]you must not make an agreement with the people who live in this land. [b]You should tear down the altars where they worship.' [c]But you have disobeyed me. Why would you do such a thing? [3] At that time [a]I also warned you, 'If you disobey, I will not drive out the Canaanites before you. They will ensnare you and their gods will [b]lure you away.'"

1:15 [a] Gen 33:11 [1] Or *blessing*. [2] Perhaps place names. 1:16 [a] Num 10:29–32; Judg 4:11, 17; 1 Sam 15:6; 1 Chr 2:55 [b] Deut 34:3; Judg 3:13 [c] Josh 12:14 [d] 1 Sam 15:6 [1] Some MSS omit *of Judah*. 1:17 [a] Judg 1:3 [b] Num 21:3; Josh 19:4 1:18 [a] Josh 11:22 1:19 [a] Josh 17:16, 18; Judg 4:3, 13 1:20 [a] Num 14:24; Josh 14:9, 14 [b] Josh 15:14; Judg 1:10 1:21 [a] Josh 15:63; Judg 1:8 1:23 [a] Gen 28:19 1:24 [a] Josh 2:12, 14 1:27 [a] Josh 17:11–13 [b] Josh 21:25 [c] Josh 17:11 1:29 [a] Josh 16:10; 1 Kgs 9:16 1:30 [a] Josh 19:10–16 1:31 [a] Josh 19:24–31 1:32 [a] Ps 106:34–35 1:33 [a] Josh 19:32–39 1:35 [a] Josh 19:42 1:36 [a] Num 34:4; Josh 15:3 2:1 [a] Exod 20:2; Judg 6:8–9 [b] Deut 1:8 [c] Gen 17:7–8; Lev 26:42, 44; Deut 7:9; Ps 89:34 2:2 [a] Exod 23:32; Deut 7:2 [b] Exod 34:12–13; Deut 12:3 [c] Ps 106:34 2:3 [a] Judg 3:6 [b] Exod 23:33; Deut 7:16; Ps 106:36

⁴When the angel of the LORD finished speaking these words to all the Israelites, the people wept loudly. ⁵They named that place Bokim and offered sacrifices to the LORD there.

The End of an Era

⁶When ᵃJoshua dismissed the people, the Israelites went to their allotted portions of territory, intending to take possession of the land. ⁷ᵃThe people worshiped the LORD throughout Joshua's lifetime and as long as the elderly men who outlived him remained alive. These men had witnessed all the great things the LORD had done for Israel. ⁸ᵃJoshua son of Nun, the LORD's servant, died at the age of 110. ⁹The people buried him in his allotted ᵃland in Timnath ᵇHeres in the hill country of Ephraim, north of Mount Gaash. ¹⁰That entire generation passed away; a new generation grew up that had not personally experienced the LORD's presence or seen what he had done for Israel.

A Monotonous Cycle

¹¹The Israelites did ᵃevil before the LORD by worshiping the Baals. ¹²They ᵃabandoned the LORD God of their ancestors who brought them out of the land of Egypt. They followed ᵇother gods—the gods of the nations who lived around them. They ᶜworshiped them and made the LORD angry. ¹³They ᵃabandoned the LORD and worshiped Baal and the Ashtoreths. ¹⁴The LORD was furious with Israel ᵃand ᵇhanded ᶜthem over to robbers who plundered them. He turned them over to their enemies who lived around them. They ᵈcould no longer withstand their enemies' attacks. ¹⁵Whenever they went out to fight, the LORD did them harm, just as he had warned and solemnly ᵃvowed he would do. They suffered greatly.

¹⁶The LORD raised up leaders¹ who delivered ᵃthem from these robbers. ¹⁷But they did not obey their leaders. Instead they prostituted themselves to other gods and worshiped them. They quickly turned aside from the path their ancestors had walked. Their ancestors had obeyed the LORD's commands, but they did not. ¹⁸When ᵃthe LORD raised up leaders ᵇfor them, the LORD was with each leader and delivered the people from their enemies while the leader remained alive. The LORD felt sorry for them when they cried out in agony because of what their harsh oppressors did to them.¹ ¹⁹When a leader died, the next generation would again act more wickedly than the previous one. They would follow after other gods, worshiping them and bowing down to them. They did not give up their practices or their stubborn ways.

A Divine Decision

²⁰The LORD was furious with Israel. He said, "This nation has ᵃviolated the terms of the covenant I made with their ancestors by disobeying me. ²¹So I will no longer remove before them any of the nations that Joshua ᵃleft unconquered when he died, ²²in order to ᵃtest Israel.¹ I want to see whether or not the people will carefully walk in the path marked out by the LORD, as their ancestors were careful to do." ²³This is why the LORD permitted these nations to remain and did not conquer them immediately; he did not hand them over to Joshua.

3 These were ᵃthe nations the LORD permitted to remain so he could use them to test Israel—he wanted to test all those who had not experienced battle against the Canaanites. ²He left those nations simply because he wanted to teach the subsequent generations of Israelites, who had not experienced the earlier battles, how to conduct holy war. ³These were the nations: the ᵃfive lords of the Philistines, all the Canaanites, the Sidonians, and the Hivites living in Mount Lebanon, from Mount Baal Hermon to Lebo Hamath. ⁴They were left to test Israel, so the LORD would know if his people would obey the commands he gave their ancestors through Moses. ⁵ᵃThe Israelites lived among the Canaanites, Hittites, Amorites, Perizzites, Hivites, and Jebusites. ⁶They took ᵃthe Canaanites'

2:6 ᵃJosh 22:6; 24:28–31   2:7 ᵃJosh 24:31   2:8 ᵃJosh 24:29   2:9 ᵃJosh 24:30   ᵇJosh 19:49–50   2:11 ᵃJudg 3:7, 12; 4:1; 6:1   2:12 ᵃDeut 31:16; Judg 8:33; 10:6   ᵇDeut 6:14   ᶜExod 20:5   2:13 ᵃJudg 10:6; Ps 106:36   2:14 ᵃDeut 31:17; Judg 3:8; Ps 106:40–42   ᵇ2 Kgs 17:20   ᶜIsa 50:1   ᵈLev 26:37; Josh 7:12–13   2:15 ᵃLev 26:14–26; Deut 28:15–68   2:16 ᵃJudg 3:9–10, 15; Ps 106:43–45   ¹Trad. judges.   2:18 ᵃJosh 1:5   ᵇGen 6:6   ¹Heb. the ones oppressing them and afflicting them.   2:20 ᵃ[Josh 23:16]   2:21 ᵃJosh 23:4–5, 13   2:22 ᵃDeut 8:2, 16; 13:3   ¹Heb. text of v. 22 simply begins with to test. For a discussion concerning three possible interpretations of this verse, see NET Bible, Full Notes Edition.   3:1 ᵃJudg 1:1; 2:21–22   3:3 ᵃJosh 13:3   3:5 ᵃPs 106:35   3:6 ᵃExod 34:15–16; Deut 7:3–4; Josh 23:12

daughters as wives and gave their daughters to the Canaanites; they worshiped their gods as well.

Othniel: A Model Leader

[7]The Israelites did [a]evil in the LORD's sight. They [b]forgot the LORD their God and worshiped the Baals and the Asherahs. [8]The LORD was furious with Israel and [a]turned them over to King Cushan [b]Rishathaim of Armon Haraim. They were Cushan Rishathaim's subjects for eight years. [9]When the Israelites cried out for [a]help to the LORD, he [b]raised up a deliverer for the Israelites who rescued them. His name was [c]Othniel son of Kenaz, Caleb's younger brother.[1] [10]The LORD's Spirit empowered him and [a]he led Israel. When he went to do battle, the LORD handed over to him King Cushan Rishathaim of Armon, and Othniel overpowered him.[1] [11]The land had rest for 40 years; then Othniel son of Kenaz died.

Deceit, Assassination, and Deliverance

[12][a]The Israelites again did evil in the LORD's sight. The LORD gave King [b]Eglon of Moab control over Israel because they had done evil in the LORD's sight. [13]Eglon formed alliances with the Ammonites and [a]Amalekites. [b]He came and defeated Israel, and they seized the city of date palm trees. [14]The Israelites were subject [a]to King Eglon of Moab for 18 years.

[15]When the Israelites cried out for [a]help to the LORD, he[1] raised up [b]a deliverer for them. His name was Ehud son of Gera the Benjaminite, a left-handed man. The Israelites sent him to King Eglon of Moab with their tribute payment. [16]Ehud made himself a sword—it had two edges and was 18 inches long. He strapped it under his coat on his right thigh. [17]He brought the tribute payment to King Eglon of Moab. (Now Eglon was a very fat man.)

[18]After Ehud brought the tribute payment, he dismissed the people who had carried it. [19]But he went back once he reached the carved images at Gilgal. He said to Eglon, "I have a secret message for you, [a]O king." Eglon said, "Be quiet!" All his attendants left. [20]When Ehud approached him, he was sitting in his well-ventilated upper room all by himself. Ehud said, "I have a message from God for you." When Eglon rose up from his seat, [21]Ehud reached with his left hand, pulled the sword from his right thigh, and drove it into Eglon's belly. [22]The handle went in after the blade, and the fat closed around the blade, for Ehud did not pull the sword out of his belly.[1] [23]As Ehud went out into the vestibule,[1] he closed the doors of the upper room behind him and locked them.

[24]When Ehud had left, Eglon's servants came and saw the locked doors of the upper room. They said, "He must be [a]relieving himself[1] in the well-ventilated inner room." [25]They waited so long they were [a]embarrassed, but he still did not open the doors of the upper room. Finally they took the key and opened the doors. Right before their eyes was their master, sprawled out dead on the floor! [26]Now Ehud had escaped while they were delaying. When he passed the carved images, he escaped to Seirah.

[27]When [a]he reached Seirah, he blew a trumpet in the Ephraimite hill [b]country. The Israelites went down with him from the hill country, with Ehud in the lead. [28]He said to [a]them, "Follow me, for the LORD is about to defeat your enemies, the Moabites!" They followed him, captured the [b]fords of the Jordan River opposite Moab, and did not let anyone cross. [29]That day they killed about 10,000 Moabites—all strong, capable warriors; not one escaped. [30]Israel humiliated Moab that day, and [a]the land had rest for 80 years.

[31]After Ehud came [a]Shamgar son of Anath. He killed 600 Philistines [b]with [c]an oxgoad. So he also delivered [d]Israel.

Deborah Summons Barak

4 [a]The Israelites again did [b]evil in the LORD's sight after Ehud's death. [2]The LORD [a]turned them over to King Jabin of Canaan, who ruled in [b]Hazor. The general of his army was [c]Sisera, who lived in

3:7 [a]Judg 2:11 [b]Deut 32:18   3:8 [a]Deut 32:30; Judg 2:14 [b]Hab 3:7   3:9 [a]Judg 3:15 [b]Judg 2:16 [c]Judg 1:13 [1]Othniel or Kenaz. 3:10 [a]Num 27:18; 1 Sam 11:6; 2 Chr 15:1 [1]Heb. *his hand was strong against Cushan Rishathaim.*   3:12 [a]Judg 2:19 [b]1 Sam 12:9   3:13 [a]Judg 5:14 [b]Deut 34:3; Judg 1:16; 2 Chr 28:15   3:14 [a]Deut 28:48   3:15 [a]Ps 78:34 [b]Judg 20:16 [1]Heb. *the LORD.* 3:19 [a]Josh 4:20   3:22 [1]Heb. *and he went out to the* [?]; LXX omits.   3:23 [1]An uncertain Heb. term.   3:24 [a]1 Sam 24:3 [1]Heb. *covering his feet;* i.e., with his outer garments while he relieves himself.   3:25 [a]2 Kgs 2:17; 8:11   3:27 [a]Judg 6:34; 1 Sam 13:3 [b]Josh 17:15   3:28 [a]Judg 7:9, 15; 1 Sam 17:47 [b]Josh 2:7; Judg 12:5   3:30 [a]Judg 3:11   3:31 [a]Judg 5:6 [b]1 Sam 17:47 [c]Judg 2:16 [d]1 Sam 4:1   4:1 [a]Judg 2:19 [b]Judg 2:11   4:2 [a]Judg 2:14 [b]Josh 11:1, 10 [c]1 Sam 12:9; Ps 83:9

[d]Harosheth Haggoyim.[1] [3]The Israelites cried out for help to the LORD because Sisera had 900 [a]chariots with iron-rimmed [b]wheels, and he cruelly oppressed the Israelites for 20 years.

[4]Now Deborah, a prophetess, wife of Lappidoth, was leading Israel at that time. [5]She would sit under the Date Palm Tree of Deborah between Ramah [a]and Bethel in the Ephraimite hill country. The Israelites would come up to her to have their disputes settled.

[6]She summoned [a]Barak son of Abinoam from [b]Kedesh in Naphtali. She said to him, "Is it not true that the LORD God of Israel is commanding you? Go, march to Mount [c]Tabor! Take with you 10,000 men from Naphtali and Zebulun. [7]I [a]will bring Sisera, the general of Jabin's army, to you at the Kishon [b]River, along with his chariots and huge army. I will hand him over to you." [8]Barak said to her, "If you go with me, I will go. But if you do not go with me, I will not go." [9]She said, "I will indeed go with you. But you will not gain fame on the expedition you are undertaking,[1] for the LORD will [a]turn Sisera over to a woman." Deborah got up and went with Barak to Kedesh. [10]Barak summoned men from [a]Zebulun and Naphtali to Kedesh, and 10,000 men followed him; Deborah went up with him as well. [11]Now Heber [a]the Kenite had moved away from the Kenites, the descendants of [b]Hobab, Moses' father-in-law. He lived near the great tree in Zaanannim near Kedesh.

[12]When Sisera heard that Barak son of Abinoam had gone up to Mount Tabor, [13]he ordered all his chariotry—900 chariots with iron-rimmed wheels—and all the troops he had with him to go from Harosheth Haggoyim to the Kishon River. [14]Deborah said to Barak, "Spring into action, for this is the day the LORD is handing Sisera over to you! [a]Has the LORD not taken the lead?" So Barak went down from Mount Tabor with 10,000 men following him. [15]The LORD routed Sisera, all his chariotry, and all his army with the edge of the sword. Sisera jumped out of his chariot and ran away on foot. [16]Now Barak chased the chariots and the army all the way to Harosheth Haggoyim. Sisera's whole army died by the edge of the sword; not even one [a]survived!

[17]Now Sisera ran away on foot to the tent of [a]Jael, wife of Heber the Kenite, for King Jabin of Hazor and the family of Heber the Kenite had made a peace treaty. [18]Jael came out to welcome Sisera. She said to him, "Stop and rest, my lord. Stop and rest with me. Don't be afraid." So Sisera stopped to rest in her tent, and she put a blanket over him. [19]He [a]said to her, "Give me a little water to drink because I'm thirsty." She opened a goatskin container of milk and gave him some milk to drink. Then she covered him up again. [20]He said to her, "Stand watch at the entrance to the tent. If anyone comes along and asks you, 'Is there a man here?' say, 'No.'" [21]Then Jael wife of Heber [a]took a tent peg in one hand and a hammer in the other. She crept up on him, drove the tent peg through his temple into the ground while he was asleep from exhaustion,[1] and he died. [22]Now Barak was chasing Sisera. Jael went out to welcome him. She said to him, "Come here and I will show you the man you are searching for." He went with her into the tent, and there he saw Sisera sprawled out dead with the tent peg through his temple.

[23]That day God humiliated King Jabin of Canaan before the Israelites. [24]Israel's power continued to overwhelm King Jabin of Canaan until they did away with him.

Celebrating the Victory in Song

5 On that day Deborah and Barak son of Abinoam [a]sang this victory song:

[2] "When the [a]leaders took the lead in Israel,
　　[b]When the people answered the call
　　　　to war—
　　Praise the LORD!
[3] [a]Hear, O [b]kings!
　　Pay attention, O rulers!
　　I will sing to the LORD!
　　I will sing to the LORD God of Israel!

[4] "O LORD, [a]when you departed from
　　Seir,

when you marched from Edom's
  plains,
  [b]the earth shook, the heavens poured
  down,
  the clouds poured down rain.
5 The mountains trembled before [a]the
  LORD, the God of Sinai;[1]
  before the LORD God of Israel.

6 "In the days of [a]Shamgar son of
  Anath,
  in the days of [b]Jael caravans
  disappeared;
  travelers had to go on winding side
  roads.
7 Warriors[1] were scarce;
  they were scarce in Israel,
  until you arose, Deborah,
  until you arose as a motherly
  protector[2] in Israel.
8 God chose [a]new leaders,[1]
  then fighters appeared in the city
  gates;[2]
  but, I swear, not a shield or spear
  could be found
  among 40 military units[3] in Israel.
9 My heart went out to Israel's
  leaders,
  to the people who answered the call
  to war.
  Praise the LORD!

10 "You who ride on light-colored
  female [a]donkeys,
  who sit on saddle blankets,
  you who walk on the road, pay
  attention!
11 Hear the sound of those who divide
  the sheep[1] among the watering
  places;
  there they tell of the LORD's
  victorious deeds,
  the victorious deeds of his warriors[2]
  in Israel.
  Then the LORD's people went down
  to the city gates—
12 "Wake [a]up, wake up, Deborah!
  Wake up, wake up, sing a song!
  Get up, Barak!

Capture your prisoners of war, son of
  Abinoam!
13 Then the survivors[1] came down to
  the mighty ones;
  the LORD's people came down to me
  as warriors.
14 They came from Ephraim, who
  uprooted [a]Amalek;
  they follow after you, Benjamin, with
  your soldiers.
  From Makir leaders came down,
  from Zebulun came the ones who
  march carrying an officer's staff.
15 Issachar's leaders were with
  Deborah;
  the men of Issachar supported Barak;
  into the valley they were sent under
  Barak's command.
  Among the clans of Reuben there
  was intense heart searching.[1]
16 Why do you remain among the
  sheepfolds,[1]
  listening to the shepherds playing
  their pipes for their flocks?
  As for the clans of Reuben—there was
  intense searching of heart.
17 [a]Gilead stayed put beyond the Jordan
  River.
  As for Dan—why did he seek
  temporary employment in the
  shipyards?
  [b]Asher remained on the seacoast;
  he stayed by his harbors.
18 The men of [a]Zebulun were not
  concerned about their lives;
  Naphtali charged onto the
  battlefields.
19 "Kings came, they fought;
  the kings of Canaan fought
  at [a]Taanach by the waters of
  Megiddo,
  but they took no silver as plunder.
20 From the sky[1] the stars fought,
  from their paths in the heavens they
  fought against Sisera.
21 The Kishon River carried [a]them off;
  the river confronted them[1]—the
  Kishon River.
  Step on the necks of the strong![2]

5:4 [b] Ps 68:8   5:5 [a] Ps 97:5   [1] Heb. *this one of Sinai.*   5:6 [a] Judg 3:31   [b] Judg 4:17   5:7 [1] Or perhaps *leaders, those living in rural areas.*   [2] Heb. *mother.*   5:8 [a] Deut 32:17   [1] Or *warriors.*   [2] Heb. *Then [?] gates.*   [3] Trad. *40,000.*   5:10 [a] Judg 10:4; 12:14   5:11 [1] Or perhaps *those who distribute the water.*   [2] Or perhaps *leaders, those living in rural areas.*   5:12 [a] Ps 57:8   5:13 [1] Probably those who responded to the call for war.   5:14 [a] Judg 3:13   5:15 [1] Maj. MSS *resolves of heart.*   5:16 [1] Or perhaps *campfires.*   5:17 [a] Josh 22:9   [b] Josh 19:29, 31   5:18 [a] Judg 4:6, 10   5:19 [a] Judg 1:27   5:20 [1] Or *from heaven.*   5:21 [a] Judg 4:7   [1] Possibly *the ancient river.*   [2] Trad. *March on, my soul, in strength!*

[22] "The horses'[1] hooves pounded the
ground;
the stallions galloped madly.[2]
[23] 'Call judgment down on Meroz,' says
the angel of the LORD;
'Be sure[1] to call judgment down on
those who live there,
because they did not come to help in
the LORD's battle,
to help in the LORD's battle against
the warriors.'

[24] "The most [a]rewarded of women
should be Jael,
the wife of Heber the Kenite!
She should be the most rewarded of
women who live in tents.
[25] He asked for water,
and she gave him milk;
in a bowl fit for a king,
she served him curds.
[26] Her left hand reached for the tent
peg,
her right hand for the workmen's
hammer.
She 'hammered' Sisera,
she shattered his skull,
she smashed his head,
she drove the tent peg through his
temple.
[27] Between her feet he collapsed,
he fell limp and was lifeless;
between her feet he collapsed and
fell,
in the spot where he collapsed,
there he fell—violently [a]killed!

[28] "Through the window she looked;
Sisera's mother cried out through
the lattice:
'Why is his chariot so slow to return?
Why are the hoofbeats of his chariot
horses delayed?'
[29] The wisest of her ladies answer;
indeed she even thinks to herself,
[30] 'No doubt they are gathering and
dividing the plunder—
a girl or two for each man to rape![1]
Sisera is grabbing up colorful cloth,
he is grabbing up colorful
embroidered cloth,
two pieces of colorful embroidered
cloth,
for the neck of the plunderer!'

[31] "May all your enemies [a]perish [b]like
this, O LORD!
But may those who love you shine
like the rising [c]sun at its [d]brightest."

And the land had rest for forty years.

Oppression and Confrontation

6 The Israelites did [a]evil in the LORD's sight, so the LORD turned them over to [b]Midian for seven years. [2]The Midianites overwhelmed Israel. Because of Midian [a]the Israelites made shelters for themselves in the hills, caves, and strongholds. [3]Whenever the Israelites planted their crops, the Midianites, Amalekites, and the [a]people from the east would attack them. [4]They invaded the land and [a]devoured its crops all the way to Gaza. They left nothing for the Israelites to eat, and they took away the sheep, oxen, and [b]donkeys. [5]When they invaded with their cattle and tents, they were as thick as locusts. Neither they nor their camels could be counted. They came to devour[1] the land. [6]Israel was so severely weakened by Midian that the Israelites cried [a]out to the LORD for help.

[7]When the Israelites cried out to the LORD for help because of Midian, [8]the LORD sent a prophet to the Israelites. He said to them, "This is what the LORD God of Israel has said: 'I brought you up from Egypt[1] and took you out of that [a]place of slavery. [9]I rescued you from Egypt's power and from the power of all who oppressed you. I [a]drove them out before you and gave their land to you. [10]I said to you, "I am the LORD your God! [a]Do not worship the gods of the Amorites, in whose land you are now living." But you have disobeyed [b]me.'"

Gideon Meets Some Visitors

[11]The angel of [a]the LORD came and sat down under the oak tree in Ophrah owned by Joash the Abiezrite. He arrived while Joash's son [b]Gideon was threshing wheat in a winepress so he could hide it from the

5:22[1] MT *horse*. [2] Heb. *galloped, galloped*; an emphatic Heb. construction. **5:23**[1] Heb. *Curse, cursing*; an emphatic Heb. construction. **5:24**[a] [Luke 1:28] **5:27**[a] Judg 4:18–21 **5:30**[1] Heb. *a womb or two for each man*. **5:31**[a] Ps 92:9 [b] 2 Sam 23:4 [c] Ps 37:6; 89:36–37 [d] Ps 19:5 **6:1**[a] Judg 2:11 [b] Num 22:4; 31:1–3 **6:2**[a] 1 Sam 13:6; Heb 11:38 **6:3**[a] Judg 7:12 **6:4**[a] Lev 26:16 [b] Deut 28:31 **6:5**[1] Heb. *destroy*. **6:6**[a] Ps 50:15; Hos 5:15 **6:8**[a] Josh 24:17 [1] Some wss *from the land of Egypt*. **6:9**[a] Ps 44:2–3 **6:10**[a] 2 Kgs 17:35, 37, 38; Jer 10:2 [b] Judg 2:1–2 **6:11**[a] Josh 17:2; Judg 6:15 [b] Judg 7:1; Heb 11:32

Midianites. [12] The [a]angel of the LORD appeared and said to him, "The LORD is [b]with you, courageous warrior!" [13] Gideon said to him, "Pardon me, but if the LORD is with us, why has such disaster overtaken us? [a]Where are all his miraculous deeds our ancestors told us about? They said, 'Did the LORD not bring us up from Egypt?' But now the LORD has [b]abandoned us and handed us over to Midian." [14] Then the LORD himself[1] turned to him and said, "You [a]have the strength. Deliver Israel from the power of the Midianites! Have I not sent you?" [15] Gideon said to him, "But Lord, how can I deliver Israel? Just look! [a]My clan is the weakest in Manasseh, and I am the youngest in my family." [16] The LORD said to him, "Ah, [a]but I will be with you! You will strike down the whole Midianite army."[1] [17] Gideon said to him, "If you really are pleased with me, then [a]give me a sign as proof that it is really you speaking with me. [18][a]Do not leave this place until I come back with a gift and present it to you." The LORD said, "I will stay here until you come back."

[19][a]Gideon went and prepared a young goat, along with unleavened bread made from an ephah of flour. He put the meat in a basket and the broth in a pot. He brought the food to him under the oak tree and presented it to him. [20] God's angel said to him, "[a]Put the meat and unleavened bread on this rock, and [b]pour out the broth." Gideon did as instructed. [21] The angel of the LORD touched the meat and the unleavened bread with the tip of his staff. [a]Fire flared up from the rock and consumed the meat and unleavened bread. The angel of the LORD then disappeared.

[22] When Gideon [a]realized that it was the angel of the LORD, he said, "Oh no! Sovereign LORD![1] I have [b]seen the angel of the LORD face-to-face!" [23] The LORD said to him, "You are [a]safe![1] Do not be afraid. You are not going to die!" [24] Gideon built an altar for the LORD there, and named it "The LORD is on friendly terms with me."[1] To this day it is still there [a]in Ophrah of the Abiezrites.

Gideon Destroys the Altar

[25] That night the LORD said to him, "Take the bull from your father's herd, as well as [a]a second bull, one that is seven years old. Pull down your father's [b]Baal altar and [c]cut down the nearby Asherah pole. [26] Then build an altar for the LORD your God on the top of this stronghold according to the proper pattern.[1] Take the second bull and offer it as a burnt sacrifice on the wood from the Asherah pole that you cut down." [27] So Gideon took 10 of his servants and did just as the LORD had told him. He was too afraid of his father's family and the men of the city to do it in broad daylight, so he waited until nighttime.

[28] When the men of the city got up the next morning, they saw the Baal altar pulled down, the nearby Asherah pole cut down, and the second bull sacrificed on the newly built altar. [29] They said to one another, "Who did this?" They investigated the matter thoroughly and concluded that Gideon son of Joash had done it. [30] The men of the city said to Joash, "Bring out your son, so we can execute him![1] He pulled down the Baal altar and cut down the nearby Asherah pole." [31] But Joash said to all those who confronted him, "Must you fight Baal's battles? Must you rescue him? Whoever takes up his cause will die by morning! If he really is a god, let him fight his own battles! After all, it was his altar that was pulled down."[1] [32] That very day Gideon's father named him Jerub [a]Baal, because he had said, "Let Baal fight with him, for it was his altar that was pulled down."

Gideon Summons an Army and Seeks Confirmation

[33] All [a]the Midianites, Amalekites, and [b]the people from the east assembled. They crossed the Jordan River and camped in the Jezreel Valley. [34] The LORD's Spirit took control of Gideon. [a]He [b]blew a trumpet, summoning the Abiezrites to follow him. [35] He sent messengers throughout Manasseh and summoned them to follow him as well. He also sent messengers throughout [a]Asher,

6:12 [a] Judg 13:3; Luke 1:11, 28 [b] Josh 1:5 6:13 [a] [Isa 59:1] [b] Deut 31:17; 2 Chr 15:2; Ps 44:9–16 6:14 [a] Josh 1:9 [1] LXX *the angel of the Lord.* 6:15 [a] 1 Sam 9:21 6:16 [a] Exod 3:12; Josh 1:5 [1] Heb. *strike down Midian as one man.* 6:17 [a] Judg 6:36–37; 2 Kgs 20:8; Ps 86:17; Isa 7:11; 38:7–8 6:18 [a] Gen 18:3, 5 6:19 [a] Gen 18:6–8 6:20 [a] Judg 13:19 [b] 1 Kgs 18:33–34 6:21 [a] Lev 9:24 6:22 [a] Gen 32:30; Exod 33:20; Judg 13:21–22 [b] Gen 16:13 [1] Heb. *Lord, LORD.* 6:23 [a] Dan 10:19 [1] Heb. *Peace to you.* 6:24 [a] Judg 8:32 [1] Heb. *The LORD is peace.* 6:25 [a] Judg 2:2 [b] Judg 3:7 [c] Exod 34:13; Deut 7:5 6:26 [1] Possibly *in a row, in a layer.* 6:30 [1] Heb. *and let him die.* 6:31 [1] Heb. *for he pulled down his altar.* 6:32 [a] Judg 7:1; 1 Sam 12:11; 2 Sam 11:21 6:33 [a] Judg 6:3 [b] Josh 17:16; Hos 1:5 6:34 [a] Judg 3:10; 1 Chr 12:18; 2 Chr 24:20 [b] Num 10:3; Judg 3:27 6:35 [a] Judg 5:17; 7:23

[b]Zebulun, and Naphtali, and they came up to meet him.

[36]Gideon said to God, "If you really intend to use me to deliver Israel, as you promised, then give me a sign as proof. [37a]Look, I am putting a wool fleece on the threshing floor. If there is dew only on the fleece, and the ground around it is dry, then I will be sure that you will use me to deliver Israel, as you promised." [38]The LORD did as he asked. When he got up the next morning, he squeezed the fleece, and enough dew dripped from it to fill a bowl. [39]Gideon said to God, "Please [a]do not get angry at me, when I ask for just one more sign. Please allow me one more test with the fleece. This time make only the fleece dry, while the ground around it is covered with dew." [40]That night God did as he asked. Only the fleece was dry and the ground around it was covered with dew.

Gideon Reduces the Ranks

7 Jerub [a]Baal (that is, Gideon) and his men got up the next morning and camped near the spring of Harod. The Midianites[1] were camped north of them near the hill of Moreh in the valley. [2]The LORD said to Gideon, "You have too many men for me to hand Midian over to you. Israel might brag, 'Our own strength has delivered us.' [3]Now, announce to the men, '[a]Whoever is shaking with fear may turn around and leave Mount Gilead.'" Twenty-two thousand men[1] went home; 10,000 remained. [4]The LORD spoke to Gideon again, "There are still too many men. Bring them down to the water, and I will thin the ranks some more. When I say, 'This one should go with you,' pick him to go; when I say, 'This one should not go with you,' do not take him." [5]So he brought the men down to the water. Then the LORD said to Gideon, "Separate those who lap the water as a dog laps from those who kneel to drink." [6]Only 300 men lapped with their hands to their mouths; the rest of the men kneeled to drink water. [7]The LORD said to Gideon, "With the 300 men who lapped I will deliver the whole army, and I will hand Midian over to you. The rest of the men should go home." [8]The men who were chosen took supplies and their trumpets. Gideon sent all the men of Israel back to their homes; he kept only 300 men. Now the Midianites were camped down below in the valley.

Gideon Reassured of Victory

[9]That [a]night the LORD said to Gideon, "Get up! Attack the camp, for I am handing it over to you. [10]But if you are afraid to attack, go down to the camp with Purah your servant [11]and listen [a]to what they are saying. Then you will be brave and attack the camp." So he went down with Purah his servant to where the sentries were guarding the camp. [12]Now the Midianites, Amalekites, and the [a]people from the [b]east covered the valley like a swarm of locusts. Their camels could not be counted; they were as innumerable as the sand on the seashore. [13]When Gideon arrived, he heard a man telling another man about a dream he had. The man said, "Look! I had a dream. I saw[1] a stale cake of barley bread rolling into the Midianite camp. It hit a tent so hard it knocked it over and turned it upside down. The tent just collapsed." [14]The other man said, "Without a doubt this symbolizes the sword of Gideon son of Joash, the Israelite. [a]God is handing Midian and all the army over to him."

Gideon Routs the Enemy

[15]When Gideon heard the report of the dream and its interpretation, he praised God. Then he went back to the Israelite camp and said, "Get up, for the LORD is handing the Midianite army over to you!" [16]He divided the 300 men into three units. He gave them all trumpets and empty jars with torches inside them. [17]He said to them, "Watch me and do as I do. Watch closely! I am going to the edge of the camp. Do as I do! [18]When I and all who are with me blow our trumpets, you also blow your trumpets all around the camp. Then say, 'For the LORD and for Gideon!'"

[19]Gideon took 100 men to the edge of the camp at the beginning of the middle watch, just after they had changed the guards. They blew their trumpets and broke the jars they were carrying. [20]All three units blew their trumpets and broke their jars.

6:35 [b]Judg 4:6, 10; 5:18   6:37 [a][Exod 4:3–7]   6:39 [a]Gen 18:32   7:1 [a]Judg 6:32   [1]Heb. *Midian*.   7:3 [a]Deut 20:8
[1]Heb. *people*; warriors are in view, and in ancient Israelite culture, these would have been only males.
7:9 [a]Gen 46:2–3; Judg 6:25   7:11 [a]Gen 24:14; 1 Sam 14:9–10   7:12 [a]Judg 6:3, 33; 8:10   [b]Judg 6:5
7:13 [1]Heb. *Look!*; the repetition is emphatic.   7:14 [a]Judg 6:14, 16

They held the torches in their left hand and the trumpets in their right. Then they yelled, "A sword for the LORD and for Gideon!" [21]They stood in order all around the camp. The whole Midianite army ran away; they shouted as they scrambled away. [22]When the 300 men [a]blew [b]their trumpets, the LORD caused the Midianites to attack one another with their swords throughout[1] the camp. The army fled to Beth Shittah on the way to Zererah. They went to the border of Abel [c]Meholah near Tabbath. [23]Israelites from [a]Naphtali, Asher, and Manasseh answered the call and chased the Midianites.

Gideon Appeases the Ephraimites

[24]Now Gideon sent messengers throughout the Ephraimite hill [a]country who announced, "Go down and head off the Midianites. Take control [b]of the fords of the streams all the way to Beth [c]Barah and the Jordan River." When all the Ephraimites had assembled, they took control of the fords all the way to Beth Barah and the Jordan River. [25]They captured the [a]two Midianite generals, [b]Oreb and Zeeb. They executed Oreb on [c]the rock of Oreb and Zeeb in the winepress of Zeeb. They chased the Midianites and brought the heads of Oreb and Zeeb to Gideon, who was now on the other side of the Jordan River.

8 The Ephraimites said to him, "Why have you done such a thing to us? You did not summon us when you went to fight [a]the Midianites!" They argued vehemently with him. [2]He said to them, "Now what have I accomplished compared to you? Even Ephraim's leftover grapes are better quality than [a]Abiezer's harvest! [3]It was to you that [a]God handed over the Midianite generals, Oreb and Zeeb! What did I accomplish to rival that?" When he said this, [b]they calmed down.

Gideon Tracks Down the Midianite Kings

[4]Now Gideon and his 300 men had crossed over [a]the Jordan River, and even though they were exhausted, they were still chasing the Midianites.[1] [5]He said to the men of [a]Sukkoth, "Give some loaves of bread to the men[1] who are following me because they are exhausted. I am chasing Zebah and Zalmunna, the kings of Midian." [6]The officials of Sukkoth said, "You have not yet [a]overpowered Zebah and Zalmunna. So why should we give bread to your army?"[1] [7]Gideon said, "Since you will not help, after [a]the LORD hands Zebah and Zalmunna over to me, I will thresh your skin with[1] desert thorns and briers." [8]He went up from there [a]to Penuel and made the same request. The men of Penuel responded the same way the men of Sukkoth had. [9]He also threatened the men of Penuel, [a]warning, "When I return victoriously, I will tear down this tower."

[10]Now Zebah and Zalmunna were in Karkor with their armies. There were about 15,000 survivors from the army of the eastern peoples; 120,000 sword-wielding soldiers had been killed. [11]Gideon went up the road of the nomads east of [a]Nobah and Jogbehah and ambushed the [b]surprised army.[1] [12]When Zebah and Zalmunna ran away, Gideon chased them and [a]captured the two Midianite kings, Zebah and Zalmunna. He had surprised their entire army.

[13]Gideon son of Joash returned from the battle by the pass of Heres. [14]He captured a young man from Sukkoth and interrogated him. The young man wrote down for him the names of Sukkoth's officials and city leaders—77 men in all. [15]He approached the men of Sukkoth and said, "Look what I have! Zebah and Zalmunna! You [a]insulted me, saying, 'You have not yet overpowered Zebah and Zalmunna. So why should we give bread to your exhausted men?'" [16]He seized the leaders of the city, along with some desert thorns [a]and briers; he then "threshed" the men of Sukkoth with them.[1] [17]He also tore down [a]the tower of [b]Penuel and executed the city's men.

[18]He said to Zebah and Zalmunna, "Describe for me the men you killed at [a]Tabor."

7:22 [a]Josh 6:4, 16, 20　[b]Ps 83:9; Isa 9:4　[c]1 Kgs 4:12　[1]MT *and throughout the camp.*　**7:23** [a]Judg 6:35　**7:24** [a]Judg 3:27　[b]Judg 3:28　[c]John 1:28　**7:25** [a]Judg 8:3　[b]Ps 83:11; Isa 10:26　[c]Judg 8:4　**8:1** [a]Judg 12:1; 2 Sam 19:41　**8:2** [a]Judg 6:11　**8:3** [a]Judg 7:24–25　[b]Prov 15:1　**8:4** [a]Judg 7:6　[1]Heb. *And Gideon arrived at the Jordan, crossing over, he and the 300 men who were with him, exhausted and chasing.*　**8:5** [a]Gen 33:17; Ps 60:6　[1]Heb. *people;* warriors are in view, and in ancient Israelite culture, these would have been only males.　**8:6** [a]1 Sam 25:11　[1]Heb. *Are the palms of Zebah and Zalmunna now in your hand, that we should give to your army bread?*　**8:7** [a]Judg 8:16　[1]Or perhaps *together with.*　**8:8** [a]Gen 32:30–31; 1 Kgs 12:25　**8:9** [a]Judg 8:17　**8:11** [a]Num 32:35, 42　[b]Judg 18:27; [1 Thess 5:3]　[1]Heb. *and attacked the army, while the army was secure;* a few MSS, LXX *trustingly.*　**8:12** [a]Ps 83:11　**8:15** [a]Judg 8:6　**8:16** [a]Judg 8:7　[1]MT *he used them* [i.e., the thorns and briers] *to teach the men of Sukkoth a lesson.*　**8:17** [a]Judg 8:9　[b]1 Kgs 12:25　**8:18** [a]Judg 4:6; Ps 89:12

They said, "They were like you. Each one looked like a king's son." [19]He said, "They were my brothers, the sons of my mother. I swear, as surely as the LORD is alive, if you had let them live, I would not kill you." [20]He ordered Jether his firstborn son, "Come on! Kill them!" But Jether was too afraid to draw his sword because he was still young. [21]Zebah and Zalmunna said to Gideon, "Come on, you strike us, for a man is judged by his strength." So Gideon [a]killed Zebah and Zalmunna, and he took the crescent-shaped ornaments that were on the necks of their camels.

Gideon Rejects a Crown but Makes an Ephod

[22]The men of Israel said to Gideon, "[a]Rule over us—you, your son, and your grandson. For you have [b]delivered us from Midian's power." [23]Gideon said to [a]them, "I will not rule over you, nor will my son rule over you. The LORD will rule over you." [24]Gideon continued, "I would like to make one request. Each of you give me an earring from the plunder you have taken." (The Midianites had gold earrings [a]because they were Ishmaelites.) [25]They said, "We are happy to give you earrings." So they[1] spread out a garment, and each one threw an earring from his plunder onto it. [26]The total weight of the gold earrings he requested came to 1,700 gold shekels. This was in addition to the crescent-shaped ornaments, jewelry, purple clothing worn by the Midianite kings, and the necklaces on the camels. [27]Gideon used all this to [a]make an ephod, which he put in his hometown of [b]Ophrah. All the Israelites prostituted themselves to it by worshiping it there. It became [c]a [d]snare to Gideon and his family.

Gideon's Story Ends

[28]The Israelites humiliated Midian; the Midianites' fighting spirit was broken. The [a]land had rest for 40 years during Gideon's time. [29]Then Jerub [a]Baal son of Joash went home and settled down. [30]Gideon fathered [a]70 sons through his many wives. [31]His concubine, who lived in Shechem, also gave him [a]a son, whom he named Abimelech,

[32]Gideon son of Joash died [a]at a very old age and was buried [b]in the tomb of his father Joash located in Ophrah of the Abiezrites.

Israel Returns to Baal Worship

[33]After Gideon died, the Israelites again prostituted themselves to the Baals. They made Baal Berith their god. [34]The Israelites [a]did not remain true to the LORD their God, who had delivered them from all the enemies who lived around them. [35a]They did not treat the family of Jerub Baal (that is, Gideon) fairly in return for all the good he had done for Israel.

Abimelech Murders His Brothers

9 Now Abimelech son of Jerub Baal went to Shechem to see [a]his mother's relatives. He said to them and to his mother's entire extended family, [2]"Tell all the leaders of Shechem this: 'Why would you want to have [a]70 men, all Jerub Baal's sons, ruling over you when you can have just one ruler? Recall that I am your own flesh and [b]blood.'" [3]His mother's [a]relatives spoke on his behalf to all the leaders of Shechem and reported his proposal. The leaders were drawn to Abimelech; they said, "He is our close relative." [4]They paid him 70 silver shekels out of the temple of Baal [a]Berith. Abimelech then used the silver to hire some [b]lawless, dangerous men as his followers. [5]He went to his [a]father's home in Ophrah and [b]murdered his half brothers, the 70 legitimate sons of Jerub Baal, on one stone. Only Jotham, Jerub Baal's youngest son, escaped because he hid. [6]All the leaders of Shechem and Beth Millo assembled and then went and made Abimelech king by the oak near the pillar in Shechem.

Jotham's Parable

[7]When Jotham heard the news, he went and stood on the top of [a]Mount Gerizim. He spoke loudly to the people below, "Listen to me, leaders of Shechem, so that God may listen to you!

[8]"The trees were determined to go out[1] and choose a king for [a]themselves. They said to the olive tree, '[b]Be our king!' [9]But

8:21 [a]Ps 83:11   8:22 [a][Judg 9:8]   [b]Judg 3:9; 9:17   8:23 [a]1 Sam 8:7; 10:19; 12:12; Ps 10:16   8:24 [a]Gen 37:25, 28   8:25 [1]LXX *he.*   8:27 [a]Judg 17:5   [b]Judg 6:11, 24   [c][Ps 106:39]   [d]Deut 7:16   8:28 [a]Judg 5:31   8:29 [a]Judg 6:32; 7:1   8:30 [a]Judg 9:2, 5   8:31 [a]Judg 9:1   8:32 [a]Gen 25:8; Job 5:26   [b]Judg 6:24; 8:27   8:34 [a]Deut 4:9; Judg 3:7; Ps 78:11, 42; 106:13, 21   8:35 [a]Judg 9:16–18   9:1 [a]Judg 8:31, 35   9:2 [a]Judg 8:30; 9:5, 18   [b]Gen 29:14   9:3 [a]Gen 29:15   9:4 [a]Judg 8:33   [b]Judg 11:3; 2 Chr 13:7; Acts 17:5   9:5 [a]Judg 6:24   [b]Judg 8:30; 9:2, 18; 2 Kgs 11:1–2   9:7 [a]Deut 11:29; 27:12; Josh 8:33; John 4:20   9:8 [a]2 Kgs 14:9   [b]Judg 8:22–23   [1]Heb. *Going they went, the trees.*

the olive tree said to them, ᵃI am not going to stop producing my oil, which is used to honor gods and men, just to sway above the other trees!'

¹⁰"So the trees said to the fig tree, 'You come and be our king!' ¹¹But the fig tree said to them, 'I am not going to stop producing my sweet figs, my excellent fruit, just to sway above the other trees!'

¹²"So the trees said to the grapevine, 'You come and be our king!' ¹³But the grapevine said to them, ᵃI am not going to stop producing my wine, which makes gods and men so happy, just to sway above the other trees!'

¹⁴"So all the trees said to the thornbush, 'You come and be our king!' ¹⁵The thornbush said to the trees, 'If you really want to choose me as your king, then come along, find safety under my ᵃbranches. Otherwise may fire blaze from the thornbush and consume the ᵇcedars of Lebanon!'

¹⁶"Now, if you have shown loyalty and integrity when you made Abimelech king, if you have done right to Jerub Baal and his family, if you have properly repaid him— ¹⁷my ᵃfather fought for you; he risked his life¹ and ᵇdelivered you from Midian's power. ¹⁸ᵃBut you have attacked my father's family today. You murdered his 70 legitimate sons on one stone and made Abimelech, the son of his ᵇfemale slave, king over the leaders of Shechem just because he is your close relative. ¹⁹So if you have shown loyalty and integrity to Jerub Baal and his family today, then may Abimelech bring you ᵃhappiness and may you bring him happiness! ²⁰But if not, may fire blaze from Abimelech and consume the leaders of Shechem and Beth Millo! May fire also blaze from the leaders of Shechem and Beth Millo and consume Abimelech!" ²¹Then Jotham ran away to ᵃBeer and lived there to escape from Abimelech his half-brother.

God Fulfills Jotham's Curse

²²Abimelech commanded Israel for three years. ²³ᵃGod sent a ᵇspirit to stir up hostility¹ between Abimelech and the leaders of Shechem. He made the leaders of Shechem disloyal to Abimelech. ²⁴ᵃHe did this so the violent deaths of Jerub Baal's 70 sons might be avenged and Abimelech, their half-brother who murdered them, might have to pay for their spilled ᵇblood, along with the leaders of Shechem who helped him murder them. ²⁵The leaders of Shechem rebelled against Abimelech by putting bandits in the hills, who robbed everyone who traveled by on the road. But Abimelech found out about it.

²⁶Gaal son of Ebed came through Shechem with his brothers. The leaders of Shechem transferred their loyalty to him.¹ ²⁷They went out to ᵃthe field, harvested their grapes, squeezed out the juice,¹ and celebrated. They came to the temple of their god and ate, drank, and cursed Abimelech. ²⁸Gaal son of Ebed said, "ᵃWho is Abimelech and who is Shechem, that we should serve him? Is he not the son of Jerub Baal, and is not Zebul the deputy he appointed? Serve the sons of ᵇHamor, the father of Shechem! But why should we serve Abimelech? ²⁹If only these men were under my command, ᵃI would get rid of Abimelech!" He challenged Abimelech,¹ "Muster your army and come out for battle!"

³⁰When Zebul, the city commissioner, heard the words of Gaal son of Ebed, he was furious. ³¹He sent messengers to Abimelech, who was in Arumah,¹ reporting, "Beware! Gaal son of Ebed and his brothers are coming to Shechem and inciting the city to rebel against you. ³²Now, come up at night with your men and set an ambush in the field outside the city. ³³In the morning at sunrise quickly attack the city. When he and his men come out to fight you, do what you can to him."

³⁴So Abimelech and all his men came up at night and set an ambush outside Shechem; they divided into four units. ³⁵When Gaal son of Ebed came out and stood at the entrance to the city's gate, Abimelech and his men got up from their hiding places. ³⁶Gaal saw the men¹ and said to Zebul, "Look, men are coming down from the tops of the hills." But Zebul said to him, "You are seeing the

---

9:9 ᵃ [John 5:23]   9:13 ᵃ Ps 104:15   9:15 ᵃ Isa 30:2; Dan 4:12; Hos 14:7   ᵇ 2 Kgs 14:9; Isa 2:13; Ezek 31:3   9:17 ᵃ Judg 7   ᵇ Judg 8:22   ¹ Heb. *threw his life out in front.*   9:18 ᵃ Judg 8:30, 35; 9:2, 5, 6   ᵇ Judg 8:31   9:19 ᵃ Isa 8:6; [Phil 3:3]   9:21 ᵃ Num 21:16   9:23 ᵃ 1 Kgs 12:15; Isa 19:14   ᵇ 1 Sam 16:14; 18:9–10; 1 Kgs 22:22; 2 Chr 18:22   ¹ Heb. *an evil spirit;* can be used in a nonethical sense of "harmful" or "dangerous."   9:24 ᵃ 1 Kgs 2:32; Esth 9:25; Matt 23:35–36   ᵇ Num 35:33   9:26 ¹ Heb. *trusted in him.*   9:27 ᵃ Judg 9:4   ¹ Heb. *stomped, trampled.*   9:28 ᵃ 1 Sam 25:10; 1 Kgs 12:16   ᵇ Gen 34:2, 6; Josh 24:32   9:29 ᵃ 2 Sam 15:4   ¹ Or perhaps *He boasted, 'Abimelech;* Heb. *said to Abimelech.*   9:31 ¹ Or perhaps *secretly, with deception.*   9:36 ¹ Heb. *the people;* warriors are in view, and in ancient Israelite culture, these would have been only males.

shadows on the hills—it just looks like men." [37]Gaal again said, "Look, men are coming down from the very center of the land. A unit is coming by way of the Oak Tree of the Diviners." [38]Zebul [a]said to him, "Where now are your bragging words, 'Who is Abimelech that we should serve him?' Are these not the men you insulted? Go out now and fight them!" [39]So Gaal led the leaders of Shechem out and fought Abimelech. [40]Abimelech chased him, and Gaal ran from him. Many Shechemites fell wounded at the entrance of the gate. [41]Abimelech went back[1] to Arumah; Zebul drove Gaal and his brothers out of Shechem.

[42]The next day the Shechemites came out to the field. When Abimelech heard about it, [43]he took his men and divided them into three units and set an ambush in the field. When he saw the people coming out of the city, he attacked and struck them down. [44]Abimelech and his units attacked and blocked the entrance to the city's gate. Two units then attacked all the people in the field and struck them down. [45]Abimelech fought against [a]the city all that day. He captured the city and killed all the people in it. Then he [b]leveled the city and spread salt over it.

[46]When all the leaders [a]of the Tower of Shechem heard the news, they went to the stronghold[1] of the temple of El Berith. [47]Abimelech heard that all the leaders of the Tower of Shechem were in one place. [48]He and all his men went up on Mount [a]Zalmon. He took an ax in his hand and cut off a tree branch. He put it on his shoulder and said to his men, "Quickly, do what you have just seen me do!" [49]So each of his men also cut off a branch and followed Abimelech. They put the branches against the stronghold and set fire to it. All the people of the Tower of Shechem died—about 1,000 men and women.

[50]Abimelech moved on to Thebez; he besieged and captured it. [51]There was a fortified tower[1] in the center of the city, so all the men and women, as well as the city's leaders, ran into it and locked the entrance. Then they went up to the roof of the tower.

[52]Abimelech came and attacked the tower. When he approached the entrance of the tower to set it on fire, [53]a woman [a]threw an upper millstone down on his head and shattered his skull. [54]He quickly called to [a]the young man who carried his weapons, "Draw your sword and kill me, so they will not say, 'A woman killed him.'" So the young man stabbed him and he died. [55]When the Israelites saw that Abimelech was dead, they went home.

[56a]God repaid Abimelech for the evil he did to his father by murdering his 70 half brothers. [57]God also repaid [a]the men of Shechem for their evil deeds. The curse spoken by Jotham son of Jerub Baal fell on them.

Stability Restored

10 After Abimelech's death, Tola son of Puah, grandson of Dodo, from the tribe of Issachar, rose [a]up to deliver Israel. He lived in Shamir in the Ephraimite hill country. [2]He led Israel for 23 years, then died and was buried in Shamir.

[3]Jair the Gileadite rose up after him; he led Israel for 22 years. [4]He had 30 sons who [a]rode on 30 donkeys and possessed 30 cities. To this day these towns are called Havvoth Jair—they are in the land of Gilead. [5]Jair died and was buried in Kamon.

The Lord's Patience Runs Short

[6]The Israelites again did evil in [a]the LORD's sight. They [b]worshiped [c]the Baals and the Ashtoreths, as well as the gods of Syria, [d]Sidon, Moab, the Ammonites, and the Philistines. They abandoned the LORD and did not worship him. [7]The LORD was furious with Israel and [a]turned them over to the [b]Philistines and [c]Ammonites. [8]They ruthlessly oppressed[1] the Israelites that eighteenth year[2]—that is, all the Israelites living east of the Jordan in Amorite [a]country in Gilead. [9]The Ammonites crossed the Jordan to fight with Judah, Benjamin, and Ephraim. Israel suffered greatly.

[10a]The Israelites cried out for help to the LORD: "We have [b]sinned against you. We abandoned our God and worshiped

9:38 [a]Judg 9:28–29   9:41 [1]Heb. *stayed.*   9:45 [a]Judg 9:20   [b]Deut 29:23; 2 Kgs 3:25   9:46 [a]Judg 8:33   [1]Perhaps the inner sanctuary or an underground chamber.   9:48 [a]Ps 68:14   9:51 [1]Or *fortress.*   9:53 [a]2 Sam 11:21   9:54 [a]1 Sam 31:4   9:56 [a]Judg 9:24; Job 31:3; Prov 5:22   9:57 [a]Judg 9:20   10:1 [a]Judg 2:16   10:4 [a]Judg 5:10; 12:14   10:6 [a]Judg 2:11; 3:7; 6:1; 13:1   [b]Judg 2:13   [c]Judg 2:12   [d]1 Kgs 11:33; Ps 106:36   10:7 [a]Judg 2:14; 4:2; 1 Sam 12:9   [b]Judg 13:1   [c]Judg 3:13   10:8 [a]Num 32:33   [1]Heb. *shattered and crushed*; an emphatic Heb. construction.   [2]Or perhaps *eighteen years.*   10:10 [a]Judg 6:6; 1 Sam 12:10   [b]Deut 1:41

the Baals." [11] The LORD said to the Israelites, "Did I not deliver you [a] from Egypt, the Amorites, the Ammonites, the Philistines, [12] the [a] Sidonians, [b] Amalek, and Midian[1] when they [c] oppressed you? You cried out for help to me, and I delivered you from their power. [13a] But since you abandoned me and worshiped other gods, I will not deliver you again. [14] Go and cry for [a] help to the gods you have chosen! Let them deliver you from trouble!" [15] But the Israelites said to the LORD, "We have sinned. You [a] do to us as you see fit, but deliver us today!" [16] They threw away the foreign gods they owned and worshiped the LORD. Finally the LORD grew tired of seeing Israel suffer [a] so much.[1]

An Outcast Becomes a General

[17] The Ammonites assembled and camped in Gilead; the Israelites gathered together and camped in [a] Mizpah. [18] The leaders of Gilead said to one another, "Who is willing to lead the charge against the Ammonites? He will [a] become the leader of all who live in Gilead!"

11 Now [a] Jephthah the [b] Gileadite was a brave warrior. His mother was a prostitute, but Gilead was his father. [2] Gilead's wife also gave him sons. When his wife's sons grew up, they made Jephthah leave and said to him, "You are [a] not going to inherit any of our father's wealth because you are another woman's son." [3] So Jephthah left his half brothers and lived in the land of [a] Tob. [b] Lawless men joined Jephthah's gang and traveled with him.

[4] It was some time after this when the [a] Ammonites fought with Israel. [5] When the Ammonites attacked, the leaders of Gilead asked Jephthah to come back from the land of Tob. [6] They said, "Come, be our commander, so we can fight with the Ammonites." [7] Jephthah said to the leaders of Gilead, "But you hated me and made me leave my father's house. Why do you come to me now, when you are in trouble?" [8a] The leaders of Gilead said to Jephthah, "That may be true,[1]

but now we [b] pledge to you [c] our loyalty.[2] Come with us and fight with the Ammonites. Then you will become the leader of all who live in Gilead." [9] Jephthah said to the leaders of Gilead, "All right. If you take me back to fight with the Ammonites and the LORD gives them to me, I will be your leader."[1] [10] The leaders of Gilead said to Jephthah, "[a] The LORD will judge any grievance you have against us[1] if we do not do as you say." [11] So Jephthah went with the leaders of Gilead. The people made him their [a] leader and commander. Jephthah repeated the terms of the agreement[1] [b] before the LORD in Mizpah.

Jephthah Gives a History Lesson

[12] Jephthah sent messengers to the Ammonite king, saying, "[a] Why have you come against me to attack my land?" [13] The Ammonite king said to Jephthah's messengers, "[a] Because Israel stole my land when [b] they came up from Egypt—from [c] the Arnon River in the south to the Jabbok River in the north, and as far west as the Jordan.[1] Now return it[2] peaceably!"

[14] Jephthah sent messengers back to the Ammonite king [15] and said to him, "This is what Jephthah says, '[a] Israel did not steal the land of Moab and the land of the Ammonites. [16] When they left Egypt, Israel traveled through the desert as far as the Red Sea and then [a] came to Kadesh. [17a] Israel sent messengers to the [b] king of Edom, saying, "Please allow us to pass through your land." But the king of Edom rejected the request. Israel sent the same request to the king of Moab, but he was unwilling to cooperate. So Israel [c] stayed at Kadesh. [18] Then Israel [a] went through the wilderness and [b] bypassed the land of Edom and the land of Moab. They traveled east of the land of Moab and camped on the other side of the Arnon River; they did not go through Moabite territory (the Arnon was Moab's border). [19a] Israel sent messengers to King Sihon, the Amorite king who ruled in Heshbon, and said to him,

10:11 [a] Judg 3:31   10:12 [a] Judg 1:31; 5:19   [b] Judg 6:3; 7:12   [c] Ps 106:42–43   [1] Heb. *Maon.*   10:13 [a] [Deut 32:15; Judg 2:12; Jer 2:13]   10:14 [a] Deut 32:37–38   10:15 [a] 1 Sam 3:18; 2 Sam 15:26   10:16 [a] 2 Chr 7:14; Jer 18:7–8   [1] Heb. *And his spirit grew short* [i.e., impatient] *with the suffering of Israel.*   10:17 [a] Gen 31:49; Judg 11:11, 29   10:18 [a] Judg 11:8, 11   11:1 [a] Heb 11:32   [b] Judg 6:12; 2 Kgs 5:1   11:2 [a] Gen 21:10; Deut 23:2   11:3 [a] 2 Sam 10:6, 8   [b] 1 Sam 22:2   11:4 [a] Judg 10:9, 17   11:8 [a] Judg 10:18   [b] [Luke 17:4]   [c] Judg 10:18   [1] Heb. *therefore, even so.*   [2] Heb. *we have returned to you.*   11:9 [1] Or perhaps *will I really be your leader?*   11:10 [a] Gen 31:49–50; Jer 29:23; 42:5   [1] Heb. *The LORD will be the one who hears between us.*   11:11 [a] Judg 11:8   [b] Judg 10:17; 20:1; 1 Sam 10:17   [1] Or *Jephthah conducted business before the LORD in Mizpah*; Heb. *spoke all his words.*   11:12 [a] 2 Sam 16:10   11:13 [a] Num 21:24–26   [b] Josh 13:9   [c] Gen 32:22   [1] Heb. *from the Arnon to the Jabbok and to the Jordan.*   [2] Heb. *them.*   11:15 [a] Deut 2:9, 19   11:16 [a] Num 13:26; 20:1   11:17 [a] Num 20:14   [b] Josh 24:9   [c] Num 20:1   11:18 [a] Deut 2:9, 18, 19   [b] Num 21:4   11:19 [a] Num 21:21; Deut 2:26–36

"Please allow us to pass through your land to our land." [20a]But Sihon did not trust Israel to pass through his territory. He assembled his whole army, camped in Jahaz, and fought with Israel. [21]The LORD God of Israel [a]handed Sihon and his whole army over to Israel, and they [b]defeated them. Israel took all the land of the Amorites who lived in that land. [22]They took [a]all the Amorite territory from the Arnon River on the south to the Jabbok River on the north, from the desert in the east to the Jordan in the west.[1] [23]Since the LORD God of Israel has driven out the Amorites before his people Israel, do you think you can just take it from them?[1] [24]You have the right to take what [a]Chemosh your god gives you, but we will take [b]the land of all whom the LORD our God has driven out before us.[1] [25]Are you really better than [a]Balak son of Zippor, king of Moab? Did he dare to quarrel with Israel? Did he dare to fight with them? [26]Israel has been living in [a]Heshbon and its nearby towns, in [b]Aroer and its nearby towns, and in all the cities along the Arnon for 300 years! Why did you not reclaim them during that time? [27]I have not done you wrong, but you are doing wrong by attacking me. May [a]the LORD, the Judge, judge this day between the Israelites and the Ammonites!'" [28]But the Ammonite king disregarded the message sent by Jephthah.

A Foolish Vow Spells Death for a Daughter

[29]The LORD's Spirit empowered Jephthah. [a]He passed through Gilead and Manasseh and went to Mizpah in Gilead. From there he approached the Ammonites. [30]Jephthah [a]made a vow to the LORD, saying, "If you really do hand the Ammonites over to me, [31]then whoever is the first to come through[1] the doors of my house to meet me when I return safely from fighting the Ammonites—he[2] will belong to the LORD, and[3] I will offer him up as [a]a burnt sacrifice."

[32]Jephthah approached the Ammonites to fight with them, and the LORD handed them over to him. [33]He defeated them from Aroer all the way to [a]Minnith—20 cities in all, even as far as Abel Keramim. He wiped them out! The Israelites humiliated the Ammonites.

[34]When Jephthah came home to [a]Mizpah, there was [b]his daughter hurrying out to meet him, dancing to the rhythm of tambourines. She was his only child; except for her he had no son or daughter. [35]When he saw her, he [a]ripped his clothes and said, "Oh no! My daughter! You [b]have completely [c]ruined me! You have brought me disaster! I made an oath to the LORD, and I cannot break it." [36]She said to him, "My father, since you made an oath to the LORD, [a]do to me as you promised. After all, [b]the LORD vindicated you before your enemies, the Ammonites." [37]She then said to her father, "Please grant me this one wish. For two months allow me to walk through the hills with my friends and mourn my virginity." [38]He said, "You may go." He permitted her to leave for two months. She went with her friends and mourned her virginity as she walked through the hills. [39]After two months she returned to her father, and he did to her as he had vowed. She died [a]a virgin.[1] Her tragic death gave rise to a custom in Israel. [40]Every year Israelite women commemorate the daughter of Jephthah the Gileadite for four days.

Civil Strife Mars the Victory

12 The Ephraimites assembled and crossed over to Zaphon. [a]They said to Jephthah, "Why did you go and fight with the Ammonites without asking us to go with you? We will burn your house down right over you!"

[2]Jephthah said to them, "My people and I were in a struggle, and the Ammonites were oppressing me greatly.[1] I asked for your help, but you did not deliver me from their power.

11:20 [a]Num 21:23; Deut 2:27   11:21 [a]Josh 24:8   [b]Num 21:24–25   11:22 [a]Deut 2:36–37   [1]Heb. *from the Arnon to the Jabbok, and from the desert to the Jordan.*   11:23 [1]Heb. *will you dispossess him* [i.e., Israel; or possibly *it*, i.e., the territory]?   11:24 [a]Num 21:29; 1 Kgs 11:7; Jer 48:7   [b][Deut 9:4–5; Josh 3:10]   [1]Heb. *Is it not so that what Chemosh your god causes you to possess, you possess, and all whom the LORD our God dispossesses before us we will possess?*   11:25 [a]Num 22:2; Josh 24:9; Mic 6:5   11:26 [a]Num 21:25–26   [b]Deut 2:36   11:27 [a]Gen 18:25   11:29 [a]Judg 3:10   11:30 [a]Gen 28:20; Num 30:2; 1 Sam 1:11   11:31 [a]Lev 27:2–3, 28; 1 Sam 1:11   [1]Heb. *the one coming out, who comes out from;* Jephthah may have envisioned an animal meeting him, because the construction of Iron Age houses would allow for an animal coming through the doors of a house.   [2]The language is fluid enough to include women and perhaps even animals.   [3]Or perhaps *or*, suggesting Jephthah makes a distinction between humans and animals.   11:33 [a]Ezek 27:17   11:34 [a]Judg 10:17; 11:11   [b]Exod 15:20; 1 Sam 18:6; Ps 68:25; Jer 31:4   11:35 [a]Gen 37:29, 34   [b]Eccl 5:2, 4, 5   [c]Num 30:2   11:36 [a]Num 30:2   [b]2 Sam 18:19, 31   11:39 [a]Judg 11:31   [1]Heb. *She had never known a man.*   12:1 [a]Judg 8:1   12:2 [1]Heb. *A fighting man was I was and my people, and the Ammonites greatly; LXX I was man fighting, and my people [also]. And the sons of Ammon were humiliating me greatly.*

[3] When I saw that you were not going to help,[1] I [a]risked my life and advanced against the Ammonites, and the LORD handed them over to me. Why have you come up to fight with me today?" [4] Jephthah assembled all the men of Gilead and they fought with Ephraim. The men of Gilead defeated Ephraim because the Ephraimites insulted them, saying, "You Gileadites [a]are refugees in Ephraim, living within Ephraim's and Manasseh's territory."[1] [5] The Gileadites captured the [a]fords of the Jordan River opposite Ephraim. Whenever an Ephraimite fugitive said, "Let me cross over," the men of Gilead asked him, "Are you an Ephraimite?" If he said, "No," [6] then they said to him, "Say [a]Shibboleth!'" If he said, "Sibboleth" (and could not pronounce the word[1] correctly), they grabbed him and executed him right there at the fords of the Jordan. On that day 42,000 Ephraimites fell dead.

[7] Jephthah led Israel for six years; then he died and was buried in his town in Gilead.[1]

Order Restored

[8] After him Ibzan of Bethlehem led Israel. [9] He had 30 sons. He arranged for 30 of his daughters to be married outside his extended family, and he arranged for 30 young women to be brought from outside as wives for his sons. Ibzan led Israel for seven years; [10] then he died and was buried in Bethlehem.

[11] After him Elon the Zebulunite led Israel for 10 years. [12] Then Elon the Zebulunite died and was buried in Aijalon in the land of Zebulun.

[13] After him Abdon son of Hillel the Pirathonite led Israel. [14] He had 40 sons and 30 grandsons who [a]rode on 70 donkeys. He led Israel for eight years. [15] Then Abdon son of Hillel the Pirathonite died and was buried [a]in Pirathon in the land of Ephraim, in the hill country of the Amalekites.

Samson's Birth

13 The Israelites again [a]did evil [b]in the LORD's sight, so the LORD handed them over to the Philistines for 40 years.

[2] There was a man named Manoah from [a]Zorah, from the Danite tribe. His wife was infertile and childless. [3] The [a]angel of the LORD appeared to the woman and said to her, "You are infertile and childless, but you will conceive and have a son. [4] Now be careful! Do [a]not drink wine or beer, and do not eat any food that will make you ritually unclean. [5] Look, you will conceive and have a son.[1] You must never [a]cut his [b]hair, for the child will be dedicated to God[2] from birth. He will [c]begin to deliver Israel from the power of the Philistines."

[6] The [a]woman went and said to her husband, "A man sent from God came to me! He [b]looked like God's angel—he was very awesome. [c]I did not ask him where he came from, and he did not tell me his name. [7] He said to me, 'Look, you will conceive and have a son. So now, do not drink wine or beer and do not eat any food that will make you ritually unclean. For the child will be dedicated to God from birth till the day he dies.'"

[8] Manoah prayed to the LORD, "Please, Lord, allow the man sent from God to visit us again, so he can teach[1] us how we should raise the child who will be born." [9] God answered Manoah's prayer. God's angel visited the woman again while she was sitting in the field. But her husband Manoah was not with her. [10] The woman ran at once and told her husband, "Come quickly, the man who visited me the other day has appeared to me!" [11] So Manoah got up and followed his wife. When he met the man, he said to him, "Are you the man who spoke to my wife?" He said, "Yes." [12] Manoah said, "Now, when your announcement comes true, how should the child be raised and what should he do?" [13] The angel of the LORD told Manoah, "Your wife should pay attention to everything I told her.[1] [14] She should not drink anything that the grapevine produces. She must [a]not drink wine or beer, and she must not eat any food that will make her ritually unclean. She should obey everything I commanded her to do." [15] Manoah said to the angel of the LORD, "Please stay here awhile, so we can prepare a young goat for you to eat." [16] The angel of

12:3 [a]1 Sam 19:5; 28:21; Job 13:14   [1]Heb. *you were no deliverer.*   12:4 [a]1 Sam 25:10   [1]Heb. *Refugees of Ephraim are you, O Gilead, in the midst of Ephraim and in the midst of Manasseh;* LXX omits all after "because."   12:5 [a]Josh 22:11   12:6 [a]Ps 69:2, 15   [1]Heb. *and could not prepare to speak.*   12:7 [1]Heb. *in the cities of Gilead.*   12:14 [a]Judg 5:10; 10:4   12:15 [a]Judg 3:13, 27; 5:14   13:1 [a]Judg 2:11   [b]Judg 10:7; 1 Sam 12:9   13:2 [a]Josh 19:41; Judg 16:31   13:3 [a]Judg 6:12   13:4 [a]Num 6:2–3, 20; Judg 13:4; Luke 1:15   13:5 [a]Num 6:5; 1 Sam 1:11   [b]Num 6:2   [c]1 Sam 7:13; 2 Sam 8:1; 1 Chr 18:1   [1]Or *you are already pregnant and will have a son.*   [2]Or *set apart to God;* trad. *Nazirite.*   13:6 [a]Gen 32:24–30   [b]Matt 28:3; Luke 9:29; Acts 6:15   [c]Judg 13:17–18   13:8 [1]LXX *enlighten.*   13:13 [1]*to everything* is emphasized in the Heb. text.   13:14 [a]Num 6:3–4; Judg 13:4

the LORD said to Manoah, "If I stay, I will not eat your food. But if you want to make a burnt sacrifice to the LORD, you should offer it." (He said this because Manoah did not know that he was the angel of the LORD.) [17]Manoah said to the angel of the LORD, "Tell us your name, so we can honor you when your announcement comes true." [18]The angel of the LORD said to him, "You should [a]not ask me my name because you cannot comprehend it." [19]Manoah took [a]a young goat and a grain offering and offered them on a rock to the LORD. The LORD's messenger did an amazing thing as Manoah and his wife watched.[1] [20]As the flame went up from the altar toward the sky, the angel of the LORD went up in it while Manoah and his wife watched. They [a]fell facedown to the ground. [21]The angel of [a]the LORD did not appear again to Manoah and his wife. After all this happened Manoah realized that the visitor had been the angel of the LORD. [22]Manoah said to his wife, "[a]We will certainly die because we have seen a supernatural being!" [23]But his wife said to him, "If the LORD wanted to kill us, he would not have accepted the burnt offering and the grain offering from us. He would not have shown us all these things or have spoken to us like this just now."

[24]Manoah's wife gave birth to a son and named him [a]Samson.[1] [b]The child grew and the LORD empowered him. [25a]The LORD's Spirit began to control him in Mahaneh Dan [b]between Zorah and [c]Eshtaol.

Samson's Unconsummated Marriage

14 Samson went down [a]to Timnah, where a Philistine girl [b]caught his eye. [2]When he got home, he told his father and mother, "A Philistine girl in Timnah has caught my eye. Now [a]get her for my wife." [3]But his father and mother said to him, "Certainly [a]you can find a wife among your relatives or among all our[1] people! You should not have to go and get a wife from the [b]uncircumcised Philistines." But Samson said to his father, "Get her for me because she is the right one for me." [4]Now his [a]father and mother did not realize this was the LORD's doing because he was looking for an opportunity to stir up trouble with the Philistines (for at that time the Philistines were ruling Israel).

[5]Samson[1] went down to Timnah. When he approached[2] the vineyards of Timnah, he saw a roaring young lion attacking him. [6]The LORD's Spirit empowered him, and [a]he tore the lion in two with his bare hands as easily as one would tear a young goat. But he did not tell his father or mother what he had done.

[7]Samson continued on down to Timnah and spoke to the girl. In his opinion, she was just the right one. [8]Sometime later, when he went back to marry her, he turned aside to see the lion's remains. He saw a swarm of bees in the lion's carcass, as well as some honey. [9]He scooped it up with his hands and ate it as he walked along. When he returned to his father and mother, he offered them some and they ate it. But he did not tell them he had scooped the honey out of the lion's [a]carcass.

[10]Then Samson's father accompanied him to Timnah for the marriage. Samson hosted a party there, for this was customary for bridegrooms to do. [11]When the Philistines saw he had no attendants, they gave him 30 groomsmen who kept him company.[1] [12]Samson said to them, "I will [a]give you a riddle. If you really can solve [b]it during the seven days the party lasts, I will give you 30 linen robes and 30 [c]sets of clothes. [13]But if you cannot solve it, you will give me 30 linen robes and 30 sets of clothes." They said to him, "Let us hear your [a]riddle." [14]He said to them,

"Out of the one who eats came
    something to eat;
out of the strong one came
    something sweet."

They could not solve the riddle for three days.

13:18 [a]Gen 32:29   13:19 [a]Judg 6:19–21 [1]Heb. *Doing an extraordinary deed while Manoah and his wife were watching.*
13:20 [a]Lev 9:24; 1 Chr 21:16; Ezek 1:28; Matt 17:6   13:21 [a]Judg 6:22   13:22 [a]Gen 32:30; Exod 33:20; Deut 5:26; Judg 6:22–23   13:24 [a]Heb 11:32 [b]1 Sam 3:19; Luke 1:80 [1]The name "Samson" appears to mean "sun-like" or "solar."
13:25 [a]Judg 3:10; 1 Sam 11:6; Matt 4:1 [b]Josh 15:33; Judg 18:11 [c]Judg 16:31   14:1 [a]Gen 38:13; Josh 15:10, 57 [b]Gen 34:2
14:2 [a]Gen 21:21   14:3 [a]Gen 24:3–4 [b]Gen 34:14; Exod 34:16; Deut 7:3 [1]Heb. *my.*   14:4 [a]Deut 28:48; Judg 13:1
14:5 [1]Heb. adds *and his father and his mother.* [2]MT *they approached.*   14:6 [a]Judg 3:10   14:9 [a]Lev 11:27
14:11 [1]Heb. *When they saw him, they gave him thirty companions and they were with him.*
14:12 [a]1 Kgs 10:1; Ezek 17:2 [b]Gen 29:27 [c]Gen 45:22; 2 Kgs 5:22   14:13 [a]Ezek 17:2

[15]On the fourth[1] day they said to Samson's bride, "[a]Trick your husband into giving the solution to the riddle. If you refuse, we will burn up you and your father's family. Did you invite us here to make us [b]poor?" [16]So Samson's bride cried on his shoulder and said, "[a]You must hate me; you do not love me! You told the young men a riddle, but you have not told me the solution." He said to her, "Look, I have not even told my father or mother. Do you really expect me to tell you?" [17]She cried on his shoulder until the party was almost over.[1] Finally, on the seventh day, he told her because she had nagged him so much. Then she told the young men the solution to the riddle. [18]On the seventh day, before the sun set, the men of the city said to him,

> "What is sweeter than honey?
> What is stronger than a lion?"

He said to them,

> "If you had not plowed with my heifer,
> you would not have solved my riddle!"

[19]The LORD's Spirit empowered him. [a]He went down to Ashkelon and killed 30 men. He took their clothes and gave them to the men who had solved the riddle. He was furious as he went back home. [20]Samson's bride [a]was then given to [b]his best man.

Samson Versus the Philistines

15 Sometime later, during the wheat harvest, Samson took a [a]young goat as a gift and went to visit his bride. He said to her father, "I want to sleep with[1] my bride in her bedroom!"[2] But her father would not let him enter. [2]Her father said, "I really thought[1] you [a]absolutely despised[2] her, so I gave her to your best man. Her younger sister is more attractive than she is. Take her instead!" [3]Samson said to them,[1] "This time I am justified in doing the Philistines harm!" [4]Samson went and captured 300 jackals and got some

torches. He tied the jackals in pairs by their tails and then tied a torch to each pair. [5]He lit the torches and set the jackals loose in the Philistines' standing grain. He burned up the grain heaps and the standing grain, as well as the vineyards and olive groves. [6]The Philistines asked, "Who did this?" They were told, "[a]Samson, the Timnite's son-in-law, because the Timnite took Samson's bride and gave her to his best man." So the Philistines went up and burned her and her father. [7]Samson said to them, "Because you did this, I will get revenge against you before I quit fighting." [8]He struck them down and defeated them.[1] Then he went down and lived for a time in the cave in the cliff of [a]Etam.

[9]The Philistines went up and invaded Judah. They arrayed themselves for battle[1] [a]in Lehi. [10]The men of Judah said, "Why are you attacking us?" The Philistines said, "We have come up to take Samson prisoner so we can do to him what he has done to us." [11]So 3,000 men of Judah went down to the cave in the cliff of Etam and said to Samson, "Do you not know that the Philistines [a]rule over us? Why have you done this to us?" He said to them, "I have only done to them what they have done to me." [12]They said to him, "We have come down to take you prisoner so we can hand you over to the Philistines." Samson said to them, "Promise me you will not kill me." [13]They said to him, "We promise! We will only take you prisoner and hand you over to them. We promise not to kill you." They tied him up with two brand [a]new ropes and led him up from the cliff. [14]When [a]he arrived in Lehi, the Philistines shouted as they approached him. But the LORD's Spirit empowered him. The ropes around his arms were like flax dissolving in fire, and they melted away from his hands. [15]He happened to see a solid jawbone of a donkey. He grabbed it and struck [a]down 1,000 men. [16]Samson then said,

> "With the jawbone of a donkey
> I have left them in heaps;[1]
> with the jawbone of a donkey
> I have struck down a thousand men!"

14:15 [a] Judg 16:5 [b] Judg 15:6 [1] MT *seventh.* 14:16 [a] Judg 16:15 14:17 [1] Heb. *the seven days* [during] *which they held the party.* 14:19 [a] Judg 3:10; 13:25 14:20 [a] Judg 15:2 [b] John 3:29 15:1 [a] Gen 38:17 [1] Heb. *I want to approach*; a euphemism for sexual relations. [2] Heb. *I will go to my wife in the bedroom.* 15:2 [a] Judg 14:20 [1] Heb. *saying, I said*; an emphatic Heb. construction. [2] Heb. *hating, you hated*; an emphatic Heb. construction. 15:3 [1] LXX *him.* 15:6 [a] Judg 14:15 15:8 [a] 2 Chr 11:6 [1] Heb. *He struck them, calf on thigh,* [with] *a great slaughter.* 15:9 [a] Judg 15:19 [1] Or *spread out.* 15:11 [a] Lev 26:25; Deut 28:43; Judg 13:1; 14:4; Ps 106:40–42 15:13 [a] Judg 16:11–12 15:14 [a] Judg 3:10; 14:6 15:15 [a] Lev 26:8; Josh 23:10; Judg 3:31 15:16 [1] Or perhaps *I have made donkeys of them, I have thoroughly skinned them, I have stormed mightily against them.*

[17]When he finished speaking, he threw the jawbone down and named that place Ramath Lehi.

[18]He was very thirsty, so he cried out to the LORD and said, "[a]You have given your servant this great victory. But now must I die of thirst and fall into the hands of these uncircumcised Philistines?" [19]So God split open the basin[1] at Lehi, and water flowed out from it. When he took a drink, [a]his strength was restored and he revived. For this reason he named the spring En Hakkore. It remains in Lehi to this very day. [20][a]Samson led Israel for [b]20 years [c]during the days of Philistine prominence.

Samson's Downfall

16 Samson went to [a]Gaza. There he saw a prostitute and slept with her.[1] [2]The Gazites were told,[1] "Samson has come here!" So they [a]surrounded the town and hid all night at the city gate, waiting for him to leave. They relaxed all night, thinking, "He will not leave until morning comes; then we will kill him!" [3]Samson spent half the night with the prostitute; then he got up in the middle of the night and left. He grabbed the doors of the city gate, as well as the two posts, and pulled them right off, bar and all. He put them on his shoulders and carried them up to the top of a hill east of Hebron.

[4]After this Samson fell in love with a woman named Delilah, who lived in the Sorek Valley. [5]The [a]rulers of the Philistines went up to visit her and said to her, "[b]Trick him! Find out what makes him so strong and how we can subdue him and humiliate him. Each one of us will give you 1,100 silver pieces."

[6]So Delilah said to Samson, "Tell me what makes you so strong and how you can be subdued and humiliated." [7]Samson said to her, "If they tie me up with seven fresh bowstrings that have not been dried, I will become weak and be just like any other man." [8]So the rulers of the Philistines brought her seven fresh bowstrings that had not been dried, and she tied him up with them. [9]They hid[1] in the bedroom and then she said to him, "The Philistines are here, Samson!" He snapped the bowstrings as easily as a thread of yarn snaps when it is put close to fire. The secret of his strength was not discovered.

[10]Delilah said to Samson, "Look, you deceived me and told me lies! Now tell me how you can be subdued." [11]He said to her, "If they tie me tightly with brand [a]new ropes that have never been used, I will become weak and be just like any other man." [12]So Delilah took new ropes and tied him with them and said to him, "The Philistines are here, Samson!" (The Philistines were hiding in the bedroom.) But he tore the ropes from his arms as if they were a piece of thread.

[13]Delilah said to Samson, "Up to now you have deceived me and told me lies. Tell me how you can be subdued." He said to her, "If you weave the seven braids of my hair[1] into the fabric on the loom[2] and secure it with the pin, I will become weak and be like any other man." [14]So she made him go to sleep, wove the seven braids of his hair into the fabric on the loom, fastened it with the pin, and said to him, "The Philistines are here, Samson!"[1] He woke up and tore away the pin of the loom and the fabric.

[15]She said to him, "[a]How can you say, 'I love you,' when you will not share your secret with me? Three times you have deceived me and have not told me what makes you so strong." [16]She nagged him every day and pressured him until he was sick to death of it. [17]Finally he [a]told her his secret. He said to her, "My hair has [b]never been cut, for I have been dedicated to God[1] from the time I was conceived. If my head were shaved, my strength would leave me; I would become weak and be just like all other men." [18]When Delilah saw that he had told her his secret, she sent for the rulers of the Philistines, saying, "Come up here again, for he has told me[1] his secret." So the rulers of the Philistines went up to visit her, bringing the silver in their hands. [19]She made him go to sleep on her lap[1] and [a]then called a man in to shave off the seven braids

15:18 [a]Ps 3:7   15:19 [a]Gen 45:27; Isa 40:29   [1]A circular-shaped depression in the land's surface.   15:20 [a]Judg 10:2; 12:7–14   [b]Judg 16:31   [c]Judg 13:1   16:1 [a]Josh 15:47   [1]Heb. *approached her*; a euphemism for sexual relations.   16:2 [a]1 Sam 23:26; Ps 118:10–12   [1]Heb. *To the Gazites, saying.*   16:5 [a]Josh 13:3   [b]Judg 14:15   16:9 [1]Heb. *And the ones lying in wait were sitting for her.*   16:11 [a]Judg 15:13   16:13 [1]Heb. *head.*   [2]Heb. *with the web.*   16:14 [1]MT vv. 13b–14a *He said to her, 'If you weave the seven braids of my head with the web.' And she fastened with the pin and said to him.*   16:15 [a]Judg 14:16   16:17 [a][Mic 7:5]   [b]Num 6:5; Judg 13:5   [1]Or *set apart to God*; trad. *Nazirite.*   16:18 [1]Ket. *her.*   16:19 [a]Prov 7:26–27   [1]Heb. *on her knees*; probably a euphemism for sexual intercourse.

of his hair.[2] She made him vulnerable[3] and his strength left him. [20]She said, "The Philistines are here, Samson!" He woke up and thought, "I will do as I did before and shake myself free." But he did not realize that the LORD [a]had left him. [21]The Philistines captured him and gouged out his [a]eyes. They brought him down to Gaza and bound him in bronze chains. He became a grinder in the prison. [22]His hair began to grow back after it had been shaved off.

Samson's Death and Burial

[23]The rulers of the Philistines gathered to offer a great sacrifice to [a]Dagon their god and to celebrate. They said, "Our god has handed Samson, our enemy, over to us." [24]When the people saw him,[1] they [a]praised their god, saying, "Our god has handed our enemy over to us, the one who ruined our land and killed so many of us!"

[25]When they really started [a]celebrating, they said, "Call for Samson so he can entertain us!" So they summoned Samson from the prison and he entertained them. They made him stand between two pillars. [26]Samson said to the young man who held his hand, "Position me so I can touch the pillars that support the temple. Then I can lean on them." [27]Now the temple was filled with men and women, and all the rulers of the Philistines were there. There were 3,000 men and women on the [a]roof watching Samson entertain. [28]Samson called to the LORD, "O Sovereign LORD,[1] [a]remember me! Strengthen me just one more time, O God, so I can get swift revenge against the Philistines for my two eyes!" [29]Samson took hold of the two middle pillars that supported the temple and he leaned against them, with his right hand on one and his left hand on the other. [30]Samson said, "Let me die with the Philistines!" He pushed hard, and the temple collapsed on the rulers and all the people in it. He killed many more people in his death than he had killed during his life. [31]His brothers and all his family went down and brought him back. They [a]buried him between Zorah and Eshtaol in the tomb of Manoah his father. He had led Israel for [b]20 years.

Micah Makes His Own Religion

17 There was [a]a man named Micah from the Ephraimite hill country. [2]He said to his mother, "You know the 1,100 pieces of silver which were stolen from you, about which I heard you pronounce [a]a curse? Look here, I have the silver. I stole it, but now I am giving it back to you." His mother said, "May the LORD reward you, my son!" [3]When he gave back to his mother the 1,100 pieces of silver, his mother said, "I solemnly dedicate[1] this silver to the LORD. It will be for my son's benefit. We will use it to [a]make a carved image and a metal image." [4]When he gave the silver back to his mother, she [a]took 200 pieces of silver to a silversmith, who made them into a carved image and a metal image. She then put them in Micah's house. [5]Now this man Micah owned a [a]shrine. He made an [b]ephod and some personal idols and hired one of his sons to serve as a priest. [6]In those days Israel had no [a]king. Each [b]man did what he considered to be right.

Micah Hires a Professional

[7]There was a young man from [a]Bethlehem in Judah. He [b]was a Levite who had been temporarily residing among the tribe of Judah. [8]This man left the town of Bethlehem in Judah to find another place to live. He came to the Ephraimite hill country and made his way to Micah's house. [9]Micah said to him, "Where do you come from?" He replied, "I am a Levite from Bethlehem in Judah. I am looking for a new place to live." [10]Micah said to him, "Stay with me. [a]Become my [b]adviser[1] and priest. I will give you 10 pieces of silver per year, plus clothes and food." [11]So the Levite agreed to stay with the man; the young man was like a son to Micah. [12]Micah [a]paid the Levite; the young man [b]became his priest and lived in Micah's house. [13]Micah said, "Now I know the LORD will make me rich because I have this Levite as my [a]priest."

16:19 [2]Heb. *head.* [3]Heb. *She began to humiliate him.*   16:20 [a]Num 14:9, 42, 43; [Josh 7:12]; 1 Sam 16:14; 18:12; 28:15–16; 2 Chr 15:2   16:21 [a]2 Kgs 25:7   16:23 [a]1 Sam 5:2   16:24 [a]Dan 5:4   [1]Perhaps Samson, but more likely an image of Dagon.   16:25 [a]Judg 9:27   16:27 [a]Deut 22:8   16:28 [a]Jer 15:15   [1]Heb. *Lord Yahweh.*   16:31 [a]Judg 13:25   [b]Judg 15:20   17:1 [a]Judg 18:2   17:2 [a]Gen 14:19   17:3 [a]Exod 20:4, 23; 34:17; Lev 19:4   [1]Heb. *dedicating, I dedicate;* an emphatic Heb. construction.   17:4 [a]Isa 46:6   17:5 [a]Judg 18:24   [b]Judg 8:27; 18:14   17:6 [a]Judg 18:1; 19:1   [b]Deut 12:8; Judg 21:25   17:7 [a]Josh 19:15; Judg 19:1; Ruth 1:1–2; Mic 5:2; Matt 2:1, 5, 6   [b]Deut 18:6   17:10 [a]Judg 18:19   [b]Gen 45:8; Job 29:16   [1]Heb. *father;* a title of honor that suggests the priest will give advice.   17:12 [a]Judg 17:5   [b]Judg 18:30   17:13 [a]Judg 18:4

The Tribe of Dan Finds an Inheritance

18 In [a]those days Israel had no king. And in those days [b]the Danite tribe was looking for a place to settle because at that time they did not yet have a place to call their own among the tribes of Israel. [2]The Danites sent out from their whole tribe five representatives, capable men from [a]Zorah and Eshtaol, [b]to spy out the land and explore it. They said to them, "Go, explore the land." They came to the Ephraimite hill country and spent the night at Micah's [c]house. [3]As they approached Micah's house, they recognized the accent[1] of the young Levite. So they stopped there and said to him, "Who brought you here? What are you doing in this place? What is your business here?" [4]He told them what Micah had done for him, saying,[1] "He [a]hired me, and I became his priest." [5]They said to him, "[a]Seek a divine oracle for us, so we can know if we will be successful on our mission." [6]The priest said to them, "[a]Go with confidence. The LORD will be with you on your mission."

[7]So the five men journeyed on and arrived in [a]Laish. They noticed that the people there were living securely, like the [b]Sidonians do, undisturbed and unsuspecting. No conqueror was troubling them in any way. They lived far from the Sidonians and had no dealings with anyone.[1] [8]When the Danites returned to their tribe in [a]Zorah and Eshtaol, their kinsmen asked them, "How did it go?" [9]They said, "Come [a]on, let's attack them, for[1] we saw their land and it is very good. You seem lethargic, but [b]don't hesitate to invade and conquer the land. [10]When you invade, you will encounter [a]unsuspecting people. The [b]land is wide! God is handing it over to you—a place that lacks nothing on earth!"

[11]So 600 Danites, fully armed, set out from Zorah and Eshtaol. [12]They went up and camped in Kiriath [a]Jearim in Judah. (To this day that place is called Camp of [b]Dan. It is west of Kiriath Jearim.) [13]From [a]there they traveled through the Ephraimite hill country and arrived at Micah's house. [14]The five men who had gone to spy out [a]the land of Laish[1] said to their kinsmen, "Do you realize that inside these houses are an ephod, some personal idols, a carved image, and a metal image? Decide now what you want to do." [15]They stopped there, went inside the young Levite's house (which belonged to Micah), and asked him how he was doing. [16]Meanwhile the [a]600 Danites, fully armed, stood at the entrance to the gate. [17]The five men who had gone to spy out [a]the land broke in and stole [b]the carved image, the ephod, the personal idols, and the metal image, while the priest was standing at the entrance to the gate with the 600 fully armed men. [18]When these men broke into Micah's house and stole the carved image, the ephod, the personal idols, and the metal image, the priest said to them, "What are you doing?" [19]They said to him, "Shut up! [a]Put your hand over your mouth and come with us! You can [b]be our adviser and priest. Wouldn't it be better to be a priest for a whole Israelite tribe than for just one man's family?" [20]The priest was happy. He took the ephod, the personal idols, and the carved image and joined the group.

[21]They turned and went on their way, but they walked behind the children, the cattle, and their possessions. [22]After they had gone a good distance from Micah's house, Micah's neighbors gathered together and caught up with the Danites. [23]When they called out to the Danites, the Danites turned around and said to Micah, "[a]Why have you gathered together?" [24]He said, "You stole my gods that I made, as well as this priest, and then went away. What do I have left? How can you have the audacity to say to me, 'What do you want?'" [25]The Danites said to him, "Don't say another word to us, or some very angry men[1] will attack you, and you and your family will die." [26]The Danites went on their way; when Micah realized they were too strong to resist, he turned around and went home.

[27]Now the Danites took what Micah had made, as well as his priest, [a]and came to Laish, where the people were undisturbed and unsuspecting. They struck them down with the sword and burned the city. [28]No one came to the rescue because the city

18:1 [a]Judg 17:6; 19:1; 21:25 [b]Josh 19:40–48   18:2 [a]Judg 13:25 [b]Num 13:17; Josh 2:1 [c]Judg 17:1   18:3 [1]Heb. *voice*.   18:4 [a]Judg 17:10, 12 [1]Heb. *He said to them, 'Such and such Micah has done for me.'*   18:5 [a]1 Kgs 22:5; [Isa 30:1]; Hos 4:12   18:6 [a]1 Kgs 22:6   18:7 [a]Josh 19:47 [b]Judg 10:12 [1]Heb. *and a thing there was not to them with men.*   18:8 [a]Judg 18:2   18:9 [a]Num 13:30; Josh 2:23–24 [b]1 Kgs 22:3 [1]LXX adds *we entered and walked around in the land as far as Laish and.*   18:10 [a]Judg 18:7, 27 [b]Deut 8:9   18:12 [a]Josh 15:60 [b]Judg 13:25   18:13 [a]Judg 18:2   18:14 [a]1 Sam 14:28 [1]LXX omits *of Laish*.   18:16 [a]Judg 18:11   18:17 [a]Judg 18:2, 14 [b]Judg 17:4–5   18:19 [a]Job 21:5; 29:9; 40:4; Mic 7:16 [b]Judg 17:10   18:23 [a]2 Kgs 6:28   18:25 [1]Heb. *bitter in spirit*.   18:27 [a]Josh 19:47

was [a]far from Sidon and they had no dealings with anyone. The city was in a valley near Beth Rehob. The Danites rebuilt the city and occupied it. [29][a]They named it [b]Dan after their ancestor, who was one of Israel's sons. But the city's name used to be Laish. [30]The Danites worshiped the carved image. Jonathan, descendant of Gershom, son of Moses,[1] and his descendants served as priests for the tribe of Dan [a]until the time of the exile. [31]They worshiped Micah's carved image the [a]whole time God's authorized shrine was in Shiloh.

Sodom and Gomorrah Revisited

19 In those days Israel had no king. There was a Levite living temporarily in the remote region of the Ephraimite hill country. [a]He acquired a concubine from [b]Bethlehem in Judah. [2]However, she got angry at him[1] and went home to her father's house in Bethlehem in Judah. When she had been there four months, [3]her husband came after her, hoping he could [a]convince her to return. He brought with him his servant and a pair of donkeys. When she brought him into her father's house and the girl's father saw him, he greeted him warmly. [4]His father-in-law, the girl's father, persuaded him to stay with him for three days, and they ate and drank together, and spent the night there. [5]On the fourth day they woke up early and the Levite got ready to leave. But the girl's father said to his son-in-law, "[a]Have a bite to eat for some energy, then you can go." [6]So the two of them sat down and had a meal together. Then the girl's father said to the man, "Why not stay another night and have a good time?" [7]When the man got ready to leave, his father-in-law convinced him to stay another night. [8]He woke up early in the morning on the fifth day so he could leave, but the girl's father said, "Get some energy! Wait until later in the day to leave." So they ate a meal together. [9]When the man got ready to leave with his concubine and his servant, his father-in-law, the girl's father, said to him, "Look! The day is almost over. Stay another night! Since the day is over, stay another night here and have a good time. You can get up early tomorrow and start your trip home." [10]But the man did not want to stay another night. He left and traveled as far as [a]Jebus (that is, Jerusalem). He had with him a pair of saddled donkeys and his concubine.[1]

[11]When they got near Jebus, it was getting quite late and the servant said to his master, "Come on, let's stop at this Jebusite city and spend the night in it." [12]But his master said [a]to him, "We should not stop at a foreign city where non-Israelites live. We will travel on to Gibeah." [13]He said to his servant, "Come on, we will go into one of the other towns and spend the night in Gibeah or [a]Ramah." [14]So they traveled on, and the sun went down when they were near Gibeah in the territory of Benjamin. [15]They stopped there and decided to spend the night in Gibeah. They came into the city and sat down in the town square, but no one [a]invited them to spend the night.

[16]But then an old man passed by, returning at the end of the day from [a]his work in the field. The man was from the Ephraimite hill country; he was living temporarily in Gibeah. (The residents of the town were Benjaminites.) [17]When he looked up and saw the traveler in the town square, the old man said, "Where are you heading? Where do you come from?" [18]The Levite said to him, "We are traveling from Bethlehem in Judah to [a]the remote region of the Ephraimite hill country. That's where I'm from. I had business in Bethlehem in Judah, but now I'm heading home.[1] But no one has invited me into their home. [19]We have enough straw and grain for our donkeys, and there is enough food and wine for me, your female servant, and the young man who is with your servants.[1] We lack nothing." [20]The old man said, "Everything is just [a]fine. I will take care of all your needs. But don't spend the night in the town square." [21][a]So he brought him to his house [b]and fed the donkeys. They washed their feet and had a meal.

[22]They were having a good [a]time, when suddenly some men of the city, some [b]good-for-nothings,[1] surrounded the house

---

18:28 [a]Judg 18:7   18:29 [a]Josh 19:47   [b]Judg 20:1; 1 Kgs 12:29–30; 15:20   18:30 [a]2 Kgs 15:29   [1]Sev. mss *Manasseh.*
18:31 [a]Deut 12:1–32; Josh 18:1, 8; Judg 19:18; 21:12   19:1 [a]Judg 17:6; 18:1; 21:25   [b]Judg 17:7; Ruth 1:1   19:2 [1]Or *was unfaithful to him.*   19:3 [a]Gen 34:3; 50:21   19:5 [a]Gen 18:5; Judg 19:8; Ps 104:15   19:10 [a]Josh 18:28; 1 Chr 11:4–5   [1]Some wss add *and his servant.*   19:12 [a]Josh 18:28   19:13 [a]Josh 18:25   19:15 [a]Matt 25:43   19:16 [a]Ps 104:23   19:18 [a]Josh 18:1; Judg 18:31; 20:18;
1 Sam 1:3, 7   [1]Heb. *I went to Bethlehem in Judah, but* [to] *the house of the LORD I am going.*   19:19 [1]Some wss *servant.*
19:20 [a]Gen 43:23; Judg 6:23; 1 Sam 25:6   19:21 [a]Gen 24:32; 43:24   [b]Gen 18:4; John 13:5   19:22 [a]Judg 16:25; 19:6, 9
[b]Deut 13:13; 1 Sam 2:12; 1 Kgs 21:10; [2 Cor 6:15]   [1]Heb. *the men of the city, men, the sons of wickedness.*

and kept beating on the door. They said to the old man who owned the house, "Send out the man who came to visit you so we can take carnal knowledge of him."[2] [23]The man who owned [a]the house went outside and said to them, "No, my brothers! [b]Don't do this wicked thing! After all, this man is a guest in my house. Don't do such a disgraceful thing! [24][a]Here are my virgin daughter and my guest's concubine. I will send them out, and you can [b]abuse them and do to them whatever you like. But don't do such a disgraceful thing to this man!" [25]The men refused to listen to him, so the Levite grabbed his concubine and made her go outside. They [a]raped her and abused her all night long until morning. They let her go at dawn. [26]The woman arrived back at daybreak and was sprawled out on the doorstep of the house where her master[1] was staying until it became light. [27]When her master[1] got up in the morning, opened the doors of the house, and went outside to start on his journey, there was the woman, his concubine, sprawled out on the doorstep of the house with her hands on the threshold. [28]He said to [a]her, "Get up, let's leave." But there was no response. He put her on the donkey and went home. [29]When he got home, he took a knife, grasped his concubine, and [a]carved her up into twelve pieces. Then he sent the pieces throughout Israel. [30]Everyone who saw the sight said, "Nothing like this has happened or been witnessed during the entire time since the Israelites left the land of Egypt![1] Take careful note of it! [a]Discuss it and speak!"

Civil War Breaks out

20 [a]All the Israelites from [b]Dan to Beer [c]Sheba and from the land of Gilead left their homes and assembled together before the LORD [d]at Mizpah. [2]The leaders[1] of all the people from all the tribes of Israel took their places in the assembly of God's people, which numbered 400,000 sword-wielding foot soldiers. [3]The Benjaminites heard that the Israelites had gone up to Mizpah. Then the Israelites said, "Explain how this wicked thing happened!" [4]The [a]Levite, the husband of the murdered woman, spoke up, "I and my concubine stopped in Gibeah in the territory of Benjamin to spend the night. [5]The leaders of Gibeah attacked me [a]and at night surrounded the house where I was staying. They wanted to kill me; instead they abused my concubine so badly that she died. [6]I took hold of my [a]concubine and carved her up and sent the pieces throughout the territory occupied by Israel because they [b]committed such an unthinkable atrocity in Israel. [7]All you Israelites, [a]make a decision here!"

[8]All Israel rose up in unison and said, "Not one of us will go home! Not one of us will return to his house! [9]Now this is what we will do to Gibeah: We will [a]attack the city as the lot dictates.[1] [10]We will take ten of every group of a hundred men from all the tribes of Israel (and a hundred of every group of a thousand, and a thousand of every group of ten thousand) to get supplies for the army. When they arrive in Gibeah of Benjamin, they will punish them for the atrocity that they committed in Israel."[1] So all the men of Israel gathered together at the city as allies.

[12]The tribes of Israel sent men throughout [a]the tribe[1] of Benjamin, saying, "How could such a wicked thing take place? [13]Now, hand over [a]the good-for-nothings in Gibeah, so we can execute them and [b]purge Israel of wickedness." But the Benjaminites refused to listen to their Israelite brothers. [14]The Benjaminites came from their cities and assembled at Gibeah to make war against the Israelites. [15]That day [a]the Benjaminites mustered from their cities 26,000 sword-wielding soldiers, besides 700 well-trained soldiers from Gibeah. [16]Among this army were 700 specially trained [a]left-handed soldiers.[1] Each one could sling a stone and hit

---

19:22 [2] Heb. *know*; a euphemism for sexual relations. **19:23** [a] Gen 19:6–7 [b] Gen 34:7; Deut 22:21; Judg 20:6, 10; 2 Sam 13:12 **19:24** [a] Gen 19:8 [b] Gen 34:2; Deut 21:14 **19:25** [a] Gen 4:1 **19:26** [1] The Heb. is a pl. of degree and emphasizes the Levite's absolute sovereignty over the woman. **19:27** [1] The Heb. is a pl. of degree and emphasizes the Levite's absolute sovereignty over the woman. **19:28** [a] Judg 20:5 **19:29** [a] Judg 20:6; 1 Sam 11:7 **19:30** [a] Judg 20:7; Prov 13:10 [1] LXX adds *And he instructed the men whom he sent out, 'Thus you will say to every male Israelite: "There has never been anything like this from the day the Israelites left Egypt till the present day."'* **20:1** [a] Josh 22:12; Judg 20:11; 21:5 [b] Judg 18:29; 1 Sam 3:20; 2 Sam 3:10; 24:2 [c] Josh 19:2 [d] Judg 10:17; 1 Sam 7:5 **20:2** [1] Heb. *the cornerstones, the supports.* **20:4** [a] Judg 19:15 **20:5** [a] Judg 19:22 **20:6** [a] Judg 19:29 [b] Josh 7:15 **20:7** [a] Judg 19:30 **20:9** [a] Judg 1:3 [1] Heb. *against her by lot.* **20:10** [1] Heb. *to do at their arrival in Geba of Benjamin according to all the disgraceful* [thing] *which he* [collective = Benjamin] *did in Israel.* **20:12** [a] Deut 13:14; Josh 22:13, 16 [1] MT *tribes.* **20:13** [a] Deut 13:13; Judg 19:22 [b] Deut 17:12; 1 Cor 5:13 **20:15** [a] Num 1:36–37; 2:23; 26:41 **20:16** [a] Judg 3:15; 1 Chr 12:2 [1] Heb. *700 choice men, bound/restricted in the right hand.*

even the smallest target. [17]The men of Israel (not counting Benjamin) had mustered 400,000 sword-wielding soldiers, every one an experienced warrior.

[18]The Israelites [a]went up to Bethel and [b]asked God, "Who should lead the charge against the Benjaminites?" The LORD said, "[c]Judah should lead." [19]The Israelites got up the next morning and moved against Gibeah. [20]The men of Israel marched out to fight Benjamin; they arranged their battle lines against Gibeah. [21]The Benjaminites attacked from Gibeah and struck down 22,000 Israelites that day.

[22]The Israelite army took heart and once more arranged their battle lines, in the same place where they had taken their positions the day before. [23]The Israelites went up and wept before [a]the LORD until evening. They asked the LORD, "Should we again march out to fight the Benjaminites, our brothers?" The LORD said, "Attack them." [24]So the Israelites marched toward the Benjaminites the next day. [25]The [a]Benjaminites again attacked them from Gibeah and struck down 18,000 sword-wielding Israelite soldiers.

[26]So all the Israelites, the whole army, [a]went up to Bethel. They wept and sat there before the LORD; they did not eat anything that day until evening. They offered up burnt sacrifices and tokens of peace to the LORD. [27]The Israelites asked [a]the LORD (for the ark of God's covenant was there in those days; [28]Phinehas son of Eleazar, son of Aaron, was serving the LORD in those days), "Should we once more march out to fight the Benjaminites our brothers, or should we quit?" The LORD said, "Attack, for tomorrow I will [a]hand them over [b]to you."

[29]So Israel [a]hid men in ambush outside Gibeah. [30]The Israelites attacked the Benjaminites the next day; they took their positions against Gibeah just as they had done before. [31]The Benjaminites attacked the army, leaving the city unguarded. They began to strike down their enemy just as they had done before. On the main roads ([a]one leads to Bethel, the other to Gibeah) and in the field, they struck down about 30 Israelites. [32]Then the Benjaminites said, "They are defeated just as before." But the Israelites said, "Let's retreat and lure them away from the city into the main roads." [33]All the men of Israel got up from their places and took their positions at Baal Tamar, while the Israelites hiding in ambush jumped out of their places west of Gibeah. [34]Then 10,000 men, well-trained soldiers from all Israel, made a frontal assault against Gibeah; the battle was fierce. [a]But the Benjaminites did not realize that disaster was at their doorstep. [35]The LORD annihilated Benjamin before Israel; the Israelites struck down that day 25,100 sword-wielding Benjaminites. [36]Then [a]the Benjaminites saw they were defeated.

The Israelites retreated before Benjamin because they had confidence in the men they had hidden in ambush outside Gibeah. [37]The men hiding in ambush made [a]a mad dash to Gibeah. They attacked and put the sword to the entire city. [38]The Israelites and the men hiding in ambush had arranged a signal. When the men hiding in ambush sent up a [a]smoke signal from the city, [39]the Israelites counterattacked. Benjamin had begun to strike down the Israelites; they struck down about 30 men. They said, "There's no doubt about it! They are totally defeated as in the earlier battle." [40]But when the signal, a pillar of smoke, began to rise up from the city, the Benjaminites [a]turned around and saw the whole city going up in a cloud of smoke that rose high into the sky. [41]When the Israelites turned around, the Benjaminites panicked because they could see that disaster was on their doorstep. [42]They retreated before the Israelites, taking the road to the wilderness. But the battle overtook them as men from the surrounding cities struck them down. [43]They surrounded the Benjaminites, chased them from Nohah,[1] and annihilated them all the way to a spot east of Geba.[2] [44]So 18,000 Benjaminites, all of them capable warriors, fell dead. [45]The rest turned and ran toward the wilderness, heading toward the cliff of [a]Rimmon. But the Israelites caught[1] 5,000 of them on the main roads. They stayed right on their heels all the way to Gidom and struck down 2,000 more. [46]That day

20:18 [a]Judg 20:23, 26 [b]Num 27:21 [c]Judg 1:1–2   20:23 [a]Judg 20:26–27   20:25 [a]Judg 20:21   20:26 [a]Judg 20:18, 23; 21:2   20:27 [a]Josh 18:1; 1 Sam 1:3; 3:3; 4:3–4   20:28 [a]Num 25:7, 13; Josh 24:33 [b]Deut 10:8; 18:5   20:29 [a]Josh 8:4   20:31 [a]Judg 21:19   20:34 [a]Josh 8:14; Job 21:13; Isa 47:11   20:36 [a]Josh 8:15   20:37 [a]Josh 8:19   20:38 [a]Josh 8:20   20:40 [a]Josh 8:20   20:43 [1]MT *resting place.* [2]Heb. *unto the opposite of Gibeah toward the east.*   20:45 [a]Josh 15:32; 1 Chr 6:77; Zech 14:10 [1]Heb. *gleaned.*

25,000 sword-wielding Benjaminites fell in battle, all of them capable warriors. [47a] But 600 survivors turned and ran away to the wilderness, to the cliff of Rimmon. They stayed there four months. [48] The Israelites returned to the Benjaminite towns and put the sword to them. They wiped out the cities, the animals, and everything they could find. They set fire to every city in their path.

Six Hundred Brides for Six Hundred Brothers

21 The Israelites had taken an oath in Mizpah, saying, "Not one of us will allow his daughter to marry a Benjaminite." [2] So the people came [a] to Bethel and sat there before God until evening, weeping loudly and uncontrollably.[1] [3] They said, "Why, O LORD God of Israel, has this happened in Israel? An entire tribe has disappeared from Israel today!"

[4] The next morning the people got up early and [a] built an altar there. They offered up burnt sacrifices and tokens of peace. [5] The Israelites asked, "Who from all the Israelite tribes has not assembled [a] before the LORD?" They had made a solemn oath that whoever did not assemble before the LORD at Mizpah must certainly be executed. [6] The Israelites regretted what had happened to their brother Benjamin. They said, "Today we cut off an entire tribe from Israel! [7] How can we find wives for those who are left? After all, we took an oath in the LORD's name not to give them our daughters as wives." [8] So they asked, "Who from all the Israelite tribes did not assemble before the LORD at Mizpah?" Now it just so happened no one from [a] Jabesh Gilead had come to the gathering. [9] When they took roll call, they noticed none of the inhabitants of Jabesh Gilead were there. [10] So the assembly sent 12,000 capable warriors against Jabesh Gilead. They commanded them, "[a] Go and kill with your swords the inhabitants of Jabesh Gilead, including the women and little children. [11] Do this: Exterminate every male, as well as every woman who has experienced a man's bed. But spare the lives of any virgins." So they did as instructed.

[12] They found among the inhabitants of Jabesh Gilead 400 young girls who were virgins who had never been intimate with a man in bed. They brought them back to the camp at [a] Shiloh in the land of Canaan. [13] The entire assembly sent messengers to the Benjaminites at the cliff of Rimmon and assured them they would not be harmed. [14] The Benjaminites returned at that time, and the Israelites gave to them the women they had spared from Jabesh Gilead. But there were not enough to go around. [15] The people [a] regretted what had happened to Benjamin because the LORD had weakened[1] the Israelite tribes. [16] The leaders of the assembly said, "How can we find wives for those who are left? After all, the Benjaminite women have been wiped out. [17] The remnant of Benjamin must be preserved. An entire Israelite tribe should not be wiped out.[1] [18] But we can't allow our daughters to marry them, [a] for the Israelites took an oath, saying, 'Whoever gives a woman to a Benjaminite will be destroyed.' [19] However, there is an annual [a] festival to the LORD in [b] Shiloh, which is north of Bethel (east of the main [c] road that goes up from Bethel to Shechem) and south of Lebonah." [20] So they commanded the Benjaminites, "Go hide in the vineyards, [21] and keep your eyes open. When you see the daughters of Shiloh coming out [a] to dance in the celebration, jump out from the vineyards. Each one of you, catch yourself a wife from among the daughters of Shiloh and then go home to the land of Benjamin. [22] When their fathers or brothers come and protest to us,[1] we'll say to them, 'Do us a favor and let them be, for we could not get each one a wife through battle. Don't worry about breaking your oath! You would only be guilty if you had voluntarily given them wives.'"[2]

[23] The Benjaminites did as instructed. They abducted 200 of the dancing girls to be their wives. They went home to their own territory, [a] rebuilt their cities, and settled down. [24] Then the Israelites dispersed from there to their respective tribal and clan territories. Each went from there to his own property. [25] In those days Israel had no [a] king. Each [b] man did what he considered to be right.

20:47 [a] Judg 21:13   21:2 [a] Judg 20:18, 26   [1] Heb. *and they lifted up their voice[s] and wept with great weeping;* an emphatic Heb. construction.   21:4 [a] Deut 12:5; 2 Sam 24:25   21:5 [a] Judg 20:1–3   21:8 [a] 1 Sam 11:1; 31:11   21:10 [a] Num 31:17; Judg 5:23; 1 Sam 11:7   21:12 [a] Josh 18:1; Judg 18:31   21:15 [a] Judg 21:6   [1] Heb. *had made a gaping hole in.*   21:17 [1] Heb. *An inheritance for the remnant belonging to Benjamin, and a tribe from Israel will not be wiped away.*   21:18 [a] Judg 11:35; 21:1   21:19 [a] Lev 23:2   [b] Deut 12:5; Josh 18:1; Judg 18:31; 1 Sam 1:3   [c] Judg 20:31   21:21 [a] Exod 15:20; Judg 11:34; 1 Sam 18:6   21:22 [1] LXX, Vg. *you.*   [2] Heb. *You did not give to them, now you are guilty.*   21:23 [a] Judg 20:48   21:25 [a] Judg 17:6; 18:1; 19:1   [b] Deut 12:8; Judg 17:6

RUTH

Ruth is a cameo story of love, devotion, and redemption set in the dark context of the days of the judges. It is the story of a Moabite woman who forsakes her pagan heritage in order to cling to the people of Israel and to the God of Israel. Because of her faithfulness in a time of national faithlessness, God rewards her by giving her a new husband (Boaz), a son (Obed), and a privileged position in the lineage of David and Christ (she is the great-grandmother of David). *Ruth* is the Hebrew title of this book. This name may be a Moabite modification of the Hebrew word *reuit*, meaning "friendship" or "association." The Septuagint entitles the book *Routh*, the Greek equivalent of the Hebrew name. The Latin title is *Ruth*, a transliteration of *Routh*.

A Family Tragedy: Famine and Death

1 During [a]the time of the judges, there [b]was a famine in the land of Judah. So a man from [c]Bethlehem in Judah went to live as a resident foreigner in the region of [d]Moab, along with his wife and two sons. [2](Now the man's name was Elimelech, his wife was Naomi, and his two sons were Mahlon and Kilion. They were of the clan of [a]Ephrath from Bethlehem in Judah.) They entered the region of Moab and settled there. [3]Sometime later Naomi's husband Elimelech died, so she and her two sons were left alone. [4]Both her sons married Moabite women. (One was named Orpah and the other Ruth.) And they continued to live there about 10 years. [5]Then Naomi's two sons, Mahlon and Kilion, also died. So the woman was left all alone—bereaved of her two children as well as her husband! [6]So she decided to return home from the region of Moab, accompanied by her daughters-in-law, because while she was living in Moab she had heard that the LORD had shown concern [a]for his people, reversing the famine by [b]providing abundant crops.

Ruth Returns with Naomi

[7]Now as she and her two daughters-in-law began to leave the place where she had been living to return to the land of Judah, [8]Naomi said to her two daughters-in-law, "Listen to me! Each of you should return to your [a]mother's home. May the LORD show[1] you the same kind of devotion that you have shown to your deceased husbands and to me. [9]May the LORD enable each of you to find [a]security in the home of a new husband." Then she kissed them goodbye, and they wept loudly. [10]But they said to her, "No! We will return with you to your people."

[11]But Naomi replied, "Go back home, my daughters! There is no reason for you to return to Judah with me. I am no longer capable of giving birth to sons who might become your husbands! [12]Go back home, my daughters! For I am too old to get married again. Even if I thought that there was hope that I could get married tonight and conceive sons, [13]surely you would not want to wait until [a]they were old enough to marry. Surely you would not remain unmarried all that time! No, my daughters, you must not return with me. For my intense suffering is too much for you to bear. For the LORD is afflicting me!"

[14]Again they wept loudly. Then Orpah kissed her mother-in-law goodbye,[1] but Ruth clung [a]tightly to her. [15]So Naomi said, "Look, your sister-in-law is returning to [a]her people and to her god. Follow your sister-in-law [b]back home!" [16]But Ruth replied,

1:1 [a]Judg 2:16–18 [b]Gen 12:10; 26:1; 2 Kgs 8:1 [c]Judg 17:8; Mic 5:2 [d]Gen 19:37   1:2 [a]Gen 35:19; 1 Sam 1:1; 1 Kgs 11:26   1:6 [a]Exod 3:16; 4:31; Jer 29:10; Zeph 2:7; Luke 1:68 [b]Ps 132:15; Matt 6:11   1:8 [a]2 Tim 1:16–18 [1]Ket. [the Lord] will do.   1:9 [a]Ruth 3:1   1:13 [a]Judg 2:15; Job 19:21; Ps 32:4; 38:2   1:14 [a][Prov 17:17] [1]LXX adds *and she returned to her people.*   1:15 [a]Judg 11:24 [b]Josh 1:15

"Stop [a]urging me to abandon [b]you!
For wherever you go, I will go.
Wherever you live, I will live.
Your people will become my people,
and your God will become my God.
17 Wherever you die, I will die—and
[a]there I will be buried.
May the LORD punish me severely if
I do not keep my promise!
Only death will be able to separate
me from you!"

18 When Naomi realized [a]that Ruth was determined to go with her, she stopped trying to dissuade her. 19 So the two of them journeyed together until they arrived in Bethlehem.

Naomi and Ruth Arrive in Bethlehem

When they entered Bethlehem, the [a]whole village was excited about their arrival. The women of the village said, "Can [b]this be Naomi?" 20 But she replied to them, "Don't call me 'Naomi'! Call me 'Mara' because the Sovereign One[1] has treated me very harshly.[2] 21 I left here full, but the LORD has caused me to return [a]empty-handed. Why do you call me 'Naomi,' seeing that the LORD has opposed me,[1] and the Sovereign One has caused me to suffer?" 22 So Naomi returned, accompanied by her Moabite daughter-in-law Ruth, who came back with her from the region of Moab. (Now they arrived in Bethlehem [a]at the beginning of the barley harvest.)

Ruth Works in the Field of Boaz

2 Now Naomi had [a]a relative[1] on her husband's side of the family named [b]Boaz. He was a wealthy, prominent man from the clan of [c]Elimelech. 2 One day Ruth the Moabite said to Naomi, "Let me go to the [a]fields so I can gather grain behind whoever permits me to do so." Naomi replied, "You may go, my daughter." 3 So Ruth went and gathered grain in the fields behind the harvesters. Now she just happened to end up in the portion of the field belonging to Boaz, who was from the clan of Elimelech.

Boaz and Ruth Meet

4 Now at that very moment, Boaz arrived from [a]Bethlehem and greeted [b]the harvesters, "May the LORD be with you!" They replied, "May the LORD bless you!" 5 Boaz asked his servant in charge of the harvesters, "To whom does this young woman belong?" 6 The servant in charge of the harvesters replied, "She's the young Moabite woman [a]who came back with Naomi from the region of Moab. 7 She asked, 'May I follow the harvesters and gather grain among the bundles?' Since she arrived she has been working hard from this morning until now[1]—except for sitting[2] in the resting hut[3] a short time."

8 So Boaz said to Ruth, "Listen carefully, my dear! Do not leave to gather grain in another field. You need not go beyond the limits of this field. You may go along beside my female workers. 9 Take note of the field where the men are harvesting and follow behind with the female workers. I will tell the men to leave you alone.[1] When you are thirsty, you may go to the water jars and drink some of the water the servants draw."

10 Ruth knelt [a]before him with her forehead to the ground and said to him, "Why are you so [b]kind and so attentive to me, even though I am a foreigner?" 11 Boaz replied to her, "I have been given a full report of [a]all that you have done for your mother-in-law following the death of your husband—how you left your father and your mother, as well as your homeland, and came to live among people you did not know previously. 12 May [a]the LORD reward your efforts! May your acts of kindness be repaid fully by the LORD God of Israel, from whom you have sought protection."[1] 13 She said, "You really are being kind to me, sir, for you have reassured and encouraged me, your servant, even [a]though I will never be like one of your servants."

14 Later during the mealtime Boaz said to her, "Come here and have some food! Dip your bread in the vinegar." So she sat down beside the harvesters. Then he handed her some roasted grain. She ate until she [a]was

1:16 [a] 2 Kgs 2:2, 4, 6   [b] Ruth 2:11–12   1:17 [a] 1 Sam 3:17; 2 Sam 19:13; 2 Kgs 6:31   1:18 [a] Acts 21:14   1:19 [a] Matt 21:10   [b] Isa 23:7; Lam 2:15   1:20 [1] Heb. *Shaddai*; trad. *the Almighty*.   [2] Or *caused me to be very bitter*.   1:21 [a] Job 1:21   [1] LXX *humbled me*.   1:22 [a] Ruth 2:23; 2 Sam 21:9   2:1 [a] Ruth 3:2, 12   [b] Ruth 4:21   [c] Ruth 1:2   [1] Ket. *friend*.   2:2 [a] Lev 19:9–10; 23:22; Deut 24:19   2:4 [a] Ruth 1:1   [b] Ps 129:7–8; Luke 1:28; 2 Thess 3:16   2:6 [a] Ruth 1:22   2:7 [1] Heb. *and she came and she stood, from then, the morning, and until now, this, her sitting* [in] *the house a little*; the meaning of this phrase is uncertain.   [2] LXX *she rested*.   [3] LXX *in the field*.   2:9 [1] Heb. *Have I not commanded the servants not to touch* [i.e., harm] *you?*   2:10 [a] 1 Sam 25:23   [b] 1 Sam 1:18   2:11 [a] Ruth 1:14–18   2:12 [a] 1 Sam 24:19; Ps 58:11   [1] Heb. *under whose wings you have sought shelter*.   2:13 [a] 1 Sam 25:41   2:14 [a] Ruth 2:18

full and saved the rest. [15]When she got up to gather grain, Boaz told his male servants, "Let her gather grain even among the bundles. Don't chase her off![1] [16]Make sure you pull out ears of grain for her and drop them so she can gather them up. Don't tell her not to!"[1] [17]So she gathered grain in the field until evening. When she threshed what she had gathered, it came to about 30 pounds of [a]barley.

Ruth Returns to Naomi

[18]She carried it back to town, and her mother-in-law saw[1] how much grain she had gathered. Then Ruth gave her the roasted grain she had saved from mealtime. [19]Her mother-in-law asked her, "Where did you gather grain today? Where did you work? May the one who [a]took notice of you be rewarded!"[1] So Ruth told her mother-in-law with whom she had worked. She said, "The name of the man with whom I worked today is Boaz." [20]Naomi said to her daughter-in-law, "May he be [a]rewarded by the LORD because he[1] [b]has shown loyalty to the living [c]on behalf of the dead!" Then Naomi said to her, "This man is a close relative of ours; he is our guardian."[2] [21]Ruth the Moabite replied, "He even told me, 'You may go along beside my servants until they have finished gathering all my harvest!'"[22]Naomi then said to her daughter-in-law Ruth, "It is good, my daughter, that you should go out to work with his female servants. That way you will not be harmed, which could happen in another field."[1] [23]So Ruth worked beside Boaz's female servants, gathering grain until the end of the barley harvest as well as the wheat harvest. After that she stayed home with her mother-in-law.

Naomi Instructs Ruth

3 At that time, Naomi, her mother-in-law, said to her, "My daughter, I must find [a]a [b]home for you so you will be secure. [2]Now Boaz, with [a]whose female servants you worked, is our close relative. Look, tonight he is winnowing barley at the threshing floor. [3]So bathe yourself, rub on some perfumed [a]oil, and get dressed up. Then go down[1] to the threshing floor. But don't let the man know you're there until he finishes his meal. [4]When he gets ready to go to sleep, take careful notice of the place where he lies down. Then go, uncover his legs,[1] and lie down[2] beside him. He will tell you what you should do." [5]Ruth replied to Naomi, "I will do everything you have told me[1] to do."

Ruth Visits Boaz

[6]So she went down to the threshing floor and did everything her mother-in-law had instructed her to do. [7]When Boaz had finished [a]his meal and was feeling satisfied, he lay down to sleep at the far end of the grain heap. Then Ruth crept up quietly, uncovered his legs,[1] and lay down beside him. [8]In the middle of the night he was startled and turned over. Now he saw a woman lying beside him![1] [9]He said, "Who are you?" She replied, "I am Ruth, your servant. Marry your servant,[1] for you are [a]a [b]guardian of the family interests."[2] [10]He said, "May you be [a]rewarded[1] by the LORD, my dear! This act of devotion is [b]greater than what you did before. For you have not sought to marry one of the young men, whether rich or poor. [11]Now, my dear, don't worry! I intend to do for you everything you propose, for everyone in the village knows that you are a [a]worthy woman.[1] [12]Now yes, it is true

2:15 [1]Heb. *do not humiliate her.*   **2:16** [1]Heb. *do not rebuke her.*   **2:17** [a]Ruth 1:22   **2:18** [1]A few mss, Syr., Vg. *she showed her mother-in-law what she had gathered.*   **2:19** [a]Ruth 2:10; [Ps 41:1]   [1]Or *blessed.*   **2:20** [a]Ruth 3:10; 2 Sam 2:5   [b]Prov 17:17   [c]Ruth 3:9; 4:4, 6   [1]Heb. *Blessed be he to the LORD, who has not abandoned his loyalty*; for a discussion of this complicated text, see *Net Bible, Full Notes Edition.*   [2]Or *redeemer*, a guardian of the family interests who has responsibility for caring for the widows of his deceased kinsmen.   **2:22** [1]Heb. *and they will not harm you in another field.*   **3:1** [a]1 Cor 7:36; 1 Tim 5:8   [b]Ruth 1:9   **3:2** [a]Ruth 2:3, 8   **3:3** [a]2 Sam 14:2   [1]Ket. *then I will go down.*   **3:4** [1]Or perhaps *the place for the feet*; because "foot" is sometimes used as a euphemism for the genitals, some believe Ruth uncovered Boaz's genitals; however, it is more likely that Ruth and Boaz did not have a sexual encounter at the threshing floor and Ruth's actions are instead symbolic and constitute a marriage proposal.   [2]Ket. *then I will lie down.*   **3:5** [1]Ket. omits *me.*   **3:7** [a]Judg 19:6, 9, 22; 2 Sam 13:28; Esth 1:10   [1]Or perhaps *feet*; because "foot" is sometimes used as a euphemism for the genitals, some believe Ruth uncovered Boaz's genitals; however, it is more likely that Ruth and Boaz did not have a sexual encounter at the threshing floor and Ruth's actions are instead symbolic and constitute a marriage proposal.   **3:8** [1]Heb. [at] *his legs*; or perhaps *feet*; because "foot" is sometimes used as a euphemism for the genitals, some believe Ruth uncovered Boaz's genitals; however, it is more likely that Ruth and Boaz did not have a sexual encounter at the threshing floor and Ruth's actions are instead symbolic and constitute a marriage proposal.   **3:9** [a]Ezek 16:8   [b]Ruth 2:20; 3:12   [1]Heb. *and spread your wing* [or *skirt*] *over your servant.*   [2]Or *redeemer*, a guardian of the family interests who has responsibility for caring for the widows of his deceased kinsmen.   **3:10** [a]Ruth 2:20   [b]Ruth 1:8   [1]Or *blessed.*   **3:11** [a]Prov 12:4; 31:10–31   [1]Or *woman of strong character.*

that I am a guardian,[1] but there is another guardian who is a [a]closer relative than I am. [13]Remain here tonight. Then in the morning, if he agrees to marry you,[1] fine, let him do so. But if he does not want to do so, I promise, [a]as surely as the LORD lives, to marry you.[2] Sleep here until morning." [14]So she slept beside him[1] until morning. She woke up while it was still dark.[2] Boaz thought, "No one must know that a woman visited the threshing floor." [15]Then he said, "Hold out the shawl you are wearing and grip it tightly." As she held it tightly, he measured out about 60 pounds[1] of barley into the shawl and put it on her shoulders. Then he[2] went into town, [16]and she returned to her mother-in-law.

Ruth Returns to Naomi

When Ruth returned to her mother-in-law, Naomi asked, "How did things turn out for you, my daughter?" Ruth told her about all the man had done for her. [17]She said, "He gave me these 60 pounds of barley, for he said to me,[1] 'Do not go to your mother-in-law empty-handed.'" [18]Then Naomi said, "Stay put, my daughter, until you know how the matter turns out. For the man will not rest until he has taken care of the matter today."

Boaz Settles the Matter

4 Now Boaz went up to [a]the village gate and sat there. Then along came the guardian[1] whom Boaz had mentioned to Ruth. Boaz said, "Come here, what's-your-name,[2] and sit down." So he came and sat down. [2]Boaz chose 10 of [a]the village leaders and said, "Sit down here!" So they sat down. [3]Then Boaz said to the guardian,[1] "Naomi, who has returned from the region of Moab, is selling the portion of land that belongs to our relative Elimelech. [4]So I am legally informing you:[1] [a]Acquire it before those [b]sitting here and [c]before the leaders of my people. If you want to exercise your right to redeem it, then do so. But if not, then tell me so I will know. For you possess the first option to redeem it; I am next in line after you." He replied, "I will redeem it." [5]Then Boaz said, "When you acquire the field from Naomi, you must also acquire Ruth the Moabite,[1] the wife of our deceased relative, in order [a]to preserve his family name by raising up a descendant who will inherit his property." [6a]The guardian said, "Then I am unable to redeem it, for I would ruin my own inheritance in that case. You may exercise my redemption option, for I am unable to redeem it." [7]([a]Now this used to be the customary way to finalize a transaction involving redemption in Israel: A man would remove his sandal and give it to the other party. This was a legally binding act in Israel.) [8]So the guardian said to Boaz, "You may acquire it," and he removed his sandal.[1] [9]Then Boaz said to the leaders and all the people, "You are witnesses today that I have acquired from Naomi all that belonged to Elimelech, Kilion, and Mahlon. [10]I have also acquired Ruth the Moabite, the wife of Mahlon, as my wife to raise up [a]a descendant who will inherit his property so the name of the deceased might not disappear from among his relatives and from his village. You are witnesses today." [11]All [a]the people who were at the gate and the elders replied, "We are witnesses. May the LORD make the woman who is entering your home like Rachel and Leah, both of whom built [b]up the house of Israel! May you prosper in [c]Ephrathah and become famous[1] in [d]Bethlehem. [12]May your family become like the family of [a]Perez—[b]whom Tamar bore to Judah—through [c]the descendants the LORD gives you by this young woman."

3:12 [a] Ruth 3:9 [1]Or *redeemer*, a guardian of the family interests who has responsibility for caring for the widows of his deceased kinsmen.   3:13 [a] Judg 8:19; Jer 4:2; 12:16 [1]Heb. *if he redeems you.* [2]Heb. *but if he does not want to redeem you, then I will redeem you, I, [as] the LORD lives.*   3:14 [1]Heb. [at] *his legs*; or perhaps *feet*; because "foot" is sometimes used as a euphemism for the genitals, some believe Ruth uncovered Boaz's genitals; however, it is more likely that Ruth and Boaz did not have a sexual encounter at the threshing floor and Ruth's actions are instead symbolic and constitute a marriage proposal. [2]Heb. *and she arose before a man could recognize his companion.*   3:15 [1]Heb. *measured out six of barley and placed upon her.* [2]Sev. MSS, Syr., Vg. *then she went.*   3:17 [1]Ket. omits *me.*   4:1 [a] Ruth 3:12 [1]Or *redeemer*, a guardian of the family interests who has responsibility for caring for the widows of his deceased kinsmen. [2]Lit. *a certain one, such and such*; an idiom used when wishing to be ambiguous.   4:2 [a]1 Kgs 21:8; Prov 31:23   4:3 [1]Or *redeemer*, a guardian of the family interests who has responsibility for caring for the widows of his deceased kinsmen.   4:4 [a] Jer 32:7–8 [b] Gen 23:18 [c] Lev 25:25 [1]Heb. *and I said* [or perhaps, *thought to myself*], '*I will* [or *must*] *uncover your ear, saying*'.   4:5 [a] Gen 38:8; Deut 25:5–6; Ruth 3:13; Matt 22:24 [1]Ket. *I acquire Ruth the Moabitess.*   4:6 [a] Ruth 3:12–13; Job 19:14   4:7 [a] Deut 25:7–10   4:8 [1]LXX adds *and gave it to him.*   4:10 [a] Deut 25:6   4:11 [a] Ps 127:3; 128:3 [b] Gen 29:25–30; Deut 25:9 [c] Gen 35:16–18 [d]1 Sam 16:4–13; Mic 5:2; Matt 2:1–8 [1]Heb. *and call a name.*   4:12 [a]1 Chr 2:4; Matt 1:3 [b] Gen 38:6–29 [c]1 Sam 2:20

A Grandson Is Born to Naomi

[13]So Boaz [a]married Ruth and slept with her. [b]The LORD enabled her to conceive and she gave birth to a son. [14]The village women said to Naomi, "May [a]the LORD be praised because he has not left you without a guardian[1] today! May he become famous in Israel! [15]He will encourage you and provide for you when you are old, for your daughter-in-law, who loves you, has given him birth. She is [a]better to you than seven sons!" [16]Naomi took the child and placed him on her lap; she became his caregiver. [17]The neighbor women gave him [a]a name, saying, "A son has been born to Naomi." They named him Obed. Now he became the father of Jesse—David's father.

Epilogue: Obed in the Genealogy of David

[18a]These are the descendants of [b]Perez: Perez was the father of Hezron, [19]Hezron was the father of Ram, Ram was the father of Amminadab, [20]Amminadab was the father of [a]Nachshon, Nachshon was the father of [b]Salmah, [21]Salmon was the father of Boaz, Boaz was the father of Obed, [22]Obed was the father of Jesse, and Jesse was the father of [a]David.

4:13 [a]Ruth 3:11 [b]Gen 29:31; 33:5; Matt 1:5   4:14 [a]Luke 1:58; [Rom 12:15]   [1]Or *redeemer*; a guardian of the family interests who has responsibility for caring for the widows of his deceased kinsmen.   4:15 [a]1 Sam 1:8   4:17 [a]Luke 1:58   4:18 [a]1 Chr 2:4–5; Matt 1:1–7 [b]Num 26:20–21   4:20 [a]Num 1:7 [b]Matt 1:4   4:22 [a]1 Chr 2:15; Matt 1:6

1 SAMUEL

The Book of 1 Samuel describes the transition of leadership in Israel from judges to kings. Three characters are prominent in the book: Samuel, the last judge and first prophet; Saul, the first king of Israel; and David, the king-elect, anointed but not yet recognized as Saul's successor. The Books of 1–2 Samuel were originally one book in the Hebrew Bible known as the "Book of Samuel" or simply "Samuel." The name *Samuel* has been variously translated "The Name of God," "His Name Is God," "Heard of God," and "Asked of God." The Septuagint divides Samuel into two books even though it is one continuous account. This division artificially breaks up the history of David. The Greek (Septuagint) title is *Bibloi Basileion,* "Books of Kingdoms," referring to the later kingdoms of Israel and Judah. First Samuel is called *Basileion Alpha,* "First Kingdoms." Second Samuel and 1–2 Kings are called "Second, Third, and Fourth Kingdoms." The Latin Vulgate originally called the books of Samuel and Kings *Libri Regum,* "Books of the Kings." Later the Latin Bible combined the Hebrew and Greek titles for the first of these books, calling it *Liber I Samuelis,* the "First Book of Samuel" or simply "First Samuel."

Hannah Is Childless

1 There was a man from Ramathaim Zophim,[1] from the hill[a] country of Ephraim. His name was [b] Elkanah. He was the son of Jeroham, the son of Elihu, the son of Tohu, the son of Zuph, [c] an Ephraimite. [2] He had [a] two wives; the name of the first was Hannah and the name of the second was Peninnah. Peninnah had children, but Hannah had no children. [3] This man would go up from his city [a] year after year[1] [b] to worship and to sacrifice to the LORD of Heaven's Armies at [c] Shiloh. (It was there that the two sons of Eli,[2] Hophni and Phinehas, served as the LORD's priests.) [4] The day came, and Elkanah [a] sacrificed.

(Now he used to give meat portions to his wife Peninnah and to all her sons and daughters. [5] But to Hannah he would give [a] a double portion because he loved Hannah,[1] although[2] the LORD had not enabled her to have children. [6] Her rival used to [a] aggravate her to the point of exasperation, just to irritate her, since the LORD had not enabled her to have children. [7] This is how it would go[1] year after year. As often as she went up to the LORD's house, Peninnah would offend her in that way.)

So she cried and refused to eat. [8] Then her husband Elkanah said to her, "Hannah, why are you crying and why won't you eat? Why are you so upset?[1] Am I not [a] better to you than 10 sons?" [9] So Hannah got up after [a] they had finished eating and drinking in Shiloh.[1,2]

At the time Eli the priest was sitting in his chair by the doorpost of the LORD's sanctuary.[3] [10] As for Hannah, she was very distressed.[1] She prayed to the LORD [a] and was, in fact, weeping.[2] [11] She [a] made a vow saying, "O LORD of Heaven's Armies, if you would truly [b] look[1] on the suffering of your servant,[2] and would [c] keep me in mind and [d] not neglect[3] your servant, and give your

---

1:1 [a] Josh 17:17–18; 24:33 [b] 1 Chr 6:27, 33–38 [c] Ruth 1:2 [1] LXX *a man from Ramathaim, a Zuphite.* 1:2 [a] Deut 21:15–17 1:3 [a] Exod 34:14, 23; Judg 21:19; 1 Sam 1:21; Luke 2:41 [b] Deut 12:5–7; 16:16 [c] Josh 18:1 [1] Heb. *from days to days.* [2] LXX *Eli and his two sons.* 1:4 [a] Deut 12:17–18 1:5 [a] Gen 16:1; 30:1–2 [1] Heb. *because Hannah he loved*; an emphatic Heb. construction. [2] Or *and* [because] *the LORD had closed her womb.* 1:6 [a] Job 24:21 1:7 [1] MT *thus he used to do.* 1:8 [a] Ruth 4:15 [1] Heb. *why is your heart displeased?* 1:9 [a] 1 Sam 3:3 [1] LXX adds *and stood before the Lord.* [2] Heb. *after eating in Shiloh, and after drinking.* [3] The Heb. term often refers to the temple; however, this story happens well before Solomon built the temple. 1:10 [a] Job 7:11 [1] Heb. *she was bitter* [in] *soul.* [2] Heb. *and weeping, she was weeping*; an emphatic Heb. construction. 1:11 [a] Gen 28:20; Num 30:6–11 [b] Ps 25:18 [1] Heb. *looking you look*; an emphatic Heb. construction. [2] Heb. *handmaid.* [3] LXX omits *and not neglect your servant.*

servant a male child, then I will dedicate him to the LORD all the days of his life. His hair will never be cut."[4]

[12]It turned out that she did a great deal of praying before the LORD. Meanwhile Eli was watching her mouth. [13]As for Hannah, she was speaking in her mind. Only her lips were moving; her voice could not be heard. So Eli thought she was a drunkard. [14]Then he[1] said to her, "How much longer do you intend to get drunk? Put away your wine!"[2] [15]But Hannah replied, "Not so, my lord! I am a woman under a great deal of stress.[1] I haven't drunk wine or beer. But I have [a]poured out my soul before the LORD. [16]Don't consider your servant a [a]wicked woman. It's just that, to this point, I have spoken from my deep pain[1] and anguish."[2]

[17]Eli replied, "[a]Go in peace, and may [b]the God of Israel grant the request that you have asked of him." [18]She said, "May I, your servant, find favor in your sight."[1] So the woman [a]went her way and got something to eat.[2] Her face no longer looked sad.[3]

[19]They got up early the next morning. Then they worshiped the LORD and returned to their home at Ramathaim.[1] Elkanah was intimate [a]with his wife Hannah, and the LORD [b]called her to mind. [20]Then Hannah became pregnant.

Hannah Dedicates Samuel to the Lord

In the course of time she gave birth to a son.[1] And she named him Samuel, thinking, "I asked the LORD for him."[2] [21]Then the man Elkanah and all his family [a]went up to make the yearly sacrifice[1] to the LORD and to keep his vow.[2] [22]But Hannah did not go up with them, because she had told her husband, "Not until the boy is weaned. Then I will [a]bring him so that he may appear before the LORD. And he will [b]remain there from then [c]on."

[23]Then her husband [a]Elkanah said to her, "Do what you think best. Stay until you have weaned him. Only may the LORD fulfill his promise."

So the woman stayed and nursed her son until she had weaned him. [24]Then she [a]took him up with her[1] as soon as she had weaned him, along with three bulls,[2] an ephah of flour, and a container of wine. She came to [b]the LORD's house at Shiloh, and the boy was with them.[3] [25]They slaughtered the bull, then [a]brought the boy to Eli.[1] [26]She said, "My lord. Just [a]as surely as you are alive, my lord, I am the woman who previously stood here with you in order to pray to the LORD. [27][a]For this boy I prayed, and the LORD has given me the request that I asked of him. [28]So I also dedicate him to the LORD. For all the days of his life he is dedicated to the LORD." Then he[1] bowed down there in [a]worship to the LORD.

Hannah Exalts the Lord in Prayer

2 Hannah [a]prayed,

"[b]My heart has rejoiced in the LORD;
  [c]my horn has been raised high
    because of the LORD.
I have loudly denounced my
    enemies.
Indeed I [d]rejoice in your deliverance.
2 No one is holy like the LORD!
There is no one other than you!
There is [a]no [b]rock[1] like our God!
3 Don't keep speaking so arrogantly.[1]
Proud talk should not come out of
    your mouth,
  for the LORD is a God who [a]knows;
he[2] evaluates what people do.
4 The bows of warriors are shattered,
  but those who stumbled have taken
    on strength.

1:11 [4]LXX adds *wine and strong drink he will not drink.*   **1:14** [1]LXX *Eli's servant.*   [2]LXX adds *And go away from the Lord's face* (i.e., presence).   **1:15** [a]Job 30:16; Ps 42:4; 62:8; Lam 2:19   [1]Or perhaps *distressed spirit, difficult of breath.*   **1:16** [a]Deut 13:13   [1]Or *lament, complaint.*   [2]Or *provocation, anger.*   **1:17** [a]Judg 18:6; 1 Sam 25:35; 2 Kgs 5:19; Mark 5:34; Luke 7:50   [b]Ps 20:3–5   **1:18** [a]Prov 15:13; Eccl 9:7; Rom 15:13   [1]LXX *Your servant [has] found favor in your sight.*   [2]Sev. MSS omit *and got something to eat*; LXX *went her way. She entered her guest room. She ate with her husband, and drank.*   [3]MT *her face, it did not belong to her any more.*   **1:19** [a]Gen 4:1   [b]Gen 21:1; 30:22   [1]Heb. *Ramah.*   **1:20** [1]MT *It happened at the turning of the days. Hannah conceived. And she gave birth to a son.*   [2]Heb. *because from the LORD I asked him*; the name "Samuel" sounds like the Heb. verb translated as "asked."   **1:21** [a]Deut 12:11; 1 Sam 1:3   [1]Heb. *sacrifice of days.*   [2]LXX adds *and all the tithes of his land.*   **1:22** [a]Luke 2:22   [b]1 Sam 1:11, 28   [c]Exod 21:6   **1:23** [a]Num 30:7, 10, 11   **1:24** [a]Num 15:9–10; Deut 12:5–6   [b]Josh 18:1; 1 Sam 4:3–4   [1]LXX *she went up with him to Shiloh.*   [2]LXX *with a three year old bull and loaves.*   [3]MT *and the boy was a boy.*   **1:25** [a]Luke 2:22   [1]LXX *They brought [him] before the Lord and his father slaughtered the sacrifice which he would bring to the Lord from time to time. And he brought the child and slaughtered the calf. And Hannah, the child's mother, brought him to Eli.*   **1:26** [a]2 Kgs 2:2, 4, 6; 4:30   **1:27** [a][Matt 7:7]   **1:28** [a]Gen 24:26, 52   [1]Some wss *they.*   **2:1** [a]Phil 4:6   [b]1 Sam 2:1–10; Ps 97:11–12; Luke 1:46–55   [c]Ps 75:10; 89:17, 24; 92:10; 112:9   [d]Ps 9:14; 13:5; 35:9; Isa 12:2–3   **2:2** [a]Deut 4:35   [b]Deut 32:4, 30, 31; 2 Sam 22:32; Ps 18:2   [1]A rocky cliff where one can seek refuge from enemies.   **2:3** [a]1 Sam 16:7   [1]Heb. *proudly, proudly*; if intentional, an emphatic Heb. construction.   [2]Ket. *and not.*

5 The well fed hire [a]themselves out to
   earn food,
   but the hungry no longer lack.
   Even the barren woman has given
   birth to seven,
   but the one with many children has
   declined.
6 The LORD both kills and gives life;
   [a]he brings down to the grave and
   raises up.
7 The LORD impoverishes and [a]makes
   wealthy;
   [b]he humbles and he exalts.
8 He lifts [a]the weak from the dust;
   he raises the poor from the ash heap
   [b]to seat them with princes—
   he bestows on them an honored
   position.
   The foundations of the earth belong
   to the LORD—
   he placed the world on them.
9 He [a]watches over his holy ones,[1]
   but the [b]wicked are made speechless
   in the darkness,[2]
   for it is not by one's own strength
   that one prevails.
10 The LORD shatters his adversaries;[1]
   he thunders against them [a]from [b]the
   [c]heavens.
   The LORD executes judgment to the
   ends of the earth.
   He will [d]strengthen his king
   and [e]exalt the power[2] of his anointed
   one."

[11]Then Elkanah went back home to
Ramah.

Eli's Sons Misuse Their Sacred Office

The boy[1] Samuel was serving the LORD
with the favor of[2] Eli the priest.[3] [12]But the
sons of Eli were [a]wicked men. [b]They did not
acknowledge the LORD's authority. [13]This
was the priests' routine with the people.
Whenever anyone was making a sacrifice,[1]
the priest's attendant would come with a
three-pronged fork in his hand, just as the
meat was boiling. [14]He would jab it into the
basin, kettle, cauldron, or pot. Everything
that the fork would bring up the priest
would take for himself. This is how they
used to treat all the Israelites who came
there[1] to [a]Shiloh.

[15]Also, before they [a]burned the fat the
priest's attendant would come and say to
the person who was making the sacrifice,
"Give some meat for the priest to roast! He[1]
won't accept boiled meat from you, but only
raw." [16]If the individual said to him, "They
should certainly burn[1] the fat away first,
then take for yourself[2] whatever you wish,"
then he would say, "No![3] Give it now! If not,
I'll take it by force!"[4] [17]The sin of these young
men[1] was very great in the [a]LORD's sight,
for they[2] [b]treated the LORD's offering with
contempt.

[18a]Now Samuel was ministering with the
favor of the LORD. The boy[1] was [b]dressed in
a linen ephod. [19]His mother used to make
him [a]a small robe and bring it to him from
time to time when she would go up with her
husband to make the annual sacrifice. [20]Eli
[a]would bless Elkanah and his wife saying,
"May the LORD establish descendants for
you from this woman in place of the one
that she [b]dedicated[1] to the LORD." Then
they[2] would go to their home. [21]And indeed
the LORD attended [a]to[1] Hannah. She got
pregnant and gave birth to three sons and
two daughters. But the boy[2] Samuel grew
[b]up before the LORD.[3]
[22]Eli was very old. And [a]he would hear

2:5 [a] Ps 113:9   2:6 [a] Deut 32:39; 2 Kgs 5:7; Job 5:18; [Rev 1:18]   2:7 [a] Deut 8:17–18; Job 1:21   [b] Job 5:11; Ps 75:7; Jas 4:10   2:8 [a] Job
42:10–12; Ps 75:7; 113:7; Luke 1:52   [b] Job 36:7; Ps 113:8   2:9 [a] Ps 37:23–24; 91:11–12; 94:18; 121:3; Prov 3:26; [1 Pet 1:5]   [b] [Rom 3:19]
[1] Ket. one.   [2] LXX granting the prayer to the one who prays; he blessed the years of the righteous.   2:10 [a] 1 Sam 7:10; 2 Sam
22:14–15; Ps 18:13–14   [b] Ps 96:13; 98:9; [Matt 25:31–32]   [c] [Matt 28:18]   [d] Ps 21:1, 7   [e] Ps 89:24   [1] Ket. adversary; LXX adds the
Lord is holy. Let not the wise boast in his wisdom, and let not the strong boast in his strength, and let not the rich boast in
his riches, but let him who boasts boast in this: to understand and know the Lord, and to practice justice and righteousness in
the midst of the land.   [2] Heb. the horn.   2:11 [1] The Heb. word often refers to a servant or apprentice in line for a position of
authority.   [2] Or perhaps under the supervision of; Heb. with [or before] the face of.   [3] This verse varies significantly among the
wss. For details, see the NET Bible, Full Notes Edition.   2:12 [a] Deut 13:13   [b] Judg 2:10; [Rom 1:28]   2:13 [1] LXX As to the right
of the priests from the people, [from] anyone sacrificing.   2:14 [a] 1 Sam 1:3   [1] LXX who came to sacrifice at Shiloh.   2:15 [a] Lev
3:3–5, 16   [1] LXX I.   2:16 [1] LXX the fat should be burned.   [2] LXX adds from any.   [3] Ket. to him.   [4] One Qum. ws adds text
similar to vv. 13–14, in which the priest's servant describes stabbing the trident into the pot to take whatever would come up.
2:17 [a] Gen 6:11   [b] [Mal 2:7–9]   [1] The Heb. word often refers to servants or apprentices in line for a position of authority.   [2] A
few mss omit the men.   2:18 [a] 1 Sam 2:11; 3:1   [b] Exod 28:4   [1] The Heb. word often refers to servants or apprentices in line for
a position of authority.   2:19 [a] 1 Sam 1:3, 21   2:20 [a] Gen 14:19   [b] 1 Sam 1:11, 27, 28   [1] MT in place of the request which he asked
of the LORD; LXX in place of the loan which you lent to the Lord.   [2] LXX the man.   2:21 [a] Gen 21:1   [b] Judg 13:24; 1 Sam 2:26;
3:19–21; Luke 1:80; 2:40   [1] Heb. to take note of.   [2] One Qum. ws omits the boy.   [3] MT with the LORD.   2:22 [a] Exod 38:8

about everything that his sons used to do to all the people of Israel and[1] how they used to go to bed with the women who were stationed at the entrance to the tent of meeting. [23]So he said to them, "Why do you do these things, these evil things that I hear about from all these people?[1] [24]No, my sons! For the report that I hear circulating[1] among the LORD's people is not good. [25]If a man sins against a man, one may appeal to [a]God on his behalf.[1] But if a man [b]sins against the LORD, who can intercede for him?" But Eli's sons would not listen to their father. Indeed the LORD had decided to kill them. [26]However, the boy[1] Samuel was growing [a]up and [b]finding favor both with the LORD and with people.

The Lord Judges the House of Eli

[27]Then a [a]man of God came to Eli and said to him, "This is what the LORD has said: '[b]I plainly[1] revealed[2] myself to your ancestor's house when they were slaves to the house of Pharaoh in Egypt.[3] [28]I [a]chose[1] your ancestor from all the tribes of Israel to be my priest, to offer sacrifice on my altar, to burn incense, and to bear the ephod before me. [b]I gave to your ancestor's house all the fire offerings made by the Israelites. [29]Why are you [a]scorning my sacrifice and my offering that I commanded for my dwelling [b]place?[1] You have honored your sons more than you have [c]me by having made yourselves fat from the best parts of all the offerings of my people Israel.'

[30]"Therefore the LORD, the God of [a]Israel, says, 'I really did say that your house and your ancestor's house would serve me forever.' But now the LORD says, 'May it never [b]be! For I will honor [c]those who honor me, but those who despise me will be cursed! [31]In fact, days are coming when I will remove your strength and [a]the strength of your father's house. There will not be an old man in your house! [32]You will see trouble in my dwelling place! Israel will experience

blessings, but there will not be [a]an old man in your[1] house for all time. [33]Any man of yours that I do not cut off from my altar, I will cause his[1] eyes to fail and will cause him grief. All those born to your family will die by the sword of man.[2] [34]This will be [a]a [b]confirming sign for you that will be fulfilled through your two sons, Hophni and Phinehas: in a single day they both will die! [35]Then [a]I [b]will raise up for [c]myself a faithful priest. He will do what is in my heart and soul. I will build for him a lasting dynasty, and he will serve my chosen one for all time. [36]Everyone who remains in your house will come to bow before him for [a]a little money and for a scrap of bread. Each will say, "Assign me to a priestly task so I can eat a scrap of bread."'"

The Call of Samuel

3 Now [a]the boy Samuel continued serving [b]the LORD under Eli's supervision. Receiving a message from the LORD was rare in those days; revelatory visions were infrequent.

[2]Eli's eyes had begun to fail, [a]so that he was unable to see well. At that time he was lying down in his place, [3]and [a]the lamp of God had not yet been extinguished. Samuel was lying down in the temple of the LORD as well; the ark of God was also there. [4]The LORD called to Samuel, and he replied, "Here I am!" [5]Then he ran to Eli and said, "Here I am, for you called me." But Eli said, "I didn't call you. Go back and lie down." So he went back and lay down. [6]The LORD again called, "Samuel!" So Samuel got up and went to Eli and said, "Here I am, for you called me." But Eli said, "I didn't call you, my son. Go back and lie down."

[7]Now Samuel [a]did not yet know the LORD; the LORD's messages had not yet been revealed to him. [8]Then the LORD called Samuel a third time. So he got up and went to Eli and said, "Here I am, for you called me!" Eli then realized that it was the LORD who was calling the boy. [9]So Eli said

---

2:22[1]LXX omits the latter half of the verse.   **2:23**[1]LXX *from all the people of the Lord.*   **2:24**[1]LXX *the report . . . is not good, so that the people do not serve God.*   **2:25** [a]Deut 1:17; 25:1–2   [b]Num 15:30   [1]LXX *they shall pray for him to the Lord.*   **2:26** [a]1 Sam 2:21   [b]Prov 3:4   [1]The Heb. word often refers to servants or apprentices in line for a position of authority.   **2:27** [a]Deut 33:1; Judg 13:6; 1 Sam 9:6; 1 Kgs 13:1   [b]Exod 4:14–16; 12:1   [1]*Or certainly.*   [2]MT *Did I actually reveal myself . . . ?*   [3]MT omits *slaves.*   **2:28** [a]Exod 28:1, 4; Num 16:5   [b]Lev 2:3, 10; 6:16; 7:7–8, 34, 35; Num 5:9   [1]Heb. *even choosing.*   **2:29** [a]Deut 32:15   [b]Deut 12:5; Ps 26:8   [c]Matt 10:37   [1]LXX *Why did you look at my incense and my sacrifice with a shameless eye?*   **2:30** [a]Exod 29:9; Num 25:13   [b]Jer 18:9–10   [c]Ps 91:14; Mal 2:9–12   **2:31** [a]1 Sam 4:11–18; 22:18–19; 1 Kgs 2:27, 35   **2:32** [a]Zech 8:4   [1]LXX, one Qum. MS *my.*   **2:33**[1]MT *your.*   [2]MT *all the increase of your house will die men.*   **2:34** [a]1 Sam 10:7–9; 1 Kgs 13:3   [b]1 Sam 4:11, 17   **2:35** [a]1 Kgs 2:35; Ezek 44:15; [Heb 2:17; 7:26–28]   [b]2 Sam 7:11, 27; 1 Kgs 11:38   [c]Ps 18:50   **2:36** [a]1 Kgs 2:27   **3:1** [a]1 Sam 2:11, 18   [b]Ps 74:9; Ezek 7:26; Amos 8:11–12   **3:2** [a]Gen 27:1; 48:10; 1 Sam 4:15   **3:3** [a]Exod 27:20–21   **3:7** [a]1 Sam 2:12; Acts 19:2; 1 Cor 13:11

to Samuel, "Go back and lie down. When he calls you, say, '[a]Speak, LORD, for your servant is listening.'" So Samuel went back and lay down in his place.

[10] Then the LORD came and stood nearby, calling as he had previously done, "Samuel! Samuel!" Samuel replied, "Speak, for your servant is listening!" [11] The LORD said to Samuel, "Look! I am about to do something in Israel; when anyone hears about it, both of his ears will tingle. [12] On that day I will carry out against Eli [a]everything that I spoke about his house—from start to finish! [13a] You[1] should tell him that I am about to [b]judge [c]his house forever because of the sin that he knew about. For his sons were cursing God,[2] and he [d]did not rebuke them. [14] Therefore I swore an oath to the house of Eli, 'The sin of the house of Eli can never be forgiven by sacrifice or by grain offering.'"

[15] So Samuel lay down until morning. Then he opened the doors of the LORD's house. But Samuel was afraid to tell Eli about the vision. [16] However, Eli called Samuel and said, "Samuel, my son!" He replied, "Here I am." [17] Eli said, "What message did he speak to you? Don't conceal it from me. [a]God will judge you severely if you conceal from me anything that he said to you!"

[18] So Samuel told him everything. He did not hold back anything from him. Eli said, "The LORD will do what he pleases." [19] Samuel continued to [a]grow, and [b]the LORD was with him. None of his prophecies fell to the ground unfulfilled. [20] All Israel [a]from Dan to Beer Sheba realized that Samuel was confirmed as a prophet of the LORD. [21] Then [a]the LORD again appeared in Shiloh, for it was in Shiloh that the LORD had revealed himself to Samuel[1] through a message from the LORD. [4] [1] Samuel revealed the word of the LORD to all Israel.

The Ark of the Covenant Is Lost to the Philistines

Then the Israelites went out to fight the Philistines. They camped at [a]Ebenezer,[1] and the Philistines camped at Aphek. [2] The [a]Philistines arranged their forces to fight Israel. As the battle spread out,[1] Israel was defeated by the Philistines, who killed about 4,000 men in the battle line in the field.

[3] When the army came back to the camp, the elders of Israel said, "Why did the LORD [a]let us be defeated today by the Philistines? Let's take with us the ark of the covenant of the LORD from Shiloh. When it is with us, it will save us[1] from the hand of our enemies."

[4] So the army sent to Shiloh, and they took from there the ark of the covenant of the LORD of Heaven's Armies, [a]who sits between [b]the cherubim. Now the [c]two sons of Eli, Hophni and Phinehas, were there with the ark of the covenant of God. [5] When the ark of the covenant of the LORD arrived at the camp, all Israel shouted so loudly that the ground shook.

[6] When the Philistines heard the sound of the shout, they said, "What is this loud shout in the camp of the Hebrews?" Then they realized that the ark of the LORD had arrived at the camp. [7] The Philistines were scared because they thought that gods had come to the camp. They said, "[a]Woe to us! We've never seen anything like this! [8] Woe to us! Who can deliver us from the hand of these mighty gods? These are the gods who struck the Egyptians with all sorts of plagues in the desert! [9a] Be strong and act like men, you Philistines, or else you will wind up serving the Hebrews the way they have served you! Act like men and fight!"

[10] So the Philistines fought. [a]Israel was defeated; they all ran home. The slaughter was very great; 30,000 foot soldiers from Israel fell in battle. [11] The ark of God was taken, and [a]the two sons of Eli, Hophni and Phinehas, were killed.

Eli Dies

[12] On that day a Benjaminite ran from the battle lines and [a]came to Shiloh. His clothes were torn, and [b]dirt was on his head. [13] When he [a]arrived in Shiloh, Eli was sitting in his chair on the lookout by the side of the road, for he was very worried about the ark of

3:9 [a] 1 Kgs 2:17   **3:12** [a] 1 Sam 2:27–36; Ezek 12:25; Luke 21:33   **3:13** [a] 1 Sam 2:29–31   [b] 1 Sam 2:22; Ezek 7:3; 18:30   [c] 1 Sam 2:12, 17, 22   [d] 1 Sam 2:23, 25   [1] MT *I will say to him.*   [2] MT *them.*   **3:17** [a] Ruth 1:17   **3:19** [a] 1 Sam 2:21   [b] Gen 21:22; 28:15; 39:2, 21, 23   **3:20** [a] Judg 20:1   **3:21** [a] 1 Sam 3:1, 4   [1] LXX adds *And Samuel was acknowledged to be a prophet of the LORD in all Israel, from one end to the other. Eli was very old and, as for his sons, their way kept getting worse and worse before the LORD.*   **4:1** [a] 1 Sam 7:12   [1] Heb. *the stone, the help.*   **4:2** [a] 1 Sam 12:9   [1] Or perhaps *and it grew fierce.*   **4:3** [a] Num 10:35; Josh 6:6–21   [1] Or perhaps *when he is with us, he will save us.*   **4:4** [a] Exod 25:18–21; 1 Sam 6:2; Ps 80:1   [b] Num 7:89   [c] 1 Sam 2:12   **4:7** [a] Exod 15:14   **4:9** [a] 1 Cor 16:13   **4:10** [a] Lev 26:17; Deut 28:15, 25; 1 Sam 4:2; 2 Sam 18:17; 19:8; 2 Kgs 14:12; 2 Chr 25:22   **4:11** [a] 1 Sam 2:32; Ps 78:60–61   **4:12** [a] 2 Sam 1:2   [b] Josh 7:6; 2 Sam 13:19; 15:32; Neh 9:1; Job 2:12   **4:13** [a] 1 Sam 1:9; 4:18

God. As the man entered the city to give his report, the whole city cried out.

[14]When Eli heard the outcry, he said, "What's this commotion?" The man quickly came and told Eli. [15]Now Eli was ninety-eight years old and [a]his eyes looked straight ahead; he was unable to see.

[16]The man said to Eli, "I am the one who came from the battle lines! Just today I fled from the battle lines!" Eli asked, "How did things go, my son?" [17]The messenger replied, "Israel has fled from the Philistines! The army has suffered a great defeat! Your two sons, Hophni and Phinehas, are dead! The ark of God has been captured!"

[18]When he mentioned the ark of God, Eli fell backward from his chair beside the gate. He broke his neck and died, for he was old and heavy. He had judged Israel for 40 years.

[19]His daughter-in-law, the wife of Phinehas, was pregnant and close to giving birth. When she heard that the ark of God was captured and that her father-in-law and her husband were dead, she doubled over and gave birth. But her labor pains were too much for her. [20]As she was dying, [a]the women who were there with her said, "Don't be afraid! You have given birth to a son!" But she did not reply or pay any attention.

[21]She named the boy [a]Ichabod, saying, "[b]The glory has departed from Israel," referring to the capture of the ark of God and the deaths of her father-in-law and her husband. [22]She said, "The glory has departed from Israel, because the ark of God has been captured."

God Sends Trouble for the Philistines Who Have the Ark

5 Now the Philistines had captured the ark of God and brought it [a]from Ebenezer to Ashdod. [2]The Philistines took the ark of God and brought it into the temple of [a]Dagon, where they positioned it beside Dagon. [3]When the residents of Ashdod got up early the next day,[1] Dagon was [a]lying on the ground before the ark of the Lord. So they took Dagon and [b]set him back in his place. [4]But when [a]they got up early the following day, Dagon was again lying on the ground before the ark of the Lord. The head of Dagon and his two hands were sheared off and were lying at the threshold. Only Dagon's body was left intact.[1] [5](For this reason, to this very day, neither Dagon's priests nor anyone else who enters Dagon's temple [a]steps on Dagon's threshold in Ashdod.)

[6]The [a]Lord attacked the residents of Ashdod severely, bringing devastation [b]on them. He struck the people of both Ashdod and the surrounding [c]area with sores.[1,2] [7]When the people of Ashdod saw what was happening, they said, "The ark of the [a]God of Israel should not remain with us, for he has attacked both us and our god Dagon!"

[8]So they assembled all the [a]leaders of the Philistines and asked, "What should we do with the ark of the God of Israel?" They replied, "The ark of the God of Israel should be moved to [b]Gath." So they moved the ark of the God of Israel.

[9]But after it had been moved [a]the Lord attacked that city as well, causing a great deal of panic. He struck all the people of that city with sores.[1] [10]So they sent the ark of God to Ekron.

But when the ark of God arrived at Ekron, the residents of Ekron cried out saying, "They have brought the ark of the God of Israel here to kill our people!" [11]So they assembled all the leaders of the Philistines and said, "Get the ark of the God of Israel out of here! Let it go back to its own place so that it won't kill us and our people!" The terror of death was throughout the entire city; God was attacking them very severely there. [12]The people who did not die were struck with sores; the city's cry for [a]help went all the way up to heaven.

The Philistines Return the Ark

6 When the ark of the Lord had been in the land of the Philistines for seven months,[1] [2]the Philistines [a]called the priests and the omen readers, saying, "What should we do with the ark of the Lord? Advise us as to how we should send it back to its place." [3]They replied, "If you are going to send

---

4:15 [a]1 Sam 3:2; 1 Kgs 14:4   4:20 [a]Gen 35:16–19   4:21 [a]1 Sam 14:3   [b]Ps 26:8; 78:61; [Jer 2:11]   5:1 [a]1 Sam 4:1; 7:12
5:2 [a]Judg 16:23–30; 1 Chr 10:8–10   5:3 [a]Isa 19:1; 46:1–2   [b]Isa 46:7   [1]LXX adds *they entered the temple of Dagon and saw.*
5:4 [a]Jer 50:2; Ezek 6:4, 6; Mic 1:7   [1]Heb. *only Dagon was left.*   5:5 [a]Zeph 1:9   5:6 [a]Exod 9:3; Deut 2:15; 1 Sam 5:7; 7:13; Ps
32:4; 145:20; 147:6   [b]1 Sam 6:5   [c]Josh 15:46–47   [1]LXX, Vg. add *And mice multiplied in their land, and the terror of death was
throughout the entire city.*   [2]Or *tumors.*   5:7 [a]1 Sam 6:5   5:8 [a]1 Sam 6:4   [b]Josh 11:22   5:9 [a]Deut 2:15; 1 Sam 5:11;
7:13; 12:15   [1]Or *tumors.*   5:12 [a]1 Sam 9:16; Jer 14:2   6:1 [1]LXX adds *and their land swarmed with mice.*
6:2 [a]Gen 41:8; Exod 7:11; Isa 2:6; 47:13; Dan 2:2; 5:7

the ark of the God of Israel back, don't send it away [a] empty. Be sure to return it with [b] a guilt offering. Then you will be healed, and you will understand why his hand has not been removed from you." [4] They inquired, "What is the guilt offering that we should send to him?"

They replied, "The Philistine leaders number five. So send [a] five gold sores and five gold mice, for it is the same plague that has afflicted both you and your leaders. [5] You should make images of the sores and images of the mice that are [a] destroying the land. You should [b] honor the God of Israel. Perhaps he will [c] release his grip on [d] you, your gods, and your land. [6] Why harden your hearts like the Egyptians and Pharaoh [a] did? When God treated them harshly, didn't the Egyptians send the Israelites on their way? [7] So now go and make [a] a new cart. Get two cows that have calves and that have never had a yoke placed on them. Harness the cows to the cart, and take their calves from them back to their stalls. [8] Then take [a] the ark of the LORD and place it on the cart, and put in a chest beside it the gold objects you are sending to him as a guilt offering. You should then send it on its way. [9] But keep an eye on it. If it should go up by the way of its own border to Beth [a] Shemesh, then he has brought this great calamity on us. But if that is not the case, then [b] we will know that it was not his hand that struck us; rather, it just happened to us by accident."

[10] So the men did as instructed. They took two cows that had calves and harnessed the cows to a cart; they also removed their calves to their stalls. [11] They put the ark of the LORD on the cart, along with the chest, the gold mice, and the images of the sores. [12] Then the cows went directly on the road to Beth Shemesh. They went along that route, bellowing more and more; they turned neither to the right nor to the left. The leaders of the Philistines were walking along behind them all the [a] way to the border of Beth Shemesh.

[13] Now the residents of Beth Shemesh were harvesting [a] wheat in the valley. When they looked up and saw the ark, they were pleased at the sight. [14] The cart was coming to the field of Joshua, who was from Beth Shemesh. It paused there near a big stone. Then they cut up the wood of the cart and offered the cows as a burnt offering to the LORD. [15] The Levites took down the ark of the LORD and the chest that was with it, which contained the gold objects. They placed them near the big stone. At that time the people of Beth Shemesh offered burnt offerings and made sacrifices to the LORD. [16] The five leaders of [a] the Philistines watched what was happening and then returned to Ekron on the same day.

[17] These are [a] the gold sores that the Philistines brought as a guilt offering to the LORD—one for each of the following cities: Ashdod, Gaza, Ashkelon, [b] Gath, and Ekron. [18] The gold mice corresponded in number to all the Philistine cities of the five leaders, from the fortified cities to hamlet villages, to greater Abel.[1] They positioned the ark of the LORD on a rock until this very day in the field of Joshua who was from Beth Shemesh.

[19] But [a] the LORD struck down some of the people of Beth Shemesh because they had looked into the ark of the LORD; he struck down 50,070[1] of the men. The people grieved because the LORD had [b] struck the people with a hard blow. [20] The residents of Beth Shemesh asked, "[a] Who is able to stand before the LORD, this holy God? To whom will the ark go up from here?"

[21] So they sent messengers to the residents of Kiriath [a] Jearim, saying, "The Philistines have returned the ark of the LORD. Come down here and take it back home with you."

7 Then the people of Kiriath [a] Jearim came and took the ark of the LORD; they brought it to the house of [b] Abinadab located on the hill. They [c] consecrated Eleazar his son to guard the ark of the LORD.

Further Conflict with the Philistines

[2] It was quite a long time—some 20 years in all—that the ark stayed at Kiriath Jearim. All the people of Israel longed for the LORD. [3] Samuel said to all the people of Israel, "If

6:3 [a] Exod 23:15; Deut 16:16   [b] Lev 5:15–16   [1] LXX, one Qum. MS add *the covenant of the LORD.*   6:4 [1] 1 Sam 5:6, 9, 12; 6:17
6:5 [a] 1 Sam 5:6   [b] Josh 7:19; 1 Chr 16:28–29; Isa 42:12; Jer 13:16; Mal 2:2; Rev 14:7   [c] 1 Sam 5:6, 11; Ps 39:10   [d] 1 Sam 5:3–4, 7
6:6 [a] Exod 12:31   6:7 [a] 2 Sam 6:3   6:8 [a] 1 Sam 6:4–5   6:9 [a] Josh 15:10; 21:16   [b] 1 Sam 6:3   6:12 [a] Num 20:19   6:13 [a] 1 Sam
12:17   6:16 [a] Josh 13:3; Judg 3:3   6:17 [a] 1 Sam 6:4   [b] 1 Sam 5:8   6:18 [1] A few MSS *villages; the large rock . . . [is witness] until
this very day.*   6:19 [a] Exod 19:21; Num 4:5, 15, 16, 20   [b] 2 Sam 6:7   [1] A few MSS *70.*   6:20 [a] Lev 11:44–45; Ps 24:3–4; Mal 3:2;
Rev 6:17   6:21 [a] Josh 9:17; 15:9, 60; 18:14; Judg 18:12; 1 Chr 13:5–6   7:1 [a] 1 Sam 6:21; Ps 132:6   [b] 2 Sam 6:3–4   [c] Lev 21:8

you are really [a]turning to the LORD with all your hearts, remove from among you the foreign gods and the images of [b]Ashtoreth. [c]Give your hearts to the LORD and [d]serve only him. Then he will deliver you from the hand of the Philistines." [4]So the Israelites removed the [a]Baals and images of Ashtoreth. They served only the LORD.

[5]Then Samuel said, "[a]Gather all [b]Israel to Mizpah, and I will pray to the LORD on your behalf." [6]After they had assembled at Mizpah, they [a]drew water and poured it out before the LORD. They [b]fasted on that day, and they confessed there, "[c]We have sinned against the LORD." So Samuel led[1] the people of Israel at Mizpah.

[7]When the Philistines heard that the Israelites had gathered at Mizpah, the leaders of the Philistines went up against Israel. When the Israelites heard about this, they were afraid of the Philistines. [8]The Israelites said to Samuel, "Keep[1] crying out to the LORD our[2] God so that he may save us from the hand of the Philistines!" [9]So Samuel took a [a]nursing lamb and offered it as a whole burnt offering to the LORD. [b]Samuel cried out to the LORD on Israel's behalf, and the LORD answered him.

[10]As Samuel was offering burnt offerings, the Philistines approached to do battle with Israel. [a]But on that day the LORD thundered loudly against the Philistines. He caused them to panic, and they were defeated by Israel. [11]Then the men of Israel left Mizpah and chased the Philistines, striking them down all the way to an area below Beth Car.

[12]Samuel [a]took a stone and placed it between Mizpah and Shen. He named it Ebenezer, saying, "Up to here the LORD has helped us." [13a]So the Philistines were defeated; they [b]did not invade Israel again. The hand of the LORD was against the Philistines all the days of Samuel.

[14]The cities that the Philistines had captured from Israel were returned to Israel, from Ekron to Gath. Israel also delivered their territory from the control of the Philistines. There was also peace between Israel and the Amorites. [15]So Samuel [a]led Israel all the days of his life. [16]Year after year he used to travel the circuit of Bethel, Gilgal, and Mizpah; he used to judge Israel in all these places. [17]Then [a]he would return to Ramah, because his home was there. He also judged Israel there and [b]built an altar to the LORD there.

Israel Seeks a King

8 In his old [a]age Samuel [b]appointed his [c]sons as judges over Israel. [2]The name of his firstborn son was Joel, and the name of his second son was Abijah. They were judges in Beer Sheba. [3]But his sons [a]did not follow his ways. Instead, they [b]made money dishonestly, [c]accepted bribes, and perverted justice.

[4]So all the elders of Israel gathered together and approached Samuel at Ramah. [5]They said to him, "Look, you are old, and your sons don't follow your ways. So now [a]appoint over us a king to lead us, just like all the other nations have."

[6]But this request [a]displeased Samuel, for they said, "Give us a king to lead us." So Samuel [b]prayed to the LORD. [7]The LORD said to Samuel, "Do everything [a]the people request of you. For it is not you that [b]they have rejected, but it is me that they have rejected as their king. [8]Just as they have done from the day that I brought them up from Egypt until this very day, they have rejected me and have served other gods. This is what they are also doing to you. [9]So now do as they say. But you must warn them and [a]make them aware of the policies of the king who will rule over them."

[10]So Samuel spoke all the LORD's words to the people who were asking him for a king. [11]He said, "[a]Here are the policies of the king who will rule over you: He will conscript your [b]sons and put them in his chariot forces and in his cavalry; they will run in front of his [c]chariot. [12]He will [a]appoint for himself leaders of thousands and leaders of fifties,[1] as

7:3 [a]Deut 30:2–10; 1 Kgs 8:48; Isa 55:7; Hos 6:1; Joel 2:12–14   [b]Judg 2:13; 1 Sam 31:10   [c]2 Chr 30:19; Job 11:13   [d]Deut 6:13; 10:20; 13:4; Josh 24:14; Matt 4:10; Luke 4:8   7:4 [a]Judg 2:11; 10:16   7:5 [a]Judg 10:17; 20:1; 1 Sam 10:17   [b]1 Sam 12:17–19   7:6 [a]2 Sam 14:14   [b]Judg 20:26; Neh 9:1–2; Dan 9:3–5; Joel 2:12   [c]Judg 10:10; 1 Sam 12:10; 1 Kgs 8:47; Ps 106:6   [1]Heb. judged.   7:8 [1]Heb. don't stop.   [2]LXX your.   7:9 [a]Lev 22:27   [b]1 Sam 12:18; Ps 99:6; Jer 15:1   7:10 [a]Josh 10:10; 2 Sam 22:14–15; Ps 18:13–14   7:12 [a]Gen 28:18; 35:14; Josh 4:9; 24:26   7:13 [a]Judg 13:1   [b]1 Sam 13:5   7:15 [a]1 Sam 12:11   7:17 [a]1 Sam 8:4   [b]Judg 21:4   8:1 [a]1 Sam 12:2   [b]Deut 16:18–19; 2 Chr 19:5   [c]Judg 10:4   8:3 [a]Jer 22:15–17   [b]Exod 18:21   [c]Exod 23:6–8; Deut 16:19; 1 Sam 12:3   8:5 [a]Deut 17:14–15; Hos 13:10–11; Acts 13:21   8:6 [a]1 Sam 12:17   [b]1 Sam 7:9   8:7 [a]Exod 16:8   [b]1 Sam 10:19   8:9 [a]1 Sam 8:11–18   8:11 [a]Deut 17:14–20   [b]1 Sam 14:52   [c]2 Sam 15:1   8:12 [a]1 Sam 22:7   [1]LXX hundreds; Syr. heads of thousands and heads of hundreds and heads of fifties and heads of tens.

well as those who plow his ground, reap his harvest, and make his weapons of war and his chariot equipment. [13]He will take your daughters to be ointment makers, cooks, and bakers. [14]He will take your best fields, vineyards, and olive groves, and give [a]them to his own servants. [15]He will demand a tenth of your seed and of the produce of your vineyards and give it to his administrators and his servants. [16]He will take your male and female servants, as well as your best cattle and your donkeys, and assign them for his own use. [17]He will demand a tenth of your flocks, and you yourselves will be his servants. [18]In that day you [a]will cry out because of your king whom you have chosen for yourselves, but the LORD won't answer you in that day."[1]

[19]But the people [a]refused to heed Samuel's warning. Instead they said, "No! There will be a king over us! [20]We will be [a]like all the other nations. Our king will judge us and lead us and fight our battles." [21]So Samuel listened to everything the people said and then reported it to the LORD. [22]The LORD said to Samuel, "[a]Do as they say and install a king over them." Then Samuel said to the men of Israel, "Each of you go back to his own city."

Samuel Meets with Saul

9 There was a Benjaminite man named [a]Kish son of Abiel, the son of Zeror, the son of Becorath, the son of Aphiah of Benjamin. Kish was a prominent person. [2]He had a son named Saul, a handsome young man. There was no one among the Israelites more handsome than he was; he stood head and shoulders above all the people.

[3]The donkeys of Saul's father Kish wandered off, so Kish said to his son Saul, "Take one of the servants with you and go look for the donkeys."[1] [4]So Saul crossed through the hill country of Ephraim, passing through the land of [a]Shalisha, but they did not find them. So they crossed through the land of Shaalim, but they were not there. Then he crossed through the land of Benjamin, and still they did not find them.

[5]When they came to the land of [a]Zuph, Saul said to his servant who was with him, "Come on, let's head back before my father quits worrying about the donkeys and becomes [b]anxious about us!" [6]But the [a]servant said to him, "Look, there is a man of God in this town. He is highly respected. [b]Everything that he says really happens. Now let's go there. Perhaps he will tell us where we should go from here." [7]So Saul said to his servant, "All right, we can go. But [a]what can we bring the man, since the food in our bags is used up? We have no gift to take to the man of God. What do we have?" [8]The servant went on to answer Saul, "Look, I happen to have in my hand a quarter shekel of silver. I will give it to the man of God and he will tell us where we should go." [9](Now it used to be in Israel that whenever someone [a]went to inquire of God he would [b]say, "Come on, let's go to the seer." For today's prophet used to be called a seer.) [10]So Saul said to his servant, "That's a good idea! Come on. Let's go." So they went to the town where the man of God was.

[11]As [a]they were going up the ascent to the town, they met some girls coming out to draw water. They said to them, "Is this where the seer is?" [12]They replied, "Yes, straight ahead! But hurry now, for [a]he came to the town today, and the people are making a sacrifice at the high place. [13]When you enter the town, you can find him before he goes up to the high place to eat. The people won't eat until he arrives, for he must bless the sacrifice. Once that happens, those who have been invited will eat. Now go on up, for[1] this is the time when you can find him."

[14]So they went up to the town. As they were heading for the middle of the town, Samuel was coming in their direction to go up to the high place. [15a]Now the day before Saul arrived, the LORD had told Samuel: [16]"At [a]this time tomorrow I will send to you [b]a man from the land of Benjamin. You must consecrate him as a leader over my people Israel. He will save my people from the hand of the Philistines. For I have looked with favor [c]on my people. Their cry has reached me."

[17]When Samuel saw Saul, the LORD said, "[a]Here is the man that I told you about.

8:14 [a]1 Kgs 21:7; [Ezek 46:18]   **8:18** [a]Prov 1:25–28; Isa 1:15; Mic 3:4   [1]LXX adds *because you have chosen for yourselves a king.*   **8:19** [a]Isa 66:4; Jer 44:16   **8:20** [a]1 Sam 8:5   **8:22** [a]1 Sam 8:7; Hos 13:11   **9:1** [a]1 Sam 14:51; 1 Chr 8:33; 9:36–39   **9:3** [1]Syr. adds *So Saul arose and went out. He took with him one of the boys and went out to look for his father's donkeys.*   **9:4** [a]2 Kgs 4:42   **9:5** [a]1 Sam 1:1   [b]1 Sam 10:2   **9:6** [a]Deut 33:1; 1 Kgs 13:1; 2 Kgs 5:8   [b]1 Sam 3:19   **9:7** [a]Judg 6:18; 13:17; 1 Kgs 14:3; 2 Kgs 4:42; 8:8   **9:9** [a]Gen 25:22   [b]2 Sam 24:11; 2 Kgs 17:13; 1 Chr 26:28; 29:29; 2 Chr 16:7, 10; Isa 30:10; Amos 7:12   **9:11** [a]Gen 24:11, 15; 29:8–9; Exod 2:16   **9:12** [a]Gen 31:54; 1 Sam 16:2   **9:13** [1]MT adds *him.*   **9:15** [a]1 Sam 15:1   **9:16** [a]Deut 17:15   [b]1 Sam 10:1   [c]Exod 2:23–25; 3:7, 9   **9:17** [a]1 Sam 16:12; Hos 13:11

He will rule over my people." [18]As Saul approached Samuel in the middle of the gate, he said, "Please tell me where the seer's house is."

[19]Samuel replied to Saul, "I am the seer! Go up in front of me to the high place! Today you will eat with me and in the morning I will send you away. I will tell you everything that you are thinking. [20]Don't be concerned about the donkeys that [a]you lost three days ago, for they have been found. Whom does all [b]Israel desire? Is it not you, and all your father's family?"

[21]Saul replied, "[a]Am I not a Benjaminite, from the [b]smallest of Israel's tribes, and is not [c]my family clan the smallest of all the clans in the tribe of Benjamin? Why do you speak to me in this way?"

[22]Then Samuel brought Saul and his servant into the room and gave them a place at the head of those who had been invited. There were about thirty people present. [23]Samuel said to the cook, "Give me the portion of meat that I gave to you—the one I asked you to keep with you."

[24]So [a]the cook picked up the leg and brought it and set it in front of Saul. Samuel said, "What was kept is now set before you! Eat, for it has been kept for you for this meeting time, from the time I said, 'I have invited the people.'" So Saul ate with Samuel that day.

[25]When [a]they came down from the high place to the town, Samuel spoke with Saul on the roof. [26]They got up at dawn and Samuel called to Saul on the roof, "Get up, so I can send you on your way." So Saul got up and the two of them—he and Samuel—went outside. [27]While they were going down to the edge of town, Samuel said to Saul, "Tell the servant to go on ahead of us." So he did.[1] Samuel then said, "You remain here awhile, so I can inform you of God's message."

Samuel Anoints Saul

10 Then [a]Samuel took [b]a small container of olive oil and poured it on Saul's head. Samuel kissed him and said, "[c]The LORD has chosen you[1] to lead [d]his people Israel! You will rule over the LORD's people and you will deliver them from the power of the enemies who surround them. This will be your sign that the LORD has chosen[2] you as leader over his inheritance.[3] [2]When you leave me today, you will find two men near [a]Rachel's tomb [b]at Zelzah on Benjamin's border. They will say to [c]you, 'The donkeys you have gone looking for have been found. Your father is no longer concerned about the donkeys but has become anxious about you two! He is asking, "What should I do about my son?"'

[3]"As you continue on from there, you will come [a]to the tall tree of Tabor. At that point three men who are going up to God at Bethel will meet you. One of them will be carrying three young goats, one of them will be carrying three round loaves of bread, and one of them will be carrying a container of wine. [4]They will ask you how you're doing and will give you two loaves of bread. You will accept them. [5]Afterward you will go to Gibeah of God, [a]where there are Philistine officials.[1] When you enter the town, you will meet a company of prophets coming down [b]from the high place. They will have harps, tambourines, flutes, [c]and lyres, and they will be prophesying. [6]Then [a]the Spirit of the LORD will rush upon [b]you and you will prophesy with them. You will be changed into a different person.

[7]"When these [a]signs have taken place, do whatever your hand finds to do, for [b]God will be with you. [8]You will go down [a]to Gilgal before me. I am going to join you there to offer burnt offerings and to make peace offerings. You should wait for [b]seven days until I arrive and tell you what to do."

Saul Becomes King

[9]As Saul turned to leave Samuel, God changed his inmost person. All these signs happened on that very day. [10]When Saul and his servant[1] arrived at Gibeah, a company of prophets was coming out to meet him. Then the Spirit of God rushed upon Saul

9:20 [a]1 Sam 9:3 [b]1 Sam 8:5, 19; 12:13   **9:21** [a]1 Sam 15:17 [b]Judg 20:46–48; Ps 68:27 [c]Judg 6:15   **9:24** [a]Exod 29:22, 27; Lev 7:32–33; Num 18:18; Ezek 24:4   **9:25** [a]Deut 22:8; 2 Sam 11:2; Luke 5:19; Acts 10:9   **9:27** [1]Some wss omit this statement.   **10:1** [a]Exod 30:23–33; 1 Sam 9:16; 16:13; 2 Kgs 9:3, 6 [b]Ps 2:12 [c]2 Sam 5:2; Acts 13:21 [d]Exod 34:9; Deut 32:9; Ps 78:71   [1]Heb. *Is it not that the LORD has anointed you?* [2]I.e., anointed. [3]MT *Is it not that the LORD has anointed you over his inheritance for a leader?*   **10:2** [a]Gen 35:16–20; 48:7 [b]Josh 18:28 [c]1 Sam 9:3–5   **10:3** [a]Gen 28:22; 35:1, 3, 7   **10:5** [a]1 Sam 13:2–3 [b]1 Sam 19:12, 20; 2 Kgs 2:3, 5, 15 [c]Exod 15:20–21; 2 Kgs 3:15; 1 Chr 25:1–6; 1 Cor 14:1 [1]Or *sentries.*   **10:6** [a]Num 11:25, 29; Judg 14:6; 1 Sam 16:13 [b]1 Sam 10:10; 19:23–24   **10:7** [a]Exod 4:8; Luke 2:12 [b]Josh 1:5; Judg 6:12; 1 Sam 3:19; [Heb 13:5]   **10:8** [a]1 Sam 11:14–15; 13:8 [b]1 Sam 13:8–10   **10:10** [1]Some wss *he.*

and [a]he prophesied [b]among them. [11]When everyone who had known him previously saw him prophesying with the prophets, the people asked one another, "What on earth has happened to the son of [a]Kish? Does even Saul belong with the prophets?" [12]A man [a]who was from there replied, "And who is their father?" Therefore this became a proverb: "Is even Saul among the prophets?" [13]When Saul had finished prophesying, he went to the high place.

[14]Saul's [a]uncle asked him and his servant, "Where did you go?" Saul replied, "To look for the donkeys. But when we realized they were lost, we went to Samuel." [15]Saul's uncle said, "Tell me what Samuel said to you." [16]Saul said to his uncle, "He assured us that the donkeys had been [a]found." But Saul did not tell him what Samuel had said about the matter of kingship.

[17]Then Samuel called the people [a]together before the LORD [b]at Mizpah. [18]He said to the Israelites, "This is what the LORD God of Israel has said, 'I brought Israel up from Egypt and I delivered you from the power of the Egyptians and from the power of all the kingdoms that oppressed you. [19a]But today you have rejected your God who saves you from all your trouble and distress. You have said, "No![1] Appoint a king over us." Now take your positions before the LORD by your tribes and by your clans.'"

[20]Then Samuel brought all the tribes of Israel near, and the tribe of Benjamin was chosen by lot. [21]Then he brought the tribe of Benjamin near by its families, and the family of Matri was chosen by lot. At last Saul son of Kish was chosen by lot. But when they looked for him, he was nowhere to be found. [22]So they [a]inquired again of the LORD, "Has the man arrived here yet?" The LORD said, "He has hidden himself among the equipment." [23]So [a]they ran and brought him from there. When he took his position among the people, he stood head and shoulders above them all. [24]Then Samuel said to all the people, "Do you see the one [a]whom the LORD has chosen? Indeed, there is no one like him among all the people." All the people shouted out, "[b]Long live the king!"

[25]Then Samuel talked to [a]the people about how the kingship would work.[1] He wrote it all down on a scroll and set it before the LORD. Then Samuel sent all the people away to their homes. [26]Even Saul went [a]to his home in Gibeah. With him went some brave men whose hearts God had touched. [27]But some wicked men said, "How can this man save us?" They despised him and did not even bring him a gift. [a]But Saul said nothing about it.[1]

Saul Comes to the Aid of Jabesh

11 [1,a]Nahash the Ammonite marched against [b]Jabesh Gilead. All the men of Jabesh Gilead said to Nahash, "[c]Make a treaty with us and we will serve you." [2]But Nahash the Ammonite said to them, "The only way I will make a treaty with you is if you let me gouge out the right eye of every one of you and in so doing [a]humiliate all Israel!"

[3]The elders of Jabesh said to him, "Leave us alone for seven days so that we can send messengers throughout the territory of Israel. If there is no one who can deliver us, we will come out voluntarily to you."

[4]When the messengers went [a]to Gibeah (where Saul lived) and informed the people of these matters, [b]all the people wept loudly. [5]Now Saul was walking behind the oxen as he came from the field. Saul asked, "What has happened to the people? Why are they weeping?" So they told him about the men of Jabesh.

[6]The Spirit of God rushed upon Saul when [a]he heard these words, and he became very angry. [7]He took a pair of oxen and [a]cut them up. Then he sent the pieces throughout the territory of Israel by the hand of messengers, [b]who said, "Whoever does not go out after Saul and after Samuel should expect this to be done to his oxen!" Then the terror of the LORD fell on the people, and they went out as one army. [8]When

10:10 [a]1 Sam 10:5   [b]1 Sam 19:20   10:11 [a]1 Sam 19:24; Amos 7:14–15; Matt 13:54–57; John 7:15; Acts 4:13   10:12 [a]John 5:30, 36   10:14 [a]1 Sam 14:50   10:16 [a]1 Sam 9:20   10:17 [a]Judg 20:1   [b]1 Sam 7:5–6   10:19 [a]1 Sam 8:7, 19; 12:12   [1]MT *to him*.   10:22 [a]1 Sam 23:2, 4, 10, 11   10:23 [a]1 Sam 9:2   10:24 [a]Deut 17:15; 1 Sam 9:16; 2 Sam 21:6   [b]1 Kgs 1:25, 39   10:25 [a]Deut 17:14–20; 1 Sam 8:11–18   [1]Heb. *the regulation of the kingship*.   10:26 [a]Judg 20:14   10:27 [a]1 Sam 11:12   [1]LXX *after about a month*.   11:1 [a]1 Sam 12:12   [b]Judg 21:8; 1 Sam 31:11   [c]Gen 26:28; 1 Kgs 20:34; Job 41:4; Ezek 17:13   [1]Some wss add a lengthy passage about Nahash here. For details, see the *NET Bible, Full Notes Edition*.   11:2 [a]Gen 34:14; 1 Sam 17:26; Ps 44:13   11:4 [a]1 Sam 10:26; 15:34; 2 Sam 21:6   [b]Gen 27:38; Judg 2:4; 20:23, 26; 21:2; 1 Sam 30:4   11:6 [a]Judg 3:10; 6:34; 11:29; 13:25; 14:6; 1 Sam 10:10; 16:13   11:7 [a]Judg 19:29   [b]Judg 21:5, 8, 10

Saul counted them at [a]Bezek, the Israelites were 300,000 strong[1] and the men [b]of Judah numbered 30,000.

[9]They said to the messengers who had come, "Here's what you should say to the men of Jabesh Gilead: 'Tomorrow deliverance will come to you when the sun is fully up.'" When the messengers went and told the men of Jabesh Gilead, they were happy. [10]The men of Jabesh said, "Tomorrow we will come out to you and you can do with us whatever you wish."

[11]The next day [a]Saul placed the people [b]in three groups. They went to the Ammonite camp during the morning watch and struck them down until the hottest part of the day. The survivors scattered; no two of them remained together.

Saul Is Established as King

[12]Then the people said to Samuel, "[a]Who were the ones asking, 'Will Saul reign over us?' Hand [b]over those men so we may execute them!" [13]But Saul said, "[a]No one will be killed on this day. For today [b]the LORD has given Israel a victory!" [14]Samuel said [a]to the people, "Come on! Let's go to Gilgal and renew the kingship there." [15]So all the people went to Gilgal, where they established Saul as king in the [a]LORD's presence. They offered up peace offerings [b]there in the LORD's presence. Saul and all the Israelites were very happy.

12 Samuel said to all Israel, "I have done everything [a]you requested. I [b]have given you a king. [2]Now look! This king [a]walks before you. As for me, I am old [b]and gray, and my sons are here with you. I have walked before you from the time of my youth till the present day. [3]Here [a]I am. Bring a charge against me before the LORD and before his chosen king. [b]Whose ox have I taken? Whose donkey have I taken? Whom have I wronged? Whom have I oppressed? From whose hand have I taken a [c]bribe so that I would [d]overlook something? Tell me, and I will return it to you!"

[4]They replied, "[a]You have not wronged us or oppressed us. You have not taken anything from the hand of anyone." [5]He said to them, "The LORD is witness against you, and his chosen king is witness this day, [a]that you have not found any reason to accuse me." They said, "He is witness!"

[6]Samuel said to the people, "The LORD is the one who chose Moses and Aaron and who brought your ancestors up from the land of Egypt. [7]Now take your positions, so I may [a]confront you before the LORD regarding all the LORD's just actions toward you and your ancestors. [8a]When Jacob entered Egypt, your ancestors cried [b]out to the LORD. The LORD [c]sent Moses and Aaron, and they led your ancestors out of Egypt and settled them in this place.

[9]"But they [a]forgot the LORD their God, so he gave them into the hand of [b]Sisera, the general in command of Hazor's army, and into the hands of the [c]Philistines and the king of [d]Moab, and they fought against them. [10]Then they cried out to the LORD and admitted, '[a]We have sinned, for we have forsaken the LORD [b]and have served the Baals and the images of Ashtoreth. Now deliver us from the hands of our enemies so that we may serve you.' [11]So the LORD sent Jerub Baal, Barak,[1] [a]Jephthah, and [b]Samuel,[2] and he delivered you from the hands of the enemies all around you, and you were able to live securely.

[12]"When you saw that King [a]Nahash of the Ammonites was advancing against [b]you, you said to me, 'No! A king will rule over us'—even though [c]the LORD your God is your king. [13]Now look! [a]Here is [b]the king you have chosen—the one that you asked for! Look, the LORD has given you a king. [14]If you [a]fear the LORD, serving him and obeying him and not rebelling against what he says, and if both you and the king who rules over you follow the LORD your God, all will be well. [15]But if you [a]don't obey the LORD and [b]rebel against what the LORD says, the hand of the LORD will be against both you and your king.[1]

11:8 [a]Judg 1:5 [b]2 Sam 24:9 [1]LXX, two Old Latin MSS 600,000.   11:11 [a]1 Sam 31:11 [b]Judg 7:16, 20   11:12 [a]1 Sam 10:27 [b]Luke 19:27   11:13 [a]1 Sam 10:27; 2 Sam 19:22 [b]Exod 14:13, 30; 1 Sam 19:5   11:14 [a]1 Sam 7:16; 10:8   11:15 [a]1 Sam 10:17 [b]Josh 8:31; 1 Sam 10:8   12:1 [a]1 Sam 8:5, 7, 9, 20, 22 [b]1 Sam 10:24; 11:14–15   12:2 [a]Num 27:17; 1 Sam 8:20 [b]1 Sam 8:1, 5   12:3 [a]1 Sam 10:1; 24:6; 2 Sam 1:14, 16 [b]Num 16:15; Acts 20:33; 1 Thess 2:5 [c]Exod 23:8 [d]Deut 16:19   12:4 [a]Lev 19:13   12:5 [a]John 18:38; Acts 23:9; 24:20   12:7 [a]Isa 1:18; Ezek 20:35; Mic 6:1–5   12:8 [a]Gen 46:5–6; Ps 105:23 [b]Exod 2:23–25 [c]Exod 3:10; 4:14–16   12:9 [a]Deut 32:18; Judg 3:7 [b]Judg 4:2 [c]Judg 3:31; 10:7; 13:1 [d]Judg 3:12–30   12:10 [a]Judg 10:10 [b]Judg 2:13; 3:7   12:11 [a]Judg 11:1 [b]1 Sam 7:13 [1]MT Bedan. [2]Tg. Gideon, Samson, Jephthah, and Samuel; Syr. Deborah, Barak, Gideon, Jephthah, and Samson.   12:12 [a]1 Sam 11:1–2 [b]1 Sam 8:5, 19, 20 [c]Judg 8:23; 1 Sam 8:7; Ps 59:13   12:13 [a]1 Sam 10:24 [b]Hos 13:11   12:14 [a]Josh 24:14   12:15 [a]Deut 28:15 [b]Lev 26:14–15; Josh 24:20; Isa 1:20 [1]MT fathers.

[16] "So now, [a] take your positions and watch this great thing that the LORD is about to do in your sight. [17] Is this not the time of the [a] wheat harvest? [b] I will call on the LORD so that he makes it thunder and [c] rain. Realize and see what a great sin [d] you have committed before the LORD by asking for a king for yourselves."

[18] So Samuel called to the LORD, and the LORD made it thunder and rain that day. [a] All the people were very afraid of both the LORD and Samuel. [19] All the people said to Samuel, "[a] Pray to the LORD your God on behalf of us—your servants—so we won't die, for we have added to all our sins by asking for a king."

[20] Then Samuel said to the people, "Don't be afraid. You have indeed sinned. However, don't turn aside from the LORD. Serve the LORD with all your heart. [21] You should not turn aside after empty things that can't profit and can't deliver, since they are empty. [22] The LORD will not abandon his people because [a] he wants to uphold [b] his great reputation. The LORD was pleased to make you his own people. [23] As far as [a] I am concerned, far be [b] it from me to sin against the LORD by ceasing to pray for you! I will instruct you in the way that is [c] good and upright. [24a] However, fear the LORD and serve him faithfully with all your heart. Just [b] look [c] at the great things he has done for you! [25] But if [a] you continue to do evil, [b] both you and your king will be swept away."

Saul Fails the Lord

13 Saul was [thirty][1] years old when he began to reign; he ruled over Israel for [forty][2] years. [2] Saul selected for himself 3,000 men from Israel. Of these 2,000 were with Saul at [a] Micmash and in the hill country of Bethel; the remaining 1,000 were with [b] Jonathan at [c] Gibeah in the territory of Benjamin. He sent all the rest of the people back home.

[3] Jonathan attacked [a] the Philistine outpost that was at [b] Geba and the Philistines heard about it. Then Saul alerted all the land saying, "Let the Hebrews pay attention!" [4] All Israel heard this message, "Saul has attacked the Philistine outpost, and now Israel is repulsive[1] to the Philistines!" So the people were summoned to join Saul at Gilgal.

[5] Meanwhile the Philistines gathered to battle with Israel. Then they went up against Israel[1] with 3,000 chariots,[2] 6,000 horsemen, and an army [a] as numerous as the sand on the seashore. They went up and camped at Micmash, east of Beth [b] Aven. [6] The men of Israel realized they had a problem because their army was hard pressed. So the army [a] hid in caves, thickets, cliffs, strongholds,[1] and cisterns. [7] Some of the Hebrews crossed over the Jordan River to the [a] land of Gad and Gilead. But Saul stayed at Gilgal; the entire army that was with him was terrified. [8] He waited for seven days, [a] the time period indicated by Samuel. But Samuel did not come to Gilgal, and the army began to abandon Saul.

[9] So Saul said, "Bring me the burnt offering and the peace offerings." Then he offered a burnt offering. [10] Just when he had finished offering the burnt offering, Samuel appeared on the scene. Saul went out to meet him and to greet him.

[11] But Samuel said, "What have you done?" Saul replied, "When I saw that the army had started to abandon me, and that you didn't come at the appointed time, and that the Philistines had assembled at Micmash, [12] I thought, 'Now the Philistines will come down on me at Gilgal and I have not sought the LORD's favor.' So I felt obligated[1] to offer the burnt offering."

[13] Then Samuel said to Saul, "[a] You have made a foolish choice! [b] You have not obeyed the commandment that the LORD your God gave you. Had you done that, the LORD would have established your kingdom over Israel forever. [14a] But now your kingdom will not continue. [b] The LORD has sought out for himself [c] a man who is loyal to him,[1] and the LORD has appointed him to be leader over his people, for you have [d] not obeyed what the LORD commanded you."

12:16 [a] Exod 14:13, 31   **12:17** [a] Gen 30:14   [b] Josh 10:12; 1 Sam 7:9–10; [Jas 5:16–18]   [c] Ezra 10:9   [d] 1 Sam 8:7   **12:18** [a] Exod 14:31   **12:19** [a] Exod 9:28; 1 Sam 7:8; [Jas 5:15; 1 John 5:16]   **12:22** [a] Deut 31:6; 1 Kgs 6:13   [b] Isa 43:21   **12:23** [a] Acts 12:5; Rom 1:9; Col 1:9; 2 Tim 1:3   [b] Ps 34:11; Prov 4:11   [c] 1 Kgs 8:36   **12:24** [a] Eccl 12:13   [b] Isa 5:12   [c] Deut 10:21   **12:25** [a] Josh 24:20   [b] Deut 28:36   **13:1** [1] MT *a son of a year*; Syr. *twenty-one*; maj. LXX MSS omit the verse.   [2] MT *two years*; Syr. omits this part of v. 1.   **13:2** [a] 1 Sam 14:5, 31   [b] 1 Sam 14:1   [c] 1 Sam 10:26   **13:3** [a] 1 Sam 10:5   [b] 2 Sam 5:25   **13:4** [1] Heb. *stinks*.   **13:5** [a] Judg 7:12   [b] Josh 7:2; 1 Sam 14:23   [1] MT omits *they went up against Israel*.   [2] MT *30,000*.   **13:6** [a] Judg 6:2; 1 Sam 14:11   [1] Or perhaps *vaults*.   **13:7** [a] Num 32:1–42   **13:8** [a] 1 Sam 10:8   **13:12** [1] Or *I forced myself*.   **13:13** [a] 2 Chr 16:9   [b] 1 Sam 15:11, 22, 28   **13:14** [a] 1 Sam 15:28; 31:6   [b] 1 Sam 16:1   [c] Ps 89:20; Acts 7:46; 13:22   [d] 1 Sam 15:11, 19   [1] Heb. *according to his heart*.

[15]Then Samuel set [a]out and went up from Gilgal[1] to Gibeah in the territory of Benjamin. Saul mustered the army that remained with him; there were about 600 men. [16]Saul, his son Jonathan, and the army that remained with them stayed in Gibeah in the territory of Benjamin, while the Philistines camped in Micmash. [17]Raiding bands went out from the camp of the Philistines in three groups. One band turned toward the road leading to [a]Ophrah by the land of Shual; [18]another band turned toward the road leading to Beth [a]Horon; and yet another band turned toward the road leading to the border that overlooks the valley of [b]Zeboyim in the direction of the desert.

[19]A blacksmith could not be found in all [a]the land of Israel, for the Philistines had said, "This will prevent the Hebrews from making swords and spears." [20]So all Israel had to go down to the Philistines in order to get their plowshares, cutting instruments, axes, and sickles[1] sharpened. [21]They charged[1] two-thirds of a shekel[2] to sharpen plowshares and cutting instruments, and one-third of a shekel[3] to sharpen picks and axes, and to set ox goads. [22]So on [a]the day of the battle no sword or spear was to be found in the hand of anyone in the army that was with Saul and Jonathan. No one but Saul and his son Jonathan had them.

Jonathan Ignites a Battle

[23a]A garrison of the Philistines had gone out to the pass at Micmash.

14 Then one day Jonathan son of Saul said to his armor-bearer, "Come on, let's go over to the Philistine garrison that is opposite us." But he did not let his father know. [2]Now Saul was sitting under a pomegranate tree in Migron, on the outskirts of [a]Gibeah. The army that was with him numbered about 600 men. [3]Now [a]Ahijah was carrying[1] an ephod. He was the son of Ahitub, who was the brother of [b]Ichabod and [c]a son of Phinehas, son of Eli, the priest of the LORD in Shiloh. The army was unaware that Jonathan had left.

[4]Now there was a steep cliff on each side of the pass through which Jonathan intended [a]to go to reach the Philistine garrison. One cliff was named Bozez, the other Seneh. [5]The cliff to the north was closer to Micmash, the one to the south closer to Geba.

[6]Jonathan said to his armor-bearer, "Come on, let's go over to the garrison of these uncircumcised [a]men. Perhaps the LORD will intervene for us. Nothing can prevent the LORD [b]from delivering, whether by many or by a few." [7]His armor-bearer said to him, "Do everything that is on your mind. Do as you're inclined. I'm with you all the way!"

[8]Jonathan replied, "All right. We'll go over to these men and fight them. [9]If they say to us, 'Stay put until we approach you,' we will stay right there and not go up to them. [10]But if they say, 'Come up against us,' we will go up. For in that case the LORD has given them into our hand—it will be a sign to us."

[11]When they made themselves known to the Philistine garrison, the Philistines said, "Look! The Hebrews are coming out of the holes in which they [a]hid themselves." [12]Then the men of the garrison said to Jonathan and his armor-bearer, "Come on up to us so we can teach you a thing or two!" Then Jonathan said to his armor-bearer, "Come up behind me, for the LORD has given them into the hand of Israel!"

[13]Jonathan crawled up on his hands and feet, with his armor-bearer following behind him. Jonathan struck [a]down the Philistines, while his armor-bearer came along behind him and killed them. [14]In this initial skirmish Jonathan and his armor-bearer struck down about 20 men in an area that measured half an acre.

[15]Then fear overwhelmed those who were in [a]the camp, those who were in [b]the field, [c]all the army in the garrison, and the raiding bands. They trembled and the ground shook. This fear was caused by God.[1]

[16]Saul's watchmen at Gibeah in the territory of Benjamin looked on as the crowd of soldiers seemed to melt away first in one direction and then in another. [17]So Saul said

---

13:15 [a]1 Sam 13:2, 6, 7; 14:2   [1]LXX, two Old Latin mss add *on his way. And the rest of the people went up after Saul to meet the warring army. When they arrived from Gilgal.*   **13:17** [a]Josh 18:23   **13:18** [a]Josh 16:3; 18:13–14   [b]Gen 14:2; Neh 11:34   **13:19** [a]Judg 5:8; 2 Kgs 24:14; Jer 24:1; 29:2   **13:20** [1]MT *plowshares.*   **13:21** [1]Heb. *the price was.*   [2]Probably a stone weight of about 0.268 ounces.   [3]Heb. *and for a third, a pick.*   **13:22** [a]Judg 5:8   **13:23** [a]1 Sam 14:1, 4   **14:2** [a]1 Sam 13:15–16   **14:3** [a]1 Sam 22:9, 11, 20   [b]1 Sam 4:21   [c]1 Sam 2:28   [1]Or *wearing*; Heb. *bearing.*   **14:4** [a]1 Sam 13:23   **14:6** [a]1 Sam 17:26, 36; Jer 9:25–26   [b]Judg 7:4, 7; 1 Sam 17:46–47; 2 Chr 14:11; [Ps 115:3; 135:6; Zech 4:6; Matt 19:26; Rom 8:31]   **14:11** [a]1 Sam 13:6; 14:22   **14:13** [a]Lev 26:8; Josh 23:10   **14:15** [a]Deut 28:7; 2 Kgs 7:6–7; Job 18:11   [b]1 Sam 13:17   [c]Gen 35:5   [1]Or *a very great fear*; Heb. *and it was by the fear of God.*

to the army that was with him, "Muster the troops and see who is no longer with us." When they mustered the troops, Jonathan and his armor-bearer were not there. [18] So Saul said to Ahijah, "Bring near the ephod,"[1] for he was at that time wearing the ephod in front of the Israelites.[2] [19] While Saul [a] spoke to the priest, the panic in the Philistines' camp was becoming greater and greater. So Saul said to the priest, "Withdraw your hand."

[20] Saul and all the army assembled and marched into battle, where they found the Philistines in [a] total panic killing one another with their swords. [21] The Hebrews who had earlier gone over to the Philistine side joined the Israelites who were with Saul and Jonathan. [22] When all the Israelites who [a] had hidden themselves in the hill country of Ephraim heard that the Philistines had fled, they too pursued them in battle. [23a] So the LORD delivered Israel that day, and the battle shifted over [b] to Beth Aven.[1]

Jonathan Violates Saul's Oath

[24] Now the men of Israel were hard pressed that day, for Saul had [a] made the army agree to this oath: "Cursed be the man who eats food before evening. I will get my vengeance on my enemies!" So no one in the army ate anything.

[25a] Now the whole army entered the forest, and there was [b] honey on the ground. [26] When the army entered the forest, they saw the honey flowing, but no one ate any of it, for the army was afraid of the oath. [27] But Jonathan had not heard about the oath his father had made the army take. He extended the end of his staff that was in his hand and dipped it in the honeycomb. When he ate it, his eyes gleamed.[1] [28] Then someone from the army informed him, "Your father put the army under a strict oath saying, 'Cursed be the man who eats food today.' That is why the army is tired." [29] Then Jonathan said, "My father has caused trouble for the land. See how my eyes gleamed[1] when I tasted just a little of this honey. [30] Certainly if the army had eaten some of the enemies' provisions that they came across today,

would not the slaughter of the Philistines have been even greater?"

[31] On that day the army struck down the Philistines from Micmash to Aijalon, and they became very tired. [32] So the army rushed greedily on[1] the[2] plunder, confiscating sheep, cattle, and calves. They slaughtered them right on the ground, and the army ate them, blood and all.

[33] Now it was reported to Saul, "Look, the army is sinning against the LORD by eating even the blood." He said, "All of you have broken the covenant![1] Roll a large stone over here[2] to me." [34] Then Saul said, "Scatter out among the army and say to them, 'Each of you bring to me your ox and sheep and slaughter them in this spot and eat. But don't sin against the LORD by eating the blood.'" So that night each one brought his ox and slaughtered it there. [35] Then Saul [a] built an altar for the LORD; it was the first time he had built an altar for the LORD.

[36] Saul said, "Let's go down after the Philistines at night; we will rout them until the break of day. We won't leave any of them alive!" They replied, "Do whatever seems best to you." But the priest said, "Let's approach God here." [37] So Saul [a] asked God, "Should I go down after [b] the Philistines? Will you deliver them into the hand of Israel?" But he did not answer him that day.

[38] Then Saul said, "All you leaders of the army [a] come here. Find out how this sin occurred today. [39] For [a] as surely as the LORD, the deliverer of Israel, lives, even if it turns out to be my own son Jonathan, he will certainly die!" But no one from the army said anything.

[40] Then he said to all Israel, "You will be on one side, and I and my son Jonathan will be on the other side." The army replied to Saul, "Do whatever you think is best."

[41] Then Saul said, "O LORD God of Israel! If this sin has been committed by me or by my son Jonathan, then, O LORD God of Israel, respond [a] with Urim. But if this sin has been committed by your people Israel, respond with Thummim."[1] Then Jonathan and Saul were indicated by lot, while the army was exonerated. [42] Then Saul said, "Cast the lot

14:18 [1] Heb. *the ark of God.* [2] Heb. *for the ark of God was in that day, and the sons of Israel.* 14:19 [a] Num 27:21
14:20 [a] Judg 7:22; 2 Chr 20:23 14:22 [a] 1 Sam 13:6 14:23 [a] Exod 14:30; 2 Chr 32:22; Hos 1:7 [b] 1 Sam 13:5 [1] LXX adds *And all the people were with Saul, about ten thousand men. And the battle extended to the entire city on mount Ephraim.*
14:24 [a] Josh 6:26 14:25 [a] Deut 9:28; Matt 3:5 [b] Exod 3:8; Num 13:27; Matt 3:4 14:27 [1] Ket. *saw.* 14:29 [1] LXX *saw.*
14:32 [1] Ket. *and they did.* [2] Ket. *spoil.* 14:33 [1] Heb. *You have acted deceptively.* [2] MT *today.* 14:35 [a] 1 Sam 7:12, 17; 2 Sam 24:25 14:37 [a] Judg 20:18 [b] 1 Sam 28:6 14:38 [a] Josh 7:14; 1 Sam 10:19 14:39 [a] 1 Sam 14:24, 44; 2 Sam 12:5
14:41 [a] Prov 16:33; Acts 1:24–26 [1] Heb. *to the LORD God of Israel: 'Give what is perfect.'*

between me and my son Jonathan!"[1] Jonathan was indicated by lot.

[43]So Saul said to Jonathan, "[a]Tell me what you have done." Jonathan told [b]him, "I used the end of the staff that was in my hand to taste a little honey. I must die!"[1] [44]Saul said, "[a]God will punish me severely if Jonathan doesn't die!"

[45]But the army said to Saul, "Should Jonathan, who won this great victory in Israel, die? May it never be! [a]As surely as the LORD lives, not a single hair of his head will fall to the ground, for [b]it is with the help of God that he has acted today." So the army rescued Jonathan from death.

[46]Then Saul stopped chasing the Philistines, and the Philistines went back home. [47]After Saul had secured his royal position over Israel, he fought against all their enemies on all sides—the Moabites, [a]Ammonites, Edomites, the kings of [b]Zobah, and the Philistines. In every direction that he turned, he was victorious.[1] [48]He fought bravely, striking [a]down the Amalekites and delivering Israel from the hand of its enemies.

Members of Saul's Family

[49]The sons of Saul were Jonathan, Ishvi, and Malki-Shua. [a]He had two daughters; the older one was named Merab and the younger [b]Michal. [50]The name of Saul's wife was Ahinoam, the daughter of Ahimaaz. The name of the general in command of his army was Abner son of Ner, Saul's [a]uncle. [51a]Kish was the father of Saul, and Ner the father of Abner was the son of Abiel. [52]There was fierce war with [a]the Philistines all the days of Saul. So whenever Saul saw anyone who was a warrior or a brave individual, he would conscript him.

Saul Is Rejected as King

15 Then Samuel said to Saul, "I was [a]the one the LORD sent to anoint you as king over his people Israel. Now listen to what the LORD says. [2]Here is what the LORD of Heaven's Armies has said: 'I carefully observed [a]how the Amalekites opposed Israel along the way when Israel came up from Egypt. [3]So go now and strike [a]down the Amalekites. Destroy everything they have. Don't spare them. Put them to death—man, woman, child, infant, ox, sheep, camel, and donkey alike.'"

[4]So Saul assembled the army and mustered them at Telaim. There were 200,000 foot soldiers and 10,000 men of Judah. [5]Saul proceeded to the city[1] of Amalek, where he set an ambush[2] in the wadi. [6]Saul said to [a]the Kenites, "[b]Go on and leave! Go down from among the Amalekites. Otherwise I will sweep [c]you away[1] with them. After all, you were kind to all the Israelites when they came up from Egypt." So the Kenites withdrew from among the Amalekites.

[7a]Then Saul struck down the Amalekites all the way from [b]Havilah to [c]Shur, which is next to Egypt. [8]He captured King Agag of [a]the Amalekites alive, but he executed all Agag's people with the sword. [9]However, Saul and the army [a]spared Agag, along with the best of the flock, the cattle, the fatlings, and the lambs, as well as everything else that was of value. They were not willing to slaughter them. But they did slaughter everything that was despised and worthless.

[10]Then the LORD's message came to Samuel: [11]"I regret that [a]I have made Saul king, for he has [b]turned away from me [c]and has not done what I told him to do." Samuel became [d]angry and he cried out to the LORD all that night.

[12]Then Samuel got up early to meet Saul the next morning. But Samuel was informed, "Saul has gone to [a]Carmel where he is setting up a monument for himself." Then Samuel left[1] and went down to Gilgal.[2] [13]When Samuel came to Saul, Saul said to him, "May the LORD [a]bless you! I have fulfilled the LORD's orders."

14:42 [1]LXX adds *Whomever the Lord will indicate by the lot, let him die! And the people said to Saul, 'It is not this word.' But Saul prevailed over the people, and they cast lots between him and between Jonathan his son.* **14:43** [a]Josh 7:19 [b]1 Sam 14:27 [1]Heb. *Look, I, I will die*; either acquiescing to his anticipated fate of death, sarcastic, or a question. **14:44** [a]Ruth 1:17; 1 Sam 25:22 **14:45** [a]2 Sam 14:11; 1 Kgs 1:52; Luke 21:18; Acts 27:34 [b][2 Cor 6:1; Phil 2:12–13] **14:47** [a]1 Sam 11:1–13 [b]2 Sam 10:6 [1]MT *he acted wickedly.* **14:48** [a]Exod 17:16; 1 Sam 15:3–7 **14:49** [a]1 Sam 31:2; 1 Chr 8:33 [b]1 Sam 18:17–20, 27; 19:12 **14:50** [a]1 Sam 10:14 **14:51** [a]1 Sam 9:1, 21 **14:52** [a]1 Sam 8:11 **15:1** [a]1 Sam 9:16; 10:1 **15:2** [a]Exod 17:8, 14; Num 24:20; Deut 25:17–19 **15:3** [a]Deut 25:19 **15:5** [1]LXX *cities.* [2]MT *and he contended.* **15:6** [a]Num 24:21; Judg 1:16; 4:11–22; 1 Chr 2:55 [b]Gen 18:25; 19:12, 14; Rev 18:4 [c]Exod 18:10, 19; Num 10:29, 32 [1]MT *I am gathering you.* **15:7** [a]1 Sam 14:48 [b]Gen 2:11; 25:17–18 [c]Gen 16:7; Exod 15:22; 1 Sam 27:8 **15:8** [a]1 Sam 15:32–33 **15:9** [a]1 Sam 15:3, 15, 19 **15:11** [a]Gen 6:6–7; 1 Sam 15:35; 2 Sam 24:16 [b]Josh 22:16; 1 Kgs 9:6 [c]1 Sam 13:13; 15:3, 9 [d]1 Sam 15:35; 16:1 **15:12** [a]Josh 15:55; 1 Sam 25:2 [1]LXX adds *he returned the chariot.* [2]LXX, one Old Latin MS add *to Saul. And behold, he was offering as a burnt offering to the LORD the best of the spoils that he had brought from the Amalekites.* **15:13** [a]Gen 14:19; Judg 17:2; Ruth 3:10; 2 Sam 2:5

[14] Samuel replied, "If that is the case, then what is this sound of sheep in my ears and the sound of cattle that I hear?" [15] Saul said, "They were brought from the Amalekites; the army spared the best of the flocks and cattle to sacrifice to the LORD our God. But everything else we slaughtered."

[16] Then Samuel said to Saul, "Wait a minute! Let me tell you what the LORD said to me last night." Saul[1] said to him, "Tell me." [17] Samuel said, "Is it not true that [a] when you were insignificant in your own eyes, you became head of the tribes of Israel? The LORD chose you as king over Israel. [18] The LORD sent you on a campaign saying, 'Go and exterminate those sinful Amalekites! Fight against them until you[1] have destroyed them.' [19] Why haven't you obeyed the LORD? Instead you have greedily rushed upon the plunder! You have done what is wrong in the LORD's estimation."

[20] Then Saul said to Samuel, "[a] But I have obeyed the LORD! I went on the campaign the LORD sent me on. I brought back King Agag of the Amalekites after exterminating the Amalekites. [21a] But the army took from the plunder some of the sheep and cattle—the best of what was to be slaughtered—to sacrifice to the LORD your God in Gilgal."

[22] Then Samuel said,

"Does the LORD take pleasure in
    burnt offerings and sacrifices
[a] as much as he does in obedience?
Certainly, obedience is better than
    sacrifice;
paying attention is better than the
    fat of rams.
[23] For rebellion is like [a] the sin of
    divination,
and presumption is like the evil of
    idolatry.
Because you have rejected the LORD's
    orders,
he has rejected you from being king."

[24] Then Saul said to Samuel, "I have sinned, for I have disobeyed what [a] the LORD commanded and your words as well. For I was afraid [b] of the army, and I obeyed their voice. [25] Now please forgive my sin. Go back with me so I can worship the LORD."

[26] Samuel said to Saul, "I will not go back with you, [a] for you have rejected the LORD's orders, and the LORD has rejected you from being king over Israel!"

[27] When Samuel turned to leave, [a] Saul grabbed the edge of his robe and it tore. [28] Samuel said to him, "[a] The LORD has torn the kingdom of Israel from you this day and has given it to one of your colleagues who is better than you! [29] The Preeminent One of Israel does not go back on his word or change his mind, for he is not a human being who changes his mind." [30] Saul again replied, "I have sinned. But please [a] honor me before the elders of my people and before Israel. Go back with me so I may worship the LORD your God." [31] So Samuel followed Saul back, and Saul worshiped the LORD.

Samuel Puts Agag to Death

[32] Then Samuel said, "Bring me King Agag of the Amalekites." So Agag came to him trembling,[1] thinking to himself, "Surely death is bitter!"[2] [33] Samuel said, "Just [a] as your sword left women childless, so your mother will be the most bereaved[1] among women." Then Samuel hacked Agag to pieces there in Gilgal before the LORD.

[34] Then Samuel went to [a] Ramah, while Saul went up to his home in [b] Gibeah of Saul. [35] Until the day he died, [a] Samuel did not see Saul again. Samuel did, however, mourn for Saul, but the LORD regretted that he had made Saul king over Israel.

Samuel Anoints David as King

16 The LORD said to Samuel, "[a] How long do you intend to mourn for Saul? I have rejected him as king over Israel.[1] [b] Fill your horn with olive oil and go. I am sending you to [c] Jesse [d] in Bethlehem, for I have selected a king for myself from among his sons."

[2] Samuel [a] replied, "How can I go? Saul will hear about it and kill me!" But the LORD said, "Take a heifer with you and say, 'I have

---

15:16 [1] Ket. *they.*   **15:17** [a] 1 Sam 9:21; 10:22   **15:18** [1] MT *they.*   **15:20** [a] 1 Sam 15:13; [Prov 28:13]   **15:21** [a] 1 Sam 15:15   **15:22** [a] Ps 50:8–9; 51:16–17; [Prov 21:3; Isa 1:11–17; Jer 7:22–23; Mic 6:6–8; Heb 10:4–10]   **15:23** [a] 1 Sam 13:14; 16:1   **15:24** [a] Num 22:34; Josh 7:20; 1 Sam 26:21; 2 Sam 12:13; Ps 51:4   [b] [Exod 23:2; Prov 29:25; Isa 51:12–13]   **15:26** [a] 1 Sam 2:30   **15:27** [a] 1 Kgs 11:30–31   **15:28** [a] 1 Sam 28:17–18; 1 Kgs 11:31   **15:30** [a] [John 5:44; 12:43]   **15:32** [1] Heb. *in bonds.*   [2] MT *Surely the bitterness of death is past.*   **15:33** [a] [Gen 9:6]; Num 14:45; Judg 1:7; [Matt 7:2]   [1] Heb. *bereaved more than* [other] *women.*   **15:34** [a] 1 Sam 7:17   [b] 1 Sam 11:4   **15:35** [a] 1 Sam 19:24   **16:1** [a] 1 Sam 15:23, 35   [b] 1 Sam 9:16; 10:1; 2 Kgs 9:1   [c] Ruth 4:18–22   [d] Ps 78:70–71; Acts 13:22   [1] Luc. adds *And the Lord said to Samuel.*   **16:2** [a] 1 Sam 9:12

come to sacrifice to the LORD.' [3]Then invite Jesse to the sacrifice, and I will show you what you should do. You will anoint for me the one I point out to you."

[4]Samuel did what the LORD told him. When he arrived in Bethlehem, the elders of the city were [a]afraid to meet him. They[1] said, "[b]Do you come in peace?" [5]He replied, "Yes, in peace. I have come to sacrifice to the LORD. [a]Consecrate yourselves and come with me to the sacrifice." So he consecrated Jesse and his sons and invited them to the sacrifice.

[6]When they arrived, Samuel noticed [a]Eliab and [b]said to himself, "Surely, here before the LORD stands his chosen king." [7]But the LORD said to Samuel, "[a]Don't be impressed by his appearance [b]or his height, for I have rejected him. God does not view things the way people do.[1] People [q]look on the outward appearance, but the LORD looks at the [d]heart."

[8]Then Jesse called Abinadab and presented him to Samuel. But Samuel said, "The LORD has not chosen this one either." [9]Then Jesse presented Shammah. But Samuel said, "The LORD has not chosen this one either." [10]Jesse presented seven of his sons to Samuel.[1] But Samuel said to Jesse, "The LORD has not chosen any of these." [11]Then Samuel asked Jesse, "Is that all the young men?" Jesse replied, "There is still the youngest one, but he's taking care of the [a]flock." Samuel said to Jesse, "Send and get him, for we cannot turn our attention to other things until he comes here."

[12]So Jesse had him brought in. Now he was [a]ruddy, [b]with attractive eyes [c]and a handsome appearance. The LORD said, "Go and anoint him. This is the one." [13]So Samuel took [a]the horn full of olive oil and anointed him in the presence of his brothers. The Spirit of the LORD rushed upon David from that day onward. Then Samuel got up and went to Ramah.

David Appears before Saul

[14][a]Now the Spirit of the LORD [b]had turned away from Saul, and an evil spirit[1] from the LORD tormented him. [15]Then Saul's servants said to him, "Look, an evil spirit from God is tormenting you. [16]Let our lord instruct his servants who are here before you to look for a man who knows how to [a]play the lyre. Then whenever the evil spirit from God comes upon you, he can play the lyre and you will feel better." [17]So Saul said to his servants, "Find me a man who plays well and bring him to me." [18]One of his attendants replied, "I have seen a son of Jesse in Bethlehem who knows how to play [a]the lyre. He is a brave warrior[1] and is articulate and handsome, for the LORD is with him."

[19]So Saul sent messengers to Jesse and said, "Send me your son David, who is out with the sheep." [20]So Jesse [a]took a donkey loaded with bread, a container of wine, and a young goat and sent them to Saul with his son David. [21]David came to Saul and [a]stood before him. Saul liked him a great deal, and he became his armor-bearer. [22]Then Saul sent word to Jesse saying, "Let David be my servant, for I am very pleased with him."

[23]So whenever the spirit from God would come upon Saul, David would take his lyre and play it. This would bring relief to Saul and make him feel better. Then the evil spirit would leave him alone.

David Kills Goliath

17 [1]The Philistines gathered their troops for battle. They assembled at [a]Socoh in Judah. They camped in Ephes Dammim, between Socoh and Azekah. [2]Saul and the Israelite army assembled and camped in the valley of Elah, where they arranged their battle lines to fight against the Philistines. [3]The Philistines were standing on one hill, and the Israelites on another hill, with the valley between them.

[4]Then a champion came out from the camp of the Philistines. His name was [a]Goliath; he was from [b]Gath. He was close to seven feet tall.[1] [5]He had a bronze helmet on his head and was wearing scale body armor. The weight of his bronze body armor was

16:4 [a]1 Sam 21:1   [b]1 Kgs 2:13; 2 Kgs 9:22   [1]MT *he.*   16:5 [a]Gen 35:2; Exod 19:10   16:6 [a]1 Sam 17:13, 28   [b]1 Kgs 12:26   16:7 [a]Ps 147:10   [b]Isa 55:8–9   [c]2 Cor 10:7   [d]1 Kgs 8:39   [1]Heb. *for not that which the man sees.*   16:10 [1]Heb. *caused seven of his sons to pass before Samuel.*   16:11 [a]2 Sam 7:8; Ps 78:70–72   16:12 [a]1 Sam 17:42   [b]Gen 39:6; Exod 2:2; Acts 7:20   [c]1 Sam 9:17   16:13 [a]Num 27:18; 1 Sam 10:6, 9, 10   16:14 [a]Judg 16:20; 1 Sam 11:6; 18:12; 28:15   [b]Judg 9:23; 1 Sam 16:15–16; 18:10; 19:9; 1 Kgs 22:19–22   [1]Or *an injurious spirit;* may refer to the character of the spirit or to its effect upon Saul.   16:16 [a]1 Sam 18:10; 19:9; 2 Kgs 3:15   16:18 [a]1 Sam 3:19; 18:12, 14   [1]Heb. *mighty man of valor and a man of war.*   16:20 [a]1 Sam 10:4, 27; Prov 18:16   16:21 [a]Gen 41:46; Prov 22:29   17:1 [a]Josh 15:35; 2 Chr 28:18   [1]LXX for chs. 17–18 is much shorter, lacking almost half the material (39 of a total of 88 vv.).   17:4 [a]2 Sam 21:19   [b]Josh 11:21–22   [1]Heb. *his height was six cubits and a span;* MT places Goliath at about 9½ feet tall while other textual wss place him at about 6 feet, 7 inches.

5,000 shekels. [6] He had bronze shin guards on his legs, and a bronze javelin was slung over his shoulders. [7] The shaft of his spear was like a weaver's beam, and the iron point of his spear weighed 600 shekels. His shield bearer was walking before him.

[8] Goliath stood and called to Israel's troops, "Why do you come out to prepare for battle? Am I not the Philistine, and are you not the [a]servants of Saul? Choose[1] for yourselves a man so he may come down to me! [9] If he is able to fight with me and strike me down, we will become your servants. But if I prevail against him and strike him down, you will become our servants and will [a]serve us." [10] Then the Philistine said, "I [a]defy Israel's troops this day! Give me a man so we can fight each other!" [11] When Saul and all the Israelites heard these words of the Philistine, they were upset and very afraid.

[12] [1] Now David was [a]the son of an [b]Ephrathite named Jesse from Bethlehem in Judah. He had [c]eight sons, and in Saul's days he was old and well advanced in years.[2] [13] Jesse's three oldest sons had followed Saul to war. The [a]names of the three sons who went to war were Eliab, his firstborn; Abinadab, the second oldest; and Shammah, the third oldest. [14] Now David was the youngest. While the three oldest sons followed Saul, [15] David was going back and forth from Saul in order [a]to care for his father's sheep in Bethlehem.

[16] Meanwhile for 40 days the Philistine approached every morning and evening and took his position. [17] Jesse said to his son David, "Take your brothers this ephah of roasted grain and these 10 loaves of bread; go quickly to the camp to your brothers. [18] Also take these 10 portions of cheese to their commanding officer. Find [a]out how your brothers are doing and bring back their pledge that they received the goods.[1] [19] They are with Saul and the whole Israelite army in the valley of Elah, fighting with the Philistines."

[20] So David got up early in the morning and entrusted the flock to someone else who would watch over it. After loading up, he went just as Jesse had instructed him. He arrived at the camp as the army was going out to the battle lines shouting its battle cry. [21] Israel and the Philistines drew up their battle lines opposite one another. [22] After David had entrusted his cargo to the care of the supply officer, he ran to the battlefront. When he arrived, he asked his brothers how they were doing. [23] As he was speaking with them, the champion named Goliath, the Philistine from Gath, was coming up from the battle lines of the Philistines. He spoke the way he usually did, and David heard it. [24] When all the men of Israel saw this man, they retreated from his presence and were very afraid.

[25] The men of Israel said, "Have you seen this man who is coming up? He does so to defy Israel. But the king [a]will make the man who can strike him down very wealthy! He will give him his daughter in marriage, and he will make his father's house exempt from tax obligations in Israel."

[26] David asked [a]the men who were standing near him, "What will be done for the man who strikes down this Philistine and frees Israel from this humiliation? For who is this [b]uncircumcised Philistine, that he [c]defies [d]the armies of the living God?" [27] The [a]soldiers told him what had been promised, saying, "This is what will be done for the man who can strike him down."

[28] When David's oldest brother Eliab heard him speaking to the men, [a]he became angry with David and said, "Why have you come down here? To whom did you entrust those few sheep in the wilderness? I am familiar with your pride and deceit! You have come down here to watch the battle."

[29] David replied, "What have [a]I done now? Can't I say anything?" [30] Then he turned from those who were nearby to someone else and [a]asked the same question, but they gave him the same answer as before. [31] When David's words were overheard and reported to Saul, he called for him.

[32] David said to Saul, "Don't [a]let anyone be discouraged.[1] [b]Your servant will go and fight this Philistine!" [33] But Saul replied to David, "[a]You aren't able to go against this Philistine and fight him. You're just a boy! He has been a warrior from his youth."

17:8 [a]1 Sam 8:17   [1]MT to eat food.   17:9 [a]1 Sam 11:1   17:10 [a]1 Sam 17:26, 36, 45; 2 Sam 21:21   17:12 [a]Ruth 4:22; 1 Sam 16:1, 18; 17:58   [b]Gen 35:19   [c]1 Sam 16:10–11; 1 Chr 2:13–15   [1]Some MSS of the LXX omit vv. 12–31.   [2]MT among men.   17:13 [a]1 Sam 16:6, 8, 9; 1 Chr 2:13   17:15 [a]1 Sam 16:11, 19; 2 Sam 7:8   17:18 [a]Gen 37:13–14   [1]Heb. and their pledge take.   17:25 [a]Josh 15:16   17:26 [a]1 Sam 11:2   [b]1 Sam 14:6; 17:36; Jer 9:25–26   [c]1 Sam 17:10   [d]Deut 5:26; 2 Kgs 19:4; Jer 10:10   17:27 [a]1 Sam 17:25   17:28 [a]Gen 37:4, 8–36; [Prov 18:19; Matt 10:36]   17:29 [a]1 Sam 17:17   17:30 [a]1 Sam 17:26–27   17:32 [a]Deut 20:1–4   [b]1 Sam 16:18   [1]Heb. Let not the heart of a man fall upon him.   17:33 [a]Num 13:31; Deut 9:2

34David replied to Saul, "Your servant has been a shepherd for his father's flock. Whenever a ªlion or bear would come and carry off a sheep from the flock, 35I would go out after it, strike it down, and rescue the sheep from its mouth. If it rose up against me, I would grab it by its jaw, strike it, and kill it. 36Your servant has struck down both the lion and the bear. This uncircumcised Philistine will be just like one of them,1 for he has defied the armies of the living God." 37David went on to say, "ªThe LORD who delivered me from the lion and the bear will also deliver me from the hand of this Philistine." Then Saul said to David, "bGo! The LORD will be with you."1

38Then Saul clothed David with his own fighting attire and put a bronze helmet on his head. He also put body armor on him. 39David strapped on his sword over his fighting attire and tried to walk around, but he was not used to them. David said to Saul, "I can't walk in these things, for I'm not used to them." So David removed them. 40He took his staff in his hand, picked out five smooth stones from the stream, placed them in the pouch1 of his shepherd's bag, took his sling in hand, and approached the Philistine.

411The Philistine, with his shield bearer walking in front of him, kept coming closer to David. 42When the Philistine looked carefully at David, he ªdespised him, for he was only a bruddy and handsome boy. 43The Philistine ªsaid to David, "Am I a dog, that you are coming after me with sticks?" Then the Philistine cursed David by his gods. 44The Philistine ªsaid to David, "Come here to me, so I can give your flesh to the birds of the sky and the wild animals of the field!"1

45But David replied to the Philistine, "You are coming against me with sword and spear and javelin. ªBut I am coming against you in the name of the LORD of Heaven's Armies, the God of Israel's armies, whom you have bdefied! 46This very day ªthe LORD will deliver you into my hand. I will strike you down and cut off your head. This day I will give the corpses of the Philistine army to the birds of the sky and the wild animals of the land. Then all the land will realize bthat Israel has a God, 47and all this assembly will know that it is not by sword or spear that ªthe LORD saves! For the battle is the LORD's, and he will deliver you into our hand."

48The Philistine drew steadily closer to David to attack him, while David quickly ªran toward the battle line to attack the Philistine.1 49David reached his hand into the bag and took out a stone. He slung it, striking the Philistine on the forehead. The stone sank deeply into his forehead, and he fell down with his face to the ground.

501David prevailed over the Philistine with just the ªsling and the stone. He struck down the Philistine and killed him. David did not even have a sword in his hand. 51David ran and stood over the Philistine. He grabbed Goliath's ªsword, drew it from its sheath,1 and after killing him, bhe cut off his head with it. When the Philistines saw their champion was dead, they ran away.

52Then the men of Israel and Judah charged forward, shouting a battle cry. They chased the Philistines to the valley1 and to the very gates of Ekron. The Philistine corpses lay fallen along the ªShaaraim road to Gath and Ekron. 53When the Israelites returned from their hot pursuit of the Philistines, they looted their camp. 54David took the head of the Philistine and brought it to Jerusalem, and he put Goliath's weapons in his tent.

551Now as Saul watched David going out to fight the Philistine, he asked ªAbner, the general in command of the army, "bWhose son is that young man, Abner?" Abner replied, "As surely as you live, O king, I don't know." 56The king said, "Find out whose son this boy is."

57So when David returned from striking down the Philistine, Abner took him and brought him before Saul. He still had the

17:34 ªJudg 14:5   17:36 1LXX adds *Should I not go and smite him, and remove today reproach from Israel? For who is this uncircumcised one?*   17:37 ª[2 Cor 1:10; 2 Tim 4:17–18]   b1 Sam 20:13; 1 Chr 22:11, 16   1Or *Go, and may the LORD be with you.*   17:40 1A receptacle of some sort and apparently a common part of a shepherd's equipment.   17:41 1Most LXX MSS omit v. 41.   17:42 ª[Ps 123:4; Prov 16:18; 1 Cor 1:27–28]   b1 Sam 16:12   17:43 ª1 Sam 24:14; 2 Sam 3:8; 9:8; 16:9; 2 Kgs 8:13   17:44 ª1 Sam 17:46; 1 Kgs 20:10–11   1Sev. MSS *earth.*   17:45 ª2 Sam 22:33, 35; 2 Chr 32:8; Ps 124:8; [2 Cor 10:4]; Heb 11:33–34   b1 Sam 17:10   17:46 ªDeut 28:26   bJosh 4:24; 1 Kgs 8:43; 18:36; 2 Kgs 19:19; Isa 52:10   17:47 ª2 Chr 20:15   17:48 ªPs 27:3   1Most LXX MSS omit the second half of v. 48.   17:50 ªJudg 3:31; 15:15; 20:16   1Most LXX MSS omit v. 50.   17:51 ª1 Sam 21:9; 2 Sam 23:21   bHeb 11:34   1Most LXX MSS omit *drew it from its sheath.*   17:52 ªJosh 15:36   1Most LXX MSS *Gath.*   17:55 ª1 Sam 14:50   b1 Sam 16:21–22   1Most LXX MSS omit 17:55–18:5.

head of the Philistine in his hand. [58] Saul [a] said to him, "Whose son are you, young man?" David replied, "I am the son of your servant Jesse in Bethlehem."

Saul Comes to Fear David

18 When David had finished talking with Saul, Jonathan and David became bound [a] together in close friendship. Jonathan loved David as much as he did his own life. [2] Saul retained David on that day [a] and did not allow him to return to his father's house. [3] Jonathan made a [a] covenant with David, for he loved him as much as he did his own life. [4] Jonathan took off the robe he was wearing and gave it to David, along with the rest of his gear including his sword, his bow, and even his belt.

[5] On every mission on which Saul sent him, David achieved success. So Saul appointed him over the men of war. This pleased not only all the army, but also Saul's servants.

[6] When [a] the men arrived after David returned from striking down the Philistine, the women from all the cities of Israel came out singing and dancing to meet King Saul. They were happy as they played their tambourines and three-stringed instruments. [7] The women who were playing the music [a] sang,

> [b] "Saul has struck down his
>   thousands,
> but David his tens of thousands!"

[8] This made Saul very angry. The statement [a] displeased him and [b] he thought, "They have attributed to David tens of thousands, but to me they have attributed only thousands. What does he lack, except the kingdom?" [9] So Saul was keeping an eye on David from that day onward.

[10] The next day an evil spirit from God rushed upon Saul [a] and [b] he prophesied[1] within his house. Now David was playing the [c] lyre as usual. There was a spear in Saul's hand, [11] and Saul [a] threw the spear, thinking, "I'll nail David to the wall!" But David escaped from him on two different occasions. [12] So Saul [a] feared David, because [b] the LORD was with David but had [c] departed from Saul. [13] Saul removed David from his presence and made him a commanding officer. David led [a] the army out to battle and back. [14] Now David achieved success in all [a] he did, for the LORD was with him. [15] When Saul saw how very successful he was, he was afraid of him. [16] But [a] all Israel and Judah loved David, for he was the one leading them out to battle and back.

[17] [1] Then Saul [a] said to David, "Here's my oldest daughter, Merab. I want to give her to you in marriage. Only be a brave warrior for me and fight [b] the battles of the LORD." For Saul thought, "There's no need for me to raise my hand against him. [c] Let it be the hand of the Philistines!"

[18] David said to Saul, "[a] Who am I? Who are my relatives or the clan of my father in Israel that I should become the king's son-in-law?" [19] When the time came for Merab, Saul's daughter, to be given to David, she instead was given in marriage to [a] Adriel, who was from [b] Meholah.

[20] [a] Now Michal, Saul's daughter, loved David. When they told Saul about this, it pleased him. [21] Saul said, "I will give her to him so that she may become a snare to him and so [a] the hand of the Philistines may be against him." So Saul said to David, "Today is the second time for [b] you to become my son-in-law."[1]

[22] Then Saul instructed his servants, "Tell David secretly, 'The king is pleased with you, and all his servants like you. So now become the king's son-in-law.'" [23] So Saul's servants spoke these words privately to David. David replied, "Is becoming the king's son-in-law something insignificant to you? I'm just a poor and lightly esteemed man!"

[24] When Saul's servants reported what David had said, [25] Saul replied, "Here is what you should say to David: 'There is nothing that the king wants as a price for the [a] bride except 100 Philistine foreskins, so that he

17:58 [a] 1 Sam 17:12   18:1 [a] Gen 44:30   18:2 [a] 1 Sam 17:15   18:3 [a] 1 Sam 20:8–17   18:6 [a] Exod 15:20–21; Judg 11:34; Ps 68:25; 149:3   18:7 [a] Exod 15:21   [b] 1 Sam 21:11; 29:5   18:8 [a] Eccl 4:4   [b] 1 Sam 15:28   18:10 [a] 1 Sam 19:24; 1 Kgs 18:29; Acts 16:16   [b] 1 Sam 16:14   [c] 1 Sam 16:23   [1] Or *he raved.*   18:11 [a] 1 Sam 19:10; 20:33   18:12 [a] 1 Sam 18:15, 29   [b] 1 Sam 16:13, 18   [c] 1 Sam 16:14; 28:15   18:13 [a] Num 27:17; 1 Sam 18:16; 29:6; 2 Sam 5:2   18:14 [a] Gen 39:2–3, 23; Josh 6:27; 1 Sam 16:18   18:16 [a] Num 27:16–17; 1 Sam 18:5; 2 Sam 5:2; 1 Kgs 3:7   18:17 [a] 1 Sam 14:49; 17:25   [b] Num 32:20, 27, 29; 1 Sam 25:28   [c] 1 Sam 18:21, 25; 2 Sam 12:9   [1] Some LXX MSS omit vv. 17–19.   18:18 [a] 1 Sam 9:21; 18:23; 2 Sam 7:18   18:19 [a] 2 Sam 21:8   [b] Judg 7:22; 2 Sam 21:8; 1 Kgs 19:16   18:20 [a] 1 Sam 18:28   18:21 [a] 1 Sam 18:17   [b] 1 Sam 18:26   [1] Most LXX MSS omit the final sentence of v. 21.   18:25 [a] Gen 34:12; Exod 22:17

can be [b]avenged of his enemies.'" (Now Saul was [c]thinking that he could kill David by the hand of the Philistines.)

[26]So his servants told David [a]these things and David agreed to become the king's son-in-law. Now the specified time had not yet expired [27]when David, along with [a]his men, went out and struck down 200 Philistine men. [b]David brought their foreskins and presented all of them to the king so that he could become the king's son-in-law. Saul then gave him his daughter Michal in marriage.

[28]When Saul realized that the LORD was with David and that his daughter Michal loved David, [29]Saul became even more afraid of him. Saul continued to be at odds with David from then on.[1] [30][1]The leaders of the Philistines would march out, and as often as they did so, David achieved more success than all of Saul's servants. His name was held in high esteem.

Saul Repeatedly Attempts to Take David's Life

19 Then Saul told his son Jonathan and all his servants to kill [a]David. But Saul's son Jonathan [b]liked David very much. [2]So Jonathan told David, "My father Saul is trying to kill you. So be careful tomorrow morning. Find a hiding place and stay in seclusion. [3]I will go out and stand beside my father in the field where [a]you are. I will speak to my father about you. When I find out what the problem is, I will let you know."

[4]So Jonathan [a]spoke on David's behalf to his father Saul. He said to him, "The king should not [b]sin against his servant David, for he has not sinned against you. On the contrary, his actions have been very beneficial for you. [5]He risked his [a]life when he struck [b]down [c]the Philistine, and the LORD gave all Israel a great victory. When you saw it, you were happy. So [d]why would you [e]sin against innocent blood by putting David to death for no reason?"

[6]Saul accepted Jonathan's advice and took an oath, "As surely as the LORD lives, he will not be put to death." [7]Then Jonathan called David and told him all these things. Jonathan brought David to Saul, and he served him [a]as he had done formerly.

[8]Now once again there was war. So David went out to fight the Philistines. He defeated them thoroughly, [a]and they ran away from him. [9]Then an evil spirit from [a]the LORD came upon Saul. He was sitting in his house with his spear in his hand, while David was playing the lyre. [10]Saul tried to nail David to the wall with the spear, but he escaped from Saul's presence, and the spear drove into the wall. David escaped quickly that night.

[11][a]Saul sent messengers to David's house to guard it and to kill him in the morning. Then David's wife Michal told him, "If you do not save yourself tonight, tomorrow you will be dead!" [12]So Michal lowered David through the window, and he ran away and escaped.

[13]Then Michal took a household idol[1] and put it on the bed. She put a quilt made of goats' hair over its head and then covered the idol with a garment. [14]When Saul sent messengers to arrest David, she said, "He's sick."

[15]Then Saul sent the messengers back to see David, saying, "Bring him up to me on his bed so I can kill him." [16]When the messengers came, they found only the idol on the bed and the quilt made of goats' hair at its head.

[17]Saul said to Michal, "[a]Why have you deceived me this way by sending my enemy away? Now he has escaped!" Michal replied to Saul, "He said to me, 'Help me get away or else I will kill you!'"[1]

[18]Now David had run away and escaped. He went to [a]Samuel in [b]Ramah and told him everything that Saul had done to him. Then he and Samuel went and stayed at Naioth. [19]It was reported to Saul saying, "David is at Naioth in Ramah." [20]So [a]Saul sent messengers to capture David. When they saw [b]a company of prophets prophesying with Samuel standing there as their leader, the Spirit of God came upon Saul's messengers, and they also [c]prophesied. [21]When it

18:25 [b]1 Sam 14:24   [c]1 Sam 18:17   18:26 [a]1 Sam 18:21   18:27 [a]1 Sam 18:13   [b]2 Sam 3:14   18:29 [1]Most LXX MSS omit the final sentence of v. 29.   18:30 [1]Most LXX MSS omit v. 30.   19:1 [a]1 Sam 8:8–9   [b]1 Sam 18:1   19:3 [a]1 Sam 20:8–13   19:4 [a]1 Sam 20:32; [Prov 31:8–9]   [b]Gen 42:22; [Prov 17:13]; Jer 18:20   19:5 [a]Judg 9:17; 12:3   [b]1 Sam 17:49–50   [c]1 Sam 11:13; 1 Chr 11:14   [d]1 Sam 20:32   [e][Deut 19:10–13]   19:7 [a]1 Sam 16:21; 18:2, 10, 13   19:8 [a]1 Sam 18:27; 23:5   19:9 [a]1 Sam 16:14; 18:10–11   19:11 [a]Judg 16:2; Ps 59:title   19:13 [1]Heb. *teraphim*; statues that represented various deities.   19:17 [a]2 Sam 2:22   [1]Heb. *Send me away! Why should I kill you?*   19:18 [a]1 Sam 16:13   [b]1 Sam 7:17   19:20 [a]1 Sam 19:11, 14; John 7:32   [b]1 Sam 10:5–6, 10; [1 Cor 14:3, 24, 25]   [c]Num 11:25; Joel 2:28

was reported to Saul, he sent more messengers, but they prophesied too. So Saul sent messengers a third time, but they also prophesied. [22] Finally Saul himself went to Ramah. When he arrived at the large cistern that is in Secu, he asked, "Where are Samuel and David?" They said, "At Naioth in Ramah."

[23] So Saul went to Naioth in Ramah.[a] The Spirit of God came upon him as well, and he walked along prophesying until he came to Naioth in Ramah. [24] He even stripped off his clothes[a] and prophesied before Samuel. He lay there[b] naked all that day and night. (For that reason it[c] is asked, "Is Saul also among the prophets?")

Jonathan Seeks to Protect David

20 David fled from Naioth in Ramah. He came to Jonathan and asked, "What have I done? What is my offense? How have I sinned before your father, that he is seeking my life?"

[2] Jonathan said to him, "By no means are you going to die! My father does nothing[1] large or small without making me aware of it. Why would my father hide this matter from me? It just won't happen!"

[3] Taking an oath, David again[1] said, "Your father is very much aware of the fact that I have found favor with you, and he has thought, 'Don't let Jonathan know about this, or he will be upset.'[a] But as surely as the LORD lives and you live, there is about one step between me and death!" [4] Jonathan replied to David, "Tell me what I can do for you."

[5] David said to Jonathan, "Tomorrow is the[a] new moon, and I am certainly expected to join the king for a meal. You must send me away so I can[b] hide in the field until the third evening from now. [6] If your father happens[a] to miss me, you should say, 'David urgently requested me to let him go to his town Bethlehem, for there is an annual sacrifice there for his entire family.' [7][a] If he should then say, 'That's fine,' then your servant is safe. But if he becomes very angry, be assured that he has decided to[b] harm me. [8] You must[a] be loyal to[b] your servant, for you have made a covenant with your servant in the LORD's name.[c] If I am guilty, you yourself kill me! Why bother taking me to your father?"

[9] Jonathan said, "Far be it from you to suggest this! If I were at all aware that my father had decided to harm you, wouldn't I tell you about it?" [10] David said to Jonathan, "Who will tell me if your father answers you harshly?" [11] Jonathan said to David, "Come on. Let's go out to the field."

When the two of them had gone out into the field, [12] Jonathan said to David, "The LORD God of Israel is my witness![1] I will feel out my father about this time the day after tomorrow. If he is favorably inclined toward David, will I not then send word to you and let you know? [13] But if my[a] father intends to do you harm, may[b] the LORD do all this and more to Jonathan if I don't let you know and send word to you, so you can go safely on your way. May the LORD[c] be with you, as he was with my father. [14] While I am still alive, extend to me the loyalty of the LORD, or else I will die. [15] Don't ever cut off[a] your loyalty to my family, not even when the LORD has cut off every one of David's enemies from the face of the earth [16] and called David's enemies to account." So Jonathan made a covenant with the house of David. [17] Jonathan once again took an oath with David, because he loved him. In fact Jonathan loved him as much as he did his own life. [18] Jonathan said to him, "[a] Tomorrow is the new moon, and you will be missed, for your seat will be empty. [19] On[a] the third day[1] you should go down quickly and come to the place where you hid yourself the day this all started. Stay near the stone Ezel. [20] I will shoot three arrows near it, as though I were shooting at a target. [21] When I send[a] a boy after them, I will say, 'Go and find the arrows.' If I say to the boy, 'Look, the arrows are on this side of you; get them,' then come back. For as surely as the LORD lives, you will be safe and there will be no problem. [22] But if I say to the boy, 'Look, the arrows are on the other side of you,' then get away. For in that case the LORD has sent you away. [23] With regard to[a] the matter that you and I discussed, the LORD is the witness between us forever."[1]

19:23[a] 1 Sam 10:10   19:24[a] Isa 20:2   [b] Mic 1:8   [c] 1 Sam 10:10–12   20:2[1] Ket. *do to him.*   20:3[a] 1 Sam 27:1; 2 Kgs 2:6   [1] LXX, Syr. omit *again.*   20:5[a] Num 10:10; 28:11–15   [b] 1 Sam 19:2–3   20:6[a] 1 Sam 16:4; 17:12; John 7:42   20:7[a] Deut 1:23; 2 Sam 17:4   [b] 1 Sam 25:17; Esth 7:7   20:8[a] Josh 2:14   [b] 1 Sam 18:3; 20:16; 23:18   [c] 2 Sam 14:32   20:12[1] Heb. *the LORD God of Israel.* 20:13[a] Ruth 1:17; 1 Sam 3:17   [b] Josh 1:5; 1 Sam 17:37; 18:12; 1 Chr 22:11, 16   [c] 1 Sam 10:7   20:15[a] 1 Sam 24:21; 2 Sam 9:1, 3, 7; 21:7 20:18[a] 1 Sam 20:5, 24   20:19[a] 1 Sam 19:2   [1] Heb. *you will do* [something] *a third time.*   20:21[a] Jer 4:2 20:23[a] 1 Sam 20:14–15   [1] Heb. *the LORD* [is] *between me and between you forever.*

[24] So David hid in the field. When the new moon came, the king sat down to eat his meal. [25] The king sat down in his usual place by the wall, with Jonathan opposite him[1] and Abner at his side. But David's place was vacant. [26] However, Saul said nothing about it that day, for he thought, "Something has happened to make him ceremonially [a]unclean. Yes, he must be unclean." [27] But the next morning, the second day of the new moon, David's place was still vacant. So Saul said to his son Jonathan, "Why has Jesse's son not come to the meal yesterday or today?"

[28] Jonathan [a]replied to Saul, "David urgently requested that he be allowed to go to Bethlehem. [29] He said, 'Permit me to go, for we are having a family sacrifice in the town, and my brother urged me to be there. So now, if I have found favor with you, let me go to see my brothers.' For that reason he has not come to the king's table."

[30] Saul became angry with Jonathan[1] and said to him, "You stupid traitor![2] Don't I realize that to your own disgrace and to the disgrace of your mother's nakedness you have chosen this son of Jesse? [31] For as long as this son of Jesse is alive on the earth, you and your kingdom will not be established. Now, send some men and bring him to me. For he is as good as dead!"

[32] Jonathan responded to his father Saul, "[a]Why should he be put to death? What has he done?" [33] Then Saul [a]threw his spear at Jonathan in order to strike him down. So Jonathan was convinced that his father had decided to kill David. [34] Jonathan got up from the table enraged. He did not eat any food on that second day of the new moon, for he was upset that his father had humiliated David.[1]

[35] The next morning Jonathan, along with a young servant, went out to the field to meet David. [36] He said to his servant, "Run, find the arrows that I am about to shoot." As the servant ran, Jonathan shot the arrow beyond him. [37] When the servant came to the place where Jonathan had shot the arrow, Jonathan called out to the servant, "Isn't the arrow farther beyond you?" [38] Jonathan called out to the servant, "Hurry! Go faster! Don't delay!" Jonathan's servant retrieved the arrow and came back to his master. [39] (Now the servant did not understand any of this. Only Jonathan and David knew what was going on.) [40] Then Jonathan gave his equipment to the servant who was with him. He said to him, "Go, take these things back to the town."

[41] When the servant had left, David got up from beside the mound,[1] knelt with his face to the ground, and bowed three times. Then they kissed each other and they both wept, especially David. [42] Jonathan said to David, "[a]Go in peace, for the two of us have sworn together in the name of the LORD saying, 'The LORD will be between me and you and between my descendants and your descendants forever.'"

David Goes to Nob

Then David got up and left, while Jonathan went back to the town of Naioth.

21 [1] David went to [a]Ahimelech the priest in Nob. Ahimelech was shaking with [b]fear when he met David, and said to him, "Why are you by yourself with no one accompanying you?" [2] David replied to Ahimelech the priest, "The king instructed me to do something, but he said to me, 'Don't let anyone know the reason I am sending you or the instructions I have given you.' I have told my soldiers to wait at a certain place. [3] Now what do you have at your disposal? Give me five loaves of bread, or whatever can be found."

[4] The priest replied to David, "I don't have any ordinary bread at my disposal. Only [a]holy bread is available, and then only [b]if your soldiers have abstained from relations with women." [5] David said to the priest, "Certainly women have been kept away from us, just as on previous occasions when I have set out. The soldiers' [a]equipment is holy, even on an [b]ordinary journey. How much more so will they be holy today, along with their equipment!"

[6] So the priest [a]gave him holy bread, for there was no bread there other than the Bread of the Presence. It had been removed from before the LORD in order to replace it with hot bread on the day it had been taken

20:25 [1] Heb. *and Jonathan arose.*   20:26 [a] Lev 7:20–21; 15:5   20:28 [a] 1 Sam 20:6   20:30 [1] Sev. MSS add *his son.* [2] Heb. *son of a perverse woman of rebelliousness.*   20:32 [a] Gen 31:36; 1 Sam 19:5; [Prov 31:9]; Matt 27:23; Luke 23:22   20:33 [a] 1 Sam 18:11; 19:10   20:34 [1] Heb. *upset concerning David for his father had humiliated him.*   20:41 [1] MT *south.*   20:42 [a] 1 Sam 1:17   21:1 [a] 1 Sam 14:3; Mark 2:26   [b] 1 Sam 16:4   21:4 [a] Exod 25:30; Lev 24:5–9; Matt 12:4   [b] Exod 19:15   21:5 [a] Exod 19:14–15; 1 Thess 4:4   [b] Lev 8:26   21:6 [a] Matt 12:3–4; Mark 2:25–26; Luke 6:3–4

away. 7(One of Saul's servants was there that day, detained before the LORD. His name was ªDoeg the Edomite, who was in charge of Saul's shepherds.) 8David said to Ahimelech, "Is there no sword or spear here at your disposal? I don't have my own sword or equipment in hand due to the urgency of the king's instructions."

David Goes to Gath

9The priest replied, "ªThe sword of Goliath ᵇthe Philistine, whom you struck down in the valley of Elah, is wrapped in a garment behind the ephod. If you wish, take it for yourself. Other than that one, there's no sword here." David said, "There's nothing like it. Give it to me." 10So on that day David arose and fled from Saul. He went to King Achish of Gath. 11The servants of Achish said to him, "Isn't this David, ªthe king of the land? Isn't he the one that they sing about when they dance, saying,

"ᵇSaul struck down his thousands,
but David his tens of thousands'?"

12David ªthought about what they said and was very afraid of King Achish of Gath. 13He altered his behavior in ªtheir presence. Since he was in their power, he pretended to be insane, making marks on the doors of the gate and letting his saliva run down his beard.

14Achish said to his servants, "Look at this madman! Why did you bring him to me? 15Do I have a shortage of fools so that you have brought me this man to display his insanity in front of me? Should this man enter my house?"

David Goes to Adullam and Mizpah

22 So David left there and ªescaped ᵇto the cave of Adullam. When his brothers and the rest of his father's family learned about it, they went down there to him. 2All those who were in trouble or owed someone money or were discontented gathered around him, ªand he became their leader. He had about ᵇ400 men with him.

3Then David went from there to Mizpah in ªMoab, where he said to the king of Moab, "Please let my father and mother stay with you until I know what God is going to do for me." 4So he had them stay with the king of Moab; they stayed with him the whole time that David was in the stronghold. 5Then ªGad the prophet said to David, "Don't stay in the stronghold. Go to the land of Judah." So David left and went to the forest of Hereth.

Saul Executes the Priests

6But Saul found out the whereabouts of David and the men who were with him. Now Saul was sitting at ªGibeah under the tamarisk tree at an elevated location with his spear in hand and all his servants stationed around him. 7Saul said to his servants, "Listen up, you Benjaminites! Is Jesse's son ªgiving fields and vineyards to all of you? Or is he making all of you[1] commanders and officers? 8For all of you have conspired against me! No one informs me when ªmy own son makes an agreement with the son of Jesse. Not one of you feels sorry for me or informs me that my own son has commissioned my own servant to hide in ambush against me, as is the case today!"

9But ªDoeg the Edomite, who had stationed himself with the servants of Saul, replied, "I saw this son of Jesse come to ᵇAhimelech son of ᶜAhitub at Nob. 10He inquired of the LORD for him ªand ᵇgave him provisions. He also gave him the sword of Goliath the Philistine."

11Then the king arranged for a meeting with the priest Ahimelech son of Ahitub and all the priests of his father's house who were at Nob. They all came to the king. 12Then Saul said, "Listen, son of Ahitub." He replied, "Here I am, my lord." 13Saul said to him, "Why have you conspired against me, you and this son of Jesse? You gave him bread and a sword and inquired of God on his behalf, so that he opposes me and waits in ambush, as is the case today!"

14Ahimelech replied to the king, "Who among all your servants is ªfaithful like David? He is the king's son-in-law, the leader of your bodyguard, and honored in your house. 15Was it just today that I began to inquire of God on his behalf? Far be it from me! The

21:7 ª1 Sam 14:47; 22:9; Ps 52:title   21:9 ª1 Sam 17:2, 50   ᵇ1 Sam 31:10   21:11 ªPs 56:title   ᵇ1 Sam 18:6–8; 29:5   21:12 ªLuke 2:19   21:13 ªPs 34:title   22:1 ªPs 57:title; 142:title   ᵇJosh 12:15; 15:35; 2 Sam 23:13   22:2 ªJudg 11:3   ᵇ1 Sam 25:13   22:3 ª2 Sam 8:2   22:5 ª2 Sam 24:11; 1 Chr 21:9; 29:29; 2 Chr 29:25   22:6 ª1 Sam 15:34   22:7 ª1 Sam 8:14   ¹MT to all of you.   22:8 ª1 Sam 18:3; 20:16, 30   22:9 ª1 Sam 21:7; 22:22; Ps 52:title   ᵇ1 Sam 21:1   ᶜ1 Sam 14:3   22:10 ªNum 27:21; 1 Sam 10:22   ᵇ1 Sam 21:6, 9   22:14 ª1 Sam 19:4–5; 20:32; 24:11

king should not accuse his servant or any of my father's house, for your servant is not aware of all this—not in whole or in part!" [16]But the king said, "[a]You will surely die, Ahimelech, you and all your father's house!" [17]Then the king said to the messengers who were stationed beside him, "Turn and kill the priests of the LORD, for they too have sided with David. They knew he was fleeing, but they did not inform me." But the king's servants [a]refused to harm the priests of the LORD.

[18]Then the king said to Doeg, "You turn and strike down the priests!" So Doeg the Edomite turned and struck down the priests. He [a]killed on that day 85[1] men who wore the linen ephod. [19a]As for Nob, the city of the priests, Doeg struck down men and women, children and infants, oxen, donkeys, and sheep—all with the sword.

[20a]But one of the sons of Ahimelech son of Ahitub [b]escaped and fled to David. His name was Abiathar. [21]Abiathar told David that Saul had killed the priests of the LORD. [22]Then David said to Abiathar, "I knew that day when Doeg the Edomite was there that he would certainly tell Saul! I am guilty[1] of all the deaths in your father's house. [23]Stay with me. Don't be afraid. Whoever[1] seeks my life is seeking your life as well. You are secure with me."

David Delivers the City of Keilah

23 They told David, "The Philistines are fighting in [a]Keilah and are looting the threshing floors." [2]So David [a]asked the LORD, "Should I go and strike down these Philistines?" The LORD said to David, "Go, strike down the Philistines and deliver Keilah."

[3]But David's men said to him, "We are afraid while we are still here in Judah. What will it be like if we go to Keilah against the armies of the Philistines?" [4]So David asked the LORD once again. But again the LORD replied, "Arise, go down to Keilah, for I will give the Philistines into your hand."

[5]So David and his men went to Keilah and [a]fought the Philistines. He took away their cattle and thoroughly defeated them. David delivered the inhabitants of Keilah.

David Eludes Saul Again

[6]Now when Abiathar son of Ahimelech had [a]fled to David at Keilah, he had brought with him an ephod. [7]When Saul was told that David had come to Keilah, Saul said, "God has delivered[1] him into my hand, for he has boxed himself into a corner by entering a city with two barred gates." [8]So Saul mustered all his army to go down to Keilah and besiege David and his men.

[9]When David realized that Saul was planning to harm him, [a]he told Abiathar the priest, "Bring the ephod." [10]Then David said, "[a]O LORD God of Israel, your servant has clearly heard that Saul is planning to come to Keilah to destroy the city because of me. [11]Will the leaders of Keilah deliver me into his hand? Will Saul come down as your servant has heard? O LORD God of Israel, please inform your servant."

Then the LORD said, "He will come down." [12]David asked, "Will the leaders of Keilah deliver me and my men into Saul's hand?" The LORD said, "They will deliver you over."

[13]So David and his men, who numbered [a]about 600, set out and left Keilah; they moved around from one place to another. When told that David had escaped from Keilah, Saul called a halt to his expedition. [14]David stayed in [a]the strongholds that were in the desert and in the hill country of the wilderness of [b]Ziph. Saul looked [c]for him all the time, but God did not deliver David into his hands. [15]David realized that Saul had come out to seek his life; at that time David was in Horesh in the wilderness of Ziph.

[16]Then Jonathan son of Saul left and went to David at Horesh. He encouraged him through God. [17]He said to him, "[a]Don't be afraid! For the hand of my father Saul cannot find you. You will rule over Israel, and I will be your second-in-command. [b]Even my father Saul realizes this." [18]When the two of them had [a]made a covenant before the LORD, David stayed at Horesh, but Jonathan went to his house.

[19]Then the Ziphites went up to Saul at Gibeah and said, "Isn't David hiding among us in the strongholds at Horesh on the hill of Hakilah, south of Jeshimon? [20]Now at

22:16 [a] Deut 24:16   **22:17** [a] Exod 1:17   **22:18** [a] 1 Sam 2:31   [1] LXX *305*; Luc., two Old Latin MSS *350*.   **22:19** [a] Josh 21:1–45; 1 Sam 22:9, 11   **22:20** [a] 1 Sam 23:6, 9; 30:7; 1 Kgs 2:26–27   [b] 1 Sam 2:33   **22:22** [1] MT *I have turned.*   **22:23** [1] Or *the one who.*   **23:1** [a] Josh 15:44; Neh 3:17–18   **23:2** [a] 1 Sam 22:10; 23:4, 6, 9; 28:6; 30:8; 2 Sam 5:19, 23   **23:5** [a] 1 Sam 19:8; 2 Sam 5:20   **23:6** [a] 1 Sam 22:20   **23:7** [1] Heb. *God has alienated him into my hand.*   **23:9** [a] Num 27:21; 1 Sam 23:6; 30:7   **23:10** [a] 1 Sam 22:19   **23:13** [a] 1 Sam 22:2; 25:13   **23:14** [a] Ps 11:1   [b] Josh 15:55; 2 Chr 11:8   [c] Ps 32:7; 54:3–4   **23:17** [a] [Ps 27:1–3; Heb 13:6]   [b] 1 Sam 20:31; 24:20   **23:18** [a] 1 Sam 18:3; 20:12–17, 42; 2 Sam 9:1; 21:7

[a]your own discretion, O king, come down. Delivering him into the king's hand will be our responsibility."

[21]Saul replied, "May you be blessed by the LORD, for you have had compassion on me. [22]Go and make further arrangements. Determine precisely where he is and who has seen him there, for I am told that he is extremely cunning. [23]Locate precisely all the places where he hides and return to me with dependable information. Then I will go with you. If he is in the land, I will find him among all the thousands of Judah."

[24]So they left and went to Ziph ahead [a]of Saul. Now David and his men were in the wilderness of Maon, in the rift valley to the south of Jeshimon. [25]Saul and his men went to look for him. But David was informed and went down to the rock and stayed in the wilderness of Maon. When Saul heard about it, he pursued David in the wilderness of Maon. [26]Saul went on one side of the mountain, while David and his men went on the other side of the mountain. David was hurrying to get away from Saul, but Saul and his men [a]were surrounding David and his men to capture them. [27a]But a messenger came to Saul saying, "Come quickly, for the Philistines have raided the land!"

[28]So Saul stopped pursuing David and went to confront the Philistines. Therefore that place is called Sela Hammahlekoth. [29]Then David went up from there and stayed in the strongholds of En [a]Gedi.

David Spares Saul's Life

24 When Saul returned from pursuing the Philistines, he was told, "Look, David is in the desert of En [a]Gedi." [2]So Saul took 3,000 select men from all Israel and [a]went to find David and his men in the region of the rocks of the mountain goats.[1] [3]He came to the sheepfolds by the road, where there was a cave. [a]Saul went into it to [b]relieve himself.

Now [c]David and his men were sitting in the recesses of the cave. [4]David's men said to him, "This is [a]the day about which the LORD said to you, 'I will give your enemy into

your hand, and you can do to him whatever seems appropriate to you.'" So David got up and quietly cut off an edge of Saul's robe. [5]Afterward [a]David's conscience bothered him because he had cut off an edge of Saul's robe. [6]He said to his men, "May [a]the LORD keep me far away from doing such a thing to my lord, who is the LORD's chosen one, by extending my hand against him. After all, he is the LORD's chosen one." [7]David [a]restrained his men with these words and did not allow them to rise up against Saul. Then Saul left the cave and started down the road.

[8]Afterward David got up and went out of the cave. He called out to Saul, "My lord, O king!" When Saul looked behind him, David kneeled down and bowed with his face to the ground. [9]David said to Saul, "[a]Why do you pay attention when men say, 'David is seeking to do you harm'? [10]Today your own eyes see how the LORD delivered you—this very day—into my hands in the cave. Some told me to kill you, but I had pity on you and said, 'I will not extend my hand against my lord, for he is the LORD's chosen one.' [11]Look, my father, and see the edge of your robe in my hand! When I cut off the edge of your robe, I didn't kill you. So realize and understand that I am [a]not planning evil or rebellion. Even though I have not sinned against you, you are waiting in [b]ambush to take my life. [12a]May the LORD judge between the two of us, and may the LORD vindicate me over you, but my hand will not be against you. [13]It's like the old proverb says: 'From evil people [a]evil proceeds.' But my hand will not be against you. [14]Who has the king of Israel come out after? Who is it that you are pursuing? A dead dog? A [a]single [b]flea? [15]May [a]the LORD be our judge and arbiter. May he [b]see and [c]arbitrate my case and deliver me from your hands."

[16]When David [a]finished speaking these words to Saul, Saul said, "Is that your voice, my son David?" Then Saul wept loudly. [17a]He said to David, "You are [b]more innocent[1] than I, for [c]you have treated me well, even though I have tried to harm you. [18]You have explained today how you have treated

23:20 [a]Ps 54:3 **23:24** [a]Josh 15:55; 1 Sam 25:2 **23:26** [a]Ps 17:9 **23:27** [a]2 Kgs 19:9 **23:29** [a]Josh 15:62; 2 Chr 20:2 **24:1** [a]1 Sam 23:19, 28, 29 **24:2** [a]1 Sam 26:2; Ps 38:12 [1]Or *the Rocks of the Mountain Goats*; if a place name. **24:3** [a]1 Sam 24:10 [b]Judg 3:24 [c]Ps 57:title; 142:title **24:4** [a]1 Sam 26:8–11 **24:5** [a]2 Sam 24:10 **24:6** [a]1 Sam 26:11 **24:7** [a]Ps 7:4; [Matt 5:44; Rom 12:17, 19] **24:9** [a]Ps 141:6; [Prov 16:28; 17:9] **24:11** [a]Judg 11:27; Ps 7:3; 35:7 [b]1 Sam 26:20 **24:12** [a]Gen 16:5; Judg 11:27; 1 Sam 26:10–23; Job 5:8 **24:13** [a][Matt 7:16–20] **24:14** [a]1 Sam 17:43; 2 Sam 9:8 [b]1 Sam 26:20 **24:15** [a]1 Sam 24:12 [b]2 Chr 24:22 [c]Ps 35:1; 43:1; 119:154; Mic 7:9 **24:16** [a]1 Sam 26:17 **24:17** [a]1 Sam 26:21 [b]Gen 38:26 [c][Matt 5:44] [1]Or *righteous*.

me well. [a]The LORD delivered me into your hand, but you did not kill me. [19]Now if a man finds his enemy, does he send him on his way in good shape? May the LORD repay you with good this day for what you have done to me. [20]Now look, [a]I realize that you will in fact be king and that the kingdom of Israel will be established in your hands. [21]So now swear to me in [a]the LORD's name [b]that you will not kill my descendants after me or destroy my name from the house of my father." [22]David promised Saul this on oath. [a]Then Saul went to his house, and David and his men went up to the stronghold.

The Death of Samuel

25 [a]Samuel died, and all Israel assembled and [b]mourned him. They buried him at his home in Ramah. Then David left and went down [c]to the wilderness of Paran.[1]

David Marries Abigail the Widow of Nabal

[2]There was a man [a]in Maon whose business was in [b]Carmel. This man was very wealthy; he owned 3,000 sheep and 1,000 goats. At that time he was shearing his sheep in Carmel. [3]The man's name was Nabal, and his wife's name was Abigail. She was both wise[1] and beautiful, but the man was harsh and his deeds were evil. He was [a]a Calebite.

[4]When David heard in the wilderness that Nabal was [a]shearing his sheep, [5]he sent 10 servants, saying to them, "Go up to Carmel to see Nabal and give him greetings in my name. [6]Then you will say to my brother,[1] [a]'Peace to you and your house! Peace to all that is yours! [7]Now I hear that they are shearing sheep for you. When your shepherds were with us, we neither insulted them [a]nor harmed them the whole time they were in Carmel. [8]Ask your own [a]servants; they can tell you! May my servants find favor in your sight, for we have come[1] at the time of a holiday. Please provide us— your servants and your son David—with whatever you can spare.'"

[9]So David's servants went and spoke all these words to Nabal in David's name. Then they paused. [10]But Nabal responded to David's servants, "[a]Who is David, and who is this son of Jesse? This is a time when many servants are breaking away from their masters! [11a]Should I take my bread and my water and my meat that I have slaughtered for my shearers and give them to these men? I don't even know where they came from!"

[12]So David's servants went on their way. When they had returned, they came and told David all these things. [13]Then David instructed his men, "Each of you strap on your sword!" So each one strapped on his sword, and David also strapped on his sword. About 400 men followed David, while 200 [a]stayed behind with the equipment.

[14]But one of the servants told Nabal's wife Abigail, "David sent messengers from the wilderness to greet our lord, but he screamed at them. [15]These men [a]were very good to us. They did not insult us, nor did we sustain any loss during the entire time we were together in the field. [16]Both night [a]and day they were a protective wall for us the entire time we were with them, while we were tending our flocks. [17]Now be aware of this, and see what you can do. For [a]disaster has been planned for our lord and his entire household. He is such a wicked person that no one tells him anything!"

[18]So Abigail quickly [a]took 200 loaves of bread, two containers of wine, five prepared sheep, five seahs of roasted grain, 100 bunches of raisins, and 200 lumps of pressed figs. She loaded them on donkeys [19]and said to her servants, "[a]Go on ahead of me. I will come after you." But she did not tell her husband Nabal.

[20]Riding on her donkey, she went down under cover of the mountain. David and his men were coming down to meet her, and she encountered them. [21]Now David had been thinking, "In vain I guarded everything that belonged to this man in the wilderness. I didn't take anything from him. But he has [a]repaid my good with evil. [22a]God will severely punish David,[1] if I leave

24:18 [a]1 Sam 26:23   24:20 [a]1 Sam 23:17   24:21 [a]Gen 21:23; 1 Sam 20:14–17   [b]2 Sam 21:6–8   24:22 [a]1 Sam 23:29   25:1 [a]1 Sam 28:3   [b]Num 20:29; Deut 34:8   [c]Gen 21:21; Num 10:12; 13:3   [1]LXX *Maon*.   25:2 [a]1 Sam 23:24   [b]Josh 15:55   25:3 [a]Josh 15:13; 1 Sam 30:14   [1]Heb. *good of insight*.   25:4 [a]Gen 38:13; 2 Sam 13:23   25:6 [a]Judg 19:20; 1 Chr 12:18; Ps 122:7; Luke 10:5   [1]MT *to the one who lives*.   25:7 [a]1 Sam 25:15, 21   25:8 [a]Neh 8:10–12; Esth 8:17; 9:19, 22   [1]MT *we have built*.   25:10 [a]Judg 9:28   25:11 [a]Judg 8:6, 15   25:13 [a]1 Sam 30:24   25:15 [a]1 Sam 25:7, 21   25:16 [a]Exod 14:22; Job 1:10   25:17 [a]1 Sam 20:7   25:18 [a]Gen 32:13; [Prov 18:16; 21:14]   25:19 [a]Gen 32:16, 20   25:21 [a]1 Sam 24:17; Ps 109:5; [Prov 17:13]   25:22 [a]Ruth 1:17; 1 Sam 3:17; 20:13, 16   [1]Heb. *Thus God will do to the enemies of David and thus he will add.*

[b]alive until morning even [c]one male[2] from all those who belong to him!"

[23]When Abigail saw David, she got [a]down quickly from the donkey, threw herself facedown before David, and bowed to the ground. [24]Falling at his feet, she said, "My lord, I accept all the guilt! But please let your female servant speak to you! Please listen to the words of your servant! [25]My lord should not pay attention to this wicked man Nabal. He simply lives up to his name! His name means 'fool,' and he is indeed foolish! But I, your servant, did not see the servants my lord sent.

[26]"Now, my lord, [a]as surely as the LORD lives and as surely as you live, it is the LORD who has kept you from shedding blood and taking [b]matters into your own hands. Now may your enemies and those who seek to harm my lord be like Nabal. [27]Now let [a]this present that your servant has brought to my lord be given to the servants who follow my lord. [28]Please forgive [a]the sin of your servant, for the LORD will certainly establish a lasting dynasty for my lord, because my lord [b]fights the battles of the LORD. May no evil be found in you all your days! [29]When someone sets out to chase you and to take your life, the life of my lord will be wrapped [a]securely in the bag of the living by the LORD your God. But he will sling away the lives of your enemies from the [b]sling's pocket! [30]The LORD will do for my lord everything that he promised you, and he will make you a [a]leader over Israel. [31]Your conscience will not be overwhelmed with guilt for having poured out innocent blood and for having taken matters into your own hands. When the LORD has granted my lord success, please remember your servant."

[32]Then David said to Abigail, "[a]Praised be the LORD, the God of Israel, who has sent you this day to meet me! [33]Praised be your good judgment! May you yourself be rewarded for having [a]prevented me this day from shedding blood and taking matters into my own hands! [34]Otherwise, as surely as the LORD, the God of Israel, lives—he who

has prevented me from harming you—if you had not come so quickly to meet me, [a]by morning's light not even one male belonging to Nabal would have remained alive!" [35]Then David took from her hand what she had brought to him. He said to her, "[a]Go back to your home in peace. Be assured that I have listened to you and [b]responded favorably."

[36]When Abigail went back to Nabal, he was [a]holding a banquet in his house like that of the king. Nabal was having a good time[1] and was very intoxicated. She told him absolutely nothing until morning's light. [37]In the morning, when Nabal was sober, his wife told him about these matters. He had a stroke and was paralyzed.[1] [38]After about 10 days the LORD [a]struck Nabal down and he died.

[39]When David heard that Nabal had died, he said, "[a]Praised be the LORD who has [b]vindicated me and avenged the insult that I suffered from Nabal! The LORD has [c]kept his servant from doing evil, and he has [d]repaid Nabal for his evil deeds." Then David sent word to Abigail and asked her to become his wife.

[40]So the servants of David went to Abigail at Carmel and said to her, "David has sent us to you to bring you back to be his wife." [41]She arose, bowed her face toward the ground, and said, "Your female servant, like a lowly servant, will [a]wash the feet of the servants of my lord." [42]Then Abigail quickly went and mounted her donkey, with five of her female servants accompanying her. She followed David's messengers and became his wife.

[43]David had also married Ahinoam from Jezreel; the two [a]of them became his wives. [44](Now Saul had given his daughter [a]Michal, David's wife, to Paltiel son of Laish, who was from [b]Gallim.)

David Spares Saul's Life Again

26 The Ziphites came to Saul at Gibeah and said, "[a]Isn't David hiding on the hill of Hakilah near Jeshimon?" [2]So Saul

25:22 [b]1 Sam 25:34   [c]1 Kgs 14:10; 21:21; 2 Kgs 9:8   [2]Heb. *one who urinates against a wall.*   25:23 [a]Josh 15:18; Judg 1:14   25:26 [a]2 Kgs 2:2   [b][Rom 12:19]   25:27 [a]Gen 33:11; 1 Sam 30:26; 2 Kgs 5:15   25:28 [a]2 Sam 7:11–16, 27; 1 Kgs 9:5; 1 Chr 17:10, 25   [b]1 Sam 18:17   25:29 [a][Ps 66:9; Col 3:3]   [b]Jer 10:18   25:30 [a]1 Sam 13:14; 15:28   25:32 [a]Gen 24:27; Exod 18:10; 1 Kgs 1:48; Ps 41:13; 72:18; 106:48; Luke 1:68   25:33 [a]1 Sam 25:26   25:34 [a]1 Sam 25:22   25:35 [a]1 Sam 20:42; 2 Sam 15:9; 2 Kgs 5:19; Luke 7:50; 8:48   [b]Gen 19:21   25:36 [a]2 Sam 13:28; Prov 20:1; Isa 5:11; Dan 5:1; [Hos 4:11]   [1]Heb. *and the heart of Nabal was good upon him.*   25:37 [1]Heb. *and his heart died within him and he became a stone.*   25:38 [a]1 Sam 26:10; 2 Sam 6:7; Ps 104:29   25:39 [a]1 Sam 25:32   [b]1 Sam 24:15; Prov 22:23   [c]1 Sam 25:26, 34   [d]1 Kgs 2:44   25:41 [a][Prov 15:33]; Luke 7:38, 44   25:43 [a]Josh 15:56   25:44 [a]1 Sam 18:20; 2 Sam 3:14   [b]Isa 10:30   26:1 [a]1 Sam 23:19; Ps 54:title

arose and went down to the wilderness of Ziph, accompanied by [a]3,000 select men of Israel, to look for David in the wilderness of Ziph. [3]Saul camped by the road on the hill of Hakilah near Jeshimon, but David was staying in the wilderness. When he realized that Saul had come to the wilderness to find him, [4]David sent scouts and verified that Saul had indeed arrived.

[5]So David set out and went to the place where Saul was camped. David saw the place where Saul and [a]Abner son of Ner, the general in command of his army, were sleeping. Now Saul was lying in the entrenchment, and the army was camped all around him. [6]David said to Ahimelech [a]the Hittite and Abishai son of Zeruiah, [b]Joab's brother, "Who will [c]go down with me to Saul in the camp?" [d]Abishai replied, "I will go down with you."

[7]So David and Abishai approached the army at night and found Saul lying asleep in the entrenchment with his spear stuck in the ground by his head. Abner and the army were lying all around him. [8]Abishai said to David, "Today [a]God has delivered your enemy into your hands. Now let me drive the spear[1] right through him into the ground with one swift jab! A second jab won't be necessary!"

[9]But David said to Abishai, "Don't kill him! Who can extend his hand against the LORD's chosen one and remain guiltless?" [10]David went on to say, "As [a]the LORD lives, the LORD himself will strike him down. Either [b]his day will come and he will die, or he will [c]go down into battle and be swept away. [11]But may [a]the LORD prevent me from extending my hand against the LORD's chosen one! Now take the spear by Saul's head and the jug of water, and let's get out of here!" [12]So [a]David took the spear and the jug of water by Saul's head, and they got out of there. No one saw them or was aware of their presence or woke up. All of them were asleep, for the LORD had caused a deep sleep to fall on them.

[13]Then David crossed to the other side and stood on the top of the hill some distance away; there was a considerable distance between them. [14]David called to the army and to Abner son of Ner, "Won't you answer, Abner?" Abner replied, "Who are you, that you have called to the king?" [15]David said to Abner, "Aren't you a man? After all, who is like you in Israel? Why then haven't you protected your lord the king? One of the soldiers came to kill your lord the king. [16]This failure on your part isn't good! As surely as the LORD lives, you people who have not protected your lord, the LORD's chosen one, are as good as dead! Now look where the king's spear and the jug of water that was by his head are!"

[17]When Saul recognized David's voice, he said, "[a]Is that your voice, my son David?" David replied, "Yes, it's my voice, my lord the king." [18]He went on to say, "[a]Why is my lord chasing his servant? What have I done? What wrong have I done? [19]So let my lord the king now listen to the words of his servant. If the LORD has incited you against me, may he take delight in an offering. But if men have instigated this, may they be cursed [a]before the LORD! For they have driven me away this day from being united with the [b]LORD's inheritance, saying, 'Go on, serve other gods!' [20]Now don't let my blood fall to the ground away from the LORD's presence, for the king of Israel has gone out to look for [a]a flea the way one looks for a partridge in the hill country."

[21]Saul [a]replied, "I have sinned. Come back, my son David. I won't harm you anymore, for you treated my life with value this day. I have behaved foolishly and have made a very terrible mistake!" [22]David replied, "Here is the king's spear! Let one of your servants cross over and get it. [23a]The LORD [b]rewards each man for his integrity and loyalty. Even though today the LORD delivered you into my hand, I was not willing to extend my hand against the LORD's chosen one. [24]In the same way that I valued your life this day, may the LORD value my life and deliver me from all danger." [25]Saul replied to David, "May you be rewarded, my son David! You will without question be [a]successful!" So David went on his way, and Saul returned to his place.

26:2 [a]1 Sam 13:2; 24:2 26:5 [a]1 Sam 14:50–51; 17:55 26:6 [a]1 Chr 2:16 [b]2 Sam 2:13 [c]Judg 7:10–11 [d]2 Sam 2:18, 24 26:8 [a]1 Sam 24:4 [1]Almost certainly Saul's own spear. 26:10 [a][Deut 32:35]; 1 Sam 25:26, 38; [Luke 18:7; Rom 12:19; Heb 10:30] [b]Gen 47:29; Deut 31:14; [Job 7:1; 14:5]; Ps 37:13 [c]1 Sam 31:6 26:11 [a]1 Sam 24:6–12; [Rom 12:17, 19] 26:12 [a]Gen 2:21; 15:12; Isa 29:10 26:17 [a]1 Sam 24:16 26:18 [a]1 Sam 24:9, 11–14 26:19 [a]Deut 4:27–28 [b]2 Sam 14:16; 20:19 26:20 [a]1 Sam 24:14 26:21 [a]Exod 9:27; 1 Sam 15:24, 30; 24:17; 2 Sam 12:13 26:23 [a]1 Sam 24:19; Ps 7:8; 18:20; 62:12 [b]2 Sam 22:21 26:25 [a]Gen 32:28; 1 Sam 24:20

David Aligns Himself with the Philistines

27 David thought to himself, "One of these days I'm going to be swept away by the hand of Saul! There is nothing better for me than to escape to the land of the Philistines. Then Saul will despair of searching for me through all the territory of Israel and I will escape from his hand."

[2] So David left [a]and crossed over [b]to King Achish son of Maoch of Gath accompanied by his 600 men. [3] David settled [a]with Achish in Gath, along with his men and their families. David had with him his two wives, Ahinoam the Jezreelite and Abigail the Carmelite, Nabal's widow. [4] When Saul learned that David had fled to Gath, he did not mount a new search for him.

[5] David said to Achish, "If I have found favor with you, let me be given a place in one of the country towns so that I can live there. Why should your servant settle in the royal city with you?" [6] So Achish gave him [a]Ziklag on that day. (For that reason Ziklag has belonged to the kings of Judah until this very day.) [7] The length of time that David [a]lived in the Philistine countryside was a year[1] and four months.

[8] Then David and his men went up and raided [a]the Geshurites, [b]the Girzites, and the [c]Amalekites. (They had been living in that land for [d]a long time, from the approach to Shur as far as the land of Egypt.) [9] When David would attack a district, he would leave neither man nor woman alive. He would take sheep, cattle, donkeys, camels, and clothing and would then go back to Achish. [10] When Achish would ask, "Where[1] did you raid today?" David would say, "[a]The Negev of Judah" or "[b]The Negev of Jerahmeel" or "The Negev of the Kenites." [11] Neither man nor woman would David leave alive so as to bring them back to Gath. He was thinking, "This way they can't tell on us, saying, 'This is what David did.'" Such was his practice the entire time that he lived in the country of the Philistines. [12] So Achish trusted David, thinking to himself, "He is really hated[1] among his own people in[2] Israel! From now on he will be my servant."

The Witch of Endor

28 In those days the Philistines gathered their troops for war in order to fight Israel. Achish said to David, "You should fully understand that you and your men must go [a]with me into the battle."[1] [2] David replied to Achish, "That being the case, you will come to know what your servant can do!" Achish said to David, "Then I will make you my bodyguard from now on."

[3] Now [a]Samuel had died, and all Israel had lamented over him and had buried him in [b]Ramah, his hometown. In [c]the meantime Saul had removed the mediums[1] and magicians from the land. [4] The Philistines assembled; they came and camped at [a]Shunem. Saul mustered all Israel and camped at [b]Gilboa. [5] When Saul saw the camp of the Philistines, he [a]was absolutely terrified. [6] So Saul inquired of [a]the Lord, but the Lord did not answer him—not by [b]dreams nor [c]by Urim nor by the prophets. [7] So Saul instructed his servants, "Find me [a]a woman who is a medium, so that I may go to her and inquire of her." His servants replied to him, "There is a woman who is a medium in Endor."

[8] So Saul disguised himself and put on [a]other clothing and left, accompanied by two of his men. They came to the woman at night and said, "Use your ritual pit to conjure up for me the one I tell you."

[9] But the woman said to him, "Look, you are aware of what Saul has done; he has removed the mediums and magicians from the land! Why are you trapping me so you can put me to death?" [10] But Saul swore an oath to her by the Lord, "As surely as the Lord lives, you will not incur guilt in this matter!" [11] The woman replied, "Who is it that I should bring up for you?" He said, "Bring up for me Samuel."

[12] When the woman saw Samuel, she cried out loudly. The woman said to Saul, "Why have you deceived me? You are Saul!" [13] The king [a]said to her, "Don't be afraid! But what

27:2 [a]1 Sam 25:13   [b]1 Sam 21:10; 1 Kgs 2:39   27:3 [a]1 Sam 25:42–43   27:6 [a]Josh 15:31; 19:5; 1 Chr 12:1; Neh 11:28   27:7 [a]1 Sam 29:3   [1]Heb. *days.*   27:8 [a]Josh 13:2, 13   [b]Josh 16:10; Judg 1:29   [c]Exod 17:8, 16; 1 Sam 15:7–8   [d]Gen 25:18; Exod 15:22   27:10 [a]1 Chr 2:9, 25   [b]Judg 1:16   [1]MT *not.*   27:12 [1]Heb. *he really stinks.*   [2]Sev. MSS omit *in.*   28:1 [a]1 Sam 29:1–2   [1]MT *in the camp.*   28:3 [a]1 Sam 25:1   [b]1 Sam 1:19   [c]Exod 22:18; Lev 19:31; 20:27; Deut 18:10–11; 1 Sam 15:23; 28:9   [1]Pits used by magicians to conjure up underworld spirits.   28:4 [a]Josh 19:18; 1 Sam 28:4; 1 Kgs 1:3; 2 Kgs 4:8   [b]1 Sam 31:1   28:5 [a]Job 18:11; [Isa 57:20]   28:6 [a]1 Sam 14:37; Prov 1:28; Lam 2:9   [b]Num 12:6; Joel 2:28   [c]Exod 28:30; Num 27:21; Deut 33:8   28:7 [a]1 Chr 10:13   28:8 [a]Deut 18:10–11; 1 Chr 10:13; Isa 8:19   28:13 [a]Exod 22:28; Ps 138:1

have you seen?" The woman replied to Saul, "I have seen a divine being[1] coming up from the ground!" [14] He [a]said to her, "What about his appearance?" She said, "An old man is coming up! He is wrapped in a robe!"

Then Saul realized it was Samuel, and he bowed his face toward the ground and kneeled down. [15] Samuel said to Saul, "Why have you [a]disturbed me by bringing me up?" Saul replied, "I am terribly troubled! The Philistines are fighting against me and [b]God has turned away from me. He [c]does not answer me anymore—not by the prophets nor by dreams. So I have called on you to tell me what I should do."

[16] Samuel said, "Why are you asking me, now that the LORD has turned away from you and has become your enemy? [17] The LORD [a]has done exactly as I prophesied! The LORD has torn the kingdom from your hand and has given it to your neighbor David! [18a] Since you did not obey the LORD and did not carry out his fierce anger against the [b]Amalekites, the LORD has done this thing to you today. [19] The LORD will hand you and Israel over to the Philistines! Tomorrow both you and your sons will be with [a]me.[1] The LORD will also hand the army of Israel over to the Philistines!"

[20] Saul quickly fell full length on the ground and was very afraid because of Samuel's words. He was completely drained of energy, having not eaten anything all that day and night. [21] When the woman came to Saul and saw how terrified he was, she said to him, "Your servant has done what you asked. I [a]took my life into my own hands and did what you told me. [22] Now it's your turn to listen to your servant! Let me set before you a bit of bread so that you can eat. When you regain your strength, you can go on your way."

[23] But he refused, saying, "I won't eat!" Both his servants and the woman urged[1] him to eat, so he gave in. He got up from the ground and sat down on the bed. [24] Now the woman had a well-fed calf at her home that she quickly slaughtered. Taking some flour, she kneaded it and baked bread without

leaven. [25] She brought it to Saul and his servants, and they ate. Then they arose and left that same night.

David Is Rejected by the Philistine Leaders

29 The Philistines assembled all [a]their troops [b]at Aphek, while Israel camped at the spring that is in Jezreel. [2] When the [a]leaders of the Philistines were passing in review at the head of their units of hundreds and thousands,[1] [b]David and his men were passing in review in the rear with Achish.

[3] The leaders of [a]the Philistines asked, "What about these Hebrews?" Achish said to the leaders of the Philistines, "Isn't this David, the servant of King Saul of Israel, who has been with me for quite some time? I have [b]found no fault with him from the day of his defection until the present time!"

[4] But the leaders of the Philistines became angry with him and said to him, "Send the man back! Let him return to the place that you assigned him! Don't let him go down with us into the [a]battle, for he might become our adversary [b]in the battle. What better way to please his lord than with the heads of these [c]men? [5] Isn't this David, [a]of whom they sang as they danced,

""[b]Saul has struck down his
thousands,
but David his tens of thousands'?"

[6] So Achish summoned David and said to him, "As surely as the LORD lives, [a]you are an honest man, and [b]I am glad to have you serving with me in the army. I have found no fault with you from the day that you first came to me until the present time. But in the opinion of the leaders, you are not reliable. [7] So turn and leave in peace. You must not do anything that the leaders of the Philistines consider improper!"

[8] But David said to Achish, "What have I done? What have you found in your servant from the day that I first came into your presence until the present time, that

28:13 [1] Heb. *gods*.   **28:14** [a] 1 Sam 15:27; 2 Kgs 2:8, 13   **28:15** [a] Isa 14:9   [b] 1 Sam 16:14; 18:12   [c] 1 Sam 28:6   **28:17** [a] 1 Sam 15:28   **28:18** [a] 1 Sam 13:9–13; 15:1–26; 1 Kgs 20:42; 1 Chr 10:13; Jer 48:10   [b] 1 Sam 15:3–9   **28:19** [a] 1 Sam 31:1–6; Job 3:17–19   [1] LXX *and tomorrow you and your sons with you will fall.*   **28:21** [a] Judg 12:3; 1 Sam 19:5; Job 13:14   **28:23** [1] MT *and they broke forth.*   **29:1** [a] 1 Sam 28:1   [b] Josh 12:18; 19:30; 1 Sam 4:1; 1 Kgs 20:30   **29:2** [a] 1 Sam 6:4; 7:7   [b] 1 Sam 28:1–2   [1] Heb. *passing by with respect to hundreds and thousands.*   **29:3** [a] 1 Sam 27:7   [b] 1 Sam 27:1–6; 1 Chr 12:19–20; Dan 6:5   **29:4** [a] 1 Sam 14:21   [b] 1 Sam 29:9   [c] 1 Chr 12:19–20   **29:5** [a] 1 Sam 21:11   [b] 1 Sam 18:7   **29:6** [a] 2 Sam 3:25; 2 Kgs 19:27   [b] 1 Sam 29:3

I shouldn't go and fight the enemies of my lord the king?" [9]Achish replied to David, "I am convinced that you are [a]as reliable as [b]the angel of God! However, the leaders of the Philistines have said, 'He must not go up with us in the battle.' [10]So get up early in the morning along with the servants of your lord [a]who have come with you.[1] When you get up early in the morning, as soon as it is light enough to see, leave."

[11]So David [a]and his men got up early in the morning to return[1] to the land of the Philistines, but the Philistines went up to Jezreel.

David Defeats the Amalekites

30 On the third day David and his men came to [a]Ziklag. Now the [b]Amalekites had raided the Negev and Ziklag. They attacked Ziklag and burned it. [2]They took captive the [a]women and all[1] who were in it, from the youngest to the oldest, but they did not kill anyone. They simply carried them off and went on their way.

[3]When David and his men came to the city, they found it burned. Their wives, sons, and daughters had been taken captive. [4]Then David and the men who were with him wept loudly until they could weep no more. [5]David's two [a]wives had been taken captive—Ahinoam the Jezreelite and Abigail the Carmelite, Nabal's widow. [6]David was very upset, for [a]the men were thinking of stoning him; each man grieved bitterly over his sons and daughters. [b]But David drew strength from the LORD his God.

[7]Then David said to [a]the priest [b]Abiathar son of Ahimelech, "Bring me the ephod." So Abiathar brought the ephod to David. [8a]David inquired of the LORD, saying, "Should I pursue this raiding band? Will I overtake them?" He said to him, "Pursue, for you will certainly overtake them and carry out a rescue!"

[9]So David went, accompanied by his 600 men. When he came to the Wadi Besor, those who were in the rear stayed there. [10]David and 400 men continued the pursuit, but 200 men who were too exhausted to cross the Wadi Besor stayed there.

[11]Then they found an Egyptian in the field and brought him to David. They gave him bread to eat and water to drink. [12]They [a]gave him a slice of pressed figs and two bunches of raisins to eat. This greatly refreshed him, for [b]he had not eaten food or drunk water for three days and three nights. [13]David said to him, "To whom do you belong, and where are you from?" The young man said, "I am an Egyptian, the servant of an Amalekite man. My master abandoned me when I was ill for three days. [14]We conducted a raid on [a]the Negev [b]of the Kerethites, on the area of Judah, and on the Negev of Caleb. We burned Ziklag." [15]David said to him, "Can you take us down to this raiding party?" He said, "Swear to me by God that you will not kill me or hand me over to my [a]master, and I will take you down to this raiding party."

[16]So he took David down, and they found them spread out over the land. They were [a]eating and drinking and enjoying themselves because of all the loot they had taken from the land of the Philistines and from the land of Judah. [17]But David struck them down from twilight until the following evening. None of them escaped, with the exception of 400 young men who got away on camels. [18]David retrieved everything the Amalekites had taken; he also rescued his two wives. [19]There was nothing missing, whether small or great. He retrieved sons and daughters, the plunder, and everything else they had taken. [a]David brought everything back. [20]David took all the flocks and herds and drove them in front of the rest of the animals. People were saying, "This is David's plunder!"

[21]Then David approached the 200 men who had been too exhausted to go with him, those whom they had left at the Wadi Besor. They went out to meet David and the people who were with him. When David approached the people, he asked how they were doing. [22]But all the evil and [a]worthless men among those who had gone with David said, "Since they didn't go with us,[1] we won't give them any of the loot we retrieved! They may take only their wives and children. Let them lead them away and be gone!"

29:9 [a]2 Sam 14:17, 20; 19:27   [b]1 Sam 29:4   **29:10** [a]1 Chr 12:19, 22   [1]LXX, two Old Latin MSS add *and you shall go to the place that I have appointed you. Don't place an evil thing in your heart, for you are good before me.*   **29:11** [a]2 Sam 4:4   [1]Heb. *to go in the morning to return; some MSS omit in the morning.*   **30:1** [a]1 Sam 27:6   [b]1 Sam 15:7; 27:8   **30:2** [a]1 Sam 27:2–3   [1]MT omits *and all.*   **30:5** [a]1 Sam 25:42–43   **30:6** [a]Exod 17:4; John 8:59   [b]1 Sam 23:16; Isa 25:4; Hab 3:17–19   **30:7** [a]1 Sam 23:2–9   [b]1 Sam 23:6   **30:8** [a]1 Sam 23:2, 4; Ps 50:15; 91:15   **30:12** [a]1 Sam 25:18; 1 Kgs 20:7   [b]Judg 15:19; 1 Sam 14:27   **30:14** [a]2 Sam 8:18; 1 Kgs 1:38, 44; Ezek 25:16; Zeph 2:5   [b]Josh 14:13; 15:13   **30:15** [a]Deut 23:15   **30:16** [a]1 Thess 5:3   **30:19** [a]1 Sam 30:8   **30:22** [a]Deut 13:13; Judg 19:22   [1]Heb. *with me.*

[23]But David said, "No! You shouldn't do this, my brothers. Look at what the LORD has given us![1] He has protected us and has delivered into our hands the raiding party that came against us. [24]Who will listen to you in this matter? The portion of the one who went down into the battle will be the same [a]as the portion of the one who remained with the equipment! Let their portions be the same!"

[25]From that time onward it was a binding ordinance for Israel, right up to the present time.

[26]When David came to Ziklag, he sent some of the plunder to the elders of Judah who were his friends, saying, "Here's a gift for you from the looting of the LORD's enemies!" [27]The gift was for those in the following locations: for those in Bethel, Ramoth [a]Negev, and [b]Jattir; [28]for those in [a]Aroer, [b]Siphmoth, [c]Eshtemoa, [29]and Racal; for those in [a]the cities of the Jerahmeelites and [b]Kenites; [30]for those in [a]Hormah, Bor Ashan, Athach, [31]and [a]Hebron; and for those in whatever other places David and his men had [b]traveled.

The Death of Saul

31 Now [a]the Philistines were fighting against Israel. The men of Israel fled from the Philistines and many of them fell dead on Mount [b]Gilboa. [2]The Philistines stayed right on the heels of Saul and his sons. They struck down Saul's sons [a]Jonathan, Abinadab, and Malki-Shua. [3]Saul himself was in [a]the thick of the battle; the archers spotted him and wounded him severely.

[4]Saul said to his armor-bearer, "Draw your sword and stab me with it! Otherwise these uncircumcised people will come, stab me, and torture me." But his armor-bearer refused to do it, because [a]he was very afraid. So Saul took his sword and [b]fell on it. [5]When his armor-bearer saw that Saul was dead, he also fell on his own sword and died with him. [6]So Saul, his three sons, his armor-bearer, and all his men died together that day.

[7]When the men of Israel who were in the valley and across the Jordan saw that the men of Israel had fled and that Saul and his sons were dead, they abandoned the cities and fled. The Philistines came and occupied them.

[8]The next day, when the Philistines came to strip loot from the corpses, they discovered Saul and his three sons lying dead on Mount Gilboa. [9]They cut off Saul's head and stripped him of his armor. They sent messengers to announce the [a]news in the temple of their idols and among their people throughout the surrounding land of the Philistines. [10]They placed Saul's armor in [a]the temple of the [b]Ashtoreths and hung his corpse on [c]the city wall of Beth [d]Shan.

[11a]When the residents of Jabesh Gilead heard what the Philistines had done to Saul, [12a]all their warriors set out and traveled throughout the night. They took Saul's corpse and the corpses of his sons from the city wall of Beth Shan and went[1] to Jabesh, where they [b]burned them. [13]They took the bones and [a]buried them under the tamarisk tree at Jabesh; then they fasted for seven days.

30:23[1]LXX *You should not do this after the LORD has delivered us.*   30:24[a]Num 31:27; Josh 22:8   30:27[a]Josh 19:8   [b]Josh 15:48; 21:14   30:28[a]Josh 13:16   [b]1 Chr 27:27   [c]Josh 15:50   30:29[1]1 Sam 27:10   [b]Judg 1:16; 1 Sam 15:6; 27:10   30:30[a]Num 14:45; 21:3; Josh 12:14; 15:30; 19:4; Judg 1:17   30:31[a]Num 13:22; Josh 14:13–15; 21:11–13; 2 Sam 2:1   [b]1 Sam 23:22   31:1[a]1 Chr 10:1–12   [b]1 Sam 28:4   31:2[a]1 Sam 14:49; 1 Chr 8:33   31:3[a]2 Sam 1:6   31:4[a]Judg 9:54; 1 Chr 10:4   [b]2 Sam 1:6, 10   31:9[a]Judg 16:23–24; 2 Sam 1:20   31:10[a]1 Sam 21:9   [b]Judg 2:13; 1 Sam 7:3   [c]2 Sam 21:12   [d]Judg 1:27   31:11[a]1 Sam 11:1–13   31:12[a]1 Sam 11:1–11; 2 Sam 2:4–7   [b]2 Chr 16:14; Jer 34:5; Amos 6:10   [1]LXX *they brought.*   31:13[a]2 Sam 2:4–5; 21:12–14

2 SAMUEL

The Book of 2 Samuel records the highlights of David's reign, first over the territory of Judah and finally over the entire nation of Israel. It traces the ascension of David to the throne, his climactic sins of adultery and murder, and the shattering consequences of those sins upon his family and the nation. See 1 Samuel for details on the titles of the Books of Samuel. The Hebrew title for both books (originally one) is "Samuel." The Greek title for 2 Samuel is *Basileion Beta*, "Second Kingdoms." The Latin title is *Liber II Samuelis*, the "Second Book of Samuel" or simply "Second Samuel."

David Learns of the Deaths of Saul and Jonathan

1 After the [a]death of Saul, when David had returned from defeating [b]the Amalekites, he stayed at Ziklag for two days. [2]On the third [a]day a man arrived from the camp of Saul [b]with his clothes torn and dirt on his head. When he approached David, the man [c]threw himself to the ground.

[3]David asked him, "Where are you coming from?" He replied, "I have escaped from the camp of Israel." [4]David inquired, "[a]How were things going? Tell me!" He replied, "The people fled from the battle and many of them fell dead. Even Saul and his son [b]Jonathan are dead!" [5]David said to the young man who was telling him this, "How do you know that Saul and his son Jonathan are dead?"[1] [6]The young man[1] said, "I just happened to be on [a]Mount Gilboa and came across [b]Saul leaning on his spear for support. The chariots and leaders of the horsemen were in hot pursuit of him. [7]When he turned around and saw me, he called out to me. I answered, 'Here I am!' [8]He asked me, 'Who are you?' I told him, 'I'm[1] an Amalekite.' [9]He said to me, 'Stand over me and finish me off! I'm very dizzy, even though I'm still alive.'[1] [10]So I stood over him and [a]put him to death, since I knew that he couldn't live in such a condition. Then I took the crown which was on

his head and the[1] bracelet which was on his arm. I have brought them here to my lord."

[11]David then grabbed his own clothes[1] and [a]tore them, as did all the men who were with him. [12]They [a]lamented and wept and [b]fasted until evening because Saul, his son Jonathan, the [c]LORD's army, and the house of Israel had fallen by the sword.

[13]David said to the young man who told this to him, "Where are you from?" He replied, "I am an Amalekite, the son of a resident foreigner." [14]David replied to him, "How is it that you were not [a]afraid to reach out your hand to destroy the LORD's anointed?" [15]Then [a]David called one of the soldiers and said, "Come here and strike him down!" So he struck him down, and he died. [16]David said to him, "[a]Your blood be on [b]your own head! Your own mouth has testified against you, saying 'I have put the LORD's anointed to death.'"

David's Tribute to Saul and Jonathan

[17]Then David chanted this lament over Saul and his son Jonathan. [18]([a]He gave [b]instructions that the people of Judah should be taught "The Bow."[1] Indeed, it is written down in the Scroll of the Upright One.)

[19] "The beauty of Israel lies slain on
    your high places!
  [a]How the mighty have fallen!

20 Don't [a]report it in Gath,
  don't spread the news in the streets
    of [b]Ashkelon,
  or [c]the daughters of [d]the Philistines
    will rejoice,
  the daughters of the uncircumcised
    will celebrate!
21 O [a]mountains of Gilboa,
  may there be no dew or rain on you,
    nor fields of grain offerings![1]
  For it was there that the shield of
    warriors was defiled;[2]
  the shield of Saul lies neglected
    [b]without oil.
22 From [a]the blood of the slain, from
    the fat of warriors,
  the bow of Jonathan was not turned
    away.
  The sword of Saul never returned
    empty.
23 Saul and Jonathan were greatly loved
    during their lives,
  and not even in their [a]deaths were
    they separated.
  They were swifter than eagles,
    [b]stronger than lions.
24 O daughters of Israel, weep over Saul,
  who clothed you in scarlet as well as
    jewelry,
  who put gold jewelry on your clothes.
25 How the warriors have fallen
  in the midst of battle!
  Jonathan lies slain on your high
    places!
26 I grieve over [a]you, my brother
    Jonathan.
  You were very dear to me.
  Your love was more special to me
    than the love of women.
27 How the warriors have fallen!
  The weapons of war are destroyed!"

David Is Anointed King

2 Afterward David [a]inquired of the LORD, "Should I go up to one of the cities of Judah?" The LORD told him, "Go up." David asked, "Where should I go?" The LORD replied, "To [b]Hebron."[2] So David went up, along with his [a]two wives, Ahinoam the Jezreelite and Abigail, formerly the wife of Nabal the Carmelite. [3]David also brought along [a]the men who were with him, each with his family. They settled in the cities[1] of Hebron. [4a]The men of Judah came and there they [b]anointed David as king over [c]the people of Judah.

David was told, "The people of Jabesh Gilead are the ones who buried Saul." [5]So David sent messengers to the people of Jabesh Gilead and told them, "May [a]you be blessed by the LORD because you have shown this kindness to your lord Saul by burying him. [6]Now may [a]the LORD show you true kindness! I also will reward you, because you have done this deed. [7]Now be courageous and prove to be valiant warriors, for your lord Saul is dead. The people of Judah have anointed me as king over them."

David's Army Clashes with the Army of Saul

[8]Now [a]Abner son of Ner, the general in command of Saul's army, had taken Saul's son Ish Bosheth and had brought him to [b]Mahanaim. [9]He appointed him king over [a]Gilead, the Geshurites,[1] [b]Jezreel, Ephraim, Benjamin, and all Israel. [10]Ish Bosheth son of Saul was forty years old when he began to rule over Israel. He ruled two years. However, the people of Judah followed David. [11]David was king in Hebron over [a]the people of Judah for seven-and-a-half years.

[12]Then Abner son of Ner and the servants of Ish Bosheth son of Saul went out from Mahanaim to [a]Gibeon. [13a]Joab son of Zeruiah and [b]the servants of David also went out and confronted them at the pool of Gibeon. One group stationed themselves on one side of the pool, and the other group on the other side of the pool. [14]Abner said to Joab, "Let the soldiers get up and fight before us." Joab said, "So be it!"

[15]So they got up and crossed over by number: 12 belonging to Benjamin and to Ish Bosheth son of Saul, and 12 from the servants of David. [16]As they grappled with one another, each one stabbed his opponent

1:20 [a]1 Sam 27:2; 31:8–13; Mic 1:10 [b]1 Sam 6:17; Jer 25:20 [c]Exod 15:20; Judg 11:34; 1 Sam 18:6 [d]1 Sam 31:4   1:21 [a]1 Sam 31:1 [b]1 Sam 10:1 [1]Luc. *your high places are mountains of death.* [2]Heb. *to abhor, to loathe.*   1:22 [a]Deut 32:42; 1 Sam 18:4   1:23 [a]1 Sam 31:2–4 [b]Judg 14:18   1:26 [a]1 Sam 18:1–4; 19:2; 20:17   2:1 [a]Judg 1:1; 1 Sam 23:2, 4, 9; 30:7–8 [b]1 Sam 30:31; 2 Sam 2:11; 5:1–3; 1 Kgs 2:11   2:2 [a]1 Sam 25:42–43; 30:5   2:3 [a]1 Sam 27:2–3; 30:1; 1 Chr 12:1 [1]Syr. *in Hebron.*   2:4 [a]1 Sam 30:26; 2 Sam 2:11; 5:5; 19:14, 41–43 [b]1 Sam 16:13; 2 Sam 5:3 [c]1 Sam 31:11–13   2:5 [a]Ruth 2:20; 3:10   2:6 [a]Exod 34:6; 2 Tim 1:16, 18   2:8 [a]1 Sam 14:50; 2 Sam 3:6 [b]Gen 32:2; Josh 21:38; 2 Sam 17:24   2:9 [a]Josh 22:9 [b]1 Sam 29:1 [1]MT *the Ashurite*; Tg. *of the house of Ashur.*   2:11 [a]2 Sam 5:5; 1 Kgs 2:11   2:12 [a]Josh 10:2–12; 18:25   2:13 [a]1 Sam 26:6; 2 Sam 8:16; 1 Chr 2:16; 11:6 [b]Jer 41:12

with his sword and they fell dead together. So that place is called the Field of Flints;[1] it is in Gibeon.

[17] Now the battle was very severe that day; Abner and the men of Israel were overcome by David's soldiers. [18] The [a]three sons of Zeruiah were there—Joab, Abishai, and [b]Asahel. (Now [c]Asahel was as quick on his feet as one of the gazelles in the field.) [19] Asahel chased Abner, without turning to the right or to the left as he followed Abner.

[20] Then Abner turned and asked, "Is that you, Asahel?" He replied, "Yes it is!" [21] Abner said to him, "Turn aside to your right or to your left. Capture one of the soldiers and take his equipment for yourself!" But Asahel was not willing to turn aside from following him. [22] So Abner spoke again to Asahel, "Turn aside from following me! I do not want to strike you to the ground. How then could I show my face in the presence of Joab your brother?" [23] But Asahel refused to turn aside. So Abner struck him [a]in the abdomen with the back end of his spear. The spear came out his back; Asahel collapsed on the spot and died there right before Abner. Everyone who came to the place where Asahel fell dead [b]paused in respect.

[24] So Joab and Abishai chased Abner. At sunset they came to the hill of Ammah near Giah on the way to the wilderness of Gibeon. [25] The Benjaminites formed their ranks behind Abner and were like a single army, standing at the top of a certain hill. [26] Then Abner called out to Joab, "Must the sword devour forever? Don't you realize that this will turn bitter in the end? When will you tell the people to turn aside from pursuing their brothers?" [27] Joab replied, "As surely as God lives, if [a]you had not said this, it would have been morning before the people would have abandoned pursuit of their brothers." [28] Then Joab blew the ram's horn and all the people stopped in their tracks. They stopped chasing Israel and ceased fighting. [29] Abner and his men went through the rift valley all that night. They crossed the Jordan River and went through the whole region of Bitron[1] and came to Mahanaim.

[30] Now Joab returned from chasing Abner and assembled all the people. Nineteen of David's soldiers were missing, in addition to Asahel. [31] But David's soldiers had slaughtered the Benjaminites and Abner's men—in all, 360 men had died! [32] They took Asahel's body and buried him in his father's tomb at [a]Bethlehem. Joab and his men then traveled all that night and reached Hebron by dawn.

3 [1] However, the [a]war was prolonged between the house of Saul and the house of David. David was becoming steadily stronger, while the house of Saul was becoming increasingly weaker.

[2] Now sons were born [a]to David in Hebron. His firstborn was Amnon, born to Ahinoam the Jezreelite. [3] His second son was Kileab, born to Abigail the widow of Nabal the Carmelite. His third son was [a]Absalom, the son [b]of Maacah daughter of King Talmai of Geshur. [4] His fourth son was [a]Adonijah, the son of Haggith. His fifth son was Shephatiah, the son of Abital. [5] His sixth son was Ithream, born to David's wife Eglah. These sons were all born to David in Hebron.

Abner Defects to David's Camp

[6] As the war continued between the house of Saul and the house of David, Abner was becoming more influential[1] in the house of Saul. [7] Now Saul had a concubine named [a]Rizpah daughter of Aiah. Ish Bosheth[1] said to Abner, "Why did you sleep with my father's concubine?"

[8] These words of Ish Bosheth [a]really angered Abner and he said, "Am I the head of a dog that belongs to Judah? This very day I am demonstrating loyalty to the house of Saul your father and to his relatives and his friends! I have not betrayed you into the hand of David. Yet you have accused me of sinning with this woman today! [9][a]God will severely judge Abner if I do not do for David exactly what the LORD [b]has promised him,[1] [10] namely, to transfer the kingdom [a]from the house of Saul and to establish the throne of David over Israel and over Judah all the way from Dan to Beer Sheba!" [11] Ish Bosheth was unable to answer Abner

2:16 [1] Heb. *Helkath Hazzurim.*   2:18 [a] 1 Chr 2:16   [b] 1 Chr 12:8; Hab 3:19   [c] Ps 18:33   2:23 [a] 2 Sam 3:27; 4:6; 20:10   [b] 2 Sam 20:12   2:27 [a] 2 Sam 2:14   2:29 [1] Or perhaps *and they traveled all morning long;* Heb. *and they went, all the Bitron.*   2:32 [a] 1 Sam 20:6   3:1 [a] 1 Kgs 14:30; [Ps 46:9]   3:2 [a] 1 Chr 3:1–4   3:3 [a] 2 Sam 15:1–10   [b] Josh 13:13; 1 Sam 27:8; 2 Sam 13:37; 14:32; 15:8   3:4 [a] 1 Kgs 1:5   3:6 [1] Heb. *was strengthening himself;* perhaps in a negative sense, suggesting Abner was overstepping the bounds of political propriety in a self-serving way.   3:7 [a] 2 Sam 21:8–11   [1] MT *and he said.*   3:8 [a] Deut 23:18; 1 Sam 24:14; 2 Sam 9:8; 16:9   3:9 [a] Ruth 1:17; 1 Kgs 19:2   [b] 1 Sam 15:28; 16:1, 12; 28:17; 1 Chr 12:23   [1] Heb. *has sworn to David;* LXX adds *in this day.*   3:10 [a] Judg 20:1; 1 Sam 3:20; 2 Sam 17:11; 1 Kgs 4:25

with even a single word because he was afraid of him.

[12]Then Abner sent messengers to David saying, "To whom does the land belong? Make an agreement with me, and I will do whatever I can to cause all Israel to turn to you." [13]So David said, "Good! I will make an agreement with [a]you. I ask only one thing from you. You will not see my face unless you bring Saul's daughter [b]Michal when you come to visit me."

[14]David sent messengers to Ish [a]Bosheth son of Saul with this demand: "Give me my wife Michal whom I acquired [b]for 100 Philistine foreskins." [15]So Ish Bosheth took her from her husband Paltiel son of Laish. [16]Her husband went along behind her, weeping all the way to [a]Bahurim. Finally Abner said to him, "Go back!" So he returned home.

[17]Abner advised the elders of Israel, "Previously you were wanting David to be your king. [18]Act now! [a]For the LORD has said to David, 'By the hand of my servant David I will save[1] my people Israel from the Philistines and from all their enemies.'"

[19]Then Abner spoke privately with the Benjaminites. Abner also went to Hebron to inform David privately of all that Israel and the entire house of [a]Benjamin had agreed to. [20]When Abner, accompanied by 20 men, came to David in Hebron, David prepared a banquet for Abner and the men who were with him. [21]Abner said to David, "Let me leave so that I may go and [a]gather all Israel to my lord the king so that they may make an agreement with you. Then you will [b]rule over all that you desire." So David sent Abner away, and he left in peace.

Abner Is Killed

[22]Now David's soldiers and Joab were coming back from a raid, bringing a great deal of plunder with them. Abner was no longer with David in Hebron, for David had sent him away and he had left in peace. [23]When Joab and all the army that was with him arrived, Joab was told: "Abner the son of Ner came to the king; he sent him away, and he left in peace!"

[24]So Joab went to the king and said, "What have you done? Abner has come to you. Why would you send him away? Now he's gone on his way![1] [25]You know Abner the son of Ner. Surely he came here to spy on [a]you and to determine when you leave and when you return[1] and to discover everything that you are doing!"

[26]Then Joab left David and sent messengers after Abner. They brought him back from the well of Sirah. (But David was not aware of it.) [27]When Abner returned [a]to Hebron, Joab took him aside at the gate as if to speak privately with him. Joab then stabbed him [b]in the abdomen and killed him, avenging the shed blood of his brother [c]Asahel.

[28]When David later heard about this, he said, "I and my kingdom are forever innocent before the LORD of the shed blood of Abner son of Ner. [29a]May his blood whirl over[1] the head of Joab and the entire house of his father![2] May the males of Joab's house[3] never cease to have someone with a running sore or a skin disease or one [b]who works at the spindle or one who falls by the sword or one who lacks food!"

[30]So Joab and his brother Abishai killed Abner, because he had killed their brother [a]Asahel in Gibeon during the battle.

[31]David instructed Joab and all the people who were with him, "[a]Tear your clothes. Put [b]on sackcloth. Lament before Abner!" Now King David followed behind the funeral pallet.[1] [32]So they buried Abner in Hebron. The king cried loudly over Abner's grave, and all the people wept too. [33]The king chanted the following lament for Abner:

"Should Abner have died like a [a]fool?
[34] Your hands were not bound,
  and your feet were not put into irons.
  You fell the way one falls before
  criminals."

All the people[1] wept over him again. [35]Then all the people came and encouraged David [a]to eat food while it was still day. But David took an oath saying, "[b]God

3:13 [a]Gen 43:3 [b]1 Sam 18:20; 19:11; 25:44; 2 Sam 6:16   3:14 [a]2 Sam 2:10 [b]1 Sam 18:25–27   3:16 [a]2 Sam 16:5; 19:16   3:18 [a]2 Sam 3:9 [1]MT *he saved.*   3:19 [a]1 Sam 10:20–21; 1 Chr 12:29   3:21 [a]2 Sam 3:10, 12 [b]1 Kgs 11:37   3:24 [1]LXX adds *in peace.*   3:25 [a]Deut 28:6; 1 Sam 29:6; Isa 37:28 [1]Heb. *your going out and your coming in*; a merism.   3:27 [a]2 Sam 20:9–10; 1 Kgs 2:5 [b]2 Sam 4:6 [c]2 Sam 2:23   3:29 [a]Deut 21:6–9; 1 Kgs 2:32–33 [b]Lev 15:2 [1]Heb. *and may they whirl over.* [2]One DSS MS *of Joab.* [3]Heb. *the house of Joab.*   3:30 [a]2 Sam 2:23   3:31 [a]Josh 7:6; 2 Sam 1:2, 11 [b]Gen 37:34 [1]A portable frame for carrying a body, technically a bier.   3:33 [a]2 Sam 13:12–13   3:34 [1]One DSS MS omits *all the people.*   3:35 [a]2 Sam 12:17; Jer 16:7–8 [b]Ruth 1:17

will punish me severely if I taste bread or anything whatsoever ^cbefore the sun sets!" ³⁶All the people noticed this and it pleased them. In fact, everything the king did pleased all the people. ³⁷All the people and all Israel realized on that day that the killing of Abner son of Ner was not done at the king's instigation.

³⁸Then the king said to his servants, "Do you not realize that a great leader has fallen this day in Israel? ³⁹Today I am weak, even though I am anointed as king. These men, the sons of Zeruiah, ^aare too much for me to bear! May ^bthe LORD punish appropriately the one who has done this evil thing!"

Ish Bosheth Is Killed

4 When Ish ^aBosheth the son of Saul heard that Abner had died in Hebron, he was very disheartened, and all Israel was ^bafraid. ²Now Saul's son[1] had two men who were in charge of raiding units; one was named Baanah and the other Recab. They were sons of Rimmon the Beerothite, who was a Benjaminite. (^aBeeroth is regarded as belonging to Benjamin, ³for the Beerothites fled to ^aGittaim and have remained there as resident foreigners until the present time.) ⁴Now Saul's son ^aJonathan had a son who was crippled in both feet. He was five years old when the news about Saul and Jonathan arrived ^bfrom Jezreel. His nurse picked him up and fled, but in her haste to get away, he fell and was injured. ^cMephibosheth was his name.

⁵Now the sons of Rimmon the Beerothite—Recab and Baanah—went at the hottest part of the day to the ^ahome of Ish Bosheth, as he was enjoying his midday rest. ⁶They entered the house under the pretense of ^agetting wheat[1] and mortally wounded him in the stomach. Then Recab and his brother Baanah escaped.

⁷They had entered the house while Ish Bosheth was resting on his bed in his bedroom. They mortally wounded him and then cut off his head. Taking his head,[1] they traveled on the way of the rift valley all that night. ⁸They brought the head of Ish Bosheth to David in Hebron, saying to the king, "Look! The head of Ish Bosheth son of Saul, your enemy ^awho sought your life! The LORD has granted vengeance to my lord the king this day against Saul and his descendants!"

⁹David replied to Recab and his brother Baanah, the sons of Rimmon the Beerothite, "As surely as the LORD lives, ^awho has delivered my life from all adversity, ¹⁰when ^asomeone told me that Saul was dead—even though he thought he was bringing good news—I seized him and killed him in Ziklag. That was the good news I gave to him! ¹¹Surely when wicked men have killed an innocent man as he slept in his own house, should I not now ^arequire his blood from your hands and remove you from the earth?"

¹²So David issued orders ^ato the soldiers and they put them to death. Then they cut off their hands and feet and hung them[1] near the pool in Hebron. But they took the head of Ish Bosheth[2] and buried it in the ^btomb of Abner[3] in Hebron.[4]

David Is Anointed King over Israel

5 All the tribes of Israel ^acame to David at Hebron saying, "Look, ^bwe are your very flesh and blood! ²In the past, when Saul was our king, ^ayou were the real leader in Israel. The LORD said to ^byou, 'You will shepherd my people Israel; you will rule over Israel.'"

³When all ^athe leaders of Israel came to the king at Hebron, King David made ^ban agreement with them in Hebron ^cbefore the LORD. They designated David as king over Israel. ⁴David was ^athirty years old ^bwhen he began to reign, and he reigned for forty years. ⁵In Hebron he reigned over Judah for ^aseven years and six months, and in Jerusalem he reigned for thirty-three years over all Israel and Judah.

David Occupies Jerusalem

⁶Then the king ^aand his men advanced to Jerusalem against ^bthe Jebusites who

3:35 ^cJudg 20:26; 2 Sam 1:12   **3:39** ^a2 Sam 19:5–7   ^b1 Kgs 2:5–6, 32–34; 2 Tim 4:14   **4:1** ^aEzra 4:4; Isa 13:7   ^bMatt 2:3   **4:2** ^aJosh 18:25   ¹MT *the son of Saul.*   **4:3** ^aNeh 11:33   **4:4** ^a2 Sam 9:3   ^b1 Sam 29:1, 11   ^c2 Sam 9:6   **4:5** ^a2 Sam 2:8–9   **4:6** ^a2 Sam 2:23; 20:10   ¹LXX *behold the house doorkeeper was cleaning wheat and became drowsy and fell asleep and the brothers Rekcha and Baana avoided notice.*   **4:7** ¹Luc. omits *his head.*   **4:8** ^a1 Sam 19:2, 10, 11; 23:15; 25:29   **4:9** ^aGen 48:16; 1 Kgs 1:29; Ps 31:7   **4:10** ^a2 Sam 1:2–16   **4:11** ^a[Gen 9:5–6; Ps 9:12]   **4:12** ^a2 Sam 1:15   ^b2 Sam 3:32   ¹*them* is supplied; presumably the corpses and not merely the detached hands and feet.   ²One DSS MS *Mephibosheth.*   ³LXX adds *the son of Ner.*   ⁴Some LXX MSS omit *in Hebron.*   **5:1** ^a1 Chr 11:1–3   ^bGen 29:14; Judg 9:2; 2 Sam 19:12–13   **5:2** ^a1 Sam 18:5, 13, 16   ^b1 Sam 16:1   **5:3** ^a2 Sam 3:17; 1 Chr 11:3   ^b2 Sam 2:4; 3:21; 2 Kgs 11:17   ^cJudg 11:11; 1 Sam 23:18   **5:4** ^aGen 41:46; Num 4:3; Luke 3:23   ^b1 Kgs 2:11; 1 Chr 26:31; 29:27   **5:5** ^a2 Sam 2:11; 1 Chr 3:4; 29:27   **5:6** ^aJudg 1:21   ^bJosh 15:63; Judg 1:8; 19:11–12

lived in the land. The Jebusites said to David, "You cannot invade this place! Even the blind and the lame will turn you back, saying, 'David cannot invade this place!'" [7] But David captured the fortress of Zion ([a]that is, the City of David). [8] David said on that day, "Whoever attacks [a]the Jebusites must approach the 'lame' and the 'blind' who are David's enemies by going through the water tunnel." For this reason it is said, "The blind and the lame cannot enter the palace."

[9] So David lived in [a]the fortress and called it the City of David. David built all around it, from the terrace inwards. [10] David's power grew steadily, for [a]the LORD God[1] of Heaven's Armies was with [b]him.

[11a] King [b]Hiram of Tyre sent messengers to David, along with cedar logs, carpenters, and stonemasons. They built a palace for David. [12] David realized that the LORD had established him as king over Israel and that he had [a]elevated his kingdom [b]for the sake of his people Israel. [13a] David married more concubines and wives from Jerusalem after he arrived from Hebron. Even more sons and daughters were born to David. [14a] These are the names of children born to him in Jerusalem: Shammua, Shobab, Nathan, [b]Solomon, [15] Ibhar, Elishua, Nepheg, Japhia, [16] Elishama, Eliada, and Eliphelet.

Conflict with the Philistines

[17a] When the Philistines heard that David had been designated king over Israel, they all went up to search for David. When David heard about it, he went down to the fortress. [18] Now [a]the Philistines had arrived and spread out in the valley of Rephaim. [19] So David [a]asked the LORD, "Should I march up against the Philistines? Will you hand them over to me?" The LORD said to David, "March up, for I will indeed hand the Philistines over to you."

[20] So David marched against Baal [a]Perazim and defeated them there. Then he said, "The LORD has burst out against my enemies like water bursts out." So he called the name of that place Baal Perazim. [21] The Philistines abandoned their idols[1] there, and David and his men [a]picked them up.

[22] The Philistines again came up and spread out in [a]the valley of Rephaim. [23] So [a]David asked the LORD what he should do. This time the LORD said to him, "Don't march straight up. Instead, circle around behind them and come against them opposite the trees.[1] [24] When you [a]hear [b]the sound of marching in the tops of the trees, act decisively. For at that moment the LORD is going before you to strike down the army of the Philistines." [25] David did just as the LORD commanded him, and he struck down the Philistines from [a]Gibeon all the way to [b]Gezer.

David Brings the Ark to Jerusalem

6 David again assembled all the best men in Israel, 30,000 in number. [2a] David and all the men [b]who were with him traveled to Baalah in Judah to bring up from there the ark of God which is called by the name of the LORD of Heaven's Armies, who sits enthroned between the cherubim that are on it. [3] They loaded [a]the ark of God on a new cart and carried it from the house of Abinadab, which was on the hill. Uzzah and Ahio, the sons of Abinadab, were guiding the new cart. [4] They brought it with [a]the ark of God from the house of Abinadab on the hill. Ahio was walking in front of the ark, [5] while David and all Israel were energetically [a]celebrating before the LORD, singing[1] and playing various stringed instruments, tambourines, rattles, and cymbals.

[6] When they arrived at the threshing floor of [a]Nacon, Uzzah reached out [b]and grabbed hold of the ark of God, because the oxen stumbled. [7] The LORD was so furious with Uzzah, he killed him on the spot[1] for his negligence.[2] He died right there beside the ark of God.

[8] David was angry because the LORD attacked Uzzah; so he called that place Perez Uzzah, which remains its name to this very day. [9a] David was afraid of the LORD that day

5:7 [a] 2 Sam 6:12, 16; 1 Kgs 2:10; 8:1; 9:24   **5:8** [a] 1 Chr 11:6–9   **5:9** [a] 2 Sam 5:7; 1 Kgs 9:15, 24   **5:10** [a] 1 Sam 17:45   [b] 1 Sam 18:12, 28   [1] LXX, one DSS MS omit *God*.   **5:11** [a] 1 Chr 14:1   [b] 1 Kgs 5:1–18   **5:12** [a] Num 24:7   [b] Isa 45:4   **5:13** [a] [Deut 17:17]; 1 Chr 3:9   **5:14** [a] 1 Chr 3:5–8   [b] 2 Sam 12:24   **5:17** [a] 1 Chr 11:16   **5:18** [a] Gen 14:5; Josh 15:8; 1 Chr 11:15; Isa 17:5   **5:19** [a] 1 Sam 23:2; 2 Sam 2:1   **5:20** [a] 1 Chr 14:11; Isa 28:21   **5:21** [a] Deut 7:5, 25   [1] LXX, Vg. *gods*.   **5:22** [a] 1 Chr 14:13   **5:23** [a] 2 Sam 5:19   [1] Or *balsam trees*.   **5:24** [a] 2 Kgs 7:6; 1 Chr 14:15   [b] Judg 4:14   **5:25** [a] 1 Chr 14:16   [b] Josh 16:10   **6:2** [a] 1 Chr 13:5–6   [b] Exod 25:22; 1 Sam 4:4; Ps 80:1   **6:3** [a] 1 Sam 26:1   **6:4** [a] 1 Sam 7:1; 1 Chr 13:7   **6:5** [a] 1 Sam 18:6–7   [1] Heb. *were celebrating before the LORD with all woods of fir.*   **6:6** [a] 1 Chr 13:9   [b] Num 4:15, 19, 20   **6:7** [1] Heb. *there.*   [2] LXX omits *his negligence.*   **6:9** [a] Deut 9:19; Ps 119:120; Luke 5:8

and said, "How will the ark of the LORD ever come to me?" [10]So David was no longer willing to bring the ark of the LORD to be with him in the [a]City of David. David left it in the house of Obed-Edom the [b]Gittite. [11]The ark of [a]the LORD remained in the house of Obed-Edom the Gittite for three months. The LORD [b]blessed Obed-Edom and all his family. [12]King David was told, "The LORD has blessed the family of Obed-Edom and everything he owns because of the ark of God." [a]So David went and joyfully brought the ark of God from the house of Obed-Edom to the City of David. [13]Those who carried the ark of the LORD took six steps and then David sacrificed an [a]ox and a fatling calf. [14]Now David, wearing a linen ephod, was [a]dancing with [b]all his strength before the LORD. [15a]David and all Israel[1] were bringing up the ark of the LORD, shouting and blowing trumpets.

[16]As the ark of the LORD entered the City of David, Saul's daughter [a]Michal looked out the window. When she saw King David leaping and dancing before the LORD, she despised him. [17]They brought [a]the ark of the LORD and put [b]it in its place[1] in the middle of the tent that David had pitched for it. Then David [c]offered burnt sacrifices and peace offerings before the LORD. [18]When David [a]finished offering the burnt sacrifices and peace offerings, he pronounced a blessing over the people in the name of the LORD of Heaven's Armies. [19]He [a]then handed out to each member of the entire assembly of Israel, both men and women, a portion of bread, a date cake, and a raisin cake. Then all the people went home. [20]When David went home to pronounce a blessing on his own house, Michal, Saul's daughter, came out to meet him. She said, "How [a]the king of Israel has distinguished himself this day! He has [b]exposed himself today before his servants' slave girls the way a vulgar [c]fool might do!"

[21]David replied to Michal, "It was before the LORD! I was celebrating before the LORD, [a]who chose me over your father and his entire family and appointed me as leader over the [b]LORD's people Israel. [22]I am willing to shame and humiliate myself even more than this. But with the slave girls whom you mentioned, let me be distinguished." [23]Now Michal, Saul's daughter, had no children [a]to the day of her death.

The Lord Establishes a Covenant with David

7 The king settled into his palace, for the LORD gave him relief from all his enemies on all sides. [2]The king [a]said to Nathan the prophet, "Look! I am living in a palace made from cedar, while the ark of God sits in the middle of a [b]tent." [3]Nathan replied to the king, "You should go[1] and do whatever you have in [a]mind, for the LORD is with you." [4]That night the LORD's message came to Nathan, [5]"Go, tell my servant David, 'This is what the LORD has said: Do you really intend to build a house for me to live in? [6]I have not lived [a]in [b]a house from the time I brought the Israelites up from Egypt to the present day. Instead, I was traveling with them and living in a tent.[1] [7]Wherever I [a]moved among all the Israelites, I did not say [b]to any of their leaders whom I appointed to care for my people Israel, "Why have you not built me a house made from cedar?"'

[8]"So now, say [a]this to my servant David, 'This is what the LORD of Heaven's Armies has said: I took you from the pasture and from your work as a shepherd to make you leader of my people Israel. [9]I was [a]with you wherever you went, [b]and I defeated all your enemies before you. Now I will make you as famous as the great men of the earth. [10]I will establish a place for my people Israel and [a]settle them there; they will live there and [b]not be disturbed anymore. Violent men will not oppress them again, as they did in the beginning [11]and during the time when [a]I appointed judges to lead my people Israel. Instead, I will give you relief from all your enemies. The LORD declares to you [b]that he himself will build a dynastic house[1] for you. [12a]When the time comes for you to [b]die, [c]I

6:10 [a]2 Sam 5:7   [b]1 Chr 13:13; 26:4–8   **6:11** [a]1 Chr 13:14   [b]Gen 30:27; 39:5   **6:12** [a]1 Chr 15:25–16:3   **6:13** [a]1 Kgs 8:5   **6:14** [a]Ps 30:11; 149:3   [b]1 Sam 2:18, 28   **6:15** [a]1 Chr 15:28   [1]Heb. *all the house of Israel.*   **6:16** [a]2 Sam 3:14   **6:17** [a]1 Chr 16:1   [b]1 Chr 15:1; 2 Chr 1:4   [c]1 Kgs 8:5, 62, 63   [1]Syr. omits *in its place.*   **6:18** [a]1 Kgs 8:14–15, 55   **6:19** [a]1 Chr 16:3   **6:20** [a]Ps 30:title   [b]2 Sam 6:14, 16   [c]Judg 9:4   **6:21** [a]1 Sam 13:14; 15:28   [b]2 Kgs 11:17   **6:23** [a]1 Sam 15:35; Isa 22:14   **7:2** [a]2 Sam 5:11   [b]Exod 26:1   **7:3** [a]1 Kgs 8:17–18; 1 Chr 22:7   [1]Sev. wss omit *should go.*   **7:6** [a]Josh 18:1; 1 Kgs 8:16   [b]Exod 40:18, 34   [1]Heb. *in a tent and in a dwelling.*   **7:7** [a]Lev 26:11–12   [b]2 Sam 5:2; [Acts 20:28]   **7:8** [a]1 Sam 16:11–12; Ps 78:70–71   **7:9** [a]1 Sam 18:14; 2 Sam 5:10   [b]1 Sam 31:6   **7:10** [a]Exod 15:17; Ps 44:2; 80:8; Jer 24:6   [b]Ps 89:22–23; Isa 60:18   **7:11** [a]Judg 2:14–16   [b]Exod 1:21; 1 Sam 25:28; 2 Sam 7:27   [1]Heb. *house.*   **7:12** [a]1 Kgs 2:1   [b]Deut 31:16; Acts 13:36   [c]1 Kgs 8:20; Ps 132:11; Matt 1:6; Luke 3:31

will raise up your descendant, one of your own sons, to succeed you, and I will establish his kingdom. [13a]He will build a house for my name, and I will [b]make his dynasty permanent. [14]I [a]will become his father and he will become [b]my son. When he sins, I will correct him with the rod of men and with wounds inflicted by human beings. [15]But my loyal love will not be removed from him [a]as I removed it from Saul, whom I removed from before you. [16]Your house and [a]your kingdom will stand before me[1] permanently; your dynasty will be permanent.'" [17]Nathan told David all these words that were revealed to him.

David Offers a Prayer to God

[18]King David went in, sat before the LORD, and said, "[a]Who am I, O Sovereign LORD, and what is my family, that you should have brought me to this point? [19]And you didn't stop there, O LORD God! You have also spoken about the future of your servant's family. [a]Is this your usual way of dealing with men,[1] O Sovereign LORD? [20]What more can David say to you? You have [a]given your servant special recognition,[1] O Sovereign LORD! [21]For the sake of your promise and according to your purpose you have done this great thing in order to reveal it to your servant. [22]Therefore [a]you are great, O Sovereign LORD, for [b]there is none like you. There is no God besides you! What we have [c]heard is true. [23]Who is like your people, Israel, a unique nation on [a]the earth? Their God went to claim a nation for himself and to make a name for himself! [b]You did great and awesome acts for your land, before your people whom you delivered for yourself from the Egyptian empire and its gods.[1] [24]You made Israel [a]your very own people for all time. You, O LORD, became their God. [25]So now, O LORD God, make this promise you have made about your servant and his family a permanent reality. Do as you promised, [26]so you may gain lasting fame, as people say, 'The LORD of Heaven's Armies is God over Israel!' The dynasty of your servant David will be established before you, [27]for you, O LORD of Heaven's Armies, the God of Israel, have told your servant, 'I will build you a dynastic house.'[1] That is why your servant has had the courage to pray this prayer to you. [28]Now, [a]O Sovereign LORD, you are the true God. May your words prove to be true![1] You have made this good promise to your servant. [29]Now be willing to bless your servant's dynasty[1] so that it may stand [a]permanently before you, for you, O Sovereign LORD, have spoken. By your blessing may your servant's dynasty be blessed from now on into the future!"

David Subjugates Nearby Nations

8 Later David defeated the Philistines and subdued them. David took Metheg Ammah from the Philistines. [2]He defeated [a]the Moabites. He made them lie on the ground and then used a rope to measure them off. He put two-thirds of them to death and spared the other third. The Moabites became David's [b]subjects and [c]brought tribute. [3]David defeated King Hadadezer son of Rehob of [a]Zobah when he came to reestablish[1] [b]his authority over the Euphrates River. [4]David seized from him 1,700 charioteers[1] and 20,000 infantrymen. David cut the hamstrings [a]of all but 100 of the chariot horses. [5a]The Arameans of Damascus came to help King Hadadezer of Zobah, but David killed 22,000 of the Arameans. [6]David placed garrisons in [a]the territory of the Arameans of Damascus; the Arameans became David's subjects and brought tribute. The LORD protected David wherever he campaigned. [7]David took [a]the golden shields that belonged to Hadadezer's servants and brought them to Jerusalem.[1] [8]From Tebah[1] and [a]Berothai, Hadadezer's cities, King David took a great deal of bronze.

[9]When King Toi of [a]Hamath heard that David had defeated the entire army of Hadadezer, [10]he sent his son Joram to King

7:13 [a]1 Kgs 5:5; 8:19; 2 Chr 6:2   [b]2 Sam 7:16; [Isa 9:7; 49:8]   7:14 [a][Heb 1:5]   [b][Ps 2:7; 89:26–27, 30]; Matt 3:17   7:15 [a]1 Sam 15:23, 28; 16:14   7:16 [a]2 Sam 7:13; Ps 89:36–37; Matt 25:31; John 12:34   [1]Heb. *you.*   7:18 [a]Gen 32:10; Exod 3:11; 1 Sam 18:18   7:19 [a][Isa 55:8–9]   [1]Heb. *and this [is] the law of man.*   7:20 [a][1 Sam 16:7]; Ps 139:1; John 21:17   [1]Heb. *and you know your servant.*   7:22 [a]Deut 10:17; 1 Chr 16:25; 2 Chr 2:5; Ps 86:10; Jer 10:6   [b]Exod 15:11; Deut 3:24; 4:35; 32:39   [c]Exod 10:2; Ps 44:1   7:23 [a]Ps 147:20   [b]Deut 9:26; 33:29   [1]Heb. *from Egypt, nations and their gods.*   7:24 [a]Gen 17:7–8; Exod 6:7; [Deut 26:18]   7:27 [1]Heb. *a house.*   7:28 [a]Exod 34:6; Josh 21:45; John 17:17   [1]Or perhaps *your words are true.*   7:29 [a]2 Sam 22:51   [1]Heb. *house.*   8:2 [a]Num 24:17   [b]2 Sam 12:31   [c]1 Sam 10:27; 1 Kgs 4:21   8:3 [a]1 Sam 14:47; 2 Sam 10:16, 19   [b]Gen 15:18; 2 Sam 10:15–19   [1]LXX *cause to stand.*   8:4 [a]Josh 11:6, 9   [1]LXX *1,000 chariots and 7,000 charioteers.*   8:5 [a]1 Kgs 11:23–25   8:6 [a]2 Sam 7:9; 8:14   8:7 [a]1 Kgs 10:16   [1]LXX adds *And Sousakim king of Egypt took them when he came up to Jerusalem in the days of Rehoboam the son of Solomon.*   8:8 [a]Ezek 47:16   [1]Heb. *Betah.*   8:9 [a]1 Kgs 8:65; 2 Kgs 14:28; 2 Chr 8:4

David to extend his best wishes and to pronounce a blessing on him for his victory over Hadadezer, for Toi had been at war with Hadadezer. He brought with him various items made of silver, gold, and bronze. [11] King David [a]dedicated these things to the LORD, along with the dedicated silver and gold that he had taken from all the nations that he had subdued, [12]including Edom,[1] Moab, the Ammonites, the [a]Philistines, and Amalek. This also included some of the plunder taken from King Hadadezer son of Rehob of Zobah.

[13]David became [a]famous when he returned from defeating the Edomites[1] in the Valley of Salt; he defeated [b]18,000 in all. [14]He placed garrisons throughout Edom,[1] and [a]all the Edomites became David's subjects. The LORD protected David wherever he campaigned. [15]David reigned over all Israel; he guaranteed justice for all his people.

David's Cabinet

[16a]Joab son of Zeruiah was general in command of the army; [b]Jehoshaphat son of Ahilud was secretary; [17a]Zadok son of Ahitub and Ahimelech son of Abiathar were priests; Seraiah was scribe; [18a]Benaiah son of Jehoiada supervised the [b]Kerethites and Pelethites; and David's sons were priests.

David Finds Mephibosheth

9 Then David asked, "Is anyone still left from the family of Saul, so that I may [a]extend kindness to him for the sake of Jonathan?"

[2]Now there was a servant from Saul's house named [a]Ziba, so he was summoned to David. The king asked him, "Are you Ziba?" He replied, "At your service." [3]The king asked, "Is [a]there not someone left from Saul's family that I may extend God's kindness to him?" Ziba said to the king, "One of Jonathan's sons is left; both of his feet are [b]crippled." [4]The king asked him, "Where is he?" Ziba told the king, "He is at the house of [a]Makir son of Ammiel in Lo Debar."

[5]So King David had him brought from the house of Makir son of Ammiel in Lo Debar.

[6]When [a]Mephibosheth son of Jonathan, the son of Saul, came to David, he bowed low with his face toward the ground. David said, "Mephibosheth?" He replied, "Yes, at your service."

[7]David said to him, "Don't be afraid, because I will certainly extend kindness to you for the sake of Jonathan your father. I will give back to you all the land that belonged to your grandfather Saul, and you will be a regular guest at my table." [8]Then Mephibosheth bowed [a]and said, "Of what importance am I, your servant, that you show regard for a dead dog like me?"

[9]Then the [a]king summoned Ziba, Saul's attendant, and said to him, "Everything that belonged to Saul and to his entire house I hereby give to your master's grandson. [10]You will cultivate the land for him—you and your sons and your servants. You will bring its produce and it will be[1] food for your master's grandson to eat. But Mephibosheth, your master's grandson, will be [a]a regular guest at my table." (Now Ziba had [b]15 sons and 20 servants.)

[11]Ziba said to the king, "Your servant will do everything that my lord the king has instructed his servant to do." So Mephibosheth was a regular guest at David's table,[1] just as though he were one of the king's sons.

[12]Now Mephibosheth had a young son [a]whose name was Mica. All the members of Ziba's household were Mephibosheth's servants. [13]Mephibosheth was living in Jerusalem, [a]for he [b]was a regular guest at the king's table. But both his feet were crippled.

David and the Ammonites

10 Later the [a]king of the Ammonites died and his son Hanun succeeded him. [2]David said, "I will express my [a]loyalty to Hanun son of [b]Nahash just as his father was loyal to me." So David sent his servants with a message expressing sympathy over his father's death. When David's servants entered the land of the Ammonites, [3]the Ammonite officials said to their lord Hanun, "Do you really think David is trying

8:11 [a]1 Kgs 7:51   8:12 [a]2 Sam 5:17–25   [1]Heb. *Aram.*   8:13 [a]2 Sam 7:9   [b]2 Kgs 14:7   [1]Heb. *Aram.*   8:14 [a]Gen 27:29, 37–40; Num 24:18; 1 Kgs 11:15   [1]MT *He placed in Edom garrisons; in all Edom he placed garrisons.*   8:16 [a]2 Sam 19:13; 20:23; 1 Chr 11:6   [b]1 Kgs 4:3   8:17 [a]1 Chr 6:4–8; 24:3   8:18 [a]1 Kgs 1:8; 1 Chr 18:17   [b]1 Sam 30:14; 1 Kgs 1:38   9:1 [a]1 Sam 18:3; 20:14–16; 2 Sam 21:7; [Prov 27:10]   9:2 [a]2 Sam 16:1–4; 19:17, 29   9:3 [a]1 Sam 20:14   [b]2 Sam 4:4   9:4 [a]2 Sam 17:27–29   9:6 [a]2 Sam 16:4; 19:24–30   9:8 [a]2 Sam 16:9   9:9 [a]2 Sam 16:4; 19:29   9:10 [a]2 Sam 9:7, 11, 13; 19:28   [b]2 Sam 19:17   [1]LXX, Syr, Vg. omit *it will be.*   9:11 [1]Heb. *my table;* Syr. *the table of the king.*   9:12 [a]1 Chr 8:34   9:13 [a]2 Sam 9:7, 10, 11; 1 Kgs 2:7; 2 Kgs 25:29   [b]2 Sam 9:3   10:1 [a]2 Sam 11:1; 1 Chr 19:1   10:2 [a]2 Sam 9:1; 1 Kgs 2:7   [b]1 Sam 11:1

to honor your father by sending these messengers to express his sympathy? No, David has sent his servants to you to get information about the city and spy on it so they can overthrow it!"

[4]So Hanun seized David's servants and shaved off half of each one's beard. He cut the lower part of their robes off so [a]that their buttocks were exposed, and then sent them away. [5]Messengers told David what had happened, so he sent them to the men who were thoroughly humiliated. The king said, "Stay in Jericho until your beards have grown again; then you may come back."

[6]When [a]the Ammonites realized that David was disgusted with them, they sent and hired 20,000 foot soldiers from Aram Beth [b]Rehob and Aram Zobah, in addition to 1,000 men from the king of [c]Maacah and 12,000 men from [d]Ish Tob.[1]

[7]When David heard [a]the news, he sent Joab and the entire army to meet them. [8]The Ammonites marched out and were deployed for battle at [a]the entrance of the city gate, while the men from Aram Zobah, Rehob, Ish Tob, and Maacah were by themselves in the field.

[9]When Joab saw that the battle would be fought on two fronts, he chose some of Israel's best men and deployed them against the Arameans. [10]He put his brother [a]Abishai in charge of the rest of the army and they were deployed against the Ammonites. [11]Joab said, "If the Arameans start to overpower me, you come to my rescue. If the Ammonites start to overpower you, I will come to your rescue. [12]Be strong! Let's fight bravely for the sake of our people and the cities of our God! The LORD will do what he decides is [a]best!"

[13]So Joab and his men marched out to do battle with the Arameans, and they fled before him. [14]When the Ammonites saw the Arameans flee, they fled before his brother Abishai and went into the city. Joab withdrew from fighting the Ammonites and returned to [a]Jerusalem.

[15]When the Arameans realized that they had been defeated by Israel, they consolidated their forces. [16]Then Hadadezer sent for Arameans from beyond the Euphrates River, and they came to Helam. Shobach, the general in command of Hadadezer's army, led them.

[17]When David was informed, he gathered all Israel, crossed the Jordan River, and came to Helam. The Arameans deployed their forces against David and fought with him. [18]The Arameans fled before Israel. David killed 700 Aramean charioteers and 40,000 foot soldiers.[1] He also struck down Shobach, the general in command of the army, who died there. [19]When all the kings who were subject to Hadadezer saw they were defeated by Israel, they made peace with Israel and became subjects [a]of Israel. The Arameans were no longer willing to help the Ammonites.

David Commits Adultery with Bathsheba

11 In the spring of the year, at the [a]time when kings[1] normally conduct wars, [b]David sent out Joab with his officers and the entire Israelite army. They defeated the Ammonites and besieged [c]Rabbah. But David stayed behind in Jerusalem. [2]One evening David got up from his bed [a]and walked around on the roof of his palace. From the roof he [b]saw a woman bathing. Now this woman was very attractive. [3]So David sent someone to inquire about the woman. The messenger said, "Isn't this Bathsheba, the daughter [a]of Eliam, the wife of Uriah the [b]Hittite?"

[4]David sent some messengers to get [a]her. She came to[1] him and he went to bed with her.[2] (Now at that time she was in the process of [b]purifying herself from her menstrual uncleanness.) Then she returned to her home. [5]The woman conceived and then sent word to David saying, "I'm pregnant."

[6]So David sent a message to Joab that said, "Send me Uriah the Hittite." So Joab sent Uriah to David. [7]When Uriah came to him, David asked about how Joab and the

10:4 [a]Isa 20:4; 47:2   10:6 [a]2 Sam 8:3, 5   [b]Judg 18:28   [c]Deut 3:14; Josh 13:11, 13   [d]Judg 11:3, 5   [1]Or perhaps *the men of Tob.*   10:7 [a]2 Sam 23:8   10:8 [a]2 Sam 10:6   10:10 [a]1 Sam 26:6; 2 Sam 3:30   10:12 [a]Deut 31:6; Josh 1:6–7, 9; Neh 4:14   10:14 [a]2 Sam 11:1   10:18 [1]Heb. *horsemen.*   10:19 [a]2 Sam 8:6   11:1 [a]1 Kgs 20:22–26   [b]1 Chr 20:1   [c]2 Sam 12:26; Jer 49:2–3; Amos 1:14   [1]One MS *messengers.*   11:2 [a]Deut 22:8; 1 Sam 9:25; Matt 24:17; Acts 10:9   [b]Gen 34:2; [Exod 20:17]; Job 31:1; [Matt 5:28]   11:3 [a]2 Sam 23:39   [b]1 Sam 26:6   11:4 [a][Lev 20:10; Deut 22:22]; Ps 51:title; [Jas 1:14–15]   [b]Lev 15:19, 28   [1]While sometimes used as a euphemism for sexual relations, here it refers only to the stage of approaching while the next verb describes the result. That she is the subject of this verb (while David is the subject of the next verb) probably indicates that the act was consensual.   [2]Heb. *he lay down with her;* a euphemism for sexual relations.

army were doing and how the campaign was going. [8]Then David said to Uriah, "Go down to your home and [a]relax." When Uriah left the palace, the king sent a gift to him. [9]But Uriah stayed at the [a]door of the palace with all[1] the servants of his lord. He did not go down to his house.

[10]So they informed David, "Uriah has not gone down to his house." So David said to Uriah, "Haven't you just arrived from a journey? Why haven't you gone down to your house?" [11]Uriah replied to David, "[a]The ark and Israel and Judah reside in temporary shelters, and [b]my lord Joab and my lord's soldiers are camping in the open field. Should I go to my house to eat and drink and go to bed with my wife? As surely as you are alive, I will not do this thing!" [12]So David said to Uriah, "Stay here another day. Tomorrow I will send you back." So Uriah stayed in Jerusalem both that day and the following one. [13]Then David summoned him. He ate and drank with him, and got him [a]drunk. But in the evening he went out to sleep on his bed [b]with the servants of his lord; he did not go down to his own house.

[14]In the morning David [a]wrote a letter to Joab and sent it with Uriah. [15]In the letter he wrote: "Station Uriah at the front in the thick of the battle and then withdraw from him so he will [a]be cut down and killed."

[16]So as Joab kept watch on the city, he stationed Uriah at the place where he knew the best enemy soldiers[1] were. [17]When the men of the city came out and fought with Joab, some of David's soldiers fell in battle. Uriah the Hittite also died.

[18]Then Joab sent a full battle report to David. [19]He instructed the messenger as follows: "When you finish giving the battle report to the king, [20]if the king becomes angry and asks you, 'Why did you go so close to the city to fight? Didn't you realize they would shoot from the wall? [21]Who struck down [a]Abimelech the son of Jerub-Besheth? Didn't a woman throw an upper millstone down on him from the wall so that he died in Thebez? Why did you go so close to the wall?' just say to him, 'Your servant Uriah the Hittite is also dead.'"

[22]So the messenger departed. When he arrived, he informed David of all the news that Joab had sent with him. [23]The messenger said to David, "The men overpowered us and attacked us in the field. But we forced them to retreat all the way to the door of the city gate. [24]Then the archers shot at your servants from the wall and some of the king's soldiers[1] died. Your servant Uriah the Hittite is also dead." [25]David said to the messenger, "Tell Joab, 'Don't let this thing upset you. There is no way to anticipate whom the sword will cut down. Press the battle against the city and conquer it.' Encourage him with these words."

[26]When Uriah's wife heard that her husband Uriah was dead, she mourned for him. [27]When the time of mourning passed, David had her brought to his palace. She [a]became his wife and she bore him [b]a son. But what David had done upset the LORD.[1]

Nathan the Prophet Confronts David

12 So [a]the LORD sent Nathan[1] to David. When he came to David, Nathan [b]said, "There were two men in a certain city, one rich and the other poor. [2]The rich man had a great many flocks and herds. [3]But the poor man had nothing except for a little lamb he had acquired. He raised it, and it grew up alongside him and his children. It used to eat his food, drink from his cup, and sleep in his arms. It was just like a daughter to him.

[4]"When a traveler arrived at the rich man's home, he did not want to use one of his own sheep or cattle to feed the traveler who had come to visit him. Instead, he took the poor man's lamb and cooked it for the man who had come to visit him."

[5]Then David became very angry at this man. He said to Nathan, "As surely as the LORD lives, the man who did this deserves to die![1] [6]Because he committed this cold-hearted crime, he must pay for the lamb four times [a]over!"[1]

[7]Nathan said to David, "You are that man! This is what the LORD God of Israel has said: 'I [a]chose you to be king over Israel and I rescued you from the hand of Saul.

11:8 [a]Gen 18:4; 19:2   11:9 [a]1 Kgs 14:27–28   [1]Luc. omits *all*.   11:11 [a]2 Sam 7:2, 6   [b]2 Sam 20:6–22   11:13 [a]Gen 19:33, 35
[b]2 Sam 11:9   11:14 [a]1 Kgs 21:8–9   11:15 [a]2 Sam 12:9   11:16 [1]Heb. *the valiant men*; the strongest or most valiant defenders
of the city that Joab and the Israelite army were besieging.   11:21 [a]Judg 9:50–54   11:24 [1]Ket. *servant*.   11:27 [a]2 Sam 12:9
[b]1 Chr 21:7; [Heb 13:4]   [1]Heb. *and the thing which David had done was evil in the eyes of the LORD*.   12:1 [a]Ps 51:title
[b]1 Kgs 20:35–41   [1]Some wss add *the prophet*.   12:5 [1]Heb. *the man doing this* [is] *a son of death*.   12:6 [a][Exod
22:1]; Luke 19:8   [1]Some wss *sevenfold*; Tg., Syr. *fortyfold*.   12:7 [a]1 Sam 16:13; 2 Sam 5:3

[8]I gave you your master's house, and put your master's wives into your arms. I also gave you the house of Israel and Judah. And if all that somehow seems insignificant, I would have given you so much more as well! [9][a]Why have you shown [b]contempt for the LORD's decrees[1] by doing evil in my[2] sight? [c]You have struck down Uriah the Hittite with the sword and you have taken his wife to be your own wife! You have killed him with the sword of the Ammonites. [10]So now [a]the sword will never depart from your house. For you have despised me by taking the wife of Uriah the Hittite as your own!' [11]This is what the LORD has said: 'I am about to bring disaster on you from inside your own household! Right before your eyes I will [a]take your wives and hand them over to your companion. He will go to bed with your wives in broad daylight! [12]Although you have acted in secret, I will do this thing before all Israel, and in broad daylight.'"

[13][a]Then [b]David exclaimed to Nathan, "I have sinned against the LORD!" Nathan replied to David, "Yes, and the LORD has forgiven your sin. You are not going to die. [14]Nonetheless, because you have treated the LORD with such contempt[1] in this matter, the son who has been born [a]to you will certainly die."

[15]Then Nathan went to his home. The [a]LORD struck the child that Uriah's wife had borne to David, and the child became very ill.[1] [16]Then David prayed to God for the child and fasted. He would even go and spend the night [a]lying on the ground. [17]The elders of his house stood over him and tried to lift him from the ground, but he was unwilling, and refused to eat food with them.

[18]On the seventh day the child died. But the servants of David were afraid to inform him that the child had died, for they said, "While the child was still alive he would not listen to us when we spoke to him. How can we tell him that the child is dead? He will do himself harm!"[1]

[19]When David saw that his servants were whispering to one another, he realized that the child was dead. So David asked his servants, "Is the child dead?" They replied, "Yes, he's dead." [20]So David got up from the ground, bathed, put on [a]oil, and changed his clothes. He went to the house of the LORD and [b]worshiped. Then, when he entered his palace, he requested that food be brought to him, and he ate.

[21]His servants said to him, "What is this that you have done? While[1] the child was still alive, you fasted and wept. Once the child was dead you got up and ate food!" [22]He replied, "While the child was still alive, I fasted and wept because I thought, 'Perhaps the LORD will show pity and the child will live.' [23]But now he is dead. Why should I fast? Am I able [a]to bring him back at this point? I will go to him, but [b]he cannot return to me!"

[24]So David comforted his wife [a]Bathsheba. [b]He came to her and went to bed with her.[1] Later she gave birth to a son, and David[2] named him Solomon. Now the LORD loved the child [25]and sent word through Nathan the prophet that he should be named Jedidiah for the LORD's sake.

David's Forces Defeat the Ammonites

[26]So [a]Joab fought against [b]Rabbah of the Ammonites and captured the royal city. [27]Joab then sent messengers to David, saying, "I have fought against Rabbah and have captured the water supply of the city. [28]So now assemble the rest of the army and besiege the city and capture it. Otherwise I will capture the city and it will be named for me."

[29]So David assembled all the army and went to Rabbah and fought against it and captured it. [30]He took [a]the crown of their king from his head—it was gold, weighed about 75 pounds,[1] and held a precious stone—and it was placed on David's head. He also took from the city a great deal of plunder. [31]He removed the people who were in it and made them labor with saws, iron picks, and iron axes, putting them to work at the brick kiln. This was his policy with all the Ammonite cities. Then David and all the army returned to Jerusalem.

12:9 [a]1 Sam 15:19 [b]Num 15:31 [c]2 Sam 11:14–17, 27 [1]Or *word, message.* [2]Ket. *his.* 12:10 [a]2 Sam 13:28; 18:14; 1 Kgs 2:25; [Amos 7:9] 12:11 [a]Deut 28:30; 2 Sam 16:21–22 12:13 [a]1 Sam 15:24 [b]2 Sam 24:10; Job 7:20; Ps 51; Luke 18:13 12:14 [a]Isa 52:5; [Ezek 36:20, 23]; Rom 2:24 [1]MT *because you have caused the enemies of the LORD to treat the LORD with such contempt.* 12:15 [a]1 Sam 25:38 [1]Heb. *and he was ill.* 12:16 [a]2 Sam 13:31 12:18 [1]Heb. *he will do harm.* 12:20 [a]Ruth 3:3; Matt 6:17 [b]Job 1:20 12:21 [1]MT *for the sake of.* 12:23 [a]Gen 37:35 [b]Job 7:8–10 12:24 [a]Matt 1:6 [b]1 Chr 22:9 [1]Heb. *and he lay with her,* a euphemism for sexual relations. [2]Qe. *she.* 12:26 [a]1 Chr 20:1 [b]Deut 3:11; 2 Sam 11:1 12:30 [a]1 Chr 20:2 [1]Heb. *and its weight* [was] *a talent of gold.*

The Rape of Tamar

13 Now David's son [a]Absalom had a beautiful sister named [b]Tamar. In the course of time David's son [c]Amnon fell madly in love with her.[1] [2]But Amnon became frustrated because he was so lovesick over his sister Tamar. For she was a virgin, and to Amnon it seemed out of the question to do anything to her.

[3]Now Amnon had a friend named Jonadab, [a]the son of David's brother Shimeah. Jonadab was a very crafty man. [4]He asked Amnon, "Why are you, the king's son,[1] so depressed every morning? Can't you tell me?" So Amnon said to him, "I'm in love with Tamar the sister of my brother Absalom." [5]Jonadab replied to him, "Lie down on your bed and pretend to be sick. When your father comes in to see you, say to him, 'Please let my sister Tamar come in so she can fix some food for me. Let her prepare the food in my sight so I can watch. Then I will eat from her hand.'"

[6]So Amnon lay down and pretended to be sick. When the king came in to see him, Amnon said to the king, "Please let my sister Tamar come in so she can [a]make a couple of cakes in my sight. Then I will eat from her hand."

[7]So David sent Tamar to the house saying, "Please go to the house of Amnon your brother and prepare some food for him." [8]So Tamar went to the house of Amnon her brother, who was lying down. She took the dough, kneaded it, made some cakes while he watched, and baked them. [9]But when she took the pan and set it before him, he refused to eat. Instead Amnon said, "Get everyone out of here!" So everyone left.[1]

[10]Then Amnon said to Tamar, "Bring the cakes into the bedroom; then I will eat from your hand." So Tamar took the cakes that she had prepared and brought them to her brother Amnon in the bedroom. [11]As [a]she brought them to him to eat, he grabbed her and said to her, "Come on! Get in bed with me,[1] my sister!"

[12]But she said to him, "No, my brother! Don't humiliate me! This just [a]isn't done in Israel! Don't do this foolish thing! [13]How could I ever be rid of my humiliation? And you would be considered one of the fools in Israel! Just speak to the king, [a]for he will not withhold me from you." [14]But he refused to listen to her. He overpowered her and [a]humiliated her by raping her. [15]Then Amnon greatly despised her. His disdain toward her surpassed the love he had previously felt toward her. Amnon said to her, "Get up and leave!"

[16]But she said to him, "No I won't, for sending me away now would be worse than what you did to me earlier!" But he refused to listen to her. [17]He called his personal attendant and said to him, "Take this woman out of my sight and lock the door behind her!" [18](Now she [a]was wearing a long robe, for this is what the king's virgin daughters used to wear.) So Amnon's attendant removed her and bolted the door behind her. [19]Then Tamar put [a]ashes on her head and tore the long robe she was wearing. She [b]put her hands on her head and went on her way, wailing as she went.

[20]Her brother Absalom said to her, "Was Amnon your brother with you? Now be quiet, my sister. He is your brother. Don't take it so seriously!"[1] Tamar, devastated, lived in the house of her brother Absalom.

[21]Now King David heard about all these things and was very angry.[1] [22]But Absalom said [a]nothing to Amnon, either bad or good, yet Absalom [b]hated Amnon because he had humiliated his sister Tamar.

Absalom Has Amnon Put to Death

[23]Two years later Absalom's sheepshearers were in Baal Hazor, near Ephraim. Absalom invited all the king's sons. [24]Then Absalom went to the king and said, "My shearers have begun their work. Let the king and his servants go with me."

[25]But the king said to Absalom, "No, my son. We shouldn't all go. We shouldn't burden you in that way." Though Absalom pressed[1] him, the king was not willing to go. Instead, David blessed him.

13:1 [a] 2 Sam 3:2–3; 1 Chr 3:2   [b] 1 Chr 3:9   [c] 2 Sam 3:2   [1] Heb. *Amnon the son of David loved her.*   13:3 [a] 1 Sam 16:9   13:4 [1] I.e., "Why are you of all people."   13:6 [a] Gen 18:6   13:9 [1] Some wss *and they removed everyone.*   13:11 [a] Gen 39:12; [Deut 27:22]; Ezek 22:11   [1] Heb. *lie with me.*   13:12 [a] [Lev 18:9–11; 20:17]   13:13 [a] Gen 20:12   13:14 [a] Lev 18:9; [Deut 22:25; 27:22]; 2 Sam 12:11   13:18 [a] Gen 37:3; Judg 5:30; Ps 45:13–14   13:19 [a] Josh 7:6; 2 Sam 1:2; Job 2:12; 42:6   [b] Jer 2:37   13:20 [1] Heb. *Don't set your heart to this thing!*   13:21 [1] LXX adds *But he did not grieve the spirit of Amnon his son, because he loved him, since he was his firstborn.*   13:22 [a] Gen 24:50; 31:24   [b] [Lev 19:17–18; 1 John 2:9, 11; 3:10, 12, 15]   13:25 [1] MT *and he broke through.*

[26]Then Absalom said, "If you will not go, then let my brother Amnon go with us." The king replied to him, "Why should he go with you?" [27]But when Absalom pressed him, he sent Amnon and all the king's sons along with him.

[28]Absalom instructed his servants, "Look! When Amnon is [a]drunk and I say to you, 'Strike Amnon down,' kill him then and there. Don't fear! Is it not I who have given you these instructions? Be strong and courageous!" [29]So Absalom's servants [a]did to Amnon exactly what Absalom had instructed. Then all the king's sons got up; each one rode away on [b]his mule and fled.

[30]While they were still on their way, the following report reached David: "Absalom has killed all the king's sons; not one of them is left!" [31]Then the king stood up and [a]tore his garments and lay [b]down on the ground. All his servants were standing there with torn garments as well.

[32][a]Jonadab, the son of David's brother Shimeah, said, "My lord should not say, 'They have killed all the young men who are the king's sons.' For only Amnon is dead. This is what Absalom has talked about from the day that Amnon humiliated his sister Tamar. [33]Now don't [a]let my lord the king be concerned about the report that has come saying, 'All the king's sons are dead.' It is only Amnon who is dead."

[34]In [a]the meantime Absalom fled. When the servant who was the watchman looked up, he saw many people coming from the west on a road beside the hill. [35]Jonadab said to the king, "Look! The king's sons have come! It's just as I said."

[36]Just as he finished speaking, the king's sons arrived, wailing and weeping. The king and all his servants wept loudly as well. [37]But Absalom fled and went to King [a]Talmai son of Ammihud of Geshur. And David[1] grieved over his son every day.

[38]After Absalom fled and went to [a]Geshur, he remained there for three years. [39]The king longed[1] to go to Absalom, for he had since been [a]consoled over the death of Amnon.

David Permits Absalom to Return to Jerusalem

14 Now Joab son of Zeruiah realized that the king longed to see[1] Absalom. [2]So Joab sent to [a]Tekoa [b]and brought from there a wise woman. He told her, "Pretend to be in mourning and put on garments for mourning. Don't anoint yourself with oil. Instead, act like a woman who has been mourning for the dead for some time. [3]Go to the king and speak to him in the following fashion." Then Joab [a]told her what to say.

[4]So the Tekoan woman went[1] to the king. She bowed [a]down with her face to the ground in deference to him and said, "Please [b]help me, O king!" [5]The king replied to her, "What do you want?"[1] She answered, "I am a [a]widow; my husband is dead. [6]Your servant has two sons. When the two of them got into a fight in the field, there was no one present who could intervene. One of them struck the other and killed him. [7]Now the entire family has risen up against your servant, saying, 'Turn over the one who struck down his brother, so that we can execute him and avenge the death[1] of his brother whom he killed. In so doing we will also destroy the heir.' They want to extinguish my remaining coal, leaving no one on the face of the earth to carry on the name of my husband."

[8]Then the king told the woman, "Go to your home. I will give instructions concerning your situation." [9]The Tekoan woman said to [a]the king, "My lord the king, let any blame fall on me [b]and on the house of my father. But let the king and his throne be innocent!"

[10]The king said, "Bring to me whoever speaks to you, and he won't bother you again!" [11]She replied, "In that case, let [a]the king invoke the name of the LORD your God so that the avenger of blood may not add to the killing! Then they will not destroy my son!" He replied, "[b]As surely as the LORD lives, not a single hair of your son's head will fall to the ground."

[12]Then the woman said, "Please permit your servant to speak to my lord the king

13:28 [a]Judg 19:6, 9, 22; Ruth 3:7; 1 Sam 25:36; Esth 1:10   **13:29** [a]2 Sam 12:10   [b]2 Sam 18:9; 1 Kgs 1:33, 38   **13:31** [a]2 Sam 1:11   [b]2 Sam 12:16   **13:32** [a]2 Sam 13:3–5   **13:33** [a]2 Sam 19:19   **13:34** [a]2 Sam 13:37–38   **13:37** [a]2 Sam 3:3; 1 Chr 3:2   [1]Heb. omits *David.*   **13:38** [a]2 Sam 14:23, 32; 15:8   **13:39** [a]Gen 38:12; 2 Sam 12:19, 23   [1]MT *David the king.*   **14:1** [1]Heb. *the heart of the king was upon.*   **14:2** [a]2 Sam 23:26; 2 Chr 11:6; Amos 1:1   [b]Ruth 3:3   **14:3** [a]Exod 4:15; 2 Sam 14:19   **14:4** [a]1 Sam 20:41; 25:23; 2 Sam 1:2   [b]2 Kgs 6:26, 28   [1]MT *and she said.*   **14:5** [a][Zech 7:10]   [1]Heb. *What to you?*   **14:7** [1]Heb. *in exchange for the life.*   **14:9** [a]Gen 27:13; 43:9; 1 Sam 25:24; Matt 27:25   [b]2 Sam 3:28–29; 1 Kgs 2:33   **14:11** [a]Num 35:19, 21; [Deut 19:4–10]   [b]1 Sam 14:45; 1 Kgs 1:52; Matt 10:30; Acts 27:34

about another matter." He replied, "Tell me." [13]The woman said, "Why have you devised something like this against God's people? When [a]the king speaks in [b]this fashion, he makes himself guilty, for the king has not brought back the one he has banished. [14]Certainly we must die, and are like water spilled on the ground that cannot be gathered up again. But God does not take [a]away life; instead he [b]devises ways for the banished to be restored. [15]I have now come to speak with my lord the king about this matter, because the people have made me fearful.[1] But your servant said, 'I will speak to the king! Perhaps the king will do what his female servant asks. [16]Yes! The king may[1] listen and deliver his female servant from the hand of the man who seeks to remove both me and my son from the [a]inheritance God has given us!' [17]So your servant said, 'May the word of my lord the king be my security, for my lord the king is like the angel of God when it comes to [a]deciding between right and wrong! May the LORD your God be with you!'"

[18]Then the king replied to the woman, "Don't hide any information from me when I question you." The woman said, "Let my lord the king speak." [19]The king said, "Did Joab put you up to all of this?" [a]The woman answered, "As surely as you live, my lord the king, there is no deviation to the right or to the left from all that my lord the king has said. For your servant Joab gave me instructions. He has put all these words in your servant's mouth. [20]Your servant Joab did this so as to change this situation. But my lord has wisdom like that of the angel of God, and knows everything that is happening [a]in the land."

[21]Then the king said to Joab, "All right! I[1] will do this thing. Go and bring back the young man Absalom!" [22]Then Joab bowed down with his face toward the ground and thanked the king. Joab said, "Today your servant knows that I have found favor in your sight, my lord the king, because the king has granted the request of your[1] servant!"

[23]So Joab got up [a]and went to Geshur and brought Absalom back to Jerusalem. [24]But the king said, "Let him go over to his own house. He may not see my face." So Absalom went over to his own house; he did not see the king's face.

[25]Now in all Israel everyone acknowledged that there was no man as handsome as Absalom. [a]From the soles of his feet to the top of his head he was perfect in appearance. [26]When he would shave his head—at the end of every year he used to shave his head, for it grew too long and he would shave it—he used to weigh the hair of his head at three pounds[1] according to the king's weight. [27][a]Absalom had three sons and one daughter, whose name was Tamar. She was a very attractive woman.[1]

[28]Absalom lived in Jerusalem for two years without seeing the king's face. [29]Then Absalom sent a message to Joab asking him to send him to the king, but Joab was not willing to come to him. So he sent a second message to him, but he still was not willing to come. [30]So he said to his servants, "Look, Joab has a portion of field adjacent to mine and he has some barley there. Go and set it on fire."[1] So Absalom's servants set Joab's portion of the field on fire.

[31]Then Joab got up and came to Absalom's house. He said to him, "Why did your servants set my portion of field on fire?" [32]Absalom said to Joab, "Look, [a]I sent a message to you saying, 'Come here so that I can send you to the king with this message: "Why have I come from Geshur? It would be better for me if I were still there."' Let me now see the face of the king. If I am at fault, let him put me to death!"

[33]So Joab went to the king and informed him. The king summoned Absalom, and he came to the king. Absalom bowed down before the king with his face toward the ground and the king [a]kissed him.

Absalom Leads an Insurrection against David

15 Some time later Absalom managed to [a]acquire a chariot and horses, as well as 50 men to serve as his royal guard. [2]Now Absalom used to get up early and stand beside the road that led to the city gate.

14:13 [a]Judg 20:2   [b]2 Sam 13:37–38   14:14 [a]Job 34:19; Matt 22:16; Acts 10:34; Rom 2:11   [b]Num 35:15   14:15 [1]LXX to see.   14:16 [a]Deut 32:9; 1 Sam 26:19; 2 Sam 20:19   [1]Or will.   14:17 [a]1 Kgs 3:9   14:19 [a]2 Sam 14:3   14:20 [a]2 Sam 14:17; 19:27   14:21 [1]Sev. MSS you.   14:22 [1]MT his.   14:23 [a]2 Sam 13:37–38   14:25 [a]Deut 28:35; Job 2:7; Isa 1:6   14:26 [1]Heb. two hundred shekels.   14:27 [a]2 Sam 13:1; 18:18   [1]LXX adds And she became a wife to Rehoboam the son of Solomon and bore to him Abia.   14:30 [1]LXX adds And the servants of Absalom burned them up. And the servants of Joab came to him, rending their garments. They said.   14:32 [a]1 Sam 20:8; [Prov 28:13]   14:33 [a]Gen 33:4; 45:15; Luke 15:20   15:1 [a]1 Kgs 1:5

Whenever anyone came by who had a [a]complaint to bring to the king for arbitration, Absalom would call out to him, "What city are you from?" The person would answer, "I, your servant, am from one of the tribes of Israel." [3]Absalom would then say to him, "Look, your claims are legitimate and appropriate. But there is no representative of the king who will listen to you." [4]Absalom would then say, "If only they would make me a judge in the land! Then everyone who had a judicial complaint could come to me and I would make sure he receives a just settlement."

[5]When someone approached to bow before him, Absalom would extend his hand and embrace him and [a]kiss him. [6]Absalom acted this way toward everyone in Israel who came to the king for justice. In this way Absalom won the loyalty of the citizens of Israel.

[7a]After four[1] years Absalom said to the king, "Let me go and repay my vow that I made to the LORD while I was in [b]Hebron. [8a]For I [b]made this vow when [c]I was living in Geshur in Aram: 'If the LORD really does allow me to return to Jerusalem, I will serve the LORD.'" [9]The king replied to him, "Go in peace." So Absalom got up and went to Hebron.

[10]Then Absalom sent spies through all the tribes of Israel who said, "When you hear the sound of the horn, you may assume that Absalom [a]rules in Hebron." [11]Now 200 men had gone with Absalom from Jerusalem. Since they were [a]invited, they [b]went naively and were unaware of what Absalom was planning. [12]While he was offering sacrifices, Absalom sent for Ahithophel the Gilonite, [a]David's adviser, to come from his city, [b]Giloh. The conspiracy was gaining momentum, and the people were [c]starting to side with Absalom.

David Flees from Jerusalem

[13]Then a messenger came to David and reported, "[a]The men of Israel are loyal to Absalom!" [14]So David said to all his servants who were with him in Jerusalem, "Come on! Let's [a]escape! Otherwise no one will be delivered from Absalom! Go immediately, or else he will quickly overtake us and bring disaster on us and kill the city's residents with the sword." [15]The king's servants replied to the king, "We will do whatever our lord the king decides."

[16]So [a]the king and all the members of his royal court set out on foot, though the king left behind [b]10 concubines to attend to the palace. [17]The king and all the people set out on foot, pausing at a spot some distance away. [18]All his servants were leaving with him, along with all the Kerethites, all the Pelethites, [a]and all the Gittites—some [b]600 men who had come on foot from Gath. They were leaving with the king.

[19]Then the king said to [a]Ittai the Gittite, "Why should you come with us? Go back and stay with the new king, for you are a foreigner and an exile from your own country. [20]It seems as [a]if you arrived just yesterday. Today should I make you wander around by going with us? I go where I must go. But as for you, go back and take your men with you. May genuine loyal love protect you!"

[21]But Ittai replied to the king, "[a]As surely as the LORD lives and as my lord the king lives, wherever my lord the king is, whether it means death or life, there I will be as well!" [22]So David said to Ittai, "Come along then." So Ittai the Gittite went along, accompanied by all his men and all the dependents who were with him.

[23]All the land was weeping loudly as all these people were leaving. As the king was crossing over the Kidron Valley, all the people were leaving on the road that leads to the [a]desert. [24a]Zadok and all the Levites who were with him were carrying the [b]ark of the covenant of God. When they positioned the ark of God, [c]Abiathar offered sacrifices until all the people had finished leaving the city.

[25]Then the king said to Zadok, "Take the ark of God back to the city. If [a]I find favor in the LORD's sight he will bring me back and enable me to see both it and [b]his dwelling place again. [26]However, if he should say, 'I do not take [a]pleasure in you,' then he will deal with me in a way that he considers appropriate."

15:2 [a]Deut 19:17   15:5 [a]2 Sam 14:33; 20:9   15:7 [a][Deut 23:21]   [b]2 Sam 3:2–3   [1]MT *forty*.   15:8 [a]1 Sam 16:2   [b]Gen 28:20–21   [c]2 Sam 13:38   15:10 [a]1 Kgs 1:34; 2 Kgs 9:13   15:11 [a]1 Sam 16:3, 5   [b]Gen 20:5   15:12 [a]2 Sam 16:15; 1 Chr 27:33; Ps 41:9; 55:12–14   [b]Josh 15:51   [c]Ps 3:1   15:13 [a]Judg 9:3; 2 Sam 15:6   15:14 [a]2 Sam 12:11; Ps 3:title   15:16 [a]Ps 3:title   [b]2 Sam 12:11; 16:21–22   15:18 [a]2 Sam 8:18   [b]1 Sam 23:13; 25:13; 30:1, 9   15:19 [a]2 Sam 18:2   15:20 [a]1 Sam 23:13   15:21 [a]Ruth 1:16–17; [Prov 17:17]   15:23 [a]2 Sam 15:28; 16:2   15:24 [a]2 Sam 8:17   [b]Num 4:15; 1 Sam 4:4   [c]1 Sam 22:20   15:25 [a][Ps 43:3]   [b]Exod 15:13; Jer 25:30   15:26 [a]Num 14:8; 2 Sam 22:20; 1 Kgs 10:9; 2 Chr 9:8; Isa 62:4

[27]The king said to Zadok the priest, "Are you a [a]seer? Go back to the city in peace! [b]Your son Ahimaaz and Abiathar's son Jonathan may go with you and Abiathar. [28]Look, [a]I will be waiting at the fords of the desert until word from you reaches me." [29]So Zadok and Abiathar took the ark of God back to Jerusalem and remained there.

[30]As David was going up the Mount of Olives, he was weeping as he went; [a]his head was covered and his feet were [b]bare. All the people who were with him also had their heads [c]covered and were [d]weeping as they went up. [31]Now David had been told, "[a]Ahithophel has sided with the conspirators who are with Absalom." So David prayed, "Make the advice of Ahithophel foolish, O Lord."

[32]When David reached the summit, where he used to worship God, Hushai the [a]Arkite met him [b]with his clothes torn and dirt on his head. [33]David [a]said to him, "If you leave with me you will be a burden to me. [34]But you [a]will be able to counter the advice of Ahithophel if you go back to the city and say to Absalom, 'I will be your servant, O king! Previously I was your father's servant, and now I will be your servant.' [35a]Zadok and Abiathar the priests will be there with you. Everything you hear in the king's palace you must tell Zadok and Abiathar the priests. [36]Furthermore, their two sons are there [a]with them, Zadok's son Ahimaaz and Abiathar's son Jonathan. You must send them to me with any information you hear."

[37]So [a]David's friend Hushai arrived in the city, just as Absalom was entering Jerusalem.

David Receives Gifts from Ziba

16 When David had gone a short way beyond the summit, Ziba the servant of Mephibosheth was there to meet him. [a]He had [b]a couple of donkeys that were saddled, and on them were 200 loaves of bread, 100 raisin cakes, 100 baskets of summer fruit, and a container of wine. [2]The king asked Ziba, "Why did you bring these things?" Ziba replied, "The donkeys are for the king's family to ride on, the loaves of bread and the summer fruit are for the attendants to eat, and the wine is for [a]those who get exhausted in the desert." [3]The king asked, "[a]Where is your master's [b]grandson?" Ziba replied to the king, "He remains in Jerusalem, for he said, 'Today the house of Israel will give back to me my grandfather's kingdom.'" [4]The king said to Ziba, "Everything that was Mephibosheth's now belongs to you." Ziba replied, "I bow before you. May I find favor in your sight, my lord the king."

Shimei Curses David and His Men

[5]Then King David reached [a]Bahurim. There a man from Saul's extended family named [b]Shimei son of Gera came out, yelling curses as he approached. [6]He threw stones at David and all of King David's servants, as well as all the people and the soldiers who were on his right and on his left. [7]As he yelled curses, Shimei said, "Leave! Leave! [a]You man of bloodshed, you wicked man! [8]The Lord has punished you for all [a]the spilled blood of the house of Saul, in whose place you rule. Now the Lord has given the kingdom into the hand of your son Absalom. Disaster has overtaken you, for you are a man of bloodshed!"

[9]Then Abishai son of Zeruiah said to the king, "Why should this [a]dead dog [b]curse my lord the king? Let me go over and cut off his head!" [10]But the king said, "[a]What do we have in common, you sons of Zeruiah? If [b]he curses because the Lord has said to him, 'Curse David!,' [c]who can say to him, 'Why have you done this?'" [11]Then David said to Abishai and to all his servants, "[a]My own son, my very own flesh and [b]blood,[1] is trying to take my life. So also now this Benjaminite! Leave him alone so that he can curse, for the Lord has spoken to him. [12]Perhaps the Lord will notice my affliction[1] and this day [a]grant me [b]good in place of his curse." [13]So David and his men went on their way. But Shimei kept going along the side of the

15:27 [a]1 Sam 9:6–9   [b]2 Sam 17:17–20   **15:28** [a]Josh 5:10; 2 Sam 17:16   **15:30** [a]2 Sam 19:4; Esth 6:12; Ezek 24:17, 23   [b]Isa 20:2–4   [c]Jer 14:3–4   [d][Ps 126:6]   **15:31** [a]Ps 3:1–2; 55:12   **15:32** [a]Josh 16:2   [b]2 Sam 1:2   **15:33** [a]2 Sam 19:35   **15:34** [a]2 Sam 16:19   **15:35** [a]2 Sam 17:15–16   **15:36** [a]2 Sam 15:27   **15:37** [a]2 Sam 16:16; 1 Chr 27:33   **16:1** [a]2 Sam 15:30, 32   [b]2 Sam 9:2; 19:17, 29   **16:2** [a]2 Sam 15:23; 17:29   **16:3** [a]2 Sam 9:9–10   [b]2 Sam 19:27   **16:5** [a]2 Sam 3:16   [b]2 Sam 19:21; 1 Kgs 2:8–9, 44–46   **16:7** [a]Deut 13:13   **16:8** [a]2 Sam 1:16; 3:28–29; 4:11–12   **16:9** [a]1 Sam 24:14; 2 Sam 9:8   [b]Exod 22:28   **16:10** [a]2 Sam 3:39; 19:22; [1 Pet 2:23]   [b]2 Kgs 18:25; [Lam 3:38]   [c][Rom 9:20]   **16:11** [a]2 Sam 12:11   [b]Gen 15:4   [1]Heb. *who came out from my entrails.*   **16:12** [a]Deut 23:5; Neh 13:2; Prov 20:22   [b]Deut 23:5; [Rom 8:28; Heb 12:10–11]   [1]MT *on my wrongdoing.*

hill opposite him, yelling curses as he threw stones and dirt at them.[1] [14] The king and all the people who were with him arrived exhausted at their destination, where David refreshed himself.

The Advice of Ahithophel

[15] Now when [a] Absalom and all the men of Israel arrived in Jerusalem, Ahithophel was with him. [16] When [a] David's friend [b] Hushai the Arkite came to Absalom, Hushai said to him, "Long live the king! Long live the king!"

[17] Absalom said to Hushai, "Do you call this loyalty to your friend? [a] Why didn't you go with your friend?" [18] Hushai replied to Absalom, "No, I will be loyal to the one whom the LORD, these people, and all the men of Israel have chosen.[1] [19] Moreover, [a] whom should I serve? Should it not be his son? Just as I served your father, so I will serve you."

[20] Then Absalom said to [a] Ahithophel, "Give us your advice. What should we do?" [21] Ahithophel replied to Absalom, "Sleep with[1] your father's [a] concubines whom he left to [b] care for [c] the palace. All Israel will hear that you have made yourself repulsive to your father. Then your followers will be motivated to support you." [22] So they pitched a tent for Absalom on the roof, and Absalom slept with[1] his father's [a] concubines in the sight of all Israel.

[23] In those days Ahithophel's advice was considered as valuable as a prophetic revelation. [a] Both David and Absalom highly regarded the advice of Ahithophel.

The Death of Ahithophel

17 Ahithophel said to Absalom, "Let me pick out 12,000 men. Then I will go and pursue David this very night. [2] When I catch up with him he will be [a] exhausted and worn out. I will rout him, and the entire army that is with him will flee. I will [b] kill only the king [3] and will bring the entire army back to you. In exchange for the life of the man you are seeking, you will get

back everyone.[1] The entire army will return unharmed."

[4] This seemed like a good idea to Absalom and to all the [a] leaders of Israel. [5] But Absalom said, "Call for Hushai the Arkite, and let's hear what he has to [a] say." [6] So Hushai came to Absalom. Absalom said to him, "Here is what Ahithophel has advised. Should we follow his advice? If not, what would you recommend?"

[7] Hushai replied to Absalom, "Ahithophel's advice is not sound this time." [8] Hushai went on to [a] say, "You know your father and his men—they are soldiers and are as dangerous as a bear out in the wild that has been robbed of her cubs. Your father is an experienced soldier; he will not stay overnight with the army. [9] At this very moment he is hiding out in one of the caves or in some other similar place. If it should turn out that he attacks our troops first, whoever hears about it will say, 'Absalom's army has been slaughtered!' [10] If that happens even the bravest soldier—one who is lion-hearted—will [a] virtually melt away. For all Israel knows that your father is a warrior and that those who are with him are brave. [11] My advice therefore is this: Let all Israel [a] from Dan to Beer Sheba—in number [b] like the sand by the sea—be mustered to you, and you lead them personally into battle. [12] We will come against him wherever he happens to be found. We will descend on him like the dew falls on the ground. Neither he nor any of the men who are with him will be spared alive—not one of them! [13] If he regroups in a city, all Israel will take up ropes to that city and [a] drag it down to the valley, so that not a single pebble will be left there!"

[14] Then Absalom and all [a] the men of Israel said, "The advice of Hushai the Arkite sounds better than the advice of Ahithophel." Now the LORD had decided to frustrate the sound advice of Ahithophel, so that the LORD could bring disaster on Absalom.

[15] Then Hushai reported to Zadok and Abiathar [a]the priests, "Here is what Ahithophel has advised Absalom and the leaders of Israel to do, and here is what I have advised. [16]Now send word quickly to David and warn him, "Don't spend the night at the fords of the wilderness tonight. [a]Instead, be sure you cross over, or else the king and everyone who is with him may be overwhelmed."

[17a]Now Jonathan and Ahimaaz were [b]staying in En [c]Rogel. A female servant would go and inform them, and they would then go and inform King David. It was not advisable for them to be seen going into the city. [18]But a young man saw them on one occasion and [a]informed Absalom. So the two of them quickly departed and went to the house of a man in Bahurim. There was a well in his courtyard, and they got down in it. [19]His wife [a]then took the covering and spread it over the top of the well and scattered some grain over it. No one was aware of what she had done.

[20]When [a]the servants of Absalom approached the woman at her home, they asked, "Where are Ahimaaz and Jonathan?" The woman replied to them, "They crossed over the stream." Absalom's men searched but did not find them, so they returned to Jerusalem.

[21]After the men had left, Ahimaaz and Jonathan climbed out of the well. Then they left and informed King David. They advised David, "Get [a]up and cross the stream quickly, for Ahithophel has devised a plan to catch you." [22]So David and all the people who were with him got up and crossed the Jordan River. By dawn there was not one person left who had not crossed the Jordan.

[23]When Ahithophel realized that [a]his advice had not been followed, he saddled his donkey and returned to his [b]house in his hometown. After setting his household in order, he [c]hanged himself. So he died and was buried in the grave[1] of his father.

[24]Meanwhile David had gone to [a]Mahanaim, while Absalom and all the men of Israel had crossed the Jordan River. [25]Absalom had made [a]Amasa general in command of the army in place of Joab. (Now Amasa was the son of an Israelite man named Jether, who had married [b]Abigail the daughter of Nahash and sister of Zeruiah, Joab's mother.) [26]The army of Israel and Absalom camped in the land of Gilead.

[27]When David came to Mahanaim, [a]Shobi the son of Nahash from Rabbah of the Ammonites, [b]Makir the son of Ammiel from Lo Debar, and [c]Barzillai the Gileadite from Rogelim [28]brought bedding, basins, and pottery utensils. They also brought food for David and all who were with him, including wheat, barley, flour, roasted grain, beans, lentils,[1] [29]honey, curds, flocks, and cheese. For they said, "The people are no doubt hungry, tired, and thirsty there [a]in the desert."

The Death of Absalom

18 David assembled the army that was with him. He [a]appointed leaders of thousands and leaders of hundreds. [2]David then sent out the army—a third under the leadership of Joab, a third under the leadership of Joab's brother Abishai son of Zeruiah, and a third under the leadership of [a]Ittai the Gittite. The king said to the troops, "I too will indeed march out with you."

[3]But the soldiers replied, "You should not do this! For if we should have to make a rapid retreat, they won't be concerned about us. Even if half of us should die, they won't be concerned. [a]But you[1] are like 10,000 of us! So it is better if you remain in the city for support." [4]Then the king said to them, "I will do whatever seems best to you."

So the king stayed beside the city gate, while all the army marched out by hundreds and by thousands. [5]The king gave this order to Joab, Abishai, [a]and Ittai: "For my sake deal gently with the young man Absalom." Now the entire army was listening when the king gave all the leaders this order concerning Absalom.

[6]Then the army marched out to the field to fight against Israel. The battle took place in the [a]forest of Ephraim. [7]The army of Israel was defeated there by David's men. The slaughter there was great that

17:15 [a]2 Sam 15:35–36   17:16 [a]2 Sam 15:28   17:17 [a]2 Sam 15:27, 36; 1 Kgs 1:42–43   [b]Josh 2:4–6   [c]Josh 15:7; 18:16   17:18 [a]2 Sam 3:16; 16:5   17:19 [a]Josh 2:4–6   17:20 [a]Exod 1:19; [Lev 19:11]; Josh 2:3–5   17:21 [a]2 Sam 17:15–16   17:23 [a]2 Sam 15:12   [b]2 Kgs 20:1   [c]Matt 27:5   [1]Orig., Luc. *house.*   17:24 [a]Gen 32:2; Josh 13:26; 2 Sam 2:8; 19:32   17:25 [a]2 Sam 19:13; 20:9–12; 1 Kgs 2:5, 32   [b]1 Chr 2:16   17:27 [a]1 Sam 11:1; 2 Sam 10:1; 12:29   [b]2 Sam 9:4   [c]2 Sam 19:31–32; 1 Kgs 2:7   17:28 [1]MT adds *roasted grain.*   17:29 [a]2 Sam 16:2, 14   18:1 [a]Exod 18:25; Num 31:14; 1 Sam 22:7   18:2 [a]2 Sam 15:19–22   18:3 [a]2 Sam 21:17   [1]MT *now.*   18:5 [a]2 Sam 18:12   18:6 [a]Josh 17:15, 18; 2 Sam 17:26

day—20,000 soldiers were killed. [8] The battle there was spread out over the whole area, and the forest consumed more soldiers than the sword devoured that day.

[9] Then Absalom happened to come across David's men. Now as Absalom was riding on [a] his mule, it went under the branches of a large oak tree. His head got caught in the oak and he was suspended in midair, while the mule he had been riding kept going.

[10] When one[1] of the men saw this, he reported it to Joab saying, "I saw Absalom hanging in an oak tree." [11] Joab replied to the man who was telling him this, "What! You saw this? Why didn't you strike him down right on the spot? I would have given you 10 pieces of silver[1] and a commemorative belt!"[2]

[12] The man replied to Joab, "Even if[1] I were receiving 1,000 pieces of silver,[2] I would not strike the king's son! In our very presence the king gave this order to you and Abishai and Ittai, 'Protect the young man Absalom [a] for my sake.'[3] [13] If I had acted at risk of my own life[1]—and nothing is hidden from the king—you would have abandoned me."

[14] Joab replied, "I will not wait around like this for you!" He took three spears in his hand and thrust them into the middle of Absalom while he was still alive in the middle of the oak tree.[1] [15] Then 10 soldiers who were Joab's armor-bearers struck Absalom and finished him off.

[16] Then Joab blew the trumpet and the army turned back from chasing Israel, for Joab had called for the army to halt. [17] They took Absalom, threw him into a large pit in the forest, and [a] stacked a huge pile of stones over him. In the meantime all the Israelite soldiers [b] fled to their homes.[1]

[18] Before this Absalom had set up a monument and dedicated it to himself in [a] the [b] King's Valley, reasoning, "I have no son who will carry on my name." He named the monument after himself, and to this day it is known as Absalom's Memorial.

David Learns of Absalom's Death

[19] Then [a] Ahimaaz the son of Zadok said, "Let me run and give the king the good news that the LORD has vindicated him before his enemies." [20] But Joab said to him, "You will not be a bearer of good news today. You will bear good news some other day, but not today, for the king's son is dead."

[21] Then Joab said to the Cushite, "Go and tell the king what you have seen." After bowing to Joab, the Cushite ran off. [22] Ahimaaz the son of Zadok again spoke to Joab, "Whatever happens, let me go after the Cushite." But Joab said, "Why is it that you want to go, my son? You have no good news that will bring you a reward." [23] But he said, "Whatever happens, I want to go!" So Joab said to him, "Then go!" So Ahimaaz ran by the way of the Jordan plain, and he passed the Cushite.

[24] Now David was sitting between the inner and [a] outer gates, and the watchman went up to the roof over the gate at the wall. When he looked, he saw a man running by himself. [25] So the watchman called out and informed the king. The king said, "If he is by himself, he brings good news." The runner came ever closer.

[26] Then the watchman saw another man running. The watchman called out to the gatekeeper, "There is another man running by himself." The king said, "This one also is bringing good news." [27] The watchman said, "It appears to me that the first runner is Ahimaaz son of Zadok." The king said, "He is a [a] good man, and he comes with good news."

[28] Then Ahimaaz called out and said to the king, "Greetings!" He bowed down before the king with his face toward the ground and said, "May the LORD your God be [a] praised because he has defeated the men who opposed my lord the king!"

[29] The king replied, "How is the young man Absalom?" Ahimaaz replied, "I saw a great deal of confusion when Joab was sending the king's servant and me, your servant, but I don't know what it was all about." [30] The king said, "Turn aside and take your place here." So he turned aside and waited.

[31] Then the Cushite arrived and said, "May my lord the king now receive the good news! The LORD has vindicated you today and delivered you from the hand of all who have

---

18:9 [a] 2 Sam 14:26   18:10 [1] One DSS MS omits *one*.   18:11 [1] Heb. *ten* [shekels] *of silver; about 4 ounces.* [2] Heb. *and a girdle.*   18:12 [a] 2 Sam 18:5   [1] MT *and not.* [2] Heb. *a thousand* [shekels] *of silver; about 25 pounds.* [3] MT *Show care, whoever you might be, for the youth Absalom.*   18:13 [1] MT *his life.*   18:14 [1] Lit. *he took three spears in his hand and thrust them into the heart of Absalom while he was still alive in the heart of the oak tree.*   18:17 [a] Deut 21:20–21; Josh 7:26; 8:29   [b] 2 Sam 19:8; 20:1, 22   [1] Heb. *and all Israel fled, each to his tent.*   18:18 [a] Gen 14:17   [b] 2 Sam 14:27   18:19 [a] 2 Sam 15:36; 17:17   18:24 [a] Judg 5:11; 2 Sam 13:34; 2 Kgs 9:17   18:27 [a] 1 Kgs 1:42   18:28 [a] 2 Sam 16:12

rebelled against you!" [32]The king asked the Cushite, "How is the young man Absalom?" The Cushite replied, "May the enemies of my lord the king and all who have plotted against you be like that young man!"

[33]The king then became very upset. He went up [a]to the upper room over the gate and wept. As he went he said, "[b]My son, Absalom! My son, my son,[1] Absalom! If only I could have died in your place! Absalom, my son, my son!"[2]

19 Joab was told, "The king is weeping and [a]mourning over Absalom." [2]So the victory of that day was turned to [a]mourning as far as all the people were concerned. For the people heard on that day, "The king is grieved over his son." [3]That day the people stole away [a]to go to the city the way people who are embarrassed steal away in fleeing from battle. [4]The king [a]covered his face and cried [b]out loudly, "My son, Absalom! Absalom, my son, my son!"

[5]So [a]Joab visited the king at his home. He said, "Today you have embarrassed all your servants who have saved your life this day, as well as the lives of your sons, your daughters, your wives, and your concubines. [6]You seem to love your enemies and hate your friends! For you have as much as declared today that leaders and servants don't matter to you. I realize now that if[1] Absalom were alive and all of us were dead today,[2] it would be all right with you. [7]So get up now and go out and give some encouragement to your servants. For I swear by the LORD that if you don't go out there, not a single man will stay here with you tonight! This disaster will be worse for you than any disaster that has overtaken you from your youth right to the present time!"

[8]So the king got up and sat at the city [a]gate. When all the people were informed that the king was sitting at the city gate, they all came before him.

David Goes Back to Jerusalem

But the Israelite soldiers had all [b]fled to their own homes. [9]All the people throughout all the tribes of Israel were arguing among themselves saying, "The king delivered us from the hand of our [a]enemies. He rescued us from the hand of the [b]Philistines, but now he has [c]fled from the land because of Absalom. [10]But Absalom, whom we anointed as our king, has died in battle. So now why do you hesitate to bring the king back?"[1]

[11]Then King David sent a message to [a]Zadok and Abiathar the priests saying, "Tell the elders of Judah, 'Why should you delay any further in bringing the king back to his palace, when everything Israel is saying has come to the king's attention.[1] [12]You are [a]my brothers—my very own flesh and blood! Why should you delay any further in bringing the king back?' [13]Say to Amasa, 'Are you not my flesh [a]and blood? [b]God will punish me severely, if from this time on you are not the commander of my army in place of Joab!'"

[14]He won over the hearts of all the men of Judah as though they were one man. Then they sent word to the king saying, "Return, you and all your servants as well." [15]So the king returned and came to the Jordan River.

Now the people of Judah had come to [a]Gilgal to meet the king and to help him [b]cross the Jordan. [16a]Shimei son of Gera the Benjaminite from Bahurim came down quickly with the men of Judah to meet King David. [17]There were 1,000 men from [a]Benjamin with him, along with [b]Ziba the servant of Saul's household, and with him his 15 sons and 20 servants. They hurriedly crossed the Jordan within sight of the king. [18]They crossed at the ford in order to help the king's household cross and to do whatever he thought appropriate.

Now after he had crossed the Jordan, Shimei son of Gera threw himself down before the king. [19]He said to the king, "[a]Don't think badly of me, my lord, and don't recall the [b]sin of your servant on the day when you, my lord the king, left Jerusalem! Please don't [c]call it to mind! [20]For I, your servant, know that I sinned, and I have come today as [a]the first of all the house of Joseph to come down to meet my lord the king."

[21]Abishai son of Zeruiah replied, "For this should not Shimei [a]be put to death? After

18:33[a]2 Sam 12:10 [b]2 Sam 19:4 [1]Some MSS omit the second *my son*. [2]Some MSS omit the second *my son*. **19:1**[a]Jer 14:2 **19:2**[a]Esth 4:3 **19:3**[a]2 Sam 17:24, 27; 19:32 **19:4**[a]2 Sam 15:30 [b]2 Sam 18:33 **19:5**[a]2 Sam 18:14 **19:6**[1]MT *not.* [2]Luc., Syr. omit *today.* **19:8**[a]2 Sam 15:2; 18:24 [b]2 Sam 18:17 **19:9**[a]2 Sam 8:1–14 [b]2 Sam 3:18 [c]2 Sam 15:14 **19:10**[1]LXX adds *And what all Israel was saying came to the king's attention.* **19:11**[a]2 Sam 15:24 [1]Heb. adds *to his house* (= palace). **19:12**[a]2 Sam 5:1; 1 Chr 11:1 **19:13**[a]2 Sam 17:25; 1 Chr 2:17 [b]Ruth 1:17 **19:15**[a]Josh 5:9; 1 Sam 11:14–15 [b]2 Sam 17:22 **19:16**[a]2 Sam 16:5; 1 Kgs 2:8 **19:17**[a]2 Sam 3:19; 1 Kgs 12:21 [b]2 Sam 9:2, 10; 16:1–2 **19:19**[a]1 Sam 22:15 [b]2 Sam 16:5–6 [c]2 Sam 13:33 **19:20**[a]Judg 1:22; 1 Kgs 11:28 **19:21**[a][Exod 22:28]

all, he [b]cursed the LORD's anointed!" [22]But David said, "[a]What do we have in common, you sons of Zeruiah? You are like my enemy today! Should anyone be put to death in Israel today? Don't I know that today I am king over Israel?" [23]The king said to Shimei, "You won't die." [a]The king vowed an oath concerning this.

[24]Now [a]Mephibosheth, Saul's grandson, came down to meet the king. From the day the king had left until the day he safely returned, Mephibosheth had not cared for his feet nor trimmed his mustache nor washed his clothes.

[25]When he came from Jerusalem to meet the king, the king asked him, "[a]Why didn't you go with me, Mephibosheth?" [26]He replied, "My lord the king, my servant deceived me! I said, 'Let me get my donkey saddled so that I can ride on it and go with the king,' for I am lame. [27]But my servant has slandered me to my lord [a]the king. [b]But my lord the king is like an angel of God. Do whatever seems appropriate to you. [28]After all, there was no one in the entire house of my grandfather who did not deserve death from my lord the king. But instead you allowed me to eat at your own table! What further claim do I have to ask the king for anything?"

[29]Then the king replied to him, "Why should you continue speaking like this? You and Ziba will inherit the field together." [30]Mephibosheth said to the king, "Let him have the whole thing! My lord the king has returned safely to his house!"

[31]Now when [a]Barzillai the Gileadite had come down from Rogelim, he crossed the Jordan with the king so he could send him on his way from there.[1] [32]But Barzillai was very old—eighty years old, in fact—and [a]he had taken care of the king when he stayed in Mahanaim, for he was a very rich man. [33]So the king said to Barzillai, "Cross over with me, and I will take care of you while you are with me in Jerusalem."

[34]Barzillai replied to the king, "How many days do I have left to my life, that I should go up with the king to Jerusalem? [35]I am now [a]eighty years old. Am I able to discern good and bad? Can I taste what I eat and drink? Am I still able to hear the voices of male and female singers? Why should I continue to be a burden to my lord the king? [36]I will cross the Jordan with the king and go a short distance. Why should the king reward me in this way? [37]Let me return so that I may die in my own town near the grave of my father and my mother. But look, here is your servant [a]Kimham. Let him cross over with my lord the king. Do for him whatever seems appropriate to you."

[38]The king replied, "Kimham will cross over with me, and I will do for him whatever I deem appropriate. And whatever you choose, I will do for you."

[39]So all the people crossed the Jordan, as did the king. After the king had [a]kissed him and blessed him, Barzillai returned to his home. [40]When the king crossed over to Gilgal, Kimham[1] crossed over with him. Now all the soldiers of Judah along with half the soldiers of Israel had helped the king cross over.[2]

[41]Then all the men of Israel began coming to the king. They asked the king, "Why did our brothers, the men of Judah, sneak the king away and [a]help the king and his household cross the Jordan—and not only him but all of David's men as well?" [42]All the men of [a]Judah replied to the men of Israel, "Because the king is our close relative! Why are you so upset about this? Have we eaten at the king's expense? Or have we misappropriated anything for our own use?" [43]The men of Israel replied to the men of Judah, "We have [a]10 shares in [b]the king, and we have a greater claim on David than you do! Why do you want[1] to curse us? Weren't we the first to suggest bringing back our king?" But the comments of the men of Judah were more severe than those of the men of Israel.

Sheba's Rebellion

20 Now a wicked man named Sheba son of Bikri, a Benjaminite, happened to be there. He blew the trumpet and said,

"[a]We have no share in David;
we have no inheritance in this son of Jesse!
[b]Every man go home,[1] O Israel!"

19:21[b] [1 Sam 26:9]   **19:22**[a]2 Sam 3:39; 16:10   **19:23**[a]1 Kgs 2:8–9, 37, 46   **19:24**[a]2 Sam 9:6; 21:7   **19:25**[a]2 Sam 16:17   **19:27**[a]2 Sam 16:3–4   [b]2 Sam 14:17, 20   **19:31**[a]2 Sam 17:27–29; 1 Kgs 2:7   [1]MT *in the Jordan.*   **19:32**[a]2 Sam 17:27–29   **19:35**[a]Ps 90:10   **19:37**[a]2 Sam 19:40; Jer 41:17   **19:39**[a]Gen 31:55; Ruth 1:14; 2 Sam 14:33   **19:40**[1]Heb. *Kimhan.*   [2]MT *they crossed over.*   **19:41**[a]2 Sam 19:15   **19:42**[a]2 Sam 19:12   **19:43**[a]1 Kgs 11:30–31   [b]Judg 8:1; 12:1   [1]Or perhaps *Why have you cursed us?*   **20:1**[a]2 Sam 19:43; 1 Kgs 12:16   [b]1 Sam 13:2; 2 Sam 18:17; 2 Chr 10:16   [1]Some wss *to his gods.*

[2] So all the [a] men of Israel deserted David and followed Sheba son of Bikri. But the men of Judah stuck by their king all the way from the Jordan River to Jerusalem.

[3] Then David went to [a] his palace in Jerusalem. The king took the 10 concubines he had left to care for the palace and placed them under confinement. Though he provided for their needs, he did not sleep with them.[1] They remained under restriction until the day they died, living out the rest of their lives as widows.

[4] Then the king said to Amasa, "[a] Call the men of Judah together for me in three days, and you be present here with them too." [5] So Amasa went out to call Judah together. But in doing so he took longer than the time that the king had allotted him.

[6] Then David said to [a] Abishai, "Now Sheba son of Bikri will cause greater disaster for us than Absalom did! Take [b] your lord's servants and pursue him. Otherwise he will secure[1] fortified cities for himself and get away from us." [7] So Joab's men, accompanied by the [a] Kerethites, the Pelethites, and [b] all the warriors, left Jerusalem to pursue Sheba son of Bikri.

[8] When they were near the big rock that is in Gibeon, Amasa came to them. Now Joab was dressed in military attire and had a dagger in its sheath belted to his waist. When he advanced, it fell out.

[9] Joab said to Amasa, "How are you, my brother?" With his right [a] hand Joab took hold of Amasa's beard as if to greet him with a kiss. [10] Amasa did not protect himself from [a] the knife [b] in Joab's other hand, and Joab stabbed him in the abdomen, causing Amasa's intestines to spill out on the ground. There was no need to stab him again; the first blow was fatal. Then Joab and his brother Abishai pursued Sheba son of Bikri.

[11] One of Joab's soldiers who stood over Amasa said, "Whoever is for Joab and whoever is for David, follow Joab!" [12] Amasa was squirming in his own blood in the middle of the path, and this man had noticed that all the soldiers stopped. Having noticed that everyone who came across Amasa stopped,

the man pulled him away from the path and into the field and threw a garment over him. [13] Once he had removed Amasa from the path, everyone followed Joab to pursue Sheba son of Bikri.

[14] Sheba traveled through all the tribes of Israel to [a] Abel of[1] Beth Maacah and all the Berite region. When they had assembled,[2] they too joined him. [15] So Joab's men came and laid siege against him in Abel of Beth Maacah. They prepared [a] a siege ramp outside the city that stood against its outer rampart. As all of Joab's soldiers were trying to break through[1] the wall so that it would collapse, [16] a wise woman called out from the city, "Listen up! Listen up! Tell Joab, 'Come near so that I may speak to you.'"

[17] When he approached her, the woman asked, "Are you Joab?" He replied, "I am." She said to him, "Listen to the words of your servant." He said, "Go ahead. I'm listening." [18] She said, "In the past they would always say, 'Let them inquire in Abel,' and that is how they settled things. [19] I represent [a] the peaceful and the faithful in Israel. You are attempting to destroy an important city[1] in Israel. Why should you swallow up the LORD's inheritance?"

[20] Joab answered, "Not at all![1] I don't intend to swallow up or destroy anything! [21] That's not the way things are. There is a man from the hill country of Ephraim named Sheba son of Bikri. He has rebelled against King David. Give me just this one man, and I will leave the city." The woman said to Joab, "This very minute his head will be thrown over the wall to you!"

[22] Then the woman went to all the people with her wise advice and they cut off Sheba's head and threw it out to Joab. Joab blew the trumpet, and his men dispersed from the city, each [a] going to his own home. Joab returned to the king in Jerusalem.

[23] Now [a] Joab was the general in command of all the army of Israel. Benaiah the son of Jehoiada was over the Kerethites and the Perethites. [24] Adoniram[1] was supervisor of the work crews. [a] Jehoshaphat son of Ahilud was the secretary. [25] Sheva was the scribe,

20:2 [a] 2 Sam 19:14   20:3 [a] 2 Sam 15:16; 16:21–22   [1] Heb. *come to them*; a euphemism for sexual relations.   20:4 [a] 2 Sam 17:25; 19:13   20:6 [a] 2 Sam 21:17   [b] 2 Sam 11:11; 1 Kgs 1:33   [1] Heb. *find*.   20:7 [a] 2 Sam 8:18; 1 Kgs 1:38, 44   [b] 2 Sam 15:18   20:9 [a] Matt 26:49; Luke 22:47   20:10 [a] 2 Sam 3:27; 1 Kgs 2:5   [b] 2 Sam 2:23   20:14 [a] 1 Kgs 15:20; 2 Kgs 15:29; 2 Chr 16:4   [1] MT adds *and*.   [2] Ket. *and they cursed him*.   20:15 [a] 2 Kgs 19:32; Ezek 4:2   [1] LXX *were devising*.   20:19 [a] 1 Sam 26:19; 2 Sam 14:16; 21:3   [1] Heb. *a city and a mother*.   20:20 [1] Heb. *Far be it, far be it from me*.   20:22 [a] 2 Sam 20:16; [Eccl 9:13–16]   20:23 [a] 2 Sam 8:16–18; 1 Kgs 4:3–6   20:24 [a] 2 Sam 8:16; 1 Kgs 4:3   [1] Heb. *Adoram*.

and [a]Zadok and Abiathar were the priests. [26a]Ira the Jairite was David's personal priest.

The Gibeonites Demand Revenge

21 During David's reign there was a famine for three consecutive years. So David [a]inquired of the LORD. The LORD said, "It is because of Saul and his blood-stained family, because he murdered the Gibeonites."

[2]So the king summoned the Gibeonites and spoke with them. (Now the Gibeonites were not descendants [a]of Israel; they were a remnant of the Amorites. The Israelites had made a promise to them, but Saul tried to kill them because of his zeal for the people of Israel and Judah.) [3]David said to [a]the Gibeonites, "What can I do for you, and how can I make amends so that you will bless the LORD's inheritance?"

[4]The Gibeonites said to him, "We[1] have no claim to silver or gold from Saul or from his family, nor would we be justified in putting to death anyone in Israel." David asked, "What then are you asking me to do for you?" [5]They replied to the king, "As for this man who exterminated us and who schemed against us so that we were destroyed and left without status throughout all the borders of Israel—[6]let seven of his male descendants be turned over [a]to us, and we will execute them before the LORD [b]in Gibeah of Saul, [c]who was the LORD's chosen one."[1] The king replied, "I will turn them over."

[7]The king had mercy on [a]Mephibosheth son of Jonathan, [b]the son of Saul, in light of the LORD's oath that had been taken between David and Jonathan son of Saul. [8]So the king took Armoni and Mephibosheth, the two sons of Aiah's daughter [a]Rizpah whom she had born to Saul, and the five sons of Saul's daughter Merab[1] whom she had born to Adriel the son of Barzillai the Meholathite. [9]He turned them over to the Gibeonites, and they executed them on a hill [a]before the LORD. The seven of them[1] died together; they were put to death during harvest time—during the first days of the beginning[2] of the barley harvest.

[10a]Rizpah the daughter of Aiah took sackcloth and spread it out for herself on a rock. [b]From the beginning of the harvest until the rain fell on them, she did not allow the birds of the air to feed on them by day, nor the wild animals by night. [11]When David was told what Rizpah daughter of Aiah, Saul's concubine, had done, [12]he went and took the bones of Saul and of his son Jonathan from the leaders of [a]Jabesh Gilead. (They had secretly taken them from the plaza at Beth Shan. It was there that [b]Philistines publicly exposed their corpses after they had killed Saul at Gilboa.) [13]David brought the bones of Saul and of Jonathan his son from there; they also gathered up the bones of those who had been executed.

[14]They buried the bones of Saul and his son Jonathan in the land of Benjamin at [a]Zela in the grave of his father Kish. After they had done everything[1] that the king had commanded, [b]God responded to their prayers[2] for the land.

Israel Engages in Various Battles with the Philistines

[15]Another battle was fought between the Philistines and Israel. So David went down with his soldiers and fought the Philistines. David became exhausted. [16]Now Ishbi-Benob, one of the descendants of Rapha,[1] had [a]a spear that weighed 300 bronze shekels, and he was armed with a new weapon.[2] He had said that he would kill David. [17]But [a]Abishai the son of Zeruiah came to David's aid, striking the Philistine down and killing him. Then David's men took an oath saying, "[b]You will not go out to battle with us again! You must not extinguish the [c]lamp of Israel!"

[18a]Later there was another battle with the Philistines, this time in Gob. On that occasion [b]Sibbekai the Hushathite killed Saph, who was one of the descendants of Rapha. [19]Yet another battle occurred with the Philistines in Gob. On that occasion [a]Elhanan [b]the son of Jair[1] the Bethlehemite killed the brother of Goliath the Gittite, the shaft of whose spear was like a weaver's beam. [20]Yet

20:25 [a]2 Sam 8:17; 1 Kgs 4:4   **20:26** [a]2 Sam 8:18   **21:1** [a]Num 27:21; 2 Sam 5:19   **21:2** [a]Josh 9:3, 15–20   **21:3** [a]1 Sam 26:19; 2 Sam 20:19   **21:4** [1]MT *to me.*   **21:6** [a]Num 25:4   [b]1 Sam 10:26   [c]1 Sam 10:24; [Hos 13:11]   [1]LXX *at Gibeon on the mountain of the LORD.*   **21:7** [a]2 Sam 4:4; 9:10   [b]1 Sam 18:3; 20:12–17; 23:18; 2 Sam 9:1–7   **21:8** [a]2 Sam 3:7   [1]MT *Michal.*   **21:9** [a]2 Sam 6:17   [1]MT *seventy.*   [2]MT *beginning of.*   **21:10** [a]2 Sam 3:7; 21:8   [b]Deut 21:23   **21:12** [a]1 Sam 31:11–13   [b]1 Sam 31:8   **21:14** [a]Josh 18:28   [b]Josh 7:26; 2 Sam 24:25   [1]Sev. MSS *according to all.*   [2]Heb. *was entreated.*   **21:16** [a]Num 13:22, 28; Josh 15:14; 2 Sam 21:18–22   [1]Perhaps a group of people, rather than an individual with this name.   [2]Heb. *a new* [thing].   **21:17** [a]2 Sam 20:6–10   [b]2 Sam 18:3   [c]2 Sam 22:29; 1 Kgs 11:36   **21:18** [a]1 Chr 20:4–8   [b]1 Chr 11:29; 27:11   **21:19** [a]2 Sam 23:24   [b]1 Sam 17:4; 1 Chr 20:5   [1]Heb. *Jaare-Oregim.*

another battle occurred in Gath. On that occasion [a]there was a large man who had six fingers on each hand and six toes on each foot, twenty-four in all! He too was a descendant of Rapha. [21]When he [a]taunted Israel, Jonathan, the son of David's brother Shimeah, killed him. [22]These four were [a]the descendants of Rapha who lived in Gath; they were killed by David and his soldiers.

David Sings to the Lord

22 David [a]sang to the LORD the words of this song when the LORD [b]rescued him from the power of all his enemies, including Saul. [2]He [a]said:

> "[b]The LORD is my high ridge,[1] my
>   [c]stronghold, my deliverer.
> [3] My God[1] is my rocky summit where [a]I
>   take shelter,
> my [b]shield, the [c]horn that saves me,
>   my [d]stronghold,
> my [e]refuge, my savior. You save me
>   from violence!
> [4] I called to the LORD, who is worthy of
>   praise,
> and I was delivered from my
>   enemies.
> [5] The waves of death engulfed me;
>   the currents[1] of chaos[2]
>   overwhelmed me.
> [6] The [a]ropes of Sheol[1] tightened
>   around me;
> the snares of death trapped me.
> [7] In my [a]distress I called to the LORD;
>   I called to my God.
> From his heavenly temple he [b]heard
>   my voice;
> he listened to my cry for help.
> [8] The earth heaved and shook;[1]
>   [a]the foundations of [b]the sky
>   trembled.
> They heaved because he was angry.
> [9] Smoke ascended from his nose;[1]

> [a]fire devoured as it came from his
>   mouth;
> he hurled down fiery coals.
> [10] He [a]made the sky sink[1] as he
>   descended;
> a thick [b]cloud was under his feet.
> [11] He mounted a winged angel and flew;
>   he glided[1] [a]on the wings of the wind.
> [12] He shrouded himself in [a]darkness,[1]
>   in thick rain clouds.[2]
> [13] From the brightness in front of him
>   came coals of fire.
> [14] The LORD [a]thundered from the sky;
>   the Most High shouted loudly.[1]
> [15] He shot [a]arrows and scattered them,
>   lightning and routed them.
> [16] The depths of the sea [a]were exposed;
>   the inner regions of the world were
>   uncovered
> by the [b]LORD's battle cry,[1]
> by the powerful breath from his
>   nose.[2]
> [17] He [a]reached down from above and
>   grabbed me;[1]
> he pulled me from the surging
>   water.[2]
> [18] He rescued me from my strong
>   enemy,
> from those who hate me,
> for they were too strong for me.
> [19] They confronted me in my day of
>   calamity,
> but the LORD [a]helped me.
> [20] He brought me out into a wide open
>   place;
> [a]he delivered me because he was
>   [b]pleased with me.
> [21] The LORD repaid me for my godly
>   deeds;[1]
> [a]he rewarded my [b]blameless
>   behavior.
> [22] For I have [a]obeyed the LORD's
>   commands;[1]
> I have not rebelled against my God.

21:20 [a]1 Chr 20:6   21:21 [a]1 Sam 17:10   21:22 [a]1 Chr 20:8   22:1 [a]Exod 15:1; Deut 31:30; Judg 5:1   [b]Ps 18:title; 34:19   22:2 [a]Ps 18   [b]Deut 32:4; 1 Sam 2:2   [c]Ps 91:2   [1]Trad. *is my rock*; pictures God as a rocky, relatively inaccessible summit where one can seek refuge from enemies.   22:3 [a]Ps 7:1; Heb 2:13   [b]Gen 15:1; Deut 33:29; Ps 84:11   [c]Luke 1:69   [d]Prov 18:10   [e]Ps 9:9; 46:1, 7, 11; Jer 16:19   [1]MT *the God of*.   22:5 [1]Heb. *a river, stream*.   [2]An epithet for death.   22:6 [a]Ps 116:3   [1]Personified as David's enemy; the underworld, place of the dead in primitive Hebrew cosmology.   22:7 [a]Ps 116:4; 120:1   [b]Exod 3:7; Ps 34:6, 15   22:8 [a]Judg 5:4; Ps 77:18; 97:4   [b]Job 26:11   [1]Pictures an earthquake, in which the earth's surface rises and falls.   22:9 [a]Deut 32:22; Ps 97:3–4; Heb 12:29   [1]Or *in his anger*.   22:10 [a]Exod 19:16–20; Isa 64:1   [b]Exod 20:21   [1]Heb. [to cause to] *bend*; [to cause to] *bow down*.   22:11 [a]Ps 104:3   [1]MT *and he appeared*.   22:12 [a]Job 36:29; Ps 97:2   [1]Heb. *he made darkness around him coverings*.   [2]Heb. *a sieve of water, clouds of clouds*.   22:14 [a]1 Sam 2:10; Job 37:2–5; Ps 29:3   [1]Heb. *offered his voice*.   22:15 [a]Deut 32:23; Josh 10:10; 1 Sam 7:10; Ps 7:13   22:16 [a]Nah 1:4   [b]Exod 15:8   [1]Heb. *rebuke*.   [2]Heb. *blast of the breath*; lit. *breath of breath*.   22:17 [a]Ps 144:7; Isa 43:2   [1]Heb. *stretched*.   [2]Heb. *mighty waters*.   22:19 [a]Isa 10:20   22:20 [a]Ps 31:8; 118:5   [b]2 Sam 15:26   22:21 [a]1 Sam 26:23; [Ps 7:8]   [b][Job 17:9]; Ps 24:4   [1]Heb. *according to my righteousness*.   22:22 [a]Gen 18:19; 2 Chr 34:33; Ps 119:3   [1]Heb. *have kept the ways of the LORD*.

23 For I am aware of all his ᵃregulations,¹
and I do not reject his rules.²
24 I was ᵃblameless before him;
I kept myself from sinning.¹
25 The LORD rewarded me for my godly
deeds;
ᵃhe took notice of my blameless
behavior.
26 You prove to be loyal to one who is
faithful;¹
you prove to be trustworthy to one
who is innocent.²
27 You prove to be reliable to one who is
blameless,
but you prove to be deceptive¹ to one
who is perverse.
28 You deliver ᵃoppressed people,
but you watch ᵇthe proud and bring
them down.¹
29 Indeed, you are my ᵃlamp,¹ LORD.
The LORD illumines the darkness
around me.
30 Indeed, with your help I can charge¹
against an army;²
by my God's power I can jump over a
ᵃwall.³
31 The one true God acts in a faithful
manner;¹
the LORD's promise ᵃis reliable;²
ᵇhe is a shield to all who take shelter
in him.
32 Indeed, ᵃwho is God besides the
LORD?
Who is a protector besides our God?
33 The one true God is my mighty
ᵃrefuge;¹
he ᵇremoves the ᶜobstacles in my
way.²
34 He ᵃgives me the agility of a deer;¹
he ᵇenables me to negotiate the
rugged terrain.²

35 He trains my hands for battle;
my arms can bend even the strongest
bow.¹
36 You give me¹ your protective shield;²
your willingness to help enables me
to prevail.
37 You ᵃwiden my path;
my feet do not slip.
38 I chase my enemies and destroy
them;
I do not turn back until I wipe them
out.
39 I wipe them out and beat them to
death;
they cannot get up;
they fall at my feet.
40 You ᵃgive me strength for battle;
you make my foes kneel before me.
41 You make my enemies ᵃretreat;¹
I destroy those who hate me.
42 They cry out,¹ but there is no one ᵃto
help them;
they cry out to the LORD, but he does
not answer them.
43 I grind them ᵃas fine as the dust of
the ground;
ᵇI crush them and stomp them like
clay in the streets.
44 You rescue me from a hostile army;¹
ᵃyou preserve me as a ᵇleader of
ᶜnations;
people over whom I had no authority
are now my subjects.²
45 Foreigners are powerless before me;¹
when they hear of my exploits, they
submit to me.
46 Foreigners lose their courage;
they shake with fear¹ as they leave
their strongholds.
47 The LORD is alive!
My ᵃProtector is praiseworthy!

22:23 ᵃ[Deut 6:6–9; 7:12]; Ps 119:30, 102 ¹Heb. *for all his regulations are before me.* ²Heb. *and his rules, I do not turn
aside from it.* 22:24 ᵃGen 6:9; 7:1; Job 1:1; [Eph 1:4; Col 1:21–22] ¹Heb. *from my sin.* 22:25 ᵃ2 Sam 22:21 22:26 ¹Or
to a faithful follower. ²Heb. *a warrior of innocence.* 22:27 ¹MT *to be tasteless, behave silly.* 22:28 ᵃPs 72:12 ᵇJob
40:11 ¹Heb. *but your eyes are upon the proud, you bring low.* 22:29 ᵃPs 119:105; 132:17 ¹Sev. wss add *you cause to
shine.* 22:30 ᵃ2 Sam 5:6–8 ¹Heb. *I will run.* ²More specifically, a raiding party or a contingent of troops. ³David uses
hyperbole to emphasize his God-given military superiority. 22:31 ᵃ[Deut 32:4]; Dan 4:37; [Matt 5:48] ᵇPs 12:6; [Prov
30:5] ¹Heb. [As for] *the God, his way is blameless.* ²Heb. *the word of the LORD is purified.* 22:32 ᵃIsa 45:5–6 22:33 ᵃPs
27:1 ᵇ[Heb 13:21] ᶜPs 101:2, 6 ¹One DSS MS *the one girding me with strength.* ²Heb. *and he sets free* [the] *blameless,
his way.* 22:34 ᵃ2 Sam 2:18; Hab 3:19 ᵇIsa 33:16 ¹Heb. [the one who] *makes his feet like* [those of] *a deer.* ²Heb. *and
on my high places he makes me walk.* 22:35 ¹Heb. *and a bow of bronze is bent by my arms*; a bow probably laminated
with bronze strips, or a purely ceremonial or decorative bow made entirely from bronze. In the latter case, the language
is hyperbolic, for such a weapon would not be functional in battle. 22:36 ¹Or *you gave me.* ²Heb. *and you give me the
shield of your deliverance.* 22:37 ᵃ2 Sam 22:20; Prov 4:12 22:40 ᵃ[Ps 18:32] 22:41 ᵃGen 49:8; Josh 10:24 ¹Heb. *and*
[as for] *my enemies, you give to me* [the] *back* [or *neck*]. 22:42 ᵃ1 Sam 28:6; Prov 1:28; Isa 1:15 ¹MT *they look about for
help.* 22:43 ᵃ2 Kgs 13:7; Ps 18:42 ᵇIsa 10:6 22:44 ᵃ2 Sam 3:1 ᵇDeut 28:13 ᶜ[Isa 55:5] ¹Heb. *from the strivings of my
people.* ²Heb. *a people whom I did not know serve me.* 22:45 ¹Or *cower in fear.* 22:46 ¹MT *and they
girded themselves.* 22:47 ᵃ[2 Sam 23:3]; Ps 89:26

The God who delivers me[1] is exalted
as king!
48 The one true God completely
vindicates me;[1]
he makes nations [a]submit to me.
49 He delivers me from my enemies;
you snatch me away from those who
attack me;
you rescue me from [a]violent men.
50 So I will give you thanks, O LORD,
before [a]the nations!
I will sing praises to [b]you.[1]
51 He gives his king magnificent
victories;[1]
[a]he is faithful to his chosen [b]ruler,
to David and to [c]his descendants
forever!"

David's Final Words

23 These are [a]the final words of David:

"[b]The oracle of David son of Jesse,
the oracle of the man raised up as
the ruler chosen by the God of Jacob,
Israel's beloved singer of songs:
2 The LORD's Spirit spoke through me;
his word was on my tongue.
3 The God of Israel spoke,
[a]the Protector of Israel spoke to me.
The one who rules fairly among men,
the one who rules [b]in the fear of God,
4 is like [a]the light of morning when the
sun comes up,
a morning in which there are no
clouds.
He is like the brightness after rain
that produces grass from the earth.
5 My dynasty is approved by God,
for he has made a perpetual
covenant with me,
arranged in all its particulars and
secured.
He always delivers me,
and brings all I desire to fruition.
6 But evil people are like thorns—
all of them are tossed away,
for they cannot be held in the hand.
7 The one who touches them
must use an iron instrument

or the wooden shaft of a spear.
They are completely burned up right
where they lie!"

David's Warriors

8 These are the names of David's warriors:
Josheb Basshebeth, a Tahkemonite, was
head of the officers.[1] He killed 800 men with
his spear in one battle.[2] 9 Next in command
was [a]Eleazar son of Dodo, the son of Ahohi.
He was one of the three warriors who were
with David when they defied the Philistines
who were assembled there for battle. When
the men of Israel retreated, 10 he stood his
ground and fought the Philistines until his
hand [a]grew so tired that it seemed stuck to
his sword. The LORD gave a great victory on
that day. When the army returned to him,
the only thing left to do was to plunder the
[b]corpses.

11 Next in command was [a]Shammah son
of Agee [b]the Hararite. When the Philistines
assembled at Lehi, where there happened
to be an area of a field that was full of lentils,
the army retreated before the Philistines.
12 But he made a stand in the middle of that
area. He defended it and defeated the Philistines; the LORD gave them a great victory.

13 At the time of the harvest [a]three[1] of [b]the
thirty leaders went down to David at [c]the
cave of Adullam. A band of Philistines was
camped in the valley of Rephaim. 14 David
was in [a]the stronghold at the time, while
a Philistine garrison was in Bethlehem.
15 David was thirsty and said, "How I wish
someone would give me some water to
drink from the cistern in Bethlehem near
the gate!" 16 So the three elite warriors broke
through the Philistine forces and drew
some water from the cistern in Bethlehem
near the gate. They carried it back to David,
but he refused to drink it. He poured it out
as a drink offering to the LORD 17 and said,
"O LORD, I will not do this! It is equivalent to
[a]the blood of the men who risked their lives
by going." So he refused to drink it. Such
were the exploits of the three elite warriors.
18 [a]Abishai son of Zeruiah, the brother
of Joab, was head of the three.[1] He killed

22:47 [1]Heb. *the God of the rock of my deliverance.*   **22:48** [a]1 Sam 24:12; Ps 144:2   [1]Heb. *The God is the one who grants vengeance to me.*   **22:49** [a]Ps 140:1, 4, 11   **22:50** [a]2 Sam 8:1–14   [b]Ps 57:7; Rom 15:9   [1]Heb. *to your name.*   **22:51** [a]Ps 144:10   [b]Ps 89:20   [c]2 Sam 7:12–16; Ps 89:29   [1]MT *tower.*   **23:1** [a]2 Sam 7:8–9; Ps 78:70–71   [b]1 Sam 16:12–13; Ps 89:20   **23:3** [a][Deut 32:4]   [b]Exod 18:21; [Isa 11:1–5]   **23:4** [a]Ps 89:36; Isa 60:1   **23:8** [1]Or perhaps *the three.*   [2]MT *Adino the Ezenite.*   **23:9** [a]1 Chr 11:12; 27:4   **23:10** [a]Judg 8:4   [b]1 Sam 30:24–25   **23:11** [a]1 Chr 11:27   [b]1 Chr 11:13–14   **23:13** [a]1 Chr 11:15   [b]1 Sam 22:1   [c]2 Sam 5:18   [1]Ket. *thirty.*   **23:14** [a]1 Sam 22:4–5   **23:17** [a][Lev 17:10]   **23:18** [a]2 Sam 21:17; 1 Chr 11:20   [1]Ket. *the third, adjutant;* a few wss *thirty.*

300 men with his spear and gained fame among the three. [19]From the three he was given honor and he became their officer, even though he was not one of the three.

[20]Benaiah son of Jehoiada was a brave warrior[1] from [a]Kabzeel who performed great exploits. [b]He struck down the two sons of Ariel of Moab.[2] He also went down and killed a lion in a cistern on a snowy day. [21]He also killed an impressive-looking Egyptian.[1] The Egyptian wielded a spear, while Benaiah attacked him with a club. He grabbed the spear out of the Egyptian's hand and killed him with his own spear. [22]Such were the exploits of Benaiah son of Jehoiada, who gained fame among the three elite warriors. [23]He received honor from the 30 warriors, though he was not one of the three elite warriors. David put him in charge of his bodyguard.

[24]Included with the 30 were the following: [a]Asahel the brother of Joab, Elhanan son of Dodo from Bethlehem, [25][a]Shammah the Harodite, Elika the Harodite, [26]Helez the Paltite, Ira son of Ikkesh from Tekoa, [27]Abiezer the Anathothite, Mebunnai the Hushathite, [28]Zalmon the Ahohite, Maharai the Netophathite, [29]Heled son of Baanah the Netophathite, Ittai son of Ribai from Gibeah in Benjamin, [30]Benaiah the Pirathonite, Hiddai from the wadis of [a]Gaash, [31]Abi-Albon the Arbathite, Azmaveth the Barhumite, [32]Eliahba the Shaalbonite, the sons of Jashen, Jonathan [33]son of [a]Shammah the Hararite, Ahiam son of Sharar the Hararite, [34]Eliphelet son of Ahasbai the Maacathite, Eliam son of [a]Ahithophel the Gilonite, [35]Hezrai the Carmelite, Paarai the Arbite, [36]Igal son of Nathan from [a]Zobah, Bani the Gadite, [37]Zelek the Ammonite, Naharai the Beerothite (the armor-bearer[1] of Joab son of Zeruiah), [38][a]Ira the Ithrite, Gareb the Ithrite, [39]and [a]Uriah the Hittite. Altogether there were 37.

David Displeases the Lord by Taking a Census

24 The LORD's anger again raged against Israel, and [a]he incited David against them, saying, "[b]Go count Israel and Judah." [2]The king told Joab, the general in command of his army, "Go through all the tribes of Israel [a]from Dan to Beer Sheba and muster the army, so [b]I may know the size of the army."

[3]Joab replied to the king, "May the LORD your God [a]make the army a hundred times larger right before the eyes of my lord the king! But why does my master the king want to do this?"

[4]But the king's edict stood, despite the objections of Joab and the leaders of the army. So Joab and the leaders of the army left the king's presence in order to muster the Israelite army.

[5]They crossed the Jordan and camped at [a]Aroer, on the south side of the city, at the wadi of Gad, near [b]Jazer. [6]Then they went on to Gilead and to the region of Tahtim Hodshi, coming to Dan [a]Jaan and on around to [b]Sidon. [7]Then they went to the fortress of [a]Tyre and all the cities of the [b]Hivites and the Canaanites. Then they went on to the Negev of Judah, to Beer Sheba. [8]They went through all the land and after nine months and twenty days came back to Jerusalem.

[9]Joab reported the number of warriors to the king. In Israel there were 800,000 sword-wielding warriors, [a]and in Judah there were 500,000 soldiers.

[10][a]David felt guilty after he had numbered the army. David said to the LORD, "I have [b]sinned greatly by doing this! Now, [c]O LORD, please remove the guilt of your servant, for I have acted very foolishly."

[11]When David got up the next morning, the LORD's message had already come to the prophet [a]Gad, David's [b]seer: [12]"Go, tell David, 'This is what the LORD has said: I am offering you three forms of judgment. Pick one of them and I will carry it out against you.'"

[13]Gad went to David and told him, "Shall [a]seven[1] years of famine come upon your land? Or shall you flee for three months from your enemies with them in hot pursuit? Or shall there be three days of plague in your land? Now decide what I should tell the one who sent me." [14]David said to Gad, "I am very upset! I prefer that we be attacked

23:20 [a]Josh 15:21   [b]Exod 15:15   [1]MT *life.*   [2]Heb. *the two of Ariel, Moab.*   **23:21** [1]MT *who.*   **23:24** [a]2 Sam 2:18; 1 Chr 27:7   **23:25** [a]1 Chr 11:27   **23:30** [a]Judg 2:9   **23:33** [a]2 Sam 23:11   **23:34** [a]2 Sam 15:12   **23:36** [a]2 Sam 8:3   **23:37** [1]Ket. *armor-bearers.*   **23:38** [a]1 Chr 2:53   **23:39** [a]2 Sam 11:3, 6   **24:1** [a]2 Sam 21:1–2   [b]Num 26:2; 1 Chr 27:23–24   **24:2** [a]Judg 20:1; 2 Sam 3:10   [b][Jer 17:5]   **24:3** [a]Deut 1:11   **24:5** [a]Deut 2:36; Josh 13:9, 16   [b]Num 32:1, 3   **24:6** [a]Josh 19:47; Judg 18:29   [b]Josh 19:28; Judg 18:28   **24:7** [a]Josh 19:29   [b]Josh 11:3; Judg 3:3   **24:9** [a]1 Chr 21:5   **24:10** [a]2 Sam 23:1   [b]2 Sam 12:13   [c]1 Sam 13:13; [2 Chr 16:9]   **24:11** [a]1 Sam 22:5   [b]1 Sam 9:9; 1 Chr 29:29   **24:13** [a]Ezek 14:21   [1]LXX *three.*

by the LORD, [a]for his mercy is great; I [b]do not want to be attacked by human hands!"

[15]So [a]the LORD sent a plague through Israel from the morning until the completion of the appointed time, and 70,000 people died from Dan to Beer Sheba. [16]When the angel extended his [a]hand to destroy Jerusalem, [b]the LORD relented from his judgment. He told the angel who was killing the people, "That's enough! Stop now!" (Now the angel of the LORD was near the threshing floor of Araunah the Jebusite.)

[17]When he saw the angel who was [a]destroying the people, David said to the LORD, "Look, it is I who have sinned and done this evil thing! As for these sheep—what have they done? Attack me and my family."

David Acquires a Threshing Floor and Constructs an Altar There

[18]So Gad went to David that day and told him, "[a]Go up and build an altar for the LORD on the threshing floor of Araunah the Jebusite." [19]So David went up as Gad instructed him to do, according to the LORD's instructions.

[20]When Araunah looked out and saw the king and his servants approaching him, he went out and bowed to the king with his face to the ground. [21]Araunah said, "Why has my lord the king come to his servant?" David replied, "To buy from you the threshing floor so I can build [a]an altar for [b]the LORD, so that the plague may be removed from the people." [22]Araunah told David, "My lord the king may take whatever he wishes and offer it. [a]Look! Here are oxen for burnt offerings, and threshing sledges and harnesses for wood. [23]I, the servant of my lord the king, give it all to the king!" Araunah also told the king, "May the LORD your God [a]show you favor!" [24]But the king said to Araunah, "No, I insist on buying it from you! I will not offer to the LORD my God burnt sacrifices that cost me nothing."

So [a]David bought the threshing floor and the oxen for 50 pieces of silver. [25]Then David built an altar for [a]the LORD there and offered burnt sacrifices and peace offerings. And the LORD accepted prayers for the land, and the plague was removed from Israel.

24:14 [a] [Ps 51:1; 103:8, 13, 14; 119:156; 130:4, 7] [b] [Isa 47:6; Zech 1:15] **24:15** [a] 1 Chr 21:14 **24:16** [a] Exod 12:23; 2 Kgs 19:35; Acts 12:23 [b] Gen 6:6; 1 Sam 15:11 **24:17** [a] 2 Sam 7:8; 1 Chr 21:17; Ps 74:1 **24:18** [a] 1 Chr 21:18 **24:21** [a] Gen 23:8–16 [b] Num 16:48, 50 **24:22** [a] 1 Sam 6:14; 1 Kgs 19:21 **24:23** [a] [Ezek 20:40–41] **24:24** [a] 1 Chr 21:24–25 **24:25** [a] 2 Sam 24:21

1 KINGS

The first half of 1 Kings traces the life of Solomon. Under his leadership Israel rises to the peak of her size and glory. Solomon's great accomplishments, including the unsurpassed splendor of the temple that he constructs in Jerusalem, bring him worldwide fame and respect. But Solomon's zeal for God diminishes in his later years as pagan wives turn his heart away from worship in the temple of God. As a result, the king with the divided heart leaves behind a divided kingdom. For the next century, the Book of 1 Kings traces the twin histories of two sets of kings and two nations of disobedient people who are growing indifferent to God's prophets and precepts. Like the two Books of Samuel, the two Books of Kings were originally one in the Hebrew Bible. The original title was *Melechim*, "Kings," taken from the first word in 1:1, *Vehamelech*, "Now King." The Septuagint artificially divided the Book of Kings in the middle of the story of Ahaziah. It called the Books of Samuel "First and Second Kingdoms" and the Books of Kings "Third and Fourth Kingdoms." The Septuagint may have divided Samuel, Kings, and Chronicles into two books each because the Greek required a greater amount of scroll space than did the Hebrew. The Latin title for these books is *Liber Regum Tertius et Quartus*, "Third and Fourth Books of Kings."

Adonijah Tries to Seize the Throne

1 King David was very [a]old; even when they covered him with blankets, he could not get warm. [2]His servants advised him, "A young virgin must be found for our master, the king,[1] to take care of the king's needs and serve as his nurse. She can also sleep with you[2] and keep our master, the king, warm." [3]So they looked through all Israel for a beautiful young woman and found [a]Abishag, a [b]Shunammite, and brought her to the king. [4]The young woman was very beautiful; she became the king's nurse and served him, but the king was not intimate with her.[1]

[5]Now [a]Adonijah, son of David and Haggith, was promoting himself, boasting, "I will be king!" [b]He managed to acquire chariots and horsemen, as well as 50 men to serve as his royal guard. [6](Now [a]his father had never corrected him[1] by saying, "Why do you do such things?" He was also very handsome and had been born right after Absalom.) [7]He collaborated with [a]Joab son of Zeruiah and with [b]Abiathar [c]the priest, and they supported him. [8]But [a]Zadok the priest, [b]Benaiah son of Jehoiada, [c]Nathan the prophet, [d]Shimei, Rei, and David's elite warriors did not ally [e]themselves with Adonijah. [9]Adonijah sacrificed sheep, cattle, and fattened steers at the Stone of Zoheleth near En [a]Rogel. He invited all his brothers, the king's sons,[1] as well as all the men of Judah, the king's servants. [10]But he did not invite Nathan the prophet, Benaiah, the elite warriors, or his brother [a]Solomon.

[11]Nathan said to Bathsheba, Solomon's mother, "Has it been reported to you that [a]Haggith's son Adonijah has become king behind our master David's back? [12]Now[1] let me give you some advice as to how you can save your life and your son Solomon's life. [13]Visit[1] King David and say to him, 'My master, O king, did you not solemnly

1:1 [a]1 Chr 23:1   1:2 [1]Heb. *let them seek for my master, the king, a young girl, a virgin.*   [2]Heb. *and she will lie down in your bosom*; might imply sexual intimacy, although v. 4b indicates David did not have sex with the young woman.   1:3 [a]1 Kgs 2:17   [b]Josh 19:18; 1 Sam 28:4   1:4 [1]Heb. *did not know her*; a euphemism for sexual relations.   1:5 [a]2 Sam 3:4   [b]2 Sam 15:1   1:6 [a]2 Sam 3:3–4; 1 Chr 3:2   [1]Heb. *did not correct him from his days.*   1:7 [a]1 Chr 11:6   [b]2 Sam 20:25   [c]1 Kgs 2:22, 28   1:8 [a]1 Kgs 2:35   [b]1 Kgs 2:25; 2 Sam 8:18   [c]2 Sam 12:1   [d]1 Kgs 4:18   [e]2 Sam 23:8   1:9 [a]Josh 15:7; 18:16; 2 Sam 17:17   [1]Some wss omit *the king's sons.*   1:10 [a]2 Sam 12:24   1:11 [a]2 Sam 3:4   1:12 [1]Heb. *now, come.*   1:13 [1]Heb. *come, go to.*

promise[2] your servant, "[a]Surely your son Solomon will be king after me; he will sit on my throne"? So why has Adonijah become king?' [14]While you are still there speaking to the king, I will arrive[1] and verify your report."

[15]So Bathsheba visited the king in his private quarters. (The king was very old, and Abishag the Shunammite was serving the king.) [16]Bathsheba bowed down on the floor before the king. The king said, "What do you want?" [17]She replied to him, "My master, [a]you swore an oath to your servant by the LORD your God, 'Solomon your son will be king after me and he will sit on my throne.' [18]But now, look, Adonijah has become king! But you, my master the king, are not even aware of it! [19]He has sacrificed many cattle, steers, and [a]sheep and has invited all the king's sons, Abiathar the priest, and Joab, the commander of the army, but he has not invited your servant Solomon. [20]Now, my master, O king, all Israel is watching anxiously to see who is named to succeed my master the king on the throne. [21]If a decision is not made, when my master the king is [a]buried with his ancestors, my son Solomon and I will be considered state criminals."

[22]Just then,[1] while she was still speaking to the king, Nathan the prophet arrived. [23]The king was told, "Nathan the prophet is here." Nathan entered and bowed before the king with his face to the floor. [24]Nathan said, "My master, O king, did you announce, 'Adonijah will be king after me; he will sit on my throne'? [25a]For today he has gone down and sacrificed many cattle, steers, and sheep and has invited all the king's sons, the army commanders, and Abiathar the priest. At this moment they are having a feast in his presence, and they have declared, '[b]Long live King Adonijah!' [26]But he did not invite me—your servant—or Zadok the priest, or Benaiah son of Jehoiada, or your servant Solomon. [27]Has my master the king authorized this without informing your servants[1] who should succeed my master the king on his throne?"

David Picks Solomon as His Successor

[28]King David responded, "Summon Bathsheba!" She came and stood before the king. [29]The king swore an oath: "[a]As certainly as the LORD lives (he who has rescued me from every danger), [30a]I will keep today the oath I swore to you by the LORD God of Israel: 'Surely Solomon your son will be king after me; he will sit in my place on my throne.'" [31]Bathsheba bowed down to the king with her face to the floor and said, "May my master, King David, live forever!"

[32]King David said, "Summon Zadok the priest, Nathan the prophet, and Benaiah son of Jehoiada." They came before the king, [33]and he told them, "[a]Take your master's servants with you, put my son Solomon on my [b]mule, and lead him down to [c]Gihon. [34]There Zadok the priest and Nathan the prophet will [a]anoint him king over Israel; then [b]blow the trumpet and declare, 'Long live King Solomon!' [35]Then follow him up as he comes and sits on my throne. He will be king in my place; I have decreed that he will be ruler over Israel and Judah." [36]Benaiah son of Jehoiada responded to the king: "So be [a]it! May the LORD God of my master the king confirm it! [37]As the LORD is with my [a]master the king, so may he be with Solomon, and may he [b]make him an even greater king than my master King David!"

[38]So Zadok the priest, Nathan the prophet, [a]Benaiah son of Jehoiada, the Kerethites, and the Pelethites went down, put Solomon on King David's mule, and led him to Gihon. [39]Zadok the priest took a horn filled with olive [a]oil[1] from the tent and [b]poured it on Solomon; the trumpet was blown [c]and all the people declared, "Long live King Solomon!" [40]All the people followed him up, playing flutes and celebrating so loudly they made the ground shake.[1]

[41]Now Adonijah and all his guests heard the commotion just as they had finished eating. When Joab heard the sound of the trumpet, he asked, "Why is there such a noisy commotion in the city?" [42]As he was still speaking, [a]Jonathan son of Abiathar

1:13 [a] 1 Kgs 1:30; 1 Chr 22:9–13   [2] Or *swear an oath to*.   1:14 [1] Heb. *I will come after you.*   1:17 [a] 1 Kgs 1:13, 30
1:19 [a] 1 Kgs 1:7–9, 25   1:21 [a] Deut 31:16; 2 Sam 7:12; 1 Kgs 2:10   1:22 [1] Heb. *look.*   1:25 [a] 1 Kgs 1:9, 19   [b] 1 Sam 10:24
1:27 [1] Sev. wss *servant.*   1:29 [a] 2 Sam 4:9; 12:5   1:30 [a] 1 Kgs 1:13, 17   1:33 [a] 2 Sam 20:6   [b] Esth 6:8   [c] 2 Chr 32:30;
33:14   1:34 [a] 1 Sam 10:1; 16:3, 12; 2 Sam 2:4; 5:3; 1 Kgs 19:16; 2 Kgs 9:3; 11:12; 1 Chr 29:22   [b] 2 Sam 15:10; 2 Kgs 9:13;
11:14   1:36 [a] Jer 28:6   1:37 [a] Josh 1:5, 17; 1 Sam 20:13   [b] 1 Kgs 1:47   1:38 [a] 2 Sam 8:18; 23:20–23   1:39 [a] Exod
30:23, 25, 32; Ps 89:20   [b] 1 Chr 29:22   [c] 1 Sam 10:24   [1] Heb. *the horn of oil.*   1:40 [1] Heb. *and all the people
went up after him, and the people were playing flutes and rejoicing with great joy and the ground split
open at the sound of them*; an exaggeration for the sake of emphasis.   1:42 [a] 2 Sam 17:17, 20

the priest arrived. Adonijah said, "Come in, for an important man like [b]you must be bringing good news."[1] [43]Jonathan replied to Adonijah: "No! Our master King David has made Solomon king. [44]The king sent with him Zadok the priest, Nathan the prophet, Benaiah son of Jehoiada, the Kerethites, and the Pelethites and they put him on the king's mule. [45]Then Zadok the priest and Nathan the prophet anointed him king in Gihon. They went up from there rejoicing, and the city is in an uproar. That is the sound you hear. [46]Furthermore, Solomon has [a]assumed the royal throne. [47]The king's servants have even come to congratulate our master King David, saying, '[a]May your God[1] make Solomon more famous than you and make him an even greater king than you!'[2] [b]Then the king leaned[3] on the bed [48]and said[1] this: 'The LORD God of Israel is worthy of praise because[2] today he has [a]placed a successor on my throne and allowed me to see [b]it.'"

[49]All of Adonijah's guests panicked; they jumped up and rushed off their separate ways. [50]Adonijah feared Solomon, so he got up and went and grabbed hold of the horns of the altar. [51]Solomon was told, "Look, Adonijah fears you; see, he has taken hold of the horns of the altar, saying, 'May King Solomon solemnly promise[1] me today that he will not kill his servant with the sword.'" [52]Solomon said, "If he is a loyal subject,[1] [a]not a hair of his head will be harmed, but if he is found to be a traitor, he will die." [53]King Solomon sent men to bring him down from the altar. He came and bowed down to King Solomon, and Solomon told him, "Go home."

David's Final Words to Solomon

2 When David was close to death, [a]he told Solomon his son: [2]"I am about to [a]die. [b]Be strong and become a man! [3]Do the job the LORD your God has assigned you by following his instructions and obeying his rules, commandments, regulations, and laws as written in the law of Moses. Then you will [a]succeed in all you do and seek to accomplish, [4]and the LORD will [a]fulfill his promise to me, '[b]If your descendants watch their step and [c]live faithfully in my presence with all their heart and being, then,' he promised, '[d]you will not fail to have a successor on the throne of Israel.'

[5]"You know what Joab son of Zeruiah [a]did to me—how he murdered two commanders of the Israelite armies, [b]Abner son of Ner and [c]Amasa son of Jether. During peacetime he struck them down as if in battle; when he shed their blood, he stained the belt on his waist and the sandals on his feet. [6]Do to him what you think is appropriate, but don't let him live long and die [a]a peaceful death.

[7]"Treat fairly the sons of [a]Barzillai of Gilead and provide for their [b]needs, because [c]they helped me when I had to flee from your brother Absalom.

[8]"Note well, you still have to contend with [a]Shimei son of Gera, [b]the [c]Benjaminite from Bahurim, who tried to call down upon me a horrible judgment when I went to Mahanaim. He came down and met me at the Jordan, and I solemnly promised him by the LORD, 'I will not strike you down with the sword.' [9]But now[1] [a]don't treat him as if he were innocent. You are a wise man and you know how to handle him; make sure he has a bloody death."

[10]Then [a]David passed away and was buried in [b]the City of David. [11]David [a]reigned over Israel forty years; he reigned in Hebron seven years, and in Jerusalem thirty-three years.

Solomon Secures the Throne

[12][a]Solomon sat on his father David's throne, and his royal [b]authority was firmly solidified.

[13]Haggith's son [a]Adonijah visited Bathsheba, Solomon's mother. She asked, "Do you come in peace?" He answered, "Yes." [14]He added, "I have something to say to you." She replied, "Speak." [15]He said, "You know

1:42 [b]2 Sam 18:27 [1]Heb. *you are a man of strength* [or *ability*] *and you bring a message* [that is] *good.*   **1:46** [a]1 Kgs 2:12; 1 Chr 29:23   **1:47** [a]1 Kgs 1:37 [b]Gen 47:31 [1]Sev. MSS omit *your.* [2]Heb. *make the name of Solomon better than your name, and make his throne greater than your throne.* [3]Or *bowed down; worshiped.*   **1:48** [a]1 Kgs 3:6; [Ps 132:11–12] [b]2 Sam 7:12 [1]Heb. *and the king said.* [2]Or *Blessed be the LORD God of Israel, who.*   **1:51** [1]Or *swear an oath to.*   **1:52** [a]1 Sam 14:45; 2 Sam 14:11; Acts 27:34 [1]Heb. *if he is a man of strength* [or *ability*].   **2:1** [a]Gen 47:29; Deut 31:14   **2:2** [a]Josh 23:14 [b]Deut 31:7, 23; 1 Chr 22:13   **2:3** [a][Deut 29:9; Josh 1:7]; 1 Chr 22:12–13   **2:4** [a]2 Sam 7:25 [b][Ps 132:12] [c]2 Kgs 20:3 [d]2 Sam 7:12–13; 1 Kgs 8:25   **2:5** [a]2 Sam 3:39; 18:5, 12, 14 [b]2 Sam 3:27; 1 Kgs 2:32 [c]2 Sam 20:10   **2:6** [a]1 Kgs 2:9; Prov 20:26   **2:7** [a]2 Sam 19:31–39 [b]2 Sam 9:7, 10; 19:28 [c]2 Sam 17:17–29   **2:8** [a]2 Sam 16:5–13 [b]2 Sam 19:18 [c]2 Sam 19:23   **2:9** [a]Exod 20:7; Job 9:28 [1]Luc., Vg. *you.*   **2:10** [a]1 Kgs 1:21; Acts 2:29; 13:36 [b]2 Sam 5:7; 1 Kgs 3:1   **2:11** [a]2 Sam 5:4–5; 1 Chr 3:4; 29:26–27   **2:12** [a]1 Kgs 1:46; 1 Chr 29:23 [b]1 Kgs 2:46; 2 Chr 1:1   **2:13** [a]1 Sam 16:4–5

that the kingdom was [a]mine and all Israel considered me king. But then the kingdom was given to my brother, for the LORD decided [b]it should be his. [16] Now I'd like to ask you for just one thing. Please don't refuse me." She said, "Go ahead and ask." [17] He said, "Please ask King Solomon if he would give me [a]Abishag the Shunammite as a wife, for he won't refuse you." [18] Bathsheba replied, "That's fine; I'll speak to the king on your behalf."

[19] So Bathsheba visited King Solomon to speak to him on Adonijah's behalf. The king got up to greet her, [a]bowed to her, and then sat on his throne. He ordered a throne to be brought for the king's mother, and she sat at his right hand. [20] She said, "I would like to ask you for just one small favor. Please don't refuse me." He said, "Go ahead and ask, my mother, for I would not refuse you." [21] She said, "Allow Abishag the Shunammite to be given to your brother Adonijah as a wife." [22] King Solomon answered his mother, "Why just request Abishag the Shunammite for him? Since he is my [a]older brother, you should also request the kingdom for him, for [b]Abiathar the priest, and for Joab son of Zeruiah!"

[23] King Solomon then swore an oath by the LORD, "[a]May God judge me severely, if Adonijah does not pay for this request with his life! [24] Now, as certainly as the LORD lives (he who made me secure, allowed me to sit on my father David's throne, and established a dynasty for me as he [a]promised), Adonijah will be executed today!" [25] King Solomon then sent [a]Benaiah son of Jehoiada, and he killed Adonijah.

[26] The king then told Abiathar the priest, "Go back to your property in [a]Anathoth. You deserve to die,[1] but today I will not kill you [b]because you did carry the ark of the Sovereign LORD before my father David and you suffered with my father through all his difficult times." [27] Solomon removed Abiathar from being a priest for the LORD, [a]fulfilling the LORD's message that he had pronounced against the family of Eli in Shiloh.

[28] When the news reached Joab (for Joab [a]had supported Adonijah, although he had not supported Absalom), he ran [b]to the tent of the LORD and grabbed hold of the horns of the altar. [29] When King Solomon heard that Joab had run to the tent of the LORD and was right there beside the altar, he ordered Benaiah son of Jehoiada, "Go, [a]strike him down." [30] When Benaiah arrived at the tent of the LORD, he said to him, "The king says, '[a]Come out!'" But he replied, "No, I will die here!" So Benaiah sent word to the king and reported Joab's reply. [31] The king told him, "[a]Do as he said! Strike him down and bury him. Take away from me and from my father's family the guilt of Joab's murderous, bloody deeds. [32] May the LORD punish him for the blood he shed; behind my father David's back he struck down [a]and murdered with the sword two men who were more innocent and morally upright than he—[b]Abner son of Ner, commander of Israel's army, and [c]Amasa son of Jether, commander of Judah's army. [33] May Joab and his descendants be perpetually guilty of their shed blood, [a]but may the LORD give perpetual peace to David, his descendants, his family, and his dynasty." [34] So Benaiah son of Jehoiada went up and executed Joab; he was buried at his home in the wilderness. [35] The king appointed Benaiah son of Jehoiada to take his place at the head of the army, and the king appointed [a]Zadok the priest to take [b]Abiathar's place.[1]

[36] Next the king summoned [a]Shimei and told him, "Build yourself a house in Jerusalem and live there, but you may not leave there to go anywhere. [37] If you ever do leave and cross [a]the Kidron Valley, know for sure that [b]you will certainly die. You will be responsible for your own death." [38] Shimei said to the king, "My master the king's proposal is acceptable. Your servant will do as you say." So Shimei lived in Jerusalem for a long time.

[39] Three years later two of Shimei's servants ran away to King [a]Achish son of Maacah of Gath. Shimei was told, "Look, your servants are in Gath." [40] So Shimei got

2:15 [a]1 Kgs 1:11, 18 [b]1 Chr 22:9–10; 28:5–7; [Dan 2:21] 2:17 [a]1 Kgs 1:3–4 2:19 [a][Exod 20:12] 2:22 [a]1 Kgs 1:6; 2:15; 1 Chr 3:2, 5 [b]1 Kgs 1:7 2:23 [a]Ruth 1:17 2:24 [a]2 Sam 7:11, 13; 1 Chr 22:10 2:25 [a]2 Sam 8:18; 1 Kgs 4:4 2:26 [a]Josh 21:18; Jer 1:1 [b]1 Sam 22:23; 23:6; 2 Sam 15:14, 29 [1]Heb. *you are a man of death*; an idiom. 2:27 [a]1 Sam 2:31–35 2:28 [a]1 Kgs 1:7 [b]1 Kgs 1:50 2:29 [a]1 Kgs 2:5–6 2:30 [a][Exod 21:14] 2:31 [a][Exod 21:14] 2:32 [a]2 Chr 21:13–14 [b]2 Sam 3:27 [c]2 Sam 20:9–10 2:33 [a][Prov 25:5] 2:35 [a]1 Sam 2:35; 1 Kgs 4:4; 1 Chr 6:53; 24:3; 29:22 [b]1 Kgs 2:27 [1]Some wss add 14 vv. here. 2:36 [a]2 Sam 16:5–13; 1 Kgs 2:8 2:37 [a]2 Sam 15:23; 2 Kgs 23:6; John 18:1 [b]Lev 20:9; Josh 2:19; 2 Sam 1:16; Ezek 18:13 2:39 [a]1 Sam 27:2

up, saddled his donkey, and went to Achish at Gath to find his servants; Shimei went and brought back his servants from Gath. ⁴¹When Solomon was told that Shimei had gone from Jerusalem to Gath and had then returned, ⁴²the king summoned Shimei and said to him, "You will recall[1] that I made you take an oath by the LORD, and I solemnly warned you, 'If you ever leave and go anywhere, know for sure that you will certainly die.' You said to me, 'The proposal is acceptable; I agree to it.' ⁴³Why then have you broken the oath you made before the LORD and disobeyed the order I gave you?" ⁴⁴Then the king said to Shimei, "You are well aware of the way you mistreated my father David. The LORD will [a]punish you for what you did. ⁴⁵But King Solomon will be empowered, and David's dynasty will endure permanently before [a]the LORD." ⁴⁶The king then gave the order to Benaiah son of Jehoiada who went and executed Shimei.

So Solomon took firm control of the [a]kingdom.

The Lord Gives Solomon Wisdom

3 [a]Solomon made an alliance by marriage with Pharaoh, king of Egypt; he married Pharaoh's daughter. He brought her [b]to [c]the City of David until [d]he could finish building his residence and the temple of the LORD and the wall around Jerusalem. ²Now the people were offering sacrifices at the high places, because in those days [a]a temple had not yet been built to honor the LORD.[1] ³Solomon [a]demonstrated his loyalty to the LORD by [b]following the practices of his father David, except that he offered sacrifices and burned incense on the high places.

⁴The king went to Gibeon to offer sacrifices, for it had [a]the most prominent of the high places. Solomon would offer up[1] 1,000 burnt sacrifices on the altar there. ⁵One night in Gibeon the LORD appeared to Solomon in [a]a dream. God said, "Tell me what [b]I should give you." ⁶[a]Solomon replied, "You demonstrated great loyalty to your servant, my father David, as he [b]served you faithfully, properly, and sincerely. You [c]have maintained this great loyalty to this day by allowing his son to sit on his throne. ⁷Now, O LORD my God, you have made your servant king in my father David's place, even though I am [a]only a young man and am inexperienced. ⁸Your servant stands among your chosen people; they are [a]a great nation that is [b]too numerous to count or number. ⁹[a]So give your servant a discerning mind[1] [b]so he can make judicial decisions for your people and [c]distinguish right from wrong. Otherwise no one is able to make judicial decisions for this great nation of yours." ¹⁰The Lord was pleased that Solomon made this request. ¹¹God said to him, "Because you asked for the ability to make wise judicial decisions, and [a]not for long life, or riches, or vengeance on your enemies, ¹²[a]I grant your request and give you a wise and discerning mind superior to that of anyone who has preceded or will succeed you. ¹³Furthermore, I am [a]giving you what you did not request—[b]riches and honor so that you will be the greatest king of your generation.[1] ¹⁴If you follow my instructions by obeying my rules and regulations, just as your father David did, then [a]I will [b]grant you long life." ¹⁵Solomon then woke [a]up and realized it was a dream. He went to Jerusalem, stood before the ark of the Lord's covenant, offered up burnt sacrifices, [b]presented peace offerings, and held a feast for all his servants.

Solomon Demonstrates His Wisdom

¹⁶Then two prostitutes came to the king and [a]stood before him. ¹⁷One of the women said, "My master, this woman and I live in the same house. I had a baby while she was with me in the house. ¹⁸Then three days after I had my baby, this woman also had a baby. We were alone; there was no one else in the house except the two of us. ¹⁹This woman's child suffocated during the night when she rolled on top of him. ²⁰She got

2:42 ¹Heb. *Is it not* [true]... ?; a rhetorical question expecting a negative answer.   2:44 [a]1 Sam 25:39; 2 Kgs 11:1, 12–16; Ps 7:16; Ezek 17:19   2:45 [a]2 Sam 7:13; [Prov 25:5]   2:46 [a]1 Kgs 2:12; 2 Chr 1:1   3:1 [a]1 Kgs 7:8; 9:24   [b]2 Sam 5:7   [c]1 Kgs 6   [d]1 Kgs 9:15, 19   3:2 [a][Deut 12:2–5, 13, 14]; 1 Kgs 11:7; 22:43   ¹Heb. *for the name of the LORD.*   3:3 [a][Rom 8:28]   [b][1 Kgs 3:6, 14]   3:4 [a]1 Kgs 9:2; 2 Chr 1:3   ¹Or *customarily offered up.*   3:5 [a]1 Kgs 9:2; 11:9; 2 Chr 1:7   [b]Num 12:6; Matt 1:20; 2:13   3:6 [a]2 Chr 1:8   [b]1 Kgs 2:4; 9:4; 2 Kgs 20:3   [c]2 Sam 7:8–17; 1 Kgs 1:48   3:7 [a]1 Chr 22:5; Jer 1:6–7   3:8 [a][Exod 19:6; Deut 7:6]   [b]Gen 13:6; 15:5; 22:17   3:9 [a]2 Chr 1:10; [Jas 1:5]   [b]Ps 72:1–2   [c]2 Sam 14:17; Isa 7:15; [Heb 5:14]   ¹Heb. *a hearing heart;* often refers to the mental faculties.   3:11 [a][Jas 4:3]   3:12 [a][1 John 5:14–15]   3:13 [a][Matt 6:33; Eph 3:20]   [b]1 Kgs 4:21, 24; 10:23; 1 Chr 29:12   ¹Heb. *so that there is not one among the kings like you all your days.*   3:14 [a][1 Kgs 6:12]   [b]Ps 91:16; Prov 3:2   3:15 [a]Gen 41:7   [b]Gen 40:20; 1 Kgs 8:65; Esth 1:3; Dan 5:1; Mark 6:21   3:16 [a]Num 27:2

up in the middle of the night and took my son from my side, while your servant was sleeping. She put him in her arms, and put her dead son in my arms. 21I got up in the morning to nurse my son, and there he was, dead! But when I examined him carefully in the morning, I realized it was not my baby." 22The other woman said, "No! My son is alive; your son is dead!" But the first woman replied, "No, your son is dead; my son is alive." Each presented her case before the king.

23The king said, "One says, 'My son is alive; your son is dead,' while the other says, 'No, your son is dead; my son is alive.'" 24The king ordered, "Get me a sword." So they placed a sword before the king. 25The king then said, "Cut the living child in two, and give half to one and half to the other!" 26The real mother spoke up to the king, for her motherly instincts were awakened. aShe said, "My master, give her the living child! Whatever you do, don't kill him!" But the other woman said, "Neither one of us will have him. Let them cut him in two!" 27The king responded, "Give the first woman the living child; don't kill him. She is the mother." 28When all Israel heard about the judicial decision which the king had rendered, they respected the king, for they realized that he possessed divine awisdom to make judicial decisions.

Solomon's Royal Court and Administrators

4 King Solomon ruled over all Israel. 2These were his officials:

Azariah son of Zadok was the priest.

3Elihoreph and Ahijah, the sons of Shisha, wrote down what happened.1

aJehoshaphat son of Ahilud was in charge of the records.

4aBenaiah son of Jehoiada was commander of the army.

Zadok and bAbiathar were priests.

5Azariah son of Nathan was supervisor of athe district governors.

bZabud son of Nathan was a priest and adviser to cthe king.

6Ahishar was supervisor of the palace.

aAdoniram son of Abda was supervisor of the work crews.

7Solomon had 12 district governors appointed throughout Israel who acquired supplies for the king and his palace. Each was responsible for one month in the year. 8These were their names:

Ben Hur was in charge of the hill country of Ephraim.

9Ben Deker was in charge of Makaz, Shaalbim, Beth Shemesh, and Elon Beth Hanan.

10Ben Hesed was in charge of Arubboth; he controlled Socoh and all the territory of Hepher.

11Ben Abinadab was in charge of Naphath Dor. (He was married to Solomon's daughter Taphath.)

12Baana son of Ahilud was in charge of Taanach and Megiddo, as well as all of Beth Shean next to Zarethan below Jezreel, from Beth Shean to Abel Meholah and on past Jokmeam.

13Ben Geber was in charge of Ramoth Gilead; ahe controlled bthe villages of Jair son of Manasseh in Gilead, as well as the region of Argob in Bashan, including 60 large walled cities with bronze bars locking their gates.

14Ahinadab son of Iddo was in charge of Mahanaim.

15aAhimaaz was in charge of Naphtali. (He married Solomon's daughter Basemath.)

16Baana son of aHushai was in charge of Asher and Aloth.

17Jehoshaphat son of Paruah was in charge of Issachar.

18aShimei son of Ela was in charge of Benjamin.

19Geber son of Uri was in charge of athe land of Gilead (the territory which had once belonged to King Sihon of the Amorites and to King Og of Bashan). He was sole governor of the area.

Solomon's Wealth and Fame

20The people of Judah and Israel were aas innumerable as the sand on the seashore; they had plenty to beat and drink and were happy. 21aSolomon ruled all the kingdoms from the Euphrates River to the land of the Philistines, as far as the border of Egypt. These kingdoms paid tribute as

3:26 aGen 43:30; Isa 49:15; Jer 31:20; Hos 11:8   3:28 a1 Kgs 3:9, 11, 12; 2 Chr 1:12; Dan 1:17; [Col 2:2–3]   4:3 a2 Sam 8:16; 20:24   1Heb. were scribes.   4:4 a1 Kgs 2:35   b1 Kgs 2:27   4:5 a1 Kgs 4:7   b2 Sam 8:18; 20:26   c2 Sam 15:37; 16:16; 1 Chr 27:33   4:6 a1 Kgs 5:14   4:13 aNum 32:41; 1 Chr 2:22   bDeut 3:4   4:15 a2 Sam 15:27   4:16 a2 Sam 15:32; 1 Chr 27:33   4:18 a1 Kgs 1:8   4:19 aDeut 3:8–10   4:20 aGen 22:17; 32:12; 1 Kgs 3:8; [Prov 14:28]   bPs 72:3, 7; Mic 4:4   4:21 aExod 34:24; 2 Chr 9:26; Ps 72:8

Solomon's subjects throughout his lifetime. [22a]Each day Solomon's royal court consumed 30 cors of finely milled flour, 60 cors of cereal, [23]10 calves fattened in the stall, 20 calves from the pasture, and 100 sheep, not to mention rams, gazelles, deer, and well-fed birds. [24]His royal court was so large because he ruled over [a]all [b]the kingdoms west of the Euphrates River from Tiphsah to Gaza; he was at peace with all his neighbors. [25]All the people of Judah and Israel [a]had security; everyone [b]from Dan to Beer Sheba enjoyed the produce of their vines and fig trees throughout Solomon's lifetime. [26a]Solomon had 4,000 stalls[1] for his chariot [b]horses and 12,000 horses. [27]The district governors acquired supplies for King Solomon and all who ate in his royal palace. Each was responsible for one month in [a]the year; they made sure nothing was lacking. [28]Each one also brought to the assigned location his quota of barley and straw for the various horses.

[29a]God gave Solomon wisdom and very great discernment; the breadth of his understanding was as infinite as the sand on the seashore. [30]Solomon was wiser than all the men [a]of [b]the east and all the sages of Egypt. [31]He was [a]wiser [b]than any man, including Ethan the Ezrahite or Heman, Calcol, [c]and Darda, the sons of Mahol. He was famous in all the neighboring nations. [32a]He composed 3,000 proverbs and 1,005 [b]songs. [33]He produced manuals on botany, describing every kind of plant, from the cedars of Lebanon to the hyssop that grows on walls. He also produced manuals on biology, describing animals, birds, insects, and fish. [34]People from all nations [a]came to hear Solomon's display of wisdom; they came from all the kings of the earth who heard about his wisdom.

Solomon Gathers Building Materials for the Temple

5 King [a]Hiram of Tyre sent messengers to Solomon when he heard that he had been anointed king in his father's place. (Hiram had always been an ally of David.) [2a]Solomon then sent this message to Hiram: [3]"[a]You know that my father David was unable to build a temple to honor the LORD[1] his God, [b]for he was busy fighting battles on all fronts while the LORD subdued his enemies. [4]But now the LORD my God has [a]made me secure on all fronts; there is no adversary or dangerous threat. [5]So I have decided to build [a]a temple to honor the LORD my God, [b]as the LORD instructed my father David, 'Your son, whom I will put on your throne in your place, is the one who will build a temple to honor me.' [6]So now order some [a]cedars of Lebanon to be cut for me. My servants will work with your servants. I will pay your servants whatever you say is appropriate, for you know that we have no one among us who knows [a]how to cut down trees like the Sidonians."

[7]When Hiram heard Solomon's message, he was very happy. He said, "The LORD is worthy of praise today because he has given David a wise son to rule over this great nation." [8]Hiram then sent this message to Solomon: "I received the message you sent to me. I will give you all the cedars and evergreens you need. [9]My servants will bring the timber down [a]from Lebanon to the sea. I will send it [b]by sea in raft-like bundles to the place you designate.[1] There I will separate the logs[2] and you can carry them away. In exchange you will supply the food I need for my royal court."

[10]So Hiram supplied the cedars and evergreens Solomon needed, [11a]and Solomon supplied Hiram annually with 20,000 cors of wheat as provision for his royal court, as well as 120,000 gallons[1] of pure[2] olive oil. [12]So the LORD gave Solomon wisdom, [a]as he had promised him. And Hiram and Solomon were at peace and made a treaty.[1]

[13]King Solomon conscripted work crews from throughout Israel, 30,000 men in all. [14]He sent them to Lebanon in shifts of 10,000 men per month. They worked in Lebanon for one month, and then spent two months at home. [a]Adoniram was supervisor of the work

---

4:22 [a]Neh 5:18   4:24 [a]Ps 72:11   [b]1 Kgs 5:4; 1 Chr 22:9   4:25 [a][Jer 23:6]   [b]Judg 20:1   4:26 [a]1 Kgs 10:26; 2 Chr 1:14   [b][Deut 17:16]   [1]Heb. *40,000 stalls.*   4:27 [a]1 Kgs 4:7   4:29 [a]1 Kgs 3:12   4:30 [a]Gen 25:6   [b]Isa 19:11–12; Acts 7:22   4:31 [a]1 Kgs 3:12   [b]1 Chr 15:19; Ps 89:title   [c]1 Chr 2:6; Ps 88:title   4:32 [a]Prov 1:1; 10:1; 25:1; Eccl 12:9   [b]Song 1:1   4:34 [a]1 Kgs 10:1; 2 Chr 9:1, 23   5:1 [a]1 Kgs 5:10, 18; 2 Chr 2:3   5:2 [a]2 Chr 2:3   5:3 [a]1 Chr 28:2–3   [b]1 Chr 22:8; 28:3   [1]Heb. *a house for the name of the LORD.*   5:4 [a]1 Kgs 4:24; 1 Chr 22:9   5:5 [a]2 Chr 2:4   [b]2 Sam 7:12–13; 1 Kgs 6:38; 1 Chr 17:12; 22:10; 28:6; 2 Chr 6:2   5:6 [a]2 Chr 2:8, 10   5:9 [a]Ezra 3:7   [b]Ezek 27:17; Acts 12:20   [1]Heb. *I will place them* [on? as?] *rafts in the sea to the place where you designate to me.*   [2]Heb. *smash them;* i.e., untie the bundles.   5:11 [a]2 Chr 2:10   [1]Heb. *twenty cors.*   [2]Or *pressed.*   5:12 [a]1 Kgs 3:12   [1]Heb. *a covenant;* a formal peace treaty or alliance.   5:14 [a]1 Kgs 12:18

crews. [15a] Solomon also had 70,000 common laborers and 80,000 stonecutters[1] in the hills, [16] besides 3,300 [a] officials[1] who supervised the workers. [17] By royal order they supplied large valuable stones in order to build the temple's foundation with [a] chiseled stone. [18] Solomon's and Hiram's construction workers, along with men from Byblos, did the chiseling and prepared the wood and stones for the building of the temple.[1]

The Building of the Temple

6 In the four hundred and eightieth year after the [a] Israelites left Egypt, in the fourth year of Solomon's reign over Israel, during the month Ziv (the second month), he began building the LORD's temple. [2] The temple King Solomon built for [a] the LORD was 90 feet long, 30 feet wide, and 45 feet high. [3] The porch in front of the main hall of the temple was 30 feet long, corresponding to the width of the temple. It was 15 feet wide, extending out from the front of the temple. [4] He made framed [a] windows for the temple. [5] He built [a] an extension all around the walls of the temple's main hall and Holy Place and constructed side rooms in it. [6] The bottom floor of the extension was 7½ feet wide, the middle floor 9 feet wide, and the third floor 10½ feet wide. He made ledges[1] on the temple's outer walls so the beams would not have to be inserted into the walls. [7] As [a] the temple was being built, only stones shaped at the quarry were used; the sound of hammers, pickaxes, or any other iron tool was not heard at the temple while it was being built. [8] The entrance to the bottom[1] level of side rooms was on the south side of the temple; stairs went up to the middle floor and then on up to the third[2] floor. [9a] He finished building the temple and covered it with rafters and boards made of cedar. [10] He built an extension all around the temple; it was 7½ feet high and it was attached to the temple by cedar beams.

[111] The LORD's message came to Solomon: [12] "As for this temple you are building, [a] if you follow my rules, observe my regulations, and obey all my commandments, [b] I will fulfill through you the promise I made to your father David. [13] I [a] will live among the Israelites and will not [b] abandon my people Israel."

[14] So Solomon finished building the temple. [15] He constructed the walls inside the temple with cedar planks; he paneled the inside with wood from the floor of the temple to the rafters[1] of the ceiling. He covered the temple floor with boards made from the wood of evergreens. [16] He built a wall 30 feet in from the rear of the temple as a partition for an inner sanctuary that would be the [a] Most Holy Place. He paneled the wall with cedar planks from the floor to the rafters.[1] [17] The main hall in front of the inner sanctuary was 60 feet long. [18] The inside of the temple was all cedar and was adorned with carvings of round ornaments and of flowers in bloom. Everything was cedar; no stones were visible.

[19] He prepared the inner sanctuary inside the temple so that the ark of the covenant of the LORD could be placed there. [20] The inner sanctuary was 30 feet long, 30 feet wide, and 30 feet high. He plated it with gold, as well as the cedar altar. [21] Solomon plated the inside of the temple with gold. He hung golden chains in front of the inner sanctuary and plated the inner sanctuary with gold. [22] He plated [a] the entire inside of the temple with gold, as well as the altar inside the inner sanctuary.

[23] In [a] the inner sanctuary he made two cherubim of olive wood; each stood 15 feet high. [24] Each of the first cherub's wings was 7½ feet long; its entire wingspan was 15 feet. [25] The second cherub also had a wingspan of 15 feet; it was identical to the first in measurements and shape. [26] Each cherub stood 15 feet high. [27] He put [a] the cherubim in the inner sanctuary of the temple. Their wings were spread out. One of the first cherub's wings touched one wall and one of the other cherub's wings touched the opposite wall. The first cherub's other wing touched the second cherub's other wing in the middle of the room. [28] He plated the cherubim with gold.

[29] On all the walls around the temple, inside and out, he [a] carved cherubim, palm trees, and flowers in bloom. [30] He plated the

floor of the temple with gold, inside and out. [31]He made doors of olive wood at the entrance to the inner sanctuary; the pillar on each doorpost was five sided. [32]On the two doors made of olive wood he carved cherubim, palm trees, and flowers in bloom, and he plated them with gold. He plated the cherubim and the palm trees with hammered gold. [33]In the same way he made doorposts of olive wood for the entrance to the main hall, only with four-sided pillars. [34]He also made [a]two doors out of wood from evergreens; each door had two folding leaves.[1] [35]He carved cherubim, palm trees, and flowers in bloom and plated them with gold, leveled out over the carvings. [36]He built the [a]inner courtyard with three rows of chiseled stones and a row of cedar beams.

[37]In the month of Ziv [a]in the fourth year of Solomon's reign the foundation was laid for the LORD's temple. [38]In the eleventh year, in the month of Bul (the eighth month) the temple was completed in accordance with all its specifications and blueprints. It took [a]seven years to build.

The Building of the Royal Palace

7 Solomon took [a]13 years to build his palace. [2]He named it "The [a]Palace of the Lebanon Forest"; it was 150 feet long, 75 feet wide, and 45 feet high. It had four rows of cedar pillars and cedar beams above the pillars. [3]The roof above the beams supported by the pillars was also made of cedar; there were 45 beams, 15 per row. [4]There were three rows of windows arranged in sets of three.[1] [5]All the entrances were rectangular in shape and they were arranged in sets of three.[1] [6]He made a colonnade 75 feet long and 45 feet wide. There was a porch in front of this and pillars and a roof in front of the porch.[1] [7]He also made a throne room, called "The Hall of Judgment," where he made judicial decisions.[1] It was paneled with cedar

from the floor to the rafters.[2] [8]The palace where he lived was constructed in a similar way. He also constructed a palace like this hall for Pharaoh's daughter, [a]whom he had married. [9]All these were built with the best[1] stones, chiseled to the right size and cut with a saw on all sides, from the foundation to the edge of the roof and from the outside to the great courtyard. [10]The foundation was made of large valuable stones, measuring either 15 feet or 12 feet.[1] [11]Above the foundation the best[1] stones, chiseled to the right size, were used along with cedar. [12]Around the great courtyard were three rows of chiseled stones and one row of cedar beams, like the [a]inner courtyard of the LORD's temple [b]and the hall of the palace.

Solomon Commissions Hiram to Supply the Temple

[13]King Solomon sent for Hiram of Tyre. [14]He was [a]the son of a widow from the tribe of Naphtali, and [b]his [c]father was a craftsman in bronze from Tyre. He had the skill and knowledge to make all kinds of works of bronze. He reported to King Solomon and did all the work he was assigned.

[15]He fashioned [a]two bronze pillars; each pillar was 27 feet high and 18 feet in circumference. [16]He made two bronze tops for the pillars; each was 7½ feet high. [17]The latticework on the tops of the pillars was adorned with ornamental wreaths and chains; the top of each pillar had seven groupings of ornaments. [18]When he made the pillars, there were two rows of pomegranate-shaped ornaments around the latticework covering the top of each pillar.[1] [19]The tops of the two pillars in the porch were shaped like lilies and were six feet high. [20]On the top of each pillar, right above the bulge beside the latticework, there were 200 pomegranate-shaped ornaments arranged in rows all the way around.[1] [21]He set up [a]the pillars on the

---

6:34 [a]Ezek 41:23–25 [1]Heb. *two of the leaves of the first door were folding, and two of the leaves of the second door were folding*; MT *curtains in second occurrence.* **6:36** [a]1 Kgs 7:12; Jer 36:10 **6:37** [a]1 Kgs 6:1 **6:38** [a]2 Sam 7:13; 1 Kgs 5:5; 6:1; 8:19 **7:1** [a]1 Kgs 3:1; 9:10; 2 Chr 8:1 **7:2** [a]1 Kgs 10:17, 21; 2 Chr 9:16 **7:4** [1]Heb. *and framed [windows in] three rows, and opening to opening three times.* **7:5** [1]Heb. *and all the entrances and the doorposts [had] four frames, and in front of opening to opening three times.* **7:6** [1]Heb. *and a porch was in front of them [i.e., the aforementioned pillars] and pillars and a roof in front of them [i.e., the aforementioned pillars and porch].* **7:7** [1]Heb. *and a porch for the throne, where he was making judicial decisions, the Porch of Judgment, he made.* [2]Heb. *from the floor to the floor.* **7:8** [a]1 Kgs 3:1; 9:24; 11:1; 2 Chr 8:11 **7:9** [1]Or *valuable.* **7:10** [1]Heb. *stones of 10 cubits and stones of 8 cubits.* **7:11** [1]Or *valuable.* **7:12** [a]1 Kgs 6:36 [b]John 10:23; Acts 3:11 **7:14** [a]2 Chr 2:14 [b]2 Chr 4:16 [c]Exod 31:3; 36:1 **7:15** [a]2 Kgs 25:17; 2 Chr 3:15; 4:12; Jer 52:21 **7:18** [1]Heb. *he made the pillars, and two rows surrounding one latticework to cover the capitals which were on top of the pomegranates, and so he did for the second latticework.* **7:20** [1]Heb. *and the capitals on the two pillars, also above, close beside the bulge which was beside the latticework, two hundred pomegranates in rows around, on the second capital.* **7:21** [a]2 Chr 3:17

porch in front of the main hall. He erected one pillar on the right side and called it Yakin; he erected the other pillar on the left side and called it Boaz. [22] The tops of the pillars were shaped like lilies. So the construction of the pillars was completed.

[23] He also made [a] the large bronze basin called "The Sea." It measured 15 feet from rim to rim, was circular in shape, and stood 7½ feet high. Its circumference was 45 feet.[1] [24] Under the rim [a] all the way around it were round ornaments arranged in settings 15 feet long. The ornaments were in two rows and had been cast with "The Sea." [25] "The Sea" stood on top of [a] twelve bulls. Three faced northward, three westward, three southward, and three eastward. "The Sea" was placed on top of them, and they all faced outward. [26] It was four fingers thick and its rim was like that of a cup shaped like a lily blossom. It could hold about 12,000 gallons.[1]

[27] He also made 10 bronze movable stands. Each stand was 6 feet long, 6 feet wide, and 4½ feet high. [28] The stands were constructed with frames between the joints. [29] On these frames and joints were ornamental lions, bulls, and cherubim. Under the lions and bulls were decorative wreaths. [30] Each stand had four bronze wheels with bronze axles and four supports. Under the basin the supports were fashioned on each side with wreaths. [31] Inside the stand was a round opening that was 18 inches deep; it had a support that was 27 inches long. On the edge of the opening were carvings in square frames. [32] The four wheels were under the frames, and the crossbars of the axles were connected to the stand. Each wheel was 27 inches high. [33] The wheels were constructed like chariot wheels; their crossbars, rims, spokes, and hubs were made of cast metal. [34] Each stand had four supports, one per side projecting out from the stand. [35] On top of each stand was a round opening three-quarters of a foot deep; there were also supports and frames on top of the stands. [36] He engraved ornamental cherubim, lions, and palm trees on the plates of the supports and frames wherever there was room, with wreaths all around. [37] He made the 10 stands in this way. All of them were cast in one mold and were identical in measurements and shape.

[38] He also made 10 bronze basins, each of which could hold about 240 gallons. Each basin was 6 feet in diameter; [a] there was one basin for each stand. [39] He put five basins on the south side of the temple and five on the north side. He put "The Sea" on the south side, in the southeast corner.

[40] Hiram also made basins, shovels, and bowls. [a] He finished all the work on the LORD's temple he had been assigned by King Solomon. [41] He made the two pillars, the two bowl-shaped tops of the pillars, the [a] latticework for the bowl-shaped tops of the two pillars, [42] the [a] 400 pomegranate-shaped ornaments for the latticework of the two pillars (each latticework had two rows of these ornaments at the bowl-shaped top of the pillar), [43] the 10 movable stands with their 10 basins, [44] the big bronze basin called "The Sea" with its 12 bulls underneath, [45] and [a] the pots, shovels, and bowls. All these items King Solomon assigned Hiram to make for the LORD's temple were made from polished bronze. [46] The [a] king had them cast in earth foundries in the region of the Jordan between [b] Sukkoth and [c] Zarethan. [47] Solomon left all these items unweighed; there were so many of them they did not [a] weigh the bronze.

[48] Solomon also made all [a] these items for [b] the LORD's temple: [c] the gold altar; the gold table on which was kept the Bread of the Presence;[1] [49] the pure gold lampstands at the entrance to the inner sanctuary (five on the right and five on the left); the gold flower-shaped ornaments, lamps, and tongs; [50] the pure gold bowls, trimming shears, basins, pans, and censers; and the gold door sockets for the inner sanctuary (the Most Holy Place) and for the doors of the main hall of the temple. [51] When King Solomon finished constructing the LORD's temple, he put the holy items that belonged to his father David (the silver, gold, and other articles) in the treasuries of the LORD's temple.

7:23 [a] 2 Kgs 25:13; 2 Chr 4:2; Jer 52:17 [1] Heb. *and a measuring line went around it 30 cubits all around.* 7:24 [a] 2 Chr 4:3 7:25 [a] 2 Chr 4:4–5; Jer 52:20 7:26 [1] Heb. *2,000 baths.* 7:38 [a] Exod 30:18; 2 Chr 4:6 7:40 [a] 2 Chr 4:11–5:1 7:41 [a] 1 Kgs 7:17–18 7:42 [a] 1 Kgs 7:20 7:45 [a] Exod 27:3; 2 Chr 4:16 7:46 [a] 2 Chr 4:17 [b] Gen 33:17; Josh 13:27 [c] Josh 3:16 7:47 [a] 1 Chr 22:3, 14 7:48 [a] Exod 37:25–26; 2 Chr 4:8 [b] Exod 37:10–11 [c] Lev 24:5–8 [1] Heb. *the bread of the face* [or presence].

Solomon Moves the Ark into the Temple

8 [1]Then [a]Solomon convened in Jerusalem Israel's elders, all the leaders of the Israelite tribes and families, [b]so they could witness the [c]transferal of the ark of the LORD's covenant from the City of David (that is, Zion). [2]All the men of Israel assembled before King Solomon during the [a]festival in the month of Ethanim (the seventh month). [3]When all Israel's elders had arrived, the priests lifted the ark. [4]The priests and Levites carried [a]the ark of the LORD, the tent of meeting, and all the holy items in the tent. [5]Now King Solomon and all the Israelites who had assembled with him went on ahead of the ark and [a]sacrificed more sheep and cattle than could be counted or numbered.

[6]The priests [a]brought the ark of the LORD's covenant to [b]its assigned place in the inner sanctuary of the temple, in the Most Holy Place, [c]under the wings of the cherubim. [7]The cherubim's wings extended over the place where the ark sat; the cherubim overshadowed the ark and its poles. [8]The poles [a]were so long their ends were visible from the Holy Place in front of the inner sanctuary, but they could not be seen from beyond that point. They have remained there to this very day. [9]There was [a]nothing in the ark [b]except the two stone tablets Moses had placed there in Horeb. It was there that the LORD made a covenant with the Israelites after [c]he brought them out of the land of Egypt. [10]Once the priests left the Holy Place, a cloud [a]filled the LORD's temple. [11]The priests could not carry out their duties because of the cloud; the [a]LORD's glory filled his temple.

[12]Then Solomon said, "[a]The LORD has said that he lives [b]in thick darkness. [13]O LORD, truly [a]I have built [b]a lofty temple for you, a place where you can live permanently." [14]Then the king turned around and pronounced a blessing [a]over the whole Israelite assembly as they stood there. [15]He said, "The LORD God of Israel is worthy of [a]praise because he has fulfilled what he [b]promised my father David. [16]He told David, 'Since the day I brought [a]my people Israel out of Egypt, I have not chosen a city from all the tribes of Israel to build a temple in which to live. But I have chosen [b]David to lead my people Israel.' [17]Now my father David had a strong desire to build a temple to honor the LORD God of Israel.[1] [18a]The LORD told my father David, 'It is right for you to have a strong desire to build a temple to honor me. [19]But [a]you will not build the temple; your very own son will build the temple for my honor.' [20]The LORD [a]has kept the promise he made. I have taken my father David's place and have occupied the throne of Israel, as the LORD promised. I have built this temple for the honor of the LORD God of Israel [21]and set up in it a place for [a]the ark containing the covenant the LORD made with our ancestors when he brought them out of the land of Egypt."

Solomon Prays for Israel

[22]Solomon stood before [a]the altar of the LORD in front of the entire assembly of Israel and spread [b]out his hands toward the sky. [23]He prayed: "O LORD, God of Israel, [a]there is no god like you in heaven above or on earth below! You maintain covenantal loyalty to your servants [b]who [c]obey you with sincerity. [24]You have kept your word to your servant, my father David; this very day you have fulfilled what you promised. [25]Now, [a]O LORD, God of Israel, keep the promise you made to your servant, my father David, when you said, 'You will never fail to have a successor ruling before me on the throne of Israel, provided that your descendants watch their step[1] and serve me as you have done.' [26a]Now, O God of Israel, may the promise you made to your servant, my father David, be realized.

[27]"[a]God does not really live on the earth![1]

8:1 [a]Num 1:4; 7:2; 2 Chr 5:2–14   [b]2 Sam 6:12–17; 1 Chr 15:25–29   [c]2 Sam 5:7; 6:12, 16   [1]One ws adds *It so happened that when Solomon finished building the Lord's temple and his own house, after twenty years.*   8:2 [a]Lev 23:34; 1 Kgs 8:65; 2 Chr 7:8–10   8:4 [1]Kgs 3:4; 2 Chr 1:3   8:5 [a]2 Sam 6:13; 2 Chr 1:6   8:6 [a]2 Sam 6:17   [b]Exod 26:33–34; 1 Kgs 6:19   [c]1 Kgs 6:27   8:8 [a]Exod 25:13–15; 37:4–5   8:9 [a]Exod 25:21; Deut 10:2   [b]Exod 25:16; Deut 10:5; Heb 9:4   [c]Exod 34:27–28   8:10 [a]Exod 40:34–35; 2 Chr 7:1–2   8:11 [a]2 Chr 7:1–2   8:12 [a]2 Chr 6:1   [b]Lev 16:2; Ps 18:11; 97:2   8:13 [a]2 Sam 7:13   [b][Exod 15:17]; Ps 132:14   8:14 [a]2 Sam 6:18; 1 Kgs 8:55   8:15 [a]1 Chr 29:10, 20; Neh 9:5; Luke 1:68   [b]2 Sam 7:2, 12, 13, 25; 1 Chr 22:10   8:16 [a]Deut 12:5; 1 Kgs 8:29   [b]1 Sam 16:1; 2 Sam 7:8; 1 Chr 28:4   8:17 [1]Heb. *to build a house for the name of the LORD God of Israel.*   8:18 [a]2 Chr 6:8–9   8:19 [a]2 Sam 7:5, 12, 13; 1 Kgs 5:3, 5; 6:38; 1 Chr 17:11–12; 22:8–10; 2 Chr 6:2   8:20 [a]1 Chr 28:5–6   8:21 [a]Deut 31:26; 1 Kgs 8:9   8:22 [a]1 Kgs 8:54; 2 Chr 6:12   [b]Exod 9:33; Ezra 9:5   8:23 [a]Exod 15:11; 2 Sam 7:22   [b][Deut 7:9; Neh 1:5; Dan 9:4]   [c][Gen 17:1; 1 Kgs 3:6]; 2 Kgs 20:3   8:25 [a]2 Sam 7:12, 16; 1 Kgs 2:4; 9:5   [1]Heb. *watch their way.*   8:26 [a]2 Sam 7:25   8:27 [a][2 Chr 2:6; Isa 66:1; Acts 7:49; 17:24]

Look, if the sky and the highest [b]heaven cannot contain you, how much less this temple I have built! [28]But respond favorably to your servant's prayer and his request for help, O LORD my God. Answer the desperate prayer your servant is presenting to you today. [29]Night and day may you watch over this temple, [a]the place where you promised you would live. May you answer your servant's prayer for this place. [30]Respond to the request of your servant [a]and your people Israel for this place. Hear from inside your heavenly dwelling place and respond favorably.[1]

[31]"When someone is accused of sinning against his neighbor [a]and the latter pronounces a curse on the alleged offender before your altar in this temple, be willing to forgive the accused if the accusation is false.[1] [32]Listen from heaven and make a just decision about your servants' claims. [a]Condemn the guilty party, declare the other innocent, and give both of them what they deserve.

[33]"The time will come [a]when your people Israel are defeated by an enemy because they sinned against you. If they come back to you, renew their allegiance to you, and pray for your help in this temple, [34]then listen from heaven, forgive the sin of your people Israel, and bring them back to the land you gave to their [a]ancestors.

[35]"The time will come [a]when the skies are shut up tightly and no rain falls because your people sinned against you. When they direct their prayers toward this place, renew their allegiance to you, and turn away from their sin because you punish[1] them, [36]then listen from heaven and forgive the sin of your servants, your people Israel. Certainly you will then [a]teach [b]them the right way to live and send rain on your land that you have given your people to possess.

[37]"The time will come [a]when the land suffers from a famine, a plague, blight and disease, or a locust invasion, or when their enemy lays siege to the cities of the land, or when some other type of plague or epidemic occurs. [38]When all your people Israel pray and ask for help, as they acknowledge their pain and spread out their hands toward this temple, [39]then listen from your heavenly dwelling place, forgive their sin, and act favorably toward each one based on your [a]evaluation of his motives. (Indeed you are the only one who can correctly evaluate the motives of all people.) [40][a]Then they will obey you throughout their lifetimes as they live on the land you gave to our ancestors.

[41]"Foreigners, who do not belong to your people Israel, will come from a distant land because of your reputation. [42]When they hear about your great reputation and your [a]ability to accomplish mighty deeds, they will come and direct their prayers toward this temple. [43]Then listen from your heavenly dwelling place and answer all the prayers of the foreigners. [a]Then all the nations of the earth will acknowledge your reputation, [b]obey you as your people Israel do, and recognize that this temple I built belongs to you.[1]

[44]"When you direct your people to march out and fight their enemies, and they direct their prayers to the LORD toward his chosen city and this temple I built for your honor, [45]then listen from heaven to their prayers for help and vindicate them.

[46]"The time will come when your people will sin against you ([a]for there is no one who is sinless!) and you will be angry with them and deliver them over [b]to their enemies, who will take them as prisoners to their own land, whether far away or close by. [47][a]When your people come to their senses in the land where they are held prisoner, they will repent and beg for your mercy in the land of their imprisonment, [b]admitting, 'We have sinned and gone astray; we have done evil.' [48]When they [a]return to you with all their heart and being in the land where they are held prisoner, and [b]direct their prayers to you toward the land you gave to

their ancestors, your chosen city, and the temple I built for your honor, [49]then listen from your heavenly dwelling place to their prayers for help and vindicate them. [50]Forgive all the rebellious acts of your sinful people and [a]cause their captors to have mercy on them. [51]After all, [a]they are your people and your special possession whom you brought [b]out of Egypt, from the middle of the iron-smelting furnace.

[52]"[a]May you be attentive to your servant's and your people Israel's requests for help and may you respond to all their prayers to you. [53]After all, you picked them out of all the nations of the earth to be your special possession, just [a]as you, O Sovereign Lord, announced through your servant Moses when you brought our ancestors out of Egypt."

[54]When Solomon finished presenting all these prayers [a]and requests to the Lord, he got up from before the altar of the Lord where he had kneeled and spread out his hands toward the sky. [55]When he stood up, he pronounced [a]a blessing over the entire assembly of Israel, saying in a loud voice: [56]"The Lord is worthy of praise because he has made Israel his people [a]secure just as [b]he promised! Not one of all the faithful promises he made through his servant Moses is left unfulfilled! [57]May the Lord our God be with us, as he was with our ancestors. [a]May he not abandon us or leave us. [58]May he [a]make us submissive,[1] so we can follow all his instructions and obey the commandments, rules, and regulations he commanded our ancestors. [59]May the Lord our God be constantly aware of these requests of mine I have presented to him, so that he might vindicate his servant and his people Israel as the need arises. [60]Then all the nations of the earth will recognize [a]that [b]the Lord is the only genuine God. [61]May [a]you demonstrate wholehearted devotion to the Lord our God by following his rules and obeying his commandments, as you are now doing."

Solomon Dedicates the Temple

[62]The king and all Israel with him were presenting sacrifices to [a]the Lord. [63]Solomon offered as peace offerings[1] to the Lord 22,000 cattle and 120,000 sheep. Then the king and all the Israelites dedicated the Lord's temple. [64]That day [a]the king consecrated the middle of the courtyard that is in front of the Lord's temple. He offered there burnt sacrifices, grain offerings, and the fat from the peace offerings, because the [b]bronze altar that stood before the Lord was too small to hold all these offerings. [65]At [a]that time Solomon and all Israel with him celebrated a festival before [b]the Lord our God for two entire [c]weeks. This great assembly included people from all over the land, from Lebo Hamath in the north to [d]the Stream of Egypt[1] in the south. [66]On the fifteenth day after the festival started, he dismissed the people. They asked God to empower the king and then went to their homes, happy and [a]content because of all the good the Lord had done for his servant David and his people Israel.

The Lord Gives Solomon a Promise and a Warning

9 After Solomon finished building the Lord's temple, the royal palace, [a]and [b]all the other construction projects he had planned, [2]the Lord appeared to Solomon [a]a second time, in the same way he had appeared to him at Gibeon. [3]The Lord [a]said [b]to him, "I have answered your prayer [c]and your request for help that you made to me. I have consecrated this temple you built by making it my permanent home; I will be constantly present there. [4]You must [a]serve me with integrity and sincerity, just [b]as your father David did. Do everything I commanded and [c]obey my rules and regulations. [5]Then I will allow your [a]dynasty to rule over Israel permanently, just as I promised your father David, 'You will not fail to have a successor on the throne of Israel.' [6]"[a]But if you or your sons ever turn away

8:50 [a][2 Chr 30:9]; Ezra 7:6; Ps 106:46; Acts 7:10   8:51 [a]Exod 32:11–12; Deut 9:26–29; Neh 1:10; [Rom 11:28–29] [b]Deut 4:20; Jer 11:4   8:52 [a]1 Kgs 8:29   8:53 [a]Exod 19:5–6   8:54 [a]2 Chr 7:1   8:55 [a]Num 6:23–26; 2 Sam 6:18; 1 Kgs 8:14   8:56 [a]1 Chr 22:18 [b]Deut 12:10; Josh 21:45; 23:14   8:57 [a]Deut 31:6; Josh 1:5; 1 Sam 12:22; [Rom 8:31–37]; Heb 13:5   8:58 [a]Ps 119:36; Jer 31:33 [1]Heb. *to bend our hearts toward him.*   8:60 [a]Josh 4:24; 1 Sam 17:46; 1 Kgs 8:43; 2 Kgs 19:19 [b]Deut 4:35, 39; 1 Kgs 18:39; [Jer 10:10–12]   8:61 [a]Deut 18:13; 1 Kgs 11:4; 15:3, 14; 2 Kgs 20:3   8:62 [a]2 Chr 7:4–10   8:63 [1]Heb. *peace offerings that he sacrificed.*   8:64 [a]2 Chr 7:7 [b]2 Chr 4:1   8:65 [a]Lev 23:34; 1 Kgs 8:2 [b]Num 34:8; Josh 13:5; Judg 3:3; 2 Kgs 14:25 [c]2 Chr 7:8 [d]Gen 15:18; Exod 23:31; Num 34:5 [1]Or *the Wadi of Egypt.*   8:66 [a]2 Chr 7:9   9:1 [a]1 Kgs 7:1 [b]2 Chr 8:6   9:2 [a]1 Kgs 3:5; 11:9; 2 Chr 1:7   9:3 [a]2 Kgs 20:5; Ps 10:17 [b]1 Kgs 8:29 [c]Deut 11:12   9:4 [a]Gen 17:1 [b]1 Kgs 11:4, 6; 15:5 [c]1 Kgs 8:61   9:5 [a]2 Sam 7:12, 16; 1 Kgs 2:4; 6:12; 8:25; 1 Chr 22:10; Matt 1:6; 25:31   9:6 [a]2 Sam 7:14–16; 2 Chr 7:19–20; Ps 89:30

from me, fail to obey the regulations and rules I instructed you to keep, and decide to serve and worship other gods, [7]then I will remove Israel from [a]the land I have given them, I will abandon this temple I have consecrated with my presence, and [b]Israel will be mocked and ridiculed[1] among all the nations. [8]This temple will become a heap of ruins;[1] everyone who passes by it will be shocked and will hiss out their scorn, saying, 'Why did the LORD do [a]this to this land and this temple?' [9]Others will then answer, 'Because they abandoned the LORD their God, who led their ancestors out of Egypt. They embraced other gods whom they worshiped and served. That is why the LORD has brought all this [a]disaster down on them.'"

Foreign Affairs and Building Projects

[10]After 20 years, during which Solomon built the LORD's temple and the royal palace, [11]King Solomon gave King [a]Hiram of Tyre 20 towns in the region of Galilee, because Hiram had supplied Solomon with cedars, evergreens, and all the gold he wanted. [12]When Hiram went out from Tyre to inspect the towns Solomon had given him, he was not pleased with them. [13]Hiram asked, "Why did you give me these towns, my friend?"[1] He called that area the region of Cabul, [a]a name which it has retained to this day. [14]Hiram had sent to the king 120 talents[1] of gold.

[15]Here are [a]the details concerning the work crews King Solomon conscripted to build the LORD's temple, his palace, the [b]terrace, the wall of Jerusalem, and the cities of [c]Hazor, [d]Megiddo, and [e]Gezer. [16](Pharaoh, king of Egypt, [a]had attacked and captured Gezer. He burned it and killed the Canaanites who lived in the city. He gave it as a wedding present to his daughter, who had married Solomon.) [17]Solomon built up Gezer, lower Beth [a]Horon, [18a]Baalath, Tadmor in the wilderness, [19]all the storage cities that belonged to him, and the cities where

[a]chariots and [b]horses were kept. He built whatever he [c]wanted in Jerusalem, Lebanon, and throughout his entire kingdom. [20a]Now several non-Israelite peoples were left in the land after the conquest of Joshua, including the Amorites, Hittites, Perizzites, Hivites, and Jebusites. [21]Their descendants remained in the land (the Israelites were unable to wipe them out completely). Solomon conscripted them for his work [a]crews, and they continue in that role to this very day. [22]Solomon did not [a]assign Israelites to these work crews; the Israelites served as his soldiers, attendants, officers, charioteers, and commanders of his chariot forces. [23]These men were also in charge of Solomon's work projects; there were a total of [a]550 men who supervised the workers. [24]Solomon built the terrace as soon as [a]Pharaoh's daughter moved up from the City of David to the palace Solomon built for [b]her.

[25a]Three times a year Solomon offered burnt offerings and peace offerings[1] on the altar he had built for the LORD, burning incense along with them before the LORD. He made the temple his official worship place.

[26a]King Solomon also built ships in Ezion [b]Geber, which is located near Elat in the land of Edom, on the shore of the Red Sea. [27]Hiram sent his fleet and some of his sailors, who were well acquainted with [a]the sea, to serve with Solomon's men. [28]They sailed to [a]Ophir, took from there 420 talents[1] of gold, and then brought them to King Solomon.

Solomon Entertains a Queen

10 When the [a]queen of Sheba heard about Solomon,[1] she came [b]to challenge him with difficult questions. [2]She arrived in Jerusalem with a great display of pomp,[1] bringing with her camels carrying spices, a very large quantity of gold, and precious gems. She visited Solomon and discussed with him everything that was on her mind. [3]Solomon answered all her questions; there was no question too

---

9:7 [a] [Lev 18:24–29]; Deut 4:26; 2 Kgs 17:23; 25:21 [b] Deut 28:37; Ps 44:14; Jer 24:9 [1] Heb. *will become a proverb and a taunt.* 9:8 [a] 2 Chr 7:21 [1] Heb. *and this house will be high* [or *elevated*]. 9:9 [a] [Deut 29:25–28] 9:11 [a] 1 Kgs 5:1 9:13 [a] Josh 19:27 [1] Heb. *my brother.* 9:14 [1] About 9,000 pounds. 9:15 [a] 1 Kgs 5:13 [b] 2 Sam 5:9; 1 Kgs 9:24 [c] Josh 11:1; 19:36 [d] Josh 17:11 [e] Josh 16:10 9:16 [a] Josh 16:10; Judg 1:29 9:17 [a] Josh 10:10; 16:3; 21:22; 2 Chr 8:5 9:18 [a] Josh 19:44; 2 Chr 8:4 9:19 [a] 1 Kgs 10:26; 2 Chr 1:14 [b] 1 Kgs 4:26 [c] 1 Kgs 9:1 9:20 [a] 2 Chr 8:7 9:21 [a] Ezra 2:55, 58; Neh 7:57 9:22 [a] [Lev 25:39] 9:23 [a] 2 Chr 8:10 9:24 [a] 1 Kgs 3:1 [b] 1 Kgs 7:8 9:25 [a] Exod 23:14–17; Deut 16:16; 2 Chr 8:12–13 [1] Or *tokens of peace.* 9:26 [a] 2 Chr 8:17–18 [b] Num 33:35; Deut 2:8; 1 Kgs 22:48 9:27 [a] 1 Kgs 5:6, 9; 10:11 9:28 [a] Job 22:24 [1] About 31,500 pounds. 10:1 [a] 2 Chr 9:1; Matt 12:42; Luke 11:31 [b] Judg 14:12; Ps 49:4; Prov 1:6 [1] Heb. adds *to the name of the LORD.* 10:2 [1] Heb. *with very great strength.*

complex for the king. [4]When the queen of Sheba saw for herself Solomon's extensive wisdom, the palace he had built, [5]the food in his banquet hall, his servants [a]and attendants, their robes, his cupbearers, and his burnt offerings which he presented in the LORD's temple, she was amazed. [6]She said to the king, "The report I heard in my own country about your wise sayings and insight was true! [7]I did not believe these things until I came and saw them with my own eyes. Indeed, I didn't hear even half the story! Your wisdom and wealth surpass what was reported to me. [8]Your attendants, who stand before you at all times and hear your wise sayings, are truly [a]happy! [9]May the LORD your God be [a]praised because he [b]favored you by placing you on the throne of Israel! Because of the LORD's eternal love for Israel, he made you king so you could make just and right decisions." [10]She [a]gave the king 120 talents[1] of gold, a very large quantity of spices, and precious gems. The quantity of spices the queen of Sheba gave King Solomon has never been matched. [11](Hiram's fleet, which carried gold from Ophir, [a]also brought from Ophir a very large quantity of fine timber and precious gems. [12]With the timber the king made supports for the LORD's temple [a]and for the royal palace and stringed instruments for the musicians. No one has seen so much of this [b]fine timber to this very day.) [13]King Solomon gave the queen of Sheba everything she requested, besides what he had freely offered her. Then she left and returned to her homeland with her attendants.

Solomon's Wealth

[14]Solomon received 666 talents[1] of gold per year, [15]besides what he collected [a]from the merchants, traders, Arabian kings, and governors of the land. [16]King Solomon made 200 large shields of hammered gold; 600 measures of gold were used for each shield. [17]He also made 300 small shields of hammered gold; [a]three minas of gold were used for each of these shields. The king placed them in the [b]Palace of the Lebanon Forest.

[18a]The king made a large throne decorated with ivory and overlaid it with pure gold. [19]There were six steps leading up to the throne, and the back of it was rounded on top. The throne had two armrests with a statue of a lion standing on each side. [20]There were 12 statues of lions on the six steps, one lion at each end of each step. There was nothing like it in any other kingdom.

[21]All of King Solomon's cups were made of gold, and [a]all the household items in the Palace of the Lebanon Forest were made of pure gold. There were no silver items, for silver was not considered very valuable in Solomon's time. [22]Along with Hiram's fleet, the king had a fleet of large [a]merchant ships[1] that sailed the sea. Once every three years the [b]fleet came into port with cargoes of gold, silver, ivory, apes, and peacocks.

[23a]King Solomon was wealthier and wiser than any of the kings of the earth. [24]Everyone[1] in the world wanted to visit Solomon to see him display his God-given wisdom. [25]Year after year visitors brought their gifts, which included items of silver, items of gold, clothes, perfume, spices, horses, and mules.

[26]Solomon accumulated chariots [a]and horses. [b]He had 1,400 chariots and 12,000 horses. He kept them in assigned cities and in Jerusalem. [27]The king made silver as plentiful in Jerusalem as stones; cedar was as plentiful as sycamore fig trees are in [a]the foothills. [28a]Solomon acquired his horses from Egypt and from Que; the king's traders purchased them from Que. [29]They paid 600 silver pieces for each chariot from Egypt [a]and 150 silver pieces for each horse. They also sold chariots and horses to all the kings of the Hittites and to the kings of Syria.

The Lord Punishes Solomon for Idolatry

11 [a]King Solomon fell in love with [b]many foreign women (besides Pharaoh's daughter), including Moabites, Ammonites, Edomites, Sidonians, and Hittites. [2]They

10:5 [a]1 Chr 26:16; 2 Chr 9:4   10:8 [a]Prov 8:34   10:9 [a]1 Kgs 5:7   [b]2 Sam 22:20   10:10 [a]Ps 72:10, 15   [1]About 9,000 pounds.   10:11 [a]1 Kgs 9:27–28; Job 22:24   10:12 [a]2 Chr 9:11   [b]2 Chr 9:10   10:14 [1]About 50,000 pounds.   10:15 [a]2 Chr 9:24; Ps 72:10   10:17 [a]1 Kgs 14:26   [b]1 Kgs 7:2   10:18 [a]1 Kgs 10:22; 2 Chr 9:17; Ps 45:8   10:21 [a]2 Chr 9:20   10:22 [a]Gen 10:4; 2 Chr 20:36   [b]1 Kgs 9:26–28; 22:48; Ps 72:10   [1]Heb. *a fleet of Tarshish* [ships]; probably large ships either made in or capable of traveling to the distant western port of Tarshish.   10:23 [a]1 Kgs 3:12–13; 4:30; 2 Chr 1:12   10:24 [1]A few wss *all the kings of the earth*.   10:26 [a]1 Kgs 4:26; 2 Chr 1:14; 9:25   [b][Deut 17:16]; 1 Kgs 9:19   10:27 [a][Deut 17:17]; 2 Chr 1:15–17   10:28 [a][Deut 17:16]; 2 Chr 1:16; 9:28   10:29 [a]Josh 1:4; 2 Kgs 7:6–7   11:1 [a][Neh 13:26]   [b][Deut 17:17]; 1 Kgs 3:1

came from nations about which the LORD had warned the Israelites, "ᵃYou must not establish friendly relations with them! If you do, they will surely shift your allegiance to their gods." But Solomon was irresistibly attracted to them.¹

3 He had 700 royal wives and 300 concubines; his wives had a powerful influence over him. 4 When Solomon became old, his wives shifted his ᵃallegiance to other gods; he ᵇwas not wholeheartedly devoted to the LORD his God, as his father David had been. 5 Solomon worshiped the Sidonian goddess ᵃAstarte and the detestable ᵇAmmonite god ᶜMilcom. 6 Solomon did evil in the LORD's sight; he did not remain loyal to¹ the LORD, as his father David had. 7 Furthermore, on ᵃthe hill east of Jerusalem Solomon built a high place for the detestable Moabite god ᵇChemosh and for ᶜthe detestable Ammonite god Milcom.¹ 8 He built high places for all his foreign wives so they could burn incense and make sacrifices to their gods.

9 The LORD was angry with Solomon because he had shifted his allegiance away from the LORD, the God of Israel, ᵃwho had appeared to him on two occasions 10 and ᵃhad warned him about this very thing, so that he would not follow other gods. But he did not obey the LORD's command. 11 So the LORD ᵃsaid to Solomon, "Because you insist on doing these things and have not kept the covenantal rules I gave you, I will surely tear the kingdom away from you and give it to your ᵇservant. 12 However, for your father David's sake I will not do this while you are alive. I will tear it away from your son's hand instead. 13ᵃBut I will not tear away the entire kingdom; I will leave your son ᵇone tribe ᶜfor my servant David's sake and for the sake of my chosen city Jerusalem."

14 The LORD brought against Solomon an enemy, Hadad the Edomite, ᵃa descendant of the Edomite king. 15ᵃDuring David's campaign against Edom, Joab, the commander of the army, while on ᵇa mission to bury the dead, killed every male in Edom. 16 For Joab and the entire Israelite army stayed there six months until they had exterminated every male in Edom. 17 Hadad,¹ who was only a small boy at the time, escaped with some of his father's Edomite servants and headed for Egypt. 18 They went from Midian to Paran; they took some men from Paran and went to Egypt. Pharaoh, king of Egypt, gave him a house and some land and supplied him with food. 19 Pharaoh liked Hadad so well he gave him his sister-in-law (Queen Tahpenes' sister) as a wife. 20 Tahpenes' sister gave birth to his son, named Genubath. Tahpenes raised¹ him in Pharaoh's palace; Genubath grew up in Pharaoh's palace among Pharaoh's sons. 21 While in Egypt Hadad heard that David had passed away and that Joab, the commander of the army, was dead. ᵃSo Hadad asked Pharaoh, "Give me permission to leave so I can return to my homeland." 22 Pharaoh said to him, "What do you lack here that makes you want to go to your homeland?" Hadad replied, "Nothing, but please give me permission to leave."

23 God also brought against Solomon another enemy, Rezon son of Eliada who had run away from his master, King ᵃHadadezer of Zobah. 24 He gathered some men and organized a raiding band. ᵃWhen David tried to kill them, they went to Damascus, where they settled down and gained control of the city. 25 He was Israel's enemy throughout Solomon's reign and, like Hadad, caused trouble. He loathed Israel and ruled over Syria.

26ᵃJeroboam son of Nebat, one of Solomon's servants, ᵇrebelled against the king. He was an Ephraimite¹ from Zeredah whose mother was a widow named Zeruah. 27 This is what prompted him to rebel against the king: ᵃSolomon built a terrace, and he closed up a gap in the wall of the city of his father David. 28 Jeroboam was a talented man; when Solomon saw that the young man was an accomplished worker, he made him the leader of the work crew from the tribe of Joseph. 29 At that time, when Jeroboam had left Jerusalem, the prophet ᵃAhijah the Shilonite met him on the road; the two of them were alone in the open country. Ahijah was wearing a brand new robe, 30 and he grabbed the robe and ᵃtore it into 12 pieces.

11:2 ᵃ Exod 34:16; [Deut 7:3–4] ¹ Heb. *Solomon clung to them for love.*   11:4 ᵃ 1 Kgs 8:61 ᵇ 1 Kgs 9:4   11:5 ᵃ Judg 2:13; 1 Kgs 11:33 ᵇ 2 Kgs 23:13 ᶜ [Lev 20:2–5]   11:6 ¹ Heb. *he did not fill up after.*   11:7 ᵃ Num 33:52 ᵇ Num 21:29; Judg 11:24 ᶜ 2 Kgs 23:13 ¹ MT *Molech.*   11:9 ᵃ 1 Kgs 3:5; 9:2   11:10 ᵃ 1 Kgs 6:12; 9:6–7   11:11 ᵃ 1 Kgs 11:31; 12:15–16 ᵇ 1 Kgs 11:31, 37   11:13 ᵃ 2 Sam 7:15; 1 Chr 17:13; Ps 89:33 ᵇ 1 Kgs 12:20 ᶜ 2 Sam 7:15–16   11:14 ᵃ 1 Chr 5:26   11:15 ᵃ 2 Sam 8:14; 1 Chr 18:12–13 ᵇ Num 24:18–19; [Deut 20:13]   11:17 ¹ Heb. *Adad.*   11:20 ¹ Heb. *weaned him.*   11:21 ᵃ 1 Kgs 2:10, 34   11:23 ᵃ 2 Sam 8:3; 10:16   11:24 ᵃ 2 Sam 8:3; 10:8, 18   11:26 ᵃ 1 Kgs 12:2 ᵇ 2 Sam 20:21 ¹ Heb. *Ephrathite.*   11:27 ᵃ 1 Kgs 9:15, 24   11:29 ᵃ 1 Kgs 12:15; 14:2; 2 Chr 9:29   11:30 ᵃ 1 Sam 15:27–28; 24:5

[31]Then he told Jeroboam, "Take 10 pieces, for this is what the LORD God of Israel has said: 'Look, I am about to tear the kingdom from Solomon's hand and I will give 10 tribes to you. [32]He will retain one tribe, for my servant David's sake and for the sake of Jerusalem, the city I have chosen out of all the tribes of Israel. [33]I am taking the kingdom from him [a]because they have[1] abandoned me and worshiped the Sidonian goddess Astarte, the Moabite god Chemosh, and the Ammonite god Milcom. They have not followed my instructions by doing what I approve and obeying my rules and regulations, as Solomon's father David did. [34]I will not take the whole kingdom from his hand. I will allow him to be ruler for the rest of his life for the sake of my chosen servant David who kept my commandments and rules. [35]I [a]will take the kingdom from the hand of his son and give 10 tribes to you. [36]I will leave his son one tribe so [a]my servant David's dynasty may continue to serve me[1] in Jerusalem, the city I have chosen as my home. [37]I will select you; you will rule over all you desire to have and you will be king over Israel. [38]You must obey[1] all [a]I command you to do, follow my instructions, do what I approve, and keep my rules and commandments, as my servant David did. Then I will be with you and [b]establish for you a lasting dynasty, as I did for David; I will give you Israel. [39]I will humiliate David's descendants because of this, but not forever.'" [40]Solomon tried to kill Jeroboam, but Jeroboam escaped to Egypt and found refuge with King [a]Shishak of Egypt. He stayed in Egypt until Solomon died.

Solomon's Reign Ends

[41]The rest of [a]the events of Solomon's reign, including all his accomplishments and his wise decisions, are recorded in the scroll called the Annals of Solomon. [42a]Solomon ruled over all Israel from Jerusalem for 40 years. [43]Then Solomon passed away and was buried in [a]the city of his father David. His son Rehoboam [b]replaced him as king.[1]

Rehoboam Loses His Kingdom

12 [a]Rehoboam traveled to [b]Shechem, for all Israel had gathered in Shechem to make Rehoboam king. [2]When [a]Jeroboam son of Nebat heard the news, he was still in [b]Egypt, where he had fled from King Solomon and had been living ever since.[2] [3]They sent for him, and Jeroboam and the whole Israelite assembly came and spoke to Rehoboam, saying, [4]"Your father made us [a]work too hard. Now if you lighten the demands he made and don't make us work as hard, we will serve you." [5]He said to them, "Go away for three days, then return to me." So the people went away.

[6]King Rehoboam consulted with the older advisers who had served his father Solomon when he had been alive. He asked them, "How do you advise me to answer these people?" [7]They said to him, "Today [a]if you will be a servant to these people and grant their request, speaking kind words to them, they will be your servants from this time forward."[1] [8]But Rehoboam rejected their advice and consulted the young advisers who served him, with whom he had grown up. [9]He asked them, "How do you advise me to respond to these people who said to me, 'Lessen the demands your father placed on us'?" [10]The young advisers with whom Rehoboam had grown up said to him, "Say this to these people who have said to you, 'Your father made us work hard, but now lighten our burden.' Say this to them: 'I am a lot harsher than my father![1] [11]My father imposed heavy demands on you; I will make them even heavier. My father punished you with ordinary whips; I will punish you with whips that really sting your flesh.'"[1]

[12]Jeroboam and all the people reported to Rehoboam on the third day, just as the king had ordered when he said, "Return to me on the third day." [13]The king responded to the people harshly. He rejected the advice of the older men [14]and followed the advice of the younger ones. He said, "My father imposed heavy demands on you; I

11:33 [a]1 Sam 7:3; 1 Kgs 11:5–8 [1]LXX, Syr., Vg. *he has.* 11:35 [a]1 Kgs 12:16–17 11:36 [a][1 Kgs 15:4; 2 Kgs 8:19] [1]Heb. *so there might be a lamp for David my servant all the days before me in Jerusalem.* 11:38 [a]Deut 31:8; Josh 1:5 [b]2 Sam 7:11, 27 [1]Heb. *If you obey.* 11:40 [a]1 Kgs 11:17; 14:25; 2 Chr 12:2–9 11:41 [a]2 Chr 9:29 11:42 [a]2 Chr 9:30 11:43 [a]1 Kgs 2:10; 2 Chr 9:31 [b]1 Kgs 14:21; 2 Chr 10:1 [1]One ws inserts *And it so happened that when Jeroboam son of Nebat heard—now he was in Egypt where he had fled from before Solomon and was residing in Egypt—he came straight to his city in the land of Sarira which is on mount Ephraim. And king Solomon slept with his fathers* before this sentence. 12:1 [a]2 Chr 10:1 [b]Judg 9:6 12:2 [a]1 Kgs 11:26 [b]1 Kgs 11:40 [1]One ws omits v. 2. [2]Heb. *and Jeroboam lived in Egypt.* 12:4 [a]1 Sam 8:11–18; 1 Kgs 4:7; 5:13–15 12:7 [a]2 Chr 10:7; [Prov 15:1] [1]Heb. *all the days.* 12:10 [1]Heb. *My little one is thicker than my father's hips; i.e., the little finger.* 12:11 [1]Heb. *I will punish you with scorpions; perhaps a torture using poisonous insects, but more likely a type of whip.*

will make them even heavier. My father punished you with ordinary whips; I will punish you with whips that really sting your flesh." [15] The king refused to listen to [a] the people, because the LORD was instigating this turn of events so that he might bring to pass the prophetic announcement he had made through Ahijah the Shilonite to Jeroboam son of Nebat.

[16] When all Israel saw that the king refused to listen to them, the people answered the king, "We have no portion in David, no share in the son of Jesse! Return to your homes, O Israel! Now, look after your own dynasty, O David!" So Israel returned to their homes. [17] (Rehoboam continued to rule over [a] the Israelites who lived in the cities of Judah.) [18] King Rehoboam [a] sent Adoniram,[1] the supervisor of the work crews, out after them, but all Israel stoned him to death. King Rehoboam managed to jump into his chariot and escape to Jerusalem. [19] So [a] Israel has been in rebellion against the Davidic dynasty to this very day. [20] When all [a] Israel heard that Jeroboam had returned, they summoned him to the assembly and made him king over all Israel. No one except the tribe of Judah remained loyal to the Davidic dynasty.

[21] When [a] Rehoboam arrived in Jerusalem, he summoned 180,000 skilled warriors from all Judah and the tribe of [b] Benjamin to attack Israel and restore the kingdom to Rehoboam son of Solomon. [22] But God told Shemaiah [a] the prophet, [23] "Say this to King Rehoboam son of Solomon of Judah, and to all Judah and Benjamin, as well as the rest of the people, [24] 'This is what the LORD has said: "Do not attack and make war with your brothers, the Israelites. Each of you go home. Indeed this thing has happened because of me."'" So they obeyed the LORD's message. They went home in keeping with the LORD's message.

Jeroboam Makes Golden Calves

[25] Jeroboam built [a] up Shechem in the Ephraimite hill country and lived there. From there he went out and built up [b] Penuel. [26] Jeroboam then thought to himself: "Now the Davidic dynasty could regain the kingdom. [27] If these people [a] go up to offer sacrifices in the LORD's temple in Jerusalem, their loyalty could shift to their former master, King Rehoboam of Judah. They might kill me and return to King Rehoboam of Judah." [28] After the king had consulted with his advisers, he [a] made two golden calves. Then [b] he said to the people, "It is too much trouble for you to go up to Jerusalem. Look, Israel, here are your gods who brought you up from the land of Egypt." [29] He put one in [a] Bethel and the other in [b] Dan. [30] This [a] caused Israel to sin; the people went to Bethel and Dan to worship the calves.[1]

[31] He built temples on the high places [a] and appointed as priests common people who were not Levites. [32] Jeroboam inaugurated a festival on [a] the fifteenth day of the eighth month, like the festival celebrated in Judah. On the altar in Bethel he offered sacrifices to the calves he had made. In Bethel he also appointed priests for the high places he had made.

A Prophet from Judah Visits Bethel

[33] On the fifteenth day of the eighth month (a date he had arbitrarily [a] chosen) Jeroboam offered sacrifices on the altar he had made in Bethel. He inaugurated a festival for the Israelites and went up to the altar to offer sacrifices. [1] Just then [a] a prophet arrived from Judah with the LORD's message for Bethel, as Jeroboam was [b] standing near the altar ready to offer a sacrifice. [2] He cried out against the altar with the LORD's message, "O altar, altar! This is what the LORD has said, 'Look, a son named [a] Josiah will be born to the Davidic dynasty. He will sacrifice on you the priests of the high places who offer sacrifices on you. Human bones will be [b] burned on you.'" [3] That [a] day he had also given a sign, saying, "This is the sign that the LORD has declared: The altar will split open and the ashes[1] on it will pour out." [4] When the king heard the

12:15 [a] Deut 2:30; Judg 14:4; 1 Kgs 12:24; 2 Chr 10:15   12:17 [a] 1 Kgs 11:13, 36; 2 Chr 11:14–17   12:18 [a] 1 Kgs 4:6; 5:14   [1] MT *Adoram.*
12:19 [a] 2 Kgs 17:21   12:20 [a] 2 Kgs 17:21   12:21 [a] 2 Chr 11:1–4   [b] 2 Sam 19:17   12:22 [a] 2 Chr 11:2; 12:5–7   12:25 [a] Gen 12:6; Judg
9:45–49; 1 Kgs 12:1   [b] Gen 32:30–31; Judg 8:8, 17   [1] One ws adds 23 vv. here.   12:27 [a] [Deut 12:5–7, 14]   12:28 [a] 2 Kgs 10:29;
17:16; [Hos 8:4–7]   [b] Exod 32:4, 8   12:29 [a] Gen 28:19   [b] Judg 18:26–31   12:30 [a] 1 Kgs 13:34; 2 Kgs 17:21   [1] MT *and the people
went before the one to Dan.*   12:31 [a] [Num 3:10; 17:1–11]; Judg 17:5; 1 Kgs 13:33; 2 Kgs 17:32; 2 Chr 11:14–15   12:32 [a] Lev
23:33–34; Num 29:12; 1 Kgs 8:2, 5   12:33 [a] Num 15:39   13:1 [a] 2 Kgs 23:17   [b] 1 Kgs 12:32–33   13:2 [a] 2 Kgs 23:15–16
[b] [Lev 26:30]   13:3 [a] Exod 4:1–5; Judg 6:17; Isa 7:14; 38:7; John 2:18; 1 Cor 1:22   [1] Heb. *the fat;* i.e.,
fat mixed with ashes from the altar.

prophet's message that he had cried out against the altar in Bethel, Jeroboam took his hand from the altar and pointed it saying, "Seize him!" Then the hand that he had pointed at him stiffened up, and he could not pull it back. [5]Meanwhile the altar split open, and the ashes[1] poured from the altar in fulfillment of the sign the prophet had given with the LORD's message. [6]The king responded to the prophet, "[a]Seek the favor of the LORD your God and pray for me, so that my hand may be restored." So the prophet sought the LORD's favor and the king's hand was restored as it was at first. [7]The [a]king then said to the prophet, "Come home with me and have something to eat, so that I may give you a gift." [8]But the prophet said to the king, "Even [a]if you were to give me half your possessions, I would not go with you. I am not allowed to eat food or drink water in this place. [9]For this is how I was commanded in the LORD's message, 'Eat no food. Drink no water. And do not return by the way [a]you came.'" [10]So he started back on another road; he did not travel back on the same road he had taken to Bethel.

[11]Now there was an [a]old prophet living in Bethel. When his sons[1] came home, they told him everything the prophet had done in Bethel that day. And they told their father all the words that he had spoken to the king. [12]Their father asked them, "Which road did he take?" His sons showed him[1] the road the prophet from Judah had taken. [13]He then told his sons, "Saddle the donkey for me." When they had saddled the donkey for him, he mounted it [14]and took off after the prophet, whom he found sitting under an oak tree. He asked him, "Are you the prophet from Judah?" He answered, "Yes, I am." [15]He then said to him, "Come home with me and eat something." [16]But he [a]replied, "I can't go back with you. I am not allowed to eat food or to drink water with you in this place. [17]For an order came to me in the LORD's message, 'Eat no food. Drink no water there. And do not return [a]by the way you came.'" [18]Then the old prophet said, "I too am a prophet like you. And an angel has told me in a message from the LORD, 'Bring him back with you to your house so he can eat food and drink water.'" But he had lied to him. [19]So the prophet went back with him. He ate food in his house and he drank water.

[20]While they were sitting at the table, the LORD's message came to the old prophet who had brought him back. [21]So he cried out to the prophet who had come from Judah, "This is what the LORD has said, 'You have rebelled against the LORD's instruction and have not obeyed the command the LORD your God gave you. [22]You went back. You ate food. And you drank water in the [a]place of which he had said to you, "Eat no food. Drink no water." Therefore your corpse will not be buried in your ancestral tomb.'"

[23]So this is what happened after he had eaten food and drunk water. The old prophet saddled the donkey for the prophet whom he had brought back. [24]So the prophet from [a]Judah travelled on. Then a lion attacked him on the road and killed him.

There was his body lying on the road, with the donkey standing next to it, and the lion just standing there by the body. [25]Then some men came passing by and saw the body lying in the road with the lion standing next to the body. They went and reported what they had seen in the city where the old prophet lived. [26]When the old prophet who had invited him to his house heard the news, he said, "It is the prophet who rebelled against the LORD. The LORD delivered him over to the lion and it tore him up and killed him, in keeping with the LORD's message that he had spoken to him." [27]He told his sons, "Saddle my donkey." So they saddled it. [28]He went and found the body lying in the road with the donkey and the lion standing beside it; the lion had neither eaten the body nor attacked the donkey. [29]The old prophet picked up the prophet's body, put it on the donkey, and brought it back. The old prophet then entered the city to mourn him and to bury him. [30]He put the body into his own tomb, and they mourned over him, saying, "[a]Ah, my brother!" [31]After he buried him, he said to his sons, "When I die, bury me in the tomb where the prophet is buried; put my bones right beside his bones, [32][a]because the message that he announced as the LORD's

13:5 [1]The fat mixed with ashes.   13:6 [a] Exod 8:8; 9:28; 10:17; Num 21:7; Jer 37:3; Acts 8:24; [Jas 5:16]   13:7 [a]1 Sam 9:7; 2 Kgs 5:15   13:8 [a] Num 22:18; 24:13; 1 Kgs 13:16–17   13:9 [a] [1 Cor 5:11]   13:11 [a]1 Kgs 13:25   [1]MT son.   13:12 [1]MT they saw.   13:16 [a]1 Kgs 13:8–9   13:17 [a]1 Kgs 20:35; 1 Thess 4:15   13:22 [a]1 Kgs 13:9   13:24 [a]1 Kgs 20:36   13:30 [a]Jer 22:18   13:32 [a]1 Kgs 13:2; 2 Kgs 23:16, 19

message against the altar in Bethel and against all the temples on the high places in the cities of the [b]north[1] will certainly be fulfilled."

A Prophet Announces the End of Jeroboam's Dynasty

[33a]After this happened, Jeroboam still did not change his evil ways; he continued to appoint common people as priests at the high places. Anyone who wanted the job he consecrated as a priest. [34]This sin caused Jeroboam's dynasty to come to [a]an end and [b]to be destroyed from the face of the earth.

14 [1]At that time Jeroboam's son Abijah became sick. [2]Jeroboam told [a]his wife, "Disguise yourself so that people cannot recognize you are Jeroboam's wife. Then go to Shiloh; Ahijah the prophet, who told me I would rule over this nation, lives there. [3]Take 10 loaves of bread, some small cakes, and [a]a container of honey and visit him. He will tell you what will happen to the boy."

[4]Jeroboam's wife did as she was told. She went to Shiloh [a]and visited Ahijah. Now Ahijah could not see; he had lost his eyesight in his old age. [5]But the LORD had told Ahijah, "Look, Jeroboam's wife is coming to find out from you what will happen to her son, for he is sick. Tell her such and such. When she comes, she will be in a disguise." [6]When Ahijah heard the sound of her footsteps as she came through the door, he said, "Come on in, wife of Jeroboam! Why are you pretending to be someone else? I have been commissioned to give you bad news. [7]Go, tell Jeroboam, 'This is what the LORD God of Israel has said: "I raised you up from among the people and made you ruler over my people Israel. [8]I [a]tore the kingdom away from the Davidic dynasty and gave it to you. But you are not like my servant David, [b]who kept my commandments and followed me wholeheartedly by doing only what I approve. [9]You have sinned more than all who came [a]before you. You went and angered me by making other gods, formed out of metal; you

[b]have completely disregarded me. [10]So [a]I am ready to bring disaster on the dynasty of Jeroboam. [b]I will cut off every last male belonging to Jeroboam in Israel, including even the [c]weak and incapacitated.[1] I will burn up the dynasty of Jeroboam, just as one burns manure until it is completely consumed. [11]Dogs will eat the members of your family [a]who die in the city, and the birds of the sky will eat the ones who die in the country.'" Indeed, the LORD has announced it!

[12]"As for you, get up and go home. [a]When you set foot in the city, the boy will die. [13]All Israel will mourn him and bury him. [a]He is the only one in Jeroboam's family who will receive a decent burial, for he is the only one in whom the LORD God of Israel found anything good. [14]The LORD will raise up a king [a]over Israel who will cut off Jeroboam's dynasty. It is ready to happen![1] [15]The LORD will attack Israel, making it like a reed that sways in the water.[1] He will [a]remove Israel from this [b]good land he gave to their ancestors and scatter them [c]beyond the Euphrates River, [d]because they angered the LORD by making Asherah poles.[2] [16]He will hand Israel over to their enemies because of the sins which Jeroboam committed and which he made Israel commit."

[17]So Jeroboam's wife got up and went back to [a]Tirzah. As she crossed the threshold of the house, the boy died. [18]All Israel buried him and mourned for him, [a]in keeping with the LORD's message that he had spoken through his servant, the prophet Ahijah.

Jeroboam's Reign Ends

[19]The rest of the events of Jeroboam's reign, including the details of his battles and rule, are recorded in the scroll called the Annals of the Kings of Israel. [20]Jeroboam ruled for 22 years; then he passed away. His son [a]Nadab replaced him as king.

Rehoboam's Reign over Judah

[21]Now [a]Rehoboam son of Solomon ruled in Judah. He was forty-one years old when

13:32 [b]1 Kgs 16:24; John 4:5; Acts 8:14   [1]Heb. *Samaria*.   13:33 [a]1 Kgs 12:31–32; 2 Chr 11:15; 13:9   13:34 [a]1 Kgs 12:30; 2 Kgs 17:21   [b][1 Kgs 14:10; 15:29–30]   14:1 [1]Some MSS omit vv. 1–20.   14:2 [a]1 Kgs 11:29–31   14:3 [a]1 Sam 9:7–8; 1 Kgs 13:7; 2 Kgs 4:42   14:4 [a]1 Kgs 11:29   14:8 [a]1 Kgs 11:31   [b]1 Kgs 11:33, 38; 15:5   14:9 [a]1 Kgs 12:28; 2 Chr 11:15   [b]2 Chr 29:6; Neh 9:26; Ps 50:17   14:10 [a]1 Kgs 15:29   [b]1 Kgs 21:21; 2 Kgs 9:8   [c]Deut 32:36; 2 Kgs 14:26   [1]Heb. *cut off from Jeroboam those who urinate against a wall* [including both those who are] *restrained and let free* [or *abandoned*] *in Israel*.   14:11 [a]1 Kgs 16:4; 21:24   14:12 [a]1 Kgs 14:17   14:13 [a]2 Chr 12:12; 19:3   14:14 [a]1 Kgs 15:27–29   [1]Heb. *This is the day. What also now?*; the meaning of the second sentence is uncertain.   14:15 [a]Deut 29:28; 2 Kgs 17:6; Ps 52:5   [b][Josh 23:15–16]   [c]2 Kgs 15:29   [d][Exod 34:13–14; Deut 12:3]   [1]Heb. *and the LORD will strike Israel as a reed sways in the water.*   [2]Or *their images of Asherah*.   14:17 [a]1 Kgs 15:21, 33; 16:6, 8, 15, 23; Song 6:4   14:18 [a]1 Kgs 14:13   14:20 [a]1 Kgs 15:25   14:21 [a]2 Chr 12:13

he became king, and he ruled for 17 years in Jerusalem, the city the LORD chose from all the tribes of Israel to be [b]his home. His mother was an Ammonite woman named Naamah.

[22][a]Judah did evil in the sight of the LORD. They made him more jealous by their sins than their ancestors had done. [23]They even built for themselves [a]high places, [b]sacred pillars, and Asherah [c]poles on every high hill and [d]under every green tree. [24]There were also male cultic prostitutes[1] in the [a]land. They committed the same horrible [b]sins as the nations that the LORD had driven out from before the [c]Israelites.

[25][a]In King Rehoboam's fifth year, King Shishak of Egypt attacked Jerusalem. [26]He took away the treasures of the LORD's temple [a]and of the royal palace; he took everything, including all the golden shields that Solomon had made. [27]King Rehoboam made bronze shields to replace them and assigned them to the officers of the royal guard who protected the entrance to the royal palace. [28]Whenever the king visited the LORD's temple, the royal guard carried them and then brought them back to the guardroom.

[29][a]The rest of the events of Rehoboam's reign, including his accomplishments, are recorded in the scroll called the Annals of the Kings of Judah. [30]Rehoboam and Jeroboam were continually at [a]war with each other. [31]Rehoboam passed away and was buried with his ancestors in the City of David. His [a]son [b]Abijah replaced him as king.

Abijah's Reign over Judah

15 In the eighteenth year of the reign of Jeroboam son of Nebat, Abijah[1] became [a]king over Judah. [2]He ruled for three years in Jerusalem. [a]His mother was [b]Maacah, the daughter of [c]Abishalom. [3]He followed all the sinful practices of [a]his father before him. He was not wholeheartedly devoted to the LORD his God, as his ancestor David had been. [4]Nevertheless [a]for David's sake the LORD his God maintained his dynasty in Jerusalem by giving him a son[1] to succeed him and by protecting Jerusalem. [5]He did this because David had [a]done what he approved and had not disregarded any of his commandments his entire lifetime, [b]except for the incident involving Uriah the Hittite. [6]Rehoboam[1] [a]and Jeroboam were continually at war with each other throughout Abijah's lifetime. [7][a]The rest of the events of Abijah's reign, including all his accomplishments, are recorded in the scroll called the Annals of the Kings of Judah. Abijah and Jeroboam had been at war with each other. [8]Abijah passed away and was buried in the City of David. His [a]son Asa replaced him as king.

Asa's Reign over Judah

[9]In the twentieth year of Jeroboam's reign over Israel, Asa became the king of Judah. [10]He ruled for 41 years in Jerusalem. His grandmother was Maacah daughter of Abishalom. [11][a]Asa did what the LORD approved as his ancestor David had done. [12]He removed the male cultic prostitutes from the [a]land and got rid of all the disgusting idols his ancestors had made. [13]He also removed [a]Maacah his grandmother from her position as queen mother because she had made a loathsome Asherah pole. Asa cut down her loathsome pole and [b]burned it in the Kidron Valley. [14][a]The high places were not eliminated, yet Asa was wholeheartedly [b]devoted to the LORD throughout his lifetime. [15]He brought the holy items that he and his father [a]had made into the LORD's temple, including the silver, gold, and other articles.

[16]Now Asa and King Baasha of Israel were continually at war with each other. [17]King [a]Baasha of Israel attacked Judah and established [b]Ramah as [c]a military outpost to prevent anyone from leaving or entering the land of King Asa of Judah. [18]Asa took all the silver and gold that was left in the treasuries

14:21 [b]1 Kgs 14:31   14:22 [a]2 Chr 12:1, 14   14:23 [a]Deut 12:2; Ezek 16:24–25   [b][Deut 16:22]   [c][2 Kgs 17:9–10]   [d]Isa 57:5; Jer 2:20   14:24 [a]Gen 19:5; Deut 23:17; 1 Kgs 15:12; 22:46; 2 Kgs 23:7   [b]Deut 20:18   [c][Deut 9:4–5]   [1]One ws *a conspiracy*.   14:25 [a]1 Kgs 11:40; 2 Chr 12:2   14:26 [a]1 Kgs 15:18; 2 Chr 12:9–11   14:29 [a]2 Chr 12:15–16   14:30 [a]1 Kgs 12:21–24; 15:6   14:31 [a]2 Chr 12:16   [b]2 Chr 12:16   15:1 [a]2 Chr 13:1   [1]One ws adds *the son of Rehoboam*.   15:2 [a]2 Chr 11:20–22   [b]2 Chr 13:2   [c]2 Chr 11:21   15:3 [a]1 Kgs 11:4; Ps 119:80   15:4 [a]2 Sam 21:17; 1 Kgs 11:32, 36; 2 Chr 21:7   [1]One ws *sons*.   15:5 [a]1 Kgs 9:4; 14:8; Luke 1:6   [b]2 Sam 11:3, 15–17; 12:9–10   15:6 [a]1 Kgs 14:30; 2 Chr 12:15–13:20   [1]A few mss *Abijam*.   15:7 [a]2 Chr 13:2–22   15:8 [a]2 Chr 14:1   15:11 [a]2 Chr 14:2   15:12 [a]Deut 23:17; 1 Kgs 14:24; 22:46   15:13 [a]2 Chr 15:16–18   [b]Exod 32:20   15:14 [a]1 Kgs 3:2; 22:43; 2 Kgs 12:3; 2 Chr 15:17–18   [b][1 Sam 16:7]; 1 Kgs 8:61; 15:3   15:15 [a]1 Kgs 7:51   15:17 [a]2 Chr 16:1–6   [b]Josh 18:25; 1 Kgs 15:21–22   [c]1 Kgs 12:26–29

of the LORD's temple and of the royal palace and handed it to his servants. He then told them to deliver it to Ben [a]Hadad son of Tabrimmon, the son of Hezion, king of Syria, ruler in [b]Damascus, along with this message: [19]"I want to make a treaty with you, like the one our fathers made. See, I have sent you silver and gold as a present. Break your treaty with King Baasha of Israel, so he will retreat from my land." [20]Ben Hadad accepted King Asa's offer and [a]ordered his army commanders to attack the cities of Israel. They conquered [b]Ijon, [c]Dan, [d]Abel Beth Maacah, and all the territory of Naphtali, including the region of Kinnereth. [21]When Baasha heard the news, he stopped fortifying Ramah and settled down in [a]Tirzah. [22]King Asa ordered all [a]the men of Judah (no exemptions were granted) to carry away the stones and wood that Baasha had used to build Ramah. King Asa used the materials to build up [b]Geba (in Benjamin) and [c]Mizpah.

[23]The rest of the events of Asa's reign, [a]including all his successes and accomplishments, as well as a record of the cities he built, are recorded in the scroll called the Annals of the Kings of Judah. Yet when he was very old he developed a foot disease. [24]Asa passed away and was buried with his ancestors in [a]the city of his ancestor David. His son [b]Jehoshaphat replaced him as king.

Nadab's Reign over Israel

[25]In the second year of Asa's reign over Judah, Jeroboam's son [a]Nadab became the king of Israel; he ruled Israel for two years. [26]He did evil in the sight of the LORD. He followed in [a]his father's footsteps and encouraged Israel to sin.

[27]Baasha son of Ahijah, from [a]the tribe of Issachar, conspired against Nadab and assassinated him in [b]Gibbethon, which was in Philistine territory. This happened while Nadab and all the Israelite army were besieging Gibbethon. [28]Baasha killed him in the third year of Asa's reign over Judah and replaced him as king. [29]When [a]he became king, he executed Jeroboam's entire family. He wiped out everyone who breathed, in keeping with the LORD's message that he had spoken through his servant Ahijah the Shilonite. [30]This happened [a]because of the sins which Jeroboam committed and which he made Israel commit. These sins angered the LORD God of Israel.

[31]The rest of the events of Nadab's reign, including all his accomplishments, are recorded in the scroll called the Annals of the Kings of Israel. [32]Asa [a]and King Baasha of Israel were continually at war with each other.

Baasha's Reign over Israel

[33]In the third year of Asa's reign over Judah, Baasha son of Ahijah became king over all Israel in Tirzah; he ruled for 24 years. [34]He did evil in [a]the sight of the LORD; he followed in Jeroboam's footsteps and encouraged Israel to sin.

16 The LORD's message against [a]Baasha came to[1] [b]Jehu son of [c]Hanani: [2]"I raised you up from the dust and made you ruler over my people Israel. Yet you followed [a]in Jeroboam's footsteps and encouraged my people Israel to sin; their sins have made me angry. [3]So I am ready to burn up[1] Baasha and his family, and make your family[2] like [a]the family of Jeroboam son of Nebat. [4]Dogs will eat the members of Baasha's family [a]who die in the city, and the birds of the sky will eat the ones who die in the country."

[5]The rest of the events of Baasha's reign, including his accomplishments and successes, [a]are recorded in the scroll called the Annals of the Kings of Israel. [6]Baasha passed away and was buried in [a]Tirzah. His son Elah replaced him as king. [7]And so it was the LORD's message came through the prophet [a]Jehu son of Hanani against Baasha and his family. This was because of all [b]the evil he had done in the LORD's view, by angering him with his deeds and becoming like Jeroboam's dynasty, and because of how he had destroyed Jeroboam's dynasty.

Elah's Reign over Israel

[8]In the twenty-sixth year of Asa's reign over Judah, Baasha's son Elah became king

15:18 [a] 2 Kgs 12:17–18; 2 Chr 16:2 [b] Gen 14:15; 1 Kgs 11:23–24 **15:20** [a] 1 Kgs 20:1 [b] 2 Kgs 15:29 [c] Judg 18:29; 1 Kgs 12:29 [d] 2 Sam 20:14–15 **15:21** [a] 1 Kgs 14:17; 16:15–18 **15:22** [a] 2 Chr 16:6 [b] Josh 21:17 [c] Josh 18:26 **15:23** [a] 2 Chr 16:11–14 **15:24** [a] 2 Chr 17:1 [b] 1 Kgs 22:41–44; Matt 1:8 **15:25** [a] 1 Kgs 14:20 **15:26** [a] 1 Kgs 12:28–33; 14:16 **15:27** [a] 1 Kgs 14:14 [b] Josh 19:44; 21:23; 1 Kgs 16:15 **15:29** [a] 1 Kgs 14:10–14 **15:30** [a] 1 Kgs 14:9, 16 **15:32** [a] 1 Kgs 15:16 **15:34** [a] 1 Kgs 13:33; 14:16 **16:1** [a] 1 Kgs 15:27 [b] 1 Kgs 16:7; 2 Chr 19:2; 20:34 [c] 2 Chr 16:7–10 [1] LXX *by the hand of.* **16:2** [a] 1 Sam 2:8; 1 Kgs 14:7 **16:3** [a] 1 Kgs 14:10; 15:29 [1] Or possibly *I am ready to sweep away Baasha and his family.* [2] Some wss *his house.* **16:4** [a] 1 Kgs 14:11; 21:24 **16:5** [a] 2 Chr 16:11 **16:6** [a] 1 Kgs 14:17; 15:21 **16:7** [a] 1 Kgs 16:1 [b] 1 Kgs 15:27, 29

over Israel; he ruled in Tirzah for two years. [9a]His servant Zimri, [b]a commander of half of his chariot force, conspired against him. While Elah was in Tirzah drinking heavily at the house of Arza, who supervised the palace in Tirzah, [10]Zimri came in and struck him dead. (This happened in the twenty-seventh year of Asa's reign over Judah.) Zimri replaced Elah as king. [11]When he became king and occupied the throne, he killed Baasha's entire family. He [a]did not spare any male belonging to him; he killed his relatives and his friends. [12]Zimri destroyed Baasha's entire family, [a]in keeping with the LORD's message which he had spoken against Baasha through Jehu the prophet. [13]This happened because of all the sins which Baasha and his son Elah committed and which they made Israel commit. They angered the LORD God of Israel [a]with their worthless idols.

[14]The rest of the events of Elah's reign, including all his accomplishments, are recorded in the scroll called the Annals of the Kings of Israel.

Zimri's Reign over Israel

[15]In the twenty-seventh year of Asa's reign over Judah, Zimri became king over Israel; he ruled for seven days [a]in Tirzah. Zimri's revolt took place while the army was deployed in Gibbethon, which was in Philistine territory. [16]While deployed there, the army received this report: "Zimri has conspired against the king and assassinated him." So all Israel made Omri, the commander of the army, king over Israel that very day in the camp. [17]Omri and all Israel went up from Gibbethon and besieged Tirzah. [18]When Zimri saw that the city was captured, he went into the fortified area of the royal palace. He set the palace on fire and died in the flames. [19]This happened because of the [a]sins he committed. He did evil in the sight of the LORD and followed in Jeroboam's [b]footsteps and encouraged Israel to continue sinning.

[20]The rest of the events of Zimri's reign, including the details of his revolt, are recorded in the scroll called the Annals of the Kings of Israel.

Omri's Reign over Israel

[21]At that time the people of Israel were divided in their loyalties. Half the people supported Tibni son of Ginath and wanted to make him king; the other half supported Omri. [22]Omri's supporters were stronger than those who supported Tibni son of Ginath. Tibni died; Omri became king.

[23]In the thirty-first year of Asa's reign over Judah, Omri became king over Israel. He ruled for twelve years, six of them in [a]Tirzah. [24]He purchased the hill of [a]Samaria from Shemer for two talents[1] of silver. He launched a construction project there and named the city he built after Shemer, the former owner of the hill of Samaria. [25a]Omri did more evil in the sight of the LORD than all who were before him. [26]He [a]followed in the footsteps of Jeroboam son of Nebat and encouraged Israel to sin; they angered the LORD God of Israel with their worthless [b]idols.

[27]The rest of the events of Omri's reign, including his accomplishments and successes, are recorded in the scroll called the Annals of the Kings of Israel. [28]Omri passed away and was buried in Samaria. His son Ahab replaced him as king.[1]

Ahab Promotes Idolatry

[29]In the thirty-eighth year of Asa's reign over Judah, Omri's son Ahab became king over Israel. Ahab son of Omri ruled over Israel for 22 years in Samaria. [30]Ahab son of Omri did more evil in the sight of the LORD than all who were before him. [31]As if following in the sinful footsteps of Jeroboam son of Nebat were not bad enough, he married Jezebel the daughter of King Ethbaal of the [a]Sidonians. Then he worshiped [b]and bowed to Baal. [32]He set up an altar for Baal in [a]the temple of Baal he had built in Samaria. [33]Ahab also made [a]an Asherah pole; he [b]did more to anger the LORD God of Israel than all the kings of Israel who were before him.

[34]During Ahab's reign, Hiel the Bethelite rebuilt Jericho. Abiram, his firstborn son, died when he laid the foundation; Segub, his youngest son, died when he erected its gates, [a]in keeping with the LORD's message that he had spoken through Joshua son of Nun.

16:9 [a]2 Kgs 9:30–33 [b]Gen 24:2; 39:4; 1 Kgs 18:3 16:11 [a]1 Sam 25:22 16:12 [a]1 Kgs 16:3 16:13 [a]Deut 32:21; 1 Sam 12:21; [Isa 41:29; Jonah 2:8; 1 Cor 8:4; 10:19] 16:15 [a]1 Kgs 15:27 16:19 [a]1 Kgs 15:26, 34 [b]1 Kgs 12:25–33 16:23 [a]1 Kgs 15:21; 2 Kgs 15:14 16:24 [a]1 Kgs 13:32; 2 Kgs 17:24; John 4:4 [1]About 150 pounds. 16:25 [a]Mic 6:16 16:26 [a]1 Kgs 16:19 [b]1 Kgs 16:13 16:28 [1]One ws adds 8 vv. here. 16:31 [a]Judg 18:7; 1 Kgs 11:1–5 [b]1 Kgs 21:25–26; 2 Kgs 10:18; 17:16 16:32 [a]2 Kgs 10:21, 26, 27 16:33 [a]2 Kgs 13:6 [b]1 Kgs 14:9; 16:29–30; 21:25 16:34 [a]Josh 6:26

Elijah Visits a Widow in Sidonian Territory

17 Elijah the Tishbite, from [a]Tishbe in Gilead, said to Ahab, "[b]As certainly as the LORD God of Israel lives (whom I [c]serve), [d]there will be no dew or rain in [e]the years ahead unless I give the command." [2]The LORD's message came to him: [3]"Leave here and travel eastward. Hide out in the Kerith Valley near the Jordan. [4]Drink from the stream; I have already told the [a]ravens to bring you food there." [5]So he carried out the LORD's message; he went and lived in the Kerith Valley near the Jordan. [6]The ravens would bring him bread and meat each morning and evening, and he would drink from the stream.

[7]After a while, the stream dried up because there had been no rain in the land. [8]The LORD's message came to him, [9]"Get up, go to [a]Zarephath in [b]Sidonian territory, and live there. I have already told a widow who lives there to provide for you." [10]So he got up and went to Zarephath. When he went through the city gate, there was a widow gathering wood. He called out to her, "Please give me a little water in a cup, so I can take a drink." [11]As she went to get it, he called out to her, "Please bring me a piece of bread." [12]She said, "As certainly as the LORD your God lives, I have no food, except for a handful of flour in a jar and a little olive oil in a jug. Right now I am gathering a couple of sticks for a fire. Then I'm going home to make one final meal for my son and myself. After we have eaten that, we will [a]die of starvation." [13]Elijah said to her, "Don't be afraid. Go and do as you planned. But first make me a small cake and bring it to me; then make something for yourself and your son. [14]For this is what the LORD God of Israel has said: 'The jar of flour will not be empty and the jug of oil will not run out until the day the LORD makes it rain on the surface of the ground.'" [15]She went and did as Elijah told her; there was always enough food for Elijah and for her and her family. [16]The jar of flour was never empty and the jug of oil never ran out, in keeping with the LORD's message that he had spoken through Elijah.

[17]After this the son of the woman who owned the house got sick. His illness was so severe he could no longer breathe. [18]She asked Elijah, "Why, prophet, have you come to me to confront me with my sin and kill my son?" [19]He said to her, "Hand me your son." He took him from her arms, carried him to the upper room where he was staying, and laid him down on his bed. [20]Then he called out to the LORD, "O LORD, my God, are you also bringing disaster on this widow I am staying with by killing her son?" [21]He stretched out over the boy three times [a]and called out to the LORD, "O LORD, my God, please let this boy's breath return to him." [22]The LORD answered Elijah's prayer; the boy's breath returned to him and he [a]lived. [23]Elijah took the boy, brought him down from the upper room to the house, and handed him to his mother. Elijah then said, "See, your son is alive!" [24]The woman [a]said to Elijah, "Now I know that you are a prophet and that the LORD's message really does come through you."

Elijah Meets the King's Servant

18 Some time later, in the third year of the famine, the LORD's message came to Elijah, "Go, make [a]an appearance before Ahab, so [b]I may send rain on the surface of the ground." [2]So Elijah went to make an appearance before Ahab.

Now the famine was severe in Samaria. [3]So Ahab summoned Obadiah, who supervised the palace. (Now Obadiah was a very loyal follower of the LORD. [4]When Jezebel was killing the LORD's prophets, Obadiah took 100 prophets and hid them in two caves in two groups of 50. He also brought them food and water.) [5]Ahab told Obadiah, "Go through the land to all the springs and valleys. Maybe we can find some grazing areas so we can keep the horses and mules alive and not have to kill some of the animals." [6]They divided up the land between them to search it; Ahab went one way by himself and Obadiah went the other way by himself.

[7]As Obadiah was traveling along, Elijah met him. When he [a]recognized him, he fell facedown to the ground and said, "Is it really

17:1 [a] Judg 12:4   [b] 1 Kgs 18:10; 22:14; 2 Kgs 3:14; 5:20   [c] Deut 10:8   [d] 1 Kgs 18:1; Jas 5:17   [e] Luke 4:25   17:4 [a] Job 38:41
17:9 [a] Obad 20; Luke 4:25–26   [b] 2 Sam 24:6   17:12 [a] Deut 28:23–24   17:21 [a] 2 Kgs 4:34–35; Acts 20:10
17:22 [a] Luke 7:14–15; Heb 11:35   17:24 [a] John 2:11; 3:2; 16:30   18:1 [a] 1 Kgs 17:1; Luke 4:25;
Jas 5:17   [b] Deut 28:12   18:7 [a] 2 Kgs 1:6–8

you, my master, Elijah?" [8]He replied, "Yes, go and say to your master, 'Elijah is back.'" [9]Obadiah said, "What sin have I committed that you are ready to hand your servant over to Ahab for execution? [10]As certainly as the LORD your God lives, my master has sent to every nation and kingdom in an effort to find you. When they say, 'He's not here,' he makes them swear an oath that they could not find you. [11]Now you say, 'Go and say to your master, "Elijah is back."' [12]But when I leave you, [a]the LORD's Spirit will carry you away so I can't find you. If I go tell Ahab I've seen you, he won't be able to find you and he will kill me. That would not be fair, because your servant has been a loyal follower of the LORD from my youth. [13]Certainly my master is aware of what I did when Jezebel was killing the LORD's prophets. I hid 100 of the LORD's prophets in two caves in two groups of 50 and I brought them food and water. [14]Now you say, 'Go and say to your master, "Elijah is back,"' but he will kill me." [15]But Elijah said, "As certainly as the LORD of Heaven's Armies[1] lives (whom I serve), I will make an appearance before him today."

Elijah Confronts Baal's Prophets

[16]When Obadiah went and informed Ahab, the king went to meet Elijah. [17]When Ahab saw Elijah, he said to him, "[a]Is it really you, the one who brings disaster [b]on Israel?" [18]Elijah replied, "[a]I have not brought disaster on Israel. But you and your father's dynasty have, by abandoning the LORD's commandments and following the Baals. [19]Now send out messengers and assemble all Israel before me at [a]Mount Carmel, as well as the 450 prophets of Baal [b]and 400 prophets of Asherah whom Jezebel supports."

[20]Ahab sent messengers to all the Israelites and had the prophets [a]assemble at Mount Carmel. [21]Elijah approached all the people and said, "[a]How long are you going to be paralyzed by indecision? If the LORD is the true God, then [b]follow him, but if Baal is, follow him!" But the people did not say a word. [22]Elijah [a]said to them: "I am the only prophet of the LORD who is left, [b]but there are 450 prophets of Baal. [23]Let them bring us two bulls. Let them choose one of the bulls for themselves, cut it up into pieces, and place it on the wood. But they must not set it on fire. I will do the same to the other bull and place it on the wood. But I will not set it on fire. [24]Then you will invoke the name of your god, and I will invoke the name of the LORD. The god who [a]responds with fire will demonstrate that he is the true God." All the people responded, "This will be a fair test."

[25]Elijah told the prophets of Baal, "Choose one of the bulls for yourselves and go first, for you are the majority. Invoke the name of your god, but do not light a fire."[1] [26]So they took a bull, as he had suggested, and prepared it. They invoked the name of Baal from morning until noon, saying, "Baal, answer us." But there was [a]no sound and no answer. They jumped around on the altar they had made.[1] [27]At noon Elijah mocked them, "Yell louder! After all, he is a god; he may be deep in thought, or perhaps he stepped out for a moment or has taken a trip. Perhaps he is sleeping and needs to be awakened." [28]So they yelled louder and, in accordance with their prescribed ritual, [a]mutilated themselves with swords and spears until their bodies were covered with blood. [29]Throughout [a]the [b]afternoon they were in an ecstatic frenzy, but there was no sound, no answer, and no response.[1]

[30]Elijah then told all the people, "Approach me." So all the people approached him. He repaired the altar of the LORD that had been torn down. [31]Then Elijah took 12 stones, corresponding to the number of tribes that descended from Jacob, to whom the LORD's message had come, "[a]Israel will be your name." [32]With the stones he constructed an altar for the LORD. Around the altar he made a trench large enough to [a]contain two seahs[1] of seed. [33]He arranged the wood, cut up the bull, and placed it on the wood. Then he said, "Fill four water jars and [a]pour the water on the offering and the wood." [34]When they had done so, he said, "Do it again." So they did it again. Then he said, "Do it a third time." So they did it a third

---

18:12 [a]2 Kgs 2:16; Ezek 3:12, 14; Matt 4:1; Acts 8:39   18:15 [1]Trad. *the LORD of Hosts.*   18:17 [a]1 Kgs 21:20   [b]Josh 7:25; Acts 16:20   18:18 [a]1 Kgs 16:30–33; [2 Chr 15:2]   18:19 [a]Josh 19:26; 2 Kgs 2:25   [b]1 Kgs 16:33   18:20 [a]1 Kgs 22:6   18:21 [a]2 Kgs 17:41; [Matt 6:24]   [b]Josh 24:15   18:22 [a]1 Kgs 19:10, 14   [b]1 Kgs 18:19   18:24 [a]1 Kgs 18:38; 1 Chr 21:26   18:25 [1]Syr. omits the last sentence.   18:26 [a]Ps 115:5; Jer 10:5; [1 Cor 8:4]   [1]MT *which he made.*   18:28 [a][Lev 19:28; Deut 14:1]   18:29 [a]Exod 29:39, 41   [b]1 Kgs 18:26   [1]Two wss add *When it was time to offer the sacrifice, Elijah the Tishbite spoke to the prophets of the abominations: 'Stand aside for the time being, and I will offer my burnt offering.' So they stood aside and departed.*   18:31 [a]Gen 32:28; 35:10; 2 Kgs 17:34   18:32 [a][Exod 20:25; Col 3:17]   [1]About 7 quarts.   18:33 [a]Judg 6:20

time. [35]The water flowed down all sides of [a]the altar and filled the trench. [36]When it was time for the evening offering, Elijah the prophet approached the altar and prayed: "O LORD [a]God of Abraham, [b]Isaac, and Israel, prove today that you are God in Israel and that I am your servant and have done all these things at your command. [37]Answer me, O LORD, answer me, so these people will know that you, O LORD, are the true God and that you are winning back their allegiance." [38]Then fire from [a]the LORD fell from the sky. It consumed the offering, the wood, the stones, and the dirt, and licked up the water in the trench. [39]When all [a]the people saw this, they threw themselves down with their faces to the ground and said, "The LORD is the true God! The LORD is the true God!" [40]Elijah told them, "[a]Seize the prophets of Baal! Don't let even one of them escape!" So they seized them, and Elijah led them down to the [b]Kishon Valley and [c]executed them there.

[41]Then Elijah told Ahab, "Go on up and eat and drink, for the sound of a heavy rainstorm can be heard." [42]So Ahab went on up to eat and drink, while Elijah climbed to [a]the top of Carmel. He bent down toward the ground and put his face between his knees. [43]He told his servant, "Go on up and look in the direction of the sea." So he went on up, looked, and reported, "There is nothing." Seven times Elijah sent him to look. [44]The seventh time the servant said, "Look, a small cloud, the size of the palm of a man's hand, is rising up from the sea." Elijah then said, "Go and tell Ahab, 'Hitch up the chariots and go down, so that the rain won't overtake you.'" [45]Meanwhile the sky was covered with dark clouds, the wind blew, and there was a heavy rainstorm. Ahab rode toward Jezreel. [46]Now the LORD energized Elijah with [a]power; he tucked his robe into his belt and ran ahead of Ahab all the way to Jezreel.

Elijah Runs for His Life

19 Ahab told Jezebel all that Elijah had done, including a detailed account of how he [a]killed all the prophets with the sword. [2]Jezebel sent a messenger to Elijah with this warning, "May the gods judge me severely if by this time tomorrow I do not take your life as you did theirs!"

[3]Elijah was afraid,[1] so he got up and fled for his life to Beer Sheba in Judah. He left his servant there, [4]while he went a day's journey into the wilderness. He went and sat down under a shrub and [a]asked the LORD to take his life: "I've had enough! Now, O LORD, take my life. After all, I'm no better than my ancestors." [5]He stretched out and fell asleep under the shrub. Suddenly an angelic messenger touched him and said, "Get up and eat." [6]He looked and right there by his head was a cake baking on hot coals and a jug of water. He ate and drank and then slept some more. [7]The angel of the LORD came back again, touched him, and said, "Get up and eat, for otherwise you won't be able to make the journey." [8]So he got up and ate and drank. That meal gave him the strength to travel [a]40 days and 40 nights until he reached [b]Horeb, the mountain of God.

[9]He went into a cave there and spent the night. Suddenly the LORD's message came to him, "Why are you here, Elijah?" [10]He answered, "[a]I have [b]been absolutely loyal to the LORD God of Heaven's Armies,[1] even though the Israelites have abandoned the covenant they made with you, torn down your altars, and [c]killed your prophets [d]with the sword. I alone am left and now they want to take my life." [11]The LORD said, "Go out and stand [a]on the mountain before the LORD. Look, the LORD is ready to [b]pass by." [c]A very powerful wind went before the LORD, digging into the mountain and causing landslides, but the LORD was not in the wind. After the windstorm there was an earthquake, but the LORD was not in the earthquake. [12]After the earthquake, there was a fire, but the LORD was not in the fire. After the fire, there was a soft whisper.[1] [13]When Elijah [a]heard it, he covered his face with his robe and went out and stood at the entrance to the cave. [b]Suddenly a voice asked him, "Why are you here, Elijah?" [14]He answered, "I have been absolutely loyal[1] to

18:35 [a]1 Kgs 18:32, 38   **18:36** [a]Gen 28:13; Exod 3:6; 4:5; [Matt 22:32]   [b]Num 16:28   **18:38** [a]Gen 15:17; Lev 9:24; 10:1–2; Judg 6:21; 2 Kgs 1:12; 1 Chr 21:26; 2 Chr 7:1; Job 1:16   **18:39** [a]1 Kgs 18:21, 24   **18:40** [a]2 Kgs 10:25   [b]Judg 4:7; 5:21   [c][Deut 13:5; 18:20]   **18:42** [a]Jas 5:17–18   **18:46** [a]2 Kgs 3:15; Isa 8:11; Ezek 3:14   **19:1** [a]1 Kgs 18:40   **19:3** [1]MT *and he saw.*   **19:4** [a]Num 11:15; Jer 20:14–18; Jonah 4:3, 8   **19:8** [a]Exod 24:18; 34:28; Deut 9:9–11, 18; Matt 4:2   [b]Exod 3:1; 4:27   **19:10** [a]Rom 11:3   [b]Num 25:11, 13; Ps 69:9   [c]1 Kgs 18:4   [d]1 Kgs 18:22; Rom 11:3   [1]Trad. *the God of hosts.*   **19:11** [a]Exod 19:20; 24:12, 18   [b]Exod 33:21–22   [c]Ezek 1:4; 37:7   **19:12** [1]Heb. *a voice, calm, soft.*   **19:13** [a]Exod 3:6; Isa 6:2   [b]1 Kgs 19:9   **19:14** [1]Or *very zealous.*

the LORD God of Heaven's Armies,[2] even though the Israelites have [a]abandoned the covenant they made with you, torn down your altars, and killed your prophets with the sword. I alone am left and now they want to take my life." [15]The LORD said to him, "Go back the way you came [a]and then head for the wilderness of Damascus. Go and anoint Hazael king over Syria. [16]You must anoint [a]Jehu son of Nimshi king over Israel, and [b]Elisha son of Shaphat from Abel Meholah to take your place as prophet. [17][a]Jehu will [b]kill anyone who escapes Hazael's sword, and [c]Elisha will kill anyone who escapes Jehu's sword. [18][a]I still have left in Israel 7,000 followers who have not bowed their knees to Baal or kissed the images of him."

[19]Elijah went from there and found Elisha son of Shaphat. He was plowing with twelve pairs of oxen; he was near the twelfth pair. Elijah passed by him and threw his [a]robe over him. [20]He left the oxen, ran after Elijah, and said, "[a]Please let me kiss my father and mother goodbye, then I will follow you." Elijah said to him, "Go back! Indeed, what have I done to you?" [21]Elisha went back and took his pair of oxen and slaughtered them. He [a]cooked the meat over a fire that he made by burning the harness and yoke. He gave the people meat and they ate. Then he got up and followed Elijah and became his assistant.

Ben Hadad Invades Israel

20 Now King Ben [a]Hadad of Syria assembled all his army, along with 32 other kings with their horses and chariots. He marched against [b]Samaria and besieged and attacked it. [2]He sent messengers to King Ahab of Israel, who was in the city. He said to him, "This is what Ben Hadad says: [3]'Your silver and your gold are mine, as well as the best of your wives and sons.'" [4]The king of Israel replied, "It is just as you say, my master, O king. I and all I own belong to you."

[5]The messengers came again and said, "This is what Ben Hadad says: 'I sent this message to you, "You must give me your silver, gold, wives, and sons." [6]But now at this time tomorrow I will send my servants to you and they will search through your palace and your servants' houses. They will carry away all your valuables.'" [7]The king of Israel summoned all the leaders of the land and said, "Notice how this man is looking for trouble. Indeed, he demanded my wives, sons, silver, and gold, and I did not resist him." [8]All the leaders and people said to him, "Do not give in or agree to his demands." [9]So he said to the messengers of Ben Hadad, "Say this to my master, the king: 'I will give you everything you demanded at first from your servant, but I am unable to agree to this latest demand.'" So the messengers went back and gave their report.

[10]Ben Hadad sent [a]another message to him, "May the gods judge me severely if there is enough dirt left in Samaria for all my soldiers to scoop up in their hands." [11]The king of Israel replied, "Tell him the one who puts on his battle gear should not [a]boast like one who is taking it off." [12]When Ben Hadad received this reply, he and the other kings were [a]drinking in their quarters. He ordered his servants, "Get ready to attack!" So they got ready to attack the city.

The Lord Delivers Israel

[13]Now a prophet [a]visited King Ahab of Israel and said, "This is what the LORD has said: 'Do you see this huge army? Look, I am going to hand it over to you this very day. Then you will know that I am the LORD.'" [14]Ahab asked, "By whom will this be accomplished?" He answered, "This is what the LORD has said, 'By the servants of the district governors.'" Ahab asked, "Who will launch the attack?" He answered, "You will."

[15]So Ahab assembled the 232 servants of the district governors. After that he assembled all the Israelite army, numbering 7,000. [16]They marched out at noon, while Ben Hadad and the 32 kings allied with him were drinking heavily [a]in their quarters. [17]The servants of the district governors led the march. When Ben Hadad sent messengers, they reported back to him, "Men are marching out of Samaria." [18]He ordered, "Whether they come in peace or to do battle, take them alive." [19]They marched out of the city with the servants of the district governors in the lead and the army behind them. [20]Each

---

19:14 [a]1 Kgs 19:10   [2]Trad. *the God of hosts.*   **19:15** [a]2 Kgs 8:8–15   **19:16** [a]2 Kgs 9:1–10   [b]1 Kgs 19:19–21; 2 Kgs 2:9–15   **19:17** [a]2 Kgs 8:12; 13:3, 22   [b]2 Kgs 9:14–10:28   [c][Hos 6:5]   **19:18** [a]Rom 11:4   **19:19** [a]1 Sam 28:14; 2 Kgs 2:8, 13, 14   **19:20** [a][Matt 8:21–22; Luke 9:61–62]; Acts 20:37   **19:21** [a]2 Sam 24:22   **20:1** [a]1 Kgs 15:18, 20; 2 Kgs 6:24   [b]1 Kgs 16:24; 2 Kgs 6:24   **20:10** [a]1 Kgs 19:2; 2 Kgs 6:31   **20:11** [a]Prov 27:1; [Eccl 7:8]   **20:12** [a]1 Kgs 20:16   **20:13** [a]1 Kgs 20:28   **20:16** [a]1 Kgs 16:9; 20:12; [Prov 20:1]

one struck down an enemy soldier; the Syrians fled and Israel chased them. King Ben Hadad of Syria escaped on horseback with some horsemen. [21]Then the king of Israel marched out and struck down the horses and chariots; he thoroughly defeated Syria.

The Lord Gives Israel Another Victory

[22]The prophet visited the king of Israel and instructed him, "Go, [a]fortify your defenses. Determine what you must do, for in the spring the king of Syria will attack you." [23]Now the advisers of the king of Syria said to him: "Their God is a god of the mountains. That's why they overpowered us. But if we fight them in the plains, we will certainly overpower them. [24]So do this: Dismiss the kings from their command, and replace them with military commanders. [25]Muster an army like the one you lost, with the same number of horses and chariots. Then we will fight them in the plains; we will certainly overpower them." He approved their plan and did as they advised.

[26]In the spring Ben Hadad mustered the Syrian army and marched to [a]Aphek to fight Israel. [27]When the Israelites had mustered and received their supplies, they marched out to face them in battle. When the Israelites deployed opposite them, they were like two small flocks of goats, but the Syrians filled the [a]land. [28]The [a]prophet [b]visited the king of Israel and said, "This is what the LORD has said: 'Because the Syrians said, "The LORD is a god of the mountains and not a god of the valleys," I will deliver this entire huge army into your control. Then you will know that I am the LORD.'"

[29]The armies were deployed opposite each other for seven days. On the seventh day the battle began, and the Israelites killed 100,000 Syrian foot soldiers in one day. [30]The remaining 27,000 ran to Aphek and went into the city, but the wall fell on them. Now Ben Hadad ran into the city and hid in an inner room. [31]His advisers said to him, "Look, we have heard that the kings of the Israelite dynasty are kind.[1] Allow us to [a]put sackcloth around our waists and ropes on our heads and surrender to the king of Israel. Maybe he will spare our lives." [32]So they put sackcloth around their waists and ropes on their heads and went to the king of Israel. They said, "Your servant Ben Hadad says, 'Please let me live!'" Ahab replied, "Is he still alive? He is my brother." [33]The men took this as a good omen and quickly accepted his offer, saying, "Ben Hadad is your brother." Ahab then said, "Go, get him." So Ben Hadad came out to him, and Ahab pulled him up into his chariot. [34]Ben Hadad said, "I will return [a]the cities my father took from your father. You may set up markets[1] in Damascus, just as my father did in Samaria." Ahab then said, "I want to make a treaty with you before I dismiss you." So he made a treaty with him and then dismissed him.

A Prophet Denounces Ahab's Actions

[35]One of [a]the members of the prophetic guild told his companion a message from the LORD, "Please wound me!" But the man refused to wound him. [36]So the prophet [a]said to him, "Because you have disobeyed the LORD, as soon as you leave me a lion will kill you." When he left him, a lion attacked and killed him. [37]He found another man and said, "Wound me!" So the man wounded him severely. [38]The prophet then went and stood by the road, waiting for the king. He also disguised himself by putting a bandage down over his eyes. [39]When the king [a]passed by, he called out to the king, "[b]Your servant went out into the heat of the battle, and then a man turned aside and brought me a prisoner. He told me, 'Guard this prisoner. If he ends up missing for any reason,[1] you will pay with your life or with a talent[2] of silver.' [40]Well, it just so happened that while your servant was doing this and that, he disappeared." The king of Israel said to him, "Your punishment is already determined by your own testimony." [41]The prophet quickly removed the bandage from his eyes, and the king of Israel recognized he was one of the prophets. [42]The prophet then said to him, "This is what the LORD has said: '[a]Because you released a man I had determined should die, you will pay with your life, and your people will suffer instead of his people.'" [43]The king of Israel [a]went home to Samaria bitter and angry.

20:22 [a]2 Sam 11:1; 1 Kgs 20:26   20:26 [a]Josh 13:4; 2 Kgs 13:17   20:27 [a]Judg 6:3–5; 1 Sam 13:5–8   20:28 [a]1 Kgs 17:18   [b]1 Kgs 20:13   20:31 [a]Gen 37:34; 2 Sam 3:31   [1]Or *merciful.*   20:34 [a]1 Kgs 15:20   [1]Heb. *streets.*   20:35 [a]2 Kgs 2:3, 5, 7, 15   20:36 [a]1 Kgs 13:24   20:39 [a]2 Sam 12:1   [b]2 Kgs 10:24   [1]Heb. *if being missed, he is missed;* an emphatic Heb. construction.   [2]About 75 pounds.   20:42 [a]1 Kgs 22:31–37   20:43 [a]1 Kgs 21:4

Ahab Murders Naboth

21 After this the following episode took place. Naboth the Jezreelite owned a vineyard in [a]Jezreel adjacent to the palace of King Ahab of Samaria. [2]Ahab said to Naboth, "Give me your [a]vineyard so I can make a vegetable garden out of it, for it is adjacent to my palace. I will give you an even better vineyard in its place, or if you prefer, I will pay you silver for it."[1] [3]But Naboth replied to Ahab, "The LORD forbid [a]that I should sell you my ancestral inheritance."

[4]So Ahab went into his palace, bitter and angry that Naboth the Jezreelite had said, "I will not sell to you my ancestral inheritance." He lay down on his bed, pouted, and would not eat. [5]Then his wife [a]Jezebel came in and said to him, "Why do you have a bitter attitude and refuse to eat?" [6]He answered her, "While I was talking to Naboth the Jezreelite, I said to him, 'Sell me your vineyard for silver, or if you prefer, I will give you another vineyard in its place.' But he said, 'I will not sell you my vineyard.'" [7]His wife Jezebel said to him, "You are the king of Israel! Get up, eat some food, and have a good time. I will get the vineyard of Naboth the Jezreelite for you."

[8]She wrote out orders, signed Ahab's name to them, and sealed them with his seal. She then sent the orders to the leaders and to the nobles who lived in Naboth's city. [9]This is what she wrote: "Observe a time of fasting and seat Naboth in front of the people. [10]Also seat two villains opposite him and have them testify, 'You [a]cursed God and the king.' Then take him out and [b]stone him to death."

[11]The men of the city, the leaders, and the nobles who lived there followed the written orders Jezebel had sent them. [12]They observed a time of fasting and put Naboth in front of [a]the people. [13]The two villains arrived and sat opposite him. Then the villains testified [a]against Naboth right before [b]the people, saying, "Naboth cursed God and the king." So they dragged him outside the city and stoned him to death. [14]Then they reported to Jezebel, "Naboth has been stoned to death."

[15]When Jezebel heard that Naboth had been stoned to death, she said to Ahab, "Get up, take possession of the vineyard Naboth the Jezreelite refused to sell you for silver, for Naboth is no longer alive; he's dead." [16]When Ahab heard that Naboth was dead,[1] he got up and went down to take possession of the vineyard of Naboth the Jezreelite.

[17a]The LORD's message came to [b]Elijah the Tishbite: [18]"Get up, go down and meet King Ahab of Israel [a]who lives in Samaria. He is at the vineyard of Naboth; he has gone down there to take possession of it. [19]Say to him, 'This is what the LORD has said: "Haven't you committed murder and taken possession of the property of the deceased?"' Then say to him, 'This is what the LORD has said: "[a]In the spot where dogs licked up Naboth's blood they will also lick up your blood—yes, yours!"'"

[20]When Elijah arrived, Ahab said to him, "So, you [a]have found me, my enemy!" Elijah replied, "I have found [b]you, because you are committed to doing evil in the sight of the LORD. [21]The LORD says, 'Look, [a]I am ready to bring disaster on you. I will [b]destroy you and cut off [c]every last male belonging to Ahab in Israel, including even the [d]weak and incapacitated.[1] [22]I will make your dynasty like those of [a]Jeroboam son of Nebat and [b]Baasha son of Ahijah because you angered me and made Israel sin.' [23]The LORD says this about Jezebel, 'Dogs will devour Jezebel by the outer wall[1] of Jezreel.' [24]As for Ahab's family, dogs will eat the ones [a]who die in the city, and the birds of the sky will eat the ones who die in the country." [25](There had never been anyone like Ahab, who was firmly committed to doing evil in [a]the sight of the LORD, urged on by his wife Jezebel. [26]He was so wicked he worshiped the disgusting idols, just as the Amorites whom the LORD had driven out from before the Israelites.)

21:1 [a] Judg 6:33; 1 Kgs 18:45–46   **21:2** [a] 1 Sam 8:14   [1] One ws adds *And it will be mine as a garden of herbs.*   **21:3** [a] [Lev 25:23; Num 36:7; Ezek 46:18]   **21:5** [a] 1 Kgs 19:1–2   **21:10** [a] [Exod 22:28; Lev 24:15–16]; Acts 6:11   [b] [Lev 24:14]   **21:12** [a] Isa 58:4   **21:13** [a] [Exod 20:16; 23:1, 7]   [b] 2 Kgs 9:26; 2 Chr 24:21; Acts 7:58–59; Heb 11:37   **21:16** [1] One ws adds *he tore his garments and put on sackcloth. After these things.*   **21:17** [a] [Ps 9:12]   [b] 1 Kgs 19:1   **21:18** [a] 1 Kgs 13:32; 2 Chr 22:9   **21:19** [a] 1 Kgs 22:38; 2 Kgs 9:26   **21:20** [a] 1 Kgs 18:17   [b] 1 Kgs 21:25; 2 Kgs 17:17; [Rom 7:14]   **21:21** [a] 1 Kgs 14:10; 2 Kgs 9:8   [b] 2 Kgs 10:10   [c] 1 Sam 25:22   [d] 1 Kgs 14:10   [1] Heb. *and I will cut off from Ahab those who urinate against a wall,* [including both those who are] *restrained and let free* [or *abandoned*] *in Israel.*   **21:22** [a] 1 Kgs 15:29   [b] 1 Kgs 16:3, 11   **21:23** [1] A few wss *the plot* [of ground] *at Jezreel.*   **21:24** [a] 1 Kgs 14:11; 16:4   **21:25** [a] 1 Kgs 16:30–33; 21:20

27When Ahab heard these words, he tore his clothes, aput on sackcloth, and fasted. He slept in sackcloth and walked around dejected. 28The LORD's message came to Elijah the Tishbite, 29"Have you noticed how Ahab shows remorse before me? Because he shows remorse before me, aI will not bring disaster on his dynasty during his lifetime, but during the reign of his son."

Ahab Dies in Battle

22 There was no war between Syria and Israel for three years. 2In the third year King aJehoshaphat of Judah came down to visit the king of Israel. 3The king of Israel said to his servants, "Surely you recognize that aRamoth Gilead belongs to us, though we are hesitant to reclaim it from the king of Syria." 4Then he asaid to Jehoshaphat, "Will you go with me to attack Ramoth Gilead?" Jehoshaphat replied to the king of Israel, "I will support you; my army and horses are at your disposal." 5But then Jehoshaphat said to Israel's king, "aPlease seek a message from the LORD this very day." 6So the king of Israel aassembled about 400 prophets and asked them, "Should I attack Ramoth Gilead or not?" They said, "Attack! The Sovereign One will hand it over to the king." 7But aJehoshaphat asked, "Is there not a prophet of the LORD still here, that we may ask him?" 8The king of Israel answered Jehoshaphat, "There is still one man through whom we can seek the LORD's will. But I despise him because he does not prophesy prosperity for me, but disaster. His name is Micaiah son of Imlah." Jehoshaphat said, "The king should not say such things." 9The king of Israel summoned an official and said, "Quickly bring Micaiah son of Imlah."

10Now the king of Israel and King Jehoshaphat of Judah were sitting on their respective thrones, dressed in their robes, at the threshing floor at the entrance of the gate of Samaria. All the prophets were prophesying before them. 11Zedekiah son of Kenaanah made iron ahorns and said, "This is what the LORD has said, 'With these you will bgore Syria until they are destroyed.'" 12All the prophets were prophesying the same, saying, "Attack Ramoth Gilead! You will succeed; the LORD will hand it over to the king." 13Now the messenger who went to summon Micaiah said to him, "Look, the prophets are in complete agreement that the king will succeed. Your words must agree with theirs; you must predict success." 14But Micaiah said, "As certainly as the LORD lives, I will say awhat the LORD tells me to say."

15When he came before the king, the king asked him, "Micaiah, should we attack Ramoth Gilead or not?" He answered him, "Attack! You will succeed; the LORD will hand it over to the king." 16The king said to him, "How many times must I make you solemnly promise in the name of the LORD to tell me only the truth?" 17Micaiah said, "I saw all Israel ascattered on the mountains like sheep that have no shepherd. Then the LORD said, 'They have no master. They should go home in peace.'" 18The king of Israel said to Jehoshaphat, "Didn't I tell you he does not prophesy prosperity for me, but disaster?" 19Micaiah asaid, "That being the case, listen to the LORD's message. I saw the LORD sitting on his throne, with all the heavenly assembly bstanding beside him on his right and on his left. 20The LORD said, 'Who will deceive Ahab, so he will attack Ramoth Gilead and die there?' One said this and another that. 21Then a spirit stepped forward and stood before the LORD. He said, 'I will deceive him.' 22The LORD asked him, 'How?' He replied, 'I will go out and be a lying spirit in the mouths of all his prophets.' The LORD said, 'Deceive and overpower him. Go out and do as ayou have proposed.' 23So now, look, athe LORD has placed a lying spirit in the mouths of all these prophets of yours, but the LORD has decreed disaster for you." 24Zedekiah son of Kenaanah approached, ahit Micaiah on the jaw, and said, "bWhich way did the LORD's Spirit go when he went from me to speak to you?" 25Micaiah replied, "Look, you will see in the day when you go into an ainner room to hide." 26Then the king of Israel said, "Take Micaiah and return him to Amon the city official and Joash the king's son. 27Say, 'This is what the king says, "Put this man in

21:27 aGen 37:34; 2 Sam 3:31; 2 Kgs 6:30   **21:29** a2 Kgs 9:25; 10:11, 17   **22:2** a1 Kgs 15:24; 2 Chr 18:2   **22:3** aDeut 4:43; Josh 21:38; 1 Kgs 4:13   **22:4** a2 Kgs 3:7   **22:5** a2 Kgs 3:11   **22:6** a1 Kgs 18:19   **22:7** a2 Kgs 3:11   **22:11** aZech 1:18–21   bDeut 33:17   **22:14** aNum 22:38; 24:13   **22:17** aNum 27:17; 1 Kgs 22:34–36; 2 Chr 18:16; Matt 9:36; Mark 6:34   **22:19** aIsa 6:1; Ezek 1:26–28; Dan 7:9   bJob 1:6; 2:1; Ps 103:20; Dan 7:10; Zech 1:10; [Matt 18:10; Heb 1:7, 14]   **22:22** aJudg 9:23; 1 Sam 16:14; 18:10; 19:9; Job 12:16; [Ezek 14:9; 2 Thess 2:11]   **22:23** a[Ezek 14:9]   **22:24** aJer 20:2   b2 Chr 18:23   **22:25** a1 Kgs 20:30

ᵃprison. Give him only a little bread and water until I safely return.'"" ²⁸Micaiah said, "If you really do safely return, ᵃthen the LORD has not spoken through me." Then he added, "Take note, all you people."

²⁹The king of Israel and King Jehoshaphat of Judah attacked Ramoth Gilead. ³⁰The king of Israel said to Jehoshaphat, "I will ᵃdisguise myself and then enter into the battle, but you wear your royal robes." So the king of Israel disguised himself and then entered into the battle. ³¹Now the ᵃking of Syria had ordered his 32 chariot ᵇcommanders, "Do not fight common soldiers or high-ranking officers; fight only the king of Israel." ³²When the chariot commanders saw Jehoshaphat, they said, "He must be the king of Israel." So they turned and attacked him, but Jehoshaphat ᵃcried out. ³³When the chariot commanders realized he was not the king of Israel, they turned away from him. ³⁴Now an archer shot an arrow at random,¹ and it struck the king of Israel between the plates of his armor. The king ordered his charioteer, "Turn around and take me from the battle line, because I'm wounded." ³⁵While the battle raged throughout the day, the king stood propped up in his chariot opposite the Syrians. He died in the evening; the blood from the wound ran down into the bottom of the chariot. ³⁶As the sun was setting, a cry went through the camp, "Each one should return to his city and to his homeland." ³⁷So the king died and was taken to Samaria, where they buried him. ³⁸They washed off the chariot at the pool of Samaria. Then the dogs licked his blood, while the prostitutes bathed, in keeping with the LORD's message that he had spoken.

³⁹The rest of ᵃthe events of Ahab's reign, including a record of his accomplishments and how he built a luxurious palace and various cities, are recorded in the scroll called the Annals of the Kings of Israel. ⁴⁰Ahab passed away. His son ᵃAhaziah replaced him as king.

Jehoshaphat's Reign over Judah

⁴¹In the fourth year of Ahab's reign over Israel, Asa's son ᵃJehoshaphat became king over Judah. ⁴²Jehoshaphat was thirty-five years old when he became king, and he reigned for 25 years in Jerusalem. His mother was Azubah, the daughter of Shilhi. ⁴³He followed in his ᵃfather Asa's footsteps and was careful to do what ᵇthe LORD approved. However, the high places were not eliminated; the people continued to offer sacrifices and burn incense on the high places. ⁴⁴ᵃJehoshaphat was also at ᵇpeace with the king of Israel.

⁴⁵The rest of the events of Jehoshaphat's reign, ᵃincluding his successes and military exploits, are recorded in the scroll called the Annals of the Kings of Judah. ⁴⁶He removed from the ᵃland any male cultic prostitutes who had managed to survive the reign of his father Asa. ⁴⁷ᵃThere was no king in Edom at this time; a governor ruled. ⁴⁸ᵃJehoshaphat ᵇbuilt a fleet of large merchant ships to travel to ᶜOphir for gold, ᵈbut they never made the voyage because they were shipwrecked in Ezion ᵉGeber. ⁴⁹Then Ahaziah son of Ahab said to Jehoshaphat, "Let my sailors join yours in the fleet," but Jehoshaphat refused.

⁵⁰ᵃJehoshaphat passed away and was buried with his ancestors in the city of his ancestor David. His son Jehoram replaced him as king.

Ahaziah's Reign over Israel

⁵¹In the seventeenth year of Jehoshaphat's reign over Judah, Ahab's son ᵃAhaziah became king over Israel in Samaria. He ruled for two years over Israel. ⁵²He did evil in the sight of the LORD and ᵃfollowed in the footsteps of his father and mother; like Jeroboam son of Nebat, he encouraged Israel to sin. ⁵³He worshiped and bowed down to Baal, angering ᵃthe LORD God of Israel just as his father had done.

2 KINGS

The Book of 2 Kings continues the drama begun in 1 Kings—the tragic history of two nations on a collision course with captivity. The author systematically traces the reigning monarchs of Israel and Judah, first by carrying one nation's history forward, then retracing the same period for the other nation. Nineteen consecutive evil kings rule in Israel, leading to the captivity by Assyria. The picture is somewhat brighter in Judah, where godly kings occasionally emerge to reform the evils of their predecessors. In the end, however, sin outweighs righteousness, and Judah is marched off to Babylon.

Elijah Confronts the King and His Commanders

1 [a]After Ahab died, Moab [b]rebelled against Israel. [2][a]Ahaziah fell through a window lattice in his upper chamber in Samaria and was injured. He sent messengers with these orders, "Go, ask Baal [b]Zebub, the god of [c]Ekron, if I will survive this injury."

[3]But the angel of the LORD told Elijah the Tishbite, "Get up; go to meet the messengers from the king of Samaria. Say this to them: 'You must think there is no God in Israel! That explains why you are on your way to seek an oracle from Baal Zebub the god of Ekron.[1] [4]Therefore this is what the LORD has said, "You will not leave the bed you lie on, for you will certainly die!"'" So Elijah went on his way.

[5]When the messengers returned to the king, he asked them, "Why have you returned?" [6]They replied, "A man came up to meet us. He told us, 'Go back to the king who sent you and tell him, "This is what the LORD has said: 'You must think there is no God in Israel! That explains why you are sending for an oracle from Baal Zebub, the god of Ekron.[1] Therefore you will not leave the bed you lie on, for you will certainly die.'"'" [7]The king asked them, "Describe the appearance of this man who came up to meet you and told you these things." [8]They replied, "He [a]was a hairy[1] man and had a leather belt tied around his waist." The king said, "He is Elijah the [b]Tishbite."

[9]The king sent a captain and his 50 soldiers to retrieve Elijah. The captain went up to him while he was sitting on the top of a hill. He told him, "Prophet, the king says, 'Come down!'" [10]Elijah replied to the captain, "If I am indeed a prophet, may fire come down from the sky and consume you and your 50 soldiers!" Fire then came down from the sky and consumed him and his 50 soldiers.

[11]The king sent another captain and his 50 soldiers to retrieve Elijah. He went up and told him,[1] "Prophet, this is what the king says, 'Come down at once!'" [12]Elijah replied to them,[1] "If I am indeed a prophet, may fire come down from the sky and consume you and your 50 soldiers!" Fire from God[2] came down from the sky and consumed him and his 50 soldiers.

[13]The king sent a third captain and his 50 soldiers. This third captain went up and fell on his knees [a]before Elijah. He begged for mercy, "Prophet, please have respect for my life and for the lives of these 50 servants of yours. [14]Indeed, fire came down from the sky and consumed the two captains who came before me, along with their men. So now, please have respect for my life." [15]The angel of the LORD said to Elijah, "Go down with him. Don't be afraid of him." So he got up and went down with him to the king.

[16]Elijah said to the king, "This is what the LORD has said, 'You sent messengers to seek an oracle from Baal Zebub, the god of Ekron.

1:1 [a] 2 Kgs 3:5   [b] 2 Sam 8:2   **1:2** [a] 1 Kgs 22:40   [b] 2 Kgs 1:3, 6, 16; Matt 10:25; Mark 3:22   [c] 1 Sam 5:10   **1:3** [1] Heb. *Is it because there is no God in Israel* [that] *you are going to inquire of Baal Zebub, the god of Ekron?*; a sarcastic rhetorical question. **1:6** [1] Heb. *Is it because there is no God in Israel* [that] *you are sending to inquire of Baal Zebub, the god of Ekron?*; a sarcastic rhetorical question.   **1:8** [a] Zech 13:4; Matt 3:4; Mark 1:6   [b] 1 Kgs 18:7   [1] Heb. *an owner of hair.*   **1:11** [1] MT *he answered and said to him.*   **1:12** [1] A few wss *him.*   [2] Or *intense fire.*   **1:13** [a] 1 Sam 26:21; Ps 72:14

Is it because there is no God in Israel from whom you can seek a message? Therefore you will not leave the bed you lie on, for you will certainly die.'"

[17] And he did die in keeping with the LORD's message that he had spoken through Elijah. In the second year of the reign of King [a]Jehoram son of Jehoshaphat over Judah, Ahaziah's brother Jehoram replaced him as king of Israel, because he had no son. [18] The rest of the events of Ahaziah's reign, including his accomplishments, are recorded in the scroll called the Annals of the Kings of Israel.

Elijah Makes a Swift Departure

2 Just before the LORD took Elijah up to heaven in [a]a windstorm, Elijah and [b]Elisha were traveling from Gilgal. [2] Elijah told Elisha, "[a]Stay here, for the LORD [b]has sent me to Bethel." But Elisha said, "As certainly as the LORD lives and as you live, I will not leave you." So they went down to Bethel. [3] Some members of [a]the prophetic guild in Bethel came out to Elisha and said, "Do you know that today the LORD is going to take your master from you?" He answered, "Yes, I know. Be quiet."

[4] Elijah said to him, "Elisha, stay here, for the LORD has sent me to Jericho." But he replied, "As certainly as the LORD lives and as you live, I will not leave you." So they went to Jericho. [5] Some members of the prophetic guild in Jericho approached Elisha and said, "Do you know that today the LORD is going to take your master from you?" He answered, "Yes, I know. Be quiet."

[6] Elijah said to him, "Stay here, for the LORD has sent me to the Jordan." But he replied, "As certainly as the LORD lives and as you live, I will not leave you." So they traveled on together. [7] The 50 members of the prophetic guild went and stood opposite them at a distance, while Elijah and Elisha stood by the Jordan. [8] Elijah took his cloak, folded [a]it up, and hit the water with it. The water divided, and the two of them crossed over on dry [b]ground.

[9] When they had crossed over, Elijah said to Elisha, "What can I do for you, before I am taken away from you?" Elisha answered, "May I receive a double portion of the prophetic spirit that energizes you?" [10] Elijah replied, "That's a difficult request! If you see me taken from you, may it be so, but if you don't, it will not happen."

[11] As they were [a]walking along and talking, suddenly a fiery chariot[1] pulled by fiery horses appeared. They [b]went between Elijah and Elisha, and Elijah went up to heaven in a windstorm. [12] While Elisha was watching, he was crying out, "[a]My father, my father! The chariot and horsemen of Israel!" Then he could no longer see him. He grabbed his clothes and tore them in two. [13] He picked up Elijah's cloak, which had fallen off him, and went back and stood on the shore of the Jordan. [14] He took the cloak that had fallen off Elijah, [a]hit the water with it, and said, "Where is the LORD, the God of Elijah?" When he hit the water, it divided and Elisha crossed over.

[15] When the members of the prophetic guild in Jericho, who were standing at a distance, saw him do this, they said, "The spirit that energized Elijah rests upon Elisha." They went to meet him and bowed down to the ground before him. [16] They said to him, "Look, there are 50 capable men with your servants. Let them go and look for your master, for the wind sent from the LORD may have carried him away and dropped him on one of the hills or in one of the valleys." But Elisha replied, "Don't send them out." [17] But they were so insistent that he became [a]embarrassed. So he said, "Send them out." They sent the 50 men out, and they looked for three days, but could not find Elijah. [18] When they came back, Elisha was staying in Jericho. He said to them, "Didn't I tell you, 'Don't go'?"

Elisha Demonstrates His Authority

[19] The men of the city said to Elisha, "Look, the city has a good location, as our master can see. But the water is bad and the land doesn't produce crops." [20] Elisha said, "Get me a new jar and put some salt in it." So they got it. [21] He went out to the spring and [a]threw the salt in. Then he said, "This is what the LORD has said, 'I have purified this water. It will no longer cause death or fail to

1:17 [a] 1 Kgs 22:50; 2 Kgs 8:16; Matt 1:8   2:1 [a] Gen 5:24; [Heb 11:5]   [b] 1 Kgs 19:16-21   2:2 [a] Ruth 1:15-16   [b] 1 Sam 1:26; 2 Kgs 2:4, 6; 4:30   2:3 [a] 1 Kgs 20:35; 2 Kgs 2:5, 7, 15; 4:1, 38; 9:1   2:8 [a] Exod 14:21-22; Josh 3:16; 2 Kgs 2:14   [b] Josh 3:17   2:11 [a] 2 Kgs 6:17; Ps 104:4   [b] Gen 5:24; Heb 11:5   [1] Or perhaps *chariots*.   2:12 [a] 2 Kgs 13:14   2:14 [a] 2 Kgs 2:8   2:17 [a] 2 Kgs 8:11   2:21 [a] Exod 15:25-26; 2 Kgs 4:41; 6:6; John 9:6

produce crops.'" [22] The water has been [a] pure to this very day, just as Elisha prophesied.

[23] He went up from there to Bethel. As he was traveling up the road, some young boys[1] came out of the city and made fun of him, saying, "Go on up, baldy! Go on up, baldy!" [24] When he turned around and saw them, he called God's judgment down [a] on them. Two female bears came out of the woods and ripped 42 of the boys to pieces. [25] From there he traveled to [a] Mount Carmel and then back to Samaria.

Moab Fights with Israel

3 In the eighteenth year of King Jehoshaphat's reign over Judah, Ahab's son [a] Jehoram became king over Israel in Samaria; he ruled for 12 years. [2] He did evil in the sight of the LORD, but not to the same degree as his father and mother. He did remove the sacred pillar of Baal [a] that his father had made. [3] Yet [a] he persisted in the sins of Jeroboam son of Nebat, who encouraged Israel to sin; he did not turn from them.[1]

[4] Now King Mesha of Moab was [a] a sheep breeder. He would send as tribute to the king of Israel 100,000 male [b] lambs and the wool of 100,000 rams. [5] When [a] Ahab died, the king of Moab rebelled against the king of Israel. [6] At that time King Jehoram left Samaria and assembled all Israel for war. [7] He sent [a] this message to King Jehoshaphat of Judah: "The king of Moab has rebelled against me. Will you fight with me against Moab?" Jehoshaphat replied, "I will join you in the campaign; my army and horses are at your disposal." [8] He then asked, "Which invasion route are we going to take?" Jehoram answered, "By the road through the wilderness of Edom." [9] So the kings of Israel, Judah, and Edom set out together. They wandered around on the road for seven days and finally ran out of water for the men and animals they had with them. [10] The king of Israel said, "Oh no! Certainly the LORD has summoned these three kings so that he can hand them over to the king of Moab!" [11a] Jehoshaphat asked, "Is there no

prophet of the LORD here that we might seek the LORD's direction?" One of the servants of the king of Israel answered, "Elisha son of Shapat is here; he used to [b] be Elijah's servant."[1] [12] Jehoshaphat said, "Yes, he receives the LORD's messages." So the king of Israel and Jehoshaphat and the king of Edom [a] went down to visit him.

[13] Elisha said to the king of Israel, "[a] Why are you here?[1] [b] Go to your [c] father's [d] prophets or your mother's prophets!" The king of Israel replied to him, "No, for the LORD is the one who summoned these three kings so that he can hand them over to Moab." [14] Elisha said, "[a] As certainly as the LORD of Heaven's Armies[1] lives (whom I serve), if I did not respect King Jehoshaphat of Judah, I would not pay attention to you or acknowledge you. [15] But now, get me [a] a musician." When the musician [b] played, [c] the LORD energized him,[1] [16] and he said, "This is what the LORD has said, '[a] Make many cisterns in this valley,'[1] [17] for this is what the LORD has said, 'You will not feel any wind or see any rain, but this valley will be full of water, and you and your cattle and animals will drink.' [18] This is an easy task for the LORD; he will also hand Moab over to you. [19] You will defeat every fortified city and every important city. You must chop down every productive tree, stop up all the springs, and cover all the cultivated land with stones."

[20] Sure enough, [a] the next morning, at the time of the morning sacrifice, water came flowing down from Edom and filled the land. [21] Now all Moab had heard that the kings were attacking, so everyone old enough to fight was mustered and placed at the border. [22] When they got up early the next morning, the sun was shining on the water. To the Moabites, who were some distance away, the water looked red like blood. [23] The Moabites said, "It's blood! The kings must have fought one another! The soldiers have struck one another down![1] Now, Moab, seize the plunder!" [24] When they approached the Israelite camp, the Israelites rose up and struck down the Moabites, who

2:22 [a] Ezek 47:8–9   **2:23** [1] Can refer to a broad age range, incl. infants as well as young men.   **2:24** [a] Deut 27:13–26   **2:25** [a] 1 Kgs 18:19–20; 2 Kgs 4:25   **3:1** [a] 2 Kgs 1:17   **3:2** [a] 1 Kgs 16:31–32   **3:3** [a] 1 Kgs 12:28–32   [1] Heb. *it.*   **3:4** [a] 2 Sam 8:2   [b] Isa 16:1–2   **3:5** [a] 2 Kgs 1:1   **3:7** [a] 1 Kgs 22:4   **3:11** [a] 1 Kgs 22:7   [b] 1 Kgs 19:21; [John 13:4–5, 13, 14]   [1] Heb. *who poured water on the hands of Elijah*; perhaps a typical task of a servant.   **3:12** [a] 2 Kgs 2:25   **3:13** [a] [Ezek 14:3]   [b] Judg 10:14; Ruth 1:15   [c] 1 Kgs 22:6–11   [d] 1 Kgs 18:19   [1] Or *What do we have in common?*; Heb. *What to me and to you?*   **3:14** [a] 1 Kgs 17:1; 2 Kgs 5:16   [1] Trad. *the LORD of hosts.*   **3:15** [a] 1 Sam 10:5   [b] 1 Sam 16:16, 23; 1 Chr 25:1   [c] Ezek 1:3; 3:14, 22; 8:1   [1] Heb. *the hand of the LORD came on him.*   **3:16** [a] Jer 14:3   [1] Heb. *making this valley cisterns, cisterns*; an emphatic Heb. construction.   **3:20** [a] Exod 29:39–40   **3:23** [1] Heb. *Each struck down his counterpart.*

then ran from them. The Israelites thoroughly defeated Moab. [25]They tore down the cities, and each man threw a stone into every cultivated field until they were covered. They stopped up every spring and chopped down every productive tree.

Only Kir [a]Hareseth was left intact, but the soldiers armed with slings surrounded it and attacked it. [26]When the king of Moab realized he was losing the battle, he and 700 swordsmen tried to break through and attack the king of Edom, but they failed. [27]So [a]he took his firstborn [b]son, who was to succeed him as king, and offered him up as a burnt sacrifice on the wall. There was an outburst of divine anger against Israel, so they broke off the attack and returned to their homeland.

Elisha Helps a Widow and Her Sons

4 Now a wife of one of [a]the prophets appealed [b]to Elisha for help, saying, "Your servant, my husband is dead. You know that your servant was a loyal follower of the LORD. Now the creditor is coming to take away my two boys to be his servants." [2]Elisha said to her, "What can I do for you? Tell me, what do you have in the house?" She answered, "Your servant has nothing in the house except a small jar of olive oil." [3]He said, "Go and ask all your neighbors for empty containers. Get as many as you can. [4]Go and close the door behind you and your sons. Pour the olive oil into all the containers; set aside each one when you have filled it." [5]So she left him and closed the door behind her and her sons. As they were bringing the containers to her, she was pouring the olive oil. [6]When the containers were full, she said to one of her sons, "Bring me another container." But he answered her, "There are no more." Then the olive oil stopped flowing. [7]She went and told the prophet. He said, "Go, sell the olive oil. Repay your creditor, and then you and your sons can live off the rest of the profit."

Elisha Gives Life to a Boy

[8]One day Elisha traveled to [a]Shunem, where a prominent woman lived. She insisted that he stop for a meal. So whenever he was passing through, he would stop in there for a meal. [9]She said to her husband, "Look, I'm sure that the man who regularly passes through here is a very special prophet. [10]Let's make a small, private upper room and furnish it with a bed, table, chair, and lamp. When he visits us, he can stay there."

[11]One day Elisha came for a visit; he went into the upper room and rested. [12]He told his servant [a]Gehazi, "Ask the Shunammite woman to come here." So he did so and she came to him. [13]Elisha said to Gehazi, "Tell her, 'Look, you have treated us with such great respect.[1] What can I do for you? Can I put in a good word for you with the king or the commander of the army?'" She replied, "I'm quite secure."[2] [14]So he asked Gehazi, "What can I do for her?" Gehazi replied, "She has no son, and her husband is old." [15]Elisha told him, "Ask her to come here." So he did so and she came and stood in the doorway. [16]He said, "About this time next year[1] you will be holding a son." She said, "No, my master! [a]O prophet, do not lie to your servant!" [17]The woman did conceive, and at the specified time the next year she gave birth to a son, just as Elisha had told her.

[18]The boy grew and one day he went out to see his father who was with the harvest workers. [19]He said to his father, "My head! My head!" His father told a servant, "Carry him to his mother." [20]So he picked him up and took him to his mother. He sat on her lap until noon and then died. [21]She went up and laid him down on the prophet's bed. She shut the door behind her and left. [22]She called to her husband, "Send me one of the servants and one of the donkeys, so I can go see the prophet quickly and then return." [23]He said, "Why do you want to go see him today? It is not the [a]new moon or the Sabbath." She said, "Everything's fine." [24]She saddled the donkey and told her servant, "Lead on. Do not stop unless I say so." [25]So she went to visit the prophet [a]at Mount Carmel. When he saw her at a distance, he said to his servant Gehazi, "Look, it's the Shunammite woman. [26]Now, run to meet her and ask her, 'Are you well? Are your husband and the boy well?'" She told Gehazi, "Everything's fine." [27]But when she reached

3:25 [a] Isa 16:7, 11; Jer 48:31, 36   3:27 [a] [Deut 18:10; Amos 2:1; Mic 6:7]   [b] 2 Kgs 8:20   4:1 [a] 1 Kgs 20:35; 2 Kgs 2:3   [b] [Lev 25:39–41, 48]; 1 Sam 22:2; Neh 5:2–5; Matt 18:25   4:8 [a] Josh 19:18   4:12 [a] 2 Kgs 4:29–31; 5:20–27; 8:4–5   4:13 [1] Heb. *you have turned trembling to us with all this trembling.*   [2] Heb. *Among my people I am living.*   4:16 [a] 2 Kgs 4:28   [1] Heb. *at this appointed time, at the time* [when it is] *reviving.*   4:23 [a] Num 10:10; 28:11; 1 Chr 23:31   4:25 [a] 2 Kgs 2:25

the prophet on the mountain, she grabbed hold of his feet. Gehazi came near to push her away, but the prophet said, "Leave her alone, for she is very upset. The LORD has kept the matter hidden from me; he didn't tell me about it." [28]She said, "[a]Did I ask my master for a son? Didn't I say, 'Don't mislead me?'" [29]Elisha told Gehazi, "[a]Tuck your robes into your belt, take my staff, and go! [b]Don't stop to exchange greetings with anyone! [c]Place my staff on the child's face." [30]The mother of the child said, "[a]As certainly as the LORD lives and as you live, I will not [b]leave you." So Elisha got up and followed her back.

[31]Now Gehazi went on ahead of them. He placed the staff on the child's face, but there was [a]no sound or response. When he came back to Elisha he told him, "The child did not wake up." [32]When Elisha arrived at the house, there was the child lying dead on his bed. [33]He [a]went in by himself [b]and closed the door. Then he prayed to the LORD. [34]He got up on [a]the bed and spread his body out over the boy; he put his mouth on the boy's mouth, his eyes over the boy's eyes, and the palms of his hands against the boy's palms. As he bent down across him, the boy's skin grew warm. [35]Elisha went back [a]and walked around in [b]the house. Then he got up on the bed again and bent down over him. The child sneezed seven times and opened his eyes. [36]Elisha called to Gehazi and said, "Get the Shunammite woman." So he did so and she came to him. He said to her, "Take your son." [37]She came in, fell at his feet, and bowed down. Then she [a]picked up her son and left.

Elisha Makes a Meal Edible

[38]Now Elisha went back to [a]Gilgal, while there was a [b]famine in the land. Some of the prophets were [c]visiting him and he told his servant, "Put the big pot on the fire and boil some stew for the prophets." [39]Someone went out to the field to gather some herbs and found a wild vine. He picked some of its fruit, enough to fill up the fold of his robe. He came back, cut it up, and threw the slices into the stew pot, not knowing they were harmful.[1] [40]The stew was poured out for the men to eat. When they ate some of the stew, they cried out, "[a]Death is in the pot, O prophet!" They could not eat it. [41]He said, "Get some flour." [a]Then he threw it into the pot and said, "Now pour some out for the men so they may eat." There was no longer anything harmful in the pot.

Elisha Miraculously Feeds a Hundred People

[42]Now a man from Baal [a]Shalisha brought some food for the prophet—20 loaves of bread made from the firstfruits of the barley harvest, as well as fresh ears of grain. Elisha said, "Set it before the people so they may eat." [43]But his attendant said, "[a]How can I feed a hundred men with this?" [b]He replied, "Set it before the people so they may eat, for this is what the LORD has said, 'They will eat and have some left over.'" [44]So he set it before them; they ate [a]and had some left over, just as in the LORD's message.

Elisha Heals a Syrian General

5 Now [a]Naaman, the [b]commander of the king of Syria's army, was esteemed and respected by his master, for through him the LORD had given Syria military victories. But this great warrior had a skin disease. [2]Raiding parties went out from Syria and took captive from the land of Israel a young girl, who became a servant to Naaman's wife. [3]She told her mistress, "If only my master were in the presence of the prophet who is in Samaria! Then he would cure him of his skin disease."

[4]Naaman went and told his master what the girl from the land of Israel had said. [5]The king of Syria said, "Go! I will send a letter to the king of Israel." So Naaman went, [a]taking with him 10 talents[1] of silver, 6,000 shekels of gold, and 10 suits of clothes. [6]He brought the letter to the king of Israel. It read: "This is a letter of introduction for my servant Naaman, whom I have sent to be cured of his skin disease." [7]When the king of Israel read the letter, he tore his clothes and said, "Am I [a]God? Can I kill or restore life? Why does he ask me to cure a man of his skin disease? Certainly you must see that he is looking for an excuse to fight me!"

4:28 [a]2 Kgs 4:16   4:29 [a]1 Kgs 18:46; 2 Kgs 9:1   [b]Luke 10:4   [c]Exod 7:19; 14:16; 2 Kgs 2:8, 14; Acts 19:12   4:30 [a]2 Kgs 2:2   [b]2 Kgs 2:4   4:31 [a]John 11:11   4:33 [a]2 Kgs 4:4; [Matt 6:6]; Luke 8:51   [b]1 Kgs 17:20   4:34 [a]1 Kgs 17:21–23; Acts 20:10   4:35 [a]1 Kgs 17:21   [b]2 Kgs 8:1, 5   4:37 [a]1 Kgs 17:23; [Heb 11:35]   4:38 [a]2 Kgs 2:1   [b]2 Kgs 8:1   [c]Luke 10:39; Acts 22:3   4:39 [1]Heb. for they did not know.   4:40 [a]Exod 10:17   4:41 [a]Exod 15:25; 2 Kgs 2:21   4:42 [a]1 Sam 9:4   4:43 [a]Luke 9:13; John 6:9   [b]Luke 9:17; John 6:11   4:44 [a]Matt 14:20; 15:37; John 6:13   5:1 [a]Luke 4:27   [b]Exod 11:3   5:5 [a]1 Sam 9:8; 2 Kgs 8:8–9   [1]About 750 pounds.   5:7 [a][Gen 30:2; Deut 32:39; 1 Sam 2:6]

[8]When Elisha the prophet heard that the king of Israel had torn his clothes, he sent this message to the king, "Why did you tear your clothes? Send him to me so he may know there is a prophet in Israel." [9]So Naaman came with his horses and chariots and stood in the doorway of Elisha's house. [10]Elisha sent out a messenger who told him, "Go and [a]wash seven times in the Jordan; your skin will be restored and you will be healed." [11]Naaman went away angry. He said, "Look, I thought for sure he would come out, stand there, invoke the name of the LORD his God, wave his hand over the area, and cure the skin disease. [12]The rivers of Damascus, the Abana and Pharpar, are better than any of the waters of Israel![1] Could I not wash in them and be healed?" So he turned around and went away angry. [13]His [a]servants approached and said to him, "O master, if the prophet had told you to do some difficult task, you would have been willing to do it. It seems you should be happy that he simply said, 'Wash and you will be healed.'" [14]So he went down and dipped in the Jordan seven times, as the prophet had instructed. His [a]skin became as smooth as a young child's and [b]he was healed.

[15]He and his entire entourage returned to the prophet. Naaman came and stood before him. He said, "For sure I know that there is [a]no God in [b]all the earth except in Israel! Now, please accept a gift from your servant." [16]But Elisha replied, "[a]As [b]certainly as the LORD lives (whom I serve), I will take nothing from you." Naaman insisted that he take it, but he refused. [17]Naaman said, "If not, then please give your servant a load of dirt, enough for a pair of mules to carry, for your servant will never again offer a burnt offering or sacrifice to a god other than the LORD. [18]May [a]the LORD forgive your servant for this one thing: When my master enters the temple of Rimmon to worship, and he leans on my arm and I bow down in the temple of Rimmon, may the LORD forgive your servant for this." [19]Elisha said to him, "Go in peace."

When he had gone a short distance,[1] [20][a]Gehazi, the prophet Elisha's servant, thought, "Look, my master did not accept what this Syrian Naaman offered him. As certainly as the LORD lives, I will run after him and accept something from him." [21]So Gehazi ran after Naaman. When Naaman saw someone running after him, he got down from his chariot to meet him and asked, "Is everything all right?" [22]He answered, "Everything is [a]fine. My master sent me with this message, 'Look, two servants of the prophets just arrived from the Ephraimite hill country. Please give them a talent[1] of silver and two suits of clothes.'" [23]Naaman said, "Please accept two talents of silver." He insisted, and tied up two talents of silver in two bags, along with two suits of clothes. He gave them to two of his servants and they carried them for Gehazi. [24]When he arrived at the hill, he took them from the servants and put them in the house. Then he sent the men on their way.

[25]When he came and stood before his master, Elisha asked him, "Where have you been, Gehazi?" He answered, "Your servant hasn't been anywhere." [26]Elisha replied, "I was there in spirit when a man turned and got down from his chariot to meet you.[1] This is not the proper [a]time to accept silver or to accept clothes, olive groves, vineyards, sheep, cattle, and male and female servants.[2] [27]Therefore Naaman's skin disease will afflict you and your descendants forever!" When Gehazi went out from his presence, his skin was as [a]white as snow.[1]

Elisha Makes an Ax Head Float

6 Some of [a]the prophets said to Elisha, "Look, the place where we meet with you is too cramped for us. [2]Let's go to the Jordan. Each of us will get a log from there, and we will build a meeting place for ourselves there." He said, "Go." [3]One of them said, "[a]Please come along with your servants." He replied, "All right, I'll come." [4]So he went with them. When they arrived at the Jordan, they started cutting down trees.

[5]As one of them was felling a tree, the ax head dropped into the water. He shouted, "Oh no, my master! It was [a]borrowed!" [6]The [a]prophet asked, "Where did it drop in?" When he showed him the spot, Elisha cut off a branch, threw it in at that spot, and made the ax head float. [7]He said, "Lift it out." So he reached out his hand and grabbed it.

Elisha Defeats an Army

[8]Now the [a]king of Syria was at war with Israel. He consulted his advisers, who said, "Invade at such and such a place." [9]But the prophet sent this message to the king of Israel, "Make sure you don't pass through this place because Syria is invading there." [10]So the king of Israel sent a message to the place the prophet had pointed out, warning it to be on its guard. This happened on several occasions. [11]This made the king of Syria upset. So he summoned his advisers and said to them, "One of us must be helping the king of Israel."[1] [12]One of his advisers said, "No, my master, O king. The prophet Elisha who lives in Israel keeps telling the king of Israel the things you say in your bedroom." [13]The king ordered, "Go, find out where he is, so I can send some men to capture him." The king was told, "He is in [a]Dothan." [14]So he sent horses and chariots there, along with a good-sized army. They arrived during the night and surrounded the city.

[15]The prophet's attendant got up early in the morning. When he went outside there was an army surrounding the city, along with horses and chariots. He said to Elisha, "Oh no, my master! What will we do?" [16]He replied, "[a]Don't be afraid, for our side outnumbers them." [17]Then Elisha prayed, "O LORD, [a]open his eyes so he can see." The LORD opened the servant's eyes, and he saw that the hill was full of [b]horses and chariots of fire all around Elisha. [18]As [a]the army approached him, Elisha prayed to the LORD, "Strike these people with blindness." The LORD struck them with blindness as Elisha requested. [19]Then Elisha said to them, "This is not the right road or city. Follow me, and I will lead you to the man you're looking for." He led them to Samaria.

[20]When they had entered Samaria, Elisha said, "O LORD, open their eyes, so they can see." The LORD opened their eyes, and they saw that they were in the middle of Samaria. [21]When the king of Israel saw them, he asked Elisha, "Should I strike them down, my [a]master?" [22]He replied, "Do not strike them down! You did not capture them with your sword or bow, so what gives you the right to strike them down? [a]Give them some food and water, so they can eat and drink and then go back to their master." [23]So [a]he threw a big banquet for them and they ate and drank. Then he sent them back to their master. After that no Syrian raiding parties again invaded the land of Israel.

The Lord Saves Samaria

[24]Later King Ben [a]Hadad of Syria assembled his entire army and attacked and besieged Samaria. [25]Samaria's food [a]supply ran out. They laid siege to it so long that a donkey's head was selling for eighty shekels of silver and a quarter of a kab of dove's droppings for five shekels of silver.

[26]While the king of Israel was passing by on the city wall, a woman shouted to him, "Help us, my master, O king!" [27]He replied, "No, let the LORD help you. How can I help you? The threshing floor and winepress are empty." [28]Then the king asked her, "What's your problem?" She answered, "This woman said to me, 'Hand over your son; we'll eat him today and then eat my son tomorrow.' [29]So [a]we boiled my son and ate him. Then I said to her the next day, 'Hand over your son and we'll eat him.' But she hid her son!" [30]When the king heard what the woman said, he [a]tore his clothes. As he was passing by on the wall, the people could see he was wearing sackcloth under his clothes. [31]Then he said, "May [a]God judge me severely if Elisha son of Shaphat still has his head by the end of the day!"

[32]Now Elisha was sitting in his house with [a]the community leaders. The king sent a messenger on ahead, but before he arrived, Elisha said to the leaders, "[b]Do you [c]realize this assassin intends to cut off my head? Look, when the messenger arrives, shut the

6:5 [a][Exod 22:14]   6:6 [a]Exod 15:25; 2 Kgs 2:21; 4:41   6:8 [a]2 Kgs 8:28–29   6:11 [1]Heb. *Will you not tell me who among us [is] for the king of Israel?*; a sarcastic rhetorical question.   6:13 [a]Gen 37:17   6:16 [a]Exod 14:13; 1 Kgs 17:13   6:17 [a]Num 22:31; Luke 24:31   [b]2 Kgs 2:11; Ps 34:7; 68:17; Zech 1:8; 6:1–7   6:18 [a]Gen 19:11; Acts 13:11   6:21 [a]2 Kgs 2:12; 5:13; 8:9   6:22 [a][Rom 12:20]   6:23 [a]2 Kgs 5:2; 6:8–9   6:24 [a]1 Kgs 20:1   6:25 [a]2 Kgs 4:38; 8:1   6:29 [a]Lev 26:27–29; Deut 28:52–57; Lam 4:10   6:30 [a]1 Kgs 21:27   6:31 [a]Ruth 1:17; 1 Kgs 19:2   6:32 [a]Ezek 8:1; 14:1; 20:1   [b]Luke 13:32   [c]1 Kgs 18:4, 13, 14; 21:10, 13

door and lean against it. His master will certainly be right behind him." ³³He was still talking to them when the messenger approached and said, "Look, the LORD is responsible for this disaster! ᵃWhy should I continue to wait for the LORD to help?"

7 ¹Elisha replied, "Listen to the LORD's message. This is what the LORD has said, 'About this time ᵃtomorrow a seah of finely milled flour will sell for a shekel and two seahs of barley for a shekel at the gate of Samaria.'" ²An officer who was the king's right-hand man responded to the prophet, "Look, even if the LORD made it rain by opening holes in the sky, could this happen ᵃso soon?" Elisha said, "Look, you will see it happen with your own eyes, but you will not eat any of the food!"

³Now four men with ᵃa skin disease were sitting at the entrance of the city gate. They said to one another, "Why are we just sitting here waiting to die? ⁴If we go into the city, we'll die of starvation, and if we stay here we'll die! So come on, let's defect to the Syrian ᵃcamp! If they spare us, we'll live; if they kill us—well, we were going to die anyway." ⁵So they started toward the Syrian camp at dusk. When they reached the edge of the Syrian camp, there was no one there. ⁶The Lord had caused the Syrian camp ᵃto hear ᵇthe sound of chariots and horses and a large army. Then they said to one another, "Look, the king of Israel has paid the kings of the Hittites and Egyptians to attack us!" ⁷So they got ᵃup and fled at dusk, leaving behind their tents, horses, and donkeys. They left the camp as it was and ran for their lives. ⁸When the men with a skin disease reached the edge of the camp, they entered a tent and had a meal. They also took some silver, gold, and clothes and went and hid it all. Then they went back and entered another tent. They looted it and went and hid what they had taken. ⁹Then they said to one another, "It's not right what we're doing! This is a day to celebrate, but we haven't told anyone. If we wait until dawn, we'll be punished. So come on, let's go and inform the royal palace." ¹⁰So they went and called out to the gatekeepers¹ of the city. They told them, "We entered the Syrian camp and there was no one there. We didn't even hear a man's voice. But the horses and donkeys are still tied up, and the tents remain up." ¹¹The gatekeepers relayed the news to the royal palace.

¹²The king got up in the night and said to his advisers, "I will tell you what the Syrians have done to us. They know we are ᵃstarving, so they left the camp and hid in the field, thinking, 'When they come out of the city, we will capture them alive and enter the city.'" ¹³One of his advisers replied, "Pick some men and have them take five of the horses that are left in the city. (Even if they are killed, their fate will be no different than that of all the Israelite people—we're all going to die!) Let's send them out so we can know for sure what's going on." ¹⁴So they picked two horsemen and the king sent them out to track the Syrian army. He ordered them, "Go and find out what's going on." ¹⁵So they tracked them as far as the Jordan. The road was filled with clothes and equipment that the Syrians had discarded in their haste. The scouts went back and told the king. ¹⁶Then the people went out and looted the Syrian camp. ᵃA seah of finely milled flour sold for a shekel, and two seahs of barley for a shekel, just as in the LORD's message.

¹⁷Now the king had placed the officer who ᵃwas his right-hand man at the city gate. When the people rushed out, they trampled him to death in the gate. This fulfilled the prophet's word which he had spoken when the king tried to arrest him. ¹⁸The prophet had told the king, "ᵃTwo seahs of barley will sell for a shekel, and a seah of finely milled flour for a shekel; this will happen about this time tomorrow in the gate of Samaria." ¹⁹But the officer had replied to the prophet, "Look, even if the LORD made it rain by opening holes in the sky, could this happen so soon?" Elisha had said, "Look, you will see it happen with your own eyes, but you will not eat any of the food!" ²⁰This is exactly what happened to him. The people trampled him to death in the city gate.

Elisha Again Helps the Shunammite Woman

8 Now Elisha advised the woman ᵃwhose son he had brought back to life, "You and your family should go and live somewhere else for ᵇa while, for the LORD has

6:33 ᵃJob 2:9   7:1 ᵃ2 Kgs 7:18–19   7:2 ᵃ2 Kgs 5:18; 7:17, 19, 20   7:3 ᵃ[Lev 13:45–46; Num 5:2–4; 12:10–14]   7:4 ᵃ2 Kgs 6:24   7:6 ᵃ2 Sam 5:24; 2 Kgs 19:7; Job 15:21   ᵇ1 Kgs 10:29   7:7 ᵃPs 48:4–6; [Prov 28:1]   7:10 ¹Heb. gatekeeper.   7:12 ᵃ2 Kgs 6:24–29   7:16 ᵃ2 Kgs 7:1   7:17 ᵃ2 Kgs 6:32; 7:2   7:18 ᵃ2 Kgs 7:1   8:1 ᵃ2 Kgs 4:18, 31–35   ᵇPs 105:16; Hag 1:11

decreed that a [c]famine will overtake the land for seven years." [2]So the woman did as the prophet said. She and her family went and lived in the land of the Philistines for seven years. [3]After seven years the woman returned from the land of the Philistines and went to ask the king to give her back her house and field. [4]Now the king was talking to [a]Gehazi, the prophet's servant, and said, "Tell me all the great things that Elisha has done." [5]While Gehazi was telling the king how Elisha had brought the dead back [a]to life, the woman whose son he had brought back to life came to ask the king for her house and field. Gehazi said, "My master, O king, this is the very woman, and this is her son whom Elisha brought back to life!" [6]The king asked the woman about it, and she gave him the details. The king assigned a eunuch to take care of her request and ordered him, "Give her back everything she owns, as well as the amount of crops her field produced from the day she left the land until now."

Elisha Meets with Hazael

[7]Elisha traveled to Damascus while King Ben [a]Hadad of Syria was sick. The king was told, "The prophet has come here." [8]So the king told [a]Hazael, "[b]Take a gift and go visit the prophet. [c]Request from him an oracle from the LORD. Ask him, 'Will I recover from this sickness?'" [9]So [a]Hazael went to visit Elisha. He took along a gift, as well as[1] 40 camel-loads of all the fine things of Damascus. When he arrived, he stood before him and said, "Your son, King Ben Hadad of Syria, has sent me to you with this question, 'Will I recover from this sickness?'" [10]Elisha said to him, "Go and tell him, 'You will surely recover,'[1] but [a]the LORD has revealed to me that he will surely die." [11]Elisha just stared at him until Hazael became uncomfortable. Then the prophet started [a]crying. [12]Hazael asked, "Why are you crying, my master?" [a]He replied, "Because [b]I know the trouble you will cause the Israelites. You will set fire to

their fortresses, kill their young men with the sword, smash their children to bits, and rip open their pregnant women." [13]Hazael said, "How could your servant, who [a]is as insignificant as a dog, accomplish this great military victory?"[1] Elisha answered, "[b]The LORD has revealed to me that you will be the king of Syria." [14]He left Elisha and went to his master. Ben Hadad asked him, "What did Elisha tell you?" Hazael replied, "He told me you would surely recover." [15]The next day Hazael took a piece of cloth, dipped it in water, and spread it over Ben Hadad's face until he died. Then Hazael replaced him as king.

Jehoram's Reign over Judah

[16]In the fifth year of the reign of Israel's [a]King Joram, son of Ahab, Jehoshaphat's son [b]Jehoram became king over Judah.[1] [17]He was [a]thirty-two years old when he became king, and he reigned for eight years in Jerusalem. [18]He followed in [a]the footsteps of the kings of Israel, just as Ahab's dynasty had done, for he married Ahab's daughter. He did evil in the sight of the LORD. [19]But the LORD [a]was unwilling to destroy Judah. He preserved Judah for the sake of his servant David to whom he had promised a perpetual dynasty.[1]

[20]During his reign [a]Edom freed themselves from Judah's control [b]and set up their own king. [21]Jehoram crossed over to Zair with all his chariots. The Edomites, who had surrounded him, attacked at night and defeated him and his chariot officers.[1] The Israelite army retreated to their homeland. [22]So Edom has remained free from Judah's control to this very day. At that same time Libnah also rebelled.

[23]The rest of the events of Jehoram's reign, including a record of his accomplishments, are recorded in the scroll called the Annals of the Kings of Judah. [24]Jehoram passed away and was buried with his ancestors in the City of David. His son [a]Ahaziah replaced him as king.

8:1 [c]2 Sam 21:1; 1 Kgs 18:2; 2 Kgs 4:38; 6:25   8:4 [a]2 Kgs 4:12; 5:20–27   8:5 [a]2 Kgs 4:35   8:7 [a]2 Kgs 6:24   8:8 [a]1 Kgs 19:15 [b]1 Sam 9:7; 1 Kgs 14:3; 2 Kgs 5:5 [c]2 Kgs 1:2   8:9 [a]1 Kgs 19:15   [1]Or perhaps *consisting of.*   8:10 [a]2 Kgs 8:15   [1]Ket. *Go, say, 'Surely you will not live.'*   8:11 [a]Luke 19:41   8:12 [a]2 Kgs 10:32; 12:17; 13:3, 7; Amos 1:3–4 [b]2 Kgs 15:16; Hos 13:16; Amos 1:13; Nah 3:10   8:13 [a]1 Sam 17:43; 2 Sam 9:8 [b]1 Kgs 19:15 [1]Heb. *Indeed, what is your servant, a dog, that he could do this great thing?*   8:16 [a]2 Kgs 1:17; 3:1 [b]2 Chr 21:3 [1]Heb. *and in the fifth year of Joram son of Ahab king of Israel, and [or while?] Jehoshaphat [was?] king of Judah, Jehoram son of Jehoshaphat king of Judah became king.*   8:17 [a]2 Chr 21:5–10   8:18 [a]2 Kgs 8:26–27   8:19 [a]2 Sam 7:13; 1 Kgs 11:36; 15:4; 2 Chr 21:7 [1]Heb. *just as he had said to him, to give to him a lamp for his sons all the days.*   8:20 [a]Gen 27:40; 2 Chr 21:8–10 [b]1 Kgs 22:47   8:21 [1]Heb. *and he arose at night and defeated Edom, who had surrounded him, and the chariot officers.*   8:24 [a]2 Chr 22:1, 7

Ahaziah Takes the Throne of Judah

25 In the twelfth year of the reign of Israel's King Joram, son of Ahab, Jehoram's son Ahaziah became king over Judah. 26 Ahaziah was [a] twenty-two years old when he became king, and he reigned for one year in Jerusalem. His mother was Athaliah, the granddaughter[1] of King Omri of Israel. 27 He followed in the footsteps of Ahab's dynasty [a] and did evil in the sight of the LORD, as Ahab's dynasty had done, for he was related to Ahab's family.

28 He joined Ahab's son Joram in a battle against King Hazael of Syria at [a] Ramoth Gilead in which the Syrians defeated Joram. 29 [a] King Joram returned to Jezreel to recover from the wounds he received from the Syrians in Ramah when he fought against King Hazael of Syria. King Ahaziah son of Jehoram of Judah went down to visit Joram son of Ahab in Jezreel, for he was ill.

Jehu Becomes King

9 Now Elisha [a] the prophet summoned a member of the prophetic guild and told him, "[b] Tuck your robes into your belt, take this container of olive oil in your [c] hand, and go to Ramoth Gilead. 2 When you arrive there, look for Jehu son of Jehoshaphat son of Nimshi and take him aside into an inner room. 3 [a] Take the container of olive oil, pour it over his head, and say, 'This is what the LORD has said, "I have designated you as king over Israel."' Then open the door and run away quickly!"

4 So the young prophet[1] went to Ramoth Gilead. 5 When he arrived, the officers of the army were sitting there. So he said, "I have a message for you, O officer." Jehu asked, "For which one of us?" He replied, "For you, O officer." 6 So Jehu got up and went inside. Then the prophet poured the olive oil on his head and said to him, "This is what the LORD God of Israel has said, 'I have designated you as king over the LORD's people Israel. 7 You will destroy the family of your master Ahab. I will get [a] revenge against Jezebel for the shed blood of my servants the prophets and for the shed blood of all the LORD's servants. 8 Ahab's [a] entire family will die. I[1] will cut off every last male belonging to Ahab in Israel, including even [b] the [c] weak and incapacitated.[2] 9 I will make Ahab's dynasty like those of [a] Jeroboam son of Nebat and [b] Baasha son of Ahijah. 10 Dogs will devour Jezebel on [a] the plot of ground in Jezreel; she will not be buried.'" Then he opened the door and ran away.

11 When Jehu rejoined [a] his master's servants, they[1] asked him, "Is everything all right? Why did this madman visit you?" He replied, "Ah, it's not important. You know what kind of man he is and the kinds of things he says." 12 But they said, "You're lying! Tell us what he said." So he told them what he had said. He also related how he had said, "This is what the LORD has said, 'I have designated you as king over Israel.'" 13 Each of them quickly [a] took off his cloak, and they spread them out at Jehu's feet on the steps.[1] The trumpet was blown and they shouted, "Jehu is king!" 14 Then Jehu son of Jehoshaphat son of Nimshi conspired against [a] Joram.

Jehu the Assassin

Now Joram had been in Ramoth Gilead with the whole Israelite army, guarding against an invasion by King Hazael of Syria. 15 But [a] King Joram had returned to Jezreel to recover from the wounds he received from the Syrians when he fought against King Hazael of Syria. Jehu told his supporters, "If you really want me to be king,[1] then don't let anyone escape from the city to go and warn Jezreel." 16 Jehu drove his chariot to Jezreel, for Joram was recuperating there. (Now King Ahaziah of Judah had come down to visit Joram.)

17 Now the watchman was standing on the tower in Jezreel and saw Jehu's troops approaching.[1] He said, "I see troops!" Joram ordered, "Send a rider out to meet them and have him ask, 'Is everything all right?'" 18 So the horseman went to meet him and said, "This is what the king says, 'Is everything

---

8:26 [a] 2 Chr 22:2 [1] Heb. *daughter*, can refer to a granddaughter. 8:27 [a] 2 Chr 22:3–4 8:28 [a] 1 Kgs 22:3, 29 8:29 [a] 2 Kgs 9:15 9:1 [a] 1 Kgs 20:35 [b] 2 Kgs 4:29; Jer 1:17 [c] 2 Kgs 8:28–29 9:3 [a] 1 Kgs 19:16 9:4 [1] Heb. *the young man, the young man, the prophet.* 9:7 [a] [Deut 32:35, 41] 9:8 [a] 1 Kgs 14:10; 21:21; 2 Kgs 10:17 [b] 1 Sam 25:22 [c] Deut 32:36; 2 Kgs 14:26 [1] LXX *you.* [2] Heb. *and I will cut off from Ahab those who urinate against a wall,* [including both those who are] *restrained and let free* [or *abandoned*] *in Israel.* 9:9 [a] 1 Kgs 14:10; 15:29; 21:22 [b] 1 Kgs 16:3, 11 9:10 [a] 1 Kgs 21:23; 2 Kgs 9:35–36 9:11 [a] Jer 29:26; Hos 9:7; Mark 3:21; John 10:20; Acts 26:24; [1 Cor 4:10] [1] MT *he.* 9:13 [a] Matt 21:7–8; Mark 11:7–8 [1] Heb. *and they hurried and took, each one his garment, and they placed* [them] *beneath him on the bone* [?] *of the steps.* 9:14 [a] 2 Kgs 8:28 9:15 [a] 2 Kgs 8:29 [1] Heb. *If this is your desire.* 9:17 [1] Heb. *the quantity* [of the men] *of Jehu, when he approached.*

all right?'" Jehu replied, "None of your business! Follow me." The watchman reported, "The messenger reached them, but hasn't started back." [19] So he sent a second horseman out to them and he said, "This is what the king says, 'Is everything all right?'" Jehu replied, "None of your business! Follow me." [20] The watchman reported, "He reached them, but hasn't started back. The one who drives the lead chariot drives like Jehu son of Nimshi; he drives recklessly." [21a] Joram ordered, "Hitch up my chariot." When his chariot had been hitched up, King Joram of Israel and King Ahaziah of Judah went out in their respective chariots to meet Jehu. They met up with him in the plot of land that had [b] once belonged to Naboth of Jezreel.

[22] When Joram saw Jehu, he asked, "Is everything all right, Jehu?" He replied, "How can everything be all right as long as your mother Jezebel promotes idolatry and pagan practices?" [23] Joram turned his chariot around and took off. He said to Ahaziah, "It's a trap, Ahaziah!" [24] Jehu aimed his bow and shot an arrow right between Joram's shoulders. The arrow went through his heart and he fell to his knees in his chariot. [25] Jehu ordered his officer Bidkar, "Pick him up and throw him into [a] the part of the field that once belonged to Naboth of Jezreel. Remember, you and I were riding together behind his father, Ahab, when the LORD pronounced this [b] oracle against him, [26] "'Know for sure that I saw the shed blood of Naboth [a] and his sons yesterday,' says the LORD, "and that I will give you what you deserve right here in this plot of land," says the LORD.' So now pick him up and throw him into this plot of land, just as in the LORD's message."

[27] When King Ahaziah of Judah saw what happened, he took off up the road to Beth Haggan. Jehu chased him and ordered, "Shoot him too." They shot him while he was driving his chariot up the ascent of Gur near Ibleam. He fled to [a] Megiddo and died there. [28] His servants took his body back to Jerusalem and buried him in his tomb with his ancestors in the City of David. [29] Ahaziah had become king over Judah in the eleventh year of Joram son of Ahab.

[30] Jehu approached Jezreel. When Jezebel heard the news, she put on some eye liner, fixed up her hair, [a] and leaned out the window. [31] When Jehu came through the gate, she said, "[a] Is everything all right, Zimri, murderer of his master?" [32] He looked up at the window and said, "Who is on my side? Who?" Two or three eunuchs looked down at him. [33] He said, "Throw her down!" So they threw her down, and when she hit the ground, her blood splattered against the wall and the horses, and Jehu drove his chariot over her. [34] He went inside and had a meal. Then [a] he said, "Dispose of this accursed woman's corpse. Bury her, for after all, she was a king's daughter." [35] But when they went to bury her, they found nothing left but the skull, feet, and palms of the hands. [36] So they went back and told him. Then he said, "It is the fulfillment of the LORD's message that he had spoken through his servant, Elijah the Tishbite, 'In the plot of land at Jezreel, dogs will devour Jezebel's flesh. [37] Jezebel's corpse will be like manure on the surface of the ground in the plot of land at Jezreel. People will not be able to even recognize her.'"

Jehu Wipes out Ahab's Family

10 Ahab had 70 sons living in Samaria. So Jehu wrote letters and sent them to Samaria to the leading officials of Jezreel and to the guardians of Ahab's dynasty. This is what the letters said, [2] "You have with you the sons of your master, chariots and horses, a fortified city, and weapons. So when this letter arrives, [3] pick the best and most capable of your master's sons, place him on his father's throne, and defend your master's dynasty."

[4] They were absolutely terrified and said, "Look, [a] two kings could not stop him! How can we?" [5] So the palace supervisor, the city commissioner, the leaders, and the guardians sent this message to Jehu, "We are your subjects! Whatever you say, we will do. We will not make anyone king. Do what you consider proper."

9:19 [1] MT *peace.*   **9:21** [a] 1 Kgs 19:17; 2 Chr 22:7   [b] 1 Kgs 21:1–14   **9:22** [1] Heb. *How* [can there be] *peace as long as the adulterous acts of Jezebel your mother and her acts of sorcery* [are] *many?*   **9:23** [1] Heb. *and Jehoram turned his hands and fled.*   **9:25** [a] 1 Kgs 21:19, 24–29   [b] Isa 13:1   **9:26** [a] 1 Kgs 21:13, 19   **9:27** [a] 2 Chr 22:7, 9   **9:30** [a] [Jer 4:30]; Ezek 23:40   [1] Heb. *she fixed her eyes with antimony*; antimony was used as a cosmetic and the narrator portrays her as a prostitute.   **9:31** [a] 1 Kgs 16:9–20; 2 Kgs 9:18–22   **9:32** [1] Heb. *two, three.*   **9:34** [a] [Exod 22:28]; 1 Kgs 16:31   **9:37** [1] Heb. *so that they will not say, "This is Jezebel."*   **10:4** [a] 2 Kgs 9:24, 27   [1] Heb. *they were very, very afraid*; an emphatic Heb. construction.

[6] He wrote them a second letter, saying, "If you are really on my side and are willing to obey me, then take the heads of your master's sons and come to me in Jezreel at this time tomorrow." Now the king had 70 sons, and the prominent men of the city were raising them. [7] When they received the letter, they seized the king's sons and [a] executed all 70 of them. They put their heads in baskets and sent them to him in Jezreel. [8] The messenger came and told Jehu, "They have brought the heads of the king's sons." Jehu said, "Stack them in two piles at the entrance of the city gate until morning." [9] In the [a] morning he went out and stood there. Then he said to all the people, "You are innocent. I conspired against my master and killed him. But who struck down all of these men? [10] Therefore take note that not one of the LORD's words which he pronounced against Ahab's dynasty will [a] fail to materialize. The LORD has done what he announced [b] through his servant Elijah." [11] Then Jehu killed all who were left of Ahab's family in Jezreel, and all his nobles, close friends, and priests. He left no survivors.

[12] Jehu then left there and set out for Samaria. While he was traveling through Beth Eked of the Shepherds, [13a] Jehu encountered the relatives of King Ahaziah of Judah. He asked, "Who are you?" They replied, "We are Ahaziah's relatives. We have come down to see how the king's sons and the queen mother's sons are doing." [14] He said, "Capture them alive!" So they captured them alive and then [a] executed all 42 of them by the cistern at Beth Eked. He left no survivors.

[15] When he left there, he met [a] Jehonadab son of [b] Rekab who had been looking for him. Jehu greeted him and asked, "Are you as committed to me as I am to you?" Jehonadab answered, "I am!" Jehu replied, "If so, [c] give me your hand." So he offered his hand and Jehu pulled him up into the chariot. [16] Jehu said, "Come with me and see how [a] zealous I am for the LORD's cause." So he[1] took him along in his chariot. [17] He went to Samaria and killed each of Ahab's remaining family members who were in Samaria until [a] he destroyed them, in keeping with the LORD's message [b] which he had announced to Elijah.

Jehu Executes the Prophets and Priests of Baal

[18] Jehu assembled all the people and said to them, "[a] Ahab worshiped Baal a little; Jehu will worship him with great devotion. [19] So now, bring to me all the [a] prophets of Baal, as well as all his servants and priests. None of them must be absent, for I am offering a great sacrifice to Baal. Any of them who fails to appear will lose his life." But Jehu was tricking them so he could destroy the servants of Baal. [20] Then Jehu ordered, "Make arrangements for a celebration for Baal." So they announced it. [21] Jehu sent invitations throughout Israel, and all the servants of Baal came; not one was absent. They arrived at the [a] temple of Baal and filled it up from end to end. [22] Jehu ordered the one who was in charge of the wardrobe, "Bring out robes for all the servants of Baal." So he brought out robes for them. [23] Then Jehu and Jehonadab son of Rekab went to the temple of Baal. Jehu said to the servants of Baal, "Make sure there are no servants of the LORD here with you; there must be only servants of Baal." [24] They went inside to offer sacrifices and burnt offerings. Now Jehu had stationed 80 men outside. He had told them, "If any of the men inside gets away, you will pay with your lives!"

[25] When he finished offering the burnt sacrifice, Jehu ordered the royal guard and officers, "Come in and strike them down! Don't let any escape!" So the royal guard and officers struck them down with the sword and left their bodies lying there. Then they entered the inner sanctuary of the temple of Baal.[1] [26] They hauled out the [a] sacred pillar of the temple of Baal and burned it. [27] They demolished the sacred pillar of Baal and the temple of Baal; it is used [a] as a latrine to this very day. [28] So Jehu eradicated Baal worship from Israel.

A Summary of Jehu's Reign

[29] However, Jehu did not repudiate [a] the sins that Jeroboam son of Nebat had encouraged Israel to commit; the golden

---

10:7 [a] Judg 9:5; 1 Kgs 21:21; 2 Kgs 11:1   10:9 [a] 2 Kgs 9:14–24   10:10 [a] 1 Sam 3:19; 1 Kgs 8:56; Jer 44:28   [b] 1 Kgs 21:17–24, 29   10:13 [a] 2 Chr 22:8   10:14 [a] 2 Chr 22:8   10:15 [a] Jer 35:6   [b] 1 Chr 2:55   [c] Ezra 10:19; Ezek 17:18   [1] Heb. *Jehonadab said, 'There is and there is. Give your hand.'*   10:16 [a] 1 Kgs 19:10   [1] MT *they.*   10:17 [a] 2 Kgs 9:8; 2 Chr 22:8   [b] 1 Kgs 21:21, 29   10:18 [a] 1 Kgs 16:31–32   10:19 [a] 1 Kgs 18:19; 22:6   10:21 [a] 1 Kgs 16:32; 2 Kgs 11:18   10:25 [1] Heb. *and they came to the city of the house of Baal.*   10:26 [a] [Deut 7:5, 25]; 1 Kgs 14:23; 2 Kgs 3:2   10:27 [a] Ezra 6:11; Dan 2:5; 3:29   10:29 [a] 1 Kgs 12:28–30; 13:33–34

calves remained in Bethel and Dan. [30]The LORD [a]said to Jehu, "[b]You have done well. You have accomplished my will and carried out my wishes with regard to Ahab's dynasty. Therefore four generations of your descendants will rule over Israel." [31]But Jehu did not carefully and wholeheartedly obey [a]the law of the LORD God of Israel. He did not repudiate the sins which Jeroboam had encouraged Israel to commit.

[32]In those days the LORD began to reduce the size of Israel's territory. [a]Hazael attacked their eastern border.[1] [33]He conquered all the land of Gilead, including the territory of Gad, Reuben, and Manasseh, extending all the way from the [a]Aroer in the Arnon Valley through [b]Gilead to Bashan.

[34]The rest of the events of Jehu's reign, including all his accomplishments and successes, are recorded in the scroll called the Annals of the Kings of Israel. [35]Jehu passed away and was buried in Samaria. His son [a]Jehoahaz replaced him as king. [36]Jehu reigned over Israel for 28 years in Samaria.

Athaliah Is Eliminated

11 When [a]Athaliah, [b]the mother of Ahaziah, saw that her son was [c]dead, she was determined to destroy the entire royal line.[1] [2]So Jehosheba, the daughter of King Jehoram[1] and sister of [a]Ahaziah, took Ahaziah's son Joash and stole him away from the rest of the royal descendants who were to be executed. She hid him and his nurse in the room where the bed covers were stored.[2] So he was hidden from Athaliah and escaped execution. [3]He hid out with his nurse in the LORD's temple for six years, while Athaliah was ruling over the land.

[4]In [a]the seventh year Jehoiada summoned the officers of the units of hundreds of the Carians and the royal bodyguard. He met with them in the LORD's temple. He made an agreement with them and made them swear an oath of allegiance in the LORD's temple. Then he showed them the king's son. [5]He ordered them, "This is what you must do. [a]One-third of the unit that is on duty during the Sabbath will guard the royal palace.

[6]Another third of you will be stationed at the Foundation[1] Gate. Still another third of you will be stationed at the gate behind the royal guard. You will take turns guarding the palace. [7]The two units who are off duty on the Sabbath will guard the LORD's temple and protect the king. [8]You must surround the king. Each of you must hold his weapon in his hand. Whoever approaches your ranks must be killed. You must accompany the king wherever he goes."

[9][a]The officers of the units of hundreds did just as Jehoiada the priest ordered. Each of them took his men, those who were on duty during the Sabbath as well as those who were off duty on the Sabbath, and reported to Jehoiada the priest. [10]The priest gave to the officers of the units of hundreds King David's spears and the shields [a]that were kept in the LORD's temple. [11]The royal bodyguard took their stations, each holding his weapon in his hand. They lined up from the south side of the temple to the north side and stood near the altar and the temple, surrounding the king. [12]Jehoiada led out the king's son and placed on him the crown and the royal [a]insignia.[1] They proclaimed him king and poured olive oil [b]on his head. They clapped their hands and cried out, "Long live the king!"

[13][a]When Athaliah heard the royal guard[1] shout, she joined the crowd at the LORD's temple. [14]Then she [a]saw the king standing by the pillar, according to custom. The officers stood beside the king with their trumpets, and all the people of the land were celebrating and blowing trumpets. Athaliah tore her clothes and screamed, "Treason, treason!" [15]Jehoiada the priest ordered the officers of the units of hundreds, who were in charge of the army, "Bring her outside the temple to the guards. Put to death by the sword anyone who follows her." The priest gave this order because he had decided she should not be executed in the LORD's temple. [16]They seized her and took her into the precincts of the royal palace through the horses' entrance. There she was executed.

10:30 [a]2 Kgs 9:6–7 [b]2 Kgs 13:1, 10; 14:23; 15:8, 12. **10:31** [1]1 Kgs 14:16 **10:32** [a]1 Kgs 19:17; 2 Kgs 8:12; 13:22 [1]Heb. *Hazael struck them down in all the territory of Israel, from the Jordan on the east.* **10:33** [a]Deut 2:36 [b]Amos 1:3–5 **10:35** [a]2 Kgs 13:1 **11:1** [a]2 Chr 22:10 [b]2 Kgs 8:26 [c]2 Kgs 9:27 [1]Heb. *she arose and she destroyed all the royal offspring.* **11:2** [a]2 Kgs 8:25 [1]Heb. *Joram.* [2]Heb. *him and his nurse in an inner room of beds.* **11:4** [a]2 Kgs 12:2; 2 Chr 23:1 **11:5** [a]1 Chr 9:25 **11:6** [1]Heb. *the gate of Sur.* **11:9** [a]2 Chr 23:8 **11:10** [a]2 Sam 8:7; 1 Chr 18:7 **11:12** [a]Exod 25:16; 31:18 [b]1 Sam 10:24 [1]Heb. *witness, testimony.* **11:13** [a]2 Kgs 8:26; 2 Chr 23:12 [1]MT *and Athaliah heard the sound of the runners, the people.* **11:14** [a]2 Kgs 23:3; 2 Chr 34:31

[17] Jehoiada [a] then drew [b] up a covenant [c] between the LORD and the king and people, stipulating that they should be loyal to the LORD. [18] All the people of the land went and demolished the [a] temple of Baal. They smashed its altars and idols to bits.[1] They [b] killed Mattan [c] the priest of Baal in front of the altar. Jehoiada the priest then placed guards at the LORD's temple. [19] He took the officers of the units of hundreds, the Carians, the royal bodyguard, and all the people of the land, and together they led the king down from the LORD's temple. They entered the royal palace through the Gate of the Royal Bodyguard, and the king sat down on the royal throne. [20] All the people of the land celebrated, for the city had rest now that they had killed Athaliah with the sword in the royal palace.

Joash's Reign over Judah

[21] Jehoash was [a] seven years old when he began to reign. [1] In Jehu's seventh year **12** [a] Jehoash became king; he reigned for 40 years in Jerusalem. His mother was Zibiah, who was from Beer Sheba. [2] Jehoash did what the LORD approved all his days when [a] Jehoiada the priest taught him. [3] But [a] the high places were not eliminated; the people continued to offer sacrifices and burn incense on the high places.

[4] Jehoash said to the priests, "I place at your disposal [a] all the consecrated silver that has been brought to the LORD's temple, including the silver collected from the [b] census tax,[1] the silver received from those who have made [c] vows,[2] and all the silver that people have [d] voluntarily contributed to the LORD's temple. [5] The priests should receive the silver they need from the treasurers and repair any damage to the temple they discover."

[6] By the twenty-third year of King Jehoash's reign the priests had still not repaired the damage to the temple. [7a] So King Jehoash summoned Jehoiada the priest along with the other priests, and said to them, "Why have you not repaired the damage to the temple? Now, take no more silver from your treasurers unless you intend to use it to repair the damage." [8] The priests agreed not to collect silver from the people and relieved themselves of personal responsibility for the temple repairs.[1]

[9] Jehoiada the priest took [a] a chest and drilled a hole in its lid. [b] He placed it on the right side of the altar near the entrance of the LORD's temple. The priests who guarded the entrance would put into it all the silver brought to the LORD's temple. [10] When they saw the chest was full of silver, the royal [a] secretary and the high priest counted the silver that had been brought to the LORD's temple and bagged it up. [11] They would then hand over the silver that had been weighed to the construction foremen assigned to the LORD's temple. They hired carpenters and builders to work on the LORD's temple, [12] as well as masons and stonecutters. They bought wood and chiseled stone to [a] repair the damage to the LORD's temple and also paid for all the other expenses. [13] The silver brought to [a] the LORD's temple was not used for silver bowls, trimming shears, basins, trumpets, or any kind of gold or silver implements. [14] It was handed over to the foremen who used it to repair the LORD's temple. [15] They did not audit [a] the treasurers who disbursed the funds to the foremen, for they were honest. [16] (The silver collected in conjunction with reparation offerings and sin offerings was not brought to [a] the LORD's temple; [b] it belonged to the priests.)

[17] At that time King [a] Hazael of Syria attacked Gath and captured it. [b] Hazael then decided to attack Jerusalem. [18] King Jehoash of Judah [a] collected all the sacred items that his ancestors Jehoshaphat, Jehoram, and Ahaziah, kings of Judah, had consecrated, as well as his own sacred items and all the gold that could be found in the treasuries of the LORD's temple and the royal palace. He sent it all to King Hazael of Syria, who then withdrew from Jerusalem.

[19] The rest of the events of Joash's reign, including all his accomplishments, are

11:17 [a] 2 Chr 23:16   [b] Josh 24:24–25; 2 Chr 15:12–15   [c] 2 Sam 5:3   [1] An emphatic Heb. construction.   11:21 [a] 2 Chr 24:1–14   12:1 [a] 2 Chr 24:1   12:2 [a] 2 Kgs 11:4   12:3 [a] 1 Kgs 15:14; 22:43; 2 Kgs 14:4; 15:35   12:4 [a] 2 Kgs 22:4   [b] Exod 30:13–16   [c] Lev 27:2–28   [d] Exod 35:5; 1 Chr 29:3–9   [1] Heb. *the silver of passing over a man.*   [2] Heb. *the silver of persons, his valuation.*   12:7 [a] 2 Chr 24:6   12:8 [1] Heb. *and not to repair the damages to the temple*; i.e., the priests hired skilled workers to repair the damage to the temple, rather than trying to make the repairs themselves.   12:9 [a] 2 Chr 23:1; 24:8   [b] Mark 12:41; Luke 21:1   12:10 [a] 2 Sam 8:17; 2 Kgs 19:2; 22:3–4, 12   12:12 [a] 2 Kgs 22:5–6   12:13 [a] 2 Chr 24:14   12:15 [a] 2 Kgs 22:7; [1 Cor 4:2]; 2 Cor 8:20   12:16 [a] [Lev 5:15, 18]   [b] [Lev 7:7; Num 18:9]   12:17 [a] 2 Kgs 8:12   [b] 2 Chr 24:23   12:18 [a] 1 Kgs 15:18; 2 Kgs 16:8; 18:15–16

recorded in the scroll called the Annals of the Kings of Judah. [20]His servants conspired against him and murdered Joash at Beth Millo, on the road that goes down to Silla. [21]His servants Jozabad son of Shimeath and Jehozabad son of Shomer murdered him. He was buried with his ancestors in the City of David. His son [a]Amaziah replaced him as king.

Jehoahaz's Reign over Israel

13 In the twenty-third year of the reign of Judah's King [a]Joash son of Ahaziah, Jehu's son [b]Jehoahaz became king over Israel. He reigned in Samaria for 17 years. [2]He did evil in the sight of the LORD. He continued in the sinful [a]ways of Jeroboam son of Nebat who had encouraged Israel to sin; he did not repudiate those sins. [3]The LORD was furious with Israel and handed [a]them over to King [b]Hazael of Syria and to Hazael's son Ben [c]Hadad for many years.

[4]Jehoahaz asked for [a]the LORD's mercy, and the LORD responded favorably, for he saw that Israel was oppressed by the king of Syria. [5]The LORD provided a deliverer for Israel, and they were freed from Syria's power. [a]The Israelites once more lived in security. [6]But they did not repudiate the sinful ways of the family of Jeroboam, who encouraged Israel to sin; they continued in those sins.[1] There was even [a]an Asherah pole standing in Samaria. [7]Jehoahaz had no army left[1] except for 50 horsemen, 10 chariots, [a]and 10,000 foot soldiers. The king of Syria had destroyed his troops and trampled on them as dust.

[8]The rest of the events of Jehoahaz's reign, including all his accomplishments and successes, are recorded in the scroll called the Annals of the Kings of Israel. [9]Jehoahaz passed away and was buried in Samaria. His son Jehoash replaced him as king.

Jehoash's Reign over Israel

[10]In the thirty-seventh year of King Jehoash's reign over Judah, Jehoahaz's son Jehoash became king over Israel. He reigned in Samaria for 16 years. [11]He did evil in the sight of the LORD. He did not repudiate the sinful ways of Jeroboam son of Nebat who encouraged Israel to sin; he continued in those sins. [12a]The rest of the events of Jehoash's reign, including [b]all [c]his accomplishments and his successful war with King Amaziah of Judah, are recorded in the scroll called the Annals of the Kings of Israel. [13]Jehoash passed [a]away and Jeroboam succeeded him on the throne. Jehoash was buried in Samaria with the kings of Israel.

Elisha Makes One Final Prophecy

[14]Now Elisha had a terminal illness. King Jehoash of Israel went down to visit him. [a]He wept before him and said, "My father, my father! The chariot and horsemen of Israel!" [15]Elisha told him, "Take a bow and some arrows," and he did so. [16]Then Elisha told the king of Israel, "Aim the bow." He did so, and Elisha placed his hands on the king's hands. [17]Elisha said, "Open the east window," and he did so. Elisha said, "Shoot!" and he did so. Elisha said, "This arrow symbolizes the victory the LORD will give you over Syria. You will annihilate Syria in [a]Aphek!" [18]Then Elisha said, "Take the arrows," and he did so. He told the king of Israel, "Strike the ground!" He struck the ground three times and stopped. [19]The prophet got angry at him and said, "If you had struck the ground five or six times, you would have annihilated Syria! [a]But now, you will defeat Syria only three times."

[20]Elisha died and was buried. Moabite [a]raiding parties invaded the land at the beginning of the year.[1] [21]One day some men were burying a man when they spotted a raiding party. So they threw the dead man into Elisha's tomb. When the body touched Elisha's bones, the dead man came to life and stood on his feet.

[22]Now King [a]Hazael of Syria oppressed Israel throughout Jehoahaz's reign. [23]But the LORD had mercy [a]on them and felt pity for them. He [b]extended his favor to them [c]because of the promise he had made to Abraham, Isaac, and Jacob. He has been unwilling to destroy them or remove them from his presence to this very day. [24]When King Hazael of Syria died, his son Ben Hadad replaced him as king. [25]Jehoahaz's son Jehoash took back from Ben Hadad son of Hazael the

12:21 [a]2 Chr 24:27   **13:1** [a]2 Kgs 12:1   [b]2 Kgs 10:35   **13:2** [a]1 Kgs 12:26–33   **13:3** [a]Judg 2:14   [b]2 Kgs 8:12   [c]Amos 1:4   **13:4** [a][Exod 3:7, 9; Judg 2:18]; 2 Kgs 14:26   **13:5** [a]2 Kgs 13:25; 14:25, 27; Neh 9:27   **13:6** [a]1 Kgs 16:33   [1]Heb. *in it he walked.*   **13:7** [a]2 Kgs 10:32   [1]Heb. *Indeed he did not leave to Jehoahaz people.*   **13:12** [a]2 Kgs 14:8–15   [b]2 Kgs 13:14–19, 25   [c]2 Kgs 14:9; 2 Chr 25:17–25   **13:13** [a]2 Kgs 14:16   **13:14** [a]2 Kgs 2:12   **13:17** [a]1 Kgs 20:26   **13:19** [a]2 Kgs 13:25   **13:20** [a]2 Kgs 3:5; 24:2   [1]MT *it came, year.*   **13:22** [a]2 Kgs 8:12–13   **13:23** [a]2 Kgs 14:27   [b][Exod 2:24–25]   [c]Gen 13:16–17; 17:2–7; Exod 32:13

cities that he had taken from his father Jehoahaz in war. Jehoash defeated him [a]three times and recovered the Israelite cities.

Amaziah's Reign over Judah

14 In [a]the second year of the reign of Israel's King Joash son of Joahaz, Joash's son [b]Amaziah became king over Judah. [2]He was twenty-five years old when he began to reign, and he reigned for twenty-nine years in Jerusalem. His mother was Jehoaddan, who was from Jerusalem. [3]He did what the LORD approved, but not like David his ancestor had done. He followed the example of his father [a]Joash. [4a]But the high places were not eliminated; the people continued to offer sacrifices and burn incense on the high places.

[5]When he had secured control of the kingdom, he executed the servants [a]who had assassinated his father. [6]But he did not execute the sons of the assassins. He obeyed the LORD's commandment as recorded in the scroll of the law of Moses, "[a]Fathers must not be put to death for what their sons do, and sons must not be put to death for what their fathers do. A man must be put to death only for his own sin."

[7]He defeated 10,000 Edomites in [a]the Salt Valley; [b]he captured Sela in battle [c]and renamed it Joktheel, a name it has retained to this very day. [8]Then Amaziah sent messengers to Jehoash son of Jehoahaz son of Jehu, king of Israel. [a]He said, "Come, let's meet face to face."[1] [9]King Jehoash of Israel sent this message back to King Amaziah of Judah, "A thornbush in Lebanon sent this message to a cedar in Lebanon, 'Give your daughter to my son as a wife.' [a]Then [b]a wild animal of Lebanon came by and trampled down the thorn. [10]You thoroughly defeated Edom, and it has gone to [a]your head! Gloat over your success, but stay in your palace. Why bring calamity on yourself? Why bring down yourself and Judah along with you?" [11]But Amaziah would not heed the warning, so King Jehoash of Israel attacked. He and King Amaziah of Judah met face to face in Beth [a]Shemesh of Judah. [12]Judah was defeated by Israel, and each man ran back home. [13]King Jehoash of Israel captured King Amaziah of Judah, son of Jehoash son of Ahaziah, in Beth Shemesh. [a]He[1] attacked Jerusalem and broke down [b]the wall of Jerusalem from the Gate of Ephraim to the Corner Gate—a distance of about 600 feet.[2] [14]He took away all [a]the gold and silver, all the items found in the LORD's temple and in the treasuries of the royal palace, and some hostages. Then he went back to Samaria.

[15a]The rest of the events of Jehoash's reign, including all his accomplishments and his successful war with King Amaziah of Judah, are recorded in the scroll called the Annals of the Kings of Israel. [16]Jehoash passed away and was buried in Samaria with the kings of Israel. His son Jeroboam replaced him as king.

[17]King [a]Amaziah son of Joash of Judah lived for 15 years after the death of King Jehoash son of Jehoahaz of Israel. [18]The rest of the events of Amaziah's reign are recorded in the scroll called the Annals of the Kings of Judah. [19]Conspirators plotted against him in Jerusalem, so [a]he fled to [b]Lachish. But they sent assassins after him, and they killed him there. [20]His body was carried back by horses, and he was buried in Jerusalem with his ancestors in the City of David. [21]All the people of Judah took [a]Azariah, who was sixteen years old, and made him king in his father Amaziah's place. [22]Azariah built up [a]Elat and restored it to Judah after the king had passed away.

Jeroboam II's Reign over Israel

[23]In the fifteenth year of the reign of Judah's King Amaziah son of Joash, Jeroboam son of Joash became king over Israel. He reigned for 41 years in Samaria. [24]He did evil in the sight of the LORD; he did not repudiate the sinful [a]ways of Jeroboam son of Nebat who encouraged Israel to sin. [25]He [a]restored the border of Israel [b]from Lebo Hamath[1] in [c]the north to the sea of the rift valley[2] in the south, just as in the message

13:25 [a]2 Kgs 13:18–19   14:1 [a]2 Kgs 13:10   [b]2 Chr 25:1–2   14:3 [a]2 Kgs 12:2   14:4 [a]2 Kgs 12:3   14:5 [a]2 Kgs 12:20
14:6 [a]Deut 24:16; [Jer 31:30; Ezek 18:4, 20]   14:7 [a]2 Chr 25:5–16   [b]2 Sam 8:13; 1 Chr 18:12; Ps 60:title   [c]Josh 15:38
14:8 [a]2 Chr 25:17–18   [1]Heb. *let us look at each other* [in the] *face.*   14:9 [a]Judg 9:8–15   [b]1 Kgs 4:33   14:10 [a]Deut 8:14; 2 Chr 32:25; [Ezek 28:2, 5, 17; Hab 2:4]   14:11 [a]Josh 19:38; 21:16   14:13 [a]Neh 8:16; 12:39   [b]Jer 31:38; Zech 14:10   [1]MT *they.*   [2]Heb. *400 cubits.*   14:14 [a]1 Kgs 7:51; 2 Kgs 12:18; 16:8   14:15 [a]2 Kgs 13:12–13   14:17 [a]2 Chr 25:25–28   14:19 [a]2 Chr 25:27   [b]Josh 10:31   14:21 [a]2 Kgs 15:13; 2 Chr 26:1   14:22 [a]1 Kgs 9:26; 2 Kgs 16:6; 2 Chr 8:17   14:24 [a]1 Kgs 12:26–33   14:25 [a]2 Kgs 10:32; 13:5, 25   [b]Num 13:21; 34:8; 1 Kgs 8:65   [c]Deut 3:17   [1]Or *entrance of Hamath*; perhaps 44 miles north of Damascus.   [2]The Dead Sea.

from the LORD God of Israel that he had announced through his servant [d]Jonah son of Amittai, the prophet from [e]Gath Hepher. [26]The LORD [a]saw Israel's intense suffering;[1] everyone was weak and incapacitated and Israel had no deliverer. [27][a]The LORD had not decreed that he would blot out Israel's memory from under heaven, so he delivered them through Jeroboam son of Joash.

[28]The rest of the events of Jeroboam's reign, including all his accomplishments, his military success in restoring Israelite control over [a]Damascus and Hamath, are recorded in the scroll called the Annals of the Kings of Israel. [29]Jeroboam passed away and was buried in Samaria with the kings of Israel. His son [a]Zechariah replaced him as king.

Azariah's Reign over Judah

15 In the twenty-seventh year of King Jeroboam's reign over Israel, Amaziah's son [a]Azariah [b]became king over Judah. [2]He was sixteen years old when he began to reign, and he reigned for 52 years in Jerusalem. His mother's name was Jecholiah, who was from Jerusalem. [3]He did what the LORD approved, just as his father Amaziah had done. [4][a]But the high places were not eliminated; the people continued to offer sacrifices and burn incense on the high places. [5]The LORD [a]afflicted the king with an illness; he suffered from a skin disease[1] until the day he [b]died. He [c]lived in separate quarters, while his son Jotham was in charge of the palace and ruled over the people of the land.

[6]The rest of the events of Azariah's reign, including all his accomplishments, are recorded in the scroll called the Annals of the Kings of Judah. [7]Azariah passed away and was buried with his ancestors in [a]the City of David. His son Jotham replaced him as king.

Zechariah's Reign over Israel

[8]In the thirty-eighth year of King Azariah's reign over Judah, Jeroboam's son [a]Zechariah became king over Israel. He reigned in Samaria for six months. [9]He did evil in the sight of the LORD, [a]as his ancestors had done. He did not repudiate the sinful ways of Jeroboam son of Nebat who encouraged Israel to sin. [10]Shallum son of Jabesh conspired against him; he assassinated him in Ibleam[1] and took his place as king. [11]The rest of the events of Zechariah's reign are recorded in the scroll called the Annals of the Kings of Israel. [12]His assassination fulfilled the LORD's message to Jehu, "Four generations of [a]your descendants will rule on Israel's throne." And that is how it happened.

[13]Shallum son of Jabesh became king in the thirty-ninth year of King Uzziah's reign over Judah. He reigned for one month in Samaria. [14]Menahem son of Gadi went up from [a]Tirzah to Samaria and attacked Shallum son of Jabesh. He killed him and took his place as king. [15]The rest of the events of Shallum's reign, including the conspiracy he organized, are recorded in the scroll called the Annals of the Kings of Israel. [16]At that time Menahem came from Tirzah and attacked [a]Tiphsah. [b]He struck down all who lived in the city and the surrounding territory, because they would not surrender. He even ripped open the pregnant women.

Menahem's Reign over Israel

[17]In the thirty-ninth year of King Azariah's reign over Judah, Menahem son of Gadi became king over Israel. He reigned for 10 years in Samaria. [18]He did evil in the sight of the LORD; he did not repudiate the sinful ways of Jeroboam son of Nebat, who encouraged Israel to sin.[1]

During his reign, [19][a]Pul king of Assyria invaded the land, and Menahem paid him 1,000 talents[1] of silver to gain his support and to [b]solidify his control of the kingdom. [20]Menahem [a]got this silver by taxing all the wealthy men in Israel; he took 50 shekels of silver from each one of them and paid it to the king of Assyria. Then the king of Assyria left; he did not stay there in the land.

[21]The rest of the events of Menahem's reign, including all his accomplishments, are recorded in the scroll called the Annals of the Kings of Israel. [22]Menahem passed away and his son Pekahiah replaced him as king.

14:25 [d] Jonah 1:1; Matt 12:39–40 [e] Josh 19:13 14:26 [a] Exod 3:7; 2 Kgs 13:4; Ps 106:44 [1] Heb. *for the LORD saw the very bitter affliction of Israel.* 14:27 [a] [2 Kgs 13:5, 23] 14:28 [a] 1 Kgs 11:24 14:29 [a] 2 Kgs 15:8 15:1 [a] 2 Kgs 15:13, 30 [b] 2 Kgs 14:21; 2 Chr 26:1, 3, 4 15:4 [a] 2 Kgs 12:3; 14:4; 15:35 15:5 [a] 2 Chr 26:19–23; Ps 78:31 [b] Isa 6:1 [c] [Lev 13:46]; Num 12:14 [1] Trad. *he was a leper.* 15:7 [a] 2 Chr 26:23 15:8 [a] 2 Kgs 14:29 15:9 [a] 2 Kgs 14:24 15:10 [1] MT *and he struck him down before the people and killed him.* 15:12 [a] 2 Kgs 10:30 15:14 [a] 1 Kgs 14:17; Song 6:4 15:16 [a] 1 Kgs 4:24 [b] 2 Kgs 8:12; Hos 13:16 15:18 [1] MT adds *all his days.* 15:19 [a] 1 Chr 5:26; Isa 66:19; Hos 8:9 [b] 2 Kgs 14:5 [1] About 75,000 pounds. 15:20 [a] 2 Kgs 23:35

Pekahiah's Reign over Israel

23 In the fiftieth year of King Azariah's reign over Judah, Menahem's son Pekahiah became king over Israel. He reigned in Samaria for two years. 24 He did evil in the sight of the LORD; he did not repudiate the sinful ways of Jeroboam son of Nebat who encouraged Israel to sin. 25 His officer Pekah son of Remaliah conspired against him. He and 50 Gileadites assassinated Pekahiah, as well as Argob and Arieh, in Samaria in the [a]fortress of the royal palace. Pekah then took his place as king.

26 The rest of the events of Pekahiah's reign, including all his accomplishments, are recorded in the scroll called the Annals of the Kings of Israel.

Pekah's Reign over Israel

27 In the fifty-second year of King Azariah's reign over Judah, [a]Pekah son of Remaliah became king over Israel. He reigned in Samaria for twenty years. 28 He did evil in the sight of the LORD; he did not repudiate the sinful ways of Jeroboam son of Nebat who encouraged Israel to sin. 29 During Pekah's reign over Israel, King Tiglath-Pileser of Assyria [a]came and captured [b]Ijon, Abel Beth Maacah, Janoah, Kedesh, Hazor, Gilead, and Galilee, including all the territory of Naphtali. He deported the people to Assyria. 30 Hoshea son of Elah conspired against Pekah son of Remaliah. He assassinated him and took his place as [a]king, in the twentieth year of the reign of Jotham son of Uzziah.

31 The rest of the events of Pekah's reign, including all his accomplishments, are recorded in the scroll called the Annals of the Kings of Israel.

Jotham's Reign over Judah

32 In the second year of the reign of Israel's King Pekah son of Remaliah, Uzziah's son [a]Jotham became king over Judah. 33 He was twenty-five years old when he began to reign, and he reigned for sixteen years in Jerusalem. His mother was Jerusha the daughter of Zadok. 34 He did what the LORD approved, just as his father Uzziah had done. 35 [a]But [b]the high places were not eliminated; the people continued to offer sacrifices and burn incense on the high places. He built the Upper Gate to the LORD's temple.

36 The rest of the events of Jotham's reign, including his accomplishments, are recorded in the scroll called the Annals of the Kings of Judah. 37 In those days the LORD prompted King [a]Rezin of Syria and [b]Pekah son of Remaliah to attack Judah. 38 Jotham passed away and was buried with his ancestors in the city of his ancestor David. His son Ahaz replaced him as king.

Ahaz's Reign over Judah

16 In the seventeenth year of the reign of Pekah son of Remaliah, Jotham's son Ahaz became king over Judah. 2 Ahaz was twenty years old when he began to reign, and he reigned for sixteen years in Jerusalem. He did not do what pleased the LORD his God, in contrast to his ancestor David. 3 He followed in [a]the footsteps of the kings of Israel. He passed his son through the fire, a horrible [b]sin practiced by the nations whom the LORD drove out from before the Israelites. 4 He offered sacrifices and burned incense on the [a]high places, [b]on the hills, and under every green tree.

5 [a]At that time King Rezin of Syria and King Pekah son of Remaliah of Israel attacked Jerusalem. They besieged Ahaz,[1] but were unable to conquer him. 6 (At that time King Rezin of Syria [a]recovered Elat for Syria; he drove the Judahites from there. Syrians[1] arrived in Elat and live there to this very day.) 7 Ahaz sent messengers to King [a]Tiglath-Pileser of Assyria, saying, "I am your servant and your dependent. March up and rescue me from the power of the king of Syria and the king of Israel, who have attacked me." 8 Then Ahaz [a]took the silver and gold that were in the LORD's temple and in the treasuries of the royal palace and sent it as tribute to the king of Assyria. 9 The king of Assyria responded favorably to his request; he attacked [a]Damascus and [b]captured it. He deported the people to [c]Kir and executed Rezin.

15:25 [a] 1 Kgs 16:18   15:27 [a] 2 Chr 28:6; Isa 7:1   15:29 [a] 2 Kgs 16:7, 10; 1 Chr 5:26   [b] 1 Kgs 15:20   15:30 [a] 2 Kgs 17:1; [Hos 10:3, 7, 15]   15:32 [a] 2 Chr 27:1   15:35 [a] 2 Kgs 15:4   [b] 2 Chr 23:20; 27:3   15:37 [a] 2 Kgs 16:5–9; Isa 7:1–17   [b] 2 Kgs 15:26–27   16:3 [a] [Lev 18:21]; 2 Kgs 17:17; 2 Chr 28:3; Ps 106:37–38; Isa 1:1   [b] [Deut 12:31]; 2 Kgs 21:2, 11   16:4 [a] 2 Kgs 15:34–35   [b] [Deut 12:2]; 1 Kgs 14:23   16:5 [a] 2 Kgs 15:37; Isa 7:1, 4   [1] I.e., Jerusalem, Ahaz's capital city.   16:6 [a] 2 Kgs 14:22; 2 Chr 26:2   [1] Sev. wss Edomites.   16:7 [a] 2 Kgs 15:29; 1 Chr 5:26; 2 Chr 28:20   16:8 [a] 2 Kgs 12:17–18; 2 Chr 28:21   16:9 [a] 2 Kgs 14:28   [b] Amos 1:5   [c] Isa 22:6; Amos 9:7

[10]When King Ahaz went to meet with King Tiglath-Pileser of Assyria in Damascus, he saw the altar there. King Ahaz sent to Uriah the priest a drawing of the altar and a blueprint for its design. [11]Uriah the priest built an altar in conformity to the plans King Ahaz had sent from Damascus. [a]Uriah the priest finished it before King Ahaz arrived back from Damascus. [12]When [a]the king arrived back from Damascus and saw the altar, he approached it and offered a sacrifice on it. [13]He offered his burnt sacrifice and his grain offering. He poured out his libation and sprinkled the blood from his peace offerings on the altar. [14]He moved [a]the bronze altar that stood in the LORD's presence from the front of the temple (between the altar and the LORD's temple) and put it on the north side of the new altar. [15]King Ahaz ordered Uriah [a]the priest, "On the large altar offer the morning burnt sacrifice, the evening grain offering, the royal burnt sacrifices and grain offering, the burnt sacrifice for all the people of the land, their grain offering, and their libations. Sprinkle all the blood of the burnt sacrifice and other sacrifices on it. The bronze altar will be for my personal use."[1][16]So Uriah the priest did exactly as King Ahaz ordered.

[17]King Ahaz took off the frames of the movable [a]stands, and removed [b]the basins from [c]them. He took "The Sea" down from the bronze bulls that supported it and put it on the stone pavement. [18]He also removed the Sabbath awning that had been built in the temple and the king's outer entranceway to the LORD's temple, on account of the king of Assyria.

[19]The rest of the events of Ahaz's reign, including his accomplishments, are recorded in the scroll called the Annals of the Kings of Judah. [20]Ahaz passed away and [a]was buried with his ancestors in the City of David. His son Hezekiah replaced him as king.

Hoshea's Reign over Israel

17 In the twelfth year of King Ahaz's reign over Judah, [a]Hoshea son of Elah became king over Israel. He reigned in Samaria for nine years. [2]He did evil in the sight of the LORD, but not to the same degree as the Israelite kings who preceded him. [3]King [a]Shalmaneser of Assyria marched up to attack him; so Hoshea [b]became his subject and paid him tribute. [4]The king of Assyria discovered that Hoshea was planning a revolt. Hoshea had sent messengers to King So of Egypt and had not sent his annual tribute to the king of Assyria. So the king of Assyria arrested him and imprisoned him. [5]The king of Assyria marched through [a]the whole land. He attacked Samaria and besieged it for three years. [6]In the [a]ninth year of Hoshea's reign, the king of Assyria captured Samaria [b]and deported the people of Israel to Assyria. He settled them in Halah, along the Habor (the river of Gozan), and in the cities of the Medes.

A Summary of Israel's Sinful History

[7]This happened because the Israelites sinned against the LORD their God, who brought them up from the land of Egypt and freed them from the power of Pharaoh king of Egypt. They [a]worshiped other gods; [8]they observed the practices of the nations whom the LORD [a]had driven out from before them, and followed the example of the kings of Israel. [9]The Israelites said things about the LORD their God that were not right. They built high places in all their towns, [a]from watchtower to fortified city. [10a]They set up sacred pillars and Asherah [b]poles [c]on every high hill and under every green tree. [11]They burned incense on all the high places just like the nations whom the LORD had driven away before them did. Their evil practices made the LORD angry. [12]They worshiped the disgusting idols in blatant disregard [a]of the LORD's command.

[13]The LORD solemnly warned Israel and Judah through all his [a]prophets and all the seers, "Turn [b]back from your evil ways; obey my commandments and rules that are recorded in the law. I ordered your ancestors to keep this law and sent my servants the prophets to remind you of its demands." [14]But they did not pay attention and [a]were as stubborn as their ancestors, who had not trusted the LORD their God. [15]They

16:11 [a]Isa 8:2   16:12 [a]2 Chr 26:16, 19   16:14 [a]Exod 27:1–2; 40:6, 29; 2 Chr 4:1   16:15 [a]Exod 29:39–41   [1]Heb. for me to seek.
16:17 [a]2 Chr 28:24   [b]1 Kgs 7:27–29   [c]1 Kgs 7:23–25   16:20 [a]2 Chr 28:27   17:1 [a]2 Kgs 15:30   17:3 [a]2 Kgs 18:9–12   [b]2 Kgs
24:1   17:5 [a]2 Kgs 18:9; Hos 13:16   17:6 [a]2 Kgs 18:10–11; Isa 7:7–9; Hos 1:4; 13:16; Amos 4:2   [b]1 Chr 5:26   17:7 [a]Judg 6:10
17:8 [a][Lev 18:3; Deut 18:9]; 2 Kgs 16:3   17:9 [a]2 Kgs 18:8   17:10 [a]1 Kgs 14:23; Isa 57:5   [b][Exod 34:12–14; Deut 16:21];
Mic 5:14   [c][Deut 12:2]; 2 Kgs 16:4   17:12 [a][Exod 20:3–5; Lev 26:1; Deut 5:7–8]   17:13 [a]Neh 9:29–30
[b][Jer 18:11; 25:5; 35:15; Ezek 18:31]   17:14 [a]Exod 32:9; 33:3; Deut 31:27; [Prov 29:1; Acts 7:51]

[a]rejected his rules, the covenant he had made with their ancestors, [b]and the laws he had commanded them to obey. They paid allegiance to[1] worthless [c]idols, and so [d]became worthless to the LORD. They copied the practices of the surrounding nations in blatant disregard of the LORD's command. [16]They abandoned all the commandments of the LORD their God; they [a]made two metal calves [b]and an Asherah pole, bowed down to all the [c]stars in the sky,[1] [d]and worshiped Baal. [17]They passed their sons [a]and daughters through the fire, and [b]practiced divination and omen reading. They [c]committed themselves to doing evil in the sight of the LORD and made him angry.

[18]So the LORD was furious with Israel and rejected them; only the tribe of Judah was left. [19][a]Judah also failed to keep the commandments of the LORD their God; they followed Israel's example. [20]So the LORD rejected all of Israel's descendants; he humiliated them and [a]handed them over to robbers, until he had thrown them from his [b]presence. [21]He tore Israel away from David's dynasty, and Jeroboam son of Nebat became [a]their king. Jeroboam drove Israel away[1] from [b]the LORD and encouraged them to commit a serious sin. [22]The Israelites followed in the sinful ways of Jeroboam and did not repudiate them. [23]Finally the LORD rejected Israel just [a]as he had warned he would do through all his servants the prophets. Israel was deported from its land to Assyria and remains there to this very day.

The King of Assyria Populates Israel with Foreigners

[24][a]The king of Assyria brought foreigners from Babylon, Cuthah, [b]Avva, Hamath, and Sepharvaim and settled them in the cities of Samaria in place of the Israelites. They took possession of Samaria and lived in its cities. [25]When they first moved in, they did not worship the LORD. So the LORD sent lions among them and the lions were killing them. [26]The king of Assyria was told, "The nations whom you deported and settled in the cities of Samaria do not know the requirements of the God of the land, so he has sent lions among them. They are killing the people because they do not know the requirements of the God of the land." [27]So the king of Assyria ordered, "Take back one of the priests whom you deported from there. He must settle there and teach them the requirements of the God of the land."[1] [28]So one of the priests whom they had deported from Samaria went back and settled in Bethel. He taught them how to worship the LORD.

[29]But each of these nations made its own gods and put them [a]in the shrines on the high places that the people of Samaria had made. Each nation did this in the cities where they lived. [30]The people from [a]Babylon made Sukkoth Benoth, the people from Cuth made Nergal, the people from Hamath made Ashima, [31]the Avvites made Nibhaz [a]and Tartak, and the Sepharvites [b]burned their sons in the fire as an offering to Adrammelech and Anammelech, the gods of Sepharvaim. [32]At the same time they worshiped the LORD. They appointed some of their own people to serve as priests in the shrines on the high places. [33]They were worshiping [a]the LORD and at the same time serving their own gods in accordance with the practices of the nations from which they had been deported.

[34]To this very day they observe their earlier practices. They do not worship the LORD; they do not obey the rules, regulations, law, and commandments that the LORD gave the descendants of Jacob, [a]whom he renamed Israel. [35]The LORD made a covenant with them and instructed them, "[a]You must not worship other gods. Do not [b]bow down to them, serve them, or offer sacrifices to them. [36]Instead you must worship the LORD, who [a]brought you up from the [b]land of Egypt by his great power and military ability; bow down to [c]him and offer sacrifices to him. [37]You must carefully obey at all times the rules, regulations, law, and commandments he wrote down for [a]you. You must

17:15 [a]Jer 44:3　[b]Exod 24:6–8; Deut 29:25　[c]Deut 32:21; 1 Kgs 16:31; [1 Cor 8:4]　[d]2 Chr 13:7; Jer 2:5; [Rom 1:21–23]　[1]Heb. *They went [or followed] after.*　**17:16** [a]Exod 32:8; 1 Kgs 12:28　[b][1 Kgs 14:15]　[c][Deut 4:19]　[d]1 Kgs 16:31; 22:53　[1]Trad. *all the host of heaven;* the heavenly lights, incl. stars and planets.　**17:17** [a][Lev 18:21]; 2 Kgs 16:3; Ezek 23:37　[b][Lev 19:26; Deut 18:10–12]　[c]1 Kgs 21:20　**17:19** [a]Jer 3:8　**17:20** [a]Judg 2:14; 2 Kgs 13:3; 15:29　[b]2 Kgs 24:20　**17:21** [a]1 Kgs 11:11, 31　[b]1 Kgs 12:20, 28　[1]Ket. *push away.*　**17:23** [a]1 Kgs 14:16; Isa 8:4　**17:24** [a]Ezra 4:2, 10　[b]2 Kgs 18:34　**17:27** [1]Heb. *and let them go and let them live there, and let him teach them the requirements of the God of the land.*　**17:29** [a]1 Kgs 12:31; 13:32　**17:30** [a]2 Kgs 17:24　**17:31** [a]Ezra 4:9　[b][Lev 18:21; Deut 12:31]　**17:33** [a]Zeph 1:5　**17:34** [a]Gen 32:28; 35:10　**17:35** [a]Judg 6:10　[b][Exod 20:5]　**17:36** [a]Exod 14:15–30　[b]Exod 6:6; 9:15　[c][Deut 10:20]　**17:37** [a]Deut 5:32

not worship other gods. [38]You must never forget the covenant I made with [a]you, and you must not worship other gods. [39]Instead you must worship the LORD your God; then he will rescue you from the power of all your enemies." [40]But they paid no attention; instead they observed their earlier practices. [41]These nations were worshiping the LORD and at the same time serving their idols; their [a]sons and grandsons are doing just as their fathers have done, to this very day.

Hezekiah Becomes King of Judah

18 In the third year of the reign of Israel's King [a]Hoshea son of Elah, Ahaz's son [b]Hezekiah became king over Judah. [2]He was twenty-five years old when he began to reign, and he reigned twenty-nine years in Jerusalem. His mother was [a]Abi, the daughter of Zechariah. [3]He did what the LORD approved, just as his ancestor David had done. [4]He eliminated [a]the high places, smashed the sacred pillars to bits, and cut down the Asherah pole. He also demolished the [b]bronze serpent that Moses had made, for up to that time the Israelites had been offering incense to it; it was called Nehushtan. [5]He [a]trusted in the LORD God of Israel; in this regard there was none like him among the kings of Judah either before or after. [6]He was loyal to the LORD and did not abandon him. [a]He obeyed the commandments that the LORD had given to Moses. [7]The LORD [a]was with him; he [b]succeeded in all his endeavors. He [c]rebelled against the king of Assyria and refused to submit to him. [8]He defeated [a]the Philistines as far as Gaza and its territory, [b]from watchtower to fortified city.

[9]In the fourth year of King Hezekiah's reign ([a]it was the seventh year of the reign of Israel's King Hoshea, son of Elah), King Shalmaneser of Assyria marched up against Samaria and besieged it. [10]After three years [a]he captured it (in the sixth year of Hezekiah's reign); in the ninth year of King Hoshea's reign over Israel, Samaria was captured. [11]The king of Assyria deported [a]the people of Israel to Assyria. He settled them [b]in Halah, along the Habor (the river of Gozan), and in the cities of the Medes. [12]This happened because they [a]did not obey the LORD their God and broke his covenant with them. They did not pay attention to and obey all that Moses, the LORD's servant, had commanded.

Sennacherib Invades Judah

[13]In the fourteenth year of [a]King Hezekiah's reign, King Sennacherib of Assyria marched up against all the fortified cities of Judah and captured them. [14]King Hezekiah of Judah sent this message to the king of Assyria, who was at Lachish, "I have violated our treaty. If you leave, I will do whatever you demand." So the king of Assyria demanded that King Hezekiah of Judah pay 300 talents[1] of silver and 30 talents of gold. [15]Hezekiah [a]gave him all the silver in the LORD's temple and in the treasuries of the royal palace. [16]At that time King Hezekiah of Judah stripped the metal overlays from the doors of the LORD's temple and from the posts that he had plated and gave them to the king of Assyria.

[17]The king of Assyria sent his commanding general, the chief eunuch, and the chief adviser from Lachish to King Hezekiah in Jerusalem, along with a large army. They went up and arrived at Jerusalem. They went and stood at the [a]conduit of the upper pool [b]which is located on the road to the field where they wash and dry cloth. [18]They summoned the king, so [a]Eliakim son of Hilkiah, the palace supervisor, accompanied by Shebna, the scribe, and Joah son of Asaph, the secretary, went out to meet them.

[19]The chief adviser said to them, "Tell Hezekiah: 'This is [a]what the great king, the king of Assyria, says: "What is your source of confidence? [20]Your claim to have a strategy and military strength is just empty talk.[1] In whom are you trusting that you would dare to rebel against me? [21][a]Now look, you must be trusting in Egypt, that splintered reed staff. If a man leans for support on it, it punctures his hand and wounds him. That is what Pharaoh king of Egypt does to all who trust in him. [22]Perhaps you will tell

17:38 [a]Deut 4:23; 6:12   **17:41** [a]2 Kgs 17:32–33   **18:1** [a]2 Kgs 17:1   [b]2 Chr 28:27; 29:1   **18:2** [a]Isa 38:5   **18:4** [a]2 Chr 31:1   [b]Num 21:5–9   **18:5** [a]2 Kgs 19:10; [Job 13:15; Ps 13:5]   **18:6** [a]Deut 10:20; Josh 23:8   **18:7** [a][2 Chr 15:2]   [b]Gen 39:2–3; 1 Sam 18:5, 14; Ps 60:12   [c]2 Kgs 16:7   **18:8** [a]1 Chr 4:41; 2 Chr 28:18; Isa 14:29   [b]2 Kgs 17:9   **18:9** [a]2 Kgs 17:3   **18:10** [a]2 Kgs 17:6   **18:11** [a]2 Kgs 17:6; Hos 1:4; Amos 4:2   [b]1 Chr 5:26   **18:12** [a]2 Kgs 17:7–18   **18:13** [a]2 Chr 32:1; Isa 36:1–39:8   **18:14** [1]About 75 pounds.   **18:15** [a]1 Kgs 15:18–19; 2 Kgs 12:18; 16:8   **18:17** [a]2 Kgs 20:20   [b]Isa 7:3   **18:18** [a]2 Kgs 19:2; Isa 22:20   **18:19** [a]2 Chr 32:10; [Ps 118:8–9]   **18:20** [1]Heb. *you say only a word of lips, counsel and might for battle.*   **18:21** [a]Isa 30:2–7; Ezek 29:6–7

me, 'We are trusting in the LORD our God.' But Hezekiah is the one [a]who eliminated his high places and altars and then told the people of Judah and Jerusalem, 'You must worship at this altar in Jerusalem.' [23]Now make a deal with my master the king of Assyria, and I will give you 2,000 horses, provided you can find enough riders for them. [24]Certainly you will not refuse one of my master's minor officials and trust in Egypt for chariots and horsemen. [25]Furthermore it was by the command of the LORD that I marched up against this place to destroy it. The LORD told me, 'March up against this land and destroy it.'"'"

[26]Eliakim son of Hilkiah, Shebna, and Joah said to [a]the chief adviser, "Speak to your servants in [b]Aramaic, for we understand it. Don't speak with us in the Judahite dialect in the hearing of the people who are on the wall." [27]But the chief adviser said to them, "My master did not send me to speak these words only to your master and to you. His message is also for the men who sit on the wall, for they will eat their own excrement and drink their own urine along with you."

[28]The chief adviser then stood there and called out loudly in the Judahite dialect, "Listen to the message of the great king, the king of Assyria. [29]This is what the king says: '[a]Don't let Hezekiah mislead you, for he is not able to rescue you from my hand![1] [30]Don't let Hezekiah talk you into trusting in the LORD when he says, "The LORD will certainly rescue us; this city will not be handed over to the king of Assyria." [31]Don't listen to Hezekiah!' For this is what the king of Assyria says, 'Send me a token of your submission and surrender to me. Then each of you may eat from his own [a]vine and fig tree and drink water from his own cistern, [32]until I come [a]and take you to a land just like your own—a land of grain and new wine, a land of bread and vineyards, a land of olive oil and honey. Then you will live and not die. Don't listen to Hezekiah, for he is misleading you when he says, "The LORD will rescue us." [33a]Have any of the gods of the nations actually rescued his land from the power of the king of Assyria? [34]Where are the gods of [a]Hamath and Arpad? Where are the gods of Sepharvaim, Hena, and [b]Ivvah? Indeed, did any gods rescue Samaria from my power? [35]Who among all the gods of the lands has rescued their lands from my power? So how can the LORD rescue Jerusalem from my power?'"[1] [36]The people were silent and did not respond, for the king had ordered, "Don't respond to him."

[37]Eliakim son of Hilkiah, the palace supervisor, accompanied by Shebna the scribe and Joah son of Asaph, the secretary, went to Hezekiah [a]with their clothes torn and reported to him what the chief adviser had **19** said. [1]When King Hezekiah heard this, he tore his clothes, put on [a]sackcloth, and went to the LORD's temple. [2]He sent Eliakim the palace supervisor, Shebna the scribe, and the leading priests, clothed in sackcloth, to the prophet Isaiah son of Amoz. [3]They told him, "This is what Hezekiah says: 'This is a day of distress, insults, and humiliation, as when a baby is ready to leave the birth canal, but the mother lacks the strength to push it through. [4a]Perhaps the LORD your God will hear all these things the chief adviser has spoken on behalf of his master, the king of Assyria, who sent him to [b]taunt the living God. When the LORD your God hears, perhaps he will [c]punish him for the things he has said. So pray for this remnant that remains.'"

[5]When King Hezekiah's servants came to Isaiah, [6a]Isaiah said to them, "Tell your master this: 'This is what the LORD has said: "Don't be [b]afraid because of the things you have heard, because the Assyrian king's [c]officers have insulted me. [7]Look, I will [a]take control of his mind;[1] he will receive a report and return to his own land. I will cut him down with a sword in his own land."'"

[8]When the chief adviser heard the king of Assyria had departed [a]from Lachish, he left and went to Libnah, where the king was campaigning. [9]The king heard that King Tirhakah of Ethiopia was marching out to fight him. [a]He again sent messengers to Hezekiah, ordering them: [10]"Tell [a]King Hezekiah of Judah this: 'Don't let your God in whom you

---

18:22 [a]2 Kgs 18:4; 2 Chr 31:1; 32:12   18:26 [a]Isa 36:11–39:8   [b]Ezra 4:7; Dan 2:4   18:29 [a]2 Chr 32:15   [1]MT *his hand.*
18:31 [a]1 Kgs 4:20, 25   18:32 [a]Deut 8:7–9; 11:12   18:33 [a]2 Kgs 19:12; Isa 10:10–11   18:34 [a]2 Kgs 19:13   [b]2 Kgs 17:24
18:35 [1]Heb. *from my hand.*   18:37 [a]Isa 33:7   19:1 [a]Ps 69:11   19:4 [a]2 Sam 16:12   [b]2 Kgs 18:35   [c]Ps 50:21
19:6 [a]Isa 37:6   [b][Ps 112:7]   [c]2 Kgs 18:17   19:7 [a]2 Kgs 19:35–37; Jer 51:1   [1]Heb. *I will put in him a spirit;*
perhaps a spiritual being that will take control of his mind or a disposition of concern and fear.
19:8 [a]2 Kgs 18:14, 17   19:9 [a]1 Sam 23:27; Isa 37:9   19:10 [a]2 Kgs 18:5

trust mislead you when he says, "Jerusalem will not be handed over to the king of Assyria." [11]Certainly you have heard how the kings of Assyria have annihilated all lands. Do you really think you will be rescued? [12a]Were the nations whom my ancestors destroyed—the nations of Gozan, Haran, Rezeph, and the people of [b]Eden in Telassar—rescued by their gods? [13a]Where are the king of Hamath, the king of Arpad, and the kings of Lair, Sepharvaim, Hena, and Ivvah?'"

[14]Hezekiah took the letter[1] from the messengers [a]and read it.[2] Then Hezekiah went up to the LORD's temple and spread it out before the LORD. [15]Hezekiah prayed before the LORD: "LORD God of Israel, [a]who is enthroned above the cherubim! [b]You alone are God over all the kingdoms of the earth. You made the sky and the earth. [16a]Pay attention, LORD, and hear! [b]Open your eyes, LORD, and observe! Listen to the message Sennacherib sent and how he taunts the living God! [17]It is true, LORD, that the kings of Assyria have destroyed the nations and their lands. [18]They have burned the gods of the nations, for they are [a]not really gods, but only [b]the product of human hands manufactured from wood and stone. That is why the Assyrians could destroy them. [19]Now, O LORD our God, rescue us from his power, so [a]that all the kingdoms of the earth will [b]know that you, LORD, are the only God."

[20]Isaiah son of Amoz sent [a]this message to Hezekiah: "This is what the LORD God of Israel has said: 'I have heard your prayer concerning King Sennacherib of Assyria. [21]This is what [a]the LORD says about him:

"'The virgin daughter Zion
despises you, she makes fun of you;
Daughter Jerusalem
shakes her head after you.
[22] Whom have you taunted and hurled
insults at?
At whom have you shouted,
and looked so arrogantly?
At [a]the Holy One of Israel!
[23] [a]Through your messengers you
taunted the Sovereign Master,

'With my many chariots
I climbed up the high mountains,
the slopes of Lebanon.
I cut down its tall cedars
and its best evergreens.
I invaded its most remote regions,
its thickest woods.
[24] I dug wells and drank
water in foreign lands.
With the soles of my feet [a]I dried up
all the rivers of Egypt.'
[25] Certainly you must have heard!
Long ago [a]I worked it out.
In ancient times I planned it;
and now I am bringing it to pass.
The plan is this:
Fortified cities will crash
into heaps of ruins.
[26] Their residents are powerless,
[a]they are terrified and ashamed.
They are as short-lived as plants in
the field,
or green vegetation.
They are as short-lived as grass on
the rooftops
when it is scorched by the east
wind.[1]
[27] I know where you [a]live
and everything you do.[1]
[28] Because you rage [a]against me,
and the uproar you create has
reached my ears,[1]
I will put my hook in your nose,
and my bridle between your lips,
and I will lead you back the way
you came."

[29]"'This will be your [a]confirmation that I have spoken the truth:[1] This year you will eat what grows wild, and next year what grows on its own from that. But in the third year you will plant seed and harvest crops; you will plant vines and consume their produce. [30]Those who remain in Judah will take root in the ground [a]and bear fruit.

[31] "'For a remnant will leave Jerusalem;
survivors will come out of Mount
Zion.

19:12 [a]2 Kgs 18:33–34   [b]Ezek 27:23   19:13 [a]2 Kgs 18:34   19:14 [a]Isa 37:14   [1]MT *letters.*   [2]MT *them.*   19:15 [a]Exod 25:22; Ps 80:1; Isa 37:16   [b][Isa 44:6]   19:16 [a]Ps 31:2; Isa 37:17   [b]1 Kgs 8:29; 2 Chr 6:40   19:18 [a][Isa 44:9–20; Jer 10:3–5]   [b]Ps 115:4; Jer 10:3; [Acts 17:29]   19:19 [a]Ps 83:18   [b]1 Kgs 8:42–43   19:20 [a]2 Kgs 20:5; Ps 65:2   19:21 [a]Jer 14:17; Lam 2:13   19:22 [a]Jer 51:5   19:23 [a]2 Kgs 18:17   19:24 [a]Isa 19:6   19:25 [a][Isa 45:7]   19:26 [a]Ps 129:6   [1]Heb. *scorched before the standing grain.*   19:27 [a]Ps 139:1–3; Isa 37:28   [1]Heb. *your going out and your coming in and how you have raged against me.*   19:28 [a]Job 41:2; Ezek 29:4; 38:4; Amos 4:2   [1]Heb. *and your complacency comes up into my ears.*   19:29 [a]Exod 3:12; 1 Sam 2:34; 2 Kgs 20:8–9; Isa 7:11–14; Luke 2:12   [1]Heb. *and this is your sign.*   19:30 [a]2 Kgs 19:4; 2 Chr 32:22–23

[a]The zeal of the LORD of Heaven's Armies[1] will accomplish this.

[32] So this is what the LORD has said about the king of Assyria:

"He will [a]not enter this city,
  nor will he shoot an arrow here.
He will not attack it with his
  shield-carrying warriors,
  nor will he build siege works
  against it.
[33] He will go back the way he came.
  He will not enter this city," says the
  LORD.

[34] "'I [a]will [b]shield this city and rescue it [c]for the sake of my reputation and because of my promise to David my servant.'"

[35] That very night the angel of the LORD went out and killed 185,000 in the Assyrian camp. When they got up early the next morning, there were all the corpses. [36] So King Sennacherib of Assyria broke camp and went on his way. He went home and stayed in [a]Nineveh. [37] One day, as he was worshiping in the temple of his god Nisroch, his sons[1] [a]Adrammelech and Sharezer [b]struck him down with the sword. They escaped to the land of Ararat; his son [c]Esarhaddon replaced him as king.

Hezekiah Is Healed

20 In [a]those days Hezekiah was stricken with a terminal illness. The prophet Isaiah son of Amoz visited him and told him, "This is what the LORD has said, 'Give your household instructions, for you are about to die; you will not get well.'" [2] He turned his face to the wall and prayed to the LORD, [3] "Please, LORD. [a]Remember how I have served you faithfully and with wholehearted devotion, and how I have carried out your will." Then Hezekiah wept bitterly.

[4] Isaiah had not yet left the middle courtyard[1] when the LORD's message came to him, [5] "Go back and tell Hezekiah, [a]the leader of my people: '[b]This is what the LORD God of [c]your ancestor David has said: "I have heard your prayer; I have seen your tears. Look, I will heal you. The day after tomorrow you will go up to the LORD's temple. [6] I [a]will add 15 years to your life and rescue you and this city from the king of Assyria. I will shield this city for the sake of my reputation and because of my promise to David my servant."'" [7] [a]Isaiah ordered, "Get a fig cake." So they did as he ordered and placed it on the ulcerated sore, and he recovered.

[8] Hezekiah had said to Isaiah, "[a]What is the confirming sign that the LORD will heal me and that I will go up to the LORD's temple the day after tomorrow?" [9] Isaiah replied, "[a]This is your sign from the LORD confirming that the LORD will do what he has said. Do you want the shadow to move ahead 10 steps or to go back 10 steps?" [10] Hezekiah answered, "It is easy for the shadow to lengthen 10 steps, but not for it to go back 10 steps." [11] Isaiah [a]the prophet called out to the LORD, and the LORD made the shadow go back 10 steps on the stairs of Ahaz.

Messengers from Babylon Visit Hezekiah

[12] At [a]that time Merodach Baladan[1] son of Baladan, king of Babylon, sent messengers with letters and a gift to Hezekiah, for he had heard that Hezekiah was ill. [13] [a]Hezekiah welcomed[1] them and showed them his whole storehouse, with its silver, gold, spices, and high quality olive oil, as well as his armory and everything in his treasuries. Hezekiah showed them everything in his palace and in his whole kingdom. [14] Isaiah the prophet visited King Hezekiah and asked him, "What did these men say? Where do they come from?" Hezekiah replied, "They come from the distant land of Babylon." [15] Isaiah asked, "What have [a]they seen in your palace?" Hezekiah replied, "They have seen everything in my palace. I showed them everything in my treasuries." [16] Isaiah said to Hezekiah, "Listen to the LORD's message, [17] 'Look, [a]a time is coming when everything in your palace and the things your ancestors have accumulated to this day will be carried away to Babylon; nothing will be left,' says the LORD. [18] '[a]Some of your

19:31 [a]2 Kgs 25:26; Isa 9:7 [1]Trad. *the LORD of hosts*. **19:32** [a]Isa 8:7–10 **19:34** [a]2 Kgs 20:6; 2 Chr 32:21 [b]Isa 31:5 [c]1 Kgs 11:12–13 **19:36** [a]Gen 10:11 **19:37** [a]2 Kgs 17:31 [b]2 Kgs 19:7; 2 Chr 32:21 [c]Ezra 4:2 [1]Ket. omits *his sons*. **20:1** [a]2 Kgs 18:13; 2 Chr 32:24; Isa 38:1–22 **20:3** [a]2 Kgs 18:3–6; Neh 13:22 **20:4** [1]Ket. *the city*. **20:5** [a]1 Sam 9:16; 10:1 [b]2 Kgs 19:20; Ps 65:2 [c]Ps 39:12; 56:8 **20:6** [a]2 Kgs 19:34; 2 Chr 32:21 **20:7** [a]Isa 38:21 **20:8** [a]Judg 6:17, 37, 39; Isa 7:11, 14; 38:22 **20:9** [a]Num 23:19; Isa 38:7–8 **20:11** [a]Josh 10:12–14; Isa 38:8 **20:12** [a]2 Kgs 8:8–9; 2 Chr 32:31; Isa 39:1–8 [1]MT *Berodach-Baladan*. **20:13** [a]2 Kgs 16:9; 2 Chr 32:27, 31 [1]Heb. *listened to*. **20:15** [a]2 Kgs 20:13 **20:17** [a]2 Kgs 24:13; 25:13–15; 2 Chr 36:10; Jer 27:21–22; 52:17 **20:18** [a]2 Kgs 24:12; 2 Chr 33:11

very own descendants whom you father will be taken away [b]and will be made [c]eunuchs in the palace of the king of Babylon.'" [19]Hezekiah said to Isaiah, "[a]The LORD's message which you have announced is appropriate." Then he added, "At least there will be peace and stability during my lifetime."

[20a]The rest of the events of Hezekiah's reign and all his accomplishments, including how he [b]built a [c]pool and conduit to [d]bring water into the city, are recorded in the scroll called the Annals of the Kings of Judah. [21a]Hezekiah passed away and his son Manasseh replaced him as king.

Manasseh's Reign over Judah

21 Manasseh [a]was twelve years old when he became king, and he reigned for fifty-five years in Jerusalem. His mother was Hephzibah. [2]He did evil [a]in the sight of the LORD and committed the same horrible sins practiced by the nations whom the LORD drove out before the Israelites. [3]He rebuilt the high places that his father Hezekiah had destroyed; he set up altars for Baal and made an [a]Asherah pole just as King Ahab of Israel had done. He bowed down to all the stars in the sky and [b]worshiped them. [4]He built altars in [a]the LORD's temple, about which the LORD had said, "Jerusalem will be my home." [5]In the [a]two courtyards of the LORD's temple he built altars for all the stars in the sky. [6]He passed his son[1] through the fire and practiced divination and omen reading. He set up [a]a ritual pit to conjure up underworld spirits and appointed magicians to supervise it. He did [b]a great amount of evil in the sight of the LORD, provoking him to anger.[2] [7]He put an idol of Asherah he had made [a]in the temple, about which the LORD had said to David and to his son Solomon, "This temple in Jerusalem, which I have chosen out of all the tribes of Israel, will be my permanent home. [8]I will not make Israel again leave the [a]land I gave to their ancestors, provided that they carefully obey all I commanded them, the whole law my servant Moses ordered

them to obey." [9]But they did not obey, and Manasseh misled them so that they sinned more than the nations whom the LORD had destroyed from before the Israelites.

[10]So the LORD announced [a]through his servants the prophets: [11]"[a]King Manasseh of Judah has committed horrible sins. [b]He has sinned more than the [c]Amorites before him and [d]has encouraged Judah to sin by worshiping his disgusting idols. [12]So [a]this is what the LORD God of Israel has said, 'I am about to bring disaster on Jerusalem and Judah. The news will reverberate in the ears of those who hear about it. [13]I will destroy Jerusalem [a]the same way [b]I did Samaria and the dynasty of Ahab.[1] I will wipe Jerusalem clean, just as one wipes a plate on both sides. [14]I will abandon this last remaining [a]tribe among my people and hand them over to their enemies; they will be plundered and robbed by all their enemies, [15]because they have done evil in my sight and have angered me from the time their ancestors left Egypt right up to this very day!'"

[16a]Furthermore Manasseh killed so many innocent people, he stained Jerusalem with their blood from end to end, in addition to encouraging Judah to sin by doing evil in the sight of the LORD.

[17]The rest of [a]the events of [b]Manasseh's reign and all his accomplishments, as well as the sinful acts he committed, are recorded in the scroll called the Annals of the Kings of Judah. [18a]Manasseh passed away and was buried in his palace garden, the garden of Uzzah, and his son Amon replaced him as king.

Amon's Reign over Judah

[19a]Amon was twenty-two years old when he became king, and he reigned for two years in Jerusalem. His mother was Meshullemeth, the daughter of Haruz, from Jotbah. [20]He did evil in the sight of the LORD, just [a]as his father Manasseh had done. [21]He followed in the footsteps of his father and worshiped and bowed down to the disgusting

20:18 [b]Dan 1:3–7   [c]Dan 1:11, 18   20:19 [a]1 Sam 3:18   20:20 [a]2 Chr 32:32   [b]Neh 3:16   [c]2 Kgs 18:17; Isa 7:3   [d]2 Chr 32:3, 30   20:21 [a]2 Kgs 16:20; 2 Chr 32:33   21:1 [a]2 Chr 33:1–9   21:2 [a]2 Kgs 16:3   21:3 [a]1 Kgs 16:31–33   [b][Deut 4:19; 17:2–5]; 2 Kgs 17:16; 23:5   21:4 [a]Jer 7:30; 32:34   21:5 [a]1 Kgs 6:36; 7:12; 2 Kgs 23:12   21:6 [a][Lev 18:21; 20:2]; 2 Kgs 16:3; 17:17   [b]Lev 19:26, 31; [Deut 18:10–14]; 2 Kgs 17:17   [1]LXX sons.   [2]Heb. and he multiplied doing what is evil in the eyes of the LORD, angering. 21:7 [a]2 Sam 7:13; 1 Kgs 8:29; 9:3; 2 Kgs 23:27; 2 Chr 7:12, 16; Jer 32:34   21:8 [a]2 Sam 7:10; [2 Kgs 18:11–12]   21:10 [a]2 Kgs 17:13   21:11 [a]2 Kgs 23:26–27; 24:3–4   [b]1 Kgs 21:26   [c]Gen 15:16   [d]2 Kgs 21:9   21:12 [a]1 Sam 3:11; Jer 19:3   21:13 [a]Lam 2:8; Amos 7:7–8   [b]2 Kgs 22:16–19; 25:4–11   [1]Heb. I will stretch out over Jerusalem the measuring line of Samaria, and the plumb line of the house of Ahab.   21:14 [a]Jer 6:9   21:16 [a]2 Kgs 24:4   21:17 [a]2 Chr 33:11–19   [b]2 Kgs 20:21   21:18 [a]2 Chr 33:20   21:19 [a]2 Chr 33:21–23   21:20 [a]2 Kgs 21:2–6, 11, 16

idols that his father had worshiped. [22]He [a]abandoned the LORD, God of his ancestors, and did not follow the LORD's instructions. [23a]Amon's servants [b]conspired against him and killed the king in his palace. [24]The people of the land [a]executed all those who had conspired against King Amon, and they made his son Josiah king in his place.

[25]The rest of Amon's accomplishments are recorded in the scroll called the Annals of the Kings of Judah.[1] [26]He was buried in his tomb in the garden of Uzzah, and his son Josiah replaced him as king.

Josiah Repents

22 Josiah [a]was eight years old when he became king, and he reigned for thirty-one years in Jerusalem. His mother was Jedidah, daughter of Adaiah, from [b]Bozkath. [2]He [a]did what the LORD approved and followed in his ancestor David's footsteps; he did not deviate to the right or the left.

[3a]In the eighteenth year of King Josiah's reign, the king sent the scribe Shaphan son of Azaliah, son of Meshullam, to the LORD's temple with these orders: [4]"Go up to Hilkiah the high priest and have him melt down[1] the silver that has been [a]brought by [b]the people to the LORD's temple and has been collected by the guards at the door. [5]Have them [a]hand it over to the construction foremen assigned to the LORD's temple. They in turn should pay the temple workers to repair it, [6]including craftsmen, builders, and masons, and should buy wood and chiseled stone for the repair work. [7]Do not audit [a]the foremen who disburse the silver, for they are honest."

[8]Hilkiah the [a]high priest informed Shaphan the scribe, "I found the scroll of the law in the LORD's temple." Hilkiah gave the scroll to Shaphan and he read it. [9]Shaphan the scribe went to the king and reported, "Your servants melted down the silver in the temple and handed it over to the construction foremen assigned to the LORD's temple." [10]Then Shaphan the scribe told the king, "Hilkiah the priest has given me a scroll." Shaphan read it out loud before the king. [11]When the king heard the words of the law scroll, he tore his clothes. [12]The king ordered Hilkiah the priest, [a]Ahikam son of Shaphan, Achbor son of Micaiah, Shaphan the scribe, and Asaiah the king's servant, [13]"Go, seek an oracle from [a]the LORD for me and the people—for all Judah. Find out about the words of this scroll that has been discovered. For the LORD's great fury has been ignited against us, because our ancestors have not obeyed the words of this scroll by doing all that it instructs us to do."[1]

[14]So Hilkiah the priest, Ahikam, Achbor, Shaphan, and Asaiah went to Huldah the prophetess, the wife of Shullam son of [a]Tikvah, the son of Harhas, the supervisor of the wardrobe. (She lived in Jerusalem in the Mishneh[1] district.) They stated their business, [15]and she said to them: "This is what the LORD God of Israel has said: 'Say this to the man who sent you to me: [16]"This [a]is what the LORD has said: 'I am about to bring disaster on this place and its residents, all the things in the scroll that the king of Judah has read. [17]This will happen [a]because they have abandoned me and offered sacrifices to other gods, angering me with all the idols they have made.[1] My anger will ignite against this place and will not be extinguished!'" [18]Say this to [a]the king of Judah, who sent you to seek an oracle from the LORD: "This is what the LORD God of Israel has said concerning the words you have heard: [19]'You displayed a sensitive [a]spirit and [b]humbled yourself before the LORD when you [c]heard how I intended to [d]make this place and its residents into an appalling example of an accursed people. You tore your clothes and wept before me, and I have heard you,' says the LORD. [20]Therefore I will allow you to die and be buried in peace. You will not have to witness [a]all the disaster I will bring on this place.""" Then they reported back to the king.

21:22 [a]Judg 2:12–13; 1 Kgs 11:33; 1 Chr 28:9   21:23 [1]1 Chr 3:14; 2 Chr 33:24–25; Matt 1:10   [b]2 Kgs 12:20; 14:19   21:24 [a]2 Kgs 14:5   21:25 [1]Heb. *As for the rest of the things of Amon which he did, are they not written on the scroll of the events of the days of the kings of Judah?*   22:1 [a]1 Kgs 13:2; 2 Chr 34:1   [b]Josh 15:39   22:2 [a]Deut 5:32; Josh 1:7   22:3 [a]2 Chr 34:8   22:4 [a]2 Kgs 12:4   [b]2 Kgs 12:9–10   [1]MT *and let them add up.*   22:5 [a]2 Kgs 12:11–14   22:7 [a]2 Kgs 12:15; [1 Cor 4:2]   22:8 [a]Deut 31:24–26; 2 Chr 34:14   22:12 [a]2 Kgs 25:22; Jer 26:24   22:13 [a][Deut 29:23–28; 31:17–18]   [1]Heb. *by doing all that is written concerning us.*   22:14 [a]2 Chr 34:22   [1]Or *second.*   22:16 [a]Deut 29:27; [Dan 9:11–14]   22:17 [a]Deut 29:25–27; 2 Kgs 21:22   [1]Or perhaps *angering me by all the things they do*; Heb. *so as to anger me with all the work of their hands.*   22:18 [a]2 Chr 34:26   22:19 [a]1 Sam 24:5; [Ps 51:17; Isa 57:15]   [b]Exod 10:3; 1 Kgs 21:29; [2 Chr 7:14]   [c]Lev 26:31–32   [d]Jer 26:6; 44:22   22:20 [a]2 Kgs 23:30; [Ps 37:37; Isa 57:1–2]

The King Institutes Religious Reform

23 The king summoned all[a] the leaders of Judah and Jerusalem. [2] The king went up to the LORD's temple, accompanied by all the people of Judah, all the residents of Jerusalem, the priests, and the prophets. All the people were there, from the youngest to the oldest. He [a]read aloud all the words of the scroll of the covenant that had been discovered in the LORD's temple. [3] The king [a]stood by the pillar and renewed the [b]covenant before the LORD, agreeing to follow the LORD and to obey his commandments, laws, and rules with all his heart and being, by carrying out the terms of this covenant recorded on this scroll. All the people agreed to keep the covenant.

[4] The king ordered Hilkiah the high [a]priest, the high-ranking priests, and the guards to bring [b]out of the LORD's temple all the items that were used in the worship of Baal, Asherah, and all the stars of the sky. The king burned them outside of Jerusalem in the terraces of Kidron, and carried their ashes to Bethel. [5] He eliminated the pagan priests whom the kings of Judah had appointed to offer sacrifices on the high places in the cities of Judah and in the area right around Jerusalem. (They offered sacrifices to Baal, the sun god, the moon god, the constellations, and [a]all the stars in the sky.) [6] He removed the Asherah pole from the LORD's temple and took it outside Jerusalem to the Kidron Valley, where he burned it. He smashed it to [a]dust and [b]then threw the dust in the public graveyard. [7] He tore down the quarters[a] of the male cultic prostitutes in the LORD's temple, [b]where [c]women were weaving shrines[1] for Asherah.

[8] He brought all the priests from the cities of Judah and ruined the high places where the priests had offered sacrifices, from [a]Geba to Beer Sheba. He tore down the high place of the goat idols[1] situated at the entrance of the gate of Joshua, the city official, on the left side of the city gate. [9] (Now [a]the priests of the high places did not go up to the altar of the LORD in Jerusalem, [b]but they did eat unleavened cakes among their fellow priests.) [10] The king ruined[a] Topheth in [b]the Valley of Ben Hinnom so [c]that no one could [d]pass his son or his daughter through the fire to Molech. [11] He removed from the entrance to the LORD's temple the statues of horses that the kings of Judah had placed there in honor of the sun god. (They were kept near the room of Nathan Melech the eunuch, which was situated among the courtyards.) He burned up the chariots devoted to the sun god. [12] The king tore down the altars the kings of Judah had set up[a] on the roof of Ahaz's upper room, as well as the altars [b]Manasseh had set up in the two courtyards of the LORD's temple. He crushed them[1] and threw the dust in the Kidron Valley. [13] The king ruined the high places east of Jerusalem, south of the Mount of Destruction, that King [a]Solomon of Israel had built for the detestable Sidonian goddess Astarte, the detestable Moabite god Chemosh, and the horrible Ammonite god Milcom. [14] He [a]smashed the sacred pillars to bits, cut down the Asherah poles, and filled those shrines with human bones.

[15] He also tore down the altar in Bethel at the high place made by Jeroboam son of Nebat, who encouraged Israel to sin. He burned all the combustible items at that high place and crushed them to dust, including the Asherah pole. [16] When Josiah turned around, he saw the tombs there on the hill. So he ordered the bones from the tombs to be brought; he burned them on the altar and defiled it, just as in the [a]LORD's message that was announced by the prophet while Jeroboam stood by the altar during a festival. Then the king turned and saw the grave of the prophet who had foretold this.[1] [17] He asked, "What is this grave marker I see?" [a]The men from the city replied, "It's the grave of the prophet who came from Judah and foretold these very things you have done to the altar of Bethel." [18] The king said, "Leave it alone! No one must touch his bones." So [a]they left his bones undisturbed, as well as the bones of the Israelite prophet buried beside him.[1]

23:1 [a]2 Sam 19:11; 2 Chr 34:29–30   23:2 [a]Deut 31:10–13   23:3 [a]2 Kgs 11:14   [b]2 Kgs 11:17   23:4 [a]2 Kgs 25:18; Jer 52:24   [b]2 Kgs 21:3–7   23:5 [a]2 Kgs 21:3   23:6 [a]Exod 32:20   [b]2 Chr 34:4   [1]Heb. *on the grave of the sons of the people.*   23:7 [a]1 Kgs 14:24; 15:12   [b]Exod 35:25–26; Ezek 16:16   [c]Exod 38:8   [1]Heb. *houses.*   23:8 [a]Josh 21:17; 1 Kgs 15:22   [1]Heb. *the high places of the gates.*   23:9 [a][Ezek 44:10–14]   [b]1 Sam 2:36   23:10 [a]Isa 30:33; Jer 7:31–32   [b]Josh 15:8   [c][Lev 18:21; Deut 18:10]; Ezek 23:37–39   [d]2 Kgs 21:6   23:12 [a]Jer 19:13; Zeph 1:5   [b]2 Kgs 21:5; 2 Chr 33:5   [1]MT *he ran from there.*   23:13 [a]1 Kgs 11:5–7   23:14 [a][Exod 23:24; Deut 7:5–25]   23:16 [a]1 Kgs 13:2   [1]MT *according to the word of the LORD which the man of God proclaimed, who proclaimed these words.*   23:17 [a]1 Kgs 13:1, 30, 31   23:18 [a]1 Kgs 13:11, 31   [1]Heb. *and they left undisturbed his bones, the bones of the prophet who came from Samaria.*

[19]Josiah also removed all the [a]shrines on the high places in the cities of Samaria. The kings of Israel had made them and angered the LORD.[1] He did to them what he had done to the high place in Bethel. [20][a]He [b]sacrificed all the priests of the high places on the altars located there, and [c]burned human bones on them. Then he returned to Jerusalem.

[21]The king ordered all the people, "[a]Observe the [b]Passover of the LORD your God, as prescribed in this scroll of the covenant." [22][a]He issued this edict because a Passover like this had not been observed since the days of the judges who led Israel; it was neglected for the entire period of the kings of Israel and Judah. [23]But in the eighteenth year of King Josiah's reign, such a Passover of the LORD was observed in Jerusalem.

[24]Josiah also got rid of [a]the ritual pits used to conjure up spirits, the magicians, personal idols, disgusting images, and all the detestable idols [b]that had appeared in the land of Judah and in Jerusalem. In this way he carried out the terms of the law recorded on the scroll that Hilkiah the priest had discovered in the LORD's temple. [25][a]No king before or after repented before the LORD as he did, with his whole heart, soul, and being in accordance with the whole law of Moses.

[26]Yet the LORD's great anger against Judah did not subside; he was still infuriated by all the things Manasseh had done. [27]The LORD announced, "[a]I will also spurn Judah, just as I spurned Israel. I will reject this city that I chose—both Jerusalem and the temple, about which I said, 'I will live there.'"

[28]The rest of the events of Josiah's reign and all his accomplishments are recorded in the scroll called the Annals of the Kings of Judah. [29]During Josiah's reign Pharaoh Necho [a]king of Egypt marched toward[1] the Euphrates River to help the king of Assyria. King Josiah marched out to fight him, but Necho killed him at [b]Megiddo when he [c]saw him. [30]His servants transported his dead body from Megiddo in a chariot and brought it to Jerusalem, where they buried him in his tomb. [a]The people of [b]the land took Josiah's son Jehoahaz, poured olive oil on his head, and made him king in his father's place.

Jehoahaz's Reign over Judah

[31][a]Jehoahaz was twenty-three years old when he became king, and he reigned three months in Jerusalem. His mother was [b]Hamutal the daughter of Jeremiah, from Libnah. [32]He did evil in the sight of the LORD as his ancestors had done. [33]Pharaoh Necho imprisoned him in Riblah in the land of [a]Hamath and prevented him from ruling in Jerusalem.[1] He imposed on the land a special tax of 100 talents[2] of silver and a talent of gold. [34]Pharaoh [a]Necho made Josiah's son Eliakim king in Josiah's place, and [b]changed his name to [c]Jehoiakim. He took Jehoahaz to Egypt, where he died. [35]Jehoiakim paid Pharaoh [a]the required amount of silver and gold, but to meet Pharaoh's demands Jehoiakim had to tax the land. He collected an assessed amount from each man among the people of the land in order to pay Pharaoh Necho.

Jehoiakim's Reign over Judah

[36][a]Jehoiakim was twenty-five years old when he became king, and he reigned for eleven years in Jerusalem. His mother was Zebidah the daughter of Pedaiah, from Rumah. [37]He did evil in the sight of the LORD as his ancestors had done.

24 [a]During Jehoiakim's reign, King Nebuchadnezzar of [b]Babylon attacked. Jehoiakim was his subject for three years, but then he rebelled against him. [2]The LORD sent against him Babylonian, Syrian, Moabite, [a]and Ammonite raiding bands; he sent them to destroy Judah, just as [b]in the LORD's message that he had announced through his servants the prophets. [3]Just as the LORD had announced, he rejected Judah [a]because of all the sins that Manasseh had committed. [4]Because he killed innocent

23:19 [a]2 Chr 34:6–7 [1]Heb. *which the kings of Israel had made, angering.* **23:20** [a]1 Kgs 13:2 [b][Exod 22:20]; 1 Kgs 18:40; 2 Kgs 10:25; 11:18 [c]2 Chr 34:5 **23:21** [a]Num 9:5; Josh 5:10; 2 Chr 35:1 [b]Exod 12:3; Lev 23:5; Num 9:2; Deut 16:2–8 **23:22** [a]2 Chr 35:18–19 **23:24** [a][Lev 19:31; 20:27]; Deut 18:11 [b]2 Kgs 22:8 **23:25** [a]2 Kgs 18:5 **23:27** [a]2 Kgs 17:18, 20; 18:11; 21:13 **23:29** [a]2 Chr 35:20; Jer 2:16; 46:2 [b]Judg 5:19; Zech 12:11 [c]2 Kgs 14:8 [1]Heb. *went up to.* **23:30** [a]2 Chr 35:24; 2 Kgs 22:20 [b]2 Chr 36:1–4 **23:31** [a]1 Chr 3:15; Jer 22:11 [b]2 Kgs 24:18 **23:33** [a]2 Chr 25:6; Jer 52:27 [1]Ket. *when [he was] ruling in Jerusalem.* [2]About 7,500 pounds of silver and 75 pounds of gold. **23:34** [a]2 Chr 36:4 [b]2 Kgs 24:17; Dan 1:7 [c]Matt 1:11 **23:35** [a]2 Kgs 23:33 **23:36** [a]2 Chr 36:5; Jer 22:18–19; 26:1 **24:1** [a]2 Chr 36:6; Jer 25:1, 9; Dan 1:1 [b]2 Kgs 20:14 **24:2** [a]Jer 25:9; 32:28; 35:11; Ezek 19:8 [b]2 Kgs 20:17; 21:12–14; 23:27 **24:3** [a]2 Kgs 21:2, 11; 23:26

people [a]and stained Jerusalem with their blood, the LORD was unwilling to forgive them.

[5]The rest of the events of Jehoiakim's reign and all his accomplishments, are recorded in the scroll called the Annals of the Kings of Judah. [6]He passed away and his [a]son Jehoiachin replaced him as king. [7]The king of Egypt did not march out from his land again, for [a]the king of Babylon conquered all [b]the territory that the king of Egypt had formerly controlled between the Stream of Egypt and the Euphrates River.

Jehoiachin's Reign over Judah

[8a]Jehoiachin was eighteen years old when he became king, and he reigned three months in Jerusalem. His mother was Nehushta the daughter of Elnathan, from Jerusalem. [9]He did evil in the sight of the LORD as his ancestors had done.

[10]At [a]that time the generals of King Nebuchadnezzar of Babylon marched to Jerusalem and besieged the city. [11]King Nebuchadnezzar of Babylon came to the city while his generals were besieging it. [12]King Jehoiachin of Judah, along with his mother, his servants, his officials, and his eunuchs surrendered to [a]the [b]king of Babylon. The king of Babylon, in the eighth year of his reign, took Jehoiachin prisoner. [13]Nebuchadnezzar took from there all the riches in the treasuries of the LORD's temple [a]and of the royal palace. He removed all the gold items that King Solomon of Israel had made for the LORD's temple, just [b]as the LORD had warned. [14]He deported all [a]the residents of Jerusalem, including all the officials and all the soldiers ([b]10,000 people in [c]all). This included all [d]the craftsmen and those who worked with metal. No one was left except for the poorest among the people of the land. [15]He deported Jehoiachin from Jerusalem to Babylon, along with [a]the king's mother and wives, his eunuchs, and the high-ranking officials of the land. [16]The king of Babylon deported to Babylon [a]all the soldiers (there were 7,000), as well as 1,000 craftsmen and metal workers. This included all the best warriors. [17]The king of Babylon made Mattaniah, Jehoiachin's uncle, king in Jehoiachin's place. [a]He [b]renamed him Zedekiah.

Zedekiah's Reign over Judah

[18a]Zedekiah was twenty-one years old when he became king, and he ruled for eleven years in Jerusalem. His mother was [b]Hamutal,[1] the daughter of Jeremiah, from Libnah. [19]He did evil in [a]the sight of the LORD, as Jehoiakim had done.

[20]What follows is a record of what happened to Jerusalem and Judah because of [a]the LORD's anger; he finally threw them out of his presence. Zedekiah rebelled against the king of Babylon. [1]So [a]King Nebuchadnezzar of Babylon came against Jerusalem with his whole army and set up camp outside it. They built siege ramps all around it. He arrived on the tenth day of the tenth month in the ninth year of Zedekiah's reign. [2]The city remained under siege until King Zedekiah's eleventh year. [3]By the ninth day of the [a]fourth month the famine in the city was so severe the residents had no food. [4]The enemy broke through [a]the city walls, and all [b]the soldiers tried to escape. They left the city during the night. They went through the gate between the two walls, which is near the king's garden. (The Babylonians were all around the city.) Then they headed for the rift valley. [5]But the Babylonian army chased after the king. They caught up with him in the rift valley plains of Jericho, and his entire army deserted him. [6]They captured the king and brought him up to the king of Babylon [a]at Riblah, where he passed sentence on him. [7]Zedekiah's sons were executed while Zedekiah was forced to watch. The king of Babylon then had Zedekiah's eyes [a]put out, bound him in bronze chains, and carried him off to Babylon.

Nebuchadnezzar Destroys Jerusalem

[8]On the seventh day of the fifth [a]month, in [b]the nineteenth year of King

24:4 [a]2 Kgs 21:16   24:6 [a]2 Chr 36:6, 8; Jer 22:18–19   24:7 [a]Jer 37:5–7 [b]Jer 46:2   24:8 [a]1 Chr 3:16; 2 Chr 36:9   24:10 [a]Dan 1:1   24:12 [a]Jer 22:24–30; 24:1; 29:1–2; Ezek 17:12 [b]2 Chr 36:10   24:13 [a]2 Kgs 20:17; Isa 39:6 [b]Jer 20:5   24:14 [a]Isa 3:2–3; Jer 24:1 [b]2 Kgs 24:16; Jer 52:28 [c]1 Sam 13:19 [d]2 Kgs 25:12   24:15 [a]2 Chr 36:10; Esth 2:6; Jer 22:24–28; Ezek 17:12   24:16 [a]Jer 52:28   24:17 [a]Jer 37:1 [b]2 Chr 36:4   24:18 [a]2 Chr 36:11; Jer 52:1 [b]2 Kgs 23:31 [1]Sev. WSS Hamital.   24:19 [a]2 Chr 36:12   24:20 [a]2 Chr 36:13; Ezek 17:15   25:1 [a]2 Chr 36:17; Jer 6:6; 34:2; Ezek 4:2; 24:1–2; Hab 1:6   25:3 [a]2 Kgs 6:24–25; Isa 3:1; Jer 39:2; Lam 4:9–10   25:4 [a]Jer 39:2 [b]Jer 39:4–7; Ezek 12:12   25:6 [a]2 Kgs 23:33; Jer 52:9   25:7 [a]Jer 39:7; Ezek 17:16   25:8 [a]Jer 52:12 [b]2 Kgs 24:12

Nebuchadnezzar of Babylon, [c]Nebuzaradan, the captain of the royal guard, who served the king of Babylon, arrived in Jerusalem. [9]He burned down [a]the LORD's temple, the royal palace, [b]and all [c]the houses in Jerusalem, including every large house. [10]The whole Babylonian army that came with the captain of the royal guard tore down the walls that surrounded Jerusalem. [11]Nebuzaradan, [a]the captain of the royal guard, deported the rest of the people who were left in the city, those who had deserted to the king of Babylon, and the rest of the craftsmen.[1] [12]But he left [a]behind some of the poor of the land and gave them fields and vineyards.

[13]The Babylonians broke [a]the two bronze [b]pillars in [c]the LORD's temple, as well as [d]the movable stands and the big bronze basin called "The Sea." They [e]took the bronze to Babylon. [14]They also took [a]the pots, shovels, trimming shears, pans, and all the bronze utensils used by the priests. [15]The captain of the royal guard took the golden and silver censers and basins. [16]The bronze of [a]the items that King Solomon made for the LORD's temple—including the two pillars, the big bronze basin called "The Sea," the twelve bronze bulls under "The Sea,"[1] and the movable stands—was too heavy to be weighed. [17]Each of [a]the pillars was about 27 feet[1] high. The bronze top of one pillar was about 4½ feet[2] high and had bronze latticework and pomegranate-shaped ornaments all around it. The second pillar with its latticework was like it.

[18a]The captain of the royal guard took [b]Seraiah, the chief priest, and [c]Zephaniah, the priest who was second in rank, and the three doorkeepers. [19]From the city he took a eunuch who was in charge of the soldiers, [a]five of the king's advisers who were discovered in the city, an official army secretary who drafted citizens for military service, and 60 citizens from the people of the land who were discovered in the city. [20]Nebuzaradan, captain of the royal guard, took them and brought them to the king of Babylon at Riblah. [21]The king of Babylon ordered them to be executed at Riblah in the territory of Hamath. So Judah was deported from its land.

Gedaliah Appointed Governor

[22]Now King Nebuchadnezzar of Babylon appointed Gedaliah son of [a]Ahikam, son of Shaphan, as governor over [b]the people whom he allowed to remain in the land of Judah. [23]All the [a]officers of the Judahite army and their troops heard that the king of Babylon had appointed Gedaliah to govern. So they came to Gedaliah at Mizpah. The officers who came were Ishmael son of Nethaniah, Johanan son of Kareah, Seraiah son of Tanhumeth the Netophathite, and Jaazaniah son of the Maacathite. [24]Gedaliah took an oath so as to give them and their troops some assurance of safety. He said, "You don't need to be afraid to submit to the Babylonian officials. Settle down in the land and submit to the king of Babylon. Then things will go well for you." [25]But in the seventh month Ishmael son of Nethaniah, son of Elishama, who was a member of the royal family, came [a]with 10 of his men and murdered Gedaliah, as well as the Judeans and Babylonians who were with him at Mizpah. [26]Then all the people, from the youngest to the oldest, as well as the army officers, left for Egypt, because they were afraid of what the Babylonians might do.

Jehoiachin in Babylon

[27a]In the thirty-seventh year of the exile of King Jehoiachin of Judah, on the twenty-seventh day of the twelfth month, King Evil Merodach of Babylon, in the first year of his reign, [b]pardoned King Jehoiachin of Judah and released him from prison. [28]He spoke kindly to him and gave him a more prestigious position than the other kings who were with him in Babylon. [29]Jehoiachin took off his prison clothes and [a]ate daily in the king's presence for the rest of his life. [30]He was given daily provisions by the king for the rest of his life until the day he died.[1]

25:8 [c]Jer 39:9   25:9 [a]2 Kgs 25:13; 2 Chr 36:19; Ps 79:1; Jer 7:14   [b]Jer 39:8   [c]Jer 17:27   25:11 [a]Isa 1:9; Jer 5:19; 39:9   [1]MT the multitude.   25:12 [a]2 Kgs 24:14; Jer 39:10; 40:7; 52:16   25:13 [a]Jer 52:17   [b]1 Kgs 7:15   [c]1 Kgs 7:27   [d]1 Kgs 7:23   [e]2 Kgs 20:17; Jer 27:19–22   25:14 [a]Exod 27:3; 1 Kgs 7:45   25:16 [a]1 Kgs 7:47   [1]MT omits the twelve bronze bulls under 'the Sea,'.   25:17 [a]1 Kgs 7:15–22; Jer 52:21   [1]Heb. 18 cubits.   [2]Heb. 3 cubits.   25:18 [a]Jer 39:9–13; 52:12–16, 24   [b]1 Chr 6:14; Ezra 7:1   [c]Jer 21:1; 29:25, 29   25:19 [a]Esth 1:14; Jer 52:25   25:22 [a]2 Kgs 22:12   [b]Isa 1:9; Jer 40:5   25:23 [a]Jer 40:7–9   25:25 [a]Jer 41:1–3   25:27 [a]2 Kgs 24:12, 15; Jer 52:31–34   [b]Gen 40:13, 20   25:29 [a]2 Sam 9:7   25:30 [1]MT omits until the day he died.

1 CHRONICLES

The Books of 1–2 Chronicles cover the same period of Jewish history described in 2 Samuel through 2 Kings, but the perspective is different. These books are no mere repetition of the same material but rather form a divine editorial on the history of God's people. While 2 Samuel and 1–2 Kings give a political history of Israel and Judah, 1–2 Chronicles present a religious history of the Davidic dynasty of Judah. The former are written from a prophetic and moral viewpoint and the latter from a priestly and spiritual perspective. The Book of 1 Chronicles begins with the royal line of David, then traces the spiritual significance of David's righteous reign. The Books of 1–2 Chronicles were originally one continuous work in the Hebrew. The title was *Dibere Hayyamim*, meaning "The Words [Accounts, Events] of the Days." The equivalent meaning today would be "The Events of the Times." Chronicles was divided into two parts in the third-century BC Greek translation of the Hebrew Bible (the Septuagint). At that time it was given the name *Paraleipomenon*, "Of Things Omitted," referring to the things left out of Samuel and Kings. Some copies add the phrase *Basileon Iouda*, "Concerning the Kings of Judah." The first Book of Chronicles was called *Paraleipomenon Primus*, "The First Book of Things Omitted." The name "Chronicles" comes from Jerome in his Latin Vulgate Bible (AD 385–405): *Chronicorum Liber*. He meant his title in the sense of the chronicles of the whole of sacred history.

Adam's Descendants

1 ªAdam, ᵇSeth, Enosh, ²Kenan, Mahalalel, Jered, ³Enoch, Methuselah, Lamech, ⁴ªNoah, Shem, Ham, and Japheth.¹

Japheth's Descendants

⁵ªThe sons of Japheth: Gomer, Magog, Madai, Javan, Tubal, Meshech, and Tiras. ⁶The sons of Gomer: Ashkenaz, Riphath,¹ and Togarmah. ⁷The sons¹ of Javan: Elishah, Tarshish, the Kittites, and the Rodanites.²

Ham's Descendants

⁸ªThe sons of Ham: Cush, Mizraim,¹ Put, and Canaan. ⁹The sons of Cush: Seba, Havilah, Sabta, Raamah, and Sabteca.

The sons of Raamah: Sheba and Dedan. ¹⁰Cush was the father ªof Nimrod, who established himself as a mighty warrior on earth.

¹¹Mizraim was the father of the Ludites, Anamites, Lehabites, Naphtuhites, ¹²Pathrusites, Casluhites (from whom the Philistines descended), and the ªCaphtorites.

¹³ªCanaan was the father of Sidon—his firstborn—and Heth, ¹⁴as well as the Jebusites, Amorites, Girgashites, ¹⁵Hivites, Arkites, Sinites, ¹⁶Arvadites, Zemarites, and Hamathites.

Shem's Descendants

¹⁷The sons of ªShem: Elam, Asshur, ᵇArphaxad, Lud, and Aram.

The sons of Aram:¹ Uz, Hul, Gether, and Meshech.

¹⁸Arphaxad was the father of Shelah, and Shelah was the father of Eber. ¹⁹Two sons were born to Eber: The first was named

1:1 ªGen 1:27; 2:7; 5:1–2, 5   ᵇGen 4:25–26; 5:3–9   1:4 ªGen 5:28–10:1   ¹LXX *Noah; the sons of Noah* [were] *Shem, Ham, and Japheth.*   1:5 ªGen 10:2–4   1:6 ¹MT *Diphath.*   1:7 ¹Or *descendants.*   ²Qe. *Dodanim.*   1:8 ªGen 10:6   ¹I.e., Egypt.   1:10 ªGen 10:8–10, 13   1:12 ªDeut 2:23   1:13 ªGen 9:18, 25–27; 10:15   1:17 ªGen 10:22–29; 11:10   ᵇLuke 3:36   ¹Heb. omits *the sons of Aram.*

Peleg, for during his lifetime the earth was divided; his brother's name was Joktan.

[20a]Joktan was the father of Almodad, Sheleph, Hazarmaveth, Jerah, [21]Hadoram, Uzal, Diklah, [22]Ebal,[1] Abimael, Sheba, [23]Ophir, Havilah, and Jobab. All these were the sons of Joktan.

[24a]Shem, Arphaxad, Shelah,[1] [25a]Eber, Peleg, Reu, [26]Serug, Nahor, Terah, [27a]Abram (that is, Abraham).

[28a]The sons of Abraham: [b]Isaac and [c]Ishmael.

[29]These were their descendants:

Ishmael's Descendants

Ishmael's firstborn [a]son was Nebaioth; the others were Kedar, Adbeel, Mibsam, [30]Mishma, Dumah, Massa, Hadad, Tema, [31]Jetur, Naphish, and Kedemah. These were the sons of Ishmael.

Keturah's Descendants

[32]The sons to whom Keturah, Abraham's concubine, gave birth: Zimran, Jokshan, Medan, Midian, Ishbak, Shuah.

[a]The sons of Jokshan: Sheba and Dedan.

[33]The sons of Midian: Ephah, Epher, Hanoch, Abida, and Eldaah. All these were the sons of Keturah.

Isaac's Descendants

[34a]Abraham was [b]the father of Isaac. The sons of Isaac: Esau and Israel.

Esau's Descendants

[35]The sons of [a]Esau: Eliphaz, Reuel, Jeush, Jalam, and Korah.

[36]The sons of Eliphaz: Teman, Omar, Zephi,[1] Gatam, Kenaz, and (by [a]Timna) Amalek.[2]

[37]The sons of Reuel: Nahath, Zerah, Shammah, and Mizzah.

The Descendants of Seir

[38a]The sons of Seir: Lotan, Shobal, Zibeon, Anah, Dishon, Ezer, and Dishan.

[39]The sons of Lotan: Hori and Homam. (Timna was Lotan's sister.)

[40]The sons of Shobal: Alyan,[1] Manahath, Ebal, Shephi,[2] and Onam.

The sons of Zibeon: Aiah and Anah.

[41]The son of Anah: [a]Dishon.

The sons of Dishon: Hamran, Eshban, Ithran, and Keran.

[42]The sons of Ezer: Bilhan, Zaavan, Jaakan.

The sons of Dishan:[1] Uz and Aran.

Kings of Edom

[43]These were the [a]kings who reigned in the land of Edom before any king ruled over the Israelites: Bela son of Beor; the name of his city was Dinhabah.

[44]When Bela died, Jobab son of Zerah from Bozrah succeeded him.

[45]When Jobab died, Husham from the land of the Temanites succeeded him.

[46]When Husham died, Hadad son of Bedad succeeded him. He struck down the Midianites in the plains of Moab; the name of his city was Avith.

[47]When Hadad died, Samlah from Masrekah succeeded him.

[48a]When Samlah died, Shaul from Rehoboth on the River succeeded him.

[49]When Shaul died, Baal Hanan son of Achbor succeeded him.

[50]When Baal Hanan died, Hadad succeeded him; the name of his city was Pai.[1] His wife was Mehetabel, daughter of Matred, daughter of Me-Zahab.

[51]Hadad died.

Tribal Chiefs of Edom

The tribal chiefs of Edom were: Timna, Alvah, Jetheth, [52]Oholibamah, Elah, Pinon, [53]Kenaz, Teman, Mibzar, [54]Magdiel, and Iram.[1] These were the tribal chiefs of Edom.

Israel's Descendants

2 These were the [a]sons of Israel: [b]Reuben, Simeon, Levi, and Judah; Issachar and Zebulun; [2]Dan, Joseph, and Benjamin; Naphtali, Gad, and Asher.

Judah's Descendants

[3]The sons of [a]Judah: Er, Onan, and Shelah. These three were born to him by [b]Bathshua,[1] a Canaanite woman. [c]Er, Judah's

1:20 [a]Gen 10:26   1:22 [1]Some MSS *Obal.*   1:24 [a]Gen 11:10–26; Luke 3:34–36   [1]Some LXX MSS *Arphaxad, Cainan, Shelah.*   1:25 [a]Gen 11:15   1:27 [a]Gen 17:5   1:28 [a]Gen 21:2–3   [b]Gen 21:2   [c]Gen 16:11, 15   1:29 [a]Gen 25:13–16   1:32 [a]Gen 25:1–4   1:34 [a]Gen 21:2   [b]Gen 25:9, 25, 26, 29; 32:28   1:35 [a]Gen 36:10–19   1:36 [a]Gen 36:12   [1]Sev. WSS *Zepho.*   [2]Heb. *and Timna and Amalek.*   1:38 [a]Gen 36:20–28   1:40 [1]A few MSS *Alvan.*   [2]A few MSS *Shepho.*   1:41 [a]Gen 36:25   1:42 [1]MT *Dishon.*   1:43 [a]Gen 36:31–43   1:48 [a]Gen 36:37   1:50 [1]Sev. WSS *Pau.*   1:54 [1]*chief* precedes each name in this list.   2:1 [a]Gen 29:32–35; 35:23, 26; 46:8–27   [b]Gen 29:32; 35:22   2:3 [a]Gen 38:3–5; 46:12; Num 26:19   [b]Gen 38:2   [c]Gen 38:7   [1]The name means "daughter of Shua."

firstborn, displeased the LORD, so the LORD killed him.

[4a] Tamar, Judah's daughter-in-law, [b] bore to him Perez and Zerah. Judah had five sons in all.

[5] The sons of [a] Perez: Hezron and Hamul.

[6] The sons of Zerah: Zimri, [a] Ethan, Heman, Kalkol, Dara[1]—five in all.

[7] The son of [a] Carmi: Achan,[1] who brought the disaster on Israel when he stole what was devoted to [b] God.

[8] The son of Ethan: Azariah.

[9] The sons born to Hezron: Jerahmeel, Ram, and Caleb.

Ram's Descendants

[10] Ram was the father [a] of Amminadab, and Amminadab was the father of Nahshon, the tribal [b] chief of Judah. [11] Nahshon was the father of Salma,[1] and Salma was the father of Boaz. [12] Boaz was the father of Obed, and Obed was the father of Jesse.

[13a] Jesse was the father of Eliab, his firstborn; Abinadab was born second, Shimea third, [14] Nethanel fourth, Raddai fifth, [15] Ozem sixth, and David [a] seventh. [16] Their sisters were Zeruiah [a] and Abigail. Zeruiah's three sons were Abshai, Joab, and Asahel. [17] Abigail bore Amasa, whose father was Jether the Ishmaelite.

Caleb's Descendants

[18] Caleb son of Hezron fathered sons by his wife Azubah (also known as Jerioth).[1] Her sons were Jesher, Shobab, and Ardon. [19] When Azubah died, Caleb married [a] Ephrath, who bore him Hur. [20] Hur was the father of Uri, and Uri was the father of [a] Bezalel.

[21] Later Hezron slept with the daughter of [a] Makir, the father of Gilead. (He had married her when he was sixty years old.) She bore him Segub. [22] Segub was the father of [a] Jair, who owned twenty-three cities in the land of Gilead. [23] ([a] Geshur and Aram captured the towns of Jair,[1] along with Kenath and its sixty surrounding towns.) All these were descendants of Makir, the father of Gilead.

[24] After Hezron's death, Caleb slept with Ephrath, his father Hezron's widow, and she bore to him [a] Ashhur the father of Tekoa.[1]

Jerahmeel's Descendants

[25] The sons of Jerahmeel, Hezron's firstborn, were Ram, the firstborn, Bunah, Oren, Ozem, and Ahijah. [26] Jerahmeel had another wife named Atarah; she was Onam's mother.

[27] The sons of Ram, Jerahmeel's firstborn, were Maaz, Jamin, and Eker.

[28] The sons of Onam were Shammai and Jada.

The sons of Shammai: Nadab and Abishur.

[29] Abishur's wife was Abihail, who bore him Ahban and Molid. [30] The sons of Nadab: Seled and Appaim. (Seled died without having sons.)

[31] The son of Appaim: Ishi.

The son of Ishi: [a] Sheshan.

The son of Sheshan: Ahlai.

[32] The sons of Jada, Shammai's brother: Jether and Jonathan. (Jether died without having sons.)

[33] The sons of Jonathan: Peleth and Zaza.

These were the descendants of Jerahmeel.

[34] Sheshan had no sons, only daughters. Sheshan had an Egyptian servant named Jarha. [35] Sheshan gave his daughter to his servant Jarha as a wife; she bore him Attai.

[36] Attai was the father of Nathan, and Nathan was the father of [a] Zabad. [37] Zabad was the father of Ephlal, and Ephlal was the father of [a] Obed. [38] Obed was the father of Jehu, and Jehu was the father of Azariah. [39] Azariah was the father of Helez, and Helez was the father of Eleasah. [40] Eleasah was the father of Sismai, and Sismai was the father of Shallum. [41] Shallum was the father of Jekamiah, and Jekamiah was the father of Elishama.

More of Caleb's Descendants

[42] The sons of Caleb, Jerahmeel's brother: his firstborn Mesha, the father of Ziph, and his second son Mareshah,[1] the father of Hebron.

[43] The sons of Hebron: Korah, Tappuah, Rekem, and Shema.

[44] Shema was the father of Raham, the

2:4 [a] Gen 38:6 [b] Matt 1:3   2:5 [a] Gen 46:12; Ruth 4:18   2:6 [a] 1 Kgs 4:31 [1] Sev. wss *Darda.*   2:7 [a] 1 Chr 4:1 [b] Josh 6:18 [1] Heb. *Achar.*   2:10 [a] Ruth 4:19–22; Matt 1:4 [b] Num 1:7; 2:3   2:11 [1] LXX *Salmon.*   2:13 [a] 1 Sam 16:6   2:15 [a] 1 Sam 16:10–11; 17:12   2:16 [a] 2 Sam 2:18   2:18 [1] Heb. *and Caleb son of Hezron fathered* [children] *with Azubah, a wife, and with Jerioth.*   2:19 [a] 1 Chr 2:50   2:20 [a] Exod 31:2; 38:22   2:21 [a] Num 27:1; Judg 5:14; 1 Chr 7:14   2:22 [a] Judg 10:3   2:23 [a] Num 32:41; Deut 3:14; Josh 13:30 [1] Or perhaps *Havvoth Jair.*   2:24 [a] 1 Chr 4:5 [1] Heb. *And after the death of Hezron in Caleb Ephrathah, and the wife of Hezron, Abijah, and she bore to him Ashhur the father of Tekoa.*   2:31 [a] 1 Chr 2:34–35   2:36 [a] 1 Chr 11:41   2:37 [a] 2 Chr 23:1   2:42 [1] Heb. *and the sons of Mareshah.*

father of Jorkeam. Rekem was the father of Shammai. ⁴⁵Shammai's son was Maon, who was the father of Beth Zur.

⁴⁶Caleb's concubine Ephah bore Haran, Moza, and Gazez. Haran was the father of Gazez.

⁴⁷The sons of Jahdai: Regem, Jotham, Geshan, Pelet, Ephah, and Shaaph.

⁴⁸Caleb's concubine Maacah bore Sheber and Tirhanah. ⁴⁹She also bore Shaaph the father of Madmannah and Sheva the father of Machbenah and Gibea. Caleb's daughter was ᵃAchsah.

⁵⁰These were the descendants of Caleb.

The sons of ᵃHur, the firstborn of Ephrath: Shobal, the father of Kiriath ᵇJearim, ⁵¹Salma, the father of Bethlehem, and Hareph, the father of Beth Gader.

⁵²The sons of Shobal, the father of Kiriath Jearim, were Haroeh, half the Manahathites, ⁵³the clans of Kiriath Jearim—the Ithrites, Puthites, Shumathites, and Mishraites. (The Zorathites and Eshtaolites descended from these groups.)

⁵⁴The sons of Salma: Bethlehem, the Netophathites, Atroth Beth Joab, half the Manahathites, the Zorites, ⁵⁵and the clans of the scribes who lived in Jabez: the Tirathites, Shimeathites, and Sucathites. These are the ᵃKenites who descended from Hammath, the father of Beth ᵇRechab.

David's Descendants

3 These were the sons of David who were born to him in Hebron:

The firstborn was ᵃAmnon, whose mother was ᵇAhinoam from ᶜJezreel;

the second was Daniel, whose mother was ᵈAbigail from Carmel;

²the third was ᵃAbsalom, whose mother was Maacah, daughter of King Talmai of Geshur;

the fourth was ᵇAdonijah, whose mother was Haggith;

³the fifth was Shephatiah, whose mother was Abital;

the sixth was Ithream, whose mother was ᵃEglah, David's wife.

⁴These six were born to David in Hebron, where ᵃhe ruled for seven years and six months.

He ruled thirty-three years ᵇin Jerusalem. ⁵These were the sons born to him in Jerusalem:

Shimea, Shobab, Nathan, ᵃand ᵇSolomon—the mother of these four was Bathsheba the daughter of Ammiel.

⁶The other nine were Ibhar, Elishua, Elpelet, ⁷Nogah, Nepheg, Japhia, ⁸Elishama, Eliada, and Eliphelet.

⁹These were all the sons of David, not counting the sons of his concubines. ᵃTamar was their sister.

Solomon's Descendants

¹⁰Solomon's son was ᵃRehoboam, followed by Abijah his son, Asa his son, Jehoshaphat his son, ¹¹Joram his son, Ahaziah his son, Joash his son, ¹²Amaziah his son, Azariah his son, Jotham his son, ¹³Ahaz his son, Hezekiah his son, Manasseh his son, ¹⁴Amon his son, Josiah his son.

¹⁵The sons of Josiah: Johanan was the firstborn; Jehoiakim was born second; Zedekiah third, and Shallum fourth.

¹⁶The sons of ᵃJehoiakim: his son Jehoiachin and his son Zedekiah.

¹⁷The sons of Jehoiachin the exile:¹ Shealtiel ᵃhis son, ¹⁸Malkiram, Pedaiah, Shenazzar, Jekamiah, Hoshama, and Nedabiah.

¹⁹The sons of Pedaiah: Zerubbabel and Shimei.

The sons of Zerubbabel: Meshullam and Hananiah. Shelomith was their sister. ²⁰The five others were Hashubah, Ohel, Berechiah, Hasadiah, and Jushab Hesed.

²¹The descendants of Hananiah: Pelatiah, Jeshaiah, the sons of Rephaiah, of Arnan, of Obadiah, and of Shecaniah.

²²The descendants of Shecaniah: Shemaiah and his sons: ᵃHattush, Igal, Bariah, Neariah, and Shaphat—six in all.

²³The sons of Neariah: Elioenai, Hizkiah, and Azrikam—three in all.

2:49 ᵃJosh 15:17   **2:50** ᵃ1 Chr 4:4   ᵇJosh 9:17; 18:14   **2:55** ᵃJudg 1:16   ᵇ2 Kgs 10:15; Jer 35:2   **3:1** ᵃ2 Sam 3:2–5   ᵇ1 Sam 25:43   ᶜJosh 15:56   ᵈ1 Sam 25:39–42   **3:2** ᵃ2 Sam 13:37; 15:1   ᵇ1 Kgs 1:5   **3:3** ᵃ2 Sam 3:5   **3:4** ᵃ2 Sam 2:11   ᵇ2 Sam 5:5   **3:5** ᵃ1 Chr 14:4–7   ᵇ2 Sam 12:24–25   **3:9** ᵃ2 Sam 13:1   **3:10** ᵃ1 Kgs 11:43; Matt 1:7–10   **3:16** ᵃMatt 1:11   **3:17** ᵃMatt 1:12   ¹Heb. *prisoner.*   **3:22** ᵃEzra 8:2

[24] The sons of Elioenai: Hodaviah, Eliashib, Pelaiah, Akkub, Johanan, Delaiah, and Anani—seven in all.

Judah's Descendants

4 The descendants of Judah: [a] Perez, Hezron, Carmi, Hur, and Shobal. [2] Reaiah the son of Shobal was the father of Jahath, and Jahath was the father of Ahumai and Lahad. These were the clans of the Zorathites.

[3] These were the sons of Etam: Jezreel, Ishma, and Idbash. Their sister was Hazzelelponi.

[4] Penuel was the father of Gedor, and Ezer was the father of Hushah. These were the descendants of [a] Hur, the firstborn of Ephrathah and the father of Bethlehem.

[5] [a] Ashhur the father of Tekoa had two wives, Helah and Naarah. [6] Naarah bore him Ahuzzam, Hepher, Temeni, and Haahashtari. These were the sons of Naarah. [7] The sons of Helah: Zereth, Zohar, Ethnan, [8] and Koz, who was the father of Anub, Hazzobebah, and the clans of Aharhel the son of Harum.

[9] Jabez was [a] more respected than his brothers. His mother had named him Jabez, for she said, "I experienced pain when I gave birth to him." [1] [10] Jabez called out to the God of Israel, "If only you would greatly bless me and expand my territory. May your hand be with me! Keep me from harm [1] so I might not endure pain." God answered his prayer.

[11] Kelub, the brother of [a] Shuhah, was the father of Mehir, who was the father of Eshton. [12] Eshton was the father of Beth Rapha, Paseah, and Tehinnah, the father of Ir Nahash. These were the men of Recah.

[13] The sons of Kenaz: [a] Othniel and Seraiah.

The sons of Othniel: Hathath and Meonothai. [1] [14] Meonothai was the father of Ophrah.

Seraiah was the father of Joab, the father of those who live in the [a] Valley of the Craftsmen, for they were craftsmen.

[15] The sons of [a] Caleb son of Jephunneh: Iru, Elah, and Naam.

The son of Elah: Kenaz.

[16] The sons of Jehallelel: Ziph, Ziphah, Tiria, and Asarel.

[17] The sons of Ezrah: Jether, Mered, Epher, and Jalon.

Mered's wife Bithiah gave birth to Miriam, Shammai, and Ishbah, the father of Eshtemoa. [18] (His Judahite wife gave birth to Jered the father of Gedor, Heber the father of Soco, and Jekuthiel the father of Zanoah.) These were the sons of Pharaoh's daughter Bithiah, whom Mered married.

[19] The sons of Hodiah's wife, the sister of Naham: the father of Keilah the Garmite, and Eshtemoa the [a] Maacathite.

[20] The sons of Shimon: Amnon, Rinnah, Ben Hanan, and Tilon.

The descendants of Ishi: Zoheth and Ben Zoheth.

[21] The sons of [a] Shelah son of Judah: Er [b] the father of Lecah, Laadah the father of Mareshah, the clans of the linen workers at Beth Ashbea, [22] Jokim, the men of Cozeba, and Joash and Saraph, both of whom ruled in Moab and Jashubi Lehem. (This information is from ancient records.) [23] They were the potters who lived in Netaim and Gederah; they lived there and worked for the king.

Simeon's Descendants

[24] The [a] descendants of Simeon: Nemuel, Jamin, Jarib, Zerah, Shaul, [25] his son Shallum, his son Mibsam, and his son Mishma.

[26] The descendants of Mishma: his son Hammuel, his son Zaccur, and his son Shimei.

[27] Shimei had sixteen sons and six daughters. But his brothers did not have many sons, so their whole clan was not as numerous as the sons of Judah. [28] They lived in Beer Sheba, Moladah, Hazar Shual, [29] Bilhah, Ezem, Tolad, [30] Bethuel, Hormah, Ziklag, [31] Beth Marcaboth, Hazar Susim, Beth Biri, and Shaaraim. These were their towns until the reign of David. [32] Their settlements also included Etam, Ain, Rimmon, Tochen, and Ashan—five towns, [33] along with all their settlements that surrounded these towns as far as Baal. [1] These were the places where they lived; they kept genealogical records.

[34] Their clan leaders were: Meshobab, Jamlech, Joshah son of Amaziah, [35] Joel, Jehu son of Joshibiah (son of Seraiah, son of Asiel), [36] Eleoenai, Jaakobah, Jeshohaiah, Asaiah,

Adiel, Jesimiel, Benaiah, [37]Ziza son of Shipi (son of Allon, son of Jedaiah, son of Shimri, son of Shemaiah). [38]These who are named above were the leaders of their clans.

Their extended families increased greatly in numbers. [39]They went to the entrance of Gedor, to the east of the valley, looking for pasture for their sheep. [40]They found fertile and rich pasture; the land was very broad, undisturbed, and peaceful. Indeed some Hamites had been living there before that. [41]The men whose names are listed came during the time of King Hezekiah of Judah and [a]attacked the Hamites' settlements, as well as the Meunites they discovered there, and they wiped them out, as can be seen to this very day. They dispossessed them, for they found pasture for their sheep there. [42]Five hundred men of Simeon, led by Pelatiah, Neariah, Rephaiah, and Uzziel, the sons of Ishi, went to the hill country of Seir [43]and defeated [a]the rest of the Amalekite refugees; they live there to this very day.

Reuben's Descendants

5 The sons of Reuben, Israel's firstborn— (Now [a]he was the firstborn, but when he [b]defiled [c]his father's bed, his rights as firstborn were given to the sons of Joseph, Israel's son. So Reuben is not listed as firstborn in the genealogical records. [2]Though [a]Judah was the strongest among his brothers and a [b]leader descended from him, the right of the firstborn belonged to Joseph.)

[3]The sons of [a]Reuben, Israel's firstborn: Hanoch, Pallu, Hezron, and Carmi.

[4]The descendants of Joel: his son Shemaiah, his son Gog, his son Shimei, [5]his son Micah, his son Reaiah, his son Baal, [6]and his son Beerah, whom King Tiglath-Pileser of Assyria carried into [a]exile. Beerah was the tribal leader of Reuben.

[7]His brothers by their clans, as listed in their genealogical records:

The leader Jeiel, Zechariah, [8]and Bela son of Azaz, son of Shema, son of Joel.

They lived in [a]Aroer as far as Nebo and Baal Meon. [9]In the east they settled as far as the entrance to the wilderness that stretches to the Euphrates River, for their cattle had [a]increased in numbers in the land of Gilead. [10]During the time of Saul they attacked the Hagrites and defeated them. They took over their territory in the entire eastern region of Gilead.

Gad's Descendants

[11]The [a]descendants of Gad lived near them in the land of [b]Bashan, as far as [c]Salecah.

[12]They included Joel the leader, Shapham the second-in-command, Janai, and Shaphat in Bashan. [13]Their relatives, listed according to their families, included Michael, Meshullam, Sheba, Jorai, Jacan, Zia, and Eber—seven in all.

[14]These were the sons of Abihail son of Huri, son of Jaroah, son of Gilead, son of Michael, son of Jeshishai, son of Jahdo, son of Buz. [15]Ahi son of Abdiel, son of Guni, was the leader of the family. [16]They lived in Gilead, in Bashan and its surrounding settlements, and in the pasturelands of [a]Sharon to their very borders. [17]All of them were listed in the genealogical records in the time of King [a]Jotham of Judah and in the time of King [b]Jeroboam of Israel.

[18]The Reubenites, Gadites, and the half-tribe of Manasseh had 44,760 men in their combined armies, warriors who carried shields and swords, were equipped with bows, and were trained for war. [19]They attacked the Hagrites, [a]Jetur, Naphish, and Nodab. [20]They received divine help in fighting them, and [a]the Hagrites and all their allies were handed over to them. They cried [b]out to God during the battle; he responded to their prayers because they trusted in him. [21]They seized the Hagrites' animals, including 50,000 camels, 250,000 sheep, and 2,000 donkeys. They also took captive 100,000 people. [22]Because God fought for [a]them, they killed many of the enemy. They dispossessed the Hagrites and lived in their land until the exile.

The Half-Tribe of Manasseh

[23]The half-tribe of Manasseh settled in the land from Bashan as far as Baal Hermon, [a]Senir, and Mount Hermon. They grew in number.

4:41 [a]2 Kgs 18:8   4:43 [a]Exod 17:14; 1 Sam 15:8; 30:17   5:1 [a]Gen 29:32; 49:3   [b]Gen 35:22; 49:4   [c]Gen 48:15, 22   5:2 [a]Gen 49:8, 10; Ps 60:7; 108:8   [b]Mic 5:2; Matt 2:6   5:3 [a]Gen 46:9; Exod 6:14; Num 26:5   5:6 [a]2 Kgs 18:11   5:8 [a]Num 32:34; Josh 12:2; 13:15–16   5:9 [a]Josh 22:8–9   5:11 [a]Num 26:15–18   [b]Josh 13:11, 24–28   [c]Deut 3:10   5:16 [a]1 Chr 27:29; Song 2:1; Isa 35:2; 65:10   5:17 [a]2 Kgs 15:5, 32   [b]2 Kgs 14:16, 28   5:19 [a]Gen 25:15; 1 Chr 1:31   5:20 [a][1 Chr 5:22]   [b]2 Chr 14:11–13   5:22 [a]2 Kgs 15:29; 17:6   5:23 [a]Deut 3:9

[24]These were the leaders of their families: Epher, Ishi, Eliel, Azriel, Jeremiah, Hodaviah, and Jahdiel. They were skilled warriors, men of reputation, and leaders of their families. [25]But they were unfaithful to the God of their ancestors and worshiped instead the gods of the native peoples whom God had destroyed before them. [26]So the God of Israel stirred up King [a]Pul of Assyria (that is, King [b]Tiglath-Pileser of Assyria), and he carried away the Reubenites, Gadites, and half-tribe of Manasseh and took them to [c]Halah, Habor, Hara, and the river of Gozan, where they remain to this very day.

Levi's Descendants

6 The sons of Levi: [a]Gershon, Kohath, and Merari.

[2]The sons of Kohath: Amram, [a]Izhar, Hebron, and Uzziel.

[3]The children of Amram: Aaron, Moses, and Miriam.

The sons of Aaron: [a]Nadab, Abihu, Eleazar, and Ithamar.

[4]Eleazar was the father of Phinehas, and Phinehas was the father of Abishua. [5]Abishua was the father of Bukki, and Bukki was the father of Uzzi. [6]Uzzi was the father of Zerahiah, and Zerahiah was the father of Meraioth. [7]Meraioth was the father of Amariah, and Amariah was the father of Ahitub. [8a]Ahitub was the father of [b]Zadok, and Zadok was the father of Ahimaaz. [9]Ahimaaz was the father of Azariah, and Azariah was the father of Johanan. [10]Johanan was the father of Azariah, [a]who served as a priest in the [b]temple Solomon built in Jerusalem. [11a]Azariah was the father of [b]Amariah, and Amariah was the father of Ahitub. [12]Ahitub was the father of Zadok, and Zadok was the father of Shallum. [13]Shallum was the father of Hilkiah, and Hilkiah was the father of Azariah. [14]Azariah was the father of [a]Seraiah, and Seraiah was the father of Jehozadak. [15]Jehozadak went into exile [a]when the LORD sent the people of Judah and Jerusalem into exile by the hand of Nebuchadnezzar.

[16]The sons of Levi: [a]Gershom, Kohath, and Merari.

[17]These are the names of the sons of Gershom: Libni and Shimei.

[18]The sons of Kohath: Amram, Izhar, Hebron, and Uzziel.

[19]The sons of Merari: Mahli and Mushi.

These are the clans of the Levites by their families.

[20]To Gershom: his son Libni, his son Jahath, his son [a]Zimmah, [21]his son Joah, his son Iddo, his son Zerah, and his son Jeatherai.

[22]The sons[1] of Kohath: his son Amminadab, his son [a]Korah, his son Assir, [23]his son Elkanah, his son Ebiasaph, his son Assir, [24]his son Tahath, his son Uriel, his son Uzziah, and his son Shaul.

[25]The sons of Elkanah: [a]Amasai, Ahimoth, [26]his son Elkanah,[1] his son Zophai, his son Nahath, [27]his son Eliab, his son Jeroham, and his son Elkanah.[1]

[28]The sons of Samuel: Joel the firstborn[1] and Abijah the second oldest.

[29]The descendants of Merari: Mahli, his son Libni, his son Shimei, his son Uzzah, [30]his son Shimea, his son Haggiah, and his son Asaiah.

Professional Musicians

[31]These are [a]the men David put in charge of music in the LORD's sanctuary, after the [b]ark was placed there. [32]They performed music before the sanctuary of the meeting tent until Solomon built the LORD's temple in Jerusalem. They carried out their tasks according to regulations.

[33]These are the ones who served along with their sons:

From the [a]Kohathites: Heman the musician, son of Joel, son of Samuel, [34]son of Elkanah, son of Jeroham, son of Eliel, son of Toah, [35]son of Zuph, son of Elkanah, son of Mahath, son of Amasai, [36]son of Elkanah, son of Joel, son of Azariah, son of Zephaniah, [37]son of Tahath, son of Assir, son of [a]Ebiasaph, son of Korah, [38]son of Izhar, son of Kohath, son of Levi, son of Israel.

[39]Serving beside him was his fellow Levite [a]Asaph, son of Berechiah, son of Shimea, [40]son of Michael, son of Baaseiah,[1] son of Malkijah, [41]son of [a]Ethni, son of Zerah, son of Adaiah, [42]son of Ethan, son of

---

5:26 [a] 2 Kgs 15:19　[b] 2 Kgs 15:29　[c] 2 Kgs 17:6; 18:11　6:1 [a] Gen 46:11; Exod 6:16; Num 26:57; 1 Chr 23:6　6:2 [a] 1 Chr 6:18, 22　6:3 [a] Lev 10:1–2　6:8 [a] 2 Sam 8:17　[b] 2 Sam 15:27　6:10 [a] 2 Chr 26:17–18　[b] 1 Kgs 6:1; 2 Chr 3:1　6:11 [a] Ezra 7:3　[b] 2 Chr 19:11　6:14 [a] 2 Kgs 25:18–21; Neh 11:11　6:15 [a] 2 Kgs 25:21　6:16 [a] Gen 46:11; Exod 6:16　6:20 [a] 1 Chr 6:42　6:22 [a] Num 16:1　[1] Or perhaps *descendants*.　6:25 [a] 1 Chr 6:35–36　6:26 [1] Ket. *Elkanah, his son, Elkanah*; Qe. *Elkanah, the sons of Elkanah*.　6:27 [1] Some LXX MSS add *Samuel his son*.　6:28 [1] Heb. omits *Joel*.　6:31 [a] 1 Chr 15:16–22, 27; 16:4–6　[b] 2 Sam 6:17; 1 Kgs 8:4; 1 Chr 15:25–16:1　6:33 [a] Num 26:57　6:37 [a] Exod 6:24　6:39 [a] 2 Chr 5:12　6:40 [1] A few wss *Maaseiah*.　6:41 [a] 1 Chr 6:21

Zimmah, son of Shimei, [43]son of Jahath, son of Gershom, son of Levi.

[44]Serving beside them were their fellow Levites, the descendants of Merari, led by Ethan, son of Kishi, son of Abdi, son of Malluch, [45]son of Hashabiah, son of Amaziah, son of Hilkiah, [46]son of Amzi, son of Bani, son of Shemer, [47]son of Mahli, son of Mushi, son of Merari, son of Levi.

[48]The rest of their fellow Levites were assigned to perform the remaining tasks at God's sanctuary. [49a]But [b]Aaron and his descendants offered sacrifices [c]on the altar for burnt offerings and on the altar for incense as they had been assigned to do in the Most Holy Sanctuary. They made atonement for Israel, just as God's servant Moses had ordered.

[50]These were the descendants of Aaron:

His [a]son Eleazar, his son Phinehas, his son Abishua, [51]his son Bukki, his son Uzzi, his son Zerahiah, [52]his son Meraioth, his son Amariah, his son Ahitub, [53]his son Zadok, and his son Ahimaaz.

[54a]These were the areas where Aaron's descendants lived:

The following belonged to the Kohathite clan, for they received the first allotment:

[55]They were allotted Hebron in [a]the territory of Judah, as well as its surrounding pasturelands. [56]([a]But the city's land and nearby towns were allotted to Caleb son of Jephunneh.) [57]The descendants of Aaron were also allotted as cities of refuge Hebron, Libnah and its pasturelands, Jattir, Eshtemoa and its pasturelands, [58]Hilez and its pasturelands, Debir and its pasturelands, [59]Ashan and its pasturelands,[1] and Beth Shemesh and its pasturelands.

[60]Within the territory of the tribe of Benjamin, they were allotted Geba and its pasturelands, Alemeth and its pasturelands, and Anathoth and its pasturelands. Their clans were allotted thirteen cities in all. [61]The rest of Kohath's descendants were allotted ten cities in the [a]territory of the half-tribe of Manasseh.

[62]The clans of Gershom's descendants received thirteen cities within the territory of the tribes of Issachar, Asher, Naphtali, and Manasseh (in Bashan).

[63]The clans of Merari's descendants were allotted [a]twelve cities within the territory of the tribes of Reuben, Gad, and Zebulun.

[64]So the Israelites gave to the Levites these cities and their pasturelands. [65]They allotted these previously named cities from the territory of the tribes of Judah, Simeon, and Benjamin.

[66]The clans of Kohath's descendants also received cities as their territory within the tribe of Ephraim. [67]They were allotted as cities of refuge Shechem [a]and its pasturelands (in the hill country of Ephraim), Gezer and its pasturelands, [68a]Jokmeam and its pasturelands, Beth Horon and its pasturelands, [69]Aijalon and its pasturelands, and Gath Rimmon and its pasturelands.

[70]Within the territory of the half-tribe of Manasseh, the rest of Kohath's descendants received Aner and its pasturelands and Bileam and its pasturelands.

[71]The following belonged to Gershom's descendants:

Within the territory of the half-tribe of Manasseh: Golan in Bashan and its pasturelands and Ashtaroth and its pasturelands.

[72]Within the territory of the tribe of Issachar: Kedesh and its pasturelands, Daberath and its pasturelands, [73]Ramoth and its pasturelands, and Anem and its pasturelands.

[74]Within the territory of the tribe of Asher: Mashal and its pasturelands, Abdon and its pasturelands, [75]Hukok and its pasturelands, and Rehob and its pasturelands.

[76]Within the territory of the tribe of Naphtali: Kedesh in Galilee and its pasturelands, Hammon and its pasturelands, and Kiriathaim and its pasturelands.

[77]The following belonged to the rest of Merari's descendants:

Within the territory of the tribe of Zebulun: Rimmono[1] and its pasturelands and Tabor and its pasturelands.

[78]Within the territory of the tribe of Reuben across the Jordan River east of Jericho: Bezer in the wilderness and its pasturelands, Jahzah and its pasturelands, [79]Kedemoth and its pasturelands, and Mephaath and its pasturelands.

[80]Within the territory of the tribe of Gad: Ramoth in Gilead and its pasturelands,

6:49 [a] Exod 28:1; [Num 18:1–8] [b] Lev 1:8–9 [c] Exod 30:7 **6:50** [a] 1 Chr 6:4–8; Ezra 7:5 **6:54** [a] Josh 21 **6:55** [a] Josh 14:13; 21:11–12 **6:56** [a] Josh 14:13; 15:13 **6:59** [1] LXX, Syr. add *Juttah and its pasturelands.* **6:61** [a] 1 Chr 6:66–70 **6:63** [a] Josh 21:7, 34–40 **6:67** [a] Josh 21:21 **6:68** [a] Josh 21:22 **6:77** [1] LXX adds *Jokneam and its pasturelands, Kartah and its pasturelands* before "Rimmono."

Mahanaim and its pasturelands, [81] Heshbon and its pasturelands, and Jazer and its pasturelands.

Issachar's Descendants

7 The sons of Issachar: [a] Tola, Puah, Jashub, and Shimron—four in all. [2] The sons of Tola: Uzzi, Rephaiah, Jeriel, Jahmai, Jibsam, and Samuel. They were leaders of [a] their families. In the time of David there were 22,600 warriors listed in Tola's genealogical records. [3] The son of Uzzi: Izrahiah.

The sons of Izrahiah: Michael, Obadiah, Joel, and Isshiah. All five were leaders. [4] According to the genealogical records of their families, they had 36,000 warriors available for battle, for they had numerous wives and sons. [5] Altogether the genealogical records of the clans of Issachar listed 87,000 warriors.

Benjamin's Descendants

[6] The sons of [a] Benjamin: [1] Bela, Beker, and Jediael—three in all.

[7] The sons of Bela: Ezbon, Uzzi, Uzziel, Jerimoth, and Iri. The five of them were leaders of their families. There were 22,034 warriors listed in their genealogical records.

[8] The sons of Beker: Zemirah, Joash, Eliezer, Elioenai, Omri, Jeremoth, Abijah, Anathoth, and Alemeth. All these were the sons of Beker. [9] There were 20,200 family leaders and warriors listed in their genealogical records.

[10] The son of Jediael: Bilhan.

The sons of Bilhan: Jeush, Benjamin, Ehud, Kenaanah, Zethan, Tarshish, and Ahishahar. [11] All these were the sons of Jediael. There were 17,200 family leaders and warriors who were capable of marching out to battle.

[12] The Shuppites and Huppites were descendants of Ir; the Hushites were descendants of Aher.

Naphtali's Descendants

[13] The [a] sons of Naphtali: Jahziel, Guni, Jezer, and Shallum[1]—sons of Bilhah.

Manasseh's Descendants

[14] The [a] sons of Manasseh: Asriel, who was born to Manasseh's Aramean concubine.

She also gave birth to [b] Makir the father of Gilead. [15] Now Makir married a wife from the Huppites and Shuppites.[1] (His sister's name was Maacah.)

[a] Zelophehad was Manasseh's second son; he had only daughters.

[16] Maacah, Makir's wife, gave birth to a son, whom she named Peresh. His brother was Sheresh, and his sons were Ulam and Rekem.

[17] The son of Ulam: [a] Bedan.

These were the sons of Gilead, son of Makir, son of Manasseh. [18] His sister Hammoleketh gave birth to Ishhod, Abiezer, and Mahlah.

[19] The sons of Shemida were Ahian, Shechem, Likhi, and Aniam.

Ephraim's Descendants

[20] The descendants of Ephraim: [a] Shuthelah, his son Bered, his son Tahath, his son Eleadah, his son Tahath, [21] his son Zabad, his son Shuthelah (Ezer and Elead were killed by the men of Gath, who were natives of the land, when they went down to steal their cattle. [22] Their father Ephraim mourned for them many days and his brothers came to console him. [23] He slept with his wife; she became pregnant and gave birth to a son. Ephraim named him Beriah because tragedy had come to his family. [24] His daughter was Sheerah, who built Lower and Upper Beth [a] Horon, as well as Uzzen Sheerah), [25] his son Rephah, his son Resheph,[1] his son Telah, his son Tahan, [26] his son Ladan, his son Ammihud, his son [a] Elishama, [27] his son Nun,[1] and his son [a] Joshua.

[28] Their [a] property and settlements included Bethel and its surrounding towns, Naaran to the east, Gezer and its surrounding towns to the west, and Shechem and its surrounding towns as far as Ayyah and its surrounding towns. [29] On the border of [a] Manasseh's territory were Beth Shean and its surrounding towns, Taanach and its surrounding towns, [b] Megiddo and its surrounding towns, and Dor and its surrounding towns. The descendants of Joseph, Israel's son, lived here.

Asher's Descendants

[30] The sons of Asher: Imnah, Ishvah, Ishvi, and Beriah. Serah was [a] their sister.

7:1 [a] Num 26:23–25   7:2 [a] 2 Sam 24:1–9; 1 Chr 27:1   7:6 [a] Gen 46:21; Num 26:38–41; 1 Chr 8:1   [1] Heb. omits *sons of.*
7:13 [a] Num 26:48–50   [1] Some MSS read *Shillem.*   7:14 [a] Num 26:29–34   [b] 1 Chr 2:21   7:15 [a] Num 26:30–33; 27:1   [1] Or perhaps *Huppim and Shuppim;* i.e., names of individuals.   7:17 [a] 1 Sam 12:11   7:20 [a] Num 26:35–37   7:24 [a] Josh 16:3, 5; 2 Chr 8:5   7:25 [1] Heb. omits *his son.*   7:26 [a] Num 10:22   7:27 [a] Exod 17:9, 14; 24:13; 33:11   [1] Heb. *Non.*
7:28 [a] Josh 16:1–10   7:29 [a] Gen 41:51; Josh 17:7   [b] Josh 17:11   7:30 [a] Gen 46:17; Num 26:44–47

[31]The sons of Beriah: Heber and Malkiel, who was the father of Birzaith.

[32]Heber was the father of Japhlet, Shomer, Hotham, and Shua their sister.

[33]The sons of Japhlet: Pasach, Bimhal, and Ashvath. These were Japhlet's sons.

[34]The sons of his brother[1] [a]Shemer: Rohgah, Hubbah,[2] and Aram.

[35]The sons of his brother Helem: Zophah, Imna, Shelesh, and Amal.

[36]The sons of Zophah: Suah, Harnepher, Shual, Beri, Imrah, [37]Bezer, Hod, Shamma, Shilshah, Ithran, and Beera.

[38]The sons of Jether: Jephunneh, Pispah, and Ara.

[39]The sons of Ulla: Arah, Hanniel, and Rizia.

[40]All these were the descendants of Asher. They were the leaders of their families, the most capable men, who were warriors and served as head chiefs. There were 26,000 warriors listed in their genealogical records as capable of doing battle.

Benjamin's Descendants (Continued)

8 Benjamin was the father of [a]Bela, his firstborn; Ashbel was born second, Aharah third, [2]Nohah fourth, and Rapha fifth.

[3]Bela's sons were Addar, Gera, Abihud, [4]Abishua, Naaman, Ahoah, [5]Gera, Shephuphan, and Huram.

[6]These were the descendants of Ehud who were leaders of the families living in [a]Geba who were forced to move to [b]Manahath: [7]Naaman, Ahijah, and Gera, who moved them. Gera was the father of Uzzah and Ahihud.

[8]Shaharaim fathered sons in Moab after he divorced his wives Hushim and Baara. [9]By his wife Hodesh he fathered Jobab, Zibia, Mesha, Malkam, [10]Jeuz, Sakia, and Mirmah. These were his sons; they were family leaders. [11]By Hushim he fathered Abitub and Elpaal.

[12]The sons of Elpaal: Eber, Misham, Shemed (who built Ono and Lod, as well as its surrounding towns), [13]Beriah, and [a]Shema. They were leaders of the families living in Aijalon and chased out the inhabitants of Gath.

[14]Ahio, Shashak, Jeremoth, [15]Zebadiah, Arad, Eder, [16]Michael, Ishpah, and Joha were the sons of Beriah.

[17]Zebadiah, Meshullam, Hizki, Heber, [18]Ishmerai, Izliah, and Jobab were the sons of Elpaal.

[19]Jakim, Zikri, Zabdi, [20]Elienai, Zillethai, Eliel, [21]Adaiah, Beraiah, and Shimrath were the sons of Shimei.

[22]Ishpan, Eber, Eliel, [23]Abdon, Zikri, Hanan, [24]Hananiah, Elam, Anthothijah, [25]Iphdeiah, and Penuel were the sons of Shashak.

[26]Shamsherai, Shechariah, Athaliah, [27]Jaareshiah, Elijah, and Zikri were the sons of Jeroham. [28]These were the family leaders listed in the genealogical records; they lived in Jerusalem.

[29]The father of Gibeon[1] lived in Gibeon; his [a]wife's name was Maacah. [30]His firstborn son was Abdon, followed by Zur, Kish, Baal,[1] Nadab, [31]Gedor, Ahio, Zeker, and Mikloth.[1]

[32]Mikloth was the father of Shimeah. They also lived near their relatives in Jerusalem.

[33][a]Ner was the father of Kish, and Kish was the father of Saul. Saul was the father of Jonathan, Malki-Shua, Abinadab, and Eshbaal.

[34]The son of Jonathan: Meribbaal. Meribbaal was the father of [a]Micah.

[35]The sons of Micah: Pithon, Melech, Tarea, and Ahaz.

[36]Ahaz was the father of Jehoaddah, and Jehoaddah was the father of Alemeth, Azmaveth, and Zimri. Zimri was the father of Moza, [37]and Moza was the father of Binea. His son was Raphah, whose son was Eleasah, whose son was Azel.

[38]Azel had six sons: Azrikam his firstborn,[1] followed by Ishmael, Sheariah,[2] Obadiah, and Hanan. All these were the sons of Azel.

[39]The sons of his brother Eshek: Ulam was his firstborn, Jeush second, and Eliphelet third. [40]The sons of Ulam were warriors who were adept archers. They had many sons and grandsons, a total of 150.

All these were the descendants of Benjamin.

9 Genealogical records were kept for [a]all Israel; they are recorded in the Scroll of the Kings of Israel.

Exiles Who Resettled in Jerusalem

The people of Judah were carried away to Babylon because of their unfaithfulness.

7:34 [a]1 Chr 7:32   [1]Heb. *the brother of.*   [2]Ket. *Jachbah.*   **8:1** [a]Gen 46:21; Num 26:38; 1 Chr 7:6   **8:6** [a]1 Chr 6:60   [b]1 Chr 2:52   **8:13** [a]1 Chr 8:21   **8:29** [a]1 Chr 9:35–38   [1]Some LXX MSS add *Jeiel.*   **8:30** [1]Some LXX MSS add *Ner.*   **8:31** [1]Heb. omits *Mikloth.*   **8:33** [a]1 Sam 14:51   **8:34** [a]2 Sam 9:12   **8:38** [1]Heb. *Bocheru.*   [2]Luc. adds *and Azariah.*   **9:1** [a]Ezra 2:59

[2]The first to resettle on their property[a]and in[b]their cities were some Israelites, priests, Levites, and temple servants. [3]Some from the tribes of Judah, Benjamin, and Ephraim and Manasseh settled in[a]Jerusalem.

[4]The settlers included: Uthai son of Ammihud, son of Omri, son of Imri, son of Bani, who was a descendant of Perez son of Judah. [5]From the Shilonites: Asaiah the firstborn and his sons. [6]From the descendants of Zerah: Jeuel. Their relatives numbered 690.

[7]From the descendants of Benjamin:

Sallu son of Meshullam, son of Hodaviah, son of Hassenuah; [8]Ibneiah son of Jeroham; Elah son of Uzzi, son of Mikri; and Meshullam son of Shephatiah, son of Reuel, son of Ibnijah. [9]Their relatives, listed in their genealogical records, numbered 956. All these men were leaders of their families.

[10a]From the priests:

Jedaiah; Jehoiarib; Jakin; [11]Azariah son of Hilkiah, son of Meshullam, son of Zadok, son of Meraioth, son of Ahitub the[a]leader in God's temple; [12]Adaiah son of Jeroham, son of Pashhur, son of Malkijah; and Maasai son of Adiel, son of Jahzerah, son of Meshullam, son of Meshillemith, son of Immer.

[13]Their relatives, who were leaders of their families, numbered 1,760. They were capable men who were assigned to carry out the various tasks of service in God's temple.

[14]From the Levites:

Shemaiah son of Hasshub, son of Azrikam, son of Hashabiah a descendant of Merari; [15]Bakbakkar; Heresh; Galal; Mattaniah son of Mika, son of[a]Zikri, son of Asaph; [16a]Obadiah son of[b]Shemaiah, son of Galal, son of Jeduthun; and Berechiah son of Asa, son of Elkanah, who lived among the settlements of the Netophathites.

[17]The gatekeepers were:

Shallum, Akkub, Talmon, Ahiman, and their brothers. Shallum was the leader; [18]he serves to this day at the King's Gate on the east. These were the gatekeepers from the camp of the descendants of Levi.

[19]Shallum son of Kore, son of Ebiasaph, son of Korah, and his relatives from his family (the Korahites) were assigned to guard the entrance to the sanctuary. Their ancestors had guarded the entrance to the LORD's dwelling place. [20a]Phinehas son of Eleazar had been their leader in earlier times, and the LORD was with him. [21a]Zechariah son of Meshelemiah was the guard at the entrance to the meeting tent.

[22]All those selected to be gatekeepers at[a]the entrances numbered 212.[b]Their names were recorded in the genealogical records of their settlements. David and Samuel the prophet[1] had appointed them to their positions. [23]They and their descendants were assigned to guard the gates of the LORD's sanctuary (that is, the tabernacle). [24]The gatekeepers were posted on all four sides—east, west, north, and south. [25]Their relatives, who lived in their settlements, came from time to time and served with them[a]for seven-day periods. [26]The four head gatekeepers, who were Levites, were assigned to guard the storerooms and treasuries in God's sanctuary. [27]They would spend the night in their posts all around God's sanctuary, for they were assigned to[a]guard it and would open it with the key every morning. [28]Some of them were in charge of the articles used by those who served; they counted them when they brought them in and when they brought them out. [29]Some of them were[a]in charge of the equipment and articles of the sanctuary, as well as the flour, wine, olive oil, incense, and spices. [30](But some of[a]the priests mixed the spices.) [31]Mattithiah, a Levite, the firstborn son of Shallum the Korahite, was in charge of baking the bread for offerings. [32]Some of the Kohathites, their relatives,[a]were in charge of preparing the bread that is displayed each Sabbath.

[33]The musicians and Levite family leaders stayed in rooms at[a]the sanctuary and were exempt from other duties, for day and night they had to carry out their assigned tasks. [34]These were the family leaders of the Levites, as listed in their genealogical records. They lived in Jerusalem.

Jeiel's Descendants

[35]Jeiel (the father of Gibeon) lived in Gibeon. His wife was[a]Maacah. [36]His firstborn son was Abdon, followed by Zur, Kish,

9:2[a]Ezra 2:70; Neh 7:73 [b]Ezra 2:43; 8:20 9:3[a]Neh 11:1–2 9:10[a]Neh 11:10–14 9:11[a]2 Chr 31:13; Jer 20:1 9:15[a]Neh 11:17 9:16[a]Neh 11:17 [b]Neh 11:17 9:20[a]Num 25:6–13; 31:6 9:21[a]1 Chr 26:2, 14 9:22[a]1 Chr 26:1–2 [b]1 Sam 9:9 [1]Heb. seer. 9:25[a]2 Kgs 11:4–7; 2 Chr 23:8 9:27[a]1 Chr 23:30–32 9:29[a]1 Chr 23:29 9:30[a]Exod 30:22–25 9:32[a]Lev 24:5–8 9:33[a]1 Chr 6:31; 25:1 9:35[a]1 Chr 8:29–32

Baal, Ner, Nadab, [37]Gedor, Ahio, Zechariah, and Mikloth. [38]Mikloth was the father of Shimeam. They also lived near their relatives in Jerusalem.

[39a]Ner was the father of Kish, and Kish was the father of Saul. Saul was the father of Jonathan, Malki-Shua, Abinadab, and Eshbaal.

[40]The son of Jonathan:

Meribbaal, who was the father of Micah.

[41]The sons of Micah:

Pithon, Melech, Tahrea, [a]and Ahaz.[1]

[42]Ahaz was the father of Jarah,[1] and Jarah was the father of Alemeth, Azmaveth, and Zimri. Zimri was the father of Moza, [43]and Moza was the father of Binea. His son was Rephaiah, whose son was Eleasah, whose son was Azel.

[44]Azel had six sons: Azrikam his first-born,[1] followed by Ishmael, Sheariah, Obadiah, and Hanan. These were the sons of Azel.

Saul's Death

10 Now [a]the Philistines fought against Israel. The Israelites fled before the Philistines and many of them fell dead on Mount Gilboa. [2]The Philistines stayed right on the heels of Saul and his sons. They struck down Saul's sons Jonathan, Abinadab, and Malki-Shua. [3]The battle was thick around Saul; the archers spotted him and wounded him. [4]Saul told his armor-bearer, "Draw your sword and stab me with it. Otherwise these uncircumcised people will come and torture me." But his armor-bearer refused to do it because he was very afraid. So Saul took the sword and fell on it. [5]When his armor-bearer saw that Saul was dead, he also fell on his sword and died. [6]So Saul and his three sons died; his whole household died together. [7]When all the Israelites who were in the valley saw that the army had fled and that Saul and his sons were dead, they abandoned their cities and fled. The Philistines came and occupied them.

[8]The next day, when the Philistines came to strip loot from the corpses, they discovered Saul and his sons lying dead on Mount Gilboa. [9]They stripped his corpse and then carried off his head and his armor.

They sent messengers throughout the land of the Philistines proclaiming the news to their idols and their people. [10]They placed his armor in [a]the temple of their gods[1] and hung his head in the temple of Dagon. [11]When all the residents of Jabesh Gilead heard about everything the Philistines had done to Saul, [12]all the [a]warriors went and recovered the bodies of Saul and his sons and brought them to [b]Jabesh. They buried their remains under the oak tree in Jabesh and fasted for seven days.

[13]So Saul died [a]because [b]he was unfaithful to the LORD and did not obey the LORD's instructions; he even tried to conjure up underworld spirits. [14]He did not seek the LORD's guidance, so the LORD killed him and [a]transferred the kingdom to David son of Jesse.

David Becomes King

11 All Israel joined David at Hebron and said, "Look, we are your very flesh and blood! [2]In the past, even when Saul was king, you were Israel's commanding general. The LORD your [a]God said to you, 'You will [b]shepherd my people Israel; you will rule over my people Israel.'" [3]When all [a]the leaders of Israel came to the king at Hebron, David made a covenant with them in Hebron before the LORD. They anointed David king over Israel, in keeping with the LORD's message that came through [b]Samuel.

David Conquers Jerusalem

[4]David and the whole Israelite army [a]advanced to Jerusalem (that is, Jebus). (The Jebusites, the land's original inhabitants, lived there.) [5]The residents of Jebus said to David, "You cannot invade this place!" But David captured the fortress of Zion (that is, the City of David). [6]David said, "Whoever attacks the Jebusites first will become commanding general!" So Joab son of Zeruiah attacked first and became commander. [7]David lived in the fortress; for this reason it is called the City of David. [8]He built up the city around it, from the terrace to the surrounding walls; Joab restored the rest of the city. [9]David's power [a]steadily grew, for the LORD of Heaven's Armies was with [b]him.

9:39 [a]1 Chr 8:33–38   **9:41** [a]1 Chr 8:35   [1]MT omits *Ahaz.*   **9:42** [1]Some wss *Jadah.*   **9:44** [1]Heb. *Bocheru.*   **10:1** [a]1 Sam 31:1–2   **10:10** [a]1 Sam 31:10   [1]Or *god.*   **10:12** [a]1 Sam 14:52   [b]2 Sam 21:12   **10:13** [a]1 Sam 13:13–14; 15:22–26   [b][Lev 19:31; 20:6]; 1 Sam 28:7   **10:14** [a]1 Sam 15:28; 2 Sam 3:9–10; 5:3; 1 Chr 12:23   **11:2** [a]1 Sam 16:1–3; Ps 78:70–72   [b]2 Sam 7:7   **11:3** [a]2 Sam 5:3   [b]1 Sam 16:1, 4, 12, 13   **11:4** [a]2 Sam 5:6   **11:9** [a]2 Sam 3:1   [b]1 Sam 16:18

David's Warriors

[10] These were [a] the leaders of David's warriors who, [b] together with all Israel, stood courageously with him in his kingdom by installing him as king, in keeping with the LORD's message concerning Israel. [11] This is the list of David's warriors:

[a] Jashobeam, a Hacmonite, was [b] head of the officers.[1] He killed 300 men with his spear in a single battle.

[12] Next in command was Eleazar son of [a] Dodo the Ahohite. He was one of the three elite warriors. [13] He was with David in Pas Dammim when the Philistines assembled there for battle. In an area of the field that was full of barley, the army retreated before the Philistines, [14] but then they made a stand in the middle of that area. They defended it and defeated the Philistines; the LORD gave them a great victory.

[15] Three of the thirty leaders [a] went down to David at the rocky cliff at the cave of Adullam, while a [b] Philistine force was camped in the Valley of Rephaim. [16] David was in the stronghold at the time, while a Philistine garrison was in Bethlehem. [17] David was thirsty and said, "How I wish someone would give me some water to drink from the cistern in Bethlehem near the city gate!" [18] So the three elite warriors broke through the Philistine forces and drew some water from the cistern in Bethlehem near the city gate. They carried it back to David, but David refused to drink it. He poured it out as a drink offering to the LORD [19] and said, "God forbid that I should do this! Should I drink the blood of these men who risked their lives?" Because they risked their lives to bring it to him, he refused to drink it. Such were the exploits of the three elite warriors.

[20] [a] Abishai the brother of Joab was head of the three[1] elite warriors. He killed 300 men with his spear and gained fame along with the three elite warriors. [21] From the three he was given double honor and he became their [a] officer, even though he was not one of them.

[22] Benaiah son of Jehoiada was a brave warrior from Kabzeel who performed great exploits. [a] He struck down the two sons of Ariel of Moab;[1] he also went down and killed a lion inside a cistern on a snowy day. [23] He even killed an Egyptian who was 7½ feet[1] tall. The Egyptian had a spear in his hand as big as the crossbeam of a weaver's loom; Benaiah attacked him with a club. He grabbed the spear out of the Egyptian's hand and killed him with his own spear. [24] Such were the exploits of Benaiah son of Jehoiada, who gained fame along with the three elite warriors. [25] He received honor from the thirty warriors, though he was not one of the three elite warriors. David put him in charge of his bodyguard.

[26] The mighty warriors were:

[a] Asahel the brother of Joab,
Elhanan son of Dodo, from Bethlehem,
[27] Shammoth the Harorite,
[a] Helez the Pelonite,
[28] [a] Ira son of Ikkesh the Tekoite,
[b] Abiezer the Anathothite,
[29] Sibbekai the Hushathite,
Ilai the Ahohite,
[30] [a] Maharai the Netophathite,
Heled son of Baanah the Netophathite,
[31] Ithai son of Ribai from Gibeah in Benjaminite territory,
[a] Benaiah the Pirathonite,
[32] Hurai from the valleys of Gaash,
Abiel the Arbathite,
[33] Azmaveth the Baharumite,
Eliahba the Shaalbonite,
[34] the sons of Hashem the Gizonite,
Jonathan son of Shageh the Hararite,
[35] Ahiam son of Sakar the Hararite,
Eliphal son of Ur,
[36] Hepher the Mekerathite,
Ahijah the Pelonite,
[37] Hezro the Carmelite,
Naarai son of Ezbai,
[38] Joel the brother of Nathan,
Mibhar son of Hagri,
[39] Zelek the Ammonite,
Naharai the Beerothite, the armor-bearer of Joab son of Zeruiah,
[40] Ira the Ithrite,
Gareb the Ithrite,
[41] [a] Uriah the Hittite,
Zabad son of Achli,
[42] Adina son of Shiza the Reubenite, leader of the Reubenites and the thirty warriors with him,

11:10 [a] 2 Sam 23:8   [b] 1 Sam 16:1, 12   11:11 [a] 1 Chr 27:2   [b] 1 Chr 12:18   [1] Ket. *the Thirty*.   11:12 [a] 1 Chr 27:4   11:15 [a] 2 Sam 23:13   [b] 2 Sam 5:18; 1 Chr 14:9   11:20 [a] 2 Sam 23:18; 1 Chr 18:12   [1] Syr. *thirty*.   11:21 [a] 2 Sam 23:19   11:22 [a] 2 Sam 23:20   [1] Heb. *the two of Ariel, Moab*.   11:23 [1] Heb. *5 cubits*.   11:26 [a] 2 Sam 23:24   11:27 [a] 2 Sam 23:26; 1 Chr 27:10   11:28 [a] 1 Chr 27:9   [b] 1 Chr 27:12   11:30 [a] 1 Chr 27:13   11:31 [a] 1 Chr 27:14   11:41 [a] 2 Sam 11

43Hanan son of Maacah,
Joshaphat the Mithnite,
44Uzzia the Ashterathite,
Shama and Jeiel, the sons of Hotham the Aroerite,
45Jediael son of Shimri,
and Joha his brother, the Tizite,
46Eliel the Mahavite,
and Jeribai and Joshaviah, the sons of Elnaam,
and Ithmah the Moabite,
47Eliel,
and Obed,
and Jaasiel the Mezobaite.

Warriors Who Joined David at Ziklag

12 aThese were the men who joined David in bZiklag, when he was banished from the presence of Saul son of Kish. (They were among the warriors who assisted him in battle. 2They were armed with bows and could shoot arrows or sling stones right- or left-handed. aThey were fellow tribesmen of Saul from Benjamin.) These were:

3Ahiezer, the leader, and Joash, the sons of Shemaah the Gibeathite; Jeziel and Pelet, the sons of Azmaveth; Berachah, Jehu the Anathothite,

4Ishmaiah the Gibeonite, one of the thirty warriors and their leader, Jeremiah, Jahaziel, Johanan, Jozabad the Gederathite,

5Eluzai, Jerimoth, Bealiah, Shemariah, Shephatiah the Haruphite,

6Elkanah, Isshiah, Azarel, Joezer, and Jashobeam, who were Korahites,

7and Joelah and Zebadiah, the sons of Jeroham from Gedor.

8Some of the Gadites joined David at the stronghold in the wilderness. They were warriors who were trained for battle; they carried shields and spears. They were aas fierce as lions and could run as quickly as gazelles across the hills. 9Ezer was the leader, Obadiah the second-in-command, Eliab the third, 10Mishmannah the fourth, Jeremiah the fifth, 11Attai the sixth, Eliel the seventh, 12Johanan the eighth, Elzabad the ninth, 13Jeremiah the tenth, and Machbannai the eleventh. 14These Gadites were military leaders; the least led a hundred men, the greatest a athousand.1 15They crossed the Jordan River in the first month, when it was overflowing its abanks, and routed those living in all the valleys to the east and west.

16Some from Benjamin and Judah also came to David's stronghold. 17David went out to meet them and said, "If you come to me in peace and want to help me, then I will make an alliance with you. But if you come to betray me to my enemies when I have not harmed you, may the God of our ancestors take notice and judge!" 18But a spirit empowered aAmasai, the leader of the group of warriors known as the Thirty, and he said:

"We are yours, O David!
We support you, O son of Jesse!
May you greatly prosper.1
May those who help you prosper.
Indeed your God helps you!"

So David accepted them and made them leaders of raiding bands.

19Some men from Manasseh joined David awhen bhe went with the Philistines to fight against Saul. (But in the end they did not help the Philistines because, after taking counsel, the Philistine lords sent David away, saying, "It would be disastrous for us if he deserts to his master Saul.") 20When David went to Ziklag, the men of Manasseh who joined him were Adnach, Jozabad, Jediael, Michael, Jozabad, Elihu, and Zillethai, leaders of 1,000 soldiers each in the tribe of Manasseh. 21They helped David fight against raiding bands, for all of athem were warriors and leaders in the army. 22Each day men came to help David until his army became very large.1

Support for David in Hebron

23The following is a record of the armed warriors who acame with their leaders and joined David in bHebron in order to cmake David king din Saul's place, in accordance with the LORD's decree:

24From Judah came 6,800 trained warriors carrying shields and spears.

25From Simeon there were 7,100 warriors.

26From Levi there were 4,600. 27Jehoiada, the leader of Aaron's descendants, brought 3,700 men with him, 28along with aZadok, a young warrior, and 22 leaders from his family.

12:1 a1 Sam 27:2   b1 Sam 27:6   12:2 aJudg 3:15; 20:16   12:8 a2 Sam 2:18   12:14 a1 Sam 18:13   1Heb. *one for a hundred the small, and the great for a thousand.*   12:15 aJosh 3:15; 4:18-19   12:18 a2 Sam 17:25   1Heb. *Peace, peace to you*; an emphatic Heb. construction.   12:19 a1 Sam 29:2   b1 Sam 29:4   12:21 a1 Sam 30:1, 9, 10   12:22 1Heb. *for at the time of day in a day they were coming to David to help him until* [there was] *a great camp like the camp of God.*   12:23 a2 Sam 2:1-4   b1 Chr 11:1   c1 Chr 10:14   d1 Sam 16:1-4   12:28 a2 Sam 8:17; 1 Chr 6:8, 53

[29] From Benjamin, Saul's tribe, [a]there were 3,000, most of whom, up to that time, had been loyal to Saul.

[30] From Ephraim there were 20,800 warriors, who had brought fame to their families.

[31] From the half-tribe of Manasseh there were 18,000 who had been designated by name to come and make David king.

[32] From Issachar there were 200 leaders and all their relatives at their command—they understood the times and knew what Israel should do.

[33] From Zebulun there were 50,000 warriors who were prepared for battle, equipped with all kinds of weapons, and ready to give their [a]undivided loyalty.

[34] From Naphtali there were 1,000 officers, along with 37,000 men carrying shields and spears.

[35] From Dan there were 28,600 men prepared for battle.

[36] From Asher there were 40,000 warriors prepared for battle.

[37] From the other side of the Jordan, from Reuben, Gad, and the half-tribe of Manasseh, there were 120,000 men armed with all kinds of weapons.

[38] All these men were warriors who were ready to march.[1] They came to Hebron to make David king over all Israel by acclamation; all the rest of the Israelites also were in [a]agreement that David should become king. [39] They spent three days feasting there with David, for their relatives had given them provisions. [40] Also their neighbors, from as far away as Issachar, Zebulun, and Naphtali, were bringing food on donkeys, camels, mules, and oxen. There were large supplies of flour, fig cakes, raisins, wine, olive oil, beef, and lamb, for Israel was celebrating.

Uzzah Meets Disaster

13 David consulted with his military [a]officers, including those who led groups of a thousand and those who led groups of a hundred. [2] David said to the whole Israelite assembly, "If you so desire and the LORD our God approves, let's spread the word to our brothers who [a]remain in all the regions of Israel, and to the priests and Levites in their cities, so they may join us. [3] Let's move the ark of our God back here, [a]for we did not seek his will throughout Saul's reign." [4] The whole assembly agreed to do this, for the proposal seemed right to all the people. [5] So [a]David assembled all Israel from the [b]Shihor River in Egypt to Lebo Hamath, to bring the ark of God [c]from Kiriath Jearim. [6] David and all Israel went up to [a]Baalah (that is, Kiriath Jearim) in Judah to bring up from there the ark of God the LORD, [b]who sits enthroned between the cherubim—the ark that is called by his Name.

[7] They transported the ark of God [a]on a new cart [b]from the house of Abinadab; Uzzah and Ahio were guiding the cart, [8] while [a]David and all Israel were energetically celebrating before God, singing and playing various stringed instruments,[1] tambourines, cymbals, and trumpets. [9] When they arrived at the threshing floor of Kidon, Uzzah reached out his hand to take hold of the ark because the oxen stumbled. [10] The LORD was so furious with Uzzah, he killed him, [a]because he reached out his hand and touched the ark. He [b]died right there before God.

[11] David was angry because the LORD attacked Uzzah; so he called that place Perez Uzzah, which remains its name to this very day. [12] David was afraid of God that day and said, "How will I ever be able to bring the ark of God up here?" [13] So David did not move the ark to the City of David; he left it in the house of Obed-Edom the Gittite. [14] The ark of God remained in Obed-Edom's house for three months; [a]the LORD blessed Obed-Edom's family and everything that belonged to him.

David's Prestige Grows

14 King [a]Hiram of Tyre sent messengers to David, along with cedar logs, stonemasons,[1] and carpenters to build a palace for him. [2] David realized that the LORD had established him as king over Israel and that he had [a]elevated his kingdom for the sake of his people Israel.

[3] In Jerusalem David married more wives and fathered more sons and daughters. [4] These are [a]the names of children born to him in Jerusalem: Shammua, Shobab,

12:29 [a] 2 Sam 2:8–9   **12:33** [a] Ps 12:2; [Jas 1:8]   **12:38** [a] 2 Chr 30:12   [1] Heb. *all these* [were] *men of war, helpers of the battle line.*   **13:1** [a] 1 Chr 11:15; 12:34   **13:2** [a] 1 Sam 31:1; Isa 37:4   **13:3** [a] 1 Sam 7:1–2   **13:5** [a] 1 Sam 7:5   [b] Josh 13:3   [c] 1 Sam 6:21; 7:1–2   **13:6** [a] Josh 15:9, 60   [b] Exod 25:22; 1 Sam 4:4; 2 Kgs 19:15   **13:7** [a] Num 4:15; 1 Sam 6:7   [b] 1 Sam 7:1   **13:8** [a] 2 Sam 6:5   [1] Heb. *with songs and with zithers* [meaning uncertain] *and with harps.*   **13:10** [a] [Num 4:15]; 1 Chr 15:13, 15   [b] Lev 10:2   **13:14** [a] 2 Sam 6:11   **14:1** [a] 2 Sam 5:11; 1 Kgs 5:1   [1] Heb. *craftsman of a wall.*   **14:2** [a] Num 24:7   **14:4** [a] 1 Chr 3:5–8

Nathan, Solomon, [5]Ibhar, Elishua, Elpelet, [6]Nogah, Nepheg, Japhia, [7]Elishama, Beeliada, and Eliphelet.

[8]When the Philistines heard that [a]David had been anointed[1] king of all Israel, all the Philistines marched up to confront him. When David heard about it, he marched out against them. [9]Now the Philistines had come and raided the Valley of Rephaim. [10]David [a]asked God, "Should I march up against the Philistines? Will you hand them over to me?" The LORD said to him, "March up! I will hand them over to you!" [11]So they marched against Baal Perazim and David defeated them there. David said, "Using me as his instrument, God has burst out against my enemies like water bursts out." So that place is called Baal Perazim. [12]The Philistines left their idols[1] there, so David ordered that they be burned.

[13]The Philistines again raided [a]the valley. [14]So David again asked God what he should do. This time God told him, "Don't march up after them; circle around them [a]and come against them in front of the trees. [15]When you hear the sound of marching in the tops of the trees, then attack. For at that moment God is going before you to strike down the army of the Philistines." [16]David did just as God commanded him, and they struck down the Philistine army from Gibeon to Gezer.

[17]So David became famous in all [a]the lands; the LORD [b]caused all the nations to fear him.

David Brings the Ark to Jerusalem

15 David constructed buildings in the City of David; he then prepared [a]a place for the ark of God and pitched a tent for it. [2]Then David said, "Only the Levites may carry the [a]ark of God, for [b]the LORD chose them to carry the ark of the LORD and to serve before him perpetually." [3]David assembled all Israel [a]at Jerusalem to bring the ark of the LORD up to the place he had prepared for it. [4]David gathered together the descendants of Aaron and the Levites:

[5]From the descendants of Kohath: Uriel the leader and 120 of his relatives.

[6]From the descendants of Merari: Asaiah the leader and 220 of his relatives.

[7]From the descendants of Gershom: Joel the leader and 130 of his relatives.

[8]From the descendants of [a]Elizaphan: Shemaiah the leader and 200 of his relatives.

[9]From the descendants of [a]Hebron: Eliel the leader and 80 of his relatives.

[10]From the descendants of Uzziel: Amminadab the leader and 112 of his relatives.

[11]David summoned the priests [a]Zadok and [b]Abiathar, along with the Levites Uriel, Asaiah, Joel, Shemaiah, Eliel, and Amminadab. [12]He told them: "You are the leaders of the Levites' families. You and your relatives must consecrate yourselves and bring the ark of the LORD God of Israel up to the place I have prepared for it. [13]The first time you did not carry it; that is why the LORD God attacked us, [a]because we did not ask him about [b]the proper way to carry it." [14]The priests and Levites consecrated themselves so they could bring up the ark of the LORD God of Israel. [15]The descendants of Levi carried the ark of God on their shoulders with poles, just as [a]Moses had commanded in keeping with the LORD's instruction.

[16]David told the leaders of the Levites to appoint some of their relatives as musicians; they were to play various instruments, including stringed instruments and cymbals, and to sing loudly and joyfully. [17]So the Levites appointed [a]Heman son of Joel; one of his relatives, [b]Asaph son of Berechiah; one of the descendants of Merari, [c]Ethan son of Kushaiah; [18]along with some of their relatives who were second in rank, including Zechariah,[1] Jaaziel, Shemiramoth, Jehiel, Unni, Eliab, Benaiah, Maaseiah, Mattithiah, Eliphelehu, Mikneiah, Obed-Edom, and Jeiel, the gatekeepers.

[19]The musicians Heman, Asaph, and Ethan were to sound the bronze cymbals; [20]Zechariah, Aziel, Shemiramoth, Jehiel, Unni, Eliab, Maaseiah, and Benaiah were to play the harps according to the [a]*alamoth* style; [21]Mattithiah, Eliphelehu, Mikneiah, Obed-Edom, Jeiel, and Azaziah were to play the lyres according to the [a]*sheminith* style, as led by the director; [22]Kenaniah, the leader

of the Levites, was in charge of transport,[1,2] for he was well-informed on this matter; [23] Berechiah and Elkanah were guardians of the ark; [24] Shebaniah, Joshaphat, Nethanel, Amasai, Zechariah, Benaiah, and Eliezer the priests [a] were to blow the trumpets before the ark of God; [b] Obed-Edom and Jehiel were also guardians of the ark.

[25] So [a] David, the leaders of Israel, and the commanders of units of a thousand went to bring up the ark of the LORD's covenant from the house of Obed-Edom with celebration. [26] When God helped the Levites who were carrying the ark of the LORD's covenant, they sacrificed seven bulls and seven rams. [27] David was wrapped in a [a] linen robe, as were all the Levites carrying the ark, the musicians, and Kenaniah the supervisor of transport and the musicians;[1] David also wore a linen ephod. [28a] All Israel brought up the ark of the LORD's covenant; they were shouting, blowing trumpets, sounding cymbals, and playing stringed instruments. [29] As the ark of the LORD's covenant entered the City of David, Michal, Saul's daughter, looked out the window. When she saw King David jumping and celebrating, she despised him.

David Leads in Worship

16 They brought [a] the ark of God and put it in the middle of the tent David had pitched for it. Then they offered burnt sacrifices and peace offerings before God. [2] When David [a] finished offering burnt sacrifices and peace offerings, he pronounced a blessing over the people in the LORD's name. [3] He then handed out to each Israelite man and woman a loaf of bread, a date cake, and a raisin cake. [4] He appointed some of the Levites to serve before the ark of the LORD, to offer [a] prayers, songs of thanks, and hymns to the LORD God of Israel. [5] Asaph was the leader and Zechariah second-in-command, followed by [a] Jeiel, Shemiramoth, Jehiel, Mattithiah, Eliab, Benaiah, Obed-Edom, and Jeiel. They were to play stringed instruments, Asaph was to sound the cymbals, [6] and the priests Benaiah and Jahaziel were to blow trumpets regularly before the ark of God's covenant.

David Thanks God

[7] That day [a] David [b] first gave to Asaph and his colleagues this song of thanks to the LORD.

[8] [a] Give thanks to the LORD!
   Call on his name!
   Make known his accomplishments
     among the nations.
[9] Sing to him! Make music to him!
   Tell about all his miraculous deeds.
[10] Boast about his holy name.
   Let the hearts of those who seek the
     LORD rejoice.
[11] Seek the LORD and the strength he
     gives.
   Seek his presence continually!
[12] Recall the miraculous deeds he
     performed,
   his mighty acts and the judgments
     he decreed,
[13] O children of Israel, God's servant,
   you descendants of Jacob, God's
     chosen ones!
[14] He is the LORD our God;
   he carries out [a] judgment throughout
     the earth.
[15] Remember continually his
     covenantal decree,
   the promise he made to a thousand
     generations—
[16] the promise he made to Abraham,
   the promise he made by oath to
     Isaac!
[17] He [a] gave it to [b] Jacob as a decree,
   to Israel as a lasting promise,
[18] saying, "To you I will give the land of
     Canaan
   as the portion of your inheritance."
[19] When they were [a] few in number,
   just a very few, and foreign residents
     within it,
[20] they wandered from nation to
     nation,
   and from one kingdom to another.
[21] He let no one oppress them;
   he [a] disciplined kings for their sake,
[22] saying, "[a] Don't touch my anointed
     ones!
   Don't harm my prophets!"

15:22 [1] MT *in* [the] *lifting up, an instructor in lifting up;* LXX *ruler/leader of the songs.* [2] Or *in charge of the singing.* **15:24** [a] [Num 10:8]; Ps 81:3 [b] 1 Chr 13:13–14 **15:25** [a] 2 Sam 6:12–13; 1 Kgs 8:1 **15:27** [a] 1 Sam 2:18, 28 [1] Heb. *the leader, the lifting up, the musicians.* **15:28** [a] Num 23:21; Josh 6:20; 1 Chr 13:8; Zech 4:7; 1 Thess 4:16 **16:1** [a] 2 Sam 6:17; 1 Chr 15:1 **16:2** [a] 1 Kgs 8:14 **16:4** [a] Ps 38:title; 70:title **16:5** [a] 1 Chr 15:18 **16:7** [a] 2 Sam 22:1; 23:1 [b] Ps 105:1–15 **16:8** [a] 1 Chr 17:19–20; Ps 105:1–15 **16:14** [a] Ps 48:10; [Isa 26:9] **16:17** [a] Gen 35:11–12 [b] Gen 28:10–15 **16:19** [a] Gen 34:30; Deut 7:7 **16:21** [a] Gen 12:17; 20:3; Exod 7:15–18 **16:22** [a] Gen 20:7; Ps 105:15

23 [a]Sing to the LORD, all the earth!
Announce every day how he delivers.
24 Tell the nations about his splendor,
tell all the nations about his
miraculous deeds.
25 For the LORD is great and certainly
worthy of praise,
he is more awesome than all gods.
26 For all the gods [a]of the nations are
worthless,[1]
but the LORD made the heavens.
27 Majestic splendor emanates from
him,
he is the source of strength and joy.
28 Ascribe to the LORD, O families of
the nations,
ascribe to the LORD splendor and
strength!
29 Ascribe to the LORD the splendor he
deserves!
Bring an offering and enter his
presence!
Worship the LORD in holy attire![1]
30 Tremble before him, all the earth!
The world is established, it cannot be
moved.
31 Let the heavens rejoice, and the
earth be happy!
Let the nations say, "The LORD
reigns!"
32 Let the sea and everything in it shout!
Let the fields and everything in them
celebrate!
33 Then let the [a]trees of the forest
shout with joy before the LORD,
for he [b]comes to judge the earth!
34 [a]Give thanks to the LORD, for he is
good
and his loyal love endures.
35 Say this prayer: "Deliver us, O God
who delivers us!
Gather us! Rescue us from the
nations!
Then we will give thanks to your holy
name,
[a]and boast about your praiseworthy
deeds."
36 May the LORD God of Israel be
[a]praised,

in [b]the future and forevermore.
Then all the people said, "We agree![1]
Praise the LORD."

David Appoints Worship Leaders

37 David left [a]Asaph and his colleagues there before the ark of the LORD's covenant to serve before the ark regularly and fulfill each day's requirements, 38 including [a]Obed-Edom and sixty-eight colleagues. Obed-Edom son of Jeduthun and Hosah were gatekeepers. 39 Zadok the priest and his fellow priests served [a]before the LORD's tabernacle [b]at the worship center[1] in Gibeon, 40 regularly offering burnt sacrifices to the LORD on the altar for burnt sacrifice, [a]morning and evening, according to what is prescribed in the law of the LORD which he charged Israel to observe. 41 Joining them were Heman, Jeduthun, and the rest of those chosen and designated by name to give thanks to the LORD. (For his loyal love endures!)[1] 42 Heman and Jeduthun were in charge of the music, including the trumpets, cymbals, and the other musical instruments used in praising God. The sons of Jeduthun guarded the entrance. 43 Then all [a]the people returned to their homes, and David went to pronounce a blessing on his family.[1]

God Makes a Promise to David

17 When David had settled into his palace, he said to Nathan the prophet, "Look, [a]I am living in a palace made from cedar, while the ark of the LORD's covenant is under a tent." 2 Nathan said to David, "You should do whatever you have in mind, for God is with you."

3 That night God told Nathan, 4 "Go, tell my servant David: 'This is what the LORD says: "You must [a]not build me a house in which to live. 5 For I have not lived in a house from the time I brought Israel up from Egypt to the present day. I have lived in a tent that has been in various places.[1] 6 Wherever I moved throughout Israel, I did not say[1] to any of the leaders whom I appointed to care for my people Israel, 'Why have you not built me a house made from cedar?'"'

16:23 [a]Ps 96:1–13   16:26 [a]Lev 19:4; [1 Cor 8:5–6]   [1]The Heb. words translated as "worthless" and "gods" sound alike.
16:29 [1]Or *holy splendor.*   16:33 [a]Isa 55:12–13   [b][Joel 3:1–14]; Zech 14:1–14; [Matt 25:31–46]   16:34 [a]2 Chr 5:13; 7:3; Ezra 3:11; Ps 106:1; 107:1; 118:1; 136:1; Jer 33:11   16:35 [a]Ps 106:47–48   16:36 [a]1 Kgs 8:15, 56; Ps 72:18   [b]Deut 27:15; Neh 8:6   [1]Trad. *amen.*
16:37 [a]1 Chr 16:4–5   16:38 [a]1 Chr 13:14   16:39 [a]1 Chr 21:29; 2 Chr 1:3   [b]1 Kgs 3:4   [1]Or *high place.*   16:40 [a][Exod 29:38–42; Num 28:3–4]   16:41 [1]Or perhaps *to the LORD with songs using the refrain, 'For his loyal love endures.'*   16:43 [a]2 Sam 6:18–20   [1]Heb. *to bless his house.*   17:1 [a]2 Sam 7:1; 1 Chr 14:1   17:4 [a][1 Chr 28:2–3]   17:5 [1]Heb. *and I was from tent to tent and from tabernacle.*   17:6 [1]Heb. *Did I say a word?*; a rhetorical question expecting a negative answer.

[7]"So now, say this to my servant David: 'This is what the LORD of Heaven's Armies says: "I took you [a]from the pasture and from your work as a shepherd to make you a leader of my people Israel. [8]I was with you wherever you went, and I defeated all your enemies before you. Now I will make you as famous as the great men of the earth. [9]I will establish a place for my people Israel and [a]settle them there; they will live there and not be disturbed anymore. Violent men will not oppress them again, as they did in the beginning [10]and during the time when I appointed judges to lead my people Israel. I will subdue all your enemies.

""I declare to you that the LORD will build a dynastic house for you! [11]When the time [a]comes for you to die, I will raise up your [b]descendant, one of your own sons, to succeed you, and I will establish his kingdom. [12a]He will build me a house, and I will make his dynasty permanent. [13]I [a]will become his father, and he will become my son. I will never withhold my loyal love from him, [b]as I withheld it from the one who ruled before you. [14]I [a]will put him in permanent charge of my house and my kingdom; his dynasty will be permanent.""" [15]Nathan told David all these words that were revealed to him.

David Praises God

[16]King David went in, sat before [a]the LORD, and said: "Who am I, O LORD God, and what is my family, that you should have brought me to this point? [17]And you did not stop there, O God! You have also spoken about the future of your servant's family. You have revealed to me what men long to know,[1] O LORD God. [18]What more can David say to you? You have honored your servant; you have given your servant special recognition. [19]O LORD, for the sake of your servant and according to your will, you have done this great thing in order to reveal your greatness. [20]O LORD, there is none like you; there is no God besides you! What we heard is true! [21]And who is like your people, Israel, [a]a unique nation in the earth? Their God went to claim a nation for himself! You made a name for yourself by doing great and awesome deeds when you drove out nations before your people whom you had delivered from the Egyptian empire and its gods. [22]You made Israel your very own nation for all time. You, O LORD, became their God. [23]So now, O LORD, may the promise you made about your servant and his family become a permanent reality! Do as you promised, [24]so it may become a reality and you may gain lasting fame, as people say, 'The LORD of Heaven's Armies is the God of Israel.'[1] The dynasty of your servant David will be established before you, [25]for you, my God, have revealed to your servant that you will build a dynasty for him. That is why your servant has had the courage to pray to you. [26]Now, O LORD, you are the true God; you have made this good promise to your servant. [27]Now you are willing to bless your servant's dynasty so that it may stand permanently before you, for you, O LORD, have blessed it and it will be blessed from now on into the future."

David Conquers the Neighboring Nations

18 Later David defeated the Philistines and subdued them. He took Gath and [a]its surrounding towns away from the Philistines.[1]

[2]He defeated the [a]Moabites; the Moabites became David's [b]subjects and brought tribute.[1]

[3a]David defeated King Hadadezer of Zobah as far as Hamath, when he went to extend his authority to the Euphrates River. [4]David seized from him 1,000 chariots, 7,000 charioteers, and 20,000 infantrymen. David cut the hamstrings of all but 100 of Hadadezer's chariot horses. [5]The [a]Arameans of Damascus came to help King Hadadezer of Zobah, but David killed 22,000 of the Arameans. [6]David placed garrisons in the territory of the Arameans of Damascus;[1] the Arameans became David's subjects and brought tribute. The LORD protected David

17:7 [a] 1 Sam 16:11–13   17:9 [a] [Deut 30:1–9; Jer 16:14–16; 23:5–8; 24:6; Ezek 37:21–27]; Amos 9:14   17:11 [a] 1 Kgs 2:10; 1 Chr 29:28   [b] 1 Kgs 5:5; 6:12; 8:19–21; [1 Chr 22:9–13; 28:20]; Matt 1:6; Luke 3:31   17:12 [a] 1 Kgs 6:38; 2 Chr 6:2; [Ps 89:20–37]   17:13 [a] 2 Sam 7:14–15; Matt 3:17; Mark 1:11; Luke 3:22; 2 Cor 6:18; Heb 1:5   [b] [1 Sam 15:23–28]; 1 Chr 10:14   17:14 [a] Ps 89:3–4; Matt 19:28; 25:31; [Luke 1:31–33]   17:16 [a] 2 Sam 7:18   17:17 [1] Heb. *and you see me like the searching of man, that which is upward.*   17:21 [a] [Deut 4:6–8, 33–38]; Ps 147:20   17:24 [1] Heb. *the LORD of Heaven's Armies* [trad. "the Lord of hosts"], *the God of Israel, Israel's God.*   18:1 [a] 2 Sam 8:1–18   [1] Heb. *the hand of the Philistines.*   18:2 [a] 2 Sam 8:2; Zeph 2:9   [b] Ps 60:8   [1] Heb. *carriers of tribute;* i.e., tribute payers.   18:3 [a] 2 Sam 8:3   18:5 [a] 2 Sam 8:5–6; 1 Kgs 11:23–25   18:6 [1] Heb. *and David placed in Aram of Damascus.*

wherever he campaigned. [7]David took the golden shields which Hadadezer's servants had carried and brought them to Jerusalem. [8]From Tibhath and Kun, Hadadezer's cities, David took a great deal of [a]bronze. ([b]Solomon used it to make the big bronze basin called "The Sea,"[1] the pillars, and other bronze items.)

[9]When King Tou of Hamath heard that David had defeated the entire army of King Hadadezer of Zobah, [10]he sent his son Hadoram to King David to extend his best wishes and to pronounce a blessing on him for his victory over Hadadezer, for Tou had been at war with Hadadezer. He also sent various [a]items made of gold, silver, and bronze. [11]King David dedicated these things to the LORD, along with the silver and gold which he had carried off from all the nations, including Edom, Moab, the [a]Ammonites, the [b]Philistines, and [c]Amalek.

[12a]Abishai son of Zeruiah killed [b]18,000 Edomites in the Valley of Salt. [13]He placed garrisons in Edom, and all [a]the Edomites became David's subjects. The LORD protected David wherever he campaigned.

David's Officials

[14]David reigned over all Israel; he guaranteed justice for all his people. [15]Joab son of Zeruiah was commanding general of the army; Jehoshaphat son of Ahilud was secretary; [16]Zadok son of Ahitub and Abimelech son of Abiathar were priests; Shavsha was scribe; [17a]Benaiah son of Jehoiada supervised the Kerethites and Pelethites; and David's sons were the king's leading officials.

David's Campaign against the Ammonites

19 Later King Nahash of the [a]Ammonites died and his son succeeded him. [2]David said, "I will express my loyalty to Hanun son of Nahash, for his father was loyal to me." So David sent messengers to express his sympathy over his father's death. When David's servants entered Ammonite territory to visit Hanun and express the king's sympathy, [3]the Ammonite officials said to Hanun, "Do you really think David is trying to honor your father by sending these messengers to express his sympathy? No, his servants have come to you so they can get information and spy out the land!"[1] [4]So Hanun seized David's servants and shaved their beards off. He cut off the lower part of their robes so that their [a]buttocks were exposed and then sent them away. [5]People came and told David what had happened to the men, so he sent messengers to meet them, for the men were thoroughly humiliated. The king said, "Stay in Jericho until your beards grow again; then you may come back."

[6]When the Ammonites realized that David was disgusted with them, Hanun [a]and the Ammonites sent 1,000 talents[1] of silver to hire chariots and charioteers from Aram Naharaim, Aram Maacah, and Zobah. [7]They hired 32,000 chariots, along with the king of Maacah and his army, who came and camped in front of Medeba. The Ammonites also assembled from their cities and marched out to do battle.

[8]When David heard the news, he sent Joab and the entire army to meet them. [9]The Ammonites marched out and were deployed for battle at the entrance to the city, while the kings who had come were by themselves in the field. [10]When Joab saw that the battle would be fought on two fronts, he chose some of Israel's best men and deployed them against the Arameans. [11]He put his brother Abishai in charge of the rest of the army, and they were deployed against the Ammonites. [12]Joab said, "If the Arameans start to overpower me, you come to my rescue. If the Ammonites start to overpower you, I will come to your rescue. [13]Be strong! Let's fight bravely for the sake of our people and the cities of our God! The LORD will do what he decides is best!" [14]So Joab and his men marched toward the Arameans to do battle, and they fled before him. [15]When the Ammonites saw the Arameans flee, they fled before Joab's brother Abishai and withdrew into the city. Joab went back to Jerusalem.

[16]When the Arameans realized they had been defeated by Israel, they sent for reinforcements from beyond the Euphrates River, led by Shophach the commanding general of Hadadezer's army. [17]When

18:8 [a]2 Sam 8:8 [b]1 Kgs 7:15, 23; 2 Chr 4:12, 15, 16 [1]Heb. *the sea of bronze.* **18:10** [a]2 Sam 8:10–12 **18:11** [a]2 Sam 10:14 [b]2 Sam 5:17–25 [c]2 Sam 1:1 **18:12** [a]2 Sam 23:18; 1 Chr 2:16 [b]2 Sam 8:13 **18:13** [a]Gen 27:29–40; Num 24:18; 2 Sam 8:14 **18:17** [a]2 Sam 8:18 **19:1** [a]1 Sam 11:1; 2 Sam 10:1–19 **19:3** [1]Heb. *Is it not to explore and to overturn and to spy out the land* (that) *his servants have come to you?* **19:4** [a]Isa 20:4 **19:6** [a]1 Chr 18:5, 9 [1]About 33.7 tons.

David was informed, he gathered all Israel, crossed the Jordan River, and marched against them. David deployed his army against the Arameans for battle and they fought against him. [18] The Arameans fled before Israel. David killed 7,000 Aramean charioteers and 40,000 infantrymen; he also killed Shophach the commanding general. [19] When Hadadezer's subjects saw they were defeated by Israel, they made peace with David and became his subjects. The Arameans were no longer willing to help the Ammonites.

20 In the spring, at the time when kings normally conduct wars, Joab led the army into battle and devastated the land of the [a]Ammonites. He went and besieged Rabbah, while [b]David stayed in Jerusalem. [c]Joab defeated Rabbah and tore it down. [2] David [a]took the crown from the head of their king[1] and wore it (its weight was a talent of gold, and it was set with precious stones). He took a large amount of plunder from the city. [3] He removed the city's residents and made them labor with saws, iron picks, and axes.[1] This was his policy with all the Ammonite cities. Then David and all the army returned to Jerusalem.

Battles with the Philistines

[4] Later there was [a]a battle with the Philistines in Gezer. At that time [b]Sibbekai the Hushathite killed Sippai, one of the descendants of the Rephaim, and the Philistines were subdued.

[5] There was another battle with the Philistines in which Elhanan son of Jair the Bethlehemite killed the brother of Goliath the Gittite,[1] whose spear had a shaft as big as the crossbeam of [a]a weaver's loom.

[6] In a battle in Gath [a]there was a large man who had six fingers on each hand and six toes on each foot—twenty-four in all! He too was a descendant of Rapha. [7] When he taunted Israel, Jonathan son of Shimea, David's brother, killed him.

[8] These were the descendants of Rapha who lived in Gath; they were killed by the hand of David and his soldiers.

The Lord Sends a Plague against Israel

21 An [a]adversary[1] opposed Israel, inciting David to count how many warriors Israel had.[2] [2] David told Joab [a]and the leaders of the army, "Go, count the number of warriors from Beer Sheba to Dan. Then bring back a report to me so I may know how many we have." [3] Joab replied, "May the LORD make his army a hundred times larger! My master, O king, do not all of them serve my master? Why does my master want to do this? Why bring judgment on Israel?"[1]

[4] But the king's edict stood, despite Joab's objections. So Joab left and traveled throughout Israel before returning to Jerusalem. [5] Joab reported to David the number of warriors. In all Israel there were 1,100,000 sword-wielding soldiers; Judah alone had 470,000 sword-wielding soldiers. [6a] Now Joab did not number Levi and Benjamin, for the king's edict disgusted him. [7] God was also offended by it, so he attacked Israel.

[8] David [a]said to God, "I have sinned greatly by doing this! Now, please remove the guilt of your servant, for I have acted very foolishly." [9] The LORD told Gad, David's [a]prophet,[1] [10] "Go, [a]tell David, 'This is what the LORD says: "I am offering you three forms of judgment from which to choose. Pick one of them."'" [11] Gad went to David and told him, "This is what the LORD says: 'Pick one of these: [12] three years of famine, [a]or three months being chased by your enemies and struck down by their swords,[1] or three days being struck down by the LORD, during which a plague will invade the land and the angel of the LORD will destroy throughout Israel's territory.' Now, decide what I should tell the one who sent me." [13] David said to Gad, "I am very upset! I prefer to be attacked by the LORD, for his [a]mercy is very great; I do not want to be attacked by men!" [14] So the LORD sent a [a]plague through Israel, and 70,000 Israelite men died.

[15] God sent an [a]angel to ravage Jerusalem. As he was doing so, the LORD watched and [b]relented from his judgment. He told the angel who was destroying, "That's enough! Stop now!"

20:1 [a] 2 Sam 11:1   [b] 2 Sam 11:2–12:25   [c] 2 Sam 12:26   20:2 [a] 2 Sam 12:30–31   [1] LXX, Vg. of Milcom.   20:3 [1] Heb. *saws.*
20:4 [a] 2 Sam 21:18   [b] 1 Chr 11:29   20:5 [a] 1 Sam 17:7; 1 Chr 11:23   [1] Heb. *Elchanan son of Jair killed Lachmi the brother of Goliath the Gittite.*   20:6 [a] 1 Sam 5:8; 2 Sam 21:20   21:1 [a] 2 Sam 24:1–25; Job 1:6   [1] Or *Satan.*   [2] Heb. *and incited David to count Israel.*   21:2 [a] 1 Chr 27:23–24   21:3 [1] Heb. *Why should it become guilt for Israel?*   21:6 [a] 1 Chr 27:24   21:8 [a] 2 Sam 24:10   21:9 [a] 1 Sam 9:9; 2 Kgs 17:13; 1 Chr 29:29; 2 Chr 16:7, 10; Isa 30:9–10; Amos 7:12–13   [1] Heb. *seer.*   21:10 [a] 2 Sam 24:12–14   21:12 [a] 2 Sam 24:13   [1] Heb. *or three months being swept away from before your enemies and the sword of your enemies overtaking.*   21:13 [a] Ps 51:1; 130:4, 7   21:14 [a] 1 Chr 27:24   21:15 [a] 2 Sam 24:16   [b] Gen 6:6

Now the angel of the Lord was standing near the threshing ᶜfloor of Ornan the Jebusite. ¹⁶David looked up and ᵃsaw the angel of the Lord standing between the earth and sky with his sword drawn and in his hand, stretched out over Jerusalem. David and the leaders, covered with sackcloth, threw themselves down with their faces to the ground. ¹⁷David said to God, "Was I not the one who decided to number the army? I am the one who sinned and committed this awful deed!¹ As for these ᵃsheep—what have they done? O Lord my God, attack me and my family, but remove the plague from your people!"

¹⁸So the ᵃangel of the Lord told Gad to instruct David to go up and build an altar for the Lord on the threshing floor of Ornan the Jebusite. ¹⁹So David went up as Gad instructed him to do in the name of the Lord. ²⁰While Ornan was threshing wheat, he turned and saw the messenger, and he and his four sons hid themselves. ²¹When David came to Ornan, Ornan looked and saw David; he came out from the threshing floor and bowed to David with his face to the ground. ²²David said to Ornan, "Sell me the threshing floor so I can build on it an altar for the Lord—I'll pay top price—so that the plague may be removed from the people." ²³Ornan told David, "You can have it! My master, the king, may do what he wants. Look, I am giving you the oxen for burnt sacrifices, the threshing sledges for wood, and the wheat for an offering. I give it all to you." ²⁴King David replied to Ornan, "No, I insist on buying it for top price.¹ I will not offer to the Lord what belongs to you or offer a burnt sacrifice that cost me nothing. ²⁵So ᵃDavid bought the place from Ornan for 600 pieces of gold.¹ ²⁶David built ᵃthere an altar to the Lord and offered burnt sacrifices and peace offerings. He called out to the Lord, and the Lord responded by sending fire from the sky and consuming the burnt sacrifice on the altar. ²⁷The Lord ordered the messenger to put his sword back into its sheath.

²⁸At that time, when David saw that the Lord responded to him at the threshing floor of Ornan the Jebusite, he sacrificed there. ²⁹Now the Lord's tabernacle (which Moses had made in the wilderness) and the altar ᵃfor burnt sacrifices were at that time at the worship center¹ in ᵇGibeon. ³⁰But David could not go before it to seek God's will, for he was afraid of the sword of the angel of the Lord. ¹David then said, "ᵃThis is the place where the temple of the Lord God will be, along with the altar for burnt sacrifices for Israel."

David Orders a Temple to Be Built

²David ordered the resident ᵃforeigners in the land of Israel to be called together. He appointed some of them to be ᵇstonecutters to chisel stones for the building of God's temple. ³David supplied a large amount of iron for the nails of the doors of the gates and for braces, more bronze than could ᵃbe weighed, ⁴and more cedar logs than could be counted. (The ᵃSidonians and Tyrians had brought a large amount of cedar logs to David.)

⁵David said, "My son ᵃSolomon is just an inexperienced young man, and the temple to be built for the Lord must be especially magnificent so it will become famous and be considered splendid by all the nations. Therefore I will make preparations for its construction." So David made extensive preparations before he died.

⁶He summoned his son Solomon and charged him to build a temple for the Lord God of Israel. ⁷David said to Solomon: "My son, ᵃI really wanted ᵇto build a temple to honor the Lord my God. ⁸But this was the Lord's message to me: 'ᵃYou have spilled a great deal of blood and fought many battles. You must not build a temple to honor me, for you have spilled a great deal of blood on the ground before me. ⁹Look, you will have a son, who will ᵃbe a peaceful man. I will give him ᵇrest from all his enemies on every side. Indeed, Solomon will be his name; I will give Israel peace and quiet during his reign. ¹⁰He will build a temple to honor me; ᵃhe will become my son, and I will become his ᵇfather. I will grant to his dynasty permanent rule over Israel.'

21:15 ᶜ 2 Chr 3:1   21:16 ᵃ Josh 5:13; 2 Chr 3:1   21:17 ᵃ 2 Sam 7:8; Ps 74:1   ¹Heb. and doing evil I did evil.   21:18 ᵃ 1 Chr 21:11–12; 2 Chr 3:1   21:24 ¹Heb. No, for buying I will buy for full silver.   21:25 ᵃ 2 Sam 24:24   ¹Heb. shekels of gold; about 15 pounds.   21:26 ᵃ Lev 9:24; Judg 6:21; 1 Kgs 18:36–38; 2 Chr 3:1; 7:1   21:29 ᵃ 1 Kgs 3:4; 2 Chr 1:3   ᵇ 1 Chr 16:39   ¹Or high place.   22:1 ᵃ Deut 12:5; 2 Sam 24:18; 1 Chr 21:18–19, 26, 28; 2 Chr 3:1   22:2 ᵃ 1 Kgs 9:20–21; 2 Chr 2:17–18   ᵇ 1 Kgs 5:17–18   22:3 ᵃ 1 Kgs 7:47; 1 Chr 22:14   22:4 ᵃ 1 Kgs 5:6–10   22:5 ᵃ 1 Kgs 3:7; 1 Chr 29:1–2   22:7 ᵃ 2 Sam 7:1–2; 1 Kgs 8:17; 1 Chr 17:1; 28:2   ᵇ Deut 12:5, 11   22:8 ᵃ 2 Sam 7:5–13; 1 Kgs 5:3; 1 Chr 28:3   22:9 ᵃ 1 Chr 28:5   ᵇ 1 Kgs 4:20, 25; 5:4   22:10 ᵃ 2 Sam 7:13; 1 Kgs 5:5; 6:38; 1 Chr 17:12–13; 28:6; 2 Chr 6:2   ᵇ Heb 1:5

[11] "Now, my son, may [a]the LORD be with you! May you succeed and build a temple for the LORD your God, just as he announced you would. [12]Only may the LORD [a]give you insight and understanding when he places you in charge of Israel, so you may obey the law of the LORD your God. [13]Then you will succeed, if you carefully obey [a]the rules and regulations which the LORD ordered Moses to give to Israel. [b]Be strong and brave! Don't be afraid and don't panic! [14]Now, look, I have made every effort to supply what is needed to build the LORD's temple. I have stored up 100,000 talents of gold, 1,000,000 talents of silver, and so much bronze and iron it cannot [a]be weighed, as well as wood and stones. Feel free to add more! [15]You also have available many workers, including stonecutters, masons, carpenters, and an innumerable array of workers who are skilled [16]in using gold, silver, bronze, and iron. Get up and begin [a]the work! May the LORD be with you!"

[17]David ordered all the [a]officials of Israel to support his son Solomon. [18]He told them, "The LORD your God is with you![1] He has made you secure on every side, for he [a]handed over to me the inhabitants of the region and the region is subdued before the LORD and his people. [19]Now seek the LORD your God wholeheartedly and with your entire being! Get up and build the sanctuary of the LORD God! Then you can [a]bring the ark of the LORD's covenant and the holy items dedicated to God's service into the temple that is built to honor the LORD."

David Organizes the Levites

23 When David was old and approaching the end of his life, he made his son [a]Solomon king over Israel.

[2]David assembled all the leaders of Israel, along with the priests and the Levites. [3]The Levites who were [a]thirty years old and up were counted; there were 38,000 men. [4]David said, "Of these, 24,000 are to [a]direct the work of the LORD's temple; 6,000 are to be [b]officials and judges; [5]4,000 are to be gatekeepers; and 4,000 are to [a]praise the LORD with the instruments [b]I supplied for worship." [6a]David divided them into groups corresponding to the sons of Levi: Gershon, Kohath, and Merari.

[7]The [a]Gershonites included Ladan and Shimei.

[8]The sons of Ladan: Jehiel the oldest, Zetham, and Joel—three in all.

[9]The sons of Shimei: Shelomoth, Haziel, and Haran—three in all.

These were the leaders of the family of Ladan.

[10]The sons of Shimei: Jahath, Zina,[1] Jeush, and Beriah. These were Shimei's sons—four in all. [11]Jahath was the oldest and Zizah the second oldest. Jeush and Beriah did not have many sons, so they were considered one family with one responsibility.

[12a]The sons of Kohath: Amram, Izhar, Hebron, and Uzziel—four in all.

[13]The sons of [a]Amram: [b]Aaron and Moses.

Aaron and his descendants were chosen on a permanent basis [c]to consecrate the most holy items, [d]to offer sacrifices before the LORD, [e]to serve him, and to praise his name. [14]The descendants of Moses [a]the man of God were considered Levites.

[15a]The sons of Moses: Gershom and Eliezer.

[16]The son of Gershom: [a]Shebuel[1] the oldest.

[17]The son of Eliezer was [a]Rehabiah, the oldest. Eliezer had no other sons, but Rehabiah had many descendants.

[18]The son of Izhar: [a]Shelomith the oldest.

[19]The sons [a]of Hebron: Jeriah the oldest, Amariah the second, Jahaziel the third, and Jekameam the fourth.

[20]The sons of Uzziel: Micah the oldest, and Isshiah the second.

[21]The sons of Merari: Mahli and Mushi. [a]The sons of Mahli: Eleazar and [b]Kish.

[22]Eleazar died without having sons; he [a]had only daughters. The sons of Kish, their cousins, [b]married them.[1]

[23a]The sons of Mushi: Mahli, Eder, and Jeremoth—three in all.

22:11[a]1 Chr 22:16   **22:12**[a]1 Kgs 3:9–12; 2 Chr 1:10   **22:13**[a][Josh 1:7–8]; 1 Chr 28:7   [b][Deut 31:7–8; Josh 1:6–7, 9; 1 Chr 28:20]   **22:14**[a]1 Chr 22:3   **22:16**[a]1 Chr 22:11   **22:17**[a]1 Chr 28:1–6   **22:18**[a]Deut 12:10; Josh 22:4; 2 Sam 7:1; [1 Kgs 5:4; 8:56]   [1]Heb. *Is not the Lord your God with you?*; a rhetorical question expecting a positive answer.   **22:19**[a]1 Kgs 8:1–11; 2 Chr 5:2–14   **23:1**[a]1 Kgs 1:33–40; 1 Chr 28:4–5   **23:3**[a]Num 4:1–3   **23:4**[a]2 Chr 2:2, 18; Ezra 3:8–9   [b]Deut 16:18–20   **23:5**[a]1 Chr 15:16   [b]2 Chr 29:25–27   **23:6**[a]Exod 6:16; Num 26:57; 2 Chr 8:14   **23:7**[a]1 Chr 26:21   **23:10**[1]A few wss *Zizah*.   **23:12**[a]Exod 6:18   **23:13**[a]Exod 6:20   [b]Exod 28:1; Heb 5:4   [c]Exod 30:7; 1 Sam 2:28   [d][Deut 21:5]   [e]Num 6:23   **23:14**[a]1 Chr 26:20–24   **23:15**[a]Exod 18:3–4   **23:16**[a]1 Chr 26:24   [1]LXX *Shubael*.   **23:17**[a]1 Chr 26:25   **23:18**[a]1 Chr 24:22   **23:19**[a]1 Chr 24:23   **23:21**[a]1 Chr 24:26   [b]1 Chr 24:29   **23:22**[a]1 Chr 24:28   [b]Num 36:6   [1]Heb. *their brothers* [i.e., relatives/cousins] *lifted them up.*   **23:23**[a]1 Chr 24:30

²⁴These were the descendants of ªLevi according to their families, that is, the leaders of families as counted and individually listed who carried out assigned tasks in the LORD's temple and were ᵇtwenty years old and up. ²⁵For David said, "The LORD God of Israel ªhas given his people rest and has permanently settled in Jerusalem. ²⁶So the Levites no longer need to ªcarry the tabernacle or any of the items used in its service." ²⁷According to David's ªfinal instructions, the Levites twenty years old or older were counted.

²⁸Their job was to help Aaron's descendants in the service of the LORD's temple. They were to take care of the courtyards, the rooms, ceremonial purification of all holy items, and other jobs related to the service of God's temple. ²⁹They also took care of ªthe bread that is displayed, ᵇthe flour for offerings, ᶜthe unleavened wafers, the round cakes, the mixing, and all the ᵈmeasuring. ³⁰They also stood in a designated place every morning and offered thanks and praise to the LORD. They also did this in the evening ³¹and whenever burnt sacrifices were offered to the LORD ªon the Sabbath and at new moon festivals and assemblies. A designated number were to serve before the LORD regularly in accordance with regulations. ³²They ªwere in ᵇcharge of the meeting tent ᶜand the Holy Place, and helped their relatives, the descendants of Aaron, in the service of the LORD's temple.

David Organizes the Priests

24 The divisions of Aaron's descendants were as follows:

ªThe sons of Aaron: Nadab, Abihu, Eleazar, and Ithamar.

²ªNadab and Abihu died before their father did; they had no sons. Eleazar and Ithamar served as priests.

³David, Zadok (a descendant of Eleazar), and ªAhimelech (a descendant of Ithamar) divided them into groups to carry out their assigned responsibilities. ⁴The descendants of Eleazar had more leaders than the descendants of Ithamar, so they divided them up accordingly; the descendants of Eleazar had sixteen leaders, while the descendants of Ithamar had eight. ⁵They divided them by lots, for there were officials of the Holy Place and officials designated by God among the descendants of both Eleazar and Ithamar. ⁶The scribe Shemaiah son of Nethanel, a Levite, wrote down their names before the king, the officials, Zadok the priest, Ahimelech son of Abiathar, and the leaders of the priestly and Levite families. One family was drawn by lot from Eleazar, and then the next from Ithamar.

⁷The first lot went to Jehoiarib,
the second to Jedaiah,
⁸the third to Harim,
the fourth to Seorim,
⁹the fifth to Malkijah,
the sixth to Mijamin,
¹⁰the seventh to Hakkoz,
the eighth to ªAbijah,
¹¹the ninth to Jeshua,
the tenth to Shecaniah,
¹²the eleventh to Eliashib,
the twelfth to Jakim,
¹³the thirteenth to Huppah,
the fourteenth to Jeshebeab,
¹⁴the fifteenth to Bilgah,
the sixteenth to Immer,
¹⁵the seventeenth to Hezir,
the eighteenth to Happizzez,
¹⁶the nineteenth to Pethahiah,
the twentieth to Jehezkel,
¹⁷the twenty-first to Jakin,
the twenty-second to Gamul,
¹⁸the twenty-third to Delaiah,
the twenty-fourth to Maaziah.
¹⁹This was the order in which they carried out their assigned responsibilities when they entered the LORD's temple, according to the regulations given them by their ancestor Aaron, just as the LORD God of Israel had instructed him.

Remaining Levites

²⁰The rest of the Levites included:
Shubael from the sons of Amram,
Jehdeiah from the sons of Shubael,
²¹the firstborn Isshiah from ªRehabiah and the sons of Rehabiah,
²²Shelomoth from the Izharites,
Jahath from the sons of Shelomoth.
²³The sons of ªHebron:¹ Jeriah, Amariah

23:24 ªNum 10:17, 21 ᵇNum 1:3; Ezra 3:8 **23:25** ª1 Chr 22:18 **23:26** ªNum 4:5, 15; 7:9; Deut 10:8 **23:27** ª2 Sam 23:1 **23:29** ªExod 25:30 ᵇLev 6:20 ᶜLev 2:1, 4 ᵈLev 19:35 **23:31** ªNum 10:10 **23:32** ª2 Chr 13:10–11 ᵇ[Num 1:53]; 1 Chr 9:27 ᶜNum 3:6–9, 38 **24:1** ªLev 10:1–6; Num 26:60–61; 1 Chr 6:3 **24:2** ªNum 3:1–4; 26:61 **24:3** ª1 Chr 18:16 **24:10** ªNeh 12:4, 17; Luke 1:5 **24:21** ª1 Chr 23:17 **24:23** ª1 Chr 23:19; 26:31 ¹Some MSS omit Hebron.

the second, Jahaziel the third, and Jekameam the fourth.

24 The son of Uzziel: Micah;
Shamir from the sons of Micah.
25 The brother of Micah: Isshiah.
Zechariah from the sons of Isshiah.
26 The sons of Merari: Mahli and Mushi.
[a] The son of Jaaziah: Beno.
27 The sons of Merari, from Jaaziah: Beno, Shoham, Zaccur, and Ibri.
28 From Mahli: Eleazar, [a] who had no sons.
29 From Kish: Jerahmeel.[1]
30 The sons of Mushi: Mahli, Eder, and Jerimoth.
[a] These were the Levites, listed by their families.

31 Like their relatives, the descendants of Aaron, they also cast lots before King David, Zadok, Ahimelech, the leaders of families, the priests, and the Levites. The families of the oldest son cast lots along with those of the youngest.

David Organizes the Musicians

25 David and the army officers selected some of the sons of [a] Asaph, Heman, and Jeduthun to prophesy as they played stringed instruments and cymbals. The following men were assigned this responsibility:

2 From the sons of Asaph: Zaccur, Joseph, Nethaniah, and Asarelah. The sons of Asaph were supervised by Asaph, who prophesied under the king's supervision.

3 From the sons of [a] Jeduthun: Gedaliah, Zeri, Jeshaiah,[1] Hashabiah, and Mattithiah— six in all, under supervision of their father Jeduthun, who prophesied as he played a harp, giving thanks and praise to the LORD.

4 From the sons of Heman: Bukkiah, Mattaniah, Uzziel, Shebuel, Jerimoth, Hananiah, Hanani, Eliathah, Giddalti, Romamti-Ezer, Joshbekashah, Mallothi, Hothir, and Mahazioth. 5 All these were the sons of Heman, the king's prophet. God had promised him these sons in order to make him [a] prestigious. God gave Heman fourteen sons and three daughters.

6 All these were under the supervision of their fathers; they were musicians in the LORD's temple, playing cymbals and stringed [a] instruments as they served in God's temple. Asaph, Jeduthun, and Heman were [b] under the supervision of the king. 7 They and their relatives, all of them skilled and trained to make music to the LORD, [a] numbered 288.

8 They cast lots to determine [a] their responsibilities—oldest as well as youngest, teacher as well as student.

9 The first lot went to Asaph's son Joseph and his relatives and sons—twelve in all,[1]
the second to Gedaliah and his relatives and sons—twelve in all,
10 the third to Zaccur and his sons and relatives—twelve in all,
11 the fourth to Izri and his sons and relatives—twelve in all,
12 the fifth to Nethaniah and his sons and relatives—twelve in all,
13 the sixth to Bukkiah and his sons and relatives—twelve in all,
14 the seventh to Jesharelah and his sons and relatives—twelve in all,
15 the eighth to Jeshaiah and his sons and relatives—twelve in all,
16 the ninth to Mattaniah and his sons and relatives—twelve in all,
17 the tenth to Shimei and his sons and relatives—twelve in all,
18 the eleventh to Azarel and his sons and relatives—twelve in all,
19 the twelfth to Hashabiah and his sons and relatives—twelve in all,
20 the thirteenth to Shubael and his sons and relatives—twelve in all,
21 the fourteenth to Mattithiah and his sons and relatives—twelve in all,
22 the fifteenth to Jerimoth and his sons and relatives—twelve in all,
23 the sixteenth to Hananiah and his sons and relatives—twelve in all,
24 the seventeenth to Joshbekashah and his sons and relatives—twelve in all,
25 the eighteenth to Hanani and his sons and relatives—twelve in all,
26 the nineteenth to Mallothi and his sons and relatives—twelve in all,
27 the twentieth to Eliathah and his sons and relatives—twelve in all,
28 the twenty-first to Hothir and his sons and relatives—twelve in all,

---

24:26 [a] Exod 6:19; 1 Chr 23:21   24:28 [a] 1 Chr 23:22   24:29 [1] Heb. *Belonging to* [i.e., from] *Kish, the sons of Kish, Jerahmeel.*
24:30 [a] 1 Chr 23:23   25:1 [a] 1 Chr 6:30, 33, 39, 44; 2 Chr 5:12   25:3 [a] 1 Chr 16:41-42   [1] Some MSS add *Shimei.*
25:5 [a] 1 Chr 16:42   25:6 [a] 1 Chr 15:16   [b] 1 Chr 15:19; 25:2   25:7 [a] 1 Chr 23:5   25:8 [a] 2 Chr 23:13
25:9 [1] Heb. *The first lot went to Asaph, to Joseph.*

[29]the twenty-second to Giddalti and his sons and relatives—twelve in all,

[30]the twenty-third to Mahazioth and his sons and relatives—twelve in all,

[31]the twenty-fourth to Romamti-Ezer and his sons and relatives—twelve in all.

Divisions of Gatekeepers

26 The divisions of the gatekeepers:

From the Korahites: Meshelemiah, son of [a]Kore, one of the sons of Asaph. [2]Meshelemiah's sons:

The firstborn [a]Zechariah, the second Jediael, the third Zebadiah, the fourth Jathniel, [3]the fifth Elam, the sixth Jehohanan, and the seventh Elihoenai.

[4a]Obed-Edom's sons:

The firstborn Shemaiah, the second Jehozabad, the third Joah, the fourth Sakar, the fifth Nethanel, [5]the sixth Ammiel, the seventh Issachar, and the eighth Peullethai. (Indeed, God blessed Obed-Edom.)

[6]His son Shemaiah also had sons, who were leaders of their families, for they were highly respected. [7]The sons of Shemaiah:

Othni, Rephael, Obed, and Elzabad. His relatives Elihu and Semakiah were also respected.

[8]All these were the descendants of Obed-Edom. They and their sons and relatives were [a]respected men, capable of doing their responsibilities. There were sixty-two of them related to Obed-Edom.

[9]Meshelemiah had sons and relatives who were respected—eighteen in all.

[10a]Hosah, one of the descendants of Merari, had sons:

The firstborn Shimri (he was not actually the firstborn, but his father gave him that status), [11]the second Hilkiah, the third Tebaliah, and the fourth Zechariah. All Hosah's sons and relatives numbered thirteen.

[12]These divisions of the gatekeepers, corresponding to their leaders, had assigned responsibilities, like their relatives, as they served in the LORD's temple.

[13]They [a]cast lots, both young and old, according to their families, to determine which gate they would be responsible for. [14]The lot for the east gate went to Shelemiah. They then cast lots for his son Zechariah, a wise adviser, and the lot for the north gate went to him. [15]Obed-Edom was assigned the south gate, and his sons were assigned the storehouses. [16]Shuppim and Hosah were assigned the west gate, along with the Shalleketh gate on the [a]upper road. One guard was adjacent to another. [17]Each day there were six Levites posted on the east, four on the north, and four on the south. At the storehouses they were posted in pairs. [18]At the court on the west there were four posted on the road and two at the court. [19]These were the divisions of the gatekeepers who were descendants of Korah and Merari.

Supervisors of the Storehouses

[20]Their fellow Levites were[1] in charge of the storehouses in God's temple and the storehouses containing consecrated items. [21]The descendants of Ladan, who were descended from Gershon through Ladan and were leaders of the families of Ladan the Gershonite, included Jehieli [22]and the sons of Jehieli, Zetham and his brother Joel. They were in charge of the storehouses in the LORD's temple.

[23]As for the [a]Amramites, Izharites, Hebronites, and Uzzielites:

[24a]Shebuel son of Gershom, the son of Moses, was the supervisor of the storehouses. [25]His relatives through Eliezer included: Rehabiah his son, Jeshaiah his son, Joram his son, Zikri his son, and [a]Shelomith[1] his son. [26]Shelomith[1] and his relatives were in charge of all the storehouses containing the consecrated items dedicated by King David, the family leaders who led units of a thousand and a hundred, and the army officers. [27]They had dedicated some of the plunder taken in battles to be used for repairs on the LORD's temple. [28]They were also in charge of everything dedicated by Samuel [a]the prophet,[1] Saul son of Kish, Abner son of Ner, and Joab son of Zeruiah; Shelomith and his relatives were in charge of everything that had been dedicated.

[29]As [a]for the Izharites: Kenaniah and his sons were given responsibilities outside the temple as [b]officers and judges over Israel. [30]As for the Hebronites: [a]Hashabiah and

26:1 [a]Ps 42:title   **26:2** [a]1 Chr 9:21   **26:4** [a]1 Chr 15:18, 21   **26:8** [a]1 Chr 9:13   **26:10** [a]1 Chr 16:38   **26:13** [a]1 Chr 24:5, 31; 25:8   **26:16** [a]1 Kgs 10:5; 2 Chr 9:4   **26:20** [1]Heb., LXX *And the Levites: Ahijah was.*   **26:23** [a]Exod 6:18; Num 3:19   **26:24** [a]1 Chr 23:16   **26:25** [a]1 Chr 23:18   [1]Ket. *Shelomoth.*   **26:26** [1]MT *Shelomoth.*   **26:28** [a]1 Sam 9:9   [1]Or *seer.*   **26:29** [a]Neh 11:16   [b]1 Chr 23:4   **26:30** [a]1 Chr 27:17

his relatives, 1,700 respected men, were assigned responsibilities in Israel west of the Jordan; they did the LORD's work and the king's service.

[31] As for the Hebronites: [a]Jeriah was the leader of the Hebronites according to the genealogical records. In the fortieth year of David's reign, they examined the records and discovered there were highly respected men in Jazer in Gilead. [32]Jeriah had 2,700 relatives who were respected family leaders. King David placed them in charge of the Reubenites, the Gadites, and the half-tribe of Manasseh; they took care of all [a]matters pertaining to God and the king.

Leaders of the Army

27 What follows is a list of Israelite family leaders and commanders of units of a thousand and a hundred, as well as their officers who served the king in various matters. Each division was assigned to serve for one month during the year; each consisted of 24,000 troops.

[2][a]Jashobeam son of Zabdiel was in charge of the first division, which was assigned the first month. His division consisted of 24,000 troops. [3]He was a descendant of Perez; he was in charge of all the army officers for the first month.

[4]Dodai the Ahohite was in charge of the division assigned the second month; Mikloth was the next in rank. His division consisted of 24,000 troops.

[5]The third army commander, assigned the third month, was [a]Benaiah son of Jehoiada the priest. He was the leader of his division, which consisted of 24,000 troops. [6]Benaiah was the leader of the thirty [a]warriors and his division; his son was Ammizabad.

[7]The fourth, assigned the fourth month, was [a]Asahel, brother of Joab; his son Zebadiah succeeded him. His division consisted of 24,000 troops.

[8]The fifth, assigned the fifth month, was the commander Shamhuth the Izrahite. His division consisted of 24,000 troops.

[9]The sixth, assigned the sixth month, was [a]Ira son of Ikkesh the Tekoite. His division consisted of 24,000 troops.

[10]The seventh, assigned the seventh month, was [a]Helez the Pelonite, an Ephraimite. His division consisted of 24,000 troops.

[11]The eighth, assigned the eighth month, was [a]Sibbekai the Hushathite, a Zerahite. His division consisted of 24,000 troops.

[12]The ninth, assigned the ninth month, was [a]Abiezer the Anathothite, a Benjaminite. His division consisted of 24,000 troops.

[13]The tenth, assigned the tenth month, was [a]Maharai the Netophathite, a Zerahite. His division consisted of 24,000 troops.

[14]The eleventh, assigned the eleventh month, was [a]Benaiah the Pirathonite, an Ephraimite. His division consisted of 24,000 troops.

[15]The twelfth, assigned the twelfth month, was Heldai the Netophathite, a descendant of Othniel. His division consisted of 24,000 troops.

[16]The officers of the Israelite tribes:

Eliezer son of Zikri was the leader of the Reubenites,

Shephatiah son of Maacah led the Simeonites,

[17][a]Hashabiah son of Kemuel led the Levites,

Zadok led the descendants of Aaron,

[18][a]Elihu, a brother of David, led Judah,

Omri son of Michael led Issachar,

[19]Ishmaiah son of Obadiah led Zebulun,

Jerimoth son of Azriel led Naphtali,

[20]Hoshea son of Azaziah led the Ephraimites,

Joel son of Pedaiah led the half-tribe of Manasseh,

[21]Iddo son of Zechariah led the half-tribe of Manasseh in Gilead,

Jaasiel son of Abner led Benjamin,

[22]Azarel son of Jeroham led Dan.

These were the commanders of the Israelite tribes.

[23]David did not count [a]the males twenty years old and under, for the LORD had promised to make Israel as numerous as the [b]stars in the sky. [24]Joab son of Zeruiah started to count the men but did not finish. God was [a]angry with Israel because of this, so the number was not recorded in the scroll[1] called The Annals of King David.

26:31 [a]1 Chr 23:19   26:32 [a]2 Chr 19:11   27:2 [a]1 Chr 11:11   27:5 [a]1 Chr 18:17   27:6 [a]2 Sam 23:20–23   27:7 [a]2 Sam 23:24; 1 Chr 11:26   27:9 [a]1 Chr 11:28   27:10 [a]1 Chr 11:27   27:11 [a]2 Sam 21:18; 1 Chr 11:29; 20:4   27:12 [a]1 Chr 11:28   27:13 [a]2 Sam 23:28; 1 Chr 11:30   27:14 [a]1 Chr 11:31   27:17 [a]1 Chr 26:30   27:18 [a]1 Sam 16:6   27:23 [a][Deut 6:3]   [b]Gen 15:5; 22:17; 26:4; Exod 32:13; Deut 1:10   27:24 [a]2 Sam 24:12–15; 1 Chr 21:1–7   [1]Heb. in the number.

Royal Officials

25 Azmaveth son of Adiel was in charge of the king's storehouses;

Jonathan son of Uzziah was in charge of the storehouses in the field, in the cities, in the towns, and in the towers.

26 Ezri son of Kelub was in charge of the field workers who farmed the land.[1]

27 Shimei the Ramathite was in charge of the vineyards;

Zabdi the Shiphmite was in charge of the wine stored in the vineyards.

28 Baal Hanan the Gederite was in charge of the olive and sycamore trees in the foothills;

Joash was in charge of the storehouses of olive oil.

29 Shitrai the Sharonite was in charge of the cattle grazing in Sharon;

Shaphat son of Adlai was in charge of the cattle in the valleys.

30 Obil the Ishmaelite was in charge of the camels;

Jehdeiah the Meronothite was in charge of the donkeys.

31 Jaziz the [a]Hagrite was in charge of the sheep.

All these were the officials in charge of King David's property.

32 Jonathan, David's uncle, was a wise adviser and scribe;

Jehiel son of Hacmoni cared for the king's sons.

33 [a]Ahithophel was the king's adviser;

[b]Hushai the Arkite was the king's confidant.[1]

34 Ahithophel was succeeded by Jehoiada son of Benaiah and by [a]Abiathar.

[b]Joab was the commanding general of the king's army.

David Commissions Solomon to Build the Temple

28 David assembled in Jerusalem all [a]the officials of Israel, including [b]the commanders of [c]the tribes, [d]the commanders of the army divisions that served the king, the commanders of units of a thousand and a hundred, the officials who were in charge of all the property and livestock of the king and his sons, the eunuchs, and the warriors, including the most skilled of them.

2 King [a]David rose to his feet and said: "Listen to me, my [b]brothers and my people. I wanted to build a temple where the ark of the LORD's covenant could be placed as a footstool for our God. I have made the preparations for building it. 3 But God said to me, '[a]You must not build a temple to honor me, for you are a warrior and have spilled [b]blood.' 4 The LORD God of Israel [a]chose me out of my father's entire family to become king over Israel and have a permanent dynasty. Indeed, he chose [b]Judah as leader, and my [c]father's family within Judah, and then he picked me out from [d]among my father's sons and made me king over all Israel. 5a From all [b]the many sons the LORD has given me, he chose Solomon my son to rule on his behalf over Israel. 6 He said to me, 'Solomon [a]your son is the one who will build my temple and my courts, for I have chosen him to become my son and I will become his father. 7 I will establish his kingdom permanently, [a]if he remains committed to obeying my commands and regulations, as you are doing this day.' 8 So now, in the sight of all Israel, the LORD's assembly, and in the hearing of our God, I say this: Carefully observe all the commands of the LORD your God, so that you may possess this good land and may leave it as a permanent inheritance for your children after you.

9 "And you, Solomon my son, [a]obey the God of your father and serve him [b]with a submissive attitude and a willing spirit, for [c]the LORD examines all minds and understands every motive of one's thoughts. [d]If you seek him, he will let you find him, but if you abandon him, he will reject you permanently. 10 Realize now that the LORD has chosen you to build a temple as his sanctuary. Be strong and do it!"

11 David gave to his son Solomon [a]the blueprints for the temple porch, its buildings, its treasuries, its upper areas, its inner

27:26 [1]Heb. *with respect to the work of the land.*   27:31 [a]1 Chr 5:10   27:33 [a]2 Sam 15:12   [b]2 Sam 15:32–37   [1]Heb. *friend.*
27:34 [a]1 Kgs 1:7   [b]1 Chr 11:6   28:1 [a]1 Chr 27:16   [b]1 Chr 27:1–2   [c]1 Chr 27:25   [d]2 Sam 23:8–39; 1 Chr 11:10–47   28:2 [a]2 Sam 7:2   [b]Ps 99:5; 132:7; [Isa 66:1]   28:3 [a]2 Sam 7:5, 13; 1 Kgs 5:3   [b][1 Chr 17:4; 22:8]   28:4 [a]1 Sam 16:6–13   [b]Gen 49:8–10; 1 Chr 5:2; Ps 60:7   [c]1 Sam 16:1   [d]1 Sam 13:14; 16:12–13; Acts 13:22   28:5 [a]1 Chr 3:1–9; 14:3–7; 23:1   [b]1 Chr 22:9; 29:1   28:6 [a]2 Sam 7:13–14; 1 Kgs 6:38; 1 Chr 22:9–10; 2 Chr 1:9; 6:2   28:7 [a]1 Chr 22:13   28:9 [a][1 Sam 12:24]; Jer 9:24; Hos 4:1; [John 17:3]   [b]2 Kgs 20:3   [c][1 Sam 16:7; 1 Kgs 8:39; 1 Chr 29:17]; Jer 11:20; 17:10; 20:12; Rev 2:23   [d]2 Chr 15:2; [Jer 29:13]   28:11 [a]1 Kgs 6:3; 1 Chr 28:19

rooms, and the room for atonement. [12]He gave him the [a]blueprints [b]of all he envisioned for the courts of the LORD's temple, all the surrounding rooms, the storehouses of God's temple, and the storehouses for the holy items.

[13]He gave him the regulations for the divisions of priests and [a]Levites, for all the assigned responsibilities within the LORD's temple, and for all the items used in the service of the LORD's temple.

[14]He gave him the prescribed weight for all the gold items to be used in various types of service in the LORD's temple, for all the silver items to be used in various types of service; [15]for the gold [a]lampstands and their gold lamps, including the weight of each lampstand and its lamps; for the silver lampstands, including the weight of each lampstand and its lamps, according to the prescribed use of each lampstand; [16]for the gold used in the display [a]tables, including the amount to be used in each table; for the silver to be used in the silver tables; [17]for the pure gold used for the meat forks, bowls, and jars; for the small gold bowls, including the weight for each bowl; for the small silver bowls, including the weight for each bowl; [18]and for the refined gold of the incense [a]altar.

He gave him the blueprint for the seat[1] of the gold [b]cherubim that spread their wings[2] and provide shelter for the ark of the LORD's covenant.

[19]David said, "All this I put in writing as [a]the LORD directed me and gave me insight regarding the details of the blueprints."

[20]David said to his son Solomon: "[a]Be strong and brave! Do it! Don't be afraid and don't panic! For [b]the LORD God, my God, is with you. He will not leave you or abandon you before all the work for the service of the LORD's temple is finished. [21]Here are [a]the divisions of the priests and Levites who will perform [b]all the service of God's temple. All the willing and skilled men are ready to assist you in all the work and perform their service. The officials and all the people are ready to follow your instructions."

The People Contribute to the Project

29 King David said to the entire assembly: "My son Solomon, the one whom God has [a]chosen, is just an inexperienced young [b]man, and the task is great, for this palace is not for man, but for the LORD God. [2]So I have made every effort to provide what is needed for the temple of my God, including the gold, silver, bronze, iron, wood, as well as a large amount of [a]onyx, settings of antimony and other stones, all kinds of precious stones, and alabaster. [3]Now, to show my commitment to the temple of my God, I donate my personal treasure of gold and silver to the temple of my God, in addition to all that I have already supplied for this holy temple. [4]This includes 3,000 talents[1] of gold from [a]Ophir and 7,000 talents of refined silver for overlaying the walls of the buildings, [5]for gold and silver items, and for all the work of the craftsmen. Who else [a]wants to contribute to the LORD today?"

[6]The leaders of [a]the families, [b]the leaders [c]of the Israelite tribes, the commanders of units of a thousand and a hundred, and the supervisors of the king's work contributed willingly. [7]They donated for the service of God's temple 5,000 talents[1] and 10,000 darics of gold, 10,000 talents of silver, 18,000 talents of bronze, and 100,000 talents of iron. [8]All who possessed precious stones donated them to the treasury of the LORD's temple, which was under the supervision of [a]Jehiel the Gershonite. [9]The people were delighted with their donations, for they contributed to the LORD with a willing attitude; King David was also very happy.

David Praises the Lord

[10]David praised the LORD before the entire assembly:[1]

"O LORD God of our father Israel, you deserve praise forevermore! [11]O LORD, [a]you are great, mighty, majestic, magnificent, glorious, and sovereign over all the sky and earth! You, LORD, have dominion and exalt yourself as the ruler of all. [12][a]You are the source of wealth and honor; you rule over all. You possess strength and might to magnify and

28:12 [a]Exod 25:40; Heb 8:5 [b]1 Chr 26:20, 28 28:13 [a]1 Chr 23:6 28:15 [a]Exod 25:31–39; 1 Kgs 7:49 28:16 [a]1 Kgs 7:48 28:18 [a]Exod 30:1–10 [b]Exod 25:18–22; 1 Sam 4:4; 1 Kgs 6:23 [1]Heb. *chariot*. [2]Heb. omits *their wings*. 28:19 [a]Exod 25:40; 1 Chr 28:11–12 28:20 [a]Deut 31:6–7; [Josh 1:6–9]; 1 Chr 22:13 [b]Josh 1:5; Heb 13:5 28:21 [a]1 Chr 24–26 [b]Exod 35:25–35; 36:1–2; 2 Chr 2:13–14 29:1 [a]1 Chr 28:5 [b]1 Kgs 3:7; 1 Chr 22:5; Prov 4:3 29:2 [a]Isa 54:11–12; Rev 21:18 29:4 [a]1 Kgs 9:28 [1]About 101 tons of gold and 235.5 tons of silver. 29:5 [a]2 Chr 29:31; [2 Cor 8:5, 12] 29:6 [a]1 Chr 27:1; 28:1 [b]1 Chr 27:25–31 [c]Exod 35:21–35 29:7 [1]About 168.3 tons of gold, 336.5 tons of silver, 605.7 tons of bronze, and 3,365 tons of iron. 29:8 [a]1 Chr 23:8 29:10 [1]Heb. *assembly, and David said.* 29:11 [a]Matt 6:13; 1 Tim 1:17; Rev 5:13 29:12 [a]Rom 11:36

give strength to all. [13] Now, our God, we give thanks to you and praise your majestic name! [14] "But who am I and who are my people that we should be in a position to contribute this much? Indeed, everything comes from you, and we have simply given back to you what is yours. [15] For [a] we are resident foreigners and temporary settlers in [b] your presence, as all our ancestors were; our days are like a shadow on the earth, without security. [16] O LORD our God, all this wealth, which we have collected to build a temple for you to honor your holy name, comes from you; it all belongs to you. [17] I know, my God, that you [a] examine thoughts and are pleased with integrity. With pure motives I contribute all this; and now I look with joy as your people who [b] have gathered here contribute to you. [18] O LORD God of our ancestors Abraham, Isaac, and Israel, always maintain these motives of your people and keep them devoted to you. [19] Make my son Solomon willing to obey your commands, rules, and regulations, and to complete building the palace for which [a] I have made [b] preparations."

[20] David told the entire assembly: "Praise the LORD your God!" So the entire assembly praised the LORD God of their ancestors; they bowed down and stretched out flat on the ground before the LORD and the king.

David Designates Solomon King

[21] The next day they [a] made sacrifices and offered burnt sacrifices to the LORD (1,000 bulls, 1,000 rams, 1,000 lambs), along with their accompanying drink offerings and many other sacrifices for all Israel. [22] They held a feast before the LORD that day and celebrated.

Then they designated Solomon, David's son, as king a second time; before the LORD they [a] anointed him as ruler and Zadok as priest. [23] Solomon sat on the LORD's throne as king in place of his father David; he was successful and all Israel was loyal to him. [24] All the officers and warriors, as well as all of King David's sons, [a] pledged their allegiance to King Solomon. [25] The LORD greatly magnified Solomon before all Israel and [a] bestowed on him greater majesty than any king of Israel before him.

David's Reign Comes to an End

[26] David son of Jesse reigned over all Israel. [27] [a] He reigned over Israel forty years; he reigned in Hebron [b] seven years and in Jerusalem thirty-three years. [28] He [a] died at a good old age, having enjoyed [b] long life, wealth, and honor. His son Solomon succeeded him. [29] King David's accomplishments, from start to finish, are recorded in the Annals of Samuel the prophet, the Annals of Nathan the prophet, and the Annals of Gad the prophet. [30] Recorded there are all the facts about his reign [a] and accomplishments, and an account of the events that involved him, Israel, and all the neighboring kingdoms.

29:15 [a] Lev 25:23; Ps 39:12; Heb 11:13–14; 1 Pet 2:11 [b] Job 14:2; Ps 90:9   29:17 [a] [1 Sam 16:7; 1 Chr 28:9] [b] Prov 11:20
29:19 [a] [1 Chr 28:9]; Ps 72:1 [b] 1 Chr 29:1–2   29:21 [a] 1 Kgs 8:62–63   29:22 [a] 1 Kgs 1:32–35, 39; 1 Chr 23:1
29:24 [a] Eccl 8:2   29:25 [a] 1 Kgs 3:13; 2 Chr 1:12; Eccl 2:9   29:27 [a] 2 Sam 5:4; 1 Kgs 2:11 [b] 2 Sam 5:5
29:28 [a] Gen 25:8 [b] 1 Chr 23:1   29:30 [a] Dan 2:21; 4:23, 25

2 CHRONICLES

The Book of 2 Chronicles parallels 1–2 Kings but virtually ignores the northern kingdom of Israel because of its false worship and refusal to acknowledge the temple in Jerusalem. Chronicles focuses on those kings who pattern their lives and reigns after the life and reign of godly King David. It gives extended treatment to such zealous reformers as Asa, Jehoshaphat, Joash, Hezekiah, and Josiah. The temple and temple worship, central throughout the book, befit a nation whose worship of God is integral to its very survival. The book begins with Solomon's glorious temple and concludes with Cyrus's edict to rebuild the temple more than 400 years later.

The Lord Gives Solomon Wisdom

1 [a]Solomon son of David solidified his royal authority, for [b]the LORD his God was with him and [c]magnified him greatly.

[2]Solomon addressed all Israel, including those who commanded units of a thousand and a hundred, [a]the judges, and all the leaders of all Israel who were heads of families. [3]Solomon and the entire assembly went to the worship center[1] in [a]Gibeon, for the tent where they met God was located there, which Moses the LORD's servant had [b]made in the wilderness. [4]([a]Now David had brought up the ark of God from Kiriath Jearim to the place he had prepared for it, for he had pitched a tent for it in Jerusalem. [5]But [a]the bronze altar made by [b]Bezalel son of Uri, son of Hur, was in front of the LORD's tabernacle. Solomon and the entire assembly prayed to him there.) [6]Solomon went [a]up to the bronze altar before the LORD which was at the meeting tent, and he offered up 1,000 burnt sacrifices.

[7]That night God appeared to [a]Solomon and said to him, "Tell me what I should give you." [8]Solomon replied to God, "You demonstrated great [a]loyalty to my father David and have made me [b]king in his place. [9]Now, LORD God, may your promise to my father David be realized,[1] [a]for you have made me king over a great nation as numerous as the [b]dust of the earth. [10]Now give me wisdom and discernment so I can effectively lead this nation.[1] Otherwise [a]no one is able to make judicial decisions for this great nation of yours."

[11a]God said to Solomon, "Because you desire this, and did not ask for riches, wealth, and honor, or for vengeance on your enemies, and because you did not ask for long life, but requested wisdom and discernment so you can make judicial decisions for my people over whom I have made you king, [12]you are granted wisdom and discernment. Furthermore I am giving you riches, wealth, and honor surpassing that of any king before or after you."

[13]Solomon left the meeting tent at the worship center in Gibeon and went to Jerusalem, where he reigned over Israel.

Solomon's Wealth

[14]Solomon accumulated chariots [a]and horses. He had 1,400 chariots and 12,000 horses. He kept them in assigned cities and in Jerusalem. [15a]The king made silver and gold as plentiful in Jerusalem as stones; cedar was as plentiful as sycamore fig trees are in the foothills. [16]Solomon acquired his horses from Egypt [a]and from Que; the king's traders purchased them from Que. [17]They paid 600 silver pieces for each chariot from Egypt and 150 silver pieces for each horse. They also sold chariots and horses to all the kings of the Hittites and to the kings of Syria.

Solomon Gathers Building Materials for the Temple

2 Solomon [a]ordered a temple to be built to honor the LORD, as well as a royal palace for himself. [2][a]Solomon had[1] 70,000 common laborers and 80,000 stonecutters in the hills, in addition to 3,600 supervisors.

[3]Solomon sent [a]a message to King Huram of Tyre: "Help me as you did my father David, when you sent him cedar logs for the construction of his palace. [4]Look, [a]I am ready [b]to build a temple to honor [c]the LORD my God and to dedicate it to him in order to burn fragrant incense before him, to set out [d]the bread that is regularly displayed, and to offer burnt sacrifices each morning and evening, and on [e]Sabbaths, new moon festivals, and at other times appointed by the LORD our God. This is something Israel must do on a permanent basis. [5]I will build a great temple, for [a]our God is greater than all gods. [6][a]Of course, who can really build a temple for him, since the sky and the highest heavens cannot contain him? Who am I that I should build him a temple! It will really be only a place to offer sacrifices before him.

[7]"Now send me a man [a]who is skilled in working with gold, silver, bronze, and iron, as well as purple-, crimson-, and blue-colored fabrics, and who knows how to engrave. He will work with my skilled craftsmen here in Jerusalem and Judah, whom my father David provided. [8][a]Send me cedars, evergreens, and algum trees from Lebanon, for I know your servants are adept at cutting down trees in Lebanon. My servants will work with your servants [9]to supply me with large quantities of timber, for I am building a great, magnificent temple. [10]Look, I will pay your servants who cut the timber 20,000 cors of ground wheat, 20,000 cors of barley, 120,000 gallons[1] of wine, [a]and 120,000 gallons of olive oil."

[11]King Huram of Tyre sent this letter to Solomon: "[a]Because the LORD loves his people, he has made you their king." [12]Huram also said, "Worthy of [a]praise is the LORD God of Israel, [b]who made the sky and the earth! He has given King David a wise son who has discernment and insight and will build a temple for the LORD, as well as a royal palace for himself. [13]Now I am sending you Huram Abi, a skilled and capable man, [14]whose [a]mother is a Danite and whose father is a Tyrian. He knows how to work with gold, silver, bronze, iron, stones, and wood, as well as purple, blue, white, and crimson fabrics. He knows how to do all kinds of engraving and understands any design given to him. He will work with your skilled craftsmen and the skilled craftsmen of my lord David your father. [15]Now let [a]my lord send to his servants the wheat, barley, olive oil, and wine he has promised; [16]we will get all the timber you need from Lebanon [a]and bring it in raft-like bundles[1] by sea to Joppa. You can then haul it on up to Jerusalem."

[17]Solomon took a census of all [a]the male resident foreigners in the land of Israel, after the census his father [b]David had taken. There were 153,600 in all. [18]He designated [a]70,000 as common laborers, 80,000 as stonecutters in the hills, and 3,600 as supervisors to make sure the people completed the work.

The Building of the Temple

3 [a]Solomon began building the LORD's temple in [b]Jerusalem on Mount Moriah, where the LORD had appeared to his father David. This was the place that David prepared at the threshing floor of [c]Ornan the Jebusite. [2]He began building on the second day of the second month of the fourth year of his reign.

[3]Solomon laid the foundation for God's temple; its length (determined according to the old standard of measure) was 90 feet, and its width 30 feet. [4]The porch in front of the main hall was 30 feet long, corresponding to the width of the temple,[1] and its height was 30 feet.[2] He plated the inside with pure gold. [5]He paneled [a]the main hall with boards made from evergreen trees and [b]plated it with fine gold, decorated with palm trees and chains. [6]He decorated the temple with precious stones; the gold he

2:1 [a]1 Kgs 5:5   2:2 [a]1 Kgs 5:15–16; 2 Chr 2:18   [1]Or perhaps *conscripted*; Heb. *counted.*   2:3 [a]1 Chr 14:1   2:4 [a]2 Chr 2:1   [b]Exod 30:7   [c]Exod 25:30; Lev 24:8   [d]Exod 29:38–42   [e]Num 28:3, 9–11   2:5 [a]Ps 135:5; [1 Cor 8:5–6]   2:6 [a]1 Kgs 8:27; 2 Chr 6:18; Isa 66:1   2:7 [a]1 Chr 22:15   2:8 [a]1 Kgs 5:6   2:10 [a]1 Kgs 5:11   [1]About 120,000 gallons; Heb. *20,000 baths.*   2:11 [a]1 Kgs 10:9; 2 Chr 9:8   2:12 [a]1 Kgs 5:7   [b]Gen 1; 2; Acts 4:24; 14:15; Rev 10:6   2:14 [a]1 Kgs 7:13–14   2:15 [a]2 Chr 2:10   2:16 [a]1 Kgs 5:8–9   [1]Or *on rafts.*   2:17 [a]1 Kgs 5:13; 2 Chr 8:7–8   [b]1 Chr 22:2   2:18 [a]2 Chr 2:2   3:1 [a]1 Kgs 6:1   [b]Gen 22:2–14   [c]1 Chr 21:18; 22:1   3:4 [1]Heb. *and the porch which was in front of the length corresponding to the width of the house, 20 cubits.*   [2]Heb. *120 cubits.*   3:5 [a]1 Kgs 6:17   [b]1 Kgs 6:15; Jer 22:14

used came from Parvaim. [7]He overlaid the temple's rafters, thresholds, walls and doors with gold; he carved decorative cherubim on the walls.

[8]He made the [a]Most Holy Place; its length was 30 feet, corresponding to the width of the temple, and its width 30 feet.[1] He plated it with 600 talents[2] of fine gold. [9]The gold nails weighed 50 shekels; he also plated the upper [a]areas with gold. [10a]In the Most Holy Place he made two images of cherubim and plated them with gold. [11]The combined wing span of the cherubim was 30 feet. One of the first cherub's wings was 7½ feet long and touched one wall of the temple; its other wing was also 7½ feet long and touched one of the second cherub's wings. [12]Likewise one of the second cherub's wings was 7½ feet long and touched the other wall of the temple; its other wing was also 7½ feet long and touched one of the first cherub's wings. [13]The combined wing-span of these cherubim was 30 feet. They stood upright, facing inward.[1] [14]He made the [a]curtain out of blue, purple, crimson, and white fabrics, and embroidered on it decorative cherubim.

[15]In front of the temple he made [a]two pillars which had a combined length of 52½ feet,[1] with each having a plated capital 7½ feet high. [16]He made ornamental chains and put them [a]on top of the pillars. He also made 100 pomegranate-shaped ornaments and arranged them within the chains. [17]He [a]set up the pillars in front of the temple, one on the right side and the other on the left. He named the one on the right Yakin and the one on the left Boaz.

4 He [a]made a bronze altar, 30 feet long, 30 feet wide, and 15 feet high. [2]He also made [a]the big bronze basin called "The Sea." It measured 15 feet from rim to rim, was circular in shape, and stood 7½ feet high. Its circumference was 45 feet. [3]Images of bulls were under it all the way around, ten every 18 inches all the way around. The bulls were in two rows [a]and had been cast with "The Sea." [4]"The Sea" stood on top of twelve [a]bulls. Three faced northward, three westward, three southward, and three eastward. "The Sea" was placed on top of them, and they all faced outward. [5]It was four fingers thick, and its rim was like that of a cup shaped like a lily blossom. It could hold 18,000 gallons.[1] [6]He made [a]ten washing basins; he put five on the south side and five on the north side. In them they rinsed the items used for burnt sacrifices; the [b]priests washed in "The Sea."

[7]He made ten gold [a]lampstands [b]according to specifications and put them in the temple, five on the right and five on the left. [8]He made ten tables and set [a]them in the temple, five on the right and five on the left. He also made 100 gold [b]bowls. [9]He made [a]the courtyard of the priests and the [b]large enclosure and its doors; he plated their doors with bronze. [10]He put "[a]The Sea" on the south side, in the southeast corner.

[11a]Huram Abi made the pots, shovels, and bowls. He finished all the work on God's temple he had been assigned by King Solomon. [12]He made [a]the two pillars, the two bowl-shaped tops of the pillars, the latticework for the bowl-shaped tops of the two pillars, [13]the [a]400 pomegranate-shaped ornaments for the latticework of the two pillars (each latticework had two rows of these ornaments at the bowl-shaped top of the pillar), [14]the ten[1] movable [a]stands with their ten[2] basins, [15]the big bronze basin called "The Sea" with its twelve bulls underneath, [16]and the pots, shovels, and meat forks. All the items King Solomon assigned [a]Huram Abi to make for the LORD's temple were made from polished bronze. [17]The king had them cast in earth foundries in the region of the Jordan between Sukkoth and Zarethan. [18a]Solomon made so many of these items they did not weigh the bronze.

[19a]Solomon also made these items for God's temple: the gold altar, the tables on which [b]the Bread of the Presence was kept, [20]the pure gold lampstands and their lamps which burned as specified at the entrance to the [a]inner sanctuary, [21]the pure

3:8 [a]Exod 26:33; 1 Kgs 6:16   [1]Heb. 20 cubits.   [2]About 40,380 pounds.   3:9 [a]1 Chr 28:11   3:10 [a]Exod 25:18–20; 1 Kgs 6:23–28   3:13 [1]Heb. and they were standing on their feet, with their faces to the house.   3:14 [a]Exod 26:31; Matt 27:51; Heb 9:3   3:15 [a]1 Kgs 7:15–20; Jer 52:21   [1]Syr. 18 cubits.   3:16 [a]1 Kgs 7:20   3:17 [a]1 Kgs 7:21   4:1 [a]Exod 27:1–2; 2 Kgs 16:14; Ezek 43:13, 16   4:2 [a]Exod 30:17–21; 1 Kgs 7:23–26   4:3 [a]1 Kgs 7:24–26   4:4 [a]1 Kgs 7:25   4:5 [1]Heb. 3,000 baths.   4:6 [a]1 Kgs 7:38, 40   [b]Exod 30:19–21   4:7 [a]1 Kgs 7:49   [b]Exod 25:31; 1 Chr 28:12, 19   4:8 [a]1 Kgs 7:48   [b]1 Chr 28:17   4:9 [a]1 Kgs 6:36   [b]2 Kgs 21:5   4:10 [a]1 Kgs 7:39   4:11 [a]1 Kgs 7:40–51   4:12 [a]1 Kgs 7:41   4:13 [a]1 Kgs 7:20   4:14 [a]1 Kgs 7:27, 43   [1]Heb. he made.   [2]Heb. he made.   4:16 [a]1 Kgs 7:45; 2 Chr 2:13   4:18 [a]1 Kgs 7:47   4:19 [a]1 Kgs 7:48–50   [b]Exod 25:30   4:20 [a]Exod 27:20–21

gold flower-shaped ornaments, lamps, and tongs, [22] the pure gold trimming shears, basins, pans, and censers, and the gold door sockets for the inner sanctuary (the Most Holy Place) and for the doors of the main hall of the temple.

5 [1] When Solomon had finished constructing the LORD's temple, he put the holy items that belonged to his father David (the silver, gold, and [a] all the other articles) in the treasuries of God's temple.

Solomon Moves the Ark into the Temple

[2a] Then Solomon convened Israel's elders—all the leaders of the Israelite tribes and families—in Jerusalem, so they could witness the transferal of the ark of the covenant of the LORD [b] from the City of David (that is, Zion). [3] All [a] the men of Israel assembled before the king during the festival in the seventh month. [4] When all Israel's elders had arrived, the [a] Levites lifted the ark. [5] The priests and Levites carried the ark, the tent where God appeared to his people, and all the holy items in the tent. [6] Now King Solomon and all the Israelites who had assembled with him went on ahead of the ark and sacrificed more sheep and cattle than could be counted or numbered.

[7] The priests brought the ark of the covenant of the LORD to its assigned place [a] in the inner sanctuary of the temple, in the Most Holy Place under the wings of the cherubim. [8] The cherubim's wings extended over the place where the ark sat; the cherubim overshadowed the ark and its poles. [9] The [a] poles were so long their ends extending out from the ark were visible from in front of the inner sanctuary, but they could not be seen from beyond that point. They have remained there to this very day. [10] There was nothing in the ark except the two tablets Moses had [a] placed there in Horeb. (It was there that the LORD made a covenant with the Israelites after he brought them out of the land of Egypt.)

[11] The priests left the Holy Place.[1] All the priests who participated had consecrated themselves, no matter which [a] division they represented. [12] All the Levites who were musicians, including Asaph, Heman, Jeduthun, [a] and their sons [b] and relatives, wore linen. They played cymbals and stringed instruments as they stood east of the altar. They were accompanied by 120 priests who blew trumpets. [13] The trumpeters and musicians played together, praising and giving thanks to the LORD. Accompanied by trumpets, cymbals, and other instruments, they loudly praised the LORD, singing: "Certainly he is good; certainly his loyal love endures!" Then a cloud filled the LORD's temple. [14] The priests could not carry out their duties because of the cloud; the LORD's splendor filled God's temple.

6 Then [a] Solomon said, "The LORD has said that he lives in thick [b] darkness. [2] O LORD, I [a] have built a lofty temple for you, a place where you can live permanently." [3] Then the king turned around and pronounced a blessing [a] over the whole Israelite assembly as they stood there. [4] He [a] said, "The LORD God of Israel is worthy of praise because he has fulfilled what he promised my father David. [5] He told David, 'Since the day I brought my people out of the land of Egypt, I have not chosen a city from all the tribes of Israel to build a temple in which to live. Nor did I choose a man as leader of my people Israel. [6a] But now I [b] have chosen Jerusalem as a place to live, and I have chosen David to lead my people Israel.' [7] Now my father David had a strong desire to build a temple to honor the LORD God of Israel. [8] The LORD told my father David, 'It is right for you to have a strong desire to build a temple to honor me. [9] But you will not build the temple; your very own son will build the temple for my [a] honor.' [10] The LORD has kept the promise he made. I have taken my father David's place and have [a] occupied the throne of Israel, as the LORD promised. I have built this temple for the honor of the LORD God of Israel [11] and set up [a] in it a place for the ark containing the covenant the LORD made with the Israelites."

[12] He stood before [a] the altar of the LORD in front of the entire assembly of Israel and spread out his hands. [13] Solomon had made a bronze platform and had placed it in the middle of the enclosure. It was 7½ feet long,

5:1 [a] 1 Kgs 7:51   5:2 [a] 1 Kgs 8:1–9; Ps 47:9   [b] 2 Sam 6:12   5:3 [a] 1 Kgs 8:2   5:4 [a] 1 Chr 15:2, 15   5:7 [a] 2 Chr 4:20   5:9 [a] Exod 25:13–15   5:10 [a] Exod 25:16; Deut 10:2, 5; 2 Chr 6:11; Heb 9:4   5:11 [a] 1 Chr 24:1–5   [1] Heb. *and when the priests went from the holy place.*   5:12 [a] Exod 32:26; 1 Chr 25:1–7   [b] 1 Chr 13:8; 15:16, 24   6:1 [a] Exod 19:9; 20:21; 1 Kgs 8:12–21   [b] [Lev 16:2]; Ps 97:2   6:2 [a] 2 Sam 7:13; 1 Chr 17:12; 2 Chr 7:12   6:3 [a] 2 Sam 6:18   6:4 [a] 1 Chr 17:5   6:6 [a] Deut 12:5–7; 2 Chr 12:13; Zech 2:12   [b] 1 Sam 16:7–13; 1 Chr 28:4   6:9 [a] 1 Chr 28:3–6   6:10 [a] 1 Kgs 2:12; 10:9   6:11 [a] 2 Chr 5:7–10   6:12 [a] 1 Kgs 8:22; 2 Chr 7:7–9

7½ feet wide, and 4½ feet high. He stood on it and then got down on his knees in front of the entire assembly of Israel. He spread out his hands toward the sky, [14]and prayed: "O LORD God of Israel, [a]there is no god like you in heaven or on earth! You maintain [b]covenantal loyalty to your servants who obey you with sincerity. [15]You have kept [a]your word to your servant, my father David; this very day you have fulfilled what you promised. [16]Now, [a]O LORD God of Israel, keep the promise you made to your servant, my father David, when you said, 'You will never fail to have a successor ruling before me on the throne of Israel, [b]provided that your descendants watch their step and obey my law as you have done.' [17]Now, O LORD God of Israel, may the promise you made to your servant David be realized.

[18]"God does not really live with humankind on the earth![1] Look, if the sky and the highest heaven cannot contain you, how much less this temple I have built! [19]But respond favorably to your servant's prayer and his request for help, O LORD my God. Answer the desperate prayer your servant is presenting to you. [20]Night and day may you [a]watch over this temple, the place where you promised you would live. May you answer your servant's prayer for this place. [21]Respond to the requests of your servant and your people Israel for this place. Hear from your heavenly dwelling place and respond favorably and [a]forgive.

[22]"When someone is accused of sinning against his neighbor and the latter pronounces a [a]curse on the alleged offender before your altar in this temple, [23]listen from heaven and make a just decision about your servants' claims. Condemn the guilty party, declare the other innocent, and give both of them what they [a]deserve.

[24]"If your people Israel are defeated by an [a]enemy because they sinned against you, then if they come back to you, renew their allegiance to you, and pray for your help before you in this temple, [25]then listen from heaven, forgive the sin of your people Israel, and bring them back to the land you gave to them and their ancestors.

[26]"The time will come when the [a]skies are shut up tightly and no rain falls because your people sinned against you. When they direct their prayers toward this place, renew their allegiance to you, and turn away from their sin because you punish[1] them, [27]then listen from heaven and forgive the sin of your servants, your people Israel. Certainly you will then teach them the right way to live and send rain on your land that you have given your people to possess.

[28]"The time will come when the land suffers from a famine, a plague, blight, and [a]disease, or a locust invasion, or when their enemy lays siege to the cities of the land, or when some other type of plague or [b]epidemic occurs. [29]When all your people Israel pray and ask for help, as they acknowledge their intense pain and spread out their hands toward this temple, [30]then listen from your heavenly dwelling place, forgive their sin, and act favorably toward each one based on your [a]evaluation of their [b]motives.[1] (Indeed you are the only one who can correctly evaluate the motives of all people.) [31]Then they will honor you by obeying you throughout their lifetimes as they live on the land you gave to our ancestors.

[32]"Foreigners [a]who do not belong to your people Israel will come from a distant land because of your great reputation and your ability to accomplish mighty deeds; they will come and direct their prayers toward this temple. [33]Then listen from your heavenly dwelling place and answer all the prayers of the foreigners. Then all the nations of the earth will acknowledge your reputation, obey you as your people Israel do, and recognize that this temple I built belongs to you.

[34]"When you direct your people to march out and fight their enemies, and they direct their prayers to you toward this chosen city and this temple I built for your honor, [35]then listen from heaven to their prayers for help and vindicate them.

[36]"The time will come when your people will sin against you (for there is [a]no one who is sinless!) and you will be angry at them and deliver them over to their enemies,

6:14 [a] [Exod 15:11; Deut 4:39]   [b] [Deut 7:9]   6:15 [a] 1 Chr 22:9–10   6:16 [a] 2 Sam 7:12, 16; 1 Kgs 2:4; 6:12; 2 Chr 7:18   [b] Ps 132:12
6:18 [1] Heb. *Indeed, can God really live with mankind on the earth?*; a rhetorical question expecting a negative answer.
6:20 [a] 2 Chr 7:15   6:21 [a] [Isa 43:25; 44:22; Mic 7:18]   6:22 [a] Exod 22:8–11   6:23 [a] [Job 34:11]   6:24 [a] 2 Kgs 21:14–15
6:26 [a] Deut 28:23–24; 1 Kgs 17:1   [1] Heb. *because you answer them.*   6:28 [a] 2 Chr 20:9   [b] [Mic 6:13]   6:30 [a] [1 Chr 28:9;
Prov 21:2; 24:12]   [b] [1 Sam 16:7]   [1] Heb. *and give to each one according to all his ways because you know his heart.*
6:32 [a] John 12:20; Acts 8:27   6:36 [a] Prov 20:9; Eccl 7:20; [Rom 3:9, 19; 5:12; Gal 3:10]; Jas 3:2; 1 John 1:8

who will [b]take them as prisoners to their land, whether far away or close by. [37]When your people come to their senses[1] in the land where they are held prisoner, they will repent and beg for your mercy in the land of their imprisonment, admitting, 'We have sinned and gone astray, we have done evil!' [38]When they return to you with all their heart and being in the land where they are held prisoner and direct their prayers toward the land you gave to their ancestors, your chosen [a]city, and the temple I built for your honor, [39]then listen from your heavenly dwelling place to their prayers for help, vindicate them, and forgive your sinful people.

[40]"Now, my God, may you be [a]attentive and responsive to the prayers offered in this place. [41]Now ascend, [a]O LORD God, to your resting [b]place, you and the ark of your strength! May your priests, O LORD God, experience your deliverance. May your loyal followers [c]rejoice in the prosperity you give. [42]O LORD God, do not reject your chosen ones![1] [a]Remember the faithful promises you made to your servant David!"

Solomon Dedicates the Temple

7 When [a]Solomon finished praying, [b]fire came down from heaven and consumed [c]the burnt offering and the sacrifices, and the LORD's splendor filled the temple. [2a]The priests were unable to enter the LORD's temple because the LORD's splendor filled the LORD's temple. [3]When all the Israelites saw the fire come down and the LORD's splendor over the temple, they got on their knees with their faces downward toward the pavement. They worshiped and gave thanks to the LORD, saying, "Certainly he is good; certainly his loyal love endures!"

[4]The king and all [a]the people were presenting sacrifices to the LORD. [5]King Solomon sacrificed 22,000 cattle and 120,000 sheep. Then the king and all the people dedicated God's temple. [6]The priests stood in their assigned spots, along with the Levites who had the musical instruments used for praising the LORD. (These were the ones King David made for giving thanks to the LORD [a]and which were used by David when [b]he offered praise, saying, "Certainly his loyal love endures.") Opposite the Levites, the priests were blowing the trumpets, while all Israel stood there. [7a]Solomon consecrated the middle of the courtyard that is in front of the LORD's temple. He offered burnt sacrifices, grain offerings,[1] and the fat from the peace offerings there because the bronze altar that Solomon had made was too small to hold all these offerings.[2] [8]At [a]that time Solomon and all Israel with him celebrated a festival for seven days. This great assembly included people [b]from Lebo Hamath in [c]the north to the Stream of Egypt in the south. [9]On the eighth day they held an assembly, for they had dedicated the altar for seven days and celebrated the festival for seven more days. [10]On the twenty-third day of the seventh [a]month, Solomon sent the people home. They left happy and contented because of the good the LORD had done for David, Solomon, and his people Israel.

The Lord Gives Solomon a Promise and a Warning

[11]After [a]Solomon finished building the LORD's temple and the royal palace and accomplished all his plans for the LORD's temple and his royal palace, [12]the LORD [a]appeared to Solomon at night [b]and said to him: "I have answered your prayer and chosen this [c]place to be my temple where sacrifices are to be made. [13a]When[1] I close up the sky so that it doesn't rain, or command locusts to devour the land's vegetation, or send a plague among my people, [14]if my people, who [a]belong to me, [b]humble themselves, pray, seek to please me,[1] and repudiate their sinful practices, [c]then I will respond from heaven, forgive their sin, and heal their land. [15]Now I will be attentive and responsive to the prayers offered in this place. [16]Now [a]I have chosen and consecrated this temple by making it my permanent home; I will be constantly present there.

6:36 [b] Deut 28:63–68   **6:37** [1] Or *stop and reflect*; Heb. *bring back to their heart.*   **6:38** [a] Dan 6:10   **6:40** [a] 2 Chr 6:20
6:41 [a] Ps 132:8–10, 16   [b] 1 Chr 28:2   [c] Neh 9:25   **6:42** [a] 2 Sam 7:15; Ps 89:49; 132:1, 8–10; Isa 55:3   [1] Heb. *do not turn away the face of your anointed ones.*   **7:1** [1] 1 Kgs 8:54   [b] Lev 9:24; Judg 6:21; 1 Kgs 18:38; 1 Chr 21:26   [c] 1 Kgs 8:10–11   **7:2** [a] 2 Chr 5:14   **7:4** [a] 1 Kgs 8:62–63   **7:6** [a] 1 Chr 15:16   [b] 2 Chr 5:12   **7:7** [a] 1 Kgs 8:64–66; 9:3   [1] Heb. omits *grain offerings.*   [2] Heb. *hold the burnt sacrifice, the grain offering, and the fat portions.*   **7:8** [a] 1 Kgs 8:65   [b] 1 Kgs 4:21, 24; 2 Kgs 14:25   [c] Josh 13:3   **7:10** [a] 1 Kgs 8:66   **7:11** [a] 1 Kgs 9:1   **7:12** [a] 1 Kgs 3:5; 11:9   [b] Deut 12:5, 11   [c] 2 Chr 6:20   **7:13** [a] Deut 28:23–24; 1 Kgs 17:1; 2 Chr 6:26–28   [1] Or *if.*   **7:14** [a] Deut 28:10; [Isa 43:7]   [b] 2 Chr 12:6–7; [Jas 4:10]   [c] 2 Chr 6:27, 30   [1] Heb. *seek my face.*   **7:16** [a] 1 Kgs 9:3; 2 Chr 6:6

[17]You must serve me [a]as your father David did. Do everything I commanded and obey my rules and regulations. [18]Then I will establish [a]your dynasty, just as I promised your father David, 'You will not fail to have a successor ruling over Israel.'

[19][a]But if you people ever turn away from me, fail to obey the regulations and rules I instructed you to keep, and decide to serve and worship other gods, [20][a]then I will remove you from my land I have given you, I will abandon this temple I have consecrated with my presence, and I will make you an object [b]of mockery and ridicule among all the nations. [21]As for [a]this temple, which was once majestic, everyone who passes by it will be [b]shocked and say, '[c]Why did the LORD do this to this land and this temple?' [22]Others will then answer, 'Because they abandoned the LORD God of their ancestors, who led them out of Egypt. They embraced other gods whom they worshiped and served. That is why he brought all this disaster down on them.'"

Building Projects and Commercial Efforts

8 After [a]twenty years, during which Solomon built the LORD's temple and his royal palace, [2]Solomon rebuilt the cities that Huram had given him and settled Israelites there. [3]Solomon went to Hamath Zobah and seized it. [4]He built up Tadmor in [a]the wilderness and all the storage cities he had built in [b]Hamath. [5]He made upper Beth Horon and [a]lower Beth Horon fortified cities with walls and barred gates, [6]and built up Baalath, all the storage cities that belonged to him, and all the cities where chariots and horses were kept. He built whatever he [a]wanted in Jerusalem, Lebanon, and throughout his entire kingdom.

[7][a]Now several non-Israelite peoples were left in the land after the conquest of Joshua, including the Hittites, Amorites, Perizzites, Hivites, and Jebusites. [8]Their descendants remained in the land (the Israelites were unable to wipe them out). Solomon conscripted them for his work crews, and they continue in that role to this very day. [9]Solomon did not assign Israelites to these work crews; the Israelites served as his soldiers, officers, charioteers, and commanders of his chariot forces. [10]These men worked for King Solomon as supervisors; there were a total of 250 of them who were in charge of the people.

[11]Solomon [a]moved Pharaoh's daughter up from the City of David to the palace he had built for her, for he said, "My wife must not live in the palace of King David of Israel, for the places where the ark of the LORD has entered are holy."

[12]Then Solomon offered burnt sacrifices to the LORD on the altar of the LORD which he had built in front of the temple's porch. [13]He observed the [a]daily requirements for sacrifices that Moses had specified for Sabbaths, new moon festivals, and the [b]three annual [c]celebrations—the Feast of Unleavened Bread, the Feast of Weeks, and the Feast of Shelters.[1] [14]As his father David had decreed, Solomon appointed the [a]divisions of [b]the priests to do their assigned tasks, the Levitical orders to lead worship and help the priests with their daily tasks, and the divisions of the [c]gatekeepers to serve at their assigned gates. This was what David the man of God had ordered. [15]They did not neglect any detail of the king's orders pertaining to the priests, Levites, and [a]treasuries.

[16]All the work ordered by Solomon was completed, from the day the foundation of the LORD's temple was laid until it was finished; the LORD's temple was completed.

[17]Then Solomon went to Ezion [a]Geber and to Elat on the coast in the land of Edom. [18]Huram sent him ships [a]and some of his sailors, men who were well acquainted with the sea. They sailed with Solomon's men to [b]Ophir and took from there 450 talents[1] of gold, which they brought back to King Solomon.

Solomon Entertains a Queen

9 When the queen of Sheba heard about Solomon, she came to challenge him with difficult questions. She arrived in Jerusalem with a great display of pomp,[1] bringing with her camels carrying spices,

7:17 [a]1 Kgs 9:4   **7:18** [a]2 Sam 7:12–16; 1 Kgs 2:4; 2 Chr 6:16   **7:19** [a]Lev 26:14, 33; [Deut 28:15, 36]   **7:20** [a]Deut 28:63–68; 2 Kgs 25:1–7   [b]Ps 44:14   **7:21** [a]2 Kgs 25:9   [b]2 Chr 29:8   [c][Deut 29:24–25; Jer 22:8–9]   **8:1** [a]1 Kgs 6:38–7:1   **8:4** [a]1 Kgs 9:17–18   [b]1 Chr 18:3, 9   **8:5** [a]1 Chr 7:24   **8:6** [a]2 Chr 7:11   **8:7** [a]Gen 15:18–21; 1 Kgs 9:20   **8:11** [a]1 Kgs 3:1; 7:8; 9:24; 11:1   **8:13** [a]Exod 29:38–42; Num 28:3, 9, 11, 26; 29:1   [b]Exod 23:14–17; 34:22–23; Deut 16:16   [c]Lev 23:1–44   [1]Trad. *the Feast of Tabernacles.*   **8:14** [a]1 Chr 24:3   [b]1 Chr 25:1   [c]1 Chr 9:17; 26:1   **8:15** [a]1 Chr 26:20–28   **8:17** [a]1 Kgs 9:26; 2 Chr 20:36   **8:18** [a]1 Kgs 9:27; 2 Chr 9:10, 13   [b]1 Chr 29:4   [1]About 30,285 pounds.   **9:1** [1]Heb. *with very great strength.*

a very large quantity of gold, and precious gems. She visited Solomon and discussed with him everything that was on her mind. [2]Solomon answered all her questions; there was no question too complex for the king. [3]When the queen of Sheba saw for herself Solomon's wisdom, the palace he had built, [4]the food in his banquet hall, his servants and attendants in their robes, his [a]cupbearers in their robes, and his burnt sacrifices which he presented in the LORD's temple,[1] she was amazed. [5]She said to the king, "The report I heard in my own country about your wise sayings and insight was true! [6]I did not believe these things until I came and saw them with my own eyes. Indeed, I didn't hear even half the story! Your wisdom surpasses what was reported to me. [7]Your attendants, who stand before you at all times and hear your wise sayings, are truly happy! [8]May the LORD your God be praised because he favored[1] you by placing you on his throne as the one ruling on his behalf. Because of your God's [a]love for Israel and his lasting commitment to them, he made you king over them so you could make just and right decisions." [9]She gave the king 120 talents[1] of gold and a very large quantity of spices and precious gems. The quantity of spices the queen of Sheba gave King Solomon has never been matched. [10](Huram's servants, aided by Solomon's servants, brought gold from Ophir, as well as fine timber and precious gems. [11]With the timber the king made steps for the LORD's temple and royal palace as well as stringed instruments for the musicians. No one had seen anything like them in the land of Judah before that.) [12]King Solomon gave the queen of Sheba everything she requested, more than what she had brought him. Then she left and returned to her homeland with her attendants.

Solomon's Wealth

[13a]Solomon received 666 talents[1] of gold per year, [14]besides what he collected from the merchants and traders. All the Arabian kings and the governors of the land also brought gold and silver to Solomon. [15]King Solomon made 200 large shields of hammered gold; 600 measures of hammered gold were used for each shield. [16]He also made 300 small shields of hammered gold; 300 measures of gold were used for each of those shields. The king placed them in the [a]Palace of the Lebanon Forest.

[17]The king made a large throne decorated with ivory and overlaid it with pure gold. [18]There were six steps leading up to the throne, and a gold footstool was attached to the throne. The throne had two armrests with a statue of a lion standing on each side. [19]There were twelve statues of lions on the six steps, one lion at each end of each step. There was nothing like it in any other kingdom.

[20]All of King Solomon's cups were made of gold, and all the household items in the Palace of the Lebanon Forest were made of pure gold. There were no silver items, for silver was not considered very valuable in Solomon's time. [21]The king had a fleet of large [a]merchant ships[1] manned by Huram's men that sailed the sea. Once every three years the fleet came into port with cargoes of gold, silver, ivory, apes, and peacocks.[2] [22]King Solomon was wealthier and wiser than any of the kings of the earth. [23]All the kings of the earth wanted to visit Solomon to see him display his God-given wisdom. [24]Year after year visitors brought their gifts, which included items of silver, items of gold, clothes, [a]perfume, spices, horses, and mules.

[25]Solomon [a]had 4,000 stalls for his chariot horses and 12,000 horses. He kept them in assigned cities and also with him in Jerusalem. [26a]He ruled all the kingdoms [b]from the Euphrates River to the land of the Philistines as far as the border of Egypt. [27]The king made silver as plentiful in Jerusalem as stones; cedar was as plentiful as sycamore fig trees are in [a]the foothills. [28]Solomon acquired horses from Egypt [a]and from all the lands.

Solomon's Reign Ends

[29a]The rest of the events of Solomon's reign, from start to finish, are recorded in the Annals of Nathan the Prophet, the

---

9:4 [a] Neh 1:11   [1] Heb. *and his upper room* [by] *which he was going up to the house of the LORD.*   9:8 [a] Deut 7:8; 2 Chr 2:11; [Ps 44:3]   [1] Or *delighted in.*   9:9 [1] About 8,076 pounds.   9:13 [a] 1 Kgs 10:14–29   [1] About 44,822 pounds.   9:16 [a] 1 Kgs 7:2   9:21 [a] 2 Chr 20:36–37; Ps 72:10   [1] Heb. *for ships belonging to the king were going* [to] *Tarshish;* large ships either made in or capable of traveling to the distant western port of Tarshish.   [2] Or perhaps *baboons, monkeys.*   9:24 [a] 1 Kgs 20:11   9:25 [a] Deut 17:16; 1 Kgs 4:26; 10:26; 2 Chr 1:14; Isa 2:7   9:26 [a] 1 Kgs 4:21   [b] Gen 15:18; Ps 72:8   9:27 [a] 1 Kgs 10:27   9:28 [a] 1 Kgs 10:28; 2 Chr 1:16   9:29 [a] 1 Kgs 11:41

Prophecy of [b]Ahijah the Shilonite, and the Vision of [c]Iddo the Seer pertaining to Jeroboam son of Nebat. [30a]Solomon ruled over all Israel from Jerusalem for forty years. [31]Then Solomon passed away and was buried in the city of his father David. His son Rehoboam replaced him as king.

The Northern Tribes Rebel

10 [a]Rehoboam traveled to Shechem, for all Israel had gathered in Shechem to make Rehoboam king. [2]When Jeroboam son of Nebat heard the news, [a]he was still in Egypt, where he had fled from King Solomon. Jeroboam returned from Egypt. [3]They sent for him, and Jeroboam and all Israel came and spoke to Rehoboam, saying, [4]"Your father made us work too hard! Now if you lighten the demands he made and don't make us work as hard, we will serve you." [5]He said to them, "Go away for three days, then return to me." So the people went away.

[6]King Rehoboam consulted with the older advisers who had served his father Solomon when he had been alive. He asked them, "How do you advise me to answer these people?" [7]They said to him, "If you are fair to these people, grant their request, and are cordial to them, they will be your servants from this time forward." [8a]But Rehoboam rejected their advice and consulted the young advisers who served him, with whom he had grown up. [9]He asked them, "How do you advise me to respond to these people who said to me, 'Lessen the demands your father placed on us'?" [10]The young advisers with whom Rehoboam had grown up said to him, "Say this to these people who have said to you, 'Your father made us work hard, but now lighten our burden'—say this to them: 'I am a lot harsher than my father![1] [11]My father imposed heavy demands on you; I will make them even heavier. My father punished you with ordinary whips; I will punish you with whips that really sting your flesh.'"[1]

[12a]Jeroboam and all the people reported to Rehoboam on the third day, just as the king had ordered when he said, "Return to me on the third day." [13]The king responded to the people harshly. He rejected the advice of the older men [14]and followed the advice of the younger ones. He said, "My father imposed heavy demands on you;[1] I will make them even heavier. My father punished you with ordinary whips; I will punish you with whips that really sting your flesh." [15]The king refused to listen to the people, because God was instigating this turn of events so that he might bring to pass the prophetic [a]announcement he had made through Ahijah the Shilonite to Jeroboam son of Nebat.

[16]When all Israel saw[1] that the king refused to listen to them, the people answered the king, "We have no portion in David—no share in the son of Jesse! Return to your homes, O Israel! Now, look after your own dynasty, O David!" So all Israel returned to their homes. [17](Rehoboam continued to rule over the Israelites who lived in the cities of Judah.) [18]King Rehoboam sent Hadoram, the supervisor of the work crews, out after them, but the Israelites stoned him to death. King Rehoboam managed to jump into his chariot and escape to Jerusalem. [19a]So Israel has been in rebellion against the Davidic dynasty to this very day.

11 When Rehoboam arrived in Jerusalem, [a]he summoned 180,000 skilled warriors from Judah and Benjamin to attack Israel and restore the kingdom to Rehoboam. [2]But the LORD's message came [a]to the prophet Shemaiah, [3]"Say this to King Rehoboam son of Solomon of Judah and to all the Israelites in Judah and Benjamin, [4]'The LORD says this: "Do not attack and make war with your brothers. Each of you go home, for I have caused this to happen."'" They obeyed the LORD and called off the attack against Jeroboam.

Rehoboam's Reign

[5]Rehoboam lived in Jerusalem; he built up these fortified cities throughout Judah: [6]Bethlehem, Etam, Tekoa, [7]Beth Zur, Soco, Adullam, [8]Gath, Mareshah, Ziph, [9]Adoraim, Lachish, Azekah, [10]Zorah, Aijalon, and Hebron. These were the fortified cities in Judah and Benjamin. [11]He fortified these cities and placed officers in them, as well

as storehouses of food, olive oil, and wine. [12]In each city there were shields and spears; he strongly fortified them. Judah and Benjamin belonged to him.

[13]The priests and Levites who lived throughout Israel supported him, no matter where they resided. [14]The Levites even left [a]their pasturelands and their property behind and came to Judah and Jerusalem, for [b]Jeroboam and his sons prohibited them from serving as the LORD's priests. [15]Jeroboam appointed his own priests to serve at [a]the worship centers[1] and to lead in [b]the worship of [c]the goat idols and calf idols he had made. [16][a]Those among all the Israelite tribes who were determined to worship the LORD God of Israel [b]followed them to Jerusalem to sacrifice to the LORD God of their ancestors. [17]They [a]supported[1] the kingdom of Judah and were loyal to[2] Rehoboam son of Solomon for three years; they followed the edicts of David and Solomon for three years.

[18]Rehoboam married Mahalath the daughter of David's son Jerimoth and of Abihail, the daughter of Jesse's son [a]Eliab. [19]She bore him sons named Jeush, Shemariah, and Zaham. [20]He later married [a]Maacah the daughter of [b]Absalom. She bore to him [c]Abijah, Attai, Ziza, and Shelomith. [21]Rehoboam loved Maacah daughter of Absalom more than his other [a]wives and concubines. He had eighteen wives and sixty concubines; he fathered twenty-eight sons and sixty daughters.

[22]Rehoboam [a]appointed [b]Abijah son of Maacah as the leader over his brothers, for he intended to name him his successor. [23]He wisely placed some of his many sons throughout the regions of Judah and Benjamin in the various [a]fortified cities. He supplied them with abundant provisions and acquired many wives for them.

12 After Rehoboam's rule was [a]established and solidified, he and all Israel rejected the law of the LORD. [2][a]Because they were unfaithful to the LORD, in King Rehoboam's fifth year, King Shishak of Egypt attacked Jerusalem. [3]He had 1,200 chariots, 60,000 horsemen, and an innumerable number of soldiers who accompanied him from Egypt, including Libyans, Sukkites, and Cushites. [4]He captured the fortified cities of Judah and marched against Jerusalem.

[5][a]Shemaiah the prophet visited Rehoboam and the leaders of Judah who were assembled in Jerusalem because of Shishak. He said to them, "This is what the LORD says: 'You have rejected me, so I have rejected you and will hand you over to Shishak.'" [6]The leaders of Israel and the king [a]humbled [b]themselves and said, "The LORD is just."[1] [7]When [a]the LORD saw that they humbled themselves, the LORD's message came to Shemaiah: "They have humbled themselves, so I will not destroy them. I will deliver them soon. My anger will not be unleashed against Jerusalem through Shishak. [8]Yet [a]they will become his subjects, so they can experience how serving me differs from serving the surrounding nations."

[9]King Shishak of Egypt attacked Jerusalem and took away the treasures of the LORD's temple and of the royal palace; he took everything, including the gold shields that [a]Solomon had [b]made. [10]King Rehoboam made bronze shields [a]to replace them and assigned them to the officers of the royal guard who protected the entrance to the royal palace. [11]Whenever the king visited the LORD's temple, the royal guards carried them and then brought them back to the guardroom.

[12]So when Rehoboam humbled himself, the LORD relented from his anger and did not annihilate him; Judah experienced some good things. [13]King [a]Rehoboam solidified his rule in Jerusalem; [b]he was forty-one years old when he became king, and he ruled for seventeen years in Jerusalem, the city the LORD chose from all the tribes of Israel to be his home. Rehoboam's mother was an [c]Ammonite named Naamah. [14]He did evil because he was not determined to follow the LORD.

[15]The events of Rehoboam's reign, from start to finish, are recorded in the Annals of Shemaiah the Prophet [a]and of Iddo the Seer that include genealogical records.

11:14 [a]Num 35:2–5　[b]1 Kgs 12:28–33; 2 Chr 13:9　**11:15** [a]1 Kgs 12:31; 13:33; 14:9; [Hos 13:2]　[b][Lev 17:7; 1 Cor 10:20]　[c]1 Kgs 12:28　[1]Heb. *for the high places.*　**11:16** [a]2 Chr 14:7　[b]2 Chr 15:9–10; 30:11, 18　**11:17** [a]2 Chr 12:1, 13　[1]Or *strengthened.*　[2]Or *strengthened.*　**11:18** [a]1 Sam 16:6　**11:20** [a]2 Chr 13:2　[b]1 Kgs 15:2　[c]1 Kgs 14:31　**11:21** [a]Deut 17:17　**11:22** [a]Deut 21:15–17　[b]2 Chr 13:1　**11:23** [a]2 Chr 11:5　**12:1** [a]1 Kgs 14:22–24　**12:2** [a]1 Kgs 11:40; 14:25　**12:5** [a]2 Chr 11:2　**12:6** [a][Jas 4:10]　[b]Exod 9:27; [Dan 9:14]　[1]Or *fair.*　**12:7** [a]1 Kgs 21:28–29　**12:8** [a]Isa 26:13　**12:9** [a]1 Kgs 14:25–26　[b]1 Kgs 10:16–17; 2 Chr 9:15–16　**12:10** [a]1 Kgs 14:27　**12:13** [a]1 Kgs 14:21　[b]2 Chr 6:6　[c]1 Kgs 11:1, 5　**12:15** [a]2 Chr 9:29; 13:22

There were wars between Rehoboam [b]and Jeroboam continually. [16]Then Rehoboam passed away and was buried in the City of David. His son [a]Abijah replaced him as king.

Abijah's Reign

13 In [a]the eighteenth year of the reign of King Jeroboam, Abijah became king over [b]Judah. [2]He ruled for three years in Jerusalem. His mother was Michaiah, the daughter of Uriel from Gibeah.

There was war between Abijah and Jeroboam. [3]Abijah launched the attack with 400,000 well-trained warriors, while Jeroboam deployed against him 800,000 well-trained warriors.

[4]Abijah ascended Mount [a]Zemaraim, in the Ephraimite hill country, and said: "Listen to me, Jeroboam and all Israel! [5]Don't you realize that the Lord God of Israel has [a]given David and his dynasty lasting dominion over Israel [b]by a formal covenant? [6]Jeroboam son of Nebat, a servant of Solomon son of David, rose up and [a]rebelled against his master. [7][a]Lawless good-for-nothing men gathered around him and conspired against Rehoboam son of Solomon, when Rehoboam was an inexperienced young [b]man and could not resist them. [8]Now you are declaring that you will resist the Lord's rule through the Davidic dynasty. You have a huge army[1] and bring with you the gold calves that Jeroboam [a]made for you as gods. [9]But you banished[1] the Lord's priests, Aaron's descendants, and the Levites, and appointed your own priests just as the surrounding nations do! Anyone who comes to consecrate himself with [a]a young bull or seven rams becomes a priest of these fake gods! [10]But as for us, the Lord is our [a]God and we have not rejected him. Aaron's descendants serve as the Lord's priests, and the Levites assist them with the work. [11]They offer burnt sacrifices to the Lord every morning [a]and every evening, along with fragrant incense. They arrange the [b]Bread of the Presence on a ritually clean table and light the lamps on the gold lampstand every evening. Certainly we are observing the Lord our God's regulations, but you have rejected him. [12]Now look, God is with us as our [a]leader. His priests are ready to blow the trumpets to signal the attack against you. You Israelites, don't fight against the Lord God of your ancestors, for you will not win!"

[13]Now Jeroboam had sent some men to ambush the Judahite army from behind. The main army was in front of the Judahite army; the ambushers were behind it. [14]The men of Judah turned around and realized they were being attacked from the front and the rear. So they cried [a]out to the Lord for help. The priests blew their trumpets, [15]and the men of Judah gave the battle cry. As the men of Judah gave the battle cry, God struck [a]down Jeroboam and all Israel before Abijah and Judah. [16]The Israelites fled from before the Judahite army, and God handed them over to the men of Judah. [17]Abijah and his army thoroughly defeated them; 500,000 well-trained Israelite men fell dead. [18]That day the Israelites were defeated; the men of Judah prevailed [a]because they relied on the Lord God of their ancestors.

[19]Abijah chased Jeroboam; he seized from him these cities: Bethel and its surrounding towns, Jeshanah and its surrounding towns, and [a]Ephron and its surrounding towns. [20]Jeroboam did not regain power during the reign of Abijah. The Lord [a]struck him down and [b]he died. [21]Abijah's power grew; he had fourteen wives and fathered twenty-two sons and sixteen daughters.

[22]The rest of [a]the events of Abijah's reign, including his deeds and sayings, are recorded in the writings of the prophet Iddo.

14 Abijah passed away and was buried in the City of David. His son [a]Asa replaced him as king. During his reign the land had rest for ten years.

Asa's Religious and Military Accomplishments

[2]Asa did what the Lord his God desired and approved. [3]He removed [a]the pagan altars [b]and the high places, smashed the sacred pillars, and cut down the Asherah poles.

12:15 [b]1 Kgs 14:30   **12:16** [a]2 Chr 11:20–22   **13:1** [a]1 Kgs 15:1   [b]1 Kgs 12:17   **13:4** [a]Josh 18:22   **13:5** [a]2 Sam 7:8–16   [b]Lev 2:13; Num 18:19   **13:6** [a]1 Kgs 11:28; 12:20   **13:7** [a]Judg 9:4   [b]2 Chr 12:13   **13:8** [a]1 Kgs 12:28; 14:9; 2 Chr 11:15; [Hos 8:4–6]   [1]Or *horde, multitude*.   **13:9** [a]2 Chr 11:13–15   [1]Heb. *Did you not banish?*; a rhetorical question expecting a positive answer.   **13:10** [a]Josh 24:15   **13:11** [a]Exod 29:38; 2 Chr 2:4   [b]Exod 25:30; Lev 24:5–9   **13:12** [a]Josh 5:13–15; [Heb 2:10]   **13:14** [a]Josh 24:7; 2 Chr 6:34–35; 14:11   **13:15** [a]1 Kgs 14:14; 2 Chr 14:12   **13:18** [a]1 Chr 5:20; 2 Chr 14:11; [Ps 22:5]   **13:19** [a]Josh 15:9   **13:20** [a]1 Sam 2:6; 25:38; Acts 12:23   [b]1 Kgs 14:20   **13:22** [a]2 Chr 9:29   **14:1** [a]1 Kgs 15:8   **14:3** [a]1 Kgs 15:14; 2 Chr 15:17   [b]1 Kgs 11:7

⁴He ordered Judah to ªseek the LORD God of their ancestors and to observe his law and commands. ⁵He removed the high places and the incense altars from all the towns of Judah. The kingdom had rest under his rule.

⁶He built fortified cities throughout Judah, for the land was at rest and there was no war during those years; the LORD ªgave him peace. ⁷He said to the people of Judah: "Let's build these cities and fortify them with walls, towers, and barred gates. The land remains ours because we have followed the LORD our God; we have followed him, and he has made us secure on all sides." So they built the cities and prospered.

⁸Asa had an army of 300,000 men from Judah, equipped with large shields and spears. He also had 280,000 men from Benjamin who carried small shields and were adept ªarchers; they were all ᵇskilled warriors. ⁹Zerah ªthe Cushite marched against them with an army of a million men and 300 chariots. He arrived at ᵇMareshah, ¹⁰and Asa went out to oppose him. They deployed for battle in the Valley of Zephathah near Mareshah.

¹¹Asa ªprayed to the LORD his God: "O LORD, there is ᵇno one but you who can help the weak when they are vastly outnumbered. Help us, O LORD our God, for we rely on you and have marched on your behalf ᶜagainst this huge army. O LORD, you are our God; don't let men prevail against you!" ¹²The LORD struck ªdown the Cushites before Asa and Judah. The Cushites fled, ¹³and Asa and his army chased them as far as ªGerar. The Cushites were wiped out; they were shattered before the LORD and his army. The men of Judah carried off a huge amount of plunder. ¹⁴They defeated all ªthe towns surrounding Gerar, for the LORD caused them to panic. The men of Judah looted all the towns, for they contained a huge amount of goods. ¹⁵They also attacked the tents of the herdsmen in charge of the livestock. They carried off many sheep and camels and then returned to Jerusalem.

15 God's Spirit came upon Azariah son of Oded. ²He met Asa and told him, "Listen to me, Asa and all Judah and Benjamin!

ªThe LORD is with you when you are loyal to him. ᵇIf you seek him, he will respond to you, but ᶜif you reject him, he will reject you. ³For a long time Israel had not sought the one true God, ªor a priest to ᵇinstruct them, or the ᶜlaw. ⁴Because of their distress, they turned back to the LORD God of Israel. They sought him, and ªhe responded to them. ⁵In those days no one could travel safely, for total chaos had overtaken all the people of the surrounding lands. ⁶ªOne nation was crushed by another, and one city by another, for God caused them to be in great turmoil. ⁷But as for you, be strong and don't get discouraged, for your work will be rewarded."

⁸When Asa heard these words and the prophecy of Oded the prophet, he was encouraged. He removed the detestable idols from the entire land of Judah and Benjamin and from the cities he had seized in the Ephraimite hill country. He repaired the altar of the LORD in front of the porch of the LORD's temple.

⁹He assembled all Judah and Benjamin, as well as the settlers¹ from Ephraim, Manasseh, and Simeon who had come to live with them. Many people from Israel had come there to live when they saw that the LORD his God was with him. ¹⁰They assembled in Jerusalem in the third month of the fifteenth year of Asa's reign. ¹¹At that time they sacrificed to the LORD some of the plunder they had brought back, including 700 head of cattle ªand 7,000 sheep. ¹²They solemnly ªagreed to seek the LORD God of their ancestors with their whole heart and being. ¹³ªAnyone who would not seek the LORD God of Israel would be executed, whether they were young or old, male or female. ¹⁴They swore their allegiance to the LORD, shouting their approval loudly and sounding trumpets and horns. ¹⁵All Judah was happy about the oath because they made the vow with their whole heart. They willingly ªsought the LORD and he responded to them. He ᵇmade them secure on every side.

¹⁶King Asa also removed ªMaacah his grandmother¹ from her position as queen mother because she had made a loathsome Asherah pole. Asa cut down her loathsome

14:4 ª [2 Chr 7:14]   **14:6** ª 2 Chr 15:15   **14:8** ª 1 Chr 12:2   ᵇ 2 Chr 13:3   **14:9** ª 2 Chr 12:2–3; 16:8   ᵇ Josh 15:44   **14:11** ª Exod 14:10; 2 Chr 13:14; [Ps 22:5]   ᵇ [1 Sam 14:6]   ᶜ 1 Sam 17:45; [Prov 18:10]   **14:12** ª 2 Chr 13:15   **14:13** ª Gen 10:19; 20:1   **14:14** ª Gen 35:5; Deut 11:25; Josh 2:9; 2 Chr 17:10   **15:2** ª [Jas 4:8]   ᵇ [1 Chr 28:9]; 2 Chr 14:4; 33:12–13; [Jer 29:13; Matt 7:7]   ᶜ 2 Chr 24:20   **15:3** ª Hos 3:4   ᵇ 2 Kgs 12:2   ᶜ Lev 10:11; 2 Chr 17:8–9   **15:4** ª [Deut 4:29]   **15:6** ª Matt 24:7   **15:9** ¹ Or *foreign residents.*   **15:11** ª 2 Chr 14:13–15   **15:12** ª 2 Kgs 23:3; 2 Chr 23:16; 34:31; Neh 10:29   **15:13** ª Exod 22:20   **15:15** ª 2 Chr 15:2   ᵇ 2 Chr 14:7   **15:16** ª 1 Kgs 15:2, 10, 13   ¹ Heb. *mother,* often used for grandparents or remote ancestors.

pole and crushed and burned it in the Kidron Valley. [17]The high places were not eliminated from Israel, yet Asa was wholeheartedly devoted to [a]the LORD throughout his lifetime. [18]He brought the holy items that his father and he had made into God's temple, including the silver, gold, and other articles.

Asa's Failures

[19]There was no more war until the thirty-fifth year of Asa's reign. **16** [1]In the thirty-sixth year of Asa's reign, King [a]Baasha of Israel attacked Judah, and he established Ramah as [b]a military outpost to prevent anyone from leaving or entering the land of King Asa of Judah. [2]Asa took all the silver and gold that was left in the treasuries of the LORD's temple and of the royal palace and sent it to King Ben Hadad of Syria, ruler in Damascus, along with this message: [3]"I want to make a treaty with you, like the one our fathers made. See, I have sent you silver and gold. Break your treaty with King Baasha of Israel, so he will retreat from my land." [4]Ben Hadad accepted King Asa's offer and ordered his army commanders to attack the cities of Israel. They conquered Ijon, Dan, Abel Maim, and all the storage cities of Naphtali. [5]When Baasha heard the news, he stopped fortifying Ramah and abandoned the project. [6]King Asa ordered all the men of Judah to carry away the stones and wood that Baasha had used to build Ramah. He used the materials to build up Geba and Mizpah.

[7]At that time [a]Hanani the prophet[1] visited King Asa of Judah and said to him: "[b]Because you relied on the king of Syria and did not rely on the LORD your God, the army of the king of Syria has escaped from your hand. [8]Did not [a]the Cushites and Libyans have a huge army with chariots and a very large number of horsemen? But when you relied on [b]the LORD, he handed them [c]over to you! [9][a]Certainly the LORD watches the whole earth carefully and is ready to strengthen those who are devoted to him. [b]You have acted foolishly in this matter; from now on [c]you will have war." [10]Asa was so angry at the prophet, he [a]put him in jail. Asa also oppressed some of the people at that time.

Asa's Reign Ends

[11]The [a]events of Asa's reign, from start to finish, are recorded in the Scroll of the Kings of Judah and Israel. [12]In the thirty-ninth year of his reign, Asa developed a foot disease, and his disease became severe. Yet even in his disease, he [a]did not seek the LORD, but only the doctors. [13][a]Asa passed away in the forty-first year of his reign. [14]He was buried in the tomb he had carved out in the City of David. They laid him to rest on a platform covered [a]with spices [b]and assorted mixtures of ointments. They made a huge bonfire to honor him.

Jehoshaphat Becomes King

17 His son [a]Jehoshaphat replaced him as king and solidified his rule over Israel. [2]He placed troops in all Judah's fortified cities and posted garrisons[1] throughout the land of [a]Judah and in the cities of Ephraim that his father Asa had seized.

[3]The LORD was with Jehoshaphat because he followed in his ancestor David's footsteps at the beginning of his reign. He did not seek the Baals, [4]but instead sought [a]the God of his ancestors and obeyed his commands, unlike the Israelites. [5]The LORD made his kingdom secure; all Judah [a]brought tribute to Jehoshaphat, [b]and he became very wealthy and greatly respected. [6]He was committed to following [a]the LORD;[1] he even removed the high places and Asherah poles from Judah.

[7]In the third year of his reign he sent his officials Ben Hail, Obadiah, Zechariah, Nethanel, and Micaiah [a]to teach in the cities of Judah. [8]They were accompanied by the Levites Shemaiah, Nethaniah, Zebadiah, Asahel, Shemiramoth, Jehonathan, Adonijah, Tobijah, and Tob-Adonijah, and by the priests Elishama and Jehoram. [9][a]They taught throughout Judah, taking with them the scroll of the law of the LORD. They traveled to all the cities of Judah and taught the people.

15:17 [a]1 Kgs 15:14; 2 Chr 14:3, 5   **16:1** [a]1 Kgs 15:17–22   [b]2 Chr 15:9   **16:7** [a]1 Kgs 16:1; 2 Chr 19:2   [b]2 Chr 32:8–10; Ps 118:9; [Isa 31:1; Jer 17:5]   [1]Heb. *seer.*   **16:8** [a]2 Chr 14:9   [b]2 Chr 12:3   [c]2 Chr 13:16, 18   **16:9** [a]Job 34:21; [Prov 5:21; 15:3; Jer 16:17; 32:19]; Zech 4:10   [b]1 Sam 13:13   [c]1 Kgs 15:32   **16:10** [a]2 Chr 18:26; Jer 20:2; Matt 14:3   **16:11** [a]1 Kgs 15:23–24; 2 Chr 14:2   **16:12** [a][Jer 17:5]   **16:13** [a]1 Kgs 15:24   **16:14** [a]Gen 50:2; Mark 16:1; John 19:39–40   [b]2 Chr 21:19; Jer 34:5   **17:1** [a]1 Kgs 15:24; 2 Chr 20:31   **17:2** [a]2 Chr 11:5   [1]Or perhaps *governors.*   **17:4** [a]1 Kgs 12:28   **17:5** [a]1 Sam 10:27; 1 Kgs 10:25   [b]2 Chr 18:1   **17:6** [a]1 Kgs 22:43; 2 Chr 15:17; 19:3; 20:33   [1]Heb. *and his heart was high in the ways of the LORD.*   **17:7** [a]2 Chr 15:3; 35:3   **17:9** [a]Deut 6:4–9; 2 Chr 35:3; Neh 8:3, 7

[10] The LORD put fear into all [a]the kingdoms surrounding Judah; they did not make war with Jehoshaphat. [11] Some of the Philistines [a]brought Jehoshaphat tribute, including a load of silver. The Arabs brought him 7,700 rams and 7,700 goats from their flocks.

[12] Jehoshaphat's power kept increasing. He built fortresses and storage cities throughout Judah. [13] He had many supplies stored in the cities of Judah and an army of skilled warriors stationed in Jerusalem. [14] These were their divisions by families:

There were 1,000 officers from Judah.[1] Adnah the commander led 300,000 skilled warriors, [15] Jehochanan the commander led 280,000, [16] and Amasiah son of Zikri, [a]who volunteered to serve the LORD, led 200,000 skilled warriors.

[17] From Benjamin, Eliada, a skilled warrior, led 200,000 men who were equipped with bows and shields, [18] and Jehozabad led 180,000 trained warriors.

[19] These were the ones who served the king, besides [a]those whom the king placed in the fortified cities throughout Judah.

Jehoshaphat Allies with Ahab

18 Jehoshaphat was very wealthy and greatly respected. He made an alliance by marriage with [a]Ahab, [2] and [a]after several years went down to visit Ahab in Samaria. Ahab slaughtered many sheep and cattle to honor Jehoshaphat and those who came with him. He persuaded him to join in an attack against Ramoth Gilead. [3] King Ahab of Israel said to King Jehoshaphat of Judah, "Will you go with me to attack Ramoth Gilead?" He replied, "I will support you; my army is at your disposal and will support you in battle." [4] Then Jehoshaphat said further to the king of Israel, "First,[1] [a]please seek an oracle from the LORD."[2] [5] So the king of Israel assembled 400 prophets and asked them, "Should we attack Ramoth Gilead or not?" They said, "Attack! God will hand it over to the king." [6] But Jehoshaphat asked, "Is there not a prophet of the LORD still here that we may ask [a]him?" [7] The king of Israel answered Jehoshaphat, "There is still one man through whom we can seek the LORD's will, but I despise him because he does not prophesy prosperity for me, but always disaster—Micaiah son of Imlah." Jehoshaphat said, "The king should not say such things!" [8] The king of Israel summoned an officer and said, "Quickly bring Micaiah son of Imlah."

[9] Now the king of Israel and King Jehoshaphat of Judah were sitting on their respective thrones, dressed in their royal robes, at the threshing floor at the entrance of the gate of Samaria. All the prophets were prophesying before them. [10] Zedekiah son of Kenaanah made iron [a]horns and said, "This is what the LORD says, 'With these you will gore Syria until they are destroyed.'" [11] All the prophets were prophesying the same, saying, "Attack Ramoth Gilead! You will succeed; the LORD will hand it over to the king." [12] Now the messenger who went to summon Micaiah said to him, "Look, the prophets are in complete agreement that the king will succeed. Your words must agree with theirs; you must predict success!" [13] But Micaiah said, "As certainly as the LORD lives, I will say [a]what my God tells me to say!"

[14] Micaiah came before the king and the king asked him, "Micaiah, should we attack Ramoth Gilead or not?" He answered him, "Attack! You will succeed; they will be handed over to you." [15] The king said to him, "How many times must I make you solemnly promise in the name of the LORD to tell me only the truth?" [16] Micaiah replied, "I saw all Israel [a]scattered on the mountains like sheep that have no [b]shepherd. Then the LORD said, 'They have no master. They should go home in peace.'" [17] The king of Israel said to Jehoshaphat, "Didn't I tell you he does not prophesy prosperity for me, but disaster?" [18] Micaiah said, "That being the case, listen to the LORD's message. I saw the LORD sitting on his [a]throne, with all the heavenly assembly standing on his right and on his left. [19] The LORD said, 'Who will deceive King Ahab of Israel, so he will attack Ramoth Gilead and die there?' One said this and another that. [20] Then a [a]spirit[1] stepped forward and stood before the LORD. He said, 'I will deceive him.' The LORD asked him,

'How?' [21]He replied, 'I will go out and be a lying spirit in the mouths of all his prophets.' The LORD said, 'Deceive and overpower him. Go out and do as you have proposed.' [22]So now, look, [a]the LORD has placed a lying spirit in the mouths of all these prophets of yours, but the LORD has decreed disaster for you." [23]Zedekiah son of Kenaanah approached, [a]hit Micaiah on the jaw, and said, "Which way did the LORD's Spirit go when he went from me to speak to you?" [24]Micaiah replied, "Look, you will see in the day when you go into an inner room to hide." [25]Then the king of Israel said, "Take Micaiah and return him to Amon the city official and Joash the king's son. [26]Say, 'This is what the king says: "[a]Put this man in prison. Give him only a little bread and water[1] until I return safely."'" [27]Micaiah said, "If you really do return safely, then the LORD has not spoken through [a]me!" Then he added, "Take note,[1] all you people."

[28]The king of Israel and King Jehoshaphat of Judah attacked Ramoth Gilead. [29]The king of Israel said to Jehoshaphat, "I will [a]disguise myself and then enter the battle, but you wear your royal attire." So the king of Israel disguised himself and they entered the battle. [30]Now the king of Syria had ordered his chariot commanders, "Do not fight common soldiers or high ranking officers; fight only the king of Israel!" [31]When the chariot commanders saw Jehoshaphat, they said, "He must be the king of Israel!" So they turned and attacked him, but Jehoshaphat [a]cried out. The LORD helped him; God lured them away from him. [32]When the chariot commanders realized he was not the king of Israel, they turned away from him. [33]Now an archer shot an arrow at random,[1] and it struck the king of Israel between the plates of his armor. The king ordered his charioteer, "Turn around and take me from the battle line, for I am wounded." [34]While the battle raged throughout the day, the king of Israel stood propped up in his chariot opposite the Syrians. He died in the evening as the sun was setting.

19

When King Jehoshaphat of Judah returned home safely to Jerusalem, [2]the prophet[1] Jehu son of Hanani confronted him; [a]he said to King Jehoshaphat, "Is it right to help the wicked and be an [b]ally of those who oppose the LORD? Because you have done this, the LORD is [c]angry with you! [3]Nevertheless you have done some [a]good things; you removed the Asherah poles from the land, and you were [b]determined to follow God."

Jehoshaphat Appoints Judges

[4]Jehoshaphat lived in Jerusalem. He went out among the people from Beer Sheba to the hill country of Ephraim and encouraged them to follow the LORD God of their [a]ancestors. [5]He appointed [a]judges throughout the land and in each of the fortified cities of Judah. [6]He told the judges, "Be careful what [a]you do, for you are not judging for men, but for the LORD, [b]who will be with you when you make judicial decisions. [7]Respect [a]the LORD and make careful decisions, for the LORD our God disapproves of injustice, [b]partiality, and bribery."

[8]In Jerusalem Jehoshaphat [a]appointed some Levites, priests, and Israelite family leaders to judge on behalf of the LORD and to settle disputes among the residents of Jerusalem.[1] [9]He commanded them: "Carry out your duties with respect for the LORD, with honesty, and with pure motives. [10]Whenever your countrymen who live in the cities bring [a]a case before you (whether it involves a violent crime or other matters related to the law, commandments, rules, and regulations), warn them that they must not sin against the LORD. If you fail to do so, God will be [b]angry with [c]you and your colleagues, but if you obey, you will be free of guilt. [11]Take note, [a]Amariah the chief priest will oversee you [b]in every matter pertaining to the LORD and Zebadiah son of Ishmael, the leader of the family of Judah, in every matter pertaining to the king. The Levites will serve as officials before you. Act courageously, and may the LORD be [c]with those who do well!"

18:22 [a]Job 12:16–17; Isa 19:12–14; Ezek 14:9   **18:23** [a]Jer 20:2; Mark 14:65; Acts 23:2   **18:26** [a]2 Chr 16:10   [1]Heb. *the bread of affliction and the water of affliction.*   **18:27** [a]Deut 18:22   [1]Heb. *Listen.*   **18:29** [a]2 Chr 35:22   **18:31** [a]2 Chr 13:14–15   **18:33** [1]Heb. *now a man drew a bow in his innocence*; i.e., without a target in mind, or at least without realizing his target was the king of Israel.   **19:2** [a]1 Sam 9:9; 1 Kgs 16:1; 2 Chr 20:34   [b]Ps 139:21   [c]2 Chr 32:25   [1]Or *seer.*   **19:3** [a]2 Chr 17:4, 6   [b]2 Chr 30:19   **19:4** [a]2 Chr 15:8–13   **19:5** [a][Deut 16:18–20]   **19:6** [a][Lev 19:15; Deut 1:17]; Ps 58:1   [b]Ps 82:1; [Eccl 5:8]   **19:7** [a][Gen 18:25; Deut 32:4]; Rom 9:17   [b][Deut 10:17–18; Job 34:19]; Acts 10:34; Rom 2:11; Gal 2:6; [Eph 6:9; Col 3:25]   **19:8** [a]Deut 16:18; 2 Chr 17:8   [1]Heb. *and to conduct a case* [or *for controversy*], *and they returned* [to] *Jerusalem.*   **19:10** [a]Deut 17:8   [b]Num 16:46   [c][Ezek 3:18]   **19:11** [a]Ezra 7:3   [b]1 Chr 26:30   [c][2 Chr 15:2; 20:17]

The Lord Gives Jehoshaphat Military Success

20 Later the [a]Moabites and [b]Ammonites, along with some of the Meunites,[1] attacked Jehoshaphat. [2]Messengers arrived and reported to Jehoshaphat, "A huge army is [a]attacking you from the other side of the Dead Sea, from the direction of Edom.[1] Look, they are in Hazazon Tamar (that is, En [b]Gedi)." [3]Jehoshaphat was afraid, so he decided to [a]seek the LORD's advice. [b]He decreed that all Judah should observe a fast. [4]The people of Judah assembled to ask for the LORD's [a]help; they came from all the cities of Judah to ask for the LORD's help.

[5]Jehoshaphat stood before the assembly of Judah and Jerusalem at the LORD's temple, in front of the new courtyard. [6]He prayed: "O LORD [a]God of our ancestors, you are the God who lives in heaven[1] and rules over all the [b]kingdoms of the nations. You possess strength and power; no one can stand [c]against you. [7]Our God, you drove out[1] the inhabitants of this land before [a]your people Israel and gave it as a permanent possession to the descendants of [b]your friend[2] Abraham. [8]They settled down in it and built in it a temple to honor you, saying, [9]'[a]If disaster comes on us in the form of military attack, judgment, plague, or famine, we will stand in front of this temple before you, for [b]you are present in this temple. We will cry out to you for help in our distress, so that you will[1] hear and deliver us.' [10]Now [a]the Ammonites, Moabites, and men from Mount Seir are coming! When Israel came from the land of Egypt, you did not allow them to invade these lands. They bypassed them and did not destroy them. [11]Look how they are repaying us! They come to drive us out of our allotted land which you assigned to us! [12]Our God, will you not [a]judge them? For we are powerless against this huge army that attacks us. We don't know what we should do; we look to you for help."

[13]All the men of Judah were standing before the LORD, along with their infants, wives, and children. [14]Then in [a]the midst of the assembly, the LORD's Spirit came upon Jachaziel son of Zechariah, son of Benaiah, son of Jeiel, son of Mattaniah, a Levite and descendant of Asaph. [15]He said: "Pay attention, all you people of Judah, residents of Jerusalem, and King Jehoshaphat! This is what the LORD says to you: '[a]Don't be afraid and don't panic[1] because of this huge army! [b]For the battle is not yours, but God's. [16]Tomorrow march down against them as they come up the Ascent of Ziz. You will find them at the end of the ravine in front of the wilderness of Jeruel. [17]You will not fight in this battle. Take [a]your positions, stand, and watch the LORD deliver you, [b]O Judah and Jerusalem. Don't be afraid and don't panic! Tomorrow march out toward them; the LORD is with you!'"

[18]Jehoshaphat bowed down with his face toward the ground, and all the people of Judah and the residents of Jerusalem fell [a]down before the LORD and worshiped him. [19]Then some Levites, from the Kohathites and Korahites, got up and loudly praised the LORD God of Israel.

[20]Early the next morning they marched out to the wilderness of Tekoa. When they were ready to march, Jehoshaphat stood up and said: "Listen to me, you people of Judah and residents of Jerusalem! [a]Trust in the LORD your God and you will be safe! Trust in the message of his prophets and you will win." [21]He met[1] with the people [a]and appointed musicians to play before the LORD and praise his majestic splendor. As they marched ahead of the warriors they said: "Give [b]thanks to the LORD, [c]for his loyal love endures."[2]

[22]When [a]they began to shout and praise, the LORD suddenly attacked[1] the Ammonites, Moabites, and men from Mount Seir who were invading Judah, and they were defeated. [23]The Ammonites and Moabites attacked [a]the men from Mount Seir and

20:1 [a]1 Chr 18:2 [b]1 Chr 19:15 [1]Heb. *Ammonites.* 20:2 [a]Gen 14:7 [b]Josh 15:62 [1]Sev. wss *from Aram.* 20:3 [a]2 Chr 19:3 [b]1 Sam 7:6; Ezra 8:21; Jer 36:9; Jonah 3:5 20:4 [a]2 Chr 14:11 20:6 [a]Deut 4:39; Josh 2:11; [1 Kgs 8:23]; Matt 6:9 [b]Ps 22:28; 47:2, 8; Dan 4:17, 25, 32 [c]1 Chr 29:12; 2 Chr 25:8; Ps 62:11; Matt 6:13 [1]Heb. *are you not God in heaven?;* a rhetorical question expecting a positive answer. 20:7 [a]Gen 13:14–17; 17:7; Exod 6:7 [b]Isa 41:8; Jas 2:23 [1]Heb. *did you not drive out . . . ?;* a rhetorical question expecting a positive answer. [2]Or perhaps *your covenantal partner.* 20:9 [a]1 Kgs 8:33, 37; 2 Chr 6:28–30 [b]2 Chr 6:20 [1]Or *may.* 20:10 [a]Num 20:21 20:12 [a]Judg 11:27; [1 Sam 3:13] 20:14 [a]Num 11:25–26; 24:2; 2 Chr 15:1; 24:20 20:15 [a]Exod 14:13–14; [Deut 1:29–30; 31:6, 8]; 2 Chr 32:7 [b]1 Sam 17:47; Zech 14:3 [1]Or perhaps *don't get discouraged.* 20:17 [a]Exod 14:13–14 [b]Num 14:9; [2 Chr 15:2; 32:8] 20:18 [a]Exod 4:31; 2 Chr 7:3; 29:28 20:20 [a]Isa 7:9 20:21 [a]1 Chr 16:29; Ps 29:2; 90:17; 96:9; 110:3 [b]1 Chr 16:34; Ps 106:1; 136:1 [c]1 Chr 16:41; 2 Chr 5:13 [1]Or *consulted.* [2]Or *is eternal.* 20:22 [a]Judg 7:22; 1 Sam 14:20 [1]Heb. *set ambushers against;* i.e., launch a surprise attack. 20:23 [a]Judg 7:22; 1 Sam 14:20

annihilated them. When they had finished off the men of Seir, they attacked and destroyed one another.[1] [24]When the men of Judah arrived at the observation post overlooking the wilderness and looked at the huge army, they saw dead bodies on the ground; there were no survivors. [25]Jehoshaphat and his men went to gather the plunder; they found a huge amount of supplies, clothing,[1] and valuable items. They carried away everything they could. There was so much plunder, it took them three days to haul it off.

[26]On the fourth day they assembled in the Valley of Berachah, where they praised the LORD. So that place is called the Valley of Berachah to this very day. [27]Then all the men of Judah and Jerusalem returned joyfully to Jerusalem with Jehoshaphat leading them; the LORD had given them reason to rejoice over their enemies. [28]They entered Jerusalem to the sound of stringed instruments and trumpets and proceeded to the temple of the LORD. [29]All [a]the kingdoms of the surrounding lands were afraid of God[1] when they heard how the LORD had fought against Israel's enemies. [30]Jehoshaphat's kingdom enjoyed peace; his [a]God made him secure on every side.

Jehoshaphat's Reign Ends

[31][a]Jehoshaphat reigned over Judah. He was thirty-five years old when he became king, and he reigned for twenty-five years in Jerusalem. His mother was Azubah, the daughter of Shilhi. [32]He followed in his father [a]Asa's footsteps and was careful to do what the LORD approved. [33]However, [a]the high places were not eliminated; the people were still not [b]devoted to the God of their ancestors.

[34]The rest of the events of Jehoshaphat's reign, from start to finish, are recorded in the Annals of Jehu son of Hanani, [a]which are included in the Scroll of the Kings of Israel.

[35]Later King [a]Jehoshaphat of Judah made an alliance with King Ahaziah of Israel, [b]who did [c]evil. [36]They agreed[1] [a]to make large seagoing merchant ships;[2] they built the ships in Ezion Geber. [37]Eliezer son of Dodavahu from Mareshah prophesied against Jehoshaphat, "Because you made an alliance with Ahaziah, [a]the LORD will shatter what you have made." The ships were wrecked and unable [b]to go to sea.

21 [a]Jehoshaphat passed away and was buried with his ancestors in the City of David. His son Jehoram replaced him as king.

Jehoram's Reign

[2]His brothers, Jehoshaphat's sons, were Azariah, Jechiel, Zechariah, Azariahu, Michael, and Shephatiah. All these were sons of King Jehoshaphat of Israel. [3]Their father gave them many presents, including silver, gold, and other precious items, along with fortified cities in Judah. But he gave the kingdom to Jehoram because he was the firstborn.

[4]Jehoram took control of his father's kingdom and became powerful. Then he killed all his brothers, as well as some of the officials of Israel. [5][a]Jehoram was thirty-two years old when he became king, and he reigned for eight years in Jerusalem. [6]He followed in the footsteps of the kings of Israel, just as [a]Ahab's dynasty had done, for he married Ahab's daughter. He did evil in the sight of the LORD. [7]But the LORD was unwilling to destroy David's dynasty because of the [a]promise[1] he had made to give [b]David a perpetual dynasty.[2]

[8]During Jehoram's reign Edom freed themselves from Judah's control and set up their own [a]king. [9]Jehoram crossed over with his officers and all his chariots. The Edomites, who had surrounded him, attacked at night and defeated him and his chariot officers.[1] [10]So Edom has remained free from Judah's control to this very day. At that same time Libnah also rebelled and freed themselves from Judah's control[1] because Jehoram rejected the LORD God of his

20:23[1] Heb. *they helped, each one his fellow, for destruction.* **20:25**[1] *MT corpses.* **20:29**[a] 2 Chr 14:14; 17:10 [1] Heb. *and the terror of God* [or perhaps *a great terror*] *was upon all the kingdoms of the lands.* **20:30**[a]1 Kgs 22:41–43; 2 Chr 14:6–7; 15:15; Job 34:29 **20:31**[a] [1 Kgs 22:41–43] **20:32**[a] 2 Chr 14:2 **20:33**[a] 2 Chr 15:17; 17:6 [b] 2 Chr 12:14; 19:3 **20:34**[a]1 Kgs 16:1, 7 **20:35**[a] 2 Chr 18:1 [b] 1 Kgs 22:48–53 [c] [2 Chr 19:2] **20:36**[a] 1 Kgs 9:26; 10:22 [1] Heb. *he made an alliance with him.* [2] Heb. *make ships to go to Tarshish; large ships either made in or capable of traveling to the distant western port of Tarshish.* **20:37**[a]1 Kgs 22:48 [b] 2 Chr 9:21 **21:1**[a]1 Kgs 22:50 **21:5**[a] 2 Kgs 8:17–22 **21:6**[a] 2 Chr 18:1 **21:7**[a] 2 Sam 7:8–17 [b] 1 Kgs 11:36; 2 Kgs 8:19; Ps 132:11 [1] Or *covenant.* [2] Heb. *which he made to David, just as he had promised to give him and his sons a lamp all the days.* **21:8**[a] 2 Kgs 8:20; 14:7, 10; 2 Chr 25:14, 19 **21:9**[1] Heb. *and he arose at night and defeated Edom, who had surrounded him, and the chariot officers.* **21:10**[1] Or *from Jehoram's control;* Heb. *from under his hand.*

ancestors. [11]He also built high places on the hills of Judah; he encouraged the residents of Jerusalem to be unfaithful to the LORD[1] and led Judah away from the LORD.

[12]Jehoram received this letter from Elijah the prophet: "This is what the LORD God of your ancestor David says: 'You have not followed in the footsteps of your father Jehoshaphat and of King Asa of Judah, [13]but have instead followed in the footsteps of the kings of Israel. You [a]encouraged the people of Judah and the residents of Jerusalem to be unfaithful to the LORD, just as the family of Ahab does in Israel. You also [b]killed your brothers, members of your father's family, who were better than you. [14]So look, the LORD is about to severely afflict your people, your sons, your wives, and all you own. [15]And you will get a serious, chronic intestinal [a]disease which will cause your intestines to come out.'"

[16]The [a]LORD [b]stirred up against Jehoram the Philistines and the [c]Arabs who lived beside the Cushites. [17]They attacked Judah and swept through it. They carried off everything they found in the royal palace, including [a]his sons and wives. None of his sons was left, except for his youngest, Ahaziah. [18]After all this happened, the LORD afflicted him with an [a]incurable intestinal disease. [19]After about two years his intestines came out because of [a]the disease, so that he died a very painful death. His people did not make a bonfire to honor him, as they had done for his ancestors.

[20]Jehoram was thirty-two years old when he became king, and he reigned eight years in Jerusalem. No one regretted his death; he was buried in the City of David, but not in the royal tombs.

Ahaziah's Reign

22 The residents of Jerusalem made his youngest son [a]Ahaziah king in his place, for the raiding party that invaded the camp with the [b]Arabs had killed all the older [c]sons. So Ahaziah son of Jehoram became king of Judah. [2]Ahaziah was twenty-two[1] years old when he became king, and he reigned for one year in Jerusalem. His mother was [a]Athaliah, the granddaughter[2] of Omri. [3]He followed in the footsteps of Ahab's dynasty, for his mother gave him evil advice. [4]He did evil in the sight of the LORD like Ahab's dynasty because, after his father's death, they gave him advice that led to his destruction. [5]He followed their advice and joined Ahab's son King Joram of Israel in a battle against King Hazael of Syria at Ramoth Gilead in which the Syrians defeated Joram. [6]Joram returned to Jezreel to recover from [a]the wounds he received from the Syrians in Ramah when he fought against King Hazael of Syria. Ahaziah[1] son of King Jehoram of Judah went down to visit Joram son of Ahab in Jezreel, because he had been wounded.[2]

[7]God brought about Ahaziah's downfall through his visit to Joram. [a]When Ahaziah arrived, he went out with Joram to meet Jehu son of Nimshi, [b]whom the LORD had commissioned to wipe out Ahab's family. [8]While Jehu was dishing out punishment to Ahab's family, he [a]discovered the officials of Judah and the sons of Ahaziah's relatives who were serving Ahaziah and killed them. [9]He looked for Ahaziah, who was captured while hiding in Samaria. They brought him to Jehu and [a]then executed him. They did give him a burial, for they reasoned, "He is the son of [b]Jehoshaphat, who [c]sought the LORD with his whole heart." There was no one in Ahaziah's family strong enough to rule in his place.

Athaliah Is Eliminated

[10a]When Athaliah the mother of Ahaziah saw that her son was dead, she was determined to destroy the entire royal line of Judah. [11]So Jehoshabeath, the daughter of King Jehoram, took Ahaziah's son [a]Joash and stole him away from the rest of the royal descendants who were to be executed. She hid him and his nurse in the room where the bed covers were stored. So Jehoshabeath the daughter of King Jehoram, wife of Jehoiada the priest and sister of Ahaziah, hid him from Athaliah so she could not execute him. [12]He remained in hiding in God's temple for six years while Athaliah was ruling over the land.

21:11 [1]Heb. *and he caused the residents of Jerusalem to commit adultery.*   21:13 [a]1 Kgs 16:31–33; 2 Kgs 9:22   [b]1 Kgs 2:32; 2 Chr 21:4   21:15 [a]2 Chr 21:18–19   21:16 [a]2 Chr 33:11; [Jer 51:11]   [b]1 Kgs 11:14, 23   [c]2 Chr 17:11   21:17 [a]2 Chr 24:7   21:18 [a]2 Chr 13:20; 21:15; Acts 12:23   21:19 [a]2 Chr 16:14   22:1 [a]2 Chr 21:17; 22:6   [b]2 Chr 21:16   [c]2 Chr 21:17   22:2 [a]2 Chr 21:6   [1]Heb. *forty-two.*   [2]Heb. *daughter; can refer to a granddaughter.*   22:6 [a]2 Kgs 9:15   [1]Most Heb. MSS *Azariah.*   [2]Heb. *because he was sick.*   22:7 [a]2 Kgs 9:21–24   [b]2 Kgs 9:6–7   22:8 [a]2 Kgs 10:10–14; Hos 1:4   22:9 [a][2 Kgs 9:27]   [b]1 Kgs 15:24   [c]2 Chr 17:4; 20:3–4   22:10 [a]2 Kgs 11:1–3   22:11 [a]2 Kgs 12:18

23

In [a]the seventh year [b]Jehoiada made a bold move. He made a pact with the officers of the units of hundreds: Azariah son of Jehoram, Ishmael son of Jehochanan, Azariah son of [c]Obed, Maaseiah son of Adaiah, and Elishaphat son of Zikri. [2]They traveled throughout Judah and assembled the Levites from all the cities of Judah, as well as the Israelite family [a]leaders.

They came to Jerusalem, [3]and the whole assembly made a covenant with the king in the temple of God. Jehoiada said to them, "The king's son will rule, just as the LORD [a]promised David's descendants. [4]This is what you must do. One-third of you priests and Levites who are on [a]duty during the Sabbath will guard the doors. [5]Another third of you will be stationed at the royal palace and still another third at the Foundation Gate. All the others will stand in the courtyards of the LORD's temple. [6]No one must enter the LORD's temple except the priests and Levites who are on duty. They may enter because they are ceremonially pure. All the others should carry out their assigned service to the LORD. [7]The Levites must surround the king. Each of you must hold his weapon in his hand. Whoever tries to enter the temple[1] must be killed. You must accompany the king wherever he goes."

[8]The Levites and all [a]the men of Judah did just as Jehoiada the priest ordered. Each of them took his men, those who were on duty during the Sabbath as well as those who were off duty on the Sabbath. Jehoiada the priest did not release his divisions from their duties. [9]Jehoiada the priest gave to the officers of the units of hundreds King David's spears and [a]shields that were kept in God's temple. [10]He placed the men at their posts, each holding his weapon in his hand. They lined up from the south side of the temple to the north side and stood near the altar and the temple, surrounding the king. [11]Jehoiada and his sons led out the king's son and placed on him the crown and the royal insignia.[1] They proclaimed him king and poured olive oil on his head.[2] They declared, "Long live the king!"

[12]When [a]Athaliah heard the royal guard shouting and praising the king, she joined the crowd at the LORD's temple. [13]Then she saw the king standing by his pillar at the entrance. The officers and trumpeters stood beside the king and all the people of the land were celebrating and blowing trumpets, and the musicians with various instruments were leading the celebration. Athaliah tore her clothes and yelled, "[a]Treason! Treason!"[1] [14]Jehoiada the priest sent out the officers of the units of hundreds, who were in charge of the army, and ordered them, "Bring her outside the temple to the guards.[1] Put the sword to anyone who follows her." The priest gave this order because he had decided she should not be executed in the LORD's temple. [15]They seized her and took her into the precincts [a]of the royal palace through the horses' entrance. There they executed her.

[16]Jehoiada then drew up a [a]covenant stipulating that he, all the people, and the king should be loyal to the LORD. [17]All the people went and demolished the temple of Baal. They smashed its altars and idols. They [a]killed Mattan the priest of Baal in front of the altars. [18]Jehoiada then assigned the duties of the LORD's temple to the priests, the Levites whom David had [a]assigned to the LORD's temple. They were responsible for offering burnt sacrifices to the LORD with joy and music, according to the [b]law of Moses and the edict of David. [19]He posted [a]guards at the gates of the LORD's temple, so no one who was ceremonially unclean in any way could enter. [20]He summoned [a]the officers of the units of hundreds, the nobles, the rulers of the people, and all the people of the land, and he then led the king down from the LORD's temple. They entered the royal palace through the Upper Gate and seated the king on the royal throne. [21]All the people of the land celebrated, for the city had rest now that they had killed Athaliah.

Joash's Reign

24

Joash [a]was seven years old when he began to reign. He reigned for forty years in Jerusalem. His mother was Zibiah, who was from Beer Sheba. [2]Joash [a]did what the LORD approved throughout the

---

23:1 [a]2 Kgs 11:4   [b]2 Kgs 12:2   [c]1 Chr 2:37–38   **23:2** [a]Ezra 1:5   **23:3** [a]2 Sam 7:12; 1 Kgs 2:4; 9:5; 2 Chr 6:16; 7:18; 21:7   **23:4** [a]1 Chr 9:25   **23:7** [1]Heb. *house.*   **23:8** [a]1 Chr 24:1–31   **23:9** [a]2 Sam 8:7   **23:11** [1]Heb. *witness, testimony.*   [2]Or *they made him king and anointed him.*   **23:12** [a]2 Chr 22:10   **23:13** [a]2 Kgs 9:23   [1]Or *Conspiracy! Conspiracy!*   **23:14** [1]Heb. *ranks.*   **23:15** [a]Neh 3:28; Jer 31:40   **23:16** [a]Josh 24:24–25; 2 Chr 15:12–15   **23:17** [a]Deut 13:6–9; 1 Kgs 18:40   **23:18** [a]1 Chr 23:6, 30, 31; 24:1   [b]Num 28:2   **23:19** [a]1 Chr 26:1–19   **23:20** [a]1 Kgs 9:22; 2 Kgs 11:19   **24:1** [a]2 Kgs 11:21; 12:1–15   **24:2** [a]2 Chr 26:4–5

lifetime of Jehoiada the priest. ³Jehoiada chose two wives for him who gave him sons and daughters.

⁴Later, Joash was determined to repair the LORD's temple. ⁵He ᵃassembled the priests and Levites and ordered them, "Go out to the cities of Judah and collect the annual quota of silver from all Israel for repairs on the temple of your God. Be quick about it!" But the Levites delayed.

⁶ᵃSo the king summoned Jehoiada the chief priest, and said to him, "Why have you not made the Levites collect from Judah and Jerusalem the tax authorized by ᵇMoses the LORD's servant and by the assembly of Israel at the ᶜtent containing the tablets of the law?" ⁷(Wicked Athaliah and her sons had broken into God's temple and used all ᵃthe holy items of the LORD's temple in their worship of the Baals.) ⁸The king ordered a chest to be made and placed outside ᵃthe gate of the LORD's temple. ⁹An edict was sent throughout Judah and Jerusalem requiring ᵃthe people to bring to the LORD the tax that Moses, God's servant, imposed on Israel in the wilderness. ¹⁰All the officials and all the people gladly brought their silver and threw it into the chest until it was full. ¹¹Whenever the Levites brought the chest to the royal accountant and they saw there was a lot of silver, the royal scribe and the accountant of the high priest emptied the chest and then took it back to its place. They went through this routine every day and collected a large amount of silver.

¹²The king and Jehoiada gave it to the construction foremen assigned to the LORD's temple. They hired carpenters and craftsmen to ᵃrepair the LORD's temple, as well as those skilled in working with iron and bronze to restore the LORD's temple. ¹³They worked hard and made the repairs. They followed the measurements specified for God's temple and restored it. ¹⁴When ᵃthey were finished, they brought the rest of the silver to the king and Jehoiada. They used it to make items for the LORD's temple, including items used in the temple service and for burnt sacrifices, pans, and various other gold and silver items. Throughout Jehoiada's lifetime, burnt sacrifices were offered regularly in the LORD's temple.

¹⁵Jehoiada grew old and died at the age of 130. ¹⁶He was buried in the City of David with the kings, because he had accomplished good in Israel and for God and his temple.

¹⁷After Jehoiada died, the officials of Judah visited the king and declared their loyalty to him. The king listened to their advice. ¹⁸They abandoned the temple of the LORD God of their ancestors and worshiped the Asherah poles and idols. Because of this sinful activity, God was ᵃangry with Judah and Jerusalem. ¹⁹The LORD ᵃsent prophets among them to lead them back to him. They warned the people, but they would not pay attention. ²⁰God's Spirit energized ᵃZechariah son of Jehoiada the priest. He stood up before the people and said to them, "This is what God says: 'ᵇWhy are you violating the commands of the LORD? You will not ᶜbe prosperous. Because you have rejected the LORD, he has rejected you!'" ²¹They plotted against him and by royal decree ᵃstoned him to death in the courtyard of the LORD's temple. ²²King Joash disregarded the loyalty Zechariah's father Jehoiada had shown him and killed Jehoiada's son. As Zechariah was dying, he said, "May the LORD take notice and seek ᵃvengeance!"

²³At ᵃthe beginning of the year the Syrian army attacked Joash and invaded Judah and Jerusalem. They wiped out all the leaders of the people and sent all the plunder they gathered to the king of Damascus. ²⁴Even though the ᵃinvading Syrian army was relatively weak, the LORD ᵇhanded over to them Judah's very large army, for the people of Judah had abandoned the LORD God of their ancestors. The Syrians ᶜgave Joash what he deserved. ²⁵When they withdrew, they left Joash badly wounded. ᵃHis servants plotted against him because of what he had done to the son¹ of Jehoiada the priest. They murdered him on his bed. Thus he died and was buried in the City of David, but not in the tombs of the kings. ²⁶The conspirators were Zabad son of Shimeath (an Ammonite woman) and Jehozabad son of Shimrith (a Moabite woman).

24:5 ᵃ 2 Kgs 12:4   24:6 ᵃ 2 Kgs 12:7   ᵇ Exod 30:12–16   ᶜ Num 1:50; Acts 7:44   24:7 ᵃ 2 Chr 21:17   24:8 ᵃ 2 Kgs 12:9   24:9 ᵃ 2 Chr 24:6   24:12 ᵃ 2 Chr 30:12   24:14 ᵃ 2 Kgs 12:13   24:18 ᵃ [Exod 34:12–14]; Judg 5:8; 2 Chr 19:2; 28:13; 29:8; 32:25   24:19 ᵃ 2 Kgs 17:13; 21:10–15; 2 Chr 36:15–16; Jer 7:25–26; 25:4   24:20 ᵃ Judg 6:34; Matt 23:35   ᵇ Num 14:41; [Prov 28:13]   ᶜ [2 Chr 15:2]   24:21 ᵃ [Neh 9:26]; Matt 23:35; Acts 7:58–59   24:22 ᵃ [Gen 9:5]   24:23 ᵃ 2 Kgs 12:17; Isa 7:2   24:24 ᵃ Lev 26:8; [Deut 32:30]; Isa 30:17   ᵇ Lev 26:25; [Deut 28:25]   ᶜ 2 Chr 22:8; Isa 10:5   24:25 ᵃ 2 Kgs 12:20–21; 2 Chr 25:3   ¹MT sons.

27The list of Joash's sons, [a]the many prophetic oracles about him, and [b]the account of his building project on God's temple are included in the record of the Scroll of the Kings. His son Amaziah replaced him as king.

Amaziah's Reign

25 Amaziah [a]was twenty-five years old when he began to reign, and he reigned for twenty-nine years in Jerusalem. His mother was Jehoaddan, who was from Jerusalem. 2He did what the LORD approved, [a]but not with wholehearted devotion.

3aWhen he had secured control of the kingdom, he executed the servants who had assassinated his father the king. 4However, [a]he did not execute their sons. He obeyed the LORD's commandment as recorded in the law scroll of Moses, "Fathers must not be executed for what their sons do, and sons must not be executed for what their fathers do. A man must be executed only for his own sin."

5Amaziah assembled the people of Judah and assigned them by families to the commanders of units of 1,000 and the commanders of units of 100 for all Judah and Benjamin. He counted those twenty years old and up and discovered there were 300,000 young men of fighting age equipped with spears and shields. 6He hired 100,000 Israelite warriors for 100 talents[1] of silver.

7But a [a]prophet visited him and said: "O king, the Israelite troops must not go with you, for the LORD is not with Israel or any of the Ephraimites. 8Even if you go and fight bravely in battle, God will defeat you before the enemy. God is [a]capable of helping or defeating." 9Amaziah asked [a]the prophet: "But what should I do about the 100 talents of silver I paid the Israelite troops?" The prophet replied, "The LORD is capable of giving you more than that." 10So Amaziah dismissed the troops that had come to him from Ephraim and sent them home. They were very angry at Judah and returned home incensed. 11Amaziah boldly led his army to [a]the Valley of Salt, where he defeated 10,000 Edomites. 12The men of Judah captured 10,000 men alive. They took them to the top of a cliff and threw them over. All the captives fell to their death. 13Now the troops Amaziah had dismissed and had not allowed to fight in the battle raided the cities of Judah from Samaria to Beth Horon. They killed 3,000 people and carried off a large amount of plunder.

14When Amaziah returned from defeating [a]the Edomites, he brought back the gods of the people of Seir and made them [b]his personal gods. He bowed down before them and offered them sacrifices. 15The LORD was angry at Amaziah and sent a prophet to him, who said, "Why are you following[1] [a]these gods[2] that [b]could not deliver their own people from your power?" 16While he was speaking, Amaziah said to him, "Did we appoint you to be a royal [a]counselor? Stop prophesying or else you will be killed!" So the prophet stopped, but added, "I know that God has decided to destroy you because you have done this thing and refused to listen to my advice."

17After King [a]Amaziah of Judah consulted with his advisers, he sent this message to the king of Israel, Joash son of Jehoahaz, the son of Jehu, "Come, face me on the battlefield."[1] 18King Joash of Israel sent this message back to King Amaziah of Judah, "A thorn bush in Lebanon sent this message to a cedar in Lebanon, 'Give your daughter to my son as a wife.' Then a wild animal of Lebanon came by and trampled down the thorn bush. 19You defeated Edom and it has gone to your head. Gloat [a]over your success,[1] but stay in your palace. Why bring calamity on yourself? Why bring down yourself and Judah along with you?"

20But Amaziah did not heed the warning, for God wanted to hand them over to Joash because they [a]followed the gods of Edom. 21So King Joash of Israel attacked. He and King Amaziah of Judah faced each other on the battlefield[1] in Beth [a]Shemesh of Judah. 22Judah was defeated by Israel, and each man ran back home. 23King Joash of Israel captured King Amaziah of Judah, son of Joash son of [a]Jehoahaz, in Beth Shemesh

24:27 [a]2 Kgs 12:18   [b]2 Kgs 12:21   25:1 [a]2 Kgs 14:1–6   25:2 [a]2 Kgs 14:4; 2 Chr 25:14   25:3 [a]2 Kgs 14:5; 2 Chr 24:25   25:4 [a]Deut 24:16; 2 Kgs 14:6; Jer 31:30; [Ezek 18:20]   25:6 [1]About 6,730 pounds.   25:7 [a]2 Chr 11:2   25:8 [a]2 Chr 14:11; 20:6   25:9 [a][Deut 8:18]; Prov 10:22   25:11 [a]2 Kgs 14:7   25:14 [a]2 Chr 28:23   [b][Exod 20:3, 5]   25:15 [a][Ps 96:5]   [b]2 Chr 25:11   [1]Heb. *seeking*; perhaps in the sense of consulting an oracle from.   [2]Heb. *the gods of the people*.   25:16 [a][1 Sam 2:25]   25:17 [a]2 Kgs 14:8–14   [1]Heb. *let us look at each other* [in the] *face*.   25:19 [a]2 Chr 26:16; 32:25; [Prov 16:18]   [1]Heb. *glorify*.   25:20 [a]2 Chr 25:14   25:21 [a]Josh 19:38   [1]Heb. *looked at each other* [in the] *face*.   25:23 [a]2 Chr 21:17; 22:1, 6

and brought him to Jerusalem. He broke down the wall of Jerusalem from the Gate of Ephraim to the Corner Gate—a distance of about 600 feet. [24] He took away all the gold and silver, all the items found in God's temple that were in the care of [a]Obed-Edom, the riches in the royal palace, and some hostages. Then he went back to Samaria.

[25] King [a]Amaziah son of Joash of Judah lived for fifteen years after the death of King Joash son of Jehoahaz of Israel. [26] The rest of the events of Amaziah's reign, from start to finish, are recorded in the Scroll of the Kings of Judah and Israel. [27] From the time Amaziah turned from following the LORD, conspirators plotted against him in Jerusalem, so he fled to Lachish. But they sent assassins after him, and they killed him there. [28] His body was carried back by horses, and he was buried with his ancestors in the City of David.[1]

Uzziah's Reign

26 All the people of Judah took Uzziah, who was sixteen years old, and made him king in his father Amaziah's place. [2] Uzziah built up Elat and restored it to Judah after King Amaziah had passed away.

[3] Uzziah was sixteen years old when he began to reign, and he reigned for fifty-two years in Jerusalem. His mother's name was Jecholiah, who was from Jerusalem. [4] He did [a]what the LORD approved, just as his father Amaziah had done. [5] He followed God during [a]the lifetime of Zechariah, who taught him how to honor God. As long as he followed the LORD, God caused him to [b]succeed.

[6] Uzziah attacked the Philistines and broke down the walls of Gath, Jabneh, and Ashdod. He built cities in the region of Ashdod and throughout Philistine territory. [7] God helped him in his campaigns against [a]the Philistines, the Arabs living in Gur Baal, and the Meunites. [8] The Ammonites [a]paid tribute to Uzziah, and his fame reached the border of Egypt, for he grew in power.

[9] Uzziah built and fortified towers in Jerusalem at the [a]Corner Gate, Valley Gate, and at the Angle. [10] He built towers in the wilderness and dug many cisterns, for he owned many herds in the foothills and on the plain. He had workers in the fields and vineyards in the hills and in Carmel, for he loved agriculture.

[11] Uzziah had an army of skilled warriors trained for battle. They were organized by divisions according to the muster rolls made by Jeiel the scribe and Maaseiah the officer under the authority of Hananiah, a royal official. [12] The total number of family leaders who led warriors was 2,600. [13] They commanded an army of 307,500 skilled and able warriors who were ready to defend the king against his enemies. [14] Uzziah supplied shields, spears, helmets, breastplates, bows, and slingstones for the entire army. [15] In Jerusalem he made war machines carefully designed to shoot arrows and large stones from the towers and corners of the walls. He became very famous, for he received tremendous support and became powerful.

[16] But once [a]he became powerful, his pride destroyed him. He disobeyed[1] the LORD his God. He entered the LORD's temple to offer incense on the incense altar. [17] [a]Azariah the priest and eighty other brave priests of the LORD followed him in. [18] They confronted King Uzziah and said to him, "It [a]is not proper for you, Uzziah, to offer incense to the LORD. That is the responsibility of the [b]priests, the descendants of Aaron, who are consecrated to offer incense. Leave the sanctuary, for you have disobeyed[1] and the LORD God will not honor you!" [19] Uzziah, who had an incense censer in his hand, became angry. While he was ranting and raving at the priests, a skin [a]disease[1] appeared on his forehead right there in front of the priests in the LORD's temple near the incense altar. [20] When Azariah the high priest and the other priests looked at him, there was a skin disease on his forehead. They hurried him out of there; even the king himself [a]wanted to leave quickly because the LORD had afflicted him. [21] [a]King Uzziah suffered from a skin disease until the day he died. He lived in separate quarters,[1] afflicted by a skin disease and banned from the LORD's temple. His son Jotham was in charge of the palace and ruled over the people of the land.

25:24 [a]1 Chr 26:15   **25:25** [a]2 Kgs 14:17–22   **25:28** [1]Heb. *Judah.*   **26:4** [a]2 Chr 24:2   **26:5** [a]2 Chr 24:2   [b][2 Chr 15:2; 20:20; 31:21]   **26:7** [a]2 Chr 21:16   **26:8** [a]2 Sam 8:2; 2 Chr 17:11   **26:9** [a]2 Kgs 14:13; 2 Chr 25:23; Neh 3:13, 19, 32; Zech 14:10   **26:16** [a][Deut 32:15]   [1]Or *was unfaithful to.*   **26:17** [a]1 Chr 6:10   **26:18** [a][Num 3:10; 16:39–40; 18:7]   [b]Exod 30:7–8; Heb 7:14   [1]Or *been unfaithful.*   **26:19** [a]Lev 13:42; Num 12:10; 2 Kgs 5:25–27   [1]Trad. *leprosy.*   **26:20** [a]Esth 6:12   **26:21** [a]2 Kgs 15:5   [1]Heb. *house of* [?].

[22]The rest of the events of Uzziah's reign, from start to finish, were recorded by the prophet [a]Isaiah son of Amoz. [23]Uzziah passed away and was buried near his ancestors in a cemetery belonging to the kings. (This was because he had a skin disease.) His [a]son Jotham replaced him as king.

Jotham's Reign

27 Jotham [a]was twenty-five years old when he began to reign, and he reigned for sixteen years in Jerusalem. His mother was Jerusha the daughter of Zadok. [2]He did what [a]the LORD approved, just as his father Uzziah had done. (He did not, however, have the audacity to enter the temple.) Yet the people were still sinning. [3]He built the Upper Gate to the LORD's temple and did a lot of work on the wall in the area known as [a]Ophel. [4]He built cities in the hill country of Judah and fortresses and towers in the forests. [5]He launched a military campaign against the king of the [a]Ammonites and defeated them. That year the Ammonites paid him 100 talents[1] of silver, 10,000 cors of wheat, and 10,000 cors of barley. The Ammonites also paid this same amount of annual tribute the next two years.

[6]Jotham grew powerful [a]because he was determined to please the LORD his God. [7]The rest of the events of Jotham's reign, including all his military campaigns and his accomplishments, are recorded in the Scroll of the Kings of Israel and Judah. [8]He was twenty-five years old when he began to reign, and he reigned for sixteen years in Jerusalem. [9]Jotham passed away and was buried in the City of David. His [a]son [b]Ahaz replaced him as king.

Ahaz's Reign

28 Ahaz [a]was twenty years old when he began to reign, and he reigned for sixteen years in Jerusalem. He did not do what pleased the LORD, in contrast to his ancestor David. [2]He followed in [a]the footsteps of the kings of Israel; he also made images of the Baals. [3]He offered sacrifices in [a]the Valley of Ben Hinnom and passed [b]his sons through the [c]fire, [d]a horrible sin practiced by the nations whom the LORD drove out before the Israelites. [4]He offered sacrifices and burned incense on the high places, on the hills, and under every green tree.

[5]The LORD his God handed him over to [a]the king of Syria. The Syrians [b]defeated him and deported many captives to Damascus. He was also handed over to the king of Israel, who thoroughly defeated him. [6]In one day [a]Pekah son of Remaliah killed 120,000 warriors in Judah [b]because they had abandoned the LORD God of their ancestors. [7]Zikri, an Ephraimite warrior, killed the king's son Maaseiah, Azrikam, the supervisor of the palace, and Elkanah, the king's second-in-command. [8]The Israelites seized from their [a]brothers 200,000 wives, sons, and daughters. They also carried off a huge amount of plunder and took it back to Samaria.

[9]Oded, a [a]prophet of the LORD, was there. He went to meet the army as they arrived in Samaria and said to them: "Look, [b]because the LORD God of your ancestors was angry with Judah, [c]he handed them over to you. You have killed them so mercilessly that God has taken notice. [10]And now you are planning to [a]enslave the people of Judah and Jerusalem. Yet are you not also guilty before the LORD your God? [11]Now listen to me! Send back those you have seized from your brothers, [a]for the LORD is very angry at you!" [12]So some of the Ephraimite family leaders, Azariah son of Jehochanan, Berechiah son of Meshillemoth, Jechizkiah son of Shallum, and Amasa son of Hadlai confronted those returning from the battle. [13]They said to them, "Don't bring those captives here! Are you planning on making us even more sinful and guilty before the LORD? Our guilt is already great, and the LORD is very angry at Israel." [14]So the soldiers released the captives and the plunder before the officials and the entire assembly. [15]Men were assigned to take the prisoners and find clothes among the plunder for those [a]who were naked. So they clothed them, supplied them with sandals, [b]gave

26:22 [a]2 Kgs 20:1; 2 Chr 32:20, 32; Isa 1:1   26:23 [a]2 Kgs 15:7; 2 Chr 21:20; 28:27; Isa 6:1   27:1 [a]2 Kgs 15:32–35   27:2 [a]2 Kgs 15:35; Ezek 20:44; 30:13   27:3 [a]2 Chr 33:14; Neh 3:26   27:5 [a]2 Chr 26:8   [1]About 6,730 pounds.   27:6 [a]2 Chr 26:5   27:9 [a]2 Kgs 15:38   [b]Isa 1:1; Hos 1:1; Mic 1:1   28:1 [a]2 Kgs 16:2–4   28:2 [a]Judg 2:11   28:3 [a]Josh 15:8   [b]2 Kgs 23:10   [c][Lev 18:21]; 2 Kgs 16:3; 2 Chr 33:6   [d][Lev 18:24–30]   28:5 [a][Isa 10:5]   [b]2 Kgs 16:5–6; [2 Chr 24:24]; Isa 7:1, 17   28:6 [a]2 Kgs 15:27   [b][2 Chr 29:8]   28:8 [a]Deut 28:25, 41; 2 Chr 11:4   28:9 [a]2 Chr 25:15   [b]Ps 69:26; [Isa 10:5; 47:6]; Ezek 25:12, 15; 26:2; Obad 10; [Zech 1:15]   [c]Ezra 9:6; Rev 18:5   28:10 [a][Lev 25:39, 42, 43, 46]   28:11 [a]Ps 78:49; Jas 2:13   28:15 [a]2 Chr 28:12   [b][Prov 25:21–22; Luke 6:27; Rom 12:20]

[c]them food and drink, and provided them with oil to rub on their skin.[1] They put the ones who couldn't walk on donkeys. They brought them back to their brothers at Jericho, the city of date palm trees, and then returned to Samaria.

[16]At [a]that time King Ahaz asked the king[1] of Assyria for help. [17]The [a]Edomites had again invaded and defeated Judah and carried off captives. [18]The Philistines had raided [a]the cities of Judah in the foothills and the Negev. They captured and settled in Beth Shemesh, Aijalon, Gederoth, Soco and its surrounding villages, Timnah and its surrounding villages, and Gimzo and its surrounding villages. [19]The LORD humiliated[1] Judah because of King Ahaz of [a]Israel, for he [b]encouraged Judah to sin and was very unfaithful to the LORD. [20]King [a]Tiglath-Pileser[1] of Assyria came, but he gave him more trouble than support. [21]Ahaz gathered riches[1] from the LORD's temple, the royal palace, and the officials and gave them to the king of Assyria, but that did not help.

[22]During his time of trouble King Ahaz was even more unfaithful to the LORD. [23]He offered sacrifices to [a]the gods of Damascus whom he thought had defeated him. He reasoned, "Since the gods of the kings of Syria helped them, I will sacrifice to them so they will help me." But they caused him and all Israel to stumble. [24]Ahaz gathered the items in God's temple and removed them. He [a]shut the doors of the LORD's temple and erected altars on every street corner in Jerusalem. [25]In every city throughout Judah he set up high places to offer sacrifices to other gods. He angered the LORD God of his ancestors.

[26][a]The rest of the events of Ahaz's reign, including his accomplishments from start to finish, are recorded in the Scroll of the Kings of Judah and Israel. [27]Ahaz passed away and was buried in the city of Jerusalem; they [a]did not bring him to the tombs of the kings of Israel. His son Hezekiah replaced him as king.

Hezekiah Consecrates the Temple

29 Hezekiah was twenty-five years old when he began to reign, and he reigned twenty-nine years in Jerusalem. His mother was Abijah, the daughter of Zechariah. [2]He did what the LORD approved, just as his ancestor David had done.

[3]In the first month of the first year of his reign, he [a]opened the doors of the LORD's temple and repaired them. [4]He brought in the priests and Levites and assembled them in the square on the east side. [5]He said to them: "Listen to me, you Levites! Now [a]consecrate yourselves, so you can consecrate the temple of the LORD God of your ancestors. Remove from the sanctuary what is ceremonially unclean. [6]For our fathers were unfaithful; they did what is evil in the sight of the LORD our God and abandoned him. They [a]turned away from the LORD's dwelling place and rejected him. [7]They closed [a]the doors of the temple porch and put out the lamps; they did not offer incense or burnt sacrifices in the sanctuary of the God of Israel. [8]The LORD was [a]angry at Judah and Jerusalem and [b]made them an appalling object of horror at which people hiss [c]out their scorn, as you can see with your own [d]eyes. [9]Look, [a]our fathers died violently, and our sons, daughters, and wives were carried off because of this. [10]Now I intend to [a]make a covenant with the LORD God of Israel, so that he may relent from his raging anger.[1] [11]My sons, do not be negligent now, for the LORD has [a]chosen you to stand in his presence, to minister to him,[1] to be his ministers,[2] and offer sacrifices."[3]

[12]The following Levites prepared to carry out the king's orders:

From the [a]Kohathites: [b]Mahath son of Amasai and Joel son of Azariah;

from the Merarites: Kish son of Abdi and Azariah son of Jehallelel;

from the Gershonites: Joah son of Zimmah and Eden son of Joah;

[13]from the descendants of Elizaphan: Shimri and Jeiel;

28:15[c] Deut 34:3; Judg 1:16 [1]Heb. *and poured oil on them.* **28:16**[a] 2 Kgs 16:7 [1]Maj. Heb. MSS *kings.* **28:17**[a] 2 Chr 21:10; Obad 10–14 **28:18**[a] 2 Chr 21:16–17; Ezek 16:27, 57 **28:19**[a] 2 Kgs 16:2; 2 Chr 21:2 [b]Exod 32:25 [1]Or *subdued.* **28:20**[a] 2 Kgs 15:29; 16:7–9; 1 Chr 5:26 [1]Heb. *Tilgath-Pilneser.* **28:21**[1]Heb. *divided up.* **28:23**[a] 2 Chr 25:14 **28:24**[a] 2 Chr 29:3, 7 **28:26**[a] 2 Kgs 16:19–20 **28:27**[a] 2 Chr 21:20; 24:25 **29:3**[a] 2 Chr 28:24; 29:7 **29:5**[a] 1 Chr 15:12; 2 Chr 29:15, 34; 35:6 **29:6**[a] [Isa 1:4]; Jer 2:27; Ezek 8:16 **29:7**[a] 2 Chr 28:24 **29:8**[a] 2 Chr 24:18 [b]2 Chr 28:5 [c]1 Kgs 9:8; Jer 18:16; 19:8; 25:9, 18; 29:18 [d]Deut 28:32 **29:9**[a] Deut 28:25; 2 Chr 28:5–8, 17 **29:10**[a] 2 Chr 15:12; 23:16 [1]Heb. *so that the rage of his anger might turn from us.* **29:11**[a] Num 3:6; 8:14; 18:2, 6; 2 Chr 30:16–17 [1]I.e., to conduct the religious rituals directed to the Lord. [2]I.e., to be his ministers for the nation. [3]Heb. *ones who cause [sacrifices] to go up in smoke.* **29:12**[a] Num 3:19–20 [b]2 Chr 31:13

from the descendants of Asaph: Zechariah and Mattaniah;

[14]from the descendants of Heman: Jehiel and Shimei;

from the descendants of Jeduthun: Shemaiah and Uzziel.

[15]They assembled their brothers and [a]consecrated themselves. Then they went in [b]to purify the LORD's temple, just as the king had ordered, in accordance with the word of the LORD. [16]The priests then entered the LORD's temple to purify it; they brought out to the courtyard of the LORD's temple every ceremonially unclean thing they discovered inside. The Levites took them out to the [a]Kidron Valley. [17]On the first day of the first month they began consecrating; by the eighth day of the month they reached the porch of the LORD's temple. For eight more days they consecrated the LORD's temple. On the sixteenth day of the first month they were finished. [18]They went to King Hezekiah and said: "We have purified the entire temple of the LORD, including the altar of burnt sacrifice and all its equipment, and the table for the Bread of the Presence and all its equipment. [19]We have prepared and consecrated all the items that King Ahaz removed during his reign when he acted unfaithfully. They are in front of the altar of the LORD."

[20]Early the next morning King Hezekiah assembled the city officials and went up to the LORD's temple. [21]They brought seven bulls, seven rams, seven lambs, and seven goats as a [a]sin offering for the kingdom, the sanctuary, and Judah. The king told the priests, the descendants of Aaron, to offer burnt sacrifices on the altar of the LORD. [22]They slaughtered the bulls, and the priests took the blood and [a]splashed it on the altar. Then they slaughtered the rams and splashed the blood on the altar; next they slaughtered the lambs and splashed the blood on the altar. [23]Finally they brought the goats for the sin offering before the king and the assembly, and they placed their [a]hands on them. [24]Then the priests slaughtered them. They offered their blood as a sin offering on the altar [a]to make atonement for all Israel because the king had decreed that the burnt sacrifice and sin offering were for all Israel.

[25]Hezekiah stationed the Levites in the LORD's temple with cymbals [a]and stringed instruments just as David, [b]Gad the king's prophet,[1] and Nathan the prophet had ordered. (The LORD had actually given these orders through his prophets.) [26]The Levites had David's musical instruments and [a]the priests had trumpets. [27]Hezekiah ordered [a]the burnt sacrifice to be offered on the altar. As they began to offer the sacrifice, they also began to sing to the LORD, accompanied by the trumpets and the musical instruments of King David of Israel. [28]The entire assembly worshiped, as the singers sang and the trumpeters played. They continued until the burnt sacrifice was completed.

[29]When [a]the sacrifices were completed, the king and all who were with him bowed down and worshiped. [30]King Hezekiah and the officials told the Levites to praise the LORD, using the psalms of David and Asaph the prophet.[1] So they joyfully offered praise and bowed down and worshiped. [31]Hezekiah said, "Now you have consecrated yourselves to the LORD. Come and bring sacrifices and [a]thank offerings to the LORD's temple." So the assembly brought sacrifices and thank offerings, and whoever [b]desired to do so brought burnt sacrifices.

[32]The assembly brought a total of 70 bulls, 100 rams, and 200 lambs as burnt sacrifices to the LORD, [33]and 600 bulls and 3,000 sheep were consecrated. [34]But there were not enough priests to skin all [a]the animals,[1] so their brothers, the Levites, helped them until the work was finished and the priests could consecrate themselves. (The Levites had been [b]more conscientious about [c]consecrating themselves than the priests.) [35]There was a large number of burnt sacrifices, as well as fat from [a]the peace offerings and drink offerings that accompanied [b]the burnt sacrifices. So the service of the LORD's temple was reinstituted.[1] [36]Hezekiah and all the people were happy about what God had done[1] for them, for it had been done quickly.

29:15 [a]2 Chr 29:5   [b]1 Chr 23:28   29:16 [a]2 Chr 15:16; 30:14   29:21 [a]Lev 4:3–14   29:22 [a]Lev 8:14–15, 19, 24; Heb 9:21   29:23 [a]Lev 4:15, 24; 8:14   29:24 [a]Lev 14:20   29:25 [a]1 Chr 16:4; 25:6   [b]2 Sam 24:11   [1]Or seer.   29:26 [a]Num 10:8, 10; 1 Chr 15:24; 16:6; 2 Chr 5:12   29:27 [a]2 Chr 23:18   29:29 [a]2 Chr 20:18   29:30 [1]Or seer.   29:31 [a]Lev 7:12   [b]Exod 35:5, 22   29:34 [a]2 Chr 35:11   [b]Ps 7:10   [c]2 Chr 29:5   [1]Heb. the burnt sacrifices.   29:35 [a]Lev 3:15–16   [b]Num 15:5–10   [1]Or established.   29:36 [1]Heb. prepared.

Hezekiah Observes the Passover

30 Hezekiah sent messages throughout Israel and Judah; he even wrote letters to Ephraim and Manasseh, summoning them to come to the LORD's temple in Jerusalem and observe a Passover celebration for the LORD God of Israel. [2]The king, his officials, and the entire assembly in Jerusalem decided to observe the Passover in the second [a]month. [3]They were unable to observe it [a]at the regular time [b]because not enough priests had consecrated themselves and the people had not assembled in Jerusalem. [4]The proposal seemed appropriate to the king and the entire assembly. [5]So they sent an edict throughout Israel from Beer Sheba to Dan, summoning the people to come and observe a Passover for the LORD God of Israel in Jerusalem, for they had not observed it on a nationwide scale as prescribed in the law. [6a]Messengers delivered the letters from the king and his officials throughout Israel and Judah.

This royal edict read: "O Israelites, [b]return to [c]the LORD God of Abraham, Isaac, and Israel, so he may return to you who have been spared from the kings of [d]Assyria. [7]Don't be [a]like your fathers and brothers who were unfaithful to the LORD God of their ancestors, provoking him to [b]destroy them,[1] as you can see. [8]Now, don't be [a]stubborn[1] like your fathers. Submit[2] to the LORD and come to his sanctuary which he has permanently consecrated. Serve the LORD your God so [b]that he might relent from his raging anger.[3] [9]For if you return to the LORD, your brothers and sons will be shown [a]mercy by their captors and return to this land. The LORD your God is [b]merciful and compassionate; he will not reject you if you [c]return to him."

[10]The messengers journeyed from city to city through [a]the land of Ephraim and Manasseh as far as Zebulun, but people mocked and ridiculed them. [11]But [a]some men from Asher, Manasseh, and Zebulun humbled themselves and came to Jerusalem. [12]In Judah God moved [a]the people to unite and carry out the edict of the king and the officers in keeping with the LORD's message. [13]A huge crowd assembled in Jerusalem to observe the Feast of [a]Unleavened Bread in the second month. [14]They removed the [a]altars in Jerusalem; they also removed all the incense altars and threw them into the [b]Kidron Valley.

[15]They slaughtered the Passover lamb on the fourteenth day of the second month. The priests and Levites were [a]ashamed, so they consecrated themselves and brought burnt sacrifices to the LORD's temple. [16]They stood at their [a]posts according to the regulations outlined in the law of Moses, the man of God. The priests were splashing the blood as the Levites handed it to them. [17]Because many in [a]the assembly had not consecrated themselves, the Levites slaughtered the Passover lambs of all who were ceremonially unclean and could not consecrate their sacrifice to the LORD. [18]The majority of the [a]many people from Ephraim, Manasseh, Issachar, and Zebulun were ceremonially unclean, [b]yet they ate the Passover in violation of what is prescribed in the law. For Hezekiah prayed for them, saying: "May the LORD, who is good, forgive [19]everyone who has [a]determined to follow God, the LORD God of his ancestors, even if he is not ceremonially clean according to the standards of the temple." [20]The LORD responded favorably to Hezekiah and forgave the people.

[21]The Israelites who were in Jerusalem observed [a]the Feast of Unleavened Bread for seven days with great joy. The Levites and priests were praising the LORD every day with all their might.[1] [22]Hezekiah expressed his appreciation to all the Levites,[1] [a]who demonstrated great skill [b]in serving the LORD. They feasted for the seven days of the festival and were making peace offerings and giving thanks to the LORD God of their ancestors.

[23]The entire assembly then decided to

30:2 [a] Num 9:10–11; 2 Chr 30:13, 15   **30:3** [a] Exod 12:6, 18   [b] 2 Chr 29:17, 34   **30:6** [a] Esth 8:14; Job 9:25; Jer 51:31   [b] [Jer 4:1; Joel 2:13]   [c] 2 Kgs 15:19, 29   [d] 2 Chr 28:20   **30:7** [a] Ezek 20:18   [b] 2 Chr 29:8   [1] Heb. *and he made them a devastation.*   **30:8** [a] Exod 32:9; Deut 10:16; Acts 7:51   [b] 2 Chr 29:10   [1] Heb. *don't stiffen your neck;* an idiom for being stubborn.   [2] Heb. *give a hand.*   [3] Heb. *so that the rage of his anger might turn from you.*   **30:9** [a] Ps 106:46   [b] [Exod 34:6; Mic 7:18]   [c] [Isa 55:7]   **30:10** [a] 2 Chr 36:16   **30:11** [a] 2 Chr 11:16; 30:18, 21   **30:12** [a] [2 Cor 3:5; Phil 2:13; Heb 13:20–21]   **30:13** [a] Lev 23:6; Num 9:11   **30:14** [a] 2 Chr 28:24   [b] 2 Chr 29:16   **30:15** [a] 2 Chr 29:34   **30:16** [a] 2 Chr 35:10, 15   **30:17** [a] 2 Chr 29:34   **30:18** [a] 2 Chr 30:1, 11, 25   [b] Exod 12:43–49; [Num 9:10]   **30:19** [a] 2 Chr 19:3   **30:21** [a] Exod 12:15; 13:6; 1 Kgs 8:65   [1] Heb. *and they were praising the LORD day by day, the Levites and the priests with instruments of strength to the LORD.*   **30:22** [a] [Deut 33:10]; 2 Chr 17:9; 35:3   [b] Ezra 10:11   [1] Heb. *and Hezekiah spoke to the heart of all the Levites.*

celebrate for seven [a]more days; so they joyfully celebrated for seven more days. [24]King Hezekiah of Judah [a]supplied 1,000 bulls and 7,000 sheep for the assembly, while the officials supplied them with 1,000 bulls and 10,000 sheep. Many priests [b]consecrated themselves. [25]The celebration included[1] the entire assembly of Judah, the priests, the Levites, the entire assembly of those [a]who came from Israel, the resident foreigners who came from the land of Israel, and those who were residents of Judah. [26]There was a great celebration in Jerusalem, unlike anything that had occurred in Jerusalem since the time of King [a]Solomon son of David of Israel. [27]The priests and Levites got up and pronounced blessings [a]on the people. The LORD responded favorably to them[1] as their prayers reached [b]his holy dwelling place in heaven.

31

When all this was over, the Israelites who were in the cities of Judah went out and [a]smashed the sacred pillars, cut down the Asherah poles, and demolished all the high places and altars throughout Judah, Benjamin, Ephraim, and Manasseh. Then all the Israelites returned to their own homes in their cities.

The People Contribute to the Temple

[2]Hezekiah appointed [a]the divisions of the priests and Levites to do their assigned tasks—to offer burnt sacrifices and present offerings and to serve, give thanks, and offer praise in the gates of the LORD's sanctuary. [3]The king contributed some of what he [a]owned for burnt sacrifices, including the morning and evening burnt sacrifices and the burnt sacrifices made on Sabbaths, new moon festivals, and at other appointed times prescribed in the [b]law of the LORD. [4]He ordered the people living in Jerusalem to contribute the [a]portion prescribed for [b]the priests and Levites so they might be obedient to the law of the LORD. [5]When [a]the edict was issued, the Israelites freely contributed the initial portion of their grain, wine, olive oil, honey, and all the produce of their fields. They brought a [b]tenth of everything, which added up to a huge

amount. [6]The Israelites and people of Judah who lived in the cities of Judah also contributed a [a]tenth of their cattle and sheep, as well as a tenth of the holy items consecrated to the LORD their God. They brought them and placed them in many heaps.[1] [7]In the third month they began piling their contributions in heaps and finished in the seventh month. [8]When Hezekiah and the officials came and saw the heaps, they praised the LORD and pronounced blessings on his people Israel.

[9]When Hezekiah asked the priests and Levites about the heaps, [10]Azariah, the head priest from the [a]family of Zadok, said to him, "[b]Since the contributions began arriving in the LORD's temple, we have had plenty to eat and have a large quantity left over. For the LORD has blessed his people, and this large [c]amount remains." [11]Hezekiah ordered that [a]storerooms be prepared in the LORD's temple. When this was done, [12]they brought in the contributions, tithes, and consecrated items that had been offered. [a]Konaniah, a Levite, was in charge of all this, assisted by his brother Shimei. [13]Jehiel, Azaziah, Nahath, Asahel, Jerimoth, Jozabad, Eliel, Ismakiah, Mahath, and Benaiah worked under the supervision of Konaniah and his brother Shimei, as directed by King Hezekiah and Azariah, the [a]supervisor of God's temple.

[14]Kore son of Imnah, a Levite and the guard on the east side, was in charge of the voluntary offerings made to God and disbursed the contributions made to the LORD and the consecrated items. [15]In the cities of the priests, [a]Eden, Miniamin, Jeshua, Shemaiah, Amariah, and Shecaniah faithfully assisted him in making disbursements to [b]their fellow priests according to their divisions, regardless of age. [16]They made disbursements to all the males three years old and up who were listed in the genealogical records—to all who would enter the LORD's temple to serve on a daily basis and fulfill their duties as assigned to their divisions. [17]They made disbursements to the priests listed in the genealogical records by their families, and to the Levites twenty years

30:23 [a]1 Kgs 8:65; 2 Chr 35:17–18   **30:24** [a]2 Chr 35:7–8   [b]2 Chr 29:34   **30:25** [a]2 Chr 30:11, 18   [1]Heb. *they rejoiced.*
30:26 [a]2 Chr 7:8–10   **30:27** [a]Num 6:23   [b]Deut 26:15; Ps 68:5   [1]Heb. *and it was heard with their voice.*   **31:1** [a]2 Kgs 18:4
31:2 [a]1 Chr 23:6; 24:1   **31:3** [a]2 Chr 35:7   [b]Num 28:1–29:40   **31:4** [a]Num 18:8; 2 Kgs 12:16; Neh 13:10; Ezek 44:29
[b]Mal 2:7   **31:5** [a]Exod 22:29; Neh 13:12   [b][Lev 27:30]; Deut 14:28; 26:12–13   **31:6** [a][Lev 27:30]; Deut 14:28   [1]Heb.
heaps, heaps; an emphatic Heb. construction.   **31:10** [a]1 Chr 6:8–9   [b][Mal 3:10]   [c]Exod 36:5   **31:11** [a]1 Kgs
6:5–8   **31:12** [a]2 Chr 35:9; Neh 13:13   **31:13** [a]1 Chr 9:11; Jer 20:1   **31:15** [a]2 Chr 29:12   [b]Josh 21:1–3, 9

old and up, according to their duties as assigned to their divisions, [18]and to all the infants, wives, sons, and daughters of the entire assembly listed in the genealogical records, for they faithfully consecrated themselves. [19]As for [a]the descendants of Aaron, the priests who lived in the outskirts of all their cities, men were [b]assigned to disburse portions to every male among the priests and to every Levite listed in the genealogical records.

[20]This is what Hezekiah [a]did throughout Judah. He did what the LORD his God considered good and right and faithful. [21]He wholeheartedly and [a]successfully reinstituted service in God's temple and obedience to the law, in order to follow his God.

Sennacherib Invades Judah

32 After [a]these faithful deeds were accomplished, King Sennacherib of Assyria invaded Judah. He besieged the fortified cities, intending to seize them. [2]When Hezekiah saw that Sennacherib had invaded and intended to attack Jerusalem, [3]he consulted with his advisers and military officers about stopping up the springs outside the city, and they supported him. [4]A large number of people gathered together and stopped up all the [a]springs and the stream that flowed through the district.[1] They reasoned, "Why should the kings of Assyria come and find plenty of water?" [5]Hezekiah energetically rebuilt every broken wall. [a]He erected towers and an outer wall and fortified the [b]terrace of the City of David. He made many weapons and shields.

[6]He appointed military officers over the army and assembled them in the square at the city gate. He [a]encouraged them, saying, [7]"Be strong and brave! Don't [a]be afraid and [b]don't panic because of [c]the king of Assyria and this huge army that is with him. We have with us one who is stronger than those who are with him. [8]He has with him mere human [a]strength, but the LORD our God is [b]with us to help us and fight our battles!" The army was encouraged by the words of King Hezekiah of Judah.

[9][a]Afterward King Sennacherib of Assyria, while attacking Lachish with all his military might, sent his messengers to Jerusalem. The message was for King Hezekiah of Judah and all the people of Judah who were in Jerusalem. It read: [10]"[a]This is what King Sennacherib of Assyria says: 'Why are you so confident that you remain in Jerusalem while it is under siege? [11]Hezekiah says, "[a]The LORD our God will rescue us from the power[1] of the king of Assyria." But he is misleading you, and you will die of hunger and thirst! [12]Hezekiah is the one who eliminated[1] the [a]LORD's high places and altars and then told Judah and Jerusalem, "At one altar you must worship and offer sacrifices." [13]Are you not aware of what I and my predecessors[1] have done to all the nations of the surrounding lands? Have the gods of the surrounding lands actually been able to rescue their lands from my power? [14]Who among all the gods of these nations whom my predecessors annihilated was able to rescue his people from my [a]power that your God would be able to rescue you from my power? [15]Now [a]don't let Hezekiah deceive you or mislead you like this. Don't believe him, for no god of any nation or kingdom has been able to rescue his people from my power or the power of my predecessors. So how can your gods rescue you from my power?'"

[16]Sennacherib's servants further insulted the LORD God and his servant Hezekiah. [17]He wrote letters mocking the LORD God of Israel and insulting him with these words: "The gods of the surrounding nations could not rescue their people from my [a]power. Neither can Hezekiah's god rescue his people from my power." [18]They called out loudly in [a]the Judahite dialect to the people of Jerusalem who were on the wall, trying to scare and terrify them so they could seize the city. [19]They talked about [a]the God of Jerusalem as if he were one of the man-made gods of the nations of the earth.

[20][a]King Hezekiah and [b]the prophet Isaiah son of Amoz prayed about this and cried out to heaven. [21]The LORD sent a messenger[1]

31:19 [a] Lev 25:34; Num 35:1–4   [b] 2 Chr 31:12–15   31:20 [a] 2 Kgs 20:3; 22:2   31:21 [a] 2 Chr 26:5; 32:30; Ps 1:3   32:1 [a] 2 Kgs 18:13–19:37; Isa 36:1–37:38   32:4 [a] 2 Kgs 20:20   [1] Heb. *the land.*   32:5 [a] Isa 22:9–10   [b] 2 Sam 5:9; 1 Kgs 9:15, 24; 11:27; 2 Kgs 12:20; 1 Chr 11:8   32:6 [a] 2 Chr 30:22; Isa 40:2   32:7 [a] [Deut 31:6]   [b] 2 Chr 20:15   [c] 2 Kgs 6:16; [Rom 8:31]   32:8 [a] [Jer 17:5; 1 John 4:4]   [b] Exod 14:13; [1 Sam 17:45–47]; 2 Chr 13:12; 20:17; [Rom 8:31]   32:9 [a] 2 Kgs 18:17   32:10 [a] 2 Kgs 18:19   32:11 [a] 2 Kgs 18:30   [1] Heb. *hand.*   32:12 [a] 2 Kgs 18:22   [1] Heb. *Did not he, Hezekiah, eliminate . . . ?;* a rhetorical question expecting a positive answer.   32:13 [1] Heb. *fathers.*   32:14 [a] [Isa 10:5–12]   32:15 [a] 2 Kgs 18:29   32:17 [a] 2 Kgs 19:12; Dan 3:15   32:18 [a] 2 Kgs 18:28; Ps 59:6   32:19 [a] 2 Kgs 19:18; [Ps 96:5; 115:4–8]   32:20 [a] 2 Kgs 19:15   [b] 2 Kgs 19:2

and [a]he wiped out all the soldiers, princes, and officers in the army of the king of Assyria. So Sennacherib returned home [b]humiliated. When he entered the temple of his god, some of his own sons struck him down with the sword. [22]The LORD delivered Hezekiah and the residents of Jerusalem from the power of King Sennacherib of Assyria and from all the other nations. He made them secure on every side.[1] [23]Many were bringing presents to the LORD in Jerusalem and precious [a]gifts to King Hezekiah of Judah. From that time on he was [b]respected by all the nations.

Hezekiah's Shortcomings and Accomplishments

[24]In those days Hezekiah was stricken with a [a]terminal illness. He prayed to the LORD, who answered him and gave him a sign confirming that he would be healed. [25]But Hezekiah was ungrateful; [a]he had a proud attitude, provoking God to be angry at him, as well as Judah and Jerusalem. [26]But [a]then Hezekiah and the residents of Jerusalem humbled themselves and abandoned their pride, and the LORD was not angry with them for the rest of Hezekiah's reign.

[27]Hezekiah was very wealthy and greatly respected. He made storehouses for his silver, gold, precious stones, spices, shields, and all his other valuable possessions. [28]He made storerooms for the harvest of grain, wine, and olive oil, and stalls for all his various kinds of livestock and his flocks.[1] [29]He built royal cities[1] and owned a large number of sheep and cattle, for [a]God gave him a huge amount of possessions.

[30a]Hezekiah dammed up the source of the waters of the Upper Gihon and directed them down to the west side of the City of David. Hezekiah [b]succeeded in all that he did. [31]So when the envoys arrived from the Babylonian officials to [a]visit him and inquire about the sign that occurred in the land, God left him alone to [b]test him in order to know his true motives.

[32]The rest of [a]the events of Hezekiah's reign, including his faithful deeds, are recorded in the vision of the prophet Isaiah son of Amoz, included in the [b]Scroll of the Kings of Judah and Israel. [33a]Hezekiah passed away and was buried on the ascent of the tombs of the descendants of David. All the people of Judah and the residents of Jerusalem buried him with great [b]honor. His son Manasseh replaced him as king.

Manasseh's Reign

33 Manasseh [a]was twelve years old when he became king, and he reigned for fifty-five years in Jerusalem. [2]He did evil in the sight of the LORD and committed the same horrible [a]sins practiced by the nations whom the LORD drove out ahead of the Israelites. [3]He rebuilt the high places that his father Hezekiah had destroyed; he set up altars for the Baals and [a]made Asherah poles. He bowed down to [b]all the stars in the sky[1] and worshiped them. [4]He built altars [a]in the LORD's temple, about which the LORD had said, "Jerusalem will be my permanent home."[1] [5]In the two courtyards of the LORD's temple, he built altars for all the stars [a]in the sky. [6a]He passed his sons through the fire[1] in the Valley of Ben Hinnom and practiced [b]divination, omen reading, and sorcery. He set [c]up a ritual pit to conjure up underworld spirits and appointed magicians to supervise it.[2] He did a great amount of evil in the sight of the LORD and angered him. [7]He put an idolatrous image [a]he had made [b]in God's temple, about which God had said to David and to his son Solomon, "This temple in Jerusalem, which I have chosen out of all the tribes of Israel, will be my permanent home. [8]I will not make Israel again leave the [a]land I gave to their ancestors provided that they carefully obey all I commanded them, the whole law, the rules and regulations given through Moses." [9]But Manasseh misled the people of Judah and the residents of Jerusalem so that they sinned more than

32:21 [a]2 Kgs 19:35; Isa 10:12–19; Zech 14:3   [b]Ps 44:7   [1]Or *an angel.*   **32:22** [1]Heb. *and he led him from all around.* **32:23** [a]2 Sam 8:10; 2 Chr 17:5; 26:8; Ps 45:12   [b]2 Chr 1:1   **32:24** [a]2 Kgs 20:1–11; Isa 38:1–8   **32:25** [a]2 Chr 24:18   **32:26** [a]Jer 26:18–19   **32:28** [1]Heb. *and stalls for all beasts and beasts, and flocks for the stalls.*   **32:29** [a]1 Chr 29:12   [1]Heb. *and cities he made for himself.*   **32:30** [a]Isa 22:9–11   [b]2 Chr 31:21   **32:31** [a]2 Kgs 20:12; Isa 39:1   [b][Deut 8:2, 16]   **32:32** [a]Isa 36—39   [b]2 Kgs 18—20   **32:33** [a]1 Kgs 1:21; 2 Kgs 20:21   [b]Ps 112:6; Prov 10:7   **33:1** [a]2 Kgs 21:1–9   **33:2** [a][Deut 18:9–12]; 2 Chr 28:3; [Jer 15:4]   **33:3** [a]Deut 16:21; 2 Kgs 23:5–6   [b]Deut 17:3   [1]Trad. *all the host of heaven;* the heavenly lights, incl. stars and planets.   **33:4** [a]Deut 12:11; 1 Kgs 8:29; 9:3; 2 Chr 6:6; 7:16   [1]Heb. *In Jerusalem my name will be permanently.*   **33:5** [a]2 Chr 4:9   **33:6** [a][Lev 18:21]; Deut 18:10; 2 Kgs 23:10; 2 Chr 28:3; Ezek 23:37, 39   [b]Deut 18:11; 2 Kgs 17:17   [c][Lev 19:31; 20:27]; 2 Kgs 21:6   [1]Or *he sacrificed his sons in the fire;* perhaps child sacrifice, though some interpret it as a less drastic cultic practice.   [2]Heb. *and he set up a ritual pit, along with a conjurer.*   **33:7** [a]2 Kgs 21:7; 2 Chr 25:14   [b]Ps 132:14   **33:8** [a]2 Sam 7:10

the nations whom the LORD had destroyed ahead of the Israelites.

[10]The LORD confronted Manasseh and his people, but they paid no attention. [11]So [a]the LORD brought against them the commanders of the army of the king of Assyria. They seized Manasseh, put hooks in his nose, [b]bound him with bronze chains, and carried him away to Babylon. [12]In his pain Manasseh asked the LORD his God for mercy and truly [a]humbled himself before the God of his ancestors. [13]When he prayed to the LORD, the LORD responded to him and answered favorably[1] his cry for mercy. The LORD brought him back to Jerusalem to his kingdom. Then Manasseh [a]realized that the LORD is the true God.

[14]After this Manasseh built up the outer wall of the City of David on the west side of the [a]Gihon in the valley to the entrance of the Fish Gate and all [b]around the terrace; he made it much higher. He placed army officers in all the fortified cities in Judah.

[15]He removed [a]the foreign gods and images from the LORD's temple and all the altars he had built on the hill of the LORD's temple and in Jerusalem; he threw them outside the city. [16]He erected the altar of the LORD and offered on it peace offerings and [a]thank offerings. He told the people of Judah to serve the LORD God of Israel. [17]However, [a]the people continued to offer sacrifices at the high places, but only to the LORD their God.

[18]The rest of [a]the events of Manasseh's reign, including his prayer to his God and the words the prophets[1] spoke to him in the name of the LORD God of Israel, are recorded in the Annals of the Kings of Israel. [19]The Annals of the Prophets include his prayer, give an account of how the LORD responded to it, record all his sins and unfaithful acts, and identify the sites where he built high places and erected Asherah poles and idols before he humbled himself. [20]Manasseh passed away and was buried in his palace. His [a]son Amon replaced him as king.

Amon's Reign

[21a]Amon was twenty-two years old when he became king, and he reigned for two years in Jerusalem. [22]He did evil in the sight of the LORD, just as his father Manasseh had done. Amon offered sacrifices to all the idols his father Manasseh had made and worshiped them. [23]He did not humble himself before the LORD [a]as his father Manasseh had done. Amon was guilty of great sin. [24a]His servants conspired against him and [b]killed him in his palace. [25]The people of the land executed all who had conspired against King Amon, and they made his son Josiah king in his place.

Josiah Institutes Religious Reforms

34 Josiah [a]was eight years old when he became king, and he reigned for thirty-one years in Jerusalem. [2]He did what the LORD approved and followed in his ancestor David's footsteps; he did not deviate to the right or the left.

[3]In the eighth year of his reign, while he was still [a]young, he began to [b]seek the God of his [c]ancestor David. In his twelfth year he began ridding Judah and Jerusalem [d]of the high places, Asherah poles, idols, and images. [4]He ordered [a]the altars of the Baals to be torn down [b]and broke the incense altars that were above them. He smashed the Asherah poles, idols, and images, crushed them, and sprinkled the dust over the tombs of those who had sacrificed to them. [5]He [a]burned the bones of the pagan priests on their [b]altars; he purified Judah and Jerusalem. [6]In the cities of Manasseh, Ephraim, and Simeon, as far as Naphtali, and in the ruins around them, [7]he tore down the altars and Asherah poles, [a]demolished the idols, and smashed all the incense altars throughout the land of Israel. Then he returned to Jerusalem.

[8]In the eighteenth year of his reign, he [a]continued his policy of purifying the land and the temple. He sent [b]Shaphan son of Azaliah, Maaseiah the city [c]official, and Joah son of Joahaz the secretary to repair the temple of the LORD his God. [9]They went to Hilkiah [a]the high priest and gave him the silver that had been brought to God's temple. The Levites who guarded the door had collected it from the people of Manasseh

33:11 [a]Deut 28:36   [b]2 Chr 36:6; Job 36:8; Ps 107:10–11   **33:12** [a]2 Chr 7:14; 32:26; [1 Pet 5:6]   **33:13** [a]1 Kgs 20:13; Ps 9:16; Dan 4:25   [1]Heb. *heard.*   **33:14** [a]1 Kgs 1:33   [b]2 Chr 27:3   **33:15** [a]2 Chr 33:3, 5, 7   **33:16** [a]Lev 7:12   **33:17** [a]2 Chr 32:12   **33:18** [a]1 Sam 9:9   [1]Or *seers.*   **33:20** [a]1 Kgs 1:21; 2 Kgs 21:18   **33:21** [a]2 Kgs 21:19–24; 1 Chr 3:14   **33:23** [a]2 Chr 33:12, 19   **33:24** [a]2 Kgs 21:23–24; 2 Chr 24:25   [b]2 Chr 25:27   **34:1** [a]2 Kgs 22:1–2; Jer 1:2; 3:6   **34:3** [a]Eccl 12:1   [b]2 Chr 15:2; [Prov 8:17]   [c]1 Kgs 13:2   [d]2 Chr 33:17–19, 22   **34:4** [a]Lev 26:30; 2 Kgs 23:4   [b]2 Kgs 23:6   **34:5** [a]1 Kgs 13:2   [b]2 Kgs 23:20   **34:7** [a]Deut 9:21   **34:8** [a]2 Kgs 22:3–20   [b]2 Kgs 25:22   [c]2 Chr 18:25   **34:9** [a]2 Kgs 12:4

and Ephraim and from all who were [b]left in Israel, as well as from all the people of Judah and Benjamin and the residents of[i] Jerusalem. [10]They handed it over to the construction foremen assigned to the LORD's temple. They in turn paid the temple workers to restore and repair it. [11]They gave money to the craftsmen and builders to buy chiseled stone and wood for the braces and rafters of the buildings that the kings of Judah had allowed to fall into disrepair.[i] [12]The men worked faithfully. Their supervisors were Jahath and Obadiah (Levites descended from Merari), as well as Zechariah and Meshullam (descendants of Kohath). The Levites, all of whom were skilled musicians, [13]supervised the laborers [a]and all the foremen on their various jobs. Some of the Levites were scribes, officials, and guards.

[14]When they took out the silver that had been brought to the LORD's temple, Hilkiah the priest [a]found the law scroll the LORD had given to Moses. [15]Hilkiah informed Shaphan the scribe, "I found the law [a]scroll in the LORD's temple." Hilkiah gave the scroll to Shaphan. [16]Shaphan brought the scroll to the king and reported, "Your servants are doing everything assigned to them. [17]They melted down the silver in the LORD's temple and handed it over to the supervisors and the construction foremen." [18]Then Shaphan the scribe told the king, "Hilkiah the priest has given me a scroll." Shaphan read it out loud before the king. [19]When the king heard the words of the law, he tore his clothes. [20]The king ordered Hilkiah, [a]Ahikam son of Shaphan, Abdon son of Micah, Shaphan the scribe, and Asaiah the king's servant, [21]"Go, ask the LORD for me and for those who remain in Israel and Judah about the words of this scroll that has been discovered. For the LORD's great fury has been ignited[i] against us because our ancestors did not [a]obey the word of the LORD by living according to all that is written in this scroll."

[22]So Hilkiah and the others sent by the king went to Huldah the prophetess, the wife of Shallum son of Tokhath, the son of Hasrah, the supervisor of the wardrobe. (She lived in Jerusalem in the Mishneh[i] district.) They stated their business,[2] [23]and she said to them: "This is what the LORD God of Israel says: 'Say this to the man who sent you to me: [24]"This is what the LORD says: 'I am about to [a]bring disaster on this place and its residents, all the curses that are recorded in the [b]scroll which they read before the king of Judah. [25]This will happen because they have abandoned me and offered sacrifices[i] to other gods, angering me with all the idols they have made.[2] My anger will ignite against this place and will not be extinguished!'" [26]Say this to the king of Judah, who sent you to seek an oracle from the LORD: "This is what the LORD God of Israel says concerning the words you have heard: [27]'You displayed a sensitive spirit and humbled yourself before God when you heard his words concerning this place and its residents. You humbled yourself before me, tore your clothes, and wept before me, and I have heard you,' says the [a]LORD. [28]'Therefore I will allow you to die and be buried in peace. You will not have to witness all the disaster I will bring on this place and its residents.'"'" Then they reported back to the king.

[29]The king summoned all [a]the leaders of Judah and Jerusalem. [30]The king went up to the LORD's temple, accompanied by all the people of Judah, the residents of Jerusalem, the priests, and the Levites. All the people were there, from the oldest to the youngest. He [a]read aloud all the words of the scroll of the covenant that had been discovered in the LORD's temple. [31]The king [a]stood by [b]his pillar[i] and renewed[2] the [c]covenant before the LORD, agreeing to follow the LORD and to obey his commandments, laws, and rules with all his heart and being, by carrying out the terms of this covenant recorded on this scroll. [32]He made all who were in Jerusalem and Benjamin agree to it. The residents of Jerusalem acted in accordance with the covenant of God, the God of their ancestors. [33]Josiah removed all the detestable [a]idols from [b]all the areas belonging to the Israelites and encouraged[i] all who were in Israel

34:9 [b]2 Chr 30:6 [i]Qe. *and they returned.* **34:11** [i]Heb. *of the houses that the kings of Judah had destroyed.* **34:13** [a]1 Chr 23:4–5 **34:14** [a]2 Kgs 22:8 **34:15** [a]Deut 31:24, 26 **34:20** [a]Jer 26:24 **34:21** [a]2 Kgs 17:15–19 [i]MT *has gushed forth.* **34:22** [i]Or *second.* [2]Heb. *and they spoke to her like this.* **34:24** [a]2 Chr 36:14–20 [b]Deut 28:15–68 **34:25** [i]Or *burned incense.* [2]Or perhaps *angering me by all the things they do;* Heb. *angering me with all the work of their hands.* **34:27** [a]2 Kgs 22:19; 2 Chr 12:7; 30:6; 33:12–13 **34:29** [a]2 Kgs 23:1–3 **34:30** [a]Neh 8:1–3 **34:31** [a]2 Chr 6:13 [b]2 Kgs 11:14; 23:3; 2 Chr 30:16 [c]2 Chr 23:16; 29:10 [i]MT *at his place.* [2]Heb. *cut;* i.e., made or agreed to. **34:33** [a]1 Kgs 11:5; 2 Chr 33:2 [b]Jer 3:10 [i]Or *caused, forced.*

to worship the LORD their God. Throughout the rest of his reign they did not turn aside from following the LORD God of their ancestors.

Josiah Observes the Passover

35 [a]Josiah observed a Passover festival for the LORD in Jerusalem. They slaughtered the Passover lambs on the [b]fourteenth day of the first month. [2]He appointed the priests to fulfill their [a]duties and [b]encouraged them to carry out their service in the LORD's temple. [3]He told the Levites, [a]who instructed all Israel about things consecrated to the LORD, "[b]Place the holy ark [c]in the temple which King Solomon son of David of Israel built. Don't carry [d]it on your shoulders. Now serve the LORD your God and his people Israel! [4]Prepare yourselves by your families [a]according to your divisions, as instructed in [b]writing by King David of Israel [c]and his son Solomon. [5a]Stand in the sanctuary and, together with the Levites, represent the family divisions of your countrymen. [6]Slaughter the Passover lambs, [a]consecrate yourselves, and make preparations for your countrymen to celebrate according to the LORD's message which came through Moses."

[7]From his own royal flocks and [a]herds, Josiah [b]supplied the people with 30,000 lambs and goats for the Passover sacrifice, as well as 3,000 cattle. [8]His [a]officials also willingly contributed to the people, priests, and Levites. Hilkiah, Zechariah, and Jehiel, the leaders of God's temple, gave the priests 2,600 Passover sacrifices and 300 cattle. [9a]Konaniah and his brothers Shemaiah and Nethanel, along with Hashabiah, Jeiel, and Jozabad, the officials of the Levites, supplied the Levites with 5,000 Passover sacrifices and 500 cattle. [10]Preparations were made, and the priests [a]stood at their posts and the [b]Levites in their divisions as prescribed by the king. [11]They slaughtered the Passover lambs and the priests [a]splashed the blood, while the Levites [b]skinned the animals. [12]They reserved the burnt [a]offerings and the cattle for the family divisions of the people to present to the LORD, as prescribed in the scroll of Moses. [13]They [a]cooked the Passover sacrifices over the open fire as prescribed and [b]cooked the consecrated offerings in pots, kettles, and pans. They quickly served them to all the people. [14]Afterward they made preparations for themselves and for the priests, because the priests, the descendants of Aaron, were offering burnt sacrifices and fat portions until evening. The Levites made preparations for themselves and for the priests, the descendants of Aaron. [15]The musicians, the descendants of Asaph, manned their posts, as [a]prescribed by David, Asaph, Heman, and Jeduthun the king's prophet.[1] The guards at the various gates did not need to leave their posts, for their fellow Levites made preparations for them. [16]So all the preparations for the LORD's service were made that day, as the Passover was observed and the burnt sacrifices were offered on the altar of the LORD, as prescribed by King Josiah. [17]So the Israelites who were present observed the Passover at that time, as well as the Feast of [a]Unleavened Bread for seven days. [18]A Passover like this had not been observed in Israel since [a]the days of Samuel the prophet. None of the kings of Israel had observed a Passover like the one celebrated by Josiah, the priests, the Levites, all the people of Judah and Israel who were there, and the residents of Jerusalem. [19]This Passover was observed in the eighteenth year of Josiah's reign.

Josiah's Reign Ends

[20a]After Josiah had done all this for the temple, King Necho of Egypt marched up to do battle at [b]Carchemish on the Euphrates River. Josiah marched out to oppose him. [21]Necho sent messengers to him, saying, "Why are you opposing me, O king of Judah? I am not attacking you today, but the kingdom with which I am at war. God told me to hurry. Stop opposing God, who is with me, or else he will destroy you." [22]But Josiah did not turn back from him; he [a]disguised himself for battle. He did not take seriously the words of Necho that he had received from God; he went to fight him in

35:1 [a]2 Kgs 23:21–22 [b]Exod 12:6; Num 9:3; Ezra 6:19 35:2 [a]2 Chr 23:18; Ezra 6:18 [b]2 Chr 29:5–15 35:3 [a]Deut 33:10; 2 Chr 17:8–9; Neh 8:7 [b]2 Chr 34:14 [c]Exod 40:21; 2 Chr 5:7 [d]1 Chr 23:26 35:4 [a]1 Chr 9:10–13 [b]1 Chr 23–26 [c]2 Chr 8:14 35:5 [a]Ps 134:1 35:6 [a]2 Chr 29:5, 15 35:7 [a]2 Chr 31:3 [b]2 Chr 30:24 35:8 [a]Num 7:2 35:9 [a]2 Chr 31:12 35:10 [a]Ezra 6:18; Heb 9:6 [b]2 Chr 5:12; 7:6; 8:14–15; 13:10; 29:25–34 35:11 [a]Exod 12:22; 2 Chr 29:22 [b]2 Chr 29:34 35:12 [a]Lev 3:3; Ezra 6:18 35:13 [a]Exod 12:8–9; Deut 16:7 [b]1 Sam 2:13–15 35:15 [a]1 Chr 25:1–6 [1]Or *seer*. 35:17 [a]Exod 12:15; 13:6; 2 Chr 30:21 35:18 [a]2 Kgs 23:22–23 35:20 [a]2 Kgs 23:29 [b]Isa 10:9; Jer 46:2 35:22 [a]1 Kgs 22:30; 2 Chr 18:29

the Plain of Megiddo. [23] Archers shot King Josiah; the king ordered his servants, "Take me out of this chariot,[1] for I am seriously wounded." [24] So [a]his servants took him out of the chariot, put him in another chariot that he owned, and brought him to Jerusalem, where he died. He was buried in the tombs of his ancestors; [b]all the people of Judah and Jerusalem mourned Josiah. [25] Jeremiah composed [a]laments for [b]Josiah which [c]all [d]the male and female singers use to mourn Josiah to this very day. It has become customary in Israel to sing these; they are recorded in the Book of Laments.

[26] The rest of the events of Josiah's reign, including the faithful acts he did in obedience to what is written in the law of the LORD [27] and his accomplishments, from start to finish, are recorded in the Scroll of the Kings of Israel and Judah.

Jehoahaz's Reign

36 The people of [a]the land took Jehoahaz son of Josiah and made him king in his father's place in Jerusalem. [2] Jehoahaz was twenty-three years old when he became king, and he reigned three months in Jerusalem. [3] The king of Egypt prevented him from ruling in Jerusalem and imposed on the land a special tax of 100 talents[1] of silver and a talent of gold. [4] The king of Egypt made Jehoahaz's brother Eliakim king over Judah and Jerusalem, and changed his name to Jehoiakim. Necho seized his brother Jehoahaz and took him to Egypt.

Jehoiakim's Reign

[5] [a]Jehoiakim was twenty-five years old when he became king, and he reigned for eleven years in Jerusalem. He did [b]evil in the sight of the LORD his God. [6] King [a]Nebuchadnezzar of Babylon attacked him, bound him with bronze chains, and [b]carried him away to Babylon. [7] [a]Nebuchadnezzar took some of the items in the LORD's temple to Babylon and put them in his palace there.

[8] The rest of the events of Jehoiakim's reign, including the horrible sins he committed and his shortcomings, are recorded in the Scroll of the Kings of Israel and Judah. His son Jehoiachin replaced him as king.

Jehoiachin's Reign

[9] [a]Jehoiachin was eighteen[1] years old when he became king, and he reigned three months and ten days in Jerusalem. He did evil in the sight of the LORD. [10] At the beginning of the year [a]King Nebuchadnezzar ordered him to be brought to Babylon, along [b]with the valuable items in the LORD's temple. In his place Nebuchadnezzar made Jehoiachin's relative[1] [c]Zedekiah king over Judah and Jerusalem.

Zedekiah's Reign

[11] [a]Zedekiah was twenty-one years old when he became king, and he ruled for eleven years in Jerusalem. [12] He [a]did evil in the sight of the LORD his God. He did not humble himself before Jeremiah the prophet, the LORD's spokesman. [13] He also [a]rebelled against King Nebuchadnezzar, who had made him vow allegiance in the name of God. He was [b]stubborn and obstinate and refused to return to the LORD God of Israel. [14] All the leaders of the priests and people became more unfaithful and committed the same horrible sins practiced by the nations. They defiled the LORD's temple which he had consecrated in Jerusalem.

The Babylonians Destroy Jerusalem

[15] The LORD God of their ancestors continually warned them through his messengers, for he felt compassion for his people [a]and his dwelling place. [16] But [a]they mocked God's messengers, [b]despised his warnings, and [c]ridiculed his prophets. Finally the LORD got very [d]angry at his people and there was no one who could prevent his judgment. [17] He brought against them [a]the king of the Babylonians, who [b]slaughtered their young men in their temple. He did not spare young men or women, or even the old and aging. God handed everyone over to him. [18] He carried away to Babylon all the items in God's temple, whether large or small, as well as what was in the

35:23 [1] Heb. *carry me away.*   35:24 [a] 2 Kgs 23:30   [b] 1 Kgs 14:18; Zech 12:11   35:25 [a] Lam 4:20   [b] Jer 22:10–11   [c] Matt 9:23   [d] Jer 22:20   36:1 [a] 2 Kgs 23:30–34   36:3 [1] About 6,730 pounds.   36:5 [a] 2 Kgs 23:36–37; 1 Chr 3:15   [b] [Jer 22:13–19]   36:6 [a] 2 Kgs 24:1; Hab 1:6   [b] [Deut 29:22–29]; 2 Chr 33:11; Jer 36:30   36:7 [a] 2 Kgs 24:13; Dan 1:1–2   36:9 [a] 2 Kgs 24:8–17   [1] Heb. *eight.*   36:10 [a] 2 Kgs 24:10–17   [b] Dan 1:1–2   [c] Jer 37:1   [1] Heb. *and he made Zedekiah his brother king.*   36:11 [a] 2 Kgs 24:18–20; Jer 52:1   36:12 [a] Jer 21:3–7; 44:10   36:13 [a] Jer 52:3; Ezek 17:15   [b] 2 Kgs 17:14; [2 Chr 30:8]   36:15 [a] Jer 7:13; 25:3–4   36:16 [a] 2 Chr 30:10; Jer 5:12–13   [b] [Prov 1:24–32]   [c] Jer 38:6; Matt 23:34   [d] 2 Chr 34:25; Ps 79:5   36:17 [a] Num 33:56; Deut 4:26; 28:49; 2 Kgs 25:1; Ezra 9:7; Isa 3:8   [b] Ps 74:20

treasuries of the LORD's temple [a]and in the treasuries of the king and his officials. [19]They burned down God's temple and tore down [a]the wall of Jerusalem. They burned all its fortified buildings and destroyed all its valuable items. [20]He deported to Babylon all who escaped the sword. They served him and his sons until the Persian kingdom rose to power. [21]This took place to fulfill the LORD's message spoken through [a]Jeremiah and lasted until the land experienced its sabbatical years. All the time of its desolation the land rested in order to fulfill the seventy years.

Cyrus Allows the Exiles to Go Home

[22a]In the first year of King Cyrus of Persia, in fulfillment of the LORD's message spoken through [b]Jeremiah, the LORD motivated[1] King [c]Cyrus of Persia to issue a proclamation[2] throughout his kingdom and also to put it in writing. It read:

[23]"[a]This is what King Cyrus of Persia says: 'The LORD God of heaven has given me all the kingdoms of the earth. He has appointed me to build a temple for him in Jerusalem, which is in Judah. Anyone of his people among you may go up there, and may the LORD his God be with him.'"

36:18 [a]2 Kgs 25:13–15; 2 Chr 36:7, 10   36:19 [a]2 Kgs 25:9; Ps 79:1, 7; Isa 1:7–8; Jer 52:13   36:21 [a]Jer 25:9–12; 27:6–8; 29:10   36:22 [a]Ezra 1:1–3   [b]Jer 29:10   [c]Isa 44:28; 45:1   [1]Heb. *stirred the spirit of.*   [2]Heb. *a voice.*   36:23 [a]Ezra 1:2–3

EZRA

Ezra continues the Old Testament narrative of 2 Chronicles by showing how God fulfills his promise to return his people to the land of promise after seventy years of exile. Israel's second exodus, this one from Babylon, is less impressive than the return from Egypt because only a remnant chooses to leave Babylon. Ezra relates the story of two returns from Babylon—the first led by Zerubbabel to rebuild the temple (chs. 1–6) and the second under Ezra's leadership to rebuild the spiritual condition of the people (chs. 7–10). Sandwiched between these two accounts is a gap of nearly six decades during which Esther lives and rules as queen in Persia. Ezra is the Aramaic form of the Hebrew word *ezer*, "Help," and perhaps means "Yahweh Helps." Ezra and Nehemiah were originally bound together as one book because Chronicles, Ezra, and Nehemiah were viewed as one continuous history. The Septuagint, a Greek-language version of the Old Testament translated in the third century BC, calls Ezra/Nehemiah *Esdras Deuteron*, "Second Esdras." First Esdras is the name of the apocryphal book of Esdras. The Latin title is *Liber Primus Esdrae*, "First Book of Ezra." In the Latin Bible, Ezra is called 1 Ezra and Nehemiah is called 2 Ezra.

The Decree of Cyrus

1 In the first year of King Cyrus of Persia, in fulfillment of the LORD's message spoken through[1] Jeremiah, the LORD motivated King Cyrus of Persia to issue a proclamation throughout his kingdom and [a]also to put it in writing. It read:

2 "This is what King Cyrus of Persia says:

"'The LORD God of heaven has given me all the kingdoms of the earth. He has [a]appointed me to build a temple for him in Jerusalem, which is in Judah. 3 Anyone of his people among you (may his God be with him!) may go up to Jerusalem, which is in Judah, and may build [a]the temple of the LORD God of Israel—he is the God who is in Jerusalem. 4 Anyone who survives in any of those places where he is a resident foreigner must be helped by his neighbors with silver, gold, equipment, and animals, along with voluntary offerings for the temple of God which is in Jerusalem.'"

The Exiles Prepare to Return to Jerusalem

5 Then the leaders of Judah and Benjamin, along with the priests and the Levites—all those whose mind [a]God had stirred—got ready to go up in order to build the temple of the LORD in Jerusalem. 6 All their neighbors assisted them with silver utensils,[1] gold, equipment, animals, and expensive gifts, not to mention all the voluntary offerings.

7 Then [a]King Cyrus brought out the vessels of the LORD's temple [b]which Nebuchadnezzar had brought from Jerusalem and had displayed in the temple of his gods. 8 King Cyrus of Persia entrusted them to Mithredath the treasurer, who counted them out to [a]Sheshbazzar the leader of the Judahite exiles.

9 The inventory of these items was as follows:

> 30 gold basins,
> 1,000 silver basins,
> 29 silver utensils,[1]
> 10 30 gold bowls,
> 410 other[1] silver bowls,
> and 1,000 other vessels.

11 All these gold and silver vessels totaled 5,400. Sheshbazzar brought them all along when the captives were brought up from Babylon to Jerusalem.

1:1 [a] Ezra 5:13–14; Isa 44:28—45:13   [1] MT *from the mouth of;* LXX *by the mouth of.*   1:2 [a] Isa 44:28; 45:1, 13   1:3 [a] 1 Kgs 8:23; 18:39; Isa 37:16; Dan 6:26   1:5 [a] [Phil 2:13]   1:6 [1] LXX *everywhere, with silver.*   1:7 [a] Ezra 5:14; 6:5; Dan 1:2; 5:2–3   [b] 2 Kgs 24:13; 2 Chr 36:7, 18   1:8 [a] Ezra 5:14, 16   1:9 [1] Heb. *knives;* but its meaning is unclear.   1:10 [1] Heb. *double, second, what is doubled, two-fold.*

The Names of the Returning Exiles

2 These are [a]the people of the province [b]who were going up, from the captives of the exile whom King Nebuchadnezzar of Babylon had forced into exile in Babylon. They returned to Jerusalem and Judah, each to his own city. [2]They came with Zerubbabel, Jeshua, Nehemiah, Seraiah, Reelaiah, Mordecai, Bilshan, Mispar, Bigvai, Rehum, and Baanah.

The number of Israelites was as follows:
[3]the descendants of Parosh: 2,172;
[4]the descendants of Shephatiah: 372;
[5]the descendants of Arah: [a]775;
[6]the descendants of Pahath [a]Moab (from the line of Jeshua and[1] Joab): 2,812;
[7]the descendants of Elam: 1,254;
[8]the descendants of Zattu: 945;
[9]the descendants of Zaccai: 760;
[10]the descendants of Bani: 642;
[11]the descendants of Bebai: 623;
[12]the descendants of Azgad: 1,222;
[13]the descendants of Adonikam: 666;
[14]the descendants of Bigvai: 2,056;
[15]the descendants of Adin: 454;
[16]the descendants of Ater (through Hezekiah): 98;
[17]the descendants of Bezai: 323;
[18]the descendants of Jorah: 112;
[19]the descendants of Hashum: 223;
[20]the descendants of Gibbar: 95.
[21]The men[1] of Bethlehem: 123;
[22]the men of Netophah: 56;
[23]the men of Anathoth: 128;
[24]the men of the family[1] of Azmaveth: 42;
[25]the men of Kiriath Jearim,[1] Kephirah and Beeroth: 743;
[26]the men of Ramah and Geba: 621;
[27]the men of Micmash: 122;
[28]the men of Bethel and Ai: 223;
[29]the descendants of Nebo: 52;
[30]the descendants of Magbish: 156;
[31]the descendants of the other [a]Elam: 1,254;
[32]the descendants of Harim: 320;
[33]the men of Lod, Hadid, and Ono: 725;
[34]the men of Jericho: 345;
[35]the descendants of Senaah: 3,630.
[36]The priests: the descendants of [a]Jedaiah (through the family of Jeshua): 973;
[37]the descendants of [a]Immer: 1,052;
[38]the descendants of [a]Pashhur: 1,247;

[39]the descendants of [a]Harim: 1,017.
[40]The Levites: the descendants of Jeshua and Kadmiel (through the line of Hodaviah): 74.
[41]The singers: the descendants of Asaph: 128.
[42]The gatekeepers:[1] the descendants of Shallum, the descendants of Ater, the descendants of Talmon, the descendants of Akkub, the descendants of Hatita, and the descendants of Shobai: 139.
[43]The temple servants: [a]the descendants of Ziha, the descendants of Hasupha, the descendants of Tabbaoth, [44]the descendants of Keros, the descendants of Siaha, the descendants of Padon, [45]the descendants of Lebanah, the descendants of Hagabah, the descendants of Akkub, [46]the descendants of Hagab, the descendants of Shalmai,[1] the descendants of Hanan, [47]the descendants of Giddel, the descendants of Gahar, the descendants of Reaiah, [48]the descendants of Rezin, the descendants of Nekoda, the descendants of Gazzam, [49]the descendants of Uzzah, the descendants of Paseah, the descendants of Besai, [50]the descendants of Asnah, the descendants of Meunim, the descendants of Nephussim, [51]the descendants of Bakbuk, the descendants of Hakupha, the descendants of Harhur, [52]the descendants of Bazluth, the descendants of Mehida, the descendants of Harsha, [53]the descendants of Barkos, the descendants of Sisera, the descendants of Temah, [54]the descendants of Neziah, and the descendants of Hatipha.
[55]The descendants of the servants of [a]Solomon: the descendants of Sotai, the descendants of [b]Hassophereth, the descendants of Peruda, [56]the descendants of Jaala, the descendants of Darkon, the descendants of Giddel, [57]the descendants of Shephatiah, the descendants of Hattil, the descendants of Pokereth Hazzebaim, and the descendants of Ami.
[58]All the temple [a]servants and the descendants of the servants of [b]Solomon: 392.
[59]These are the ones that came up from Tel Melah, Tel Harsha, Kerub, Addon, and Immer (although they were unable to certify their family connection or their ancestry, as to whether they really were from Israel):

2:1[a]Neh 7:6–73; Jer 32:15; 50:5; Ezek 14:22 [b]2 Kgs 24:14–16; 25:11; 2 Chr 36:20 2:5[a]Neh 7:10 2:6[a]Neh 7:11 [1]MT omits and. 2:21[1]MT the sons of. 2:24[1]MT the sons of. 2:25[1]MT Kiriath Arim. 2:31[a]Ezra 2:7 2:36[a]1 Chr 24:7–18 2:37[a]1 Chr 24:14 2:38[a]1 Chr 9:12 2:39[a]1 Chr 24:8 2:42[1]MT the sons of the gatekeepers. 2:43[a]1 Chr 9:2; Ezra 7:7 2:46[1]Ket. Shamlai. 2:55[a]1 Kgs 9:21 [b]Neh 7:57–60 2:58[a]Josh 9:21, 27; 1 Chr 9:2 [b]1 Kgs 9:21

⁶⁰the descendants of Delaiah, the descendants of Tobiah, and the descendants of Nekoda: 652.

⁶¹And from among¹ the priests: the descendants of ᵃHobaiah, the descendants of Hakkoz, and the descendants of ᵇBarzillai (who had taken a wife from the daughters of Barzillai the Gileadite and was called by that name). ⁶²They searched ᵃfor their records in the genealogical materials, but did not find them. They were therefore excluded¹ from the priesthood. ⁶³The governor instructed them not to eat any of the sacred food until there was a priest who could consult the ᵃUrim and Thummim.

⁶⁴ᵃThe entire group numbered 42,360, ⁶⁵not counting their male and female servants, who numbered 7,337. They also had 200 male and female singers ⁶⁶and 736 horses, 245 mules, ⁶⁷435 camels, and 6,720 donkeys. ⁶⁸When they came to the LORD's temple in Jerusalem, ᵃsome of the family leaders offered voluntary offerings for the temple of God in order to rebuild it on its site. ⁶⁹As they were able, they gave to the ᵃtreasury for this work 61,000 drachmas¹ of gold, 5,000 minas of silver, and 100 priestly robes.

⁷⁰The priests, the Levites, ᵃsome of the people, the singers, the gatekeepers, and the temple servants lived in their towns, and all the rest of Israel lived in their towns.

The Altar Is Rebuilt

3 When the ᵃseventh month arrived and the Israelites were living in their¹ towns, the people assembled in Jerusalem. ²Then Jeshua the son of ᵃJozadak ᵇand his priestly colleagues and Zerubbabel son of ᶜShealtiel and his colleagues started to build the altar of the God of Israel so they could offer burnt offerings on it as ᵈrequired by the law of Moses the man of God. ³They established the altar on its foundations, even though they were in terror of the local peoples, and they offered ᵃburnt offerings on it to the LORD, both the morning and the evening offerings. ⁴They observed ᵃthe ᵇFeast ᶜof Shelters as required and offered the proper

number of daily burnt offerings according to the requirement for each day.⁵Afterward they offered the ᵃcontinual burnt offerings and those for the new moons and those for all the holy assemblies of the LORD and all those that were being voluntarily offered to the LORD.⁶From the first day of the seventh month they began to offer burnt offerings to the LORD. However, the LORD's temple was not at that time established.

Preparations for Rebuilding the Temple

⁷So they provided money for the masons and carpenters, and ᵃfood, beverages, and olive oil for the people of Sidon and Tyre, so that they would bring cedar timber from Lebanon to the seaport at ᵇJoppa, ᶜin accord with the edict of King Cyrus of Persia. ⁸In the second year after they had come to the temple of God in Jerusalem, in the second month, ᵃZerubbabel the son of Shealtiel ᵇand Jeshua the son of Jozadak initiated the work, along with the rest of their associates, the priests and the Levites, and all those who were coming to Jerusalem from the exile. They appointed the Levites who were at least twenty years old to take charge of the work on the LORD's temple. ⁹So Jeshua appointed both his sons and his relatives, Kadmiel and his sons (the sons of Yehudah), to take charge of the workers in the temple of God, along with the sons of Henadad, their sons, and their relatives the Levites. ¹⁰When ᵃthe builders established the LORD's temple, the priests, ceremonially attired and with their clarions, and the Levites (the sons of Asaph) with their cymbals, stood to praise the LORD according to the ᵇinstructions left by King David of Israel. ¹¹With antiphonal response they sang, praising ᵃand glorifying the LORD:

"ᵇFor he is good;
his loyal love toward Israel is ᶜforever."

All the people gave a loud shout as they praised the LORD when the temple of the

2:61 ᵃ Neh 7:63   ᵇ 2 Sam 17:27; 1 Kgs 2:7   ¹ MT *and from the sons of.*   **2:62** ᵃ Num 3:10   ¹ Heb. *they were desecrated.* **2:63** ᵃ Exod 28:30; Num 27:21   **2:64** ᵃ Neh 7:66; Isa 10:22   **2:68** ᵃ Ezra 1:6; 3:5; Neh 7:70   **2:69** ᵃ 1 Chr 26:20; Ezra 8:25–35 ¹ Or perhaps *daric;* a Persian gold coin.   **2:70** ᵃ Ezra 6:16–17; Neh 7:73   **3:1** ᵃ Neh 7:73; 8:1–2   ¹ MT *in the towns.*   **3:2** ᵃ 1 Chr 6:14–15; Ezra 4:3; Neh 12:1, 8; Hag 1:1; 2:2   ᵇ Ezra 2:2; 4:2–3; 5:2   ᶜ 1 Chr 3:17   ᵈ Deut 12:5–6   **3:3** ᵃ Num 28:3   **3:4** ᵃ Lev 23:33–43; Neh 8:14–18; Zech 14:16   ᵇ Exod 23:16   ᶜ Num 29:12–13   **3:5** ᵃ Exod 29:38; Num 28:3, 11, 19, 26; Ezra 1:4; 2:68; 7:15–16; 8:28   **3:7** ᵃ 1 Kgs 5:6, 9; 2 Chr 2:10; Acts 12:20   ᵇ 2 Chr 2:16; Acts 9:36   ᶜ Ezra 1:2; 6:3   **3:8** ᵃ Ezra 3:2; 4:3 ᵇ 1 Chr 23:4, 24   **3:10** ᵃ 1 Chr 16:5–6   ᵇ 1 Chr 6:31; 16:4; 25:1   **3:11** ᵃ Exod 15:21; 2 Chr 7:3; Neh 12:24 ᵇ 1 Chr 16:34; Ps 136:1   ᶜ 1 Chr 16:41; Jer 33:11

LORD was established. [12]Many of the priests, the Levites, and the [a]leaders—older people who had seen with their own eyes the former temple while it was still established— were weeping loudly, and many others raised their voice in a joyous shout. [13]People were unable to tell the difference between the sound of joyous shouting and the sound of the people's weeping, for the people were shouting so loudly that the sound was heard a long way off.

Opposition to the Building Efforts

4 When [a]the enemies of Judah and Benjamin learned that the former exiles were building a temple for the LORD God of Israel, [2]they came to Zerubbabel and the leaders and said to them, "Let us help you build, for like you we seek your God and we have been sacrificing to him[1] from the time of King Esarhaddon of Assyria, who brought us here." [3]But Zerubbabel, Jeshua, and the rest of the leaders of Israel said to them, "[a]You have no right[1] to help us build the temple of our God. We will build it by ourselves for the LORD God of Israel, just as [b]King Cyrus, the king of Persia, has commanded us." [4]Then [a]the local people began to discourage the people of Judah and to dishearten them from building. [5]They were hiring advisers to oppose them, so as to frustrate their plans, throughout the time of King Cyrus of Persia until the reign of King [a]Darius of Persia.

Official Complaints Are Lodged against the Jews

[6]At the beginning of the reign of Ahasuerus they filed an accusation against the inhabitants of Judah and Jerusalem. [7]And during the reign of [a]Artaxerxes, Bishlam, Mithredath, Tabeel, and the rest of their colleagues[1] wrote to King Artaxerxes of Persia. This letter[2] was first written in [b]Aramaic but then translated.

[What follows is in Aramaic.]

[8]Rehum the commander and Shimshai the scribe wrote a letter concerning[1] Jerusalem to King Artaxerxes as follows: [9]From Rehum [a]the commander, Shimshai the scribe, and the rest of their colleagues— the judges, the rulers, the officials, the secretaries, the Erechites, the Babylonians, the people of Susa (that is, the Elamites), [10]and the rest of the nations whom the great [a]and noble Ashurbanipal[1] deported [b]and settled in the cities[2] of Samaria and other places in Trans-Euphrates.[3] [11](This is a copy of the letter they sent to him.)

"To King Artaxerxes, from your servants in Trans-Euphrates: [12]Now let the king be aware that the Jews who came up to us from you have gone to Jerusalem. They are rebuilding that [a]rebellious and odious city. They are completing its [b]walls and repairing its foundations. [13]Let the king also be aware that if this city is built and its walls are completed, no more [a]tax, custom, or toll will be paid, and the royal treasury will suffer loss. [14]In light of the fact that we are loyal to the king,[1] and since it does not seem appropriate to us that the king should sustain damage, we are sending the king this information [15]so that he may initiate a search of the records of his predecessors and discover in those records[1] that this city is rebellious and injurious to both kings and provinces, producing internal revolts from long ago. It is for this very reason that this city was destroyed. [16]We therefore are informing the king that if this city is rebuilt and its walls are completed, you will not retain control of this portion of Trans-Euphrates."

[17]The king sent the following response:

"To Rehum the commander, Shimshai the scribe, and the rest of their colleagues who live in Samaria and other parts of Trans-Euphrates: Greetings! [18]The letter you sent to us has been translated and read in my presence. [19]So I gave orders, and it was determined[1] that this city from long ago has been engaging in insurrection against kings. It has continually engaged in rebellion and revolt. [20]Powerful kings have been over Jerusalem who [a]ruled throughout the entire [b]Trans-Euphrates and who were the beneficiaries of tribute, custom, and toll. [21]Now give orders that these men cease their work and that this city not be rebuilt until such time as I so instruct. [22]Exercise appropriate

3:12 [a]Ezra 2:68   4:1 [a]Ezra 4:7–9   4:2 [1]Ket. *and not.*   4:3 [a]Neh 2:20   [b]Ezra 1:1–4   [1]Heb. *not to you and to us.*   4:4 [a]Ezra 3:3
4:5 [a]Ezra 5:5; 6:1   4:7 [a]Ezra 7:1, 7, 21   [b]2 Kgs 18:26   [1]Ket. *colleague.*   [2]MT *the text of the letter.*   4:8 [1]Or perhaps *against.*
4:9 [a]2 Kgs 17:30–31   4:10 [a]2 Kgs 17:24; Ezra 4:1   [b]Ezra 4:11, 17; 7:12   [1]Aram. *Osnappar,* another name for Ashurbanipal.
[2]MT *the city.*   [3]Aram. *beyond the river,* a technical designation for the region west of the Euphrates.   4:12 [a]2 Chr 36:13
[b]Ezra 5:3, 9   4:13 [a]Ezra 4:20; 7:24   4:14 [1]Aram. *we eat the salt of the palace.*   4:15 [1]Aram. *Discover . . . and*
learn.   4:19 [1]Aram. *and they searched and found.*   4:20 [a]1 Kgs 4:21; 1 Chr 18:3; Ps 72:8   [b]Gen 15:18; Josh 1:4

caution so that there is no negligence in this matter. Why should danger increase to the point that the king sustains damage?"

[23] Then, as soon as the copy of the letter from King Artaxerxes was read in the presence of Rehum, Shimshai the scribe, and their colleagues, they proceeded promptly to the Jews in Jerusalem and stopped them with threat of armed force.[l]

[24] So the work on the temple of God in Jerusalem came to a halt. It remained halted until the second year of the reign of King Darius of Persia.

Tattenai Appeals to Darius

5 Then the prophets [a]Haggai and [b]Zechariah son of Iddo prophesied concerning the Jews who were in Judah and Jerusalem in the name of the God of Israel who was over them. [2] Then [a]Zerubbabel [b]the son of Shealtiel and Jeshua the son of Jozadak began to rebuild the temple of God in Jerusalem. The prophets of God were with them, supporting them.

[3] At that time [a]Tattenai governor of Trans-Euphrates, Shethar-Bozenai, and their colleagues came to them and asked, "[b]Who gave you authority to rebuild this temple and to complete this structure?"[l] [4] They[l] [a]also asked them, "What are the names of the men who are building this edifice?"[5] But God was watching over [a]the elders of Judah, and they were not stopped until a report could be dispatched to Darius and a [b]letter could be sent back concerning this.

[6] This is [a]a copy of the letter that Tattenai governor of Trans-Euphrates, Shethar-Bozenai, and his colleagues (who were the officials of Trans-Euphrates) sent to King Darius. [7] The report they sent to him was written as follows:

"To King Darius: All greetings! [8] Let it be known to the king that we have gone to the province of Judah, to the temple of the great God. It is being built with large stones, and timbers are being placed in the walls. This work is being done with all diligence and is prospering in their hands. [9] We inquired of those elders, asking them, '[a]Who gave you the authority to rebuild this temple and to complete this structure?' [10] We also inquired

of their names in order to inform you, so that we might write the names of the men who were their leaders. [11] They responded to us in the following way: 'We are servants of the God of heaven [a]and earth. We are rebuilding the temple which was previously built many years ago. A great king of Israel built it and completed it. [12] But after our ancestors angered the God of heaven, he delivered them into the hands of King [a]Nebuchadnezzar of Babylon, the Chaldean, who destroyed this temple and exiled the people to Babylon. [13] But in the first year of King [a]Cyrus of Babylon, King Cyrus enacted a decree to rebuild this temple of God. [14] Even [a]the gold and silver vessels of the temple of God that Nebuchadnezzar had taken from the temple in Jerusalem and had brought to the palace of Babylon—even those things King Cyrus brought from the palace of Babylon and presented to a man by the name of Sheshbazzar whom he had appointed as governor. [15] He said to him, "Take these vessels and go deposit them in the temple in Jerusalem, and let the house of God be rebuilt in its proper location." [16] Then this Sheshbazzar went and [a]laid the foundations of the temple of God in Jerusalem. From that time to the present moment [b]it has been in the process of being rebuilt, although it is not yet finished.'

[17] "Now if the king is so inclined, [a]let a search be conducted in the royal archives there in Babylon in order to determine whether King Cyrus did in fact issue orders for this temple of God to be rebuilt in Jerusalem. Then let the king send us a decision concerning this matter."

Darius Issues a Decree

6 So Darius the king issued orders, [a]and they searched in the archives of the treasury which were deposited there in Babylon. [2] A scroll was found in the citadel[l] of Ecbatana which is in the province of [a]Media, and it was inscribed as follows:

"Memorandum: [3] In the first year of his reign, King Cyrus gave [a]orders concerning the temple of God in Jerusalem: 'Let the temple be rebuilt as a place where sacrifices are offered. Let its foundations be

4:23 [l] Aram. *by force and power.*   **5:1** [a] Hag 1:1   [b] Zech 1:1   **5:2** [a] Ezra 3:2; Hag 1:12   [b] Ezra 6:14; Hag 2:4   **5:3** [a] Ezra 5:6; 6:6   [b] Ezra 1:3; 5:9   [l] Or perhaps *wall.*   **5:4** [a] Ezra 5:10   [l] MT *We said.*   **5:5** [a] 2 Chr 16:9; Ezra 7:6, 28; Ps 33:18   [b] Ezra 6:6   **5:6** [a] Ezra 4:7–10   **5:9** [a] Ezra 5:3–4   **5:11** [a] 1 Kgs 6:1, 38   **5:12** [a] 2 Kgs 24:2; 25:8–11; 2 Chr 36:17; Jer 52:12–15   **5:13** [a] Ezra 1:1   **5:14** [a] Ezra 1:7–8; 6:5; Dan 5:2   **5:16** [a] Ezra 3:8–10; Hag 2:18   [b] Ezra 6:15   **5:17** [a] Ezra 6:1–2   **6:1** [a] Ezra 5:17   **6:2** [a] 2 Kgs 17:6   [l] MT *in the in citadel.*   **6:3** [a] Ezra 1:1; 5:13

set in place.[1] Its height is to be 90 feet and its width 90 feet,[2] [4a]with three layers of large stones and one[1] layer of timber. The [b]expense is to be subsidized by the royal treasury. [5]Furthermore, let [a]the gold and silver vessels of the temple of God, which Nebuchadnezzar brought from the temple in Jerusalem and carried to Babylon, be returned and brought to their proper place in the temple in Jerusalem. Let them be deposited in the temple of God.'

[6]"[a]Now Tattenai governor of Trans-Euphrates, Shethar-Bozenai, and their colleagues, the officials of Trans-Euphrates—all of you stay far away from there. [7]Leave the work on this temple of God alone.[1] Let the governor of the Jews and the elders of the Jews rebuild this temple of God in its proper place.

[8]"I also hereby issue orders as to what you are to do with those elders of the Jews in order to rebuild this temple of God. From the royal treasury, from the taxes of Trans-Euphrates, the complete costs are to be given to these men so that there may be no interruption of the work. [9]Whatever is needed—whether oxen or rams or lambs for burnt offerings for the God of heaven or wheat or salt or wine or oil, as required by the priests who are in Jerusalem—must be given to them daily without any neglect, [10]so [a]that they may be offering incense to the God of heaven and may be praying for the good fortune of the king and his family. [11]"I hereby give orders that if anyone changes this directive [a]a beam is to be pulled out from his house and he is to be raised up and impaled on it, and his house is to be reduced to a rubbish heap[1] for this indiscretion.[2] [12]May God who makes his [a]name to reside there overthrow any king or nation who reaches out to cause such change so as to destroy this temple of God in Jerusalem. I, Darius, have given orders. Let them be carried out with precision!"

The Temple Is Finally Dedicated

[13]Then Tattenai governor of Trans-Euphrates, Shethar-Bozenai, and their colleagues acted accordingly—with precision, just as Darius the king had given instructions. [14]The elders of the Jews continued building and prospering, while at the same time Haggai the prophet and Zechariah the [a]son of Iddo continued prophesying. They built and brought it to completion by the command of the God of Israel and by the command of [b]Cyrus and [c]Darius and [d]Artaxerxes king of Persia. [15]They finished this temple on the third day of the month Adar, which is the sixth year of the reign of King Darius.

[16]The people of Israel—[a]the priests, the Levites, and the rest of the exiles—observed the dedication of this temple of God with joy. [17]For the dedication of this temple of God they [a]offered 100 bulls, 200 rams, 400 lambs, and 12 male goats for the sin of all Israel, according to the number of the tribes of Israel. [18]They appointed the priests by their [a]divisions and the Levites by their [b]divisions over the worship of God at Jerusalem, in accord with the book of Moses. [19]The exiles observed the Passover [a]on the fourteenth day of the first month. [20]The priests and the Levites had [a]purified themselves, every last one, and they all were ceremonially pure. They [b]sacrificed the Passover lamb for all the exiles, for their colleagues the priests, and for themselves. [21]The Israelites who were returning from the exile ate it, along with all those who had joined them in separating themselves from the [a]uncleanness of the nations of the land to seek the Lord God of Israel. [22]They observed the [a]Feast of Unleavened Bread for seven days with joy, for the Lord had given them joy and had [b]changed the opinion [c]of the king of Assyria toward them so that he assisted them in the work on the temple of God, the God of Israel.

The Arrival of Ezra

7 Now after these things had happened, during the reign of King [a]Artaxerxes of Persia, Ezra came up from Babylon. Ezra was the [b]son of Seraiah, who was [c]the son of Azariah, who was the son of [d]Hilkiah, [2]who was the son of Shallum, who was the son of Zadok, who was the son of Ahitub, [3]who was the son of Amariah, who was the son of Azariah,

who was the son of Meraioth, [4]who was the son of Zerahiah, who was the son of Uzzi, who was the son of Bukki, [5]who was the son of Abishua, who was the son of Phinehas, who was the son of Eleazar, who was the son of Aaron the chief priest. [6]This [a]Ezra is the one who came up from Babylon. He was [b]a scribe who was skilled in the law of Moses which the LORD God of Israel had given. The king supplied him with everything he requested, for the hand of the LORD his God was on him. [7]In the seventh year of King Artaxerxes, Ezra brought up[1] to Jerusalem [a]some of [b]the Israelites and some of [c]the priests, the Levites, the attendants, the gatekeepers, and the temple servants. [8]He entered Jerusalem in the fifth month of the seventh year of the king. [9]On the first day of the first month he had determined to make[1] the ascent from Babylon, and on the first day of the fifth month he arrived at Jerusalem, for the good hand of his God was on him. [10]Now Ezra had dedicated himself to the [a]study of the law of the LORD, to its observance, and to [b]teaching its statutes and judgments in Israel.

Artaxerxes Gives Official Endorsement to Ezra's Mission

[11]What follows is a copy of the letter that King Artaxerxes gave to Ezra the priestly scribe. Ezra was a scribe in matters pertaining to the commandments of the LORD and his statutes over Israel:

[12]"Artaxerxes, [a]king of kings, to Ezra the priest, [b]a scribe of the law of the God of heaven: [13]I have now issued a decree that anyone in my kingdom from the people of Israel—even the priests and Levites—who wishes to do so may go up with you to Jerusalem. [14]You are authorized by the king and his [a]seven advisers to inquire concerning Judah and Jerusalem, according to the law of your God which is in your possession, [15]and to bring silver and gold which the king and his advisers have freely contributed to the God of Israel, [a]who resides in Jerusalem, [16]along with all the silver [a]and gold that you may collect throughout all the province of Babylon and the [b]contributions of the people and the priests for the temple of their God which is in Jerusalem. [17]With this money you should be sure to purchase bulls, rams, and lambs, along with the appropriate [a]meal offerings and libations. You should [b]bring them to the altar of the temple of your God which is in Jerusalem. [18]You may do whatever seems appropriate to you and your colleagues with the rest of the silver and the gold, in keeping with the will of your God. [19]Deliver to the God of Jerusalem the vessels that are given to you for the service of the temple of your God. [20]The rest of the needs for the temple of your God that you may have to supply, you may do so from the royal treasury.

[21]"I, King Artaxerxes, hereby issue orders to all the treasurers of Trans-Euphrates that you precisely execute all that Ezra the priestly scribe of the law of the God of heaven may request of you—[22]up to 100 talents of silver, 100 cors of wheat, 100 baths of wine, 100 baths of olive oil,[1] and unlimited salt. [23]Everything that the God of heaven has required should be precisely done for the temple of the God of heaven. Why should there be wrath against the empire of the king and his sons? [24]Furthermore, be aware of the fact that you have no authority to impose tax, tribute, or toll on any of the priests, the Levites, the musicians, the doorkeepers, the temple servants, or the attendants at the temple of this God.

[25]"Now you, Ezra, in keeping with the wisdom of your God which you possess, [a]appoint judges[1] and court officials who can arbitrate cases on behalf of all the people who are in Trans-Euphrates who [b]know the laws of your God. Those who do not know this law should be taught. [26]Everyone who does not observe both the law of your God and the law of the king will be completely liable to the appropriate penalty, whether it is death or banishment or confiscation of property or detainment in prison."

[27][a]Blessed be the LORD God of our fathers, [b]who so moved in the heart of the king to so honor the temple of the LORD which is in Jerusalem! [28]He [a]has also conferred his favor on me before [b]the king, his advisers, and all the influential leaders of the king. I gained strength as the hand of the LORD my God was on me, and I gathered leaders from Israel to go up with me.

7:6 [a]Ezra 7:11–12, 21 [b]Ezra 7:9, 28; 8:22   7:7 [a]Ezra 8:1–14 [b]Ezra 8:15 [c]Ezra 2:43; 8:20 [1]MT *they came up.*   7:9 [1]MT *foundation.*   7:10 [a]Ps 119:45 [b]Deut 33:10; Ezra 7:6, 25; Neh 8:1–8; [Mal 2:7]   7:12 [a]Ezek 26:7; Dan 2:37 [b]Ezra 4:10   7:14 [a]Esth 1:14   7:15 [a]2 Chr 6:2; Ezra 6:12; Ps 135:21   7:16 [a]Ezra 8:25 [b]1 Chr 29:6, 9   7:17 [a]Num 15:4–13 [b]Deut 12:5–11   7:22 [1]MT reverses *olive oil* and *baths.*   7:25 [a]Exod 18:21–22; Deut 16:18 [b]2 Chr 17:7; Ezra 7:10; [Mal 2:7; Col 1:28] [1]LXX *scribes.*   7:27 [a]1 Chr 29:10 [b]Ezra 6:22; [Prov 21:1]   7:28 [a]Ezra 9:9 [b]Ezra 5:5; 7:6, 9; 8:18

The Leaders Who Returned with Ezra

8 These are the leaders and those enrolled with them by genealogy who were coming up with me from Babylon during the reign of King Artaxerxes: [2]from the descendants of Phinehas, Gershom;

from the descendants of Ithamar, Daniel;

from the descendants of David, [a]Hattush [3]the son of Shecaniah;[1]

from the descendants of [a]Parosh, Zechariah, and with him were enrolled by genealogy 150 men;

[4]from the descendants of Pahath [a]Moab, Eliehoenai son of Zerahiah, and with him 200 men;

[5]from the descendants of Zattu,[1] Shecaniah son of Jahaziel, and with him 300 men;

[6]from the descendants of Adin, Ebed son of Jonathan, and with him 50 men;

[7]from the descendants of Elam, Jeshaiah son of Athaliah, and with him 70 men;

[8]from the descendants of Shephatiah, Zebadiah son of Michael, and with him 80 men;

[9]from the descendants of Joab, Obadiah son of Jehiel, and with him 218 men;

[10]from the descendants of Bani,[1] Shelomith son of Josiphiah, and with him 160 men;

[11]from the descendants of [a]Bebai, Zechariah son of Bebai, and with him 28 men;

[12]from the descendants of Azgad, Johanan son of Hakkatan, and with him 110 men;

[13]from the descendants of Adonikam there were the latter ones.[1] Their names were Eliphelet, Jeuel, and Shemaiah, and with them 60 men;

[14]from the descendants of Bigvai, Uthai, and Zaccur,[1] and with them 70 men.

The Exiles Travel to Jerusalem

[15]I had them assemble at the canal that flows toward Ahava, and we camped there for three days. I observed that the people and the priests were present, but I found no [a]Levites there. [16]So I sent for Eliezer, Ariel, Shemaiah, Elnathan, Jarib, Elnathan, Nathan, Zechariah, and [a]Meshullam, who were leaders, and Joiarib and Elnathan, who were teachers. [17]I sent them to Iddo, who was the leader in the place called Casiphia. I told them what to say to Iddo and his relatives,[1] who were the temple servants in Casiphia, so they would bring us attendants for the temple of our God.

[18]Due to the fact that the good hand of our God was on us, they [a]brought us a skilled man, from the descendants of Mahli the son of Levi son of Israel. This man was Sherebiah, who was accompanied by his sons and brothers, 18 men; [19]and [a]Hashabiah, along with Jeshaiah from the descendants of Merari, with his brothers and their sons, 20 men; [20a]and some of the temple servants that David and his officials had established for the work of the Levites—220 of them. They were all designated by name.

[21]I [a]called for a fast there by the Ahava Canal, so that we might [b]humble ourselves before our God and seek from him a [c]safe journey for us, our children, and all our property. [22]I was embarrassed to request [a]soldiers and horsemen from [b]the king to protect us from the enemy along the way, because we had said to the king, "The [c]good hand of our God is on everyone who is seeking him, but his great anger is [d]against everyone who [e]forsakes him." [23]So we fasted and prayed to our God about this, and he [a]answered us.

[24]Then I set apart 12 of the leading priests, together with[1] Sherebiah, Hashabiah, and 10 of their brothers, [25]and I weighed out to [a]them the silver, the gold, and the vessels intended for the temple of our God—items that the king, his advisers, his officials, and all Israel who were present had contributed. [26]I weighed out to them: 650 talents of silver, silver vessels worth 100 talents, 100 talents of gold, [27]20 gold bowls worth 1,000 darics, and 2 exquisite vessels of gleaming bronze, as valuable as gold. [28]Then I said to them, "You are [a]holy to the LORD, just as these vessels are [b]holy. The silver and the gold are a voluntary offering to the LORD, the God of your fathers. [29]Be careful with them and protect them, until you weigh them out before the [a]leading priests and the Levites and the family leaders of Israel in Jerusalem, in the storerooms of the temple of the LORD.

8:2 [a]1 Chr 3:22; Ezra 2:68   8:3 [a]Ezra 2:3   [1]MT *from the sons of Shecaniah.*   8:4 [a]Ezra 10:30   8:5 [1]MT omits *of Zattu.*   8:10 [1]MT omits *Bani.*   8:11 [a]Ezra 10:28   8:13 [1]Or *those who came later.*   8:14 [1]Ket. *and Zabbud.*   8:15 [a]Ezra 7:7; 8:2   8:16 [a]Ezra 10:15   8:17 [1]MT *his brother.*   8:18 [a]2 Chr 30:22; Neh 8:7   8:19 [a]Neh 12:24   8:20 [a]Ezra 2:43; 7:7   8:21 [a]1 Sam 7:6; 2 Chr 20:3   [b]Lev 16:29; 23:29; Isa 58:3, 5   [c]Ps 5:8   8:22 [a]1 Cor 9:15   [b]Ezra 7:6, 9, 28   [c]Ps 33:18–19; 34:15, 22; Rom 8:28]   [d]Ps 34:16]   [e]2 Chr 15:2]   8:23 [a][1 Chr 5:20]; 2 Chr 33:13; Isa 19:22   8:24 [1]MT *to Sherebiah Hashabiah.*   8:25 [a]Ezra 7:15–16   8:28 [a]Lev 21:6–9; Deut 33:8   [b]Lev 22:2–3; Num 4:4, 15, 19, 20   8:29 [a]Ezra 4:3

[30]Then the priests and the Levites took charge of the silver, the gold, and the vessels that had been weighed out, to transport them to Jerusalem to the temple of our God. [31]On [a]the twelfth day of the first month we began traveling from the Ahava Canal to go to Jerusalem. The hand of our God was on us, and he delivered us from our enemies and from bandits along the way. [32]So we [a]came to Jerusalem, and we stayed there for three days. [33]On the fourth day we weighed [a]out the silver, the gold, and the vessels in the house of our God into the care of Meremoth son of Uriah, the priest, and Eleazar son of Phinehas, who were accompanied by [b]Jozabad son of Jeshua and Noadiah son of Binnui, who were Levites. [34]Everything was verified by number and by weight, and the total weight was written down at that time.

[35]The exiles who were [a]returning from the captivity [b]offered burnt offerings to the God of Israel—12 bulls for all Israel, 96 rams, 77 male lambs, along with 12 male goats as a sin offering. All this was a burnt offering to the LORD. [36]Then they presented the [a]decrees of the king to the king's satraps and to the governors of Trans-Euphrates, who assisted the people and the temple of God.

A Prayer of Ezra

9 Now when these things had been completed, the leaders approached me and said, "The people of Israel, the priests, and the Levites have not [a]separated themselves from the local residents who practice detestable things similar to those of the Canaanites, the Hittites, the Perizzites, the Jebusites, the Ammonites, the Moabites, the Egyptians, and the Amorites. [2]Indeed, they have [a]taken some of their daughters as wives for themselves and for their sons, so that the [b]holy race has become [c]intermingled with the local residents. Worse still, the leaders and the officials have been at the forefront of all this unfaithfulness!" [3]When [a]I heard this report, I tore my tunic and my robe and ripped out some of the hair from my head and beard. Then I sat down, quite [b]devastated. [4]Everyone who [a]held the words of the God of Israel in awe[1] gathered around me because of the unfaithful acts of the people of the exile. Devastated, I continued to sit there until the [b]evening offering.

[5]At the time of the evening offering I got up from my self-abasement, with my tunic and robe torn, and then dropped to my knees and [a]spread my hands to the LORD my God. [6]I prayed:

"O my God, I [a]am ashamed and embarrassed to lift my face to you, my God! For [b]our iniquities have climbed higher than our heads, and our guilt extends to the heavens. [7]From the days of our fathers until this very day our guilt has been great. Because of our iniquities [a]we, along with our kings and[1] priests, have been delivered over by the local kings to [b]sword, captivity, plunder, and [c]embarrassment—right up to the present time.

[8]"But now briefly we have received mercy from the LORD our God, in that he has left us a remnant and has given us a secure position[1] in his holy place. Thus our God has [a]enlightened our eyes and has given us a little relief in our time of servitude. [9a]Although we are slaves, our God has not abandoned us in our servitude. [b]He [c]has extended kindness to us in the sight of the kings of Persia, in that he has revived us to restore the temple of our God and to raise up its ruins and to give us a protective wall in Judah and Jerusalem.

[10]"And now what are we able to say after this, our God? For we have forsaken your commandments [11]which you commanded us through your servants the prophets with these words: 'The land that you are entering to possess is a land [a]defiled by the impurities of the local residents! With their abominations they have filled it from one end to the other with their filthiness. [12]Therefore [a]do not give your daughters in marriage to their sons, and do not take their daughters in marriage for your sons. Do not [b]ever seek their peace or welfare, so that you may be strong and may eat the good of the land and may [c]leave it as an inheritance for your children forever.'

[13]"Everything that has happened to us has come about because of our wicked actions and our great guilt. Even so, our God, you [a]have exercised restraint toward our iniquities and have given us a remnant such as this. [14]Shall we once [a]again break your commandments and intermarry with these abominable peoples? Would you not [b]be so angered by us that you would wipe us out, with no survivor or remnant? [15]O LORD God of Israel, [a]you are righteous, for we are left as a remnant this day. [b]Indeed, we stand before you in our guilt. However, because of this guilt no one can really stand before you."

The People Confess Their Sins

10 While Ezra was praying and confessing, weeping and throwing himself to the ground [a]before the temple of God, a very large crowd of Israelites—men, women, and children alike—gathered around him. The people wept [b]loudly. [2]Then Shecaniah son of Jehiel, from the descendants of Elam,[1] addressed Ezra:

"We have been [a]unfaithful to our God by marrying[2] foreign women from the local peoples. Nonetheless, there is still hope for Israel in this regard. [3]Therefore let us [a]enact a covenant with our God to send away all these women and their offspring, in keeping with your counsel, my lord, and that of those who [b]respect[1] [c]the commandments of our God. And let it be done according to the [d]law. [4]Get up, for this matter concerns you. We are with you, so [a]be strong and act decisively!"

[5]So Ezra got up and made the leading priests and Levites and all Israel take an [a]oath to carry out this plan. And they all took a solemn oath. [6]Then Ezra got up from in front of the temple of God and went to the room of Jehohanan son of Eliashib. While he stayed[1] there, he did not [a]eat food or drink water, for he was in mourning over the infidelity of the exiles.

[7]A proclamation was circulated throughout Judah and Jerusalem that all the exiles were to be assembled in Jerusalem. [8]Everyone who did not come within three days would thereby forfeit all his property, in keeping with the counsel of the officials and the elders. Furthermore, he himself would be excluded from the assembly of the exiles.

[9]All the men of Judah and Benjamin were gathered in Jerusalem within the three days. (It was in the ninth month, on the twentieth day of that month.) [a]All the people sat in the square at the temple of God, trembling because of this matter and because of the rains.

[10]Then Ezra the priest stood up and said to them, "You have behaved in an unfaithful manner by taking foreign wives! This has contributed to the guilt of Israel. [11]Now [a]give praise to the LORD God of your fathers, and do his will. [b]Separate yourselves from the local residents and from these foreign wives."

[12]All the assembly replied in a loud voice: "We will do just as you have said! [13]However, the people are numerous and it is the rainy season. We are unable to stand here outside. Furthermore, this business cannot be resolved in a day or two, for we have sinned greatly in this matter. [14]Let our leaders take steps[1] on behalf of all [a]the assembly. Let all those in our towns who have married foreign women come at an appointed time, and with them the elders of each town and its judges, until the hot anger of our God is turned away from us in this matter."

[15]Only Jonathan son of Asahel and Jahzeiah son of Tikvah were against this, assisted by [a]Meshullam and Shabbethai the Levite. [16]So the exiles proceeded accordingly. Ezra the priest separated out[1] by name men who were [a]leaders in their family groups. They sat down to consider this matter on the first day of the tenth month, [17]and on the first day of the first month they finished considering all the men who had married foreign wives.

Those Who Had Taken Foreign Wives

[18]It was determined that from the descendants of the priests, the following had taken foreign wives: from the descendants of [a]Jeshua son of Jozadak, and his brothers:

9:13 [a][Ps 103:10]   **9:14** [a][John 5:14; 2 Pet 2:20]   [b]Deut 9:8   **9:15** [a]Neh 9:33; Dan 9:14   [b]1 Cor 15:17   **10:1** [a]2 Chr 20:9   [b]Neh 8:1–9   [1]Heb. *with much weeping.*   **10:2** [a]Ezra 10:10, 13, 14, 17, 18; Neh 13:23–27   [1]Ket. *eternity.*   [2]Heb. *in that we have given a dwelling to.*   **10:3** [a]2 Chr 34:31   [b]Ezra 9:4   [c]Deut 7:2–3   [d]Deut 24:1–2   [1]Heb. *who tremble at.*   **10:4** [a]1 Chr 28:10   **10:5** [a]Ezra 10:12, 19; Neh 5:12; 13:25   **10:6** [a]Deut 9:18   [1]MT *and he went.*   **10:9** [a]1 Sam 12:18; Ezra 9:4; 10:3   **10:11** [a][Lev 26:40–42]; Josh 7:19; [Prov 28:13]   [b]Ezra 10:3   **10:14** [a]2 Kgs 23:26; 2 Chr 28:11–13; 29:10; 30:8   [1]Heb. *stand.*   **10:15** [a]Ezra 8:16; Neh 3:4   **10:16** [a]Ezra 4:3   [1]MT *were separated.*   **10:18** [a]Ezra 5:2; Hag 1:1, 12; 2:4; Zech 3:1; 6:11

Maaseiah, Eliezer, Jarib, and Gedaliah. [19] (They[a] gave their word to send away their wives; their guilt[b] offering was a ram from the flock for their[c] guilt.)

[20] From the descendants of Immer: Hanani and Zebadiah.

[21] From the descendants of Harim: Maaseiah, Elijah, Shemaiah, Jehiel, and Uzziah.

[22] From the descendants of Pashhur: Elioenai, Maaseiah, Ishmael, Nethanel, Jozabad, and Elasah.

[23] From the Levites: Jozabad, Shimei, Kelaiah (also known as Kelita), Pethahiah, Judah, and Eliezer.

[24] From the singers: Eliashib. From the gatekeepers: Shallum, Telem, and Uri.

[25] From the Israelites: from the[a] descendants of Parosh: Ramiah, Izziah, Malkijah, Mijamin, Eleazar, Malkijah, and Benaiah.

[26] From the descendants of Elam: Mattaniah, Zechariah, Jehiel, Abdi, Jeremoth, and Elijah.

[27] From the descendants of Zattu: Elioenai, Eliashib, Mattaniah, Jeremoth, Zabad, and Aziza.

[28] From the[a] descendants of Bebai: Jehohanan, Hananiah, Zabbai, and Athlai.

[29] From the descendants of Bani: Meshullam, Malluch, Adaiah, Jashub, Sheal, and Jeremoth.

[30] From the[a] descendants of Pahath Moab: Adna, Kelal, Benaiah, Maaseiah, Mattaniah, Bezalel, Binnui, and Manasseh.

[31] From[1] the descendants of Harim: Eliezer, Ishijah, Malkijah, Shemaiah, Shimeon, [32] Benjamin, Malluch, and Shemariah.

[33] From the descendants of Hashum: Mattenai, Mattattah, Zabad, Eliphelet, Jeremai, Manasseh, and Shimei.

[34] From the descendants of Bani: Maadai, Amram, Uel, [35] Benaiah, Bedeiah, Keluhi, [36] Vaniah, Meremoth, Eliashib, [37] Mattaniah, Mattenai, and Jaasu.

[38] From[1] the descendants of Binnui: Shimei, [39] Shelemiah, Nathan, Adaiah, [40] Machnadebai, Shashai, Sharai, [41] Azarel, Shelemiah, Shemariah, [42] Shallum, Amariah, and Joseph.

[43] From the descendants of Nebo: Jeiel, Mattithiah, Zabad, Zebina, Jaddai, Joel, and Benaiah.

[44] All these had taken foreign wives, and some of them also had children by these women.[1]

10:19[a] 2 Kgs 10:15 [b] Lev 6:4, 6 [c] Lev 5:6, 15 10:25[a] Ezra 2:3; 8:3; Neh 7:8 10:28[a] Ezra 8:11 10:30[a] Ezra 8:4 10:31[1] MT *and the sons of.* 10:38[1] MT *and Bani and Binnui.* 10:44[1] This final statement is difficult in its syntax and meaning. Some translate it as *and they sent these wives and children away.*

NEHEMIAH

Nehemiah, contemporary of Ezra and cupbearer to the king in the Persian palace, leads the third and last return to Jerusalem after the Babylonian exile. His concern for the welfare of Jerusalem and its inhabitants prompts him to take bold action. Granted permission to return to his homeland, Nehemiah challenges his countrymen to arise and rebuild the shattered wall of Jerusalem. In spite of opposition from without and abuse from within, the task is completed in only fifty-two days, a feat even the enemies of Israel must attribute to God's enabling. By contrast, the task of reviving and reforming the people of God within the rebuilt wall demands years of Nehemiah's godly life and leadership. The Hebrew for Nehemiah is *Nehemyah*, "Comfort of Yahweh." The book is named after its chief character whose name appears in the opening verse. The combined Books of Ezra/Nehemiah are given the Greek title *Esdras Deuteron*, "Second Esdras" in the Septuagint, a third-century BC Greek-language translation of the Hebrew Old Testament. The Latin title of Nehemiah is *Liber Secundus Esdrae*, "Second Book of Ezra" (Ezra was the first). At this point, it is considered a separate book from Ezra and is later called *Liber Nehemiae*, "Book of Nehemiah."

A Prayer of Nehemiah

1 These are the words of [a]Nehemiah son of Hacaliah:

It so happened that in the month of Kislev, in the [b]twentieth year, I was in [c]Susa the citadel. **2** [a]Hanani, who was one of my relatives, along with some of the men from Judah, came to me, and I asked them about the Jews who had escaped and had survived the exile, and about Jerusalem.

3 They said to me, "The remnant that remains from the exile there in the [a]province are experiencing considerable adversity and [b]reproach. [c]The wall of Jerusalem lies breached, and its gates have been burned down!"

4 When I heard these things I sat down abruptly, crying and mourning for several days. I continued fasting and praying before the God of heaven. **5** Then I said, "Please, O [a]LORD God of heaven, great and [b]awesome God, who keeps his loving covenant with those who love him and obey his commandments, **6** may [a]your ear be attentive and your eyes be open to hear the prayer of your servant that I am praying to you today throughout both day and night on behalf of your servants the Israelites. I am [b]confessing the sins of the Israelites that we have committed against you—both I myself and my family have sinned. **7** [a]We have behaved corruptly against you, [b]not obeying the commandments, the statutes, and the judgments that you commanded your servant Moses. **8** Please recall the word you commanded your servant Moses: '[a]If you act unfaithfully, I will scatter you among the nations. **9** [a]But if you repent[1] and obey my commandments and do them, then even if your dispersed people are in the most remote location,[2] I will gather them from there and bring them to the place I have chosen for my name to reside.' **10** [a]They are your servants and your people, whom you have redeemed by your mighty strength and by your powerful hand. **11** Please, Lord, listen attentively to the prayer of your servant and to the prayer of your servants who

1:1 [a]Neh 10:1 [b]Neh 2:1 [c]Esth 1:1–2, 5; Dan 8:2   **1:2** [a]Neh 7:2   **1:3** [a]Neh 7:6 [b]Neh 2:17 [c]Neh 2:17   **1:5** [a]Dan 9:4 [b]Neh 4:14   **1:6** [a]1 Kgs 8:28–29; 2 Chr 6:40; Dan 9:17–18 [b]Ezra 10:1; Neh 9:2; Dan 9:20   **1:7** [a]Ps 106:6; Dan 9:5 [b]Deut 28:15   **1:8** [a]Lev 26:33; Deut 4:25–27; 28:63–67   **1:9** [a]Lev 26:39; [Deut 4:29–31; 30:2–5] [1]Heb. *turn to me.* [2]Heb. *at the end of the heavens.*   **1:10** [a]Exod 32:11; Deut 9:29; Dan 9:15

take [a]pleasure in showing respect to[1] your name. Grant your servant success today and show compassion to me in the presence of this man."

Now I was [b]cupbearer for the king.

Nehemiah Is Permitted to Go to Jerusalem

2 Then in the month of Nisan, in the twentieth year of [a]King Artaxerxes, when [b]wine was brought to me,[1] I took the wine and gave it to the king. Previously[2] I had not been depressed in the king's presence. [2]So the king said to me, "Why do you appear to be depressed when you aren't sick? What can this be other than [a]sadness of heart?" This made me very fearful.

[3]I replied to [a]the king, "O king, live forever! Why would I not appear dejected when the city with the graves of my ancestors lies desolate and its gates destroyed by [b]fire?" [4]The king responded, "What is it you are seeking?" Then I quickly [a]prayed to the God of heaven [5]and said to the king, "If the king is so inclined and if your servant has found favor in your sight, dispatch me to Judah, to the city with the graves of my ancestors, so that I can rebuild it." [6]Then the king, with his consort[1] sitting beside him, replied, "How long would your trip [a]take, and when would you return?" Since the king was pleased to send me, I gave him a time. [7]I said to the king, "If the king is so inclined, let him give me letters for the [a]governors of Trans-Euphrates[1] that will enable me to travel safely until I reach Judah, [8]and a letter for Asaph the keeper of the king's nature preserve, so that he will give me timber for beams for the gates of the fortress adjacent [a]to the temple and for the city wall[1] and for the house to which [b]I go." So the king granted me these requests, for the good hand of my God was on me. [9]Then I went to the governors of Trans-Euphrates, and I presented to them the letters from the king. The king had sent with me officers of the army and horsemen. [10]When [a]Sanballat the Horonite and Tobiah the Ammonite official heard all this, they were very displeased

that someone had come to seek benefit for the Israelites.

Nehemiah Arrives in Jerusalem

[11]So I [a]came to Jerusalem. When I had been there for three days, [12]I got up during the night, along with a few men who were with me. But I did not tell anyone what my God was putting on my heart to do for Jerusalem. There were no animals with me, except for the one I was riding. [13]I proceeded [a]through the Valley Gate by night, in the direction of the Well of the Dragons and the Dung Gate, inspecting[1] the walls of Jerusalem that had been breached and its gates that had been destroyed by fire. [14]I passed on to the Gate of the [a]Well and the [b]King's Pool, where there was not enough room for my animal to pass with me. [15]I continued up the [a]valley during the night, inspecting the wall. Then I turned back and came to the Valley Gate, and so returned. [16]The officials did not know where I had gone or what I had been doing, for up to this point I had not told any of the Jews or the priests or the nobles or the officials or the rest of the workers. [17]Then I [a]said to them, "You see the problem that we have—Jerusalem is desolate and its gates are burned. Come on! Let's rebuild the wall of Jerusalem so that this reproach will not continue." [18]Then I related to [a]them how the good hand of my God was on me and what the king had said to me. Then they replied, "Let's begin rebuilding right away!" So they [b]readied themselves for this good project. [19]But when Sanballat the Horonite, Tobiah the Ammonite official, and Geshem the Arab heard all this, they derided us and expressed contempt toward us. They said, "What is this you are doing? Are you rebelling against the king?" [20]I responded to them by saying, "The God of heaven will prosper us. We his servants will start the rebuilding.[1] [a]But you have no just or ancient right in Jerusalem."

The Names of the Builders

3 Then [a]Eliashib the high priest [b]and his priestly colleagues[1] arose and built the Sheep Gate. They dedicated it and erected

1:11 [a] Isa 26:8; [Heb 13:18] [b] Gen 40:21; Neh 2:1 [1]Heb. *fear. face*; e.g., not being sad in front of the king. 2:2 [a] Prov 15:13 Neh 1:3 2:4 [a] Neh 1:4 2:6 [a] Neh 5:14; 13:6 [1]Or *queen.* 2:7 [a] Ezra 7:21; 8:36 [1]Heb. *beyond the river.* 2:8 [a] Neh 3:7 [b] Ezra 5:5; 7:6, 9, 28; Neh 2:18 [1]Sev. wss *walls.* 2:10 [a] Neh 2:19; 4:1 2:11 [a] Ezra 8:32 2:13 [a] 2 Chr 26:9; Neh 3:13 [1]LXX *breaking.* 2:14 [a] Neh 3:15 [b] 2 Kgs 20:20 2:15 [a] 2 Sam 15:23; Jer 31:40 2:17 [a] Neh 1:3; Ps 44:13; 79:4; Jer 24:9; Ezek 5:14–15; 22:4 2:18 [a] Neh 2:8 [b] 2 Sam 2:7 2:20 [a] Ezra 4:3; Neh 6:16 [1]Heb. *will arise and build.* 3:1 [a] Neh 3:20; 12:10; 13:4, 7, 28 [b] John 5:2 [1]Heb. *his brothers the priests.*

its doors, working [c]as far as the Tower of the Hundred[2] and[3] the Tower of [d]Hananel. [2]The men of Jericho built adjacent to it, and Zaccur son of Imri built adjacent to [a]them.

[3]The sons of Hassenaah rebuilt [a]the Fish Gate. They laid its beams and [b]positioned its doors, its bolts, and its bars. [4a]Meremoth son of Uriah, the son of Hakoz, worked on the section adjacent to them. [b]Meshullam son of Berechiah the son of Meshezabel worked on the section next to them. And Zadok son of Baana worked on the section adjacent to them. [5]The men of Tekoa worked on [a]the section adjacent to them, but their town leaders would not assist[1] with the work of their master.[2]

[6]Joiada son of Paseah and Meshullam son of Besodeiah worked on [a]the Jeshanah Gate. They laid its beams and positioned its doors, its bolts, and its bars. [7]Adjacent to them worked Melatiah the Gibeonite and Jadon the Meronothite, who were [a]men of Gibeon and Mizpah. These towns were under the [b]jurisdiction of the governor of Trans-Euphrates. [8]Uzziel son of Harhaiah, a member of the goldsmiths' guild, worked on the section adjacent to him. Hananiah, a member of the perfumers' guild, worked on the section adjacent to him. They plastered the city wall of Jerusalem as far as the [a]Broad Wall. [9]Rephaiah son of Hur, head of a half district of Jerusalem, worked on the section adjacent to them. [10]Jedaiah son of Harumaph worked on the section adjacent to them opposite his house, and Hattush son of Hashabneiah worked on the section adjacent to him. [11]Malkijah son of Harim and [a]Hasshub son of Pahath Moab worked on another section and the Tower of the Ovens. [12]Shallum son of Hallohesh, head of a half district of Jerusalem, worked on the section adjacent to him, assisted by his daughters.[1]

[13]Hanun and [a]the residents of Zanoah worked on [b]the Valley Gate. They rebuilt it and positioned its doors, its bolts, and its bars, in addition to working on 1,500 feet of the wall as far as the Dung Gate.

[14]Malkijah son of Recab, head of the district of Beth [a]Hakkerem, worked on the Dung Gate. He rebuilt it and positioned its doors, its bolts, and its bars.

[15]Shallun son of Col-Hozeh, head of [a]the district of Mizpah, worked on the Fountain Gate. He rebuilt it, put on its roof, and positioned its doors, its bolts, and its bars. In addition, he rebuilt the wall of the Pool of [b]Siloam, by the [c]royal garden, as far as the steps that go down from the City of David. [16]Nehemiah son of Azbuk, head of a half district of Beth Zur, worked after him as far as the tombs of David and the [a]artificial pool and the House of the Warriors.

[17]After him the Levites worked—Rehum son of Bani and[1] after him Hashabiah, head of half the district of Keilah, for his district. [18]After him their relatives worked—Binnui[1] son of Henadad, head of a half district of Keilah. [19]Adjacent to him Ezer son of Jeshua, head of Mizpah, worked on another section, opposite the ascent to the armory at the [a]buttress. [20]After him Baruch son of Zabbai worked on another section, from the buttress to the door of the house of Eliashib the high priest. [21]After him Meremoth son of Uriah, the son of Hakkoz, worked on another section from the door of Eliashib's house to the end of it.

[22]After him the priests worked, men of the nearby district. [23]After them Benjamin and Hasshub worked opposite their house. After them Azariah son of Maaseiah, the son of Ananiah, worked near his house. [24]After him [a]Binnui son of Henadad worked on [b]another section, from the house of Azariah to the buttress and the corner. [25]After him Palal son of Uzai worked[1] opposite the buttress and the tower that protrudes from the upper palace of the [a]court of the guard. After him Pedaiah son of Parosh [26]and [a]the temple servants who were living on [b]Ophel worked[1] up to [c]the area opposite the Water Gate toward the east and the protruding tower. [27]After them the men of Tekoa worked on another section, from opposite the great protruding tower to the wall of Ophel.

[28]Above the [a]Horse Gate the priests

worked, each in front of his house. [29]After them Zadok son of Immer worked opposite his house, and after him Shemaiah son of Shecaniah, guard at the East Gate, worked. [30]After him[1] Hananiah son of Shelemiah, and Hanun, the sixth son of Zalaph, worked on another section. After them Meshullam son of Berechiah worked opposite his quarters. [31]After him Malkijah, one of the goldsmiths, worked as far as the house of the temple servants and the traders, opposite the Inspection Gate, and up to the room above the corner. [32]And between the room above the corner and the [a]Sheep Gate the goldsmiths and traders worked.

Opposition to the Work Continues

4 Now [a]when Sanballat heard that we were rebuilding the wall he became angry and was quite upset. He derided the Jews, [2]and in the presence of his colleagues[1] and the army of Samaria he said, "What are these feeble Jews doing? Will they be left to themselves? Will they again offer sacrifice? Will they finish this in a day? Can they bring these burnt stones to life again from piles of dust?"

[3]Then [a]Tobiah the Ammonite, who was close by, said, "If even a fox were to climb up on what they are building, it would break down their wall of stones!"

[4a]Hear, O our God, for we are despised. [b]Return their reproach on their own head. Reduce them to plunder in a land of exile! [5]Do not cover their iniquity, and [a]do not wipe out their sin from your sight, for they have bitterly offended the builders.

[6]So we rebuilt the wall, and the entire wall was joined together up to half its height. The people were enthusiastic in their work.

[7]When Sanballat, Tobiah, [a]the Arabs, the Ammonites, and the people of Ashdod heard that the restoration of the walls of Jerusalem had moved ahead and that the breaches had begun to be closed, they were very angry. [8]All of them [a]conspired together to move with armed forces[1] against Jerusalem and to create a disturbance in it. [9]So [a]we prayed to our God and stationed a guard to protect against them both day and night. [10]Then those in Judah said, "The strength of the laborers has failed! The debris is so great that we are unable to rebuild the wall."

[11]Our adversaries also boasted, "Before they are aware or anticipate anything, we will come in among them and kill them, and we will bring this work to a halt!"

[12]So it happened that the Jews who were living near them came and warned us repeatedly about all the schemes[1] they were plotting[2] against us.

[13]So I stationed people at the lower places behind the wall in the exposed places. I stationed the people by families, with their swords, spears, and bows. [14]When I had made an inspection, I stood up and said to the nobles, the officials, and the rest of the people, "[a]Don't be afraid of them. Remember the [b]great and awesome Lord, and [c]fight on behalf of your brothers, your sons, your daughters, your wives, and your families!"

[15]It so happened [a]that when our adversaries heard that we were aware of these matters, God frustrated their intentions. Then all of us returned to the wall, each to his own work. [16]From that day forward, half my men were doing the work and half were taking up spears,[1] shields, bows, and body armor. Now the officers were behind all the people of Judah [17]who were rebuilding the wall. Those who were carrying loads did so by keeping one hand on the work and the other on their weapon. [18]The builders, to a man, had their swords strapped to their sides while they were building. But the trumpeter remained with me.

[19]I said to the nobles, the officials, and the rest of the people, "The work is demanding and extensive, and we are spread out on the wall, far removed from one another. [20]Wherever you hear the sound of the trumpet, gather there with us. [a]Our God will fight for us!"

[21]So we worked on, with half holding spears, from dawn till dusk. [22]At that time I instructed the people, "Let every man and his coworker spend the night in Jerusalem and let them be guards for us by night and workers by day." [23]We did not change clothes—not I, nor my relatives, nor

3:30 [1]MT *after me.*   **3:32** [a]Neh 3:1; 12:39   **4:1** [a]Neh 2:10, 19   **4:2** [1]Heb. *brothers.*   **4:3** [a]Neh 2:10, 19   **4:4** [a]Ps 123:3–4   [b]Ps 79:12; Prov 3:34   **4:5** [a]Ps 69:27–28; 109:14–15; Jer 18:23   **4:7** [a]Neh 2:19   **4:8** [a]Ps 83:3–5   [1]Heb. *to fight.*   **4:9** [a][Ps 50:15]   **4:12** [1]MT *from every place.*   [2]MT *you turn.*   **4:14** [a][Num 14:9]; Deut 1:29   [b][Deut 10:17]   [c]2 Sam 10:12   **4:15** [a]Job 5:12   **4:16** [1]MT *and spears.*   **4:20** [a]Exod 14:14, 25; Deut 1:30; 3:22; 20:4; Josh 23:10; 2 Chr 20:29

my workers, nor the watchmen who were with me. Each had his weapon, even when getting a drink of water.[1]

Nehemiah Intervenes on behalf of the Oppressed

5 Then there was a great [a]outcry from the people and their wives against their fellow [b]Jews. [2]There were those who said, "With our sons and daughters, we are many. We must obtain grain in order to eat and stay alive." [3]There were others who said, "We are putting up our fields, our vineyards, and our houses as collateral in order to obtain grain during the famine." [4]Then there were those who said, "We have borrowed money to pay our taxes to the king on our fields and our vineyards. [5]And now, though we share the same flesh and blood as [a]our fellow countrymen and our children [b]are just like their children, still we have found it necessary to subject our sons and daughters to slavery. Some of our daughters have been subjected to slavery, while we are powerless to help, since our fields and vineyards now belong to other people."

[6]I was very angry when I heard their outcry and these complaints. [7]I considered these things carefully and then registered a complaint with the wealthy and the officials. I said to them, "Each [a]one of you is seizing the collateral[1] from your own countrymen!" Because of them I called for a great public assembly. [8]I said to them, "To the extent possible we have bought [a]back our fellow Jews who had been sold to the Gentiles. But now you yourselves want to sell your own countrymen, so that we can then buy them back!" They were utterly silent, and could find nothing to say.

[9]Then [a]I[1] said, "The thing that you are doing is wrong! Should you not conduct yourselves in the fear of our God in order to avoid the reproach of the Gentiles who are our enemies? [10]Even I and my relatives and my associates[1] are lending them money and grain. But let us abandon this practice of seizing collateral![2] [11]This very day return to them their fields, their vineyards, their

olive trees, and their houses, along with the interest[1] that you are exacting from them on the money, the grain, the new wine, and the olive oil."

[12]They replied, "We will return these things, [a]and we will no longer demand anything from them. We will do just as you say." Then I called the priests and made the wealthy and the officials swear to do what had been promised. [13]I also shook out my garment, and [a]I said, "In this way may God shake out from his house and his property every person who does not carry out this matter. In this way may [b]he be shaken out and emptied!" All the assembly replied, "So be it!" and they praised the LORD. Then the people did as they had promised.

[14]From the day that [a]I was appointed[1] governor[2] in the land of Judah, that is, from the twentieth year until the thirty-second year of King Artaxerxes—twelve years in all—neither I nor my relatives [b]ate the food allotted to the governor. [15]But the former governors who preceded me had burdened the people and had taken food and [a]wine from them, in addition to 40 shekels of silver. Their associates were also domineering over the people. But I did not behave in this way, due to my [b]fear of God. [16]I gave myself to the [a]work on this wall, without even purchasing a field. All my associates were gathered there for the work.

[17]There were 150 Jews and officials who dined with me routinely, in addition to those who came to us from the [a]nations all around us. [18]Every day one ox, six select sheep, and some birds were prepared for me, and every ten days all kinds of wine in abundance. Despite all this [a]I [b]did not require the food allotted to the governor, for the work was demanding on this people.

[19]Please [a]remember me for good, O my God, for all that I have done for this people.

Opposition to the Rebuilding Efforts Continues

6 When Sanballat, Tobiah, Geshem the Arab, and the rest of our enemies heard that I had rebuilt the wall and no breach

4:23 [1]Heb. *a man, his weapon, the waters.*   **5:1** [a]Lev 25:35–37; Neh 5:7–8   [b]Deut 15:7   **5:5** [a]Isa 58:7   [b]Exod 21:7; [Lev 25:39]   **5:7** [a][Exod 22:25; Lev 25:36; Deut 23:19–20]; Ezek 22:12   [1]Heb. *taking a creditor's debt*; probably the collateral (pledge) collected by a creditor.   **5:8** [a]Lev 25:48   **5:9** [a]Lev 25:36   [1]Ket. *and he said.*   **5:10** [1]Heb. *servants.*   [2]Heb. *this debt*; probably the collateral (pledge) collected by a creditor.   **5:11** [1]MT *and the hundredth.*   **5:12** [a]Ezra 10:5; Jer 34:8–9   **5:13** [a]Matt 10:14; Acts 13:51; 18:6   [b]2 Kgs 23:3   **5:14** [a]Neh 2:1; 13:6   [b][1 Cor 9:4–15]   [1]MT *he appointed me.*   [2]MT *their governor.*   **5:15** [a]2 Cor 11:9; 12:13   [b]Neh 5:9   **5:16** [a]Neh 4:1; 6:1   **5:17** [a]2 Sam 9:7; 1 Kgs 18:19   **5:18** [a]1 Kgs 4:22   [b]Neh 5:14–15   **5:19** [a]2 Kgs 20:3; Neh 13:14, 22, 31

remained in it (even [a]though up to that time I had not positioned doors in the gates), [2]Sanballat and Geshem [a]sent word to me saying, "Come on! Let's set up a time to meet together at Kephirim[1] in the plain of [b]Ono." Now they [c]intended to do me harm.

[3]So I sent messengers to them saying, "I am engaged in an important work, and I am unable to come down. Why should the work come to a halt when I leave it to come down to you?" [4]They contacted me four times in this way, and I responded the same way each time.

[5]The fifth time that Sanballat sent his assistant to me in this way, he had an open letter in his hand. [6]Written in it were the following words:

"Among the nations it is rumored (and Geshem[1] has substantiated this) [a]that you and the Jews have intentions of revolting, and for this reason you are building the wall. Furthermore, according to these rumors you are going to become their king. [7]You have also established prophets to announce in Jerusalem on your behalf, 'We have a king in Judah!' Now the king is going to hear about these rumors. So come on, let's talk about this."

[8]I sent word back to him, "We are not engaged in these activities you are describing. All of this is a figment of your imagination."

[9]All of them were wanting to scare us, supposing, "Their hands will grow slack from the work, and it won't get done."

So now, strengthen my hands!

[10]Then I went to the house of Shemaiah son of Delaiah, the son of Mehetabel. He was confined to his home. He said, "Let's set up a time to meet in the house of God, within the temple. Let's close the doors of the temple, for they are coming to kill you. It will surely be at night that they will come to kill you."

[11]But I replied, "Should a man like me run away? Would someone like me flee to the temple in order to save his life? I will not go!" [12]I recognized [a]the fact that God had not sent him, for he had spoken the prophecy against me as a hired agent of Tobiah and Sanballat. [13]He had been hired to scare me so that I would do this and thereby sin.

They would thus bring reproach on me and I[1] would be discredited.

[14]Remember, O [a]my God, Tobiah and Sanballat in light of these actions of theirs—also Noadiah the [b]prophetess and the other prophets who have been trying to scare me!

The Rebuilding of the Wall Is Finally Completed

[15]So the wall was completed on the twenty-fifth day of Elul, in just fifty-two days. [16]When all our enemies heard and all [a]the nations who were around us saw[1] this, they were greatly disheartened. They knew that this work had been accomplished with the help of our God.

[17]In those days the aristocrats of Judah repeatedly sent letters to Tobiah, and responses from Tobiah were repeatedly coming to them. [18]For many [a]in Judah had sworn allegiance to him, because he was the son-in-law of Shecaniah son of Arah. His son Jonathan had married the daughter of [b]Meshullam son of Berechiah. [19]They were telling me about his good deeds and then taking back to him the things I said. Tobiah, on the other hand, sent letters in order to scare me.

7 When the wall had been rebuilt and I had [a]positioned the doors, and the gatekeepers, the singers, and the Levites had been appointed, [2]I then put in charge over Jerusalem my brother [a]Hanani and Hananiah the chief [b]of the citadel, for he was a faithful man and [c]feared God more than many do. [3]I[1] said to them, "The gates of Jerusalem must not be opened in the early morning, until those who are standing guard close the doors and lock them. Position residents of Jerusalem as guards, some at their guard stations and some near their homes." [4]Now the city was spread out and large, and there were not a [a]lot of people in it. At that time houses had not been rebuilt. [5]My God placed it on my heart to gather the leaders, the officials, and the ordinary people so they could be enrolled on the basis of genealogy. I found the genealogical records of those who had formerly returned. Here is what I found written in that record:

[6]These are [a]the people of the province who returned from the captivity of the exiles,

6:1 [a] Neh 3:1, 3   **6:2** [a] Prov 26:24–25   [b] 1 Chr 8:12; Neh 11:35   [c] Ps 37:12, 32   [1] Or perhaps *in* [one of] *the villages.*   **6:6** [a] Neh 2:19   [1] Heb. *Gashmu.*   **6:12** [a] Ezek 13:22   **6:13** [1] MT *to them.*   **6:14** [a] Neh 13:29   [b] Ezek 13:17   **6:16** [a] Ps 126:2   [1] *to fear.*   **6:18** [a] Neh 13:4, 28   [b] Ezra 10:15; Neh 3:4   **7:1** [a] Neh 6:1, 15   **7:2** [a] Neh 1:2   [b] Neh 2:8; 10:23   [c] Exod 18:21   **7:3** [1] Ket. *and he said.*   **7:4** [a] Deut 4:27   **7:6** [a] Ezra 2:1–70

whom King Nebuchadnezzar of Babylon had forced into exile.[1] They returned to Jerusalem and to Judah, each to his own city. [7]They came with [a]Zerubbabel, Jeshua, Nehemiah, Azariah, Raamiah, Nahamani, Mordecai, Bilshan, Mispereth, Bigvai, Nehum, and Baanah.

The number of Israelite men was as follows:

[8]the descendants of Parosh: 2,172;

[9]the descendants of Shephatiah: 372;

[10]the descendants of Arah: 652;

[11]the descendants of Pahath Moab (from the line of Jeshua and Joab): 2,818;

[12]the descendants of Elam: 1,254;

[13]the descendants of Zattu: 845;

[14]the descendants of Zaccai: 760;

[15]the descendants of Binnui: 648;

[16]the descendants of Bebai: 628;

[17]the descendants of Azgad: 2,322;

[18]the descendants of Adonikam: 667;

[19]the descendants of Bigvai: 2,067;

[20]the descendants of Adin: 655;

[21]the descendants of Ater (through Hezekiah): 98;

[22]the descendants of Hashum: 328;

[23]the descendants of Bezai: 324;

[24]the descendants of Harif: 112;

[25]the descendants of Gibeon: 95;

[26]The men of Bethlehem and Netophah: 188;

[27]the men of Anathoth: 128;

[28]the men of the family of Azmaveth: 42;

[29]the men of Kiriath Jearim, Kephirah, and Beeroth: 743;

[30]the men of Ramah and Geba: 621;

[31]the men of Micmash: 122;

[32]the men of Bethel and Ai: 123;

[33]the men of the other Nebo: 52;

[34]the descendants of the other [a]Elam: 1,254;

[35]the descendants of Harim: 320;

[36]the descendants of Jericho: 345;

[37]the descendants of Lod, Hadid, and Ono: 721;

[38]the descendants of Senaah: 3,930;

[39]The priests: the descendants of [a]Jedaiah (through the family of Jeshua): 973;

[40]the descendants of [a]Immer: 1,052;

[41]the descendants of [a]Pashhur: 1,247;

[42]the descendants of [a]Harim: 1,017.

[43]The Levites: the descendants of Jeshua (through Kadmiel, through the line of Hodaviah): 74.

[44]The singers: the descendants of Asaph: 148.

[45]The gatekeepers: the descendants of Shallum, the descendants of Ater, the descendants of Talmon, the descendants of Akkub, the descendants of Hatita, and the descendants of Shobai: 138.

[46]The temple servants: the descendants of Ziha, the descendants of Hasupha, the descendants of Tabbaoth, [47]the descendants of Keros, the descendants of Sia, the descendants of Padon, [48]the descendants of Lebanah, the descendants of Hagabah, the descendants of Shalmai, [49]the descendants of Hanan, the descendants of Giddel, the descendants of Gahar, [50]the descendants of Reaiah, the descendants of Rezin, the descendants of Nekoda, [51]the descendants of Gazzam, the descendants of Uzzah, the descendants of Paseah, [52]the descendants of Besai, the descendants of Meunim, the descendants of Nephussim, [53]the descendants of Bakbuk, the descendants of Hakupha, the descendants of Harhur, [54]the descendants of Bazluth, the descendants of Mehida, the descendants of Harsha, [55]the descendants of Barkos, the descendants of Sisera, the descendants of Temah, [56]the descendants of Neziah, the descendants of Hatipha.

[57]The descendants of the servants of Solomon: the descendants of Sotai, the descendants of Sophereth, the descendants of Perida, [58]the descendants of Jaala, the descendants of Darkon, the descendants of Giddel, [59]the descendants of Shephatiah, the descendants of Hattil, the descendants of Pokereth Hazzebaim, and the descendants of Amon.

[60]All the temple servants and the descendants of the servants of Solomon, 392.

[61]These are the ones who came up from Tel Melah, Tel Harsha, Kerub, Addon, and Immer (although they were unable to certify their family connection or their ancestry, as to whether they were really from Israel):

[62]the descendants of Delaiah, the descendants of Tobiah, and the descendants of Nekoda, 642.

[63]And from among the priests: the descendants of Hobaiah, the descendants of Hakkoz, and the descendants of Barzillai (who had married a woman from the daughters of Barzillai the Gileadite and was called

by that name). [64] They searched for their records in the genealogical materials, but none were found. They were therefore excluded[1] from the priesthood. [65] The governor instructed them not to eat any of the sacred food until there was a priest who could consult the Urim and Thummim.

[66] The entire group numbered 42,360— [67] not counting their 7,337 male and female servants. They also had 245 male and female singers. [68] They had 736 horses, 245 mules, [69] 435 camels, and 6,720 donkeys. [70] Some of [a] the family leaders contributed to the work. The governor contributed to the treasury 1,000 gold drachmas,[1] 50 bowls, and 530 priestly garments. [71] Some of the family leaders gave to the project treasury [a] 20,000 gold drachmas and 2,200 silver minas. [72] What the rest of the people gave amounted to 20,000 gold drachmas, 2,000 silver minas, and 67 priestly garments.

[73] The priests, the Levites, the gatekeepers, the singers, some of the people, the temple servants, and all the rest of Israel lived in their cities.

The People Respond to the Reading of the Law

When the seventh month arrived and the Israelites were settled in their towns,[1] **8** [1] all [a] the people gathered together[1] [b] in the plaza which was in front of the Water Gate. They asked Ezra the [c] scribe to bring the book of the law of Moses which the LORD had commanded Israel. [2] So Ezra [a] the priest brought the law before the assembly which included men and women and all those able to understand what they heard. (This happened [b] on the first day of the seventh month.) [3] So he [a] read it before the plaza in front of the Water Gate from dawn till noon before the men and women and those children who could understand. All the people were eager to hear the book of the law.

[4] Ezra the scribe stood on a towering wooden platform constructed for this purpose. Standing near him on his right were Mattithiah, Shema, Anaiah, Uriah, Hilkiah, and Masseiah. On his left were Pedaiah,

Mishael, Malkijah, Hashum, Hashbaddanah, Zechariah, and Meshullam. [5] Ezra opened the book in plain view of all the people, for he was elevated above all the people. When he opened the book, all the people [a] stood up. [6] Ezra blessed the LORD, the great God, and all the people [a] replied "Amen! Amen!" as they lifted their hands. Then they [b] bowed down and worshiped the LORD with their faces to the ground.

[7] Jeshua, Bani, Sherebiah, Jamin, Akkub, Shabbethai, Hodiah, Maaseiah, Kelita, Azariah, Jozabad, Hanan, and Pelaiah—all of whom were Levites[1]—were teaching the people the law, as the people remained standing. [8] They read from the book of God's law, explaining it[1] and imparting insight. Thus the people gained understanding from what was read.

[9] Then Nehemiah the governor, Ezra the priestly scribe, [a] and the Levites who were imparting understanding to the people said to all of them, "[b] This day is holy to the LORD your God. [c] Do not mourn or weep." For all the people had been weeping when they heard the words of the law. [10] He said to them, "Go [a] and eat delicacies and drink sweet drinks and send portions to those for whom nothing is prepared. For this day is holy to our Lord. Do not grieve, for the joy of the LORD is your strength."

[11] Then the Levites quieted all the people saying, "Be quiet, for this day is holy. Do not grieve." [12] So all the people departed to eat and drink and to [a] share their food with others and to enjoy tremendous joy, for they had gained [b] insight in the matters that had been made known to them.

[13] On the second day of the month the family leaders met with Ezra the scribe, together with all the people, the priests, and the Levites, to consider the words of the law. [14] They discovered written in the law that the LORD had commanded through Moses that the Israelites should live in temporary [a] shelters during the festival of the seventh month, [15] and [a] that they should make a proclamation and [b] disseminate this message in all their cities and in Jerusalem: "Go to the hill

<hr>

7:64 [1] Heb. *they were desecrated.*   7:69 [1] Most MSS omit v. 68. final part of v. 73 is best understood as belonging with 8:1.   7:70 [a] Neh 8:9   [1] Heb. *darics.*   7:71 [a] Ezra 2:69   7:73 [1] The
8:2 [a] [Deut 31:11–12]; Neh 8:9   [b] Lev 23:24; Num 29:1–6   8:3 [a] Deut 31:9–11; 2 Kgs 23:2   8:5 [a] Judg 3:20; 1 Kgs 8:12–14
8:1 [a] Ezra 3:1   [b] Neh 3:26   [c] Ezra 7:6   [1] Heb. *like one man.*
8:6 [a] Neh 5:13; [1 Cor 14:16]   [b] Exod 4:31; 12:27; 2 Chr 20:18   8:7 [1] MT adds *and.*   8:8 [1] Heb. *to make distinct, to divide in parts, to interpret, to translate.*   8:9 [a] Ezra 2:63; Neh 7:65, 70; 10:1   [b] Lev 23:24; Num 29:1
[c] Deut 16:14; Eccl 3:4   8:10 [a] [Deut 26:11–13]; Esth 9:19, 22; Rev 11:10   8:12 [a] Neh 8:10
[b] Neh 8:7–8   8:14 [a] Lev 23:34, 40, 42; Deut 16:13   8:15 [a] Lev 23:4   [b] Deut 16:16

country and bring ᶜback olive branches and branches of wild olive trees, myrtle trees, date palms, and other leafy trees to construct temporary shelters, as it is written."

¹⁶So the people went out and brought these things back and constructed temporary shelters for themselves, each on his ᵃroof and in his courtyard and in the courtyards of the temple of God and in the plaza of the ᵇWater Gate ᶜand the plaza of the Ephraim Gate. ¹⁷So all the assembly which had returned from the exile constructed temporary shelters and lived in them. The Israelites had not done so from the days of Joshua son of Nun until that day. Everyone experienced very ᵃgreat joy. ¹⁸Ezra read in the book of the law of God ᵃday by day, from the first day to the last. They observed the festival for ᵇseven days, and on the ᶜeighth day they held an assembly as was required.

The People Acknowledge Their Sin before God

9 On the twenty-fourth day of ᵃthis same month the Israelites assembled; they were fasting ᵇand wearing sackcloth, their heads covered with dust. ²Those truly of Israelite descent separated from all the foreigners, standing and ᵃconfessing their sins and the iniquities of their ancestors. ³For one-fourth of the day they stood in their place and ᵃread from the book of the law of the LORD their God, and for another fourth they were confessing their sins and worshiping the LORD their God. ⁴Then the Levites—Jeshua, Binnui,¹ Kadmiel, Shebaniah, Bunni, Sherebiah, Bani, and Kenani—stood on the steps and called out loudly to the LORD their God. ⁵The Levites—Jeshua, Kadmiel, Bani, Hashabneiah, Sherebiah, Hodiah, Shebaniah, and Pethahiah—said, "Stand up and bless the LORD ᵃyour God!"

"May you be blessed, O LORD our God, from age to age.¹ May your glorious name be blessed; may it be lifted up above all blessing and praise. ⁶You alone are the LORD. ᵃYou made ᵇthe heavens, even the highest heavens, along with ᶜall their multitude of stars,

the earth and all that is on it, the seas and all that is in them. You impart ᵈlife to them all, and the multitudes of heaven worship you. ⁷"You are the LORD God who chose ᵃAbram and brought him forth from Ur of the Chaldeans. You changed his name to ᵇAbraham. ⁸When you perceived that his heart was ᵃfaithful toward you, you established a ᵇcovenant with him to give his descendants the land of the Canaanites, the Hittites, the Amorites, the Perizzites, the Jebusites, and the Girgashites. You ᶜhave fulfilled your promise, for you are righteous.

⁹"You saw the affliction of our ancestors in Egypt, and ᵃyou ᵇheard their cry at the Red Sea. ¹⁰You ᵃperformed awesome signs against Pharaoh, against his servants, and against all the people of his land, for you knew that the Egyptians had ᵇacted presumptuously against them. You ᶜmade for yourself a name that is celebrated to this day. ¹¹You split the sea before them, ᵃand they crossed through the sea on dry ground. But you threw their pursuers into the depths, like ᵇa stone into surging waters. ¹²You ᵃguided them with a pillar of cloud by day and with a pillar of fire by night to illumine for them the path they were to travel.

¹³"You came down on Mount Sinai and spoke with them from heaven. ᵃYou provided them with ᵇjust judgments, true laws, and good statutes and commandments. ¹⁴You made known to them your ᵃholy Sabbath; you issued commandments, statutes, and laws to them through Moses your servant. ¹⁵You ᵃprovided bread from heaven for them in their time of hunger, and you brought ᵇforth water from the rock for them in their time of thirst. You told them to enter in order to possess the land that you had sworn to give them.

¹⁶"But they—our ancestors—behaved presumptuously; they ᵃrebelled and did not obey your commandments. ¹⁷They refused to obey and did not recall your miracles that you had performed among them. Instead, ᵃthey rebelled ᵇand appointed a leader to return to their bondage in Egypt.¹

8:15 ᶜLev 23:40   8:16 ᵃDeut 22:8   ᵇNeh 12:37   ᶜ2 Kgs 14:13; Neh 12:39   8:17 ᵃ2 Chr 30:21   8:18 ᵃDeut 31:11   ᵇLev 23:36   ᶜNum 29:35   9:1 ᵃNeh 8:2   ᵇJosh 7:6; 1 Sam 4:12; 2 Sam 1:2; Job 2:12   9:2 ᵃNeh 1:6   9:3 ᵃNeh 8:7–8   9:4 ¹Heb. *Bani.*   9:5 ᵃ1 Chr 29:13   ¹MT omits *May you be blessed, O LORD our God;* LXX adds *And Ezra said* at the beginning of v. 6.   9:6 ᵃGen 1:1; Exod 20:11; Rev 14:7   ᵇ[Deut 10:14]; 1 Kgs 8:27   ᶜGen 2:1   ᵈ[Ps 36:6]   9:7 ᵃGen 11:31   ᵇGen 17:5   9:8 ᵃGen 15:6; 22:1–3; [Jas 2:21–23]   ᵇGen 15:18   ᶜJosh 23:14   9:9 ᵃExod 2:25; 3:7   ᵇExod 14:10   9:10 ᵃExod 7–14   ᵇExod 18:11   ᶜJer 32:20   9:11 ᵃExod 14:20–28   ᵇExod 15:1, 5   9:12 ᵃExod 13:21–22   9:13 ᵃExod 20:1–18   ᵇ[Rom 7:12]   9:14 ᵃGen 2:3; Exod 16:23; 20:8; 23:12   9:15 ᵃExod 16:14–17; John 6:31   ᵇExod 17:6; Num 20:8; [1 Cor 10:4]   9:16 ᵃDeut 1:26–33; 31:27; Neh 9:29   9:17 ᵃPs 78:11, 42–45   ᵇNum 14:4; Acts 7:39   ¹MT *in their rebellion.*

But you are a God of forgiveness, [c]merciful and compassionate, slow to get angry and unfailing in your loyal love.[2] You did not abandon them, [18]even [a]when they made a cast image of a calf for themselves and said, 'This is your God who brought you up from Egypt,' or when they committed atrocious blasphemies.

[19]"Due to your [a]great compassion you did not abandon them in the wilderness. The [b]pillar of cloud did not stop guiding them in the path by day, nor did the pillar of fire stop illuminating for them by night the path on which they should travel. [20]You imparted your [a]good Spirit to instruct them. You did not withhold your [b]manna from their mouths; you provided [c]water for their thirst. [21]For [a]40 years you sustained them. Even in the wilderness they never lacked anything. Their [b]clothes did not wear out and their feet did not swell.

[22]"You gave them kingdoms and peoples, and you allocated them to every corner of the land. They inherited the land of King [a]Sihon of Heshbon[1] and the land of King Og of Bashan. [23]You multiplied [a]their descendants like the stars of the sky. You brought them to the land you had told their ancestors to enter in order to possess. [24]Their descendants entered and possessed [a]the land. [b]You subdued before them the Canaanites who were the inhabitants of the land. You delivered them into their hand, together with their kings and the peoples of the land, to deal with as they pleased. [25]They captured fortified cities and [a]fertile land. They took possession of [b]houses full of all sorts of good things—wells previously dug, vineyards, olive trees, and fruit trees in abundance. They ate until they were full and [c]grew fat. They enjoyed to the full your great [d]goodness.

[26]"Nonetheless they grew disobedient and rebelled against you; they [a]disregarded your law. They killed your [b]prophets who had solemnly admonished them in order to cause them to return to you. They committed atrocious blasphemies. [27]Therefore you delivered them into [a]the hand of their adversaries, who oppressed them. But in the time of their distress they called to you, and you [b]heard from heaven. In [c]your abundant compassion you provided them with deliverers to rescue them from their adversaries.

[28]"Then, when [a]they were at rest again, they went back to doing evil before you. Then you abandoned them to their enemies, and they gained dominion over them. When they again cried out to you, in your compassion you heard from heaven and rescued them time and [b]again. [29]And you solemnly admonished them in order to return them to your law, but they behaved presumptuously and did not obey your commandments. They sinned against your ordinances—those by [a]which an individual, if he obeys them, will live. They boldly turned from you;[1] they rebelled and did not obey. [30]You prolonged your kindness with them for many years, and you solemnly admonished them by your Spirit [a]through your prophets. Still they paid no attention, so you delivered them into [b]the hands of the neighboring peoples. [31]However, due to [a]your abundant mercy you did not do away with them altogether; you did not abandon them. For you are a merciful and compassionate God.

[32]"So now, our God—the great, [a]powerful, and awesome God, who keeps covenant fidelity—do not regard as inconsequential all the hardship that has befallen us—our kings, our leaders, our priests, our prophets, our ancestors, and all your people—[b]from the days of the kings of Assyria until this very day. [33]You are righteous with regard to all that has happened to us, for [a]you have acted faithfully. It is [b]we who have been in the wrong! [34]Our kings, our leaders, our priests, and our ancestors have not kept your law. They have not paid attention to your commandments or your testimonies by which you have solemnly admonished them. [35]Even when they were in their kingdom and benefiting from your incredible goodness that you had lavished on them in the spacious and fertile land you had set

9:17 [c] Joel 2:13   [2] Ket. adds *and.*   9:18 [a] Exod 32:4–8, 31   9:19 [a] Ps 106:45   [b] Exod 13:20–22; 1 Cor 10:1   9:20 [a] Num 11:17   [b] Exod 16:14–16   [c] Exod 17:6   9:21 [a] Deut 2:7   [b] Deut 8:4; 29:5   9:22 [a] Num 21:21–35   [1] Most mss *the land of Sihon and the land of the king of Heshbon.*   9:23 [a] Gen 15:5; 22:17; Heb 11:12   9:24 [a] Josh 1:2–4   [b] Josh 18:1; [Ps 44:2–3]   9:25 [a] Num 13:27   [b] Deut 6:11; Josh 24:13   [c] [Deut 32:15]   [d] Hos 3:5   9:26 [a] 1 Kgs 14:9; Ps 50:17   [b] 1 Kgs 18:4; 19:10; Matt 23:37; Acts 7:52   9:27 [a] Judg 2:14; Ps 106:41   [b] Ps 106:44   [c] Judg 2:18   9:28 [a] Judg 3:12   [b] Ps 106:43   9:29 [a] Lev 18:5; Rom 10:5; [Gal 3:12]   [1] Heb. *they gave a stubborn shoulder.*   9:30 [a] [Acts 7:51]; 1 Pet 1:11   [b] Isa 5:5   9:31 [a] Jer 4:27; [Rom 11:2–5]   9:32 [a] [Exod 34:6–7]   [b] 2 Kgs 15:19; 17:3–6; Ezra 4:2, 10   9:33 [a] Ps 119:137; [Dan 9:14]   [b] Ps 106:6; [Dan 9:5–6, 8]

before them, they did [a]not serve you, nor did they turn from their evil practices. [36]"So today [a]we are slaves! In the very land you gave to our ancestors to eat its fruit and to enjoy its good things—we are slaves. [37]Its abundant produce goes to the kings you have placed over us due to our sins. They rule over our bodies and our livestock as they see [a]fit, and we are [b]in great distress!

The People Pledge to Be Faithful

[38]"Because of all this we are entering [a]into a binding covenant in written form; our leaders, our Levites, and our priests have affixed their names on the sealed [b]document."

10 On [a]the sealed documents were the following names:

Nehemiah the governor, son of Hacaliah, along with Zedekiah,
[2a]Seraiah, Azariah, Jeremiah,
[3]Pashhur, Amariah, Malkijah,
[4]Hattush, Shebaniah, Malluch,
[5]Harim, Meremoth, Obadiah,
[6]Daniel, Ginnethon, Baruch,
[7]Meshullam, Abijah, Mijamin,
[8]Maaziah, Bilgai, and Shemaiah. These were the priests.
[9]The Levites were as follows:
Jeshua son of Azaniah, Binnui of the sons of Henadad, Kadmiel.
[10]Their colleagues[1] were as follows: Shebaniah, Hodiah, Kelita, Pelaiah, Hanan,
[11]Mica, Rehob, Hashabiah,
[12]Zaccur, Sherebiah, Shebaniah,
[13]Hodiah, Bani, and Beninu.
[14]The leaders of the people were as follows:
[a]Parosh, Pahath Moab, Elam, Zattu, Bani,
[15]Bunni, Azgad, Bebai,
[16]Adonijah, Bigvai, Adin,
[17]Ater, Hezekiah, Azzur,
[18]Hodiah, Hashum, Bezai,
[19]Hariph, Anathoth, Nebai,
[20]Magpiash, Meshullam, Hezir,
[21]Meshezabel, Zadok, Jaddua,
[22]Pelatiah, Hanan, Anaiah,
[23]Hoshea, Hananiah, Hasshub,
[24]Hallohesh, Pilha, Shobek,
[25]Rehum, Hashabnah, Maaseiah,
[26]Ahiah, Hanan, Anan,
[27]Malluch, Harim, and Baanah.

[28]"[a]Now the rest of the people—the priests, the Levites, the gatekeepers, the singers, the temple attendants, [b]and all those who have separated themselves from the neighboring peoples because of the law of God, along with their wives, their sons, and their daughters, all of whom are able to understand—[29]hereby participate with their colleagues the town leaders [a]and enter [b]into a curse and an oath to adhere to the law of God which was given through Moses the servant of God, and to obey carefully all the commandments of the LORD our Lord, along with his ordinances and his statutes.

[30]"We will not give [a]our daughters in marriage to the neighboring peoples, and we will not take their daughters in marriage for our sons. [31a]We will not buy[1] on the Sabbath or on a holy day from the neighboring peoples who bring their wares and all kinds of grain to sell on the Sabbath day. We will let the fields lie fallow every [b]seventh year, and we will cancel every loan. [32]We accept responsibility for fulfilling the commands to give[1] [a]one-third of a shekel each year for the work of the temple of our God, [33]for [a]the loaves of presentation and for the [b]regular grain offerings and regular burnt offerings, for the Sabbaths, for the new moons, for the appointed meetings, for the holy offerings, for the sin offerings to make atonement for Israel, and for all the work of the temple of our God.

[34]"We—the priests, the Levites, and the people—have [a]cast lots concerning the wood offerings, to bring them to the temple of our God according to our families at the designated times year by year to burn on the altar of the LORD our God, as is written in the law. [35]We also accept responsibility for bringing the firstfruits of our land and the firstfruits of every fruit tree year by year [a]to the temple of the LORD. [36]We also accept responsibility, as is written in the law, for bringing the [a]firstborn of our sons and our cattle and the firstborn of our herds and of our flocks to the temple of our God, to the priests who are ministering in the temple of our God. [37]We

9:35 [a]Deut 28:47   9:36 [a]Deut 28:48; Ezra 9:9   9:37 [a]Deut 28:33, 51   [b]Deut 28:48   9:38 [a]2 Kgs 23:3; 2 Chr 29:10; Ezra 10:3   [b]Neh 10:1   10:1 [a]Neh 1:1   10:2 [a]Neh 12:1–21   10:10 [1]Heb. brothers.   10:14 [a]Ezra 2:3   10:28 [a]Ezra 2:36–43   [b]Ezra 9:1; Neh 13:3   10:29 [a]Deut 29:12; Neh 5:12; Ps 119:106   [b]2 Kgs 23:3; 2 Chr 34:31   10:30 [a]Exod 34:16; Deut 7:3; [Ezra 9:12]   10:31 [a]Exod 20:10; Lev 23:3; Deut 5:12   [b]Exod 23:10–11; Lev 25:4; Jer 34:14   [1]Heb. take.   10:32 [a]Exod 30:11–16; 38:25–26; 2 Chr 24:6, 9; Matt 17:24   [1]MT adds upon us.   10:33 [a]Lev 24:5; 2 Chr 2:4   [b]Num 28; 29   10:34 [a]Lev 6:12   10:35 [a]Exod 23:19; 34:26; Lev 19:23; Num 18:12; Deut 26:1–2   10:36 [a]Exod 13:2, 12, 13; Lev 27:26–27; Num 18:15–16

will also bring the first of our coarse meal, of our contributions, of the fruit of every tree, of new wine, and of olive oil [a]to [b]the priests at the storerooms of the temple of our God, along with a tenth of the produce[1] of our land to the Levites, for the Levites are the ones who collect the tithes in all the cities where we work. [38]A priest of Aaron's line will be with the Levites [a]when [b]the Levites collect the tithes, and the Levites will bring up a tenth of the tithes to the temple of our God, to the storerooms of the treasury. [39]The Israelites [a]and the Levites will bring the contribution of the grain, the new wine, and the olive oil to the storerooms where the utensils of the sanctuary are kept, and where the priests who minister stay, along with the gatekeepers and the singers. We will not [b]neglect the temple of our God."

The Population of Jerusalem

11 So [a]the leaders of the people settled in Jerusalem, while the rest of the people cast lots to bring one out of every ten to settle in Jerusalem, the holy city, while the other nine remained in other cities. [2]The people gave their blessing on all the men who volunteered to settle [a]in Jerusalem.

[3]These are [a]the provincial leaders who settled in Jerusalem. (While other Israelites, the priests, the Levites, the temple [b]attendants, and the [c]sons of the servants of Solomon settled in the cities of Judah, each on his own property in their cities, [4]some of the descendants of Judah and some of the descendants of [a]Benjamin settled in Jerusalem.)

Of the descendants of Judah:

Athaiah son of Uzziah, the son of Zechariah, the son of Amariah, the son of Shephatiah, the son of Mahalalel, from the descendants of [b]Perez; [5]and Maaseiah son of Baruch, the son of Col-Hozeh, the son of Hazaiah, the son of Adaiah, the son of Joiarib, the son of Zechariah, from the descendants of Shelah.[1] [6]The sum total of the descendants of Perez who were settling in Jerusalem was 468 exceptional men.

[7]These are the descendants of Benjamin:

Sallu son of Meshullam, the son of Joed, the son of Pedaiah, the son of Kolaiah, the son of Maaseiah, the son of Ithiel, the son of Jeshaiah, [8]and his followers, Gabbai and Sallai—928 in all. [9]Joel son of Zicri was the officer in charge of them, and Judah son of Hassenuah was second-in-command over the city.

[10]From the priests:

Jedaiah son [a]of Joiarib, Jakin, [11]Seraiah son of Hilkiah, the son of Meshullam, the son of Zadok, the son of Meraioth, the son of Ahitub, supervisor in the temple of God, [12]and their colleagues[1] who were carrying out work for the temple—822; and Adaiah son of Jeroham, the son of Pelaliah, the son of Amzi, the son of Zechariah, the son of Pashhur, the son of Malkijah, [13]and his colleagues who were heads of families—242; and Amashsai son of Azarel, the son of Ahzai, the son of Meshillemoth, the son of Immer, [14]and his colleagues[1] who were exceptional men—128. The officer over them was Zabdiel the son of Haggedolim.

[15]From the Levites:

Shemaiah son of Hasshub, the son of Azrikam, the son of Hashabiah, the son of Bunni; [16a]Shabbethai and [b]Jozabad, leaders of [c]the Levites, were in charge of the external work for the temple of God; [17]Mattaniah son of Mica, the son of Zabdi, the son of Asaph, the praise[1] leader who led in thanksgiving and prayer; Bakbukiah, second among his colleagues; and Abda son of Shammua, the son of Galal, the son of Jeduthun. [18]The sum total of [a]the Levites in the holy city was 284.

[19]And the gatekeepers:

Akkub, Talmon, and their colleagues who were guarding the gates—172.

[20]And the rest of the Israelites, with the priests and the Levites, were in all the cities of Judah, each on his own property.

[21a]The temple attendants were living on Ophel, and Ziha and Gishpa were over them.

[22]The overseer of the Levites in Jerusalem was Uzzi son of Bani, the son of Hashabiah, the son of Mattaniah, the son of Mica. He was one of Asaph's descendants, who were the singers responsible for the service of the temple of God. [23]For they were under royal orders which determined their [a]activity day by day.

10:37 [a] Lev 23:17; Num 15:19; 18:12; Deut 18:4; 26:2   [b] Lev 27:30; Num 18:21; Mal 3:10   [1] Heb. *a tithe of our land.*   **10:38** [a] Num 18:26   [b] 1 Chr 9:26; 2 Chr 31:11   **10:39** [a] Neh 13:10–11   [b] [Heb 10:25]   **11:1** [a] Neh 10:18; Matt 4:5; 5:35; 27:53   **11:2** [a] Judg 5:9; 2 Chr 17:16   **11:3** [a] 1 Chr 9:2–3   [b] Ezra 2:43   [c] Ezra 2:55   **11:4** [a] 1 Chr 9:3   [b] Gen 38:29   **11:5** [1] MT *the son of the Shilionite.*   **11:10** [a] 1 Chr 9:10   **11:12** [1] Heb. *brothers.*   **11:14** [1] MT *and their.*   **11:16** [a] Ezra 10:15   [b] Ezra 8:33   [c] 1 Chr 26:29   **11:17** [1] MT *the beginning.*   **11:18** [a] Neh 11:1   **11:21** [a] 2 Chr 27:3; Neh 3:26   **11:23** [a] Ezra 6:8–9; 7:20

24Pethahiah son of Meshezabel, one of the descendants of aZerah son of Judah, was an adviser to bthe king in every matter pertaining to the people.

25As for the settlements with their fields, some of the people of Judah settled in Kiriath aArba and its neighboring villages,1 in Dibon and its villages, in Jekabzeel and its settlements, 26in Jeshua, in Moladah, in Beth Pelet, 27in Hazar Shual, in Beer Sheba and its villages, 28in Ziklag, in Meconah and its villages, 29in En Rimmon, in Zorah, in Jarmuth, 30Zanoah, Adullam and their settlements, in Lachish and its fields, and in Azekah and its villages. So they were encamped from Beer Sheba to the Valley of Hinnom.

31Some of the descendants of1 Benjamin settled in Geba,2 Micmash, Aija, Bethel and its villages, 32in Anathoth, Nob, and Ananiah, 33in Hazor, Ramah, and Gittaim, 34in Hadid, Zeboyim, and Neballat, 35in Lod, Ono, and1 athe Valley of the Craftsmen. 36Some of the Judean divisions of the Levites settled in Benjamin.

The Priests and the Levites Who Returned to Jerusalem

12 These are the apriests and Levites who returned with bZerubbabel son of Shealtiel and Jeshua: cSeraiah, Jeremiah, Ezra, 2Amariah, Malluch, Hattush, 3Shecaniah, Rehum, Meremoth, 4Iddo, Ginnethon,1 aAbijah, 5Mijamin, Moadiah, Bilgah, 6Shemaiah, Joiarib, Jedaiah, 7Sallu, Amok, Hilkiah, and Jedaiah. These were the leaders of the priests and their colleagues1 in the days of aJeshua.

8And the Levites: Jeshua, Binnui, Kadmiel, Sherebiah, Judah, and Mattaniah, awho together with his colleagues was in charge of the songs of thanksgiving. 9Bakbukiah and Unni,1 their colleagues, stood opposite them in the services.

10Jeshua was the father of Joiakim, Joiakim was the father of Eliashib, Eliashib was the father of Joiada, 11Joiada was the father of Jonathan, and Jonathan was the father of Jaddua.

12In the days of Joiakim, these were the priests who were aleaders of the families: of Seraiah, Meraiah; of Jeremiah, Hananiah; 13of Ezra, Meshullam; of Amariah, Jehohanan; 14of Malluch, Jonathan; of Shecaniah,1 Joseph; 15of Harim, Adna; of Meremoth,1 Helkai; 16of Iddo,1 Zechariah; of Ginnethon, Meshullam; 17of Abijah, Zicri; of Miniamin and1 of Moadiah, Piltai; 18of Bilgah, Shammua; of Shemaiah, Jehonathan; 19of Joiarib, Mattenai; of Jedaiah, Uzzi; 20of Sallu,1 Kallai; of Amok, Eber; 21of Hilkiah, Hashabiah; of Jedaiah, Nethanel.

22As for the Levites, in the days of Eliashib, Joiada, Johanan, and Jaddua the aheads of families were recorded, as were the priests during the reign of Darius the Persian. 23The descendants of Levi were recorded in the Book of the aChronicles as heads of families up to the days of Johanan son of Eliashib. 24And the leaders of the Levites were Hashabiah, Sherebiah, Jeshua son of Kadmiel, and their colleagues, who stood opposite them to offer apraise and thanks, one bcontingent corresponding to the other, as specified by David the man of God.

25Mattaniah, Bakbukiah, Obadiah, Meshullam, Talmon, and Akkub were gatekeepers who were guarding the storerooms at the gates. 26These all served in athe days of Joiakim son of Jeshua, bthe son of Jozadak, and in the days of Nehemiah the governor and of Ezra the priestly scribe.

The Wall of Jerusalem Is Dedicated

27At athe dedication of the wall of Jerusalem, they sought out the Levites from all the places they lived to bring them to Jerusalem to celebrate the dedication joyfully with songs of thanksgiving and songs accompanied by cymbals, harps, and lyres. 28The singers were also assembled from the district around Jerusalem and from the asettlements of the Netophathites 29and from Beth Gilgal and from the fields of Geba and Azmaveth, for the singers had built settlements for themselves around Jerusalem. 30When the priests and Levites had apurified themselves, they purified the people, the gates, and the wall.

11:24 aGen 38:30 b1 Chr 18:17   11:25 aJosh 14:15 1Heb. *its daughters.*   11:31 1MT *the sons of.* 2Heb. *from Geba.*   11:35 a1 Chr 4:14 1MT omits *and.*   12:1 aEzra 2:1–2; 7:7 bNeh 7:7; Matt 1:12–13 cNeh 10:2–8   12:4 aLuke 1:5 1Most MSS *Ginnethoi.*   12:7 aEzra 3:2; Hag 1:1; Zech 3:1 1Heb. *brothers.*   12:8 aNeh 11:17   12:9 1Ket. *Unno.*   12:12 aNeh 7:70–71; 8:13; 11:13   12:14 1Most MSS *Shebaniah.*   12:15 1MT *Meraioth.*   12:16 1MT *Adaia.*   12:17 1Or *of Miniamin . . .; of Moadiah, Piltai;* where the name of the leader of the family of Miniamin has dropped out of the text due to a problem in transmission.   12:20 1MT *Sallai.*   12:22 a1 Chr 24:6   12:23 a1 Chr 9:14–22   12:24 aNeh 11:17 bEzra 3:11   12:26 aNeh 8:9 bEzra 7:6, 11   12:27 aDeut 20:5; Neh 7:1; Ps 30:title   12:28 a1 Chr 9:16   12:30 aEzra 6:20; Neh 13:22, 30

[31]I brought the leaders of Judah up [a]on top of the wall, and I appointed two large choirs [b]to give thanks. One was to proceed[1] on the top of the wall southward toward the Dung Gate. [32]Going after them were Hoshaiah, half the leaders of Judah, [33]Azariah, Ezra, Meshullam, [34]Judah, Benjamin, Shemaiah, Jeremiah, [35]some of the priests [a]with trumpets, Zechariah son of Jonathan, the son of Shemaiah, the son of Mattaniah, the son of Micaiah, the son of Zaccur, the son of Asaph, [36]and his colleagues—Shemaiah, Azarel, Milalai, Gilalai, Maai, Nethanel, Judah, and Hanani—with [a]musical [b]instruments of David the man of God. (Ezra the scribe led them.) [37][a]They went over [b]the Fountain Gate and continued directly up the steps of the [c]City of David on [d]the ascent to the wall. They passed the house of David and continued on to the Water Gate toward the east.

[38]The second choir was proceeding[1] in [a]the opposite direction. I followed them, along with half the people, on top of the wall, past the [b]Tower of [c]the Ovens to the Broad Wall, [39]over the Ephraim Gate, the Jeshanah Gate, the Fish Gate, the Tower of Hananel, [a]and [b]the Tower of [c]the Hundred, to [d]the Sheep Gate. [e]They stopped at [f]the Gate of the Guard.

[40]Then the two choirs that gave thanks took their stations in the temple of God. I did also, along with half the officials with me, [41]and the priests—Eliakim, Maaseiah, Miniamin, Micaiah, Elioenai, Zechariah, and Hananiah, with their trumpets—[42]and also Maaseiah, Shemaiah, Eleazar, Uzzi, Jehohanan, Malkijah, Elam, and Ezer. The choirs sang loudly under the direction of Jezrahiah. [43]And on that day they offered great sacrifices and rejoiced, for God had given them great joy. The women and children also rejoiced. The rejoicing in Jerusalem could be heard from [a]far away.

[44]On that day men were appointed over the storerooms for the contributions, firstfruits, [a]and [b]tithes, to gather into them from[1] the fields of the cities the portions prescribed by the law for the priests and the Levites, for the people of Judah took delight in the priests and Levites who were ministering. [45]They performed the service of their God and the service of purification, along with the singers and gatekeepers, [a]according to the commandment of David and[1] his son Solomon. [46]For long ago, in the days of David [a]and Asaph, there had been directors for the singers and for the songs of praise and thanks to God. [47]So in [a]the days of Zerubbabel [b]and in the days of Nehemiah, all Israel was contributing the portions for the singers and gatekeepers, according to the daily need. They also set aside[1] the portion for the Levites, and the Levites set aside the portion for the descendants of Aaron.

Further Reforms by Nehemiah

13 On that day [a]the book of Moses was read aloud in the hearing of the people. They found written in it [b]that no Ammonite or Moabite may ever enter the assembly of God, [2]for they had not met the Israelites with food and water, but instead had [a]hired Balaam to curse them. (Our God, [b]however, turned the curse into blessing.) [3]When they heard the law, they removed from Israel all who were of mixed ancestry.

[4]But before this time, [a]Eliashib the priest, a relative of [b]Tobiah, had been appointed over the storerooms[1] of the temple of our God. [5]He made for him a large storeroom [a]where previously they had been keeping the grain offering, the incense, and the vessels, along with the tithes of the grain, the new wine, and the olive oil as commanded for the Levites, the singers, the gatekeepers, and the offering for the priests.

[6]During all this time I was not in Jerusalem, [a]for in the thirty-second year of King Artaxerxes of Babylon, I had gone back to the king. After some time I had requested leave of the king, [7]and I returned to Jerusalem. Then I discovered the evil that Eliashib had [a]done for Tobiah by supplying him with a storeroom in the courts of the temple of God. [8]I was very upset, and I threw all of Tobiah's household possessions out of the storeroom. [9]Then I gave instructions that the storerooms should be [a]purified, and I brought back the equipment of the temple

---

12:31 [a] Neh 12:38   [b] Neh 2:13; 3:13   [1] MT *and processions.*   **12:35** [a] Num 10:2, 8   **12:36** [a] 1 Chr 23:5   [b] 2 Chr 29:26–27   **12:37** [a] Neh 2:14; 3:15   [b] Neh 3:15   [c] 2 Sam 5:7–9   [d] Neh 3:26; 8:1, 3, 16   **12:38** [a] Neh 12:31   [b] Neh 3:11   [c] Neh 3:8   [1] MT *the one proceeding.*   **12:39** [a] 2 Kgs 14:13; Neh 8:16   [b] Neh 3:6   [c] Neh 3:3   [d] Neh 3:1   [e] Neh 3:32   [f] Jer 32:2   **12:43** [a] Ezra 3:13   **12:44** [a] 2 Chr 31:11–12; Neh 13:5, 12, 13   [b] Neh 10:37–39   [1] MT *to the fields.*   **12:45** [a] 1 Chr 25; 26   [1] One ws omits *and.*   **12:46** [a] 1 Chr 25:1; 2 Chr 29:30   **12:47** [a] Num 18:21, 24   [b] Num 18:26   [1] Heb. *were sanctifying.*   **13:1** [a] [Deut 31:11–12]; 2 Kgs 23:2; Neh 8:3, 8; 9:3; Isa 34:16   [b] Deut 23:3–4   **13:2** [a] Num 22:5; Josh 24:9–10   [b] Num 23:1; 24:10; Deut 23:5   **13:4** [a] Neh 12:10   [b] Neh 2:10; 4:3; 6:1   [1] MT *storeroom.*   **13:5** [a] Neh 12:44   **13:6** [a] Neh 5:14–16   **13:7** [a] Neh 13:1, 5   **13:9** [a] 2 Chr 29:5, 15, 16

of God, along with the grain offering and the incense.

[10]I also discovered that the portions for the Levites had [a]not been provided, and that as a result the Levites and the singers who performed [b]this work had all gone off to their fields. [11]So [a]I registered a complaint with the leaders, asking, "[b]Why is the temple of God neglected?" Then I gathered them and reassigned them to their positions.

[12]Then all of Judah brought [a]the tithe of the grain, the new wine, and the olive oil to the storerooms. [13]I gave instructions[1] that Shelemiah the priest, Zadok the scribe, [a]and a certain Levite named Pedaiah be put in charge of the storerooms, and that Hanan son of Zaccur, the son of Mattaniah, be their assistant,[2] for they were regarded as [b]trustworthy. It was then their responsibility to oversee the distribution to their colleagues.[3]

[14]Please [a]remember me for this, O my God, and do not wipe out the kindness that I have done for the temple of my God and for its services!

[15]In those days I saw people in Judah treading winepresses [a]on the Sabbath, bringing in heaps of grain and loading them onto donkeys, along with wine, grapes, figs, and all kinds of loads, and bringing them to Jerusalem on the Sabbath day. So [b]I warned them on the day that they sold these provisions. [16]The people from Tyre who lived there were bringing fish and all kinds of merchandise and were selling it on the Sabbath to the people of Judah—and in Jerusalem, of all places! [17]So I registered a complaint with the nobles of Judah, saying to them, "What is this evil thing that you are doing, profaning the Sabbath day? [18]Isn't this the way your ancestors [a]acted, causing our God to bring on them and on this city all this misfortune? And now you are causing even more wrath on Israel, profaning the Sabbath like this!"

[19]When the evening shadows [a]began to fall on [b]the gates of Jerusalem before the Sabbath, I ordered the doors to be closed. I further directed that they were not to be opened until after the Sabbath. I positioned some of my young men at the gates so that no load could enter on the Sabbath day. [20]The traders and sellers of all kinds of merchandise spent the night outside Jerusalem once or twice. [21]But I warned them and said, "Why do you spend the night by the wall? If you repeat this, I will forcibly remove you!" From that time on they did not show up on the Sabbath. [22]Then I directed [a]the Levites to purify themselves and come and guard the gates in order to keep the Sabbath day holy.

For this please remember me, O my God, and have pity on me in keeping with your great love.

[23]Also in those days I saw the men of Judah who [a]had married women from [b]Ashdod, Ammon, and Moab. [24]Half their children spoke the language of Ashdod (or the language of one of the other peoples mentioned[1]) and were unable to speak the language of Judah. [25]So I entered a [a]complaint with them. I called down a curse on them, and I struck some of the men and pulled out their hair. I had them [b]swear by God saying, "You will not marry off your daughters to their sons, and you will not take any of their daughters as wives for your sons or for yourselves. [26][a]Was it not because of things like these that King Solomon of Israel sinned? Among [b]the many nations there was no king like him. He was loved by his God, and God made him king over all Israel. But the foreign wives made even him sin! [27]Should we then in your case hear that you do all this great evil, thereby being [a]unfaithful to our God by marrying foreign wives?"

[28]Now one [a]of the sons of Joiada son of Eliashib the high priest was a son-in-law of [b]Sanballat the Horonite. So I banished him from my sight.

[29]Please [a]remember [b]them, O my God, because they have defiled the priesthood, the covenant of the priesthood,[1] and the Levites.

[30][a]So I purified them of everything foreign, and I [b]assigned specific duties to the priests and the Levites. [31]I also provided for [a]the wood offering at the appointed times and also for the firstfruits.

Please [b]remember me for good, O my God.

13:10 [a]Neh 10:37; Mal 3:8 [b]Num 35:2 13:11 [a]Neh 13:17, 25 [b]Neh 10:39 13:12 [a]Neh 10:38; 12:44 13:13 [a]2 Chr 31:12 [b]1 Cor 4:2 [1]MT and I appointed over the storeroom. [2]Heb. on their hand. [3]Heb. brothers. 13:14 [a]Neh 5:19; 13:22, 31 13:15 [a][Exod 20:10] [b]Neh 10:31; [Jer 17:21] 13:18 [a]Ezra 9:13; [Jer 17:21] 13:19 [a]Lev 23:32 [b]Jer 17:21–22 13:22 [a]1 Chr 15:12; Neh 12:30 13:23 [a][Exod 34:16; Deut 7:3–4]; Ezra 9:2; Neh 10:30 [b]Neh 4:7 13:24 [1]Heb. people and people. 13:25 [a]Prov 28:4 [b]Ezra 10:5; Neh 10:29–30 13:26 [a]1 Kgs 11:1–2 [b]1 Kgs 11:4–8 13:27 [a][Ezra 10:2]; Neh 13:23 13:28 [a]Neh 12:10, 12 [b]Neh 4:1, 7; 6:1–2 13:29 [a]Neh 6:14 [b]Mal 2:4, 11, 12 [1]A few wss the priests. 13:30 [a]Neh 10:30 [b]Neh 12:1 13:31 [a]Neh 10:34 [b]Neh 13:14, 22

ESTHER

God's hand of providence and protection on behalf of his people is evident throughout the Book of Esther though his name does not appear once. Haman's plot creates grave danger for the Jews and is countered by the courage of beautiful Esther and the counsel of her wise cousin Mordecai, resulting in a great deliverance. The Feast of Purim becomes an annual reminder of God's faithfulness on behalf of his people. Esther's Hebrew name was *Hadassah*, "Myrtle" (2:7), but her Persian name *Ester* was derived from the Persian word for "Star" (*stara*). The Greek title for this book is *Esther*, and the Latin title is *Hester*.

The King Throws a Lavish Party

1 The following events happened in the days of [a]Ahasuerus. (I am referring to that Ahasuerus who used to rule [b]over 127 provinces extending all the way [c]from India to Ethiopia.) [2]In those days, as King Ahasuerus [a]sat on his royal throne in [b]Susa the citadel, [3]in the third year of his reign he [a]provided a banquet for all his officials and his servants. The army of Persia and Media was present, as well as the nobles and the officials of the provinces.

[4]He displayed the riches of his royal glory and the splendor of his majestic greatness for a lengthy period of time—180 days, to be exact! [5]When those days[1] were completed, the king then provided a seven-day[2] banquet for all the people who were present in Susa the citadel, for those of highest standing to the most lowly. It was held in the court located in the garden of the royal palace. [6]The furnishings included white linen and blue curtains hung by cords of the finest linen and purple wool on silver rings, alabaster columns, gold and silver [a]couches displayed on a floor made of valuable stones of alabaster, mother-of-pearl, and mineral stone. [7]Drinks were served [a]in golden containers, all of which differed from one another. Royal wine was available in abundance at the king's expense. [8]There were no restrictions on the drinking, for the king had instructed all his supervisors that they should do as everyone so desired.

[9]Queen Vashti also gave a banquet for the women in King Ahasuerus' royal palace.

Queen Vashti Is Removed from Her Royal Position

[10]On the seventh day, as King Ahasuerus was feeling the effects of the wine, he ordered Mehuman, Biztha, [a]Harbona, Bigtha, Abagtha, Zethar, and Carcas, the seven eunuchs who attended him, [11]to bring Queen Vashti into the king's presence wearing her royal high turban. He wanted to show the people and the officials her beauty, for she was very attractive. [12]But Queen Vashti refused to come at the king's bidding conveyed through the eunuchs. Then the king became extremely angry, and his rage consumed him.

[13]The king then inquired of the [a]wise men [b]who were discerners of the times—for it was the royal custom to confer with all those who were proficient in laws and legalities. [14]Those who were closest to him were Carshena, Shethar, Admatha, Tarshish, Meres, Marsena, and Memucan. These men were the [a]seven officials of Persia and Media [b]who saw the king on a regular basis[1] and had the most prominent offices in the kingdom. [15]The king asked, "By law, what should be done to Queen Vashti in light of the fact that she has not obeyed the instructions of King Ahasuerus conveyed through the eunuchs?"

[16]Memucan then replied to the king and

1:1 [a] Ezra 4:6; Dan 9:1 [b] Esth 8:9 [c] Dan 6:1   1:2 [a] 1 Kgs 1:46 [b] Neh 1:1; Dan 8:2   1:3 [a] Gen 40:20; Esth 2:18   1:5 [1] LXX *the days of the wedding.* [2] LXX *six.*   1:6 [a] Esth 7:8; Ezek 23:41; Amos 2:8; 6:4   1:7 [a] Esth 2:18   1:10 [a] Esth 7:9   1:13 [a] Jer 10:7; Dan 2:12; Matt 2:1 [b] 1 Chr 12:32   1:14 [a] Ezra 7:14 [b] 2 Kgs 25:19; [Matt 18:10] [1] Heb. *seers of the face of the king.*

the officials, "The wrong of Queen Vashti is not against the king alone, but against all the officials and all the people who are throughout all the provinces of King Ahasuerus. [17]For the matter concerning the queen will spread to all the women, leading them to [a]treat their husbands with contempt, saying, 'When King Ahasuerus gave orders to bring Queen Vashti into his presence, she would not come.' [18]And this very day the noble ladies of Persia and Media who have heard the matter concerning the queen will respond in the same way to all the royal officials, and there will be more than enough contempt and anger. [19]If the king is so inclined, let a royal edict go forth from him, and let it be written in the laws of Persia and Media that [a]cannot be repealed that Vashti may not come into the presence of King Ahasuerus, and let the king convey her royalty to another who is more deserving than she. [20]And let the king's decision that he will enact be disseminated throughout all his kingdom, vast though it is.[1] Then all the women will give [a]honor to their husbands, from the most prominent to the lowly."

[21]The matter seemed appropriate to the king and the officials. So the king acted on the advice of Memucan. [22]He sent letters throughout all the royal provinces, [a]to each province according to its own script and to each people according to their own language, that every man should [b]be ruling his family and should be speaking the language of his own people.[1]

Esther Becomes Queen in Vashti's Place

2 When these things had been accomplished and the rage of King Ahasuerus had diminished, he remembered Vashti and [a]what she had done and what had been decided against her. [2]The king's servants who attended him said, "Let a search be conducted on the king's behalf for attractive young women. [3]And let the king appoint officers throughout all the provinces of his kingdom to gather all the attractive young women to Susa the citadel, to the harem under the authority of Hegai, the king's eunuch who oversees the women, and let him provide whatever cosmetics they desire. [4]Let the young woman whom the king finds most attractive become queen in place of Vashti." This seemed like a good idea to the king, so he acted accordingly.

[5]Now there happened to be a Jewish man in Susa the citadel whose name was Mordecai. He was the son of Jair, the son of Shimei, the son of [a]Kish, a Benjaminite, [6a]who had been taken into exile from Jerusalem with the captives who had been carried into exile with Jeconiah king of Judah, whom Nebuchadnezzar king of Babylon had taken into exile. [7]Now he was acting as the guardian of Hadassah (that [a]is, Esther), the daughter of his uncle, for neither her father nor her mother was alive. This young woman was very attractive and had a beautiful figure. When her father and mother died, Mordecai had raised her as if she were his own daughter.

[8]It so happened that when the king's edict and his law became known many young women were [a]taken to Susa the citadel to be placed under the authority of Hegai. Esther also was taken to the royal palace to be under the authority of Hegai, who was overseeing the women. [9]This young woman pleased him, and she found favor with him. He quickly provided her with her cosmetics and her rations; he also provided her with the seven specially chosen young women who were from the palace. He then transferred her and her young women to the best quarters in the harem.

[10]Now [a]Esther had not disclosed her people or her lineage, for Mordecai had instructed her not to do so. [11]And day after day Mordecai used to walk back and forth in front of the court of the harem in order to learn how Esther was doing and what might happen to her.

[12]At the end of the twelve months that were required for the women,[1] when the turn of each young woman arrived to go to King Ahasuerus—for in this way they had to fulfill their time of cosmetic treatment: six months with oil of myrrh, and six months with perfume and various ointments used by women—[13]the woman would go to the king in the following way: Whatever she

---

1:17 [a][Eph 5:33]   1:19 [a]Esth 8:8; Dan 6:8   1:20 [a][Eph 5:33; Col 3:18; 1 Pet 3:1]   [1]LXX omits *vast though it is.*   1:22 [a]Esth 3:12, 8:9   [b][Eph 5:22–24; 1 Tim 2:12]   [1]LXX omits *and should be speaking the language of his own people.*   2:1 [a]Esth 1:19–20   2:5 [a]1 Sam 9:1   2:6 [a]2 Kgs 24:14–15; 2 Chr 36:10, 20; Jer 24:1   2:7 [a]Esth 2:15   2:8 [a]Esth 2:3   2:10 [a]Esth 2:20   2:12 [1]LXX omits *that were required for the women.*

asked for would be provided for her to take with her from the harem to the royal palace. [14]In the evening she went, and in the morning she returned to a separate part of the harem, to the authority of Shaashgaz, the king's eunuch who was overseeing the concubines. She would not go back to the king unless the king was pleased with her[1] and she was requested by name.

[15]When it became [a]the turn of Esther, daughter of Abihail, the uncle of Mordecai (who had raised her as if she were his own daughter), to go to the king, she did not request anything except what Hegai the king's eunuch, who was overseer of the women, had recommended. Yet Esther met [b]with the approval of all who saw her. [16]Then Esther was taken to King Ahasuerus at his royal residence in the tenth[1] month (that is, the month of Tebeth) in the seventh[2] year of his reign. [17]And the king loved Esther more than all the other women, and she met with his loving approval[1] more than all the other young women.[2] So he placed the royal high [a]turban on her head and appointed her queen in place of Vashti. [18]Then the king [a]prepared a large banquet for all his officials and his servants—it was actually Esther's banquet. He also set aside a holiday for the provinces, and he provided for offerings at the king's expense.[1]

Mordecai Learns of a Plot against the King

[19]Now when the young women were being gathered again,[1] Mordecai was sitting at the king's gate. [20][a]Esther was still not divulging her lineage or her people, just as Mordecai had instructed her.[1] Esther continued to do whatever Mordecai said, just as she had done when he was raising her.

[21]In those days while Mordecai was sitting at the king's gate, Bigthan and Teresh,[1] two of the king's eunuchs who protected the entrance, became angry and plotted to assassinate King Ahasuerus. [22]When Mordecai learned of the conspiracy, he informed Queen Esther,[1] and Esther told the king in Mordecai's name. [23]The king [a]then had the matter investigated and, finding it to be so, had the two conspirators hanged on a gallows.[1] It was then recorded in the daily chronicles in the king's presence.

Haman Conspires to Destroy the Jews

3 Some time later King Ahasuerus promoted Haman the son of Hammedatha, the [a]Agagite, exalting him and setting his position above that of all the officials who were with him. [2]As a result, all the king's servants who were at the king's gate were bowing and paying homage to Haman, for the king had so commanded. However, Mordecai did not bow, nor did he pay him homage.

[3]Then the servants of the [a]king who were at the king's gate asked Mordecai, "Why are you violating the king's commandment?" [4]And after they had spoken to him day after day without his paying any attention to them, they informed Haman to see whether this attitude on Mordecai's part would be permitted. Furthermore, he had disclosed to them that he was a Jew.

[5]When Haman saw that Mordecai was not bowing or paying homage to him, he was [a]filled with rage. [6]But the thought of striking out against Mordecai alone was repugnant to him, for he had been informed of the identity of Mordecai's people.[1] So Haman [a]sought to destroy all the Jews (that is, the people of Mordecai)[2] who were in all the kingdom of Ahasuerus.

[7]In [a]the first month (that is, the month of Nisan), in the twelfth year of King Ahasuerus' reign, *pur* (that is, the lot) was cast before Haman in order to determine a day and a month.[1] It turned out to be the twelfth month (that is, the month of Adar).

[8]Then Haman said to King Ahasuerus, "There is a particular people that is dispersed and spread among [a]the inhabitants[1] throughout all the provinces of your kingdom whose laws differ from those of all other peoples. Furthermore, they do not observe the king's laws. It is not appropriate

for the king to provide a haven for them. [9] If the king is so inclined, let an edict be issued to destroy them. I will pay 10,000 talents of silver to be conveyed to the king's treasuries for the officials who carry out this business."

[10] So the king [a] removed [b] his signet ring from his hand and gave it to Haman the son of Hammedatha, the Agagite, who was hostile [c] toward the Jews. [11] The king replied to Haman, "Keep your money, and do with those people whatever you wish."

[12] So [a] the royal scribes were summoned [b] in the first month, on the thirteenth day of the month. [c] Everything Haman commanded was written to the king's satraps and governors who were in every province and to the officials of every people, province by province according to its script and people by people according to their language. In the name of King Ahasuerus it was written and sealed with the king's signet ring. [13] Letters were [a] sent by the runners to all the [b] king's provinces stating that they should destroy, kill, and annihilate all the Jews, from youth [c] to elderly, both women and children, on a particular day, namely the thirteenth day[1] of the twelfth month (that is, the month of Adar), and to loot and plunder their possessions. [14] A copy of this edict [a] was to be presented as law throughout every province; it was to be made known to all the inhabitants,[1] so that they would be prepared for this day. [15] The messengers scurried forth with [a] the king's order. The edict was issued in Susa the citadel. While the king and Haman sat down to drink, the city of Susa was in an uproar.

Esther Decides to Risk Everything in Order to Help Her People

4 Now when Mordecai became aware of all that had been done, he [a] tore his garments [b] and put on sackcloth and ashes. He went out into the city, crying [c] out in a loud and bitter voice. [2] But he went no farther than the king's gate, for no one was permitted to enter the king's gate clothed in sackcloth. [3] Throughout each and every province where the king's edict and law were announced there was considerable mourning among the Jews, along with fasting, weeping, and sorrow. Sackcloth and ashes were characteristic of many. [4] When Esther's female attendants and her eunuchs came and informed her about Mordecai's behavior, the queen was overcome with anguish. Although she sent garments for Mordecai to put on so that he could remove his sackcloth, he would not accept them. [5] So Esther called for Hathach, one of the king's eunuchs who had been placed at her service, and instructed him to find out the cause and reason for Mordecai's behavior. [6] So Hathach went to Mordecai at the plaza of the city in front of the king's gate. [7] Then Mordecai related to him everything that had happened to him, even [a] the specific amount of money that Haman had offered to pay to the king's treasuries for the Jews to be destroyed. [8] He [a] also gave him a written copy of the law that had been disseminated in Susa for their destruction so that he could show it to Esther and talk to her about it. He also gave instructions that she should go to the king to implore him and petition him on behalf of her people. [9] So Hathach returned and related Mordecai's instructions to Esther.

[10] Then Esther replied to Hathach with instructions for Mordecai: [11] "All [a] the servants of [b] the king and the people of the king's provinces know that there is only one law applicable [c] to any man or woman who comes [d] uninvited to the king in the inner court—that person will be put to death, unless the king extends to him the gold scepter, permitting him to be spared. Now I have not been invited to come to the king for some 30 days." [12] When Esther's reply was conveyed to Mordecai, [13] he said to take back this answer to Esther: "Don't imagine that because you are part of the king's household you will be the one Jew who will escape. [14] If you keep quiet at this time, liberation and protection for the Jews will appear[1] from another source,[2] while you and your father's household perish. It may very well be that you have achieved royal status for such a time as this!"

[15] Then Esther sent this reply to Mordecai: [16] "Go, assemble all the Jews who are

3:10 [a] Gen 41:42 [b] Esth 8:2, 8 [c] Esth 7:6 3:12 [a] Esth 8:9 [b] Esth 1:22 [c] 1 Kgs 21:8; Esth 8:8–10 3:13 [a] 2 Chr 30:6; Esth 8:10, 14 [b] Esth 8:12 [c] Esth 8:11, 9:10 [1] LXX omits on the thirteenth day. 3:14 [a] Esth 8:13–14 [1] Heb. peoples. 3:15 [a] Esth 8:15; [Prov 29:2] 4:1 [a] 2 Sam 1:11; Esth 3:8–10; Jonah 3:5–6 [b] Josh 7:6; Ezek 27:30 [c] Gen 27:34 4:7 [a] Esth 3:9 4:8 [a] Esth 3:14–15 4:11 [a] Esth 5:1, 6:4 [b] Dan 2:9 [c] Esth 5:2, 8:4 [d] Esth 2:14 4:14 [1] Heb. stand. [2] Heb. place.

found in Susa, and fast on my behalf. Don't eat and don't drink for [a]three days, night or day. My female attendants [b]and I will also fast in the same way. Afterward I will go to the king, even though it violates the law. If I perish, I perish."

[17]So Mordecai set out to do everything that Esther had instructed him.

Esther Appeals to the King for Help

5 It so happened that on the third day Esther put [a]on her royal attire and stood in [b]the inner court of the palace, opposite the king's quarters. The king was sitting on his royal throne in the palace, opposite the entrance. [2]When the king saw Queen Esther standing in the court, [a]she met with his approval. [b]The king extended to Esther the gold scepter that was in his hand, and Esther approached and touched the end of the scepter.

[3]The king said to her, "What is on your mind, Queen Esther? What is your request? Even as much as half the kingdom will be given to you."

[4]Esther replied, "If the king is so inclined, let the king and Haman come today to the banquet that I have prepared for the king." [5]The king replied, "Find Haman quickly so that we can do as Esther requests."

So the king and Haman went to the banquet that Esther had prepared. [6]While at [a]the banquet of wine, the king said to Esther, "[b]What is your request? It shall be given to you. What is your petition? Ask for as much as half the kingdom, and it shall be done."

[7]Esther responded, "My request and my petition is this: [8]If I have found favor in the king's sight and if the king is inclined to grant my request and approve my petition, let the king and Haman come tomorrow to the [a]banquet that I will prepare for them. At that time I will do as the king wishes."

Haman Expresses His Hatred of Mordecai

[9]Now Haman went forth that day [a]pleased and very much encouraged. But when Haman saw Mordecai [b]at the king's gate, and he did not rise or tremble in his presence, Haman was filled with rage toward Mordecai. [10]But Haman [a]restrained himself and went on to his home.

He then sent for his friends to join him, along with his wife Zeresh. [11]Haman [a]then recounted to them his fabulous wealth, his many sons, and how the king had magnified him and [b]exalted him over the king's other officials and servants. [12]Haman said, "Furthermore, Queen Esther invited only me to accompany the king to the banquet that she prepared. And also tomorrow I am invited along with the king. [13]Yet all this fails to satisfy me so long as I have to see Mordecai the Jew sitting at the king's gate."

[14]Haman's wife Zeresh and all his friends said to him, "Have a [a]gallows 75 feet high built, and in the morning [b]tell [c]the king that Mordecai should be hanged on it. Then go with the king to the banquet contented."

It seemed like a good idea to Haman, so he had the gallows built.

The Turning Point: The King Honors Mordecai

6 Throughout that night [a]the king was unable to sleep, so he asked for the book containing the historical records to be brought. As the records were being read in the king's presence, [2]it was found written that Mordecai had disclosed that Bigthana and Teresh, two of the king's eunuchs who guarded the entrance, had plotted to assassinate King Ahasuerus.

[3]The king asked, "What great honor was bestowed on Mordecai because of this?" The king's attendants who served him responded, "Not a thing was done for him."

[4]Then [a]the king said, "Who is that in the courtyard?" Now Haman had come [b]to the outer courtyard of the palace to suggest that the king hang Mordecai on the gallows that he had constructed for him. [5]The king's attendants said to him, "It is Haman who is standing in the courtyard." The king said, "Let him enter."

[6]So Haman [a]came in, and the king said to him, "What should be done for the man whom the king wishes to honor?" Haman thought to himself, "Who is it that the king would want to honor more than me?" [7]So Haman said to the king, "For the man whom the king wishes to honor, [8]let them bring

[a]royal attire which the king himself has worn and a horse on which the king himself has ridden—one bearing the royal insignia.[1] [9]Then let this clothing [a]and this horse be given to one of the king's noble officials. Let him[1] then clothe the man whom the king wishes to honor, and let him lead him about through the plaza of the city on the horse, calling[2] before him, 'So shall it be done to the man whom the king wishes to honor!'"

[10]The king then said to Haman, "Go quickly! Take the clothing and the horse, just as you have described, and do as you just indicated to Mordecai the Jew, who sits at the king's gate. Don't neglect a single thing of all that you have said."

[11]So Haman took the clothing and the horse, and he clothed Mordecai. He led him about on the horse throughout the plaza of the city, calling before him, "So shall it be done to the man whom the king wishes to honor!"

[12]Then Mordecai again sat at the king's gate, while Haman hurried [a]away to his home, mournful [b]and with a veil over his head. [13]Haman then related to his wife Zeresh and to all his friends everything that had happened to [a]him. These wise men,[1] along with his wife Zeresh, said to him, "If indeed this Mordecai before whom you have begun to fall is Jewish, you will not prevail against him. No, you will surely fall before him!"

[14]While [a]they were still speaking with him, the king's eunuchs arrived. They quickly brought Haman to the banquet that Esther had prepared.

The King Has Haman Executed

7 So the king and Haman came to dine with Queen Esther. [2]On the second day of the banquet of wine the king asked Esther, "[a]What is your request, Queen Esther? It shall be granted to you. And what is your petition? Ask for up to half the kingdom, and it shall be done."

[3]Queen Esther replied, "If I have met with your approval, O king, and if the king is so inclined, grant me my life as my request, and my people as my petition. [4]For we have been [a]sold—both I and my people—to

destruction and to slaughter and to annihilation. If we had simply been sold as [b]male and female slaves, I would have remained silent, for such distress would not have been sufficient for troubling the king."

[5]Then King Ahasuerus responded[1] to Queen Esther, "Who is this individual? Where is this person to be found who is presumptuous enough[2] to act in this way?"

[6]Esther replied, "The oppressor and [a]enemy is this evil Haman!"

Then Haman became terrified in the presence of the king and queen. [7]In rage the king arose from the banquet of wine and withdrew to the palace garden. Meanwhile, Haman stood to beg Queen Esther for his life, for he realized that the king had now determined a catastrophic end for him.

[8]When [a]the king returned from the palace garden to the banquet of wine, Haman was throwing himself down[1] on the couch where Esther was lying. The king exclaimed, "Will he also attempt to rape the queen while I am still in the building?"

As these words left the king's mouth, they [b]covered Haman's face. [9a]Harbona, one of the king's eunuchs, said, "Indeed, there is [b]the gallows that Haman made for Mordecai, who spoke [c]out on the king's behalf. It stands near Haman's home and is 75 feet high."

The king said, "Hang him on it!" [10]So [a]they [b]hanged Haman on the very gallows that he had prepared for Mordecai. The king's rage then abated.

The King Acts to Protect the Jews

8 On that same day King Ahasuerus gave the estate of Haman, that [a]adversary of the Jews, to Queen Esther. Now Mordecai had come before the king, for Esther had revealed [b]how he was related to her. [2]The king then removed [a]his signet ring (the very one he had taken back from Haman) and gave it to Mordecai. And Esther designated Mordecai to be in charge of Haman's estate.

[3]Then Esther again spoke with the king, falling at his feet. She wept and begged him for mercy that he might nullify the evil of Haman the Agagite and the plot that he had intended against the Jews. [4]When [a]the king

6:8 [a]1 Kgs 1:33 [1]LXX omits *one bearing the royal insignia.* 6:9 [a]Gen 41:43 [1]MT *and they will clothe.* [2]Heb. *and let them call.* 6:12 [a]2 Chr 26:20 [b]2 Sam 15:30; Jer 14:3–4 6:13 [a][Gen 12:3]; Zech 2:8 [1]Some wss *his friends.* 6:14 [a]Esth 5:8 7:2 [a]Esth 5:6 7:4 [a]Esth 3:9, 4:7 [b]Deut 28:68 7:5 [1]MT adds *and he said.* [2]Heb. *has so filled his heart.* 7:6 [a]Esth 3:10 7:8 [a]Esth 1:6 [b]Job 9:24 [1]Heb. *falling.* 7:9 [a]Esth 1:10 [b]Esth 5:14; [Ps 7:16; Prov 11:5–6] [c]Esth 6:2 7:10 [a][Ps 7:16; 94:23; Prov 11:5–6] [b]Ps 37:35–36; Dan 6:24 8:1 [a]Esth 7:6 [b]Esth 2:7, 15 8:2 [a]Esth 3:10 8:4 [a]Esth 4:11, 5:2

extended to Esther the gold scepter, she arose and stood before the king.

[5]She said, "If the king is so inclined, and if I have met with his approval, and if the matter is agreeable to the king, and if I am attractive to him, let an edict be written rescinding those [a]recorded intentions of Haman the son of Hammedatha, the Agagite,[1] which he wrote in order to destroy the Jews who are throughout all the king's provinces. [6]For how can I watch [a]the calamity that will befall my people, and how can I watch the destruction of my relatives?"

[7]King Ahasuerus [a]replied to Queen Esther and to Mordecai the Jew, "Look, I have already given Haman's estate to Esther, and he has been hanged on the gallows because he took hostile action against the Jews. [8]Now write in the king's name whatever in your opinion is appropriate concerning the Jews and seal it with the king's signet ring. Any decree that is written in the king's name and sealed with the king's signet ring [a]cannot be rescinded."

[9][a]The king's scribes were quickly summoned—in the third month (that is, the month of Sivan), on the twenty-third day. They wrote out everything that Mordecai instructed to the Jews, and to the satraps, and the governors, and the officials of the provinces all the way [b]from [c]India to Ethiopia—127 provinces in all—to each province in its own script and to each people in their own language, and to the Jews according to their own script and their own language. [10]Mordecai wrote in the name of King Ahasuerus [a]and sealed it with the king's signet ring. He then sent letters by couriers, who rode royal horses that were very swift.

[11]The king thereby allowed [a]the Jews who were in every city to assemble and to stand up for themselves—to [b]destroy, to kill, and to annihilate any army of whatever people or province that should become their adversaries, including their women and children, and to confiscate their property. [12]This was to take place [a]on a certain day throughout all the provinces of King Ahasuerus—namely, on the thirteenth day of the twelfth month (that is, the month of Adar). [13]A copy of the edict [a]was to be presented as law throughout each and every province and made known to all peoples, so that the Jews might be prepared on that day to avenge themselves on their enemies. [14]The couriers who were riding the royal horses went forth with the king's edict without delay. And the law was presented in Susa the citadel as well.

[15]Now Mordecai went out from [a]the king's presence in blue and white royal attire, with a large golden crown and a purple linen mantle. The city of Susa shouted with joy. [16]For the Jews there was [a]radiant happiness and joyous honor. [17]Throughout every province [a]and throughout every city where the king's edict and his law arrived, the Jews experienced happiness and joy, banquets and holidays. Many of the resident peoples[1] pretended to [b]be Jews,[2] because the [c]fear of the Jews had overcome them.

The Jews Prevail over Their Enemies

9 In the twelfth month (that is, the month of Adar), on its thirteenth day, the edict of the [a]king and his law were to be executed. It was on this day that [b]the enemies of the Jews had supposed that they would gain [c]power over them. But contrary to expectations, the Jews gained power over their enemies. [2]The Jews assembled themselves in their cities throughout all [a]the provinces of King Ahasuerus to strike out against those who were [b]seeking their harm. No one was able to stand before them, for dread of them fell on all the peoples. [3]All the officials of the provinces, the satraps, the governors, and those who performed the king's business were assisting the Jews, for the dread of Mordecai had fallen on them. [4]Mordecai was of high rank in the king's palace, and word about him was spreading throughout all the provinces. His influence[1] continued to become greater and greater.

[5]The Jews struck all their enemies with the sword, bringing death and destruction, and they did as they pleased with their enemies. [6]In [a]Susa the citadel the Jews killed and destroyed 500 men. [7]In addition, they

also killed Parshandatha, Dalphon, Aspatha, [8]Poratha, Adalia, Aridatha, [9]Parmashta, Arisai, Aridai, and Vaizatha, [10]the 10 sons of Haman son of Hammedatha, [a]the enemy of the Jews. [b]But they did not confiscate their property.

[11]On that same day the number of those killed in Susa the citadel was brought to the king's attention. [12]Then the king said to Queen Esther, "In Susa the citadel the Jews have killed and destroyed 500 men and the 10 sons of Haman. [a]What then have they done in the rest of the king's provinces? What is your request? It shall be given to you. What other petition do you have? It shall be done."

[13]Esther replied, "If the king is so inclined, let the Jews who are [a]in Susa [b]be permitted to act tomorrow also according to today's law, and let them hang the 10 sons of Haman on the gallows."

[14]So the king issued orders for this to be done. A law was passed in Susa, and the ten sons of Haman were hanged. [15]The Jews who were in Susa then assembled on [a]the fourteenth day of the month of Adar, and they killed 300 men in Susa. [b]But they did not confiscate their property.

[16]The rest of [a]the Jews who were throughout the provinces of the king assembled in order to stand up for themselves and to have rest from their enemies. They killed 75,000[1] of their adversaries, [b]but they did not confiscate their property. [17]All this happened on the thirteenth day of the month of Adar. They then rested on the fourteenth day and made it a day for banqueting and happiness.

The Origins of the Feast of Purim

[18]But the Jews who were in Susa assembled [a]on the thirteenth and fourteenth days, and rested on the fifteenth, making it a day for banqueting and happiness. [19]This is why the Jews who are in the rural country—those who live in rural villages—set [a]aside the fourteenth day of the month of Adar for happiness, banqueting, a holiday, and [b]sending gifts to one another.

[20]Mordecai wrote these matters down and sent letters to all the Jews who were throughout all the provinces of King Ahasuerus, both near and far, [21]to have them observe the fourteenth and the fifteenth days of the month of Adar each year [22]as the time when the Jews gave themselves rest from their enemies—the month when their trouble was turned to happiness and their mourning to a holiday. These were to be days of banqueting, happiness, [a]sending gifts to one another, and providing for the [b]poor.

[23]So the Jews committed themselves to continuing what they had begun to do and to what Mordecai had written to them. [24]For Haman the son of Hammedatha, the Agagite, the enemy of all the Jews, [a]had devised plans against the Jews to destroy them. He had cast *pur* (that is, the lot) in order to afflict and destroy them. [25]But [a]when the matter came to the king's attention, the king gave written orders that Haman's evil intentions that he had devised against the Jews should [b]fall on his own head. He and his sons were hanged on the gallows. [26]For [a]this reason these days are known as *Purim*, after the name of *pur*. Therefore, because of the account found in this letter and what they had faced in this regard and what had happened to them, [27]the Jews established as binding on themselves, their descendants, and all who [a]joined their company that they should observe these two days without fail, just as written and at the appropriate time on an annual basis. [28]These days were to be remembered and to be celebrated in every generation and in every family, every province, and every city. The Jews were not to fail to observe these days of Purim; the remembrance of them was not to cease among their descendants.

[29]So Queen [a]Esther, the daughter of Abihail, and Mordecai the Jew wrote with full authority to confirm this [b]second[1] letter about Purim. [30]Letters were sent[1] to all [a]the Jews in the 127 provinces of the empire of Ahasuerus—words of true peace—[31]to establish these days of Purim in their proper times, just as Mordecai the Jew and Queen Esther had established, and just as they had established both for themselves and their descendants, matters pertaining to [a]fasting

9:10 [a] Esth 5:11; 9:7–10; Job 18:19; 27:13–15; Ps 21:10 [b] Esth 8:11 **9:12** [a] Esth 5:6, 7:2 **9:13** [a] Esth 8:11, 9:15 [b] 2 Sam 21:6, 9 **9:15** [a] Esth 8:11, 9:2 [b] Esth 9:10 **9:16** [a] Esth 9:2 [b] Esth 8:11 [1] Some MSS *15,000*; Luc. *70,100*. **9:18** [a] Esth 9:11, 15 **9:19** [a] Esth 8:16–17 [b] Neh 8:10, 12; Esth 9:22 **9:22** [a] Neh 8:10; Esth 9:19 [b] [Deut 15:7–11]; Job 29:16 **9:24** [a] Esth 3:6–7, 9:26 **9:25** [a] Esth 7:4–10; 8:3; 9:13–14 [b] Esth 7:10 **9:26** [a] Esth 9:20 **9:27** [a] Esth 8:17; [Isa 56:3, 6]; Zech 2:11 **9:29** [a] Esth 2:15 [b] Esth 8:10; 9:20–21 [1] LXX, Syr. omit *second*. **9:30** [a] Esth 1:1 [1] MT *and he sent*. **9:31** [a] Esth 4:3, 16

and lamentation. [32]Esther's command established these matters of Purim, and the matter was officially recorded.

Mordecai's Fame Increases

10 King Ahasuerus [a]then imposed forced labor on the land and on the coastlands of the sea. [2]Now all the actions carried out under his authority and his great achievements, along with an exact statement concerning the greatness of Mordecai, whom the king promoted, are they not written in the Book of the [a]Chronicles of the Kings of Media and Persia? [3]Mordecai the Jew was [a]second only to King Ahasuerus. He was the highest-ranking Jew, and he was admired by his numerous relatives. He worked enthusiastically [b]for the good of his people and was an advocate for the welfare of all his descendants.

10:1 [a]Gen 10:5; Ps 72:10; Isa 11:11; 24:15   10:2 [a]Esth 6:1   10:3 [a]Gen 41:40, 43, 44; 2 Chr 28:7   [b]Neh 2:10; Ps 122:8–9

JOB

Job is perhaps the oldest book of the Bible. Set in the period of the patriarchs (Abraham, Isaac, Jacob, and Joseph), it tells the story of a man who loses everything—his wealth, his family, his health—and wrestles with the question *Why?* The book begins with a heavenly debate between God and Satan, moves through three cycles of earthly debates between Job and his friends, and concludes with a dramatic divine diagnosis of Job's problem. In the end, Job acknowledges God's sovereignty in his life and receives more than he had before his trials. *Iyyob* is the Hebrew title for this book, and the name has two possible meanings. If derived from the Hebrew word for "persecution," it means "Persecuted One." It is more likely that it comes from the Arabic word meaning "to come back" or "repent." If so, it may be defined "Repentant One." Both meanings apply to the book. The Greek title is *Iob*, and the Latin title is *Iob*.

I. THE PROLOGUE (1:1–2:13)

Job's Good Life

1 There was a man [a]in the land of Uz whose name was [b]Job. And that man was [c]blameless[1] and upright, one who [d]feared God and turned away from evil. [2]Seven sons and three daughters were born to him. [3]His possessions[1] included 7,000 sheep, 3,000 camels, 500 yoke of oxen, and 500 female donkeys; in addition he had a very great household. Thus he was the greatest of all the people in the east.

[4]Now his sons used to go and hold a feast in the house of each one in turn, and they would send and invite their three sisters to eat and to drink with them. [5]When the days of their feasting were finished, Job would send for them [a]and sanctify them; he would get up early in the morning and offer burnt offerings according to the number of them all. For Job thought, "Perhaps my children have sinned and [b]cursed[1] God in their hearts." This was Job's customary practice.

Satan's Accusation of Job

[6]Now [a]the day came when the sons of God came to present themselves before the LORD—and Satan also arrived among them. [7]The LORD said to Satan, "Where have you come from?" And Satan answered the LORD, "From roving about on the earth, and from walking back and forth across it." [8]So the LORD said to Satan, "Have you considered my servant Job? There is no one like him on the earth, a blameless and upright man, one who fears God and turns away from evil."

[9]Then Satan answered the LORD, "Is it for nothing that Job fears God? [10]Have you[1] not made [a]a hedge around him and his household and all that he has on every side? [b]You have blessed the work of his hands, and his livestock have increased in the land. [11a]But extend your hand and strike everything he has, and he will no doubt [b]curse you to your face!"

[12]So the LORD said to Satan, "All right then, everything he has is in your power. Only do not extend your hand against the man himself!"[1] So Satan went out from the presence of the LORD.

Job's Integrity in Adversity

[13]Now the day came [a]when Job's sons and daughters were eating and drinking wine in

---

1:1 [a] 1 Chr 1:17   [b] Ezek 14:14, 20; Jas 5:11   [c] Gen 6:9; 17:1; [Deut 18:13]   [d] [Prov 16:6]   [1] This Heb. word does not mean he was sinless, but rather that he wholeheartedly tried to please God and had integrity.   1:3 [1] Heb. *cattle, livestock, possessions*.
1:5 [a] Gen 8:20; [Job 42:8]   [b] 1 Kgs 21:10, 13   [1] Lit. *to bless*; the writer or a scribe has substituted the word "curse" with the word "bless" to avoid the expression "curse God."   1:6 [a] Job 2:1   1:10 [a] Job 29:2–6; Ps 34:7; Isa 5:2   [b] [Ps 128:1–2; Prov 10:22]   [1] An emphatic Heb. construction.   1:11 [a] Job 2:5; 19:21   [b] Isa 8:21; Mal 3:13–14
1:12 [1] An emphatic Heb. construction.   1:13 [a] [Eccl 9:12]

their oldest brother's house, [14]and a messenger came to Job, saying, "The oxen were plowing and the donkeys were grazing beside them, [15]and the Sabeans swooped down and carried them all away, and they killed the servants with the sword! And I—only I alone—escaped to tell you!"

[16]While this one was still speaking, another messenger arrived and said, "The fire of God has fallen from heaven and has burned up the sheep and the servants—it has consumed them! And I—only I alone—escaped to tell you!"

[17]While this one was still speaking another messenger arrived and said, "The Chaldeans formed three bands and made a raid on the camels and carried them all away, and they killed the servants with the sword! And I—only I alone—escaped to tell you!"

[18]While this one was still speaking another messenger arrived and said, "[a]Your sons and your daughters were eating and drinking wine in their oldest brother's house, [19]and suddenly a great wind swept across the wilderness and struck the four corners of the house, and it fell on the young people, and they died! And I—only I alone—escaped to tell you!"

[20]Then Job got up and [a]tore his robe. He shaved his head, and then he [b]threw himself down with his face to the ground. [21]He said, "[a]Naked I came from my mother's womb, and naked I will return there. The LORD [b]gives, and the LORD takes away. May the name of the LORD be [c]blessed!" [22]In all this Job did not [a]sin, nor did he charge God with moral impropriety.[1]

Satan's Additional Charge

2 Again [a]the day came when the sons of God came to present themselves before the LORD, and Satan also arrived among them to present himself before the LORD.[1] [2]And the LORD said to [a]Satan, "Where have you come from?" Satan answered the LORD, "From roving about on the earth, and from walking back and forth across it." [3]Then the LORD [a]said to Satan, "Have you considered my servant Job? For there is no one like him on the earth, a pure and upright man, one who fears God and turns away from evil. And he still holds [b]firmly [c]to his integrity, so that you stirred me up to destroy him without reason."

[4]But Satan answered the LORD, "Skin for skin! Indeed, a man will give up[1] all that he has to save his life. [5a]But extend your hand and strike his [b]bone and his flesh, and he will no doubt curse you to your face!"

[6a]So the LORD said to Satan, "All right, he is in your power; only preserve his life."

Job's Integrity in Suffering

[7]So Satan went out [a]from the presence of the LORD, and he afflicted Job with a malignant ulcer from the soles of his feet to the top of his head. [8]Job took a shard of broken pottery to scrape himself with [a]while he was sitting among the ashes.

[9]Then his wife said to him, "Are you still holding firmly to your integrity? Curse[1] God, and die!" [10]But he replied, "You're talking like one of the godless women would do! Should we receive what is good from God, and not [a]also receive what is evil?" [b]In all this Job did not [c]sin by what he said.[1]

The Visit of Job's Friends

[11]When Job's three friends heard about all this calamity that had happened to him, each of them came from his own country—Eliphaz the [a]Temanite, Bildad the [b]Shuhite, [c]and Zophar the Naamathite. They met together to come to show sympathy for him and to console him. [12]But when they gazed intently from a distance but did not recognize him, they began to weep loudly. Each of them tore his robes, and they [a]threw dust into the air over their heads. [13]Then they sat down with him on the ground for [a]seven days and seven nights, yet no one spoke a word to him, for they saw that his pain was very great.

1:18 [a]Job 1:4, 13   1:20 [a]Gen 37:29, 34; Josh 7:6; Ezra 9:3   [b][1 Pet 5:6]   1:21 [a][Ps 49:17; Eccl 5:15]; 1 Tim 6:7   [b]Eccl 5:19; [Jas 1:17]   [c]Eph 5:20; [1 Thess 5:18]   1:22 [a]Job 2:10   [1]Lit. *and he did not give unseemliness to God.*   2:1 [a]Job 1:6–8   [1]Some wss omit *to present himself before the LORD.*   2:2 [a]Job 1:7   2:3 [a]Job 1:1, 8   [b]Job 27:5–6   [c]Job 9:17   2:4 [1]LXX *make full payment, pay a full price.*   2:5 [a]Job 1:11   [b]Job 19:20   2:6 [a]Job 1:12   2:7 [a]Isa 1:6   2:8 [a]Job 42:6; Jer 6:26; Ezek 27:30; Jonah 3:6; Matt 11:21   2:9 [1]Lit. *to bless*; the writer or a scribe has substituted the word "curse" with the word "bless" to avoid the expression "curse God."   2:10 [a]Job 1:21–22; [Heb 12:6; Jas 5:10–11]   [b]Job 1:22; [Jas 1:12]   [c]Ps 39:1   [1]Heb. *sin with his lips.*   2:11 [a]Gen 36:11; 1 Chr 1:36; Job 6:19; Jer 49:7; Obad 9   [b]Gen 25:2; 1 Chr 1:32   [c]Job 42:11; Rom 12:15   2:12 [a]Josh 7:6; Neh 9:1; Lam 2:10; Ezek 27:30   2:13 [a]Gen 50:10; Ezek 3:15

II. JOB'S DIALOGUE WITH HIS FRIENDS (3:1–27:23)

Job Regrets His Birth

3 After this Job opened his mouth and cursed the day he was born. [2] Job spoke up[1] and said:

[3] "Let the day on which I was born perish,
and the night that said,
 '[a] A man[1] has been conceived!'
[4] That day—let it be darkness;
let not God on high regard it,
nor let light shine on it!
[5] Let darkness and [a] the deepest shadow claim it;
let a cloud settle on it;
let whatever blackens the day terrify it.
[6] That night—let darkness seize it;
let it not be included among the days of the year;
let it not enter among the number of the months!
[7] Indeed, let that night be barren;
let no shout of joy penetrate it!
[8] Let those [a] who curse the day curse it—
those who are prepared to rouse Leviathan.
[9] Let its morning stars be darkened;
let it wait[1] for daylight but find none,
nor let it see the first rays of dawn,
[10] because it did not shut the doors of my mother's womb on me,
nor did it hide trouble from my eyes.

Job Wishes He Had Died at Birth

[11] "Why did I not die at birth,
and [a] why did I not expire as I came out of the womb?
[12] Why did the knees welcome me,
and [a] why were there two breasts that I might nurse at them?
[13] For now I would be lying down and would be quiet,
I would be asleep and then at peace
[14] with kings and counselors of the earth

who [a] built for themselves places now desolate,
[15] or with princes who possessed gold,
who filled their palaces with silver.
[16] Or why was [a] I not buried like a stillborn infant,
like infants who have never seen the light?
[17] There the wicked cease from turmoil,[1]
and there the weary are at [a] rest.
[18] There [a] the prisoners relax together;
they do not hear the voice of the oppressor.
[19] Small and great are there,
and the slave is free from his master.[1]

Longing for Death

[20] "Why does God give light to one who is in misery,
and life to those whose soul is [a] bitter,
[21] to those who [a] wait for death that does not come,
and search for it more than for [b] hidden treasures,
[22] who rejoice even to jubilation,
and are exultant when they find the [a] grave?
[23] Why is light given to [a] a man whose way is hidden,
and whom God has hedged in?
[24] For my sighing comes in place of my food,
and my groanings[1] flow forth like water.
[25] For the very thing I [a] dreaded has happened to me,
and what I feared has come upon me.
[26] I have no ease; I have no quietness;
I cannot rest; turmoil has come upon me."[1]

Eliphaz Begins to Speak

4 Then Eliphaz the Temanite answered:

[2] "If someone should attempt a word with you,
will you be impatient?
But who can refrain from speaking?
[3] Look, you [a] have instructed[1] many;

3:2 [1] Sev. wss *and he answered*; LXX *saying*. **3:3** [a] Job 10:18–19; Jer 20:14–18 [1] The Heb. word usually distinguishes a man as strong, distinct from children and women. **3:5** [a] Job 10:21–22; Jer 13:16; Amos 5:8 **3:8** [a] Jer 9:17 **3:9** [1] I.e., with eager expectation and preparation. **3:11** [a] Job 10:18–19 **3:12** [a] Gen 30:3 **3:14** [a] Job 15:28; Isa 58:12 **3:16** [a] Ps 58:8 **3:17** [a] Job 17:16 [1] Heb. *to be agitated, excited.* **3:18** [a] Job 39:7 **3:19** [1] Lit. *masters*; a pl. of majesty. **3:20** [a] 2 Kgs 4:27 **3:21** [a] Rev 9:6 [b] Prov 2:4 **3:22** [a] Job 7:15–16 **3:23** [a] Job 19:8; Ps 88:8; Lam 3:7 **3:24** [1] The Heb. word normally describes the roaring of a lion. **3:25** [a] [Job 9:28; 30:15] **3:26** [1] Lit. *and trouble came.* **4:3** [a] Isa 35:3 [1] Heb. *to correct.*

you have strengthened feeble hands.
4 Your words [a]have supported those
who stumbled,
and you have strengthened the knees
that gave way.[1]
5 But now the same thing comes to
you,
and you are discouraged;
it strikes you,
and you are terrified.
6 Is not [a]your piety [b]your confidence,
and your blameless ways your hope?[1]
7 Call to mind now:
[a]Who,[1] being innocent, ever
perished?
And where were upright people ever
destroyed?
8 Even as I have seen, [a]those who plow
iniquity
and those who sow trouble reap the
same.
9 By the breath of God they perish,
and by the blast of his anger they are
consumed.
10 There is [a]the roaring of the lion
and the growling[1] of the young lion,
but the teeth of the young lions are
broken.
11 The mighty lion perishes for lack of
prey,
and [a]the cubs of the lioness are
scattered.

Ungodly Complainers Provoke God's Wrath

12 "Now a word was stealthily brought
to me,
and my ear caught a whisper of it.
13 In the [a]troubling thoughts of the
dreams in the night
when a deep sleep[1] falls on men,
14 dread gripped me and [a]trembling,
which made all my bones shake.
15 Then a breath of air[1] passes by my
face;
it makes the hair of my flesh
stand up.

16 It stands still,[1]
but I cannot recognize its
appearance;
an image is before my eyes,
and I hear a murmuring voice:
17 'Is a mortal man righteous before
God?
Or a man pure before his Creator?
18 If God [a]puts no trust in his servants
and attributes folly to his angels,
19 how much more to those who live in
houses of clay,
whose foundation is in the dust,
who are crushed like a moth?
20 They are destroyed between morning
and evening;
[a]they perish forever without anyone
regarding it.
21 Is not their excess wealth taken away
from them?[1]
They die, yet without attaining
wisdom.'

5 "Call now! Is there anyone who will
answer you?[1]
To which of the holy ones will you
turn?
2 For wrath kills the foolish person,
and anger slays the silly one.
3 I myself[1] have seen the fool [a]taking
root,
but suddenly I cursed his place of
residence.
4 His children are [a]far from safety,
and they are crushed at [b]the place
where judgment is rendered,[1]
nor is there anyone to deliver them.
5 The hungry eat up his harvest,
and take it even from behind the
thorns,
and the thirsty pant for their wealth.
6 For evil does not come up from the
dust,
nor does trouble spring up from the
ground,
7 but people are [a]born to trouble,
as surely as the sparks fly upward.

4:4 [a] Isa 35:3 [1] Or feeble knees; lit. the bowing [or tottering] knees. 4:6 [a] Job 1:1 [b] Prov 3:26 [1] Lit. your hope and the integrity of your ways. 4:7 [a] [Job 8:20; 36:6–7; Ps 37:25] [1] An emphatic Heb. construction. 4:8 [a] [Job 15:31, 35; Prov 22:8; Hos 10:13; Gal 6:7] 4:10 [a] Job 5:15; Ps 58:6 [1] Heb. voice. 4:11 [a] Job 29:17; Ps 34:10 4:13 [a] Job 33:15 [1] This Heb. word is used in Genesis when God caused a deep sleep to fall on Adam and in Jonah when the prophet was asleep during the storm. 4:14 [a] Hab 3:16 4:15 [1] Or spirit; the implication is that it was something Eliphaz felt—what he saw follows in v. 16. 4:16 [1] LXX I arose and perceived it not, I looked and there was no form before my eyes, but I only heard a breath and a voice. 4:18 [a] Job 15:15 4:20 [a] Ps 90:5–6 4:21 [1] LXX for he blows on them and they are withered; Tg. Is it not by their lack of righteousness that they have been deprived of all support? 5:1 [1] Or Is anyone listening to you? 5:3 [a] [Ps 37:35–36]; Jer 12:1–3 [1] An emphatic Heb. construction. 5:4 [a] Ps 119:155 [b] Ps 109:12 [1] Heb. in the gate; the city gate was the place of both business and justice. 5:7 [a] Job 14:1

Blessings for the One Who Seeks God

8 "But[1] as for me,[2] I would seek God,
   and to God I would set forth my case.
9 He does great and unsearchable
      things,
   marvelous things without number;
10 he gives rain on [a]the earth,
   and sends water on the fields;[1]
11 he sets [a]the lowly on high,
   that those who mourn are raised to
      safety.
12 He frustrates [a]the plans of the crafty[1]
   so that their hands cannot
      accomplish
   what they had planned.
13 He catches the [a]wise in their own
      craftiness,
   and the counsel of the cunning is
      brought to a quick end.
14 They meet with darkness in the
      daytime,
   and grope about in the noontime as
      if it were night.
15 So [a]he saves from the sword that
      comes from their mouth,
   even the poor from the hand of the
      powerful.
16 [a]Thus the poor have hope,
   and iniquity shuts its mouth.

17 "Therefore, blessed[1] is the man
      whom God corrects,
   so do not despise the discipline of
      the Almighty.
18 [a]For he[1] wounds, but he also bandages;
   he strikes, but his hands also heal.
19 [a]He will deliver you from six
      calamities;
   yes, in seven[1] [b]no evil will touch you.
20 In time of [a]famine he will redeem
      you from death,
   and in time of war from the power of
      the sword.
21 [a]You will be protected from
      malicious gossip
   and will not be afraid of the
      destruction when it comes.
22 You will laugh at destruction and
      famine[1]

and need not be afraid of the [a]beasts
      of the earth.
23 [a]For you will have a pact with the
      stones of the field,
   and the wild animals will be at peace
      with you.
24 And you will know that your home
      will be secure,
   and when you inspect your domains,
   you will not be missing anything.
25 You will also know that [a]your
      children[1] will be numerous
   and your descendants [b]like the grass
      of the earth.
26 You will come to [a]your grave in a full
      age,
   As stacks of grain are harvested in
      their season.
27 Look, we have [a]investigated this, so it
      is true.
   Hear it, and apply it for your own
      good."

Job Replies to Eliphaz

6 Then Job responded:

2 "Oh, if only my grief could be
      weighed,
   and my misfortune laid on the scales
      too!
3 But because it is heavier than the
      sand of the sea,
   that is why my words have been wild.
4 [a]For [b]the arrows of the Almighty are
      within me;
   my spirit drinks their poison;
   God's sudden terrors are arrayed
      [c]against[1] me.

Complaints Reflect Suffering

5 "Does the [a]wild donkey bray when it
      is near grass?
   Or does the ox bellow over its fodder?
6 Can food that is tasteless be eaten
      without salt?
   Or is there any taste in the white of
      an egg?
7 I[1] have refused to touch such things;
   they are like loathsome food to me.

5:8 [1] A strong adversative. [2] An emphatic Heb. construction.　5:10 [a] [Job 36:27–29; 37:6–11; 38:26] [1] Heb. *outside.* 5:11 [a] Ps 113:7　5:12 [a] Neh 4:15 [1] Or *shrewd.* 5:13 [a] [Job 37:24; 1 Cor 3:19]　5:15 [a] Job 4:10–11; Ps 35:10　5:16 [a] 1 Sam 2:8; Ps 107:41–42　5:17 [1] Or *happy.* 5:18 [a] [Deut 32:39; 1 Sam 2:6–7]; Isa 30:26; Hos 6:1 [1] An emphatic Heb. construction. 5:19 [a] Ps 34:19; 91:3; [1 Cor 10:13] [b] Ps 91:10; [Prov 24:16] [1] The numerical ladder, "six . . . seven," shows completeness. 5:20 [a] Ps 33:19–20; 37:19　5:21 [a] Job 5:15; Ps 31:20　5:22 [a] Hos 2:18 [1] LXX *the unrighteous and the lawless.* 5:23 [a] Ps 91:12　5:25 [a] Ps 112:2 [b] Ps 72:16 [1] Heb. *your seed.* 5:26 [a] [Prov 9:11; 10:27]　5:27 [a] Ps 111:2　6:4 [a] Job 16:13; Ps 38:2 [b] Ps 88:15–16 [c] Job 30:15 [1] Heb. *to set in battle array.* 6:5 [a] Job 39:5–8　6:7 [1] Trad. *my soul.*

A Cry for Death

8 "Oh that my request would be
 realized,
 and that God would grant me what I
 long for!
9 And that God would be willing to
 crush me,
 that he would let loose his hand
 and kill me.
10 Then [a]I would yet have my comfort,
 [b]then I would rejoice,
 in spite of pitiless pain,
 for I have not concealed the words of
 the Holy One.
11 What is my strength, that I should
 wait?
 And what is my end,
 that I should prolong my life?
12 Is my strength like that of stones?
 Or is my flesh made of bronze?
13 Is not my power to help myself
 nothing,
 and has not every resource been
 driven from me?

Disappointing Friends

14 "To the one in despair, kindness[1]
 should come from his friend
 even if he forsakes the fear of the
 Almighty.
15 [a]My brothers have been as
 treacherous as a seasonal stream,
 and as the riverbeds of the
 intermittent streams
 that flow away.[1]
16 They are dark because of ice;
 snow is piled up over them.
17 When they are scorched, they dry up,
 when it is hot, they vanish from their
 place.
18 Caravans turn aside from their
 routes;
 they go into the wasteland[1] and
 perish.
19 The caravans of [a]Tema looked
 intently for these streams;
 the traveling merchants of [b]Sheba
 hoped for them.
20 They were [a]distressed[1]
 because each one had been so
 confident;

they arrived there, but were
 disappointed.
21 For now [a]you have become like these
 streams that [b]are no help;
 you see a terror and are afraid.

Friends' Fears

22 "Have I ever said, 'Give me
 something,
 and from your fortune make gifts in
 my favor'?
23 Or, 'Deliver me from the enemy's
 power,
 and from the hand of tyrants ransom
 me'?

No Sin Discovered

24 "Teach me, and I, for my part,[1] will be
 silent;
 explain to me how I have been
 mistaken.
25 How painful are honest words!
 But what does your reproof prove?
26 Do you intend to criticize mere
 words,
 and treat the words of a despairing
 man as wind?
27 Yes, you would gamble for the
 fatherless,
 and [a]auction off your friend.

Other Explanation

28 "Now then, be good enough to look
 at me;
 and I will not lie to your face!
29 Relent,[1] let there be no falsehood;
 [a]reconsider, for my [b]righteousness is
 intact!
30 Is there any falsehood on my lips?
 Can my mouth[1] not discern evil
 things?

The Brevity of Life

7 "Does not [a]humanity have hard service
 on earth?
 Are not their days also like the days
 of a hired man?
2 Like a servant longing for the
 evening shadow,
 and like a hired man looking for his
 wages,

6:10 [a]Acts 20:20 [b][Lev 19:2; Isa 57:15] 6:14 [1]Or *loyalty.* 6:15 [a]Ps 38:11 [1]Or *pass away, overflow.* 6:18 [1]The Heb. word was used in Genesis to mean without shape or structure. 6:19 [a]Gen 25:15; Isa 21:14; Jer 25:23 [b]1 Kgs 10:1; Ps 72:10; Ezek 27:22–23 6:20 [a]Jer 14:3 [1]Heb. *to be ashamed, disappointed, distressed.* 6:21 [a]Job 13:4 [b]Ps 38:11 6:24 [1]An emphatic Heb. construction. 6:27 [a]Ps 57:6 6:29 [a]Job 17:10 [b]Job 27:5–6; 34:5 [1]Lit. *return.* 6:30 [1]Heb. *my palate.* 7:1 [a][Job 14:5, 13, 14]; Ps 39:4

3 thus I have been made to inherit
  [a]months of futility,[1]
  and nights of sorrow
  have been appointed to me.
4 If I lie down, I say, '[a]When will I
    arise?'
  And the night stretches on,
  and I toss and turn restlessly
  until the day dawns.
5 My body is clothed [a]with worms and
    dirty scabs;
  my skin is broken and festering.
6 My days are swifter than a weaver's
    shuttle,
  and they come to an end without
    hope.[1]
7 Remember that [a]my life is but a
    breath,
  that my eyes will never again see
    happiness.
8 [a]The eye of him who sees me now
    will see me no more;
  your eyes will look for me, but I will
    be gone.
9 As a cloud is dispersed and [a]then
    disappears,
  so the one who goes down to the
    grave[1]
  does not come up again.
10 He returns [a]no more to his house,
   nor does his place of residence know
     him anymore.

Job Remonstrates with God

11 "Therefore, I will [a]not refrain my
     mouth;
   I will speak in the anguish of my
     spirit;
   I will [b]complain in the bitterness of
     my soul.
12 Am I the sea, or the creature of the
     deep,[1]
   that you must put me under guard?
13 [a]If I say, 'My bed will comfort me,
   my couch will ease my complaint,'
14 then you scare me with dreams
   and terrify me with visions,
15 so that I would prefer strangling
   and death more than life.[1]

16 I loathe [a]it; I do not want to live
     forever;
   leave me alone, for [b]my days are a
     vapor!

Insignificance of Humans

17 "What is mankind that you make so
     much of them,
   and that you pay attention to them?
18 And that you visit[1] them every
     morning,
   and try them every moment?
19 Will you never look away from me,
   will you not let me alone
   long enough to swallow my spittle?
20 If I have sinned—what have I [a]done to
     you,
   O watcher of men?
   Why [b]have you set me as your target?
   Have I become a burden to you?
21 And why do you not pardon my
     transgression
   and take away my iniquity?
   For now I will lie down in the dust,
   and you will seek me diligently,
   but I will be gone."

Bildad's First Speech to Job

8 Then Bildad the Shuhite spoke up and
  said:

2 "How long will you speak these
     things,
   seeing that the words of your mouth
   are like a great wind?
3 Does God pervert justice?
   Or [a]does the Almighty pervert what
     is right?
4 If [a]your children sinned against him,
   he gave them over to the penalty[1] of
     their sin.
5 But [a]if you will look to God
   and make your supplication to the
     Almighty,
6 if you become pure and upright,
   even now he will rouse himself for
     you
   and will restore your righteous
     home.

7:3 [a][Job 15:31] [1]Heb. *vanity, deception, nothingness, futility*. 7:4 [a]Deut 28:67; Job 7:13–14 7:5 [a]Isa 14:11 7:6 [a]A wordplay is present based on this Heb. word's relation to *thread, cord*; his life is coming to an end for "lack of thread"/for "lack of hope." 7:7 [a]Job 7:16; Ps 78:39; 89:47 7:8 [a]Job 8:18; 20:9 7:9 [a]2 Sam 12:23 [1]Heb. *the grave, death, Sheol*; the realm of departed spirits. 7:10 [a]Ps 103:16 7:11 [a]Ps 39:1, 9 [b]1 Sam 1:10 7:12 [1]Or *whale, dragon, monster of the deep*. 7:13 [a]Job 9:27 7:15 [1]Lit. *more than my bones*. 7:16 [a]Job 10:1 [b]Ps 62:9 7:18 [1]I.e., a divine intervention for blessing or cursing that changes the destiny of the one visited. 7:20 [a]Ps 36:6 [b]Ps 21:12 8:3 [a]Gen 18:25; [Deut 32:4; 2 Chr 19:7; Job 34:10, 12; 36:23; 37:23]; Rom 3:5 8:4 [a]Job 1:5, 18, 19 [1]Heb. *into the hand of their rebellion*. 8:5 [a][Job 5:17–27; 11:13]

7 Your beginning will seem so small,
  since your future will [a]flourish.[1]

8 "For inquire now of the [a]former
    generation,
  and pay attention to the findings
  of their ancestors;

9 For [a]we were born yesterday and do
    not have knowledge,
  since our days on earth are but a
    shadow.

10 Will they not[1] instruct you and speak
    to you,
  and bring forth words
  from their understanding?

11 Can the papyrus plant grow tall
    where there is no marsh?
  Can reeds flourish without water?

12 [a]While they are still beginning to
    flower
  and not ripe for cutting,
  they can wither away
  faster than any grass.

13 Such is the destiny of all who [a]forget
    God;
  the hope of the [b]godless[1] perishes,

14 whose trust is in something futile,
  whose security is a spider's web.

15 He leans against his house, but it
    does not hold up;
  [a]he takes hold of it, but it does not
    stand.

16 He is a well-watered plant in the sun;
  its shoots spread[1] over its garden.[2]

17 It wraps its roots around a heap of
    stones,
  and it looks for a place among stones.

18 If he is uprooted from his place,
  then that place will disown him,
    saying,
  '[a]I have never seen you!'

19 Indeed, this is the joy of his way,
  and [a]out of the earth others spring up.

20 "Surely, [a]God does not reject a
    blameless man,
  nor does he grasp the hand
  of the evildoers.

21 He will yet fill your mouth with
    laughter
  and your lips with gladness.

22 Those who hate you will be [a]clothed
    with shame,
  and the tent of the wicked will be no
    more."

Job's Reply to Bildad

9 Then Job answered:

2 "Truly, I know that this is so.
  But how can a [a]human be [b]just
    before God?

3 If someone wishes to contend with
    him,
  he cannot answer him one time in a
    thousand.

4 [a]He is wise in heart and mighty in
    strength—
  who has resisted him and remained
    safe?

5 He who removes mountains suddenly,
  who overturns them in his anger,

6 he who [a]shakes the earth out of its
    place
  so that its [b]pillars tremble,

7 he who commands the sun, and it
    does not shine[1]
  and seals up the stars,

8 he alone spreads out [a]the heavens
  and treads on the waves of the sea.

9 He makes [a]the Bear, Orion, and the
    Pleiades,
  and the constellations of the
    southern sky;

10 [a]he does great and unsearchable
    things,
  and wonderful things without
    number.

11 If he passes by me, [a]I cannot see him;
  if he goes by, I cannot perceive him.

12 [a]If he snatches away, who can turn
    him back?
  Who dares to say to him, 'What are
    you doing?'

13 God does not restrain his anger;
  under him [a]the helpers of Rahab lie
    crushed.[1]

8:7 [a] Job 42:12 [1] Heb. to flourish, grow considerably. 8:8 [a] Deut 4:32; 32:7; Job 15:18; 20:4 8:9 [a] Gen 47:9; [1 Chr 29:15]; Job 7:6; [Ps 39:5; 102:11; 144:4] 8:10 [1] Lit. Is it not they; an emphatic Heb. construction. 8:12 [a] Ps 129:6 8:13 [a] Ps 9:17 [b] Job 11:20; 18:14; 27:8; Ps 112:10; [Prov 10:28] [1] Or hypocrite. 8:15 [a] Job 8:22; 27:18; Ps 49:11 8:16 [1] Heb. its shoot goes out. [2] LXX out of his corruption. 8:18 [a] Job 7:10 8:19 [a] Ps 113:7 8:20 [a] Job 4:7 8:22 [a] Ps 35:26; 109:29 9:2 [a] [Job 4:17; 15:14–16; Ps 143:2; Rom 3:20] [b] [Hab 2:4; Rom 1:17; Gal 3:11; Heb 10:38] 9:4 [a] Job 36:5 9:6 [a] Isa 2:19, 21; Hag 2:6; Heb 12:26 [b] Job 26:11 9:7 [1] Heb. sunrise. 9:8 [a] Gen 1:6; Job 37:18; Ps 104:2–3; Isa 40:22 9:9 [a] Gen 1:16; Job 38:31; Amos 5:8 9:10 [a] Job 5:9 9:11 [a] [Job 23:8–9; 35:14] 9:12 [a] [Isa 45:9; Dan 4:35; Rom 9:20] 9:13 [a] Job 26:12 [1] Heb. to be prostrate, to crouch.

The Impossibility of Facing God in Court

14 "How much less, then, can I answer him
and choose my words to argue with him.
15 Although I am innocent,
I could not answer him;
I could only plead with my judge [a]for mercy.
16 If I summoned him and he answered me,
I would not believe
that he would be listening to my voice—
17 he who crushes me [a]with a tempest
and multiplies my wounds for no reason.
18 He does not allow me to recover my breath,
for he fills me with bitterness.
19 If it is a matter of strength,
most certainly he is the strong one!
And if it is a matter of justice,
he will say, 'Who will summon me?'
20 Although I am innocent,
my mouth would condemn me;
although I am blameless,
it would declare me perverse.
21 I am blameless. I do not know myself.[1]
I despise my life.

Accusation of God's Justice

22 "It is all one![1] That is why I say,
'[a]He destroys the blameless and the guilty.'
23 If a scourge brings sudden death,[1]
he mocks at the despair of the innocent.
24 If a land[1] has been given
into the hand of a wicked man,
he covers the faces of its judges;
if it is not he, then who is it?

Renewed Complaint

25 "My days are swifter than a runner,
they speed by without seeing happiness.
26 They glide by [a]like reed boats,
like an eagle that swoops down on its prey.

27 If [a]I say, 'I will forget my complaint,
I will change my expression and be cheerful,'
28 I dread all my [a]sufferings,
for [b]I know that you do not hold me blameless.
29 If I am guilty,
why then weary myself in vain?
30 If [a]I wash myself with snow-melt water
and make my hands clean with lye,
31 then you plunge me into a slimy pit
and my own clothes abhor me.
32 For [a]he is not a human being like I am,
that I might answer him,
that we might come together in judgment.
33 [a]Nor is there an arbiter between us,
who might lay his hand on us both,
34 [a]who would take his rod away from me
so that his terror would not make me afraid.
35 Then would I speak and not fear him,
but it is not so with me.

An Appeal for Revelation

10 "I am weary of my life;
I will complain freely without restraint;[1]
I will speak in the bitterness of my [a]soul.
2 I will say to God, 'Do not condemn me;
tell me why you are contending[1] with me.'
3 Is it good for you to oppress,
to despise the work of your hands,
while you smile
on the schemes of the wicked?

Motivations of God

4 "Do you have eyes of flesh,
or [a]do you see as a human being sees?
5 Are your days like the days of a mortal,
or your years like the years of a mortal,
6 that you must search out my iniquity
and inquire about my sin,

9:15 [a] Job 10:15; 23:1–7   9:17 [a] Job 2:3   9:21 [1] Perhaps meaning "I do not care."   9:22 [a] [Eccl 9:2–3]; Ezek 21:3 [1] LXX omits *It is all one.*   9:23 [1] LXX *for the worthless die, but the righteous are laughed to scorn.*   9:24 [1] Or *earth.*   9:26 [a] Job 39:29; Hab 1:8   9:27 [a] Job 7:13   9:28 [a] Ps 119:120 [b] Exod 20:7   9:30 [a] [Jer 2:22]   9:32 [a] Eccl 6:10; [Isa 45:9; Jer 49:19; Rom 9:20]   9:33 [a] [1 Sam 2:25]; Job 9:19; Isa 1:18   9:34 [a] Job 13:20–21; Ps 39:10   10:1 [a] 1 Kgs 19:4; Job 7:16; Jonah 4:3 [1] Heb. *to abandon, let go, let slip.*   10:2 [1] Heb. *to dispute, contend, strive, quarrel*; often in the legal sense.   10:4 [a] [1 Sam 16:7; Job 28:24; 34:21]

7 although you know that I am not
  guilty,
  and that there is no one who can
  deliver[1]
  out of your hand?

Contradictions in God's Dealings

8 "Your hands have shaped me and
  made me,
  but now [a]you [b]destroy me completely.
9 Remember [a]that you have made me
  as with the clay;
  will you return me to dust?
10 [a]Did you not pour me out like milk
  and curdle me like cheese?
11 You clothed me with skin and flesh
  and knit me together with bones and
  sinews.
12 You gave me life and favor,
  and your intervention[1] watched over
  my spirit.

13 "But these things you have concealed
  in your heart;
  I know that this is with you:
14 If I sinned, then [a]you would
  watch me,
  and you would not acquit me of my
  iniquity.
15 If I am guilty, [a]woe to me,
  and if I am innocent, I cannot lift my
  head;
  I am full of shame
  and satiated with my affliction.
16 If I lift myself up,
  [a]you hunt me as a fierce lion,
  and again you display your power
  against me.
17 You bring new witnesses against me
  and increase your anger against me;
  relief troops come against me.

An Appeal for Relief

18 "Why then did you bring me out
  from the womb?
  I should have died,
  and no eye would have seen me!
19 I should have been as though I had
  never existed;
  I should have been carried
  right from the womb to the grave!

20 Are not my days few?
  Cease, then, and leave me alone
  that I may find [a]a little comfort,
21 before I depart, never [a]to return,
  to the [b]land of darkness
  and the deepest shadow,
22 to the land of utter darkness,
  like the deepest darkness,
  and the deepest shadow and disorder,
  where even the light is like darkness."

Zophar's First Speech to Job

11 Then Zophar the Naamathite spoke
  up and said:

2 "Should not this[1] abundance of words
  be answered,
  or should this talkative man
  be vindicated?
3 Should people remain silent at your
  idle talk,[1]
  and should no one rebuke you when
  you mock?
4 For you have said, '[a]My teaching is
  flawless,
  and I am pure in your sight.'
5 But if only God would speak,
  if only he would open his lips against
  you
6 and reveal to you the secrets of
  wisdom—
  for true wisdom has two sides—
  so that you would know
  that [a]God has forgiven some of your
  sins.

7 "Can you discover the essence of God?
  [a]Can you find out the perfection of
  the Almighty?
8 It is higher than the heavens—what
  can you do?
  It is deeper than Sheol[1]—what can
  you know?
9 Its measure is longer than the earth
  and broader than the sea.
10 If he comes by and confines you
  and convenes a court,
  then who can prevent him?
11 For [a]he[1] knows deceitful men;
  when he sees evil, will he not
  consider it?

10:7 [1] Heb. *and there is no deliverer.*   10:8 [a] Job 10:3; Ps 119:73   [b] [Job 9:22]   10:9 [a] Gen 2:7; Job 33:6   10:10 [a] [Ps 139:14–16]
10:12 [1] Or *providence;* trad. *visitation.*   10:14 [a] Job 7:20; Ps 139:1   10:15 [a] Job 10:7; Isa 3:11   10:16 [a] Isa 38:13; Lam 3:10; Hos
13:7   10:20 [a] Ps 39:5   10:21 [a] Ps 88:12   [b] Ps 23:4   11:2 [1] MT *abundance;* Sev. wss *great.*   11:3 [1] Heb. *chatter, pratings,*
boastings.   11:4 [a] Job 6:30   11:6 [a] [Ezra 9:13]   11:7 [a] Job 33:12–13; 36:26; [Eccl 3:11; Rom 11:33]
11:8 [1] Or *deeper than hell.*   11:11 [a] [Ps 10:14]   [1] An emphatic Heb. construction.

12 But an ᵃempty man will become wise,
  when a wild donkey's colt is born a
    human being.

13 "As for you,¹ if you ᵃprove faithful,
  and if you ᵇstretch out your hands
    toward him,
14 if iniquity is in your hand—put it far
    away,
  and do not let evil reside in your
    tents.
15 For ᵃthen you will lift up your face
  without blemish;
  you will be securely established
  and will not fear.
16 For you¹ will ᵃforget your trouble;
  you will remember it
  like water that has flowed away.
17 And life will be brighter than the
    noonday;
  though there be darkness,
  it will be like the morning.
18 And you will be secure because there
    is hope;
  you will be protected
  and will ᵃtake your rest in safety.
19 You will lie down with no one to
    make you afraid,
  and many will seek your favor.¹
20 But ᵃthe eyes of ᵇthe wicked fail,
  and escape eludes them;
  their one hope is to breathe their
    last."

Job's Reply to Zophar

12 Then Job answered:

2 "Without a doubt you are the people,
  and wisdom will die with you.
3 I also have understanding as well as
    you;
  I am not ᵃinferior to you.
  Who does not know such things as
    these?
4 I am a ᵃlaughingstock to my friends,
  I, who ᵇcalled on God and whom he
    answered—
  a righteous and blameless man
  is a laughingstock!

5 For calamity, there is derision
  (according to the ideas of the
    fortunate)—
  a fate for ᵃthose whose feet slip.
6 But ᵃthe tents of robbers are peaceful,
  and those who provoke God are
    confident—
  who carry their god in their hands.

Knowledge of God's Wisdom

7 "But now, ask the animals and they
    will teach you,
  or the birds of the sky and they will
    tell you.
8 Or speak to the earth and it will
    teach you,
  or let the fish of the sea declare to
    you.
9 Which of all these does not know
  that the hand of the LORD¹ has done
    this?
10 ᵃIn his hand is the life of every
    creature
  and the ᵇbreath of all the human
    race.
11 Does not the ear test words,
  as the tongue tastes food?
12 Is not wisdom found among the
    aged?
  Does not long life bring
    understanding?
13 With God are ᵃwisdom and power;
  counsel and understanding are his.
14 If ᵃhe tears down, it cannot be
    rebuilt;
  if he imprisons a person, there is no
    escape.
15 If he holds ᵃback the waters, then
    they dry up;¹
  if he releases them, they destroy² the
    land.
16 With him are strength and prudence;
  both the one who goes astray
  and the one who misleads are his.
17 He leads counselors away stripped
  and makes judges into fools.¹
18 He loosens the bonds¹ of kings
  and binds a loincloth around their
    waist.

11:12 ᵃ [Ps 39:5]; Rom 1:22   11:13 ᵃ [1 Sam 7:3]   ᵇ Ps 88:9   ¹ An emphatic Heb. construction.   11:15 ᵃ Job 22:26; Ps 119:6; [1 John 3:21]   11:16 ᵃ Isa 65:16   ¹ An emphatic Heb. construction.   11:18 ᵃ Lev 26:5–6; Ps 3:5; Prov 3:24   11:19 ¹ Heb. *they will stroke your face*; a picture of a child stroking the face of the parent.   11:20 ᵃ Lev 26:16; Deut 28:65; Job 17:5   ᵇ Job 18:14; [Prov 11:7]   12:3 ᵃ Job 13:2   12:4 ᵃ Job 21:3   ᵇ Ps 91:15   12:5 ᵃ Prov 14:2   12:6 ᵃ [Job 9:24; 21:6–16; Ps 73:12; Jer 12:1; Mal 3:15]   12:9 ¹ A few MSS *God.*   12:10 ᵃ [Acts 17:28]   ᵇ Job 27:3; 33:4   12:13 ᵃ Job 9:4; 36:5   12:14 ᵃ Job 11:10; Isa 25:2   12:15 ᵃ Deut 11:17; [1 Kgs 8:35–36]   ¹ LXX *he will dry the earth.*   ² Heb. *to overthrow, destroy, overwhelm*; used in Genesis for the destruction of Sodom.   12:17 ¹ Or *makes mad.*   12:18 ¹ MT *discipline.*

¹⁹ He leads priests away stripped
and overthrows the potentates.
²⁰ He deprives ᵃthe trusted advisers of
speech
and takes away the discernment of
elders.
²¹ He pours contempt on noblemen
and disarms ᵃthe powerful.
²² He ᵃreveals the deep things of
darkness
and brings deep shadows¹ into the
light.
²³ He makes nations great and destroys
ᵃthem;
he extends the boundaries of nations
and disperses them.
²⁴ He deprives the leaders of the earth
of their understanding;
he ᵃmakes them wander
in a trackless desert waste.
²⁵ They grope about in darkness
without light;
ᵃhe makes them ᵇstagger like
drunkards.

Job Pleads His Cause to God

13 "Indeed, my eyes have seen all this;
my ears have heard and
understood it.
² ᵃWhat you know, I¹ know also;
I am not inferior to you!
³ ᵃBut I wish to speak to the
Almighty,¹
and I desire to argue my case with
God.
⁴ But ᵃyou, however, are inventors of
lies;
all of you are worthless physicians!
⁵ If only you would keep completely
silent!
For you, that would be wisdom.
⁶ Listen now to my argument,
and be attentive to my lips'
contentions.
⁷ Will you speak wickedly on God's
behalf?
ᵃWill you speak deceitfully for him?
⁸ Will you show him partiality?
Will you argue the case for God?

⁹ Would it turn out well if he would
examine you?
Or as one deceives a man would you
deceive him?
¹⁰ He would certainly rebuke you
if you secretly showed partiality.
¹¹ Would not his splendor terrify you
and the fear he inspires fall on you?
¹² Your maxims are proverbs of ashes;¹
your defenses are defenses of clay.

¹³ "Refrain from talking with me so that
I may speak;
then let come to me what may.
¹⁴ Why ᵃdo I put myself in peril,¹
and take my life in my hands?
¹⁵ Even ᵃif he slays me, I will hope in
him;
I will surely defend my ways to his
face.
¹⁶ Moreover, this will become my
deliverance,
for no godless ᵃperson would come
before him.
¹⁷ Listen carefully to my words;
let your ears be attentive to my
explanation.
¹⁸ See now, I have prepared my case;
I know that I am ᵃright.¹
¹⁹ ᵃWho will contend with me?
If anyone can, I will be silent and die.
²⁰ Only in two things spare me, ᵃO God,
and then I will not hide from your
face:
²¹ Remove your hand far from me
and stop making me afraid ᵃwith
your terror.
²² Then call, and I will ᵃanswer,
or I will speak, and you respond
to me.
²³ How many are my iniquities and
sins?
Show me my transgression and my
sin.
²⁴ ᵃWhy do you hide your face
and ᵇregard me as your enemy?
²⁵ ᵃDo you wish to torment a
windblown leaf
and chase after dry chaff?¹

12:20 ᵃ Job 32:9   12:21 ᵃ [Job 34:19]; Ps 107:40; [Dan 2:21]   12:22 ᵃ Dan 2:22; [1 Cor 4:5] ¹ Trad. *shadow of death.*
12:23 ᵃ Isa 9:3; 26:15   12:24 ᵃ Ps 107:4   12:25 ᵃ Job 5:14; 15:30; 18:18 ᵇ Ps 107:27   13:2 ᵃ Job 12:3 ¹ An emphatic Heb.
construction.   13:3 ᵃ Job 23:3; 31:35 ¹ Heb. *El Shaddai.*   13:4 ᵃ Job 6:21; [Jer 23:32]   13:7 ᵃ Job 27:4; 36:4   13:12 ¹ Perhaps
proverbs that are/have become ashes; something that may have been useful, but now is worthless.   13:14 ᵃ Job
18:4 ¹ Heb. *why do I take my flesh in my teeth?*   13:15 ᵃ Ps 23:4; [Prov 14:32]   13:16 ᵃ Job 8:13   13:18 ᵃ [Rom 8:34] ¹ Or
vindicated; an emphatic Heb. construction.   13:19 ᵃ Job 7:21; 10:8; Isa 50:8   13:20 ᵃ Job 9:34   13:21 ᵃ Job 9:34; Ps 39:10
13:22 ᵃ Job 9:16; 14:15   13:24 ᵃ [Deut 32:20]; Ps 13:1 ᵇ Lam 2:5   13:25 ᵃ Isa 42:3 ¹ Heb. *chaff, stubble*; a wisp of straw.

²⁶ For you write down bitter things
    against me
and cause me to inherit the sins of
    my youth.
²⁷ And ^ayou put my feet in the stocks
and you watch all my movements;¹
you put marks on the soles of my
    feet.
²⁸ So I waste away like something
    rotten,
like a garment eaten by moths.

The Brevity of Life

14 "Man, born of woman,
    lives but a few days, and they are
    ^afull of trouble.
² He grows up like a flower and ^athen
    withers away;
he flees like a shadow and does not
    remain.
³ Do you fix your eye¹ on such a one?
And ^ado you ^bbring me before you for
    judgment?
⁴ Who ^acan make a clean thing come
    from an unclean?
No one!
⁵ ^aSince man's days are determined,
the number of his months is under
    your control;¹
you have set his limit, and he cannot
    pass it.
⁶ Look ^aaway from him and let him
    desist,
until he fulfills his time ^blike a hired
    man.

The Inevitability of Death

⁷ "But there is hope for a tree:
If it is cut down, it will sprout again,
and its new shoots will not fail.
⁸ Although its roots may grow old in
    the ground
and its stump begins to die in the
    soil,
⁹ at the scent of water it will flourish
and put forth shoots like a new plant.
¹⁰ But man dies and is powerless;
    ^ahe expires—and where is he?
¹¹ As water disappears from the sea,¹
or a river drains away and dries up,

¹² so man lies down and does
    not rise;
until the heavens are no more,¹
they will not awake
nor arise from their sleep.

The Possibility of Another Life

¹³ "O that you would hide me in Sheol,
and conceal me till your anger has
    passed!
O that you would set me a time
and then remember me!
¹⁴ If a man ^adies, will he live again?¹
All the days of my hard service I will
    wait
until my release comes.
¹⁵ You will call and I¹—I will answer ^ayou;
you will long for the creature you
    have made.

The Present Condition

¹⁶ "Surely now ^ayou count my steps;
then you would not mark my sin.
¹⁷ My offenses would be sealed up in a
    bag;
you would cover over ^amy sin.
¹⁸ But as a mountain falls away and
    crumbles,
and as a rock will be removed from
    its place,
¹⁹ as water wears away stones,
and torrents wash away the soil,
so you destroy man's hope.
²⁰ You overpower him once for all,
    and he departs;
you change his appearance
and send him away.
²¹ If his sons are honored,
    ^ahe does not know it;
if they are brought low,
he does not see it.
²² His flesh only has pain for him,
and he mourns for himself."

Eliphaz's Second Speech

15 Then ^aEliphaz the Temanite answered:

² "Does a wise man answer with
    blustery knowledge,
or fill his belly with the east wind?

13:27 ^a Job 33:11   ¹ Heb. *ways, roads, paths.*   **14:1** ^a Job 5:7; Eccl 2:23   **14:2** ^a Job 8:9; Ps 90:5–6, 9; 102:11; 103:15; 144:4; Isa 40:6; Jas 1:10–11; 1 Pet 1:24   **14:3** ^a Ps 8:4; 144:3   ^b [Ps 143:2]   ¹ Heb. *open the eye on*; an idiom meaning to prepare to judge someone.   **14:4** ^a [Job 15:14; 25:4; Ps 51:2, 5, 10; John 3:6; Rom 5:12; Eph 2:3]   **14:5** ^a Job 7:1; 21:21; Heb 9:27   ¹ Heb. [is] *with you.*   **14:6** ^a Job 7:16, 19; Ps 39:13   ^b Job 7:1   **14:10** ^a Job 10:21–22   **14:11** ¹ Or *lake.*   **14:12** ¹ Sev. wss *till the heavens wear out.*   **14:14** ^a Job 13:15   ¹ LXX *he will live again.*   **14:15** ^a Job 13:22   ¹ An emphatic Heb. construction.   **14:16** ^a Job 10:6, 14; 13:27; 31:4; 34:21; Ps 56:8; 139:1–3; Prov 5:21; [Jer 32:19]   **14:17** ^a Deut 32:32–34   **14:21** ^a Eccl 9:5; Isa 63:16   **15:1** ^a Job 4:1

3 Does he argue with useless talk,
  with words that have no value in
  them?
4 But you even break off piety
  and hinder[1] meditation before God.
5 Your sin inspires your mouth;
  you choose the language of the crafty.
6 Your own mouth condemns [a]you,
  not I;
  your own lips testify against you.

7 "Were you the first man ever [a]born?
  Were you brought forth before the
  hills?
8 [a]Do you listen in on God's secret
  council?
  Do you limit wisdom to yourself?
9 [a]What do you know that we don't
  know?
  What do you understand that we
  don't understand?[1]
10 [a]The gray-haired and the aged are on
  our side,
  men far older than your father.
11 Are God's consolations too trivial for
  you,
  or a word spoken in gentleness to
  you?
12 Why has your heart carried you away,
  and why do your eyes flash,
13 when you turn your rage[1] against God
  and allow such words to escape from
  your mouth?
14 What is man that he should be pure,
  or one born of woman, that he
  should be righteous?
15 If God places no trust in his holy ones,
  [a]if even the heavens are not pure in
  his eyes,
16 [a]how much less man, [b]who is
  abominable and corrupt,
  who drinks in evil like water!
17 I will explain to you;
  listen to me,
  and what I have seen, I will declare,
18 what wise men declare,
  hiding nothing,
  [a]from the tradition of their
  ancestors,

19 to whom alone the land was given
  when [a]no foreigner passed among
  them.
20 All his days the wicked man suffers
  torment,
  throughout the number of the years
  that are stored up for the tyrant.
21 Terrifying sounds fill his ears;
  [a]in a time of peace marauders[1] attack
  him.
22 He does not expect to [a]escape from
  darkness;
  he is marked for the sword;
23 he wanders [a]about—food for
  vultures—
  he knows [b]that the day of darkness is
  at hand.
24 Distress and anguish terrify him;
  they prevail against him
  like a king ready to launch an attack,
25 for he stretches out his hand against
  God,
  and vaunts himself against the
  Almighty,
26 defiantly charging against him
  with a thick, strong shield!
27 Because he covered his face with fat
  and made his hips bulge with fat,
28 he lived in ruined towns
  and in houses where no one lives,
  where they are ready to crumble into
  heaps.[1]
29 He will not grow rich,
  and his wealth will not [a]endure,
  nor will his possessions spread over
  the land.
30 He will not escape the darkness;
  a flame will wither his shoots,
  and he will depart
  [a]by the breath of God's mouth.
31 Let him not [a]trust in what is
  worthless,
  deceiving himself;
  for worthlessness will be his reward.
32 [a]Before his time he will be paid in
  full,
  and his branches will not flourish.
33 Like a vine he will let his sour grapes
  fall,[1]

and like an olive tree
he will shed his blossoms.
34 For the company of the godless is
barren,
and fire consumes the tents of those
who accept bribes.
35 [a]They conceive trouble and bring
forth evil;
their belly prepares deception."

Job's Reply to Eliphaz

16 Then Job replied:

2 "I have heard many things like these
before.
What [a]miserable comforters are you
all!
3 Will there be an end to your windy
words?
Or what provokes you that you
answer?
4 I also could speak like you,
if you were in my place;
I could pile up words against you,
and I could [a]shake my head at you.
5 But I would strengthen you with my
words;
comfort from my lips would bring
you relief.

Abandonment by God and Man

6 "But if I speak, my pain is not relieved,
and if I refrain from speaking,
how much of it goes away?
7 Surely now he has [a]worn me out;
you [b]have devastated my entire
household.
8 You have seized me,
and it has become a [a]witness;
my leanness[1] has risen up against me
and testifies against me.
9 His anger has torn me and
persecuted me;
[a]he has gnashed at me with his teeth;
[b]my adversary locks his eyes on me.
10 People have [a]opened their mouths
against me;
they have [b]struck my cheek in scorn;
they unite together against me.

11 God abandons me to evil men,[1]
and throws me into the hands of
wicked men.
12 I was in peace, and he has
[a]shattered me.
He has seized me by the neck and
crushed me.
He has made me his target;
13 his archers surround me.
Without pity he pierces my kidneys
and pours out my gall on the ground.
14 He breaks through against me, time
and time again;
he rushes against me like a warrior.
15 I have sewed sackcloth on my skin
and [a]buried my horn[1] in the dust;
16 my face is reddened because of
weeping,
and on my eyelids there is a deep
darkness,
17 although there is no violence in my
hands
and my prayer is pure.

An Appeal to God as Witness

18 "O earth, do not cover my blood,
nor [a]let there be a secret place for my
cry.
19 Even now [a]my witness is in heaven;
my advocate is on high.
20 My intercessor is my friend
as my eyes pour out tears[1] to God;
21 [a]and he contends with God on behalf
of man
as a man pleads for his friend.
22 For the years that lie ahead are few,
and then I will [a]go on the way of no
return.[1]

17 My spirit is broken,
my days have faded out;
[a]the grave awaits me.
2 Surely mockery is with me;
my eyes must dwell on their [a]hostility.
3 Set my pledge beside you.
Who else [a]will put up security
for me?
4 Because you have closed their minds
to [a]understanding,
therefore you will not exalt them.

15:35 [a] Ps 7:14; Isa 59:4; [Hos 10:13]   16:2 [a] Job 13:4; 21:34   16:4 [a] Ps 22:7; 109:25; Lam 2:15; Zeph 2:15; Matt 27:39
16:7 [a] Job 7:3   [b] Job 16:20; 19:13–15   16:8 [a] Job 10:17   [1] Or *lie, deceit.*   16:9 [a] Job 10:16–17; 19:11; Hos 6:1   [b] Job 13:24; 33:10
16:10 [a] Ps 22:13; 35:21   [b] Isa 50:6; Lam 3:30; Mic 5:1; Matt 26:67; Mark 14:65; Luke 22:63; Acts 23:2   16:11 [1] Heb. *child.*
16:12 [a] Job 9:17   16:15 [a] Job 30:19; Ps 7:5   [1] Drawn from the animal world, the image conveys strength, pride, and victory.
16:18 [a] Job 27:9; [Ps 66:18]   16:19 [a] Gen 31:50; Rom 1:9; Phil 1:8; 1 Thess 2:5   16:20 [1] Heb. *to drip, stream, flow.*   16:21 [a] Job
31:35; Eccl 6:10; [Isa 45:9; Rom 9:20]   16:22 [a] Job 10:21; Eccl 12:5   [1] Heb. *I will not return.*   17:1 [a] Ps 88:3–4
17:2 [a] 1 Sam 1:6; Job 12:4; 17:6; 30:1, 9; 34:7   17:3 [a] Prov 6:1; 17:18; 22:26   17:4 [a] Job 12:20; 32:9

5 If a man denounces his friends for
   personal gain,
   the eyes of his children will [a]fail.
6 He [a]has made me a byword[1] to
   people;
   I am the one in whose face they spit.
7 My eyes have grown dim with grief;
   [a]my whole frame is but a shadow.
8 Upright men are appalled at this;
   the innocent man is troubled with
      the godless.
9 But the righteous man holds to his
      [a]way,
   and the one with [b]clean hands grows
      stronger.

Anticipation of Death

10 "But turn, all of you, and [a]come now!
   I will not find a wise man among you.
11 My days have passed; [a]my plans are
      shattered,
   even the desires of my heart.
12 These men change night into day;
   they say, 'The light is near
   in the face of darkness.'
13 If I hope for the grave to be my home,
   if I spread out my bed in darkness,
14 if I cry out to corruption, 'You are my
      father,'
   and to the worm, 'My mother,' or 'My
      sister,'
15 where then is my [a]hope?
   And my hope, who sees it?
16 Will it go down [a]to the barred gates[1]
      of death?
   Will we [b]descend[2] together into the
      dust?"

Bildad's Second Speech

18 Then [a]Bildad the Shuhite answered:

2 "How long until you make an end of
      words?
   You must consider, and then we can
      talk.
3 Why should we be regarded [a]as
      beasts,
   and considered stupid in your sight?

4 You who tear [a]yourself to pieces in
      your anger,
   will the earth be abandoned for your
      sake?
   Or will a rock be moved from its
      place?
5 "Yes, [a]the lamp of the wicked is
      extinguished;
   his flame of fire does not shine.
6 The light in his tent grows dark;
   his lamp above him is extinguished.
7 His vigorous steps are restricted,
   and [a]his own counsel throws him
      down.
8 For [a]he has been thrown into a net
      by his feet,
   and he wanders into a mesh.
9 A [a]trap[1] seizes him by the heel;
   a snare grips him.
10 A rope is hidden for him on the
      ground,
   and a trap for him lies on the path.
11 [a]Terrors frighten him on all sides
   and dog his every step.
12 Calamity is hungry for him,
   and [a]misfortune is ready at his side.[1]
13 It eats away parts of his skin;
   the most terrible death devours his
      limbs.
14 He is dragged from [a]the security of
      his tent,
   and marched off to the king of
      terrors.
15 Fire resides in his tent;
   over his residence burning sulfur is
      scattered.
16 Below [a]his roots dry up,
   and his branches wither above.
17 His memory perishes from [a]the
      earth
   he has no name in the land.
18 He is driven from light into darkness
   and is banished from the world.
19 He has [a]neither children nor
      descendants[1] among his people,
   no survivor in those places he once
      stayed.

17:5 [a] Job 11:20   17:6 [a] Job 30:9   [1] The Heb. word is related to the word translated "proverb" in the Bible.   17:7 [a] Ps 6:7;
31:9   17:9 [a] Prov 4:18   [b] Ps 24:4   17:10 [a] Job 6:29   17:11 [a] Job 7:6   17:15 [a] Job 7:6; 13:15; 14:19; 19:10   17:16 [a] Jonah 2:6
[b] Job 3:17–19; 21:33   [1] Heb. bars, bolts.   [2] Or will our rest be together in the dust?   18:1 [a] Job 8:1   18:3 [a] Ps 73:22
18:4 [a] Job 13:14   18:5 [a] Job 21:17; Prov 13:9; 20:20; 24:20   18:7 [a] Job 5:12–13; 15:6   18:8 [a] Job 22:10; Ps 9:15; 35:8;
Isa 24:17–18   18:9 [a] Job 5:5   [1] The snare of the fowler; a bird trap.   18:11 [a] Job 20:25; Jer 6:25   18:12 [a] Job
15:23   [1] I.e., misfortune is right there to destroy him whenever there is the opportunity.   18:14 [a] Job 11:20
18:16 [a] Job 29:19   18:17 [a] Job 24:20; [Ps 34:16]; Prov 10:7   18:19 [a] Job 27:14–15; Isa 14:22   [1] These Heb.
terms are always together and form an alliteration that is hard to capture in English.

20 People of the west are appalled ᵃat
   his fate;
   people of the east are seized with
   horror, saying,
21 'Surely such is the residence of an
   evil man;
   and this is the place of one who has
   not known God.'"

Job's Reply to Bildad

19

Then Job answered:

2 "How long will you torment me
   and crush me with your words?
3 These ten times you have been
   reproaching me;
   you are not ashamed to attack me.
4 But even if it were true that I have
   erred,
   my error remains solely my concern!
5 If indeed you would ᵃexalt yourselves
   above me
   and plead my disgrace against me,
6 know then that ᵃGod has
   wronged me
   and encircled me with his net.

Job's Abandonment and Affliction

7 "If I cry out,[1] 'Violence!'
   I receive no answer;
   I cry for help,
   but there is no justice.
8 ᵃHe has blocked my way so I cannot
   pass
   and has set darkness over my paths.
9 He has stripped me of my honor
   and has taken ᵃthe crown off my
   head.
10 He tears me down on every side until
   I perish;
   he uproots my ᵃhope like an
   uprooted tree.
11 Thus his anger burns against me,
   and ᵃhe considers me among his
   enemies.
12 His troops advance together;
   they throw up a siege ramp
   against me,
   and they camp around my tent.

Job's Forsaken State

13 "He has put my relatives far from me;
   my acquaintances only turn away
   from me.
14 My kinsmen have failed me;
   my friends have forgotten me.
15 My guests and my servant girls
   consider me a stranger;
   I am a foreigner[1] in their eyes.
16 I summon my servant, but he does
   not respond,
   even though I implore him with my
   own mouth.
17 My breath is repulsive to my wife;
   I am loathsome to my brothers.
18 Even ᵃyoungsters have scorned me;
   when I get up, they scoff at me.
19 ᵃAll my closest friends detest me;
   and those whom I love have turned
   against me.
20 My bones stick to ᵃmy skin and my
   flesh;[1]
   I have escaped alive with only the
   skin of my teeth.
21 Have pity on me, my friends, have
   pity on me,
   for the hand of God has struck me.
22 Why do you ᵃpursue me like God
   does?
   Will you never be satiated with my
   flesh?

Job's Assurance of Vindication

23 "O that my words were written down!
   O that they were written on a scroll!
24 O that with an iron chisel and with
   lead
   they were engraved in a rock forever!
25 As for me, I know that my Redeemer[1]
   lives,
   and that as the last
   he will stand upon the earth.
26 And after my ᵃskin has been
   destroyed,
   yet in my flesh[1] I will see God,
27 whom I will see for myself,
   and whom my own eyes will behold,
   and not another.
   My heart[1] grows faint within me.

18:20 ᵃ Ps 37:13; Jer 50:27; Obad 12   19:5 ᵃ Ps 35:26; 38:16; 55:12–13   19:6 ᵃ Job 16:11   19:7 [1] LXX *I laugh at reproach.*
19:8 ᵃ Job 3:23; Ps 88:8; Lam 3:7, 9   19:9 ᵃ Job 12:17, 19; Ps 89:44   19:10 ᵃ Job 17:14–16   19:11 ᵃ Job 13:24; 33:10   19:15 [1] A
person from another race or from a strange land.   19:18 ᵃ 2 Kgs 2:23; Job 17:6   19:19 ᵃ Ps 38:11; 55:12–13   19:20 ᵃ Job 16:8;
33:21; Ps 102:5; Lam 4:8   [1] I.e., "I am nothing but skin and bones."   19:22 ᵃ Job 13:24–25; 16:11; 19:6; Ps 69:26   19:25 [1] Or *my
Vindicator; the near kinsman who will pay off one's debts, defend the family, avenge a killing, and marry the widow of
the deceased (see the Book of Ruth).*   19:26 ᵃ [Ps 17:15]; Matt 5:8; 1 Cor 13:12; [1 John 3:2]   [1] Heb. *and from my flesh*; either
"separated from my flesh" or "in/with my flesh."   19:27 [1] Heb. *kidneys*; a poetic expression for the seat of emotions.

28 If you say, 'How we will pursue him,
  since the root of the trouble is found
    in him!'[1]
29 Fear the sword yourselves,
  for wrath brings the punishment by
    the sword,
  so that you may know
  that there is judgment."

Zophar's Second Speech

20 Then [a]Zophar the Naamathite answered:

2 "This is why my troubled thoughts
    bring me back—
  because of my feelings within me.
3 When I hear a reproof that
    dishonors me,
  then my understanding prompts me
    to answer.
4 "Surely you know[1] that it has been
    from [a]old,
  ever since humankind was placed on
    the earth,
5 that the elation of the wicked is
    brief,
  the joy of the godless lasts but [a]a
    [b]moment.
6 Even [a]though his stature reaches to
    the heavens
  and his head touches the clouds,
7 he will perish forever, like his own
    excrement;
  those who used to see him will say,
  'Where is he?'
8 Like a dream he flies away, never
    again to be found,
  and [a]like a vision of the night he is
    put to flight.
9 People who had seen him will not see
    him again,
  and the place where he was
  will recognize him no longer.
10 His sons must recompense the poor;
  his own hands must return his
    wealth.
11 His bones[1] were full of [a]his youthful
    vigor,
  [b]but that vigor will lie down with
    him in the dust.

12 "If evil is sweet in his mouth
  and he hides it under his tongue,
13 if he retains it for himself
  and does not let it go,
  and holds it fast in his mouth,
14 his food is turned sour in his
    stomach;[1]
  it becomes the venom of serpents
    within him.
15 The wealth that he consumed he
    vomits up,
  God will make him throw it out of his
    stomach.
16 He sucks the poison of serpents;
  the fangs of a viper kill him.
17 He will not look on [a]the streams,
  the rivers that are the torrents
  of honey and butter.
18 He gives back the ill-gotten gain
  without assimilating it;
  he will not enjoy the wealth from his
    commerce.
19 For he has oppressed the poor and
    abandoned them;
  he has seized a house which he did
    not build.
20 For he knows no satisfaction in his
    appetite;[1]
  he does not let anything he desires
    escape.
21 Nothing is left for him to devour;
  that is why his prosperity does not
    last.
22 In the fullness of his sufficiency,
  distress overtakes him.
  The full force of misery will come
    upon him.
23 While he is filling his belly,
  God sends his burning anger against
    him
  and rains down his blows upon him.
24 If [a]he flees from an iron weapon,
  then an arrow from a bronze bow
    pierces him.
25 When [a]he pulls it out and it comes
    out of his back,
  the gleaming point out of his liver,
  [b]terrors come over him.
26 Total darkness waits to receive his
    treasures;
  [a]a fire that has not been kindled

19:28 [1]MT *in me.*   20:1 [a]Job 11:1   20:4 [a]Job 8:8; 15:10   [1]Heb. *Do you not know?*   20:5 [a]Ps 37:35–36   [b][Job 8:13; 13:16; 15:34; 27:8]   20:6 [a]Isa 14:13–14   20:8 [a]Ps 73:20; 90:5   20:11 [a]Job 13:26   [b]Job 21:26   [1]Often used for the whole person.   20:14 [1]Or *bowels;* Heb. *in his loins, within him.*   20:17 [a]Ps 36:8; Jer 17:8   20:20 [1]Heb. *belly.*   20:24 [a]Isa 24:18; Amos 5:19   20:25 [a]Job 16:13   [b]Job 18:11, 14   20:26 [a]Ps 21:9

will consume him and devour what is
   left in his tent.
27 The heavens reveal his iniquity;
   the earth rises up against him.
28 A flood will carry off his house,
   rushing waters on the day of God's
   [a]wrath.
29 Such [a]is the lot God allots the wicked,
   and the heritage of his appointment
   from God."

Job's Reply to Zophar

21 Then Job answered:

2 "Listen carefully to my words;
   let this be[1] the consolation you
      offer me.
3 Bear with me and I[1] will speak,
   and after I have spoken you may
      [a]mock.
4 Is my complaint against a man?
   If so, why should I not be impatient?
5 Look at me and be appalled;
   [a]put your hands over your mouths.
6 For, when I think about this, I am
     terrified
   and my body feels a shudder.

The Wicked Prosper

7 "[a]Why do the wicked go on living,
   grow old, even increase in power?
8 Their children[1] are firmly established
     in their presence,
   their offspring before their eyes.
9 Their houses are safe and without
      fear;
   and no rod of punishment from God
     is upon them.
10 Their bulls breed [a]without fail;
   their cows calve and do not miscarry.
11 They allow their children to run like
     a flock;
   their little ones dance about.
12 They sing to the accompaniment of
      tambourine and harp,
   and make merry to the sound of the
      flute.
13 They live out[1] their years in prosperity
   and go down[2] to the grave in peace.

14 [a]So they say to God, 'Turn away
     from us!
   We do not want to know your ways.
15 [a]Who is the Almighty, that we should
     serve him?
   [b]What would we gain
   if we were to pray[1] to him?'
16 But [a]their prosperity is not their own
     doing.
   The counsel of the wicked is far
     from me!

How Often Do the Wicked Suffer?

17 "How often is the lamp of the wicked
     extinguished?
   How often does their misfortune
     come upon them?
   How often does God [a]apportion pain
     to them in his anger?
18 How often are [a]they like straw before
     the wind
   and like chaff swept away by a
     whirlwind?
19 You may say, 'God stores up a man's
     punishment [a]for his children!'[1]
   Instead let him repay the man
     himself
   so that he may be humbled!
20 Let his own eyes see his destruction;
   [a]let him drink of the anger of the
     Almighty.
21 For what is his interest in his home
     after his death,[1]
   when the number of his months
     has been broken off?
22 Can anyone teach God knowledge,
   since he judges those that are on
     high?

Death Levels Everything

23 "One man dies in his full vigor,
   completely secure and prosperous,
24 his body well nourished,
   and the marrow of his bones moist.
25 And another man dies in bitterness
     of soul,
   never having tasted[1] anything good.
26 Together they [a]lie down in the dust,
   and worms cover over them both.

20:28 [a] Job 20:15; 21:30   20:29 [a] Job 27:13; 31:2–3   21:2 [1] LXX *that I may not have this consolation from you.*   21:3 [a] Job 16:10 [1] An emphatic Heb. construction.   21:5 [a] Judg 18:19; Job 13:5; 29:9; 40:4   21:7 [a] Job 12:6; Ps 17:10, 14; 73:3, 12; [Jer 12:1]; Hab 1:13, 16   21:8 [1] Heb. *their seed.*   21:10 [a] Exod 23:26   21:13 [1] Ket. *they wear out.* [2] MT *they are frightened* [or *broken*].   21:14 [a] Job 22:17   21:15 [a] Exod 5:2; Job 22:17; 34:9 [b] Job 35:3; Mal 3:14 [1] Heb. *to meet with request, intercede, interpose.*   21:16 [a] Job 22:18; Ps 1:1; Prov 1:10   21:17 [a] [Job 31:2–3; Luke 12:46]   21:18 [a] Ps 1:4; 35:5; Isa 17:13; Hos 13:3   21:19 [a] [Exod 20:5]; Jer 31:29; Ezek 18:2 [1] Heb. *his sons.*   21:20 [a] Ps 75:8; Isa 51:17; Jer 25:15; Rev 14:10; 19:15   21:21 [1] Heb. *after him.*   21:25 [1] Heb. *eaten what is good;* i.e., he died without having enjoyed the good life.   21:26 [a] Job 3:13; 20:11; Eccl 9:2

Futile Words, Deceptive Answers

27 "Yes, I know what you are thinking,
the schemes by which you would
wrong me.
28 For you say,
'Where now is the nobleman's house,
and where are the tents in which the
wicked lived?'
29 Have you never questioned those
who travel the roads?
Do you not recognize their
accounts[1]—
30 that the evil man is spared
from the day of his [a]misfortune,
that he is delivered
from the day of God's wrath?
31 No one denounces his conduct to his
face;
no one repays him for what he has
done.
32 And when he is carried to the tombs
and watch is kept over the funeral
mound,
33 the clods of the torrent valley are
sweet to him;
behind him [a]everybody follows in
procession,
and before him goes a countless
throng.
34 So how can you console me with your
futile words?
Nothing is left of your answers but
deception!"

Eliphaz's Third Speech

22 Then [a]Eliphaz the Temanite
answered:

2 "Is it to God that [a]a strong man is of
benefit?
Is it to him that even a wise man is
profitable?
3 Is it of any special benefit to the
Almighty
that you should be righteous,
or is it any gain to him
that you make your ways blameless?
4 Is it because of your piety that he
rebukes you
and goes to judgment with you?

5 Is not your wickedness great
and is there no end to your iniquity?
6 "For you took pledges from your
brothers
for no reason,
and you stripped the clothing from
the naked.[1]
7 You gave the weary no water to drink
and from the hungry you withheld
food.
8 Although you were a powerful man,
owning land,
an honored man[1] living on it,
9 you sent widows away empty-handed,
and the arms of the orphans you
crushed.
10 That is why snares surround you,
and why sudden fear terrifies you,
11 why it is so dark you cannot see,
and why a flood of [a]water covers you.
12 "Is not God on high in heaven?
And see the lofty stars, how high
they are!
13 But you have said, '[a]What does God
know?
Does he judge through such deep
darkness?
14 [a]Thick clouds are a veil for him, so he
does not see us,
as he goes back and forth
in the vault of heaven.'
15 Will you keep to the old path
that evil men have walked—
16 men who [a]were carried off before
their time,
when the flood was poured out
on their foundations?
17 They were saying to God, 'Turn away
from us,'
and, 'What can [a]the Almighty do to us?'
18 But it was he who filled their houses
with good things—
yet the counsel of the wicked
was far from me.[1]
19 The righteous see [a]their destruction
and rejoice;
the innocent mock them scornfully,
saying,

21:29 [1] LXX *Ask those who go by the way, and do not disown their signs.*   21:30 [a] Job 20:29; [Prov 16:4; 2 Pet 2:9]
21:33 [a] Heb 9:27   22:1 [a] Job 4:1; 15:1; 42:9   22:2 [a] Job 35:7; [Ps 16:2; Luke 17:10]   22:6 [1] I.e., people who are
poorly clothed; either he made them naked by stripping their garments off, or they were already in rags.
22:8 [1] Lit. *the one lifted up of face.*   22:11 [a] Job 38:34; Ps 69:1–2; 124:5; Lam 3:54   22:13 [a] Ps 73:11
22:14 [a] Ps 139:11–12   22:16 [a] Job 14:19; 15:32; Ps 90:5; Isa 28:2; Matt 7:26–27   22:17 [a] Job 21:14–15
22:18 [1] LXX *from him.*   22:19 [a] Ps 52:6; 58:10; 107:42

20 'Surely our enemies[1] are destroyed,
    and fire consumes their wealth.'

21 "Reconcile yourself with God,
    and [a]be at peace with him;
    in this way your prosperity will be
        good.
22 Accept [a]instruction[1] from his mouth
    and store up his words in your heart.
23 If you return to the Almighty, you
        will be built up;[1]
    if you remove wicked behavior far
        from your tent,
24 and [a]throw[1] your gold in the dust—
    your gold of Ophir
        among the rocks in the ravines—
25 then the Almighty himself will be
        your gold,
    and the choicest silver for you.
26 Surely then you will [a]delight yourself
        in the Almighty
    and will lift up your face toward God.
27 You will pray to him, and he will hear
        [a]you,
    and you will fulfill your vows to him.
28 Whatever you decide on a matter,
    it will be established for you,
    and light will shine on your ways.
29 When people are brought low and
        you say,
    'Lift [a]them up!'
    then he will save the downcast;
30 he will deliver even someone who is
        not innocent,[1]
    who will escape[2] through the
        cleanness of your hands."

Job's Reply to Eliphaz

23 Then Job answered:

2 "Even today my [a]complaint is still
        bitter;[1]
    his[2] hand is heavy despite my
        groaning.
3 [a]O that I knew where I might find
        him,
    that I could come to his place of
        residence!

4 I would lay out my case before him
    and fill my mouth with arguments.
5 I would know with what words he
        would answer me
    and understand what he would say
        to me.
6 Would he contend[1] with me with
        great power?
    No, he [a]would only pay attention
        to me.
7 There an upright person
    could present his case before him,
    and I would be delivered forever
        from my judge.

The Inaccessibility and Power of God

8 "If I go to the east, he is not there,
    and to the west, yet I do not perceive
        him.
9 In the north when he is at work,[1]
    I do not see him;
    when he turns to the south,
    I see no trace of him.
10 But [a]he knows [b]the pathway that I
        take;
    if he tested me, I would come forth
        like gold.
11 [a]My feet have followed his steps
        closely;
    I have kept to his way and have not
        turned aside.
12 I have not departed from the
        [a]commands of [b]his lips;
    I have treasured the words of his
        mouth more than my allotted
        portion.[1]
13 But he [a]is unchangeable,[1] and who
        can change him?
    Whatever he has desired, he does.
14 For he fulfills his [a]decree against me,
    and many such things are his plans.
15 That is why I am terrified in his
        presence;
    when I consider, I am afraid because
        of him.
16 Indeed, God has [a]made my heart
        faint;
    the Almighty has terrified me.

22:20 [1] LXX *possessions.*   22:21 [a] [Ps 34:10]; Isa 27:5   22:22 [a] Job 6:10; 23:12; Prov 2:6   [1] Heb. *torah.*   22:23 [1] LXX *humble yourself.*   22:24 [a] 2 Chr 1:15   [1] Thd., Syr. *and you will esteem.*   22:26 [a] Job 27:10; Ps 37:4; Isa 58:14   22:27 [a] Job 11:13; 33:26; [Isa 58:9–11]   22:29 [a] Job 5:11; [Matt 23:12; Jas 4:6; 1 Pet 5:5]   22:30 [1] Heb. *island of the innocent* or *him that is not innocent.* [2] MT *he will escape* [or *be delivered*]; Thd. *you will be delivered.*   23:2 [a] Job 7:11   [1] MT *rebellious.* [2] MT, Vg., Tg. *my hand is heavy on my groaning.*   23:3 [a] Job 13:3, 18; 16:21; 31:35   23:6 [a] Isa 57:16   [1] Heb. *to quarrel, dispute, contend;* often in a legal context.   23:9 [1] Syr. *I seek him;* LXX *[when] he turns.*   23:10 [a] [Ps 1:6; 139:1–3]   [b] [Ps 17:3; 66:10; Jas 1:12]   23:11 [a] Job 31:7; Ps 17:5   23:12 [a] Job 6:10; 22:22   [b] Ps 44:18   [1] LXX, Latin *in my bosom.*   23:13 [a] [Ps 115:3]   [1] MT *But he [is] in one.*   23:14 [a] [1 Thess 3:2–4]   23:16 [a] Ps 22:14

17 Yet I have not been silent because of
    the darkness,
    because of the thick darkness
    that covered my face.

The Apparent Indifference of God

24 "Why are [a]times not appointed by
    the Almighty?[1]
    Why do those who know him not see
    his [b]days?
2 Men move boundary [a]stones;
    they seize the flock and pasture
    them.[1]
3 They drive away the orphan's donkey;
    they [a]take the widow's ox as a pledge.
4 They turn the needy from the
    pathway,
    and the [a]poor of the land hide
    themselves together.
5 Like[1] wild donkeys in the wilderness,
    they go out to their labor seeking
    diligently for food;
    the arid rift valley[2] provides food for
    them and for their children.
6 They reap fodder in the field
    and glean in the vineyard of the
    wicked.
7 They [a]spend the night naked because
    they lack clothing;
    they have no covering against the
    cold.
8 They are soaked by mountain rains
    and [a]huddle in the rocks because
    they lack shelter.
9 The fatherless child is snatched from
    the breast;
    the infant of the poor is taken as a
    pledge.[1]
10 They go about naked, without
    [a]clothing,
    and go hungry while they carry the
    sheaves.
11 They press out the olive oil between
    the rows of olive trees;
    they tread the winepresses while
    they are thirsty.
12 From the city the dying[1] groan,
    and the wounded[2] cry out for help,

but God charges no one with
    wrongdoing.[3]
13 There are those who rebel against
    the light;
    they do not know its ways,
    and they do not stay on its paths.
14 Before daybreak [a]the murderer
    rises up;
    he kills the poor and the needy;
    in the night he is like a thief.
15 And [a]the eye of the adulterer
    watches for the twilight,
    [b]thinking, 'No eye can see me,'
    and covers his face with a mask.
16 In [a]the dark the robber breaks into
    houses,
    but by day they shut themselves in;
    they do not know the light.
17 For all of them, the morning is to
    them like deep darkness;
    they are friends with the terrors of
    darkness.
18 "You say, 'He is foam on the face of
    the waters;
    their portion of the land is cursed
    so that no one goes to their vineyard.
19 The drought as well as the heat
    snatch up the melted snow;
    so the grave[1] snatches up the sinner.[2]
20 The womb forgets him,
    [a]the worm feasts on him,
    no longer will he be remembered.
    Like a tree, wickedness will be
    broken down.
21 He preys on[1] the barren and childless
    woman
    and does not treat the widow well.
22 But God drags off the mighty by his
    power;
    when God rises up against him, he
    has no faith in his life.
23 God may let them rest in a feeling of
    security,
    but he [a]is constantly watching all
    their ways.
24 They are exalted for a little while,
    and then they are gone;

24:1 [a] [Acts 1:7] [b] [Isa 2:12]; Jer 46:10; [Obad 15]; Zeph 1:7 [1]LXX *Why are times hidden from the Almighty?* 24:2 [a] [Deut 19:14; 27:17]; Prov 22:28; 23:10; Hos 5:10 [1]LXX *and their shepherd.* 24:3 [a] [Deut 24:6, 10, 12, 17]; Job 22:6, 9 24:4 [a] Job 29:16; Prov 28:28 24:5 [1]MT *behold.* [2]The rift valley extends from Galilee to the Gulf of Aqaba, but likely only the section south of the Dead Sea. 24:7 [a] Exod 22:26–27; [Deut 24:12–13]; Job 22:6; [Jas 2:15–16] 24:8 [a] Lam 4:5 24:9 [1]MT *they take as a pledge upon the poor.* 24:10 [a] Job 31:19 24:12 [1]MT *from the city of men they groan.* [2]Heb. *the souls of the wounded.* [3]MT *folly; tastelessness* (cf. 1:22). 24:14 [a] Ps 10:8 24:15 [a] Prov 7:7–10 [b] Ps 10:11 24:16 [a] [John 3:20] 24:19 [1]Or *Sheol.* [2]Heb. *The grave [ ] they have sinned.* 24:20 [a] Job 18:17; Ps 34:16; Prov 10:7 24:21 [1]LXX *oppressed.* 24:23 [a] Ps 11:4; [Prov 15:3]

they are brought low like all others
  and gathered in,
and like a head of grain they are cut
  off.'

25 "If this is not so, who can prove me a
  liar
and reduce my words to nothing?"

Bildad's Third Speech

25 Then [a]Bildad the Shuhite answered:

2 "Dominion and awesome might
  belong to God;
he establishes peace in his heights.
3 Can [a]his armies be numbered?
On whom does his light[1] not rise?
4 How then can a human being be
  righteous before God?
[a]How can one born of a woman be
  [b]pure?
5 If even the moon is not bright,
and the stars are not pure as far as he
  is [a]concerned,
6 how much less [a]a mortal man, who is
  but a maggot—
a son of man, who is only a worm!"

Job's Reply to Bildad

26 Then Job replied:

2 "How you have helped the powerless!
How you have saved the person who
  has no strength!
3 How you have advised the one
  without wisdom,
and abundantly revealed your insight!
4 To whom did you utter these words?
And whose spirit has come forth
  from your mouth?

A Better Description of God's Greatness

5 "The dead tremble—
those beneath the waters
and all that live in them.
6 The [a]underworld[1] is naked before God;
the place of destruction lies
  uncovered.
7 He spreads out [a]the northern skies
  over empty space;

he suspends the earth on nothing.
8 He locks [a]the waters in his clouds,
and the clouds do not burst with the
  weight of them.
9 He conceals the face of the full
  moon,[1]
shrouding it with his clouds.
10 He marks out [a]the horizon on the
  surface of the waters
as a boundary between light and
  darkness.
11 The pillars of the heavens tremble
and are amazed at his rebuke.
12 By his power [a]he stills the sea;
by his wisdom he cut Rahab the great
  sea monster to pieces.
13 [a]By his breath [b]the skies became fair;
his hand pierced the fleeing serpent.
14 Indeed, these are but the outer
  fringes of his ways!
How faint is the whisper we hear of
  him!
But who can understand the thunder
  of his power?"

A Protest of Innocence

27 And Job took up his discourse again:

2 "As surely as God lives, [a]who has
  denied me justice,
the Almighty, who has made my life
  bitter—
3 for while my spirit is still in me,
and the breath from God is in my
  nostrils,
4 my lips will not speak wickedness,
and my tongue will whisper no
  deceit.
5 I [a]will never declare that you three
  are in the right;
until I die, I will not set aside my
  integrity!
6 I will [a]maintain [b]my righteousness
and never let it go;
my conscience will not reproach me
for as long as I live.

The Condition of the Wicked

7 "May my enemy be like the wicked,
my adversary like the unrighteous.[1]

25:1 [a] Job 8:1; 18:1   25:3 [a] Jas 1:17   [1] LXX *his ambush.*   25:4 [a] Job 4:17; 15:14; Ps 130:3; 143:2   [b] [Job 14:4]   25:5 [a] Job 15:15
25:6 [a] Ps 22:6   26:6 [a] [Ps 139:8]; Prov 15:11; [Heb 4:13]   [1] Heb. *Sheol.*   26:7 [a] Job 9:8; Ps 24:2; 104:2   26:8 [a] Job 37:11;
Prov 30:4   26:9 [1] MT *throne.*   26:10 [a] [Job 38:1–11]; Ps 33:7; 104:9; Prov 8:29; Jer 5:22   26:12 [a] Exod 14:21; Job 9:13;
Isa 51:15; [Jer 31:35]   26:13 [a] [Job 9:8]; Ps 33:6   [b] Isa 27:1   27:2 [a] Job 34:5   27:5 [a] Job 2:9; 13:15   27:6 [a] Job 2:3; 33:9
[b] Acts 24:16   27:7 [1] LXX *No, but let my enemies be as the overthrow of the ungodly, and they that rise up
against me as the destruction of transgressors.*

8 [a]For what hope does the godless have
  when he is cut off,
  when God takes away his life?
9 [a]Does God listen to his cry
  when distress overtakes him?
10 Will he find delight in the Almighty?
  [a]Will he call out to God at all times?
11 I will teach you about the power of
  God;
  what is on the Almighty's mind I will
  not conceal.
12 If you yourselves have all seen this,
  Why in the world do you continue
  this meaningless talk?
13 This [a]is the portion of the wicked man
  allotted by God,
  the inheritance that evildoers
  receive
  from the Almighty.
14 [a]If his children increase—it is for the
  sword!
  His offspring never have enough to
  eat.[1]
15 Those who survive him are buried by
  [a]the plague,
  and their[1] widows do not mourn for
  them.
16 If he piles up silver like dust
  and stores up clothing like mounds
  of clay,
17 what [a]he stores up a righteous man
  will wear,
  and an innocent man will inherit his
  silver.
18 The house he builds is as fragile as a
  moth's cocoon,
  [a]like a hut that a watchman has made.
19 He goes to bed wealthy, but will do so
  [a]no more.[1]
  When he opens his eyes, it is all gone.
20 [a]Terrors overwhelm him like a flood;
  at night a whirlwind carries him off.
21 The east wind carries him away, and
  he is gone;
  it sweeps him out of his place.
22 It hurls itself against him without
  [a]pity
  as he flees headlong from its power.
23 It claps its hands at him in derision
  and hisses him away from his place.

III. JOB'S SEARCH FOR WISDOM (28:1–28)

No Known Road to Wisdom

28 "Surely there is a mine for silver
  and a place where gold is refined.
2 Iron is taken from the ground,
  and rock is poured out as copper.
3 Man puts an end to the darkness;
  he searches the farthest recesses
  for the ore in the deepest darkness.
4 Far from where people live he sinks a
  shaft,
  in places travelers have long
  forgotten,
  far from other people he dangles and
  sways.
5 The earth, from which food comes,
  is overturned below as though by
  fire;
6 a place whose stones are sapphires
  that contain dust of gold;
7 a hidden path no bird of prey
  knows—
  no falcon's eye has spotted it.
8 Proud beasts have not set foot on it,
  and no lion has passed along it.
9 On the flinty rock man has set to
  work with his hand;
  he has overturned mountains at
  their bases.[1]
10 He has cut out channels through the
  rocks;
  his eyes have spotted every precious
  thing.
11 He has searched[1] the sources of the
  rivers,
  and what was hidden he has brought
  into the light.

No Price Can Buy Wisdom

12 "But wisdom—where can it be found?
  Where is the place of understanding?
13 Mankind does not know its [a]place;[1]
  it cannot be found in the land of the
  living.
14 The deep says, 'It is not with me.'
  And [a]the sea says, 'It is not with me.'
15 Fine gold [a]cannot be given in
  exchange for it,

27:8 [a]Matt 16:26; Luke 12:20   27:9 [a]Job 35:12–13; Ps 18:41; Prov 1:28; 28:9; [Isa 1:15]; Jer 14:12; Ezek 8:18; [Mic 3:4; John 9:31; Jas 4:3]   27:10 [a]Job 22:26–27; [Ps 37:4; Isa 58:14]   27:13 [a]Job 20:29   27:14 [a]Deut 28:41; Esth 9:10; Hos 9:13   [1]Heb. *will not be satisfied with bread/food.*   27:15 [a]Ps 78:64   [1]LXX *their widows.*   27:17 [a]Prov 28:8; [Eccl 2:26]   27:18 [a]Isa 1:8; Lam 2:6   27:19 [a]Job 7:8, 21; 20:7   [1]MT *he is gathered.*   27:20 [a]Job 18:11   27:22 [a]Jer 13:14; Ezek 5:11; 24:14   28:9 [1]Heb. *from/at* [their] *root* [or base].   28:11 [1]MT *binds up* or *dams up.*   28:13 [a]Prov 3:15   [1]LXX *its way.*   28:14 [a]Job 28:22   28:15 [a]Prov 3:13–15; 8:10–11, 19

nor can its price be weighed out in
   silver.
16 It cannot be measured out for
   purchase with the gold of Ophir,
   with precious onyx or sapphires.
17 Neither [a]gold nor crystal can be
   compared with it,
   nor can a vase[1] of gold match its
   worth.
18 Of coral and jasper no mention will
   be made;
   the price of wisdom is more than
   [a]pearls.
19 The topaz of Cush[1] cannot be
   compared with it;
   it cannot be purchased with pure
   [a]gold.

God Alone Has Wisdom

20 "But wisdom—where does it come
   [a]from?
   Where is the place of understanding?
21 For it has been hidden
   from the eyes of every living
   creature,
   and from the birds of the sky it has
   been concealed.
22 [a]Destruction[1] and Death say,
   'With our ears we have heard a rumor
   about where it can be found.'
23 God understands the way to it,
   and he alone knows its place.
24 For he looks to the ends of the earth
   and [a]observes everything under the
   heavens.
25 [a]When he made the force of the wind
   and measured the waters with a
   gauge,
26 when he [a]imposed a limit for the
   rain,
   and a path for the thunderstorm,
27 then he looked at wisdom and
   assessed its value;
   he established[1] it and examined it
   closely.
28 And [a]he said to mankind,
   'The fear of the Lord[1]—that is
   wisdom,
   and to turn away from evil is
   understanding.'"

IV. JOB'S CONCLUDING SOLILOQUY (29:1–31:40)

Job Recalls His Former Condition

29 Then Job continued his speech:
2 "O that I could be as I was
   in the months now [a]gone,
   in the days when God watched
   [b]over me,
3 when [a]he caused his lamp
   to shine upon my head,
   and by his light
   I walked through darkness;
4 just as I was in my most productive
   time,
   when God's intimate friendship[1] was
   experienced in my tent,
5 when the Almighty was still with me
   and my children were around me;
6 when [a]my steps were [b]bathed with
   butter
   and the rock poured out for me
   streams of olive oil!
7 When I went out to the city gate
   and secured my seat in the public
   square,
8 the young men would see me and
   step aside,[1]
   and the old men would get up and
   remain standing;
9 the chief men refrained from talking
   and [a]covered their mouths with their
   hands;
10 the voices of the nobles fell silent,
   and their [a]tongues stuck to the roof
   of their mouths.

Job's Benevolence

11 "As soon as the ear heard these
   things, it blessed me,
   and when the eye saw them, it bore
   witness to me;
12 for [a]I rescued the poor who cried out
   for help,
   and the orphan who had no one to
   assist him;
13 the blessing of the dying man
   descended on me,
   and I made the widow's heart rejoice;

28:17 [a]Prov 8:10; 16:16 [1]Some wss have a plural here. 28:18 [a]Prov 3:15; 8:11 28:19 [a]Prov 8:19 [1]Or *Ethiopia*; the region of the upper Nile, rather than modern Ethiopia. 28:20 [a]Job 28:12; [Ps 111:10; Prov 1:7; 9:10] 28:22 [a]Job 28:14 [1]Heb. *Abaddon*. 28:24 [a][Ps 11:4; 33:13–14; 66:7; Prov 15:3] 28:25 [a]Ps 135:7 28:26 [a]Job 37:3; 38:25 28:27 [1]Sev. mss *he discerned it*. 28:28 [a][Deut 4:6; Ps 111:10; Prov 1:7; 9:10; Eccl 12:13] [1]Sev. medieval mss *LORD*. 29:2 [a]Job 1:1–5 [b]Job 1:10 29:3 [a]Job 18:6 29:4 [1]LXX, Syr. *when God protected my tent*. 29:6 [a]Gen 49:11; Deut 32:14; Job 20:17 [b]Deut 32:13; Ps 81:16 29:8 [1]Heb. *to hide, withdraw*. 29:9 [a]Job 21:5 29:10 [a]Ps 137:6 29:12 [a]Job 31:16–23; [Ps 72:12; Prov 21:13; 24:11]

14 I put on ᵃrighteousness and it
clothed me;
my just dealing¹ was like a robe and a
turban;
15 I was ᵃeyes for the blind
and feet for the lame;
16 I was a father to the needy,
and ᵃI investigated the case of the
person I did not know;
17 I broke ᵃthe fangs of the wicked,
and made him drop his prey from his
teeth.

Job's Confidence

18 "Then ᵃI thought, 'I will die in my
own home,¹
my days as numerous as the grains of
sand.²
19 My roots reach the water,
and the dew lies on ᵃmy branches all
night long.
20 My glory will always be fresh in me,
and my ᵃbow ever new in my hand.'

Job's Reputation

21 "People listened to me and waited
silently;
they kept silent for my advice.
22 After I had spoken, they did not
respond;
my words fell on them drop by drop.
23 They waited for me as people wait
for ᵃthe rain,
and they opened their mouths as for
the spring rains.
24 If I smiled at them, they hardly
believed it;
and they did not cause the light of
my face to darken.
25 I chose the way for them
and sat as their chief;
I lived like a king among his troops;
I was like one who comforts
mourners.

Job's Present Misery

30 "But now they mock me, those who
are younger than I,
whose fathers I disdained too much
to put with my sheep dogs.

2 Moreover, the strength of their
hands—
what use was it to me?
Those whose strength had perished,
3 gaunt with want and hunger,
they would roam the parched land,
by night a desolate waste.
4 By the brush they would gather
herbs from the salt marshes,
and the root of the broom tree was
their food.
5 They were banished from the
community—
people shouted at them
as they would shout at thieves—
6 so that they had to live
in the dry stream beds,
in the holes of the ground, and
among the rocks.
7 They brayed like animals among the
bushes
and were huddled together under
the nettles.
8 Sons of senseless and nameless
people,
they were driven out of the land with
whips.

Job's Indignities

9 "And now I have become their taunt
song;
I have become ᵃa byword among
them.
10 They detest me and maintain their
distance;
they do not hesitate ᵃto spit in my
face.
11 Because God has untied my tent cord
and afflicted me,
people throw off all restraint in my
presence.
12 On my right ᵃthe young rabble rise up;
they drive me from place to place
and build up siege ramps against me.
13 They destroy my path;
they succeed in destroying me¹
without anyone assisting them.
14 They come in as through a wide
breach;
amid the crash they come rolling in.

29:14 ᵃ Deut 24:13; Job 27:5–6; Ps 132:9; [Isa 59:17; 61:10; Eph 6:14] ¹ Heb. *my justice, my judgment.* 29:15 ᵃ Num 10:31
29:16 ᵃ Prov 29:7 29:17 ᵃ Ps 58:6; Prov 30:14 29:18 ᵃ Ps 30:6 ¹ MT *with my nest;* LXX *My age shall grow old as the stem
of a palm tree, I shall live a long time;* Vg. *In my nest I shall die and like the palm tree increase my days.* ² LXX *like the
palm tree or like the phoenix.* 29:19 ᵃ Job 18:16 29:20 ᵃ Gen 49:24; Ps 18:34 29:23 ᵃ [Zech 10:1] 30:9 ᵃ Job 17:6;
Ps 69:12; Lam 3:14, 63 30:10 ᵃ Num 12:14; Deut 25:9; Job 17:6; Isa 50:6; Matt 26:67; 27:30
30:12 ᵃ Job 19:12 30:13 ¹ MT *they further my misfortune.*

15 Terrors are turned loose on me;
they drive away[1] my honor like the
wind,
and as a cloud my deliverance has
passed away.

Job's Despondency

16 "And now my soul pours itself out
within me;[1]
days of suffering take hold of me.
17 Night pierces my bones;[1]
my gnawing pains never cease.
18 With great power God grasps my
clothing;
he binds me like the collar of my
tunic.
19 He has flung me into the mud,
and I have come to resemble dust
and ashes.
20 I cry [a]out to you, but you do not
answer me;
I stand up, and you only look at me.
21 You have become cruel to me;
with the strength of your hand you
[a]attack me.[1]
22 You pick me up on the wind and
make me ride on it;
you toss me about in the storm.
23 I know that you are bringing me to
death,
to the [a]meeting place for all the
living.

The Contrast with the Past

24 "Surely one does not stretch out his
hand
against a broken man[1]
when he cries for help in his distress.
25 [a]Have I not wept for the unfortunate?
Was not my soul grieved for the
poor?
26 [a]But when I hoped for good, trouble
came;
when I expected light, then darkness
came.
27 My heart[1] is in turmoil unceasingly;
the days of my affliction confront me.

28 I go about blackened, but not by the
sun;
[a]in the assembly I stand up and cry
for help.
29 I have become a brother to jackals
and a [a]companion of ostriches.
30 My skin has turned dark on me;
[a]my body[1] is hot with fever.
31 My harp is used for mourning
and my flute for the sound of
weeping.

Job Vindicates Himself

31 "I made a covenant with my eyes;
how then could I entertain
thoughts against a virgin?
2 What then would be one's [a]lot from
God above,
one's heritage from the Almighty on
high?
3 Is it not misfortune for the unjust
and disaster for those who work
iniquity?
4 [a]Does he not see my ways
and count all my steps?
5 If I have walked in falsehood
and if my foot has hastened to
deceit—
6 let him weigh me with honest scales;
then God will discover my [a]integrity.
7 If [a]my footsteps have strayed from
the way,
if my heart has gone after my eyes,
or if anything has defiled my hands,
8 then [a]let me sow and let another eat,
and let my crops be uprooted.
9 If my heart has been enticed by a
woman,
and I have lain in wait at my
neighbor's door,
10 then let my wife turn the millstone
for another [a]man,
and may other men commit adultery
with her.[1]
11 For [a]I would have committed a
shameful act,
an iniquity to be judged.

30:15 [1]LXX *my hope is gone like the wind.*   30:16 [1]Either he is wasting away (i.e., his life is being poured out), or
he is grieving.   30:17 [1]MT adds *upon me.*   30:20 [a]Job 19:7   30:21 [a]Job 10:3; 16:9, 14; 19:6, 22   [1]LXX *you scourged/
whipped me.*   30:23 [a][Heb 9:27]   30:24 [1]MT *surely not against a ruinous heap will he* [God] *put forth his* [God's] *hand.*
30:25 [a]Ps 35:13-14; Rom 12:15   30:26 [a]Job 3:25-26; Jer 8:15   30:27 [1]Heb. *my loins, my bowels, my innermost being.*
30:28 [a]Job 30:31; Ps 38:6; 42:9; 43:2   30:29 [a]Ps 44:19; 102:6; Mic 1:8   30:30 [a]Ps 119:83; Lam 4:8; 5:10   [1]Heb. *my
bones.*   31:2 [a]Job 20:29   31:4 [a][2 Chr 16:9]; Job 24:23; 28:24; 34:21; 36:7; [Prov 5:21; 15:3; Jer 32:19]   31:6 [a]Job
23:10; 27:5-6   31:7 [a]Num 15:39; [Eccl 11:9]; Ezek 6:9; [Matt 5:29]   31:8 [a]Lev 26:16; Deut 28:30, 38; Job 20:18;
Mic 6:15   31:10 [a]Deut 28:30; 2 Sam 12:11; Jer 8:10   [1]Heb. *kneel down over her;* a euphemism for
sexual relations.   31:11 [a]Gen 38:24; [Lev 20:10; Deut 22:22]; Job 31:28

¹² For it is a fire that devours even to
　　　Destruction,¹
　　and it would uproot all my harvest.

¹³ "If I have ᵃdisregarded the right of
　　　my male servants
　　or my female servants
　　when they disputed with me,
¹⁴ then what will I do when ᵃGod
　　　confronts me in judgment;
　　when he intervenes,
　　how will I respond to him?
¹⁵ Did not the one who made me in the
　　　womb make them?
　　ᵃDid not the same one form us in the
　　　womb?
¹⁶ If I have refused to give the poor
　　　what they desired,
　　or caused the eyes of the widow to
　　　ᵃfail,
¹⁷ if I ate my morsel of bread myself,
　　and did not share any of it with
　　　orphans—
¹⁸ but from my youth I raised the
　　　orphan like a father,
　　and from my mother's womb I
　　　guided the widow—
¹⁹ if I have seen anyone about to perish
　　　for lack of clothing,
　　or a poor man without a coat,
²⁰ whose heart did not ᵃbless me
　　as he warmed himself with the fleece
　　　of my sheep,
²¹ if ᵃI have raised my hand to vote
　　　against the orphan,
　　when I saw my support in the court,¹
²² then let my arm fall from the
　　　shoulder,
　　let my arm be broken off at the
　　　socket.
²³ For the ᵃcalamity from God was a
　　　terror to me,¹
　　and by reason of his majesty I was
　　　powerless.

²⁴ "If ᵃI have put my confidence in gold
　　or said to pure gold,
　　　'You are my security!'
²⁵ if ᵃI have rejoiced because of the
　　　extent of my wealth,

　　or because of the great wealth my
　　　hand had gained,
²⁶ if ᵃI looked at the sun when it was
　　　shining,
　　and the moon advancing as a
　　　precious thing,
²⁷ so that my heart was secretly enticed,
　　and my hand threw them a kiss from
　　　my mouth,
²⁸ then this also would be iniquity to be
　　　judged,
　　for I would have been false to God
　　　above.
²⁹ If ᵃI have rejoiced over the
　　　misfortune of my enemy
　　or exulted because calamity¹ found
　　　him—
³⁰ ᵃI have not even permitted my mouth
　　　to sin
　　by asking for his life through a curse—
³¹ if the members of my household
　　　have never said,
　　'If only there were someone
　　who has not been satisfied from Job's
　　　meat!'—
³² ᵃbut no stranger had to spend the
　　　night outside,
　　for I opened my doors to the traveler—
³³ if I have covered my transgressions
　　　ᵃas men do,
　　by hiding iniquity in my heart,
³⁴ because I was terrified of the great
　　　ᵃmultitude,
　　and the contempt of families
　　　terrified me,
　　so that I remained silent
　　and would not go outdoors—

Job's Appeal

³⁵ "ᵃIf only I had someone to hear me!
　　Here is my signature—
　　let the Almighty answer me!
　　If only I had an indictment¹
　　ᵇthat my accuser had written.
³⁶ Surely I would wear it proudly on my
　　　shoulder,
　　I would bind it on me like a crown;
³⁷ I would give him an accounting of my
　　　steps;
　　like a prince I would draw near to him.

31:12 ¹Heb. to Abaddon.　31:13 ᵃ[Deut 24:14–15]　31:14 ᵃ[Ps 44:21]　31:15 ᵃJob 34:19; Prov 14:31; 22:2; [Mal 2:10]　31:16 ᵃJob 29:12　31:20 ᵃ[Deut 24:13]　31:21 ᵃJob 22:9　¹Heb. gate; the city gate was the place of both business and justice.　31:23 ᵃIsa 13:6　¹LXX For the terror of God restrained me.　31:24 ᵃ[Matt 6:19–20; Mark 10:23–25]　31:25 ᵃJob 1:3, 10; Ps 62:10　31:26 ᵃ[Deut 4:19; 17:3]; Ezek 8:16　31:29 ᵃ[Prov 17:5; 24:17]; Obad 12　¹Heb. evil; anything that harms, interrupts, or destroys life.　31:30 ᵃ[Matt 5:44]　31:32 ᵃGen 19:2–3　31:33 ᵃGen 3:10; [Prov 28:13]　31:34 ᵃExod 23:2　31:35 ᵃJob 19:7; 30:20, 24, 28　ᵇJob 13:22, 24; 33:10　¹Heb. a scroll; containing the accusations of Job's legal adversary.

Job's Final Solemn Oath

38 "If my land cried out against me
  and all its furrows wept together,
39 if [a]I have eaten its produce without
    paying,
  or [b]caused the death[1] of its owners,
40 then let [a]thorns sprout up in place of
    wheat,
  and in place of barley, noxious weeds."

The words of Job are ended.

V. THE SPEECHES OF ELIHU
(32:1–37:24)

Elihu's First Speech

32 So these three men refused to answer Job further, because he was [a]righteous in his[1] own eyes. [2]Then Elihu son of Barakel the [a]Buzite, of the family of Ram, became very angry. He was angry with Job for [b]justifying himself rather than God.[1] [3]With Job's three friends he was also angry because they could not find an answer, and so declared Job guilty. [4]Now Elihu had waited before speaking[1] to Job because the others were older than he was. [5]But when Elihu saw that the three men had no further reply, he became very angry.

Elihu Claims Wisdom

[6]So Elihu son of Barakel the Buzite spoke up:

  "I am [a]young, but you are elderly;
  that is why I was fearful
  and afraid to explain to you what I
    know.
7 I said to myself, 'Age should speak,
  and length of years should make
    wisdom known.'
8 But it is a spirit in people,
  [a]the breath of the Almighty,
  that makes them understand.
9 It is not the [a]aged who are wise,
  nor old men who understand what is
    right.
10 Therefore I say, 'Listen[1] to me.
  I, even I, will explain what I know.'
11 Look, I waited for you to speak;

I listened closely to your wise
  thoughts,[1] while you were
  searching for words.
12 Now I was paying you close attention,
  yet there was no one proving Job
    wrong,
  not one of you was answering his
    statements.
13 [a]So do not say, 'We have found
    wisdom.
  God will refute him, not man.'
14 Job has not directed his words to me,
  and so I will not reply to him with
    your arguments.[1]

Job's Friends Failed to Answer

15 "They are dismayed and cannot
    answer anymore;
  they have nothing left to say.
16 And I have waited. But because they
    do not speak,
  because they stand there and answer
    no more,
17 I too will answer my part;
  I too will explain what I know.
18 For I am full of words,
  and the spirit within me
    constrains me.
19 Inside I am like wine that has no
    outlet,
  like new wineskins[1] ready to burst!
20 I will speak, so that I may find relief;
  I will open my lips, so that I may
    answer.
21 I will not show partiality to any
    person,
  nor will I confer a title on anyone.
22 For I do not know how to give
    honorary titles;
  if I did, my Creator would quickly do
    away [a]with me.[1]

Elihu Invites Job's Attention

33 "But now, O Job, listen to my words,
  and hear everything I have to say.
2 See now, I have opened my mouth;
  my tongue in my mouth has spoken.
3 My words come from the
    uprightness of my heart,
  and my lips will utter knowledge
    sincerely.

31:39 [a]Job 24:6, 10–12; [Jas 5:4]   [b]1 Kgs 21:19   [1]Some wss *grieved*.   **31:40** [a]Gen 3:18   **32:1** [a]Job 6:29; 31:6; 33:9   [1]Sev. wss *in their eyes*.   **32:2** [a]Gen 22:21   [b]Job 27:5–6   [1]LXX, Latin *before God*.   **32:4** [1]MT *he waited for Job with words*.   **32:6** [a]Lev 19:32   **32:8** [a]1 Kgs 3:12; 4:29; [Job 35:11; 38:36; Prov 2:6; Eccl 2:26; Dan 1:17; 2:21; Matt 11:25; Jas 1:5]   **32:9** [a][1 Cor 1:26]   **32:10** [1]Maj. MSS sing. imperative (addressed to Job); two MSS pl.   **32:11** [1]Heb. *understanding*.   **32:13** [a][Jer 9:23; 1 Cor 1:29]   **32:14** [1]Heb. *your words*.   **32:19** [1]LXX *like smith's bellows*.   **32:22** [a]Job 27:8   [1]Heb. *quickly carry me away*.

4 The Spirit of God has made me,
    and [a]the breath of the Almighty gives
    me life.
5 Reply to me, if you can;
    set your arguments in order
    before me
    and take your stand.
6 [a]Look, I am just like you in relation
    to God;
    I too have been molded from clay.
7 [a]Therefore no fear of me should
    terrify you,
    nor should my pressure[1] be heavy on
    you.

Elihu Rejects Job's Plea of Innocence

8 "Indeed, you have said in my hearing
    (I heard the sound of the words!):
9 'I am pure, [a]without transgression;
    I am clean and have no iniquity.
10 Yet God finds occasions with me;
    [a]he regards me as his enemy.
11 He puts my feet in shackles;
    [a]he watches closely all my paths.'
12 Now in this, you are not right—I
    answer you,
    for God is greater than a human
    being.[1]
13 Why do you [a]contend against him,
    that he does not answer all a
    person's[1] words?

Elihu Disagrees with Job's View of God

14 "[a]For God speaks, the first time in
    one way,
    the second time in another,
    though a person does not perceive it.
15 In a dream, a night vision,
    when deep sleep falls on people
    as they sleep [a]in their beds,
16 then [a]he gives a revelation[1] to people
    and terrifies them with warnings,[2]
17 to turn a person from his sin,[1]
    and to cover a person's pride.
18 He spares a person's life from
    corruption,
    his very life from crossing over the
    river.
19 Or a person is chastened[1] by pain on
    his [a]bed

and with the continual strife of his
    bones,
20 [a]so that his life loathes [b]food
    and his soul rejects appetizing fare.
21 His flesh wastes away from sight,
    and his bones, which were not seen,
    are easily visible.[1]
22 He draws near to the place of
    corruption,
    and his life to the messengers of
    death.
23 If there is an angel beside him,
    one mediator out of a thousand,
    to tell a person what constitutes his
    uprightness,
24 and if God is gracious to him and says,
    'Spare him from going down
    to the place of corruption,
    I have found a ransom for him,'
25 then his flesh is restored like a
    youth's;
    he returns to the days of his youthful
    vigor.
26 He entreats God, and God delights in
    him;
    he sees God's face with rejoicing,
    and God restores to him his
    righteousness.
27 That person sings to others, [a]saying:
    '[b]I have sinned and falsified what is
    right,
    but I was not punished according to
    what I deserved.
28 He [a]redeemed my life
    from going down to the place of
    corruption,
    and my life sees the light!'

Elihu's Appeal to Job

29 "Indeed, God does all these things,
    twice, three times, in his dealings
    with a person,
30 [a]to turn back his life from the place
    of corruption,
    that he may be enlightened with the
    light of life.
31 Pay attention, Job—listen to me;
    be silent, and I will speak.
32 If you have any words, reply to me;
    speak, for I want to justify you.

33:4 [a] [Gen 2:7]; Job 32:8   33:6 [a] Job 4:19   33:7 [a] Job 9:34   [1] LXX *hand.*   33:9 [a] Job 10:7   33:10 [a] Job 13:24; 16:9
33:11 [a] Job 13:27; 19:8   33:12 [1] LXX *he that is above men is eternal.*   33:13 [a] Job 40:2; [Isa 45:9]   [1] MT *all his word.*
33:14 [a] Job 33:29; 40:5; Ps 62:11   33:15 [a] [Num 12:6]   33:16 [a] [Job 36:10, 15]   [1] Lit. *he uncovers the ear of men.*
[2] Heb. *and seals their bonds;* LXX *appearances of fear.*   33:17 [1] LXX *from his iniquity;* MT *deed.*   33:19 [a] Job
30:17   [1] LXX [God] *chastens.*   33:20 [a] Ps 107:18   [b] Job 3:24; 6:7   33:21 [1] Heb. *are laid bare.*   33:27 [a] [2 Sam
12:13; Prov 28:13; Luke 15:21; 1 John 1:9]   [b] [Rom 6:21]   33:28 [a] Isa 38:17   33:30 [a] Ps 56:13

33 If not, you ªlisten to me;
  be silent, and I will teach you wisdom."

Elihu's Second Speech

34 Elihu answered:

2 "Listen to my words, you wise men;
  hear me, you learned men.
3 ªFor the ear assesses words
  as the mouth[1] tastes food.
4 Let us evaluate for ourselves what is
    right;
  let us come to know among ourselves
    what is good.
5 For Job says, 'ªI am innocent,
  but ᵇGod turns away my right.
6 Concerning my right, ªshould I lie?
  My wound is incurable,
  although I am without transgression.'
7 Who is there like Job,
  ªwho drinks derision like water?
8 He goes about in company with
    evildoers;
  he goes along with wicked men.
9 For ªhe says, 'It does not profit a man
  when he makes his delight with God.'

God Is not Unjust

10 "Therefore, listen to me, you men of
    understanding.
  ªFar be it from God to do wickedness,
  from the Almighty to do evil.
11 For he repays a person ªfor his work,
  and according to the conduct of a
    person,
  he causes the consequences to find
    him.
12 Indeed, in truth, God does not act
    wickedly,
  and the Almighty does not ªpervert
    justice.
13 Who entrusted to him the earth?
  And who put him over the whole
    world?
14 If God were to set his heart on it,[1]
  and gather ªin his spirit and his breath,
15 ªall flesh would perish together,
  and human beings would return to
    dust.

God Is Impartial and Omniscient

16 "If you have understanding, listen to
    this,
  hear what I have to say.
17 ªDo you really think
  that one who hates justice can
    govern?
  And will you declare ᵇguilty
  the supremely Righteous One,
18 ªwho says to a king,[1] 'Worthless man,'
  and to nobles, 'Wicked men,'
19 who shows no partiality to princes,
  and does not take note of the rich
    more than the poor
  because all of them are the work of
    ªhis hands?
20 In a moment they die, ªin the middle
    of the night;
  people are shaken, and they pass
    away.
  The mighty are removed effortlessly.
21 For his eyes are on the ways of an
    individual;
  he observes all a person's steps.
22 ªThere is no darkness, and no deep
    darkness,
  where evildoers can hide themselves.
23 For he does not still consider a
    person,
  that he should come before God in
    judgment.
24 He shatters ªthe great without
    inquiry[1]
  and sets up others in their place.
25 Therefore, he knows their deeds;
  he overthrows them in the night,
  and they are crushed.
26 He strikes them for their wickedness
  in a place where people can see,
27 because they have ªturned away from
    following him
  and have not understood any of his
    ways,
28 so that they ªcaused the cry of the
    poor
  to come before him,
  so that he ᵇhears the cry of the needy.
29 But if God is quiet, who can condemn
    him?

33:33 ªPs 34:11   34:3 ªJob 6:30; 12:11   [1]Or *palate*.   34:5 ªJob 13:18; 33:9   ᵇJob 27:2   34:6 ªJob 6:4; 9:17   34:7 ªJob 15:16
34:9 ªMal 3:14   34:10 ª[Gen 18:25; Deut 32:4; 2 Chr 19:7]; Job 8:3; 36:23; Ps 92:15; Rom 9:14   34:11 ªJob 34:25; Ps 62:12;
[Prov 24:12; Jer 32:19]; Ezek 33:20; [Matt 16:27]; Rom 2:6; [2 Cor 5:10; Rev 22:12]   34:12 ªJob 8:3   34:14 ªJob 12:10;
Ps 104:29; [Eccl 12:7]   [1]LXX, Syr. *if he* [God] *recalls*.   34:15 ª[Gen 3:19]; Job 10:9; [Eccl 12:7]   34:17 ª2 Sam 23:3;
Job 34:30   ᵇJob 40:8   34:18 ªExod 22:28   [1]Heb. *Does one say*.   34:19 ª[Deut 10:17; Acts 10:34; Rom 2:11–12]
34:20 ªExod 12:29; Job 34:25; 36:20   34:22 ª[Ps 139:11–12; Amos 9:2–3]   34:24 ªJob 12:19; [Dan 2:21]   [1]Heb.
[with] *no investigation*.   34:27 ª1 Sam 15:11   34:28 ªJob 35:9; Jas 5:4   ᵇ[Exod 22:23]; Job 22:27

If he hides his face, then who can see
    him?
Yet he is over the individual and the
    nation alike,
30 so that the godless man should not
    rule
and not lay snares for the people.

Job Is Foolish to Rebel

31 "Has anyone said to God,
'I have endured chastisement,
but I will not act wrongly any more;
32 teach me what I cannot see;[1]
if I have done evil, I will do so no
    more'?
33 Is it your opinion that God should
    recompense it,
because you reject this?
But you must choose, and not I,
so tell us what you know.
34 Men of understanding say to me—
any wise man listening to me says—
35 that [a]Job speaks without knowledge
and his words are without
    understanding.
36 But[1] Job will be tested to the end,
because his answers are like those of
    wicked men.
37 For he adds [a]transgression to his sin;
in our midst he claps his hands
and multiplies his words against God."

Elihu's Third Speech

35 Then Elihu answered:

2 "Do you think this to be just
when you say, 'My right before God'?
3 But [a]you say, 'What will it profit you,'
and, 'What do I gain by not sinning?'
4 I[1] will reply to [a]you,
and to your friends with you.
5 Gaze [a]at the heavens and see;
consider the clouds, which are higher
    than you.
6 If you sin, how does it affect God?
If your transgressions are many,
what does it do to him?
7 [a]If you are righteous, what do you
    give to God,

or what does he receive from your
    hand?
8 Your wickedness affects only a
    person like yourself,
and your righteousness only other
    people.

9 "People cry out
[a]because of the excess of oppression;
they cry out for help
because of the power of the mighty.
10 But no one says, '[a]Where is God, my
    Creator,
[b]who gives songs in the night,
11 who [a]teaches us more than[1] the wild
    animals of the earth,
and makes us wiser than the birds of
    the sky?'
12 Then they cry out—but [a]he does not
    answer—
because of the arrogance of the
    wicked.
13 [a]Surely it is an empty cry—God does
    not hear it;
the Almighty does not take notice
    of it.
14 How much [a]less, then,
when [b]you say that you do not
    perceive him,
that the case is before him
and you are waiting for him!
15 And further, when you say
that his anger does not [a]punish,[1]
and that he does not know
    transgression!
16 So Job opens his mouth to no
    purpose;
without knowledge [a]he multiplies
    words."

Elihu's Fourth Speech

36 Elihu said further:

2 "Be patient with me a little longer,
and I will instruct you,
for I still have words to speak on
    God's behalf.
3 With my knowledge I will speak
    comprehensively,[1]

34:32 [1] Heb. *what I do not see.*   **34:35** [a] Job 35:16; 38:2   **34:36** [1] MT *my father.*   **34:37** [a] Job 7:11; 10:1   **35:3** [a] Job 21:15; 34:9
35:4 [a] Job 34:8   [1] An emphatic Heb. construction.   **35:5** [a] Gen 15:5; [Job 22:12; Ps 8:3]   **35:7** [a] Job 22:2; Ps 16:2; Prov 9:12;
[Luke 17:10]; Rom 11:35   **35:9** [a] Job 34:28   **35:10** [a] Isa 51:13   [b] Job 8:21; Ps 42:8; 77:6; 149:5; Acts 16:25   **35:11** [a] Job 36:22;
Ps 94:12; [Isa 48:17]; Jer 32:33; [1 Cor 2:13]   [1] Or *teaches us by the beasts.*   **35:12** [a] Prov 1:28   **35:13** [a] Job 27:9;
[Prov 15:29; Isa 1:15]; Jer 11:11; [Mic 3:4]   **35:14** [a] Job 9:11   [b] [Ps 37:5–6]   **35:15** [a] Ps 89:32   [1] Heb. *to visit;*
a divine intervention for blessing or cursing that changes the destiny of the one visited.
35:16 [a] Job 34:35; 38:2   **36:3** [1] Heb. *I will carry my knowledge to-from afar.*

and to my Creator I will ascribe
  righteousness.
4 For in truth, my words are not false;
  it is one complete in knowledge
  who is with you.
5 Indeed, God is mighty, and ªhe does
    not despise people;
  he is mighty, and firm in his intent.
6 He does not allow the wicked to live,
  but he gives justice to the ªpoor.
7 He does not take his eyes off ªthe
    righteous;
  but with kings on ᵇthe throne
  he seats the righteous and exalts
    them forever.
8 But ªif they are bound in chains
  and held captive by the cords of
    affliction,
9 then he reveals to them what they
    have done
  and their transgressions,
  that they were behaving proudly.
10 And ªhe reveals this for correction
  and says that they must turn¹ from
    evil.
11 If they obey and serve him,
  they live ªout their days in prosperity
  and their years in pleasantness.
12 But if they refuse to listen,
  they pass over the river of death
  and expire without ªknowledge.
13 The godless at heart nourish anger;
  they do not cry out even when he
    binds them.
14 ªThey die in their youth,
  and their life ends among the male
    cultic prostitutes.
15 He delivers the afflicted by their
    afflictions;
  he reveals himself to them by their
    suffering.
16 And surely, he drew you from the
    mouth of distress,
  ªto ᵇa wide place, unrestricted,
  and to the comfort of your table
  filled with rich ᶜfood.
17 But now you are preoccupied with
    the judgment due the ªwicked;
  judgment and justice take hold of
    you.

18 Be ªcareful that no one entices you
    with riches;
  do not let a large bribe turn you
    aside.
19 ªWould your wealth sustain you,
  so that you would not be in distress,
  even all your mighty efforts?
20 Do not long for the cover of night
  to drag people away from their
    homes.
21 Take heed; ªdo not turn to evil,
  for because of this ᵇyou have been
    tested by affliction.
22 Indeed, God is exalted in his power;
  who is a teacher like him?
23 ªWho has prescribed his ways for
    him?
  Or said to him, 'You have done what
    is ᵇwicked'?
24 Remember to ªextol his work,
  which people have praised in song.
25 All humanity has seen it;
  people gaze on it from afar.

The Work and Wisdom of God

26 "Yes, God is great—beyond our
    knowledge!
  The number of his years is
    unsearchable.
27 He ªdraws up drops of water;
  they distill the rain into its mist,
28 ªwhich the clouds pour down
  and shower on humankind
    abundantly.
29 Who can understand the spreading
    of the clouds,
  the thunderings of his pavilion?
30 See how he ªscattered¹ his lightning
    about him;
  he has covered the depths² of the sea.
31 It is ªby these that he judges the
    nations
  and ᵇsupplies food in abundance.
32 With his hands ªhe covers the
    lightning
  and directs it against its target.
33 ªHis thunder announces the coming
    storm,
  the cattle also, concerning the
    storm's approach.

36:5 ª Job 12:13, 16; 37:23; [Ps 99:2–5]   36:6 ª Job 5:15   36:7 ª [Ps 33:18; 34:15]   ᵇ Job 5:11; Ps 113:8   36:8 ª Ps 107:10
36:10 ª Job 33:16; 36:15   ¹ One of the two major Heb. words for "repent."   36:11 ª Job 21:13; [Isa 1:19–20]   36:12 ª Job 4:21
36:14 ª Ps 55:23   36:16 ª Ps 18:19; 31:8; 118:5   ᵇ Ps 23:5   ᶜ Ps 36:8   36:17 ª Job 22:5, 10, 11   36:18 ª Ps 49:7   36:19 ª [Prov
11:4]   36:21 ª Job 36:10; [Ps 31:6; 66:18]   ᵇ Job 36:8, 15; [Heb 11:25]   36:23 ª Job 34:13; [Isa 40:13–14]   ᵇ [Deut 32:4]; Job 8:3
36:24 ª [Ps 92:5; Rev 15:3]   36:27 ª Job 5:10; 37:6, 11; 38:28; Ps 147:8   36:28 ª [Prov 3:20]   36:30 ª Job 37:3   ¹ Heb. to
spread.   ² Heb. roots.   36:31 ª [Acts 14:17]   ᵇ Gen 9:3; Ps 104:14–15   36:32 ª Ps 147:8   36:33 ª 1 Kgs 18:41; Job 37:2

37 At this also my heart pounds
and leaps from its place.
2 Listen carefully to the thunder of his
voice,
to the rumbling that proceeds from
his mouth.
3 Under the whole heaven he lets it go,
even his lightning to the far corners
of the earth.
4 After [a]that a voice roars;
he thunders with an exalted voice,
and he does not hold back his
lightning bolts
when his voice is heard.
5 God thunders with his voice in
marvelous ways;
[a]he does great things beyond our
understanding.
6 For to [a]the snow he says, 'Fall to earth,'
and to the torrential rains, 'Pour
down.'
7 He causes everyone to stop working,
so [a]that [b]all people[1] may know his
work.
8 The wild animals [a]go to their lairs,
and in their dens they remain.
9 A tempest blows out from its
chamber,
icy cold from the driving winds.[1]
10 [a]The breath of God produces ice,
and the breadth of the waters freeze
solid.
11 He loads the clouds with moisture;
he scatters his lightning through the
clouds.
12 The clouds go round in circles,
wheeling about according to his plans,
to carry [a]out all that he commands
them
over the face of the whole inhabited
world.
13 Whether it is for punishment,
or for his land,
or for mercy,
[a]he causes it to find its mark.

14 "Pay attention to this, Job!
Stand still and [a]consider the wonders
God works.
15 Do you know how God commands
them,
how he makes lightning flash in his
storm cloud?
16 [a]Do you know about the balancing of
the clouds,
that wondrous activity of [b]him who
is perfect in knowledge?
17 You, whose garments are hot
when the earth is still because of the
south wind,
18 will you, with him, [a]spread out the
[b]clouds,
solid as a mirror of molten metal?
19 Tell us what we should say to him.
We cannot prepare a case[1]
because of the darkness.
20 Should he be informed that I want to
speak?
If a man speaks, surely he will be
swallowed up!
21 But now, the sun cannot be looked at—
it is bright in the skies—
after a wind passed and swept the
clouds away.
22 From the north he comes in golden
splendor;
around God is awesome majesty.
23 As for the Almighty, [a]we cannot
attain to him!
[b]He is great in power,
but justice and abundant
righteousness he does not oppress.
24 Therefore people [a]fear him,
for he does not regard all the [b]wise in
heart."

VI. THE DIVINE SPEECHES (38:1–42:6)

The Lord's First Speech

38 Then the LORD answered Job [a]out of
the whirlwind:

2 "Who is this [a]who darkens counsel
with [b]words without knowledge?
3 [a]Get ready for a difficult task like a
man;

37:4 [a] Ps 29:3   37:5 [a] Job 5:9; 9:10; 36:26; Rev 15:3   37:6 [a] Ps 147:16–17   37:7 [a] Ps 109:27   [b] Ps 19:3–4   [1] MT *all men whom he made*; i.e., all men of his making.   37:8 [a] Job 38:40; Ps 104:21–22   37:9 [1] Heb. *from the scatterers*; the north winds that bring cold air, ice, snow, and hard rains.   37:10 [a] Job 38:29–30; Ps 147:17–18   37:12 [a] Job 36:32; Ps 148:8   37:13 [a] Exod 9:18, 23; 1 Sam 12:18–19   37:14 [a] Ps 111:2   37:16 [a] Job 36:29   [b] Job 36:4   37:18 [a] Gen 1:6; [Isa 44:24]   [b] Job 9:8; Ps 104:2; [Isa 45:12; Jer 10:12; Zech 12:1]   37:19 [1] Heb. *to arrange, set in order.*   37:23 [a] [Job 11:7–8; Rom 11:33–34; 1 Tim 6:16]   [b] [Job 9:4; 36:5]   37:24 [a] [Matt 10:28]   [b] [Job 5:13; Matt 11:25]; 1 Cor 1:26   38:1 [a] Exod 19:16; Job 40:6   38:2 [a] Job 34:35; 42:3   [b] 1 Tim 1:7   38:3 [a] Job 40:7

I will question you,
and you will inform me.

God's Questions to Job

4 "ᵃWhere were you
when I laid the foundation of the
earth?
Tell me, if you possess understanding.
5 Who set its measurements—if you
know—
or who stretched a measuring line
across it?
6 On what were its bases set,
or who laid its cornerstone—
7 when ᵃthe morning stars sang in
chorus,
and all the sons of God shouted for
joy?

8 "Who shut up the sea with ᵃdoors
when it burst forth, coming out of
the womb,
9 when I made the storm clouds its
garment
and thick darkness its swaddling band,
10 when ᵃI prescribed¹ its limits
and set in place its bolts and doors,
11 when I said, 'To here you may come
and no farther,
here your proud waves will be
confined'?
12 Have you ever in your life
ᵃcommanded the morning,
or made the dawn know its place,
13 that it might seize ᵃthe corners of the
earth
and shake the wicked out of it?
14 The earth takes shape like clay under
a seal;
its features are dyed¹ like a garment.
15 Then from the wicked the ᵃlight is
withheld,
and ᵇthe arm raised in violence is
broken.
16 Have you ᵃgone to the springs that
fill the sea
or walked about in the recesses of
the deep?
17 Have ᵃthe gates of death been
revealed to you?

Have you seen the gates of deepest
darkness?
18 Have you considered the vast
expanses of the earth?
Tell me, if you know it all.

19 "In what direction does light reside,
and darkness, where is its place,
20 that you may take them to their
borders
and perceive the pathways to their
homes?
21 You know, for you were born before
them;
and the number of your days is great!
22 Have you entered ᵃthe storehouse of
the snow
or seen the armory¹ of the hail,
23 which ᵃI reserve for the time of
trouble,
for the day of war and battle?
24 In what direction is lightning
dispersed,
or the east winds scattered over the
earth?
25 Who carves out ᵃa channel for the
heavy rains
and a path for the rumble of thunder,
26 to cause it to rain on an uninhabited
land,
a wilderness where there are no
human beings,
27 to satisfy a devastated and desolate
land,
and ᵃto cause it to sprout with
vegetation?
28 Does the rain ᵃhave a father,
or who has fathered the drops of the
dew?
29 From whose womb does the ice
emerge,
and the ᵃfrost from the sky, who gives
birth to it,
30 when the waters become hard like
stone,
when the surface of the deep is
frozen ᵃsolid?
31 Can you tie the bands of the
ᵃPleiades
or release the cords of Orion?

38:4 ᵃJob 15:7; Ps 104:5   38:7 ᵃJob 1:6   38:8 ᵃGen 1:9; Ps 33:7; 104:9; Prov 8:29; [Jer 5:22]   38:10 ᵃJob 26:10   ¹MT *and I broke.*   38:12 ᵃ[Ps 74:16; 148:5]   38:13 ᵃJob 34:25; Ps 104:35   38:14 ¹MT *they stand up like a garment.*   38:15 ᵃJob 18:5; [Prov 13:9]   ᵇ[Num 15:30]; Ps 10:15; 37:17   38:16 ᵃ[Ps 77:19]; Prov 8:24   38:17 ᵃPs 9:13   38:22 ᵃPs 135:7   ¹The same Heb. term is translated "storehouse" in the first line.   38:23 ᵃExod 9:18; Josh 10:11; Isa 30:30; Ezek 13:11, 13; Rev 16:21   38:25 ᵃJob 28:26   38:27 ᵃPs 104:13–14; 107:35   38:28 ᵃJob 36:27–28; [Ps 147:8; Jer 14:22]   38:29 ᵃ[Job 37:10]; Ps 147:16–17   38:30 ᵃ[Job 37:10]   38:31 ᵃJob 9:9; Amos 5:8

[32] Can you lead out
the constellations in their seasons
or guide the Bear with its cubs?
[33] Do you know [a]the laws of the
heavens,
or can you set up their rule over the
earth?
[34] Can you raise your voice to the clouds
so that a flood of water covers you?[1]
[35] Can you send out lightning bolts, and
they go?
Will they say to you, 'Here we are'?
[36] [a]Who has put wisdom in the heart
or has imparted understanding to
the mind?
[37] Who by wisdom can count the clouds,
and who can tip over the water jars
of heaven,
[38] when the dust hardens into a mass,
and the clumps of earth stick
together?

[39] "Do you hunt prey for the lioness
and satisfy the appetite of the lions
[40] when they crouch in their dens,
when they wait in ambush in the
thicket?
[41] [a]Who prepares prey for the raven,
when its young cry out to God
and wander about for lack of food?

39

"Are you acquainted with the way
the [a]mountain goats[1] give birth?
Do you watch as [b]the wild deer give
birth to their young?
[2] Do you count the months they must
fulfill,
and do you know the time they give
birth?
[3] They crouch; they bear their young;
they bring forth the offspring they
have carried.
[4] Their young grow strong and grow up
in the open;
they go off and do not return to
them.
[5] Who let the wild donkey go free?
Who released the bonds of the
donkey,
[6] [a]to whom I appointed the arid rift
valley for its home,

the salt wastes as its dwelling place?
[7] It scorns the tumult in the town;
it does not hear the shouts of a
driver.
[8] It ranges the hills as its pasture
and searches after [a]every green plant.
[9] Is the [a]wild ox willing to be your
servant?
Will it spend the night at your
feeding trough?
[10] Can you bind the wild ox to a furrow
with its rope;
will it till the valleys, following after
you?
[11] Will you rely on it because its
strength is great?
Will you commit your labor to it?
[12] Can you count[1] on it to bring in[2] your
grain
and gather the grain to your
threshing floor?

[13] [1]"The wings of the ostrich flap with
joy,
but are they the pinions and
plumage of a stork?
[14] For she leaves her eggs on the ground
and lets them be warmed on the soil.
[15] She forgets that a foot might crush
them
or that a wild animal might trample
them.
[16] She is harsh with her young,
as if they were not hers;
she is unconcerned about the
uselessness of her labor.
[17] For God deprived her of wisdom
and did not [a]impart understanding
to her.
[18] But as soon as she springs up,
she laughs at the horse and its rider.

[19] "Do you give the horse its strength?
Do you clothe its neck with a mane?
[20] Do you make it leap like a locust?
Its proud neighing is terrifying!
[21] It[1] paws [a]the ground in the valley,
exulting mightily;
it goes out to meet the weapons.
[22] It laughs at fear and is not dismayed;
it does not shy away from the sword.

38:33 [a] [Ps 148:6]; Jer 31:35–36   38:34 [1] LXX *answer you.*   38:36 [a] [Job 9:4; 32:8; Ps 51:6; Eccl 2:26; Jas 1:5]   38:41 [a] Ps 147:9;
[Matt 6:26; Luke 12:24]   39:1 [a] Deut 14:5; 1 Sam 24:2; Ps 104:18   [b] Ps 29:9   [1] Or *ibex.*   39:6 [a] Job 24:5; Jer 2:24; Hos 8:9
39:8 [a] Gen 1:29   39:9 [a] Num 23:22; Deut 33:17; Ps 22:21; 29:6; 92:10; Isa 34:7   39:12 [1] Or *believe.*   [2] Ket. [that] *he
will return.*   39:13 [1] LXX omits this section on the ostrich.   39:17 [a] Job 35:11   39:21 [a] Jer 8:6   [1] MT *They paw.*

23 On it the quiver rattles;
  the lance and javelin flash.
24 In excitement and impatience it
    consumes the ground;[1]
  it cannot stand still when the
    trumpet is blown.
25 At the sound of the trumpet, it says,
    'Aha!'
  And from a distance it catches the
    scent of battle,
  the thunderous shouting of
    commanders,
  and the battle cries.

26 "Is it by your understanding that the
    hawk soars
  and spreads its wings toward the
    south?
27 Is it at your command that the [a]eagle
    soars
  and builds its nest on high?
28 It lives on a rock and spends the
    night there,
  on a rocky crag and a fortress.
29 From there it spots its prey;
  its eyes gaze intently from a distance.
30 And its young ones devour the blood,
  and [a]where the dead carcasses are,
    there it is."

Job's Reply to God's Challenge

40 Then the LORD [a]answered Job:

2 "Will [a]the one who contends with the
    Almighty correct him?
  Let the person who [b]accuses God give
    him an answer!"

3 Then Job answered the LORD:
4 "Indeed, [a]I am completely
    unworthy—how could I reply to
    you?
  I put my hand over my mouth to
    silence myself.
5 I have spoken once, but I cannot
    answer;
  twice, but I will say no more."

The Lord's Second Speech

6 Then [a]the LORD answered Job from the
whirlwind:

7 "Get ready for a [a]difficult task like a
    man.
  I will question you, and you will
    inform me.
8 Would you indeed annul my justice?
  [a]Would you declare me guilty so that
    you might be right?
9 Do you [a]have an arm as powerful as
    God's,
  and can you thunder with a voice like
    his?
10 Adorn yourself, [a]then, with majesty
    and excellency,
  and clothe yourself with glory and
    honor.
11 Scatter abroad the abundance of
    your anger.
  Look at every proud man and bring
    him low.
12 Look at every proud [a]man and abase
    him;
  crush the wicked on the spot.
13 Hide them in the dust together;
  imprison them in the grave.
14 Then I myself will acknowledge to you
  that your own right hand can save
    you.

The Description of Behemoth

15 "Look now at Behemoth, which I
    made as I made you;
  it eats grass like the ox.
16 Look at its strength in its loins
  and its power in the muscles of its
    belly.
17 It makes its tail stiff like a cedar;
  the sinews of its thighs are tightly
    wound.
18 Its bones are tubes of bronze,
  its limbs like bars of iron.
19 It ranks first among the [a]works of God;
  the One who made it
  has furnished it with a sword.[1]
20 For the hills [a]bring it food,
  where all the wild animals play.
21 Under the lotus trees it lies,
  in the secrecy of the reeds and the
    marsh.
22 The lotus trees conceal it in their
    shadow;
  the poplars by the stream conceal it.

39:24 [1] A metaphor for the horse's running.   **39:27** [a] Prov 30:18–19   **39:30** [a] Matt 24:28; Luke 17:37   **40:1** [a] Job 38:1
40:2 [a] Job 9:3; 10:2; 33:13   [b] Job 13:3; 23:4   **40:4** [a] Job 29:9; Ps 39:9   **40:6** [a] Job 38:1   **40:7** [a] Job 42:4   **40:8** [a] Job 16:11;
19:6; [Ps 51:4; Rom 3:4]   **40:9** [a] Job 37:4; [Ps 29:3–4]   **40:10** [a] Ps 93:1; 104:1   **40:12** [a] 1 Sam 2:7; [Isa 2:12; 13:11]; Dan
4:37   **40:19** [a] Job 26:14   [1] MT *let the one who made him draw near* [with] *his sword.*   **40:20** [a] Ps 104:14

²³ If the river rages, it is not disturbed;
it is secure, though the Jordan
should surge up to its mouth.
²⁴ Can anyone catch it by its eyes
or pierce its nose with a snare?

The Description of Leviathan

41 ¹ "Can you pull in [a]Leviathan with a hook
and tie down its tongue with a rope?
² Can you [a]put a cord through its nose
or pierce its jaw with a hook?
³ Will it make numerous supplications
to you;
will it speak to you with tender
words?
⁴ Will it make a pact with you,
so you could take it as your slave for
life?
⁵ Can you play with it, like a bird,
or tie it on a leash for your girls?
⁶ Will partners bargain for it?
Will they divide it up among the
merchants?
⁷ Can you fill its hide with harpoons
or its head with fishing spears?
⁸ If you lay your hand on it,
you will remember the fight.
Do not do it again![l]
⁹ See, his expectation is wrong;
he is laid low even at the sight of it.
¹⁰ Is it not fierce when it is awakened?
Who is he, then, who can stand
before it?[1]
¹¹ [a]Who has confronted me that [b]I
should repay?
Everything under heaven belongs
to me!
¹² I will not keep silent about its limbs,
and the extent of its might,
and the grace of its arrangement.
¹³ Who can uncover its outer
covering?[1]
Who can penetrate to the inside of
its armor?
¹⁴ Who can open the doors of its
mouth?
Its teeth all around are fearsome.
¹⁵ Its back[1] has rows of shields,
shut up closely together as with a
seal;

¹⁶ each one is so close to the next
that no air can come between them.
¹⁷ They lock tightly together, one to the
next;
they cling together and cannot be
separated.
¹⁸ Its snorting throws out flashes of
light;
its eyes are like the red glow of dawn.
¹⁹ Out of its mouth go flames;
sparks of fire shoot forth!
²⁰ Smoke streams from its nostrils
as from a boiling pot over burning
rushes.
²¹ Its breath sets coals ablaze,
and a flame shoots from its mouth.
²² Strength lodges in its neck,
and despair runs before it.
²³ The folds of its flesh are tightly
joined;
they are firm on it, immovable.
²⁴ Its heart[1] is hard as rock,
hard as a lower millstone.
²⁵ When it rises up, the mighty are
terrified;
at its thrashing about they
withdraw.
²⁶ Whoever strikes it with a sword
will have no effect,
nor with the spear, arrow, or dart.
²⁷ It regards iron as straw
and bronze as rotten wood.
²⁸ Arrows do not make it flee;
slingstones become like chaff to it.
²⁹ A club is counted as a piece of straw;
it laughs at the rattling of the lance.
³⁰ Its underparts are the sharp points
of potsherds;
it leaves its mark in the mud
like a threshing sledge.
³¹ It makes the deep boil like a
cauldron
and stirs up the sea like a pot of
ointment,
³² It leaves a glistening wake behind it;
one would think the deep had a head
of white hair.
³³ The likes of it is not on earth,
a creature without fear.
³⁴ It looks on every haughty being;
it is king over all that are proud."

41:1 [a] Ps 74:14; 104:26; Isa 27:1   **41:2** [a] 2 Kgs 19:28; Isa 37:29   **41:8** [1] LXX *You will lay a hand on it, [though] remembering the battle that [be]comes in its body, don't let it happen again.*   **41:10** [1] MT *before me.*   **41:11** [a] [Rom 11:35]   [b] Exod 19:5; [Deut 10:14; Job 9:5–10; 26:6–14]; Ps 24:1; 50:12; 1 Cor 10:26, 28   **41:13** [1] Heb. *the face of his garment.*   **41:15** [1] MT *his pride.*   **41:24** [1] I.e., he is cruel and fearless.

Job's Confession

42
Then Job answered the LORD:

2 "I know that you can ᵃdo all things;
no purpose of yours can be thwarted;
3 you asked, 'ᵃWho is this who darkens
counsel without knowledge?'
But ᵇI have declared without
understanding
things too wonderful for me to know.
4 You ᵃsaid, 'Pay attention, and I will
speak;
I will question you, and you will
answer me.'
5 I had heard ᵃof you by the hearing of
the ear,
but now my eye has seen you.
6 Therefore I ᵃdespise myself,
and I repent in dust and ashes!"

VII. THE EPILOGUE (42:7–17)

Job's Restoration

7 After the LORD had spoken these things to Job, he said to Eliphaz the Temanite, "My anger is stirred up against you and your two friends because you have not spoken about me what is right, as my servant Job has. 8 So now take ᵃseven bulls and seven rams and ᵇgo to my servant Job and offer a burnt offering for yourselves. And my servant Job will ᶜintercede for you, and I will respect him,¹ so that I do not deal with you according to your folly, because you have not spoken about me what is right, as my servant Job has."

9 So they went, Eliphaz the Temanite, Bildad the Shuhite, and Zophar the Naamathite, and did just as the LORD had told them; and the LORD had respect for Job.

10 So the LORD restored what Job had lost after he prayed for his friends, ᵃand the LORD doubled all that had belonged to Job. 11 So they came to him, ᵃall his brothers and sisters and all who had known him before, and they dined¹ with him in his house. They comforted him and consoled him for all the trouble the LORD had brought on him, and each one gave him a piece of silver and a gold ring.

12 So ᵃthe LORD blessed the second part of Job's life more than the first. He had ᵇ14,000 sheep, 6,000 camels, 1,000 yoke of oxen, and 1,000 female donkeys. 13 And ᵃhe also had seven sons and three daughters. 14 The first daughter he named Jemimah, the second Keziah, and the third Keren-Happuch. 15 Nowhere in all the land could women be found who were as beautiful as Job's daughters, and their father granted them an inheritance alongside their brothers.

16 After this Job ᵃlived 140 years; he saw his children and their children to the fourth generation. 17 And so Job died, old and ᵃfull of days.

42:2 ᵃ Gen 18:14; [Matt 19:26; Mark 10:27; 14:36; Luke 18:27] 42:3 ᵃ Job 38:2 ᵇ Ps 40:5; 131:1; 139:6 42:4 ᵃ Job 38:3; 40:7 42:5 ᵃ Job 26:14; [Rom 10:17] 42:6 ᵃ Ezra 9:6; Job 40:4 42:8 ᵃ Num 23:1 ᵇ [Matt 5:24] ᶜ Gen 20:17; [Jas 5:15 16; 1 John 5:16] ¹ Heb. *I will lift up his face.* 42:10 ᵃ Deut 30:3; Ps 14:7; 85:1–3; 126:1 42:11 ᵃ Job 19:13 ¹ Heb. *ate bread.* 42:12 ᵃ Job 1:10; 8:7; Jas 5:11 ᵇ Job 1:3 42:13 ᵃ Job 1:2 42:16 ᵃ Job 5:26; Prov 3:16 42:17 ᵃ Gen 15:15; 25:8; Job 5:26

PSALMS

The Book of Psalms is the largest and perhaps most widely used book in the Bible. It explores the full range of human experience in a very personal and practical way. Its 150 songs run from the creation through the patriarchal, theocratic, monarchical, exilic, and postexilic periods. The tremendous breadth of subject matter in the Psalms includes jubilation, war, peace, worship, judgment, messianic prophecy, praise, and lament. The Psalms were set to the accompaniment of stringed instruments and served as the temple hymnbook and devotional guide for the Jewish people. The psalms were gradually collected and the book originally unnamed, perhaps due to the great variety of material. It came to be known as *Sepher Tehillim*—"Book of Praises"—because almost every psalm contains some note of praise to God. The Septuagint uses the Greek word *Psalmoi* as its title for this book, meaning "Poems Sung to the Accompaniment of Musical Instruments." It also calls it the *Psalterium* ("A Collection of Songs"), and this word is the basis for the term *psalter*. The Latin title is *Liber Psalmorum*, "Book of Psalms."

BOOK 1 (PSALMS 1–41)

1
How blessed [a] is the one[1] who does
  not follow the advice of the wicked,
[b] or stand in the pathway with
  sinners,
or sit in the assembly of scoffers.
2 Instead[1] he finds pleasure in obeying
  the LORD's commands;
he meditates on [a] his [b] commands day
  and night.
3 He is like a tree [a] planted by flowing
  streams;
it yields its fruit at the proper time,
and its leaves never fall off.
He succeeds [b] in everything he
  attempts.
4 Not so with the wicked!
Instead[1] they are [a] like wind-driven
  chaff.
5 For this reason the wicked cannot
  withstand judgment,
nor can sinners join the assembly of
  the godly.

6 Certainly [a] the LORD guards the way
  of the godly,
but the way of the wicked ends in
  destruction.[1]

2
Why [a] do the nations rebel?
Why are the countries devising plots
  that will fail?
2 The kings of the earth form a united
  front;
the [a] rulers collaborate
against the LORD and his anointed
  [b] king.
3 They say, "Let's tear off the shackles
  they've put on [a] us.
Let's free ourselves from their ropes."
4 The one enthroned in heaven laughs
  in disgust;
the Lord taunts them.
5 Then he angrily speaks to them
and terrifies them in his rage,
  saying,
6 "I myself[1] have installed my king
on Zion, my holy hill."

1:1 [a] Prov 4:14 [b] Ps 26:4–5; Jer 15:17 [1] Heb. [Oh] *the happiness* [of] *the man*; Heb. wisdom literature often assumes and reflects the male-oriented perspective of ancient Israelite society, but the principle is certainly applicable to all people. 1:2 [a] Ps 119:14, 16, 35 [b] [Josh 1:8] [1] A Heb. expression of strong contrast. 1:3 [a] [Ps 92:12–14]; Jer 17:8; Ezek 19:10 [b] Gen 39:2–3, 23; Ps 128:2 1:4 [a] Job 21:18; Ps 35:5; Isa 17:13 [1] A Heb. expression of strong contrast. 1:6 [a] Ps 37:18; [Nah 1:7; John 10:14; 2 Tim 2:19] [1] Heb. *but the way of the wicked perishes*; their course of life or their sinful behavior. 2:1 [a] Acts 4:25–26 2:2 [a] [Matt 12:14; 26:3–4, 59–66; 27:1–2; Mark 3:6; 11:18] [b] [John 1:41] 2:3 [a] Luke 19:14 2:6 [1] An emphatic Heb. construction.

7 The king says, "I will announce the
    LORD's decree. He said to me:
  'ªYou are my son. This very day I have
    become your father.
8 Ask me,
  and I will give you the nations as
    your inheritance,
  the ends of the earth as your
    personal property.
9 You will break them[1] with an iron
    scepter;[2]
  ªyou will smash them like a potter's
    jar.'"
10 So now, you kings, do what is wise;
  you rulers of the earth, submit to
    correction.
11 Serve the LORD in fear.
  Repent in terror.
12 Give sincere homage.
  Otherwise he will be angry,
  and you will die because of your
    behavior,
  when ªhis anger quickly ignites.
  How ᵇblessed are all who take shelter
    in him!

*A psalm of David, written when
he fled from his son Absalom.*

3 LORD, how numerous are my enemies!
  Many attack me.
2 Many say about me,
  "God will not deliver him."   *Selah*
3 But you, LORD, ªare a shield that
    protects me;
  you are my glory and ᵇthe one who
    restores me.[1]
4 To ªthe LORD I cried out,
  and he answered me from his
    ᵇholy hill.   *Selah*
5 I rested and slept;
  ªI awoke, for the LORD protects me.
6 I am not ªafraid of the multitude of
    people
  who attack me from all directions.
7 Rise up, LORD!
  Deliver me, my God!
  Yes, you will strike all my enemies on
    the jaw;

you will break the teeth of the wicked.
8 The LORD ªdelivers;
  you show favor to your people.[1]
                                   Selah

*For the music director, to be accompanied
by stringed instruments; a psalm of David.*

4 When I call out, answer me,
  O God who vindicates me.
  Though I am hemmed in, you will
    lead me into a wide, open place.
  Have mercy on me and respond to
    my prayer.
2 You men, how long will you try to
    turn my honor into shame?
  How long will you love what is
    worthless
  and search for what is deceptive?
                                   Selah
3 Realize that ªthe LORD shows the
    godly special favor;
  the LORD responds when I cry out to
    him.
4 ªTremble with fear and do not sin.
  ᵇMeditate as you lie in bed, and
    repent of your ways.   *Selah*
5 Offer ªthe prescribed sacrifices
  and trust in the LORD.
6 Many say, "Who can show us
    anything good?"
  Smile upon us, ªLORD!
7 You make me ªhappier
  than those who have abundant grain
    and wine.
8 I ªwill lie down and sleep peacefully,
  ᵇfor you, LORD, make me safe and
    secure.

*For the music director, to be accompanied
by wind instruments; a psalm of David.*

5 ªListen to what I say, LORD!
  Carefully consider my complaint!
2 Pay attention to my cry for help,
  my King and my God,
  for I am praying to you!
3 LORD, ªin the morning you will
    hear[1] me;

2:7 ª Matt 3:17; Mark 1:1, 11; Luke 3:22; John 1:18; Acts 13:33; [Heb 1:5; 5:5]   2:9 ª Ps 89:23; 110:5–6; [Rev 2:26–27; 12:5; 19:15]   [1] LXX *you will shepherd them* (cf. Rev 2:27; 12:5; 19:15).   [2] Or *staff, rod.*   2:12 ª [Rev 6:16–17]   ᵇ [Ps 5:11; 34:22]   3:3 ª Ps 5:12; 28:7   ᵇ Ps 9:13; 27:6   [1] Heb. [the one who] *lifts my head*; a general strengthening of the psalmist or restoration to his former position.   3:4 ª Ps 4:3; 34:4   ᵇ Ps 2:6; 15:1; 43:3   3:5 ª Lev 26:6; Ps 4:8; Prov 3:24   3:6 ª Ps 23:4; 27:3   3:8 ª Ps 28:8; 35:3; [Isa 43:11]   [1] Heb. *upon your people* [is] *your blessing.*   4:3 ª [2 Tim 2:19]   4:4 ª [Ps 119:11; Eph 4:26]   ᵇ Ps 77:6   4:5 ª Deut 33:19; Ps 51:19   4:6 ª Num 6:26; Ps 80:3, 7, 19   4:7 ª Ps 97:11–12; Isa 9:3; Acts 14:17   4:8 ª Job 11:19; Ps 3:5   ᵇ [Lev 25:18]; Deut 12:10   5:1 ª Ps 4:1   5:3 ª Ps 55:17; 88:13   [1] Or *LORD, in the morning hear me.*

in the morning I will present my case
to you and then wait expectantly
for an answer.
4 Certainly you are not a God who
approves of evil;
evil people cannot dwell with you.
5 Arrogant [a]people cannot [b]stand in
your presence;[1]
you hate all who behave wickedly.
6 You destroy liars;
the LORD despises [a]violent and
deceitful people.
7 But as for me, because of your great
faithfulness I will enter your house;
I will bow down toward your holy
temple as I worship you.
8 LORD, [a]lead me in your righteousness
because of those who wait to
ambush me,
remove the obstacles in the way in
which you are guiding me.
9 For[1] they do not speak [a]the truth;
their stomachs are like the place of
destruction,
their throats like an open grave,
their tongues like a steep slope
leading into it.
10 Condemn them, O God!
May their own schemes be their
downfall.
Drive them away because of their
many acts of insurrection,
for they have rebelled against you.
11 But may all who take shelter in you
be happy.
May they continually shout for joy.
Shelter them so that those who are
loyal to you may rejoice.
12 Certainly you reward[1] the godly,
LORD.
Like a shield you protect them in
your good favor.

For the music director, to be accompanied
by stringed instruments, according
to the sheminith style;[1] a psalm of David.

6 LORD, [a]do not rebuke me in your
anger.
Do not discipline me in your raging
fury.

2 Have mercy on me, LORD, for I am
frail.
[a]Heal me, LORD, for my bones are
shaking.
3 I am absolutely [a]terrified,
and you, LORD—how long will this
continue?
4 Relent, LORD, rescue me!
Deliver me because of your
faithfulness.
5 [a]For no one remembers you in the
realm of death.
In Sheol who gives you thanks?
6 I am exhausted as I groan.
All night long I drench my bed in
tears;
my tears saturate the cushion
beneath me.
7 My eyes grow dim from suffering;
they grow weak because of all [a]my
enemies.
8 Turn [a]back from me, all you who
behave wickedly,
for the LORD has [b]heard the sound of
my weeping.
9 The LORD has heard my appeal for
mercy;
the LORD has accepted my
prayer.
10 They will be humiliated and
absolutely terrified.
All my enemies will turn back and
be suddenly humiliated.

A musical composition by David,
which he sang to the LORD concerning
a Benjaminite named Cush.

7 O LORD my God, in you [a]I have taken
shelter.
[b]Deliver me from all who chase me.
Rescue me!
2 [a]Otherwise they will rip me to shreds
like a lion;
they will tear me to bits and no one
will be able to rescue me.
3 O LORD my God, [a]if I have done what
they say,
or am guilty of unjust [b]actions,
4 or [a]have wronged my ally,
or helped his lawless enemy,

5 may an enemy relentlessly chase me
  and catch me;
may he trample me to death
and leave me lying dishonored
  in the dust.   *Selah*
6 Stand up angrily, LORD.
  ^aRise up with raging fury against my
  enemies.
Wake up for my sake, and execute
  the judgment you have decreed for
  them.[1]
7 The countries are assembled all
  around you;[1]
take once more your rightful place
  over them.
8 The LORD judges the nations.
  ^aVindicate me, LORD, because ^bI am
  innocent,
because I am blameless, O Exalted
  One.
9 May the evil deeds of the wicked
  come to an end.
But make the innocent secure,
  ^aO righteous God,
you who examine inner thoughts
  and motives.
10 The Exalted God is my shield,
  the one who delivers the morally
  ^aupright.[1]
11 God is a just judge;
  he is angry throughout the day.
12 If a person does not repent, God will
  ^awield his sword.
He has prepared to shoot his bow.
13 He has prepared deadly weapons to
  use against him;
he gets ready to shoot flaming arrows.
14 ^aSee the one who is pregnant with
  wickedness,
who conceives destructive plans,
and gives birth to harmful lies—
15 he digs ^aa pit[1]
and then falls into the hole he has
  made.
16 He becomes the victim of ^ahis own
  destructive plans—

and the violence he intended for
  others falls on his own head.
17 I will thank the LORD for his justice;
  I will sing praises to the LORD Most
  High!

---

*For the music director, according
to the* gittith *style;[1] a psalm of David.*

8 O LORD, our Lord,
how ^amagnificent is your reputation
  throughout the earth!
You ^breveal your majesty in the
  heavens above.[1]
2 From the ^amouths of children and
  nursing babies
you have ordained praise on account
  of your adversaries,
so that you might put an end to ^bthe
  vindictive enemy.
3 When I ^alook up at the heavens,
  which your fingers made,
and see the moon and the stars,
  which you set in place,
4 Of ^awhat importance is the human
  race,[1] that you should notice them?
Of what importance is mankind,[2]
  that you should pay attention ^bto
  them?
5 You made them a little less than the
  heavenly beings.[1]
You crowned mankind with honor
  and majesty.
6 you appoint them to rule over ^ayour
  creation;
^byou have placed everything under
  their authority,
7 including all the sheep and cattle,
  as well as the wild animals,
8 the birds in the sky, the fish in the
  sea,
and everything that moves through
  the currents of the seas.
9 O ^aLORD, our Lord,
how magnificent is your reputation
  throughout the earth!

7:6 ^aPs 35:23; 44:23   [1]Heb. *Wake up to me* [with the] *judgment* [which] *you have commanded*; LXX *my God* instead of
"for my sake."   **7:7** [1]Or perhaps *may the assembly of the peoples surround you*; Heb. *and the assembly of the peoples
surrounds you.*   **7:8** ^aPs 26:1; 35:24; 43:1   ^bPs 18:20; 35:24   **7:9** ^a[1 Sam 16:7]   **7:10** ^aPs 97:10–11; 125:4   [1]Heb. *pure of
heart*; the seat of one's moral character and motives.   **7:12** ^aDeut 32:41   **7:14** ^aJob 15:35; Isa 59:4; [Jas 1:15]   **7:15** ^a[Job
4:8]; Ps 57:6   [1]Heb. *a pit he digs and he excavates it*; apparently the imagery of hunting is employed.   **7:16** ^aEsth 9:25;
Ps 140:9   **8** [1]Probably a musical style or type of instrument.   **8:1** ^aPs 148:13   ^bPs 113:4   [1]Heb. *which, give, your majesty
on the heavens.*   **8:2** ^aMatt 21:16; [1 Cor 1:27]   ^bPs 44:16   **8:3** ^aPs 111:2   **8:4** ^aJob 7:17–18; [Heb 2:6–8]   ^b[Job 10:12]
[1]Heb. *What is man*[kind]*?*; used in a collective sense for the human race.   [2]Heb. *and the son of man*; used in
a collective sense for human beings.   **8:5** [1]Heb. *elohim*; the one true God, false gods, or the heavenly
beings.   **8:6** ^a[Gen 1:26, 28]   ^b[1 Cor 15:27; Eph 1:22; Heb 2:8]   **8:9** ^aPs 8:1

For the music director, according to the alumoth-labben style;[1] a psalm of David.

9 I will thank the LORD with all my heart!
I will tell about all your amazing deeds.
[2] I will be happy and [a]rejoice in [b]you.
I will sing praises to you, O Most High.
[3] When my enemies turn back,
they trip and are defeated before you.
[4] For you defended my just cause;
from your throne you pronounced a just decision.
[5] You terrified the nations with your battle cry.
You destroyed the wicked;
you permanently wiped out all memory of them.
[6] The enemy's cities have been reduced to permanent ruins.
You destroyed their cities;[1]
all memory of the enemies has [a]perished.
[7] [a]But the LORD rules forever;
he reigns in a just manner.
[8] He judges [a]the world fairly;
he makes just legal decisions for the nations.
[9] Consequently the LORD provides [a]safety for the oppressed;
he provides safety in times of trouble.
[10] Your loyal [a]followers trust in you,
for you, LORD, do not abandon those who seek your help.[1]
[11] Sing praises to the LORD, who rules in Zion.
[a]Tell the nations what he has done.
[12] For the one who takes revenge against murderers took notice of the oppressed;
[a]he did not overlook their cry for help
[13] when they prayed:
"Have mercy on me, LORD!
See how I am oppressed by those who hate me,

O one who can snatch me away from the gates of death!
[14] Then I will tell about all your praiseworthy acts;
in the gates of Daughter Zion I will [a]rejoice because of your deliverance."
[15] The nations fell into [a]the pit they had made;
their feet were caught in the net they had hidden.
[16] The LORD [a]revealed himself;
he accomplished justice.
The wicked were ensnared by their own actions.   [b]*Higgaion.*[1] *Selah*
[17] The wicked are turned back and sent to Sheol;[1]
this is the destiny of all the nations [a]that ignore God,
[18] for the needy are not permanently ignored,
the hopes of the oppressed are not [a]forever dashed.
[19] Rise up, LORD!
Don't let men be defiant.
May the nations be judged in your presence.
[20] Terrify them, LORD.
Let the nations know they are mere mortals.   *Selah*

10 Why, LORD, do you stand far off?
Why do you pay no attention during times of trouble?
[2] The wicked arrogantly chase the oppressed;
the oppressed are trapped by the schemes the wicked have dreamed up.
[3] Yes,[1] the wicked man [a]boasts because he gets what he wants;
the one who robs others [b]curses and rejects the LORD.
[4] The wicked man is so arrogant he always [a]thinks,
"God won't hold me accountable; he doesn't care."
[5] He is secure at all times.
He has no regard for your commands;[1]
he disdains all his enemies.

9[1] A few MSS *according to the death* [of the son]; LXX *according to alumoth.* The phrase probably refers to a particular tune or musical style.   **9:2** [a] Ps 5:11; 104:34   [b] [Ps 83:18; 92:1]   **9:6** [a] [Ps 34:16]   [1] Heb. *you uprooted cities.*   **9:7** [a] Ps 102:12, 26; Heb 1:11   **9:8** [a] [Ps 96:13; 98:9; Acts 17:31]   **9:9** [a] Ps 32:7; 46:1; 91:2   **9:10** [a] Ps 91:14   [1] Heb. *the ones who seek you.*   **9:11** [a] Ps 66:16; 107:22   **9:12** [a] [Gen 9:5; Ps 72:14]   **9:14** [a] Ps 13:5; 20:5; 35:9   **9:15** [a] Ps 7:15–16   **9:16** [a] Exod 7:5   [b] Ps 92:3   [1] Probably a technical musical term.   **9:17** [a] Job 8:13; Ps 50:22   [1] Heb. *the wicked turn back to Sheol.*   **9:18** [a] Ps 9:12; 12:5   **10:3** [a] Ps 49:6; 94:3–4   [b] Prov 28:4   [1] Or *for.*   **10:4** [a] Ps 14:1; 36:1   **10:5** [1] Heb. [on a] *height, your judgments from before him.*

6 [a]He says to [b]himself,[1]
"I will never be shaken,
because I experience no calamity."
7 His mouth [a]is full of curses and
[b]deceptive, harmful words;
his tongue injures and destroys.
8 He waits in ambush near the villages;
in hidden places he kills the
innocent.
His eyes look for some unfortunate
victim.
9 He lies in ambush in a hidden place,
like a lion in a thicket.
He lies in ambush, waiting to catch
the oppressed;
he catches the oppressed by pulling
in his net.
10 His victims are crushed and beaten
down;
they are trapped in his sturdy nets.
11 He says to himself,
"God overlooks it;
he does not pay attention;
he never notices."
12 Rise up, LORD!
O God, strike him down.[1]
Do not forget the oppressed.
13 Why does the wicked man reject
God?
He says to himself, "You will not hold
me accountable."
14 You have taken [a]notice,
for you always see one who inflicts
pain and suffering.
The unfortunate victim [b]entrusts his
cause to [c]you;
you deliver the fatherless.
15 Break the arm of the wicked and evil
man.
Hold him accountable for his wicked
deeds,
which he thought you would not
discover.
16 The LORD rules forever!
[a]The nations are driven out of his
land.
17 LORD, you have heard the request of
the oppressed;
you make them feel secure because
you listen to their prayer.

18 You defend the fatherless and
oppressed,
so that mere mortals may no longer
terrorize them.

For the music director, by David.

11 In [a]the LORD I have taken shelter.
How can you say to me,
"Flee to a mountain like a bird.[1]
2 For look, [a]the wicked prepare their
bows,
they put their arrows on the strings,
to shoot in the darkness at the
morally upright.[1]
3 [a]When the foundations are
destroyed,
what can the godly accomplish?"
4 The LORD is in his holy temple;
the [a]LORD's throne [b]is in heaven.
His eyes watch;
his eyes examine all people.
5 The LORD approves [a]of the godly,
but he hates the wicked and those
who love to do violence.
6 May he rain down burning coals[1] and
brimstone on the wicked!
[a]A whirlwind is what they deserve.
7 Certainly[1] the LORD is just;
he [a]rewards godly deeds.
The upright will experience his favor.

*For the music director, according
to the* sheminith *style;[1] a psalm of David.*

12 Deliver, LORD!
For the godly have [a]disappeared;
people of integrity have vanished.
2 People lie to one another;
[a]they flatter and deceive.
3 May the LORD cut off all flattering
lips,
and the tongue that boasts!
4 They say, "We speak persuasively;
we know how to flatter and boast.
Who is our master?"
5 "Because of the violence done to the
oppressed,
because of the painful cries of the
needy,

10:6 [a]Ps 49:11; [Eccl 8:11] [b]Rev 18:7 [1]Heb. *he says in his heart/mind.* 10:7 [a][Rom 3:14] [b]Ps 55:10–11 10:12 [1]Heb. *lift up your hand.* 10:14 [a][Ps 11:4] [b][2 Tim 1:12] [c]Ps 68:5; Hos 14:3 10:16 [a]Ps 29:10 11:1 [a]Ps 56:11 [1]Ket. *flee* [masc. pl.!] to your [masc. pl.!] *mountain, bird.* 11:2 [a]Ps 64:3–4 [1]Heb. *pure of heart*; the seat of one's moral character and motives. 11:3 [a]Ps 82:5; 87:1; 119:152 11:4 [a]Ps 2:4; [Isa 66:1]; Matt 5:34; 23:22; [Acts 7:49]; Rev 4:2 [b][Ps 33:18; 34:15–16] 11:5 [a]Gen 22:1; [Jas 1:12] 11:6 [a]1 Sam 1:4; Ps 75:8; Ezek 38:22 [1]MT *traps, fire, and brimstone.* 11:7 [a]Ps 33:5; 45:7 [1]Or *for.* 12 [1]Perhaps a particular style of music. 12:1 [a][Isa 57:1]; Mic 7:2 12:2 [a]Ps 10:7; 41:6

I will spring into action," says the
   LORD.
"I will provide the safety they so
   desperately desire."
6 The LORD's words are absolutely
   [a]reliable.
They are as untainted as silver
   purified in a furnace on the
   ground,
where it is thoroughly refined.
7 You, LORD, will protect them;
you will continually shelter each one
   from these evil people,
8 for the wicked seem to be
   everywhere,
when people promote evil.

For the music director, a psalm of David.

13 How long, LORD, will you continue
   to ignore me?
[a]How long will you pay no attention
   to me?
2 How long must I worry,
and suffer in broad daylight?
How long will my enemy gloat
   over me?
3 Look at me! Answer me, O LORD my
   God!
[a]Revive me, or else I will die.
4 Then my enemy will say, "I have
   defeated him."
Then my foes will rejoice because I
   am shaken.
5 But I trust in your faithfulness.
May I rejoice because of your
   deliverance.
6 I will sing praises to the LORD
when he vindicates me.

For the music director, by David.

14 [a]Fools say to themselves, "There is
   no God."
They sin and commit evil deeds;
none of them does what is right.
2 The LORD looks down from heaven
   at [a]the human race,
to see if there is anyone who is wise
   and seeks God.
3 Everyone rejects God;

[a]they are all morally corrupt.
None of them does what is right,
   not even one.
4 All those who behave wickedly [a]do
   not understand—
those who devour my people as if
   they were eating bread
and do not call out to the LORD.
5 They are absolutely terrified,
for God defends the godly.
6 You want to humiliate the oppressed,
   even though the LORD is their
   [a]shelter.
7 [a]I wish the deliverance of Israel
   would come from Zion!
[b]When the LORD restores the
   well-being of his people,
may Jacob rejoice,
may Israel be happy!

A psalm of David.

15 LORD, [a]who may be a guest in your
   home?
Who may live on your holy hill?
2 Whoever lives a blameless life,
does what is right,
and speaks [a]honestly.
3 He [a]does not slander,
[b]or do harm to others,
or insult his neighbor.
4 [a]He despises a reprobate,
but honors the LORD's loyal
   followers.[1]
He [b]makes firm commitments and
   does not renege on his promise.
5 He does not charge interest when he
   lends his money.
He does not take bribes to testify
   against the innocent.
The one who lives like this will never
   be shaken.

A prayer[1] of David.

16 Protect me, O God, for [a]I have taken
   shelter in you.
2 I say to the LORD, "You are the Lord,
   [a]my only source of well-being."
3 As for God's chosen people [a]who are
   in the land,

12:6 [a]2 Sam 22:31; Ps 18:30; 119:140; Prov 30:5   13:1 [a]Job 13:24; Ps 89:46   13:3 [a]1 Sam 14:29; Ezra 9:8; Job 33:30; Ps 18:28
14:1 [a]Ps 10:4; 53:1   14:2 [a]Ps 33:13–14; 102:19; Rom 3:11   14:3 [a]Rom 3:12   14:4 [a]Ps 79:6; Isa 64:7; Jer 10:25; Amos 8:4; Mic
3:3   14:6 [a]Ps 9:9; 40:17; 46:1; 142:5   14:7 [a]Ps 53:6; [Rom 11:25–27]   [b]Deut 30:3; Job 42:10   15:1 [a]Ps 24:3–5   15:2 [a]Zech
8:16; [Eph 4:25]   15:3 [a][Lev 19:16–18]   [b]Exod 23:1   15:4 [a]Esth 3:2   [b]Lev 5:4   [1]Heb. *those who fear the LORD.*
16 [1]The meaning of the Heb. term is uncertain.   16:1 [a]Ps 56–60   16:2 [a]Job 35:7   16:3 [a]Ps 119:63

and the leading officials I admired so
    much—
4 their troubles multiply;
    they desire other gods.
  I will not pour out drink offerings of
    [a]blood to their gods,
  [b]nor will I make vows in the name of
    their gods.
5 LORD, you give me stability and
    prosperity;
  you make my future secure.[1]
6 It is as if I have been given fertile
    fields
  or received a beautiful tract of land.
7 I will praise the LORD who
    guides me;
  yes, during the night I reflect and
    learn.[1]
8 I constantly trust [a]in the LORD;
  because he is at my right hand, I will
    not be shaken.
9 So my heart rejoices
  and I am happy;
    my life is safe.
10 [a]You will not abandon me to Sheol;
  you will not allow your faithful
    follower to see the Pit.[1]
11 You lead me in the [a]path of life.
  I experience absolute joy in your
    presence;
  you always give me sheer delight.

A prayer of David.

17 LORD, consider my just cause.
    Pay attention to my cry for help.
  Listen to the prayer
  I sincerely offer.
2 Make a just decision on my behalf.
  Decide what is right.
3 You have scrutinized my inner
    motives;
  [a]you have examined me during the
    night.
  You have carefully evaluated me, but
    you find no sin.
  I am determined I will [b]say nothing
    sinful.[1]

4 As for the actions of people—
    just as you have commanded,
  I have not followed in the footsteps
    of violent men.
5 I carefully [a]obey your commands;
  I do not deviate from them.
6 I call to you because you [a]will answer
    me, O God.
  Listen to me!
  Hear what I say!
7 Accomplish awesome, faithful deeds,
  you who powerfully deliver those
    who look to you for protection
    from their enemies.
8 Protect me as you would protect the
    pupil of your eye.[1]
  Hide me in the shadow of your wings.
9 Protect me from the wicked men
    who attack me,
  my enemies who crowd around me
    for the kill.
10 They are [a]calloused;
  they [b]speak arrogantly.
11 They attack me, now they surround
    me;[1]
  they intend to throw me to the
    ground.
12 He is like a lion that wants to tear its
    prey to bits,
  like a young lion crouching in hidden
    places.
13 Rise up, LORD!
  Confront him. Knock him down.
  Use your sword to rescue me from
    the wicked man.
14 LORD, use your power to deliver me
    from these murderers,[1]
  from the murderers of this world.
  They enjoy prosperity;
  you overwhelm them with the riches
    they desire.
  They have many children,
  and leave their wealth to their
    offspring.[2]
15 As for me, because [a]I am [b]innocent I
    will see your face;
  when I [c]awake you will reveal
    yourself to me.[1]

16:4 [a]Ps 106:37–38 [b][Exod 23:13]; Josh 23:7 16:5 [1]Heb. *you take hold of my lot.* 16:7 [1]Heb. *yes,* [during] *nights my kidneys instruct* [or *correct*] *me;* the kidneys are viewed as the seat of the psalmist's moral character. 16:8 [a][Acts 2:25–28] 16:10 [a]Ps 49:15; 86:13; Acts 2:31–32; Heb 13:20 [1]Often used as a title for Sheol. 16:11 [a]Ps 139:24; [Matt 7:14] 17:3 [a]Job 23:10; Ps 66:10; Zech 13:9; [1 Pet 1:7] [b]Ps 39:1 [1]Heb. *you tested me, you do not find, I plan, my mouth will not cross over.* 17:5 [a]Job 23:11; Ps 44:18; 119:133 17:6 [a]Ps 86:7; 116:2 17:8 [1]Heb. *Protect me like the pupil, a daughter of an eye.* 17:10 [a]Ezek 16:49 [b][1 Sam 2:3] 17:11 [1]Heb. *our steps, now they surround me.* 17:14 [1]Heb. *from men* [by] *your hand, LORD.* [2]Heb. *they are satisfied* [with] *sons and leave their abundance to their children.* 17:15 [a][1 John 3:2] [b]Ps 4:6–7; 16:11 [c][Isa 26:19] [1]Heb. *I will be satisfied, when I awake,* [with] *your form.*

For the music director, by the LORD's servant David, who sang to the LORD the words of this song when the LORD rescued him from the power of all his enemies, including Saul.

18 He said:
"[a]I love you, LORD, my source of strength![1]

2 The LORD is my high ridge, my stronghold, my deliverer.
My God is my rocky summit where [a]I take shelter,
my shield, the horn that saves me, and my refuge.

3 I called to the LORD, [a]who is worthy of praise,
and I was delivered from my enemies.

4 The waves[1] of death engulfed me, [a]the currents of chaos overwhelmed me.

5 The ropes of Sheol tightened around me,
the snares of death trapped me.

6 In my distress I called to the LORD;
I cried out to my God.
From his heavenly temple he heard my voice;
he listened to my cry for help.[1]

7 The earth heaved and shook.
[a]The roots of the mountains trembled;
they heaved because he was angry.

8 Smoke ascended from his nose;
fire devoured as it came from his mouth.
He hurled down fiery coals.

9 He made [a]the sky sink as he descended;
a thick cloud was under his feet.

10 He mounted [a]a winged angel[1] and flew;
[b]he glided on the wings of the wind.

11 He shrouded himself in darkness,[1]
in thick rain clouds.[2]

12 [a]From the brightness in front of him came
hail and fiery coals.[1]

13 The LORD thundered in the sky;
the Most High shouted.[1]

14 He shot his arrows and scattered [a]them,
many lightning bolts and routed them.

15 The depths of the sea[1] were exposed;
the inner regions of the world were uncovered
by your battle cry,[2] LORD,
by the powerful breath from your nose.

16 He [a]reached down from above and took hold of me;
he pulled me from the surging water.

17 He rescued me from my strong enemy,
from those who hate me,
for they were too strong for me.

18 They confronted me in my day of calamity,
but the LORD helped me.

19 He brought me out into a wide open place;
[a]he delivered me because he was pleased with me.

20 The LORD repaid me for my godly deeds;
[a]he rewarded my blameless behavior.

21 For I have obeyed the LORD's commands;
I have not rebelled against my God.

22 For I am aware of all his regulations,
and I do not reject his rules.

23 I was innocent before him,
and kept myself from sinning.

24 The LORD rewarded me [a]for my godly deeds;
he took notice of my blameless behavior.

25 You prove to be loyal [a]to one who is faithful;
you prove to be trustworthy to one who is innocent.

26 You prove to be reliable [a]to one who is blameless,
but you prove to be deceptive to one who is perverse.

27 For you deliver oppressed people,
but you bring down those who have a [a]proud look.

18:1 [a] 2 Sam 22 [1] Heb. *my strength.* 18:2 [a] Heb 2:13 18:3 [a] Ps 76:4; Rev 5:12 18:4 [a] Ps 116:3 [1] Heb. *ropes.* 18:6 [1] Heb. *and my cry for help before him came into his ears.* 18:7 [a] Acts 4:31 18:9 [a] Ps 144:5 18:10 [a] Ps 80:1; 99:1 [b] [Ps 104:3] [1] Heb. *a cherub.* 18:11 [1] Heb. *he made darkness his hiding place around him, his covering.* [2] Heb. *darkness of water, clouds of clouds.* 18:12 [a] Ps 97:3; 140:10; Hab 3:11 [1] Heb. *from the brightness in front of him his clouds came, hail and coals of fire.* 18:13 [1] MT adds *hail and coals of fire.* 18:14 [a] Josh 10:10; Ps 144:6; Isa 30:30; Hab 3:11 18:15 [1] MT *water.* [2] Or *rebuke.* 18:16 [a] Ps 144:7 18:19 [a] Ps 4:1; 31:8; 118:5 18:20 [a] 1 Sam 24:19; [Job 33:26]; Ps 7:8 18:24 [a] 1 Sam 26:23; Ps 18:20 18:25 [a] [1 Kgs 8:32; Ps 62:12]; Matt 5:7 18:26 [a] [Lev 26:23–28]; Prov 3:34 18:27 [a] [Ps 101:5]; Prov 6:17

28 [a]Indeed,[1] you light my lamp, LORD.
My God illuminates the darkness
around me.
29 Indeed,[1] with your help I can charge
against an army;
by my God's power I can jump over a
wall.
30 The one true God acts in a faithful
manner;
the LORD's promise [a]is reliable.
[b]He is a shield [c]to all who take
shelter in him.
31 [a]Indeed,[1] who is God besides the
LORD?
Who is a protector besides our God?
32 The one true God [a]gives me strength;
he removes the obstacles in my way.
33 He gives me [a]the agility of a deer;
he [b]enables me to negotiate the
rugged terrain.
34 He trains my hands for battle;
my arms can bend even [a]the
strongest bow.
35 You give me your protective shield;
your right hand supports me.
Your willingness to help enables me
to prevail.
36 You widen my path;
my feet do not slip.
37 I chase my enemies and catch them;
I do not turn back until I wipe them
out.
38 I beat them to death;
they fall at my feet.
39 You give me strength for battle;
you make my foes kneel before me.
40 You make my enemies retreat;[1]
I destroy those who hate me.
41 They cry out, but there is no one to
help them;
they cry out to the LORD, but he does
not answer them.
42 I grind them [a]as fine windblown dust;
I beat them underfoot[1] like clay in
the streets.
43 You rescue me from a hostile army.
[a]You [b]make me a leader of nations;
people over whom I had no authority
are now my subjects.

44 When they hear of my exploits, they
submit to me.
Foreigners are powerless before me.
45 Foreigners lose [a]their courage;
they shake with fear as they leave
their strongholds.[1]
46 The LORD is alive!
My Protector[1] is praiseworthy.
The God who delivers me is exalted
as king.
47 The one true God completely
vindicates me;
he makes nations submit to me.
48 He delivers me from my enemies.
[a]You snatch me away from those who
attack me;
you rescue me from violent men.
49 So I will give you thanks before [a]the
nations, O LORD.
I will sing praises to you.
50 He [a]gives his king magnificent
victories;
he is faithful to his chosen ruler,
to David and his descendants[1]
forever."

For the music director, a psalm of David.

19 The [a]heavens declare the glory of
God;
the [b]sky displays his handiwork.
2 Day after day it speaks out;
night after night it reveals his
greatness.
3 There is no actual speech or word,
nor is its voice literally heard.
4 Yet its voice[1] echoes throughout [a]the
earth;
its words carry to the distant horizon.
In the sky he has pitched a tent for
the sun.
5 Like [a]a bridegroom it emerges from
its chamber;
like a strong man it enjoys running
its course.
6 It emerges from the distant horizon,
and goes from one end of the sky to
the other;
nothing can escape its heat.

18:28 [a]1 Kgs 15:4; Job 18:6; [Ps 119:105] [1]Or *for*. **18:29** [1]Or *for*. **18:30** [a][Deut 32:4]; Rev 15:3 [b]Ps 12:6; 119:140; [Prov 30:5] [c][Ps 17:7] **18:31** [a][Deut 32:31, 39; 1 Sam 2:2; Ps 86:8–10; Isa 45:5] [1]Or *for*. **18:32** [a][Ps 91:2] **18:33** [a]2 Sam 2:18; Hab 3:19 [b]Deut 32:13; 33:29 **18:34** [a]Ps 144:1 **18:40** [1]Heb. *and [as for] my enemies, you give to me [the] back [or neck]*. **18:42** [a]Zech 10:5 [1]MT *I empty them out*. **18:43** [a]2 Sam 8; Ps 89:27 [b]Isa 52:15 **18:45** [a]Mic 7:17 [1]Heb. *their prisons*. **18:46** [1]Heb. *my rocky cliff*. **18:48** [a]Ps 27:6; 59:1 **18:49** [a]2 Sam 22:50; Rom 15:9 **18:50** [a]2 Sam 7:12; Ps 21:1; 144:10 [1]Or *offspring*; Heb. *seed*. **19:1** [a]Isa 40:22; [Rom 1:19–20] [b]Gen 1:6–7 **19:4** [a]Rom 10:18 [1]MT *their measuring line*. **19:5** [a]Eccl 1:5

7 The law of ᵃthe LORD is perfect
  and preserves one's life.
  The rules set down by the LORD¹ are
  reliable
  and impart wisdom ᵇto the
  inexperienced.
8 The LORD's precepts are fair
  and make one joyful.
  The LORD's commands¹ are pure
  and give insight for life.
9 The commands to fear the LORD are
  right
  and endure forever.
  The judgments given by the LORD
  are trustworthy
  and absolutely just.
10 They are of greater value than ᵃgold,
  than even a great amount of pure
  gold;
  they bring greater delight than
  honey,
  than even the sweetest honey from a
  honeycomb.
11 Yes, your servant finds moral
  guidance there;
  those who obey them receive a rich
  reward.
12 Who can know all his errors?¹
  Please do not ᵃpunish me for sins I
  am unaware of.
13 Moreover, keep me from committing
  flagrant ᵃsins;
  do not allow such sins to ᵇcontrol me.
  Then I will be blameless
  and innocent of blatant rebellion.
14 ᵃMay my words and my thoughts
  be acceptable in your sight,
  O LORD, my sheltering rock and my
  ᵇredeemer.

For the music director, a psalm of David.

20 May the LORD answer you when
you are in trouble;
  may the God of Jacob make you
  secure.
2 May he send you help from his
  temple;¹
  from Zion may he give you
  support.

3 May he take notice of all your
  offerings;
  may he accept¹ your burnt
  sacrifice.   *Selah*
4 May he grant your heart's desire;
  may he ᵃbring all your plans to pass.
5 Then we will shout for joy over your
  victory;
  we will rejoice¹ in the name of our
  God.
  May the LORD grant all your
  requests.
6 Now I am sure that the LORD will
  deliver his chosen king;
  he will intervene for him from his
  holy, heavenly temple,
  and display his mighty ability to
  deliver.¹
7 Some trust in chariots and others in
  ᵃhorses,
  but we depend on¹ the LORD our God.
8 They will fall down,
  but we will stand firm.
9 The LORD will deliver the king;
  he will answer us when we call to
  him for help!

For the music director, a psalm of David.

21 O LORD, the king rejoices in the
strength you give;
  he takes great delight in the
  deliverance you provide.
2 You grant him his heart's desire;
  you do not refuse his ᵃrequest.¹
                                Selah
3 For you bring him rich blessings;
  you place a golden crown on his head.
4 ᵃHe asked you to sustain his life,
  and you have granted him long life
  and an enduring dynasty.
5 Your deliverance brings him great
  honor;
  you give him majestic splendor.
6 For ᵃyou grant him lasting blessings;
  you give him great joy by allowing
  him into your presence.
7 For the king trusts in the LORD,
  and because of the Most High's
  faithfulness he is not shaken.

19:7 ᵃ Ps 111:7; [Rom 7:12] ᵇ Ps 119:130 ¹ Trad. *the testimony of the LORD*; i.e., the demands of God's covenant law. 19:8 ¹ Heb. *command; the law as a whole.* 19:10 ᵃ Ps 119:72, 127; Prov 8:10–11, 19 19:12 ᵃ [Ps 51:1–2] ¹ Heb. *Errors who can discern?*; a rhetorical question. 19:13 ᵃ Num 15:30 ᵇ Ps 119:133; [Rom 6:12–14] 19:14 ᵃ Ps 51:15 ᵇ Ps 31:5; Isa 47:4 20:2 ¹ Heb. *from [the] temple.* 20:3 ¹ Heb. *consider as fat.* 20:4 ᵃ Ps 21:2 20:5 ¹ Heb. *raise a banner.* 20:6 ¹ Heb. *with mighty acts of deliverance of his right hand.* 20:7 ᵃ Deut 20:1; Ps 33:16–17; Prov 21:31; Isa 31:1 ¹ LXX *we will boast.* 21:2 ᵃ 2 Sam 7:26–29 ¹ Heb. *and the request of his lips you do not refuse.* 21:4 ᵃ Ps 61:5–6; 133:3 21:6 ᵃ Ps 16:11; 45:7

8 You prevail over[1] all your enemies;
  your power is too great for those who
  hate you.
9 You burn them up like a fiery furnace
  when you appear.
  The LORD angrily devours them;
  the fire consumes them.
10 You destroy their offspring[1] from the
  earth,
  their descendants[2] from among the
  human race.
11 Yes, they intend to do you harm;
  they dream up a scheme, but they do
  not succeed.
12 For you make them retreat
  when you aim your arrows at them.
13 Rise up, O LORD, in strength!
  We will sing and praise your power.

For the music director,
according to the tune "Morning
Doe"; a psalm of David.

22 My [a]God, my God, why have you
  abandoned me?
  I groan in prayer, but help seems far
  away.
2 My God, I cry out during the day,
  but you do not answer,
  and during the night my prayers do
  not let up.
3 You are holy;
  you sit as king receiving the [a]praises
  of Israel.
4 In you our ancestors trusted;
  they trusted in you and you rescued
  them.
5 To you [a]they cried out, and they were
  saved;
  in you they trusted and they were
  not disappointed.
6 But I [a]am [b]a worm, not a man;
  people insult me and despise me.
7 [a]All who see me taunt me;
  they mock me and shake their
  heads.
8 They say,
  "Commit yourself to [a]the LORD!
  [b]Let the LORD rescue him!

Let the LORD deliver him, for he
  delights in him."
9 [a]Yes, you are the one who brought
  me out from the womb
and made me feel secure on my
  mother's breasts.
10 I have been dependent on [a]you since
  birth;
from the time I came out of my
  mother's womb you have been my
  God.
11 Do not remain far away from me,
  for trouble is near and I have no one
  to help me.
12 [a]Many bulls surround me;
  powerful bulls of [b]Bashan hem me in.
13 [a]They open their mouths to
  devour me
  like a roaring lion that rips its prey.[1]
14 My strength drains away like water;
  all my bones are dislocated.
  My heart is like wax;
  it melts away inside me.
15 The roof of [a]my mouth[1] is as dry as a
  piece of pottery;
  [b]my tongue sticks to my gums.
  You set me in the dust of death.
16 Yes, wild dogs surround me—
  a gang of evil men crowd around me;
  like a lion [a]they pin my hands and
  feet.[1]
17 I can count all my bones;
  my enemies are gloating over me in
  triumph.
18 They are dividing up my clothes
  among themselves;
  [a]they are rolling dice for my
  garments.
19 But you, O LORD, do not remain far
  away.
  You are my source of strength. Hurry
  and help me!
20 Deliver me from the sword.
  Save [a]my life from the claws of the
  wild dogs.
21 [a]Rescue me from the mouth of the
  lion
and from the horns of the wild oxen.
  [b]You have answered me.

21:8 [1]Heb. *your hand finds*; an idiom picturing the king grabbing hold of his enemies and defeating them.   21:10 [1]Heb.
fruit. [2]Heb. *seed.*   22:1 [a][Matt 27:46; Mark 15:34]   22:3 [a]Deut 10:21; Ps 148:14   22:5 [a]Isa 49:23   22:6 [a]Job 25:6; Isa
41:14   [b]Ps 109:25; [Isa 53:3]; Matt 27:39–44   22:7 [a]Matt 27:39; Mark 15:29   22:8 [a]Matt 27:43; Luke 23:35   [b]Ps 91:14
22:9 [a][Ps 71:5-6]   22:10 [a][Isa 46:3; 49:1]; Luke 1:35   22:12 [a]Ps 22:21; 68:30   [b]Deut 32:14   22:13 [a]Job 16:10; Ps 35:21;
Lam 2:16; 3:46   [1]Heb. *a lion ripping and roaring.*   22:15 [a]Prov 17:22   [b]John 19:28   [1]Heb. *my strength.*   22:16 [a]Isa 53:7;
Matt 27:35; John 20:25   [1]MT *like a lion, my hands and my feet*; LXX *they dug my hands and feet.*   22:18 [a]Matt 27:35;
Mark 15:24; Luke 23:34; John 19:24   22:20 [a]Ps 35:17   22:21 [a]2 Tim 4:17   [b]Isa 34:7

22 I [a]will declare your name to [b]my
    countrymen.
  In the middle of the assembly I will
    praise you.
23 You loyal followers of the LORD,
    praise him.
  All [a]you descendants of Jacob, honor
    him.
  All you descendants of Israel, stand
    in awe of him.
24 For [a]he did not despise or detest the
    suffering of the oppressed.
  He did not ignore him;
  when he cried out to him, he
    responded.
25 You are the reason I offer praise in
    the great assembly;
  I will fulfill [a]my [b]promises before the
    LORD's loyal followers.
26 Let the oppressed eat and be filled.
  Let those who seek his help praise
    the LORD.
  May you live forever!
27 Let all the people of the earth
    acknowledge the LORD and turn to
    him.
  Let all the nations[1] worship you.
28 [a]For the LORD is king
  and rules over the nations.
29 All the thriving people of the earth
    will join the celebration and
    worship;
  [a]all those who are descending into
    the grave will bow before him,
  including those who cannot preserve
    their lives.
30 A whole generation[1] will serve him;
  they will tell the next generation
    about the Lord.
31 They will come and tell about his
    saving deeds;
  they will tell a future generation
    what he has accomplished.

A psalm of David.

23

  The LORD is [a]my shepherd,
  [b]I lack nothing.
2 He takes me to lush pastures,
  [a]he leads me to refreshing water.
3 He restores my strength.
  [a]He leads me down the right paths
  for the sake of his reputation.[1]
4 Even when I must walk through [a]the
    darkest valley,[1]
  [b]I fear no danger,[2]
  [c]for you are with me;
  your rod and your staff reassure me.
5 You [a]prepare a feast before me
  in plain sight of my enemies.
  You [b]refresh my head with oil;
  my cup is completely full.
6 Surely your goodness and
    faithfulness will pursue me all my
    days,
  and I will live in the LORD's house for
    the rest of my life.[1]

A psalm of David.

24

  The LORD owns the [a]earth and all
  it contains,
  the world and all who live in it.
2 For he set its [a]foundation upon the
    seas,
  and established it upon the ocean
    currents.
3 Who is allowed to ascend the
    mountain of the LORD?
  [a]Who may go up to his holy dwelling
    place?
4 The one whose deeds are [a]blameless
  [b]and whose motives are pure,
  who does not lie,
  or make [c]promises with no intention
    of keeping them.
5 Such godly people are rewarded by
    the LORD,
  and vindicated by the God who
    delivers them.
6 Such purity characterizes the people
    who [a]seek his favor,
  Jacob's descendants, who pray
    to him.   *Selah*
7 [a]Look up, you gates.
  Rise up, you eternal doors.
  Then the majestic king will enter.
8 Who is this majestic king?

22:22 [a] Matt 4:23; Mark 1:21, 39; Heb 2:12 [b] [Rom 8:29]   22:23 [a] Ps 135:19–20   22:24 [a] Ps 31:22; Heb 5:7   22:25 [a] Ps 35:18;
40:9–10 [b] Ps 61:8; Eccl 5:4   22:27 [1] Heb. *families of the nations.*   22:28 [a] [Ps 47:7]; Obad 21; [Zech 14:9]; Matt 6:13
22:29 [a] Ps 17:10; 45:12; Hab 1:16   22:30 [1] Heb. *offspring.*   23:1 [a] Ps 78:52; 80:1; [Isa 40:11]; Ezek 34:11–12; [John 10:11;
1 Pet 2:25; Rev 7:16–17] [b] [Ps 34:9–10; Phil 4:19]   23:2 [a] Ps 65:11–13; Ezek 34:14   23:3 [a] Ps 5:8; 31:3; Prov 8:20 [1] Heb.
name.   23:4 [a] Job 3:5; 10:21–22; 24:17; Ps 44:19 [b] [Ps 3:6; 27:1] [c] Ps 16:8; [Isa 43:2] [1] Trad. *shadow of death.* [2] Trad. *evil.*
23:5 [a] Ps 104:15 [b] Ps 92:10; Luke 7:46   23:6 [1] Trad. *forever.*   24:1 [a] 1 Cor 10:26, 28   24:2 [a] Ps 89:11   24:3 [a] Ps 15:1–5
24:4 [a] [Job 17:9]; Ps 26:6 [b] Ps 51:10; 73:1; [Matt 5:8] [c] Ps 15:4   24:6 [a] Ps 27:4, 8   24:7 [a] Ps 118:20; Isa 26:2

The LORD who is strong and mighty.
The LORD who is mighty in [a]battle.
9 Look up, you gates.
Rise up, you eternal doors.
Then the majestic king will enter.
10 Who is this majestic king?
The LORD of Heaven's Armies.[1]
He is the majestic king.　　　*Selah*

By David.

25 O LORD, I come before [a]you in prayer.
2 My God, I [a]trust in you.
Please do not [b]let me be humiliated;
do not let my enemies triumphantly rejoice over me.
3 Certainly none who rely on you will be humiliated.
Those who deal in treachery will be thwarted and humiliated.
4 Make me [a]understand your ways, O LORD.
Teach me your paths.
5 Guide me into your truth and teach me.
For you are the God who delivers me;
on you I rely all day long.
6 Remember [a]your compassionate and faithful deeds, O LORD,
for you have always acted in this manner.
7 Do not hold against me [a]the sins of my youth [b]or my rebellious acts.
Because you are faithful to me,
extend to me your favor, O LORD.
8 The LORD is both kind and fair;
that is why he teaches sinners the right way to live.
9 May he show the humble what is right.
May he teach the humble his way.
10 The LORD always proves faithful and reliable[1]
to those who follow the demands of his covenant.
11 For the sake of your reputation,[1] [a]O LORD,
forgive my sin, because it is great.

12 The LORD shows his faithful followers
the way they should live.
13 They experience his favor;
[a]their descendants[1] inherit the land.
14 The LORD's loyal followers receive his guidance,
and [a]he reveals his covenantal demands to them.
15 I continually look to the LORD for help,
for he will free [a]my feet from the enemy's net.
16 [a]Turn toward me and have mercy on me,
for I am alone and oppressed.
17 Deliver me from my distress;[1]
rescue me from my suffering.
18 [a]See my pain and suffering.
Forgive all my sins.
19 Watch my enemies, for they outnumber me;
they hate me and want to harm me.
20 Protect me and deliver me!
Please do not let me be humiliated,
for I have taken shelter in you.
21 May integrity and godliness protect me,
for I rely on you.
22 O God, [a]rescue Israel
from all their distress!

By David.

26 Vindicate [a]me, O LORD,
for I [b]have [c]integrity,[1]
and I trust in the LORD without wavering.
2 [a]Examine me, O LORD, and test me.
Evaluate my inner thoughts and motives.
3 For [a]I am ever aware of your faithfulness,
and your loyalty continually motivates me.
4 I do not [a]associate with deceitful men,
or consort with those who are dishonest.

24:8 [a]Rev 19:13–16   24:10 [1]Trad. *the LORD of hosts.*   25:1 [a]Ps 86:4; 143:8   25:2 [a]Ps 34:8   [b]Ps 13:4; 41:11   25:4 [a]Exod 33:13; Ps 5:8; 27:11; 86:11; 119:27; 143:8   25:6 [a]Ps 103:17; 106:1   25:7 [a]Job 13:26; [Jer 3:25]   [b]Ps 51:1   25:10 [1]Heb. *all the paths of the LORD are faithful and trustworthy.*   25:11 [a]Ps 31:3; 79:9; 109:21; 143:11   [1]Heb. *name.*   25:13 [a][Prov 19:23]   [1]Or *offspring*; Heb. *seed.*   25:14 [a][Prov 3:32; John 7:17]   25:15 [a][Ps 123:2; 141:8]   25:16 [a]Ps 69:16   25:17 [1]Heb. *the distresses of my heart, they make wide.*   25:18 [a]2 Sam 16:12; Ps 31:7   25:22 [a][Ps 130:8]   26:1 [a]Ps 7:8   [b]2 Kgs 20:3; [Prov 20:7]   [c][Ps 13:5; 28:7]   [1]Heb. *for I in my integrity walk.*   26:2 [a]Ps 17:3; 139:23   26:3 [a]2 Kgs 20:3; Ps 86:11   26:4 [a]Ps 1:1; Jer 15:17

5 I [a]hate the mob of evil men,
and do not associate[1] with the
wicked.
6 I maintain a pure lifestyle,
so I can appear before your altar,
O LORD,
7 to give you thanks,
and to tell about all your amazing
deeds.
8 O LORD, [a]I love the temple where you
live,
the place where your splendor is
revealed.
9 [a]Do not sweep me away with sinners,
or execute me along with violent
people,
10 who are always ready to do wrong
or offer a [a]bribe.
11 But I have integrity.
Rescue me and have mercy on me!
12 [a]I am safe,
and among the worshipers I will
praise the LORD.

By David.

27 The LORD is my [a]light and my
salvation.
I fear no one.
The [b]LORD protects my life.
I am afraid of no one.
2 When evil men attack me
to devour my flesh,
when my adversaries and enemies
attack me,
they stumble and fall.
3 [a]Even when an army is deployed
against me,
I do not fear.
Even when war is imminent,
I remain confident.
4 I have asked the LORD for one
[a]thing—
this is what I desire!
I want to [b]live in the LORD's house all
the days of my life,
so I can gaze at the splendor of the
LORD
and contemplate in his temple.

5 He will surely[1] give me shelter [a]in the
day of danger;
he will hide me in his home.
He will [b]place me on an inaccessible
rocky summit.
6 Now I will triumph
over [a]my enemies who surround me.
I will offer sacrifices in his dwelling
place and shout for joy.
I will sing praises to the LORD.
7 Hear me, O LORD, when I cry out.
Have mercy on me and answer me.
8 My heart tells me to pray to you,[1]
and I do pray to you, O LORD.
9 Do not reject me.
[a]Do not push your servant away in
anger.
You are my deliverer.
Do not forsake or abandon me,
O God who vindicates me.
10 [a]Even if my father and mother
abandoned me,
the LORD would take me in.
11 [a]Teach me how you want me to live,[1]
LORD;
lead me along a level path because of
those who wait to ambush me.
12 Do not turn me over to my enemies,
for [a]false witnesses who want to
destroy me testify against me.
13 Where would [a]I be if I did not believe
I would experience
the LORD's favor in the land of the
living?
14 Rely on the LORD!
Be strong and confident!
[a]Rely on the LORD!

By David.

28 To you, [a]O LORD, I cry out!
My Protector,[1] do not ignore me.
[b]If you do not respond to me,
I will join those who are descending
into the grave.[2]
2 Hear my plea for mercy [a]when I cry
out [b]to you for help,
when I lift my hands toward your
holy temple.

26:5 [a] Ps 31:6; 139:21 [1] Heb. *sit.*   26:8 [a] Ps 27:4; 84:1–4, 10   26:9 [a] Ps 28:3   26:10 [a] 1 Sam 8:3   26:12 [a] Ps 40:2   27:1 [a] Ps 18:28; 84:11; [Isa 60:19–20; Mic 7:8] [b] Exod 15:2; Ps 62:7; 118:14; Isa 12:2; 33:2   27:3 [a] Ps 3:6   27:4 [a] Ps 26:8; 65:4 [b] Luke 2:37   27:5 [a] Ps 31:20; 91:1 [b] Ps 40:2 [1] Or *for he will.*   27:6 [a] Ps 3:3   27:8 [1] Heb. *concerning you my heart says, "Seek my face".*   27:9 [a] Ps 69:17; 143:7   27:10 [a] Isa 49:15   27:11 [a] Ps 25:4; 86:11; 119:33 [1] Heb. *teach me your way.*   27:12 [a] Deut 19:18; Ps 35:11; Matt 26:60; Mark 14:56; John 19:33   27:13 [a] Job 28:13; Ps 52:5; 116:9; 142:5; Isa 38:11; Jer 11:19; Ezek 26:20   27:14 [a] Ps 25:3; 37:34; 40:1; 62:5; 130:5; Prov 20:22; Isa 25:9; [Hab 2:3]   28:1 [a] Ps 35:22; 39:12; 83:1 [b] Ps 88:4; 143:7; Prov 1:12 [1] Heb. *my rocky summit.* [2] Heb. *the pit.*   28:2 [a] Ps 5:7 [b] Ps 138:2

3 Do not drag me away with evil men,
with those [a]who behave wickedly,
who talk so friendly to their
neighbors,
while they plan to harm them.
4 Pay them back for their evil deeds.
[a]Pay them back for what they do.
Punish them.
5 For [a]they do not understand the
LORD's actions,
or the way he carries out justice.
The LORD will permanently
demolish them.
6 The LORD deserves praise,
for he has heard my plea for mercy.
7 The LORD [a]strengthens and
protects me;
I [b]trust in him with all my heart.
I am rescued and my heart is full of
joy;
I will sing to him in gratitude.
8 The LORD strengthens his people;
he protects and [a]delivers his chosen
king.
9 Deliver [a]your people.
Empower the nation that belongs to
you.[1]
Care for them like [b]a shepherd and
carry them in your arms at all
times!

A psalm of David.

29 Acknowledge the LORD, you
heavenly beings,[1]
acknowledge the LORD's majesty and
power.
2 Acknowledge [a]the majesty of the
LORD's reputation.
Worship the LORD in holy attire.
3 The LORD's shout is heard over [a]the
water;
the majestic God thunders,
the LORD appears over the surging
water.[1]
4 The LORD's shout is powerful;
the LORD's shout is majestic.
5 The LORD's shout breaks [a]the
cedars;

the LORD shatters the cedars of
Lebanon.
6 He makes [a]them skip like a calf,
Lebanon and [b]Sirion like a young ox.
7 The LORD's shout strikes with
flaming fire.
8 The LORD's shout shakes the
wilderness;
the LORD shakes the wilderness of
[a]Kadesh.
9 The LORD's shout bends the large
trees[1]
and strips the leaves from the forests.
Everyone in his temple says,
"Majestic!"
10 The [a]LORD sits enthroned over [b]the
engulfing waters;
the LORD sits enthroned as the
eternal king.
11 The LORD gives his people strength;
[a]the LORD grants his people security.

*A psalm, a song used at the dedication
of the temple; by David.*

30 I will praise you, O LORD, for you
lifted me up
and did not allow my enemies to
[a]gloat over me.
2 O LORD my God,
I cried out to you and you
[a]healed me.
3 O LORD, [a]you pulled me up from
Sheol;
you rescued me from among those
descending into the grave.
4 [a]Sing to the LORD, you faithful
followers of his;
give thanks to his holy name.
5 For [a]his anger lasts only a brief
moment,
and [b]his good favor restores one's life.
One may experience sorrow during
the night,
but joy arrives in the morning.
6 In my self-confidence I said,
"I will never be shaken."
7 O LORD, in [a]your good favor you
made me secure.

28:3 [a]Ps 12:2; 55:21; 62:4; Jer 9:8   28:4 [a][Ps 62:12]; 2 Tim 4:14; [Rev 18:6; 22:12]   28:5 [a]Isa 5:12   28:7 [a]Ps 18:2; 59:17
[b]Ps 13:5; 112:7   28:8 [a]Ps 20:6   28:9 [a][Deut 9:29; 32:9; 1 Kgs 8:51; Ps 33:12]; 106:40   [b]Deut 1:31; Isa 63:9   [1]Heb. *your
inheritance.*   29:1 [1]Heb. *sons of gods* or *sons of God.*   29:2 [a]2 Chr 20:21; Ps 110:3   29:3 [a][Job 37:4–5]; Ps 18:13; Acts 7:2
[1]Trad. *many waters*; perhaps a reference to the Mediterranean Sea.   29:5 [a]Judg 9:15; 1 Kgs 5:6; Ps 104:16; Isa 2:13; 14:8
29:6 [a]Ps 114:4   [b]Deut 3:9   29:8 [a]Num 13:26   29:9 [1]Heb. *the deer.*   29:10 [a]Gen 6:17; Job 38:8, 25   [b]Ps 10:16
29:11 [a]Ps 28:8; 68:35; [Isa 40:29]   30:1 [a]Ps 25:2   30:2 [a]Ps 6:2; 103:3; [Isa 53:5]   30:3 [a]Ps 86:13   30:4 [a]Ps
97:12   30:5 [a]Ps 103:9; Isa 26:20; 54:7–8   [b]Ps 63:3   30:7 [a][Deut 31:17; Ps 104:29; 143:7]

Then you rejected me[1] and I was
   terrified.
8 To you, O LORD, I cried out;
   I begged the Lord for mercy:
9 "What profit is there in taking my life,
   in my descending into the Pit?[1]
   Can the dust of the grave praise you?
   Can it declare your loyalty?
10 Hear, O LORD, and have mercy on me.
   O LORD, deliver me."
11 Then [a]you turned my lament into
   dancing;
   you removed my sackcloth and
      covered me with joy.
12 So now my heart will sing to you and
   not be silent;
   O LORD my God, I will always give
      thanks to you.

For the music director, a psalm of David.

31 In [a]you, O LORD, I have taken
   shelter.
   Never let me be humiliated.
   Vindicate me by rescuing me.
2 [a]Listen to me.
   Quickly deliver me.
   Be my protector and refuge,[1]
   a stronghold where I can be safe.
3 For you are my high ridge and my
   stronghold;
   [a]for the sake of your own reputation[1]
   you lead me and guide me.
4 You will free me from the net they
   hid for me,
   for you are my place of refuge.
5 Into your hand [a]I entrust my life;
   you will rescue me, O LORD, the
   [b]faithful God.
6 I hate those [a]who serve worthless
   idols,
   but I trust in the LORD.
7 I will be happy and rejoice in your
   faithfulness,
   because you notice my pain
   and you are [a]aware of how distressed
      I am.
8 You do not deliver me over to the
   power of the enemy;

[a]you enable me to stand in a wide
   open place.
9 Have mercy on me, LORD, for I am in
   distress!
   [a]My eyes grow dim[1] from suffering.
   I have lost my strength.
10 For my life nears its end in pain;
   my years draw to a close as I groan.
   My strength fails me because of my
      sin,
   and my bones become brittle.
11 Because of all my [a]enemies, people
   disdain me;
   my neighbors are appalled by my
      suffering[1]—
   [b]those who know me are horrified by
      my condition;
   those who see me in the street run
      away from me.
12 I am forgotten, [a]like a dead man no
   one thinks about;
   I am regarded as worthless, like a
      broken jar.
13 [a]For I hear what so many are saying,
   the terrifying [b]news that comes from
      every direction.
   When they plot together against me,
   they figure out how they can [c]take
      my life.
14 But I trust in you, O LORD!
   I declare, "You are my God!"
15 You [a]determine my destiny.
   Rescue me from the power of my
      enemies and those who chase me.
16 [a]Smile on your servant.
   Deliver me because of your
      faithfulness.
17 O LORD, [a]do not [b]let me be
   humiliated,
   for I call out to you.
   May evil men be humiliated.
   May they go wailing to the grave.
18 [a]May lying lips be silenced—
   lips that [b]speak defiantly against the
      innocent
   with arrogance and contempt.
19 [a]How great is your favor,
   which you store up for your loyal
      followers.[1]

30:7 [1] Heb. *you hid your face*; an idiom that can mean to ignore or to reject.   **30:9** [1] Or *Sheol*.   **30:11** [a] Eccl 3:4; Isa 61:3;
Jer 31:4   **31:1** [a] Ps 22:5   **31:2** [a] Ps 17:6; 71:2; 86:1; 102:2   [1] Heb. *become for me a rocky summit of refuge.*   **31:3** [a] [Ps 18:2]
[1] Heb. *name.*   **31:5** [a] Luke 23:46   [b] [Deut 32:4]; Ps 71:22   **31:6** [a] Jonah 2:8   **31:7** [a] [John 10:27]   **31:8** [a] [Ps 4:1; 18:19]
31:9 [a] Ps 6:7   [1] Or perhaps *are swollen.*   **31:11** [a] [Isa 53:4]   [b] Ps 64:8   [1] Heb. *and to my neighbors, exceedingly.*   **31:12** [a] Ps
88:4–5   **31:13** [a] Ps 50:20; Jer 20:10   [b] Lam 2:22   [c] Ps 62:4; Matt 27:1   **31:15** [a] [Job 14:5; 24:1]   **31:16** [a] Ps 4:6; 80:3
31:17 [a] Ps 25:2, 20   [b] [1 Sam 2:9]; Ps 94:17; 115:17   **31:18** [a] Ps 109:2; 120:2   [b] [1 Sam 2:3]; Ps 94:4; [Jude 15]
31:19 [a] Ps 145:7; [Rom 2:4; 11:22]   [1] Heb. *for those who fear you.*

In plain sight of everyone you
    bestow it on those who take
    shelter in you.
20 You hide them with [a]you, where they
    are safe from the attacks of men;[1]
  [b]you conceal them in a shelter, where
    they are safe from slanderous
    attacks.
21 The LORD deserves praise
    for [a]he demonstrated his amazing
    faithfulness to me when I was
    besieged by enemies.[1]
22 I jumped to conclusions and said,
    "I am cut off from your presence!"
  But you heard my plea for mercy
    when I cried out to you for help.
23 Love the LORD, all you faithful
    followers of his!
  The LORD protects those who have
    integrity,
  but he pays back in full the one who
    acts arrogantly.
24 [a]Be strong and confident,
  all you who wait on the LORD.

By David; a well-written song.[1]

32 How blessed is the one whose
    rebellious [a]acts are forgiven,
  whose sin is pardoned.
2 How blessed is the one[1] whose
    wrongdoing the LORD [a]does not
    punish,
  [b]in whose spirit there is no deceit.
3 When I refused to confess my sin,
  my whole body wasted away,
  while I groaned in pain all day long.
4 For day and night [a]you
    tormented me;
  you tried to destroy me[1] in the
    intense heat of summer.   *Selah*
5 Then [a]I confessed my sin;
  I no longer covered up my
    wrongdoing.
  I said, "I will confess my rebellious
    acts to the LORD."
  And then you forgave my sins.   *Selah*

6 [a]For this reason every one of your
    faithful followers should [b]pray to
    you
  while there is a window of
    opportunity.
  Certainly when the surging water
    rises,
  it will not reach them.
7 You are my hiding place;
  [a]you protect me from distress.
  You surround me with shouts
    of [b]joy from those celebrating
    deliverance.   *Selah*
8 I will instruct and teach you about
    how you should live.
  I will advise you as I look you in the
    eye.
9 Do not be[1] like an unintelligent
    [a]horse or mule,
  which will not obey you
  unless they are controlled by a bridle
    and bit.
10 An evil person suffers [a]much pain,
  but [b]the LORD's faithfulness
    overwhelms the one who trusts in
    him.
11 Rejoice in the LORD and [a]be happy,
    you who are godly!
  Shout for joy, all you who are morally
    upright!

33 You godly ones, shout for joy
    because of the LORD!
  It is appropriate for the morally
    upright to offer him praise.
2 Give thanks to the LORD with the
    harp.
  Sing to him to the accompaniment of
    a ten-stringed instrument.
3 Sing to him a new song.
  Play skillfully as you shout out your
    praises to him.
4 For the LORD's decrees are just,
  and everything he does is fair.
5 He promotes[1] equity and justice;
  the LORD's faithfulness extends
    throughout the earth.

31:20 [a] [Ps 27:5; 32:7]   [b] Job 5:21   [1] Heb. *you hide them in the hiding place of your face from the attacks of man.*
31:21 [a] [Ps 17:7]   [1] Heb. *for he caused his faithfulness to be amazing to me in a besieged city.*   **31:24** [a] [Ps 27:14]   **32** [1] Or *a contemplative song, a song imparting moral wisdom*; the meaning of the Heb. word is uncertain.   **32:1** [a] [Ps 85:2; 103:3]; Rom 4:7–8   **32:2** [a] [2 Cor 5:19]   [b] John 1:47   [1] Heb. *man*; Heb. wisdom literature often assumes and reflects the male-oriented perspective of ancient Israelite society, but the principle is certainly applicable to all people.   **32:4** [a] 1 Sam 5:6; Ps 38:2; 39:10   [1] Heb. *my [?] was turned.*   **32:5** [a] 2 Sam 12:13; Ps 38:18; [Prov 28:13; 1 John 1:9]   **32:6** [a] [1 Tim 1:16]   [b] Ps 69:13; Isa 55:6   **32:7** [a] Ps 9:9   [b] Exod 15:1; Judg 5:1; [Ps 40:3]   **32:9** [a] Prov 26:3   [1] The verb is pl.; the psalmist addresses the whole group.   **32:10** [a] Ps 16:4; [Prov 13:21; Rom 2:9]   [b] [Ps 5:11–12]; Prov 16:20   **32:11** [a] Ps 64:10; 68:3; 97:12   **33:5** [1] Heb. *loves.*

6 By the LORD's decree the heavens
     were made,
   and ᵃby the breath of his mouth all
     the starry ᵇhosts.
7 He piles up ᵃthe water of the sea;
   he puts the oceans in storehouses.
8 Let the whole earth fear¹ the LORD.
   Let all who live in the world stand in
     awe of him.
9 For ᵃhe spoke, and it came into
     existence.
   He issued the decree, and it stood
     firm.
10 The LORD frustrates ᵃthe decisions of
     the nations;
   he nullifies the plans of the peoples.
11 The LORD's decisions stand forever;
   his plans abide throughout ᵃthe ages.
12 How blessed is the nation whose God
     is the LORD,
   the people whom he has ᵃchosen to
     be his special possession.
13 The LORD watches from heaven;
   ᵃhe sees all people.
14 From the place where he lives he
     looks carefully
   at all the earth's inhabitants.
15 He is ᵃthe one who forms every
     human heart,
   and takes note of all their actions.
16 No king is delivered by his vast army;
   a warrior is ᵃnot saved by his great
     might.
17 A horse ᵃdisappoints those who trust
     in it for victory;
   despite its great strength, it cannot
     deliver.
18 ᵃLook, the LORD takes notice of his
     loyal followers,¹
   those who wait for him to
     demonstrate his faithfulness
19 by saving their lives from death
   and sustaining them during times of
     famine.
20 We wait for the LORD;
   he is our deliverer and shield.

21 For our hearts rejoice in him,
   for we trust in his holy name.
22 May we experience your faithfulness,
     O LORD,
   for we wait for you.

*By David, when he pretended to be
insane before Abimelech, causing
the king to send him away.¹*

34 I will ᵃpraise the LORD at all times;
   my mouth will continually praise
     him.
2 I will boast in the LORD;
   let the oppressed hear and rejoice.
3 Magnify the LORD with me.
   Let us praise his name together.
4 I ᵃsought the LORD's help¹ and he
     answered me;
   he delivered me from all my fears.
5 Look to him and be radiant;
   do not let your faces be ashamed.¹
6 This oppressed man cried out and
     the LORD heard;
   he saved him from all his troubles.
7 The angel of ᵃthe LORD ᵇcamps
     around
   the LORD's loyal followers and
     delivers them.
8 ᵃTaste and see that the LORD is good.
   How ᵇblessed is the one¹ who takes
     shelter in him.
9 Fear the LORD, you chosen people of
     his,
   for those who fear him lack
     nothing.
10 Even young lions sometimes lack
     food and are hungry,
   ᵃbut those who seek the LORD lack
     no good thing.
11 Come ᵃchildren. Listen to me.
   I will teach you what it means to fear
     the LORD.
12 ᵃDo you want to really live?
   Would you love to live a long, happy
     life?

33:6 ᵃGen 1:6–7; Ps 148:5; [Heb 11:3; 2 Pet 3:5]   ᵇGen 2:1   **33:7** ᵃGen 1:9; Job 26:10; 38:8   **33:8** ¹Probably demonstrating respect for the Lord's power and authority.   **33:9** ᵃGen 1:3; Ps 148:5   **33:10** ᵃ[Ps 2:1–3]; Isa 8:10; 19:3   **33:11** ᵃ[Job 23:13; Prov 19:21]   **33:12** ᵃ[Exod 19:5; Deut 7:6]; Ps 28:9   **33:13** ᵃJob 28:24; [Ps 14:2]   **33:15** ᵃ[2 Chr 16:9]; Job 34:21; [Jer 32:19]   **33:16** ᵃPs 44:6; 60:11; [Jer 9:23–24]   **33:17** ᵃ[Ps 20:7; 147:10; Prov 21:31]   **33:18** ᵃ[Job 36:7]; Ps 32:8; 34:15; [1 Pet 3:12]   ¹Heb. *look, the eye of the LORD* [is] *toward the ones who fear him*; indicates recognition and the bestowing of favor.   **34** ¹Heb. *By David, when he changed his sense before Abimelech and he drove him away and he went.*   **34:1** ᵃ[Eph 5:20; 1 Thess 5:18]   **34:4** ᵃ[2 Chr 15:2; Ps 9:10; Matt 7:7; Luke 11:9]   ¹Heb. *I sought the LORD.*   **34:5** ¹MT *they looked to him and were radiant; let their faces not be ashamed.*   **34:7** ᵃ[Ps 91:11]; Dan 6:22   ᵇ2 Kgs 6:17   **34:8** ᵃPs 119:103; [Heb 6:5]; 1 Pet 2:3   ᵇPs 2:12   ¹Heb. *man*; Heb. wisdom literature often assumes and reflects the male-oriented perspective of ancient Israelite society, but the principle is certainly applicable to all people.   **34:10** ᵃ[Ps 84:11]   **34:11** ᵃPs 32:8   **34:12** ᵃ[1 Pet 3:10–12]

¹³ Then make sure you don't speak evil
words
or use ^adeceptive speech.
¹⁴ Turn ^aaway from evil and do what is
right.
Strive ^bfor peace and promote it.
¹⁵ The LORD pays attention to ^athe godly
and hears their cry for help.
¹⁶ But ^athe LORD opposes evildoers
and wipes out all memory of them
from the earth.
¹⁷ The godly cry out and ^athe LORD
hears;
he saves them from all their troubles.
¹⁸ The LORD is near ^athe brokenhearted;
he delivers those who are
discouraged.
¹⁹ The godly face ^amany dangers,
^bbut the LORD saves them from each
one of them.
²⁰ He protects all his bones;
^anot one of them is broken.
²¹ Evil people ^aself-destruct;
those who hate the godly are
punished.
²² The LORD ^arescues his servants;
all who take shelter in him escape
punishment.

By David.

35 O LORD, fight those who fight
with me.
Attack those who attack me.
² Grab your small shield and large
shield,
and rise up to help me.
³ Use your spear and lance against
those who chase me.
Assure me with these words: "I am
your deliverer."
⁴ ^aMay those who seek my life be
embarrassed and humiliated.
May those who plan to harm me be
^bturned back and ashamed.
⁵ ^aMay they be like wind-driven chaff,
as the angel of the LORD attacks them.
⁶ May their path be ^adark and slippery,
as the angel of the LORD chases them.

⁷ I did not harm them, but they ^ahid a
net to catch me
and dug a pit to trap me.¹
⁸ Let ^adestruction take them by
surprise.
Let the net they hid catch them.
Let them fall into destruction.
⁹ Then I will rejoice in the LORD
and be happy because of his
deliverance.
¹⁰ With ^aall my strength I will say,
"^bO LORD, who can compare to you?
You rescue¹ the oppressed from those
who try to overpower them,
the oppressed and needy from those
who try to rob them."
¹¹ Violent men perjure themselves,
and falsely accuse me.
¹² They repay me evil for ^athe good I
have done;
I am overwhelmed with sorrow.
¹³ When they were sick, I wore sackcloth,
and refrained from eating food.
(If I am lying, may my prayers go
unanswered.)
¹⁴ I mourned for them as I would for a
friend or my brother.
I bowed down in sorrow as if I were
mourning for my mother.
¹⁵ But when I stumbled, they rejoiced
and gathered together;
they gathered together to
ambush me.
They tore at me without stopping to
rest.¹
¹⁶ When I tripped, they taunted me
relentlessly,¹
and tried to bite me.
¹⁷ O Lord, how long are you going to
watch this?
Rescue me from their destructive
attacks;
guard my life from the young lions.
¹⁸ Then I will give you thanks in the
great assembly;
I will praise you before a large crowd
of people.
¹⁹ Do not ^alet those who are my enemies
for no reason gloat over me.

34:13 ^a [Eph 4:25]   **34:14** ^a Ps 37:27; Isa 1:16–17   ^b [Rom 14:19; Heb 12:14]   **34:15** ^a Job 36:7; [Ps 33:18]   **34:16** ^a Lev 17:10; Jer 44:11; Amos 9:4   **34:17** ^a Ps 34:6; 145:19   **34:18** ^a [Ps 145:18]   **34:19** ^a Prov 24:16   ^b Ps 34:4, 6, 17   **34:20** ^a John 19:33, 36   **34:21** ^a Ps 94:23; 140:11; Prov 24:16   **34:22** ^a 1 Kgs 1:29   **35:4** ^a Ps 40:14–15; 70:2–3   ^b Ps 129:5   **35:5** ^a Job 21:18; Ps 83:13; Isa 29:5   **35:6** ^a Ps 73:18; Jer 23:12   **35:7** ^a Ps 9:15   ¹Heb. *for without cause they hid for me a pit of their net, without cause they dug for my life.*   **35:8** ^a [Ps 55:23]; Isa 47:11; [1 Thess 5:3]   **35:10** ^a Ps 51:8   ^b [Exod 15:11]; Ps 71:19; 86:8; [Mic 7:18]   ¹Heb. [the one who] *rescues.*   **35:12** ^a Ps 38:20; 109:5; Jer 18:20; John 10:32   **35:15** ¹Heb. *they tore and did not keep quiet.*   **35:16** ¹MT *as profane* [ones] *of mockers of food.*   **35:19** ^a Ps 69:4; 109:3; Lam 3:52; [John 15:25]

Do not let those who hate me
    without cause carry out their
    wicked schemes.
20 For they do not try to make peace
    with others,
but plan ways to deceive those who
    live peacefully in the land.
21 They are ready to devour me;
they say, "Aha! Aha! We've got you!"[1]
22 But you take notice, LORD; do not be
    silent!
O Lord, do not remain far away
    from me.
23 Rouse yourself, wake up and
    vindicate me.
My God and Lord, defend my just
    cause.
24 Vindicate me by your justice, O LORD
    my God.
Do not let them gloat over me.
25 Do not let them say to themselves,
    "Aha! We have what we wanted!"[1]
Do not let them say, "We have
    devoured him."
26 May those who rejoice in my
    troubles be totally embarrassed
    and ashamed.
May those who arrogantly taunt
    me be [a]covered with shame and
    humiliation.
27 [a]May those who desire my vindication
    shout for joy and rejoice.
May they continually say, "May the
    LORD be praised, for he wants his
    servant to be secure."
28 Then I will tell others about your
    justice,
and praise you all day long.

*For the music director, an oracle,
written by the LORD's servant David.*[1]

36 An evil man is rebellious to [a]the
    core.
He does not fear God,
2 for he is too proud
to recognize and give up his sin.
3 The words [a]he speaks are sinful and
    deceitful;

he does not care about doing what is
    wise and right.
4 While [a]he lies [b]in bed he plans ways
    to sin.
He is committed to a sinful lifestyle;[1]
he does not reject what is [c]evil.
5 O LORD, your loyal love reaches to
    the sky,
your faithfulness to the clouds.
6 Your justice is like the highest
    mountains,
[a]your fairness like the deepest sea;
you, LORD, preserve mankind and the
    animal kingdom.
7 How precious is your loyal love,
    O God!
The human race finds shelter under
    your wings.[1]
8 They are filled with food from your
    house,
and you allow them to drink from
    [a]the river of your delicacies.
9 [a]For with you is the [b]fountain of life;
in your light we see light.
10 Extend your loyal love to your
    faithful followers,
and vindicate the morally upright.
11 Do not let arrogant men overtake me,
or let evil men make me homeless.
12 I can see the evildoers! They have
    fallen.
They have been knocked down and
    are unable to get up.

By David.

37 Do not fret when wicked men seem
    to succeed.
[a]Do not envy evildoers.
2 For they will quickly dry up [a]like
    grass,
and wither away like plants.
3 Trust in the LORD and do what is
    right.
Settle in the land and maintain your
    integrity.[1]
4 Then you will take [a]delight in the
    LORD,
and he will answer your [b]prayers.

35:21[1]Heb. *our eye sees*; apparently, an idiom meaning to "look in triumph" or "gloat over."   35:25[1]Heb. *Aha! Our desire!*;
to triumph over him.   35:26[a]Ps 109:29   35:27[a]Rom 12:15   36[1]One could translate the superscription and first verse
together as, *Here is a poem written as I reflected on the rebellious character of evil men.*   36:1[a]Rom 3:18   36:3[a]Ps 94:8;
Jer 4:22   36:4[a]Prov 4:16; [Mic 2:1] [b]Isa 65:2 [c][Ps 52:3; Rom 12:9] [1]Heb. *he takes a stand in a way* [that is] *not good.*
36:6[a]Job 11:8; Ps 77:19; [Rom 11:33]   36:7[1]Heb. *and the sons of man in the shadow of your wings find shelter.*   36:8[a]Ps 63:5;
65:4; Isa 25:6; Jer 31:12–14   36:9[a][Jer 2:13; John 4:10, 14] [b][1 Pet 2:9]   37:1[a]Ps 73:3; [Prov 23:17; 24:19]   37:2[a]Job 14:2; Ps
90:5–6; 92:7; Jas 1:11   37:3[1]Heb. *tend integrity.*   37:4[a]Job 22:26; Ps 94:19; Isa 58:14 [b]Ps 21:2; 145:19; [Matt 7:7–8]

5 ᵃCommit your future to the LORD.
   Trust in him, and he will act on your
      behalf.
6 ᵃHe will vindicate you in broad
      daylight,
   and publicly defend your just cause.
7 ᵃWait patiently for the LORD!
   Wait confidently[1] for him!
   Do not fret over the apparent
      ᵇsuccess of a sinner,
   a man who carries out wicked
      schemes.
8 Do not ᵃbe angry and frustrated.
   ᵇDo not fret. That only leads to
      trouble.
9 Wicked men will be wiped out,
   but those who rely on the LORD are
      the ones who will ᵃpossess the land.
10 Evil men will soon disappear;
   ᵃyou will stare at the spot where they
      once were, but they will be gone.
11 ᵃBut the oppressed will possess the
      land
   and enjoy great prosperity.
12 Evil men plot against the godly
   ᵃand viciously attack them.
13 The Lord laughs in disgust at ᵃthem,
   for he knows that their day ᵇis
      coming.
14 Evil men draw their swords
   and prepare their bows,
   to bring down the oppressed and
      needy,
   and to slaughter those who are godly.
15 Their swords will pierce their own
      hearts,
   and their bows will be broken.
16 The little bit ᵃthat a godly man owns
      is better than
   the wealth of many evil men,
17 for evil men will lose their power,
   but the LORD sustains the godly.
18 The LORD watches over the innocent
      day by day,
   and they possess a permanent
      inheritance.
19 They will not be ashamed when hard
      times come;

   when famine comes they will have
      enough to eat.
20 But evil men will die;
   the LORD's enemies will be
      incinerated[1]—
   they will go up in smoke.
21 Evil men borrow, but do not repay
      ᵃtheir debt,
   but the godly show compassion and
      are generous.
22 ᵃSurely those favored by the LORD
      will possess the land,
   but those rejected by him will be
      wiped out.
23 The LORD grants success to ᵃthe one
   whose behavior he finds
      commendable.[1]
24 ᵃEven if he trips, he will not fall
      headlong,
   for the LORD holds his hand.
25 I was once young, now I am old.
   I have never seen the godly
      abandoned,
   or their children[1] forced to search for
      food.
26 All day long ᵃthey show compassion
      and lend to others,
   and their children[1] are blessed.
27 Turn away from evil. Do what is right.
   Then you will enjoy lasting security.
28 For the LORD promotes justice,
   and never abandons his faithful
      followers.
   They are permanently secure,
   but the children[1] of the wicked are
      wiped out.
29 The godly will possess ᵃthe land
   and will dwell in it permanently.
30 ᵃThe godly speak wise words
   and promote justice.
31 The law of their God controls their
      thinking;
   their feet do not slip.
32 The wicked set an ᵃambush for the
      godly
   and try to kill them.
33 But the LORD does not surrender the
      godly,

37:5 ᵃ [Ps 55:22; Prov 16:3; 1 Pet 5:7]   37:6 ᵃ Job 11:17; [Isa 58:8, 10]   37:7 ᵃ Ps 40:1; 62:5; [Lam 3:26]   ᵇ [Ps 73:3–12]   [1] MT *writhe with fear, suffer.*   37:8 ᵃ [Eph 4:26]   ᵇ Ps 73:3   37:9 ᵃ Ps 25:13; Prov 2:21; [Isa 57:13; 60:21; Matt 5:5]   37:10 ᵃ Job 7:10; Ps 37:35–36   37:11 ᵃ [Matt 5:5]   37:12 ᵃ Ps 35:16   37:13 ᵃ Ps 2:4; 59:8   ᵇ 1 Sam 26:10; Job 18:20   37:16 ᵃ Prov 15:16; 16:8; [1 Tim 6:6]   37:20 [1] MT *like what is precious among the pastures/rams.*   37:21 ᵃ Ps 112:5, 9   37:22 ᵃ [Prov 3:33] 37:23 ᵃ [1 Sam 2:9]; Ps 40:2; 66:9; 119:5   [1] Or *The LORD grants success to the one who desires to obey his commands*; Heb. *from the LORD the steps of a man are established, and in his way he delights.*   37:24 ᵃ Prov 24:16   37:25 [1] Or *offspring*; Heb. *seed.*   37:26 ᵃ [Deut 15:8]; Ps 37:21   [1] Or *offspring*; Heb. *seed.*   37:28 [1] Or *offspring*; Heb. *seed.* 37:29 ᵃ Ps 37:9; Prov 2:21   37:30 ᵃ [Matt 12:35]   37:32 ᵃ Ps 10:8; 17:11

or allow them to be condemned in a
    court of law.
34 [a]Rely on the LORD. Obey his
    commands.
  Then he will permit you to possess
    the land;
  you will see the demise of the
    wicked.
35 I have seen ruthless, wicked people
  growing in influence, like a green
    tree grows in its native soil.
36 But then one passes by, and suddenly
    they have disappeared.
  I looked for them, but they could not
    be found.
37 Take note of the one who has
    integrity. Observe the upright.
  For the one who promotes peace has
    a future.
38 [a]Sinful rebels are totally destroyed;
  the wicked have no future.
39 But the LORD delivers the godly;
  he protects them [a]in times of
    trouble.
40 The LORD helps [a]them and rescues
    them;
  he rescues them from the wicked
    and delivers them,
  for they seek his protection.

A psalm of David, written
to get God's attention.

38 O LORD, do not continue [a]to
    [b]rebuke me in your anger.
  Do not continue to punish me in
    your raging fury.
2 For your arrows pierce me,
  and your hand presses me down.
3 My whole body is sick because of
    your judgment;
  I am deprived of health because of
    my sin.
4 For my sins overwhelm me;
  like a heavy load, they are too much
    for me to bear.
5 My wounds are infected and starting
    to smell,
  because of my foolish sins.
6 I am dazed[1] and completely
    humiliated;
  all day long I walk around mourning.

7 For I am overcome with shame,
  and my whole body is sick.
8 I am numb with pain and severely
    battered;
  I groan loudly because of the anxiety
    I feel.
9 O Lord, you understand my heart's
    desire;
  my groaning is not hidden from you.
10 My heart beats quickly;
  my strength leaves me.
  I can hardly see.
11 Because of my condition, even my
    friends and acquaintances keep
    their distance;
  my neighbors [a]stand far away.
12 Those who seek my life try to entrap
    me;[1]
  those who want to harm me speak
    destructive words.
  All day long they say deceitful things.
13 But I am like a deaf man—I hear
    nothing;
  I am like a mute who cannot speak.
14 I am like a man who cannot hear
  and is incapable of arguing his
    defense.
15 Yet [a]I wait for you, O LORD!
  You will respond, O Lord, my God!
16 I have prayed for deliverance,
    because otherwise they will gloat
    over me;
  when my foot slips they will
    arrogantly taunt me.
17 [a]For I am about to stumble,
  and I am in constant pain.
18 Yes,[1] I [a]confess my [b]wrongdoing,
  and I am concerned about my sins.
19 But those who are my enemies for no
    reason are numerous;
  those who hate me without cause
    outnumber me.
20 They repay me evil for the good I
    have done;
  though I have tried to do good
    to them, they hurl accusations
    at me.
21 Do not abandon me, O LORD.
  My God, do not remain far away
    from me.
22 Hurry and help me, O Lord, my
    deliverer.

37:34 [a]Ps 27:14; 37:9   **37:38** [a][Ps 1:4–6; 37:20, 28]   **37:39** [a]Ps 9:9; 37:19   **37:40** [a]Ps 22:4; Isa 31:5; Dan 3:17; 6:23   **38:1** [a]Ps 70:title [b]Ps 6:1   **38:6** [1]Lit. *to bend.*   **38:11** [a]Ps 31:11; 88:18   **38:12** [1]Heb. *lay snares.*   **38:15** [a][Ps 39:7]   **38:17** [a]Ps 51:3   **38:18** [a]Ps 32:5 [b][2 Cor 7:9–10] [1]Or *for.*

For the music director,
Jeduthun; a psalm of David.

39 I decided, "I will watch what I say
and make sure I do not sin with my
[a]tongue.
I will put a muzzle over my mouth
while in the presence of an evil
person."
2 I was stone [a]silent;
I held back the urge to speak.
My frustration grew;
3 my anxiety intensified.
As I thought about it, I became
impatient.
Finally I spoke these words:
4 "O LORD, help me understand my
mortality
and the brevity of life.
Let me realize how quickly my life
will pass.
5 Look, you make my days short lived,[1]
and my life span is nothing from
your perspective.
Surely all people, even those who
seem secure, are nothing but
[a]vapor. *Selah*
6 Surely people go through life as mere
ghosts.
Surely they accumulate worthless
wealth
without knowing who will eventually
haul it away."[1]
7 But now, O Lord, upon what am I
relying?
You are my only [a]hope!
8 Deliver me from all my sins of
rebellion.
Do not make me [a]the object of fools'
insults.
9 I am [a]silent and cannot open my
mouth
because of what [b]you have done.
10 Please [a]stop wounding me.
You have almost beaten me to death.
11 You severely discipline people for
their sins;

like a moth you slowly devour their
strength.[1]
Surely all people are a mere
vapor. *Selah*
12 Hear my prayer, O LORD.
Listen to my cry for help.
Do not ignore my sobbing.
For I am [a]a resident foreigner with
you,
a temporary settler,[1] just as all my
ancestors were.
13 [a]Turn your angry gaze away from me,
so I can be happy
before I pass away.

For the music director, a psalm of David.

40 I [a]relied completely[1] on the LORD,
and he turned toward me
and heard my cry for help.
2 He lifted me out of [a]the watery pit,
out of the slimy mud.
He [b]placed my feet on a rock
and gave me secure footing.
3 He gave me reason to sing a new
song,
praising our God.
May many see what God has done,
so that [a]they might swear allegiance
to him and trust in the LORD.
4 How [a]blessed is the one who trusts in
the LORD
and does not seek help from the
proud or from liars.
5 O LORD, my God, you have
accomplished many [a]things;
you have done amazing things [b]and
carried out your purposes for us.
No one can thwart you.
I want to declare your deeds and talk
about them,
but they are too numerous to
recount.
6 Receiving [a]sacrifices and offerings
are not your primary concern.[1]
You make that quite clear to me.

39:1 [a] Job 2:10; Ps 34:13; [Jas 3:5–12] **39:2** [a] Ps 38:13 **39:5** [a] Ps 62:9; [Eccl 6:12] [1] Heb. *Look, handbreadths you make my days*; equivalent to the width of four fingers, one of the smallest measures used by ancient Israelites. **39:6** [1] Heb. *Surely* [in] *vain they strive, he accumulates and does not know who gathers them.* **39:7** [a] Ps 38:15 **39:8** [a] Ps 44:13; 79:4; 119:22 **39:9** [a] Ps 39:2 [b] 2 Sam 16:10; Job 2:10 **39:10** [a] Job 9:34; 13:21 **39:11** [1] Heb. *you cause to dissolve, like a moth, his desired* [thing]. **39:12** [a] Gen 47:9; Lev 25:23; 1 Chr 29:15; Ps 119:19; Heb 11:13; 1 Pet 2:11 [1] The Heb. terms for "resident foreigner" and "temporary settler" have similar meanings and are not used here with the technical distinctions of most references in the Mosaic Law. **39:13** [a] Job 7:19; 10:20–21; 14:6; Ps 102:24 **40:1** [a] Ps 25:5; 27:14; 37:7 [1] Heb. *relying, I relied*; an emphatic Heb. construction. **40:2** [a] Ps 69:2, 14; Jer 38:6 [b] Ps 27:5 **40:3** [a] Ps 32:7; 33:3 **40:4** [a] Ps 34:8; 84:12 **40:5** [a] Job 9:10 [b] Ps 139:17; [Isa 55:8] **40:6** [a] [1 Sam 15:22]; Ps 51:16; Isa 1:11; [Jer 6:20; 7:22–23]; Amos 5:22; [Mic 6:6–8; Heb 10:5–9] [1] Heb. *sacrifice and offering you do not desire*; an exaggeration for emphasis.

You do not ask for burnt sacrifices
    and sin offerings.
7 Then I say,
"Look, I come!
What is written in the scroll pertains
    to me.
8 I want to do what pleases you, my
    God.
Your law [a]dominates my thoughts."
9 I have told the great assembly about
    your [a]justice.
Look, [b]I spare no words.
O LORD, you know this is true.
10 I have not [a]failed to tell about your
    justice;
I spoke about your reliability and
    deliverance.
I have not neglected to tell the great
    assembly about your loyal love and
    faithfulness.
11 O LORD, you do not withhold your
    compassion from me.
May your loyal love and faithfulness
    continually protect me!
12 For innumerable dangers
    surround me.
[a]My sins overtake me
so I am unable to see;
they outnumber the hairs of my head
so my strength fails me.[1]
13 Please [a]be willing, O LORD, to
    rescue me!
O LORD, hurry and help me!
14 [a]May those who are trying to snatch
    away my life
be totally embarrassed and
    ashamed.
May those who want to harm me
be turned back and ashamed.
15 May those who say to me, "Aha! Aha!"
be [a]humiliated and disgraced.
16 [a]May all those who seek you be
    happy and rejoice in you.
May those who love to experience
    your deliverance [b]say continually,
"May the LORD be praised!"
17 [a]I am oppressed and needy.
May the Lord pay attention to me.
You are my helper and my deliverer.
O my God, do not delay.

For the music director, a psalm of David.

41 How blessed is the one who treats
    the poor properly.
When trouble comes, may the LORD
    deliver him.
2 May the LORD protect him and save
    his life.
May he be blessed[1] in the land.
Do not turn him over to his enemies.
3 The LORD supports him on his
    sickbed;
you have healed him from his illness.
4 As for me, I said:
"O LORD, have mercy on me!
[a]Heal me, for I have sinned against
    you.
5 My enemies ask this cruel question
    about me,[1]
'When will he finally die and be
    forgotten?'
6 When someone comes to visit, he
    pretends to be friendly;
he thinks of ways to defame me,
and when he leaves he slanders me.
7 All who hate me whisper insults
    about me to one another;
they plan ways to harm me.
8 They say,
'An awful disease overwhelms him,
and now that he is bedridden he will
    never recover.'
9 [a]Even my close friend [b]whom I
    trusted,
he who shared meals with me, has
    turned against me.
10 As for you, O LORD, have mercy on
    me and raise me up,
so I can pay them back!"
11 By this I know that you are pleased
    with me,
for my enemy does not triumph
    over me.
12 As for me, you uphold me because of
    my integrity;
you [a]allow me permanent access to
    your presence.
13 The LORD God of Israel deserves
    [a]praise
in the future and forevermore.
We agree! We agree!

40:8 [a] [Ps 37:31; Jer 31:33; 2 Cor 3:3] **40:9** [a] Ps 22:22, 25 [b] Ps 119:13 **40:10** [a] Acts 20:20, 27 **40:12** [a] Ps 38:4; 65:3 [1] Heb. *and my heart abandons me*; the seat of emotional strength and courage. **40:13** [a] Ps 70:1 **40:14** [a] Ps 35:4, 26; 70:2; 71:13 **40:15** [a] Ps 73:19 **40:16** [a] Ps 70:4 [b] Ps 35:27 **40:17** [a] Ps 70:5; 86:1; 109:22 **41:2** [1] LXX *and may he bless him* or *and he will bless him.* **41:4** [a] Ps 6:2; 103:3; 147:3 **41:5** [1] Heb. *my enemies speak evil concerning me.* **41:9** [a] 2 Sam 15:12; Job 19:13, 19 [b] Ps 55:12, 14, 20; Jer 20:10; Obad 7; [Mic 7:5]; Matt 26:14–16, 21–25, 47–50; John 13:18, 21–30; Acts 1:16–17 **41:12** [a] [Job 36:7; Ps 21:6; 34:15] **41:13** [a] Ps 72:18–19; 89:52; 106:48; 150:6

BOOK 2 (PSALMS 42–72)

For the music director, a well-written song[1] by the Korahites.

42 As a deer longs for streams of water,
so I long for you, O God!
2 [a]I thirst for God,
for the [b]living God.
I say, "When will I be able to go and
appear in God's presence?"
3 [a]I cannot eat; I weep day and night.
All day long they say to me, "[b]Where
is your God?"
4 I [a]will remember and weep.
For [b]I was once walking along with
the great throng to the temple of
God,
shouting and giving thanks along
with the crowd as we celebrated
the holy festival.[1]
5 [a]Why are you depressed, O my soul?
Why are you upset?
[b]Wait for God!
For I will again give thanks
to my God for his saving
intervention.[1]
6 I am depressed,
so I will pray to you while in the
region of the upper Jordan,[1]
from Hermon,[2] from Mount Mizar.[3]
7 One deep stream [a]calls out to
another at the sound of your
waterfalls;
all your billows and waves
overwhelm me.
8 By day the LORD [a]decrees his loyal
love,
and by night he gives me a song,
a prayer[1] to the God of my life.
9 I will pray to God, my high ridge:
"[a]Why do you ignore me?
Why must I walk around mourning
because my enemies oppress me?"

10 My enemies' taunts cut me to the
bone,[1]
as they say to me all day long, "Where
is your God?"
11 [a]Why are you depressed, O my soul?
Why are you upset?
Wait for God!
For I will again give thanks
to my God for his saving
intervention.[1]

43 Vindicate [a]me, O God!
[b]Fight for me against an ungodly
nation.
Deliver me from deceitful and evil
men.
2 For you are the God who shelters me.
[a]Why do you reject me?
Why must I walk around mourning
because my enemies oppress me?
3 [a]Reveal [b]your light and your
faithfulness.
They will lead me;
they will escort me back to your holy
hill,
and to the place where you live.
4 Then I will go to the altar of God,
to the God who gives me ecstatic joy,
so that I may express my thanks to
you, O God, my God, with a harp.
5 Why are you depressed, O my soul?
[a]Why are you upset?
Wait for God!
For I will again give thanks
to my God for his saving
intervention.[1]

*For the music director, by the Korahites;
a well-written song.[1]*

44 O God, we have clearly heard;
[a]our ancestors[1] have told us
what you did in their days,
in ancient times.

42[1]Or *a contemplative song, a song imparting moral wisdom*; the meaning of the Heb. word is uncertain.   **42:2** [a] Ps 63:1; 84:2; 143:6; [Jer 10:10]   [b] Rom 9:26; 1 Thess 1:9   **42:3** [a] Ps 80:5; 102:9   [b] Ps 79:10; 115:2; Joel 2:17; Mic 7:10   **42:4** [a] 1 Sam 1:15; Job 30:16   [b] Ps 55:14; 122:1; Isa 30:29   [1]Heb. *for I was passing by with the throng [?], I was walking with [?] them to the house of God; with a voice of a ringing shout and thanksgiving a multitude was observing a festival.*   **42:5** [a] Ps 42:11; 43:5   [b] Ps 71:14; Lam 3:24   [1]Heb. *for again I will give him thanks, the saving acts of his face.*   **42:6** [1]Heb. *therefore I will remember you from the land of Jordan.*   [2]Heb. *Hermons.*   [3]Probably a proper name, designating a particular mountain in the Hermon region; it appears only here in the OT.   **42:7** [a] Ps 69:1–2; 88:7; Jonah 2:3   **42:8** [a] Deut 28:8   [1]A few medieval MSS *praise.*   **42:9** [a] Ps 38:6   **42:10** [1]Heb. *with a shattering in my bones my enemies taunt me*; a few wss *like a shattering.*   **42:11** [a] Ps 43:5   [1]Heb. *for again I will give him thanks, the saving acts of my face and my God.*   **43:1** [a] [Ps 26:1; 35:24]   [b] 1 Sam 24:15; Ps 35:1   **43:2** [a] Ps 42:9   **43:3** [a] [Ps 40:11]   [b] Ps 3:4   **43:5** [a] Ps 42:5, 11   [1]Heb. *for again I will give him thanks, the saving acts of my face and my God.*   **44**[1]Or *a contemplative song, a song imparting moral wisdom*; the meaning of the Heb. word is uncertain.   **44:1** [a] [Exod 12:26–27; Deut 6:20]; Judg 6:13; Ps 78:3   [1]Heb. *fathers* (also in v. 2).

2 You, by ᵃyour power, defeated nations
and settled our fathers on their
land;
you crushed the people living there
and enabled our ancestors to
occupy it.
3 For ᵃthey did not conquer the land by
their swords,
and they did not prevail by their
strength,
but rather by your power, strength,
and good favor,
for you were partial to them.
4 You are my king, ᵃO God.
Decree[1] Jacob's deliverance.
5 By your ᵃpower we will drive back our
enemies;
by your strength we will trample
down our foes.
6 For ᵃI do not trust in my bow,
and I do not prevail by my sword.
7 For you deliver us from our enemies;
you humiliate those who hate us.
8 In God we boast all day long,
and we will ᵃcontinually give
thanks to your name. *Selah*
9 But ᵃyou rejected and
embarrassed us.
You did not go into battle with our
armies.
10 You made us ᵃretreat from the
enemy.
Those who hate us take whatever
they want from us.
11 You handed us over like sheep to be
eaten;
ᵃyou ᵇscattered us among the
nations.
12 You sold ᵃyour people for a pittance;[1]
you did not ask a high price for them.
13 ᵃYou made us an object of disdain to
our neighbors;
those who live on our borders taunt
and insult us.
14 ᵃYou ᵇmade us an object of ridicule
among the nations;
foreigners treat us with contempt.

15 All day long I feel humiliated
and am overwhelmed with shame,
16 ᵃbefore the vindictive enemy
who ridicules and insults me.
17 ᵃAll this has happened to us, even
though we have not rejected you[1]
or violated your covenant with us.
18 We have not been unfaithful,
ᵃnor have we disobeyed your
commands.
19 Yet you have battered us, leaving us a
heap of ruins overrun by wild dogs;
you have covered us ᵃwith darkness.
20 If we had rejected our God,
and spread out our hands in prayer
to another god,
21 ᵃwould not God discover it,
for he knows a person's secret
thoughts?
22 ᵃYet because of you we are killed all
day long;
we are treated like sheep at the
slaughtering block.
23 Rouse yourself! Why do you sleep,
O Lord?
ᵃWake up! Do not reject us forever.
24 ᵃWhy do you look the other way,[1]
and ignore the way we are oppressed
and mistreated?
25 For we lie in the dirt,
with ᵃour bellies pressed to the
ground.
26 Rise up and help us.
Rescue us because of your loyal love.

*For the music director, according
to the tune of "Lilies";[1] by the Korahites,
a well-written poem,[2] a love song.*

45 My heart is stirred by a beautiful
song.
I say, "I have composed this special
song for the king;
my tongue is as skilled as the stylus
of an experienced scribe."
2 You are the most handsome of all
men.

44:2ᵃ Exod 15:17; 2 Sam 7:10; Jer 24:6; Amos 9:15   44:3ᵃ [Deut 8:17–18]; Josh 24:12   44:4ᵃ [Ps 74:12]   [1]LXX *the one who
commands/decrees.*   44:5ᵃ Deut 33:17; [Dan 8:4]   44:6ᵃ [1 Sam 17:47]; Ps 33:16; [Hos 1:7]   44:8ᵃ Ps 34:2; [Jer 9:24]
44:9ᵃ Ps 60:1   44:10ᵃ Lev 26:17; Josh 7:8, 12; Ps 89:43   44:11ᵃ Ps 44:22; Rom 8:36   ᵇ Lev 26:33; Deut 4:27; 28:64;
Ps 106:27; Ezek 20:23   44:12ᵃ Isa 52:3–4; Jer 15:13   [1]Heb. *for what is not wealth.*   44:13ᵃ Ps 79:4; 80:6; Jer 24:9
44:14ᵃ Deut 28:37   ᵇ Job 16:4   44:16ᵃ Ps 8:2   44:17ᵃ Dan 9:13   [1]Heb. *we have not forgotten you*; worshiping false
gods and thereby refusing to recognize God's sovereignty.   44:18ᵃ Job 23:11   44:19ᵃ [Ps 23:4]   44:21ᵃ Job 31:14;
[Ps 139:1–2; Jer 17:10]   44:22ᵃ Rom 8:36   44:23ᵃ Ps 7:6   44:24ᵃ Job 13:24   [1]Heb. *Why do you hide your face?*; an
idiom that can mean ignore or reject.   44:25ᵃ Ps 119:25   45[1]Heb. *according to lilies*; perhaps a tune title
or musical style, suggestive of romantic love.   [2] Or *a contemplative song, a song imparting
moral wisdom*; the meaning of the Heb. word is uncertain.

You speak in an impressive and
   fitting [a]manner.
For this reason God grants you
   continual blessings.
3 Strap your [a]sword [b]to your thigh,
   O warrior.
Appear in your [c]majestic splendor.
4 Appear in your majesty [a]and be
   victorious.
Ride forth for the sake of what is right,
on behalf of justice.
Then your right hand will
   accomplish mighty acts.
5 Your arrows are sharp
and penetrate the hearts of the
   king's enemies.
Nations fall at your feet.[1]
6 Your throne, [a]O God, is permanent.
The [b]scepter of your kingdom is a
   scepter of justice.
7 You love justice and hate evil.
For this reason God, your God,[1] has
   [a]anointed you
with the oil of [b]joy, elevating you
   above your companions.
8 All your garments are perfumed with
   myrrh, aloes, and cassia.
From the luxurious palaces[1] comes
   the music of stringed instruments
   that makes you happy.
9 [a]Princesses are among your honored
   women.
Your bride stands [b]at your right
   hand, wearing jewelry made with
   gold from Ophir.
10 Listen, O princess.
Observe and pay attention!
[a]Forget your homeland[1] and your
   family.
11 Then the king will [a]be attracted by
   your beauty.
After all, he is your master. Submit
   to him.
12 Rich people from Tyre
will seek your favor by bringing a gift.
13 The princess looks absolutely
   magnificent,

decked out in pearls and clothed in a
   brocade trimmed with gold.[1]
14 In embroidered robes [a]she is
   escorted to the king.
Her attendants, the maidens of
   honor who follow her,
are led before you.
15 They are bubbling with joy as they
   walk in procession
and enter the royal palace.
16 Your sons will carry on the dynasty of
   your ancestors;
you will make them princes
   throughout the land.
17 I [a]will proclaim your greatness
   through the coming years,
then the nations will praise you
   forever.

For the music director, by the Korahites;
according to the alamoth *style; a song.*

46 God is our strong [a]refuge;
he is truly our helper in times of
   trouble.
2 For this reason we do not fear when
   the earth shakes,
and the mountains tumble into the
   depths of the sea,
3 [a]when its waves crash and foam,
and the mountains shake before
   the surging sea.   *Selah*
4 The [a]river's channels bring joy to the
   [b]city of God,
the special, holy dwelling place of the
   Most High.
5 God lives [a]within it, it cannot be
   moved.[1]
God rescues it at the break of dawn.
6 Nations are in uproar, kingdoms are
   overthrown.
God gives a shout, [a]the earth
   dissolves.[1]
7 The [a]Lord of Heaven's Armies is on
   our side.
The God of Jacob is our
   stronghold.   *Selah*

45:2 [a] Luke 4:22 45:3 [a] [Isa 49:2; Heb 4:12]; Rev 1:16 [b] [Isa 9:6] [c] Jude 25 45:4 [a] Rev 6:2 45:5 [1] Heb. *your arrows are sharp—peoples beneath you fall—in the heart of the enemies of the king*; the choppy style reflects the poet's excitement. 45:6 [a] [Ps 93:2]; Heb 1:8–9 [b] [Num 24:17] 45:7 [a] Ps 2:2 [b] Ps 21:6; Heb 1:8–9 [1] Because the name Yahweh ("Lord") is relatively rare in Pss 42–83, this compounding of Elohim may be an alternative form of the compound name "the Lord my/your/our God." 45:8 [1] Heb. *the palaces of ivory*; palaces with ivory panels and furniture decorated with ivory inlays, a high level of luxury. 45:9 [a] Song 6:8 [b] 1 Kgs 2:19 45:10 [a] Deut 21:13; Ruth 1:16–17 [1] Heb. *your people.* 45:11 [a] Ps 95:6; [Isa 54:5] 45:13 [1] Heb. *within, from settings of gold, her clothing.* 45:14 [a] Song 1:4 45:17 [a] Mal 1:11 46:1 [a] Ps 62:7–8 46:3 [a] [Ps 93:3–4] 46:4 [a] [Ezek 47:1–12] [b] Ps 48:1, 8; Isa 60:14 46:5 [a] [Deut 23:14; Isa 12:6]; Ezek 43:7; Hos 11:9; [Joel 2:27; Zeph 3:15; Zech 2:5, 10, 11; 8:3] [1] Or *it will not be moved.* 46:6 [a] Ps 2:1–2 [1] Or *melts.* 46:7 [a] Num 14:9; 2 Chr 13:12

8 Come, Witness the exploits of the
  LORD,
who brings devastation to the earth.
9 He brings an end to wars throughout
  [a]the earth.
[b]He shatters [c]the bow and breaks the
  spear;
he burns the shields with fire.[1]
10 He says, "Stop your [a]striving and
  recognize that I am God.
I will be exalted over the nations! I
  will be exalted over the earth!"
11 The LORD of Heaven's Armies is on
  our side![1]
The God of Jacob is our
  stronghold!   *Selah*

For the music director,
by the Korahites; a psalm.

47 All you nations, clap your hands.
     Shout out to God in celebration.
2 For the LORD Most High is
  awe-inspiring;
he is the great [a]king who rules the
  whole earth!
3 [a]He subdued nations beneath us
and countries under our feet.
4 He picked out for us a special [a]land
to be a source of pride for Jacob,
  whom he loves.   *Selah*
5 [a]God has ascended his throne
  amid loud shouts;
the LORD has ascended amid the
  blaring of ram's horns.
6 Sing to God! Sing!
Sing to our king! Sing!
7 [a]For God is king of the whole earth.
[b]Sing a well-written song.[1]
8 [a]God reigns over the nations.
God [b]sits on his [c]holy throne.
9 The nobles of [a]the nations
  assemble,
along with the people of the God
  of Abraham,[1]
[b]for God has authority over the
  rulers of the earth.
He is highly exalted.

A song, a psalm by the Korahites.

48 The LORD is great and certainly
     worthy of praise
in the [a]city of our God, his holy hill.
2 It is lofty and pleasing to look [a]at,
a source of joy to the whole earth.
Mount Zion resembles the peaks of
  Zaphon;
it is the city of the great king.
3 God is in its fortresses;
he reveals himself as its defender.
4 For look, [a]the kings assemble;
they advance together.
5 As soon as they see, they are
  shocked;
they are terrified, they quickly
  retreat.
6 Look at them shake uncontrollably,
like a woman writhing in
  childbirth.
7 With an east wind
you shatter the large [a]ships.[1]
8 We heard about God's mighty deeds;
  now we have seen them,
in the city of the LORD of Heaven's
  Armies,[1]
in the city of our God.
God [a]makes it permanently
  secure.   *Selah*
9 Within [a]your temple
we reflect on your loyal love, O God.
10 The praise [a]you receive as far away
  as the ends of the earth
is worthy of your reputation,
  O God.
You execute justice.
11 Mount Zion rejoices;
the towns[1] of Judah are happy,
because of your acts of judgment.
12 Walk around Zion. Encircle it.
Count its towers.
13 Consider its defenses.
Walk through its fortresses,
so you can [a]tell the next generation
  about it.
14 For God, our God, is our defender
  forever.
[a]He guides us.

46:9 [a] Isa 2:4 [b] Ps 76:3 [c] Ezek 39:9 [1] Heb. *wagons he burns with fire.* **46:10** [a] [Isa 2:11, 17] **46:11** [1] Heb. *the LORD of hosts is with us.* **47:2** [a] Deut 7:21; Neh 1:5; Ps 76:12 **47:3** [a] Ps 18:47 **47:4** [a] [1 Pet 1:4] **47:5** [a] Ps 68:24–25 **47:7** [a] Zech 14:9 [b] 1 Cor 14:15 [1] Or *a contemplative song, a song imparting moral wisdom*; the meaning of the Heb. word is uncertain. **47:8** [a] 1 Chr 16:31 [b] Ps 97:2 [c] Ps 48:1 **47:9** [a] [Rom 4:11–12] [b] [Ps 89:18] [1] MT omits *along with.* **48:1** [a] Ps 46:4; 87:3; Matt 5:35 **48:2** [a] Ps 50:2 **48:4** [a] 2 Sam 10:6, 14 **48:7** [a] 1 Kgs 10:22; Ezek 27:25 [1] Heb. *the ships of Tarshish*; probably large ships either made in or capable of traveling to and from the distant western port of Tarshish. **48:8** [a] [Ps 87:5; Isa 2:2]; Mic 4:1 [1] Heb. *the LORD of hosts.* **48:9** [a] Ps 26:3 **48:10** [a] [Deut 28:58]; Josh 7:9; Mal 1:11 **48:11** [1] Heb. *daughters.* **48:13** [a] [Ps 78:5–7] **48:14** [a] Isa 58:11

For the music director,
a psalm by the Korahites.

49 Listen to this, all you nations.
Pay attention, all you inhabitants
of the world.

2 Pay attention, all you people,
both rich and poor.

3 I will declare a wise saying;
I will share my profound thoughts.

4 I will learn a song that imparts
wisdom;
I will then sing my insightful song to
the accompaniment of a harp.

5 Why should I be afraid in times of
trouble,
when the sinful deeds of deceptive
men threaten to overwhelm me?[1]

6 They [a]trust in their wealth
and boast in their great riches.

7 Certainly a man cannot rescue his
brother;
he cannot [a]pay God an adequate
ransom price

8 (the ransom price for a human life is
too high,
and people go to [a]their final destiny),

9 so that he might continue to live
forever
and [a]not experience death.[1]

10 Surely one sees that even wise
people die;
fools and spiritually insensitive
people all pass away
and leave their wealth to others.

11 Their grave becomes their
permanent residence,
their eternal dwelling place.[1]
They [a]name their lands after
themselves,

12 but, despite their wealth, people do
not last.
They are like animals that perish.

13 This is the destiny of [a]fools,
and of those who approve of
their philosophy. *Selah*

14 They will travel to Sheol like
sheep,
with death as [a]their shepherd.[1]

The godly will rule over them when
the day of vindication dawns.[2]
Sheol will consume their bodies,
[b]and they will no longer live in
impressive houses.

15 But God [a]will rescue my life from the
power of Sheol;
certainly he will [b]pull me to
safety. *Selah*

16 Do not be afraid when a man
becomes rich
and his wealth multiplies.

17 For he will take nothing with him
when he dies;
his wealth will not follow him down
into the grave.

18 He pronounces this blessing on
himself while [a]he is alive:
"May men praise you, for you have
done well."

19 But he will join his ancestors;
they will never again see the [a]light
of day.

20 Wealthy people do not understand;
they are like animals that [a]perish.

A psalm by Asaph.

50 [a]El, God, the LORD has spoken,
and summoned the earth to come
from the east and west.

2 From Zion, the most beautiful of all
places,
[a]God has come in splendor.

3 "May our God come
[a]and not be silent."
Consuming fire goes ahead of him,
and all around him a storm rages.

4 He summons [a]the heavens above,
as well as the earth, so that he might
judge his people.

5 He says:
"Assemble [a]my covenant people
before me,
[b]those who ratified a covenant with
me by sacrifice."

6 The [a]heavens declare his fairness,
for [b]God is judge. *Selah*

49:5 [1] MT *the iniquity of my heels surrounds me.*   **49:6** [a] Job 31:24; Ps 52:7; [Prov 11:28; Mark 10:23–24]   **49:7** [a] Job 36:18–19
49:8 [a] [Matt 16:26]   **49:9** [a] Ps 89:48   [1] Or *Sheol;* Heb. *see the Pit.*   **49:11** [a] Gen 4:17; Deut 3:14   [1] Heb. *their inward part* [is]
their houses [are] *permanent, their dwelling places for a generation and a generation.*   **49:13** [a] [Luke 12:20]   **49:14** [a] Ps
47:3; [Dan 7:18; 1 Cor 6:2; Rev 2:26]   [b] Job 4:21   [1] Heb. *death will shepherd them.*   [2] Heb. *will rule over them in the morning;*
a metaphor for a time of deliverance and vindication after the dark "night" of trouble.   **49:15** [a] [Hos 13:4]; Mark 16:6–7;
Acts 2:31–32   [b] Ps 73:24   **49:18** [a] Deut 29:19; Luke 12:19   **49:19** [a] Job 33:30   **49:20** [a] Eccl 3:19   **50:1** [a] Isa 9:6
50:2 [a] Deut 33:2; Ps 80:1   **50:3** [a] Lev 10:2; Num 16:35; [Ps 97:3]   **50:4** [a] Deut 4:26; 31:28; 32:1;
Isa 1:2   **50:5** [a] Deut 33:3   [b] Exod 24:7   **50:6** [a] [Ps 97:6]   [b] Ps 75:7

7 He says:
  "[a]Listen, my people. I am speaking!
  Listen, Israel. I am accusing you.
  I am God, your God!
8 I am not [a]condemning you because
    of your sacrifices,
  [b]or because of your burnt sacrifices
    that you continually offer me.
9 [a]I do not need to take a bull from
    your household
  or goats from your sheepfolds.
10 For every wild animal in the forest
    belongs to me,
  as well as the cattle that graze on a
    thousand hills.
11 I keep track of every bird in the hills,
  and the insects of the field are
    mine.
12 Even if I were hungry, I would not tell
    you,
  [a]for the world and all it contains
    belong to me.
13 Do [a]I eat the flesh of bulls?
  Do I drink the blood of goats?
14 Present to God a thank [a]offering.
  [b]Repay your vows to the Most High.
15 Pray [a]to me when you are in trouble.
  I will deliver you, and you will
    honor me."
16 God says this to the evildoer:
  "How can you declare my commands,
  and talk about my covenant?
17 [a]For you hate instruction
  and reject my words.
18 When you see a thief, you [a]join him;
  you [b]associate with men who are
    unfaithful to their wives.
19 You do damage with words,
  and use [a]your tongue to deceive.
20 You plot against your brother;
  you slander your own brother.
21 When [a]you did these things, I was
    silent,
  so you thought I was exactly like you.
  But now I will condemn you
  and state my case against you.
22 Carefully consider this, you who
    [a]reject God.[1]

Otherwise I will rip you to shreds
  and no one will be able to rescue you.
23 Whoever presents a thank offering
    honors me.
  [a]To whoever obeys my commands, I
    will reveal my power to deliver."

*For the music director, a psalm
of David, written when Nathan
the prophet confronted him after
David's affair with Bathsheba.*[1]

51 Have mercy on me, [a]O God, because
  of your loyal love.
  Because of your great compassion,
    wipe away my rebellious acts.
2 [a]Wash away my wrongdoing.
  Cleanse me of my sin.
3 For I am aware of my rebellious acts;
  I am forever conscious of my sin.
4 Against you—you above all—[a]I have
    [b]sinned;
  I have done what is evil in your sight.
  So you are just when you confront
    me;[1]
  you are right when you condemn me.
5 [a]Look, I was guilty of sin from birth,
  a sinner the moment my mother
    conceived me.
6 Look, you desire integrity in the
    inner man;
  you want me to possess wisdom.
7 [a]Cleanse me with hyssop and I will be
    pure;
  wash me and I will be [b]whiter than
    snow.
8 Grant me the ultimate joy of being
    forgiven.
  [a]May the bones you crushed rejoice.
9 Hide your face from my sins.
  Wipe away all my guilt.
10 [a]Create for me a pure heart, O God.
  Renew a resolute spirit within me.
11 Do not reject me.
  Do not take your [a]Holy Spirit away
    from me.
12 Let me again experience the joy of
    your deliverance.

50:7 [a]Exod 20:2   50:8 [a]Jer 7:22   [b]Isa 1:11; [Hos 6:6]   50:9 [a]Ps 69:31   50:12 [a]Exod 19:5; [Deut 10:14; Job 41:11]; 1 Cor 10:26   50:13 [a][Ps 51:15–17]   50:14 [a]Hos 14:2; Heb 13:15   [b]Num 30:2; Deut 23:21   50:15 [a]Job 22:27; [Zech 13:9]   50:17 [a]Neh 9:26; Rom 2:21   50:18 [a][Rom 1:32]   [b]1 Tim 5:22   50:19 [a]Ps 52:2   50:21 [a][Rom 2:4]   50:22 [a][Job 8:13]   [1]Heb. [you who] *forget God*; i.e., forgetting about his commandments and not respecting his moral authority.   50:23 [a]Gal 6:16   51 [1]Heb. *a psalm by David, when Nathan the prophet came to him when he had gone to Bathsheba.*   51:1 [a][Isa 43:25; 44:22; Acts 3:19; Col 2:14]   51:2 [a]Jer 33:8; Ezek 36:33; [Heb 9:14; 1 John 1:7, 9]   51:4 [a]2 Sam 12:13   [b][Luke 5:21]   [1]Heb. *when you speak.*   51:5 [a][Job 14:4; Ps 58:3; John 3:6; Rom 5:12]   51:7 [a]Exod 12:22; Lev 14:4; Num 19:18; Heb 9:19   [b][Isa 1:18]   51:8 [a][Matt 5:4]   51:10 [a][Ezek 18:31; Eph 2:10]   51:11 [a][Luke 11:13]

Sustain me by giving me the desire
  to [a]obey.
13 Then I will teach rebels your
  merciful ways,
and sinners will turn to you.
14 Rescue me from the guilt of
  murder, O God, the God who
  delivers me.
Then my tongue will shout for joy
  because of your righteousness.
15 O Lord, give me the words.
Then my mouth will praise you.
16 Certainly[1] [a]you do not want a
  sacrifice, or else I would offer it;
you do not desire a burnt sacrifice.
17 [a]The sacrifice God desires is a
  humble spirit—
O God, a humble and repentant
  heart[1] you will not reject.
18 Because you favor Zion, do what is
  good for her.
Fortify the walls of Jerusalem.
19 Then you will accept [a]the proper
  sacrifices, burnt sacrifices and
  whole offerings;
then bulls will be sacrificed on your
  altar.

*For the music director, a well-written
song[1] by David. It was written
when Doeg the Edomite went
and informed Saul: "David has
arrived at the home of Ahimelech."*

52 Why do you boast about your evil
  plans, [a]O powerful man?
God's loyal love protects me all day
  long.
2 Your tongue carries out your
  destructive plans;
it is as effective as a sharp razor,
  O deceiver.
3 You love evil more than good,
lies more than speaking the
  truth. *Selah*
4 You love to use all the words that
  destroy,
and the tongue that deceives.
5 Yet God will make you a permanent
  heap of ruins.

He will scoop you up and remove you
  from your home;
he will uproot you from the land
  of the living. *Selah*
6 When the godly see this, they will be
  filled with awe,
and will mock the evildoer, saying:
7 "Look, here is the man who would
  not make[1] God his protector.
He trusted in his great wealth
and was confident about his plans to
  destroy others."
8 But [a]I am like a flourishing olive tree
  in the house of God;
I continually trust in God's loyal love.
9 I will continually thank you when
  you execute judgment;
I will rely on you,[1] for your loyal
  followers know you are good.

*For the music director, according
to the* machalath *style;[1]
a well-written song[2] by David.*

53 [a]Fools say to themselves, "[b]There is
  no God."
They sin and commit evil deeds;
none of them does what is right.
2 God looks down from heaven at the
  human race,
to see if there is anyone who is wise
  and [a]seeks God.
3 Everyone rejects God;
they are all morally corrupt.
None of them does what is right,
not even one!
4 All those who behave wickedly do
  [a]not understand—
those who devour my people as if
  they were eating bread
and do not call out to God.
5 [a]They are absolutely terrified,
even by things that do not normally
  cause fear.
For God annihilates those who attack
  you.
You are able to humiliate them
  because God has rejected them.
6 [a]I wish the deliverance of Israel
  would come from Zion!

51:12[a] [2 Cor 3:17]   **51:16**[a] [1 Sam 15:22]; Ps 50:8–14; [Mic 6:6–8]   [1]Or *For.*   **51:17**[a] Ps 34:18; [Isa 57:15]; 66:2   [1]Heb. *a broken and crushed heart.*   **51:19**[a] Ps 4:5   **52**[1]Or *a contemplative song, a song imparting moral wisdom;* the meaning of the Heb. word is uncertain.   **52:1**[a] Ezek 22:9   **52:7**[1]Or *does not make.*   **52:8**[a] Jer 11:16   **52:9**[1]Heb. *your name.*   **53**[1]Perhaps a particular style of music, a tune title, or a musical instrument.   [2]Or *a contemplative song, a song imparting moral wisdom;* the meaning of the Heb. word is uncertain.   **53:1**[a] Ps 10:4   [b] Rom 3:10–12   **53:2**[a] [2 Chr 15:2]   **53:4**[a] Jer 4:22   **53:5**[a] Lev 26:17, 36; Prov 28:1   **53:6**[a] Ps 14:7

When God restores the well-being of
　　his people,
may Jacob rejoice,
may Israel be happy!

For the music director, to be accompanied
by stringed instruments; a well-written
song[1] by David. It was written when
the Ziphites came and informed
Saul: "David is hiding with us."

54 O God, deliver me by your name.
　　Vindicate me by your power.
2　O God, listen to my prayer.
　Pay attention to what I say.
3　For foreigners[1] attack me;
　ruthless men, who do not respect
　　God, seek my life.　　　　*Selah*
4　Look, God is my deliverer.
　The Lord is among those who
　　support me.
5　May those who wait to ambush me
　　be repaid for their evil.
　As a demonstration of your
　　faithfulness, destroy them.
6　With a freewill offering I will
　　sacrifice to you.
　I will give thanks to your name,
　　O Lord, for it is good.
7　Surely he rescues me from all trouble,
　[a]and I triumph over my enemies.

For the music director, to be
accompanied by stringed instruments;
a well-written song[1] by David.

55 Listen, O God, to my prayer.
　　Do not ignore my appeal for mercy.
2　Pay attention to me and answer me.
　I [a]am so upset and distressed, I am
　　beside myself,
3　because of what the enemy says,
　and because of how the wicked
　　pressure me,
　[a]for they hurl trouble down upon me[1]
　and angrily attack me.
4　[a]My heart beats violently within me;
　the horrors of death overcome me.
5　Fear and panic overpower me;

terror overwhelms me.
6　I say, "I wish I had wings like a dove.
　I would fly away and settle in a safe
　　place.
7　Look, I will escape to a distant place;
　I will stay in the wilderness.　　*Selah*
8　I will hurry off to a place that is safe
　from the strong wind and the gale."
9　Confuse them,[1] O Lord.
　Frustrate their plans.
　For I see [a]violence and conflict in the
　　city.
10　Day and night they walk around on
　　its walls,
　while [a]wickedness and destruction
　　are within it.
11　Disaster is within it;
　[a]violence and deceit do not depart
　　from its public square.
12　Indeed, it is not an enemy who
　　insults me,
　[a]or else I could bear it;
　it is not one who hates me who
　　arrogantly [b]taunts me,
　or else I could hide from him.
13　But it is you, a man like me,
　[a]my close friend in whom I confided.
14　We would share personal thoughts
　　with each other;
　in God's temple we would [a]walk
　　together among the crowd.
15　May death destroy them.[1]
　May they [a]go down alive into Sheol.
　For evil is in their dwelling place and
　　in their midst.
16　As for me, I will call out to God,
　and the Lord will deliver me.
17　During the [a]evening, morning, and
　　noontime
　I will lament and moan,
　and he will hear me.
18　He will rescue me and protect me
　　from those who attack me,
　even though they greatly
　　outnumber me.
19　God, the one who has reigned as king
　　from long ago,
　will hear and humiliate them.[1]
　　　　　　　　　　　　　　Selah

54:1[1]Or *a contemplative song, a song imparting moral wisdom*; the meaning of the Heb. word is uncertain.　54:3[1]Sev. medieval mss *proud ones*.　54:7[a]Ps 59:10　55:1[1]Or *a contemplative song, a song imparting moral wisdom*; the meaning of the Heb. word is uncertain.　55:2[a]Isa 38:14; 59:11; Ezek 7:16　55:3[a]2 Sam 16:7-8　[1]MT *to sway*; Ket. *let him rain down*.　55:4[a]Ps 116:3　55:9[a]Jer 6:7　[1]Trad. *swallow*; in the sense of devour or destroy.　55:10[a]Ps 10:7　55:11[a]Ps 10:7　55:12[a]Ps 41:9　[b]Ps 35:26; 38:16　55:13[a]2 Sam 15:12　55:14[a]Ps 42:4　55:15[a]Num 16:30, 33　[1]Ket. *May devastation [be] upon them.*　55:17[a]Dan 6:10; Luke 18:1; Acts 3:1; 10:3, 30　55:19[1]Heb. *God will hear and answer them, even [the] one who sits [from] ancient times.*

They refuse to change,
and do not fear God.
20 He attacks his friends;
he breaks his solemn promises to
them.
21 His words are as smooth as butter,
but [a]he harbors animosity in his
heart.
His words seem softer than oil,
but they are really like sharp swords.
22 [a]Throw your burden upon [b]the LORD,
and he will sustain you.[1]
He will never allow the godly to be
shaken.
23 But you, [a]O God, will bring them
down to the deep Pit.[1]
Violent and deceitful people will not
live even half [b]a normal life-span.
But as for me, I trust in you.

8 You keep track of my misery.
Put my tears in your leather
container.
[a]Are they not recorded in your scroll?
9 My enemies will turn back when I
cry out to you for help;
I know that [a]God is on my side.
10 In God—I boast in his promise—
in the LORD—I boast in his promise—
11 in God I trust; I am not afraid.
What can mere men do to me?
12 I am obligated to fulfill the vows I
made to you, O God;
I will give you the thank offerings
you deserve,
13 [a]when you deliver my life from death.
You keep my feet from stumbling,[1]
so that I might serve God as I [b]enjoy
life.

*For the music director, according
to the yonath-elem-rekhoqim style;[1]
a prayer[2] of David, written when
the Philistines captured him in Gath.*

56

Have mercy [a]on me, O God, for men
are attacking me.
All day long hostile enemies are
tormenting me.
2 Those who anticipate my defeat
[a]attack me all day long.
Indeed,[1] many are fighting against
me, O Exalted One.
3 When I am afraid,
I trust in you.
4 In God—[a]I boast in his promise—
in God I trust; I am not afraid.
What can mere men do to me?
5 All day long they cause me trouble;
they make a habit of plotting my
demise.
6 They stalk and lurk;
they watch my every step,
as they prepare to take my life.
7 Because they are bent on violence, do
not let them escape.[1]
In your anger bring down the
nations, O God.

*For the music director, according
to the al-tashcheth style;[1] a prayer[2]
of David, written when he fled
from Saul into the cave.*

57

Have mercy on me, O God. Have
mercy on me.
For in you [a]I have taken shelter.
In the shadow of your wings I take
shelter
until trouble passes.
2 I cry out for help to God Most High,
to the God [a]who vindicates me.
3 May [a]he send help from heaven and
deliver me
from my enemies who hurl
insults.   *Selah*
May God send his loyal love and
faithfulness.
4 I am surrounded by lions;
I lie down among those [a]who want to
devour me,[1]
men whose teeth are spears and
arrows,
whose tongues are sharp swords.
5 [a]Rise up above the sky, O God.
May your splendor cover the whole
earth.

55:21 [a] Ps 28:3; 57:4; [Prov 5:3–4; 12:18]   55:22 [a] [Ps 37:5; Matt 6:25–34; Luke 12:22–31; 1 Pet 5:7]   [b] Ps 37:24   [1] Sing.
55:23 [a] Ps 5:6   [b] Prov 10:27   [1] Or *Sheol*; Heb. *well of the pit.*   56 [1] Heb. *silent dove, distant ones*; perhaps a particular style
of music, a tune title, or a type of musical instrument.   [2] The meaning of the Heb. term is uncertain.   56:1 [a] Ps 57:1
56:2 [a] Ps 57:3   [1] Or *for.*   56:4 [a] Ps 118:6; Isa 31:3; [Heb 13:6]   56:7 [1] Heb. *because of wickedness, deliver them.*   56:8 [a] [Mal
3:16]   56:9 [a] [Ps 118:6; Rom 8:31]   56:13 [a] Ps 116:8–9   [b] Job 33:30   [1] Heb. *are not my feet* [kept] *from stumbling?*; a
rhetorical question expecting the answer, "of course they are!"   57 [1] Heb. *do not destroy*; perhaps a particular style of
music, a tune title, or a musical instrument.   [2] The meaning of the Heb. term is uncertain.   57:1 [a] Isa 26:20
57:2 [a] [Ps 138:8]   57:3 [a] Ps 144:5, 7   57:4 [a] Prov 30:14   [1] Or perhaps *those who are aflame.*   57:5 [a] Ps 108:5

6 They have prepared a net to trap me;
    I am discouraged.
  ᵃThey have dug a pit for me.
  They will fall into it.   *Selah*
7 ᵃI am determined, O God. I am
    determined.
  I will sing and praise you.
8 Awake, ᵃmy soul![1]
  Awake, O stringed instrument and
    harp!
  I will wake up at dawn.
9 I ᵃwill give you thanks before the
    nations, O Lord.
  I will sing praises to you before
    foreigners.
10 ᵃFor your loyal love extends beyond
    the sky,
  and your faithfulness reaches the
    clouds.
11 ᵃRise up above the sky, O God.
  May your splendor cover the whole
    earth.

For the music director,
according to the al-tashcheth
style; a prayer[1] of David.

58 Do you rulers really pronounce just
    decisions?
  Do you judge people fairly?
2 No! You plan how to do what is
    unjust;
  you deal out violence in the
    earth.
3 The wicked turn aside from
    birth;
  liars go astray as soon as ᵃthey are
    born.
4 ᵃTheir venom is like that of a
    snake,
  like a deaf serpent that does not
    hear,
5 that does not respond ᵃto the
    magicians,
  or to a skilled snake charmer.
6 O God, ᵃbreak the teeth in their
    mouths!
  Smash the jawbones of the lions,
    O Lord.

7 Let them disappear like water that
    flows away.
  ᵃLet them wither like grass.[1]
8 Let them be ᵃlike a snail that melts
    away as it moves along.
  Let them be like stillborn babies that
    never see the sun.
9 Before the kindling is even placed
    under your ᵃpots,
  he will sweep it away along with both
    the raw and cooked meat.
10 The godly will rejoice when they see
    ᵃvengeance carried out;
  ᵇthey will bathe their feet in the
    blood of the wicked.
11 ᵃThen observers will say,
  "Yes indeed, the godly are rewarded.
  Yes indeed, there is a God who
    ᵇjudges in the earth."

For the music director, according
to the al-tashcheth *style;[1] a prayer[2]*
of David, written when Saul sent men
to surround his house and murder him.

59 Deliver me from my enemies, my
    God.
  Protect me from those who
    attack me.
2 Deliver me from evildoers.
  Rescue me from violent men.
3 For look, ᵃthey wait to ambush me;
  powerful men stalk me,
  but not because I have rebelled or
    sinned, O Lord.
4 Though I have done nothing wrong,
    they are anxious to attack.
  Spring into ᵃaction and help me.
  Take notice of me.
5 You, O Lord God of Heaven's Armies,
    the God of Israel,
  rouse yourself and punish all the
    nations.
  Have no mercy on any treacherous
    evildoers.   *Selah*
6 ᵃThey return in the evening;
  they growl like dogs
  and prowl around outside
    the city.

57:6 ᵃPs 9:15   57:7 ᵃPs 108:1–5   57:8 ᵃPs 16:9   [1]Heb. *glory* or perhaps *my liver*; like the heart, the liver is viewed as the seat of one's emotions.   57:9 ᵃPs 108:3   57:10 ᵃPs 103:11   57:11 ᵃPs 57:5   58 [1]The meaning of the Heb. term is uncertain.   58:3 ᵃ[Ps 53:3; Isa 48:8]   58:4 ᵃEccl 10:11   58:5 ᵃJer 8:17   58:6 ᵃJob 4:10   58:7 ᵃJosh 2:11; 7:5; Ps 112:10; Isa 13:7; Ezek 21:7   [1]MT *he treads his arrows like they are cut off/dry up.*   58:8 ᵃJob 3:16   58:9 ᵃPs 118:12; Eccl 7:6   58:10 ᵃ[Deut 32:43]; Jer 11:20   ᵇPs 68:23   58:11 ᵃPs 92:15; Prov 11:18; [2 Cor 5:10]   ᵇPs 50:6; 75:7   59 [1]Heb. *do not destroy*; perhaps a particular style of music, a tune title, or a musical instrument.   [2]The meaning of the Heb. term is uncertain.   59:3 ᵃPs 56:6   59:4 ᵃPs 35:23   59:6 ᵃPs 59:14

7 Look, they hurl insults at me
and openly threaten to [a]kill me,
for they say,
"[b]Who hears?"
8 But [a]you, O LORD, laugh in disgust at
them;
you taunt all the nations.
9 You are my source of strength. I will
wait [a]for you.[1]
For God is my refuge.
10 The God who loves [a]me will
help [b]me;
God will enable me to triumph over
my enemies.
11 Do not strike them dead suddenly,
because then my people might forget
the lesson.
Use your power to make them
homeless vagabonds and then
bring them down,
O Lord who shields us.
12 [a]They speak sinful words.
So let them be trapped by their own
pride
and by the curses and lies they
speak.
13 Angrily [a]wipe them out. Wipe them
out so they vanish.
[b]Let them know that God rules
over Jacob and to the ends of the
earth. *Selah*
14 They return in the evening;
they growl like dogs
and prowl around outside the city.
15 They [a]wander around looking for
something to eat;
they refuse to sleep until they are
full.
16 As for me, I will sing about your
strength;
I will praise your loyal love in the
morning.
For you are my refuge
and my place of shelter when I face
trouble.
17 You are my [a]source of strength. I will
sing praises to you.[1]
For God is my refuge, the God who
loves me.

*For the music director, according
to the shushan-eduth style;[1] a prayer[2]
of David written to instruct others. It was
written when he fought against Aram
Naharaim and Aram Zobah. That was
when Joab turned back and struck down
12,000 Edomites[3] in the Valley of Salt.*

60 O God, [a]you have rejected us.
You suddenly turned on us in your
anger.
Please restore us!
2 You made the earth quake; you split
it open.
[a]Repair its breaches, for it is ready to
fall.
3 You have made [a]your people
experience hard times;
[b]you have made us drink intoxicating
wine.
4 You have given [a]your loyal followers a
rallying flag,
so that they might seek safety
from the bow. *Selah*
5 Deliver by your power and answer me,
so [a]that the ones you love may be
safe.
6 God has [a]spoken in his sanctuary:
"I will triumph. I will parcel [b]out
[c]Shechem;
[d]the Valley of Sukkoth I will measure
off.
7 Gilead belongs to me,
as does Manasseh.
[a]Ephraim is my helmet,
[b]Judah my royal scepter.
8 [a]Moab is my washbasin.
I will make Edom serve me.
I will shout in triumph [b]over
[c]Philistia."[1]
9 Who will lead me into the fortified
city?
Who will bring me to Edom?
10 Have you not rejected us, [a]O God?
[b]O God, you do not go into battle
with our armies.
11 Give us help against the enemy,
[a]for any help men might offer is futile.
12 By God's [a]power we will conquer;
he will trample down our enemies.

59:7 [a] Ps 57:4; Prov 12:18 [b] Job 22:13; Ps 10:11 **59:8** [a] Prov 1:26 **59:9** [a] [Ps 62:2] [1] Heb. *his strength, for you I will watch.*
59:10 [a] Ps 21:3 [b] Ps 54:7 **59:12** [a] Prov 12:13 **59:13** [a] Ps 104:35 [b] Ps 83:18 **59:15** [a] Job 15:23 **59:17** [a] Ps 18:1 [1] Heb. *my
strength, to you I will sing praises.* **60** [1] Heb. *lily of the testimony*; perhaps a particular music style or a tune title. [2] The
meaning of the Heb. term is uncertain. [3] Heb. *12,000 of Edom*; or perhaps *Aram*. **60:1** [a] Ps 44:9 **60:2** [a] [2 Chr 7:14]; Isa
30:26 **60:3** [a] Ps 71:20 [b] Isa 51:17, 22; Jer 25:15 **60:4** [a] Ps 20:5; Isa 5:26; 11:12; 13:2 **60:5** [a] Ps 108:6–13 **60:6** [a] Ps 89:35
[b] Josh 1:6 [c] Gen 12:6 [d] Josh 13:27 **60:7** [a] Deut 33:17 [b] [Gen 49:10] **60:8** [a] 2 Sam 8:2 [b] 2 Sam 8:14; Ps 108:9 [c] 2 Sam 8:1
[1] Heb. *over me, O Philistia, shout in triumph.* **60:10** [a] Ps 108:11 [b] Josh 7:12 **60:11** [a] Ps 118:8; 146:3 **60:12** [a] Num 24:18

*For the music director, to be
played on a stringed instrument;
written by David.*

61 O God, hear my cry for help.
Pay attention to my prayer.
2 From the remotest place on earth
I call out to you in my despair.
Lead me up to a rocky summit where
I can be safe.
3 Indeed,[1] you [a]are my shelter,
a strong tower that protects me from
the enemy.
4 I [a]will be a permanent guest in your
home;
I will find shelter in the protection
of your wings. *Selah*
5 For you, O God, hear my vows;
you grant me the reward that
belongs to your loyal followers.[1]
6 Give the king long life.
Make his lifetime span several
generations.
7 May he reign forever before God.
Decree that your loyal love [a]and
faithfulness should protect
him.
8 Then I will sing praises to your name
continually,
as I fulfill my vows day after day.

*For the music director,
Jeduthun; a psalm of David.*

62 For God alone I patiently wait;
he is the one who delivers me.
2 He alone is my protector and
deliverer.
He is my refuge; I will not be
[a]upended.
3 How long will you threaten a man
[a]like me?
All of you are murderers,
as dangerous as a leaning wall or an
unstable fence.
4 They spend all their time planning
how to bring their victim down.
They [a]love to use deceit;
they pronounce blessings with their
mouths,
but inwardly they utter curses. *Selah*

5 Patiently wait for God alone, my soul!
For he is the one who gives me hope.
6 He alone is my protector and
deliverer.
He is my refuge; I will not be shaken.
7 [a]God delivers me and exalts me;
God is my strong protector and my
shelter.
8 Trust in him at all times, you people!
[a]Pour out your hearts before him.
God is our shelter. *Selah*
9 [a]Men are nothing but a mere breath;
human beings are unreliable.
When they are weighed in the scales,
all of them together are lighter than
air.
10 Do not trust in what you can gain by
oppression.
Do not put false confidence in what
you can gain by robbery.
[a]If wealth increases, do not become
attached to it.
11 God has declared one principle;
two principles I have heard:
God is strong,
12 and [a]you, O Lord, demonstrate loyal
love.
For you repay men for what they do.

*A psalm of David, written when he
was in the Judean wilderness.*

63 O God, you are [a]my God. I long for
you.
My soul thirsts for you,
my flesh yearns for you,
in a dry and parched land where
there is no water.
2 Yes, in the sanctuary I have seen
[a]you,
and witnessed your power and
splendor.
3 [a]Because[1] experiencing your loyal
love is better than life itself,
my lips will praise you.
4 For this reason [a]I will praise you
while I live;
in your name I will lift up my hands.
5 As with choice meat you satisfy my
soul.
My mouth joyfully praises you,

61:3 [a]Prov 18:10 [1]Or *for*. 61:4 [a]Ps 91:4 61:5 [1]Heb. *you grant the inheritance of those who fear your name; to have
a healthy respect for his revealed reputation, which in turn motivates one to obey his commands.* 61:7 [a]Ps 40:11
62:2 [a]Ps 55:22 62:3 [a]Isa 30:13 62:4 [a]Ps 28:3 62:7 [a][Jer 3:23] 62:8 [a]1 Sam 1:15; Ps 42:4; Lam 2:19 62:9 [a]Job 7:16; Ps
39:5; Isa 40:17 62:10 [a]Job 31:25; [Mark 10:24; Luke 12:15; 1 Tim 6:10] 62:12 [a][Matt 16:27]; Rom 2:6; 1 Cor 3:8 63:1 [a]Ps
42:2; [Matt 5:6] 63:2 [a]Ps 27:4 63:3 [a]Ps 138:2 [1]Or *Indeed, your loyal love is better.* 63:4 [a]Ps 28:2; 143:6

6 whenever [a]I remember you on my
  bed,
and think about you during the
  nighttime hours.
7 For you are my deliverer;
under your wings[1] I rejoice.
8 My soul pursues you;
your right hand upholds me.
9 Enemies seek to destroy my life,
but they will descend into the depths
  of the earth.
10 Each one will be handed over to the
  sword;
their corpses will be eaten by jackals.
11 But the king will rejoice in God;
[a]everyone who takes oaths in his
  name will boast,
for the mouths of those who speak
  lies will be shut up.

For the music director, a psalm of David.

64 Listen to me, O God, as I offer my
  lament!
Protect my life from the enemy's
  terrifying attacks.[1]
2 Hide me from the plots of evil men,
from the crowd of evildoers.
3 They sharpen their tongues like
  swords;
they aim their arrows, [a]a slanderous
  charge,
4 in order to shoot down the innocent
  in secluded places.
They shoot at him suddenly and are
  unafraid of retaliation.
5 They encourage one another to carry
  out their evil deed.
[a]They plan how to hide snares
and boast, "Who will see them?"
6 They devise unjust schemes;
they disguise[1] a well-conceived plot.
Man's inner thoughts cannot be
  discovered.
7 But God will shoot at them;
suddenly they will be wounded by an
  arrow.
8 Their slander will bring about their
  demise.[1]
[a]All who see them will shudder,

9 and all people will fear.[1]
They will [a]proclaim what God has
  done,
and reflect on his deeds.
10 The godly will rejoice in [a]the LORD
and take shelter in him.
All the morally upright will boast.

For the music director,
a psalm of David, a song.

65 Praise awaits you, O God, in Zion.
Vows made to you are fulfilled.
2 You hear prayers;
all people approach you.
3 Our record of sins overwhelms me,
but you forgive our acts of rebellion.
4 How [a]blessed is the one whom you
  [b]choose
and allow to live in your palace courts.
May [c]we be satisfied with the good
  things of your house—
your holy palace.
5 You answer our prayers by
  performing awesome acts of
  deliverance,
O God, our savior.
All the ends of the earth trust in you,
as well as those living across the wide
  seas.[1]
6 You created the mountains by your
  power
and demonstrated your strength.
7 [a]You calmed the raging seas
[b]and their roaring waves,
as well as the commotion made by
  the nations.
8 Even those living in the remotest
  areas are awestruck by your acts;
you cause those living in the east and
  west to praise you.[1]
9 You visit the earth and [a]give it rain;
you make it rich and fertile.
God's streams are full of water;
you provide grain for [b]the people of
  the earth,
for you have prepared the earth in
  this way.
10 You saturate its furrows,
and soak its plowed ground.

63:6 [a] Ps 42:8   **63:7** [1] Heb. *in the shadow of your wings.*   **63:11** [a] Deut 6:13; [Isa 45:23; 65:16]   **64:1** [1] Heb. *from the terror of* [the] *enemy.*   **64:3** [a] Ps 58:7   **64:5** [a] Ps 10:11; 59:7   **64:6** [1] MT *we are finished.*   **64:8** [a] Ps 31:11   [1] MT *and they caused him* [or it] *to stumble upon them, their tongue.*   **64:9** [a] Jer 50:28; 51:10   [1] Sev. medieval MSS *and they will see.*   **64:10** [a] Job 22:19; Ps 32:11   **65:4** [a] Ps 33:12   [b] Ps 4:3   [c] Ps 36:8   **65:5** [1] Heb. *and* [the] *distant sea.*   **65:7** [a] Matt 8:26   [b] Isa 17:12–13   **65:8** [1] Heb. *the goings out of the morning and the evening you cause to shout for joy;* the sunrise and sunset.   **65:9** [a] [Deut 11:12]; Jer 5:24   [b] Ps 46:4; 104:13; 147:8

With rain showers you soften its soil,[1]
and make its crops grow.
11 You crown the year with your good
blessings,
and you leave abundance in your
wake.
12 The pastures in the wilderness
glisten with moisture,
and the hills are clothed with joy.
13 The meadows are [a]clothed with
sheep,
and the valleys are covered with
grain.
They shout joyfully, yes, they sing.

For the music director, a song, a psalm.

66 Shout out [a]praise to God, all the
earth!
2 Sing praises about the majesty of his
reputation.[1]
Give him the honor he deserves!
3 Say to God:
"How [a]awesome are your deeds!
Because of your great power your
enemies cower in fear before you.
4 [a]All the earth worships you
and sings praises to you.
They sing praises to your name."
Selah
5 Come and witness God's exploits!
His acts on behalf of people are
awesome.
6 He turned [a]the sea into dry land;
[b]they passed through the river on
foot.[1]
Let us rejoice in him there.
7 He rules by his power forever;
he watches[1] the nations.
Stubborn rebels should not exalt
themselves. *Selah*
8 Praise our God, you nations.
Loudly proclaim his praise.
9 He preserves our lives
and does not allow our feet to slip.
10 For[1] [a]you, [b]O God, tested us;
you purified us like refined silver.
11 You led us into a trap;
[a]you caused us to suffer.

12 You allowed men to ride over our
heads;
we passed through fire and water,
but [a]you brought us out into a wide
open place.[1]
13 I [a]will enter your temple [b]with burnt
sacrifices;
I will fulfill the vows I made to you,
14 which my lips uttered
and my mouth spoke when I was in
trouble.
15 I will offer up to you fattened
animals as burnt sacrifices,
along with the smell of sacrificial
rams.
I will offer cattle and goats. *Selah*
16 Come! Listen, all you who are loyal to
God.
I will declare what he has done for me.
17 I cried out to him for help
and praised him with my tongue.
18 If [a]I had harbored sin in my heart,
the Lord would not have listened.
19 However, God heard;
he listened to my prayer.
20 God deserves praise,
for he did not reject my prayer
or abandon his love for me.

*For the music director, to be accompanied
by stringed instruments; a psalm, a song.*

67 May God show [a]us his favor and
bless us.
May he smile on us. *Selah*
2 Then those living on earth will know
what [a]you are like;
all nations will know how [b]you
deliver your people.
3 Let the nations thank you, O God.
Let all the nations thank you.
4 Let foreigners rejoice and celebrate.
For [a]you execute justice among the
nations
and govern the people living on
earth. *Selah*
5 Let the nations thank you, O God.
Let all the nations thank you.
6 [a]The earth yields its crops.

65:10 [1]Heb. *soften it.*   **65:13** [a]Isa 44:23; 55:12   **66:1** [a]Ps 100:1   **66:2** [1]Heb. *his name.*   **66:3** [a]Ps 65:5   **66:4** [a]Ps 117:1;
Zech 14:16   **66:6** [a]Exod 14:21   [b]Josh 3:14–16   [1]Some understand this as an allusion to Israel's crossing the Jordan River;
however, the Heb. term does not always refer to a river; it can be used of sea currents. Thus, this line may refer to the
Red Sea crossing.   **66:7** [1]Heb. *his eyes watch.*   **66:10** [a]Job 23:10; Ps 17:3   [b][Isa 48:10; Zech 13:9; Mal 3:3; 1 Pet 1:7]   [1]Or
indeed.   **66:11** [a]Lam 1:13; Ezek 12:13   **66:12** [a]Isa 51:23   [1]MT *saturation.*   **66:13** [a]Ps 100:4; 116:14, 17–19   [b][Eccl 5:4]
66:18 [a]Job 27:9; [Prov 15:29; 28:9]; Isa 1:15; [John 9:31; Jas 4:3]   **67:1** [a]Num 6:25   **67:2** [a]Acts 18:25   [b]Isa 52:10;
Titus 2:11   **67:4** [a][Ps 96:10, 13; 98:9]   **67:6** [a]Lev 26:4; Ps 85:12; [Ezek 34:27]; Zech 8:12

May God, our God, bless us.
7 May God bless us.
Then all the ends of the earth will
give him the honor he deserves.

For the music director,
by David, a psalm, a song.

68 [a]God springs into action.
His enemies scatter;
his adversaries run from him.
2 As smoke is driven away by the wind,
so you drive them away.
[a]As wax melts before fire,
so the wicked are destroyed before
God.
3 But the godly are happy;
they rejoice before God
and are overcome with joy.
4 Sing to God! Sing praises to
his name.
[a]Exalt the one who rides on the
clouds.[1]
For the LORD is his name.[2]
Rejoice before him.
5 He is [a]a father to the fatherless
and an advocate for widows.
God rules from his holy dwelling
place.
6 [a]God settles in [b]their own homes
those who have been deserted;
[c]he frees prisoners and grants them
prosperity.
But sinful rebels live in the desert.
7 O God, [a]when you lead your people
into battle,
when you march through the
wastelands, *Selah*
8 the earth shakes.
Yes, the heavens pour down rain
before God, the God of Sinai,[1]
before God, the God of Israel.
9 O God, [a]you cause abundant showers
to fall on your chosen people.
When they are tired, you sustain
them,
10 for [a]you live among them.
You sustain the oppressed with your
good blessings, O God.

11 The Lord speaks;
many, many women spread the good
news.
12 [a]Kings leading armies run away—they
run away![1]
The lovely lady of the house divides
up the loot.
13 [a]When [b]you lie down among the
sheepfolds,
the wings of the dove are covered
with silver
and with glittering gold.
14 [a]When the Sovereign One[1] scatters
kings,
let it snow on Zalmon.
15 The mountain of Bashan is a
towering mountain;[1]
the mountain of Bashan is a
mountain with many peaks.
16 Why do you look with envy,
O mountains with many peaks,
at the mountain where God has
decided to live?
Indeed the LORD will live there
permanently.
17 God has countless chariots;
[a]they number in the thousands.
The Lord comes from Sinai in holy
splendor.[1]
18 You ascend on high;
[a]you have taken many captives.
[b]You receive tribute[1] from men,
including even sinful rebels.
Indeed, [c]the LORD God lives there.
19 The Lord deserves praise.
Day after day he carries our
burden,
the God who delivers us. *Selah*
20 Our God is a God who delivers;
the LORD, the Sovereign Lord, can
rescue from death.
21 Indeed, [a]God strikes [b]the heads of
his enemies,
the hairy foreheads of those who
persist in rebellion.
22 The Lord says,
"I will retrieve them from Bashan.
I will bring them [a]back [b]from the
depths of the sea,

68:1 [a]Num 10:35 **68:2** [a][Isa 9:18]; Hos 13:3 **68:4** [a]Deut 33:26 [1]Trad. *deserts.* [2]Heb. *in the LORD his name.* **68:5** [a][Ps 10:14, 18; 146:9] **68:6** [a]Ps 107:4-7 [b]Acts 12:6-11 [c]Ps 107:34 **68:7** [a]Exod 13:21; [Hab 3:13] **68:8** [1]Heb. *this one of Sinai;* perhaps indicating that the Lord rules from Sinai. **68:9** [a]Lev 26:4; Deut 11:11; Job 5:10; Ezek 34:26 **68:10** [a]Deut 26:5; Ps 74:19 **68:12** [a]Num 31:8; Josh 10:16; Judg 5:19 [1]An emphatic Heb. construction. **68:13** [a]Ps 81:6 [b]Ps 105:37 **68:14** [a]Josh 10:10 [1]Heb. *Shaddai.* **68:15** [1]Heb. *a mountain of God;* i.e., a mountain fit for God. **68:17** [a]Deut 33:2; Dan 7:10 [1]MT *the Lord [is] among them, Sinai, in holiness.* **68:18** [a]Mark 16:19; Acts 1:9; Eph 4:8; Phil 2:9; Col 3:1; Heb 1:3 [b]Judg 5:12 [c][1 Tim 1:13] [1]Or *gifts.* **68:21** [a]Hab 3:13 [b]Ps 55:23 **68:22** [a]Num 21:33; Deut 30:1-9; Amos 9:1-3 [b]Exod 14:22

23 so [a]that your feet may stomp in their
   blood,
   [b]and your dogs may eat their portion
   of the enemies' corpses."
24 They see your processions, O God—
   the processions of my God, my
   king, who marches along in holy
   splendor.
25 Singers walk in front;
   musicians follow playing [a]their
   stringed instruments,[1]
   in the midst of young women playing
   tambourines.
26 In your large assemblies praise God,
   [a]the LORD, in the assemblies of
   Israel.
27 There is little Benjamin, their ruler,
   and [a]the princes of Judah in their
   robes,
   along with the princes of Zebulun
   and the princes of Naphtali.
28 God has [a]decreed that you will be
   powerful.
   O God, you who have acted on our
   behalf, demonstrate your power.
29 Because of your temple in Jerusalem,
   [a]kings bring tribute to you.
30 Sound your battle cry against [a]the
   wild beast of the reeds,
   and the nations that assemble like a
   herd of calves led by bulls.
   They humble [b]themselves and offer
   gold and silver as tribute.[1]
   God scatters the nations that like to
   do battle.
31 They come with red [a]cloth from
   Egypt.
   [b]Ethiopia[1] voluntarily offers tribute
   to God.
32 O [a]kingdoms of the earth, sing to
   God.
   Sing praises to the Lord,   *Selah*
33 to the one [a]who rides through the
   sky from ancient times.[1]
   Look! He thunders [b]loudly.
34 [a]Acknowledge God's power,
   his sovereignty over Israel,
   and the power he reveals in
   the skies.

35 You are awe inspiring, [a]O God, as you
   emerge from your holy temple.
   It is the God of Israel who gives the
   people power and strength.
   God deserves praise!

*For the music director, according
to the tune of "Lilies"; by David.*

69 Deliver me, O God,
   for [a]the water has reached my neck.
2 I [a]sink into the deep mire
   where there is no solid ground;
   I am in deep water,
   and the current overpowers me.
3 I am exhausted from [a]shouting for
   help.
   [b]My throat is sore;[1]
   my eyes grow tired from looking for
   my God.
4 Those who [a]hate me without cause
   are more numerous than the hairs of
   my head.
   Those who want to destroy me,
   my enemies for no reason,
   outnumber me.
   They make me repay what I did not
   steal.
5 O God, you are aware of my foolish
   sins;
   my guilt is not hidden from you.
6 Let none who rely on you be
   disgraced because of me,
   O Sovereign LORD of Heaven's
   Armies.
   Let none who seek you be ashamed
   because of me,
   O God of Israel.
7 For I suffer humiliation for your sake
   and am thoroughly disgraced.
8 My own brothers treat me [a]like a
   stranger;
   they act as if I were a foreigner.
9 [a]Certainly zeal for your house
   consumes me;
   I endure the insults of those who
   insult you.
10 I weep and refrain from eating food,
   which causes others to insult me.

68:23 [a]Ps 58:10   [b]1 Kgs 21:19; Jer 15:3   **68:25** [a]1 Chr 13:8   [1]Heb. *after* [are] *the stringed instrument players.*   **68:26** [a]Deut 33:28; Isa 48:1   **68:27** [a]Judg 5:14; 1 Sam 9:21   **68:28** [a]Ps 42:8; Isa 26:12   **68:29** [a]1 Kgs 10:10, 25; 2 Chr 32:23; Ps 45:12; 72:10; Isa 18:7   **68:30** [a]Ps 22:12   [b]2 Sam 8:2   [1]Heb. *with pieces* [?] *of silver.*   **68:31** [a]Isa 19:19–23   [b]Isa 45:14; Zeph 3:10   [1]Heb. *Cush.*   **68:32** [a][Ps 67:3–4]   **68:33** [a]Deut 33:26; Ps 18:10   [b]Ps 46:6; Isa 30:30   [1]Heb. *to the one who rides through the skies of skies of ancient times.*   **68:34** [a]Ps 29:1   **68:35** [a]Ps 76:12   **69:1** [a]Job 22:11; Jonah 2:5   **69:2** [a]Ps 40:2   **69:3** [a]Ps 6:6   [b]Deut 28:32; Ps 119:82, 123; Isa 38:14   [1]Or perhaps *raw*; Heb. *burned, inflamed.*   **69:4** [a]Ps 35:19; John 15:25   **69:8** [a]Isa 53:3; Mark 3:21; Luke 8:19; John 7:3–5   **69:9** [a]John 2:17

11 I wear sackcloth
    and they ridicule me.
12 Those who sit at the city gate gossip
        about me;
    [a]drunkards mock me in their songs.
13 O LORD, may you hear my prayer and
        be favorably disposed to me.
    O God, because of your great loyal
        love,
    answer me with your faithful
        deliverance.
14 Rescue me from the mud. Don't let
        me sink.
    Deliver me from those who hate me,
    from the deep water.
15 Don't let the current overpower me.
    Don't let the deep swallow me up.
    Don't let the Pit[1] devour me.
16 Answer me, O LORD, for your loyal
        love is good.
    Because of your great compassion,
        turn toward me.
17 Do not ignore your servant,
    for I am in trouble. Answer me right
        away.
18 Come near me and redeem me.
    Because of my enemies, rescue me.
19 You know how I am insulted,
        humiliated, and disgraced;
    you can see all [a]my enemies.
20 Their [a]insults are painful[1] and make
        me lose heart;
    I look for sympathy, but receive none,
    for [b]comforters, but find none.
21 They put bitter poison into my food,
    [a]and to quench my thirst they give
        me vinegar to drink.
22 [a]May their dining table become a
        trap before them.
    May it be a snare for that group of
        friends.[1]
23 [a]May their eyes be blinded.
    Make them shake violently.
24 [a]Pour out your judgment on them.
    May your raging anger overtake
        them.
25 [a]May their camp become desolate,
    their tents uninhabited.
26 For they harass the one whom [a]you
        discipline;

they spread the news about the
    suffering of those whom you
    punish.
27 [a]Hold them accountable for all their
        sins.
    Do not vindicate them.
28 May their names [a]be deleted from
        the scroll of the living.
    Do not let their names be listed with
        the godly.
29 I am oppressed and suffering.
    O God, deliver and protect me.
30 I [a]will sing praises to God's name.
    I will magnify him as I give him
        thanks.
31 [a]That will please the LORD more
        than an ox or a bull
    with horns and hooves.
32 The oppressed look on—let [a]them
        rejoice.
    [b]You who seek God, may you be
        encouraged.
33 For the LORD listens to the needy;
    he does not despise [a]his captive
        people.
34 [a]Let the heavens [b]and the earth
        praise him,
    along with the seas and everything
        that swims in them.
35 [a]For God will deliver Zion
    and rebuild the cities of Judah,
    and his people will again live in them
        and possess Zion.
36 The descendants of his servants will
        inherit it,
    and those who are loyal to him will
        live in it.

For the music director, by David;
written to get God's attention.

70 O God, please be willing [a]to
    rescue me.
    [b]O LORD, hurry and help me.
2 [a]May those who are trying to
        take my life
    be embarrassed and ashamed.
    May those who want to
        harm me
    be turned back and ashamed.

69:12 [a]Job 30:9   69:15 [1]Heb. *well.*   69:19 [a]Ps 22:6–7; Heb 12:2   69:20 [a]Isa 63:5   [b]Job 16:2   [1]Heb. *break my heart;* the origin of the psalmist's emotions.   69:21 [a]Matt 27:34, 48; Mark 15:23, 36; Luke 23:36; John 19:28–30   69:22 [a]Rom 11:9–10   [1]Heb. *and to the friends for a snare.*   69:23 [a]Isa 6:9–10   69:24 [a][Jer 10:25; 1 Thess 2:16]   69:25 [a]Matt 23:38; Luke 13:35; Acts 1:20   69:26 [a][Isa 53:4; 1 Pet 2:24]   69:27 [a]Neh 4:5; [Rom 1:28]   69:28 [a][Exod 32:32]; Phil 4:3; [Rev 3:5; 13:8]   69:30 [a][Ps 28:7]   69:31 [a]Ps 50:13–14, 23; 51:16   69:32 [a]Ps 34:2   [b]Ps 22:26   69:33 [a][Ps 68:6]; Eph 3:1   69:34 [a]Ps 96:11; Isa 44:23; 49:13   [b]Isa 55:12   69:35 [a]Ps 51:18; Isa 44:26   70:1 [a]Ps 38:title   [b]Ps 40:13–17   70:2 [a]Ps 35:4, 26

3 [a]May those who say, "Aha! Aha!"
be driven back and disgraced.
4 May all those who seek you be happy
and rejoice in you.
May those who love to experience[1]
your deliverance say continually,
"May God be praised!"
5 [a]I am oppressed and needy.
O God, hurry to me.
You are my helper and my deliverer.
O LORD, do not delay.

71 In [a]you, O LORD, I have taken
shelter.
Never let me be humiliated.
2 [a]Vindicate me by rescuing me.
[b]Listen to me. Deliver me.
3 Be my protector and refuge,[1]
a stronghold where I can [a]be safe.[2]
For you are my high ridge [b]and my
stronghold.
4 My God, [a]rescue me from the power
of the wicked,
from the hand of the cruel oppressor.
5 For you are [a]my hope;
O Sovereign LORD, I have trusted in
you since I was young.
6 [a]I have leaned on you since birth;
you pulled me[1] from my mother's
womb.
I praise you continually.
7 [a]Many are appalled when they see me,
but you are my secure shelter.
8 I praise you constantly
and speak of your splendor all day
long.
9 Do not reject me in my old age.
When my strength fails, do not
abandon me.
10 For my enemies talk about me;
those waiting for [a]a chance to kill me
plot my demise.
11 They say, "God has abandoned him.
Run and seize him, for there is no
one who will rescue him."
12 O [a]God, do not remain far away
from me.
My God, hurry and help me.
13 May my accusers be humiliated and
defeated.

May those who want to harm me be
covered with scorn and disgrace.
14 As for me, I will wait continually,
and will continue to praise you.
15 I will tell about your justice,
and all day long proclaim your
salvation,
though I cannot fathom its full
extent.
16 I will come and tell about the mighty
acts of the Sovereign LORD.
I will proclaim your justice—yours
alone.
17 O God, you have taught me since I
was [a]young,
and I am still declaring your amazing
deeds.
18 Even [a]when I am old and gray,
O God, do not abandon me,
until I tell the next generation about
your strength
and those coming after me about
your power.[1]
19 Your justice, [a]O [b]God, extends to the
skies above;
you have done great things.
O God, who can compare to you?
20 Though [a]you have allowed me to
experience much trouble and
distress,
revive me once again.
Bring me up once again[1] from the
depths of the earth.
21 Raise me to a position of great honor.
Turn and comfort me.
22 I will express my thanks to you [a]with
a stringed instrument,
praising your faithfulness, [b]O my
God.
I will sing praises to you
accompanied by a harp,
O Holy One of Israel.
23 My lips will shout for joy. Yes,[1] I will
sing your praises.
I will praise you when you rescue me.
24 All day long my tongue will also tell
about your justice,
for those who want to harm me
will be embarrassed and
ashamed.

70:3 [a]Ps 40:15   70:4 [1]Heb. those who love.   70:5 [a]Ps 72:12–13   71:1 [a]Ps 25:2–3   71:2 [a]Ps 31:1   [b]Ps 17:6   71:3 [a]Ps 31:2–3
[b]Ps 44:4   [1]Heb. become for me a rocky summit of a dwelling place.   [2]Heb. to enter, continually you commanded to deliver me.
71:4 [a]Ps 140:1, 3   71:5 [a]Jer 14:8; 17:7, 13, 17; 50:7   71:6 [a]Ps 22:9–10; Isa 46:3   [1]MT to cut off.   71:7 [a]Isa 8:18; Zech 3:8;
1 Cor 4:9   71:10 [a]2 Sam 17:1   71:12 [a]Ps 35:22   71:17 [a]Deut 4:5; 6:7   71:18 [a][Isa 46:4]   [1]Heb. until I declare your arm
to a generation, to everyone who comes your power.   71:19 [a]Deut 3:24; Ps 57:10   [b]Ps 35:10   71:20 [a]Ps 60:3
[1]Heb. you return, you bring me up.   71:22 [a]Ps 92:1–3   [b]2 Kgs 19:22; Isa 1:4   71:23 [1]Or when.

For[1] *Solomon.*

72 O God, grant the king the ability to make just decisions.
Grant the king's son the ability to make fair decisions.
2 Then [a]he will judge your people fairly
and your oppressed ones equitably.
3 The mountains will bring news of peace to [a]the people,
and the hills will announce justice.
4 He will defend [a]the oppressed among the people;
he will deliver the children of the poor
and crush the oppressor.
5 People will fear you as long [a]as the sun and moon remain in the sky,
for generation after generation.
6 He will descend like rain on [a]the mown grass,
like showers that drench the earth.
7 During his days the godly will flourish;
peace will prevail as long as the moon remains in the sky.
8 May [a]he rule from sea to sea,
and from the Euphrates River[1] to the ends of the earth.
9 [a]Before him the [b]coastlands will bow down,
and his enemies will lick the dust.
10 The kings of Tarshish and [a]the coastlands will offer gifts;
the kings of Sheba and Seba will bring tribute.
11 [a]All kings will bow down to him;
all nations will serve him.
12 For he [a]will rescue the needy when they cry out for help,
and the oppressed who have no defender.
13 He will take pity on the poor and needy;
the lives of the needy he will save.
14 From harm and violence he will defend them;[1]
he will [a]value their lives.

15 May he live! May they offer him gold from [a]Sheba.
May they continually pray for him.
May they pronounce blessings on him all day long.
16 May there be [a]an abundance of grain in the earth;
on the tops of the mountains may it sway.
May its fruit trees flourish like the forests of Lebanon.
May its crops[1] be as abundant as the grass of the earth.[2]
17 May [a]his fame endure.
May his dynasty last as long as the sun remains in the sky.
May they use his name when they formulate their blessings.
May [b]all nations consider him to be favored by God.
18 The LORD God, the God of Israel, deserves [a]praise.
He alone accomplishes amazing things.
19 His glorious name deserves [a]praise forevermore.
May his majestic splendor fill the whole earth.
We agree! We agree![1]
20 This collection of the prayers of David son of Jesse ends here.[1]

BOOK 3 (PSALMS 73–89)

A psalm by Asaph.

73 Certainly God is good to Israel,
and to those whose motives are pure.
2 But as for me, my feet almost slipped;
my feet almost slid out from [a]under me.[1]
3 [a]For I envied those who are proud,
as I observed the prosperity of the [b]wicked.
4 For they suffer no pain;
their bodies are strong and well fed.[1]

72:1 Or *Of Solomon.*   72:2 [a] [Isa 9:7; 11:2–5; 32:1]   72:3 [a] Ps 85:10   72:4 [a] Isa 11:4   72:5 [a] Ps 72:7, 17; 89:36   72:6 [a] Deut 32:2; 2 Sam 23:4; Hos 6:3   72:8 [a] Exod 23:31; [Isa 9:6; Zech 9:10]   [1] Heb. *the river.*   72:9 [a] Ps 74:14; Isa 23:13   [b] Isa 49:23; Mic 7:17   72:10 [a] 1 Kgs 10:2; 2 Chr 9:21   72:11 [a] Isa 49:23   72:12 [a] Job 29:12   72:14 [a] 1 Sam 26:21; [Ps 116:15]   [1] Or *redeem their lives.*   72:15 [a] Isa 60:6   72:16 [a] 1 Kgs 4:20   [1] MT *from the city.*   [2] MT *May there be an abundance of grain in the earth, / and on the tops of the mountains! / May its [or his?] fruit [trees?] rustle like [the trees of] Lebanon! / May they flourish from the city, like the grass of the earth!*   72:17 [a] [Ps 89:36]   [b] Luke 1:48   72:18 [a] 1 Chr 29:10   72:19 [a] [Neh 9:5]   [1] Heb. *surely and surely*; i.e., "amen and amen"; probably a congregational response of agreement to the preceding statement.   72:20 [1] Heb. *the prayers of David, son of Jesse, are concluded*; apparently a remnant of an earlier collection of psalms or an earlier edition of the Psalter.   73:2 [a] Job 12:5   [1] Heb. *to pour out.*   73:3 [a] Ps 37:1, 7; [Prov 23:17]   [b] Job 21:5–16; Jer 12:1   73:4 [1] MT *for there are no pains at their death, and fat* [is] *their body.*

5 They are immune to [a]the trouble
  common to men;
  they do not suffer as other men do.
6 Arrogance is their necklace,
  and violence covers them [a]like
  clothing.
7 Their prosperity causes them to do
  wrong;[1]
  [a]their thoughts are sinful.
8 They mock and say evil things;
  [a]they proudly [b]threaten violence.
9 They speak as if they rule [a]in
  heaven,
  and lay claim to the earth.
10 Therefore they have more than
  enough food to eat
  [a]and even suck up the water of the
  sea.[1]
11 They say, "[a]How does God know what
  we do?
  Is the Most High aware of what
  goes on?"
12 Take a good look. This is what the
  wicked are like,
  those who always have it so easy and
  get richer and richer.
13 I concluded, "Surely in [a]vain I have
  kept my motives pure
  and maintained a pure lifestyle.
14 I suffer all day long
  and am punished every morning."
15 If I had publicized these thoughts,
  I would have betrayed your people.
16 When I tried to make sense of this,
  it was troubling to me.
17 Then I entered the precincts of God's
  temple
  and understood the [a]destiny of the
  wicked.
18 Surely [a]you put them in slippery
  places;
  you bring them down to ruin.
19 How desolate they become in a mere
  moment.
  Terrifying judgments make their
  demise complete.
20 They are like a dream after one
  wakes up.
  O Lord, when you awake you will
  despise them.

21 Yes, my spirit was bitter,
  and my insides felt sharp pain.
22 I was [a]ignorant and lacked insight;
  I was as senseless as an animal before
  you.
23 But I am continually with you;
  you hold my right hand.
24 You guide me by [a]your wise advice,
  and then you will lead me to a
  position of honor.
25 [a]Whom do I have in heaven but you?
  On earth there is no one I desire but
  you.
26 My flesh and [a]my heart may grow
  weak,
  but God always protects my heart
  and gives me [b]stability.
27 Yes, look! [a]Those far from you die;
  you destroy everyone who is
  unfaithful to you.
28 But as for me, God's presence is all I
  need.
  I have made the Sovereign LORD my
  shelter,
  as I [a]declare all the things you have
  done.

A well-written song[1] by Asaph.

74 Why, O God, have you permanently
  rejected us?
  Why does your anger burn against
  the sheep of your pasture?
2 Remember your people whom you
  acquired in ancient times,
  whom you rescued so they could be
  your very own nation,
  as well as Mount Zion, where you
  dwell.
3 Hurry to the permanent ruins,
  and to all the damage the enemy has
  done to the temple.
4 Your enemies roar in the middle of
  [a]your sanctuary;
  [b]they set up their battle flags.
5 They invade like lumberjacks
  swinging their axes in a thick forest.
6 And now they are tearing down all its
  engravings
  with axes and crowbars.

73:5 [a]Job 21:9   73:6 [a]Ps 109:18   73:7 [a]Job 15:27; Jer 5:28   [1]MT *it goes out from fatness their eye.*   73:8 [a]Ps 53:1   [b]2 Pet 2:18; Jude 16   73:9 [a]Rev 13:6   73:10 [a][Ps 75:8]   [1]Heb. *therefore his people return to here, and waters of abundance are sucked up by them.*   73:11 [a]Job 22:13   73:13 [a]Job 21:15; 35:3; Mal 3:14   73:17 [a][Ps 37:38; 55:23]   73:18 [a]Ps 35:6   73:22 [a]Ps 92:6   73:24 [a]Ps 32:8; 48:14; Isa 58:11   73:25 [a][Phil 3:8]   73:26 [a]Ps 84:2   [b]Ps 16:5   73:27 [a][Ps 119:155]   73:28 [a]Ps 116:10; 2 Cor 4:13   74 [1]Or *a contemplative song, a song imparting moral wisdom;* the meaning of the Heb. word is uncertain.   74:4 [a]Lam 2:7   [b]Num 2:2

7 They set your sanctuary on fire;
  they desecrate your dwelling place
    by knocking it to the ground.
8 They say to themselves,
  "We will oppress all of them."
  [a]They burn down all the places in the
    land where people worship God.
9 We do not see any signs of God's
    presence;
  [a]there are no longer any prophets,
  and we have no one to tell us how
    long this will last.
10 How long, O God, will the adversary
    hurl insults?
  Will the enemy blaspheme your
    name forever?
11 [a]Why do you remain inactive?
  Intervene and destroy him.[1]
12 But [a]God has been my king from
    ancient times,
  performing acts of deliverance on
    the earth.
13 You destroyed the sea by [a]your
    strength;
  you shattered the heads of the sea
    monster in the water.
14 You crushed the heads of Leviathan;
  you fed him to the people who live
    along the coast.
15 You broke open the spring and the
    stream;
  [a]you dried up perpetually flowing
    rivers.
16 You established the cycle of day and
    night;
  [a]you put the moon and sun in place.
17 You set [a]up all the boundaries[1] of the
    earth;
  [b]you created the cycle of summer
    and winter.
18 Remember how the enemy hurls
    insults, O LORD,
  and how a foolish nation blasphemes
    your name.
19 Do not hand the life of your dove
    over to a wild animal.
  Do not continue to disregard the
    lives of your oppressed people.

20 [a]Remember your covenant promises,[1]
  for the dark regions of the earth are
    full of places where violence rules.
21 Do not let the afflicted be turned
    back in shame.
  Let the oppressed and poor praise
    your name.
22 Rise up, O God. Defend your honor.
  Remember how fools insult you all
    day long.
23 Do not disregard what your enemies
    say
  or the unceasing shouts of those who
    defy you.

*For the music director, according
to the al-tashcheth style;[1]
a psalm of Asaph, a song.*

75 We give thanks to you, [a]O God. We
  give thanks.
  You reveal your presence;
  people tell about your amazing
    deeds.
2 God says,
  "At the appointed times,
  I judge fairly.
3 When the earth and all its
    inhabitants dissolve in fear,
  I make its pillars secure."   *Selah*
4 I say to the proud, "[a]Do not be
    proud,"
  and to the wicked, "Do not be so
    confident of victory.[1]
5 Do not be so certain you have won.
  Do not speak with your head held so
    high.
6 For victory does not come from the
    east or west,
  or from the wilderness.
7 For [a]God is [b]the judge.
  He brings one down and exalts
    another.
8 For the LORD holds [a]in his hand a
    cup
  full of foaming wine mixed with
    spices,
  and pours it out.

74:8 [a] Ps 83:4   **74:9** [a] 1 Sam 3:1; Lam 2:9; Ezek 7:26; Amos 8:11   **74:11** [a] Lam 2:3   [1] Heb. *Why do you draw back your hand,
even your right hand? From the midst of your chest, destroy!*   **74:12** [a] Ps 44:4   **74:13** [a] Exod 14:21   **74:15** [a] Exod 17:5–6;
Num 20:11; Ps 105:41; Isa 48:21   **74:16** [a] Job 38:12   **74:17** [a] Deut 32:8; Acts 17:26   [b] Gen 8:22   [1] Probably geographical
boundaries, such as mountains, rivers, and seacoasts, but because the day-night cycle has just been mentioned (v. 16)
and the next line speaks of the seasons, possibly the divisions of the seasons.   **74:20** [a] Gen 17:7–8; Lev 26:44–45   [1] Heb.
look at the covenant.   **75** [1] Heb. *do not destroy*; perhaps a particular style of music, a tune title, or a musical instrument.
75:1 [a] Ps 57:title   **75:4** [a] [1 Sam 2:3]; Ps 94:4   [1] Heb. *do not lift up a horn*; signifies military victory.   **75:7** [a] Ps 50:6
[b] 1 Sam 2:7; Ps 147:6; Dan 2:21   **75:8** [a] Job 21:20; Ps 60:3; Jer 25:15; Rev 14:10; 16:19

Surely all the wicked of the earth
will slurp it up and drink it to its very
last drop."
9 As for me, I will continually tell what
you have done;
I will sing praises to the God of Jacob.
10 God says,
"I will bring down [a]all [b]the power of
the wicked;
the godly will [c]be victorious."[1]

For the music director, to be
accompanied by stringed instruments;
a psalm of Asaph, a song.

76 God has revealed himself in [a]Judah;
in Israel his reputation[1] is great.
2 He lives in Salem;
he dwells in Zion.
3 There he shattered the arrows,
the shield, the sword, and the rest
of the weapons of war. Selah
4 You shine brightly and reveal your
majesty,
as you descend from the hills where
you killed your prey.
5 The bravehearted[1] were plundered;
[a]they "fell asleep."
All [b]the warriors were helpless.
6 At the sound of your [a]battle cry,
O God of Jacob,
both rider and horse "fell asleep."
7 You are awesome! Yes, you!
[a]Who can withstand your intense
anger?[1]
8 From heaven [a]you announced what
[b]their punishment would be.
The earth[1] was afraid and silent
9 when God [a]arose to execute
judgment,
and to deliver all the oppressed of
the earth. Selah
10 [a]Certainly your angry judgment upon
men will bring you praise;
you reveal your anger in full measure.
11 [a]Make vows to the LORD your God
and repay them.
[b]Let all those who surround him
bring tribute to the awesome one.

12 He humbles princes;
[a]the kings of the earth regard him as
awesome.

For the music director, Jeduthun;
a psalm of Asaph.

77 I will cry out [a]to God and call for
help.
I will cry out to God and he will pay
attention to me.
2 In my time of trouble I sought the
Lord.
I kept my hand raised in prayer
throughout the night.[1]
I refused to be comforted.
3 I said, "I will remember God while I
groan;
I will think about him while my
strength leaves me." Selah
4 You held my eyelids open;
I was troubled and could not speak.
5 I thought about the days of old,
about ancient times.
6 I said, "During the night I will
remember the song I once sang;
I will think very carefully."
I tried to make sense of what was
happening.
7 I asked, "Will the Lord reject me
forever?
Will he never again show me his
favor?
8 Has his loyal love disappeared
forever?
Has his [a]promise failed forever?
9 Has God forgotten to be merciful?
Has his anger stifled his
compassion?" Selah
10 Then I said, "I am sickened by the
thought
that the Most High might become
inactive.[1]
11 I will remember the works of the
LORD.
Yes, I will remember the amazing
things you did long ago.
12 I will think about all you have done;
I will reflect upon your deeds."

75:10 [a] Ps 101:8; Jer 48:25 [b] Ps 89:17; 148:14 [c] 1 Sam 2:1 [1] Heb. *and all the horns of the wicked I will cut off, the horns of the godly will be lifted up.* 76:1 [a] Ps 48:1, 3 [1] Heb. *name.* 76:5 [a] Isa 10:12; 46:12 [b] Ps 13:3 [1] Heb. *strong of heart.* 76:6 [a] Exod 15:1–21; Ezek 39:20; Nah 2:13; Zech 12:4 76:7 [a] [Ezra 9:15; Nah 1:6; Mal 3:2; Rev 6:17] [1] Heb. *and who can stand before you from the time of your anger?* 76:8 [a] Exod 19:9 [b] 1 Chr 16:30; 2 Chr 20:29 [1] I.e., its inhabitants. 76:9 [a] [Ps 9:7–9] 76:10 [a] Exod 9:16; Rom 9:17 76:11 [a] [Eccl 5:4–6] [b] 2 Chr 32:22–23 76:12 [a] Ps 68:35 77:1 [a] Ps 39:title 77:2 [1] Heb. *my hand [at] night was extended and was not growing numb.* 77:8 [a] [2 Pet 3:8–9] 77:10 [1] Heb. *And I said, "This is my wounding, the changing of the right hand of the Most High".*

13 O God, your deeds are [a]extraordinary.
    What god can compare to our great
    God?[1]
14 You are the God who does amazing
    things;
  you have revealed your strength
    among the nations.
15 You delivered your people by your
    strength—
  the children of Jacob and Joseph.
                                Selah
16 The waters saw you, O God,
  the waters saw you and [a]trembled.
  Yes, the depths of the sea shook with
    fear.
17 The clouds poured down rain;
  the skies thundered.
  Yes, your arrows[1] flashed about.
18 Your thunderous voice was heard in
    the wind;
  the lightning bolts lit up the world.
  The earth trembled and shook.
19 You walked through the sea;
  you passed through the surging
    waters,
  but left no footprints.
20 You led your people like a flock of
    sheep,
  by the hand of Moses and Aaron.

A well-written song[1] by Asaph.

78

Pay attention, my people, to my
instruction.
Listen to the words [a]I speak.
2 I will sing a song that imparts
    [a]wisdom;
  I will make insightful observations
    about the past.
3 What we have heard and learned—
  that which our ancestors have told
    us—
4 we will not hide from their
    descendants.
  [a]We will [b]tell the next generation
  about the LORD's praiseworthy acts,
  about his strength and the amazing
    things he has done.

5 He [a]established a rule[1] in Jacob;
  [b]he set up a law in Israel.
  He commanded our ancestors
  to make his deeds known to their
    descendants,
6 so [a]that the next generation, children
    yet to be born,
  might know about them.
  They will grow up and tell their
    descendants about them.
7 Then they will place their confidence
    in God.
  They will not forget the works of God,
  and they will obey his commands.
8 Then they will not be like their
    ancestors,
  who were [a]a stubborn [b]and rebellious
    generation,
  [c]a generation that was not
    committed
  and faithful to God.
9 The Ephraimites were armed with
    bows,
  but they retreated in the day of
    battle.
10 They did not keep their covenant
    with God,
  and [a]they refused to obey his law.
11 They [a]forgot what he had done,
  the amazing things he had shown
    them.
12 [a]He did [b]amazing things in the sight
    of their ancestors,
  in the land of Egypt, in the region of
    Zoan.
13 He divided [a]the sea and led [b]them
    across it;
  he made the water stand in a heap.
14 [a]He led them with a cloud by day
  and with the light of a fire all night
    long.
15 He broke open rocks in [a]the
    wilderness
  and gave them enough water to fill
    the depths of the sea.
16 He caused [a]streams to flow from the
    rock
  and made the water flow like rivers.

77:13 [a] Ps 73:17   [1] Heb. *Who [is] a great god like God?*; a rhetorical question expecting the answer, "no one!"   **77:16** [a] Exod 14:21; Hab 3:8, 10   **77:17** [1] I.e., lightning.   **78** [1] Or *a contemplative song, a song imparting moral wisdom*; the meaning of the Heb. word is uncertain.   **78:1** [a] Ps 74:title   **78:2** [a] Matt 13:34–35   **78:4** [a] Exod 12:26–27; Deut 4:9; 6:7; Job 15:18; Isa 38:19; Joel 1:3   [b] Exod 13:8, 14   **78:5** [a] Ps 147:19   [b] Deut 4:9; 11:19   [1] I.e., God's command that the older generation teach their children about God's mighty deeds in the nation's history.   **78:6** [a] Ps 102:18   **78:8** [a] 2 Kgs 17:14; 2 Chr 30:7; Ezek 20:18   [b] Exod 32:9; Deut 9:7, 24; 31:27; Judg 2:19; Isa 30:9   [c] Job 11:13; Ps 78:37   **78:10** [a] 2 Kgs 17:15   **78:11** [a] Ps 106:13   **78:12** [a] Exod 7–12   [b] Num 13:22; Isa 19:11; 30:4; Ezek 30:14   **78:13** [a] Exod 14:21   [b] Exod 15:8   **78:14** [a] Exod 13:21   **78:15** [a] Exod 17:6; Num 20:11; Isa 48:21; [1 Cor 10:4]   **78:16** [a] Num 20:8, 10, 11

17 Yet they continued to sin against
  him
  and rebelled ᵃagainst the Most High
  in the desert.
18 They willfully challenged God¹
  by asking for food to satisfy their
  appetite.
19 ᵃThey insulted God, saying,
  "Is God really able to give us food in
  the wilderness?
20 ᵃYes, he struck a rock and water
  flowed out;
  streams gushed forth.
  But can he also give us food?
  Will he provide meat for his people?"
21 When the LORD heard this, he ᵃwas
  furious.
  A fire broke out against Jacob,
  and his anger flared up against Israel,
22 because they ᵃdid not have faith in
  God
  and did not trust his ability to
  deliver them.
23 He gave ᵃa command to the clouds
  above
  and opened the doors in the sky.
24 ᵃHe rained down manna for them to
  eat;
  he gave them the grain of ᵇheaven.
25 Man ate the food of the mighty ones.
  He sent them more than enough to
  eat.
26 He brought ᵃthe east wind through
  the sky
  and by his strength led forth the
  south wind.
27 He rained down meat on them like
  dust,
  birds as numerous as the sand on the
  seashores.
28 He caused them to fall right in the
  middle of their camp,
  all around their homes.
29 ᵃThey ate until they were beyond full;
  he gave them what they desired.
30 They were not yet filled up;
  their food was still in their mouths
31 when the anger of God flared up
  against them.

He killed some of the strongest of
  them;
  he brought the young men of Israel
  to their knees.
32 Despite all this, ᵃthey continued to
  sin,
  and ᵇdid not trust him to do amazing
  things.
33 So ᵃhe caused them to die unsatisfied
  and filled with terror.
34 When ᵃhe struck them down, they
  sought his favor;
  they turned back and longed for God.
35 They remembered that ᵃGod was
  ᵇtheir protector
  and that God Most High was their
  deliverer.
36 But they ᵃdeceived him with their
  words
  and lied to him.
37 They were not really committed to
  him,
  and they were unfaithful to his
  covenant.
38 ᵃYet he is ᵇcompassionate.
  ᶜHe forgives sin and does not
  destroy.
  He often holds back his anger
  and does not stir up his fury.
39 He remembered that ᵃthey were
  made of flesh
  and were like ᵇa wind ᶜthat blows
  past and does not return.
40 How often they ᵃrebelled against him
  in the wilderness
  and insulted him in the wastelands.
41 They ᵃagain challenged God
  and offended the Holy One of Israel.
42 They did not remember what he had
  done,¹
  how he delivered them from the
  enemy,
43 when he performed his awesome
  deeds in Egypt
  and his acts of judgment in the
  region of Zoan.
44 He ᵃturned their rivers into blood,
  and they could not drink from their
  streams.

78:17 ᵃDeut 9:22; Isa 63:10; Heb 3:16   78:18 ¹Heb. *and they tested God in their heart,* the center of their volition.
78:19 ᵃExod 16:3; Num 11:4; 20:3; 21:5   78:20 ᵃNum 20:11   78:21 ᵃNum 11:1   78:22 ᵃDeut 1:32; 9:23; [Heb 3:18]
78:23 ᵃGen 7:11; [Mal 3:10]   78:24 ᵃExod 16:4   ᵇJohn 6:31   78:26 ᵃNum 11:31   78:29 ᵃNum 11:19–20   78:32 ᵃNum
14:16–17   ᵇNum 14:11; Ps 78:11, 22   78:33 ᵃNum 14:29, 35   78:34 ᵃNum 21:7; [Hos 5:15]   78:35 ᵃ[Deut 32:4, 15]   ᵇ[Exod
15:13]; Deut 7:8; Isa 41:14; 44:6; 63:9   78:36 ᵃExod 24:7–8; Ezek 33:31   78:38 ᵃ[Num 14:18–20]   ᵇExod 34:6   ᶜ[Isa 48:9]
78:39 ᵃJob 10:9; Ps 103:14–16   ᵇJohn 3:6   ᶜ[Job 7:7, 16; Jas 4:14]   78:40 ᵃPs 95:8–10; [Eph 4:30]; Heb 3:16
78:41 ᵃNum 14:22; Deut 6:16   78:42 ¹Heb. *his hand.*   78:44 ᵃExod 7:20

45 He sent swarms of biting insects
against ᵃthem,
as well as ᵇfrogs that overran their
land.
46 He gave their crops to the
grasshopper,
the fruit of their labor to the ᵃlocust.
47 He destroyed ᵃtheir vines with hail
and their sycamore-fig trees with
driving rain.
48 He rained hail down on their ᵃcattle
and hurled lightning bolts down on
their livestock.
49 His raging anger lashed out against
them.
He sent fury, rage, and trouble
as messengers who bring disaster.
50 He sent his anger in full force.
He did not spare them from death;
he handed their lives over to
destruction.
51 He struck down all the ᵃfirstborn in
Egypt,
the firstfruits of their reproductive
power in the tents of Ham.
52 Yet he brought out his people like
sheep;
he led them through the wilderness
like ᵃa flock.
53 He ᵃguided them safely along, and
they were not afraid;
but the sea ᵇcovered their enemies.
54 He brought them to the border of his
holy ᵃland,
to this mountainous land that his
right hand acquired.
55 He drove ᵃthe nations out from
before them;
he ᵇassigned them their tribal
allotments
and allowed the tribes of Israel to
settle down.
56 ᵃYet they challenged and defied God
Most High
and did not obey his commands.¹
57 They were unfaithful and acted as
treacherously as their ancestors;
they were as unreliable as a
malfunctioning bow.

58 ᵃThey made him angry with their
pagan shrines
and made him jealous with their
idols.
59 God heard and was angry;
he completely rejected Israel.
60 ᵃHe abandoned the sanctuary at
Shiloh,
the tent where he lived among men.
61 He allowed the symbol of his strong
presence to be captured;
he gave the symbol of his splendor
into the ᵃhand of the enemy.
62 He delivered his people over to ᵃthe
sword
and was angry with his chosen
nation.
63 Fire consumed ᵃtheir young men,
and their virgins remained
unmarried.¹
64 Their priests fell by ᵃthe sword,
but ᵇtheir widows did not weep.
65 But then the Lord awoke from his
sleep;
he was ᵃlike a warrior in a drunken
rage.¹
66 He drove his enemies back;
ᵃhe made them a permanent target
for insults.
67 He rejected the tent of Joseph;
he did not choose the tribe of
Ephraim.
68 He chose the tribe of Judah
and Mount Zion, ᵃwhich he loves.
69 He made his ᵃsanctuary as enduring
as the heavens above,¹
as secure as the earth, which he
established permanently.
70 He chose David, his servant,
and took him from ᵃthe
sheepfolds.
71 He took him away from following
ᵃthe mother sheep,
and made him the shepherd of Jacob,
his people,
and of Israel, his chosen nation.
72 David cared for them with ᵃpure
motives;
he led them with skill.

78:45 ᵃExod 8:24   ᵇExod 8:6   78:46 ᵃExod 10:14   78:47 ᵃExod 9:23–25   78:48 ᵃExod 9:19   78:51 ᵃExod 12:29–30
78:52 ᵃPs 77:20   78:53 ᵃExod 14:19–20   ᵇExod 14:27–28   78:54 ᵃExod 15:17   78:55 ᵃJosh 11:16–23; Ps 44:2   ᵇJosh
13:7; 19:51; 23:4   78:56 ᵃJudg 2:11–13   ¹Heb. his testimonies.   78:58 ᵃDeut 32:16, 21; Judg 2:12; 1 Kgs 14:9; Isa 65:3
78:60 ᵃ1 Sam 4:11; Jer 7:12–14; 26:6–9   78:61 ᵃJudg 18:30   78:62 ᵃJudg 20:21; 1 Sam 4:10   78:63 ᵃJer 7:34; 16:9; 25:10
¹Heb. were not praised; i.e., in wedding songs.   78:64 ᵃ1 Sam 4:17; 22:18   ᵇJob 27:15; Ezek 24:23   78:65 ᵃIsa 42:13   ¹Heb.
like a warrior overcome with wine.   78:66 ᵃ1 Sam 5:6   78:68 ᵃ[Ps 87:2]   78:69 ᵃ1 Kgs 6:1–38   ¹Heb. and he built like
the exalting [ones] his sanctuary.   78:70 ᵃ1 Sam 16:11–12; 2 Sam 7:8   78:71 ᵃ2 Sam 7:8; [Isa 40:11]   78:72 ᵃ1 Kgs 9:4

A psalm of Asaph.

79 O God, foreigners have invaded [a]your chosen land;
[b]they have polluted your holy temple
and turned Jerusalem into a heap of
  ruins.
2 They have given [a]the corpses of your
  servants
to the birds of the sky,
the flesh of your loyal followers
to the beasts of the earth.
3 They have made their blood flow like
  water
all around Jerusalem, and there is no
  one to bury them.
4 We have become an object of disdain
  to our [a]neighbors;
those who live on our borders taunt
  and insult us.
5 How long will this go on, [a]O LORD?
Will you stay angry forever?
How long will your [b]rage burn like
  fire?
6 [a]Pour out your anger on the nations
  that [b]do not acknowledge you,
on the [c]kingdoms that do not pray
  to you.
7 For they have devoured Jacob
and destroyed his home.
8 [a]Do not hold us accountable for the
  sins of earlier generations.
Quickly send your compassion our
  way,
for we are in serious trouble.
9 Help us, [a]O God, our deliverer!
For the sake of your glorious
  reputation, rescue us.
Forgive our sins for the sake of your
  reputation.
10 [a]Why should the nations say, "Where
  is their God?"
Before our very eyes may the shed
  blood of your servants
be avenged among the nations.
11 Listen to [a]the painful cries of the
  prisoners.
Use your great strength to set free
  those condemned to die.
12 Pay back our neighbors in [a]full.

May they be insulted [b]the same way
  they insulted you, O Lord.
13 Then [a]we, your people, the sheep of
  your pasture,
will continually thank you.[1]
[b]We will tell coming generations of
  your praiseworthy acts.

*For the music director, according
to the shushan-eduth style;
a psalm of Asaph.*

80 O Shepherd of Israel, pay
  attention,
[a]you who lead Joseph [b]like a flock of
  sheep.
You who sit enthroned above the
  cherubim, reveal your splendor.
2 In the sight of [a]Ephraim, Benjamin,
  and Manasseh reveal your power.
Come and deliver us.
3 O God, [a]restore [b]us.
Smile on us. Then we will be
  delivered.
4 O LORD God of Heaven's Armies,
[a]how long will you remain angry at
  your people while they pray to
  you?
5 You have given them tears as food;
[a]you have made them drink tears by
  the measure.
6 You have made our neighbors
  dislike us
and our enemies insult us.
7 O God of Heaven's Armies, restore us.
Smile on us. Then we will be
  delivered.
8 You uprooted [a]a vine from Egypt;
[b]you drove out nations and
  transplanted it.
9 You cleared the ground for it;
it took root
and filled the land.
10 The mountains were covered by its
  shadow,
the highest cedars by its [a]branches.
11 Its branches reached the
  Mediterranean Sea,[1]
and its shoots the Euphrates River.[2]

79:1 [a] Ps 74:2 [b] 2 Kgs 25:9–10; 2 Chr 36:17–19; Jer 26:18; 52:12–14; Mic 3:12 **79:2** [a] Deut 28:26; Jer 7:33; 19:7; 34:20 **79:4** [a] Ps 44:13; [Dan 9:16] **79:5** [a] Ps 74:1, 9 [b] [Zeph 3:8] **79:6** [a] Jer 10:25; [Zeph 3:8] [b] Isa 45:4–5; 1 Thess 4:5; [2 Thess 1:8] [c] Ps 53:4 **79:8** [a] Isa 64:9 **79:9** [a] Jer 14:7, 21 **79:10** [a] Ps 42:10 **79:11** [a] Ps 102:20 **79:12** [a] Gen 4:15; Lev 26:21; Prov 6:31; Isa 30:26 [b] Ps 74:10, 18, 22 **79:13** [a] Ps 74:1; 95:7 [b] Isa 43:21 [1] Or, hyperbolically, *will thank you forever.* **80:1** [a] [Exod 25:20–22]; 1 Sam 4:4; 2 Sam 6:2 [b] Ps 77:20 **80:2** [a] Ps 78:9, 67 **80:3** [a] Lam 5:21 [b] Num 6:25; Ps 4:6 **80:4** [a] Ps 79:5 **80:5** [a] Ps 42:3; Isa 30:20 **80:8** [a] [Isa 5:1, 7]; Jer 2:21; Ezek 15:6; 17:6; 19:10 [b] Ps 44:2; Acts 7:45 **80:10** [a] Lev 23:40 **80:11** [1] Heb. *to [the] sea.* [2] Heb. *to [the] river.*

12 Why did you break down its walls,
  so that all who pass by pluck its fruit?
13 The wild boars of the forest ruin it;
  the insects of the field feed on it.
14 O God of Heaven's Armies, come back.
  Look down from heaven and take
    [a]notice.
  Take care of this vine,
15 the root your right hand planted,
  the shoot you made to grow.[1]
16 It is burned and cut down.
  May those who did this die because
    you are displeased with them.
17 [a]May you give support to the one you
    have chosen,
  to the one whom you raised up for
    yourself.
18 Then we will not turn away from you.
  Revive us and we will pray to you.
19 O Lord God of Heaven's Armies,
    restore us.
  Smile on us. Then we will be
    delivered.

*For the music director, according
to the gittith style;[1] by Asaph.*

81 Shout for joy to God, our source of
  strength!
  Shout out to the God of Jacob!
2 Sing a song and play the tambourine,
  the pleasant-sounding harp, and the
  ten-stringed instrument.
3 Sound the ram's horn on the day of
    the new moon
  and on the day of the full moon when
    our festival begins.
4 For observing the festival [a]is a
    requirement for Israel;
  it is an ordinance given by the God of
    Jacob.
5 He decreed it as a regulation in
    Joseph,
  when [a]he attacked the land of Egypt.
  I heard a voice I did not recognize.
6 It said: "I removed the burden from
    his shoulder;
  his hands were released from holding
    the basket.

7 In [a]your [b]distress you called out and I
    rescued you.
  I answered you from a dark
    thundercloud.
  I [c]tested you at the waters of
    Meribah.   *Selah*
8 I said, '[a]Listen, my people!
  I will warn you.
  O Israel, if only you would obey me!
9 There must be no [a]other[1] god among
    you.
  You must not worship a foreign god.
10 I am the Lord, your God,
  the one who brought you out of the
    land of Egypt.
  Open your mouth [a]wide and I will
    fill it.'
11 But my people did not obey me;
  Israel did not submit to me.
12 [a]I gave them over to their stubborn
    desires;
  they did what seemed right to them.
13 If only my people would obey me!
  If only Israel would keep my
    commands!
14 Then I would quickly subdue their
    enemies,
  and attack their adversaries."
15 (May those who hate [a]the Lord
    cower in fear before him.
  May they be permanently
    humiliated.)[1]
16 "I would feed Israel the best wheat,
  and would satisfy your appetite with
    honey [a]from the rocky cliffs."

A psalm of Asaph.

82 God [a]stands in [b]the assembly of El;[1]
  in the midst of the gods he renders
    judgment.
2 He says, "[a]How long will you make
    unjust legal decisions
  and show favoritism to the
    wicked?   *Selah*
3 Defend the cause of the poor and the
    fatherless.
  Vindicate the oppressed and
    [a]suffering.

80:14 [a] Isa 63:15   80:15 [1] Heb. *and upon a son you strengthened for yourself.*   80:17 [a] Ps 89:21   81 [1] Probably a musical style or type of instrument.   81:4 [a] Lev 23:24; Num 10:10   81:5 [a] Deut 28:49; Ps 114:1; Jer 5:15   81:7 [a] Exod 2:23; 14:10; Ps 50:15   [b] Exod 19:19; 20:18   [c] Exod 17:6–7; Num 20:13   81:8 [a] [Ps 50:7]   81:9 [a] [Exod 20:3; Deut 5:7; 32:12]; Ps 44:20; [Isa 43:12]   [1] Heb. *different, illicit.*   81:10 [a] Exod 20:2; Deut 5:6   81:12 [a] [Job 8:4; Acts 7:42; Rom 1:24, 26]   81:15 [a] Rom 1:30   [1] Heb. *and may their time be forever.*   81:16 [a] Job 29:6   82:1 [a] [2 Chr 19:6; Eccl 5:8]   [b] Ps 82:6   [1] Either God himself, a superlative ("God stands in the great assembly"), or the Canaanite high god El.   82:2 [a] [Deut 1:17]; Prov 18:5   82:3 [a] [Deut 24:17; Isa 11:4; Jer 22:16]

4 Rescue the poor and needy.
  Deliver them from the power of the
    wicked.
5 They neither know nor understand.
  They stumble around in the dark,
  while all the [a]foundations of the
    earth crumble.
6 I thought, '[a]You are gods;
  all of you are sons of the Most High.'
7 Yet you will die like mortals;
  you will fall like all the other rulers."[1]
8 Rise up, [a]O God, and execute
    judgment on the earth!
  For you own all the nations.

A song, a psalm of Asaph.

83 O God, [a]do not be silent.
Do not ignore us. Do not be
  inactive, O God.
2 For look, [a]your enemies are making a
    commotion;
  those who hate you are hostile.
3 They carefully plot [a]against your
    people,
  and make plans to harm the ones you
    cherish.
4 They say, "Come on, [a]let's annihilate
    them so they are no longer a
    nation.
  Then the name of Israel will be
    remembered no more."
5 Yes,[1] they devise a unified strategy;
  they form an alliance against you.
6 It includes [a]the tents of Edom and
    the Ishmaelites,
  Moab and the Hagrites,
7 Gebal, Ammon, and Amalek,
  Philistia, and the inhabitants
    of Tyre.
8 Even Assyria has allied with them,
  lending its strength to the
    descendants of Lot.   *Selah*
9 Do to them as you did to [a]Midian—
  as you did to [b]Sisera and Jabin at the
    Kishon River.
10 They were destroyed at Endor;
  their corpses were like manure on
    the ground.
11 Make their nobles like [a]Oreb and
    Zeeb,

and all their rulers like [b]Zebah and
    Zalmunna,
12 who said, "Let's take over the
    pastures of God."
13 O my [a]God, make them [b]like dead
    thistles,[1]
  like dead weeds blown away by the
    wind.
14 Like the fire that burns down the
    forest,
  or the flames that consume the
    mountainsides,
15 chase them with your gale winds
  and terrify them with your
    windstorm.
16 Cover their faces with shame,
  so they might seek you, O LORD.
17 May they be humiliated and
    continually terrified.
  May they die in shame.
18 Then they will know [a]that [b]you alone
    are [c]the LORD,
  the Most High over all the earth.

*For the music director, according
to the gittith style;[1] written
by the Korahites, a psalm.*

84 [a]How [b]lovely is the place where
you live,
  O LORD of Heaven's Armies!
2 I desperately want to be
  in the courts of the LORD's temple.
  [a]My heart and my entire being shout
    for joy
  to the living God.
3 Even the birds find a home there,
  and the swallow builds a nest
  where she can protect her young
  near your altars, O LORD of Heaven's
    Armies,
  my King and my God.
4 How blessed are those who live in
    your [a]temple
  and praise you continually.   *Selah*
5 How blessed are those who find their
    strength in you
  and long to travel the roads that lead
    to your temple.
6 As they pass through the Baca Valley,
  he provides a spring for them.[1]

82:5 [a]Ps 11:3   82:6 [a]John 10:34   82:7 [1]Heb. *like one of the rulers.*   82:8 [a]Ps 2:8; [Rev 11:15]   83:1 [a]Ps 28:1   83:2 [a]Ps 81:15;
Isa 17:12; Acts 4:25   83:3 [a][Ps 27:5]   83:4 [a]Esth 3:6, 9; Jer 11:19; 31:36   83:5 [1]Or *for.*   83:6 [a]2 Chr 20:1, 10, 11   83:9 [a]Num
31:7; Judg 7:22   [b]Judg 4:15–24; 5:20–21   83:11 [a]Judg 7:25   [b]Judg 8:12–21   83:13 [a]Isa 17:13   [b]Job 21:18; Ps 35:5; Isa 40:24; Jer
13:24   [1]Or *tumbleweed.*   83:18 [a]Ps 59:13   [b]Exod 6:3   [c][Ps 92:8]   84 [1]Probably a musical style or type of instrument.
84:1 [a]Ps 8:title   [b]Ps 27:4; 46:4–5   84:2 [a]Ps 42:1–2   84:4 [a][Ps 65:4]   84:6 [1]MT *a spring they make it.*

The rain even covers it with pools ᵃof
  water.²
7 They are sustained as they travel
    along;
  each one ᵃappears before God in Zion.
8 O Lᴏʀᴅ God of Heaven's Armies,
  hear my prayer.
  Listen, O God of Jacob.   *Selah*
9 O ᵃGod, take notice of our shield.¹
  Show concern for your chosen king.
10 Certainly spending just one day in
    your temple courts is better
  than spending a thousand elsewhere.
  I would rather stand at the entrance
    to the temple of my God
  than live in the tents of the wicked.
11 For the Lᴏʀᴅ God is our ᵃsovereign
    ᵇprotector.
  The Lᴏʀᴅ bestows favor and ᶜhonor;
  he withholds no good thing from
    those who have integrity.
12 O Lᴏʀᴅ of Heaven's Armies,
  how ᵃblessed are those who trust in
    you.

*For the music director, written
by the Korahites, a psalm.*

85 O Lᴏʀᴅ, you showed favor to your
    land;
  you restored the well-being ᵃof Jacob.
2 You pardoned the wrongdoing of
    your people;
  you forgave all their sin.   *Selah*
3 You withdrew all your fury;
  you turned back from your raging
    anger.
4 ᵃRestore us, O God our deliverer.
  Do not be displeased with us.
5 Will you stay mad at us forever?
  ᵃWill you remain angry throughout
    future generations?
6 Will you not ᵃrevive us once more?
  Then your people will rejoice in you.
7 O Lᴏʀᴅ, show us your loyal love.
  Bestow on us your deliverance.
8 I will listen to what God the Lᴏʀᴅ
    says.
  For he will make¹ peace with his
    people, his faithful followers.

Yet they must not return to their
  foolish ways.
9 Certainly ᵃhis loyal followers will
    soon experience his deliverance;
  then his splendor will again appear
    in our land.
10 Loyal love and faithfulness meet;
  ᵃdeliverance and peace greet each
    other with a kiss.
11 Faithfulness grows from the ground,
  and deliverance looks down from the
    sky.
12 ᵃYes, the Lᴏʀᴅ will bestow his good
    blessings,
  and our land will yield its crops.
13 Deliverance goes before him,
  and prepares a pathway for him.

A prayer of David.

86 Listen, O Lᴏʀᴅ. Answer me.
    For I am oppressed and needy.
2 Protect me, for I am loyal.
  You are my God; deliver your servant
    who trusts in you.
3 Have mercy on me, O Lord,
  for I cry out to you all day long.
4 Make your servant glad,
  ᵃfor to you, O Lord, I pray.
5 Certainly,¹ ᵃO Lord, you are kind and
    forgiving,
  and show great faithfulness to all
    who cry out to you.
6 O Lᴏʀᴅ, hear my prayer.
  Pay attention to my plea for mercy.
7 In my time of trouble I cry out to
    you,
  for you will answer me.
8 None can compare to you ᵃamong
    the gods, O Lord.
  Your exploits are incomparable.
9 All the nations, whom you created,
  will come and worship you, O Lord.
  They will honor your name.
10 For you are great and ᵃdo amazing
    things.
  ᵇYou alone are God.
11 O Lᴏʀᴅ, ᵃteach me how you want me
    to live.¹
  Then I will obey your commands.

84:6 ᵃ2 Sam 5:22–25 ²MT *blessings.* 84:7 ᵃExod 34:23; Deut 16:16 84:9 ᵃGen 15:1 ¹I.e., the Davidic king, who, as God's vice-regent, was the human protector of the people. 84:11 ᵃIsa 60:19–20; Mal 4:2; Rev 21:23 ᵇGen 15:1 ᶜPs 34:9–10 84:12 ᵃ[Ps 2:12; 40:4] 85:1 ᵃPs 42:title 85:4 ᵃPs 80:3, 7 85:5 ᵃPs 79:5 85:6 ᵃHab 3:2 85:8 ¹Heb. *speak.* 85:9 ᵃIsa 46:13 85:10 ᵃPs 72:3; [Isa 32:17]; Luke 2:14 85:12 ᵃ[Ps 84:11; Jas 1:17] 86:4 ᵃPs 25:1; 143:8 86:5 ᵃPs 130:7; 145:9; [Joel 2:13] ¹Or *for.* 86:8 ᵃ[Exod 15:11]; 2 Sam 7:22; 1 Kgs 8:23; Ps 89:6; Jer 10:6 86:10 ᵃ[Exod 15:11] ᵇDeut 6:4; Isa 37:16; Mark 12:29; 1 Cor 8:4 86:11 ᵃPs 27:11; 143:8 ¹Heb. *teach me your way*; i.e., the moral principles God expects the psalmist to follow.

Make me wholeheartedly committed
   to you.
12 O Lord, my God, I will give you
   thanks with my whole heart.
I will honor your name continually.
13 For you will extend your great loyal
   love to me
and will deliver my life from the
   depths of Sheol.[1]
14 O God, arrogant men attack me;
a gang of ruthless men, who do not
   respect you, seek my life.
15 But [a]you, O Lord, are a
   compassionate and merciful God.
You are patient and demonstrate
   great loyal love and faithfulness.
16 Turn toward me and have mercy
   on me.
Give your servant your strength.
Deliver this son of your female
   servant.
17 Show me evidence of your favor.
Then those who hate me will see it
   and be ashamed,
for you, O Lord, will help me and
   comfort me.

Written by the Korahites; a psalm, a song.

87 The Lord's city is in the holy
   hills.
2 The Lord loves [a]the gates of Zion
more than all the dwelling places
   of Jacob.
3 People say wonderful things about
   you,[1]
   [a]O city of God.   *Selah*
4 I mention Rahab and Babylon to my
   followers.
Here are Philistia and Tyre, along
   with Ethiopia.[1]
It is said of them, "This one was born
   there."
5 But it is said of Zion's residents,
"Each one of these was born in her,
and the Most High makes her
   secure."
6 The Lord writes in the census [a]book
   of the nations,
"This one was born there."   *Selah*

7 As for the singers, as well as the
   pipers—
all of them sing within your walls.[1]

*A song, a psalm written by the Korahites,
for the music director, according
to the machalath-leannoth
style; a well-written song[1]
by Heman the Ezrahite.*

88 O Lord [a]God who delivers me,
   by day I cry out
and at night I pray before you.
2 Listen to my prayer.
Pay attention to my cry for help.
3 For my life is filled with troubles,
and I am ready to enter Sheol.
4 They treat me [a]like those who
   descend into the grave.[1]
I am like a helpless man,
5 adrift among the dead,
like corpses lying in the grave
whom you remember no more
and who are cut off from your power.
6 You place me in the lowest regions of
   the Pit,
in the dark places, in the watery
   depths.
7 Your anger bears down on me,
and [a]you overwhelm me with all
   your waves.   *Selah*
8 You cause those who know me to
   keep their distance;
[a]you make me an [b]appalling sight to
   them.
I am trapped and cannot get free.
9 My eyes grow weak because of
   oppression.
I call out to you, O [a]Lord, all day
   long;
I spread out my hands in prayer to
   you.
10 Do you accomplish amazing things
   for the dead?
Do the departed spirits[1] rise up
   and give you thanks?   *Selah*
11 Is your loyal love proclaimed in the
   grave,
or your faithfulness in the place of
   the dead?[1]

86:13 [1] Or *lower Sheol.*   86:15 [a] Exod 34:6; [Ps 86:5]   87:2 [a] Ps 78:67–68   87:3 [a] Isa 60:1   [1] Or *wonderful things are announced concerning you;* Heb. *glorious things are spoken about you.*   87:4 [1] Heb. *Cush.*   87:6 [a] Isa 4:3   87:7 [1] Heb. *and singers, like pipers, all my springs* [are] *in you.*   88:1 Or *a contemplative song, a song imparting moral wisdom; the meaning of the Heb. word is uncertain.*   88:1 [a] Ps 27:9; [Luke 18:7]   88:4 [a] Ps 31:12   [1] Heb. *the pit.*   88:7 [a] Ps 42:7   88:8 [a] Job 19:13, 19; Ps 31:11; 142:4   [b] Lam 3:7   88:9 [a] Ps 86:3   88:10 [1] Heb. *Rephaim; those who occupy the land of the dead.*   88:11 [1] Heb. *in Abaddon;* a name for Sheol.

12 Are your amazing deeds experienced
    in the dark region,
  or your deliverance in the land of
    oblivion?
13 As for me, I cry out to you, O LORD;
  in the morning my prayer confronts
    you.
14 O LORD, why do you reject me,
  and pay no attention to me?
15 I am oppressed and have been on the
    verge of death since my youth.
  I have been subjected to your horrors
    and am numb with pain.
16 Your anger overwhelms me;
  your terrors destroy me.
17 They surround me like water all day
    long;
  they join forces and encircle me.
18 ᵃYou cause my friends and neighbors
    to keep their distance;
  those who know me leave me alone
    in the darkness.

  A well-written song[1]
  by Ethan the Ezrahite.

89 I will sing continually about the
  LORD's faithful deeds;
  to future generations I will proclaim
    your faithfulness.
2 For I say, "Loyal love is permanently
    established;
  in the skies ᵃyou set up your
    faithfulness."
3 The LORD ᵃsaid,
  "I have made a covenant with my
    chosen one;
  I have made a promise on ᵇoath to
    David, my servant:
4 'I will give you an eternal dynasty
  and establish your throne throughout
    future generations.'"   *Selah*
5 O LORD, ᵃthe heavens praise your
    amazing deeds,
  as well as your faithfulness in the
    angelic assembly.
6 ᵃFor who in the skies can compare to
    the LORD?

Who is like the LORD among the
    heavenly beings,[1]
7 a ᵃGod who is honored in the great
    angelic assembly,
  and more awesome than all who
    surround him?
8 O LORD God of Heaven's Armies![1]
  Who is strong like you, O LORD?
  Your faithfulness surrounds you.
9 You rule over the proud sea.
  When its waves surge, ᵃyou calm them.
10 You crushed the Proud One[1] and
    killed it;
  with ᵃyour strong arm you scattered
    your enemies.
11 The heavens belong to you, as does
    ᵃthe earth.
  You made the world and all it
    contains.
12 You created the north and the south.
  ᵃTabor and ᵇHermon rejoice in your
    name.
13 Your arm is powerful,
  your hand strong,
  your right hand victorious.
14 Equity and justice are the foundation
    of your throne.
  Loyal love and faithfulness
    characterize your rule.
15 How blessed are the people who
    worship you!
  ᵃO LORD, they experience your favor.
16 They rejoice in your name all day long,
  and are vindicated by your justice.
17 For you give them splendor and
    strength.
  By your favor we are victorious.
18 For our shield belongs to the LORD,
  our king to the Holy One of Israel.
19 Then you spoke through a vision to
    your faithful followers[1] and said:
  "I have placed a young hero[2] over a
    warrior;
  I have raised up a young man from
    the people.
20 I have ᵃdiscovered David, my servant.
  With my holy oil I have anointed him
    as king.

88:18 ᵃJob 19:13; Ps 31:11; 38:11   89 ¹Or *a contemplative song, a song imparting moral wisdom*; the meaning of the Heb. word is uncertain.   89:2 ᵃ[Ps 119:89–90]   89:3 ᵃ1 Kgs 8:16   ᵇ2 Sam 7:11; 1 Chr 17:10–12   89:5 ᵃ[Ps 19:1]   89:6 ᵃPs 86:8; 113:5   ¹Heb. *sons of gods, sons of God*.   89:7 ᵃPs 76:7, 11   89:8 ¹Trad. *God of hosts*.   89:9 ᵃPs 65:7; 93:3–4; 107:29   89:10 ᵃExod 14:26–28; Ps 87:4; Isa 30:7; 51:9   ¹Heb. *Rahab*; perhaps alluding to Egypt and the exodus or the sea (or the mythological sea creature), which symbolizes the disruptive forces of the world.   89:11 ᵃ[Gen 1:1; 1 Chr 29:11]   89:12 ᵃJosh 19:22; Judg 4:6; Jer 46:18   ᵇDeut 3:8; Josh 11:17; 12:1; Song 4:8   89:15 ᵃLev 23:24; Num 10:10; Ps 98:6   89:19 ¹Sev. medieval MSS *follower*.   ²MT *I have placed help on a warrior* or *I have strengthened a warrior*.   89:20 ᵃ1 Sam 13:14; 16:1–12; Acts 13:22

21 [a]My hand will support him,
and my arm will strengthen him.
22 No enemy will be able to exact
tribute from him;
a violent oppressor will not be able
to humiliate him.
23 I will crush his enemies before him;
I will strike down those who hate
him.
24 He will experience my faithfulness
and loyal love,
and by my name he will win victories.
25 I will [a]place his hand over the sea,
his right hand over the rivers.[1]
26 He will call out to me,
'You are [a]my [b]father, my God, and the
protector who delivers me.'
27 I will appoint him to be [a]my firstborn
son,
[b]the most exalted of the earth's
kings.
28 I will always extend [a]my loyal love to
him,
and my covenant with him is
secure.
29 I will give him [a]an eternal [b]dynasty
and make his throne as enduring as
the skies above.
30 If his sons [a]reject my law
and disobey my regulations,
31 if they break my rules
and do not keep my commandments,
32 I will punish their rebellion by
beating them with a club,
their sin by inflicting them with
bruises.
33 [a]But I will not remove my loyal love
from him
nor be unfaithful to my promise.
34 I will not break my covenant
or go back [a]on what I promised.
35 Once and for all I have vowed [a]by my
own holiness,
I will never deceive David.
36 His dynasty will last forever.
[a]His throne will endure before me,
like the sun;
37 it will remain stable, like the moon.

His throne will endure like the
skies." Selah
38 But you have spurned and [a]rejected
him;
you are angry with your chosen king.[1]
39 You have repudiated [a]your covenant
with your servant;
you have thrown his crown to the
ground.
40 You have broken down all his walls;
you have made his strongholds a
heap of ruins.
41 All who pass by have [a]robbed him;
he has become an object of disdain
to his neighbors.
42 You have allowed his adversaries to
be victorious
and all his enemies to rejoice.
43 You turn back his sword from the
adversary[1]
and have not sustained him in battle.
44 You have brought to an end his
splendor[1]
and have knocked his throne to the
ground.
45 You have cut short his youth
and have covered him with
shame. Selah
46 How long, O LORD, will this last?
Will you remain hidden forever?
Will your anger continue to burn like
fire?
47 Take note of my brief lifespan.
Why do you make all people so
[a]mortal?
48 No man can live on without
experiencing [a]death
or deliver his life from the power
of Sheol. Selah
49 Where are your earlier faithful deeds,
[a]O Lord,[1]
the ones performed [b]in accordance
with your reliable oath to David?
50 Take note, [a]O Lord,[1] of the way your
servants are taunted
and of how I must bear so many
insults from people.
51 [a]Your enemies, O LORD, hurl insults;

89:21 [a] Ps 80:17   89:25 [a] Ps 72:8   [1] Perhaps the Mediterranean and Euphrates; however, more likely symbols for hostile powers that oppose God and the king.   89:26 [a] 2 Sam 7:14; [1 Chr 22:10]; Jer 3:19   [b] 2 Sam 22:47   89:27 [a] Exod 4:22; Ps 2:7; Jer 31:9; [Col 1:15, 18]   [b] Num 24:7; [Ps 72:11]; Rev 19:16   89:28 [a] Isa 55:3   89:29 [a] [1 Kgs 2:4; Isa 9:7]; Jer 33:17   [b] Deut 11:21   89:30 [a] Ps 119:53   89:33 [a] 2 Sam 7:14-15   89:34 [a] [Num 23:19]; Jer 33:20-22   89:35 [a] [1 Sam 15:29]; Amos 4:2; [Titus 1:2]   89:36 [a] [Luke 1:33]   89:38 [a] Deut 32:19   [1] Heb. your anointed one.   89:39 [a] Ps 74:7; Lam 5:16   89:41 [a] Ps 80:12   89:43 [1] Heb. you turn back, rocky summit, his sword.   89:44 [1] MT from his splendor.   89:47 [a] Ps 62:9   89:48 [a] [Eccl 3:19]   89:49 [a] [2 Sam 7:15]; Jer 30:9; Ezek 34:23   [b] Ps 54:5   [1] Sev. medieval MSS the LORD.   89:50 [a] Ps 69:9, 19   [1] Sev. medieval MSS the LORD.   89:51 [a] Ps 74:10, 18, 22

they insult your chosen king as they
    dog his footsteps.[1]
52 The LORD deserves [a]praise
    forevermore!
    We agree! We agree![1]

BOOK 4 (PSALMS 90–106)

A prayer of Moses, the man of God.

90 O Lord, [a]you have been our
    protector through all generations.
2 Even [a]before the mountains came
    into existence,
  or you brought the world into being,
  you were the eternal God.
3 You make mankind [a]return to the
    dust,
  and say, "Return, O people."
4 Yes,[1] in your eyes a thousand years
  are like yesterday that quickly passes,
  [a]or like one of the divisions of the
    nighttime.
5 You bring their lives to an end and
  [a]they "fall asleep."
  In [b]the morning they are like the
  grass that sprouts up:
6 In the morning it glistens and
    sprouts up;
  at evening time it withers and
    dries up.
7 Yes,[1] we are consumed by your anger;
  we are terrified by your wrath.
8 You are aware of our sins;
  [a]you even know about our hidden
    [b]sins.
9 Yes,[1] throughout all our days we
  experience your raging fury;
  the years of our lives pass quickly,
  like a sigh.
10 The days of our lives add up to 70
    years,
  or 80, if one is especially strong.
  But even one's best years are marred
  by trouble and oppression.
  Yes,[1] they pass quickly and we fly
    away.
11 Who can really fathom the intensity
  of your anger?

Your raging fury causes people to
    fear you.[1]
12 So teach us to consider our mortality,
  [a]so that we might live wisely.
13 Turn back toward us, O LORD.
  How long must this suffering last?
  [a]Have pity on your servants.
14 Satisfy us in the morning with your
    loyal love.
  Then we will shout for joy and be
  happy all our days.
15 Make us happy in proportion to the
  days you have afflicted us,
  in proportion to the years we have
  experienced trouble.
16 May [a]your servants see your work.
  May their sons see your majesty.
17 [a]May our Sovereign God extend his
  favor to us.
  [b]Make our endeavors successful.
  Yes, make them successful.

91 As for you, the one [a]who lives in the
  shelter of the Most High,
  and resides in the protective shadow
  of the Sovereign One—
2 I say [a]this about the LORD, my
  shelter and my stronghold,
  my God in whom I trust—
3 he will certainly rescue you from [a]the
  snare of the hunter
  and from the destructive plague.
4 He will [a]shelter you with his wings;[1]
  you will find safety under his wings.
  His faithfulness is like a shield or a
  protective wall.
5 [a]You need not fear the terrors of the
    night,
  the arrow that flies by day,
6 the plague that stalks in the
    darkness,
  or the disease that ravages at noon.
7 Though a thousand may fall beside
    you,
  and a multitude on your right side,
  it will not reach you.
8 Certainly you will see [a]it with your
  very own eyes—
  you will see the wicked paid back.

89:51 [1]Heb. [by] *which your enemies, O LORD, taunt,* [by] *which they taunt* [at] *the heels of your anointed one.* **89:52** [a]Ps 41:13 [1]Heb. *surely and surely;* i.e., "amen and amen"; probably a congregational response of agreement to the preceding statement. **90:1** [a][Deut 33:27; Ezek 11:16] **90:2** [a]Job 15:7; [Prov 8:25–26] **90:3** [a]Gen 3:19; Job 34:14–15 **90:4** [a]2 Pet 3:8 [1]Or *for.* **90:5** [a]Ps 73:20 [b]Isa 40:6 **90:7** [1]Or *for.* **90:8** [a]Ps 50:21; [Jer 16:17] [b]Ps 19:12; [Eccl 12:14] **90:9** [1]Or *for.* **90:10** [1]Or *for.* **90:11** [1]Heb. *and like your fear* [is] *your raging fury.* **90:12** [a]Deut 32:29; Ps 39:4 **90:13** [a]Exod 32:12; Deut 32:36 **90:16** [a][Deut 32:4]; Hab 3:2 **90:17** [a]Ps 27:4 [b]Isa 26:12 **91:1** [a]Ps 27:5; 31:20; 32:7 **91:2** [a]Ps 142:5 **91:3** [a]Ps 124:7; Prov 6:5 **91:4** [a]Ps 17:8 [1]MT *wing.* **91:5** [a][Job 5:19; Ps 112:7; Isa 43:2] **91:8** [a]Ps 37:34; Mal 1:5

9 For you have taken refuge in the
    LORD,
  [a]my shelter, the Most High.
10 No harm will overtake you;
  [a]no illness will come near your home.
11 [a]For he will order his angels
    to protect you in all you do.
12 They will lift you up in their hands,
    so you will not slip and fall on a
      stone.
13 You will subdue a lion and a snake;
    you will trample underfoot a young
      lion and a serpent.
14 The LORD says,
  "Because he is devoted to me, I will
      deliver him;
    I will protect him because he is loyal
  [a]to me.
15 When he calls [a]out to me, [b]I will
      answer him.
    I will be with him when he is in
      trouble;
    I will rescue him and bring him
      honor.
16 I will satisfy him with long life
    and will let him see my salvation."

A psalm; a song for the Sabbath day.

92 It is [a]fitting to thank the LORD,
  and to sing praises to your name,
  O Most High.
2 It is fitting to [a]proclaim your loyal
    love in the morning
  and your faithfulness during the
      night,
3 to the accompaniment of a
      ten-stringed instrument and a
      lyre,
    to the accompaniment of the
      meditative [a]tone of the harp.
4 For you, O LORD, have made me
      happy by your work.
    I will sing for joy because of what you
      have done.
5 How great are [a]your works, [b]O LORD!
    Your plans are very intricate!
6 The [a]spiritually insensitive do not
      recognize this;
    the fool does not understand this.

7 When [a]the wicked sprout up like
      grass,
    and all the evildoers glisten,
    it is so that they may be annihilated.
8 [a]But you, O LORD, reign forever.
9 Indeed,[1] look at your enemies,
    O LORD.
    Indeed,[2] look at how your enemies
      perish.
    All the evildoers are scattered.
10 You exalt [a]my horn like that of a
      wild ox.
    I am [b]covered with fresh oil.
11 [a]I gloat in triumph over those who
      tried to ambush me;
    I hear the defeated cries of the evil
      foes who attacked me.
12 The godly grow like a palm tree;
  [a]they grow high like a cedar in
      Lebanon.
13 Planted in the LORD's house,
    they grow in the courts of our God.
14 They bear fruit even when they are
      old;
    they are filled with vitality and have
      many leaves.
15 So [a]they proclaim that [b]the LORD, my
      Protector,
    is just and never unfair.

93 The [a]LORD reigns.
  [b]He is robed in majesty.
  The LORD is robed;
  he wears strength around his waist.
  Indeed, the world is established; it
      cannot be moved.
2 Your throne has been secure from
      ancient times;
  [a]you have always been king.
3 The waves roar, O LORD,
    the waves roar,
    the waves roar and crash.
4 Above [a]the sound of the surging
      water,
    and the mighty waves of the sea,
    the LORD sits enthroned in majesty.
5 The rules you set down[1] are
      completely reliable.
    Holiness aptly adorns your house,
    O LORD, forever.

91:9 [a] Ps 91:2   91:10 [a] [Prov 12:21]   91:11 [a] Ps 34:7; Matt 4:6; Luke 4:10; [Heb 1:14]   91:14 [a] [Ps 9:10]   91:15 [a] Job 12:4; Ps 50:15   [b] Isa 43:2   92:1 [a] Ps 147:1   92:2 [a] Ps 89:1   92:3 [a] 1 Chr 23:5   92:5 [a] Ps 40:5; [Rev 15:3]   [b] Ps 139:17–18; [Isa 28:29; Rom 11:33–34]   92:6 [a] Ps 73:22   92:7 [a] Job 12:6; Ps 37:1–2; Jer 12:1–2; [Mal 3:15]   92:8 [a] [Ps 83:18]   92:9 [1] Or *for.* [2] Or *for.*   92:10 [a] Ps 89:17   [b] Ps 23:5   92:11 [a] Ps 54:7   92:12 [a] Num 24:6; Ps 52:8; Jer 17:8; Hos 14:5–6   92:15 [a] [Deut 32:4]   [b] [Rom 9:14]   93:1 [a] Ps 96:10   [b] Ps 65:6   93:2 [a] Ps 45:6; [Lam 5:19]   93:4 [a] Ps 65:7   93:5 [1] Trad. *your testimonies*; the demands of God's covenant law.

94

O Lord, the God who avenges!
ªO God who avenges, reveal your
   splendor.
2 Rise up, O ªjudge of the earth.
   Pay back the proud.
3 O Lord, ªhow long will the wicked,
   how long will the wicked
      celebrate?
4 They spew ªout threats and speak
      defiantly;
   all the evildoers boast.
5 O Lord, they crush your people;
   they oppress the nation that belongs
      to you.
6 They kill the widow and the resident
      foreigner,
   and they murder the fatherless.
7 ªThen they say, "The Lord does not
      see this;
   the God of Jacob does not take notice
      of it."
8 Take notice of this, you ignorant
      people.
   You fools, when will you ever
      understand?
9 Does ªthe one who makes the human
      ear not hear?
   Does the one who forms the human
      eye not see?
10 Does the one who disciplines the
      nations not punish?
   He is the one who imparts
      knowledge to human beings!
11 The Lord ªknows that peoples'
      thoughts
   are morally bankrupt.
12 How blessed is the one whom you
      ªinstruct, O Lord,
   the one whom you teach from your
      law
13 in order to protect him from times of
      trouble,
   until the wicked are destroyed.
14 Certainly¹ the Lord does not forsake
      his people;
   he does not abandon the nation that
      belongs to him.
15 For justice will prevail,
   and all the morally upright will be
      vindicated.

16 Who will rise up to defend me
      against the wicked?
   Who will stand up for me against the
      evildoers?
17 If the Lord had not helped me,
   I would soon have dwelt in the
      silence of death.
18 If I say, "My foot is slipping,"
   your loyal love, O Lord, supports me.
19 When worries threaten to
      overwhelm me,
   your soothing touch makes me happy.
20 Cruel rulers are not your allies,
   those who make oppressive laws.
21 They conspire against the blameless
   and condemn to death the ªinnocent.
22 But the Lord will protect me,
   and my God will shelter me.
23 He will pay them back for their sin.
   He will destroy them because of¹
      their evil;
   the Lord our God will destroy them.

95

Come, let us sing for joy to the Lord.
Let us shout out praises to our
   Protector who delivers us.
2 Let us enter his presence with
      thanksgiving.
   Let us shout out to him in
      ªcelebration.
3 For ªthe Lord is a great God,
   a great king who is superior to all
      gods.
4 The depths of the earth are in his
      hand,¹
   and the mountain peaks belong to
      him.
5 The sea is his, for ªhe made it.
   His hands formed the dry land.
6 Come, let ªus bow down and worship.
   Let us kneel before the Lord, our
      Creator.
7 For he is our God;
   ªwe are the people of his pasture,
   the sheep he owns.
   ᵇToday, if only you would obey him.
8 He says, "Do not be stubborn like
      they were at Meribah,
   like they were that day at ªMassah in
      the wilderness,¹

94:1 ª Deut 32:35; [Isa 35:4; Nah 1:2; Rom 12:19]   94:2 ª [Gen 18:25]   94:3 ª [Job 20:5]   94:4 ª Ps 31:18; Jude 15   94:7 ª Job 22:13; Ps 10:11   94:9 ª [Exod 4:11; Prov 20:12]   94:11 ª Job 11:11; 1 Cor 3:20   94:12 ª [Deut 8:5; Job 5:17; Ps 119:71; Prov 3:11–12; Heb 12:5–6]   94:14 ¹ Or for.   94:21 ª [Exod 23:7]; Ps 106:38; [Prov 17:15]; Matt 27:4   94:23 ¹ Or in.   95:2 ª Eph 5:19; Jas 5:13   95:3 ª [Ps 96:4; 1 Cor 8:5–6]   95:4 ¹ Within the sphere of his authority.   95:5 ª Gen 1:9–10; Jonah 1:9   95:6 ª 2 Chr 6:13; Dan 6:10; [Phil 2:10]   95:7 ª Ps 79:13   ᵇ Heb 3:7–11, 15; 4:7   95:8 ª Exod 17:2–7; Num 20:13   ¹ Heb. *do not harden your heart[s] as [at] Meribah, as [in] the day of Massah in the wilderness.*

9 where ªyour ancestors challenged my
    authority
  and tried my patience, even though
    they had ᵇseen my work.
10 For ª40 years I was continually
    disgusted with that generation,
  and I said, 'These people desire to go
    astray;
  they do not obey my commands.'
11 So ªI made a vow in my anger,
  'They will never enter into the resting
    place I had set aside for them.'"

96

ªSing to the LORD a new song.
Sing to the LORD, all the earth.
2 Sing to the LORD. Praise his name.
  Announce every day how he delivers.
3 Tell the nations about his splendor.
  Tell all the nations about his
    amazing deeds.
4 For ªthe LORD is great and ᵇcertainly
    worthy of praise;
  ᶜhe is more awesome than all gods.
5 For ªall the gods of the nations are
    worthless,¹
  ᵇbut the LORD made the sky.
6 Majestic splendor emanates from
    him;
  his sanctuary is firmly established
    and ªbeautiful.
7 Ascribe to the LORD, O families of
    the nations,
  ªascribe to the LORD splendor and
    strength.
8 Ascribe to the LORD the splendor he
    deserves.
  Bring an offering and enter his
    courts.
9 Worship the LORD ªin holy attire.
  Tremble before him, all the earth.
10 Say among ªthe nations, "ᵇThe LORD
    reigns!
  The world is established; it cannot be
    moved.
  He judges the nations fairly."
11 Let the sky rejoice, and the earth be
    happy.

ªLet the sea and everything in it
    shout.
12 Let the fields and everything in them
    celebrate.
  Then let the trees of the forest shout
    with joy
13 before ªthe LORD, for he comes.
  For he comes to judge the earth.
  He judges the world fairly
  and the nations in accordance with
    his justice.

97

The LORD ªreigns.
Let the earth be happy.
Let the many coastlands rejoice.
2 Dark ªclouds surround him;
  ᵇequity and justice are the
    foundation of his throne.
3 ªFire goes before him;
  on every side it burns up his enemies.
4 ªHis lightning bolts light up the
    world;
  the earth sees and trembles.
5 The mountains melt like wax before
    ªthe LORD,
  before the Lord of the whole earth.
6 The sky declares his justice,
  and all ªthe nations see his splendor.
7 ªAll who ᵇworship idols are ashamed,
  those who boast about worthless
    idols.
  All the gods bow down before him.
8 Zion hears and rejoices,
  the towns¹ of Judah are happy,
  because of your judgments, O LORD.
9 For you, ªO LORD, are the Most High
    over the whole earth;
  ᵇyou are elevated high above all gods.
10 You who love the LORD, ªhate evil!
  ᵇHe protects ᶜthe lives of his faithful
    followers;
  he delivers them from the power of
    the wicked.
11 The godly bask in the ªlight;
  the morally upright experience joy.
12 You godly ones, ªrejoice in the LORD.
  Give thanks to his holy name.

95:9 ª Ps 78:18; [1 Cor 10:9]   ᵇ Num 14:22   95:10 ª Acts 7:36; 13:18; Heb 3:10, 17   95:11 ª Num 14:23, 28–30; Deut 1:35;
Heb 4:3, 5   96:1 ¹ 1 Chr 16:23–33   96:4 ª Ps 145:3   ᵇ Ps 18:3   ᶜ Ps 95:3   96:5 ª 1 Chr 16:26; [Jer 10:11]   ᵇ Ps 115:15; Isa 42:5
¹ A wordplay is present involving "gods" (Heb. elohim) and "worthless" (Heb. elilim).   96:6 ª Ps 29:2   96:7 ª 1 Chr
16:28–29; Ps 29:1–2   96:9 ª 1 Chr 16:29; 2 Chr 20:21; Ps 29:2   96:10 ª Ps 93:1; 97:1; [Rev 11:15; 19:6]   ᵇ Ps 67:4   96:11 ª Ps
69:34; Isa 49:13   96:13 ª [Rev 19:11]   97:1 ª [Ps 96:10]   97:2 ª Exod 19:9; Deut 4:11; 1 Kgs 8:12; Ps 18:11   ᵇ [Ps 89:14]
97:3 ª Ps 18:8; Dan 7:10; Hab 3:5   97:4 ª Exod 19:18   97:5 ª Ps 46:6; Amos 9:5; Mic 1:4; Nah 1:5   97:6 ª Ps 19:1
97:7 ª [Exod 20:4]   ᵇ [Heb 1:6]   97:8 ¹ Heb. daughters.   97:9 ª Ps 83:18   ᵇ Exod 18:11; Ps 95:3; 96:4
97:10 ª [Ps 34:14; Prov 8:13; Amos 5:15; Rom 12:9]   ᵇ Ps 31:23; 145:20; Prov 2:8   ᶜ Ps 37:40;
Jer 15:21; Dan 3:28   97:11 ª Job 22:28; Ps 112:4; Prov 4:18   97:12 ª Ps 33:1

A psalm.

98

[a]Sing to the LORD a new song,
for he [b]performs amazing deeds.
His right hand and his mighty arm
accomplish deliverance.
2 The LORD demonstrates his power to
deliver;
in [a]the sight of the nations he reveals
[b]his justice.
3 He remains loyal and faithful to the
family of Israel.
[a]All the ends of the earth see our God
deliver us.
4 Shout out praises to the LORD, all the
earth.
Break out in a joyful shout and sing!
5 Sing to the LORD accompanied by a
harp,
accompanied by a harp and the
sound of music.
6 With trumpets and the blaring of the
ram's horn,
shout out praises before the king, the
LORD.
7 Let the sea and everything in it
shout,
along with the world and those who
live in it.
8 Let the rivers clap their hands!
Let the mountains sing in unison
9 before the LORD.
[a]For he comes to judge the earth.
He judges the world fairly,[1]
and the nations in a just manner.

99

The LORD reigns!
[a]The nations tremble.
He sits enthroned above the
cherubim;
the earth shakes.
2 The LORD is elevated in Zion;
he is exalted over all the nations.
3 Let them praise your great and
awesome name.
He is holy!
4 The king is strong;
he loves justice.
You ensure that legal decisions will
be made fairly;[1]
you promote justice and equity in
Jacob.

5 Praise the LORD our God.
Worship before his footstool.
He is holy!
6 Moses and Aaron were among his
priests;
Samuel was one of those who [a]prayed
to him.
They prayed to the LORD and he
answered them.
7 He spoke to them from a pillar of
cloud;
they obeyed his regulations and the
ordinance he gave them.
8 O LORD our God, you answered them.
They found you to be a forgiving God,
but also one who punished their
sinful deeds.
9 Praise the LORD our God!
Worship on his holy hill,
for the LORD our God is holy.

A thanksgiving psalm.

100

Shout out [a]praises to the LORD,
[b]all the earth!
2 Worship the LORD with joy.
Enter his presence with joyful
singing.
3 Acknowledge that the LORD is God.
He made us and [a]we belong to him,
we are his people, the sheep of his
pasture.
4 [a]Enter his gates with thanksgiving
and his courts with praise.
Give him thanks.
Praise his name.
5 For the LORD [a]is good.
His loyal love endures,
and he is faithful through all
generations.

A psalm of David.

101

I will sing about loyalty and
justice.
To you, O LORD, I will sing praises.
2 I will walk in the way of integrity.
When will you come to me?
I will [a]conduct my business with
integrity in the midst of my
palace.[1]

98:1 [a] Ps 33:3; Isa 42:10   [b] Exod 15:11; Ps 77:14   98:2 [a] Isa 52:10; [Luke 1:77; 2:30–31]   [b] Isa 62:2; Rom 3:25   98:3 [a] [Isa 49:6];
Luke 3:6; [Acts 13:47; 28:28]   98:9 [a] [Ps 96:10, 13]   [1] Or *will judge.*   99:1 [a] Exod 25:22; 1 Sam 4:4; Ps 80:1   99:4 [1] Heb.
you establish fairness.   99:6 [a] 1 Sam 7:9; 12:18   100:1 [a] Ps 145:title   [b] Ps 95:1   100:3 [a] Ps 95:7; [Isa 40:11];
Ezek 34:30–31   100:4 [a] Ps 66:13; 116:17–19   100:5 [a] Ps 136:1   101:2 [a] 1 Kgs 11:4   [1] Heb. *I will
walk about in the integrity of my heart in the midst of my house.*

3 I ᵃwill not even consider doing what
  is dishonest.
  I hate doing evil;
  I will have no part of it.¹
4 I will have nothing to do with a
  perverse person;
  I will not ᵃpermit evil.
5 I will destroy anyone who slanders
  his neighbor in secret.
  I will not tolerate anyone who has
  a haughty demeanor and an
  arrogant attitude.¹
6 I will favor the honest people of the
  land
  and allow them to live with me.
  Those who walk in the way of
  integrity will attend me.
7 Deceitful people will not live in my
  palace.
  Liars will not be welcome in my
  presence.
8 Each ᵃmorning I will destroy all the
  wicked people in the land
  and remove all evildoers ᵇfrom the
  city of the LORD.

The prayer of an oppressed man,
as he grows faint and pours out
his lament before the LORD.

102 O LORD, hear my prayer.
  Pay attention to my cry for help.
2 ᵃDo not ignore me in my time of
  trouble.
  Listen to me.
  When I call out to you, quickly
  answer me.
3 For my days go ᵃup in smoke,
  and my bones are charred as in a
  fireplace.
4 My heart is parched and withered
  like grass,
  for I am unable to eat food.
5 Because of the anxiety that makes
  me groan,
  my bones protrude from my skin.
6 I am like an owl¹ in the wilderness;
  I am like a screech owl among the
  ruins.
7 I stay awake;

  I am like a solitary bird on a roof.
8 All day long my enemies taunt me;
  those who mock me use my name in
  their curses.
9 For I eat ashes as if they were bread,
  and mix my drink with my tears,
10 because of your anger and raging
  fury.
  Indeed,¹ you pick me up and throw
  me away.
11 My days are coming to an end,
  and I am withered like grass.
12 But you, O LORD, rule forever,
  and your reputation endures.
13 You will rise up and have compassion
  on Zion.
  For it is time to have mercy on her,
  for the appointed time has come.
14 Indeed,¹ your servants take delight in
  her stones
  and feel compassion for the dust of
  her ruins.
15 The nations will ᵃrespect the
  reputation of the LORD,
  and all the kings of the earth will
  respect his splendor
16 when ᵃthe LORD rebuilds Zion
  and reveals his splendor,
17 when ᵃhe responds to the prayer of
  the destitute
  and does not reject their request.
18 The account of his intervention
  will be ᵃrecorded for future
  ᵇgenerations;
  people yet to be born will praise the
  LORD.
19 For he will ᵃlook down from his
  sanctuary above;
  from heaven the LORD will look
  toward earth,
20 in order ᵃto hear the painful cries of
  the prisoners
  and to set free those condemned to
  die,
21 so they may ᵃproclaim the name of
  the LORD in Zion
  and praise him in Jerusalem
22 ᵃwhen the nations gather together,
  and the kingdoms pay tribute to the
  LORD.

101:3 ᵃ Ps 97:10 ¹ Heb. *it* [i.e., the doing of evil deeds] *does not cling to me.* 101:4 ᵃ [Ps 119:115] 101:5 ¹ Heb. [one who has]
pride of eyes and wideness [i.e., arrogance] *of heart, him I will not endure.* 101:8 ᵃ [Ps 75:10]; Jer 21:12 ᵇ Ps 48:2, 8
102:2 ᵃ Ps 27:9; 69:17 102:3 ᵃ Jas 4:14 102:6 ¹ Some type of bird that was typically found near ruins. 102:10 ¹ Or *for.*
102:14 ¹ Or *for.* 102:15 ¹ 1 Kgs 8:43 102:16 ᵃ [Isa 60:1–2] 102:17 ᵃ Neh 1:6; Ps 22:24 102:18 ᵃ Deut 31:19;
[Rom 15:4; 1 Cor 10:11] ᵇ Ps 22:31 102:19 ᵃ Deut 26:15; Ps 14:2 102:20 ᵃ Ps 79:11 102:21 ᵃ Ps 22:22
102:22 ᵃ [Isa 2:2–3; 49:22–23; 60:3]; Zech 8:20–23

23 He has taken away my strength in
 the middle of life;
 he has cut ᵃshort my days.
24 I say, "O my God, please do not take
 me away ᵃin the middle of my life.
 ᵇYou endure through all generations.
25 ᵃIn earlier times you established the
 earth;
 the skies are your handiwork.
26 They will perish,
 but you will endure.
 ᵃThey will wear out like a garment;
 like clothes you will remove them
 and they will disappear.
27 But ᵃyou remain;
 your years do not come to an end.
28 The children of your servants will
 settle down here,
 and ᵃtheir descendants¹ will live
 securely in your presence."

By David.

103 Praise ᵃthe LORD, O my soul.
 With all that is within me, praise
 his holy name.
2 Praise the LORD, O my soul.
 Do not forget all his kind deeds.
3 He is the one ᵃwho forgives all your
 sins,
 who ᵇheals all your diseases,
4 who delivers your life from the Pit,¹
 ᵃwho crowns you with his loyal love
 and compassion,
5 who satisfies ᵃyour life with good
 things,¹
 so your youth is renewed like an
 eagle's.
6 The LORD does what is fair,
 and executes justice for all the
 oppressed.
7 The LORD revealed his faithful acts
 to Moses,
 his deeds to ᵃthe Israelites.
8 The LORD is compassionate and
 merciful;

ᵃhe is patient and demonstrates
 great loyal love.
9 ᵃHe does not always accuse
 and does not stay angry.
10 He does not deal with us as our sins
 deserve;
 ᵃhe does not repay us as our
 misdeeds deserve.
11 For as the skies are high above the
 earth,
 so his loyal love towers over his
 faithful followers.
12 As ᵃfar as the eastern horizon is from
 the west,
 so he removes the guilt of our
 rebellious actions from us.
13 As ᵃa father has compassion on his
 children,¹
 so the LORD has compassion on his
 faithful followers.
14 For he knows what we are made of;
 he realizes we are made of clay.
15 A person's life ᵃis like grass.¹
 Like a flower in the field it flourishes,
16 ᵃbut when the hot wind blows, ᵇit
 disappears,
 and one can no longer even spot the
 place where it once grew.
17 But the LORD continually shows
 loyal love to his faithful followers
 and is faithful to their descendants,
18 to those who keep his covenant,
 who are careful ᵃto obey his
 commands.
19 The LORD has established ᵃhis
 throne in heaven;
 his kingdom extends over
 everything.
20 ᵃPraise the LORD, you angels of his,
 you powerful warriors who carry ᵇout
 his decrees
 and obey his orders.
21 Praise the LORD, all ᵃyou warriors of
 his,
 you servants of his who carry out his
 desires.

102:23 ᵃJob 21:21   102:24 ᵃ[Ps 39:13]; Isa 38:10   ᵇJob 36:26; [Ps 90:2]; Hab 1:12   102:25 ᵃ[Gen 1:1; Neh 9:6; Heb 1:10–12]
102:26 ᵃIsa 34:4; 51:6; Matt 24:35; [2 Pet 3:7, 10–12]; Rev 20:11   102:27 ᵃ[Isa 41:4; 43:10; Mal 3:6; Heb 13:8]; Jas 1:17
102:28 ᵃPs 69:36   ¹Or *offspring*; Heb. *seed*.   103:1 ᵃPs 104:1, 35   103:3 ᵃPs 130:8; Isa 33:24   ᵇ[Exod 15:26]; Ps 147:3; [Isa
53:5]; Jer 17:14   103:4 ᵃ[Ps 5:12]   ¹Or *Sheol*.   103:5 ᵃ[Isa 40:31]   ¹Heb. *who satisfies with the good of your ornaments.*
103:7 ᵃExod 33:12–17; Ps 147:19   103:8 ᵃ[Exod 34:6–7; Num 14:18]; Deut 5:10; Neh 9:17; Ps 86:15; Jer 32:18; Jonah 4:2;
Jas 5:11   103:9 ᵃ[Ps 30:5; Isa 57:16]; Jer 3:5; [Mic 7:18]   103:10 ᵃ[Ezra 9:13; Lam 3:22]   103:12 ᵃ[2 Sam 12:13; Isa 38:17;
43:25; Zech 3:9; Heb 9:26]   103:13 ᵃMal 3:17   ¹Or *sons*; the Heb. term sometimes refers to children in general.
103:15 ᵃIsa 40:6–8; Jas 1:10–11; 1 Pet 1:24   ¹Heb. [as for] *mankind, like grass* [are] *his days*; used here generically
of human beings.   103:16 ᵃ[Isa 40:7]   ᵇJob 7:10   103:18 ᵃ[Deut 7:9]; Ps 25:10   103:19 ᵃ[Ps 47:2;
Dan 4:17, 25]   103:20 ᵃPs 148:2   ᵇ[Matt 6:10]   103:21 ᵃ[Heb 1:14]

22 Praise the LORD, all that he has
      made,[1]
   in all the regions of his kingdom.
   Praise the LORD, O my soul.

104

Praise [a]the LORD, O my soul!
O LORD my God, you are
   magnificent.
You are robed in splendor and
   majesty.
2 He covers himself with light as if it
      were a garment.
   He stretches out the skies like a tent
      curtain
3 and lays [a]the beams of the upper
      rooms of his palace on the rain
      clouds.
   He makes the clouds his chariot
   and travels on the wings of the wind.
4 He makes the winds his messengers
   and the flaming fire his attendant.[1]
5 He established the earth on its
      foundations;
   it will never be moved.
6 The watery deep [a]covered it[1] like a
      garment;
   the waters reached above the
      mountains.
7 Your shout made the waters retreat;
   at the sound of your thunderous
      voice they hurried off—
8 as the mountains rose up
   and the valleys went down—
   to the place you appointed for them.
9 You set [a]up [b]a boundary for them
      that they could not cross,
   so that they would not cover the
      earth again.
10 He turns springs into streams;
   they flow between the mountains.
11 They provide water for all the
      animals in the field;
   the wild donkeys quench their thirst.
12 The birds of the sky live beside them;
   they chirp among the bushes.
13 He waters [a]the mountains from [b]the
      upper rooms of his palace;
   the earth is full of the fruit you cause
      to grow.
14 He provides grass[1] for [a]the cattle
   and crops for people to cultivate,

so they can produce [b]food from the
   ground
15 as well as [a]wine that makes people
      glad,
   and olive oil to make their faces
      shine
   as well as bread that sustains them.
16 The trees of the LORD receive all the
      rain they need,
   the cedars of Lebanon that he
      planted,
17 where the birds make nests
   near the evergreens in which the
      herons live.
18 The wild goats live in the high
      mountains;
   the rock badgers find safety in the
      [a]cliffs.
19 He made [a]the moon to mark the
      months,
   and the [b]sun sets according to a
      regular schedule.
20 [a]You make it dark and night comes,
   during which all the beasts of the
      forest prowl around.
21 The lions roar for prey,
   seeking [a]their food from God.
22 When the sun rises, they withdraw
   and sleep in their dens.
23 People then go out to do their work,
   and they labor until evening.
24 How many living things [a]you have
      made, O LORD!
   You have exhibited great skill in
      making all of them;
   the earth is full of the living [b]things
      you have made.
25 Over here is the deep, wide sea,
   which teems with innumerable
      swimming creatures,
   living things both small and large.
26 The ships travel there,
   and over here swims the [a]whale you
      made to play in it.
27 [a]All your creatures wait for you
   to provide them with food on a
      regular basis.
28 You give food to them and they
      receive it;
   you open your hand and they are
      filled with food.

103:22 [1] Heb. *all his works.*   **104:1** [a] Ps 103:1   **104:3** [a] [Amos 9:6]   **104:4** [1] Heb. *and his attendants a flaming fire.*
104:6 [a] Gen 1:6   [1] Heb. *you covered it.*   **104:9** [a] Job 26:10; Ps 33:7; [Jer 5:22]   [b] Gen 9:11–15   **104:13** [a] Ps 147:8   [b] Jer 10:13
104:14 [a] Gen 1:29   [b] Job 28:5   [1] Heb. *causes the grass to sprout up.*   **104:15** [a] Judg 9:13; Ps 23:5; Prov 31:6; Eccl 10:19
104:18 [a] Lev 11:5   **104:19** [a] Gen 1:14   [b] Job 38:12; Ps 19:6   **104:20** [a] [Ps 74:16; Isa 45:7]   **104:21** [a] Job 38:39   **104:24** [a] Ps
40:5; Prov 3:19; [Jer 10:12]; 51:15   [b] Ps 65:9   **104:26** [a] Job 41:1; Isa 27:1   **104:27** [a] Job 36:31; Ps 136:25

29 When [a]you ignore them, they panic.
  When you take away their life's
    breath,
  they die and return to dust.
30 When [a]you send your life-giving
    breath, they are created,
  and you replenish the surface of the
    ground.
31 May the splendor of the LORD
    endure.
  May the LORD find [a]pleasure in the
    living things he has made.
32 He looks down on the earth and it
    [a]shakes;
  [b]he touches the mountains and they
    start to smolder.
33 I [a]will sing to the LORD as long as I
    live;
  I will sing praise to my God as long as
    I exist.
34 May my [a]thoughts be pleasing to him.
  I will rejoice in the LORD.
35 May [a]sinners disappear from the
    earth,
  and the wicked vanish.
  Praise the LORD, O my soul.
  Praise the LORD.

105

Give thanks to the LORD.
Call on his name.
  [a]Make known his accomplishments
    among the nations.
2 Sing to him.
  Make music to him.
  [a]Tell about all his miraculous deeds.
3 Boast about his holy name.
  Let the hearts of those who seek the
    LORD rejoice.
4 Seek the LORD and the strength he
    gives.
  [a]Seek his presence continually.
5 [a]Recall the miraculous deeds he
    performed,
  his mighty acts and the judgments
    he decreed,
6 O children[1] of Abraham,[2] God's
    servant,
  you descendants[3] of Jacob, God's
    chosen ones.

7 He [a]is the LORD our God;
  he carries out judgment throughout
    the earth.
8 He always [a]remembers his covenantal
    decree,
  the promise he made to a thousand
    generations—
9 the promise [a]he made to Abraham,
  the promise he made by oath to Isaac.
10 He gave it to Jacob as a decree,
  to Israel as a lasting promise,
11 saying, "[a]To you I will give the land of
    Canaan
  as the portion of your inheritance."
12 [a]When they were few in number,
  just [b]a very few, and resident
    foreigners within it,
13 they wandered from nation to
    nation,
  and from one kingdom to another.
14 He let no one oppress [a]them;
  [b]he disciplined kings for their sake,
15 saying, "Don't touch my chosen ones.
  Don't harm my prophets."
16 He called down a famine upon [a]the
    earth;
  he cut off all the food [b]supply.
17 He sent a man [a]ahead of them—
  Joseph [b]was sold as a servant.
18 [a]The shackles hurt his feet;
  his neck was placed in an iron collar,
19 until [a]the time when his prediction
    came true.
  The LORD's word proved him right.
20 The king authorized his release;
  [a]the ruler of nations set him free.
21 [a]He put him in charge of his palace,
  and made him manager of all his
    property,
22 giving him authority to imprison his
    officials
  and to teach his advisers.
23 [a]Israel moved to Egypt;
  Jacob lived for a time[1] [b]in the land of
    Ham.
24 The LORD made his people very
    fruitful
  and made [a]them more numerous
    than their enemies.

104:29 [a]Job 34:15; [Eccl 12:7]   104:30 [a]Isa 32:15   104:31 [a]Gen 1:31; Prov 8:31   104:32 [a]Hab 3:10   [b]Exod 19:18; Ps 144:5   104:33 [a]Ps 63:4   104:34 [a]Ps 19:14   104:35 [a]Ps 37:38   105:1 [a]Ps 145:12   105:2 [a]Ps 119:27   105:4 [a]Ps 27:8   105:5 [a]Ps 77:11   105:6 [1]Or offspring; Heb. seed.   [2]A few MSS Israel.   [3]Heb. sons.   105:7 [a][Isa 26:9]   105:8 [a]Luke 1:72   105:9 [a]Gen 17:2; Luke 1:73; [Gal 3:17]; Heb 6:17   105:11 [a]Gen 13:15; 15:18   105:12 [a]Gen 34:30; [Deut 7:7]   [b]Gen 23:4; Heb 11:9   105:14 [a]Gen 35:5   [b]Gen 12:17   105:16 [a]Gen 41:54   [b]Lev 26:26; Isa 3:1; Ezek 4:16   105:17 [a][Gen 45:5]   [b]Gen 37:28, 36; Acts 7:9   105:18 [a]Gen 40:15   105:19 [a]Gen 39:11–21; 41:25, 42, 43   105:20 [a]Gen 41:14   105:21 [a]Gen 41:40–44   105:23 [a]Gen 46:6; Acts 7:15   [b]Ps 78:51   [1]Heb. lived as a resident foreigner.   105:24 [a]Exod 1:7, 9

25 He caused [a]the Egyptians to hate his
people
and to mistreat his servants.
26 He sent his servant Moses,
and Aaron, whom [a]he had chosen.
27 They [a]executed his miraculous signs
among them
and his amazing deeds in the land
of Ham.
28 He made it dark;
Moses and Aaron did not disobey
his orders.
29 He turned [a]the Egyptians' water into
blood
and killed their fish.
30 Their land was overrun by frogs,
which even got into [a]the rooms of
their kings.
31 He ordered flies to come;
gnats invaded [a]their whole
territory.
32 He sent hail along with [a]the rain;
there was lightning in their land.[1]
33 He destroyed [a]their vines and fig
trees
and broke the trees throughout their
territory.
34 [a]He ordered locusts to come,
innumerable grasshoppers.
35 They ate all the vegetation in their
land
and devoured the crops of their
fields.
36 He struck down all [a]the firstborn in
[b]their land,
the firstfruits of their reproductive
power.
37 He brought his people out [a]enriched
with silver and gold;
none of his tribes stumbled.
38 [a]Egypt was happy when they left,
for they were afraid of them.
39 He spread out a cloud for a cover,
and provided a fire to light up [a]the
night.
40 They asked for food, and [a]he sent
quail;
he [b]satisfied them with food from
the sky.[1]

41 [a]He opened up a rock and water
flowed out;
a river ran through dry regions.
42 Yes,[1] he remembered the sacred
promise
he made to Abraham [a]his servant.
43 When he led his people out, they
rejoiced;
his chosen ones shouted with joy.
44 He handed [a]the territory of nations
over to them,
and they took possession of what
other peoples had produced,
45 so [a]that they might keep his
commands
and obey his laws.
Praise the LORD.

106

Praise the LORD.
Give thanks to the LORD, for he
is good,
and his loyal love endures.
2 Who can adequately recount the
LORD's mighty acts
or relate all his praiseworthy deeds?
3 How blessed are those who promote
justice
and [a]do what is right [b]all the time.
4 [a]Remember me, O LORD, when you
show favor to your people.
Pay attention to me, when you
deliver,
5 so I may see the prosperity of your
chosen ones,
rejoice along with your nation,
and boast along with the people who
belong to you.
6 We have sinned like our ancestors;
[a]we have done wrong, we have done
evil.
7 Our ancestors in Egypt failed to
appreciate your miraculous deeds.
They failed to remember your many
acts of loyal love,
and they rebelled at the sea, by the
Red Sea.[1]
8 Yet he delivered them for the sake of
his reputation[1]
[a]that he might reveal his power.

105:25 [a] Exod 1:8–10; 4:21   105:26 [a] Exod 3:10; 4:12–15   105:27 [a] Exod 7–12; Ps 78:43   105:29 [a] Exod 7:20–21; Ps 78:44
105:30 [a] Exod 8:6   105:31 [a] Exod 8:16–17   105:32 [a] Exod 9:23–25   [1] Heb. *fire of flames* [was] *in their land.*   105:33 [a] Ps
78:47   105:34 [a] Exod 10:4   105:36 [a] Exod 12:29; 13:15; Ps 135:8; 136:10   [b] Gen 49:3   105:37 [a] Exod 12:35–36   105:38 [a] Exod
12:33   105:39 [a] Exod 13:21; Neh 9:12; Ps 78:14; Isa 4:5   105:40 [a] Exod 16:12   [b] Ps 78:24   [1] *Or bread of heaven*; manna.
105:41 [a] Exod 17:6; Num 20:11; Ps 78:15; 114:8; Isa 48:21; [1 Cor 10:4]   105:42 [a] Gen 15:13–14; Ps 105:8   [1] *Or for.*   105:44 [a] Josh
11:16–23; 13:7; Ps 78:55   105:45 [a] [Deut 4:1, 40]   106:3 [a] Ps 15:2   [b] [Gal 6:9]   106:4 [a] Ps 119:132   106:6 [a] 1 Kgs 8:47; [Ezra
9:7; Neh 1:7; Jer 3:25; Dan 9:5]   106:7 [1] Heb. *Reed Sea* (also in vv. 9, 22).   106:8 [a] Exod 9:16   [1] Heb. *his name.*

9 He shouted at ᵃthe Red Sea and it
   dried up;
     ᵇhe led them through the deep water
     as if it were a desert.
10 He ᵃdelivered them from the power
     of the one who hated them
   and rescued them from the power of
     the enemy.
11 The water covered ᵃtheir enemies;
   not even one of them survived.
12 ᵃThey believed his promises;
   they sang praises to him.
13 They quickly forgot what ᵃhe had
     done;
   they did not wait for his instructions.
14 ᵃIn the wilderness they had an
     insatiable craving for meat;
   they challenged God¹ in the
     wastelands.
15 ᵃHe granted their request,
   then ᵇstruck them with a disease.
16 In ᵃthe camp they resented Moses
   and Aaron the LORD's holy priest.
17 The earth opened up and swallowed
     Dathan;
   it engulfed ᵃthe group led by Abiram.
18 Fire burned their group;
   the ᵃflames scorched the wicked.
19 ᵃThey made an image of a calf at
     Horeb
   and worshiped a metal idol.
20 They traded their majestic God
   for ᵃthe image of an ox that eats
     grass.
21 They rejected the God who delivered
     them,
   the one who performed great deeds
     in Egypt,
22 amazing feats in the land of Ham,
   mighty acts by the Red Sea.
23 ᵃHe threatened to destroy them,
   but Moses, his chosen one,
     ᵇinterceded with him
   and turned back his destructive
     anger.
24 They rejected ᵃthe fruitful land;
   they ᵇdid not believe his promise.

25 ᵃThey grumbled in their tents;
   they did not obey the LORD.
26 So ᵃhe made a solemn vow¹
   that he would make them die in the
     wilderness,
27 ᵃmake their descendants die among
     the nations,
   and scatter them among foreign
     lands.
28 They worshiped Baal of Peor
   and ate sacrifices offered to ᵃthe
     dead.
29 They made the LORD angry by their
     actions,
   and a plague broke out among them.
30 Phinehas took a stand and
     intervened,
   and ᵃthe plague subsided.
31 This was credited to Phinehas as a
     righteous act
   ᵃfor all generations to come.
32 They made him angry by ᵃthe waters
     of Meribah,
   and Moses suffered because of them,
33 ᵃfor they aroused his temper,
   and he spoke rashly.
34 They did not destroy ᵃthe nations,
   as the LORD had commanded them
     to do.
35 ᵃThey mixed in with the nations
   and learned their ways.
36 ᵃThey worshiped their idols,
   ᵇwhich became a snare to them.
37 ᵃThey sacrificed their sons and
     daughters to ᵇdemons.
38 They shed innocent blood—
   ᵃthe blood of their sons and
     daughters,
   whom they sacrificed to the idols of
     Canaan.
   The land was polluted by bloodshed.
39 They were ᵃdefiled by their deeds
   and unfaithful in their actions.
40 So ᵃthe LORD was angry with ᵇhis
     people
   and despised the people who
     belonged to him.

106:9 ᵃExod 14:21; Ps 18:15; Isa 51:10; Nah 1:4   ᵇIsa 63:11–13   106:10 ᵃExod 14:30   106:11 ᵃExod 14:27–28; 15:5   106:12 ᵃExod 15:1–21   106:13 ᵃExod 15:24; 16:2; 17:2   106:14 ᵃNum 11:4; 1 Cor 10:6   ¹Heb. *they tested God.*   106:15 ᵃNum 11:31   ᵇIsa 10:16   106:16 ᵃNum 16:1–3   106:17 ᵃNum 16:31–32; Deut 11:6   106:18 ᵃNum 16:35, 46   106:19 ᵃExod 32:1–4; Deut 9:8; Acts 7:41   106:20 ᵃJer 2:11; Rom 1:23   106:23 ᵃExod 32:10; Deut 9:19   ᵇEzek 22:30   106:24 ᵃDeut 8:7; Jer 3:19; Ezek 20:6   ᵇDeut 1:32; 9:23; [Heb 3:18–19]   106:25 ᵃNum 14:2, 27; Deut 1:27   106:26 ᵃEzek 20:15–16; [Heb 3:11, 18]   ¹Heb. *and he lifted his hand to [or concerning] them.*   106:27 ᵃLev 26:33; Ezek 20:23   106:28 ᵃNum 25:3; Deut 4:3; Hos 9:10   106:30 ᵃNum 25:7–8   106:31 ᵃGen 15:6; Num 25:11–13   106:32 ᵃNum 20:3–13; Ps 81:7   106:33 ᵃNum 20:3, 10   106:34 ᵃJudg 1:21   106:35 ᵃJudg 3:5–6   106:36 ᵃJudg 2:12   ᵇDeut 7:16   106:37 ᵃ[Deut 12:31; 32:17–18]; 2 Kgs 16:3; 17:17; Ezek 16:20–21; [1 Cor 10:20]   ᵇ[Lev 17:7]   106:38 ᵃ[Num 35:33; Isa 24:5; Jer 3:1–2]   106:39 ᵃ[Lev 18:24]; Ezek 20:18   106:40 ᵃJudg 2:14; Ps 78:59   ᵇ[Deut 9:29; 32:9]

41 He handed ᵃthem over to the
    nations,
  and those who hated them ruled
    over them.
42 Their enemies oppressed them;
  they were subject to their authority.
43 ᵃMany times he ᵃ delivered them,
  but they had a rebellious attitude
  and degraded themselves by their
    sin.
44 Yet ᵃhe took notice of their distress,
  when he heard their cry for help.
45 He remembered his covenant with
    them
  ᵃand ᵇrelented because of his great
    loyal love.
46 He caused all ᵃtheir conquerors
  to have pity on them.
47 ᵃDeliver us, O Lᴏʀᴅ, our God.
  Gather us from among the nations.
  Then we will give thanks to your holy
    name,
  and boast about your praiseworthy
    deeds.
48 The Lᴏʀᴅ God of Israel deserves
    ᵃpraise,
  in the future and forevermore.
  Let all the people say, "We agree!¹
  Praise the Lᴏʀᴅ!"

BOOK 5 (PSALMS 107–150)

107 Give thanks to the Lᴏʀᴅ, for he
    is good,
  and his loyal love endures.
2 Let those delivered by the Lᴏʀᴅ
    speak out,
  those whom he delivered from the
    power of the enemy
3 and ᵃgathered from foreign lands,
  from east and west,
  from north and south.
4 They wandered through ᵃthe
    wilderness, in a wasteland;¹
  they found no road to a city in which
    to live.
5 They were hungry and thirsty;
  they fainted from exhaustion.

6 They cried out to ᵃthe Lᴏʀᴅ in their
    distress;
  he delivered them from their
    troubles.
7 He led them on a ᵃlevel road
  that they might find a city in which
    to live.
8 ᵃLet them give thanks to the Lᴏʀᴅ
    for his loyal love
  and for the amazing things he has
    done for people.
9 For ᵃhe has satisfied those who
    thirst,
  and those who hunger he has filled
    with food.¹
10 They ᵃsat in utter darkness,
  ᵇbound in painful iron chains
11 because they had rebelled ᵃagainst
    God's commands
  and rejected ᵇthe instructions of the
    Most High.
12 So he used suffering to humble
    them;
  they stumbled and ᵃno one helped
    them up.
13 They cried out to the Lᴏʀᴅ in their
    distress;
  he delivered them from their
    troubles.
14 He brought ᵃthem out of the utter
    darkness
  and tore off their shackles.
15 Let them give thanks to the Lᴏʀᴅ for
    his loyal love
  and for the amazing things he has
    done for people.
16 For he ᵃshattered the bronze gates
  and hacked through the iron bars.
17 They acted like fools in their
    rebellious ᵃways
  and suffered because of their sins.
18 They lost ᵃtheir appetite for all
    food,
  and they ᵇdrew near the gates of
    death.
19 They cried out to the Lᴏʀᴅ in their
    distress;
  he delivered them from their
    troubles.

106:41 ᵃJudg 2:14; [Neh 9:27]   **106:43** ᵃJudg 2:16; [Neh 9:27]   **106:44** ᵃJudg 3:9; 6:7; 10:10   **106:45** ᵃ[Lev 26:41–42]
ᵇJudg 2:18   **106:46** ᵃ1 Kgs 8:50; [2 Chr 30:9]; Ezra 9:9; Neh 1:11; Jer 42:12   **106:47** ᵃ1 Chr 16:35–36   **106:48** ᵃPs 41:13
¹Trad. *amen;* Heb. *surely.*   **107:3** ᵃIsa 43:5–6; Jer 29:14; 31:8–10; [Ezek 39:27–28]   **107:4** ᵃNum 14:33; 32:13; [Deut 2:7;
32:10]; Josh 5:6; 14:10   ¹MT *on a wasteland of a road.*   **107:6** ᵃPs 50:15; [Hos 5:15]   **107:7** ᵃEzra 8:21; Ps 5:8; Jer 31:9
107:8 ᵃPs 107:15, 21   **107:9** ᵃ[Ps 34:10; Luke 1:53]   ¹Heb. *and* [the] *hungry throat he has filled* [with] *good.*   **107:10** ᵃ[Isa
42:7; Mic 7:8; Luke 1:79]   ᵇJob 36:8   **107:11** ᵃLam 3:42   ᵇ[Ps 73:24]   **107:12** ᵃPs 22:11   **107:14** ᵃPs 68:6   **107:16** ᵃIsa
45:1–2   **107:17** ᵃ[Isa 65:6–7; Jer 30:14–15]; Lam 3:39; Ezek 24:23   **107:18** ᵃJob 33:20   ᵇJob 33:22

20 He sent ᵃthem an assuring word and
  ᵇhealed them;
he ᶜrescued them from the pits
  where they were trapped.¹
21 Let them give thanks to the LORD for
  his loyal love
and for the amazing things he has
  done for people.
22 ᵃLet them present thank offerings,
and loudly ᵇproclaim what he has
  done.
23 Some traveled on the sea in ships
and carried cargo over the vast waters.
24 They witnessed the acts of the LORD,
his amazing feats on the deep water.
25 He gave the order ᵃfor a windstorm,
and it stirred up the waves of the sea.
26 They reached up to ᵃthe sky,
then dropped into the depths.
The sailors' strength¹ left them
  because the danger was so great.
27 They swayed and staggered like
  drunks,
and all their skill proved ineffective.
28 They cried out to the LORD in their
  distress;
he delivered them from their troubles.
29 He calmed ᵃthe storm,
and the waves grew silent.
30 The sailors rejoiced because the
  waves grew quiet,
and he led them to the harbor they
  desired.
31 ᵃLet them give thanks to the LORD
  for his loyal love
and for the amazing things he has
  done for people.
32 Let them exalt him ᵃin the assembly
  of the people.
Let them praise him in the place
  where the leaders preside.
33 He ᵃturned streams into a desert,
springs of water into arid land,
34 and a ᵃfruitful land into a barren
  place,
because of the sin of its inhabitants.
35 As for his people, ᵃhe turned a desert
  into a pool of water
and a dry land into springs of water.

36 He allowed the hungry to settle
  there,
and they established a city in which
  to live.
37 They cultivated fields
and planted vineyards,
which yielded a harvest of fruit.
38 He blessed¹ ᵃthem so that they
  became very numerous.
He would not allow their cattle to
  decrease in ᵇnumber.
39 As for their enemies, they decreased
  in ᵃnumber and were beaten down,
because of painful distress and
  suffering.
40 He would pour contempt upon
  princes,
and ᵃhe made them wander in a
  wasteland with no road.
41 ᵃYet he protected the needy from
  oppression
and cared ᵇfor his families like a flock
  of sheep.
42 When ᵃthe godly see this, they rejoice,
and every ᵇsinner shuts his mouth.
43 ᵃWhoever is wise, let him take note
  of these things.
Let them consider the LORD's acts of
  loyal love.

A song, a psalm of David.

108
I am determined, O ᵃGod.
I will sing and praise you with
  my whole heart.
2 ᵃAwake, O stringed instrument and
  harp.
I will wake up at dawn.
3 I will give you thanks before the
  nations, O LORD.
I will sing praises to you before
  foreigners.
4 For your loyal love extends beyond
  the sky,
and your faithfulness reaches the
  clouds.
5 ᵃRise up above the sky, O God.
May your splendor cover the whole
  earth.

107:20 ᵃMatt 8:8 ᵇ2 Kgs 20:5; Ps 30:2 ᶜJob 33:28, 30 ¹Heb. *he rescued from their traps.* 107:22 ᵃLev 7:12; Ps 50:14; Heb
13:15 ᵇPs 9:11 107:25 ᵃJonah 1:4 107:26 ᵃPs 22:14 ¹Or *courage*; trad. *their soul*; Heb. *their being.* 107:29 ᵃPs 89:9;
Matt 8:26; Luke 8:24 107:31 ᵃPs 107:8, 15, 21 107:32 ᵃPs 22:22, 25 107:33 ᵃ1 Kgs 17:1, 7; Isa 50:2 107:34 ᵃGen 13:10;
Deut 29:23 107:35 ᵃPs 114:8; [Isa 41:17–18] 107:38 ᵃGen 12:2; 17:16, 20 ᵇExod 1:7; [Deut 7:14] ¹I.e., endued
with sexual potency, made fertile. 107:39 ᵃ2 Kgs 10:32 107:40 ᵃJob 12:21, 24 107:41 ᵃ1 Sam 2:8;
[Ps 113:7–8] ᵇPs 78:52 107:42 ᵃJob 5:15–16 ᵇJob 5:16; Ps 63:11; [Rom 3:19] 107:43 ᵃPs 64:9;
Jer 9:12; [Hos 14:9] 108:1 ᵃPs 57:7–11 108:2 ᵃPs 57:8–11 108:5 ᵃPs 57:5, 11

6 Deliver by your power and
  answer me,
 so [a]that the ones you love may be
  safe.
7 God has spoken in his sanctuary:
 "I will triumph! I will parcel out
  Shechem;
 the Valley of Sukkoth I will measure
  off.
8 Gilead belongs to me,
 as does Manasseh.
 Ephraim is my helmet,
 [a]Judah my royal scepter.
9 Moab is my washbasin.
 I will make Edom serve me.[1]
 I will shout in triumph over
  Philistia."
10 Who will lead me into the fortified
  city?
 [a]Who will bring me to Edom?
11 Have you not rejected us, O God?
 O God, you do not go into battle with
  our armies.
12 Give us help against the enemy,
 for any help men might offer is futile.
13 [a]By God's power we will conquer;
 he will trample down our enemies.

For the music director, a psalm of David.

109

O God whom I praise, [a]do not
ignore me.
2 For they say cruel and deceptive
  things to me;
 they [a]lie to me.
3 They surround me and say hateful
  things;
 they attack me for no reason.
4 They repay my love with accusations,
 but I continue to pray.
5 They repay me evil for good
 and hate for love.
6 Appoint [a]an evil man to testify
  against him.
 May an accuser stand at his right
  side.
7 When he is judged, he will be found
  guilty.
 Then his prayer will be regarded as
  sinful.

8 May his days be [a]few.
 May another take his job.
9 [a]May his children be fatherless,
 and his wife a widow.
10 May his children roam around
  begging,
 asking for handouts as they leave
  their ruined home.
11 [a]May the creditor seize[1] all he owns.
 May strangers loot his property.
12 May no one show him kindness.
 May no one have compassion on his
  fatherless children.
13 [a]May his descendants be cut off.
 May the [b]memory of them be
  wiped out by the time the next
  generation arrives.
14 [a]May his ancestors' sins [b]be
  remembered by the LORD.
 May his mother's sin not be forgotten.
15 May the LORD be constantly aware of
  them
 and [a]cut off the memory of his
  children from the earth.
16 For he never bothered to show
  kindness;
 he harassed the oppressed and needy
 and killed the disheartened.
17 He loved to curse others, so those
  curses have come upon him.
 He had no desire to bless anyone, so
 he [a]has experienced no blessings.
18 He made cursing a way of life,
 so curses [a]poured into his stomach
  like water
 and seeped into his bones like oil.
19 May a curse attach itself to him, like
 a garment one puts on,
 or a belt one wears continually.
20 May the LORD repay my accusers in
  this way,
 those who say evil things about[1] me.
21 O Sovereign LORD,
 intervene on my behalf for the sake
  of your reputation.
 Because your loyal love is good,
 deliver me.
22 For I am oppressed and needy,
 and my heart beats violently
  within me.[1]

108:6 [a] Ps 60:5–12 **108:8** [a] [Gen 49:10] **108:9** [1] Heb. *over Edom I will throw my sandal*; a metaphor perhaps for taking possession of, or a master throwing his dirty sandal to a servant so the latter might dust it off. **108:10** [a] Ps 60:9 **108:13** [a] Ps 60:12 **109:1** [a] Ps 83:1 **109:2** [a] Ps 27:12 **109:6** [a] Zech 3:1 **109:8** [a] [Ps 55:23]; John 17:12 **109:9** [a] Exod 22:24 **109:11** [a] Neh 5:7; Job 5:5; 18:9 [1] Heb. *lay snares for.* **109:13** [a] Job 18:19; Ps 37:28 [b] Prov 10:7 **109:14** [a] [Exod 20:5; Num 14:18]; Isa 65:6; [Jer 32:18] [b] Neh 4:5; Jer 18:23 **109:15** [a] Job 18:17; [Ps 34:16] **109:17** [a] Prov 14:14; [Matt 7:2] **109:18** [a] Num 5:22 **109:20** [1] Or *against.* **109:22** [1] MT *pierced, wounded.*

23 I am fading away [a]like a shadow at
　　the end of the day;
　I am shaken off like a locust.
24 I am so starved my [a]knees shake;
　I have turned into skin and bones.
25 I [a]am disdained by them.
　When [b]they see me, they shake their
　　heads.
26 Help me, O LORD my God.
　Because you are faithful to me,
　　deliver me.
27 Then they will realize this is your
　　work[1]
　and [a]that you, LORD, have
　　accomplished it.
28 [a]They curse, but [b]you will bless.
　When they attack, they will be
　　humiliated,
　but your servant will rejoice.
29 [a]My accusers will be covered with
　　shame
　and draped in humiliation as if it
　　were a robe.
30 I [a]will thank the LORD profusely.
　In the middle of a crowd I will praise
　　him,
31 because [a]he stands at the right hand
　　of the needy
　to deliver him from those who
　　threaten his life.

A psalm of David.

110 Here is the LORD's [a]proclamation[1]
to my lord:
"Sit down at my right hand until
　I make your enemies your
　[b]footstool."
2 The LORD extends your dominion
　　from Zion.
　[a]Rule in the midst of your enemies.
3 Your people willingly follow [a]you
　　when you go [b]into battle.
　On the holy hills[1] at sunrise the dew
　　of your youth belongs to you.
4 The LORD makes this promise on
　　oath and [a]will not revoke it:

"You are an eternal [b]priest after the
　pattern of [c]Melchizedek."
5 O Lord, [a]at your right hand
　he strikes down [b]kings in the day he
　　unleashes his anger.
6 He executes judgment against [a]the
　　nations.
　He fills the valleys with corpses;
　he shatters their heads over the vast
　　battlefield.
7 From [a]the stream along the road he
　　drinks;
　then he lifts up his head.

111 Praise the LORD!
[a]I will give thanks to the LORD
　　with my whole heart,
in the assembly of the godly and the
　congregation.
2 [a]The LORD's deeds are great,
　eagerly [b]awaited by all who desire
　　them.
3 His work is [a]majestic and glorious,
　and his faithfulness endures[1] forever.
4 He does amazing things that will be
　　remembered;
　[a]the LORD is merciful and
　　compassionate.
5 He gives food to his faithful followers;
　he always remembers his covenant.
6 He announced that he would do
　　mighty deeds for his people,
　giving them a land that belonged to
　　other nations.
7 His acts are characterized by
　　[a]faithfulness and justice;
　all his precepts are reliable.
8 [a]They are forever firm
　and should be faithfully and properly
　　carried [b]out.
9 He delivered his people;
　[a]he ordained that his covenant be
　　observed forever.
　His name is [b]holy and awesome.
10 To obey [a]the LORD is the
　　fundamental principle for wise
　　living;[1]

109:23 [a] Ps 102:11   109:24 [a] Heb 12:12   109:25 [a] Ps 22:7; Jer 18:16; Lam 2:15   [b] Matt 27:39; Mark 15:29   109:27 [a] Job 37:7   [1] Heb. *that your hand* [is] *this.*   109:28 [a] 2 Sam 6:11–12   [b] Isa 65:14   109:29 [a] Job 8:22; Ps 35:26   109:30 [a] Ps 35:18; 111:1   109:31 [a] [Ps 16:8]   110:1 [a] Matt 22:44; Mark 12:36; 16:19; Luke 20:42–43; Acts 2:34–35; Col 3:1; Heb 1:13   [b] [1 Cor 15:25; Eph 1:22]   [1] Used frequently of a formal divine announcement through a prophet.   110:2 [a] [Ps 2:9; Dan 7:13–14]   110:3 [a] Judg 5:2; Neh 11:2   [b] 1 Chr 16:29; Ps 96:9   [1] Heb. *in splendor of holiness.*   110:4 [a] [Num 23:19]   [b] [Zech 6:13]   [c] [Heb 5:6, 10; 6:20]   110:5 [a] [Ps 16:8]   [b] Ps 2:5, 12; [Rom 2:5; Rev 6:17]   110:6 [a] Ps 68:21   110:7 [a] [Isa 53:12]   111:1 [a] Ps 35:18   111:2 [a] Ps 92:5   [b] Ps 143:5   111:3 [a] Ps 145:4–5   [1] Or *stands.*   111:4 [a] [Ps 86:5]   111:7 [a] [Rev 15:3]   111:8 [a] Isa 40:8; Matt 5:18   [b] [Rev 15:3]   111:9 [a] Luke 1:68   [b] Luke 1:49   111:10 [a] Job 28:28; [Prov 1:7; 9:10]; Eccl 12:13   [1] Heb. *the beginning of wisdom* [is] *the fear of the LORD.*

all who carry out his precepts acquire
   good moral insight.
He will receive praise forever.

112 Praise the LORD!
How blessed is the one who obeys
   the LORD,
who takes great [a]delight in keeping
   his commands.
2 [a]His descendants[1] will be powerful on
   the earth;
the godly will be blessed.
3 His house contains [a]wealth and riches;
his integrity endures.
4 [a]In the darkness a light shines for the
   godly,
for each one who is merciful,
   compassionate, and just.
5 It goes well for the one who
   generously lends money
[a]and conducts his business honestly.
6 For [a]he will never be shaken;
others will always remember one
   who is just.
7 He does not fear bad news.
[a]He[1] is confident; he trusts in the
   LORD.
8 His [a]resolve[1] is firm; [b]he will not
   succumb to fear
before he looks in [c]triumph on his
   enemies.
9 He generously gives to the needy;
his integrity endures.
He will be vindicated and honored.
10 When the wicked see this, they will
   worry;
they will grind their teeth in
   frustration and melt away.
The desire of the wicked will perish.

113 [a]Praise the LORD.
Praise, you servants of the LORD,
praise the name of the LORD.
2 May the LORD's name be [a]praised
now and forevermore.
3 [a]From east to west
the LORD's name is deserving of
   praise.

4 The LORD is [a]exalted over all the
   nations;
[b]his splendor reaches beyond the sky.
5 Who can compare to the LORD our
   God,
[a]who sits on a high throne?
6 [a]He bends down to look
at the sky and the earth.
7 He raises [a]the poor from the dirt
and lifts up the [b]needy from the
   garbage pile
8 that he might [a]seat him with
   princes,
with the princes of his people.
9 He makes [a]the barren woman of the
   family
a happy mother of children.[1]
Praise the LORD.

114 When [a]Israel left Egypt,
when the family of Jacob left a
   foreign nation behind,
2 [a]Judah became his sanctuary,
Israel his kingdom.
3 The sea looked and fled;
[a]the [b]Jordan River turned back.
4 The mountains skipped like rams,
[a]the hills like lambs.
5 [a]Why do you flee, O sea?
Why do you turn back, O Jordan
   River?
6 Why do you skip like rams,
   O mountains,
like lambs, O hills?
7 Tremble, O earth, before the Lord—
before the God of Jacob,
8 [a]who turned a rock into a pool of
   water,
a hard rock into springs of water.

115 Not [a]to us, O LORD, not to us,
but to your name bring honor,
for the sake of your loyal love and
   faithfulness.
2 Why should the nations say,
"Where is their God?"
3 [a]Our God is in heaven.
He does whatever he pleases.

112:1 [a] Ps 128:1   **112:2** [a] [Ps 102:28]   [1] Or *offspring*; Heb. *seed.*   **112:3** [a] Prov 3:16; 8:18; [Matt 6:33]   **112:4** [a] Job 11:17; Ps
97:11   **112:5** [a] Ps 37:26; [Luke 6:35]   **112:6** [a] Prov 10:7   **112:7** [a] [Prov 1:33]   [1] Heb. *his heart;* the seat of the volition and
emotions.   **112:8** [a] Heb 13:9   [b] [Ps 27:1; 56:11]; Prov 1:33; 3:24; [Isa 12:2]   [c] Ps 59:10   [1] Heb. *his heart;* the seat of the volition.
113:1 [a] Ps 135:1   **113:2** [a] [Dan 2:20]   **113:3** [a] Isa 59:19; Mal 1:11   **113:4** [a] Ps 97:9; 99:2   [b] [Ps 8:1]   **113:5** [a] Ps 89:6; [Isa 57:15]
113:6 [a] [Ps 11:4; Isa 57:15]   **113:7** [a] 1 Sam 2:8; Ps 107:41   [b] Ps 72:12   **113:8** [a] [Job 36:7]   **113:9** [a] 1 Sam 2:5; Isa 54:1   [1] Heb. *sons.*
114:1 [a] Exod 12:51; 13:3   **114:2** [a] Exod 6:7; 19:6; 25:8; 29:45–46; Deut 27:9   **114:3** [a] Exod 14:21; Ps 77:16
[b] Josh 3:13–16   **114:4** [a] Exod 19:18; Judg 5:5; Ps 29:6; Hab 3:6   **114:5** [a] Hab 3:8   **114:8** [a] Exod 17:6;
Num 20:11; Ps 107:35   **115:1** [a] [Isa 48:11]; Ezek 36:32   **115:3** [a] [1 Chr 16:26]

4 ᵃTheir idols are made of silver and
  gold—
  they are man-made.
5 They have mouths, but cannot
  speak;
  eyes, but cannot see;
6 ears, but cannot hear;
  noses, but cannot smell;
7 hands, but cannot touch;
  feet, but cannot walk.
  They cannot even clear their throats.
8 ᵃThose who make them will end up
  like them,
  as will everyone who trusts in them.
9 O Israel, trust in the ᵃLORD.
  ᵇHe is their deliverer and protector.
10 O family of Aaron, trust in the LORD.
  He is their deliverer and protector.
11 You loyal followers of the LORD, trust
  in the LORD.
  He is their deliverer and protector.
12 The LORD takes notice of us; he will
  bless—
  he will bless the family of Israel,
  he will bless the family of Aaron.
13 ᵃHe will bless his loyal followers,
  both young and old.
14 May he increase your numbers,
  yours and your children's.
15 May you be ᵃblessed by the LORD,
  the Creator of heaven and earth.
16 The heavens belong to the LORD,
  but the earth he has given to
  mankind.
17 The dead do not praise ᵃthe LORD,
  nor do any of those who descend into
  the silence of death.¹
18 ᵃBut we will praise the LORD
  now and forevermore.
  Praise the LORD!

116 I ᵃlove the LORD
because he heard my plea for
  mercy
2 and listened to me.
  As long as I live, I will call to him
  when I need help.
3 The ropes of death tightened
  around me,
  ᵃthe snares of Sheol confronted me.

I was confronted with trouble and
  sorrow.
4 I called on the name of the LORD,
  "Please, LORD, rescue my life!"
5 The LORD is ᵃmerciful and ᵇfair;
  our God is compassionate.
6 The LORD protects¹ the untrained;
  I was in serious trouble and he
  delivered me.
7 Rest once more, my soul,
  for ᵃthe LORD has vindicated you.¹
8 ᵃYes,¹ LORD, you rescued my life from
  death,
  kept my eyes from tears
  and my feet from stumbling.
9 I will serve the LORD
  ᵃin the land of the living.
10 I had ᵃfaith when I said,
  "I am severely oppressed."
11 I rashly declared,
  "All men are ᵃliars."
12 How can I repay the LORD
  for all his acts of kindness to me?
13 I will celebrate my deliverance
  and call on the name of the LORD.
14 I ᵃwill fulfill my vows to the LORD
  before all his people.
15 The LORD ᵃvalues
  the lives of his faithful followers.
16 Yes, LORD! ᵃI am indeed your servant;
  I am your servant, ᵇthe son of your
  female servant.
  You saved me from death.
17 I will present a thank offering to you,
  and call on ᵃthe name of the LORD.
18 I will fulfill my vows to the LORD
  before all his people,
19 in the ᵃcourts of the LORD's temple,
  in your midst, O Jerusalem.
  Praise the LORD!

117 Praise ᵃthe LORD, all you nations.
Applaud him, all you foreigners.
2 For his loyal love towers over us,
  and ᵃthe LORD's faithfulness endures.
  Praise the LORD.

118 Give thanks to the LORD, ᵃfor he
is good,
  and his loyal love endures.

115:4 ᵃDeut 4:28; 2 Kgs 19:18; Isa 37:19; 44:10, 20; Jer 10:3   115:8 ᵃPs 135:18; Isa 44:9–11   115:9 ᵃPs 118:2–3   ᵇPs 33:20
115:13 ᵃPs 128:1, 4   115:15 ᵃ[Gen 14:19]   115:17 ᵃPs 6:5; 88:10–12; [Isa 38:18]   ¹Heb. silence.   115:18 ᵃPs 113:2; Dan 2:20
116:1 ᵃPs 18:1   116:3 ᵃPs 18:4–6   116:5 ᵃ[Ps 103:8]   ᵇ[Ezra 9:15]; Neh 9:8; [Ps 119:137; 145:17; Jer 12:1; Dan 9:14]   116:6 ¹Heb.
guards.   116:7 ᵃPs 13:6   ¹Heb. to repay.   116:8 ᵃPs 56:13   ¹Or for.   116:9 ᵃPs 27:13   116:10 ᵃ2 Cor 4:13   116:11 ᵃPs 31:22
116:14 ᵃPs 116:18   116:15 ᵃPs 72:14; [Rev 14:13]   116:16 ᵃPs 119:125; 143:12   ᵇPs 86:16   116:17 ᵃLev 7:12; Ps 50:14; 107:22
116:19 ᵃPs 96:8   117:1 ᵃRom 15:11   117:2 ᵃ[Ps 100:5]   118:1 ᵃ2 Chr 5:13; 7:3; Ezra 3:11; [Ps 136:1–26]

2 ᵃLet Israel say,
  "Yes, his loyal love endures."
3 Let the family of Aaron say,
  "Yes, his loyal love endures."
4 Let the loyal followers of the LORD
    say,
  "Yes, his loyal love endures."
5 In my ᵃdistress I cried out to the
    LORD.
  The LORD answered me and put me
    in a wide open place.
6 ᵃThe LORD is on my side; I am not
    afraid.
  What can people do to me?
7 ᵃThe LORD ᵇis on my side as my
    helper.
  I look in triumph on those who
    hate me.
8 ᵃIt is better to take shelter in the
    LORD
  than to trust in people.
9 ᵃIt is better to take shelter in the
    LORD
  than to trust in princes.
10 All the nations surrounded me.
  Indeed, in the name of the LORD¹ I
    pushed them away.
11 They ᵃsurrounded me, yes, they
    surrounded me.
  Indeed, in the name of the LORD I
    pushed them away.
12 They surrounded me ᵃlike bees.
  But they disappeared as quickly as a
    fire among thorns.
  Indeed, in the name of the LORD ᵇI
    pushed them away.
13 "You aggressively attacked me and
    tried to knock me down,
  but the LORD helped me.
14 The LORD gives me strength and
    protects me;
  ᵃhe has become my deliverer."
15 They celebrate deliverance in the
    tents of the godly.
  The LORD's right hand conquers.

16 The LORD's right hand gives victory;
  ᵃthe LORD's right hand conquers.
17 I ᵃwill not die, but live,
  and I will ᵇproclaim what the LORD
    has done.¹
18 The LORD ᵃseverely punished me,
  but he did not hand me over to death.
19 ᵃOpen for me the gates of the just
    king's temple.
  I will enter through them and give
    thanks to the LORD.
20 This ᵃis the LORD's gate—
  the godly enter ᵇthrough it.
21 I will give you thanks, for you
    ᵃanswered me,
  and have become my deliverer.
22 The stone that ᵃthe builders
    discarded
  has become the cornerstone.
23 This is the LORD's work.
  We consider it amazing!
24 This is the day the LORD has brought
    about.¹
  We will be happy and rejoice in it.
25 Please, LORD, deliver!
  Please, LORD, grant us success!
26 May the one who comes in the name
    of the LORD be ᵃblessed.
  We will pronounce blessings on you
    in the LORD's temple.
27 The LORD is God, and he has
    delivered us.
  Tie the offering¹ with ropes
  to the horns of the altar.
28 You are my God, and I will give ᵃyou
    thanks.
  You are my God, and I will praise you.
29 Give thanks to the LORD, for he is
    good
  and his loyal love endures.

א (ALEF)

119

¹How blessed are those ᵃwhose
  actions are blameless,
who obey the law of the LORD.

118:2 ᵃ [Ps 115:9]   118:5 ᵃ Ps 120:1   118:6 ᵃ Ps 27:1; 56:9; [Rom 8:31; Heb 13:6]   118:7 ᵃ Ps 54:4   ᵇ Ps 59:10   118:8 ᵃ 2 Chr 32:7–8; Ps 40:4; Isa 31:1, 3; 57:13; Jer 17:5   118:9 ᵃ Ps 146:3   118:10 ¹ I.e., by the Lord's power.   118:11 ᵃ Ps 88:17   118:12 ᵃ Deut 1:44   ᵇ Eccl 7:6; Nah 1:10   118:14 ᵃ Exod 15:2; Isa 12:2   118:16 ᵃ Exod 15:6   118:17 ᵃ [Ps 6:5]; Hab 1:12   ᵇ Ps 73:28   ¹ Heb. *the works of the LORD*.   118:18 ᵃ Ps 73:14; Jer 31:18; [1 Cor 11:32]; 2 Cor 6:9   118:19 ᵃ Isa 26:2   118:20 ᵃ Ps 24:7   ᵇ Isa 35:8; [Rev 21:27; 22:14–15]   118:21 ᵃ Ps 116:1   118:22 ᵃ Matt 21:42; Mark 12:10–11; Luke 20:17; Acts 4:11; [Eph 2:20; 1 Pet 2:7–8]   118:24 ¹ Heb. *this is the day the LORD has made*; the day of deliverance that the psalmist and people celebrate.   118:26 ᵃ Matt 21:9; 23:39; Mark 11:9; Luke 13:35; 19:38   118:27 ¹ Heb. *festival*.   118:28 ᵃ Exod 15:2; Isa 25:1   119 ¹ This psalm is divided into twenty-two sections (corresponding to the letters of the Heb. alphabet), each of which is made of eight verses. Each of the verses in the first section (vv. 1–8) begins with the letter alef (א), the first letter of the Heb. alphabet. Each verse in section two (vv. 9–16) begins with the second letter of the alphabet, each verse in section three (vv. 17–24) with the third letter, etc. This pattern creates a sense of order and completeness and may have facilitated memorization.   119:1 ᵃ Ps 128:1; [Ezek 11:20; 18:17]; Mic 4:2

2 How blessed are those [a]who observe
   his rules
and seek him with all their heart,
3 [a]who, moreover, do no wrong,
   but follow in his footsteps.
4 You demand that your precepts
   be carefully kept.
5 If only I were predisposed
   to keep your statutes.
6 [a]Then I would not be ashamed,
   if I were focused on all your
      commands.
7 I will give you sincere thanks
   when I learn your just regulations.
8 I will keep your statutes.
   Do not completely abandon me.

ב (BET)
9 How can a young person[1] maintain a
      pure life?
   By guarding it according to your
      instructions.
10 With all my heart I [a]seek you.
   Do not allow me to stray from your
      commands.
11 In my heart I store up [a]your words,
   so I might not sin against you.
12 You deserve praise, O LORD.
   Teach me your statutes.
13 With my lips I [a]proclaim
   all the regulations you have revealed.
14 I rejoice in the lifestyle prescribed by
      your rules
   as if they were riches of all kinds.
15 I will meditate on your precepts
   and focus on your behavior.
16 I find [a]delight in your statutes;
   I do not forget your instructions.

ג (GIMEL)
17 [a]Be kind to your servant.
   Then I will live and keep your
      instructions.
18 Open my eyes so I can truly see
   the marvelous things in your law.
19 I am a [a]resident foreigner in this
      land.
   Do not hide your commands
      from me.

20 [a]I desperately long to know
   your regulations at all times.
21 You reprimand arrogant people.
   Those who stray from your
      commands are doomed.
22 [a]Spare me shame and humiliation,
   for I observe your rules.
23 Though rulers plot and slander me,
   your servant meditates on your
      statutes.
24 Yes, I find delight in your rules;
   they give me guidance.

ד (DALET)
25 [a]I collapse in the dirt.
   [b]Revive me with your word.
26 I told you about my ways and you
      answered me.
   [a]Teach me your statutes.
27 Help me to understand what your
      precepts mean.
   Then I can meditate on your
      marvelous teachings.
28 [a]I collapse from grief.
   Sustain me by your word.
29 Remove me from the path of deceit.
   Graciously give me your law.
30 I choose the path of faithfulness;
   I am committed to your regulations.
31 I hold fast to your rules.
   O LORD, do not let me be ashamed.
32 I run along the path of your
      commands,
   for you [a]enable me to do so.

ה (HE)
33 [a]Teach me, O LORD, the lifestyle
      prescribed by your statutes
   so that I might observe it
      continually.
34 Give me understanding so that [a]I
      might observe your law
   and keep it with all my heart.
35 Guide me in the path of your
      commands,
   for I delight to walk in it.
36 Give me a desire for your rules,
   rather than for wealth gained
      [a]unjustly.

119:2 [a]Deut 6:5; 10:12; 11:13; 13:3   119:3 [a][1 John 3:9; 5:18]   119:6 [a]Job 22:26   119:9 [1]Heb. *young man*; Heb. wisdom literature often assumes and reflects the male-oriented perspective of ancient Israelite society, but the principle is certainly applicable to all people.   119:10 [a]2 Chr 15:15   119:11 [a]Ps 37:31; Luke 2:19   119:13 [a]Ps 34:11   119:16 [a]Ps 1:2   119:17 [a]Ps 116:7   119:19 [a]Gen 47:9; Lev 25:23; 1 Chr 29:15; Ps 39:12; Heb 11:13   119:20 [a]Ps 42:1–2; 63:1; 84:2   119:22 [a]Ps 39:8   119:25 [a]Ps 44:25   [b]Ps 143:11   119:26 [a]Ps 25:4; 27:11; 86:11   119:28 [a]Ps 107:26   119:32 [a]1 Kgs 4:29; Isa 60:5; 2 Cor 6:11, 13   119:33 [a][Matt 10:22; Rev 2:26]   119:34 [a][Prov 2:6; Jas 1:5]   119:36 [a]Ezek 33:31; [Mark 7:20–23]; Luke 12:15; [Heb 13:5]

37 ᵃTurn my eyes ᵇaway from what is
worthless.
Revive me with your word.
38 ᵃConfirm to your servant your
promise,¹
which you made to the one who
honors you.
39 Take away the insults that I dread.
Indeed,¹ your regulations are good.
40 Look, I long for your precepts.
Revive me with your deliverance.

ו (VAV)
41 May I experience your loyal love,
O LORD,
and your deliverance, as you promised.
42 Then I will have a reply for the one
who insults me,
for I trust in your word.
43 Do not completely deprive me of a
truthful testimony,
for I await your justice.
44 Then I will keep your law continually
now and for all time.
45 I will be ᵃsecure,
for I seek your precepts.
46 I ᵃwill speak about your regulations
before kings
and not be ashamed.
47 I will find delight in your commands,
which I love.
48 I will lift my hands to¹ your
commands,
which I love,
and I will meditate on your statutes.

ז (ZAYIN)
49 Remember your word to your servant,
for you have given me hope.
50 This is what ᵃcomforts me in my
trouble,
for your promise revives me.
51 Arrogant people do nothing but scoff
at me.
Yet I do not turn aside from your law.
52 I remember your ancient regulations,
O LORD, and console myself.
53 ᵃRage takes hold of me because of
the wicked,
those who reject your law.

54 Your statutes have been my songs
in the house where I live.
55 I remember your name ᵃduring the
night, O LORD,
and I will keep your law.
56 This has been my practice,
for I observe your precepts.

ח (KHET)
57 The LORD is my source of security.
I have determined to follow ᵃyour
instructions.
58 I seek your favor with all my heart.
Have mercy on me as you promised.
59 I ᵃconsider my actions
and follow your rules.
60 I keep your commands eagerly
and without delay.
61 The ropes of the wicked tighten
around me,
but I do not forget your law.
62 In the middle of the night I arise to
thank you
for your just ᵃregulations.
63 I am a friend to all your loyal followers
and to those who keep your precepts.
64 O LORD, your loyal love fills ᵃthe
earth.
Teach me your statutes!

ט (TET)
65 You are good to your servant,
O LORD, just as you promised.
66 Teach me proper discernment and
ᵃunderstanding.
For I consider your commands to be
reliable.
67 Before I was ᵃafflicted I used to stray
off,
but now I keep your instructions.
68 You are ᵃgood and you do good.
Teach me your statutes.
69 Arrogant people ᵃsmear my
reputation with lies,
but I observe your precepts with all
my heart.
70 Their hearts are calloused,
but ᵃI find delight in your law.
71 It was good for me to suffer
so that I might learn your statutes.

119:37 ᵃ Isa 33:15   ᵇ Prov 23:5   119:38 ᵃ 2 Sam 7:25   ¹ Heb. *word.*   119:39 ¹ Or *for.*   119:45 ᵃ Prov 4:12   119:46 ᵃ Ps 138:1;
Matt 10:18; Acts 26   119:48 ¹ In prayer, as a desire to receive and appropriate the law, or as an act of praising God's
commands.   119:50 ᵃ Job 6:10; [Rom 15:4]   119:53 ᵃ Exod 32:19; Ezra 9:3; Neh 13:25   119:55 ᵃ Ps 63:6   119:57 ᵃ Num
18:20; Ps 16:5; Jer 10:16; Lam 3:24   119:59 ᵃ Mark 14:72; Luke 15:17   119:62 ᵃ Acts 16:25   119:64 ᵃ Ps 33:5
119:66 ᵃ Phil 1:9   119:67 ᵃ Prov 3:11; Jer 31:18–19; [Heb 12:5–11]   119:68 ᵃ Ps 106:1; 107:1; [Matt 19:17]
119:69 ᵃ Job 13:4; Ps 109:2   119:70 ᵃ Deut 32:15; Job 15:27; Ps 17:10; Isa 6:10; Jer 5:28; Acts 28:27

72 [a]The law you have revealed is more
   important to me
than thousands of pieces of gold and
   silver.

י (YOD)
73 Your hands made me and formed me.
Give me understanding so that I
   might learn [a]your commands.
74 [a]Your loyal followers will be glad
   when they see me,
for I find hope in your word.
75 I know, LORD, [a]that your regulations
   are just.
You disciplined me because of your
   faithful devotion to me.
76 May your loyal love console me,
as you promised your servant.
77 May I experience your compassion
   so I might live.
For I find delight in your law.
78 May the arrogant [a]be humiliated, for
   they have slandered me.
But I meditate on your precepts.
79 May your loyal followers turn to me,
those who know your rules.
80 May I be fully committed to your
   statutes,
so that I might not be ashamed.

כ (KAF)
81 [a]I desperately long for your
   deliverance.
I find hope in your word.
82 My eyes grow tired as I wait for your
   promise to be fulfilled.
I say, "When will you comfort me?"
83 For [a]I am like a wineskin dried up in
   smoke.
I do not forget your statutes.
84 [a]How long must your servant endure
   this?
[b]When will you judge those who
   pursue me?
85 [a]The arrogant dig pits to trap me,
which violates your law.
86 All your commands are reliable.
I am pursued without [a]reason.
   Help me!
87 They have almost destroyed me here
   on the earth,

but I do not reject your precepts.
88 Revive me with your loyal love
that I might keep the rules you have
   revealed.

ל (LAMED)
89 O LORD, your instructions [a]endure;
they stand secure in heaven.
90 You demonstrate your faithfulness to
   all generations.
You established the earth and it
   stood firm.
91 Today they stand firm by [a]your
   decrees,
for all things are your servants.
92 If I had not found encouragement in
   your law,[1]
I would have died in my sorrow.
93 I will never forget your precepts,
for by them you have revived me.
94 I belong to you. Deliver me!
For I seek your precepts.
95 The wicked prepare to kill me,
yet I concentrate on your rules.
96 I [a]realize that everything has its
   limits,
but your commands are beyond full
   comprehension.

מ (MEM)
97 O how [a]I love your law!
All day long I meditate on it.
98 Your commandments make me
   [a]wiser than my enemies,
for I am always aware of them.
99 I have more insight than all my
   teachers,
[a]for I meditate on your rules.
100 I am more [a]discerning than those
   older than I,
for I observe your precepts.
101 I stay away from every evil path,
so that I might keep your
   instructions.
102 I do not turn aside from your
   regulations,
for you teach me.
103 [a]Your words are sweeter
in my mouth than honey!
104 Your precepts give me discernment.
Therefore I hate all deceitful actions.

119:72 [a]Ps 19:10; Prov 8:10–11, 19   119:73 [a]Job 10:8; 31:15; [Ps 139:15–16]   119:74 [a]Ps 34:2   119:75 [a][Heb 12:10]
119:78 [a]Ps 25:3   119:81 [a]Ps 73:26; 84:2   119:83 [a]Job 30:30   119:84 [a]Ps 39:4   [b]Rev 6:10   119:85 [a]Ps 35:7;
Prov 16:27; Jer 18:22   119:86 [a]Ps 35:19   119:89 [a]Ps 89:2; Isa 40:8; Matt 24:35; [1 Pet 1:25]   119:91 [a]Jer 33:25
119:92 [1]Heb. *if your law had not been my delight.*   119:96 [a]Matt 5:18   119:97 [a]Ps 1:2   119:98 [a]Deut 4:6
119:99 [a][2 Tim 3:15]   119:100 [a][Job 32:7–9]   119:103 [a]Ps 19:10; Prov 8:11

נ (NUN)

105 a Your word is a lamp to walk by
   and a light to illumine my path.[1]
106 I have vowed and solemnly sworn
   to keep your just a regulations.
107 I am suffering terribly.
   O LORD, revive me with your word.
108 O LORD, please accept a the freewill
   offerings of my praise.
   Teach me your regulations.
109 a My life is in continual danger,
   but I do not forget your law.
110 a The wicked lay a trap for me,
   but I do not wander from your
   precepts.
111 I claim a your rules as my permanent
   possession,
   for they give me joy.
112 I am determined to obey your
   statutes
   at all times, to the very end.

ס (SAMEK)

113 I hate people with divided
   loyalties,
   but I love your law.
114 You are my hiding place and my
   shield.
   I find hope in a your word.
115 Turn a away from me, you evil men,
   so that I can observe the commands
   of my God.
116 Sustain me as you promised, so that I
   will live.
   Do not disappoint me.
117 Support me so that I will be
   delivered.
   Then I will focus on your statutes
   continually.
118 You despise all who stray from your
   statutes,
   for such people are deceptive and
   unreliable.[1]
119 You remove all the wicked of the
   earth a like slag.
   Therefore I love your rules.
120 a My body trembles because I fear
   you;
   I am afraid of your judgments.

ע (AYIN)

121 I do what is fair and right.
   Do not abandon me to my
   oppressors.
122 a Guarantee the welfare of your
   servant.
   Do not let the arrogant b oppress me.
123 My eyes grow tired as I wait for your
   deliverance,
   for your reliable promise to be
   fulfilled.
124 Show your servant your loyal love.
   Teach me your statutes.
125 I am your servant. a Give me insight,
   so that I can understand your rules.
126 It is time for the LORD to act—
   they break your law.
127 a For this reason I love your commands
   more than gold, even purest gold.
128 For this reason I carefully follow all
   your precepts.
   I hate all deceitful actions.

פ (PE)

129 Your rules are marvelous.
   Therefore I observe them.
130 Your instructions are a doorway
   through which light shines.
   They give insight to the a untrained.
131 I open my mouth and a pant,
   because I long for your commands.
132 a Turn toward me and extend mercy
   to me,
   b as you typically do to your loyal
   followers.
133 a Direct my steps by your word.
   Do not b let any sin dominate me.
134 a Deliver me from oppressive men,
   so that I can keep your precepts.
135 a Smile on your servant.
   Teach me your statutes!
136 Tears a stream down from my eyes,
   because people do not keep your law.

צ (TSADE)

137 You are a just, O LORD,
   and your judgments are fair.
138 The rules a you impose are just
   and absolutely reliable.

119:105 a Prov 6:23 [1] Heb. [is] *a lamp for my foot and a light for my path.* 119:106 a Neh 10:29 119:108 a Hos 14:2;
Heb 13:15 119:109 a Judg 12:3; Job 13:14 119:110 a Ps 140:5 119:111 a Deut 33:4 119:114 a [Ps 32:7] 119:115 a Ps 6:8;
Matt 7:23 119:118 [1] Heb. *for their deceit* [is] *falsehood.* 119:119 a Isa 1:22, 25; Ezek 22:18–19 119:120 a Job 4:14;
Hab 3:16 119:122 a Job 17:3; Heb 7:22 119:125 a Ps 116:16 119:127 a Ps 19:10 119:130 a [Ps 19:7]; Prov 1:4
119:131 a Ps 42:1 119:132 a Ps 106:4 b Ps 51:1; [2 Thess 1:6] 119:133 a Ps 17:5 b [Ps 19:13; Rom 6:12]
119:134 a Luke 1:74 119:135 a Num 6:25; Ps 4:6 119:136 a Jer 9:1, 18; 14:17; Lam 3:48; Ezek 9:4
119:137 a Ezra 9:15; Neh 9:33; Jer 12:1; Lam 1:18; Dan 9:7, 14 119:138 a [Ps 19:7–9]

139 My zeal consumes[1] me,
  for [a]my enemies forget your
    instructions.
140 Your word is absolutely pure,
  and [a]your servant loves it.
141 I am insignificant and despised,
  yet I do not forget your precepts.
142 Your justice endures,
  and your law is [a]reliable.
143 Distress and hardship confront me,
  yet I find delight in your commands.
144 Your rules remain just.
  Give me insight so that I can live.

ק (QOF)
145 I cried out with all my heart, "Answer
    me, O LORD!
  I will observe your statutes."
146 I cried out to you, "Deliver me,
  so that I can keep your rules."
147 I am up before dawn [a]crying for help.
  I find hope in your word.
148 [a]My eyes anticipate the nighttime
    hours
  so that I can meditate on your word.
149 Listen to me because of your loyal
    love.
  O LORD, revive me, as you
    typically do.
150 Those who are eager to do wrong
    draw near;
  they are far from your law.
151 You are [a]near, O LORD,
  and all your commands are reliable.
152 I learned long ago that
  you ordained your rules to [a]last.

ר (RESH)
153 See my pain and rescue me.
  For [a]I do not forget your law.
154 [a]Fight for me and defend me.
  Revive me with your word.
155 The wicked have no chance for
    deliverance,
  for they do not seek your statutes.
156 Your compassion is great, O LORD.
  Revive me, as you typically do.
157 The enemies who chase me are
    numerous.
  Yet I do not turn [a]aside from your
    rules.

158 I take note of the treacherous and
    despise them,
  because they do not keep your
    instructions.
159 See how I love your precepts.
  O LORD, revive me with your loyal
    love.
160 Your instructions are totally
    reliable;
  all your just regulations endure.

שׁ (SIN/SHIN)
161 Rulers pursue me for no reason,
  yet [a]I am more afraid of disobeying
    your instructions.
162 I rejoice in your instructions,
  like one who finds much plunder.
163 I hate and despise deceit;
  I love your law.
164 Seven times[1] a day I praise you
  because of your just regulations.
165 Those who love your law are
    [a]completely secure;
  nothing causes them to stumble.
166 I hope for your deliverance, O [a]LORD,
  and I obey your commands.
167 I keep your rules;
  I love them greatly.
168 I keep your precepts and rules,
  [a]for you are aware of everything I do.

ת (TAV)
169 Listen to my cry for help, O LORD.
  [a]Give me insight by your word.
170 Listen to my appeal for mercy.
  Deliver me, as you promised.
171 May praise flow freely from [a]my lips,
  for you teach me your statutes.
172 May my tongue sing about your
    instructions,
  for all your commands are just.
173 May your hand help me,
  for [a]I choose to obey your precepts.
174 I long for your [a]deliverance, [b]O LORD;
  I find delight in your law.
175 May I live and praise you.
  May your regulations help me.
176 I have wandered off [a]like a lost
    sheep.
  Come looking for your servant,
  for I do not forget your commands.

119:139 [a]Ps 69:9; John 2:17 [1]Heb. *destroys.* 119:140 [a]Ps 12:6 119:142 [a][Ps 19:9; John 17:17] 119:147 [a]Ps 5:3 119:148 [a]Ps 63:1, 6 119:151 [a][Ps 145:18]; Isa 50:8 119:152 [a]Luke 21:33 119:153 [a]Lam 5:1 119:154 [a]1 Sam 24:15; Mic 7:9 119:157 [a]Ps 44:18 119:161 [a]1 Sam 24:11; 26:18 119:164 [1]Used rhetorically to suggest thoroughness. 119:165 [a]Prov 3:2; [Isa 26:3; 32:17] 119:166 [a]Gen 49:18 119:168 [a]Job 24:23; Prov 5:21 119:169 [a]Ps 119:27, 144 119:171 [a]Ps 119:7 119:173 [a]Josh 24:22; Luke 10:42 119:174 [a]Ps 119:166 [b]Ps 119:16, 24 119:176 [a][Isa 53:6]; Jer 50:6; Matt 18:12; Luke 15:4; [1 Pet 2:25]

A song of ascents.

120

In [a] my distress I cried out
to the LORD and he
answered me.
2 I said, "O LORD, rescue me
from those who lie with their lips
and those who deceive with their
tongues."
3 How will he severely punish you,
you deceptive talker?
4 Here's how! With the sharp arrows of
warriors,
with arrowheads forged over the hot
coals.[1]
5 How miserable I am.
For I have lived temporarily[1] in
[a] Meshech;
I have resided among the tents of
Kedar.
6 For too long I have had to reside
with those who hate peace.
7 I am committed to peace,
but when I speak, they want to
make war.

A song of ascents.

121

I look up toward the hills.
From where does my help
come?
2 [a] My help comes from the LORD,
the Creator of heaven and earth.
3 May [a] he not allow your foot
to slip.
May your Protector not sleep.
4 Look! Israel's Protector
does not sleep or slumber.
5 The LORD is [a] your protector;
the LORD is the shade [b] at your
right hand.
6 The sun will not harm you
by day,
or [a] the moon by night.
7 The LORD will [a] protect you from
all harm;
he will protect your life.
8 The LORD will [a] protect you in all
you do,
now and forevermore.

A song of ascents; by David.

122

I was glad because they said
to me,
"We will go to the LORD's temple."
2 Our feet are standing
inside your gates, O Jerusalem.
3 Jerusalem is [a] a city designed
to accommodate an assembly.[1]
4 The tribes go up [a] there,
[b] the tribes of the LORD,
where it is required that Israel
give thanks to the name of the LORD.
5 [a] Indeed,[1] the leaders sit there on
thrones and make legal decisions,
on the thrones of the house of David.
6 [a] Pray for the peace of Jerusalem.
May those who love her prosper.
7 May there be peace inside your
defenses
and prosperity inside your fortresses.[1]
8 For the sake of my brothers and my
neighbors
I will say, "May there be peace in you."
9 For the sake of the temple of the
LORD our God
I will [a] pray for you to prosper.

A song of ascents.

123

I look up toward you,
the one enthroned[1] [a] in heaven.
2 Look, as the eyes of servants look to
the hand of their master,
as the eyes of a female servant look
to the hand of her mistress,
[a] so our eyes will look to the LORD,
our God, until he shows us favor.
3 Show us favor, O LORD, show us favor!
For we have had our fill of
humiliation, and then some.
4 We have had our fill
of the taunts of the self-assured,
of the contempt of the proud.

A song of ascents; by David.

124

"If the LORD had not been on
our [a] side"—
[b] let Israel say this.—

120:1 [a] Jonah 2:2   120:4 [1] Heb. *with coals of the wood of the broom plant.*   120:5 [a] Gen 10:2; 1 Chr 1:5; Ezek 27:13; 38:2–3; 39:1   [1] Heb. *I live as a resident foreigner.*   121:2 [a] [Ps 124:8]   121:3 [a] 1 Sam 2:9; Prov 3:23, 26   121:5 [a] Isa 25:4   [b] Ps 16:8   121:6 [a] Ps 91:5; Isa 49:10; Jonah 4:8; Rev 7:16   121:7 [a] Ps 41:2   121:8 [a] Deut 28:6; [Prov 2:8; 3:6]   122:3 [a] 2 Sam 5:9   [1] Heb. *Jerusalem, which is built like a city which is joined to her together.*   122:4 [a] Exod 23:17; Deut 16:16   [b] Exod 16:34   122:5 [a] Deut 17:8; 2 Chr 19:8   [1] Or *for.*   122:6 [a] Ps 51:18   122:7 [1] Jerusalem.   122:9 [a] Neh 2:10; Esth 10:3   123:1 [a] Ps 121:1; 141:8   [1] Heb. *sitting.*   123:2 [a] Ps 25:15   124:1 [a] Ps 118:6; [Rom 8:31]   [b] Ps 129:1

2 if the LORD had not been on our side,
   when men attacked us,
3 they would have ᵃswallowed us alive,
   when their anger raged against us.
4 The water would have overpowered us;
   the current would have
      overwhelmed us.
5 The raging water
   would have overwhelmed us.
6 The LORD deserves praise,
   for he did not hand us over as prey to
      their teeth.
7 We escaped with ᵃour lives, like ᵇa
      bird from a hunter's snare.
   The snare broke, and we escaped.
8 ᵃOur deliverer is the LORD,
   the Creator of heaven and earth.

A song of ascents.

125
Those who trust in the LORD are
like Mount Zion,
which cannot be moved and will
   endure forever.
2 As the mountains surround
      Jerusalem,
so the LORD surrounds his people,
now and forevermore.
3 Indeed,¹ ᵃthe scepter of a wicked king
      will not settle
upon the allotted land of the godly.
Otherwise the godly
might do what is wrong.
4 Do good, O LORD, to those who are
      good,
to the morally upright.¹
5 As for those who are bent on
      traveling a sinful ᵃpath,
may the LORD remove them, along
   with those who behave wickedly.
May Israel experience ᵇpeace.

A song of ascents.

126
When ᵃthe LORD restored the
ᵇwell-being of Zion,
we thought we were dreaming.
2 At that time we laughed loudly

and shouted for joy.
At that time the nations said,
"The LORD has accomplished great
   things for these people."
3 The LORD did indeed accomplish
   great things for us.
We were happy.
4 O LORD, restore our well-being,
just as the streams in the arid south
   are replenished.
5 ᵃThose who shed tears as they plant
   will shout for joy when they reap the
      harvest.
6 The one who weeps as he walks
   along, carrying his bag of seed,
will certainly come in with a shout
   of ᵃjoy, carrying his sheaves of grain.

A song of ascents; by Solomon.

127
If ᵃthe LORD does not build a
house,
then those who build it work in vain.
If the LORD does not guard a city,
then the watchman stands guard in
   vain.
2 It is vain for you to rise early, come
      home late,
and ᵃwork so hard for your food.
Yes, he provides for those whom he
   loves even when they sleep.
3 Yes, ᵃsons¹ are a gift from ᵇthe LORD;
the fruit of the womb is a ᶜreward.
4 Sons born during one's youth
are like arrows in a warrior's hand.
5 How ᵃblessed is ᵇthe man who fills
   his quiver with them.
They will not be put to shame when
   they confront enemies at the city
      gate.

A song of ascents.

128
How blessed ᵃis every one of the
LORD's loyal followers,
each one who keeps his commands.
2 ᵃYou¹ will eat what you worked so
   hard to grow.

124:3 ᵃNum 16:30; Ps 56:1–2; 57:3; Prov 1:12   124:7 ᵃPs 91:3   ᵇProv 6:5; Hos 9:8   124:8 ᵃ[Ps 121:2]   125:3 ᵃProv 22:8;
Isa 14:5   ¹Or *for.*   125:4 ¹Heb. *pure of heart;* the seat of one's moral character and motives.   125:5 ᵃProv 2:15; Isa 59:8
ᵇPs 128:6; [Gal 6:16]   126:1 ᵃPs 85:1; Jer 29:14; Hos 6:11; Joel 3:1   ᵇActs 12:9   126:5 ᵃIsa 35:10; 51:11; 61:7; Jer 31:9; [Gal 6:9]
126:6 ᵃIsa 61:3   127:1 ᵃ[Ps 121:3–5]   127:2 ᵃ[Gen 3:17, 19]   127:3 ᵃ[Gen 33:5; Josh 24:3–4; Ps 113:9]   ᵇDeut 7:13; 28:4;
Isa 13:18   ᶜ[Ps 113:9]   ¹Some prefer to translate this as *children,* but "sons" are plainly in view here, as in ancient
Israelite culture sons were the "arrows" that gave a man security in his old age, for they could defend the family
interests at the city gate, where the legal and economic issues of the community were settled.   127:5 ᵃPs
128:2–3   ᵇJob 5:4; Prov 27:11   128:1 ᵃPs 119:1   128:2 ᵃIsa 3:10   ¹The representative God-fearing man.

You will be blessed and [b]secure.
3 Your wife will be [a]like a fruitful vine
    in the inner rooms of your house;
    your [b]children will be [c]like olive
        branches,
    as they sit all around your table.
4 Yes indeed, the man who fears the
        LORD
    will be blessed in this way.
5 May [a]the LORD bless you from Zion
    that you might see Jerusalem prosper
    all the days of your life
6 and that you might [a]see your
        grandchildren.
    May Israel experience [b]peace.[1]

A song of ascents.

129
"Since my youth they have often
    [a]attacked me,"
    [b]let Israel say.
2 "Since my youth they have often
        attacked me,
    but they have not defeated me.
3 The plowers plowed my back;
    they made their furrows long.
4 The LORD is just;
    he cut the ropes of the wicked."
5 May all who hate Zion
    be humiliated and turned back.
6 May they be like the [a]grass on the
        rooftops,
    which withers before one can even
        pull it up,
7 which cannot fill the reaper's hand
    or the lap of the one who gathers the
        grain.
8 Those who pass by will not say,
    "May you experience [a]the LORD's
        blessing!
    We pronounce a blessing on you in
        the name of the LORD."

A song of ascents.

130
From the deep water[1] I cry out to
    you, [a]O LORD.
2 O Lord, listen to me.
    Pay attention to my plea for mercy.

3 [a]If you, O LORD, were to keep track of
        sins,
    O Lord, who could [b]stand before you?
4 But[1] you are willing to [a]forgive
    so that [b]you might be honored.
5 I rely on the LORD.
    [a]I rely on him with my whole [b]being;
    I wait for his assuring word.
6 [a]I yearn for the Lord,
    more than watchmen do for the
        morning,
    yes, more than watchmen do for the
        morning.
7 O Israel, [a]hope in the LORD,
    for the LORD exhibits loyal love
    and is more than willing to deliver.
8 He will deliver[1] Israel
    from all [a]their sins.

A song of ascents, by David.

131
O LORD, my heart is not proud,
    nor do [a]I have a haughty look.
    I do not have great aspirations,
    or concern myself with things that
        are beyond me.
2 Indeed,[1] [a]I have calmed and quieted
        myself
    like a weaned child with its mother;
    I am content like a young child.
3 O Israel, [a]hope in the LORD
    now and forevermore!

A song of ascents.

132
O LORD, for David's sake
    remember
    all his strenuous effort
2 and how he made [a]a vow to [b]the LORD,
    and swore an oath to the Powerful
        One of Jacob.
3 He said, "I will not enter my own
        home,[1]
    or get into my bed.
4 I will [a]not allow my eyes to sleep
    or my eyelids to slumber,
5 until I [a]find a place for the LORD,
    a fine dwelling place for the Powerful
        One of Jacob."

128:2 [b]Deut 4:40   128:3 [a]Ezek 19:10   [b]Ps 127:3–5   [c]Ps 52:8; 144:12   128:5 [a]Ps 134:3   128:6 [a]Gen 48:11; 50:23; Job 42:16; Ps 103:17; [Prov 17:6]   [b]Ps 125:5   [1]Heb. *peace* [be] *upon Israel.*   129:1 [a][Jer 1:19; 15:20]; Matt 16:18; 2 Cor 4:8–9   [b]Ps 124:1   129:6 [a]Ps 37:2   129:8 [a]Ruth 2:4   130:1 [a]Lam 3:55   [1]Heb. *depths.*   130:3 [a][Ps 143:2]   [b][Nah 1:6; Mal 3:2]; Rev 6:17   130:4 [a][Exod 34:7; Neh 9:17; Ps 86:5; Isa 55:7; Dan 9:9]   [b][1 Kgs 8:39–40; Jer 33:8–9]   [1]Or *surely.*   130:5 [a][Ps 27:14]   [b]Ps 119:81   130:6 [a]Ps 119:147   130:7 [a]Ps 131:3   130:8 [a][Ps 103:3–4]; Luke 1:68; Titus 2:14   [1]Or *redeem.*   131:1 [a]Jer 45:5; [Rom 12:16]   131:2 [a][Matt 18:3; 1 Cor 14:20]   [1]Or *but.*   131:3 [a][Ps 130:7]   132:2 [a]Ps 65:1   [b]Gen 49:24; Isa 49:26; 60:16   132:3 [1]Heb. *the tent of my house.*   132:4 [a]Prov 6:4   132:5 [a]1 Kgs 8:17; 1 Chr 22:7; Ps 26:8; Acts 7:46

6 Look, we heard about it [a]in
Ephrathah;
[b]we found it [c]in the territory of Jaar.
7 Let us go to his dwelling place.
[a]Let us worship before his footstool.
8 [a]Ascend, O LORD, to your resting
place,
you and [b]the ark of your strength.
9 May your priests [a]be clothed with
integrity.
May your loyal followers shout for
joy.
10 For the sake of David, your servant,
do not reject your chosen king.
11 The LORD made a reliable promise to
David;[1]
[a]he will not go back on his word.
[b]He said, "I will place one of your
descendants on your throne.
12 If your sons keep my covenant
and the rules I teach them,
their sons will also sit on your throne
forever."
13 [a]Certainly[1] the LORD has chosen
Zion;
he decided to make it his home.
14 He said, "[a]This will be my resting
place forever;
I will live here, for I have chosen it.
15 I [a]will abundantly supply what she
needs;
I will give her poor all the food they
need.
16 I [a]will protect her priests,
[b]and her godly people will shout
exuberantly.
17 [a]There [b]I will make David strong;[1]
I have determined that my chosen
king's dynasty will continue.
18 I will [a]humiliate his enemies,
and his crown will shine."

A song of ascents; by David.

133 Look! How good and how
pleasant it is
when [a]brothers truly live in unity.
2 It is like fine oil poured on the head,

which flows down the beard—
Aaron's beard,
and then flows down his garments.
3 It is like the dew of [a]Hermon,
which flows down upon [b]the hills of
Zion.
Indeed,[1] that is where the LORD has
decreed
a blessing will be available—eternal
life.

A song of ascents.

134 Attention! Praise the LORD,
all you servants of the LORD
who serve in the LORD's temple
during the night.
2 [a]Lift your hands toward the sanctuary
and praise the LORD.
3 May the LORD, the Creator of heaven
and earth,
bless you from Zion.

135 [a]Praise the LORD.
Praise the name of the LORD.
Offer praise, you servants of the
LORD,
2 [a]who serve in [b]the LORD's temple,
in the courts of the temple of our
God.
3 Praise [a]the LORD, [b]for the LORD is
good.
Sing praises to his name, for it is
pleasant.
4 Indeed,[1] [a]the LORD has chosen Jacob
for himself,
Israel to be his special possession.
5 Yes,[1] I know [a]the LORD is great,
and our Lord is superior to all gods.
6 He does [a]whatever he pleases
in heaven and on earth,
in the seas and all the ocean depths.
7 He causes [a]the clouds to arise from
[b]the end of the earth,
makes lightning bolts accompany the
rain,
and brings the wind out of his
[c]storehouses.

132:6 [a]1 Sam 17:12   [b]1 Sam 7:1 [c]1 Chr 13:5   **132:7** [a]Ps 5:7; 99:5   **132:8** [a]Num 10:35 [b]Ps 78:61   **132:9** [a]Job 29:14
132:11 [a][Ps 89:3–4, 33; 110:4]   [b]2 Sam 7:12; [1 Kgs 8:25; 2 Chr 6:16; Luke 1:69; Acts 2:30]   [1]Heb. *the LORD swore an oath to
David [in] truth.*   **132:13** [a][Ps 48:1–2]   [1]Or *for.*   **132:14** [a]Ps 68:16; Matt 23:21   **132:15** [a]Ps 147:14   **132:16** [a]2 Chr 6:41; Ps
132:9; 149:4   [b]1 Sam 4:5; Hos 11:12   **132:17** [a]Ezek 29:21; Luke 1:69   [b]1 Kgs 11:36; 15:4; 2 Kgs 8:19; 2 Chr 21:7; Ps 18:28   [1]Heb.
there I will cause a horn to sprout for David; signifies military victory.   **132:18** [a]Job 8:22; Ps 35:26   **133:1** [a]Gen 13:8; Heb
13:1   **133:3** [a]Deut 4:48   [b]Lev 25:21; Deut 28:8; Ps 42:8   [1]Or *for.*   **134:2** [a][1 Tim 2:8]   **135:1** [a]Ps 113:1   **135:2** [a]Luke 2:37
[b]Ps 116:19   **135:3** [a][Ps 119:68]   [b]Ps 147:1   **135:4** [a][Exod 19:5]; Mal 3:17; [Titus 2:14; 1 Pet 2:9]   [1]Or *for.*   **135:5** [a]Ps 95:3;
97:9   [1]Or *for.*   **135:6** [a]Ps 115:3   **135:7** [a]Jer 10:13   [b]Job 28:25–26; 38:24–28   [c]Jer 51:16

8 He struck down [a]the firstborn of
   Egypt,
  including both men and animals.
9 [a]He performed awesome deeds and
   acts of judgment
  in your midst, [b]O Egypt,
  against Pharaoh and all his servants.
10 [a]He defeated many nations,
  and killed mighty kings—
11 Sihon, king of the Amorites,
  and Og, king of Bashan,
  and [a]all the kingdoms of Canaan.
12 He gave their [a]land as an inheritance,
  as an inheritance to Israel his people.
13 O LORD, [a]your name endures,
  your reputation, O LORD, lasts.
14 [a]For the LORD vindicates his people
  and has compassion on his servants.
15 The nations' idols are made of silver
   and gold;
  [a]they are man-made.
16 They have mouths, but cannot speak,
  eyes, but cannot see,
17 and ears, but cannot hear.
  Indeed, they cannot breathe.
18 Those who make them will end up
   like them,
  as will everyone who trusts in them.
19 O family of Israel, [a]praise the LORD.
  O family of Aaron, praise the LORD.
20 O family of Levi, praise the LORD.
  You loyal followers of the LORD,
   praise the LORD.
21 The LORD deserves praise in Zion—
  he who dwells in Jerusalem.
  Praise the LORD.

136 Give thanks to the LORD, [a]for he
  is good,
  for his loyal love endures.
2 Give thanks to [a]the God of gods,
  for his loyal love endures.
3 Give thanks to the Lord of lords,
  for his loyal love endures.
4 To the one [a]who performs
   magnificent, amazing deeds all by
   himself,
  for his loyal love endures.

5 To the one who used wisdom [a]to
   make the heavens,
  for his loyal love endures.
6 [a]To the one who spread out the earth
   over the water,
  for his loyal love endures.
7 [a]To the one who made the great
   lights,
  for his loyal love endures,
8 [a]the sun to rule by day,
  for his loyal love endures,
9 the moon and stars to rule by night,
  for his loyal love endures.
10 [a]To the one who struck down the
   firstborn of Egypt,
  for his loyal love endures,
11 [a]and led Israel out from their midst,
  for his loyal love endures,
12 [a]with a strong hand and an
   outstretched arm,
  for his loyal love endures.
13 [a]To the one who divided the Red Sea[1]
   in two,
  for his loyal love endures,
14 and led Israel through its midst,
  for his loyal love endures,
15 [a]and tossed Pharaoh and his army
   into the Red Sea,
  for his loyal love endures.
16 [a]To the one who led his people
   through the wilderness,
  for his loyal love endures.
17 [a]To the one who struck down great
   kings,
  for his loyal love endures,
18 [a]and killed powerful kings,
  for his loyal love endures,
19 [a]Sihon, king of the Amorites,
  for his loyal love endures,
20 [a]Og, king of Bashan,
  for his loyal love endures,
21 and gave their [a]land as an inheritance,
  for his loyal love endures,
22 as an inheritance to Israel his servant,
  for his loyal love endures.
23 To the one who [a]remembered us
   when we were down,
  for his loyal love endures,

135:8 [a]Exod 12:12; Ps 78:51　135:9 [a]Exod 7:10; Deut 6:22; Ps 78:43　[b]Ps 136:15　135:10 [a]Num 21:24; Ps 136:17　135:11 [a]Josh 12:7-24　135:12 [a]Ps 78:55; 136:21-22　135:13 [a][Exod 3:15; Ps 102:12]　135:14 [a]Deut 32:36　135:15 [a][Ps 115:4-8]　135:19 [a][Ps 115:9]　136:1 [a]1 Chr 16:34; Jer 33:11　136:2 [a][Deut 10:17]　136:4 [a]Deut 6:22; Job 9:10; Ps 72:18　136:5 [a]Gen 1:1, 6-8; Prov 3:19; Jer 51:15　136:6 [a]Gen 1:9; Ps 24:2; [Isa 42:5]; Jer 10:12　136:7 [a]Gen 1:14-18　136:8 [a]Gen 1:16　136:10 [a]Exod 12:29; Ps 135:8　136:11 [a]Exod 12:51; 13:3, 16　136:12 [a]Exod 6:6; Deut 4:34; 5:15; 7:19; 9:29; 11:2; 2 Kgs 17:36; 2 Chr 6:32; Jer 32:17　136:13 [a]Exod 14:21　[1]Heb. Reed Sea (also in v. 15).　136:15 [a]Exod 14:27　136:16 [a]Exod 13:18; 15:22; Deut 8:15　136:17 [a]Ps 135:10-12　136:18 [a]Deut 29:7　136:19 [a]Num 21:21　136:20 [a]Num 21:33　136:21 [a]Josh 12:1　136:23 [a]Gen 8:1; Deut 32:36; Ps 113:7

24 and [a]snatched us away from our
    enemies,
  for his loyal love endures.
25 To the one [a]who gives food to all
    living things,
  for his loyal love endures.
26 Give thanks to the God of heaven,
  for his loyal love endures!

137

By the rivers of Babylon
we sit down and weep
when we remember Zion.
2 On the poplars in her midst
  we hang our harps,
3 for there our captors ask us to
    compose songs;
  those who [a]mock us demand that we
    be happy, saying:
  "Sing for us a song about Zion!"
4 How can we sing a song to the Lord
  in a foreign land?
5 If I forget you, O Jerusalem,
  may my right hand be crippled.
6 May my [a]tongue stick to the roof of
    my mouth,
  if I do not remember you,
  and do not give Jerusalem priority
  over whatever gives me the most joy.
7 Remember, O Lord, what [a]the
    Edomites did
  on the day Jerusalem fell.
  They said, "Tear it down, tear it down,
  right to its very foundation!"
8 O daughter Babylon, soon to be
    devastated,
  how blessed will be the one [a]who
    repays you
  for what you dished out to us.
9 How blessed will be the one who
    grabs your babies
  and [a]smashes them on a rock.

By David.

138

I will give you thanks with all my
heart;
[a]before the heavenly assembly[1] I will
  sing praises to you.
2 I [a]will bow down [b]toward your holy
    temple

and give thanks to your name,
  because of your loyal love and
    faithfulness,
  for you have [c]exalted your promise
    above the entire sky.[1]
3 When I cried out for help, you
    answered me.
  You made me bold and energized me.
4 Let [a]all the kings of the earth give
    thanks to you, O Lord,
  when they hear the words you speak.
5 Let them sing about the Lord's
    deeds,
  for the Lord's splendor is
    magnificent.
6 [a]Though [b]the Lord is exalted, he
    looks after the lowly,
  and from far away humbles the
    proud.
7 [a]Even when I must walk in the midst
    of danger, you revive me.
  You oppose my angry enemies,
  and your right hand delivers me.
8 [a]The Lord avenges me.
  [b]O Lord, your loyal love endures.
  Do not abandon those whom you
    have made.

For the music director, a psalm of David.

139

O Lord, [a]you examine me and
know me.
2 You know when I sit down and when
    I get up;
  even from far away [a]you [b]understand
    my motives.
3 You carefully observe me when I
    travel or when I lie down to rest;
  [a]you are aware of everything I do.
4 Certainly[1] my tongue does not frame
    a word
  without [a]you, O Lord, being
    thoroughly aware of it.
5 You squeeze me in from behind and
    in front;
  you place your hand on me.
6 [a]Your knowledge is beyond my
    comprehension;
  it is so far beyond me, I am unable to
    fathom it.

136:24 [a]Ps 44:7   136:25 [a]Ps 104:27; 145:15   137:3 [a]Ps 79:1   137:6 [a]Job 29:10; Ps 22:15; Ezek 3:26   137:7 [a]Jer 49:7–22; Lam 4:21; Ezek 25:12–14; 35:2; Amos 1:11; Obad 10–14   137:8 [a]Isa 13:1–6; 47:1   137:9 [a]2 Kgs 8:12; Isa 13:16; Hos 13:16; Nah 3:10   138:1 [a]Ps 119:46   [1]Either the angelic assembly or the pagan gods.   138:2 [a]Ps 28:2   [b]1 Kgs 8:29   [c]Isa 42:21   [1]MT *for you have made great over all your name your word.*   138:4 [a]Ps 102:15   138:6 [a][Ps 113:4–7]   [b]Prov 3:34; [Isa 57:15]; Luke 1:48; [Jas 4:6; 1 Pet 5:5]   138:7 [a][Ps 23:3–4]   138:8 [a]Ps 57:2; [Phil 1:6]   [b]Job 10:3, 8   139:1 [a]Ps 17:3; Jer 12:3   139:2 [a]2 Kgs 19:27   [b]Isa 66:18; Matt 9:4   139:3 [a]Job 14:16; 31:4   139:4 [a][Heb 4:13]   [1]Or *for.*   139:6 [a]Job 42:3; Ps 40:5

7 Where can I go to escape your Spirit?
[a]Where can I flee to escape your
presence?
8 If [a]I were to ascend to heaven, you
would be there.
[b]If I were to sprawl out in Sheol,
there you would be.
9 If I were to fly away on the wings of
the dawn
and settle down on the other side of
the sea,
10 even there your hand would
guide me,
your right hand would grab hold
of me.
11 If I were to say, "Certainly the
darkness will cover me,
and the light will turn to night all
around me,"
12 even [a]the darkness is not too dark for
you to see,
and the night is as bright as day;
darkness and light are the same to
you.
13 Certainly you made my mind and
heart;[1]
you wove me together in my
mother's womb.
14 I will give you thanks because your
deeds are awesome and amazing.[1]
You knew me thoroughly;[2]
15 [a]my bones were not hidden from you,
when[1] I was made in secret
and sewed together in the depths of
the earth.
16 Your eyes saw me when I was inside
the womb.
All the days ordained for me
were recorded in your scroll
before one of them came into
existence.
17 How difficult it is for me to fathom
your thoughts about me, [a]O God!
How vast is their sum total.
18 If I tried to count them,
they would outnumber the grains of
sand.
Even if I finished counting them,

I would still have to contend with
you.[1]
19 If only you would [a]kill the wicked,
O God!
Get [b]away from me, you violent men!
20 They rebel against you[1] and act
deceitfully;
your enemies lie.[2]
21 O LORD, [a]do I not hate those who
hate you
and despise those who oppose you?[1]
22 I absolutely hate them;
they have become my enemies.
23 [a]Examine me, O God, and probe my
thoughts.
Test me, and know my concerns.
24 See if there is any idolatrous way
in me,
and [a]lead me in the everlasting way.[1]

For the music director, a psalm of David.

140

O LORD, rescue me from wicked
men.
Protect me from violent men,
2 who plan ways to harm me.
All day long [a]they stir up conflict.[1]
3 Their tongues wound like a serpent;
a viper's [a]venom is behind their
lips.   *Selah*
4 O LORD, [a]shelter me from the power
of the wicked.
Protect me from violent men,
who plan to knock me over.
5 Proud men hide a [a]snare for me;
evil men spread a net by the path.
They set traps for me.   *Selah*
6 I say to the LORD, "You are my God."
O LORD, pay attention to my plea for
mercy.
7 O Sovereign LORD, my strong
deliverer,
you shield my head in the day of
battle.
8 O LORD, do not let the wicked have
their way.
Do not allow their plan to succeed
when they attack.   *Selah*

139:7 [a][Jer 23:24; Amos 9:2–4]   139:8 [a][Amos 9:2–4]   [b][Job 26:6; Prov 15:11]   139:12 [a]Job 26:6; 34:22; [Dan 2:22; Heb 4:13]
139:13 [1]Heb. *my kidneys*; the seat of one's emotions and moral character.   139:14 [1]Heb. *because awesome things, I am
distinct, amazing [are] your works*; LXX, a few wss *you are amazing*.   [2]Heb. *and my being knows very much*.   139:15 [a]Job
10:8–9; Eccl 11:5   [1]Heb. *which*.   139:17 [a][Ps 40:5; Rom 11:33]   139:18 [1]Heb. *I awake and I [am] still with you*.   139:19 [a][Isa
11:4]   [b]Ps 119:115   139:20 [1]Heb. *they speak [of] you*.   [2]Heb. *lifted up for emptiness, your cities*.   139:21 [a]2 Chr 19:2
[1]Heb. *who raise themselves up against you*.   139:23 [a]Job 31:6; Ps 26:2   139:24 [a]Ps 5:8; 143:10   [1]*Or in the ancient
path*; perhaps the moral path prescribed by the Lord at the beginning of Israel's history.   140:2 [a]Ps 56:6
[1]Heb. *they attack [for] war*.   140:3 [a]Ps 58:4; Rom 3:13; Jas 3:8   140:4 [a]Ps 71:4   140:5 [a]Ps 35:7; Jer 18:22

9 As for the heads of those who
surround me—
may the harm done by their lips
overwhelm them.
10 [a]May he rain down fiery coals upon
them.
May he throw them into the fire.
From bottomless pits they will not
escape.
11 A slanderer will not endure on[1] the
earth;
calamity will hunt down a violent
man and strike him down.
12 I know that the LORD [a]defends the
cause of the oppressed
and vindicates the poor.
13 Certainly the godly will give thanks
to your name;
the morally upright will live in your
presence.

A psalm of David.

141 O LORD, I cry out to you. Come
quickly to me.
Pay attention to me when I cry out
to you.
2 May you accept my prayer like incense,
my uplifted hands like [a]the evening
offering.
3 O LORD, place a guard on my [a]mouth.
Protect the opening of my lips.
4 Do not let me have evil desires
or participate in sinful activities
with men who behave wickedly.
I will not eat their delicacies.
5 [a]May the godly strike me in love and
correct me.
May my head not refuse choice oil.
Indeed, my prayer is a witness
against their evil deeds.[1]
6 They will be thrown over the side of
a cliff by their judges.
They will listen to my words, for they
are pleasant.
7 As when one plows and breaks up the
soil,[1]
so our bones are scattered at the
mouth of Sheol.

8 Surely I am looking to you,
O Sovereign LORD.
In you I take shelter.
Do not expose me to danger.
9 Protect me from [a]the snare they have
laid for me
and the traps the evildoers have set.
10 [a]Let the wicked fall into their own
nets,
while I escape.

*A well-written song[1] by David, when
he was in the cave; a prayer.*

142 To the LORD [a]I cry out;
to the LORD I plead for mercy.
2 I pour out my lament before him;
I tell him about my troubles.
3 Even when my strength [a]leaves me,
you watch my footsteps.
In the path where I walk
they have [b]hidden a trap for me.
4 Look to the right and see.
No one cares about me.
I have nowhere to run;
no one is concerned about my life.
5 I cry out to you, O LORD;
I say, "You are my shelter,
my security[1] in the land of the living."
6 Listen to my cry for help,
for I am in serious trouble.
Rescue me from those who chase me,
for they are stronger than I am.
7 Free me from prison
that I may give [a]thanks to your name.
Because of me the godly will
assemble,
for you will vindicate me.

A psalm of David.

143 O LORD, hear my prayer.
Pay attention to my plea for help.
Because of your faithfulness and
justice, answer me.
2 Do not sit in judgment on your
servant,
[a]for no one alive is innocent before
you.

140:10 [a]Ps 11:6   140:11 [1]Heb. *be established in.*   140:12 [a]1 Kgs 8:45; Ps 9:4   141:2 [a]Ps 134:2; [1 Tim 2:8]   141:3 [a][Prov 13:3; 21:23]   141:5 [a][Prov 9:8; Eccl 7:5; Gal 6:1]   [1]Heb. *for still, and my prayer [is] against their evil deeds.*   141:7 [1]Heb. *like splitting and breaking open in the earth*; perhaps suggesting that he and other godly individuals are as good as dead; their bones are scattered about like dirt that is dug up and tossed aside.   141:9 [a]Ps 119:110   141:10 [a]Ps 35:8   142 [1]Or *a contemplative song, a song imparting moral wisdom*; the meaning of the Heb. word is uncertain.   142:1 [a]Ps 32:title   142:3 [a]Ps 77:3   [b]Ps 141:9   142:5 [1]Heb. *my portion.*   142:7 [a]Ps 34:1–2   143:2 [a][Exod 34:7]; Job 4:17; 9:2; 25:4; Ps 130:3; Eccl 7:20; [Rom 3:20–23; Gal 2:16]

3 Certainly my enemies chase me.
  They smash me into the ground.
  They force me to live in dark regions,
    like those who have been dead for
    ages.
4 [a]My strength leaves me;[1]
  I am absolutely shocked.
5 I recall the old days.
  [a]I meditate on all you have done;
  I reflect on your accomplishments.
6 I spread [a]my hands out to you in
    prayer;
  my soul thirsts for you in a parched
    land.[1]   *Selah*
7 Answer me quickly, LORD.
  My strength is fading.
  Do not reject me,
  or I will join those descending into
    the grave.[1]
8 May [a]I hear about your loyal love in
    the morning,
  for I trust in you.
  Show me the way I should go,
  [b]because [c]I long for you.
9 Rescue me from my enemies, O LORD.
  I run to you for protection.
10 [a]Teach me to do what pleases you,
  for you are my God.
  May your kind presence
  lead me into a level land.
11 O LORD, for the sake of your
    reputation,[1] [a]revive me.
  Because of your justice, rescue me
    from trouble.
12 As a demonstration of your loyal
    love, destroy my enemies.
  Annihilate all who threaten my life,
  for I am your servant.

By David.

144

The LORD, my Protector,[1]
deserves praise—
the one [a]who trains my hands for
  battle
and my fingers for war,
2 who loves me and is my stronghold,
  my refuge and my deliverer,
  my shield and the one in whom I
    take shelter,

who makes nations submit to me.
3 O [a]LORD, of what importance is the
    human race that you should notice
    them?
  Of what importance is mankind that
    you should be concerned about
    them?[1]
4 People are like [a]a vapor,
  their days like a shadow that
    disappears.
5 O LORD, make the sky [a]sink and
    come down.
  [b]Touch the mountains and make
    them smolder.
6 [a]Hurl lightning bolts and scatter the
    enemy.
  Shoot your arrows and rout them.
7 Reach down from above.
  Grab me and rescue me from the
    surging water,[1]
  from the power of foreigners
8 who [a]speak lies
  and make false promises.
9 O God, I will [a]sing a new song to you.
  Accompanied by a ten-stringed
    instrument, I will sing praises to
    you,
10 the one [a]who delivers kings
  and rescued David his servant from a
    deadly sword.
11 Grab me and rescue me from the
    power of foreigners
  who speak lies
  and make false promises.
12 Then our sons will be like plants,
  that quickly grow to full size.
  Our daughters will be like corner
    pillars,
  carved like those in [a]a palace.
13 Our storehouses will be full,
  providing all kinds of food.
  Our sheep will multiply by the
    thousands
  and fill our pastures.[1]
14 Our cattle will be weighted down
    with produce.
  No one will break through our walls,
  no one will be taken captive,
  and there will be no terrified cries in
    our city squares.

143:4 [a]Ps 77:3 [1]Heb. *my spirit grows faint.* **143:5** [a]Ps 77:5, 10, 11 **143:6** [a]Ps 63:1 [1]Heb. *my soul like a faint land for you;* MT *my soul thirsts for you, as a parched land does for water/rain.* **143:7** [1]Heb. *the pit.* **143:8** [a]Ps 46:5 [b]Ps 5:8 [c]Ps 25:1 **143:10** [a]Ps 25:4–5 **143:11** [a]Ps 119:25 [1]Heb. *name.* **144:1** [a]2 Sam 22:35; Ps 18:34 [1]Heb. *my rocky summit.* **144:3** [a]Job 7:17; Ps 8:4; Heb 2:6 [1]Heb. *take account of him.* **144:4** [a]Ps 39:11 **144:5** [a]Ps 18:9; Isa 64:1 [b]Ps 104:32 **144:6** [a]Ps 18:13–14 **144:7** [1]Heb. *mighty waters;* the psalmist's powerful foreign enemies, as well as the realm of death they represent. **144:8** [a]Ps 12:2 **144:9** [a]Ps 33:2–3; 40:3 **144:10** [a]Ps 18:50 **144:12** [a]Ps 128:3 **144:13** [1]Heb. *in outside places.*

15 How [a]blessed are the people who
  experience these things.
  How blessed are the people whose
  God is the LORD.

A psalm of praise; by David.

145 I will extol you, my God, O King.
  I will [a]praise your name
    continually.
2 Every day I will praise you.
  I will praise your name continually.
3 The LORD is [a]great and certainly
    worthy of praise.
  No one can fathom [b]his greatness.
4 [a]One generation will praise your
    deeds to another
  and tell about your mighty acts.
5 I will focus on your honor and
    majestic splendor
  and your amazing deeds.
6 They will proclaim the power of your
    awesome acts.
  I will declare your great deeds.
7 They will talk about the fame of your
    great kindness
  and sing about your justice.
8 The LORD is merciful and
    compassionate;
  [a]he is patient[1] and demonstrates
    great loyal love.
9 The LORD is good to all
  and has compassion on all [a]he has
    made.
10 [a]All your works will give thanks to
    you, LORD.
  Your loyal followers will praise you.
11 They will proclaim the splendor of
    your kingdom;
  they will tell about your power,
12 so that mankind[1] might acknowledge
    your mighty acts
  and the majestic splendor of your
    kingdom.
13 Your kingdom is an eternal kingdom,
  and [a]your dominion endures through
    all generations.

14 [1]The LORD supports all who fall
  and lifts up all who are bent over.
15 Everything looks to you in
    anticipation,
  and you provide [a]them with food on
    a regular basis.[1]
16 You open your [a]hand
  and fill every living thing with the
    food it desires.
17 The LORD is just in all his actions
  and exhibits love in all he does.
18 [a]The LORD is near all who cry out to
    him,
  all who cry out to him [b]sincerely.
19 He satisfies the desire of his loyal
    followers;
  he hears their cry for help and
    delivers them.
20 The LORD protects all those who love
    him,
  but [a]he destroys all the wicked.
21 My mouth will praise the LORD.
  Let all who live praise his holy name
    forever.

146 [a]Praise the LORD.
  Praise the LORD, O my soul.
2 I will praise the LORD as long as [a]I
    live.
  I will sing praises to my God as long
    as I exist.
3 [a]Do not trust in princes,
  or in human beings, who cannot
    deliver.
4 [a]Their life's breath departs, they
    return to the ground.
  On that day their plans die.
5 How [a]blessed is the one whose
    helper is the God of Jacob,
  whose hope is in the LORD his God.
6 The one [a]who made heaven and
    earth,
  the sea, and all that is in them,
  who remains forever faithful,
7 [a]vindicates [b]the oppressed,
  and gives food to the hungry.
  The LORD releases the imprisoned.

144:15 [a]Deut 33:29; [Ps 33:12; Jer 17:7] 145:1 [a]Ps 100:title 145:3 [a][Ps 147:5] [b]Job 5:9; 9:10; 11:7; Isa 40:28; [Rom 11:33]
145:4 [a]Isa 38:19 145:8 [a][Exod 34:6–7; Num 14:18]; Ps 86:5, 15 [1]Heb. *slow to anger.* 145:9 [a][Ps 100:5]; Jer 33:11; Nah 1:7;
[Matt 19:17; Mark 10:18] 145:10 [a]Ps 19:1 145:12 [1]Heb. *the sons of man.* 145:13 [a]Dan 2:44; 4:3; [1 Tim 1:17; 2 Pet 1:11]
145:14 [1]Ps 145 is an acrostic, with each verse begins with a successive letter of the Heb. alphabet. The MT, however,
lacks a verse beginning with the letter *nun.* Sev. wss add a verse beginning with this letter: *The Lord is reliable in
all his words, and faithful in all his deeds.* 145:15 [a]Ps 104:27 [1]Heb. *and you give to them their food in its season.*
145:16 [a]Ps 104:21, 28 145:18 [a][Deut 4:7] [b][John 4:24] 145:20 [a][Ps 31:23] 146:1 [a]Ps 103:1 146:2 [a]Ps 104:33
146:3 [a][Isa 2:22] 146:4 [a][Eccl 12:7] 146:5 [a]Jer 17:7 146:6 [a]Gen 1:1; Exod 20:11; Acts 4:24; Rev 14:7
146:7 [a]Ps 103:6 [b]Ps 107:10; Isa 61:1

8 The LORD gives sight to [a]the blind.
   [b]The LORD lifts up all who are bent
      over.
   The LORD loves the godly.
9 The LORD protects [a]the resident
      foreigner.
   He lifts up the fatherless and the
      widow,
   [b]but he opposes the wicked.
10 The LORD rules forever,
   your God, O Zion, throughout [a]the
      generations to come.
   Praise the LORD!

147 Praise the LORD,
   for [a]it is good to sing praises to
      our God.
   Yes,[1] [b]praise is pleasant and
      appropriate.
2 The LORD [a]rebuilds Jerusalem
   and [b]gathers the exiles of Israel.
3 He [a]heals the brokenhearted
   and bandages their wounds.
4 He counts [a]the number of the stars;
   he names all of them.
5 Our Lord is [a]great and has [b]awesome
      power;[1]
   there [c]is no limit to his wisdom.
6 The LORD lifts up [a]the oppressed,
   but knocks the wicked to the ground.
7 Offer to the LORD a song of thanks.
   Sing praises to our God to the
      accompaniment of a harp.
8 [a]He covers the sky with clouds,
   provides the earth with rain,
   and causes grass to grow on the
      hillsides.
9 He gives food to [a]the animals
   and [b]to the young ravens when they
      chirp.
10 He is not enamored with [a]the
      strength of a horse,
   nor is he impressed by the warrior's
      strong legs.[1]
11 The LORD takes delight in his
      faithful followers
   and in those who wait for his loyal
      love.

12 Extol the LORD, O Jerusalem.
   Praise your God, O Zion.
13 For he makes the bars of your gates
      strong.
   He blesses your children within you.
14 He brings peace to your territory.
   [a]He abundantly [b]provides for you[1]
      the best grain.
15 He sends his command through [a]the
      earth;
   swiftly his order reaches its
      destination.
16 He sends [a]the snow that is white like
      wool;
   he spreads the frost that is white like
      ashes.
17 He throws his hailstones like crumbs.
   Who can withstand the cold wind he
      sends?
18 He [a]then orders it all to melt;
   he breathes on it, and the water flows.
19 [a]He proclaims [b]his word to Jacob,
   his statutes and regulations to Israel.
20 He has not done so with any [a]other
      nation;
   they are not aware of his regulations.
   Praise the LORD!

148 Praise the LORD.
   Praise the LORD from the sky.
   Praise him in the heavens.
2 Praise him, all his angels.[1]
   Praise him, all his heavenly assembly.
3 Praise him, O sun and moon.
   Praise him, all you shiny stars.
4 Praise him, [a]O highest heaven
   and [b]you waters above the sky.
5 Let [a]them praise the name of the
      LORD,
   for he gave the command and they
      came into existence.
6 He [a]established them so they would
      endure;
   he issued a decree that will not be
      revoked.
7 Praise the LORD from the earth,
   [a]you sea creatures and all you ocean
      depths,

146:8 [a] Matt 9:30; [John 9:7, 32, 33] [b] Luke 13:13 146:9 [a] Deut 10:18; Ps 68:5 [b] Ps 147:6 146:10 [a] Exod 15:18; Ps 10:16; [Rev 11:15] 147:1 [a] Ps 92:1 [b] Ps 33:1 [1] Or *for.* 147:2 [a] Ps 102:16 [b] Deut 30:3; Isa 11:12; 56:8; Ezek 39:28 147:3 [a] [Ps 51:17]; Isa 61:1; Luke 4:18 147:4 [a] Isa 40:26 147:5 [a] Ps 48:1 [b] Nah 1:3 [c] Isa 40:28 [1] Heb. *and great of strength.* 147:6 [a] Ps 146:8–9 147:8 [a] Job 38:26; Ps 104:13 147:9 [a] Job 38:41 [b] [Matt 6:26] 147:10 [a] Ps 33:16–17 [1] Heb. *he does not desire the strength of the horse, he does not take delight in the legs of the man.* 147:14 [a] Isa 54:13; 60:17–18 [b] Ps 132:15 [1] Heb. *satisfies you with.* 147:15 [a] [Ps 107:20] 147:16 [a] Job 37:6 147:18 [a] Job 37:10 147:19 [a] Deut 33:4; Ps 103:7 [b] Mal 4:4 147:20 [a] Deut 4:32–34; [Rom 3:1–2] 148:2 [1] Or *heavenly messengers.* 148:4 [a] Deut 10:14; 1 Kgs 8:27; [Neh 9:6] [b] Gen 1:7 148:5 [a] Gen 1:1, 6 148:6 [a] Ps 89:37; [Jer 31:35–36; 33:20, 25] 148:7 [a] Isa 43:20

8 O fire and hail, snow and clouds,
  O stormy wind that carries out his
    orders,
9 you ᵃmountains and all you hills,
  you fruit trees and all you cedars,
10 you animals and all you cattle,
  you creeping things and birds,
11 you kings of the earth and all you
    nations,
  you princes and all you leaders[1] on
    the earth,
12 you young men and young women,
  you elderly, along with you children.
13 Let them praise the ᵃname of the
    LORD,
  for his name alone is exalted;
  his majesty extends over the earth
    and sky.
14 He ᵃhas made his people victorious
  and given ᵇall his ᶜloyal followers
    reason to praise—
  the Israelites, the people who are
    close to him.
  Praise the LORD!

149

Praise the LORD.
ᵃSing to the LORD a new song.
Praise him in the assembly of the
  godly.
2 Let Israel rejoice in their Creator.
  Let the people of Zion delight in
    their ᵃKing.
3 Let them praise his name with
    dancing.
  ᵃLet them sing praises to him
  to the accompaniment of the
    tambourine and harp.
4 For ᵃthe LORD takes delight in his
    people;
  ᵇhe exalts the oppressed by
    delivering them.

5 Let the godly rejoice because of their
    vindication.
  Let them shout for joy upon their
    beds.
6 May the ᵃpraises of God be in their
    mouths
  and a two-edged sword in their
    hands,
7 in order to take revenge on the
    nations
  and punish foreigners.
8 The godly bind their enemies' kings
    in chains
  and their nobles in iron shackles,
9 and execute the judgment ᵃto
  which their enemies have been
    sentenced.
  All ᵇhis loyal followers will be
    vindicated.
  Praise the LORD.

150

ᵃPraise the LORD!
Praise God in his sanctuary;
praise him in the sky, which testifies
  to his strength!
2 Praise him for his mighty acts;
  praise him for his surpassing
    ᵃgreatness!
3 Praise him with the blast of
    the horn;
  praise him with the lyre and the
    harp!
4 Praise him with the tambourine
    and with dancing;
  praise him with stringed
    instruments and the flute!
5 Praise him with loud cymbals;
  praise him with clanging cymbals!
6 Let everything that has breath
    praise the LORD!
  Praise the LORD!

148:9 ᵃ Isa 44:23; 49:13   148:11 ¹ Or *judges.*   148:13 ᵃ Ps 8:1   148:14 ᵃ 1 Sam 2:1; Ps 75:10   ᵇ Ps 149:9   ᶜ Lev 10:3; Eph 2:17
149:1 ᵃ Ps 33:3   149:2 ᵃ Judg 8:23; Zech 9:9; Matt 21:5   149:3 ᵃ Exod 15:20; Ps 81:2   149:4 ᵃ Ps 35:27   ᵇ Ps 132:16; Isa 61:3
149:6 ᵃ Heb 4:12; Rev 1:16   149:9 ᵃ Deut 7:1–2; Ezek 28:26   ᵇ Ps 148:14; 1 Cor 6:2   150:1 ᵃ Ps 145:5–6   150:2 ᵃ Deut 3:24

PROVERBS

The key word in Proverbs is *wisdom*, "the ability to live life skillfully." A godly life in an ungodly world, however, is no simple assignment. Proverbs provides God's detailed instructions for his people to deal successfully with the practical affairs of everyday life: how to relate to God, parents, children, neighbors, and government. Solomon, the principal author, uses a combination of poetry, parables, pithy questions, short stories, and wise maxims to give in strikingly memorable form the common sense and divine perspective necessary to handle life's issues. Because Solomon, the pinnacle of Israel's wise men, was the principal contributor, the Hebrew title of this book is *Mishle Shelomoh*, "Proverbs of Solomon" (1:1). The Greek title is *Paroimiai Salomontos*, "Proverbs of Solomon." The Latin title *Liber Proverbiorum*, "Book of Proverbs," combines the words *pro* ("for") and *verba* ("words") to describe the way the proverbs concentrate many words into a few. The rabbinical writings called Proverbs *Sepher Hokhmah*, "Book of Wisdom."

Introduction to the Book

1 The [a]proverbs[1] of Solomon, son of
David, king of Israel:
2 To learn wisdom and moral
instruction,[1]
to discern wise counsel.
3 To receive moral instruction in
skillful living,
with righteousness, justice, and
equity.
4 To impart shrewdness[1] to the morally
[a]naive,[2]
a discerning plan to the young
person.
5 (Let the wise [a]also hear and gain
instruction,
and let the discerning acquire
guidance!)
6 To discern the meaning of a proverb
and a parable,
the sayings of the wise and their
[a]riddles.[1]

Introduction to the Theme of the Book

7 Fearing [a]the LORD[1] is the beginning[2]
of discernment,
but fools have despised wisdom and
moral instruction.
8 Listen, [a]my child,[1] to the instruction
from your father,
and do not forsake the teaching from
your mother.
9 For they will be like an [a]elegant
garland on your head,
and like pendants around your neck.

Admonition to Avoid Easy but Unjust Riches

10 My child, if sinners try to entice you,
[a]do not consent![1]
11 If they say, "Come with us!
We will [a]lie in wait[1] to shed blood;[2]
we will ambush an innocent person
capriciously.
12 We will swallow them alive [a]like Sheol,

1:1 [a]1 Kgs 4:32; Prov 10:1; 25:1; Eccl 12:9 [1]A short pithy statement, object lesson drawn from experience, saying or by-word, or an oracle of future blessing. 1:2 [1]Heb. *instruction*; physical or parental discipline/chastisement, verbal warning/exhortation, or moral training/instruction. 1:4 [a]Prov 9:4 [1]A shrewd plan of action, viewed positively or negatively. [2]Heb. *the naive, simpleton.* 1:5 [a]Prov 9:9 1:6 [a]Num 12:8; Ps 78:2; Dan 8:23 [1]Enigmatic sayings for which the meaning is obscure or hidden, such as a riddle, allegory, perplexing moral problem, perplexing question, or ambiguous saying. 1:7 [a]Job 28:28; Ps 111:10; Prov 9:10; 15:33; [Eccl 12:13] [1]Heb. *fear of the LORD*; reverential submission to his will. [2]Heb. *beginning, chief thing.* 1:8 [a]Prov 4:1 [1]Heb. *my son*; it is likely that collections of proverbs were designed for the training of the youthful prince, but in the canon, the term "son" would mean a disciple, for all are to learn wisdom when young. 1:9 [a]Prov 3:22 1:10 [a]Gen 39:7–10; Deut 13:8; Ps 50:18; [Eph 5:11] [1]A few medieval MSS *do not go with them.* 1:11 [a]Prov 12:6; Jer 5:26 [1]Used for planning murder, kidnapping, and seduction. [2]Heb. *for blood.* 1:12 [a]Ps 28:1

those full of vigor like those going
   down to the Pit.
[13] We will seize all kinds of precious
   wealth;
we will fill our houses with plunder.
[14] Join with us!
We will all share equally in what we
   steal."
[15] My child, [a]do not go down their way,
   [b]withhold yourself[1] from their path;
[16] [a]for they are eager to inflict harm,
   and they hasten to shed blood.[1]
[17] Surely it is futile to spread a net
   in plain sight of any bird,
[18] but these men lie in wait for their
   own blood;
they ambush their own lives!
[19] [a]Such are the ways of all who gain
   profit unjustly;
it takes away the life of those who
   obtain it!

Warning against Disregarding Wisdom

[20] [a]Wisdom calls out in the street,
   she shouts loudly in the plazas;
[21] at the head of the noisy streets[1] she
   calls,
in the entrances of the gates in the
   city she utters her words:
[22] "How long will you simpletons love
   naiveté?
How long have mockers delighted in
   mockery?
And how long will fools hate
   knowledge?
[23] You should respond to my rebuke.
Then [a]I would pour out my thoughts[1]
   to you;
I would make my words known to
   you.
[24] However, [a]because I called but you
   refused to listen,
because I stretched out my hand but
   no one was paying attention,
[25] and you [a]neglected all my advice,
and did not comply with my rebuke,
[26] so [a]I myself will laugh when disaster
   strikes you;
I will mock when what you dread
   comes,
[27] when what [a]you dread comes like a
   whirlwind,
and disaster strikes you like a
   devastating storm,
when distressing trouble comes on
   you.
[28] Then they will call to me, but I will
   not answer;
they will diligently seek me, but they
   will not find me.
[29] Because they [a]hated moral
   knowledge
and did not [b]choose to fear the
   LORD,[1]
[30] they did not comply with my advice;
   [a]they spurned all my rebuke.
[31] Therefore [a]they will eat from the
   fruit of their way,
and they will be stuffed full of their
   own counsel.
[32] For the waywardness[1] of the
   simpletons will kill them,
and the careless ease of fools will
   destroy them.
[33] But the one who listens to me will
   live in [a]security
and [b]will be at ease from the dread of
   harm."

Benefits of Seeking Wisdom

2 My child,[1] if you receive my words,
and store [a]up my commands inside
   yourself,
[2] by making your ear attentive to
   wisdom
and by turning your heart to
   understanding,
[3] indeed, if you call out for
   discernment—
shout loudly for understanding—
[4] [a]if you seek it like silver
and search for it like hidden
   treasure,
[5] then you will understand how to
   fear [a]the LORD,[1]
and you will discover knowledge
   about God.
[6] [a]For the LORD gives wisdom,
and from his mouth comes
   knowledge and understanding.

1:15 [a] Ps 1:1; Prov 4:14 [b] Ps 119:101 [1] Heb. *your foot.* **1:16** [a] Prov 6:17–18; [Isa 59:7]; Rom 3:15 [1] Sev. wss omit this verse. **1:19** [a] Prov 15:27; [1 Tim 6:10] **1:20** [a] Prov 8:1; 9:3; [John 7:37] **1:21** [1] LXX *walls.* **1:23** [a] Isa 32:15; Joel 2:28; [John 7:39] [1] Heb. *my spirit.* **1:24** [a] Isa 65:12; 66:4; Jer 7:13; Zech 7:11 **1:25** [a] Ps 107:11; Luke 7:30 **1:26** [a] Ps 2:4 **1:27** [a] [Prov 10:24–25] **1:29** [a] Job 21:14; Prov 1:22 [b] Ps 119:173 [1] Heb. *the fear of the LORD.* **1:30** [a] Ps 81:11; Prov 1:25 **1:31** [a] Job 4:8; Prov 5:22–23; 22:8; Isa 3:11; Jer 6:19 **1:32** [1] Heb. *turning away*; moral defection and apostasy. **1:33** [a] Prov 3:24–26 [b] Ps 112:7 **2:1** [a] [Prov 4:21] [1] Heb. *my son.* **2:4** [a] [Prov 3:14] **2:5** [a] [Jas 1:5–6] [1] Heb. *the fear of the LORD.* **2:6** [a] 1 Kgs 3:9, 12; [Job 32:8; Jas 1:5]

⁷ He stores up effective counsel for
  ᵃthe upright
  and is like a shield for those who live
    with integrity,
⁸ to guard the paths of the righteous
  and to ᵃprotect the way of his pious
    ones.¹
⁹ Then you will understand
    righteousness and justice
  and equity—every¹ good way.
¹⁰ For wisdom will enter your heart,
  and moral knowledge will be
    attractive¹ to you.
¹¹ Discretion will protect you;
  ᵃunderstanding will guard you
¹² to deliver you from the way of the
    wicked,¹
  from those speaking perversity,
¹³ who leave the upright paths
  to ᵃwalk on the dark ways,
¹⁴ ᵃwho delight in doing evil;
  they rejoice in perverse evil,
¹⁵ whose paths are morally crooked
  and ᵃwho are devious in their ways,
¹⁶ to deliver you from ᵃthe adulterous
    woman,¹
  ᵇfrom the loose woman² who has
    flattered you with her words,
¹⁷ who leaves the husband from her
    younger days
  and has ignored her marriage
    covenant¹ made before God.
¹⁸ For she has set¹ ᵃher house by death
  and her paths by the place of the
    departed spirits.²
¹⁹ None who go in to her will return,
  nor will they reach the paths of life.
²⁰ So you will walk in the way of good
    people
  and will keep on the paths of the
    righteous.

²¹ For the upright will reside in the
    ᵃland,
  and those with integrity will remain
    in it,
²² but the wicked will be removed¹ from
    the land,
  and the treacherous will be torn
    away from it.

Exhortations to Seek Wisdom and Walk with the Lord

3 My child,¹ do not forget my teaching,
  ᵃbut let your heart keep my
    commandments,
² for they will provide¹ a long and full
    life
  and ᵃwell-being² for you.
³ Do not let mercy and truth leave you;
  ᵃbind them around your neck,
  ᵇwrite them on the tablet of your
    heart.
⁴ Then you will find favor ᵃand good
    understanding
  in the sight of God and people.
⁵ ᵃTrust in the LORD with all your
    heart,
  ᵇand do not rely on your own
    understanding.
⁶ Acknowledge him ᵃin all your ways,¹
  and he will make your paths straight.
⁷ Do not be wise in your own
    ᵃestimation;
  fear the LORD and turn away from
    evil.
⁸ This will bring healing to your body¹
  and ᵃrefreshment to your inner self.²
⁹ ᵃHonor the LORD from your wealth
  and from the firstfruits of all your
    crops;
¹⁰ ᵃthen your barns will be filled
    completely,¹

2:7 ᵃ[Ps 84:11]; Prov 30:5   **2:8** ᵃ[1 Sam 2:9]; Ps 66:9 ¹Ket. *one.*   **2:9** ¹Further explains and defines the preceding triad of righteous attributes.   **2:10** ¹Heb. *pleasant*; being physically attracted to one's lover or to a close friend.   **2:11** ᵃProv 4:6; 6:22   **2:12** ¹Heb. *bad, harmful, painful.*   **2:13** ᵃPs 82:5; Prov 4:19; [John 3:19–20]   **2:14** ᵃProv 10:23; Jer 11:15; [Rom 1:32]   **2:15** ᵃPs 125:5; [Prov 21:8]   **2:16** ᵃProv 5:20; 6:24; 7:5   ᵇProv 5:3 ¹Heb. *strange woman*; sometimes refers to people who are ethnically foreign to Israel, but it often refers to what is morally estranged from God or his covenant people. ²Heb. *alien woman*; may refer to a non-Israelite or an Israelite who is unknown or unfamiliar. Perhaps used here for a harlot or promiscuous woman who is morally alienated from God and moral society.   **2:17** ¹Heb. *the covenant*; could refer to the Mosaic covenant that prohibits adultery.   **2:18** ᵃProv 7:27 ¹LXX *She has placed her house near death.* ²Heb. *to the departed spirits, to the Rephaim*; refers to spirits of the dead who are inhabitants of Sheol.   **2:21** ᵃPs 37:3   **2:22** ¹Heb. *cut off*; die prematurely, be excommunicated from the community, or be separated eternally in judgment.   **3:1** ᵃDeut 8:1 ¹Heb. *my son* (also in vv. 11, 21).   **3:2** ᵃPs 119:165; Prov 4:10 ¹Heb. *They will add to you.* ²Heb. *shalom*; meaning "welfare," "health," or "prosperity," and may be used of physical health and personal well-being. It is the experience of positive blessing and freedom from negative harm and catastrophe.   **3:3** ᵃExod 13:9; Deut 6:8; Prov 6:21 ᵇProv 7:3; Jer 17:1; [2 Cor 3:3]   **3:4** ᵃ1 Sam 2:26; Luke 2:52; Rom 14:18   **3:5** ᵃ[Ps 37:3, 5]; Prov 22:19 ᵇProv 23:4; [Jer 9:23–24]   **3:6** ᵃ[1 Chr 28:9]; Prov 16:3; [Phil 4:6; Jas 1:5] ¹A person's course of life, actions, and undertakings.   **3:7** ᵃRom 12:16   **3:8** ᵃJob 21:24 ¹Heb. *your navel*; LXX *your body.* ²Heb. *your bones.*   **3:9** ᵃExod 22:29; Deut 26:2; [Mal 3:10]   **3:10** ᵃDeut 28:8 ¹LXX *with grain.*

and your vats will overflow with new
wine.
11 [a]My child, do not despise discipline
from the Lord,
and do not loathe his rebuke.
12 For the Lord disciplines those he
loves,
[a]just as a father[1] disciplines the son
in whom he delights.

Blessings of Obtaining Wisdom

13 [a]Blessed is the one who has found
wisdom
and the one who obtains
understanding.
14 [a]For her benefit[1] is more profitable[2]
than silver,
and her gain is better than gold.
15 She is more precious than rubies,
and none of the things you desire can
compare with her.
16 [a]Long life is in her right hand;
in her left hand are riches and honor.
17 Her ways are very pleasant,
and all [a]her paths are peaceful.
18 She is like [a]a tree of life to those who
grasp onto her,
and everyone who takes hold of her
will be blessed.
19 By wisdom [a]the Lord laid the
foundation of the earth;[1]
he established the heavens by
understanding.
20 By his knowledge the primordial sea
was [a]broken open,
so that the clouds drip down dew.
21 My child, do not let them escape
from your sight;
safeguard sound wisdom and
discretion.
22 So they will become life for your soul
and grace around your neck.
23 [a]Then you will walk on your way with
security,
and you will not stumble.
24 When you lie down[1] you will not be
filled with fear;

when you lie down your sleep will be
pleasant.
25 [a]Do not be afraid of sudden disaster
or when destruction overtakes the
wicked;
26 for the Lord will be the source of
your confidence,
and he will guard your foot from
being caught in a trap.

Wisdom Demonstrated in Relationships with People

27 [a]Do not withhold good from those
who need it
when you[1,2] have the ability to help.
28 [a]Do not say to your neighbor, "Go!
Return tomorrow
and I will give it," when you have it
with you at the time.
29 Do not plot evil against your neighbor
when he dwells by you
unsuspectingly.
30 [a]Do not accuse anyone without
legitimate cause
if he has not treated you wrongly.
31 Do not envy a violent man,
and [a]do not choose any of his ways;
32 for one who goes astray is an
abomination to the Lord,
[a]but he reveals his intimate counsel
to the upright.
33 The Lord's curse is on [a]the
household of [b]the wicked,
but he blesses the home of the
righteous.[1]
34 [a]With[1] arrogant scoffers[2] he is scornful,
yet he shows favor to the humble.[3]
35 The wise inherit honor,
but he holds fools up to[1] public
contempt.

Admonition to Follow Righteousness and Avoid Wickedness

4 Listen, children, to a father's
instruction,
and pay attention so that you may
gain discernment.

3:11 [a] Job 5:17; Ps 94:12; Heb 12:5–6; Rev 3:19   3:12 [a] Deut 8:5; Prov 13:24   [1] MT *and like a father the son in whom he delights*;
LXX *and scourges every son he receives.*   3:13 [a] Prov 8:32, 34, 35   3:14 [a] Job 28:13   [1] Heb. *profit*; the financial profit of traveling
merchants.   [2] Heb. *profit*; repeated for emphasis and creating a wordplay.   3:16 [a] Prov 8:18; [1 Tim 4:8]   3:17 [a] [Matt 11:29]
3:18 [a] Gen 2:9; Prov 11:30; 13:12; 15:4; Rev 2:7   3:19 [a] Ps 104:24; Prov 8:27   [1] Heb. *founded the earth.*   3:20 [a] Gen 7:11
3:23 [a] [Ps 37:24; 91:11–12]; Prov 10:9   3:24 [1] LXX *sit down.*   3:25 [a] Ps 91:5; 1 Pet 3:14   3:27 [a] Rom 13:7; [Gal 6:10]   [1] Ket. *your
hands.*   [2] Heb. *your hand.*   3:28 [a] Lev 19:13; Deut 24:15   3:30 [a] Prov 26:17; [Rom 12:18]   3:31 [a] Ps 37:1; Prov 24:1   3:32 [a] Ps
25:14   3:33 [a] Lev 26:14, 16; Deut 11:28; Zech 5:3–4; Mal 2:2   [b] Job 8:6; Ps 1:3   [1] The Heb. is structured chiastically (AB:BA):
The curse of the Lord / is on the house of the wicked // but the home of the righteous / he blesses.   3:34 [a] Jas 4:6; 1 Pet 5:5
[1] LXX omits *with*; MT *if.*   [2] Heb. *with those who mock he will mock*; the repetition connotes poetic justice; the
punishment fits the crime.   [3] Ket. *afflicted.*   3:35 [1] MT *he lifts up*; LXX, Vg. *but fools exalt shame.*

2 Because I hereby give you good
   instruction,
do not forsake my teaching.

3 When I was a son to my father,
   a [a]tender, only child[1] before my
   mother,
4 he taught me, and [a]he said to me:
   "Let your heart lay hold of my words;
   [b]keep my commands so that you will
   live.
5 Acquire wisdom, [a]acquire
   understanding;
do not forget and do not turn aside
   from the words I speak.
6 Do not forsake wisdom, and she will
   protect you;
[a]love her, and she will guard you.
7 [a]Wisdom is supreme—so acquire
   wisdom,
and whatever you acquire, acquire
   understanding![1]
8 Esteem her [a]highly and she will exalt
   you;
she will honor you if you embrace her.
9 She will place [a]a fair garland on your
   head;
she will bestow a beautiful crown on
   you."
10 Listen, my child,[1] [a]and accept my
   words
so that the years of your life will be
   many.
11 I hereby [a]guide you in the way of
   wisdom,
and I lead you in upright paths.
12 When [a]you walk, your steps will not
   be hampered,
[b]and when you run, you will not
   stumble.
13 Hold on to instruction, do not let it go;
protect it, because it is your life.
14 [a]Do not enter the path of the wicked
or walk in the way of those who are
   evil.
15 Avoid it, do not go on it;
turn away from it, and go on.

16 [a]For they cannot sleep unless they
   cause harm;
they are robbed of sleep until they
   make someone stumble.
17 Indeed they have eaten bread gained
   from wickedness
and drink wine obtained from
   violence.
18 [a]But the path of the righteous [b]is like
   the bright morning light,
growing brighter and brighter until
   full day.
19 The way of [a]the wicked is like gloomy
   darkness;
they do not know what they stumble
   over.

20 My child, pay attention to my words;
listen attentively to my sayings.
21 Do not let them depart from your
   sight;
guard[1] them within your heart,
22 for they are life to those who find
   them
and healing to one's entire body.
23 Guard your heart[1] with all vigilance,
for from it are the sources of [a]life.
24 Remove perverse speech from your
   mouth;
keep devious talk far from your lips.
25 Let your eyes look directly in front of
   you,
and let your gaze[1] look straight
   before you.
26 Make the path for your [a]feet level,
so that all your ways may be
   established.
27 Do not turn to the right or to the left;
turn yourself away from evil.[1]

Admonition to Avoid Seduction to Evil

5 My child,[1] be attentive to my wisdom;
pay close attention to my
   understanding,
2 in order to safeguard discretion
and that your lips [a]may guard
   knowledge.

4:3 [a]1 Chr 29:1   [1]LXX *obedient and beloved.*   4:4 [a]1 Chr 28:9; Eph 6:4   [b]Prov 7:2   4:5 [a]Prov 2:2–3   4:6 [a]2 Thess 2:10
4:7 [a]Prov 3:13–14; Matt 13:44   [1]LXX *omits this verse.*   4:8 [a]1 Sam 2:30   4:9 [a]Prov 3:22   4:10 [a]Prov 3:2   [1]Heb. *my son*
(likewise in v. 20).   4:11 [a]1 Sam 12:23   4:12 [a]Job 18:7; Ps 18:36   [b][Ps 91:11]; Prov 3:23   4:14 [a]Ps 1:1; Prov 1:15   4:16 [a]Ps 36:4;
Mic 2:1   4:18 [a]Isa 26:7; Matt 5:14, 45; Phil 2:15   [b]2 Sam 23:4   4:19 [a]1 Sam 2:9; [Job 18:5–6]; Prov 2:13; [Isa 59:9–10; Jer 23:12];
John 12:35   4:21 [1]Or *keep.*   4:23 [a][Matt 12:34; 15:18–19; Mark 7:21; Luke 6:45]   [1]One's inner self, will, understanding, or
mind.   4:25 [1]Heb. *your eyelids.*   4:26 [a]Prov 5:21; Heb 12:13   4:27 [1]LXX adds *For the way of the right hand God knows,
but those of the left hand are distorted; and he himself will make straight your paths and guide your goings in peace.*
5:1 [1]Heb. *my son;* the image of the adulterous woman probably represents all kinds of folly (through
personification), and even in this particular folly the temptation works both ways.   5:2 [a]Mal 2:7

3 [a]For the lips of the adulterous
  woman drip honey,
  and her seductive words[1] are
  [b]smoother than olive oil,
4 but in the end she is bitter as
  wormwood,
  sharp as a two-edged sword.
5 Her feet go down to death;
  [a]her steps lead straight to the grave.
6 Lest[1] she should make level the path
  leading to life,
  her paths have wandered, but she is
  not able to discern it.
7 So now, children, listen to me;
  do not turn aside from the words I
  speak.
8 Keep yourself far from her,
  and do not go near the door of her
  house,
9 lest you give your vigor to others
  and your years to a cruel person,
10 lest strangers devour your strength[1]
  and your labor benefit another man's
  house.
11 And at the end of your life you will
  groan
  when your flesh and your body are
  wasted away.
12 And you will say, "How I hated
  discipline!
  My heart spurned reproof!
13 For I did not obey my teachers,
  and I did not heed my instructors.
14 I almost came to complete ruin
  in the midst of the whole
  congregation!"
15 Drink water from your own cistern
  and running water from your own
  well.
16 Should your springs be dispersed
  outside,
  your streams of water in the wide
  plazas?[1]
17 Let them be for yourself alone
  and not for strangers with you.
18 May your fountain be blessed,
  and may you rejoice in [a]the wife you
  married in your youth[1]—
19 a loving doe, [a]a graceful deer;

may her breasts satisfy you at all
  times;
may you be captivated by her love
  always.
20 But why should you be captivated,
  my son, by [a]an adulteress,
  and embrace the bosom of a
  different woman?[1]
21 [a]For the ways of a person are in front
  of the LORD's eyes,
  and the LORD weighs all that person's
  paths.
22 The wicked will be captured by [a]his
  own iniquities,
  and he will be held by the cords of
  his own sin.[1]
23 He will die because [a]there was no
  discipline;
  because of the greatness of his folly
  he will reel.

Admonitions and Warnings against Dangerous and Destructive Acts

6 My child, [a]if you have made a pledge
  for your neighbor,[1]
  if you have become a guarantor for a
  stranger,
2 if you have been ensnared by the
  words you have uttered
  and have been caught by the words
  you have spoken,
3 then, my child, do this in order to
  deliver yourself,
  because you have fallen into your
  neighbor's power:
  Go, humble yourself,
  and appeal firmly to your neighbor.
4 [a]Permit no sleep to your eyes
  or slumber to your eyelids.
5 Deliver yourself like a gazelle from a
  snare[1]
  and like a bird from the trap[2] of the
  fowler.
6 [a]Go to the ant, you sluggard;
  observe her ways and be wise!
7 It has no commander,
  overseer, or ruler,
8 yet it would prepare its food in the
  summer;

it gathered at the harvest what it will
    eat.[1]
9 [a]How long, you sluggard, will you lie
    there?
  When will you rise from your sleep?
10 A little sleep, a little slumber,
  a little folding of the hands to relax,
11 [a]and your poverty will come like a
    robber,
  and your need like an armed man.
12 A worthless and wicked person
  walks around saying perverse things;
13 [a]he winks with his eyes,
  signals with his feet,
  and points with his fingers;
14 he plots evil with perverse thoughts
    in his [a]heart;
  [b]he spreads contention at all times.
15 Therefore, his disaster will come
    [a]suddenly;
  in an instant he will [b]be broken, and
    there will be no remedy.
16 There are six things that the LORD
    hates,
  even seven things that are an
    abomination to him:
17 haughty eyes, [a]a lying tongue,
  [b]and [c]hands that shed innocent blood,
18 a [a]heart that devises wicked plans,
  [b]feet that are swift to run[1] to evil,
19 a [a]false witness who pours out lies,
  and a person who [b]spreads discord
    among family members.
20 [a]My child,[1] guard the commands of
    your father
  and do not forsake the instruction of
    your mother.
21 [a]Bind them on your heart
    continually;
  fasten them around your neck.
22 When you walk about, they will guide
    you;
  [a]when you lie down, [b]they will watch
    over you;
  when you wake up, they will talk to
    you.

23 [a]For the commandments are like a
    lamp;
  instruction is like a light,
  and rebukes of discipline are like the
    road leading to life
24 by keeping you from the evil woman,[1]
  from the smooth [a]tongue of the
    loose woman.
25 Do not lust in your heart for her
    beauty,
  and [a]do not let her captivate you
    with her alluring eyes;
26 for on account of [a]a prostitute one is
    brought down to a loaf of bread,
  but the wife of another man [b]preys
    on your precious life.
27 Can a man hold fire against his chest
  without burning his clothes?
28 Can a man walk on hot coals
  without scorching his feet?
29 So it is with the one who sleeps with[1]
  his neighbor's wife;
  no one who touches her will escape
    punishment.
30 People do not despise a thief when
    he steals
  to fulfill his need when he is hungry.
31 Yet if [a]he is caught he must repay
    seven times over;
  he might even have to give all the
    wealth of his house.
32 A man who commits adultery with a
    woman [a]lacks sense;
  whoever does it destroys his own
    life.
33 He will be beaten and despised,
  and his reproach will not be wiped
    away;
34 for [a]jealousy kindles a husband's
    rage,
  and he will not show mercy when he
    takes revenge.
35 He will not consider any
    compensation;[1]
  he will not be willing, even if you
    multiply the compensation.

6:8 [1]LXX adds *Or, go to the bee and learn how diligent she is and how seriously she does her work—her products kings and private persons use for health—she is desired and respected by all—though feeble in body, by honoring wisdom she obtains distinction.*   6:9 [a]Prov 24:33–34   6:11 [a]Prov 10:4   6:13 [a]Job 15:12; Ps 35:19; Prov 10:10   6:14 [a]Prov 3:29; Mic 2:1   [b]Prov 6:19   6:15 [a]Prov 24:22; Isa 30:13; 1 Thess 5:3   [b]Jer 19:11   6:17 [a]Ps 101:5; Prov 21:4   [b]Ps 120:2; Prov 12:22   [c]Deut 19:10; Prov 28:17; Isa 1:15   6:18 [a]Gen 6:5; Ps 36:4; Prov 24:2; Jer 18:18; Mark 14:1, 43–46   [b]2 Kgs 5:20–27; Isa 59:7; Rom 3:15   [1]MT *make haste to run;* LXX omits *run.*   6:19 [a]Ps 27:12; Prov 19:5, 9; Matt 26:59–66   [b]Prov 6:14; 1 Cor 1:11–13; [Jude 3, 4, 16–19]   6:20 [a]Eph 6:1   [1]Heb. *my son;* the image of the adulterous woman probably represents all kinds of folly (through personification), and even in this particular folly the temptation works both ways.   6:21 [a]Prov 3:3   6:22 [a][Prov 3:23]   [b]Prov 2:11   6:23 [a]Ps 19:8; 2 Pet 1:19   6:24 [a]Prov 2:16   [1]LXX *wife of a neighbor.*   6:25 [a]Matt 5:28   6:26 [a]Gen 39:14   [b]Ezek 13:18   6:29 [1]Heb. *approaches;* used as a euphemism for sexual relations.   6:31 [a]Exod 22:1–4   6:32 [a]Prov 7:7   6:34 [a]Prov 27:4; Song 8:6   6:35 [1]MT *he will not lift the face of all of compensation.*

Admonition to Avoid the Wiles of the Adulteress

7 My child,[1] devote yourself to my words
and store [a]up my commands inside yourself.
2 [a]Keep my [b]commands[1] so that you may live,
and obey my instruction as your most prized possession.
3 [a]Bind them on your forearm;
write them on the tablet of your heart.
4 Say to wisdom, "You are my sister,"
and call understanding a close relative
5 so [a]that they may keep you from the adulterous woman,
from the loose woman[1] who has flattered you with her words.
6 For at the window of my house
through my window lattice I looked out,
7 and I saw among the naive—
I discerned among the youths[1]—
a young man who [a]lacked sense.[2]
8 He was passing by the street near her corner,
making his way along the road to her house
9 in the twilight, the [a]evening,
in the dark of the night.
10 Suddenly[1] a woman came out to meet him!
She was dressed like a prostitute and with secret intent.
11 (She is loud and rebellious;
[a]she does not remain at home—
12 at one time outside, at another in the wide plazas,
and by every corner she lies in wait.)
13 So she grabbed him and kissed him,
and with a bold expression she said to him,
14 "I have meat from my peace offerings at home;[1]
today I have fulfilled my vows!
15 That is why I came out to meet you,

to look for you, and I found you!
16 I have spread my bed with elegant coverings,
with richly colored fabric from [a]Egypt.
17 I have perfumed my bed
with myrrh, aloes, and cinnamon.
18 Come, let's drink deeply of lovemaking[1] until morning;
let's delight ourselves with love's pleasures.
19 For my husband is not at home;
he has gone on a journey of some distance.
20 He has taken a bag of money with him;
he will not return until the end of the month."
21 She turned him aside with [a]her persuasions;
[b]with her smooth talk she was enticing him along.
22 Suddenly he was going after her
like an ox that goes to the slaughter,
like a stag prancing into a trapper's snare
23 till an arrow pierces his liver—
like [a]a bird hurrying into a trap,
and he does not know that it will cost him his life.[1]
24 So now, sons, listen to me,
and pay attention to the words I speak.
25 Do not let your heart turn aside to her ways—
do not wander into her pathways;
26 for she has brought down many [a]fatally wounded,
and all those she has slain are many.
27 [a]Her house is the way to the grave,[1]
going down to the chambers of death.

The Appeal of Wisdom

8 Does not [a]wisdom call out?
Does not understanding raise her voice?

7:1 [a]Prov 2:1 [1]Heb. *my son*; the image of the adulterous woman probably represents all kinds of folly (through personification), and even in this particular folly the temptation works both ways. 7:2 [a]Lev 18:5; Prov 4:4; [Isa 55:3] [b]Deut 32:10; Ps 17:8; Zech 2:8 [1]LXX adds *My son, fear the LORD and you will be strong, and besides him, fear no other* before v. 2. 7:3 [a]Deut 6:8; Prov 6:21 7:5 [a]Prov 2:16; 5:3 [1]Heb. *strange woman*; sometimes refers to people who are ethnically foreign to Israel, but it often refers to what is morally estranged from God or his covenant people. 7:7 [a][Prov 6:32; 9:4, 16] [1]MT *among the sons*; Syr., Tg., Vg. *among the fools*. [2]Heb. *mind, heart.* 7:9 [a]Job 24:15 7:10 [1]An emphatic Heb. construction. 7:11 [a]Prov 9:13; 1 Tim 5:13 7:14 [1]Heb. *peace offerings are with me.* 7:16 [a]Isa 19:9; Ezek 27:7 7:18 [1]Heb. *loves.* 7:21 [a]Prov 5:3 [b]Ps 12:2 7:23 [a]Eccl 9:12 [1]Heb. *for/about/over his life*; could refer to moral corruption and social disgrace rather than physical death. 7:26 [a]Neh 13:26 7:27 [a]Prov 2:18; 5:5; 9:18; [1 Cor 6:9–10; Rev 22:15] [1]Heb. *Sheol.* 8:1 [a]Prov 1:20–21; 9:3; [1 Cor 1:24]

2 At the top of the prominent places along the way,
at the intersection of the paths she has taken her stand;

3 beside the gates opening into the city,
at the entrance of the doorways she cries out:

4 "To you, O people, I call out,
and my voice calls to all mankind.

5 You who are naive, discern wisdom!
And you fools, understand discernment!

6 Listen, for I will speak [a]excellent things,[1]
and my lips will utter[2] what is right.

7 For my mouth speaks truth,
and my lips hate wickedness.

8 All the words of my mouth are righteous;
there is nothing in them twisted or crooked.

9 All of them are clear[1] to the discerning
and upright to those who find knowledge.

10 Receive my instruction rather than silver,
and knowledge rather than choice gold.

11 [a]For wisdom is better than rubies,
and desirable things cannot be compared to her.

12 "I, wisdom, have dwelt with prudence,
and I find knowledge and discretion.

13 The fear of [a]the LORD is to hate evil;
I hate arrogant [b]pride and [c]the evil way
and perverse utterances.

14 Counsel and sound [a]wisdom belong to me;
I possess understanding and might.

15 By me, kings reign,
and [a]by me, potentates decree righteousness;

16 by me, princes rule,
as well as nobles and all righteous judges.[1]

17 I [a]will love [b]those who love me,
and those who seek me diligently will find me.

18 [a]Riches and honor are with me,
long-lasting wealth and righteousness.

19 My fruit is better than the purest gold,
and my harvest is better than choice silver.

20 I walk in the path of righteousness,
in the pathway of justice,

21 that I may cause those who love me to inherit wealth,
and that I may fill their treasuries.[1]

22 The LORD created me as [a]the beginning of his works,[1]
before his deeds of long ago.

23 From [a]eternity I have been fashioned,
from the beginning, from before the world existed.

24 When there were no deep oceans I was born,
when there were no springs overflowing with water;

25 before the mountains were set in place—
[a]before the hills—I was born,

26 before he made the earth and its fields,
or the top soil of the world.

27 When he established the heavens, I was there;
when he marked out the horizon over the face of the deep,

28 when he established the clouds above,
when he secured the fountains of the deep,[1]

29 when [a]he gave [b]the sea his decree
that the waters should not pass over his command,
when he marked out the foundations of the earth,

8:6 [a] Prov 22:20 [1] MT *nobles.* [2] Heb. *opening of my lips.*   8:9 [1] Heb. *front of.*   8:11 [a] Job 28:15; Ps 19:10; 119:127; Prov 3:14–15; 4:5, 7; 16:16   8:13 [a] Prov 3:7; 16:6 [b] 1 Sam 2:3; [Prov 16:17–18; Isa 13:11] [c] Prov 4:24   8:14 [a] Eccl 7:19; 9:16   8:15 [a] 2 Chr 1:10; Prov 29:4; Dan 2:21; [Matt 28:18]; Rom 13:1   8:16 [1] Sev. MSS *sovereigns* [princes], *all the judges of the earth;* LXX *sovereigns . . . rule the earth.*   8:17 [a] 1 Sam 2:30; [Ps 91:14]; Prov 4:6; [John 14:21] [b] Prov 2:4–5; John 7:37; Jas 1:5   8:18 [a] Prov 3:16; [Matt 6:33]   8:21 [1] LXX adds *If I declare to you the things of daily occurrence, I will remember to recount the things of old.*   8:22 [a] Job 28:26–28; Ps 104:24; Prov 3:19; [John 1:1] [1] Heb. *his way;* an idiom for the actions of God.   8:23 [a] [Ps 2:6]   8:25 [a] Job 15:7–8   8:28 [1] MT *when* [they] *grew strong.*   8:29 [a] Gen 1:9–10; Job 38:8–11; Ps 33:7; 104:9; Jer 5:22 [b] Job 28:4, 6; Ps 104:5

[30] [a]then I was beside him as [b]a master craftsman,
and I was his delight day by day,
rejoicing before him at all times,
[31] rejoicing in the habitable part of his earth,
and delighting in its people.

[32] "So now, children, listen to me;
[a]blessed are those who keep my ways.
[33] Listen to my instruction[1] so that you may be wise,
and do not neglect it.
[34] [a]Blessed is the one who listens to me,
watching at my doors day by day,
waiting beside my doorway.
[35] For the one who finds me has found[1] life
and [a]received favor from the LORD.
[36] But the one who misses me[1] brings [a]harm to himself;
all who hate[2] me love death."

The Consequences of Accepting Wisdom or Folly

9 Wisdom has [a]built her house;
she has carved out its seven pillars.
[2] She has prepared her meat, [a]she has mixed her wine;
[b]she also has arranged her table.
[3] She has sent out her female servants;
she calls out on the highest places of the city.
[4] "Whoever is naive, let him turn in here."
To those [a]who lack understanding, she has said,
[5] "[a]Come, eat some of my food,
and drink some of the wine I have mixed.
[6] Abandon your foolish ways[1] so that you may live,
and proceed in the way of understanding."

[7] Whoever corrects a mocker is asking for insult;
whoever reproves a wicked person receives abuse.
[8] [a]Do not [b]reprove a mocker, or he will hate you;
reprove a wise person, and he will love you.
[9] Give instruction to [a]a wise person,
and he will become wiser still;
teach a righteous person, and he will add to his learning.
[10] The beginning of wisdom is to fear [a]the LORD,
and acknowledging the Holy One is understanding.
[11] [a]For because of me your days will be many,
and years will be added to your life.
[12] If you are wise, you are wise to your own advantage,
but [a]if you have mocked, you alone must[1] bear it.[2]
[13] The [a]woman called Folly is brash;
she is naive and does not know anything.[1]
[14] And she has sat down at the door of her house,
on a seat at the highest point of the city,
[15] calling out to those who are passing by her in the way,
who go straight on their way.
[16] "Whoever is naive, let him turn in here,"
To those [a]who lack understanding she has said,[1]
[17] "[a]Stolen waters are sweet,
and food obtained in secret[1] is pleasant!"
[18] But [a]they do not realize that the dead are there,
that her guests are in the depths of the grave.[1]

8:30 [a][John 1:1–3, 18] [b][Matt 3:17] **8:32** [a]Ps 119:1–2; 128:1; Prov 29:18; Luke 11:28 **8:33** [1]Heb. *discipline.* **8:34** [a]Prov 3:13, 18 **8:35** [a]Prov 3:4; 12:2; [John 17:3] [1]Ket. *the one who finds me are finders of life.* **8:36** [a]Prov 20:2 [1]Heb. *the one sinning* [against] *me.* [2]I.e., rejected. **9:1** [a][Matt 16:18; 1 Cor 3:9–10; Eph 2:20–22; 1 Pet 2:5] **9:2** [a]Matt 22:4 [b]Prov 23:30 **9:4** [a]Ps 19:7 **9:5** [a]Song 5:1; Isa 55:1; [John 6:27] **9:6** [1]Or *fools.* **9:8** [a]Prov 15:12; Matt 7:6 [b]Ps 141:5; Prov 10:8 **9:9** [a][Matt 13:12] **9:10** [a]Job 28:28; Ps 111:10; Prov 1:7 **9:11** [a]Prov 3:2, 16 **9:12** [a]Job 35:6–7; Prov 16:26 [1]Or *you . . . will bear it.* [2]LXX adds *Forsake folly, that you may reign forever; and seek discretion and direct understanding in knowledge.* **9:13** [a]Prov 7:11 [1]LXX *A foolish and impudent woman comes to lack a morsel, she who knows not shame;* Syr. *a woman lacking in discretion, seductive;* Tg. *a foolish woman and a gadabout, ignorant, and she knows not good;* Vg. *a woman foolish and noisy, and full of wiles, and knowing nothing at all.* **9:16** [a]Prov 7:7–8 [1]LXX *she exhorts saying.* **9:17** [a]Prov 20:17 [1]Or *food eaten in secret;* Heb. *bread of secrecies.* **9:18** [a]Prov 2:18; 7:27 [1]LXX adds *But turn away, linger not in the place, neither set your eye on her: for thus will you go through alien water, but abstain from alien water, drink not from an alien fountain, that you may live long, that years of life may be added to you.*

The First Collection of Solomonic Proverbs

10 The proverbs of [a]Solomon:

[b]A wise child makes a father rejoice,[1]
but a foolish child is a grief to his
mother.

2 [a]Treasures gained by wickedness do
not profit,
[b]but righteousness delivers from
death.

3 The LORD satisfies [a]the appetite of
the righteous,
but he thwarts the craving of the
wicked.

4 The one who is lazy becomes poor,
but [a]the one who works diligently
becomes wealthy.

5 The one who gathers crops in the
[a]summer is [b]a wise[1] son,
but the one who sleeps during
harvest is a shameful son.

6 Blessings are on the head of the
righteous,
but the speech of the wicked
conceals violence.

7 The memory of [a]the righteous is a
blessing,
but the reputation of the wicked will
rot.

8 The wise person accepts
instructions,
[a]but the one who speaks foolishness[1]
will come to ruin.

9 The one who conducts himself in
integrity will live securely,
but [a]the one who behaves perversely
will be found out.

10 The one who winks[1] his eye causes
trouble,
and the one who speaks foolishness[2]
will come to ruin.

11 The speech of the righteous is a
fountain of life,
but the speech of the wicked
conceals violence.

12 Hatred stirs up dissension,
but [a]love covers all transgressions.

13 Wisdom is found in the words of the
discerning person,
but the one who [a]lacks sense will be
disciplined.[1]

14 Those who are wise store up
knowledge,
but foolish speech leads to imminent
destruction.

15 The wealth of a rich [a]person is like a
fortified city,
but the poor are brought to ruin by[1]
their poverty.

16 The reward that the righteous
receive is [a]life;
the recompense that the wicked
receive is judgment.

17 The one who heeds instruction[1] is on
the way to life,
but the one who rejects rebuke goes
astray.

18 The one who [a]conceals hatred utters
lies,
and the one [b]who spreads slander is
certainly a fool.

19 When words abound, transgression is
[a]inevitable,[1]
but [b]the one who restrains his words
is wise.

20 What the righteous say is like the
best silver,
but what the wicked think is of little
value.

21 The teaching of the righteous feeds
many,
but fools die[1] for lack of sense.

22 The blessing from [a]the LORD makes a
person rich,
and he adds no sorrow[1] to it.

23 Carrying out a wicked scheme is
enjoyable [a]to a fool,

10:1 [a]Prov 1:1; 25:1   [b]Prov 15:20; 17:21, 25; 19:13; 29:3, 15   [1]The Heb. verb tense describes habitual action; proverbs are general maxims, and not necessarily absolutes or universal truths. One may normally expect to find what the proverb notes, and one should live according to its instructions in the light of those expectations, but one should not be surprised if, from time to time, there is an exception.   10:2 [a]Ps 49:7; Prov 11:4; 21:6; Ezek 7:19; [Luke 12:19–20]   [b]Dan 4:27   10:3 [a]Ps 34:9–10; 37:25; Prov 28:25; [Matt 6:33]   10:4 [a]Prov 19:15   10:5 [a]Prov 6:8   [b]Prov 19:26   [1]Heb. prudent.   10:7 [a]Ps 112:6; Eccl 8:10   10:8 [a]Prov 10:10   [1]Heb. fool of lips.   10:9 [a][Ps 23:4; Prov 3:23; 28:18; Isa 33:15–16]   10:10 [1]I.e., habitually winking maliciously as a secretive sign to those conspiring evil.   [2]Heb. the fool of lips.   10:12 [a]Prov 17:9; [1 Cor 13:4–7; Jas 5:20]; 1 Pet 4:8   10:13 [a]Prov 26:3   [1]Heb. a rod is for the back of the one lacking heart.   10:15 [a]Job 31:24; Ps 52:7; Prov 18:11; [1 Tim 6:17]   [1]Heb. is their poverty.   10:16 [a]Prov 6:23   10:17 [1]Heb. discipline.   10:18 [a]Prov 26:24   [b]Ps 15:3; 101:5   10:19 [a]Job 11:2; [Prov 18:21]; Eccl 5:3   [b]Prov 17:27; [Jas 1:19; 3:2]   [1]Heb. does not cease.   10:21 [1]The contrast is between enhancing life and ruining life; fools ruin their lives and the lives of others by their lack of discipline and knowledge.   10:22 [a]Gen 24:35; 26:12; Deut 8:18; Ps 37:22; Prov 8:21   [1]Heb. toil; i.e., the pain and sorrow that is the result of toil and labor.   10:23 [a]Prov 2:14; 15:21

and so is wisdom for the one who has
  discernment.
24 What ᵃthe wicked fears will come on
  him;
  what ᵇthe righteous desire will be
  granted.
25 When ᵃthe storm passes through,
  ᵇthe wicked are swept away,¹
  but the righteous are an everlasting
  foundation.
26 Like vinegar to the teeth and like
  smoke to the eyes,
  so is the sluggard to those who send
  him.
27 Fearing ᵃthe LORD prolongs life,
  but ᵇthe life span of the wicked will
  be shortened.
28 The hope of the righteous is joy,
  but the ᵃexpectation of the wicked
  perishes.
29 The way of the LORD¹ is like a
  stronghold for the upright,²
  but it is ᵃdestruction to evildoers.
30 The righteous will never be moved,
  but ᵃthe wicked will not inhabit the
  land.
31 The speech¹ of ᵃthe righteous bears
  the fruit of wisdom,
  but the one who speaks perversion
  will be destroyed.
32 The lips of the righteous know what
  is pleasing,
  but the speech of the wicked is
  perverse.

11 The LORD abhors ᵃdishonest
  scales,
  but an accurate weight¹ is his delight.
2 After pride came, ᵃdisgrace followed;
  but wisdom came with humility.
3 The integrity of ᵃthe upright guides
  them,
  but the crookedness of the
  treacherous destroys them.
4 ᵃWealth does not profit in the day of
  wrath,
  but ᵇrighteousness delivers from
  death.

5 The righteousness of the blameless
  will make their way smooth,
  but the wicked will fall through their
  own ᵃwickedness.
6 The righteousness of the upright will
  deliver them,
  but the treacherous will be ensnared
  by their own desires.¹
7 When a wicked person dies, his¹
  expectation ᵃperishes,
  and hope based on power has
  perished.
8 A righteous person was delivered out
  of trouble,
  ᵃthen a wicked person took his place.
9 With his speech the godless person
  destroys his neighbor,
  but by knowledge the righteous will
  be delivered.
10 When the righteous do well, the city
  rejoices;
  ᵃwhen the wicked perish, there is joy.
11 A city is ᵃexalted by the blessing
  provided from the upright,
  but it is destroyed by the counsel of
  the wicked.
12 The one who denounces his neighbor
  lacks sense,¹
  but a discerning person keeps silent.
13 The one who goes ᵃabout slandering
  others reveals secrets,
  but the one who is trustworthy
  ᵇconceals a matter.
14 ᵃWhen there is no guidance a nation
  falls,
  but there is success in the abundance
  of counselors.
15 The one who has put up security
  ᵃfor a stranger will surely have
  trouble,
  but whoever avoids¹ shaking hands is
  secure.
16 A generous woman gains honor,
  and ruthless men seize wealth.¹
17 ᵃA kind person benefits himself,
  but a cruel person brings himself
  trouble.¹

10:24 ᵃJob 15:21; Prov 1:27; Isa 66:4 ᵇPs 145:19; Prov 15:8; Matt 5:6; [1 John 5:14–15] 10:25 ᵃPs 37:9–10 ᵇPs 15:5; Prov 12:3;
Matt 7:24–25 ¹Heb. *the wicked are not.* 10:27 ᵃProv 9:11 ᵇJob 15:32 10:28 ᵃJob 8:13 10:29 ᵃPs 1:6 ¹LXX *the fear of
the LORD.* ²Heb. *for the one with integrity.* 10:30 ᵃPs 37:22; Prov 2:21 10:31 ᵃPs 37:30; Prov 10:13 ¹Heb. *the mouth.*
11:1 ᵃLev 19:35–36; Deut 25:13–16; Prov 20:10, 23; Mic 6:11 ¹Heb. *a perfect stone;* used for measuring amounts of silver on
the scales in economic transactions. 11:2 ᵃProv 16:18; 18:12; 29:23 11:3 ᵃProv 13:6 11:4 ᵃProv 10:2; Ezek 7:19; Zeph 1:18
ᵇGen 7:1 11:5 ᵃProv 5:22 11:6 ¹LXX *ungodliness will fall into* [the hands of] *unrighteousness* or *encounters injustice.*
11:7 ᵃProv 10:28 ¹LXX *When the righteous dies, hope does not perish; but the boasting by the ungodly perishes.* 11:8 ᵃProv
21:18 11:10 ᵃProv 28:12 11:11 ᵃProv 14:34 11:12 ¹Heb. *lacking of mind.* 11:13 ᵃLev 19:16; Prov 20:19; 1 Tim 5:13 ᵇProv
19:11 11:14 ᵃ1 Kgs 12:1 11:15 ᵃProv 6:1–2 ¹Heb. *hates;* i.e., to reject. 11:16 ¹LXX adds *She who hates virtue makes a
throne for dishonor; the idle will be destitute of means.* 11:17 ᵃ[Matt 5:7; 25:34–36] ¹Heb. *brings trouble to his flesh.*

18 The wicked person earns deceitful
  wages,
but ᵃthe one who sows righteousness
  reaps a genuine reward.
19 True righteousness leads to ᵃlife,
but the one who pursues evil pursues
  it to his own ᵇdeath.
20 The LORD abhors those who are
  perverse in heart,
but those who are blameless in their
  ways are his delight.
21 ᵃBe assured that ᵇthe evil person will
  not be unpunished,
but the descendants of the righteous
  have escaped harm.
22 Like a gold ring in a pig's snout
is a beautiful woman who rejects
  discretion.¹
23 The desire of the righteous ᵃis only
  good,
but the expectation of the wicked is
  wrath.¹
24 One ᵃperson is generous and yet
  grows more wealthy,
but another withholds more than he
  should and comes to poverty.
25 A generous person will be enriched,
and ᵃthe one who provides water for
  others will himself be satisfied.
26 People will curse the one who
  withholds grain,
but they will ᵃpraise the one who
  sells it.
27 The one who diligently seeks good
  seeks favor,
ᵃbut the one who searches for evil—it
  will come to him.
28 The one who trusts in his ᵃriches will
  fall,
but ᵇthe righteous will flourish like a
  green leaf.
29 The one who troubles his family ᵃwill
  inherit nothing,
and the fool will be a ᵇservant to the
  wise person.
30 The fruit of ᵃthe righteous is like a
  tree producing life,
and the one who wins souls is wise.¹

31 ᵃIf the righteous are recompensed on
  earth,¹
how much more the wicked sinner!

12 The one who loves discipline loves
  knowledge,
but the one who hates reproof is
  stupid.
2 A good person obtains favor from the
  LORD,
but the LORD¹ condemns a person
  with wicked schemes.
3 No one can be established through
  wickedness,
but a righteous ᵃroot cannot be
  moved.
4 A noble wife is the crown of her
  ᵃhusband,
but the wife who acts shamefully is
  ᵇlike rottenness in his bones.
5 The plans of the righteous are just;
the counsels of the wicked are
  deceitful.
6 The words of ᵃthe wicked lie in wait
  to shed innocent blood,
ᵇbut the words of the upright will
  deliver them.
7 The wicked are overthrown and
  perish,
but ᵃthe righteous household will
  stand.
8 A person will be praised in
  accordance with his wisdom,
ᵃbut the one with a bewildered mind
  will be despised.
9 ᵃBetter is a person of humble
  standing who works for
  himself,¹
than one who pretends to be
  somebody important yet has no
  food.
10 A righteous person ᵃcares for¹ the life
  of his animal,
but even the most compassionate
  acts of the wicked are cruel.
11 ᵃThe one who works his field will
  have plenty of ᵇfood,
but whoever chases daydreams lacks
  sense.

11:18 ᵃHos 10:12; [Gal 6:8–9]; Jas 3:18   **11:19** ᵃProv 10:16; 12:28   ᵇProv 21:16; [Rom 6:23; Jas 1:15]   **11:21** ᵃProv 16:5   ᵇPs 112:2;
Prov 14:26   **11:22** ¹Heb. *taste*; i.e., physical taste, intellectual discretion, or ethical judgment.   **11:23** ᵃProv 10:28; Rom 2:8–9
¹LXX *will perish.*   **11:24** ᵃPs 112:9; Prov 13:7; 19:17   **11:25** ᵃProv 3:9–10; [2 Cor 9:6–7]   **11:26** ᵃJob 29:13   **11:27** ᵃEsth 7:10; Ps
7:15–16; 57:6   **11:28** ᵃJob 31:24   ᵇPs 1:3; Jer 17:8   **11:29** ᵃEccl 5:16   ᵇProv 14:19   **11:30** ᵃProv 14:25; [Dan 12:3; 1 Cor 9:19–22;
Jas 5:20]   ¹LXX, Syr. *but the one who takes away lives* [= kills people] *is violent.*   **11:31** ᵃJer 25:29   ¹LXX *If the righteous
be scarcely saved.*   **12:2** ¹Heb. *but he condemns.*   **12:3** ᵃ[Prov 10:25]   **12:4** ᵃProv 31:23; 1 Cor 11:7   ᵇProv 14:30; Hab 3:16
12:6 ᵃProv 1:11, 18   ᵇProv 14:3   **12:7** ᵃPs 37:35–37; Prov 11:21; Matt 7:24–27   **12:8** ᵃ1 Sam 25:17; Prov 18:3   **12:9** ᵃProv 13:7
¹MT *has a servant or is a servant for himself.*   **12:10** ᵃDeut 25:4   ¹Heb. *knows.*   **12:11** ᵃGen 3:19   ᵇProv 28:19

12 The wicked person has desired the
   stronghold of the wicked,
but the root of the righteous will
   yield fruit.[1]
13 The evil person is ensnared by [a]the
   transgression of his speech,
[b]but the righteous person escapes
   out of trouble.
14 A person will be [a]satisfied with good
   from the fruit of his words,[1]
[b]and the work of his hands will be
   rendered to him.
15 The way of a fool is right in his own
   opinion,
but [a]the one who listens to advice is
   wise.
16 A fool's [a]annoyance is known at once,[1]
but the prudent conceals dishonor.
17 [a]The faithful witness tells what is
   right,
but a false witness speaks deceit.
18 Speaking recklessly is like [a]the
   thrusts of a sword,
but the words of the wise bring
   healing.
19 The one who tells the truth will
   endure forever,
[a]but the one who lies will last only
   for a moment.
20 Deceit is in the heart of those who
   plot evil,
but those who promote peace have
   joy.
21 [a]No harm will be directed at the
   righteous,
but the wicked are filled with
   calamity.
22 The LORD abhors a person who
   [a]lies,[1]
but those who deal truthfully are his
   delight.
23 The shrewd person [a]conceals
   knowledge,
but foolish people proclaim folly.
24 The diligent person will rule,
but [a]the slothful[1] will be put to forced
   labor.

25 [a]Anxiety in a person's [b]heart weighs
   him down,
but an encouraging[1] word brings him
   joy.
26 The righteous person is cautious in
   his friendship,
but the way of the wicked leads them
   astray.
27 The lazy person does not roast[1] his
   prey,
but personal possessions are
   precious to the diligent.
28 In the path of righteousness there is
   life,
but another path[1] leads to death.[2]

13 A wise son accepts his father's
   discipline,[1]
[a]but a scoffer has never listened to
   rebuke.
2 From the fruit of his speech [a]a
   person eats good things,
but the treacherous desire the fruit
   of violence.[1]
3 [a]The one who guards his words
   guards his life;
whoever is talkative will come to
   ruin.
4 The appetite of [a]the sluggard craves
   but gets nothing,
but the desire of the diligent will be
   abundantly satisfied.
5 The righteous person will reject
   anything false,
but the wicked person will act in
   shameful disgrace.[1]
6 [a]Righteousness guards the one who
   lives with integrity,
but wickedness overthrows the
   sinner.
7 [a]There is one who pretends to be rich
   and yet has nothing;
another pretends to be poor and yet
   possesses great wealth.
8 The ransom of a person's life is his
   wealth,
thus the poor person has never
   heard[1] a threat.

12:12 [1]LXX *the root of the righteous endures.* 12:13 [a] Prov 18:7 [b] [2 Pet 2:9] 12:14 [a] Prov 13:2; 15:23; 18:20 [b] Job 34:11;
Prov 1:31; 24:12; [Isa 3:10–11]; Hos 4:9 [1]Heb. *fruit of the lips.* 12:15 [a] Prov 3:7; Luke 18:11 12:16 [a] Prov 11:13; 29:11 [1]Heb. *on
the day, the same day.* 12:17 [a] Prov 14:5 12:18 [a] Ps 57:4; Prov 4:22; 15:4 12:19 [a] [Ps 52:4–5]; Prov 19:9 12:21 [a] Ps 91:10;
Prov 1:33; 1 Pet 3:13 12:22 [a] Prov 6:17; 11:20; Rev 22:15 [1]Heb. *lips of lying.* 12:23 [a] Prov 13:16 12:24 [a] Prov 10:4 [1]Heb.
slack, negligent, deceptive. 12:25 [a] Prov 15:13 [b] Isa 50:4 [1]Heb. *good; what is beneficial for life, promotes life, creates
life, or protects life.* 12:27 [1]LXX, Syr., Vg. *a lazy person cannot catch his prey.* 12:28 [1]LXX *the ways of the revengeful
[lead] to death.* [2]MT *no death.* 13:1 [a] Isa 28:14–15 [1]A few medieval MSS, LXX, Syr. *a wise son listens to/obeys his father.*
13:2 [a] Prov 12:14 [1]LXX *the souls of the wicked perish untimely.* 13:3 [a] Ps 39:1; Prov 21:23; [Jas 3:2] 13:4 [a] Prov 10:4
13:5 [1]LXX *is ashamed and without confidence;* Tg. *is ashamed and put to the blush;* Vg. *confounds and will be
confounded.* 13:6 [a] Prov 11:3, 5, 6 13:7 [a] [Prov 11:24; 12:9; Luke 12:20–21] 13:8 [1]Heb. *has not heard.*

9 The light of the righteous shines
  brightly,
  [a]but the lamp of the wicked goes out.[1]
10 With pride comes only [a]contention,
  but wisdom is with the well-advised.[1]
11 [a]Wealth gained quickly[1] will dwindle
  away,
  but the one who gathers it little by
  little will become rich.[2]
12 Hope deferred makes the heart sick,
  but a longing fulfilled is like a tree of
  life.
13 The one who [a]despises instruction
  will pay the penalty,
  but whoever esteems direction will
  be rewarded.[1]
14 Instruction from [a]the wise is like a
  life-giving fountain,
  to turn a person from deadly snares.
15 Keen insight wins [a]favor,
  but the conduct[1] of the treacherous
  ends in destruction.[2]
16 [a]Every shrewd person acts with
  knowledge,
  but a fool displays his folly.
17 An [a]unreliable messenger falls into
  trouble,
  but a faithful envoy brings healing.
18 The one who neglects discipline ends
  up in poverty and shame,
  but [a]the one who accepts reproof is
  honored.
19 A desire fulfilled will be sweet to the
  soul,
  but fools abhor turning away from
  evil.
20 The one who associates with the wise
  grows wise,[1]
  but a companion of fools suffers harm.
21 [a]Calamity pursues sinners,
  but prosperity rewards the righteous.
22 A good person leaves an inheritance
  for his grandchildren,

but [a]the wealth of a sinner is stored
  up for the righteous.
23 [a]Abundant food may come from the
  field of the poor,
  but it is swept away by injustice.[1]
24 The one who spares his rod hates his
  child,[1]
  but [a]the one who loves his child is
  diligent in disciplining him.
25 The righteous has enough food to
  satisfy his appetite,
  but [a]the belly of the wicked will be
  empty.

14 Every wise woman has built her
  household,
  but a foolish woman tears it down
  with her own hands.
2 The one who walks in his
  uprightness fears the LORD,
  [a]but the one who is perverted in his
  ways despises him.
3 In the speech of a fool is a rod for his
  back,[1]
  [a]but the words[2] of the wise protect
  them.
4 Where there are no oxen, the feeding
  trough is clean,
  but an abundant harvest is produced
  by strong oxen.
5 A [a]truthful witness does not lie,
  but a false witness breathes out [b]lies.
6 The scorner sought wisdom—there
  was none,
  but [a]understanding was easy for a
  discerning person.
7 Walk[1,2] abreast with a foolish person,
  and you do not understand[3] [a]wise
  counsel.
8 The wisdom of the shrewd person is
  to discern his way,
  but the folly of fools is deception.
9 [a]Fools mock[1] at reparation,[2]
  but among the upright there is favor.

10 The heart knows its own bitterness,
and with its joy no one else can
share.
11 The household of ªthe wicked will be
destroyed,
but the tent[1] of the upright will
flourish.
12 There is a way that seems right to a
person,
but its end is ªthe way that leads to
ᵇdeath.[1]
13 Even in laughter ªthe heart may ache,
and the end[1] of joy may be grief.
14 The backslider will be paid ªback
from his own ways,
but a good person will be rewarded
ᵇfor his.
15 A naive person will believe anything,
but the shrewd person discerns his
steps.
16 A wise person is ªcautious and turns
from evil,
but a fool throws off restraint and is
overconfident.
17 A person who has a quick temper will
do foolish things,
and a person with crafty schemes
will be hated.[1]
18 The naive have inherited folly,
but the shrewd will be crowned with
knowledge.
19 Bad people have bowed before good
people,
and wicked people have bowed at the
gates of someone righteous.
20 ªA poor person will be disliked[1] even
by his neighbors,
but those who ᵇlove the rich are
many.
21 The one who despises his neighbor
sins,
ªbut whoever is kind to the needy is
blessed.
22 Do not those who devise evil go
astray?
But those who plan good exhibit
faithful covenant love.
23 In all hard work there is profit,

but merely talking about it only
brings poverty.
24 The crown of the wise is their riches,[1]
but the folly[2] of fools is folly.
25 A truthful witness rescues ªlives,
but one who testifies falsely betrays
them.[1]
26 In the fear of the LORD one has
strong confidence,
and it will be a refuge for his
children.
27 The fear of ªthe LORD is like a
life-giving fountain,
to turn people from deadly snares.
28 A king's glory is the abundance of
people,
but the lack of subjects is the ruin of
a ruler.
29 Someone with great understanding
is slow to anger,
but ªthe one who has a quick temper
exalts folly.
30 A tranquil spirit revives the body,[1]
but ªenvy is ᵇrottenness to the
bones.[2]
31 The one who oppresses ªthe poor has
insulted ᵇhis Creator,
but whoever honors him shows favor
to the needy.
32 An evil person will be thrown down
through his wickedness,
but a righteous person takes refuge
in his integrity.[1]
33 Wisdom rests in the heart of the
discerning;
it is not known[1] in the inner parts of
fools.
34 Righteousness exalts a ªnation,
but sin is a disgrace to any people.
35 ªThe king shows favor to a wise
servant,
but his wrath falls on one who acts
shamefully.

15 A ªgentle response turns ᵇaway
anger,
but a harsh word stirs up wrath.[1]
2 The tongue of the wise treats
knowledge correctly,

14:11 ªJob 8:15 [1] I.e., the contents of the tent: families. 14:12 ªProv 16:25 ᵇProv 12:15 [1] LXX the depths of Hades.
14:13 ªProv 5:4; Eccl 2:1–2 [1] Heb. and its end, joy, is grief. 14:14 ªProv 1:31; 12:15 ᵇProv 13:2; 18:20 14:16 ªJob
28:28; Ps 34:14; Prov 22:3 14:17 [1] LXX endures. 14:20 ªProv 19:7 ᵇProv 19:4 [1] Heb. hated. 14:21 ªPs 112:9; [Prov
19:17] 14:24 [1] LXX crafty. [2] LXX lifestyle. 14:25 ª[Ezek 3:18–21] [1] MT but he breathes lies, deceit. 14:27 ªProv 13:14
14:29 ªProv 16:32; 19:11; Eccl 7:9; Jas 1:19 14:30 ªPs 112:10 ᵇProv 12:4; Hab 3:16 [1] Heb. is the life of the flesh. [2] Heb.
rottenness of bones. 14:31 ªProv 17:5; Matt 25:40; 1 John 3:17 ᵇ[Job 31:15; Prov 22:2] 14:32 [1] MT in his death.
14:33 [1] Tg. folly is in the heart of fools; MT it [wisdom] is known. 14:34 ªProv 11:11 14:35 ªMatt 24:45–47
15:1 ªProv 25:15 ᵇ1 Sam 25:10 [1] Heb. raises anger.

^abut the mouth of the fool spouts out folly.

3 The eyes of ^athe LORD are in every place,
keeping watch on those who are evil and those who are good.

4 Speech that heals is like a life-giving tree,
but a perverse speech breaks the spirit.

5 A fool rejects his ^afather's discipline,
^bbut whoever heeds reproof shows good sense.[1]

6 In the house of the righteous is abundant wealth,
but the income of the wicked will be ruined.

7 The lips of the wise spread[1] knowledge,
but not so the heart of fools.

8 The LORD abhors ^athe sacrifice of the wicked,
but the prayer of the upright pleases him.

9 The LORD abhors the way of the wicked,
but he will love those who ^apursue righteousness.

10 ^aSevere discipline is for ^bthe one who abandons the way;
the one who hates reproof will die.

11 ^aDeath and Destruction[1] are before ^bthe LORD—
how much more the hearts of humans!

12 ^aThe scorner will not love one who corrects him;
he will not go to[1] the wise.

13 A joyful ^aheart makes the face cheerful,
but ^bby a painful heart the spirit is broken.

14 The discerning mind seeks knowledge,
but the mouth of fools feeds on folly.

15 All the days of the afflicted are bad,[1]
^abut one with a cheerful heart has a continual feast.

16 ^aBetter is little with the fear of the LORD
than great wealth and turmoil with it.

17 ^aBetter a meal of vegetables where there is love
than a fattened ox where there is hatred.

18 A quick-tempered person stirs up dissension,
but one who is slow to ^aanger calms a quarrel.

19 The way of ^athe sluggard is like a hedge of thorns,
but the path of the upright is like a highway.

20 A wise child brings joy to his ^afather,
but a foolish person despises his mother.

21 ^aFolly is a joy to one who lacks sense,[1]
^bbut one who has understanding follows an upright course.

22 Plans fail when there is no counsel,
but ^awith abundant advisers they are established.

23 A person ^ahas joy in giving an appropriate answer,
and a word at the right time—how good it is!

24 The path of life is upward for ^athe wise person,
to keep him from going downward to Sheol.

25 The LORD tears down ^athe house of ^bthe proud,
but he maintains the boundaries of the widow.

26 The LORD abhors ^athe plans of the wicked,
^bbut pleasant words are pure.[1]

27 ^aThe one who is greedy for gain[1] troubles his household,
but whoever hates bribes will live.

28 The heart of the righteous ^aconsiders how to answer,[1]

15:2 ^aProv 12:23   15:3 ^a2 Chr 16:9; Job 34:21; Prov 5:21; Jer 16:17; 32:19; Zech 4:10; Heb 4:13   15:5 ^aProv 10:1   ^bProv 13:18
[1]Heb. *is prudent.*   15:7 [1]One wss *guard, keep*; LXX *bind.*   15:8 ^aProv 21:27; Eccl 5:1; Isa 1:11; Jer 6:20; Mic 6:7   15:9 ^aProv
21:21   15:10 ^a1 Kgs 22:8   ^bProv 5:12   15:11 ^aJob 26:6; Ps 139:8   ^b1 Sam 16:7; 2 Chr 6:30; Ps 44:21; Acts 1:24   [1]Heb. *Sheol
and Abaddon*; the remote underworld and all the mighty powers that reside there.   15:12 ^aProv 13:1; Amos 5:10; 2 Tim
4:3   [1]LXX *with the wise.*   15:13 ^aProv 12:25   ^bProv 17:22   15:15 ^aProv 17:22   [1]Or *evil, catastrophic.*   15:16 ^aPs 37:16;
Prov 16:8; Eccl 4:6; 1 Tim 6:6   15:17 ^aProv 17:1   15:18 ^aProv 26:21   15:19 ^aProv 22:5   15:20 ^aProv 10:1   15:21 ^aProv
10:23   ^bEph 5:15   [1]Heb. *lacking of mind.*   15:22 ^aProv 11:14   15:23 ^aProv 25:11; Isa 50:4   15:24 ^aPhil 3:20; [Col 3:1–2]
15:25 ^aProv 12:7; Isa 2:11   ^bPs 68:5–6   15:26 ^aProv 6:16, 18   ^bPs 37:30   [1]LXX *the sayings of the pure are held in
honor*; Vg. *pure speech will be confirmed by him as very beautiful.*   15:27 ^aIsa 5:8; [Jer 17:11]   [1]Heb. *the one
who gains*; i.e., a person who is always making the big deal, getting the larger cut, or in a hurry
to get rich.   15:28 ^a1 Pet 3:15   [1]LXX *the hearts of the righteous meditate faithfulness.*

but the mouth of the wicked pours
   out evil things.
29 The LORD is far from [a]the wicked,
   but [b]he hears the prayer of the
      righteous.
30 A bright look[1,2] brings joy to the
      heart,
   and good news gives health to the
      body.
31 The person who hears the reproof
      that leads to life
   is at home among the wise.
32 The one who refuses correction
      despises himself,
   but whoever listens to reproof
      acquires understanding.
33 The fear of [a]the LORD provides wise
      instruction,
   and [b]before honor comes humility.[1]

16 The [a]intentions of the heart belong
      to a man,
   [b]but the answer of the tongue comes
      from the LORD.
2 All a person's ways seem right in his
      own [a]opinion,
   but the LORD evaluates the motives.[1]
3 [a]Commit[1] your works to the LORD,
   and your plans will be established.
4 The [a]LORD has worked everything for
      his own ends—
   even the wicked for the day of
      disaster.
5 The LORD abhors [a]every arrogant
      person;[1]
   rest assured that they will not go
      unpunished.[2]
6 Through loyal love and truth
      [a]iniquity is appeased;
   through fearing the LORD one avoids
      evil.
7 When a person's ways are pleasing to
      the LORD,
   he even reconciles his enemies to
      himself.[1]

8 [a]Better to have a little with
      righteousness
   than to have abundant income
      without justice.
9 A person [a]plans his course,
   [b]but the LORD directs his steps.
10 The divine verdict is in the words of
      the king;
   his pronouncements[1] must not
      act treacherously against
      justice.
11 [a]Honest scales and balances are from
      the LORD;
   all the weights in the bag are his
      handiwork.
12 Doing wickedness is [a]an abomination
      to kings,
   because a throne is established in
      righteousness.
13 The delight of a king[1] is [a]righteous
      counsel,
   and he will love the one who speaks
      uprightly.
14 A king's wrath is like a messenger of
      death,
   but a wise person [a]appeases it.
15 In the light of the king's face[1] there is
      life,
   and his favor is like the [a]clouds of the
      spring rain.
16 [a]How much better it is to acquire
      wisdom than gold;
   to acquire understanding is more
      desirable than silver.
17 The highway of the upright is to turn
      away from evil;
   the one who guards his way
      safeguards his life.[1]
18 Pride goes before destruction
   and a haughty spirit before a fall.
19 It is better to be lowly in spirit with
      the afflicted
   than to share the spoils[1] with the
      proud.

15:29 [a] Ps 10:1; 34:16   [b] Ps 145:18; [Jas 5:16]   **15:30** [1] LXX *the eye that sees beautiful things.*   [2] Heb. *light of the eyes*; perhaps the gleam in the eyes of the one who tells good news.   **15:33** [a] Prov 1:7   [b] Prov 18:12   [1] Heb. *[is] humility.*   **16:1** [a] Jer 10:23   [b] Matt 10:19   **16:2** [a] Prov 21:2   [1] Heb. *spirits.*   **16:3** [a] Ps 37:5; Prov 3:6; [1 Pet 5:7]   [1] LXX, Tg. *reveal.*   **16:4** [a] Isa 43:7; Rom 11:36   **16:5** [a] Prov 6:17; 8:13   [1] Heb. *everyone of proud of heart*; the attitude of someone's spirit.   [2] LXX adds *The beginning of a good way is to do justly, // and it is more acceptable with God than to do sacrifices; // he who seeks the LORD will find knowledge with righteousness, // and they who rightly seek him will find peace.*   **16:6** [a] Dan 4:27; Luke 11:41   **16:7** [1] Heb. *even his enemies he makes to be at peace with him.*   **16:8** [a] Ps 37:16; Prov 15:16   **16:9** [a] Prov 19:21   [b] Ps 37:23; Prov 20:24; Jer 10:23   **16:10** [1] Heb. *his mouth.*   **16:11** [a] Lev 19:36   **16:12** [a] Prov 25:5   **16:13** [a] Prov 14:35   [1] MT *kings.*   **16:14** [a] Prov 25:15   **16:15** [a] Zech 10:1   [1] Heb. *the light of the face of the king*; the king's brightened face, his delight in what is taking place.   **16:16** [a] Prov 8:10–11, 19   **16:17** [1] LXX adds three lines after v. 17a and one after v. 17b: *The paths of life turn aside from evils, and the ways of righteousness are length of life; he who receives instruction will be prosperous, and he who regards reproofs will be made wise; he who guards his ways preserves his soul, and he who loves his life will spare his mouth.*   **16:19** [1] Heb. *than to divide plunder.*

20 The one who deals wisely in a matter
    will find success,
  and blessed[1] is the one who [a]trusts in
    the LORD.
21 The one who is wise in heart is called
    discerning,
  and kind speech increases
    persuasiveness.
22 Insight is like a life-giving fountain[1]
    to the one who possesses it,
  but folly leads to the discipline of
    fools.
23 A wise person's heart makes his
    speech wise,
  and it adds persuasiveness to his
    words.
24 Pleasant words are like a honeycomb,
  sweet to the soul and healing to the
    bones.
25 There is a way that seems right to a
    person,
  but its end is the way that leads to
    [a]death.
26 A laborer's appetite has labored for
    [a]him,
  for his hunger has pressed him to
    work.[1]
27 A wicked scoundrel[1] digs up evil,
  and his slander is like a scorching
    [a]fire.
28 A perverse person [a]spreads
    dissension,
  and a gossip separates the closest
    friends.
29 A violent person entices his neighbor,
  and then leads him down a path that
    is terrible.[1]
30 The one who winks his eyes devises
    perverse things,
  and one who compresses his lips has
    accomplished evil.
31 Gray hair is like a crown of glory;
  it is attained in [a]the path of
    righteousness.
32 [a]Better to be slow to anger than to be
    a mighty warrior,
  and one who controls his temper[1] is
    better than one who captures a city.

33 The dice are thrown into the lap,
  but their every decision is from the
    LORD.

17 Better is [a]a dry crust of bread[1] where
    there is quietness
  than a house full of feasting with
    strife.
2 A [a]servant who acts wisely will rule
    over an heir who behaves shamefully
  and will share the inheritance along
    with the relatives.
3 The crucible is for refining silver and
    the furnace is for gold;
  likewise the LORD tests hearts.
4 One who acts wickedly pays
    attention to evil counsel;
  a liar listens[1] to a malicious tongue.
5 The one who mocks [a]the poor has
    insulted his Creator;
  whoever rejoices over disaster will
    not go [b]unpunished.
6 Grandchildren are like a crown to the
    elderly,
  and the glory[1] of [a]children is their
    parents.[2]
7 Excessive speech is not becoming for
    a fool;
  how much less are lies for a ruler!
8 A bribe works like a charm for the
    one who offers it;
  in whatever he does he succeeds.
9 [a]The one who forgives an offense
    seeks love,
  but whoever repeats a matter
    separates close friends.
10 A [a]rebuke makes a greater
    impression on a discerning person
  than a hundred blows on a fool.
11 An evil person seeks only rebellion,[1]
  and so a cruel messenger will be sent
    against him.
12 It is better for [a]a person to meet a
    mother bear being robbed of her
    cubs
  than to encounter a fool in his folly.
13 As for the one who [a]repays evil for
    good,
  evil will not leave his house.

16:20 [a]Ps 34:8; Jer 17:7 [1]Trad. *happy*; the heavenly bliss that comes from knowing one is right with God and following God's precepts. 16:22 [1]Heb. *fountain of life*. 16:25 [a]Prov 14:12 16:26 [a][Eccl 6:7; John 6:35] [1]LXX *he drives away ruin*. 16:27 [a][Jas 3:6] [1]Heb. *a man of belial*. 16:28 [a]Prov 17:9 16:29 [1]Heb. *not good*; a deliberate understatement for the sake of emphasis. 16:31 [a]Prov 20:29 16:32 [a]Prov 14:29; 19:11 [1]Heb. *who rules his spirit*. 17:1 [a]Prov 15:17 [1]I.e., a simple, humble meal. 17:2 [a]Prov 10:5 17:4 [1]Heb. *to feed*. 17:5 [a]Prov 14:31 [b]Job 31:29; Prov 24:17; Obad 12; 1 Cor 13:6 17:6 [a][Ps 127:3; 128:3] [1]Heb. *beauty, glory*; i.e., the glorying that children do. [2]LXX adds *To the faithful belongs the whole world of wealth, but to the unfaithful not an obulus*. 17:9 [a][Prov 10:12; 1 Cor 13:5–7; Jas 5:20] 17:10 [a]Prov 10:17; [Mic 7:9] 17:11 [1]LXX *contention*. 17:12 [a]2 Sam 17:8; Hos 13:8 17:13 [a]Ps 109:4–5; Jer 18:20; Rom 12:17; 1 Thess 5:15; [1 Pet 3:9]

14 Starting a quarrel is like letting out
    water;[1,2]
  [a]abandon strife before it breaks out!
15 The one who acquits [a]the guilty
    and the one who condemns the
      innocent—
  both of them are an abomination to
    the LORD.
16 What's the point of a fool having
    money in hand
  to buy wisdom when his head is
    empty?
17 A friend loves [a]at all times,
  and a relative[1] is born to help in
    adversity.
18 The one who [a]lacks sense strikes
    hands in pledge
  and puts up financial security for his
    neighbor.
19 The one who loves a quarrel loves
    transgression;
  whoever builds his gate high seeks
    destruction.
20 The one who [a]has a perverse heart
    does not find good,
  and the one who is deceitful in
    speech falls into trouble.
21 Whoever brings a fool into the world
    does so to his grief,
  and the father of a fool has no joy.
22 A [a]cheerful heart brings good
    healing,
  but a crushed spirit dries up the
    bones.
23 A wicked person receives a bribe
    secretly
  to pervert the ways of justice.
24 [a]Wisdom is directly in front of the
    discerning person,
  but the eyes of a fool run to the ends
    of the earth.
25 A [a]foolish child is a grief to his father
  and bitterness to the mother who
    bore him.
26 It is terrible to punish a righteous
    person,
  and to flog honorable men is wrong.[1]

27 The truly wise person restrains his
    words,
  and [a]the one who stays calm is
    discerning.
28 [a]Even a fool who remains silent is
    considered wise,
  and the one who holds his tongue is
    deemed discerning.

18 One who has isolated himself seeks
    his own desires;[1]
  he rejects all sound judgment.
2 A fool takes no pleasure in
    understanding
  but only in disclosing what is on his
    mind.
3 When a wicked person arrives,
    contempt shows up with him,
  and with shame comes a reproach.
4 The words of a person's mouth[1] are
    like deep waters,
  and [a]the fountain of wisdom is like a
    flowing brook.
5 It is terrible[1] to show partiality to the
    wicked
  by depriving a righteous man of
    [a]justice.
6 The lips of a fool enter into strife,
  and his mouth invites a flogging.
7 The mouth of [a]a fool is his ruin,
  and his lips are a snare for his [b]life.
8 The words of a gossip are like choice
    morsels,
  and [a]they have gone down into the
    person's innermost being.[1]
9 The one who is slack in his work
  is a brother to one who destroys.
10 The name of the LORD is like a strong
    [a]tower;
  the righteous person runs to it and is
    set safely on high.[1]
11 The wealth of a rich person is like a
    strong city,
  and it is like a high wall in his
    imagination.
12 [a]Before destruction the heart of a
    person is proud,
  but humility comes before honor.

17:14 [a][Prov 20:3; 1 Thess 4:11] [1]LXX *Giving authority to words is the beginning of strife.* [2]Heb. *Someone who releases water is the beginning of a quarrel.* 17:15 [a]Exod 23:7; Prov 24:24; Isa 5:23 17:17 [a]Ruth 1:16; Prov 18:24 [1]Heb. *a brother.* 17:18 [a]Prov 6:1 17:20 [a]Jas 3:8 17:22 [a]Prov 12:25; 15:13, 15 17:24 [a]Eccl 2:14 17:25 [a]Prov 10:1; 15:20; 19:13 17:26 [1]Or *contrary to what is right*; Heb. [is] *against uprightness.* 17:27 [a]Prov 10:19; Jas 1:19 17:28 [a]Job 13:5 18:1 [1]LXX *seeks his own occasion.* 18:4 [a]Prov 10:11 [1]LXX *in a person's heart.* 18:5 [a]Lev 19:15; Deut 1:17; 16:19; Ps 82:2; Prov 17:15 [1]Heb. *not good*; a deliberate understatement for the sake of emphasis. 18:7 [a]Ps 64:8; 140:9; Prov 10:14 [b]Eccl 10:12 18:8 [a]Prov 12:18 [1]Heb. *they have gone down* [into] *the dark/inner chambers of the belly.* 18:10 [a]2 Sam 22:2–3, 33; Ps 18:2; 61:3; 91:2; 144:2 [1]Heb. *is high, inaccessible*; stresses the effect of the trust—security, being out of danger. 18:12 [a]Prov 15:33; 16:18

13 The one who gives an answer before
   he listens—
that is his folly and his shame.
14 A person's spirit sustains him
   through sickness—
but who can bear a crushed spirit?
15 The discerning person acquires
   knowledge,
and the wise person seeks
   knowledge.
16 A person's gift [a]makes room for him
and leads him before important
   people.
17 The first to state his case seems
   right,
until his opponent begins to
   cross-examine him.
18 A toss of a [a]coin ends disputes
and settles the issue[1] between strong
   opponents.
19 A relative offended is harder to reach
   than[1] a strong city,
and disputes are like the barred
   gates[2] of a fortified citadel.
20 From the fruit of [a]a person's mouth
   his stomach will be satisfied;
with the product of his lips he will be
   satisfied.
21 [a]Death and life are in the power of
   the tongue,
and those who love its use will eat its
   fruit.
22 The one who has found a good[1] wife
   has found what goodness is[2]
and obtained a delightful gift from
   [a]the LORD.[3]
23 A poor person makes supplications,
but a rich man answers [a]harshly.
24 There are companions who harm one
   another,
   [a]but there is a friend[1] who sticks
   closer than a brother.

19 Better [a]is a poor person who walks
   in his integrity
than one who is perverse in his
   speech and is a fool.[1]

2 It is dangerous[1] to have zeal without
   knowledge,
and the one who acts hastily makes
   poor choices.
3 A person's folly subverts his way,
and his heart rages against the LORD.
4 [a]Wealth adds many friends,
but a poor person is separated from
   his friend.
5 A [a]false witness will not go
   unpunished,
and the one who spouts out lies will
   not escape punishment.
6 Many people entreat the favor of a
   generous person,[1]
and everyone is the friend of the
   person who gives gifts.
7 All the relatives of [a]a poor person
   hate him;
how much more do his friends [b]avoid
   him—
one who chases words, which are
   nothing.[1]
8 The one who acquires understanding
   loves himself;
the one who preserves
   understanding [a]will prosper.
9 A false witness will not go
   unpunished,
and the one who spouts out lies will
   perish.
10 Luxury is not appropriate [a]for a fool;
how much less for a servant to rule
   over princes!
11 [a]A person's wisdom[1] has made him
   slow to anger,
   [b]and it is his glory to overlook an
   offense.
12 A king's wrath is like [a]the roar of a
   lion,
but his favor is [b]like dew on
   the grass.
13 A foolish child[1] is the ruin of his
   [a]father,
   [b]and a contentious wife is like a
   constant dripping.[2]

18:16 [a]Gen 32:20–21; 1 Sam 25:27; Prov 17:8; 21:14   18:18 [a][Prov 16:33]   [1]Heb. *makes a separation, decides.*   18:19 [1]LXX
A brother helped is like a stronghold, but disputes are like bars of a citadel.   [2]Heb. *bars.*   18:20 [a]Prov 12:14; 14:14
18:21 [a]Prov 12:13; 13:3; Matt 12:37   18:22 [a]Gen 2:18; [Prov 12:4; 19:14]   [1]MT omits *good.*   [2]LXX *grace/favor.*   [3]LXX adds
Whoever puts away a good wife puts away good, and whoever keeps an adulteress is foolish and ungodly.   18:23 [a]Jas
2:3, 6   18:24 [a]Prov 17:17; [John 15:14–15]   [1]*From the root meaning "to love."*   19:1 [a]Prov 28:6   [1]Syr., Tg. *rich.*   19:2 [1]Heb.
not good; a deliberate understatement for the sake of emphasis.   19:4 [a]Prov 14:20   19:5 [a]Exod 23:1; Deut 19:16–19;
Prov 6:19; 21:28   19:6 [1]Heb. *the face of a generous man.*   19:7 [a]Prov 14:20   [b]Ps 38:11   [1]This section features 374 two-line
proverbs and this one three-line proverb. For an explanation of the challenges of this line, see *NET Bible, Full Notes
Edition.*   19:8 [a]Prov 16:20   19:10 [a]Prov 30:21–22   19:11 [a]Jas 1:19   [b]Prov 16:32; [Matt 5:44]; Eph 4:32; Col 3:13
[1]Or *prudence.*   19:12 [a]Prov 16:14   [b]Gen 27:28; Deut 33:28; Ps 133:3; Hos 14:5; Mic 5:7   19:13 [a]Prov 10:1
[b]Prov 21:9, 19   [1]Heb. *a foolish son.*   [2]LXX *vows paid out of hire of a harlot are not pure.*

14 A ªhouse ᵇand wealth are inherited
 from parents,
 but a prudent wife is from the LORD.
15 ªLaziness brings on a deep sleep,
 and the idle person will go hungry.
16 The one who obeys commandments
 guards¹ his life;
 ªthe one who despises his ways will
 die.²
17 The one who is gracious to ªthe poor
 lends to the LORD,
 and the LORD will repay him for his
 good deed.
18 ªDiscipline your child, for there is
 hope,
 but do not set your heart on causing
 his death.¹
19 A person with great anger bears the
 penalty,
 but if you deliver him from it once,
 you will have to do it again.
20 Listen to advice and receive
 ªdiscipline,
 that you may become wise by the
 end of your life.¹
21 There are many plans in a person's
 mind,
 but it is ªthe counsel of the LORD
 that will stand.
22 What is desirable for a person is to
 show loyal love,
 and a poor person is better than a liar.
23 Fearing ªthe LORD leads to life,
 and one who does so will live
 satisfied; he will not be afflicted by
 calamity.
24 The ªsluggard has plunged his hand
 into the dish,
 and he will not even bring it back to
 his mouth!
25 Flog a scorner, and as a result the
 simpleton ªwill learn prudence;
 ᵇcorrect a discerning person, and
 as a result he will understand
 knowledge.
26 The one who robs his ªfather and
 chases away his mother

is a son¹ who brings shame and
 disgrace.
27 If you stop listening to instruction,
 my child,
 you will stray from the words of
 knowledge.
28 A crooked witness scorns justice,
 and ªthe mouth of the wicked
 devours iniquity.
29 Penalties¹ have been prepared for
 scorners,
 ªand floggings for the backs of fools.

20 Wine ªis a mocker and strong drink
 is a brawler;
 whoever goes astray by them is not
 wise.
2 The king's terrifying anger is like the
 roar of a lion;
 whoever provokes him sins against
 himself.
3 ªIt is an honor for a person to cease
 from strife,
 but every fool quarrels.
4 The sluggard will not plow during
 ªthe planting season,
 so at harvest time ᵇhe asks for grain
 but has nothing.
5 Counsel in a person's heart is like
 deep water,
 but an understanding person draws
 it out.
6 Many people profess their loyalty,
 but a faithful person—who can find?
7 ªThe righteous person behaves in
 integrity;
 blessed are ᵇhis children after him.
8 A king sitting on the throne to
 judge
 separates out all evil with his eyes.
9 ªWho can say, "I have kept my heart¹
 clean;
 I am pure from my sin"?
10 Diverse weights and ªdiverse
 measures—
 the LORD abhors both of them.
11 Even a young man is ªknown by his
 actions,

19:14 ª 2 Cor 12:14   ᵇ Prov 18:22   19:15 ª Prov 6:9   19:16 ª Prov 13:13; 16:17; Luke 10:28; 11:28   ¹ There is a wordplay present: *The one who obeys* (Heb. *shomer*) *commandments guards* (Heb. *shomer*) *his life.*   ² Ket. *will be put to death.*   19:17 ª Deut 15:7–8; Job 23:12–13; Prov 28:27; Eccl 11:1; Matt 10:42; 25:40; [2 Cor 9:6–8]; Heb 6:10   19:18 ª Prov 13:24   ¹ LXX *do not lift up your soul to excess.*   19:20 ª Ps 37:37   ¹ Heb. *become wise in your latter end.*   19:21 ª Ps 33:10–11; Prov 16:9; Isa 46:10; Heb 6:17   19:23 ª Prov 14:27; [1 Tim 4:8]   19:24 ª Prov 15:19   19:25 ª Deut 13:11   ᵇ Prov 9:8   19:26 ª Prov 17:2   ¹ "Child" does not fit the context of this verse. In the ancient world a "son" was more likely than a daughter to behave as stated.   19:28 ª Job 15:16   19:29 ª Prov 26:3   ¹ LXX *scourges.*   20:1 ª Gen 9:21; Prov 23:29–35; Isa 28:7; Hos 4:11   20:3 ª Prov 17:14   20:4 ª Prov 10:4   ᵇ Prov 19:15   20:7 ª 2 Cor 1:12   ᵇ Ps 37:26   20:9 ª [1 Kgs 8:46; 2 Chr 6:36]; Job 9:30–31; 14:4; [Ps 51:5; Eccl 7:20; Rom 3:9; 1 John 1:8]   ¹ Both motives and thoughts.   20:10 ª Deut 25:13   20:11 ª Matt 7:16

whether his activity is pure and
  whether it is right.
12 The ear that hears and [a]the eye that
  sees—
  the LORD has made them both.
13 [a]Do not love sleep, lest you become
  impoverished;
  open your eyes so that you might be
  satisfied with food.[1]
14 "It's worthless! It's worthless!"[1] says
  the buyer,
  but when he goes on his way, he
  boasts.
15 There is gold and an abundance of
  rubies,
  but words of knowledge are like a
  precious jewel.
16 [a]Take a man's garment when he has
  given security for a stranger,
  and hold him in pledge on behalf of
  strangers.
17 [a]Bread gained by deceit[1] tastes sweet
  to a person,
  but afterward his mouth will be filled
  with gravel.
18 [a]Plans are established [b]by counsel,
  so make war with guidance.
19 The one who goes about gossiping
  reveals secrets;
  [a]therefore do not associate with
  someone [b]who is always opening
  his mouth.
20 The one [a]who curses [b]his father and
  his mother,
  his lamp[1] will be extinguished in the
  blackest[2] darkness.
21 An [a]inheritance gained easily[1] in the
  beginning
  [b]will not be blessed in the end.
22 [a]Do not say, "I will pay back evil!"
  [b]Wait for the LORD, so that he may
  vindicate you.
23 The LORD abhors differing weights,
  and dishonest scales are wicked.[1]

24 The steps of a person[1] are ordained
  by the LORD—
  so how can anyone understand his
  own way?
25 It is a snare for a person to rashly cry,
  "Holy!"
  and only afterward to consider what
  he has vowed.
26 A wise king [a]separates out[1] the
  wicked;
  he turns the threshing wheel over
  them.
27 The human spirit is like [a]the lamp[1] of
  the LORD,
  searching all his innermost parts.
28 Loyal [a]love and truth preserve a king,
  and his throne is upheld by loyal love.
29 The glory of young men is [a]their
  strength,
  and the splendor of old men is gray
  hair.
30 Beatings and wounds cleanse away[1]
  evil,
  and floggings cleanse the innermost
  being.

21 The king's heart is in the hand of
  the LORD like channels of water;
  he turns it wherever he wants.
2 [a]All a person's ways seem right in his
  own opinion,
  [b]but the LORD evaluates his thoughts.
3 To do righteousness and justice
  is more acceptable [a]to the LORD than
  sacrifice.
4 Haughty eyes [a]and a proud heart—
  what the wicked cultivate[1] is sin.
5 The plans of [a]the diligent lead only
  to plenty,
  but everyone who is hasty comes
  only to poverty.[1]
6 [a]Making a fortune by a lying tongue
  is like a vapor driven back and
  forth;
  they seek death.[1]

20:12 [a]Exod 4:11; Ps 94:9   20:13 [a]Rom 12:11 [1]Heb. *bread*.   20:14 [1]Heb. [It is] *bad*, [it is] *bad*.   20:16 [a]Prov 22:26
20:17 [a]Prov 9:17 [1]Heb. *bread of deceit*; food gained through dishonest means.   20:18 [a]Prov 24:6 [b]Luke 14:31
20:19 [a]Prov 11:13 [b]Rom 16:18   20:20 [a]Exod 21:17; Lev 20:9; Prov 30:11; Matt 15:4 [b]Job 18:5–6; Prov 24:20 [1]I.e., his life.
[2]LXX, Syr., Latin *the pupil of the eyes*.   20:21 [a]Prov 28:20 [b]Hab 2:6 [1]Ket. *gotten by greed*.   20:22 [a][Deut 32:35]; Prov
17:13; 24:29; [Rom 12:17–19]; 1 Thess 5:15; [1 Pet 3:9] [b]2 Sam 16:12   20:23 [1]Heb. *not good*; a deliberate understatement
for the sake of emphasis.   20:24 [1]Heb. *the steps of a man*; but the line seems to have a wider, more general application.
20:26 [a]Ps 101:8 [1]Heb. *winnows*; the king will separate good people from bad people like wheat is separated from
chaff.   20:27 [a]1 Cor 2:11 [1]Functioning as a conscience, enabling people to know and please God, and directing them in
choices that will be life-giving.   20:28 [a]Ps 101:1; Prov 21:21   20:29 [a]Prov 16:31   20:30 [1]LXX *blows and contusions fall on*
evil men, and stripes penetrate their inner beings; Latin *the bruise of a wound cleanses away evil things*.   21:2 [a]Prov 16:2
[b]Prov 24:12; Luke 16:15   21:3 [1]1 Sam 15:22; Prov 15:8; Isa 1:11, 16, 17; Hos 6:6; [Mic 6:7–8]   21:4 [a]Prov 6:17
[1]MT *the tillage of the wicked*; Sev. wss *the lamp of the wicked*.   21:5 [a]Prov 10:4 [1]Heb. *lack, need,*
thing needed.   21:6 [a]2 Pet 2:3 [1]Heb. *seekers of death*.

7 The violence done by the wicked will
    drag them away
  because they have refused to do what
    is right.
8 The way of the guilty person is
    devious,
  but as for the pure, his way is
    upright.
9 It is better to live on [a]a corner of the
    housetop
  than to share a house with a
    quarrelsome wife.[1]
10 The appetite of [a]the wicked has
    desired evil;
  his neighbor is shown no favor in his
    eyes.
11 When a scorner is punished, the
    naive becomes wise;
  when a wise [a]person is instructed, he
    gains knowledge.
12 The Righteous One[1] considers[2] the
    house of the wicked;
  he overthrows the wicked to their
    ruin.
13 The one [a]who shuts his ears to the
    cry of the poor,
  he too will cry out and will not be
    answered.
14 A gift given in secret subdues anger,
  and a bribe given secretly subdues
    strong wrath.[1]
15 Doing justice brings joy to the
    righteous
  and terror to those who do evil.
16 The one who wanders from the way
    of wisdom
  will end up in the company of the
    [a]departed.
17 The one who loves pleasure will be a
    poor person;[1]
  whoever loves wine and anointing oil
    will not be rich.
18 The wicked become a ransom for the
    righteous,
  and the treacherous are taken in the
    place of the upright.
19 It is better to live in the wilderness

than with a quarrelsome and easily
    provoked woman.
20 There is desirable treasure and olive
    oil in [a]the dwelling of the wise,
  but a foolish person devours all he has.
21 [a]The one who pursues righteousness
    and love
  finds life, bounty, and honor.
22 A wise [a]man went up against the city
    of the mighty
  and brought down the stronghold in
    which they trust.
23 The one [a]who guards his mouth and
    his tongue
  keeps his life from troubles.
24 A proud and arrogant person, whose
    name is "Scoffer,"
  acts[1] with overbearing pride.
25 What the sluggard [a]desires will kill
    him,
  for his hands have refused to work.
26 All day long he has craved greedily,
  but the righteous person [a]gives and
    does not hold back.
27 The wicked person's sacrifice is an
    abomination;
  how much more when [a]he brings it
    with evil intent![1]
28 A lying witness will perish,
  but the one who reports accurately
    speaks forever.
29 A wicked person has put on a bold
    face,
  but as for the upright, he establishes[1]
    his ways.
30 There is no wisdom and [a]there is no
    understanding,
  and there is no counsel against the
    LORD.
31 A horse is prepared for the day of
    battle,
  but the [a]victory is from the LORD.[1]

22 A [a]good name is to be chosen
    rather than great wealth,
  good favor more than silver or gold.
2 The [a]rich and the poor are met
    together;

21:9 [a]Prov 19:13 [1]Heb. *a wife of contentions*.   21:10 [a]Jas 4:5   21:11 [a]Prov 19:25   21:12 [1]Perhaps a human being, although
it would have to refer to a judge or ruler with the right to destroy the wicked. Many interpret this as a reference to God.
[2]Heb. *to consider, give attention to, ponder*; the careful scrutiny given to the household of the wicked before judgment is
poured out on them.   21:13 [a][Matt 7:2; 18:30–34]; Jas 2:13; 1 John 3:17   21:14 [1]LXX *he who withholds a gift stirs up violent
wrath*.   21:16 [a]Ps 49:14   21:17 [1]Heb. *a man of poverty*.   21:20 [a]Ps 112:3; Prov 8:21   21:21 [a]Prov 15:9; Matt 5:6; [Rom 2:7];
1 Cor 15:58   21:22 [a]2 Sam 5:6–9; Prov 24:5; Eccl 7:19; 9:15–16   21:23 [a]Prov 12:13; 13:3; 18:21; [Jas 3:2]   21:24 [1]Heb. *does*.
21:25 [a]Prov 13:4   21:26 [a][Prov 22:9; Eph 4:28]   21:27 [a]Prov 15:8; Isa 66:3; Jer 6:20; Amos 5:22   [1]Heb. *plan, device,
wickedness*.   21:29 [1]LXX *he understands/he discerns*.   21:30 [a]Isa 8:9–10; [Jer 9:23–24]; Acts 5:39; 1 Cor 3:19–20
21:31 [a]Ps 3:8; Jer 3:23; [1 Cor 15:57]   [1]Heb. *of the LORD*.   22:1 [a][Prov 10:7]; Eccl 7:1   22:2 [a]Prov 29:13

the [b]LORD is the Creator of them
  both.
3 A shrewd person saw danger[1] and hid
  himself,
but the naive passed on by and [a]paid
  for it.
4 The reward for humility and fearing
  the LORD
is riches and honor and life.
5 Thorns and snares are in the path of
  the perverse,
but the one who guards himself
  keeps far from them.
6 [a]Train a child in the way that he
  should go,
and when he is old he will not turn
  from it.
7 The [a]rich rule over the poor,
and the borrower is servant[1] to the
  lender.
8 The one who sows iniquity will reap
  [a]trouble,
and the rod of his fury[1] will end.
9 [a]A generous person will be [b]blessed,
for he has given some of his food to
  the poor.
10 [a]Drive out the scorner and
  contention will leave;
strife and insults will cease.[1]
11 The one who loves a pure [a]heart
and whose speech is gracious—the
  king will be his friend.
12 The eyes of the LORD watched over a
  cause
and subverted the words of the
  treacherous person.
13 The sluggard has said, "[a]There is a
  lion outside!
I will be killed in the middle of the
  streets!"[1]
14 The mouth of an adulteress is like a
  deep pit;
[a]the one against whom [b]the LORD is
  angry will fall into it.[1]
15 Folly is bound up in [a]the heart of a
  child,
but the rod of discipline will drive it
  far from him.

16 The one who oppresses the poor to
  increase his own gain
and the one who gives to the
  rich—both end up only in poverty.

The Sayings of the Wise

17 Incline your ear and listen to the
  words of the wise,
and apply your mind to my
  instruction.
18 For it is pleasing if you keep these
  sayings within you,
and they are ready on your lips.
19 So that your confidence may be in
  the LORD,
I hereby make them known to you
  today—even you.
20 Have I not written thirty sayings for
  you,
sayings of counsel and knowledge,
21 to show you true and reliable words,
so [a]that you may give accurate
  answers to those who sent you?
22 Do not exploit a poor person because
  he is [a]poor
and do not crush the needy in court,[1]
23 [a]for the LORD will plead their case
and will rob the life of those who are
  robbing them.
24 Do not make friends with an angry
  person,
and do not associate with a [a]wrathful
  person,
25 lest you learn his ways
and entangle yourself in a snare.
26 [a]Do not be one who strikes hands in
  pledge
or who puts up security for debts.
27 If you do not have enough to pay,
your bed[1] will be taken right out from
  under you!
28 [a]Do not move an ancient boundary
  stone
that was put in place by your
  ancestors.
29 You have seen a person skilled in his
  work—
he will take his position before kings;

22:2 [b] Job 31:15; [Prov 14:31]   22:3 [a] Prov 27:12; Isa 26:20   [1] Heb. evil.   22:6 [a] Eph 6:4; 2 Tim 3:15   22:7 [a] Prov 18:23; Jas 2:6
[1] Or slave; perhaps referring to the practice of people selling themselves into slavery to pay off debts.   22:8 [a] Job 4:8
[1] LXX the punishment of his deeds; LXX adds A man who is cheerful and a giver God blesses.   22:9 [a] 2 Cor 9:6   [b] [Prov
19:17]   22:10 [a] Ps 101:5   [1] LXX adds when he sits in council he insults everyone.   22:11 [a] Ps 101:6   22:13 [a] Prov 26:13
[1] LXX murderers in the street.   22:14 [a] Prov 2:16; 5:3; 7:5   [b] Eccl 7:26   [1] Heb. will fall there.   22:15 [a] Prov 13:24; 23:13-14
22:21 [a] Luke 1:3-4   22:22 [a] Exod 23:6; Job 31:16-21; Zech 7:10   [1] Heb. in the gate; the place of business and for settling
legal disputes.   22:23 [a] 1 Sam 24:12; Ps 12:5; 140:12   22:24 [a] Prov 29:22   22:26 [a] Prov 11:15   22:27 [1] The individual's last
possession (like the English expression "the shirt off his back").   22:28 [a] Deut 19:14; 27:17; Job 24:2; Prov 23:10

he will not take his position before
obscure people.

23 When you sit down to eat with a
ruler,
consider carefully what is before you,
² and put a knife to your throat
if you possess a large appetite.
³ Do not crave that ruler's delicacies,
for that food is deceptive.
⁴ ªDo not wear yourself out to become
rich;
ᵇbe wise enough to restrain yourself.
⁵ When you gaze upon riches,¹ they are
gone,
for they surely make wings for
themselves
and fly off into the sky like an eagle!
⁶ Do not ªeat the food of a stingy person,
do not crave his delicacies;
⁷ for ªhe is¹ like someone who has
calculated the cost in his mind.
"Eat and drink," he says to you,
but his heart is not with you;
⁸ you will vomit up the little bit you
have eaten
and will have wasted your pleasant
words.
⁹ Do not speak in the ears of a fool,
for he will despise the ªwisdom of
your words.
¹⁰ Do not move an ancient boundary
stone
or take over the fields of the
fatherless,
¹¹ ªfor their Protector is strong;
he will plead their case against you.
¹² Apply your heart to instruction
and your ears to the words of
knowledge.
¹³ ªDo not withhold discipline from a
child;
even if you strike him with the rod,
he will not die.
¹⁴ If you strike him with the rod,
you will deliver him from death.¹
¹⁵ My child, if your heart is wise,
then my heart also will be glad;

¹⁶ my soul¹ will rejoice
when your lips speak what is right.
¹⁷ ªDo not let your heart envy sinners,
but rather ᵇbe zealous in fearing the
LORD all the time.
¹⁸ ªFor surely there is a future,
and your hope will not be cut off.
¹⁹ Listen, my child,¹ and be wise,
and guide your heart on the right
way.
²⁰ ªDo not spend time among
drunkards,
among those who eat too much
meat,
²¹ because drunkards and gluttons
become impoverished,
and drowsiness clothes them with
rags.
²² ªListen to your father who gave you
life,
and do not despise your mother
when she is old.
²³ ªAcquire truth and do not sell it—
wisdom, and discipline, and
understanding.
²⁴ The ªfather of a righteous person will
rejoice greatly;
whoever fathers a wise child will
have joy in him.
²⁵ May your father and your mother
have joy;
may she who bore you rejoice.
²⁶ Give me your heart, my son,¹
and let your eyes observe my ways;
²⁷ ªfor a prostitute is like a deep pit;
a harlot is like a narrow well.
²⁸ Indeed, ªshe lies in wait like a robber
and increases the unfaithful among
men.
²⁹ Who has woe? ªWho ᵇhas sorrow?
Who has contentions? Who has
complaints?
Who has wounds without cause?
Who has dullness of the eyes?
³⁰ Those who linger over wine,
ªthose who go looking for ᵇmixed
wine.

23:4 ª [Prov 28:20; Matt 6:19; 1 Tim 6:9–10; Heb 13:5] ᵇ Rom 12:16 **23:5** ¹ Ket. *do your eyes fly* [light] *on it?* **23:6** ª Deut 15:9; Prov 28:22 **23:7** ª Prov 12:2 ¹ Heb. *For, as he has calculated in his soul, so he is;* LXX *Eating and drinking with him is as if one should swallow a hair; do not introduce him to your company nor eat bread with him.* **23:9** ª Prov 9:8; Matt 7:6 **23:11** ª Prov 22:23 **23:13** ª Prov 13:24 **23:14** ¹ Heb. *Sheol;* perhaps social as well as physical. **23:16** ¹ Heb. *my kidneys;* the innermost being, the soul, the central location of the passions. **23:17** ª Ps 37:1; Prov 24:1, 19 ᵇ Prov 28:14 **23:18** ª [Ps 37:37] **23:19** ¹ Heb. *my son,* but the immediate context does not limit this to male children. **23:20** ª Prov 20:1; 23:29–30; Isa 5:22; Matt 24:49; [Luke 21:34]; Rom 13:13; [Eph 5:18] **23:22** ª Prov 1:8; Eph 6:1 **23:23** ª Prov 4:7; 18:15; [Matt 13:44] **23:24** ª Prov 10:1 **23:26** ¹ Heb. *my son;* "child" is not used because advice to avoid women who are prostitutes follows. **23:27** ª Prov 22:14 **23:28** ª Prov 7:12; Eccl 7:26 **23:29** ª Isa 5:11, 22 ᵇ Gen 49:12 **23:30** ª 1 Sam 25:36; Prov 20:1; 21:17; Isa 5:11; 28:7; [Eph 5:18] ᵇ Ps 75:8

³¹ Do not look on the wine when it is
  red,
  when it sparkles in the cup,
  when it goes down smoothly.
³² Afterward it bites like a snake
  and stings like a viper.
³³ Your eyes will see strange things,
  and your mind will speak perverse
  things.
³⁴ And you will be like one who lies
  down in the midst of the sea,
  and like one who lies down on the
  top of the rigging.
³⁵ You will say, "ᵃThey have struck me,
  but ᵇI am not harmed!
  They beat me, but I did not know it!
  When will I awake? I will look for
  another drink."

24 Do not ᵃenvy evil people¹
  do not desire to be with them;
² for their hearts contemplate violence,
  and their lips speak harm.
³ By wisdom a house is built,
  and through understanding it is
  established;
⁴ by knowledge its rooms are filled
  with all kinds of precious and
  pleasing treasures.
⁵ A wise ᵃwarrior is strong,
  and a man of knowledge makes his
  strength stronger;
⁶ ᵃfor with guidance you wage your war,
  and with numerous advisers there is
  victory.
⁷ ᵃWisdom is unattainable¹ for a fool;
  in court he does not open his mouth.
⁸ The one who ᵃplans to do evil
  will be called a scheming person.
⁹ A foolish scheme is sin,
  and the scorner is an abomination to
  people.¹
¹⁰ You have slacked ᵃoff in the day of
  trouble—
  your strength is small!
¹¹ ᵃDeliver those being taken away to
  death,
  and hold back those slipping to the
  slaughter.

¹² If you say, "But we did not know
  about this,"
  won't ᵃthe one who evaluates hearts
  discern it?
  Won't the one who guards your life
  realize
  and repay each person ᵇaccording to
  his deeds?
¹³ ᵃEat honey, my child, for it is good,
  and honey from the honeycomb is
  sweet to your taste.
¹⁴ Likewise, know that wisdom is sweet
  to your ᵃsoul;
  if you have found it, you have a future,
  and your hope will not be cut off.
¹⁵ Do not lie in wait like the wicked¹
  against the place where the
  righteous live;
  do not assault his home.
¹⁶ ᵃIndeed a righteous person will fall
  seven times, and then get up again,
  ᵇbut the guilty will collapse in
  calamity.
¹⁷ Do not rejoice when your enemy falls,
  and when he stumbles ᵃdo not let
  your heart rejoice,
¹⁸ lest the LORD see it, and be
  displeased,
  and turn his wrath away from him.
¹⁹ ᵃDo not fret because of evil people
  or be envious of wicked people,
²⁰ for the evil person has no future,
  and the lamp of the wicked will be
  extinguished.
²¹ ᵃFear the LORD, my child,¹ as well as
  the king,
  and do not associate with rebels,
²² for suddenly their destruction will
  overtake them,
  and who knows the ruinous
  judgment both the LORD and the
  king can bring?

Further Sayings of the Wise
²³These sayings also are from the wise:

To show ᵃpartiality¹ in judgment is
  terrible:

23:35 ᵃProv 27:22; Jer 5:3   ᵇEph 4:19   **24:1** ᵃPs 1:1; 37:1; Prov 23:17   ¹Heb. *evil men*; the context indicates a generic sense.   **24:5** ᵃProv 21:22; Eccl 9:16   **24:6** ᵃLuke 14:31   **24:7** ᵃPs 10:5; Prov 14:6   ¹MT *wisdom to the fool is corals*; i.e., an unattainable treasure.   **24:8** ᵃProv 6:14; 14:22; Rom 1:30   **24:9** ¹Heb. *to a man.*   **24:10** ᵃDeut 20:8; Job 4:5; Jer 51:46; Heb 12:3   **24:11** ᵃPs 82:4; Isa 58:6–7; 1 John 3:16   **24:12** ᵃ1 Sam 16:7; Prov 21:2   ᵇJob 34:11; Ps 62:12; Rev 2:23; 22:12   **24:13** ᵃPs 19:10; 119:103; Prov 25:16; Song 5:1   **24:14** ᵃPs 19:10; 58:11; Prov 23:18   **24:15** ¹Or *O wicked man.*   **24:16** ᵃJob 5:19; [Ps 34:19; 37:24; Mic 7:8]   ᵇEsth 7:10; Amos 5:2   **24:17** ᵃJob 31:29; Ps 35:15, 19; [Prov 17:5]; Obad 12   **24:19** ᵃPs 37:1   **24:21** ᵃ[Rom 13:7; 1 Pet 2:17]   ¹Heb. *my son*, but there is no indication in the immediate context that this should be limited only to male children.   **24:23** ᵃLev 19:15; Deut 1:17; 16:19; [John 7:24]   ¹Heb. *to recognize faces.*

24 The one who says to [a]the guilty, "You
   are innocent,"
   peoples will curse him, and nations
   will denounce him.
25 But there will be [a]delight[1] for those
   who convict[2] the guilty,
   and a pleasing blessing will come on
   them.
26 Like a kiss on the lips
   is the one who gives an honest
   answer.
27 [a]Establish your work outside and get
   your fields ready;
   afterward build your house.
28 Do not be a witness against your
   neighbor without cause,
   and [a]do not deceive with your words.
29 Do not say, "I will [a]do to him just as
   he has done to me;
   I will pay him back according to what
   he has done."
30 I passed by the field of a sluggard,
   by the vineyard of one who lacks
   sense.
31 I saw[1] that thorns had grown up [a]all
   over it;
   the ground was covered with weeds,
   and its stone wall was broken down.
32 Then I scrutinized it. I was putting
   my mind to it—
   I saw; I took in a lesson:
33 "A little sleep, [a]a little slumber,
   a little folding of the hands to relax,
34 [a]and your poverty will come like a
   bandit,
   and your need like an armed robber."

Proverbs of Solomon Collected by Hezekiah

25 [a]These also are proverbs of Solomon,
which the men of King Hezekiah of
Judah copied:

2 It is the glory of God to conceal a
   matter,
   and [a]it is the glory of a king to search
   out a matter.
3 As the heaven is high and the earth is
   deep

so the hearts of kings are
   unsearchable.
4 [a]Remove the dross from the silver,
   and material for the silversmith will
   emerge;
5 remove the wicked from before the
   king,
   and his throne will be established in
   [a]righteousness.
6 Do not honor yourself before the
   king,
   and do not stand in the place of great
   men;
7 for it is better [a]for him to say to you,
   "Come up here,"
   than to put you lower before a prince,
   whom your eyes have seen.
8 Do not go out hastily to litigation,
   or what will you [a]do afterward
   when your neighbor puts you to
   shame?
9 When you [a]argue a case with your
   neighbor,
   do not reveal the secret of another
   person,
10 lest the one who hears it put you to
   shame
   and your infamy[1] will never go away.
11 Like apples of gold in settings of silver,
   so is a word skillfully [a]spoken.
12 Like an earring of gold and an
   ornament of fine gold,
   so is a wise reprover to the ear of the
   one who listens.
13 [a]Like the cold of snow in the time of
   harvest,
   so is a faithful messenger to those
   who send him,
   for he refreshes the heart of his
   masters.
14 Like cloudy [a]skies and wind that
   produce no rain,
   so is the [b]one who boasts of a gift not
   given.
15 [a]Through patience a ruler can be
   persuaded,
   and a soft tongue can break a bone.
16 You have found[1] honey—eat only
   what is sufficient for you,

24:24 [a]Prov 17:15; Isa 5:23   24:25 [a]Prov 28:23 [1]Heb. *to be pleasant, delightful.* [2]Heb. *to decide, adjudge, prove;*
either reproving the wicked for what they do or convicting them in a legal setting.   24:27 [a]1 Kgs 5:17; Prov 27:23–27
24:28 [a]Lev 6:2–3; 19:11; Eph 4:25   24:29 [a][Prov 20:22; Matt 5:39–44; Rom 12:17–19]   24:31 [a]Gen 3:18 [1]Trad. *and, lo.*
24:33 [a]Prov 6:9–10   24:34 [a]Prov 6:9–11   25:1 [a]1 Kgs 4:32   25:2 [a]Deut 29:29; Rom 11:33   25:4 [a]2 Tim 2:21   25:5 [a]Prov
16:12; 20:8   25:7 [a]Luke 14:7–11   25:8 [a]Prov 17:14; Matt 5:25   25:9 [a][Matt 18:15]   25:10 [1]Heb. *infamy, defamation,*
evil report, whispering.   25:11 [a]Prov 15:23; Isa 50:4   25:13 [a]Prov 13:17   25:14 [a]Jude 12 [b]Prov 20:6
25:15 [a]Prov 15:1   25:16 [1]Or *Have you found honey?*, *If/When you find honey.*

lest you become stuffed with it and
    vomit it up.
17 Don't set foot too frequently in your
    neighbor's house,
lest he become weary of you and hate
    you.
18 Like [a]a club or a sword or a sharp
    arrow,
so is the one who testifies against his
    neighbor as a false witness.
19 Like a bad tooth or a foot out of joint,
so is confidence[1] in an unfaithful
    person at the time of trouble.
20 Like one who takes off a garment on
    a cold day[1]
or like vinegar poured on soda,
so is one who [a]sings songs to a heavy
    heart.
21 If your enemy is hungry, give him
    food to eat,
and [a]if he is thirsty, give him water to
    drink,
22 for you will heap coals of fire on his
    head,
[a]and the LORD will reward you.
23 The north wind brings forth [a]rain,
and a gossiping tongue brings forth
    an angry look.
24 It is better to live on a corner of the
    housetop
than in a house in company [a]with a
    quarrelsome wife.[1]
25 Like cold water to a weary person,
so is [a]good news from a distant land.
26 Like a muddied spring and a polluted
    well,
so is a righteous person who gives
    way before the wicked.
27 It is not good [a]to eat too much
    honey,
nor is it honorable for people to seek
    their own glory.
28 Like a city that is broken down and
    without a wall,
so is a [a]person who cannot control
    his temper.

26 Like snow in summer or rain in
    harvest,
so honor is not fitting for [a]a fool.

2 Like [a]a fluttering bird or like a flying
    swallow,
so a curse without cause does not
    come to rest.
3 A whip for the horse [a]and a bridle for
    the donkey,
and a rod for the backs of fools!
4 Do not answer a fool according to his
    folly,
lest you yourself also be like him.
5 [a]Answer a fool according to his folly,
lest he be wise in his own opinion.
6 Like cutting off the feet or drinking
    violence,
so is sending a message by the hand
    of a fool.
7 Like legs dangle uselessly from the
    lame,
so a proverb dangles in the mouth of
    fools.
8 Like tying a stone in a sling,
so is giving honor to a fool.
9 Like a thorn has gone up into the
    hand of a drunkard,
so a proverb has gone up into the
    mouth of a fool.
10 Like an archer who wounds at
    random,
so is the one who hires a fool or hires
    any passerby.
11 Like [a]a dog that returns to its vomit,
[b]so a fool repeats his folly.
12 [a]You have seen a man wise in his own
    opinion—
there is more hope for a fool than for
    him.
13 The sluggard has said,[1] "There is a
    lion in the road!
A lion in the streets!"
14 Like a door that turns on its hinges,
so a sluggard turns on his bed.
15 The [a]sluggard has plunged his hand
    in the dish;
he is too lazy to bring it back to his
    mouth.
16 The sluggard is wiser in his own
    opinion
than seven people who respond with
    good sense.[1]

25:18 [a] Ps 57:4; Prov 12:18   25:19 [1] Heb. *Confidence, treacherous ones in a day of trouble.*   25:20 [a] Dan 6:18   [1] LXX *Like vinegar is bad for a wound, so a pain that afflicts the body afflicts the heart. Like a moth in a garment, and a worm in wood, so the pain of a man wounds the heart.*   25:21 [a] Exod 23:4–5; 2 Kgs 6:22; 2 Chr 28:15; Matt 5:44; Rom 12:20   25:22 [a] 2 Sam 16:12; [Matt 6:4, 6]   25:23 [a] Ps 101:5   25:24 [a] Prov 19:13   [1] This proverb is identical with 21:9.   25:25 [a] Prov 15:30   25:27 [a] Prov 27:2; [Luke 14:11]   25:28 [a] Prov 16:32   26:1 [1] 1 Sam 12:17   26:2 [a] Num 23:8; Deut 23:5; 2 Sam 16:12   26:3 [a] Ps 32:9; Prov 19:29   26:5 [a] Matt 16:1–4; Rom 12:16   26:11 [a] 2 Pet 2:22   [b] Exod 8:15   26:12 [a] Prov 29:20; Luke 18:11–12; [Rev 3:17]   26:13 [1] Heb. *to say, think.*   26:15 [a] Prov 19:24   26:16 [1] Heb. *taste, judgment.*

17 Like one who grabs a wild dog by the
 ears,
 so is the person passing by who
 becomes furious over a quarrel not
 his own.
18 Like a madman who shoots
 firebrands and deadly arrows,
19 so [a]is a person who has deceived his
 neighbor,
 and said, "Was I not only joking?"
20 Where there is no wood, a fire goes
 out,
 and where there is no gossip,
 contention ceases.
21 Like charcoal is to burning coals, and
 wood to fire,
 so is [a]a contentious person to kindle
 strife.
22 The words of a gossip are like choice
 morsels;
 and they have gone down into a
 person's innermost being.[1]
23 Like a coating of glaze over
 earthenware
 are fervent lips with an evil heart.
24 The one who hates others disguises
 it with his lips,
 but he stores up deceit within him.
25 When [a]he speaks graciously, do not
 believe him,
 for there are seven abominations
 within him.
26 Though his hatred may be concealed
 by deceit,
 his evil will be uncovered in the
 assembly.
27 The one [a]who digs a pit will fall into it;
 the one who rolls a stone—it will
 come back on him.
28 A lying tongue hates those crushed
 by it,
 and a flattering mouth works [a]ruin.

27 Do not boast about tomorrow;
 for you [a]do not know what a day
 may bring forth.
2 [a]Let another[1] praise you, and not
 your own mouth;
 someone else, and not your own lips.

3 A stone is heavy and sand is weighty,
 but vexation by a fool is more
 burdensome than the two of them.
4 Wrath is cruel and anger is
 overwhelming,
 but [a]who can stand before jealousy?[1]
5 Better is [a]open rebuke
 than hidden love.
6 Faithful are the wounds of a friend,
 but the kisses of an enemy are
 [a]excessive.
7 The one whose appetite[1] is satisfied
 loathes honey,
 but to the hungry mouth[2] every
 bitter thing is sweet.
8 Like a bird that wanders from its
 nest,
 so is a person who wanders from his
 home.
9 Ointment and incense make the
 heart rejoice,
 likewise the sweetness of one's friend
 from sincere counsel.
10 Do not forsake your friend and your
 father's friend,
 and do not enter your brother's
 house in the day of your disaster;
 a neighbor nearby is [a]better than a
 brother far away.
11 Be wise, my son, and make my heart
 glad,
 so [a]that I may answer anyone who
 taunts me.
12 A shrewd person saw danger—he hid
 himself;
 the naive passed right on by—they
 had to [a]pay for it.
13 Take a man's garment when he has
 given security for a stranger,
 and hold him in pledge on behalf of a
 stranger.[1]
14 If someone blesses his neighbor with
 a loud voice early in the morning,
 it will be counted as a curse to him.
15 A [a]continual dripping on a rainy
 day—
 a contentious wife makes herself like
 that.[1]

26:19 [a]Eph 5:4   26:21 [a]Prov 15:18   26:22 [1]This proverb is identical to 18:8.   26:25 [a]Ps 28:3; Prov 26:23; Jer 9:8
26:27 [a]Esth 7:10; Ps 7:15; Prov 28:10; Eccl 10:8   26:28 [a]Prov 29:5   27:1 [a]Luke 12:19–21; Jas 4:13–16   27:2 [a]Prov 25:27;
2 Cor 10:12, 18; 12:11   [1]Heb. *a stranger*, a person outside familiar and accepted circles who would be objective.   27:4 [a]Prov
6:34; 1 John 3:12   [1]Probably the negative sense of envy rather than the positive sense of zeal.   27:5 [a][Prov 28:23]; Gal
2:14   27:6 [a]Matt 26:49   27:7 [1]Trad. *soul*; the whole person with all his appetites.   [2]Trad. *soul*.   27:10 [a]Prov 17:17; 18:24
27:11 [a]Prov 10:1; 23:15–26   27:12 [a]Prov 22:3   27:13 [1]Or *for a strange woman*; someone from outside the community
and not well-known.   27:15 [a]Prov 19:13   [1]LXX *Drops drive a man out of his house on a wintry day; so a
railing woman also drives him out of his own house.*

16 Whoever contains her has contained
   the wind
or can grasp oil with his right hand.[1]
17 As iron sharpens iron,
   so a person sharpens his friend.
18 The one [a]who tends a fig tree will eat
   its fruit,
and whoever takes care of his master
   will be honored.
19 As in water the face is reflected as a
   face,
so a person's heart reflects the
   person.
20 As [a]Death and Destruction are never
   satisfied,
so [b]the eyes of a person are never
   satisfied.[1]
21 As [a]the crucible is for silver and the
   furnace is for gold,
so a person must put his praise to
   the test.
22 [a]If you should pound the fool in the
   mortar
among the grain with the pestle,
his foolishness would not depart
   from him.
23 Pay careful attention to the
   condition of your [a]flocks,
set your mind on your herds,
24 for riches do not last forever,
nor does a crown last from
   generation to generation.
25 [a]When the hay is removed and new
   grass appears,
and the grass from the hills is
   gathered in,
26 the lambs will be for your clothing,
and the goats will be for the price of
   a field.
27 And there will be enough goat's milk
   for your food,
for the food of your household,
and for the sustenance of your
   servant girls.

28 The wicked [a]person fled, though no
   one was pursuing,
but the righteous person can be as
   confident as a lion.

2 When a country is rebellious it has
   many princes,
but by someone who is discerning
   and knowledgeable[1] order is
   maintained.[2]
3 A poor person[1] who oppresses the
   [a]weak
is like a driving rain without food.
4 Those who forsake the law praise the
   wicked,
but [a]those who keep the law contend
   with them.
5 [a]Evil people[1] do not understand
   justice,
but [b]those who seek the LORD
   understand it all.
6 A poor person who walks in his
   integrity is better
than one who is perverse in his ways
   even though he is rich.
7 The one who keeps the law[1] is a
   discerning child,
but a companion of gluttons brings
   shame to his parents.
8 The one who increases his wealth by
   increasing interest
gathers it for someone who is
   gracious to the needy.
9 The one who turns away his ear from
   hearing the law,
[a]even his prayer is an abomination.
10 The one [a]who leads the upright
   astray in an evil way
will himself fall into his own pit,
[b]but the blameless will inherit what
   is good.
11 A rich person is wise in his own
   opinion,
but a discerning poor person can
   evaluate him properly.
12 When the righteous rejoice, great is
   the [a]glory,
but when the wicked rise to power,
   people are sought out.
13 The one who covers his
   transgressions will not prosper,
but whoever confesses [a]them and
   forsakes them will find mercy.

27:16 [1]LXX the north wind is a severe wind, but by its name is termed auspicious.   27:18 [a] 2 Kgs 18:31; Song 8:12; Isa 36:16; [1 Cor 3:8; 9:7–13]; 2 Tim 2:6   27:20 [a] Prov 30:15–16; Hab 2:5   [b] Eccl 1:8; 4:8   [1]LXX adds He who fixes his eye is an abomination to the LORD, and the uninstructed do not restrain their tongues.   27:21 [a] Prov 17:3   27:22 [a] Prov 23:35; 26:11; Jer 5:3   27:23 [a] Prov 24:27   27:25 [a] Ps 104:14   28:1 [a] Lev 26:17, 36; Ps 53:5   28:2 [1]Heb. a man who understands [and] knows.   [2]LXX It is the fault of a violent man that quarrels start, but they are settled by a man of discernment.   28:3 [a] Matt 18:28   [1]LXX A courageous man oppresses the poor with impieties.   28:4 [a] Ps 49:18; Rom 1:32   28:5 [a] Ps 92:6; Isa 6:9; 44:18   [b] Ps 119:100; Prov 2:9; John 17:17; 1 Cor 2:15; [1 John 2:20, 27]   [1]Heb. men of evil; the context does not limit this to males.   28:7 [1]Either instruction by the father or the Mosaic law.   28:9 [a] Ps 66:18; 109:7; Prov 15:8   28:10 [a] Ps 7:15; Prov 26:27   [b] [Matt 6:33; Heb 6:12; 1 Pet 3:9]   28:12 [a] Prov 11:10; 29:2   28:13 [a] Ps 32:3–5; 1 John 1:8–10

[14] Blessed is the one who is always
cautious,
but whoever hardens his heart will
fall into evil.
[15] [a]Like a roaring lion or a roving bear,
so [b]is a wicked ruler over a poor
people.
[16] The prince who is a great [a]oppressor
lacks wisdom,
but the one who hates unjust gain
will prolong his days.
[17] The one who is tormented by the
murder of [a]another will flee to the
pit;[1]
let no one support him.
[18] The one who walks blamelessly will
be delivered,
but whoever is perverse in his ways
will fall at once.
[19] [a]The one who works his land will be
satisfied with food,[1]
but whoever chases daydreams will
have his fill of poverty.
[20] A faithful person will have an
abundance of blessings,
[a]but the one who hastens to gain
riches will not go unpunished.
[21] [a]To show partiality is terrible,[1]
for [b]a person will transgress over the
smallest piece of bread.
[22] The stingy person hastens after
riches
and does not know that [a]poverty will
overtake him.
[23] The one who reproves [a]another will
in the end find more favor
than the one who flatters with the
tongue.
[24] The one who robs [a]his father and
mother and says, "There is no
transgression,"
is a companion to the one who
destroys.
[25] The greedy person stirs up
dissension,
but [a]the one who trusts in the LORD
will prosper.
[26] The one who [a]trusts in his own heart
is a fool,

but the one who walks in wisdom
will escape.
[27] The one who gives to [a]the poor will
not lack,
but whoever shuts his eyes to them
will receive many curses.
[28] When the wicked gain control,
[a]people hide themselves,
but when they perish, the righteous
increase.

29 The [a]one who stiffens his neck
after numerous rebukes
will suddenly be destroyed without
remedy.
[2] When the righteous become
numerous, the [a]people rejoice;
when [b]the wicked rule, the people
groan.
[3] The man who loves wisdom brings
joy to his father,
but whoever associates with
prostitutes wastes his wealth.
[4] A king brings stability to a land[1] by
justice,
but one who exacts tribute tears it
down.
[5] The one who [a]flatters his neighbor
spreads a net for his steps.
[6] In the transgression of an evil person
there is a snare,
but a righteous person can sing and
rejoice.
[7] The righteous person cares for the
legal rights of the poor;
the wicked person does not
understand such knowledge.
[8] Scornful people [a]inflame a city,
but those who are wise turn away
wrath.
[9] When a wise person goes to court
with a foolish person,
there is no peace [a]whether he is
angry or laughs.
[10] Bloodthirsty people[1] hate someone
with integrity;
as for [a]the upright, they seek his
life.
[11] A fool lets fly with all his [a]temper,
but a wise person keeps it back.

28:15 [a]Prov 19:12; 1 Pet 5:8   [b]Exod 1:14; Prov 29:2; Matt 2:16   28:16 [a]Eccl 10:16; Isa 3:12   28:17 [a]Gen 9:6   [1]Perhaps the place of detention for prisoners, or death.   28:19 [a]Prov 12:11; 20:13   [1]Or will have plenty of food (Heb. bread). 28:20 [a]Prov 13:11; 20:21; 23:4; 1 Tim 6:9   28:21 [a]Prov 18:5   [b]Ezek 13:19   [1]Heb. not good; a deliberate understatement for the sake of emphasis.   28:22 [a]Prov 21:5   28:23 [a]Prov 27:5-6   28:24 [a]Prov 18:9   28:25 [a]Prov 13:10   28:26 [a]Prov 3:5 28:27 [a]Deut 15:7; Prov 19:17; 22:9   28:28 [a]Job 24:4   29:1 [a]2 Chr 36:16; Prov 6:15   29:2 [a]Esth 8:15; Prov 28:12   [b]Esth 4:3 29:4 [1]Or country.   29:5 [a]Prov 26:28   29:8 [a]Prov 11:11   29:9 [a]Matt 11:17   29:10 [a]Gen 4:5-8; 1 John 3:12 [1]Heb. men of bloods.   29:11 [a]Prov 14:33

12 If a ruler listens to lies,
   all his ministers will be wicked.
13 The poor person and [a]the oppressor
   have this in common:
   The LORD gives light to the eyes of
   them both.
14 If a king judges the [a]poor in truth,
   his throne will be established
   forever.
15 A rod and reproof impart [a]wisdom,
   but a child who is unrestrained
   brings shame to his mother.
16 When the wicked increase,
   transgression increases,
   but the righteous will see their
   [a]downfall.
17 Discipline your child, and he will give
   you rest;
   he will bring you happiness.
18 [a]When there is no prophetic vision
   the people cast off restraint,
   but the one who keeps the law,
   [b]blessed is he!
19 A servant cannot be corrected by
   words,
   for although[1] he understands, there
   is no answer.
20 You have seen someone[1] who is hasty
   in his words—
   [a]there is more hope for a fool than
   for him.
21 If someone pampers his servant
   from youth,
   he will be a weakling in the end.
22 An [a]angry person stirs up
   dissension,
   and a wrathful person is abounding
   in transgression.
23 A person's pride will bring him low,
   but one who [a]has a lowly spirit will
   gain honor.
24 Whoever shares with a thief is his
   own enemy;
   [a]he hears the oath to testify, but does
   not talk.
25 The fear of people[1] becomes a snare,
   but whoever trusts in [a]the LORD will
   be set on high.

26 Many [a]people seek the face of a ruler,
   but it is from the LORD that one
   receives justice.
27 An unjust person is an abomination
   to the righteous,
   and the one who lives an upright life
   is an abomination to the wicked.

The Words of Agur

30 The words of Agur, the son of
   Jakeh; an oracle:
   This man says to Ithiel, to Ithiel and
   to Ukal:
2 [a]Surely[1] I am more brutish than any
   other human being,
   and I do not have human
   understanding;
3 I have not learned wisdom,
   nor can I have [a]knowledge of the
   Holy One.
4 Who has ascended into heaven, and
   then descended?
   [a]Who has gathered up the winds in
   his fists?
   [b]Who has bound up the waters in his
   cloak?
   Who has established all the ends of
   the earth?
   What is his name, and what is his
   son's name? Surely[1] you can know!
5 [a]Every word of God is purified;
   [b]he is like a shield for those who take
   refuge in him.
6 [a]Do not add to his words,
   lest he reprove you and prove you to
   be a liar.
7 Two things I have asked from you;
   do not refuse me before I die:
8 Remove falsehood and lies far
   from me;
   do not give me poverty or riches;
   [a]feed me with my allotted portion of
   bread,
9 lest I become satisfied and act
   deceptively
   and say, "Who is the LORD?"
   Or [a]lest I become poor and steal
   and demean[1] the name of my God.

29:13 [a][Matt 5:45]   29:14 [a]Ps 72:4; Isa 11:4   29:15 [a]Prov 22:15   29:16 [a]Ps 37:34; Prov 21:12   29:18 [a]1 Sam 3:1; Ps 74:9; Amos 8:11–12   [b]Prov 8:32; John 13:17   29:19 [1]Heb. *for he understands, but there is no answer.*   29:20 [a]Prov 26:12   [1]Heb. *a man; although the context does not indicate this should be limited to males.*   29:22 [a]Prov 26:21   29:23 [a]Job 22:29; Prov 15:33; 18:12; Isa 66:2; Dan 4:30; Matt 23:12; Luke 14:11; 18:14; Acts 12:23; [Jas 4:6–10; 1 Pet 5:5–6]   29:24 [a]Lev 5:1   29:25 [a]Gen 12:12; 20:2; Luke 12:4; John 12:42–43   [1]Heb. *the fear of man; although the context does not indicate this should be limited to males.*   29:26 [a]Ps 20:9   30:2 [a]Ps 73:22; Prov 12:1   [1]Or *indeed, truly.*   30:3 [a][Prov 9:10]   30:4 [a][Ps 68:18; John 3:13]   [b]Job 38:4; Ps 104:3; Isa 40:12   [1]Or *indeed, truly.*   30:5 [a]Ps 12:6; 19:8; 119:140   [b]Ps 18:30; 84:11; 115:9–11   30:6 [a]Deut 4:2; 12:32; Rev 22:18   30:8 [a]Job 23:12; Matt 6:11; [Phil 4:19]   30:9 [a]Deut 8:12–14; Neh 9:25–26; Hos 13:6   [1]Heb. *to take hold of, seize.*

¹⁰ Do not slander a servant to his master,
lest he curse you, and you are found
guilty.
¹¹ There is a generation who curse their
[a]fathers
and do not bless their mothers.
¹² There is [a]a generation who are pure
in their own opinion
and yet are not washed from their
filthiness.
¹³ There is a generation whose eyes are
so [a]lofty
and whose eyelids are lifted up
disdainfully.
¹⁴ There is a generation whose teeth
are like swords
and whose molars[1] are like knives
to devour [a]the poor from the earth
and the needy from among the
human race.
¹⁵ The leech has two daughters:
"Give! Give!"
There are three things that will
never be satisfied,
four that have never said, "Enough"—
¹⁶ the grave, [a]the barren womb;
earth has not been satisfied with
water;
and fire has never said, "Enough!"
¹⁷ The eye that mocks at a [a]father
and despises obeying a mother—
the ravens of the valley will peck it
out,
and the young vultures will eat it.
¹⁸ There are three things that are too
wonderful for me,
four that I do not understand:
¹⁹ the way of an eagle in the sky,
the way of a snake on a rock,
the way of a ship in the sea,
and the way of a man with a woman.
²⁰ This is the way of an adulterous
woman:
She has eaten and wiped her mouth
and has said, "I have not done wrong."
²¹ Under three things the earth has
trembled,
and under four things it cannot
bear up:

²² [a]under a servant who becomes king,
under a fool who becomes stuffed
with food,
²³ under an unloved woman who
becomes married,
and under a female servant who
dispossesses[1] her mistress.
²⁴ There are four things on earth that
are small,
but they are exceedingly wise:
²⁵ Ants are creatures with little
strength,
but [a]they prepare their food in the
summer;
²⁶ rock badgers[1] are creatures with little
power,
but [a]they make their homes in the
crags;
²⁷ locusts have no king,
but they all go forward by ranks;
²⁸ a lizard you can catch with the hand,
but it gets into the palaces of the
king.[1]
²⁹ There are three things that are
magnificent in their step,
four things that move about
magnificently:
³⁰ a lion, mightiest of the beasts,
who does not retreat from anything;
³¹ a strutting rooster, a male goat,
and a king with his army around him.[1]
³² If you have done foolishly by exalting
yourself
or if you have planned evil,
[a]put your hand over your mouth!
³³ For as the churning of milk produces
butter
and as punching the nose produces
blood,
so stirring up anger produces strife.

The Words of Lemuel

31 The words of King Lemuel, an oracle
that his mother taught him:

² O my [a]son, O son of my womb,
O son of my vows,
³ [a]do not give your strength [b]to
women,

30:11 [a] Exod 21:17; Prov 20:20   30:12 [a] [Prov 16:2]; Isa 65:5; Luke 18:11; [Titus 1:15–16]   30:13 [a] Ps 131:1; Prov 6:17; Isa 2:11;
5:15   30:14 [a] Job 29:17; Ps 52:2   [1] Heb. *teeth, jaw teeth, jawbone*; a different Heb. word than the one in the previous line.
30:16 [a] Prov 27:20; Hab 2:5   30:17 [a] Gen 9:22; Lev 20:9; Prov 20:20   30:22 [a] Prov 19:10; Eccl 10:7   30:23 [1] The Heb. verb
means either to possess or to dispossess; often the process of possessing meant the dispossessing of something already
there.   30:25 [a] Prov 6:6   30:26 [a] Lev 11:5; Ps 104:18   [1] Or *hyraxes*.   30:28 [1] Trad. *kings' palaces*.   30:31 [1] LXX *a king
haranguing his people*; Tg. *a king who stands up before his people and addresses them*.   30:32 [a] Job 21:5; 40:4;
Mic 7:16   31:2 [a] Isa 49:15   31:3 [a] Prov 5:9   [b] Deut 17:17; 1 Kgs 11:1; Neh 13:26; Prov 7:26; Hos 4:11

nor your ways to that which ruins
    kings.
4 It is not for kings, O Lemuel,
    [a]it is not for kings to drink wine
    or for rulers to crave strong drink,[1]
5 [a]lest they drink and forget what is
    decreed
    and remove from all the poor their
    legal rights.
6 [a]Give strong drink to the one who is
    perishing
    and wine to those who are bitterly
    distressed;[1]
7 let them drink and forget their
    poverty,
    and remember their misery no more.
8 [a]Open your mouth on behalf of those
    unable to speak,
    for the legal rights of all the dying.
9 Open your mouth, [a]judge in
    righteousness,
    and plead the [b]cause of the poor and
    needy.

The Wife of Noble Character

10 [a]Who can find a wife[1] of noble
    character?
    For her value is far more than
    rubies.[2]
11 Her husband's heart has trusted her,
    and he does not lack the dividends.
12 She has rewarded him with good and
    not harm
    all the days of her life.
13 She sought out wool and flax,
    then worked happily with her hands.
14 She was like the merchant ships;
    she would bring in her food from
    afar.
15 Then [a]she rose while it was still
    night,
    and [b]provided food for her
    household and a portion to her
    female servants.
16 She considered a field and bought it;
    from her own income she planted a
    vineyard.
17 She clothed herself in might,
    and she strengthened her arms.

18 She perceived that her merchandise
    was good.
    Her lamp would not go out in the
    night.
19 She extended her hands to the spool,
    and her hands grasped the spindle.
20 [a]She opened her hand to the poor,
    and extended her hands to the
    needy.
21 She would not fear for her household
    in winter,
    because all her household were
    clothed with scarlet,
22 because she had made coverings for
    herself;
    and because her clothing was fine
    linen and purple.
23 Her husband is well known in the
    city gate
    when [a]he sits with the elders of the
    land.
24 She made linen garments then sold
    them
    and traded belts to the merchants;[1]
25 her clothing was strong and
    splendid;
    and she laughed at the time
    to come.
26 She has opened her mouth with
    wisdom,
    with loving instruction[1] on her
    tongue.
27 Watching over the ways of her
    household,
    she would not eat the bread of
    idleness.
28 Her children have risen and called
    her blessed;
    her husband also has praised her:
29 "Many daughters have done valiantly,
    but you have surpassed them all!"
30 Charm is deceitful and beauty is
    fleeting.
    A woman who fears the LORD—she
    makes herself praiseworthy.
31 Give her credit for what she has
    accomplished,
    and let her works praise her in the
    city gates.

31:4 [a]Eccl 10:17 [1]Probably barley beer. 31:5 [a]Hos 4:11 31:6 [a]Ps 104:15 [1]Heb. *to the bitter of soul.* 31:8 [a]Job 29:15–16; Ps 82 31:9 [a]Lev 19:15; Deut 1:16 [b]Job 29:12; Isa 1:17; Jer 22:16 31:10 [a]Ruth 3:11; Prov 12:4; 19:14 [1]This poem forms an acrostic, with the first line beginning with א (*alef*), the first letter in the Heb. alphabet, and each following line beginning with a subsequent letter. [2]Heb. *gems.* 31:15 [a]Prov 20:13; Rom 12:11 [b]Luke 12:42 31:20 [a]Deut 15:11; Job 31:16–20; Prov 22:9; Rom 12:13; Eph 4:28; Heb 13:16 31:23 [a]Prov 12:4 31:24 [1]Heb. *to the Canaanites;* the Phoenician traders who survived the wars and continued to do business down to the exile. 31:26 [1]Or *faithful teaching, teaching with kindness.*

ECCLESIASTES

The key word in Ecclesiastes is "futile" as in the futile emptiness of trying to be happy apart from God. The Teacher (traditionally taken to be Solomon—1:1, 12—the wisest, richest, most influential king in Israel's history) looks at life "on earth" (1:9) and, from the human perspective, declares it all to be empty. Power, popularity, prestige, pleasure—nothing can fill the God-shaped void in man's life but God himself! But once seen from God's perspective, life takes on meaning and purpose, causing Solomon to exclaim, *Eat … drink … rejoice … do good … live joyfully … fear God … keep his commandments!* Skepticism and despair melt away when life is viewed as a daily gift from God. The Hebrew title *Qoheleth* is a rare term found only in Ecclesiastes (1:1–2, 12; 7:27; 12:8–10). It comes from the word *qahal*, "to convoke an assembly, to assemble." Thus it means "one who addresses an assembly," "a preacher." The Septuagint used the Greek word *Ekklesiastes* as its title for this book. Derived from the word *ekklesia*, "assembly," "congregation," "church," it simply means "Preacher." The Latin title *Ecclesiastes* means "Speaker Before an Assembly."

Title

1 The words of the Teacher,[1] the son of David, [a]king in Jerusalem:

Introduction: Utter Futility

2 "Futile! [a]Futile!" laments the Teacher.
"Absolutely futile! Everything is
    futile!"[1]

Futility Illustrated from Nature

3 [a]What benefit do people get from all
        the effort
which they expend on earth?[1]
4 A generation comes and a generation
        goes,
    [a]but the earth remains the same
        through the ages.
5 The sun rises and [a]the sun sets;
    it hurries away to a place from which
        it rises again.
6 The wind goes to [a]the south and
        circles around to the north;
    round and round the wind goes and
        on its rounds it returns.
7 [a]All the streams flow into the sea, but
        the sea is not full,
    and to the place where the streams
        flow, there they will flow again.
8 All this monotony is tiresome; no
        one can bear to describe it.
    [a]The eye is never satisfied with
        seeing, nor is the ear ever content
        with hearing.
9 [a]What exists now is what will be,
    and what has been done is what will
        be done;
    there is nothing truly new on earth.
10 Is there anything about which
        someone can say, "Look at this! It is
        new"?
    It was already done long ago, before
        our time.[1]
11 No one remembers the former
        events,
    [a]nor will anyone remember the
        events that are yet to happen;
    they will not be remembered by the
        future generations.

1:1 [a]Prov 1:1   [1]The convener of the assembly; a leader, speaker, teacher, or preacher of the assembly; or a member of the assembly.   1:2 [a]Ps 39:5–6; 62:9; 144:4; Eccl 12:8   [1]"Futile" (Heb. *hevel*) is repeated five times within the eight Heb. words of this verse for emphasis. It is the key word in Ecclesiastes, but it should not be translated the same way in every place.   1:3 [a]Eccl 2:22; 3:9   [1]Heb. *under the sun*.   1:4 [a]Ps 104:5; 119:90   1:5 [a]Ps 19:4–6   1:6 [a]Eccl 11:5; John 3:8   1:7 [a][Ps 104:8–9; Jer 5:22]   1:8 [a]Prov 27:20; Eccl 4:8   1:9 [a]Eccl 3:15   1:10 [1]Heb. *in the ages long ago before us*.   1:11 [a]Eccl 2:16

Futility of Secular Accomplishment

12 I, the Teacher, have been king over
Israel in Jerusalem.
13 I decided to carefully[1] and
thoroughly examine
all that has been accomplished on
earth.
I concluded: God has given people [a]a
burdensome task
that keeps them occupied.
14 I reflected on everything that is
accomplished by man on earth,
and I concluded: Everything he
has accomplished is futile[1]—like
chasing the wind!
15 What is bent cannot be straightened,
and [a]what is missing cannot be
supplied.

Futility of Secular Wisdom

16 I thought to myself,
"I have become [a]much wiser than any
of my predecessors who ruled over
Jerusalem;
I have acquired much wisdom and
knowledge."
17 So I decided to discern the benefit
of wisdom [a]and knowledge over
foolish behavior and ideas;
however, I concluded that even this
endeavor is like trying to chase the
wind.[1]
18 For with great wisdom comes great
frustration;
whoever [a]increases his knowledge
merely increases his heartache.

Futility of Self-Indulgent Pleasure

2 I thought to myself,

"Come now, [a]I will try self-indulgent
[b]pleasure to see if it [c]is worthwhile."
But I found[1] that it also is futile.
2 I said of partying, "It is folly,"
and of self-indulgent pleasure, "It
accomplishes nothing!"
3 I thought deeply about the effects of
[a]indulging myself with wine
(all the while my mind was guiding
me with wisdom)

and the effects of behaving foolishly,[1]
so that I might discover what is
[b]profitable
for people to do on earth[2] during the
few days of their lives.

Futility of Materialism

4 I increased my possessions:
I built [a]houses for myself;
I planted vineyards for myself.
5 I designed royal gardens[1] and parks
for myself,
and I planted all kinds of fruit trees
in them.
6 I constructed pools of water for myself,
to irrigate my grove of flourishing
trees.
7 I purchased male and female slaves,
and I owned slaves who were born in
my house;
I also possessed more livestock—both
herds and flocks—
than any of my predecessors in
Jerusalem.
8 I also amassed [a]silver and gold for
myself,
as well as valuable treasures taken
from kingdoms and provinces.
I acquired male singers and female
singers for myself,
and what gives a man sensual
delight—a harem of beautiful
concubines.
9 So I was far wealthier than all my
[a]predecessors in Jerusalem,
yet I maintained my objectivity.
10 I did not restrain myself from getting
whatever [a]I wanted;
I did not deny myself anything that
would bring me pleasure.
So all my accomplishments gave me
joy;[1]
this was my reward for all my effort.
11 Yet when I reflected on everything I
had accomplished
and on all the effort that I had
expended to accomplish it,
I concluded:[1] "All these achievements
and possessions are ultimately
[a]profitless—

1:13 [a] [Eccl 7:25; 8:16–17]   [1] Heb. *with wisdom*.   1:14 [1] Heb. *hevel*.   1:15 [a] Eccl 7:13   1:16 [a] 1 Kgs 3:12–13; Eccl 2:9   1:17 [a] Eccl
2:3, 12; 7:23, 25; [1 Thess 5:21]   [1] Heb. *striving of wind*.   1:18 [a] Eccl 12:12   2:1 [a] Luke 12:19   [b] Prov 14:13; [Eccl 7:4; 8:15]
[c] Eccl 1:2   [1] Lit. *Behold!*   2:3 [a] Eccl 1:17   [b] [Eccl 3:12–13; 5:18; 6:12]   [1] Heb. *embracing folly*.   [2] Heb. *under the heavens*.
2:4 [a] 1 Kgs 7:1–12   2:5 [1] Not vegetable gardens, but orchards, in the same way the "garden" of Eden was actually
an orchard filled with fruit trees.   2:8 [a] 1 Kgs 9:28; 10:10, 14, 21   2:9 [a] Eccl 1:16   2:10 [a] Eccl 3:22; 5:18; 9:9
[1] Heb. *So my heart was joyful from all my toil.*   2:11 [a] Eccl 1:3, 14   [1] Heb. *Behold!*

like chasing the wind!
There is nothing gained from them
on earth."[2]

Wisdom Is Better than Folly

12 Next, I decided to consider wisdom,
as well as foolish behavior [a]and
ideas.
For what more can the king's
successor do than what the king[1]
has already [b]done?
13 I realized that wisdom is [a]preferable
to folly,
just as light is preferable to darkness:
14 The wise man can see where [a]he
is going, but [b]the fool walks in
darkness.
Yet I also realized that the same fate
happens to them both.
15 So I thought to myself, "The fate of
the fool will happen even to me!
Then what did I gain by becoming so
excessively wise?"
So I lamented to myself,
"The benefits of wisdom are
ultimately meaningless!"
16 For the wise man, like the fool,
will [a]not be remembered for very
long,
because in the days to come, both
will already have been forgotten.
Alas, the wise man dies—just like the
fool!
17 So I loathed[1] life because what
happens on earth seems awful to me;
for all the benefits of wisdom are
futile—like chasing the wind.

Futility of Being a Workaholic

18 So [a]I loathed all the fruit of my
effort,[1]
for which I worked so hard on earth,
because I must leave it behind in the
hands of my successor.
19 Who knows if he will be a wise man
or a fool?
Yet he will be master over all the
fruit of my labor
for which I worked so wisely on
earth.
This also is futile!

20 So I began to despair about all the
fruit of my labor
for which I worked so hard on earth.
21 For a man may do his work with
wisdom, knowledge, and skill;
however, he must hand over the fruit
of his labor as an inheritance
to someone else who did not work
for it.
This also is futile, and an awful
injustice!

Painful Days and Restless Nights

22 [a]What does a man acquire from all
his labor
and from the anxiety that
accompanies his toil on earth?
23 For all day long[1] his work produces
[a]pain and frustration,
and even at night his mind cannot
relax.
This also is futile!

Enjoy Work and Its Benefits

24 There is [a]nothing better for people
than[1] to eat and drink,
and to find enjoyment in their work.
I also perceived that this ability to
find enjoyment comes from God.
25 For no one can eat and drink
or experience joy apart from him.[1]
26 For to the one who pleases him, God
gives [a]wisdom, knowledge, and joy,
but to [b]the sinner, he gives the task
of amassing wealth—
only to give it to the one who pleases
God.
This task of the wicked is futile—like
chasing the wind!

A Time for All Events in Life

3 For everything there is an appointed
time,
and an appropriate [a]time for every
activity on earth:
2 A time to be born, [a]and a time to die;
a time to plant, and a time to uproot
what was planted;
3 a time to kill, and a time to heal;
a time to break down, and a time to
build up;

2:11 [2] Heb. *under the sun.*   2:12 [a] Eccl 1:17; 7:25   [b] Eccl 1:9   [1] Heb. *they have done it;* LXX, Syr. *he has done.*   2:13 [a] Eccl 7:11, 14, 19; 9:18; 10:10   2:14 [a] Prov 17:24; Eccl 8:1   [b] Ps 49:10; Eccl 9:2–3, 11   2:16 [a] Eccl 1:11; 4:16   2:17 [1] Or *I hated.*   2:18 [a] Ps 49:10   [1] Heb. *I hated all my toil for which I had toiled.*   2:22 [a] Eccl 1:3; 3:9   2:23 [a] Job 5:7; 14:1   [1] Heb. *all his days.*   2:24 [a] Eccl 3:12–13, 22; Isa 56:12; Luke 12:19; 1 Cor 15:32; [1 Tim 6:17]   [1] MT *that he should eat.*   2:25 [1] MT *more than I.*   2:26 [a] Job 32:8; Prov 2:6; Jas 1:5   [b] Job 27:16–17; Prov 28:8   3:1 [a] Eccl 3:17; 8:6   3:2 [a] Job 14:5; Heb 9:27

4 a time to [a]weep, and a time to laugh;
  a time to mourn, and a time to dance.
5 A time to throw [a]away stones, and a
    time to gather stones;
  a time to embrace, and a time to
    refrain from embracing;
6 a time to search, and a time to give
    something up as lost;
  a time to keep, and a time to throw
    away;
7 a time to rip, [a]and a time to sew;
  a time to keep silent, and a time to
    [b]speak.
8 A time to love, and a time to [a]hate;
  a time for war, and a time for peace.

Man Is Ignorant of God's Timing

9 What benefit can [a]a worker gain from
    his toil?
10 I have observed the burden
    that God has [a]given to people to keep
    them occupied.
11 God has made everything fit
    beautifully in its appropriate time,
  but he has also placed ignorance[1] in
    the human heart
  [a]so that people cannot discover what
    God has ordained,
  from the beginning to the end of
    their lives.

Enjoy Life in the Present

12 I have concluded that there is
    nothing [a]better for people
  than to be happy and to enjoy
    themselves as long as they live,
13 and also that [a]everyone should eat
    and drink, and find enjoyment in
    all his toil,
  for these things are a gift from God.

God's Sovereignty

14 I also know that whatever God does
    will endure forever;
  [a]nothing can be added to it, and
    nothing taken away from it.
  God has made it this way, so that
    men will fear him.
15 [a]Whatever exists now has already
    been, and whatever will be has
    already been;

for God will seek to do again what
  has occurred in the past.

The Problem of Injustice and Oppression

16 I saw [a]something else on earth:
  In the place of justice, there was
    wickedness,
  and in the place of fairness, there was
    wickedness.
17 I thought to myself, "[a]God will
    judge both the righteous and the
    wicked;
  for there is an appropriate time for
    every activity,
  and there is a time of judgment for
    every deed."
18 I also thought to myself, "It is for the
    sake of people,
  so God can clearly show them that
    they are like animals.
19 For the fate of humans and the fate
    of animals are the same:
  As one dies, so dies the other; both
    have the same breath.
  There is no advantage [a]for humans
    over animals,
  for both are fleeting.
20 Both go to the same place;
  both come from the dust,
  and to dust both return.
21 [a]Who really knows if the human
    spirit ascends upward,
  and the animal's spirit descends into
    the earth?"
22 [a]So I perceived there is nothing
    better than for people to enjoy
    their work
  because [b]that is their reward;
  [c]for who can show them what the
    future holds?[1]

Evil Oppression on Earth

4 So I again considered all the
  [a]oppression that continually
    occurs on earth.
  This is what I saw:[1]
  The oppressed were in tears, but no
    one was comforting them;
  no one delivers them from the power
    of their oppressors.

3:4 [a] Rom 12:15   3:5 [a] Joel 2:16; 1 Cor 7:5   3:7 [a] Amos 5:13   [b] Prov 25:11   3:8 [a] Prov 13:5; Luke 14:26   3:9 [a] Eccl 1:3
3:10 [a] Eccl 1:13   3:11 [a] Job 5:9; Eccl 7:23; 8:17; Rom 11:33   [1] Heb. *darkness*; perhaps *eternity, the future.*   3:12 [a] Eccl 2:3, 24
3:13 [a] Eccl 2:24   3:14 [a] Jas 1:17   3:15 [a] Eccl 1:9   3:16 [a] Eccl 5:8   3:17 [a] Gen 18:25; Ps 96:13; Eccl 11:9; [Matt 16:27; Rom 2:6–10;
2 Cor 5:10; 2 Thess 1:6–9]   3:19 [a] Ps 49:12, 20; 73:22; [Eccl 2:16]   3:21 [a] Eccl 12:7   3:22 [a] Eccl 2:24; 5:18   [b] Eccl 2:10   [c] Eccl
6:12; 8:7   [1] Heb. *what will be after him, afterward.*   4:1 [a] Job 35:9; Ps 12:5; Eccl 3:16; 5:8; Isa 5:7   [1] Heb. *and behold.*

2 [a]So I considered those who are dead
    and gone[1]
more fortunate than those who are
    still alive.
3 [a]But better than both is the one who
    has not been born
and has not seen the evil things that
    are done on earth.

Labor Motivated by Envy

4 Then I considered all the skillful
    work that is done:
Surely it is nothing more than
    competition between one person
    and another.
This also is profitless—like chasing
    the wind.
5 The fool folds his hands and does no
    work,
so [a]he has nothing to eat but his own
    flesh.
6 [a]Better is one handful with some rest
than two hands full of toil and
    chasing the wind.

Labor Motivated by Greed

7 So I again considered another futile
    thing on earth:
8 A man who is all alone with no
    companion—
he has no children nor siblings;
yet there is no end to all his toil,
and [a]he is never satisfied with
    [b]riches.
He laments, "For whom am I toiling
    and depriving myself of [c]pleasure?"
This also is futile and a burdensome
    task![1]

Labor Is Beneficial When Its Rewards Are Shared

9 Two people are better than one
because they can reap more benefit[1]
    from their labor.
10 For if they fall, one will help his
    companion up,
but pity the person who falls down
    and has no one to help him up.
11 Furthermore, if two lie down
    together, they can keep each other
    warm,

but how can one person keep warm
    by himself?
12 Although an assailant may
    overpower one person,
two can withstand him.
Moreover, a three-stranded cord is
    not quickly broken.

Labor Motivated by Prestige Seeking

13 A poor but wise youth is better than
    an old and foolish king
who no longer knows how to receive
    advice.
14 For he came out of prison to become
    king,
even though he had been born poor in
    what would become his kingdom.
15 I considered all the living who walk
    on earth,
as well as the successor who would
    arise in his place.
16 There is no end to all the people nor
    to the past generations,[1]
yet future generations will not
    rejoice in him.
This also is profitless and like
    chasing the wind.

Rash Vows

5 Be careful what you [a]do when you go
    to the temple of God;
draw near to listen rather [b]than to
    offer a sacrifice[1] like fools,
for they do not realize that they are
    doing wrong.
2 Do not be [a]rash with your mouth or
    hasty in your heart to bring up a
    matter [b]before God,
for God is in heaven and you are on
    earth!
Therefore, let your words be few.
3 Just [a]as dreams come when there are
    many cares,
so the rash vow of a fool occurs when
    there are many words.
4 [a]When you make a vow to God, do
    not delay in paying it.
For God takes no pleasure in fools:
[b]Pay what you vow!
5 It is [a]better for you not to vow
than to vow and not pay it.

4:2 [a]Job 3:17–18 [1]Heb. *the dead who had already died.* **4:3** [a]Job 3:11–22; Eccl 6:3; Luke 23:29 **4:5** [a]Prov 6:10; 24:33 **4:6** [a]Prov 15:16–17; 16:8 **4:8** [a]Prov 27:20; Eccl 5:10; [1 John 2:16] [b]Ps 39:6 [c]Eccl 2:18–21 [1]Heb. *misfortune, injustice, wrong.* **4:9** [1]Heb. *a good reward.* **4:16** [1]Heb. *those who were before them.* **5:1** [a]Exod 3:5; Isa 1:12 [b][1 Sam 15:22]; Ps 50:8; Prov 15:8; 21:27; [Hos 6:6] [1]I.e., the thank offering and free will offering. **5:2** [a]Prov 20:25 [b]Prov 10:19; Matt 6:7 **5:3** [a]Prov 10:19 **5:4** [a]Num 30:2; Deut 23:21–23; Ps 50:14; 76:11 [b]Ps 66:13–14 **5:5** [a]Prov 20:25; Acts 5:4

6 Do not let your [a]mouth cause you to
    sin,
  and do not tell the priest,[1,2] "It was a
    mistake!"
  Why make God angry at you
  so that he would destroy the work of
    your hands?
7 Just as there is futility in many
    dreams,
  so also in many words.
  Therefore, [a]fear God.

Government Corruption

8 If you [a]see the extortion of the poor,
  or the perversion of justice and
    fairness in the government,[1]
  do not be astonished by the matter.
  For the high [b]official is watched by a
    higher official,
  and there are higher ones over them!
9 The produce of the land is seized by
    all of them,
  even the king is served by the fields.[1]

Covetousness

10 The one who loves money will never
    be satisfied with money;
  he who loves wealth will never be
    satisfied with his income.
  This also is futile.
11 When someone's prosperity
    increases, those who consume it
    also increase;
  so what does its owner gain, except
    that he gets to see it with his eyes?
12 The sleep of the laborer is
    pleasant—whether he eats little or
    much—
  but the wealth of the rich will not
    allow him to sleep.

Materialism Thwarts Enjoyment of Life

13 [a]Here is a misfortune on earth[1] that I
    have seen:
  Wealth hoarded by its owner to his
    own misery.
14 Then that wealth was lost through
    bad luck;
  although he fathered a son, he has
    nothing left to give him.

15 Just [a]as he came forth from his
    mother's womb, naked will he
    return as he came,
  and he will take nothing in his hand
    that he may carry away from his
    toil.
16 This is another misfortune:
  Just as he came, so will he go.
  [a]What did he gain from toiling for
    the wind?
17 Surely, [a]he ate in darkness every day
    of his life,
  and he suffered greatly with sickness
    and anger.

Enjoy the Fruit of Your Labor

18 I have seen personally what is
    the only beneficial and
    appropriate course of action
  [a]for people:
  to eat and drink, and find enjoyment
    in all their hard work on earth
  during the few days of their life that
    God has given them,
  for this is their reward.
19 To [a]every man whom God has given
    wealth and possessions,
  he has also given him the ability
  to eat from them, to receive his
    reward, and to find enjoyment in
    his toil;
  these things are the [b]gift of God.
20 For he does not think[1] much about
    the fleeting days of his life
  because God keeps him preoccupied
    with the joy he derives from his
    activity.

Not Everyone Enjoys Life

6 Here is another misfortune that I
    have seen on earth,
  and it weighs heavily on people:
2 God gives a man riches, property,
    and wealth
  [a]so that he lacks nothing that his
    heart desires,
  [b]yet God does not enable him to
    enjoy[1] the fruit of his labor—
  instead, someone else enjoys it!
  This is fruitless and a grave
    misfortune.

5:6 [a] Prov 6:2 [1] MT *messenger;* LXX *God.* [2] Heb. *the messenger.* 5:7 [a] [Eccl 12:13] 5:8 [a] Eccl 3:16 [b] [Ps 12:5; 58:11; 82:1] [1] Heb. *in the province.* 5:9 [1] The king takes care of the security of the cultivated land, the king is in favor of a prosperous agricultural policy, or the king exploits the poor farmers. 5:13 [a] Eccl 6:1–2 [1] Heb. *under the sun.* 5:15 [a] Job 1:21; Ps 49:17; 1 Tim 6:7 5:16 [a] Eccl 1:3 5:17 [a] Ps 127:2 5:18 [a] Eccl 2:10; 3:22 5:19 [a] [Eccl 6:2] [b] Eccl 2:24; 3:13 5:20 [1] Heb. *to remember.* 6:2 [a] Job 21:10; Ps 17:14; 73:7 [b] Luke 12:20 [1] Heb. *to eat of it.*

3 Even if a man fathers a hundred
  children and lives many years,
even if he lives a long, long time, but
  cannot enjoy his prosperity—
even if he were to live forever—
  [a]I would [b]say, "A stillborn child is
  better off than he is."
4 Though the stillborn child came
  into the world for no reason and
  departed into darkness,
though its name is shrouded in
  darkness,
5 though it never saw the light of day
  nor knew anything,
yet it has more rest than that man—
6 if he should live a thousand years
  twice, yet does not enjoy his
  prosperity.
For both of them [a]die!
7 [a]All man's labor is for nothing more
  than to fill his stomach—
yet his appetite is never satisfied!
8 So what advantage does a wise man
  have over a fool?
And what advantage does a pauper
  gain by knowing how to survive?
9 It is better to be content with [a]what
  the eyes can see
than for one's heart always to crave
  more.
This continual longing is futile—like
  chasing the wind.

The Futile Way Life Works

10 Whatever has happened was
  [a]foreordained,
  [b]and what happens to a person was
  also foreknown.
It is useless for him to argue with
  God about his fate
because God is more powerful than
  he is.
11 The more one argues with words, the
  less he accomplishes.
How does that benefit him?
12 For no one knows [a]what is best for a
  person during his life—
during the few days of his fleeting
  life—
for they pass away like a shadow.

Nor can anyone tell him what
  the future will hold for him on
  earth.

Life Is Brief and Death Is Certain

7 A [a]good reputation[1] is better than
  precious perfume;
likewise, the day of one's death
  is better than the day of one's
  [b]birth.
2 It is better to go to a funeral
  than a feast.
For death is the destiny of every
  person,[1]
and the living should take this to
  [a]heart.
3 Sorrow is better than laughter
  because sober reflection is good [a]for
  the heart.
4 The heart of the wise is in the house
  of mourning,
but the heart of fools is in the house
  of merrymaking.

Frivolous Living Versus Wisdom

5 [a]It is better for a person to receive a
  rebuke from those who are wise
  than to listen to the song of fools.
6 [a]For like the crackling of
  quick-burning thorns[1] under a
  cooking pot,
so is the laughter of the fool.
This kind of folly also is useless.[2]

Human Wisdom Overturned
by Adversity

7 Surely oppression can turn [a]a wise
  person into a fool;
likewise, a bribe corrupts[1] the
  heart.
8 The end of a matter is better than
  its beginning;
likewise, patience is better than
  pride.
9 [a]Do not let yourself be quickly
  provoked,[1]
for anger resides in the lap of fools.
10 Do not say, "Why were the old days
  better than these days?"
for it is not wise to ask that.

6:3 [a]2 Kgs 9:35; Isa 14:19–20; Jer 22:19 [b]Job 3:16; Ps 58:8; Eccl 4:3 6:6 [a]Eccl 2:14–15 6:7 [a]Prov 16:26 6:9 [a]Eccl
11:9 6:10 [a]Eccl 1:9; 3:15 [b]Job 9:32; Isa 45:9; Jer 49:19 6:12 [a]Ps 102:11; Jas 4:14 7:1 [a]Prov 22:1 [b]Eccl 4:2 [1]Heb. *name*.
7:2 [a][Ps 90:12] [1]Heb. *all men, every man*. 7:3 [a][2 Cor 7:10] 7:5 [a]Ps 141:5; [Prov 13:18; 15:31–32] 7:6 [a]Eccl 2:2 [1]Twigs
from wild thorn bushes that were used as fuel for quick heat, but burned out quickly before a cooking pot could be
properly heated. [2]Or *fleeting*; Heb. *hevel*. 7:7 [a]Exod 23:8; Deut 16:19; [Prov 17:8, 23] [1]MT *to destroy*.
7:9 [a]Prov 14:17; Jas 1:19 [1]Heb. *Do not be hasty in your spirit to become angry*.

Wisdom Can Lengthen One's Life

11 Wisdom, like an inheritance, is a
good thing;
it benefits those who see the light of
day.
12 For wisdom provides [a]protection,
just as money provides protection.
But the advantage of knowledge is
this:
Wisdom preserves the [b]life of its
owner.

Wisdom Acknowledges God's Orchestration of Life

13 Consider the work of God:
For [a]who can make straight what he
has bent?
14 In times of prosperity be joyful,
but [a]in times of adversity[1] consider
this:
God has made one as well as the
other,
so that no one can discover what the
future holds.

Exceptions to the Law of Retribution

15 During [a]the days of my fleeting life I
have seen both of these things:
Sometimes a righteous person
dies prematurely in spite of his
righteousness,
and sometimes a wicked person lives
long in spite of his evil deeds.
16 So [a]do not be excessively righteous
[b]or excessively wise;
otherwise you might be disappointed.
17 Do not be excessively wicked and do
not be a fool;
otherwise you might die before your
time.
18 It is best to take hold of one warning
without letting go of the other
warning;
for the one who [a]fears God will follow
both warnings.

Wisdom Needed because No One Is Truly Righteous

19 [a]Wisdom gives a wise person more
protection[1]
than ten rulers in a city.

20 [a]For[1] there is not one truly righteous
person on the earth
who continually does good and never
sins.
21 Also, do not pay attention to
everything that people say;
otherwise, you might even hear your
servant cursing you.
22 For you know in your own heart
that you also have cursed others
many times.

Human Wisdom Is Limited

23 I have [a]examined all this by wisdom;
I said, "I am determined to
comprehend this"—but it was
beyond my grasp.[1]
24 Whatever [a]has happened is beyond
human understanding;
it is far deeper than anyone can
fathom.[1]

True Righteousness and Wisdom Are Virtually Nonexistent

25 I [a]tried to understand, examine, and
comprehend
the role of wisdom in the scheme of
things,
and to understand the stupidity of
wickedness and the insanity of folly.
26 I discovered this:
More bitter than death is the kind of
woman who is like [a]a hunter's snare;
her heart is like a hunter's net, and
her hands are like prison chains.
The man who pleases God escapes her,
but the sinner is captured by her.
27 The Teacher says:
I discovered this while trying to
discover [a]the scheme of things,
item by item.
28 What I have continually sought, I
have not found;
I have found only [a]one upright man
among a thousand,
but I have not found one upright
woman among all of them.
29 This alone have I discovered: God
made humankind upright,
but [a]they have sought many evil
schemes.

7:12 [a] Eccl 9:18 [b] Prov 3:18 **7:13** [a] Job 12:14 **7:14** [a] Deut 28:47 [1] Heb. *the day of evil.* **7:15** [a] Eccl 8:12–14 **7:16** [a] Prov 25:16;
Phil 3:6 [b] Rom 12:3 **7:18** [a] Eccl 3:14; 5:7; 8:12–13 **7:19** [a] Prov 21:22; Eccl 9:13–18 [1] Heb. *gives strength.* **7:20** [a] 1 Kgs 8:46;
2 Chr 6:36; Prov 20:9; Rom 3:23; 1 John 1:8 [1] Or *indeed.* **7:23** [a] Rom 1:22 [1] Or *but it eluded me*; Heb. *but it was far from
me.* **7:24** [a] Job 28:12; 1 Tim 6:16 [1] Heb. *It is deep, deep—who can find it?*; the repetition of "deep" emphasizes the degree of
incomprehensibility. **7:25** [a] Eccl 1:17 **7:26** [a] Prov 5:3–4 **7:27** [a] Eccl 1:1–2 **7:28** [a] Job 33:23 **7:29** [a] Gen 3:6–7

Human Government Demonstrates Limitations of Wisdom

8 Who is [a]a wise person? Who knows
[b]the solution to a problem?[1]
A person's wisdom brightens his
appearance and softens[2] his harsh
countenance.
2 Obey the king's command,[1]
because you took an oath [a]before
God to be loyal to him.
3 Do not rush out of the king's presence
in haste—[a]do not delay when the
matter is unpleasant,[1]
for he can do whatever he pleases.
4 Surely the king's authority is absolute;
no one can say to him, "What are you
doing?"
5 Whoever obeys his command will
not experience harm,
and a wise person knows the proper
time and procedure.
6 For there is a proper time and
procedure [a]for every matter,
for the oppression of the king is
severe upon his victim.
7 [a]Surely no one knows the future,
and no one can tell another person
what will happen.
8 Just as [a]no one has power over the
wind to restrain it,
so [b]no one has power over the day of
his death.
Just as no one can be discharged
during the battle,[1]
so wickedness cannot rescue the
wicked.
9 While applying my mind to
everything that happens in this
world,[1] I have seen all this:
Sometimes one person dominates
other people to their harm.

Contradictions to the Law of Retribution

10 Not only that, but I have seen the
wicked approaching[1] and entering
the temple,
and as they left the holy temple, they
boasted[2] in the city that they had
done so.
This also is an enigma.[3]
11 When [a]a sentence is not executed at
once against a crime,
the human heart is encouraged to do
evil.
12 Even [a]though a sinner might
[b]commit a hundred crimes and
still live a long time,
yet I know that it will go well with
God-fearing people—for they stand
in fear before him.
13 But it will not go well with the
wicked,
nor will they prolong their days like
a shadow,
because they do not stand in fear
before God.
14 Here is another enigma[1] that occurs
on earth:
Sometimes there are righteous
people who [a]get what the wicked
deserve,
and sometimes there are wicked
people who get what the
[b]righteous deserve.
I said, "This also is an enigma."

Enjoy Life in Spite of Its Injustices

15 So I recommend the enjoyment of
life,
for there is nothing better on earth
for a [a]person to do except to eat,
drink, and enjoy life.
So joy will accompany him in his toil
during the days of his life that God
gives him on earth.

Limitations of Human Wisdom

16 When I tried[1] to gain wisdom
and to observe the activity on earth—
even though it prevents anyone from
sleeping day or night—
17 then I discerned [a]all that God has
done:

8:1 [a] Prov 4:8–9; Acts 6:15   [b] Deut 28:50   [1] Heb. *a thing.*   [2] MT *changes;* LXX *hates.*   8:2 [a] Exod 22:11; 2 Sam 21:7; 1 Chr 29:24; Ezek 17:18; [Rom 13:5]   [1] MT *I obey the king's command.*   8:3 [a] Eccl 10:4   [1] Or *do not stand up for a bad cause.*
8:6 [a] Eccl 3:1, 17   8:7 [a] Prov 24:22; Eccl 6:12   8:8 [a] Ps 49:6–7; Job 14:5   [b] Deut 20:5–8   [1] Heb. *There is no discharge in war.*
8:9 [1] Heb. *that is done under the sun.*   8:10 [1] MT *they were buried, and they came, and from the place;* LXX *to the tombs they are brought, and from the place.*   [2] MT *and they were forgotten.*   [3] Heb. *hevel;* the sense is derived from the concept of breath, vapor, or wind that cannot be seen.   8:11 [a] Ps 10:6; 50:21; Isa 26:10   8:12 [a] Isa 65:20; [Rom 2:5–7]   [b] [Deut 4:40; Ps 37:11, 18, 19; Prov 1:32–33; Isa 3:10; Matt 25:34, 41]   8:14 [a] Ps 73:14   [b] Eccl 2:14; 7:15; 9:1–3   [1] Or *vanity* (again at the end of this verse); Heb. *hevel;* the sense is derived from the concept of breath, vapor, or wind that cannot be seen.
8:15 [a] Eccl 2:24   8:16 [1] Heb. *I applied my heart.*   8:17 [a] Job 5:9; Ps 73:16; Eccl 3:11; Rom 11:33

No one really comprehends what
    happens on earth.
Despite all human efforts to discover
    it, no one can ever grasp it.
Even if a wise person claimed that he
    understood,
he would not really comprehend[1] it.

Everyone Will Die

9 So I reflected on all this, attempting
    to clear it all up.
I concluded [a]that the righteous and
    the wise, as well as their works, are
    in the hand of God;
whether a person will be loved or
    hated—
no one knows what lies ahead.
2 Everyone [a]shares the same fate—
    the righteous and the wicked,
    the good and the bad,[1]
    the ceremonially clean and unclean,
    those who offer sacrifices and those
      who do not.
What happens to the good person,
    also happens to the sinner;
what happens to those who make
    vows, also happens to those who
    are afraid to make vows.
3 This is the unfortunate fact[1] about
    everything that happens on
    earth:
The same fate awaits everyone.
In addition to this, the hearts of all
    people are full of evil,
and there is folly in their hearts
    during their lives—then they die.

Better to Be Poor but Alive than Rich but Dead

4 But whoever is among the living has
    hope;
a live dog is better than a dead lion.
5 For [a]the living know that [b]they will
    die, but the dead do not know
    anything;
they have no further reward—and
    even the memory of them
    disappears.[1]
6 What they loved, as well as what they
    hated and envied, perished long
    ago,
and they no longer have a part in
    anything that happens on earth.

Life Is Brief, so Cherish Its Joys

7 Go, [a]eat your food with joy,
    and drink your wine with a happy
    heart,
because God has already approved
    your works.
8 Let your clothes always be white,
    and do not spare precious ointment
    on your head.
9 Enjoy life with your beloved wife[1]
    during all the days of your fleeting
    life
that God has given you on earth
    during all your fleeting days;[2]
[a]for that is your reward in life and in
    your burdensome work on earth.
10 [a]Whatever you find to do with your
    hands,
do it with all your [b]might,
because there is neither work nor
    planning nor knowledge nor
    wisdom in the grave,[1]
the place where you will
    eventually go.

Wisdom Cannot Protect against Seemingly Chance Events

11 Again, I observed this on the earth:
The race is not always won by the
    swiftest,
the battle is not always won by the
    strongest;
prosperity does not always belong to
    those who are the wisest;
wealth does not always belong to
    those who are the most discerning,
nor does success always come to
    those with the most knowledge—
for time [a]and [b]chance may overcome
    them all.
12 Surely, no [a]one knows his appointed
    time.
Like fish that are caught in a deadly[1]
    net and like birds that are caught
    in a snare—
just like them, all people are
    [b]ensnared at an unfortunate[2] time
    that falls upon them suddenly.

8:17 [1] Heb. *he cannot find, he does not find.*   **9:1** [a] Deut 33:3; Job 12:10; Eccl 8:14   **9:2** [a] Gen 3:17–19; Job 21:7; Ps 73:3, 12, 13; Mal 3:15   [1] MT *the good.*   **9:3** [1] Heb. *evil.*   **9:5** [a] Job 14:21; Isa 63:16   [b] Job 7:8–10; Eccl 1:11; 2:16; 8:10; Isa 26:14   [1] Heb. *for their memory is forgotten.*   **9:7** [a] Eccl 8:15   **9:9** [a] Eccl 2:10   [1] Heb. *the wife whom you love.*   [2] Sev. wss omit *all your fleeting days.*   **9:10** [a] [Col 3:17]   [b] Rom 12:11; Col 3:23   [1] Heb. *Sheol.*   **9:11** [a] Jer 9:23; Amos 2:14–15   [b] 1 Sam 6:9   **9:12** [a] Eccl 8:7   [b] Prov 29:6; Luke 12:20, 39; 17:26; 1 Thess 5:3   [1] Heb. *bad, evil;* the moral connotation hardly fits here.   [2] Heb. *evil.*

Most People Are not Receptive to Wise Counsel

13 This is what I also observed about wisdom on earth,[1]
and it is a great burden to me:
14 [a]There was once a small city with a few men in it,
and a mighty king attacked it, besieging it and building strong siege works against it.
15 However, a poor but wise man lived in the city,
and he could have delivered the city by his wisdom,
but no one listened to that poor man.
16 So I concluded that wisdom is better than [a]might,
but a poor man's wisdom is despised; no one ever listens to his advice.

Wisdom Versus Fools, Sin, and Folly

17 The words of the wise are heard in quiet,
more than the shouting of a ruler is heard among fools.
18 Wisdom is better than weapons of war,
but [a]one sinner can destroy much that is good.

10 One dead fly[1] makes the perfumer's ointment give off a rancid stench,
so a little folly can outweigh much wisdom.

Wisdom Can Be Nullified by the Caprice of Rulers

2 A wise person's good sense protects him,[1]
but a fool's lack of sense leaves him vulnerable.
3 Even when [a]a fool walks along the road he lacks sense
and shows everyone what a fool he is.
4 If the anger of the ruler flares up against you, [a]do not resign from your position,
for a [b]calm response can undo great offenses.
5 I have seen another misfortune on the earth:
It is an error a ruler makes.[1]

6 [a]Fools are placed in many positions of authority,
while wealthy men sit in lowly positions.
7 I have seen slaves [a]on horseback
and princes walking on foot like slaves.

Wisdom Is Needed to Avert Dangers in Everyday Life

8 [a]One who digs a pit may fall into it,
and one who breaks through a wall may be bitten by a snake.
9 One who quarries stones may be injured by them;
one who splits logs may be endangered by them.
10 If an iron axhead is blunt and a workman does not sharpen its edge,
he must exert a great deal of effort;
so wisdom has the advantage of giving success.
11 If the snake should bite before it is charmed,
the snake charmer[1] is in trouble.

Words and Works of Wise Men and Fools

12 The words of a wise person win him favor,
but [a]the words of a fool are self-destructive.
13 At the beginning his words are foolish
and at the end his talk is wicked madness,
14 yet [a]a fool keeps on babbling.
No one knows [b]what will happen;
who can tell him what will happen in the future?
15 The toil of a stupid fool wears him out,
because he does not even know the way to the city.

The Problem with Foolish Rulers

16 [a]Woe to you, O land, when your king is childish[1]
and your princes feast in the morning.

9:13 [1]Heb. *under the sun.* 9:14 [a]2 Sam 20:16–22 9:16 [a]Eccl 7:12, 19 9:18 [a]Josh 7:1–26; 2 Kgs 21:2–17 10:1 [1]Or *dead flies; Heb. flies of death.* 10:2 [1]Heb. *a wise man's heart is at his right hand;* an idiom for the place of protection. 10:3 [a]Prov 13:16; 18:2 10:4 [a]Eccl 8:3 [b]1 Sam 25:24–33; Prov 25:15 10:5 [1]Heb. *like an error that comes forth from the presence of a ruler.* 10:6 [a]Esth 3:1 10:7 [a]Prov 19:10; 30:22 10:8 [a]Ps 7:15; Prov 26:27 10:11 [1]Heb. *the master of the tongue.* 10:12 [a]Prov 10:32; Luke 4:22 10:14 [a][Prov 15:2]; Eccl 5:3 [b]Eccl 3:22; 8:7 10:16 [a]Isa 3:4–5; 5:11 [1]Or *a servant.*

17 Blessed are you, O land, when your
  king is the son of nobility,
  and your ªprinces feast at the proper
  time—with self-control and not in
  drunkenness.
18 Because of laziness the roof caves in,
  and because of idle hands[1] the house
  leaks.
19 Feasts are made for laughter,
  and ªwine makes life merry,
  but money is the answer for
  everything.
20 Do not curse a king even in your
  thoughts,
  and ªdo not curse the rich while in
  your bedroom;
  for a bird might report what you are
  thinking,
  or some winged creature might
  repeat your words.

Ignorance of the Future Demands Diligence in the Present

11 Send your grain ªoverseas,
  ᵇfor after many days you will get a
  return.
2 ªDivide your merchandise among
  seven ᵇor even eight investments,
  for you do not know what calamity
  may happen on earth.
3 If the clouds are full of rain, they will
  empty themselves on the earth,
  and whether a tree falls to the south
  or to the north, the tree will lie
  wherever it falls.
4 He who watches the wind will not sow,
  and he who observes the clouds will
  not reap.
5 Just as ªyou do not know the path of
  the wind
  ᵇor how the bones form in the womb
  of a pregnant woman,
  so you do not know the work of God
  who makes everything.
6 Sow your seed in the morning,
  and do not stop working until the
  evening;[1]
  for you do not know which activity
  will succeed—

whether this one or that one, or
  whether both will prosper equally.

Life Should Be Enjoyed because Death Is Inevitable

7 Light is sweet,
  and it is pleasant for a person ªto see
  the sun.[1]
8 So, if a man lives many years, let him
  ªrejoice in them all,
  but let him ᵇremember that the days
  of darkness[1] will be many—all that
  is about to come is obscure.[2]

Enjoy Life to the Fullest under the Fear of God

9 Rejoice, young man, while you are
  young,
  and let your heart cheer you in the
  days of your youth.
  ªFollow the impulses of your heart
  and the desires of your eyes,
  but know that ᵇGod will judge your
  motives and actions.
10 Banish emotional stress from your
  mind
  and ªput away pain from your body;
  ᵇfor youth and the prime of life are
  fleeting.[1]

Fear God Now because Old Age and Death Come Quickly

12 So ªremember your Creator in the
  days of your youth—
  before the difficult[1] days come
  and the years draw near ᵇwhen you
  will say, "I have no pleasure in
  them";
2 before the sun and the light of the
  moon and the stars grow dark,
  and the clouds disappear after the
  rain;
3 when those who keep watch over the
  house begin to tremble,
  and the virile men begin to stoop over,
  and the grinders begin to cease
  because they grow few,
  and those who look through the
  windows grow dim,

10:17 ª Prov 31:4; Isa 5:11   **10:18** [1] Heb. *lowering of hands.*   **10:19** ª Judg 9:13; Ps 104:15; Eccl 2:3   **10:20** ª Exod 22:28; Acts 23:5
11:1 ª Isa 32:20   ᵇ [Deut 15:10; Prov 19:17; Matt 10:42; 2 Cor 9:8; Gal 6:9–10; Heb 6:10]   **11:2** ª Ps 112:9; Matt 5:42; Luke 6:30;
[1 Tim 6:18–19]   ᵇ Eph 5:16   **11:5** ª John 3:8   ᵇ Ps 139:14   **11:6** [1] "Morning" and "evening" form a merism, a figure of speech
using two polar extremes to include everything in between.   **11:7** ª Eccl 7:11   [1] An idiom meaning to be alive.   **11:8** ª Eccl
9:7   ᵇ Eccl 12:1   [1] The onset of old age and the inevitable experience of death.   [2] Heb. *hevel*; the sense is derived from the
concept of breath, vapor, or wind that cannot be seen.   **11:9** ª Num 15:39; Job 31:7; Eccl 2:10   ᵇ Eccl 3:17; 12:14; [Rom 14:10]
11:10 ª 2 Cor 7:1; 2 Tim 2:22   ᵇ Ps 39:5   [1] Heb. *hevel.*   **12:1** ª 2 Chr 34:3; Prov 22:6; Lam 3:27   ᵇ 2 Sam 19:35   [1] Heb. *evil.*

4 and [a]the doors along the street are shut;
when the sound of the grinding mill[1] grows low,
and one is awakened by the sound of a bird,
and all their songs grow faint,

5 and they are afraid of heights and the dangers in the street;
the almond blossoms grow white,
and the grasshopper drags itself along,
and the caper berry[1] shrivels up[2]—
because man goes to [a]his eternal home,
and [b]the mourners go about in the streets—

6 before the silver cord is removed,
or the golden bowl is broken,
or the pitcher is shattered at the well,
or the water wheel is broken at the cistern—

7 and [a]the dust returns to the earth as it was,
[b]and the life's breath returns to God [c]who gave it.

Concluding Refrain: The Teacher Restates His Thesis

8 "Absolutely [a]futile!"[1] laments the Teacher,
"All these things are futile!"[2]

Concluding Epilogue: The Teacher's Advice Is Wise

9 Not only was the Teacher wise,
but he also taught knowledge to the people;
he carefully evaluated and arranged many proverbs.

10 The Teacher sought to find delightful words
and to write[1] accurately truthful sayings.

11 The words of the sages are like prods,[1]
and the collected sayings are like firmly fixed nails;
they are given by one shepherd.

Concluding Exhortation: Fear God and Obey His Commands

12 Be warned, my son, of anything in addition to them.
There is no end to the making of many books,
and [a]much study is exhausting to the body.

13 Having heard everything, I have reached this conclusion:
[a]Fear God and keep his commandments,
because this is the whole duty of man.

14 For [a]God will evaluate every deed,
including every secret thing, whether good or evil.

12:4 [a]2 Sam 19:35 [1]Where grain is ground into flour; the term is used as a double entendre, figuratively describing the loss of one's teeth at the onset of old age. 12:5 [a]Job 17:13 [b]Gen 50:10; Jer 9:17 [1]An aphrodisiac in the ancient Near East. [2]MT *burst*; LXX *is scattered*; Syr. *is broken up*; Sym. *are enjoyed*. 12:7 [a]Gen 3:19; Job 34:15; Ps 90:3 [b]Eccl 3:21 [c]Num 16:22; 27:16; Job 34:14; Isa 57:16; Zech 12:1 12:8 [a]Ps 62:9 [1]Heb. *futility of futilities*. [2]"Futile" (Heb. *hevel*) is repeated three times within the six Heb. words of this verse for emphasis. 12:10 [1]MT, LXX *what was written*; sev. medieval MSS *he wrote*. 12:11 [1]Or *goads*. 12:12 [a]Eccl 1:18 12:13 [a][Deut 6:2; 10:12]; Mic 6:8 12:14 [a]Eccl 11:9; Matt 12:36; [Acts 17:30–31; Rom 2:16; 1 Cor 4:5; 2 Cor 5:10]

SONG OF SOLOMON

The Song of Solomon is a love song written by Solomon and abounding in metaphors and oriental imagery. Historically it depicts the wooing and wedding of a shepherdess by King Solomon and the joys and heartaches of wedded love. Allegorically it pictures Israel as God's betrothed bride (Hos 2:19–20) and the church as the bride of Christ. As human life finds its highest fulfillment in the love of man and woman, so spiritual life finds its highest fulfillment in the love of God for his people and Christ for his church. The book reads like scenes in a drama with three main speakers: the bride (the Beloved), the king (Solomon), and a chorus (the maidens). The Hebrew title *Shir Hashirim* comes from 1:1, "Solomon's Most Excellent Love Song." The Greek title *Asma Asmaton* and the Latin *Canticum Canticorum* also mean "Song of Songs" or "The Best Song." The name *Canticles* ("Songs") is derived from the Latin title. Because Solomon is mentioned in 1:1, the book is also known as the Song of Solomon.

Title/Superscription

1 Solomon's[1] Most Excellent[2] Love [a]Song.

The Desire for Love

The Beloved to Her Lover:[1]

2 Oh, how I wish you would kiss me
   passionately!
   [a]For your lovemaking[2] is more
   delightful than wine.
3 The fragrance of your colognes is
   delightful;
   your name is like the finest perfume.
   No wonder the young women adore
   you!
4 [a]Draw me after you; let us hurry!
   May the king bring me into his[1]
   bedroom chambers!

The Maidens to the Lover:
[b]We will rejoice and delight in you;
we will praise[2] your love more than
wine.

The Beloved to Her Lover:
How rightly the young women adore
you!

The Country Maiden and the Daughters of Jerusalem

The Beloved to the Maidens:

5 I am dark but lovely, O maidens of
   Jerusalem,
   dark like the tents of Qedar,
   lovely like the tent curtains of
   Salmah.[1]
6 Do not stare at me because I am
   dark,
   for the sun has burned my skin.
   My brothers[1] were angry with me;
   they made me the keeper of the
   vineyards.
   Alas, my own [a]vineyard I could not
   keep!

The Shepherd and the Shepherdess

The Beloved to Her Lover:

7 Tell me, O you whom my heart loves,
   where do you pasture your sheep?
   Where do you rest your sheep during
   the midday heat?
   Tell me lest I wander around
   beside the flocks of your
   companions!

1:1 [a]1 Kgs 4:32 [1]Probably "which is written by Solomon," but could be "which is dedicated for Solomon" or "which is about/concerning Solomon." [2]Heb. *the song of songs*; could also mean a song composed of several songs.
1:2 [a]Song 4:10 [1]The headings identifying the speakers have been supplied; "The Lover" refers to a young man, while "the Beloved" refers to a young woman. Because the Song appears to be a collection of individual love songs, the same man and woman may not have been in mind. [2]LXX, Vg. *your breasts*. 1:4 [a]Hos 11:4; John 6:44; 12:32 [b]Phil 3:12–14 [1]Syr., Sym. *your chambers*. [2]Or *remember*; trad. *we will remember*.
1:5 [1]MT *Solomon*. 1:6 [a]Song 8:11–12 [1]Heb. *the sons of my mother*.

The Lover to His Beloved:

8 If ᵃyou do not know, O most beautiful
  of women,
simply follow the tracks of my
  flock,
and pasture your little lambs
beside the tents of the shepherds.

The Beautiful Mare and the Fragrant Myrrh

The Lover to His Beloved:

9 O ᵃmy beloved, you are like a mare
among Pharaoh's stallions.
10 Your cheeks are beautiful with
  ornaments;
ᵃyour neck is lovely with strings of
  jewels.
11 We will make for you gold
  ornaments
studded with silver.

The Beloved about Her Lover:

12 While the king was at his banqueting
  table,
my nard gave forth its fragrance.
13 My beloved is like a fragrant pouch
  of myrrh
spending the night¹ between my
  breasts.
14 My beloved is like a cluster of henna
  blossoms
in the vineyards of En Gedi.

Mutual Praise and Admiration

The Lover to His Beloved:

15 ᵃOh, how beautiful you are, my
  beloved!
Oh, how beautiful you are!
Your eyes are like doves!

The Beloved to Her Lover:

16 Oh, how ᵃhandsome you are, my
  lover!
Oh, how delightful¹ you are!
The lush foliage is our canopied
  bed;
17 the cedars are the beams of our
  bedroom chamber;
the pines are the rafters of our
  bedroom.

The Lily among the Thorns and the Apple Tree in the Forest

The Beloved to Her Lover:

2 I am a meadow flower¹ from Sharon,
a lily from the valleys.

The Lover to His Beloved:

2 Like a lily among the thorns,
so is my darling among the
  maidens.

The Beloved about Her Lover:

3 Like an apple tree among the trees of
  the forest,
so ᵃis my beloved among the young
  men.
I delight to sit in his shade,
and his fruit is sweet to my taste.¹

The Banquet Hall for the Lovesick

The Beloved about Her Lover:

4 He brought me¹ into the banquet hall,
and he looked² at me lovingly.
5 Sustain me with raisin cakes,
refresh me with apples,
for I am faint with love.

The Double Refrain: Embracing and Adjuration

6 His left hand ᵃis under my head,
and his right hand embraces me.

The Beloved to the Maidens:

7 I ᵃadmonish you, O maidens of
  Jerusalem,
by the gazelles and by the young
  does¹ of the open fields:
Do not awaken or arouse love until it
  pleases!

The Arrival of the Lover

The Beloved about Her Lover:

8 Listen! My lover is approaching!
Look! Here he comes,
leaping over the mountains,
bounding over the hills!
9 ᵃMy lover is like a gazelle or a young
  stag.
Look! There he stands behind our
  wall,

1:8 ᵃSong 5:9   1:9 ᵃSong 2:2, 10, 13; 4:1, 7; John 15:14   1:10 ᵃEzek 16:11   1:13 ¹Or *resting between my breasts.*
1:15 ᵃSong 4:1; 5:12   1:16 ᵃSong 5:10–16   ¹Probably physical attractiveness but could be personal character.
2:1 ¹Heb. *meadow-saffron*; trad. *rose.*   2:3 ᵃSong 4:16; Rev 22:1–2   ¹Heb. *my palate.*   2:4 ¹Sev. medieval MSS,
LXX, Syr. *Bring me!*   ²MT *his banner over me is love*; sev. medieval MSS, LXX *Set love before me!*
2:6 ᵃSong 8:3   2:7 ᵃSong 3:5; 8:4   ¹Trad. *hinds*; female deer, generally less than
three years old.   2:9 ᵃProv 6:5; Song 2:17

gazing through the window,
peering through the lattice.

The Season of Love and the Song of the Turtledove

The Lover to His Beloved:

10 My lover spoke to me, saying:
"Arise, my darling;
My beautiful one, come away with me!
11 Look! The winter has passed,
the winter rains are over and gone.
12 Blossoms have appeared in the land;
the time for pruning and singing has
come;
the voice of the turtledove is heard
in our land.
13 The fig tree has ripened its figs;
the vines have blossomed and give
off their fragrance.
Arise, come away my darling;
my beautiful one, come away
with me!"

The Dove in the Clefts of En Gedi

The Lover to His Beloved:

14 O my [a]dove, in the clefts of the rock,
in the hiding places of the mountain
crags,
[b]let me see your face;
let me hear your voice;
for your voice is sweet,
and your face is lovely.

The Foxes in the Vineyard

The Beloved to Her Lover:

15 Catch [a]the foxes for us,
the little foxes,
that ruin the vineyards—
for our vineyard is in bloom.

Poetic Refrain: Mutual Possession

The Beloved about Her Lover:

16 [a]My lover is mine and I am his;
he grazes among the lilies.

The Gazelle and the Rugged Mountains

The Beloved to Her Lover:

17 [a]Until the dawn arrives and the
shadows flee,
turn, my beloved—
be [b]like a gazelle or a young stag
on the mountain gorges.[1]

The Lost Lover Is Found

The Beloved about Her Lover:

3 All [a]night long on my bed
I longed for my lover.
I longed for him, but he never
appeared.[1]
2 "I will arise and look all around
throughout the town,
and throughout the streets and
squares;
I will search for my beloved."
I searched for him, but I did not find
him.
3 The night watchmen found me—[a]the
ones who guard the city walls.
"Have you seen my beloved?"[1]
4 Scarcely had I passed them by
when I found my beloved!
I held onto him tightly and would
not let him go
until I brought him to my mother's
[a]house,
to the bedroom chamber of the one
who conceived me.

The Adjuration Refrain

The Beloved to the Maidens:

5 I [a]admonish you, O maidens of
Jerusalem,
by the gazelles and by the young does
of the open fields:
"Do not awaken or arouse love until
it pleases!"

The Royal Wedding Procession

The Speaker:

6 [a]Who is this coming up from the
wilderness
like a column of smoke,
like a fragrant billow of myrrh and
frankincense,
every kind of fragrant powder[1] of
the traveling merchants?
7 Look! It is Solomon's portable
couch!
It is surrounded by sixty warriors,
some of Israel's mightiest warriors.
8 All of them are skilled with a sword,
well trained in the art of warfare.
Each has his sword at his side,
to guard against the terrors of the
night.

2:14 [a] Song 5:2 [b] Song 8:13   2:15 [a] Ps 80:13; Ezek 13:4; Luke 13:32   2:16 [a] Song 6:3   2:17 [a] Song 4:6 [b] Song 8:14 [1] Or perhaps *mountains of Bethar*; no known mountain range was called this.   3:1 [a] Isa 26:9 [1] LXX adds *I called him, but he did not answer me.*   3:3 [a] Song 5:7; Isa 21:6–8, 11, 12 [1] Heb. *the one whom my soul loves—have you seen* [him]; an emphatic Heb. construction.   3:4 [a] Song 8:2   3:5 [a] Song 2:7; 8:4   3:6 [a] Song 8:5 [1] Heb. *scent-powders, ground spice.*

9 King Solomon made a sedan chair for
   himself
of wood imported from Lebanon.
10 Its posts were made of silver;
   its back was made of gold.
Its seat was upholstered with purple
   wool;
its interior was inlaid with leather by
   the maidens of Jerusalem.
11 Come out, O maidens of Zion,
   and gaze upon King Solomon!
He is wearing the crown with which
   his mother crowned him
on his wedding day,
on the most joyous day of his life!

The Wedding Night: Praise of the Bride

The Lover to His Beloved:

4 Oh, [a]you are beautiful, my darling!
Oh, you are beautiful!
Your eyes behind your veil are like
   doves.
Your hair is like a [b]flock of female goats
descending from Mount Gilead.
2 [a]Your teeth are like a flock of newly
   shorn sheep
coming up from the washing place;[1]
each of them has a twin,
and not one of them is missing.
3 Your lips are like a scarlet thread;
[a]your mouth is lovely.
Your forehead behind your veil
is like a slice of pomegranate.
4 [a]Your neck is like the tower of David
built with courses of stones;
one thousand shields are hung on it—
all shields of valiant warriors.
5 [a]Your two breasts are like two fawns,
twins of the gazelle
grazing among the lilies.
6 Until the dawn arrives
and the shadows flee,
[a]I will go up to the mountain of myrrh
and to the hill of frankincense.
7 You are altogether beautiful, my
   darling!
There is no blemish in [a]you!

The Wedding Night: Beautiful as Lebanon

8 Come with me from Lebanon, my
   bride;

come with me from Lebanon.
Descend from the crest of
   Amana,
from the top of Senir, the summit
   of Hermon,
from the lions' dens
[a]and the mountain haunts of the
   leopards.
9 You have stolen my heart, my sister,
   my bride!
You have stolen my heart with one
   glance of your eyes,
with one jewel of your necklace.
10 How delightful is your love, my sister,
   my bride!
[a]How much better is your love than
   wine;
the fragrance of your perfume is
   better than any spice!
11 Your lips drip sweetness like the
   honeycomb, my bride;
[a]honey and milk are under your
   tongue.
The fragrance of your garments is
[b]like the fragrance of Lebanon.

The Wedding Night: The Delightful Garden

The Lover to His Beloved:

12 You are a locked garden, my sister,
   my bride;
you are an enclosed spring, a
   sealed-up fountain.
13 Your shoots are a royal garden full of
   pomegranates
with choice fruits:
henna with nard,
14 nard and saffron,
calamus and cinnamon with every
   kind of spice,
myrrh and aloes with all the finest
   spices.[1]
15 You are a garden spring,
a well of [a]fresh water flowing down
   from Lebanon.

The Beloved to Her Lover:

16 Awake, O north wind; come, O south
   wind!
Blow on my garden so that its
   fragrant spices may send out their
   sweet smell.

4:1 [a] Song 1:15; 5:12   [b] Song 6:5   4:2 [a] Song 6:6   [1] Or *the watering-hole, watering-place.*   4:3 [a] Song 6:7   4:4 [a] Song 7:4
4:5 [a] Prov 5:19; Song 7:3   4:6 [a] Song 2:17   4:7 [a] Song 1:15; Eph 5:27   4:8 [a] Deut 3:9; 1 Chr 5:23; Ezek 27:5
4:10 [a] Song 1:2, 4   4:11 [a] Prov 24:13–14; Song 5:1   [b] Gen 27:27; Hos 14:6–7   4:14 [1] Or *with all the
finest balsam trees.*   4:15 [a] Zech 14:8; John 4:10; 7:38

May my beloved come into his
 garden
and eat its delightful [a]fruit!

The Lover to His Beloved:

5 I [a]have entered my garden, O my
 [b]sister, my [c]bride;
I have gathered my myrrh with my
 balsam spice.
I have eaten my honeycomb and my
 honey;
I have drunk my wine and my milk!

The Poet to the Couple:

Eat, [d]friends, and drink!
Drink freely, O lovers!

The Trials of Love: The Beloved's Dream of Losing Her Lover

The Beloved about Her Lover:

2 I was asleep, but my mind[1] was
 dreaming.
Listen! My lover is knocking at [a]the
 door!

The Lover to His Beloved:

"Open for me, my sister, my darling,
my dove, my flawless one!
My head is drenched with dew,
my hair with the dampness of the
 night."

The Beloved to Her Lover:

3 "I have already taken off my
 robe—must I put it on again?
I have already washed my feet—must
 I soil them again?"
4 My lover thrust his hand[1] through
 the hole,
and my feelings[2] were stirred for him.
5 I arose to open for my beloved;
my hands dripped with myrrh—
my fingers flowed with myrrh
on the handles of the lock.
6 I opened for my beloved,
but my lover had already turned and
 gone away.
[a]I fell into despair when he departed.
I looked for him but did not find
 him;
I called him, but he did not
 answer me.

7 The watchmen found me as [a]they
 made their rounds in the city.
They beat me; they bruised me;
they took away my cloak, those
 watchmen on the walls!

The Triumph of Love: The Beloved Praises Her Lover

The Beloved to the Maidens:

8 I admonish you, O maidens of
 Jerusalem—
If you find my beloved, what will you
 tell him?
Tell him that I am lovesick!

The Maidens to the Beloved:

9 Why is [a]your beloved better than
 others,
O most beautiful of women?
Why is your beloved better than
 others,
that you would admonish us in this
 manner?

The Beloved to the Maidens:

10 My beloved is dazzling and ruddy;
he stands out in comparison to
 all other men.
11 His head is like the purest gold.
His hair is curly—black like a
 raven.
12 [a]His eyes are like doves by streams
 of water,
washed in milk, mounted like
 jewels.
13 His cheeks are like garden beds full
 of balsam trees yielding perfume.
His lips are like lilies dripping with
 drops of myrrh.
14 His arms are like rods of gold set
 with chrysolite.
His abdomen is like polished ivory
 inlaid with sapphires.
15 His legs are like pillars of marble set
 on bases of pure gold.
His appearance is like Lebanon,
 choice as its cedars.
16 His mouth is very sweet;
he is totally desirable.
This is my beloved!
This is my companion, O maidens of
 Jerusalem!

4:16 [a]Song 7:13   5:1 [a]Song 4:16   [b]Song 4:9   [c]Song 4:11   [d]Luke 15:7, 10; John 3:29   5:2 [a]Rev 3:20   [1]Heb. *my heart; represents emotions or thoughts.*   5:4 [1]Possibly a euphemism for the male sexual organ.   [2]Heb. *my inward parts, my intestines, my bowels.*   5:6 [a]Song 3:1   5:7 [a]Song 3:3   5:9 [a]Song 1:8; 6:1   5:12 [a]Song 1:15; 4:1

The Lost Lover Found

The Maidens to the Beloved:

6 Where has [a]your beloved gone,
O most beautiful among women?
Where has your beloved turned?
Tell us, that we may seek him with
you.

The Beloved to the Maidens:

2 My beloved has gone down to his
[a]garden,
to the flowerbeds of balsam spices,
to graze in the gardens,
and to gather lilies.

Poetic Refrain: Mutual Possession

The Beloved about Her Lover:

3 I am my lover's, and my lover [a]is
mine;
he grazes among the lilies.

The Renewal of Love

The Lover to His Beloved:

4 My darling, you are as beautiful as
Tirzah,
as lovely as Jerusalem,
as awe-inspiring as bannered armies.
5 Turn your eyes away from me—
they overwhelm me!
Your hair is [a]like a flock of goats
descending from Mount Gilead.
6 [a]Your teeth are like a flock of sheep
coming up from the washing;
each has its twin;
not one of them is missing.
7 [a]Like a slice of pomegranate
is your forehead behind your veil.
8 There may be sixty queens,
and eighty concubines,
and young [a]women without number.
9 But she is unique,
my dove, my perfect [a]one!
She is the special daughter of her
mother;
she is the favorite of the one who
bore her.
The maidens saw her and
complimented her;
the queens and concubines praised
her:

10 "Who is this who appears like the
dawn?
Beautiful as the moon,[1] bright as the
sun,
[a]awe-inspiring as the stars in
procession?"

The Return to the Vineyards

The Lover to His Beloved:

11 I went down [a]to the orchard of
walnut trees,
to look for the blossoms of the valley,
to see if the vines had budded
or if the pomegranates were in
bloom.
12 I was beside myself with joy!
There please give me your myrrh,[1]
O daughter of my princely people.[2]

The Love Song and Dance

The Lover to His Beloved:

13 Turn, turn, O Perfect One!
Turn, turn, that I[1] may stare at you!

The Beloved to Her Lover:
Why do you gaze upon the Perfect
One
like the dance of the Mahanaim?[2]

The Lover to His Beloved:

7 How beautiful are [a]your sandaled
feet,
O nobleman's daughter!
The curves of your thighs are like
jewels,
the work of the hands of a master
craftsman.
2 Your navel[1] is a round mixing bowl—
may it never lack mixed wine!
Your belly is a mound of wheat,
encircled by lilies.
3 [a]Your two breasts are like two fawns,
twins of a gazelle.
4 Your neck is like a tower made of
ivory.
[a]Your eyes are the pools in Heshbon
by the gate of Bath Rabbim.
Your nose is like the tower of
Lebanon
overlooking Damascus.

6:1 [a]Song 1:8; 5:9   6:2 [a]Song 4:16; 5:1   6:3 [a]Song 2:16; 7:10   6:5 [a]Song 4:1   6:6 [a]Song 4:2   6:7 [a]Song 4:3   6:8 [a]Song 1:3   6:9 [a]Song 2:14; 5:2   6:10 [a]Song 6:4   [1]Lit. *the white one.*   6:11 [a]Song 7:12   6:12 [1]MT *chariots;* LXX *There I will give my breasts to you!*   [2]Sev. mss, LXX, Vg. *Amminadab.*   6:13 [1]Heb. *we;* in ancient Near Eastern love literature, plural verbs and pronouns were often used in reference to individuals.   [2]A few mss, LXX *in/like the dances;* Sym. *in the injury.*   7:1 [a]Ps 45:13   7:2 [1]Or perhaps *vulva.*   7:3 [a]Song 4:5   7:4 [a]Song 4:4

5 Your head crowns you like Mount
  Carmel.
  The locks of your hair are like royal
    tapestries—
  the king is held captive in its
    tresses!
6 How beautiful you are! How lovely,
  O love, with your delights![1]

The Palm Tree and the Palm Tree Climber

The Lover to His Beloved:

7 Your stature is like a palm tree,
  and your breasts are like clusters of
    grapes.[1]
8 I want to climb the palm tree
  and take hold of its fruit stalks.
  May your breasts be like the clusters
    of grapes,
  and may the fragrance of your breath
    be like apples!
9 May your mouth be like the best
    wine,
  flowing smoothly for my beloved,
  gliding gently over our lips as we
    sleep together.[1]

Poetic Refrain: Mutual Possession

The Beloved about Her Lover:

10 I am my beloved's,
   and he [a]desires me!

The Journey to the Countryside

The Beloved to Her Lover:

11 Come, my beloved; let us go to the
     countryside;
   let us spend the night in the
     villages.
12 Let us rise early to go to the
     vineyards,
   to [a]see if the vines have budded,
   to see if their blossoms have
     opened,
   if the pomegranates are in
     bloom—
   there I will give you my love.
13 The [a]mandrakes send out their
     fragrance;
   over our door is every delicacy,
   both new and old, which I have
     stored up for you, my lover.

The Beloved's Wish Song

The Beloved to Her Lover:

8 Oh, how I wish you were my little
    brother,
  nursing at my mother's breasts;
  if I saw you outside, I could kiss you—
  surely no one would despise me!
2 I would lead you and bring you to my
    mother's [a]house,
  the one who taught me.[1]
  I would give you [b]spiced wine[2] to drink,
  the nectar of my pomegranates.[3]

Double Refrain: Embracing and Adjuration

The Beloved about Her Lover:

3 His left hand [a]is under my head,
  and his right hand embraces me.

The Beloved to the Maidens:

4 I [a]admonish you, O maidens of
    Jerusalem:
  "Do not arouse or awaken love until
    it pleases!"

The Awakening of Love

The Maidens about His Beloved:

5 Who is this coming up from the
    wilderness,
  leaning on her beloved?

The Beloved to Her Lover:

Under the apple tree I aroused you;
there your mother conceived you;
there she [a]who bore you was in labor
  of childbirth.

The Nature of True Love

The Beloved to Her Lover:

6 [a]Set me like a cylinder seal over your
    heart,
  like a signet[1] on your arm.
  For love is as strong as death;
  [b]passion is as unrelenting as Sheol.
  Its flames burst forth;
  it is a blazing flame.
7 Surging waters cannot quench love;
  floodwaters[1] cannot overflow it.
  [a]If someone were to offer all his
    possessions to buy love,
  the offer would be utterly despised.

7:6 [1] Some wss *daughter of delights* or *delightful daughter.*   7:7 [1] Or *clusters of figs.*   7:9 [1] MT *lips of those who sleep;* LXX *my lips and my teeth.*   7:10 [a] Song 2:16; 6:3   7:12 [a] Song 6:11   7:13 [a] Gen 30:14   8:2 [a] Song 3:4   [b] Prov 9:2   [1] LXX *I would bring you to the house of my mother, to the chamber of the one who bore me.*   [2] Or *wine, that is, spiced mixture;* i.e., ground herbs added to wine.   [3] MT *pomegranate.*   8:3 [a] Song 2:6   8:4 [a] Song 2:7; 3:5   8:5 [a] Song 3:6   8:6 [a] Isa 49:16; Jer 22:24; Hag 2:23   [b] Prov 6:34–35   [1] Lit. *cylinder-seal, seal.*   8:7 [a] Prov 6:35   [1] Heb. *rivers.*

The Brother's Plan and the Sister's Reward

The Beloved's Brothers:

8 We have a little sister,
and as yet she has no breasts.
What shall [a]we do for our sister
on the day when she is spoken for?

9 If she is a wall,
we will build on her a battlement of
  silver;
but if she is a door,
we will barricade her with boards of
  cedar.

The Beloved:

10 I was a wall,
and my breasts were like fortress
  towers.
Then I found favor[1] in his eyes.

Solomon's Vineyard and the Beloved's Vineyard

The Beloved to Her Lover:

11 Solomon had a vineyard at Baal
  Hamon;
[a]he leased out the vineyard to those
  who maintained it.
Each was to bring 1,000 shekels of
  silver for its fruit.

12 My vineyard, which belongs to me, is
  at my disposal alone.
The thousand shekels belong to you,
  O Solomon,
and 200 shekels belong to those who
  maintain it for its fruit.

Epilogue: The Lover's Request and His Beloved's Invitation

The Lover to His Beloved:

13 O you who stay in the gardens,
my companions are listening
  attentively for your
  voice;
[a]let me be the one to hear it!

The Beloved to Her Lover:

14 Make haste, my beloved!
Be like [a]a gazelle or a young
  stag
on the mountains of spices.

8:8 [a] Ezek 23:33   8:10 [1] Heb. *peace*; a wordplay is used here in that she found "favor" (Heb. *shalom*) in the eyes of Solomon (Heb. *shelomoh*, v. 11).   8:11 [a] Matt 21:33   8:13 [a] Song 2:14   8:14 [a] Rev 22:17, 20

ISAIAH

I saiah is like a miniature Bible. The first thirty-nine chapters (like the thirty-nine books of the Old Testament) are filled with judgment upon immoral and idolatrous people. Judah has sinned; the surrounding nations have sinned; the whole earth has sinned. Judgment must come, for God cannot allow such blatant sin to go unpunished forever. But the final twenty-seven chapters (like the twenty-seven books of the New Testament) declare a message of hope. The Messiah is coming as a Savior and a Sovereign to bear a cross and to wear a crown. Isaiah's prophetic ministry, spanning the reigns of four kings of Judah, covers at least forty years. *Yesha'yahu* and its shortened form *Yeshaiah* mean "Yahweh Is Salvation." This name is an excellent summary of the contents of the book. The Greek form in the Septuagint is *Hesaias,* and the Latin form is *Esaias* or *Isaias.*

Heading

1 Here is the [a]message about Judah and Jerusalem that was revealed to Isaiah son of Amoz during the [b]time when Uzziah, Jotham, Ahaz, and Hezekiah reigned over Judah.[1]

Obedience, not Sacrifice

2 [a]Listen, O heavens,
pay attention, O earth!
For the LORD speaks:
"I raised children, I brought them up,
but they have rebelled against me!
3 [a]An ox recognizes its owner,
a donkey recognizes where its owner
  puts its food;
but Israel [b]does not recognize me,
my people do not understand."
4 Beware sinful [a]nation,
the people weighed down by evil
  deeds.
They are offspring who do wrong,
children who do wicked things.
They have abandoned the LORD,
and rejected the Holy One of Israel.
They are alienated from him.
5 Why do you insist on being battered?
[a]Why do you continue to rebel?
Your head has a massive wound,
your whole heart is sick.

6 From the soles of your feet to your
  head,
there is no spot that is unharmed.
There are only bruises, cuts,
and open wounds.
They have not been cleansed or
  bandaged,
nor have they been treated with olive
  oil.
7 Your land is devastated,
[a]your cities burned with fire.
Right before your eyes your crops
are being destroyed by foreign
  invaders.
They leave behind devastation and
  destruction.
8 Daughter Zion is left isolated,
like [a]a hut in [b]a vineyard
or a shelter in a cucumber field;
she is a besieged city.[1]
9 [a]If the LORD of Heaven's Armies had
  not left us a few survivors,
we would have quickly been like
  [b]Sodom,
we would have become like
  Gomorrah.
10 Listen to the LORD's message,
you leaders [a]of Sodom!
Pay attention to our God's rebuke,
people of Gomorrah!

11 "Of what importance to me are your
    many ᵃsacrifices?"
  says the LORD.
  "I have had my fill of burnt sacrifices,
  of rams and the fat from steers.
  The blood of bulls, lambs, and goats
  I do not want.
12 When you enter my presence,
  do you actually think I want this—
  animals trampling on my courtyards?
13 Do not bring any more ᵃmeaningless[1]
    offerings;
  I consider your incense detestable!
  You observe new moon festivals,
    Sabbaths, and convocations,
  but I cannot tolerate sin-stained
    celebrations!
14 I hate your ᵃnew moon festivals and
    assemblies;
  they are ᵇa burden
  that I am tired of carrying.
15 When you spread out your hands in
    prayer,
  I look the other way;
  ᵃwhen you offer your many prayers,
  I do not listen
  because your hands are covered with
    blood.
16 ᵃWash! Cleanse yourselves!
  Remove your sinful deeds
  from my sight.
  ᵇStop sinning.
17 Learn to do what is right.
  Promote justice.
  Give the oppressed reason to
    celebrate.
  Take up the cause of the orphan.
  Defend the rights of the widow.

18 "Come, let's consider your options,"[1]
    says the LORD.
  "Though your sins have stained you
    like the color red,
  you can become white like snow;
  though they are ᵃas easy to see as
    ᵇthe color scarlet,
  you can become white like wool.
19 If you have a willing attitude and
    obey,
  then you will again eat the good
    crops of the land.

20 But if you refuse and rebel,
  you will be devoured by the sword."
  Know ᵃfor certain that the LORD has
    spoken.

Purifying Judgment

21 ᵃHow tragic that the once-faithful city
  has become a prostitute!
  She was once a center of justice;
  fairness resided in her—
  but now only ᵇmurderers!
22 Your[1] silver has become scum,
  ᵃyour beer is diluted with water.
23 ᵃYour officials are rebels,
  they ᵇassociate with thieves.
  All of them love bribery,
  and look for payoffs.
  They ᶜdo not take up the cause of the
    orphan
  or defend the rights of the widow.
24 Therefore, the ᵃSovereign LORD of
    Heaven's Armies,
  the Powerful One of Israel, says this:
  "Ah, I will seek vengeance against my
    adversaries,
  I will take revenge against my
    enemies.
25 I will attack you;
  I will purify your metal with ᵃflux.
  I will remove all your slag.
26 I will reestablish honest judges ᵃas in
    former times,
  wise advisers as in earlier days.
  Then ᵇyou will be called, 'The Just
    City,
  Faithful Town.'"
27 Zion will be freed by justice
  and her returnees by righteousness.
28 All rebellious sinners will be
    ᵃshattered,
  those who abandon the LORD will
    perish.
29 Indeed, they[1] will be ashamed of the
    sacred trees
  you find so desirable;
  you will be embarrassed because of
    the sacred orchards
  where you choose to worship.
30 For you will be like a tree whose
    leaves wither,
  like an orchard that is unwatered.

1:11 ᵃ[1 Sam 15:22]   1:13 ᵃMatt 15:9   [1]Or *worthless, vain.*   1:14 ᵃNum 28:11   ᵇLam 2:6   1:15 ᵃProv 1:28   1:16 ᵃJer 4:14   ᵇRom 12:9   1:18 ᵃIsa 43:26; Mic 6:2   ᵇPs 51:7; [Isa 43:25]; Rev 7:14   [1]Trad. *let us reason together.*   1:20 ᵃIsa 40:5; 58:14; Mic 4:4; [Titus 1:2]   1:21 ᵃIsa 57:3–9; Jer 2:20   ᵇMic 3:1–3   1:22 ᵃJer 6:28   [1]I.e., Jerusalem's.   1:23 ᵃHos 9:15   ᵇProv 29:24   ᶜIsa 10:2; Jer 5:28; Ezek 22:7; Zech 7:10   1:24 ᵃDeut 28:63   1:25 ᵃIsa 48:10; Ezek 22:19–22; Mal 3:3   1:26 ᵃJer 33:7–11   ᵇIsa 33:5; Zech 8:3   1:28 ᵃJob 31:3; Ps 9:5; [Isa 66:24; 2 Thess 1:8–9]   1:29 [1]Some wss *you.*

31 The powerful will be like a thread of
  yarn,
  [a]their deeds like a spark;
  both will burn together,
  and no one will put out the [b]fire.

The Future Glory of Jerusalem

2 Here is the message about Judah and
  Jerusalem that was revealed to Isaiah
son of Amoz.

2 In future days
  the mountain of the LORD's temple
    will endure[1]
  as the most important of mountains
  and will be the most prominent of
    hills.
  All the nations will stream to [a]it;
3 many peoples will [a]come and say,
  "Come, let us go up to the LORD's
    mountain,
  to the temple of the God of Jacob,
  so he can teach us his requirements,
  and we can follow his standards."
  [b]For Zion will be the center for moral
    instruction;
  the LORD's message will issue from
    Jerusalem.
4 He will judge disputes between
    nations;
  he will settle cases for many peoples.
  They will beat their swords into
    plowshares,
  and their spears into pruning hooks.
  Nations will not take up the sword
    against other nations,
  and they will no longer train for war.
5 O descendants of Jacob,
  come, let us [a]walk in the LORD's
    guiding light.

The Lord's Day of Judgment

6 Indeed, O LORD, you have abandoned
    your people,
  the descendants of Jacob.
  For diviners from the east are
    everywhere;[1]
  they consult omen [a]readers like the
    Philistines do.
  Plenty of foreigners are around.

7 Their land is full of gold and silver;
  there is no end to [a]their wealth.
  Their land is full of horses;
  there is no end to their chariots.
8 Their land is full of worthless idols;
  they worship [a]the product of their
    own hands,
  what their own fingers have
    fashioned.
9 Men bow down to them in homage,
  they lie flat on the ground in worship.
  Don't spare them!
10 Go [a]up into the rocky cliffs,
  hide in the ground.
  Get away from the dreadful
    judgment of the LORD,[1]
  from his royal splendor!
11 Proud men will be brought [a]low,
  arrogant men will be humiliated;
  the LORD alone will be exalted
  [b]in that day.
12 Indeed, the LORD of Heaven's Armies
    has planned a day of judgment
  for all the high and mighty;
  for all who are proud—they will be
    humiliated;
13 for all [a]the cedars of Lebanon
  that are so high and mighty,
  for all the oaks of Bashan,
14 for all the tall mountains,
  [a]for all the high hills,
15 for every high tower,
  for every fortified wall,
16 for all the large ships,[1]
  [a]for all the impressive ships.
17 Proud men will be humiliated,
  arrogant men will be brought low;
  the LORD alone will be exalted
  in that day.
18 The worthless idols will be
    completely eliminated.
19 They will go into [a]caves in the rocky
    cliffs
  and into holes in the ground
  trying to [b]escape the dreadful
    judgment of the LORD
  and his royal splendor,
  when he rises up [c]to terrify the earth.
20 At that time men will throw
  their silver and gold idols,

1:31 [a]Ezek 32:21 [b]Isa 66:24; Matt 3:12; Mark 9:43 2:2 [a]Mic 4:1 [1]Or be established. 2:3 [a]Jer 50:5; [Zech 8:21–23; 14:16–21] [b]Luke 24:47 2:5 [a]Eph 5:8 2:6 [a]Deut 18:14 [1]Heb. they are full from the east. 2:7 [a]Deut 17:16; Isa 30:16; 31:1; Mic 5:10 2:8 [a]Isa 40:19–20; Jer 2:28 2:10 [a]Isa 2:19, 21; Rev 6:15–16 [1]Heb. from the dread of the LORD; get away is supplied. 2:11 [a]Prov 16:5; Isa 5:15 [b]Hos 2:16 2:13 [a]Isa 14:8; Zech 11:1–2 2:14 [a]Isa 30:25 2:16 [a]1 Kgs 10:22; Isa 23:1, 14; 60:9 [1]Heb. the ships of Tarshish; probably referring to large ships either made in or capable of traveling to the distant western port of Tarshish. 2:19 [a]Hos 10:8; [Rev 9:6] [b][2 Thess 1:9] [c]Ps 18:7; Isa 2:21; 13:13; 24:1, 19, 20; Hag 2:6–7; Heb 12:26

which they made for themselves to
  worship,
into the caves where rodents and
  bats live,
21 so they themselves can go into the
  crevices of the rocky cliffs
and the openings under the rocky
  overhangs,
trying to escape the dreadful
  judgment of the LORD
and his royal splendor,
when he rises up to terrify the earth.[1]
22 [a]Stop trusting in human beings,
  whose life's [b]breath is in their
  nostrils.
For why should they be given special
  consideration?

A Coming Leadership Crisis

3 Look, [a]the Sovereign LORD of
  Heaven's Armies
is about to remove from Jerusalem
  and Judah
every source of security, including[1]
all the food and water,
2 [a]the mighty men and warriors,
  judges and prophets,
  omen readers and leaders,
3 captains of groups of 50,
  the respected citizens,
advisers and those skilled in magical
  arts,
and those who know incantations.
4 The LORD says, "I will make [a]youths
  their officials;
malicious young men will rule over
  them.
5 The people will treat each other
  harshly;
men will oppose each other;
  neighbors will fight.
Youths will proudly defy the elderly
and riffraff will challenge those who
  were once respected.
6 Indeed, a man will grab his brother
right in his father's house and say,
'You own a coat—
you be our leader!
This heap of ruins will be under your
  control.'
7 At that time the brother will shout,

'I am no doctor,
I have no food or coat in my house;
don't make me a leader of the
  people!'"
8 [a]Jerusalem certainly stumbles,
  Judah falls,
for their words and their actions
  offend the LORD;
they rebel against his royal
  authority.[1]
9 The look on their faces testifies to
  their guilt;
like the people of [a]Sodom they
  openly boast of their sin.
Woe to them!
For they bring disaster on
  themselves.
10 Tell the innocent it will go well with
  them,
[a]for they will be rewarded for what
  they have done.
11 Woe to the wicked sinners!
For they will get exactly what they
  deserve.
12 Oppressors treat my people cruelly;
creditors rule over them.[1]
My people, your leaders mislead you;
they give you confusing directions.
13 The LORD takes his position [a]to
  judge;
he stands up to pass sentence on his
  people.[1]
14 The LORD comes to pronounce
  judgment
on [a]the leaders of his people and
  their officials.
He says, "It is you who have ruined
  the vineyard!
You have stashed in your houses
what you have stolen from the
  poor.
15 Why do you [a]crush my people
and grind the faces of the poor?"
The Sovereign LORD of Heaven's
  Armies has spoken.

Washing Away Impurity

16 The LORD says,
"The women of Zion are proud.
They walk with their heads high
and flirt with their eyes.

2:21 [1] Or *land.*   2:22 [a] Ps 146:3; Jer 17:5   [b] Job 27:3   3:1 [a] Lev 26:26   [1] Heb. *support and support;* the masc. and fem. forms
of the noun are placed side-by-side to emphasize completeness.   3:2 [a] 2 Kgs 24:14; Isa 9:14–15; Ezek 17:12–13   3:4 [a] Eccl
10:16   3:8 [a] 2 Chr 36:16–17; Mic 3:12   [1] Heb. *to rebel* [against] *the eyes of his majesty.*   3:9 [a] Gen 13:13; Isa 1:10–15
3:10 [a] Ps 128:2   3:12 [1] Heb. *My people, his oppressors, he deals severely, and women rule over them.*
3:13 [a] Isa 66:16; Hos 4:1; Mic 6:2   [1] MT *nations.*   3:14 [a] Matt 21:33   3:15 [a] Mic 3:2–3

They skip along
and the jewelry on their ankles
    jingles.[1]
17 So the Lord will [a]afflict the foreheads
    of Zion's women with skin
    diseases;
  the LORD will [b]make the front of
    their heads bald."

[18]At that time the Lord will remove their beautiful ankle jewelry, neck ornaments, crescent-shaped [a]ornaments, [19]earrings, bracelets, veils, [20]headdresses, ankle ornaments, sashes, sachets, amulets, [21]rings, nose rings, [22]festive dresses, robes, shawls, purses, [23]garments, vests, head coverings, and gowns.[1]

24 A putrid stench will replace the
    smell of spices,
  a rope will replace a belt,
  [a]baldness will replace braided locks
    of hair,
  a sackcloth garment will replace a
    fine robe,
  and a prisoner's brand will replace
    beauty.
25 Your men will fall by the sword,
  your strong men will die in battle.
26 Her gates will mourn and lament;
  deprived of [a]her people, she will sit
    on the ground.

4 Seven women will grab hold of
  one man at that time.
  They will say, "We will [a]provide [b]our
    own food,
  we will provide our own clothes;
  but let us belong to you—
  take away our shame!"

Cleansing and Protection from the Lord

2 At that time
  [a]the crops given by the LORD will
    bring admiration and honor;
  the produce of the land will be a
    source of pride and delight
  to those who remain in Israel.
3 Those remaining in Zion, those left
    in Jerusalem,

[a]will be called "holy,"
  all in Jerusalem who are [b]destined to
    live.[1]
4 At that time [a]the Lord will wash the
    excrement from Zion's women,
  he will rinse the bloodstains from
    Jerusalem's midst,
  as he comes to judge
  and to bring devastation.
5 Then the LORD will [a]create
  over all Mount Zion
  and over its convocations
  a cloud and smoke by day
  and a bright flame of fire by night;
  indeed a canopy will accompany [b]the
    LORD's glorious presence.
6 By day it will be a shelter to provide
    shade from the heat,
  as well as safety and protection from
    the heavy downpour.

A Love Song Gone Sour

5 I will sing to my love—
  [a]a song to my lover about his
    vineyard.
  My love had a vineyard
  on a fertile hill.
2 He built a hedge around it, removed
    its stones,
  and planted a vine.
  He built a tower in the middle of it
  and constructed a winepress.
  He waited for it to produce edible
    grapes,
  but it produced [a]sour ones instead.[1]
3 So now, residents of Jerusalem,
  people of Judah,
  you [a]decide between me and my
    vineyard!
4 What more can [a]I do for my vineyard
  beyond what I have already done?
  When I waited for it to produce
    edible grapes,
  why did it produce sour ones
    instead?
5 Now [a]I will inform you
  what I am about to do to my
    vineyard:
  I will remove its hedge and turn it
    into pasture,

3:16 [1]Heb. *and with their feet they jingle.* **3:17** [a]Deut 28:27 [b]Jer 13:22 **3:18** [a]Judg 8:21, 26 **3:23** [1]The precise meaning of many of the words in this list is uncertain. **3:24** [a]Isa 22:12; Ezek 27:31; Amos 8:10 **3:26** [a]Jer 14:2; Lam 1:4 **4:1** [a]2 Thess 3:12 [b]Luke 1:25 **4:2** [a]Isa 12:1–6; [Jer 23:5]; Zech 3:8 **4:3** [a]Isa 60:21 [b]Phil 4:3 [1]Heb. *all who are written down for life in Jerusalem.* **4:4** [a]Mal 3:2–3 **4:5** [a]Exod 13:21–22; Num 9:15–23 [b]Zech 2:5 **5:1** [a]Ps 80:8; Jer 2:21; Matt 21:33; Mark 12:1; Luke 20:9 **5:2** [a]Deut 32:6 [1]Heb. *wild grapes.* **5:3** [a][Rom 3:4] **5:4** [a]2 Chr 36:15–16; Jer 2:5; 7:25–26; Mic 6:3; Matt 23:37 **5:5** [a]2 Chr 36:19; Ps 80:12; 89:40–41

I will break its wall and allow animals
  to graze there.
6 I will make it a [a]wasteland;
  no one will prune its vines or hoe its
    ground,
  and thorns and [b]briers will grow
    there.
  I will order the clouds
  not to drop any rain on it.
7 Indeed, Israel is the vineyard of the
    LORD of Heaven's Armies,
  the people of Judah are the cultivated
    place in which he took delight.
  He waited for justice, but look what
    he got—disobedience!
  He waited for fairness, but look what
    he got—cries for help!

Disaster Is Coming

8 Beware, those who accumulate
    [a]houses,
  who also accumulate field after field
  until there is no land left,
  and you are the only landowners
    remaining within the land.
9 The LORD of Heaven's Armies told
    me this:
  "Many houses will [a]certainly become
    desolate,
  large, impressive houses will have no
    one living in them.
10 Indeed, a large vineyard[1] will produce
    just a few [a]gallons,[2]
  and enough seed to yield several
    bushels will produce less than a
    bushel."
11 [a]Beware, those who get up early to
    drink beer,
  those who keep drinking long after
    dark
  until they are intoxicated with wine.
12 They have stringed instruments,
    tambourines, flutes,
  and wine at [a]their parties.
  So [b]they do not recognize what the
    LORD is doing,
  they do not perceive what he is
    bringing about.
13 [a]Therefore my people will be
    deported

because of their lack of
  [b]understanding.
  Their leaders will have nothing to eat,
  their masses will have nothing to
    drink.
14 So Death will open up its throat,
  and open wide its mouth;
  Zion's dignitaries and masses will
    descend into it,
  including those who revel and
    celebrate within her.
15 Men will be humiliated,
  they will be brought low;
  the proud will be brought low.
16 The LORD of Heaven's Armies will be
    [a]exalted when he punishes,
  the holy God's authority will be
    recognized when he judges.
17 Lambs will graze as if in [a]their
    pastures,
  amid the ruins the rich sojourners
    will graze.[1]
18 Beware, those who pull evil along
    using cords of emptiness are as
    good as dead,
  who pull sin as with cart ropes.[1]
19 [a]They say, "Let him hurry, let him act
    quickly,
  so we can see;
  let the plan of the Holy One of Israel
    take shape and come to pass,
  then we will know it!"
20 Beware, those who call evil good and
    good evil,
  who turn darkness into light and
    light into darkness,
  who turn bitter into sweet and sweet
    into bitter.
21 Beware, those who think they are
    [a]wise,
  those who think they possess
    understanding.
22 Beware, those who are champions at
    drinking,
  who display great courage when
    mixing strong drinks.
23 They [a]pronounce the guilty innocent
    for a payoff,
  they ignore the just cause of the
    innocent.

5:6 [a] 2 Chr 36:19–21   [b] Isa 7:19–25; Jer 25:11   5:8 [a] Jer 22:13–17; Mic 2:2; Hab 2:9–12   5:9 [a] Isa 22:14   5:10 [a] Ezek 45:11   [1] Heb. *a ten-yoke vineyard*; a unit of square measure of unknown size that would take ten teams of oxen to plow in a certain period of time.   [2] Heb. *one bath*.   5:11 [a] Prov 23:29–30; Eccl 10:16–17; Isa 5:22   5:12 [a] Amos 6:5   [b] Job 34:27; Ps 28:5   5:13 [a] 2 Kgs 24:14–16   [b] Isa 1:3; 27:11; Hos 4:6   5:16 [a] Isa 2:11   5:17 [a] Isa 10:16   [1] MT *and ruins, fatlings, resident foreigners, will eat.*   5:18 [1] MT *Woe to those who pull evil with the ropes of emptiness, and, as [with] ropes of a cart, sin.*   5:19 [a] Jer 17:15; Amos 5:18   5:21 [a] Prov 3:7; Rom 1:22; 12:16; [1 Cor 3:18–20]   5:23 [a] Exod 23:8; Prov 17:15; Isa 1:23; Mic 3:11; 7:3

24 Therefore, [a]as flaming fire devours straw
and dry grass disintegrates in [b]the flames,
so their root will rot,
and their flower will blow away like dust.
For they have rejected the law of the LORD of Heaven's Armies,
they have spurned the commands of the Holy One of Israel.
25 So [a]the LORD is furious with his people;
[b]he lifts his hand and strikes them.
The mountains shake,
and corpses lie like manure in the middle of the streets.
Despite all this, his anger does not subside,
and his hand is ready to strike again.[1]
26 He lifts a signal flag for a distant nation,[1]
[a]he [b]whistles for it to come from [c]the far regions of [d]the earth.
Look, they come quickly and swiftly.
27 None tire or stumble,
they don't stop to nap or sleep.
They don't loosen their belts
or unstrap their sandals to rest.
28 [a]Their arrows are sharpened,
and all their bows are prepared.
The hooves of their horses are hard as flint,
and their chariot wheels are like a windstorm.
29 Their roar is like a lion's;
they roar like young lions.
They growl and seize their prey;
they drag it away and no one can come to the rescue.
30 At that time they will growl over their prey,
it will sound like sea waves crashing against rocks.
One will look [a]out over the land and see the darkness of disaster,
clouds will turn the light into darkness.

Isaiah's Commission

6 In the year of [a]King Uzziah's death, I [b]saw the Lord seated on a high, elevated throne. The hem of his robe filled the temple. [2]Seraphs[1] stood over him; each one had six wings. [a]With two wings they covered their faces, with two they covered their feet, and they used the remaining two to fly. [3]They called out to one another, "[a]Holy, holy, holy is [b]the LORD of Heaven's Armies! His majestic splendor fills the entire earth!" [4]The sound of their voices shook the door frames, and the temple was filled with smoke.

[5]I said, "Woe to me! I am destroyed, for my lips are contaminated by [a]sin, and I live among people whose lips are contaminated by sin. My eyes have seen the king, the LORD of Heaven's Armies." [6]But [a]then one of the seraphs flew toward me. In his hand was a hot coal he had taken from the altar with tongs. [7]He [a]touched my mouth with it and said, "Look, this coal has touched your lips. Your evil is removed; your sin is forgiven." [8]I heard the voice of the Lord say, "Whom will I send? Who will go on our behalf?" I answered, "Here I am, send me!" [9]He said, "Go and [a]tell these people:

"'Listen continually, but don't understand.
Look continually, but don't perceive.'
10 Make [a]the hearts of these people calloused;
make their ears deaf and their eyes blind.
[b]Otherwise they might see with their eyes and hear with their ears,
their hearts might understand
and they might repent and be healed."
11 I replied, "How long, Lord?" He said,
"[a]Until cities are in ruins and unpopulated,
and houses are uninhabited,
and the land is ruined and devastated,
12 and [a]the LORD has sent the people off to a distant place,
and the very heart of the land is completely abandoned.

5:24 [a]Exod 15:7 [b]Job 18:16   5:25 [a]2 Kgs 22:13, 17; Isa 66:15 [b]Ps 18:7; Isa 64:3; Jer 4:24; Nah 1:5 [1]Heb. *in all this his anger is not turned, and still his hand is outstretched.*   5:26 [a]Isa 11:10, 12 [b]Isa 7:18; Zech 10:8 [c]Mal 1:11 [d]Joel 2:7 [1]MT *for nations from a distance.*   5:28 [a]Jer 5:16   5:30 [a]Isa 8:22; Jer 4:23–28; Joel 2:10; Luke 21:25–26   6:1 [a]2 Kgs 15:7; 2 Chr 26:23; Isa 1:1 [b]John 12:41; Rev 4:2–3; 20:11   6:2 [a]Ezek 1:11 [1]Lit. *burning ones*; perhaps suggesting a fiery or serpentine appearance.   6:3 [a]Rev 4:8 [b]Num 14:21; Ps 72:19   6:5 [a]Exod 6:12, 30   6:6 [a]Rev 8:3   6:7 [a]Jer 1:9; Dan 10:16   6:9 [a]Isa 43:8; Matt 13:14; Mark 4:12; Luke 8:10; John 12:40; Acts 28:26; Rom 11:8   6:10 [a]Ps 119:70; Mark 6:1–6; Acts 7:51; Rom 10:1–4 [b]Jer 5:21   6:11 [a]Mic 3:12   6:12 [a]2 Kgs 25:21; Isa 5:9

[13] Even if only a tenth of [a]the people
  remain in the land,
  it will again be destroyed,
  like one of the large sacred trees or
  an Asherah pole,
  when a sacred pillar on a high place[1]
  is thrown down.[2]
  That sacred pillar symbolizes the
  special chosen family."

Ahaz Receives a Sign

7 During the reign of [a]Ahaz son of Jotham, son of Uzziah, king of Judah, King Rezin of Syria and King Pekah son of Remaliah of Israel marched up to Jerusalem to do battle, but they were unable to prevail against [b]it. [2]It was reported to the family of David, "Syria has allied with Ephraim." They and their people were emotionally shaken, just as the trees of the forest shake before the wind. [3]So the LORD told Isaiah, "Go out with your son Shear Jashub[1] and meet Ahaz at the end of the conduit of the upper pool that is located on the road to the field where they wash and dry cloth. [4]Tell him, 'Make sure you stay [a]calm! Don't be afraid. Don't be intimidated by these two stubs of smoking logs, or by the raging anger of Rezin, Syria, and the son of Remaliah. [5]Syria has plotted with Ephraim and the son of Remaliah to bring about your demise. [6]They say, "Let's attack Judah, terrorize it, and conquer it. Then we'll set up the son of Tabeel as its king." [7]For this reason the Sovereign LORD says:

"'[a]It will not take place;
  it will not happen.
[8] [a]For Syria's leader is Damascus,
  and the leader of Damascus is Rezin.
  Within 65 years Ephraim will no
  longer exist as a nation.
[9] Ephraim's leader is Samaria,
  and Samaria's leader is the son of
  Remaliah.
  [a]If your faith does not remain firm,
  then you will not remain secure.'"

[10]The LORD again spoke to Ahaz: [11]"[a]Ask for a confirming sign from the LORD your God. You can even ask for something miraculous." [12]But Ahaz responded, "I don't want to ask; I don't want to put the LORD to a test." [13]So Isaiah replied, "Pay attention, family of David. Do you consider it too insignificant to try the patience of men? Is that why you are also trying the patience of my God? [14]For this reason the Lord himself will give you a confirming sign.[1] [a]Look, this young [b]woman[2] is about to conceive and will give birth to [c]a son. You, young woman, will name him Immanuel. [15]He will eat sour milk and honey, which will help him know how to reject evil and choose what is right. [16]Here is why this will be so: [a]Before the child knows how to reject evil and choose what is right, the land whose [b]two kings you fear will be desolate. [17]The LORD will bring on you, your people, and your [a]father's family a time unlike any since [b]Ephraim departed from Judah—the king of Assyria!"

[18]At that time the LORD [a]will whistle for flies from the distant streams of Egypt and for bees from the land of Assyria. [19]All of [a]them will come and make their home in the ravines between the cliffs and in the crevices of the cliffs, in all the thornbushes, and in all the watering holes. [20]At that time the Lord will use a [a]razor [b]hired from the banks of the Euphrates River,[1] the king of Assyria, to shave the hair off the head and private parts; it will also shave off the beard. [21]At that time a man will keep alive a young cow from the herd and a couple of goats. [22]From the abundance of milk they produce, he will have sour milk for his meals. Indeed, everyone left in the heart of the land will eat sour milk and honey. [23]At that time every place where there had been 1,000 vines worth 1,000 silver shekels will be overrun [a]with thorns and briers. [24]With bow and arrow people will hunt there, for the whole land will be covered with thorns and briers. [25]They will stay away from all

6:13 [a] Deut 7:6; Ezra 9:2 [1] MT *in them*; LXX omits. [2] MT *in felling*.   7:1 [a] 2 Chr 28 [b] 2 Kgs 16:5, 9   7:3 [1] This name means "a remnant will return."   7:4 [a] Exod 14:13; Isa 30:15; Lam 3:26   7:7 [a] 2 Kgs 16:5; Isa 8:10; Acts 4:25–26   7:8 [a] 2 Sam 8:6; 2 Kgs 17:6   7:9 [a] 2 Chr 20:20; Isa 5:24   7:11 [a] Matt 12:38   7:14 [a] Matt 1:23; Luke 1:31; John 1:45; Rev 12:5 [b] [Isa 9:6] [c] Isa 8:8, 10 [1] The Heb. term can refer to a miraculous event (see v. 11), but it does not carry this sense inherently. [2] Trad. *virgin*; because Matt 1:23 quotes this verse in connection with Jesus' birth, it is often translated here as *virgin*, but that is not the inherent meaning of the Heb. word. Rather, the Heb. term seems to focus on age. Translating it here as "young woman," however, does not negate Jesus' virgin birth. For a fuller discussion of this issue, see *NET Bible, Full Notes Edition*.   7:16 [a] Isa 8:4 [b] 2 Kgs 15:30   7:17 [a] 2 Chr 28:19–20; Isa 8:7–8; 10:5–6 [b] 1 Kgs 12:16   7:18 [a] Isa 5:26   7:19 [a] Isa 2:19; Jer 16:16   7:20 [a] 2 Kgs 16:7; 2 Chr 28:20 [b] Isa 10:5, 15 [1] Heb. *the river*.   7:23 [a] Isa 5:6

the hills that were cultivated for fear of the thorns and briers. Cattle will graze there, and sheep will trample on them.

A Child Is Born for a Sign

8 The Lord told me, "Take a large tablet and [a]inscribe these words on it with an ordinary stylus: 'Maher Shalal Hash Baz.' [2]Then I will summon as my reliable witnesses [a]Uriah the priest and Zechariah son of Jeberekiah." [3]I then approached the prophetess for marital relations;[1] she conceived and gave birth to a son. The Lord told me, "Name him Maher Shalal Hash Baz, [4a]for before [b]the child knows how to cry out 'My father' or 'My mother,' the wealth of Damascus and the plunder of Samaria will be carried off by the king of Assyria."

[5]The Lord spoke to me again: [6]"These people have rejected the gently flowing waters of [a]Shiloah and melt [b]in fear over Rezin and the son of Remaliah. [7]So look, the Lord is bringing up against them the turbulent and mighty waters of the Euphrates River[1]—the king of Assyria and all his majestic power. It will reach flood stage and overflow its banks. [8]It will spill into Judah, flooding and engulfing, as it [a]reaches to the necks of its victims. He will spread his wings out over your entire land, O [b]Immanuel."

[9] You will [a]be broken, O nations;
  you will be shattered!
  Pay attention, all you distant lands of
    the earth.
  Get ready for battle, and you will be
    shattered!
  Get ready for battle, and you will be
    shattered!
[10] [a]Devise your strategy, [b]but it will be
    thwarted.
  Issue your orders, but they will not
    be executed!
  [c]For God is with us!

The Lord Encourages Isaiah

[11]Indeed this is what the Lord told me quite forcefully. He warned me not to act like these people:[1]

[12] "Do not say, 'Conspiracy,' every time
    these people say the word.
  Don't be afraid of what scares them;
    don't be terrified.
[13] You must recognize the authority of
    the Lord of Heaven's Armies.[1]
  He is the one you must respect;
  he is the one you must fear.
[14] He will become a sanctuary,
  but a stone that makes a person trip
  and a rock that makes one stumble—
  to [a]the two houses of [b]Israel.
  He will become a trap and a snare
  to the residents of Jerusalem.
[15] Many will [a]stumble over the stone
    and the rock,
  and will fall and be seriously injured,
  and will be ensnared and captured."
[16] Tie up the scroll as legal evidence,
  seal the official record of God's
    instructions, and give it to my
    followers.
[17] I will wait patiently for the Lord,
  who has [a]rejected the family of
    Jacob;
  [b]I will wait for him.
[18] [a]Look, I and the sons whom the
    Lord has given me [b]are reminders
    and object lessons[1] in Israel, sent
    from the Lord of Heaven's Armies,
    who lives on Mount Zion.

Darkness Turns to Light as an Ideal King Arrives

[19]They will say to you, "Seek [a]oracles at the pits used to conjure up underworld spirits, from the magicians [b]who chirp and mutter incantations. Should people not [c]seek oracles from their gods, by asking the dead about the destiny of the living?" [20a]Then you must recall [b]the Lord's instructions and the prophetic testimony of what would happen. Certainly they say such things because their minds are spiritually darkened. [21]They will pass through the land destitute and starving. Their hunger will make them angry, and they will [a]curse their king and their God as they look upward. [22]When one looks out

8:1 [a]Isa 30:8; Hab 2:2   **8:2** [a]2 Kgs 16:10   **8:3** [1]Lit. *draw near to, approach*; a euphemism for sexual relations.   **8:4** [a]2 Kgs 17:6; Isa 7:16   [b]2 Kgs 15:29   **8:6** [a]John 9:7   [b]Isa 7:1–2   **8:7** [1]Heb. *the mighty and abundant waters of the river.*   **8:8** [a]Isa 30:28   [b]Isa 7:14; Matt 1:23   **8:9** [a]Joel 3:9   **8:10** [a]Isa 7:7; Acts 5:38   [b]Isa 7:14   [c]Rom 8:31   **8:11** [1]Heb. *he warned me against (or from) walking in the way of these people, saying.*   **8:13** [1]Heb. *the Lord of Heaven's Armies* [trad. *the Lord of hosts*], *him you must set apart*; an emphatic Heb. construction.   **8:14** [a]Isa 4:6; 25:4; Ezek 11:16   [b]Luke 2:34; 20:17; Rom 9:33; 1 Pet 2:8   **8:15** [a]Matt 21:44   **8:17** [a]Deut 31:17; Isa 54:8   [b]Hab 2:3   **8:18** [a]Heb 2:13   [b]Ps 71:7   [1]Or *signs and portents.*   **8:19** [a]1 Sam 28:8   [b]Isa 29:4   [c]Ps 106:28   **8:20** [a]Isa 1:10; 8:16; Luke 16:29   [b]Isa 8:22; Mic 3:6   **8:21** [a]Rev 16:11

over the land, he sees distress and darkness,
gloom[1] and anxiety, darkness and people
9 forced from the land. [1a]The gloom will
be dispelled for those who were anxious.

In [b]earlier times he humiliated
the land of Zebulun,
and the land of Naphtali;
but [c]now he brings honor
to the way of the sea,
the region beyond the Jordan,
and Galilee of the nations.
2 [a]The people walking in darkness
see a bright light;
light shines
on those who live in a land of deep
darkness.[1]
3 You have enlarged the nation;
you give them great joy.[1]
They rejoice in your presence
as harvesters rejoice;
as warriors celebrate [a]when they
divide up the plunder.
4 For their oppressive yoke
and the club that strikes their
shoulders,
the cudgel the oppressor uses on
them,
you have shattered, as in the day of
[a]Midian's defeat.
5 Indeed every boot that marches and
shakes the earth
and every garment dragged through
blood
is used as fuel for the fire.
6 [a]For a child has been born to us,
a [b]son has been given to us.
[c]He shoulders responsibility
and is called
[d]Wonderful Adviser,
[e]Mighty God,
Everlasting Father,[1]
[f]Prince of Peace.
7 His dominion will be vast,[1]
and [a]he will bring immeasurable
prosperity.
He will rule on David's throne
and over David's kingdom,[2]

establishing it and strengthening it
by promoting justice and fairness,
from this time forward and
forevermore.
The [b]zeal of the LORD of Heaven's
Armies will accomplish this.

God's Judgment Intensifies

8 The Lord decreed judgment on
[a]Jacob,
and it fell on Israel.
9 All the people were aware of it,
the people of Ephraim and those
living in Samaria.
Yet with pride and an arrogant
attitude, they said,
10 "The bricks have fallen,
but we will rebuild with chiseled
stone;
the sycamore fig trees have been cut
down,
but we will replace them with cedars."
11 Then the LORD provoked their
adversaries to attack them,[1]
he stirred up their enemies—
12 Syria from the east,
and the Philistines from the west;
they gobbled up Israelite territory.
Despite all this, his anger does not
subside,
and his hand is ready to strike again.[1]
13 The people did not return to the one
who struck them,
they did not seek reconciliation with
the LORD of Heaven's Armies.
14 So the LORD cut off Israel's head and
tail,
both the shoots and stalk [a]in one day.
15 The leaders and the highly respected
people are the head,
the prophets who teach lies are the
tail.
16 The leaders of this nation were
misleading people,
and [a]the people being led were
destroyed.
17 So the Lord was not pleased with
their young men,

8:22 [1] The precise meaning of the term is uncertain.   9:1 [a] Isa 8:22   [b] 2 Kgs 15:29; 2 Chr 16:4   [c] Matt 4:13–16   9:2 [a] Matt
4:16; Luke 1:79; 2 Cor 4:6; Eph 5:8   [1] Trad. *shadow of death.*   9:3 [a] Judg 5:30   [1] Ket. *You multiply the nation, you do not
make great the joy.*   9:4 [a] Judg 7:22   9:6 [a] [Isa 7:14; Luke 2:11]; John 1:45   [b] Luke 2:7; [John 3:16; 1 John 4:9]   [c] [Matt 28:18;
1 Cor 15:25]; Rev 12:5   [d] Judg 13:18   [e] Titus 2:13   [f] Eph 2:14   [1] This title must not be taken in an anachronistic Trinitarian
sense; rather, in its original context the title pictures the king as the protector of his people.   9:7 [a] Dan 2:44; Matt 1:1,
6; Luke 1:32–33; John 7:42   [b] Isa 37:32   [1] MT *to the abundance of.*   [2] Heb. *over the throne of David, and over his kingdom.*
9:8 [a] Gen 32:28   9:11 [1] Heb. *adversaries of Rezin against him* [them].   9:12 [1] Heb. *in all this his anger is not turned,
and still his hand is outstretched.*   9:14 [a] Rev 18:8   9:16 [a] Isa 3:12; Mic 3:1, 5, 9; Matt 15:14

he took no pity on their orphans and
  widows;
  [a]for the whole nation was godless[1]
    and did wicked things,
every mouth was speaking
  disgraceful words.
Despite all this, his anger does not
  subside,
and his hand is ready to strike again.
18 For evil [a]burned like a fire,
  it consumed thorns and briers;
  it burned up the thickets of the forest,
  and they went up in smoke.
19 Because of [a]the anger of the LORD
    of Heaven's Armies, the land was
    scorched,
  and the people became fuel for the
    fire.
  People had [b]no compassion on one
    another.
20 They devoured on the right, but were
    still hungry;
  they ate on the left, but were not
    satisfied.
  People even ate the flesh of their
    own arm!
21 Manasseh fought against Ephraim,
  and Ephraim against Manasseh;
  together they fought [a]against Judah.
  Despite all this, his anger does not
    subside,
  and his hand is ready to strike again.

10 Beware, those who [a]enact unjust
    policies
  those who are always instituting
    unfair regulations,
2 to keep the poor from getting fair
    treatment
  and to deprive the oppressed among
    my people of justice,
  so they can steal what widows own
  and loot what belongs to orphans.[1]
3 [a]What will you do on judgment day,
  when destruction arrives from a
    distant [b]place?
  To whom will you run for help?
  Where will you leave your wealth?
4 You will have no place to go, except
    to kneel with the [a]prisoners

[b]or to fall among those who have
    been killed.
Despite all this, his anger does not
    subside,
and his hand is ready to strike again.

The Lord Turns on Arrogant Assyria

5 "Beware, Assyria, [a]the club I use to
    vent my anger,
  a cudgel with which I angrily punish.
6 I sent him against [a]a godless nation,
  [b]I ordered him to attack the people
    with whom I was angry,
  to take plunder and to carry away
    loot,
  to trample them down like dirt in
    the streets.
7 [a]But he does not agree with this;
  his mind does not reason this way,
  for his goal is to destroy
  and to eliminate many nations.
8 [a]Indeed, he says:
  'Are not my officials all kings?
9 Is not [a]Calneh [b]like Carchemish?
  Hamath [c]like Arpad?
  Samaria like Damascus?
10 I overpowered kingdoms ruled by
    idols,
  whose carved images were more
    impressive than Jerusalem's or
    Samaria's.
11 As I have done to Samaria and its
    idols,
  so I will do to Jerusalem and its
    idols.'"[1]

12 But when the Lord finishes judging
Mount [a]Zion and Jerusalem, then he [b]will
punish the king of Assyria for what he has
proudly planned and for the arrogant attitude he displays. [13a]For he says:

"By my strong hand I have
    accomplished this,
by my strategy that I devised.
I invaded the territory of nations
and looted their storehouses.
Like a mighty conqueror,[1] I brought
    down rulers.

9:17 [a]Isa 5:25 [1]Or *defiled, profane.* 9:18 [a]Ps 83:14; [Isa 1:7; 10:17]; Nah 1:10; Mal 4:1 9:19 [a]Isa 8:22 [b]Mic 7:2, 6
9:21 [a]2 Chr 28:6, 8; Isa 11:13 10:1 [a]Ps 58:2 10:2 [1]Heb. *so that widows are their plunder, and they can loot orphans.*
10:3 [a]Job 31:14 [b]Isa 5:26 10:4 [a]Isa 24:22 [b]Isa 5:25 10:5 [a]Jer 51:20 10:6 [a]Isa 9:17 [b]2 Kgs 17:6; Jer 34:22
10:7 [a]Gen 50:20; Mic 4:11–12; Acts 2:23–24 10:8 [a]2 Kgs 19:10 10:9 [a]Gen 10:10; Amos 6:2 [b]2 Chr 35:20
[c]2 Kgs 16:9 10:11 [1]Heb. *Is it not* [true that] *just as I have done to Samaria and its idols, so I will do to*
Jerusalem and its idols? 10:12 [a]2 Kgs 19:31; Isa 28:21 [b]2 Kgs 19:35; 2 Chr 32:21; Jer 50:18
10:13 [a][2 Kgs 19:22–24]; Isa 37:24–27; Ezek 28:4; Dan 4:30 [1]Ket. *a strong one.*

14 [a]My hand discovered the wealth of
 the nations, as if it were in a nest;
 as one gathers up abandoned eggs,
 I gathered up the whole earth.
 There was no wing flapping
 or open mouth chirping."
15 Does an ax exalt itself over [a]the one
 who wields it
 or a saw magnify itself over the one
 who cuts with it?
 As if a scepter should brandish the
 one who raises it
 or a staff should lift up what is not
 made of wood!
16 For this reason the Sovereign LORD
 of Heaven's Armies
 will make his healthy ones emaciated.
 His majestic glory will go up in smoke.[1]
17 The Light of Israel will become a fire,
 their Holy One will become a flame;
 [a]it will burn and consume the
 Assyrian king's briers
 and his thorns in one day.
18 The splendor of [a]his forest and his
 orchard
 will be completely destroyed,
 as when a sick man's life ebbs away.[1]
19 There will be so few trees left in his
 forest,
 a child will be able to count them.

20 At that time those left in Israel, those
who remain of the family of Jacob, [a]will no
longer rely on a foreign leader that abuses
them. Instead they will truly rely on the
LORD, the Holy One of Israel. 21 A remnant will
come back, a remnant of Jacob, to the [a]mighty
God. 22 [a]For though your people, [b]Israel, are as
numerous as the sand on the seashore, only
a remnant will come back. Destruction has
been decreed; just punishment[1] is about to
engulf you. 23 [a]The Sovereign LORD of Heav-
en's Armies is certainly ready to carry out the
decreed destruction throughout the land.

24 So here is what the Sovereign LORD
of Heaven's Armies says: "My people who
live in Zion, [a]do not be afraid of Assyria,
even though they beat you with a club and
lift their cudgel against you as [b]Egypt did.
25 For very soon my fury[1] will subside, [a]and
my anger will be directed toward their destruction." 26 The LORD of [a]Heaven's Armies
is about to beat them with a whip, similar to
the way he struck down [b]Midian at the rock
of Oreb. He will use his staff against the sea,
lifting it up [c]as he did in Egypt.[1]

27 At that time
 [a]the LORD will remove their burden
 from your shoulders
 and their yoke from your neck;
 the yoke will be taken off because
 your neck will be too large.[1]
28 They attacked Aiath,
 moved through Migron,
 depositing their supplies at Micmash.
29 They went through [a]the pass,
 spent the night at Geba.
 Ramah trembled,
 [b]Gibeah of Saul ran away.
30 Shout out, daughter [a]of Gallim!
 Pay attention, [b]Laishah!
 Answer her, Anathoth![1]
31 [a]Madmenah flees,
 the residents of Gebim have hidden.
32 This very day, standing in [a]Nob,
 they [b]shake [c]their fist at Daughter
 Zion's mountain[1]—
 at the hill of Jerusalem.
33 Look, the Sovereign LORD of
 Heaven's Armies
 is ready to cut off the branches with
 terrifying power.
 The tallest trees will be cut down,
 the loftiest ones will be brought low.
34 The thickets of the forest will be
 chopped down with an ax,
 and mighty Lebanon will fall.

An Ideal King Establishes a Kingdom of Peace

11 [a]A shoot will grow out of [b]Jesse's
 root stock,
 [c]a bud will sprout[1] from his roots.

10:14 [a] Job 31:25   10:15 [a] Jer 51:20   10:16 [1] Heb. *and in the place of his glory burning will burn, like the burning of fire.*
10:17 [a] Isa 9:18   10:18 [a] 2 Kgs 19:23   [1] The precise meaning of this line is uncertain.   10:20 [a] 2 Kgs 16:7   10:21 [a] [Isa 9:6]
10:22 [a] Rom 9:27–28   [b] Isa 6:13   [1] This Heb. word often means *righteousness.*   10:23 [a] Isa 28:22; Dan 9:27; Rom 9:28
10:24 [a] Isa 7:4; 12:2   [b] Exod 14   10:25 [a] Isa 10:5; 26:20; Dan 11:36   [1] MT only *fury.*   10:26 [a] 2 Kgs 19:35   [b] Judg 7:25; Isa 9:4
[c] Exod 14:26–27   [1] MT *and his staff* [will be] *against the sea, and he will lift it in the way* [or *manner*] *of Egypt.*   10:27 [a] Ps
105:15; [1 John 2:20]   [1] Heb. *and the yoke will be destroyed* [pulled down] *because of fatness.*   10:29 [a] 1 Sam 13:23
[b] 1 Sam 11:4   10:30 [a] 1 Sam 25:44   [b] Judg 18:7   [1] MT *Poor* [is] *Anathoth.*   10:31 [a] Josh 15:31   10:32 [a] 1 Sam 21:1;
Neh 11:32   [b] Isa 13:2   [c] Isa 37:22   [1] Ket. *a mountain of a house, Zion.*   11:1 [a] [Zech 6:12]; Rev 5:5
[b] [Isa 9:7; 11:10]; Matt 1:5; [Acts 13:23]   [c] Isa 4:2   [1] MT *will bear fruit.*

2 The LORD's Spirit will rest on him—
  a Spirit that gives extraordinary
    wisdom,[1]
  a Spirit that provides [a]the ability to
    execute plans,
  a Spirit that produces absolute
    loyalty to the LORD.[2]
3 He will take delight in obeying the
    LORD.
  He will not judge by mere
    appearances
  or make decisions on the basis of
    hearsay.
4 He will treat the poor fairly
  and make [a]right decisions for the
    downtrodden of the earth.
  He will [b]strike the earth with the rod
    of his mouth[1]
  and order the wicked to be executed.[2]
5 Justice will be like a belt around his
    waist,
  integrity will be like a belt around
    his hips.
6 A wolf will reside with a lamb,
  and a leopard will lie down with a
    young goat;
  an ox and a young lion will graze
    [a]together,[1]
  as a small child leads them along.
7 A cow and a bear will graze together,
  their young will lie down together.
  A lion, like an ox, will eat straw.
8 A baby will play
  over the hole of a snake;
  over the nest[1] of a serpent
  an infant will put his hand.
9 They will no longer injure or destroy
  on my entire royal mountain.[1]
  For there will be universal
    submission to [a]the LORD's
    sovereignty,
  just as [b]the waters completely cover
    the sea.

Israel Is Reclaimed and Reunited

10 At that time [a]a [b]root from Jesse will stand like a signal [c]flag for the nations. [d]Nations will look to him for guidance, and his residence will be majestic. [11]At that time the Lord will again lift his hand[1] to reclaim the remnant of his people [a]from Assyria, Egypt, Pathros, Cush,[2] Elam, Shinar,[3] Hamath, and the seacoasts.

12 He will lift a signal flag for [a]the
    nations;
  he will gather Israel's dispersed
    people
  and assemble Judah's scattered
    people
  from the four corners of the earth.
13 Ephraim's jealousy will end,
  and Judah's hostility will be
    eliminated.
  Ephraim will no longer be jealous of
    Judah,
  and Judah will no longer be hostile
    toward Ephraim.
14 They will swoop down on [a]the
    Philistine hills to the west;
  together they will loot the people of
    the east.
  They will take over Edom and Moab,
  and the Ammonites will be their
    subjects.
15 The LORD [a]will divide the gulf of the
    Egyptian Sea;
  he will wave his hand over the
    Euphrates River[1] and send a strong
    wind;
  he will turn it into seven dried-up
    streams
  and enable them to walk across in
    their sandals.
16 There will be a highway leading out
    of Assyria
  for [a]the remnant of his people,
  just [b]as there was for Israel,
  when they went up from the land of
    Egypt.

12 At that time you will say:
  "[a]I praise you, O LORD,
  for even though you were angry
    with me,
  your anger subsided, and you
    consoled me.

11:2 [a] [Isa 42:1; 48:16; 61:1; Matt 3:16]; Mark 1:10; Luke 3:22; [John 1:32] [1] Heb. *a spirit of wisdom and understanding.* [2] Heb. *a spirit of knowledge and fear of the Lord.* 11:4 [a] Rev 19:11 [b] Job 4:9; Isa 30:28, 33; Mal 4:6; 2 Thess 2:8 [1] MT *and he will strike the earth with the scepter of his mouth.* [2] Heb. *and by the breath of his lips he will kill the wicked.* 11:6 [a] Hos 2:18 [1] MT *and an ox, and a young lion, and a fatling together.* 11:8 [1] MT *place of light.* 11:9 [a] Job 5:23; Isa 65:25; Ezek 34:25; Hos 2:18 [b] Ps 98:2–3; Isa 45:6; Hab 2:14 [1] Heb. *in all my holy mountain;* probably Mount Zion/Jerusalem or the entire land of Israel. 11:10 [a] Isa 2:11 [b] Isa 11:1; Rom 15:12 [c] Isa 27:12–13 [d] Rom 15:10 11:11 [a] Isa 19:23–25; Hos 11:11; Zech 10:10 [1] MT *the Lord will again, a second time, his hand.* [2] Or *Ethiopia.* [3] Or *Babylonia.* 11:12 [a] John 7:35 11:14 [a] Isa 63:1; Dan 11:41; Joel 3:19; Amos 9:12 11:15 [a] Isa 50:2; 51:10–11; Zech 10:10–11 [1] Heb. *the river.* 11:16 [a] Isa 19:23 [b] Exod 14:29 12:1 [a] Isa 2:11

2 Look, God is my deliverer!
   I will trust in him and not fear.
   [a]For the [b]LORD gives me strength
      and protects me;[1]
   he has become my deliverer."
3 Joyfully you will draw [a]water
   from the springs of deliverance.
4 At that time you will say:
   "[a]Praise the LORD!
   Ask him for help!
   [b]Publicize his mighty acts among the
      nations.
   Make it known that he is [c]unique.
5 [a]Sing to the LORD, for he has done
      magnificent things;
   let this be known throughout the
      earth.
6 [a]Cry out and shout for joy, O citizens
      of Zion,
   for [b]the Holy One of Israel acts
      mightily among you!"

The Lord Will Judge Babylon

13 This is an [a]oracle[1] about Babylon that
   Isaiah son of Amoz saw:

2 On a bare hill [a]raise a signal flag;
   shout to them,
   [b]wave your hand
   so they might enter the gates of the
      princes!
3 I have given orders to [a]my chosen
      soldiers;
   I have summoned the warriors
      through whom I will vent my
      anger—
   my [b]boasting, arrogant ones.
4 There is a loud [a]noise on the
      mountains—
   it sounds like a large army!
   There is great commotion among the
      kingdoms—
   nations are being assembled!
   The LORD of Heaven's Armies is
      mustering
   forces for battle.
5 They come from a distant land,
   from the horizon.

It is the [a]LORD with his instruments
      of judgment
   coming to destroy the whole [b]earth.
6 Wail, [a]for the LORD's day of judgment
      is near;
   [b]it comes with all the destructive
      power of the Sovereign One.
7 For this reason all hands hang limp,
   every human heart loses its courage.[1]
8 They panic—
   [a]cramps and pain seize hold of them
   like those of a woman who is
      straining to give birth.
   They look at one another in
      astonishment;
   their faces are flushed red.
9 Look, [a]the LORD's day of judgment is
      coming;
   [b]it is a day of cruelty and savage,
      raging anger,
   destroying the earth
   and annihilating its sinners.
10 Indeed the stars in the sky and their
      constellations
   no longer give out their light;
   the sun is [a]darkened as soon as it
      rises,
   and the moon does not shine.
11 I will [a]punish the world for [b]its evil
   and wicked people for their sin.
   I will put an end to the pride of the
      insolent,
   I will bring down the arrogance of
      tyrants.
12 I will make human beings more
      scarce than pure gold
   and people more scarce than gold
      from Ophir.
13 So I will shake [a]the heavens,[1]
   and [b]the earth will shake loose from
      its foundation,
   because of the fury of the LORD of
      Heaven's Armies,
   in the day he vents his raging anger.
14 Like a frightened gazelle
   or a sheep with no shepherd,
   each will turn toward home,
   each will run to his homeland.

12:2 [a]Ps 83:18   [b]Exod 15:2; Ps 118:14   [1]MT *for my strength and protection* [is] *the LORD, the LORD.*   12:3 [a][John 4:10, 14;
7:37-38]   12:4 [1]1 Chr 16:8; Ps 105:1   [b]Ps 145:4-6   [c]Ps 34:3   12:5 [a]Exod 15:1; Ps 98:1; Isa 24:14; 42:10-11; 44:23
12:6 [a]Isa 52:9; 54:1; Zeph 3:14-15   [b]Ps 89:18   13:1 [a]Jer 50; 51; Matt 1:11; Rev 14:8   [1]A technical term introducing
a message from the Lord.   13:2 [a]Isa 18:3   [b]Isa 10:32   13:3 [a]Joel 3:11   [b]Ps 149:2   13:4 [a]Isa 17:12; Joel 3:14
13:5 [a]Isa 42:13   [b]Isa 24:1; 34:2   13:6 [a]Isa 2:12; Ezek 30:3; Amos 5:18; Zeph 1:7; Rev 6:17   [b]Isa 10:25; Job 31:23;
Joel 1:15   13:7 [1]Heb. *melts.*   13:8 [a]Ps 48:6   13:9 [a]Mal 4:1   [b]Ps 104:35; Prov 2:22   13:10 [a]Isa 24:21-23;
Ezek 32:7; Joel 2:31; Matt 24:29; Mark 13:24; Luke 21:25   13:11 [a]Isa 26:21   [b][Isa 2:17]
13:13 [a]Isa 34:4; 51:6; Hag 2:6   [b]Ps 110:5; Lam 1:12   [1]Or *the sky.*

¹⁵ Everyone who is caught will be
stabbed;
everyone who is seized will die by the
sword.
¹⁶ Their children will be smashed to
pieces before their very eyes;
their houses will be looted
and their wives raped.
¹⁷ Look, I am stirring up the Medes to
attack them;
they are not concerned about silver,
nor are they interested in gold.
¹⁸ Their arrows will cut young men to
ribbons;¹
they have no compassion on a
person's offspring;
they will not look with pity on
children.
¹⁹ Babylon, the most admired of
kingdoms,
the Chaldeans' source of honor ᵃand
pride,
will be destroyed by God
just as ᵇSodom and Gomorrah were.
²⁰ ᵃNo one will live there again;
no one will ever reside there again.¹
No bedouin will camp there,
no shepherds will rest their flocks
there.
²¹ ᵃWild animals will rest there,
the ruined houses will be full of
hyenas.
Ostriches will live there,
wild goats will skip among the ruins.
²² Wild dogs will yip in ᵃher ruined
fortresses,
jackals will yelp in the once-splendid
palaces.¹
Her time is almost up,
her days will not be prolonged.

14 The LORD ᵃwill certainly have compassion on Jacob;¹ he ᵇwill again choose
Israel as his special people and restore
ᶜthem to their land. Resident foreigners will
join them and unite with the family of Jacob.
²Nations will take them ᵃand bring them
back to their own place. Then the family of

Israel will make foreigners their servants
as they settle in the LORD's ᵇland. They will
make their captors captives and rule over
the ones who oppressed them. ³When the
LORD gives you relief from your suffering
and anxiety and from the hard labor that
you were made to perform, ⁴you ᵃwill taunt
the king of Babylon with these words:

"Look how the oppressor has met his
end!
Hostility has ceased!
⁵ The LORD has broken ᵃthe club of the
wicked,
the scepter of rulers.
⁶ It furiously struck down nations
with unceasing blows.¹
It angrily ruled over nations,
oppressing them without restraint.
⁷ The whole earth rests and is quiet;
they break into song.
⁸ The evergreens ᵃalso rejoice over
your demise,
as do the cedars of Lebanon, singing,
'Since you fell asleep,
no woodsman comes up to chop us
down!'
⁹ ᵃSheol below is stirred up about you,
ready to meet you when you arrive.
It rouses the spirits of the dead for
you,
all the former leaders of the earth;¹
it makes all the former kings of the
nations
rise from their thrones.
¹⁰ All of them ᵃrespond to you, saying:
'You too have become weak like us!
You have become just like us!
¹¹ Your splendor has been brought
down to Sheol,
as well as the sound of your stringed
instruments.
You lie on a bed of maggots,
with a blanket of worms over you.'

¹² "Look ᵃhow you have fallen from the
sky,
O shining one, son of the dawn!

13:18 ¹ Heb. *and bows cut to bits young men.*   13:19 ᵃ Isa 14:4; Dan 4:30; Rev 18:11–16, 19, 21   ᵇ Gen 19:24; Deut 29:23; Jer
50:40; Amos 4:11   13:20 ᵃ Jer 50:3   ¹ Heb. *she will not be inhabited forever, and she will not be dwelt in to generation
and generation (i.e., forever).*   13:21 ᵃ Isa 34:11–15; Zeph 2:14; Rev 18:2   13:22 ᵃ Jer 51:33   ¹ MT *wild dogs will yip
among his widows, and jackals in the palaces of pleasure.*   14:1 ᵃ Ps 102:13; Isa 49:13, 15; 54:7–8   ᵇ Isa 41:8–9;
Zech 1:17; 2:12   ᶜ Isa 60:4–5, 10   ¹ Or *For the Lord will have compassion.*   14:2 ᵃ Isa 49:22; 60:9; 66:20
ᵇ Isa 60:14   14:4 ᵃ Isa 13:19; Hab 2:6   14:5 ᵃ Ps 125:3   14:6 ¹ Heb. *it was striking down nations in fury*
[with] *a blow without ceasing.*   14:8 ᵃ Isa 55:12; Ezek 31:16   14:9 ᵃ Ezek 32:21   ¹ Heb. *all the
rams of the earth.*   14:10 ᵃ Ezek 32:21   14:12 ᵃ Isa 34:4; Luke 10:18; [Rev 12:7–9]

You have been cut down to the
    ground,
  O conqueror of the nations!
13 You [a]said to yourself,
  [b]'I will climb up to the sky.
  Above the stars of El
    I will set up my throne.
  I will rule on the [c]mountain of
    assembly
  [d]on the remote slopes of Zaphon.
14 I [a]will climb up to the tops of the
    clouds;
  I will make myself like the Most High!'
15 But you were brought down to Sheol,
  to the remote slopes of the Pit.[1]
16 Those who see you stare at you,
  they look at you carefully, thinking:
  'Is this the man who shook the earth,
  the one who made kingdoms
    tremble?
17 Is this the one who made the world
    like a wilderness,
  who ruined its cities
  and refused to free his prisoners so
    they could return home?'
18 As for all the kings of the nations,
  all of them[1] lie down in splendor,
  each in his own tomb.
19 But you have been thrown out of
    your grave
  like a shoot that is thrown away.
  You lie among the slain,
  among those who have been slashed
    by the sword,
  among those headed for the stones
    of the Pit,[1]
  as if you were a mangled corpse.
20 You will not be buried with [a]them,
  because you destroyed your land
  and killed your people.

  "The offspring of the wicked
  will never be mentioned again.
21 Prepare to execute his sons
  for the sins their ancestors have
    committed.
  They must not rise up and take
  possession of the earth
  or fill the surface of the world with
    cities.

22 "I will rise up against [a]them,"
  says the LORD of Heaven's Armies.
  "I will blot out all remembrance
  of Babylon and destroy all her
    [b]people,[1]
  including the offspring she
    produces,"
  says the LORD.
23 "I will turn her into a place that is
  overrun with wild [a]animals
  and covered with pools of stagnant
    water.
  I will get rid of her, just as one
  sweeps away dirt with a broom,"
  says the LORD of Heaven's Armies.

24 The LORD of Heaven's Armies makes
    this solemn vow:
  "Be sure of this:
  Just as I have intended, so it will be;
  just as I have planned, it will
    [a]happen.
25 I will break [a]Assyria in my land,
  [b]I will trample them underfoot on
    my hills.
  Their yoke will be removed from my
    people,
  the burden will be lifted from their
    shoulders.
26 This is the [a]plan I have devised for
    the whole earth;
  my hand is ready to strike all the
    nations."
27 Indeed,[1] the LORD of Heaven's
    Armies has a [a]plan,
  and who can possibly frustrate it?
  His hand is ready to strike,
  and who can possibly stop it?

The Lord Will Judge the Philistines

28 This oracle came in the year that [a]King
Ahaz died:

29 Don't [a]be so happy, all you
    Philistines,
  just because the club that beat you
    has been broken!
  For [b]a viper will grow out of the
    serpent's root,
  and its fruit will be a darting adder.

14:13 [a] Ezek 28:2; Matt 11:23 [b] Dan 8:10; 2 Thess 2:4 [c] Ezek 28:14 [d] Ps 48:2 14:14 [a] Isa 47:8; 2 Thess 2:4 14:15 [1] Heb. cistern. 14:18 [1] DSS omits all of them. 14:19 [1] Heb. cistern. 14:20 [a] Job 18:19; Ps 21:10; 109:13; Isa 1:4; 31:2 14:22 [a] Prov 10:7; Isa 26:14; Jer 51:62 [b] 1 Kgs 14:10 [1] Heb. I will cut off from Babylon name and remnant. 14:23 [a] Isa 34:11; Zeph 2:14 14:24 [a] Isa 43:13 14:25 [a] Mic 5:5-6; Zeph 2:13 [b] Isa 10:27; Nah 1:13 14:26 [a] Isa 23:9; Zeph 3:6, 8 14:27 [a] 2 Chr 20:6; Job 9:12; 23:13; Ps 33:11; Prov 19:21; 21:30; Isa 43:13; Dan 4:31, 35 [1] Or For. 14:28 [a] 2 Kgs 16:20; 2 Chr 28:27 14:29 [a] 2 Chr 26:6 [b] 2 Kgs 18:8

30 The poor will graze in my pastures;[1]
   the needy will rest securely.
But I will kill your root by famine;
   it will put to death all your survivors.[2]
31 Wail, O city gate!
   Cry out, O city!
Melt with fear, all you Philistines!
For out of the north comes a cloud of
   smoke,
and there are no stragglers in its
   ranks.
32 How will [a]they respond to [b]the
   messengers of this nation?
Indeed, the LORD has made Zion
   secure;
the oppressed among his people will
   find safety in her.

The Lord Will Judge Moab

15 This is an [a]oracle about Moab:
   Indeed, in a night it is devastated,
[b]Ar of [c]Moab is destroyed!
Indeed, in a night it is devastated,
Kir of Moab is destroyed!
2 They went up to the temple;
   the people of [a]Dibon went up to the
      high places to lament.
Because of what happened to Nebo
   and Medeba, Moab wails.
Every head is shaved bare,
every beard is trimmed off.
3 In their streets they wear sackcloth;
   on their roofs and in their town
      squares
all of them wail;
they fall down [a]weeping.
4 The people of Heshbon and Elealeh
   cry out;
their voices are heard as far away as
   [a]Jahaz.
For this reason Moab's soldiers shout
   in distress;
their courage wavers.[1]
5 My heart cries out because of Moab's
   plight
and for the fugitives stretched out
   as far as Zoar and Eglath
   Shelishiyah.

For they weep as they make their
   way up the ascent of Luhith;
they loudly lament their demise on
   the road to Horonaim.
6 For the waters [a]of Nimrim are gone;
   the grass is dried up,
the vegetation has disappeared,
and there are no plants.
7 For this reason what they have made
   and stored up,
they carry over the Stream of the
   Poplars.
8 Indeed, the cries of distress echo
   throughout Moabite territory;
their wailing can be heard in Eglaim
   and Beer Elim.
9 Indeed, the waters of Dimon[1] are full
   of blood!
Indeed, I will heap even more trouble
   on Dimon.
A [a]lion will attack the Moabite
   fugitives
and the people left in the land.

16 Send rams as tribute to [a]the ruler of
   the land,[1]
[b]from Sela in the wilderness
to the hill of Daughter Zion.
2 At the fords of the [a]Arnon
   the Moabite women are like a [b]bird
   that flies about when forced from its
      nest.
3 "Bring a plan, make a decision.
Provide some shade in the middle of
   the day.[1]
Hide the fugitives! Do not betray the
   one who tries to escape.
4 Please let the Moabite fugitives live
   among you.
Hide them from the destroyer!"
Certainly[1] the one who applies
   pressure will cease;
the destroyer will come to an end;
those who trample will disappear[2]
   from the earth.
5 Then a trustworthy king will be
   established;
[a]he will rule in a reliable manner,
this one from David's family.

14:30 [1]MT *the firstborn of the poor will graze.*   [2]Heb. *your remnant.*   14:32 [a]Ps 87:1, 5   [b]Zech 11:11   15:1 [a]2 Kgs 3:4   [b]Deut 2:9; Num 21:28   [c]Isa 15:1–16:14; Jer 25:21; 48:1–47; Amos 2:1–3; Zeph 2:8–11   15:2 [a]Lev 21:5; Jer 48:37   15:3 [a]Jer 48:38   15:4 [a]Num 21:28; 32:3; Jer 48:34   [1]MT *For this reason the soldiers of Moab shout; his inner being quivers for him.*   15:6 [a]Num 32:36   15:9 [a]2 Kgs 17:25; Jer 50:17   [1]DSS *Dibon.*   16:1 [a]2 Kgs 3:4; Ezra 7:17   [b]2 Kgs 14:7; Isa 42:11   [1]MT *Send a ram [to] the ruler of the land.*   16:2 [a]Num 21:13   [b]Prov 27:8   16:3 [1]Heb. *Make your shade like night in the midst of noonday;* "shade" *symbolizes shelter and the heat of noonday represents the intense suffering of the Moabites.*   16:4 [1]Or *for, when.*   [2]MT *they will be finished, the one who tramples, from the earth.*   16:5 [a][Isa 9:6–7; 32:1; 55:4; Dan 7:14; Mic 4:7; Luke 1:33; Rev 11:15]

He will be sure to [b]make just decisions
and will be experienced in executing [c]justice.
6 We have heard about Moab's [a]pride—
their great arrogance—
their boasting, pride, and excess.
[b]But their boastful claims are empty.
7 So Moab wails over its demise—
they all [a]wail!
Completely devastated, they moan
about what has happened to the raisin cakes [b]of Kir Hareseth.
8 For [a]the fields of Heshbon are dried up,
as well as [b]the vines of Sibmah.
The rulers of the nations trample all over its vines,
which reach Jazer and spread to the wilderness;
their shoots spread out and cross the [c]sea.
9 So I weep [a]along with Jazer
over the vines of Sibmah.
I will saturate you with my tears,
Heshbon and Elealeh,
for the conquering invaders shout triumphantly
over your fruit and crops.[1]
10 [a]Joy and happiness disappear from the orchards,
and in the vineyards no one rejoices or shouts;
no one treads out juice in the wine vats—
I have brought the joyful shouts to an end.
11 So [a]my heart constantly sighs for Moab, like the strumming of a harp,
my inner being sighs for Kir Hareseth.[1]
12 When [a]the Moabites plead with all their might at their high places
and enter their temples to pray, their prayers will be ineffective.

13 This is the message the LORD previously announced about Moab. 14 Now the LORD makes this announcement: "Within exactly three years Moab's splendor will disappear, along with all her many people; there will be only [a]a few insignificant survivors left."

The Lord Will Judge Damascus

17 This is an [a]oracle about Damascus:
"Look, Damascus is no longer a city,
it is a heap of ruins!
2 The cities of [a]Aroer are abandoned.
They will be used for herds,
which will lie down there in [b]peace.[1]
3 Fortified cities will disappear from Ephraim,
and Damascus will lose its kingdom.
[a]The survivors in Syria
will end up like the splendor of the Israelites,"
says the LORD of Heaven's Armies.
4 "At that time
Jacob's splendor will be greatly diminished,
and [a]he will become skin and bones.
5 It will be as when one gathers the grain harvest
and his hand gleans the ear of grain.
[a]It will be like one gathering the ears of grain
in the Valley of Rephaim.
6 [a]There will be some left behind,
as when an olive tree is beaten—
two or three ripe olives remain toward the very top,
four or five on its fruitful branches,"
says the LORD God of Israel.
7 At that time men will [a]trust in their Creator;
they will depend on the Holy One of Israel.
8 They will no longer trust in the altars their hands made,
or depend on the Asherah poles and incense altars their [a]fingers made.[1]
9 At that time their fortified cities will be
like the abandoned summits of the Amorites,
which they abandoned because of the Israelites;
there will be desolation.

16:5 [b] Ps 72:2 [c] Isa 9:7   16:6 [a] Jer 48:29; Amos 2:1; Obad 3, 4; Zeph 2:8, 10 [b] Isa 28:15   16:7 [a] Jer 48:20 [b] 2 Kgs 3:25; Jer 48:31   16:8 [a] Isa 24:7 [b] Isa 16:9 [c] Jer 48:32   16:9 [a] Isa 15:4 [1] Heb. *for over your fruit and over your harvest shouting has fallen.*   16:10 [a] Isa 24:8; Jer 48:33   16:11 [a] Isa 15:5; 63:15; Jer 48:36; Hos 11:8; Phil 2:1 [1] Heb. *Kir Heres.*   16:12 [a] Isa 15:2   16:14 [a] Job 7:1; 14:6; Isa 21:16   17:1 [a] Gen 14:15; 15:2; 2 Kgs 16:9; Jer 49:23; Amos 1:3–5; Zech 9:1; Acts 9:2   17:2 [a] Num 32:34 [b] Jer 7:33 [1] Heb. *and they lie down, and there is no one scaring* [them].   17:3 [a] Isa 7:16; 8:4   17:4 [a] Isa 10:16   17:5 [a] Isa 17:11; Jer 51:33; Joel 3:13; Matt 13:30   17:6 [a] Deut 4:27; Isa 24:13; Obad 5   17:7 [a] Isa 10:20; Hos 3:5; Mic 7:7   17:8 [a] Isa 2:8; 31:7 [1] Heb. *and that which his fingers made he will not see, the Asherah poles and the incense altars.*

[10] For you ignore [a]the God who rescues you;
you pay no attention to your strong protector.
So this is what happens:
You cultivate beautiful plants
and plant exotic vines.
[11] The day you begin cultivating, you do what you can to make it grow;
the morning you begin planting, you do what you can to make it sprout.
Yet the harvest will disappear[1] in the day of disease
and incurable pain.
[12] Beware, you many nations massing together,
those who make a commotion as loud as the roaring of the sea's waves.
Beware, you people making such an uproar,
those who make an uproar as loud as the roaring of powerful waves.
[13] Though these people make an uproar as loud as the roaring of powerful waves,
when he [a]shouts at[1] them, they will flee to a distant land,
driven [b]before the wind like dead weeds on the hills
or like dead thistles before a strong gale.
[14] In the evening there is sudden terror;
by morning they vanish.
This is the fate of those who try to plunder us,
the destiny of those who try to loot us!

The Lord Will Judge a Distant Land in the South

18 Beware, land of buzzing wings,
the one beyond the rivers of Cush,
[2] that sends messengers by sea,
who glide over the water's surface in boats made of papyrus.
Go, you swift messengers,
to a nation of tall, smooth-skinned people,
to a people that are feared far and wide,
to a nation strong and victorious,
whose land rivers divide.
[3] All you who live in the world,
who reside on the earth,
you will see a signal flag raised on the mountains;
you will hear a trumpet being blown.
[4] For this is what the LORD has told me:
"I will wait[1] and watch from my place,
like scorching heat produced by the sunlight,
like a cloud of mist in the heat[2] of harvest."
[5] For before the harvest, when the bud has sprouted
and the ripening fruit appears,
he will cut off the unproductive shoots with pruning knives;
he will prune the tendrils.
[6] They will all be left for the birds of the hills
and the wild animals;
the birds will eat them during the summer,
and all the wild animals will eat them during the winter.
[7] At [a]that time
tribute will be brought to the LORD of Heaven's Armies
by a people that are tall and smooth-skinned,
a people that are feared far and wide,
a nation strong and victorious,
whose land rivers divide.
The tribute will be brought to the place where the LORD of Heaven's Armies has chosen to reside, on Mount Zion.[1]

The Lord Will Judge Egypt

19 This is an [a]oracle about Egypt:
Look, the LORD [b]rides on a swift-moving cloud
and approaches Egypt.
[c]The idols of Egypt tremble before him;
the Egyptians lose their courage.
[2] "I will [a]provoke civil strife in Egypt:
brothers will fight with one another,
as will neighbors,
cities, and kingdoms.

17:10 [a] Ps 68:19; Isa 51:13 **17:11** [1] MT *a heap of harvest.* **17:13** [a] Ps 9:5; Isa 41:11 [b] Ps 83:13; Hos 13:3 [1] Or *rebukes.*
18:4 [1] Or *be quiet, inactive.* [2] Some wss *the day.* **18:7** [a] Ps 68:31; 72:10; Isa 16:1; Zeph 3:10; Mal 1:11; Acts 8:27–38
[1] Heb. *place of the name of the LORD who commands armies* [trad. *the LORD of hosts*], *Mount Zion.*
19:1 [a] Jer 9:25–26; Ezek 29:1–30:19; Joel 3:19 [b] Ps 18:10; 104:3; Matt 26:64; Rev 1:7 [c] Exod 12:12;
Jer 43:12 **19:2** [a] Judg 7:22; 1 Sam 14:16, 20; 2 Chr 20:23; Matt 10:21, 36

3 The Egyptians will panic,
  and I will confuse their strategy.
  They will seek ᵃguidance from the
    idols and from the spirits of the
    dead,
  from the pits used to conjure up
    underworld spirits, and from the
    magicians.
4 I will hand Egypt over ᵃto a harsh
    master;
  a powerful king will rule over them,"
  says the Sovereign LORD of Heaven's
    Armies.
5 The water of ᵃthe sea will be dried up,
  and the river will dry up and be
    empty.¹
6 The canals will stink;
  the streams ᵃof Egypt will trickle and
    then dry up;
  the bulrushes and reeds will decay,
7 along with the plants by the mouth
    of the river.
  All the cultivated land near the river
  will turn to dust and be blown away.
8 The fishermen will mourn and
    lament;
  all those who cast a fishhook into the
    river,
  and those who spread out a net on
    the water's surface will grieve.
9 Those who make clothes from
    ᵃcombed flax will be embarrassed;
  those who weave will turn pale.
10 Those who make cloth will be
    demoralized;¹
  all the hired workers will be
    depressed.
11 The officials of ᵃZoan are nothing but
    fools;
  Pharaoh's wise advisers give stupid
    advice.
  ᵇHow dare you say to Pharaoh,
  "I am one of the sages,
  one well versed in the writings of the
    ancient kings"?
12 But ᵃwhere, oh where, are your wise
    men?¹
  Let them tell you, let them find out

what the LORD of Heaven's Armies
    has ᵇplanned for Egypt.
13 The officials of Zoan are fools,
  ᵃthe officials of Memphis¹ are misled;
  the rulers of her tribes lead Egypt
    astray.
14 The LORD ᵃhas made them
    undiscerning;
  they lead Egypt astray in all she does,
  so that she is like a drunk sliding
    around in his own vomit.
15 Egypt will not be able to do a thing,
  head or tail, shoots or stalk.

¹⁶At that time the Egyptians¹ will ᵃbe like women. They will tremble and fear because the LORD of Heaven's Armies brandishes his fist against them. ¹⁷The land of Judah will humiliate Egypt. Everyone who hears about Judah will be afraid because of what the LORD of Heaven's Armies is ᵃplanning to do to them.

¹⁸At that time five cities in the land of Egypt will ᵃspeak the language of Canaan and swear ᵇallegiance to the LORD of Heaven's Armies. One will be called the City of the Sun.¹ ¹⁹At that time ᵃthere will be an altar for the ᵇLORD in the middle of the land of Egypt, as well as a sacred pillar dedicated to the LORD at its border. ²⁰It will become a visual reminder in the land of Egypt of the LORD of Heaven's Armies. When they cry out to the LORD because of oppressors, he will send them a ᵃdeliverer and defender who will rescue them. ²¹The LORD will ᵃreveal himself to the Egyptians, and they ᵇwill acknowledge the LORD's authority at that time. They will present sacrifices and offerings; they will make vows to the LORD and fulfill them. ²²The LORD will strike Egypt, striking and then healing them. They will turn to the LORD, and he will listen to their prayers and ᵃheal them.

²³At that time ᵃthere will be a highway from Egypt to Assyria. The Assyrians will visit Egypt, and the Egyptians will visit Assyria. The Egyptians and Assyrians will ᵇworship together. ²⁴At that time Israel will

19:3 ᵃ1 Chr 10:13; Isa 8:19; 47:12; Dan 2:2   19:4 ᵃIsa 20:4; Jer 46:26; Ezek 29:19   19:5 ᵃIsa 50:2; Jer 51:36; Ezek 30:12   ¹Heb. *will dry up and be dry*; an emphatic Heb. construction.   19:6 ᵃ2 Kgs 19:24   19:9 ᵃ1 Kgs 10:28; Prov 7:16; Ezek 27:7   19:10 ¹Heb. *crushed.*   19:11 ᵃNum 13:22; Ps 78:12, 43; Isa 30:4   ᵇGen 41:38–39; 1 Kgs 4:29–30; Acts 7:22   19:12 ᵃ1 Cor 1:20   ᵇPs 33:11   ¹Heb. *Where are they? Where are your wise men?*; an emphatic Heb. construction.   19:13 ᵃJer 2:16; Ezek 30:13   ¹Heb. *Noph.*   19:14 ᵃ1 Kgs 22:22; Isa 29:10   19:16 ᵃJer 51:30; Nah 3:13   ¹Heb. *Egypt.*   19:17 ᵃIsa 14:24; Dan 4:35   19:18 ᵃZeph 3:9   ᵇIsa 45:23   ¹MT *City of Destruction.*   19:19 ᵃGen 28:18; Exod 24:4; Josh 22:10, 26, 27; Isa 56:7; 60:7   ᵇPs 68:31   19:20 ᵃIsa 43:11   19:21 ᵃ[Isa 2:3–4; 11:9]   ᵇIsa 56:7; 60:7; Zech 14:16–18; Mal 1:11   19:22 ᵃDeut 32:39; Isa 30:26; 57:18; [Heb 12:11]   19:23 ᵃIsa 11:16; 35:8; 49:11; 62:10   ᵇIsa 27:13

be the third member of the group, along with Egypt and Assyria, and will be a recipient of blessing in the earth.[1] [25]The LORD of Heaven's Armies will pronounce a blessing over [a]the earth, saying, "Blessed be my people, Egypt, and the work of my hands, Assyria, and my special possession, Israel!"

20 The LORD revealed the following message during the year in which King Sargon of Assyria sent his commanding [a]general to Ashdod, and he fought against it and captured it. [2]At that time [a]the LORD announced through Isaiah son of Amoz: "[b]Go, remove the sackcloth from your waist and take your sandals off your feet." He did as instructed and walked around in undergarments[1] and barefoot. [3]Later the LORD explained, "In the same way that my servant Isaiah has walked around in undergarments and barefoot [a]for the past three years, as an object lesson and omen pertaining to Egypt and Cush, [4]so the [a]king of Assyria will lead away the captives of Egypt and the exiles of Cush, both young and old. They will be in undergarments and barefoot, [b]with the buttocks exposed; the Egyptians will be publicly humiliated. [5a]Those who put their hope in Cush and took pride in Egypt will be afraid and embarrassed. [6]At that time those who live on this coast will say, 'Look what has happened to our source of hope to whom we fled for [a]help, expecting to be rescued from the king of Assyria! How can we escape now?'"

The Lord Will Judge Babylon

21 This is an oracle about the wilderness by the Sea:

Like strong [a]winds blowing in the
   south,[1]
one invades from the wilderness,
from a land that is feared.
[2] I have received a distressing message:
"[a]The deceiver deceives,
the destroyer destroys.
Attack, you Elamites!
Lay siege, you Medes!
I will put an end to all the groaning."
[3] For this reason [a]my stomach churns;
[b]cramps overwhelm me

like the contractions of a woman in
   labor.
I am disturbed by what I hear,
horrified by what I see.
[4] My heart palpitates,
I shake in fear;
[a]the twilight I desired
has brought me terror.
[5] [a]Arrange the table,
lay out the carpet,
eat and drink!
Get up, you officers,
smear oil on the shields!

[6]For this is what the Lord has told me:

"Go, post a guard!
He must report what he sees.
[7] When he sees chariots,
teams of horses,
riders on donkeys,
riders on camels,
he must be alert,
very alert."
[8] Then the guard[1] cries out:
"On the [a]watchtower, O Lord,
I stand all day long;
at my post
I am stationed every night.
[9] Look what's coming!
A charioteer,
a team of horses."
When questioned, he replies,
"[a]Babylon has [b]fallen, fallen!
All the idols of her gods lie shattered
on the ground!"
[10] [a]O my downtrodden people, crushed
like stalks on the threshing floor,
what I have heard
from the LORD of Heaven's Armies,
the God of Israel,
I have reported to you.

Bad News for Seir

[11] [a]This is an oracle about Dumah:
Someone calls to me from [b]Seir,
"Watchman, what is left of the
   night?
Watchman, what is left of the
   night?"

19:24 [1]Or land.   19:25 [a]Deut 14:2; Ps 100:3; Isa 29:23; Hos 2:23; [Eph 2:10]   20:1 [a]2 Kgs 18:17   20:2 [a]Zech 13:4; Matt 3:4 [b]1 Sam 19:24; Mic 1:8 [1]The Heb. word sometimes means "naked."   20:3 [a]Isa 8:18   20:4 [a]Isa 19:4 [b]2 Sam 10:4; Isa 3:17; Jer 13:22; Mic 1:11   20:5 [a]2 Kgs 18:21; Isa 30:3–5; 31:1; Ezek 29:6–7   20:6 [a]Isa 30:5, 7   21:1 [a]Zech 9:14 [1]Or in the Negev.   21:2 [a]Isa 33:1   21:3 [a]Isa 15:5; 16:11 [b]Isa 13:8   21:4 [a]Deut 28:67   21:5 [a]Jer 51:39; Dan 5:5   21:8 [a]Hab 2:1 [1]Heb. the lion.   21:9 [a]Isa 13:19; 47:5, 9; 48:14; Jer 51:8; Dan 5:28, 31; Rev 14:8; 18:2 [b]Isa 46:1; Jer 50:2; 51:44   21:10 [a]Jer 51:33; Mic 4:13   21:11 [a]Gen 25:14; 1 Chr 1:30; Josh 15:52 [b]Gen 32:3; Jer 49:7; Ezek 35:2; Obad 1

12 The watchman replies,
 "Morning is coming, but then night.
 If you want to ask, ask;
 come back again."

The Lord Will Judge Arabia

13 This is an oracle about Arabia:
 In [a]the thicket [b]of Arabia you spend
    the night,
 you Dedanite caravans.
14 Bring out some water for the thirsty.
 You who live in the land of Tema,
 bring some food for the fugitives.
15 For they flee from the swords—
 from the drawn sword,
 and from the battle-ready bow,
 and from the severity of the battle.

16 For this is what the Lord has told me:
"Within exactly one year all the splendor of
[a]Kedar will come to an end. 17 Just a handful
of archers, the warriors of Kedar, will be left."
Indeed,[1] the LORD God of Israel has spoken.

The Lord Will Judge Jerusalem

22 This is an oracle about the Valley
 of Vision:
 What is the reason
 that all of you go up to the rooftops?
2 The noisy city is full of [a]raucous
    sounds;
 the town is filled with revelry.
 Your slain were not cut down by the
    sword;
 they did not die in battle.
3 All your leaders ran away together—
 they fled to a distant place;
 all your refugees were captured
    together—
 they were captured without a single
    arrow being shot.
4 So [a]I say:
 "Don't look at me!
 I am weeping bitterly.
 Don't try to console me
 concerning the destruction of my
    defenseless people."
5 [a]For the Sovereign LORD of Heaven's
    Armies
 has planned a day of panic, defeat,
    and confusion.

 In the Valley of Vision[1] people shout
 and cry out to the hill.
6 The [a]Elamites picked up the quiver
 and came with chariots and
    horsemen;
 the men of [b]Kir prepared[1] the shield.
7 Your very best valleys were full of
    chariots;
 horsemen confidently took their
    positions at the gate.
8 They removed [a]the defenses [b]of
    Judah.
 At that time you looked
 for the weapons in the House of the
    Forest.
9 You saw the many breaks
 in the walls of the City of David;
 [a]you stored up water in the lower pool.
10 You counted the houses in Jerusalem
 and demolished houses so you could
 have material to reinforce the wall.
11 [a]You made a reservoir between the
    two walls
 for the water of the old [b]pool—
 but you did not trust in the one who
    made it;
 you did not depend on the one who
 formed it long ago.
12 At that time the Sovereign LORD
 of Heaven's Armies [a]called [b]for
 weeping and mourning,
 for shaved heads and sackcloth.
13 But look, there is outright celebration!
 You say, "Kill the ox and slaughter
    the sheep,
 eat meat and [a]drink wine.
 Eat and drink, for tomorrow we die!"

14 The LORD of Heaven's Armies told me
this: "Certainly this sin will not be forgiv-
en as long as you live," says [a]the Sovereign
LORD of Heaven's Armies.

15 This is what the Sovereign LORD of
 Heaven's Armies says:
 "Go visit this administrator, [a]Shebna,
 who supervises the palace, and tell
    him:
16 'What right do you have to be here?
 What relatives do you have buried
    here?

21:13 [a]Jer 25:24; 49:28 [b]Gen 10:7; 1 Chr 1:9, 32; Jer 25:23; Ezek 27:15   21:16 [a]Ps 120:5; Song 1:5; Isa 42:11; 60:7; Ezek 27:21
21:17 [1]Or for.   22:2 [a]Isa 32:13   22:4 [a]Jer 4:19   22:5 [a]Isa 37:3   [1]The Heb. suggests that this phrase goes with what
precedes.   22:6 [a]Jer 49:35   [b]Isa 15:1   [1]Heb. Kir uncovers.   22:8 [a]2 Kgs 18:15–16   [b]1 Kgs 7:2; 10:17   22:9 [a]2 Kgs 20:20;
2 Chr 32:4; Neh 3:16   22:11 [a]Neh 3:16   [b]2 Kgs 20:20; 2 Chr 32:3–4   22:12 [a]Isa 32:11; Joel 1:13; 2:17   [b]Ezra 9:3; Isa 15:2;
Mic 1:16   22:13 [a]Isa 5:11, 22; 28:7–8; Luke 17:26–29   22:14 [a]Isa 5:9   22:15 [a]2 Kgs 18:37; Isa 36:3

Why do you chisel out a tomb for
  yourself here?
He chisels out his burial site in an
  elevated place,
he carves out his tomb on a cliff.
[17] Look, the LORD will throw you far
  away, you mere man!
He will wrap you up tightly.
[18] He will wind [a]you up tightly into a ball
and throw you into a wide, open land.
There you will die,
and there with you will be your
  impressive chariots,[1]
which bring disgrace to the house of
  your master.
[19] I will remove you from your office;
  you will be thrown down from your
  position.

[20]"At that time I will summon my servant [a]Eliakim, son of Hilkiah. [21]I will put your robe on him, tie your belt around him, and transfer your authority to him. He will become a protector of the residents of Jerusalem and of the people of Judah. [22]I will place the key to the house of David on his [a]shoulder. When he opens the door, no one can close it; when he closes the door, no one can [b]open it. [23]I will [a]fasten him like a peg into a solid place; he will bring honor and respect to his father's family. [24]His father's family will gain increasing prominence because of him, including the offspring and the offshoots. All the small containers, including the bowls and all the jars, will hang from this peg.[1]

[25]"At that time," says the LORD of Heaven's Armies, "the peg fastened into a solid place will come loose. It will be cut off and fall, and the load hanging on it will be cut off." Indeed,[1] the LORD has spoken.

The Lord Will Judge Tyre

23 This is an [a]oracle about Tyre:
Wail, you large ships,[1]
for the port is too devastated to
  enter![2]

From the land of Cyprus[3] this news is
  announced to them.
[2] Lament, you residents of the coast,
you merchants of Sidon who travel
  over the sea,
whose agents sail over [3]the deep
  waters.[1]
Grain from the Shihor region,[2]
crops grown near the Nile [a]she
  receives;
she is the trade center of the nations.
[4] Be ashamed, O Sidon,
for the sea says this, O fortress of the
  sea:
"I have not gone into labor
or given birth;
I have not raised young men
or brought up young women."
[5] [a]When the news reaches Egypt,
they will be shaken by what has
  happened to Tyre.
[6] Travel to Tarshish!
Wail, you residents of the coast!
[7] Is this really your [a]boisterous city
whose origins are in the distant past
and whose feet led her to a distant
  land to reside?
[8] Who planned this for royal Tyre,
whose merchants are princes,
whose traders are [a]the dignitaries of
  the earth?
[9] The LORD of Heaven's Armies
  [a]planned it—
to dishonor the [b]pride that comes
  from all her beauty,
to humiliate all the dignitaries of the
  earth.
[10] Daughter Tarshish, travel back to
  your land, as one crosses the Nile;
there is no longer any marketplace
  in Tyre.[1]
[11] The LORD stretched out his hand
  over the sea,
he shook kingdoms;
he gave the order
to destroy Canaan's fortresses.
[12] He said,

22:18 [a]Isa 2:7 [1]Heb. *and there the chariots of your splendor.* **22:20** [a]2 Kgs 18:18; Isa 36:3, 22; 37:2 **22:22** [a]Isa 9:6 [b]Job 12:14; Rev 3:7 **22:23** [a]Ezra 9:8; Zech 10:4 **22:24** [1]Heb. *all the small vessels, from the vessels that are bowls to all the vessels that are jars;* the picture is that of a single peg holding the weight of all kinds of containers. **22:25** [1]Or *for.* **23:1** [a]Jer 25:22; 47:4; Ezek 26—28; Amos 1:9; Zech 9:2, 4 [1]Heb. *the ships of Tarshish;* probably referring to large ships either made in or capable of traveling to the distant western port of Tarshish. [2]MT *for it is destroyed, from a house, from entering.* [3]Heb. *the Kittim.* **23:3** [a]Ezek 27:3–23 [1]MT (vv. 2b–3a) *merchant of Sidon, the one who crosses the sea, they filled you, and on the deep waters.* [2]Heb. *seed of Shihor;* probably the east branch of the Nile. **23:5** [a]Isa 19:16 **23:7** [a]Isa 22:2; 32:13 **23:8** [a]Ezek 28:2, 12 **23:9** [a]Isa 14:26 [b]Job 40:11–12; Isa 13:11; 24:4; Dan 4:37 **23:10** [1]MT *Cross over your land, like the Nile, daughter of Tarshish, there is no more waistband.*

"You will no longer celebrate,
oppressed virgin daughter Sidon!
Get up, travel to Cyprus,
but you will find no relief there."
[13] Look at the land of the [a]Chaldeans,
these people who have lost their
identity!
The Assyrians have made it a home
for [b]wild animals.
They erected their siege towers,
demolished its fortresses,
and turned it into a heap of ruins.
[14] [a]Wail, you large ships,
for your fortress is destroyed!

[15] At that time Tyre will be forgotten for 70 years, the typical life span of a king. At the end of 70 years Tyre will try to attract attention again, like the prostitute in the popular song:

[16] "Take the harp,
go through the city,
forgotten prostitute!
Play it well,
play lots of songs,
so you'll be noticed."

[17] At the end of 70 years the LORD will revive[1] Tyre. She will start making money again by selling her services to all the earth's kingdoms. [18] Her profits and earnings [a]will be set apart for the LORD. They will not be stored up or accumulated, for her profits will be given to those who live in the LORD's presence and will be used to purchase large quantities of food and beautiful clothes.

The Lord Will Judge the Earth

24 Look, the LORD is ready to
devastate the earth
and leave it in ruins;
he will mar its surface
and scatter its inhabitants.
[2] Everyone will suffer—the [a]priest [b]as
well as the people,
the master as well as the servant,
the elegant lady as well as the female
attendant,
the seller as well as the buyer,
the borrower as well as the lender,
the creditor as well as the debtor.
[3] The earth will be completely
devastated
and thoroughly ransacked.
For the LORD has decreed this
judgment.
[4] The earth dries up and withers,
the world shrivels up and withers;
the [a]prominent people of the earth
fade away.
[5] The earth is defiled by its
inhabitants,
for [a]they have [b]violated laws,
disregarded the regulation,
and broken the [c]permanent treaty.[1]
[6] So a treaty curse devours [a]the earth;
its inhabitants pay for their guilt.
This is why the inhabitants of the
earth disappear,
and are reduced to just a handful of
people.
[7] The new wine dries up,
[a]the vines shrivel up,
all those who like to celebrate groan.
[8] The happy sound [a]of the
tambourines stops,
the revelry of those who celebrate
comes to a halt,
the happy sound of the harp ceases.
[9] They no longer sing and drink wine;
the beer tastes bitter to those who
drink it.
[10] The ruined town[1] is shattered;
all the houses are shut up tight.
[11] They howl in the streets because of
what happened to the wine;
all joy turns to sorrow;
celebrations disappear from the
earth.
[12] The city is left in ruins;
the gate is reduced to rubble.
[13] This is what will happen throughout
the earth,
among the nations.
[a]It will be like when they beat an
olive tree,
and just a few olives are left at the
end of the harvest.
[14] They lift their voices and shout
joyfully;

23:13 [a]Isa 47:1 [b]Ps 72:9 **23:14** [a]Ezek 27:25–30 **23:17** [1]Heb. *visit* [with favor]. **23:18** [a]Exod 28:36; Zech 14:20–21 **24:2** [a]Hos 4:9 [b]Ezek 7:12–13 **24:4** [a]Isa 25:11 **24:5** [a]Gen 3:17; Num 35:33; Isa 9:17; 10:6 [b]Isa 59:12 [c]1 Chr 16:14–19; Ps 105:7–12 [1]Or *everlasting covenant.* **24:6** [a]Mal 4:6 **24:7** [a]Isa 16:8–10; Joel 1:10, 12 **24:8** [a]Isa 5:12, 14; Jer 7:34; 16:9; 25:10; Ezek 26:13; Hos 2:11; Rev 18:22 **24:10** [1]Heb. *the city of chaos.* **24:13** [a][Isa 17:5–6; 27:12]

they praise the majesty of the LORD
in the west.
15 So in the east[1] [a]extol [b]the LORD,
along the seacoasts extol the fame[2]
of the LORD God of Israel.
16 From [a]the ends of the earth we hear
songs—
the Just One is majestic.
But I say, "I'm wasting away! I'm
wasting away! I'm doomed!
Deceivers deceive, deceivers
thoroughly deceive!"[1]
17 [a]Terror, pit, and snare
are ready to overtake you,
inhabitants of the earth!
18 The one who runs away from [a]the
sound of [b]the terror
will fall into the pit;
the one who climbs out of the pit
will be trapped by the snare.
For the floodgates of the heavens are
opened up
and the foundations of the earth
shake.
19 The earth is broken in pieces,
[a]the earth is ripped to shreds,
the earth shakes violently.
20 The earth will [a]stagger around like a
drunk;
it will sway back and forth like a hut
in a windstorm.
Its sin will weigh it down,
and it will fall and never get up again.

The Lord Will Become King

21 At that time [a]the LORD will punish
the heavenly forces in the heavens
and the earthly kings on the earth.
22 They will be imprisoned in a pit,
locked up in a prison,
and after staying there for a long
time, they will be punished.
23 The full [a]moon will be covered up,
the bright sun will be darkened;
for the LORD of Heaven's Armies will
[b]rule[1]
on [c]Mount Zion in Jerusalem
in the presence of his assembly, in
majestic splendor.

25 O LORD, you are my God!
[a]I will exalt you in praise, I will
extol your fame.
[b]For [c]you have done extraordinary
things,
and executed plans made long ago
exactly as you decreed.
2 Indeed,[1] you [a]have made the city into
a heap of rubble,
the fortified town into a heap of
ruins;
the fortress of foreigners[2] is no
longer a city,
it will never be rebuilt.
3 So a strong nation will [a]extol you;
the towns of powerful nations will
fear you.
4 For you [a]are a protector for the poor,
a protector for the needy in their
distress,
a shelter from the rainstorm,
a shade from the heat.
Though the breath of tyrants is like a
winter rainstorm,[1]
5 like heat in a dry land,
you humble the boasting foreigners.
Just as the shadow of a cloud causes
the heat to subside,
so he causes the song of tyrants to
cease.
6 The LORD of Heaven's Armies will
hold a banquet for [a]all the nations
on [b]this mountain.
At this banquet [c]there will be plenty
of meat and aged wine—
tender meat and choicest wine.
7 On this mountain [a]he will swallow up
the shroud that is over all the
peoples,
the woven covering that is over all
the nations;
8 he will swallow [a]up death
permanently.
The Sovereign LORD will [b]wipe away
the tears from every face,
and remove his people's disgrace
from all the earth.
Indeed, the LORD has announced it![1]
9 At that time they will say,

24:15 [a]Isa 25:3 [b]Mal 1:11 [1]MT *in the lights.* [2]Heb. *name.* **24:16** [a]Isa 21:2; 33:1; Jer 3:20; 5:11 [1]V. 16b is a classic example of Heb. wordplay involving repetition of sound to draw attention to the prophet's lament. **24:17** [a]Jer 48:43; Amos 5:19 **24:18** [a]Gen 7:11 [b]Ps 18:7; 46:2; Isa 2:19, 21; 13:13 **24:19** [a]Jer 4:23 **24:20** [a]Isa 19:14; 24:1; 28:7 **24:21** [a]Ps 76:12 **24:23** [a]Isa 13:10; 60:19; Ezek 32:7; Joel 2:31; 3:15 [b]Rev 19:4, 6 [c][Heb 12:22] [1]Or *take his throne, become king.* **25:1** [a]Exod 15:2 [b]Ps 98:1 [c]Num 23:19 **25:2** [a]Isa 21:9; 23:13; Jer 51:37 [1]Or *For.* [2]LXX *the insolent.* **25:3** [a]Isa 24:15; Rev 11:13 **25:4** [a]Isa 4:6 [1]MT *like a rainstorm of a wall.* **25:6** [a][Dan 7:14; Matt 8:11] [b][Isa 2:2–4; 56:7] [c]Prov 9:2; Matt 22:4 **25:7** [a]2 Cor 3:15; [Eph 4:18] **25:8** [a][Hos 13:14; 1 Cor 15:54; Rev 20:14] [b]Isa 30:19; Rev 7:17; 21:4 [1]Heb. *has spoken.*

"Look, here is our God!
ᵃWe waited for him, and he
delivered us.
Here is the LORD! ᵇWe waited for
him.
Let's rejoice and celebrate his
deliverance!"
10 For the LORD's power will make this
mountain secure.
ᵃMoab will be trampled down where
it stands,
as a heap of straw is trampled down
in¹ a manure pile.
11 Moab will spread out its hands in the
middle of it,
just as a swimmer spreads his hands
to swim;
the LORD will bring down Moab's
ᵃpride as it spreads its hands.
12 The fortified ᵃcity (along with the
very tops of your walls) he will
knock down,
he will bring it down, he will throw it
down to the dusty ground.

Judah Will Celebrate

26 At ᵃthat time this song will be sung
in the land of Judah:
"We have a strong city!
The LORD's deliverance, like walls
and a rampart, makes it secure.
2 ᵃOpen the gates so a righteous nation
can enter—
one that remains trustworthy.
3 You keep ᵃcompletely safe the people
who maintain their faith,
for they trust in you.
4 Trust in the LORD from this time
ᵃforward,
even in YAH, the LORD, an enduring
protector!¹
5 Indeed,¹ ᵃthe LORD knocks down
those who live in a high place,
he brings down an elevated town;
he brings it down to the ground,
he throws it down to the dust.
6 It is trampled underfoot
by the feet of the oppressed,
by the soles of the poor."

God's People Anticipate Vindication

7 The way ᵃof the righteous is level,
the path of the righteous that you
prepare is straight.¹
8 Yes, as your judgments unfold,
O LORD, we ᵃwait for you.
We desire your fame and reputation
to grow.
9 I look for you during the night;
my spirit ᵃwithin me seeks you at
dawn;
for when your judgments come upon
the earth,
those who live in the world learn
about justice.
10 ᵃIf ᵇthe wicked are shown mercy,
they do not learn about justice.
Even in a land where right is
rewarded, they act unjustly;¹
they do not see the LORD's majesty
revealed.
11 O LORD, you are ready to act,
but ᵃthey don't even notice.
They will see and be put to shame
by your angry judgment against
humankind;
yes, fire will consume your enemies.
12 O LORD, you make us secure,
for even all we have accomplished
you have done for us.
13 O LORD, our God,
ᵃmasters other than you have
ruled us,
but we praise your name alone.
14 The dead do not come back to life,
the spirits of the dead do not rise.
That is because you came in
judgment and destroyed them,
you wiped ᵃout all memory of them.
15 You have ᵃmade the nation larger,
O LORD;
you have made the nation larger and
revealed your splendor;
you have extended all the borders of
the land.
16 O LORD, ᵃin distress they looked for
you;
they uttered incantations because of
your discipline.¹

25:9 ᵃGen 49:18; Isa 8:17; 26:8; [Titus 2:13] ᵇPs 20:5 25:10 ᵃIsa 16:14; Jer 48:1–47; Ezek 25:8–11; Amos 2:1–3; Zeph 2:9 ¹Ket. *in the water of.* 25:11 ᵃIsa 24:4; 26:5 25:12 ᵃIsa 26:5 26:1 ᵃIsa 2:11; 12:1 26:2 ᵃPs 118:19–20 26:3 ᵃIsa 57:19; [Phil 4:6–7] 26:4 ᵃIsa 12:2; 45:17 ¹MT *for in Yah, the LORD, an everlasting rock.* 26:5 ᵃIsa 25:11–12 ¹Or *For.* 26:7 ᵃPs 37:23 ¹MT *upright, the path of the righteous you make level.* 26:8 ᵃIsa 25:9; 33:2 26:9 ᵃPs 63:6; Song 3:1; Isa 50:10; Luke 6:12 26:10 ᵃEccl 8:12; [Rom 2:4] ᵇPs 143:10 ¹Heb. *land of uprightness they act unjustly.* 26:11 ᵃJob 34:27; Ps 28:5; Isa 5:12 26:13 ᵃ2 Chr 12:8 26:14 ᵃEccl 9:5; Isa 14:22 26:15 ᵃIsa 9:3 26:16 ᵃIsa 37:3; Hos 5:15 ¹The meaning of this verse is unclear and appears to read lit. *O LORD, in distress they visit you, they pour out [?] an incantation, your discipline to them.*

17 As when ᵃa pregnant woman gets
        ready to deliver
    and strains and cries out because of
        her labor pains,
    so were we because of you, O LORD.
18 We were pregnant, we strained,
    we gave birth, as it were, to wind.
    We cannot produce deliverance on
        ᵃthe earth;
    no people are born to populate the
        world.
19 Your dead will come back to life;
    ᵃyour corpses will rise up.
    Wake ᵇup and shout joyfully, you who
        live in the ground!
    For you will grow like plants
        drenched with the morning dew,
    and the earth will bring forth its
        dead spirits.
20 Go, my people! ᵃEnter your inner
        rooms!
    Close your doors behind you!
    Hide ᵇfor a little while,
    until his angry judgment is over.
21 For look, the LORD is coming out of
        the place where he lives
    to punish the sin of those who live
        on the earth.
    The earth will display the blood shed
        on it;
    it will no longer cover up its slain.

27 At that time the LORD will punish
    with his destructive,¹ great, and
        powerful sword
    ᵃLeviathan ᵇthe fast-moving serpent,
    Leviathan the squirming serpent;
    he will kill the sea monster.
2 When that time comes,
    ᵃsing ᵇabout a delightful vineyard!
3 "I, the LORD, protect ᵃit;
    I water it regularly.
    I guard it night and day,
    so no one can harm it.
4 I am not angry.
    I wish I could confront some ᵃthorns
        and briers!
    Then I would march against them for
        battle;

I would set them all on fire,
5 unless they became my subjects
    and made peace with me;
    let them ᵃmake peace with me."¹

6 The time is coming when Jacob will
        take root;¹
    Israel will blossom and grow
        branches.
    The produce will fill the surface of
        the world.
7 Has the LORD struck down Israel ᵃas
        he did their oppressors?
    Has Israel been killed like their
        enemies?
8 When you summon her for divorce,
        you prosecute her;
    he drives her away with his strong
        ᵃwind in ᵇthe day of the east wind.
9 So in this way Jacob's sin will be
        forgiven,¹
    and this is how they will show they
        are finished sinning:
    They will make all the stones of the
        altars
    like crushed limestone,
    and the Asherah poles and the
        incense altars will no longer stand.
10 For the fortified city is left ᵃalone;
    it is a deserted settlement
    and abandoned like the wilderness.
    Calves graze there;
    they lie down there
    and eat its branches bare.
11 When ᵃits branches get brittle, they
        break;
    women come and use them for
        kindling.
    For these people lack understanding,
    therefore the one who made them
        has ᵇno compassion on ᶜthem;
    the one who formed them has no
        mercy on them.

12 At that time the LORD will shake the
tree, from the Euphrates River¹ to the
Stream of Egypt. Then you will be gathered
ᵃup one by one, O Israelites. 13ᵃAt that time a

26:17 ᵃIsa 13:8; [John 16:21]   26:18 ᵃPs 17:14   26:19 ᵃIsa 25:8; [Ezek 37:1–14]   ᵇ[Dan 12:2]; Hos 13:14   26:20 ᵃExod
12:22–23; [Ps 91:1, 4]   ᵇ[Ps 30:5; Isa 54:7–8; 2 Cor 4:17]   27:1 ᵃGen 3:1; Ps 74:13–14; Rev 12:9, 15   ᵇIsa 51:9; Ezek 29:3;
32:2   ¹Heb. hard, severe.   27:2 ᵃIsa 5:1   ᵇPs 80:8; Isa 5:7; Jer 2:21   27:3 ᵃ1 Sam 2:9; Ps 121:4–5; Isa 31:5; [John 10:28]
27:4 ᵃ2 Sam 23:6; Isa 9:18   27:5 ᵃJob 22:21; Isa 26:3, 12; [Rom 5:1; 2 Cor 5:20]   ¹MT he makes peace with me; peace
he makes with me.   27:6 ¹MT the coming ones, let Jacob take root.   27:7 ᵃIsa 10:12, 17; 30:30–33   27:8 ᵃJob 23:6;
Ps 6:1; Jer 10:24; 30:11; 46:28; [1 Cor 10:13]   ᵇ[Ps 78:38]   27:9 ¹Or be atoned for.   27:10 ᵃIsa 5:6, 17; 32:14;
Jer 26:18   27:11 ᵃDeut 32:28; Isa 1:3   ᵇIsa 9:17   ᶜDeut 32:18; Isa 43:1, 7; 44:2, 21, 24
27:12 ᵃ[Isa 11:11; 56:8]   ¹Heb. the river.   27:13 ᵃIsa 2:11

large trumpet will be blown, and [b]the ones lost in the land of Assyria will come, as well as the refugees in the land of [c]Egypt. They will [d]worship the LORD on the holy mountain in Jerusalem.

The Lord Will Judge Ephraim

28 The splendid crown of Ephraim's drunkards is doomed,
the withering flower, its beautiful splendor,[1]
situated at the head of a rich valley,
the crown of those overcome with wine.

2 Look, the Lord sends a strong, powerful one.
With the force of a hailstorm or a destructive windstorm,
with the might of a driving, torrential rainstorm,
he will knock that crown to the ground with his hand.

3 The splendid crown of Ephraim's drunkards
will be trampled underfoot.

4 The withering flower, its beautiful splendor,
situated at the head of a rich valley,
will be like an early fig before harvest—
as soon as someone notices it,
he grabs it and swallows it.

5 At that time the LORD of Heaven's Armies will become a beautiful crown
and a splendid diadem for the remnant of his people.

6 He will give discernment to the one who makes judicial decisions
and strength to those who defend the city from attackers.

7 Even [a]these men stagger because of wine;
they stumble around because of beer—
priests and prophets stagger because of beer,
they are confused because of wine,
they stumble around because of beer;
they stagger while seeing prophetic visions,
they totter while making legal decisions.

8 Indeed, all the tables
are covered with vomit,
with filth, leaving no clean place.

9 [a]Who is the LORD trying to teach?
To whom is he explaining a message?
To those just weaned from milk!
To those just taken from their mother's breast![1]

10 [a]Indeed, they will hear meaningless gibberish,
senseless babbling,
a syllable here, a syllable there.

11 For with [a]mocking lips and a foreign tongue
he will speak to these people.

12 In the past he said to them,
"This is where security can be [a]found.
Provide security for the one who is exhausted.
This is where rest can be found."
But they refused to listen.

13 So the LORD's message to them will sound like
meaningless gibberish,
senseless babbling,
a syllable here, a syllable there.
As a result, they will fall on their backsides when they try to walk,
and be injured, ensnared, and captured.

The Lord Will Judge Jerusalem

14 Therefore, listen to the LORD's message,
you who mock,
you rulers of these people
who reside in Jerusalem.

15 For you say,
"We have made a treaty with death,
with Sheol we have made an agreement.
When the overwhelming judgment sweeps by
it will not reach us.
[a]For we have made a lie our refuge,
we have hidden ourselves in a deceitful word."

16 Therefore, this is [a]what the Sovereign LORD, says:

27:13 [b] Lev 25:9; 1 Chr 15:24; Matt 24:31; Rev 11:15   [c] Isa 19:21–22   [d] [Isa 2:3]; Zech 14:16; [Heb 12:22]   **28:1** [1] Heb. *the beauty of his splendor.*   **28:7** [a] Isa 56:10, 12   **28:9** [a] Jer 6:10   [1] Heb. *from the breasts.*   **28:10** [a] [2 Chr 36:15; Neh 9:30; Jer 25:3–4; 35:15; 44:4]   **28:11** [a] Isa 33:19; 1 Cor 14:21   **28:12** [a] Isa 30:15; Jer 6:16; [Matt 11:28–29]   **28:15** [a] Isa 9:15; Ezek 13:22; Amos 2:4   **28:16** [a] Gen 49:24; Ps 118:22; Isa 8:14–15; Matt 21:42; Mark 12:10; Luke 20:17; Acts 4:11; Rom 9:33; 10:11; Eph 2:20; 1 Pet 2:6–8

"Look, I am laying a stone in Zion,
an approved[1] stone,
set in place as a precious cornerstone
for the foundation.
The one who maintains his faith will
not panic.
[17] I will make justice the measuring line,
fairness the plumb line;
hail will sweep away the unreliable
refuge,
the floodwaters will overwhelm the
hiding place.
[18] Your treaty with death will be
dissolved;
your agreement with Sheol will not
last.
When the overwhelming judgment
sweeps by,
you will be overrun by it.
[19] Whenever it sweeps by, it will
overtake you;
indeed,[1] every morning it will
sweep by,
it will come through during the day
and the night."
When this announcement is
understood,
it will cause nothing but terror.
[20] For the bed is too short to stretch
out on,
and the blanket is too narrow to
wrap around oneself.
[21] For the LORD will rise up, as he did at
Mount [a]Perazim;
he will rouse himself, as he did in the
Valley of [b]Gibeon,
to accomplish [c]his work,
his peculiar work,
to perform his task,
his strange task.
[22] So now, do not mock,
or your [a]chains will become heavier!
For I have heard a message about
decreed destruction,
from the Sovereign LORD of Heaven's
Armies against the entire land.
[23] Pay attention and listen to my
message.
Be attentive and listen to what I have
to say!
[24] Does a farmer just keep on plowing
at planting time?

Does he keep breaking up and
harrowing his ground?
[25] Once he has leveled its surface,
does he not scatter the seed of the
caraway plant,
sow the seed of the cumin plant,
and plant the wheat, barley, and
grain in their designated places?[1]
[26] His God instructs him;
he teaches him the principles of
agriculture.
[27] Certainly[1] caraway seed is not
threshed with a sledge,
nor is the wheel of a cart rolled over
cumin seed.
Certainly caraway seed is beaten
with a stick
and cumin seed with a flail.
[28] Grain is crushed,
though one certainly does not thresh
it forever.
The wheel of one's wagon rolls
over it,
but his horses do not crush it.
[29] This also comes from the LORD of
Heaven's Armies,
[a]who gives supernatural guidance
and imparts great wisdom.

Ariel Is Besieged

29 Ariel is as good as dead—
Ariel, the [a]town David besieged!
Keep observing your annual rituals;
celebrate your festivals on schedule.
[2] I will threaten Ariel,
and she will mourn intensely
and become like an altar hearth
before me.
[3] I will lay siege to you on all sides;[1]
I will besiege you with troops;[2]
I will raise siege works against you.
[4] You will fall;
while lying on the ground you will
speak;
from the dust where you lie, your
words will be heard.
Your voice will sound like a spirit
speaking from the underworld;
from the dust you will chirp as if
muttering an incantation.
[5] But the horde of [a]invaders will be
like fine dust,

28:16 [1]Trad. tested.   28:19 [1]Or for.   28:21 [a]2 Sam 5:20; 1 Chr 14:11   [b]Josh 10:10, 12; 2 Sam 5:25; 1 Chr 14:16   [c][Lam 3:33; Luke 19:41–44]   28:22 [a]Isa 10:22; Dan 9:27   28:25 [1]MT *place wheat [?], and barley [?], and grain in its territory.*
28:27 [1]Or *For.*   28:29 [a]Ps 92:5; Isa 9:6; Jer 32:19   29:1 [a]Ezek 24:6, 9   29:3 [1]LXX *like David.*
[2]Or perhaps *towers.*   29:5 [a]Isa 25:5

the horde of tyrants like [b]chaff that
is blown away.
It will happen suddenly, [c]in a flash.
6 [a]Judgment will come from the LORD
of Heaven's Armies,
accompanied by thunder,
[b]earthquake, and a loud noise,
by a strong gale, a windstorm, and a
consuming flame of fire.
7 It will be like a dream, a night vision.
[a]There will be [b]a horde from all the
nations that fight against Ariel,
those who attack her and her
stronghold and besiege her.
8 It will be like a hungry man
dreaming that he is eating,
only to awaken and find that his
stomach is empty.
[a]It will be like a thirsty man
dreaming that he is drinking,
only to awaken and find that he is still
weak and his thirst unquenched.
So it will be for the horde from all
the nations
that fight against Mount Zion.

God's People Are Spiritually Insensitive

9 You will be shocked and amazed!
You are totally blind!
[a]They are drunk, [b]but not because of
wine;
they stagger, but not because of beer.
10 For [a]the LORD has poured out on you
a strong urge to sleep deeply.
He has [b]shut your eyes (you
prophets),
and covered your heads (you seers).

[11]To you this entire prophetic revelation[1] is like words in [a]a sealed scroll. When
they [b]hand it to one who can read and say,
"Read this," he responds, "I can't, because it
is sealed." [12]Or when they hand the scroll to
one who can't read and say, "Read this," he
says, "I can't read."

13 The Lord says,
"[a]These people say they are loyal
to me;

they say wonderful things about me,
but they are not really loyal to me.
Their worship consists of
nothing but man-made ritual.
14 [a]Therefore I will again do an amazing
thing for these people—
an absolutely extraordinary deed.
Wise men will have nothing to say,
the sages will have no explanations."
15 Those who try to hide their plans
from the LORD are as good as [a]dead,
who do their work in secret and boast,
"Who sees us? Who knows what we're
doing?"
16 Your thinking is perverse!
Should the potter be regarded as
clay?
Should the thing [a]made say about its
maker, "He didn't make me"?
Or should the pottery say about the
potter, "He doesn't understand"?

Changes Are Coming

17 In just a very short time
[a]Lebanon will turn into an orchard,
and the orchard will be considered a
forest.
18 At that time[1] the deaf will be able to
hear words read from a scroll,
and the eyes of the [a]blind will be able
to see through deep darkness.
19 The downtrodden will again rejoice
in [a]the LORD;
[b]the poor among humankind will
take delight in the Holy One of
Israel.
20 For tyrants will disappear,
those who taunt will vanish,
and all those who love to [a]do wrong
will be eliminated—
21 those who bear false testimony
against [a]a person,
who entrap the one who arbitrates at
the city gate
and deprive the innocent of justice
[b]by making false charges.
22 So this is what the LORD, the one
[a]who delivered Abraham, has said
to the family of Jacob:

29:5 [b]Job 21:18; Isa 17:13   [c]Isa 30:13; 47:11; 1 Thess 5:3   **29:6** [a]Isa 28:2; 30:30   [b]1 Sam 2:10; Zech 14:4; Matt 24:7; Mark 13:8;
Luke 21:11; Rev 16:18-19   **29:7** [a]Isa 37:36; Mic 4:11-12; Zech 12:9   [b]Job 20:8   **29:8** [a]Ps 73:20   **29:9** [a]Isa 28:7-8   [b]Isa 51:21
29:10 [a]Ps 69:23; Isa 6:9-10; Mic 3:6; Rom 11:8   [b]Ps 69:23; Isa 6:10   **29:11** [a]Isa 8:16   [b]Dan 12:4, 9; [Matt 13:11-16]; Rev
5:1-5, 9   [1]Heb. *vision*.   **29:13** [a]Ps 78:36; Ezek 33:31; Matt 15:8-9; Mark 7:6-7   **29:14** [a]Isa 6:9-10; 28:21; Hab 1:5
29:15 [a]Isa 30:1   **29:16** [a]Isa 45:9; Jer 18:1-6; [Rom 9:19-21]   **29:17** [a]Isa 32:15   **29:18** [a]Isa 35:5; Matt 11:5;
Mark 7:37   [1]Or *In that day*.   **29:19** [a][Ps 25:9; 37:11; Isa 11:4; 61:1; Matt 5:5; 11:29]   [b]Isa 14:30; [Matt 5:3;
11:5; Jas 2:5]   **29:20** [a]Isa 59:4; Mic 2:1   **29:21** [a]Amos 5:10, 12   [b]Prov 28:21   **29:22** [a]Josh 24:3

"Jacob will no longer be [b]ashamed;
their faces will no longer show their
embarrassment.[1]
23 For when [a]they see their children,
whom I will produce among them,
they will honor my name.
They will honor the Holy One of
Jacob;
they will respect the God of Israel.
24 Those [a]who stray morally will gain
understanding;
those who complain will acquire
insight.

Egypt Will Prove Unreliable

30 "The rebellious children are as
good as dead," says the LORD,
"those [a]who make plans without
consulting me,
who form alliances without
consulting my Spirit,
and thereby compound their sin.
2 [a]They travel down to Egypt
without seeking my will,
seeking Pharaoh's protection,
and looking for safety in Egypt's
protective shade.[1]
3 But Pharaoh's protection will bring
you nothing but shame
and [a]the safety of Egypt's protective
shade nothing but humiliation.
4 Though his officials are in [a]Zoan
and his messengers arrive at Hanes,
5 [a]all will be put to shame
because of a nation that cannot help
them,
who cannot give them aid or help,
but only shame and disgrace."
6 This is an oracle about [a]the animals
in [b]the Negev:
Through a land of distress and
danger,
inhabited by lionesses and roaring
lions,[1]
by snakes and darting adders,
they transport their wealth on the
backs of donkeys,
their riches on the humps of camels,
to a nation that cannot help them.

7 Egypt is totally incapable of helping.
[a]For this reason I call her
"Proud one[1] who is silenced."
8 Now go, [a]write it down on a tablet in
their presence;
inscribe it on a scroll
so that it might be preserved for a
future time
as an enduring witness.
9 For these are rebellious people—
they are lying children,
children unwilling to obey the
LORD's law.
10 [a]They[1] say to the visionaries, "See no
more visions!"
and to the seers, "Don't relate
messages to us about what is right!
[b]Tell us nice things;
relate deceptive messages.
11 Turn aside from the way;
stray off the path.
Remove from our presence the Holy
One of Israel."

12 For this reason this is what the Holy
One of Israel says:
"You have [a]rejected this message;
you trust instead in your ability to
oppress and trick,
and rely on that kind of behavior.
13 So this sin will become your
downfall.
You will be [a]like a high wall
that bulges and cracks and is ready to
collapse;
it [b]crumbles suddenly, in a flash.
14 It shatters in pieces like a clay jar,
so shattered to bits that none of it
can be salvaged.
Among its fragments one cannot find
a shard large enough
to scoop a hot coal from a fire
or to skim off water from a cistern."

15 For this is what the Sovereign LORD, the
Holy One of Israel says:

"If you repented and patiently waited
for me, you would be delivered;

29:22 [b] Isa 45:17   [1] Heb. *and his face will no longer be pale.*   29:23 [a] [Isa 45:11; 49:20–26; Eph 2:10]   29:24 [a] Isa 28:7
30:1 [a] Isa 29:15   30:2 [a] Isa 31:1; Jer 43:7   [1] Heb. *to seek protection in the protection of Pharaoh, and to seek refuge in the
shade of Egypt.*   30:3 [a] Isa 20:5; Jer 37:5, 7   30:4 [a] Isa 19:11   30:5 [a] Jer 2:36   30:6 [a] Isa 57:9; Hos 8:9; 12:1   [b] Deut 8:15; Isa
14:29   [1] Heb. [a land of] *a lioness and a lion, from them.*   30:7 [a] Jer 37:7   [1] Heb. *Rahab,* which appears elsewhere as a name
for Egypt and for a mythical sea monster symbolic of chaos.   30:8 [a] Hab 2:2   30:10 [a] Isa 5:20; Jer 11:21; Amos 2:12; Mic
2:6   [b] 1 Kgs 22:8, 13; Jer 6:14; 23:17, 26; Ezek 13:7; Mic 2:11; Rom 16:18; 2 Tim 4:3–4   [1] Heb. *who.*   30:12 [a] Lev 26:43; Num
15:31; Prov 1:30; 13:13; Isa 5:24; Ezek 20:13, 16, 24; Amos 2:4   30:13 [a] 1 Kgs 20:30; Ps 62:3–4; Isa 58:12   [b] Isa 29:5

if you calmly trusted ªin me, you
    would find strength,
 ᵇbut you are unwilling.
16 You say, 'No, we will flee on horses,'
    so you will indeed flee.
 You say, 'We will ride on fast horses,'
    so your pursuers will be fast.
17 ªOne thousand will scurry at the
    battle cry of one enemy soldier;
 at the battle cry of five enemy
    soldiers you will all run away,
 until the remaining few are as
    isolated
 as a flagpole on a mountaintop
 or a signal flag on a hill."

The Lord Will not Abandon His People

18 For this reason the LORD is ready to
    ªshow you mercy;
 he sits on his throne, ready to have
    compassion on you.
 Indeed, the LORD is a just God;
 all who ᵇwait for him in faith will be
    ᶜblessed.
19 For people will live in Zion;
 in Jerusalem you will ªweep no more.
 When he hears your cry of despair, he
    will indeed show you mercy;
 when he hears it, he will ᵇrespond to
    you.
20 The Lord will give you distress to eat
 and suffering to drink;
 but your teachers will no longer be
    hidden;
 your eyes will see ªthem.
21 You[1] will hear a word spoken behind
    you, saying,
 "This is the correct way, walk in it,"
 whether you are heading to the right
    or the left.
22 You will desecrate ªyour silver-plated
    idols
 and ᵇyour gold-plated images.
 You will throw them away as if they
    were a menstrual rag,
 saying to them, "Get out!"
23 He will water ªthe seed you plant in
    the ground,
 and the ground will produce crops in
    abundance.

At that time your cattle will graze in
    wide pastures.
24 The oxen and donkeys used in
    plowing[1]
 will eat seasoned feed winnowed
    with a shovel and pitchfork.
25 On every high mountain
 and every high hill
 there will be streams flowing with
    water,
 at the time of ªgreat slaughter when
    the fortified towers collapse.
26 The light of ªthe full moon will be
    like the sun's glare,
 and the sun's glare will be seven
    times brighter,
 like the light of seven days,
 when the LORD binds up his people's
    fractured bones
 and heals their severe wound.
27 Look, the name of the LORD comes
    from a distant place
 in raging anger and awesome
    splendor.
 He speaks angrily,
 and his word is like destructive fire.[1]
28 ªHis ᵇbattle cry overwhelms like a
    flooding river
 that reaches one's neck.
 He shakes the nations in a sieve that
    isolates the chaff;
 he puts a bit into the mouth of
    the nations and leads them to
    destruction.
29 You will sing
 as you do in ªthe evening when you
    are celebrating a festival.
 You will be happy like one who plays
    a flute
 as he goes to the mountain of the
    LORD, the Rock who shelters Israel.
30 ªThe LORD will give ᵇa mighty shout
 and intervene in power,
 with furious anger and flaming,
    destructive fire,
 with a driving rainstorm and
    hailstones.
31 Indeed, the LORD's shout will shatter
    Assyria;
 he will beat them with a ªclub.

30:15 ªPs 116:7; Isa 7:4; 28:12　ᵇMatt 23:37　30:17 ªLev 26:36; Deut 28:25; 32:30; Josh 23:10; [Prov 28:1]　30:18 ªIsa 33:2
ᵇIsa 26:8　ᶜPs 2:12; 34:8; Prov 16:20; Jer 17:7　30:19 ªIsa 25:8　ᵇPs 50:15; Isa 65:24; [Matt 7:7–11]　30:20 ª1 Kgs 22:27;
Ps 127:2　30:21 ¹Heb. your ears.　30:22 ª2 Chr 31:1; Isa 2:20; 31:7　ᵇHos 14:8　30:23 ª[Matt 6:33]; 1 Tim 6:8
30:24 ¹Heb. that work the ground.　30:25 ªIsa 2:10–21; 34:2　30:26 ª[Isa 60:19–20; Rev 21:23; 22:5]
30:27 ¹Heb. his lips are full of anger, and his tongue is like consuming fire.　30:28 ªIsa 11:4; 2 Thess 2:8
ᵇ2 Kgs 19:28; Isa 37:29　30:29 ª[Isa 2:3]　30:30 ªIsa 29:6　ᵇIsa 28:2　30:31 ªIsa 10:5, 24

32 Every blow from his punishing
  cudgel[1]
with which the LORD will beat them
will be accompanied by music from
  the tambourine and harp,
and he will attack them with his
  [a]weapons.
33 For[1] the burial place is already
  prepared;[2]
it has been made deep and wide [a]for
  the king.
The firewood is piled high on it.
The LORD's breath, like a stream
  flowing with brimstone,
will ignite it.

Egypt Will Disappoint

31 Those [a]who go down to Egypt for
  help are as good as dead;
those who [b]rely on war horses
and trust in Egypt's many chariots
and in their many, many horsemen.
But they do [c]not rely on the Holy
  One of Israel
and do not seek help from the LORD.
2 Yet he too is wise and he [a]will bring
  disaster;
he does not retract his decree.
He will attack the wicked nation
and the nation that helps those who
  commit sin.
3 The Egyptians are mere humans, not
  God;
their horses are made of flesh, not
  spirit.
The LORD will strike with his hand;
the one who helps will stumble
and the one being helped will fall.
[a]Together they will perish.

The Lord Will Defend Zion

4 Indeed, this is what the LORD [a]has
  said to me:
"The LORD will be like a growling
  lion,
like a young lion growling over its
  prey.
Though a whole group of shepherds
  gathers against it,
it is not afraid of their shouts

or intimidated by their yelling.
In this same way the LORD of
  Heaven's Armies will descend
to do battle on Mount Zion and on
  its hill.
5 [a]Just as birds hover over a nest,
so the LORD of Heaven's Armies will
  protect Jerusalem.
He will protect and deliver it;
as he passes over he will rescue it."

[6]You Israelites! Return to the one you
have so [a]blatantly rebelled against! [7]For at
that time every one will get rid of[1] the silver
and gold idols your hands [a]sinfully made.

8 "Assyria will [a]fall by a sword, but not
  one human made;
a sword not made by humankind will
  [b]destroy them.
They will run away from this sword
and their young men will be forced
  to do hard labor.
9 They will surrender [a]their
  stronghold because of fear;
their officers will be afraid of the
  LORD's battle flag."
This is what the LORD says—
the one whose fire is in Zion,
whose firepot is in Jerusalem.

Justice and Wisdom Will Prevail

32 Look, [a]a king will promote fairness;[1]
  officials will promote justice.
2 Each of them will be like [a]a shelter
  from the wind
and a refuge from a rainstorm;
like streams of water in a dry region
and like the shade of a large cliff in a
  parched land.
3 [a]Eyes will no longer be blind
and ears will be attentive.
4 The mind that acts rashly will
  [a]possess discernment,
and the tongue that stutters will
  speak with ease and clarity.
5 A fool will no longer be called
  honorable;
a deceiver will no longer be called
  principled.

30:32 [a]Isa 11:15 [1]MT *every blow from a founded [i.e., appointed?] cudgel.* 30:33 [a]2 Kgs 23:10; Jer 7:31 [1]Or *indeed.*
[2]MT *for arranged from before [or yesterday] is [?].* 31:1 [a]Isa 30:1–2 [b]Deut 17:16; Ps 20:7; Isa 2:7; 30:16 [c]Isa 9:13;
Dan 9:13; Amos 5:4–8 31:2 [a]Num 23:19; Jer 44:29 31:3 [a]Isa 20:6 31:4 [a]Num 24:9; Hos 11:10; Amos 3:8
31:5 [a]Deut 32:11; Ps 91:4 31:6 [a]Hos 9:9 31:7 [a]1 Kgs 12:30 [1]Heb. *reject.* 31:8 [a]2 Kgs 19:35–36
[b]Isa 37:36 31:9 [a]Isa 37:37 32:1 [a]Ps 45:1 [1]Heb. *will reign according to fairness.*
32:2 [a]Isa 4:6 32:3 [a]Isa 29:18; 35:5 32:4 [a]Isa 29:24

6 For a fool speaks disgraceful things;
  his mind plans out sinful [a]deeds.[1]
He commits godless deeds
and says misleading things about the
    LORD;
he gives the hungry nothing to
    satisfy their appetite
and gives the thirsty nothing to
    drink.
7 A deceiver's methods are evil;
he dreams up evil plans
to ruin the poor with [a]lies,
even when the needy are in the right.
8 An honorable man makes honorable
    plans;
his honorable character gives him
    security.

The Lord Will Give True Security

9 You complacent[1] women,
get up and listen to me!
You carefree daughters,
pay attention to what I say!
10 In a year's time
you carefree ones will shake with fear,
for the grape harvest[1] will fail,
and the fruit harvest will not arrive.
11 Tremble, you complacent ones!
Shake with fear, you carefree ones!
Strip off your clothes and expose
    yourselves—
put sackcloth around your waists.
12 Mourn over the field,[1]
over the delightful fields
and the fruitful vine.
13 Mourn over the land of my people,
which is overgrown with thorns and
    briers,
and over all the [a]once-happy houses
in [b]the city filled with revelry.
14 [a]For the fortress is neglected;
the once-crowded city is abandoned.
Hill and watchtower
are permanently uninhabited.
Wild donkeys love to go there,
and flocks graze there.
15 This desolation will continue until
new life is poured out on us from
    heaven.

[a]Then [b]the wilderness will become
    an orchard[1]
and the orchard will be considered a
    forest.
16 Justice will settle down in the
    wilderness
and fairness will live in the orchard.
17 [a]Fairness will produce peace
and result in lasting security.
18 My people will live [a]in peaceful
    settlements,
in secure homes,
and in safe, quiet places.
19 [a]Even if the forest is destroyed
and the city is annihilated,
20 you will be blessed,
you who plant seed by all [a]the banks
    of the streams,
you who let your ox and donkey
    graze.[1]

The Lord Will Restore Zion

33 The destroyer is as good as dead,
you [a]who have not been destroyed!
The deceitful one is as good as dead,
the one whom others have not
    deceived!
[b]When you are through [c]destroying,
    you will be destroyed;
when you finish deceiving, others
    will deceive you!
2 LORD, be merciful to us! [a]We wait for
    you.
Give us strength each morning.
Deliver us when distress comes.
3 The nations run away when they
    hear [a]a loud noise;
the nations scatter when you spring
    into action!
4 Your plunder disappears as if locusts
    were eating it;
they swarm over it like locusts.
5 The LORD is exalted,
indeed,[1] [a]he lives in heaven;
he fills Zion with justice and fairness.
6 He is your constant source of
    stability;
he abundantly provides safety and
    great wisdom;

32:6 [a]Prov 24:7–9 [1]Heb. *and his heart commits sin.* 32:7 [a]Jer 5:26–28; Mic 7:3 32:9 [1]Or *self-assured.* 32:10 [1]Or perhaps *olive.* 32:12 [1]MT *over mourning breasts.* 32:13 [a]Isa 7:23–25; Hos 9:6 [b]Isa 22:2 32:14 [a]Isa 27:10 32:15 [a]Isa 11:2; Ezek 39:29; [Joel 2:28] [b]Ps 107:35; Isa 29:17 [1]This Heb. term may refer to fertile land, an orchard, a garden of vines, a plantation of trees, or fresh grain. 32:17 [a]Ps 119:165; Isa 2:4; Rom 14:17; Jas 3:18 32:18 [a]Isa 11:10; 14:3; 30:15; [Hos 2:18–23; Zech 2:5; 3:10] 32:19 [a]Isa 30:30 32:20 [a][Eccl 11:1]; Isa 30:23–24 [1]Heb. *who set free the foot of the ox and donkey.* 33:1 [a]Isa 21:2; Hab 2:8 [b]Rev 13:10 [c]Isa 10:12; 14:25; 31:8 33:2 [a]Isa 25:9; 26:8 33:3 [a]Isa 17:13 33:5 [a]Ps 97:9 [1]Or *for.*

he gives all this to those who fear
him.
7 Look, ambassadors cry out in ªthe
streets;
messengers sent to make peace weep
bitterly.
8 Highways are empty;
ªthere are no travelers.¹
Treaties are broken;
witnesses are despised;²
human life is treated with disrespect.
9 The land dries up and ªwithers away;
the forest of Lebanon shrivels up¹
and decays.
Sharon is like the arid rift valley;
Bashan and Carmel are parched.
10 "ªNow I will rise up," says the LORD.
"Now I will exalt myself;
now I will magnify myself.
11 You conceive straw,
ªyou give birth to chaff;
your breath is a fire that destroys
you.
12 The nations will be burned to ashes;
ªlike thornbushes that have been cut
down, they will be set on fire.
13 You who are far away, listen to what I
have done!
ªYou who are close by, recognize my
strength."
14 Sinners are afraid in Zion;
panic grips the godless.
They say, "Who among us can coexist
with destructive ªfire?
Who among us can coexist with
unquenchable fire?"
15 The one who ªlives uprightly
and speaks honestly,
the one who refuses to profit from
oppressive measures
and rejects a bribe,
the one who does not plot violent
crimes
and does ᵇnot seek to harm others—
16 this is the person who will live in a
secure place;
he will find safety in the rocky,
mountain strongholds;
he will have food

and a constant supply of water.
17 You will see a king in his ªsplendor;
you will see a wide land.
18 Your mind will recall the terror you
experienced,
and you will ask yourselves, "ªWhere
is the scribe?
Where is the one who weighs the
money?
Where is the one who counts the
towers?"
19 You will no longer see a defiant
people
whose language ªyou do not
comprehend,
whose derisive speech you do not
ᵇunderstand.
20 Look ªat Zion, the city where we hold
religious festivals!
You will see ᵇJerusalem,
a peaceful settlement,
a tent that stays ᶜput;
ᵈits stakes will never be pulled up;
none of its ropes will snap in two.
21 Instead the LORD will rule there as
our mighty king.
Rivers and wide streams will flow
through it;
no war galley will enter;
no large ships will sail through.¹
22 For the LORD, our ªruler,
the LORD, our ᵇcommander,
ᶜthe LORD, our king—
he will deliver us.
23 Though at this time your ropes are
slack,
the mast is not secured,
and the sail¹ is not unfurled,
at that time you will divide up a great
quantity of loot;
even the lame will drag off plunder.
24 No resident of Zion will say, "I am ill";
ªthe people who live there will have
their sin forgiven.

The Lord Will Judge Edom

34 Come ªnear, you nations, and
listen!
Pay attention, you people!

33:7 ª 2 Kgs 18:18, 37   33:8 ª Judg 5:6   ¹ Heb. *the one passing by on the road ceases.*   ² MT *he despises cities.*   33:9 ª Isa 24:4
¹ Heb. *Lebanon is ashamed.*   33:10 ª Ps 12:5; Isa 2:19, 21   33:11 ª [Ps 7:14; Isa 26:18; 59:4; Jas 1:15]   33:12 ª Isa 9:18
33:13 ª Ps 48:10; Isa 49:1   33:14 ª Isa 30:27, 30; Heb 12:29   33:15 ª Ps 15:2; 24:3–4; Isa 58:6–11   ᵇ Ps 119:37
33:17 ª Ps 27:4   33:18 ª 1 Cor 1:20   33:19 ª 2 Kgs 19:32   ᵇ Deut 28:49–50; Isa 28:11; Jer 5:15   33:20 ª Ps 48:12
ᵇ Ps 46:5; 125:1; Isa 32:18   ᶜ Isa 37:33   ᵈ Isa 54:2   33:21 ¹ Heb. *and a mighty ship will not pass through it.*
33:22 ª [Acts 10:42]   ᵇ Isa 1:10; 51:4, 7; Jas 4:12   ᶜ Ps 89:18; Isa 25:9; 35:4; Zech 9:9   33:23 ¹ Or *perhaps
flag.*   33:24 ª Isa 40:2; Jer 50:20; Mic 7:18–19; 1 John 1:7–9   34:1 ª Ps 49:1; Isa 41:1; 43:9

The earth and everything it contains
  must listen,
the world and everything that lives
  in it.
2 For the LORD is angry at all the
  nations
and furious with all their armies.
He will annihilate them and
  [a]slaughter them.
3 Their slain will be left unburied,
  [a]their corpses will stink;
the hills will soak up their blood.[1]
4 [a]All the stars in the sky will fade
  away,[1]
the sky will roll up like a scroll;
all its stars will wither,
like [b]a leaf withers and falls from a
  vine
or a fig withers and falls from a tree.
5 He says, "Indeed, [a]my sword has
  slaughtered heavenly powers.
Look, it now descends on Edom,
on the people I will annihilate in
  judgment."
6 The [a]LORD's sword is dripping with
  blood,
it is covered with fat;
it drips with [b]the blood of young
  rams and goats
and is covered with the fat of rams'
  kidneys.
For the LORD is holding a sacrifice in
  Bozrah,
a bloody slaughter in the land of
  Edom.
7 Wild oxen will be slaughtered along
  with them,
as well as strong bulls.
Their land is drenched with blood,
their soil is covered with fat.
8 For the LORD has planned a day of
  [a]revenge,
a time when he will repay Edom for
  her hostility toward Zion.[1]
9 [a]Edom's streams will be turned into
  pitch
and her soil into brimstone;

her land will become burning pitch.
10 Night and day [a]it will burn;
its smoke will ascend continually.
Generation after generation it will be
  a wasteland,
and no one will ever pass through it
  again.
11 [a]Owls and wild animals will live
  [b]there,
all kinds of wild birds will settle in it.
The LORD will stretch out over her
the measuring line of ruin
and the plumb line[1] of destruction.
12 Her nobles will have nothing left to
  call a kingdom,
and all her officials will disappear.
13 Her fortresses will be overgrown
  with [a]thorns;
thickets and weeds will grow in her
  fortified [b]cities.
Jackals will settle there;
ostriches will live there.[1]
14 Wild animals and wild dogs will
  congregate there;
wild goats will bleat to one another.
Yes, nocturnal animals[1] will rest
  there
and make for themselves a nest.
15 Owls[1] will make nests and lay eggs
  there;
they will hatch them and protect
  them.
Yes, hawks[2] will gather there,
each with its mate.
16 Carefully read [a]the scroll of the
  LORD!
Not one of these creatures will be
  missing,
none will lack a mate.
For the LORD has issued the decree,[1]
and his own Spirit gathers them.
17 He assigns them their allotment;
he measures out their assigned
  place.
They will live there permanently;
they will settle in it through
  successive generations.

34:2 [a]Isa 13:5   34:3 [a]Joel 2:20; Amos 4:10   [1]Heb. *hills will dissolve from their blood.*   34:4 [a]Ps 102:26; Isa 13:13; Ezek 32:7–8; Joel 2:31; Matt 24:29; 2 Pet 3:10   [b]Isa 14:12   [1]Heb. *and all the host of heaven will rot;* Qum. adds *and the valleys will be split open.*   34:5 [a]Deut 32:41–42; Jer 46:10; Ezek 21:3–5   34:6 [a]Isa 66:16   [b]Zeph 1:7   34:8 [a]Isa 63:4   [1]Or perhaps *repay Edom and vindicate Zion;* Heb. *a year of repayment for the strife of Zion.*   34:9 [a]Deut 29:23; Ps 11:6; Isa 30:33   34:10 [a]Rev 14:11; 18:18; 19:3   34:11 [a]Isa 14:23; Zeph 2:14; Rev 18:2   [b]2 Kgs 21:13; Lam 2:8   [1]Heb. *stones;* i.e., the stones used in a plumb bob.   34:13 [a]Isa 32:13; Hos 9:6   [b]Isa 13:21   [1]Heb. *and she will be a settlement for wild dogs, a dwelling place for ostriches.*   34:14 [1]The precise meaning of this Heb. word is unclear, though in this context it certainly refers to some type of wild animal or bird.   34:15 [1]The precise meaning of this Heb. word is uncertain.   [2]The precise meaning of this Heb. word is uncertain, though it appears to refer to some type of bird of prey, perhaps a vulture.   34:16 [a][Mal 3:16]   [1]MT *for a mouth, it has commanded;* some wss *his mouth* [has commanded] or *the mouth of the LORD* [has commanded].

The Land and Its People Are Transformed

35 Let the [a]wilderness and desert be happy;
let the arid rift [b]valley rejoice and
bloom like a lily!
2 Let [a]it richly bloom;
let it rejoice and shout with delight!
It is given the [b]grandeur of Lebanon,
the splendor of Carmel and Sharon.
They will see the grandeur of the
LORD,
the splendor of our God.
3 [a]Strengthen the hands that have
gone limp,
steady the knees that shake.
4 Tell those who panic,
"Be strong! Do not fear!
Look, your God comes to [a]avenge;
with divine retribution he comes to
[b]deliver you."
5 Then blind [a]eyes will open,
deaf ears will hear.
6 Then the [a]lame will leap like a deer,
the mute [b]tongue will shout for joy;
for [c]water will burst forth in the
wilderness,
streams in the arid rift valley.
7 The dry soil will become a pool of
water,
[a]the parched ground springs of water.
Where jackals once lived and
sprawled out,
grass, reeds, and papyrus will grow.
8 A [a]thoroughfare will be [b]there—
it will be called the Way of Holiness.[1]
The unclean will not travel on it;
it is reserved for those authorized to
use it—
fools will not stray into it.
9 [a]No lions will be there,
no ferocious wild animals will be
on it—
they will not be found there.
Those delivered from bondage will
travel on it,
10 those whom the LORD has
[a]ransomed will return that way.
They will enter Zion with a happy
shout.

Unending joy will crown them,
happiness and joy will overwhelm
them;
[b]grief and suffering will disappear.

Sennacherib Invades Judah

36 In the fourteenth year of King Hezekiah's reign, King Sennacherib of Assyria marched up against all the fortified [a]cities of Judah and captured them. 2The king of Assyria sent his chief adviser from Lachish to King Hezekiah in Jerusalem, along with a large army. The chief adviser stood at the conduit of the upper pool that is located on the road to the field where they wash and dry cloth.[1] 3[a]Eliakim son of Hilkiah, the palace supervisor, accompanied by [b]Shebna the scribe and Joah son of Asaph, the secretary, went out to meet him.

4The chief adviser said to them, "Tell Hezekiah: 'This is what [a]the great king, the king of Assyria, says: "What is your source of confidence? 5Your claim to have a strategy and military strength is just empty talk. In whom are you trusting, that you would dare to rebel against me? 6Look, you must be trusting in Egypt, that splintered reed [a]staff. If someone leans on it for support, it punctures his hand and wounds him. That is what Pharaoh king of Egypt does to all who [b]trust in him! 7Perhaps you will tell me, 'We are trusting in the LORD our God.' But Hezekiah is the one who eliminated his high places and altars and then told the people of Judah and Jerusalem, 'You must worship at this altar.' 8Now make a deal with my master the king of Assyria, and I will give you 2,000 horses, provided you can find enough riders for them. 9Certainly you will not refuse one of my master's minor officials and trust in Egypt for chariots and horsemen. 10Furthermore it was by the command of the LORD that I marched up against this land to destroy it. The LORD told me, 'March up against this land and destroy it!'"'"

11Eliakim, Shebna, and Joah said to the chief adviser, "Speak to your servants in Aramaic, for we understand it. Don't speak

35:1 [a]Isa 32:15; 55:12 [b]Isa 41:19; 51:3   35:2 [a]Isa 32:15 [b]Isa 40:5   35:3 [a]Job 4:3–4; Heb 12:12   35:4 [a]Isa 34:8 [b]Ps 145:19; Isa 33:22   35:5 [a]Isa 29:18; Matt 9:27; John 9:6–7   35:6 [a]Matt 11:5; 15:30; John 5:8–9; Acts 8:7 [b]Isa 32:4; Matt 9:32; 12:22 [c]Isa 41:18; [John 7:38]   35:7 [a]Isa 34:13   35:8 [a]Isa 19:23 [b]Isa 52:1; Joel 3:17; [Matt 7:13–14]; 1 Pet 1:15–16; Rev 21:27 [1]MT and there will be there a road and a way, and the Way of Holiness it will be called.   35:9 [a]Lev 26:6; [Isa 11:7, 9]; Ezek 34:25 35:10 [a]Isa 51:11 [b]Isa 25:8; 30:19; 65:19; [Rev 7:17; 21:4]   36:1 [a]2 Kgs 18:13, 17; 2 Chr 32:1   36:2 [1]Trad. the fuller's field; Heb. the field of the washer.   36:3 [a]Isa 22:20 [b]Isa 22:15   36:4 [a]2 Kgs 18:19   36:6 [a]Ezek 29:6 [b]Ps 146:3; Isa 30:3, 5, 7

with us in the Judahite dialect[1] in the hearing of the people who are on the wall." [12]But the chief adviser said, "My master did not send me to speak these words only to your master and to you. His message is also for the men who sit on the wall, for they will eat their own excrement and drink their own urine along with you!"

[13]The chief adviser then stood there and called out loudly in the Judahite dialect, "Listen to the message of the great king, the king of Assyria. [14]This is what the king says: 'Don't let Hezekiah mislead you, for he is not able to rescue you! [15]Don't let Hezekiah talk you into trusting in the LORD by saying, "The LORD will certainly rescue us; this city will not be handed over to the king of Assyria." [16]Don't listen to Hezekiah!' For this is what the king of Assyria says, 'Send me [a]a token of your submission and surrender to me. Then each of you may eat from his own vine and fig tree and drink water from his own cistern, [17]until I come and take you to a land just like your own—a land of grain and new wine, a land of bread and vineyards. [18]Hezekiah is misleading you when he says, "The LORD will rescue us." Have any of the [a]gods of the nations rescued their lands from the power of the king of Assyria? [19]Where are the gods of Hamath and Arpad? Where are the gods of Sepharvaim? Indeed, did any gods rescue [a]Samaria from my power? [20]Who among all the gods of these lands have rescued their lands from my power? So how can the LORD rescue Jerusalem from my power?'" [21]They were silent and did not respond, for the king had ordered, "Don't respond to him."

[22]Eliakim son of Hilkiah, the palace supervisor, accompanied by Shebna the scribe and Joah son of Asaph, the secretary, went to Hezekiah with their clothes torn and reported to him what the chief adviser had said.

37 When King Hezekiah heard this, he tore his clothes, put on sackcloth, and went to the LORD's temple. [2]Eliakim the palace supervisor, Shebna the scribe, and the leading priests, clothed in sackcloth, sent this message to the prophet Isaiah son of Amoz: [3]"This is what Hezekiah says:

'This is a day of [a]distress, insults, and humiliation, as when a baby is ready to leave the birth canal but the mother lacks the strength to push it through. [4]Perhaps the LORD your God will hear all these things the chief adviser has spoken on behalf of his master, the king of Assyria, who sent him to [a]taunt the living God. When the LORD your God hears, perhaps he will punish him for the things he has said.[1] So pray for this remnant that remains.'"

[5]When King Hezekiah's servants came to Isaiah, [6]Isaiah said to them, "Tell your master this: 'This is what the LORD has said: "Don't be afraid because of the things you have heard—these insults the king of Assyria's servants have hurled against me. [7]Look, I will take control of his mind; he will receive a report and return to his own land. I will cut him down with a sword in his own land."'"

[8]When the chief adviser heard the king of Assyria had departed from Lachish, he left and went to Libnah, where the king was campaigning. [9]The king heard that King Tirhakah of Ethiopia[1] was marching out to fight him. He again sent messengers to Hezekiah, ordering them: [10]"Tell King Hezekiah of Judah this: 'Don't let your God in whom you trust mislead you when he says, "Jerusalem will not be handed over to the king of Assyria." [11]Certainly you have heard how the kings of Assyria have annihilated all lands. Do you really think you will be rescued? [12]Were the nations whom my predecessors[1] destroyed—the nations of Gozan, Haran, Rezeph, and the people of Eden in Telassar—rescued by their [a]gods? [13]Where is the king of [a]Hamath or the king of Arpad or the kings of Lair, Sepharvaim, Hena, and Ivvah?'"

[14]Hezekiah took the letter[1] from the messengers and read it. Then Hezekiah went up to the LORD's temple and spread it out before the LORD. [15]Hezekiah prayed before the LORD: [16]"O LORD of Heaven's Armies, O God of Israel, who is enthroned on the cherubim! You [a]alone are God over all the kingdoms of the earth. You made the sky[1] and the earth. [17][a]Pay attention, LORD, and [b]hear! Open your eyes, LORD, and observe!

36:11[1]Or *in Hebrew.*   **36:16**[a]1 Kgs 4:25; Mic 4:4; Zech 3:10   **36:18**[a]2 Kgs 19:12; Isa 37:12   **36:19**[a]2 Kgs 17:6   **37:3**[a]Isa 22:5; 26:16; 33:2   **37:4**[a]Isa 36:15, 18, 20   [1]Heb. *and rebuke the words which the LORD your God hears.*   **37:9**[1]Heb. *Cush.*   **37:12**[a]Isa 36:18–19   [1]Heb. *fathers.*   **37:13**[a]Isa 49:23   **37:14**[1]MT *letters.*   **37:16**[a]Isa 43:10–11   [1]Or *the heavens.*   **37:17**[a]2 Chr 6:40; Ps 17:6; Dan 9:18   [b]Ps 74:22

Listen to this entire message Sennacherib sent and how he taunts the living God! [18] It is true, LORD, that the kings of Assyria have destroyed all the nations and their [a]lands. [19] They have burned the gods of the nations, for they are [a]not really gods, but only the product of human hands manufactured from wood and stone. That is why the Assyrians could destroy them. [20] Now, O LORD our God, [a]rescue us from his power, so all the kingdoms of the earth may [b]know that you alone are the LORD."

[21] Isaiah son of Amoz sent this message to Hezekiah: "This is what the LORD God of Israel has said: 'As to what you have prayed to me concerning King Sennacherib of Assyria, [22] this is what the LORD says about him:

"'The virgin daughter Zion
    despises you—she makes fun of you;
    daughter Jerusalem
    shakes her head after you.

[23] "'Whom have you taunted and hurled
    insults at?
At whom have you shouted
    and looked so arrogantly?
At the Holy One of Israel!
[24] Through your messengers you
    taunted the Lord,
"With my many chariots I climbed up
    the high mountains,
    the slopes of Lebanon.
I cut down its tall cedars
    and its best evergreens.
I invaded its remotest regions,
    its thickest woods.
[25] I dug wells
    and drank water.[1]
With the soles of my feet I dried up
    all the rivers of Egypt."'

[26] "Certainly you must have heard!
[a]Long ago I worked it out,
    in ancient times I planned it,
    and now I am bringing it to pass.
The plan is this:
Fortified cities will crash
    into heaps of ruins.
[27] Their residents are powerless;[1]
    they are terrified and ashamed.

They are as short-lived as plants in
    the field
or green vegetation.
They are as short-lived as grass on
    the rooftops
when it is scorched by the east wind.[2]
[28] I know where you live
    and everything you do
    and how you rage against me.[1]
[29] Because you rage [a]against me
    and the uproar you create has
    reached my ears,[1]
I will put my hook in your nose,
    and my bit between your lips,
    and I will lead you back
    the way you came.

[30] "This will be your reminder that I have spoken the truth: This year you will eat what grows wild, and next year what grows on its own. But the year after that you will plant seed and harvest crops; you will plant vines and consume their produce. [31] Those who remain in Judah will take root in the ground and bear fruit.

[32] "For a remnant will leave Jerusalem;
    survivors will come out of Mount
    Zion.
The [a]zeal of the LORD of Heaven's
    Armies[1] will accomplish this.

[33] "So this is what the LORD says about
    the king of Assyria:
"'He will not enter this city,
    nor will he shoot an arrow here.
He will not attack it with his
    shielded warriors,
    nor will he build siege works
    against it.
[34] He will go back the way he came—
    he will not enter this city,' says the
    LORD.
[35] I will [a]shield this city and rescue it
    for the sake of my reputation and
    because of my promise to [b]David
    my servant."

[36] The [a]angel of the LORD went out and killed 185,000 troops in the Assyrian camp. When they got up early the next morning,

37:18 [a] 2 Kgs 15:29; 16:9; 17:6, 24; 1 Chr 5:26   37:19 [a] Isa 40:19–20   37:20 [a] Isa 33:22   [b] Ps 83:18   37:25 [1] DSS foreign waters.   37:26 [a] Isa 25:1; 40:21; 45:21   37:27 [1] Heb. short of hand.   [2] MT scorched before the standing grain.   37:28 [1] LXX omits and how you rage against me; Qum. omits it in v. 29.   37:29 [a] 2 Kgs 19:35–37; 2 Chr 32:21; Isa 30:28; Ezek 38:4   [1] MT and your complacency comes up into my ears.   37:32 [a] 2 Kgs 19:31; Isa 9:7; 59:17; Joel 2:18; Zech 1:14   [1] Trad. the LORD of hosts.   37:35 [a] 2 Kgs 20:6; Isa 31:5; 38:6   [b] 1 Kgs 11:13   37:36 [a] 2 Kgs 19:35; Isa 10:12, 33, 34

there were all the corpses! [37]So King Sennacherib of Assyria broke camp and went on his way. He went home and stayed in Nineveh. [38]One day, as he was worshiping in the temple of his god Nisroch, his sons Adrammelech and Sharezer struck him down with the sword. They ran away to the land of Ararat; his son [a]Esarhaddon replaced him as king.

The Lord Hears Hezekiah's Prayer

38 In [a]those days Hezekiah was stricken with a terminal illness.[1] The prophet Isaiah son of Amoz visited him and told him, "This is what the LORD says, 'Give instructions to your household, for you are about to die; you will not get well.'" [2]Hezekiah turned his face to the wall and prayed to the LORD, [3]"Please, LORD. [a]Remember how I have served you faithfully and with wholehearted devotion, and how I have carried out [b]your will." Then Hezekiah wept bitterly.[1]

[4]The LORD's message came to Isaiah, [5]"Go and tell Hezekiah: 'This is what the LORD God of your ancestor David says: "I have heard your prayer; I have seen your tears. Look, I will add 15 years to your life. [6]I [a]will also rescue you and this city from the king of Assyria. I will shield this city."'" [7]Isaiah replied, "This is your sign from [a]the LORD confirming that the LORD will do what he has said: [8]Look, I will make the shadow go back 10 steps on the stairs of Ahaz." And then the shadow went back 10 steps.

Hezekiah's Song of Thanks

[9]This is the prayer of King Hezekiah of Judah when he was sick and then recovered from his illness:

[10] "I thought,
'In the middle of my life I must walk
    through the gates of Sheol,
I am deprived of the rest of my years.'

[11] "I thought,
'[a]I will no longer see the LORD in the
    land of the living,

I will no longer look on humankind
    with the inhabitants of the world.
[12] My dwelling place is removed and
    taken away from me
as a shepherd's tent.
I rolled up [a]my life like a weaver rolls
    cloth;[1]
from the loom he cuts me off.
You turn day into night and end my
    life.
[13] I cry out until morning;
like a lion he shatters all my bones;
you turn day into night and end my
    life.
[14] Like a swallow or a thrush [a]I chirp,
I coo like a dove;
my eyes grow tired from looking up
    to the sky.
O Lord, I am oppressed;
help me!
[15] What can [a]I say?
He has decreed and acted.
I will walk slowly all my years
because I am overcome with grief.
[16] O Lord, your decrees can give men life;
may years of life be restored to me.[1]
Restore my health and preserve my
    life.'
[17] "Look, the grief I experienced was for
    my benefit.
You delivered me[1] from the Pit of
    oblivion.
For you removed all my sins from
    your sight.
[18] Indeed[1] [a]Sheol does not give you
    thanks;
death does not praise you.
Those who descend into the Pit do
    not anticipate your faithfulness.
[19] The living person, [a]the living person,
    he gives you thanks,
as I do today.
A father tells his sons about your
    faithfulness.
[20] The LORD is about to deliver me,
and we will celebrate with music
for the rest of our lives in the LORD's
    temple."

37:38 [a]Ezra 4:2   38:1 [a]2 Kgs 20:1-6, 9-11; 2 Chr 32:24; Isa 38:1-8   [1]Heb. *was sick to the point of dying.*   38:3 [a]Neh 13:14   [b]2 Kgs 18:5-6; Ps 26:3   [1]Heb. *wept with great weeping.*   38:6 [a]2 Kgs 19:35-37; 2 Chr 32:21; Isa 31:5; 37:35   38:7 [a]Judg 6:17, 21, 36-40; 2 Kgs 20:8; Isa 7:11   38:11 [a]Ps 27:13; 116:9   38:12 [a]Job 7:6   [1]Heb. *I rolled up, like a weaver, my life.*   38:14 [a]Isa 59:11; Ezek 7:16; Nah 2:7   38:15 [a]Job 7:11; 10:1; Isa 38:17   38:16 [1]The translation offered here is purely speculative because the text is difficult and obscure. It reads lit. *O Lord, on account of them* [the suffix is masc. pl.], *they live, and to all in them* [the suffix is fem. pl.], *life of my spirit.*   38:17 [1]MT *you loved my soul.*   38:18 [a]Ps 6:5; 30:9; 88:11; 115:17; [Eccl 9:10]   [1]Or *For.*   38:19 [a]Deut 4:9; 6:7; Ps 78:3-4

[21]([a]Isaiah ordered, "Let them take a fig cake and apply it to the ulcerated sore and he will get well." [22a]Hezekiah said, "What is the confirming sign that I will go up to the LORD's temple?")

Messengers from Babylon Visit Hezekiah

39 At [a]that time Merodach Baladan son of Baladan, king of Babylon, sent letters and a gift to Hezekiah, for he heard that Hezekiah had been ill and had recovered. [2]Hezekiah welcomed them [a]and showed them his storehouse with its silver, gold, spices, and high-quality olive oil, as well as his whole armory and everything in his treasuries. Hezekiah showed them everything in his palace and in his whole kingdom. [3]Isaiah the prophet visited King Hezekiah and asked him, "What did these men say? Where do they come from?" Hezekiah replied, "They come from the [a]distant land of Babylon." [4]Isaiah asked, "What have they seen in your palace?" Hezekiah replied, "They have seen everything in my palace. I showed them everything in my treasuries." [5]Isaiah said to Hezekiah, "Listen to the message of the LORD of Heaven's Armies: [6]'Look, a time is coming [a]when everything in your palace and the things your ancestors[1] have accumulated to this day will be carried away to Babylon; nothing will be left,' says the LORD. [7]'Some of your very own [a]descendants whom you father will be taken away and will be made eunuchs in the palace of the king of Babylon.'" [8]Hezekiah said to Isaiah, "[a]The LORD's message that you have announced is appropriate." Then he thought, "For[1] there will be peace and stability during my lifetime."

The Lord Returns to Jerusalem

40 "Comfort, comfort my people," says your God.
2 "Speak kindly to Jerusalem and tell her
that her time of warfare is over,
that her punishment is completed.
[a]For the LORD has made her pay
double for all her sins."
3 A voice cries out,

"In [a]the wilderness [b]clear [c]a way for the LORD;
build a level road through the rift valley for our God.
4 Every valley must be elevated
and every mountain and hill leveled.
[a]The rough terrain will become a level plain,
the rugged landscape a wide valley.
5 The [a]splendor of the LORD will be revealed,
and all people[1] will see it at the same time.
For[2] the LORD has decreed it."
6 A voice says, "Cry out!"
Another asks, "What should I cry out?"
The first voice responds: "[a]All people are like grass,
and all their promises are like the flowers in the field.
7 The grass dries up,
the flowers wither,
when the wind sent by the LORD blows on them.
Surely humanity is like grass.
8 The grass dries up,
[a]the flowers wither,
but the decree of our God is forever reliable."
9 Go up on a high mountain, O herald Zion.
Shout out loudly, O herald Jerusalem!
Shout, don't be afraid!
Say to the towns of Judah,
"Here is your God!"
10 Look, the Sovereign LORD comes as a victorious warrior;
[a]his military power establishes [b]his rule.
Look, his reward is with him;
his prize goes before him.
11 Like a [a]shepherd he tends his flock;
he gathers up the lambs with his arm;
he carries them close to his heart;
he leads the ewes along.

The Lord Is Incomparable

12 [a]Who has measured out the waters in the hollow of his hand,

38:21 [a] 2 Kgs 20:7   **38:22** [a] 2 Kgs 20:8   **39:1** [a] 2 Kgs 20:12–19; 2 Chr 32:31; Isa 39:1–8   **39:2** [a] 2 Chr 32:25, 31; Job 31:25   **39:3** [a] Deut 28:49; Jer 5:15   **39:6** [a] 2 Kgs 24:13; 25:13–15; Jer 20:5   [1] Heb. *fathers*.   **39:7** [a] Dan 1:1–7   **39:8** [a] 1 Sam 3:18   [1] Or *surely*.   **40:2** [a] Isa 61:7   **40:3** [a] Matt 3:3; Mark 1:3; Luke 3:4–6; John 1:23   [b] [Mal 3:1; 4:5–6]   [c] Ps 68:4   **40:4** [a] Isa 45:2   **40:5** [a] Isa 35:2   [1] Heb. *flesh*.   [2] Or *indeed*.   **40:6** [a] Job 14:2; Jas 1:10; 1 Pet 1:24–25   **40:8** [a] [John 12:34]   **40:10** [a] Isa 59:16, 18   [b] Isa 62:11; Rev 22:12   **40:11** [a] Jer 31:10; [Ezek 34:23, 31]; Mic 5:4; [John 10:11, 14–16; Heb 13:20; 1 Pet 2:25]   **40:12** [a] Prov 30:4

or carefully[1] measured the sky,[2]
or carefully weighed the soil of the
    earth,
or weighed the mountains in a
    balance,
or the hills on scales?
13 [a]Who comprehends the mind of the
    LORD,
or gives him instruction as his
    counselor?
14 From whom does he receive
    directions?
Who [a]teaches him the correct way to
    do things,
or imparts knowledge to him,
or instructs him in skillful design?
15 Look, the nations are like a drop in a
    bucket;
they are regarded as dust on the
    scales.
He lifts the coastlands as if they were
    dust.
16 Not even Lebanon could supply
    enough firewood for a sacrifice;
its wild animals would not provide
    enough burnt offerings.
17 All the nations are [a]insignificant
    before him;
[b]they are regarded as absolutely
    nothing.
18 To whom can you [a]compare God?
To what image can you liken him?
19 [a]A craftsman casts an idol;
a metalsmith overlays it with gold
and forges silver chains for it.
20 To make a contribution one selects
    wood that will not rot;
he then seeks a skilled craftsman
[a]to make[1] an idol that will not fall over.
21 Do you not know?
Do you not hear?
Has it not been told to you since the
    very beginning?
[a]Have you not understood from the
    time the earth's foundations were
    made?
22 He is the one who sits on the earth's
    horizon;
its inhabitants are like grasshoppers
    before him.

He is the one who stretches [a]out the
    sky like a thin curtain,
and spreads it out like a pitched [b]tent.
23 He is the one who reduces [a]rulers to
    nothing;
he makes the earth's leaders
    insignificant.
24 Indeed, they are barely planted;
yes, they are barely sown;
yes, they barely take root in the earth,
and then he blows on them, causing
    them to dry up,
and the wind carries them away like
    straw.
25 "To whom can you compare me?
    Whom do I resemble?"
says the Holy One.
26 Look up at [a]the sky!
Who created all these heavenly lights?
He is the one who leads out their
    ranks;[1]
he calls them all by name.
Because of his absolute power and
    awesome strength,
not one of them is missing.
27 [a]Why do you say, Jacob,
Why do you say, Israel,
"The LORD is not aware of what is
    happening to me;
my God is not concerned with my
    vindication"?
28 Do you not know?
Have you not heard?
The LORD [a]is an eternal God,
the Creator of the whole earth.
He does not get tired or weary;
there is no limit to his wisdom.
29 He gives strength to those who are
    tired;
to the ones who lack power, he gives
    renewed energy.
30 Even youths get tired and weary;
even strong young men clumsily
    stumble.
31 But those who [a]wait for the LORD's
    help find renewed strength;
they rise up as if they had eagles'
    wings,
they run without growing weary,
they walk without getting tired.

40:12 [1]Heb. *with a span*; the distance between the ends of the thumb and the little finger of the spread hand. [2]Or *the heavens.* 40:13 [a]Job 21:22; Rom 11:34; [1 Cor 2:16] 40:14 [a]Job 36:22-23 40:17 [a]Dan 4:35 [b]Ps 62:9 40:18 [a]Exod 8:10; 15:11; 1 Sam 2:2; Isa 46:5; [Mic 7:18]; Acts 17:29 40:19 [a]Ps 115:4-8; Isa 41:7; 44:10; Hab 2:18-19 40:20 [a]1 Sam 5:3-4; Isa 41:7; 46:7; Jer 10:3 [1]Or *set up.* 40:21 [a]Ps 19:1; Isa 37:26; Acts 14:17; Rom 1:19 40:22 [a]Job 9:8; Ps 104:2; Isa 42:5; 44:24; Jer 10:12 [b]Job 36:29; Ps 19:4 40:23 [a]Job 12:21; Ps 107:40; Isa 34:12; [1 Cor 1:26-29] 40:26 [a]Ps 147:4 [1]Heb. *the one who brings out by number their host.* 40:27 [a]Isa 54:7-8 40:28 [a]Ps 147:5; Eccl 11:5; Rom 11:33 40:31 [a]Isa 30:15; 49:23

The Lord Challenges the Nations

41 "Listen to me in [a]silence, you
coastlands![1]
Let the nations find renewed
strength!
Let them approach and then speak;
let us [b]come together for debate.[2]

2 Who stirs up this one [a]from the east?
Who officially commissions him for
service?
He [b]hands nations over to him
and enables him to subdue kings.
He makes them like dust with his
sword,
like windblown straw with his bow.

3 He pursues them and passes by
unharmed;
he advances with great speed.

4 Who acts and carries out decrees?
[a]Who summons [b]the successive
generations from the beginning?
I, the LORD, am present at the very
beginning,
and at the very end—I am the one.

5 The coastlands see and are afraid;
the whole earth[1] trembles;
they approach and come.

6 They help [a]one another;
one says to the other, 'Be strong!'

7 The craftsman encourages the
metalsmith,
the one who wields the hammer
encourages the one who pounds
on the anvil.
He approves the quality of the
welding,
and nails it down [a]so [b]it won't fall
over.

The Lord Encourages His People

8 "You, my servant Israel,
Jacob, whom I have [a]chosen,
offspring of Abraham my [b]friend,

9 you whom I am bringing back from
the earth's extremities
and have summoned from the
remote regions—
I told you, 'You are my servant.'
I have chosen you and not rejected
you.

10 Don't be [a]afraid, [b]for I am with you!
Don't be frightened, for I am your
God!
I strengthen you—
yes, I help you—
yes, I uphold you with my victorious
right hand!

11 Look, all who were angry at you will
be [a]ashamed and humiliated;
your adversaries will be reduced to
nothing and perish.

12 When you will look for your
opponents, you will not find them;
your enemies will be reduced to
absolutely nothing.

13 For I am the LORD your God,
the one who takes hold of your right
hand,
who says to you, 'Don't be afraid, I am
helping you.'

14 Don't be afraid, despised,
[a]insignificant Jacob,[1]
men of Israel.
I am helping you," says the LORD,
your Protector,[2] the Holy One of
Israel.

15 "Look, [a]I am making you like a sharp
threshing sledge,
new and double-edged.
You will thresh the mountains and
crush them;
you will make the hills like straw.

16 You will [a]winnow them and the wind
will blow them away;
the wind will scatter them.
You will rejoice in the LORD;
you will [b]boast in the Holy One of
Israel.

17 The oppressed and the poor look for
water, but there is none;
their tongues are parched from
thirst.
I, the LORD, will respond to their
prayers;
I, the God of Israel, will not [a]abandon
them.

18 I will make [a]streams flow down the
slopes
and produce springs in the middle of
the valleys.

41:1 [a] Hab 2:20; Zech 2:13 [b] Isa 1:18 [1] Or *islands.* [2] Or perhaps *judgment.*   41:2 [a] Isa 46:11 [b] Gen 14:14; Isa 45:1, 13
41:4 [a] Isa 41:26 [b] Rev 1:8, 17; 22:13   41:5 [1] Heb. *the ends of the earth.*   41:6 [a] Isa 40:19   41:7 [a] Isa 44:13 [b] Isa 40:19
41:8 [a] Deut 7:6; 10:15; Ps 135:4; [Isa 43:1] [b] 2 Chr 20:7; Jas 2:23   41:10 [a] Isa 41:13–14; 43:5 [b] [Deut 31:6]   41:11 [a] Exod
23:22; Isa 45:24; 60:12; Zech 12:3   41:14 [a] Job 25:6; Ps 22:6 [1] Heb. *O worm Jacob.* [2] Heb. *your kinsman redeemer,* a
protector of the extended family's interests.   41:15 [a] Mic 4:13; Hab 3:12; [2 Cor 10:4]   41:16 [a] Jer 51:2
[b] Isa 45:25   41:17 [a] Ps 94:14; Rom 11:2   41:18 [a] Isa 35:6–7; 43:19; 44:3

I will turn the [b]wilderness into a pool
    of water
  and the arid land into springs.
[19] I will make cedars, acacias, myrtles,
    and olive trees grow in the
    wilderness;
  I will make evergreens, firs, and
    cypresses grow together in the arid
    rift [a]valley.
[20] I will do this so people will observe
    and recognize,
  so they will pay attention and
    understand
  [a]that the LORD's power has
    accomplished this,
  and that the Holy One of Israel has
    brought it into being.

The Lord Challenges the Pagan Gods

[21] "Present your argument," says the
    LORD.
  "Produce your evidence," says Jacob's
    [a]King.
[22] "Let them produce evidence! [a]Let
    them tell us what will happen!
  Tell us about your earlier predictive
    oracles,[1]
  so we may examine them and see
    how they were fulfilled.
  [b]Or decree for us some future events!
[23] Predict [a]how future events will turn
    out,[1]
  so we might know you are gods.
  Yes, [b]do something good or
    something bad,
  so we might be frightened and in
    awe.
[24] Look, [a]you are nothing, and your
    accomplishments are nonexistent;
  the one who chooses to worship you
    is disgusting.
[25] I have stirred up one out of [a]the
    north [b]and he advances,
  one from the eastern horizon who
    prays in my name.
  He steps on rulers as if they were
    clay,
  like a potter treading the clay.
[26] [a]Who decreed this from the
    beginning, so we could know?

Who announced it ahead of time, so
    we could say, 'He's correct'?
  Indeed, none of them decreed it.
  Indeed, none of them announced it.
  Indeed, no one heard you say
    anything!
[27] [a]I [b]first decreed to Zion, 'Look, here's
    what will happen!'
  I sent a herald to Jerusalem.
[28] [a]I look, but there is no one,
  among them there is no one who
    serves as an adviser
  that I might ask questions and
    receive answers.
[29] [a]Look, all of them are nothing,[1]
  their accomplishments are
    nonexistent;
  their metal images lack any real
    substance.

The Lord Commissions His Special Servant

42 "Here is [a]my servant whom I
    support,
  my chosen one in whom I take
    [b]pleasure.
  [c]I have placed my Spirit on him;
  he will make just decrees for the
    nations.
[2] He will not cry out or shout;
  he will not publicize himself in the
    streets.
[3] A crushed reed he will not break,
  a dim wick he will not extinguish;
  he will faithfully make just decrees.
[4] He will not grow dim or be crushed
  before establishing justice on the
    earth;
  the [a]coastlands will wait in
    anticipation for his decrees."[1]
[5] This is what the true God, the LORD,
    says—
  the one [a]who created the sky and
    stretched it out,
  the one [b]who fashioned the
    earth and everything that
    lives on it,
  the one who gives breath to the
    people on it,
  and life to those who live on it:

41:18 [b]Ps 107:35   41:19 [a]Isa 35:1   41:20 [a]Job 12:9; Isa 66:14   41:21 [a]Isa 43:15   41:22 [a]Isa 45:21   [b]Isa 43:9   [1]Heb. *As for the former things, tell us what they are!*   41:23 [a]Isa 42:9; 44:7–8; 45:3; [John 13:19]   [b]Jer 10:5   [1]Heb. *Declare the coming things, with respect to the end.*   41:24 [a]Ps 115:8; Isa 44:9; [Rom 3:10–20; 1 Cor 8:4]   41:25 [a]Ezra 1:2   [b]Isa 41:2; Jer 50:3   41:26 [a]Isa 43:9   41:27 [a]Isa 41:4   [b]Isa 40:9; Nah 1:15   41:28 [a]Isa 63:5   41:29 [a]Isa 41:24   [1]MT *deception.*   42:1 [a]Isa 43:10; 49:3, 6; Matt 12:18; [Phil 2:7]   [b]Matt 3:17; 17:5; Mark 1:11; Luke 3:22; Eph 1:6   [c][Isa 11:2]; Matt 3:16; [Luke 4:18–19, 21]; John 3:34   42:4 [a][Gen 49:10]   [1]Or *his law.*   42:5 [a]Isa 44:24; Zech 12:1   [b]Job 12:10; 33:4; Isa 57:16; Dan 5:23; Acts 17:25

6 "I, the LORD,[a] officially commission
   you;
  I take hold of your [b] hand.
  I protect you [c] and make you a
   covenant mediator for people
  and a light to the nations,[1]
7 to open blind eyes,
  [a] to release prisoners from dungeons,
  those who live [b] in [c] darkness from
   prisons.

The Lord Intervenes

8 "I am the LORD! That is my name!
  I will not share my [a] glory with
   anyone else
  or the praise due me with idols.
9 Look, my earlier predictive oracles
   have come to pass;
  now I announce new events.
  Before they begin to occur,
  I reveal them to you."

10 [a] Sing to the LORD a brand new song!
   Praise him from the horizon of the
    earth,
   you who go down to the sea and
    everything that lives in it,
   [b] you coastlands and those who live
    there.
11 Let the wilderness and its cities
    shout out,
   the towns where the nomads of
    Kedar live.
   Let the residents of Sela shout
    joyfully;
   let them shout loudly from the
    mountaintops.
12 Let them give the LORD the honor he
    deserves;
   let them praise his deeds in the
    coastlands.
13 The LORD emerges like a hero,
   like a warrior he inspires himself for
    battle;
   he shouts, [a] yes, he yells,
   he shows his enemies his power.
14 "I have been inactive for a long
    time;
   I kept quiet and held back.
   Like a woman in labor I groan;
   I pant and gasp.

15 I will make the trees on the
    mountains and hills wither up;
   I will dry up all their vegetation.
   I will turn streams into islands[1]
   and dry up pools of water.
16 I will lead the blind along an
    unfamiliar way;
   I will guide them down paths they
    have never traveled.[1]
   I will turn the darkness in front of
    them into light
   and level out the rough ground.
   This is what I will do for them.
   I will not abandon them.
17 Those who trust in idols
   will [a] turn back and be utterly
    humiliated,
   those who say to metal images, 'You
    are our gods.'

The Lord Reasons with His People

18 "Listen, you deaf ones!
   Take notice, you blind ones!
19 My servant is [a] truly blind,
   my messenger is truly deaf.
   My covenant partner, the servant of
    the LORD, is truly blind.
20 You see many things, [a] but don't
    comprehend;
   their ears are open, but do not hear."
21 The LORD wanted to exhibit his
    justice
   by magnifying his law and
    displaying it.
22 But these people are looted and
    plundered;
   all of them are trapped in pits[1]
   and held captive in prisons.
   They were carried away as loot with
    no one to rescue them;
   they were carried away as plunder,
    and no one says, "Bring that
    back!"
23 Who among you will pay attention to
    this?
   Who will listen attentively in the
    future?
24 Who handed Jacob over to the
    robber?
   Who handed Israel over to the
    looters?

42:6 [a] Isa 43:1 [b] Isa 49:8 [c] Isa 49:6; Luke 2:32; [Acts 10:45; 13:47; Gal 3:14] [1] Or *the Gentiles*. 42:7 [a] Isa 35:5 [b] Isa 61:1;
Luke 4:18; [2 Tim 2:26; Heb 2:14] [c] Isa 9:2 42:8 [a] Exod 20:3–5; Isa 48:11 42:10 [a] Ps 33:3; 40:3; 98:1 [b] Ps 107:23
42:13 [a] Isa 31:4 42:15 [1] MT *I will turn streams into coastlands* [or *islands*]. 42:16 [1] Heb. *in paths they do not
know I will make them walk*. 42:17 [a] Ps 97:7; Isa 1:29; 44:11; 45:16 42:19 [a] Isa 43:8; Ezek 12:2; [John
9:39, 41] 42:20 [a] Rom 2:21 42:22 [1] MT *young men*.

Was it not the LORD, against whom
we sinned?
They refused to follow his
commands;
they disobeyed his law.
25 So he poured out his fierce anger on
them,
along ªwith the devastation[1] of war.
Its flames encircled them, but they
did not realize it;
it burned against them, but they did
not take it to ᵇheart.

The Lord Will Rescue His People

43 Now, this is what the LORD says,
the one who created you, ªO Jacob,
and formed you, O ᵇIsrael:
"Don't be afraid, for I will protect you.
I call you by name, you are mine.
2 When you pass through the waters, I
am with you;
ªwhen you pass through the streams,
they ᵇwill not overwhelm you.
When you ᶜwalk through the fire, you
will not be burned;
the flames will not harm you.
3 For ªI am the LORD your God,
the Holy One of Israel, your deliverer.
I have handed over Egypt as a
ransom price,
Ethiopia and Seba in place of you.
4 Since you are precious and special in
my sight
and I ªlove you,
I will hand over people in place of
you,
nations in place of your life.
5 Don't be ªafraid, for I am with you.
From the east I will bring your
descendants;
from the west I will ᵇgather you.
6 I will say to the ªnorth, 'Hand them
over!'
and to the south, 'Don't hold any
back!'
Bring my sons from distant lands,
and my daughters from the remote
regions of the earth,
7 everyone who ªbelongs to me,

whom ᵇI created for my glory,
whom I formed—yes, whom I made."

The Lord Declares His Sovereignty

8 Bring ªout the people who are blind,
even though they have eyes,
those who are ᵇdeaf, even though
they have ears!
9 All nations gather together,
the peoples assemble.
ªWho among them announced this?
Who predicted earlier events for us?[1]
Let them produce their witnesses to
testify they were right;
let them listen and affirm, "It is true."
10 "You are my witnesses," says the
LORD,
"my servant whom I have chosen
so that ªyou may consider ᵇand
ᶜbelieve in me,
and understand that I am he.
No god was formed before me,
and none will outlive me.
11 I, I ªam the LORD,
and there is no deliverer besides me.
12 I decreed and delivered and
proclaimed,
and there was no other god among
you.
You are my witnesses," says the LORD,
"that ªI am God.
13 From this day ªforward I am he;
no one can deliver from my power;
I will act, and who can ᵇprevent it?"

The Lord Will Do Something New

14 This is what the LORD says,
your Protector, the Holy One of
Israel:
"For your sake I send to Babylon
and make them all fugitives,
turning the Babylonians' joyful
shouts into mourning songs.[1]
15 I am the LORD, your Holy One,
the one who created Israel, your
ªKing."
16 This is what the LORD says,
the one who ªmade a road through
the sea,

42:25 ª 2 Kgs 25:9   ᵇIsa 29:13   ¹Heb. *strength.*   **43:1** ªIsa 43:5; 44:6   ᵇIsa 42:6; 45:4   **43:2** ª[Ps 66:12; 91:3]   ᵇ[Deut 31:6]; Jer 30:11   ᶜDan 3:25   **43:3** ª[Prov 11:8; 21:18]   **43:4** ªIsa 63:9   **43:5** ªIsa 41:10; 44:2; Jer 30:10; 46:27–28   ᵇIsa 54:7   **43:6** ªIsa 49:12   **43:7** ªIsa 63:19; Jas 2:7   ᵇPs 100:3; Isa 29:23; [John 3:2–3; 2 Cor 5:17; Eph 2:10]   **43:8** ªIsa 6:9; 42:19; Ezek 12:2   ᵇIsa 29:18   **43:9** ªIsa 41:21–22, 26   ¹Heb. *and the former things he was causing us to hear?*   **43:10** ªIsa 44:8   ᵇIsa 55:4   ᶜIsa 41:4; 44:6   **43:11** ªIsa 45:21; Hos 13:4   **43:12** ªDeut 32:16; Ps 81:9   **43:13** ªPs 90:2; Isa 48:16   ᵇJob 9:12; Isa 14:27   **43:14** ¹Lit. *as for the Babylonians, in ships their joyful shout;* i.e., the Lord caused the Babylonians to flee for safety in the ships in which they took such great pride.   **43:15** ªIsa 41:20–21   **43:16** ªExod 14:16, 21, 22; Ps 77:19; Isa 51:10

a [b]pathway through the surging waters,
17 the one who led chariots and horses
to destruction,
together with a mighty army.
They fell down, never to rise again;
they were extinguished, put out like
a burning wick:
18 "Don't remember these earlier events;[1]
[a]don't recall these former events.
19 "Look, I am about to do something [a]new.
Now [b]it begins to happen! Do you not recognize it?
Yes, I will make a road in the wilderness
and paths in the wastelands.
20 The [a]wild animals honor me,
the jackals and ostriches,
because I put water in the wilderness
and streams in the wastelands
to quench the thirst of my chosen people,
21 the people [a]whom I formed for myself,
so they might praise [b]me.

The Lord Rebukes His People

22 "But you did not call for me, O Jacob;
you did not long for me, O Israel.
23 You did not bring me lambs for [a]your burnt offerings;
you did not honor me with your sacrifices.
I did not burden you with offerings;
I did not make you weary by demanding incense.
24 You did not buy me aromatic reeds;[1]
you did not present to me the fat of your sacrifices.
Yet you burdened me with your sins;
you [a]made me weary with your evil deeds.
25 I, I am the one who [a]blots out your rebellious deeds [b]for my sake;
your sins I do not remember.
26 Remind me of what happened. Let's debate!
You, prove to me that you are right!
27 The father of your nation sinned;
your spokesmen rebelled against me.
28 So [a]I defiled your holy princes,
and handed Jacob over to destruction,
and subjected Israel to humiliating abuse.

The Lord Will Renew Israel

44 "Now, listen, Jacob my servant,
Israel whom I have chosen!"
2 This is what the LORD, the one who made you, says—
the one who formed you in the womb and helps you:
"Don't be afraid, my servant Jacob,
Jeshurun, whom I have chosen.
3 For I will pour water on the parched ground
and cause streams to flow on the dry land.
I will pour my Spirit on your offspring
and my blessing on your children.
4 They will sprout up like a tree in the grass,
like poplars beside channels of water.
5 One will say, 'I belong to the LORD,'
and another will use the name 'Jacob.'
One will write on his hand, 'The LORD's,'
and use the name 'Israel.'"

The Absurdity of Idolatry

6 This [a]is what the LORD, Israel's King, says,
their Protector,[1] the LORD of Heaven's Armies:
"I am the first and I am the last,
there is no God but me.
7 [a]Who is like me? Let him make his claim!
Let him announce it and explain it to me—
since I established an ancient people[1]—
let them announce future events.
8 Don't panic! Don't be afraid!

43:16 [b] Josh 3:13   43:18 [a] Jer 16:14   [1] Heb. *the former things.*   43:19 [a] Isa 42:9; 48:6; [2 Cor 5:17; Rev 21:5]   [b] Exod 17:6; Num 20:11; Deut 8:15; Ps 78:16; Isa 35:1, 6   43:20 [a] Isa 48:21   43:21 [a] Ps 102:18; Isa 42:12; [Luke 1:74–75; Eph 1:5–6; 1 Pet 2:9]   [b] Jer 13:11   43:23 [a] Amos 5:25   43:24 [a] Ps 95:10; Isa 1:14; 7:13; Ezek 6:9; Mal 2:17   [1] Or *calamus.*   43:25 [a] Isa 44:22; Jer 50:20; [Acts 3:19]   [b] Ezek 36:22   43:28 [a] Ps 79:4; Jer 24:9; Dan 9:11; Zech 8:13   44:6 [a] Isa 41:4; [Rev 1:8, 17; 22:13]   [1] Heb. *his kinsman redeemer;* a protector of the extended family's interests.   44:7 [a] Isa 41:4, 22, 26   [1] MT *from (the time) I established an ancient people, and the coming things.*

Did I not tell [a]you beforehand and
  decree it?
You are my witnesses! Is [b]there any
  God but me?
There is no other sheltering rock; I
  know of none.
9 [a]All who form idols are nothing;
  [b]the things in which they delight are
  worthless.
Their witnesses cannot see;
they recognize nothing, so they are
  put to shame.
10 Who forms [a]a god and casts an idol
that will prove worthless?
11 Look, all his associates will be put to
  [a]shame;
the craftsmen are mere humans.
Let them all assemble and take their
  stand.
They will panic and be put to shame.
12 A blacksmith works with his tool
and forges metal over [a]the coals.
He forms it[1] with hammers;
he makes it with his strong arm.
He gets hungry and loses his energy;
he drinks no water and gets tired.
13 A carpenter takes measurements;
he marks out an outline of its form;
he scrapes it with chisels
and marks it with a compass.
He patterns it after the human form,
like a well-built human being,
and puts it in a shrine.
14 He cuts down cedars
and acquires a cypress[1] or an oak.
He gets trees from the forest;
he plants a cedar and the rain makes
  it grow.
15 A man uses it to make a fire;
he takes some of it and warms
  himself.
Yes, he kindles a fire and bakes bread.
Then he makes a god and worships it;
he makes an idol and bows down to it.
16 Half of it he burns in the fire—
over that half he cooks meat;
he roasts a meal and fills himself.
Yes, he warms himself and says,
'Ah! I am warm as I look at the fire.'

17 With the rest of it he makes a god, his
  idol;
he bows down to it and worships it.
He prays to it, saying,
'Rescue me, for you are my god!'
18 [a]They do not [b]comprehend or
  understand,
for their eyes are blind and cannot
  see;
their minds do not [c]discern.
19 No one [a]thinks to himself,
nor do they comprehend or
  understand and say to themselves:
'I burned half of it in the fire—
yes, I baked bread over the coals;
I roasted meat and ate it.
With the rest of it should I make a
  disgusting idol?
Should I bow down to dry wood?'
20 He feeds on [a]ashes;[1]
his deceived mind misleads him.
He cannot rescue himself,
nor does he say, 'Is this not a false
  [b]god I hold in my right hand?'
21 Remember these things, O Jacob,
O Israel, for you are my servant.
I formed you to be my servant;
O Israel, I will not [a]forget you!
22 I remove the [a]guilt of your
  [b]rebellious deeds as if they were a
  cloud,
the guilt of your sins as if they were
  a cloud.
Come back to me, for I protect you."
23 Shout for [a]joy, O sky, for the LORD
  intervenes;
shout out, you subterranean regions[1]
  of the earth.
O mountains, give a joyful shout;
you too, O forest and all your trees!
For the LORD protects Jacob;
he [b]reveals his splendor through
  Israel.

The Lord Empowers Cyrus

24 This is what the LORD, [a]your
  Protector, says,
[b]the one [c]who formed you in the
  womb:

44:8 [a]Isa 43:10, 12   [b]Deut 4:35; 32:39; 1 Sam 2:2; 2 Sam 22:32; Isa 45:5; Joel 2:27   44:9 [a]Isa 41:24   [b]Ps 115:4   44:10 [a]Isa
41:29; Jer 10:5; Hab 2:18; Acts 19:26   44:11 [a]Ps 97:7; Isa 1:29; 42:17   44:12 [a]Isa 40:19; Jer 10:3–5   [1]Perhaps an idol being
fashioned by the blacksmith.   44:14 [1]What type of tree this Heb. word refers to is uncertain.   44:18 [a]Isa 45:20   [b][Ps
81:12]; Isa 6:9–10; 29:10; 2 Thess 2:11   [c]Jer 10:14   44:19 [a]Isa 46:8   44:20 [a]Job 15:31; Hos 4:12; Rom 1:21–22; 2 Thess 2:11;
2 Tim 3:13   [b]Isa 57:11; 59:3–4, 13; Rom 1:25   [1]Or perhaps *he eats on an ash heap.*   44:21 [a]Isa 49:15   44:22 [a]Isa 43:25
[b]Isa 43:1; 1 Cor 6:20; [1 Pet 1:18–19]   44:23 [a]Ps 69:34; Isa 42:10; 49:13; Jer 51:48; Rev 18:20   [b]Isa 49:3; 60:21
[1]Heb. *lower regions*; i.e., Sheol.   44:24 [a]Isa 43:14   [b]Isa 43:1   [c]Job 9:8

"I am the LORD, who made everything,
who alone stretched out the sky,
who fashioned the earth all by myself,
25 who [a]frustrates the omens [b]of the empty talkers
[c]and humiliates the omen readers,
who overturns the counsel of the wise men
and makes their advice seem foolish,
26 who fulfills the oracles of his prophetic servants[1]
and brings to pass the announcements of his messengers,
[a]who says about Jerusalem, 'She will be inhabited,'
and about the towns of Judah, 'They will be rebuilt,
her ruins I will raise up,'
27 [a]who says to the deep sea, 'Be dry!
I will dry up your sea currents,'
28 who commissions [a]Cyrus, the one I appointed as shepherd[1]
to carry out all my wishes
and to decree concerning Jerusalem, 'She will be rebuilt,'
and concerning the temple, 'It will be reconstructed.'

45 "This is what the LORD says to his chosen one,[1]
to [a]Cyrus, whose [b]right hand I hold
in order [c]to subdue nations before him
and [d]disarm kings,
to open doors before him
so gates remain unclosed:

2 'I will go before you
[a]and level [b]mountains.
Bronze doors I will shatter
and iron bars I will hack through.
3 I will give you hidden treasures,
riches stashed away in secret places,
so you may recognize [a]that I am the LORD,
the one who [b]calls you by name, the God of Israel.
4 For the sake of my servant [a]Jacob,

Israel, my chosen one,
I call you by name
and give you a title of respect, even though you do not submit to me.
5 I [a]am [b]the LORD, [c]I have no peer,
there is no God but me.
I arm you for battle, even though you do not recognize me.
6 I do this so people will recognize from east to west
[a]that there is [b]no God but me;
I am the LORD, I have no peer.
7 I am the one who forms light
and [a]creates darkness;
the one who brings about peace
and creates calamity.
I am the LORD, who accomplishes all these things.
8 O sky, [a]rain down from above!
Let the clouds send down showers of deliverance!
Let the earth absorb it so salvation may grow
and deliverance may sprout up along with it.
I, the LORD, create it.'"

The Lord Gives a Warning

9 One who argues with [a]his Creator is in grave danger,
one who is like [b]a mere shard among the other shards on the ground!
The clay should not say to the potter,
"What in the world are you doing?
Your work lacks skill!"
10 Danger awaits one who says to his father,
"What in the world are you fathering?"
and to his mother,
"What in the world are you bringing forth?"
11 This is what the LORD says,
the Holy One of Israel, the one who formed him,
concerning things to come:[1]
"How dare you [a]question me about [b]my children!
How dare you tell me what to do with [c]the work of my own hands!

44:25 [a] Isa 47:13 [b] Jer 50:36 [c] 2 Sam 15:31; Job 5:12–14; Ps 33:10; Isa 29:14; Jer 51:57; 1 Cor 1:20, 27   44:26 [a] Zech 1:6; Matt 5:18 [1] Heb. *the word of his servant.*   44:27 [a] Jer 50:38; 51:36   44:28 [a] 2 Chr 36:22; Ezra 1:1; Isa 45:13 [1] Heb. *my shepherd.*   45:1 [a] Isa 44:28 [b] Ps 73:23; Isa 41:13 [c] Dan 5:30 [d] Job 12:21; Isa 45:5 [1] Heb. *anointed.*   45:2 [a] Isa 40:4 [b] Ps 107:16   45:3 [a] Isa 41:23 [b] Exod 33:12   45:4 [a] Isa 44:1   45:5 [a] Deut 4:35; 32:39; Isa 44:8 [b] Isa 45:14, 18 [c] Ps 18:32   45:6 [a] Ps 102:15; Isa 37:20; Mal 1:11 [b] [Isa 11:9; 52:10]   45:7 [a] Isa 31:2; 47:11; Amos 3:6   45:8 [a] Ps 85:11   45:9 [a] Isa 64:8 [b] Jer 18:6; Rom 9:20–21   45:11 [a] Isa 8:19 [b] Jer 31:9 [c] Isa 29:23; 60:21; 64:8 [1] MT *the one who formed him, the coming things.*

12 I made the earth;
  [a]I [b]created the people who live on it.
  It was me—my hands stretched out
    the sky.
  I give orders to [c]all the heavenly
    lights.
13 It [a]is me—I stir him up and
    commission him;
  I will make all his ways level.
  He will [b]rebuild my city;
  he will send my exiled people home,
  but [c]not for a price or a bribe,"
  says the LORD of Heaven's Armies.

The Lord Is the Nations' Only Hope

14 This is what [a]the LORD says:

"The profit of Egypt and the revenue
    of Ethiopia,
  along with the Sabeans, those tall
    men,
  will be brought to you and become
    yours.
  They will walk [b]behind you, coming
    along in chains.
  They will bow down to you
  and pray to you:
  '[c]Truly God is with[1] you; [d]he has no
    peer;
  there is no other God!'"
15 Yes, you are a God [a]who keeps hidden,
  O God of Israel, deliverer!
16 They will all be [a]ashamed and
    embarrassed;
  those who fashion idols will all be
    humiliated.
17 [a]Israel will be delivered once and for
    [b]all by the LORD;
  you will never again [c]be ashamed or
    humiliated.
18 For this is what the LORD says,
  the one [a]who created the sky—
  he is the true God,
  the one who formed the earth and
    made it;
  he established it,
  he did not create it without order,
  he formed it to be [b]inhabited:
  "[c]I am the LORD, I have no peer.

19 I have not spoken in [a]secret,
  [b]in some hidden place.
  I did not tell Jacob's descendants,
  'Seek me in vain!'
  I am the LORD,
  the one who speaks honestly,
  who makes reliable announcements.
20 Gather together and come!
  Approach together, you refugees
    from [a]the nations.
  Those who carry wooden idols know
    nothing,
  those who pray to a god that cannot
    deliver.
21 Tell me! Present the evidence![1]
  Let them consult with one another.
  [a]Who predicted this in the past?
  Who announced it [b]beforehand?
  Was it not I, the LORD?
  I have no peer, there is no God
    but me,
  a God who vindicates and delivers;
  there is none but me.
22 Turn to me so you can be delivered,
  [a]all you who live in the earth's
    remote regions!
  For I am God, and I have no peer.
23 I solemnly make [a]this oath—
  what I say is true and reliable:
  'Surely every [b]knee will bow to me,
  [c]every tongue will solemnly affirm;[1]
24 they will say about me,
  "Yes, the LORD is a powerful
    [a]deliverer."'"
  [b]All who are angry at him will cower
    before him.
25 All the descendants of Israel will be
    [a]vindicated by the LORD
  and will boast in him.

The Lord Carries His People

46 Bel kneels down,
  Nebo bends low.
  Their [a]images weigh down animals
    and beasts.
  Your heavy images are burdensome
    to tired animals.
2 Together they bend low and kneel
    down;

45:12 [a] Isa 42:5; Jer 27:5 [b] Gen 1:26 [c] Gen 2:1; Neh 9:6 **45:13** [a] Isa 41:2 [b] 2 Chr 36:22; Isa 44:28 [c] [Rom 3:24] **45:14** [a] Ps 68:31; 72:10–11; Isa 14:1; 49:23; 60:9–10, 14, 16; Zech 8:22–23 [b] Ps 149:8 [c] Jer 16:19; Zech 8:20–23; 1 Cor 14:25 [d] Isa 45:5 [1] Or perhaps *among*. **45:15** [a] Ps 44:24; Isa 57:17 **45:16** [a] Isa 44:11 **45:17** [a] Isa 26:4; [Rom 11:26] [b] Isa 51:6 [c] Isa 29:22 **45:18** [a] Isa 42:5 [b] Gen 1:26; Ps 115:16; Acts 17:26 [c] Isa 45:5 **45:19** [a] Deut 30:11 [b] Ps 19:8; Isa 45:23; 63:1 **45:20** [a] Isa 44:9; 46:7; Jer 10:5 **45:21** [a] Isa 41:22; 43:9 [b] Isa 44:8 [1] Heb. *Declare! Bring near!* **45:22** [a] Ps 22:27; 65:5 **45:23** [a] Gen 22:16; Isa 62:8; [Heb 6:13] [b] Rom 14:11; [Phil 2:10] [c] Deut 6:13; Ps 63:11; Isa 19:18; 65:16 [1] Heb. *swear*. **45:24** [a] Isa 54:17; [Jer 23:5; 1 Cor 1:30] [b] Isa 41:11 **45:25** [a] Isa 45:17 **46:1** [a] Jer 10:5

they are unable to rescue the
images;
they themselves head off into
captivity.
3 "Listen to me, [a]O family of Jacob,[1]
all you who are left from the family
of Israel,
you who have been carried from
birth,
you who have been supported from
the time you left the womb.
4 Even when you are old, [a]I [b]will take
care of you,
even when you have gray hair, I will
carry you.
I made you and I will support you;
I will carry you and rescue you.
5 To whom can you compare and
liken me?
Tell me whom you think I resemble,
so we can be compared!
6 Those who empty out gold from a
purse
and weigh out silver on [a]the scale
hire a [b]metalsmith, who makes it
into a god.
They then bow down and worship it.
7 They put it on their shoulder and
carry it;
[a]they put it in its place and it just
stands there;
it does not[1] move from its place.
Even when [b]someone cries out to it,
it does not reply;
it does not deliver him from his
distress.
8 Remember this, so you can be brave.
[a]Think about it, you rebels!
9 [a]Remember what I accomplished in
antiquity.
Truly I am God, I have no peer;
I am God, and there is none like me,
10 who [a]announces the end from the
beginning
and reveals beforehand what has not
yet occurred;
who says, '[b]My plan will be realized,
I will accomplish what I desire;'

11 who summons an eagle[1] [a]from the
east,
from a distant land, one [b]who
[c]carries out my plan.
Yes, I have decreed,
yes, I will bring it to pass;
I have formulated a plan,
yes, I will carry it out.
12 Listen to me, you [a]stubborn people,
you [b]who distance yourselves from
doing what is right.
13 I am [a]bringing my deliverance near,
it is not far away;
I am bringing my [b]salvation near, it
does not wait.
I will save Zion;
I will adorn Israel with my splendor.

Babylon Will Fall

47 "Fall [a]down! [b]Sit in the dirt,
O virgin daughter [c]Babylon!
Sit on the ground, not on a throne,
O daughter of the Babylonians!
Indeed,[1] you will no longer be called
delicate and pampered.
2 Pick [a]up millstones and grind flour.
Remove your veil,
strip off your skirt,
expose your legs,
cross the streams.
3 Let [a]your naked body be exposed.
Your shame [b]will be on display!
I will get revenge;
I will not have pity on anyone,"
4 says [a]our Protector—
the LORD of Heaven's Armies is his
name,
the Holy One of Israel.[1]
5 "Sit [a]silently! Go to a hiding place,
[b]O daughter of the Babylonians!
Indeed, you will no longer be called
'Queen of kingdoms.'
6 I was angry at my people;
[a]I [b]defiled my special [c]possession
and handed them over to you.
You showed them no mercy;
you even placed a very heavy burden
on old people.

46:3 [a] Deut 32:11; Ps 71:6; Isa 63:9 [1] Heb. *house of Jacob.*   46:4 [a] Mal 3:6 [b] Ps 48:14   46:6 [a] Isa 40:19; 41:6; Jer 10:4 [b] Isa 44:12   46:7 [a] Isa 45:20; 46:1; Jer 10:5 [b] Isa 45:20 [1] Or perhaps *cannot.*   46:8 [a] Isa 44:19   46:9 [a] Deut 32:7; Isa 42:9; 65:17 46:10 [a] Isa 45:21; 48:3 [b] Ps 33:11; Prov 19:21; 21:30; Isa 14:24; 25:1; Acts 5:39; Heb 6:17   46:11 [a] Isa 41:2, 25 [b] Isa 44:28 [c] Num 23:19 [1] Or, more generally, *a bird of prey.*   46:12 [a] Ps 76:5; Isa 48:4; Zech 7:11–12; Mal 3:13 [b] [Rom 10:3]   46:13 [a] [Rom 1:17] [b] Isa 62:11; Joel 3:17; [1 Pet 2:6]   47:1 [a] Jer 48:18 [b] Isa 3:26 [c] Isa 14:18–23; Jer 25:12; 50:1—51:64 [1] Or *For.*   47:2 [a] Exod 11:5; Jer 25:10   47:3 [a] Isa 3:17; 20:4 [b] [Rom 12:19]   47:4 [a] Jer 50:34 [1] MT *Our redeemer—the LORD of armies* [trad. *the LORD of hosts*] *is his name, the Holy One of Israel.*   47:5 [a] 1 Sam 2:9 [b] Isa 13:19; [Dan 2:37]; Rev 17:18   47:6 [a] 2 Sam 24:14 [b] Isa 43:28 [c] Deut 28:49–50

7 You [a]said,
  'I will rule forever as permanent
      queen!'
  You did not [b]think about these
      things;
  you did [c]not consider how it would
      turn out.
8 So now, listen to this,
  O one who lives so lavishly,
  who lives securely,
  who says to herself,
  'I am unique! No one can compare
      to me!
  I will never have to live as a widow;
  I will never lose my children.'
9 Both of these will come upon you
  suddenly, [a]in one day!
  You will lose your children and be
      widowed.
  You will be overwhelmed by these
      tragedies,[1]
  despite your many incantations
  and your numerous amulets.
10 You were complacent in your evil
      deeds;
  you thought, 'No one [a]sees me.'
  Your self-professed wisdom and
      knowledge lead you astray,
  when you say, 'I am unique! No one
      can compare to me!'
11 Disaster will overtake you;
  you will not know how to charm it
      away.
  Destruction will fall on you;
  you will not be able to appease it.
  [a]Calamity will strike you [b]suddenly,
  before you recognize it.
12 Persist in trusting your amulets
  and your many incantations,
  which you have faithfully recited
      since your youth!
  Maybe you will be successful—
  maybe you will scare away disaster.
13 You are tired out from listening to so
      much advice.
  Let them take their stand—
  the ones who see omens in
      the sky,
  who gaze at the stars,
  who make monthly predictions—

let them rescue [a]you from [b]the
    disaster that is about to overtake
    you!
14 Look, they are like straw
  that the fire burns [a]up;
  they cannot rescue themselves
  from the heat of the flames.
  There are no coals to warm them,
  no firelight to enjoy.
15 They will disappoint [a]you,[1]
  those you have so faithfully dealt
      with since your youth.
  Each strays off in his own direction,
  leaving no one to rescue you."

The Lord Appeals to the Exiles

48 Listen to this, O family of Jacob,[1]
  you who are called by the name
      "Israel,"
  and are descended from Judah,[2]
  who take oaths in the name of the
      LORD
  and invoke the God of Israel—
  but [a]not in an honest and just
      manner.
2 Indeed, they live in the holy city;
  they [a]trust in the God of Israel,
  whose name is the LORD of Heaven's
      Armies.
3 "I [a]announced events [b]beforehand,
  I issued the decrees and made the
      predictions;
  suddenly I acted and they came to
      pass.
4 I did this because I know how
  stubborn [a]you are.
  Your neck muscles are like iron
  and your forehead like bronze.
5 I announced them to you
      beforehand;
  before they happened, I predicted
      them for you,
  so you could never say,
  'My image did these things,
  my idol, my cast image, decreed
      them.'
6 You have heard; now look at all the
      evidence!
  Will you not admit that what I say is
      true?

47:7 [a]Rev 18:7 [b]Isa 42:25; 46:8 [c]Deut 32:29; Jer 5:31; Ezek 7:2–3   47:9 [a]Ps 73:19; 1 Thess 5:3; Rev 18:8 [1]Heb. *according to their fullness, they will come upon you.*   47:10 [a]Isa 29:15; Ezek 8:12; 9:9   47:11 [a]Isa 13:6; Jer 51:8, 43; Luke 17:27; 1 Thess 5:3 [b]Isa 29:5   47:13 [a]Isa 57:10 [b]Isa 8:19; 44:25; 47:9; Dan 2:2, 10   47:14 [a][Isa 10:17]; Jer 51:58   47:15 [a]Rev 18:11 [1]Heb. *So they will be to you.*   48:1 [a]Isa 58:2; Jer 4:2; 5:2 [1]Heb. *house of Jacob.* [2]MT *and from the waters of Judah came out.*   48:2 [a]Isa 10:20; Jer 7:4; 21:2; Mic 3:11; Rom 2:17   48:3 [a]Isa 44:7–8; 46:10 [b]Josh 21:45; Isa 42:9   48:4 [a]Exod 32:9; Deut 31:27; Ezek 2:4; 3:7

From this point on I am announcing
  to you new events
that are previously unrevealed and
  you do not know about.
7 Now they come into being, not in the
    past;
before today you did not hear about
    them,
so you could not say,
  'Yes,[1] I know about them.'
8 You did not [a]hear,
you do not know,
you were not told beforehand.
For I know that you are very
    deceitful;
you were labeled a rebel from birth.
9 For the sake of my reputation I hold
    back my anger;
[a]for the sake of my [b]prestige I
    restrain myself from destroying
    you.
10 Look, [a]I have refined you, but not as
    silver;
I have purified you[1] in the [b]furnace of
    misery.
11 For my sake alone I will act,
for [a]how can [b]I allow my name to be
    defiled?
I will not share my glory with anyone
    else!
12 Listen to me, O Jacob,
[a]Israel, whom I summoned.
I am the one;
I am present at the very [b]beginning
and at the very end.
13 Yes, [a]my hand founded the earth;
my [b]right hand spread out the sky.
I summon them;
they stand together.
14 All of you, [a]gather [b]together and
    listen!
Who among them announced these
    things?
The LORD's ally[1] will carry out his
    desire against Babylon;
he will exert his power against the
    Babylonians.
15 I, [a]I have spoken—

yes, I have summoned him;
I lead him and he will succeed.
16 Approach me—[a]listen to this!
From [b]the very first I have not
    spoken in secret;
when it happens, I am there."
So now, the Sovereign LORD has
    sent me, accompanied by his
    Spirit.
17 This is what [a]the LORD, your
    Protector, says,
the Holy One of Israel:
"I am the LORD your God,
[b]who teaches you how to succeed,
who leads you in the way you
    should go.
18 [a]If only you had obeyed my
    commandments,
prosperity would have flowed to you
    like a river,[1]
deliverance would have come to you
    like [b]the waves of the sea.
19 Your descendants would have been
    as numerous as sand
and [a]your children like its granules.
Their name would not have been cut
    off
and eliminated from my presence.
20 [a]Leave Babylon!
Flee from the Babylonians!
Announce it with a shout of joy!
Make this known—
proclaim it throughout the earth!
Say, 'The LORD [b]protects his servant
    Jacob.
21 They do not thirst as he leads them
    through dry regions;
he makes water flow out of [a]a rock
    for them;
he splits open a rock and water flows
    out.'
22 There will be no prosperity for [a]the
    wicked," says the LORD.

Delivery of the Exiles

49 Listen [a]to me, you coastlands!
Pay attention, you people who live
    far away!

48:7 [1] Heb. look.   48:8 [a] Deut 9:7, 24; Ps 58:3; Isa 46:3, 8   48:9 [a] Ps 79:9; 106:8; Isa 43:25; Ezek 20:9, 14, 22, 44   [b] [Neh 9:30–31]; Ps 78:38; Isa 30:18; 65:8   48:10 [a] Ps 66:10; Jer 9:7   [b] Deut 4:20; 1 Kgs 8:51; Jer 11:4   [1] MT I have chosen you.
48:11 [a] Lev 22:2, 32; Deut 32:26–27; Ezek 20:9   [b] Isa 42:8   48:12 [a] Deut 32:39   [b] Isa 44:6; [Rev 22:13]   48:13 [a] Exod 20:11; Ps 102:25; Isa 42:5; 45:12, 18; Heb 1:10–12   [b] Isa 40:26   48:14 [a] Isa 45:1   [b] Isa 44:28; 47:1–15   [1] Or friend, covenant partner.
48:15 [a] Isa 45:1–2   48:16 [a] Isa 45:19   [b] Isa 61:1; Zech 2:8–9, 11   48:17 [a] Isa 43:14   [b] Ps 32:8; Isa 49:9–10   48:18 [a] Deut 5:29; Ps 81:13   [b] Deut 28:1–14; Ps 119:165; Isa 32:16–18; 66:12   [1] Heb. like a river your peace would have been.   48:19 [a] Gen 22:17; Isa 10:22; 44:3–4; 54:3; Jer 33:22; Hos 1:10   48:20 [a] Jer 50:8; 51:6, 45; Zech 2:6–7; Rev 18:4   [b] [Exod 19:4–6]
48:21 [a] Exod 17:6; Ps 105:41   48:22 [a] [Isa 57:21]   49:1 [a] Isa 41:1

[b]The LORD summoned me from
  birth;
he commissioned me when my
  mother brought me into the world.
2 He made [a]my mouth like a sharp
  sword,
he hid me [b]in the hollow of his [c]hand;
he made me like a sharpened arrow,
he hid me in his quiver.
3 He said to me, "[a]You are my servant,
Israel, through whom [b]I will reveal
  my splendor."
4 But I thought, "I have worked in vain;
I have expended my energy for
  absolutely nothing."
But [a]the LORD will vindicate me;
my God will reward me.
5 So now the LORD says,
the one who formed me from birth
  to be [a]his servant—
he did this to restore Jacob to himself,
so that Israel might be gathered to
  him;
and I will be honored in the LORD's
  sight,
for my God is my source of strength—
6 he says, "Is it too insignificant a task
  for you to be my servant,
to reestablish the tribes of Jacob,
and restore the remnant of Israel?
I will make you a [a]light to the nations,
so you can bring my deliverance to
  the remote regions of the earth."
7 This is what the LORD,
the [a]Protector of Israel, their Holy
  One, says
to the one who is despised[1] and
  rejected by nations,[2]
a servant of rulers:
"[b]Kings will see and rise in respect,
princes will bow down,
because of the faithful LORD,
the Holy One of Israel who has
  chosen you."

8 This is what the LORD says:

"At the time I decide to show my
  [a]favor, I will respond to you;
in the day of deliverance I will help
  you;
I will protect you [b]and make you a
  covenant mediator for people,
to rebuild the land
and to reassign the desolate
  property.
9 You will say [a]to the prisoners, 'Come
  out,'
and to those who are in dark
  dungeons, 'Emerge.'
They will graze beside the roads;
on all the slopes they will find
  pasture.
10 They will not [a]be hungry [b]or thirsty;
the sun's oppressive heat [c]will not
  beat down on them,
for one who has compassion on them
  will guide them;
he will lead them to springs of water.
11 I [a]will make all my mountains into a
  road;
I will construct my roadways."
12 Look, they come from far away!
Look, some come from [a]the north
  and west,
and others from the land of Sinim.[1]
13 Shout for [a]joy, O sky![1]
Rejoice, O earth!
Let the mountains give a joyful
  shout!
For the LORD consoles his people
and shows compassion to the
  oppressed.

The Lord Remembers Zion

14 "[a]Zion said, 'The LORD has
  abandoned me,
the Lord has forgotten me.'
15 Can [a]a woman forget her baby who
  nurses at her breast?
Can she withhold compassion from
  the child she has borne?
Even if mothers were to forget,
I could never forget you!
16 Look, [a]I have inscribed your name[1]
  on my palms;
your walls are constantly before me.
17 Your children hurry back,

49:1 [b]Jer 1:5; Matt 1:20; Luke 1:35; John 1:14; 10:36   49:2 [a]Isa 11:4; Hos 6:5; [Heb 4:12]; Rev 1:16; 2:12   [b]Isa 51:16   [c]Ps 45:5   49:3 [a][Isa 41:8; 42:1; Zech 3:8]   [b]Isa 44:23; Matt 12:18; [John 13:31–32; 14:13; 15:8; 17:4; Eph 1:6]   49:4 [a][Ezek 3:19]   49:5 [a]Matt 23:37; [Rom 11:25–29]   49:6 [a]Isa 42:6; 51:4; [Luke 2:32]; Acts 13:47; [Gal 3:14]   49:7 [a][Ps 22:6; Isa 53:3; Matt 26:67; 27:41]; Mark 15:29; Luke 23:35   [b][Isa 52:15]   [1]MT to [one who] despises life; DSS to the one despised with respect to life.   [2]Heb. nation.   49:8 [a]Ps 69:13; 2 Cor 6:2   [b]Isa 42:6   49:9 [a]Isa 61:1; Zech 9:12; Luke 4:18   49:10 [a]Isa 33:16; 48:21; Rev 7:16   [b]Ps 121:6   [c]Ps 23:2; Isa 40:11; 48:17   49:11 [a]Isa 40:4   49:12 [a]Isa 43:5–6   [1]DSS Syene.   49:13 [a]Isa 44:23   [1]Or O heavens.   49:14 [a]Isa 40:27   49:15 [a]Ps 103:13; Mal 3:17   49:16 [a]Exod 13:9; Song 8:6; Hag 2:23   [1]Heb. you.

while those who destroyed and
devastated you depart.
[18] Look all around you!
All of them gather to you.
As surely as [a]I live," says the LORD,
"you will certainly wear all of them
like jewelry;
you will put them on [b]as if you were
a bride.
[19] Yes, your land lies in ruins;
it is desolate and devastated.
But now you [a]will be too small to
hold your residents,
and those who devoured you will be
far away.
[20] Yet [a]the children born during your
time of bereavement
will say within your hearing,
'This place is too cramped for us,
make room for us so we can live here.'
[21] Then you will think to yourself,
'Who bore these children for me?
I was bereaved and barren,
dismissed and divorced.
Who raised these children?
Look, I was left all alone;
where did these children come
from?'"

[22] This is [a]what the Sovereign LORD says:

"Look I will raise my hand to the
nations;
I will raise my signal flag to the
peoples.
They will bring your sons in their
arms
and carry your daughters on their
shoulders.
[23] [a]Kings will be your children's[l]
guardians;
their princesses will nurse your
children.
With their faces to the ground they
will bow down to you,
and they will [b]lick the dirt on your
feet.
Then you will recognize that I am the
LORD;
those who wait patiently [c]for me are
not put to shame.

[24] Can spoils be taken from [a]a warrior,
or captives be rescued from a
conqueror?[1]
[25] Indeed," says the LORD,
"captives will be taken from a
warrior;
spoils will be rescued from a
conqueror.
I will oppose your adversary
and I will rescue your children.
[26] I will make your oppressors [a]eat their
own flesh;
they will get drunk on their own
[b]blood, as if it were wine.
Then [c]all humankind will recognize
that
I am the LORD, your Deliverer,
your Protector, the Powerful One of
Jacob."

50 This is what [a]the LORD says:
"Where is your mother's divorce
certificate
by which I divorced her?
Or to which of my [b]creditors did I sell
[c]you?
Look, you were sold because of your
sins;
because of your rebellious acts I
divorced your mother.
[2] Why does no one challenge me when
I come?
Why does no one respond when I
call?
Is my hand too weak to deliver you?
Do I lack the power to rescue you?
Look, with a mere [a]shout I can dry up
the sea;
I can turn streams into a desert,
so the fish rot away and die
from lack of water.
[3] I can clothe the sky [a]in darkness;
I can cover it with sackcloth."

The Servant Perseveres

[4] The Sovereign LORD has given me
[a]the capacity to be his spokesman,
so that I know how to help the
[b]weary.[1]
He wakes me up every morning;
he makes me alert so I can listen
attentively as disciples do.

49:18 [a] Isa 60:4; John 4:35 [b] Prov 17:6 **49:19** [a] Isa 54:1–2; Zech 10:10 **49:20** [a] Isa 60:4 **49:22** [a] Isa 60:4
49:23 [a] Ps 72:11; Isa 52:15 [b] Ps 72:9; Mic 7:17 [c] Ps 34:22; [Rom 5:5] [1] Heb. *your*. **49:24** [a] Matt 12:29; Luke 11:21–22
[1] MT *a righteous* [one]. **49:26** [a] Isa 9:20 [b] Rev 14:20 [c] Ps 9:16; Isa 60:16 **50:1** [a] Deut 24:1; Jer 3:8
[b] Deut 32:30; 2 Kgs 4:1; Neh 5:5 [c] Isa 52:3 **50:2** [a] Ps 106:9; Nah 1:4 **50:3** [a] Exod 10:21
50:4 [a] Exod 4:11 [b] Matt 11:28 [1] Heb. *to know* [?] *the weary with a word*.

5 The Sovereign LORD [a]has spoken to
  me clearly;[1]
I have not [b]rebelled,
I have not turned back.
6 I offered my back to those who
  attacked,
  my jaws to those who tore out my
    beard;
  [a]I did not hide [b]my face
from insults and [c]spitting.
7 But the [a]Sovereign LORD helps me,
so I am not humiliated.
For that reason I am steadfastly
  resolved;
I know I will not be put to shame.
8 The one who vindicates me is close by.
Who dares to argue with me? Let us
  confront each [a]other!
Who is my accuser? Let him
  challenge me!
9 Look, the Sovereign LORD helps me.
Who dares to condemn me?
[a]Look, all of [b]them will wear out like
  clothes;
a moth will eat away at them.
10 Who among you fears the LORD?
Who obeys his servant?
Whoever [a]walks in deep darkness,
without light,
should trust in the name of the LORD
and rely on his God.
11 Look, all of you who start a fire
and who equip yourselves with
  flaming arrows,
walk in the light[1] of the fire you
  started
and among the flaming arrows you
  ignited!
[a]This is what you will receive
  from me:
You will lie down [b]in a place of pain.

There Is Hope for the Future

51 "Listen to me, [a]you who pursue
  godliness,
who seek the LORD.
Look at the rock from which you
  were chiseled,

at the quarry from which you were
  dug.
2 [a]Look at Abraham, your father,
and Sarah, who gave you birth.
When I summoned him, he was a
  lone individual,
but I [b]blessed him and gave him
  numerous descendants.
3 Certainly the LORD will [a]console
  Zion;
he will console all her ruins.
He will make her wilderness [b]like
  Eden,
her arid rift valley like the garden of
  the LORD.
Happiness and joy will be restored
  to her,
thanksgiving and the sound of music.
4 Pay attention to me, my people.
Listen to me, my people!
[a]For[1] I will issue [b]a decree,
I will make my justice a light to the
  nations.
5 I am ready to vindicate,
I am ready to deliver,
I will establish justice among the
  nations.
The coastlands wait patiently for me;
they wait in anticipation for the
  revelation of [a]my power.
6 Look [a]up at [b]the sky.
Look at [c]the earth below.
For the sky will dissipate like smoke,
and the earth will wear out like
  clothes;
its residents will die like gnats.
But the deliverance I give is
  [d]permanent;
the vindication I provide will not
  disappear.[1]
7 Listen to me, you who know what is
  right,
you people who are aware of my law.
Don't be afraid of the [a]insults of men;
[b]don't be discouraged because of
  their abuse.
8 For a moth will eat away at [a]them
  like clothes;

50:5 [a] Ps 40:6; Isa 35:5 [b] Matt 26:39; Mark 14:36; Luke 22:42; John 8:29; 14:31; 15:10; Acts 26:19; [Phil 2:8; Heb 5:8; 10:7] [1] Or perhaps *makes me obedient*; lit. *has opened for me an ear.* 50:6 [a] Matt 27:26; John 18:22 [b] Matt 26:67; 27:30; Mark 14:65; 15:19 [c] Lam 3:30 50:7 [a] Ezek 3:8–9; Luke 9:51 50:8 [a] Acts 2:24; [Rom 8:32–34] 50:9 [a] Job 13:28; Ps 102:26; Heb 1:11 [b] Isa 51:6, 8 50:10 [a] Ps 23:4 50:11 [a] [John 9:39] [b] Ps 16:4 [1] Or perhaps *flame.* 51:1 [a] [Rom 9:30–32] 51:2 [a] Rom 4:1–3; Heb 11:11 [b] Gen 24:35; Deut 1:10; Ezek 33:24 51:3 [a] Isa 40:1; 52:9; Ps 102:13 [b] Gen 13:10; Joel 2:3 51:4 [a] Isa 2:3 [b] Isa 42:6 [1] Or *certainly.* 51:5 [a] Isa 46:13 51:6 [a] Isa 40:26 [b] Ps 102:25–26; Isa 13:13; 34:4; Matt 24:35; Heb 1:10–12; 2 Pet 3:10 [c] Isa 24:19–20; 50:9; Heb 1:10–12 [d] Isa 45:17 [1] Heb. *not be shattered* [or *dismayed*]. 51:7 [a] Ps 37:31; Jer 31:33; [Heb 10:16] [b] Isa 25:8; 54:4; [Matt 5:11–12; 10:28; Acts 5:41] 51:8 [a] Isa 50:9

a clothes moth will devour them like
    wool.
But the vindication I provide will be
    permanent;
the deliverance I give will last."
9 Wake [a]up! Wake up!
Clothe yourself with strength, O arm
    of the LORD!
Wake up [b]as in former times, as in
    antiquity.
Did you not smash the Proud [c]One?
Did you not wound the sea
    [d]monster?[1]
10 Did you not dry [a]up the sea,
the waters of the great deep?
Did you not make a path through the
    depths of the sea,
so those delivered from bondage
    could cross over?
11 Those whom [a]the LORD has
    ransomed will return;
they will enter Zion with a happy
    shout.
Unending joy will crown them,
happiness and joy will overwhelm
    them;
grief and suffering will disappear.
12 "I, I am the one [a]who consoles you.
Why are you afraid [b]of mortal men,
of mere human beings who are as
    short-lived as grass?
13 Why do [a]you forget the LORD, [b]who
    made you,
who stretched out the sky[1]
    [c]and founded the earth?
Why do you constantly tremble all
    day long
at the anger of the oppressor,
when he makes plans to destroy?
Where is the anger of the
    oppressor?
14 The one who suffers will soon be
    released;
he will not die in prison,[1]
he will not go hungry.
15 I am the LORD your God,
who churns [a]up the sea so that its
    waves surge.
The LORD of Heaven's Armies is his
    name!

Zion's Time to Celebrate

16 "I [a]commission you as my
    spokesman;
[b]I cover you with the palm of my
    hand
to establish[1] the sky and to found the
    earth,
to say to Zion, 'You are my people.'"
17 Wake [a]up! Wake up!
Get up, O Jerusalem!
You drank from the cup the LORD
    passed to you,
which was full of his anger.
You drained dry
the goblet full of intoxicating wine.
18 There was no one to lead her
among all the children she bore;
there was no one to take her by the
    hand
among all the children she raised.
19 [a]These double disasters confronted
    you.
But who feels sorry for you?
Destruction and devastation,
famine and sword.
But who consoles you?[1]
20 Your children faint;
they lie at the head of every street
like an antelope in a snare.
They are left in a stupor by the
    LORD's anger,
by the battle cry of [a]your God.
21 So listen to this, oppressed one,
who is drunk, [a]but not from wine.
22 This is what your Sovereign LORD,
    even your God who [a]judges his
    people says:
"Look, I have removed from your
    hand
the cup of intoxicating wine,[1]
the goblet full of my anger.
You will no longer have to drink it.
23 [a]I will put it into the hand of your
    tormentors
who said to you, 'Lie down, so we can
    walk over you.'
You made your back like the
    ground
and like the street for those who
    walked over you."

52 Wake up! Wake up!
Clothe yourself with strength,
    O Zion!
Put on your beautiful clothes,
    O Jerusalem, holy city.
For uncircumcised [a]and unclean
    pagans
    will no longer invade you.
2 Shake [a]off the dirt!
    Get up, captive[1] Jerusalem.
Take [b]off the iron chains around your
    neck,
    O captive daughter Zion.

3For this is what the Lord says:

"[a]You were sold for nothing,
    and you will [b]not be redeemed for
    money."

4For this is what the Sovereign Lord says:

"In the beginning my people went to
    live temporarily in [a]Egypt;
Assyria oppressed them for no good
    reason.
5 And now, what do we have here?"
    says the Lord.
"Indeed my people have been carried
    away for nothing,
those who rule over them taunt,"
    says the Lord,
"and my name is constantly
    [a]slandered all day long.
6 For this reason my people will know
    my name;
for this reason they will know at that
    time that I am the one who says,
    'Here I am.'"
7 [a]How delightful it is to see
    approaching over the mountains
the feet of a messenger who
    announces peace,
a messenger who brings good news,
    who announces deliverance,
who says to Zion, "[b]Your God reigns!"
8 Listen, your watchmen shout;
    in unison they shout for joy,
for they see with their very own eyes
    the Lord's return to Zion.

9 In unison give a joyful shout,
    O ruins of Jerusalem!
For the Lord consoles his people;
    he protects Jerusalem.
10 The Lord reveals his royal power
    in [a]the sight of [b]all the nations;
the entire earth sees
    our God deliver.
11 Leave! [a]Leave! Get out of there!
    Don't touch anything unclean!
    Get out of it!
Stay pure, you who carry the Lord's
    holy items.[1]
12 Yet do not depart quickly
    or leave in a panic.
For the Lord goes before [a]you;
    the God of Israel is your rear guard.

The Lord Will Vindicate His Servant

13 Look, [a]my servant will succeed!
    [b]He will be elevated, lifted high, and
    greatly exalted—
14 (just as many were horrified by the
    sight of you)
he was so disfigured he no longer
    [a]looked like a man;
his form was so marred he no longer
    looked human—
15 so now he will startle many nations.
Kings will be shocked by his
    exaltation,
for they will witness [a]something
    unannounced to them,
and they will understand something
    they had not heard about.

53 Who would have believed what we
    just heard?
When was the Lord's power[1]
    revealed through him?
2 He sprouted up like a twig before
    God,
like a root out of parched soil;
he had no stately form or majesty
    that might catch our attention,
no special appearance that we should
    want to follow him.
3 [a]He was despised and rejected by
    people,
one who experienced pain and was
    [b]acquainted with illness;

52:1 [a]Neh 11:1; Isa 48:2; 64:10; Zech 14:20–21; Matt 4:5; [Rev 21:2–27]   52:2 [a]Isa 3:26   [b]Isa 9:4; 10:27; 14:25; Zech 2:7   [1]Several wss sit.   52:3 [a]Ps 44:12; Jer 15:13   [b]Isa 45:13   52:4 [a]Gen 46:6   52:5 [a]Ezek 36:20, 23; Rom 2:24   52:7 [a]Isa 40:9; 61:1; Nah 1:15; Rom 10:15; Eph 6:15   [b]Ps 93:1; Isa 24:23   52:10 [a]Ps 98:1–3   [b]Luke 3:6   52:11 [a]Isa 48:20; Jer 50:8; Zech 2:6–7; 2 Cor 6:17   [1]Heb. the vessels of the LORD.   52:12 [a]Exod 12:11, 33; Deut 16:3   52:13 [a]Isa 42:1   [b]Isa 57:15; Phil 2:9   52:14 [a]Ps 22:6–7; Matt 26:67; 27:30; John 19:3   52:15 [a]Num 19:18–21; Ezek 36:25   53:1 [1]Heb. the arm of the LORD.   53:3 [a]Ps 22:6; [Isa 49:7; Matt 27:30–31; Luke 18:31–33; 23:18]   [b][Heb 4:15]

people hid their faces from him;
he was despised, and ^cwe considered
  him insignificant.
4 But ^ahe lifted up our illnesses,
he carried our pain;
even though we thought he was
  being punished,
attacked by God, and afflicted for
  something he had done.
5 He was ^awounded because of our
  rebellious deeds,
crushed because of our sins;
he endured punishment that made
  us well;
because of his ^bwounds we have been
  healed.
6 All of us had wandered off like sheep;
each of us had strayed off on his own
  path,
but the LORD caused the sin of all of
  us to attack him.
7 He was treated harshly and afflicted,
but ^ahe did not even open his mouth.
Like a lamb led to ^bthe slaughtering
  block,
like a sheep silent before her
  shearers,
he did not even open his mouth.
8 He was led ^aaway after an unjust
  trial—
but who even cared?
Indeed, ^bhe was cut off from the land
  of the living;
because of the rebellion of his own
  people he was wounded.
9 They intended to bury him with
  criminals,[1]
but he ended up in ^aa rich man's
  tomb
because he had committed no
  violent deeds,
nor had he spoken ^bdeceitfully.
10 Though the LORD desired to crush
  him ^aand make him ill,
once restitution is made,
he will see descendants and enjoy
  long life,
and the LORD's purpose will be
accomplished through him.

11 Having suffered, he will reflect on his
  work,
he will be satisfied when he
  understands what he has done.
"^aMy ^bservant will ^cacquit many,
for he carried their sins.
12 So I will assign him a portion with
  ^athe multitudes,
he will divide the spoils of victory
  with the powerful,
because he willingly submitted[1] to
  death
^band was ^cnumbered with the rebels,
when he lifted up the sin of many
and intervened on behalf of the
  rebels."

Zion Will Be Secure

54 "Shout for joy, O barren ^aone who
has not given birth!
Give a joyful shout and cry out, you
  who have not been in labor!
For the children of the desolate one
  are more numerous
than the children of the married
  woman," says the LORD.
2 Make your tent ^alarger,
stretch your tent curtains farther out!
Spare no effort,
lengthen your ropes,
and pound your stakes deep.
3 For you will spread out to the right
  and to the left;
your children will ^aconquer[1] nations
and will resettle desolate cities.
4 Don't be afraid, for you will not be
  put to shame.
^aDon't be intimidated, for you will
  not be humiliated.
You will forget about the shame you
  experienced in your youth;
you will no longer remember the
  disgrace of your abandonment.
5 ^aFor your husband is ^bthe one who
  made you—
the LORD of Heaven's Armies is his
  name.
He is your Protector, the Holy One of
  Israel.

53:3 ^c [John 1:10–11]   53:4 ^a [Matt 8:17; Heb 9:28; 1 Pet 2:24]   53:5 ^a [Isa 53:10; Rom 4:25; 1 Cor 15:3–4]   ^b [1 Pet 2:24–25]   53:7 ^a Matt 26:63; 27:12–14; Mark 14:61; 15:5; Luke 23:9; John 19:9   ^b Acts 8:32–33; Rev 5:6   53:8 ^a Matt 27:11–26; Luke 23:1–25   ^b [Dan 9:26]   53:9 ^a Matt 27:57–60; Luke 23:33   ^b 1 Pet 2:22; 1 John 3:5   ¹ Heb. one assigned his grave with criminals.   53:10 ^a John 1:29; Acts 2:24; [2 Cor 5:21]   53:11 ^a [1 John 2:1]   ^b Isa 42:1   ^c [Acts 13:38–39; Rom 5:15–18]   53:12 ^a Ps 2:8   ^b Col 2:15   ^c Matt 27:38; Mark 15:28; Luke 22:37; 2 Cor 5:21   ¹ Heb. because he laid bare his life.   54:1 ^a Gal 4:27   54:2 ^a Isa 49:19–20   54:3 ^a Isa 14:2; 49:22–23; 60:9   ¹ Or take possession of.   54:4 ^a Isa 41:10   54:5 ^a Jer 3:14; Hos 2:19   ^b Zech 14:9; Rom 3:29

He is called "God of the entire earth."
6 "Indeed, the LORD will call you back
like ᵃa wife who has been abandoned
and suffers from depression,
like a young wife when she has been
rejected," says your God.
7 "For a short ᵃtime I abandoned you,
but with great compassion I will
gather you.
8 In a burst of anger I rejected you[1]
momentarily,
ᵃbut with lasting devotion I will have
compassion on you,"
says your Protector, the LORD.
9 "As far as I am concerned, this is like
in ᵃNoah's time,[1]
when I vowed that the waters of
Noah's flood would never again
cover the earth.
In the same way I have vowed that I
will not be angry at ᵇyou or shout
at you.
10 Even if ᵃthe mountains are removed
and the hills displaced,
my devotion will not be removed
from you,
nor will my covenant of friendship be
displaced,"
says the LORD, the one who has
compassion on you.
11 "O afflicted one, driven away, and
unconsoled!
Look, I am about to set your stones
in ᵃantimony
and lay your foundation with lapis
lazuli.
12 I will make your pinnacles out of
gems,
your gates out of beryl,
and your outer wall out of beautiful
stones.
13 All your children will be ᵃfollowers of
the LORD,
and your children will enjoy ᵇgreat
prosperity.
14 You will be reestablished when I
vindicate you.
You will not experience oppression;

indeed, you will not be afraid.
You will not be terrified,[1]
for nothing frightening will come
near you.
15 If anyone dares to challenge you, it
will not be my doing!
Whoever tries to challenge you will
be ᵃdefeated.
16 Look, I create the craftsman,
who fans the coals into a fire
and forges a weapon.
I create the destroyer so he might
devastate.
17 No weapon forged to be used against
you will ᵃsucceed;
you will refute everyone who tries to
accuse you.
This is what the LORD will do for his
servants—
I will vindicate them,"
says the LORD.

The Lord Gives an Invitation

55 "Hey,[1] ᵃall who are thirsty, ᵇcome to
the water!
You who have no money, come!
Buy and eat!
Come! Buy wine and milk
without money and without cost.
2 Why pay money for something that
will not nourish you?
Why spend your hard-earned
money on something that
will not satisfy?
Listen carefully to me and eat what is
nourishing!
Enjoy fine food.
3 Pay attention and ᵃcome to me.
Listen, so you can live.
Then I will make ᵇan unconditional
covenantal promise to[1] you,
just like the ᶜreliable covenantal
promises I made to David.
4 Look, I ᵃmade him ᵇa witness to
nations,
a ruler and commander of nations."
5 ᵃLook, you will summon nations you
did not previously know;

54:6 ᵃ Isa 62:4   54:7 ᵃ [Isa 43:5; 56:8]   54:8 ᵃ Isa 55:3; Jer 31:3   [1] Heb. *I hid my face from you.*   54:9 ᵃ Gen 8:21; 9:11; [2 Pet 3:6–7]   ᵇ Isa 12:1; Ezek 39:29   [1] MT, LXX *waters of Noah.*   54:10 ᵃ Ps 46:2; Isa 51:6; Matt 5:18   54:11 ᵃ 1 Chr 29:2; Job 28:16; Rev 21:18–19   54:13 ᵃ Jer 31:34; [John 6:45; 1 Cor 2:10]; 1 Thess 4:9; [1 John 2:20]   ᵇ Ps 119:165   54:14 [1] Heb. *from terror.*   54:15 ᵃ Isa 41:11–16   54:17 ᵃ Isa 17:12–14; 29:8   55:1 ᵃ [Matt 5:6; John 4:14; 7:37; Rev 21:6; 22:17]   ᵇ [Matt 13:44; Rev 3:18]   [1] This Heb. word was used in funeral laments and often precedes judgment oracles, but here it appears to be a simple interjection, designed to grab attention.   55:3 ᵃ Matt 11:28   ᵇ Isa 54:8; 61:8; Jer 32:40   ᶜ 2 Sam 7:8; Ps 89:28; [Acts 13:34]   [1] Or *an eternal covenant with.*   55:4 ᵃ [John 18:37; Rev 1:5]   ᵇ [Jer 30:9; Ezek 34:23; Dan 9:25]   55:5 ᵃ Isa 52:15; Eph 2:11–12

nations that did not previously know
    you will run to you,
because of the LORD your God,
the Holy One of Israel,
  [b]for he bestows honor on you.

6 [a]Seek the LORD while he [b]makes
    himself available;
  call to him while he is nearby!

7 [a]The wicked need to [b]abandon their
    lifestyle
  and sinful people their plans.
They should return to the LORD, and
    he will show mercy to them,
and to their God, for he will freely
    forgive them.

8 "Indeed,[1] my plans are not like your
    plans,
  and my deeds are not like your
    deeds," says the LORD,

9 "for just as the sky[1] is higher than the
    earth,
so my deeds are superior to your
    deeds
and my plans superior to your plans.

10 The rain and snow fall from the sky
  and do not return,
but instead water the earth
and make it produce and yield crops,
and provide seed for the planter and
    food for those who must eat.

11 [a]In the same way, the promise that I
    make
does not return to me, having
    accomplished nothing.
No, it is realized as I desire
and is [b]fulfilled as I intend."

12 Indeed you will go out with joy;
you will be led along in peace;
the mountains and hills will give a
    joyful shout [a]before you,
and [b]all the trees in the field will clap
    their hands.

13 Evergreens will grow in place [a]of
    thornbushes;
firs will grow in place of nettles;
[b]they will be a monument to the
    LORD,
a permanent reminder that will
    remain.

The Lord Invites Outsiders to Enter

56 This is what the LORD says,
  "Promote[1] justice! Do what is right!
[a]For I am ready to deliver you;
I am ready to vindicate you openly.

2 The people [a]who do this will be
    blessed,
the people who commit themselves
    to obedience,
who observe the Sabbath and do not
    defile it,
who refrain from doing anything
    that is wrong.

3 No foreigner who becomes a follower
  of [a]the LORD should say,
'The LORD will certainly exclude me
    from his people.'
The [b]eunuch should not say,
'Look, I am like a dried-up tree.'"

[4]For this is what the LORD says:

"For the eunuchs who observe my
    Sabbaths
and choose what pleases me
and are faithful to my covenant,

5 I will set up within [a]my temple [b]and
    my walls a monument[1]
that will be better than sons and
    daughters.
I will set up a permanent monument
    for them that will remain.

6 As for foreigners who become
    followers of the LORD and serve
    him,
who love the name of the LORD and
    want to be his servants—
all who observe the Sabbath and do
    not defile it,
and who are faithful to my covenant—

7 I will [a]bring them to my holy
    mountain;
I will make them happy in the
    [b]temple where people pray to me.
[c]Their burnt offerings and sacrifices
    will be [d]accepted on [e]my altar,
[f]for my temple will be known as a
    temple where all nations may
    pray."[1]

55:5 [b]Isa 60:9   55:6 [a]Matt 5:25; 25:11; John 7:34; 8:21; 2 Cor 6:2; [Heb 3:13] [b]Ps 32:6; Isa 49:8   55:7 [a]Isa 1:16 [b]Ps 130:7; Jer 3:12   55:8 [1]Or *For.*   55:9 [1]Or *the heavens.*   55:11 [a]Isa 45:23; Matt 24:35 [b]Isa 46:9–11   55:12 [a]Isa 35:10 [b]1 Chr 16:33   55:13 [a]Isa 41:19 [b]Mic 7:4   56:1 [a]Isa 46:13; Matt 3:2; 4:17; Rom 13:11–12 [1]Heb. *guard.*   56:2 [a]Exod 20:8–11; 31:13–17; Isa 58:13; Jer 17:21–22; Ezek 20:12, 20   56:3 [a]Isa 14:1; [Eph 2:12–19] [b]Deut 23:1; Jer 38:7; Acts 8:27   56:5 [a]1 Tim 3:15 [b][1 John 3:1–2] [1]Heb. *a hand and a name.*   56:7 [a][Isa 2:2–3; 60:11; Mic 4:1–2] [b]Matt 21:13; Mark 11:17; Luke 19:46 [c][Rom 12:1; Heb 13:15; 1 Pet 2:5] [d]Isa 60:7 [e]Matt 21:13 [f][Mal 1:11] [1]Heb. *for my house will be called a house of prayer for all the nations.*

8 The Sovereign LORD says this,
the one ᵃwho gathers the dispersed
of Israel:
"I will still gather them up."

The Lord Denounces Israel's Paganism

9 ᵃAll you wild animals in the fields,
come and devour,
all you wild animals in the forest!
10 All their watchmen are ᵃblind,
ᵇthey are unaware.
All of them are like mute dogs,
unable to bark.
They pant, lie down,
and love to snooze.
11 The dogs have big appetites;
they are ᵃnever full.
They are shepherds who have no
understanding;
they all go their own way,
each one looking for monetary gain.
12 Each one says,
"Come on, I'll get some wine!
Let's guzzle some ᵃbeer!
ᵇTomorrow will be just like today!
We'll have everything we want!"

57 The godly¹ perish,
but no one cares.
ᵃHonest people disappear,
when no one minds
that the godly disappear because of
evil.
2 Those who live uprightly enter a
place of peace;
they rest on ᵃtheir beds.¹

3 "But approach, ᵃyou sons of omen
readers,
you offspring of adulteresses and
prostitutes!¹
4 At whom are you laughing?
At whom are you opening your
mouth
and sticking out your tongue?
You are the children of rebels,
the offspring of liars,
5 you who inflame your lusts among
the oaks and ᵃunder every green
tree,

who ᵇslaughter children near the
streams under the rocky overhangs.
6 Among the smooth ᵃstones of the
stream are the idols you love;
they, they are the object of your
devotion.
You pour out liquid offerings to them,
you make an offering.
Because of these ᵇthings how can I
relent from judgment?
7 On every high, elevated hill ᵃyou
prepare your bed;
you go up there to offer sacrifices.
8 Behind the door and doorpost ᵃyou
put your symbols.
Indeed,¹ you depart from me² and
go up
and invite them into bed with you.
You purchase favors from them;³
you love their bed,
and gaze longingly on their naked
bodies.
9 You take olive oil as tribute to ᵃyour
king,
along with many perfumes.
You send your ᵇmessengers to a
distant place;
you go all the way to Sheol.
10 Because of the long distance you
must travel, you get tired,
but you do not say, 'I give up.'¹
You get renewed energy,
so you don't collapse.
11 Whom are you worried about?
Whom do you fear, that you would
act so deceitfully
and not remember me
or think about me?
Because I have been silent for so long,
you are not afraid ᵃof me.
12 I will denounce your so-called
righteousness and your deeds,
but they will not help you.
13 When you cry out for help, let your
idols help you!
The wind blows them all away,
a breeze carries them away.
But the one who looks to me for help
will inherit the land

and will have access to[1] my holy
  mountain."

14 He says,
  "Build it! Build it! Clear [a] a way!
  Remove all the obstacles out of the
    way of my people!"

15 For this is what the high and exalted
    one says,
  the one [a] who rules forever, whose
    name [b] is holy:
  "[c] I dwell in an exalted and holy place,
  but also with the discouraged and
    humiliated,
  in order [d] to cheer up the humiliated
  and to encourage the discouraged.

16 For I will not be hostile [a] forever
  or perpetually angry,
  for then man's spirit would grow
    faint before me,
  the life-giving breath [b] I created.

17 I was angry because of their sinful
    greed;
  [a] I attacked them and [b] angrily
    rejected them,
  yet they remained disobedient [c] and
    stubborn.[1]

18 I have seen their behavior,
  but [a] I will heal them. [b] I will lead[1] them,
  and I will provide comfort to them
    and those who mourn with them.

19 I am [a] the one who gives them reason
    [b] to celebrate.[1]
  Complete prosperity[2] is available
    both to those who are far away and
    those who are nearby,"
  says the LORD, "and I will heal them.

20 [a] But the wicked are like a surging sea
  that is unable to be quiet;
  its waves toss up mud and sand.

21 There will be no prosperity," says my
  God, "for [a] the wicked."

The Lord Desires Genuine Devotion

58 "Shout loudly! Don't be quiet!
  Yell as loudly as a trumpet!
  [a] Confront my people with their
    rebellious deeds;
  confront Jacob's family with their sin.

2 They seek me day after day;
  they want to know my requirements,
  like a nation that does what is right
  and does not reject the law of their
    God.
  They ask me for just decrees;
  they want to be near God.

3 They lament, '[a] Why don't you notice
    when we fast?
  Why don't you pay attention when
    we [b] humble ourselves?'
  Look, at the same time you fast, you
    satisfy your selfish desires,
  you oppress your workers.

4 Look, your fasting is accompanied by
    arguments, brawls,
  and fistfights.[1]
  Do not fast as you do today,
  trying to make your voice heard [a] in
    heaven.

5 Is this really the kind of fasting [a] I
    [b] want?
  Do I want a day when people merely
    humble themselves,
  bowing their heads like a reed
  and stretching out on sackcloth and
    ashes?
  Is this really what you call a fast,
  a day that is pleasing [c] to the LORD?

6 No, this is the kind of fast I want:
  I want you to [a] remove the sinful
    chains,
  [b] to tear away the ropes of the
    burdensome yoke,
  [c] to set free the oppressed,
  and to break every burdensome
    yoke.

7 I want you [a] to share your food with
    the hungry
  and to provide shelter for homeless,
    oppressed people.
  [b] When [c] you see someone naked,
    clothe them!
  Don't turn your back on your own
    flesh and blood.

8 Then your light will shine like [a] the
    sunrise;
  your restoration will quickly arrive;

57:13 [1] Heb. *possess, own.*   57:14 [a] Isa 40:3; 62:10; Jer 18:15   57:15 [a] Job 6:10; Luke 1:49   [b] Ps 68:35; Zech 2:13   [c] Ps 34:18;
51:17; Isa 66:2   [d] Ps 147:3; Isa 61:1–3   57:16 [a] Ps 85:5; 103:9; [Mic 7:18]   [b] Num 16:22; Job 34:14; Heb 12:9   57:17 [a] Isa 2:7; 56:11;
Jer 6:13   [b] Isa 8:17; 45:15; 59:2   [c] Isa 9:13   [1] Heb. *and he walked* [as an] *apostate in the way of his heart.*   57:18 [a] Jer 3:22
[b] Isa 61:2   [1] Ket. *I will give them rest.*   57:19 [a] Isa 6:7; 51:16; 59:21; Heb 13:15   [b] Acts 2:39; Eph 2:17   [1] MT *one who creates fruit
of lips.*   [2] Heb. *Peace, peace;* the repetition emphasizes the degree.   57:20 [a] Job 15:20; Prov 4:16; Jude 13   57:21 [a] Isa 48:22
58:1 [a] Mic 3:8   58:3 [a] Mal 3:13–18; Luke 18:12   [b] Lev 16:29; 23:27   58:4 [1] Kgs 21:9   [1] Heb. *and for striking with a sinful fist.*
58:5 [a] Zech 7:5   [b] Lev 16:29   [c] Esth 4:3; Job 2:8; Dan 9:3   58:6 [a] Luke 4:18–19   [b] Neh 5:10–12   [c] Jer 34:9   58:7 [a] Ezek 18:7;
  Matt 25:35   [b] Job 31:19–22; Jas 2:14–17   [c] Gen 29:14; Neh 5:5   58:8 [a] Job 11:17

your godly behavior[1] will go before
    you,
and [b]the LORD's splendor will be your
    rear guard.
9 Then you will call out, and the LORD
    will respond;
you will cry out, and he will reply,
    'Here I am.'
You must remove the burdensome
    yoke from among you
and stop pointing fingers and
    [a]speaking sinfully.
10 You must actively help the hungry
    and feed the oppressed.
Then your light will dispel the
    darkness,
and your darkness will be
    transformed into noonday.
11 The LORD will continually lead you;
he will feed you even in parched
    regions.
He will give you renewed strength,
    and you will be like a well-watered
    garden,
like a spring that continually
    produces water.
12 Your perpetual ruins will be rebuilt;
you will reestablish the ancient
    foundations.
You will be called, 'The one who
    repairs broken walls,
the one who makes the streets
    inhabitable again.'[1]
13 You must[1] observe the Sabbath
rather than doing anything [a]you
    please on my holy day.
You must look forward to the
    Sabbath
and treat the LORD's holy day with
    respect.
You must treat it with respect by
    refraining from your normal
    activities
and by refraining from your selfish
    pursuits and from making
    business deals.
14 Then you will find joy in your
    relationship to [a]the LORD,
and I will [b]give you great
    prosperity,

and cause crops to grow on [c]the land
    I gave to your ancestor Jacob."
Know for certain that the LORD has
    spoken.

Injustice Brings Alienation from God

59 Look, the LORD's hand is not too
    [a]weak[1] to deliver you;
his ear is not too deaf to hear you.[2]
2 But your sinful acts have alienated
    you from your God;
your sins have caused him to
    reject you and [a]not listen to
    your prayers.
3 For [a]your hands are stained with
    blood
and your fingers with sin;
your lips speak lies,
your tongue utters malicious words.
4 No one is concerned about justice;
no one sets forth his case truthfully.
[a]They depend on false words and tell
    lies;
they conceive of oppression
and give birth to sin.
5 They hatch the eggs of a poisonous
    snake
and spin a spider's web.
Whoever eats their eggs will die,
a poisonous snake is hatched.
6 Their webs cannot be used for
    clothing;
they cannot cover themselves with
    what they make.
[a]Their deeds are sinful;
they commit violent crimes.
7 [a]They are eager to do evil,
quick to shed [b]innocent blood.
[c]Their thoughts are sinful;
they crush and [d]destroy.
8 They are unfamiliar with [a]peace;
their deeds are unjust.[1]
[b]They use deceitful methods,
and whoever deals with them is
    unfamiliar with peace.

Israel Confesses Its Sin

9 For this reason deliverance is far
    from us
and salvation does not reach us.

58:8 [b] Exod 14:19; Isa 52:12   [1] Or *righteousness*.   **58:9** [a] Ps 12:2; Isa 59:13   **58:12** [1] MT *the one who restores paths for dwelling*.   **58:13** [a] Exod 31:16–17; 35:2–3; Isa 56:2, 4, 6; Jer 17:21–27   [1] Lit. *if you*.   **58:14** [a] Job 22:26; Isa 61:10   [b] Deut 32:13; 33:29; Isa 33:16; Hab 3:19   [c] Isa 1:20; 40:5; Mic 4:4   **59:1** [a] Num 11:23; Isa 50:2; Jer 32:17   [1] Heb. *short*.   [2] Heb. *or his ear too heavy* [i.e., *dull*] *to hear*.   **59:2** [a] Isa 1:15   **59:3** [a] Isa 1:15, 21; Jer 2:30, 34; Ezek 7:23; Hos 4:2   **59:4** [a] Job 15:35; Ps 7:14; Isa 33:11   **59:6** [a] Job 8:14   **59:7** [a] Prov 1:16; Rom 3:15   [b] Prov 6:17   [c] Isa 55:7   [d] Rom 3:16–17   **59:8** [a] Isa 57:20–21   [b] Ps 125:5; Prov 2:15   [1] Heb. *a way of peace they do not know, and there is no justice in their pathways*.

[a]We wait for light, but see only
darkness;
we wait for a bright light, but live in
deep darkness.
10 We grope along the wall like the
blind,
[a]we grope like those who cannot see;
we stumble at noontime as if it were
evening.
Though others are strong, we are like
dead men.[1]
11 We all growl like bears,
we [a]coo mournfully like doves;
we wait for deliverance, but there is
none,
for salvation, but it is far from us.
12 For you are aware of our many
rebellious [a]deeds,
and our sins testify against us;
indeed, we are aware of our
rebellious deeds;
we know our sins all too well.
13 We have rebelled and tried to deceive
the LORD;
we turned back [a]from following our
God.
We stir up oppression and rebellion;
we tell lies we concocted in our
minds.
14 Justice is driven back;
godliness stands far off.
Indeed,[1] honesty stumbles in the city
square
and morality is not even able to
enter.
15 Honesty has disappeared;
the one who tries to avoid evil is
[a]robbed.
The LORD watches and is displeased,
for there is no justice.

The Lord Intervenes

16 He sees [a]there is no advocate;
he is [b]shocked that no one
intervenes.
So [c]he takes matters into his own
hands;[1]
his desire for justice drives him on.
17 He wears his desire [a]for justice like
body armor,

and his desire to deliver is like a
helmet on his head.
He puts on the garments of
vengeance
and wears zeal like a robe.
18 [a]He repays them for what they have
done,
dispensing angry judgment to his
adversaries
and punishing his enemies.
He repays the coastlands.
19 [a]In the west, people respect[1] the
LORD's reputation;
in the east they recognize his
splendor.
For he comes [b]like a rushing stream
driven on by wind sent from the
LORD.[2]
20 "A protector comes to Zion,
to those in Jacob who repent of [a]their
rebellious deeds," says the LORD.

21"As for me, this is my promise to them,"
says the LORD. "My Spirit, who is upon you,
and my words, which I have placed in your
mouth, will not depart from your mouth
or from the mouths of your children and
descendants from this time forward," says
the LORD.

Zion's Future Splendor

60 "Arise! [a]Shine! For your light
arrives!
[b]The splendor of the LORD shines on
you!
2 For, look, darkness covers the earth
and deep darkness covers the
nations,
but the LORD shines on you;
his splendor appears over you.
3 [a]Nations come to your light,
kings to your bright light.
4 [a]Look all around you!
[b]They all gather and come to you—
your sons come from far away,
and your daughters are escorted by
guardians.
5 Then you will look and smile,[1]
you will be excited and your heart
will swell with pride.

59:9 [a] Jer 8:15   59:10 [a] Deut 28:29; Job 5:14; Amos 8:9   [1] Heb. *among the strong, like dead men.*   59:11 [a] Isa 38:14; Ezek 7:16
59:12 [a] Isa 24:5; 58:1   59:13 [a] Matt 12:34   59:14 [1] Or *for.*   59:15 [a] Isa 5:23; 10:2; 29:21; 32:7   59:16 [a] Isa 41:28; 63:5; 64:7;
Ezek 22:30   [b] Mark 6:6   [c] Ps 98:1; Isa 63:5   [1] Heb. *and his arm delivers for him.*   59:17 [a] Eph 6:14, 17; 1 Thess 5:8
59:18 [a] Isa 63:6; Rom 2:6   59:19 [a] Ps 113:3; Mal 1:11   [b] Rev 12:15   [1] Heb. *fear;* a few MSS *see.*   [2] Heb. *the wind of
the LORD drives it on.*   59:20 [a] Rom 11:26   60:1 [a] Eph 5:14   [b] Mal 4:2   60:3 [a] Isa 49:6, 23; Rev 21:24
60:4 [a] Isa 49:18   [b] Isa 49:20–22   60:5 [1] Or *shine, be radiant.*

For [a]the riches of distant lands will
  belong to you,
and the wealth of nations will come
  to you.
6 Camel caravans will cover your roads,[1]
  young camels from Midian and
    [a]Ephah.
  All the merchants of [b]Sheba will
    come,
  bringing [c]gold and incense
  and singing praises to the LORD.
7 All the sheep of [a]Kedar will be
    gathered to you;
  the rams of Nebaioth will be
    available to you as sacrifices.
  They will go up on my altar
    [b]acceptably,[1]
  and [c]I will bestow honor on my
    majestic temple.
8 Who are these who float along like a
    cloud,
  who fly like doves to their shelters?
9 Indeed, the coastlands look eagerly
    for me;
  the large ships[1] are in the lead,
  bringing your sons from far away,
  along with their silver and gold,
  to honor the LORD your God,
  the Holy One of Israel, [a]for he has
    [b]bestowed honor on you.
10 Foreigners will rebuild your walls;
  [a]their kings will serve you.
  Even though I struck you down in my
    anger,
  I will restore my favor [b]and have
    compassion on you.
11 Your gates will remain open at [a]all
    times;
  they will not be shut during the day
    or at night
  so that the wealth of nations may be
    delivered,
  with their kings leading the way.
12 Indeed,[1] nations [a]or kingdoms that
    do not serve you will perish;
  such nations will definitely be
    destroyed.
13 The splendor of Lebanon will come
    to you,

its evergreens, firs, and cypresses
  [a]together,
to beautify my palace;
I will bestow honor on my throne
  room.
14 The children [a]of your oppressors will
    come [a]bowing to you;
  [b]all who treated you with disrespect
    will bow down at your feet.
  They will call you, 'The City of the
    LORD,
  [c]Zion of the Holy One of Israel.'
15 You were once abandoned
  and despised, with no one passing
    through,
  but I will make you a permanent
    source of pride
  and joy to coming generations.
16 You [a]will drink the milk of nations;
  you will nurse at the breasts of kings.
  Then you will recognize that I, the
    LORD, am your Deliverer,
  your Protector, the Powerful One of
    Jacob.
17 Instead of bronze, I will bring you
    gold;
  instead of iron, I will bring you silver;
  instead of wood, I will bring you
    bronze;
  instead of stones, I will bring you iron.
  I will make prosperity your overseer,
  and vindication your sovereign ruler.
18 Sounds of violence will no longer be
    heard in [a]your land,
  or the sounds of destruction and
    devastation within your borders.
  You will name your walls,
    'Deliverance'
  and your gates, 'Praise.'
19 The [a]sun will no longer supply light
    for [b]you by day,
  nor will the moon's brightness shine
    on you;
  the LORD will be your permanent
    source of light—
  the splendor of your God will shine
    upon you.
20 Your sun will no longer set;
  [a]your moon will not disappear;

60:5 [a] [Rom 11:25–27]   60:6 [a] Gen 25:4   [b] Gen 25:3; Ps 72:10   [c] Isa 61:6; Matt 2:11   [1] Heb. *an abundance of camels will cover you.*   60:7 [a] Gen 25:13   [b] Isa 56:7   [c] Isa 60:13; Hag 2:7, 9   [1] Heb. *they will go up on acceptance* [on] *my altar.*   60:9 [a] Ps 72:10   [b] [Gal 4:26]   [1] Heb. *the ships of Tarshish;* probably referring to large ships either made in or capable of traveling to the distant western port of Tarshish.   60:10 [a] Isa 14:1–2; 61:5; Zech 6:15   [b] Isa 49:23; Rev 21:24   60:11 [a] Isa 26:2; 60:18; 62:10; Rev 21:25–26   60:12 [a] Isa 14:2; Zech 14:17; Matt 21:44   [1] Or *For.*   60:13 [a] Isa 35:2   60:14 [a] Isa 45:14   [b] Isa 49:23; Rev 3:9   [c] [Heb 12:22; Rev 14:1]   60:16 [a] Isa 43:3   60:18 [a] Isa 26:1   60:19 [a] Rev 21:23; 22:5   [b] Isa 41:16; 45:25; Zech 2:5   60:20 [a] Amos 8:9

the LORD will be your permanent
   source of light;
your time[1] of sorrow will be over.
21 All your people will be godly;
   they will possess the land
     permanently.
   I will plant them like [a]a shoot;
   [b]they will be [c]the product of my
     labor,
   through whom I reveal my
     splendor.
22 The [a]least of you will multiply into a
     thousand;
   the smallest of you will become a
     large nation.
   When the right time comes, I the
     LORD will quickly do this!"

The Lord Will Rejuvenate His People

61 The [a]Spirit of the Sovereign LORD is
   upon me,
   because the LORD [b]has chosen me.
   He has commissioned me [c]to
     encourage the poor,
   to help the brokenhearted,
   to decree the [d]release of captives
   and the freeing of prisoners,
2 to announce the year when the LORD
   will show his favor,
   the day when our God will seek
     vengeance,
   [a]to console all who mourn,
3 to strengthen those who mourn in
     Zion
   by giving them a turban, instead of
     ashes,
   oil symbolizing joy,[1] instead of
     mourning,
   a garment symbolizing praise,
     instead of discouragement.
   They will be called oaks of
     righteousness,
   trees planted by the LORD [a]to reveal
     his splendor.
4 They will [a]rebuild the perpetual
     ruins
   and restore the places that were
     desolate;
   they will reestablish the ruined
     cities,

   the places that have been desolate
     since ancient times.
5 "[a]Foreigners will take care of your
     sheep;
   foreigners will work in your fields
     and vineyards.
6 [a]You will be called, 'the LORD's
     priests,
   servants of our God.'
   [b]You will enjoy[1] the wealth of nations
   and boast about the riches you
     receive from them.
7 Instead [a]of shame, you will get a
     double portion;
   instead of humiliation, they will
     rejoice over the land they receive.
   Yes,[1] they will possess a double
     portion in their land
   and experience lasting joy.
8 For [a]I, the LORD, love [b]justice
   [c]and hate robbery and sin.
   I will repay them because of my
     faithfulness;
   I will make a permanent covenant
     with them.
9 Their descendants will be known
     among the nations,
   their offspring among the peoples.
   All who see them will recognize [a]that
   the LORD has blessed them."
10 I [a]will greatly rejoice in [b]the LORD;
   I will be overjoyed because of my
     God.
   For he clothes me in garments of
     deliverance;
   he puts on me [c]a robe symbolizing
     vindication.
   I look like a bridegroom when
     he wears a turban as a priest
     would;
   I look like a bride when she puts on
     her jewelry.
11 For just as the ground produces its
     crops
   and a garden yields its produce,
   so the Sovereign LORD will cause
     [a]deliverance to grow
   and give his people reason to
     [b]praise him in the sight of all the
     nations.

60:20 [1]Heb. *days.* 60:21 [a]Isa 52:1; Rev 21:27 [b]Ps 37:11; Matt 5:5 [c]Isa 61:3; [Matt 15:13; John 15:2] 60:22 [a]Matt 13:31–32 61:1 [a]Isa 11:2; Matt 3:17; Luke 4:18–19; John 1:32; 3:34 [b]Ps 45:7; Matt 11:5; Luke 7:22 [c]Ps 147:3 [d]Isa 42:7; [Acts 10:43] 61:2 [a]Lev 25:9 61:3 [a]Ps 30:11 [1]Heb. *oil of joy.* 61:4 [a]Isa 49:8; 58:12; Ezek 36:33; Amos 9:14 61:5 [a][Eph 2:12] 61:6 [a]Exod 19:6 [b]Isa 60:5, 11 [1]Heb. *eat.* 61:7 [a]Isa 40:2; Zech 9:12 [1]Heb. *therefore.* 61:8 [a]Ps 11:7 [b]Isa 1:11, 13 [c]Gen 17:7; Ps 105:10; Isa 55:3; Jer 32:40 61:9 [a]Isa 65:23 61:10 [a]Hab 3:18 [b]Ps 132:9, 16 [c]Isa 49:18; Rev 21:2 61:11 [a]Ps 72:3; 85:11 [b]Isa 60:18; 62:7

The Lord Takes Delight in Zion

62 For the sake of Zion I will not be
silent;
for the sake of Jerusalem I will not be
quiet,
until her vindication shines
brightly
and her deliverance burns like a
torch.
2 ᵃNations will see your vindication,
and all ᵇkings ᶜyour splendor.
You will be called by a new name
that the LORD himself will give you.
3 You will be ᵃa majestic crown in the
hand of the LORD,
a royal turban in the hand of your
God.
4 ᵃYou will no longer be called,
"ᵇAbandoned,"
and your land will no longer be called
"ᶜDesolate."
Indeed,¹ you will be called "My
Delight is in Her"
and your land "Married."
For the LORD will take delight in you,
and your land will be married to him.
5 As a young man marries a young
woman,
ᵃso your sons will marry you.
As a bridegroom rejoices over a
bride,
so your God will rejoice over you.
6 I post watchmen on your walls,
O Jerusalem;
they should keep ᵃpraying all day and
all night.
You who pray to the LORD, don't be
silent!
7 Don't ᵃallow him to rest until he
reestablishes Jerusalem,
until he makes Jerusalem the pride
of the earth.
8 The LORD swears an oath by his right
hand,
by his strong arm:
"I will never again ᵃgive your grain
to your enemies as food,
and foreigners will not drink your
wine,
which you worked hard to produce.

9 "But those who harvest the ᵃgrain
will eat it,
and will praise the LORD.
Those who pick the grapes will drink
the wine
in the courts of my holy sanctuary."
10 Come through! Come through the
gates!
ᵃPrepare the way for the people!
Build it—build the roadway!
Remove the stones.
ᵇLift a signal flag for the nations.
11 Look, the LORD announces to the
entire earth:
"ᵃSay to Daughter Zion,
'Look, your deliverer comes!
Look, his ᵇreward is with him,
and his reward goes before him!'"
12 They will be called, "The Holy People,
the Ones Protected¹ by the LORD."
You will be called, "Sought After,
City Not Abandoned."

The Victorious Divine Warrior

63 Who is this who comes from Edom,
dressed in bright red, coming from
Bozrah?
Who is this one wearing royal attire,
who marches confidently¹ because of
his great strength?
"It is I, the one who announces
vindication,
and who is able to deliver!"
2 Why are your clothes red?
Why do you look like someone who
has stomped on grapes in a vat?¹
3 "I have stomped ᵃgrapes in the
winepress all by myself;
no one from the nations joined me.
I stomped on them in my anger;
I trampled them down in my rage.
Their juice splashed on my garments
and stained all my clothes.
4 For I looked forward to the ᵃday of
vengeance,
and then payback time arrived.
5 I looked, but there was no one to
help;
ᵃI was shocked because ᵇthere was no
one offering support.

62:2 ᵃIsa 60:3   ᵇPs 102:15–16; 138:4–5; 148:11, 13.   ᶜIsa 62:4, 12; 65:15   **62:3** ᵃIsa 28:5; Zech 9:16; 1 Thess 2:19   **62:4** ᵃHos
1:10; 1 Pet 2:10   ᵇIsa 49:14; 54:6–7   ᶜIsa 54:1   ¹Or *for.*   **62:5** ᵃIsa 65:19   **62:6** ᵃIsa 52:8; Jer 6:17; Ezek 3:17; 33:7   **62:7** ᵃIsa
60:18; 61:11; Jer 33:9; Zeph 3:19–20   **62:8** ᵃLev 26:16; Deut 28:31, 33; Judg 6:3–6; Isa 1:7; Jer 5:17   **62:9** ᵃDeut 12:12; 14:23, 26
62:10 ᵃIsa 40:3; 57:14   ᵇIsa 11:12   **62:11** ᵃZech 9:9; Matt 21:5; John 12:15   ᵇIsa 40:10; [Rev 22:12]   **62:12** ¹Or *the redeemed of
the LORD.*   **63:1** ¹MT *he stoops, bends.*   **63:2** ¹Heb. *and your garments like one who treads in a vat?*   **63:3** ᵃLam 1:15;
Rev 14:19–20; 19:15   **63:4** ᵃIsa 34:8; 35:4; 61:2; Jer 51:6   **63:5** ᵃIsa 41:28; 59:16   ᵇ[John 16:32]

So my right [c]arm accomplished
    deliverance;
my raging anger drove me on.
6 I trampled nations in my anger;
I made them drunk in my rage;
I splashed their blood on the
    ground."

A Prayer for Divine Intervention

7 I will tell of the faithful acts of the
    LORD,
of the LORD's praiseworthy deeds.
I will tell about all the LORD did
    for us,
the many good things he did for the
    family of Israel,
because of his compassion and great
    faithfulness.
8 He said, "Certainly they will be my
    people,
children who are not disloyal."
He became their deliverer.
9 Through all that they suffered, he
    suffered too.
The messenger sent from his very
    presence delivered them.
[a]In his love [b]and mercy [c]he protected
    them;
he lifted them up and carried them
    throughout ancient times.
10 But they [a]rebelled and [b]offended his
    Holy Spirit,
[c]so he turned into an enemy
and fought against them.
11 His people [a]remembered the ancient
    times.
Where is the one who [b]brought them
    up out of the sea,
along with the shepherd of[1] his flock?
[c]Where is the one who placed his
    Holy Spirit among them,
12 the one who made his majestic
    power available to Moses,
who [a]divided the water before them,
gaining for himself a lasting
    reputation,
13 [a]who led them through the deep
    water?
Like a horse running through the
    wilderness they did not stumble.

14 As an animal that goes down [a]into a
    valley to graze,
so the Spirit of the LORD granted
    them rest.
In this way[1] you guided your
    people,
gaining for yourself an honored
    reputation.
15 Look [a]down [b]from heaven and take
    notice,
from your holy, majestic palace!
Where are your zeal and power?
Do not hold back your tender
    compassion!
16 For you are our father,
[a]though Abraham does not know us
and Israel does not recognize us.
You, LORD, are our father;
you have been called our Protector
    from ancient times.
17 Why, LORD, do you make us stray
    from your ways
and make our minds stubborn so
    that we do not obey you?
Return for the sake of your servants,
the tribes of your inheritance!
18 For a short time [a]your special[1] nation
    possessed a land,
but then [b]our adversaries knocked
    down your holy sanctuary.
19 We existed from ancient times,
but you did not rule over them;
they were not your subjects.

64 If only you would tear apart the
    sky[1] and come down!
The mountains would tremble
[a]before you!
2 As when fire ignites dry wood
or fire makes water boil,
let your adversaries know who you
    are,
and may the nations shake at your
    presence!
3 When [a]you performed awesome
    deeds that took us by surprise,
you came down, and the mountains
    trembled before you.
4 Since ancient times no one has heard
    or perceived,
no eye has seen any God besides you,

63:5 [c]Ps 98:1; Isa 59:16　63:9 [a]Judg 10:16　[b]Exod 14:19　[c]Exod 19:4　63:10 [a]Exod 15:24　[b]Num 14:11; Ps 78:40; Acts 7:51; 1 Cor 10:1–11　[c]Exod 23:21; Ps 106:40　63:11 [a]Ps 106:44–45　[b]Exod 14:30　[c]Num 11:17, 25, 29; Hag 2:5　[1]The Heb. text is pl., perhaps referring to Moses, Aaron, and the Israelite tribal leaders at the time of the exodus.　63:12 [a]Exod 14:21–22; Josh 3:16; Isa 11:15; 51:10　63:13 [a]Ps 106:9　63:14 [a]2 Sam 7:23　[1]Or so.　63:15 [a]Deut 26:15; Ps 80:14　[b]Ps 33:14　63:16 [a]Deut 32:6　63:18 [a]Deut 7:6　[b]Ps 74:3–7; Isa 64:11　[1]Or holy.　64:1 [a]Exod 19:18; Ps 18:9; 144:5; Mic 1:3–4; [Hab 3:13]　[1]Or the heavens.　64:3 [a]Exod 34:10

who intervenes for those who wait
　　for him.
5 You assist those who delight [a]in
　　doing what is right,
who observe your commandments.
Look, you were angry because we
　　violated them continually.
How then can we be saved?[1]
6 We are all like one who is unclean,
all [a]our so-called righteous acts are
　　like [b]a menstrual rag in your sight.
We all wither like a leaf;
our sins carry us away like the wind.
7 No one invokes your name,
or makes an effort[1] to take hold of you.
For you have rejected us
and handed us over to our own sins.[2]
8 Yet, LORD, you are our father.
We are the clay, and you are our
　　[a]potter;
we are all the product of your labor.
9 LORD, do not be too angry!
Do not hold our sins against us
　　continually.
Take a good look at your people, at
　　all of us.
10 Your chosen cities have become a
　　wilderness;
Zion has become a wilderness,
Jerusalem, a desolate ruin.
11 Our holy temple, [a]our pride and joy,
the place where our ancestors
　　praised you,
has been burned with fire;
all our prized possessions have been
　　destroyed.
12 [a]In light of all this,[1] how can you still
　　hold back, LORD?
How can you be silent and continue
　　to humiliate us?

The Lord Will Distinguish Between Sinners and the Godly

65 "I [a]made myself available to those
　　who did not ask for me;
I appeared to those who did not look
　　for me.
I said, 'Here I am! Here I am!'
to [b]a nation that did not invoke my
　　name.

2 I spread out my hands all day long
to my [a]rebellious people,
who [b]lived in a way that is morally
　　unacceptable
and who did what they desired.
3 These people continually and
　　blatantly offend me
as they sacrifice in their sacred
　　orchards[1]
and burn incense on brick altars.
4 [a]They sit among the tombs
and keep watch all night long.
They eat pork
and broth[1] from unclean sacrificial
　　meat is in their pans.
5 [a]They say, 'Keep to yourself!
Don't get near me, for I am holier
　　than you!'
These people are like smoke in my
　　nostrils,
like a fire that keeps burning all day
　　long.
6 Look, [a]I have decreed:[1]
[b]I will not keep silent, [c]but will pay
　　them back;
I will pay them back exactly what
　　they deserve,
7 for your sins and your ancestors'
　　sins," says [a]the LORD.
"Because they burned incense on the
　　mountains
[b]and offended me on the hills,
I will punish them in full measure."
8 This is [a]what the LORD says:

"When juice is discovered in [b]a
　　cluster of grapes,
someone says, 'Don't destroy it, for it
　　contains juice.'
So I will do for the sake of my
　　servants—
I will not destroy everyone.
9 I will bring forth descendants from
　　Jacob
and from Judah people to take
　　possession of my mountains.
My chosen [a]ones will take possession
　　of the land;
my servants will live there.

64:5 [a]Mal 3:6 [1]Some wss *we were delivered*; LXX *we were evil/we deceived*. 64:6 [a][Phil 3:9] [b]Ps 90:5–6; Isa 1:30
64:7 [1]Or *rouses himself*. [2]MT *and you caused us to melt in the hand of our sin*. 64:8 [a]Isa 29:16; 45:9; Jer 18:6; [Rom 9:20–21] 64:11 [a]Ezek 24:21 64:12 [a]Isa 42:14 [1]Heb. *because of these*. 65:1 [a]Rom 9:24; 10:20 [b]Isa 63:19 65:2 [a]Isa 1:2, 23 [b]Isa 42:24 65:3 [1]Or *gardens*. 65:4 [a]Deut 18:11 [1]Ket. *fragment*. 65:5 [a]Matt 9:11; Luke 7:39; 18:9–12
65:6 [a]Deut 32:34 [b]Ps 50:3 [c]Ps 79:12 [1]Heb. *Look, it is written before me*. 65:7 [a]Exod 20:5 [b]Isa 57:7;
Ezek 20:27–28 65:8 [a]Joel 2:14 [b]Isa 1:9; Amos 9:8–9 65:9 [a]Matt 24:22

10 [a]Sharon will become a pasture for
  sheep,
and [b]the Valley of Achor a place
  where cattle graze;[1]
they will belong to my people, who
  [c]seek me.
11 But as for you who abandon the
  LORD
and forget about worshiping at [a]my
  holy [b]mountain,
who prepare a feast for the god called
  'Fortune,'
and fill up wine jugs for the god
  called 'Destiny'—
12 I predestine you to die by the sword,
all of you will kneel down at the
  slaughtering block,
[a]because I called to you, and you did
  not respond;
I spoke and you did not listen.
You did evil before me;
  you chose to do what displeases me."

13 So this is what the Sovereign LORD says:

"Look, my servants will eat, but you
  will be hungry.
Look, my servants will drink, but you
  will be thirsty.
Look, my servants will rejoice, but
  you will be humiliated.
14 Look, my servants will shout for joy
  as happiness fills their hearts.
But you will cry out as sorrow fills
  your hearts;
you will [a]wail because your spirits
  will be crushed.
15 Your names will live on in the curse
  [a]formulas of [b]my chosen ones.
The Sovereign LORD will kill you,
but he will [c]give his servants another
  name.
16 Whoever pronounces a blessing in
  the earth[1]
will do [a]so in [b]the name of the
  faithful God;
whoever makes an oath in the earth
will do so in the name of the faithful
  God.

For past problems will be forgotten;
I will no longer think about them.
17 For look, I am ready to create
[a]new heavens and a new earth!
The former ones[1] will not be
  remembered;
no one will think about them
  anymore.
18 But be happy and rejoice forevermore
over what I am about to create!
For look, I am ready to create
  Jerusalem to be a source of joy,
and her people to be a source of
  happiness.
19 Jerusalem [a]will bring me joy,
and my people will bring me
  happiness.
The [b]sound of weeping or cries of
  sorrow
will never be heard in her again.
20 Never again will one of her infants
  live just a few days
or an old man die before his time.[1]
Indeed, no one will die before the age
  of one hundred;
anyone who fails to reach the age of
  one hundred will be considered
  cursed.
21 They will build houses and live in
  them;
[a]they will plant vineyards and eat
  their fruit.
22 No longer will they build a house
  only to have [a]another live in it,
or plant [b]a vineyard only to have
  another eat its fruit,
for [c]my people will live as long as trees,
and my chosen ones will enjoy to the
  fullest what they have produced.
23 They will not work in vain
[a]or give birth to children that will
  experience disaster.[1]
For [b]the LORD will bless their
  children
and their descendants.
24 Before they even call out, I will
  respond;
while they are still speaking, I will
  [a]hear.

65:10 [a]Isa 33:9 [b]Josh 7:24; Hos 2:15 [c]Isa 55:6 [1]Heb. *a resting place for cattle.* 65:11 [a]Isa 56:7 [b]Ezek 23:41; [1 Cor 10:21]
65:12 [a]2 Chr 36:15-16; Prov 1:24; Isa 41:28; 50:2; 66:4; Jer 7:13 65:14 [a]Matt 8:12; Luke 13:28 65:15 [a]Jer 29:22; Zech 8:13
[b]Isa 65:9, 22 [c][Acts 11:26] 65:16 [a]Ps 72:17; Jer 4:2 [b]Deut 6:13; Zeph 1:5 [1]Or *in the land.* 65:17 [a]Isa 51:16; 66:22;
[2 Pet 3:13]; Rev 21:1 [1]Or perhaps *the former things.* 65:19 [a]Isa 62:4-5 [b]Isa 35:10; 51:11; Rev 7:17; 21:4 65:20 [1]Heb.
or an old [man] *who does not fill out his days.* 65:21 [a]Ezek 28:26; 45:4; Hos 11:11; Amos 9:14 65:22 [a]Isa
62:8-9 [b]Ps 92:12 [c]Isa 65:9, 15 65:23 [a]Hos 9:12 [b]Isa 61:9; [Jer 32:38-39; Acts 2:39] [1]Heb. *and they
will not give birth to horror.* 65:24 [a]Isa 30:19; Dan 9:20-23

25 A ^awolf ^band a lamb will graze
together;
a lion, like an ox, will eat straw,
and a snake's food will be dirt.
They will no longer injure or destroy
on my entire royal mountain," says
the LORD.

66 This is what the LORD says:
"The ^aheavens are my throne
and the earth is my footstool.
Where then is the house you will
build for me?
Where is the place where I will rest?
2 My hand made them;
that is how they came to be," says the
LORD.

"I show special favor to the humble
and ^acontrite,
who respect what I have to say.¹
3 The one who slaughters a bull also
strikes down a man;
^athe one who sacrifices ^ba lamb also
breaks a dog's neck;
the one who presents an offering
includes pig's blood with it;
the one who offers incense also
praises an idol.
They have decided to behave this
way;
they enjoy these disgusting practices.
4 So I will choose severe punishment
for them;
I will bring on them what they dread
^abecause I called, and no one
responded.
I spoke and they did not listen.
They did evil before me;
they chose to do what displeases me."
5 Listen to the LORD's message,
you who respect his word!

"Your countrymen, who ^ahate you
and exclude you, supposedly for the
sake of my name,
say, 'May the LORD be glorified,
then ^bwe will witness your joy.'
But they will be put to shame.
6 The sound of battle comes from the
city;
the sound comes from the temple!

It is the sound of the LORD paying
back his enemies.
7 Before she goes into labor, she gives
birth!
Before her contractions begin, she
delivers a boy!
8 Who has ever heard of such a thing?
Who has ever seen this?
Can a country be brought forth in
one day?
Can a nation be born in a single
moment?
Yet as soon as Zion goes into labor
she gives birth to sons!
9 Do I bring a baby to the birth
opening and then not deliver it?"
asks the LORD.
"Or do I bring a baby to the point of
delivery and then hold it back?"
asks your God.
10 "Be happy for Jerusalem
and rejoice with her, all you who love
her!
Share in her great joy,
all you who have mourned over her!
11 For you will nurse from her satisfying
breasts and be nourished;
you will feed with joy from her
milk-filled breasts."

12 For ^athis is what the LORD says:

"Look, I am ready to extend to her
prosperity that will flow like a
river,
the riches of nations will flow into
her like a stream that floods its
banks.
You will ^bnurse from her breast and
be ^ccarried at her side;
you will play on her knees.
13 As a mother ^aconsoles a child,
so I will console you,
and you will be consoled over
Jerusalem."
14 When ^ayou see this, you will be
happy,
and you will be revived.
The LORD will reveal his power to his
servants
and his anger to his enemies.

65:25 ^a Isa 11:6–9 ^b Gen 3:14; Mic 7:17   66:1 ^a 1 Kgs 8:27; 2 Chr 6:18; Ps 11:4; Matt 5:34; Acts 17:24   66:2 ^a Ps 34:18;
51:17 ¹ Heb. *humble and the lowly in spirit and the one who trembles at my words.*   66:3 ^a [Isa 1:10–17; 58:1–7;
Mic 6:7–8] ^b Deut 23:18   66:4 ^a Prov 1:24; Isa 65:12; Jer 7:13   66:5 ^a Ps 38:20; Isa 60:15; [Luke 6:22–23]
^b [2 Thess 1:10; Titus 2:13]   66:12 ^a Isa 48:18; 60:5 ^b Isa 60:16 ^c Isa 49:22; 60:4   66:13 ^a Isa 51:3;
[2 Cor 1:3–4]   66:14 ^a Ezek 37:1

[15] [a]For look, the LORD comes with fire;
his chariots come like a windstorm
to reveal his raging anger,
his battle cry, and his flaming arrows.
[16] For the LORD judges all humanity[1]
with fire and [a]his sword;
the LORD will kill [b]many.

[17] "As for [a]those who consecrate and ritually purify themselves so they can follow their leader and worship in the sacred orchards, those who eat the flesh of pigs and other disgusting creatures, like mice—they will all be destroyed together," says the LORD. [18]"I hate their deeds and [a]thoughts! So I am coming[1] to [b]gather all the nations and ethnic groups;[2] they will come and witness my splendor. [19]I [a]will perform [b]a mighty act among them and then send some of those who remain to the nations—to Tarshish, Pul, Lud (known for its archers), Tubal, Javan, and to the distant coastlands that have not heard about me or seen my splendor. They will tell the nations of my splendor. [20]They will bring back all your countrymen from all the nations as an offering to the LORD. They will bring them on horses, in chariots, in wagons, on mules, and on camels to my holy hill Jerusalem," says the LORD, "just as the Israelites [a]bring offerings to the LORD's temple in ritually pure containers. [21]And I will choose some of them as [a]priests and Levites," says the LORD. [22]"For just as [a]the new heavens and the new earth I am about to make will remain standing before me," says the LORD, "so your descendants and your name will remain. [23]From one month to the next and from one Sabbath to the next, [a]all people[1] will come to worship me," says the LORD. [24]"They will go out and observe the corpses of those who rebelled against me, for the [a]maggots that eat them will not die, and the fire that consumes them will not die out. All people will find the sight abhorrent."

66:15 [a]Isa 9:5; [2 Thess 1:8]   66:16 [a]Isa 27:1   [b]Isa 34:6   [1]Heb. *flesh.*   66:17 [a]Isa 65:3–8   66:18 [a]Isa 59:7   [b]Isa 45:22–25; Jer 3:17   [1]MT *and I, their deeds and their thoughts, am coming.*   [2]Heb. *and the tongues.*   66:19 [a]Luke 2:34   [b]Mal 1:11   66:20 [a]Isa 49:22   66:21 [a]Exod 19:6; Isa 61:6; 1 Pet 2:9; Rev 1:6   66:22 [a]Isa 65:17; Heb 12:26–27; 2 Pet 3:13; Rev 21:1   66:23 [a]Zech 14:17–21   [1]Heb. *all flesh.*   66:24 [a]Isa 14:11; Mark 9:44, 46, 48

JEREMIAH

The Book of Jeremiah is the prophecy of a man divinely called in his youth from the priest-city of Anathoth. A heartbroken prophet with a heartbreaking message, Jeremiah labors far more than forty years proclaiming a message of doom to the stiff-necked people of Judah. Despised and persecuted by his countrymen, Jeremiah bathes his harsh prophecies in tears of compassion. His broken heart causes him to write a broken book that is difficult to arrange chronologically or topically. But through his sermons and signs, he faithfully declares that surrender to God's will is the only way to escape calamity. *Yirmey-ahu* or *Yirmeyah* literally means "Yahweh Throws," perhaps in the sense of laying a foundation. It may effectively mean "Yahweh Establishes, Appoints, or Sends." The Greek form of the Hebrew name in the Septuagint is *Hieremias*, and the Latin form is *Jeremias*.

The Superscription

1 The [a]following is a record of what Jeremiah son of Hilkiah prophesied. He was one of the priests who lived at Anathoth in the territory of the tribe of Benjamin. [2]The LORD's message came to him in the thirteenth year that [a]Josiah son of Amon ruled over Judah. [3]It also came in the days of [a]Jehoiakim, son of Josiah, king of Judah, and continued [b]until the eleventh year of Zedekiah, son of Josiah, king of Judah, [c]until the people of Jerusalem were taken [d]into exile in the fifth month of that year.

Jeremiah's Call and Commission

[4]The LORD's message came to me,

[5] "Before I [a]formed you [b]in your
    mother's womb, I chose you.[1]
Before you were born, I [c]set you
    apart.
I appointed you to be a prophet to
    the nations."

[6]I answered, "[a]Oh, Sovereign LORD, Really I do not know how to speak well enough for that, for I am too young."[1] [7]The LORD said to me, "Do not say, 'I am too young.'

But go to whomever I send you and say [a]whatever I tell you. [8][a]Do not be [b]afraid of those to whom I send you, for I will be with you to protect you," says the LORD. [9]Then the LORD reached out his hand and [a]touched my mouth and said to me, "I will most assuredly give you the words you are to speak for me. [10]Know for certain [a]that I hereby give you the authority to announce to nations and kingdoms that they will be [b]uprooted and torn down, destroyed and demolished, rebuilt and firmly planted."

Visions Confirming Jeremiah's Call and Commission

[11]Later the LORD's message came to me, "What do you see, Jeremiah?" I answered, "I see a branch of an almond tree." [12]Then the LORD said, "You have observed correctly. This means I am watching to make sure my threats are carried out."[1]

[13]The LORD's [a]message came to me a second time, "What do you see?" I answered, "I see a pot of boiling water; it is tipped away from the north." [14]Then the LORD said, "From the [a]north destruction will break out on all who live in the land. [15]For I will soon [a]summon all the peoples of the kingdoms of

the north," says the LORD. "They will come and their kings will set up their thrones near the entrances of the gates of Jerusalem. They will attack all the walls surrounding it and all the towns in Judah. [16]In this way I will pass sentence on [a]the people of Jerusalem and Judah because of all their wickedness. For they rejected me and offered [b]sacrifices to other gods, worshiping what they made with their own [c]hands.

[17]"But you, Jeremiah, [a]get yourself ready![1] Go and tell these people everything I instruct you to say. [b]Do not be terrified of them, or I will give you good reason to be terrified of them. [18]I, the LORD, hereby promise to [a]make you as strong as a fortified city, an iron pillar, and a bronze wall. You will be able to stand up against all who live in the land, including the kings of Judah, its officials, its priests, and all the people of the land. [19]They will attack you but they will not be able to overcome you, for I will be with you to rescue you," says the LORD.

The Lord Recalls Israel's Earlier Faithfulness

2 The LORD's message came to me, [2]"Go and declare in the hearing of the people of Jerusalem: 'This is what the LORD says: "I have fond memories of you, how devoted you were to me in your early [a]years. I remember how you loved me like a new bride; you followed me through the wilderness, through a land that had never been planted. [3a]Israel was set apart to the LORD; they were like [b]the firstfruits of a harvest to him. [c]All who tried to devour them were punished; disaster [d]came upon them," says the LORD.'"

The Lord Reminds Them of the Unfaithfulness of Their Ancestors

[4] Now listen to the LORD's message, you descendants of Jacob, all you family groups from the nation of Israel.
[5] This is what the LORD says:

"[a]What fault could your ancestors [b]have possibly found in me that they strayed so far from me? They paid allegiance to worthless idols, and so became worthless to me.
[6] They did not ask, 'Where is the LORD who delivered us out of Egypt, who [a]brought us through [b]the wilderness, through a land of valleys and gorges,[1] through a land of desert and deep darkness,[2] through a land in which no one travels, and where no one lives?'
[7] I brought you into [a]a fertile land so you could enjoy its fruits and its rich bounty. But when you entered my land, you [b]defiled it; you made the land I call my own loathsome to me.
[8] Your priests did not ask, 'Where is the LORD?' Those responsible for teaching my [a]law did not really know me. Your rulers rebelled against me. Your prophets prophesied in [b]the name of the god Baal.[1] They all worshiped idols that could not help them.

The Lord Charges Contemporary Israel with Spiritual Adultery

[9] "So, once more [a]I will state my case against you," says the LORD. "I will also state it against your children and grandchildren.
[10] Go west across the sea to the coasts of Cyprus and see. Send someone east to Kedar and have them look carefully. See if such a [a]thing as this has ever happened:
[11] Has [a]a nation ever changed its gods

1:16 [a]Deut 28:20; Jer 17:13 [b]Isa 65:3–4; Jer 7:9 [c]Isa 37:19; Jer 2:28 **1:17** [a]1 Kgs 18:46; 2 Kgs 4:29; Job 38:3; Luke 12:35; [1 Pet 1:13] [b]Ezek 2:6 [1]Heb. *gird up your loins*. **1:18** [a]Isa 50:7; Jer 6:27; 15:20 **2:2** [a]Ezek 16:8; Hos 2:15 **2:3** [a][Exod 19:5–6; Deut 7:6; 14:2] [b]Jas 1:18; Rev 14:4 [c]Jer 12:14 [d]Gen 12:3; Isa 41:11; Jer 30:15–16; 50:7 **2:5** [a]Isa 5:4; Mic 6:3 [b]2 Kgs 17:15; Jer 8:19; [Jonah 2:8]; Rom 1:21 **2:6** [a]Exod 20:2; Isa 63:11 [b]Deut 8:15; 32:10 [1]Heb. *a land of the rift valley and gorges*; the rift valley extends from Galilee to the Gulf of Aqaba. Biblical references are usually to sections of the rift valley, such as the Jordan Valley, the region of the Dead Sea, or the portion south of the Dead Sea. [2]Trad., but mistakenly, *shadow of death*. **2:7** [a]Num 13:27 [b]Num 35:33; Isa 24:5; Hos 4:3 **2:8** [a]Rom 2:20 [b]Jer 23:13 [1]Heb. *by Baal*. **2:9** [a]Jer 2:35; Ezek 20:35–36; Mic 6:2 **2:10** [a]Jer 18:13 **2:11** [a]Mic 4:5

(even though they are [b]not really
  gods at all)?
  [c]But my people have exchanged me,
    their glorious God,
  for a god that cannot help them at
    all!
12 Be amazed at this, O heavens.
  Be shocked and utterly
    dumbfounded,"
  says the LORD.
13 "Do so because my people have
    committed a double wrong:
  They have rejected me,
  the [a]fountain of life-giving water,
  and they have dug cisterns for
    themselves,
  cracked cisterns that cannot even
    hold water.

Israel's Reliance on Foreign Alliances (not on God)

14 "Israel is not [a]a slave, is he?
  He was not born into slavery, was he?
  If not, why then is he being carried
    off?
15 Like lions his enemies roar
    victoriously over him;
  [a]they raise their voices in triumph.[1]
  They have laid his land waste;
  his cities have been burned down
    and deserted.
16 Even the soldiers from Memphis and
    [a]Tahpanhes
  have cracked your skulls, people of
    Israel.[1]
17 You [a]have brought all this on
    yourself, Israel,
  by deserting [b]the LORD your God
  when he was leading you along the
    right path.
18 What good will it do you [a]then to go
    down to Egypt
  to seek help from the [b]Egyptians?
  What good will it do you to go over to
    [c]Assyria
  to seek help from the Assyrians?[1]
19 Your own wickedness will bring
    [a]about your punishment.

Your unfaithful acts will bring down
    discipline on you.
  Know, then, and realize how utterly
    harmful
  it was for you to reject me, the LORD
    your God,
  to show no respect for me,"
  says the Sovereign LORD of Heaven's
    Armies.

The Lord Expresses His Exasperation at Judah's Persistent Idolatry

20 "Indeed,[1] long ago you threw [a]off my
    authority
  and refused to be subject to me.
  [b]You said, 'I will not serve you.'[2]
  Instead, you gave yourself to other
    gods [c]on every high hill
  and under every green tree,
  like [d]a prostitute sprawls out before
    her lovers.
21 I [a]planted you in [b]the land
  like a special vine of the very best
    stock.
  Why in the world have you turned
    into something like a wild vine
  that produces rotten, foul-smelling
    grapes?[1]
22 You can try to wash away your guilt
    with a strong detergent.
  You can use as much soap as you
    want.
  But the [a]stain of your guilt is still
    there for me to see,"
  says the Sovereign LORD.
23 "[a]How can you say, 'I have not made
    myself unclean.
  I have not paid allegiance to the gods
    called Baal.'
  Just look at the way you have
    behaved in the Valley of
    Hinnom![1]
  Think about the things you have
    done there!
  You are like a flighty, young female
    camel
  that rushes here and there,
    crisscrossing its path.

2:11 [b]Ps 115:4; Isa 37:19   [c]Ps 106:20; Rom 1:23   2:13 [a]Ps 36:9; Jer 17:13; [John 4:14]   2:14 [a][Exod 4:22]   2:15 [a]Isa 1:7; Jer 50:17   [1]Heb. *Lions shout over him; they give out* [raise] *their voices.*   2:16 [a]2 Kgs 23:29–37; Jer 43:7–9   [1]MT *have grazed your skulls.*   2:17 [a]Jer 4:18   [b]Deut 32:10   2:18 [a]Isa 30:1–3   [b]Josh 13:3   [c]Hos 5:13   [1]Heb. *to drink water from the River.* 2:19 [a]Isa 3:9; Jer 4:18; Hos 5:5   2:20 [a]Lev 26:13   [b]Exod 19:8; Josh 24:18; Judg 10:16; 1 Sam 12:10   [c]Deut 12:2; Isa 57:5, 7; Jer 3:6   [d]Exod 34:15   [1]Or *For.*   [2]Ket. *I will not transgress.*   2:21 [a]Exod 15:17; Ps 44:2; 80:8; Isa 5:2   [b]Deut 32:32; Isa 5:4   [1]Heb. *I planted you as a choice vine, all of it true seed. How then have you turned into a putrid thing to me, a strange* [or *wild*] *vine.*   2:22 [a]Job 14:16–17; Jer 17:1–2; Hos 13:12   2:23 [a]Prov 30:12   [1]Heb. *Look at your way in the valley; where Baal and Molech were worshiped and child sacrifice was practiced.*

24 You are like a wild female donkey
  brought up in the wilderness.
In her lust she sniffs the wind to get
  the scent of a male.
No one can hold her back when she
  is in heat.
None of the males need wear
  themselves out chasing
  after her.
At mating time she is easy to find.
25 Do not chase after other gods until
  your shoes wear out
and your throats become dry.
But you say, 'It is useless for you to
  try and stop me
because I love those ᵃforeign gods
  and want to pursue them!'
26 Just as a thief has to suffer dishonor
  when he is caught,
so the people of Israel will suffer
  dishonor for what they have done.
So will their kings and officials,
their priests and their ᵃprophets.
27 They say to a wooden idol, 'You are
  my father.'
They say to a ᵃstone image, 'You gave
  birth to me.'
Yes, they have turned away from me
  instead of turning to me.
Yet when they are in ᵇtrouble, they
  say, 'Come and save us!'
28 But ᵃwhere are the gods you made for
  yourselves?
Let them save you when you are ᵇin
  trouble.
The sad fact is that¹ you have as many
  gods
as you have towns, Judah.
29 Why do you try to refute me?
All of you have rebelled against me,"
says the LORD.
30 "It did no good for me to ᵃpunish
  your people.
They did not respond ᵇto such
  correction.
You ᶜslaughtered your prophets
like a voracious lion."

31 You people of this generation,
  listen to the LORD's message:

"Have I been like a wilderness to you,
  Israel?
Have I been like a dark and
  dangerous land to you?
Why then do you say, 'ᵃWe are free to
  wander.
We will not come to you anymore?'
32 Does ᵃa young woman forget to put
  on her jewels?
Does a bride forget to put on her
  bridal attire?
But my people have forgotten me
for more days than can even be
  counted.

33 "My, how good you have become
  at chasing after your lovers!
Why, you could even teach
  prostitutes a thing or two!
34 Even your ᵃclothes are stained with
  the lifeblood of the poor who had not
  done anything wrong;
you did not catch them breaking into
  your homes.
Yet, in spite of all these things you
  have done,
35 ᵃyou say, 'ᵇI have not done anything
  wrong,
so the LORD cannot really ᶜbe angry
  with me any more.'
But, watch out! I will bring down
  judgment on you
because you say, 'I have not
  committed any sin.'
36 ᵃWhy do ᵇyou constantly go about
changing your political allegiances?
You will get no help from Egypt
just ᶜas you got no help from Assyria.
37 Moreover, ᵃyou will come away from
  Egypt
with your hands covering your faces
  in sorrow and shame
because the LORD will not allow your
  reliance on them to be successful
and you will ᵇnot gain any help from
  them.¹

3 "If ᵃa man divorces his wife
  and she leaves him and becomes
  another man's wife,

2:25 ᵃJer 3:13   2:26 ᵃIsa 28:7; Jer 5:31   2:27 ᵃJer 3:9   ᵇJudg 10:10; Isa 26:16; Hos 5:15   2:28 ᵃDeut 32:37; Judg 10:14   ᵇ2 Kgs 17:30–31; Jer 11:13   ¹Heb. for, indeed.   2:30 ᵃIsa 9:13   ᵇIsa 1:5; Jer 5:3; 7:28   ᶜNeh 9:26; Jer 26:20–24; Acts 7:52; 1 Thess 2:15   2:31 ᵃDeut 32:15; Jer 2:20, 25   2:32 ᵃPs 106:21; Isa 17:10; Jer 3:21; 13:25; Hos 8:14   2:34 ᵃ2 Kgs 21:16; 24:4; Ps 106:38; Jer 7:6; 19:4   2:35 ᵃJer 2:23, 29; Mal 2:17; 3:8   ᵇJer 2:9   ᶜ[Prov 28:13; 1 John 1:8, 10]   2:36 ᵃJer 31:22; Hos 5:13; 12:1   ᵇIsa 30:3   ᶜ2 Chr 28:16   2:37 ᵃ2 Sam 13:19; Jer 14:3–4   ᵇJer 37:7–10   ¹Heb. The LORD has rejected those you trust in; you will not prosper by/from them.   3:1 ᵃDeut 24:1–4

he may not take her back again.
Doing that would utterly defile the
  [b]land.
But you, Israel, have given yourself as
  [c]a prostitute to many gods.
So what makes you think you can
  return to me?"
says the LORD.

2 "Look up at [a]the hilltops and
  consider this.[1]
Where have you not been ravished?
You waited for those gods like a thief
  lying in wait in the wilderness.
You defiled the land [b]by your wicked
  prostitution to other gods.

3 That is why the [a]rains have been
  withheld
and the spring rains have not come.
Yet in spite of this you are obstinate
  as [b]a prostitute.
You refuse to be ashamed of what
  you have done.

4 Even now you say to me, 'You are my
  [a]father!
You have been [b]my faithful
  companion ever since I was young.

5 You [a]will not always be angry with
  me, will you?
You will not be mad at me forever,
  will you?'
That is what you say,
but you continually do all the evil
  that you can."[1]

[6]When Josiah was king of Judah, the
LORD said to me, "Jeremiah, you have no
doubt seen what [a]wayward Israel has done.
You have seen how she went up to every
high hill and under every green tree to give
herself like a prostitute to other gods. [7a]Yet
even after she had done all that, I thought
that she might come back to me. But she
did not. Her [b]sister, unfaithful Judah, saw
what she did. [8]She also saw[1] that, because
of wayward Israel's adulterous worship of
other gods, I sent her away and gave her
divorce papers. But still her unfaithful sister Judah was not afraid, and she too went
and gave herself like a prostitute to other

gods. [9]Because she took her prostitution so
lightly, she [a]defiled the land through her
adulterous worship of gods made of wood
and [b]stone. [10]In spite of all this, Israel's sister, unfaithful Judah, has not turned back
to me [a]with any sincerity; she has only pretended to do so," says the LORD. [11]Then the
LORD said to me, "Under the circumstances,
[a]wayward Israel could even be considered
less guilty than unfaithful Judah.

The Lord Calls on Israel and Judah to Repent

[12]"Go and shout this message to my people in [a]the countries in the north.[1] Tell
them:

'Come back to me, wayward Israel,'
  says the LORD.
'I will not continue to look on you
  with displeasure.
For I am [b]merciful,' says the LORD.
'I will not be angry with you forever.

13 [a]However, you must confess that you
  have done wrong
and that you have rebelled against
  the LORD your God.
You must confess that you have
  [b]given yourself to[1] [c]foreign gods
  [d]under every green tree
and have not obeyed my commands,'
  says the LORD.

[14]"Come back to me, my wayward sons,"
says the LORD, "[a]for I am your true master. If you do, I will take [b]one of you from
each town and two of you from each family
group, and I will bring you back to [c]Zion. [15]I
will give you [a]leaders[1] who will be faithful
to me. They will [b]lead you with knowledge
and insight. [16]In those days, your population will greatly [a]increase in the land. At
that time," says the LORD, "people will no
longer talk about having the ark that contains the LORD's covenant [b]with us.[1] They
will not call it to mind, remember it, or
miss it. No, that will not be done anymore!
[17]At that time the city of Jerusalem will be
called the LORD's throne. All nations will

3:1 [b] Jer 2:7 [c] Jer 2:20; Ezek 16:26   3:2 [a] Deut 12:2; Jer 2:20; 3:21; 7:29 [b] Prov 23:28 [1] Heb. *and see.*   3:3 [a] Lev 26:19; Jer
14:3–6 [b] Zeph 3:5   3:4 [a] Ps 71:17; Prov 2:17 [b] Jer 2:2; Hos 2:15   3:5 [a] Ps 103:9; [Isa 57:16]; Jer 3:12 [1] Heb. *You do the evil and
you are able.*   3:6 [a] Jer 7:24   3:7 [a] 2 Kgs 17:13 [b] Jer 3:11; Ezek 16:47–48   3:8 [1] MT *I saw.*   3:9 [a] Jer 2:7 [b] Isa 57:6; Jer 2:27
3:10 [a] Jer 12:2; Hos 7:14   3:11 [a] Ezek 16:51–52   3:12 [a] 2 Kgs 17:6 [b] Ps 86:15; Jer 12:15; 31:20; 33:26 [1] Heb. *Go and proclaim
these words to the north.*   3:13 [a] Lev 26:40; Deut 30:1–2; [Prov 28:13; 1 John 1:9] [b] Ezek 16:15 [c] Jer 2:25 [d] Deut 12:2 [1] MT
your ways.   3:14 [a] Jer 31:32; Hos 2:19–20 [b] Jer 31:6 [c] [Rom 11:5]   3:15 [a] Jer 23:4; 31:10; [Ezek 34:23]; Eph 4:11
[b] Acts 20:28 [1] Heb. *shepherds.*   3:16 [a] Isa 49:19; Jer 23:3 [b] Isa 65:17 [1] Heb. *the ark of the covenant.*

gather there in Jerusalem [a]to honor the LORD's name. They will no longer [b]follow the stubborn inclinations of their own evil hearts. [18]At that time [a]the nation of Judah and [b]the nation of Israel will be reunited. [c]Together they will come back from a land in the north to the land that I gave to your ancestors as a permanent possession.

[19] "I thought to myself,
'Oh [a]what a joy it would be for me to
    treat you like a son!
What a joy it would be for me to give
    you a pleasant land,
the most beautiful piece of property
    there is in all the world!'
I thought you would call me 'Father'
and would never cease being loyal
    to me.
[20] But, you [a]have been unfaithful to me,
    nation of Israel,
like an unfaithful wife who has left
    her husband,"
says the LORD.
[21] "A noise is heard on [a]the hilltops.
It is the sound of the people of Israel
    crying and pleading to their gods.
Indeed they have followed sinful
    ways;
they have forgotten to be true to the
    LORD their God.
[22] Come back to me, you wayward
    people.
I want to [a]cure your waywardness.[1]
Say, 'Here we are. We come to you
because you are the LORD our God.
[23] We [a]know our noisy worship of false
    gods
on the hills and mountains did not
    help us.
We [b]know that the LORD our God
is the only one who can deliver Israel.
[24] From earliest times our worship of
    that shameful god, Baal,
has taken away all that our ancestors
    worked [a]for.
It has taken away our flocks and our
    herds
and even our sons and daughters.

[25] Let us acknowledge our shame.
Let us bear the disgrace that we
    deserve.
[a]For we [b]have sinned against the
    LORD our God,
both we and our ancestors.
From earliest times to this very day
we have not obeyed the LORD our
    God.'

4 "If you, Israel, want to come [a]back,"
    says the LORD,
"if you want to come back to me,
you must get those disgusting idols
    out of my sight
and must no longer go astray.
[2] You must be truthful, honest, [a]and
    upright
when you take an oath [b]saying, 'As
    surely as [c]the LORD lives!'
If you do, the nations will pray to be
    as blessed by him as you are
and will [d]make him the object of
    their boasting."
[3] Yes, this is what the LORD has said
to the people of Judah and Jerusalem:
"[a]Break up your unplowed ground,
    [b]do not cast seeds among thorns.
[4] Commit [a]yourselves to the LORD;
dedicate your hearts to me
people of Judah and inhabitants of
    Jerusalem.
Otherwise, my anger will blaze up
like a flaming fire against you
that no one will be able to
    extinguish.
That will happen because of the evil
    you have done."

Warning of Coming Judgment

[5]The LORD said,

"Announce this in Judah and
    proclaim it in Jerusalem:
'[a]Sound the trumpet[1] throughout the
    land!'
Shout out loudly,
'Gather [b]together! Let us flee into the
    fortified cities!'

3:17 [a]Isa 60:9 [b]Deut 29:19; Jer 7:24   3:18 [a]Isa 11:13; Jer 50:4; Ezek 37:16–22; Hos 1:11 [b]Jer 31:8 [c]Amos 9:15   3:19 [a]Ps 106:24   3:20 [a]Isa 48:8   3:21 [a]Isa 15:2   3:22 [a]Jer 30:17; 33:6; Hos 6:1; 14:4 [1]Or I will forgive your apostasies; Heb. I will [or want to] heal your apostasies.   3:23 [a]Ps 121:1–2 [b]Ps 3:8; Prov 21:31; Jer 17:14; 31:7; Jonah 2:9   3:24 [a]Jer 11:13; 14:20; Hos 9:10   3:25 [a]Ezra 9:6–7 [b]Jer 22:21   4:1 [a]Jer 3:1, 22; 15:19; Joel 2:12   4:2 [a]Deut 10:20; Isa 45:23; 65:16; Jer 12:16 [b]Isa 48:1; Zech 8:8 [c][Gen 22:18]; Ps 72:18; Isa 65:16; Jer 3:17; [Gal 3:8] [d]Isa 45:25; Jer 9:24; 1 Cor 1:31; 2 Cor 10:17   4:3 [a]Hos 10:12 [b]Matt 13:7   4:4 [a]Deut 10:16; 30:6; Jer 9:25–26; [Rom 2:28–29; Col 2:11]   4:5 [a]Jer 6:1; Hos 8:1 [b]Josh 10:20; Jer 8:14 [1]Heb. ram's horn.

6 Raise a signal flag that tells people to
    go to Zion.
  Run for safety! Do not delay!
  For I am about to bring disaster out
    of the [a]north.
  It will bring great destruction.
7 Like a lion that has come up from its
    lair,
  [a]the one who destroys nations has
    set out from his home base.
  [b]He is coming out [c]to lay your land
    waste.
  Your cities will become ruins and lie
    uninhabited.
8 So put [a]on sackcloth!
  Mourn and wail, saying,
  'The fierce anger of the LORD
  has not turned away from us!'
9 When this happens," says the LORD,
  "the king and his officials will lose
    their courage.
  The priests will be struck with
    horror,
  and the prophets will be speechless
    in astonishment."

[10]In response to all this I said, "Ah, Sovereign LORD, you have [a]surely allowed the people of Judah and Jerusalem to be deceived by those who [b]say, 'You will be safe!' But in fact a sword is already at our throats."

11 At [a]that time the people of Judah and
    Jerusalem will be told,
  "A scorching wind will sweep down
  from the hilltops in the wilderness
    on my dear people.
  It will not be a gentle breeze
  for winnowing the grain and blowing
    away the chaff.
12 No, a [a]wind too strong for that will
    come at my bidding.
  Yes, even now I, myself, am calling
    down judgment on them.
13 Look! The enemy [a]is approaching like
    gathering clouds.
  The roar of [b]his chariots is like that
    of a whirlwind.
  His horses move more swiftly than
    eagles."

  I cry out, "We are doomed,[1] for we
    will be destroyed!"
14 O people of Jerusalem, [a]purify your
    hearts from evil
  so that you may yet be delivered.
  How long will you continue to
    harbor up
  wicked schemes within you?
15 For messengers are coming,
    heralding disaster,
  [a]from the city of Dan and from the
    hills of Ephraim.
16 They are saying,
  "Announce to the surrounding
    nations,
  'The enemy is coming!'[1]
  Proclaim this message to Jerusalem:
  'Those who besiege cities[2] are
    coming from a [a]distant land.
  They are ready to raise the battle cry
    against the towns in Judah.'
17 They will surround Jerusalem
  [a]like men guarding a field
  because they have rebelled
    against me,"
  says the LORD.
18 "The way [a]you have lived and the
    things you have done
  will bring this on you.
  This is the punishment you deserve,
    and it will be painful indeed.
  The pain will be so bad it will pierce
    your heart."

[19]I said,

  "Oh, the feeling in the [a]pit of my
    stomach!
  I writhe in anguish.
  Oh, the pain in my heart!
  My heart pounds within me.
  I cannot keep silent.
  For I hear the sound of the trumpet;[1]
  the sound of the battle cry pierces
    my soul![2]
20 I see one [a]destruction after another
    taking place,
  so that the whole land lies
    in ruins.
  I see our tents suddenly destroyed,

4:6 [a]Jer 1:13–15; 6:1, 22; 50:17   4:7 [a]2 Kgs 24:1; Dan 7:4   [b]Jer 25:9; Ezek 26:7–10   [c]Isa 1:7; 6:11; Jer 2:15   4:8 [a]Isa 22:12; Jer 6:26   4:10 [a]2 Kgs 25:10–12; Ezek 14:9; 2 Thess 2:11   [b]Jer 5:12; 14:13   4:11 [a]Jer 51:1; Ezek 17:10; Hos 13:15   4:12 [a]Jer 1:16   4:13 [a]Isa 5:28   [b]Deut 28:49; Lam 4:19; Hos 8:1; Hab 1:8   [1]Heb. *Woe to us!*   4:14 [a]Prov 1:22; Isa 1:16; Jer 13:27; Jas 4:8   4:15 [a]Jer 8:16; 50:17   4:16 [a]Isa 39:3; Jer 5:15   [1]MT *Look!* or *Behold!*   [2]Heb. *Besiegers.*   4:17 [a]2 Kgs 25:1, 4   4:18 [a]Ps 107:17; Isa 50:1; Jer 2:17, 19   4:19 [a]2 Kgs 25:11; 2 Chr 36:20; Isa 15:5; 16:11; 21:3; 22:4; Jer 9:1, 10; 20:9   [1]Heb. *ram's horn.*   [2]Ket. *for the sound of the ram's horn I have heard* [or *you have heard*] *my soul* followed by *the battle cry.*   4:20 [a]Ps 42:7; Ezek 7:26

their curtains torn down in a mere
  instant.[1]
21 How long must I see the enemy's
    battle flags
and hear the military signals of their
    bugles?"

22The LORD answered,

"This will happen because my people
    are foolish.
[a]They do not know me.
They are like children who have no
    sense.
They have no understanding.
They are skilled at doing evil.
They do not know how to do good."

23 I looked at the land and saw that [a]it
    was an empty wasteland.
[b]I looked up at the sky, and its light
    had vanished.
24 I looked at the [a]mountains and saw
    that they were shaking.
All the hills were swaying back and
    forth!
25 I looked and saw that there were no
    more people
and that [a]all the birds in the sky had
    flown away.
26 I looked and saw that the fruitful
    land had become a [a]desert
and that all the cities had been laid
    in ruins.
The LORD had brought this all about
because of his blazing anger.
27 All this will happen because the
    LORD said,
"The whole land will be desolate;
however, I will not completely
    destroy it.
28 Because of this, [a]the land will mourn
and the sky above will grow black.
For I have made my [b]purpose known,
and [c]I will not relent or turn back
    from carrying it out."
29 At the sound of the approaching
    horsemen and archers
the people of every town will flee.

Some of them will hide in the
    thickets.
Others will climb up among the rocks.
All the cities will be deserted.
No one will remain in them.
30 And [a]you, Zion, city doomed to
    destruction,
you accomplish nothing by wearing a
    beautiful dress,
decking yourself out in jewels of gold,
and putting on eye shadow![1]
You are making yourself beautiful for
    nothing.
Your lovers spurn you.
They want to kill you.
31 In fact, I hear a cry like that of a
    woman in labor,
a cry of anguish like that of a woman
    giving birth to her first baby.
It is the cry of Daughter Zion gasping
    for breath,
reaching [a]out for help, saying, "I am
    done in!
My life is ebbing away before these
    murderers!"

Judah Is Justly Deserving of Coming Judgment

5 The LORD said,

"Go up and down through the streets
    of Jerusalem.
Look around and see for yourselves.
Search through its public squares.
See [a]if any of you can find a single
    person
who deals honestly and tries to be
    truthful.
[b]If you can, then I will not punish
    this city.
2 [a]These people make promises in [b]the
    name of the LORD.
But the fact is,[1] what they [c]swear to is
    really a lie."
3 LORD, I know [a]you look for
    faithfulness.
But even when you [b]punish these
    people, [c]they feel no remorse.

4:20 [1]Perhaps meaning the defenses of Israel's cities and towns have offered no more resistance than nomads' tents,
or the destruction of their homes and the resultant feeling of homelessness and loss of even elementary protection.
4:22 [a]Jer 9:3; 13:23; Rom 16:19; 1 Cor 14:20   4:23 [a]Isa 24:19   [b]Gen 1:2   4:24 [a]Isa 5:25; Jer 10:10; Ezek 38:20   4:25 [a]Jer
9:10; 12:4; Zeph 1:3   4:26 [a]Jer 9:10   4:28 [a]Isa 5:30; 50:3; Joel 2:30–31   [b]Isa 46:10–11; [Dan 4:35]   [c][Num 23:19]; Jer 7:16;
23:30; 30:24   4:30 [a]Jer 22:20, 22; Lam 1:2, 19; Ezek 23:9–10, 22   [1]Heb. *enlarging your eyes with antimony*; a black powder
used as eyeliner.   4:31 [a]Isa 1:15; Lam 1:17   5:1 [a]Ezek 22:30   [b]Gen 18:23–32   5:2 [a]Isa 48:1; Titus 1:16   [b]Jer 4:2   [c]Jer 7:9
[1]MT *Therefore.*   5:3 [a]2 Kgs 25:1; [2 Chr 16:9; Jer 16:17]   [b]Isa 1:5; 9:13; Jer 2:30   [c]Isa 9:13; Jer 7:28; Zeph 3:2

Even when you nearly destroy them,
    they refuse to be corrected.
They have become as hardheaded as
    a rock.[1]
They refuse to change their ways.
4 I thought, "Surely it is only [a]the
    ignorant poor who act this way.
They act like fools because they do
    not know what the LORD demands.
They do not know what their God
    requires of them.
5 I will go to [a]the leaders
and speak with them.
Surely they know what the LORD
    demands.
Surely they know what their God
    requires of them."[1]
Yet all of them, too, have [b]rejected his
    authority
and refuse to submit to him.
6 So like [a]a lion from the thicket, their
    enemies will kill them.
Like [b]a wolf from the rift [c]valley, they
    will destroy them.
Like a leopard, they will lie in wait
    outside their cities
and totally destroy anyone who
    ventures out.
For they have rebelled so much
and done so many unfaithful things.

7 The LORD asked,

"How can I leave you unpunished,
    Jerusalem?
Your people have rejected me
and have [a]worshiped gods [b]that are
    not gods at all.
Even though I supplied all their
    needs, they were like an unfaithful
    wife to me.
They went flocking to the houses of
    prostitutes.
8 [a]They are like lusty, well-fed stallions.
Each of them lusts after[1] his
    neighbor's wife.
9 I will surely punish them for doing
    such things!" says the LORD.
"I will surely bring [a]retribution on
    such a nation as this!"

10 The LORD commanded the enemy,
"March through the vineyards of
    Israel and Judah and ruin them.
But do not destroy them [a]completely.
Strip off their branches
for these people do not belong to the
    LORD.
11 For [a]the nations of Israel and Judah
have been very unfaithful to me,"
says the LORD.
12 "These people have denied what [a]the
    LORD says.
They have said, 'That is [b]not so!
No harm will come to us.
We will not experience war and
    famine.[1]
13 The prophets will prove to be full of
    wind.
The LORD has not spoken through
    them.[1]
So, let what they say happen to
    them.'"

14 Because of that, the LORD God of Heaven's Armies said to me:

"Because these people have spoken
    like this,
I will make the words that I put in
    your mouth like fire.
And I will make this people like
    wood,
which the fiery judgments you speak
    will burn up."
15 The LORD says, "Listen,[1] nation of
    Israel!
I am about to bring a [a]nation [b]from
    far away to attack you.
It will be a nation that was founded
    long ago
and has lasted for a long time.
It will be a nation whose language
    you will not know.
Its people will speak words that you
    will not be able to understand.
16 All its soldiers are strong and mighty.
Their arrows will send you to your
    grave.[1]
17 They will eat up your [a]crops and your
    food.

5:3 [1] Heb. *They made their faces as hard as a rock.*   5:4 [a] Isa 27:11; Jer 8:7; Hos 4:6   5:5 [a] Mic 3:1   [b] Exod 32:25; Ps 2:3; Jer 2:20   [1] Heb. *the judgment* [or *ordinance*] *of their God.*   5:6 [a] Jer 4:7   [b] Ps 104:20; Ezek 22:27; Hab 1:8; Zeph 3:3   [c] Hos 13:7   5:7 [a] Josh 23:7; Jer 12:16; Zeph 1:5   [b] Deut 32:21; Jer 2:11; Gal 4:8   5:8 [a] Jer 13:27; 29:23; Ezek 22:11   [1] Heb. *neighs after.*   5:9 [a] Jer 9:9   5:10 [a] Jer 4:27   5:11 [a] Jer 3:6–7, 20   5:12 [a] 2 Chr 36:16; Jer 4:10   [b] Jer 14:13   [1] Heb. *we will not see the sword and famine.*   5:13 [1] Heb. *the word is not in them.*   5:15 [a] Deut 28:49; Isa 5:26; Jer 1:15; 6:22   [b] Isa 39:3; Jer 4:16   [1] Heb. *Behold!*   5:16 [1] Heb. *his quiver* [is] *an open grave.*   5:17 [a] Lev 26:16; Deut 28:31, 33; Jer 8:16; 50:7, 17

They will kill off your sons and your
daughters.
They will eat up your sheep and your
cattle.
They will destroy your vines and
your fig trees.
Their weapons will batter down
the fortified cities you trust in.

[18] "Yet even then [a]I will not completely
destroy you," says the LORD. [19] "So then, Jeremiah, when your people ask, '[a]Why has the
LORD our God done all this to us?' tell them,
'It is because you [b]rejected me and served
foreign gods in [c]your own land. So you must
serve foreigners in a land that does not belong to you.'

[20] "Proclaim this message among the
descendants of Jacob.
Make it known throughout Judah.
[21] Tell them: 'Hear this,
you [a]foolish people who have no
understanding,
who have eyes but do not discern,
who have ears but do not perceive:
[22] "[a]You should fear me!" says the LORD.
"You should tremble in awe
before me!
I made the sand to be a [b]boundary
for the sea,
a permanent barrier that it can never
cross.
Its waves may roll, but they can never
prevail.
They may roar, but they can never
cross beyond that boundary."
[23] But these people have stubborn and
rebellious hearts.
They have turned aside and gone
their own way.
[24] They do not say to themselves,
"Let us revere the LORD our God.
It is he [a]who gives us the [b]autumn
rains and [c]the spring rains at the
proper time.
It is he who assures us of the regular
weeks of harvest."
[25] Your misdeeds have stopped these
things from coming.

[a]Your sins have deprived you of my
bounty.'
[26] Indeed, there are wicked scoundrels
among my people.
They [a]lie in wait like bird catchers
hiding in ambush.
They set deadly traps to catch
people.
[27] Like a cage filled with the birds that
have been caught,
their houses are filled with the gains
of their fraud and deceit.
That is how they have gotten so rich
and powerful.
[28] That is how they have grown [a]fat and
sleek.[1]
[b]There is no limit to the evil things
they do.
They do not plead the cause of the
fatherless in such a way as to
win it.
They do not defend the rights of the
poor.
[29] I will certainly punish them for
doing such things!" says the LORD.
"I will certainly bring retribution on
such [a]a nation as this!
[30] Something horrible and [a]shocking
is going on in the land of Judah:
[31] The prophets prophesy [a]lies.
The priests exercise power by their
own authority.
And my people [b]love to have it this
way.
But they will not be able to help you
when the time of judgment comes!

The Destruction of Jerusalem Depicted

6 "Run for safety, people of Benjamin!
Get out of Jerusalem!
Sound the trumpet[1] in Tekoa!
Light the signal fires at Beth
[a]Hakkerem!
[b]For disaster lurks out of the north;
it will bring great destruction.
[2] I will destroy Daughter Zion,
who is as delicate and defenseless as
a young maiden.
[3] Kings will attack her with their
armies.[1]

5:18 [a]Jer 30:11; Amos 9:8   **5:19** [a]Deut 29:24–29; 1 Kgs 9:8–9; Jer 13:22; 16:10–13   [b]Jer 1:16; 2:13   [c]Deut 28:48; Jer 16:13
5:21 [a]Isa 6:9; Jer 6:10; Ezek 12:2; Matt 13:14; John 12:40; Acts 28:26; Rom 11:8   **5:22** [a]Deut 28:58; Ps 119:120; Jer 2:19; 10:7; [Rev
15:4]   [b]Job 26:10   **5:24** [a]Ps 147:8; Jer 14:22; [Matt 5:45]; Acts 14:17   [b]Deut 11:14; Joel 2:23; Jas 5:7   [c][Gen 8:22]   **5:25** [a]Jer 3:3
5:26 [a]Ps 10:9; Prov 1:11; Jer 18:22; Hab 1:15   **5:28** [a]Deut 32:15   [b]Isa 1:23; Jer 7:6; 22:3; Zech 7:10   [1]The meaning of this
Heb. word is uncertain.   **5:29** [a]Jer 5:9; Mal 3:5   **5:30** [a]Jer 23:14; Hos 6:10; 2 Tim 4:3   **5:31** [a]Jer 14:14; Ezek 13:6
[b]Mic 2:11   **6:1** [a]Neh 3:14   [b]Jer 4:6   [1]Heb. *ram's horn.*   **6:3** [1]Heb. *Shepherds and their flocks will attack it.*

They will encamp in siege all around
  her.
Each of them will [a]devastate the
  portion assigned to him.
4 They will say, '[a]Prepare to do [b]battle[1]
  against it!
Come on! Let's attack it at noon!'
But later they will say, 'Woe to us!
For the day is almost over,
and the shadows of evening are
  getting long.
5 So come on, let's go ahead and attack
  it by night
and destroy all its fortified buildings.'
6 All this is because the LORD of
  Heaven's Armies has said:
'Cut down the trees around Jerusalem
and build up a siege ramp against its
  walls.
This is the city that is to be punished.
Nothing but oppression happens in it.
7 As [a]a well continually pours out fresh
  water,
  so it continually pours out wicked
  deeds.[1]
Sounds of [b]violence and destruction
  echo throughout it.[2]
All I see are sick and wounded
  people.'
8 So take warning, Jerusalem,
or I will abandon you in disgust
and make you desolate,
a place where no one can live."

[9]This is what the LORD of Heaven's Armies said to me:

"Those who remain in Israel will be
like the grapes thoroughly gleaned
  from a vine.
So go over them again, as though you
  were a grape harvester
passing your hand over the branches
  one last time."

[10]I answered,

"Who would listen
if I spoke to them and warned them?
Their [a]ears are so closed

that [b]they cannot hear!
Indeed, the LORD's message is
  offensive to them.
They do not like it at all.
11 I am as full of anger as you are, LORD.
  [a]I am tired of trying to hold it in."

The LORD answered,

"Vent it, then, [b]on the children who
  play in the street
and on the young men who are
  gathered together.
Husbands and wives are to be
  included,
as well as the old and those who are
  advanced in years.
12 Their houses will be turned over to
  others
as will [a]their fields and their wives.
For I will unleash my power
against those who live in this land,"
  says the LORD.
13 "That is because, from the least
  important to the most important
  of them,
all of them are greedy for dishonest
  [a]gain.
Prophets and [b]priests alike,
all of them practice deceit.
14 They [a]offer only superficial help
for the harm my people have suffered.
They [b]say, 'Everything will be all
  right!'
But everything is not all right!
15 Are they [a]ashamed because they
  have done such shameful things?
No, they are not at all ashamed.
They do not even know how to blush!
So they will die, just like others have
  died.
They will be brought to ruin when I
  punish them,"
says the LORD.

[16]The LORD said to his people:

"You are standing at the crossroads.
  So consider your path.
Ask where the [a]old, reliable paths[1] are.

6:3 [a] 2 Kgs 25:1–4; Jer 4:17; 12:10   6:4 [a] Jer 51:27; Joel 3:9   [b] Jer 15:8; Zeph 2:4   [1] Heb. *Sanctify war.*   6:7 [a] Isa 57:20   [b] Ps 55:9
[1] Heb. *As a well makes cool/fresh its water, she makes cool/fresh her wickedness;* Ket. *cistern.*   [2] Heb. *Violence and
destruction are heard in it.*   6:10 [a] Exod 6:12; Jer 5:21; 7:26; [Acts 7:51]   [b] Jer 8:9; 20:8   6:11 [a] Jer 20:9   [b] Jer 9:21
6:12 [a] Deut 28:30; Jer 8:10; 38:22   6:13 [a] Isa 56:11; Jer 8:10; 22:17   [b] Jer 5:31; 23:11; Mic 3:5, 11   6:14 [a] Jer 8:11–15;
Ezek 13:10   [b] Jer 4:10; 23:17   6:15 [a] Jer 3:3; 8:12   6:16 [a] Isa 8:20; Jer 18:15; Mal 4:4; Luke 16:29
[1] Heb. *the ancient path;* i.e., the path the Lord set out in ancient times.

Ask where the path is that leads to
  blessing and follow it.
If you do, you will find [b]rest for your
  souls."
But they said, "We will not follow it!"

[17]The LORD said,

"I appointed prophets as [a]watchmen
  to warn you,[1] saying,
'Pay [b]attention to the warning sound
  of the trumpet!'"
But they said, "We will not pay
  attention!"

[18]So the LORD said,

"Hear, you nations!
Be witnesses and take note of what
  will happen to these people.
[19] [a]Hear this, you peoples of the earth:
'Take note! I am about to bring
  [b]disaster on [c]these people.
It will come as punishment for their
  scheming.
For they have paid no attention to
  what I have said,
and they have rejected my law.
[20] [a]I take no delight when they offer up
  to me
frankincense that comes [b]from
  Sheba
or [c]sweet-smelling cane imported
  from a faraway land.
I cannot accept the burnt offerings
  they bring me.
I get no pleasure from the sacrifices
  they offer to me.'"

[21]So, this is what the LORD says:

"I will assuredly make these people
  stumble to their doom.
Parents and children will stumble
  and fall to their destruction.
Friends and neighbors will die."

[22]This is what the LORD says:

"Beware! An army is coming from a
  land in the [a]north.

A mighty nation is stirring into
  action in faraway parts of the
  earth.
[23] Its soldiers are armed with bows and
  spears.
They are cruel and show no mercy.
They sound like the [a]roaring sea
as they ride forth on their horses.
Lined up in formation like men going
  into battle
to attack you, Daughter Zion."
[24] The people cry out, "We have heard
  reports about them.
We have become helpless with fear!
[a]Anguish grips us,
agony like that of a woman giving
  birth to a baby!
[25] Do not go out into the countryside.
Do not travel on the roads.
For the enemy is there with sword in
  hand.
They are spreading terror
  everywhere."
[26] So I said, "Oh, my dear people, put
  [a]on sackcloth
[b]and roll in ashes.
[c]Mourn with painful sobs
as though you had lost your only
  child.
For any moment now that
  destructive army
will come against us."

[27]The LORD [a]said to me,

"I have made you like a metal assayer
to test my people like ore.
You are to observe them
and evaluate how they behave."

[28]I reported,

"All of them are [a]the most stubborn
  of rebels![1]
They are as hard as [b]bronze or iron.
[c]They go about telling lies.
They all deal corruptly.
[29] The fiery bellows of judgment burn
  fiercely.
But there is too much dross to be
  removed.

6:16 [b]Matt 11:29   6:17 [a]Isa 21:11; 58:1; Jer 25:4; Ezek 3:17; Hab 2:1   [b]Deut 4:1 [1]Heb. *I appointed watchmen over you.*
6:19 [a]Isa 1:2   [b]Jer 19:3, 15   [c]Prov 1:31   6:20 [a]Ps 40:6; 50:7–9; Isa 1:11; 66:3; Amos 5:21; Mic 6:6–7   [b]Isa 60:6
[c]Isa 43:24   6:22 [a]Jer 1:15; 10:22; 50:41–43   6:23 [a]Isa 5:30   6:24 [a]Jer 4:31; 13:21; 49:24   6:26 [a]Jer 4:8
[b]Jer 25:34; Mic 1:10   [c]Amos 8:10; [Zech 12:10]   6:27 [a]Jer 1:18   6:28 [a]Jer 5:23   [b]Ezek 22:18
[c]Jer 9:4 [1]Or *arch rebels, hardened rebels*; lit. *rebels of rebels.*

The process of refining them has
 proved useless.
The wicked have not been purged.
[30] They are regarded as 'arejected silver'
 because the LORD rejects them."

Faulty Religion and Unethical Behavior Will Lead to Judgment

7 The LORD said to Jeremiah: [2]"aStand in the gate of the LORD's temple and proclaim this message: 'Listen to the LORD's message, all you people of Judah who have passed through these gates to worship the LORD. [3]The LORD of Heaven's Armies, the God of Israel, says: aChange the way you have been living and do what is right. If you do, I will allow you to continue to live in this land.[1] [4]aStop putting your confidence in the false belief that says, "We are safe! The temple of the LORD is here! The temple of the LORD is here! The temple of the LORD is here!"[1] [5]You must change the way you have been living and do what is right. You amust treat one another fairly. [6]Stop oppressing resident aforeigners who live in your land, children who have lost their fathers, and women who have lost their husbands. Stop killing innocent people in this land. Stop paying allegiance to other gods. That will only bring about your ruin. [7a]If you stop doing bthese things, I will allow you to continue to live in this land that I gave to your ancestors as a lasting possession.

[8]"'But just look at you! You are putting your confidence in a afalse belief that will not deliver you. [9a]You steal.[1] You murder. You commit adultery. You lie when you swear on oath. You sacrifice to the god Baal. You pay allegiance bto other gods whom you have not previously known. [10]Then you come aand stand in my presence in this temple bI have claimed as my own and say, "We are safe!" You think you are so safe that you go on doing all those hateful sins! [11]Do you think athis temple I have claimed as my own is to be a bhideout for robbers?[1] You had better take note! I have seen for myself what you have done! says the LORD. [12]So, go to the place in Shiloh where I allowed amyself to be worshiped in the early days. See bwhat I did to it because of the wicked things my people Israel did. [13]You also have done all these things, says the LORD, and aI have spoken to you over and over again. But you have not listened! You have refused to respond when I bcalled you to repent! [14]So I will destroy this temple that I have claimed as my own, this temple that you are trusting to protect you. I will destroy this place that I gave to you and your ancestors, just like I destroyed aShiloh. [15]And I will drive you out of my sight just like I drove out your relatives, athe people of Israel.'

[16]"But as for you, Jeremiah, ado not pray bfor these people. Do not raise a cry of prayer for them! Do not plead with me to save them, because I will not listen to you. [17]Do you see what they are doing in the towns of Judah and in the streets of Jerusalem? [18]Children are agathering firewood, fathers are building fires with it, and women are mixing dough to bake cakes to offer to the goddess they call the Queen of Heaven. They are also bpouring out drink offerings to other gods. They seem to do all this just to trouble me. [19a]But I am not really the one being troubled! says the LORD. Rather they are bringing trouble on themselves to their own shame![1] [20]So, the Sovereign LORD says, my raging fury will be poured out on this land. It will be poured out on human beings and animals, on trees and crops. And it will burn like a fire that cannot be extinguished.

[21]"The LORD of Heaven's Armies, the God of Israel, says to the people of Judah: 'You might as well go ahead and aadd the meat of your burnt offerings to that of the other sacrifices and eat it, too! [22a]Consider this:[1] When I spoke to your ancestors after I brought them out of Egypt, I did not merely give them commands about burnt offerings and sacrifices. [23]I also explicitly commanded them: "aObey me. bIf you do, I will be your God and you will be my people.

6:30 [a] Isa 1:22; Jer 7:29   7:2 [a] Jer 17:19; 26:2   7:3 [a] Jer 4:1; 18:11; 26:13   [1] Heb. place.   7:4 [a] Jer 7:8; Mic 3:11   [1] Heb. The temple of the LORD, the temple of the LORD, the temple of the LORD are these (i.e., these buildings); the triple repetition marks a kind of emphasis.   7:5 [a] 1 Kgs 6:12; Jer 21:12; 22:3   7:6 [a] Deut 6:14–15; Jer 13:10   7:7 [a] Deut 4:40   [b] Jer 3:18   7:8 [a] Jer 5:31; 14:13–14   7:9 [a] 1 Kgs 18:21; Hos 4:1-2; Zeph 1:5   [b] Exod 20:3; Jer 7:6; 19:4   [1] Heb. Will you steal . . . then say, 'We are safe'?   7:10 [a] Ezek 23:39   [b] Jer 7:11, 14; 32:34; 34:15   7:11 [a] Isa 56:7   [b] Matt 21:13; Mark 11:17; Luke 19:46   [1] Heb. Is this house . . . a den/cave of robbers in your eyes?   7:12 [a] Josh 18:1; Judg 18:31   [b] 1 Sam 4:10; Ps 78:60; Jer 26:6   7:13 [a] 2 Chr 36:15; Jer 11:7   [b] Prov 1:24; Isa 65:12; 66:4   7:14 [a] 1 Sam 4:10-11; Ps 78:60; Jer 26:6, 9   7:15 [a] Ps 78:67; Hos 7:13; 9:13; 12:1   7:16 [a] Exod 32:10; Deut 9:14; Jer 11:14   [b] Jer 15:1   7:18 [a] Jer 44:17   [b] Jer 19:13   7:19 [a] Deut 32:16, 21   [1] Heb. Is it not themselves to their own shame?; this rhetorical question expects a positive answer.   7:21 [a] Isa 1:11; Jer 6:20; Hos 8:13; Amos 5:21–22   7:22 [a] 1 Sam 15:22; Ps 51:16; [Hos 6:6]   [1] Heb. For.   7:23 [a] Exod 15:26; 16:32; Deut 6:3   [b] [Exod 19:5–6]; Lev 26:12; [Jer 11:4; 13:11]

Live exactly the way I tell you and things will go well with you." [24][a]But they did not listen to me or pay any attention to me. They [b]followed the stubborn inclinations of their own wicked hearts. They acted worse and worse instead of better. [25]From the time your ancestors departed the land of Egypt until now, I [a]sent my servants the prophets to you again and again, day after day.[1] [26][a]But your ancestors did not listen to me nor pay attention to me. They became [b]obstinate and were more wicked than even their own forefathers.'"

[27]Then the LORD said to me, "When [a]you tell them all this, they will not listen to you. When you call out to them, they will not respond to you. [28]So tell them: 'This is a nation that has [a]not obeyed the LORD their God and has not accepted correction. [b]Faithfulness is nowhere to be found in it. These people do not even profess it anymore.[1] [29]So mourn, you people of this nation. [a]Cut off your hair and throw it away. Sing a song of mourning on the hilltops. For the LORD has decided to reject and forsake this generation that has provoked his wrath!'"

[30]The LORD says, "I have rejected them because [a]the people of Judah have done what I consider evil. They have set up their disgusting idols in the temple that I have claimed for my own and have defiled it. [31]They have also built places of worship in a [a]place called Topheth in the Valley of Ben Hinnom so that they can [b]sacrifice their sons and daughters by fire. That is something [c]I never commanded them to do! Indeed, it never even entered my mind to command such a thing! [32]So, watch out!'[1] says [a]the LORD. "The time will soon come when people will no longer call those places Topheth [b]or the Valley of Ben Hinnom. But they will call that valley the Valley of Slaughter, and they will bury so many people in Topheth that they will run out of room. [33]Then the dead [a]bodies of these people will be left on the ground for the birds and wild animals to eat. There will not be any survivors to scare them away. [34]I will put an [a]end to [b]the sounds of joy and gladness or the glad celebration of brides and grooms throughout the towns of Judah and the streets of Jerusalem. For the whole land will become a desolate wasteland."

8 The LORD says, "When that time comes, the bones of the kings of Judah and its leaders, the bones of the priests and prophets, and of all the other people who lived in Jerusalem will be dug up from their graves. [2]They will be spread out and exposed to the sun, the moon, and the stars.[1] These are things they adored and served, things to [a]which they paid allegiance, from which they sought guidance and worshiped. The bones of these people will [b]never be regathered and reburied. They will be like manure used to fertilize the ground. [3]However, I will leave some of these wicked people alive and banish them to other places. But wherever these people who survive may go, they will wish they had [a]died rather than lived," says the LORD of Heaven's Armies.

Willful Disregard of God Will Lead to Destruction

[4]The LORD said to me,

"Tell them, 'The LORD says,
Do people not get back up when they
  fall down?
Do they not turn around when they
  go the wrong way?
[5] Why, then, do these people of
  Jerusalem
continually turn away from me in
  apostasy?
[a]They hold fast to their deception.
[b]They refuse to turn back to me.
[6] I have [a]listened to them very
  carefully,
but they do not speak honestly.
[b]None of them regrets the evil he has
  done.
None of them says, "I have done
  wrong!"
All of them persist in their own
  wayward course

7:24 [a]Ps 81:11; Jer 11:8 [b]Deut 29:19; Jer 9:14 **7:25** [a]2 Chr 36:15; Jer 25:4; 29:19; Mark 12:1–10; Luke 11:47–49 [1]MT *day.* **7:26** [a]Jer 11:8 [b]Neh 9:17 **7:27** [a]Jer 1:7; 26:2; 37:14–15; 43:1–4; Ezek 2:7 **7:28** [a]Jer 5:3 [b]Jer 9:3 [1]Heb. *Faithfulness has vanished. It is cut off from their lips.* **7:29** [a]Job 1:20; Isa 15:2; Jer 48:37; Mic 1:16 **7:30** [a]2 Kgs 21:4; 2 Chr 33:3–5, 7; Jer 32:34–35; Ezek 7:20; Dan 9:27; 11:31 **7:31** [a]2 Kgs 23:10; Jer 19:5; 32:35 [b]Lev 18:21; 2 Kgs 17:17; Ps 106:38 [c]Deut 17:3 **7:32** [a]Jer 19:6 [b]2 Kgs 23:10; Jer 19:11 [1]Heb. *Therefore, behold!* **7:33** [a]Jer 9:22; 19:11; Ezek 6:5 **7:34** [a]Isa 24:7–8; Jer 16:9; 25:10; Ezek 26:13; Hos 2:11; Rev 18:23 [b]Lev 26:33; Isa 1:7; Jer 4:27 **8:2** [a]2 Kgs 23:5; Jer 19:13; Ezek 8:16; Zeph 1:5; Acts 7:42 [b]Jer 22:19 [1]Some wss *and all the host of heaven.* **8:3** [a]Job 3:21–22; 7:15–16; Jonah 4:3; Rev 9:6 **8:5** [a]Jer 9:6 [b]Jer 5:3 **8:6** [a]Ps 14:2; [Isa 30:18; Mal 3:16; 2 Pet 3:9] [b]Ezek 22:30; Mic 7:2; Rev 9:20

like a horse charging recklessly into
    battle.
7 Even [a]the stork knows
when it is time to move on.[1]
The turtledove, swallow, and crane
recognize the normal times for their
    migration.
But [b]my people pay no attention
to[2] what I, the LORD, require of them.
8 How can you say, "We are wise!
We have the law of the LORD"?
The truth is, those who teach it have
    used their writings
to make it say what it does not really
    mean.
9 Your wise men will be put to shame.
[a]They will be dumbfounded and be
    brought to judgment.
Since they have rejected the LORD's
    message,
[b]what wisdom do they really have?
10 So [a]I will give their wives to other men
and their fields to new owners.
For from the least important to the
    most important of them,
all of them are greedy for dishonest
    [b]gain.
Prophets and priests alike
all practice deceit.
11 They [a]offer only superficial help
for the hurt my dear people have
    suffered.
They say, "Everything will be all
    [b]right!"
But everything is not all right.[1]
12 Are they [a]ashamed because they
    have done such disgusting things?
No, they are not at all ashamed!
They do not even know how to blush.
So they will die just like others have
    died.
They will be brought to ruin when I
    punish them,
says the LORD.
13 I will take away their harvests, says
    the LORD.
There will be no grapes [a]on their
    vines.
There will be no [b]figs on their fig
    trees.

Even the leaves on their trees will
    wither.
The crops that I gave them will be
    taken away.'"

Jeremiah Laments over the Coming Destruction

14 The people say,

"Why are we just sitting here?
Let us gather [a]together inside the
    fortified cities.
Let us at least die there fighting,
since the LORD our God has
    condemned us to die.
He has condemned us to drink the
poison [b]waters of judgment
because we have sinned against him.
15 We [a]hoped for good fortune, but
    nothing good has come of it.
We hoped for a time of relief, but
    instead we experience terror.
16 The snorting of the enemy's horses
is already being heard in the city of
    [a]Dan.
The sound of the neighing of their
    stallions
causes the whole land to tremble
    with fear.
They are coming to destroy the land
    and everything in it.
They are coming to destroy the cities
    and everyone who lives in them."

17 The LORD says,

"Yes indeed, I am sending an enemy
    against you
that will be like poisonous snakes
    that cannot be [a]charmed away.[1]
And they will inflict fatal wounds on
    you."

18 Then I said,

"There is no cure for my grief!
I am sick at heart!
19 I [a]hear my dear people crying out
throughout the length and breadth
    of the land.

8:7 [a] Prov 6:6–8; Song 2:12; Isa 1:3; Matt 16:2–3   [b] Jer 5:4; 9:3   [1] Heb. *its appointed time.*   [2] Heb. *do not know.*   8:9 [a] Isa 19:11; Jer 6:15; [1 Cor 1:27]   [b] Isa 44:25; Jer 4:22   8:10 [a] Deut 28:30; Amos 5:11; Zeph 1:13   [b] Isa 56:11; 57:17; Jer 6:13   8:11 [a] Jer 6:14   [b] Ezek 13:10   [1] Heb. *They say, 'Peace! Peace!' and there is no peace!*   8:12 [a] Ps 52:1, 7; Isa 3:9; Jer 3:3; 6:15; Zeph 3:5   8:13 [a] Jer 5:17; 7:20; Joel 1:17   [b] Matt 21:19; Luke 13:6   8:14 [a] Jer 4:5   [b] Deut 29:18; Ps 69:21; Jer 9:15; Lam 3:19; Matt 27:34   8:15 [a] Jer 14:19   8:16 [a] Judg 18:29; Jer 4:15   8:17 [a] Ps 58:4–5   [1] Heb. *I am sending against you snakes, poisonous ones which cannot be charmed.*   8:19 [a] Isa 39:3; Jer 5:15

They are crying, 'Is the LORD no
  longer in Zion?
Is her divine King[1] no longer there?'"
The LORD answers,
"Why then do they provoke me to
  anger with their images,
with their worthless foreign idols?"
20 "They cry, 'Harvest time has come
  and gone and the summer is over,
and still we have not been
  delivered.'
21 [a]My heart is crushed because my
  dear people are being crushed.
I go about crying and [b]grieving. I am
  overwhelmed with dismay.
22 There is still medicinal [a]ointment
  available in Gilead!
There is still a physician there![1]
Why then have my dear people
  not been restored to health?

9 I [a]wish that my head were a well full
  of water
and my eyes were a fountain full of
  tears!
If they were, I could cry day and
  night
for those of my dear people who have
  been killed.
2 I wish I had a lodging place in [a]the
  wilderness
where I could spend some time
  like a weary traveler.
Then I would desert my people
and walk away from them
because they are all unfaithful to
  God,
a congregation[1] of people that has
  been disloyal to him."

The Lord Laments That He Has No Choice but to Judge Them

3 The LORD says,

"These people are like soldiers who
  have readied their bows.
Their tongues are always ready to
  shoot out lies.
[a]They have become powerful in the
  land,
but they have not done so by honest
  means.
Indeed, they do one evil [b]thing after
  another
and [c]do not pay attention to me.[1]
4 [a]Everyone must be on his guard
  around his friends.
He must not even trust any of his
  relatives.
For every one of them will find some
  way to cheat him.
And all his friends will [b]tell lies about
  him.
5 One friend [a]deceives another,
and no one tells the truth.
These people have trained
  themselves to tell lies.
They do wrong and are unable to
  repent.
6 They do one act of violence after
  another,
and one deceitful thing after
  another.[1]
They refuse to pay attention to me,"
says the LORD.

7 Therefore the LORD of Heaven's [a]Armies
says:

"I will now purify them in the fires of
  affliction and test them.
The wickedness of my dear people
  has left me no choice.
What else can I do?'[1]
8 Their tongues are like deadly arrows.
They are always telling [a]lies.
Friendly [b]words for their neighbors
  come from their mouths,
but their minds are thinking up
  ways to trap them.[1]
9 I will certainly punish them for
  doing such things!" says the
  LORD.
"I will certainly bring retribution
  on such [a]a nation as this!"

8:19 [1]Heb. *her King.*   8:21 [a]Jer 9:1 [b]Jer 14:2; Joel 2:6; Nah 2:10   8:22 [a]Gen 37:25; Jer 46:11 [1]Heb. *Is there no balm in Gilead? Is there no physician there?*; these rhetorical questions expect a positive answer.   9:1 [a]Isa 22:4; Jer 10:19; Lam 2:18   9:2 [a]Jer 5:7–8; 23:10; Hos 4:2 [1]Or *bunch.*   9:3 [a]Ps 64:3; Isa 59:4; Jer 9:8; Hos 4:1–2 [b]Jer 4:22; 13:23 [c]Judg 2:10; 1 Sam 2:12; Jer 4:22; Hos 4:1; 1 Cor 15:34 [1]Or *do not acknowledge me;* Heb. *do not know me.*   9:4 [a]Ps 12:2; Prov 26:24–25; Jer 9:8; Mic 7:5–6 [b]Ps 15:3; Prov 10:18; Jer 6:28   9:5 [a]Ps 36:3–4; Isa 59:4   9:6 [1]MT (vv. 5d–6b) *doing wrong they weary themselves. Your sitting in the midst of deceit; in deceit they refuse to know me;* LXX (vv. 5d–6b) *they do wrong and they do not cease to turn themselves around. Usury upon usury and deceit upon deceit. They do not want to know me.*   9:7 [a]Isa 1:25; Jer 6:27; Mal 3:3 [1]Heb. *For how else shall I deal because of the wickedness of the daughter of my people;* MT omits *wickedness.*   9:8 [a]Ps 12:2 [b]Ps 55:21 [1]Heb. *With his mouth a person speaks peace to his neighbor, but in his heart he sets an ambush for him.*   9:9 [a]Isa 1:24; Jer 5:9, 29

The Coming Destruction Calls for Mourning

[10] I said,

"I will weep and mourn [a] for the
grasslands on the mountains;
I will sing a mournful song for the
pastures in the wilderness
because they are so scorched no one
travels through them.
The sound of livestock is no longer
heard there.
Even the birds in the sky and the
wild animals in the fields
have fled and are gone."

[11] The LORD [a] said,

"I will [b] make Jerusalem a heap of
ruins.
Jackals will make their home there. [1]
I will destroy the towns of Judah
so that no one will be able to live in
them."

[12] I said,

"[a] Who is wise enough to understand
why this has happened?
Who has a word from the LORD that
can explain it?
Why does the land lie in ruins?
Why is it as scorched as a desert
through which no one travels?"

[13] The LORD answered, "This has happened because these people have rejected my laws that I gave them. They have [a] not obeyed me or followed those laws. [14] Instead they have followed the stubborn inclinations of their own hearts. They have paid allegiance to the gods called Baal, [1] as their fathers taught them to do. [15] So then, listen to what I, the LORD of Heaven's Armies, the God of Israel, say, 'I will make these people [a] eat the bitter food of suffering and drink the poison water of judgment. [16] I will [a] scatter them among nations that neither they nor their ancestors have known anything about. I will send people chasing after them with swords until I have destroyed them.'"

[17] The LORD of Heaven's Armies told me to say to this people:

"Take note of what I say.
Call for [a] the women who mourn for
the dead!
Summon those who are the most
skilled at it!"
[18] I said, "Indeed, let them come quickly
and sing a song of [a] mourning for us.
Let them wail loudly until tears
stream from our own eyes
and our eyelids overflow with water.
[19] For the sound of wailing is soon to be
heard in Zion,
'We are utterly ruined! We are
completely disgraced!
For we have left [a] our land,
for our houses have been torn down!'"

[20] I said,

"So now, you wailing women, listen to
the LORD's message.
Open your ears to the message from
his mouth.
Teach your daughters this mournful
song,
and let every woman teach her
neighbor this lament.
[21] 'Death has climbed in through our
windows.
It has entered into our fortified
houses.
It has taken away our children who
play in [a] the streets.
It has taken away our young men
who gather in the city squares.'
[22] Tell your daughters and neighbors,
'The LORD says:
"The dead bodies of people will lie
scattered everywhere
like manure scattered on [a] a field.
They will lie scattered on the ground
like grain that has been cut down but
has not been gathered."'"

[23] The LORD says,

"Wise people should not boast that
they are wise.

9:10 [a] Jer 4:26; Hos 4:3   9:11 [a] Isa 25:2; Jer 19:3, 8; 26:9   [b] Isa 13:22; 34:13   [1] Heb. a heap of ruins, a haunt for jackals.
9:12 [a] Ps 107:43; Isa 42:23; Hos 14:9   9:13 [a] Jer 3:25; 7:24   9:14 [1] Heb. the Baals; either the pagan gods or the
images of Baal.   9:15 [a] Ps 80:5   9:16 [a] Lev 26:33; Deut 28:64; Jer 15:2-4   9:17 [a] 2 Chr 35:25; Job 3:8;
Eccl 12:5; Amos 5:16; Matt 9:23   9:18 [a] Isa 22:4; Jer 9:1; 14:17   9:19 [a] Lev 18:28   9:21 [a] 2 Chr 36:17;
Jer 6:11; 18:21; Ezek 9:5-6   9:22 [a] Ps 83:10; Isa 5:25; Jer 8:1-2

Powerful people should not boast
that they are [a]powerful.
Rich people should not boast that
they are rich.
24 If people want to boast, they should
boast about this:
They should boast that they
understand and know me.
They should boast that they know
and understand
that I, the LORD, act out of
faithfulness, fairness, and justice
in the earth
and that I desire people to do these
things,"
says the LORD.

25 The LORD says, "Watch out![1] The [a]time is soon coming when I will punish all those who are circumcised only in the flesh. 26 That is, I will punish the Egyptians, the Judeans, the Edomites, the Ammonites, the Moabites, and all the desert people who [a]cut their hair short at the temples. I will do so because none of the people of those nations are really [b]circumcised in the LORD's sight. Moreover, none of the people of Israel are circumcised when it comes to their hearts."

The Lord, not Idols, Is the Only Worthy Object of Worship

10 You people of Israel, listen to what the LORD has to say to you. 2 The LORD says:

"[a]Do not start following pagan
religious practices.
Do not be in awe of signs that occur
in the sky
even though the nations hold them
in awe.
3 For the religion of these people is
worthless.
They cut down a tree in the forest,
and a craftsman makes it into an idol
with his tools.
4 He decorates it with overlays of
silver and gold.
He uses hammer and nails to [a]fasten
it together

so that it will not fall over.
5 Such idols are like scarecrows in a
cucumber field.
[a]They cannot talk.
They must be [b]carried
because [c]they cannot walk.
Do not be afraid of them
because they cannot hurt you.
And they do not have any power to
help you."
6 I said,

"There is no one [a]like you, LORD.
You are great,
and you are renowned for your
power.
7 Everyone should revere you, [a]O King
of all nations,[1]
because you deserve to be revered.
For there is no one like you
[b]among any of the wise people of the
nations nor among any of their
kings.
8 The people of those nations [a]are
both stupid and foolish.
Instruction from a wooden idol is
worthless!
9 Hammered-out silver is brought
from Tarshish
and [a]gold is brought from Ufaz[1] to
cover those idols.
[b]They are the handiwork of
carpenters and goldsmiths.
They are clothed in blue and purple
clothes.
They are all made by skillful workers.
10 The LORD is [a]the only true God.
He is the living God and the
[b]everlasting King.
When he shows his anger, the earth
shakes.
None of the nations can stand up to
his fury.
11 You people of Israel should tell those
nations this:
'[a]These gods did not make heaven
and earth.
They will disappear from the earth
and from under the heavens.'[1]

[12] The LORD is the one who by his
power made the earth.
He is the one who by his wisdom
[a]established the world.
And by his understanding, he spread
out the skies.
[13] When his voice thunders, the
heavenly ocean roars.
[a]He makes the clouds rise from the
far-off horizons.
He makes the lightning flash out in
the midst of the rain.
He unleashes the wind from the
places where he stores it.
[14] All these [a]idolaters[1] will prove to be
[b]stupid and ignorant.
[c]Every goldsmith will be disgraced by
the idol he made.
[d]For the image he forges is merely a
sham.[2]
There is no breath in any of those
idols.
[15] They are worthless, mere objects to
be mocked.
When the time comes to punish
them, they will be destroyed.
[16] The LORD, who is [a]the inheritance
of Jacob's descendants, is not like
them.
He is the one who created everything.
And the people of [b]Israel are those
[c]he claims as his own.
His name is the LORD of Heaven's
Armies."

Jeremiah Laments for and Prays for the People Soon to Be Judged

[17] "Gather your belongings [a]together
and prepare to leave the land,
you people of Jerusalem who are
being besieged.[1]
[18] For the LORD says, 'I will now [a]throw
out
those who live in this land.
I will bring so much trouble on them
[b]that they will actually feel it.'
[19] And I cried out, 'We are [a]doomed!
Our wound is severe!'
We once thought, 'This is [b]only an
[c]illness.

And we will be able to bear it.'
[20] [a]But our tents have been destroyed.
The ropes that held them in place
have been ripped apart.
Our children are gone and are not
coming back.
There is [b]no survivor to put our tents
back up,
no one left to hang their tent
curtains in place.
[21] For our leaders[1] are stupid.
They have not sought the LORD's
advice.
So they do not act wisely,
and the people they are responsible
for have all been [a]scattered.
[22] Listen! News is coming even now.
The rumble of a great army is heard
approaching from a land in the
[a]north.
It is coming to turn the towns of
Judah into rubble,
places [b]where only jackals live.
[23] LORD, we know that people do not
control their own [a]destiny.
It is not in their power to determine
what will happen to them.
[24] [a]Correct us, LORD, but only in due
measure.
Do not punish us in anger, or you will
reduce us to nothing.
[25] [a]Vent your anger on the nations that
do not acknowledge you.
Vent it on the peoples [b]who do not
worship you.[1]
For they have [c]destroyed the people
of Jacob.
They have completely destroyed
them
and left their homeland in utter
ruin."

The People Have Violated Their Covenant with God

11 The LORD said to Jeremiah: [2]"Hear the
terms of the covenant I made with
Israel and pass them on to the people of
Judah and the citizens of Jerusalem. [3]Tell
them that the LORD, the God of Israel, says,
'Anyone who does not keep the terms of the

10:12 [a] Ps 93:1   10:13 [a] Job 38:34   10:14 [a] Jer 51:17   [b] Prov 30:2   [c] Isa 42:17; 44:11   [d] Hab 2:18   [1] Heb. *Every man.*   [2] Or *nothing but a phony god*; Heb. *a lie/falsehood.*   10:16 [a] Ps 16:5; Jer 51:19; Lam 3:24   [b] Deut 32:9; Ps 74:2   [c] Isa 47:4   10:17 [a] Jer 6:1   [1] Heb. *you who are living in/under siege.*   10:18 [a] 1 Sam 25:29; 2 Chr 36:20   [b] Ezek 6:10   10:19 [a] Jer 8:21   [b] Ps 77:10   [c] Mic 7:9   10:20 [a] Jer 4:20; Lam 2:4   [b] Jer 31:15; Lam 1:5   10:21 [a] Jer 23:2   [1] Heb. *the shepherds.*   10:22 [a] Jer 5:15   [b] Jer 9:11   10:23 [a] Prov 16:1; 20:24   10:24 [a] Ps 6:1; 38:1; Jer 30:11   10:25 [a] Ps 79:6–7; Zeph 3:8   [b] Job 18:21; 1 Thess 4:5; [2 Thess 1:8]   [c] Jer 8:16   [1] Heb. *who do not call on your name.*

covenant will be under a [a]curse. [4]Those are the terms that I charged your ancestors to keep[1] when I brought them out of Egypt, that place that was like an iron-smelting furnace. I said at that time, "[a]Obey me and carry out the terms of the covenant exactly as I commanded you. If you do, you will be my people and I will be your God. [5]Then I will keep the [a]promise I swore on [b]oath to your ancestors to give them a land flowing with milk and honey."[1] That is the very land that you still live in today.'" And I responded, "Amen. Let it be so, Lord."

[6]The Lord said to me, "Announce all the following words in the towns of Judah [a]and in the streets of Jerusalem: 'Listen to the terms of my covenant with you and carry them out! [7]For [a]I solemnly warned your ancestors to obey me. I warned them again and again, ever since I delivered them out of Egypt until this very day. [8a]But they did not listen to me or pay any attention to me! Each [b]one of them followed the stubborn inclinations of his own wicked heart. So I brought on them all the punishments threatened in the covenant because they did not carry out its terms as I commanded them to do.'"

[9]The Lord [a]said to me, "The people of Judah and the citizens of Jerusalem have plotted rebellion against me. [10]They have gone back to [a]the evil ways of their ancestors of old who refused to obey what I told them. They, too, have paid allegiance to other gods and worshiped them. Both the nation of Israel and the nation of Judah have violated the covenant I made with their ancestors. [11]So I, the Lord, say this: 'I will soon bring disaster on them that they will not be able to escape! When they cry out to me for help, I will not listen to them. [12]Then those living in the towns of Judah and in Jerusalem will go and cry out for [a]help to the gods to whom they have been sacrificing. However, those gods will by no means be able[1] to save them when disaster strikes them. [13]This is in spite of the fact that the people of Judah have as many gods as they have [a]towns and the citizens of Jerusalem have set up as many altars to sacrifice to that disgusting god, Baal, as they have streets in the city!' [14]But as for you, Jeremiah, [a]do not pray for these people. Do not raise a cry of prayer for them. For I will not listen to them when they call out to me for help when disaster strikes them."[1]

[15]The Lord says to the people of Judah,

"[a]What right do you have to be in my
    temple, my beloved people?
Many of you have [b]done wicked
    things.[1]
Can your acts of treachery be so
    easily canceled by [c]sacred offerings
that you take [d]joy in doing evil even
    while you make them?

[16] I, the Lord, once called you a
    [a]thriving olive tree,
one that produced beautiful fruit.
But I will set you on fire,
fire that will blaze with a mighty
    roar.
Then all your branches will be good
    for nothing.

[17] For though I, the Lord of Heaven's
    Armies, planted you in the land,
I now decree that disaster will come
    on you
because the nations of Israel and
    Judah have done evil
and have made me angry by offering
    sacrifices to the god Baal."

A Plot against Jeremiah Is Revealed and He Complains of Injustice

[18] The Lord gave me knowledge, that I
    might have understanding.
Then he showed me what the people
    were doing.

[19] Before this I had been like [a]a docile
    lamb ready to be led to [b]the
    slaughter.
I did not know they were making
    plans to kill me.[1]
I did not know they were saying,
"Let's destroy the tree along with its
    fruit!

11:3 [a] Deut 27:26; [Jer 17:5]; Gal 3:10   11:4 [a] Lev 26:3; Deut 11:27; Jer 7:23 [1] Heb. *does not listen . . . this covenant which I commanded your fathers.*   11:5 [a] Exod 13:5; Deut 7:12; Ps 105:9; Jer 32:22 [b] Exod 3:8 [1] Or *a land of fertile fields and fine pastures.*   11:6 [a] Deut 17:19; [Rom 2:13]; Jas 1:22   11:7 [a] Jer 35:15   11:8 [a] Jer 7:26 [b] Jer 13:10   11:9 [a] Ezek 22:25; Hos 6:9   11:10 [a] 1 Sam 15:11; Jer 3:10–11; Ezek 20:18   11:12 [a] Deut 32:37; Jer 44:17 [1] Heb. *saving they will not save;* an emphatic Heb. construction.   11:13 [a] 2 Kgs 23:13; Jer 2:28   11:14 [a] Exod 32:10; Jer 7:16; 14:11; [1 John 5:16] [1] Some wss *on account of.*   11:15 [a] Ps 50:16 [b] Ezek 16:25 [c] [Titus 1:15] [d] Prov 2:14 [1] Heb. *her doing the wicked thing the many* or *doing it, the wicked thing, the many.* For an explanation of this uncertain line, see *NET Bible, Full Notes Edition.*   11:16 [a] Ps 52:8; [Rom 11:17]   11:19 [a] Ps 83:4; Jer 18:18 [b] Ps 27:13 [1] Heb. *against me.*

Let's remove Jeremiah[2] from the
world of the living
so people will not even be reminded
of him anymore."

20So I said,

"O LORD of Heaven's Armies, you are
a just judge!
You [a]examine people's hearts and
minds.
I want to see you [b]pay them back for
what they have done
because I trust you to vindicate my
cause."

21Then the LORD told me about some men
from [a]Anathoth[1] who were threatening to
kill me.[2] They had threatened, "Stop prophesying in the name of the LORD or we will
kill you!" 22So the LORD of Heaven's Armies
said, "I will surely punish them! Their young
men will be killed in battle.[1] Their sons and
daughters will [a]die of starvation. 23Not one
of [a]them will survive. I will bring disaster on
those men from Anathoth who threatened
you. A day of reckoning is coming for them."

Jeremiah Appeals to God

12 LORD, you have always been fair
whenever I have complained to you.
However, I would like to speak with
you about the disposition of
justice.
Why [a]are wicked people successful?[1]
[b]Why do all dishonest people have
such easy lives?
2 You plant them like trees, and they
put down their roots.
They grow prosperous and are very
fruitful.
They always talk about [a]you,
but they really care nothing about
you.
3 But you, LORD, [a]know all about me.
You watch me and [b]test my devotion
to you.
Drag [c]these wicked men away like
sheep to be slaughtered!

Appoint a time when they will be
killed!
4 How long must [a]the land be parched
and [b]the grass in every field be
withered?
How long must the animals and the
birds die
because of the wickedness of the
people who live in this land?
[c]For these people boast,
"God will not see what happens to
us."[1]

God Answers Jeremiah

5The LORD answered,

"If you have raced on foot against
men and [a]they have worn you out,
how will you be able to compete with
horses?
And if you feel secure only in safe
and open country,
how will you manage in the thick
undergrowth along the Jordan
River?
6 As a matter of fact, even [a]your own
brothers
and the members of your own family
have betrayed you as well.
Even they have plotted to [b]do away
with you.
So do not trust them even when they
say kind things to you.

7 "I will abandon my nation.
I will forsake the people I call my
own.
I will turn my beloved people
over to the power of their enemies.
8 The people I call my own have turned
on me
like a lion in the forest.
They have roared defiantly at me,
so I will treat them as though I [a]hate
them.[1]
9 The people I call my own attack me
like birds of prey or like hyenas.[1]
But other birds of prey are all around
them.

11:19 [2] Heb. *cut it* [or *him*] *off.*   11:20 [a] 1 Sam 16:7; 1 Chr 28:9; Ps 7:9   [b] Jer 15:15   11:21 [a] Jer 1:1; 12:5–6   [1] Heb. *the men of Anathoth.*   [2] MT *your life.*   11:22 [a] Jer 9:21   [1] Heb. *will die by the sword.*   11:23 [a] Jer 23:12; Hos 9:7; Mic 7:4   12:1 [a] Ezra 9:15; Ps 51:4; Jer 11:20   [b] Job 12:6; Jer 5:27–28; Hab 1:4; Mal 3:15   [1] Heb. *Why does the way* [= course of life] *of the wicked prosper?*   12:2 [a] Isa 29:13; Ezek 33:31; Matt 15:8; Mark 7:6   12:3 [a] Ps 17:3   [b] Ps 7:9; 11:5; Jer 11:20   [c] Jer 17:18; 50:27; Jas 5:5   12:4 [a] Jer 23:10; Hos 4:3   [b] Jer 9:10; Hos 4:3; Hab 3:17   [c] Ps 107:34   [1] LXX *God does not see what we are doing.*   12:5 [a] Josh 3:15; 1 Chr 12:15   12:6 [a] Gen 37:4–11; Job 6:15; Ps 69:8; Jer 9:4–5   [b] Ps 12:2; Prov 26:25   12:8 [a] Hos 9:15; Amos 6:8   [1] Or *so I will reject her.*   12:9 [1] Or *like speckled birds of prey.*

Let all the nations gather together
like wild beasts.
Let them [a]come and destroy these
people I call my own.
10 Many foreign [a]rulers will ruin the
land where I planted [b]my people.
They will trample all over my chosen
land.
They will turn my beautiful land
into a desolate wilderness.
11 They will lay it waste.
It will lie parched and [a]empty
before me.
The whole land will be laid waste,
but [b]no one living in it will pay any
heed.
12 A destructive army will come
marching
over the hilltops in the wilderness.
For the LORD will use them as his
destructive weapon
against everyone from one end of the
land to the other.
No one will be safe.
13 My people will sow wheat, but will
harvest weeds.
[a]They will work until they are
exhausted, but will get nothing
from it.
They will be disappointed in their
harvests
because the LORD will take them
away in his fierce anger.[1]

14 "I, the LORD, also have something to
say concerning the wicked nations who
surround my land and have attacked and
[a]plundered the land that I gave to my people as a permanent possession. I say: 'I will
[b]uproot the people of those nations from
their land, and I will free the people of
Judah who have been taken there.'[1] 15 But after I have uprooted [a]the people of those nations, I will relent [b]and have pity on them.
I will restore the people of each of those
nations to their own lands and to their
own country. 16 But they must make sure
[a]to learn to follow the religious practices of
my people. Once they taught my people to

swear their oaths using the name of the god
Baal. But then, they must swear oaths using
my name, saying, "As surely as the LORD
lives, I swear." If they do these things, then
they will be [b]included among the people I
call my own. 17 But I will completely uproot
and destroy any of those nations that will
not pay [a]heed,'" says the LORD.

An Object Lesson from Ruined Linen Shorts

13 The LORD said to me, "Go and buy
some linen shorts[1] and put them on.
Do not put them in water." 2 So I bought the
shorts in keeping with the LORD's instructions and put them on.[1] 3 Then the LORD's
message came to me again, 4 "Take the
shorts that you bought and are wearing and
go at once to Perath. Bury the shorts there
in a crack in the rocks." 5 So I went and buried them at Perath as the LORD had ordered
me to do. 6 Many days later the LORD said to
me, "Go at once to Perath and get the shorts
I ordered you to bury there." 7 So I went to
Perath and dug up the shorts from the place
where I had buried them. I found that they
were ruined; they were good for nothing.

8 Then the LORD's message came to me,
9 "I, the LORD, say: '[a]This shows how I will
ruin the highly exalted position in which
Judah and Jerusalem take [b]pride. 10 These
wicked people [a]refuse to obey what I have
said. They [b]follow the stubborn inclinations
of their own hearts and pay allegiance to
other gods by worshiping and serving them.
So they will become just like these linen
shorts that are good for nothing. 11 For,' I
say, 'just as shorts cling tightly to a person's
body, so I bound [a]the whole nation of Israel
and the whole nation of Judah tightly to
me.' I intended [b]for them to be my special
people and to bring me fame, [c]honor, and
praise. But they would [d]not obey me.

12 "So tell them, 'The LORD, the God of
Israel, says: "Every wine jar is made to be
filled with wine."' And they will probably
say to you, 'Do you not think we know that
every wine jar is supposed to be filled with
wine?' 13 Then tell them, 'The LORD says:

12:9 [a] Lev 26:22   12:10 [a] Jer 6:3; 23:1   [b] Ps 80:8–16; Isa 5:1–7   12:11 [a] Jer 10:22; 22:6   [b] Isa 42:25   12:13 [a] Lev 26:16; Deut
28:38; Mic 6:15; Hag 1:6   [1] Heb. *be disappointed in their harvests from the fierce anger of the LORD.*   12:14 [a] Jer 2:3; 50:11–12;
Zech 2:8   [b] Deut 30:3; Ps 106:47; Isa 11:11–16; Jer 32:37   [1] Heb. *I will uproot the house of Judah from their midst.*   12:15 [a] Jer
31:20; Lam 3:32; Ezek 28:25   [b] Amos 9:14   12:16 [a] [Jer 4:2]; Zeph 1:5   [b] [Eph 2:20–21; 1 Pet 2:5]   12:17 [a] Ps 2:8–12; Isa 60:12
13:1 [1] Or *girdle, waistband, waistcloth, sash, belt, loincloth*; a short, skirt-like garment reaching from the waist to the
knees.   13:2 [1] Heb. *on my loins.*   13:9 [a] Lev 26:19   [b] [Isa 2:10–17; 23:9]; Zeph 3:11   13:10 [a] Jer 16:12   [b] Jer 7:24; 16:12
13:11 [a] [Exod 19:5–6; Deut 32:10–11]   [b] Jer 33:9   [c] Isa 43:21   [d] Ps 81:11; Jer 7:13, 24, 26

"[a]I will soon fill all the people who live in this land with stupor. I will also fill the kings from David's dynasty,[1] the priests, the prophets, and the citizens of Jerusalem with stupor. [14]And [a]I will smash them like wine bottles against one another, children and parents alike. I will not show any pity, mercy, or compassion. Nothing will keep me from destroying them,' says the LORD."

[15]Then I said to the people of Judah:

"Listen and pay attention! Do not be
  arrogant!
For the LORD has spoken.
[16] [a]Show the LORD your God the
  respect that is due him.
Do it before he brings the [b]darkness
  of disaster.
Do it before you stumble into
  distress
like a traveler on the mountains at
  twilight.
Do it before he turns the light of
  deliverance you [c]hope for
into [d]the darkness and gloom of
  exile.
[17] But if you will not pay attention to
  this warning,
I will [a]weep alone because of your
  arrogant pride.
I will weep bitterly, and my eyes will
  overflow with tears
because you, the LORD's flock, will be
  carried into exile."

[18]The LORD told me:

"Tell [a]the king and the queen mother,
'Surrender your thrones,
for your glorious crowns
will be removed from your heads.
[19] The gates of the towns in southern
  Judah will be shut tight.
No one will be able to go in or out of
  them.
All Judah will be carried off into
  exile.
They will be completely carried off
  into exile.'"

[20]Then I said,

"Look up, Jerusalem, and see
the enemy that is coming from the
  [a]north.
Where now is the flock of people that
  were entrusted to your care?
Where now are the 'sheep' that you
  take such pride in?
[21] What will you say when the LORD
  appoints as rulers over you those
  allies
that you, yourself, had actually
  prepared as such?
Then anguish and [a]agony will grip
  you
like that of a woman giving birth to
  a baby.
[22] You will probably ask yourself,
'[a]Why have these things happened
  to me?
Why have I been treated like a
  disgraced adulteress
whose skirt has been torn off and her
  limbs exposed?'[1]
It is because [b]you have sinned so
  much.
[23] But there is little hope for you ever
  doing good,
you who are so accustomed to doing
  evil.
Can an Ethiopian[1] change the color
  of his skin?
Can a leopard remove its spots?

[24]"The LORD says,

'That is why I will [a]scatter your
  people [b]like chaff
that is blown away by a desert wind.
[25] [a]This is your fate,
the destiny to which I have
  appointed you
because you have forgotten me
and have trusted in false [b]gods.
[26] So [a]I will pull your skirt up over your
  face
and expose you to shame like a
  disgraced adulteress!

13:13 [a]Ps 60:3; 75:8; Isa 51:17; 63:6; Jer 25:27; 51:7, 57   [1]Heb. *who sit on David's throne.*   13:14 [a]2 Chr 36:17; Ps 2:9; Isa 9:20–21; Jer 19:9–11   13:16 [a]Josh 7:19; Ps 96:8; Mal 2:2   [b]Isa 5:30; 8:22; Amos 8:9   [c]Isa 59:9   [d]Ps 44:19; Jer 2:6   13:17 [a]Ps 119:136; Jer 9:1; 14:17; Luke 19:41–42   13:18 [a]2 Kgs 24:12; Jer 22:26   13:20 [a]Jer 10:22; 46:20   13:21 [a]Jer 6:24   13:22 [a]Jer 16:10   [b]Isa 47:2; Ezek 16:37; Nah 3:5   [1]Heb. *Your skirt has been uncovered, and your heels have been treated with violence.*   13:23 [1]These are Cushites, inhabitants of a region along the upper Nile south of Egypt.   13:24 [a]Lev 26:33; Jer 9:16; Ezek 5:2, 12   [b]Ps 1:4; Hos 13:3   13:25 [a]Job 20:29; Ps 11:6; Matt 24:51   [b]Jer 10:14   13:26 [a]Lam 1:8; Ezek 16:37; Hos 2:10

27 People of Jerusalem, I have seen your
adulterous worship,
your shameless prostitution to, and
your lustful [a]pursuit of, other gods.
I have seen your disgusting acts of
worship
[b]on the hills throughout the
countryside.
You are doomed to destruction![1]
How long will you continue to be
unclean?'"

A Lament over the Ravages of Drought

14 This was the LORD's message to Jeremiah about the drought.

2 "The people of Judah are in mourning.
The people in [a]her cities are pining
away.
They lie on the ground [b]expressing
[c]their sorrow.
Cries of distress come up to me from
Jerusalem.
3 The leading men of the cities send
their servants for water.
They go to the cisterns, but they do
not find any water there.
They return with their containers
empty.
[a]Disappointed [b]and dismayed, they
bury their faces in their hands.
4 They are dismayed because the
ground is cracked
because there has been [a]no rain in
the land.
The farmers, too, are dismayed
and bury their faces in their hands.
5 Even the doe abandons her newborn
fawn in the field
because there is no grass.
6 Wild donkeys stand on [a]the hilltops
and pant for breath like jackals.
Their eyes are strained looking for
food,
because there is none to be found."

7 Then I said,

"[a]O LORD, intervene for the honor of
your name

even though our sins speak out
against us.[1]
Indeed, we have turned away from
you many times.
We have sinned against you.
8 You have been the [a]object of Israel's
hopes.
You have saved them when they were
in trouble.
Why have you become like a resident
foreigner in the land?
Why have you become like a traveler
who only stops in to spend the
night?
9 Why should you be like someone
[a]who is helpless,
like [b]a champion who cannot save
anyone?
You are indeed with us,
and we belong to you.[1]
Do not abandon us!"

10 Then [a]the LORD spoke about these people.

"They truly love to go astray.
They cannot keep from running away
from me.
So I am not pleased with them.
I will now call to mind the wrongs
they have done
and punish them for their sins."

Judgment for Believing the Misleading Lies of the False Prophets

11 Then the LORD said to me, "[a]Do not pray
for good to come to these people! 12 Even
[a]if they fast, I will not hear their cries for
help. Even [b]if they offer burnt [c]offerings
and grain offerings, I will not accept them.
Instead, I will kill them through wars, famines, and plagues."

13 Then I said, "Oh, Sovereign LORD, look![1]
[a]The prophets are telling them that you
said, 'You will not experience war or suffer
famine. I will give you lasting peace and
[b]prosperity in this land.'"

14 Then [a]the LORD [b]said to me, "Those
prophets are prophesying lies while claiming my authority! I did not send them. I did

13:27 [a] Jer 5:7–8   [b] Isa 65:7; Jer 2:20; Ezek 6:13   [1] Heb. *Woe to you!*   14:2 [a] 2 Kgs 25:3; Isa 3:26   [b] Jer 8:21   [c] 1 Sam 5:12; Jer 11:11;
46:12; Zech 7:13   14:3 [a] Job 6:20; Ps 40:14   [b] 2 Sam 15:30   14:4 [a] Jer 3:3; Ezek 22:24   14:6 [a] Job 39:5–6; Jer 2:24   14:7 [a] Ps
25:11; Jer 14:21   [1] Or *bear witness against us, can be used as evidence against us*; Heb. *testify against.*   14:8 [a] Jer 17:13
14:9 [a] Isa 59:1   [b] Exod 29:45; Lev 26:11; Ps 46:5; Jer 8:19   [1] Heb. *Your name is called upon us.*   14:10 [a] [Jer 44:21–23];
Hos 8:13   14:11 [a] Exod 32:10; Jer 7:16; 11:14   14:12 [a] Prov 1:28; [Isa 1:15; 58:3–6]; Ezek 8:18; Mic 3:4; Zech 7:13
[b] Jer 6:20   [c] Jer 9:16   14:13 [a] Jer 4:10   [b] Jer 8:11; 23:17   [1] Heb. *Behold.*   14:14 [a] Jer 27:10   [b] Jer 29:8–9

not commission them. I did not speak to them. They are prophesying to these people false visions, worthless predictions, and the ^cdelusions of their own mind. ¹⁵I did not send those prophets, though they claim to be prophesying in my name. They may be saying, 'No war or famine will happen in this ^aland.' But I, the LORD, say this about them: 'War and starvation will kill those prophets.' ¹⁶The people to whom ^athey are prophesying will die through war and famine. Their bodies will be thrown out into the streets of Jerusalem, and there will be no one to bury them. This will happen to the men and their wives, their sons, and their daughters. For I will pour out on them the destruction they deserve."¹

Lament over Present Destruction and Threat of More to Come

¹⁷"Tell these people this, Jeremiah:

'My eyes overflow with tears
day and night without ceasing.
^aFor my people, my dear children,
have suffered a crushing blow.
They have suffered a serious wound.
¹⁸ If I go out into ^athe countryside,
I see those who have been killed in
battle.
If I go into the city,
I see those who are sick because of
starvation.
For both prophet and ^bpriest—
they go peddling in the land
but they are not humbled.'"

¹⁹Then I said,

"LORD, ^ahave you completely rejected
^bthe nation of Judah?
Do you despise the city of Zion?
Why have you struck us with such
force
that ^cwe are beyond recovery?¹
We hope for peace, but nothing good
has come of it.
We hope for a time of relief from
our troubles, but experience
terror.

²⁰ LORD, we confess that we have been
wicked.
We confess that our ^aancestors have
done wrong.
^bWe have indeed sinned against you.
²¹ For the honor of your name, do not
treat Jerusalem with contempt.
Do not treat with disdain the place
where your glorious throne sits.
Be ^amindful of your covenant with
us. Do not break it.
²² ^aDo any of ^bthe worthless idols of the
nations cause rain to ^cfall?
Do the skies themselves send
showers?
Is it not you, O LORD our God, who
does this?
So we put our hopes in you
because you alone do all this."

15 Then the LORD said to me, "^aEven if ^bMoses and ^cSamuel stood before me pleading for these people, I would not feel pity for them! Get them away from me! Tell them to go away! ²If they ask you, 'Where should we go?' tell them the LORD says this:

'Those who are destined to die of
disease will go to death by disease.
Those who are destined to die in war
will go to death in war.
Those who are destined to die of
starvation will go to death by
starvation.
Those who are destined to go into
^aexile will go into exile.'

³"I will ^apunish ^bthem in four different ways: I will have war kill them; I will have dogs drag off their dead bodies; I will have birds and wild beasts devour and destroy their corpses. ⁴I will make all the people in all the kingdoms of the world horrified at what has happened to them because of what Hezekiah's son ^aManasseh, king of Judah, did in Jerusalem."
⁵The LORD cried out,

"Who in the world will have pity on
you, Jerusalem?

14:14 ^cJer 23:16; Ezek 12:24   **14:15** ^aJer 5:12; Ezek 14:10   **14:16** ^aPs 79:2–3; Jer 7:32; 15:2–3   ¹Heb. *their evil.*   **14:17** ^aIsa 37:22; Jer 8:21; Lam 1:15; 2:13   **14:18** ^aJer 6:25; Lam 1:20; Ezek 7:15   ^bJer 23:11   **14:19** ^aJer 6:30; 7:29; 12:7; Lam 5:22   ^bJer 15:18   ^cJob 30:26; Jer 8:15; 1 Thess 5:3   ¹Heb. *Why have you struck us and there is no healing for us.*   **14:20** ^aNeh 9:2; Ps 32:5; Jer 3:25   ^bPs 106:6; Jer 8:14; 14:7; Dan 9:8   **14:21** ^aPs 106:45   **14:22** ^aZech 10:1   ^bDeut 32:21   ^c1 Kgs 17:1; Jer 5:24   **15:1** ^aPs 99:6; Ezek 14:14   ^bExod 32:11–14; Num 14:13–20; Ps 99:6   ^c1 Sam 7:9   **15:2** ^aJer 9:16; 16:13   **15:3** ^aLev 26:16, 21, 25; Jer 12:3; Ezek 14:21   ^bJer 7:33   **15:4** ^a2 Kgs 24:3–4

Who will grieve over you?
Who will stop long enough
    to inquire about how you are doing?[1]
6 I, the LORD, say: 'a You people have
    deserted me;
you keep turning your back b on me.'
So c I have unleashed my power
    against you and have begun to
    destroy you.
I have grown tired of feeling sorry for
    you!"

7 The LORD continued,

"In every town in the land I will
    purge them
like straw blown away by the wind.
I will destroy my people.
I will kill off their children.
I will a do so because they did not
    change their behavior.
8 Their widows will become in my
    sight more numerous
than the grains of sand on the
    seashores.
At noontime I will bring a destroyer
    against the mothers of their young
    men.
I will cause anguish and terror
    to fall a suddenly upon them.
9 The mother who had seven children
    will grow faint.
All the breath will go out of her.
Her pride and joy will be taken from
    her in the prime of their life.
It will seem as if the sun had set
    while it was still day.
a She will suffer shame and
    humiliation.
I will cause any of them who are still
    left alive
to be killed in war by the onslaughts
    of their enemies,"
says the LORD.

Jeremiah Complains about His Lot and the Lord Responds

10 I said,

"a Oh, mother, how I regret that you
    ever gave birth to me!

I am always starting arguments and
    quarrels with the people of this
    land.
I have not lent money to anyone, and
    I have not borrowed from anyone.
Yet all these people are treating me
    with contempt."[1]

11 The LORD said,

"Jerusalem, I will surely send you
    away for your own good.
I will surely[1] bring a the enemy upon
    you in a time of trouble and
    distress.
12 Can you people who are like iron and
    bronze
break that iron fist from the north?
13 I will give away your wealth and your
    treasures as a plunder.
I will give it away free of charge for
    the sins you have committed
    throughout your land.
14 I will make you serve your enemies[1]
    a in a land that you know nothing
    about.
For my anger is like a b fire that will
    burn against you."

15 I said,

"LORD, a you know how I suffer.
b Take thought of me and care
    c for me.
Pay back for me those who have been
    persecuting me.
Do not be so patient with them that
    you allow them to kill me.
Be mindful of how I have put up with
    their insults for your sake.
16 As your words came to me, I a drank
    them in,
and they filled my heart with joy and
    happiness
because I belong to b you, O LORD
    God of Heaven's Armies.
17 I a did not spend my time in the
    company of other people,
laughing and having a good time.
I stayed to myself because I felt
    obligated to you

and because I was filled with anger at
what they had done.
18 Why must I continually suffer such
painful [a]anguish?
Why must I endure the sting of their
insults like an incurable wound?
Will you let me down when I need
you,
[b]like a brook one goes to for water
but that cannot be relied on?"[1]

19 Because of this, the LORD said,

"You must repent of such words and
thoughts!
[a]If you do, I will restore you to the
privilege of [b]serving me.
If you say what is worthwhile instead
of what is worthless,
I will again allow you to be my
spokesman.
They must become as you have been.
You must not become like them.
20 I will make you as strong as a [a]wall to
these people,
a fortified wall of bronze.
[b]They will attack you,
but they will not be able to overcome
you.
For I will be with you to rescue you
and deliver you,"
says the LORD.
21 "I will deliver you from the power of
the wicked.
I will free you from the clutches of
violent people."

Jeremiah Forbidden to Marry, to Mourn, or to Feast

16 The LORD's message came to me, [2]"Do
not get married and do not have children here in this land. [3]For I, the LORD, tell
you what will happen to the children who
are born here in this land and to the men and
women who are their mothers and fathers.
[4]They will die of deadly [a]diseases. No one
will [b]mourn for them. They will not be [c]bur-
ied. Their dead bodies will lie [d]like manure
spread on the ground. They will be killed in

war or die of starvation. Their [e]corpses will
be food for the birds and wild animals.
[5]"Moreover I, the LORD, tell you: '[a]Do not
go into a house where they are having a funeral meal. Do not go there to mourn and
express your sorrow for them. For I have
stopped showing them my good favor,[1] my
love, and my compassion. I, the LORD, so
affirm it! [6]Rich and poor alike will die in this
land. They will [a]not be buried or mourned.
People will not [b]cut their bodies or shave off
their hair to show their grief for them. [7]No
one will take any food to those who mourn
for the dead to comfort them. No one will
give them any wine to [a]drink to console
them for the loss of their father or mother.
[8]"'Do not go to a house where people are
feasting and sit down to eat and drink with
them either. [9]For [a]I, the LORD of Heaven's
Armies, the God of Israel, tell you what will
happen. I will put an end to the sounds of
joy and gladness, to the glad celebration
of brides and grooms in this land. You and
the rest of the people will live to see this
happen.'

The Lord Promises Exile but Also Restoration

[10]"When you tell these people about all
this, they will undoubtedly ask you, '[a]Why
has the LORD threatened us with such great
disaster? What wrong have we done? What
sin have we done to offend the LORD our
God?' [11]Then tell them that the LORD says,
'It is [a]because your ancestors rejected me
and paid allegiance to[1] other gods. They
have served them and worshiped them. But
they have rejected me and not obeyed my
law. [12]And you have acted even more [a]wick-
edly than your ancestors! [b]Each one of you
has followed the stubborn inclinations of
your own wicked heart and not obeyed me.
[13]So I will throw you out of this land into a
land that neither you nor your ancestors
have ever known. [a]There you must worship
other gods day and night, for [b]I will show
you no mercy.'
[14]"Yet I, the LORD, say: 'A new [a]time will
certainly come. People now affirm their

15:18 [a] Job 34:6; Jer 10:19; 30:15; Mic 1:9   [b] Job 6:15   [1] Heb. *Will you be to me like a deceptive* (brook), *like waters which do not
last* [*or are not reliable*].   15:19 [a] Jer 4:1; Zech 3:7   [b] 1 Kgs 17:1; Jer 15:1   15:20 [a] Jer 1:18; 6:27; Ezek 3:9   [b] Ps 46:7; Isa 41:10;
Jer 1:8, 19; 20:11; 37:21; 38:13; 39:11–12   16:4 [a] Jer 15:2   [b] Jer 22:18; 25:33   [c] Jer 14:16; 19:11   [d] Ps 83:10; Jer 8:2; 9:22   [e] Ps 79:2;
Isa 18:6; Jer 7:33; 34:20   16:5 [a] Ezek 24:17, 22, 23   [1] Heb. *my peace.*   16:6 [a] Jer 22:18   [b] Lev 19:28; Deut 14:1; Jer 41:5; 47:5
16:7 [a] Prov 31:6   16:9 [a] Isa 24:7–8; Jer 7:34; 25:10; Ezek 26:13; Hos 2:11; Rev 18:23   16:10 [a] Deut 29:24; 1 Kgs 9:8; Jer 5:19
16:11 [a] Deut 29:25; 1 Kgs 9:9; 2 Chr 7:22; Neh 9:26–29; Jer 22:9   [1] Heb. *followed after.*   16:12 [a] Jer 7:26   [b] Jer 3:17;
18:12   16:13 [a] Deut 4:26; 28:36, 63   [b] Jer 15:14   16:14 [a] Isa 43:18; Jer 23:7–8; [Ezek 37:21–25]

oaths with "I swear as surely as the LORD lives who delivered the people of Israel out of Egypt." [15] But in that time they will affirm them with "I swear as surely as the LORD lives who delivered the people of Israel from the land of the [a]north and from all the other lands where he had [b]banished them." At that time I will bring them back to the land I gave their ancestors.

[16] "But for now [a]I, the LORD, say: 'I will send many enemies who will catch these people like fishermen. After that I will send others who will hunt them out like hunters from all the mountains, all the hills, and the crevices in the rocks. [17] For I [a]see everything they do. Their wicked ways are not hidden from me. Their sin is not hidden away where I cannot see it. [18] Before I restore them[1] I will punish them in [a]full for their sins and [b]the wrongs they have done. For they have polluted my land with the lifeless statues of their disgusting idols. They have filled the land I have claimed as my own with their detestable idols.'

[19] Then I said,

"LORD, you give me strength and
    protect me.
You are the one I can run to for safety
    when I am in trouble.
Nations from all over the earth
will come to you and say,
'Our ancestors had nothing but false
    gods—
worthless idols that could not [a]help
    them at all.'
[20] Can people make their own gods?
No, what they make are not gods at
    all."

[21] The LORD said,

"So I will now let this wicked people
    know—
I will let them know [a]my mighty
    power in judgment.
Then they will know that my name is
    the LORD.

17 [1] "The sin of Judah is [a]engraved with
    an iron [b]chisel
on their stone-hard hearts.
It is [c]inscribed with a diamond point
on the horns of their altars.
[2] Their children are always thinking
    about their[1] altars
and their sacred poles dedicated to
    the goddess [a]Asherah,
set up beside the green trees on the
    high hills
[3] and on the mountains and in the
    fields.[1]
I will give your wealth and all your
    treasures away as plunder.
I will give it away as the price for
    the sins you have committed
    throughout your land.
[4] You will lose your hold on [a]the land
    that I gave to [b]you as a permanent
    possession.
I will make you serve your enemies
    in a land that you know nothing
    about.
For you have made my anger burn like
    a fire that will never be put out."[1]

Individuals Are Challenged to Put Their Trust in the Lord

[5] The LORD says,

"I will put a [a]curse on people
who trust in mere human beings,
who depend on mere flesh and
    [b]blood for their strength,
and whose hearts have turned away
    from the LORD.
[6] They will be [a]like [b]a shrub[1] [c]in the
    arid rift valley.
They will not experience good things
    even when they happen.
It will be as though they were
    growing in the stony wastes in the
    wilderness,
in a salt land where no one can live.
[7] My [a]blessing is on those people who
    trust in me,
who put their confidence in me.

16:15 [a] Jer 3:18 [b] Jer 24:6; 30:3; 32:37 **16:16** [a] Amos 4:2; Hab 1:15 **16:17** [a] 2 Chr 16:9; Job 34:21; Ps 90:8; Prov 5:21; Jer 23:24; 32:19; Zech 4:10; [Luke 12:2; 1 Cor 4:5]; Heb 4:13 **16:18** [a] Isa 40:2; Jer 17:18; Rev 18:6 [b] [Ezek 43:7] [1] Heb. *First.* **16:19** [a] Isa 44:10 **16:21** [a] Exod 15:3; Ps 83:18; Isa 43:3; Jer 33:2; Amos 5:8 **17:1** [a] Jer 2:22 [b] Job 19:24 [c] Prov 3:3; 7:3; Isa 49:16; 2 Cor 3:3 [1] The chapter division, which was not a part of the original text, obscures the fact that there is no new speech here. **17:2** [a] Judg 3:7 [1] Many mss *your* [masc. pl.]. **17:3** [1] MT *hills. My mountain in the open field* [alluding to Jerusalem] *and your wealth . . . I will give.* **17:4** [a] Jer 16:13 [b] Isa 5:25; Jer 15:14 [1] A few mss *a fire is kindled in my anger.* **17:5** [a] Ps 146:3; Isa 30:1–2; 31:1 [b] Isa 31:3 **17:6** [a] Jer 48:6 [b] Job 20:17 [c] Deut 29:23; Job 39:6 [1] A kind of juniper, which is a short shrub with minute leaves that look like scales. **17:7** [a] Ps 2:12; 34:8; 125:1; 146:5; Prov 16:20; [Isa 30:18]; Jer 39:18

8 They will be [a]like a tree planted near
  a stream
whose roots spread out toward the
  water.
It has nothing to fear when the heat
  comes.
Its leaves are always green.
It has no need to be concerned in a
  year of drought.
It does not stop bearing fruit.
9 The human [a]mind is more deceitful
  than anything else.
It is incurably bad. Who can
  understand it?
10 I, the LORD, [a]probe into people's
  minds.
I examine people's hearts.
I deal with each person according to
  how he has behaved.
I give them what they deserve based
  on what they have done.
11 The person who gathers wealth by
  unjust means
is like the partridge that broods over
  eggs but does not hatch them.
Before his life is half over, he [a]will
  lose his ill-gotten [b]gains.[1]
At the end of his life, it will be clear
  he was a fool."

Jeremiah Appeals to the Lord for Vindication

12 Then I said,

"LORD, from the very beginning
you have been seated on your
  glorious throne on high.
You are the place where we can find
  refuge.
13 You are [a]the one in whom Israel may
  find hope.
[b]All who leave you will suffer shame.
Those who turn away from you will
  be [c]consigned to the netherworld.[1]
For they have rejected you, the LORD,
  the [d]fountain of life.
14 LORD, grant me relief from my
  suffering
so that I may have some relief;

rescue me from those who
  persecute me
so that I may be rescued, for [a]you
  give me reason to praise!
15 Listen to what they are saying to me,
'[a]Where are the things the LORD
  threatens us with?
May it please happen!'
16 But [a]I have not pestered you to bring
  disaster.[1]
I have not desired the time of
  irreparable devastation.
You know that.
You are fully aware of every word
  that I have spoken.
17 Do not cause me dismay!
[a]You are my source of safety in times
  of trouble.
18 May those who persecute me be
  disgraced.
Do not [a]let me be disgraced.
May they be dismayed.
[b]Do not let me be dismayed.
Bring days of disaster on them.
Bring [c]on them the destruction they
  deserve."

Observance of the Sabbath Day Is a Key to the Future

19 The LORD told me, "Go and stand in the People's Gate through which the kings of Judah enter and leave the city. Then go and stand in all the other gates of the city of Jerusalem. 20 And then announce to them, '[a]Listen to the LORD's message, you kings of Judah, and everyone from Judah, and all you citizens of Jerusalem, those who pass through these gates. 21 The LORD says, Be very careful if you value your lives! Do not carry any loads in through the gates of Jerusalem on the Sabbath day. 22 Do not carry any loads out of your houses or do any work on the Sabbath day. But observe the Sabbath day as a day set apart to the LORD,[1] as I [a]commanded your ancestors. 23 [a]Your ancestors, however, did not listen to me or pay any attention to me. They stubbornly refused to pay attention or to

17:8 [a]Job 8:16; [Ps 1:3; Ezek 31:3–9]   17:9 [a][Eccl 9:3]; Matt 15:19; [Mark 7:21–22]   17:10 [a]1 Sam 16:7; 1 Chr 28:9; Ps 7:9; 139:23–24; Prov 17:3; Jer 11:20; 20:12; Rom 8:27; Rev 2:23   17:11 [a]Ps 55:23   [b]Luke 12:20   [1]Heb. *lose it.*   17:13 [a]Jer 14:8   [b][Ps 73:27; Isa 1:28]   [c]Luke 10:20   [d]Jer 2:13   [1]Or *to the world of the dead*; or perhaps *will be as though their names were written in the dust*; Heb. *will be written in the dust.*   17:14 [a]Deut 10:21; Ps 109:1   17:15 [a]Isa 5:19; Ezek 12:22; 2 Pet 3:4   17:16 [a]Jer 1:4–12   [1]MT *I have not hastened from being a shepherd after you.*   17:17 [a]Jer 16:19; Nah 1:7   17:18 [a]Ps 35:4; 70:2; Jer 15:10; 18:18   [b]Ps 25:2   [c]Jer 11:20   17:20 [a]Ps 49:1–2; Jer 19:3–4   17:22 [a]Exod 20:8; 31:13; Ezek 20:12   [1]Heb. *But sanctify* [or *set apart as sacred*] *the Sabbath day.*   17:23 [a]Jer 7:24, 26

respond to any discipline.' 24 The LORD says, 'You must make sure to obey me. You must not bring any loads through the gates of this city on the ᵃSabbath day. You must set the Sabbath day apart to me. You must not do any work on that day. 25 If you do this, ᵃthen the kings and princes who follow in David's succession and ride in chariots or on horses will continue to enter through these gates, as well as their officials and the people of Judah and the citizens of Jerusalem. This city will always be filled with people.¹ 26 Then people will come here from ᵃthe towns in Judah, from ᵇthe villages surrounding Jerusalem, from ᶜthe territory of Benjamin, from the foothills, from the southern hill country, and from the southern part of Judah. They will come bringing offerings to the temple of the LORD: burnt offerings, ᵈsacrifices, grain offerings, and incense along with their thank offerings. 27 But you must obey me and set the Sabbath day apart to me. You must not carry any loads ᵃin through the gates of Jerusalem on the Sabbath day. If you disobey, I will set the gates of Jerusalem on fire. It will burn down all the fortified dwellings in Jerusalem ᵇand no one will be able to ᶜput it out.'"

An Object Lesson from the Making of Pottery

18 The LORD said to Jeremiah: 2 "Go down at once to the potter's house. I will speak to you further there." 3 So I went down to the potter's house and found him working at his wheel. 4 Now and then there would be something wrong with the pot he was molding from the clay with his hands. So he would rework the clay into another kind of pot as he saw fit.¹

5 Then the LORD's message came to me, 6 "I, the LORD, say: 'O nation of Israel, ᵃcan I not deal with you ᵇas this potter deals with the clay? In my hands, you, O nation of Israel, are just like the clay in this potter's hand.' 7 There are times, Jeremiah, when I threaten to uproot, tear down, and destroy a nation or kingdom. 8 But ᵃif that ᵇnation I threatened stops doing wrong, I will cancel the destruction I intended to do to it. 9 And there are times when I promise to build up and establish a nation or kingdom. 10 But if that nation does what displeases me and does not obey me, then I will cancel the good I promised to do to it. 11 So now, tell the people of Judah and the citizens of Jerusalem this: The LORD says, 'I am preparing to bring disaster on you! I am making plans to punish you. So, every one of you, ᵃstop the evil things you have been doing. ᵇCorrect the way you have been living and do what is right.' 12 But they just keep saying, 'We do not care what you say! We will do whatever we want to do! We will continue to behave wickedly and ᵃstubbornly!'"

13 Therefore, the LORD says,

"ᵃAsk the people of other ᵇnations
   whether they have heard of anything
   like this.
Israel should have been like a virgin,
but she has done something utterly
   revolting!
14 Does the snow ever completely
   vanish from the rocky slopes of
   Lebanon?
Do the cool waters from those
   distant mountains ever cease to
   flow?
15 Yet my people have forgotten ᵃme
   and offered sacrifices to worthless
   idols.
This makes them stumble along in
   the way they live
and leave the ᵇold reliable path of
   their fathers.
They have left them to walk in
   bypaths,
in roads that are not smooth and
   level.
16 So their land will become an object
   of ᵃhorror.
People will forever ᵇhiss out their
   scorn over it.
All who pass that way will be filled
   with horror
and will shake their heads in
   derision.

17:24 ᵃ Exod 16:23–30; 20:8–10; Num 15:32–36; Deut 5:12–14; Neh 13:15; [Isa 58:13]   17:25 ᵃ Jer 22:4   ¹ Heb. *will be inhabited forever.*   17:26 ᵃ Jer 33:13   ᵇ Zech 7:7   ᶜ Judg 1:9   ᵈ Ps 107:22; 116:17; Jer 33:11   17:27 ᵃ Jer 21:14; Lam 4:11; Amos 1:4, 7, 10, 12   ᵇ 2 Kgs 25:9; 2 Chr 36:19; Jer 39:8; 52:13; Amos 2:5   ᶜ Jer 7:20; Ezek 20:47   18:4 ¹ Heb. *as it was right in his eyes to do* [or *work it*].   18:6 ᵃ Isa 45:9; Rom 9:20–21   ᵇ Isa 64:8   18:8 ᵃ Jer 7:3–7; 12:16; [Ezek 18:21; 33:11]   ᵇ [Ps 106:45]; Jer 26:3; [Hos 11:8; Joel 2:13]; Jonah 3:10   18:11 ᵃ 2 Kgs 17:13; Isa 1:16–19; Jer 4:1; Acts 26:20   ᵇ Jer 7:3–7   18:12 ᵃ Jer 3:17; 23:17   18:13 ᵃ Isa 66:8; Jer 2:10–11; 1 Cor 5:1   ᵇ Jer 5:30; Hos 6:10   18:15 ᵃ Jer 2:13, 32   ᵇ Jer 6:16   18:16 ᵃ Jer 19:8   ᵇ 1 Kgs 9:8; Lam 2:15; Mic 6:16

[17] I [a]will scatter them before their
enemies
like dust blowing in front of [b]a
[c]burning east wind.
I will turn my back on them and not
look favorably on them[1]
when disaster strikes them."

Jeremiah Petitions the Lord to Punish Those Who Attack Him

[18]Then some people said, "[a]Come on! Let us consider how to deal with Jeremiah! There will still be priests to instruct us, wise men to give us advice, and prophets to declare God's word. Come on! Let's bring charges against him and get rid of him! Then we will not need to pay attention to anything he says."

[19]Then I said,

"LORD, pay attention to me.
Listen to what my enemies are
saying.[1]
[20] [a]Should good be paid back with evil?
Yet they are virtually [b]digging a pit to
kill me.
Just remember how I [c]stood before
you
pleading on their behalf
to keep you from venting your anger
on them.
[21] So [a]let their children die of
starvation.
Let them be cut down by the sword.
Let their wives lose their husbands
and [b]children.
Let the older men die of disease
and the younger men die by the
sword in battle.
[22] Let cries of terror be heard in their
houses
when you send bands of raiders
unexpectedly to plunder them.
For they have virtually dug a pit to
capture me
and have hidden traps for me to step
into.
[23] But you, LORD, know
all their plots to kill me.

Do not pardon their crimes!
Do not ignore their sins as though
you had erased them.
Let them be brought down in defeat
before you.
Deal with them while you are still
[a]angry!"[1]

An Object Lesson from a Broken Clay Jar

19 The LORD told Jeremiah, "Go and buy a clay jar from a potter. Take with you[1] some of the leaders of the people and some of the leaders of the priests. [2]Go out to [a]the part of the Hinnom Valley that is near the entrance of the Potsherd Gate. Announce there what I tell you. [3]Say, 'Listen to the LORD's message, you kings of Judah [a]and citizens of Jerusalem! This is what the LORD of Heaven's Armies, the God of Israel, has said, "Look here! I am about to bring a disaster on this place that will make the ears of everyone who hears about it [b]ring. [4]I will do so because these people [a]have rejected me and have defiled this place. [b]They have offered sacrifices in it to other gods that neither they nor their ancestors nor the kings of Judah knew anything about. They have filled it with the blood of innocent children. [5]They have built places here for worship of [a]the god Baal so that they could sacrifice their children as burnt offerings to him in the fire. Such sacrifices are something [b]I never commanded them to make. They are something I never told them to do! Indeed, such a thing never even entered my mind. [6]So I, [a]the LORD, say: 'The time will soon come that people will no longer call this place Topheth or the Hinnom Valley. But they will call this valley the Valley of Slaughter! [7]In this place I will thwart the plans of the people of Judah [a]and Jerusalem. I will deliver them over to the power of their enemies who are seeking to kill them. They will die by the sword at the hands of their enemies. I will make their dead [b]bodies food for the birds and wild beasts to eat. [8]I will make this city an object of [a]horror, a thing to be hissed at. All who pass by it will

18:17 [a]Jer 13:24 [b]Ps 48:7 [c]Jer 2:27 [1]Heb. *I will show them* [my] *back and not* [my] *face; MT I will look on their back and not on their faces.* **18:18** [a]Jer 11:19 **18:19** [1]Heb. *the voice of my adversaries.* **18:20** [a]Ps 109:4 [b]Ps 35:7; 57:6; Jer 5:26 [c]Jer 14:7–15:1 **18:21** [a]Ps 109:9–20; Jer 11:22; 14:16 [b]Jer 15:7–8; Ezek 22:25 **18:23** [a]Jer 7:20 [1]Heb. *in the time of your anger.* **19:1** [1]MT omits *Take with you.* **19:2** [a]Josh 15:8; 2 Kgs 23:10; Jer 7:31; 32:35 **19:3** [a]Jer 17:20 [b]1 Sam 3:11; 2 Kgs 21:12 **19:4** [a]Deut 28:20; Isa 65:11; Jer 2:13, 17, 19; 15:6; 17:13 [b]2 Kgs 21:12; Jer 2:34; 7:6 **19:5** [a]Num 22:41; Jer 7:31; 32:35 [b]Lev 18:21; 2 Kgs 17:17; Ps 106:37–38 **19:6** [a]Josh 15:8; Jer 7:32 **19:7** [a]Lev 26:17; Deut 28:25; Jer 15:2, 9 [b]Ps 79:2; Jer 7:33; 16:4; 34:20 **19:8** [a]Jer 18:16; 49:13; 50:13

be filled with horror and will hiss out their scorn because of all the disasters that have happened to it. [9]I will reduce the people of this city to desperate straits during the siege imposed on it by their enemies who are seeking to kill them. I will make them so desperate that they will eat the [a]flesh of their own sons and daughters and the flesh of one another.'"'

[10]The LORD continued, "Now break [a]the jar in front of those who have come here with you. [11]Tell them the LORD of Heaven's Armies says, 'I will do just as Jeremiah has done. I will smash this nation and this city as though it were a potter's vessel that is broken beyond repair. The dead will be buried here in Topheth until there is no more room to [a]bury them.' [12]I, the LORD, say: 'That is how I will deal with this city and its citizens. I will make it like Topheth. [13]The houses in Jerusalem and the houses of the kings of Judah will be defiled by dead bodies just [a]like this place, Topheth. For they offered sacrifice to the stars and poured out drink offerings to other gods on the [b]roofs of those houses.'"

[14]Then Jeremiah left Topheth where [a]the LORD had sent him to give that prophecy. He went to the LORD's temple and stood in its courtyard and called out to all the people. [15]"The LORD of Heaven's Armies, [a]the God of Israel, says, 'I will soon bring on this city and all the towns surrounding it all the disaster I threatened to do to it. I will do so because they have stubbornly refused to pay any attention to what I have said!'"

Jeremiah Is Flogged and Put in a Cell

20 Now [a]Pashhur son of [b]Immer heard Jeremiah prophesy these things. He was the priest who was chief of security in the LORD's temple. [2]When he heard Jeremiah's prophecy, he had the prophet flogged. Then he put him in the stocks[1] that were at the Upper [a]Gate of Benjamin in the LORD's temple. [3]But the next day Pashhur released Jeremiah from the stocks. When he did, Jeremiah said to him, "The LORD's name for you is not 'Pashhur' but 'Terror is Everywhere.'[1] [4]For the LORD says, 'I will [a]make both you and your friends terrified of what will happen to you. You will see all of them die by the swords of their enemies. I will hand all the people of Judah over to the king of Babylon. He will carry some of them away into exile in Babylon, and he will kill others of them with the sword. [5]I [a]will hand over all the wealth of this city to their enemies. I will hand over to them all the fruits of the labor of the people of this city and all their prized possessions, as well as all the treasures of the kings of Judah. Their enemies will seize it all as plunder and [b]carry it off to Babylon. [6]You, Pashhur, and all your household will go into exile in Babylon. You will die there, and you will be buried there. The same thing will happen to all your friends to whom you have [a]prophesied lies.'"

Jeremiah Complains about the Reaction to His Ministry

[7] LORD, [a]you coerced me [b]into being a
    prophet,
and I allowed you to do it.
You overcame my resistance and
    prevailed over me.
Now I have become a constant
    laughingstock.
Everyone ridicules me.
[8] For whenever [a]I prophesy, I must cry
    out,
"Violence and destruction are
    coming!"
This message from the LORD has
    made me
an object of continual insults and
    derision.
[9] Sometimes I think, "I will make no
    mention of his message.
I will not speak as his messenger
    anymore."
But then his message becomes like
    a fire
locked up inside of me, [a]burning [b]in
    my heart and soul.
I grow weary of trying to hold it in;
I cannot contain it.

19:9 [a]Lev 26:29; Deut 28:53, 55; Isa 9:20; Lam 4:10; Ezek 5:10   19:10 [a]Jer 51:63–64   19:11 [a]Jer 7:32   19:13 [a]2 Kgs 23:10; Ps 74:7; 79:1; Jer 52:13; Ezek 7:21–22   [b]2 Kgs 23:12; Jer 32:29; Zeph 1:5   19:14 [a]2 Chr 20:5; Jer 26:2–8   19:15 [a]Neh 9:17, 29; Jer 7:26; 17:23   20:1 [a]Ezra 2:37–38   [b]1 Chr 24:14   20:2 [a]Jer 37:13; Zech 14:10   [1]The meaning of this word is uncertain. 20:3 [1]This name is translated, rather than transliterated, to connect it clearly with the explanation that follows. 20:4 [a]Jer 21:4–10   20:5 [a]2 Kgs 20:17; 2 Chr 36:10; Jer 3:24; 27:21–22   [b]Isa 39:6   20:6 [a]Jer 14:13-15; Lam 2:14 20:7 [a]Jer 1:6–7   [b]Job 12:4; Lam 3:14   20:8 [a]Jer 6:7   20:9 [a]Job 32:18–20; Ps 39:3; Jer 4:19; 23:9; [Ezek 3:14]; Acts 4:20   [b]Job 32:18; Jer 6:11; Acts 18:5

¹⁰ I hear many whispering words of
   intrigue against me.
Those who would cause me terror
   are everywhere!
They are saying, "Come on, let's
   publicly denounce him!"
All my so-called friends are just
   watching ᵃfor
something that would lead to my
   ᵇdownfall.¹
They say, "Perhaps he can be enticed
   into slipping up,
so we can prevail over him and get
   our revenge on him."
¹¹ But the LORD is ᵃwith me to help me
   like an awe-inspiring warrior.
Therefore those who persecute
   me will fail and will not ᵇprevail
   over me.
They will be thoroughly disgraced
   because they did not succeed.
Their disgrace will ᶜnever be
   forgotten.
¹² O LORD of Heaven's Armies, you test
   and ᵃprove the righteous.
You see into people's hearts and
   minds.
Pay them back for what they have
   done
because I trust you to vindicate my
   cause.
¹³ Sing to ᵃthe LORD! Praise the LORD!
For he rescues the oppressed from
   the clutches of evildoers.
¹⁴ ᵃCursed be the day I was born!
May that day not be blessed when
   my mother gave birth to me.
¹⁵ Cursed be the man
who made my father very glad
when he brought him the news
that a baby boy had been born to
   him!
¹⁶ May that man be like the cities
   that the LORD ᵃdestroyed without
   showing any mercy.
May he ᵇhear a cry of distress in the
   morning
and a battle cry at noon.

¹⁷ ᵃFor he did not kill me before I came
   from the womb,
making my pregnant mother's womb
   my grave forever.
¹⁸ ᵃWhy did I ever come forth from my
   mother's womb?
All I ᵇexperience is trouble and grief,
and I spend my days in shame.

The Lord Will Hand Jerusalem over to Enemies

21 The LORD spoke to Jeremiah when ᵃKing Zedekiah sent to him ᵇPashhur son of Malkijah and the priest ᶜZephaniah son of Maaseiah. Zedekiah sent them to Jeremiah to ask, ²"ᵃPlease ask the LORD to come and help us, because King Nebuchadnezzar¹ of Babylon is attacking us. Maybe the LORD will perform one of his miracles as in times past and make him stop attacking us and leave." ³Jeremiah answered them, "Tell Zedekiah ⁴that the LORD, the God of ᵃIsrael, says, 'The forces at your disposal¹ are now outside the walls fighting against King Nebuchadnezzar of Babylon and the Babylonians who have you under siege. I will gather those forces back inside the city. ⁵In anger, in fury, and in wrath I ᵃmyself will fight against you with my ᵇmighty power and great strength. ⁶I will kill everything living in Jerusalem, people and animals alike. They will die from terrible diseases. ⁷Then ᵃI, ᵇthe LORD, promise that I will hand over King Zedekiah of Judah, his officials, and any of the people who survive the war, starvation, and disease. I will hand them over to King Nebuchadnezzar of Babylon and to their enemies who want to kill them. He will slaughter them with the sword. He will not show them any mercy, compassion, or pity.'

⁸"But tell the people of Jerusalem that the LORD says, 'ᵃI will give you a choice between two courses of action. One will result in life; the other will result in death. ⁹Those who ᵃstay in this city will die in battle or of starvation or disease. Those who leave the city and surrender to the Babylonians who

20:10 ᵃPs 31:13 ᵇJob 19:19; Ps 41:9; 55:13–14; Luke 11:53–54 ¹Heb. *watching my stumbling* [for me to stumble]. 20:11 ᵃJer 1:18–19 ᵇJer 15:20; 17:18 ᶜJer 23:40 20:12 ᵃPs 7:9; 11:5; 17:3; 139:23; [Jer 11:20; 17:10] 20:13 ᵃPs 35:9–10; 109:30–31 20:14 ᵃJob 3:3; Jer 15:10 20:16 ᵃGen 19:25 ᵇJer 18:22 20:17 ᵃJob 3:10–11 20:18 ᵃJob 3:20; Jer 15:10 ᵇLam 3:1 21:1 ᵃ2 Kgs 24:17–18; Jer 32:1–3; 37:1; 52:1–3 ᵇ1 Chr 9:12; Jer 38:1 ᶜ2 Kgs 25:18; Jer 29:25; 37:3 21:2 ᵃExod 9:28; 1 Sam 9:9; Jer 37:3, 7; Ezek 14:7; 20:1–3 ¹"Nebuchadrezzar" is the dominant spelling of this name. 21:4 ᵃIsa 13:4; Jer 39:3; Lam 2:5, 7; Zech 14:2 ¹Heb. *the weapons that are in your hand.* 21:5 ᵃJer 32:24; 33:5; Isa 63:10 ᵇExod 6:6; Deut 4:34; Jer 6:12 21:7 ᵃ2 Kgs 25:5–7, 18–21; Jer 37:17; 39:5; 52:9 ᵇDeut 28:50; 2 Chr 36:17; Jer 13:14; Ezek 7:9; Hab 1:6–10 21:8 ᵃDeut 30:15, 19; Isa 1:19–20 21:9 ᵃJer 38:2

are besieging it will [b]live. They will escape with their lives. [10]For I, the LORD, say that I am [a]determined not to deliver this [b]city but to bring disaster on it. It will be handed over to the king of Babylon, and he will [c]destroy it with fire.'"

Warnings to the Royal Court

[11]The LORD told me to say to the royal court of Judah:

"Listen to the LORD's message,
[12] O royal family descended from David.
The LORD says:
'See to [a]it that people each day are
    judged fairly.
Deliver those who have been robbed
    from those who oppress them.
Otherwise, my wrath will blaze out
    [b]against you.
It will burn like a fire that cannot be
    put out
because of the evil that you have done.
[13] Listen, you who [a]sit enthroned above
    the valley on a rocky plateau.
I am opposed to you,' says the LORD.
'You boast, "No [b]one can swoop down
    on us.
No one can penetrate into our places
    of refuge."
[14] But I will punish you as your deeds
    [a]deserve,'
says the LORD.
'[b]I will set fire to your palace;
it will burn up everything around it.'"

22 The LORD told me, "Go down to the palace of the king of Judah. Give him a message from me there. [2]Say: '[a]Listen, O king of Judah who follows in David's succession. You, your officials, and your subjects who pass through the gates of this palace must listen to the LORD's message. [3]The LORD says, "[a]Do what is just and right. Deliver those who have been robbed from those[1] who oppress them. Do not exploit or mistreat resident foreigners who live in your land, children who have no [b]fathers, or widows.[2] Do not kill innocent people in this land. [4]If you are careful to obey these commands, [a]then the kings who follow in David's succession and ride in chariots or on horses will continue to come through the gates of this palace, as will their officials and their subjects. [5]But, [a]if you do not obey these commands, I solemnly swear that this palace will become a pile of rubble. I, the LORD, affirm it!'"

[6]"For the LORD says concerning the palace of the king of Judah,

"'This place looks like a veritable
    forest of [a]Gilead to me.
It is like the wooded heights of
    Lebanon in my eyes.
But I swear that I will make it like a
    wilderness
whose towns have all been deserted.
[7] I will send men against it to
    destroy it
with their axes [a]and hatchets.
They will hack up its fine cedar
    panels and columns
and throw them into the fire.'

[8]"'People from other nations will pass by this city. They will ask one another, "[a]Why has the LORD done such a thing to this great city?" [9]The answer will come back, "It is [a]because they broke their covenant with the LORD their God and worshiped and served other gods."

Judgment on Jehoahaz

[10] "'Do not weep for [a]the king [b]who was
    killed.
Do not grieve for him.
But weep mournfully for the king
    who has gone into exile.
For he will never return to see his
    native land again.

[11]"'For the LORD has spoken about [a]Shallum son of Josiah, [b]who succeeded his father as king of Judah but was carried off into exile. He has said, "He will never return to this land. [12]For he will die in the country where they took him as a captive. He will never see this land again."

21:9 [b]Jer 39:18   21:10 [a]Lev 17:10; Jer 44:11, 27; Amos 9:4 [b]Jer 38:3 [c]2 Kgs 25:9; 2 Chr 36:19; Jer 34:2, 22; 37:10   21:12 [a]Ps 72:1; Isa 1:17; Jer 22:3; Zech 7:9 [b]Ps 101:8; Zeph 3:5   21:13 [a][Jer 23:30–32; Ezek 13:8] [b]2 Sam 5:6–7; Jer 49:4; Lam 4:12; Obad 3, 4   21:14 [a]Prov 1:31; Isa 3:10–11; Jer 17:10; 32:19 [b]2 Chr 36:19; Isa 10:16, 18; Jer 11:16; 17:27; 52:13; Ezek 20:47–48   22:2 [a]Jer 17:20   22:3 [a]Isa 58:6; Jer 21:12; [Mic 6:8]; Zech 7:9; 8:16; Matt 23:23 [b]Jer 7:6; Zech 7:10   [1]Heb. *from the hand* [or *power*] *of.*   [2]Heb. *aliens, orphans, or widows.*   22:4 [a]Jer 17:25   22:5 [a]Matt 23:38; Heb 6:13, 17   22:6 [a]Gen 37:25; Num 32:1; Song 4:1   22:7 [a]Jer 21:14   22:8 [a]Deut 29:24–26; 1 Kgs 9:8–9; 2 Chr 7:20–22; Jer 16:10   22:9 [a]2 Kgs 22:17; 2 Chr 34:25; Jer 11:3   22:10 [a]2 Kgs 22:20 [b]Jer 14:17; 22:11; Lam 3:48   22:11 [a]1 Chr 3:15 [b]2 Kgs 23:34; 2 Chr 36:4; Ezek 19:4

Judgment on Jehoiakim

13 "'Sure to be [a]judged is the king [b]who
  builds his palace using injustice
and treats people unfairly while
  adding its upper rooms.
He makes his countrymen work for
  him for nothing.
He does not pay them for their labor.
14 He says, "I will build myself a large
  palace
with spacious upper rooms."
He cuts windows in its walls,
panels it with cedar, and paints its
  rooms red.
15 Does [a]it make you any more of a king
that you outstrip everyone else in
  building with cedar?
Just think about your father.
He was content that he had food and
  drink.
He did what was just and right.
So things went well with him.
16 He upheld the cause of the poor and
  needy.
So things went well for Judah.'
The LORD says,
'That is a good example of what it
  means to know me.
17 But you are always thinking and
  looking
for ways to increase your wealth by
  dishonest means.
Your eyes and your heart are set
on killing some innocent person
and committing fraud and
  oppression.'"[1]

18 So [a]the LORD has this to say about Josiah's son, King Jehoiakim of Judah:

"People will not mourn for him,
  saying,
'This [b]makes me sad, my brother!
This makes me sad, my sister!'
They will not mourn for him,
  saying,
'Poor, poor lord! Poor, poor majesty!'
19 He will be left unburied just like a
  dead donkey.

His body will be dragged off and
  thrown outside [a]the gates of
  Jerusalem.

Warning to Jerusalem

20 "People of Jerusalem, go up to
  Lebanon and cry out in mourning.
Go to the land of Bashan and cry out
  loudly.
Cry out in mourning from the
  mountains of Moab.[1]
For your allies have all been defeated.
21 While you were feeling secure [a]I gave
  you warning.
But you said, 'I refuse to listen to
  you.'
That is the way you have acted from
  your earliest history onward.
Indeed, you have never paid
  attention to me.
22 My judgment will carry off all [a]your
  leaders like a storm wind!
Your allies will go into captivity.
Then you will certainly be disgraced
  and put to shame
because of all the wickedness you
  have done.
23 You may feel as secure as a bird
  nesting in [a]the cedars of Lebanon.
But O how you[1] will groan when the
  pains of judgment come on you.
They will be like those of a woman
  giving birth to a baby."

Jeconiah Will Be Permanently Exiled

24 The LORD says, "As surely as I am the
living God, you, Jeconiah,[1] king of Judah, son
of Jehoiakim, will not be the earthly representative of my authority. Indeed, I will
take that right away from you. 25 I will [a]hand
you over to those who want to take your life
and of whom you are afraid. I will hand you
over to King Nebuchadnezzar of Babylon
and his Babylonian soldiers. 26a I will force
you and your mother who gave you birth
into exile. You will be exiled to a country
where neither of you were born, and you will
both die there. 27 You will never come back
to this land that you will long to return to!

22:13 [a] 2 Kgs 23:35; Jer 17:11; Ezek 22:13   [b] Lev 19:13; Deut 24:14–15; Mic 3:10; Hab 2:9; Jas 5:4   22:15 [a] 2 Kgs 23:25; Ps 128:2;
Isa 3:10; Jer 7:23; 42:6   22:17 [1] Heb. *Your eyes and your heart do not exist except for dishonest gain and for innocent blood
to shed [it] and for fraud and for oppression to do* [them].   22:18 [a] Jer 16:4, 6   [b] 1 Kgs 13:30   22:19 [a] 1 Kgs 21:23–24; 2 Chr
36:6; Jer 36:30; Dan 1:2   22:20 [1] Heb. *from Abarim*; the mountain range in Moab from which Moses viewed the
promised land (cf. Deut 32:49).   22:21 [a] Jer 3:24–25; 32:30   22:22 [a] Jer 23:1   22:23 [a] Jer 6:24   [1] Heb. *You
who dwell in Lebanon, you who are nested in its cedars, how you.*   22:24 [1] Heb. *Coniah.*
22:25 [a] 2 Kgs 24:15–16; Jer 34:20   22:26 [a] 2 Kgs 24:15; Jer 10:18; 16:13

28 "This [a]man, Jeconiah, will be like a
broken pot someone threw away.
He will be like a clay vessel that no
one wants.
Why will he and his children be
forced into exile?
Why will they be thrown out into a
country they know nothing about?
29 O Land, land, land [a]of Judah!
Listen to the LORD's message."

30 The LORD says,

"Enroll this man in the register as
though he were [a]childless.
Enroll him as a man who will not
enjoy success during his lifetime.
For [b]none of his sons will succeed in
occupying the throne of David
or ever succeed in ruling over Judah."

New Leaders over a Regathered Remnant

23 The LORD says, "The leaders of my people are sure [a]to be judged. They were supposed to watch over my people like shepherds watch over their sheep. But they are causing my people to be destroyed and scattered." [2]So the LORD God of Israel has this to say about the leaders who are ruling over his people: "You have caused my people to [a]be dispersed and driven into exile. You have not taken care of them. So I will punish you for the evil that you have done. I, the LORD, affirm it! [3]Then [a]I myself will regather those of my people who are still alive from all the countries where I have driven them. I will bring them back to their homeland. They will greatly increase in number. [4]I will install [a]rulers over them who will care for them. Then they will no longer need to fear or be terrified. None of them will turn up missing. I, the LORD, promise it!

5 "I, [a]the LORD, promise that [b]a new
time will certainly come
when I will raise up for them a
righteous branch, a descendant of
David.

He will rule over them with wisdom
and understanding
and will do what is just and right in
the land.
6 Under his rule Judah will enjoy
safety
and Israel will live [a]in security.
This is the name he [b]will go by:
'The LORD has provided us with
justice.'

7 "So I, [a]the LORD, say: 'A new time will certainly come. People now affirm their oaths with, "I swear as surely as the LORD lives who delivered the people of Israel out of Egypt." [8]But at that time they will affirm them with, "I swear as surely as the LORD lives who delivered the descendants of the former nation of Israel[1] from the [a]land of the north and from all the other lands where he had banished[2] them." At that time they will live in their own [b]land.'"

Oracles against the False Prophets

9 Here is what the LORD says concerning the false prophets:

"My heart and my mind are deeply
disturbed.
I tremble all [a]over.
I am like a drunk person,
like a person who has had too much
wine,
because of the way the LORD
and his holy word are being
mistreated.
10 For [a]the land is full of people
unfaithful to him.[1]
They live wicked lives, and they
misuse their power.
So the land is dried up [b]because it is
under his curse.[2]
[c]The pastures in the wilderness are
withered."

11 Moreover, the LORD says,

"[a]Both the prophets and priests are
godless.

22:28 [a] Ps 31:12; Jer 48:38; Hos 8:8   22:29 [a] Deut 32:1; Isa 1:2; 34:1; Mic 1:2   22:30 [a] 1 Chr 3:16–17; Matt 1:12   [b] Ps 94:20; Jer 36:30   23:1 [a] Isa 56:9–12; Jer 10:21   23:2 [a] Exod 32:34   23:3 [a] Isa 11:11–12, 16; Jer 32:37   23:4 [a] Jer 3:15; [Ezek 34:23]   23:5 [a] Isa 4:2; 11:1; 40:10–11; Jer 33:14; [Dan 9:24; Zech 6:12]; Matt 1:1, 6; Luke 3:31; [John 1:45; 7:42]   [b] Ps 72:2; Isa 9:7; 32:1, 18; [Dan 9:24]   23:6 [a] Deut 33:28; Jer 30:10; Zech 14:11   [b] Jer 32:37   23:7 [a] Isa 43:18–19; Jer 16:14   23:8 [a] Isa 43:5–6; Ezek 34:13; Amos 9:14–15   [b] Gen 12:7; Jer 16:14–15; 31:8   [1] Heb. *descendants of the house of Israel.*   [2] MT *I had banished them.*   23:9 [a] Jer 8:18; Hab 3:16   23:10 [a] Jer 9:2   [b] Hos 4:2; Mal 3:5   [c] Ps 107:34; Jer 9:10   [1] Heb. *adulterers.*   [2] LXX, Syr. *because of these.*   23:11 [a] Jer 6:13; Zeph 3:4

[b]I have even found them doing evil in
my temple.
12 So [a]the paths they follow [b]will be
dark and slippery.
They will stumble and fall headlong.
For I will bring disaster on them.
A day of reckoning is coming for
them."
The LORD affirms it!
13 The LORD says, "I saw [a]the prophets
of Samaria
doing something that was disgusting.
They prophesied in the name of the
god Baal
and led my people Israel astray.
14 But I see [a]the prophets of Jerusalem
doing something just as shocking.
They are unfaithful to me
and continually prophesy lies.
So they [b]give encouragement to
people who are doing evil,
with the result that they do not stop
their evildoing.
I consider all of them as bad as the
people of [c]Sodom,
and the citizens of Jerusalem as bad
as the people of Gomorrah.[1]
15 So then I, the LORD of Heaven's
Armies,
have something to say concerning
the prophets of Jerusalem:
'I will make these prophets eat the
bitter [a]food of suffering
and drink the poison water of
judgment.
For the prophets of Jerusalem are
the reason
that ungodliness has spread
throughout the land.'"

16 The LORD of Heaven's Armies says to
[a]the people of Jerusalem:

"Do not listen to what
those prophets are saying to you.
They are filling you with false
hopes.
They are reporting visions of their
own imaginations,

not something the LORD has given
them to say.
17 They continually say to those who
reject what the LORD has said,[1]
'Things will go well for [a]you!'[2]
They say to all those who [b]follow the
stubborn inclinations of their own
hearts,
'Nothing bad will happen to you!'
18 Yet which of [a]them has ever stood in
the LORD's inner circle
so they could see and hear what he
has to say?[1]
Which of them have ever paid
attention or listened to what he
has said?
19 But just watch![1] The wrath of the
LORD
will come like a [a]storm!
Like a raging storm it will rage
down
on the heads of those who are
wicked.
20 The [a]anger of the LORD will not turn
back
until he has fully carried out his
[b]intended purposes.
In future days
you people will come to understand
this clearly.
21 I [a]did not send those prophets,
yet they were in a hurry to give their
message.
I did not tell them anything,
yet they prophesied anyway.
22 But if they had stood in my inner
circle,
they would have proclaimed my
message to my people.
They would have caused my people
to [a]turn from their wicked ways
and stop doing the evil things they
are doing.
23 Do you people think that I am some
local deity
and not the transcendent God?" the
LORD asks.
24 "Do you really think anyone can
[a]hide himself

23:11 [b]Jer 7:30; 32:34; Ezek 8:11; 23:39   23:12 [a]Ps 35:6; [Prov 4:19]; Jer 13:16   [b]Jer 11:23   23:13 [a]1 Kgs 18:18–21; Jer 2:8
23:14 [a]Jer 29:23   [b]Jer 23:22; Ezek 13:22–23   [c]Gen 18:20; Deut 32:32; Isa 1:9–10   [1]Heb. *All of them are to me like
Sodom and its* [Jerusalem's] *inhabitants like Gomorrah.*   23:15 [a]Deut 29:18; Jer 9:15   23:16 [a]Jer 14:14; Ezek 13:3, 6
23:17 [a]Jer 8:11; Ezek 13:10; Zech 10:2   [b]Deut 29:19; Jer 3:17   [c]Jer 5:12; Amos 9:10; Mic 3:11   [1]MT *who reject me, "The
LORD has spoken".*   [2]Heb. *You will have peace.*   23:18 [a]Job 15:8–9; [Jer 23:22; 1 Cor 2:16]   [1]Heb. *his word.*
23:19 [a]Jer 25:32; 30:23; Amos 1:14   [1]Heb. *Behold!*   23:20 [a]2 Kgs 23:26–27; Jer 30:24   [b]Gen 49:1
23:21 [a]Jer 14:14; 23:32; 27:15   23:22 [a]Jer 25:5   23:24 [a][Ps 139:7]; Amos 9:2–3

where I cannot see him?" the LORD asks.

"[b]Do you not know that I am everywhere?" the LORD asks.

[25]The LORD says, "I have heard what those prophets who are prophesying lies in my name are saying. They are saying, 'I have had a dream! I have had a dream!' [26]Those prophets are just prophesying lies. They are prophesying the delusions of their own minds. [27]How long will they go on plotting to make my people forget who I am through the dreams they tell one another? That is just [a]as bad as what their ancestors did when they forgot who I am by worshiping the god Baal. [28]Let the prophet who has had a dream go ahead and tell his dream. Let the person who has received my message report that message faithfully. What is like straw cannot compare to what is like grain! I, the LORD, affirm it! [29]My message is like a [a]fire that purges dross. It is like a hammer that breaks a rock in pieces. I, the LORD, so affirm it! [30]So [a]I, the LORD, affirm that I am opposed to those prophets who steal messages from one another that they claim are from me. [31]I, the LORD, affirm that I am opposed [a]to those prophets who are using their own tongues to declare, 'The LORD declares.' [32]I, the LORD, affirm that I am opposed to those prophets who dream up [a]lies and report them. They are misleading my people with [b]their reckless lies. I did not send them. I did not commission them. They are not [c]helping these people at all. I, the LORD, affirm it!"

[33]The LORD said to me, "Jeremiah, when one of [a]these people, or a prophet, or a priest asks you, 'What burdensome message do you have from the LORD?' Tell them, 'You are the burden,[1] and I will cast you away. I, the LORD, affirm it! [34]I will punish any prophet, priest, or other person who says, "The LORD's message is burdensome." I will punish both that person and his whole family.'"

[35]So I, Jeremiah, tell you, "Each of you people should say to his friend or his relative, 'How did the LORD answer? Or what did the LORD say?' [36]You must no longer say that the LORD's message is burdensome. For what is 'burdensome' really pertains to what a person himself says. You are [a]misrepresenting the words of our God, the living God, the LORD of Heaven's Armies. [37]Each of you should merely ask the prophet, 'What answer did the LORD give you?' Or, 'What did the LORD say?' [38]But just suppose you continue to say, 'The message of the LORD is burdensome.' Here is what the LORD says will happen: 'I sent word to you that you must not say, "The LORD's message is burdensome." But you used the words, "The LORD's message is burdensome," anyway. [39]So[1] [a]I will carry you far off[2] and throw you away. I will send both you and the city I gave to you and to your ancestors out of my sight. [40]I will bring on you lasting shame [a]and lasting [b]disgrace that will never be forgotten!'"

Good Figs and Bad Figs

24 The [a]LORD showed me two baskets of figs sitting before his temple. This happened after [b]King Nebuchadnezzar of Babylon deported Jehoiakim's son, King [c]Jeconiah of Judah. He deported him and the leaders of Judah from Jerusalem, along with the craftsmen and metal workers, and took them to Babylon. [2]One basket had very good-looking figs in it. They looked like those that had ripened early. The other basket had very bad-looking figs in it, so [a]bad they could not be eaten. [3]The LORD said to me, "What do you see, Jeremiah?" I answered, "I see figs. The good ones look very good. But the bad ones look very bad, so bad that they cannot be eaten."

[4]The LORD's message came to me, [5]"I, the LORD, the God of Israel, say: 'The exiles of Judah whom I sent away from here to the land of Babylon are like those good figs. I consider them to be good. [6]I [a]will look after [b]their welfare and will restore them to this land. There I will build them up and will not tear them down. I will plant them firmly in the land and will not uproot them.

23:24 [b] [1 Kgs 8:27]; Ps 139:7   **23:27** [a] Judg 3:7   **23:29** [a] Jer 5:14   **23:30** [a] Deut 18:20; Ps 34:16; Jer 14:14–15; Ezek 13:8–9   **23:31** [a] Ezek 13:9   **23:32** [a] Jer 20:6; 27:10; Lam 2:14; 3:37   [b] Zeph 3:4   [c] Jer 7:8; Lam 2:14   **23:33** [a] Isa 13:1; Nah 1:1; Hab 1:1; Zech 9:1; Mal 1:1   [1] MT *What burden?*   **23:36** [a] Deut 4:2   **23:39** [a] Hos 4:6   [1] Heb. *But if you say, 'The burden of the LORD,' therefore this is what the LORD says, 'Because you said this word, "The burden of the LORD," even though I sent unto saying, "you shall not say, 'The burden of the Lord,' therefore".*   [2] Maj. MSS *I will totally forget* [or *certainly forget*] *you.*   **23:40** [a] Jer 20:11; Ezek 5:14–15   [b] Mic 3:5–7   **24:1** [a] Amos 7:1, 4; 8:1   [b] 2 Kgs 24:12–16; 2 Chr 36:10   [c] Jer 22:24–28; 29:2   **24:2** [a] Isa 5:4, 7; Jer 29:17   **24:6** [a] Jer 12:15; 29:10; Ezek 11:17   [b] Jer 32:41; 33:7; 42:10

[7]I will give them the desire to [a]acknowledge that I am the LORD. I will be their God, and they will be [b]my people. For they will wholeheartedly return to me.'

[8]"I, the LORD, also solemnly assert: 'King Zedekiah of Judah, his officials, and the people who remain in Jerusalem or who have gone to live in Egypt are like those bad [a]figs. [b]I consider them to be just like [c]those bad figs that are so bad they cannot be eaten. [9]I will bring such disaster on them that all the kingdoms of the earth will be horrified. I will make them an object of reproach, a proverbial example of disaster. I will make them an object of ridicule, an example [a]to be used in curses. That is how they will be remembered wherever I banish them. [10]I will bring war, starvation, and disease on them until they are completely destroyed from the land I gave them and their ancestors.'"

Seventy Years of Servitude for Failure to Give Heed

25 [a]In the fourth year that [b]Jehoiakim son of Josiah was king of Judah, the LORD spoke to Jeremiah[1] concerning all the people of Judah. (That was the same as the first year that Nebuchadnezzar was king of Babylon.) [2]So the prophet Jeremiah spoke to all the people of Judah and to all the people who were living in Jerusalem. [3]"For the last 23 years, [a]from the thirteenth year that Josiah son of Amon was ruling in Judah until now, the LORD's messages have come to me, and I have told them to you over and over again. [b]But you would not listen. [4]Over and over again the LORD has sent his servants the prophets to you. But you have not listened or paid attention.[1] [5]He said through them, 'Each of you must [a]turn from your wicked ways and stop doing the evil things you are doing. If you do, I will allow you to continue to live here in the land that I gave to you and your ancestors as a lasting possession. [6]Do not pay allegiance to other gods and worship and serve them. Do not make me angry by the things that you do. Then I will not cause you any harm.' [7]So, now the LORD says, 'You have not listened to me. But you have made me angry by the things that you have done. Thus you have brought harm on yourselves.'

[8]"Therefore, the LORD of Heaven's Armies says, 'You have not listened to what I said. [9]So I, the LORD, affirm that I will send for [a]all the peoples of the north and [b]my servant, King Nebuchadnezzar of Babylon. I will bring them against this land and its inhabitants and all the nations that surround it. I will utterly destroy the land, its inhabitants, and all the surrounding nations and [c]make them everlasting ruins. I will make them objects of horror and hissing scorn. [10]I will put an end to the [a]sounds of joy and gladness and [b]the glad celebration of brides and grooms in these lands. I will put an end to the sound of people grinding meal. I will put an end to lamps shining in their houses. [11]This whole area will become a desolate wasteland. These nations will be subject to the king of Babylon for 70 [a]years.' [12]"But [a]when the seventy years are over, I will punish the king of Babylon [b]and his nation for their sins. I will make the land of Babylon an everlasting ruin. I, the LORD, affirm it! [13]I will bring on that land everything that I said I would. I will bring on it everything that is written in this book. I will bring on it everything that Jeremiah has prophesied against all the nations. [14]For many nations and great kings will make slaves of the king of Babylon and his nation too. I will repay them [a]for all they have done.'"

Judah and the Nations Will Experience God's Wrath

[15]So the LORD, the God of Israel, spoke to me in a vision: "Take this cup from my hand. It is filled with the [a]wine of my wrath. Take it and make the nations to whom I send you drink it. [16]When [a]they have drunk it, they will stagger to and fro and act insane. For I will send wars sweeping through them."

[17]So I took the cup from the LORD's hand. I made all the nations to whom he sent me drink the wine of his wrath. [18]I [a]made [b]Jerusalem and the cities of Judah, its kings and

its officials drink it. I did it so Judah would become a ruin. I did it so Judah, its kings, and its officials would become an object of horror and of hissing scorn, an example used in curses. Such is already becoming the case! [19] I made all these other people drink it: Pharaoh, king of Egypt; his attendants, his officials, his people, [20] the foreigners living in Egypt; all [a] the kings of the land of Uz; all the kings of the land of the [b] Philistines, [c] the people of Ashkelon, Gaza, Ekron, the people who had been left alive from Ashdod; [21] all the people of [a] Edom, Moab, Ammon; [22] all the kings of [a] Tyre, all the kings of Sidon; all the kings of the coastlands along the [b] sea; [23] the people of [a] Dedan, Tema, Buz, all the desert people who cut their hair short at the temples; [24] all the kings of Arabia who[1] live in the desert; [25] all the kings of Zimri; all the kings of [a] Elam; all the kings of [b] Media; [26] [a] all the kings of the north, whether near or far from one another; and all the other kingdoms that are on the face of the earth. After all of them have drunk the wine of the LORD's wrath, the king of Babylon[1] must drink it.

[27] Then the LORD said to me, "Tell them that the LORD of Heaven's Armies, the God of Israel, says, '[a] Drink this cup until you get drunk and vomit. Drink until you fall down and can't get up. For I will send wars sweeping through you.' [28] If they refuse to take the cup from your hand and drink it, tell them that the LORD of Heaven's Armies says,[1] 'You most certainly must drink it! [29] For take note, [a] I am already beginning to bring disaster on the city that [b] I call my own. So how can you [c] possibly avoid being punished? You will not go unpunished. For I am proclaiming war against all who live on the earth. I, the LORD of Heaven's Armies, affirm it!'

[30] "Then, Jeremiah, make the following prophecy against them:

'Like a lion about to attack, the LORD
    will [a] roar from the heights of
    heaven;
    from [b] his holy dwelling on high he
    will roar loudly.

He will roar mightily against [c] his
    [d] land.
He will shout in triumph, like
    those stomping juice from the
    grapes,
    against all those who live on the
    earth.
[31] The sounds of [a] battle will resound to
    [b] the ends of the earth.
For the LORD will bring charges
    against the nations.
He will pass judgment on all
    humankind
    and will hand the wicked over to be
    killed in war.'
    The LORD so affirms it!
[32] The LORD of [a] Heaven's Armies says,
    'Disaster will soon come on one
    nation after another.
A mighty storm of military
    destruction is rising up
    from the distant parts of the earth.'
[33] [a] Those who have been killed by the
    LORD at that time
    will be scattered from one end of the
    earth to the other.
They will not be mourned [b] over,
    gathered up, [c] or buried.
Their dead bodies will lie scattered
    over the ground like manure.
[34] [a] Wail and cry out in anguish, you
    rulers!
Roll in the dust, you who shepherd
    flocks of people!
The time for you to be slaughtered
    has come.
You will lie scattered and fallen like
    broken pieces of fine pottery.
[35] The leaders will not be able to run
    away and hide.
The shepherds of the flocks will not
    be able to escape.
[36] Listen to the cries of anguish of the
    leaders.
Listen to the wails of the shepherds
    of the flocks.
They are wailing because the LORD
    is about to destroy their lands.

25:20 [a] Job 1:11; Lam 4:21   [b] Jer 47:1–7; Ezek 25:16–17   [c] Isa 20:1   25:21 [a] Jer 49:7   25:22 [a] Jer 47:4; Zech 9:2–4   [b] Jer 49:23   25:23 [a] Isa 21:13; Jer 49:7–8   25:24 [1] LXX *people of mixed origin*.   25:25 [a] Gen 10:22; Isa 11:11; Jer 49:34   [b] Isa 13:17; Jer 51:11, 28   25:26 [a] Jer 50:9   [1] Heb. *the king of Sheshach*; "Sheshach" is a code name for Babylon formed by substituting the last letter of the Heb. alphabet for the first, the next to the last for the second, and so on.   25:27 [a] Jer 25:16; Hab 2:16   25:28 [1] Heb. *Tell them, 'Thus says the LORD'*.   25:29 [a] [Prov 11:31]; Isa 10:12; Jer 13:13; Ezek 9:6; [Luke 23:31; 1 Pet 4:17]   [b] Dan 9:18   [c] Ezek 38:21   25:30 [a] Isa 42:13; Joel 3:16; Amos 1:2   [b] Ps 11:4   [c] 1 Kgs 9:3; Ps 132:14   [d] Isa 16:9; Jer 48:33   25:31 [a] Hos 4:1; Mic 6:2   [b] Isa 66:16; Joel 3:2   25:32 [a] Jer 23:19; 30:23   25:33 [a] Isa 34:2–3; 66:16   [b] Jer 16:4, 6; Ezek 39:4, 17   [c] Ps 79:3; Jer 8:2; Rev 11:9   25:34 [a] Jer 4:8; 6:26; Ezek 27:30

37 Their peaceful dwelling places will be
laid waste
by the fierce anger of the LORD.
38 The LORD is like a lion who has left
his lair.
So their lands will certainly be laid
waste
by the warfare of the oppressive
nation[1]
and by the fierce anger of the LORD."

Jeremiah Is Put on Trial as a False Prophet

26 The LORD spoke to Jeremiah at the beginning of the reign[1] of Josiah's son, King Jehoiakim of Judah. [2]The LORD said, "Go stand in [a]the courtyard of the LORD's temple. Speak out to [b]all the people who are coming from the towns of Judah to worship in the LORD's temple. Tell them everything I command you to tell them. [c]Do not leave out a single word. [3][a]Maybe they will pay attention and each of them will stop living the evil way they do. If they do that, then I will [b]forgo destroying them as I had intended to do because of the wicked things they have been doing. [4]Tell them that the LORD says, 'You must obey me; you must live according to the way [a]I have instructed you in my laws. [5]You must pay attention to the exhortations of my servants the prophets. I have sent them to you over and over again. But you have not paid any attention to them. [6]If you do not obey me, then I will do to this temple what I did to [a]Shiloh. [b]And I will make this city an example to be used in curses by people from all the nations on the earth.'"

[7]The priests, the prophets, and all the people heard Jeremiah say these things in the LORD's temple. [8]Jeremiah had just barely finished saying all the LORD had commanded him to say to all the people when all at once some of the priests, the prophets, and the people grabbed him and shouted, "You deserve to die![1] [9]How dare you claim the LORD's authority to prophesy such things! How dare you claim his authority to prophesy that this temple will become like Shiloh and that this city will [a]become an uninhabited ruin!" Then all the people crowded around Jeremiah in the LORD's temple.

[10]However, some of the officials of Judah heard about what was happening,[1] and they rushed up to the LORD's temple from the royal palace. They set up court at the entrance of the New Gate of the LORD's temple. [11]Then the priests and the prophets made their charges before the officials and all the people. They said, "This man should be condemned to [a]die because he prophesied against this city. You have heard him do so with your own ears."

[12]Then Jeremiah made his defense before all the officials and all the people. "The LORD sent me to prophesy everything you have heard me say against this temple and against this city. [13]But [a]correct the way you have been living and do what is right. Obey the LORD your God. If you do, the LORD will forgo destroying you as he threatened he would. [14]As to my case, [a]I am in your power. Do to me what you deem fair and proper. [15]But you should take careful note of this: If you put me to death, you will bring on yourselves and this city and those who live in it the guilt of murdering an innocent man. For the LORD has sent me to speak all this where you can hear it. That is the truth!"

[16]Then the officials and all the people rendered their verdict to the priests and the prophets. They said, "This man should not be condemned to die. For he has spoken to us under the authority of the LORD our God." [17]Then some of [a]the elders of Judah stepped forward and spoke to all the people gathered there. They said, [18]"[a]Micah from Moresheth prophesied during the time Hezekiah was king of Judah. He told all the people of Judah, 'The LORD of Heaven's Armies says,

"[b]Zion will become a plowed field.
Jerusalem will become a pile of
[c]rubble.

25:38 [1]MT *the anger of the oppressor.*   26:1 [1]Possibly, but perhaps unlikely, the part of the year remaining from the death or deposing of the previous king until the beginning of the calendar year, when the new king officially ascended the throne. In this case, it would refer to September, 609 BC, when Jehoiakim was placed on the throne as a puppet king by Pharaoh Necho (2 Kgs 23:34–35), to April, 608 BC, when he would have been officially celebrated as king.   26:2 [a]2 Chr 24:20–21; Jer 19:14   [b]Deut 4:2; Jer 43:1; Ezek 3:10; Matt 28:20; [Rev 22:19]   [c]Acts 20:27   26:3 [a]Isa 1:16–19; Jer 36:3–7   [b]Jer 18:8; Jonah 3:9   26:4 [a]Lev 26:14–15; Deut 28:15; 1 Kgs 9:6; Isa 1:20; Jer 17:27; 22:5   26:6 [a]1 Sam 4:10–11; Ps 78:60; Jer 7:12, 14   [b]2 Kgs 22:19; Isa 65:15; Jer 24:9   26:8 [1]Or *You must certainly die!*; an emphatic Heb. construction.   26:9 [a]Jer 9:11   26:10 [1]Heb. *these things.*   26:11 [a]Jer 38:4   26:13 [a]Jer 7:3; [Joel 2:13]; Jonah 3:8   26:14 [a]Jer 38:5   26:17 [a]Acts 5:34   26:18 [a]Mic 1:1   [b]Mic 3:12   [c]Neh 4:2; Ps 79:1; Jer 9:11

The temple mount will become a
mere wooded ridge.'"

[19]"King Hezekiah and all the people of
Judah [a]did not put him to death, did they?
Did not Hezekiah show reverence for the
LORD and [b]seek the LORD's favor?[1] Did not
the LORD [c]forgo destroying them as he
threatened he would? [d]But we are on the
verge of bringing great disaster on ourselves."

[20]Now there was another man who
prophesied as the LORD's representative
against this city and this land just as Jeremiah did. His name was Uriah son of Shemaiah from Kiriath Jearim. [21]When King
Jehoiakim and all his bodyguards and
officials heard what he was prophesying,
the king sought to have him executed. But
Uriah found out about it and fled to Egypt
out of fear.[1] [22]However, King Jehoiakim sent
some men to Egypt, including Elnathan
son of Achbor, [23]and they brought Uriah
back from there. They took him to King
Jehoiakim, who had him executed and had
his body thrown into the burial place of the
common people.

[24]However, Ahikam son of Shaphan used
his influence to keep Jeremiah from being
handed over and executed by [a]the people.

Jeremiah Counsels Submission to Babylon

27 The LORD spoke to Jeremiah early
in the reign of Josiah's son, [a]King
Zedekiah of Judah.[1] [2]The LORD told me,
"Make [a]a yoke out of leather straps and
wooden crossbars and put it on your neck.
[3]Use it to send messages to the kings of
Edom, Moab, Ammon, Tyre, and Sidon.
Send them through the envoys who have
come to Jerusalem to King Zedekiah of
Judah. [4]Charge them to give their masters
a message from me. Tell them, 'The LORD
of Heaven's Armies, the God of Israel, says
to give your masters this message: [5]"I made
the earth and the people and [a]animals on
it by my mighty power and great strength,[1]
and I give it to whomever I see fit. [6a]I have

at this time placed all these nations of
yours under the power of [b]my servant, King
Nebuchadnezzar of Babylon. I have even
made all [c]the wild animals subject to him.
[7]All nations must serve him and his [a]son
and grandson [b]until the time comes for his
own nation to fall. Then many nations [c]and
great kings will in turn subjugate Babylon.
[8]But suppose a nation or a kingdom will not
be subject to King Nebuchadnezzar of Babylon. Suppose it will not submit to the yoke
of servitude to him. I, the LORD, affirm that
I will punish that nation. I will use the king
of Babylon to punish it with war, starvation,
and disease until I have destroyed it.[1] [9]So do
not listen to your prophets or to those who
claim to predict the future by divination, by
dreams, by consulting the dead, or by practicing magic. They keep telling you, 'You do
not need to be subject to the king of Babylon.' [10]Do not listen to them, because their
prophecies are [a]lies. Listening to them will
only cause you to be taken far away from
your native land. I will drive you out of your
country and you will die in exile. [11]Things
will go better for the nation that submits to
the yoke of servitude to the king of Babylon
and is subject to him. I will leave that nation
in its native land. Its people can continue to
farm it and live in it. I, the LORD, affirm it!"'"

[12]I told King [a]Zedekiah of Judah the same
thing. I said, "Submit to the yoke of servitude to the king of Babylon. Be subject to
him and his people. Then you will continue to live. [13]There is no reason [a]why you
and your people should die in war or from
starvation or disease. That's what the LORD
says will happen to any nation that will not
be subject to the king of Babylon. [14]'Do not
listen to the prophets who are telling you
that you [a]do not need to serve the king of
[b]Babylon. For they are prophesying lies to
you. [15]For I, the LORD, affirm that I did [a]not
send them. They are prophesying lies to
you in my name. If you listen to them, I will
drive you and the prophets who are prophesying lies out of the land and you will all
die in exile.'"

26:19 [a]2 Chr 32:26; Isa 37:1, 4, 15–20 [b]2 Kgs 20:1–19 [c]Exod 32:14; 2 Sam 24:16; Jer 18:8 [d][Acts 5:39] [1]A Heb. idiom of
"stroking" or "patting the face" of someone, seeking to gain his favor. **26:21** [1]Heb. *Uriah heard and feared and fled and
entered Egypt.* **26:24** [a]2 Kgs 22:12–14; Jer 39:14; 40:5–7 **27:1** [a]Jer 27:3, 12, 20; 28:1 [1]MT *At the beginning of the reign of
Josiah's son, Jehoiakim king of Judah.* **27:2** [a]Jer 28:10, 12; Ezek 4:1; 12:3; 24:3 **27:5** [a]Ps 115:15; 146:6; Isa 45:12 [1]Heb. *my
great power and my outstretched arm.* **27:6** [a]Jer 28:14 [b]Jer 25:9; 43:10; Ezek 29:18, 20 [c]Jer 28:14; Dan 2:38 **27:7** [a]2 Chr
36:20 [b]Jer 25:12; 50:27; [Dan 5:26]; Zech 2:8–9 [c]Jer 25:14 **27:8** [1]Heb. *I will punish that nation until I have destroyed
them* [i.e., its people] *by his hand.* **27:10** [a]Jer 23:16, 32; 28:15 **27:12** [a]Jer 28:1; 38:17 **27:13** [a][Prov 8:36]; Jer 27:8;
38:23; [Ezek 18:31] **27:14** [a]Jer 23:16 [b]Jer 14:14; 23:21; 29:8–9; Ezek 13:22 **27:15** [a]Jer 23:21; 29:9

[16]I also told [a]the priests and all the people, "The LORD says, 'Do not listen to what your prophets are saying. They are prophesying to you that the valuable articles taken from the LORD's temple will be brought back from Babylon very soon. But they are prophesying a lie to you. [17]Do not listen to them. Be subject to the king of Babylon. Then you will continue to live. Why should this city be made a pile of rubble?'" [18]I also told them, "If they are really prophets and the LORD is speaking to them, let them pray earnestly to the LORD of Heaven's Armies. Let them plead with him not to let the valuable articles that are still left in the LORD's temple, in the royal palace of Judah, and in Jerusalem be taken away to Babylon. [19]For the LORD of Heaven's Armies has already spoken about the two bronze pillars, the large bronze basin called 'The Sea,' and the movable bronze stands. He has already spoken about the rest of the valuable articles that are left [a]in this city. [20]He has already spoken about these things that King Nebuchadnezzar of Babylon did not take away when he [a]carried Jehoiakim's son King Jeconiah of Judah and the nobles of Judah and Jerusalem away as captives from Jerusalem to Babylon. [21]Indeed, the LORD of Heaven's Armies, the God of Israel, has already spoken about the valuable [a]articles that are left in the LORD's temple, in the royal palace of Judah, and in Jerusalem. [22]He has said, 'They will be carried [a]off to Babylon. They will remain there until it is time for me to show consideration [b]for them [c]again.[1] Then I will bring them back and restore them to this place. I, the LORD, affirm this!'

Jeremiah Confronted by a False Prophet

28 The following events occurred in that same year, early in the reign of King Zedekiah of Judah. To be more precise, [a]it was the fifth month of the [b]fourth year of his reign. The prophet Hananiah son of [c]Azzur, who was from Gibeon, spoke to Jeremiah in the LORD's temple in the presence of the priests and all the people: [2]"The LORD of Heaven's Armies, [a]the God of Israel, says, 'I will break the yoke of servitude to the king of Babylon. [3]Before two years are [a]over, I will bring back [b]to this place everything that King Nebuchadnezzar of Babylon took from it and carried away to Babylon. [4]I will also bring back to this place Jehoiakim's son King Jeconiah of Judah and all the exiles who were taken to Babylon.' Indeed, the LORD affirms, 'I will break the yoke of servitude to the king of Babylon.'"

[5]Then the prophet Jeremiah responded to the prophet Hananiah in the presence of the priests and all the people who were standing in the LORD's temple. [6]The prophet Jeremiah said, "[a]Amen! May the LORD do all this! May the LORD make your prophecy come true! May he bring back to this place from Babylon all the valuable articles taken from the LORD's temple and the people who were carried into exile. [7]But listen to what I say to you and to all these people. [8]From earliest times, the prophets who preceded you and me invariably prophesied war, disaster,[1] and plagues against many countries and great kingdoms. [9]So if [a]a prophet prophesied peace and [b]prosperity, it was only known that the LORD truly sent him when what he prophesied came true."

[10]The prophet Hananiah then took the [a]yoke off the prophet Jeremiah's neck and broke it. [11]Then he spoke up in the presence of all the people. "The LORD says, 'In the same way I will break the yoke of servitude of all the nations to King Nebuchadnezzar of Babylon before two years are over.'" After he heard this, the prophet Jeremiah departed and went on his way.

[12]But shortly after the prophet Hananiah had broken the yoke off the prophet Jeremiah's neck, the LORD's message came to Jeremiah. [13]"Go and tell Hananiah that the LORD says,[1] 'You have indeed broken the wooden yoke. But you have only succeeded in replacing it with an iron one! [14]For the LORD of Heaven's [a]Armies, the God of [b]Israel, says, "I have put an irresistible yoke of servitude on all these nations so they will serve King Nebuchadnezzar of Babylon. And they will indeed serve him. I have even given him control over the wild animals."'"

27:16 [a]2 Kgs 24:13; 2 Chr 36:7, 10; Jer 28:3; Dan 1:2 **27:19** [a]1 Kgs 7:15; 2 Kgs 25:13–17; Jer 52:17, 20, 21 **27:20** [a]2 Kgs 24:14–15; 2 Chr 36:10, 18; Jer 24:1 **27:21** [a]Jer 20:5 **27:22** [a]2 Kgs 25:13; 2 Chr 36:18 [b]2 Chr 36:21; Jer 29:10; 32:5 [c]Ezra 1:7; 7:19 [1]This Heb. verb is used in the sense of taking note of something and acting according to what is noticed.
28:1 [a]Jer 27:1 [b]Jer 51:59 [c]Ezek 11:1 **28:2** [a]Jer 27:12 **28:3** [a]Jer 27:16 [b]2 Kgs 24:13; Dan 1:2 **28:6** [a]1 Kgs 1:36; Ps 41:13; Jer 11:5 **28:8** [1]LXX omits disaster, and plagues. **28:9** [a]Deut 18:22 [b]Jer 23:17; Ezek 13:10, 16 **28:10** [a]Jer 27:2 **28:13** [1]Heb. Hananiah, 'Thus says the LORD. **28:14** [a]Deut 28:48; Jer 27:7–8 [b]Jer 27:6

[15]Then the prophet Jeremiah told the prophet Hananiah, "Listen, Hananiah! The LORD did not send [a]you! You are making these people trust in a [b]lie. [16]So the LORD says, 'I will most assuredly remove you from the face of the earth. You will [a]die this very year because you have counseled [b]rebellion against the LORD.'"

[17]In the seventh month of that very same year the prophet Hananiah died.

Jeremiah's Letter to the Exiles

29 The prophet Jeremiah sent [a]a letter to the exiles Nebuchadnezzar had carried off from Jerusalem to Babylon. It was addressed to the elders who were left among the exiles, to the priests, to the prophets, and to all the other people who were exiled in Babylon. [2]He sent it after King [a]Jeconiah, the queen [b]mother, the palace officials,[1] the leaders of Judah and Jerusalem, the craftsmen, and the metal workers had been exiled from Jerusalem. [3]He sent it with Elasah son of [a]Shaphan and Gemariah son of Hilkiah. King Zedekiah of Judah had sent these men to Babylon to King Nebuchadnezzar of Babylon. The letter said:

[4]"The LORD of Heaven's Armies, the God of Israel, says to all those he sent into exile to Babylon from Jerusalem, [5]'Build houses and settle down. Plant gardens and eat what they produce. [6]Marry and have sons and daughters. Find wives for your sons and allow your daughters to get married so that they too can have sons and daughters. Grow in number; do not dwindle away. [7]Work to see that the city where I sent you as exiles enjoys peace [a]and prosperity. Pray to the LORD for it. For as it prospers you will prosper.'

[8]"For the LORD of Heaven's Armies, the God of Israel, says, 'Do not let the prophets among you or those who claim to be able to predict the future by divination [a]deceive you. And do not pay any attention to the dreams that you are encouraging them to dream. [9]They are prophesying [a]lies to you and claiming my authority to do so. But I did not send them. I, the LORD, affirm it!'

[10]"For the LORD says, 'Only when the [a]seventy years of Babylonian rule are over will I again take up consideration for you. Then I will fulfill my gracious promise to you and [b]restore you to your homeland. [11]For I know what I have planned for you,' says the LORD. 'I have plans to prosper you, not to harm you. I have plans to give you a future filled with hope.[1] [12]When you call out [a]to me and come to me in prayer, I will [b]hear your prayers. [13]When [a]you seek me in prayer and worship, you will find me available to you. If you seek me [b]with all your heart and soul, [14]I [a]will make myself [b]available to you,' says the LORD. 'Then I will reverse your plight and will regather you from all the nations and all the places where I have exiled you,' says the LORD. 'I will bring you back to the place from which I exiled you.'

[15]"You say, 'The LORD has raised up prophets of good news for us here in Babylon.' [16]But just listen to what [a]the LORD has to say about the king who occupies David's throne and all your fellow countrymen who are still living in this city of Jerusalem and were not carried off into exile with you. [17]The LORD of Heaven's Armies says, 'I will bring war, starvation, and disease on them. I will treat them like figs that are so [a]rotten they cannot be eaten. [18]I [a]will [b]chase after them with war, starvation, and disease. I will make all the kingdoms of the earth horrified at what happens to them. I will make them examples of those who are cursed, objects of horror, hissing scorn, and ridicule among all the nations where I exile them. [19]For they have not [a]paid attention to what I said to them through my servants the prophets whom I sent to them over and over again,' says the LORD. 'And you exiles have not paid any attention to them either,' says the LORD. [20]'So pay attention to the LORD's message, all you exiles whom I have sent to Babylon from Jerusalem.'

[21]"The LORD of Heaven's Armies, the God of Israel, also has something to say about

28:15 [a]Jer 20:6; 29:31; Lam 2:14; Ezek 13:22; Zech 13:3 [b]Jer 27:10; 29:9 **28:16** [a]Jer 20:6 [b]Deut 13:5; Jer 29:32 **29:1** [a]Jer 27:20 **29:2** [a]2 Kgs 24:12–16; 2 Chr 36:9–10; Jer 22:24–28 [b]2 Kgs 24:12, 15; Jer 13:18 [1]This Heb. term is often mistakenly understood to refer to a "eunuch." **29:3** [a]2 Chr 34:8 **29:7** [a]Ezra 6:10; Neh 1:4–11; Dan 9:16; 1 Tim 2:2 **29:8** [a]Jer 14:14; 23:21; 27:14–15; Eph 5:6 **29:9** [a]Jer 28:15; 37:19 **29:10** [a]2 Chr 36:21–23; Ezra 1:1–4; Jer 25:12; 27:22; Dan 9:2; Zech 7:5 [b][Jer 24:6–7]; Zeph 2:7 **29:11** [1]Or *the future you hope for;* Heb. *a future and a hope.* **29:12** [a]Ps 50:15; Jer 33:3; Dan 9:3 [b]Ps 145:19 **29:13** [a]Lev 26:39–42; Deut 30:1–3 [b]1 Chr 22:19; 2 Chr 22:9; Jer 24:7 **29:14** [a][Deut 4:7]; Ps 32:6; 46:1; [Isa 55:6–7]; Jer 24:7 [b]Isa 43:5–6; Jer 23:8; 32:37 **29:16** [a]Jer 38:2–3, 17–23 **29:17** [a]Jer 24:3, 8–10 **29:18** [a]Deut 28:25; 2 Chr 29:8; Jer 15:4; 24:9; 34:17; Ezek 12:15 [b]Jer 26:6; 42:18 **29:19** [a]Jer 25:4; 26:5; 35:15

Ahab son of Kolaiah and Zedekiah son of Maaseiah, who are prophesying [a]lies to you and claiming my authority to do so. 'I will hand them over to King Nebuchadnezzar of Babylon, and he will execute them before your very eyes. [22]And all the exiles of Judah who are in Babylon will use them as examples when they put [a]a curse on anyone. They will say, "May the LORD treat you like Zedekiah and Ahab [b]whom the king of Babylon roasted to death in the fire!" [23]This will happen to them because [a]they have done what is shameful in Israel. They have committed adultery with their neighbors' wives and have spoken lies while claiming my authority. They have spoken words that I did not command them to speak. I [b]know what they have done. I have been a witness to it,' says the LORD."

A Response to the Letter and a Subsequent Letter

[24]The LORD told Jeremiah, "Tell Shemaiah the Nehelamite[1] [25]that the LORD of Heaven's Armies, the God of Israel, has a message for him. Tell him, 'On your own initiative you sent a letter [a]to the priest Zephaniah son of Maaseiah and to all the other priests and to all the people in Jerusalem. In your letter you said to Zephaniah, [26]"The LORD has made you priest in place of Jehoiada.[1] He has put you in [a]charge in the LORD's temple of controlling[2] any [b]lunatic who pretends to be a prophet. And it is your duty to [c]put any such person in the stocks with an iron collar around his neck. [27]You should have reprimanded Jeremiah from Anathoth who is pretending to be a prophet among you! [28]For he has even sent a message to us here in Babylon. He wrote and told us, 'You will be there a long time. Build houses and settle down. Plant gardens and eat what they produce.'"'"

[29]Zephaniah the priest read that letter to the prophet Jeremiah. [30]Then the LORD's message came to Jeremiah: [31]"Send [a]a message to all the exiles in Babylon. Tell them, 'The LORD has spoken about Shemaiah the Nehelamite: "Shemaiah has spoken to you as a prophet even though I did not send him. He is making you trust in a [b]lie. [32]Because he has done this,"[1] the LORD says, "I will punish Shemaiah the Nehelamite and his whole family. There will not [a]be any of them left to experience the good things that I will do for my people. I, the LORD, affirm it! For he counseled rebellion against the LORD."'"

Introduction to the Book of Consolation

30 The LORD spoke to Jeremiah. [2]"The LORD God of Israel says, 'Write everything that I am about to tell you in a scroll. [3]For [a]I, the LORD, affirm that the time will come when I will reverse the plight of my people, Israel [b]and Judah,' says the LORD. 'I will bring them back to the land I gave their ancestors, and they will take possession of it once again.'"

Israel and Judah Will Be Delivered after a Time of Deep Distress

[4]So here is what the LORD has to say about Israel and Judah.

[5]Yes, here is what he says:

"You hear cries of panic and of terror;
there is no peace in sight.
[6] Ask yourselves this and consider it
carefully:
Have you ever seen a man give birth
to a baby?
Why then do [a]I see all these strong
men
grabbing their stomachs in pain like
a woman giving birth?
And why do their faces
turn so deathly pale?
[7] [a]Alas, what a terrible time of trouble
it is!
There has never been any like it.
It is a time of trouble for the
descendants of Jacob,
but [b]some of them will be rescued
out of it.

29:21 [a] Jer 14:14–15; Lam 2:14; 2 Pet 2:1   **29:22** [a] Gen 48:20; Isa 65:15   [b] Dan 3:6, 21   **29:23** [a] Jer 23:14   [b] [Prov 5:21; Jer 16:17]; Mal 3:5; [Heb 4:13]   **29:24** [1] It is unclear whether this is a family name or a place name.   **29:25** [a] 2 Kgs 25:18; Jer 21:1   **29:26** [a] Jer 20:1   [b] 2 Kgs 9:11; Hos 9:7; Mark 3:21; John 10:20; Acts 26:24; [2 Cor 5:13]   [c] Jer 20:1–2; Acts 16:24   [1] Heb. *in place of Jehoiada the priest.*   [2] Heb. *The LORD has appointed you priest in place of the priest Jehoiada to be overseer in the house of the LORD for/over;* MT *The LORD has . . . to be overseers* [in] *the house of the LORD for/over.*   **29:31** [a] Jer 28:15   [b] Ezek 13:8–16, 22, 23   **29:32** [a] Jer 28:16   [1] Heb. *Therefore.*   **30:3** [a] Ps 53:6; Jer 29:14; 30:18; 32:44; Ezek 39:25; Amos 9:14; Zeph 3:20   [b] Jer 16:15; Ezek 20:42; 36:24   **30:6** [a] Jer 4:31; 6:24   **30:7** [a] [Isa 2:12]; Hos 1:11; Joel 2:11; Amos 5:18; Zeph 1:14   [b] Lam 1:12; Dan 9:12; 12:1

8 When the time for them to be
    rescued comes,"
  says the LORD of Heaven's Armies,
  "I will rescue you from foreign
    subjugation.
  I will deliver you from captivity.[1]
  Foreigners will then no longer
    subjugate them.
9 But they will be subject to the LORD
    their God
  and to the [a]Davidic ruler whom I will
    raise [b]up as king over them.
10 So I, the LORD, tell you not to be
    afraid,
  you descendants of Jacob, my
    servants.
  [a]Do not be terrified, people of Israel.
  For I will rescue you and your
    descendants
  [b]from a faraway land where you are
    captives.
  The descendants of Jacob will return
    to their land and enjoy peace.
  They will be secure, and no one will
    terrify them.
11 For I, the LORD, affirm that
  I will be with [a]you and will rescue
    you.
  [b]I will completely destroy all the
    nations where I scattered you.
  But I will not completely destroy you.
  I will indeed discipline you, but only
    in due measure.
  I will not allow you to go entirely
    unpunished."

The Lord Will Heal the Wounds of Judah

12 Moreover, the LORD says to the people
of Zion:

  "[a]Your injuries are incurable;
  your wounds are severe.
13 There is no one to plead [a]your cause.
  There are no remedies for your
    wounds.[1]
  There is no healing for you.
14 [a]All your allies have abandoned you.
  They no longer have any concern for
    you.

  For I have attacked you like an
    enemy would.
  I have chastened you cruelly.
  For your wickedness is so great
    and your sin is so much.
15 Why [a]do you complain about your
    injuries,
  that your pain is incurable?
  I have done all this to you
  because your wickedness is so great
    and your sin is so much.
16 But [a]all who destroyed you will be
    destroyed.
  All your enemies will go into [b]exile.
  Those who plundered you will be
    [c]plundered.
  I will cause those who pillaged you to
    be [d]pillaged.
17 Yes, I will restore you to health.
  I will heal your wounds.
  I, the LORD, affirm it!
  [a]For you have been called an
    outcast,
  Zion, whom no one cares for."

The Lord Will Restore Israel and Judah

18 The LORD says:

  "I will restore the ruined houses of
    the descendants of Jacob.
  I will show compassion on their
    ruined homes.
  Every city will be rebuilt on its
    former ruins.
  Every fortified dwelling will occupy
    its traditional site.
19 Out of those places you [a]will hear
    songs of thanksgiving
  and the sounds of laughter and
    merriment.
  I will increase their number, and
    they will not dwindle away.
  I will bring them honor, and they will
    no longer be despised.
20 The descendants of Jacob will enjoy
    their former privileges.
  Their community will be
    reestablished in my favor,
  and I will punish all who try to
    oppress them.

21 One of their own people will be their
  leader.
 Their ruler will come from their own
  number.
 I will invite him to approach me,
  ᵃand he will do so.
 For no one would dare approach me
  on his own.
 I, the LORD, affirm it!
22 Then you will again be ᵃmy people,
  and I will be your God.
23 Just watch! The wrath of the LORD
  will come like a ᵃstorm.
 Like a raging storm it will rage
  down
 on the heads of those who are
  wicked.
24 The anger of the LORD will not turn
  back
 until he has fully carried out his
  ᵃintended purposes.
 In future days you will come to
  understand this.

31 At that time I will be ᵃthe God of all
  the clans of ᵇIsrael,
 and they will be my people.
 I, the LORD, affirm it!"

Israel Will Be Restored and Join Judah in Worship

2The LORD says:

 "The people of ᵃIsrael who survived
 death at the hands of the enemy
 will find favor in the wilderness
 as they journey to find rest for
  themselves.
3 In a faraway land¹ the LORD ᵃwill
  ᵇmanifest himself to them.
 He will say to them, 'I have loved you
  with an everlasting love.
 That is why I have ᶜcontinued to be
  faithful to you.
4 I ᵃwill rebuild you, my dear children
  Israel,
 so that you will once again be
  built up.
 Once again you will take up the
  ᵇtambourine

and join in the happy throng of
  dancers.
5 Once again ᵃyou will plant vineyards
  on the hills of Samaria.
 Those who plant them
 will once again enjoy their fruit.
6 Yes, a time is coming
 when watchmen will call out on the
  mountains of Ephraim,
 "ᵃCome! Let us go to Zion
 to worship the LORD our God!'""

7Moreover, the LORD says:

 "ᵃSing for joy for the descendants of
  Jacob.
 Utter glad shouts for that foremost
  of the nations.
 Make your praises heard.¹
 Then say, 'LORD, rescue your people.
 Deliver those of Israel who remain
  alive.'²
8 Then I will reply, 'I will bring
 them back ᵃfrom the land of
  the north.
 I will ᵇgather them in from the
  distant parts of the earth.
 Blind and lame people will come
  with them,
 so will pregnant women and women
  about to give birth.
 A vast throng of people will come
  back here.
9 They will come back shedding tears
  of contrition.
 I will bring them back praying
  prayers of repentance.
 I will lead them besides streams of
  water,
 along smooth paths where ᵃthey will
  never stumble.
 I will do this because I am Israel's
  father;
 Ephraim is my ᵇfirstborn son.'

10 "Listen to the LORD's message,
  O nations.
 Proclaim it in the faraway lands
  along the sea.

30:21ᵃGen 49:10   30:22ᵃExod 6:7; Jer 32:38; Ezek 36:28; Hos 2:23; Zech 13:9   30:23ᵃJer 23:19–20; 25:32   30:24ᵃGen 49:1   31:1ᵃJer 30:24   ᵇJer 30:22   31:2ᵃExod 33:14; Num 10:33; Deut 1:33; Josh 1:13; Ps 95:11; Isa 63:14   31:3ᵃDeut 4:37; 7:8; Mal 1:2   ᵇIsa 43:4; Rom 11:28   ᶜHos 11:4   ¹Either distance in location or time.   31:4ᵃJer 33:7   ᵇExod 15:20; Judg 11:34; Ps 149:3   31:5ᵃPs 107:37; Isa 65:21; Ezek 28:26; Amos 9:14   31:6ᵃ[Isa 2:3; Jer 31:12; 50:4–5; Mic 4:2]   31:7ᵃIsa 12:5–6
¹Perhaps the exiles, who are viewed as being in the process of returning and praying for their fellow countrymen.
²LXX, Tg. *The LORD will rescue his people. He will deliver those of Israel who remain alive.*   31:8ᵃJer 3:12, 18; 23:8
ᵇDeut 30:4; Isa 43:6; Ezek 20:34, 41; 34:13   31:9ᵃ[Ps 126:5; Jer 50:4]   ᵇExod 4:22

Say, 'The one who scattered Israel
 [a]will regather them.
He will watch over his people like a
 shepherd watches over his flock.'
11 For [a]the LORD will rescue the
 descendants of Jacob.
He will secure their release [b]from
 those who had overpowered them.
12 They will come and shout for joy on
 Mount Zion.
[a]They will be radiant with joy
 over [b]the good things the LORD
 provides,
the grain, the fresh wine, the olive oil,
the young sheep, and the calves he
 has given to them.
They will be like a [c]well-watered
 garden
[d]and will not grow faint or weary any
 more.
13 The LORD says, 'At that time young
 women will dance and be glad.
Young men and old men will rejoice.[1]
I will turn their grief into gladness.
I will give them comfort and joy in
 place of their sorrow.
14 I will provide the priests with
 abundant provisions.
My people will be filled to the full
 with the good things I provide.'

[15] The LORD [a]says:

"A sound is heard in [b]Ramah,
a sound of [c]crying in bitter grief.
It is [d]the sound of Rachel weeping for
 her children
and refusing to be comforted,
 because her children are gone."
16 The LORD says to her,
"Stop [a]crying! Do not shed any more
 tears.
For your heartfelt repentance[1] will be
 rewarded.
Your children will return from the
 land of the enemy.
I, the LORD, affirm it!
17 Indeed, there is [a]hope for your
 posterity.

Your children will return to their
 own territory.
I, the LORD, affirm it!
18 I have indeed heard the people of
 Israel say mournfully,
'We were like a calf untrained to the
 yoke.
You [a]disciplined us, and we learned
 from it.
Let us come [b]back to you and we will
 do so,
for you are the LORD our God.
19 For [a]after we turned away from you
 we repented.
After we came to our senses we
 struck our thigh in sorrow.
We are [b]ashamed and humiliated
because of the disgraceful things we
 did previously.'
20 Indeed, [a]the people of [b]Israel are my
 dear children.
They are the children I take delight
 in.[1]
For even though I must often rebuke
 them,
I still remember them with fondness.
So I am deeply moved with pity for
 them
and will surely have compassion on
 them.
I, the LORD, affirm it!
21 I will say, 'My dear children of Israel,
 [a]keep in mind
the road you took when you were
 carried off.
Mark off in your minds the
 landmarks.
Make a mental note of telltale signs
 marking the way back.
Return, my dear children of Israel.
Return to these cities of yours.
22 How long will you vacillate,
you who were once like an unfaithful
 daughter?
For I, the LORD, promise to bring
 about something new on the
 earth,
something as unique as [a]a woman
 protecting [b]a man!'"[1]

31:10 [a] Isa 40:11; Ezek 34:12–14   31:11 [a] Isa 44:23; 48:20; Jer 15:21; 50:19   [b] Isa 49:24   31:12 [a] Ezek 17:23   [b] Hos 3:5   [c] Isa 58:11
[d] Isa 35:10; 65:19; [John 16:22; Rev 21:4]   31:13 [1] MT young men and old men together.   31:15 [a] Matt 2:17–18   [b] Josh 18:25;
Judg 4:5; Isa 10:29; Jer 40:1   [c] Gen 37:35   [d] Jer 10:20   31:16 [a] [Isa 25:8; 30:19]   [1] Heb. your work.   31:17 [a] Jer 29:11
31:18 [a] Job 5:17; Ps 94:12   [b] Ps 80:3, 7, 19; Jer 17:4; Lam 5:21; [Acts 3:26]   31:19 [a] Deut 30:2   [b] Ezek 36:31; [Zech
12:10]   31:20 [a] Gen 43:30; Deut 32:36; Judg 10:16; Isa 63:15; Hos 11:8   [b] Isa 57:18; Jer 3:12; 12:15; [Hos 14:4];
Mic 7:18   [1] Heb. Is Ephraim a dear son to me or a child of delight?   31:21 [a] Jer 50:5   31:22 [a] Jer
2:18, 23, 36   [b] Jer 3:6, 8, 11, 12, 14, 22   [1] The meaning of this last line is uncertain.

Judah Will Be Restored

[23]The LORD of Heaven's Armies, [a]the God of Israel, says,

> "I will restore the people of Judah to
> their land and to their towns.
> When I do, they will again say of
> Jerusalem,
> 'May the LORD bless you, you holy
> [b]mountain,
> the place where righteousness dwells.'
> [24] The land of Judah will be [a]inhabited
> by people who live in its towns,
> as well as by farmers and shepherds
> with their flocks.
> [25] I will fully satisfy the needs of those
> who are weary
> and fully refresh the souls of those
> who are faint.
> [26] Then they will say, 'Under these
> conditions I can enjoy [a]sweet sleep
> when I wake up and look around.'[1]

Israel and Judah Will Be Repopulated

[27]"Indeed, a [a]time is coming,"[1] says the LORD, "when I will cause people and animals to sprout up in the lands of Israel and Judah. [28]In the past I saw to it [a]that they were uprooted and [b]torn down, that they were destroyed and demolished and brought disaster. But now I will see [c]to it that they are built up and firmly planted. I, the LORD, affirm it!

The Lord Will Make a New Covenant with Israel and Judah

[29]"[a]When that time comes, people will no longer say, 'The parents have eaten sour grapes, but the children's teeth have grown numb.' [30a]Rather, each person will die for his own sins. The teeth of the person who eats the sour grapes will themselves grow numb.

[31]"Indeed, a [a]time is coming," says the LORD, "when I will make a new covenant with the people of Israel and Judah. [32]It [a]will not be like the old covenant that I made with their ancestors when I delivered them from Egypt. For they violated that covenant, even though I was like a faithful husband to them," says the LORD. [33]"[a]But [b]I will make [c]a new covenant with the whole nation of Israel after I plant them back in the land," says the LORD. "I will put my law within them and write it on their hearts and minds. I will be their God, and they will be my people. [34]"People will no longer need to teach their neighbors and relatives to know me. For all of them, from [a]the least [b]important to the most important, will know me," says the LORD. "For I will forgive their sin and will no longer call to mind the wrong they have done."

The Lord Guarantees Israel's Continuance

[35] The LORD has made a promise to Israel.

> He promises it as the one [a]who fixed
> [b]the sun to give light by day
> and [c]the moon and stars to give light
> by night.
> He promises it as the one who stirs
> up the sea so that its waves roll.
> His name is the LORD of Heaven's
> Armies.
> [36] The LORD affirms, "The descendants
> of Israel will not
> cease forever to be a nation in my
> sight.
> That could only happen if the fixed
> ordering of the heavenly lights
> were to cease to operate before me."
> [37] The LORD says, "[a]I will not reject all
> the descendants of Israel
> because of all that they have done.
> That could only happen if the
> heavens above could be measured
> or the foundations of the earth
> below could all be explored,"[1]
> says the LORD.

Jerusalem Will Be Enlarged

[38]"Indeed a time is coming,"[1] says the LORD, "when the city of Jerusalem will be

31:23 [a]Ps 122:5–8; Isa 1:26 [b][Zech 8:3] **31:24** [a]Jer 33:12 **31:26** [a]Prov 3:24 [1]Or *When I, Jeremiah, heard this, I woke up and looked around. My sleep had been very pleasant.* **31:27** [a]Ezek 36:9–11; Hos 2:23 [1]Heb. *Behold days are coming!* **31:28** [a]Jer 44:27; Dan 9:14 [b]Jer 1:10; 18:7 [c]Jer 24:6 **31:29** [a]Lam 5:7; Ezek 18:2–3 **31:30** [a]Deut 24:16; 2 Chr 25:4; Isa 3:11; [Ezek 18:4, 20; Gal 6:5, 7] **31:31** [a]Jer 32:40; 33:14; Ezek 37:26; Heb 8:8–12; 10:16–17 **31:32** [a]Deut 1:31; Isa 63:12 **31:33** [a]Jer 32:40; Heb 10:16 [b]Ps 40:8; [Ezek 11:19; 36:26–27; 2 Cor 3:3] [c]Jer 24:7; 30:22; 32:38 **31:34** [a]Isa 11:9; 54:13; Jer 24:7; Hab 2:14; [John 6:45; 1 Cor 2:10; 1 John 2:20] [b]Jer 33:8; 50:20; Mic 7:18; [Acts 10:43; 13:39; Rom 11:27] **31:35** [a]Gen 1:14–18; Deut 4:19; Ps 72:5, 17; 89:2, 36; 119:91 [b]Isa 51:15 [c]Jer 10:16 **31:37** [a]Isa 40:12; Jer 33:22 [1]Heb. *If the heavens above could be measured or the foundations of the earth below be explored, then also I could reject all the seed of Israel for all they have done.* **31:38** [1]Ket. omits *is coming.*

rebuilt as my special city. It will be built [a]from the Tower of Hananel westward to the Corner Gate. [39]The boundary line will extend beyond that, straight west from [a]there to the Hill of Gareb and then turn southward to Goah. [40]The whole valley where dead bodies and sacrificial ashes are thrown, and all the terraced fields out [a]to the Kidron Valley on the east as far north as the corner of the Horse Gate, will be included within this city that is sacred to the LORD. The city will never again be torn down or destroyed."

Jeremiah Buys a Field

32 In the tenth year that Zedekiah was [a]ruling over Judah the LORD spoke to Jeremiah. That was the same as the eighteenth year of Nebuchadnezzar.

[2]Now at that time, the armies of the [a]king of Babylon were besieging Jerusalem. The prophet Jeremiah was confined in the courtyard of the guardhouse attached to the royal palace of Judah. [3]For King Zedekiah had confined Jeremiah there after he had reproved him for prophesying as he did. He had asked Jeremiah, "Why do you keep [a]prophesying these things? Why do you keep saying that the LORD says, 'I will hand this city over to the king of Babylon? I will let him capture it. [4]King Zedekiah of Judah will not escape from the Babylonians. He will certainly be handed over to the king of Babylon. He must answer personally to the king of Babylon and confront him [a]face to face. [5]Zedekiah will be carried off to Babylon and will remain there [a]until I have fully dealt with him. I, the LORD, affirm it! Even if you continue to fight against the Babylonians, you cannot win.'"

[6]So now, Jeremiah said, "The LORD's message came to me, [7]'Hanamel, the son of your uncle Shallum, will come to you soon. He will say to you, "Buy my field at Anathoth because you are [a]entitled as my closest relative to buy it."' [8]And then my cousin Hanamel did come to me in the courtyard of the guardhouse in keeping with the LORD's message. He said to me, 'Buy my field that is at Anathoth in the territory of the tribe of Benjamin. Buy it for yourself since you are entitled as my closest relative to take possession of it for yourself.' When this happened, I recognized that the LORD had indeed spoken to me. [9]So I bought the field at Anathoth from my cousin Hanamel. I weighed [a]out seven ounces of silver and gave it to him to pay for it. [10]I signed the deed of purchase, sealed it, and had some men serve as witnesses to the purchase. I weighed out the silver for him on a scale. [11]There were two copies of the deed of purchase. One was sealed and contained the order of transfer and the conditions of purchase. The other was left unsealed. [12]I took both copies of the deed of purchase and gave them to [a]Baruch son of Neriah, the son of Mahseiah. I gave them to him in the presence of my cousin[1] Hanamel, the [b]witnesses who had signed the deed of purchase, and all the Judeans who were housed in the courtyard of the guardhouse. [13]In the presence of all these people I instructed [a]Baruch, [14]'The LORD of Heaven's Armies, the God of Israel, says, "Take these documents, both the sealed copy of the deed of purchase and the unsealed copy. Put them in a clay jar so that they may be preserved for a long time to come."' [15]For the LORD of Heaven's Armies, the God of Israel, says, 'Houses, fields, and vineyards will again be [a]bought in this land.'

Jeremiah's Prayer of Praise and Bewilderment

[16]"After I had given the copies of the deed of purchase to Baruch son of Neriah, I prayed to the LORD, [17]'Oh, Sovereign LORD, [a]you did indeed make heaven and earth by your mighty power and great strength. Nothing is too hard for you! [18]You show unfailing [a]love to thousands. But you also punish children for [b]the sins of [c]their parents. You are the great and powerful God whose name is the LORD of Heaven's Armies. [19]You plan [a]great things and you do mighty deeds. [b]You see everything people do. You reward each of them for the way they live and for the things they do. [20]You did [a]miracles and amazing deeds in the land of Egypt that

31:38 [a]Neh 3:1; 12:39; Zech 14:10 **31:39** [a]Ezek 40:8; Zech 2:1–2 **31:40** [a]2 Kgs 11:16; 2 Chr 23:15; Neh 3:28 **32:1** [a]2 Kgs 25:1–2; Jer 39:1–2 **32:2** [a]Neh 3:25; Jer 33:1; 37:21; 39:14 **32:3** [a]Jer 26:8–9 **32:4** [a]Jer 39:5 **32:5** [a]Jer 27:22 **32:7** [a]Lev 25:24–25, 32; Ruth 4:4 **32:9** [a]Gen 23:16; Zech 11:12 **32:12** [a]Jer 36:4 [b]Isa 8:2 [1]Maj. Heb. MSS *my uncles.* **32:13** [a]Jer 36:4 **32:15** [a]Ezra 2:1; [Jer 31:5, 12, 14]; Amos 9:14–15; Zech 3:10 **32:17** [a]2 Kgs 19:15; Ps 102:25; Isa 40:26–29; Jer 27:5 **32:18** [a]Exod 20:6; 34:7; Deut 5:9–10 [b]Ps 50:1; [Isa 9:6]; Jer 20:11 [c]Jer 10:16 **32:19** [a]Isa 28:29 [b]Job 34:21; Ps 33:13; Prov 5:21; Jer 16:17 **32:20** [a]Exod 9:16; 1 Chr 17:21; Isa 63:12; Jer 13:11; Dan 9:15

have had lasting effect. By this means you gained both in Israel and among humankind a renown that lasts to this day. [21]You used your mighty power and your great strength to perform miracles and amazing deeds and to bring great terror on the Egyptians. By this means you brought your people Israel out of the land of Egypt. [22]You kept the promise [a]that you swore on oath to their ancestors. You gave them a land flowing with milk and honey. [23]But when [a]they came in and took possession of it, they did not obey you or live as you had instructed them. They did not do anything that you commanded them to do. So you brought all this disaster on them. [24]Even now siege ramps have been built up around [a]the city in order to capture it. War, starvation, and disease are sure to make the city fall into the hands of the Babylonians who are attacking it. LORD, you threatened that this would happen. Now you can see that it is already taking place. [25]The city is sure to fall into the hands of the Babylonians. Yet, in spite of this, you, Sovereign LORD, have said to me, "Buy that field with silver and have the transaction legally witnessed."'"

The Lord Answers Jeremiah's Prayer

[26]The LORD's message came to Jeremiah: [27]"I am the LORD, the [a]God of all humankind. There is, indeed, nothing too difficult for me. [28]Therefore I, the LORD, say: 'I will indeed hand this city over to King Nebuchadnezzar of Babylon and the Babylonian army. They will capture it. [29]The Babylonian soldiers that are attacking this city will break into it and [a]set it [b]on fire. They will burn it down along with the houses where people have made me angry by offering sacrifices to the god Baal and by pouring out drink offerings to other gods on their rooftops. [30]This will happen because the people of Israel and Judah [a]have repeatedly done what displeases me from their earliest history until now and because they have repeatedly made me angry by the things they have done. I, the LORD, affirm it! [31]This will happen because the people of this city

have aroused my anger and my wrath since the time they built it until now. They have made me [a]so angry that I am determined to remove it from my sight. [32]I am determined to do so because [a]the people of Israel and Judah have made me angry with all [b]their wickedness—they, their kings, their officials, their priests, their prophets, and especially the people of Judah and the citizens of Jerusalem have done this wickedness. [33]They have turned [a]away from me instead of turning to me. [b]I tried over and over again to instruct them, but they did not listen and respond to correction. [34]They set [a]up their disgusting idols in the temple that I have claimed for my own and defiled it. [35]They built places of worship for the god Baal in the Valley of Ben Hinnom so that they could sacrifice [a]their sons and daughters to the god [b]Molech. Such a disgusting practice was not something [c]I commanded them to do. It never even entered my mind to command them to do such a thing! So Judah is certainly liable for punishment.'

[36]"You and your people are right in saying, 'War, starvation, and disease are sure to make this city fall into the hands of the king of Babylon.' But now I, the LORD God of Israel, have something further to say about this city: [37]'I will certainly [a]regather my people from all the countries where I have exiled them in my anger, fury, and great wrath. I will bring them back [b]to this place and allow them to live here in safety. [38]They will be [a]my people, and I will be their God. [39]I will [a]give them a single-minded purpose to live in a way that always shows respect for me. They will want to do that for their own good and the good of the children who descend from them. [40]I [a]will make a [b]lasting covenant[1] with them that I will never stop doing good to them. I will fill their hearts and minds with respect for me so that they will never again turn away from me. [41]I [a]will take [b]delight in doing good to them. I will faithfully and wholeheartedly plant them firmly in the land.'

[42]"For I, the LORD, say: 'I will surely bring on these people all the good fortune that I

32:22 [a]Exod 3:8, 17; Deut 1:8; Ps 105:9–11; Jer 11:5   **32:23** [a][Neh 9:26]; Jer 11:8; [Dan 9:10–14]   **32:24** [a]Jer 14:12; Ezek 14:21
32:27 [a][Num 16:22]   **32:29** [a]2 Chr 36:19; Jer 21:10; 37:8, 10; 52:13   [b]Jer 19:13   **32:30** [a]Deut 9:7–12; Isa 63:10; Jer 2:7; 3:25;
7:22–26; Ezek 20:28   **32:31** [a]2 Kgs 23:27; 24:3; Jer 27:10   **32:32** [a]Ezra 9:7; Isa 1:4, 6; Dan 9:8   [b]Jer 23:14   **32:33** [a]Jer 2:27;
7:24   [b]Jer 7:13   **32:34** [a]2 Kgs 21:1-7; Jer 7:10–12, 30; 23:11; Ezek 8:5–6   **32:35** [a]2 Chr 28:2–3; 33:6; Jer 7:31; 19:5   [b]Lev 18:21;
1 Kgs 11:33; 2 Kgs 23:10; Acts 7:43   [c]Jer 7:31   **32:37** [a]Deut 30:3; Jer 23:3; 29:14; 31:10; 50:19; Ezek 37:21   [b]Jer 33:16   **32:38** [a][Jer
24:7; 30:22; 31:33]   **32:39** [a][Jer 24:7; Ezek 11:19]   **32:40** [a]Isa 55:3; Jer 31:31; Ezek 37:26   [b]Deut 31:6, 8; [Ezek 39:29; Jer
31:33]   [1]Heb. *an everlasting covenant.*   **32:41** [a]Deut 30:9; Isa 62:5; 65:19; Zeph 3:17   [b]Jer 24:6; 31:28; Amos 9:15

am hereby promising them. I will be [a]just as sure to do that as I have been in bringing all this great disaster on them. [43]You and your people[1] are saying that this land will become desolate, uninhabited by either people or animals. You are saying that it will be handed over to the Babylonians. But fields will again be bought in this land. [44]Fields will again be bought with silver, and deeds of purchase signed, sealed, and witnessed. This will happen in [a]the [b]territory of Benjamin, the villages surrounding Jerusalem, the towns in Judah, the southern hill country, the foothills, and southern Judah. For I will restore them to their land. I, the LORD, affirm it!'"

The Lord Promises a Second Time to Restore Israel and Judah

33 The [a]LORD's message came to Jeremiah a second time while he was still confined in the courtyard of the guardhouse. [2]"I, [a]the LORD, do these things. I, the LORD, form the plan to bring them about. I am known as the LORD. I say to you, [3]'[a]Call on me in prayer, and I will answer you. I will show you great and mysterious things that you still do not know about.' [4]For I, [a]the LORD God of Israel, have something more to say about the houses in this city and the royal buildings of Judah that have been torn down for defenses against the siege ramps and military incursions of the Babylonians: [5]'The defenders of the city will go out and fight with the Babylonians. But they will only [a]fill those houses and buildings with the dead bodies of the people that I will kill in my anger and my wrath. That will happen because I have decided to turn my back on this city on account of the wicked things they have done. [6]But [a]I will most surely heal the wounds of this city and restore it and its people to health. I will show them abundant peace and security. [7]I [a]will restore Judah and Israel and will rebuild them [b]as they were in days of old. [8]I will [a]purify them from all the sin that they committed against me. I will forgive all their sins that they committed in

rebelling against me. [9]All [a]the nations will hear about all the good things that I will do for them. This city will bring me fame, honor, and praise before them for the joy that I bring it. The nations will tremble in [b]awe at all the peace and prosperity that I will provide for it.'

[10]"I, the LORD, say: 'You and your people are saying about this place, "It lies in ruins. There are no people or animals in it." That is true. The towns [a]of Judah and the streets of Jerusalem will soon be desolate, uninhabited either by people or by animals. But happy sounds will again be heard in these places. [11]Once again there will be [a]sounds of joy and gladness and the glad celebrations of brides and grooms. Once again people will bring their thank offerings to the temple of the LORD and will say, "Give [b]thanks to [c]the LORD of Heaven's Armies. For the LORD is good and his unfailing love lasts forever." For I, the LORD, affirm that I will restore the land to what it was in days of old.'

[12]"I, the LORD of Heaven's Armies, say: 'This place will [a]indeed lie in ruins. There will be no people or animals in it. But there will again be in it and in its towns sheepfolds where shepherds can rest their sheep. [13]I, the LORD, say that shepherds will once [a]again count their sheep as they [b]pass into the fold. They will do this in all the towns in the hill country, the foothills,[1] the Negev, the territory of Benjamin, the villages surrounding Jerusalem, and the towns of Judah.'

The Lord Reaffirms His Covenant with David, Israel, and Levi

[14]"I, the LORD, affirm: 'The time will [a]certainly come when [b]I will fulfill my gracious promise concerning the nations of Israel and Judah. [15]In those days and at that time I will raise up for them a righteous [a]descendant of David.

"'He will do what is just and right in the land. [16]Under his rule Judah will enjoy safety and Jerusalem will live in security. At that time Jerusalem will be called "The LORD has provided us with justice." [17]For I, the LORD,

32:42 [a] Jer 31:28; Zech 8:14–15   **32:43** [1] Heb. *you*; pl.   **32:44** [a] Jer 17:26   [b] Jer 33:7, 11   **33:1** [a] Jer 32:2–3   **33:2** [a] Exod 15:3; [Jer 10:16]; Amos 5:8; 9:6   **33:3** [a] Ps 91:15; [Isa 55:6–7]; Jer 29:12   **33:4** [a] Isa 22:10; Jer 32:24; Ezek 4:2; 21:22; Hab 1:10   **33:5** [a] 2 Kgs 23:14; Jer 21:4–7; 32:5   **33:6** [a] Jer 30:17; Hos 6:1   **33:7** [a] Ps 85:1; Jer 30:3; 32:44; Amos 9:14   [b] Isa 1:26; Jer 24:6; 30:20; 31:4, 28; 42:10; Amos 9:14–15   **33:8** [a] Ps 51:2; Isa 44:22; Jer 50:20; Ezek 36:25, 33; Mic 7:18–19; Zech 13:1; [Heb 9:11–14]   **33:9** [a] Isa 62:7; Jer 13:11   [b] Isa 60:5   **33:10** [a] Jer 32:43   **33:11** [a] Jer 7:34; 16:9; 25:10; Rev 18:23   [b] 1 Chr 16:8; 2 Chr 5:13; Ezra 3:11; Ps 136:1; Isa 12:4   [c] Lev 7:12; Ps 107:22; 116:17; Heb 13:15   **33:12** [a] Isa 65:10; [Jer 31:24; 50:19; Ezek 34:12–15; Zeph 2:6–7]   **33:13** [a] Jer 17:26; 32:44   [b] Lev 27:32; [Luke 15:4]   [1] The transition region between the hill country and the coastal plains.   **33:14** [a] Jer 23:5; 31:27, 31   [b] Isa 32:1; Jer 29:10; 32:42; Ezek 34:23–25; Hag 2:6–9   **33:15** [a] Isa 4:2; 11:1; Jer 23:5; Zech 3:8; 6:12–13

promise: "David will never [a]lack a successor to occupy the throne over the nation of Israel. [18]Nor will the Levitical [a]priests ever lack someone to stand before me and continually offer [b]up burnt offerings, sacrifice cereal offerings, and offer the other sacrifices.""'

[19]The LORD's message came to Jeremiah another time: [20]"I, the LORD, make the following promise: 'I have made a covenant with the day and with the night that they will always come at their proper times. Only if you people[1] could break that covenant [21]could [a]my covenant with my servant David and my covenant with the Levites ever be broken. So David will by all means always have a descendant to occupy his throne as king and the Levites will by all means always have priests who will minister before me. [22]I will make [a]the children who follow one another in the line of my servant David very [b]numerous. I will also make the [c]Levites who minister before me very numerous. I will make them all as numerous as the stars in the sky and as the sands that are on the seashore.'"

[23]The LORD's message came to Jeremiah another time: [24]"You have surely noticed what these people are saying, haven't you? They are saying, 'The LORD has rejected the two families of Israel and Judah that he chose.' So they have little [a]regard that my people will ever again be a nation. [25]But I, the LORD, make the following promise: 'I have made a covenant governing the coming of day and night. I have [a]established the fixed laws governing heaven and earth. [26]Just as surely as I have done this, so [a]surely will I never reject the descendants of Jacob. Nor will I ever refuse to choose one of my servant David's descendants to rule over the descendants of Abraham, Isaac, and Jacob. Indeed, I will restore them and show mercy to them.'"

The Lord Makes an Ominous Promise to Zedekiah

34 The LORD's message came to Jeremiah while King Nebuchadnezzar of Babylon was attacking Jerusalem and [a]the towns around it with a large army. This army consisted of troops from his own army and from the kingdoms and peoples of the lands under his dominion. [2]This is what the LORD God of Israel told Jeremiah,[1] "Go, [a]speak to [b]King Zedekiah of Judah. Tell him, 'This is what the LORD has said: "Take note! I am going to hand this city over to the king of Babylon, and he will burn it down. [3]You [a]yourself will not escape his clutches but will certainly be captured and handed over to him. You must confront the king of Babylon face to face and answer to [b]him personally. Then you must go to Babylon."' [4]However, listen to the LORD's message, King Zedekiah of Judah. This is what the LORD has said: 'You will not die in battle or be executed. [5]You will die a peaceful death. [a]They will burn incense at your burial just as they did at the burial of your ancestors, the former kings who preceded you. They will [b]mourn for you, saying, "Alas, master!" Indeed, you have my own word on this. I, the LORD, affirm it!'"

[6]The prophet Jeremiah told all these things to King Zedekiah of Judah in Jerusalem. [7]He did this while [a]the army of the king of Babylon was attacking Jerusalem and the cities of Lachish and Azekah. He was attacking these cities because they were the only fortified cities of Judah that were still holding out.

The Lord Threatens to Destroy Those Who Wronged Their Slaves

[8]The LORD spoke to Jeremiah after King Zedekiah had made a covenant with all the people in Jerusalem to grant their slaves their [a]freedom. [9]Everyone was supposed to free their male and female Hebrew slaves. No one was supposed to keep [a]a fellow Judean enslaved. [10]All the people and their leaders had agreed to this. They had agreed to free their male and female slaves and not keep them enslaved any longer. They originally complied with the covenant and freed them. [11]But later they changed their minds. They took back their male and female slaves that they had freed and forced them to be slaves again. [12]The LORD's message came to Jeremiah, [13]"The LORD God of Israel has a message

33:17 [a]2 Sam 7:16; 1 Kgs 2:4; Ps 89:29; [Luke 1:32]   33:18 [a]Num 3:5–10; Deut 18:1; 24:8; Josh 3:3; Ezek 44:15 [b][Rom 12:1; 15:16; 1 Pet 2:5, 9; Rev 1:6]   33:20 [1]Heb. you.   33:21 [a]2 Sam 23:5; 2 Chr 7:18; 21:7; Ps 89:34   33:22 [a]Gen 15:5; 22:17; Jer 31:37 [b]Jer 30:19; Ezek 36:10–11 [c]Isa 66:21; Jer 33:18   33:24 [a]Neh 4:2–4; Esth 3:6–8; Ps 44:13–14; 83:4; Ezek 36:2   33:25 [a]Ps 74:16; 104:19   33:26 [a]Jer 31:37   34:1 [a]Jer 1:15; 25:9; Dan 2:37–38   34:2 [a]2 Chr 36:11–12; Jer 22:1–2; 37:1–2 [b]2 Kgs 25:9; Jer 21:10; 32:3, 28   [1]Heb. told him.   34:3 [a]2 Kgs 25:4–5; Jer 21:7; 52:7–11 [b]2 Kgs 25:6–7; Jer 32:4; 39:5–6   34:5 [a]2 Chr 16:14; 21:19 [b]Jer 22:18   34:7 [a]2 Kgs 18:13; 19:8; 2 Chr 11:5, 9   34:8 [a]Exod 21:2; Lev 25:10; Neh 5:1–13; Isa 58:6; Jer 34:14, 17   34:9 [a]Neh 5:11

for you: 'I made a [a]covenant with your ancestors when I brought them out of Egypt where they had been slaves. It stipulated, [14]"Every [a]seven years each of you must free any fellow Hebrews who have sold themselves to you. After they have served you for six years, you shall set them free." But your ancestors did not obey me or pay any attention to me. [15]Recently, however, you yourselves showed a change of heart and did what is pleasing to me. You granted your fellow countrymen their freedom, and you [a]made a covenant to that effect [b]in my presence in the house that I have claimed for my own. [16]But then you turned right around and showed [a]that you did not honor me. Each of you took back your male and female slaves, whom you had freed as they desired, and you forced them to be your slaves again. [17]So I, the LORD, say: "You have not really obeyed me and granted freedom [a]to your neighbor and fellow countryman. Therefore, I will grant you freedom, the freedom to die in war, or by starvation, or disease. I, the LORD, affirm it! I will make all the kingdoms of the earth [b]horrified at what happens to you. [18]I will punish those people who have violated their covenant with me. I will make them like [a]the calf they cut in two and passed between its pieces. I will do so because they did not keep the terms of the covenant they made in my presence. [19]I will punish the leaders of Judah and Jerusalem, the court officials, the priests, and all the other people of the land who passed between the pieces of the calf. [20]I will [a]hand them over to their enemies who want to kill them. Their [b]dead bodies will become food for the birds and the wild animals. [21]I will also hand King Zedekiah of Judah and his officials over to their enemies who want to kill them. [a]I will hand them over to the army of the king of Babylon, even though they have temporarily withdrawn from attacking you. [22]For I, the LORD, affirm that I will soon give the order and bring them back to this city. They will fight against it and capture it and burn it down. I will also make the towns of Judah desolate so that there will [a]be no one [b]living in them.""""

Judah's Unfaithfulness Contrasted with the Rechabites' Faithfulness

35 The LORD spoke to Jeremiah when Jehoiakim son of Josiah was ruling over Judah: [2]"Go to the [a]Rechabite community. Invite [b]them to come into one of the side rooms of the LORD's temple and offer them some wine to drink." [3]So I went and got Jaazaniah son of Jeremiah the grandson of Habazziniah, his brothers, all his sons, and all the rest of the Rechabite community. [4]I took [a]them to the LORD's temple. I took them into the room where the disciples of the prophet Hanan son of Igdaliah stayed. That room was next to the one where the temple officers stayed and above the room where Maaseiah son of Shallum, one of the doorkeepers of the temple, stayed. [5]Then I set cups and pitchers full of wine in front of the members of the Rechabite community and said to them, "Have some wine." [6]But they answered, "We do not drink wine because our ancestor [a]Jonadab son of Rechab commanded us not to. He told us, 'You and your children must [b]never drink wine. [7]Do not build houses. Do not plant crops. Do not plant [a]a vineyard or own one. Live in tents all your lives. If you do these things you will live a long time in the land that you wander about on.' [8]We and our wives and our sons and daughters have [a]obeyed everything our ancestor Jonadab son of Rechab commanded us. We have never drunk wine. [9]We have not built any houses to live in. We do not own any vineyards, fields, or crops. [10]We have lived in tents. We have obeyed our ancestor Jonadab and done exactly as he commanded us. [11]But when King Nebuchadnezzar of Babylon invaded the land we said, 'Let's get up and [a]go to Jerusalem to get away from the Babylonian[1] and Aramean armies.' That is why we are staying here in Jerusalem."

[12]Then the LORD's message came to Jeremiah. [13]The LORD of Heaven's Armies, the God of Israel, told him, "Go and speak to the people of Judah and the citizens of Jerusalem. Tell them, 'I, the LORD, say: "You must [a]learn a lesson from this about

34:13 [a] Exod 24:3, 7, 8; Deut 5:2–3, 27; Jer 31:32   **34:14** [a] Exod 21:2; 23:10; Deut 15:12; 1 Kgs 9:22   **34:15** [a] 2 Kgs 23:3; Neh 10:29   [b] Jer 7:10   **34:16** [a] Exod 20:7; Lev 19:12   **34:17** [a] Jer 32:24, 36   [b] Deut 28:25, 64; Jer 29:18   **34:18** [a] Gen 15:10, 17   **34:20** [a] 2 Kgs 25:19–21; Jer 22:25   [b] Deut 28:26; 1 Sam 17:44, 46; 1 Kgs 14:11; 16:4; Ps 79:2; Jer 7:33; 16:4; 19:7   **34:21** [a] Jer 37:5–11; 39:4–7   **34:22** [a] Jer 37:8, 10   [b] Jer 9:11; 44:2, 6   **35:2** [a] 2 Sam 4:2; 2 Kgs 10:15; 1 Chr 2:55   [b] 1 Kgs 6:5, 8; 1 Chr 9:26, 33   **35:4** [a] 2 Kgs 12:9; 25:18; 1 Chr 9:18–19   **35:6** [a] 2 Kgs 10:15, 23   [b] Lev 10:9; Num 6:2–4; Judg 13:7, 14; Prov 31:4; Ezek 44:21; Luke 1:15   **35:7** [a] Exod 20:12; Eph 6:2–3   **35:8** [a] [Prov 1:8–9; 4:1–2, 10; 6:20; Eph 6:1; Col 3:20]   **35:11** [a] Jer 4:5–7; 8:14   [1] Heb. Chaldean.   **35:13** [a] [Isa 28:9–12]; Jer 6:10; 17:23; 32:33

obeying what I say. [14]Jonadab son of Rechab ordered his descendants not to drink wine. His orders have been carried out. To this day his descendants have drunk no wine because they have obeyed what their ancestor commanded them. [a]But [b]I have spoken to you over and over again, but you have not obeyed me. [15]I sent all my [a]servants the prophets to warn you over and over again. They said, 'Every one of you, stop [b]doing the evil things you have been doing and do what is right.[1] Do not pay allegiance to other gods and worship them. Then you can continue to [c]live in this land that I gave to you and your ancestors.' But you did not pay any attention or listen to me. [16]Yes, the descendants of Jonadab son of Rechab have carried out the orders that their [a]ancestor gave them. But you people have not obeyed me! [17]So I, the LORD God of Heaven's Armies, the God of Israel, say: 'I will soon bring on Judah and all the citizens of Jerusalem all the disaster that I threatened to bring on them. I will do this [a]because I spoke to them but they did not listen. I called out to them but they did not answer.'"'"

[18]Then Jeremiah spoke to the Rechabite community, "The LORD of Heaven's Armies, the God of Israel says, 'You have obeyed the orders of your ancestor Jonadab. You have followed all his instructions. You have done exactly as he commanded you.' [19]So the LORD of Heaven's Armies, the God of Israel, says, 'Jonadab son of Rechab will never lack a male descendant to [a]serve me.'"

Jehoiakim Burns the Scroll Containing the Lord's Messages

36 The LORD spoke to Jeremiah in the [a]fourth year that Jehoiakim son of Josiah was ruling over Judah: [2]"Get a [a]scroll. [b]Write on it everything I have told you to say about Israel, Judah, and [c]all the other nations since I began to speak to you in the reign of [d]Josiah until now. [3]Perhaps when the people of Judah hear about all the disaster I intend to bring on them, they will all stop [a]doing the evil things they have been

doing. If they do, I will forgive their sins and the wicked things they have done."

[4]So Jeremiah [a]summoned [b]Baruch son of Neriah. Then, Baruch wrote down in a scroll all the LORD's words that he had told to Jeremiah[1] as they came from his mouth. [5]Then Jeremiah told Baruch, "I am no longer allowed to go into the LORD's temple. [6]So you go [a]there the next time all the people of Judah come in from their towns to fast in the LORD's temple. Read out loud where all of them can hear you what I told you the LORD said, which you wrote in the scroll. [7]Perhaps then they will ask the LORD for mercy and will all stop doing the evil things they have been doing. For the LORD has threatened to bring great anger and wrath against these people."

[8]So Baruch son of Neriah did exactly what the prophet Jeremiah told him to do. He read what the LORD had said from the scroll in the temple of the LORD. [9]All the people living in Jerusalem and all the people who came into Jerusalem from the towns of Judah observed a fast before the LORD. The fast took place in the ninth month of the fifth year that Jehoiakim son of Josiah was ruling over Judah. [10]At that time Baruch went into the temple of the LORD. He stood in the entrance of the room of Gemariah the son of Shaphan who had been the royal secretary. That room was in the upper court near the [a]entrance of the New Gate. There, where all the people could hear him, he read from the scroll what Jeremiah had said.[1]

[11]Micaiah, who was the son of Gemariah and the grandson of Shaphan, heard Baruch read from the scroll everything the LORD had said. [12]He went down to the chamber of the royal secretary in the king's palace and found all the court officials in session there. [a]Elishama the royal secretary, Delaiah son of Shemaiah, [b]Elnathan son of Achbor, Gemariah son of Shaphan, Zedekiah son of Hananiah, and all the other officials were seated there. [13]Micaiah told them everything he had heard Baruch read from

---

35:14[a] 2 Chr 36:15 [b] Jer 7:13; 25:3   **35:15**[a] Jer 26:4–5; 29:19 [b] [Isa 1:16–17]; Jer 18:11; 25:5–6; [Ezek 18:30–32]; Acts 26:20 [c] Jer 7:7; 25:5–6 [1] Heb. *Turn, each of you, from his [= your] wicked way and make good your deeds.*   **35:16**[a] [Heb 12:9] **35:17**[a] Prov 1:24; Isa 65:12; 66:4; Jer 7:13   **35:19**[a] [Exod 20:12]; Jer 15:19; [Luke 21:36; Eph 6:2–3]   **36:1**[a] 2 Kgs 24:1; 2 Chr 36:5–7; Jer 25:1, 3; 45:1; Dan 1:1   **36:2**[a] Isa 8:1; Ezek 2:9; Zech 5:1 [b] Jer 30:2; Hab 2:2 [c] Jer 25:15 [d] Jer 25:3   **36:3**[a] [Deut 30:2, 8; 1 Sam 7:3]; Isa 55:7; Jer 18:8; Jonah 3:8   **36:4**[a] Jer 32:12 [b] Jer 45:1 [1] Heb. *him.*   **36:6**[a] Lev 16:29; 23:27–32; Acts 27:9   **36:10**[a] Jer 26:10 [1] Heb. *And Baruch read from the scroll the words of Jeremiah in the house of the LORD in (i.e., in the entrance of) the room of Gemariah, son of Shaphan the scribe, in the upper court at the entrance of the New Gate in the house of the LORD in the ears of all the people.*   **36:12**[a] Jer 41:1 [b] Jer 26:22

the scroll in the hearing of the people. [14] All the officials sent Jehudi, who was the son of Nethaniah, the son of Shelemiah, the son of Cushi, to Baruch. They ordered him to tell Baruch, "Come here and bring with you the scroll you read in the hearing of the people." So Baruch son of Neriah went to them, carrying the scroll in his hand. [15] They said to him, "Please sit down and read it to us." So Baruch sat down and read it to them. [16] When they had heard it all, they expressed their alarm to one another. Then they said to Baruch, "We must certainly give the king a report about everything you have read!" [17] Then they asked Baruch, "How did you come to write all these words? Do they actually come from Jeremiah's mouth?" [18] Baruch answered, "Yes, they came from his own mouth. He dictated all these words to me, and I wrote them down in ink on this scroll." [19] Then the officials said to Baruch, "You and Jeremiah must go and hide. You must not let anyone know where you are."

[20] The officials put the scroll in the room of Elishama, the royal secretary, for safekeeping. Then they went to the court and reported everything to the king. [21] The king sent Jehudi to get the scroll. He went and got it from the room of Elishama, the royal secretary. Then he himself read it to the king and all the officials who were standing around him. [22] Since it was [a] the ninth month of the year, the king was sitting in his winter quarters.[1] A fire was burning in the firepot in front of him. [23] As soon as Jehudi had read three or four columns of the scroll, the king[1] would cut them off with a penknife and throw them on the fire in the firepot. He kept doing so until the whole scroll was burned up in the fire. [24] Neither he nor any of his attendants showed any alarm when they heard all that had been read. [a] Nor did they [b] tear their clothes to show any grief or sorrow. [25] The king did not even listen to Elnathan, Delaiah, and Gemariah, who had urged him not to burn the scroll. [26] He also ordered Jerahmeel, who was one of the royal princes, Seraiah son of Azriel, and Shelemiah son of Abdeel to arrest the scribe Baruch and the prophet Jeremiah. However, the LORD hid them.

Baruch and Jeremiah Write Another Scroll

[27] The LORD's message came to Jeremiah after the king had burned the scroll with the words Baruch had written down at Jeremiah's dictation. [28] "Get another scroll and write on it everything that was written on the original scroll that King Jehoiakim of Judah burned. [29] Tell King Jehoiakim of Judah, 'The LORD says, "You burned the scroll. You asked Jeremiah, 'How dare you write in this scroll that the king of Babylon will certainly come and destroy this land and wipe [a] out all the people and animals on it?'" [30] So [a] the LORD says concerning King Jehoiakim of Judah, "None of his line will occupy the throne of David. His dead body will be thrown out to be exposed to scorching heat by day and frost by night. [31] I will punish him and his descendants and the officials who serve him for the wicked things they have done. I will bring on them, the citizens of Jerusalem and the people of Judah, all the disaster that I told them about and that they ignored."'" [32] Then Jeremiah got another scroll and gave it to the scribe Baruch son of Neriah. As Jeremiah dictated, Baruch wrote on this scroll everything that had been on the scroll that King Jehoiakim of Judah burned in the fire. They also added on this scroll several other messages of the same kind.

Introduction to Incidents during the Reign of Zedekiah

37 [a] Zedekiah son of Josiah succeeded Jeconiah[1] son of Jehoiakim as king. He was elevated to the throne of the land of Judah by King Nebuchadnezzar of Babylon. [2] [a] Neither he nor the officials who served him nor the people of Judah paid any attention to what the LORD said through the prophet Jeremiah.

The Lord Responds to Zedekiah's Hope for Help

[3] King Zedekiah sent Jehucal son of Shelemiah and the priest [a] Zephaniah son of Maaseiah to the prophet Jeremiah to say, "Please [b] pray to the LORD our God on our behalf." [4] (Now Jeremiah had not yet been put in

---

36:22 [a] Judg 3:20; Amos 3:15 [1] Heb. *in the autumn house.* 36:23 [1] Heb. *he;* perhaps Jehudi instead. 36:24 [a] [Ps 36:1]; Jer 36:16 [b] Gen 37:29, 34; 2 Sam 1:11; 1 Kgs 21:27; 2 Kgs 19:1–2; 22:11; Isa 36:22; 37:1; Jonah 3:6 36:29 [a] Jer 25:9–11; 26:9 36:30 [a] Jer 22:30 37:1 [a] 2 Kgs 24:17; 1 Chr 3:15; 2 Chr 36:10; Jer 22:24 [1] Heb. *Coniah.* 37:2 [a] 2 Kgs 24:19–20; 2 Chr 36:12–16; [Prov 29:12] 37:3 [a] Jer 21:1–2; 29:25; 52:24 [b] 1 Kgs 13:6; Jer 42:2; Acts 8:24

prison. So he was still free to come and go among the people as he pleased. [5]At that time the Babylonian forces had temporarily given up their siege against Jerusalem. They had had it under siege, but withdrew when they heard that the army of [a]Pharaoh had set out from Egypt.) [6]The LORD's message came to the prophet Jeremiah, [7]"This is what the LORD God of Israel has said, 'This is what you must say to the king of Judah [a]who sent you to seek my help. "Beware, Pharaoh's army that was on its way to help you is about to go back home to Egypt. [8]Then the Babylonian forces will return. They will attack the city [a]and will capture it and burn it down. [9]Moreover, I, the LORD, warn you not to deceive yourselves into thinking that the Babylonian forces will go away and leave you alone. For they will not go away. [10]For even if you were to defeat all the Babylonian [a]forces fighting against you so badly that only wounded men were left lying in their tents, they would get up and burn this city down.""""

Jeremiah Is Charged with Deserting, Arrested, and Imprisoned

[11]The following events also occurred while the Babylonian forces had temporarily withdrawn from Jerusalem because the army of Pharaoh was coming. [12]Jeremiah started to leave Jerusalem to go to the territory of Benjamin. He wanted to make sure he got his share of the property that was being divided up among his family there. [13]But he only got as far as the Benjamin Gate. There an officer in charge of the guards named Irijah, who was the son of Shelemiah and the grandson of Hananiah, stopped him. He seized Jeremiah and said, "You are deserting to the Babylonians!" [14]Jeremiah answered, "That's a lie! I am not deserting to the Babylonians." But Irijah would not listen to him. Irijah put Jeremiah under arrest and took him to the officials. [15]The officials were very angry with Jeremiah. They had him flogged [a]and put in prison in the [b]house of Jonathan, the royal secretary, which they had converted into a place for confining prisoners. [16]So Jeremiah was put in prison in a cell in [a]the dungeon in Jonathan's house. He was kept there for a long time. [17]Then King Zedekiah had him brought to the palace. There he questioned him privately and asked him, "Is there any message from the LORD?" Jeremiah answered, "Yes, there is." Then he announced, "You will be [a]handed over to the king of Babylon." [18]Then Jeremiah asked King Zedekiah, "What crime have I committed against you, or the officials who serve you, or the people of Judah? What have I done to make you people throw me into prison? [19]Where now are the prophets who prophesied to you that the king of Babylon would not attack you or this land? [20]But now please listen, your royal Majesty, and grant my plea for mercy. Do not send me back to the house of Jonathan, the royal secretary. If you do, I will die there." [21]Then King Zedekiah ordered that Jeremiah be committed [a]to the courtyard of the guardhouse. He also ordered that a loaf of bread be given to him every day from the bakers' street [b]until all the bread in the city was gone. So Jeremiah was kept in the courtyard of the guardhouse.

Jeremiah Is Charged with Treason and Put in a Cistern to Die

38 Now Shephatiah son of Mattan, Gedaliah son of Pashhur, [a]Jehucal son of Shelemiah, and [b]Pashhur son of Malkijah had [c]heard the things that Jeremiah had been telling the people. They had heard him say, [2]"The LORD says, 'Those who stay in this city will die in battle or of starvation or disease. Those who leave [a]the city and surrender to the Babylonians[1] will live. They will escape with their lives.'" [3]They had also heard him say, "The LORD says, '[a]This city will [b]certainly be handed over to the army of the king of Babylon. They will capture it.'" [4]So these officials said to the king, "This man must be put to death. For he is demoralizing the soldiers who are left in the city as well as all the other people there by these things he is saying. This man is not seeking to help these people but is trying to harm them." [5]King Zedekiah said to them, "Very well, you can do what you want with him. For I cannot do anything

37:5 [a]2 Kgs 24:7; Jer 37:7; Ezek 17:15 **37:7** [a]Isa 36:6; Jer 21:2; Ezek 17:17 **37:8** [a]2 Chr 36:19; Jer 34:22 **37:10** [a]Lev 26:36–38; Isa 30:17; Jer 21:4–5 **37:15** [a]Jer 20:2; [Matt 21:35] [b]Gen 39:20; 2 Chr 16:10; 18:26; Jer 38:26; Acts 5:18 **37:16** [a]Jer 38:6 **37:17** [a]2 Kgs 25:4–7; Jer 21:7; Ezek 12:12–13; 17:19–21 **37:21** [a]Jer 32:2; 38:13, 28 [b]2 Kgs 25:3; Jer 38:9; 52:6 **38:1** [a]Jer 37:3 [b]Jer 21:1 [c]Jer 21:8 **38:2** [a]Jer 21:9 [1]Heb. *those who go out to the Chaldeans.* **38:3** [a]Jer 21:10; 32:3 [b]Jer 34:2

to stop you." [6]So the officials took Jeremiah and put him in the cistern of Malkijah, one of the royal princes, that was in the courtyard of the guardhouse. There was no water in the cistern, only mud. [a]So when they lowered Jeremiah into the cistern with ropes he sank in the mud.

An Ethiopian Official Rescues Jeremiah from the Cistern

[7][a]An Ethiopian, Ebed Melech, a court official in the royal palace, heard that Jeremiah had been put in the cistern. While the king was holding court at the Benjamin Gate, [8]Ebed Melech departed the palace and went to speak to the king. He said to him, [9]"Your royal Majesty, those men have been very wicked in all that they have done to the prophet Jeremiah. They have thrown him into a cistern, and he is sure to die of starvation there because there is [a]no food left in the city." [10]Then the king gave Ebed Melech the Ethiopian the following order: "Take 30[1] men with you from here and go pull the prophet Jeremiah out of the cistern before he dies." [11]So Ebed Melech took the men with him and went to a room under the treasure room in the palace. He got some worn-out clothes and old rags[1] from there and let them down by ropes to Jeremiah in the cistern. [12]Ebed Melech called down to Jeremiah, "Put these rags and worn-out clothes under your armpits to pad the ropes." Jeremiah did as Ebed Melech instructed. [13]So they pulled Jeremiah up from the cistern with ropes. Jeremiah, however, still [a]remained confined to the courtyard of the guardhouse.

Jeremiah Responds to Zedekiah's Request for Secret Advice

[14]Some time later Zedekiah sent and had Jeremiah brought to him at the third entrance of the LORD's temple. The king said to Jeremiah, "I would like to [a]ask you a question. Do not hide anything from me when you answer." [15]Jeremiah said to Zedekiah, "If I answer you, you will certainly kill me. If I give you advice, you will not listen to me." [16]So King Zedekiah made a secret promise to Jeremiah and sealed it with an oath. He promised, "As surely as the LORD lives [a]who has given us life and breath, I promise you this: I will not kill you or hand you over to those men who want to kill you."

[17]Then Jeremiah said to Zedekiah, "The LORD God of Heaven's Armies, the God of Israel, says, 'You must [a]surrender [b]to the officers of the king of Babylon. If you do, your life will be spared and this city will not be burned down. Indeed, you and your whole family will be spared. [18]But if [a]you do not surrender to the officers of the king of Babylon, this city will be handed over to the Babylonians, and they will burn it down. You yourself will not escape from them.'" [19]Then King Zedekiah said to Jeremiah, "I am afraid of the Judeans who have [a]deserted to the Babylonians. The Babylonians might hand me over to them, and they will [b]torture me." [20]Then Jeremiah answered, "You will not be handed over to them. Please obey the LORD by doing what I have been telling you. Then all will go [a]well with you, and your life will be spared. [21]But if you refuse to surrender, the LORD has shown me a vision of what will happen. Here is what I saw: [22]All the [a]women who are left in the royal palace of Judah will be led out to the officers of the king of Babylon. They will taunt you saying:

"'Your trusted friends misled you;
they have gotten the best of you.
Now that your feet are stuck in the mud,
they have turned their backs on you.'

[23]"All your wives and your [a]children will be turned over to the Babylonians. [b]You yourself will not escape from them but will be captured by the king of Babylon. This city will be burned down."[1]

[24]Then Zedekiah told Jeremiah, "Do not let anyone know about the conversation we have had. If you do, you will die. [25]The officials may hear that I have talked with you. They may come to you and say, 'Tell us what you said to the king and what the king said to you. Do not hide anything from us. If you do, we will kill you.' [26]If they do [a]this, tell them, 'I was pleading with the king not [b]to send me back to die in the dungeon of

---

38:6 [a]Jer 37:21; Lam 3:55   38:7 [a]Jer 39:16   38:9 [a]Jer 37:21   38:10 [1]One MS *three.*   38:11 [1]Heb. *worn-out clothes and worn-out rags.*   38:13 [a]Neh 3:25; Jer 37:21; Acts 23:35; 24:27; 28:16, 30   38:14 [a]Jer 21:1–2; 37:17   38:16 [a]Num 16:22; Isa 57:16; Zech 12:1; [Acts 17:25, 28]   38:17 [a]2 Kgs 24:12   [b]Jer 39:3   38:18 [a]Jer 32:4; 34:3   38:19 [a]Jer 39:9   [b]1 Sam 31:4   38:20 [a]Jer 40:9   38:22 [a]Jer 8:10   38:23 [a]Jer 39:6; 41:10   [b]Jer 39:5   [1]Maj. Heb. MSS *and you will burn down this city.*   38:26 [a]Jer 37:20   [b]Jer 37:15

Jonathan's house.'" [27] All the officials did indeed come and question Jeremiah. He told them exactly what the king had instructed him to say. They stopped questioning him any further because no one had actually heard their conversation. [28] So [a] Jeremiah remained confined in the courtyard of the guardhouse until the day Jerusalem was captured.

The Fall of Jerusalem and Its Aftermath

The following events occurred when Jerusalem was captured.[1]

39 King Nebuchadnezzar of Babylon came against Jerusalem with his whole army and laid siege to it. The siege began in the tenth month of the [a] ninth year that Zedekiah ruled over Judah. [2] It lasted until the ninth day of the fourth month of Zedekiah's [a] eleventh year. On that day they broke through the city walls. [3] Then Nergal Sharezer of Samgar, Nebo Sarsekim (who was a chief officer), Nergal Sharezer (who was a high official), and all [a] the other officers of the king of Babylon came and set up quarters in the Middle Gate. [4] When King Zedekiah of Judah and all his [a] soldiers saw them, they tried to escape. They departed from the city during the night. They took a path through the king's garden and passed out through the gate between the two walls. Then they headed for the rift valley. [5] But the Babylonian army chased after them. They caught up [a] with Zedekiah in the plains of Jericho[1] and captured him. They took him to King Nebuchadnezzar of Babylon at [b] Riblah in the territory of Hamath, and Nebuchadnezzar passed sentence on him there. [6] There at Riblah the king of Babylon had Zedekiah's sons put to death while Zedekiah was forced to [a] watch. The king of Babylon also had all the [b] nobles of Judah put to death. [7] Then [a] he had Zedekiah's eyes put out and had him bound in chains to be led off to Babylon. [8][a] The Babylonians burned [b] down the royal palace, the temple of the LORD, and the people's homes,[1] and they tore down the [c] wall of Jerusalem. [9] Then Nebuzaradan, [a] the captain of the royal guard, took captive the rest of the people who were left in the city. He carried them off to Babylon along with the [b] people who had deserted to him.[1] [10] But he left behind in the land of Judah some of the [a] poor people who owned nothing. He gave them fields and vineyards at that time.

[11] Now King Nebuchadnezzar of Babylon had issued orders concerning Jeremiah. He had passed them on through Nebuzaradan, the captain of his royal guard, [12] "Find Jeremiah and look out for him. Do not do anything to [a] harm him, but do with him whatever he tells you." [13] So Nebuzaradan (the captain of the royal guard), Nebushazban (who was a chief officer), Nergal Sharezer (who was a high official), and all the other officers of the king of Babylon [14] sent and had Jeremiah brought from the courtyard of the guardhouse. They turned him over [a] to Gedaliah, the son of [b] Ahikam and the grandson of Shaphan, to take him home with him. But Jeremiah stayed among the people.

Ebed Melech Is Promised Deliverance because of His Faith

[15] Now the LORD's message had come to Jeremiah while he was still confined in the courtyard of the guardhouse, [16] "Go and tell Ebed [a] Melech the [b] Nubian,[1] 'This is what the LORD of Heaven's Armies, the God of Israel, has said, "I will carry out against this city what I promised. It will mean disaster and not good fortune for it. When that disaster happens, you will be there to see it. [17] But I will rescue you when it happens. I, the LORD, affirm it! You will not be handed over to those whom you fear. [18] I will certainly save [a] you. You will not fall victim to violence. You will escape with your life [b] because you trust in me. I, the LORD, affirm it!"'"

38:28 [a] [Ps 23:4]; Jer 37:21; 39:14 [1] Some WSS omit this line.   39:1 [a] 2 Kgs 25:1–12; Jer 52:4; Ezek 24:1–2   39:2 [a] Jer 1:3   39:3 [a] Jer 1:15; 38:17   39:4 [a] 2 Kgs 25:4; Isa 30:16; Jer 52:7; Amos 2:14   39:5 [a] Jer 21:7; 32:4; 38:18, 23 [b] 2 Kgs 23:33; Jer 52:9, 26, 27 [1] The sloping plains of the rift valley basin north of the Dead Sea, in this case, west of the Jordan in the vicinity of Jericho.   39:6 [a] Deut 28:34 [b] Jer 34:19–21   39:7 [a] 2 Kgs 25:7; Jer 52:11; Ezek 12:13   39:8 [a] 2 Kgs 25:9; Jer 38:18; 52:13 [b] Jer 21:10 [c] 2 Kgs 25:10; Neh 1:3; Jer 52:14 [1] MT omits *the temple of the LORD*; LXX omits vv. 4–13.   39:9 [a] 2 Kgs 25:8, 11, 12, 20 [b] Jer 38:19 [1] MT *And the rest of the people who were left in the city and the deserters who had deserted to him and the rest of the people Nebuzaradan, the captain of the guard, carried into exile to Babylon.*   39:10 [a] Jer 40:7   39:12 [a] Jer 1:18–19; 15:20–21   39:14 [a] Jer 40:5 [b] 2 Kgs 22:12, 14; 2 Chr 34:20; Jer 26:24   39:16 [a] Jer 38:7, 12 [b] Jer 21:10; [Dan 9:12; Zech 1:6] [1] Trad. *Ethiopian*; Heb. *Cushite.*   39:18 [a] Jer 21:9; 45:5 [b] 1 Chr 5:20; Ps 37:40; [Jer 17:7–8]

Jeremiah Is Set Free a Second Time

40 The LORD spoke to Jeremiah [a]after Nebuzaradan the captain of the royal guard had set him free at Ramah. He had taken him there in chains along with all the people from Jerusalem and Judah who were being carried off to exile to Babylon. [2]The captain of the royal guard took Jeremiah aside and [a]said to him, "The LORD your God threatened this place with this disaster. [3]Now he has brought it about. The LORD has done just as he threatened to do. This disaster has happened [a]because you people sinned against the LORD and did not obey him. [4]But now, Jeremiah, today [a]I will set you free from the chains on your wrists. If you would like to come to Babylon with me, come along and I will take care of you. But if you prefer not to come to Babylon with me, you are not required to do so. You are free to go [b]anywhere in the land you want to go. Go wherever you choose." [5]Before Jeremiah could turn to leave, the captain of the guard added, "Go back[1] to [a]Gedaliah, the son of Ahikam and grandson of Shaphan, [b]whom the king of Babylon appointed to govern the towns of Judah. Go back and live with him among the people. Or go wherever else you choose." Then the captain of the guard gave Jeremiah some food and a present and let him go. [6a]So Jeremiah went to Gedaliah son of Ahikam at [b]Mizpah and lived there with him. He stayed there to live among the people who had been left in the land of Judah.

A Small Judean Province Is Established at Mizpah

[7]Now some of the officers of the Judean army [a]and [b]their troops had been hiding in the countryside. They heard that the king of Babylon had appointed Gedaliah son of Ahikam to govern the country. They also heard that he had been put in charge over the men, women, and children from the poorer classes of the land who had not been carried off into exile in Babylon. [8]So all these officers and their troops came to Gedaliah at Mizpah. The officers who came were [a]Ishmael son of Nethaniah, [b]Johanan and Jonathan the sons of Kareah, Seraiah son of Tanhumeth, the sons of Ephai the Netophathite, and [c]Jezaniah son of the [d]Maacathite. [9]Gedaliah, the son of Ahikam and grandson of Shaphan, took an oath so as to give them and their troops some assurance of safety. "Do not be afraid to submit to the Babylonians. Settle down in the land and submit to the king of Babylon. Then things will go [a]well for you. [10]I for my part will stay at Mizpah to represent you before the Babylonians whenever they come to us. You for your part go ahead and harvest the wine, the dates, the figs, and the olive oil, and store them in jars. Go ahead and settle down in the towns that you have taken over." [11]Moreover, all the Judeans who were in Moab, Ammon, Edom, and all the other countries heard what had happened. They heard that the king of Babylon had allowed some people to stay in Judah and that he had appointed Gedaliah, the son of Ahikam and grandson of Shaphan, to govern them. [12]So all these Judeans [a]returned to the land of Judah from the places where they had been scattered. They came to Gedaliah at Mizpah. Thus they harvested a large amount of wine and dates and figs.

Ishmael Murders Gedaliah and Carries Off the Judeans at Mizpah as Captives

[13]Johanan, son of Kareah, and all the officers of the troops that had been hiding in the open country came to Gedaliah at Mizpah. [14]They said to him, "Are you at all aware that King [a]Baalis of Ammon has sent Ishmael son of Nethaniah to kill you?" But Gedaliah son of Ahikam would not believe them. [15]Then Johanan son of Kareah spoke privately to Gedaliah there at Mizpah, "Let me go and kill Ishmael the son of Nethaniah before anyone knows about it. Otherwise he will kill you and all the Judeans who have rallied around you will be scattered. Then what [a]remains of Judah will disappear." [16]But Gedaliah son of Ahikam said to Johanan son of Kareah, "Do not do that because what you are saying about Ishmael is not true."

40:1 [a]Jer 39:9, 11   40:2 [a]Jer 50:7   40:3 [a]Deut 29:24–25; Jer 50:7; Dan 9:11; [Rom 2:5]   40:4 [a]Jer 39:12   [b]Gen 20:15   40:5 [a]Jer 39:14   [b]2 Kgs 25:22; Jer 41:10   [1]MT *and he was not yet turning. "Or return* [imperative] *to Gedaliah"*; LXX omits v. 4 after "I will take care of you" and begins v. 5 with *But if not, run and return to Gedaliah*; Vg. *and don't come with me but stay with Gedaliah*; Syr. *But if you are remaining, then return to Gedaliah.*   40:6 [a]Jer 39:14   [b]Judg 20:1; 1 Sam 7:5; 2 Chr 16:6   40:7 [a]2 Kgs 25:23–24   [b]Jer 39:10   40:8 [a]Jer 41:1–10   [b]Jer 41:11; 43:2   [c]Jer 42:1   [d]Deut 3:14; Josh 12:5; 2 Sam 10:6   40:9 [a]Jer 27:11; 38:17–20   40:12 [a]Jer 43:5   40:14 [a]Jer 41:10   40:15 [a]Jer 42:2

41

But in the seventh month Ishmael, the son of Nethaniah and grandson of Elishama, who was [a] a member of the royal family and had been one of Zedekiah's chief officers, came with 10 of his men to Gedaliah son of Ahikam at [b] Mizpah. While they were eating a meal together with him there at Mizpah, [2] Ishmael son of Nethaniah and the 10 men who were with him stood up, pulled out their swords, and [a] killed Gedaliah, the son of [b] Ahikam and grandson of Shaphan. Thus Ishmael killed the man that the king of Babylon had [c] appointed to govern the country. [3] Ishmael also killed all the Judeans who were with Gedaliah at Mizpah and the Babylonian soldiers who happened to be there.

[4] On the day after Gedaliah had been murdered, before anyone even knew about it, [5] 80 men arrived from Shechem, Shiloh, and Samaria. [a] They had shaved off their beards, torn their clothes, and cut themselves to show they were mourning. They were carrying grain offerings and incense to present at the temple of the LORD in Jerusalem. [6] Ishmael son of Nethaniah went out from Mizpah to meet them. He was pretending to cry as he walked along. When he met them, he said to them, "Come with me to meet Gedaliah son of Ahikam." [7] But as soon as they were inside the city, Ishmael son of Nethaniah and the men who were with him [a] slaughtered them and threw their bodies in a cistern. [8] But there were 10 men among them who said to Ishmael, "Do not kill us. For we will give you the stores of wheat, barley, olive oil, and honey we have hidden in a field." [1] So he spared their lives and did not kill them along with the rest. [9] Now [a] the cistern where Ishmael threw all the dead bodies of those he had killed was a large one that King Asa had constructed as part of his defenses against King Baasha of Israel. Ishmael son of Nethaniah filled it with dead bodies. [10] Then Ishmael took captive all the people who were still left [a] alive in Mizpah. This included [b] the royal princesses and all [c] the rest of the people in Mizpah that Nebuzaradan, the captain of the royal guard, had put under the authority of Gedaliah son of Ahikam. Ishmael son of Nethaniah took all these people captive and set out to cross over to the Ammonites.

Johanan Rescues the People Ishmael Had Carried Off

[11] [a] Johanan son of Kareah and all the army officers who were with him heard about all the atrocities that Ishmael son of Nethaniah had committed. [12] So [a] they took all their troops and went to fight against Ishmael son of Nethaniah. They caught up with him near the large pool at Gibeon. [13] When all the people that Ishmael had taken captive saw Johanan son of Kareah and all the army officers with him, they were glad. [14] All those people that Ishmael had taken captive from Mizpah turned and went over to Johanan son of Kareah. [15] But Ishmael son of Nethaniah managed to escape from Johanan along with eight of his men, and he went on over to Ammon.

[16] Johanan son of Kareah and all the army officers who were with him led off all the people who had been left [a] alive at Mizpah. They had rescued them from Ishmael son of Nethaniah after he killed Gedaliah son of Ahikam. They led off the men, women, children, soldiers, and court officials whom they had brought away from Gibeon. [17] They set out to go to [a] Egypt to get away from the Babylonians, but stopped at Geruth Kimham near Bethlehem. [18] They were afraid of what the Babylonians might do because Ishmael son of Nethaniah had killed Gedaliah son of Ahikam, [a] whom the king of Babylon had appointed to govern the country.

The Survivors Ask the Lord for Advice but Refuse to Follow It

42

Then all the army officers, including [a] Johanan son of Kareah and Jezaniah son of Hoshaiah and all the people of every class, went to the prophet Jeremiah. [2] They said to him, "[a] Please grant our request and [b] pray to the LORD your God for [c] all those of us who are still left alive here. For, as you yourself can see, there are only a few of us left out of the many there were before. [3] Pray that [a] the LORD your God will tell us where

41:1 [a] 2 Kgs 25:25   [b] Jer 40:6, 10   41:2 [a] 2 Sam 3:27; 20:9–10; 2 Kgs 25:25; Ps 41:9; 109:5; John 13:18   [b] Jer 26:24   [c] Jer 40:5   41:5 [a] 1 Sam 1:7; 2 Kgs 25:9; Neh 10:34–35   41:7 [a] Ps 55:23; Isa 59:7; Ezek 22:27; 33:24, 26   41:8 [1] Heb. *For we have hidden stores of wheat, barley, olive oil, and honey in a field.*   41:9 [a] 1 Kgs 15:22; 2 Chr 16:6   41:10 [a] Jer 40:11–12   [b] Jer 43:6   [c] Jer 40:14   41:11 [a] Jer 40:7–8, 13–16   41:12 [a] 2 Sam 2:13   41:16 [a] Jer 40:11–12; 43:4–7   41:17 [a] Jer 43:7   41:18 [a] Jer 40:5   42:1 [a] Jer 40:8, 13; 41:11   42:2 [a] Jer 15:11   [b] Exod 8:28; 1 Sam 7:8; 12:19; 1 Kgs 13:6; Isa 37:4; Jer 37:3; Acts 8:24; [Jas 5:16]   [c] Lev 26:22; Deut 28:62; Isa 1:9; Lam 1:1   42:3 [a] Ezra 8:21

we should go and what we should do." [4]The prophet Jeremiah answered them, "Agreed! I will indeed pray to the Lord your God as you have [a]asked. I will tell you everything the Lord replies in response to you. I will not [b]keep anything back from you." [5]They answered Jeremiah, "May the Lord be a true and faithful witness against us if we do not do just as the Lord your God sends you to tell us to do. [6]We will [a]obey what the Lord our God to whom we are sending you tells us to do. It does not matter whether we like what he tells us or not. We will obey what he tells us to do so [b]that things will go well for us."

[7]Ten days later the Lord's message came to Jeremiah. [8]So Jeremiah summoned Johanan son of Kareah and all the army officers who were with him and all the people of every class. [9]Then Jeremiah said to them, "You sent me to the Lord God of Israel to make your request known to him. Here is what he says to you: [10]'If you [a]will only stay in this land, I will build you up. I will not tear you down. I will firmly plant you.[1] I will not uproot you. For I am filled with [b]sorrow because of the disaster that I have brought on you. [11]Do not be afraid of the king of Babylon whom you now fear. Do not be afraid of him because I will be with you to save you and to rescue you from his power. I, the Lord, affirm it! [12]I [a]will have compassion on you so that he in turn will have mercy on you and allow you to return to your land.'

[13]"You must not disobey the Lord [a]your God by saying, 'We will not stay in this land.' [14]You must not say, 'No, we will not stay. Instead we will go and live in the land of [a]Egypt where we will not face war, or hear the enemy's trumpet calls, or starve for lack of food.' [15]If you people who remain in Judah do that, then listen to the Lord's message. This is what the Lord of Heaven's Armies, the God of Israel, has said, 'If you are [a]so determined[1] to go to Egypt that [b]you go and settle there, [16]the [a]wars you fear will catch up with you there in the land of Egypt. The starvation you are worried about will follow you there to Egypt. You will die there. [17]All the people who are determined to go and settle in Egypt will die from war, starvation, or disease. [a]No one will survive or escape the disaster I will bring on them.' [18]For[1] the Lord of Heaven's Armies, the God of Israel, says, 'If you go to Egypt, I will pour [a]out my wrath on [b]you just as I poured out my anger and wrath on the citizens of Jerusalem. You will become an object of horror and ridicule, an example of those who have been cursed and that people use in pronouncing a curse. You will never see this place again.'

[19]"The Lord has told you people who remain in Judah, '[a]Do not go to Egypt.' Be very sure of this: I warn you here and now. [20]You are making a fatal mistake. For you sent me to the Lord your God and asked me, 'Pray to the Lord our God for us. Tell us what the Lord our God says, and we will do it.' [21]This day I have told you what he said. But you do [a]not want to obey the Lord your God by doing what he sent me to tell you. [22]So now be very sure of this: You will die from war, starvation, or disease in the place where you want to go and live."

43 Jeremiah finished telling all the people all these [a]things the Lord their God had sent him to tell them. [2]Then Azariah son of Hoshaiah, Johanan son of Kareah, and other arrogant men said to Jeremiah, "You are telling [a]a lie! The Lord our God did not send you to tell us, 'You must not go to Egypt and settle there.' [3]But [a]Baruch son of Neriah is stirring you up against us. He wants to hand us over to the Babylonians so that they will kill us or carry us off into exile in Babylon." [4]So Johanan son of Kareah, all the army officers, and all the rest of the people did [a]not obey the Lord's command to stay in the land of Judah. [5]Instead Johanan son of Kareah and [a]all the army officers led off all the Judean remnant who had come back to live in the land of Judah from all the nations where they had been scattered. [6]They also led off all [a]the men, women, children, [b]and royal princesses that Nebuzaradan, the captain of the royal guard, had left with Gedaliah, the son of Ahikam and grandson of Shaphan; this

42:4 [a] 1 Kgs 22:14; Jer 23:28   [b] 1 Sam 3:17–18; Ps 40:10; Acts 20:20   **42:6** [a] Exod 24:7; Deut 5:27; Josh 24:24   [b] Deut 5:29, 33; 6:3; Jer 7:23   **42:10** [a] Jer 24:6; 31:28; 33:7; Ezek 36:36   [b] Deut 32:36; [Jer 18:8]   [1] Or *I will firmly plant you in the land, I will establish you.*   **42:12** [a] Neh 1:11; Ps 106:46; Prov 16:7   **42:13** [a] Jer 44:16   **42:14** [a] Isa 31:1; Jer 41:17; 43:7   **42:15** [a] Deut 17:16; Jer 44:12–14   [b] Luke 9:51   [1] Heb. *set your face to.*   **42:16** [a] Jer 44:13, 27; Ezek 11:8; Amos 9:1–4   **42:17** [a] Jer 44:14, 28   **42:18** [a] 2 Chr 36:16–19; Jer 7:20   [b] Deut 29:21; Isa 65:15; Jer 18:16; 24:9; 26:6; 29:18, 22; 44:12   [1] Or *Indeed.*   **42:19** [a] Deut 17:16; Isa 30:1–7   **42:21** [a] Isa 30:1–7   **43:1** [a] Jer 42:9–18   **43:2** [a] Jer 42:1   **43:3** [a] Jer 36:4; 45:1   **43:4** [a] 2 Kgs 25:26   **43:5** [a] Jer 40:11–12   **43:6** [a] Jer 41:10   [b] Jer 39:10; 40:7

included the prophet Jeremiah and Baruch son of Neriah. [7a]They went on to Egypt because they refused to obey the LORD, and came to [b]Tahpanhes.

Jeremiah Predicts That Nebuchadnezzar Will Plunder Egypt and Its Gods

[8]At Tahpanhes the LORD's [a]message came to Jeremiah: [9]"Take some large stones and bury them in the mortar of the clay pavement at the entrance of Pharaoh's residence here in Tahpanhes. Do it while the people of Judah present there are watching. [10]Then tell them, 'The LORD of Heaven's Armies, the God of Israel, says, "I will bring [a]my servant King Nebuchadnezzar of Babylon. I will set his throne over these stones that I have buried. He will pitch his royal tent over them. [11a]He will come and attack Egypt. [b]Those who are destined to die of disease will die of disease. Those who are destined to be carried off into exile will be carried off into exile. Those who are destined to die in war will die in war.[1] [12]He will set fire[1] to [a]the temples of the gods of Egypt. He will burn their gods or carry them off as captives. He will pick Egypt clean like a shepherd picks the lice from his clothing. He will leave there unharmed.[2] [13]He will demolish the sacred pillars in the temple of the sun in Egypt and will burn down the temples of the gods of Egypt."'"

The Lord Will Punish the Judean Exiles in Egypt for Their Idolatry

44 The LORD spoke to Jeremiah concerning all the Judeans who were living in the land of Egypt, those in [a]Migdol, [b]Tahpanhes, [c]Memphis, and in the region of southern [d]Egypt: [2]"The LORD of [a]Heaven's Armies, the God of Israel, says, 'You have seen all the disaster I brought on Jerusalem and all the towns of Judah. Indeed, they now lie in ruins and are deserted. [3]This happened because of the wickedness the people living there did. They made me angry by [a]worshiping and offering sacrifices to other gods whom neither they nor you nor your ancestors previously knew. [4]I sent my servants the prophets to you people over and over [a]again warning you not to do this disgusting thing I hate. [5]But the people of Jerusalem and Judah would not listen or pay any attention. They would not stop the wickedness they were doing nor quit sacrificing to other gods. [6]So my anger and my wrath were poured out and burned like a fire through the towns of Judah and the streets of Jerusalem. That is why they have become the desolate ruins that they are today.'

[7]"So now the LORD God of Heaven's Armies, the God of Israel, asks, 'Why will you do such great harm to yourselves? Why should every man, woman, child, and baby of yours be destroyed from the midst of Judah? Why should you leave yourselves without [a]a remnant? [8]That is [a]what will result from your making me angry by what you are doing. You are making me angry by sacrificing to other gods here in the land of Egypt where you live. You will be destroyed for doing that! You will become an example used in curses and an object of ridicule among all the nations of the earth. [9]Have you forgotten all the wicked things that have been done in the towns of Judah and in the streets of Jerusalem by your ancestors, by the kings of Judah and their wives, and by you and your wives? [10]To this day your people have [a]shown no contrition! They have not [b]revered me nor followed the laws and statutes I commanded you and your ancestors.'

[11]"Because of [a]this, the LORD of Heaven's Armies, the God of Israel, says, 'I am determined to bring disaster on you, even to the point of destroying all the Judeans here. [12]I will see to it that all [a]the Judean remnant that was determined to go and live in [b]the land of Egypt will be destroyed. Here in the land of Egypt they will fall in battle[1] or perish from starvation. People of every class will die in war or from starvation. They will become an object of horror and ridicule, an example of those who have been cursed

43:7 [a] Jer 42:19   [b] Jer 2:16; 44:1   **43:8** [a] Jer 44:1–30   **43:10** [a] Jer 25:9; 27:6; Ezek 29:18, 20   **43:11** [a] Isa 19:1–25; Jer 25:15–19; 44:13; 46:1–2, 13–26; Ezek 29:19–20   [b] Jer 15:2; Zech 11:9   [1] Heb. *those to death to death, and those to captivity to captivity, and those to the sword to the sword.*   **43:12** [a] Exod 12:12; Isa 19:1; Jer 46:25; Ezek 30:13   [1] MT *I will set fire to.*   [2] Heb. *in peace/wholeness/well-being/safety.*   **44:1** [a] Exod 14:2; Jer 46:14   [b] Jer 43:7; Ezek 30:18   [c] Isa 19:13; Jer 2:16; 46:14; Ezek 30:13, 16; Hos 9:6   [d] Isa 11:11; Ezek 29:14; 30:14   **44:2** [a] Isa 6:11; Jer 4:7; 9:11; 34:22; Mic 3:12   **44:3** [a] Deut 13:6; 32:17   **44:4** [a] 2 Chr 36:15; Jer 7:25; 25:4; 26:5; 29:19; Zech 7:7   **44:7** [a] Num 16:38; Jer 7:19; [Ezek 33:11]; Hab 2:10   **44:8** [a] 1 Kgs 9:7–8; 2 Chr 7:20; Jer 42:18   **44:10** [a] 2 Chr 36:12; Jer 6:15; 8:12; Dan 5:22   [b] [Prov 28:14]   **44:11** [a] Lev 17:10; 20:5–6; Jer 21:10; Amos 9:4   **44:12** [a] Jer 42:15–17, 22   [b] Isa 65:15; Jer 42:18   [1] Heb. *fall by the sword.*

and that people use in pronouncing a curse. [13a]I will punish those who live in the land of Egypt with war, starvation, and disease, just as I punished Jerusalem. [14a]None of the Judean remnant who have come to live in the land of Egypt will escape or survive to return to the land of Judah. Though they [b]long to return and live there, none of them shall return except a few fugitives.'"

[15]Then all the men who were aware that their wives were sacrificing to other gods, as well as all their wives, answered Jeremiah—there was a great crowd of them representing all the people who lived in northern and southern Egypt—[16]"We will not listen to what you claim the LORD has spoken to us! [17]Instead we will do [a]everything we vowed we would do. We will sacrifice and pour out drink offerings to the goddess called the [b]Queen of Heaven just as we and our ancestors, our kings, and our leaders previously did in the towns of Judah and in the streets of Jerusalem. For then we had plenty of food, were well off, and had no troubles.[1] [18]But ever since we stopped sacrificing and pouring out drink offerings to the Queen of Heaven, we have been in great need. Our people have died in wars or of starvation." [19]The women added,[1] "We did indeed sacrifice [a]and pour out drink offerings to the Queen of Heaven. But it was with the full knowledge and approval of our husbands that we made cakes in her image and poured out drink offerings to her."

[20]Then Jeremiah replied to all the people, both men and women, who responded to him in this way: [21]"The LORD did indeed remember and call to mind what you did! He remembered the incense you and your ancestors, your kings, your leaders, and all the rest of the people of the land offered to other gods in the towns of Judah and in the streets of Jerusalem. [22]Finally the LORD could no longer endure your wicked deeds and the disgusting things you did. That is why your land [a]has become the desolate, uninhabited ruin that it is today. That is why it has become a proverbial example used in curses. [23]You have sacrificed to other gods. You have sinned against [a]the LORD! You have not obeyed the LORD! You have not followed his laws, his statutes, and his decrees. That is why this disaster that is evident to this day has happened to you."

[24]Then Jeremiah spoke to all the people, particularly to all the women, "Listen to the LORD's message, all you people of Judah who are in Egypt. [25]This is what the LORD of Heaven's Armies, the God of Israel, has said, 'You women have confirmed by your actions what you vowed with your lips! You said, "We will certainly carry out our vows to sacrifice and pour out drink offerings to the Queen of Heaven." Well, then fulfill your vows! Carry them out!'[1] [26]But [a]listen to the LORD's message, all you people of Judah who are living in the land of Egypt: The LORD says, 'I hereby swear by my own [b]great name that none of the people of Judah who are living anywhere in Egypt will ever again invoke [c]my name in their oaths! Never again will any of them use it in an oath saying, "As surely as the Sovereign LORD lives." [27]I will indeed see to it that disaster, not prosperity, happens to them. [a]All the people of Judah who are in the land of Egypt will die in war or from starvation until not one of them is left. [28]Some who survive the [a]battle will return to the land of Judah from the land of Egypt. But they will be very few indeed! Then the Judean remnant who have come to live in the land of Egypt will know whose word proves true, mine or theirs.' [29]Moreover the LORD says, 'I will make something happen to prove that I will punish you in this place. I will do it so that you will know that my threats to bring disaster on you [a]will prove true. [30]I, the LORD, [a]promise that I will hand Pharaoh Hophra king of Egypt over to his enemies who are seeking to kill him. I will do that just as surely as I handed King [b]Zedekiah of Judah over to King Nebuchadnezzar of Babylon, his enemy who was seeking to kill him.'"

Baruch Is Rebuked but Also Comforted

45 The prophet Jeremiah [a]spoke to [b]Baruch son of Neriah while he was writing down in a scroll the words that Jeremiah spoke to him. (This happened in the

44:13 [a] Jer 43:11   **44:14** [a] [Isa 4:2; 10:20]; Jer 44:28; [Rom 9:27]   [b] Jer 22:26–27   **44:17** [a] Num 30:12; Deut 23:23; Judg 11:36   [b] 2 Kgs 17:16; Jer 7:18   [1] Heb. *saw [or experienced] no disaster/trouble/harm.*   **44:19** [a] Jer 7:18   [1] MT omits *And the women added.*   **44:22** [a] Jer 25:11, 18, 38   **44:23** [a] 1 Kgs 9:9; Neh 13:18; Jer 44:2; Dan 9:11–12   **44:25** [1] Heb. *Carry out your vows!*   **44:26** [a] Gen 22:16; Deut 32:40–41; Jer 22:5; Amos 6:8; Heb 6:13   [b] Jer 10:6   [c] Neh 9:5; Ps 50:16; Ezek 20:39   **44:27** [a] Jer 1:10; 31:28; Ezek 7:6   **44:28** [a] Isa 10:19; 27:12–13   **44:29** [a] [Ps 33:11]   **44:30** [a] Jer 46:25–26; Ezek 29:3; 30:21   [b] 2 Kgs 24:4–7; Jer 39:5   **45:1** [a] Jer 36:1, 4, 32   [b] Jer 32:12, 16; 43:3

ᶜfourth year that Jehoiakim son of Josiah was ruling over Judah.) ²Jeremiah said, "The LORD God of Israel has a message for you, Baruch. ³'You have said, 'I feel so hopeless!ⁱ For the LORD has added sorrow to my suffering. I am worn ᵃout from groaning. I can't find any rest.'"'

⁴The LORD told Jeremiah, "Tell Baruch,ⁱ 'The LORD says, "I am about to tear down ᵃwhat I have built and to uproot what I have planted. I will do this throughout the whole earth. ⁵Are you ᵃlooking for great things for yourself? Do not look for such things. For I, the LORD, affirm that I am about to bring disaster on all humanity. But I will allow you to escape with your ᵇlife wherever you go."'"

Prophecies against Foreign Nations

46 ¹This was ᵃthe LORD's message to the prophet Jeremiah about the nations.

The Prophecy about Egypt's Defeat at Carchemish

²He spoke about ᵃEgypt and ᵇthe army of Pharaoh Necho king of Egypt, which was encamped along the Euphrates River at Carchemish. Now this was the army that King Nebuchadnezzar of Babylon ᶜdefeated in the ᵈfourth year that Jehoiakim son of Josiah was ruling over Judah:

3   "Fall into ranks with your shields
    ready!
  Prepare to march into battle!
4   Harness the horses to the chariots;
  mount your horses!
  Take your positions with helmets on;
  readyⁱ your spears!
  ᵃPut on the armor!

5   "What do I see?
  The soldiers are frightened.
  They are retreating.
  They are being scattered.
  They have fled for refuge
  without looking back.
  ᵃTerror is all around them,"ⁱ says the
    LORD.
6   "But even the swiftest cannot get
  away.

  Even the strongest cannot escape.
  There in the north by the Euphrates
    River
  they have ᵃstumbled and fallen in
  defeat.
7   Who is this that rises ᵃlike the Nile,
  like its streams turbulent at flood
    stage?
8   Egypt rises like the Nile,
  like its streams turbulent at flood
    stage.
  Egypt said, 'I will arise and cover the
    earth.
  I will destroy cities and the people
    who inhabit them.'
9   Go ahead and charge into battle, you
    horsemen!
  Drive furiously, you charioteers!
  Let the soldiers march out into
    battle,
  those from Ethiopia and Libya ᵃwho
    carry shields,
  and those from Lydia who are armed
    with the bow.
10   But that day belongs to ᵃthe
    Sovereign LORD of Heaven's
    Armies.
  It is a day of reckoning when ᵇhe will
    pay back his adversaries.
  His sword will devour them until its
    appetite is satisfied.
  It will drink its fill from their blood!
  Indeed it will be ᶜa sacrifice for
    the Sovereign LORD of Heaven's
    Armies
  in the land of the north by the
    Euphrates River.
11   Go up ᵃto Gilead and get medicinal
    ointment,
  ᵇyou dear poor people of Egypt.
  But it will prove useless no matter
    how much medicine you use;
  there will be no healing for you.
12   The nations have heard of your
    shameful ᵃdefeat.
  Your cries of distress fill the earth.
  One soldier has stumbled over
    another,
  and both of them have fallen down
    defeated."

45:1 ᶜ Jer 25:1; 36:1; 46:2 45:3 ᵃ Ps 6:6; 69:3; [2 Cor 4:1, 16; Gal 6:9] ¹ Heb. *Woe to me!* 45:4 ᵃ Isa 5:5; Jer 1:10; 11:17; 18:7–10; 31:28 ¹ Heb. *Thus you shall say to him* [i.e., Baruch]. 45:5 ᵃ Jer 25:17–26 ᵇ Jer 21:9; 38:2; 39:18 46:1 ᵃ Jer 25:15 46:2 ᵃ Jer 25:17–19; Ezek 29:2–32:32 ᵇ 2 Kgs 23:33–35 ᶜ 2 Kgs 23:29; 24:7; 2 Chr 35:20 ᵈ Jer 45:1 46:4 ᵃ Isa 21:5; Jer 51:11–12; Joel 3:9; Nah 2:1; 3:14 ¹ LXX *to hold before oneself* or *to present arms.* 46:5 ᵃ Jer 49:29 ¹ Heb. *Terror is all around.* 46:6 ᵃ Jer 46:12, 16; Dan 11:19 46:7 ᵃ Isa 8:7–8; Jer 47:2; Dan 11:22 46:9 ᵃ Isa 66:19 46:10 ᵃ Isa 13:6; Joel 1:15 ᵇ Deut 32:42; Isa 31:8; Jer 12:12 ᶜ Isa 34:6; Zeph 1:7; Ezek 39:17 46:11 ᵃ Isa 47:1; Jer 31:4, 21 ᵇ Ezek 30:21 46:12 ᵃ Jer 2:36; Nah 3:8–10

The Lord Predicts That Nebuchadnezzar Will Attack and Plunder Egypt

[13] The LORD spoke to the prophet Jeremiah about Nebuchadnezzar coming to [a]attack the land of Egypt:

[14] "Make an announcement throughout Egypt.
Proclaim it in [a]Migdol, Memphis, and [b]Tahpanhes.
'Take your positions and prepare to do battle.
For the enemy army is destroying all the nations around you.'[1]
[15] Why will your soldiers[1] be defeated?
They will not stand because I, the LORD, will thrust them down.
[16] I will make many stumble.
They will fall over [a]one another in their hurry to flee.[1]
They will say, 'Get up!
[b]Let's go back to our own people.
Let's go back to our homelands because the enemy is coming to destroy us.'
[17] There at home they will say, 'Pharaoh king of Egypt is just a big noise!
He has let the most opportune moment pass by.'
[18] I the King, [a]whose name is the LORD of Heaven's Armies, swear this:
'I swear as surely as I live that a conqueror is coming.
He will be as imposing as Mount Tabor is among the mountains,
as Mount Carmel is against the backdrop of the sea.
[19] Pack [a]your bags for exile,
you inhabitants of poor dear Egypt.[1]
For Memphis will be laid waste.
It will lie in ruins and be uninhabited.
[20] Egypt is like a beautiful young [a]cow.
But northern armies will attack her like swarms of stinging flies.
[21] Even her mercenaries will prove to be like pampered, well-fed calves.
For [a]they too will turn and run away.
They will not stand their ground when the time for them to be destroyed comes,
the time for them to be punished.
[22] Egypt will run away, hissing like a snake,
as the enemy comes marching up in force.
They will come against [a]her with axes as if they were woodsmen chopping down trees.
[23] The population of Egypt is like a vast, impenetrable forest.
But I, the LORD, affirm that the enemy will [a]cut them down.
For those who chop them down will be more numerous than [b]locusts.
They will be too numerous to count.
[24] Poor dear Egypt will be put to shame.
She will be handed over to [a]the people from the north.'"

[25] The LORD of Heaven's Armies, the God of Israel, says, "I will punish Amon, the god of [a]Thebes. [b]I will punish Egypt, its gods, and its kings. I will punish Pharaoh and all who [c]trust in him.[1] [26]I will [a]hand them over to Nebuchadnezzar and his troops, who want to kill them. But later [b]on, people will live in Egypt again as they did in former times. I, the LORD, affirm it!"

A Promise of Hope for Israel

[27] "You descendants of Jacob, my servants, do not be afraid;
do not be terrified, people of Israel.
For I will [a]rescue you and your descendants
from the faraway lands where you are captives.
The descendants of Jacob will return to their land and enjoy peace.
They will be secure, and no one will terrify them.

46:13 [a] Isa 19:1; Jer 43:10–11; Ezek 29:1–21   46:14 [a] Jer 44:1   [b] Ezek 30:18   [1] Heb. *For the sword devours those who surround you.*   46:15 [1] Or perhaps *Apis has fled*; the bull god of Memphis.   46:16 [a] Lev 26:36–37; Jer 46:6   [b] Jer 51:9   [1] LXX (vv. 15a–16) *Why has Apis fled from you? Your choice calf [i.e., Apis] has not remained. For the Lord has paralyzed him. And your multitudes have fainted and fallen; and each one said to his neighbor.*   46:18 [a] Isa 47:4; Jer 48:15; Mal 1:14   46:19 [a] Jer 48:18   [1] Heb. *inhabitants of daughter Egypt.*   46:20 [a] Hos 10:11   46:21 [a] [Ps 37:13]; Jer 50:27   46:22 [a] [Isa 29:4]   46:23 [a] Isa 10:34   [b] Judg 6:5; 7:12; Joel 2:25   46:24 [a] Jer 1:15   46:25 [a] Ezek 30:14–16; Nah 3:8   [b] Exod 12:12; Jer 43:12–13; Ezek 30:13; Zeph 2:11   [c] Isa 30:1–5; 31:1–3   [1] Heb. *Behold, I will punish Amon of No and Pharaoh and Egypt and its gods and its kings and Pharaoh and all who trust in him.*   46:26 [a] Jer 44:30; Ezek 32:11   [b] Ezek 29:8–14   46:27 [a] Isa 11:11; Jer 23:3–4; Mic 7:12

28 I, the LORD, tell you not to be [a]afraid,
  you descendants of Jacob, my servant,
  for I am with you.
  Though I completely destroy all the
    nations where I scatter you,
  I will not completely destroy you.
  I will indeed [b]discipline you but only
    in due measure.
  I will not allow you to go entirely
    unpunished."

Judgment on the Philistine Cities

47 This was the [a]LORD's message to the prophet Jeremiah about the Philistines [b]before Pharaoh attacked Gaza:

2 "Look! Enemies are gathering in the
    north like [a]water rising in a river.[1]
  They will be like an overflowing
    stream.
  They will overwhelm the whole
    country and everything in it like a
    flood.
  They will overwhelm the cities and
    their inhabitants.
  People will cry [b]out in alarm.
  Everyone living in the country will
    cry out in pain.
3 Fathers will [a]hear the hoofbeats of
    the enemies' horses,
  the clatter of their chariots and the
    rumbling of their wheels.
  They will not turn back to save their
    children
  because they will be paralyzed with
    fear.
4 For the time has come
  to destroy all the [a]Philistines.
  The time has come to destroy all the
    help
  that remains for [b]Tyre and Sidon.
  For I, [c]the LORD, will destroy the
    Philistines,
  that remnant that came from the
    island of [d]Crete.
5 The people of Gaza will shave their
    [a]heads in mourning.
  The people of [b]Ashkelon will be
    struck dumb.

How long will you gash yourselves to
    show your sorrow,
  you who remain of Philistia's power?
6 How long will you cry out, 'Oh,
    [a]sword of the LORD,
  how long will it be before you stop
    killing?
  Go back into your sheath;
  stay there and rest!'
7 But how can it rest
  when [a]I, the LORD, have given it
    orders?
  I have ordered it to attack
  the people of Ashkelon and the
    [b]seacoast."

Judgment against Moab

48 The LORD of Heaven's Armies, the God of Israel, spoke about [a]Moab:

"Sure to be judged is [b]Nebo! Indeed,[1]
    it will be destroyed.
  [c]Kiriathaim will suffer disgrace. It
    will be captured!
  Its fortress will suffer disgrace. It will
    be torn down!
2 People will [a]not praise Moab
    anymore.
  The enemy will capture [b]Heshbon
  and plot how to destroy Moab,
  saying, 'Come, let's put an end to that
    nation!'
  City of [c]Madmen, you will also be
    destroyed.
  A destructive army will march
    against you.
3 Cries of anguish will arise in
    [a]Horonaim,
  'Oh, the ruin and great destruction!'
4 "Moab will be crushed.
  Her children will cry out in distress.
5 Indeed they will climb the slopes of
    Luhith,
  weeping continually as they go.
  [a]For on the road down to
    Horonaim
  they will hear the cries of distress
  over the destruction.[1]

46:28 [a] Jer 10:24; Amos 9:8–9 [b] Jer 30:11   47:1 [a] Isa 14:29–31; Ezek 25:15–17; Zeph 2:4–5; Zech 9:6 [b] Amos 1:6   47:2 [a] Isa 8:7–8; Jer 46:7–8 [b] Jer 1:14 [1] Heb. *Behold! Waters are rising from the north.*   47:3 [a] Judg 5:22; Jer 8:16; Nah 3:2   47:4 [a] Isa 14:29–31 [b] Isa 23:1–18; Jer 25:22; Ezek 26:1–21; 28:20–24; Amos 1:9–10; Zech 9:2–4 [c] Ezek 25:16; Amos 1:8 [d] Gen 10:14; Deut 2:23; Amos 9:7   47:5 [a] Jer 48:37; Mic 1:16; Zeph 2:4 [b] Judg 1:18; Jer 25:20; Amos 1:7–8; Zech 9:5   47:6 [a] Deut 32:41; Judg 7:20; Jer 12:12; Ezek 21:3–5   47:7 [a] Isa 10:6; Ezek 14:17 [b] Mic 6:9   48:1 [a] Isa 15:1–16:14; 25:10; Ezek 25:8–11; Amos 2:1–3; Zeph 2:8–11 [b] Isa 15:2 [c] Num 32:37; Jer 48:23; Ezek 25:9 [1] Heb. *Woe to Nebo for it is destroyed.*   48:2 [a] Isa 16:14 [b] Isa 15:4; Jer 49:3 [c] Isa 10:31   48:3 [a] Isa 15:5; Jer 48:5, 34   48:5 [a] Isa 15:5 [1] Heb. *the distresses of the cry of destruction.*

6 They will hear, 'Run! Save yourselves;
even if you must be like a lonely
   [a]shrub in the wilderness!'[1]

7 "Moab, you trust in the things you do
   and in your [a]riches.
So you too will be conquered.
Your god [b]Chemosh will go into exile
along with his [c]priests and his officials.
8 The destroyer will come against
   every town.
Not one town will escape.
[a]The towns in the valley will be
   destroyed.
The cities on the high plain will be
   laid waste.
I, the LORD, have spoken.
9 Set [a]up a gravestone for Moab,
for it will certainly be laid in ruins!
Its cities will be laid waste
and become uninhabited.
10 A [a]curse on anyone who is lax in
   doing the LORD's work!
A curse on anyone who keeps from
   carrying out his destruction!

11 "From its earliest days Moab [a]has
   lived undisturbed.
It has never been taken into exile.
Its people are like wine allowed to
   settle undisturbed on its dregs,
never poured out from one jar to
   another.
They are like wine that tastes like it
   always did,
whose aroma has remained
   unchanged.
12 But the time is coming when I will
   send
men against Moab who will empty
   it out.
They will empty the towns of their
   people,
then will lay those towns in ruins.
I, the LORD, affirm it!
13 The people of Moab will be
   disappointed by their god
   [a]Chemosh.
They will be [b]as disappointed as the
   people of Israel were

when they put their trust in the calf
   god at [c]Bethel.
14 How can you men of Moab say, '[a]We
   are heroes,
men who are mighty in battle?'
15 Moab will be destroyed. Its towns
   will be invaded.
Its finest young men will be
   slaughtered.
I, [a]the King, the LORD of Heaven's
   Armies, affirm it!
16 Moab's destruction is at hand.
Disaster will come on it quickly.
17 Mourn for that nation, all you
   nations living around it,
all you nations that know of its fame.
Mourn and say, 'Alas, its powerful
   influence has been broken!
Its glory and power have been done
   away with!'
18 Come down from your place of
   honor;
sit on the dry ground, you who live in
   [a]Dibon.[1]
For the one who will destroy Moab
   will attack you;
he will destroy your fortifications.
19 You who live in [a]Aroer,
[b]stand by the road and watch.
Question the man who is fleeing and
   the woman who is escaping.
Ask them, 'What has happened?'
20 They will answer, 'Moab is disgraced,
   for it has fallen!
[a]Wail and cry out in mourning!
Announce along the [b]Arnon River
   that Moab has been destroyed.'

21 "Judgment will come on the cities on the high plain: on Holon, Jahzah, and Mephaath; 22 on Dibon, Nebo, and Beth Diblathaim; 23 on Kiriathaim, Beth Gamul, and Beth Meon; 24 on [a]Kerioth and Bozrah. It will come on all the towns of Moab, both far and near. 25 [a]Moab's might will be crushed. Its [b]power will be broken. I, the LORD, affirm it!

26 "Moab has vaunted itself against me.
So [a]make him drunk with the wine of
   my wrath

48:6 [a] Jer 17:6 [1] LXX *Be like a wild donkey in the desert!* 48:7 [a] Ps 52:7; Isa 59:4; Jer 9:23; [1 Tim 6:17] [b] Num 21:29; Judg 11:24; Jer 48:13 [c] Jer 49:3 48:8 [a] Jer 6:26 48:9 [a] Ps 55:6 48:10 [a] Judg 5:23; 1 Sam 15:3, 9; 1 Kgs 20:42 48:11 [a] Zeph 1:12 48:13 [a] 1 Kgs 11:7 [b] Hos 10:6 [c] 1 Kgs 12:29; 13:32–34; Hos 8:5–6 48:14 [a] Isa 16:6 48:15 [a] Jer 46:18; 51:57; Mal 1:14 48:18 [a] Num 21:30; Josh 13:9, 17; Isa 15:2; Jer 48:22 [1] Heb. *inhabitant of Daughter Dibon.* 48:19 [a] Deut 2:36; Josh 12:2; Isa 17:2 [b] 1 Sam 4:13–14, 16 48:20 [a] Isa 16:7 [b] Num 21:13 48:24 [a] Jer 48:41; Amos 2:2 48:25 [a] Ps 75:10; Zech 1:19–21 [b] Ezek 30:21 48:26 [a] Jer 25:15

until he splashes around in his own
    vomit,
until others treat him as a
    laughingstock.
27 For did not you people of Moab laugh
    at the people of Israel?
Did you think that they were nothing
    but thieves,
that you shook your head in contempt
every time you talked about them?
28 Leave your towns, you inhabitants of
    Moab.
Go and ᵃlive in ᵇthe cliffs.
Be like a dove that makes its nest
high on the sides of a ravine.
29 I have heard how ᵃproud the people
    of Moab are,
I know how haughty they are.
I have heard how arrogant, proud,
    and ᵇhaughty they are,
what a high opinion they have of
    themselves.
30 I, the LORD, affirm that ᵃI know how
    arrogant they are.
But their pride is ill founded.
Their boastings will prove to be false.
31 So ᵃI will weep with sorrow for Moab.
I will cry out in sadness for all Moab.
I will moan for the people of Kir
    Heres.
32 I will weep ᵃfor the grapevines of
    Sibmah
just like the town of ᵇJazer weeps
    over them.¹
Their branches once spread as far as
    the Dead Sea.
They reached as far as the town of
    Jazer.²
The destroyer will ravage
her fig, date, and grape crops.
33 ᵃJoy and gladness will disappear
from the fruitful land of Moab.
I will stop the flow of wine from the
    winepresses.
No one will stomp on the grapes
    there and shout for joy.
The shouts there will be shouts of
    soldiers,
not the shouts of those making wine.

34 Cries of anguish raised ᵃfrom
    Heshbon and ᵇElealeh
will be sounded as far as Jahaz.
They will be sounded ᶜfrom Zoar
    as far as Horonaim and Eglath
    Shelishiyah.
For even the waters of Nimrim will
    be dried up.
35 I will put an end in Moab
to those who make offerings at her
    places of worship.
I will put an end to those who
    sacrifice to ᵃother gods.
I, the LORD, affirm it!
36 So ᵃmy heart moans for Moab
like a flute playing a funeral song.
Yes, like a flute playing a funeral
    song,
my heart moans for ᵇthe people of
    Kir Heres.
For the wealth they have gained will
    perish.
37 For ᵃall of them will shave their
    heads in mourning.
They will all cut off their beards to
    show their sorrow.
They will all make gashes in their
    hands.
They will all put ᵇon sackcloth.
38 On all the ᵃhousetops in Moab
and in all its public squares,
there will be nothing but mourning.
For I will ᵇbreak Moab like an
    unwanted jar.
I, the LORD, affirm it!
39 Oh, how shattered Moab will be!
Oh, how her people will wail!
Oh, how she will turn away in shame!
Moab will become an object of
    ridicule,
a terrifying sight to all the nations
    that surround her."

40 For the LORD says,
"Look! ᵃLike an eagle with ᵇoutspread
    wings
a nation will swoop down on Moab.
41 Her towns will be captured;
her fortresses will be taken.

48:28 ᵃPs 55:6–7 ᵇSong 2:14 48:29 ᵃIsa 16:6; Zeph 2:8, 10 ᵇJer 49:16 48:30 ᵃIsa 16:6; Jer 50:36 48:31 ᵃIsa 15:5;
16:7, 11 48:32 ᵃIsa 16:8–9 ᵇNum 21:32; Isa 16:10 ¹MT *From/With the weeping of Jazer I will weep for you, vine of
Sibmah. Your tendrils crossed over the sea. They reached unto the sea of Jazer. Upon your summer fruit and your
vintage [grape harvest] the destroyer has fallen.* ²Or *reached the sea of Jazer.* 48:33 ᵃIsa 16:10; Jer 25:10;
Joel 1:12 48:34 ᵃIsa 15:4–6 ᵇNum 32:3, 37 ᶜIsa 15:5–6 48:35 ᵃIsa 15:2; 16:12 48:36 ᵃIsa 15:5; 16:11
ᵇIsa 15:7 48:37 ᵃIsa 15:2–3; Jer 16:6; 41:5; 47:5 ᵇGen 37:34; Isa 15:3; 20:2 48:38 ᵃIsa 15:3
ᵇJer 22:28 48:40 ᵃDeut 28:49; Jer 49:22; Hos 8:1; Hab 1:8 ᵇIsa 8:8

At that time [a]the soldiers of Moab
  will be frightened
like a woman in labor.

[42] Moab will be destroyed and no
  longer be [a]a nation
because she has vaunted herself
  against the LORD.

[43] [a]Terror, pits, and traps are in store
  for the people who live in Moab.
I, the LORD, affirm it!

[44] Anyone who flees at the sound of
  terror
will fall into a pit.
Anyone who climbs out of the pit
will be caught in a [a]trap.
For the [b]time is coming
when I will punish the people of
  Moab.
I, the LORD, affirm it!

[45] In the [a]shadows of the walls of
  Heshbon
those trying to escape will stand
  helpless.
For a fire will burst forth from
  Heshbon.
Flames will shoot out from the
  former territory of [b]Sihon.
They will burn the foreheads of the
  people of Moab,
the skulls of those war-loving people.

[46] Moab, you are [a]doomed!
You people who worship Chemosh
  will be destroyed.
Your sons will be taken away
  captive.
Your daughters will be carried away
  into exile.

[47] Yet [a]in future days
I will reverse Moab's ill fortune,"
says the LORD.

The judgment against Moab ends here.

Judgment against Ammon

49 The LORD spoke about the [a]Ammon-
ites:

"Do you think there are not any
  people of the nation of Israel
  remaining?
Do you think there are not any of
  them remaining to reinherit their
  land?
Is that why you people who worship
  the god Milcom[1]
have taken possession of the
  territory of [b]Gad and live in his
  cities?

[2] Because you did [a]that,
I, the LORD, affirm that a time is
  coming
when I will make [b]Rabbah, the
  capital city of Ammon,
hear the sound of the battle cry.
It will become a mound covered with
  ruins.[1]
Its villages will be burned to the
  ground.
Then Israel will take back its land
from those who took their land from
  them.
I, the LORD, affirm it!

[3] Wail, you people in [a]Heshbon,
  because Ai in Ammon is
  destroyed.
Cry out in anguish, you people in the
  villages surrounding[1] Rabbah.
Put [b]on sackcloth and cry out in
  mourning.
Run about covered with gashes.[2]
For your god Milcom will go into
  exile
along with his [c]priests and officials.

[4] Why [a]do you brag about your great
  power?
Your power is ebbing away, you
  [b]rebellious people of Ammon,
who trust in your [c]riches and [d]say,
'Who would dare to attack us?'

[5] I will bring terror on you from every
  side,"
says the Sovereign LORD of Heaven's
  Armies.
"You will be scattered in every
  direction.
No one will gather the fugitives back
  together.

[6] Yet in days to [a]come
I will reverse Ammon's ill fortune."
says the LORD.

48:41 [a] Isa 13:8; 21:3; Jer 30:6; Mic 4:9–10   48:42 [a] Ps 83:4; Jer 48:2   48:43 [a] Isa 24:17–18; Lam 3:47   48:44 [a] 1 Kgs 19:17; Isa 24:18; Amos 5:19 [b] Jer 11:23   48:45 [a] Num 21:28–29 [b] Num 21:21, 26; Ps 135:11   48:46 [a] Num 21:29   48:47 [a] Jer 49:6, 39   49:1 [a] Deut 23:3–4; 2 Chr 20:1; Jer 25:21; Ezek 21:28–32; 25:1–7 [b] Amos 1:13–15; Zeph 2:8–11 [1] MT *Malcom.*   49:2 [a] Amos 1:13–15 [b] Ezek 25:5 [1] Heb. *a desolate tel.*   49:3 [a] Jer 48:2 [b] Isa 32:11; Jer 48:37 [c] Jer 48:7 [1] Or *you women of Rabbah;* Heb. *daughters of Rabbah*; it is difficult to tell whether the word "daughters" is literal or figurative. [2] MT *run back and forth among the walls.*   49:4 [a] Jer 9:23 [b] Jer 3:14 [c] Jer 48:7 [d] Jer 21:13   49:6 [a] Jer 48:47

Judgment against Edom

[7] The LORD of Heaven's Armies spoke about Edom:

> "Is wisdom no longer to be found [a]in
>   Teman?
> Can Edom's counselors not give her
>   any good advice?
> Has all their [b]wisdom turned bad?
> [8] Turn and flee! Take up refuge in
>   remote places,
> you people who live in [a]Dedan.
> For I will bring disaster on the
>   descendants of Esau.
> I have decided it is time for me to
>   punish them.[1]
> [9] If grape pickers came to pick your
>   grapes,
> would they not leave a few grapes
>   behind?
> [a]If robbers came at night,
> would they not pillage only what
>   they needed?
> [10] [a]But I will strip everything away from
>   Esau's descendants.
> I will uncover [b]their hiding places so
>   they cannot hide.
> Their children, relatives, and
>   neighbors will all be destroyed.
> Not one of them will be left!
> [11] Leave your orphans behind, and I
>   will keep them alive.
> Your widows, too, can depend on me."

[12] For the LORD says, "If even [a]those who did not deserve to drink from the cup of my wrath must drink from it, do you think you will go unpunished? You will not go unpunished, but must certainly drink from the cup of my wrath. [13] For [a]I solemnly swear," says the LORD, "that [b]Bozrah will become a pile of ruins. It will become an object of horror and ridicule, an example to be used in curses. All the towns around it will lie in ruins forever."

> [14] I [a]said, "I have heard a message from
>   the LORD.
> A messenger has been sent among
>   the nations to say,

> 'Gather your armies and march out
>   against her!
> Prepare to do battle with her!'"
> [15] The LORD says to Edom,
> "I will certainly make you small
>   among nations.
> I will make you despised by all
>   humankind.
> [16] The terror you inspire in others
> and the [a]arrogance of your heart
>   have deceived you.
> You may make your home in the
>   clefts of the rocks;
> you may occupy the highest places in
>   the hills.
> But even if you made your home
>   where the eagles [b]nest,
> [c]I would bring you down from there,"
> says the LORD.
> [17] "Edom will become an object of
>   horror.
> [a]All who pass by it will be filled with
>   horror;
> they will hiss out their scorn
> because of all the disasters that have
>   happened to it.
> [18] [a]Edom will be destroyed like Sodom
>   and Gomorrah
> and the towns that were around them.
> No one will live there.
> No human being will settle in it,"
> says the LORD.
> [19] "A lion coming [a]up from [b]the thick
>   undergrowth along the Jordan
> scatters the sheep in the pastureland
>   around it.
> So too I will chase the Edomites off
>   their land.
> Then I will appoint over it
> [c]whomever I choose.
> For there is no [d]one like me, and
>   there is no one who can call me to
>   account.
> There is no ruler who can stand up
>   against me.
> [20] So listen to what I, [a]the LORD, have
>   planned against Edom,
> what I intend to do to the people
>   who live in Teman.

49:7 [a] Gen 25:30; 32:3; Isa 34:5–6; Jer 25:21; Ezek 25:12–14; 35:1–15; Joel 3:19; Amos 1:11–12; Obad 1–9, 15, 16 [b] Gen 36:11; Job 2:11 **49:8** [a] Isa 21:13; Jer 25:23 [1] Heb. *For I will bring the disaster of Esau upon him, the time when I will punish him*; Esau was the progenitor of the tribes and nation of Edom (cf. Gen 36:1, 8–9, 19). **49:9** [a] Obad 5, 6 **49:10** [a] Obad 5, 6; Mal 1:3 [b] Isa 17:14 **49:12** [a] Jer 25:29; Obad 16 **49:13** [a] Gen 22:16; Isa 45:23; Jer 44:26; Amos 6:8 [b] Gen 36:33; 1 Chr 1:44; Isa 34:6; 63:1; Amos 1:12 **49:14** [a] Obad 1–4 **49:16** [a] Jer 48:29 [b] Job 39:27; Isa 14:13–15 [c] Amos 9:2 **49:17** [a] Jer 18:16; 49:13; 50:13; Ezek 35:7 **49:18** [a] Gen 19:24–25; Deut 29:23; Jer 50:40; Amos 4:11; Zeph 2:9 **49:19** [a] Jer 50:44 [b] Josh 3:15; Jer 12:5 [c] Exod 15:11; Isa 46:9 [d] Job 41:10 **49:20** [a] Isa 14:24, 27; Jer 50:45

Their little ones will be dragged off.
I will completely destroy their land
    because of what they have done.
21 The people of [a]the earth will quake
    when they hear of their downfall.[1]
Their cries of anguish will be heard
    all the way to the Gulf of Aqaba.[2]
22 Look! Like an eagle with outspread
    wings,
a nation will soar up and swoop down
    on Bozrah.
At that time [a]the soldiers of Edom
    will be as fearful
as a woman in labor."

Judgment against Damascus

23[a]The LORD spoke about Damascus:

"The people of [b]Hamath and Arpad
    will be dismayed
because they have heard bad news.
Their courage will melt away because
    of worry.
Their hearts will not be able to rest.[1]
24 The people of Damascus will lose
    heart and turn to flee.
Panic will grip them.
Pain and [a]anguish will seize them
like a woman in labor.
25 How deserted will that once-famous
    city be,
that city that was once filled with joy!
26 [a]For her young men will fall in her
    city squares.
All her soldiers will be destroyed at
    that time,"
says the LORD of Heaven's Armies.
27 "I [a]will set fire to the walls of
    Damascus;
it will burn up the palaces of Ben
    Hadad."

Judgment against Kedar and Hazor

28The LORD spoke about Kedar and the
kingdoms of Hazor that King Nebuchadnezzar of Babylon conquered:

"Army of Babylon, go and attack
    Kedar.

Lay waste those who live [a]in [b]the
    eastern desert.
29 Their [a]tents and their flocks will be
    taken away.
Their tent curtains, equipment, and
    camels will be carried off.
People will shout to them,
    '[b]Terror is all around you!'"
30 The LORD says, "Flee quickly, you
    who live in Hazor.
Take up refuge in remote places.
For King Nebuchadnezzar of Babylon
    has laid out plans to attack you.
He has formed his strategy on how to
    defeat you."
31 The LORD says, "Army of Babylon, go
    and attack
a nation that lives in peace and
    security.
[a]They have no gates or walls to
    protect them.
They [b]live all alone.
32 Their camels will be taken as
    plunder.
Their vast herds will be taken as
    spoil.
I will [a]scatter to the four winds
those desert peoples who cut their
    hair short at the temples.
I will bring disaster against them
from every direction," says the LORD.
33 "Hazor will become [a]a permanent
    wasteland,
a place where only jackals live.
No one will live there.
No human being will settle in it."

Judgment against Elam

34This was the LORD's message to the
prophet Jeremiah about [a]Elam, which
came [b]early in the reign of King Zedekiah
of Judah.

35The LORD of Heaven's Armies said:

"I will kill all [a]the archers of Elam,
who are the chief source of her
    military might.
36 I will cause enemies to blow through
    Elam from every direction

49:21 [a]Jer 50:46; Ezek 26:15, 18 [1]Heb. *At the sound of their downfall the earth will quake.* [2]Heb. *the Red Sea;* the Gulf of Aqaba formed the northeastern arm. 49:22 [a]Jer 48:40–41 49:23 [a]Isa 17:1–3; Amos 1:3, 5; Zech 9:1–2 [b]Jer 39:5; Zech 9:2 [1]MT *Hamath and Arpad are dismayed. They melt away because they have heard bad news. Anxiety is in the sea; it [the sea] cannot be quiet.* 49:24 [a]Isa 13:8; Jer 4:31; 6:24; 48:21 49:26 [a]Jer 50:30; Amos 4:10 49:27 [a]Amos 1:4 49:28 [a]Gen 25:13; Ps 120:5; Isa 21:16–17; Jer 2:10; Ezek 27:21 [b]Judg 6:3; Job 1:3 49:29 [a]Ps 120:5 [b]Jer 46:5 49:31 [a]Ezek 38:11 [b]Num 23:9; Deut 33:28; Mic 7:16 49:32 [a]Ezek 5:10 49:33 [a]Jer 9:11; 10:22; Zeph 2:9, 12–15; Mal 1:3 49:34 [a]Gen 10:22; Jer 25:25; Ezek 32:24; Dan 8:2 [b]2 Kgs 24:17–18; Jer 28:1 49:35 [a]Ps 46:9; Isa 22:6

like the winds blowing in from the
    four quarters of heaven.
I will scatter the people of Elam to
    the four winds.
There will not be any nation where
    the refugees of Elam will not go.
37 I [a]will make the people of Elam
    terrified of their enemies,
who are seeking to kill them.
I will vent my fierce anger
and bring disaster upon them," says
    the LORD.
"I will send armies chasing after them
until I have completely destroyed
    them.
38 I will [a]establish my sovereignty over
    Elam.[1]
I will destroy their king and their
    leaders," says the LORD.
39 "Yet [a]in future days
I will reverse Elam's ill fortune,"
says the LORD.

Judgment against Babylon

50 The LORD spoke concerning Babylon
and the land of Babylonia through
the prophet Jeremiah.

2 "Announce the news among the
    nations! Proclaim it!
Signal for people to pay attention.
Declare the news! Do not hide it! Say:
'Babylon will be [a]captured.
[b]Bel will be put to shame.
Marduk will be dismayed.
Babylon's idols will be put to shame;
[c]her disgusting images will be
    dismayed.
3 [a]For [b]a nation from the north will
    attack Babylon;
it will lay her land waste.
People and animals will flee out of it.
No one will inhabit it.'

4 "When that time comes," says [a]the
    LORD,
"the people of Israel and Judah will
    return to the land together.
They will come back [b]with tears of
    repentance

as they seek the LORD their God.
5 They will [a]ask the way to Zion;
they will turn their faces toward it.
They will come and bind themselves
    to the LORD
in a lasting covenant that will never
    be forgotten.

6 "My people have been [a]lost sheep.
Their shepherds have allowed them
    to go [b]astray.
[c]They have wandered around in the
    mountains.
They have roamed from one
    mountain and hill to another.
They have forgotten their resting
    place.
7 All who encountered them
    [a]devoured them.
[b]Their enemies who did this said,
    '[c]We are not liable for punishment!
For those people have sinned against
    [d]the LORD, [e]their true pasture.
They have sinned against the LORD
    in whom their ancestors trusted.'

8 "People of Judah, get [a]out of Babylon
    quickly!
Leave the land of Babylonia!
Be the first to depart.
Be like the male goats that lead the
    herd.
9 [a]For I will rouse into action and bring
    against Babylon
a host of mighty nations from the
    land of the north.
They will set up their battle lines
    against her.
They will come from the north and
    capture her.
Their arrows will be like a skilled
    soldier
who does [b]not return from the battle
    empty-handed.
10 Babylonia will be plundered.
Those who plunder it will take [a]all
    they want,"
says the LORD.
11 "People of Babylonia, you plundered
    my people.

49:37 [a] Jer 9:16　**49:38** [a] Jer 43:10　[1] Or *I will sit in judgment over Elam*; Heb. *I will set up my throne in Elam.*　**49:39** [a] Jer 48:47　**50:2** [a] Isa 21:9　[b] Isa 46:1; Jer 51:44　[c] Jer 43:12–13　**50:3** [a] Jer 51:48; Dan 5:30–31　[b] Isa 13:17–18, 20　**50:4** [a] Ezra 2:1; Isa 11:12–13; Jer 3:18; 31:31; 33:7; Hos 1:11　[b] Ezra 3:12–13; [Ps 126:5]; Jer 31:9; [Zech 12:10]　**50:5** [a] Jer 31:31　**50:6** [a] Isa 53:6; [Ezek 34:15–16]; Matt 9:36; 10:6; 1 Pet 2:25　[b] Jer 23:1; Ezek 34:2　[c] [Jer 2:20; 3:6, 23]　**50:7** [a] Ps 79:7　[b] Jer 40:2–3; Zech 11:5　[c] Jer 2:3; Dan 9:16　[d] [Ps 90:1; 91:1]　[e] Ps 22:4; Jer 14:8; 17:13　**50:8** [a] Isa 48:20; Jer 51:6, 45; Zech 2:6–7; [Rev 18:4]　**50:9** [a] Jer 15:14; 51:27　[b] 2 Sam 1:22　**50:10** [a] [Rev 17:16]

That made you happy and glad.
You frolic about like calves in [a]a
pasture.
Your joyous sounds are [b]like the
neighs of a stallion.
12 But Babylonia will be put to great
shame.
The land where you were born will be
disgraced.
Indeed, Babylonia will become the
least important of all nations.
It will become a dry and barren
[a]desert.
13 After I vent my wrath on it, Babylon
will be uninhabited.
It will be [a]totally desolate.
All who pass by will be filled with
horror and will hiss out their
scorn
because of all the disasters that have
happened to it.
14 "Take up your battle positions all
around Babylon,
all you soldiers who are armed with
bows.
Shoot all your arrows at her! Do not
hold any back![1]
For she has sinned against the
LORD.
15 Shout the battle cry from all around
the city.
She will throw [a]up [b]her hands in
surrender;
her towers will fall.
Her walls will be torn down.
Because [c]I, the LORD, am wreaking
revenge,
take out your vengeance on her!
Do to her as she has done!
16 Kill all the farmers who sow the seed
in the land of Babylon;
kill all those who wield the sickle at
harvest time.
Let [a]all the foreigners return to their
own people.
Let them hurry back to their own
lands
to escape destruction by that enemy
army.

17 "The people of Israel are like
[a]scattered sheep
that lions have chased away.
First [b]the king of Assyria devoured
[c]them.
Now, last of all, King
[d]Nebuchadnezzar of Babylon has
gnawed their bones.
18 So I, the LORD of Heaven's Armies,
the God of Israel, say:
'I will punish the king of Babylon and
his land
just as I punished the king of
[a]Assyria.
19 [a]But I will restore the flock of Israel
to their own pasture.
They will graze on Mount Carmel
and the land of Bashan.
They will eat until they are full
on the hills of Ephraim and the land
of Gilead.
20 When that time comes,
no guilt will be found in Israel.
No sin will be found in Judah.
For I will forgive those of [a]them I
have allowed to survive.
I, the LORD, affirm it!'"
21 The LORD says,
"Attack the land of Merathaim
and the people who live in [a]Pekod.
Pursue, kill, and completely destroy
them!
Do just as [b]I have commanded you!
22 The noise of [a]battle can be heard in
the land of Babylonia.
There is the sound of great
destruction.
23 Babylon hammered [a]the whole world
to pieces.
But see how that 'hammer' has been
broken and shattered![1]
See what an object of horror
Babylon has become among the
nations!
24 I set a trap for you, Babylon;
you were [a]caught before you knew it.
You [b]fought against me;
so you were found and captured.
25 I have opened up [a]the place where
my weapons are stored.

50:11 [a]Isa 47:6 [b]Hos 10:11   50:12 [a]Jer 51:43   50:13 [a]Jer 49:17   50:14 [1]Heb. *Shoot at her! Don't save any arrows!*
50:15 [a]1 Chr 29:24; 2 Chr 30:8; Lam 5:6; Ezek 17:18 [b]Jer 51:58 [c]Jer 51:6, 11   50:16 [a]Isa 13:14; Jer 51:9   50:17 [a]2 Kgs
24:10, 14 [b]Jer 2:15 [c]2 Kgs 15:29; 17:6; 18:9-13 [d]2 Kgs 24:10-14; 25:1-7   50:18 [a]Isa 10:12; Ezek 31:3, 11, 12; Nah 3:7, 18, 19
50:19 [a]Isa 65:10; Jer 33:12; Ezek 34:13   50:20 [a]Num 23:21; Isa 43:25; [Jer 31:34; Mic 7:19]   50:21 [a]Ezek 23:23 [b]2 Sam 16:11;
2 Kgs 18:25; 2 Chr 36:23; Isa 10:6; 44:28; 48:14   50:22 [a]Jer 51:54   50:23 [a]Isa 14:6; Jer 51:20-24 [1]Heb. *How broken and
shattered is the hammer of all the earth!*   50:24 [a]Jer 51:8, 31; Dan 5:30 [b][Isa 45:9]   50:25 [a]Isa 13:5

I have brought out the weapons for
  carrying out my wrath.
For I, the Sovereign LORD of Heaven's
  Armies,
have work to carry out in the land of
  Babylonia.
26 Come from far away and attack
  Babylonia!
Open up the places where she stores
  her grain.
Pile her up in ruins. Destroy her
  completely!
Do not leave anyone alive!
27 Kill all her [a]soldiers.
  Let them be slaughtered.
They are doomed, for [b]their day of
  reckoning has come,
the time for them to be punished.
28 Listen! Fugitives and refugees
  are coming from the land of
  Babylon.
They are coming to Zion to [a]declare
  there
how the LORD our God is getting
  revenge,
getting revenge for what they have
  done to his temple.

29 "Call for archers to come against
  Babylon!
Summon against her all who draw
  the bow.
Set up camp all around the city.
Do not allow anyone to escape!
[a]Pay her back [b]for what she has done.
Do to her what she has done to
  others.
For she has proudly defied me,
  the Holy One of Israel.
30 So [a]her young men will fall in her city
  squares.
All her soldiers will be destroyed at
  that time,"
says the LORD.
31 "Listen! I am opposed to you, you
  proud city,"
says the Sovereign LORD of Heaven's
  Armies.
"Indeed, your day of reckoning has
  come,
the time when I will punish you.

32 You will stumble and fall, you [a]proud
  [b]city;
no one will help you get up.
I will set fire to your towns;
it will burn up everything that
  surrounds you."
33 The LORD of Heaven's Armies says,
"The people of Israel are oppressed.
So too are the people of Judah.
All those who took them captive are
  holding them prisoners.
They refuse to set them free.
34 But [a]the one who will rescue [b]them is
  strong.
His name is the LORD of Heaven's
  Armies.
He will strongly champion their
  [c]cause.
As a result he will bring peace and
  rest to the earth,
but trouble and turmoil to the
  people who inhabit Babylonia.

35 "Destructive forces will come
  [a]against the Babylonians," says the
  LORD.
"They will come against the people
  who inhabit Babylonia,
against [b]her leaders and her men of
  wisdom.
36 Destructive forces will come [a]against
  her false prophets;
they will be shown to be fools!
Destructive forces will come against
  her soldiers;
they will be filled with terror!
37 Destructive forces will come against
  her horses and her chariots.
Destructive forces will come against
  all [a]the foreign troops within her;[1]
[b]they will be as frightened as women!
Destructive forces will come against
  her treasures;
they will be taken away as plunder!
38 A drought will come upon her [a]land;
her rivers and canals will be dried
  up.[1]
All this will happen because her land
  is filled with idols.
Her people act like madmen because
  of those idols they fear.

50:27 [a]Ps 22:12; Isa 34:7; Jer 46:21 [b]Ps 37:13; Jer 48:44; Ezek 7:7   50:28 [a]Ps 149:6–9; Jer 51:10   50:29 [a]Ps 137:8; Jer 51:56;
[2 Thess 1:6]; Rev 18:6 [b][Isa 47:10]   50:30 [a]Isa 13:18; Jer 49:26; 51:4   50:32 [a]Isa 26:5; Mal 4:1 [b]Jer 21:14   50:34 [a]Prov
23:11; Isa 43:14; Jer 15:21; 31:11; Rev 18:8 [b]Isa 47:4 [c]Jer 51:36; Mic 7:9   50:35 [a]Dan 5:30 [b]Isa 47:13; Jer 51:57   50:36 [a]Isa
44:25; Jer 48:30   50:37 [a]Jer 25:20; Ezek 30:5 [b]Jer 51:30; Nah 3:13 [1]Or in the country, in her armies;
Heb. in her midst.   50:38 [a]Isa 44:27; Jer 51:36; Rev 16:12 [1]LXX, Syr. sword.

39 [a]Therefore desert creatures and
     jackals will live there;
   ostriches too will dwell in [b]it.
   But no people will ever live there
     again;
   no one will dwell there for all time to
     come.[1]
40 I will destroy Babylonia just [a]as I did
     Sodom and Gomorrah and the
     neighboring towns.
   No one will live there;
   no human being will [b]settle in it,"
   says the LORD.
41 "[a]Look! An army is about to come
     from the north.
   A mighty nation and many kings are
     stirring into action
   in faraway parts of the earth.
42 Its soldiers are armed with bows and
     spears.
   [a]They are cruel and show no mercy.
   [b]They sound like [c]the roaring sea
   as they ride forth on their horses.
   Lined up in formation like men going
     into battle,
   they are coming against you, fair
     Babylon.
43 The king of Babylon will become
     paralyzed with fear
   when he [a]hears news of their coming.
   Anguish will grip him,
   agony like that of a woman giving
     [b]birth to a baby.

44 "A lion coming [a]up from the thick
     undergrowth along the Jordan
   scatters the sheep in the pastureland
     around it.
   So too I will chase the Babylonians
     off their land;
   then I will appoint over it
     [b]whomever I choose.
   For there is no one like me.
   There is no one who can call me to
     account.
   There is no ruler that can stand up
     against me.

45 So listen to what I, [a]the LORD, have
     planned against Babylon,
   [b]what I intend to do to the people
     who inhabit the land of Babylonia.
   Their little ones will be dragged off
     like sheep.
   I will completely destroy their land
     because of what they have done.
46 The people of the earth will quake
     when they hear Babylon has been
     captured.
   Her cries of anguish will be heard by
     the other [a]nations."

51 The LORD says:
   "I will cause a destructive wind to
     blow
   against [a]Babylon [b]and the people
     who inhabit Babylonia.
2 I will send [a]people to winnow
     Babylonia like a wind blowing
     away chaff.
   They will winnow her and strip her
     land bare.
   This will happen when they come
     against her from every direction,
   when it is time to destroy her.
3 Do not give her archers time to
     string their bows
   or to put on their coats of armor.[1]
   Do not spare any of her young men.
   [a]Completely [b]destroy her whole
     army.
4 Let them fall slain in the [a]land of
     Babylonia,
   mortally wounded in the streets of
     her cities.

5 "For Israel and Judah will [a]not be
     forsaken
   by their God, the LORD of Heaven's
     Armies.
   For the land of Babylonia is full of
     guilt
   against the Holy One of Israel.
6 Get [a]out of Babylonia quickly, you
     foreign people.
   Flee to save your lives.

50:39 [a] Isa 13:21–22; 34:14; Jer 51:37; Rev 18:2   [b] Isa 13:20; Jer 25:12   [1] Heb. *It will never again be inhabited nor dwelt in unto generation and generation.*   50:40 [a] Gen 19:24–25; Isa 13:19; Jer 49:18; [Luke 17:28–30]; 2 Pet 2:6; Jude 7   [b] Isa 13:20   50:41 [a] Isa 13:2–5; Jer 6:22; 25:14; 51:27   50:42 [a] Jer 6:23   [b] Isa 13:18   [c] Isa 5:30   50:43 [a] Jer 51:31   [b] Jer 6:24   50:44 [a] Jer 49:19–21   [b] Job 41:10; Jer 49:19   50:45 [a] [Ps 33:11; Isa 14:24]; Jer 51:10–11   [b] Jer 51:29   50:46 [a] Rev 18:9   51:1 [a] Isa 47:1; Jer 50:1   [b] 2 Kgs 19:7; Jer 4:11; Hos 13:15   51:2 [a] Isa 41:16; Jer 15:7; Matt 3:12   51:3 [a] Jer 50:14, 29   [b] Jer 50:21   [1] Ket. *Against let him string. Let him string, the one who strings his bow, and against let him raise himself up in his coat of armor;* many MSS omit the second *let him string;* LXX *Let the archer bend his bow, and let the one who has armor put it on;* a few MSS *Let the archer ready his bow against it, and let him array himself against it in his coat of mail;* many MSS *Let the archer not string the bow, and let him not array himself in his armor.*   51:4 [a] Jer 49:26; 50:30, 37   51:5 [a] [Isa 54:7–8; Jer 33:24–26; 46:28]   51:6 [a] Jer 50:8; Rev 18:4

Do not let yourselves be killed
   because of her sins,
for it ᵇis time for ᶜthe LORD to wreak
   his revenge.
He will pay Babylonia back for what
   she has done.
7 Babylonia had been ᵃa gold cup in
   ᵇthe LORD's hand;
she had made the whole world
   drunk.
The nations had drunk from the
   wine of her wrath,
so they have all gone mad.
8 But suddenly Babylonia will ᵃfall and
   be destroyed.
Cry out in ᵇmourning over it!
ᶜGet medicine for her wounds;
perhaps she can be healed!
9 Foreigners living there will say,
'We tried to heal her, but she could
   not be healed.
ᵃLet's leave Babylonia and each go
   back to his own country.
ᵇFor judgment on her will be vast in
   its proportions.
It will be like it is piled up to heaven,
   stacked up into the clouds.'
10 The exiles from Judah will say,
'The LORD has brought ᵃabout a great
   deliverance for us!
Come on, let's go and ᵇproclaim in
   Zion
what the LORD our God has done!'

11 "Sharpen your arrows!
Fill your quivers!
The LORD will arouse ᵃa spirit of
   hostility in ᵇthe kings of Media,
ᶜfor ᵈhe intends to destroy
   Babylonia.
For that is how the LORD will get his
   revenge—
how he will get his revenge for the
   Babylonians' destruction of his
   temple.
12 ᵃGive the signal to attack Babylon's
   wall!
Bring more guards;
post them all around the city.
Put men in ambush,

for the LORD will do what he has
   planned.
He will do what he said he would do
   to the people of Babylon.¹

13 "You ᵃwho live along the rivers of
   Babylon,
the time of your end has come.
You who are rich in plundered
   treasure,
it is time for your lives to be cut off.
14 The LORD of Heaven's Armies has
   solemnly sworn,
'I will fill your land with enemy
   soldiers.
ᵃThey will swarm over it like
   locusts.
They will raise ᵇup shouts of victory
   over it.'
15 He is ᵃthe one who by his power
   made the earth.
ᵇHe is the one who by his wisdom
   fixed the world in place;
by his understanding, he spread out
   the heavens.
16 When his voice thunders, ᵃthe waters
   in the heavens roar.
He makes the clouds rise from the
   far-off horizons;
he makes the lightning flash out in
   the midst of the rain.
He unleashes the wind from the
   places where he stores it;
17 all ᵃidolaters will prove to be stupid
   and ignorant.
Every goldsmith will be disgraced by
   the idol he made.
ᵇFor the image he forges is merely a
   sham;
there is no breath in any of those
   idols.
18 They are worthless, objects to be
   ridiculed.
When the time comes to punish
   them, they will be destroyed.
19 The LORD, who is the portion of the
   descendants of Jacob, is not like
   them.
For he is the one who created
   everything,

51:6 ᵇJer 50:15   ᶜJer 25:14   51:7 ᵃJer 25:15; Hab 2:16; Rev 17:4   ᵇRev 14:8   51:8 ᵃIsa 21:9; Jer 50:2; Rev 14:8; 18:2   ᵇ[Isa 48:20]; Rev 18:9, 11, 19   ᶜJer 46:11   51:9 ᵃIsa 13:14; Jer 46:16; 50:16   ᵇEzra 9:6; Rev 18:5   51:10 ᵃPs 37:6; Mic 7:9   ᵇ[Isa 40:2]; Jer 50:28   51:11 ᵃJer 46:4, 9; Joel 3:9–10   ᵇIsa 13:17   ᶜJer 50:45   ᵈJer 50:28   51:12 ᵃNah 2:1; 3:14   ¹Heb. *For the LORD has both planned and done what he said concerning the people living in Babylon.*   51:13 ᵃRev 17:1, 15   51:14 ᵃJer 49:13; Amos 6:8   ᵇJer 50:15   51:15 ᵃGen 1:1, 6; Jer 10:12–16   ᵇJob 9:8; Ps 104:2; Isa 40:22   51:16 ᵃPs 135:7; Jer 10:13   51:17 ᵃ[Isa 44:18–20]; Jer 10:14   ᵇJer 50:2

including the people of Israel whom
  he claims as his own.
His name is the LORD of Heaven's
  Armies.

20 "Babylon,[1] [a]you are my war club,
  my weapon for battle.
I used you to smash nations.
I used you to destroy kingdoms.
21 I used you to smash horses and their
  riders.
I used you to smash chariots and
  their drivers.
22 I used you to smash men and women.
I used you to smash old [a]men and
  young men.
I used you to smash young men and
  young women.
23 I used you to smash shepherds and
  their flocks.
I used you to smash farmers and
  their teams of oxen.
I used you to smash governors and
  leaders.

24 "But I will repay Babylon
  [a]and all who live in Babylonia
for all the wicked things they did in
  Zion
right before the eyes of you Judeans,"
  says the LORD.
25 The [a]LORD says, "Beware! I am
  opposed to you, Babylon!
You are like [b]a destructive mountain
  that destroys all the earth.
I will unleash my power against you;
I will roll you off the cliffs and
  make you like a burned-out
  mountain.
26 No one will use any of your stones as
  a cornerstone;
no one will use any of them in the
  foundation of his house.
For you will lie desolate forever,"
  says the LORD.
27 "[a]Raise up battle flags throughout
  the lands.
Sound the trumpets calling the
  nations to do battle.

[b]Prepare [c]the nations to do battle
  against Babylonia.
Call for these kingdoms to attack her:
  Ararat, Minni, and Ashkenaz.
Appoint a commander to lead the
  attack.[1]
Send horses against her like a swarm
  of locusts.
28 Prepare the nations to do battle
  against her.
Prepare the kings of the Medes.
Prepare their governors and all their
  leaders.
Prepare all the countries they rule to
  do battle against her.[1]
29 The earth will tremble and writhe in
  agony;
for the LORD will carry out his [a]plan.
He plans [b]to make the land of
  Babylonia
a wasteland where no one lives.
30 The soldiers of Babylonia will stop
  fighting.
[a]They will remain in [b]their fortified
  cities.
They will lose their strength to do
  battle.
They will be as frightened as women.
The houses in her cities will be set
  on fire.
The gates of her cities will be broken
  down.
31 One runner after another will come
  to the king of Babylon;
[a]one messenger after another will
  come bringing news.[1]
They will bring news to the king of
  Babylon
that his whole city has been captured.
32 They will report that [a]the fords have
  been captured,
the reed marshes have been burned,
the soldiers are terrified.
33 For the LORD of Heaven's Armies, the
  God of Israel, says,
'Fair Babylon will be [a]like [b]a
  threshing floor
that has been trampled flat for
  harvest.

51:20 [a]Isa 10:5, 15; Jer 50:23 [1]Or *Media*; Heb. *You are my war club*; Babylon has been referred to as a hammer.
51:22 [a]2 Chr 36:17; Isa 13:15–16   51:24 [a]Jer 50:15, 29   51:25 [a]Isa 13:2; Zech 4:7 [b]Rev 8:8   51:27 [a]Isa 13:2; Jer 50:2; 51:12
[b]Jer 25:14 [c]Jer 50:41–42 [1]The translation of this line is uncertain.   51:28 [1]MT *Consecrate the nations against her, the
kings of the Medes, her governors and prefects, and all the land of his dominion.*   51:29 [a]Jer 50:45 [b]Isa 13:19–20;
47:11; Jer 50:13; 51:26, 43   51:30 [a]Isa 19:16; Jer 48:41 [b]Isa 45:1–2; Lam 2:9; Amos 1:5; Nah 3:13   51:31 [a]Jer 50:24
[1]Heb. *Runner will run to meet runner and*; i.e., a relay of messengers carrying news.   51:32 [a]Jer 50:38
51:33 [a]Isa 21:10; Dan 2:35; Amos 1:3; Mic 4:13 [b]Isa 17:5; Hos 6:11; Joel 3:13; Rev 14:15

The time for her to be cut down and
  harvested
will come very soon.'

34 "King Nebuchadnezzar of Babylon
  ªdevoured me and drove my people
  out.
Like a monster from the deep he
  swallowed me.
He filled his belly with my riches;
he made me an ᵇempty dish.
He completely cleaned me out."
35 The person who lives in Zion says,
"May Babylon pay for the violence
  done to me and to my relatives."
Jerusalem says,
"May those living in Babylonia pay
  for the bloodshed of my people."
36 Therefore the LORD says,
"ªI ᵇwill stand up for your cause.
I will pay the Babylonians back for
  what they have done to you.
I will dry up their sea;
I will make their springs run dry.¹
37 ªBabylon will become a heap of ruins.
Jackals will make their home there.¹
It will become ᵇan object of horror
  and of hissing scorn,
a place where no one lives.
38 The Babylonians are all like lions
  roaring for prey;
they are like lion cubs growling for
  something to eat.
39 When ªtheir appetites are all
  stirred up,
I will set out a banquet for them.
I will make them drunk
so that they will pass out,
they will fall asleep forever,
they will never wake up,"
says the LORD.
40 "I will lead them off to be slaughtered
like lambs, rams, and male goats.

41 "See how ªBabylon has been captured!
See how ᵇthe pride of the whole
  earth has been taken!
See what an object of horror
Babylon has become among the
  nations!

42 ªThe sea has swept over Babylon.
She has been covered by a multitude
  of its waves.
43 ªThe towns of Babylonia have
  become heaps of ruins.
She has become a dry and barren
  desert.
ᵇNo one lives in those towns any
  more;
no one even passes through them.
44 I will punish the god ªBel in Babylon.
I will make him spit out what ᵇhe has
  swallowed.
The nations will not come streaming
  to him any longer.
Indeed, the walls of Babylon will fall.

45 "Get out of Babylon, ªmy people!
Flee to save your lives
from the fierce anger of the LORD!¹
46 Do not lose your courage ªor become
  afraid
because of the reports that are heard
  in the land.
For a report will come in one year.
Another report will follow it in the
  next.
There will be violence in the land
with ruler fighting against ruler.

47 "So the time will certainly come
when I will punish the idols of
  Babylon.
Her whole land will be put to shame.
All her mortally wounded will
  collapse in her midst.
48 Then heaven and earth and all that is
  in ªthem
will sing ᵇfor joy over Babylon.
For destroyers from the north will
  attack it,"
says the LORD.
49 "Babylon must fall
because of the Israelites she has
  killed,
just as the earth's mortally wounded
  fell
because of Babylon.
50 ªYou who have escaped the sword,
go, do not delay.

51:34 ªJer 50:17   ᵇIsa 24:1–3   51:36 ª[Ps 140:12]; Jer 50:34   ᵇJer 50:38   ¹Heb. *I will dry up her* [Babylon's] *sea and make her fountain dry.*   51:37 ªIsa 13:22; Jer 50:39; [Rev 18:2]   ᵇJer 25:9, 11   ¹Heb. *a heap of ruins, a haunt for jackals.*   51:39 ªJer 51:57   51:41 ªJer 25:26   ᵇIsa 13:19; Jer 49:25; [Dan 4:30]   51:42 ªIsa 8:7–8; Jer 51:55; Dan 9:26   51:43 ªJer 50:39–40   ᵇIsa 13:20   51:44 ªJer 50:2; Isa 46:1   ᵇJer 50:15   51:45 ªIsa 48:20; [Jer 50:8, 28; 51:6; Rev 18:4]   ¹Heb. *Go out from her* [Babylon's] *midst, my people. Save each man his life from the fierce anger of the LORD.*   51:46 ª2 Kgs 19:7; Isa 13:3–5   51:48 ªIsa 44:23; 48:20; 49:13; Rev 18:20   ᵇJer 50:3, 41   51:50 ªJer 44:28

[b]Remember the LORD in a faraway
  land.
Think about Jerusalem.[1]
51 'We are ashamed because [a]we [b]have
  been insulted.
Our faces show our disgrace.
For foreigners have invaded
  the holy rooms in the LORD's
  temple.'
52 Yes, but the time will certainly
  come," says the LORD,
"when I will punish her idols.
Throughout her land the mortally
  wounded will groan.
53 [a]Even if Babylon climbs high into the
  sky
  and fortifies her elevated stronghold,
I will send destroyers against her,"
  says the LORD.

54 Cries of anguish will come from
  Babylon,
[a]the sound of great destruction from
  the land of the Babylonians.
55 For the LORD is ready to destroy
  Babylon,
and put an end to her loud noise.
Their waves will roar like turbulent
  waters.
They will make a deafening noise.
56 For a destroyer is attacking Babylon.
Her warriors will be captured;
  their bows will be broken.
[a]For the LORD is a God who punishes;
  he pays back in full.
57 "I will make her officials and wise
  [a]men drunk,
along with her governors, leaders,
  and warriors.
[b]They will fall asleep forever and
  never wake up,"
says the King whose name is the
  LORD of Heaven's Armies.

58 This is what the LORD of Heaven's Armies says,

"Babylon's thick wall will be
  [a]completely demolished.
Her high gates will be set on fire.

[b]The peoples strive for what does not
  satisfy.
The nations grow weary trying to get
  what will be destroyed."

59 This is the order Jeremiah the prophet gave to Seraiah son of [a]Neriah, son of
Mahseiah, when he went to King Zedekiah
of Judah in Babylon during the fourth year
of his reign. (Seraiah was a quartermaster.)
60 Jeremiah [a]recorded on one scroll all the
judgments that would come upon Babylon—
all these prophecies written about Babylon.
61 Then Jeremiah said to Seraiah, "When you
arrive in Babylon, make sure you read aloud
all these prophecies. 62 Then say, '[a]O LORD,
you have announced that you will destroy
this place so that no people or animals live in
it any longer. Certainly it will lie desolate forever!' 63 When you finish reading this scroll
aloud, tie [a]a stone to it and throw it into the
middle of the Euphrates River. 64 Then say,
'In the same way Babylon will sink and never
rise again because of the disaster I am ready
to bring upon her; they will grow faint.'"
The prophecies of Jeremiah end here.

The Fall of Jerusalem

52 Zedekiah was [a]twenty-one years old
when he became king, and he ruled
in Jerusalem for 11 years. His mother's name
was Hamutal daughter of Jeremiah, from
[b]Libnah. 2 He did what displeased the LORD
just as Jehoiakim had done.
3 What follows is a record of what happened to Jerusalem and Judah because of the
LORD's anger when he drove them out of his
sight. Zedekiah [a]rebelled against the king of
Babylon. 4 King Nebuchadnezzar of Babylon
came against Jerusalem with his whole army
and set up camp outside it. They built siege
ramps all around it. He arrived on the tenth
day of the tenth month in the [a]ninth year
that Zedekiah ruled over Judah. 5 The city
remained under siege until Zedekiah's eleventh year. 6 By the ninth day of the fourth
month the famine in the city was so severe
the residents had no food. 7 They broke
through the city walls, and all the soldiers
tried to escape. They left the city during the

51:50 [b][Deut 4:29–31]; Ezek 6:9 [1]Heb. *let Jerusalem go up upon your heart*; the "heart" is often viewed as the seat of one's
mental faculties and thought life. 51:51 [a]Ps 44:15; 79:4 [b]Ps 74:3–8; Jer 52:13; Lam 1:10 51:53 [a]Gen 11:4; Job 20:6; [Ps
139:8–10; Isa 14:12–14]; Jer 49:16; Amos 9:2; Obad 4 51:54 [a]Jer 50:22 51:56 [a]Ps 94:1; Jer 50:29 51:57 [a]Jer 50:35 [b]Jer
46:18; 48:15 51:58 [a]Jer 50:15 [b]Hab 2:13 51:59 [a]Jer 32:12 51:60 [a]Isa 30:8; Jer 36:2 51:62 [a]Isa 13:20; 14:22–23; Jer
50:3, 39 51:63 [a]Jer 19:10–11; Rev 18:21 52:1 [a]2 Kgs 24:18; 2 Chr 36:11 [b]Josh 10:29; 2 Kgs 8:22; Isa 37:8
52:3 [a]2 Chr 36:13 52:4 [a]2 Kgs 25:1; Jer 39:1; Ezek 24:1–2; Zech 8:19

night. They went through the gate between the two walls that is near the king's garden. (The Babylonians had the city surrounded.) Then they headed for the rift valley. [8] But the Babylonian army chased after the king. They caught up with Zedekiah in the plains of Jericho, and his entire army deserted him. [9a] They captured him and brought him up to the king of Babylon at Riblah in the territory of Hamath, and he passed sentence on him there. [10] The king of Babylon had Zedekiah's sons put to death while Zedekiah was forced to watch.[a] He also had all the nobles of Judah put to death there at Riblah. [11] He had Zedekiah's eyes[a] put out and had him bound in chains. Then the king of Babylon had him led off to Babylon, and he was imprisoned there until the day he died.

[12a] On the tenth day of the fifth month, in the nineteenth year of King Nebuchadnezzar of Babylon, [b] Nebuzaradan, the captain of the royal guard who served the king of Babylon, arrived in Jerusalem. [13] He burned down the LORD's temple, the royal palace, and all the houses in Jerusalem, including every large house. [14] The whole Babylonian army that came with the captain of the royal guard tore down the walls that surrounded Jerusalem. [15] Nebuzaradan, [a] the captain of the royal guard, took into exile some of the poor, the rest of the people who remained in the city, those who had deserted to the king of Babylon, and the rest of the craftsmen. [16] But he left behind some of the poor and gave them fields and vineyards.

[17] The Babylonians broke[a] the two[b] bronze pillars in the temple of the LORD, as well as the movable stands and the large bronze basin called "The Sea." They took all the bronze to Babylon. [18] They also took[a] the pots, shovels, trimming shears, basins, pans, and all the bronze utensils used by the priests. [19] The captain of the royal guard took the gold and silver bowls, censers, basins, pots, lampstands, pans, and vessels. [20] The bronze of [a] the items that King Solomon made for the LORD's temple (including the two pillars, the large bronze basin called "The Sea," the 12 bronze bulls under "The Sea," and the movable stands[1]) was too heavy to be weighed.

[21] Each of the [a] pillars was about 27 feet[1] high, about 18 feet[2] in circumference, three inches thick, and hollow. [22] The bronze top of one pillar was about 7½ feet[1] high and had bronze latticework and pomegranate-shaped ornaments all around it. The second pillar with its pomegranate-shaped ornaments was like it. [23] There were 96 pomegranate-shaped ornaments on the sides; in [a] all there were 100 pomegranate-shaped ornaments over the latticework that went around it.

[24] The captain of [a] the royal guard took Seraiah the chief priest, [b] Zephaniah the priest who was second in rank, and the three doorkeepers. [25] From the city he took an official who was in charge of the soldiers, seven of the king's advisers who were discovered in the city, an official army secretary who drafted citizens for military service, and 60 citizens who were discovered in the middle of the city. [26] Nebuzaradan, the captain of the royal guard, took them and brought them to the king of Babylon at Riblah. [27] The king of Babylon ordered them to be executed at Riblah in the territory of Hamath.

So Judah was taken into exile away from its land. [28] Here is [a] the official record of the number of people Nebuchadnezzar carried [b] into exile: In the seventh year, [c] 3,023 Jews; [29a] in Nebuchadnezzar's eighteenth year, 832 people from Jerusalem; [30] in Nebuchadnezzar's twenty-third year, Nebuzaradan, the captain of the royal guard, carried into exile 745 Judeans. In all, 4,600 people went into exile.

Jehoiachin in Exile

[31a] In the thirty-seventh year of the exile of King Jehoiachin of Judah, on the twenty-fifth day of the twelfth month, King Evil Merodach of Babylon, in the first year of his reign, [b] pardoned King Jehoiachin of Judah and released him from prison. [32] He spoke kindly to him and gave him a more prestigious position than the other kings who were with him in Babylon. [33] Jehoiachin took off his prison clothes[a] and ate daily in the king's presence for the rest of his life. [34] He was given daily provisions by the king of Babylon for the rest of his life until the day he died.

52:9[a] 2 Kgs 25:6; Jer 32:4; 39:5   **52:10**[a] Ezek 12:13   **52:11**[a] Ezek 12:13   **52:12**[a] 2 Kgs 25:8–21 [b] Jer 39:9   **52:15**[a] Jer 39:9
52:17[a] Jer 27:19 [b] 1 Kgs 7:15, 23, 27, 50   **52:18**[a] Exod 27:3; 1 Kgs 7:40, 45; 2 Kgs 25:14   **52:20**[a] 1 Kgs 7:47; 2 Kgs 25:16
[1] MT *the twelve bronze bulls under the movable stands.*   **52:21**[a] 1 Kgs 7:15; 2 Kgs 25:17; 2 Chr 3:15 [1] Heb. *18 cubits.*
[2] Heb. *12 cubits.*   **52:22**[1] Heb. *5 cubits.*   **52:23**[a] 1 Kgs 7:20   **52:24**[a] 2 Kgs 25:18; 1 Chr 6:14; Ezra 7:1 [b] Jer 21:1; 29:25
52:28[a] 2 Kgs 24:2 [b] 2 Kgs 24:12 [c] 2 Kgs 24:14   **52:29**[a] 2 Kgs 25:11; Jer 39:9   **52:31**[a] 2 Kgs 25:27–30
[b] Gen 40:13, 20; Ps 3:3; 27:6   **52:33**[a] 2 Sam 9:7, 13; 1 Kgs 2:7

LAMENTATIONS

amentations describes the funeral of a city. It is a tear-stained portrait of the once-proud Jerusalem now reduced to rubble by the invading Babylonian hordes. In a five-poem dirge, Jeremiah exposes his emotions. A death has occurred; Jerusalem lies barren. Jeremiah writes his lament in acrostic or alphabetical fashion. Beginning with the first letter *A* (*aleph*), he progresses verse by verse through the Hebrew alphabet, literally weeping from *A* to *Z*. And then, in the midst of this terrible holocaust, Jeremiah triumphantly cries out, "Your faithfulness is abundant!" (3:23). In the face of death and destruction, with life seemingly coming apart, Jeremiah turns tragedy into a triumph of faith. God has never failed him in the past. God has promised to remain faithful in the future. In the light of the God he knows and loves, Jeremiah finds hope and comfort. The Hebrew title of this book comes from the first word of chapters 1, 2, and 4: *Ekah*, "Alas." Another Hebrew word, *Ginoth* ("Elegies" or "Lamentations"), has also been used as the title because it better represents the contents of the book. The Greek title *Threnoi* means "Dirges" or "Laments," and the Latin title *Threni* ("Tears" or "Lamentations") was derived from this word. The subtitle in Jerome's Vulgate reads: "*Id est lamentations Jeremiae prophetae,*" and this became the basis for the English title "The Lamentations of Jeremiah."

The Prophet Speaks

א (ALEF)

1 [1]Alas! The city once full of people
now sits all alone!
The prominent lady among the
    nations
has become a widow!
The [a]princess who once ruled the
    provinces[2]
has become a forced laborer![3]

ב (BET)

2 She [a]weeps bitterly at [b]night;
tears stream down her cheeks.
She has no one to comfort her
among all her lovers.
All her friends have betrayed her;
they have become her enemies.

ג (GIMEL)

3 [a]Judah has departed into exile
under affliction and harsh
    oppression.

[b]She lives among the nations;
she has found no resting [c]place.
All who pursued her overtook
    her
in narrow straits.

ד (DALET)

4 The roads to Zion mourn
because no one travels to the
    festivals.
All her city gates are [a]deserted;
her priests groan.
Her virgins grieve;[1]
she is in bitter anguish!

ה (HE)

5 Her foes subjugated her;
her enemies are at ease.
For the LORD afflicted her
[a]because of her many acts of
    rebellion.
Her [b]children went away
captive before the enemy.

1:1 [a]1 Kgs 4:21; Ezra 4:20; Jer 31:7   [1]LXX, Vg. add *And it came to pass after Israel had been taken captive and Jerusalem had been laid waste, Jeremiah sat weeping and lamented this lament over Jerusalem, and said.*   [2]Heb. *princess among the provinces.*   [3]Heb. *conscripted worker;* a population subject to forced labor and/or heavy taxes.   **1:2** [a]Jer 13:17   [b]Job 7:3   **1:3** [a]Jer 52:27   [b]Lam 2:9   [c]Deut 28:65   **1:4** [a]Isa 27:10   [1]LXX *are led away.*   **1:5** [a]Jer 30:14–15; Dan 9:7, 16   [b]Jer 52:28

ו (VAV)
6 All of Daughter Zion's splendor
has departed.
Her leaders became like deer;
they found no pasture,
so they were too exhausted to escape
from the hunter.

ז (ZAYIN)
7 Jerusalem ᵃremembers,
when she became a poor homeless
person,
all her treasures
that she owned in days of old.
When her people fell into an enemy's
grip,¹
none of her allies came to her rescue.²
Her enemies gloated over her;
they sneered at her downfall.³

ח (KHET)
8 ᵃJerusalem committed terrible sin;
therefore she became an object of
scorn.
All who admired her have despised
her
because ᵇthey have seen her
nakedness.
She groans aloud
and turns away in shame.

ט (TET)
9 Her menstrual flow¹ has soiled her
clothing;
she ᵃdid not consider the
consequences of her sin.
Her demise was astonishing,
and there was no one to comfort her.
She cried, "Look, O LORD, on my²
affliction
because my enemy boasts!"

י (YOD)
10 An enemy grabbed
all her valuables.¹
Indeed she watched in horror as
Gentiles
invaded her holy temple—

those whom you had commanded:
"ᵃThey must ᵇnot enter your
assembly place."

כ (KAF)
11 All her people groaned
as ᵃthey searched for a morsel of
bread.
They exchanged their valuables
for just enough food
to stay alive.

Jerusalem Speaks
"Look, O LORD! Consider
that I have become worthless!"

ל (LAMED)
12 Is it nothing to you, all you who pass
by on the road?
Look and see!
Is there any pain like mine?
The Lord has afflicted me,
he has inflicted it on me
when he burned with anger.

מ (MEM)
13 He sent down fire
into my bones, and it overcame¹
them.
He spread ᵃout a trapper's net for my
feet;
he made me turn back.
He has made me desolate;
I am faint all day long.

נ (NUN)
14 My sins are bound around my neck
like a yoke;¹
ᵃthey are fastened together by his
hand.
He has placed his yoke² on my neck;
he has sapped my strength.
The Lord³ has handed me over
to those whom I cannot resist.

ס (SAMEK)
15 He rounded up all my mighty ones;
ᵃthe Lord¹ did this in² my midst.

1:7 ᵃPs 137:1 ¹Heb. *into the hand of.* ²Heb. *and there was no helper for her,* an idiom to describe the plight of a city whose allies refuse to help ward off a powerful attacker. ³LXX *her dwelling.* 1:8 ᵃ[1 Kgs 8:46] ᵇJer 13:22; Ezek 16:37; Hos 2:10 1:9 ᵃDeut 32:29; Isa 47:7; Jer 5:31 ¹Heb. *uncleanness*; refers in general to the state of ritual uncleanness and specifically to (1) sexual uncleanness, (2) filthy material, (3) ritual uncleanness, (4) menstrual uncleanness, and (5) polluted meat. ²Some wss *her affliction.* 1:10 ᵃPs 74:4–8; Isa 64:10–11; Jer 51:51 ᵇDeut 23:3; Neh 13:1 ¹Ket. *her desired things.* 1:11 ᵃJer 38:9; 52:6 1:13 ᵃEzek 12:13; 17:20 ¹LXX *it descended against them.* 1:14 ᵃDeut 28:48 ¹Some wss *watch is kept upon my transgression.* ²MT *they went up.* ³Many wss *the LORD.* 1:15 ᵃIsa 63:3; [Rev 14:19] ¹Many wss *the LORD* (both occurrences). ²LXX *from.*

He summoned an assembly
 against me
to shatter my young men.
The Lord has stomped like grapes
the virgin daughter, Judah.

ע (AYIN)

16 I weep because of these things;
[a]my eyes[1,2] flow with tears.
For there is no one in sight who can
 comfort me
or encourage me.
My children[3] are desolated
because an enemy has prevailed.

The Prophet Speaks

פ (PE)

17 [a]Zion spread out her hands,
but there is no one to comfort her.
The LORD has issued a decree against
 Jacob;
his [b]neighbors[1] have become his
 enemies.
Jerusalem has become
like filthy garbage in their midst.

Jerusalem Speaks

צ (TSADE)

18 The LORD is [a]right to judge me!
Yes, I [b]rebelled against his
 commands.
Please listen, all you nations,[1]
and look at my suffering!
My young women and men
have gone into exile.

ק (QOF)

19 I called for my lovers,
but they had deceived me.
My priests and my elders
perished in the city.
Truly they had searched for food
to keep themselves alive.[1]

ר (RESH)

20 Look, O LORD! I am distressed;
my [a]stomach is in knots!
My heart is pounding inside me.

Yes, I was terribly rebellious!
Out in the [b]street the sword bereaves
 a mother of her children;
inside the house death is present.

ש (SIN/SHIN)

21 They have heard[1] that I groan,
yet there is no one to comfort me.
All my enemies have heard of my
 trouble;
they are [a]glad that you have brought
 it about.
Bring about[2] [b]the day of judgment
 that you promised
so that they may end up like me!

ת (TAV)

22 Let all their wickedness come before
 you;
afflict them
just as you have afflicted me
because of all my acts of rebellion.
For my groans are many,
and my heart is sick with sorrow.

The Prophet Speaks

א (ALEF)

2 Alas! The Lord[1] has [a]covered
Daughter Zion with his anger.
[b]He has thrown down [c]the splendor
 of Israel
from heaven to earth;
he did not protect [d]his temple
when he displayed his anger.[2]

ב (BET)

2 The Lord[1] destroyed [a]mercilessly[2]
all [b]the homes of Jacob's descendants.
In his anger he tore down
the fortified cities of Daughter Judah.
He knocked to the ground and
 humiliated
the kingdom and its rulers.

ג (GIMEL)

3 In fierce anger[1] [a]he destroyed
[b]the whole army[2] of Israel.
He withdrew his right hand

1:16 [a] Ps 69:20; Eccl 4:1; Jer 13:17; Lam 2:18 [1] MT *my eye, my eye; eye.* [2] Heb. *My eye, my eye;* an emphatic Heb. construction.
[3] Heb. *my sons.* 1:17 [a] [Isa 1:15]; Jer 4:31 [b] 2 Kgs 24:2–4; Jer 12:9 [1] Heb. *his neighbors;* the surrounding nations. 1:18 [a] Neh
9:33; Ps 119:75; Dan 9:7, 14 [b] 1 Sam 12:14–15; Jer 4:17 [1] Ket. *peoples.* 1:19 [1] LXX adds *but they did not find it.* 1:20 [a] Job
30:27; Isa 16:11; Jer 4:19; Lam 2:11; Hos 11:8 [b] Deut 32:25; Ezek 7:15 1:21 [a] Ps 35:15; Jer 48:27; 50:11; Lam 2:15; Obad 12
[b] Isa 13; [Jer 46] [1] LXX *Hear!* [2] MT, LXX *you brought.* 2:1 [a] [Lam 3:44] [b] Matt 11:23 [c] 2 Sam 1:19 [d] 1 Chr 28:2;
Ps 99:5; Ezek 43:7 [1] Many mss *the LORD.* [2] Heb. *in the day of his anger.* 2:2 [a] Ps 21:9; Lam 3:43 [b] Ps 89:39–40;
Isa 43:28 [1] Many mss *the LORD.* [2] Sev. wss *and he has shown no mercy.* 2:3 [a] Ps 74:11; Jer 21:4–5
[b] Ps 89:46 [1] Some wss *His anger.* [2] Heb. *every horn of Israel.*

as the enemy attacked.
He was like a raging fire in the land
   of Jacob;
it consumed everything around it.

ד (DALET)
4 He prepared his bow like an enemy;
his right hand was [a]ready to shoot.
Like a foe he killed [b]everyone,
even our strong young men;
he has poured out his anger like fire
on the tent of Daughter Zion.

ה (HE)
5 The Lord,[1] like an enemy,
   destroyed Israel.
[a]He destroyed all [b]her palaces;
he ruined her fortified cities.
He made everyone in Daughter
   Judah
mourn and lament.

ו (VAV)
6 He destroyed his temple [a]as if it were
   a vineyard;[1]
he destroyed his appointed meeting
   place.
The LORD has made those in Zion
   forget
both the festivals and the Sabbaths.
In his fierce anger he has [b]spurned
both king and priest.

ז (ZAYIN)
7 The Lord[1] rejected his altar
and [a]abhorred his temple.[2]
[b]He handed over to the enemy
Jerusalem's palace walls;
the enemy shouted in the LORD's
   temple
as if it were a feast day.

ח (KHET)
8 The LORD was determined to tear
   down
Daughter Zion's [a]wall.
[b]He prepared to knock it down;
he did not withdraw his hand from
   destroying.

He made the ramparts and fortified
   walls lament;
together they mourned their ruin.

ט (TET)
9 Her city gates have fallen to the
   ground;
he [a]smashed to bits the bars that
   lock [b]her gates.[1]
Her king and princes were taken into
   exile;
[c]there is no more guidance available.
As for her [d]prophets,
they no longer receive a vision from
   the LORD.

י (YOD)
10 The elders of Daughter Zion
[a]sit[1] on the ground in silence.
They have [b]thrown dirt on their
   heads;
they have [c]dressed in sackcloth.
Jerusalem's young women[2] stare
   down at the ground.

כ (KAF)
11 My eyes are worn out from
   weeping;
[a]my stomach is in knots.
[b]My heart[1] is poured out on [c]the
   ground
due to the destruction of my helpless
   people;
children and infants faint
in the town squares.

ל (LAMED)
12 Children say to their mothers,
"Where are food and drink?"
They faint like a wounded warrior
in the city squares.
They die slowly
in their mothers' arms.

מ (MEM)
13 With what can I equate[1] you?
To what can I compare you,
[a]O Daughter Jerusalem?
To what can I liken you[2]

2:4 [a] Isa 63:10 [b] Ezek 24:25   2:5 [a] Jer 30:14 [b] 2 Kgs 25:9; Jer 52:13; Lam 2:2 [1] Many MSS *the LORD*.   2:6 [a] Isa 1:8; Jer 52:13 [b] Isa 43:28 [1] MT *like a garden*.   2:7 [a] Ezek 24:21 [b] Ps 74:3–8 [1] Many MSS *the LORD*. [2] Heb. *his sanctuary*.   2:8 [a] Jer 52:14 [b] [2 Kgs 21:13; Isa 34:11; Amos 7:7–9]   2:9 [a] Jer 51:30 [b] Deut 28:36; 2 Kgs 24:15; 25:7; Lam 1:3; 4:20 [c] 2 Chr 15:3 [d] Ps 74:9; Mic 3:6 [1] Heb. *her bars*.   2:10 [a] Job 2:13; Isa 3:26 [b] Job 2:12; Ezek 27:30 [c] Isa 15:3; Jonah 3:6–8 [1] Sev. wss *they have sat* [down]. [2] Heb. *the virgins of Jerusalem*.   2:11 [a] Ps 6:7; Lam 3:48 [b] Job 16:13; Ps 22:14 [c] Lam 4:4 [1] Heb. *my liver*, viewed as the seat of the emotions.   2:13 [a] Lam 1:12; Dan 9:12 [1] MT [How] *can I testify for you?* [2] LXX *Who will save you so that he might comfort you?*

so that I might comfort you, O Virgin
  Daughter Zion?
Your wound is as deep as the sea.[3]
Who can heal you?

ב (NUN)
[14] Your [a]prophets saw visions for you
  that were worthless whitewash.
They failed to [b]expose your sin
  so as to restore your fortunes.
They saw [c]oracles for you
  that were worthless lies.

ס (SAMEK)
[15] All who passed by on the road
  [a]clapped their [b]hands to mock you.[1]
[c]They sneered and shook their heads
  at Daughter Jerusalem.
"Ha! Is this the city they called
  'the perfection of beauty,
  the source of joy of the whole earth!'?"

פ (PE)
[16] [a]All your enemies
  gloated over you.
They sneered and gnashed their teeth;
  they said, "[b]We have destroyed her!
Ha! We have waited a long time for
    this [c]day.
  [d]We have lived to see it!"

ע (AYIN)
[17] The LORD has done what he [a]planned;
  he has fulfilled his promise
  that he threatened long ago:
He has overthrown you without
    mercy
  and has enabled the enemy to [b]gloat
    over you;
he has exalted your adversaries'
    power.

צ (TSADE)
[18] Cry out[1] from your heart to the Lord,[2]
  O wall of Daughter Zion!
Make your tears flow like a river
  all day and all night long![3]

Do not rest;
  do not [a]let your tears stop!

ק (QOF)
[19] Get up! [a]Cry out in the night
  when the night watches start!
[b]Pour out your heart like [c]water
  before the face of the Lord!
Lift up your hands to him
  for your children's lives;
they are fainting from hunger
  at every street corner.

Jerusalem Speaks

ר (RESH)
[20] Look, [a]O LORD! Consider!
  Whom have you ever afflicted like
    this?
Should women eat their offspring,[1]
  their healthy infants?
Should priest and prophet
  be killed in the Lord's[2] sanctuary?

ש (SIN/SHIN)
[21] The young [a]boys and old men
  lie dead on the ground in the streets.
My young women and my young men
  have fallen by the [b]sword.
You killed them when you were
    angry;
  you slaughtered them without
    mercy.

ת (TAV)
[22] As if it were a feast day, you call
  enemies to terrify me on every side.
On [a]the day of the LORD's anger
  no one escaped or survived.
My enemy has finished [b]off
  [c]those healthy infants whom I bore
    and raised.[1]

The Prophet Speaks

א (ALEF)
3 I am the man[1] who has experienced
    affliction
  from the rod of the LORD's wrath.

2:13 [3]LXX *a cup.*   2:14 [a]Jer 2:8; 23:25–29; 29:8–9; 37:19; Ezek 13:2   [b]Isa 58:1; Ezek 23:36; Mic 3:8   [c]Jer 23:33–36; Ezek 22:25, 28   2:15 [a]1 Kgs 9:8; Job 27:23; Jer 18:16; Ezek 25:6; Nah 3:19   [b]2 Kgs 19:21; Ps 44:14   [c][Ps 48:2; 50:2]; Ezek 16:14 [1]Heb. *clap their hands at you;* an expression of malicious glee, derision, and mockery.   2:16 [a]Job 16:9–10; Ps 22:13; Lam 3:46   [b]Ps 56:2; 124:3; Jer 51:34   [c]Lam 1:21; [Obad 12–15]   [d]Ps 35:21   2:17 [a]Lev 26:16   [b]Ps 38:16   2:18 [a]Jer 14:17; Lam 1:16 [1]MT *their heart cried out to the Lord.*   [2]Many MSS *the LORD.*   [3]Heb. *day and night;* a merism which encompasses everything in between two polar opposites.   2:19 [a]Ps 119:147   [b]1 Sam 1:15; Ps 42:4; 62:8   [c]Isa 51:20   [1]Many MSS *the LORD.*   2:20 [a]Lev 26:29; Deut 28:53; Jer 19:9; Lam 4:10; Ezek 5:10   [1]Heb. *their fruit.*   [2]Many MSS *the LORD.*   2:21 [a]2 Chr 36:17; Jer 6:11   [b]Jer 18:21   2:22 [a]Ps 31:13; Isa 24:17; Jer 6:25   [b]Jer 16:2–4; 44:7   [c]Hos 9:12   [1]An emphatic Heb. construction.   3:1 [1]A strong man, distinguished from women, children, and other non-combatants whom he is to defend.

2 He drove me into captivity and made
    me walk
  in darkness and not light.
3 He repeatedly attacks me;
  he turns his hand[1] against me all day
    long.

בּ (BET)

4 He has made ᵃmy mortal skin waste
    away;
  he has ᵇbroken my bones.
5 He has besieged and surrounded me
  with bitter hardship.
6 ᵃHe has made me reside in deepest
    darkness
  like those who died long ago.

גּ (GIMEL)

7 He has walled me in so that I cannot
    get out;
  ᵃhe has weighted me down with
    heavy prison chains.
8 Also, ᵃwhen I cry out desperately for
    help,
  he has shut out my prayer.[1]
9 He has blocked every road I take
  with a wall of hewn stones;
  he has made every path impassable.

דּ (DALET)

10 To me ᵃhe is like a bear lying in
    ambush,
  like a hidden lion stalking its prey.
11 He has obstructed my paths and
    ᵃtorn me to pieces;
  he has made me desolate.
12 He drew his bow and ᵃmade me
  the target for his arrow.

הּ (HE)

13 He shot his arrows
  into my heart.[1]
14 I have become the ᵃlaughingstock of
    all people,[1]
  ᵇtheir mocking song all day long.
15 He has given me my fill of bitter
    ᵃherbs
  and made me drunk with bitterness.

ו (VAV)

16 He ground my teeth in gravel;
  he trampled me in the dust.
17 I am deprived[1] of peace;
  I have forgotten what happiness is.
18 ᵃSo I said, "My endurance has
    expired;
  I have lost all hope of deliverance
    from the LORD."

ז (ZAYIN)

19 Remember[1] my impoverished and
    homeless condition,
  which is a bitter poison.
20 I continually think about this,
  and I am depressed.
21 But this I call to mind;
  therefore I have ᵃhope:

ח (KHET)

22 ᵃThe LORD's loyal kindness[1] never
    ceases;[2]
  his compassions never ᵇend.
23 They are fresh ᵃevery morning;
  your faithfulness is abundant!
24 "My ᵃportion is the LORD," I have
    said to myself,
  so I will put my ᵇhope in him.

ט (TET)

25 The LORD is good to those who
    trust ᵃin him,
  to the one who seeks him.
26 It is good to wait patiently
  for deliverance from the LORD.
27 ᵃIt is good for a man
  to bear the yoke while he is
    young.

י (YOD)

28 ᵃLet a person sit alone in silence,
  when the LORD is disciplining
    him.
29 ᵃLet him bury his face in the dust;
  perhaps there is hope.
30 Let him offer his cheek to the one
    who hits him;
  ᵃlet him have his fill of insults.

3:3 [1]An idiom denoting hostility.   3:4 ᵃJob 16:8   ᵇPs 51:8; Isa 38:13   3:6 ᵃ[Ps 88:5–6; 143:3]   3:7 ᵃJob 3:23; 19:8; Hos 2:6
  3:8 ᵃJob 30:20; Ps 22:2   [1]Or *he has shut his ears to my prayer.*   3:10 ᵃIsa 38:13   3:11 ᵃJob 16:12–13; Jer 15:3; Hos 6:1
  3:12 ᵃJob 7:20; 16:12; Ps 38:2   3:13 [1]Heb. *my kidneys;* often portrayed as the most sensitive and vital part of person.
  3:14 ᵃPs 22:6–7; 123:4; Jer 20:7   ᵇJob 30:9; Ps 69:12; Lam 3:63   [1]MT *my people.*   3:15 ᵃJer 9:15   3:17 [1]LXX *he deprived.*
  3:18 ᵃPs 31:22   3:19 [1]LXX *I remembered.*   3:21 ᵃPs 130:7   3:22 ᵃ[Mal 3:6]   ᵇPs 78:38; [Jer 3:12; 30:11]   [1]When this Heb.
    word is used of the Lord, it is often connected to his covenant loyalty.   [2]MT *we are* [not] *cut off.*   3:23 ᵃIsa 33:2;
    Zeph 3:5   3:24 ᵃPs 16:5; 73:26; 119:57; Jer 10:16   ᵇJer 17:17; Mic 7:7   3:25 ᵃPs 130:6; Isa 30:18   3:27 ᵃPs 94:12
    3:28 ᵃJer 15:17   3:29 ᵃJob 42:6   3:30 ᵃJob 16:10; Isa 50:6; [Matt 5:39; 26:67]; Mark 14:65; Luke 22:63

 כ (KAF)

31 For the Lord[1] will not
reject us[a] forever.
32 Though he causes us grief, he then
has compassion on us
according to the abundance of his
loyal kindness.[1]
33 For[a] he is not predisposed to afflict
or to grieve people.

ל (LAMED)

34 To crush underfoot
all the earth's prisoners,
35 to deprive a person of his rights
in the presence of the Most High,
36 to defraud a person in a lawsuit—
[a]the Lord[1] does not approve of such
things!

מ (MEM)

37 Whose command was ever fulfilled
unless the Lord[1] decreed it?
38 Is it not from the mouth of the
Most High that everything
comes—
both[a]calamity and blessing?
39 [a]Why should[b] any living person
complain
when punished for his sins?[1]

נ (NUN)

40 Let us carefully examine our ways,
and let us return to the LORD.
41 [a]Let us lift up our hearts[1] and our
hands
to God in heaven:
42 "[a]We[1] have blatantly rebelled;
you[2] have not forgiven."

ס (SAMEK)

43 You shrouded yourself with anger
and then pursued us;
you killed without mercy.
44 You shrouded yourself with a cloud
so that no prayer could get
through.
45 You make us like filthy[a]scum
in the estimation of the nations.

פ (PE)

46 [a]All our enemies have gloated
over us;
47 [a]panic and pitfall have come
upon us,
[b]devastation and destruction.
48 Streams of tears flow from[a]my
eyes
because my people are destroyed.

ע (AYIN)

49 Tears flow from[a]my eyes and will
not stop;
there will be no break
50 until the LORD[a]looks down from
heaven
and sees what has happened.
51 What my eyes see grieves me—
all the suffering of the daughters
in my city.

צ (TSADE)

52 For no good reason my enemies
hunted me down like a bird.
53 They shut me up[a]in a pit
and[b]threw stones at me.
54 [a]The waters closed over my head;
[b]I thought I was about to die.

ק (QOF)

55 I have called on your name, O LORD,
from the deepest[a]pit.
56 You heard my plea:
"Do not close[a]your ears to my cry for
relief!"
57 You came near on the day I called to
you;
you said, "[a]Do not fear!"

ר (RESH)

58 O Lord,[1] you[a]championed my cause;
[b]you redeemed my life.
59 You have seen the wrong done to me,
O LORD;
[a]pronounce judgment on my
behalf!
60 You have seen all their vengeance,
all their[a]plots against me.[1]

3:31 [a] Ps 77:7; 94:14; [Isa 54:7–10] [1] Many MSS the LORD. 3:32 [1] Vg. kindnesses. 3:33 [a] [Ps 119:67, 71, 75; Isa 28:21; Ezek 33:11; Heb 12:10] 3:36 [a] [Jer 22:3; Hab 1:13] [1] Many MSS the LORD. 3:37 [1] Many MSS the LORD. 3:38 [a] Job 2:10; [Isa 45:7]; Jer 32:42; Amos 3:6; [Jas 3:10–11] 3:39 [a] Prov 19:3 [b] Jer 30:15; Mic 7:9; [Heb 12:5–6] [1] Ket. his sin. 3:41 [a] Ps 86:4 [1] MT heart. 3:42 [a] Neh 9:26; Jer 14:20; Dan 9:5 [1] Heb. We—we have sinned; an emphatic Heb. construction. [2] Heb. You—you have not forgiven; an emphatic Heb. construction. 3:45 [a] 1 Cor 4:13 3:46 [a] Job 30:9–10; Ps 22:6–8; Lam 2:16 3:47 [a] Isa 24:17–18; Jer 48:43–44 [b] Isa 51:19 3:48 [a] Jer 4:19; 14:17; Lam 2:11 3:49 [a] Ps 77:2; Jer 14:17 3:50 [a] Ps 80:14; Isa 63:15; Lam 5:1 3:53 [a] Jer 37:16 [b] Dan 6:17 3:54 [a] Ps 69:2; Jonah 2:3–5 [b] Isa 38:10 3:55 [a] Jer 38:6–13 3:56 [a] Ps 3:4 3:57 [a] Isa 41:10, 14; Dan 10:12 3:58 [a] Ps 35:1; Jer 51:36 [b] Ps 71:23 [1] Many MSS the LORD. 3:59 [a] Ps 9:4 3:60 [a] Jer 11:19 [1] MT to me.

ש (SIN/SHIN)
61 You have heard their taunts, O LORD,
   all their plots against me.
62 My assailants revile and conspire
   against me all day long.
63 Watch them from morning to
      ᵃevening;
   I am the object of their mocking
      songs.

ת (TAV)
64 Pay them back ᵃwhat they deserve,
      O LORD,
   according to what they¹ have done.
65 Give them a distraught heart;¹
   may your curse be on them!
66 Pursue them in anger and eradicate
      them
   ᵃfrom under the LORD's ᵇheaven.

The Prophet Speaks

א (ALEF)
4 Alas! Gold has lost its luster;
   pure gold loses value.
   Jewels are scattered
   on every street corner.

ב (BET)
2 The precious sons of Zion
   were worth their weight in gold—
   ᵃAlas!—but now they are treated like
      broken clay pots,
   made by a potter.

ג (GIMEL)
3 Even the jackals nurse their young
   at their breast,
   but my people are cruel,
   ᵃlike ostriches in the wilderness.

ד (DALET)
4 The infant's tongue sticks
   to ᵃthe roof of its mouth due to thirst;
   little children beg for bread,¹
   but no one gives them even a morsel.

ה (HE)
5 Those who once feasted on delicacies
   are now starving to death in the
      streets.

Those who grew up wearing
   expensive clothes
are now ᵃdying amid garbage.

ו (VAV)
6 The punishment of my people
   exceeds ᵃthat of Sodom,
   which was ᵇoverthrown in a moment
   with no one to help her.

ז (ZAYIN)
7 Our consecrated ones¹ were brighter
      than snow,
   whiter than milk;
   their bodies more ruddy than corals,
   their hair like lapis lazuli.

ח (KHET)
8 Now ᵃtheir appearance is darker than
      soot;
   they are not recognized in the streets.
   Their skin has shriveled on their
      bones;
   it is dried up, like tree bark.

ט (TET)
9 Those who die by the sword are
      better off
   than those who die of hunger,
   those who waste away,
   struck down from lack of ᵃfood.

י (YOD)
10 The hands of ᵃtenderhearted women
   cooked their ᵇown children,
   who became their ᶜfood,
   when my people were destroyed.

כ (KAF)
11 The LORD fully vented his wrath;
   ᵃhe poured out his fierce anger.
   ᵇHe started a fire in Zion;
   it consumed her foundations.

ל (LAMED)
12 Neither the kings of the earth
   nor the people of the lands ever
      thought
   that enemy or foe could ᵃenter
   the gates of Jerusalem.

3:63 ᵃPs 139:2   3:64 ᵃPs 28:4; Jer 11:20; 2 Tim 4:14   ¹Heb. *their hands.*   3:65 ¹This Heb. word's meaning is debated.
3:66 ᵃDeut 25:19; Jer 10:11   ᵇPs 8:3   4:2 ᵃIsa 30:14; Jer 19:11; [2 Cor 4:7]   4:3 ᵃJob 39:14–17   4:4 ᵃPs 22:15   ¹Or perhaps
food.   4:5 ᵃJob 24:8   4:6 ᵃEzek 16:48   ᵇGen 19:25; Jer 20:16   4:7 ¹Heb. *Nazirites;* the Nazirites were consecrated
under a vow to refrain from wine, contact with the dead, and cutting their hair.   4:8 ᵃJob 19:20; Ps 102:5
4:9 ᵃJer 16:4   4:10 ᵃLev 26:29; Deut 28:57; 2 Kgs 6:29; Jer 19:9; Lam 2:20; Ezek 5:10   ᵇIsa 49:15
ᶜDeut 28:57   4:11 ᵃJer 7:20; Lam 2:17; Ezek 22:31   ᵇDeut 32:22; Jer 21:14   4:12 ᵃJer 21:13

מ (MEM)

13 [a]But it happened due to the sins of
her prophets
and the iniquities of her priests,
[b]who poured out in her midst
the blood of the righteous.

נ (NUN)

14 They wander blindly[1] through [a]the
streets,
defiled by the blood they shed,
while no one dares
to touch their garments.

ס (SAMEK)

15 People cry to them, "Turn away! You
are [a]unclean!
Turn away! Turn away! Don't
touch us!"
So they have fled and wander about;
but the nations say, "They may not
stay here any longer."

פ (PE)

16 The Lord himself has scattered
[a]them;
he no longer watches over them.
They did not honor the priests;[1]
they did not show favor to the elders.[2]

The People of Jerusalem Lament

ע (AYIN)

17 Our eyes continually failed us
as we looked in vain for help.
From [a]our watchtowers we watched
for a nation that could not rescue us.

צ (TSADE)

18 [a]Our enemies hunted us down at
every step
so that we could not walk about in
[b]our streets.
Our end drew near, our days were
numbered,
for our end had come!

ק (QOF)

19 Those who pursued us were [a]swifter
than eagles[1] in the sky.[2]

They chased us over the mountains;
they ambushed us in the
wilderness.

ר (RESH)

20 Our very life [a]breath—the Lord's
anointed king—
[b]was caught in their traps,
of whom we thought,
"Under his protection we will survive
among the nations."

The Prophet Speaks

שׁ (SIN/SHIN)

21 Rejoice and be glad for now, O people
of [a]Edom,
who reside in [b]the land of Uz.
But the cup of judgment will pass to
you also;
you will get drunk and take off your
clothes.

ת (TAV)

22 O people of Zion, your punishment
will come to an end;
[a]he will not prolong your exile.
But, O people of Edom, [b]he will
punish your sin
and reveal your offenses!

The People of Jerusalem Pray

5 O [a]Lord, reflect on what has
happened to us;
consider[1] and look at [b]our disgrace.
2 Our inheritance is turned over to
strangers;
foreigners now occupy [a]our homes.
3 We have become fatherless orphans;
our mothers have become [a]widows.
4 We must pay money for our own
water;
we must buy our own wood at a steep
price.
5 We are pursued—[a]they are breathing
down our necks;
we are weary and have no rest.
6 [a]We have submitted[1] [b]to Egypt and
[c]Assyria
in order to buy food to eat.

4:13 [a]Jer 5:31; Ezek 22:26, 28; Zeph 3:4   [b]Jer 2:30; 26:8–9; Matt 23:31   4:14 [a]Jer 2:34   [1]LXX to rise; Syr. her nobles.
4:15 [a]Lev 13:45–46   4:16 [a]Lam 5:12   [1]Some wss he did not lift up.   [2]Some wss he did not show favor.   4:17 [a]2 Kgs
24:7   4:18 [a]2 Kgs 25:4   [b]Ezek 7:2–3, 6; Amos 8:2   4:19 [a]Deut 28:49   [1]Probably the griffin-vulture.   [2]Or the heavens.
4:20 [a]Gen 2:7   [b]Jer 52:9; Ezek 12:13   4:21 [a]Ps 83:3–6   [b]Jer 25:15; Obad 10   4:22 [a][Isa 40:2; Jer 33:7–8]   [b]Ps 137:7
5:1 [a]Ps 89:50   [b]Ps 79:4; Lam 2:15   [1]Heb. Look!   5:2 [a]Ps 79:1   5:3 [a]Exod 22:24; Jer 15:8; 18:21   5:5 [a]Deut 28:48;
Jer 28:14   5:6 [a]Gen 24:2   [b]Hos 9:3; 12:1   [c]Jer 2:18; Hos 5:13   [1]Heb. we have given the hand;
a Semitic idiom for placing oneself in a subservient position as vassal.

7 [a]Our forefathers sinned and are dead,
but we[1] suffer their punishment.
8 Slaves rule over us;
there is no one to rescue us from
their power.
9 At the risk of our lives we get our food
because robbers lurk[1] in the
wilderness.
10 Our skin is as hot as an oven
due to a fever from hunger.
11 They [a]raped women in Zion,
virgins in the towns of Judah.
12 Princes were hung by their hands;
elders were mistreated.
13 The young men [a]perform menial
labor;
boys stagger from their labor.[1]
14 The elders are gone from the city
gate;
the young men have stopped playing
their [a]music.

15 Our hearts no longer have any joy;
our dancing is turned to [a]mourning.
16 [a]The crown has fallen from our head;
woe to us, for we have sinned!
17 Because of this, our hearts are sick;
[a]because of these things, we can
hardly see through our tears.
18 For wild animals are prowling over
Mount Zion,
which lies [a]desolate.
19 But you, O LORD, [a]reign forever;
[b]your throne endures from
generation to generation.
20 Why do you keep on forgetting[1] us?
[a]Why do you forsake us so long?
21 Bring us [a]back to yourself, O LORD, so
that we may return[1] to you;
renew our life as in days before,
22 unless you have utterly rejected us
and are angry with us beyond
measure.

5:7 [a]Jer 31:29 [1]Ket. *we.* 5:9 [1]Heb. *because of the sword.* 5:11 [a]Isa 13:16; Zech 14:2 5:13 [a]Judg 16:21 [1]Heb. *boys trip over wood.* 5:14 [a]Isa 24:8; Jer 7:34 5:15 [a]Jer 25:10; Amos 8:10 5:16 [a]Job 19:9; Ps 89:39; Jer 13:18 5:17 [a]Ps 6:7 5:18 [a]Isa 27:10 5:19 [a]Ps 9:7; Hab 1:12 [b]Ps 45:6 5:20 [a]Ps 13:1; 44:24 [1]I.e., not to pay attention to or to ignore. 5:21 [a]Ps 80:3, 7, 19; Jer 31:18 [1]Ket. *and we will return.*

EZEKIEL

Ezekiel, a priest and a prophet, ministers during the darkest days of Judah's history: the seventy-year period of Babylonian captivity. Carried to Babylon before the final assault on Jerusalem, Ezekiel uses prophecies, parables, signs, and symbols to dramatize God's message to his exiled people. Though they are like dry bones in the sun, God will reassemble them and breathe life into the nation once again. Present judgment will be followed by future glory so that "you will know that I am the LORD" (6:7). The Hebrew name *Yehezke'l* means "God Strengthens" or "Strengthened by God." Ezekiel is indeed strengthened by God for the prophetic ministry to which he is called (3:8–9). The name occurs twice in this book and nowhere else in the Old Testament. The Greek form in the Septuagint is *Iezekiel*, and the Latin form in the Vulgate is *Ezechiel*.

A Vision of God's Glory

1 In [a]the thirtieth year, on [b]the fifth day of the fourth month, while I was among the exiles at the Kebar River, the heavens opened and I saw a divine [c]vision. [2](On the fifth day of the month—it was the fifth year of King Jehoiachin's exile—[3]the LORD's message came to [a]the priest Ezekiel the son of Buzi, at the Kebar River in the land of the Babylonians. The hand of the LORD came on him there.)

[4]As I [a]watched, I noticed a windstorm coming from the north—an enormous cloud, with lightning flashing, such that bright light rimmed it and came from[1] it like glowing amber from the middle of a fire. [5a]In the fire[1] were what looked like four living beings. [b]In [c]their appearance they had human form, [6]but each had four faces and four wings. [7]Their legs were straight, but the soles of their feet were [a]like calves' feet. They gleamed like polished bronze. [8]They had human hands[1] under [a]their wings on their four sides. As for the faces and wings of the four of them, [9]their wings touched each other; they did not turn as they moved, but went straight [a]ahead.

[10]Their faces had this appearance: Each of [a]the four [b]had [c]the face of [d]a man, with the face of [e]a lion on the right, the face of an ox on the left, and also the face of an eagle.[1] [11]Their wings were spread out above them; each had [a]two wings touching the wings of one of the other beings on either side and two wings covering their bodies. [12]Each moved straight ahead—wherever the spirit would go, they would go, without turning as they went. [13]In the middle[1] of the living beings was something [a]like[2] burning coals of fire or like torches. It moved back and forth among the living beings. It was bright, and lightning was flashing out of the fire. [14]The [a]living beings moved backward and forward as quickly as flashes of lightning.[1]

[15]Then I looked,[1] and I saw [a]one wheel on the ground beside each of the four beings. [16]The appearance of [a]the wheels and their construction[1] was [b]like gleaming jasper,[2] and all four wheels looked alike. Their structure was like a wheel within a wheel. [17]When they moved they would go in any of the four directions they faced without turning as they moved. [18]Their rims were

1:1 [a]Ezek 3:15, 23; 10:15　[b]Matt 3:16; Mark 1:10; Luke 3:21; Acts 7:56; 10:11; Rev 4:1; 19:11　[c]Exod 24:10; Num 12:6; Isa 1:1; 6:1; Ezek 8:3; Dan 8:1–2　1:3 [a]1 Kgs 18:46; 2 Kgs 3:15; Ezek 3:14, 22　1:4 [a]Isa 21:1; Jer 23:19; 25:32; Ezek 13:11, 13　[1]LXX *in its midst.*　1:5 [a]Ezek 10:15, 17, 20; Rev 4:6–8　[b]Ezek 10:8　[c]Ezek 10:14　[1]MT *from its midst.*　1:7 [a]Dan 10:6; Rev 1:15　1:8 [a]Ezek 10:8, 21　[1]MT *his hand.*　1:9 [a]Ezek 1:12; 10:20–22　1:10 [a]Ezek 10:14; Rev 4:7　[b]Num 2:10　[c]Num 2:3　[d]Num 2:18　[e]Num 2:25　[1]MT adds *and their faces.*　1:11 [a]Isa 6:2; Ezek 1:23　1:13 [a]Ps 104:4; Rev 4:5　[1]MT *and the form of the creatures.*　[2]MT *their appearance was like burning coals of fire.*　1:14 [a]Zech 4:10; [Matt 24:27; Luke 17:24]　[1]LXX omits v. 14.　1:15 [a]Ezek 10:9　[1]MT adds *at the living beings.*　1:16 [a]Ezek 10:9–10　[b]Dan 10:6　[1]LXX omits *and their construction.*　[2]Heb. *Tarshish stone;* the meaning of this term is uncertain.

high and awesome,[1] and the rims of all four wheels were [a]full of eyes all around. [19]When the living beings moved, the wheels beside them moved; [a]when the living beings rose up from the ground, the wheels rose up too. [20]Wherever the spirit would go, they would go,[1] and the wheels would rise up beside them because the spirit of the living being was in the wheel. [21]When the living beings moved, the wheels moved, and when they stopped moving, the wheels stopped.[1] When they rose up from the ground, the wheels rose up from the ground; the wheels rose up beside them because the spirit of the living being was in the wheel.

[22]Over [a]the heads of the living beings was something like a platform, glittering awesomely like [b]ice, stretched out [c]over their heads. [23]Under the platform their wings were stretched out, each toward the other. Each of the beings also had two wings covering[1] its body. [24]When they moved, I heard the sound of their wings—it was like the sound of rushing waters, or the voice of the Sovereign One, or the tumult of an army. [a]When [b]they stood still, they lowered their wings.

[25]Then there was a voice from above the platform over their heads when they stood still.[1] [26]Above the platform over their heads was something like [a]a sapphire shaped like a throne. High above on the throne was a form that appeared to be a man. [27]I saw an amber glow [a]like a fire enclosed all around[1] from his waist up. From his waist down I saw something that looked like fire. There was a brilliant light around it, [28]like the appearance of a rainbow in the clouds after the rain. This was the appearance of the surrounding brilliant light; it looked [a]like the glory of the LORD. When [b]I saw [c]it, I threw myself face down, and I heard a voice speaking.

Ezekiel's Commission

2 He said to me, "Son of man, [a]stand on your feet and I will speak with you." [2]As [a]he spoke to me,[1] a wind came into me and stood me on my feet, and I heard the one speaking to me.

[3]He said to me, "Son of man, I am sending you to the house[1] of Israel, to rebellious nations[2] who have [a]rebelled against me; both [b]they and their fathers have revolted[3,4] against me to this very day. [4][a]The people to whom I am sending you are obstinate and hard-hearted,[1] and you must say to them, 'This is what the Sovereign LORD says.' [5]And [a]as for them, whether they listen or not—for they are a [b]rebellious house—they [c]will know that a prophet has been among them. [6]But you, son of man, [a]do not fear them, and do not fear their words. Even though [b]briers and thorns surround you and you live among scorpions—[c]do not fear their words and do not be terrified of the looks they give you, for they are a rebellious house! [7][a]You must speak my words to them whether they listen or not, for they are rebellious. [8]As for you, son of man, listen to what I am saying to you: Do not rebel like that rebellious house! Open your mouth and [a]eat what I am giving you."

[9]Then I looked [a]and [b]realized a hand was stretched out to me, and in it was a written scroll. [10]He unrolled it before me, and it had writing on the front and back; written on it were laments, mourning, and woe.

3 He said to me, "Son of man, [a]eat what you see in front of you—eat this scroll—and then go and speak to the house of Israel." [2]So I opened my mouth and he fed me the scroll.

[3]He said to me, "Son of man, feed your stomach and fill your belly with this scroll I am giving to you." So I [a]ate it,[1] and it was sweet [b]like honey in my mouth.

[4]He said to me, "Son of man, go to the

1:18 [a]Ezek 10:12; [Zech 4:10]; Rev 4:6, 8 [1]MT *and fear belonged to them.* **1:19** [a]Ezek 10:16–17 **1:20** [1]MT adds *the spirit would go.* **1:21** [1]LXX *when it went, they went; when it stood, they stood.* **1:22** [a]Ezek 10:1 [b]Rev 4:6 [c]Ezek 10:1 **1:23** [1]Heb. *each had two wings covering and each had two wings covering.* **1:24** [a]Ezek 3:13; 10:5 [b]Job 37:4–5; Ps 29:3–4; 68:33 **1:25** [1]MT adds *when they stood still, they lowered their wings.* **1:26** [a]Ezek 10:1 **1:27** [a]Ezek 8:2 [1]LXX omits *like a fire enclosed all around.* **1:28** [a][Gen 9:13]; Rev 4:3; 10:1 [b]Ezek 3:23; 8:4 [c]Gen 17:3; Ezek 3:23; Dan 8:17; Acts 9:4; Rev 1:17 **2:1** [a]Dan 10:11; Acts 9:6 **2:2** [a]Ezek 3:24; Dan 8:18 [1]LXX omits *as he spoke to me.* **2:3** [a]Ezek 5:6; 20:8, 13, 18 [b]1 Sam 8:7–8; Jer 3:25; Ezek 20:18, 21, 30 [1]MT *sons of.* [2]LXX omits *to rebellious nations.* [3]LXX omits *have revolted.* [4]The strongest Heb. word available for expressing a covenant violation. **2:4** [a]Ps 95:8; Isa 48:4; Jer 5:3; 6:15; Ezek 3:7 [1]LXX omits *obstinate and hard-hearted.* **2:5** [a]Isa 6:9–10; Ezek 3:11, 26, 27; [Matt 10:12–15; Acts 13:46] [b]Ezek 3:26 [c]Ezek 33:33; [Luke 10:10–11; John 15:22] **2:6** [a]Isa 51:12; Jer 1:8, 17; Ezek 3:9; Luke 12:4 [b][2 Sam 23:6–7; Isa 9:18]; Jer 6:28; Ezek 28:24; Mic 7:4 [c]Ezek 3:9; [1 Pet 3:14] **2:7** [a]Jer 1:7, 17; [Ezek 3:10, 17] **2:8** [a]Ezek 3:1–3; Rev 10:9 **2:9** [a]Jer 1:9; [Ezek 8:3] [b]Jer 36:2; Ezek 3:1; Rev 5:1–5; 10:8–11 **3:1** [a]Ezek 2:8–9 **3:3** [a]Jer 15:16; Rev 10:9 [b]Ps 19:10; 119:103 [1]Heb. *I ate.*

house of Israel and speak my words to them. [5]For you are not being sent to a people of unintelligible speech and difficult language, but to the house of Israel—[6]not to many peoples of unintelligible speech and difficult language, whose words you cannot understand. Surely if[1] I [a]had sent you to them, they would listen to you! [7]But the house of Israel is unwilling to listen to you, [a]because they are not willing to listen to me, [b]for the whole house of Israel is hard-headed and hardhearted.

[8]"I have made your face adamant to match their faces, and your forehead hard to match their foreheads. [9]I have made your forehead harder than flint—[a]like diamond! [b]Do not fear them or be terrified of the looks they give you, for they are a rebellious house."

[10]And he said to me, "Son of man, take all my words that I speak to you to heart and listen carefully. [11]Go to the exiles, to your fellow countrymen, and speak to them. Say to them, 'This is [a]what the Sovereign LORD says,' whether they pay attention or not."

Ezekiel before the Exiles

[12]Then a wind lifted me up and I heard a great rumbling sound behind me as [a]the [b]glory of the LORD rose from its place, [13]and the [a]sound of the living beings' wings brushing against each other, and the sound of the wheels alongside them, a great rumbling sound. [14]A wind lifted me up and carried me away. I went bitterly, my spirit full of fury, and [a]the hand of the LORD rested powerfully[1] on me. [15]I came to the [a]exiles at Tel Abib, who lived by the Kebar River. I sat dumbfounded among them there, where they were living, for seven days.

[16]At the end of seven days the LORD's message [a]came to me: [17]"[a]Son of [b]man, I have appointed you a watchman for the house of Israel. Whenever you hear a word from my mouth, you must give them a [c]warning from me. [18]When I say to the wicked, 'You will certainly die,' and you do not warn him—you do not speak out to warn the wicked to turn from his wicked lifestyle so that he may live—that wicked person will die for his iniquity, but I will hold you accountable for his death. [19]But as for you, if you warn the wicked and he does not turn from his wicked deed and from his wicked lifestyle, he will die for his iniquity [a]but you will have saved your own life.

[20]"When a righteous [a]person turns from his righteousness and commits iniquity, and I set an obstacle before him, he will die. If you have not warned him, he will die for his sin. The righteous deeds he performed will not be considered, but I will hold you accountable for his death. [21]However, if you warn the righteous person not to sin, and he does not sin, he will certainly live because he was warned, and you will have saved your own life."

Isolated and Silenced

[22]The hand of [a]the LORD rested on me there, and he said [b]to me, "Get up, go out to the valley, and I will speak with you there." [23]So I got up and went out to [a]the valley, and the glory of the LORD was standing there, just like the glory I had [b]seen by the Kebar River, [c]and I threw myself face down.

[24]Then a wind came into me and stood me on my feet. [a]The LORD spoke to me and said, "Go shut yourself in your house. [25]As for you, son of man, [a]they will put ropes on you and tie you up with them, so you cannot go out among them. [26]I [a]will make your tongue stick to the roof of your mouth so that you will be silent and [b]unable to reprove them, [c]for they are a rebellious house. [27a]But when I speak with you, I will loosen your tongue and you must say to them, 'This is [b]what the Sovereign LORD says.' Those who listen will listen, but the indifferent will refuse, for they are a rebellious house.

Ominous Object Lessons

4 "And you, son of man, take a brick and set it in front of you. Inscribe a city on it—Jerusalem. [2a]Lay siege to it! Build siege works against it. Erect a siege ramp against it! Post soldiers outside it and station

3:6 [a]Jonah 3:5–10; Matt 11:21 [1]MT *if not.*   3:7 [a]John 15:20–21 [b]Ezek 2:4   3:9 [a]Isa 50:7; Jer 1:18; Mic 3:8 [b]Jer 1:8, 17; Ezek 2:6   3:11 [b]Ezek 2:5, 7   3:12 [a]1 Kgs 18:12; Ezek 8:3; Acts 8:39 [b]Ezek 1:28; 8:4   3:13 [a]Ezek 1:24; 10:5   3:14 [a]2 Kgs 3:15; Ezek 1:3; 8:1 [1]Heb. *was on me heavily.*   3:15 [a]Job 2:13; Ps 137:1   3:16 [a]Jer 42:7   3:17 [a]Ezek 33:7–9 [b]Isa 52:8; 56:10; Jer 6:17 [c][Lev 19:17; Prov 14:25]; Isa 58:1   3:19 [a]Isa 49:4–5; Ezek 14:14, 20; Acts 18:6; 20:26; 1 Tim 4:16   3:20 [a]Ps 125:5; Ezek 18:24; 33:18; Zeph 1:6   3:22 [a]Ezek 1:3 [b]Ezek 8:4   3:23 [a]Ezek 1:28; Acts 7:55 [b]Ezek 1:1 [c]Ezek 1:28   3:24 [a]Ezek 2:2   3:25 [a]Ezek 4:8   3:26 [a]Ezek 24:27; Luke 1:20, 22 [b]Hos 4:17; Amos 8:11 [c]Ezek 2:5–7   3:27 [a]Exod 4:11–12; Ezek 24:27; 33:22 [b]Ezek 3:11   4:2 [a]Jer 6:6; Ezek 21:22

battering rams around it. ³Then for your part take an iron frying pan and set it up as an iron wall between you and the city. Set your face toward it. It is to be under ªsiege; you are to besiege it. ᵇThis is a sign for the house of Israel.

⁴"Also for your part lie on your left side and place the iniquity of the house of Israel on it. For the number of days you lie on your side you will bear their iniquity. ⁵I have determined that the number of the years of their iniquity are to be the number of days for you—390 days.¹ ªSo bear the iniquity of the house of Israel.

⁶"When you have completed these days, then lie down a second time, but on your right side, and bear the iniquity of the house of Judah 40 days—I have assigned one day for each year. ⁷You must turn your face toward the siege of Jerusalem with your arm bared and prophesy against it. ⁸ªLook here: I will tie you up with ropes, so you cannot turn from one side to the other until you complete the days of your siege.

⁹"As for you, take wheat, barley, beans, lentils, millet, and spelt, put them in a single container, and make food from them for yourself. For the same number of days that you lie on your side—390 days¹—you will eat it. ¹⁰The food you eat will be eight ounces a day by weight; you must eat it at fixed times. ¹¹And you must drink water by measure, a pint and a half; you must drink it at fixed times. ¹²And you must eat the food as you would a barley cake. You must bake it in front of them over a fire made with dried human excrement." ¹³And the LORD said, "This is how the people of Israel will eat their unclean food among the nations where I will banish them."

¹⁴And I said, "ªAh, Sovereign LORD, I have never been ceremonially defiled before. I have never eaten ᵇa carcass or an animal torn by wild beasts; from my youth up, ᶜunclean meat¹ has never entered my mouth."

¹⁵So he said to me, "All right then, I will substitute cow's manure instead of human excrement. You will cook your food over it."

¹⁶Then he said to me, "Son of man, I am about to remove the bread ªsupply in Jerusalem. They will ᵇeat their bread ration anxiously, and they will ᶜdrink their water ration in terror ¹⁷because they will lack bread and water. Each one will be terrified, and they will rot for their iniquity.

5 "As for you, son of man, take ªa sharp sword and use it as a barber's razor. Shave off some of the hair from your head and your beard. Then take scales and divide up the hair you cut off. ²Burn a third of it in the fire inside the city when the days of ªyour siege are completed. Take a third and slash it with a sword all around ᵇthe city. Scatter a third to ᶜthe wind, and I will unleash a sword behind ᵈthem. ³But take a few strands of hair from those and tie them in the ends of ªyour garment. ⁴Again, take more of them and ªthrow them into the fire, and burn them up. From there a fire will spread to all the house of Israel.

⁵"This is what the Sovereign LORD says: This is Jerusalem; I placed her in the center of the nations with countries all around her. ⁶Then she defied my regulations and my statutes, becoming more wicked than the nations and the countries around her. Indeed, they have rejected my regulations, and they do not follow my statutes.

⁷"Therefore this is what the Sovereign LORD says: Because you are more arrogant than the nations around you, you have ªnot followed my statutes and have not carried out my regulations. You have not even¹ carried out the regulations of the nations around you!

⁸"Therefore this is what the Sovereign LORD says: I—even I—am against you, and I will execute judgment¹ among you while the nations watch. ⁹I will do to you what I have never done before ªand will never do again because of all your abominable practices. ¹⁰Therefore, fathers ªwill eat their sons within you, Jerusalem, and sons will eat their fathers. I will execute judgments on you, and I will ᵇscatter any survivors to the winds.

4:3 ªJer 39:1–2; Ezek 5:2 ᵇEzek 12:6, 11; 24:24, 27   4:5 ªNum 14:34 ¹LXX *190 days*.   4:8 ªEzek 3:25   4:9 ¹LXX *190 days*. 4:14 ªActs 10:14 ᵇExod 22:31; Lev 17:15; 22:8; Ezek 44:31 ᶜDeut 14:3; Isa 65:4; 66:17 ¹Perhaps sacrificial meat not eaten by the appropriate time.   4:16 ªLev 26:26; Ps 105:16; Isa 3:1; Ezek 5:16; 14:13 ᵇEzek 4:10–11; 12:19 ᶜEzek 4:11   5:1 ªLev 21:5; Isa 7:20; Ezek 44:20   5:2 ªEzek 5:12 ᵇEzek 4:1 ᶜEzek 4:8–9 ᵈLev 26:25; Lam 1:20   5:3 ªJer 40:6; 52:16   5:4 ªJer 41:1–2; 44:14   5:7 ª2 Kgs 21:9–11; 2 Chr 33:9; Jer 2:10–11; Ezek 16:47 ¹Some wss omit *not even*.   5:8 ¹The Heb. text uses wordplay here as "execute" is the same Heb. word as "carried out" in v. 7, and "judgment" is the same Heb. word as "regulations" in v. 7. The point seems to be that God would "carry out judgments" against those who refused to "carry out" his "laws."   5:9 ªLam 4:6; Dan 9:12; [Amos 3:2]; Matt 24:21   5:10 ªLev 26:29; Deut 28:53; 2 Kgs 6:29; Jer 19:9; Lam 2:20; 4:10 ᵇLev 26:33; Deut 28:64; Ps 44:11; Ezek 5:2, 12; 6:8; 12:14; Amos 9:9; Zech 2:6; 7:14

[11] "Therefore, as surely as I live, says the Sovereign LORD, because you [a]defiled my sanctuary with all your [b]detestable idols and with all your abominable practices, I will withdraw; [c]my eye will not pity you, nor will I spare you. [12] A [a]third of your people [b]will die of plague or be overcome by [c]the famine within you. A third of your people will fall by the sword surrounding you, and a third I will scatter to the winds. I will unleash a sword behind them. [13] Then my anger will [a]be fully vented; I will exhaust my rage on them, [b]and I will be appeased. Then they will know that I, the LORD, have spoken in my jealousy when I have fully vented my rage against them.

[14] "I [a]will make you desolate and an object of scorn among the nations around you, in the sight of everyone who passes by. [15] You will be[1] an object [a]of scorn and taunting, a prime [b]example of destruction among the nations around you when I execute judgments against you in anger and [c]raging fury. I, the LORD, have spoken! [16] I will [a]shoot against them deadly, destructive arrows of famine, which I will shoot to destroy you. I will prolong a famine on you and will remove the bread [b]supply.[1] [17] I will send famine and [a]wild beasts against you, and they will take your children from you. [b]Plague and bloodshed will overwhelm you, and I will bring a sword against you. I, the LORD, have spoken!"

Judgment on the Mountains of Israel

6 The LORD's message came to me: [2] "Son of man, [a]turn toward the [b]mountains of Israel and prophesy against them. [3] Say, '[a]Mountains of Israel, hear the word of the Sovereign LORD! This is what the Sovereign LORD says to the mountains and the hills, to the ravines and the valleys: I am bringing a sword against you, and I will destroy your high places. [4] Your altars [a]will be ruined and your incense altars will be broken. I will throw down your slain in front of your idols. [5] I will place the corpses of the people of Israel in front of their idols,[1] and I will scatter your bones around your altars. [6] In all your dwellings, the cities will be laid waste and the high places ruined so that your altars will be laid waste and ruined, your idols will be shattered and demolished, your incense altars will be broken down, and your works wiped out. [7] The slain will fall among [a]you and then you will know that I am the LORD.

[8] "'[a]But I will spare some of you. Some will escape the sword when you are [b]scattered in foreign lands. [9] Then your survivors will [a]remember me among the [b]nations where they are exiled. They will realize how I was crushed [c]by their unfaithful heart that turned from me and by their eyes that lusted after their idols. [d]They will loathe themselves because of the evil they have done and because of all their abominable practices. [10] They will know that I am the LORD; my threats to bring this catastrophe on them were not empty.

[11] "'This is what the Sovereign LORD says: [a]Clap your hands, stamp your feet, and say, "Ah!" because of all the evil, abominable practices of the house of Israel, [b]for they will fall by the sword, famine, and pestilence. [12] The one far away will die by pestilence, the one close by will fall by the sword, and whoever is left and has escaped these will die by famine. I will fully vent my rage against them. [13] Then you will know that I am the LORD when their dead lie [a]among their idols around their altars, [b]on every high hill and on all the mountaintops, [c]under every green tree and every leafy oak—the places where they have offered fragrant incense to all their idols. [14] I will [a]stretch out my hand against them and make the land [b]a desolate waste from the wilderness to Riblah,[1] in all the places where they live. Then they will know that I am the LORD.'"

The End Arrives

7 The LORD's message came to me: [2] "You, son of [a]man—this is what the Sovereign LORD says to the land of Israel: An end! The

5:11 [a] 2 Chr 36:14; [Jer 7:9–11]; Ezek 8:5–6, 16   [b] Ezek 11:21   [c] Ezek 7:4, 9; 8:18; 9:10   **5:12** [a] Jer 15:2; 21:9; Ezek 6:12   [b] Jer 9:16; [Ezek 6:8]   [c] Jer 43:10–11; 44:27; Ezek 5:2; 12:14   **5:13** [a] Lam 4:11; Ezek 6:12; 7:8   [b] [Deut 32:36]; Isa 1:24   **5:14** [a] Lev 26:31; Neh 2:17   **5:15** [a] Deut 28:37; 1 Kgs 9:7; Ps 79:4; Jer 24:9; Lam 2:15   [b] [Isa 26:9]; Jer 22:8–9; 1 Cor 10:11   [c] Isa 66:15–16; Ezek 5:8; 25:17   [1] Maj. MSS *it will be.*   **5:16** [a] Deut 32:23   [b] Lev 26:26; Ezek 4:16; 14:13   [1] Heb. *break the staff of bread*; the bread supply is compared to a staff used for support.   **5:17** [a] Lev 26:22; Deut 32:24; Ezek 14:21; 33:27; 34:25; Rev 6:8   [b] Ezek 38:22   **6:2** [a] Ezek 20:46; 21:2; 25:2   [b] Ezek 36:1   **6:3** [a] Lev 26:30   **6:4** [a] Lev 26:30   **6:5** [1] LXX omits *I will place the corpses of the people of Israel in front of their idols.*   **6:7** [a] Ezek 7:4, 9   **6:8** [a] Jer 44:28; Ezek 5:2, 12; 12:16; 14:22   [b] Ezek 5:12   **6:9** [a] [Deut 4:29]; Ps 137; Jer 51:50   [b] Ps 78:40; Isa 7:13; 43:24; Hos 11:8   [c] Num 15:39; Ezek 20:7, 24   [d] Lev 26:39; Job 42:6; Ezek 20:43; 36:31   **6:11** [a] Ezek 21:14   [b] Ezek 5:12   **6:13** [a] Jer 2:20; 3:6   [b] 1 Kgs 14:23; 2 Kgs 16:4; Ezek 20:28; Hos 4:13   [c] Isa 57:5   **6:14** [a] Isa 5:25; Ezek 14:13; 20:33–34   [b] Num 33:46   [1] Vg. *Riblah.*   **7:2** [a] Ezek 7:3, 5, 6; 11:13; Amos 8:2, 10; [Matt 24:6, 13, 14]

end is coming on the four corners of the land![1] [3]The end is now upon you, and [a]I will release my anger against you. I will judge you according to your behavior; I will hold you accountable for all your abominable practices. [4][a]My eye will not pity you; I will not spare you. For I will hold you responsible for your behavior, and you will suffer [b]the consequences of your abominable practices. Then you will know that I am the LORD!

[5]"This is what the Sovereign LORD says: A [a]disaster[1]—a one-of-a-kind[2] disaster—is coming! [6]An end comes—the end comes! It has awakened against you! Look, it is coming![1] [7][a]Doom is coming upon you who live in [b]the land! The time is coming, the day is near. There are sounds of tumult, not shouts of joy, on the mountains.[1] [8]Soon now I will [a]pour out my rage on you; I will fully vent my anger against you. I will judge you according to your behavior. I will hold you accountable for all your abominable practices. [9]My eye will not pity you; I will not spare[1] you. For your behavior I will hold you accountable, and you will suffer the consequences of your abominable practices. Then you will know that it is I, the LORD, who is striking you.

[10]"Look, the day! Look, it is coming! [a]Doom has gone out! The staff has budded, pride has blossomed! [11][a]Violence has grown into a staff that supports wickedness. [b]Not one of them will be left[1]—not from their crowd, not from their wealth, not from their prominence. [12]The time has come; the day has struck! The customer should not [a]rejoice, nor the seller [b]mourn; for divine wrath comes against their whole crowd. [13]The customer will no longer pay the seller[1] while both parties are alive, for the vision against their whole crowd will not be revoked. Each person, for his iniquity, will fail to preserve his life.

[14]"They have blown the trumpet and everyone is ready, but no one goes to battle, because my anger is against their whole crowd. [15]The sword is outside; pestilence and famine are inside [a]the house. Whoever is in the open field will die by the sword, and famine and pestilence will consume everyone in the city. [16]Their [a]survivors will escape to the mountains and become like doves of the valleys; all of them will moan—each one for his iniquity. [17]All their [a]hands will hang limp; their knees will be wet with urine. [18]They will wear sackcloth, terror will cover them; shame will [a]be on all their faces, and all their heads will be shaved bald. [19]They will discard their [a]silver in the streets, and their gold will be treated like filth. Their silver and gold will not be able to deliver them on the day of the LORD's fury. They will not satisfy their hunger or fill their stomachs because their wealth was the obstacle leading to their iniquity. [20]They rendered the beauty of his ornaments into pride,[1] and with it they made their abominable images—their detestable idols. Therefore I will render it filthy to them. [21]I will give it to foreigners as [a]loot, to the world's wicked ones as plunder, and they will desecrate it. [22]I will turn my face away from them, and they will desecrate my treasured place. Vandals will enter it and desecrate it. [23](Make [a]the chain,[1] because the land is full of murder and the city is full of violence.) [24]I will bring the most [a]wicked of the nations, and they will take possession of their houses. [b]I will put an end to the arrogance of the strong, and their sanctuaries will be desecrated. [25]Terror is coming! They will seek peace, but find none. [26][a]Disaster after disaster will come, and one rumor after another. They will seek a vision from a prophet; priestly instruction will disappear, along with counsel from [b]the elders. [27]The king will mourn and the prince will be clothed with shuddering; the hands of the people of the land will tremble. Based on their behavior I will deal with them, and by their standard of justice I will judge them. Then they will know that I am the LORD!"

7:2 [1]Or earth.   7:3 [a][Rom 2:6]   7:4 [a]Ezek 5:11   [b]Ezek 12:20   7:5 [a]2 Kgs 21:12–13; Nah 1:9   [1]The Heb. term often refers to moral evil but can also mean calamity or disaster.   [2]Sev. MSS disaster after disaster.   7:6 [1]LXX omits all but the end is come.   7:7 [a]Ezek 7:10   [b]Zeph 1:14–15   [1]LXX neither tumult nor birth pains.   7:8 [a]Ezek 20:8, 21   7:9 [1]The Heb. term often refers to moral evil but can also mean calamity or disaster.   7:10 [a]Ezek 7:7   7:11 [a]Jer 6:7   [b]Jer 16:5–6; Ezek 24:16, 22   [1]LXX he will crush the wicked rod without confusion or haste.   7:12 [a]Prov 20:14; 1 Cor 7:30   [b]Isa 24:2   7:13 [1]MT The seller will not return to the sale.   7:15 [a]Deut 32:25; Jer 14:18; Lam 1:20; Ezek 5:12   7:16 [a]Ezra 9:15; Isa 37:31; Ezek 6:8; 14:22   7:17 [a]Isa 13:7; Jer 6:24; Ezek 21:7; Heb 12:12   7:18 [a]Isa 3:24; 15:2–3; Jer 48:37; Ezek 27:31; Amos 8:10   7:19 [a]Prov 11:4; Jer 15:13; Zeph 1:18   7:20 [1]MT he set up the beauty of his ornament as pride.   7:21 [a]2 Kgs 24:13; Jer 20:5   7:23 [a]2 Kgs 21:16   [1]LXX and they will make carnage.   7:24 [a]Ezek 21:31; 28:7   [b]2 Chr 7:20; Ezek 24:21   7:26 [a]Deut 32:23; Isa 47:11; Jer 4:20   [b]Ps 74:9; Lam 2:9; Ezek 20:1, 3; Mic 3:6

A Desecrated Temple

8 In [a]the sixth year, in [b]the sixth month, on the fifth of the month,[1] as I was sitting in my house with the elders of Judah sitting in front of me, the hand of the Sovereign LORD seized me. [2a]As [b]I watched, I noticed a form that appeared to be a man.[1] From his waist downward was something like fire,[2] and from his waist upward something like a brightness,[3] like an amber glow. [3]He [a]stretched out [b]the form[1] of a hand and grabbed me by a lock of hair on my head. Then a wind lifted me up between the earth and sky and [c]brought me to Jerusalem by divine visions, to the door of the inner gate that faces north [d]where the statue that [e]provokes to jealousy was located. [4]Then I perceived that the [a]glory of the God of Israel was there, as in the vision I had [b]seen earlier in the valley.

[5]He said to me, "Son of man, look up toward the north." So I looked up toward the north, and I noticed to the north of the altar gate was this statue of jealousy at the entrance.

[6]He said to me, "Son of man, do you see what they are doing—the great [a]abominations that the people of Israel are practicing here, to drive me far from my sanctuary? But you will see greater abominations than these!"

[7]He brought me to the entrance of the court, and as I watched, I noticed a hole in the wall. [8]He said to me, "Son of man, dig into the wall." So I dug into the wall and discovered a doorway.

[9]He said to me, "Go in and see the evil abominations they are practicing here." [10]So I went in and looked. I noticed every [a]figure of [b]creeping thing and beast—detestable images—and every idol of the house of Israel, engraved on the wall all around. [11a]Seventy men from the elders of the house of Israel (with Jaazaniah son of Shaphan standing among them) were standing in front of them, each with a censer in his hand, and fragrant vapors from a cloud of incense were swirling upward.

[12]He said to me, "Do you see, son of man, what [a]the elders of the house of Israel are doing in the dark, each in the chamber of his idolatrous images? For they think, 'The LORD does not see us! The LORD has abandoned the land!'" [13]He said to me, "You will see them practicing even greater abominations!"

[14]Then he brought me to the entrance of the north gate of the LORD's house. I noticed women sitting there weeping for Tammuz. [15]He said to me, "Do you see this, son of man? You will see even greater abominations than these!"

[16]Then he brought me to the inner court of the LORD's house. Right there at the entrance to the LORD's temple, [a]between the porch and the altar, [b]were about 25[1] men [c]with [d]their backs to the LORD's temple, facing east—they were worshiping the sun toward the east!

[17]He said to me, "Do you see, son of man? Is it a trivial thing that the house of Judah commits these abominations they are practicing here? For they have [a]filled the land with violence and provoked me to anger still further. Look, they are putting the branch to their nose! [18a]Therefore I will act with fury! My [b]eye will not pity them nor will I spare them. When they have [c]shouted in my ears, I will not listen to them."

The Execution of Idolaters

9 Then he shouted in my ears, "Approach,[1] you who are to visit destruction on the city, each with his destructive weapon in his hand!" [2]Next I noticed six men coming from the direction of the upper gate that faces north, each with his war club in his hand. Among them was [a]a man dressed in linen with a writing kit at his side. They came and stood beside the bronze altar.

[3]Then [a]the glory of the God of Israel went up from the cherub where it had rested to the threshold of the temple. He called to the man dressed in linen who had the writing kit at his side. [4]The LORD [a]said to him,

8:1 [a]Ezek 14:1; 20:1; 33:31 [b]Ezek 1:3; 3:22 [1]LXX *in the fifth month.*   8:2 [a]Ezek 1:26–27 [b]Ezek 1:4, 27 [1]MT *fire.* [2]LXX *from his waist to below was fire.* [3]LXX omits *like a brightness.*   8:3 [a]Dan 5:5 [b]Ezek 3:14; Acts 8:39 [c]Ezek 11:1, 24; 40:2 [d]Jer 7:30; 32:34; Ezek 5:11 [e]Exod 20:4; Deut 32:16, 21 [1]The Heb. word is normally used as an architectural term. 8:4 [a]Ezek 3:12; 9:3 [b]Ezek 1:28; 3:22–23 8:6 [a]2 Kgs 23:4–5; Ezek 5:11; 8:9, 17 8:10 [a]Exod 20:4; Deut 4:16–18 [b]Rom 1:23 8:11 [a]Num 11:16, 25; Luke 10:1 8:12 [a]Ps 14:1; Isa 29:15; Ezek 9:9 8:16 [a]Joel 2:17 [b]Ezek 11:1 [c]2 Chr 29:6; Jer 2:27; 32:33; Ezek 23:39 [d]Deut 4:19; 2 Kgs 23:5, 11; Job 31:26; Jer 44:17 [1]LXX *twenty.* 8:17 [a]Ezek 9:9; Amos 3:10; Mic 2:2 8:18 [a]Ezek 5:13; 16:42; 24:13 [b]Ezek 5:11; 7:4, 9; 9:5, 10 [c]Prov 1:28; Isa 1:15; Jer 11:11; 14:12; Mic 3:4; Zech 7:13 9:1 [1]Heb. *they approached.* 9:2 [a]Lev 16:4; Ezek 10:2; Rev 15:6 9:3 [a]Ezek 3:23; 8:4; 10:4, 18; 11:22–23 9:4 [a]Exod 12:7, 13; Ezek 9:6; [2 Cor 1:22; 2 Tim 2:19]; Rev 7:2–3; 9:4; 14:1

"Go through the city of Jerusalem and put a mark on the foreheads of the people [b]who moan and groan over all the abominations practiced in it."

[5]While I listened, he said to the others, "Go through the city after him and [a]strike people [b]down; do not let your eye pity nor spare anyone! [6]Old men, young men, young women, little children, and women—[a]wipe them out! But [b]do not touch anyone who has the mark. [c]Begin at my sanctuary!" [d]So they began with the elders who were at the front of the temple.

[7]He said to them, "Defile the temple and fill the courtyards with corpses. Go!" So they went out and struck people down throughout the city. [8]While they were striking them down, I was left alone, and I [a]threw myself face down and cried out, "[b]Ah, Sovereign LORD! Will you destroy the entire remnant of Israel when you pour out your fury on Jerusalem?"

[9]He said to me, "[a]The sin of [b]the house of Israel and Judah is extremely great; [c]the land is full of murder, and the city is full of corruption, for they say, 'The LORD has abandoned the land, and the LORD does not see!' [10]But as for me, my [a]eye [b]will not pity them nor will I spare them; I hereby repay them for what they have done."

[11]Next I noticed the man dressed in linen with the writing kit at his side bringing back word: "I have done just as you commanded me."

God's Glory Leaves the Temple

10 As I watched, I saw on the [a]platform above the top of the cherubim something like a sapphire, resembling the shape of a throne, appearing above them. [2]The LORD said to [a]the man dressed in linen, "Go between the wheelwork[1] underneath the cherubim.[2] Fill your hands with burning [b]coals from among the cherubim and [c]scatter them over the city." He went as I watched.

[3](The cherubim were standing on the south side of the temple when the man went in, and a [a]cloud filled the inner court.) [4]Then [a]the glory of [b]the LORD arose from the cherub and moved to the threshold of the temple. The temple was filled with the cloud while the court was filled with the brightness of the LORD's [c]glory. [5]The [a]sound of [b]the wings of the cherubim could be heard from the outer court, like the sound of the Sovereign God when he speaks.

[6]When the LORD commanded the man dressed in linen, "Take fire from within the wheelwork, from among the cherubim," the man went in and stood by one of the wheels. [7]Then one of the cherubim stretched out his hand toward the fire that was among the cherubim. He took some and put it into the hands of the man dressed in linen, who took it and left. [8](The cherubim appeared to have [a]the form[1] of human hands under their wings.)

[9a]As I watched, I noticed four wheels by the cherubim, one wheel beside each cherub; the wheels gleamed like [b]jasper. [10]As for their appearance, all four of them looked the same, something like a wheel within a wheel. [11a]When they moved, they would go in any of the four directions they faced without turning as they moved; in the direction the head would turn they would follow without turning as they moved, [12]along with their entire bodies,[1] their backs, their hands, and their wings. The wheels of the four of them were [a]full of eyes all around. [13]As for their wheels, they were called "the wheelwork" as I listened. [14]Each of the cherubim had four faces: The first was the face of [a]a cherub, the second that of a man, the third that of a lion, and the fourth that of an eagle.

[15]The cherubim rose up; [a]these were the living beings I saw at the Kebar River. [16]When the cherubim moved, the wheels moved beside them; [a]when the cherubim spread their wings to rise from the ground, the wheels did not move from their side. [17]When the cherubim stood still, the wheels stood still, and [a]when they rose up, the

9:4 [b]Ps 119:53, 136; Jer 13:17; Ezek 6:11; 21:6; 2 Cor 12:21; 2 Pet 2:8   9:5 [a]Ezek 7:9   [b]Ezek 5:11   9:6 [a]2 Chr 36:17   [b]Exod 12:23; Rev 9:4   [c]Jer 25:29; Amos 3:2; [Luke 12:42; 1 Pet 4:17]   [d]Ezek 8:11–12, 16   9:8 [a]Num 14:5; 16:4, 22, 45; Josh 7:6   [b]Ezek 11:13; Amos 7:2–6   9:9 [a]2 Kgs 21:16; Jer 2:34; Ezek 8:17   [b]Job 22:13; Ezek 8:12   [c]Ps 10:11; Isa 29:15   9:10 [a]Isa 65:6; Ezek 5:11; 7:4; 8:18   [b]Ezek 11:21; Hos 9:7   10:1 [a]Ezek 1:22, 26   10:2 [a]Ezek 9:2–3; Dan 10:5   [b]Ps 18:10–13; Isa 6:6; Ezek 1:13   [c]Rev 8:5   [1]The Heb. term often refers to chariot wheels.   [2]MT cherub.   10:3 [a]1 Kgs 8:10–11   10:4 [a]Ezek 1:28   [b]1 Kgs 8:10; Ezek 43:5   [c]Ezek 11:22–23   10:5 [a][Job 40:9]; Ezek 1:24; [Rev 10:3]   [b][Ps 29:3]   10:8 [a]Ezek 1:8; 10:21   [1]The Heb. word is normally used as an architectural term.   10:9 [a]Ezek 1:15   [b]Ezek 1:16   10:11 [a]Ezek 1:17   10:12 [a]Rev 4:6, 8   [1]LXX omits along with their entire bodies.   10:14 [a]1 Kgs 7:29, 36; Ezek 1:6, 10, 11; Rev 4:7   10:15 [a]Ezek 1:3, 5   10:16 [a]Ezek 1:19   10:17 [a]Ezek 1:12, 20, 21

wheels rose up with them, for the spirit of the living beings[1] was in the wheels.

[18]Then [a]the glory of the LORD moved [b]away from the threshold of the temple and stopped above the cherubim. [19]The cherubim spread [a]their wings, and they rose up from the earth while I watched (when they went, the wheels went alongside them). They stopped at the entrance to the [b]east gate of the LORD's temple as the glory of the God of Israel hovered above them.

[20]These were the living creatures that [a]I saw at the Kebar River underneath the God of Israel; I knew that they were cherubim. [21]Each had four faces; [a]each had four wings and the form of human hands under the wings. [22]As for [a]the form of their faces, [b]they were the faces whose appearance I had seen at the Kebar River. Each one moved straight ahead.

The Fall of Jerusalem

11 A wind lifted me up and brought me to [a]the east gate of [b]the LORD's temple [c]that faces the east. There, at the entrance of the gate, I noticed 25 men. Among them I saw Jaazaniah son of Azzur and Pelatiah son of Benaiah, officials of the people. [2]The LORD said to me, "Son of man, these are the men who plot evil and give wicked advice in this city. [3]They say,[1] 'The time is not [a]near to build houses; the city [b]is a cooking pot, and we are the meat in it.' [4]Therefore, prophesy against them! Prophesy, son of man!"

[5]Then [a]the [b]Spirit of the LORD came upon me and said to me, "Say: 'This is what the LORD says: This is what you are thinking, O house of Israel; I know what goes through your minds. [6]You have killed many people in this city; [a]you have filled its streets with corpses.' [7]Therefore, this is what the Sovereign LORD says: 'The corpses [a]you have dumped in the midst of the city are the meat, and this city is the cooking pot, [b]but I will take you out of it.'[1] [8]You [a]fear the sword, so the sword I will bring against you,' declares the Sovereign LORD.

[9]'But I will take you out of the city. And I will hand you over to foreigners. I will [a]execute judgments on you. [10]You will die by the sword; I will judge [a]you at [b]the border of Israel. [c]Then you will know that I am the LORD. [11]This [a]city will not be a cooking pot for you, and you will not be meat within it; I will judge you at the border of Israel. [12]Then you will know that I am the LORD, whose statutes you [a]have not followed and whose regulations you have not carried out. Instead you have behaved according to the regulations of the nations around you!'"

[13]Now, while I was prophesying, [a]Pelatiah son of [b]Benaiah died. Then I threw myself face down and cried out with a loud voice, "Alas, Sovereign LORD! You are completely wiping out the remnant of Israel!"[1]

[14]Then the LORD's message came to me: [15]"Son of man, your brothers,[1] your relatives,[2] and the whole house of Israel, all of them are those to whom the inhabitants of Jerusalem have said, 'They have gone far away[3] from the LORD; to us this land has been given as a possession.'

[16]"Therefore say: 'This is what the Sovereign LORD says: Although I have removed them far away among the nations and have dispersed them among the countries, I have been a little sanctuary for them among the lands where they have gone.'

[17]"Therefore say: '[a]This is what the Sovereign LORD says: When I regather you from the peoples and assemble you from the lands where you have been dispersed, I will give you back the country of Israel.'

[18]"When they return to it, they will remove from it all its [a]detestable things and all its abominations. [19]I [a]will give them one [b]heart and I will put a new spirit within [c]them;[1] I will remove the hearts of stone from their bodies and I will give them tender hearts, [20]so [a]that they may follow my statutes [b]and observe my regulations and carry them out. Then they will be my people, and I will be their God. [21]But those whose hearts are devoted to detestable

---

10:17 [1] Heb. *living creature.*   **10:18** [a] Ezek 10:4   [b] Hos 9:12   **10:19** [a] Ezek 11:22   [b] Ezek 11:1   **10:20** [a] Ezek 1:22   **10:21** [a] Ezek 1:6, 8; 10:14; 41:18–19   **10:22** [a] Ezek 1:10   [b] Ezek 1:9, 12   **11:1** [a] Ezek 3:12, 14   [b] Ezek 10:19   [c] Ezek 8:16   **11:3** [a] Ezek 12:22, 27; 2 Pet 3:4   [b] Jer 1:13; Ezek 11:7, 11; 24:3, 6   [1] Or *think.*   **11:5** [a] Ezek 2:2; 3:24   [b] [Jer 16:17; 17:10]   **11:6** [a] Isa 1:15; Ezek 7:23; 22:2–6, 9, 12, 27   **11:7** [a] Ezek 24:3, 6; Mic 3:2–3   [b] 2 Kgs 25:18–22; Jer 52:24–27; Ezek 11:9   [1] MT *he brought out.*   **11:8** [a] Jer 42:16   **11:9** [a] Ezek 5:8   **11:10** [a] 2 Kgs 25:19–21; Jer 39:6; 52:10   [b] 1 Kgs 8:65; 2 Kgs 14:25   [c] Ps 9:16; Ezek 6:7; 13:9, 14, 21, 23   **11:11** [a] Ezek 11:3, 7   **11:12** [a] Lev 18:3, 24; Deut 12:30–31; Ezek 8:10, 14, 16   **11:13** [a] Acts 5:5   [b] Ezek 9:8   [1] LXX presents this as a question.   **11:15** [1] MT *your brothers, your brothers.*   [2] MT *your redemption-men;* LXX, Syr. *your fellow exiles.*   [3] MT *go far!*   **11:17** [a] Isa 11:11–16; Jer 3:12, 18; 24:5; Ezek 20:41–42; 28:5   **11:18** [a] Ezek 37:23   **11:19** [a] Jer 32:39; Ezek 36:26; Zeph 3:9   [b] Ps 51:10; [Jer 31:33]; Ezek 18:31   [c] Zech 7:12; [Rom 2:4–5]   [1] MT *you.*   **11:20** [a] Ps 105:45   [b] Jer 24:7; Ezek 14:11; 36:28; 37:27

ᵃthings and abominations, I hereby repay them for what they have done, says the Sovereign Lord."

²²Then the cherubim ᵃspread their wings with their wheels alongside them while the glory of the God of Israel hovered above them. ²³The glory of ᵃthe Lord rose up from within the city and stopped over the mountain east of it. ²⁴Then a wind lifted me up and carried me to ᵃthe exiles in Babylonia, in the vision given to me by the Spirit of God.

Then the vision I had seen went up from me. ²⁵So I told the exiles everything the Lord had shown me.

Previewing the Exile

12 The Lord's message came to me: ²"Son of ᵃman, you are living in the midst of ᵇa rebellious house. They have eyes to see, but do not see, and ears to hear, but do not hear, because they are a rebellious house.

³"Therefore, son of man, pack up your belongings as if for exile. During the day, while they are watching, pretend to go into exile. Go from where you live to another place. Perhaps they will understand, although they are a rebellious house. ⁴Bring out your belongings packed for exile during the day while they are watching. And go out at evening, while they are watching, as if for exile. ⁵While they are watching, dig a hole in the wall and carry your belongings out through it. ⁶While they are watching, raise your baggage onto your shoulder and carry it out in the dark. You must cover your face so that you cannot see the ground because I have made you an object lesson to the house of Israel."

⁷So I did just as I was commanded. I carried out my belongings packed for exile during the day, and at evening I dug myself a hole through the wall with my hands. I went out in the darkness, carrying my baggage on my shoulder while they watched.

⁸The Lord's message came to me in the morning: ⁹"Son of man, has not ᵃthe house of Israel, that rebellious house, said to you, 'ᵇWhat are you doing?' ¹⁰Say to them, 'This is what the Sovereign Lord says: The prince will raise this ᵃburden in Jerusalem,¹ and all the house of Israel within it.'² ¹¹Say, 'ᵃI am an object lesson for you. Just as I have done, so it will be done to them; ᵇthey will go into exile and captivity.'

¹²"The prince who is among ᵃthem will raise his belongings onto his shoulder in darkness and will go out. He¹ will dig a hole in the wall to leave through. He will cover his face so that he cannot see the land with his eyes. ¹³But I will throw my ᵃnet over ᵇhim, and he will be caught in my snare. I will bring him to Babylon, the land of the Chaldeans (but he will not see it), and there he will die. ¹⁴All ᵃhis ᵇretinue—his attendants and his troops—I will scatter to every wind; I will unleash a sword behind them.

¹⁵"Then they will know that I am ᵃthe Lord when I disperse them among the nations and scatter them among foreign countries. ¹⁶ᵃBut I will let a small number of them survive the sword, famine, and pestilence, so that they can confess all their abominable practices to the nations where they go. Then they will know that I am the Lord."

¹⁷The Lord's message came to me: ¹⁸"Son of man, ᵃeat your bread with trembling and drink your water with anxious shaking. ¹⁹Then say to the people of the land, 'This is what the Sovereign Lord says about the inhabitants of Jerusalem and of the land of Israel: They will eat their bread with anxiety and drink their water in fright, for their land will ᵃbe stripped bare of all it contains ᵇbecause of the violence of all who live in it. ²⁰The inhabited towns will be left in ruins, and the land will be devastated. Then you will know that I am the Lord.'"

²¹The Lord's message came to me: ²²"Son of man, what is this proverb you have in ᵃthe land of Israel, 'The days pass slowly, and every vision fails'? ²³Therefore tell ᵃthem, 'This is what the Sovereign Lord says: I hereby end this proverb; they will not recite it in Israel any longer.' But say to them, 'The days are at hand when every vision will be

11:21 ᵃEzek 9:10   11:22 ᵃEzek 1:19   11:23 ᵃEzek 8:4; 9:3   11:24 ᵃEzek 8:3; 2 Cor 12:2–4   12:2 ᵃIsa 1:23; Ezek 2:3, 6–8   ᵇIsa 6:9; 42:20; Jer 5:21; Matt 13:13–14; Mark 4:12; 8:18; [Luke 8:10; John 9:39–41; 12:40]; Acts 28:26; Rom 11:8   12:9 ᵃEzek 2:5   ᵇEzek 17:12; 24:19   12:10 ᵃMal 1:1   ¹MT *The prince, the load/oracle, this, in Jerusalem.*   ²MT *within them.*   12:11 ᵃEzek 12:6   ᵇ2 Kgs 25:4–5, 7   12:12 ᵃ2 Kgs 25:4; Jer 39:4; 52:7; Ezek 12:6   ¹MT *they.*   12:13 ᵃJob 19:6; Jer 52:9; Lam 1:13; Ezek 17:20   ᵇ2 Kgs 25:7; Jer 52:11; Ezek 17:16   12:14 ᵃ2 Kgs 25:4; Ezek 5:10   ᵇEzek 5:2, 12   12:15 ᵃ[Ps 9:16]; Ezek 6:7, 14; 12:16, 20   12:16 ᵃ2 Kgs 25:11, 22; Ezek 6:8–10   12:18 ᵃLam 5:9; Ezek 4:16   12:19 ᵃJer 10:22; Ezek 6:6–7, 14; Mic 7:13; Zech 7:14   ᵇPs 107:34   12:22 ᵃJer 5:12; Ezek 11:3; 12:27; Amos 6:3; 2 Pet 3:4   12:23 ᵃPs 37:13; Joel 2:1; Zeph 1:14

fulfilled. [24] For there will [a] no longer be any [b] false visions or flattering omens amidst the house of Israel. [25] For I, [a] the LORD, will speak. Whatever word I speak will be [b] accomplished. It will not be delayed any longer. Indeed in your days, O rebellious house, I will speak the word and accomplish it, declares the Sovereign LORD.'"

[26] The LORD's message came to me: [27] "Take note, [a] son of man, the house of Israel is saying, 'The vision that he sees is [b] for distant days; he is prophesying about the far future.' [28] [a] Therefore say to them, 'This is what the Sovereign LORD says: None of my words [b] will be delayed any longer! The word I speak will come to pass, declares the Sovereign LORD.'"

False Prophets Denounced

13 Then the LORD's message came to me: [2] "Son of man, prophesy [a] against the prophets of Israel who are now prophesying. Say to the prophets [b] who prophesy from their [c] imagination: 'Listen to the LORD's message! [3] This is what the Sovereign LORD says: Woe to the foolish prophets who follow their own spirit but have seen nothing! [4] Your prophets have become [a] like jackals among the ruins, O Israel. [5] You [a] have not gone up in the breaks in the wall, nor repaired a wall for the house of Israel that it would stand strong in the battle on the day of the LORD. [6] They see delusion and their omens are a lie. [a] They say, "The LORD declares," though the LORD has [b] not sent them; yet they expect their word to be confirmed. [7] Have you not seen a false vision and announced a lying omen when you say, "The LORD declares," although I myself never spoke?

[8] "'Therefore, this is what the Sovereign LORD says: Because you have spoken false words and forecast delusion, look, I am against you,[1] declares the Sovereign LORD. [9] My hand will be [a] against the prophets who see delusion and [b] announce lying omens. They will not be included in the council of my people, [c] nor be written in the registry of the house of Israel, [d] nor enter [e] the land of Israel. Then you will know that I am the Sovereign LORD.

[10] "'This is because they have led my people astray saying, "All is [a] well," when things are not well. When anyone builds a wall without mortar, they [b] coat it with whitewash. [11] Tell [a] the ones who coat it with whitewash that it will fall. When there is a deluge of rain, hailstones will fall and a violent wind will break out. [12] When the wall has collapsed, people will ask you, "Where is the whitewash you coated it with?"

[13] "'Therefore this is what the Sovereign LORD says: In my rage I will make a violent wind break out. In my anger there will be a deluge of rain and hailstones in destructive fury. [14] I will break down [a] the wall you coated with whitewash and knock it to the ground so that its foundation is exposed. When it falls you will be destroyed beneath it, and you will know that I am the LORD. [15] I will vent my rage against the wall and against those who coated it with whitewash. Then I will say to you, "The wall is no more and those who whitewashed it are no more—[16] those prophets of Israel who would prophesy about Jerusalem and would [a] see visions of peace for it, when there was no peace," declares the Sovereign LORD.'

[17] "As for you, son of man, [a] turn toward the daughters of your people [b] who are prophesying from their imagination. Prophesy against them [18] and say 'This is what the Sovereign LORD says: Woe to those who sew bands on all their wrists and make headbands for heads of every size to [a] entrap people's lives! Will you entrap my people's lives, yet preserve your own lives? [19] You have profaned me among my people [a] for handfuls of barley and scraps of bread. You have put to death people who should not die and kept alive those who should not live by your lies to my people, who listen to lies!

[20] "'Therefore, this is what the Sovereign LORD says: Take note that I am against your wristbands with which you entrap people's lives like birds. I will tear them from your arms and will release the people's lives, which you hunt like birds. [21] I will tear off

12:24 [a] Jer 14:13–16; Ezek 13:6; Zech 13:2–4 [b] Lam 2:14 12:25 [a] [Isa 55:11]; Dan 9:12; [Luke 21:33] [b] Num 23:19; [Isa 14:24] 12:27 [a] Ezek 12:22 [b] Dan 10:14 12:28 [a] Ezek 12:23, 25 [b] Jer 4:7 13:2 [a] Isa 28:7; Jer 23:1–40; Lam 2:14; Ezek 22:25–28 [b] Ezek 13:17 [c] Jer 14:14; 23:16, 26 13:4 [a] Song 2:15 13:5 [a] Ps 106:23; [Jer 23:22]; Ezek 22:30 13:6 [a] Jer 29:8; Ezek 22:28 [b] Jer 27:8–15 13:8 [1] Or I challenge you; perhaps a formula for challenging someone to combat or a duel. 13:9 [a] Jer 23:30 [b] Jer 20:3–6 [c] Ezra 2:59, 62; Neh 7:5; [Ps 69:28] [d] Jer 20:3–6 [e] Ezek 11:10, 12 13:10 [a] Jer 6:14; 8:11 [b] Ezek 22:28 13:11 [a] Ezek 38:22 13:14 [a] Ezek 13:9, 21, 23; 14:8 13:16 [a] Jer 6:14; 8:11; 28:9; Ezek 13:10 13:17 [a] Ezek 20:46; 21:2 [b] Ezek 13:2; Rev 2:20 13:18 [a] [2 Pet 2:14] 13:19 [a] 1 Sam 2:15–17; Prov 28:21; Mic 3:5; Rom 16:18; 1 Pet 5:2

your headbands and rescue my people from your power; they will no longer be prey in your hands. [a]Then you will know that I am the LORD. [22]This is because you have disheartened the righteous person with [a]lies (although I have not grieved him), and because you have [b]encouraged the wicked person not to turn from his evil conduct and preserve his life. [23]Therefore [a]you will no longer see false visions and practice divination. I will rescue my people from your power, and you[1] will know that I am the LORD.'"

Well-Deserved Judgment

14 Then some [a]men from Israel's elders came to me and sat down in front of me. [2]The LORD's message came to me: [3]"Son of man, these men have erected their idols in their hearts and placed the obstacle leading to their iniquity right before their faces. [a]Should I really allow them to seek me? [4]Therefore speak to them and say to them, 'This is what the Sovereign LORD says: When anyone from the house of Israel erects his idols in his heart and sets the obstacle leading to his iniquity before his face, and then consults a prophet, I, the LORD, am determined to answer him personally according to the enormity of his idolatry. [5]I will do this in order to capture the hearts of the house of Israel, who have alienated themselves from me on account of all their idols.'

[6]"Therefore say to the house of Israel, 'This is what the Sovereign LORD says: [a]Return! Turn from your idols, and turn your faces away from your abominations. [7]For when anyone from the house of Israel, or the resident foreigner who lives in Israel, separates himself from me and erects his idols in his heart and sets the obstacle leading to his iniquity before his face, and then consults a prophet to seek something from me, I, the LORD, am determined to answer him personally. [8]I [a]will set my face against that person and will make him an object [b]lesson and a byword and will cut him off from among my people. [c]Then you will know that I am the LORD.

[9]"'As for the prophet, if he is made [a]a fool by being deceived into speaking a prophetic word—I, the LORD, have made a fool of that prophet, and I will stretch out my hand against him and destroy him from among my people Israel. [10]They will bear their punishment; the punishment of the one who sought an oracle will be the same as the punishment of the prophet who gave it [11]so that the house of Israel will [a]no longer go astray from me, nor continue to defile themselves by all their sins. They will be my people, and I will be their God, declares the Sovereign LORD.'"

[12]The LORD's message came to me: [13]"Son of man, suppose a country sins against me by being unfaithful and I stretch out my hand against it, cut off its bread [a]supply,[1] cause famine to come on it, and kill both people and animals. [14a]Even if these three men, Noah, Daniel, and Job, were in it, they would save only their own lives [b]by their righteousness, declares the Sovereign LORD.

[15]"Suppose I were to send [a]wild animals through the land and kill its children, leaving it desolate, without travelers due to the wild animals. [16]Even if these three men were in it, as surely as I live, declares the Sovereign LORD, they could not save their own sons or daughters; they would save only their own lives, and the land would become [a]desolate.

[17]"Or suppose [a]I were to bring a sword against that land and say, 'Let a sword pass through the land,' and I were to kill both people and animals. [18]Even if these three men were in it, as surely as I live, declares the Sovereign LORD, they could not save their own sons or daughters—they would save only their own lives.

[19]"Or suppose I were to send [a]a plague into that land and [b]pour out my rage on it with bloodshed, killing both people and animals. [20]Even if Noah, Daniel, and Job were in it, as surely as I live, declares the Sovereign LORD, they could not save their own son or daughter; they would save only their own lives by their righteousness.

13:21 [a] Ezek 13:9 **13:22** [a] Jer 28:15 [b] Jer 23:14 **13:23** [a] Ezek 12:24; 13:6; Mic 3:5–6; Zech 13:3 [1] The false prophetesses. **14:1** [a] 2 Kgs 6:32; Ezek 8:1; 20:1; 33:31 **14:3** [a] 2 Kgs 3:13; Isa 1:15; Jer 11:11; Ezek 20:3, 31 **14:6** [a] 1 Sam 7:3; Neh 1:9; Isa 2:20; 30:22; 55:6–7; Ezek 18:30 **14:8** [a] Lev 17:10; 20:3, 5, 6; Jer 44:11; Ezek 15:7 [b] Num 26:10; Deut 28:37; Ezek 5:15 [c] Ezek 6:7; 13:14 **14:9** [a] 1 Kgs 22:23; Job 12:16; Isa 66:4; Jer 4:10; 2 Thess 2:11 **14:11** [a] Ps 119:67, 71; Jer 31:18–19; [Heb 12:11]; 2 Pet 2:15 **14:13** [a] Lev 26:26; 2 Kgs 25:3; Isa 3:1; Jer 52:6; Ezek 4:16; 5:16 [1] Heb. *break its staff of bread*; the bread supply is compared to a staff used for support. **14:14** [a] Jer 15:1 [b] [Prov 11:4] **14:15** [a] Lev 26:22; Num 21:6; Ezek 5:17; 14:21 **14:16** [a] Ezek 15:8; 33:28–29 **14:17** [a] Lev 26:25; Ezek 5:12; 21:3–4; 29:8; 38:21 **14:19** [a] 2 Sam 24:15; Ezek 38:22 [b] Ezek 7:8

[21] "For [a]this is what the Sovereign LORD says: How much worse will it be when I send my four terrible judgments—sword, famine, wild animals, and plague—to Jerusalem to kill both people and animals! [22a]Yet some survivors will be left in it, sons and daughters who will be [b]brought out. They will come out to [c]you, and when you see their behavior and their deeds, you will be consoled about the catastrophe I have brought on Jerusalem—for everything I brought on it. [23]They will console you when you see their behavior and their deeds, because you will know that [a]it was not without reason that I have done everything that I have done in it, declares the Sovereign LORD."

Burning a Useless Vine

15 The LORD's message came to me: [2]"Son of man, of all the woody branches among the trees of the forest, what happens to the wood of the vine? [3]Can wood be taken from it to make anything useful? Or can anyone make a peg from it to hang things on? [4]No! [a]It is thrown in the fire for fuel; when the fire has burned up both ends of it and it is charred in the middle, will it be useful for anything? [5]Indeed! If it was not made into anything useful when it was whole, how much less can it be made into anything when the fire has burned it up and it is charred? [6]"Therefore, this is what the Sovereign LORD says: Like the wood of the vine is among the trees of the forest that I have provided as fuel for the fire—so I will provide the residents of Jerusalem as fuel. [7]I [a]will set my face against them—although [b]they have escaped from [c]the fire, the fire will still consume them! Then you will know that I am the LORD, when I set my face against them. [8]I will make the land desolate because they have acted unfaithfully, declares the Sovereign LORD."

God's Unfaithful Bride

16 The LORD's message came to me: [2]"Son of man, confront Jerusalem with her abominable practices [3]and say, 'This is what the Sovereign LORD says to Jerusalem: Your origin [a]and [b]your birth were in the land of the Canaanites; your father was an Amorite and your mother a Hittite. [4]As for your birth, [a]on the day you were born your umbilical cord was not cut, nor were you washed in water; you were certainly not rubbed down with salt, nor wrapped with blankets. [5]No eye took pity on you to do even one of these things for you to spare you; you were thrown out into the open field because you were detested on the day you were born.

[6]"I passed by you and saw you kicking around helplessly in your blood. I said to you as you lay there in your blood, "Live!" I said to you as you lay there in your blood, "Live!" [7]I made you [a]plentiful like sprouts in a field; you grew tall and came of age so that you could wear jewelry. Your breasts had formed and your hair had grown, but you were still naked and bare.

[8]"Then I passed by you and watched you, noticing that you had reached the age for love. I spread my cloak over you and covered your nakedness. I swore a [a]solemn [b]oath to you and entered into a marriage [c]covenant with [d]you, declares the Sovereign LORD, and you became mine.

[9]"Then I bathed you in water, washed the blood off you, and anointed you with fragrant oil. [10]I dressed you in embroidered clothing and put fine leather sandals on your feet. I wrapped you with fine linen and covered you with silk. [11]I adorned you with jewelry. I [a]put bracelets on your [b]hands and a necklace around your neck. [12]I put a ring in your nose, earrings on your ears, and a beautiful crown on your head. [13]You were adorned with gold and silver, while [a]your clothing was of fine linen, silk, and embroidery. You ate the finest flour, honey, and olive oil. You became extremely [b]beautiful and attained the position of royalty. [14]Your fame spread among the nations because of [a]your beauty; your beauty was perfect because of the splendor that I bestowed on you, declares the Sovereign LORD.

[15]"But you trusted in your beauty and capitalized on your fame by becoming [b]a

14:21 [a] Ezek 5:17; 33:27; Amos 4:6–10; Rev 6:8   **14:22** [a] 2 Kgs 25:11–12; Ezra 2:1; Ezek 12:16; 36:20   [b] Ezek 6:8   [c] Ezek 20:43   **14:23** [a] Jer 22:8–9   **15:4** [a] [John 15:6]   **15:7** [a] Lev 26:17; [Ps 34:16]; Jer 21:10; Ezek 14:8   [b] Isa 24:18   [c] Ezek 7:4   **16:3** [a] Ezek 21:30   [b] Gen 15:16; Deut 7:1; Josh 24:15; Ezek 16:45   **16:4** [a] Hos 2:3   **16:6** [1] A few wss omit the second *I said to you as you lay there in your blood, "Live!"*.   **16:7** [a] Exod 1:7; Deut 1:10   **16:8** [a] Ruth 3:9; Jer 2:2   [b] Gen 22:16–18   [c] Exod 24:6–8   [d] [Exod 19:5]; Jer 2:2; Ezek 20:5; [Hos 2:19–20]   **16:11** [a] Gen 24:22, 47; Isa 3:19; Ezek 23:42   [b] Gen 41:42; Prov 1:9   **16:13** [a] Deut 32:13–14   [b] Ps 48:2   **16:14** [a] Ps 50:2; Lam 2:15   **16:15** [a] Deut 32:15; Jer 7:4; Mic 3:11   [b] Isa 1:21; 57:8; Jer 2:20; 3:2, 6, 20; Ezek 23:11–20; Hos 1:2

prostitute. You offered your sexual favors to every man who passed by so that your beauty became his. [16]You took some of [a]your clothing and made for yourself decorated high places; you engaged in prostitution on them. You went to him to become his.[1] [17]You also took your beautiful jewelry, made of my gold and my silver I had given to you, and made for yourself male images and engaged in prostitution[1] with them. [18]You took your embroidered clothing and used it to cover them; you offered my olive oil and my incense to them. [19]As for [a]my food that I gave you—the fine flour, olive oil, and honey I fed you—you placed it before them as a soothing aroma. That is exactly what happened, declares the Sovereign LORD.

[20]"[a]You took your sons and your daughters whom you bore to me and you sacrificed them as food for the idols to eat. As if your prostitution was not enough, [21]you slaughtered my children and sacrificed them to the idols. [22]And with all your abominable practices and prostitution you did not remember the days of your [a]youth [b]when you were naked and bare, kicking around in your blood.

[23]"After all your evil—"Woe! Woe to you!" declares the Sovereign LORD—[24]you built [a]yourself a chamber and put [b]up a pavilion in every public square. [25]At the head of every street you erected your pavilion, and you disgraced your beauty when you spread your legs to every passerby and multiplied your promiscuity. [26]You engaged in prostitution with [a]the Egyptians, your lustful neighbors,[1] multiplying your promiscuity and provoking me to anger. [27]So see here, I have stretched out my hand against you and cut off your rations. I have delivered you into [a]the power of those who hate you, the daughters of the Philistines, who were ashamed of your obscene conduct. [28]You engaged in prostitution with the [a]Assyrians because your desires were insatiable; you prostituted yourself with them and yet you were still not satisfied. [29]Then you multiplied your promiscuity to the land of merchants, [a]Babylonia, but you were not satisfied there either.

[30]"How sick is your heart, declares the Sovereign LORD, when you perform all these acts, the deeds of a bold prostitute. [31]When [a]you built your chamber at the head of every street and put up your pavilion in every public square, you were not like a prostitute, because you scoffed at [b]payment.

[32]"Adulterous wife, who prefers strangers instead of her own husband! [33]All prostitutes receive payment, but instead [a]you give gifts to every one of your lovers. You bribe them to come to you from all around for your sexual favors! [34]You were different from other prostitutes because no one solicited you. When you gave payment and no payment was given to you, you became the opposite!

[35]"Therefore, you prostitute, listen to the LORD's message! [36]This is what [a]the Sovereign LORD says: Because your lust was poured out and your nakedness was uncovered in your prostitution with your lovers, and because of all your detestable idols, and because of the blood of your children you have given to them, [37]therefore, take note: [a]I am about to gather all your lovers whom you enjoyed, both all those you loved and all those you hated. I will gather them against you from all around, and I will expose your nakedness to them, and they will see all your nakedness. [38]I will punish you as an adulteress and [a]murderer deserves. I will avenge your bloody deeds with furious rage. [39]I will give [a]you into their hands, and [b]they will destroy your chambers and tear down your pavilions. They will strip you of your clothing and take your beautiful jewelry and leave you naked and bare. [40][a]They will summon [b]a mob who will stone you and hack you in pieces with their swords. [41]They will [a]burn down your houses and [b]execute judgments on you in front of many women. Thus I will put a [c]stop to your prostitution, and you will no longer give gifts to your

16:16 [a] 2 Kgs 23:7; Ezek 7:20; Hos 2:8   [1] MT *not coming* [pl.] *and he will not.*   16:17 [1] Or perhaps *and worshiped them.*
16:19 [a] Hos 2:8   16:20 [a] 2 Kgs 16:3; Ps 106:37; Isa 57:5; Jer 7:31; Ezek 20:26   16:22 [a] Jer 2:2; Hos 11:1   [b] Ezek 16:4-6
16:24 [a] Jer 11:13; Ezek 16:31, 39; 20:28-29   [b] Ps 78:58; Isa 57:7; Jer 2:20; 3:2   16:26 [a] Ezek 16:26; 20:7-8   [1] Heb. *your neighbors, large of flesh*; "flesh" is used here of the genitals, perhaps referring simply to their size or to the idea that they are lustful.   16:27 [a] 2 Chr 28:18; Isa 9:12; Ezek 16:57   16:28 [a] 2 Kgs 16:7, 10-18; 2 Chr 28:16, 20-23; Jer 2:18, 36; Ezek 23:12; Hos 10:6   16:29 [a] Ezek 23:14-17   16:31 [a] Ezek 16:24, 39   [b] Isa 52:3   16:33 [a] Isa 30:6; 57:9; Ezek 16:41; Hos 8:9-10
16:36 [a] Jer 2:34; Ezek 16:20   16:37 [a] Jer 13:22, 26; Lam 1:8; Ezek 23:9-10, 22, 29; Hos 2:10; 8:10; Nah 3:5   16:38 [a] Gen 9:6; Exod 21:12; Ezek 16:20, 36   16:39 [a] Ezek 16:24, 31   [b] Ezek 23:26; Hos 2:3   16:40 [a] Ezek 23:45-47; Hab 1:6-10   [b] John 8:5, 7   16:41 [a] Deut 13:16; 2 Kgs 25:9; Jer 39:8; 52:13   [b] Ezek 5:8; 23:10, 48   [c] Ezek 23:27

clients. [42]I [a]will exhaust my rage on you, and then my fury will turn from you. I will calm down and no longer be angry.

[43]"'Because [a]you [b]did not remember the days of your youth and have enraged me with all these deeds, I hereby repay you for what you have done, declares the Sovereign LORD. Have you not engaged in prostitution on top of all your other abominable practices?

[44]"'Observe—everyone who quotes proverbs will quote this proverb about you: "Like mother, like daughter." [45]You are the daughter of your mother, who detested her husband and her sons, and you are the [a]sister of [b]your sisters, who detested their husbands and their sons. Your mother was a Hittite and your father an Amorite. [46]Your older sister was Samaria, who lived north[1] of [a]you with her daughters, and your younger sister, who lived south[2] of you, was Sodom with her daughters. [47]Have [a]you not copied their behavior and practiced their abominable deeds? In a short time you became even more depraved in all your conduct than they were! [48]As surely as I live, declares the Sovereign LORD, [a]your sister Sodom and her daughters never behaved as wickedly as you and your daughters have behaved.

[49]"'See here—this was the iniquity of your sister Sodom: She and her daughters had majesty, [a]abundance of food, and enjoyed carefree ease, but they did not help the poor and needy. [50]They were haughty and [a]practiced [b]abominable deeds before me. Therefore, when I saw it I removed them. [51]Samaria has not committed [a]half the sins you [b]have; you have done more abominable deeds than they did. You have made your sisters appear righteous with all the abominable things you have done. [52]So now, bear your disgrace, because you have given your sisters reason to justify their behavior. Because the sins you have committed were more abominable than those of your sisters; they have become more righteous than you. So now, be ashamed and bear the disgrace of making your sisters appear righteous.

[53]"'I will restore [b]their fortunes, the fortunes of Sodom and her daughters, and the fortunes of Samaria and her daughters (along with your fortunes among them), [54]so that [a]you may bear your disgrace and be ashamed of all you have done in consoling them. [55]As for your sisters, Sodom and her daughters will be restored to their former status, Samaria and her daughters will be restored to their former status, and you and your daughters will be restored to your former status. [56]In your days of majesty, was not Sodom your sister a byword in your mouth, [57]before your evil was exposed? Now you have become an object of [a]scorn to [b]the daughters of Aram[1] and all those around her and to the daughters of the Philistines—those all around you who despise you. [58]You must bear [a]your punishment for your obscene conduct and your abominable practices, declares the LORD.

[59]"'For this is what the Sovereign LORD says: I will deal with you according to what you have done when you [a]despised your oath by breaking your covenant. [60]Yet I will [a]remember the [b]covenant I made with you in the days of your youth, and I will establish a lasting covenant with you. [61]Then [a]you will remember your conduct and be ashamed when you receive your older and younger sisters. I will give them to you as [b]daughters, [c]but not on account of my covenant with you. [62]I will establish my covenant with you, [a]and then you will know that I am the LORD. [63]Then you will [a]remember, be ashamed, [b]and remain silent because of your disgrace when I make atonement for all you have done, declares the Sovereign LORD.'"

A Parable of Two Eagles and a Vine

17 The LORD's message came to me: [2]"Son of man, offer a riddle and tell a [a]parable to the house of Israel. [3]Say to them: 'This is [a]what the Sovereign LORD says:

"'A great eagle with broad wings, long feathers,

16:42 [a] 2 Sam 24:25; Ezek 5:13; 21:17; Zech 6:8 **16:43** [a] Ps 78:42; Ezek 16:22 [b] Ezek 9:10; 11:21; 22:31 **16:45** [a] Ezek 23:2–4 [b] Ezek 16:3 **16:46** [a] Deut 32:32; Isa 1:10 [1] Heb. *left.* [2] Heb. *right.* **16:47** [a] 2 Kgs 21:9; Ezek 5:6–7 **16:48** [a] Isa 3:9; Lam 4:6; Matt 10:15; 11:24; Rev 11:8 **16:49** [a] Gen 13:10; Isa 22:13; Amos 6:4–6 **16:50** [a] Gen 13:13; 18:20; 19:5 [b] Gen 19:24 **16:51** [a] Ezek 23:11 [b] Jer 3:8–11; Matt 12:41 **16:53** [a] Isa 1:9; [Ezek 16:60] [b] Jer 20:16 **16:54** [a] Ezek 14:22 **16:57** [a] 2 Kgs 16:5; 2 Chr 28:18; Isa 7:1; Ezek 5:14–15; 22:4 [b] Ezek 16:27 [1] Many wss *Edom.* **16:58** [a] Ezek 23:49 **16:59** [a] Ezek 17:13 **16:60** [a] Lev 26:42–45; Ps 106:45 [b] Isa 55:3; Jer 32:40; 50:5; Ezek 37:26 **16:61** [a] Jer 50:4–5; Ezek 20:43; 36:31 [b] Isa 54:1; 60:4; [Gal 4:26] [c] Jer 31:31 **16:62** [a] Hos 2:19–20 **16:63** [a] Ezek 36:31–32; Dan 9:7–8 [b] Ps 39:9; [Rom 3:19] **17:2** [a] Ezek 20:49; 24:3 **17:3** [a] Jer 48:40; Ezek 17:12; Hos 8:1

with full plumage that was multihued,
came to Lebanon and [b]took the top
of the cedar.
4 He plucked off its topmost shoot;
he brought it to a land of merchants
and planted it in a city of traders.
5 He took one of the seedlings of the
[a]land,
placed it in a cultivated plot;
a shoot by abundant water,
[b]like a willow he planted it.
6 It sprouted and became a vine,
spreading low to the ground;
its branches turning toward him, its
roots were under itself.
So it became a vine; it produced
shoots and sent out branches.

7 "'There was another great eagle
with broad wings and thick plumage.
Now [a]this vine twisted its roots
toward him
and sent its branches toward him
to be watered from the soil where it
was planted.
8 In a good field, by abundant waters, it
was planted
to grow branches, bear fruit, and
become a beautiful vine.'

9 "Say to them: 'This is what the Sovereign
LORD says:

"'[a]Will it prosper?
Will he not rip out its roots
and cause its fruit to rot and wither?
All its foliage will wither.
No strong arm or large army
will be needed to pull it out by its
roots.
10 Consider! It is planted, but [a]will it
prosper?
Will it not wither completely when
the east wind blows on it?
Will it not wither in the soil where it
sprouted?'"

11 Then the LORD's message came to me:
12 "Say to [a]the rebellious house of Israel:
'Don't you know what [b]these things mean?'

Say: 'See here, the king of Babylon came to
Jerusalem and took her king and her officials prisoner and brought them to himself
in Babylon. [13]He took one from the royal
family,[1] made [a]a treaty with him, [b]and put
him under oath. He then took the leaders
of the land [14]so it would be a lowly kingdom
that could not rise on its own but had to
keep its treaty with him in order to stand.
[15]But this one from Israel's royal family
rebelled against [a]the king of Babylon by
sending his emissaries to Egypt to obtain
horses and [b]a large army. [c]Will he prosper?
Will the one doing these things escape? Can
he break the covenant and escape?

16 "'As surely as [a]I live, declares the Sovereign LORD, surely in the city of the king who
crowned him, whose oath he despised and
whose covenant he broke—in the middle of
Babylon he will die! [17]Pharaoh with his great
army and mighty horde will [a]not help him
in battle, [b]when siege ramps are erected
and siege walls are built to kill many people. [18]He despised the oath by breaking the
covenant. Take note—he [a]gave his promise
and did all these things. He will not escape!

19 "'Therefore this is what the Sovereign
LORD says: As surely as I live, I will certainly
repay him for despising my oath and breaking my covenant! [20]I will [a]throw my net over
him and he will be caught in my snare; I will
bring him to Babylon and [b]judge him there
because of the unfaithfulness he committed
against me. [21a]All the choice men[1] among his
troops will die by the sword, and the survivors will be [b]scattered to every wind. Then
you will know that I, the LORD, have spoken!

22 "'This is what the Sovereign LORD says:

"'I will take a sprig from the lofty [a]top
of the [b]cedar and plant it.[1]
I will pluck from the top one of its
tender twigs;
I myself will [c]plant it on a high and
lofty mountain.
23 I will plant it [a]on a high mountain of
Israel,
and it will raise branches and
produce fruit and become a
beautiful cedar.

17:3 [b] 2 Kgs 24:12   17:5 [a] Deut 8:7–9   [b] Isa 44:4   17:7 [a] Ezek 17:15   17:9 [a] 2 Kgs 25:7   17:10 [a] Ezek 19:12; Hos 13:15
17:12 [a] Ezek 2:3–5; 12:9   [b] 2 Kgs 24:11–16; Ezek 1:2; 17:3   17:13 [a] 2 Kgs 24:17; Jer 37:1; Ezek 17:5   [b] 2 Chr 36:13   [1]Or descendants;
Heb. seed.   17:15 [a] 2 Kgs 24:20; 2 Chr 36:13; Jer 52:3; Ezek 17:7   [b] Deut 17:16; Isa 31:1, 3; 36:6, 9   [c] Ezek 17:9   17:16 [a] Jer 52:11;
Ezek 12:13   17:17 [a] Jer 37:7; Ezek 29:6   [b] Jer 52:4; Ezek 4:2   17:18 [a] 1 Chr 29:24; Lam 5:6   17:20 [a] Ezek 12:13   [b] Jer 2:35;
Ezek 20:36   17:21 [a] Ezek 12:14   [b] Ezek 12:15; 22:15   [1] Maj. MSS fugitives.   17:22 [a] [Isa 11:1; Jer 23:5; Zech 3:8]
[b] Isa 53:2   [c] [Ps 2:6]   [1] LXX omits and plant it.   17:23 [a] [Isa 2:2–3]; Ezek 20:40; [Mic 4:1]

Every bird will live [b]under it;
every winged creature will live in the shade of its branches.
[24] All the trees of the field will know that I am the LORD.
I make the high tree low; I raise up the low tree.
I make the green tree wither, and I make the dry tree sprout.
I, the LORD, [a]have spoken, and [b]I will do it!'"

Individual Retribution

18 The LORD's message came to me: [2]"What do you mean by quoting this proverb concerning the land of Israel:

"'The [a]fathers eat sour grapes,
And the children's teeth become numb?'

[3]"As surely as I live, declares the Sovereign LORD, you will not quote this proverb in Israel anymore! [4]Indeed! All lives are [a]mine—[b]the life of the father as well as the life of the son is mine. The one who sins will die.

[5]"Suppose a man is righteous. He practices what is just and right; [6]does not eat pagan [a]sacrifices on the mountains or pray to the idols of the house of Israel; does not [b]defile his neighbor's wife; does not [c]approach a woman for marital relations[1] during her period; [7]does not [a]oppress anyone, but gives the debtor back whatever was given in [b]pledge; does not commit robbery,[1] but [c]gives his bread to the hungry and [d]clothes the naked; [8]does not engage in [a]usury or charge interest, but refrains from wrongdoing; [b]promotes true justice between men; [9]and follows my statutes and observes my regulations by carrying them out.[1] That man is righteous; he will certainly [a]live, declares the Sovereign LORD.

[10]"Suppose such [a]a man has a violent son who sheds blood and does any of these things mentioned previously[11](though the father did not do any of them). He eats pagan sacrifices on the mountains, defiles his neighbor's wife, [12]oppresses the poor and the needy, commits robbery, does not give back what was given in pledge, prays to idols, [a]performs abominable acts, [13]engages in usury, and charges interest. Will he live? He will not! Because he has done all these abominable deeds he will certainly die. He will bear the responsibility for [a]his own death.

[14]"But suppose he in turn has a son who notices all the sins his father commits, considers them, and does not follow his father's example. [15a]He does not eat pagan sacrifices on the mountains, does not pray to the idols of the house of Israel, does not defile his neighbor's wife, [16]does not oppress anyone or keep what has been given in pledge, does not commit robbery, gives his food to the hungry and clothes the naked, [17]refrains from wrongdoing,[1] does not engage in usury or charge interest, carries out my regulations, and follows my statutes. He will not die for his father's iniquity; he will surely live. [18]As for his [a]father, because he practices extortion, robs his brother, and does what is not good among his people, he will die for his iniquity.

[19]"Yet you say, 'Why [a]should the son not suffer for his father's iniquity?' When the son does what is just and right, and observes all my statutes and carries them out, he will surely live. [20]The person who sins is [a]the one who will die. A son will not suffer for his [b]father's iniquity, and a [c]father will not suffer for his son's iniquity; the righteous person will be judged according to his righteousness [d]and the wicked person according to his wickedness.

[21]"But [a]if the wicked person turns from all the sin he has committed and observes all my statutes and does what is just and right, he will surely live; he will not die. [22a]None of the sins he has committed will be held against him; because of the righteousness he has done, he will [b]live. [23]Do I actually

17:23 [b] Ezek 31:6; Dan 4:12   17:24 [a] Ezek 37:3; Amos 9:11; Luke 1:52; [Rom 11:23–24]   [b] Ezek 22:14   18:2 [a] Jer 31:29; Lam 5:7   18:4 [a] Num 16:22; 27:16; Isa 42:5; 57:16   [b] Ezek 18:20; [Rom 6:23]   18:6 [a] Ezek 22:9   [b] Lev 18:20; 20:10   [c] Lev 18:19; 20:18   [1] Heb. *draw near to, approach*; used as a euphemism for sexual relations.   18:7 [a] Exod 22:21; Lev 19:15; 25:14   [b] Exod 22:26; Deut 24:12   [c] Deut 15:7, 11; Ezek 18:16; [Matt 25:35–40]; Luke 3:11   [d] Isa 58:7   [1] Seizure of property, usually by the rich.   18:8 [a] Exod 22:25; Lev 25:36; Deut 23:19; Neh 5:7; Ps 15:5   [b] Deut 1:16; Zech 8:16   18:9 [a] Ezek 20:11; Amos 5:4; [Hab 2:4; Rom 1:17]   [1] MT *to do with integrity*.   18:10 [a] Gen 9:6; Exod 21:12; Num 35:31   18:12 [a] 2 Kgs 21:11; Ezek 8:6, 17   18:13 [a] Lev 20:9, 11–13, 16, 27; Ezek 3:18; Acts 18:6   18:15 [a] Ezek 18:6   18:17 [1] MT *restrains his hand from the poor*.   18:18 [a] Ezek 3:18   18:19 [a] Exod 20:5; Deut 5:9; 2 Kgs 23:26; 24:3–4   18:20 [a] 2 Kgs 14:6; 22:18–20; Ezek 18:4   [b] Deut 24:16; 2 Kgs 14:6; 2 Chr 25:4; Jer 31:29–30   [c] 1 Kgs 8:32; Isa 3:10–11; [Matt 16:27]   [d] Rom 2:6–9   18:21 [a] Ezek 18:27; 33:12, 19   18:22 [a] Isa 43:25; Jer 50:20; Ezek 18:24; 33:16; Mic 7:19   [b] [Ps 18:20–24]

delight in the death of the wicked, declares the Sovereign LORD? [a]Do I not prefer that he turn from his wicked conduct and live?

[24]"But if a righteous man turns away from his righteousness and practices wrongdoing according to all the abominable practices the wicked carry out, will [a]he live? [b]All his righteous acts will not be remembered; because of the unfaithful acts he has done and the sin he has committed, he will die. [25]"Yet you say, '[a]The Lord's conduct is unjust!' Hear, O house of Israel: Is my conduct unjust? Is it not your conduct that is unjust? [26]When a righteous person turns back from his righteousness and practices wrongdoing, [a]he will die for it; because of the wrongdoing he has done, he will die. [27]When a wicked person turns from the wickedness [a]he has committed and does what is just and right, he will preserve his life. [28]Because he [a]considered and turned from all the sins he had done, he will surely live; he will not die. [29a]Yet the house of Israel says, 'The Lord's conduct is unjust!' Is my conduct unjust, O house of Israel? Is it not your conduct that is unjust?

[30]"[a]Therefore, I will judge each person according to his conduct,[1] O house of Israel, declares the Sovereign LORD. [b]Repent and turn from all your wickedness; then it will not be an obstacle leading to iniquity. [31]Throw away all your sins you have committed and fashion yourselves [a]a [b]new heart and a new spirit! Why should you die, O house of Israel? [32]For [a]I take no delight in the death of anyone, declares the Sovereign LORD. Repent and [b]live!

Lament for the Princes of Israel

19 "And you, sing [a]a lament for the princes of Israel, [2]and say:

"What a lioness was your mother
  among the lions!
She lay among young lions; she
  reared her cubs.
[3] She reared one of [a]her cubs; he
  became a young lion.

He learned to tear prey; he devoured
  people.
[4] The nations heard about him; he was
  trapped in their pit.
They brought him with hooks to the
  land of [a]Egypt.

[5] "'When she realized that she waited
  in vain, her hope was lost.
She took [a]another of her cubs and
  made him a young lion.
[6] He walked about among [a]the lions;
  he [b]became a young lion.
He learned to tear prey; he devoured
  people.
[7] He broke down[1] their strongholds[2]
  and devastated their cities.
The land and everything in it was
  frightened at the sound of his
  roaring.
[8] The nations—[a]the surrounding
  regions—attacked him.
[b]They threw their net over him; he
  was caught in their pit.
[9] They put him in a collar with hooks;[1]
  [a]they brought him to [b]the king of
  Babylon;
they brought him to prison[2]
so that his voice would not be heard
any longer on the mountains of Israel.

[10] "'Your mother was [a]like a vine in your
  vineyard,[1] planted by water.
It was [b]fruitful and full of branches
  because it was well-watered.
[11] Its boughs were strong, fit for rulers'
  scepters; it reached up into the
  clouds.
It stood out because of its height and
  its many branches.
[12] But it was [a]plucked up in anger; it
  was thrown down to the ground.
The [b]east wind dried up its fruit;
its strong branches broke off and
  withered—
a fire consumed them.
[13] Now it is planted in the wilderness,
  in a dry and thirsty land.

18:23 [a]Lam 3:33; [Ezek 18:32; 33:11; 1 Tim 2:4; 2 Pet 3:9]   18:24 [a]1 Sam 15:11; 2 Chr 24:2, 17–22; Ezek 3:20; 18:26; 33:18   [b][2 Pet 2:20]   18:25 [a]Ezek 18:29; 33:17, 20; Mal 2:17; 3:13–15   18:26 [a]Ezek 18:24   18:27 [a]Ezek 18:21   18:28 [a]Ezek 18:14   18:29 [a]Ezek 18:25   18:30 [a]Ezek 7:3; 33:20   [b]Matt 3:2; Rev 2:5   [1]Heb. ways.   18:31 [a]Isa 1:16; 55:7; Eph 4:22–23   [b]Ps 51:10; Jer 32:39; Ezek 11:19; 36:26   18:32 [a]Lam 3:33; Ezek 33:11; [2 Pet 3:9]   [b][Prov 4:2, 5, 6]   19:1 [a]Ezek 26:17; 27:2   19:3 [a]Ezek 19:2; 2 Kgs 23:31–32   19:4 [a]2 Kgs 23:33–34; 2 Chr 36:4   19:5 [a]2 Kgs 23:34   19:6 [a]2 Kgs 24:8–9   [b]Ezek 19:3   19:7 [1]MT knew.   [2]MT widows.   19:8 [a]2 Kgs 24:2, 11   [b]Ezek 19:4   19:9 [a]2 Chr 36:6; Jer 22:18   [b]Ezek 6:2   [1]Or They put him in a neck stock with hooks.   [2]MT net.   19:10 [a]Ezek 17:6   [b]Deut 8:7–9   [1]MT in your blood.   19:12 [a]Jer 31:27–28   [b]Ezek 17:10; Hos 13:5

14   A [a]fire has gone out from its branch;
     it has consumed its shoot and its
       fruit.
     No strong branch was left in it, nor a
       scepter to rule.'

"[b]This is a lament song, and has become
a lament song."

Israel's Rebellion

20 In the seventh year, in the fifth
month, on the tenth of the month,
[a]some of the elders of Israel came to seek
the LORD, and they sat down in front of me.
[2]The LORD's message came to me: [3]"Son of
man, speak to the elders of [a]Israel, and tell
them: 'This is what the Sovereign LORD says:
Are you coming to seek me? As surely as
I live, I will not allow you to seek me, declares the Sovereign LORD.' [4]Are you willing
to pronounce judgment on them? Are you
willing to pronounce judgment, son of man?
Then confront them with the abominable
practices of their fathers, [5]and say to them:

"[a]This is what the Sovereign LORD says:
On the day I chose Israel I swore to the
descendants of the house of Jacob and
made myself [b]known to them [c]in the land
of Egypt. I swore to them, "I am the LORD
your God." [6]On that day I swore [a]to bring
them out of the land of Egypt to a land that
I had picked out for them, a land [b]flowing
with milk and honey, [c]the most beautiful of
all lands. [7]I said to [a]them, "Each of you must
get rid of [b]the detestable idols you keep before you, and do not defile yourselves with
the idols of Egypt; I am the LORD your God."
[8]But they rebelled against me and refused
to listen to me; no one got rid of their detestable idols, nor did they abandon the
idols of Egypt. Then I decided to [a]pour out
my rage on them and fully vent my anger
against them in the midst of the land of
Egypt. [9a]I acted for the sake of my reputation, so that I would not be profaned before
the nations among whom they lived, before
whom I [b]revealed myself by bringing them
out of the land of Egypt.

[10]"'So I brought them out of the land of
Egypt and led them to the wilderness. [11]I
gave them my statutes [a]and revealed my
regulations to them. The one who carries
them out will live by them! [12]I also gave
them my [a]Sabbaths as a reminder of our
relationship, so that they would know that
I, the LORD, sanctify them. [13]But the house
of Israel [a]rebelled against me in the wilderness; they did not follow my statutes
and they [b]rejected my regulations ([c]the
one who obeys them will live by them),
and they utterly [d]desecrated my Sabbaths.
So I decided to pour out my rage on them
in the [e]wilderness and destroy them. [14a]I
acted for the sake of my reputation, so that
I would not be profaned before the nations
in whose sight I had brought them out. [15]I
also swore to them [a]in the wilderness that
I would not bring them to the land I had
given them—a land [b]flowing with milk and
honey, [c]the most beautiful of all lands. [16]I
did this [a]because they rejected my regulations, did not follow my statutes, and
desecrated my Sabbaths; for [b]their hearts
followed their idols. [17]Yet I had pity on them
and did not destroy them, so I did not make
an end of them in [a]the wilderness.

[18]"'But I said to their children in the
wilderness, "Do not follow the practices
of your fathers; do not observe their regulations, nor defile yourselves with their
idols. [19]I am the LORD your God; follow
my statutes, observe my regulations, and
carry them out. [20]Treat my Sabbaths as
[a]holy[1] and they will be a reminder of our
relationship, and then you will know that
I am the LORD your God." [21]But [a]the children rebelled against me, did not follow my
statutes, did not observe my regulations
by carrying them out (the one who obeys
them will live by them), and desecrated my
Sabbaths. [b]I decided to pour out my rage
on them and fully vent my anger against
them in the wilderness. [22]But I refrained
from doing so and acted instead for the
sake of my reputation, so that I would not
be profaned before the nations in whose

19:14 [a] Judg 9:15; 2 Kgs 24:20; Ezek 17:18 [b] Lam 2:5   20:1 [a] Ezek 8:1, 11, 12; 14:1   20:3 [a] Ezek 7:26; 14:3   20:5 [a] Exod 6:6–8;
Deut 7:6 [b] Exod 3:8; 4:31; Deut 4:34 [c] Exod 20:2   20:6 [a] Exod 3:8, 17; Deut 8:7–9; Jer 32:22 [b] Exod 3:8 [c] Exod 3:8, 17;
13:5; 33:3; Ps 48:2; Jer 11:5; 32:22; Ezek 20:15; Dan 8:9; Zech 7:14   20:7 [a] 2 Chr 15:8 [b] Lev 18:3; Deut 29:16; Josh 24:14
20:8 [a] Ezek 7:8   20:9 [a] Num 14:13 [b] Josh 2:10; 9:9–10   20:11 [a] Deut 4:8; Neh 9:13; Ps 147:19   20:12 [a] Exod 20:8;
Deut 5:12; Neh 9:14   20:13 [a] Num 14:22; Ps 78:40; Ezek 20:8 [b] Prov 1:25 [c] Lev 18:5 [d] Exod 16:27 [e] Num 14:29;
Ps 106:23   20:14 [a] Ezek 20:9, 20   20:15 [a] Num 14:28; Ps 95:11; 106:26 [b] Exod 3:8 [c] Ezek 20:6   20:16 [a] Ezek
20:13, 24 [b] Num 15:39; Ps 78:37; Amos 5:25; Acts 7:42   20:17 [a] [Ps 78:38]   20:20 [a] Isa 58:13–14;
Jer 17:22 [1] Or *set apart my Sabbaths.*   20:21 [a] Num 25:1; Deut 9:23 [b] Lev 18:5

sight I had brought them out. [23]I also swore to them [a]in the wilderness that I would scatter them among the nations and disperse them throughout the lands. [24]I did this [a]because they did not observe my regulations, they rejected my statutes, they desecrated my Sabbaths, and [b]their eyes were fixed on their fathers' idols. [25]I also gave them decrees that were not good and [a]regulations by which they could not live. [26]I declared them to be defiled because of their sacrifices—they caused all their firstborn to pass [a]through the fire—so that [b]I might devastate them, so that they would know that I am the LORD.'

[27]"Therefore, speak to the house of Israel, son of man, and tell them, 'This is what the Sovereign LORD says: In this way too your fathers [a]blasphemed me when they were unfaithful to me. [28]I brought them to [a]the land that I swore to give them, but whenever they saw any high hill or leafy tree, they offered their sacrifices there and presented the offerings that provoked me to anger. They offered their [b]soothing aroma there and poured out their drink offerings. [29]So I said to them, "What is this high place you go to?"' (So it is called "High Place" to this day.)

[30]"Therefore say to the house of Israel, 'This is what the Sovereign LORD says: Will you defile yourselves like your [a]fathers and engage in prostitution with detestable [b]idols? [31]When [a]you present your sacrifices—when you make your sons pass through the fire—you defile yourselves with all your idols to this very day. Will I allow you to seek me, [b]O house of Israel? As surely as I live, declares the Sovereign LORD, I will not allow you to seek me!

[32]"'[a]What you plan will never happen. You say, "We will be like the nations, like the clans of the lands, who serve gods of wood and stone."[1] [33]As surely as [a]I live, declares the Sovereign LORD, with a powerful hand and an outstretched arm and with an outpouring of rage, I will be king over you. [34]I will bring you out from the nations and will gather you from the lands where you are scattered, with a powerful hand and an outstretched arm and with an outpouring of rage! [35]I [a]will bring you into the wilderness of the nations, and there I will enter into judgment with you face-to-face. [36a]Just as I entered into judgment with your fathers in the wilderness of the land of Egypt, so I will enter into judgment with you, declares the Sovereign LORD. [37]I will make you [a]pass under the shepherd's staff, and I will bring you into the bond of the [b]covenant. [38]I [a]will eliminate from among you [b]the rebels and those who revolt against me. I will bring them out from the land where they have been residing, but they will not come to the land of Israel. Then you will know that I am the LORD.

[39]"'As for you, [a]O house of Israel, this is what the Sovereign LORD says: Each of you go and serve your idols, if you will not listen to me. [b]But my holy name will not be profaned again by your sacrifices and your idols. [40]For there [a]on my holy mountain, the high mountain of Israel, declares the Sovereign LORD, [b]all the house of [c]Israel will serve me, all of them in the land. I will accept them there, and there I will seek your contributions and your choice gifts, with all your holy things. [41]When I bring you out from the nations and gather you from the lands where you are scattered, I will accept you along with your [a]soothing aroma. I will display my holiness among you in the sight of the nations. [42]Then you will know that I am [a]the LORD [b]when I bring you to the land of Israel, to the land I swore to give to your fathers. [43]And [a]there [b]you will remember your conduct and all your deeds by which you defiled yourselves. You will despise yourselves because of all the evil deeds you have done. [44]Then you will know that I am [a]the LORD, when I deal with you [b]for the sake of my reputation and not according to your wicked conduct and corrupt deeds, O house of Israel, declares the Sovereign LORD.'"

20:23 [a]Lev 26:33; Deut 28:64; Ps 106:27; Jer 15:4   20:24 [a]Ezek 20:13, 16   [b]Ezek 6:9   20:25 [a]Ps 81:12; Rom 1:24; 2 Thess 2:11   20:26 [a]2 Kgs 17:17; 2 Chr 28:3; Jer 32:35; Ezek 16:20   [b]Ezek 6:7; 20:12, 20   20:27 [a]Num 15:30; Isa 65:7; Rom 2:24   20:28 [a]1 Kgs 14:23; Ps 78:58; Isa 57:5-7; Jer 3:6; Ezek 6:13   [b]Ezek 16:19   20:30 [a]Judg 2:19   [b]Jer 7:26; 16:12   20:31 [a]Ps 106:37-39; Jer 7:31; Ezek 16:20; 20:26   [b]Ezek 20:3   20:32 [a]Ezek 11:5   [1]Heb. serving wood and stone.   20:33 [a]Jer 21:5   20:35 [a]Jer 2:9, 35; Ezek 17:20   20:36 [a]Num 14:21-23, 28   20:37 [a]Lev 27:32; Jer 33:13   [b]Ps 89:30-34; Ezek 16:60, 62   20:38 [a]Ezek 34:17; Amos 9:9-10; Zech 13:8-9; [Mal 3:3; 4:1-3; Matt 25:32]   [b]Jer 44:14   20:39 [a]Judg 10:14; Ps 81:12; Amos 4:4   [b]Isa 1:13-15; Ezek 23:38   20:40 [a]Isa 2:2-3; Ezek 17:23; Mic 4:1   [b]Ezek 37:22   [c]Isa 56:7; 60:7; Ezek 43:27; Zech 8:20-22; Mal 3:4; [Rom 12:1]   20:41 [a]Eph 5:2; Phil 4:18   20:42 [a]Ezek 36:23; 38:23   [b]Ezek 11:17; 34:13; 36:24   20:43 [a]Ezek 16:61   [b]Lev 26:39; Ezek 6:9; Hos 5:15   20:44 [a]Ezek 24:24   [b]Ezek 36:22

Prophecy against the South

[45]The LORD's message came to me: [46]"aSon of man, turn toward[1] the south,[2] and speak out against the south. Prophesy against the open scrub land of the Negev, [47]and say to the scrub land of the Negev, 'aListen to the LORD's message! This is what the Sovereign LORD has said: Look here, I am about to start a fire in you, and it will devour bevery green tree and every dry tree in you. The flaming fire will not be extinguished, and the whole surface of the ground cfrom the Negev to the north will be scorched by it. [48]And everyone will see that I, the LORD, have burned it; it will not be extinguished.'"

[49]Then I said, "O Sovereign LORD! They are saying of me, 'Does he not simply speak in eloquent figures of aspeech?'"

The Sword of Judgment

21 The LORD's message came to me: [2]"aSon of man, turn toward Jerusalem and speak bout against the sanctuaries. Prophesy against the land of Israel [3]and say to them, 'This is what the LORD says: Look, aI am against you. I will draw my sword from its sheath and cut off from you both the brighteous and the wicked. [4]Because I will cut off afrom you both the righteous and the wicked, my sword will go out from its sheath against everyone from the south[1] to the north. [5]Then everyone will know that I am the LORD, who drew my sword from its sheath—it will not be sheathed again!'

[6]"And you, son of man, agroan with an aching heart and bitterness; groan before their eyes. [7]When they ask you, 'Why are you groaning?' you will reply, 'Because of the report that has come. aEvery heart will melt with fear and every hand will be limp; everyone will faint, and every knee will be wet with urine.' Pay attention—it is coming and it will happen, declares the Sovereign LORD."

[8]The LORD's message came to me: [9]"Son of aman, prophesy and say: 'This is what the Lord says:

"'A sword, a sword is sharpened
and also polished.
[10] It is sharpened for slaughter;
it is polished to flash like lightning!

"'Should we rejoice in the scepter of my son? No! The sword despises every tree!

[11] "'He gave it to be polished,
to be grasped in athe hand—
the sword is sharpened, it is
polished—
giving it into the hand of the
executioner.
[12] Cry out and moan, son of man,
for it is wielded against my people,
against all the princes of Israel.
They are delivered up to the sword,
along with my people.
Therefore, astrike your thigh.

[13]"'For testing will come, aand what will happen when bthe scepter, which the sword despises, is no more? declares the Sovereign LORD.'

[14] "And you, son of man, prophesy,
and aclap your hands together.
Let the sword strike twice, even
three times!
It is ba sword for slaughter,
a sword for the great slaughter
surrounding them.
[15] So hearts melt awith fear and many
stumble.
At all their gates I have stationed the
sword for slaughter.
Ah! It is made to flash, it is drawn for
slaughter!
[16] Cut asharply on the right!
Swing to the left,
wherever your edge is appointed to
strike.
[17] I too will aclap my hands together,
bI will exhaust my rage;
I, the LORD, have spoken."

[18]The LORD's message came to me: [19]"You, son of man, mark out two routes for the

---

20:46 a Ezek 21:2; Amos 7:16   [1]Heb. *set your face toward.*   [2]Or *the way toward the south, the way toward Teman*; Teman is in the south and may be a location or the direction.   **20:47** a Isa 9:18–19; Jer 21:14   b Luke 23:31   c Ezek 21:4   **20:49** a Ezek 12:9; 17:2; Matt 13:13; John 16:25   **21:2** a Ezek 20:46   b Amos 7:16   **21:3** a Jer 21:13; Ezek 5:8; Nah 2:13; 3:5   b Job 9:22   **21:4** a Jer 12:12; Ezek 20:47   [1]Heb. *Negev*; the Negev is the south country.   **21:6** a Isa 22:4; Jer 4:19; Luke 19:41   **21:7** a Ezek 7:17   **21:9** a Deut 32:41; Ezek 5:1; 21:15, 28   **21:11** a Ezek 21:19   **21:12** a Jer 31:19   **21:13** a Job 9:23; 2 Cor 8:2   b Ezek 21:27   **21:14** a Num 24:10; Ezek 6:11   b 1 Kgs 20:30   **21:15** a Ezek 21:10, 28   **21:16** a Ezek 14:17   **21:17** a Ezek 22:13   b Ezek 5:13; 16:42; 24:13

king of Babylon's sword to take; both of them will originate in a single land. Make a signpost and put it at the beginning of the road leading to the city. [20]Mark out the routes for the sword to take: '[a]Rabbah of the Ammonites' and 'Judah with Jerusalem in it.'[1] [21]For the king of Babylon stands at the fork in the road at the head of the two routes. He looks for omens: He shakes arrows, he consults idols,[1] he examines animal livers. [22]Into his right hand comes the portent for Jerusalem—to set up battering rams, to give the signal for slaughter, to [a]shout out the battle cry, [b]to set up battering rams against the gates, to erect a siege ramp, and to build a siege wall. [23]But those in Jerusalem will view it as [a]a false omen. They have sworn solemn oaths, but the king of Babylon will accuse them of violations in order to seize them.

[24]"Therefore this is what the Sovereign LORD says: 'Because you have brought up your own guilt by uncovering your transgressions and revealing your sins through all your actions, for this reason you will be taken by force.

[25] "'As for you, [a]profane and wicked
    prince of Israel,
  [b]whose day has come, the time of
    final punishment,
[26] this is what the Sovereign LORD
    says:
  Tear off the turban;[1]
  take off the crown!
  Things must change.
  [a]Exalt the lowly;
  bring low the exalted!
[27] A total ruin [a]I will make it!
  Indeed, this will not be
  until he comes to whom is the right,
    and [b]I will give it to him.'

[28]"As for you, son of man, prophesy and say, 'This is what the Sovereign LORD says [a]concerning the Ammonites and their coming humiliation:

"'A sword, a sword drawn for
    slaughter,
  polished to consume, to flash like
    lightning—
[29] while [a]seeing false visions about you
  and reading lying omens about you—
  to place you on the necks of the
    profane wicked,
  [b]whose day has come,
  the time of final punishment.
[30] [a]Return [b]it to its sheath!
  [c]In the place where you were created,
  in your native land, I will judge you.
[31] I will [a]pour out my anger on you;
  the fire of my fury I will [b]blow on you.
  I will hand you over to brutal men,
  who are skilled in [c]destruction.
[32] You will become fuel for the fire—
  [a]your blood will stain the middle of
    the land;
  you will no longer be remembered,
  for I, the LORD, have spoken.'"

The Sins of Jerusalem

22 The LORD's message came to me: [2]"As for you, son of man, are you [a]willing to pronounce judgment? Are you willing to pronounce judgment on [b]the bloody city? Then confront her with all her abominable deeds! [3]Then say, 'This is what the Sovereign LORD says: O city, who spills [a]blood within herself (which brings on her doom), and who makes herself idols (which results in impurity), [4]you are guilty because of the blood you [a]shed and defiled by [b]the idols you made. You have hastened the day of your doom; the end of your years has come. Therefore I will make you an object of scorn to the nations, an object to be mocked by all lands. [5]Those both near and far from you will mock you, you with your bad reputation, full of turmoil.

[6]"'See how each of [a]the princes of Israel living within you has used his authority to shed blood. [7]They have treated father and mother with contempt within you; they have [a]oppressed the resident foreigner

21:20 [a]Deut 3:11; Jer 49:2; Ezek 25:5; Amos 1:14   [1]MT *Judah in fortified Jerusalem*.   21:21 [1]Personal idols that were apparently used for divination purposes.   21:22 [a]Jer 51:14   [b]Ezek 4:2   21:23 [a]Ezek 17:16, 18   21:25 [a]2 Chr 36:13; Jer 52:2; Ezek 12:10; 17:19   [b]Ezek 21:29   21:26 [a]Luke 1:52   [1]Elsewhere, the turban is worn by priests, but here a royal crown is in view.   21:27 [a]Gen 49:10; [Luke 1:32–33; John 1:49]   [b]Ps 2:6; 72:7, 10; [Jer 23:5–6; Ezek 34:24; 37:24]   21:28 [a]Jer 25:21; 49:1–6; Ezek 25:1–7; Amos 1:13; Zeph 2:8–11   21:29 [a]Jer 27:9; Ezek 12:24; 13:6–9; 22:28   [b]Job 18:20; Ps 37:17; Isa 10:3; Ezek 7:2–3, 7   21:30 [a]Jer 47:6–7   [b]Gen 15:14   [c]Ezek 16:3   21:31 [a]Ezek 7:8   [b]Ps 18:15; Isa 30:33; Ezek 22:20–21; Hag 1:9   [c]Jer 6:22–23; 51:20–21; Hab 1:6–10   21:32 [a]Ezek 25:10   22:2 [a]Ezek 20:4   [b]Nah 3:1   22:3 [a]Ezek 24:6–7   22:4 [a]2 Kgs 21:16; Ezek 24:7–8   [b]Deut 28:37; 1 Kgs 9:7; Ezek 5:14; Dan 9:16   22:6 [a]Isa 1:23; Ezek 22:27; Mic 3:1–3; Zeph 3:3   22:7 [a]Exod 22:22; Jer 5:28; Ezek 22:25; Mal 3:5

among you; they have wronged the orphan and the widow[1] within you. [8]You have despised my holy things and [a]desecrated my Sabbaths! [9]Slanderous [a]men shed blood [b]within you. Those who live within you eat pagan sacrifices on the mountains; they commit obscene acts among you. [10]They have sexual [a]relations with their father's wife within you;[1] they violate women during their menstrual period within you. [11]One commits an abominable act [a]with his neighbor's wife; [b]another obscenely defiles his daughter-in-law; another violates his sister—his father's [c]daughter—within you. [12]They take bribes within you to shed blood. You engage in usury and charge interest; you extort money from your neighbors. You have forgotten me, declares [a]the Sovereign LORD.

[13]"'See, I [a]strike my hands together at the dishonest profit you have made and at the bloodshed they have done among you. [14]Can your heart endure or [a]can your hands be strong when [b]I deal with you? I, the LORD, have spoken, and I will do it! [15]I [a]will scatter you among the nations and disperse you among various countries; I will [b]remove your impurity from you. [16]You will be profaned within [a]yourself in the sight of the nations; then you will know that I am the LORD.'"

[17]The LORD's message came to me: [18]"Son of man, [a]the house of Israel has become slag to me. All of them are like bronze, tin, iron, and lead in the [b]furnace; they are the worthless slag of silver. [19]Therefore this is what the Sovereign LORD says: 'Because all of you have become slag, look out! I am about to gather you in the middle of Jerusalem. [20]As silver, bronze, iron, lead, and tin are gathered in a furnace so that the fire can blow on them to [a]melt them, so I will gather you in my anger and in my rage. I will deposit you there and melt you. [21]I will gather you and blow on you with the fire of my fury, and you will be melted in it. [22]As silver is melted in a furnace, so you will be melted in it, and you will know that I, the LORD, have [a]poured out my anger on you.'"

[23]The LORD's message came to me: [24]"Son of man, say to her: 'You are a land that receives [a]no rain[1] or showers in the day of my anger.' [25]Her princes within her are like a roaring lion tearing its prey; [a]they [b]have devoured lives. [c]They take away riches and valuable things; they have made many women widows within it. [26a]Her priests abuse my law and have desecrated my holy things. They do not distinguish between the holy and the profane or recognize any distinction between the unclean and the clean. They ignore my Sabbaths, and I am [b]profaned [c]in their midst. [27]Her [a]officials are like wolves in her midst rending their prey—shedding blood and destroying lives—so they can get dishonest profit. [28a]Her prophets coat their messages with whitewash. They [b]see false visions and announce [c]lying omens for them, saying, 'This is what the Sovereign LORD says,' when the LORD has not spoken. [29]The people of the land have [a]practiced extortion and committed robbery. They have wronged the poor and needy; they have oppressed the resident foreigner and denied them justice.

[30]"[a]I looked for a man from among them who would [b]repair the wall and [c]stand in the gap before me on behalf of the land, so that I would not destroy it, but I found no one. [31]So I have [a]poured my anger on them and destroyed them with [b]the fire of my fury. I hereby repay them for what they have done, declares the Sovereign LORD."

Two Sisters

23 The LORD's message came to me: [2]"Son of man, there were [a]two women who were daughters of the same mother. [3]They engaged in prostitution in Egypt; in their youth [a]they engaged in prostitution. [b]Their breasts were squeezed there; lovers fondled their virgin nipples

22:7 [1] I.e., all who were poor and vulnerable to economic exploitation.   22:8 [a] Lev 19:30   22:9 [a] Lev 19:16; Jer 9:4   [b] Ezek 18:6, 11   22:10 [a] Lev 18:7-8   [1] Heb. *The nakedness of a father one uncovers within you;* an idiom for sexual intercourse, likely with a wife of one's father apart from one's mother, such as a stepmother.   22:11 [a] Lev 18:20; Jer 5:8; Ezek 18:11   [b] Lev 18:15   [c] Lev 18:9   22:12 [a] Exod 23:8; Deut 16:19; 27:25; Mic 7:2-3   22:13 [a] Ezek 21:17   22:14 [a] Ezek 21:7   [b] Ezek 17:24   22:15 [a] Deut 4:27; Neh 1:8; Ezek 20:23; Zech 7:14   [b] Ezek 23:27, 48   22:16 [a] Ps 9:16   22:18 [a] Ps 119:119; Isa 1:22; Jer 6:28; Lam 4:1   [b] Prov 17:3; Isa 48:10   22:20 [a] Isa 1:25; Jer 9:7   22:22 [a] Ezek 20:8, 33; Hos 5:10   22:24 [a] Isa 9:13; Jer 2:30; Ezek 24:13; Zeph 3:2   [1] MT *that is not cleansed.*   22:25 [a] Jer 11:9; Hos 6:9   [b] Matt 23:14   [c] Mic 3:11; Zeph 3:3-4   22:26 [a] Jer 32:32; Lam 4:3; Mal 2:8   [b] 1 Sam 2:29   [c] Lev 10:10   22:27 [a] Isa 1:23; Ezek 22:6; Mic 3:1-3, 9-11; Zeph 3:3   22:28 [a] Ezek 13:10   [b] Ezek 13:6-7   [c] Jer 23:25-32; Ezek 21:29   22:29 [a] Exod 23:9; Lev 19:33; Rom 2:8-9]   23:2 [a] Jer 3:7-8; Ezek 16:44-46   23:3 [a] Lev 17:7; Josh 24:14; Jer 3:9   [b] Ezek 16:22

there. [4]Oholah was the name of the older and Oholibah[1] the name of [a]her younger sister. [b]They became mine and gave birth to sons and daughters. Oholah is Samaria, and Oholibah is Jerusalem.

[5]"Oholah engaged in prostitution while she was mine. She lusted after her lovers, the [a]Assyrians—warriors [6]clothed in blue, governors and officials, all of them desirable young men, horsemen riding on horses. [7]She bestowed her sexual favors on them; all of them were the choicest young men of Assyria. She defiled herself with all whom she desired—with all their idols. [8]She did not abandon the prostitution she had practiced in Egypt, for in her youth men went to bed[1] with her, fondled her virgin breasts, and ravished her. [9]Therefore I handed her over to her lovers, the [a]Assyrians for whom she lusted. [10]They exposed her nakedness, seized her sons and daughters, and killed her with the sword. She became notorious among women, and they executed judgments against her.

[11]"Her sister Oholibah watched this, but [a]she became more corrupt in her lust than her sister had been, and her acts of prostitution were more numerous than those of her sister. [12]She lusted after the [a]Assyrians—[b]governors and officials, warriors in full armor, horsemen riding on horses, all of them desirable young men. [13]I saw that she was defiled; both of them followed the same path. [14]But she increased her prostitution. She saw men carved on the wall, images of the [a]Chaldeans carved in bright red, [15]wearing belts on their waists and flowing turbans on their heads, all of them looking like officers, the image of Babylonians whose native land is Chaldea. [16a]When she saw them, she lusted after them and sent [b]messengers to them in Chaldea. [17]The Babylonians crawled into bed with her. They defiled her with their lust; after she was defiled by them, she became disgusted with them. [18]When she lustfully exposed her nakedness, [a]I was [b]disgusted with her, just as I had been disgusted with her sister. [19]Yet she increased her prostitution, remembering the days of her youth [a]when she engaged in prostitution in the land of Egypt. [20]She lusted after her lovers there, whose genitals were like those of donkeys[1] and whose emission was like that of stallions. [21]This is how you assessed the obscene conduct of your youth, when the [a]Egyptians fondled your nipples and squeezed your young breasts.

[22]"Therefore, Oholibah, this is what the Sovereign LORD says: Look here, I am about to stir up against you the lovers with whom you were disgusted; I will bring them against you from every side: [23]the Babylonians and all the Chaldeans, [a]Pekod, Shoa, and Koa, and [b]all the Assyrians with them, desirable young men, all of them governors and officials, officers and nobles, all of them riding on horses. [24]They will attack you with weapons,[1] chariots, wagons, and with a huge army; they will array themselves against you on every side with large shields, small shields, and helmets. I will assign them the task of judgment; they will punish you according to their laws. [25]I will direct my jealous [a]anger against you, and they will deal with you in rage. They will cut off your nose and your ears, and your survivors will die by the sword. They will seize your sons and daughters, and your survivors will be consumed by fire. [26a]They will strip your clothes off you and take away your beautiful jewelry. [27]So [a]I will put an end to your obscene conduct and your [b]prostitution that you have practiced in the land of Egypt. You will not seek their help or remember Egypt anymore.

[28]"For this is what the Sovereign LORD says: Look here, I am about to deliver you over to [a]those whom you hate, to those with whom you were disgusted. [29a]They will treat you with hatred, take away all you have labored for,[1] and [b]leave you naked and bare. Your nakedness will be exposed, just as when you engaged in prostitution and obscene conduct. [30]I will do these things to you because you engaged in prostitution with the nations, polluting yourself with

23:4 [a] Jer 3:6–7   [b] Ezek 16:8, 20   [1] Oholah means "her tent," and Oholibah means "my tent is in her."   23:5 [a] 2 Kgs 15:19; 16:7; 17:3; Ezek 16:28; Hos 5:13; 8:9–10   23:8 [1] Heb. *lied down with*; can imply going to bed to sleep or can be a euphemism for sexual relations.   23:9 [a] 2 Kgs 17:3   23:11 [a] Jer 3:8–11; Ezek 16:51–52   23:12 [a] 2 Kgs 16:7–8; Ezek 16:28   [b] Ezek 23:6, 23   23:14 [a] Jer 50:2; Ezek 8:10; 16:29   23:16 [a] 2 Kgs 24:1   [b] Isa 57:9   23:18 [a] Jer 6:8   [b] Ps 78:59; 106:40; Jer 12:8   23:19 [a] Lev 18:3; Ezek 23:2   23:20 [1] Heb. *She lusted after their concubines (?), whose flesh was the flesh of donkeys.*   23:21 [a] Ezek 16:26   23:23 [a] Jer 50:21   [b] Ezek 23:12   23:24 [1] The precise meaning of this Heb. word is uncertain.   23:25 [a] Exod 34:14; Ezek 5:13; 8:17–18; Zeph 1:18   23:26 [a] Isa 3:18–23; Ezek 16:39   23:27 [a] Ezek 16:41; 22:15   [b] Ezek 23:3, 19   23:28 [a] Jer 21:7–10; Ezek 16:37–41   23:29 [a] Deut 28:48; Ezek 23:25–26, 45–47   [b] Ezek 16:39   [1] Heb. *labor.*

their idols. [31] You have followed the ways of your sister, so I will place her [a]cup of judgment in your hand. [32] This is what the Sovereign LORD says: '[a]You will drink your sister's deep and wide cup; you will be scorned and derided, for it holds a great deal. [33] You will be overcome by drunkenness and sorrow. The cup of your sister Samaria is a cup of horror and desolation. [34] You will [a]drain it dry, gnaw its pieces, and tear out your breasts, for I have spoken, declares the Sovereign LORD.'

[35] "Therefore this is what the Sovereign LORD says: Because you [a]have forgotten me and completely [b]disregarded me, you must bear now the punishment for your obscene conduct and prostitution."

[36] The LORD said to me: "Son of man, are you willing to pronounce [a]judgment on Oholah and Oholibah? Then [b]declare to them their abominable deeds! [37] For they have committed adultery, and [a]blood is on their hands. They have committed adultery with their idols; and their sons, [b]whom they bore to me, they have passed through the fire as food to their idols. [38] Moreover, they have done this to me: In the very same day they [a]desecrated my sanctuary and [b]profaned my Sabbaths. [39] On the same day they slaughtered their sons for their idols, they came to my sanctuary to desecrate it. This is what they have done in the middle of my house.

[40] "They even sent for men from far away; when the messenger arrived, those men set out. For them you [a]bathed, [b]painted your eyes, and decorated yourself with jewelry. [41] You sat on a magnificent [a]couch, with a table arranged in [b]front of it where you placed my incense and my olive oil. [42] The sound of a carefree crowd accompanied her, including all kinds of men; even Sabeans[1] were brought from the desert. The sisters put bracelets on their wrists and beautiful crowns on their heads. [43] Then I said about the one worn out by adultery, 'Now they will commit immoral acts with her.' [44] They slept with her the way someone sleeps with a prostitute. In this way they slept with Oholah and Oholibah, promiscuous women. [45] But upright men will [a]punish them appropriately for their adultery and bloodshed, because they are adulteresses and [b]blood is on their hands.

[46] "For this is what the Sovereign LORD says: Bring [a]up an army against them and subject them to terror and plunder. [47] That army will pelt [a]them with stones and slash them with their swords; [b]they will kill their sons and daughters and burn their houses. [48] I [a]will put an end to the obscene conduct in the land; all the women will learn [b]a lesson from this and not engage in obscene conduct. [49] They will repay you for your obscene conduct, and you will be [a]punished for idol worship. [b]Then you will know that I am the Sovereign LORD."

The Boiling Pot

24 The LORD's message came to me in the ninth year, in the tenth month, on the tenth day of the month: [2] "Son of man, write down the name of [a]this day, this very day. The king of Babylon has laid siege to Jerusalem this very day. [3] Recite [a]a proverb to this rebellious house and say to them, 'This is what the Sovereign LORD says:

"'Set on the pot, set it on,
 pour water in it too;
[4] add the pieces of meat to it,
 every good piece,
 the thigh and the shoulder;
 fill it with choice bones.
[5] Take the choice bone of the flock,
 heap up wood under it;
 boil rapidly,
 and boil its bones in it.

[6] "'Therefore this is what [a]the Sovereign LORD says:

Woe to the city of bloodshed,
 the pot whose rot is in it,
 whose rot has not been removed
 from it!

23:31[a]2 Kgs 21:13; Jer 7:14–15; 25:15; Ezek 23:33   23:32[a]Ezek 22:4–5   23:34[a]Ps 75:8; Isa 51:17   23:35[a]Isa 17:10; Jer 3:21; Ezek 22:12; Hos 8:14; 13:6   [b]1 Kgs 14:9; Jer 2:27; 32:33; Neh 9:26   23:36[a]Jer 1:10; Ezek 20:4; 22:2   [b]Isa 58:1; Ezek 16:2; Mic 3:8   23:37[a]Ezek 16:38   [b]Ezek 16:20–21, 36, 45; 20:26, 31   23:38[a]2 Kgs 21:4, 7; Ezek 5:11; 7:20   [b]Ezek 22:8   23:40[a]Ruth 3:3   [b]2 Kgs 9:30; Jer 4:30   23:41[a]Esth 1:6; Isa 57:7; Amos 2:8; 6:4   [b]Prov 7:17; Ezek 16:18–19; Hos 2:8   23:42[1]Or *drunkards*; Sheba is in modern-day Yemen.   23:45[a]Ezek 16:38   [b]Ezek 23:37   23:46[a]Ezek 16:40   23:47[a]Lev 20:10; Ezek 16:40   [b]2 Chr 36:17, 19; Ezek 24:21   23:48[a]Ezek 22:15   [b]Deut 13:11; Ezek 22:15; 2 Pet 2:6   23:49[a]Isa 59:18; Ezek 23:35   [b]Ezek 20:38, 42, 44; 25:5   24:2[a]2 Kgs 25:1; Jer 39:1; 52:4   24:3[a]Ezek 17:12   24:6[a]2 Kgs 24:3–4; Ezek 22:2–3, 27; Mic 7:2; Nah 3:1

Empty it piece by piece.
No [b] lot has fallen on it.
7 For her blood was in it;
[a] she poured it on an exposed rock;
she did not pour it on the ground to
cover it up with dust.
8 To arouse anger, to take vengeance,
[a] I have placed her blood on an
exposed rock so that it cannot be
covered up.

9 "'Therefore this is what the Sovereign
LORD says:

[a] Woe to the city of bloodshed!
I will also make the pile high.
10 Pile up the wood, kindle the fire;
cook the meat well, mix in the spices,
and let the bones be charred.
11 Set the empty pot on the coals,
until [a] it becomes hot and its copper
glows,
until its uncleanness melts within it
and its rot [1] is consumed.
12 It has tried my patience;
yet its thick rot is not removed
from it.
Subject its rot to the fire!
13 You mix [a] uncleanness with obscene
conduct.
I tried to cleanse you, but you are
[b] not clean.
You will not be cleansed from your
uncleanness
until [c] I have exhausted my anger on
you.

14 "'I, the LORD, have spoken; judgment
[a] is coming and [b] I will act! I will not relent,
[c] or show pity, or be sorry! I will judge you [1]
according to your conduct and your deeds,
declares the Sovereign LORD.'"

Ezekiel's Wife Dies

15 The LORD's message came to me: 16 "Son
of man, realize that I am about to take the
delight of your eyes away from you with a
jolt, but you must [a] not mourn or weep or

shed tears. 17 Groan to moan for the dead,
but do not [a] perform mourning rites. [b] Bind
on your turban and [c] put your sandals on
your feet. [d] Do not cover your lip and do not
eat food brought by others."

18 So I spoke to the people in the morning, and my wife died in the evening. In the
morning [1] I acted just as I was commanded.
19 Then the people said to me, "[a] Will you
not tell us what these things you are doing
mean for us?"

20 So I said to them: "The LORD's message
came to me: 21 Say to the house of [a] Israel,
'This is what the Sovereign LORD says: Realize I am about to desecrate my sanctuary—
the source of your confident pride, the
object in which your eyes delight, [b] and
your life's passion. Your very own sons and
daughters whom you have left behind will
die by the sword. 22 Then [a] you will do as I
have done: You will not cover your lip or
eat food brought by others. 23 Your turbans
will be on [a] your heads and [b] your sandals on
your feet; you will not mourn or weep, but
you will rot for your iniquities [1] and groan
among yourselves. 24 [a] Ezekiel will be an object lesson for you; you will do all that he
has done. When it happens, then you will
know that I am the Sovereign LORD.'

25 "And you, son of man, this is what will
happen on [a] the day I take from them their
stronghold—their beautiful source of joy,
the object in which their eyes delight, and
the main concern of their lives, as well as
their sons and daughters: 26 On that day
a fugitive will come to you to report the
news. 27 On that day you will be able to speak
again; you will talk with the fugitive and
be silent no [a] longer. You will be an object
lesson for them, and they will know that I
am the LORD."

A Prophecy against Ammon

25 The LORD's message came to me:
2 "Son of man, [a] turn toward the Ammonites [1] and prophesy [b] against them. 3 Say
to the Ammonites, 'Hear the word of the
Sovereign LORD. This is what the Sovereign

24:6 [b] 2 Sam 8:2; Joel 3:3; Obad 11; Nah 3:10   24:7 [a] Lev 17:13; Deut 12:16   24:8 [a] [Matt 7:2]   24:9 [a] Ezek 24:6; Nah
3:1; Hab 2:12   24:11 [a] Ezek 22:15   [1] Or *rust*.   24:13 [a] Ezek 23:36–48   [b] Jer 6:28–30; Ezek 22:24   [c] Ezek 5:13; 8:18; 16:42
24:14 [a] [1 Sam 15:29]   [b] Num 23:19; Ps 33:9; Isa 55:11   [c] Ezek 5:11   [1] Maj. MSS *they will judge you*.   24:16 [a] Jer 16:5   24:17 [a] Jer
16:5   [b] Lev 10:6; 21:10   [c] 2 Sam 15:30   [d] Mic 3:7   24:18 [1] Almost certainly the following morning.   24:19 [a] Ezek 12:9; 37:18
24:21 [a] Jer 7:14; Lam 2:7; Ezek 7:20, 24   [b] Jer 6:11; 16:3–4; Ezek 23:25, 47   24:22 [a] Jer 16:6–7   24:23 [a] Job 27:15; Ps 78:64
[b] Lev 26:39; Ezek 33:10   [1] Or *in your punishment*.   24:24 [a] Isa 20:3; Ezek 4:3; 12:6, 11; Luke 11:29–30   24:25 [a] Ps 48:2;
50:2; Ezek 24:21   24:27 [a] Ezek 3:26; 33:22   25:2 [a] Ezek 35:2   [b] Jer 49:1; Ezek 21:28; Amos 1:13–15;
Zeph 2:9   [1] Heb. *the sons of Ammon*; Ammon was located to the east of Israel.

LORD says: You said "Aha!" about my sanctuary when it was desecrated, about the land of Israel when it was made desolate, and about the house of Judah when they went into exile. [4]So take note, I am about to make you slaves of the tribes of the east. They will make camps among you and pitch their tents among you. They will eat your fruit and drink your milk. [5]I will make [a]Rabbah [b]a pasture for camels and Ammon a resting place for sheep. [c]Then you will know that I am the LORD. [6]For this is what the Sovereign LORD says: Because you [a]clapped your hands, stamped your feet, and [b]rejoiced with intense scorn over the land of Israel, [7]take note—I have [a]stretched out my hand against you, and I will hand you over as plunder to the nations. I will cut you off from the peoples and make you perish from the lands. I will destroy you; then you will know that I am the LORD.'"

A Prophecy against Moab

[8]"This is what the Sovereign LORD says: '[a]Moab and [b]Seir say, "Look, the house of Judah is like all the other nations." [9]So look, I am about to open up Moab's flank, eliminating the cities, including its frontier cities, the beauty of the land—Beth Jeshimoth, Baal Meon, and [a]Kiriathaim. [10]I will hand it over, along with the Ammonites, [a]to the tribes of the east, so that the Ammonites will no longer be remembered among the nations. [11]I will execute judgments against Moab. Then they will know that I am the LORD.'"

A Prophecy against Edom

[12]"This is what the Sovereign LORD says: 'Edom has taken vengeance against the house of Judah; they have made themselves fully culpable by taking vengeance on them. [13]So this is what the Sovereign LORD says: I will stretch out my hand against Edom, and I will kill the people and animals within her,[1] and I will make her desolate; from Teman to Dedan they will die by the sword. [14]I [a]will exact my vengeance upon Edom by the hand of my people Israel. They will

carry out in Edom my anger and rage; they will experience my vengeance, declares the Sovereign LORD.'"

A Prophecy against Philistia

[15]"This is what [a]the Sovereign LORD says: 'The Philistines have exacted merciless revenge,[1] showing intense scorn in their effort to destroy Judah with unrelenting hostility. [16]So [a]this is what the Sovereign LORD says: Take note, I am about to stretch out my hand against the Philistines. I will kill the [b]Kerethites [c]and destroy those who remain on the seacoast. [17]I will [a]exact great vengeance upon them with angry rebukes. Then they will know that I am the LORD, when I exact my vengeance upon them.'"

A Prophecy against Tyre

26 In the eleventh year, on the first day of the month, the LORD's message came to me: [2]"Son of man, [a]because Tyre has said about Jerusalem, '[b]Aha, the gateway of the peoples is broken; it has swung open to me. I will become rich, now that she has been destroyed,' [3]therefore this is what the Sovereign LORD says: Look, I am against you,[1] O Tyre! I will bring up many nations against you, as the sea brings up its waves. [4]They will destroy the walls of Tyre and break down her towers. I will scrape her soil from her and [a]make her a bare rock. [5]She will be a place where [a]fishing nets are spread, surrounded by the sea. For I have spoken, declares the Sovereign LORD. She will become plunder for the nations, [6]and her daughters who are in [a]the field will be slaughtered by the sword. Then they will know that I am the LORD.

[7]"For this is what the Sovereign LORD says: Take note that I am about to bring King [a]Nebuchadrezzar[1] of Babylon, [b]king of kings, against Tyre from the north, with horses, chariots, and horsemen, an army and hordes of people. [8]He will kill your daughters in the field with the sword. He will [a]build a siege wall against you, erect a siege ramp against you, and raise a great shield

25:5 [a]Deut 3:11; 2 Sam 12:26; Jer 49:2; Ezek 21:20 [b]Isa 17:2 [c]Ezek 24:24   25:6 [a]Job 27:23; Lam 2:15; Nah 3:19; Zeph 2:15 [b]Ezek 36:5   25:7 [a]Ezek 35:3   25:8 [a]Isa 15:6; Jer 48:1; Amos 2:1–2 [b]Ezek 35:2, 5   25:9 [a]Num 32:3, 38; Josh 13:17; 1 Chr 5:8; Jer 48:23   25:10 [a]Ezek 25:4   25:13 [1]Heb. and I will cut off from her man and beast.   25:14 [a]Isa 11:14   25:15 [a]2 Chr 28:18 [1]Heb. have acted with vengeance and taken vengeance with vengeance; an emphatic Heb. construction.   25:16 [a]Zeph 2:4 [b]1 Sam 30:14 [c]Jer 47:4   25:17 [a]Ezek 5:15   26:2 [a]2 Sam 5:11; Isa 23:1; Jer 25:22; Amos 1:9; Zech 9:2 [b]Ezek 25:3   26:3 [1]Or I challenge you; perhaps a formula for challenging someone to combat or a duel.   26:4 [a]Ezek 26:14   26:5 [a]Ezek 27:32 26:6 [a]Ezek 25:5   26:7 [a]Jer 27:3–6; Ezek 29:18 [b]Ezra 7:12; Isa 10:8; Jer 52:32; Dan 2:37, 47 [1]"Nebuchadrezzar" is the dominant spelling of this name.   26:8 [a]Jer 52:4; Ezek 21:22

against you. [9]He will direct the blows of his battering rams against your walls and tear down your towers with his weapons. [10]He will cover you with the dust kicked up by his many horses. Your walls will shake from the noise of the horsemen, wheels, and chariots when he enters your gates like those who invade through a city's broken walls. [11]With his [a]horses' hooves he will trample all your streets. He will kill your people with the sword, and your strong pillars will tumble down to the ground. [12]They will steal your wealth and loot your merchandise. They will tear down your walls and destroy your luxurious homes. Your stones, your trees, and your soil he will throw [a]into the water. [13]I [a]will silence the noise of [b]your songs; the sound of your harps will be heard no more. [14]I [a]will make you a bare rock; you will be a place where fishing nets are spread. You will never be built again, for I, the LORD, have spoken, declares the Sovereign LORD.

[15]"This is what the Sovereign LORD says to Tyre: Oh, how the coastlands will [a]shake at the sound of your fall, when the wounded groan at the massive slaughter in your midst! [16]All the [a]princes of [b]the sea will vacate their thrones. They will remove their robes and strip off their embroidered clothes; they will clothe themselves with trembling. They will sit on the ground; they will [c]tremble continually and [d]be shocked at what has happened to you. [17]They will sing this [a]lament over you:

"'How you have perished—you have
  vanished from the seas,
O renowned city, once [b]mighty in the
  sea,
she and her inhabitants, who spread
  their terror!
[18] Now [a]the coastlands will tremble on
  the day of your fall;
the coastlands by the sea will be
  terrified by your passing.'[1]

[19]"For this is what the Sovereign LORD says: When I make you desolate like the uninhabited cities, when I bring up the deep over you and the surging waters overwhelm you, [20]then [a]I will [b]bring you down to bygone people, to be with those who descend to the Pit. I will make you live in the lower parts of the earth among the primeval ruins, with those who descend to the Pit, so that you will not be inhabited or stand in the land of the living. [21]I [a]will bring terrors on you, and you will be no more! [b]Though you are sought after, you will never be found again, declares the Sovereign LORD."

A Lament for Tyre

27 The LORD's message came to me: [2]"You, son of man, sing [a]a lament for Tyre. [3]Say to Tyre, [a]who sits at the entrance[1] of the sea, [b]merchant to the peoples on many coasts, [c]This is what the Sovereign LORD says:

"'O Tyre, you have said, "I am
  perfectly beautiful."
[4] Your borders are in the heart of the
  seas;
your builders have perfected your
  beauty.
[5] They crafted all your planks out of fir
  trees from [a]Senir;[1]
they took a cedar from Lebanon to
  make your mast.
[6] They made your oars from [a]oaks of
  Bashan;
[b]they made your deck with cypress
  wood[1] from the coasts of Cyprus.[2]
[7] Fine linen from Egypt, woven with
  patterns, was used for your sail
to serve as your banner;
blue and purple from the coastlands
  of Elishah were used for your
  deck's awning.
[8] The leaders[1] of Sidon and Arvad were
  your rowers;
your skilled men, O Tyre, were your
  captains.
[9] The elders of [a]Gebal and her skilled
  men were within you, mending
  cracks;

26:11 [a] Hab 1:8   26:12 [a] Ezek 27:27, 32   26:13 [a] Isa 14:11; 24:8; Jer 7:34; 25:10; Amos 6:5   [b] Isa 23:16; Ezek 28:13; Rev 18:22   26:14 [a] Ezek 26:4–5   26:15 [a] Jer 49:21; Ezek 27:28   26:16 [a] Isa 23:8   [b] Job 2:13   [c] Ezek 32:10; Hos 11:10   [d] Ezek 27:35   26:17 [a] Ezek 27:2–36; Rev 18:9   [b] Josh 19:29; Isa 23:4   26:18 [a] Ezek 26:15   [1] Heb. *from your going out.*   26:20 [a] Ezek 32:18   [b] Ezek 32:23   26:21 [a] Ezek 27:36; 28:19   [b] Ps 37:10, 36; Ezek 28:19   27:2 [a] Ezek 26:17   27:3 [a] Ezek 26:17; 28:2   [b] Isa 23:3   [c] Ezek 28:12   [1] Heb. *entrances;* perhaps because Tyre had two main harbors.   27:5 [a] Deut 3:9; 1 Chr 5:23; Song 4:8   [1] Perhaps for the hull or deck.   27:6 [a] Isa 2:12–13; Zech 11:2   [b] Gen 10:4; Isa 23:1, 12; Jer 2:10   [1] Heb. *Your deck they made ivory, daughter of Assyria.*   [2] Heb. *from the coastlands* (or *islands*) *of Kittim;* generally understood as Cyprus, where the Phoenicians had a trading colony on the southeast coast.   27:8 [1] MT *the residents of.*   27:9 [a] Josh 13:5; 1 Kgs 5:18; Ps 83:7

all the ships of the sea and their
mariners were within you to trade
for your merchandise.
10 Men of Persia, Lud, and Put were in
your army, men of war.
They hung shield and helmet on you;
they gave you your splendor.
11 The Arvadites joined ᵃyour army on
your walls all around,
and the Gammadites were in your
towers.
They hung their quivers on your
walls all around;
they perfected your beauty.

12 "'ᵃTarshish was your trade partner because of your abundant wealth; they exchanged silver, iron, tin, and lead for your products. 13ᵃJavan, Tubal, and Meshech were your clients; they exchanged ᵇslaves and bronze items for your merchandise. 14Beth ᵃTogarmah exchanged horses, chargers, and mules for your products. 15The ᵃDedanites were your clients. Many coastlands were your customers; they paid you with ivory tusks and ebony. 16Edom¹ was your trade partner because of the abundance of your goods; they exchanged turquoise, purple, embroidered work, fine linen, coral, and rubies for your products. 17Judah and the land of Israel were your clients; they traded wheat from ᵃMinnith, millet, honey, olive oil, and ᵇbalm for your merchandise. 18Damascus was your trade partner because of the abundance of your goods and of all your wealth: wine from Helbon, white wool from Zahar, 19and casks of wine¹ from Izal they exchanged for your products. Wrought iron, cassia, and sweet cane were among your merchandise. 20ᵃDedan was your client in saddlecloths for riding. 21Arabia and all the princes of ᵃKedar were your trade partners; for lambs, rams, and goats they traded with you. 22The merchants of ᵃSheba and Raamah engaged in trade with you; they traded the best kinds of spices along with precious stones and gold for your products. 23ᵃHaran, Kanneh, Eden, merchants from ᵇSheba, Asshur, and

Kilmad were your clients. 24They traded with you choice garments, purple clothes and embroidered work, and multicolored carpets bound and reinforced with cords; these were among your merchandise. 25The ᵃships of Tarshishᵃ were the transports for your merchandise.

"'So you were filled and weighed
down ᵇin the heart of the seas.
26 Your rowers have brought you into
surging waters.
ᵃThe east wind has wrecked you in
the heart of the seas.
27 Your ᵃwealth, products, and
merchandise, your sailors and
captains,
your ship's carpenters, your
merchants,
and all your fighting men within you,
along with all your crew who are in
you,
will fall into the heart of the seas on
the day of your downfall.
28 At the sound of your captains' cries
the waves will surge;
29 They will descend from their
ships—all ᵃwho handle the oar,
the sailors and all the sea
captains—they will stand on the
land.
30 They will lament loudly over you and
cry bitterly.
They will ᵃthrow dust on their heads
and roll in the ashes;
31 they will tear out their hair because
of you and put on sackcloth,
and they will weep bitterly over you
with intense mourning.
32 As they wail they will lament over
you, chanting:
"Who was like Tyre, like ᵃa tower in
the midst of the sea?"
33 When your products went out from
the seas,
you satisfied many peoples;
with the abundance of your wealth
and merchandise
you enriched the kings of the earth.

27:11 ᵃ Ezek 27:3   27:12 ᵃ Gen 10:4; 2 Chr 20:36; Ezek 38:13   27:13 ᵃ Gen 10:2; Isa 66:19; Ezek 27:19   ᵇ Joel 3:3–6; Rev 18:13   27:14 ᵃ Gen 10:3; Ezek 38:6   27:15 ᵃ Gen 10:7; Isa 21:13   27:16 ¹ LXX man.   27:17 ᵃ Judg 11:33; 1 Kgs 5:9, 11; Ezra 3:7; Acts 12:20   ᵇ Jer 8:22   27:19 ¹ MT leaves v. 18 as an incomplete sentence and begins v. 19 and Dan and Javan [Ionia] from Uzal.   27:20 ᵃ Gen 25:3   27:21 ᵃ Gen 25:13; Isa 60:7; Jer 49:28   27:22 ᵃ Gen 10:7; 1 Kgs 10:1–2; Ps 72:10; Isa 60:6; Ezek 38:13   27:23 ᵃ Gen 11:31; 2 Kgs 19:12; Isa 37:12   ᵇ Gen 25:3   27:25 ᵃ Ps 48:7; Isa 2:16   ᵇ Ezek 27:4   27:26 ᵃ Ps 48:7; Jer 18:17; Acts 27:14   27:27 ᵃ [Prov 11:4]   27:29 ᵃ Rev 18:17   27:30 ᵃ 1 Sam 4:12; 2 Sam 1:2; Job 2:12; Lam 2:10; Rev 18:19   27:32 ᵃ Ezek 26:17

34 Now [a]you are wrecked by the seas, in
the depths of the waters;
[b]your merchandise and all your
company have sunk along with you.
35 [a]All the inhabitants of the coastlands
are shocked at you,
and their kings are horribly
afraid—their faces are troubled.
36 The traders among the peoples hiss
at you;
you have become a horror, and [a]will
be no [b]more.'"

A Prophecy against the King of Tyre

28 The LORD's message came to me:
[2]"Son of man, say to the prince of
Tyre, 'This is what the Sovereign LORD says:

"'Your heart is proud and you said, "[a]I
am a god;
I sit in the seat of gods, in the heart
of the seas"—
yet [b]you are a man and not a god,
though you [c]think you are godlike.
3 Look, [a]you are wiser than Daniel;
no secret is hidden from you.
4 By your wisdom and understanding
you have gained [a]wealth for
yourself;
you have amassed gold and silver in
your treasuries.
5 [a]By your great skill[1] in trade you have
increased your wealth,
and your heart is proud because of
your wealth.

6 "'Therefore this is what the
Sovereign LORD says:
Because you think you are godlike,
7 I am about to bring [a]foreigners
against you, [b]the most terrifying of
nations.
They will draw their swords against
the grandeur made by your
wisdom,
and they will defile your splendor.
8 They will bring you down to the [a]Pit,
and you will die violently in the
heart of the seas.

9 Will you still [a]say, "I am a god," before
the one who kills you—
though you are a man and not a god—
when you are in the power of those
who wound you?
10 You will die [a]the death of the
uncircumcised by the hand of
foreigners;
for I have spoken, declares the
Sovereign LORD.'"

11 The LORD's message came to me: 12"Son
of man, sing [a]a lament for the king of Tyre,
and say to him, 'This is what the Sovereign
LORD says:

"'[b]You were the sealer of perfection,
full of wisdom, and perfect in beauty.
13 You were in [a]Eden, the garden of God.
Every precious stone was [b]your
covering,
the ruby, topaz, and emerald,
the chrysolite, onyx, and jasper,
the sapphire, turquoise, and beryl;
your settings and mounts were made
of gold.
On the day you were created they
were prepared.
14 I placed you there with an anointed
guardian[1] [a]cherub;
you were on [b]the holy mountain of
God;
you walked about amidst fiery
stones.
15 You were blameless in your behavior
from the day you were created,
until [a]sin was discovered in you.
16 In the abundance [a]of your trade you
were filled with violence, and you
sinned;
so I defiled you and banished you
from the mountain of God—
the guardian cherub expelled you
from the midst of the stones of
fire.
17 Your [a]heart was proud because of
your beauty;
you corrupted your wisdom on
account of your splendor.

27:34 [a]Ezek 26:19   [b]Ezek 27:27   27:35 [a]Isa 23:6; Ezek 26:15–16   27:36 [a]Jer 18:16; Zeph 2:15   [b]Ps 37:10, 36; Ezek 28:19
28:2 [a]Jer 49:16; Ezek 31:10   [b]Isa 14:14; 47:8; Ezek 28:9; 2 Thess 2:4   [c]Ezek 27:3–4   28:3 [a]Ezek 14:14; Dan 1:20; 2:20–23, 28;
5:11–12; Zech 9:3   28:4 [a]Ezek 27:33; Zech 9:1–3   28:5 [a]Ps 62:10; Zech 9:3   [1]Or wisdom.   28:7 [a]Ezek 26:7   [b]Ezek 7:24;
21:31; 30:11; Hab 1:6–8   28:8 [a]Isa 14:15   28:9 [a]Ezek 28:2   28:10 [a]1 Sam 17:26, 36; Ezek 31:18; 32:19, 21, 25, 27   28:12 [a]Ezek
27:2   [b]Ezek 27:3; 28:3   28:13 [a]Gen 2:8; Isa 51:3; Ezek 31:8–9; 36:35   [b]Ezek 26:13   28:14 [a]Exod 25:20; Ezek 28:16   [b]Isa
14:13; Ezek 20:40   [1]The meaning of the Heb. phrase is uncertain; it also occurs in Exod 25:20 in reference to the
cherubim covering the ark.   28:15 [a][Isa 14:12]   28:16 [a]Ezek 28:14   28:17 [a]Ezek 28:2, 5

I threw you down to the ground;
I placed you before kings, that they
   might see you.
18 By the multitude of your iniquities,
   through the sinfulness of your
   trade,
you desecrated your sanctuaries.
So I drew fire out from within you;
it consumed you,
and I turned you to ashes on the earth
before the eyes of all who saw you.
19 All who know [a]you among the
   peoples are shocked at you;
   you have become terrified and will
   be no [b]more.'"

A Prophecy against Sidon

20 The LORD's message came to me: 21 "Son of man, [a]turn [b]toward Sidon and prophesy against it. 22 Say, 'This is what [a]the Sovereign LORD says:

"'Look, I am against you, Sidon,
and I will magnify myself in your
   midst.
Then they will know that I am the
   LORD
when I execute judgments on her
and [b]reveal my sovereign power[1] in
   her.
23 [a]I will send a plague into the city and
   bloodshed into its streets;
the slain will fall within it, by the
   sword that attacks it from every
   side.
Then they will know that I am the
   LORD.

24 "No longer will [a]Israel suffer from the sharp briers or painful thorns of all who surround and [b]scorn them. Then they will know that I am the Sovereign LORD.

25 "'This is what the Sovereign LORD says: When I [a]regather the house of Israel from the peoples where they are dispersed, I will [b]reveal my sovereign power over them in the sight of the nations, and they will live in their land that I gave to my servant Jacob. 26 They will [a]live securely in it; they will [b]build houses and [c]plant vineyards. They will live securely when I execute my judgments on all those who scorn them and surround them. Then they will know that I am the LORD their God.'"

A Prophecy against Egypt

29 In the tenth year, in the tenth month, on the twelfth day of the month, the LORD's message came to me: 2 "Son of man, [a]turn toward Pharaoh king of Egypt and prophesy [b]against him and against all Egypt. 3 Tell them, 'This is what the Sovereign LORD says:

"'Look, I am against you, Pharaoh
   king of Egypt,
the great [a]monster lying in the midst
   of its waterways,
[b]who has said, "My Nile is my own, I
   made it for myself."
4 I [a]will put hooks in your jaws
and stick the fish of your waterways
   to your scales.
I will haul you up from the midst of
   your waterways,
and all the fish of your waterways
   will stick to your scales.
5 I will leave you in the wilderness,
you and all the fish of your
   waterways;
you will fall in the open [a]field and will
   not be gathered up or collected.[1]
I have given [b]you as food to the
   beasts of the earth and the [c]birds
   of the skies.
6 Then all those living in Egypt will
   know that I am the LORD
because they were a reed [a]staff for
   the house of Israel;
7 when they grasped you with their
   hand,[1] you broke and tore their
   shoulders,
and [a]when they leaned on you, you
   splintered and caused their legs to
   be unsteady.

8 "'Therefore, this is [a]what the Sovereign LORD says: Look, I am about to bring a

28:19 [a] Ezek 26:21 [b] Ezek 27:36 **28:21** [a] Ezek 6:2; 25:2; 29:2 [b] Gen 10:15, 19; Isa 23:2, 4, 12; Ezek 27:8; 32:30 **28:22** [a] Ps 9:16 [b] Ezek 28:25 [1] Or *reveal my holiness.* **28:23** [a] Ezek 38:22 **28:24** [a] Num 33:55; Josh 23:13; Isa 55:13; Ezek 2:6 [b] Ezek 16:57; 25:6–7 **28:25** [a] Ps 106:47; Isa 11:12–13; Jer 32:37; Ezek 11:17; 20:41; 34:13; 37:21 [b] Ezek 28:22 **28:26** [a] Jer 23:6; Ezek 36:28 [b] Isa 65:21; Jer 32:15, 43, 44; Amos 9:13–14 [c] Jer 31:5; Amos 9:14 **29:2** [a] Ezek 28:21 [b] Isa 19:1; Jer 25:19; 46:2, 25; Ezek 30:1–32:32; Joel 3:19 **29:3** [a] Ps 74:13–14; Isa 37:1; 51:9; Ezek 32:2 [b] Ezek 28:2 **29:4** [a] 2 Kgs 19:28; Isa 37:29; Ezek 38:4 **29:5** [a] Ezek 32:4–6 [b] Jer 8:2; 16:4; 25:33 [c] Jer 7:33; 34:20; Ezek 39:4 [1] Some wss *buried.* **29:6** [a] 2 Kgs 18:21; Isa 36:6; Ezek 17:15 **29:7** [a] Jer 37:5, 7, 11; Ezek 17:17 [1] Ket. *by your hand.* **29:8** [a] Jer 46:13; Ezek 14:17; 32:11–13

sword against you, and I will kill every person and every animal. [9] The land of Egypt will become a [a] desolate ruin. Then they will know that I am the LORD.

"'Because he said, "The Nile is mine and I made it," [10] I am against you [a] and your waterways. I will turn the land of Egypt into an utter desolate ruin [b] from Migdol to Syene, as far as the border with Ethiopia. [11] No human foot will pass through it, and [a] no animal's foot will pass through it; it will be uninhabited for 40 years. [12] I [a] will turn the land of Egypt into a desolation in the midst of desolate lands; for 40 years her cities will lie desolate in the midst of ruined cities. I will [b] scatter Egypt among the nations and disperse them among foreign countries.

[13] "'For this is what the Sovereign LORD says: At the [a] end of 40 years I will gather Egypt from the peoples where they were scattered. [14] I will restore the fortunes of Egypt and will bring them back[1] to the land of Pathros, to the land of their origin; there they will be an [a] insignificant kingdom. [15] It will be the most insignificant of the kingdoms; it will never again exalt itself over the nations. I will make them so small that they will not rule over the nations. [16] It will never again be Israel's source of confidence, but a reminder of how [a] they sinned by turning to Egypt for help. Then they will know that I am the Sovereign LORD.'"

[17] In the twenty-seventh year, in the first month, on the first day of the month, the LORD's message came to me: [18] "Son of man, King [a] Nebuchadrezzar[1] of Babylon made his army labor hard against Tyre. Every head was rubbed [b] bald and every shoulder rubbed bare; yet he and his army received no wages from Tyre for the work he carried out against it. [19] Therefore this is what the Sovereign LORD says: Look, I am about to give the land of Egypt to King [a] Nebuchadrezzar of Babylon. He will carry off her wealth, capture her loot, and seize her plunder; it will be his army's wages. [20] I have given him the land of Egypt as his compensation for attacking Tyre, because they [a] did

it for me, declares the Sovereign LORD. [21] On that day [a] I will make Israel powerful, and I will give you the [b] right to be heard among them. Then they will know that I am the LORD."

A Lament over Egypt

30 The LORD's message came to me: [2] "Son of man, prophesy and say, 'This is what the Sovereign LORD says:

"'[a] Wail, "Alas, the day is here!"
[3] For [a] the day is near,
the day of the LORD is near;
it will be a day of storm clouds,[1]
it will be a time of judgment for the
nations.
[4] A sword will come against Egypt
and panic will [a] overtake Ethiopia
when the slain fall in Egypt
and they carry away [b] her wealth
and dismantle her foundations.

[5] Ethiopia, Put, Lud, [a] all the foreigners, Libya, and the people of the covenant land will die by the sword along with them.

[6] "'This is what the LORD says:
Egypt's supporters will fall;
her confident pride will crumble.
[a] From Migdol to Syene they will die
by the sword within her,
declares the Sovereign LORD.
[7] They will be desolate among desolate
lands,
and their cities will be among ruined
cities.
[8] They will know that I am the LORD
when I ignite a fire in Egypt
and all her allies are defeated.

[9] "'On that day [a] messengers will go out from me in ships to frighten overconfident Ethiopia; panic will overtake them on the day of Egypt's doom; for beware—it is coming!

[10] "'This [a] is what the Sovereign LORD says:

29:9 [a] Ezek 30:7–8   **29:10** [a] Ezek 30:12   [b] Ezek 30:6   **29:11** [a] Jer 43:11–12; 46:19; Ezek 32:13   **29:12** [a] Jer 25:15–19; 27:6–11; Ezek 30:7, 26   [b] Jer 46:19; Ezek 30:23, 26   **29:13** [a] Isa 19:23; Jer 46:26   **29:14** [a] Ezek 17:6, 14   [1] Some wss *I will cause to inhabit.*   **29:16** [a] Isa 30:2–3; 36:4, 6; Lam 4:17; Ezek 17:15; 29:6   **29:18** [a] Jer 25:9; 27:6; Ezek 26:7–12   [b] Jer 48:37; Ezek 27:31   [1] "Nebuchadrezzar" is the dominant spelling of this name.   **29:19** [a] Jer 43:10–13; Ezek 30:10   **29:20** [a] Isa 10:6–7; 45:1–3; Jer 25:9   **29:21** [a] 1 Sam 2:10; Ps 92:10; 132:17   [b] Ezek 24:27; Amos 3:7–8; [Luke 21:15]   **30:2** [a] Isa 13:6; 15:2; Ezek 21:12; Joel 1:5, 11, 13   **30:3** [a] Ezek 7:7, 12; Joel 2:1; Obad 15; Zeph 1:7   [1] Heb. *a day of clouds*; recalling the appearance of God at Mount Sinai (Exod 19:9, 16, 18).   **30:4** [a] Ezek 29:19   [b] Jer 50:15   **30:5** [a] Jer 25:20, 24   **30:6** [a] Ezek 29:10   **30:9** [a] Isa 18:1–2   **30:10** [a] Ezek 29:19

I will put an end to the hordes of
   Egypt,
by the hand of King Nebuchadrezzar[1]
   of Babylon.
[11] He and his people with him,
   [a]the most terrifying of the nations,
will be brought there to destroy the
   land.
They will draw their swords against
   Egypt
and fill the land with corpses.
[12] I [a]will dry up the waterways
   and [b]hand the land over to evil men.
I will make the land and everything
   in it desolate by the hand of
   foreigners.
I, the LORD, have spoken!

[13] "'This is what the Sovereign LORD
   says:
I will [a]destroy [b]the [c]idols,
and put an end to the gods of
   Memphis.
There will no longer be a prince from
   the land of Egypt;
so I will make the land of Egypt
   fearful.
[14] I will desolate [a]Pathros,
I will ignite a fire in [b]Zoan,
[c]and I will execute judgments on
   Thebes.
[15] I [a]will pour out my anger upon
   Pelusium,[1]
the stronghold of Egypt;
I will cut off the hordes of Thebes.
[16] I will [a]ignite a fire in Egypt;
Syene[1] will writhe in agony,
Thebes will be broken down,
and Memphis will face enemies
   every day.
[17] The young men of On and of Pi
   Beseth will die by the sword;
and the cities will go into captivity.
[18] In Tahpanhes the day will be dark
when I break the yoke of Egypt there.
Her confident pride will cease within
   her;
[a]a cloud will cover her, and her
   daughters will go into captivity.

[19] I will [a]execute judgments on Egypt.
Then they will know that I am the
LORD.'"

[20]In the eleventh year, in the first month,
on the seventh day of the month, the LORD's
message came to me: [21]"Son of man, I have
[a]broken the arm of Pharaoh king of Egypt.
Look, [b]it has not been bandaged for healing or set with a dressing so that it might
become strong enough to grasp a sword.
[22]Therefore this is what the Sovereign LORD
says: Look, [a]I am against Pharaoh king of
Egypt, and I will [b]break his arms, the strong
arm and the broken one, and I will make the
sword drop from his hand. [23]I [a]will scatter
the Egyptians among the nations and disperse them among foreign countries. [24]I will
strengthen the arms of the king of Babylon,
and I will place my sword in his hand, but I
will break the arms of Pharaoh, and he will
groan like the fatally wounded before the
king of Babylon. [25]I will strengthen [a]the
arms of the king of Babylon, but the arms of
Pharaoh will fall limp. Then they will know
that I am the LORD when I place my sword
in the hand of the king of Babylon and he
extends it against the land of Egypt. [26]I [a]will
scatter the Egyptians among the nations
and disperse them among foreign countries.
Then they will know that I am the LORD."

A Cedar in Lebanon

31 In the [a]eleventh year, in the third
month, on the first day of the month,
the LORD's message came to me: [2]"Son of
man, say to Pharaoh king of Egypt and his
hordes:

"'[a]Who are you like in your greatness?
[3] Consider Assyria, a cedar [a]in
   Lebanon,
with beautiful branches, like a forest
   giving shade,
and extremely tall;
its top reached into the clouds.
[4] The water made it grow;
underground springs made it grow
   tall.

30:10 [1]"Nebuchadrezzar" is the dominant spelling of this name.   30:11 [a]Ezek 28:7; 31:12   30:12 [a]Isa 19:5–6   [b]Isa 19:4
30:13 [a]Isa 19:1; Jer 43:12; 46:25; Zech 13:2   [b]Zech 10:11   [c]Isa 19:16   30:14 [a]Isa 11:11; Jer 44:1, 15; Ezek 29:14   [b]Ps 78:12, 43;
Isa 19:11, 13   [c]Jer 46:25; Ezek 30:15–16; Nah 3:8–10   30:15 [a]Jer 46:25   [1]Heb. *Sin*; a city commonly identified with
   Pelusium, a fortress on Egypt's northeastern frontier.   30:16 [a]Ezek 30:8   [1]MT *Sin*.   30:18 [a]Jer 2:16
   30:19 [a][Ps 9:16]; Ezek 5:8; 25:11   30:21 [a]Jer 48:25   [b]Jer 46:11   30:22 [a]Jer 46:25; Ezek 29:3   [b]Ps 37:17
   30:23 [a]Ezek 29:12; 30:17–18, 26   30:25 [a]Ps 9:16   30:26 [a]Ezek 29:12   31:1 [a]Jer 52:5–6; Ezek
   30:20; 32:1   31:2 [a]Ezek 31:18   31:3 [a]Isa 10:33–34; Ezek 17:3–4, 22; 31:16; Dan 4:10, 20–23

Rivers flowed all around [a] the place it
  was planted,
while smaller channels watered all
  the trees of the field.
5 Therefore [a] it grew taller than all the
  trees of the field;
its boughs grew large and its
  branches grew long,
because of the plentiful water in its
  shoots.
6 All the [a] birds of the sky nested in its
  boughs;
under its branches all the beasts of
  the field gave birth;
in its shade all the great nations
  lived.
7 It was beautiful in its loftiness, in the
  length of its branches;
for its roots went down deep to
  plentiful waters.
8 The cedars in the [a] garden of God
  could not eclipse it,
nor could the fir trees[1] match its
  boughs;
the plane trees were as nothing
  compared to its branches;
no tree in the garden of God could
  rival its beauty.
9 I made it beautiful with its many
  branches;
all the trees of Eden, in the garden of
  God, envied it.

10 "'Therefore this is what the Sovereign
LORD says: Because [a] it was tall in stature,
and its top reached into the clouds, and it
was proud of its height, [11] I gave it over to
the [a] leader of the nations. He has judged
it thoroughly, as its sinfulness deserves. I
have thrown it out. [12] Foreigners from [a] the
most terrifying [b] nations have cut it down
and left it to lie there on the mountains.
In all the valleys its branches have fallen,
and its boughs lie [c] broken in the ravines
of the land. All the peoples of the land have
departed from its shade and left it. [13] On [a] its
ruins all the birds of the sky will live, and
all the wild animals will walk on its branches. [14] For this reason no watered trees will
grow so tall; their tops will not reach into

[a] the clouds, nor will the well-watered ones
grow that high. For all of them have been
appointed [b] to die in the lower parts of the
earth; they will be among mere mortals,
with those who descend to the Pit.
15 "'This is what the Sovereign LORD says:
On the day it [a] went down to Sheol I caused
observers to lament. I covered it with the
deep and held back its rivers; its plentiful
water was restrained. I clothed Lebanon
in black for it, and all the trees of the field
wilted because of it. [16] I made the nations
[a] shake at the sound of its [b] fall, when I threw
it down to Sheol, along with those who descend to the Pit. Then all the trees of Eden,
the choicest and the best of Lebanon, all
that [c] were well-watered, were comforted
in the earth below. [17] Those who [a] lived in
its shade, its allies among the nations, also
went down with it to Sheol, to those killed
by the sword. [18] Which of the trees of Eden
was like you in majesty and loftiness? You
will be brought down with the trees of Eden
[a] to the lower parts of the earth; [b] you will
lie among the uncircumcised, with those
killed by the sword! This is what will happen to Pharaoh and all his hordes, declares
the Sovereign LORD.'"

Lamentation over Pharaoh and Egypt

32 In the [a] twelfth year, in the twelfth
  month, on the first of the month, the
LORD's message came to me: [2] "Son of man,
sing [a] a lament for Pharaoh king of Egypt,
and say to him:

"'[b] You were like a lion among the
  nations,
but [c] you are a monster [d] in the seas;
you thrash about in your streams,
stir up the water with your feet,
and [e] muddy your[1] streams.

3 "'This is what the Sovereign LORD says:

"'I will [a] throw my net over you in the
  assembly of many peoples;
and they will haul you up in my
  dragnet.
4 I [a] will leave you on the ground,

31:4 [a] Jer 51:36; Ezek 29:3–9   31:5 [a] Dan 4:11   31:6 [a] Ezek 17:23; 31:13; Dan 4:12, 21; Matt 13:32   31:8 [a] Gen 2:8–9; 13:10; Isa
51:3; Ezek 28:13; 31:16, 18   [1] Or cypress trees.   31:10 [a] 2 Chr 32:25; Isa 10:12; 14:13–14; Ezek 28:17; Dan 5:20   31:11 [a] Ezek
30:10; Dan 5:18–19   31:12 [a] Ezek 28:7; 30:11; 32:12   [b] Ezek 32:5; 35:8   [c] Ezek 30:24–25   31:13 [a] Isa 18:6; Ezek 32:4   31:14 [a] Ps
82:7   [b] Ezek 32:18   31:15 [a] Ezek 32:22–23   31:16 [a] Ezek 26:15; Hag 2:7   [b] Isa 14:8; Hab 2:17   [c] Ezek 32:31   31:17 [a] Lam 4:20
31:18 [a] Ezek 32:19   [b] Jer 9:25–26; Ezek 28:10; 32:19, 21   32:1 [a] Ezek 31:1; 33:21   32:2 [a] Ezek 27:2   [b] Jer 4:7; Ezek 19:2–6;
Nah 2:11–13   [c] Isa 27:1; Ezek 29:3   [d] Jer 46:7–8   [e] Ezek 34:18   [1] MT their.   32:3 [a] Ezek 12:13; 17:20   32:4 [a] Ezek 29:5

I will fling you on the open field,
I will allow all the birds of the sky to
settle on you,
[b]and I will permit all the wild animals[1]
to gorge themselves on you.
5 I will put your flesh [a]on the
mountains,
and fill the valleys with your
maggot-infested carcass.[1]
6 I will drench the land with the flow
of your blood up to the mountains,
and the ravines will be full of your
blood.
7 When [a]I extinguish you, I will cover
the sky;
I will darken its stars.
I will cover the sun with a cloud,
and the moon will not shine.
8 I will darken all the lights in the sky
over you,
and I will darken your land,
declares the Sovereign LORD.
9 I will disturb many peoples
when I bring about your destruction
among the nations,
among countries you do not know.
10 I will shock many peoples with you,
and their kings will shiver with
horror because of you.
When I brandish my sword before
them,
every moment each one will tremble
for his life, on [a]the day of your fall.

11 "[a]For this is what the Sovereign LORD
says:

"'The sword of the king of Babylon
will attack you.
12 By [a]the swords of [b]the mighty
warriors I will cause your hordes
to fall—
all of them are the most terrifying
among the nations.
They will devastate the pride of
Egypt,
and all its hordes will be destroyed.
13 I will destroy all its cattle beside [a]the
plentiful waters;

and no human foot will disturb the
waters again,
nor will the hooves of cattle disturb
them.
14 Then I will make their waters calm
and will make their streams flow like
olive oil, declares the Sovereign
LORD.
15 When I turn [a]the land of Egypt into
desolation
and the land is destitute of
everything that fills it,
when I strike all those who live in it,
then they will know that I am the
LORD.'
16 This is a lament; they will [a]chant it.
The daughters of the nations will
chant it.
They will chant it over Egypt and
over all her hordes,
declares the Sovereign LORD."

17 In the twelfth year, on the fifteenth day of
the month, the LORD's message came to me:
18 "Son of man, wail[1] over the horde of Egypt.
Bring it down; bring her and the daughters
of powerful nations down to the lower parts
of the earth, along with those who descend
to the Pit. 19 Say to them,[1] 'Whom [a]do you
surpass in beauty? [b]Go down and be laid to
rest with the uncircumcised!' 20 They will fall
among those killed by the sword. The sword
is drawn; they [a]carry her and all her hordes
away. 21 The bravest of [a]the warriors will speak
to him from the midst of Sheol along with
his allies, saying: 'The uncircumcised have
come down; they lie still, killed by the sword.'
22 "[a]Assyria is there with all her assembly
around her grave, all of them struck down
by the sword. 23 Their graves are located in
the remote slopes of the Pit. [a]Her assembly
is around her grave, all of them struck down
by the sword, those who [b]spread terror in
the land of the living.
24 "[a]Elam is there with all her hordes
around her grave; all of them struck down
by the sword. They went down uncircumcised to the lower parts of the earth, those
[b]who spread terror in the land of the living.

32:4 [b]Isa 18:6; Ezek 31:13   [1]Heb. *the beasts of the field.*   32:5 [a]Ezek 31:12   [1]MT *your height.*   32:7 [a]Isa 13:10; Joel 2:31;
3:15; Amos 8:9; Matt 24:29; Mark 13:24; Luke 21:25; Rev 6:12–13; 8:12   32:10 [a]Ezek 26:16   32:11 [a]Jer 46:26; Ezek 30:4
32:12 [a]Ezek 28:7; 30:11; 31:12   [b]Ezek 29:19   32:13 [a]Ezek 29:11   32:15 [a]Exod 7:5; 14:4, 18; Ps 9:16; Ezek 6:7
32:16 [a]2 Sam 1:17; 2 Chr 35:25; Jer 9:17; Ezek 26:17   32:18 [1]The Heb. verb is used as a response to death.
32:19 [a]Jer 9:25–26; Ezek 31:2, 18   [b]Ezek 28:10   [1]LXX places this verse after v. 21.   32:20 [a]Ps 28:3
32:21 [a]Isa 1:31; 14:9–10; Ezek 32:27   32:22 [a]Ezek 31:3, 16   32:23 [a]Isa 14:15   [b]Ezek 32:24–27, 32
32:24 [a]Gen 10:22; 14:1; Isa 11:11; Jer 25:25; 49:34–39   [b]Ezek 32:23

Now they will bear their shame with those who descend to the Pit. [25]Among the dead they have made a [a]bed for her, along with all her hordes around her grave. All of them are uncircumcised, killed by the sword, for their terror had spread in the land of the living. They bear their shame along with those who descend to the Pit; they are placed among the dead.

[26]"[a]Meshech Tubal is there, along with all her hordes around her grave. All of them are [b]uncircumcised, killed by the sword, for they spread their terror in the land of the living. [27]They do not lie with [a]the fallen warriors of ancient times,[1] who went down to Sheol with their weapons of war, having their swords placed under their heads and their shields on their bones,[2] when the terror of these warriors was in the land of the living.

[28]"But as for you, in the midst of the uncircumcised you will be broken, and you will lie with those killed by the sword.

[29]"[a]Edom is there with her kings and all her princes. Despite their might they are laid with those killed by the sword; they lie with the uncircumcised and those who descend to the Pit.

[30]"All [a]the leaders of the north are there, along with all the [b]Sidonians; despite their might they have gone down in shameful terror with the dead. They lie uncircumcised with those killed by the sword and bear their shame with those who descend to the Pit.

[31]"Pharaoh will see them and be [a]consoled over all his hordes who were killed by the sword, Pharaoh and all his army, declares the Sovereign LORD. [32]Indeed, I terrified him in the land of the living, yet he will lie in the midst of the uncircumcised with those killed by the sword, Pharaoh and all his hordes, declares the Sovereign LORD."

Ezekiel Israel's Watchman

33 The LORD's message came to me: [2]"Son of man, speak to your people, and say to [a]them, 'Suppose I bring a sword against the land, and the people of the land take one man from their borders and make him their [b]watchman. [3]He sees the sword coming against the land, blows the trumpet,[1] and warns the people, [4]but there is one who hears the sound of the trumpet yet does [a]not heed the warning. Then the sword comes and sweeps him away. He will be responsible for [b]his own death. [5]He heard the sound of the trumpet but did not heed the warning, so he is responsible for himself. If he had heeded the warning, he would have saved his life. [6]But suppose [a]the watchman sees the sword coming and does not blow the trumpet to warn the people. Then the sword comes and takes one of their lives. He is swept away for his iniquity, but I will hold the watchman accountable for that person's death.'

[7]"As for you, [a]son of man, I have made you a watchman for the house of Israel. Whenever you hear a word from my mouth, you must warn them on my behalf. [8]When I say to the wicked, 'O wicked man, you must certainly die,' and you do not warn the wicked about his behavior, the wicked man will die for his iniquity, but I will hold you accountable for his death. [9]But if you warn the wicked man to change his behavior, and he refuses to change, he will die for his iniquity, but you have saved your own life.

[10]"And you, son of man, say to the house of Israel, 'This is what you have said: "Our rebellious acts and our sins have caught up with us, and we are wasting away because of them. [a]How then can we live?"' [11]Say to them, 'As surely as [a]I live, declares the Sovereign LORD, I take no pleasure in the death of the wicked, but prefer that the wicked [b]change his behavior and live. Turn back, turn back from your evil deeds! [c]Why should you die, O house of Israel?'

[12]"And you, son of man, say to your people, 'The [a]righteousness of [b]the righteous will not deliver him if he rebels.[1] As for the wicked, his wickedness will not make him stumble if he turns from it. The righteous will not be able to live by his righteousness if he sins.'[2] [13]Suppose I tell the righteous that he will certainly live, [a]but he becomes

32:25 [a] Ps 139:8   **32:26** [a] Gen 10:2; Ezek 27:13; 38:2–3; 39:1   [b] Ezek 32:19   **32:27** [a] Isa 14:18–19   [1] MT *of the uncircumcised.* [2] Heb. *and their iniquities were over their bones.*   **32:29** [a] Isa 9:5–6; 34:5–6; Jer 49:7–22; Ezek 25:12–14   **32:30** [a] Jer 1:15; 25:26; Ezek 38:6, 15; 39:2   [b] Jer 25:22; Ezek 28:21–23   **32:31** [a] Ezek 14:22; 31:16   **33:2** [a] Ezek 3:11   [b] 2 Sam 18:24–25; 2 Kgs 9:17; Hos 9:8   **33:3** [1] Heb. *shofar;* a ram's horn rather than a brass instrument.   **33:4** [a] 2 Chr 25:16; Jer 6:17; Zech 1:4   [b] Ezek 18:13; 35:9; [Acts 18:6]   **33:6** [a] Ezek 33:8   **33:7** [a] Isa 62:6; Ezek 3:17–21   **33:10** [a] Isa 49:14; Ezek 37:11   **33:11** [a] [2 Sam 14:14; Lam 3:33]; Ezek 18:23, 32; Hos 11:8; [2 Pet 3:9]   [b] Ezek 18:21, 30; [Hos 14:1, 4; Acts 3:19]   [c] [Isa 55:6–7]; Jer 3:22; Ezek 18:30–31; Hos 14:1; [Acts 3:19]   **33:12** [a] Ezek 3:20; 18:24, 26   [b] [2 Chr 7:14]; Ezek 18:21; 33:19   [1] Heb. *in the day of his rebellion;* i.e., a godly person rejecting what is good and becoming sinful.   [2] Heb. *in the day of his sin.*   **33:13** [a] Ezek 3:20; 18:24

confident in his righteousness and commits iniquity. None of his righteous deeds will be remembered; because of the iniquity he has committed he will die. [14]Suppose I say to the wicked, 'You must certainly die,' but [a]he turns from his sin and does what is just and right. [15]He [a]returns what was taken in pledge, pays back what he has stolen, and follows the statutes that [b]give life, committing no iniquity. [c]He will certainly live—he will not die. [16a]None of the sins he has committed will be counted against him. He has done what is just and right; he will certainly live.

[17]"[a]Yet your people say, 'The behavior of the Lord is not right,' when it is their behavior that is not right. [18]When a righteous man turns from his godliness and commits iniquity, [a]he will die for it. [19]When the wicked turns from his sin and does what is just and right, he will live because of it. [20]Yet you say, '[a]The behavior of the Lord is not right.' House of Israel, I will judge each of you according to his behavior."

The Fall of Jerusalem

[21]In the twelfth year [a]of our exile, in the tenth month, on the fifth of the month, [b]a refugee came to me from Jerusalem saying, "[c]The city has been defeated!"[1] [22]Now [a]the hand of the LORD had been on me the evening before the refugee reached me, but the LORD [b]opened my mouth by the time the refugee arrived in the morning; he opened my mouth and I was able to speak once more. [23]The LORD's message came to me: [24]"Son of man, [a]the ones living in these [b]ruins in the land of Israel are saying, '[c]Abraham was only one man, yet he possessed the land, [d]but we are many; surely the land has been given to us for a [e]possession.' [25]Therefore say to them, 'This is what the Sovereign LORD says: [a]You eat the meat with the blood still in it, pray to your idols, and [b]shed blood. Do you really think you will possess the [c]land? [26]You rely on your swords and commit abominable

deeds; each of you [a]defiles his neighbor's wife. Will you possess the land?'

[27]"This is what you must say to them, 'This is what the Sovereign LORD says: As surely as I live, [a]those [b]living in the ruins will die by the sword, those in the open field I will give to the wild beasts for food, and those who are in the strongholds and [c]caves will die of disease. [28a]I will turn the land into a desolate ruin; her confident [b]pride will come to an end. [c]The mountains of Israel will be so desolate no one will pass through them. [29]Then they will know that I am the LORD when I turn the land into a desolate ruin because of all the abominable deeds they have committed.'

[30]"But as for you, son of man, your people (who are [a]talking about you by the walls and at the doors of the houses) say to one another, 'Come hear the word that comes from the LORD.' [31]They come to you in crowds, and [a]they [b]sit in front of you as my people. They [c]hear your words, but do not obey them. [d]For they talk lustfully, and [e]their heart is set on their own advantage.[1] [32]Realize that to them you are like a sensual song, a beautiful voice, and skilled musician. They hear your words, but they do [a]not obey them. [33]When all this comes true—[a]and it certainly will—then [b]they will know that a prophet was among them."

A Prophecy against False Shepherds

34 The LORD's message came to me: [2]"Son of man, prophesy against the shepherds of Israel; prophesy, and say to them—to the shepherds: 'This is what the Sovereign LORD says: [a]Woe to the shepherds of Israel who have been feeding themselves! Should not shepherds feed the flock? [3]You eat the fat, [a]you clothe yourselves with the wool, you [b]slaughter the choice animals, but you do not feed the sheep! [4]You have not [a]strengthened the weak, healed the sick, bandaged the injured, brought back the strays, or [b]sought the lost, but with [c]force and harshness you have ruled over them.

33:14 [a] [Isa 55:7]; Jer 18:7–8; Ezek 3:18–19; 18:27; Hos 14:1, 4   **33:15** [a] Ezek 18:7   [b] Exod 22:1–4; Lev 6:2, 4, 5; Num 5:6–7; Luke 19:8   [c] Lev 18:5; Ps 119:59; 143:8; Ezek 20:11, 13, 21   **33:16** [a] [Isa 1:18; 43:25]; Ezek 18:22   **33:17** [a] Ezek 18:25, 29   **33:18** [a] Ezek 18:26   **33:20** [a] Ezek 18:25, 29   **33:21** [a] Ezek 1:2   [b] Ezek 24:26   [c] 2 Kgs 25:4   [1] Heb. *smitten.*   **33:22** [a] Ezek 1:3; 8:1; 37:1   [b] Ezek 24:27   **33:24** [a] Ezek 34:2   [b] Ezek 36:4   [c] Isa 51:2; [Acts 7:5; Rom 4:12]   [d] Mic 3:11; [Matt 3:9; John 8:39]   [e] Ezek 11:15   **33:25** [a] Gen 9:4; Lev 3:17; 7:26; 17:10–14; 19:26; Deut 12:16, 23; 15:23   [b] Ezek 22:6, 9   [c] Deut 29:28   **33:26** [a] Ezek 18:6; 22:11   **33:27** [a] Ezek 33:24   [b] Ezek 39:4   [c] Judg 6:2; 1 Sam 13:6; Isa 2:19   **33:28** [a] Jer 44:2, 6, 22; Ezek 36:34–35   [b] Ezek 7:24; 24:21   [c] Ezek 6:2–3, 6   **33:30** [a] Isa 29:13; Ezek 14:3; 20:3, 31   **33:31** [a] Ezek 14:1   [b] Ezek 8:1   [c] Isa 58:2   [d] Ps 78:36–37; Isa 29:13; Jer 12:2; 1 John 3:18   [e] [Matt 13:22]   [1] Heb. *unjust gain.*   **33:32** [a] [Matt 7:21–28; Jas 1:22–25]   **33:33** [a] 1 Sam 3:20   [b] Ezek 2:5   **34:2** [a] Jer 23:1; Ezek 22:25; Mic 3:1–3, 11; Zech 11:17   **34:3** [a] Isa 56:11; Zech 11:16   [b] Ezek 33:25–26; Mic 3:1–3; Zech 11:5   **34:4** [a] Zech 11:16   [b] Matt 9:36; 10:16; 18:12–13; Luke 15:4   [c] [1 Pet 5:3]

[5a]They were [b]scattered because they had no shepherd, [c]and they became food for every wild beast. [6]My sheep [a]wandered over all the mountains and on every high hill. My sheep were scattered over the entire face of the earth with no one looking or searching for them.

[7]"Therefore, you shepherds, listen to the LORD's message: [8]As surely as I live, declares the Sovereign LORD, my sheep have become prey and have become food for all the wild beasts. There was no shepherd, and my shepherds did not search for my flock, [a]but fed themselves and did not feed my sheep. [9]Therefore, you shepherds, listen to the LORD's message. [10]This is what the Sovereign LORD says: Look, [a]I am [b]against the shepherds, and I will demand my sheep from their hand. I will no longer let them be shepherds; the shepherds will not [c]feed themselves anymore. I will [d]rescue my sheep from their mouths, so that they will no longer be food for them.

[11]"For this is what the Sovereign LORD says: Look, I myself will search for my sheep and seek them out. [12]As a [a]shepherd seeks out his flock when he is [b]among his scattered sheep, so I will seek out my flock. I will rescue them from all the places where they have been scattered on a cloudy, dark day. [13]I [a]will bring them out from among the peoples and gather them from foreign countries; I will bring them to their own land. I will feed them on the mountains of Israel, by the streams and all the inhabited places of the land. [14]In a good pasture [a]I will feed them; [b]the mountain heights of Israel will be their pasture. There they will lie down in a lush pasture, and they will feed on rich grass on the mountains of Israel. [15]I myself will feed my sheep and I myself will make them lie down, declares the Sovereign LORD. [16]I [a]will seek [b]the lost and [c]bring back the strays; I will bandage the injured and strengthen the sick, but the fat and the strong I will destroy. I will feed them—with judgment!

[17]"As for you, my sheep, this is what the Sovereign LORD says: Look, I am about to judge between one sheep and another, between rams and goats. [18]Is it not enough for you to feed on the good pasture that you must trample the rest of your pastures with your feet? When you drink clean water, must you muddy the rest of the water by trampling it with your feet? [19]As for my sheep, they must eat what you trampled with your feet and drink what you have muddied with your feet!

[20]"Therefore, this is what the Sovereign LORD says to them: Look, I myself will judge between the fat sheep and the lean sheep. [21]Because you push with your side and your shoulder, and thrust your horns at all the weak sheep until you scatter them abroad, [22]I will save my sheep; they will no longer be prey. I will judge between one sheep and another.

[23]"I will set one [a]shepherd over them, and he will feed them—namely, [b]my servant David. He will feed them and will be their shepherd. [24]I, the LORD, [a]will be their God, [b]and my servant David will be prince among them; I, the LORD, have spoken!

[25]"I [a]will make [b]a covenant of peace with them and [c]will rid the land of wild beasts, so that they can live securely in the wilderness and even sleep in the woods. [26]I will turn them and the regions around [a]my hill into [b]a blessing. I will make [c]showers come down in their season; they will be showers that bring blessing. [27]The trees of [a]the field will yield their fruit and the earth will yield its crops. They will live securely on their land; they will know that I am the LORD, when I [b]break the bars of their yoke and rescue them from the hand of those who [c]enslaved them. [28]They will no longer be prey for [a]the nations, and the wild beasts will not devour them. They will live securely, and no one will make them afraid. [29]I will prepare for them a healthy[1] [a]planting. They will [b]no longer be victims of famine in the land and will [c]no longer bear the insults of

34:5 [a]Ezek 33:21 [b]Num 27:17; 1 Kgs 22:17; Jer 10:21; Matt 9:36; Mark 6:34 [c]Isa 56:9; Jer 12:9 34:6 [a]Jer 40:11–12; 50:6; Ezek 7:16; 1 Pet 2:25 34:8 [a]Ezek 34:2, 10 34:10 [a]Jer 21:13; 52:24–27; Ezek 5:8; 13:8; Zech 10:3 [b]Ezek 3:18; Heb 13:17 [c]Ezek 34:2, 8 [d]Ps 72:12–14; Ezek 13:23 34:12 [a]Jer 31:10 [b]Jer 13:16; Ezek 30:3; Joel 2:2 34:13 [a]Isa 65:9–10; Jer 23:3; Ezek 11:17; 20:41; 28:25; 36:24; 37:21–22 34:14 [a]Ps 23:2; Jer 3:15; [John 10:9] [b]Jer 33:12 34:16 [a]Isa 40:11; Mic 4:6; [Matt 18:11; Mark 2:17; Luke 5:32] [b]Isa 10:16; Amos 4:1 [c]Jer 10:24 34:23 [a][Isa 40:11; Jer 23:4–5]; Hos 1:11; [John 10:11; Heb 13:20; 1 Pet 2:25; 5:4] [b]Jer 30:9; Ezek 37:24; Hos 3:5 34:24 [a]Exod 29:45; Ezek 37:25 [b]Isa 55:3; Jer 30:9; Ezek 37:24–25; Hos 3:5 34:25 [a]Ezek 37:26 [b]Lev 26:6; Job 5:22–23; Isa 11:6–9; Hos 2:18 [c]Jer 23:6 34:26 [a]Isa 56:7 [b]Gen 12:2; Isa 19:24; Zech 8:13 [c]Ps 68:9 34:27 [a]Lev 26:4; Ps 85:12; Isa 4:2 [b]Lev 26:13; Isa 52:2–3; Jer 2:20 [c]Jer 25:14 34:28 [a]Jer 30:10; Ezek 39:26 34:29 [a][Isa 11:1] [b]Ezek 36:29 [c]Ezek 36:3, 6, 15 [1]MT for a name.

the nations. [30] Then they [a]will know that I, the LORD their God, am with them and that they are [b]my people, the house of Israel, declares the Sovereign LORD. [31] And you, my [a]sheep, the sheep of my pasture, are my people, and I am your God, declares the Sovereign LORD.'"

Prophecy against Mount Seir

35 The LORD's message came to me: [2] "Son of man, turn toward[1] [a]Mount Seir and [b]prophesy against it. [3] Say to [a]it, 'This is what the Sovereign LORD says:

"'Look, I am against you, Mount Seir;
I will stretch out my hand against
 you
and turn you into a desolate ruin.
[4] I will lay waste your cities,
and you will become desolate.
Then you will know that I am the
 LORD!

[5] "'You have shown unrelenting hostility and poured the people of Israel onto the blades of [a]a sword at the time of their calamity, at the time of their final punishment. [6] Therefore, as surely as I live, declares the Sovereign LORD, I will subject you to [a]bloodshed, and bloodshed will pursue you. [b]Since you did not hate bloodshed, bloodshed will pursue you. [7] I will turn Mount Seir into a desolate ruin;[1] I will cut off from it the [a]one who passes through or returns. [8] I will fill its mountains with its dead; on your hills and in your valleys and in all your ravines, those killed by the sword will fall. [9] I [a]will turn you into a perpetual desolation, and your cities will not be inhabited. [b]Then you will know that I am the LORD.

[10] "'You said, "These two nations, these two lands will be mine, and we will [a]possess[b]them," (although the LORD was there); [11] therefore, as surely as [a]I live, declares the Sovereign LORD, I will deal with you according to your anger and your envy, by which you acted spitefully against them. I will reveal myself to them when I judge you.

[12] Then you will know that I, [a]the LORD, have [b]heard all the [c]insults you spoke against the mountains of Israel, saying, "They are desolate; they have been given to us for food." [13] You exalted yourselves against me [a]with your speech and hurled many [b]insults against me—I have heard them all! [14] This is what [a]the Sovereign LORD says: While the whole earth rejoices, I will turn you into a desolation. [15] As you rejoiced over the inheritance of the house of Israel because it [a]was [b]desolate, so will I deal with you—you will be desolate, Mount Seir, and all Edom—all of it! Then they will know that I am the LORD.'"

Blessings on the Mountains of Israel

36 "As for you, son of man, prophesy to the [a]mountains of Israel, and say: 'O mountains of Israel, listen to the LORD's message! [2] This is what [a]the Sovereign LORD says: [b]The enemy has spoken against you, saying "Aha!" and, "The ancient heights[1] [c]have become our property!"' [3] So prophesy [a]and say: 'This is what the Sovereign LORD says: Surely because they have made you desolate and crushed you from all directions, so that you have become the property of the rest of the nations, and have become the subject of [b]gossip and slander among the people, [4] therefore, O mountains of Israel, hear the word of the Sovereign LORD. This is what the Sovereign LORD says to the mountains and hills, the ravines and valleys, and to the desolate ruins and the abandoned cities that have become prey and an object of [a]derision to the rest of the nations round about; [5] therefore, this is what the Sovereign LORD says: [a]Surely I have spoken in the fire of my zeal against the rest of the nations and against all Edom, [b]who with great joy and utter contempt have made my land their property and prey, because of its pasture.'

[6] "Therefore prophesy concerning the land of Israel, and say to the mountains and hills, the ravines and valleys, 'This is what the Sovereign LORD says: Look, I have spoken in my zeal and in my anger because

34:30 [a] Ezek 34:24   [b] Ps 46:7, 11; Ezek 14:11; 36:28   **34:31** [a] Ps 100:3; Jer 23:1; [John 10:11]   **35:2** [a] Gen 36:8; Deut 2:5; Jer 25:21; 49:7–22; Ezek 25:12–14; Joel 3:19; Amos 1:11–12; Obad 1–9, 15, 16   [b] Amos 1:11   [1] Heb. *set your face against.*   **35:3** [a] Ezek 6:14   **35:5** [a] Ezek 25:12   **35:6** [a] Isa 63:1–6; Ezek 16:38; 32:6   [b] Ps 109:17   **35:7** [a] Judg 5:6   [1] Maj. MSS *desolate, desolate.*   **35:9** [a] Jer 49:13; Ezek 25:13   [b] Ezek 36:11   **35:10** [a] Ps 83:4–12; Ezek 36:2, 5   [b] [Ps 48:1–3; 132:13–14]; Isa 12:6; Ezek 48:35; Zeph 3:15   **35:11** [a] [Matt 7:2; Jas 2:13]   **35:12** [a] Ps 9:16   [b] Zeph 2:8   [c] Isa 52:5   **35:13** [a] [1 Sam 2:3]   [b] Ezek 36:3   **35:14** [a] Isa 65:13–14   **35:15** [a] Obad 12, 15   [b] Jer 50:11; Lam 4:21   **36:1** [a] Ezek 6:2–3   **36:2** [a] Jer 33:24; Ezek 25:3; 26:2   [b] Deut 32:13; Ps 78:69; Isa 58:14; Hab 3:19   [c] Ezek 35:10   [1] Or *high places.*   **36:3** [a] Deut 28:37; 1 Kgs 9:7; Lam 2:15; Dan 9:16   [b] Ps 44:13–14; Jer 18:16; Ezek 35:13   **36:4** [a] Ps 79:4; Jer 48:27   **36:5** [a] Deut 4:24; Ezek 38:19   [b] Ezek 35:10, 12

you have ᵃendured the insults of the nations. ⁷ So this is what the Sovereign LORD says: Iᵃvow that the nations around you will ᵇendure insults as well.

⁸ "But you, mountains of Israel, will grow your branches and bear your fruit for my people Israel, for they will arrive soon. ⁹ For indeed, I am on your side; I will turn to you, and you will be plowed and planted. ¹⁰ I will multiply your people—ᵃthe whole house of Israel, all of it. The cities will be populated and the ruins rebuilt. ¹¹ I ᵃwill increase the number of people and animals on you; they will increase and be fruitful. I will cause you to be inhabited as in ancient times and will ᵇdo more good for you than at ᶜthe beginning of your history. Then you will know that I am the LORD. ¹² I will lead people, my people Israel, across you; ᵃthey will possess you, and you will become their inheritance. No longer will you ᵇbereave them of their children.

¹³ "This is what the Sovereign LORD says: Because they are saying to ᵃyou, "You are a devourer of men and bereave your nation of children," ¹⁴ therefore you will no longer devour people and no longer bereave your nation of children, declares the Sovereign LORD. ¹⁵ I will ᵃno longer subject you to the nations' insults; no longer will you bear the shame of the peoples, and no longer will you bereave¹ your nation, declares the Sovereign LORD.'"

¹⁶ The LORD's message came to me: ¹⁷ "Son of man, when ᵃthe house of Israel was living on ᵇtheir own land, they defiled it by their behavior and their deeds. In my sight their behavior was like the uncleanness of a woman having her monthly period. ¹⁸ So I poured my anger on them because of the blood they shed on the land and because of the idols with which they defiled it. ¹⁹ I ᵃscattered them among the nations; they were dispersed throughout foreign countries. ᵇIn accordance with their behavior and their deeds I judged them. ²⁰ But when they arrived in the nations where they went, they ᵃprofaned my holy name. It was said of them, 'These are the people of the LORD, yet they have departed from his land.' ²¹ I was concerned ᵃfor my holy reputation, which the house of Israel profaned among the nations where they went.

²² "Therefore say to the house of Israel, 'This is what the Sovereign LORD says: It is not for your sake that I am about to act, O house of Israel, ᵃbut for the sake of my holy reputation, which you profaned among the nations where you went. ²³ I will ᵃmagnify my great name that has been profaned among the nations, which you have profaned among them. The nations will know that I am the LORD, declares the Sovereign LORD, when I magnify myself among you in their sight.

²⁴ "'I ᵃwill take you from the nations and gather you from all the countries; then I will bring you to your land. ²⁵ ᵃI will sprinkle you with pure water, and you will be clean ᵇfrom all your impurities. I will purify you from all your idols. ²⁶ I will give you a ᵃnew heart, and I will put a new spirit within you. I will remove the heart of stone from your body and give you a heart of flesh. ²⁷ I will put my ᵃSpirit within you; I will take the initiative, and you will obey my statutes and carefully observe my regulations. ²⁸ Then you will live in ᵃthe land I gave to ᵇyour fathers; you will be my people, and I will be your God. ²⁹ I will ᵃsave you from all your uncleanness. ᵇI will call for the grain and multiply it; I will not ᶜbring a famine on you. ³⁰ I will multiply the fruit of the trees ᵃand the produce of the fields, so that you will never again suffer the disgrace of famine among the nations. ³¹ Then ᵃyou ᵇwill remember your evil behavior and your deeds that were not good; you will loathe yourselves on account of your sins and your abominable deeds. ³² Understand that it is ᵃnot for your sake I am about to act, declares the Sovereign LORD. Be ashamed and embarrassed by your behavior, O house of Israel.

³³ "'This is what the Sovereign LORD says:

36:6 ᵃ Ps 74:10; 123:3–4; Ezek 34:29   36:7 ᵃ Ezek 20:5   ᵇ Jer 25:9, 15, 29   36:10 ᵃ Isa 58:12; 61:4; Amos 9:14   36:11 ᵃ Jer 31:27; 33:12   ᵇ Job 42:12; Isa 51:3   ᶜ Ezek 35:9; 37:6, 13   36:12 ᵃ Obad 17   ᵇ Jer 15:7; Ezek 22:12, 27   36:13 ᵃ Num 13:32   36:15 ᵃ Isa 60:14; Ezek 34:29   ¹ MT *you will cause to stumble.*   36:17 ᵃ Lev 18:25, 27, 28; Jer 2:7   ᵇ Lev 15:19   36:19 ᵃ Deut 28:64; Ezek 5:12; 22:15; Amos 9:9   ᵇ Ezek 7:3; 18:30; 39:24; [Rom 2:6]   36:20 ᵃ Isa 52:5; Ezek 12:16; Rom 2:24   36:21 ᵃ Ezek 20:9, 14   36:22 ᵃ Ps 106:8; Ezek 20:44   36:23 ᵃ Isa 5:16; Ezek 20:41; 28:22   36:24 ᵃ Isa 43:5–6; Ezek 34:13; 37:21   36:25 ᵃ Num 19:17–19; Ps 51:7; Isa 52:15; Heb 9:13, 19; 10:22   ᵇ Jer 33:8   36:26 ᵃ Ps 51:10; Jer 32:39; Ezek 11:19; [John 3:3]   36:27 ᵃ Isa 44:3; 59:21; Ezek 11:19; 37:14; [Joel 2:28–29]   36:28 ᵃ Ezek 28:25; 37:25   ᵇ Jer 30:22; Ezek 11:20; 37:27   36:29 ᵃ Zech 13:1; [Matt 1:21; Rom 11:26]   ᵇ Ps 105:16   ᶜ Ezek 34:27, 29; Hos 2:21–23   36:30 ᵃ Lev 26:4; Ezek 34:27   36:31 ᵃ Ezek 16:61, 63   ᵇ Lev 26:39; Ezek 6:9; 20:43   36:32 ᵃ Deut 9:5

In the day I cleanse you from all your sins, I will populate the cities, [a]and the ruins will be rebuilt. [34]The desolate land will be plowed, instead of being desolate in the sight of everyone who passes by. [35]They will say, "This desolate land has become like the garden of [a]Eden; the ruined, desolate, and destroyed cities are now fortified and inhabited." [36]Then the [a]nations that remain around you will know that I, the LORD, have rebuilt the ruins and replanted what was desolate. I, the LORD, have spoken—and I will do it!'

[37]"This [a]is what the Sovereign LORD says: I will allow the house of Israel to ask me to do this for them: I will [b]multiply their people like sheep. [38]Like the sheep for offerings, like the sheep of Jerusalem during her appointed feasts, so the ruined cities will be filled with flocks of people. Then they will know that I am the LORD."

The Valley of Dry Bones

37 The [a]hand[1] of the LORD was on me, and he brought me out by the Spirit of the LORD and placed me [b]in the midst of the valley, and it was full of bones. [2]He made me walk all around among them. I realized there were a great many bones in the valley, and they were very dry. [3]He said to me, "Son of man, can these bones live?" I said to him, "Sovereign LORD, [a]you know." [4]Then he said to me, "Prophesy over these bones, and tell them: 'Dry bones, listen to the LORD's message. [5]This is what the Sovereign LORD says to these bones: Look, I am about to infuse breath into you and you will live. [6]I will put tendons[1] on you and muscles over you and will cover you with skin; I will put breath in you, and you will live. [a]Then you will know that I am the LORD.'"

[7]So I prophesied as I was commanded. There was a sound when I prophesied—I heard a rattling, and the bones came together, bone to bone. [8]As I watched, I saw tendons on them, then muscles appeared, and skin covered over them from above, but there was no breath in them.

[9]He said to me, "Prophesy to the breath—prophesy, son of man—and say to the breath: 'This is what the Sovereign LORD says: [a]Come from the four winds, O breath, and breathe on these corpses so that they may live.'" [10]So I prophesied as I was [a]commanded, and the breath came into them; they lived and stood on their feet, an extremely great army.

[11]Then he said to me, "Son of man, these bones are [a]all the house of Israel. Look, they are saying, '[b]Our bones are dry, our hope has perished; we are cut off.' [12]Therefore [a]prophesy, and tell them, 'This is what the Sovereign LORD says: Look, I am about to open your graves and will raise you from your graves, my people. I will [b]bring you to the land of Israel. [13]Then you will know that I am the LORD, when I open your graves and raise you from your graves, my people. [14]I [a]will place my breath in you and you will live; I will give you rest in your own land. Then you will know that I am the LORD—I have spoken and I will act, declares the LORD.'"

[15]The LORD's message came to me: [16]"As for you, son of man, [a]take one branch and write on it, 'For Judah and for [b]the Israelites associated with him.' Then take another branch and write on it, 'For Joseph, the branch of Ephraim, and all the house of Israel associated with him.' [17a]Join them as one stick; they will be as one in your hand. [18]When your people say to you, '[a]Will you not tell us what these things mean?' [19]tell them, 'This is what the Sovereign LORD [a]says: Look, I am about to take [b]the branch of Joseph that is in the hand of Ephraim and the tribes of Israel associated with him, and I will place them on the stick of Judah and make them into one stick—they will be one in my hand.' [20]The sticks you write on will [a]be in your hand in front of them. [21]Then tell them, '[a]This is what the Sovereign LORD says: Look, I am about to take the Israelites from among the nations where they have gone. I will gather them from round about and bring them to their land. [22]I [a]will make them [b]one nation in the land, on the

36:33 [a]Ezek 36:10   36:35 [a]Isa 51:3; Ezek 28:13; Joel 2:3   36:36 [a]Ezek 17:24; 22:14; 37:14; Hos 14:4–9   36:37 [a]Ezek 14:3; 20:3, 31   [b]Ezek 36:10   37:1 [a]Ezek 1:3   [b]Ezek 3:14; 8:3; 11:24; Acts 8:39   [1]Or *power*.   37:3 [a][Deut 32:39; 1 Sam 2:6; John 5:21; Rom 4:17; 2 Cor 1:9]   37:6 [a]Isa 49:23; Ezek 6:7; 35:12; Joel 2:27; 3:17   [1]The exact anatomical feature is uncertain.   37:9 [a][Ps 104:30]   37:10 [a]Rev 11:11   37:11 [a]Jer 33:24; Ezek 36:10   [b]Ps 141:7; Isa 49:14   37:12 [a]Deut 32:39; 1 Sam 2:6; Isa 26:19; 66:14; [Dan 12:2]; Hos 13:14   [b]Ezek 36:24   37:14 [a]Isa 32:15; Ezek 36:27; [Joel 2:28–29]; Zech 12:10   37:16 [a]Num 17:2–3   [b]2 Chr 11:12–13, 16; 15:9; 30:11, 18   37:17 [a]Isa 11:13; Jer 50:4; Ezek 37:22–24; Hos 1:11; Zeph 3:9   37:18 [a]Ezek 12:9; 24:19   37:19 [a]Zech 10:6   [b]Ezek 37:16–17   37:20 [a]Ezek 12:3   37:21 [a]Isa 43:5–6; Jer 32:37; Ezek 36:24; Amos 9:14–15   37:22 [a]Isa 11:13; Jer 3:18; Hos 1:11   [b]Ezek 34:23; John 10:16

mountains of Israel, and one king will rule over them all. They will never again be two nations and never again be divided into two kingdoms. [23]They will not defile themselves with their idols, their detestable things, and all their rebellious deeds. I will save them from all their unfaithfulness[1] by which [a]they [b]sinned. I will purify them; they will become my people, and I will become their God.

[24]"My servant [a]David will be king over them; there will be one shepherd for all of them. [b]They will follow my regulations and carefully observe my statutes. [25]They will live in [a]the land I gave to my servant Jacob, in which your fathers lived; they will live in it—they and their children and their grandchildren [b]forever. David [c]my servant will be prince over them forever. [26]I will [a]make a covenant of peace with them; it will be a perpetual covenant with them. I will establish them, [b]increase their numbers, and place my [c]sanctuary among them forever. [27]My dwelling place will be with them; I will be their God, and they will be [a]my people. [28]Then, when my sanctuary is among [a]them forever, the nations will know that I, the LORD, [b]sanctify Israel.'"

A Prophecy against Gog

38 The LORD's message came to me: [2]"[a]Son of man, [b]turn toward [c]Gog, of the land of [d]Magog, the chief prince of [e]Meshech and Tubal. Prophesy against him [3]and say: 'This is what the Sovereign LORD says: Look, I am against you, Gog, chief prince of Meshech and Tubal. [4]I [a]will turn you around, put hooks into your jaws, and bring you out with all your army, horses, and horsemen, all of them fully armed, [b]a great company with shields of different types, [c]all of them armed with swords. [5]Persia, Ethiopia, and Put are with them, all of them with shields and helmets. [6]They are joined by [a]Gomer with all its troops and by Beth [b]Togarmah from the remote parts of the north with all its troops—many peoples are with you.

[7]"Be [a]ready and stay ready, you and all your companies assembled around you, and be a guard for them.[1] [8]After many days you will be summoned; in the latter years you will come to [a]a [b]land restored from [c]the ravages of war, from many peoples gathered on the mountains of Israel that had long been in ruins. Its people were brought out from the peoples, and all of them will be [d]living securely. [9]You will advance; you will come [a]like a storm. You will be like a cloud covering the [b]earth, you, all your troops, and the many other peoples with you.

[10]"This is what the Sovereign LORD says: On that day thoughts will come into your mind, and you will devise an evil plan. [11]You will say, "I will invade[1] [a]a land of unwalled towns; I will advance [b]against those living quietly in security—all of them living without walls and barred gates—[12]to loot [a]and plunder, to attack the inhabited ruins and the people gathered from the nations, who are acquiring cattle and goods, who live at the center[1] of the earth." [13]a Sheba and [b]Dedan and the traders of Tarshish with all its young warriors will say to you, "Have you come to loot? Have you assembled your armies to plunder, to carry away silver and gold, to take away cattle and goods, to haul away a great amount [c]of spoils?"'

[14]"Therefore, prophesy, [a]son of man, and say to Gog: 'This is what the Sovereign LORD says: On that day when my people Israel are [b]living securely, you will take notice [15]and come from your place, from [a]the remote parts of the north, you and many peoples with you, all of them riding on horses, a great company and a vast army. [16]You will advance against my people Israel like a cloud covering the earth. In future days I will bring you against my land so that the nations may [a]acknowledge me, when before their eyes I [b]magnify myself through you, O Gog.

[17]"This is what the Sovereign LORD says: Are you the one of whom I spoke in former days by my servants the prophets of Israel,

37:23 [a] Ezek 36:25 [b] Ezek 36:28–29 [1] MT *their dwellings.* **37:24** [a] Isa 40:11; [Jer 23:5; 30:9]; Ezek 34:23–24; Hos 3:5; [Luke 1:32] [b] [John 10:16] **37:25** [a] Ezek 36:28 [b] Isa 60:21; Joel 3:20; Amos 9:15 [c] Ps 89:3–4; John 12:34 **37:26** [a] Ps 89:3; Isa 55:3; [Jer 32:40] [b] Jer 30:19; Ezek 36:10 [c] [2 Cor 6:16] **37:27** [a] Lev 26:11; [John 1:14]; Rev 21:3 **37:28** [a] Ezek 36:23 [b] Exod 31:13; Ezek 20:12 **38:2** [a] Ezek 39:1 [b] Ezek 35:2–3 [c] Ezek 38:1–39:24; Rev 20:8 [d] Gen 10:2; Ezek 39:6; Rev 20:8 [e] Ezek 32:26 **38:4** [a] 2 Kgs 19:28; Ezek 29:4 [b] Isa 43:17 [c] Ezek 23:12 **38:6** [a] Gen 10:2 [b] Gen 10:3; Ezek 27:14 **38:7** [a] Isa 8:9–10; Jer 46:3–4 [1] I.e., Gog. **38:8** [a] Deut 4:30; Isa 24:22 [b] Ezek 34:13 [c] Ezek 36:1, 4 [d] Jer 23:6; Ezek 34:25; 39:26 **38:9** [a] Isa 28:2 [b] Jer 4:13 **38:11** [a] Zech 2:4 [b] Jer 49:31 [1] Heb. *go up against.* **38:12** [a] Ezek 38:8 [1] Perhaps "high point" or "top." **38:13** [a] Ezek 27:22 [b] Ezek 27:15, 20 [c] Ezek 27:12 **38:14** [a] Isa 4:1 [b] Jer 23:6; Ezek 38:8, 11; [Zech 2:5, 8] **38:15** [a] Ezek 39:2 **38:16** [a] Ezek 35:11 [b] Isa 5:16; 8:13; 29:23; Ezek 28:22

who prophesied in those days that I would bring you against them? [18]On that day, when Gog invades the land of Israel, declares the Sovereign LORD, my rage will mount up in my anger. [19]In my zeal, [a]in the fire of my fury, I declare that on that day there will be [b]a great earthquake in the land of Israel. [20]The fish of [a]the sea, [b]the birds of the sky, the wild beasts, all the things that creep on the ground, and all people who live on the face of the earth will shake at my presence. The mountains will topple, the cliffs will fall, and every wall will fall to the ground. [21]I will [a]call for [b]a sword to attack Gog on all my mountains, declares the Sovereign LORD; [c]every man's sword will be against his brother. [22]I will [a]judge him with [b]plague and bloodshed. [c]I will rain down on him, his troops, and the many peoples who are with him [d]a torrential downpour, hailstones, fire, and brimstone. [23]I will exalt and [a]magnify myself; I will reveal myself before many nations. Then they will know that I am the LORD.'

39 "As for [a]you, son of man, prophesy against Gog, and say: 'This is what the Sovereign LORD says: Look, I am against you, O Gog, chief prince of Meshech and Tubal! [2]I will [a]turn you around and drag you along; I will [b]lead you up from the remotest parts of the north and bring you against the mountains of Israel. [3]I will knock your bow out of your left hand and make your arrows fall from your right hand. [4]You will fall dead on the mountains of Israel, [a]you and all your troops and the people who are [b]with you. I give you as food to every kind of bird and every wild beast. [5]You will fall dead in the open field; for I have spoken, declares the Sovereign LORD. [6]I will send fire on Magog [a]and those who live securely in [b]the coastlands; then they will know that I am the LORD.

[7]"[a]I will make my holy name known in the midst of my people Israel; I will not let my holy name be [b]profaned anymore. [c]Then the nations will know that I am the LORD,

the Holy One of Israel. [8][a]Realize that it is coming and it will be done, declares the Sovereign LORD. It is the day I have spoken about.

[9]"Then those who live in the cities of Israel will go out and use the weapons for kindling—the shields, bows and arrows, war clubs and spears—they will burn them for seven years. [10]They will not need to take wood from the field or cut down trees from the forests because they will make fires with the weapons. They will take the loot from those who looted them [a]and seize the plunder of those who plundered them, declares the Sovereign LORD.

[11]"On that day I will assign Gog a grave in Israel. It will be the valley of those who travel east of the sea; it will block the way of the travelers. There they will bury Gog and all his horde; they will call it the Valley of Hamon Gog.[1] [12]For seven months Israel will bury them, [a]in order to cleanse the land. [13]All the people of the land will bury them, and it will be a [a]memorial for them on the day [b]I magnify myself, declares the Sovereign LORD. [14]They will designate men [a]to scout continually through the land, burying those who remain on the surface of the ground, in order to cleanse it. They will search for seven full months. [15]When the scouts survey the land and see a human bone, they will place a sign by it, until those assigned to burial duty have buried it in the valley of Hamon Gog. [16](A city by the name of Hamonah[1] will also be there.) They will [a]cleanse the land.'

[17]"As for you, son of man, this is what the Sovereign LORD [a]says: Tell every kind of bird and every wild beast: '[b]Assemble and come! Gather from all around to my [c]slaughter that I am going to make for you, a great slaughter [d]on the mountains of Israel! You will eat flesh and drink blood. [18][a]You will eat the flesh of warriors and drink the blood of the princes of the earth—the rams, lambs, goats, and bulls, all of them fattened [b]animals of Bashan. [19]You will eat fat until you

38:19 [a]Deut 32:21–22; Ps 18:7–8; Ezek 36:5–6; [Nah 1:2]; Heb 12:29 [b]Ps 89:46 38:20 [a]Hos 4:3 [b]Jer 4:24; Nah 1:5–6 38:21 [a]Ps 105:16 [b]Ezek 14:17 [c]Judg 7:22; 1 Sam 14:20; 2 Chr 20:23; Hag 2:22 38:22 [a]Isa 66:16; Jer 25:31 [b]Ezek 5:17 [c]Ps 11:6; Isa 30:30; Ezek 13:11 [d]Rev 16:21 38:23 [a]Ezek 36:23 39:1 [a]Ezek 38:2–3 39:2 [a]Ezek 38:8 [b]Ezek 38:15 39:4 [a]Ezek 38:4, 21 [b]Ezek 33:27 39:6 [a]Ezek 38:22; Amos 1:4, 7, 10; Nah 1:6 [b]Ps 72:10; Isa 66:19; Jer 25:22 39:7 [a]Ezek 39:25 [b]Lev 18:21; Ezek 36:23 [c]Ezek 38:16 39:8 [a]Rev 16:17; 21:6 39:10 [a]Isa 14:2; 33:1; Mic 5:8; Hab 2:8 39:11 [1]The name means "horde of Gog." 39:12 [a]Deut 21:23; Ezek 39:14, 16 39:13 [a]Jer 33:9; Zeph 3:19–20 [b]Ezek 28:22 39:14 [a]Ezek 39:12 39:16 [a]Ezek 39:12 [1]This name appears to be a fem. form of "horde," used in the name Hamon Gog. 39:17 [a]Isa 56:9; [Jer 12:9]; Ezek 39:4; Rev 19:17–18 [b]Isa 18:6 [c]Isa 34:6–7; Jer 46:10; Zeph 1:7 [d]Ezek 39:4 39:18 [a]Ezek 29:5; Rev 19:18 [b]Deut 32:14; Ps 22:12

are full and drink blood until you are drunk at my slaughter that I have made for you. [20a]You will fill up at my table [b]with horses and charioteers, with warriors and all the soldiers,' declares the Sovereign LORD.

[21]"I [a]will display [b]my majesty among the nations. All the nations will witness the judgment I have executed and the power I have exhibited among them. [22a]Then the house of Israel will know that I am the LORD their God, from that day forward. [23]The nations will know that [a]the house of [b]Israel went into exile due to their iniquity, for they were unfaithful to me. So I hid my face from them and [c]handed them over to their enemies; all of them died by the sword. [24]According to their uncleanness and rebellion [a]I have dealt with them, and I hid my face from them.

[25]"Therefore this is what the Sovereign LORD says: [a]Now I will restore the fortunes of Jacob, and I will have mercy on the [b]entire house of Israel. I will be zealous for my holy name. [26a]They will bear their shame for all their unfaithful acts against me, when they [b]live securely on their land with no one to make them afraid. [27a]When I have brought them back from the peoples and gathered them from the countries of their enemies, I will magnify myself [b]among them in the sight of many nations. [28]Then they will know that I am [a]the LORD their God because I sent them into exile among the nations and then gathered them into their own land. I will not leave any of them in exile any longer. [29a]I will no longer hide my face from them, when I [b]pour out my Spirit on the house of Israel, declares the Sovereign LORD."

Vision of the New Temple

40 In [a]the twenty-fifth year of our exile, at [b]the beginning of the year, on the tenth day of the month, in the fourteenth year after the city was struck down, on this very day, the hand of the LORD was on me, and he brought me there. [2]By [a]divine visions he brought me to the land of Israel and [b]placed me on a very high mountain, and on it was a structure like a city, to the south. [3]When he brought me there, [a]I saw a man whose appearance was like bronze, with a linen cord and a measuring stick in his hand. [b]He was [c]standing in the gateway. [4]The man said to me, "[a]Son of man, watch closely, listen carefully, and pay attention to everything I show you, for you have been brought here so that I can show it to you. [b]Tell the house of Israel everything you see."

[5]I [a]saw a wall all around the outside of the temple. In the man's hand was a measuring stick 10½ feet[1] long. He measured the thickness of the wall as 10½ feet and its height as 10½ feet. [6]Then he went to the gate facing [a]east. He climbed its steps and measured the threshold of the gate as 10½ feet deep. [7]The alcoves were 10½ feet long and 10½ feet wide; between the alcoves were 8¾ feet. The threshold of the gate by the porch of the gate facing inward was 10½ feet. [8]Then he measured the porch of the gate facing inward as 10½ feet. [9]He measured the porch of the gate as 14 feet and its jambs as 3½ feet; the porch of the gate faced inward. [10]There were three alcoves on each side of the east gate; the three had the same measurement, and the jambs on either side had the same measurement. [11]He measured the width of the entrance of the gateway as 17½ feet and the length of the gateway as 22¾ feet. [12]There was a barrier in front of the alcoves, 1¾ feet on either side; the alcoves were 10½ feet on either side. [13]He measured the gateway from the roof of one alcove to the roof of the other, a width of 43¾ feet from one entrance to the opposite one. [14]He measured the porch[1] at 105 feet high; the gateway went all around to the jamb of the courtyard. [15]From the front of the entrance gate to the porch of the inner gate was 87½ feet. [16]There were [a]closed windows toward the alcoves and toward their jambs within the gate all around, and likewise for the porches. There were

39:20 [a] Ps 76:5–6; Ezek 38:4; Hag 2:22 [b] Rev 19:18 **39:21** [a] Exod 9:16; Isa 37:20; Ezek 36:23; 38:23 [b] Exod 7:4 **39:22** [a] Exod 39:7, 28 **39:23** [a] Jer 22:8–9; 44:22; Ezek 36:18–20, 23 [b] Deut 31:17; Isa 1:15; 59:2; Ezek 39:29 [c] Lev 26:25 **39:24** [a] 2 Kgs 17:7; Jer 2:17, 19; 4:18; Ezek 36:19 **39:25** [a] Isa 27:12–13; Jer 30:3, 18; Ezek 34:13; 36:24 [b] Jer 31:1; Ezek 20:40; Hos 1:11 **39:26** [a] Dan 9:16 [b] Lev 26:5–6 **39:27** [a] Ezek 28:25–26 [b] Ezek 36:23–24; 38:16 **39:28** [a] Ezek 34:30 **39:29** [a] Isa 54:8–9 [b] Isa 32:15; Ezek 36:27; 37:14; [Joel 2:28; Zech 12:10]; Acts 2:17 **40:1** [a] 2 Kgs 25:1–4; Jer 39:2–3; 52:4–7; Ezek 33:21 [b] Ezek 1:3; 3:14, 22; 37:1 **40:2** [a] Ezek 1:1; 3:14; 8:3; 37:1; Dan 7:1, 7 [b] [Isa 2:2–3]; Ezek 17:23; 20:40; 37:22; [Mic 4:1]; Rev 21:10 **40:3** [a] Ezek 1:7; Dan 10:6; Rev 1:15 [b] Ezek 47:3; Zech 2:1–2 [c] Rev 11:1; 21:15 **40:4** [a] Ezek 44:5 [b] Ezek 43:10 **40:5** [a] [Isa 26:1]; Ezek 42:20 [1] Heb. *a measuring stick of 6 cubits,* [each] *a cubit and a handbreadth.* **40:6** [a] Ezek 43:1 **40:14** [1] MT *jambs.* **40:16** [a] 1 Kgs 6:4; Ezek 41:16, 26

windows all around the inside, and on each jamb were decorative [b]palm trees.

[17]Then [a]he brought me to the outer court. I saw [b]chambers there and a pavement made for the court all around; [c]30 chambers faced the pavement. [18]The pavement was beside the gates, corresponding to the length of the gates; this was the lower pavement. [19]Then he measured the width from before the lower gate to the front of the exterior of the inner court as 175 feet on the east and on the north.

[20]He measured the length and width of the gate of the outer court that faces north. [21]Its alcoves, three on each side, and its jambs and porches had the same measurement as the first gate; 87½ feet long and 43¾ feet wide. [22]Its windows, its porches, and its decorative palm trees had the same measurement as the gate that faced east. Seven steps led up to it, and its porch was in front of them. [23]Opposite the gate on the north and the east was a gate of the inner court; he measured the distance from gate to gate at 175 feet.

[24]Then he led me toward the south. I saw a gate on the south. He measured its jambs and its porches; they had the same dimensions as the others. [25]There were windows all around it and its porches, like the windows of the others, 87½ feet long and 43¾ feet wide. [26]There were seven steps going up to it; its porches were in front of them. It had decorative palm trees on its jambs, one on either side. [27]The inner court had a gate toward the south; he measured it from gate to gate toward the south as 175 feet.

[28]Then he brought me to the inner court by the south gate. He measured the south gate; it had the same dimensions as the others. [29]Its alcoves, its jambs, and its porches had the same dimensions as the others, and there were windows all around it and its porches; its length was 87½ feet and its width 43¾ feet. [30]There were porches all around, 43¾ feet long and 8¾ feet wide. [31]Its porches faced the outer court, and decorative palm trees were on its jambs, and its stairway had eight steps.

[32]Then he brought me to the inner court on the east side. He measured the gate; it had the same dimensions as the others. [33]Its alcoves, its jambs, and its porches had the same dimensions as the others, and there were windows all around it and its porches; its length was 87½ feet and its width 43¾ feet. [34]Its porches faced the outer court, it had decorative palm trees on its jambs, and its stairway had eight steps.

[35]Then he brought me to the north gate, and he measured it; it had the same dimensions as the others—[36]its alcoves, its jambs, and its porches. It had windows all around it; its length was 87½ feet and its width 43¾ feet. [37]Its jambs[1] faced the outer court, and it had decorative palm trees on its jambs on either side, and its stairway had eight steps.

[38]There was a chamber with its door by the porch of the gate;[1] there they [a]washed the burnt offering. [39]In [a]the porch of [b]the gate were two tables on either side on which to slaughter the burnt offering, the sin offering, and the guilt offering. [40]On the outside of the porch as one goes up at the entrance of the north gate were two tables, and on the other side of the porch of the gate were two tables. [41]Four tables were on each side of the gate, eight tables on which the sacrifices were to be slaughtered. [42]The four tables for the burnt offering were of carved stone, 32 inches long, 32 inches wide, and 21 inches high. They would put the instruments that they used to slaughter the burnt offering and the sacrifice on them. [43]There were hooks[1] 3 inches[2] long fastened in the house all around, and on the tables was the flesh of the offering.

[44]On [a]the outside of the inner gate were chambers for the singers of the inner court, one at the side of the north gate facing south, and the other at the side of the south[1] gate facing north. [45]He said to me, "This chamber that faces south is for [a]the priests who keep charge of the temple,[1] [46]and the chamber that faces north is for the priests [a]who keep charge of the altar. These are the descendants of [b]Zadok, from the descendants of Levi, who may approach the LORD to minister to him." [47]He measured the court as a square 175 feet long and 175 feet wide; the altar was in front of the temple.

40:16 [b]1 Kgs 6:29, 32, 35; 2 Chr 3:5; Ezek 40:22, 26, 31, 34, 37; 41:18–20, 25, 26   **40:17** [a]Ezek 10:5; 42:1; 46:21; Rev 11:2   [b]1 Kgs 6:5; 2 Chr 31:11; Ezek 40:38   [c]Ezek 45:5   **40:37** [1]LXX *porches.*   **40:38** [a]2 Chr 4:6   [1]MT *jambs of the gates.*   **40:39** [a]Lev 4:2–3   [b]Lev 5:6; 6:6; 7:1   **40:43** [1]Some wss *shelves.*   [2]Heb. *one handbreadth.*   **40:44** [a]1 Chr 6:31–32; 16:41–43; 25:1–7   [1]MT *east.*   **40:45** [a]Lev 8:35; Num 3:27–28, 32, 38; 18:5; 1 Chr 9:23; 2 Chr 13:11; Ps 134:1   [1]Heb. *the house.*   **40:46** [a]Lev 6:12–13; Num 18:5; Ezek 44:15   [b]1 Kgs 2:35; Ezek 43:19; 44:15–16

⁴⁸Then he brought me to the ªporch of the temple and measured the jambs of the porch as 8¾ feet on either side; the width of the gate was 24½ feet, and the sides¹ were 5¼ feet on each side. ⁴⁹The length of ªthe porch was 35 feet and the width 19¼ feet; steps¹ led up to it, and there were ᵇpillars beside the jambs on either side.

The Inner Temple

41 Then he ªbrought me to the outer sanctuary and measured the jambs; the jambs were 10½ feet wide on each side. ²The width of the entrance was 17½ feet, and the sides¹ of the entrance were 8¾ feet on each side. He measured the length of the outer sanctuary as 70 feet and its width as 35 feet.

³Then he went into the inner sanctuary and measured the jambs of the entrance as 3½ feet, the entrance as 10½ feet, and the width of the entrance as 12¼ feet. ⁴Then ªhe measured its length as 35 feet and its width as 35 feet, before the outer sanctuary. He said to me, "This is the Most Holy Place."

⁵Then he measured the wall of the temple¹ as 10½ feet and the width of the side chambers as 7 feet, all around the temple. ⁶The side chambers were in three stories, one above ªthe other, 30 in each story. There were offsets in the wall all around to serve as supports for the side chambers, so that the supports were ᵇnot in the wall of the temple. ⁷The side chambers surrounding the temple were wider at each successive story, for the structure surrounding the temple went up story by story all around the temple. For this reason the width of the temple increased as it went up, and one went up from the lowest story to the highest by the way of the middle story.

⁸I ªsaw that the temple had a raised platform all around; the foundations of the side chambers were a full measuring stick of 10½ feet high. ⁹The width of the outer wall of the side chambers was 8¾ feet, and the open area between the side chambers of the temple ¹⁰and the chambers of the court was 35 feet in width all around the temple

on every side. ¹¹There were entrances from the side chambers toward the open area, one entrance toward the north, and another entrance toward the south; the width of the open area was 8¾ feet all around.

¹²The building that was facing the temple courtyard at the west side was 122½ feet wide; the wall of the building was 8¾ feet thick all around, and its length 157½ feet. ¹³Then he measured the temple as ª175 feet long, the courtyard of the temple and the building and its walls as 175 feet long, ¹⁴and also the width of the front of the temple and the courtyard on the east as 175 feet.

¹⁵Then he measured the length of the building facing the courtyard at the rear of the temple, with its ªgalleries on either side as 175 feet.

The interior of the outer sanctuary and the porch of the court,¹ ¹⁶as well as ªthe thresholds, narrow windows, and galleries all around on three sides facing the threshold, were paneled with ᵇwood all around, from the ground up to the windows (now the windows were covered), ¹⁷to the space above the entrance, to the inner room, and on the outside and on all the walls in the inner room and outside, by measurement.¹ ¹⁸It was made ªwith cherubim and decorative palm ᵇtrees, with a palm tree between each cherub. Each cherub had two faces: ¹⁹ªa human face toward the palm tree on one side and a lion's face toward the palm tree on the other side. They were carved on the whole temple all around; ²⁰from the ground to the area above the entrance, cherubim and decorative palm trees were carved on the wall of the outer sanctuary. ²¹The ªdoorposts of the outer sanctuary were square. In front of the sanctuary one doorpost looked just like the other. ²²The altar was of wood, 5¼ feet high, with its length 3½ feet; its corners, its length,¹ and its walls were of wood. ªHe said to me, "This is ᵇthe table that is ᶜbefore the LORD." ²³The outer sanctuary and ªthe inner sanctuary each had a double door. ²⁴Each of the ªdoors had two leaves, two swinging leaves; two leaves for one door and two leaves for the other. ²⁵On the doors

40:48 ª 1 Kgs 6:3; 2 Chr 3:4 ¹MT *the width of the gate was 3 cubits.* **40:49** ª 1 Kgs 6:3 ᵇ 1 Kgs 7:15–22; 2 Chr 3:17; Jer 52:17–23; [Rev 3:12] ¹LXX *ten steps.* **41:1** ª Ezek 40:2–3, 17 **41:2** ¹MT *the width of the gate was 3 cubits.* **41:4** ª 1 Kgs 6:20; 2 Chr 3:8 **41:5** ¹Heb. *house.* **41:6** ª 1 Kgs 6:5–10 ᵇ 1 Kgs 6:6, 10 **41:8** ª Ezek 40:5 **41:13** ª Ezek 40:47 **41:15** ª Ezek 42:3, 5 ¹A few MSS *and its outer court.* **41:16** ª 1 Kgs 6:4; Ezek 40:16, 25 ᵇ 1 Kgs 6:15 **41:17** ¹LXX does not have *by measurement.* **41:18** ª 1 Kgs 6:29; 2 Chr 3:7 ᵇ 2 Chr 3:5; Ezek 40:16 **41:19** ª Ezek 1:10; 10:14 **41:21** ª 1 Kgs 6:33; Ezek 40:9, 14, 16; 41:1 **41:22** ª Exod 30:1–3; 1 Kgs 6:20; Rev 8:3 ᵇ Exod 25:23, 30; Lev 24:6; Ezek 23:41; 44:16; Mal 1:7, 12 ᶜ Exod 30:8 ¹LXX *base.* **41:23** ª 1 Kgs 6:31–35 **41:24** ª 1 Kgs 6:34

of the outer sanctuary were carved cherubim and palm trees, like those carved on the walls, and there was a canopy of wood on the front of the outside porch. [26]There were [a]narrow windows and decorative palm trees on either side of the side walls of the porch; this is what the side chambers of the temple and the canopies were like.

Chambers for the Temple

42 Then he led me out to the outer court, toward the north, and [a]brought me to the chamber that was opposite the courtyard and opposite the building on the [b]north. [2]Its length was 175 feet on the north side,[1] and its width 87½ feet. [3]Opposite the 35 feet that belonged to the inner court, and opposite the [a]pavement that belonged to the outer court, [b]gallery faced gallery in the three stories. [4]In front of the chambers was a walkway on the inner side, 17½ feet wide at a distance of 1¾ feet,[1] and their entrances were on the north. [5]Now the upper chambers were narrower, because the galleries took more space from them than from the lower and middle chambers of the building. [6]For they were in three stories and had no pillars like the pillars of the courts; therefore, the upper chambers were set back from the ground more than the lower and middle ones. [7]As for the outer wall by the side of the chambers, toward the outer court facing the chambers, it was 87½ feet long. [8]For the chambers on the outer court were 87½ feet long, while those facing the temple were [a]175 feet long. [9]Below these chambers was a passage on the east side as one enters from the outer court.

[10]At the beginning of the wall of the court toward the south,[1] facing the courtyard and the building, were chambers [11]like those on [a]the north with a passage in front of them. The chambers that were toward the south were the same length and width as those on the north, and had matching exits and entrances and arrangements. [12]There was an opening at the head of the passage, the passage in front of the corresponding wall toward the east when one enters.

[13]Then [a]he said to me, "The north chambers and the south chambers that face the courtyard are holy chambers where the priests who approach the Lord will eat the most holy offerings. There they will place the most holy offerings—the grain offering, the sin offering, and the guilt offering, because the place is holy. [14a]When the priests enter, then they will not go out from the sanctuary to the outer court without taking off their garments in which they minister, for these are holy; they will put on other garments, then they will go near the places where the people are."

[15]Now when he had finished measuring the interior of the temple, he led me out by the gate that faces [a]east and measured all around. [16]He measured the east side with the measuring stick as 875 feet by the measuring stick. [17]He measured the north side as 875 feet by the measuring stick. [18]He measured the south side as 875 feet by the measuring stick. [19]He turned to the west side and measured 875 feet by the measuring stick. [20]He measured [a]it on all four sides. It had a wall around it, [b]875 feet long and 875 feet wide, to separate the holy and common places.

The Glory Returns to the Temple

43 Then he brought me to the gate [a]that faced toward the east. [2]I saw the glory of the God of Israel coming from the east; the sound was like that of rushing water, [a]and the earth radiated [b]his glory. [3]It was [a]like the vision I saw when he[1] came [b]to destroy the city, and the vision I saw [c]by the Kebar River. I threw myself face down. [4a]The glory of the Lord came into the temple by way of the gate that faces east. [5]Then a wind lifted me up and brought me to [a]the inner court; I watched [b]the glory of the Lord filling the temple.

[6]I [a]heard someone speaking to me from the temple, while the man was standing beside me. [7]He said to me: "Son of man, this is [a]the place of my throne and [b]the place for the soles of my feet, [c]where I will live among the people of Israel forever. The

41:26 [a] Ezek 40:16   42:1 [a] Ezek 41:1   [b] Ezek 40:20   42:2 [1] Heb. *the door of the north.*   42:3 [a] Ezek 40:17   [b] Ezek 41:15–16;
42:5   42:4 [1] LXX, Syr. *100 cubits.*   42:8 [a] Ezek 41:13–14   42:10 [1] MT *east.*   42:11 [a] Ezek 42:4   42:13 [a] Lev 2:3, 10; 6:14,
17, 25   42:14 [a] Ezek 44:19   42:15 [a] Ezek 40:6; 43:1   42:20 [a] [Isa 60:18]; Ezek 40:5; Zech 2:5   [b] Ezek 45:2; Rev 21:16
43:1 [a] Ezek 10:19; 46:1   43:2 [a] Ezek 11:23   [b] Ezek 1:24; Rev 1:15; 14:2   43:3 [a] Ezek 1:4–28   [b] Jer 1:10; Ezek 9:1, 5; 32:18
[c] Ezek 1:28; 3:23   [1] Heb. *I.*   43:4 [a] Ezek 10:19; 11:23   43:5 [a] Ezek 3:12, 14; 8:3; 2 Cor 12:2–4   [b] Ezek 40:34; 1 Kgs 8:10–11
43:6 [a] Ezek 1:26; 40:3   43:7 [a] Ps 99:1; Isa 60:13   [b] 1 Chr 28:2; Ps 99:5   [c] Exod 29:45; Ps 68:16; 132:14;
Ezek 37:26–28; Joel 3:17; [John 1:14; 2 Cor 6:16]

house of Israel will [d]no longer profane my holy name, [e]neither they nor their kings, by their spiritual prostitution or by the pillars of their kings set up when they die. [8a]When they placed their threshold by my threshold and their doorpost by my doorpost, with only the wall between me and them, they profaned my holy name by the abominable deeds they committed. So I consumed them in my anger. [9]Now they must put away their spiritual prostitution and the pillars of their kings far from me, and then I will live among them forever.

[10]"As for you, son of man, [a]describe the temple to the house of Israel, so that they will be ashamed of their sins and measure the pattern. [11]When they are ashamed of all that they have done, make known to them the design of the temple—its pattern, its exits and entrances, and its whole design—all its [a]statutes, its entire design, and all its laws; write it all down in their sight, so that they may observe its entire design and all its statutes and [b]do them.

[12]"This is [a]the law of the temple: The entire area on top of the mountain all around will be most holy. Indeed, this is the law of the temple.

The Altar

[13]"And these are the measurements of the [a]altar:[1] Its base is 1¾ feet high and 1¾ feet wide, and its border 9 inches[2] on its edge. This is to be [b]the height[3] of the altar. [14]From the base of the ground to the lower ledge is 3½ feet, and the width 1¾ feet; and from the smaller ledge to the larger ledge, 7 feet, and the width 1¾ feet; [15]and the altar hearth, 7 feet, and from the altar hearth four [a]horns projecting upward. [16]Now the altar hearth is a perfect [a]square, 21 feet long and 21 feet wide. [17]The ledge is 24½ feet long and 24½ feet wide on four sides; the border around [a]it is 10½ inches, and its surrounding base 1¾ feet. Its steps face east."

[18]Then he said to me: "Son of man, this is what the Sovereign LORD says: These are the statutes of the altar: On the day it is built to offer up [a]burnt offerings on

it and to sprinkle blood on it, [19]you will give [a]a young bull for a sin offering to [b]the Levitical priests who are descended from [c]Zadok, who approach me to minister to me, declares the Sovereign LORD. [20]You will take some of its blood and place it on the four horns of the altar, on the four corners of the ledge, and on the border all around; you will purify it and make atonement for it. [21]You will also take the bull for the sin offering, and it will be [a]burned in the appointed place in the temple, [b]outside the sanctuary.

[22]"On the second day, you will offer a male goat without blemish for a sin offering. They will purify the altar just as they purified it with the bull. [23]When you have finished purifying it, you will offer an unblemished young bull and an unblemished ram from the flock. [24]You will present [a]them before the LORD, and the priests will scatter salt on them and offer them up as a burnt offering to the LORD.

[25]"For [a]seven days you will provide every day a goat for a sin offering; a young bull and a ram from the flock, both without blemish, will be provided. [26]For seven days they will make atonement for the altar and cleanse it, so they will consecrate it. [27a]When the prescribed period is over, on the eighth day and thereafter the priests will offer up on the altar your burnt offerings and your peace offerings; I will [b]accept you, declares the Sovereign LORD."

The Closed Gate

44 Then he brought me back by way of the outer gate of the sanctuary that faces east, but it was shut. [2]The LORD said to me: "This gate will [a]be shut; it will not be opened, and no one will enter by it. For the LORD, the God of Israel, has entered by it; therefore it will remain shut. [3]Only the [a]prince may sit in it to [b]eat a sacrificial meal before the LORD; he will enter by way of the porch of the gate and will go out by the same way."

[4]Then he brought me by way of the north gate to the front of the temple. As I

43:7 [d]Ezek 39:7 [e]Lev 26:30; Jer 16:18; Ezek 6:5, 13 43:8 [a]2 Kgs 16:14; 21:4–5, 7; Ezek 8:3; 23:39; 44:7 43:10 [a]Ezek 40:4 43:11 [a]Ezek 44:5 [b]Ezek 11:20 43:12 [a]Ezek 40:2 43:13 [a]Exod 27:1–8; 2 Chr 4:1 [b]Ezek 41:8 [1]Heb. the measurements of the altar by cubits, the cubit being a cubit and a handbreadth. [2]Heb. one span. [3]MT bulge, protuberance, mound. 43:15 [a]Exod 27:2; Lev 9:9; 1 Kgs 1:50 43:16 [a]Exod 27:1 43:17 [a]Exod 20:26 43:18 [a]Exod 40:29 43:19 [a]Exod 29:10; Lev 8:14; Ezek 45:18–19 [b]Ezek 44:15–16 [c]1 Kgs 2:35; Ezek 40:46 43:21 [a]Exod 29:14; Lev 4:12 [b]Heb 13:11 43:24 [a]Lev 2:13; Num 18:19; [Mark 9:49–50; Col 4:6] 43:25 [a]Exod 29:35; Lev 8:33 43:27 [a]Lev 9:1–4 [b]Ezek 20:40–41; [Rom 12:1; 1 Pet 2:5] 44:2 [a]Ezek 43:2–4 44:3 [a]Gen 31:54; Exod 24:9–11; [1 Cor 10:18] [b]Ezek 46:2, 8

watched, I [a]noticed the glory of the LORD filling the LORD's temple, [b]and I threw myself face down. [5]The LORD said to me: "[a]Son of man, pay attention, watch closely, and listen carefully to everything I tell you concerning all the [b]statutes of the LORD's house and all its laws. Pay attention to the entrances[1] to the temple with all the exits of the sanctuary. [6]Say to the [a]rebellious,[1] to the house of Israel, 'This is what the Sovereign LORD says: Enough of all your abominable practices, O house of Israel! [7a]When you bring [b]foreigners, those [c]uncircumcised in heart and in flesh, into [d]my sanctuary, you desecrate it—even my house—when you offer my food, [e]the fat and the blood. You[1] have broken my covenant by all your abominable practices. [8]You have not [a]kept charge of my holy things, but you have assigned foreigners to keep charge of my sanctuary for you. [9]This is what the Sovereign LORD says: [a]No foreigner who is uncircumcised in heart and flesh among all the foreigners who are among the people of Israel will enter into my sanctuary.

[10]"[a]But the Levites who went far from me, straying off from me after their idols when Israel went astray, will be responsible for their sin. [11]Yet [a]they will be ministers in my sanctuary, having oversight at [b]the gates of the temple, and serving the temple. They will slaughter the burnt offerings and the sacrifices for the people, and they will stand before them to minister to them. [12]Because they [a]used to minister to them before their idols and became a sinful obstacle to the house of Israel, consequently I have made a [b]vow concerning them, declares the Sovereign LORD, that they will be responsible for their sin. [13a]They will not come near me to serve me as priest, nor will they come near any of my holy things, the things that are most sacred. They will [b]bear the shame of the abominable deeds they have committed. [14]Yet I will appoint them to [a]keep charge of the temple, all its service, and all that will be done in it.

The Levitical Priests

[15]"[a]But [b]the Levitical priests, the descendants of Zadok who kept the charge of my sanctuary [c]when the people of Israel went astray from me, will approach me to minister to me; they will stand before me to offer me the [d]fat and the blood, declares the Sovereign LORD. [16]They will [a]enter [b]my sanctuary and approach my table to minister to me; they will keep my charge.

[17]"When [a]they enter the gates of the inner court, they must wear linen garments; they must not have any wool on them when they minister in the inner gates of the court and in the temple. [18]Linen turbans will be on their heads and linen undergarments will be around their waists; [a]they must not bind themselves with anything that causes sweat. [19]When [a]they go out to the outer court to the people, they must remove the garments they were ministering in and place them in the holy chambers; they must put on other garments so that they will [b]not transmit holiness to the people with their garments.

[20]"[a]They must not shave their heads nor let their hair grow [b]long; they must only trim their heads. [21a]No priest may drink wine when he enters the inner court. [22]They must not marry a [a]widow or a divorcee, but they may marry a virgin from the house of Israel or a widow who is a priest's widow. [23]Moreover, [a]they will teach my people the difference between the holy and the common and show them how to [b]distinguish between the ceremonially unclean and the clean.

[24]"In a controversy they will act as judges; they will judge [a]according to my ordinances. They will keep my laws [b]and my statutes regarding all my appointed festivals and will observe my Sabbaths.

[25]"They must not come near a dead person or they will be defiled; however, for father, mother, son, daughter, brother, or unmarried sister, they may defile themselves. [26a]After a priest has become ceremonially

44:4 [a] Isa 6:3; Ezek 3:23; 43:5 [b] Ezek 1:28; 43:3 **44:5** [a] Deut 32:46; Ezek 40:4 [b] Deut 12:32; Ezek 43:10–11 [1] MT *entrance*. **44:6** [a] Ezek 2:5 [1] LXX *house of rebellion*. **44:7** [a] Ezek 43:8; Acts 21:28 [b] Lev 22:25 [c] Lev 26:41; Deut 10:16; Jer 4:4; 9:26; [Acts 7:51] [d] Lev 21:17 [e] Lev 3:16 [1] MT *they*. **44:8** [a] Lev 22:2; Num 18:7 **44:9** [a] Ezek 44:7; Joel 3:17; Zech 14:21 **44:10** [a] 2 Kgs 23:8; Ezek 48:11 **44:11** [a] 2 Chr 29:34; 30:17 [b] Num 16:9 **44:12** [a] Isa 9:16; Mal 2:8 [b] Ps 106:26 **44:13** [a] Num 18:3; 2 Kgs 23:9 [b] Ezek 32:30 **44:14** [a] Num 18:4; 1 Chr 23:28–32; Ezek 44:11 **44:15** [a] Ezek 40:46 [b] [1 Sam 2:35]; 2 Sam 15:27; Ezek 43:19; 48:11 [c] Ezek 44:10 [d] Lev 3:16–17; 17:5–6; Ezek 44:7 **44:16** [a] Num 18:5, 7, 8 [b] Ezek 41:22; Mal 1:7, 12 **44:17** [a] Exod 28:39–43; 39:27–29; Rev 19:8 **44:18** [a] Exod 28:40; 39:28; Isa 3:20; Ezek 24:17, 23 **44:19** [a] Lev 6:10; 16:4, 23, 24; Ezek 42:14 [b] Exod 30:29; Lev 6:27; Ezek 46:20; [Matt 23:17] **44:20** [a] Lev 21:5 [b] Num 6:5 **44:21** [a] Lev 10:9 **44:22** [a] Lev 21:7, 13, 14 **44:23** [a] Lev 10:10–11; Ezek 22:26; Hos 4:6; Mic 3:9–11; Zeph 3:4; Hag 2:11–13; Mal 2:6–8 [b] Lev 20:25 **44:24** [a] Deut 17:8–9; 1 Chr 23:4; 2 Chr 19:8–10 [b] Ezek 22:26 **44:26** [a] Num 6:10; 19:11, 13–19

clean, they[1] must count off a period of seven days for him. 27 On [a]the day he enters the sanctuary [b]into the inner court to serve in the sanctuary, he must offer his sin offering, declares the Sovereign LORD.

28 "This will be their inheritance: I [a]am their inheritance, and you must give them no [b]property in Israel; I am their property. 29 They may eat [a]the grain offering, the sin offering, and the guilt offering, and [b]every devoted thing in Israel will be theirs. 30 The [a]first of [b]all the firstfruits and all contributions of any kind will be for the priests; you will also give [c]to the priest the first portion of your dough, so that a blessing may rest on your house. 31 The priests will not eat any bird or animal that has died a natural [a]death or was torn to pieces by a wild animal.

The Lord's Portion of the Land

45 "When you allot the land as an inheritance, you will offer an allotment to the LORD, a holy portion from the land; the length will be 8¼ miles[1] and the width 3⅓ miles.[2] This entire area will be holy. 2 Of this area a square [a]875 feet by 875 feet will be designated for the sanctuary, with 87½ feet set aside for its open space round about. 3 From this measured area you will measure a length of 8¼ miles and a width of 3⅓ miles; [a]in it will be the sanctuary, the Most Holy Place. 4 It will be [a]a holy portion of the land; it will be for the priests, the ministers of the sanctuary who approach the LORD to minister to him. It will be a place for their houses and a holy place for the sanctuary.[1] 5 [a]An area [b]8¼ miles in length and 3⅓ miles in width will be for the Levites, who minister at the temple, as the place for the cities[1] in which they will live.

6 "Alongside the portion set apart as the holy allotment, [a]you will allot for the city an area 1⅔ miles wide and 8¼ miles long; it will be for the whole house of Israel.

7 "For [a]the prince there will be land on both sides of the holy allotment and the allotted city, on the west side and on the east side; it will be comparable in length to one of the portions, from the west border to the east border 8 of the land. This will be his property in Israel. [a]My princes will no longer oppress my people, but the land will be allotted to the house of Israel according to their tribes.

9 "This is what the Sovereign LORD says: [a]Enough, you princes of Israel! Put [b]away violence and destruction and do what is just and right. Put an end to your evictions of my people, declares the Sovereign LORD. 10 You must use [a]just balances, a just dry measure (an ephah),[1] and a just liquid measure (a bath).[2] 11 The dry and liquid measures will be the same: The bath will contain a tenth of a homer, and the ephah a tenth of a homer; the homer will be the standard measure. 12 The [a]shekel will be 20 gerahs. Sixty shekels will be a mina for you.

13 "This is the offering you must offer: a sixth of an ephah from a homer of wheat, a sixth of an ephah from a homer of barley, 14 and as the prescribed portion of olive oil, one-tenth of a bath from each cor (which is ten baths or a homer, for ten baths make a homer); 15 and one sheep from each flock of 200, from the watered places of Israel, for a grain offering, burnt offering, and peace offering, [a]to make atonement for them, declares the Sovereign LORD. 16 All the people of the land will contribute to this offering for the prince of Israel. 17 It will be the duty of the [a]prince to provide the burnt offerings, the grain offering, and the drink offering at festivals, on the new moons and Sabbaths, at all the appointed feasts of the house of Israel; he will provide the sin offering, the grain offering, the burnt offering, and the peace offerings to make atonement for the house of Israel.

18 "This is what the Sovereign LORD says: In the first month, on the first day of the month, you must take an unblemished young bull and [a]purify the sanctuary. 19 The priest will take some of [a]the blood of the sin offering and place it on the doorpost of the temple, on the four corners of the ledge of

44:26 [1] LXX, Syr. *He.*   44:27 [a] Lev 5:3, 6; Num 6:9–11   [b] Ezek 44:17   44:28 [a] Num 18:20; Deut 10:9; 18:1–2; Josh 13:14, 33   [b] Ezek 45:4   44:29 [a] Lev 7:6   [b] Lev 27:21, 28; Num 18:14   44:30 [a] Exod 13:2; 22:29; 23:19; Num 3:13; 18:12   [b] Num 15:20; Neh 10:37   [c] Prov 3:9; [Mal 3:10]   44:31 [a] Exod 22:31; Lev 22:8; Deut 14:21; Ezek 4:14   45:1 [1] Heb. *25,000 cubits.*   [2] LXX *20,000 cubits.*   45:2 [a] Ezek 42:20   45:3 [a] Ezek 48:10   45:4 [a] Ezek 48:10–11   [1] LXX *open land.*   45:5 [a] Ezek 48:13   [b] Ezek 40:17   [1] MT *twenty.*   45:6 [a] Ezek 48:15   45:7 [a] Ezek 48:21   45:8 [a] [Isa 11:3–5]; Jer 22:17; Ezek 22:27   45:9 [a] Ezek 44:6   [b] Jer 22:3; Zech 8:16   45:10 [a] Lev 19:36; Deut 25:15; Prov 16:11; Amos 8:4–6; Mic 6:10–11   [1] ½ bushel.   [2] 5½ gallons.   45:12 [a] Exod 30:13; Lev 27:25; Num 3:47   45:15 [a] Lev 1:4; 6:30   45:17 [a] Ezek 46:4–12   45:18 [a] Lev 16:16, 33; Ezek 43:22, 26   45:19 [a] Lev 16:18–20; Ezek 43:20

the altar, and on the doorpost of the gate of the inner court. [20]This is what you must do on the seventh day of the month [a]for anyone who sins inadvertently or through ignorance; so you will make atonement for the temple.

[21]""[a]In the first month, on the fourteenth day of the month, you will celebrate the Passover, and for the seven days of the festival bread made without yeast will be eaten. [22]On [a]that day the prince will provide for himself and for all the people of the land a bull for a sin offering. [23]And during the [a]seven days of the feast he will provide as [b]a burnt offering to the LORD seven bulls and seven rams, all without blemish, on each of the seven days, and a male goat daily for a sin offering. [24]He will provide as [a]a grain offering an ephah for each bull, an ephah for each ram, and a gallon[1] of olive oil for each ephah of grain. [25]In the seventh month, on the fifteenth day of the month, at the [a]feast, he will make the same provisions for the sin offering, burnt offering, and grain offering, and for the olive oil, for the seven days.

The Prince's Offerings

46 ""This is what the Sovereign LORD says: The gate of the inner court that faces east will be closed six [a]working days, but on the Sabbath day it will be opened and on the day of the new moon it will be opened. [2]The prince will enter by way of [a]the porch of the gate from the outside and will stand by the doorpost of the gate. The priests will provide his burnt offering and his peace offerings, and he will bow down at the threshold of the gate and then go out. But the gate will not be closed until evening. [3]The people of the land will bow down at the entrance of that gate before the LORD on the Sabbaths and on the new moons. [4]The burnt offering that [a]the prince will offer to the LORD on the [b]Sabbath day will be six unblemished lambs and one unblemished ram. [5]The grain offering will be [a]an ephah with the ram, and the grain offering with the lambs will be as much as he is able to give, and a gallon of olive oil with an ephah. [6]On the day of the new moon he will offer an unblemished young bull and six lambs and a ram, all without blemish. [7]He will provide a grain offering: an ephah with the bull and an ephah with the ram, and with the lambs as much as he wishes, and a gallon of olive oil with each ephah of grain. [8]When the prince enters, [a]he will come by way of the porch of the gate and will go out the same way.

[9]""When the people of the land [a]come before the LORD at the appointed feasts, whoever enters by way of the north [b]gate to worship will go out by way of the south gate; whoever enters by way of the south gate will go out by way of the north gate. No one will return by way of the gate they entered but will go out straight ahead. [10]When they come in, the prince will come in with them, and when they go out, he will go out.

[11]""At [a]the festivals and at the appointed feasts the grain offering will be an ephah with the bull and an ephah with the ram, and with the lambs as much as one is able, and a gallon of olive oil with each ephah of grain. [12]When the prince provides [a]a freewill offering, a burnt offering, or peace offerings as a voluntary offering to the LORD, the gate facing east will be opened for him, and he will provide his burnt offering and his peace offerings just as he did on the Sabbath. Then he will go out, and the gate will be closed after he goes out.

[13]""[a]You[1] will provide a lamb a year old without blemish for a burnt offering daily to the LORD; morning by morning he will provide it. [14]And you[1] will provide a grain offering with it morning by morning, a sixth of an ephah and a third of a gallon of olive oil to moisten the choice flour, as a grain offering to the LORD; this is a perpetual statute. [15]Thus they will provide the lamb, the grain offering, and the olive oil morning by morning as a [a]perpetual burnt offering.

[16]""This is what the Sovereign LORD says: If the prince should give a gift to one of his sons as his inheritance, it will belong to his sons; it is their property by inheritance. [17]But if [a]he gives a gift from his inheritance to one of his servants, it will be his until the year of liberty; then it will revert to the

45:20 [a]Lev 4:27; Ps 19:12   45:21 [a]Exod 12:18; Lev 23:5–6; Num 9:2–3; 28:16–17; Deut 16:1   45:22 [a]Lev 4:14   45:23 [a]Lev 23:8   [b]Num 28:15, 22, 30; 29:5, 11, 16, 19   45:24 [a]Num 28:12–15; Ezek 46:5, 7   [1]Heb. *a hin of oil.*   45:25 [a]Lev 23:34; Num 29:12; Deut 16:13; 2 Chr 5:3; 7:8, 10   46:1 [a]Exod 20:9   46:2 [a]Ezek 44:3   46:4 [a]Ezek 45:17   [b]Num 28:9–10   46:5 [a]Num 28:12; Ezek 45:24; 46:7, 11   46:8 [a]Ezek 44:3; 46:2   46:9 [a]Exod 23:14–17; 34:23; Deut 16:16–17; Ps 84:7; Mic 6:6   [b]Ezek 48:31, 33   46:11 [a]Ezek 46:5, 7   46:12 [a]Ezek 44:3; 46:1–2, 8   46:13 [a]Exod 29:38; Num 28:3–5   [1]LXX, Vg. *He.*   46:14 [1]Some wss *he.*   46:15 [a]Exod 29:42; Num 28:6   46:17 [a]Lev 25:10

prince. His inheritance will only remain with his sons. [18]The prince will not take away any of [a]the people's inheritance by oppressively removing them from their property. He will give his sons an inheritance from his own possessions so that my people will not be scattered, each from his own property.'"

[19]Then he brought me through the entrance, which was at the side of the gate, into the holy [a]chambers for the priests, which faced north. There I saw a place at the extreme western end. [20]He said to me, "This is the place where the priests will [a]boil the guilt offering and the sin offering and where they will [b]bake the grain offering, so that they do not bring them out [c]to the outer court to transmit holiness to the people."

[21]Then he brought me out to the outer court and led me past the four corners of the court, and I noticed that in every corner of the court there was another court. [22]In the four corners of the court were small courts, 70 feet in length and 52½ feet in width; the four were all the same size. [23]There was a row of masonry around each of the four courts, and places for boiling offerings were made under the rows all around. [24]Then he said to me, "These are the houses for boiling, where the ministers of the temple [a]boil the sacrifices of the people."

Water from the Temple

47 Then he brought me back to the entrance of the temple. I noticed that [a]water was flowing from under the threshold of the temple toward the east (for the temple faced east). The water was flowing down from under the right side of the temple, from south of the altar. [2]He led me out by way of the north gate and brought me around the outside of the outer gate that faces toward the [a]east; I noticed that the water was trickling out from the south side.

[3]When [a]the man went out toward the east with a measuring line in his hand, he measured 1,750 feet, and then he led me through water, which was ankle deep. [4]Again he measured 1,750 feet and led me through the water, which was now knee deep. Once more he measured 1,750 feet and led me through the water, which was waist deep. [5]Again he measured 1,750 feet, and it was a river I could not cross, for the water had risen; it was deep enough to swim in, a river that could not be crossed. [6]He said to me, "Son of man, have you seen this?"

Then he led me back to the bank of the river. [7]When I had returned, I noticed a vast number of [a]trees on the banks of the river, on both sides. [8]He said to me, "These waters go out toward the eastern region and flow down into the rift valley; when they enter the Dead Sea,[1] where the sea is stagnant, the waters become fresh. [9]Every living creature that swarms where the river flows will live; there will be many fish, for these waters flow there. It will become fresh, and everything will live where the river flows. [10]Fishermen will stand beside it; from En Gedi to En Eglaim they will spread nets. They will catch many kinds [a]of fish, like the fish of the Great Sea. [11]But its swamps and its marshes will not become fresh; they will remain salty. [12a]On both sides of [b]the river's banks, every kind of tree will grow for food. Their leaves will not wither nor will their fruit fail, but they will bear fruit every month because their water source flows from the sanctuary. Their fruit will be for food and their leaves for [c]healing."

Boundaries for the Land

[13]This is what the Sovereign LORD says: "Here are the [a]borders you will observe as you allot the land to the 12 tribes of Israel. ([b]Joseph will have two portions.) [14]You must divide it equally just as I [a]vowed to give it to your forefathers; this land will be [b]assigned as your inheritance.

[15]"This will be [a]the border of the land: On the north side, from the Great Sea by way of Hethlon to the entrance of [b]Zedad; [16a]Hamath, [b]Berothah, Sibraim, which is between the border of Damascus and the border of Hamath, as far as Hazer Hattikon, which is on the border of Hauran. [17]The border will run from the sea to Hazar [a]Enan, at the border of Damascus, and on the north is the

46:18 [a]Ezek 45:8   46:19 [a]Ezek 42:13   46:20 [a]2 Chr 35:13   [b]Lev 2:4–5, 7   [c]Ezek 44:19   46:24 [a]Ezek 46:20   47:1 [a]Ps 46:4; Isa 30:25; 55:1; [Jer 2:13]; Joel 3:18; Zech 13:1; 14:8; [Rev 22:1, 17]   47:2 [a]Ezek 44:1–2   47:3 [a]Ezek 40:3   47:7 [a][Isa 60:13, 21; 61:3; Ezek 47:12; Rev 22:2]   47:8 [1]Heb. *the sea.*   47:10 [a]Num 34:3; Josh 23:4; Ezek 48:28   47:12 [a]Ezek 47:7; [Rev 22:2]   [b]Job 18:16; [Ps 1:3; Jer 17:8]   [c][Rev 22:2]   47:13 [a]Num 34:1–29   [b]Gen 48:5; 1 Chr 5:1; Ezek 48:4–5   47:14 [a]Gen 12:7; 13:15; 15:7; 17:8; 26:3; 28:13; Deut 1:8; Ezek 20:5–6, 28, 42   [b]Ezek 48:29   47:15 [a]Ezek 48:1   [b]Num 34:7–8   47:16 [a]Num 34:8   [b]2 Sam 8:8   47:17 [a]Num 34:9; Ezek 48:1

border of Hamath. This is the north side. ¹⁸On the east side, between Hauran and Damascus, and between Gilead and the land of Israel, will be the Jordan. You will measure from the border to the eastern sea. This is the east side. ¹⁹On ᵃthe south side it will run from Tamar to the waters of Meribah Kadesh, the river, to the Great Sea. This is the south side. ²⁰On the west side the Great Sea will be the boundary to a point opposite Lebo Hamath. This is the west side.

²¹"This is how you will ᵃdivide this land for yourselves among the tribes of Israel. ²²You must ᵃallot it as ᵇan inheritance among yourselves and for ᶜthe resident foreigners who live among you, who have fathered sons among you. You must treat them as native-born among the people of Israel; they will be allotted an inheritance with you among the tribes of Israel. ²³In whatever tribe the resident foreigner lives, there you will give him his inheritance," declares the Sovereign LORD.

The Tribal Portions

48 "These are the names of the tribes: ᵃFrom the northern end beside the road of Hethlon to Lebo Hamath, as far as Hazar Enan (which is on the border of Damascus, toward the north beside Hamath), extending from the east side to the west, ᵇDan will have one portion. ²Next to the border of Dan, from the east side to the west side, ᵃAsher will have one portion. ³Next to the border of Asher from the east side to the west side, ᵃNaphtali will have one portion. ⁴Next to the border of Naphtali from the east side to the west side, ᵃManasseh will have one portion. ⁵Next to the border of Manasseh from the east side to the west side, ᵃEphraim will have one portion. ⁶Next to the border of Ephraim from the east side to the west side, ᵃReuben will have one portion. ⁷Next to the border of Reuben from the east side to the west side, ᵃJudah will have one portion.

⁸"Next to ᵃthe border of Judah from the east side to the west side will be the allotment you must set apart. It is to be 8¼ miles wide and the same length as one of the tribal portions, from the east side to the west side; the ᵇsanctuary will be in the middle of it. ⁹The allotment you set apart to the LORD will be 8¼ miles in length and 3⅓ miles in width. ¹⁰These will be the allotments for the holy portion: for the priests, toward the north 8¼ miles in length, toward the west 3⅓ miles in width, toward the east 3⅓ miles in width, and toward the south 8¼ miles in length; the sanctuary of the LORD will be in the middle. ¹¹This will be for the priests who are set apart from the descendants of Zadok who kept my charge and did not go astray when the people of Israel strayed off, as the ᵃLevites did. ¹²It will be their portion from the allotment of the land, a ᵃMost Holy Place, next to the border of the Levites.

¹³"Alongside the border of the priests, the ᵃLevites will have an allotment 8¼ miles in length and 3⅓ miles in width. The whole length will be 8¼ miles and the width 3⅓ miles. ¹⁴They must not sell or exchange any of it; they must not transfer this choice portion of ᵃland, for it is set apart to the LORD.

¹⁵"The remainder, 1⅔ miles in width and 8¼ miles in length, will be for common use by ᵃthe city, ᵇfor houses and for open space. The city will be in the middle of it; ¹⁶these will be its measurements: The north side will be 1½ miles, the south side 1½ miles, the east side 1½ miles, and the west side 1½ miles. ¹⁷The city will have open spaces: On the north there will be 437½ feet, on the south 437½ feet, on the east 437½ feet, and on the west 437½ feet. ¹⁸The remainder of the length alongside the holy allotment will be 3⅓ miles to the east and 3⅓ miles toward the west, and it will be beside the holy allotment. Its produce will be for food for the workers of the city. ¹⁹The workers of ᵃthe city from all the tribes of Israel will cultivate it. ²⁰The whole allotment will be 8¼ miles square; you must set apart the holy allotment with the possession of the city.

²¹"The rest, on both sides of ᵃthe holy allotment ᵇand the property of the city, will belong to the prince. Extending from the 8¼ miles of the holy allotment to the east border and westward from the 8¼ miles

47:19 ᵃNum 20:13; Deut 32:51; Ps 81:7; Ezek 48:28   47:21 ᵃEzek 45:1   47:22 ᵃNum 26:55–56   ᵇ[Eph 3:6; Rev 7:9–10]   ᶜ[Acts 11:18; 15:9; Gal 3:28; Eph 2:12–14; Col 3:11]   48:1 ᵃEzek 47:15   ᵇJosh 19:40–48   48:2 ᵃJosh 19:24–31   48:3 ᵃJosh 19:32–39   48:4 ᵃJosh 13:29–31; 17:1–11, 17, 18   48:5 ᵃJosh 16:5–10; 17:8–10, 14–18   48:6 ᵃJosh 13:15–23   48:7 ᵃJosh 15:1–63; 19:9   48:8 ᵃEzek 45:1–6   ᵇ[Isa 12:6; 33:20–22]; Ezek 45:3–4   48:11 ᵃEzek 40:46; 44:15   48:12 ᵃEzek 45:4   48:13 ᵃEzek 45:5   48:14 ᵃExod 22:29; Lev 27:10, 28, 33; Ezek 44:30   48:15 ᵃEzek 45:6   ᵇEzek 42:20   48:19 ᵃEzek 45:6   48:21 ᵃEzek 34:24; 45:7; 48:22   ᵇEzek 48:8, 10

to the west border, alongside the portions, it will belong to the prince. The holy allotment and the sanctuary of the temple will be in the middle of it. [22]The property of the Levites and of the city will be in the middle of that which belongs to the prince. The portion between the border of Judah and the border of [a]Benjamin will be for the prince.

[23]"As for the rest of the tribes: From the east side to the west side, Benjamin will have one portion. [24]Next to the border of Benjamin, from the east side to the west side, [a]Simeon will have one portion. [25]Next to the border of Simeon, from the east side to the west side, [a]Issachar will have one portion. [26]Next to the border of Issachar, from the east side to the west side, [a]Zebulun will have one portion. [27]Next to the border of Zebulun, from the east side to the west side, [a]Gad will have one portion. [28]Next to [a]the border of Gad, at the south side, the border will run from Tamar to the waters of Meribah Kadesh, to the Stream of Egypt,[1] and on to the [b]Great Sea. [29]This [a]is the land that you will allot to the tribes of Israel, and these are their portions, declares the Sovereign LORD.

[30]"These are the exits of the city: On the north side, 1½ miles by measure, [31]the gates of [a]the city will be named for the tribes of Israel. There will be three gates to the north: one gate for Reuben, one gate for Judah, and one gate for Levi. [32]On the east side, 1½ miles in length, there will be three gates: one gate for Joseph, one gate for Benjamin, and one gate for Dan. [33]On the south side, 1½ miles by measure, there will be three gates: one gate for Simeon, one gate for Issachar, and one gate for Zebulun. [34]On the west side, 1½ miles in length, there will be three gates: one gate for Gad, one gate for Asher, and one gate for Naphtali. [35]The circumference of [a]the city will be 6 miles. The name of the city from that day forward will be: 'The LORD Is There.'"

48:22 [a] Josh 18:21–28   **48:24** [a] Josh 19:1–9   **48:25** [a] Josh 19:17–23   **48:26** [a] Josh 19:10–16   **48:27** [a] Josh 13:24–28
48:28 [a] Gen 14:7; 2 Chr 20:2; Ezek 47:19   [b] Ezek 47:10, 15, 19, 20   [1] Trad. *the Brook of Egypt; Egypt* is supplied.
48:29 [a] Ezek 47:14, 21, 22   **48:31** [a] [Rev 21:10–14]   **48:35** [a] Isa 12:6; 14:32; 24:23; Jer 3:17; 8:19; 14:9;
Ezek 35:10; Joel 3:21; Zech 2:10; Rev 21:3; 22:3

DANIEL

D aniel's life and ministry bridge the entire seventy-year period of Babylonian captivity. Deported to Babylon at the age of sixteen and handpicked for government service, Daniel becomes God's prophetic mouthpiece to the Gentile and Jewish world declaring God's present and eternal purpose. Nine of the twelve chapters in his book revolve around dreams, including God-given visions involving trees, animals, beasts, and images. In both his personal adventures and prophetic visions, Daniel shows God's guidance, intervention, and power in the affairs of men. The name *Daniye'l* or *Dani'el* means "God Is My Judge," and the book is, of course, named after the author and principal character. The Greek form *Daniel* in the Septuagint is the basis for the Latin and English titles.

Daniel Finds Favor in Babylon

1 In the third year of the reign of King [a]Jehoiakim of Judah, King Nebuchadnezzar of Babylon advanced against Jerusalem and laid it under siege. [2]Now the Lord delivered King Jehoiakim of Judah into his power, along with [a]some of the vessels[1] of the temple of God. He brought them [b]to the [c]land of Babylonia to the temple of his god and put the vessels in the treasury of his god.

[3]The king commanded Ashpenaz, who was in charge of his court officials, to choose [a]some of the Israelites who were of royal and noble descent—[4]young men [a]in [b]whom there was no physical defect and who were handsome, well versed in all kinds of wisdom, well educated and having keen insight, and who were capable of entering the king's royal service—and to teach them the literature and language of the Babylonians.[1] [5]So the king assigned them a daily ration from his royal delicacies and from the wine he himself drank. They were to be trained for the next three years. At the end of that time they were to [a]enter the king's service. [6]As it turned out, among these young men[1] were some from Judah: Daniel, Hananiah, Mishael, and Azariah. [7a]But [b]the overseer of the court officials renamed them. He gave[1]

Daniel the name Belteshazzar, Hananiah he named Shadrach, Mishael he named Meshach, and Azariah he named Abednego.

[8]But Daniel made up his mind that he would not defile himself [a]with the royal delicacies or the royal wine. He therefore asked the overseer of the court officials for permission not to defile himself. [9]Then [a]God made the overseer of the court officials sympathetic to Daniel. [10]But he responded to Daniel, "I fear my master the king. He is the one who has decided your food and drink. What would happen if he saw that you looked malnourished in comparison to the other young men your age? If that happened, you would endanger my life[1] with the king!" [11]Daniel then spoke to the warden whom the overseer of the court officials had appointed over Daniel, Hananiah, Mishael, and Azariah: [12]"Please test your servants for 10 days by providing us with some vegetables to eat and water to drink. [13]Then compare our appearance with that of the young men who are eating the royal delicacies; deal with us in light of what you see." [14]So the warden agreed to their proposal and tested them for 10 days.

[15]At the end of the 10 days their appearance was better and their bodies were healthier[1] than all the young men who had

1:1 [a] 2 Kgs 24:1–2; 2 Chr 36:5–7; Jer 25:1; 52:12–30   1:2 [a] 2 Chr 36:7; Jer 27:19–20; Dan 5:2   [b] Gen 10:10; 11:2; Isa 11:11; Zech 5:11   [c] 2 Chr 36:7   [1] Or *utensils, articles.*   1:3 [a] 2 Kgs 20:17–18; Isa 39:7   1:4 [a] Lev 24:19–20   [b] Acts 7:22   [1] Heb. *Chaldeans.*   1:5 [a] Gen 41:46; 1 Sam 16:22; 1 Kgs 10:8; Dan 1:19   1:6 [1] Heb. *among them.*   1:7 [a] Gen 41:45; 2 Kgs 24:17   [b] Dan 2:26; 4:8; 5:12   [1] LXX, Vg. omit *He gave.*   1:8 [a] Lev 11:47; Deut 32:38; Ezek 4:13; Hos 9:3   1:9 [a] Gen 39:21; 1 Kgs 8:50; [Job 5:15–16]; Ps 106:46; [Prov 16:7]; Acts 7:10; 27:3   1:10 [1] Heb. *my head;* presumably an implicit reference to capital punishment.   1:15 [1] Heb. *fat of flesh.*

been eating the royal delicacies. [16]So the warden removed the delicacies and the wine from their diet and gave them a diet of vegetables instead. [17]Now as for these four young men, [a]God endowed them with [b]knowledge and skill in all sorts of literature and wisdom—and Daniel had [c]insight into all kinds of visions and dreams.

[18]When the time appointed by the king arrived, the overseer of the court officials brought them into Nebuchadnezzar's presence. [19]When [a]the king spoke with them, he did not find among the entire group anyone like Daniel, Hananiah, Mishael, or Azariah. So they entered the king's service. [20]In every matter of wisdom [a]and[1] insight the king asked them about, he found them to be 10 times better than any of the magicians and astrologers that were in his entire empire. [21]Now Daniel lived [a]on until the first year of Cyrus the king.

Nebuchadnezzar Has a Disturbing Dream

2 In the second year of his[1] reign Nebuchadnezzar had many dreams. His mind was disturbed, [a]and he suffered from insomnia. [2]The king issued an order to summon [a]the magicians, astrologers, sorcerers, and wise men[1] in order to explain his dreams to him. So they came and awaited the king's instructions.

[3]The king told them, "I have had a dream, and I am anxious to understand the dream." [4]The wise men replied [a]to the king: [What follows is in Aramaic] "O king, live forever! Tell your servants the dream, and we will disclose its interpretation." [5]The king replied[1] to the wise men, "My decision is firm. If you do not inform me of both the dream and its interpretation, you will be [a]dismembered and your homes reduced to rubble! [6][a]But if you can disclose the dream and its interpretation, you will receive from me gifts, a reward, and considerable honor. So disclose to me the dream and its interpretation." [7]They again replied, "Let the king inform us of the dream; then we will disclose its interpretation." [8]The king

replied, "I know for sure that you are attempting to gain time, because you see that my decision is firm. [9]If you don't inform me of the dream, there is only one thing that is going to happen to you. For you have agreed among yourselves to report to me something false and deceitful until such time as things might change. So tell me the dream, and I will have confidence that you can disclose its interpretation."

[10]The wise men replied to the king, "There is no man on earth who is able to disclose the king's secret, for no king, regardless of his position and power, has ever requested such a thing from any magician, astrologer, or wise man. [11]What the king is asking is too difficult, and no one exists who can disclose it to the king, except [a]for the gods—but they don't live among mortals!"[1]

[12]Because of this the king got furiously angry and gave orders to destroy all the wise men of Babylon. [13]So a decree went out, and the wise men were about to be executed. They also sought [a]Daniel and his friends so that they could be executed.

[14]Then Daniel spoke with prudent counsel to Arioch, who was in charge of the king's executioners and who had gone out to execute the wise men of Babylon. [15]He inquired of Arioch the king's deputy, "Why is the decree from the king so urgent?" Then Arioch informed Daniel about the matter. [16]So Daniel went in and[1] requested the king to grant him time, that he might disclose the interpretation to the king. [17]Then Daniel went to his home and informed his friends Hananiah, Mishael, and Azariah of the matter. [18]He asked them to pray for mercy from the God of heaven concerning this mystery so [a]that he and his friends would not be destroyed along with the rest of the wise men of Babylon. [19]Then [a]in a night vision the mystery was revealed to Daniel. So Daniel praised the God of heaven, [20]saying:

"Let the name of God be [a]praised
   [b]forever and ever,
   for wisdom and power belong to him.

1:17 [a]1 Kgs 3:12, 28; 2 Chr 1:10–12; [Luke 21:15; Jas 1:5–7]   [b]Acts 7:22   [c]Num 12:6; 2 Chr 26:5; Dan 5:11–12, 14; 10:1   1:19 [a]Gen 41:46; [Prov 22:29]; Dan 1:5   1:20 [a]1 Kgs 10:1   [1]MT wisdom of insight.   1:21 [a]Dan 6:28; 10:1   2:1 [a]Gen 40:5–8; 41:1, 8; Job 33:15–17; Dan 2:3; 4:5   [1]Heb. Nebuchadnezzar's.   2:2 [a]Gen 41:8; Exod 7:11; Isa 47:12–13; Dan 1:20; 2:10, 27; 4:6; 5:7   [1]Heb. Chaldeans.   2:4 [a]1 Kgs 1:31; Dan 3:9; 5:10; 6:6, 21   2:5 [a]2 Kgs 10:27; Ezra 6:11; Dan 3:29   [1]Aram. answered and said.   2:6 [a]Dan 5:16   2:11 [a]Gen 41:39; Dan 5:11   [1]Aram. whose dwelling is not with flesh.   2:13 [a]Dan 1:19–20   2:16 [1]Thd., Syr. omit went in and.   2:18 [a][Dan 9:9; Matt 18:19]   2:19 [a]Num 12:6; Job 33:15; [Prov 3:32]; Amos 3:7   2:20 [a]Ps 113:2   [b][1 Chr 29:11–12; Job 12:13; Ps 147:5; Jer 32:19; Matt 6:13; Rom 11:33]

21 He changes times and seasons,
   deposing some kings
   and establishing [a]others.
   [b]He gives wisdom to [c]the wise;
   he imparts knowledge to those with
      understanding;
22 he reveals deep and hidden things.
   [a]He knows what is in [b]the darkness,
   and [c]light resides with him.
23 O God of my fathers, I acknowledge
      and glorify you,
   for you have bestowed wisdom and
      power on me.
   Now you have enabled me to
      understand what we [a]requested
      from you.
   For you have enabled us to
      understand the king's dilemma."

24 Then Daniel went in to see Arioch (whom the king had appointed to destroy the wise men of Babylon). He came[1] and said to him, "Don't destroy the wise men of Babylon! Escort me to the king, and I will disclose the interpretation to him."

25 So Arioch quickly ushered Daniel into the king's presence, saying to him, "I have found a man from the captives of Judah who can make known the interpretation to the king." 26 The king then asked Daniel (whose name was also Belteshazzar), "Are you able to make known to me the dream that I saw, as well as its interpretation?" 27 Daniel replied to the king, "The mystery that the king is asking about is such that no wise men, astrologers, magicians, or diviners can possibly disclose it to the king. 28 [a]However, there is a God in heaven who reveals mysteries,[1] and he has made known to King Nebuchadnezzar [b]what will happen in the times to come. The dream and the visions you had while lying on your bed are as follows:

29 "As for you, O king, while you were in your bed your thoughts turned to future things. The revealer of mysteries has made known to you what will take place. 30 As for me, this mystery was revealed to me not because I possess more wisdom than any other living person, [a]but so that the king may [b]understand the interpretation and comprehend the thoughts of your mind.

31 "You, O king, were watching as a great statue—one of impressive size and extraordinary brightness—was standing before you. Its appearance caused alarm. 32 [a]As for that statue, its head was of fine gold, its chest and arms were of silver, its belly and thighs were of bronze. 33 Its legs were of iron; its feet were partly of iron and partly of clay. 34 You were watching as a stone was cut out,[1] but [a]not by human hands. It struck the statue on its iron and clay feet, breaking them in pieces. 35 [a]Then the iron, clay, bronze, silver, and gold were broken in pieces without distinction and became [b]like chaff from the summer threshing floors that the wind carries away. [c]Not a trace of them could be found. But the stone that struck the statue [d]became [e]a large mountain that filled the entire earth. 36 This was the dream. Now we will set forth before the king its interpretation.

Daniel Interprets Nebuchadnezzar's Dream

37 "[a]You, O king, are the king of kings. The God of heaven has granted you sovereignty, power, strength, and honor. 38 Wherever human beings, wild animals,[1] [a]and birds of the sky live—he has given them into [b]your power. He has given you authority over them all. You are the head of gold. 39 Now after you [a]another kingdom will arise, one [b]inferior to yours. Then a third kingdom, one of bronze, will rule in all the earth. 40 Then [a]there will be a fourth kingdom, one strong like iron. Just like iron breaks in pieces and shatters everything, and as iron breaks in pieces[1] all these metals, so it will break in pieces and crush the others. 41 In that you were seeing feet and toes[1] partly of wet clay and partly of iron, so this will be a divided kingdom. Some of the strength of iron will be in it, for you saw iron mixed with wet clay. 42 In that the toes of the feet

2:21 [a] Ps 31:15; Esth 1:13; Dan 2:9; 7:25 [b] Job 12:18; [Ps 75:6–7; Jer 27:5; Dan 4:35] [c] 1 Kgs 3:9–10; 4:29; [Jas 1:5] 2:22 [a] Job 12:22; Ps 25:14; [Prov 3:22] [b] Job 26:6; Ps 139:12; [Isa 45:7; Jer 23:24; Heb 4:13] [c] [Ps 36:9]; Dan 5:11, 14; [1 Tim 6:16; Jas 1:17; 1 John 1:5] 2:23 [a] Ps 21:2, 4; Dan 2:18, 29, 30 2:24 [1] Some wss omit *came*. 2:28 [a] Gen 40:8; Amos 4:13 [b] Gen 49:1; Isa 2:2; Dan 10:14; Mic 4:1 [1] Aram. *a revealer of mysteries*; a quasi-title for God in Daniel. 2:30 [a] Acts 3:12 [b] Dan 2:47 2:32 [a] Dan 2:38, 45 2:34 [a] Dan 8:25; [Zech 4:6]; 2 Cor 5:1; Heb 9:24 [1] Some wss add *from a mountain*. 2:35 [a] Dan 7:23–27; [Rev 16:14] [b] Ps 1:4; Isa 17:13; 41:15–16; Hos 13:3 [c] Ps 37:10, 36 [d] [Isa 2:2–3]; Mic 4:1 [e] Ps 80:9 2:37 [a] Ezra 7:12; Isa 47:5; Jer 27:6–7; Ezek 26:7; Hos 8:10 2:38 [a] Ps 50:10–11; Jer 27:6; Dan 4:21–22 [b] Dan 2:32 [1] Aram. *the beasts of the field*. 2:39 [a] Dan 5:28, 31 [b] Dan 2:32 2:40 [a] Dan 7:7, 23 [1] Thd., Vg. omit *and as iron breaks in pieces*. 2:41 [1] LXX omits *and toes*.

were partly of iron and partly of clay, the latter stages of this kingdom will be partly strong and partly fragile. [43]And[1] in that you saw iron mixed with wet clay, so people will be mixed with one another[2] without adhering to one another, just as iron does not mix with clay. [44]In [a]the days of those kings the God of heaven will raise up an everlasting kingdom that will not be destroyed and a kingdom that will not be left to another people. It will break in pieces and bring about the demise of all these kingdoms. But [b]it will stand forever. [45]You saw that [a]a stone was cut from a mountain, but not by human hands; it smashed the iron, bronze, clay, silver, and gold into pieces. The great God has made known to the king what will occur in the future. The dream is certain, and its interpretation is reliable."

[46a]Then King Nebuchadnezzar bowed down with his face to the ground [b]and paid homage to Daniel. He gave orders to offer sacrifice and incense to him. [47]The king replied to Daniel, "Certainly [a]your [b]God is a God of gods and Lord of kings and revealer of mysteries, for you were able to reveal this mystery!" [48a]Then the king elevated Daniel to high position [b]and bestowed on him many marvelous gifts. He granted him authority over the entire province of Babylon and made him the [c]main prefect over all the wise men of Babylon. [49]And at Daniel's request, the king appointed Shadrach, Meshach, [a]and Abednego over the administration of the province of Babylon. Daniel himself served in the king's court.

Daniel's Friends Are Tested

3 King Nebuchadnezzar had a golden statue made. It was 90 feet[1] tall and 9 feet[2] wide. He erected it on the plain of Dura in the province of Babylon. [2]Then King Nebuchadnezzar sent out a summons to assemble the satraps, prefects, governors, counselors, treasurers, judges, magistrates, and all the other authorities of the province to attend the dedication of the statue that he had erected. [3]So the satraps, prefects, governors, counselors, treasurers, judges, magistrates, and all the other provincial

authorities assembled for the dedication of the statue that King Nebuchadnezzar had erected. They were standing in front of the statue that Nebuchadnezzar had erected.[1]

[4]Then the herald made a [a]loud proclamation: "To you, O peoples, nations, and language groups, the following command is given: [5]When you hear the sound of the horn, flute, zither, trigon, harp, pipes, and all kinds of music, you must bow down and pay homage to the golden statue that King Nebuchadnezzar has erected. [6]Whoever does not bow down and pay homage will immediately [a]be thrown into the midst of a furnace of blazing fire!" [7]Therefore when they all heard the sound of the horn, flute, zither, trigon, harp, pipes, and all kinds of music, all the peoples, nations, and language groups began bowing down and paying homage to the golden statue that King Nebuchadnezzar had erected.

[8]Now at that time certain Chaldeans [a]came forward and brought malicious accusations against[1] the Jews. [9]They said [a]to King Nebuchadnezzar, "O king, live forever! [10]You have issued an edict, O king, that everyone must bow down and pay homage to the golden statue when they hear the sound of the horn, flute, zither, trigon, harp, pipes, and all kinds of music. [11]And whoever does not bow down and pay homage must be thrown into the midst of a furnace of blazing fire. [12]But [a]there are Jewish men whom you appointed over the administration of the province of Babylon—Shadrach, Meshach, and Abednego—and these men have [b]not shown proper respect to you, O king. They don't serve your gods, and they don't pay homage to the golden statue that you have erected."

[13]Then Nebuchadnezzar in a fit of [a]rage demanded that they bring Shadrach, Meshach, and Abednego before him. So they brought them before the king. [14]Nebuchadnezzar said to them, "Is it true, Shadrach, Meshach, and Abednego, that you don't serve my gods and that you don't pay homage to the golden statue that I erected? [15]Now if you are ready, when you hear the sound of the horn, flute, zither, trigon, harp,

---

2:43 [1]Ket. omits And. [2]Aram. with the seed of men. 2:44 [a]Dan 2:28, 37 [b]Ps 2:9; Isa 60:12; Dan 2:34–35; [1 Cor 15:24] 2:45 [a]Dan 2:35; Isa 28:16 2:46 [a]Dan 3:5, 7; Acts 10:25; 14:13; Rev 19:10; 22:8 [b]Lev 26:31; Ezra 6:10 2:47 [a]Dan 3:28–29; 4:34–37 [b][Deut 10:17] 2:48 [a][Prov 14:35; 21:1] [b]Dan 2:6 [c]Dan 4:9; 5:11 2:49 [a]Dan 1:7; 3:12 3:1 [1]Aram. 60 cubits. [2]Aram. 6 cubits. 3:3 [1]LXX, Thd. omit that Nebuchadnezzar had erected. 3:4 [a]Dan 4:1; 6:25 3:6 [a]Jer 29:22; Ezek 22:18–22; Matt 13:42, 50; Rev 9:2; 13:15; 14:11 3:8 [a]Ezra 4:12–16; Esth 3:8–9; Dan 6:12–13 [1]Aram. ate the pieces of; a rather vivid idiom for slander. 3:9 [a]Dan 2:4; 5:10; 6:6, 21 3:12 [a]Dan 2:49 [b]Dan 1:8; 6:12–13 3:13 [a]Dan 2:12; 3:19

pipes,[a] and all kinds of music, you must bow down and pay homage to the statue that I had made. If you don't pay homage to it, you will immediately be thrown into the midst of the furnace of blazing fire. Now, who is that god who can rescue you from my power?" [16] Shadrach, Meshach, and Abednego replied to King Nebuchadnezzar,[1] "[a]We do not need to give you a reply concerning this. [17] If[1] our [a]God whom we are serving exists, he is able to [b]rescue us from the furnace of blazing fire, and he will rescue us, O king, from your power as well. [18] But if he does not, let it be known to you, O king, that we don't serve your gods, and we will not pay [a]homage to the golden statue that you have erected."

[19] Then Nebuchadnezzar was filled with rage, and his disposition changed[1] toward Shadrach, Meshach, and Abednego. He gave orders to heat the furnace seven times hotter than it was normally heated. [20] He ordered strong soldiers in his army to tie up Shadrach, Meshach, and Abednego and to throw them into the furnace of blazing fire. [21] So those men were tied up while still wearing their cloaks, trousers, turbans, and other clothes, and were thrown into the furnace of blazing fire. [22] But since the king's command was so urgent, and the furnace was so excessively hot, the men who escorted Shadrach, Meshach, and Abednego were killed[1] by the leaping flames. [23] But those three men, Shadrach, Meshach, and Abednego, fell into the furnace of blazing fire while still securely bound.

God Delivers His Servants

[24] Then King Nebuchadnezzar was startled and quickly got up. He said to his ministers, "Wasn't it three men that we tied up and threw into the fire?" They replied to the king, "For sure, O king." [25] He answered, "But I see four men, untied and walking [a]around in [b]the midst of the fire! No harm has come to them! And the appearance of the fourth is like that of a god!" [26] Then Nebuchadnezzar approached the door of the furnace of blazing fire. He called out, "Shadrach, Meshach, and Abednego, servants of the [a]most high God, come out! Come here!"

Then Shadrach, Meshach, and Abednego emerged from the fire. [27] Once the satraps, prefects, governors, and ministers of the king had gathered around, they saw that those men were physically unharmed by the fire. The hair of their heads was not singed, nor were their trousers damaged. Not even the smell of fire was to be found [a]on them!

[28] Nebuchadnezzar exclaimed, "Praised be the God of Shadrach, Meshach, and Abednego, who has sent forth his [a]angel and has rescued his servants who trusted in him, ignoring the edict of the king and giving up their bodies rather than serve or pay homage to any god other than their God! [29] I hereby decree that any people, nation, [a]or language group that blasphemes the [b]God of Shadrach, Meshach, or Abednego will be [c]dismembered and his home reduced to rubble! For there exists no other god who can deliver in this way." [30] Then Nebuchadnezzar promoted Shadrach, Meshach, and Abednego in the province of Babylon.

4 King Nebuchadnezzar, [a]to all peoples, nations, and language groups that live in all the land: "Peace and prosperity! [2] I am delighted to tell you about the signs and wonders [a]that the most high God has done for me.

[3] "[a]How great are his signs!
How mighty are his wonders!
His kingdom will last forever,[1]
[b]and his authority continues from
one generation to the next."

Nebuchadnezzar Dreams of a Tree Chopped Down

[4] I, Nebuchadnezzar, was relaxing in my home, living luxuriously in my palace. [5] I saw [a]a dream that frightened me badly. The things I imagined while lying on my bed—these visions of my mind—were [b]terrifying me. [6] So I issued an order for all the wise men of Babylon to be brought before me

3:15 [a] Exod 5:2; 2 Kgs 18:35; Isa 36:18–20; Dan 2:47   3:16 [a] [Matt 10:19]   [1] MT answered and said to the king, "O Nebuchadnezzar".   3:17 [a] Job 5:19; [Ps 27:1–2; Isa 26:3–4]; Jer 1:8; 15:20–21; Dan 6:19–22   [b] 1 Sam 17:37; Jer 1:8; 15:20–21; 42:11; Dan 6:16, 19–22; Mic 7:7; 2 Cor 1:10   [1] Some wss omit If.   3:18 [a] Job 13:15   3:19 [1] Aram. the appearance of his face was altered.   3:22 [1] The Aram. verb is active.   3:25 [a] [Ps 91:3–9]; Isa 43:2   [b] Job 1:6; 38:7; [Ps 34:7]; Dan 3:28   3:26 [a] [Dan 4:2–3, 17, 34, 35]   3:27 [a] [Isa 43:2]; Heb 11:34   3:28 [a] [Ps 34:7–8]; Isa 37:36; [Jer 17:7]; Dan 6:22–23; Acts 5:19; 12:7   3:29 [a] Dan 6:26   [b] Dan 2:46–47; 4:34–37   [c] Ezra 6:11; Dan 2:5   4:1 [a] Ezra 4:17; Dan 3:4; 6:25   4:2 [a] Dan 3:26   4:3 [a] 2 Sam 7:16; Ps 89:35–37; Dan 6:27; 7:13–14; [Luke 1:31–33]   [b] [Dan 2:44; 4:34; 6:26]   [1] Aram. kingdom is an everlasting kingdom.   4:5 [a] Dan 2:28–29   [b] Dan 2:1

so that they could make known to me the interpretation of the dream. [7]When [a]the magicians, astrologers, wise men, and diviners entered, I recounted the dream for them. But they were unable to make known its interpretation to me. [8]Later Daniel entered (whose name [a]is Belteshazzar after the name of my god, and [b]in whom there is a spirit of the holy gods). I recounted the dream for him as well, [9]saying, "Belteshazzar, [a]chief of the magicians, in whom I know there to be a spirit of the holy gods and whom no mystery baffles, consider[1] my dream that I saw and set forth its interpretation! [10]Here [a]are the visions of my mind[1] while I was on my bed.

> "While I was watching,
> there was a tree in the middle of the land.[2]
> It was enormously tall.
> [11] The tree grew large and strong.
> Its top reached far into the sky;
> it could be seen from the borders of all the land.
> [12] Its foliage was attractive and its fruit plentiful;
> on it [a]there was food enough for all.
> Under it the wild animals used to seek shade,
> and in its branches the birds of the sky used to nest.
> All creatures used to feed themselves from it.

> [13] "While I [a]was [b]watching in my mind's visions on my bed,
> a holy sentinel came down from heaven.
> [14] He called out loudly[1] as follows:
> '[a]Chop down the tree and lop off its branches!
> Strip off its foliage
> and scatter its fruit!
> [b]Let the animals flee from under it
> and the birds from its branches.
> [15] But leave its taproot in the ground,
> with a band of iron and bronze around it

> surrounded by the grass of the field.
> Let it become damp with the dew of the sky,
> and let it live with the animals in the grass of the land.
> [16] Let his mind[1] be altered from that of a human being,
> and let an animal's mind be given to him,
> and let seven periods of [a]time go by for him.
> [17] This announcement is by the decree of the sentinels;
> this decision is by the pronouncement of the holy ones,
> [a]so [b]that[1] those who are alive may understand
> that the Most High has authority over human kingdoms,
> and he [c]bestows them on whomever he wishes.
> He establishes over them even the [d]lowliest of human beings.'

[18]"This is the dream that I, King Nebuchadnezzar, saw. Now you, Belteshazzar, declare its[1] interpretation, [a]for none of the wise men in my kingdom are able to make known to me the interpretation. But you can do so, [b]for a spirit of the holy gods is in you."

Daniel Interprets Nebuchadnezzar's Dream

[19]Then Daniel ([a]whose name is also Belteshazzar) was upset for a brief time; his thoughts were [b]alarming him. [c]The king said, "Belteshazzar, don't let the dream and its interpretation alarm you." But Belteshazzar replied, "Sir, if only the dream were for your enemies and its interpretation applied to your adversaries! [20]The tree that you saw that grew large and strong, whose top reached to [a]the sky, and that could be seen in all the land, [21]whose foliage was attractive and its fruit plentiful, and from which there was food available for all, under whose branches wild animals used to live, and in whose branches birds of the sky used

---

4:7 [a]Dan 2:2   4:8 [a]Dan 1:7   [b]Isa 63:11; Dan 2:11; 4:18; 5:11, 14   4:9 [a]Dan 2:48; 5:11   [1]MT *visions.*   4:10 [a]Ezek 31:3; Dan 4:20   [1]LXX omits *the visions of my mind.*   [2]Or *a tree at the center of the earth.*   4:12 [a]Jer 27:6; Ezek 17:23; 31:6; Lam 4:20   4:13 [a][Dan 4:17, 23]   [b]Deut 33:2; Ps 89:7; Dan 8:13; Zech 14:5; Jude 14   4:14 [a]Ezek 31:10–14; Dan 4:23; [Matt 3:10; 7:19; Luke 13:7–9]   [b]Ezek 31:12–13; Dan 4:12   [1]Aram. *in strength.*   4:16 [a]Dan 11:13; 12:7   [1]Aram. *its heart.*   4:17 [a]Ps 9:16; 83:18   [b]Dan 2:21; 4:25, 32; 5:21   [c]Jer 27:5–7; Ezek 29:18–20; Dan 2:37; 5:18   [d]1 Sam 2:8; Dan 11:21   [1]MT *until.*   4:18 [a]Gen 41:8, 15; Dan 5:8, 15   [b]Dan 4:8–9; 5:11, 14   [1]Ket. *the.*   4:19 [a]Dan 4:8   [b]Jer 4:19; Dan 7:15, 28; 8:27   [c]2 Sam 18:32; Jer 29:7; Dan 4:24; 10:16   4:20 [a]Dan 4:10–12

to nest—[22]it is you, O king! For you have become great and strong. Your greatness is such that [a]it reaches to heaven [b]and your authority to the ends of the earth. [23]As for the king seeing [a]a holy sentinel coming down from heaven [b]and saying, 'Chop down the tree and destroy it, but leave its taproot in the ground, with a band of iron and bronze around it, surrounded by the grass of the field. Let it become damp with the dew of the sky, and let it live with the wild animals, until seven periods of time go by for him'—[24]this is the interpretation, O king. It is the decision of the Most High that this has happened to my lord the king. [25]You will be [a]driven from human society, and you will live with the wild animals. You will be [b]fed grass like oxen, and you will become damp with the dew of the sky. Seven periods of time will pass by for you [c]before you understand that the Most High is ruler over human kingdoms and [d]gives them to whomever he wishes. [26]They said to leave the taproot of the tree, for your kingdom will be restored to you when you come to understand that [a]heaven rules. [27]Therefore, O king, may my advice be pleasing to you. [a]Break away from your sins by doing what is right, and from your iniquities by showing mercy to the poor. [b]Perhaps your prosperity will be prolonged."[1]

[28]Now all this happened to King Nebuchadnezzar. [29]After 12 months, he happened to be walking around on the battlements of the royal palace of Babylon. [30]The king uttered these [a]words: "Is this not the great Babylon that I have built for a royal residence by my own mighty strength and for my majestic honor?" [31][a]While these words were still on the king's lips, [b]a voice came down from heaven: "It is hereby announced to you, King Nebuchadnezzar, that your kingdom has been removed from you! [32]You will be driven from human society, and you will live with [a]the wild animals. You will be fed grass like oxen, and seven periods of time will pass by for you before you understand that the Most High is ruler over human kingdoms and gives them to whomever he wishes."

[33]Now in that very moment[1] this pronouncement about Nebuchadnezzar came true. He was driven from human society, he ate grass like oxen, and his body became damp with the dew of the sky, until his hair became long like an eagle's feathers and his nails like a bird's claws.

[34]But [a]at the end of the appointed time I, Nebuchadnezzar, looked up toward heaven, and my sanity returned to me.

I extolled the Most High,
  and I praised and glorified the one
    [b]who lives forever.
For his authority is [c]an everlasting
    authority,
  and his kingdom extends from one
    generation to the next.
[35] [a]All [b]the inhabitants of the earth are
    regarded as nothing.
He does as he wishes with the army
  of heaven
and with those who inhabit the
  earth.
  [c]No one slaps his hand
  and says to him, "[d]What have you
    done?"

[36]At that time my sanity returned [a]to me. I was restored[1] to the honor of my kingdom, and my splendor returned to me. My ministers and my nobles were seeking me out, and I was [b]reinstated[2] over my kingdom. I [c]became even greater than before. [37]Now I, Nebuchadnezzar, [a]praise and exalt and glorify the King of heaven, for [b]all his deeds are right [c]and his ways are just. He is able to bring down those who live in pride.

Belshazzar Sees Mysterious Handwriting on a Wall

5 King Belshazzar [a]prepared a great banquet for 1,000 of his nobles, and he was drinking wine in front of them all. [2]While under the influence of the wine, Belshazzar issued an order to bring in the gold and

4:22 [a]Dan 2:37–38 [b]Jer 27:6–8   4:23 [a]Dan 4:13–15 [b]Dan 5:21   4:25 [a]Dan 4:32; 5:21 [b]Ps 106:20 [c]Ps 83:18; Dan 4:2, 17, 32 [d]Jer 27:5   4:26 [a]Matt 21:25; Luke 15:18   4:27 [a][Prov 28:13]; Isa 55:7; Ezek 18:21–22; [Rom 2:9–11; 1 Pet 4:8] [b][Ps 41:1–3]; Isa 58:6–7, 10 [1]Aram. *if there may be a lengthening to your prosperity.*   4:30 [a]Prov 16:18; Isa 13:19; Dan 5:20   4:31 [a]Dan 5:5; Luke 12:20 [b]Dan 4:24   4:32 [a][Dan 4:25]   4:33 [1]Aram. *hour.*   4:34 [a]Dan 4:26 [b]Ps 102:24–27; Dan 6:26; 12:7; [Rev 4:10] [c][Ps 10:16]; Dan 2:44; 7:14; Mic 4:7; [Luke 1:33]   4:35 [a]Ps 39:5; Isa 40:15, 17 [b]Ps 115:3; 135:6; Dan 6:27 [c]Job 34:29; Isa 43:13 [d]Job 9:12; Isa 45:9; Jer 18:6; Rom 9:20; [1 Cor 2:16]   4:36 [a]Dan 4:26 [b]2 Chr 20:20 [c]Job 42:12; [Prov 22:4; Matt 6:33] [1]MT *my honor.* [2]MT *it was established.*   4:37 [a]Dan 2:46–47; 3:28–29 [b]Deut 32:4; [Ps 33:4]; Isa 5:16; [Rev 15:3] [c]Exod 18:11; Job 40:11–12; Dan 5:20   5:1 [a]Esth 1:3; Isa 22:12–14

silver vessels—the ones that Nebuchadnezzar his father[1] had confiscated from the temple in Jerusalem—so that the king and his nobles, together with his wives and his concubines, could drink from them. [3]So they brought the gold and silver [a]vessels that had been confiscated from the temple, the house of God in Jerusalem, and the king and his nobles, together with his wives and concubines, drank from them. [4]As they drank wine, they praised the gods of gold [a]and silver, bronze, iron, wood, and stone.

[5]At that very moment the [a]fingers of a human hand appeared and wrote on the plaster of the royal palace wall, opposite the lampstand. The king was watching the back of the hand that was writing. [6]Then all the color drained from the king's face, and he became alarmed. The joints of his hips gave way, and his [a]knees began knocking together. [7]The king called out loudly to summon [a]the astrologers, wise men, and diviners. [b]The king proclaimed to the wise men of Babylon that anyone who could read this inscription [c]and disclose its interpretation would be clothed in purple and have a golden collar placed on his neck and be third ruler in the kingdom.

[8]So all the king's wise men came in, [a]but they were unable to read the writing or to make known its[1] interpretation to the king. [9]Then King Belshazzar was very [a]terrified, and he was visibly shaken. His nobles were completely dumbfounded.

[10]Due to the noise caused by the king and his nobles, the queen mother then entered the banquet room. She said, "O king, live forever! Don't be alarmed! Don't be shaken! [11]There is a man in your kingdom who has within him a spirit of [a]the holy gods. In the days of your father, he proved to have insight, discernment, and wisdom like that of the gods.[1] King Nebuchadnezzar your father appointed him chief of the magicians, astrologers, wise men, and diviners.[2] [12]Thus there was found in this man Daniel, [a]whom the king renamed Belteshazzar, an extraordinary spirit, knowledge, and skill to interpret dreams, explain riddles, and solve difficult problems. Now summon Daniel, and he will disclose the interpretation."

[13]So Daniel was brought in before the king. The king said to Daniel, "Are you that Daniel who is one of the captives of Judah, whom my father the king brought from Judah? [14]I have heard about you, how [a]there is a spirit of the gods in you, and how you have insight, discernment, and extraordinary wisdom. [15]Now [a]the wise men and[1] astrologers were brought before me to read this writing and make known to me its interpretation. But they were unable to disclose the interpretation of the message. [16]However, I have heard that you are able to provide interpretations and to solve difficult problems. [a]Now if you are able to read this writing and make known to me its interpretation, you will wear purple and have a golden collar around your neck and be third ruler in the kingdom."

Daniel Interprets the Handwriting on the Wall

[17]But Daniel replied to the king, "Keep your gifts, and give your rewards to someone else. However, I will read the writing for the king and make known its interpretation. [18]As for you, O king, [a]the most high God bestowed on your father Nebuchadnezzar a kingdom, greatness, honor, and majesty. [19]Due to the greatness that he bestowed on him, [a]all peoples, nations, and language groups were trembling with fear before him. He [b]killed whom he wished, he spared whom he wished, he exalted whom he wished, and he brought low whom he wished. [20a]And when his mind became arrogant and his spirit filled with pride, he was deposed from his royal throne, and his honor was removed from him. [21]He was [a]driven from human society; his mind was changed to that of an animal. He lived with the wild donkeys, he was fed grass like oxen, and his body became damp with the dew of the sky, [b]until he came to understand that the most high God rules over human kingdoms, and he appoints over them whomever he wishes.

5:2 [1]Or *ancestor, predecessor.*   5:3 [a]2 Chr 36:10   5:4 [a]Isa 42:8; Dan 5:23; Rev 9:20   5:5 [a]Dan 4:31   5:6 [a]Ezek 7:17; 21:7   5:7 [a]Dan 4:6–7; 5:11, 15   [b]Isa 47:13   [c]Dan 6:2–3   5:8 [a]Gen 41:8; Dan 2:27; 4:7; 5:15   [1]Ket. *and the interpretation.*   5:9 [a]Job 18:11; Isa 21:2–4; Jer 6:24; Dan 2:1; 5:6   5:11 [a]Dan 2:48; 4:8–9, 18   [1]Thd. omits *and wisdom like that of the gods.*   [2]MT adds *your father the king.*   5:12 [a]Dan 1:7; 4:8   5:14 [a]Dan 4:8–9, 18; 5:11–12   5:15 [a]Dan 5:7–8   [1]Or *the.*   5:16 [a]Dan 5:7, 29   5:18 [a]Jer 27:5–7; Dan 2:37–38; 4:17, 22, 25   5:19 [a]Jer 27:7   [b]Dan 2:12–13; 3:6   5:20 [a]Exod 9:17; Job 15:25; Isa 14:13–15; Dan 4:30, 37   5:21 [a]Job 30:3–7; Dan 4:32–33   [b]Exod 9:14–16; Ps 83:17–18; Ezek 17:24; [Dan 4:17, 34, 35]

[22]"But you, his son Belshazzar, [a]have not humbled yourself, although you knew all this. [23a]Instead, you have exalted yourself against the Lord of heaven. You brought before you the [b]vessels from his temple, [c]and you and your nobles, together with your wives and concubines, drank wine from them. You praised the gods of silver, gold, bronze, iron, wood, and stone—gods that cannot see or hear or comprehend. But you have not glorified the God who has in his control your very breath and all your ways! [24]Therefore the palm of a hand was sent from him, and this writing was inscribed.

[25]"This is the writing that was inscribed: MENE, MENE,[1] TEQEL, and PHARSIN.[2] [26]This is the interpretation of the words: As for *Mene*[1]—God has numbered your kingdom's days and brought it to an end. [27]As for *Teqel*—[a]you are weighed on the balances and found to be lacking. [28]As for *Peres*—your kingdom is divided and given over to the [a]Medes and [b]Persians."

[29]Then, on Belshazzar's orders, Daniel was clothed in purple, [a]a golden collar was placed around his neck, and he was proclaimed third ruler in the kingdom. [30]And [a]that very night Belshazzar, the Babylonian king, was killed. [31a]So Darius the Mede took control of the kingdom when he was about sixty-two years old.

Daniel Is Thrown into a Lions' Den

6 It seemed like a good idea to Darius to appoint over the kingdom 120 satraps[1] who would be in charge of the entire kingdom. [2]Over them would be three supervisors, one of whom was Daniel. These satraps were accountable to them, so that the king's interests might not incur damage. [3]Now this Daniel was distinguishing himself above the other supervisors and the satraps, [a]for he had an extraordinary spirit. In fact, the king intended to appoint him over the entire kingdom. [4]Consequently the [a]supervisors and satraps were trying to find some pretext against Daniel in connection with administrative matters. But they were unable to find any such damaging evidence because he was trustworthy and guilty of no negligence or corruption. [5]So these men concluded, "We won't find any pretext against this man Daniel unless it is in connection with the law of his God."

[6]So these supervisors and satraps came by collusion[1] to the [a]king and said to him, "O King Darius, live forever! [7]To all the supervisors of the kingdom, the prefects, satraps, counselors, and governors it seemed like a good idea for a royal edict to be issued and an interdict to be enforced. For the next 30 days anyone who prays to any god or human other than you, [a]O king, should be thrown into a den of lions. [8]Now let the king issue a written interdict[1] so that it cannot be altered, according to the [a]law of the Medes and Persians, which cannot be changed." [9]So King Darius issued the written interdict.

[10]When Daniel realized that a written decree had been issued, he entered his home, where the windows in his upper room opened [a]toward Jerusalem. [b]Three times daily he was[1] kneeling and offering prayers and thanks to his God just as he had been accustomed to do previously. [11]Then those officials who had gone to the king came by collusion and found Daniel praying and asking for help before his God. [12]So they approached the king [a]and said to him,[1] "Did you not issue an edict to the effect that for the next 30 days anyone who prays to any god [b]or human other than to you, O king, would be thrown into a den of lions?" The king replied, "That is correct, according to the law of the Medes and Persians, which cannot be changed." [13]Then they said to the king, "Daniel, [a]who is one of the captives from Judah, pays no attention to you, [b]O king, or to the edict that you issued. Three times daily he offers his prayer."

[14]When the king heard this, he [a]was very upset and began thinking about how he might rescue Daniel. Until late afternoon[1]

5:22 [a]Exod 10:3; 2 Chr 33:23; 36:12   5:23 [a]Dan 5:3–4   [b]Exod 40:9; Num 18:3; Isa 52:11; Heb 9:21   [c]Ps 139:3; Prov 20:24; [Jer 10:23]   5:25 [1]Thd. omits one MENE.   [2]Thd. PERES.   5:26 [1]A measure of weight.   5:27 [a]Job 31:6; Ps 62:9; Jer 6:30   5:28 [a]Isa 21:2; Dan 5:31; 9:1   [b]Dan 6:28; Acts 2:9   5:29 [a]Dan 5:7, 16   5:30 [a]Jer 51:31, 39, 57   5:31 [a]Dan 2:39; 9:1   6:1 [1]Officials placed in charge of a region of the empire who were answerable to a supervisor, who in turn answered to Darius.   6:3 [a]Dan 5:12   6:4 [a]Eccl 4:4   6:6 [a]Neh 2:3; Dan 2:4; 6:21   [1]The meaning of the Aram. word is widely disputed.   6:7 [a]Ps 59:3; 62:4; 64:2–6   6:8 [a]Esth 1:19; 8:8; Dan 6:12, 15   [1]Aram. *establish a written interdict and inscribe a written decree.*   6:10 [a][1 Kgs 8:29–30, 46–48; Ps 5:7; Jonah 2:4   [b]Ps 55:17; Acts 2:1–2, 15; [Phil 4:6]; 1 Thess 5:17–18   [1]MT *he.*   6:12 [a]Dan 3:8–12; Acts 16:19–21   [b]Esth 1:19; Dan 6:8, 15   [1]MT adds *about the edict of the king.*   6:13 [a]Dan 1:6; 5:13   [b]Esth 3:8; Dan 3:12; Acts 5:29   6:14 [a]Mark 6:26   [1]Aram. *the entrances of the sun.*

he was struggling to find a way to rescue him. [15]Then those men came by collusion to [a]the king and[1] said to him, "Recall, O king, that it is a law of the Medes and Persians that no edict or decree that the king issues can be changed." [16]So the king gave the order, and Daniel was brought and thrown into a den of lions. The king consoled Daniel by saying, "Your God whom you continually serve will rescue you!" [17]Then a stone was brought and placed over [a]the opening to the den. The king sealed it with his signet ring [b]and with those of his nobles so that nothing could be changed with regard to Daniel. [18]Then the king departed to his palace. But he spent the night without eating, and no diversions[1] were brought to him. He was unable to sleep.

God Rescues Daniel from the Lions

[19]In the morning, at the earliest sign of daylight, the [a]king got up and rushed to the lions' den. [20]As he approached the den, he called out to Daniel in [a]a worried voice, "Daniel, servant of the living God, was your God whom you continually serve able to rescue you from the lions?"

[21]Then Daniel [a]spoke to the king, "O king, live forever! [22a]My God sent his angel and [b]closed the lions' mouths so that they have not harmed me because I was found to be innocent before him. Nor have I done any harm to you, O king."

[23]Then the king was delighted and gave an order to haul Daniel up from the den. So Daniel was hauled up out of the den. He had no injury of any kind [a]because he had trusted in his God. [24]The king gave another order, [a]and those men who had maliciously accused[1] Daniel were brought and thrown into [b]the lions' den—they, their children, and their wives.[2] They did not even reach the bottom of the den before the lions overpowered them and crushed all their bones.

[25a]Then King Darius wrote to all the peoples, nations, and language groups who were living in all the land: "Peace and prosperity!

[26]I have [a]issued an edict that throughout all the dominion of my kingdom people are to revere and fear the God of Daniel.

"[b]For he is the living God;
  he endures forever.
His kingdom will not be [c]destroyed;
  his authority is forever.
[27] He rescues [a]and delivers
  and performs signs and wonders
  in the heavens and on the earth.
He has rescued Daniel from the
  power of the lions!"

[28]So this Daniel prospered during the reign of Darius [a]and the reign of [b]Cyrus the Persian.

Daniel Has a Vision of Four Animals Coming up from the Sea

7 In the first year of King Belshazzar of Babylon, [a]Daniel had a dream filled with [b]visions while he was lying on his bed. Then he wrote down the dream in summary fashion. [2]Daniel explained: "I was watching in my vision during the night as the four winds of the sky[1] were stirring up the great sea. [3]Then four large beasts [a]came up from the sea; they were different from one another.

[4]"The first one was [a]like a lion with eagles' wings. As I watched, its wings were pulled off, and it was lifted up from the ground. It was made to stand on two feet like a human [b]being, and a human mind was given to it. [5]"Then [a]a second beast appeared, like a bear. It was raised up on one side, and there were three ribs in its mouth between its teeth.[1] It was told, 'Get up and devour much flesh!'

[6]"After these things, as I was watching, another beast like a leopard appeared, with [a]four bird-like wings on its back. This beast had four heads, and ruling authority was given to it.

[7]"After these things, [a]as I was watching in the night visions [b]a fourth beast appeared—one dreadful, terrible, and very strong. It

6:15 [a]Esth 8:8; Ps 94:20–21; Dan 6:8, 12   [1]Thd. omits *came by collusion to the king and.*   6:17 [a]Lam 3:53   [b]Matt 27:66
6:18 [1]The meaning of the Aram. word is uncertain, with suggestions including *music, dancing girls, concubines, table,* and *food,* thus, this translation is deliberately vague.   6:19 [a]Dan 3:24   6:20 [a]Gen 18:14; Num 11:23; Jer 32:17; Dan 3:17; [Luke 1:37]   6:21 [a]Dan 2:4; 6:6   6:22 [a]Num 20:16; Isa 63:9; Dan 3:28; Acts 12:11; [Heb 1:14]   [b]Ps 91:11–13; 2 Tim 4:17; Heb 11:33   6:23 [a]Heb 11:33   6:24 [a]Deut 19:18–19; Esth 7:10   [b]Deut 24:16; 2 Kgs 14:6; Esth 9:10   [1]Aram. *had eaten the pieces of,* a rather vivid idiom for slander.   [2]LXX specifies only the two overseers, together with their families.   6:25 [a]Ezra 1:1–2; Esth 3:12; 8:9; Dan 4:1   6:26 [a]Ezra 6:8–12; 7:13; Dan 3:29   [b]Dan 4:34; 6:20; Hos 1:10; Rom 9:26   [c]Dan 2:44; 4:3; 7:14, 27; [Luke 1:33]   6:27 [a]Dan 4:2–3   6:28 [a]Dan 1:21   [b]Ezra 1:1–2   7:1 [a]Num 12:6; [Amos 3:7]   [b][Dan 2:28]   7:2 [1]Or *the heavens.*   7:3 [a]Dan 7:17; Rev 13:1; 17:8   7:4 [a]Deut 28:49; 2 Sam 1:23; Jer 48:40; Ezek 17:3; Hab 1:8   [b]Dan 4:16, 34   7:5 [a]Dan 2:39   [1]LXX omits *between its teeth.*   7:6 [a]Dan 8:8, 22   7:7 [a]Dan 2:40   [b]Dan 2:41; Rev 12:3; 13:1

had two large rows of iron teeth. It devoured and crushed, and anything that was left it trampled with its feet. It was different from all the beasts that came before it, and it had 10 horns.

8 "As I was contemplating the horns, [a]another horn—a small one—came up between them, and three [b]of the former horns were torn out by the roots to make room for it. This horn had eyes resembling human eyes [c]and a mouth speaking arrogant things.

9 "While [a]I was watching,

> thrones were set up,
> and [b]the Ancient of Days took [c]his
>   seat.
> His attire was white like snow;
> the hair of his head was like lamb's
>   wool.
> His throne was ablaze with fire,
> and [d]its wheels were all aflame.
> 10 A river of fire [a]was [b]streaming forth
>   and proceeding from his presence.
> Many thousands were ministering
>   to him;
> many tens of thousands stood ready
>   to serve him.
> [c]The court convened,
> and the books were opened.

11 "Then [a]I kept on watching because of the arrogant words of the horn that was speaking. I was watching[1] until the beast was killed and its body destroyed and thrown into the flaming fire. 12 As for the rest of the beasts, their ruling authority had already been removed, though they were permitted to go on living for a time and a season.

> 13 "I was watching in the night visions,
>   and with[1] the clouds of the sky,[2]
> [a]one like a son of man was
>   approaching.
> He went up to the Ancient of Days
>   and was escorted before him.
> 14 [a]To him was given ruling authority,
>   honor, and sovereignty.
> All [b]peoples, nations, [c]and language
>   groups were serving him.

> His authority is eternal and will not
>   pass away.
> His kingdom will not be destroyed.

An Angel Interprets Daniel's Vision

15 "As for me, Daniel, my spirit was distressed, and the visions of my mind were alarming me. 16 I approached one of those standing nearby and asked him about the meaning of all this. So he spoke with me and revealed to me the interpretation of the vision:[1] 17 'These large beasts, which are four in number, represent four kings who will arise from the earth. 18 The holy ones of [a]the Most High will receive the kingdom and will take possession of the kingdom forever and ever.'

19 "Then I wanted to know the meaning of the fourth beast, which was different from all the others. It was very dreadful, with two rows of iron teeth and bronze claws, and it devoured, crushed, and trampled anything that was left with its feet. 20 I also wanted to know the meaning of the 10 horns on its head, and of that other horn that came up and before which three others fell. This was the horn that had eyes and a mouth speaking arrogant things, whose appearance was more formidable than the others. 21 While I was watching, that horn began to wage war against the holy ones [a]and was defeating them, 22 until the Ancient of Days arrived [a]and judgment was rendered[1] in favor of the holy ones of the Most High. Then the time came for the holy ones to take possession of the kingdom.

23 "This is [a]what he told me:

> 'The fourth beast means that there
>   will be a fourth kingdom on earth
> that will differ from all the other
>   kingdoms.
> It will devour all the earth
>   and will trample and crush it.
> 24 The 10 horns mean that 10 kings
>   will arise from that kingdom.
> [a]Another king will arise after them,
> but he will be different from the
>   earlier ones.
> He will humiliate[1] three kings.

7:8 [a]Dan 8:9 [b]Rev 9:7 [c]Ps 12:3; Rev 13:5–6 7:9 [a][Rev 20:4] [b]Ps 90:2 [c]Ps 104:2; Rev 1:14 [d]Ezek 1:15 7:10 [a]Ps 50:3; Isa 30:33; 66:15 [b]Deut 33:2; 1 Kgs 22:19; Ps 68:17; Rev 5:11 [c]Dan 12:1; [Rev 20:11–15] 7:11 [a][Rev 19:20; 20:10] [1]LXX, Thd. omit *I was watching*. 7:13 [a]Ezek 1:26; [Matt 24:30; 26:64; Mark 13:26; 14:62; Luke 21:27; Rev 1:7, 13; 14:14] [1]LXX *upon*. [2]Or *the heavens*. 7:14 [a]Ps 2:6–8; Dan 7:27; [Matt 28:18; John 3:35–36; 1 Cor 15:27; Eph 1:22; Phil 2:9–11; Rev 1:6; 11:15] [b]Dan 3:4 [c]Ps 145:13; Mic 4:7; [Luke 1:33]; John 12:34; Heb 12:28 7:16 [1]Aram. *matter*. 7:18 [a]Ps 149:5–9; Isa 60:12–14; Dan 7:14; [2 Tim 2:11; Rev 2:26–27; 20:4; 22:5] 7:21 [a]Rev 11:7; 13:7; 17:14 7:22 [a][Rev 1:6] [1]Some wss *the Ancient of Days rendered judgment*. 7:23 [a]Dan 2:40 7:24 [a]Dan 7:7; Rev 13:1; 17:12 [1]Or *subjugate*.

25 He will speak words against ᵃthe
  Most High.
  He will ᵇharass[1] the holy ones of the
  Most High continually.
  His intention will ᶜbe to change
  times established by law.
  ᵈThe holy ones will be delivered into
  his hand
  ᵉfor a time, times, and half a time.
26 But the court will convene, and his
  ruling authority will be removed—
  destroyed and abolished forever!
27 Then the ᵃkingdom, authority,
  and greatness of the kingdoms under
  the whole heaven
  will be delivered to the people of the
  holy ones of the Most High.
  ᵇHis kingdom is ᶜan eternal kingdom;
  all authorities will serve him and
  obey him.'

28"This is the conclusion of the matter. As for me, Daniel, my thoughts troubled me greatly, and the color drained ᵃfrom my face. But I ᵇkept the matter to myself."

Daniel Has a Vision of a Goat and a Ram

8 In ᵃthe third year of King Belshazzar's reign, a vision appeared to me, Daniel, after the one that had appeared to me previously. ²In this vision I saw myself in ᵃSusa the citadel, which is located in the province of Elam. In the vision I saw myself at the Ulai Canal.[1] ³I looked up and saw a ram with two horns standing at the canal. Its two horns were both ᵃlong, but one was longer than the other. The longer one was coming up after the shorter one. ⁴I saw that the ram was ᵃbutting westward, northward, and southward. No animal was able to stand before it, and there was none who could deliver from its power. It did as it pleased and acted arrogantly.

⁵While I was contemplating all this, a male goat was coming from the west over the surface of all the land without touching the ground. This goat had a conspicuous

ᵃhorn between its eyes. ⁶It came to the two-horned ram that I had seen standing beside the canal and rushed against it with raging strength. ⁷I saw it approaching the ram. It went into a fit of rage against the ram and struck it and broke off its two horns. The ram had no ability to resist it. The goat hurled the ram to the ground and trampled it. No one could deliver the ram from its power. ⁸The male goat acted even more arrogantly. But no sooner had the large horn become strong than it was broken, and there arose ᵃfour conspicuous horns in its place, extending toward the four winds of the sky.

⁹From one of them came ᵃa small horn, but it grew ᵇto be very great toward the south and the east and toward the beautiful ᶜland. ¹⁰It grew so great it reached the army of heaven, ᵃand it brought about ᵇthe fall of some of the army and some of the stars to the ground, where ᶜit trampled them. ¹¹It also acted arrogantly against ᵃthe Prince of ᵇthe army, from whom the daily sacrifice was removed ᶜand whose sanctuary was thrown down. ¹²ᵃThe army was given over,[1] along with the daily sacrifice, in the course of his sinful rebellion. It hurled[2] ᵇtruth to the ground and ᶜenjoyed success.

¹³Then I ᵃheard a holy one speaking. Another holy one said to the one who was speaking, "To what period of time does the vision pertain—this vision concerning the daily sacrifice and the destructive act of rebellion and the giving over of both the sanctuary and army to be trampled?" ¹⁴He said to me, "To 2,300 evenings and mornings; then the sanctuary will be put right again."

An Angel Interprets Daniel's Vision

¹⁵While I, Daniel, ᵃwas watching the vision, I sought to understand it. Now ᵇone who appeared to be a man was standing before me. ¹⁶Then I heard a human voice coming from ᵃbetween the banks of the Ulai. It called out, "ᵇGabriel, enable this person to understand the vision." ¹⁷So he approached the place where I was standing. As he came,

7:25 ᵃIsa 37:23; Dan 11:36; Rev 13:1–6 ᵇRev 17:6 ᶜDan 2:21 ᵈRev 13:7; 18:24 ᵉDan 12:7; Rev 12:14 ¹Aram. *wear out.*
7:27 ᵃIsa 54:3; Dan 7:14, 18, 22; Rev 20:4 ᵇ2 Sam 7:16; Ps 89:35–37; Isa 9:7; Dan 2:44; 4:34; 7:14; [Luke 1:33–34]; John 12:34; [Rev 11:15; 22:5] ᶜPs 2:6–12; 22:27; 72:11; 86:9; Isa 60:12; Rev 11:1 7:28 ᵃDan 8:27 ᵇLuke 2:19, 51 8:1 ᵃDan 7:1 8:2 ᵃNeh 1:1; Esth 1:2, 2:8 ¹Heb. *stream, river,* apparently a sizable artificial canal in Susa. 8:3 ᵃDan 7:5 8:4 ᵃDan 5:19 8:5 ᵃDan 8:8, 21; 11:3 8:8 ᵃDan 7:6; 8:22; 11:4 8:9 ᵃDan 11:21 ᵇDan 11:25 ᶜPs 48:2 8:10 ᵃDan 11:28 ᵇIsa 14:13; Jer 48:26 ᶜRev 12:4 8:11 ᵃ2 Kgs 19:22–23; 2 Chr 32:15–17; Isa 37:23; Dan 8:25; 11:36–37 ᵇJosh 5:14 ᶜEzek 46:14; Dan 11:31; 12:11 8:12 ᵃDan 11:31 ᵇPs 119:43; Isa 59:14 ᶜDan 8:4; 11:36 ¹MT *was being given/will be given.* ²Two MSS, LXX *truth was hurled to the ground.* 8:13 ᵃDan 4:13, 23; 1 Pet 1:12 8:15 ᵃ1 Pet 1:10 ᵇEzek 1:26 8:16 ᵃDan 12:6–7 ᵇDan 9:21; Luke 1:19, 26

I felt terrified and [a]fell flat on the ground. Then he said to me, "Understand, son of man, that the vision pertains to the time of the end." [18a]As he spoke with me, I fell into a trance with my face to the ground. [b]But he touched me and stood me upright.

[19]Then he said, "I am going to [a]inform you about what will happen in the latter time of wrath, for the vision pertains to the appointed time of the end. [20]The ram that you saw with the two horns stands for the kings of Media and Persia. [21]The male goat [a]is the king of Greece,[1] and the large horn between its eyes is the first king. [22]The horn that [a]was broken and in whose place there arose four others stands for four kingdoms that will arise from his nation, though they will not have his strength. [23]Toward the end of their rule, when rebellious acts[1] are complete, [a]a rash and deceitful king will arise. [24]His power will be great, [a]but it will not be by his strength alone. He will cause terrible destruction. He will be successful in what he undertakes. He will destroy powerful people [b]and [c]the people of the holy ones. [25]By his treachery he will succeed through deceit. He will have an arrogant attitude, and he will destroy many who are unaware of his schemes. He will rise up [a]against [b]the Prince of princes, yet he will be broken [c]apart—but not by human agency. [26]The vision of [a]the evenings and mornings that was told to you is correct. But you should seal up the vision, for it refers to a time many days from now."

[27]I, Daniel, was exhausted [a]and sick for days. Then I got up and again carried out the king's business. But I was astonished at the vision, and there was no one to explain it.

Daniel Prays for His People

9 In the first year [a]of Darius son of Ahasuerus,[1] who was of Median descent and who had been appointed king over the Babylonian[2] empire—[2]in the first year of his reign[1] I, Daniel, came to understand from the sacred books that the number of years for the fulfilling of the desolation of Jerusalem, which had come as the LORD's message to the prophet [a]Jeremiah, would be 70 years. [3]So I turned my attention to [a]the Lord God to implore him by prayer and requests, with fasting, sackcloth, and ashes. [4]I prayed to the LORD my God, confessing in this way:

"O [a]Lord, great and awesome God who is faithful to his covenant with those who love him and keep his commandments, [5]we have sinned! [a]We have done what is wrong and wicked; we have rebelled by turning away from your commandments and standards. [6]We have [a]not paid attention to your servants the prophets, who spoke by your authority to our kings, our leaders, and our ancestors, and to all the inhabitants of the land as well.

[7]"You are [a]righteous, O Lord, but we are humiliated this day—the people of Judah and the inhabitants of Jerusalem and all Israel, both near and far away in all the countries in which you have scattered them because they have behaved unfaithfully toward you. [8]O LORD, we have been humiliated—our kings, our leaders, and our ancestors—because we have sinned against you. [9a]Yet the Lord our God is compassionate and forgiving, even though we have rebelled against him. [10]We have not obeyed the LORD our God by living according to his laws[1] that he set before us through his servants the prophets. [11]"[a]All Israel has broken your [b]law and turned away by not obeying you. Therefore you have poured out on us the judgment solemnly threatened in the law of Moses the servant of God, for we have sinned against you. [12]He has carried [a]out his threats[1] against us and our rulers who were over us by bringing great calamity on us—what has happened to Jerusalem has never been equaled under all heaven! [13]Just [a]as it is written in the law of Moses, so all this calamity has come on us. Still we have not tried to pacify the LORD our God by turning back from our sin and by seeking wisdom from your

---

8:17 [a] Ezek 1:28; 44:4; Dan 2:46; Rev 1:17   8:18 [a] Dan 10:9; Luke 9:32   [b] Ezek 2:2; Dan 10:10, 16, 18   8:19 [a] Hab 2:3   8:21 [a] Dan 11:3   [1] Heb. *Javan.*   8:22 [a] Dan 11:4   8:23 [a] Deut 28:50   [1] MT *the rebels.*   8:24 [a] Rev 17:13   [b] Dan 11:36   [c] Dan 7:25   8:25 [a] Dan 11:21   [b] Dan 11:36; Rev 19:19–20   [c] Job 34:20; Lam 4:6   8:26 [a] Ezek 12:27; Dan 12:4, 9; Rev 22:10   8:27 [a] Dan 7:28; 8:17; Hab 3:16   9:1 [a] Dan 1:21   [1] LXX *Xerxes.*   [2] Heb. *was made king over the kingdom of the Chaldeans.*   9:2 [a] 2 Chr 36:21; Ezra 1:1; Jer 25:11–12; 29:10; Zech 7:5   [1] Thd. omits *in the first year of his reign.*   9:3 [a] Neh 1:4; Dan 6:10; 10:15   9:4 [a] Exod 20:6   9:5 [a] 1 Kgs 8:47–48; Neh 9:33; Ps 106:6; Isa 64:5–7; Jer 14:7   9:6 [a] 2 Chr 36:15; Jer 44:4–5   9:7 [a] Neh 9:33   9:9 [a] [Neh 9:17; Ps 130:4, 7]   9:10 [1] LXX, Vg. *law.*   9:11 [a] Isa 1:3–6; Jer 8:5–10   [b] Lev 26:14; Neh 1:6; Ps 106:6   9:12 [a] Isa 44:26; Jer 44:2–6; Lam 2:17; Zech 1:6   [1] Heb. *he has fulfilled his word(s), which he spoke.*   9:13 [a] Lev 26:14–45; Deut 28:15–68; Lam 2:17

reliable moral standards.[1] [14]The LORD was mindful of [a]the calamity, and he brought it on us. For the LORD our God is just in all he has done, and we have not obeyed him.

[15]"Now, [a]O Lord our God, who brought your people out of the [b]land of Egypt with great power and made a name for yourself that is remembered to this day—we have sinned and behaved wickedly. [16]O Lord, [a]according to all [b]your justice, please turn your raging anger away from your city Jerusalem, your holy mountain. For due to our sins [c]and the iniquities of our ancestors, [d]Jerusalem and your people [e]are mocked by all our neighbors.

[17]"So now, our God, accept the prayer [a]and requests of your servant, and show favor to your devastated sanctuary [b]for your own sake. [18]Listen attentively, my [a]God, [b]and hear! Open your eyes and look on our desolated ruins[1] and the city called by your name. For it is not because of our own righteous deeds that we are praying to you, but because your compassion is abundant. [19]O Lord, hear! O Lord, forgive! O Lord, pay attention, and act! Don't delay, for your own sake, O my God! For your city and your people are called by your name."

Gabriel Gives to Daniel a Prophecy of 70 Weeks

[20]While I was still speaking and praying, confessing my sin and the sin of my people Israel and presenting my request before the LORD my God concerning his holy mountain—[21]yes, while I was still praying, the man [a]Gabriel, whom I had seen previously in a vision, was approaching me in my state of extreme weariness, around the time of the evening offering. [22]He spoke with me, instructing me as follows: "Daniel, I have now come to impart understanding to you. [23]At the beginning of your requests a message went out, and I have come to convey it to you, for you are of great value in God's sight.[1] Therefore [a]consider the message and understand the vision:

[24] "Seventy weeks[1] have been determined
    concerning your people and your
    holy city
    [a]to put an end [b]to[2] rebellion,
    to bring sin to completion,
    to atone for iniquity,
    to bring in perpetual righteousness,
    to seal up the prophetic vision,
    [c]and to anoint a Most Holy Place.
[25] So know and understand:
    From the issuing of the command to
    restore and rebuild
    Jerusalem until an anointed [a]one, a
    prince arrives,
    [b]there will be a period of seven
    weeks[1] and sixty-two weeks.
    It will again be built, with plaza and
    moat,
    but in distressful times.
[26] Now after the sixty-two weeks,
    an anointed [a]one will be cut off and
    have nothing.
    As for the city and the sanctuary,
    the people of the coming prince will
    destroy[1] them.
    [b]But his end will come speedily like
    a flood.
    Until [c]the end of the war that has
    been decreed
    there will be destruction.
[27] He will confirm [a]a covenant with
    [b]many for one week.
    But in the middle of that week
    he will bring sacrifices and offerings
    to a halt.
    On the wing of abominations will
    come one who destroys,
    until the decreed end is poured out
    on the one who destroys."

An Angel Appears to Daniel

10 In the third[1] year of King Cyrus of Persia a message was revealed to Daniel (who was also [a]called Belteshazzar). This message was true and concerned

9:13 [1]Heb. *by your truth.* **9:14** [a]Neh 9:33 **9:15** [a]Exod 32:11; 1 Kgs 8:51; Neh 1:10 [b]Exod 14:18; Neh 9:10; Jer 32:20 **9:16** [a]1 Sam 12:7; Ps 31:1; Mic 6:4–5 [b]Ps 87:1–3; Dan 9:20; Joel 3:17; Zech 8:3 [c]Exod 20:5 [d]Ps 122:6; Jer 29:7; Lam 2:16 [e]Ps 79:4 **9:17** [a]Num 6:24–26; Ps 80:3, 7, 19 [b]Lam 5:18 **9:18** [a]Isa 37:17 [b]Exod 3:7 [1]Heb. *desolations.* **9:21** [a]Dan 8:16; Luke 1:19, 26 **9:23** [a]Matt 24:15 [1]Or *a precious treasure.* **9:24** [a]2 Chr 29:24; [Isa 53:10]; Acts 10:43; [Rom 5:10]; Heb 9:12, 14 [b]Rev 14:6 [c]Ps 45:7 [1]Heb. *sevens*; elsewhere, the term is used of a literal seven-day week. Gabriel unfolds the future as if it were a calendar of successive weeks and most understand the reference here as seventy "sevens" of years, or a total of 490 years. [2]Ket. *to seal up.* **9:25** [a]Luke 2:1–2; John 1:41; 4:25 [b]Isa 55:4 [1]Heb. *sevens.* **9:26** [a][Isa 53:8]; Matt 27:50; Mark 9:12; 15:37; [Luke 23:46; 24:26]; John 19:30; Acts 8:32 [b][1 Pet 2:21] [c]Matt 22:7 [1]A few wss *the city and the sanctuary will be destroyed with the coming prince.* **9:27** [a]Isa 42:6 [b][Matt 26:28] **10:1** [a]Dan 1:7 [1]LXX *first.*

a great war. He understood the message and gained insight by the vision.

[2] In those days I, Daniel, was mourning for three whole weeks. [3] I ate no choice food, no meat or wine came to my lips, nor did I anoint myself with oil until the end of those three weeks.

[4] On the twenty-fourth day of the first month I was beside the great river, the Tigris. [5] I looked up and saw a man clothed in [a]linen; around his waist was a [b]belt made of gold from Ufaz.[1] [6] His body resembled yellow jasper,[1] [a]and his face had an appearance like lightning. His eyes were like blazing torches; his arms and feet had the gleam of polished bronze. His voice thundered forth like the sound of a large crowd.

[7] Only I, Daniel, saw the vision; the men who were with me did not see it. On the contrary, they were overcome with fright and ran away to hide. [8] I alone was left to see this great vision. My strength drained from me, and my vigor disappeared; I was without energy. [9] I listened to his voice,[1] and as I did so I fell into a trance-like sleep with my face to the ground. [10][a]Then a hand touched me and set me on my hands and knees.[1] [11] He said to me, "Daniel, [a]you are of great value. Understand the words that I am about to speak to you. So stand up, for I have now been sent to you." When he said this to me, I stood up shaking. [12] Then he said to me, "[a]Don't be afraid, Daniel, for from the very first day [b]you applied your mind to understand and to humble yourself before your God, your words were heard. I have come in response to your words. [13] However, the prince of the kingdom of Persia was opposing me for 21 days. [a]But [b]Michael, one of the leading princes, came to help me, because I was left there[1] with the kings of Persia. [14] Now [a]I have come to help you understand what will happen to your people in future days, [b]for the vision pertains to days to come."

[15] While he was [a]saying this to me, I was flat on the ground and unable to speak. [16] Then [a]one who appeared to be a human being[1] was [b]touching [c]my lips. I opened my mouth and started to speak, saying to the one who was standing before me, "Sir, due to the vision, anxiety has gripped me and I have no strength. [17] How, sir, am I able to speak with you? My strength is gone, and I am breathless." [18] Then the one who appeared to be a human being touched me again and strengthened me. [19][a]He said to me, "Don't be [b]afraid, you who are highly valued.[1] Peace be to you! Be strong! Be really strong!" When he spoke to me, I was strengthened. I said, "Sir, you may speak now, for you have given me strength." [20] He said, "Do you know why [a]I have come to you? Now I am about to return to engage in battle with the prince of Persia. When I go, the prince of Greece is coming. [21] However, I will first tell you what is written in a dependable book. (There is no one who strengthens me against these princes, [a]except Michael your prince.

11 "And [a]in the first year of [b]Darius the Mede, I stood to strengthen him and to provide protection for him.) [2] Now I will tell you the truth.

The Angel Gives a Message to Daniel

"Three more kings will arise for Persia. Then a fourth king will be unusually rich, more so than all who preceded him. When he has amassed power through his riches, he will stir up everyone against the kingdom of Greece. [3] Then [a]a powerful king will arise, exercising great authority and [b]doing as he pleases. [4] Shortly after [a]his rise to power, his kingdom will be broken up and distributed toward the four winds of the sky[1]—but not to his posterity [b]or with the authority he exercised, for his kingdom will be uprooted and distributed to others besides these.

[5] "Then the king of the south and one of his subordinates will grow strong. His subordinate will resist him and will rule a kingdom greater than his. [6] After some years have passed, they will form an alliance. Then the daughter of the king of the

10:5 [a] Ezek 9:2; 10:2 [b] Rev 1:13; 15:6 [1] The location and the exact form of the Heb. name are uncertain. **10:6** [a] [Rev 1:15] [1] Heb. *tarshish*. **10:9** [1] LXX, Syr. omit *I listened to his voice*. **10:10** [a] Dan 9:21 [1] Thd. omits *my hands*. **10:11** [a] Dan 9:23 **10:12** [a] Rev 1:17 [b] Dan 9:3–4, 22, 23; Acts 10:4 **10:13** [a] Dan 10:20 [b] Dan 10:21; 12:1; Jude 9; [Rev 12:7] [1] Thd. *I left him [Michael] there*. **10:14** [a] Gen 49:1; Deut 31:29; Dan 2:28 [b] Dan 8:26; 10:1 **10:15** [a] Dan 8:18; 10:9 **10:16** [a] Dan 8:15 [b] Jer 1:9; Dan 10:10 [c] Dan 10:8–9 [1] LXX, DSS *something that looked like a man's hand*. **10:19** [a] Dan 10:11 [b] Judg 6:23; Isa 43:1; Dan 10:12 [1] Heb. *treasured man*. **10:20** [a] Dan 10:13 **10:21** [a] Dan 10:13; Jude 9; [Rev 12:7] **11:1** [a] Dan 9:1 [b] Dan 5:31 **11:3** [a] Dan 7:6; 8:5 [b] Dan 8:4; 11:16, 36 **11:4** [a] Jer 49:36; Ezek 37:9; Dan 7:2; 8:8; Zech 2:6; Rev 7:1 [b] Dan 8:22 [1] Or *the heavens*.

south will come to the king of the north to make an agreement, but she will not retain her power, nor will he continue in his strength.[1] She, together with the one who brought her, her child,[2] and her benefactor will all be delivered over at that time.

[7]"There will arise in his place one from her family line who will come against their army and will enter the stronghold of the king of the north and will move against them successfully. [8]He will also take their gods into captivity to Egypt, along with their cast images and prized utensils of silver and gold. Then he will withdraw for some years from the king of the north. [9]Then the king of the north will advance against the empire of the king of the south, but will withdraw to his own land. [10]His sons will wage war, mustering [a]a large army that will advance like an overflowing river and carrying the battle all the way [b]to the enemy's fortress.

[11]"Then the king of the south will be enraged and will march out to fight against the king of the north, who will also muster a large [a]army, but that army will be delivered into his hand. [12]When the army is taken away, the king of the south will become arrogant. He will be responsible for the death of thousands and thousands of people, but he will not continue to prevail. [13]For the king of the north will again muster an army, one larger than before. At the end of some years he will advance with a huge army and enormous supplies.

[14]"In those times many will oppose the king of the south. Those who are violent[1] among your own people will rise up in confirmation of the vision, but they will [a]falter. [15]Then the king of the north will advance and will [a]build siege mounds and capture a well-fortified city. The forces of the south will not prevail, not even his finest contingents. They will have no strength to prevail. [16]The one advancing against him will do as he pleases, and [a]no one will be able to stand before him. He will prevail in the beautiful land, and its annihilation will be within his power. [17]His intention will [a]be to come with the strength of his entire kingdom, and he

will form alliances.[1] He will give the king of the south a daughter in marriage in order to destroy the kingdom, but it will [b]not turn out to his advantage. [18]Then he will turn his attention to the coastal regions and will capture many of them. But a commander will bring his shameful conduct to a halt; in addition, he will make him pay for his shameful conduct.[1] [19]He will then turn his attention to the fortresses of his own land, but he will [a]stumble [b]and fall, not to be found again. [20]There will arise after him one who will send out an exactor of tribute to enhance the splendor of the kingdom, but after a few days he will be destroyed, though not in anger or battle.

[21]"Then there will arise in his place [a]a despicable person to whom the royal honor has not been rightfully conferred. He will come on the scene in a time of prosperity and will seize the kingdom through deceit. [22]Armies will be suddenly swept away in defeat before him; both they [a]and a covenant leader will be destroyed. [23]After entering into an alliance with him, [a]he will behave treacherously; he will ascend to power with only a small force. [24]In a time of prosperity for the most productive areas of the province, he will come and accomplish what neither his fathers nor their fathers accomplished. He will distribute loot, spoils, and property to his followers, and he will devise plans against fortified cities, but not for long. [25]He will rouse his strength and enthusiasm[1] against the king of the south with a large army. The king of the south will wage war with a large and very powerful army, but he will not be able to prevail because of the plans devised against him. [26]Those who share the king's fine food will attempt to destroy him, and his army will be swept away; many will be killed in battle. [27]These two kings, their minds[1] filled with evil intentions, will trade lies with one another at the same table. But it will not succeed, for there is still an end at the appointed [a]time. [28]Then the king of the north will return to his own land with much property. His mind will be set against the holy covenant. He will take action, and then return to his own

11:6 [1]Heb. *and his arm*; some understand this as the descendants of the king of the north.   [2]MT *the one who begot her.* **11:10** [a]Isa 8:8; Jer 46:7–8; 51:42; Dan 9:26; 11:26, 40   [b]Dan 11:7   **11:11** [a][Ps 33:10, 16]   **11:14** [a]Job 9:13   [1]Heb. *sons of violence*; "son(s)" is sometimes used idiomatically to indicate that someone is characterized by a quality.   **11:15** [a]Jer 6:6; Ezek 4:2; 17:17   **11:16** [a]Josh 1:5   **11:17** [a]2 Kgs 12:17; 2 Chr 20:3; Ezek 4:3, 7   [b]Dan 9:26   [1]MT *uprightness.*   **11:18** [1]Heb. *his shameful conduct he will return to him.*   **11:19** [a]Ps 27:2; Jer 46:6   [b]Job 20:8; Ps 37:36; Ezek 26:21   **11:21** [a]Dan 7:8   **11:22** [a]Dan 8:10–11   **11:23** [a]Dan 8:25   **11:25** [1]Heb. *heart.*   **11:27** [a]Dan 8:19; Hab 2:3   [1]Heb. *heart.*

land. [29]At an appointed time he will again invade the south, but this latter visit will not turn out the way the former one did. [30]The ships of Kittim will come against him, leaving him disheartened. He will turn back and direct his indignation against the holy covenant. He will return and honor those who [a]forsake the holy covenant. [31]His forces will rise up [a]and profane the fortified sanctuary, stopping the daily sacrifice. In its place they will set up the abomination that causes desolation. [32]Then with smooth words he will defile those who have rejected the covenant. But the people who are loyal to their God will act valiantly. [33]These who are wise among the people will teach the masses. However, they will fall by the sword and by the flame, and they will be imprisoned and plundered for some time. [34]When they stumble, they will be granted some help. But many will unite with them deceitfully. [35]Even some of the wise will stumble, resulting in their refinement, purification, and cleansing until the time of the end, for it is still for the appointed time.

[36]"Then the king will do as he pleases. He will [a]exalt and magnify himself above every deity, and he will utter presumptuous things against the God of gods. He will succeed until the time of wrath is completed, for what has been decreed must occur. [37]He will not respect[1] the gods of his fathers—not even the god loved by women. He will not respect any god; he will elevate himself above them all. [38]What he will honor is a god of fortresses—a god his fathers did not acknowledge he will honor with gold, silver, valuable stones, and treasured commodities. [39]He will attack mighty fortresses, aided by a foreign deity. To those who recognize him he will grant considerable honor. He will place them in authority over many people, and he will parcel out land for a price.

[40]"At the [a]time of the end the king of the south will attack him. Then the king of the north will storm against him with chariots, [b]horsemen, and a large armada of ships. He will invade lands, passing through them [c]like an overflowing river. [41]Then he will enter the beautiful land. Many will fall, but these will escape: [a]Edom, Moab, and the Ammonite leadership. [42]He will extend his power[1] against other lands; the land of [a]Egypt will not escape. [43]He will have control over the hidden stores of gold and silver, as well as all the treasures of Egypt. Libyans and Ethiopians[1] will submit to him. [44]But reports will trouble him from the east and north, and he will set out in a tremendous rage to destroy and wipe out many. [45]He will pitch his royal tents between [a]the seas toward the beautiful holy mountain. But he will come to his end, with no one to help him.

12

"At that time Michael,
  the great prince who watches over
    your people,
  will arise.
There will be [a]a time of distress
  unlike any other from the nation's
    beginning
  up to that time.
But at that time your own people,
  [b]all those whose names are found
    [c]written in the book,
  will escape.

[2] Many of those who sleep
  in the dusty ground will awake—
  [a]some to everlasting life,
  [b]and others to shame and everlasting
    abhorrence.
[3] But the wise will [a]shine
  like the brightness of the heavenly
    expanse.
  [b]And those bringing many to
    righteousness
  will be [c]like the stars forever and
    ever.

[4]"But you, Daniel, close up these words and seal the book until the time of the end. Many will dash about, and knowledge will increase."

[5]I, Daniel, watched as two others stood there, one on each side of the [a]river. [6]One said to the man clothed in [a]linen who was above the waters of the river, "When will the end of these wondrous events occur?" [7]Then I heard the man clothed in linen who was over the waters of the river as [a]he raised

11:30 [a] Gen 10:4; Num 24:24; Isa 23:1, 12; Jer 2:10   11:31 [a] Dan 8:11–13; 12:11   11:36 [a] Dan 7:8, 25   11:37 [1] Heb. *consider.*
11:40 [a] Dan 11:27, 35; 12:4, 9   [b] Ezek 38:4; Rev 9:16   [c] Isa 21:1   11:41 [a] Isa 11:14   11:42 [a] Joel 3:19   [1] Heb. *hand.*   11:43 [1] Or
Nubians; Heb. *Cushites.*   11:45 [a] Ps 48:2   12:1 [a] Isa 26:20; Jer 30:7; Ezek 5:9; Dan 9:12; Matt 24:21; Mark 13:19   [b] Rom 11:26
[c] Exod 32:32; Ps 56:8   12:2 [a] [Matt 25:46; John 5:28–29; Acts 24:15]   [b] [Isa 66:24; Rom 9:21]   12:3 [a] Prov 3:35; Dan 11:33, 35;
Matt 13:43   [b] Prov 11:30; [Jas 5:19–20]   [c] 1 Cor 15:41   12:5 [a] Dan 10:4   12:6 [a] Ezek 9:2; Dan 10:5   12:7 [a] Deut 32:40

both his right and left hands to the sky and made an oath by the one [b]who lives forever: "It is for [c]a time, times, [d]and half a time. [e]Then, when the power of the one who shatters[1] the holy people has been exhausted, all these things will be finished."

[8]I heard, but I did not understand. So I said, "Sir, what will happen after these things?" [9]He said, "Go, Daniel. For these matters are closed and sealed until the time of the end. [10][a]Many will be purified, made clean, and refined, [b]but [c]the wicked will go on being wicked. None of the wicked will understand, though the wise will understand. [11]From the time that the daily sacrifice is removed and the abomination that causes desolation is set in place, there are 1,290 days. [12]Blessed is the one who waits and attains to the 1,335 days. [13]But you should go your way until the end.[1] You will rest, [a]and then at the end of the days you will arise to receive what you have been allotted."

12:7 [b]Dan 4:34 [c]Dan 7:25; Rev 12:14 [d]Luke 21:24 [e]Dan 8:24 [1]MT to shatter the hand. 12:10 [a]Zech 13:9 [b]Isa 32:6–7; Rev 22:11 [c]Dan 12:3; Hos 14:9; John 7:17; 8:47 12:13 [a]Ps 1:5 [1]LXX omits until the end.

HOSEA

Hosea ministers to the northern kingdom of Israel (also called Ephraim, after its largest tribe). Outwardly the nation is enjoying a time of prosperity and growth but inwardly, moral corruption and spiritual adultery permeate the people. Hosea, instructed by God to marry a woman named Gomer, finds his domestic life to be an accurate and tragic dramatization of the unfaithfulness of God's people. During his half century of prophetic ministry, Hosea repeatedly echoes his threefold message: God abhors the sins of his people, judgment is certain, but God's loyal love stands firm. The names *Hosea, Joshua,* and *Jesus* are all derived from the same Hebrew root word: the word *hoshea* means "salvation," but *Joshua* and *Jesus* include an additional idea: "Yahweh Is Salvation." As God's messenger, Hosea offers the possibility of salvation only if the nation will turn from idolatry back to God. Israel's last king, Hoshea, has the same name as the prophet even though the English Bible spells them differently. Hosea in the Greek and Latin is *Osee.*

Superscription

1 ¹This is the LORD's message that came to Hosea son of Beeri during the time of ªUzziah, ᵇJotham, ᶜAhaz, and ᵈHezekiah, kings of Judah, and during the time of ᵉJeroboam son of Joash, king of Israel.

Symbols of Sin and Judgment: The Prostitute and Her Children

²When the LORD first spoke through¹ Hosea, he said to him, "ªGo marry a prostitute² who will bear illegitimate children conceived through prostitution because ᵇthe nation continually commits spiritual prostitution by turning away from the LORD." ³So Hosea married Gomer, the daughter of Diblaim. Then she conceived and gave birth to a son for him. ⁴Then the LORDªsaid to Hosea, "Name him 'Jezreel,' because in ᵇa little while I will punish the dynasty of Jehu on account of the bloodshed in the valley of Jezreel, and I will put an end to the kingdom¹ of Israel. ⁵At that time, ªI will destroy the military power of Israel in the valley of Jezreel."

⁶She conceived again and gave birth to a daughter. Then the LORD said to him, "Name her 'No Pity' (Lo-Ruhamah) because I will no longer have pity on the nation of Israel. ªFor I will certainly not forgive their guilt. ⁷ªBut ᵇI will have pity on the nation of Judah. I will deliver them by the LORD their God; I will not deliver them by the warrior's bow, by sword, by military victory, by chariot horses, or by chariots."

⁸When she had weaned "No Pity" (Lo-Ruhamah), she conceived again and gave birth to another son. ⁹Then the LORD said: "Name him 'Not My People' (Lo-Ammi) because you¹ are not my people, and I am not your God.

The Restoration of Israel

¹⁰"However, in ªthe future the number of the people of Israel will be like the ᵇsand of the sea that can be neither measured nor numbered. Although it was said to them, 'You are not my ᶜpeople,' it will be said to them, 'You are ᵈchildren of the living God!'

1:1 ª 2 Chr 26; Isa 1:1; Amos 1:1 ᵇ 2 Kgs 15:5, 7, 32–38; 2 Chr 27; Mic 1:1 ᶜ 2 Kgs 16:1–20; 2 Chr 28 ᵈ 2 Kgs 18–20; 2 Chr 29:1–32:33; Mic 1:1 ᵉ 2 Kgs 13:13; 14:23–29; Amos 1:1 ¹ The textual problems in Hosea are virtually unparalleled in the OT. For an explanation of this issue, see *NET Bible, Full Notes Edition.* **1:2** ª Hos 3:1 ᵇ Deut 31:16; Judg 2:17; Ps 73:27; Jer 2:13; Ezek 16:1–59; 23:1–49 ¹ Or *by, with.* ² Heb. *a wife/woman of harlotries*; possibly a temple prostitute serving at a Baal temple. **1:4** ª 2 Kgs 10:11 ᵇ 2 Kgs 15:8–10; 17:6, 23; 18:11 ¹ Heb. *the kingdom of the house of Israel.* **1:5** ª 2 Kgs 15:29 **1:6** ª 2 Kgs 17:6 **1:7** ª 2 Kgs 19:29–35; Isa 30:18; 37:36–37 ᵇ Ps 44:3–7; [Zech 4:6] **1:9** ¹ The pl. form refers to the people of Israel as a whole. **1:10** ª Gen 22:17; 32:12; Jer 33:22 ᵇ 1 Pet 2:10 ᶜ Rom 9:26 ᵈ Isa 63:16; 64:8; [John 1:12]

[11]Then [a]the people of Judah and the people of Israel will be gathered together. They will appoint for themselves one leader, and will flourish in the land. Certainly, the day of Jezreel will be great!

2 "Then you will call your brother, 'My People' (Ammi)! You will call your sister, 'Pity' (Ruhamah)!

Idolatrous Israel Will Be Punished Like a Prostitute

2 "Plead earnestly[1] with your mother
(for [a]she is not my wife, and I am not
her husband),
so that she might put an end to her
adulterous [b]lifestyle
and turn away from her sexually
immoral behavior.
3 Otherwise, [a]I will strip her naked
and expose her like she was when
she was [b]born.
I will turn her land into a wilderness
and make her country a parched land,
so that I might kill her with [c]thirst.
4 I will have no pity on her [a]children
because they are children conceived
in adultery.[1]
5 For their mother has committed
adultery;
she [a]who conceived them has acted
shamefully.
For she said, 'I will seek out my lovers;
they are the ones who give me my
bread and my water,
my wool, my flax, my olive oil, and
my wine.'

The Lord's Discipline Will Bring Israel Back

6 "Therefore, [a]I will soon fence her in
with thorns;
I will wall her in so that she cannot
find her way.
7 Then she [a]will pursue her lovers, but
she will not catch them;
she will seek them, but she will not
find them.
Then she will say,
'I will go back to my [b]husband,[1]

because I was better off then than I
am now.'

Agricultural Fertility Withdrawn from Israel

8 "Yet[1] until now she has refused to
[a]acknowledge that I[2] was the one
who gave her the grain, the new wine,
and the olive oil;
and that it was I who lavished on her
the silver and gold—
that they used in worshiping Baal!
9 Therefore, I will take back my grain
during the harvest time
and my new wine when it ripens;
I will take away my wool and my flax
that I had provided in order to clothe
her.
10 Soon [a]I will expose her lewd
nakedness in front of her lovers,
and no one will be able to rescue her
from me!
11 I [a]will put an end to all her
celebrations:
her annual religious festivals,
monthly new moon celebrations,
and weekly Sabbath festivities—
all her appointed festivals.
12 I will destroy her vines and fig trees,
about which she said, 'These are my
wages for prostitution
that my lovers gave to me!'
I will turn her cultivated vines and
fig trees into an uncultivated
thicket,
so that wild animals will devour
them.
13 I will punish her for the festival days
when she burned incense to the Baal
idols;
she adorned herself with earrings
and jewelry,
and went after her lovers,
but she forgot me!"[1] says the LORD.

Future Repentance and Restoration of Israel

14 "However, in the future I will allure
her;

1:11 [a]Isa 11:11–13; Jer 3:18; 50:4; [Ezek 34:23; 37:15–28]   2:2 [a]Isa 50:1   [b]Ezek 16:25   [1]Heb. *Plead with your mother; plead!*; an emphatic Heb. construction.   2:3 [a]Jer 13:22, 26; Ezek 16:37–39   [b]Ezek 16:4–7, 22   [c]Jer 14:3; Amos 8:11–13   2:4 [a]John 8:41   [1]Heb. *sons of adulteries.*   2:5 [a]Ezek 23:5; Hos 2:8, 12   2:6 [a]Job 19:8; Lam 3:7, 9   2:7 [a]Luke 15:17–18   [b]Isa 54:5–8; Jer 2:2; 3:1; Ezek 16:8; 23:4   [1]Heb. *to my man, the first*; perhaps meaning "my first husband," although this implies there was more than one husband involved. The text refers to multiple lovers, but not necessarily husbands.   2:8 [a]Isa 1:3; Ezek 16:19   [1]Or *For, But.*   [2]An emphatic Heb. construction.   2:10 [a]Ezek 16:37   2:11 [a]Jer 7:34; 16:9; Hos 3:4; Amos 5:21; 8:10   2:13 [1]An emphatic Heb. construction.

I will lead her back into the
wilderness
and speak tenderly to her.
[15] From[a] there I will give back her
vineyards to her
and turn[b] the 'Valley of Trouble'[1] into
an 'Opportunity for Hope.'
There she will sing[c] as she did when
she was young,
when she came up from the land of
Egypt.
[16] At that time," declares the LORD,
"you will call me,[1] 'My husband';
you will never again call me,[2] 'My
master.'
[17] For[a] I will remove the names of the
Baal idols from your lips,
so that you will never again utter
their names!

New Covenant Relationship with Repentant Israel

[18] "At that time I will make a[a] covenant
for them[b] with the wild animals,
the birds of the air, and the creatures
that crawl on the ground.
[c] I will abolish the warrior's bow and
sword—
that is, every weapon of
warfare—from the land,
and I will allow them to live securely.
[19] I will commit myself to you forever;
I will commit myself to you in
righteousness and justice,
in steadfast love and tender
compassion.
[20] I will commit myself to[a] you in
faithfulness;
then you will acknowledge[1] the LORD.[2]

Agricultural Fertility Restored to the Repentant Nation

[21] "At that[a] time, I will willingly
respond," declares the LORD.
"I will respond to the sky,
and the sky will respond to the
ground;
[22] then the ground will respond to the
grain, the new wine, and the olive
oil;
and they will respond to 'God Plants'
(Jezreel)!
[23] Then[a] I will plant her as my own in
the[b] land.
[c] I will have pity on 'No Pity'
(Lo-Ruhamah).
I will say to 'Not My People'
(Lo-Ammi), 'You are my people!'
And he will say, 'You are my God!'"

An Illustration of God's Love for Idolatrous Israel

3 The LORD said to me, "Go, show love to
your wife[1] again, even though she loves[2]
another [a] man and continually commits
adultery. Likewise, the LORD loves the Israelites although they turn to other gods
and love to offer raisin cakes to idols." [2] So
I paid 15 shekels of silver and about seven
bushels of barley[1,2] to purchase her. [3] Then
I told her, "You must [a] live with me many
days; you must not commit adultery or
become joined to another man, and I also
will wait for you." [4] For the Israelites must
live many days [a] without a king or prince,
without sacrifice or sacred fertility pillar,
without [b] ephod or [c] idols. [5] Afterward, the
Israelites will turn and[a] seek the LORD their
God and their[b] Davidic king. Then they will
submit to the LORD in fear and receive his
blessings in[c] future days.

The Lord's Covenant Lawsuit against the Nation Israel

4 Listen to the LORD's message, you
Israelites!
For the LORD has a covenant
[a] lawsuit[1] against the people of
Israel.
For there is neither faithfulness nor
loyalty in the land,
nor do they[b] acknowledge God.
[2] There is only cursing, lying, murder,
stealing, and adultery.

2:15 [a] Josh 7:26 [b] Jer 2:1–3; Ezek 16:8–14 [c] Exod 15:1 [1] Heb. *Valley of Achor*, so named because of the incident recorded in Josh 7:1–26. 2:16 [1] Some wss *she will call me.* [2] Some wss *she will not call me.* 2:17 [a] Exod 23:13; Josh 23:7; Ps 16:4 2:18 [a] Job 5:23; Isa 11:6–9; Ezek 34:25 [b] Isa 2:4; Ezek 39:1–10 [c] Lev 26:5; Isa 32:18; Jer 23:6; Ezek 34:25 2:20 [a] [Jer 31:33–34]; Hos 6:6; 13:4; [John 17:3] [1] Or *know*; the Heb. word in this use can mean to obey. [2] Sev. MSS *that it is I*; Vg. *know who I am.* 2:21 [a] Isa 55:10; Zech 8:12; [Mal 3:10–11] 2:22 [1] "Jezreel" creates a powerful wordplay involving the similar sounding "Israel" and the Heb. term for "to plant, sow." 2:23 [a] Jer 31:27; Amos 9:15 [b] Hos 1:6 [c] Hos 1:10; Zech 13:9; Rom 9:25–26; [Eph 2:11–22]; 1 Pet 2:10 3:1 [a] Jer 3:20 [1] Heb. *a woman*; probably Gomer. [2] MT *who is loved by.* 3:2 [1] LXX *a homer of barley and a measure of wine.* [2] Heb. *a homer of barley and a lethech of barley.* 3:3 [a] Deut 21:13 3:4 [a] Hos 10:3 [b] Exod 28:4–12; 1 Sam 23:9–12 [c] Gen 31:19, 34; Judg 17:5; 18:14, 17; [1 Sam 15:23] 3:5 [a] Jer 50:4 [b] Jer 30:9; Ezek 34:24 [c] [Isa 2:2–3]; Jer 31:9 4:1 [a] Isa 1:18; Hos 12:2; Mic 6:2 [b] Jer 4:22 [1] The Heb. noun can be used for nonlegal disputes or legal lawsuits.

They resort to violence and
   bloodshed.
3 Therefore [a]the land will mourn,
   and all its inhabitants will perish.
   The wild animals, the birds of the sky,
   and even the fish in the sea will
   perish.

The Lord's Dispute against the Sinful Priesthood

4 Do not let anyone accuse or contend
   against anyone else,
   for my case is against you priests![1,2]
5 You stumble day and night,
   and the false prophets stumble with
   you;
   you have destroyed your own people.[1]
6 You have destroyed [a]my people
   by failing to acknowledge me!
   [b]Because you refuse to
   acknowledge me,
   I will reject you as my priests.
   Because you reject the law of your
   God,
   I will reject your descendants.
7 The more the [a]priests increased in
   numbers,
   the more they rebelled against me.
   They have turned[1] their glorious
   calling
   into a shameful disgrace!
8 They feed on the sin offerings of my
   people;
   their appetites long for their iniquity!
9 I will deal with the people and
   priests together:
   [a]I will punish them both for their
   ways,
   and I will repay them for their deeds.
10 They will eat, but not be satisfied;
   [a]they will engage in prostitution, but
   not increase in numbers
   because they have abandoned the
   LORD
   by pursuing other gods.

Judgment of Pagan Idolatry and Cultic Prostitution

11 Old and new wine
   take [a]away the understanding of my
   people.

12 They consult their wooden [a]idols,
   and [b]their diviner's staff answers
   with an oracle.
   The wind of prostitution blows them
   astray;
   they commit spiritual adultery
   against their God.
13 They sacrifice on [a]the mountaintops
   and burn offerings on [b]the hills;
   they sacrifice under oak, poplar, and
   terebinth,
   because their shade is so pleasant.
   As a result, your daughters have
   become cult prostitutes,
   and your daughters-in-law commit
   adultery!
14 I will not punish your daughters
   when they commit prostitution,
   nor your daughters-in-law when they
   commit adultery.
   For the men consort with harlots;
   they sacrifice with temple
   prostitutes.
   [a]It is true: "A people that lacks
   understanding will come to
   ruin!"

Warning to Judah: Do not Join in Israel's Apostasy

15 Although you, [a]O Israel, commit
   adultery,
   do not let Judah become guilty!
   Do not journey to Gilgal.
   Do not go up to Beth [b]Aven.
   Do [c]not swear, "As surely as the LORD
   lives!"
16 Israel has rebelled like a stubborn
   heifer!
   Soon the LORD will put them out to
   pasture
   like a lamb in a broad field.
17 Ephraim has attached himself to
   idols;
   Do not go near him!

The Shameful Sinners Will Be Brought to Shame

18 They consume their alcohol,
   then engage in cult prostitution;
   they dearly love their shameful
   behavior.

4:3 [a] Isa 24:4; 33:9; Jer 4:28; 12:4; Amos 5:16; 8:8   4:4 [1] MT, LXX *And your people [are] like those who contend against the priest.* [2] Heb. *priest.*   4:5 [1] MT *and I will destroy your mother.*   4:6 [a] Isa 5:13   [b] Ezek 22:26   4:7 [a] 1 Sam 2:30; Mal 2:9   [1] MT *I will change, exchange.*   4:9 [a] Isa 24:2; Jer 5:30–31; 2 Tim 4:3–4   4:10 [a] Lev 26:26; Isa 65:13; Mic 6:14; Hag 1:6   4:11 [a] Prov 20:1; Isa 5:12; 28:7   4:12 [a] Jer 2:27   [b] Isa 44:19–20   4:13 [a] Isa 1:29; 57:5, 7; Jer 2:20; Ezek 6:13; 20:28   [b] Amos 7:17; [Rom 1:28–32]   4:14 [a] Deut 23:18   4:15 [a] Hos 9:15; 12:11   [b] 1 Kgs 12:29; Josh 7:2; Hos 10:8   [c] Jer 5:2; 44:26; Amos 8:14

19 A whirlwind has wrapped ^athem in
its wings;
^bthey will be brought to shame
because of their idolatrous
worship.

Announcement of Sin and Judgment

5 Hear this, ^ayou priests!
Pay attention, you Israelites!
Listen closely, O king!
For judgment is about to overtake
you.[1]
For you were like a trap to Mizpah,
like a net spread out to catch Tabor.
2 Those who revolt are ^aknee-deep in
slaughter,
but I will discipline them all.
3 I know ^aEphraim all too well;
the evil of Israel is not hidden
from me.
For ^byou have engaged in
prostitution, O Ephraim;
Israel has defiled itself.[1]
4 Their wicked deeds do not allow
^athem to return to their God;
for a spirit of idolatry is in them,
and they do not acknowledge the
LORD.
5 The ^aarrogance of Israel testifies
against it;
Israel and Ephraim will be
overthrown because of their
iniquity.
Even Judah will be brought down
with them.

The Futility of Sacrificial Ritual without Moral Obedience

6 Although ^athey bring their flocks and
herds
to seek the favor of the LORD,
they will not find him—
he has withdrawn himself from
them!
7 They have committed treason
against the LORD
because they bore illegitimate
children.
Soon the new moon festival will
devour them and their fields.

The Prophet's Declaration of Judgment

8 ^aBlow the ram's horn in Gibeah!
Sound the trumpet in Ramah!
Sound the alarm in Beth ^bAven;
tremble in fear,[1] O Benjamin!
9 Ephraim will be ruined in the day of
judgment.
What I am declaring to the tribes of
Israel will certainly take place!

The Oppressors of the Helpless Will Be Oppressed

10 The princes of Judah are like those
who ^amove boundary markers.
I will pour out my rage on them like
a torrential flood.[1]
11 Ephraim will be ^aoppressed, crushed
under judgment,
because he was determined to
pursue worthless idols.[1]

The Curse of the Incurable Wound

12 I will be ^alike a moth to Ephraim,
like wood rot to the house of Judah.
13 When Ephraim saw his sickness
and Judah saw his ^awound,
then Ephraim turned ^bto Assyria
and begged its great king[1] for help.
But he will not be able to heal you.
He cannot cure your wound!

The Lion Will Carry Israel Off into Exile

14 I ^awill be ^blike a lion to Ephraim,
like a young lion to the house of
Judah.
I myself will tear them to pieces;
then I will carry them off, and no one
will be able to rescue them!
15 Then I will return again to my lair
until they have suffered their
punishment.
Then they will seek me;
in their distress they will earnestly
seek me.

Superficial Repentance Breeds False Assurance of God's Forgiveness

6 Come on! Let's return to ^athe LORD.
^bHe himself has torn us to pieces,
but he will heal us!

4:19 ^aJer 51:1 ^bIsa 1:29   5:1 ^aHos 6:9 ¹Heb. *for the judgment is to you.*   5:2 ^aIsa 29:15; Hos 4:2; 6:9   5:3 ^aAmos 3:2; 5:12 ^bHos 4:17 ¹Or *has become corrupt.*   5:4 ^aHos 4:12   5:5 ^aHos 7:10   5:6 ^aProv 1:28; Isa 1:15; Jer 11:11; Ezek 8:18; Mic 3:4; John 7:34   5:8 ^aHos 8:1; Joel 2:1 ^bJosh 7:2 ¹MT *behind you, O Benjamin.*   5:10 ^aDeut 19:14; 27:17 ¹Heb. *like water.*   5:11 ^aDeut 28:33 ¹The meaning of the Heb. term is uncertain.   5:12 ^aProv 12:4   5:13 ^aJer 30:12–15 ^b2 Kgs 15:19; Hos 7:11; 10:6 ¹MT *a contentious king.*   5:14 ^aPs 7:2; Lam 3:10; Hos 13:7–8 ^bPs 50:22   6:1 ^aDeut 32:39; Hos 5:14 ^bJer 30:17; Hos 14:4

He has injured[1] us,
but he will bandage our wounds!
2 He will restore us in [a]a very short
  time;
he will heal us in a little while,[1]
so that we may live in his presence.
3 So [a]let us search for him!
Let us seek to know the LORD!
He will come to our rescue [b]as
  certainly as [c]the appearance of the
  dawn,
as certainly as the winter rain comes,
as certainly as the spring rain that
  waters the land.

Transitory Faithfulness and Imminent Judgment

4 What am I going to do with you,
  O Ephraim?
What am I going to do with you,
  O Judah?
For your faithfulness is as fleeting as
  the morning mist;
it disappears as quickly as dawn's
  dew.
5 Therefore, I will certainly cut you
  into pieces at [a]the hands of the
  prophets;
I will certainly kill you in fulfillment
  of my oracles of judgment,
for my judgment[1] will come forth like
  the light of the dawn.
6 For I delight in [a]faithfulness, [b]not
  simply in sacrifice;
I delight in [c]acknowledging God, not
  simply in whole burnt offerings.

Indictments against the Cities of Israel and Judah

7 At Adam[1] they broke the covenant;
Oh how they were unfaithful to me!
8 [a]Gilead is a city full of evildoers;
its streets are stained with bloody
  footprints!
9 The company of [a]priests is like a gang
  of robbers,
lying in ambush to pounce on a
  victim.
They commit [b]murder on the road to
  Shechem;
they have done heinous [c]crimes!

10 I have seen a disgusting thing in the
  house of Israel:
There Ephraim commits prostitution
  with other gods,
and Israel defiles itself.
11 I have appointed a time to reap
  judgment for you also, O Judah!

If Israel Would Repent of Sin, God Would Relent of Judgment

Whenever I want to restore the
  fortunes of my people,

7 whenever I want to heal Israel,
[a]the sin of Ephraim is revealed,
and the evil deeds of Samaria are
  exposed.
For they do what is wrong;
thieves break into houses,
and gangs rob people out in the
  streets.
2 They do not [a]realize
that I remember all their wicked
  deeds.
Their evil deeds have now
  surrounded them;
their sinful deeds are always
  before me.

Political Intrigue and Conspiracy in the Palace

3 The royal advisers delight the [a]king
[b]with their evil schemes;
the princes make him glad with their
  lies.
4 They are all like bakers;[1]
[a]they are like a smoldering oven;
they are like a baker who does not
  stoke the fire
until the kneaded dough is ready for
  baking.
5 At the celebration of their king,[1]
his princes become inflamed with
  [a]wine;
they conspire with evildoers.
6 They approach him, all the while
  plotting against him.
Their hearts are like an oven;
their anger smolders all night long,
but in the morning it bursts into a
  flaming fire.
7 All of them are blazing like an oven;

6:1 [1]Heb. *has struck*.   6:2 [a]Luke 24:46; Acts 10:40; [1 Cor 15:4]   [1]Heb. *on the third day*.   6:3 [a]Isa 54:13   [b]2 Sam 23:4   [c]Ps 72:6; Joel 2:23   6:5 [a][Jer 23:29]   [1]MT *and your judgments* [are] *a light* [that] *goes forth*.   6:6 [a]Matt 9:13; 12:7   [b]Isa 1:12–13; [Mic 6:6–8]   [c][John 17:3]   6:7 [1]Or *Like Adam; Like* [sinful] *men*.   6:8 [a]Hos 12:11   6:9 [a]Hos 5:1   [b]Jer 7:9–10; Hos 4:2   [c]Ezek 22:9; 23:27; Hos 2:10   7:1 [a]Ezek 23:4–8; Hos 5:1   7:2 [a]Ps 25:7; Jer 14:10; 17:1; Hos 8:13; 9:9; Amos 8:7   7:3 [a]Hos 1:1   [b]Mic 7:3; [Rom 1:32]   7:4 [a]Jer 9:2; 23:10   [1]MT *adulterers*.   7:5 [a]Isa 28:1, 7   [1]MT *our king*.

they devour their rulers.
All their kings fall,
and [a]none of them call on me!

Israel Lacks Discernment and Refuses to Repent

8 Ephraim [a]has mixed itself like flour
  among the nations;
Ephraim is like a ruined cake of
  bread that is scorched on one
  side.[1]
9 [a]Foreigners are consuming what
  his strenuous labor produced,
but he does not recognize it.
His head is filled with gray hair,
but he does not realize it.
10 The [a]arrogance of Israel testifies
  against him,
yet [b]they refuse to return to the
  LORD their God.
In spite of all this they refuse to seek
  him.

Israel Turns to Assyria and Egypt for Help

11 [a]Ephraim has been like a dove,
easily deceived and lacking
  discernment.
[b]They called to Egypt for help;
they turned to [c]Assyria for
  protection.
12 I will [a]throw my bird net over them
  while they are flying;
[b]I will bring them down like birds in
  the sky;
I will discipline them when I hear
  them flocking together.

Israel Has Turned Away from the Lord

13 Woe to them! For they have fled
  from me!
[a]Destruction to them! For they have
  rebelled against me!
I want to deliver them,
but they have lied to me.
14 They do not pray to me,
but howl in distress on their beds;
[a]they slash themselves[1] for grain and
  new [b]wine,
but turn away from me.

15 Although I trained and strengthened
  them,
they plot evil against me!
16 They turn to Baal;[1]
[a]they are like an unreliable bow.
Their leaders will fall by the sword
because their prayers to Baal have
  made me [b]angry.
So people will [c]disdain them in the
  land of Egypt.

God Will Raise up the Assyrians to Attack Israel

8 Sound the alarm!
An eagle[1] looms over the temple of
  the LORD!
For they have broken their covenant
  with me
and have rebelled against my law.
2 [a]Israel cries out to me,
"My God, [b]we acknowledge you!"
3 But Israel has rejected what is
  morally good;
so an enemy will pursue him.

The Political and Cultic Sin of Israel

4 They enthroned kings without my
  consent.
[a]They appointed princes without my
  approval.
They made idols out of their silver
  and gold,
but they will be destroyed!
5 O Samaria, he has rejected your calf
  idol.
My anger burns against them!
They will not survive much longer
  without being punished,
even though they are Israelites!
6 That idol was made by a
  [a]workman—it is not God!
The calf idol of Samaria will be
  broken to bits.

The Fertility Cultists Will Become Infertile

7 They sow [a]the wind,
and so they will reap the whirlwind!
The stalk does not have any standing
  grain;

7:7 [a] Isa 64:7   7:8 [a] Ps 106:35 [1] Heb. *a cake of bread not turned.*   7:9 [a] Isa 1:7; 42:25; Hos 8:7   7:10 [a] Hos 5:5 [b] Isa 9:13
7:11 [a] Hos 11:11 [b] Isa 30:3 [c] Hos 5:13; 8:9   7:12 [a] Ezek 12:13 [b] Lev 26:14; Deut 28:15; 2 Kgs 17:13   7:13 [a] Exod 18:8; Mic 6:4
7:14 [a] Job 35:9–10; Ps 78:36; Jer 3:10; Zech 7:5 [b] Judg 9:27; Amos 2:8 [1] MT *they assemble themselves.*   7:16 [a] Ps 78:57
[b] Ps 73:9; Dan 7:25; Mal 3:13–14 [c] Deut 28:68; Ezek 23:32; Hos 8:13; 9:3 [1] MT *they turn, but not upward;* LXX *they turn to nothing.*   8:1 [1] Or perhaps *A vulture.*   8:2 [a] Ps 78:34; Hos 5:15; 7:14 [b] Titus 1:16   8:4 [a] 1 Kgs 12:20; 2 Kgs 15:23, 25; Hos 13:10–11   8:6 [a] Isa 40:19   8:7 [a] Prov 22:8

it will not produce any flour.
Even if it were to yield grain,
[b]foreigners would swallow it all up.
8 [a]Israel will be swallowed up among
the nations;
they will be like a worthless piece of
pottery.

Israel's Hired Lovers

9 They [a]have gone up to Assyria,
like [b]a wild donkey that wanders off.
Ephraim has hired prostitutes as
lovers.
10 Even though they have [a]hired lovers
among [b]the nations,
I will soon gather them together for
judgment.
Then they will begin to waste away
under the oppression of a mighty
king.[1]

Sacrifices Ineffective without Moral Obedience

11 Although Ephraim has built many
altars for sin offerings,
these have become altars for sinning.
12 I spelled out my law for him in great
detail,
but [a]they regard it as something
totally unknown to them.
13 They offer up sacrificial gifts to me
and eat [a]the meat,
[b]but the LORD does not accept their
sacrifices.
[c]Soon he will remember their
wrongdoing;
he will punish their sins,
and they will return to Egypt.
14 Israel has [a]forgotten [b]his Maker and
built royal palaces,
and Judah has built many [c]fortified
[d]cities.
But I will send fire on their cities;
it will consume their royal citadels.

Fertility Cult Festivals Have Intoxicated Israel

9 O Israel, [a]do not rejoice jubilantly
like the nations,
for you are unfaithful to your God.
You love to receive a prostitute's
[b]wages
on all the floors where you thresh
your grain.
2 Threshing floors and wine vats will
not feed the people,[1]
and new wine only deceives them.

Assyrian Exile Will Reverse the Egyptian Exodus

3 They will not remain in [a]the LORD's
land.
Ephraim will return to Egypt;
they will eat ritually unclean food in
Assyria.
4 They will not pour out drink
offerings of wine to the LORD;
they [a]will not please him with their
[b]sacrifices.
Their sacrifices will be like bread
eaten while in mourning;
all those who eat them will make
themselves ritually unclean.
For their bread will be only to satisfy
their appetite;
it will not come into the temple of
the LORD.
5 So what will you do on the festival
day,
on the festival days of the LORD?

No Escape for the Israelites This Time

6 Look! Even if they flee from the
destruction,
Egypt will take hold of them,
and Memphis will bury them.
The [a]weeds will inherit the silver
they treasure—
thornbushes will occupy their
homes.
7 The [a]time of judgment is about to
arrive!
The time of retribution[1] is imminent!
Israel will be humbled![2]

Israel Rejects Hosea's Prophetic Exhortations

The prophet is considered a [b]fool—
[c]the inspired man[3] is viewed as a
madman—

8:7 [b]Hos 7:9   8:8 [a]2 Kgs 17:6; Jer 51:34   8:9 [a]Hos 7:11; 12:1; Jer 2:24   [b]Ezek 16:33–34   8:10 [a]Ezek 16:37; 22:20   [b]Isa 10:8;
Ezek 26:7; Dan 2:37   [1]Heb. *a king of princes.*   8:12 [a][Deut 4:6–8]; Ps 119:18; 147:19–20   8:13 [a]Zech 7:6   [b]Jer 14:10; Hos 6:6;
9:4; 1 Cor 4:5   [c]Hos 9:9; Amos 8:7; Luke 12:2   8:14 [a]Deut 32:18; [Hos 2:13; 4:6; 13:6]   [b]Isa 29:23   [c]Num 32:17; 2 Kgs 18:13
[d]Jer 17:27   9:1 [a]Isa 22:12–13; Hos 10:5   [b]Jer 44:17   9:2 [1]Heb. *them.*   9:3 [a][Lev 25:23]; Jer 2:7   9:4 [a]Jer 6:20   [b]Hos 8:13;
Amos 5:22   9:6 [a]Isa 5:6; 7:23; Hos 10:8   9:7 [a]Isa 10:3; Jer 10:15; Mic 7:4; Luke 21:22   [b]Lam 2:14; [Ezek 13:3, 10]
[c]Mic 2:11   [1]Heb. *the days of the retribution.*   [2]MT *Let them know.*   [3]Heb. *the man of the Spirit.*

because of the multitude of your sins
and your intense animosity.
8 The prophet is a[a] watchman over
Ephraim on behalf of God,
yet traps are laid for him along all his
paths;
animosity rages against him in the
land[1] of his God.

The Best of Times, the Worst of Times
9 They have sunk deep into corruption
as in[a] the days of[b] Gibeah.
He will remember their wrongdoing.
He will repay them for their sins.
10 When I found Israel, it was like
finding grapes in the[a] wilderness.
I viewed your ancestors like an early
[b] fig on a fig tree in its first season.
Then they came to Baal[c] Peor, and
[d] they dedicated themselves to
shame—
they became as detestable as what
they loved.

The Fertility Worshipers Will Become Infertile
11 Ephraim will be like a bird;
what they value will fly away.
They will not bear children—
they will not enjoy pregnancy—
they will not even conceive!
12 Even if they raise their children,
I will take away every last one of
them.
[a] Woe to them!
For I will turn away from them.
13 Ephraim,[a] as I have seen, has given
their children for prey;[1]
Ephraim will bear his sons for
slaughter.
14 Give them, O LORD—
[a] what will you give them?
Give them wombs that miscarry,
and breasts that cannot nurse!
15 Because of all their evil in[a] Gilgal,
I hate them there.
On account of their evil deeds,
I will drive them out of my land.
I will no longer love them;
[b] all their rulers are rebels.

16 Ephraim will be struck[a] down—
their root will be dried up;
they will not yield any fruit.
Even if they do bear children,
I will kill their precious offspring.
17 My God will reject them,
for they have not obeyed him;
so they will be[a] fugitives among the
nations.

Israel Is Guilty of Fertility Cult Worship
10 Israel was a[a] fertile vine
that yielded fruit.
As his fruit multiplied,
[b] he multiplied altars to Baal.
As his land prospered,
they adorned the fertility pillars.
2 Their hearts are[a] slipping;
soon they will be punished for their
guilt.
The LORD will break their altars;
he will completely destroy their
fertility pillars.

The Lord Will Punish Israel by Removing Its Kings
3 Very soon they will say, "We have no
king
since we did not fear the LORD.
But what can a king do for us
anyway?"
4 They utter empty words,
taking false oaths and making empty
agreements.
Therefore legal disputes sprout up
[a] like poisonous weeds in the furrows
of a plowed field.

The Calf Idol and Idolaters of Samaria Will Be Exiled
5 The inhabitants[1] of Samaria will
lament[2] over the calf[a] idol[3] of Beth
Aven.
Its people will mourn over it;
its idolatrous priests will wail[4]
over it,
because its[b] splendor will be taken
from them into exile.
6 Even the calf idol will be carried to
Assyria

9:8 a Jer 6:17; 31:6; Ezek 3:17; 33:7 1 Heb. *house*; either the temple/official sanctuaries or the land of Israel. 9:9 a Hos 10:9
b Judg 19:22 9:10 a Jer 2:2 b Isa 28:4; Mic 7:1 c Num 25:3; Ps 106:28 d Ps 81:12 9:12 a Deut 31:17; Hos 7:13 9:13 a Ezek
26—28 1 MT *Ephraim as I have seen like Tyre is planted in a meadow.* 9:14 a Luke 23:29 9:15 a Hos 4:15; 12:11 b Isa 1:23;
Hos 5:2 9:16 a Hos 5:11 9:17 a Lev 26:33 10:1 a Nah 2:2 b Jer 2:28; Hos 8:11; 12:11 10:2 a 1 Kgs 18:21; Zeph 1:5;
[Matt 6:24] 10:4 a Deut 31:16-17; 2 Kgs 17:3-4; Amos 5:7 10:5 a 1 Kgs 12:28-29; Hos 8:5-6; 13:2
b Hos 9:11 1 MT *inhabitant.* 2 MT *to dread.* 3 MT *calves.* 4 MT *they will rejoice.*

as tribute for the great king.[1]
Ephraim will be disgraced;
Israel will be put to shame because
of its wooden idol.
7 Samaria and its king will be carried
off
like a twig on the surface of the
waters.
8 The [a]high places of [b]the "House of
Wickedness"[1] will be destroyed;
it is [c]the place where Israel sins.
Thorns and thistles will grow up over
its altars.
Then they will say to the mountains,
"Cover us!"
and to the hills, "Fall on us!"

Failure to Learn from the Sin and Judgment of Gibeah

9 "O Israel, you have sinned since the
time of [a]Gibeah,
and there you have remained.
Did not [b]war overtake the evildoers
in Gibeah?
10 When I please, I will discipline them;
I will gather [a]nations together to
attack them,
to bind them in chains for their two
sins.[1]

Fertility Imagery: Plowing, Sowing, and Reaping

11 "Ephraim [a]was a well-trained heifer
who loved to thresh grain;
I myself put a fine yoke[1] on her neck.
I will harness Ephraim.
Let Judah plow![2]
Let Jacob break up the unplowed
ground for himself!
12 Sow righteousness for yourselves,
reap unfailing love.
[a]Break up the unplowed ground for
yourselves,
for it is time to seek the LORD,
until he [b]comes and showers
deliverance on you.
13 But [a]you have plowed wickedness;
you have reaped injustice;
you have eaten the fruit of deception.

Because you have depended on your
chariots;[1]
you have relied on your many
warriors.

Bethel Will Be Destroyed Like Beth Arbel

14 "The roar of battle will rise against
your people;
all your fortresses will be devastated,
just as Shalman devastated[1] Beth
Arbel on the day of battle,
when mothers were dashed to the
ground with their children.
15 So will it happen to you, O Bethel,
because of your great wickedness!
When that day dawns,
the king of Israel will be destroyed.

Reversal of the Exodus: Return to Egypt and Exile in Assyria

11 "When [a]Israel was a young man, I
loved him like a son,
and I summoned my [b]son[1] out of
Egypt.
2 But the more I summoned[1] them,
the farther they [a]departed from me.[2]
They sacrificed to the Baal idols
and burned incense to images.
3 Yet [a]it was [b]I who led Ephraim;
I took them by the arm,
but they did not acknowledge
that I had healed them.
4 I drew them [a]with leather cords,
[b]with straps of hide;
I lifted the yoke from their neck[1]
and gently fed them.
5 They will return to Egypt!
Assyria will rule over them
because they refuse to repent!
6 A sword will flash in their cities;
it will destroy the bars of their city
gates,
and will devour them in their
fortresses.
7 My people are obsessed with turning
away [a]from me;
they call to Baal,[1] but he will never
exalt them!

10:6 [1]MT *a king who contends* [?] *let him contend!* 10:8 [a]Hos 4:15 [b]Deut 9:21; 1 Kgs 13:34 [c]Isa 2:19; Luke 23:30; Rev 6:16 [1]MT *high places of Aven;* sev. MSS *high places of Beth Aven.* 10:9 [a]Hos 9:9 [b]Judg 20 10:10 [a]Jer 16:16 [1]Ket. *for their two eyes.* 10:11 [a][Jer 50:11; Hos 4:16; Mic 4:13] [1]MT *upon a fine* [thing]? [2]Or *Judah will plow.* 10:12 [a]Jer 4:3 [b]Hos 6:3 10:13 [a][Job 4:8; Prov 22:8; Gal 6:7–8] [1]MT *in your own way.* 10:14 [1]Heb. *as the devastation of Shalman.* 11:1 [a]Matt 2:15 [b]Exod 4:22–23 [1]LXX *his sons.* 11:2 [a]2 Kgs 17:13–15 [1]MT *they.* [2]MT *them.* 11:3 [a]Deut 1:31; 32:10–11 [b]Exod 15:26 11:4 [a]Lev 26:13 [b]Exod 16:32; Ps 78:25 [1]Or *cheek;* Heb. *their jaws.* 11:7 [a]Jer 3:6–7; 8:5 [1]MT *they call upwards to him; a few* WSS *they cry out because of* [their] *yoke.*

The Divine Dilemma: Judgment or Mercy?

8 "How can I give you up,[a] O Ephraim?
How can I surrender you, O Israel?
How can I treat you like[b] Admah?
How can I make you like Zeboyim?
I have had a change of heart.
All my tender compassions are
aroused.
9 I cannot carry out my fierce anger!
I cannot totally destroy Ephraim!
Because I am God, and not man—the
Holy One among you—
I will not come in wrath!

God Will Restore the Exiles to Israel

10 "He will roar like a lion,
and[a] they will follow the LORD;
when he roars,
his children will come trembling
from the west.
11 They will return in fear and
trembling
[a] like birds from Egypt,
like doves from Assyria,
[b] and I will settle them in their
homes," declares the LORD.

God's Lawsuit against Israel: Breach of Covenant

12 Ephraim has surrounded me with
lies;
the house of Israel has surrounded
me with deceit.
But Judah still roams about with God;
he remains faithful to the Holy One.

12 Ephraim continually feeds[a] on the
wind;
he chases the east wind all day;
he multiplies lies and violence.
They make treaties with Assyria
and send olive[b] oil as tribute to
Egypt.
2 The LORD also has a covenant
lawsuit[1] against Judah;
[a] he will punish Jacob according to his
ways
and repay him according to his
deeds.

Israel Must Return to the God of Jacob

3 In the womb he attacked his brother;
in his manly vigor he[a] struggled with
God.
4 He struggled with an angel and
prevailed;
he wept and begged for his favor.
He found God at[a] Bethel,
and there he spoke with him![1]
5 As for the LORD God Almighty,
the LORD is the name by[a] which he is
remembered!
6 [a] But you must return to your God,
by maintaining love and justice
and by waiting for your God to return
to you.

The Lord Refutes Israel's False Claim of Innocence

7 The businessmen love to cheat;
they use[a] dishonest scales.
8 Ephraim boasts, "I am very rich!
I have become wealthy![1]
In all that I have done to gain my
wealth,[2]
no one can accuse me of any offense
that is actually sinful."[3]

9 "I am the LORD your God who
brought you out of Egypt;
[a] I will make you live in tents again as
in the days of old.
10 I spoke to the prophets;
[a] I myself revealed many visions;
I spoke in parables through the
prophets."
11 Is there idolatry in[a] Gilead?
Certainly its inhabitants[1] will come
to nothing!
Do they sacrifice bulls in[b] Gilgal?
Surely their altars will be like stones
heaped up on a plowed field!

Jacob in Aram, Israel in Egypt, and Ephraim in Trouble

12 Jacob[a] fled to the country of Aram,
then[b] Israel worked to acquire a wife;
he tended sheep to pay for her.

11:8 [a] Jer 9:7 [b] Gen 14:8; 19:24–25; Deut 29:23   11:10 [a] Isa 31:4; [Joel 3:16]; Amos 1:2   11:11 [a] Isa 11:11; 60:8; Hos 7:11 [b] Ezek 28:25–26; 34:27–28   12:1 [a] Job 15:2–3; Hos 8:7 [b] Isa 30:6   12:2 [a] Hos 4:1; Mic 6:2. [1] The Heb. noun can be used for nonlegal disputes or legal lawsuits.   12:3 [a] Gen 32:24–28   12:4 [a] [Gen 28:12–19; 35:9–15] [1] MT *us*.   12:5 [a] Exod 3:15   12:6 [a] Hos 14:1; Mic 6:8   12:7 [a] Prov 11:1; Amos 8:5; Mic 6:11   12:8 [1] Heb. *I have found wealth for myself.* [2] LXX *his labors.* [3] MT [in] *all my gains, they will not find guilt in me that would be sin;* LXX *in all his labors, he cannot offset his guilt that is sin.*   12:9 [a] Lev 23:42   12:10 [a] 2 Kgs 17:13; Jer 7:25   12:11 [a] Hos 6:8 [b] Hos 9:15
[1] Heb. *they.*   12:12 [a] Gen 28:5; Deut 26:5 [b] Gen 29:20, 28

13 The LORD brought Israel out of
Egypt [a]by a prophet,
and due to a prophet[1] Israel was
preserved alive.
14 But Ephraim bitterly [a]provoked him
to anger;
so he will hold him accountable for
the blood he has shed;
his Lord will repay him for the
contempt he has shown.

Baal Worshipers and Calf Worshipers to Be Destroyed

13 When Ephraim spoke, there was
terror;
he was exalted[1] in Israel,
but he became guilty by worshiping
Baal and died.
2 Even now they persist in sin!
They make metal images for
themselves,
idols that they skillfully fashion from
their own silver;
all of them are nothing but the work
of craftsmen.
There is a saying about them:[1]
"Those who sacrifice to the calf idol
are calf kissers!"
3 Therefore they will disappear [a]like
the morning mist,
like early morning dew that
evaporates,
like chaff that is blown away from a
threshing floor,
like smoke that disappears through
an open window.

Well-Fed Israel Will Be Fed to Wild Animals

4 But [a]I am [b]the LORD your God,
who brought you out of Egypt.
Therefore, you must not
acknowledge any God but me.
Except for me there is no Savior.
5 I cared for[1] you [a]in the wilderness,
[b]in the dry desert where no water was.[2]
6 When they were fed,[1] they became
satisfied;

[a]when they were satisfied, they
became proud;
as a result, they forgot me!
7 So [a]I will pounce on them like [b]a lion;
like a leopard I will lurk by the path.
8 I will attack them [a]like a bear robbed
of her cubs—
I will rip open their chests.
I will devour them there like a lion—
like a wild animal would tear them
apart.

Israel's King Unable to Deliver the Nation

9 I will destroy you,[1] O Israel!
Who[2] is there to help you?
10 Where[1] [a]then is [b]your king,
that he may save you in all your
cities?
Where are your rulers for whom you
asked, saying,
"Give me a king and princes"?
11 I granted you a [a]king in my anger,
and I will take him away in my
wrath!

Israel's Punishment Will not Be Withheld Much Longer

12 The punishment of Ephraim has
been decreed;
his punishment is being stored up
for [a]the future.
13 The labor pains of a woman will
overtake him,
but [a]the baby will lack wisdom;
when the time arrives,
he will not come out of the womb!

The Lord Will not Relent from the Threatened Judgment

14 Will I deliver them [a]from the power
of Sheol? No, I will not!
Will I redeem them from death? No,
I will not!
O Death, bring on your plagues![1]
O Sheol, bring on your destruction![2]
My eyes will not show any
[b]compassion!

12:13 [a] Exod 12:50–51; 13:3; Ps 77:20; Isa 63:11–12; Mic 6:4 [1] Heb. *by a prophet.* 12:14 [a] Ezek 18:10–13 13:1 [1] MT *he exalted.*
13:2 [1] Or *It is said of them—those men who sacrifice, 'They kiss calves!';* Heb. *They say about them.* 13:3 [a] Ps 1:4; Isa
17:13; Dan 2:35 13:4 [a] Isa 43:11 [b] Isa 43:11; 45:21–22; [1 Tim 2:5] 13:5 [a] Deut 2:7; 32:10 [b] Deut 8:15 [1] MT *I knew.* [2] Heb.
land of intense drought, intensely thirsty land. 13:6 [a] Deut 8:12, 14; 32:13–15; Jer 5:7 [1] MT *according to their pasturage.*
13:7 [a] Lam 3:10; Hos 5:14 [b] Jer 5:6 13:8 [a] 2 Sam 17:8; Prov 17:12 13:9 [1] MT *he destroyed you.* [2] MT *but in me is your help.*
13:10 [a] Deut 32:38 [b] 1 Sam 8:5–6 [1] MT *I want to be* [your king]. 13:11 [a] 1 Sam 8:7; 10:17–24 13:12 [a] Deut 32:34–35;
Job 14:17; [Rom 2:5] 13:13 [a] Isa 13:8; Mic 4:9–10 13:14 [a] [1 Cor 15:54–55] [b] Jer 15:6 [1] Heb. *Where, O Death,
are your plagues?* [2] Heb. *Where, O Sheol, is your destruction?*

The Capital of the Northern Empire Will Be Destroyed

15 Even though he flourishes like [a]a
    reed plant,[1]
a scorching east wind will come,
a wind from the LORD rising up from
    the desert.
As a result, his spring will dry up;[2]
his well will become dry.
That wind will spoil all his delightful
    foods
in the containers in his storehouse.

16 Samaria will be held guilty
because she [a]rebelled against her God.
They will fall by the sword;
their infants will be dashed to the
    ground—
their pregnant women will be
    [b]ripped open.

Prophetic Call to Genuine Repentance

14 [a]Return, O Israel, to the LORD your
    God,
for your sin has been your downfall!
2 Return to the LORD and repent!
Say to him: "Completely forgive our
    iniquity;
accept our penitential prayer,
that we may offer the praise of our
    lips as sacrificial [a]bulls.[1]
3 Assyria cannot save us;
we will [a]not ride warhorses.
[b]We will never again say, 'Our gods,'
to what our own hands have made.
[c]For only you will show compassion
    to Orphan Israel!"[1]

Divine Promise to Relent from Judgment and to Restore Blessings

4 "I will heal their [a]waywardness
and [b]love them freely,
for my anger will turn away from
    them.
5 I will be like the [a]dew to Israel;
he will blossom like a lily;
he will send down his roots like a
    cedar of Lebanon.
6 His young shoots will grow;
[a]his splendor will be like an olive
    tree;
[b]his fragrance like a cedar of
    Lebanon.
7 [a]People will reside again in his shade;
they will plant and harvest grain in
    abundance.
They will blossom like a vine,
and his fame will be like the wine
    from Lebanon.
8 O Ephraim, I do not want to
    have anything to do with idols
    anymore!
I will answer him and care for him.
I am like a luxuriant cypress tree;
[a]your fruitfulness comes from me!"

Concluding Exhortation

9 Who is wise?
Let him discern [a]these things!
Who is discerning?
Let him understand them!
For the ways of the LORD are right;
the godly walk in them,
but in them the rebellious stumble.

13:15 [a] Gen 41:6; Jer 4:11–12; Ezek 17:10; 19:12 [1] MT *he flourishes* [as] *a son of brothers; some* WSS *he causes division between brothers.* [2] MT *will be ashamed.* 13:16 [a] 2 Kgs 18:12 [b] 2 Kgs 15:16 14:1 [a] Hos 12:6; [Joel 2:13] 14:2 [a] [Ps 51:16–17; Hos 6:6; Heb 13:15] [1] LXX *fruit.* 14:3 [a] Hos 7:11; 10:13; 12:1 [b] [Ps 33:17]; Isa 31:1 [c] Ps 10:14; 68:5 [1] Heb. *For the orphan is shown compassion by you.* 14:4 [a] Jer 14:7 [b] [Eph 1:6] 14:5 [a] Job 29:19; Prov 19:12; Isa 26:19 14:6 [a] Ps 52:8; 128:3 [b] Gen 27:27 14:7 [a] Dan 4:12 14:8 [a] [John 15:4] 14:9 [a] [Ps 111:7–8; Prov 10:29]; Zeph 3:5

JOEL

Disaster strikes the southern kingdom of Judah without warning. An ominous black cloud descends upon the land—the dreaded locusts. In a matter of hours, every living green thing has been stripped bare. Joel, God's spokesman during the reign of Joash (835–796 BC), seizes this occasion to proclaim God's message. Although the locust plague has been a terrible judgment for sin, God's future judgments during the day of the Lord will make that plague pale by comparison. In that day, God will destroy his enemies but bring unparalleled blessing to those who faithfully obey him. The Hebrew name *Yo'el* means "Yahweh Is God." This name is appropriate to the theme of the book, which emphasizes God's sovereign work in history. The courses of nature and nations are in his hand. The Greek equivalent is *Ioel*, and the Latin is *Joel*.

Introduction

1 This is the Lord's message that came to [a]Joel the son of Pethuel:

A Locust Plague Foreshadows the Day of the Lord

2 Listen to this, you elders;
  pay attention, all inhabitants of the
    land.
  [a]Has anything like this ever
    happened in your whole life[1]
  or in the lifetime of your ancestors?
3 [a]Tell your children about it;
  have your children tell their children,
  and their children the following
    generation.
4 What the *gazam*-locust left the
    'arbeh-locust consumed;
  [a]what the *'arbeh*-locust left the
    yeleq-locust consumed;
  and what the *yeleq*-locust left the
    hasil-locust consumed.

5 Wake up, you [a]drunkards, and weep!
  Wail, all you wine drinkers,
  because the sweet wine has been
    taken away from you.
6 For [a]a nation has invaded my land,
  mighty and without number.

Their teeth are lion's teeth;
  they have the fangs of a lioness.
7 They have [a]destroyed my vines;[1]
  they have turned my fig trees into
    mere splinters.
  They have completely stripped off
    the bark and thrown it aside;
  the twigs are stripped bare.

A Call to Lament

8 Wail like [a]a young virgin [b]clothed in
    sackcloth,
  lamenting the death of her husband
    to be.
9 No one brings grain offerings or
    drink offerings
  to [a]the temple of the Lord
    anymore.
  So the priests, those who serve the
    Lord, are in [b]mourning.
10 The crops of [a]the fields have been
    destroyed.[1]
  [b]The ground is in mourning because
    the grain has perished.
  The fresh wine has dried up;
    the olive oil languishes.
11 [a]Be distressed, farmers;
  wail, vinedressers, over the wheat
    and the barley.

1:1 [a] Acts 2:16   1:2 [a] Jer 30:7; Joel 2:2   [1] Heb. *days.*   1:3 [a] Exod 10:2; Ps 78:4; Isa 38:19   1:4 [a] Deut 28:38; Joel 2:25; Amos 4:9   1:5 [a] Isa 5:11; 28:1; Hos 7:5   1:6 [a] Prov 30:25; Joel 2:2, 11, 25   1:7 [a] Isa 5:6; Amos 4:9   [1] Heb. *vine* and *fig tree*; either the prophet speaks in the first-person sing. about his own vine to personalize the description, or the voice of God speaks, and these do double duty, representing the foliage being destroyed and the nation.   1:8 [a] Isa 22:12   [b] Prov 2:17; Jer 3:4   1:9 [a] Hos 9:4; Joel 1:13; 2:14   [b] Joel 2:17   1:10 [a] Jer 12:11; Hos 3:4   [b] Isa 24:7   [1] Both "the fields have been destroyed" and "the ground is in mourning" are alliterative Heb. constructions.   1:11 [a] Jer 14:3–4; Amos 5:16

For the harvest of the field has
  perished.
[12] The vine has dried up;
  [a]the fig tree languishes—
the pomegranate, date, and apple[1] as
  well.
In fact, all the trees of the field have
  dried up.
Indeed, the [b]joy of the people has
  dried up!

[13] Get [a]dressed and lament, you priests.
Wail, you who minister at the altar.
Come, spend the night in sackcloth,
  you servants of my God,
because no one brings grain offerings
  or drink offerings
to the temple of your God anymore.
[14] Announce a [a]holy [b]fast;
proclaim a sacred assembly.
Gather the elders and[1] [c]all the
  inhabitants of the land
to the temple of the LORD your God,
and cry out to the LORD.
[15] How [a]awful that day will be!
For [b]the day of the LORD is near;
it will come as destruction from the
  Divine Destroyer.[1]
[16] Our food has been [a]cut off right
  before our eyes!
There is no longer any [b]joy or
  gladness in the temple of our God.
[17] The grains of seed have shriveled
  beneath their shovels.[1]
Storehouses have been decimated,
and granaries have been torn down
because the grain has dried up.
[18] Listen to [a]the cattle groan!
The herds of livestock wander
  around in confusion
because they have no pasture.
Even the flocks of sheep are
  suffering.

[19] To you, [a]O LORD, I call out for help,
for [b]fire has burned up the pastures
  of the wilderness,

flames have razed[1] all the trees in the
  fields.
[20] Even the wild animals cry [a]out to
  you,
for [b]the river beds have dried up;
fire has destroyed the pastures of the
  wilderness.

The Locusts' Devastation

2 Blow [a]the trumpet in Zion;
  [b]sound [c]the alarm signal on my holy
  mountain!
Let all the inhabitants of the land
  shake with fear,
for the day of the LORD is about to
  come.
Indeed,[1] it is near!
[2] It will be [a]a [b]day of dreadful darkness,
a day of foreboding storm clouds,
like blackness[1] spread over [c]the
  mountains.
It is a huge and powerful army—
there has never been anything like it
  ever before,
and there will not be anything like it
  for many generations to come!

[3] Like fire [a]they devour everything in
  their path;
[b]a flame blazes behind them.
The land looks like the Garden of
  Eden before them,
but behind them there is only a
  desolate wilderness—
for nothing escapes them!
[4] [a]They look like horses;[1]
they charge ahead like war horses.
[5] [a]They sound like chariots rumbling
  over mountain tops,
like the crackling of blazing fire
  consuming stubble,
like the noise of a mighty army being
  drawn up for battle.
[6] People[1] writhe in fear when they see
  them.
  [a]All their faces turn pale with fright.
[7] They charge like warriors;

1:12 [a] Joel 1:10; Hab 3:17 [b] Isa 16:10; 24:11; Jer 48:33 [1] Or perhaps *apricot, citron, quince.* 1:13 [a] Jer 4:8; Ezek 7:18 1:14 [a] 2 Chr 20:3; Joel 2:15–16 [b] Lev 23:36 [c] 2 Chr 20:13 [1] MT, LXX omit *and.* 1:15 [a] [Isa 13:9; Jer 30:7]; Amos 5:16 [b] Isa 13:6; Ezek 7:2–12 [1] There is a wordplay in Heb. here with the word used for "destruction" (*shod*) and the term used for God (*shadday*). 1:16 [a] Isa 3:1; Amos 4:6 [b] Deut 12:7; Ps 43:4 1:17 [1] Qum. MS *the heifers decay in* [their] s[talls]; LXX *the heifers leap in their stalls.* 1:18 [a] 1 Kgs 8:5; Jer 12:4; 14:5–6; Hos 4:3 1:19 [a] [Ps 50:15]; Mic 7:7 [b] Jer 9:10; Amos 7:4 [1] Heb. *a flame has set ablaze.* 1:20 [a] Job 38:41; Ps 104:21; 147:9; Joel 1:18 [b] 1 Kgs 17:7; 18:5 2:1 [a] Jer 4:5; Joel 2:15; Zeph 1:16 [b] Num 10:5 [c] Joel 1:15; 2:11, 31; 3:14; [Obad 15]; Zeph 1:14 [1] Or *for.* 2:2 [a] Joel 2:10, 31; Amos 5:18; Zeph 1:15 [b] Joel 1:6; 2:11, 25 [c] Exod 10:14; Lam 1:12; Dan 9:12; 12:1; Joel 1:2 [1] MT *morning.* 2:3 [a] Gen 2:8; Isa 51:3; Ezek 36:35 [b] Exod 10:5, 15; Ps 105:34–35; Zech 7:14 2:4 [a] Rev 9:7 [1] Heb. *Like the appearance of horses* [is] *its appearance.* 2:5 [a] Rev 9:9 2:6 [a] Isa 13:8; Jer 8:21; Lam 4:8; Nah 2:10 [1] Or *nations.*

they scale walls like soldiers.
Each one proceeds on his course;
they do not alter[1] their [a]path.
8 They do not jostle one another;
each of them marches straight ahead.
They burst through the city defenses[1]
and do not break ranks.
9 They rush into the city;
they scale its walls.
They climb up into the houses;
they go [a]in through the windows
  [b]like a thief.
10 The earth quakes before [a]them;
  [b]the sky reverberates.
The sun and the moon grow dark;
the stars refuse to shine.
11 The voice of [a]the LORD thunders as
he leads his army.
Indeed, his warriors are
innumerable;[1]
Surely his command is carried out!
Yes, the [b]day of the LORD is awesome
and very terrifying—[c]who can
survive it?

An Appeal for Repentance

12 "Yet even now," the LORD says,
"[a]return to me with all your heart—
with fasting, weeping, and mourning.
13 [a]Tear [b]your hearts,
not just your garments."
Return to the LORD your God,
for he is [c]merciful and
compassionate,
slow to anger and boundless in
loyal love—often relenting from
calamitous punishment.
14 [a]Who knows?
[b]Perhaps he will be [c]compassionate
and grant a reprieve,
and leave blessing in his wake[1]—
a meal offering and a drink offering
for you to offer to the LORD your
God!

15 [a]Blow the trumpet in Zion.
Announce a [b]holy fast;
proclaim a sacred assembly.
16 Gather the people;
[a]sanctify an assembly!
Gather the elders;
gather the children and the nursing
infants.
[b]Let the bridegroom come out from
his bedroom
and the bride from her private
quarters.
17 Let the priests, those who serve the
LORD, weep
from the vestibule all the way back to
the altar.
Let them say, "Have pity, O LORD, on
your people;
please do not turn over your
inheritance to [a]be mocked,
to become [b]a proverb among the
nations.
[c]Why should it be said among the
peoples,
'Where is their God?'"

The LORD's Response

18 Then the LORD [a]became zealous for
his land;
he had compassion on his people.
19 The LORD responded to his people,
"Look! I am about to restore your
[a]grain
as well as fresh wine and olive oil.
You will be fully satisfied.[1]
I will never again make you an object
of mockery among the nations.
20 I [a]will remove [b]the one from the
north far from you.
I will drive him out [c]to a dry and
desolate place.
Those in front will be driven
eastward into the Dead Sea,[1]
and those in back westward into the
Mediterranean Sea.[2]
His stench will rise up as a foul
smell."
Indeed, the LORD has accomplished
great things!

21 Do not fear, my land.
Rejoice and be glad
because the LORD has accomplished
great things!
22 Do not fear, wild animals.
For[a] the pastures of the wilderness
are again green with grass.
Indeed, the trees bear their fruit;
the fig tree and the vine yield to
their fullest.
23 Citizens of Zion, rejoice!
Be[a] glad because of what the LORD
your God has done!
For he has given to you the early
rains as vindication.
He has sent to you the rains—
both the early and the late rains as
formerly.
24 The threshing floors are full of grain;
the vats overflow with fresh wine
and olive oil.

25 "I will make up for the years
[a] that the *'arbeh*-locust consumed
your crops—
the *yeleq*-locust, the *hasil*-locust, and
the *gazam*-locust—
my great army that I sent against
you.
26 You will have plenty to[a] eat,
and your hunger will be fully
satisfied;
you will praise the name of the LORD
your God,
who has acted wondrously in your
behalf.
My people will never again be put to
[b] shame.
27 You will be[a] convinced that[b] I am in
the midst of Israel.
I am the LORD your God; there is no
other.
My people will never again be put to
shame.

An Outpouring of the Spirit

28 "[a] After all of this
[b] I will pour out my Spirit on all kinds
of people![1]

[c] Your sons and[d] daughters will
prophesy.
Your elderly will have prophetic
dreams;
your young men will see visions.
29 Even on male and female[a] servants
I will pour out my Spirit in those days.
30 I[a] will produce portents both in the
sky[1] and on the earth—
blood, fire, and columns of smoke.
31 The sunlight will be turned to
darkness
and[a] the moon to the color of blood,
[b] before the day of the LORD comes—
that great and terrible day!
32 It will so happen that
everyone[a] who calls on the name of
the LORD will be delivered.
For on Mount Zion and[b] in Jerusalem
[c] there will be those who survive,
just as the LORD has promised;
the remnant will be those whom the
LORD will call.

The LORD Plans to Judge the Nations

3 "For look![a] In those[1] days and at that
time
I will return the exiles to Judah and
Jerusalem.
2 Then[a] I[b] will gather all the nations
and bring them down to the Valley of
Jehoshaphat.
I will enter into judgment against
them there
concerning my people Israel who are
my inheritance,
whom they scattered among the
nations.
They partitioned my land,
3 and they[a] cast lots for my people.
They traded a boy for a prostitute;
they sold a little girl for wine so they
could drink.
4 Why are[a] you doing these things to
me, Tyre and Sidon?
Are you trying to get even with me,
land of Philistia?
If you are, I will very quickly repay
you for what you have done!

2:22 [a] Joel 1:19   2:23 [a] Deut 11:14; Isa 41:16; Jer 5:24; Hab 3:18; Zech 10:7   2:25 [a] Joel 1:4–7; 2:2–11   2:26 [a] Lev 26:5; Deut 11:15; Isa 62:9 [b] Isa 45:17   2:27 [a] Lev 26:11–12; [Joel 3:17, 21] [b] [Isa 45:5–6]   2:28 [a] Ezek 39:29; Acts 2:17–21 [b] Zech 12:10 [c] Isa 54:13 [d] Acts 21:9 [1] Heb. *all flesh*.   2:29 [a] [1 Cor 12:13; Gal 3:28]   2:30 [a] Matt 24:29; Mark 13:24–25; Luke 21:11, 25, 26; Acts 2:19 [1] Or *in the heavens*.   2:31 [a] Isa 13:9–10; 34:4; Joel 2:10; 3:15; Matt 24:29; Mark 13:24; Luke 21:25; Acts 2:20; Rev 6:12–13 [b] Isa 13:9; Zeph 1:14–16; [Mal 4:1, 5, 6]   2:32 [a] Jer 33:3; Acts 2:21; Rom 10:13 [b] Isa 46:13; [Rom 11:26] [c] Isa 11:11; Jer 31:7; [Mic 4:7]; Rom 9:27   3:1 [a] Jer 30:3; Ezek 38:14 [1] One ws *in that day*.   3:2 [a] Isa 66:18; Mic 4:12; Zech 14:2 [b] Isa 66:16; Jer 25:31; Ezek 38:22   3:3 [a] Obad 11; Nah 3:10   3:4 [a] Isa 14:29–31; Jer 47:1–7; Ezek 25:15–17; Amos 1:6–8; Zech 9:5–7

5 For you took my silver and my gold
  and brought my precious valuables
    to your own palaces.
6 You sold Judeans and Jerusalemites
    to the Greeks,
  removing them far from their own
    country.
7 Look! [a]I am rousing them from that
    place to which you sold them.
  I will repay you for what you have
    done!
8 I will sell your sons and daughters to
    the people of Judah.
  They will sell them to the [a]Sabeans,
    [b]a nation far away."
  Indeed, the LORD has spoken.

Judgment in the Valley of Jehoshaphat

9 [a]Proclaim this among the nations:
  "Prepare for a holy war!
  Call out the warriors!
  Let all these fighting men approach
    and attack!
10 [a]Beat your plowshares into swords
  and your pruning hooks into spears.
  Let the weak say, 'I too am a warrior!'
11 Lend [a]your aid and come,
  all you surrounding nations,
  and gather yourselves[1] to that
    place."

  Bring down, O LORD, your warriors!
12 "Let the nations be roused and let
    them go up
  to the Valley of Jehoshaphat,
  for there I will sit in [a]judgment on all
    the surrounding nations.
13 Rush forth [a]with [b]the sickle, for the
    harvest is ripe!
  Come, stomp the grapes, for the
    [c]winepress is full!
  The vats overflow.
  Indeed, their evil is great!"

14 Crowds, great crowds are in [a]the
    Valley of Decision,
  for the day of the LORD is near in the
    Valley of Decision!
15 The sun and moon are darkened;
  the stars withhold[1] their brightness.
16 The LORD roars from Zion;
  from Jerusalem his voice bellows out.
  The heavens and the earth shake.
  [a]But the LORD is a refuge for his
    people;
  he is a stronghold for the citizens of
    Israel.

The Lord's Presence in Zion

17 "You will be convinced that I, the
    LORD, am your God,
  dwelling on Zion, my [a]holy mountain.
  Jerusalem will be holy—
  conquering armies will no longer
    pass through it.
18 On that day the mountains will drip
    with sweet wine,[1]
  and the hills will flow with milk.
  All the dry stream beds of Judah will
    flow with water.
  A [a]spring will flow out from the
    temple of the LORD,
  watering the Valley of Acacia Trees.[2]
19 Egypt will be desolate,
  and Edom will be a desolate
    wilderness
  because of the violence they did to
    the people of Judah,
  in whose land they shed innocent
    blood.
20 But Judah will reside securely
    forever,
  and Jerusalem will be secure from
    one generation to the next.
21 I will avenge[1] their blood that I had
    not previously [a]acquitted."
  It is the LORD who dwells in Zion!

3:7 [a] Isa 43:5–6; Jer 23:8; Zech 9:13   3:8 [a] Ezek 23:42   [b] Jer 6:20   3:9 [a] Jer 6:4; Ezek 38:7; Mic 3:5   3:10 [a] [Isa 2:4; Mic 4:3] 3:11 [a] Ps 103:20; Isa 13:3   [1] MT *they will gather themselves.*   3:12 [a] [Ps 96:13]; Isa 2:4   3:13 [a] [Matt 13:39]; Rev 14:15   [b] Jer 51:33; Hos 6:11   [c] [Isa 63:3]; Lam 1:5; Rev 14:19   3:14 [a] Joel 2:1   3:15 [1] Heb. *gather in.*   3:16 [a] [Isa 51:5–6]   3:17 [a] Obad 16; Zech 8:3   3:18 [a] Ps 46:4; Ezek 47:1; Zech 14:8; [Rev 22:1]   [1] Or perhaps *new wine.*   [2] Heb. *Valley of Shittim*; the exact location is uncertain but would be a very arid and dry place. Joel's point is that the stream will proceed to the most dry and barren of locations in the vicinity of Jerusalem.   3:21 [a] Isa 4:4   [1] MT *I will acquit.*

AMOS

Amos prophesies during a period of national optimism in Israel. Business is booming, and boundaries are bulging. But below the surface, greed and injustice are festering. Hypocritical religious motions have replaced true worship, creating a false sense of security and a growing callousness to God's disciplining hand. Famine, drought, plagues, death, destruction—nothing can force the people to their knees. Amos, the farmer-turned-prophet, unflinchingly lashes out at sin, trying to visualize the nearness of God's judgment and mobilize the nation to repentance. The nation, like a basket of rotting fruit, stands ripe for judgment because of its hypocrisy and spiritual indifference. The name *Amos* is derived from the Hebrew root *amas,* "to lift a burden, to carry." Thus his name means "Burden" or "Burden-Bearer." Amos bears up under his divinely given burden of declaring judgment to rebellious Israel. The Greek and Latin titles are both transliterated in English as *Amos.*

Introduction

1 The following is a record of what Amos prophesied.[1] He was one of the [a]herdsmen from [b]Tekoa. These prophecies about Israel were revealed to him during the time of King [c]Uzziah of Judah and King [d]Jeroboam son of Joash of Israel, two years before the [e]earthquake.

God Will Judge the Surrounding Nations

[2]Amos said:

> "The LORD comes [a]roaring out of Zion;
> from Jerusalem he comes bellowing!
> The shepherds' pastures wilt;
> the summit of [b]Carmel withers."

[3]This is what the LORD says:

> "Because [a]Damascus has committed
> three crimes—
> make that four![1]—I will not revoke my
> decree of judgment.
> They ripped [b]through Gilead like
> threshing sledges with iron teeth.

[4] [a]So I will set Hazael's house on fire;
> fire will consume Ben [b]Hadad's
> fortresses.

[5] I will break the bar on the [a]gate of
> Damascus.
> I will remove the ruler from Wicked
> Valley,[1]
> the one who holds the royal scepter
> from Beth Eden.[2]
> The people of Aram will be deported
> to Kir."
> The LORD has spoken!

[6]This is what the LORD says:

> "Because [a]Gaza has committed three
> crimes—
> make that four!—I will not revoke my
> decree of judgment.
> They deported a whole community
> and sold them to Edom.

[7] [a]So I will set Gaza's city wall on fire;
> fire will consume her fortresses.

[8] I will remove the ruler [a]from Ashdod,
> the one who holds the royal scepter
> from Ashkelon.

1:1[a]2 Kgs 3:4; Amos 7:14 [b]2 Sam 14:2; Jer 6:1 [c]2 Kgs 15:1–7; 2 Chr 26:1–23; Isa 1:1; Hos 1:1 [d]2 Kgs 14:23–29; Amos 7:10 [e]Zech 14:5 [1]Heb. *The words of Amos.* 1:2[a]Isa 42:13; Jer 25:30; Joel 3:16 [b]1 Sam 25:2; Isa 33:9 1:3[a]Isa 8:4; 17:1–3; Jer 49:23–27; Zech 9:1 [b]2 Kgs 10:32–33 [1]Heb. *Because of three violations of Damascus, even because of four.* 1:4[a]Jer 49:27; 51:30 [b]1 Kgs 20:1; 2 Kgs 6:24 1:5[a]2 Kgs 14:28; Isa 8:4; Jer 51:30; Lam 2:9 [1]Heb. *valley of wickedness*; perhaps a geographical location but probably a derogatory epithet for Damascus and the kingdom of Aram. [2]Perhaps Bit Adini, an Aramean state located near the Euphrates River, or perhaps a sarcastic epithet meaning "house of pleasure." 1:6[a]1 Sam 6:17; Jer 47:1, 5; Zeph 2:4 1:7[a]Jer 47:1 1:8[a]Jer 47:5; Zeph 2:4

I will ^bstrike Ekron with my hand;
  ^cthe rest of the Philistines will also
    die."
The Sovereign LORD has spoken!

⁹This is what the LORD says:

"Because ^aTyre has committed three
  crimes—
make that four—I will not revoke my
  decree of judgment.
They sold a whole community[1] to
  Edom;
they failed to observe a treaty of
  brotherhood.
¹⁰ So I will set fire to Tyre's city wall;
  fire will consume her fortresses."

¹¹This is what the LORD says:

"Because ^aEdom has committed
  three crimes—
make that four—I will not revoke my
  decree of judgment.
He chased his ^bbrother with a sword;
  he wiped out his allies.
In his anger he tore them apart
  without stopping to rest;[1]
in his fury he relentlessly attacked
  them.
¹² So ^aI will set Teman on fire;
  fire will consume Bozrah's fortresses."

¹³This is what ^athe LORD says:

"Because the Ammonites have
  committed three crimes—
make that four—I will not revoke my
  decree of judgment.
They ripped open Gilead's pregnant
  women
so they could expand their territory.
¹⁴ So I will set fire to ^aRabbah's city wall;
  fire will consume her fortresses.
War cries will be heard on the day of
  battle;
^ba strong gale will blow on the day of
  the windstorm.

¹⁵ Ammon's[1] king will be deported;
  ^ahe and his officials[2] will be carried
    off together."
The LORD has spoken!

² This is what the LORD says:

"Because Moab has committed three
  crimes—
make that four—I will not revoke my
  decree of judgment.
They ^aburned the bones of Edom's
  king into lime.
² So I will set Moab on fire,
  and it will consume ^aKerioth's
    fortresses.
Moab will perish in the heat of battle[1]
  amid war cries and the blaring of the
    ram's horn.
³ I will remove Moab's leader;
  I will kill all Moab's officials with
    him."
^aThe LORD has spoken!

⁴This is what the LORD says:

"Because ^aJudah has committed
  three covenant transgressions—
make that four—^bI will not revoke my
  decree of judgment.
They rejected the LORD's law;
  they did not obey his commands.
Their false gods,
  to ^cwhich their fathers were loyal,
led them astray.
⁵ ^aSo I will set Judah on fire,
  and it will consume Jerusalem's
    fortresses."

God Will Judge Israel

⁶This is what the LORD says:

"Because ^aIsrael has committed three
  covenant transgressions—
make that four—I will not revoke my
  decree of judgment.
^bThey sold the innocent for silver,
  the ^cneedy for a pair of sandals.

1:8 ^bPs 81:14 ^cIsa 14:29–31; Jer 47:1–7; Ezek 25:16; Joel 3:4–8; Zeph 2:4–7; Zech 9:5–7   1:9 ^aIsa 23:1–18; Jer 25:22; Ezek 26:2–4; Joel 3:4–8 ¹Heb. [group of] *exiles*.   1:11 ^aIsa 21:11; Jer 49:8; Ezek 25:12–14; Mal 1:2–5 ^bNum 20:14–21; 2 Chr 28:17; Obad 10–12 ¹Heb. *his anger tore continually*; the word picture is that of a vicious predator's feeding frenzy.   1:12 ^aJer 49:7, 20; Obad 9, 10   1:13 ^aJer 49:1; Ezek 25:2; Zeph 2:8–9   1:14 ^aDeut 3:11; 1 Chr 20:1; Jer 49:2 ^bEzek 21:22; Amos 2:2   1:15 ^aJer 49:3 ¹Heb. *their*. ²Or *princes*.   2:1 ^a2 Kgs 3:26–27   2:2 ^aJer 48:24, 41 ¹Or *the tumult*.   2:3 ^aNum 24:17; Jer 48:7   2:4 ^a2 Kgs 17:19; Hos 12:2; Amos 3:2 ^bIsa 9:15–16; 28:15; Jer 16:19; Hab 2:18 ^cJer 9:14; 16:11–12; Ezek 20:13, 16, 18   2:5 ^aJer 17:27; Hos 8:14   2:6 ^aJudg 2:17–20; 2 Kgs 17:7–18; 18:12; Ezek 22:1–13, 23–29 ^bIsa 29:21 ^cJoel 3:3; Amos 4:1; 5:11; 8:6; Mic 2:2; 3:3

7 They trample on the dirt-covered
   heads of the poor;[1]
 they [a]push the destitute [b]away.
 A man and his father go [c]to the same
   girl;[2]
 in this way they show disrespect for
   my moral purity.
8 They stretch out on clothing seized
   as collateral;
 they do so right [a]beside every altar!
 They drink wine bought with the
   fines they have levied;
 they do so right in the temple of
   their God![1]
9 For Israel's sake I destroyed the
   [a]Amorites.
 They were as [b]tall as cedars
 and as strong as oaks,
 but I [c]destroyed the fruit on their
   branches
 and their roots in the ground.
10 I brought you up from the land of
   Egypt;
 [a]I [b]led you through the wilderness
   for 40 years
 so you could take the Amorites' land
   as your own.
11 I made some of your sons [a]prophets
 and some of your young men
   [b]Nazirites.[1]
 Is this not true, you Israelites?"
 The LORD is speaking.
12 "But you made the Nazirites drink
   wine;
 you [a]commanded the prophets, 'Do
   not prophesy!'
13 [a]Look! I will press you down,
 like a cart loaded down with grain
   presses down.
14 [a]Fast runners will find no place to
   hide;
 strong men will have [b]no strength
   left;
 warriors will not be able to save their
   lives.
15 Archers will not hold their ground;
 fast runners will not save their lives,
 nor will those who ride horses.

16 Bravehearted warriors will run away
   naked in that day."
 The LORD is speaking.

Every Effect Has Its Cause

3 Listen, you Israelites, to this message
that the LORD is proclaiming against
you! This message is for the entire clan I
brought up from the land of Egypt:

2 "I have chosen [a]you alone from all
   [b]the clans of the earth.
 Therefore I will punish you for all
   your sins."
3 Do two walk together without having
   met?
4 Does a lion roar in the woods if he
   has not cornered his prey?
 Does a young lion bellow from
   his den if he has not caught
   something?
5 Does a bird swoop down into a trap
   on the ground if there is no bait?
 Does a trap spring up from the
   ground unless it has surely caught
   something?
6 If an alarm sounds[1] in a city, do
   people not fear?
 [a]If disaster overtakes a city, is the
   LORD not responsible?
7 Certainly [a]the Sovereign LORD
   does nothing without first
   revealing his plan to his
   servants the prophets.
8 A lion has roared! [a]Who is not afraid?
 The Sovereign LORD has spoken.
 Who can refuse to prophesy?

Samaria Will Fall

9 Make this announcement in the
   fortresses of Ashdod
 and in the fortresses in the land of
   Egypt.
 Say this:
 "Gather on the hills around Samaria!
 Observe the many acts of violence
   taking place within the city,
 the oppressive deeds[1] occurring in it."

2:7 [a] Amos 5:12   [b] Lev 18:6–8; Ezek 22:11   [c] Lev 20:3; Ezek 36:20–22   [1] Or perhaps *they trample the heads of the poor into the dust of the ground;* Heb. *those who stomp on the dirt of the ground on the head of the poor.*   [2] Heb. *go to the girl.*
2:8 [a] 1 Cor 8:10   [1] Or *gods.*   2:9 [a] Gen 15:16; Num 21:25; Deut 2:31; Josh 10:12   [b] Ezek 31:3   [c] Isa 5:24; Ezek 17:9; [Mal 4:1]
2:10 [a] Exod 12:51; Amos 3:1; 9:7   [b] Deut 2:7   2:11 [a] Num 12:6   [b] Num 6:2–3; Judg 13:5   [1] Or perhaps *religious devotees.*
2:12 [a] Isa 30:10; Jer 11:21; Amos 7:13, 16; Mic 2:6   2:13 [a] Isa 1:14   2:14 [a] Jer 46:6   [b] Ps 33:16; Jer 9:23   3:2 [a] [Gen 18:19;
Exod 19:5–6; Deut 7:6; Ps 147:19]   [b] Jer 14:10; Ezek 20:36; Dan 9:12; Matt 11:22; [Rom 2:9]   3:6 [a] Isa 45:7   [1] Heb. *If
the ram's horn is blown.*   3:7 [a] Gen 6:13; 18:17; [Jer 23:22]; Dan 9:22; [John 15:15]   3:8 [a] Jer 20:9; [Mic 3:8];
Acts 4:20; 1 Cor 9:16   3:9 [1] Or perhaps *the oppressed.*

10 "They [a]do not know how to do what
   is right," the LORD says.
   "They store up the spoils of
   destructive violence in their
   fortresses.
11 Therefore," says the Sovereign LORD,
   "an enemy will encircle the land.[1]
   He will take away your power;
   your fortresses will be looted."

12 This is what the LORD says:

   "Just as a shepherd salvages from the
   lion's mouth a couple of leg bones
   or a piece of an ear,
   so the Israelites who live in Samaria
   will be salvaged.
   They will be left with just a corner of
   a bed,
   and a part of a couch.
13 Listen and warn the family of Jacob!"
   The Sovereign LORD, the God who
   commands armies, is speaking!

14 "Certainly when I punish Israel for
   their covenant transgressions,
   I will destroy[1] [a]Bethel's altars.
   The horns of the altar will be cut off
   and fall to the ground.
15 I will destroy both [a]the winter and
   summer houses.
   [b]The [c]houses filled with ivory[1] will be
   ruined;
   the great houses will be swept away."
   The LORD is speaking!

4 Listen to this message, you [a]cows of
   Bashan who live on Mount Samaria!
   You oppress the [b]poor;
   you crush the needy.
   You say to your husbands,
   "Bring us more to [c]drink!"
2 The Sovereign LORD confirms this
   oath by his own holy character:
   "Certainly [a]the time is approaching
   when you will be carried away in
   baskets,
   every last one of you[1] in fishermen's
   pots.

3 Each of [a]you will go straight through
   the gaps in the walls;
   you will be thrown out toward
   Harmon."
   The LORD is speaking.

Israel Has an Appointment with God

4 "Go [a]to Bethel and rebel!
   At [b]Gilgal rebel some more!
   [c]Bring [d]your sacrifices in the
   morning,
   your tithes on the third day!
5 Burn a thank [a]offering of bread made
   with yeast!
   Make a public display of your
   voluntary offerings!
   For you love to do this, you Israelites."
   [b]The Sovereign LORD is speaking.

6 "But surely I gave[1] you no food to eat
   in all your cities;
   you lacked food everywhere you
   lived.
   Still you did not come back to me."
   The LORD is speaking.

7 "I withheld rain from you three
   months before the harvest.
   I gave rain to one city, but not to
   another.
   One field would get rain, but the field
   that received no rain dried up.
8 People from two or three cities
   staggered into one city to get
   water,
   but remained thirsty.
   Still you did not come back to me."
   The LORD is speaking.

9 "I destroyed your crops[1] [a]with blight
   and disease.
   Locusts kept devouring your
   orchards, vineyards, fig trees, and
   olive trees.
   Still you did not come back to me."
   [b]The LORD is speaking.

10 "I sent against you [a]a plague like one
   of the Egyptian plagues.

3:10 [a] Ps 14:4; Jer 4:22; Amos 5:7; 6:12   3:11 [1] MT *an enemy and around the land* or possibly *an enemy, and all about the land!*   3:14 [a] 2 Kgs 23:15; Hos 10:5–8, 14, 15; Amos 4:4   [1] Heb. *punish.*   3:15 [a] Jer 36:22   [b] Judg 3:20   [c] 1 Kgs 22:39; Ps 45:8   [1] Heb. *houses of ivory*; these houses were not made of ivory, but had ivory panels and furniture decorated with ivory inlays.   4:1 [a] Ps 22:12; Ezek 39:18   [b] Amos 2:6   [c] Prov 23:20   4:2 [a] Ps 89:35   [1] *Or your children.*   4:3 [a] Ezek 12:5   4:4 [a] Ezek 20:39; Amos 3:14   [b] Hos 4:15   [c] Num 28:3; Amos 5:21–22   [d] Deut 14:28   4:5 [a] Lev 7:13   [b] Lev 22:18; Deut 12:6   4:6 [1] An emphatic Heb. construction.   4:9 [a] Deut 28:22; Hag 2:17   [b] Joel 1:4, 7; Amos 7:1–2   [1] Heb. *you.*   4:10 [a] Exod 9:3, 6; Lev 26:25; Deut 28:27, 60; Ps 78:50

I killed your young men with the
  sword,
along with the horses you had
  captured.
I made the stench from the corpses
  rise up into your nostrils.
Still you did not come back to me."
The LORD is speaking.

11 "I overthrew some of you the way
  God overthrew ªSodom and
  Gomorrah.[1]
You were like a burning stick
  snatched from the flames.
Still you did not come back to me."
The LORD is speaking.

12 "Therefore this is what I will do to
  you, Israel.
Because I will do this to you,
  ªprepare to meet your God, Israel!"

13 For here ªhe is!
He formed the mountains and
  created the wind.
He reveals his plans to men.
He turns the dawn into darkness
and marches on the heights of the
  earth.
The LORD God of Heaven's Armies[1] is
  his name!

Death Is Imminent

5 Listen to this funeral song I am ready to
sing about you, family of Israel:

2 "The virgin Israel has fallen down
  and will not get up again.
She is abandoned on her own land
  with no one to help her get up."

3 The Sovereign LORD says this:

"The city that marches out with a
  thousand soldiers will have only a
  hundred left;
the town that marches out with
  a hundred soldiers will have
  only ten left for the family of
  Israel."

4 The LORD says this to the family of Israel:

"ªSeek me so you can live!
5 Do not seek ªBethel.
Do not visit Gilgal.
Do not journey down to Beer ᵇSheba.
For the people of Gilgal will certainly
  be carried into exile,
and ᶜBethel will become a place
  where disaster abounds."

6 ªSeek the LORD so you can live!
Otherwise he will break out like fire
  against Joseph's family;
the fire will consume,
and no one will be able to quench it
  and save Bethel.
7 The Israelites ªturn justice into
  bitterness;
they throw what is fair and right to
  the ground.

8 But there is one who made the
  constellations ªPleiades ᵇand
  Orion;
he can turn the darkness into
  morning
and daylight into night.
He ᶜsummons ᵈthe water of the seas
and pours it out on the earth's
  surface.
The LORD is his name!
9 He flashes destruction down upon
  the strong
so that destruction overwhelms the
  fortified places.

10 The Israelites hate anyone who
  arbitrates at ªthe city gate;
they ᵇdespise anyone who speaks
  honestly.
11 Therefore, ªbecause ᵇyou make the
  poor pay taxes on their crops
and exact a grain tax from them,
you will not live in the houses you
  built with chiseled stone,
nor will you drink the wine from
  the fine vineyards you
  planted.

4:11 ª Gen 19:24–25; Deut 29:23; Isa 13:19; Jer 49:18; Lam 4:6   [1] Or perhaps *like the great* [or *disastrous*] *overthrow of Sodom and Gomorrah*; Heb. *like God's overthrow of Sodom and Gomorrah.*   4:12 ª Jer 5:22   4:13 ª Isa 47:4; Jer 10:16   [1] Trad. *God of Hosts.*   5:4 ª [Deut 4:29; 2 Chr 15:2; Jer 29:13]   5:5 ª 1 Kgs 12:28–29; Amos 4:4   ᵇ Gen 21:31–33; Amos 8:14   ᶜ Hos 4:15   5:6 ª [Isa 55:3, 6, 7; Amos 5:14]   5:7 ª Amos 6:12   5:8 ª Job 9:9; 38:31   ᵇ Ps 104:20   ᶜ Job 38:34   ᵈ [Amos 4:13]   5:10 ª Isa 29:21; 66:5; Amos 5:15   ᵇ 1 Kgs 22:8; Isa 59:15; Jer 17:16–18   5:11 ª Amos 2:6   ᵇ Deut 28:30, 38, 39; Mic 6:15; Zeph 1:13; Hag 1:6

12 Certainly[1] I am aware [a]of your many
  rebellious acts
  and your numerous sins.
  You [b]torment the innocent, you take
  bribes,
  and you deny justice [c]to the needy at
  the city gate.
13 For this reason whoever is smart
  keeps quiet in such a time,
  for it is an evil time.

14 Seek good and not evil so you can
  live!
  Then the LORD God of Heaven's
  Armies just might be with you,
  [a]as you claim he is.
15 [a]Hate what is wrong, love what is
  right.
  Promote[1] justice at the [b]city gate.
  Maybe the LORD God of Heaven's
  Armies will have mercy on those
  who are left from Joseph.

16Because of Israel's sins this is what the
Lord, the LORD God of Heaven's Armies,
says:

  "In all the squares there will be
  wailing;
  in all the streets they will mourn the
  dead.
  They will tell the field workers to
  lament
  [a]and the professional mourners to
  wail.
17 In all the [a]vineyards there will be
  wailing,
  for I will pass through your midst,"
  says the LORD.

The Lord Demands Justice

18 [a]Woe[1] to those who wish for [b]the day
  of the LORD!
  Why do you want the LORD's day of
  judgment to come?
  It will bring darkness, not light.
19 Disaster will be inescapable,

  [a]as if a man ran from a lion only to
  meet a bear,
  then escaped into a house,
  leaned his hand against the wall,
  and was bitten by a poisonous snake.
20 Don't you realize the LORD's day of
  judgment will bring darkness, not
  light—
  gloomy blackness, not bright light?

21 "I absolutely [a]despise your [b]festivals!
  I get no pleasure from your religious
  assemblies.
22 [a]Even if you offer me burnt and grain
  offerings, I will not be satisfied;
  I will not look with favor on your
  peace offerings of fattened calves.
23 Take away from me your noisy songs;
  I don't want to hear the music of
  your stringed instruments.
24 [a]Justice must flow like torrents of
  water,
  righteous actions like a stream that
  never dries up.

25 You [a]did not bring me sacrifices and
  grain offerings during the 40 years
  you spent in the wilderness, family
  of Israel.
26 You will pick up [a]your images of
  Sikkuth,[1] your king,[2]
  and Kiyyun,[3] your star god, which you
  made for yourselves,
27 and I will drive you into exile
  [a]beyond Damascus," says the LORD.
  He is called the God of Heaven's
  Armies.

The Party Is over for the Rich

6 Woe [a]to those who live in [b]ease in
  Zion,
  to those who feel [c]secure on Mount
  Samaria.
  They think of themselves as the elite
  class of the [d]best nation.
  The family of Israel looks to them for
  leadership.

5:12 [a]Hos 5:3 [b]Isa 1:23; 5:23; Amos 2:6 [c]Isa 29:21 [1]Or *for*.   5:14 [a]Mic 3:11   5:15 [a]Ps 97:10; Rom 12:9 [b]Joel 2:14 [1]Heb. *set up, establish*; in the ancient Near East it was the responsibility of the king to establish justice.   5:16 [a]2 Chr 35:25; Jer 9:17   5:17 [a]Exod 12:12   5:18 [a]Isa 5:19; Jer 17:15; Joel 1:15; 2:1, 11, 31 [b]Isa 5:30; Joel 2:2 [1]The Heb. word was used when mourning the dead. The prophet either engages in role playing and mourns the death of the nation in advance or sarcastically taunts those who hold to this misplaced belief.   5:19 [a]Job 20:24; Isa 24:17–18; Jer 48:44   5:21 [a]Isa 1:11–16; Amos 4:4–5; 8:10 [b]Lev 26:31; Jer 14:12; Hos 5:6   5:22 [a]Isa 66:3; Mic 6:6–7   5:24 [a]Jer 22:3; Ezek 45:9; Hos 6:6; Mic 6:8   5:25 [a]Deut 32:17; Josh 24:14; Neh 9:18–21; Acts 7:42–43   5:26 [a]1 Kgs 11:33 [1]Apparently Sakkuth, a Mesopotamian star god. [2]LXX, Vg. *Moloch*. [3]Apparently the Mesopotamian god Kayamanu, or Saturn.   5:27 [a]2 Kgs 17:6; Amos 7:11, 17; Mic 4:10   6:1 [a]Luke 6:24 [b]Ps 123:4; Isa 32:9–11; Zeph 1:12 [c]Isa 31:1; Jer 49:4 [d]Exod 19:5; Amos 3:2

2 [a]They say to the people:
"Journey over to [b]Calneh and look
    at it;
then go from there to
    [c]Hamath-Rabbah;[1]
then go down to Gath of the
    Philistines.
[d]Are they superior to our two
    kingdoms?
Is their territory larger than yours?"
3 You refuse to believe a day of
    [a]disaster will come,
but you establish a reign of violence.
4 They lie around on beds decorated
    with ivory
and sprawl out on their couches.
They eat lambs from the flock
and calves from the middle of the
    pen.
5 [a]They sing to the tune of stringed
    instruments;
like David they invent [b]musical
    instruments.
6 They [a]drink wine from sacrificial
    bowls
and pour the very best oils on
    themselves.
Yet they are not concerned over the
    ruin of Joseph.
7 Therefore they will now be the [a]first
    to go into exile,
and the religious banquets where
    they sprawl on couches will end.

8 The Sovereign Lord confirms this
    oath by his very own life.
[a]The Lord God of Heaven's Armies is
    speaking:
"I despise Jacob's arrogance;
I hate [b]their fortresses.
I will hand over to their enemies the
    city of Samaria and everything
    in it."

9 If 10 men are left in one house, they
too will die. 10 When their close relatives,
the ones who will burn the corpses, pick
up their bodies to remove the bones from
the house, they will say to anyone who is in
the inner rooms of the house, "Is anyone
else with you?" He will respond, "No one."
Then he will say, "Hush! Don't invoke the
Lord's name!"

11 Indeed, look! [a]The Lord is giving
    [b]the command.[1]
He will smash the large house
    to bits
and the small house into little
    pieces.
12 Can horses run on rocky cliffs?
Can one plow the sea with oxen?[1]
Yet [a]you have turned justice into a
    poisonous plant
and the fruit of righteous actions
    into a bitter plant.
13 You are happy because you
    conquered Lo Debar.
You say, "Did we not conquer
    Karnaim by our own power?"
14 "Look! [a]I am about to bring a nation
    against you, family of Israel,"
the Lord, the God who commands
    armies, is speaking.
"They will oppress you all the way
    from [b]Lebo Hamath to the stream
    of the rift valley."

Symbolic Visions of Judgment

7 The Sovereign Lord showed me this: I
saw him making locusts just as the crops
planted late were beginning to sprout. (The
crops planted late sprout after the royal
harvest.) 2 When they had completely consumed the earth's vegetation, I said,

"Sovereign Lord, forgive Israel!
How can Jacob survive?
He is too weak!"

3 The Lord decided not to do this. "It will
not happen," [a]the Lord said.
4 The Sovereign Lord showed me this:
I saw the Sovereign Lord summoning a
shower of fire.[1] It consumed the great deep
and devoured the fields. 5 I said,

"Sovereign Lord, stop!
How can Jacob survive?
He is too weak!"

6:2 [a]Jer 2:10 [b]Gen 10:10; Isa 10:9 [c]1 Kgs 8:65; 2 Kgs 18:34 [d]Nah 3:8 [1]Or *Great Hamath, Hamath the great*; Heb. *rabbah* means "great." 6:3 [a]Amos 5:18 6:5 [a]Isa 5:12; Amos 5:23 [b]1 Chr 15:16; 16:42 6:6 [a]Amos 2:8; 4:1 6:7 [a]Amos 5:27 6:8 [a]Gen 22:16; Jer 51:14; Amos 4:2; 8:7; Heb 6:13–17 [b]Ps 47:4; Ezek 24:21; Amos 8:7 6:11 [a]Isa 55:11 [b]2 Kgs 25:9; Amos 3:15 [1]Or *is issuing the decree.* 6:12 [a]1 Kgs 21:7–13; Isa 59:13–14; Hos 10:4; Amos 5:7, 11, 12 [1]Heb. *Does one plow with oxen?* 6:14 [a]Jer 5:15 [b]Num 34:7–8; 1 Kgs 8:65; 2 Kgs 14:25 7:3 [a]Deut 32:36; Jer 26:19; Hos 11:8; Amos 5:15; Jonah 3:10; [Jas 5:16] 7:4 [1]Heb. *summoning to contend with fire, summoning fire to contend.*

[6]The LORD decided not to do this. The Sovereign LORD said, "This will not happen either."

[7]He showed me this: I saw the Lord standing by a tin wall holding tin in his hand. [8]The LORD [a]said to me, "What do you see, Amos?" [b]I said, "Tin." The Lord then said,

> "Look, I am about to place tin among
>   my people Israel.
> I will no longer overlook their sin.
> [9] Isaac's centers of worship[1] will
>   become desolate;
> Israel's holy places will be in ruins.
> I will attack Jeroboam's dynasty with
>   [a]the sword."

Amos Confronts a Priest

[10]Amaziah the [a]priest of [b]Bethel sent this message to King [c]Jeroboam of Israel: "Amos is conspiring against you in the very heart of the kingdom of Israel! The land cannot endure all his prophecies. [11]As a matter of fact,[1] Amos is saying this: 'Jeroboam will die by the sword, and Israel will [a]certainly be carried into exile away from its land.'"

[12]Amaziah then said to Amos, "Leave, you visionary![1] Run away to the land of Judah. Earn your living and prophesy there! [13a]Don't prophesy at Bethel any longer, [b]for a royal temple and palace are here."

[14]Amos replied to [a]Amaziah, "I was not a prophet by profession. No, I was a [b]herdsman who also took care of sycamore fig trees. [15]Then the LORD took me from tending flocks and gave me this commission, 'Go! [a]Prophesy to my people Israel.' [16]So now listen to the LORD's message! You say, '[a]Don't prophesy against Israel! Don't preach[1] against the family of Isaac!'

[17]"[a]Therefore this is what the LORD says:

> '[b]Your wife will become a prostitute
>   in the streets,
> and your sons and daughters will die
>   violently.
> Your land will be given to others,

and you will die in a [c]foreign land. Israel will certainly be carried into exile away from its land.'"

More Visions and Messages of Judgment

8 The Sovereign LORD showed me this: I saw a basket of summer fruit. [2]He said, "What do you see, Amos?" I replied, "A basket of summer fruit." [a]Then the LORD [b]said to me, "The end has come for my people Israel! I will no longer overlook their sins. [3]The women singing in [a]the temple[1] will wail in that day."

> [b]The Sovereign LORD is speaking.
> "There will be many corpses littered
>   everywhere! Be quiet!"
> [4] Listen to this, you who trample the
>   needy
> and do away with the destitute in the
>   land.

[5]You say,

> "When will [a]the new moon festival be
>   over, so we can sell grain?
> When will the Sabbath end, so we
>   can open up the grain bins?
> We're eager to sell less for [b]a higher
>   price,[1]
> and to cheat the buyer with [c]rigged
>   scales!
> [6] We're eager to trade [a]silver for the
>   poor,
> a pair of sandals for the needy.
> We want to mix in some chaff with
>   the grain!"

[7]The LORD confirms this oath by [a]the arrogance of Jacob:

> "[b]I swear I will never forget all you
>   have done!
> [8] Because of this the earth will quake,
> and [a]all who live in it will mourn.
> The whole earth will rise [b]like the
>   Nile River;[1]

7:8 [a]2 Kgs 21:13; Isa 28:17; 34:11; Lam 2:8 [b]Mic 7:18   7:9 [a]Gen 46:1; Hos 10:8; Mic 1:5 [1]Trad. *the high places.*   7:10 [a]1 Kgs 12:31–32; 13:33 [b]1 Kgs 13:32; Amos 4:4 [c]2 Kgs 14:23   7:11 [a]Amos 5:27; 6:7 [1]Or *for.*   7:12 [1]Trad. *seer,* a synonym for "prophet," though it may carry a derogatory tone here.   7:13 [a]Amos 2:12; Acts 4:18 [b]1 Kgs 12:29, 32; Amos 7:9   7:14 [a]1 Kgs 20:35; 2 Kgs 2:5; 2 Chr 19:2 [b]2 Kgs 3:4; Amos 1:1; Zech 13:5   7:15 [a]Amos 3:8   7:16 [a]Deut 32:2; Ezek 21:2; Mic 2:6 [1]Lit. *to drip*; it might carry a derogatory tone here.   7:17 [a]Jer 28:12; 29:21, 32 [b]Isa 13:16; Lam 5:11; Hos 4:13; Zech 14:2 [c]2 Kgs 17:6; Ezek 4:13; Hos 9:3   8:2 [a]Ezek 7:2 [b]Amos 7:8   8:3 [a]Amos 5:23 [b]Amos 6:9–10 [1]Or *palace.*   8:5 [a]Exod 31:13–17; Neh 13:15 [b]Mic 6:10–11 [c]Lev 19:35–36; Deut 25:13–15 [1]Heb. *to make small the ephah and to make great the shekel.*   8:6 [a]Amos 2:6   8:7 [a]Deut 33:26, 29; Ps 68:34; Amos 6:8 [b]Ps 10:11; Hos 7:2; 8:13   8:8 [a]Hos 4:3 [b]Jer 46:7–8; Amos 9:5 [1]MT *like the light.*

it will surge upward and then grow
    calm, like the Nile in Egypt.
9 In [a]that day," says the Sovereign
    LORD, "I will make the sun set at
    noon
and make the earth dark in the
    middle of the day.
10 I will turn your festivals into
    funerals[1]
and all your songs into funeral dirges.
I will make everyone wear funeral
    clothes
and cause every head to be shaved
    bald.
I will make you [a]mourn as if you had
    lost your only son;
when it ends it will indeed have been
    [b]a [c]bitter day.
11 Be certain [a]of this, the time is
    coming," says the Sovereign LORD,
"when I will send a famine through
    the land—
not a shortage of food or water
but an end to divine revelation.[1]
12 People will stagger from sea to sea,
and from the north around to the
    east.
They will wander about looking for a
    message from the LORD,
but they will [a]not find any.
13 In that day your beautiful young
    women and your young men will
    faint from thirst.
14 These are the ones who now take
    [a]oaths[1] in [b]the name of the sinful
    idol goddess of Samaria.
They vow, 'As surely as your god
    lives, O Dan,' or, 'As surely as your
    beloved one[2] lives, O Beer [c]Sheba!'
But they will fall down and not get
    up again."

9 I saw the Lord standing by the altar and
he said,

"Strike the tops of the support
    pillars,[1] so the thresholds shake!
[a]Knock [b]them down on the heads of
    all the people,

and I will kill the survivors with the
    sword.
No one will be able to run away;
no one will be able to escape.
2 Even if they could dig down into the
    netherworld,[1]
my hand would pull them up from
    there.
Even if they could climb up to
    heaven,
I would drag them down from there.
3 Even if they were to [a]hide on the top
    of Mount Carmel,
I would hunt them down and take
    them from there.
Even if they tried to hide from me at
    the bottom of the sea,
from there I would command the Sea
    Serpent to bite them.
4 Even when [a]their [b]enemies drive
    them into captivity,
from there I will command the sword
    to kill them.
I will not let them out of my sight;
they will experience disaster, not
    prosperity."
5 The Sovereign LORD of Heaven's
    Armies will do this.
He touches the earth and it
    [a]dissolves;
all who live on it mourn.
The whole earth rises like the Nile
    River
[b]and then grows calm like the Nile in
    Egypt.
6 He builds the upper rooms of his
    palace[1] in heaven
and sets its foundation supports on
    the earth.
He [a]summons [b]the water of the sea
and pours it out on the earth's
    surface.
The LORD is his name.
7 "You Israelites are just like the
    Ethiopians in my sight," says the
    LORD.
"Certainly I brought Israel up from
    the land of Egypt,

8:9 [a]Job 5:14; Isa 13:10; 59:9–10; Jer 15:9; [Mic 3:6]; Matt 27:45; Mark 15:33; Luke 23:44   8:10 [a]Lam 5:15; Ezek 7:18   [b]Isa 15:2–3; Jer 48:37; Ezek 27:31   [c]Jer 6:26; [Zech 12:10]   [1]Heb. *mourning.*   8:11 [a]1 Sam 3:1; 2 Chr 15:3; Ps 74:9; Ezek 7:26; Mic 3:6   [1]Heb. *not a hunger for food or a thirst for water, but for hearing the words of the LORD.*   8:12 [a]Hos 5:6   8:14 [a]Hos 4:15   [b]Deut 9:21   [c]Amos 5:5   [1]Heb. *those who swear.*   [2]MT *As surely as the way* [to] *Beer Sheba lives, As surely as the way lives, O Beer Sheba.*   9:1 [a]Ps 68:21; Hab 3:13   [b]Amos 2:14   [1]Or *the capitals.*   9:2 [1]Heb. *into Sheol*; i.e., the land of the dead, localized in Heb. thought in the earth's core or the grave.   9:3 [a]Jer 23:24   9:4 [a]Lev 26:33   [b]Lev 17:10; Jer 21:10; 39:16; 44:11   9:5 [a]Ps 104:32; 144:5; Isa 64:1; Mic 1:4   [b]Amos 8:8   9:6 [a]Amos 5:8   [b]Amos 4:13; 5:27   [1]MT *his steps.*

but I also brought the [a]Philistines
   from [b]Caphtor and the Arameans
   from [c]Kir.
8 Look, [a]the Sovereign LORD is
   watching the sinful nation,
and [b]I will destroy it from the face of
   the earth.
But I will not completely destroy the
   family of Jacob," says the LORD.
9 "For look, I am giving a command,
and I will shake the family of Israel
   together with all the nations.
It will resemble a sieve being shaken,
when not even a pebble falls to the
   ground.[1]
10 All the sinners among my people will
   die by the sword—
the ones [a]who say, 'Disaster will not
   come near, it will not confront us.'

The Restoration of the Davidic Dynasty

11 "In that day I will rebuild the
   collapsing hut of David.
I will seal its gaps,
   repair its ruins,
and restore it to what it was like in
   days [a]gone by.

12 As [a]a result they will conquer those
   left in [b]Edom[1]
and all the nations subject to my
   rule."
The LORD, who is about to do this, is
   speaking.
13 "Be sure of this, [a]the time is coming,"
   says [b]the LORD,
"when the plowman will catch up to
   the reaper,
and the one who stomps the grapes
   will overtake the planter.
Juice will run down the slopes;
it will flow down all the hillsides.
14 I [a]will bring back my people,
   Israel;
[b]they will rebuild the cities lying in
   rubble and settle down.
They will plant vineyards and drink
   the wine they produce;
they will grow orchards and eat the
   fruit they produce.
15 I will plant them on their [a]land,
and they will never again be
   uprooted from the land I have
   given them,"
says the LORD your God.

9:7 [a] Jer 47:4 [b] Deut 2:23 [c] Amos 1:5   9:8 [a] Jer 44:27; Amos 9:4 [b] Jer 5:10; 30:11; [Joel 2:32]; Amos 3:12; [Obad 16, 17]
9:9 [1] Heb. *like being shaken with a sieve, and a pebble does not fall to the ground.*   9:10 [a] [Isa 28:15]; Jer 5:12; Amos 6:3
9:11 [a] Acts 15:16–18   9:12 [a] Obad 19 [b] Num 24:18; Isa 11:14 [1] Heb. *take possession of the remnant of Edom.*   9:13 [a] Lev 26:5
[b] Joel 3:18   9:14 [a] Ps 53:6; Isa 60:4; Jer 30:3, 18 [b] Isa 61:4   9:15 [a] Isa 60:21; Ezek 34:28; 37:25

OBADIAH

A struggle that began in the womb between twin brothers, Esau and Jacob, eventuates in a struggle between their respective descendants, the Edomites and the Israelites. For the Edomites' stubborn refusal to aid Israel, first during the time of wilderness wandering (Num 20:14–21) and later during a time of invasion, they are roundly condemned by Obadiah. This little-known prophet describes their crimes, tries their case, and pronounces their judgment: total destruction. The Hebrew name *Obadyah* means "Worshiper of Yahweh" or "Servant of Yahweh." The Greek title in the Septuagint is *Obdiou*, and the Latin title in the Vulgate is *Abdias*.

God's Judgment on Edom

1 The vision that Obadiah saw.[1]
The Sovereign LORD says this
[a]concerning Edom:

Edom's Approaching Destruction

[b]We have heard a report from the
LORD.
An envoy was sent among the
nations, saying,
"Arise! Let us make war against
Edom!"
2 The LORD says, "Look! I will make
you a weak nation;
you will be greatly despised!
3 Your [a]presumptuous heart has
deceived [b]you—
you who reside in the safety of the
rocky cliffs,[1]
whose home is high in the
mountains.
You think to yourself,
'No one can bring me down to the
ground!'
4 [a]Even if you were to soar high like an
eagle,
even if you[1] were to [b]make your nest
among the stars,
I can bring you down even from
there!" says the LORD.

5 "If [a]thieves came to rob you during
the night,[1]

they [b]would steal only as much as
they wanted.
If grape pickers came to harvest your
vineyards,
they would leave some behind for
the poor.
But you will be totally destroyed!
6 How the people of Esau[1] will be
thoroughly plundered!
Their hidden valuables will be
ransacked!
7 All your allies will force you from
your homeland![1]
Your treaty partners will deceive you
and overpower you.
Your trusted friends will set an
ambush for you
that will take you by [a]surprise!

8 "At that time," the LORD says,
"[a]I will destroy the wise sages of
Edom,
the advisers from Esau's mountain.
9 Your [a]warriors will be shattered,
O [b]Teman,
so that everyone[1] will be destroyed
from Esau's mountain!

Edom's Treachery against Judah

10 "Because you [a]violently slaughtered
[b]your relatives, the people of Jacob,
shame will cover you, and you will be
destroyed forever.

1 [a]Isa 21:11; Ezek 25:12; Joel 3:19; Mal 1:3   [b]Jer 49:14–16; Obad 1–4   [1]Heb. *the vision of Obadiah.*   3 [a]Isa 16:6; Jer 49:16   [b]Isa 14:13–15; Rev 18:7   [1]Heb. *in the concealed places of the rock.*   4 [a]Job 20:6   [b]Hab 2:9; Mal 1:4   [1]MT *and your nest be set among the stars.*   5 [a]Jer 49:9   [b]Deut 24:21   [1]Heb. *If thieves came to you, or if plunderers of the night,* an emphatic Heb. construction.   6 [1]I.e., the Edomites.   7 [a]Isa 19:11; Jer 49:7   [1]Heb. *to the border.*   8 [a][Job 5:12–14]; Isa 29:14   9 [a]Ps 76:5   [b]Gen 36:11; 1 Chr 1:45; Job 2:11; Jer 49:7   [1]Heb. *a man.*   10 [a]Gen 27:41; Ezek 25:12; Amos 1:11   [b]Ezek 35:9; Joel 3:19

11 You [a]stood aloof while strangers took
  his army[1] captive
and foreigners advanced to his gates.
When they [b]cast lots over Jerusalem,
you behaved as though you were in
  league with them.
12 You should not have [a]gloated when
  your relatives suffered calamity.
You should not have [b]rejoiced over
  the people of Judah when they
  were destroyed.[1]
You should not have boasted when
  they suffered adversity.
13 You should not have entered the
  city of my people when they
  experienced distress.
You should not have joined in
  gloating over their misfortune
  when they suffered distress.
You should not have looted their
  wealth when they endured distress.
14 You should not have stood at the
  fork in the road[1] to slaughter those
  trying to escape.
You should not have captured their
  refugees when they suffered
  adversity.

The Coming Day of the Lord

15 "For the day of the LORD is
  approaching [a]for all the nations!
Just [b]as you have done, so it will be
  done to you.
You will get exactly what your deeds
  deserve.
16 [a]For just as you have drunk on my
  holy mountain,
so all the nations will drink
  continually.
They will drink, and they will gulp
  down;
they will be as though they had never
  been.

17 But on Mount Zion there will be [a]a
  remnant of those who escape,
and it will be a holy place once again.
The descendants of Jacob will
  conquer[1]
those who had conquered them.[2]
18 The [a]descendants of Jacob will be a
  fire
and the descendants of Joseph a
  flame.
The descendants of Esau will be like
  stubble.
They will burn them up and devour
  them.
There will not be a single survivor of
  the descendants of Esau!"
Indeed, the LORD has spoken it.
19 The people of the Negev will take
  possession of Esau's mountain,
[a]and the people of the foothills will
  take
possession of the land of the
  Philistines.
They will also take possession of
  the territory of Ephraim and the
  territory of Samaria,
and the people of Benjamin will take
  possession of Gilead.
20 The exiles of this fortress of the
  people of Israel
will take possession of what
  belongs to
the people of Canaan, as far [a]as
  Zarephath,
and the exiles of Jerusalem who are
  in Sepharad
will take possession of the towns of
  the Negev.
21 Those who have been [a]delivered[1] will
  go up on Mount Zion
in order to rule over Esau's
  mountain.
Then the LORD will reign as [b]King!

11 [a] Ps 83:5–8; Amos 1:6, 9 [b] Joel 3:3; Nah 3:10 [1] Or perhaps, *wealth*; the Heb. word is somewhat ambiguous here.
12 [a] Mic 4:11; 7:10 [b] [Prov 17:5]; Ezek 35:15; 36:5 [1] Heb. *in the day of their destruction.*   14 [1] The meaning of the Heb. word
is uncertain.   15 [a] Ezek 30:3; [Joel 1:15; 2:1, 11, 31; Amos 5:18, 20] [b] Jer 50:29; 51:56; Hab 2:8   16 [a] Joel 3:17   17 [a] Isa 14:1–2;
Joel 2:32; Amos 9:8 [1] Heb. *dispossess.* [2] MT *their possessions.*   18 [a] Isa 5:24; 9:18–19; Zech 12:6   19 [a] Zeph 2:7
20 [1] Kgs 17:9; Luke 4:26   21 [a] [Jas 5:20] [b] Ps 22:28; [Dan 2:44; 7:14; Zech 14:9; Rev 11:15] [1] MT *deliverers.*

JONAH

Nineveh is northeast; Tarshish is west. When God calls Jonah to preach repentance to the wicked Ninevites, the prophet knows that God's mercy may follow. He refuses the assignment and heads for Tarshish instead. But once God has gotten his attention (by tossing him out of the boat and into the water) and has demonstrated his protection (by moving him out of the water and into the fish), Jonah realizes God is serious about his command. Nineveh must hear the word of the Lord, therefore Jonah goes. Because the preaching is a success, the preacher grows angry and discouraged and he must learn firsthand of God's compassion for sinful people. *Yonah* is the Hebrew word for "dove." The Septuagint hellenized this word into *Ionas*, and the Latin Vulgate used the title *Jonas*.

Jonah Tries to Run from the Lord

1 The Lord's message came to [a]Jonah son of Amittai, [2]"Go immediately[1] to [a]Nineveh, that [b]large capital city, and announce judgment against[2] its people because [c]their wickedness has come to my attention."

[3]Instead, Jonah immediately headed off[1] to Tarshish to escape from the commission of the Lord. He traveled to [a]Joppa and found a merchant ship heading to [b]Tarshish. So he paid the fare and went aboard[2] it to go with them to Tarshish, far away [c]from the Lord.

[4]But [a]the Lord hurled a powerful[1] wind on the sea. Such a violent tempest arose on the sea that the ship threatened to break up![2] [5]The sailors were so afraid that each cried out [a]to his own god[1] and they flung the ship's cargo overboard to make the ship lighter.

Jonah, meanwhile, had gone down into the hold below deck,[2] had lain down, and was sound asleep. [6]The ship's captain approached him and said, "What are you doing asleep? Get up! Cry [a]out to your god! [b]Perhaps your god might take notice of us so that we might not die!"

[7]The sailors said to one another, "Come on, let's [a]cast lots to find out whose fault it is that this disaster has overtaken us." So they cast lots, and Jonah was singled out. [8]They said to him, "[a]Tell us, whose fault is it that this disaster has overtaken us?[1] What's your occupation? Where do you come from? What's your country? And who are your people?"

[9]He said to them, "I am a Hebrew, and I worship the Lord,[1] the God of heaven, [a]who made the sea and the dry land." [10]Hearing this, the men became even more afraid and said to him, "What have you done?" (The men said this because they knew that he was trying to escape from the Lord, because he had previously told them.[1]) [11]Because the storm was growing worse and worse, they said to him, "What should we do to you so that the sea will calm down for us?"

[12]He said to them, "[a]Pick me up and throw me into the sea so that the sea will calm

1:1 [a]2 Kgs 14:25; Matt 12:39–41; 16:4; Luke 11:29–30, 32 · 1:2 [a]Isa 37:37 [b]Gen 10:11–12; 2 Kgs 19:36; Jonah 4:11; Nah 1:1; Zeph 2:13 [c]Gen 18:20; Hos 7:2 [1]Heb. *Arise, go*; an emphatic Heb. construction. [2]Heb. *cry out against it*; a technical term referring to what a prophet must say. · 1:3 [a]Josh 19:46; 2 Chr 2:16; Ezra 3:7; Acts 9:36, 43 [b]Isa 23:1 [c]Gen 4:16; Job 1:12; 2:7 [1]Heb. *he arose to flee*; a wordplay on the Lord's command (Heb. "Arise! Go!") in v. 2. But Jonah did not "arise to go" to Nineveh; he "arose to flee" to Tarshish. [2]Heb. *he went down into it.* · 1:4 [a]Ps 107:25 [1]Heb. *great.* [2]Heb. *the ship considered breaking apart*; personifies the ship to emphasize the ferocity of the storm. · 1:5 [a]1 Sam 24:3 [1]Or *gods*; either a pl. of number ("gods") or a pl. of majesty ("god"). They each might have looked to a particular god for help in trouble. [2]Or *of the ship.* · 1:6 [a]Ps 107:28 [b]Joel 2:14 · 1:7 [a]Josh 7:14; 1 Sam 14:41–42; Prov 16:33 · 1:8 [a]Josh 7:19; 1 Sam 14:43 [1]Heb. *On whose account is this calamity upon us?* · 1:9 [a][Neh 9:6]; Ps 146:6; Acts 17:24 [1]Heb. *The Lord, the God of heaven, I fear*; an unusual Heb. construction emphasizing the object of his worship. · 1:10 [1]Heb. *because he had told them.* · 1:12 [a]John 11:50

down for you, because I know it's my fault you are in this severe storm."

[13]Instead, they tried to row back to land, [a]but they were not able to do so because the storm kept growing worse and worse. [14]So they cried out to the LORD, "Oh, please, LORD, [a]don't let us die on account of this man! Don't hold us guilty of shedding innocent blood. After all, you, LORD, [b]have done just as you pleased." [15]So they picked Jonah up [a]and threw him into the sea, and the sea stopped raging. [16]The men [a]feared the LORD greatly and earnestly vowed to offer lavish sacrifices to the LORD.[1]

Jonah Prays

[17]The LORD sent a huge fish to swallow [a]Jonah, and Jonah was in the stomach of the fish three days and three nights.

2 Jonah prayed to the LORD his God from the stomach of the fish [2]and said,

"I called [a]out to the LORD from my
    distress,
  [b]and he answered me;
from the belly of Sheol I cried out for
    help,
and you heard my prayer.
[3] [a]You threw me into the deep waters,[1]
  into the middle of the sea;
the ocean current engulfed me;
  [b]all the mighty waves you sent swept
    over me.
[4] [a]I thought I had been banished from
    your sight
and that I would never again[1] see
    your holy temple.[2]
[5] [a]Water engulfed me up to my neck;
the deep ocean surrounded me;
seaweed[1] was wrapped around my
    head.
[6] I went down to the very bottoms of
    the mountains;
the gates of the netherworld[1] barred
    me in forever,
but you brought [a]me up from the Pit,
  O LORD, my God.

[7] When my life was ebbing away, I
    called out to[1] the LORD.
  [a]And my prayer came to you, to your
    holy temple.
[8] Those who worship [a]worthless idols
    forfeit the mercy that could be
    theirs.
[9] But as for me, I promise to offer
  a [a]sacrifice to you with a public
    declaration of praise;[1]
  I will surely do what I have
    [b]promised.
  [c]Salvation belongs to the [d]LORD!"

[10]Then the LORD commanded the fish and it vomited Jonah out onto dry land.

The People of Nineveh Respond to Jonah's Warning

3 The LORD's message came to Jonah a second time, [2]"Go immediately to Nineveh, that large city, and proclaim to it the message that I tell you." [3]So Jonah went immediately to Nineveh, in keeping with the LORD's message. Now Nineveh was an enormous city[1]—it required three days to walk through it! [4]Jonah began to enter [a]the city by going one day's walk, announcing, "At the end of 40 days, Nineveh will be overthrown!"

[5]The [a]people of Nineveh believed in God, and they declared a fast and put on sackcloth, from the greatest to the least of them. [6]When the news reached the king of Nineveh, he got up from his throne, took off his royal robe, put on sackcloth, [a]and sat on ashes. [7]He issued [a]a proclamation and said, "In Nineveh, by the decree of the king and his nobles: No human or animal, cattle or sheep, is to taste anything; they must not eat and they must not drink water. [8]Every person and animal must put on sackcloth and must cry earnestly to God, and everyone must turn from [a]their evil way of living[1] and from the violence that they do. [9][a]Who knows? Perhaps God might be willing to change his mind and relent and turn from his fierce anger so that we might not die."

1:13 [a] [Prov 21:30]   1:14 [a] Deut 21:8   [b] Ps 115:3; [Dan 4:35]   1:15 [a] [Ps 89:9; 107:29]; Luke 8:24   1:16 [a] Mark 4:41; Acts 5:11   [1]Heb. *The men feared the LORD* [with] *a great fear, they sacrificed sacrifices, and they vowed vows.*   1:17 [a] [Matt 12:40; Luke 11:30]   2:2 [a] 1 Sam 30:6; Ps 120:1; Lam 3:55   [b] Ps 65:2   2:3 [a] Ps 88:6   [b] Ps 42:7   [1]Heb. *the deep.*   2:4 [a] Ps 31:22; Jer 7:15   [1]Tg. *However, I shall look again upon your holy temple*; Thd. *How shall I again look at your holy temple?*   [2]Heb. *Will I ever see your holy temple again?*; this rhetorical question expects a negative response.   2:5 [a] Ps 69:1; Lam 3:54   [1]LXX *end.*   2:6 [a] Job 33:28; [Ps 16:10; Isa 38:17]   [1]Heb. *the earth.*   2:7 [a] 2 Chr 30:27; Ps 18:6   [1]Heb. *remembered.*   2:8 [a] 2 Kgs 17:15; Ps 31:6; Jer 10:8   2:9 [a] Ps 50:14, 23; Jer 33:11; Hos 14:2   [b] Job 22:27; [Eccl 5:4–5]   [c] Ps 3:8; [Isa 45:17]   [d] [Jer 3:23]   [1]A few Tg. MSS *with the sound of hymns of thanksgiving.*   3:3 [1]Heb. *was a great city to God/gods.*   3:4 [a] [Deut 18:22]   3:5 [a] [Matt 12:41; Luke 11:32]   3:6 [a] Job 2:8   3:7 [a] 2 Chr 20:3; Dan 3:29; Joel 2:15   3:8 [a] Isa 59:6   [1]Heb. *evil way.*   3:9 [a] 2 Sam 12:22; Joel 2:14; Amos 5:15

[10]When God saw their actions—that they turned from their evil way of living—God relented concerning [a]the judgment he had threatened them with and did not destroy them.

Jonah Responds to God's Kindness

4 This displeased Jonah terribly and he became very angry. [2]He prayed to the LORD and said, "Oh, LORD, this is just what I thought would happen when I was in my own country.[1] This is what I tried to prevent by attempting to [a]escape to Tarshish, because I knew that you are a [b]gracious and compassionate God, slow to anger and abounding in mercy, and one who relents concerning threatened judgment. [3a]So now, LORD, kill me instead, because [b]I would rather die than live!"[1] [4]The LORD said, "Are you really so very angry?"

[5]Jonah left the city and sat down east of it. He made a shelter for himself there and sat down under it in the shade to see what would happen to the city. [6]The LORD God appointed a little plant and caused it to grow up over Jonah to be a shade over his head to rescue[1] him from his misery. Now Jonah was very delighted[2] about the little plant.

[7]So God sent a worm at dawn the next day, and it attacked the little plant so that it dried up. [8]When the sun began to shine, God sent a hot[1] east wind. So the sun beat down on Jonah's head, and he grew faint. So he despaired of life and said, "[a]I would rather die than live!"

[9]God said to Jonah, "Are you really so very angry about the little plant?" And he said, "I am as angry as I could possibly be!"[1] [10]The LORD said, "You were upset about this little plant, something for which you did not work, nor did you do anything to make it grow. It grew up overnight and died the next day. [11]Should I not be more concerned about Nineveh, this enormous city? There are more than 120,000 people in it [a]who do not know right from wrong, as well as many animals."

3:10 [a]Exod 32:14; Jer 18:8; Amos 7:3, 6   4:2 [a]Jonah 1:3   [b]Exod 34:6; Num 14:18; Ps 86:5, 15; Joel 2:13   [1]Heb. *Is this not my saying while I was in my own country?*; this rhetorical question expects a positive answer.   4:3 [a]1 Kgs 19:4; Job 6:8–9   [b]Jonah 4:8   [1]Heb. *better my death than my life.*   4:6 [1]LXX *to shade.*   [2]Heb. *he rejoiced with great joy*; an emphatic Heb. construction.   4:8 [a]Jonah 4:3   [1]MT *autumnal.*   4:9 [1]Heb. *unto death*; an idiom meaning "to the extreme."   4:11 [a]Deut 1:39; Isa 7:16

MICAH

Micah, called from his rustic home to be a prophet, leaves his familiar surroundings to deliver a stern message of judgment to the princes and people of Jerusalem. Burdened by the abusive treatment of the poor by the rich and influential, the prophet turns his verbal rebukes upon any who use their social or political power for personal gain. One-third of Micah's book exposes the sins of his countrymen, another third pictures the punishment God is about to send, and the final third holds out the hope of restoration once that discipline has ended. Through it all, God's righteous demands upon his people are clear: "to carry out justice, to love faithfulness, and to live obediently before your God" (6:8). The name *Michayahu* ("Who Is Like Yahweh?") is shortened to *Michaia*. In 7:18, Micah hints at his own name with the phrase "Who is a God like you?" The Greek and Latin titles of this book are *Michaias* and *Micha*.

Introduction

1 This is the LORD's message that came to [a]Micah of Moresheth during the time of [b]Jotham, Ahaz, and Hezekiah, kings of Judah, which he saw concerning Samaria and Jerusalem.

The Judge Is Coming

2 Listen, all you nations!
  Pay attention, all inhabitants of earth!
  The Sovereign LORD will act[1] as a
    witness against you;
  the Lord will accuse you from [a]his
    majestic palace.[2]
3 Look, the LORD is coming out of his
    dwelling place!
  He will descend and march on the
    earth's mountaintops!
4 The mountains will crumble beneath
    him,
  and [a]the valleys will split apart
  like wax before a fire,
  like water dumped down a steep
    slope.

5 All this is because of Jacob's rebellion
  and the sins of the nation of Israel.
  And just what is Jacob's rebellion?
  Isn't it Samaria's doings?

And what is Judah's sin?[1]
  Isn't it Jerusalem's doings?

6 "I will turn [a]Samaria into a heap of
    ruins in an open field,
  into a place for planting vineyards.
  I will dump the rubble of her walls[1]
    down into the valley
  and lay [b]bare her foundations.
7 All her carved idols will be smashed
    to pieces;
  all her metal cult [a]statues will be
    destroyed by fire.
  I will make a waste heap of all her
    images.
  Since[1] she gathered the metal as a
    prostitute collects her [b]wages,
  the idols will become a prostitute's
    wages again."
8 For [a]this reason I will mourn and wail;
  I will walk around barefoot and
    without my outer garments.
  I will howl like a wild dog
  and screech like an owl.
9 For Samaria's disease[1] is incurable.
  [a]It has infected Judah;
  it has spread to the leadership[2] of my
    people
  and even to Jerusalem!

1:1 [a] [2 Pet 1:21]; Jer 26:18   [b] 2 Kgs 15:5, 7, 32–38; 2 Chr 27:1–9; Isa 1:1; Hos 1:1   1:2 [a] [Ps 11:4]   [1] MT *may he act.*   [2] Or *his holy temple*; the Lord's dwelling in heaven rather than the temple in Jerusalem.   1:4 [a] Amos 9:5   1:5 [1] MT *What are Judah's high places?*   1:6 [a] 2 Kgs 19:25; Mic 3:12   [b] Ezek 13:14   [1] Heb. *her stones.*   1:7 [a] Hos 2:5   [b] Deut 23:18; Isa 23:17   [1] Or *for.*   1:8 [a] Ps 102:6   1:9 [a] 2 Kgs 18:13; Isa 8:7–8   [1] MT *diseases.*   [2] Heb. *the gate*; kings and civic leaders typically conducted important business at the city gate.

10 Don't [a]spread the news in Gath.
    Don't shed even a single tear.
    In Beth Leaphrah roll about in
        mourning in the dust![1]
11 Residents of Shaphir, pass by in
        nakedness and humiliation!
    The residents of Zaanan have not
        escaped.
    Beth Ezel mourns,
    "He takes from you what he desires."
12 Indeed, the residents of Maroth hope
        for something good to happen,
    though the LORD has sent [a]disaster
        against the city of Jerusalem.
13 Residents of [a]Lachish, hitch the
        horses to the chariots!
    You influenced Daughter Zion to sin,
    for Israel's rebellious deeds can be
        traced [b]back to you!
14 Therefore you will have to [a]say
        farewell[1] to Moresheth Gath.
    The residents of [b]Achzib will be as
        disappointing
    as a dried up well to the kings of
        Israel.
15 Residents of [a]Mareshah, a conqueror
        will attack you;
    the leaders of Israel shall flee to
        [b]Adullam.
16 Shave your heads [a]bald as you mourn
        for the children you [b]love;
    shave your foreheads as bald as an
        eagle,[1]
    for they are [c]taken from you into
        exile.

Land Robbers Will Lose Their Land

2 Beware wicked schemers,
    those who devise calamity as they lie
        in bed.
    As soon as [a]morning dawns they
        carry out their plans,
    because they have the power to
        do so.
2 They confiscate the fields they
        [a]desire
    and seize the houses they want.
    They defraud people of their homes

and deprive people of the land they
    have inherited.

3 Therefore the LORD says this:

"Look, I am devising disaster for this
    [a]nation!
It will be like a yoke from which you
    cannot free your neck.[1]
You will no longer walk proudly,
    for it will be a time of [b]catastrophe.
4 In that day people will sing this
        taunt song to you—
    they will mock you with this [a]lament:
    'We are completely destroyed;
    they sell off the property of my
        people.
    How they remove it from me!
    They assign our fields to the
        conqueror.'"
5 Therefore no one will assign you land
    in the LORD's community.

6 "Don't preach with such impassioned
        rhetoric," they say excitedly.[1]
    "These prophets should not preach
        of such things;
    we will not be overtaken by
        humiliation."
7 Does the family of Jacob say,
    "The LORD's patience can't be
        exhausted—
    he would never do such things"?
    To be sure, my commands bring a
        reward
    for those who obey them,
8 but you rise up as an enemy against
        my people.[1]
    You steal a robe from a friend,[2]
    from those who pass by peacefully as
        if returning from a war.
9 You wrongly evict widows[1] among
        my people from their cherished
        homes.
    You defraud their children of their
        prized inheritance.
10 But you are the ones who will be
        forced to leave![1]

1:10 [a]2 Sam 1:20 [1]Or *wallow*. 1:12 [a]Isa 59:9–11; Jer 14:19; Amos 3:6 1:13 [a]Josh 10:3; 2 Kgs 14:19; 18:14; Isa 36:2 [b]Ezek 23:11 1:14 [a]2 Sam 8:2 [b]Josh 15:44 [1]Heb. *you will give a dowry to*; Lachish is compared to a father who presents wedding gifts to his daughter as she leaves to take up residence with her husband. 1:15 [a]Josh 15:44 [b]2 Chr 11:7 1:16 [a]Job 1:20 [b]Lam 4:5 [c]2 Kgs 17:6; Amos 7:11, 17; [Mic 4:10] [1]Or *a vulture*. 2:1 [a]Hos 7:6–7 2:2 [a]Isa 5:8 2:3 [a]Exod 20:5; Jer 8:3; Amos 3:1–2 [b]Amos 5:13 [1]Heb. *from which you will not remove your neck; It will be like a yoke* is supplied. 2:4 [a]2 Sam 1:17 2:6 [1]Heb. *'Do not foam at the mouth,' they foam at the mouth*; probably refers in a derogatory way to their impassioned style of delivery. 2:8 [1]Heb. *Recently my people rise up as an enemy*. [2]Heb. *From the front of a garment glory* [perhaps *a robe*] *you strip off*. 2:9 [1]Heb. *women*. 2:10 [1]Heb. *Arise and go!*

For this land is not [a]secure;
sin will thoroughly destroy it!
11 If a lying windbag should come and
    say,
'I'll [a]promise you blessings of wine
    and beer,'
he would be just the right preacher
    for these people!

The Lord Will Restore His People

12 "I [a]will certainly gather all of you,
    O Jacob,
[b]I will certainly assemble those
    Israelites who remain.
I will bring them together like sheep
    in a fold,[1]
like a flock in [c]the middle of a
    pasture;[2]
they will be so numerous that they
    will make a lot of noise.
13 The one who can break through
    barriers will lead them out;
they will break out, pass through [a]the
    gate, and leave.
Their king will advance before them;
the LORD himself will lead them."[1]

God Will Judge Judah's Sinful Leaders

3 I said,
"Listen, you leaders of Jacob,
you [a]rulers of the nation of [b]Israel!
You ought to know what is just,
2 yet you hate what is good
and love what is evil.
You flay my people's skin[1]
and rip the flesh from their bones.
3 You [a]devour my people's flesh,
strip off their skin,
and crush their bones.
You chop them up [b]like flesh in a
    pot[1]—
like meat in a kettle.
4 Someday these sinful leaders will cry
    to [a]the LORD for help,
but he will not answer them.
He will hide his face from them at
    that time,
because they have done such wicked
    deeds."

5 This is what the LORD has said [a]about
the prophets who mislead my people,
"If someone gives them enough to
    [b]eat,
they offer an oracle of peace.[1]
But if someone does not give them
    food,
they are ready to declare war on him.
6 [a]Therefore night will fall, and you
    will receive no visions;
it will grow dark, and you will no
    longer be able to read the omens.
[b]The sun will set on these prophets,
and the daylight will turn to
    darkness over their heads.
7 The prophets[1] will be ashamed;
the omen readers will be humiliated.
All of them will cover their mouths,
[a]for they will receive no divine
    oracles."

8 But I am full of the courage that the
    LORD's Spirit gives
and have a strong commitment [a]to
    justice.
This enables me to confront Jacob
    with its rebellion
and Israel with its sin.
9 Listen to this, you leaders of the
    family of Jacob,
you rulers of the nation of Israel!
You hate justice
and pervert all that is right.
10 [a]You build Zion through bloody
    [b]crimes,
Jerusalem through unjust violence.
11 Her leaders take bribes when they
    decide legal cases,
[a]her priests proclaim rulings for
    profit,
and [b]her prophets read omens for
    pay.
[c]Yet they claim to trust the LORD and
    say,
"The LORD is among us.
Disaster will not overtake[1] us!"
12 Therefore, because of you, Zion will
    be plowed [a]up like a field,

2:10 [a] Deut 12:9 **2:11** [a] Isa 30:10; Jer 5:30–31; 2 Tim 4:3–4 **2:12** [a] [Mic 4:6–7] [b] Jer 31:10 [c] Ezek 33:22; 36:37 [1] MT *Bozrah.* [2] MT *its pasture.* **2:13** [a] [Hos 3:5] [1] Heb. *the LORD* [will be] *at their head.* **3:1** [a] Ezek 22:27 [b] Ps 82:1–5; Jer 5:4–5 **3:2** [1] Heb. *their skin from upon them.* **3:3** [a] Ps 14:4; 27:2; Zeph 3:3 [b] Ezek 11:3, 6, 7 [1] MT *and they chop up as in a pot.* **3:4** [a] Ps 18:41; Prov 1:28; Isa 1:15; Jer 11:11 **3:5** [a] Isa 56:10–11; Jer 6:13; Ezek 13:10, 19 [b] Matt 7:15 [1] Heb. *those who bite with their teeth and cry out, 'peace.'* **3:6** [a] Isa 8:20–22; 29:10–12 [b] Isa 29:10; [Jer 23:33–40]; Ezek 13:23 **3:7** [a] Amos 8:11 [1] Or *seers.* **3:8** [a] Isa 58:1 **3:10** [a] Jer 22:13, 17 [b] Ezek 22:27; Hab 2:12 **3:11** [a] Isa 1:23; Mic 7:3 [b] Jer 6:13 [c] Isa 48:2; Jer 7:4 [1] Or *come upon.* **3:12** [a] Jer 26:18

[b]Jerusalem will become a heap of
  ruins,
and [c]the Temple Mount will become
  a hill overgrown with brush!

Better Days Ahead for Jerusalem

4 And in future days the LORD's
  Temple Mount will be the most
  important mountain of all;[1]
[a]it will be more prominent than
  other hills.
People will stream to it.

2 Many nations will come, saying,
"Come on! Let's go up to the LORD's
  mountain,
to the temple of Jacob's God,
so he can teach us his ways
and we can live by his laws."
For instruction will proceed from
  Zion,
the LORD's message from Jerusalem.

3 He will arbitrate between many
  peoples
and settle disputes between many
  distant nations.
They will beat their swords into
[a]plowshares
and their spears into pruning hooks.
Nations will [b]not use weapons against
  other nations,
and they will no longer train for war.

4 [a]Each will sit under his own grapevine
or under his own fig tree without any
  fear.
The LORD of Heaven's Armies has
  decreed it.

5 Though all the nations follow their
  respective gods,
[a]we will follow the LORD our God
  forever.

Restoration Will Follow Crisis

6 "In that day," says the LORD, "[a]I [b]will
  gather the lame
and assemble the outcasts whom I
  injured.
7 I will [a]transform the lame into the
  nucleus of a new nation
and those far off into a mighty nation.

The LORD [b]will reign over them on
  Mount Zion,
from that day forward and
  forevermore.
8 As for you, watchtower for the flock,[1]
fortress of Daughter Zion—
your former dominion will be
  restored,
the sovereignty that belongs to
  Daughter Jerusalem."

9 Jerusalem, why are you now shouting
  so loudly?
Has your king [a]disappeared?
Has your wise leader been destroyed?
Is this why [b]pain grips you as if you
  were a woman in labor?
10 Twist and strain,[1] Daughter Zion, as if
  you were in labor!
For you will leave the city
and live in the open field.
You will go to [a]Babylon,
but there you will be rescued.
There the [b]LORD will [c]deliver you
from the power of your enemies.
11 Many nations have [a]now assembled
  against you.
They say, "Jerusalem must be
  desecrated,
so we can [b]gloat over Zion!"
12 But [a]they do not know what the
  LORD is planning;
they do not understand his strategy.
He has gathered them [b]like stalks
  of grain to be threshed at the
  threshing floor.
13 "Get [a]up and [b]thresh, Daughter [c]Zion!
For I will give you iron horns;
I will give you bronze hooves,
and you will crush many nations."
You will devote to [d]the LORD the
  spoils you take from them
and dedicate their wealth to the
  sovereign Ruler of the whole earth.[1]

5 But now slash yourself, daughter
  surrounded by soldiers!
We are besieged!
With a scepter they [a]strike Israel's
  ruler
on the side of his face.

3:12 [b] Ps 79:1; Jer 9:11   [c] Mic 4:1–2   4:1 [a] Isa 2:2–4; Ezek 17:22; Dan 2:28; 10:14; Hos 3:5   [1] Heb. *will be established as the head of the mountains.*   4:3 [a] Isa 2:4; Joel 3:10   [b] Ps 72:7   4:4 [a] 1 Kgs 4:25; Zech 3:10   4:5 [a] Zech 10:12   4:6 [a] Ezek 34:16 [b] Ps 147:2   4:7 [a] Mic 2:12   [b] [Isa 9:6; 24:23; Luke 1:33; Rev 11:15]   4:8 [1] Heb. *Migdal Eder;* perhaps a place name.   4:9 [a] Jer 8:19   [b] Isa 13:8; Jer 30:6   4:10 [a] 2 Chr 36:20; Amos 5:27   [b] [Isa 45:13; Mic 7:8–12]   [c] Ezra 1:1–3; 2:1; Ps 18:17 [1] Or perhaps *scream.*   4:11 [a] Lam 2:16   [b] Obad 12   4:12 [a] [Isa 55:8–9]   [b] Isa 21:10   4:13 [a] Jer 51:33; [Zech 12:1–8; 14:14]   [b] Isa 41:15   [c] Isa 18:7   [d] Zech 4:14   [1] Heb. *and their wealth to the master of all the earth.* 5:1 [a] 1 Kgs 22:24; Job 16:10; Lam 3:30; Matt 27:30; Mark 15:19

A King Will Come and a Remnant Will Prosper

2 As for you, [a]Bethlehem [b]Ephrathah,
    seemingly insignificant [c]among the
      [d]clans of Judah—
    from you a king will emerge who will
      [e]rule over Israel on my behalf,
    one [f]whose origins are in the distant
      past.
3 So [a]the LORD will hand the people of
      Israel over to their enemies
    until the time when the woman in
      labor gives birth.
    Then the rest of the king's
      countrymen will return
    to be reunited with the people of
      Israel.
4 He will assume his post and
      [a]shepherd the people by the
      LORD's strength,
    by the sovereign authority of the
      LORD his God.
    They will live securely, for at that
      time he will be honored[1]
    even in the distant regions of the
      earth.
5 He will give us peace.
    Should the Assyrians try to invade
      our land
    and attempt to set foot in our
      fortresses,
    we will send against them seven
      shepherd-rulers,
    make that eight commanders.
6 They will rule the land of Assyria
      with the sword,
    the land of [a]Nimrod with a drawn
      sword.[1]
    Our king will [b]rescue us from the
      Assyrians
    should they attempt to invade our
      land
    and try to set foot in our territory.
7 Those survivors from[1] Jacob will live
    in [a]the midst of many nations.
    They will be [b]like the dew the LORD
      sends,
    like the rain on the grass,
    that does not hope for men to come
    or wait around for humans
      to arrive.

8 Those survivors from Jacob will live
      among the nations,
    in the midst of many peoples.
    They will be like a [a]lion among the
      animals of the forest,
    like a young lion among the flocks of
      sheep,
    which attacks when it passes
      through.
    It rips its prey and there is no one to
      stop it.
9 Lift your hand triumphantly against
      your adversaries;
    may all your enemies be destroyed!

The Lord Will Purify His People

10 "In that day," says the LORD,
    "I will destroy your [a]horses from your
      midst
    and smash your [b]chariots.
11 I will destroy the cities of your land
    and tear down all your fortresses.
12 I will remove the sorcery that you
      practice,
    and you will no longer have omen
      [a]readers living among you.
13 I will remove [a]your idols and sacred
      pillars from your midst;
    you will [b]no longer worship what
      your own hands made.
14 I will uproot your images of Asherah[1]
      from your midst
    and destroy your idols.
15 With furious anger I will carry [a]out
      vengeance
    on the nations that do not
      obey me."

The Lord Demands Justice, not Ritual

6 Listen to what the LORD says:

    "Get up! Defend yourself before the
      mountains.
    Present your case before the hills."
2 [a]Hear the LORD's accusation, you
      mountains,
    you enduring foundations of the
      earth.
    For the LORD has a case against his
      people;
    [b]he has a dispute with Israel!

5:2 [a] Isa 11:1; Matt 2:6; Luke 2:4, 11; John 7:42 [b] Gen 35:19; 48:7; Ruth 4:11 [c] 1 Sam 23:23 [d] Exod 18:25 [e] [Gen 49:10; Isa 9:6] [f] Ps 90:2; [John 1:1] 5:3 [a] Mic 4:7; 7:18 5:4 [a] [Isa 40:11; 49:9; Ezek 34:13–15, 23, 24]; Mic 7:14 [1] Heb. be great. 5:6 [a] Gen 10:8–11 [b] Isa 14:25; Luke 1:71 [1] MT in her gates. 5:7 [a] Mic 5:3 [b] Gen 27:28; Deut 32:2; Ps 72:6; Hos 14:5 [1] Heb. the remnant of. 5:8 [a] Gen 49:9; Num 24:9 5:10 [a] Deut 17:16 [b] Isa 2:7; 22:18; Hos 14:3 5:12 [a] Deut 18:10–12; Isa 2:6 5:13 [a] Zech 13:2 [b] Isa 2:8 5:14 [1] Or Asherah poles. 5:15 [a] [2 Thess 1:8] 6:2 [a] Ps 50:1, 4 [b] [Isa 1:18]; Hos 12:2

3 "My people, how [a]have I wronged
   you?
   How have I [b]wearied you?
   Answer me!
4 In [a]fact, I brought you up from the
   land of Egypt;
   I delivered you from that place of
   slavery.
   I sent Moses, Aaron, and Miriam to
   lead you.
5 My people, recall how King [a]Balak of
   Moab planned to harm you,[1]
   how Balaam son of Beor responded
   to him.
   Recall how you journeyed from
   Shittim to Gilgal,
   so you might acknowledge that [b]the
   LORD has treated you fairly."

6 With what should I enter the LORD's
   presence?
   With what should I bow before the
   sovereign God?
   Should I enter his presence with
   burnt offerings,
   with year-old calves?
7 [a]Will the LORD accept a thousand
   rams
   or ten thousand [b]streams of olive oil?
   Should I give him my firstborn child
   as payment for my rebellion,
   my offspring—my own flesh and
   blood—for my sin?[1]
8 He has [a]told you, [b]O man, what is
   good,
   and what the LORD really wants from
   you:
   He wants you to carry out justice, to
   love faithfulness,
   and to live obediently before your
   God.

9 Listen! The LORD is calling to the
   city!
   It is wise to respect your authority,
   O LORD.
   Listen, O nation, and those
   assembled in the city![1]

10 "I will not overlook, O sinful house,
   the dishonest gain you have
   hoarded away
   or the smaller-than-standard
   measure I hate so much.
11 I do not condone [a]the use of rigged
   scales
   or a bag of deceptive weights.
12 The city's wealthy people readily
   resort to [a]violence;
   her inhabitants tell lies;
   [b]their tongues speak deceptive words.
13 I will strike you brutally[1]
   and destroy you because of your sin.
14 You will eat, but not be satisfied.
   Even if [a]you have the strength[1] to
   overtake some prey,
   you will not be able to carry it away;
   if you do happen to carry away
   something,
   I will deliver it over to the sword.
15 You will plant [a]crops, but will not
   harvest them;
   you will squeeze oil from the olives,
   but you will have no oil to rub on
   your bodies;
   you will squeeze juice from the
   grapes, but you will have no wine
   to drink.
16 You [a]follow [b]Omri's edicts
   and all the practices of Ahab's
   dynasty;
   you follow their policies.
   Therefore I will make you an
   appalling sight;[1]
   the city's inhabitants will be taunted
   derisively,
   and nations will [c]mock all of you."[2]

Micah Laments Judah's Sin

7 Woe is me!
   For I am like those gathering fruit
   and those [a]harvesting grapes,
   when there is no grape cluster to eat
   and no fresh figs that [b]my stomach
   craves.
2 Faithful [a]men have disappeared from
   the land;

6:3 [a] Isa 5:4; Jer 2:5, 31   [b] Isa 43:22–23; Mal 1:13   6:4 [a] [Deut 4:20]   6:5 [a] Num 22:5–6; Josh 24:9   [b] Judg 5:11   [1] Heb. remember what Balak . . . planned.   6:7 [a] Ps 50:9; Isa 1:11   [b] Job 29:6   [1] Heb. the fruit of my body for the sin of my soul. 6:8 [a] [Deut 10:12; 1 Sam 15:22]; Hos 6:6; 12:6   [b] Gen 18:19; Isa 1:17   6:9 [1] MT Listen, tribe [or staff], and who appointed it; v. 10 then begins with still or again; LXX who will set the city in order?   6:11 [a] Lev 19:36; Hos 12:7   6:12 [a] Isa 1:23; 5:7; Amos 6:3–4; Mic 2:1–2   [b] Jer 9:2–6, 8; Hos 7:13; Amos 2:4   6:13 [1] Heb. and I, even I, will make you sick, [by] striking you. 6:14 [a] Lev 26:26   [1] Heb. and your filth is inside you.   6:15 [a] Deut 28:38–40; Amos 5:11; Zeph 1:13; Hag 1:6   6:16 [a] 1 Kgs 16:30; 21:25–26; 2 Kgs 21:3; Hos 5:11   [b] 1 Kgs 16:25–26   [c] Isa 25:8   [1] Heb. destruction, ruin.   [2] MT my people. 7:1 [a] Isa 17:6   [b] Isa 28:4; Hos 9:10   7:2 [a] Ps 12:1; Isa 57:1

there are no godly men left.
They all wait in ambush to shed
    blood;[1]
they hunt their own brother with a
    net.
3 They are experts at doing evil;
government officials and judges take
    [a]bribes,
prominent men announce what they
    wish,
and then they plan it out.
4 The best of them is [a]like a thorn;
their godly are like a thornbush.[1]
Woe[2] to your watchmen;
your appointed punishment is on
    the way.
The time of their confusion is now.
5 Do not rely on a friend;
[a]do not trust a companion!
Even with the one who lies [b]in your
    arms,
do not share secrets!
6 For a [a]son thinks his father is a fool,
a daughter challenges[1] her mother,
and a daughter-in-law her
    mother-in-law;
a man's enemies are his own family.
7 But I will keep watching for the
    LORD;
I will [a]wait for the God who
    delivers me.
My God will listen to me.

Jerusalem Will Be Vindicated

8 My enemies, [a]do not gloat over me!
Though I have fallen, I will get up.
Though I sit in darkness, the LORD
    will be my light.
9 I must endure the LORD's fury,
for [a]I have sinned against him.
But then he will defend my [b]
    cause
and accomplish justice on my behalf.
He will lead me out into the light;
I will witness his deliverance.
10 When my enemies see this, they will
    be covered with [a]shame.
They say to me, "[b]Where is the LORD
    your God?"

I will gloat over them;
then they will be trampled down
like mud in the streets.
11 It will be a day for rebuilding your
    [a]walls;
in that day your boundary will be
    extended.

A Closing Prayer

12 In that day people will come to you
from Assyria as far as[1] Egypt,
from Egypt as far as [a]the Euphrates
    River,[2]
from the seacoasts and the
    mountains.
13 The earth will become desolate
because of what its inhabitants have
    done.
14 Shepherd your people with
    your rod,[1]
the flock that belongs to you,
the one that lives alone in a [a]thicket,
in the midst of a pastureland.[2]
Allow them to graze in Bashan and
    Gilead,
as they did in the old days.
15 "As in the days when you departed
    from the land of Egypt,
I will show you miraculous [a]deeds."
16 Nations will see this and be
    disappointed by [a]all their
    strength;
[b]they will put their hands over their
    mouths
and act as if they were deaf.
17 They will lick the [a]dust like a snake,
like serpents crawling on [b]the
    ground.
[c]They will come trembling from
    their strongholds
to the LORD our God;
they will be terrified of you.
18 Who is a God like you?
[a]Who [b]forgives sin
and pardons [c]the rebellion
of those who remain among his
    people?
Who does not stay angry forever,
but delights in showing loyal [d]love?

7:2 [1] Heb. *for bloodshed.*   7:3 [a] Amos 5:12; Mic 3:11   7:4 [a] Isa 55:13; Ezek 2:6   [1] MT *a godly* [person] *from a thorn bush.*
[2] MT *day of your watchmen.*   7:5 [a] Jer 9:4   [b] Deut 28:56   7:6 [a] Matt 10:36; Mark 3:21; Luke 8:19; John 7:5   [1] Heb. *rises up
against.*   7:7 [a] Ps 130:5; Isa 25:9; Lam 3:24–25   7:8 [a] Prov 24:17; Obad 12; [Acts 10:43]   7:9 [a] Lam 3:39–40; [2 Cor 5:21]
[b] Jer 50:34   7:10 [a] Ps 35:26   [b] Ps 42:3   7:11 [a] Isa 54:11; [Amos 9:11]   7:12 [a] [Isa 11:16; 19:23–25]   [1] MT *and the cities* [of Egypt].
[2] Heb. *the River.*   7:14 [a] Isa 37:24   [1] I.e., a shepherd's rod or a scepter.   [2] Or *in the midst of Carmel*; perhaps a place name.
7:15 [a] Exod 34:10   7:16 [a] Isa 26:11   [b] Job 21:5   7:17 [a] Ps 72:9; [Isa 49:23]   [b] Ps 18:45   [c] Jer 33:9   7:18 [a] Exod 15:11
[b] Exod 34:6–7, 9; Isa 43:25; Jer 50:20   [c] Mic 4:7   [d] [Ezek 33:11]

19 Who will once again have mercy
on us?
Who will conquer our evil deeds?
Who will hurl[1] all our[2] sins into the
depths of the sea?

20 You will be loyal to Jacob
and extend [a]your loyal love to
Abraham,
[b]which you promised on oath to our
ancestors in ancient times.

7:19 [1] MT *and you will throw.*   [2] MT *their.*   7:20 [a] Luke 1:72–73 [b] Ps 105:9

NAHUM

From everyone who has been given much, much will be required" (Luke 12:48). Nineveh had been given the privilege of knowing the one true God. Under Jonah's preaching this great Gentile city had repented, and God had graciously stayed his judgment. Yet 100 years later, Nahum proclaims the downfall of this same city. The Assyrians have forgotten their revival and have returned to their habits of violence, idolatry, and arrogance. As a result, Babylon will so destroy the city that no trace of it will remain—a prophecy fulfilled in painful detail. The Hebrew word *nahum* ("comfort," "consolation") is a shortened form of Nehemiah ("Comfort of Yahweh"). The destruction of the capital city of Assyria is a message of comfort and consolation to Judah and all who live in fear of the Assyrians' cruelty. The title of this book in the Greek and Latin Bibles is *Naoum* and *Nahum*.

Introduction

1 This is an oracle about Nineveh; the book of the vision of Nahum the Elkoshite:[1]

God Takes Vengeance against His Enemies

2 The LORD is a [a]zealous and avenging God;
the LORD is avenging and very angry.
The LORD takes vengeance against his foes;
he sustains his rage against his enemies.
3 The LORD is [a]slow to anger but [b]great in power;
[c]the LORD will certainly not allow the wicked to go unpunished.

The Divine Warrior Destroys His Enemies but Protects His People

He marches out in the whirlwind and the raging storm;
dark storm clouds billow like dust under his feet.
4 He shouts a battle cry against [a]the sea and makes it dry up;
he makes all the rivers run dry.
[b]Bashan and Carmel wither;
the blossom of Lebanon withers.

5 The mountains tremble before him;
the hills convulse;
the earth is laid waste before him;
the world and all its inhabitants are laid waste.
6 No one can withstand his indignation!
No one can resist his fierce anger!
His wrath is poured out like volcanic fire,
boulders are broken up as he approaches.[1]
7 The LORD is good—
indeed, [a]he is a fortress[1] in time of distress,
and [b]he protects those who seek refuge in him.
8 But with an overwhelming flood he will make a complete end of Nineveh;[1]
he will drive his enemies into darkness.

Denunciation and Destruction of Nineveh

9 Whatever you plot against the LORD, he will completely destroy![1]
Distress will not arise [a]a second time.

1:1 [1] Or *Nahum of Elkosh.*   1:2 [a] Exod 20:5; Josh 24:19   1:3 [a] Exod 34:6–7; Neh 9:17; Ps 103:8   [b] [Job 9:4]   [c] Ps 18:17   1:4 [a] Josh 3:15–16; Ps 106:9; Isa 50:2; Matt 8:26   [b] Isa 33:9   1:6 [1] Heb. *before him.*   1:7 [a] Ps 25:8; 37:39–40; 100:5; [Jer 33:11]; Lam 3:25   [b] Ps 1:6; John 10:14; 2 Tim 2:19   [1] LXX *to those who trust* [him].   1:8 [1] MT, DSS *her place*; LXX *those who rise up* [against him]; Aquila *adversaries.*   1:9 [a] Ps 2:1; Nah 1:11   [1] Or *The LORD will completely foil whatever you plot against him, Whatever you may think about the LORD, he* [always] *brings everything to a conclusion.*

[10] Surely they will be totally consumed
[a]like entangled thornbushes,[1]
like [b]the drink of drunkards,
like very dry stubble.
[11] From you, O Nineveh, one has
marched forth who plots evil
against the LORD,
a wicked military strategist.

Oracle of Deliverance to Judah

[12]This is what the LORD says:

"Even though they are powerful—
and what is more, even though their
army is numerous[1]—
nevertheless, they will be destroyed[2]
and trickle away![3]
Although I afflicted you,
I will afflict you no more.
[13] And now, I will break Assyria's yoke
bar from your neck;
I will tear apart the shackles that are
on you."

Oracle of Judgment against the King of Nineveh

[14] The LORD has issued a decree against
you:
"Your dynasty will come to an end.
I will destroy the idols and images in
the temples of your gods.
I will desecrate your [a]grave, because
you are [b]accursed!"

Proclamation of the Deliverance of Judah

[15] Look! A herald is [a]running on the
mountains!
A messenger is proclaiming
deliverance:[1]
"Celebrate your sacred festivals,
O Judah!
Fulfill your sacred vows to praise
God!
For never again will the wicked[2]
Assyrians invade you;
they have been completely
destroyed."

Proclamation of the Destruction of Nineveh

2 An enemy who will scatter you,
Nineveh, has advanced against
you!
Guard the rampart!
Watch the road!
Prepare yourselves for battle![1]
Muster your mighty strength!
[2] For the LORD is about to restore the
majesty of Jacob,
as well as the majesty of Israel,
though their enemies have
plundered them
and have destroyed their fields.[1]

Prophetic Vision of the Fall of Nineveh

[3] The shields of his warriors are dyed
red;[1]
the mighty soldiers are dressed in
scarlet garments.
The chariots are in[2] flashing metal
fittings[3]
on the day of battle;
the soldiers brandish their spears.[4]
[4] The chariots race madly through the
streets,
they rush back and forth in the broad
plazas;
they look[1] like lightning bolts,
they dash here and there like flashes
of lightning.
[5] The commander orders[1] his officers;
they stumble as they advance;
they rush to the city wall,[2,3]
and they set up the covered siege
tower.
[6] The sluice gates[1] are opened;
the royal palace is deluged and
dissolves.
[7] Nineveh is taken into exile and is led
away;
her slave girls moan[1] like doves while
they beat their breasts.[2]
[8] Nineveh was like a pool of water
throughout her days,[1]
but now her people[2] are running
away;

1:10 [a]2 Sam 23:6; Mic 7:4   [b]Isa 5:24; 10:17; Mal 4:1   [1]Syr. *your princes are rebels.*   1:12[1]LXX *ruler of many waters;* Syr. *to the rulers of many waters.*   [2]Heb. *they will be sheared.*   [3]MT *and he [?] will pass away.*   1:14[a]Ezek 32:22–23   [b]Nah 3:6
1:15[a]Isa 40:9; 52:7; Rom 10:15   [1]Heb. *a messenger of peace.*   [2]LXX *to old age.*   2:1[1]Heb. *Make strong your loins;* either tucking the ends of the outer garment into the belt to shorten it for fighting in battle, preparing oneself physically for the onslaught of the enemy, or both.   2:2[1]Heb. *their vine-branches.*   2:3[1]LXX *from man.*   [2]Sev. MSS *like.*   [3]LXX, Vg. *reins.*
[4]MT *the cypresses.*   2:4[1]Heb. *Their appearance is like.*   2:5[1]LXX *And their mighty men will be remembered.*   [2]MT *her wall.*   [3]Heb. *to her wall;* referring to Nineveh.   2:6[1]Or *river dam gates.*   2:7[1]LXX *and her maidservants were led away.*   [2]LXX *moaning in their hearts.*   2:8[1]MT *from her days;* LXX *her waters.*   [2]Heb. *they.*

she cries out: "Stop! Stop!"—
but no one turns back.
9 Her conquerors cry out:
"Plunder the silver! Plunder the
[a]gold!"
There is no end to the treasure—
riches of every kind of precious thing.
10 Destruction, devastation, and
desolation!
Hearts faint, knees tremble;
every stomach churns, all their faces
have turned pale!

Taunt against the Once-Mighty Lion

11 Where now is the den of the [a]lions[1]
and the feeding place of the young
lions,
where the lion, lioness, and lion cub
once prowled
and no one disturbed them?
12 The lion tore apart as much prey as
his cubs needed
and strangled prey for his lionesses;
he [a]filled his lairs with prey
and his dens with torn flesh.

Battle Cry of the Divine Warrior

13 "I am [a]against you!" declares the
LORD of Heaven's Armies:[1]
"I will burn your chariots[2] with fire;
the sword will devour your young
lions.
You will no longer prey upon the
land;
the voices of your [b]messengers[3] will
no longer be heard."

Reason for Judgment: Sins of Nineveh

3 Woe to the city guilty of [a]bloodshed!
She is full of lies;
she is filled with plunder;
she has hoarded her spoil!

Portrayal of the Destruction
of Nineveh

2 The chariot drivers will crack their
whips;[1]
the chariot wheels will shake the
ground.

The chariot horses will gallop;
the war chariots will bolt forward!
3 The charioteers will charge ahead;
their swords[1] will flash
and their spears will glimmer!
There will be many people slain;
there will be piles of the dead
and countless casualties[2]—
so many that people will stumble
over the corpses.

Taunt against the Harlot City

4 Because you have acted like a wanton
prostitute—
a seductive mistress who practices
sorcery,[1]
who enslaves[2] nations by her
harlotry,
and entices peoples by her sorcery—
5 "I am [a]against you," declares the
LORD of Heaven's [b]Armies.
"I will strip off your clothes!
I will show your nakedness to the
nations
and your shame to the kingdoms.
6 I will pelt you with filth;[1]
I will [a]treat you with contempt;
I will [b]make you a public spectacle.
7 Everyone who sees you [a]will turn
away from you in disgust;
they will say, '[b]Nineveh has been
devastated!
[c]Who will lament for her?'
There will be no one to comfort
you!"[1]

Nineveh Will Suffer the Same Fate
as Thebes

8 You [a]are no more secure than
[b]Thebes—
she was located on the banks of the
Nile;
the waters surrounded her—
her rampart was the sea,
the water was her wall.
9 Cush and Egypt had limitless
strength;[1]
[a]Put and the Libyans[2] were among
her[3] allies.

2:9 [a] Ezek 7:19; Zeph 1:18 2:11 [a] Job 4:10–11; Ezek 19:2–7 [1] Or *What has become of the den of the lions?* 2:12 [a] Isa 10:6; Jer 51:34 2:13 [a] Jer 21:13; Ezek 5:8; Nah 3:5 [b] 2 Kgs 18:17–25; 19:9–13, 23 [1] Trad. *the LORD of hosts*; an abbreviation of a longer title "Yahweh, the God of Armies." [2] LXX *abundance.* [3] LXX *deeds.* 3:1 [a] Ezek 22:2–3; 24:6–9; Hab 2:12 3:2 [1] Heb. *the sound of a whip.* 3:3 [1] Heb. *a sword.* [2] LXX *to her nations.* 3:4 [1] Heb. *fair of form, a mistress of sorceries.* [2] MT *the one who sells/betrays* [nations]. 3:5 [a] Jer 50:31; Ezek 26:3; Nah 2:13 [b] Isa 47:2–3; Jer 13:26 3:6 [a] Nah 1:14 [b] Heb 10:33 [1] Heb. *detestable things.* 3:7 [a] Rev 18:10 [b] Jonah 3:3; 4:11 [c] Isa 51:19; Jer 15:5 [1] LXX *her.* 3:8 [a] Amos 6:2 [b] Jer 46:25; Ezek 30:14–16 3:9 [a] Gen 10:6; Jer 46:9; Ezek 27:10 [1] Or *Cush was limitless and Egypt was strong.* [2] Heb. *Lubim.* [3] MT, DSS *your.*

[10] Yet she went into captivity as an
exile;
even [a]her infants were smashed to
pieces[1] [b]at the head of every street.
They [c]cast lots for her nobility;[2]
all her dignitaries were bound with
chains.
[11] You too will act like [a]drunkards;
you will go into hiding;
you too will seek refuge from the
enemy.

The Assyrian Defenses Will Fail

[12] All your fortifications will be like [a]fig
trees with first-ripe fruit:
If they are shaken, their figs will fall
into the mouth of the eater.
[13] Your warriors will be like women in
[a]your midst;
the gates of your land will be wide
open to your enemies;
fire will consume the bars [b]of your
gates.
[14] Draw yourselves water for a siege!
[a]Strengthen your fortifications!
Trample the mud[1] and tread the clay!
Make mud bricks to strengthen your
walls!
[15] There the fire will consume you;
the sword will cut you down;
it will devour you like the young
[a]locust would.

The Assyrian Defenders Will Flee

Multiply yourself like the young
locust;
multiply yourself like the flying
locust!
[16] Increase your [a]merchants more than
the stars of heaven!
They are like the young locust that
sheds its skin and flies away.
[17] Your courtiers are like locusts,
[a]your officials are like a swarm of
locusts!
They encamp in the walls on a cold
day,
yet when the sun rises, they fly
away,
and no one knows where they are.[1]

Concluding Dirge

[18] Your shepherds are sleeping, [a]O [b]king
of Assyria.
Your officers are slumbering!
Your people are [c]scattered like sheep
on the mountains,
and there is no one to regather them.
[19] Your destruction is like an incurable
wound;
[a]your demise is like a fatal injury.
[b]All who hear what has happened to
you will clap their hands for joy,
for no one ever escaped your endless
cruelty!

3:10 [a] Ps 137:9; Isa 13:16; Hos 13:16 [b] Lam 2:19 [c] Joel 3:3; Obad 11 [1] LXX *they will be smashed to pieces.* [2] LXX *for all her nobles.* 3:11 [a] Isa 49:26; Jer 25:27; Nah 1:10 3:12 [a] Rev 6:12–13 3:13 [a] Isa 19:16; Jer 50:37; 51:30 [b] Ps 147:13; Jer 51:30 3:14 [a] Nah 2:1 [1] Heb. *go into the mud.* 3:15 [a] Joel 1:4 3:16 [a] Rev 18:3, 11–19 3:17 [a] Rev 9:7 [1] LXX *Woe to them!* 3:18 [a] Exod 15:16; Ps 76:5–6; Isa 56:10; Jer 51:57 [b] Jer 50:18; Ezek 31:3 [c] 1 Kgs 22:17; Isa 13:14 3:19 [a] Jer 46:11; Mic 1:9 [b] Job 27:23; Lam 2:15; Zeph 2:15

HABAKKUK

Habakkuk ministers during the death throes of the nation of Judah. Although repeatedly called to repentance, the nation stubbornly refuses to change its sinful ways. Habakkuk, knowing the hardheartedness of his people, asks God how long this intolerable condition can continue. God replies that the Babylonians will be his chastening rod upon the nation—an announcement that sends the prophet to his knees. He acknowledges that the just in any generation shall live by faith (2:4), not by sight. Habakkuk concludes by praising God's wisdom even though he does not fully understand God's ways. *Habaqquq* is an unusual Hebrew name derived from the verb *habaq*, "embrace." Thus his name probably means "One Who Embraces" or "Clings." At the end of his book, this name becomes appropriate because Habakkuk chooses to cling firmly to God regardless of what happens to his nation (3:16–19). The Greek title in the Septuagint is *Ambakouk*, and the Latin title in Jerome's Vulgate is *Habacuc*.

Habakkuk Complains to the Lord

1 This is the oracle that the prophet Habakkuk saw:

2 How long, LORD, must I cry for help?
But you do not listen!
I call out to you, "[a]Violence!"
But you do [b]not deliver!

3 Why do you force me to witness
injustice?
Why do you put up with wrongdoing?
Destruction and violence
confront me;
conflict is present and one must
endure strife.

4 For this reason the law lacks power,[1]
and justice is never carried out.
Indeed,[2] the [a]wicked intimidate the
innocent.
For this reason justice is perverted.

The Lord's Surprising Answer

5 "[a]Look at the nations and pay
attention!
You will be shocked and amazed!
For I will do something in your
lifetime[1]
that you will not believe even though
you are forewarned.

6 Look, I am about to [a]empower the
Babylonians,
that ruthless and greedy[1] [b]nation.
They sweep across the surface of the
earth,
seizing dwelling places that do not
belong to them.

7 They are frightening and terrifying;
they decide for themselves what is
right.

8 Their horses are [a]faster than
leopards
and more alert than wolves in the
desert.
Their horses gallop,
their horses come a great distance;
like [b]vultures[1] they swoop down
quickly to devour their prey.

9 All of them intend to do violence;
every face is determined.
They take prisoners as easily as one
scoops up sand.

10 They mock kings
and laugh at rulers.
They laugh at every fortified city;

1:2 [a] Mic 2:1–2; 3:1–3 [b] [Job 21:5–16]   1:4 [a] Jer 12:1 [1] Heb. *the law is numb*; like a hand that has "fallen asleep." [2] Or *for*.
1:5 [a] Isa 29:14; Ezek 12:22–28 [1] Heb. *for a work working in your days*.   1:6 [a] Deut 28:49–50; 2 Kgs 24:2; 2 Chr 36:17;
Jer 4:11–13; Mic 4:10 [b] Ezek 7:24; 21:31 [1] Or perhaps *impetuous, rash*; Heb. *hasty, quick*.   1:8 [a] Jer 4:13
[b] Job 9:26; 39:29–30; Lam 4:19; Ezek 17:3; Hos 8:1; Matt 24:28; Luke 17:37 [1] Or *eagle*.

they build siege ramps and capture
them.
[11] They sweep by like the wind and
pass on.
But the one who considers himself [a]a
god will be held guilty."

Habakkuk Voices Some Concerns

[12] LORD, you have been active [a]from
ancient times;
my sovereign God,[1] [b]you are
immortal.[2]
LORD, you have made them your
instrument of judgment.
Protector, you have appointed
them as your instrument of
[c]punishment.
[13] You are too just to tolerate evil;
you are unable to condone
wrongdoing.
So why do you put up with such
treacherous people?
Why do you say nothing when
the wicked devour[1] those more
righteous than they are?
[14] You made people like fish in the sea,
like animals in the sea that have no
ruler.
[15] The Babylonian tyrant pulls them all
up with a fishhook;
he hauls them in with his throw net.
When he catches them in his
dragnet,
he is very happy.
[16] Because of his success [a]he offers
sacrifices to his throw net
and burns incense to his dragnet;
for because of them he has plenty of
food
and more than enough to eat.
[17] Will he then[1] continue to fill and
empty his throw net?
Will he always destroy nations and
spare none?

2 I will [a]stand at my watch post;
I will remain stationed on the city
wall.
I will keep watching so I can see what
he says to me

and can know how I should answer
when he counters my argument.

The Lord Assures Habakkuk

[2] The LORD responded:

"Write [a]down this message.[1]
Record it legibly on tablets
so the one who announces it may
read it easily.
[3] For [a]the message is a witness to what
is decreed;
it gives reliable testimony about how
matters will turn out.
Even if the message is not fulfilled
right away, wait [b]patiently;
for it will [c]certainly come to pass—it
[d]will not arrive late.
[4] Look, the one whose desires are not
upright will faint from exhaustion,
but the person of [a]integrity will live[1]
because of his faithfulness.
[5] Indeed, wine will betray the proud,
restless man!
His appetite is as [a]big as Sheol's;
like death, he is never satisfied.
He gathers all the nations;
he seizes all peoples.

The Proud Babylonians Are as Good as Dead

[6] "But all these nations will someday
taunt him
and ridicule him with proverbial
sayings:
'Woe to the one who accumulates[1]
what does not belong to him
(how long will this go on?)—
he who gets rich by extortion!'
[7] Your creditors will suddenly attack;
those who terrify you will spring into
action,
and they will rob you.[1]
[8] [a]Because you robbed many countries,
all who are left among the nations
will rob you.
You have shed human blood
and committed violent acts against
lands, cities, and those who live in
them.

1:11 [a]Dan 5:4   1:12 [a]Deut 33:27; Ps 90:2; 93:2; Mal 3:6   [b]Isa 10:5-7; Mal 3:5   [c]Jer 25:9   [1]Heb. *My God, my holy one.*   [2]MT *we will not die.*   1:13 [1]Or *swallow up.*   1:16 [a]Deut 8:17   1:17 [1]Or *therefore.*   2:1 [a]Isa 21:8, 11   2:2 [a]Isa 8:1   [1]Heb. [the] *vision.*   2:3 [a]Dan 8:17, 19; 10:14   [b][Heb 10:37-38]   [c]Ps 27:13-14; [Jas 5:7-8; 2 Pet 3:9]   [d]Ezek 12:24-25   2:4 [a][John 3:36]; Rom 1:17; Heb 10:38   [1]Or *will be preserved*; probably referring to physical preservation through both the present oppression and the coming judgment.   2:5 [a]Prov 27:20; 30:16; Isa 5:11-15   2:6 [1]Or *increases.*   2:7 [1]Heb. *and you will become their plunder.*   2:8 [a]Isa 33:1; Jer 27:7; Ezek 39:10; Zech 2:8

9 "The one who builds his house by
  unjust gain is as good as dead.
He does this so he can [a]build his nest
  way up high
and escape the clutches of disaster.
10 Your schemes will bring shame to
  your house.
Because you destroyed many nations,
  you will self-destruct.
11 For the stones in the walls will cry out,
and the wooden rafters will answer
  back.

12 "Woe to the one who builds a city by
  bloodshed—
he who starts a town by unjust deeds.
13 Be sure of this! The LORD of Heaven's
  Armies has decreed:
The nations' efforts will go up in
  smoke;
their exhausting work will be for
  nothing.
14 For recognition of the LORD's
  sovereign majesty will fill the earth
just as the waters fill up the sea.

15 "Woe to you who force your neighbor
  to drink wine—
you who make others intoxicated
by forcing them to drink from the
  bowl of your furious anger[1]
so you can look at their naked bodies.
16 But you will become drunk[1] with
  shame, not majesty.
Now it is your turn to drink and
  expose your uncircumcised
  foreskin![2]
The cup of wine in the LORD's right
  hand is coming to you,
and disgrace will replace your
  majestic glory!
17 For you will pay in full for your
  violent acts against Lebanon;
terrifying judgment will come upon
  you
because of the way you destroyed the
  wild animals living there.[1]
You have shed human blood
and committed violent acts against
  lands, cities, and those who live in
  them.

18 What good is an idol? Why would a
  craftsman make it?
What good is a metal image that
  gives misleading oracles?
Why would its creator place his trust
  in it
and make such mute, worthless
  things?
19 Woe to the one who says to wood,
  'Wake up!'—
he who says to speechless stone,
  'Awake!'
Can it give reliable guidance?[1]
It is overlaid with gold and silver;
  it has no life's breath inside it.
20 But the LORD is in his majestic palace.
  The whole earth is speechless in his
  presence!"

Habakkuk's Vision of the Divine Warrior

3 This is a prayer of Habakkuk the
  prophet:

2 LORD, I have heard the report of
  what you did;
I am awed, LORD, by what you
  accomplished.
In our time repeat those deeds;[1]
in our time reveal them again.
But when you cause turmoil,
  remember to show us mercy!
3 God comes from Teman,
the Holy One from Mount Paran.
  Selah[1]
His splendor has covered the skies,
  the earth is full of his glory.
4 His brightness will be as lightning;
a two-pronged lightning bolt flashing
  from his hand.
This is the outward display of his
  power.
5 Plague will go before him;
pestilence will march right behind
  him.
6 He took his battle position [a]and
  shook[1] the earth;
with a mere look he frightened the
  nations.
The ancient mountains
  disintegrated;

2:9 [a] Jer 49:16; Obad 4   2:15 [1] Heb. *pouring out your anger and also making drunk, pouring out your anger and* [by] *rage
making drunk.*   2:16 [1] Heb. *are filled.*   [2] DSS *stumble.*   2:17 [1] MT *and the violence against the animals* [which] *he terrified.*
2:19 [1] This statement should be taken as a rhetorical question anticipating a negative answer.   3:2 [1] Heb. *revive it*; i.e.,
"your work."   3:3 [1] The meaning of this musical term is unknown.   3:6 [a] Nah 1:5   [1] Trad. *measure.*

the primeval hills were flattened.
His are ancient roads.
7 I saw the tents of Cushan
overwhelmed by trouble;
the tent curtains of the land of
Midian were shaking.
8 Was the LORD mad at the rivers?
Were you angry with the rivers?
Were you enraged at the sea?
Such that you would climb into your
horse-drawn chariots,[1]
your victorious chariots?
9 Your bow is ready for action;
you commission your arrows.   *Selah*
You cause flash floods on the earth's
surface.
10 When the mountains see you, they
shake.
The torrential downpour sweeps
through.
The great deep shouts out;
it [a]lifts its hands high.
11 The [a]sun and moon stand still in
their courses;
the flash of your arrows drives them
away,[1]
the bright light of your
lightning-quick spear.
12 You furiously stomp on the earth;
you angrily trample down the
nations.
13 You march out to deliver your
people,
to deliver your special servant.
You strike the leader of the wicked
nation,
laying him open from the lower
body to the neck.   *Selah*

14 You pierce the heads of his warriors
with a spear.[1]
They storm forward to scatter us;
they shout with joy as if they were
plundering the poor with no
opposition.
15 But [a]you trample on the sea with
your horses,
on the surging, raging waters.[1]

Habakkuk Declares His Confidence

16 I listened and [a]my stomach churned;
the sound made my lips quiver.
My frame went limp, as if my bones
were decaying,
and I shook as I tried to walk.[1]
I long for the day of distress
to come upon the people who
attack us.
17 When the fig tree does not bud,
and there are no grapes on the
vines;
when the olive trees do not produce
and the fields yield no crops;
when the sheep disappear[1] from the
pen
and there are no cattle in the stalls—
18 I will [a]rejoice because of the LORD;
I will be happy because of the God
who delivers me!
19 The Sovereign LORD is my source of
strength.
He gives me the agility of a [a]deer;
he enables me to [b]negotiate the
rugged terrain.

(This prayer is for the song leader. It is to
be accompanied by stringed instruments.)

3:8 [1] Heb. *you mount your horses.*   **3:10** [a] Exod 14:22   **3:11** [a] Josh 10:12–14   [1] Or *at the light of your arrows they vanish.*
3:14 [1] Heb. *his shafts.*   **3:15** [a] Ps 77:19; Hab 3:8   [1] Heb. *the foaming of the mighty* [or *many*] *waters.*   **3:16** [a] Ps 119:120
[1] Heb. *beneath me I shook, which.*   **3:17** [1] Or *are cut off.*   **3:18** [a] Isa 41:16; 61:10   **3:19** [a] 2 Sam 22:34; Ps 18:33
[b] Deut 32:13; 33:29

ZEPHANIAH

During Judah's hectic political and religious history, reform comes from time to time. Zephaniah's forceful prophecy may be a factor in the reform that occurs during Josiah's reign—a revival that produces outward change but does not fully remove the inward heart of corruption that characterizes the nation. Zephaniah hammers home his message repeatedly that the day of the Lord, Judgment Day, is coming, and God will deal with the malignancy of sin. Israel and her Gentile neighbors will soon experience the crushing hand of God's wrath. But after the chastening process is complete, blessing will come in the person of the Messiah, who will be the cause for praise and singing. *Tsephan-yah* means "Yahweh Hides" or "Yahweh Has Hidden." Zephaniah was evidently born during the latter part of the reign of King Manasseh; his name may mean that he was "hidden" from Manasseh's atrocities. The Greek and Latin title is *Sophonias*.

Introduction

1 This is the LORD's message that came to Zephaniah son of Cushi, son of Gedaliah, son of Amariah, son of Hezekiah during the time of [a]Josiah son of Amon, king of Judah:

The Lord's Day of Judgment Is Approaching

2 "I will destroy everything from the
  face of the earth," says the LORD.
3 "I [a]will destroy people and animals;
  I will destroy the birds in the sky
  and the fish in the sea.
  (The idolatrous images of these
    creatures will be destroyed along
    with evil people.)
  I will remove humanity from the face
    of the earth," says the LORD.
4 "I will attack Judah
  and all who live in Jerusalem.
  [a]I will remove from this place every
    trace of Baal worship,[1]
  as well as the very memory of the
    pagan priests.[2]
5 I will remove those [a]who worship the
    stars in the sky from their rooftops,
  those who swear allegiance to the
    LORD[1] while taking oaths in the
    name of their 'king,'

6 and [a]those who turn their backs on
    the LORD
  and do not want the LORD's help or
    guidance."
7 Be silent [a]before the Sovereign LORD,
  [b]for [c]the LORD's day of judgment[1] is
    almost here.
  The LORD has prepared a sacrificial
    meal;
  he has ritually purified his guests.
8 "On [a]the day of the LORD's sacrificial
    meal,
  I will punish the princes and the
    king's sons,
  and all who wear foreign styles of
    clothing.
9 On that day I will punish all who
    [a]leap over the threshold,
  who fill the house of their master
    with wealth taken by violence and
    deceit.[1]
10 On that day," says [a]the LORD,
  "a loud cry will go up from the Fish
    Gate,
  wailing from the city's newer district,
  and a loud crash from the hills.
11 [a]Wail, you who live in the market
    district,
  for all the merchants[1] will disappear

1:1 [a]2 Kgs 22:1–2; 2 Chr 34:1–33; Jer 1:2; 22:11   1:3 [a]Hos 4:3   1:4 [a]2 Kgs 23:5; Hos 10:5   [1]Heb. *the remnant of Baal*.   [2]Heb. *of the pagan priests with the priests*.   1:5 [a]2 Kgs 23:12; Jer 19:13   [1]MT *those who worship, those who swear allegiance to the LORD*.   1:6 [a]Isa 1:4; Jer 2:13   1:7 [a]Hab 2:20; Zech 2:13   [b]Isa 13:6   [c]Deut 28:26; Isa 34:6; Jer 46:10; Ezek 39:17–19   [1]Heb. *the day of the LORD*.   1:8 [a]Jer 39:6   1:9 [a]1 Sam 5:5   [1]Heb. *who fill . . . with violence and deceit*.   1:10 [a]2 Chr 33:14; Neh 3:3; 12:39   1:11 [a]Jas 5:1   [1]Or perhaps *Canaanites*.

and those who count money will be removed.

12 At that time I will search through Jerusalem with lamps.
I will punish the people who are
[a]entrenched in their sin,
those [b]who think to themselves,
'The LORD neither rewards nor punishes.'

13 Their wealth will be stolen
and their houses ruined!
They will [a]not live in the houses they have built,
nor will they drink the wine from the vineyards they have planted.

14 The LORD's great day of judgment is almost here;
it is approaching very rapidly!
[a]There will be a bitter sound on the LORD's day of judgment;
at that time warriors will cry out in battle.

15 That day will be [a]a day of God's anger,
a day of distress and hardship,
a day of devastation and ruin,
a day of darkness and gloom,
a day of clouds and dark skies,

16 a day of [a]trumpet blasts and battle cries.
Judgment will fall on the fortified cities and the high corner towers.

17 I will bring distress on the people
and they will [a]stumble like blind men,
for they have sinned against the LORD.
Their blood will be poured out like dirt;
their flesh will be scattered like manure.

18 [a]Neither their silver nor their gold will be able to deliver them
in the day of the LORD's angry judgment.
The whole earth will be consumed by his fiery wrath.
Indeed,[1] he will bring terrifying destruction on all who live on the earth."

The Prophet Warns the People

2 Bunch yourselves together like straw, you undesirable nation,

2 before God's decree becomes reality
and the day of opportunity
disappears like windblown chaff,
before the LORD's raging anger overtakes you—
before the day of the LORD's angry judgment overtakes you!

3 [a]Seek the LORD's [b]favor, all you humble people of the land who have obeyed his commands![1]
Strive to do what is right! Strive to be humble!
Maybe you will be protected on the day of the LORD's angry judgment.

Judgment on Surrounding Nations

4 Indeed,[1] [a]Gaza will be deserted
and Ashkelon will become [b]a heap of ruins.
Invaders will drive away the people of Ashdod by noon,
and Ekron will be overthrown.

5 Beware, you who live by [a]the sea, the people who came from Crete.[1]
The LORD's message is against you, [b]Canaan, land of the Philistines:
"I will destroy everyone who lives there!"

6 The seacoast will be used as pasture [a]lands by the shepherds
and as pens for their flocks.

7 Those who are left from [a]the kingdom of Judah will take possession of it.
By the sea[1] they will graze,
in the houses of Ashkelon they will lie down in the evening,
for the LORD their God will intervene [b]for them and [c]restore their prosperity.

8 "I have heard Moab's taunts
and the [a]Ammonites' insults.
[b]They taunted my people
and verbally harassed those living in Judah.

1:12 [a] Jer 48:11; Amos 6:1 [b] Ps 94:7   1:13 [a] Deut 28:39   1:14 [a] Jer 30:7; Joel 2:1, 11   1:15 [a] Isa 22:5   1:16 [a] Isa 27:13; Jer 4:19
1:17 [a] Deut 28:29   1:18 [a] Ezek 7:19 [1] Or *for.*   2:3 [a] Ps 105:4; Amos 5:6 [b] Ps 76:9 [1] Or perhaps *who have promoted the justice God demands.*   2:4 [a] Jer 47:1, 5; Amos 1:7–8; Zech 9:5 [b] Jer 6:4 [1] Or *for.*   2:5 [a] Ezek 25:15–17 [b] Josh 13:3
[1] Heb. *Kerethites*; a people who originally came from Crete and settled alongside the Philistines in the coastal areas of Canaan.   2:6 [a] Isa 17:2   2:7 [a] [Mic 5:7–8] [b] Luke 1:68 [c] Jer 29:14 [1] Heb. *on them.*
2:8 [a] Jer 48:27; Amos 2:1–3 [b] Ezek 25:3; Amos 1:13

9 Therefore, as surely as I live," says the
  LORD of Heaven's Armies, the God
  of Israel,
  "be certain that ᵃMoab will become
    like Sodom
  and ᵇthe Ammonites like Gomorrah.
  They will be ᶜoverrun by weeds,
  filled with salt pits,
  and permanently desolate.
  Those of my people who are left will
    plunder their belongings;
  those who are left in Judah will take
    possession of their land."
10 This is how they will be repaid ᵃfor
    their arrogance,
  for they taunted and verbally
    harassed the people of the LORD of
    Heaven's Armies.
11 The LORD will terrify ᵃthem,
  for¹ he will weaken all the gods of the
    earth.
  All the distant nations will worship
    the LORD in their own lands.
12 "You Ethiopians¹ will also die by ᵃmy
    sword!"
13 The LORD will attack the north
  and ᵃdestroy Assyria.
  He will make Nineveh a heap of
    ruins;
  it will be as barren as the desert.
14 Flocks and herds will lie down in the
    middle of it,
  as well as ᵃevery kind of wild animal.
  ᵇOwls will sleep in the tops of its
    support pillars;
  they will hoot through the windows.
  Rubble will cover the thresholds;
  even the ᶜcedar work¹ will be exposed
    to the elements.
15 This is how the once-proud city will
    end up—
  the city ᵃthat was so secure.
  She thought to herself, "I am
    unique! No one can compare
    to me!"
  What ᵇa heap of ruins she has
    become, ᶜa place where wild
    animals live!
  Everyone who passes by her taunts
    her¹ and ᵈshakes his fist.

Jerusalem Is Corrupt

3 Beware to the filthy, stained city;
  the city filled with oppressors!
2 She is disobedient;
  she has refused correction.
  She does not trust the LORD;
  she has not sought the advice of her
    God.
3 Her princes¹ are as fierce as roaring
    lions;
  ᵃher rulers are as hungry as wolves
    ᵇin the desert,
  who completely devour their prey by
    morning.
4 Her ᵃprophets are proud;
  they are deceitful men.
  Her priests have defiled what is holy;
  they have ᵇbroken God's laws.
5 The just LORD resides within her;
  ᵃhe commits no unjust acts.
  Every morning he reveals his
    justice.
  At dawn he appears without fail.
  Yet the unjust know no shame.

The Lord's Judgment Will Purify

6 "I destroyed nations;
  their walled cities are in ruins.
  I turned their streets into ruins;
  no one passes through them.
  Their cities are desolate;
  no one lives there.
7 I thought, 'ᵃCertainly you will
    respect me!
  Now you will accept correction!'
  If she had done so, her home would
    not be destroyed
  by all the punishments I have
    threatened.
  But they eagerly ᵇsinned
  in everything they did.¹
8 Therefore you must wait ᵃpatiently
    for me," says the LORD,
  "for the day when I attack and take
    plunder.
  I have decided to ᵇgather nations
    together
  and assemble kingdoms,
  so I can pour out my fury on them—
  ᶜall my raging anger.

2:9 ᵃIsa 15:1–9; Jer 48:1–47 ᵇAmos 1:13 ᶜDeut 29:23 2:10 ᵃIsa 16:6 2:11 ᵃGen 10:5 ¹Or certainly. 2:12 ᵃPs 17:13 ¹Heb.
Cushites; the people from the region south of Egypt, i.e., Nubia or northern Sudan. 2:13 ᵃIsa 10:5–27; 14:24–27; Mic 5:5–6
2:14 ᵃIsa 13:21 ᵇIsa 14:23; 34:11 ᶜJer 22:14 ¹The meaning of this Heb. word is unclear. 2:15 ᵃIsa 47:8 ᵇRev 18:7 ᶜLam
2:15 ᵈNah 3:19 ¹Heb. hisses, whistles. 3:3 ᵃEzek 22:27 ᵇJer 5:6; Hab 1:8 ¹Or officials. 3:4 ᵃHos 9:7 ᵇEzek 22:26;
Mal 2:7–8 3:5 ᵃJer 3:3 3:7 ᵃJer 8:6 ᵇGen 6:12 ¹Heb. But they got up early, they made corrupt all their actions.
3:8 ᵃProv 20:22; Mic 7:7; Hab 2:3 ᵇIsa 66:18; Ezek 38:14–23; Joel 3:2; Mic 4:12; Matt 25:32 ᶜZeph 1:18

For[1] the whole earth will be
consumed
by my fiery anger.
⁹ Know for sure [a] that I will then enable
the nations to give me acceptable
praise.
All of them will invoke the LORD's
name when they pray
and will worship him in unison.
¹⁰ [a] From beyond the rivers of Ethiopia,[1]
those who pray to me, my dispersed
people,
will bring me tribute.
¹¹ In that day you will not be ashamed
of all your rebelliousness
against me,
for then I will remove from your
midst those who proudly [a] boast,
and you will never again be arrogant
on my holy hill.
¹² I will [a] leave in your midst a humble
and meek group of people,
and they will find safety in the
LORD's presence.
¹³ The Israelites who remain will not
act deceitfully.
[a] They will not lie,
and [b] a deceitful tongue will not be
found in their mouths.
Indeed, they will graze peacefully
like sheep [c] and lie down;
no one will terrify them."
¹⁴ Shout for [a] joy, Daughter Zion!
Shout out, Israel!
Be happy and boast with all your
heart, Daughter Jerusalem!

¹⁵ The LORD has removed [a] the
judgment against you;
he has turned back your enemy.
[b] Israel's king, the LORD, is in your
midst!
You no longer need to fear disaster.
¹⁶ On that day they will say to
Jerusalem,
"Don't be afraid, Zion!
Your hands must not be paralyzed
from panic!
¹⁷ The LORD your God is [a] in your midst;
[b] he is a warrior who can deliver.
He takes great delight in you;
he renews you by his love;[1]
he shouts for joy over you."
¹⁸ "As for those who [a] grieve because
they cannot attend the festivals—
I took them away from you;
they became tribute and were a
source of shame to you.
¹⁹ Look, at that time I will deal with
those who mistreated you.
I will rescue the [a] lame sheep
and gather together the scattered
sheep.
I will take away their humiliation
and make the whole earth admire
and respect them.
²⁰ At that [a] time I will lead you—
at the time I gather you together.
Be sure of this![1] I will make all the
nations of the earth respect and
admire you
when you see me restore you," says
the LORD.

3:8 [1] Or *certainly*.   3:9 [a] Isa 19:18; 57:19   3:10 [a] Ps 68:31; Isa 18:1; Acts 8:27   [1] Or *Nubia*; Heb. *Cush*; the region south of Egypt, i.e., Nubia or northern Sudan.   3:11 [a] Isa 2:12; 5:15; Matt 3:9   3:12 [a] Isa 14:32; Zech 13:8–9   3:13 [a] Isa 10:20–22; [Mic 4:7]   [b] Isa 60:21   [c] Zech 8:3, 16; Rev 14:5   3:14 [a] Isa 12:6   3:15 [a] [John 1:49]   [b] Ezek 48:35; [Rev 7:15]   3:17 [a] Zeph 3:5, 15   [b] Deut 30:9; Isa 62:5; 65:19; Jer 32:41   [1] MT *he remains silent in his love*.   3:18 [a] Lam 2:6   3:19 [a] [Ezek 34:16; Mic 4:6–7]   3:20 [a] Isa 11:12; Ezek 28:25; Amos 9:14   [1] Or *for*.

HAGGAI

With the Babylonian exile in the past and a newly returned group of Jews in the land, the work of rebuilding the temple can begin. Yet sixteen years after the process is begun, the people have yet to finish the project because their personal affairs have interfered with God's business. Haggai preaches a fiery series of sermonettes designed to stir up the nation to complete the temple. He calls the builders to renewed courage in the Lord, renewed holiness of life, and renewed faith in God who controls the future. The etymology and meaning of *Haggay* is uncertain, but it is probably derived from the Hebrew word *hag*, "festival." It may also be an abbreviated form of *haggiah*, "festival of Yahweh." Thus Haggai's name means "Festal" or "Festive," possibly because he was born on the day of a major feast such as Temporary Shelters (Haggai's second message takes place during that feast, 2:1). The title in the Septuagint is *Aggaios*, and in the Vulgate it is *Aggaeus*.

Introduction

1 On [a]the first day of the sixth month of King Darius' second year, the LORD's message came through[1] the prophet [b]Haggai to [c]Zerubbabel son of Shealtiel, governor of Judah, and to the high priest [d]Joshua son of [e]Jehozadak:

The Accusation of Indifference against the People

[2]This is what the LORD of Heaven's Armies has said: "These people have said, 'The time for rebuilding the LORD's temple has not yet come.'" [3]The LORD's message [a]came through the prophet Haggai as follows: [4]"Is it [a]right for you to live in richly paneled houses while my temple is in ruins? [5]Here then, this is what the LORD of Heaven's Armies has said: 'Think carefully about what you are doing. [6]You have [a]planted much, but have harvested little. You eat, but are never filled. You drink, but are still thirsty. You put on [b]clothes, but are not warm. Those who earn wages end up with holes in their money bags.'"

Consequences of the Failure to Rebuild the Temple

[7]Moreover, this is what the LORD of Heaven's Armies has said: "Pay close attention to these things also. [8]Go up to the hill [a]country and bring back timber to build[1] the temple. Then I will be pleased and honored," says the LORD. [9]"You expected a large harvest, but instead there was little. And when [a]you would [b]bring it home, I would blow it right away. Why?" asks the LORD of Heaven's Armies. "Because my temple remains in ruins, thanks to each of you favoring his own house! [10]This is why [a]the sky has held back its dew and the earth its produce. [11]Moreover, I have [a]called for a drought that will affect the fields, the hill country, the grain, new wine, fresh olive oil, and everything that grows from the ground; it also will harm people, animals, and [b]everything they produce."

The Response of the Leaders and the People

[12]Then Zerubbabel son of Shealtiel and [a]the high priest Joshua son of Jehozadak, along with the whole remnant of the people, obeyed the LORD their God. They responded favorably to the message of the prophet Haggai, who spoke just as the LORD their God had instructed him, and the people began to respect the LORD.[1] [13]Then [a]Haggai, the LORD's messenger, spoke the LORD's announcement to the people: "I am

---

1:1 [a]Ezra 4:24; Hag 2:10; Zech 1:1, 7   [b]Ezra 5:1; 6:14   [c]1 Chr 3:19; Ezra 2:2; Neh 7:7; Zech 4:6; Matt 1:12–13   [d]Ezra 5:2–3; Zech 6:11   [e]1 Chr 6:15   [1]Heb. *by the hand of*; the prophet is only an instrument of the Lord.   1:3 [a]Ezra 5:1   1:4 [a]2 Sam 7:2   1:6 [a]Deut 28:38–40; Hos 8:7; Hag 1:9–10; 2:16–17   [b]Zech 8:10   1:8 [a]Ezra 3:7   [1]Heb. *and build the house.*   1:9 [a]Hag 2:16   [b]Hag 2:17   1:10 [a]Lev 26:19; Deut 28:23; 1 Kgs 8:35; Joel 1:18–20   1:11 [a]1 Kgs 17:1; 2 Kgs 8:1   [b]Hag 2:17   1:12 [a]Ezra 5:2   [1]Heb. *people feared from before the LORD.*   1:13 [a][Matt 28:20; Rom 8:31]

with you," decrees the LORD. [14] So [a]the LORD energized and encouraged Zerubbabel son of Shealtiel, [b]governor of Judah, the high priest Joshua son of Jehozadak, [c]and the whole remnant of the people. They came and worked on the temple of their God, the LORD of Heaven's Armies. [15] This took place on the twenty-fourth day of the sixth month of King Darius' second year.

The Glory to Come

2 On the twenty-first day of the seventh month, the LORD's message came through[1] the prophet Haggai again: [2] "Ask the following questions to[1] Zerubbabel son of Shealtiel, governor of Judah, the high priest Joshua son of Jehozadak, and the remnant of the people: [3] '[a]Who among you survivors saw the former splendor of [b]this temple? How does it look to you now? Isn't it nothing by comparison?' [4] Even so, take heart, [a]Zerubbabel," decrees the LORD. "Take heart, Joshua son of Jehozadak, the high priest. And take heart all you citizens of the land," decrees the LORD, "and begin to work. For I am with you," decrees the LORD of Heaven's Armies. [5] "Do not fear, because [a]I made a promise to your ancestors when they left Egypt, and [b]my Spirit even now testifies to you." [6] Moreover, this is what the LORD of Heaven's Armies has said: "In just a little while[1] I will [a]once [b]again shake the sky and the earth, the sea and the dry ground. [7] I will also shake up all [a]the nations, and they will offer their treasures; then I will fill this temple with [b]glory." So the LORD of Heaven's Armies has said. [8] "The silver and gold will be mine," decrees the LORD of Heaven's Armies. [9] "The future splendor of this temple will be greater than that of former times,"[1] [a]the LORD of Heaven's Armies has declared. "And in this place I will give [b]peace," decrees the LORD of Heaven's Armies.

The Promised Blessing

[10] On the twenty-fourth day of the ninth month of Darius' second year, the LORD's message came to the prophet Haggai: [11] "This is what the LORD of Heaven's Armies has said, '[a]Ask the priests about the law. [12] If someone carries holy meat in a fold of his garment and that fold touches bread, a boiled dish, wine, olive oil, or any other food, will that item become holy?'" The priests answered, "It will not." [13] Then Haggai asked, "If a person who is ritually [a]unclean because of touching a dead body comes in contact with one of these items, will it become unclean?" The priests answered, "It will be unclean."

[14] Then Haggai responded, "'The people of this nation are unclean in my sight,' decrees the LORD. 'And [a]so is all their effort; everything they offer is also unclean. [15] Now therefore reflect carefully [a]on the recent past, before one stone was laid on another in the LORD's temple. [16] From that time [a]when one came expecting a heap of 20 measures, there were only 10; when one came to the wine vat to draw out 50 measures from it, there were only 20. [17] I struck all the products of your labor [a]with blight, disease, and hail, and yet you brought [b]nothing to me,'[1] says the LORD. [18] 'Think carefully about [a]the past: from today, the twenty-fourth day of the ninth month, to the day work on the temple of the LORD was resumed, think about it. [19] The seed [a]is still in the storehouse, isn't it? And the vine, fig tree, pomegranate, and olive tree have not produced. Nevertheless, from today on I will [b]bless you.'"

Zerubbabel the Chosen One

[20] Then the LORD spoke to Haggai a second time on the twenty-fourth day of the month: [21] "Tell Zerubbabel [a]governor of Judah: '[b]I am ready to shake the sky and the earth. [22] I [a]will overthrow royal thrones and shatter the [b]might of earthly kingdoms. I will overthrow chariots and those who ride them, and horses and their riders will fall as people kill one another. [23] On that day,' says the LORD of Heaven's Armies, 'I will take you, Zerubbabel son of Shealtiel, my servant,' says the LORD, '[a]and [b]I will make you like a signet ring, for I have chosen you,' says the LORD of Heaven's Armies."

1:14 [a] 2 Chr 36:22; Ezra 1:1 [b] Hag 2:21 [c] Ezra 5:2, 8; Neh 4:6 **2:1** [1] DSS to. **2:2** [1] Heb. say to. **2:3** [a] Ezra 3:12–13 [b] Zech 4:10 **2:4** [a] Deut 31:23; 1 Chr 22:13; 28:20; Zech 8:9; Eph 6:10 **2:5** [a] Exod 29:45–46 [b] [Neh 9:20]; Isa 63:11, 14 **2:6** [a] Heb 12:26 [b] [Joel 3:16] [1] LXX yet once. **2:7** [a] Gen 49:10; Mal 3:1 [b] 1 Kgs 8:11; Isa 60:7; Zech 2:5 **2:9** [a] [John 1:14] [b] Ps 85:8–9; Luke 2:14; [Eph 2:14] [1] Heb. greater will be the latter splendor of this house than the former. **2:11** [a] Lev 10:10–11; Deut 33:10; Mal 2:7 **2:13** [a] Lev 22:4–6; Num 19:11, 22 **2:14** [a] [Titus 1:15] **2:15** [a] Hag 1:5, 7; 2:18 **2:16** [a] Hag 1:6, 9; Zech 8:10 **2:17** [a] Deut 28:22; 1 Kgs 8:37; Amos 4:9 [b] Hag 1:11 [1] Heb. and there was not with you to me; likely the harvests were so poor that the people took care of only themselves, leaving no offering for the Lord. **2:18** [a] Ezra 5:1–2, 16; Zech 8:9 **2:19** [a] Zech 8:12 [b] Ps 128:1–6; Jer 31:12, 14; [Mal 3:10] **2:21** [a] Ezra 5:2; Hag 1:1, 14; Zech 4:6–10 [b] Hag 2:6–7; [Heb 12:26–27] **2:22** [a] [Dan 2:44; Rev 19:11–21] [b] Ps 46:9; Ezek 39:20; Mic 5:10; Zech 9:10 **2:23** [a] Song 8:6; Jer 22:24 [b] Isa 42:1; 43:10

ZECHARIAH

For a dozen years or more, the task of rebuilding the temple has been half completed. God commissions Zechariah to encourage the people to fulfill their responsibility. Rather than exhorting them to action with strong words of rebuke, Zechariah seeks to encourage them to action by reminding them of the future importance of the temple. The temple must be built, for one day the Messiah's glory will inhabit it. But future blessing is contingent upon present obedience. The people are not merely building a building; they are building the future. With that as their motivation, they can plunge into the building project with wholehearted zeal, for their Messiah is coming. *Zekar-yah* means "Yahweh Remembers" or "Yahweh Has Remembered." This theme dominates the whole book: Israel will be blessed because Yahweh remembers the covenant he made with the fathers. The Greek and Latin version of his name is *Zacharias*.

Introduction

1 In the eighth month [a]of Darius' second year, the LORD's message came [b]to the prophet Zechariah, son of Berechiah son of [c]Iddo: [2]"The LORD was very angry with your ancestors. [3]Therefore say [a]to the people: The LORD of Heaven's Armies says, 'Turn to me,' says the LORD of Heaven's Armies, 'and I will turn to you,' says the LORD of Heaven's Armies. [4]Do not be like your [a]ancestors, to whom the former prophets called out, saying, 'This is what the LORD of Heaven's Armies has said, "[b]Turn now from your evil wickedness."' But they would by no means obey me," says the LORD. [5]"As for your ancestors, where are they? And did the prophets live forever? [6]But have [a]my words and statutes, which I commanded my servants the prophets, not outlived your fathers? Then they paid attention and confessed, 'The LORD of Heaven's Armies has indeed done what he said he would do to [b]us, because of our sinful ways.'"

The Introduction to the Visions

[7]On the twenty-fourth day of the eleventh month, the month Shebat, in Darius' second year, the LORD's message came to the prophet Zechariah, son of Berechiah son of Iddo:

The Content of the First Vision

[8]I [a]was attentive that night and saw a man seated on a red [b]horse that stood among some myrtle trees[1] in the ravine. Behind him were red, sorrel, and white horses.

The Interpretation of the First Vision

[9]Then I asked one nearby, "What are these, sir?" The angelic messenger[1] who replied to me said, "I will show you what these are." [10]Then the man standing among the myrtle trees spoke up and said, "[a]These are the ones whom the LORD has sent to walk about on the earth." [11a]The riders then agreed with the angel of the LORD, who was standing among the myrtle trees, "We have been walking about on the earth, and now everything is at rest and quiet." [12]The angel of the LORD then asked, "[a]O LORD of Heaven's Armies, how long before you have compassion on Jerusalem and [b]the other cities of Judah that you have been so angry with for these 70 years?" [13]The LORD then addressed [a]good, comforting words to the angelic messenger who was speaking to me. [14]Turning to me, the messenger then

1:1 [a]Ezra 4:24; 6:15; Hag 1:1; Zech 7:1 [b]Ezra 5:1; 6:14; Zech 7:1; Matt 23:35; Luke 11:51 [c]Neh 12:4, 16   1:3 [a]Isa 31:6; 44:22; [Mic 7:19; Mal 3:7–10; Luke 15:20; Jas 4:8]   1:4 [a]2 Chr 36:15–16 [b]Isa 31:6; Jer 3:12; 18:11; Ezek 18:30; [Hos 14:1]   1:6 [a][Isa 55:11] [b]Lam 1:18; 2:17   1:8 [a]Isa 55:13; Zech 6:2; [Rev 6:4] [b][Zech 6:2–7; Rev 6:2] [1]LXX *mountains.*   1:9 [1]Heb. *messenger, angel.*   1:10 [a][Heb 1:14]   1:11 [a][Ps 103:20–21]   1:12 [a]Ps 74:10; Jer 12:4; Hab 1:2 [b]2 Chr 36:21; Jer 25:11–12; 29:10; Dan 9:2; Zech 7:5   1:13 [a]Jer 29:10

said, "Cry out that the LORD of Heaven's Armies says, 'I am very much ªmoved for Jerusalem and for Zion. ¹⁵But ªI am greatly displeased with the nations that take my grace for granted. I was a little displeased with them, but they have only made things worse for themselves.

The Oracle of Response

¹⁶"'Therefore,'ªthis is what the LORD has said, 'I have become compassionate toward Jerusalem and will rebuild my ᵇtemple in it,' says the LORD of Heaven's Armies. 'Once more ᶜa surveyor's ᵈmeasuring line will be stretched out over Jerusalem.' ¹⁷Speak up again with ªthe message of the LORD of Heaven's Armies: 'My cities ᵇwill once more overflow with prosperity, and once more the LORD will comfort Zion and validate his choice of Jerusalem.'"

Vision Two: The Four Horns

¹⁸Once again I looked and this time I saw four ªhorns. ¹⁹So I asked the angelic messenger who spoke with me, "What are ªthese?" He replied, "These are the horns that have scattered Judah, Israel, and Jerusalem." ²⁰Next the LORD showed me four blacksmiths. ²¹I asked, "What are these going to do?" He answered, "These ªhorns are the ones that have scattered Judah so that there is no one to be ᵇseen. But the blacksmiths have come to terrify Judah's enemies¹ and cut off the horns of the nations that have thrust themselves against the land of Judah in order to scatter its people."

Vision Three: The Surveyor

2 I looked ªagain, and there was a man with a measuring line in his hand. ²I asked, "Where are you going?" He replied, "ªTo measure Jerusalem in order to determine its width and its length." ³At this point the angelic messenger who spoke to me went out, and another messenger came to meet him ⁴and said to him, "Hurry, speak to this young man as follows: 'ªJerusalem will no longer be enclosed by walls because of the multitude of people and animals there. ⁵But I,' the LORD ªsays, 'will be ᵇa wall of fire surrounding Jerusalem and the source of glory in her midst.'"

⁶"You there! Flee ªfrom the northland!" says the LORD, "for like the four winds of heaven¹ I have scattered you," says the LORD. ⁷"ªEscape, Zion, you who live among the Babylonians!" ⁸For the LORD of Heaven's Armies says: "For his own glory he has sent me to the nations that plundered you—for anyone who ªtouches you touches the pupil of his eye. ⁹Yes, look here, I am about to ªpunish them so that they will be looted by their own slaves." Then ᵇyou will know that the LORD of Heaven's Armies has sent me.

¹⁰"Sing ªout and be happy, Zion my daughter! For look, ᵇI have come; I will settle in your midst," says the LORD. ¹¹"ªMany nations will ᵇjoin themselves to the LORD on the day of salvation, and they will also be ᶜmy¹ people. Indeed, I will settle in the midst of ᵈyou all. Then you will know that the LORD of Heaven's Armies has sent me to you. ¹²The LORD will ªtake possession of Judah as his portion in the holy land and he will choose Jerusalem once again. ¹³Be silent in the LORD's presence, all people everywhere,¹ for he is ªbeing moved to action in his holy dwelling place."

Vision Four: The Priest

3 Next I saw ªJoshua the high priest standing before the angel of the LORD, with ᵇSatan¹ standing at his right hand to accuse him. ²The LORD said to Satan, "May ªthe LORD rebuke you, Satan! May the LORD, who ᵇhas chosen Jerusalem, rebuke you! ᶜIsn't this man like a burning stick snatched from the fire?" ³Now Joshua was dressed in ªfilthy clothes as he stood there before the angel. ⁴The angel spoke up to those ªstanding all around, "Remove his filthy clothes." Then he said to Joshua, "I have freely forgiven your iniquity and will dress you in

1:14 ª Joel 2:18; Zech 8:2   1:15 ª Isa 47:6   1:16 ª [Isa 12:1; 54:8; Zech 2:10; 8:3]   ᵇ Ezra 6:14–15; Hag 1:4; Zech 4:9   ᶜ 2 Chr 36:23; Ezra 1:2–3; Isa 44:28   ᵈ Zech 2:1–3   1:17 ª [Isa 40:1–2; 51:3]   ᵇ Isa 14:1; Zech 2:12   1:18 ª [Lam 2:17]   1:19 ª Ezra 4:1, 4, 7   1:21 ª [Ps 75:10]   ᵇ Ps 75:4–5   ¹ Heb. terrify them.   2:1 ª Jer 31:39; Ezek 40:3; 47:3; Zech 1:16   2:2 ª Rev 11:1   2:4 ª Jer 31:27   2:5 ª [Isa 26:1]   ᵇ [Isa 60:19]   2:6 ª Isa 48:20   ¹ Or of the sky.   2:7 ª Isa 48:20; Jer 51:6; [Rev 18:4]   2:8 ª Deut 32:10; Ps 17:8   2:9 ª Isa 19:16   ᵇ Zech 4:9   2:10 ª Isa 12:6   ᵇ [Lev 26:12]   2:11 ª [Isa 2:2–3]   ᵇ Zech 3:10   ᶜ Exod 12:49   ᵈ Ezek 33:33   ¹ LXX, Syr. his people and he will settle.   2:12 ª [Deut 32:9]; Ps 33:12; Jer 10:16   2:13 ª Hab 2:20; Zeph 1:7   ¹ Heb. all flesh.   3:1 ª Ezra 5:2; Hag 1:1; Zech 6:11   ᵇ 1 Chr 21:1; Job 1:6; Ps 109:6; [Rev 12:9–10]   ¹ This Heb. term suggests not so much a personal name as an epithet, namely, "the adversary."   3:2 ª Mark 9:25; [Jude 9]   ᵇ [Rom 8:33]   ᶜ Amos 4:11; Jude 23   3:3 ª Ezra 9:15; Isa 64:6   3:4 ª Gen 3:21; Isa 61:10

fine clothing." [5]Then I spoke up, "Let a clean [a]turban be put on his head." So they put a clean turban on his head and clothed him, while the angel of the LORD stood nearby. [6]Then the angel of the LORD exhorted Joshua solemnly: [7]"The LORD of Heaven's Armies says, 'If you follow my ways and [a]keep my requirements, you will be able to preside [b]over my temple and attend to my courtyards, and I will allow you to come and go among these others who are [c]standing by you. [8]Listen now, [a]Joshua the high priest, both you and your colleagues who are sitting before you, all of you are a symbol that I am about to introduce [b]my servant, the [c]Branch. [9]As for the stone I have set before Joshua—[a]on the one stone there are [b]seven eyes. [c]I am about to engrave an inscription on it,' says the LORD of Heaven's Armies, 'to the effect that I will remove the iniquity of this land in a single day. [10]In that day,' says the LORD of Heaven's Armies, 'everyone will [a]invite his friend to fellowship [b]under his vine and under his fig tree.'"

Vision Five: The Menorah

4 The angelic messenger who had been speaking with me [a]then returned and woke me, [b]as a person is wakened from sleep. [2]He [a]asked me, "What do you see?" I replied,[1] "I see [b]a menorah of pure gold with a receptacle at the top. There are seven lamps at the top, with seven[2] pipes going to the lamps. [3]There are also [a]two olive trees beside it, one on the right of the receptacle and the other on the left." [4]Then I asked the messenger who spoke with me, "What are these, sir?" [5]He replied, "Don't you know what these are?" So I responded, "No, sir." [6]Therefore he told me, "This is the LORD's message to [a]Zerubbabel: '[b]Not by strength and not by power, but by my Spirit,' says the LORD of Heaven's Armies.

Oracle of Response

[7]"What are [a]you, you great mountain? Because of Zerubbabel you will become a level plain! And [b]he will bring forth the temple capstone [c]with shoutings of 'Grace! Grace!' because of this." [8]Moreover, the LORD's message came to me as follows: [9]"The hands of Zerubbabel [a]have laid the foundations of this temple, and his hands will complete it. Then [b]you will know that the [c]LORD of Heaven's Armies has sent me to you. [10]For who dares make light of [a]small beginnings? These seven eyes will joyfully look on [b]the tin tablet in Zerubbabel's hand. These are the eyes of the LORD, which constantly range across the whole earth."

[11]Next I asked the messenger, "What are these [a]two olive trees on the right and the left of the menorah?" [12]Before he could reply I asked again, "What are these two extensions of the olive trees, which are emptying out the golden oil through the two golden pipes?" [13]He replied, "Don't you know what these are?" And I said, "No, sir." [14]So he said, "[a]These are the two anointed ones [b]who stand by the Lord of the whole earth."

Vision Six: The Flying Scroll

5 Then I turned to look, and there was a flying [a]scroll! [2]Someone asked me, "What do you see?" I replied, "I see a flying scroll 30 feet long and 15 feet wide."[1] [3]The speaker went on to say, "This is a [a]curse traveling across the whole earth. For example, according to the curse whoever steals will be removed from the community; or on the other hand (according to the curse) whoever swears falsely will suffer the same fate." [4]"I will send it out," says the LORD of Heaven's Armies, "and it will enter the house of the [a]thief and of [b]the person who swears falsely in my name. [c]It will land in the middle of his house and destroy both timber and stones."

Vision Seven: The Ephah

[5]After this the angelic messenger who had been speaking to me went out and said, "Look, see what is leaving." [6]I asked, "What is it?" And he replied, "It is a basket for measuring grain[1] that is moving away

3:5 [a]Exod 29:6   3:7 [a]Lev 8:35; Ezek 44:16   [b]Deut 17:9, 12   [c]Zech 3:4   3:8 [a]Ps 71:7   [b]Isa 42:1   [c]Isa 11:1; 53:2; Jer 23:5; 33:15; Zech 6:12   3:9 [a][Zech 4:10; Rev 5:6]   [b]Ps 118:22   [c]Jer 31:34; 50:20; Zech 3:4   3:10 [a]Zech 2:11   [b]1 Kgs 4:25; Isa 36:16; Mic 4:4   4:1 [a]Zech 1:9; 2:3   [b]Dan 8:18   4:2 [a]Rev 1:12   [b]Exod 25:37; [Rev 4:5]   [1]MT *he*.   [2]MT, Qum. MSS *seven and seven*. 4:3 [a]Rev 11:3–4   4:6 [a]Hag 1:1   [b]Isa 30:1; Hos 1:7; Hag 2:4–5   4:7 [a]Ps 114:4, 6; Isa 40:4; Jer 51:25; Nah 1:5; Zech 14:4–5; [Matt 21:21]   [b]Ps 118:22   [c]Ezra 3:10–11, 13; Ps 84:11   4:9 [a]Ezra 3:8–10; 5:16; Hag 2:18   [b]Zech 2:9, 11; 6:15   [c][Isa 43:16]; Zech 2:8 4:10 [a]Neh 4:2–4; Amos 7:2, 5; Hag 2:3   [b]2 Chr 16:9; Prov 15:3; Zech 3:9   4:11 [a]Zech 4:3; Rev 11:4   4:14 [a]Rev 11:4   [b]Zech 3:1–7   5:1 [a]Jer 36:2; Ezek 2:9; Rev 5:1   5:2 [1]Heb. *20 cubits . . . 10 cubits*.   5:3 [a]Mal 4:6   5:4 [a]Exod 20:15; Lev 19:11   [b]Exod 20:7; Lev 19:12; Isa 48:1; Jer 5:2; Zech 8:17; Mal 3:5   [c]Lev 14:34–35; Job 18:15   5:6 [1]Heb. [This is] *the ephah*.

from here." Moreover, he said, "This is their 'eye'[2] throughout all the earth." [7]Then a round lead cover was raised up, revealing a woman sitting inside the basket. [8]He then said, "This woman represents wickedness," and he pushed her down into the basket and placed the lead cover on top. [9]Then I looked again and saw two women going forth with the wind in their wings (they had wings like those of a [a]stork), and they lifted up the basket between the earth and the sky. [10]I asked the [a]messenger who was speaking to me, "Where are they taking the basket?" [11]He replied, "To [a]build a temple for her in [b]the land of Babylonia. When it is finished, she will be placed there in her own residence."

Vision Eight: The Chariots

6 Once more I looked, and this time I saw four chariots emerging from between two mountains of bronze. [2]Harnessed to the first chariot were [a]red horses, to the second [b]black horses, [3]to the third white horses, and to the fourth spotted horses, all of them strong.[1] [4]Then I asked the angelic messenger who was speaking with me, "What are these, sir?" [5]The messenger replied, "[a]These are the four spirits of heaven going out after [b]presenting themselves before the Lord of all the earth. [6]The chariot with [a]the black horses is going to the north country, and the white ones are going after them, but the spotted ones are going to the south country. [7]All these strong ones are scattering; they have sought permission to go and [a]walk about over the earth." The Lord had said, "Go! Walk about over the earth!" So they are doing so. [8]Then he cried out to me, "Look! The ones going to the northland have brought [a]me peace about the northland."

A Concluding Oracle

[9]The LORD's message came to me as follows: [10]"Choose some people from among the exiles, namely, Heldai, Tobijah, and Jedaiah, all who have come from Babylon, and when you have done so go to the house of Josiah son of Zephaniah. [11]Then take some silver [a]and gold to make a crown and set it on the head of [b]Joshua the high priest, the son of Jehozadak. [12]Then say to him, '[a]The LORD of Heaven's Armies says, "Look—here is the man whose name is [b]Branch,[1] who will sprout up from his place [c]and build the temple of the LORD. [13]Indeed, he will build the temple of the LORD, and he will be clothed in splendor, sitting as king on his throne. Moreover, there will be [a]a priest with him on his throne and [b]they will see eye to eye on everything. [14]The crown will then be turned over to Helem, Tobijah, Jedaiah, and Hen son of Zephaniah as a memorial in the temple of the LORD. [15]Then [a]those who are far away will come and build the temple of the LORD so that you may know that the LORD of Heaven's Armies has sent me to you. This will all come to pass if you completely obey the voice of the LORD your God.""'

The Hypocrisy of False Fasting

7 In King Darius' fourth year, on the fourth day of Kislev, the ninth month, the LORD's message came to Zechariah. [2]Now the people of Bethel had sent Sharezer and Regem-Melech and their companions to seek the LORD's favor [3]by [a]asking both [b]the priests of the temple of the LORD of Heaven's Armies and the prophets, "Should we weep in the fifth month, fasting as we have done over the years?" [4]The message of the LORD of Heaven's Armies then came to me, [5]"Speak to all the people and priests of the land as follows: 'When you [a]fasted [b]and lamented [c]in the fifth and seventh months through all these 70 years, did you truly fast [d]for me—for me, indeed? [6]And now [a]when you eat and drink, are you not doing so for yourselves? [7]Should you not have obeyed the words that the LORD cried out through the [a]former prophets when Jerusalem was peacefully inhabited and her surrounding cities, [b]the Negev, and the foothills were also populated?'"

[8]Again the LORD's message came to

5:6 [2] LXX, Syr. *iniquity.*   **5:9** [a] Lev 11:13, 19; Ps 104:17; Jer 8:7   **5:10** [a] Zech 5:5   **5:11** [a] Jer 29:5, 28   [b] Gen 10:10; Isa 11:11; Dan 1:2   **6:2** [a] Zech 1:8; Rev 6:4   [b] Rev 6:5   **6:3** [1] Aquila, Syr. *red.*   **6:5** [a] [Ps 104:4; Heb 1:7, 14]   [b] 1 Kgs 22:19; Dan 7:10; Zech 4:14; Luke 1:19   **6:6** [a] Jer 1:14; Ezek 1:4   **6:7** [a] Gen 13:17; Zech 1:10   **6:8** [a] Eccl 10:4   **6:11** [a] Exod 29:6   [b] Ezra 3:2; Hag 1:1; Zech 3:1   **6:12** [a] John 1:45   [b] Isa 4:2; 11:1; Jer 23:5; 33:15; Zech 3:8   [c] [Matt 16:18; Eph 2:20; Heb 3:3]   [1] This term derives from the Heb. verb "will sprout up," which describes the rise of the Messiah. In the immediate context, this refers to Zerubbabel, but it ultimately refers to Jesus (cf. John 19:5).   **6:13** [a] Isa 22:24   [b] Ps 110:4; [Heb 3:1]   **6:15** [a] Isa 57:19; [Eph 2:13]   **7:3** [a] Deut 17:9; Mal 2:7   [b] Zech 8:19   **7:5** [a] [Isa 58:1–9]   [b] Jer 41:1   [c] Zech 1:12   [d] [Rom 14:6]   **7:6** [a] Deut 12:7; 14:26; 1 Chr 29:22   **7:7** [a] Isa 1:16–20; Jer 7:5, 23; Zech 1:4   [b] Jer 17:26

Zechariah: [9]"The Lord of Heaven's Armies said, '[a]Exercise true judgment and show brotherhood and compassion to each other. [10]You must not oppress the [a]widow, the orphan, the resident foreigner, or the poor, nor should anyone secretly plot evil against his fellow citizen.'

[11]"But they refused to pay attention, turning away stubbornly and [a]stopping their ears so they could not hear. [12]Indeed, they made their [a]hearts as hard as diamond, so that they could not obey the law of Moses and the other words the Lord of Heaven's Armies had sent by his Spirit through the former prophets. Therefore, the Lord of Heaven's Armies poured out great wrath.

[13]"'Just as I called out, but [a]they would not obey, so they will call out, but I will not listen,' the Lord of Heaven's Armies says. [14]'Rather, [a]I will sweep them away in a storm into all the nations they are not familiar with.' Thus the land became desolate because of them, with no one crossing through or returning, for they had made the fruitful land a waste."

The Blessing of True Fasting

8 Then the message of the Lord of Heaven's Armies came to me as follows: [2]"The Lord of Heaven's [a]Armies says, 'I am very much concerned for Zion; indeed, I am so concerned for her that my rage will fall on those who hurt her.' [3]The Lord says, '[a]I have returned to Zion and will [b]live within Jerusalem. Now Jerusalem will be called "truthful city," "mountain of [c]the Lord of Heaven's Armies," "holy mountain."' [4]Moreover, the Lord of Heaven's Armies says, '[a]Old men and women will once more live in the plazas of Jerusalem, each one leaning on a cane because of advanced age. [5]And the streets of the city will be [a]full of boys and girls playing. [6]And,' says the Lord of Heaven's Armies, 'though such a thing may seem to be difficult in the opinion of the small community of those days, [a]will it also appear difficult to me?' asks the Lord of Heaven's Armies.

[7]"The Lord of Heaven's [a]Armies asserts, 'I am about to save my people from the lands of the east and the west. [8]And I will [a]bring them to settle within Jerusalem. [b]They will be my people, and [c]I will be their God, in truth and righteousness.'

[9]"The Lord of Heaven's Armies also says, '[a]Gather strength, you who are listening to [b]these words today from the mouths of the prophets who were there at the founding of the house of the Lord of Heaven's Armies, so that the temple might be built. [10]Before that time there was no [a]compensation for man or animal, nor was there any relief from adversity for those who came and went, because I had pitted everybody—each one—against everyone else. [11a]But I will be different now to this remnant of my people from the way I was in those days,' says the Lord of Heaven's Armies, [12]'for [a]there will be a peaceful time of sowing, [b]the vine will produce its fruit, and the ground its yield, and the skies[1] will rain down dew. Then I will allow the remnant of my people to possess all these things. [13]And it will come [a]about that just as [b]you, both Judah and Israel, were a curse to the nations, so I will save you and you will be a blessing. Do not be afraid! Instead, be strong.'

[14]"For the Lord of Heaven's Armies says, 'As I had planned to hurt you when your fathers made me angry,' says the Lord of Heaven's Armies, '[a]and I was not sorry, [15]so, to the contrary, I have planned in these days to do good to Jerusalem and Judah—do not fear! [16]These are the things you must [a]do: [b]Speak the truth, each of you, to one another. Practice true and righteous judgment in your courts. [17a]Do not plan evil in your hearts against one another. Do not favor a false oath—these are all things that I hate,' says the Lord."

[18]The message of the Lord of Heaven's Armies came to me as follows: [19]"The Lord of Heaven's Armies says, '[a]The fast of [b]the fourth, fifth, [c]seventh, [d]and tenth months will become [e]joyful and happy, pleasant feasts [f]for the house of Judah; so love

7:9 [a]Isa 58:6–7; Jer 7:28   **7:10** [a]Exod 22:22; Ps 72:4; Isa 1:17; Jer 5:28   **7:11** [a]Jer 17:23; Acts 7:57   **7:12** [a]Ezek 11:19   **7:13** [a]Prov 1:24–28; Isa 1:15; Jer 11:11; Mic 3:4   **7:14** [a]Lev 26:33; Deut 4:27; 28:64; Neh 1:8   **8:2** [a]Joel 2:18; Nah 1:2; Zech 1:14   **8:3** [a]Zech 1:16   [b]Zech 2:10–11   [c][Isa 2:2–3]   **8:4** [a]1 Sam 2:31; Isa 65:20   **8:5** [a]Jer 30:19–20   **8:6** [a][Gen 18:14; Luke 1:37]   **8:7** [a]Ps 107:3; Isa 11:11; Ezek 37:21   **8:8** [a]Zeph 3:20; Zech 10:10   [b][Jer 30:22; 31:1, 33; Zech 13:9]   [c]Jer 4:2   **8:9** [a]Ezra 5:1–2; 6:14; Zech 4:9   [b]Hag 2:18   **8:10** [a]Hag 1:6, 9   **8:11** [a][Ps 103:9]; Isa 12:1; Hag 2:15–19   **8:12** [a]Ps 67:6   [b]Hag 1:10   [1]Or *the heavens.*   **8:13** [a]Jer 42:18   [b]Gen 12:2; Ruth 4:11–12; Isa 19:24–25; Ezek 34:26; [Zeph 3:20]   **8:14** [a][2 Chr 36:16]   **8:16** [a]Zech 7:9–10   [b]Ps 15:2; [Prov 12:17–19]; Zech 8:3; [Eph 4:25]   **8:17** [a]Prov 3:29; Jer 4:14; Zech 7:10   **8:19** [a]Jer 52:6   [b]Jer 52:12   [c]2 Kgs 25:25; Jer 41:1–2   [d]Jer 52:4   [e]Esth 8:17   [f]Zech 8:16; Luke 1:74–75

truth and peace.' [20]The LORD of Heaven's Armies says, 'It will someday come to pass that people—residents of many cities—will come. [21]The inhabitants of one will go to another and say, "[a]Let's go up at once to ask the favor of the LORD, to seek the LORD of Heaven's Armies. Indeed, I'll go with you."' [22a]Many peoples and powerful nations will come to Jerusalem to seek the LORD of Heaven's Armies and to ask his favor. [23]The LORD of Heaven's Armies says, 'In those days 10 people [a]from all languages and nations will grasp hold [b]of—indeed, grab—the robe of one Jew and say, "Let us go with you, for we have heard [c]that God is with you."'"

The Coming of the True King

9 This is an oracle, the LORD's message concerning the land of Hadrach, with its focus on [a]Damascus:

[b]The eyes of all humanity, especially of the tribes of Israel, are toward the LORD, [2]as are those of [a]Hamath also, which adjoins Damascus, [b]Tyre, and [c]Sidon, though they consider themselves to be very [d]wise. [3]Tyre built herself a fortification and piled up silver like dust and gold like the mud of the streets. [4]Nevertheless [a]the Lord will evict [b]her and shove her fortifications into the sea—she will be consumed by fire. [5]Ashkelon will see and be afraid; Gaza will be in great anguish, as will [a]Ekron, for her hope will have been dried up. Gaza will lose her king, and Ashkelon will no longer be inhabited. [6]A mongrel people will live [a]in Ashdod, for I will greatly humiliate the [b]Philistines. [7]I will take away their abominable religious practices; then those who survive will become a community of believers in our God, like a clan in Judah, and Ekron will be like the Jebusites. [8]Then [a]I will surround my temple to protect it like a guard from anyone crossing back and forth; so no one will cross over against them anymore as an oppressor, for now I myself have seen it.

[9] Rejoice [a]greatly, daughter of Zion!
Shout, daughter of Jerusalem!
Look! [b]Your king is coming to you:
He is legitimate and victorious,
humble and riding on a donkey—
on a young donkey, the foal of a
female donkey.
[10] I [a]will remove[1,2] the chariot from Ephraim
and the warhorse from Jerusalem,
and the [b]battle bow will be removed.
Then he will announce peace to the nations.
His dominion will be [c]from sea to sea
and from the Euphrates River[3] to the ends of the earth.

[11]Moreover, as for you, because of our covenant relationship secured with blood, I will release your [a]prisoners from the waterless pit. [12]Return to the stronghold, [a]you prisoners, with hope; today I declare that I will return [b]double what was taken from you. [13]I will bend Judah as my bow; I will load the bow with Ephraim, my arrow. I will stir up your sons, Zion, against your sons, Greece, and I will make you, Zion, like a warrior's sword.

[14]Then the LORD will appear above them, and [a]his arrow will shoot forth like lightning; the Sovereign LORD will blow the trumpet and will proceed in the southern storm winds. [15]The LORD of Heaven's Armies will [a]guard them, and they will prevail and overcome with sling stones. Then they will drink and will become noisy like drunkards, full like the sacrificial basin or like the corners of the altar. [16]On that day the LORD their God will [a]deliver them as [b]the flock of his people, for they are the precious stones of a crown sparkling over his land. [17a]How precious and [b]fair! [c]Grain will make the young men flourish, and new wine the young women.

The Restoration of the True People

10 Ask [a]the LORD for [b]rain in [c]the season of the late spring rains—the LORD who causes thunderstorms—and he will give everyone showers of rain and green growth in the field. [2]For the household [a]gods have spoken wickedness, the soothsayers have

8:21[a] [Isa 2:2–3; Mic 4:1–2]   **8:22**[a] Isa 60:3; 66:23; [Zech 14:16–21]   **8:23**[a] Isa 3:6   [b] [Isa 45:14]   [c] 1 Cor 14:25   **9:1**[a] Isa 17:1; Jer 23:33   [b] Amos 1:3–5   **9:2**[a] Jer 49:23   [b] Isa 23; Jer 25:22; 47:4; Ezek 26; Amos 1:9–10   [c] 1 Kgs 17:9   [d] Ezek 28:3   **9:4**[a] Isa 23:1   [b] Ezek 26:17   **9:5**[a] Zeph 2:4–5   **9:6**[a] Amos 1:8; Zeph 2:4   [b] Ezek 25:15–17   **9:8**[a] [Ps 34:7]   **9:9**[a] Zeph 3:14–15; Zech 2:10   [b] [Ps 110:1; Isa 9:6–7; Jer 23:5–6]; Matt 21:5; Mark 11:7, 9; Luke 19:38; John 12:15   **9:10**[a] Hos 1:7; Mic 5:10   [b] Ps 46:9; Isa 2:4; Hos 2:18; Mic 4:3   [c] Ps 72:8   [1] LXX *He will remove.*   [2] Heb. *cut off.*   [3] Heb. *the river.*   **9:11**[a] Isa 42:7   **9:12**[a] Isa 49:9; Jer 17:13; Heb 6:18–20   [b] Isa 61:7   **9:14**[a] Ps 18:14; Hab 3:11   **9:15**[a] Isa 37:35; Zech 12:8   **9:16**[a] Jer 31:10–11   [b] Isa 62:3; Mal 3:17   **9:17**[a] [Ps 31:19]   [b] [Ps 45:1–16]   [c] Joel 3:18   **10:1**[a] [Jer 14:22]   [b] [Deut 11:13–14]   [c] [Joel 2:23]   **10:2**[a] Jer 10:8

seen a [b]lie, and the dreamers have disclosed emptiness and give [c]comfort in vain. Therefore the people set out like [d]sheep and become scattered [e]because they have no shepherd. [3]"I am enraged at the [a]shepherds [b]and [c]will punish the lead goats.

"For the LORD of Heaven's Armies has brought blessing to his flock, the house of Judah, and [d]will transform them into his majestic warhorse. [4]From him will come [a]the cornerstone, [b]the wall peg, the battle bow, and every ruler. [5]And they will be like warriors trampling the mud of the streets in battle. They will fight, for the LORD will be with them, and will defeat the enemy cavalry.

[6]"I (says the LORD) [a]will strengthen the kingdom of Judah and deliver the people of Joseph[1] and [b]will bring them back because of my compassion for them. They will be as though I had never rejected them, for I am the LORD their God, and therefore I will hear them. [7]The Ephraimites will be like warriors and will [a]rejoice as if they had drunk wine. Their children will see it and rejoice; they will celebrate in the things of the LORD. [8]I will [a]signal for them [b]and gather them, for I have already redeemed them; then they will become as numerous as they were before. [9]Though [a]I scatter them among the nations, they will [b]remember in far-off places—they and their children will survive and return. [10]I [a]will bring them back from Egypt and gather them from Assyria. [b]I will bring them to the lands of Gilead and Lebanon, and there will not be enough room for them. [11]The LORD will cross [a]the sea of storms and will calm its turbulence. [b]The depths of [c]the Nile will dry up, the pride of Assyria will be humbled, and the domination of Egypt will be no more. [12]Thus I will strengthen them by my power,[1] and [a]they will walk about[2] in my name," says the LORD.

The History and Future of Judah's Wicked Kings

11 Open [a]your gates, Lebanon, so that the fire may consume your cedars.

[2] Howl, fir tree,
because the [a]cedar has fallen;
the majestic trees have been
   destroyed.
Howl, oaks of Bashan,
because the impenetrable [b]forest has
   fallen.

[3] Listen to the howling of [a]shepherds,
because their magnificence has been
   destroyed.
Listen to the roaring of young lions,
because the thickets of the Jordan
   have been devastated.

[4]The LORD my God says this: "Shepherd the flock set aside for slaughter. [5]Those who buy them slaughter them and are not held guilty; those who sell them [a]say, 'Blessed be the LORD, for I am rich.' Their own shepherds have [b]no compassion for them. [6]Indeed, I will no longer have compassion on the people of the land," says the LORD, "but instead I will turn every last person over to his neighbor and his king. They will devastate the land, and I will not deliver it from them."

[7]So I began to shepherd [a]the flock destined for slaughter, the most afflicted[1] of all the flock. Then I took two staffs, calling one "Pleasantness" and the other "Union," and I tended the flock. [8]Next [a]I eradicated the three shepherds in one month, for I ran out of patience with them and, indeed, they detested me as well. [9]I then said, "I will not shepherd you. What is to die, [a]let it die, and what is to be eradicated, let it be eradicated. As for those who survive, let them eat each other's flesh!"

[10]Then I took my staff "Pleasantness" and cut it in two to annul my covenant that I had made with all the people. [11]So it was annulled that very day, and [a]then the most afflicted of the flock who kept faith with me knew that it was the LORD's message. [12]Then I said to them, "If it seems good to you, pay me my wages, but if not, forget it." So they weighed [a]out my payment—30 pieces of silver. [13]The LORD then said to me,

10:2 [b]Jer 27:9; [Ezek 13]   [c]Job 13:4   [d]Jer 50:6, 17   [e]Ezek 34:5–8; Matt 9:36; Mark 6:34   **10:3** [a]Jer 25:34–36; Ezek 34:2; Zech 11:17   [b]Ezek 34:17   [c]Luke 1:68   [d]Song 1:9   **10:4** [a]Isa 28:16   [b]Isa 22:23   **10:6** [a]Jer 3:18; Ezek 37:21   [b]Zech 13:9   [1]Or *the kingdom of Israel*; Heb. *the house of Joseph*.   **10:7** [a]Ps 104:15   **10:8** [a]Isa 5:26   [b]Isa 49:19; Ezek 36:37; Zech 2:4   **10:9** [a]Hos 2:23   [b]Deut 30:1   **10:10** [a]Isa 11:11; Hos 11:11   [b]Isa 49:19–20   **10:11** [a]Isa 11:15   [b]Isa 14:25; Zeph 2:13   [c]Ezek 30:13   **10:12** [a]Mic 4:5   [1]Heb. *I will strengthen them in the LORD*.   [2]LXX, Syr. *they will glory*.   **11:1** [a]Zech 10:10   **11:2** [a]Ezek 31:3   [b]Isa 32:19   **11:3** [a]Jer 25:34–36   **11:5** [a]Deut 29:19; Hos 12:8; 1 Tim 6:9   [b]Ezek 34:2–3   **11:7** [a]Jer 39:10; Zeph 3:12; Matt 11:5   [1]LXX *to the merchants of*.   **11:8** [a]Hos 5:7   **11:9** [a]Jer 15:2   **11:11** [a]Zeph 3:12; Matt 27:50; Mark 15:37; Luke 23:46; Acts 8:32   **11:12** [a]Gen 37:28; Exod 21:32; Matt 26:15; 27:9–10

"Throw to the [a]potter that exorbitant sum at which they valued me!" So I took the 30 pieces of silver and threw them to the potter at the temple of the LORD. [14]Then I cut the second staff "Union" in two in order to annul the covenant of brotherhood between Judah and Israel.

[15]Again the LORD said to me, "Take up once more the equipment of a foolish shepherd. [16]Indeed, I am about to raise up a shepherd in the land who will not take heed of the sheep headed to slaughter, will not seek the scattered, and will not heal the injured. Moreover, he will not nourish the one that is healthy, but instead will eat the meat of the fat sheep and tear [a]off their hooves.

[17]   "[a]Woe to the worthless shepherd
      who abandons the flock!
   May a sword fall on his arm and his
      right eye!
   May his arm wither completely away
      and his right eye become completely
      blind!"

The Repentance of Judah

12 This is an oracle, the LORD's message concerning Israel: The LORD—he [a]who stretches out the heavens and lays the foundations of the earth, who [b]forms the human spirit within a person[1]—says, [2]"I [a]am about to make Jerusalem a cup that brings dizziness to all the surrounding nations; indeed, Judah will also be included when Jerusalem is besieged. [3]Moreover, on that day I will make Jerusalem [a]a [b]heavy burden for all the nations, and all who try to carry it will be seriously injured; yet all the peoples of the earth will be assembled against it. [4]On that day," says the LORD, "[a]I will strike every horse with confusion and its rider with madness. I will pay close attention to the house of Judah, but will strike all the horses of the nations with blindness. [5]Then the leaders of Judah will say to themselves, 'The inhabitants of Jerusalem are a means of strength to us through their God, the LORD of Heaven's Armies.' [6]On that day [a]I will make the leaders of Judah like an igniter among sticks and a burning torch among sheaves, and they will burn up all the surrounding nations right and left. Then the people of Jerusalem will settle once more in their place, the city of Jerusalem. [7]The LORD also will deliver the homes of Judah first, so that the splendor of the kingship of David and of the people of Jerusalem may not exceed that of Judah. [8]On that day the LORD himself will defend the inhabitants of Jerusalem, so that the weakest among them will be like mighty David, and the dynasty of David will be like God, like the angel of the LORD before them. [9]So on that day I will set out to [a]destroy all the nations that come against Jerusalem.

[10]"I will pour out on the kingship of David [a]and the population of Jerusalem a spirit of grace and supplication so that they will [b]look to me,[1] the one they have pierced. They will lament for him [c]as one laments for an only son, and there will be a bitter cry for him like the bitter cry for a firstborn. [11]On that day the [a]lamentation in Jerusalem will be as great as the lamentation at Hadad Rimmon[1] in the plain of Megiddo. [12]The [a]land will mourn, each clan by itself—the clan of the royal household of David by itself and their wives by themselves; the clan of the family of [b]Nathan by itself and their wives by themselves; [13]the clan of the descendants of Levi by itself and their wives by themselves; and the clan of the Shimeites by itself and their wives by themselves; [14]all the clans that remain, each separately with their wives.

The Refinement of Judah

13 "In that [a]day there will be [b]a fountain opened up for the dynasty of David and the people of Jerusalem to cleanse them from sin and [c]impurity. [2]And also on that day," says [a]the LORD of Heaven's Armies, "I will remove the names of the idols from the land and they will never again be remembered. Moreover, I will remove the

11:13 [a] Matt 27:3–10; Acts 1:18–19   **11:16** [a] Ezek 34:1–10; Mic 3:1–3   **11:17** [a] Jer 23:1; Ezek 34:2; Zech 10:2; 11:15; John 10:12–13   **12:1** [a] Isa 42:5; 44:24   [b] Num 16:22; [Eccl 12:7; Isa 57:16]; Heb 12:9   [1] Heb. *the spirit of man within him.*   **12:2** [a] Isa 51:17   **12:3** [a] Zech 12:4, 6, 8; 13:1   [b] Matt 21:44   **12:4** [a] Ps 76:6; Ezek 38:4   **12:6** [a] Isa 10:17–18; Obad 18; Zech 11:1   **12:9** [a] Hag 2:22   **12:10** [a] Jer 31:9; 50:4; Ezek 39:29; [Joel 2:28–29]   [b] John 19:34, 37; 20:27; [Rev 1:7]   [c] Jer 6:26; Amos 8:10   [1] A few MSS *to the one whom.*   **12:11** [a] [Matt 24:30]; Acts 2:37; [Rev 1:7]   [1] A compound of the names of two Canaanite deities, the gods of storm and thunder respectively, but the grammar seems to demand that this is a place name, perhaps where Judah lamented the death of good king Josiah.   **12:12** [a] [Matt 24:30; Rev 1:7]   [b] Luke 3:31   **13:1** [a] Acts 10:43; [Rev 21:6–7]   [b] Ps 36:9; [Heb 9:14; 1 John 1:7]   [c] Num 19:17; Isa 4:4; Ezek 36:25   **13:2** [a] Jer 23:14–15; 2 Pet 2:1

prophets and the unclean spirit from the land. ³Then, if anyone prophesies in spite of this, his father and mother to whom he was born will say to him, 'You ᵃcannot live, for you lie in the name of the LORD.' Then his father and mother to whom he was born will run him through with ᵇa sword when he prophesies.

⁴"Therefore, on ᵃthat day each prophet will be ashamed of his vision when he prophesies and will no longer wear the hairy garment of a prophet to deceive the people. ⁵ᵃInstead he will say, 'I am no prophet; indeed, I am a farmer, for a man has made me his indentured servant since my youth.' ⁶Then someone will ask him, 'What are these wounds on your chest?' and he will answer, 'Some that I received in the house of my friends.'

7 "Awake, sword, against ᵃmy shepherd,
       against the man ᵇwho is my
          associate,"
    says the LORD of Heaven's Armies.
    "ᶜStrike ᵈthe shepherd that the flock
       may be scattered;
    I will turn my hand against the
       insignificant ones.
8 It will happen in all the land," says
       the LORD,
    "that ᵃtwo-thirds of the people in it
       will be cut off and die,
    ᵇbut one-third will be left in it.
9 Then I will bring the remaining third
       into the fire;
    I will ᵃrefine them like silver is
       refined
    and will test them like gold is tested.
    ᵇThey ᶜwill call on my name and I will
       answer;
    I will say, 'These are my people,'
    and they will say, 'The LORD is our
       God.'"

The Sovereignty of the Lord

14 A day of ᵃthe LORD is about to come when your possessions¹ will be divided as plunder in your midst. ²For ᵃI will gather all the nations against Jerusalem to wage war; the city will be taken, its houses plundered, and the women raped. Then half of the city will go into exile, but the remainder of the people will not be taken away.

³Then the LORD will go to battle and fight against those nations, just as he fought battles in ancient days. ⁴On that day his feet will stand ᵃon the Mount of Olives that lies to the east of Jerusalem, and the Mount of Olives will be split ᵇin half from east to west, leaving a great valley. Half the mountain will move northward and the other half southward. ⁵Then you will escape¹ through my mountain valley, for the valley of the mountains will extend to Azal. Indeed, you will flee as you fled from the ᵃearthquake in the days of King Uzziah of Judah. Then the LORD my God will come with ᵇall his holy ones with him. ⁶On that day there will be no light—the sources of light in the heavens will congeal. ⁷It will happen in one day—a day known to the LORD—not in the day or the night, but in the ᵃevening there will be light. ⁸Moreover, on that day living ᵃwaters will flow out from Jerusalem, half of them to the eastern sea and half of them to the western sea; it will happen both in summer and in winter.

⁹The LORD will then be ᵃking over all ᵇthe earth. In that day the LORD will be seen as one with a single name. ¹⁰All the land will change and become like the rift valley from Geba to Rimmon, south of Jerusalem. Jerusalem will be raised up and will ᵃstay in its own place from the Benjamin Gate to the site of the First Gate ᵇand on to the Corner Gate, and from the Tower of Hananel to the royal winepresses. ¹¹And people will settle there, and there will ᵃno longer be the threat of divine extermination—Jerusalem will dwell in security.

¹²But this will be the nature of the plague with which the LORD will strike all the nations that have fought against Jerusalem: Their flesh will decay while they stand on their feet, their eyes will rot away in their sockets, and their tongues will dissolve in their mouths. ¹³On ᵃthat day there will be great confusion from the LORD among

13:3 ᵃDeut 18:20; [Ezek 14:9] ᵇDeut 13:6–11; [Matt 10:37] **13:4** ²Kgs 1:8; Isa 20:2; Matt 3:4 **13:5** ᵃAmos 7:14 **13:7** ᵃIsa 40:11; Ezek 34:23–24; 37:24; Mic 5:2, 4 ᵇ[John 10:30] ᶜMatt 26:31, 56, 67; Mark 14:27; 1 Pet 5:4; Rev 7:16–17 ᵈLuke 12:32 **13:8** ᵃIsa 6:13; Ezek 5:2, 4, 12 ᵇ[Rom 11:5] **13:9** ᵃ1 Pet 1:6–7 ᵇPs 50:15; Zeph 3:9; [Zech 12:10] ᶜJer 30:22; Hos 2:23 **14:1** ᵃ[Isa 13:6, 9; Joel 2:1; Mal 4:1] ¹Heb. *your plunder.* **14:2** ᵃJoel 3:2; Zech 12:2–3 **14:4** ᵃEzek 11:23; Acts 1:9–12 ᵇJoel 3:12 **14:5** ᵃIsa 29:6; Amos 1:1 ᵇJoel 3:11 ¹LXX *will be stopped up.* **14:7** ᵃIsa 30:26 **14:8** ᵃEzek 47:1–12; Joel 3:18; [John 7:38; Rev 22:1–2] **14:9** ᵃ[Jer 23:5–6; Rev 11:15] ᵇ[Eph 4:5–6]; Deut 6:4 **14:10** ᵃJer 30:18; Zech 12:6 ᵇNeh 3:1; Jer 31:38 **14:11** ᵃJer 31:40 **14:13** ᵃ1 Sam 14:15, 20

them; they will seize each other and attack one another violently. [14] Moreover, Judah will fight at Jerusalem, [a]and the wealth of all the surrounding nations will be gathered up[1]—gold, silver, and clothing in great abundance. [15a]This is the kind of plague that will devastate horses, mules, camels, donkeys, and all the other animals in those camps.

[16]Then all who survive from all the nations that came to attack Jerusalem will [a]go up annually to [b]worship [c]the King, the LORD of Heaven's Armies, and to observe the Feast of Shelters. [17a]But if any of the nations anywhere on earth refuse to go up to Jerusalem to worship the King, the LORD of Heaven's Armies, they will get no rain. [18]If the [a]Egyptians will not do so, [b]they will get no rain—instead there will be the kind of plague that the LORD inflicts on any nations that do not go up to celebrate the Feast of Shelters. [19]This will be the punishment of Egypt and of all nations that do not go up to celebrate the Feast of Shelters.

[20]On that day the bells of the horses will bear the inscription "[a]Holy to the LORD." The cooking [b]pots in the LORD's temple will be as holy as the bowls in front of the altar. [21]Every cooking pot in Jerusalem and Judah will become holy in the sight of the LORD of Heaven's Armies, so that all who offer sacrifices may come and use some of them to boil their sacrifices in them. On that day there will no longer be a [a]Canaanite [b]in the house of the LORD of Heaven's Armies.

14:14 [a] Ezek 39:10, 17   [1] Or *collected* (which might suggest a form of taxation), *confiscated* (which might imply seizure of property against someone's will).   **14:15** [a] Zech 14:12   **14:16** [a] [Isa 2:2–3; 60:6–9; 66:18–21; Mic 4:1–2]   [b] Isa 27:13   [c] Lev 23:34–44; Neh 8:14; Hos 12:9; John 7:2   **14:17** [a] Isa 60:12   **14:18** [a] Isa 19:21   [b] Deut 11:10   **14:20** [a] Exod 28:36; 39:30; Isa 23:18; Jer 2:3   [b] Ezek 46:20   **14:21** [a] Isa 35:8; Ezek 44:9; Joel 3:17; Rev 21:27; 22:15   [b] [Eph 2:19–22]

MALACHI

Malachi, a prophet in the days of Nehemiah, directs his message of judgment to a people plagued by corrupt priests, wicked practices, and a false sense of security in their privileged relationship with God. Using the question-and-answer format, Malachi probes deeply into their problems of hypocrisy, infidelity, mixed marriages, divorce, false worship, and arrogance. So sinful has the nation become that God's words to the people no longer have any impact. For 400 years after Malachi's ringing condemnations, God remains silent. Only with the coming of John the Baptist (prophesied in 3:1) does God again communicate to his people through a prophet's voice. The meaning of the name *Mal'aki* ("My Messenger") is probably a shortened form of *Mal'akya*, "Messenger of Yahweh," and it is appropriate to the book that speaks of the coming of the "messenger" ("messenger" is mentioned three times in 2:7; 3:1). The Septuagint used the title *Malachias* even though it also translated it "By the Hand of His Messenger." The Latin title is *Maleachi*.

Introduction and God's Election of Israel

1 This is an oracle, the LORD's message to Israel through Malachi:[1]

[2]"I have shown love to you," says the LORD, but you say, "How have you shown love to us?"

"Esau was Jacob's brother," the LORD [a]explains, "yet I chose [b]Jacob [3]and rejected Esau. I [a]turned Esau's mountains into a deserted wasteland and gave his territory to the wild jackals."

[4]Edom says, "Though we are devastated, we will once again build the ruined places." So the LORD of Heaven's Armies responds, "They indeed may build, but I will [a]overthrow. They will be known as the land of evil, the people with whom the LORD is permanently displeased. [5]Your eyes will see it, and [a]then you will say, 'May the LORD be magnified[1] even beyond the border of Israel!'"

The Sacrilege of Priestly Service

[6]"A son naturally [a]honors his father and a slave respects his master. [b]If I am your father, where is my honor? If I am your master, where is my respect? The LORD of Heaven's Armies asks you this, you priests who make light of my name! But you reply, 'How have we made light of your name?' [7]You are offering [a]improper sacrifices on my altar, yet you ask, 'How have we offended you?' By treating [b]the table of the LORD as if it is of no importance. [8]For [a]when you offer blind animals as a sacrifice, is that not wrong? And when you offer the lame and sick, is that not wrong as well? Indeed, try offering them to your governor! Will he be pleased with you[1] or [b]show you favor?" asks the LORD of Heaven's Armies. [9]"But now plead for God's favor that he might be gracious to us." "With this kind of offering in your hands, how can he be pleased with you?" asks the LORD of Heaven's Armies.

[10]"I wish that one of you would close the temple doors, [a]so that you no [b]longer would light useless fires on my altar. I am not pleased with you," says the LORD of Heaven's Armies, "and I will no longer accept an offering from you. [11]For [a]from the east to the west my name will be great [b]among the nations. [c]Incense and pure offerings will be offered [d]in my name everywhere, [e]for my name will be great among the nations," says

---

1:1 [1]There is question as to whether this is a personal name or "my messenger," the literal meaning of the Heb. 1:2 [a]Deut 4:37; 7:8; 23:5; Isa 41:8–9; [Jer 31:3]; John 15:12 [b]Rom 9:13 1:3 [a]Jer 49:18; Ezek 35:9, 15 1:4 [a]Jer 49:16–18 1:5 [a]Ps 35:27; Mic 5:4 [1]Or *Great is the LORD.* 1:6 [a][Exod 20:12]; Prov 30:11, 17; [Matt 15:4–8; Eph 6:2–3] [b][Isa 63:16; 64:8]; Jer 31:9; Luke 6:46 1:7 [a]Deut 15:21 [b]Ezek 41:22 1:8 [a]Lev 22:22; Deut 15:19–23 [b][Job 42:8] [1]LXX, Vg. *with it.* 1:10 [a]1 Cor 9:13 [b]Isa 1:11 1:11 [a]Isa 59:19 [b]Isa 60:3, 5 [c]1 Tim 2:8 [d]Rev 8:3 [e]Isa 66:18–19

the Lord of Heaven's Armies. [12]"But you are profaning it by saying that [a]the table of the Lord is common and its offerings despicable. [13]You also say, 'How [a]tiresome it is.' You turn up your nose at it," says the Lord of Heaven's Armies, "and instead bring what is stolen, lame, or sick. You bring these things for an offering! [b]Should I accept this from you?" asks the Lord. [14]"There will be harsh condemnation for [a]the hypocrite who has [b]a valuable male [c]animal in his flock but vows and sacrifices something inferior to the Lord. For I am a great king," says the Lord of Heaven's Armies, "and my name is awesome among the nations."

The Sacrilege of the Priestly Message

2 "Now, you [a]priests, this commandment is for you. [2]If you do not listen and take seriously the need to honor my name," says the Lord of Heaven's Armies, "[a]I will send judgment on you and turn your blessings into curses—indeed, I have [b]already done so because you are not taking it to heart. [3]I am about to discipline your children[1] and will spread [a]offal on your faces, the very offal produced at your festivals, and you will be carried [b]away along with it. [4]Then you will know that I sent this commandment to you so that my covenant may continue to be with Levi," says the Lord of Heaven's Armies. [5]"My covenant with him was designed to bring life and peace. I gave its statutes to him to fill him with awe, and he indeed revered me and stood in awe before me. [6]He taught what was true; sinful words were not found on his lips. [a]He walked with me in peace and integrity, and he [b]turned many people away from sin. [7]For the lips of a priest should preserve knowledge of sacred things, and people should seek instruction from him because he is the messenger of the Lord of Heaven's Armies. [8]You, however, [a]have turned from the way. [b]You have caused many to violate the law;[1] you have corrupted the covenant with Levi," says the Lord of Heaven's Armies. [9]"Therefore, [a]I have caused you to be ignored and belittled before all people to the extent that you are not following after me and are showing [b]partiality in your instruction."

The Rebellion of the People

[10]Do we not all [a]have one father? Did not one God create us? Why do we betray one another, thus making light of the covenant of our ancestors? [11]Judah has become disloyal, and unspeakable sins have been committed in Israel and Jerusalem. For Judah has [a]profaned the holy things that the Lord loves and has turned to a foreign god! [12]May the Lord cut off from the community of Jacob every last person [a]who does this,[1] as well as the person who presents improper offerings to the Lord of Heaven's Armies!

[13]You also do this: You cover the altar of the Lord with tears as you weep and groan, because he no longer pays any attention to the offering nor accepts it favorably from you. [14]Yet you ask, "Why?" [a]The Lord is testifying against you on behalf of the wife you married when you were young, to whom you have become unfaithful even though she is your companion and wife by law. [15]No one who has even a small portion of the Spirit in him does this. What [a]did our ancestor do when seeking a child from [b]God? Be attentive, then, to your own spirit, for one should not be disloyal to the wife he took in his youth. [16]"I hate divorce," says [a]the Lord God of Israel, "and the one who is guilty of violence,"[1] says the Lord of Heaven's Armies. "Pay attention to your conscience, and do not be unfaithful."

Resistance to the Lord through Self-Deceit

[17]You have wearied the Lord with [a]your words. But you say, "How have we wearied him?" Because you say, "[b]Everyone who does evil is good in the Lord's opinion, and he delights in them," or, "Where is the God of justice?"[1] 3"I am about to send my messenger,[1] who [a]will [b]clear [c]the way before me. Indeed, the Lord you are seeking will suddenly come to his temple, and

1:12 [a]Mal 1:7   1:13 [a]Isa 43:22   [b]Lev 22:20   1:14 [a]Mal 1:8   [b]Lev 22:18–20   [c]Ps 47:2   2:1 [a]Mal 1:6   2:2 [a][Lev 26:14–15; Deut 28:15]   [b]Mal 3:9   2:3 [a]Exod 29:14   [b]1 Kgs 14:10   [1]LXX, Vg. *I am about to take away your arm.*   2:6 [a]Deut 33:10   [b]Jer 23:22; [Jas 5:20]   2:8 [a]Jer 18:15   [b]Num 25:12–13; Neh 13:29; Ezek 44:10   [1]The Torah or the priestly instruction just mentioned.   2:9 [a]1 Sam 2:30   [b]Deut 1:17; Mic 3:11; 1 Tim 5:21   2:10 [a]Jer 31:9; 1 Cor 8:6; [Eph 4:6]   2:11 [a]Ezra 9:1–2; Neh 13:23   2:12 [a]Neh 13:29   [1]Heb. *every man who does this, him who is awake and him who answers;* LXX *until he is humbled.*   2:14 [a]Prov 5:18; Jer 9:2; Mal 3:5   2:15 [a]Gen 2:24; Matt 19:4–5   [b]Ezra 9:2; [1 Cor 7:14]   2:16 [a]Deut 24:1; [Matt 5:31; 19:6–8]   [1]Heb. *him who covers his garment with violence.*   2:17 [a]Isa 43:22, 24   [b]Isa 5:20; Zeph 1:12   3:1 [a]Matt 11:10; Mark 1:2; Luke 1:76; 7:27; John 1:23; 2:14–15   [b][Isa 40:3]   [c]Hab 2:7   [1]The same Heb. form as the prophet's name.

the messenger of the covenant, whom you long for, is certainly coming," says the LORD of Heaven's Armies.

[2] Who can endure [a]the day of his coming? [b]Who can keep standing [c]when he appears? For he will be like a refiner's fire, like a launderer's soap. [3]He will act like a refiner and purifier of silver and will cleanse [a]the Levites and refine them like gold and silver. Then they will [b]offer the LORD a proper offering. [4]The offerings of Judah and Jerusalem will be pleasing to [a]the LORD as in former times and years past.

[5]"I will come to you [a]in judgment. I will be quick to testify against those who practice divination; those who commit adultery; those who break promises; and those who [b]exploit workers, [c]widows, and orphans, who refuse to help the resident foreigner and in this way show they do not fear me," says the LORD of Heaven's Armies.

Resistance to the Lord through Selfishness

[6]"Since, [a]I, [b]the LORD, do not go back on my promises, you, sons of Jacob, have not perished. [7]From the days of [a]your ancestors you have ignored my commandments[1] and have not kept them. [b]Return to me, and I will return to you," says the LORD of Heaven's Armies. "[c]But you say, 'How should we return?' [8]Can a person rob[1] God? You are [a]indeed robbing me, but you say, 'How are we robbing you?' In tithes and contributions! [9]You are bound for judgment because you are robbing me—this whole nation is guilty.

[10]"[a]Bring the entire tithe into the storehouse so that there may be food in my temple. Test me in this matter," says the LORD of Heaven's Armies, "[b]to see if I will not open for you the [c]windows of heaven and [d]pour out blessing for you until there is no room for it all. [11]Then I will stop [a]the plague from ruining your crops, and the vine will not lose its fruit before harvest," says the LORD of Heaven's Armies. [12]"All [a]nations will call you blessed, for you indeed will live in a delightful land," says the LORD of Heaven's Armies.

Resistance to the Lord through Self-Sufficiency

[13]"You have criticized me sharply," says the LORD, "but [a]you ask, 'How have we criticized you?' [14][a]You have said, 'It is useless to serve God. How have we been helped[1] by keeping his requirements and going about like mourners before the LORD of Heaven's Armies? [15]So now [a]we consider the arrogant to be blessed; indeed, those who practice evil are successful. In fact, those who [b]challenge God escape!'"

[16]Then those [a]who respected the LORD [b]spoke to one [c]another, and the LORD took notice. A scroll was prepared before him in which were recorded the names of those who respected the LORD and honored his name. [17]"They will belong to me," says [a]the LORD of Heaven's Armies, "in the day when I prepare my own special [b]property. [c]I will spare them as a man spares his son who serves him. [18]Then once more you will see that I make a distinction between [a]the righteous and the wicked, between the one who serves God and the one who does not.

4 "For indeed [a]the day is coming, burning like a furnace, and all [b]the arrogant evildoers will be [c]chaff. The coming day will burn them up," says the LORD of Heaven's Armies. "It will not [d]leave them even a root or branch. [2]But for you who [a]respect my name, the [b]sun of vindication will rise with healing wings, and you will skip about like calves released from the stall. [3]You will trample on the wicked, for they will be like ashes under the soles of [a]your feet on the day that I am preparing," says the LORD of Heaven's Armies.

Restoration through the Lord

[4]"Remember the [a]law of my servant Moses, to whom at Horeb I gave rules and regulations for all Israel to obey.[1] [5]Look, I will send you [a]Elijah the prophet [b]before the great and terrible day of the LORD arrives. [6]He will encourage [a]fathers and their children to return to me, so that I will not come and [b]strike the [c]earth with judgment."

3:2 [a]Jer 10:10; Joel 2:11; Nah 1:6; [Mal 4:1]   [b]Isa 33:14; Ezek 22:14; Rev 6:17   [c]Isa 4:4; Zech 13:9; [Matt 3:10–12; 1 Cor 3:13–15]
3:3 [a]Isa 1:25; Dan 12:10; Zech 13:9   [b][1 Pet 2:5]   3:4 [a]Mal 1:11   3:5 [a]Lev 19:12; Zech 5:4; [Jas 5:12]   [b]Lev 19:13; Jas 5:4   [c]Exod 22:22   3:6 [a][Num 23:19; Rom 11:29; Jas 1:17]   [b][Lam 3:22]   3:7 [a]Acts 7:51   [b]Zech 1:3   [c]Mal 1:6   [1]Or statutes.   3:8 [a]Neh 13:10–12   [1]LXX deceive.   3:10 [a]Prov 3:9–10   [b]1 Chr 26:20   [c]Gen 7:11   [d]2 Chr 31:10   3:11 [a]Amos 4:9   3:12 [a]Dan 8:9   3:13 [a]Mal 2:17   3:14 [a]Job 21:14   [1]Heb. What [is the] profit.   3:15 [a]Ps 73:12   [b]Ps 95:9   3:16 [a]Ps 66:16   [b]Heb 3:13   [c]Ps 56:8   3:17 [a]Exod 19:5; Deut 7:6; Isa 43:21; [1 Pet 2:9]   [b]Isa 62:3   [c]Ps 103:13   3:18 [a][Ps 58:11]   4:1 [a]Ps 21:9; [Nah 1:5–6; Mal 3:2–3; 2 Pet 3:7]   [b]Mal 3:18   [c]Isa 5:24; Obad 18   [d]Amos 2:9   4:2 [a]Mal 3:16   [b]Matt 4:16; Luke 1:78; Acts 10:43; 2 Cor 4:6; Eph 5:14   4:3 [a]Mic 7:10   4:4 [a]Exod 20:3   [1]Heb. which I commanded him in Horeb concerning all Israel, statutes and ordinances.
4:5 [a][Matt 11:14; 17:10–13; Mark 9:11–13; Luke 1:17]; John 1:21   [b]Joel 2:31   4:6 [a]Zech 1:17   [b]Zech 14:12   [c]Zech 5:3

THE
NEW TESTAMENT

MATHEW

Matthew is the Gospel written by a Jew to Jews about a Jew. Matthew is the writer, his countrymen are the readers, and Jesus Christ is the subject. Matthew's design is to present Jesus as the King of the Jews, the long-awaited Messiah. Through a carefully selected series of Old Testament quotations, Matthew documents Jesus Christ's claim. His genealogy, baptism, messages, and miracles all point to the same inescapable conclusion: Christ is King. Even in his death, seeming defeat is turned to victory by the resurrection, and the message again echoes forth: the King of the Jews lives. At an early date this Gospel was given the title *Kata Matthaion*, "According to Matthew." As this title suggests, other Gospel accounts were known at that time (the word "Gospel" was added later). Matthew ("Gift of the Lord") was also surnamed Levi (Mark 2:14; Luke 5:27).

The Genealogy of Jesus Christ

1 This is the record of the [a]genealogy of Jesus Christ, [b]the son of David, [c]the son of Abraham.

[2a]Abraham was the father of [b]Isaac, Isaac the father of Jacob, Jacob the father of [c]Judah and his brothers, [3a]Judah the father of [b]Perez and Zerah (by Tamar), Perez the father of Hezron, Hezron the father of Ram, [4]Ram the father of Amminadab, Amminadab the father of Nahshon, Nahshon the father of Salmon, [5]Salmon the father of [a]Boaz (by Rahab), Boaz the father of Obed (by Ruth), Obed the father of Jesse, [6]and [a]Jesse the father of [b]David the king.

David was the father of Solomon (by the wife of Uriah), [7a]Solomon the father of Rehoboam, Rehoboam the father of [b]Abijah, Abijah the father of Asa,[1] [8]Asa the father of [a]Jehoshaphat, Jehoshaphat the father of Joram, Joram the father of [b]Uzziah, [9]Uzziah the father of Jotham, Jotham the father of [a]Ahaz, Ahaz the father of Hezekiah, [10a]Hezekiah the father of Manasseh, Manasseh the father of Amon,[1] Amon the father of [b]Josiah, [11]and [a]Josiah the father of Jeconiah and his brothers, at the time of the [b]deportation to Babylon.

[12]After the deportation to Babylon, [a]Jeconiah became the father of Shealtiel, Shealtiel the father of [b]Zerubbabel, [13]Zerubbabel the father of Abiud, Abiud the father of Eliakim, Eliakim the father of Azor, [14]Azor the father of Zadok, Zadok the father of Achim, Achim the father of Eliud, [15]Eliud the father of Eleazar, Eleazar the father of Matthan, Matthan the father of Jacob, [16]and Jacob the father of Joseph, the husband of [a]Mary, by whom Jesus was born, who is called Christ.[1]

[17]So all the generations from Abraham to David are fourteen generations, and from David to the deportation to Babylon, fourteen generations, and from the deportation to Babylon to Christ, fourteen generations.

The Birth of Jesus Christ

[18]Now the [a]birth of Jesus Christ happened this way. While his mother Mary was engaged to Joseph, but before they came together, she was found to be pregnant [b]through the Holy Spirit. [19]Because Joseph, her husband [a]to be, was a righteous man, and because he did not want to disgrace her, he intended to divorce her privately. [20]When he had contemplated this, an[1] angel of the Lord appeared to him in a

1:1 [a]Luke 3:23   [b]2 Sam 7:12–16; Ps 132:11; Isa 9:6; 11:1; Jer 23:5; [Matt 1:18; Luke 3:23, 31]; John 7:42; Acts 2:30; [Rom 1:3]; Rev 22:16   [c]Gen 12:3; 22:18; [Gal 3:16]   1:2 [a]Gen 21:2, 12   [b]Gen 25:26; 28:14   [c]Gen 29:35   1:3 [a]Gen 38:27; 49:10   [b]Ruth 4:18–22; 1 Chr 2:1–15; Matt 1:3–6   1:5 [a]Ruth 2:1; 4:1–13   1:6 [a]1 Sam 16:1; Isa 11:1, 10   [b]2 Sam 7:12; 12:24; Isa 9:7   1:7 [a]1 Kgs 11:43; 1 Chr 3:10   [b]2 Chr 11:20   [1]Many sig. wss *Asaph*.   1:8 [a]1 Chr 3:10   [b]2 Kgs 15:13   1:9 [a]2 Kgs 15:38   1:10 [a]2 Kgs 20:21   [b]1 Kgs 13:2   [1]Many sig. wss *Amos*.   1:11 [a]1 Chr 3:15–16   [b]2 Kgs 24:14–16; Jer 27:20; Matt 1:17   1:12 [a]1 Chr 3:17   [b]Ezra 3:2; Neh 12:1; Hag 1:1   1:16 [a]Matt 13:55; Mark 6:3   [1]Or *Messiah*; both "Christ" (Grk.) and "Messiah" (Heb., Aram.) mean "one who has been anointed."   1:18 [a]Matt 12:46; Luke 1:27   [b]Isa 7:14; 49:5; Luke 1:35   1:19 [a]Deut 24:1; John 8:4–5   1:20 [1]Grk. *behold, an angel*.

dream and said, "Joseph, son of David, do not be afraid to take Mary as your wife [a]because the child conceived in her is from the Holy Spirit. [21]She will give birth to [a]a son and you will name him Jesus [b]because he will save his people from their sins." [22]This all happened so that what was spoken by the Lord through the prophet would be fulfilled: [23]"[a]*Look! The virgin will conceive and give birth to a son, and they will name him Emmanuel,*"[1] which means "*God with us.*"[2] [24]When Joseph awoke from sleep he did what the angel of the Lord told him. He took his wife, [25]but did not have marital relations with [a]her until she gave birth to a son, whom he named Jesus.

The Visit of the Wise Men

2 After [a]Jesus was born in Bethlehem in Judea, in the time of King Herod, wise men [b]from the East came to Jerusalem [2]saying, "[a]Where is the one who is born king of the Jews? For we saw [b]his star when it rose and have come to worship him." [3]When King Herod heard this he was alarmed, and all Jerusalem with him. [4]After assembling all [a]the chief priests and experts in the [b]law,[1] [c]he asked them where the Christ[2] was to be born. [5]"In Bethlehem of Judea," they said, "for it is written this way by the prophet:

6 '[a]*And you, Bethlehem, in the land of Judah,*
   are in no way least among the rulers of Judah,
   for out of you will come a ruler [b]who will shepherd my people Israel.'"[1]

[7]Then Herod privately summoned the wise men and determined from them when the [a]star had appeared. [8]He sent them to Bethlehem and said, "Go and look carefully for the child. When you find him, inform me so that I can go and worship him as well." [9]After listening to the king they left, and once again the star they saw when it rose led them until it stopped above the place where the child was. [10]When they saw the star they shouted joyfully. [11]As [a]they came into the house and saw the child with Mary his mother, they bowed down and worshiped him. They opened their treasure boxes and gave him gifts of gold, frankincense, and myrrh. [12]After being warned [a]in a dream not to return to Herod, they went back by another route to their own country.

The Escape to Egypt

[13]After they had gone, an angel of the Lord appeared to Joseph in a dream and said, "Get up, take the child and his mother and flee to Egypt, and stay there until I tell you, for Herod is going to look for the child to kill him." [14]Then he got up, took the child and his mother during the night, and went to Egypt. [15]He stayed there until Herod died. In this way what was spoken by the Lord through the prophet was fulfilled: "*I called my Son out [a]of Egypt.*"[1]

[16]When Herod saw that he had been tricked by the wise men, he became enraged. He sent men to kill all the children in Bethlehem and throughout the surrounding region from the age of two and under, according to the time he had learned from the wise men. [17]Then what was spoken by Jeremiah the prophet was fulfilled:

18 "*A [a]voice was heard in Ramah,*
    weeping and loud wailing,[1]
    Rachel weeping for her children,
    and she did not want to be comforted,
    because they were gone."[2]

The Return to Nazareth

[19]After Herod had died, an angel of the Lord appeared in a dream to Joseph in Egypt [20a]saying, "Get up, take the child and his mother, and go to the land of Israel, for those who were [b]seeking the child's life are dead." [21]So he got up and took the child and his mother and returned to the land of Israel. [22]But when he heard that Archelaus was reigning over Judea in place of his father Herod, he was afraid to go there. After being warned in a [a]dream, he went [b]to the regions of Galilee. [23]He came to a town called [a]Nazareth and lived there. Then [b]what had been

1:20 [a]Luke 1:35   1:21 [a][Isa 7:14; 9:6–7]; Luke 1:31; 2:21   [b]Luke 2:11; John 1:29; [Acts 4:12; 5:31; 13:23, 38; Rom 5:18–19; Col 1:20–23]   1:23 [a]Isa 7:14   [1]Isa 7:14   [2]Isa 8:8, 10 LXX   1:25 [a]Exod 13:2; Luke 2:7, 21   2:1 [a]Mic 5:2; Luke 2:4–7   [b]Gen 25:6; 1 Kgs 4:30   2:2 [a]Luke 2:11   [b][Num 24:17; Isa 60:3]   2:4 [a]2 Chr 36:14   [b]2 Chr 34:13   [c]Mal 2:7   [1]Or *and scribes of the people.*   [2]Or *Messiah*; both "Christ" (Grk.) and "Messiah" (Heb., Aram.) mean "one who has been anointed."   2:6 [a]Mic 5:2; John 7:42   [b]Gen 49:10; [Rev 2:27]   [1]Mic 5:2   2:7 [a]Num 24:17   2:11 [a]Ps 72:10; Isa 60:6   2:12 [a][Job 33:15–16]; Matt 1:20   2:15 [a]Num 24:8; Hos 11:1   [1]Hos 11:1   2:18 [a]Jer 31:15   [1]LXX *lamentation, weeping, and loud wailing.*   [2]Jer 31:15   2:20 [a]Luke 2:39   [b]Matt 2:16   2:22 [a]Matt 2:12–13, 19   [b]Matt 3:13; Luke 2:39   2:23 [a]Luke 1:26; 2:39; John 1:45–46   [b]Judg 13:5

spoken by the prophets was fulfilled, that Jesus would be called a Nazarene.[1]

The Ministry of John the Baptist

3 In those days [a]John the Baptist came [b]into the wilderness of Judea proclaiming, 2"Repent, for [a]the kingdom of heaven is near." 3For [a]he is the one about whom the prophet Isaiah had spoken:

> "*The voice of one shouting in the wilderness,*
> '[b]*Prepare the way for the Lord, make his paths straight.*'"[1]

4Now [a]John wore clothing made from camel's hair with a leather belt around his waist, and his diet consisted of [b]locusts and [c]wild honey. 5[a]Then people from Jerusalem, as well as all Judea and all the region around the Jordan, were going out to him, 6[a]and he was baptizing them in the Jordan River as they confessed their sins.

7But when he saw many Pharisees and Sadducees coming to his baptism, he said to them, "You [a]offspring of vipers! Who warned you to flee from [b]the coming wrath? 8Therefore produce fruit that proves your repentance, 9and don't think you can say to yourselves, '[a]We have Abraham as our father.' For I tell you that God can raise up children for Abraham from these stones! 10Even now the ax is laid at the root of the trees, [a]and every tree that does not produce good fruit will be cut down and thrown into the fire.

11"[a]I baptize you with water, for repentance, but the one coming after me is more powerful than I am—I am not worthy to carry [b]his sandals! He will baptize you with the Holy Spirit and fire. 12His winnowing fork [a]is in his hand, and he will clean out his threshing floor and will gather his wheat into the storehouse, but the chaff he will [b]burn up with inextinguishable fire!"

The Baptism of Jesus

13[a]Then Jesus came [b]from Galilee to John to be baptized by him in the Jordan River. 14But John[1] tried to prevent him, saying, "I need to be baptized by you, and yet you come to me?" 15So Jesus replied to him, "Let it happen now, for it is right for us to fulfill all righteousness." Then John yielded to him. 16After Jesus was baptized, just as he was coming up out of the water, the[1] heavens opened[2] [a]and he saw [b]the Spirit of God descending like a dove and coming to rest on him. 17[a]And a voice from heaven said,[1] "[b]This is my one dear Son;[2] in him I take great delight."

The Temptation of Jesus

4 Then [a]Jesus was led by [b]the Spirit into the wilderness to be tempted by the devil. 2After he fasted 40 days and 40 nights he was famished. 3The tempter came and said to him, "If you are the Son of God, command these stones to become bread."[1] 4But he answered, "It is written, '[a]*Man does not live by bread alone, but by every word that comes from the mouth of God.*'"[1] 5Then the devil took him [a]to the holy city, had him stand on the highest point of the temple, 6and said to him, "If you are [a]the Son of God, throw yourself down. For it is written, '[b]*He will command his angels concerning you*'[1] and '[b]*with their hands they will lift you up, so that you will not strike your foot against a stone.*'"[2] 7Jesus said to him, "Once again it is written: '[a]*You are not to put the Lord your God to the test.*'"[1] 8Again, the devil took him to a very high mountain, and [a]showed him all the kingdoms of the world and their grandeur. 9And he said to him, "I will give you all these things if you throw yourself to the ground and worship me." 10Then Jesus said to him, "Go away,[1] Satan! For it is written: '[a]*You are to worship the Lord your God and serve* only *him.*'"[2] 11Then the devil [a]left him, and [b]angels came and began ministering to his needs.

2:23 [1] An expression of scorn rooted in the OT.   3:1 [a] Matt 3:1–12; Mark 1:3–8; Luke 3:2–17; John 1:6–8, 19–28 [b] Josh 14:10   3:2 [a] Dan 2:44; Mal 4:6; Matt 4:17; Mark 1:15; Luke 1:17; 10:9; 11:20; 21:31   3:3 [a] Isa 40:3; Luke 3:4; John 1:23 [b] Luke 1:76 [1] Isa 40:3   3:4 [a] 2 Kgs 1:8; Zech 13:4; Matt 11:8; Mark 1:6 [b] Lev 11:22 [c] 1 Sam 14:25–26   3:5 [a] Mark 1:5   3:6 [a] Acts 19:4, 18   3:7 [a] Matt 12:34; Luke 3:7–9 [b] [Rom 5:9; 1 Thess 1:10]   3:9 [a] John 8:33; Acts 13:26; [Rom 4:1, 11, 16; Gal 3:29]   3:10 [a] [Ps 92:12–14]; Matt 7:19; Luke 13:7, 9; [John 15:6]   3:11 [a] Mark 1:4, 8; Luke 3:16; John 1:26; Acts 1:5 [b] [Isa 4:4; John 20:22; Acts 2:3–4; 1 Cor 12:13]   3:12 [a] Mal 3:3 [b] Mal 4:1; Matt 13:30   3:13 [a] Matt 3:13–17; Mark 1:9–11; Luke 3:21–22; John 1:31–34 [b] Matt 2:22   3:14 [1] ‡ Earliest MSS omit *John*.   3:16 [a] Mark 1:10 [b] [Isa 11:2]; Luke 3:22; John 1:32; Acts 7:56 [1] Grk. *behold the heavens.* [2] ‡ Maj. WSS add *to/before him.*   3:17 [a] John 12:28 [b] Ps 2:7; Isa 42:1; Mark 1:11; Luke 1:35; 9:35; Col 1:13 [1] Grk. *behold, a voice from the heavens, saying.* [2] Grk. *my beloved Son.*   4:1 [a] Matt 4:1–11; Mark 1:12; Luke 4:1 [b] Ezek 3:14; Acts 8:39   4:3 [1] Grk. *say that these stones should become bread.*   4:4 [a] Deut 8:3 [1] Deut 8:3   4:5 [a] Neh 11:1, 18; Dan 9:24; Matt 27:53   4:6 [a] Ps 91:11 [b] Ps 91:12 [1] Ps 91:11 [2] Ps 91:12   4:7 [a] Deut 6:16 [1] Deut 6:16   4:8 [a] [Matt 16:26; 1 John 2:15–17]   4:10 [a] Deut 6:13; 10:20; Josh 24:14 [1] Maj. WSS add *behind me.* [2] Deut 6:13   4:11 [a] [Jas 4:7] [b] Matt 26:53; Luke 22:43; [Heb 1:14]

Preaching in Galilee

[12] [a]Now when Jesus heard that John had been imprisoned, he went into Galilee. [13]While in Galilee, he moved from Nazareth to make his home in Capernaum by the sea, in the region of Zebulun and Naphtali, [14]so that what was spoken by the prophet Isaiah would be fulfilled:

[15] *"Land of Zebulun and land of Naphtali,*
[a]the way by the sea, beyond the Jordan, Galilee of the Gentiles—
[16] *[a]the people who sit in darkness have seen a great light,*
and on those who sit in the region and shadow of death a light has dawned."[1]

[17][a]From that time Jesus began to preach this message: "[b]Repent, for the kingdom of heaven is near!"

The Call of the Disciples

[18]As he was walking by the Sea of Galilee he saw two brothers, Simon (called Peter) [a]and Andrew his brother, casting [b]a net into the sea (for they were fishermen). [19]He [a]said to them, "Follow me, and I will turn you into fishers of people!"[1] [20][a]They left their nets immediately and followed him. [21]Going on from there he saw two other brothers, James the son of Zebedee and his brother John, [a]in a boat with their father Zebedee, mending their nets. Then he called them. [22]They immediately left the boat and their father and followed him.

Jesus' Healing Ministry

[23]Jesus went throughout all of Galilee, [a]teaching in their synagogues, preaching [b]the gospel of the kingdom, [c]and healing every kind of disease and sickness among the people. [24]So a report about him spread throughout Syria. People[1] [a]brought to him all who suffered with various illnesses and afflictions, those who had seizures, paralytics, and those possessed by demons, and he healed them. [25]And [a]large crowds followed him from Galilee, the Decapolis, Jerusalem, Judea, and beyond the Jordan River.

The Beatitudes

5 When [a]he saw the crowds, he went up the mountain. After he sat down his disciples came to him. [2]Then he began to [a]teach them by saying:

[3] "[a]Blessed are the poor in spirit, for the kingdom of heaven belongs to them.
[4] [a]Blessed are those who mourn, for they will be comforted.
[5] [a]Blessed are the meek, for [b]they will inherit the earth.
[6] Blessed are those who [a]hunger and thirst [b]for righteousness, for they will be satisfied.
[7] Blessed are the merciful, [a]for they will be shown mercy.
[8] [a]Blessed are the pure in heart, for [b]they will see God.
[9] Blessed are the peacemakers, for they will be called the children of God.
[10] [a]Blessed are those who are persecuted for righteousness, for the kingdom of heaven belongs to them.
[11] [a]Blessed are you when people insult you and persecute you and say all kinds of [b]evil things about you falsely[1] on account of me.
[12][a]Rejoice and be glad because your reward is great in heaven, for they persecuted the prophets before you in the same [b]way.

Salt and Light

[13]"You are the salt of the earth. [a]But if salt loses its flavor, how can it be made salty again? It is no longer good for anything

4:12 [a]Matt 14:3; Mark 1:14; Luke 3:20; John 4:43   4:15 [a]Isa 9:1–2   4:16 [a]Isa 42:7; Luke 2:32   [1]Isa 9:1   4:17 [a]Mark 1:14–15 [b]Matt 3:2; 10:7   4:18 [a]Matt 4:18–22; Mark 1:16–20; Luke 5:2–11; John 1:40–42   [b]Matt 10:2; 16:18; John 1:40–42   4:19 [a]Luke 5:10   [1]Grk. men.   4:20 [a]Matt 19:27; Mark 10:28   4:21 [a]Mark 1:19   4:23 [a]Ps 22:22; Matt 9:35; Mark 1:21; 6:2; 10:1; Luke 4:15; 6:6; 13:10; John 6:59; 18:20   [b][Matt 24:14]; Mark 1:14; Luke 4:43; 8:1; 16:16   [c]Mark 1:34; Luke 4:40; 7:21; Acts 10:38 4:24 [a]Mark 1:32–33; Luke 4:40   [1]Grk. And they.   4:25 [a]Matt 5:1; 8:1, 18; Mark 3:7–8   5:1 [a]Matt 14:23; 15:29; 17:1; Mark 3:13; Luke 6:17; 9:28; John 6:3, 15   5:2 [a][Matt 7:29]; Mark 10:1; 12:35; John 8:2   5:3 [a]Prov 16:19; Isa 66:2; Luke 6:20–23 5:4 [a]Isa 61:2–3; Luke 6:21; [John 16:20]; Acts 16:34; [2 Cor 1:7]; Rev 21:4   5:5 [a]Ps 37:11; Isa 29:19   [b][Rom 4:13]   5:6 [a]Luke 1:53; Acts 2:4   [b][Isa 55:1; 65:13; John 4:14; 6:48; 7:37]   5:7 [a]Ps 41:1; Mark 11:25   5:8 [a]Ps 15:2; 24:4; Heb 12:14   [b]Acts 7:55–56; 1 Cor 13:12   5:10 [a][2 Cor 4:17]; 1 Pet 3:14   5:11 [a]Luke 6:22   [b]1 Pet 4:14   [1]A few MSS omit bearing witness falsely.   5:12 [a]Luke 6:23; Acts 5:41; 1 Pet 4:13–14   [b]2 Chr 36:16; Neh 9:26; Matt 23:37; Acts 7:52; 1 Thess 2:15; Heb 11:35–37; Jas 5:10   5:13 [a]Mark 9:50; Luke 14:34

except to be thrown out and trampled on by people! [14a]You are the light of the world. A city located on a hill cannot be hidden. [15]People do not [a]light a lamp and put it under a basket but on a lampstand, and it gives light to all in the house. [16]In the same way, let your light shine before people, so [a]that they can see your good deeds and give [b]honor to your Father in heaven.

Fulfillment of the Law and Prophets

[17][a]"Do not think that I have come to abolish the law or the prophets. I have not come to abolish these things but to fulfill them. [18]I tell you the truth, until heaven and earth pass away not the smallest letter or stroke of a letter[1] will pass from the law until everything takes place. [19]So anyone [a]who breaks one of the least of these commands and teaches others to do so will be called least in the kingdom of heaven, but whoever obeys them and teaches others to do so will be called great in the kingdom of heaven. [20]For I tell you, unless your righteousness goes beyond that of [a]the experts in the law[1] and the Pharisees, you will never enter the kingdom of heaven!

Anger and Murder

[21]"You have heard that it was said to an older generation, '[b]Do not murder,'[1] and 'whoever murders will be subjected to judgment.' [22]But I say to you that [a]anyone who is angry with [b]a brother[1] will be subjected to judgment. And whoever insults[2] a brother will be brought before the council,[3] and whoever says 'Fool' will be sent to fiery hell. [23]So then, [a]if you bring your gift to the altar and there you remember that your brother has something against you, [24a]leave your gift there in front of the altar. First go and be reconciled to your brother and then come and present your gift. [25]Reach [a]agreement quickly with your accuser [b]while on the way to court, or he may hand you over to the judge, and the judge hand you over to the warden, and you will be thrown into prison.

[26]I tell you the truth, you will never get out of there until you have paid the last penny!

Adultery

[27]"You have heard that it was said, '**Do not commit adultery.**'[1] [28]But I say to you that whoever looks [a]at a woman to desire her has already committed adultery with her in his heart. [29a]If your right eye causes you to sin, [b]tear it out and throw it away! It is better to lose one of your members than to have your whole body thrown into hell. [30]If your right hand causes you to sin, cut it off and throw it away! It is better to lose one of your members than to have your whole body go into hell.

Divorce

[31]"It was said, '[a]**Whoever divorces his wife must give her a legal document.**'[1] [32]But I say to you that [a]everyone who divorces his wife, except for immorality, makes her commit adultery, and whoever marries a divorced woman commits adultery.

Oaths

[33]"Again, you have heard that [a]it was said to an older generation, '**Do not break an oath, but fulfill [b]your vows to the Lord.**'[1] [34]But I say to you, [a]do not take oaths at all—not by heaven because it is the throne of [b]God, [35]not by earth because it is his footstool, and not by Jerusalem because it is [a]the city of the great King. [36]Do not take an oath by your head because you are not able to make one hair white or black. [37a]Let your word be 'Yes, yes' or 'No, no.' More than this is from the evil one.[1]

Retaliation

[38]"You have heard that it was said, '[a]**An eye for an eye and a tooth for a tooth.**'[1] [39a]But I say to you, do not resist the evildoer. [b]But whoever strikes you on the[1] right cheek, turn the other to him as well. [40]And if someone wants to sue you and take your tunic, let him have your coat also. [41]And if anyone

5:14 [a][Prov 4:18; John 8:12]; Phil 2:15 **5:15** [a]Mark 4:21; Luke 8:16; Phil 2:15 **5:16** [a]1 Pet 2:12 [b][John 15:8]; 1 Cor 14:25 **5:17** [a]Rom 10:4 **5:18** [1]Grk. *Not one iota or one serif.* **5:19** [a][Jas 2:10] **5:20** [a][Rom 10:3] [1]Or *and scribes of the people.* **5:21** [1]Exod 20:13; Deut 5:17 **5:22** [a][1 John 3:15] [b][Jas 2:20; 3:6] [1]Many MSS add *without cause.* [2]Grk. *whoever says to his brother 'Raca,';* a word of contempt meaning "fool, empty head." [3]Grk. *the Sanhedrin.* **5:23** [a]Matt 8:4 **5:24** [a][Job 42:8; 1 Tim 2:8; 1 Pet 3:7] **5:25** [a][Prov 25:8]; Luke 12:58–59 [b][Ps 32:6; Isa 55:6] **5:27** [1]Exod 20:14; Deut 5:17 **5:28** [a]2 Sam 11:2–5; Job 31:1; Prov 6:25; [Matt 15:19; Jas 1:14–15] **5:29** [a]Mark 9:43 [b][Col 3:5] **5:31** [a]Deut 24:1; [Jer 3:1]; Mark 10:2 [1]Deut 24:1 **5:32** [a][Matt 19:9; Mark 10:11; Luke 16:18; Rom 7:3]; 1 Cor 7:11 **5:33** [a]Matt 23:16 [b][Exod 20:7]; Lev 19:12; Num 30:2 [1]Lev 19:12 **5:34** [a]Matt 23:16; Jas 5:12 [b]Isa 66:1 **5:35** [a]Ps 48:2; [Matt 5:2, 19; 6:10] **5:37** [a][Col 4:6]; Jas 5:12 [1]Or a general reference to evil. **5:38** [a]Exod 21:24; Lev 24:20; Deut 19:21 [1]Exod 21:24; Lev 24:20 **5:39** [a][Prov 20:22]; Luke 6:29; [Rom 12:17; 1 Cor 6:7; 1 Pet 3:9] [b]Isa 50:6; Lam 3:30 [1]‡ Many MSS *your.*

[a]forces you to go one mile, go with him two. [42]Give to the one who asks you, and do not reject the one who wants to borrow [a]from you.

Love for Enemies

[43]"You have heard that it was said, '*Love [a]your neighbor*'[1] [b]and 'hate your enemy.' [44]But I say to you, [a]love your enemy and[1] pray [b]for those who persecute you, [45]so that you may be like your [a]Father in heaven, since he causes the sun to rise on the evil and the good, and sends rain on the righteous and the unrighteous. [46][a]For if you love those who love you, what reward do you have? Even the tax collectors do the same, don't they? [47]And if you only greet your brothers, what more do you do? Even the Gentiles do the same, don't they? [48]So [a]then, be perfect, [b]as your heavenly Father is perfect.

Pure-Hearted Giving

6 "Be[1] careful not to display your righteousness merely to be seen by people. Otherwise you have no reward with your Father in heaven. [2]Thus [a]whenever you do charitable giving,[1] do not blow a trumpet before you, as the hypocrites do in synagogues and on streets so that people will praise them. I tell you the truth, they have their reward! [3]But when you do your giving, do not let your left hand know what your right hand is doing, [4]so that your gift may be in secret. And your Father, who sees in secret, [a]will reward you.[1]

Private Prayer

[5]"Whenever you pray, do not be like the hypocrites because they love to pray while standing in synagogues and on street corners so that people can see them. Truly I say to you, they have their reward! [6]But whenever you pray, [a]go into your inner room, close the door, and pray to your Father in secret. And your Father, who sees in secret, will reward you.[1] [7]When you pray, [a]do not babble repetitiously like the Gentiles [b]because they think that by their many words they will be heard. [8]Do not be like them, for your Father [a]knows what you need before you ask him. [9]So pray this [a]way:

> "[b]Our Father in heaven, may your
> [c]name be honored,[1]
> [10] may [a]your kingdom come,
> may your will be done on earth [b]as it
> is in heaven.
> [11] Give us today our [a]daily bread,
> [12] and [a]forgive us our debts, as we
> ourselves have forgiven our
> debtors.
> [13] [a]And do not lead us into temptation,
> but [b]deliver us from the evil one.[1]

[14]"[a]For if you forgive others their sins, your heavenly Father will also forgive you. [15]But [a]if you do not forgive others, your Father will not forgive you your sins.

Proper Fasting

[16][a]When you fast, do not look sullen like the hypocrites, for they make their faces unattractive so that people will see them fasting. I tell you the truth, they have their reward! [17]When you fast, [a]anoint your head and wash your face, [18]so that it will not be obvious to others when you are fasting, but only to your Father who is in secret. And your Father, who sees in secret, will reward you.

Lasting Treasure

[19]"[a]Do not accumulate for yourselves treasures on earth, where moth and devouring insect[1] destroy and where thieves break in and steal. [20][a]But accumulate for yourselves treasures in heaven, where moth and devouring insect do not destroy, and thieves do not break in and steal. [21]For where your treasure is, there your heart will be also.

5:41[a] Matt 27:32   **5:42**[a] Deut 15:7–11; Luke 6:30–34; 1 Tim 6:18   **5:43**[a] Lev 19:18 [b] Deut 23:3–6; Ps 41:10 [1] Lev 19:18
5:44[a] Luke 6:27; Rom 12:14 [b] Luke 23:34; Acts 7:60; 1 Cor 4:12; 1 Pet 2:23 [1] Maj. MSS *bless those who curse you, do good to those who hate you, and pray for those who mistreat you.*   **5:45**[a] Job 25:3; Ps 65:9–13; Luke 12:16–17; Acts 14:17   **5:46**[a] Luke 6:32   **5:48**[a] Gen 17:1; Lev 11:44; 19:2; Luke 6:36; [Col 1:28; 4:12]; Jas 1:4; 1 Pet 1:15 [b] Eph 5:1   **6:1**[1] ‡ Sev. MSS begin this verse with *But, now.*   **6:2**[a] Rom 12:8 [1] Grk. *give alms.*   **6:4**[a] Luke 14:12–14 [1] Some MSS add *openly.*   **6:6**[a] 2 Kgs 4:33 [1] Some MSS add *openly.*   **6:7**[a] Eccl 5:2 [b] 1 Kgs 18:26   **6:8**[a] [Rom 8:26–27]   **6:9**[a] Matt 6:9–13; Luke 11:2–4; [John 16:24; Eph 6:18; Jude 20] [b] [Matt 5:9, 16] [c] Mal 1:11 [1] Grk. *may your name be held in reverence, may your name be considered holy.*   **6:10**[a] Matt 26:42; Luke 22:42; Acts 21:14 [b] Ps 103:20   **6:11**[a] [Job 23:12]; Prov 30:8; Isa 33:16; Luke 11:3   **6:12**[a] [Matt 18:21–22]   **6:13**[a] [Matt 26:41; 1 Cor 10:31; 2 Pet 2:9; Rev 3:10] [b] John 17:15; [2 Thess 3:3]; 2 Tim 4:18; [1 John 5:18] [1] Maj. MSS add *for yours is the kingdom and the power and the glory forever, amen.*   **6:14**[a] [Matt 7:2]; Mark 11:25; [Eph 4:32; Col 3:13]   **6:15**[a] Matt 18:35; Jas 2:13   **6:16**[a] Isa 58:3–7; Luke 18:12   **6:17**[a] Ruth 3:3; 2 Sam 12:20; Dan 10:3   **6:19**[a] Prov 23:4; [1 Tim 6:17; Heb 13:5]; Jas 5:1 [1] Grk. *eating, consuming;* trad. *rust.*   **6:20**[a] Matt 19:21; Luke 12:33; 18:22; 1 Tim 6:19; 1 Pet 1:4

22"[a]The eye is the lamp of the body. If then your eye is healthy, your whole body will be full of light. 23But if your eye is diseased, your whole body will be full of darkness. If then the light in you is darkness, how great is the darkness!

24"No one can serve two masters, for either he will hate the one and love the other, or he will be devoted to the one and despise the other. You [a]cannot serve God and money.

Do not Worry

25"Therefore I tell you, [a]do not worry[1] about your life, what you will eat or drink, or about your body, what you will wear. Isn't there more to life than food and more to the body than clothing? 26[a]Look at the birds in the sky: They do not sow, or reap, or gather into barns, yet your heavenly Father feeds them. Aren't you more valuable than they are? 27And which of you by worrying can add even one hour to his life? 28Why do you worry about clothing? Think about how the flowers of the field grow; they do not work or spin. 29Yet I tell you that not even Solomon in all his glory was clothed like one of these! 30And if this is how God clothes the wild grass, which is here today and tomorrow is tossed into the fire to heat the oven, won't he clothe you even more, you people of little faith? 31So then, don't worry saying, 'What will we eat?' or 'What will we drink?' or 'What will we wear?' 32For the unconverted[1] pursue these things, and your heavenly Father knows that you need them. 33But above all [a]pursue his kingdom[1] and righteousness, and all these things will be given to you as well. 34So then, do not worry about tomorrow, for tomorrow will worry about itself. Today has enough trouble of its own.

Do not Judge

7 "Do [a]not judge so that you will not be judged. 2For by the standard you judge you will be judged, [a]and the measure you use will be the measure you receive. 3Why do you see the speck in your brother's eye, [a]but fail to see the beam of wood in your own? 4Or how can you say to your brother, 'Let me remove the speck from your eye,' while there is a beam in your own? 5You hypocrite! First remove the beam from your own eye, and then you can see clearly to remove the speck from your brother's eye. 6Do not give what is holy to [a]dogs or throw your pearls before pigs; otherwise they will trample them under their feet and turn around and tear you to pieces.

Ask, Seek, Knock

7"[a]Ask and it will be given to you; seek and you will find; knock and the door will be opened for you. 8For [a]everyone who asks receives, and the one who seeks finds, and to the one who knocks, the door will be opened. 9Is there anyone among you who, if his son asks [a]for bread, will give him a stone? 10Or if he asks for a fish, will give him a snake? 11If you then, although you [a]are evil, know how to give good gifts to your children, how much more will your Father in heaven give good gifts to those who ask him! 12In everything, treat others as you would want them to treat you, for [a]this fulfills the law and the prophets.

The Narrow Gate

13"[a]Enter through the narrow gate because the gate is wide and the way is spacious that leads to destruction, and there are many who enter through it. 14How narrow is the gate and difficult the way that leads to life, and there are few who find it!

A Tree and Its Fruit

15"Watch [a]out for false prophets, [b]who come to you in sheep's clothing but inwardly are voracious wolves. 16[a]You will recognize them by their fruit. Grapes are [b]not gathered from thorns or figs from thistles, are they?[1] 17In the same way, [a]every good tree bears good fruit, but the bad[1] tree bears bad fruit. 18A good tree is not able to bear

6:22 [a]Luke 11:34–35   6:24 [a]Luke 16:9, 11, 13   6:25 [a][Ps 55:22]; Luke 12:22; [Phil 4:6; 1 Pet 5:7]   [1]Or *not be anxious*, and throughout the paragraph.   6:26 [a]Job 38:41; Ps 147:9; Matt 10:29; Luke 12:24   6:32 [1]Or *unbelievers*; Grk. *Gentiles*.
6:33 [a]1 Kgs 3:13; Luke 12:31; [1 Tim 4:8]   [1]‡ Maj. mss *the kingdom of God and his righteousness.*   7:1 [a]Matt 7:1–5; Luke 6:37; Rom 14:3; [1 Cor 4:3–4]   7:2 [a]Mark 4:24; Luke 6:38   7:3 [a]Luke 6:41   7:6 [a]Prov 9:7–8; Acts 13:45   7:7 [a][Matt 21:22; Mark 11:24]; Luke 11:9–13; 18:1–8; [John 15:7; Jas 1:5–6; 1 John 3:22]   7:8 [a]Prov 8:17; Jer 29:12   7:9 [a]Luke 11:11   7:11 [a]Gen 6:5; 8:21; Ps 84:11; Isa 63:7; [Rom 8:32; Jas 1:17]; 1 John 3:1   7:12 [a]Matt 22:40; Rom 13:8; Gal 5:14; [1 Tim 1:5]   7:13 [a]Luke 13:24
7:15 [a]Deut 13:3; Jer 23:16; Ezek 22:28; Mark 13:22; [Luke 6:26]; Rom 16:17; Eph 5:6; [Col 2:8; 2 Pet 2:1; 1 John 4:1–3]   [b]Mic 3:5   7:16 [a]Matt 7:20; 12:33; Luke 6:44; Jas 3:12   [b]Luke 6:43   [1]A rhetorical question expecting a negative answer.   7:17 [a]Jer 11:19; Matt 12:33   [1]Grk. *rotten, diseased*; also v. 18.

bad fruit, nor a bad tree to bear good fruit. [19a]Every tree that does not bear good fruit is cut down and thrown into the fire. [20]So then, you will recognize them by their fruit.

Judgment of Pretenders

[21]"Not everyone who says to me, '[a]Lord, Lord,' will enter into the kingdom of heaven—only the one who [b]does the will of my Father in heaven. [22]On that day, many will say to me, 'Lord, Lord, [a]didn't we prophesy in your name, and cast out demons in your name, and do many powerful deeds in your name?' [23a]Then I will declare to them, 'I never knew you. Go [b]away from me, you lawbreakers!'

Hearing and Doing

[24]"Everyone [a]who hears these words of mine and does them is like a wise man who built his house on rock. [25]The rain fell, the flood came, and the winds beat against that house, but it did not collapse because its foundation had been laid on rock. [26]Everyone who hears these words of mine and does not do them is like a foolish man who built his house on sand. [27]The rain fell, the flood came, and the winds beat against that house, and it collapsed—it was utterly destroyed!"

[28]When Jesus finished saying these things, [a]the crowds were amazed by his teaching, [29a]because he taught them like one who had authority, not like their experts in the law.

Cleansing a Leper

8 After he came down from the mountain, large crowds followed him. [2a]And a leper[1] approached and bowed [b]low before him, saying, "Lord, if you are willing, you can make me clean." [3]He stretched out his hand and touched him saying, "I am willing. Be clean!" Immediately his leprosy [a]was cleansed. [4]Then Jesus said to him, "[a]See that you do not speak to anyone, but go, show yourself to the priest, and bring the offering that [b]Moses [c]commanded, as a testimony to them."

Healing the Centurion's Servant

[5a]When he entered Capernaum, a [b]centurion came to him asking for help: [6]"Lord, my servant[1] is lying at home paralyzed, in terrible anguish." [7]Jesus said to him, "I will come and heal him." [8]But the [a]centurion replied, "Lord, I am not worthy to have you come under my roof! Instead, just say the word and my servant will be healed. [9]For I too am a man under authority, with soldiers under me. I say to this one, 'Go!' and he goes, and to another 'Come!' and he comes, and to my slave 'Do this!' and he does it." [10]When Jesus heard this he was amazed and said to those who followed him, "I tell you the truth, I have not found such faith in anyone in Israel! [11]I tell you, [a]many will come from the east and west to share the banquet with Abraham, Isaac, and Jacob in the kingdom of heaven, [12]but [a]the sons of the kingdom [b]will be thrown out into the outer darkness, where there will be weeping and gnashing of teeth." [13]Then Jesus said to the centurion, "Go; just as you believed, it will be done for you." And the servant[1] was healed at that hour.

Healings at Peter's House

[14a]Now when Jesus entered Peter's house, he saw [b]his mother-in-law lying down, sick with a fever. [15]He touched her hand, and the fever left her. Then she got up and began to serve them. [16]When it was evening, many demon-possessed people were brought to him. [a]He drove out the spirits with a word, and healed all who were sick. [17]In this way what was spoken by [a]the prophet Isaiah was fulfilled:

"He took our weaknesses and carried our diseases."[1]

Challenging Professed Followers

[18]Now when Jesus saw a large crowd[1] around him, he gave orders to go to the other side of the lake. [19a]Then an expert in the law came to him and said, "Teacher, I will follow you wherever you go." [20]Jesus

7:19 [a]Matt 3:10; Luke 3:9; [John 15:2, 6]   7:21 [a]Hos 8:2; Matt 25:11; Luke 6:46; Acts 19:13   [b]Rom 2:13; Jas 1:22   7:22 [a]Num 24:4   7:23 [a]Matt 25:12; Luke 13:25; [2 Tim 2:19]   [b]Ps 5:5; 6:8; [Matt 25:41]; Luke 13:27   7:24 [a]Matt 7:24–27; Luke 6:47–49   7:28 [a]Matt 13:54; Mark 1:22; 6:2; Luke 4:32; John 7:46   7:29 [a][John 7:46]   8:2 [a]Matt 8:2–4; Mark 1:40–45; Luke 5:12–14   [b]Matt 2:11; 9:18; 15:25; John 9:38; Acts 10:25   [1]Grk. *And behold, a leper.*   8:3 [a]Matt 11:5; Luke 4:27   8:4 [a]Matt 9:30; Mark 5:43; Luke 4:41; 8:56; 9:21   [b]Lev 14:3–4, 10; Mark 1:44; Luke 5:14   [c]Lev 14:4–32; Deut 24:8   8:5 [a]Luke 7:1–3   [b]Matt 27:54; Acts 10:1   8:6 [1]Possibly a personal servant.   8:8 [a]Luke 15:19, 21   8:11 [a][Gen 12:3; Isa 2:2–3; 11:10]; Mal 1:11; Luke 13:29; [Acts 10:45; 11:18; 14:27; Rom 15:9–13; Eph 3:6]   8:12 [a][Matt 21:43]   [b]Matt 13:42, 50; 22:13; 24:51; 25:30; Luke 13:28; 2 Pet 2:17; Jude 13   8:13 [1]‡ Maj. MSS *his servant.*   8:14 [a]Matt 8:14–16; Mark 1:29–31; Luke 4:38–39   [b]1 Cor 9:5   8:16 [a]Mark 1:32–34; Luke 4:40–41   8:17 [a]Isa 53:4; 1 Pet 2:24   [1]Isa 53:4   8:18 [1]‡ Many MSS *large crowds.*   8:19 [a]Matt 8:19–22; Luke 9:57–58

said to him, "Foxes have dens, and the birds in the sky[1] have nests, but the Son of Man has no place to lay his head." [21]Another of [a]the[1] disciples said to him, "Lord, [b]let me first go and bury my father." [22]But Jesus said to him, "Follow me, and let the dead bury their own dead."

Stilling of a Storm

[23]As he got into the boat, his disciples followed him. [24a]And a great storm developed on the sea so that the waves began to swamp the boat. But he was asleep. [25]So they came and woke him up saying, "Lord, save us! We are about to die!" [26]But [a]he said to them, "Why are you cowardly, you people of little faith?" Then he got up and rebuked[1] the winds and the sea, and it was dead calm. [27]And the men were amazed and said, "What sort of person is this? Even the winds and the sea obey him!"

Healing the Gadarene Demoniacs

[28]When [a]he came to the other side, to the region of the Gadarenes,[1] two demon-possessed men coming from the tombs met him. They were extremely violent, so that no one was able to pass by that way. [29]They cried out, "Son of God, leave us alone! Have you come here to torment us before the time?" [30]A large herd of pigs was feeding some distance from them. [31]Then the demons begged him, "If you drive us out, send us into the herd of pigs." [32]And he said, "Go!" So they came out and went into the pigs, and the herd rushed down the steep slope into the lake and drowned in the water. [33]The herdsmen ran off, went into the town, and told everything that had happened to the demon-possessed men. [34]Then [a]the entire town came out to meet Jesus. And when they saw him, they begged him to leave their region.

Healing and Forgiving a Paralytic

9 After getting into a boat he crossed to the other side [a]and came to his own town. [2]Just [a]then some people brought to him a paralytic lying on a stretcher.[1] [b]When Jesus saw their faith, he said to the paralytic, "Have courage, son! Your sins are forgiven." [3]Then some of the experts in the law said to themselves, "This man is blaspheming!" [4]When Jesus perceived their thoughts he said, "Why do you respond with evil [a]in your hearts? [5]Which is easier, to say, 'Your sins are forgiven' or to say, 'Stand up and walk'? [6]But so that you may know that the Son of Man has authority on earth to forgive sins"—then he said to the paralytic—"Stand up, take your stretcher, and go home." [7]So he stood up and went home. [8]When the crowd saw this, they were [a]afraid[1] and honored God who had given such authority to men.

The Call of Matthew; Eating with Sinners

[9]As Jesus went on from there, he saw a man named Matthew sitting at the tax booth.[1] "Follow me," he said to him. [a]So he got up and followed him. [10]As Jesus was having a meal in Matthew's house, many tax collectors [a]and sinners came and ate with Jesus and his disciples. [11]When the Pharisees saw this they said to his disciples, "Why does your teacher eat with [a]tax collectors and [b]sinners?" [12]When Jesus heard this he said, "Those who are healthy don't need a physician, but those who are sick do. [13]Go and learn what [a]this saying means: *'I want mercy and not sacrifice.'*[1] For I did not come to call the righteous, [b]but sinners."

The Superiority of the New

[14]Then John's disciples came to Jesus and asked, "[a]Why do we and the Pharisees fast often, but your disciples don't fast?" [15]Jesus said to them, "[a]The wedding guests cannot mourn while the bridegroom is with them, can they? But the days are coming when the bridegroom will be taken from them, and [b]then they will fast. [16]No one sews a patch of unshrunk cloth on an old garment because the patch will pull away from the garment and the tear will be worse. [17]And no one pours new wine into old wineskins; otherwise the skins burst and the wine is spilled

8:20 [1]Or *the wild birds.*   8:21 [a]Luke 9:59–60   [b]1 Kgs 19:20   [1]‡ Maj. mss *his.*   8:24 [a]Mark 4:37; Luke 8:23–25   8:26 [a]Ps 65:7; 89:9; 107:29   [1]Or *commanded.*   8:28 [a]Mark 5:1–4; Luke 8:26–33   [1]Many mss *Gergesenes, Gerasenes.*   8:34 [a]Deut 5:25; 1 Kgs 17:18; Amos 7:12; Luke 5:8; Acts 16:39   9:1 [a]Matt 4:13; 11:23; Mark 5:21   9:2 [a]Mark 2:3–12; Luke 5:18–26   [b]Matt 8:10   [1]Or *couch, cot, stretcher, bier;* trad. *on a bed.*   9:4 [a]Ps 139:2; Matt 12:25; Mark 12:15; Luke 5:22; 6:8; 9:47; 11:17   9:8 [a]Matt 8:27; John 7:15   [1]Maj. mss *marveled/were amazed.*   9:9 [a]Mark 2:14; Luke 5:27   [1]Or *tax office.*   9:10 [a]Mark 2:15; Luke 5:29   9:11 [a]Matt 11:19; Mark 2:16; Luke 5:30; 15:2   [b][Gal 2:15]   9:13 [a]Hos 6:6; [Mic 6:6–8]; Matt 12:7   [b]Mark 2:17; Luke 5:32; 1 Tim 1:15   [1]Hos 6:6   9:14 [a]Mark 2:18; Luke 5:33–35; 18:12   9:15 [a]John 3:29   [b]Acts 13:2–3; 14:23

out and the skins are destroyed. Instead they put new wine into new wineskins and both are preserved."

Restoration and Healing

[18a] As he was saying these things, a leader[1] came, bowed low before him, and said, "My daughter has just died, but come and lay your hand on her and she will live." [19] Jesus and his [a]disciples got up and followed him. [20] But [a]a woman who had been suffering from a hemorrhage for 12 years came up behind him and [b]touched the edge of his cloak. [21] For she kept saying to herself, "If only I touch his cloak, I will be healed." [22] But when Jesus turned and saw her he said, "Have courage, daughter! [a]Your faith has made you well." And the woman was healed from that hour. [23] When Jesus entered the leader's house [a]and saw [b]the flute players and the disorderly crowd, [24] he said, "Go away, for the girl is not dead but asleep!" And they began making fun of him. [25] But when the crowd had been forced outside,[1] he went in and gently [a]took her by the hand, and the girl got up. [26] And the [a]news of this spread throughout that region.

Healing the Blind and Mute

[27] As Jesus went on from there, [a]two blind men began to follow him, shouting, "Have mercy on us, [b]Son of David!" [28] When he went into the house, the blind men came to him. Jesus said to them, "Do you believe that I am able to do this?" They said to him, "Yes, Lord." [29] Then he touched their eyes saying, "Let it be done for you according to your faith." [30] And their eyes were opened. Then Jesus sternly warned them, "See [a]that no one knows about this!" [31a] But they went out and spread the news about him throughout that entire region.

[32] As they were going away, [a]a man who was demon-possessed and unable to speak[1] was brought to him. [33] After the demon was cast out, the man who had been mute began to speak. The crowds were amazed and said, "Never has anything like this been seen in Israel!" [34] But [a]the Pharisees said, "By the ruler of demons he casts out demons!"

Workers for the Harvest

[35] Then Jesus went throughout all the towns and villages, [a]teaching in their synagogues, preaching the good news of the kingdom, and healing every kind of disease and sickness. [36a] When he saw the crowds, he had compassion on them because they were bewildered and helpless,[1] [b]like sheep without a shepherd. [37] Then he said to his disciples, "[a]The harvest is plentiful, but the workers are few. [38a] Therefore ask the Lord of the harvest to send out workers into his harvest-ready fields."

Sending out the 12 Apostles

10 Jesus called his twelve disciples and gave them authority over unclean spirits so they could cast them out and heal every kind of disease and sickness. [2] Now these are [a]the names of the 12 apostles: first, Simon (called Peter), and Andrew his brother; James son of Zebedee and John his brother; [3] Philip and Bartholomew; Thomas and Matthew the tax collector; James the son of Alphaeus, and Thaddaeus;[1] [4a] Simon the Zealot[1] and Judas [b]Iscariot, who betrayed him.[2]

[5] Jesus sent out these 12, instructing them as follows: "[a]Do not go on a road that leads to Gentile regions and do not enter any Samaritan town. [6a] Go instead to the [b]lost sheep of the house of Israel. [7a] As you go, preach this message: '[b]The kingdom of heaven is near!' [8] Heal the sick, raise the dead,[1] cleanse lepers, cast out demons. [a]Freely you received, freely give. [9] Do not [a]take gold, silver, or [b]copper in your belts; [10] no bag[1] for the journey; or an extra tunic or sandals or staff; [a]for the worker deserves

9:18 [a] Mark 5:22–43; Luke 8:41–56 [1] Grk. *ruler*. **9:19** [a] Matt 10:2–4 **9:20** [a] Mark 5:25; Luke 8:43 [b] Num 15:38; Deut 22:12; Matt 14:36; 23:5; Mark 6:56 **9:22** [a] Matt 9:29; 15:28; Mark 5:34; 10:52; Luke 7:50; 8:48; 17:19; 18:42 **9:23** [a] Mark 5:38; Luke 8:51 [b] 2 Chr 35:25; Jer 9:17; 16:6; Ezek 24:17 **9:25** [a] Matt 8:3, 15; Mark 1:31 [1] Or *been expelled*. **9:26** [a] Matt 4:24; Mark 1:28, 45; Luke 4:14, 37; 5:15; 7:17 **9:27** [a] Matt 20:29–34 [b] Matt 15:22; Mark 10:47; Luke 18:38–39 **9:30** [a] Matt 8:4; Luke 5:14 **9:31** [a] Mark 7:36 **9:32** [a] Matt 12:22, 24; Luke 11:14 [1] Grk. *a man mute, demon-possessed*; perhaps a causal relationship, but not explicit. **9:34** [a] Matt 12:24; Mark 3:22; Luke 11:15; John 7:20 **9:35** [a] Matt 4:23 **9:36** [a] Mark 6:34 [b] Num 27:17; 1 Kgs 22:17; Ezek 34:5; Zech 10:2; Mark 6:34 [1] Or perhaps *they had been bewildered and helpless*. **9:37** [a] Luke 10:2; John 4:35 **9:38** [a] [Matt 28:19–20; Eph 4:11–12]; 2 Thess 3:1 **10:2** [a] John 1:42 **10:3** [1] Some wss *Lebbaeus, Judas Zelotes*. **10:4** [a] Luke 6:15; Acts 1:13 [b] Matt 26:14; Luke 22:3; John 13:2, 26 [1] Grk. *the Cananean*; unrelated to Cana or Canaan; derived from the Aram. term for "enthusiast, zealot." [2] Grk. *who even betrayed him*. **10:5** [a] Matt 4:15 **10:6** [a] Matt 15:24; Acts 13:46 [b] Isa 53:6; Jer 50:6 **10:7** [a] Luke 9:2 [b] Matt 3:2; Luke 10:9 **10:8** [a] [Acts 8:18] [1] Some wss omit *raise the dead*. **10:9** [a] 1 Sam 9:7; Mark 6:8 [b] Mark 6:8 **10:10** [a] Luke 10:7; [1 Cor 9:4–14]; 1 Tim 5:18 [1] Or *no traveler's bag, no beggar's bag*.

his provisions. [11a]Whenever you enter a town or village, find out who is worthy there and stay with them until you leave. [12]As you enter the house, greet those within it. [13]And [a]if the house is worthy, let your peace come on it, [b]but if it is not worthy, let your peace return to you. [14a]And if anyone will not welcome you or listen to your message, [b]shake the dust off your feet as you leave that house or that town. [15]I tell you the truth, [a]it will be more bearable for the region of Sodom and Gomorrah on the day of judgment than for that town!

Persecution of Disciples

[16]"[a]I[1] am sending you out like sheep surrounded by wolves, [b]so be wise as serpents and [c]innocent as doves. [17]Beware of people, because [a]they will hand you over to councils and [b]flog you in their synagogues. [18]And [a]you will be brought before governors and kings because of me, as a witness to them and to the Gentiles. [19a]Whenever they hand you over for trial, do not worry about how to speak or what to say, for what you should say will be given to you at that time. [20a]For it is not you speaking, but the Spirit of your Father speaking through you.

[21]"[a]Brother will hand over brother to death, and a father his child. Children will rise against parents and have them put to death. [22]And [a]you will be hated by everyone because of my name. [b]But the one who endures to the end will be saved! [23a]Whenever they persecute you in [b]one town, flee to another! I tell you the truth, you will not finish going through all the towns of Israel [c]before the Son of Man comes.

[24]"A disciple is not [a]greater than his teacher, nor a slave greater than his master. [25]It is enough for [a]the disciple to become like his teacher, and the slave like his master. If they have called the head of the house 'Beelzebul,' how much worse will they call the members of his household!

Fear God, not Man

[26]"Do not be afraid of them, [a]for nothing is hidden that will not be revealed,[1] and nothing is secret that will not be made known. [27]What I [a]say to you in the dark, tell in the light, and what is whispered in your ear, proclaim from the housetops. [28a]Do not be afraid of those who kill the body but cannot kill the soul. Instead, [b]fear the one who is able to destroy both soul and body in hell. [29]Aren't two [a]sparrows sold for a penny? Yet not one of them falls to the ground apart from your Father's will.[1] [30a]Even all the hairs on your head are numbered. [31]So do not be afraid; you are more valuable than many sparrows.

[32]"Whoever, [a]then, acknowledges me before people, [b]I will acknowledge before my Father in heaven. [33a]But whoever denies me before people, I will deny him also before my Father in heaven.

Not Peace, but a Sword

[34]"[a]Do not think that I have come to bring peace to the earth. I have not come to bring peace but a sword! [35]For I have come to [a]set *a man against his father, a daughter against her mother, and a daughter-in-law against her mother-in-law,* [36]*and [a]a man's enemies will be the members of his household.*[1]

[37]"Whoever loves [a]father or mother more than me is not worthy[1] of me, and whoever loves son or daughter more than me is not worthy of me. [38a]And whoever does not take up his cross and follow me is not worthy of me. [39a]Whoever finds his life will lose it, and whoever loses his life because of me will find it.

Rewards

[40]"Whoever receives you receives me, and whoever receives me receives [a]the one who sent me. [41]Whoever receives a [a]prophet in the name of a prophet will receive a prophet's reward. Whoever receives a righteous

10:11[a]Luke 10:8   10:13[a]Luke 10:5   [b]Ps 35:13   10:14[a]Mark 6:11; Luke 9:5   [b]Neh 5:13; Luke 10:10–11; Acts 13:51   10:15[a]Matt 11:22, 24   10:16[a]Luke 10:3   [b]2 Cor 12:16; Eph 5:15; Col 4:5   [c][Phil 2:14–16]   [1]Grk. *Behold I.*   10:17[a]Matt 23:34; Mark 13:9; Luke 12:11   [b]Acts 5:40; 22:19; 26:11   10:18[a]Acts 12:1; 2 Tim 4:16   10:19[a]Mark 13:11; Luke 12:11–12; 21:14–15   10:20[a]2 Sam 23:2; [2 Tim 4:17]   10:21[a]Mic 7:6; Luke 21:16   10:22[a]Matt 24:9; Luke 21:17; John 15:18   [b][Dan 12:12]; Matt 24:13; Mark 13:13   10:23[a]Matt 2:13; Acts 8:1   [b][Matt 24:14; Mark 13:10]   [c]Matt 16:28   10:24[a]Luke 6:40; John 15:20   10:25[a]Mark 3:22; Luke 11:15, 18, 19; John 8:48, 52   10:26[a]Mark 4:22; Luke 8:17; 12:2–3; [1 Cor 4:5]   [1]Passive voice (and next verb) probably for rhetorical effect.   10:27[a]Luke 12:3; Acts 5:20   10:28[a]Luke 12:4; [1 Pet 3:14]   [b]Isa 8:13; Matt 5:22; Luke 12:5   10:29[a]Luke 12:6–7   [1]Or *ground without the knowledge and consent of your Father.*   10:30[a]1 Sam 14:45; 2 Sam 14:11; 1 Kgs 1:52; Luke 21:18; Acts 27:34   10:32[a]Ps 119:46; Luke 12:8; [Rom 10:9]   [b][Rev 3:5]   10:33[a][Mark 8:38; Luke 9:26]; 2 Tim 2:12   10:34[a][Luke 12:49]   10:35[a]Mic 7:6; Matt 10:21; Luke 12:53   10:36[a]Ps 41:9; 55:13; John 13:18   [1][Mic 7:6]   10:37[a]Deut 33:9; Luke 14:26   [1]Or *not worthy to be my disciple.*   10:38[a][Matt 16:24; Mark 8:34; Luke 9:23; 14:27]   10:39[a]Matt 16:25; Mark 8:35; Luke 9:24; 17:33; John 12:25   10:40[a]Mark 9:37; Luke 9:48; John 12:44; Gal 4:14   10:41[a]1 Kgs 17:10; 2 Kgs 4:8

person in the name of a righteous person will receive a righteous person's reward. [42a]And whoever gives only a cup of cold water to one of these little ones in the name of a disciple, I tell you the truth, he will never lose his reward."

11 When Jesus had finished instructing his 12 disciples, he went on from there to [a]teach and preach in their towns.

Jesus and John the Baptist

[2a]Now when John heard [b]in prison about the deeds Christ[1] had done, he sent his disciples to ask a question: [3]"Are you the one [a]who is to come, or should we look for another?" [4]Jesus answered them, "Go tell John what you hear and see: [5]The blind see, [a]the lame walk, lepers are cleansed, [b]the deaf hear, the dead are raised, and the poor have good news proclaimed to them [6]—and blessed is anyone who [a]takes no offense at me!"

[7]While they were going away, Jesus began to speak to the crowd about John: "What did you go out into the wilderness to see? [a]A reed [b]shaken by the wind? [8]What did you go out to see? A man dressed in soft clothing? Look, those who wear soft clothing are in the palaces of kings! [9]What did you go out to see? A prophet? Yes, I tell you, [a]and more than a prophet! [10]This is the one about whom it is written:

"'Look, I am sending my messenger
ahead of you,
who will prepare your way before you.'"[1]

[11]"I tell you the truth, among those born of women, no one has arisen greater than John the Baptist. Yet the one who is least in the kingdom of heaven is greater than he is! [12]From the days of John the Baptist until now the kingdom of heaven has suffered violence, [a]and forceful people lay hold of it. [13a]For all the prophets and the law prophesied until John appeared. [14]And if you are willing to accept it, he is [a]Elijah, who is to come. [15a]The one who has ears had better listen!"[1]

[16]"[a]To what should I compare this generation? They are like children sitting in the marketplaces who call out to one another,

[17] "'We played the flute for you, yet you
did not dance;
we wailed in mourning, yet you did
not weep.'

[18]For John came neither eating nor drinking, and they say, 'He has a demon!' [19]The Son of [a]Man came eating and drinking, and they say, 'Look at him, a glutton and a drunk, a friend of tax collectors and sinners!' [b]But wisdom is vindicated by her deeds."[1]

Woes on Unrepentant Cities

[20a]Then Jesus began to criticize openly the cities in which he had done many of his miracles because they did not repent. [21]"Woe to you, Chorazin! Woe to you, Bethsaida! If the miracles done [a]in you had been done in Tyre and Sidon, they would have repented long ago in sackcloth and ashes. [22]But [a]I tell you, it will be more bearable for Tyre and Sidon on the day of judgment than for you! [23]And you, Capernaum, will you be exalted to heaven? [a]No, you will be thrown down to Hades! For if the miracles done among you had been done in Sodom, it would have continued to this day. [24]But I tell you, it will be more bearable for the region of Sodom on the day of judgment than for you!"

Jesus' Invitation

[25a]At that time Jesus said, "I praise [b]you, Father, Lord of heaven [c]and earth, because you have hidden these things from the wise and intelligent, and have revealed them to little children. [26]Yes, Father, for this was your gracious will.[1] [27]All [a]things have been handed over to me by my Father. No one knows the Son except the Father, and [b]no one knows the Father except the Son and anyone to whom the Son decides to reveal him. [28]Come to [a]me, all you who are weary and burdened, and I will give you rest.

10:42[a] [Matt 25:40]; Mark 9:41; Heb 6:10   **11:1**[a] Matt 9:35; Luke 23:5   **11:2**[a] Luke 7:18–35   [b] Matt 4:12; 14:3; Mark 6:17; Luke 9:7   [1] A few MSS *Jesus*.   **11:3**[a] Gen 49:10; Num 24:17; Deut 18:15, 18; Dan 9:24; John 6:14   **11:5**[a] Isa 29:18; 35:4–6; John 2:23   [b] Ps 22:26; Isa 61:1; Luke 4:18; Jas 2:5   **11:6**[a] Isa 8:14–15; [Rom 9:32]; 1 Pet 2:8   **11:7**[a] Luke 7:24   [b] [Eph 4:14]   **11:9**[a] Matt 14:5; 21:26; Luke 1:76; 20:6   **11:10**[1] Mal 3:1; Exod 23:20   **11:12**[a] Luke 16:16   **11:13**[a] Mal 4:4–6   **11:14**[a] Mal 4:5; Matt 17:10–13; Mark 9:11–13; Luke 1:17; John 1:21   **11:15**[a] Matt 13:9; Luke 8:8; Rev 2:7, 11, 17, 29; 3:6, 13   [1] Trad. *let him hear*.   **11:16**[a] Luke 7:31   **11:19**[a] Matt 9:10   [b] Luke 7:35; John 2:1–11   [1] Maj. WSS *children*.   **11:20**[a] Luke 10:13–15, 18   **11:21**[a] Jonah 3:6–8   **11:22**[a] Matt 10:15; 11:24   **11:23**[a] Isa 14:13; Lam 2:1; Ezek 26:20; 31:14; 32:18, 24   **11:25**[a] Luke 10:21–22   [b] Ps 8:2; 1 Cor 1:19; [2 Cor 3:14]   [c] Matt 16:17   **11:26**[1] Grk. *for to do thus was well-pleasing before you.*   **11:27**[a] Matt 28:18; Luke 10:22; John 3:35; 13:3; 1 Cor 15:27   [b] John 1:18; 6:46; 10:15   **11:28**[a] [John 6:35–37]

[29] Take my yoke on you [a]and learn from me because I am gentle and [b]humble in heart, [c]and you will find rest for your souls. [30a]For my yoke is easy to bear, and my load is not hard to carry."

Lord of the Sabbath

12 At that time [a]Jesus went through the grain fields on a Sabbath. His disciples were hungry, and they began to [b]pick heads of wheat[1] and eat them. [2]But when the Pharisees saw this they said to him, "Look, your disciples are doing what is against the law to do on the Sabbath." [3]He said to them, "Haven't you read [a]what David did when he and his companions were hungry—[4]how he entered the house of God and ate[1] the sacred bread, which was against the law for him or his [a]companions to eat, [b]but only for the priests? [5]Or have you not read in the [a]law that the priests in the temple desecrate the Sabbath and yet are not guilty? [6]I tell you that something greater than the temple is here. [7]If you had known what [a]this means: '*I want mercy and not sacrifice,*'[1] you would not have condemned the innocent. [8]For the Son of Man is lord[1] of the Sabbath."

[9a]Then Jesus left that place and entered their synagogue. [10]A man was there who had a withered hand. And they asked Jesus, "[a]Is it lawful to heal on the Sabbath?" so that they could accuse him. [11]He said to them, "Would not any one of you, if he had one sheep that fell into a pit on the Sabbath, take hold of it and lift it out? [12]How much more valuable is a person than a sheep! So it is lawful to do good on the Sabbath." [13]Then he said to the man, "Stretch out your hand." He stretched it out and it was restored, as healthy as the other. [14]But [a]the Pharisees went out and plotted against him, as to how they could assassinate him.

God's Special Servant

[15]Now [a]when Jesus learned of this, he went away from there. Great crowds[1] followed him, [b]and he healed them all. [16]But he sternly [a]warned them not to make him known. [17]This fulfilled what was spoken by the prophet Isaiah:

[18] "*Here is my servant whom [a]I have chosen,*
the one I love, in whom I take great delight.
I will put my Spirit on him, and he will proclaim justice to the nations.
[19] *He will not quarrel or cry out, nor will anyone hear his voice in the streets.*
[20] *He will not break a bruised reed or extinguish a smoldering wick, until he brings justice to victory.*
[21] *And in his name the Gentiles[1] will hope.*"[2]

Jesus and Beelzebul

[22a]Then they brought to him a demon-possessed man who was blind and mute. Jesus healed him so that he could speak and see. [23]All the crowds were amazed and said, "Could this one be the [a]Son of David?" [24a]But when the Pharisees heard this they said, "He does not cast out demons except by the power of Beelzebul, the ruler of demons!" [25]Now when Jesus[1] [a]realized what they were thinking, he said to them, "Every kingdom divided against itself is destroyed, and no town or house divided against itself will stand. [26]So if[1] Satan casts out Satan, he is divided against himself. How then will his kingdom stand? [27]And if I cast out demons by Beelzebul, by whom do your sons cast them out? For this reason they will be your judges. [28]But if I cast out demons by the Spirit of God, [a]then the kingdom of God has already overtaken[1] you. [29]How [a]else can someone enter a strong man's house and steal his property, unless he first ties up the strong man? Then he can thoroughly plunder the house. [30]Whoever is not with me is against me, and whoever does not gather with me scatters. [31]For this reason I tell you, people will be forgiven for [a]every sin

11:29 [a] [John 13:15]; Eph 4:2; [Phil 2:5; 1 Pet 2:21; 1 John 2:6] [b] Zech 9:9; [Phil 2:7–8] [c] Jer 6:16 **11:30** [a] [1 John 5:3] **12:1** [a] Mark 2:23; Luke 6:1–5 [b] Deut 23:25 [1] Or *heads of grain.* **12:3** [a] Exod 31:15; 35:2; 1 Sam 21:6 **12:4** [a] Exod 25:30; Lev 24:5 [b] Exod 29:32; Lev 8:31; 24:9 [1] ‡ Some wss *they . . . ate.* **12:5** [a] Num 28:9; [John 7:22] **12:7** [a] [1 Sam 15:22; Hos 6:6; Mic 6:6–8]; Matt 9:13 [1] Hos 6:6 **12:8** [1] An emphatic Grk. construction. **12:9** [a] Mark 3:1–6; Luke 6:6–11 **12:10** [a] Luke 13:14; 14:3; John 9:16 **12:14** [a] Ps 2:2; Matt 27:1; Mark 3:6; [Luke 6:11]; John 5:18; 10:39; 11:53 **12:15** [a] Matt 10:23; Mark 3:7 [b] Matt 19:2 [1] A few MSS only *many* or only *crowds.* **12:16** [a] Matt 8:4; 9:30; 17:9 **12:18** [a] Matt 3:17; 17:5 **12:21** [1] Or *the nations.* [2] Isa 42:1–4 **12:22** [a] Matt 9:32; [Mark 3:11]; Luke 11:14–15 **12:23** [a] Matt 9:27; 21:9 **12:24** [a] Matt 9:34; Mark 3:22; Luke 11:15 **12:25** [a] Matt 9:4; John 2:25; Rev 2:23 [1] A few wss omit *Jesus.* **12:26** [1] A rhetorical question expecting a negative answer. **12:28** [a] [Dan 2:44; 7:14; Luke 1:33]; 11:20; [17:20–21; 1 John 3:8] [1] It has arrived or is now arriving. **12:29** [a] Isa 49:24; [Luke 11:21–23] **12:31** [a] Mark 3:28–30; Luke 12:10; [Heb 6:4–6; 10:26, 29; 1 John 5:16]

and blasphemy, [b]but the blasphemy against the Spirit will not be forgiven. [32]Whoever [a]speaks a word against the Son of Man will be forgiven. But whoever speaks against the Holy [b]Spirit will not be forgiven, either in this age or in the age to come.

Trees and Their Fruit

[33]"Make a tree good and [a]its fruit will be good, or make a tree bad and its fruit will be bad, for a tree is known by its fruit. [34a]Offspring of vipers! How are you able to say anything good, since you are evil? [b]For the mouth speaks from what fills the heart. [35]The good person brings good things out of his good treasury, and the evil person brings evil things out of his evil treasury. [36]I tell you that on the day of judgment, people will give an account for every worthless word they speak. [37]For by your words you will be justified, and by your words you will be condemned."

The Sign of Jonah

[38a]Then some of the experts in the law along with some Pharisees answered him, "Teacher, we want to see a sign from you." [39]But he answered them, "An evil and [a]adulterous generation asks for a sign, but no sign will be given to it except the sign of the prophet Jonah. [40a]For just as Jonah was *in the belly of the huge fish for three days and three nights,*[1] so the Son of Man will be in the heart of the earth for three days and three nights. [41]The people of Nineveh will stand up at [a]the judgment with this generation and [b]condemn it [c]because they repented when Jonah preached to them—and now, something greater than Jonah is here! [42]The queen of [a]the South will rise up at the judgment with this generation and condemn it because she came from the ends of the earth to hear the wisdom of Solomon—and now, something greater than Solomon is here!

The Return of the Unclean Spirit

[43]"[a]When an unclean spirit goes out of a person, it passes through waterless places looking for rest but does not find it. [44]Then it says, 'I will return to the home I left.' When it returns, it finds the house empty, swept clean, and put in order. [45]Then it goes [a]and brings with it seven other spirits more evil than itself, and they go in and live there, so the last state of that person is worse than the first. It will be that way for this evil generation as well!"

Jesus' True Family

[46]While Jesus was still speaking to the crowds,[1] his mother and [a]brothers came and stood outside, asking to speak to him. [47][1]Someone told him, "Look, [a]your mother and your brothers are standing outside wanting to speak to you." [48]To the one who had said this, Jesus replied, "Who is my mother and who are my brothers?" [49]And pointing toward his disciples he said, "Here[1] are my mother and my [a]brothers! [50]For [a]whoever does the will of my Father in heaven is my brother and sister and mother."

The Parable of the Sower

13 On that day after Jesus went out of the house, he sat by the lake. [2a]And such a large crowd gathered around [b]him that he got into a boat to sit while the whole crowd stood on the shore. [3]He told them many things in parables, saying: "Listen! A sower went out to sow. [4]And as he sowed, some seeds fell along the path, and the birds came and devoured them. [5]Other seeds fell on rocky ground where they did not have much soil. They sprang up quickly because the soil was not deep. [6]But when the sun came up, they were scorched, and because they did not have sufficient root, they withered. [7]Other seeds fell among the thorns, and they grew up and choked them. [8]But other seeds fell on good soil [a]and produced grain, some a hundred times as much, some sixty, and some thirty. [9a]The one who has ears had better listen!"[1]

[10]Then the disciples came to him and said, "Why do you speak to them in parables?"

12:31 [b]Acts 7:51   12:32 [a]Matt 11:19; 13:55; John 7:12, 52   [b]1 Tim 1:13   12:33 [a]Matt 7:16–18; Luke 6:43–44; [John 15:4–7]   12:34 [a]Matt 3:7; 23:33; Luke 3:7   [b]1 Sam 24:13; Isa 32:6; [Matt 15:18]; Luke 6:45; Eph 4:29; [Jas 3:2–12]   12:38 [a]Matt 16:1; Mark 8:11; Luke 11:16; John 2:18; 1 Cor 1:22   12:39 [a]Isa 57:3; Matt 16:4; Mark 8:38; [Luke 11:29–32]; John 4:48   12:40 [a]Jonah 1:17; Luke 24:46; Acts 10:40; 1 Cor 15:4   [1]Jonah 1:17   12:41 [a]Jonah 3:5; Luke 11:32   [b]Jer 3:11; Ezek 16:51; [Rom 2:27]   [c]Jonah 3:5   12:42 [a]1 Kgs 10:1–13; 2 Chr 9:1; Luke 11:31   12:43 [a]Luke 11:24–26   12:45 [a]Mark 5:9; Luke 11:26; [Heb 6:4–8; 10:26; 2 Pet 2:20–22]   12:46 [a]Matt 13:55; Mark 6:3; John 2:12; 7:3, 5; Acts 1:14; 1 Cor 9:5; Gal 1:19   [1]Grk. *crowds, behold, his mother.*   12:47 [a]Matt 13:55–56; John 2:12; Acts 1:14   [1]A few MSS omit this verse.   12:49 [a]John 20:17; [Rom 8:29]   [1]Grk. *Behold my mother and my brothers.*   12:50 [a]John 15:14; [Gal 5:6; 6:15; Col 3:11; Heb 2:11]   13:2 [a]Luke 8:4   [b]Luke 5:3   13:8 [a]Gen 26:12; Matt 13:23   13:9 [a]Matt 11:15; Mark 4:9; Rev 2:7, 11, 17, 29; 3:6, 13, 22   [1]Trad. *let him hear.*

[11] He replied, "You have been given the [a]opportunity to know[1] the secrets of the kingdom of heaven, but they have not. [12][a]For whoever has will be given more, and will have an abundance. But whoever does not have, even what he has will be taken from him. [13]For this reason I speak to them in parables: Although they see they do not see, and although they hear they do not hear nor do they understand. [14]And concerning them the prophecy of Isaiah is fulfilled that says:

> "**'You will listen [a]carefully yet will
>   never understand,
>   you will look closely yet will never
>   comprehend.**
> [15] **For the heart of this people has
>   become dull;
>   they [a]are hard of hearing,
>   and they have [b]shut their eyes,
>   so that they would not see with their
>   eyes
>   and hear with their ears
>   and understand with their hearts
>   and turn, and I would [c]heal them.'[1]**

[16]"But your eyes are [a]blessed because they see, and your ears because they hear. [17]For I tell you the truth, many prophets and righteous people longed to see what you see but did not see it, and to hear what you hear but did not hear it.

[18]"So listen to [a]the parable of the sower: [19]When anyone hears the word about the kingdom and does not understand it, the evil one comes and snatches what was sown in his heart; this is the seed sown along the path. [20]The seed sown on rocky ground is the person who hears the word and immediately [a]receives it with joy. [21]But he has no root in himself and does not endure; when [a]trouble or persecution comes because of [b]the word, immediately he falls away. [22][a]The seed sown [b]among thorns is the person who hears the word, but worldly cares and the seductiveness of wealth choke the word, so

it produces nothing. [23]But as for the seed sown on good soil, this is the person who hears the word and understands. He bears [a]fruit, yielding a hundred, sixty, or thirty times what was sown."[1]

The Parable of the Weeds

[24]He presented them with another parable: "The kingdom of heaven is like a person who sowed good seed in his field. [25]But while everyone was sleeping, an enemy came and sowed darnel[1] among the wheat and went away. [26]When the plants sprouted and produced grain, then the darnel also appeared. [27]So the slaves of the landowner came and said to him, 'Sir, didn't you sow good seed in your field? Then where did the darnel come from?' [28]He said, 'An enemy has done this!' So the slaves replied, 'Do you want us to go and gather it?' [29]But he said, 'No, since in gathering the darnel you may uproot the wheat along with it. [30]Let both grow together until the harvest. At harvest time I will tell the reapers, "First collect the darnel and tie it in bundles to be burned, but then [a]gather the wheat into my barn."'"

The Parable of the Mustard Seed

[31]He gave [a]them another parable: "The kingdom of heaven is like a mustard seed that a man took and sowed in his field. [32]It is the smallest of all the seeds, but when it has grown it is the greatest garden plant and becomes a [a]tree, so that the wild birds come and nest in its branches."

The Parable of the Yeast

[33]He told them [a]another parable: "The kingdom of heaven is like yeast that a woman took and mixed [b]with three measures of flour until all the dough had risen."

The Purpose of Parables

[34]Jesus spoke [a]all these things in parables to the crowds; he did not speak to them without a parable. [35]This [a]fulfilled what was spoken by the prophet:[1]

13:11 [a] [Matt 11:25; 16:17]; Mark 4:10–11; [John 6:65; 1 Cor 2:10; Col 1:27; 1 John 2:20, 27] [1] Grk. *to you it has been given to know*; an emphatic Grk. construction.   13:12 [a] Matt 25:29; Mark 4:25; Luke 8:18; 19:26   13:14 [a] Isa 6:9–10; Ezek 12:2; Mark 4:12; Luke 8:10; John 12:40; Acts 28:26–27; Rom 11:8; [2 Cor 3:14–15]   13:15 [a] Ps 119:70; Zech 7:11; 2 Tim 4:4; Heb 5:11 [b] Luke 19:42 [c] Acts 28:26–27 [1] Isa 6:9–10   13:16 [a] [Prov 20:12; Matt 16:17]; Luke 10:23–24; [John 20:29]   13:18 [a] Mark 4:13–20; Luke 8:11–15   13:20 [a] Isa 58:2; Ezek 33:31–32; John 5:35   13:21 [a] [Acts 14:22] [b] Matt 11:6; 2 Tim 1:15   13:22 [a] Matt 19:23; Mark 10:23; Luke 18:24; 1 Tim 6:9; 2 Tim 4:10 [b] Jer 4:3   13:23 [a] [John 15:5]; Phil 1:11; Col 1:6 [1] Or *Who indeed bears fruit and yields, in one instance a hundred times, in another, sixty times, in another, thirty times.*   13:25 [1] Or *sowed poisonous weeds.*   13:30 [a] Matt 3:12   13:31 [a] [Isa 2:2–3; Mic 4:1]; Mark 4:30; Luke 13:18–19   13:32 [a] Ps 104:12; Ezek 17:22–24; 31:3–9; Dan 4:12   13:33 [a] Luke 13:20–21 [b] [1 Cor 5:6; Gal 5:9]   13:34 [a] Mark 4:33–34; John 10:6; 16:25   13:35 [a] Ps 78:2 [1] A few sig. MSS add *Isaiah.*

"[b]*I will open my mouth in parables,*
I will announce what has been hidden
from the foundation of the world."[2]

Explanation for the Disciples

[36]Then he left the crowds and went into the house. And his disciples came to him saying, "Explain to us the parable of the darnel in the field." [37]He answered, "The one who sowed the good seed is the Son of Man. [38]The field is [a]the world and [b]the good seed are the people[1] of the kingdom. The poisonous weeds are the people of the evil one, [39]and [a]the enemy who sows them is the devil. The harvest is the end of the age, and the reapers are angels. [40]As the poisonous weeds are collected and burned with fire, so it will be at the end of the age. [41]The Son of Man will send his angels, [a]and they will gather from his kingdom everything that causes sin as well as all lawbreakers. [42a]They will *throw them into the fiery furnace,*[1] where [b]there will be weeping and gnashing of teeth. [43a]Then *the righteous will shine like* [b]*the sun in the kingdom of their Father.*[1] The one who has ears had better listen!

Parables on the Kingdom of Heaven

[44]"The kingdom of heaven is like a treasure, hidden in a field, that a person found and hid. Then because of joy he went and [a]sold all that he had and [b]bought that field. [45]"Again, the kingdom of heaven is like a merchant searching for fine pearls. [46]When he found [a]a pearl of great value, he went out and sold everything he had and bought it.

[47]"Again, the kingdom of heaven is like a net that was cast into the sea that [a]caught all kinds of fish. [48]When it was full, they pulled it ashore, sat down, and put the good fish into containers and threw the bad away. [49]It will be this way at the end of the age. Angels will come and [a]separate the evil from the righteous [50]and *throw them into the fiery furnace,*[1] where there will be weeping and gnashing of teeth.

[51]"Have you understood all these things?" They replied, "Yes." [52]Then he said to them, "Therefore every expert [a]in the law[1] who has been trained for the kingdom of heaven is like the owner of a house who brings out of his treasure what is new and old."

Rejection at Nazareth

[53]Now when Jesus finished these parables, he moved on from there. [54]Then he came to his hometown and began to teach the people in their synagogue. They were astonished [a]and said, "Where did this man get such wisdom and miraculous powers? [55]Isn't [a]this the carpenter's son? Isn't [b]his mother named Mary? And aren't his brothers [c]James, Joseph, Simon, and Judas? [56]And aren't all his sisters here with us? So where did he get all this?" [57]And so they took offense [a]at him. But Jesus said to them, "A prophet is not without honor except in his hometown and in his own house." [58]And [a]he did not do many miracles there because of their unbelief.

The Death of John the Baptist

14 At that time [a]Herod the tetrarch heard reports about Jesus, [2]and he said to his servants, "This is John the Baptist. He has been raised from the dead! And because of this, miraculous powers are at work in him." [3a]For Herod had arrested John, bound him,[1] and put him in prison on account of Herodias, his brother Philip's wife, [4]because John had repeatedly told him, "[a]It is not lawful for you to have her." [5]Although Herod wanted to kill John, he feared the crowd [a]because they accepted John as a prophet. [6]But on Herod's birthday, the daughter of Herodias danced before them and pleased Herod, [7]so much that he promised with an oath to give her whatever she asked. [8]Instructed by her mother, she said, "Give me the head of John the Baptist here on a platter." [9]Although it grieved the king because of his oath and the dinner guests, he commanded it to be given. [10]So he sent and had John beheaded in the prison. [11]His head was brought on a platter and given to the girl, and she brought it to her

13:35 [b] Rom 16:25–26; 1 Cor 2:7; Eph 3:9; Col 1:26 [2] Ps 78:2 **13:38** [a] Matt 24:14; 28:19; Mark 16:15; Luke 24:47; Rom 10:18; Col 1:6 [b] Gen 3:15; John 8:44; Acts 13:10 [1] Grk. *the sons of the kingdom.* **13:39** [a] Joel 3:13; Rev 14:15 **13:41** [a] Matt 18:7; 2 Pet 2:1–2 **13:42** [a] Matt 3:12; Rev 19:20; 20:10 [b] Matt 8:12; 13:50 [1] Dan 3:6 **13:43** [a] [Dan 12:3; 1 Cor 15:42–43, 58] [b] Matt 13:9 [1] [Dan 12:3] **13:44** [a] Phil 3:7–8 [b] [Isa 55:1; Rev 3:18] **13:46** [a] Prov 2:4; 3:14–15; 8:10, 19 **13:47** [a] Matt 22:9–10 **13:49** [a] Matt 25:32 **13:50** [1] [Dan 3:6] **13:52** [a] Song 7:13 [1] Or *every scribe.* **13:54** [a] Ps 22:22; Matt 2:23; Mark 6:1; Luke 4:16; John 7:15 **13:55** [a] Isa 49:7; Mark 6:3; [Luke 3:23]; John 6:42 [b] Matt 12:46 [c] Mark 15:40 **13:57** [a] Luke 4:24; John 4:44 **13:58** [a] Mark 6:5–6; John 5:44, 46, 47 **14:1** [a] Mark 6:14–29; Luke 9:7–9 **14:3** [a] Matt 4:12; Mark 6:17; Luke 3:19–20 [1] ‡ Sig. wss omit *him.* **14:4** [a] Lev 18:16; 20:21 **14:5** [a] Matt 21:26; Luke 20:6

mother. [12]Then John's disciples came and took the body and buried it and went and told Jesus.

The Feeding of the 5,000

[13]Now [a]when Jesus heard this he went away from there privately in a boat to an isolated place. But when the crowd heard about it, they followed him on foot from the towns. [14]As he got out he saw the large crowd, and he had compassion on them and healed their sick. [15a]When evening arrived, his disciples came to him saying, "This is an isolated place[1] and the hour is already late. Send the crowds away so that they can go into the villages and buy food for themselves." [16]But he[1] replied, "They don't need to go. You[2] give them something to eat." [17]They said to him, "We have here only five loaves and two fish." [18]"Bring them here to me," he replied. [19]Then [a]he instructed the crowds to sit down on the grass. He took the five loaves and two fish, and looking up to heaven he gave thanks and broke the loaves. He gave them to the disciples, who in turn gave them to the crowds. [20]They all ate and were satisfied, and they picked up the broken pieces left over, 12 baskets full. [21]Not counting women and children, there were about 5,000 men who ate.

Walking on Water

[22]Immediately Jesus made the disciples get into the boat and go ahead of him to the other side, while he dispersed the crowds. [23a]And after he sent the crowds away, he went up the mountain by himself to pray. When evening came, he was there alone. [24]Meanwhile the boat, already far from land,[1] was taking a beating from the waves because the wind was against it. [25]As the night was ending,[1] Jesus came to them walking on the sea. [26]When the disciples saw him [a]walking on the water they were terrified and said, "It's a ghost!" and cried out with fear. [27]But immediately Jesus[1] spoke to them: "Have [a]courage! It is I. Do not be afraid." [28]Peter said to him, "Lord, if it is you, order me to come to you on the water." [29]So he said, "Come." Peter got out of the boat, walked on the water, and came toward Jesus. [30]But when he saw the strong wind he became afraid. And starting to sink, he cried out, "Lord, save me!" [31]Immediately Jesus reached out his hand and caught him, saying to him, "You of [a]little faith, why did you doubt?" [32]When they went up into the boat, the wind ceased. [33]Then those who were in the boat worshiped him, saying, "Truly [a]you are the Son of God."

[34a]After they had crossed over, they came to land at Gennesaret. [35]When the people there recognized him, they sent word into all the surrounding area, and they brought all their sick to him. [36]They begged him if they could only [a]touch the edge of his cloak, and [b]all who touched it were healed.

Breaking Human Traditions

15 Then Pharisees and experts in [a]the law came from Jerusalem to Jesus and said, [2]"[a]Why do your disciples disobey the tradition of the elders? For they don't wash their hands when they eat." [3]He answered them, "And why do you disobey the commandment of God because of your tradition? [4]For God said,[1] '[a]**Honor your** [b]**father and mother**'[2] and '**Whoever insults his father or mother must be put to death.**'[3] [5]But you say, 'If someone tells his father or mother, "[a]Whatever help you would have received from me is given to God,"[1] [6]he does not need to honor his father.'[1] You have nullified the word of God on account of your tradition. [7a]Hypocrites! Isaiah prophesied correctly about you when he said,

[8] "'[a]**This people honors me with their lips,**
    but their hearts are far from me,
[9]   **and they worship me in vain,**
    [a]**teaching as doctrines the commandments of men.'**"[1]

14:13 [a] Matt 10:23; 12:15; Mark 6:32–44; Luke 9:10–17; John 6:1–2   **14:15** [a] Mark 6:35; Luke 9:12   [1] Or *a desert.*   **14:16** [1] ‡ Maj. of wss *Jesus.*   [2] An emphatic Grk. construction.   **14:19** [a] 1 Sam 9:13; Matt 15:36; 26:26; Mark 6:41; 8:7; 14:22; Luke 24:30; Acts 27:35; [Rom 14:6]   **14:23** [a] Mark 6:46; Luke 9:28; John 6:15   **14:24** [1] Grk. *The boat was already many stades from the land*; a stade was about 607 ft. (185 m.) long.   **14:25** [1] Grk. *In the fourth watch of the night*; 3:00–6:00 a.m.   **14:26** [a] Job 9:8   **14:27** [a] Acts 23:11; 27:22, 25, 36   [1] A few wss omit *Jesus.*   **14:31** [a] Matt 6:30; 8:26   **14:33** [a] Ps 2:7; Matt 16:16; 26:63; Mark 1:1; Luke 4:41; John 1:49; 6:69; 11:27; Acts 8:37; Rom 1:4   **14:34** [a] Mark 6:53; Luke 5:1   **14:36** [a] [Mark 5:24–34]   [b] Matt 9:20; Mark 3:10; [Luke 6:19]; Acts 19:12   **15:1** [a] Mark 7:1; John 1:19; Acts 25:7   **15:2** [a] Mark 7:5   **15:4** [a] Exod 20:1, 12; Lev 19:3; [Deut 5:16]; Prov 23:22; [Eph 6:2–3]   [b] Exod 21:17; Lev 20:9; Deut 27:16; Prov 20:20; 30:17   [1] Maj. MSS *commanded, saying.*   [2] Exod 20:12; Deut 5:16   [3] Exod 21:17; Lev 20:9   **15:5** [a] Mark 7:11–12   [1] Grk. *is a gift*; i.e., dedicated to God.   **15:6** [1] Maj. MSS add *or mother.*   **15:7** [a] Mark 7:6   **15:8** [a] Ps 78:36; Isa 29:13; Ezek 33:31   **15:9** [a] Isa 29:13; [Col 2:18–22]; Titus 1:14   [1] Isa 29:13

True Defilement

[10]Then he called the crowd to him and said, "Listen [a]and understand. [11]What defiles a person is [a]not what goes into the mouth; it is what comes out of the mouth that defiles a person." [12]Then the disciples came to him and said, "Do you know that when the Pharisees heard this saying they were offended?" [13]And he replied, "[a]Every plant that my heavenly Father did not plant will be uprooted. [14]Leave them! [a]They are blind guides.[1] If someone who is blind leads another who is blind, both will fall into a pit." [15a]But Peter said to him, "Explain this parable to us." [16]Jesus said, "Even after all this, [a]are you still so foolish? [17]Don't you understand that [a]whatever goes into the mouth enters the stomach and then passes out into the sewer? [18]But the things that come out of the mouth come from the heart, and these things defile a person. [19a]For out of the heart come evil ideas, murder, adultery, sexual immorality, theft, false testimony, slander. [20]These are the things that defile a person; it is not eating with unwashed hands that defiles a person."

A Canaanite Woman's Faith

[21]After going out from there, Jesus went to the region of Tyre [a]and Sidon. [22]A[1] Canaanite woman from that area came and cried out, "Have mercy on me, Lord, [a]Son of David! My daughter is horribly demon-possessed!" [23]But he did not answer her a word. Then his disciples came and begged him, "Send her away because she keeps on crying out after us." [24]So he answered, "[a]I was sent only to the lost sheep of the house of Israel." [25]But she came and bowed down before him and said, "Lord, help me!" [26]"It is not right to take the children's bread and throw it to the [a]dogs,"[1] he said. [27]"Yes, Lord," she replied, "but even the dogs eat the crumbs that fall from their masters' table." [28]Then Jesus answered her, "Woman, your faith is [a]great! Let what you want be done for you." And her daughter was healed from that hour.

Healing Many Others

[29]When he left there, [a]Jesus went along the Sea of Galilee. Then he went up a mountain, where he sat down. [30a]Then large crowds came to him bringing with them the lame, blind, crippled, mute, and many others. They laid them at his [b]feet, and he healed them. [31]As a result, the crowd was amazed when they saw the mute speaking, the crippled healthy, the lame walking, and the blind seeing, and they [a]praised the God of Israel.

The Feeding of the 4,000

[32a]Then Jesus called his disciples and said, "I have compassion on the crowd because they have already been here with me three days and they have nothing to eat. I don't want to send them away hungry since they may faint on the way." [33a]The disciples said to him, "Where can we get enough bread in this desolate place to satisfy so great a crowd?" [34]Jesus said to them, "How many loaves do you have?" They replied, "Seven—and a few small fish." [35]After instructing the crowd to sit down on the ground, [36]he took [a]the seven loaves and the fish, and after giving thanks, he broke them and began giving them to the disciples, who then [b]gave them to the crowds. [37]They all ate and were satisfied, and they picked up the broken pieces left over, seven baskets full. [38]Not counting children and women,[1] there were 4,000 men who ate. [39]After sending away the crowd, he got into the boat [a]and went to the region of Magadan.

The Demand for a Sign

16 Now when the [a]Pharisees and Sadducees came to test Jesus, they asked him to show them a sign from heaven. [2]He said, "When evening comes you say, 'It will be fair weather because the sky is red,' [3]and in the morning, 'It will be stormy today because the sky is red and darkening.' You know how to judge correctly the appearance of the sky, but you cannot evaluate the signs of the times. [4]A wicked [a]and

15:10 [a]Mark 7:14　**15:11** [a][Acts 10:15; Rom 14:14, 17, 20; 1 Tim 4:4; Titus 1:15]　**15:13** [a][Isa 60:21; 61:3; John 15:2; 1 Cor 3:12–13]　**15:14** [a]Isa 9:16; Mal 2:8; Matt 23:16, 24; Luke 6:39; Rom 2:19　[1]‡ Maj. MSS add *of the blind.*　**15:15** [a]Mark 7:17　**15:16** [a]Matt 16:9; Mark 7:18　**15:17** [a][1 Cor 6:13]　**15:19** [a]Gen 6:5; 8:21; Prov 6:14; Jer 17:9; Mark 7:21; [Rom 1:29–32; Gal 5:19–21]　**15:21** [a]Mark 7:24–30　**15:22** [a]Matt 1:1; 22:41–42　[1]Grk. *And behold a Canaanite.*　**15:24** [a]Matt 10:5–6; [Rom 15:8]　**15:26** [a]Matt 7:6; Phil 3:2　[1]Or *lap dogs, house dogs.*　**15:28** [a]Luke 7:9　**15:29** [a]Matt 15:29–31; Mark 7:31–37　**15:30** [a]Isa 35:5–6; Matt 11:5; Luke 7:22　[b]Mark 7:25; Luke 7:38; 8:41; 10:39　**15:31** [a]Luke 5:25–26; 19:37–38　**15:32** [a]Mark 8:1–10　**15:33** [a]2 Kgs 4:43　**15:36** [a]Matt 14:19; 26:27; Luke 22:17, 19; John 6:11, 23; Acts 27:35; [Rom 14:6]　[b]1 Sam 9:13; Luke 22:19　**15:38** [1]‡ Maj. wss *women and children.*　**15:39** [a]Mark 8:10　**16:1** [a]Matt 12:38; Mark 8:11; Luke 11:16; 12:54–56; 1 Cor 1:22　**16:4** [a]Prov 30:12; Matt 12:39; Luke 11:29; 24:46

adulterous generation asks for a sign, but no sign will be given to it except the sign of Jonah." Then he left them and went away.

The Yeast of the Pharisees and Sadducees

[5]When the disciples went to the other side, they forgot to take bread. [6]"Watch out," Jesus said to them, "beware of the yeast of the Pharisees and Sadducees." [7]So they began to discuss this among themselves, saying, "It is because we brought no bread." [8]When Jesus learned of this, he said, "You who have such little faith! Why are you arguing among yourselves about having no bread? [9]Do you still not understand? [a]Don't you remember the five loaves for the 5,000, and how many baskets you took up? [10a]Or the seven loaves for the 4,000 and how many baskets you took up? [11]How could you not understand that I was not speaking to you about bread? But beware of the yeast of the Pharisees and Sadducees!" [12]Then they understood that he had not told them to be on guard against the yeast in bread, but against the teaching of the Pharisees and Sadducees.

Peter's Confession

[13]When Jesus came to the area of Caesarea Philippi, he asked his disciples, "[a]Who do people say that the Son of Man is?" [14]They answered, "[a]Some say John the Baptist, others Elijah, and others Jeremiah or [b]one of the prophets." [15]He said to them, "But who do [a]you say that I am?" [16]Simon Peter answered, "[a]You are the Christ, the Son of the living God." [17]And Jesus answered him, "You are blessed, Simon son of Jonah, [a]because flesh and blood[1] did not reveal this to you, but [b]my Father in heaven! [18]And I tell [a]you that you are Peter, and [b]on this rock I will build my church, and [c]the gates of Hades[1] will not overpower it. [19]I will give you the keys of the kingdom of heaven. Whatever you bind on earth will have been bound in heaven, [a]and whatever you release on earth will have been released in heaven." [20a]Then he instructed his disciples not to tell anyone that he was the Christ.[1]

First Prediction of Jesus' Death and Resurrection

[21]From that time on Jesus began [a]to show his disciples that he must go to Jerusalem and suffer many things at the hands of the elders, chief priests, and experts in the law, and be killed and on the third day be raised. [22]So Peter took him aside and began to rebuke him: "God forbid,[1] Lord! This must not happen to you!" [23]But he turned and said to Peter, "Get behind me, [a]Satan! [b]You are a stumbling block to me because you are not setting your mind on God's interests, but on man's." [24a]Then Jesus said to his disciples, "If anyone wants to become my follower, he must deny himself, take up his cross, and [b]follow me. [25]For [a]whoever wants to save his life will lose it, but whoever loses his life because of me will find it. [26]For what does it [a]benefit a person if he gains the whole world but forfeits his life? Or [b]what can a person give in exchange for his life? [27]For [a]the Son of Man will come [b]with his angels in the glory of his Father, [c]and then *he will reward each person according to what he has done.*[1] [28]I tell you [a]the truth, there are some standing here who will not experience[1] death before they see the Son of Man coming in his kingdom."

The Transfiguration

17 Six days [a]later Jesus took with him Peter, James, and John the brother of James, and led them privately up a high mountain. [2]And he was transfigured before them. His face shone like the sun, and his clothes became white as light. [3]Then Moses and Elijah also appeared before them, talking with him. [4]So Peter said to Jesus, "Lord, it is good for us to be here. If you want, I will make[1] three shelters—one

16:9 [a]Matt 14:15–21; Mark 6:30–44; Luke 9:10–17; John 6:1–14   16:10 [a]Matt 15:32–38; Mark 8:1–9   16:13 [a]Mark 8:27; Luke 9:18   16:14 [a]Matt 14:2; Luke 9:7–9   [b]Matt 21:11   16:15 [a]John 6:67   16:16 [a]Matt 14:33; Mark 8:29; Luke 9:20; John 6:69; 11:27; Acts 8:37; 9:20; Heb 1:2, 5; 1 John 4:15   16:17 [a][Eph 2:8]   [b][Matt 11:27; 1 Cor 2:10]; Gal 1:16   [1]Any human or Peter's own intuition.   16:18 [a]John 1:42   [b]Acts 2:41; [Eph 2:20; Rev 21:14]   [c]Job 33:17; Ps 9:13; 107:18; Isa 38:10   [1]Or *the power of death.*   16:19 [a]Matt 18:18; John 20:23   16:20 [a]Matt 17:9; Mark 8:30; Luke 9:21   [1]Maj. mss *Jesus, the Christ, Christ Jesus.*   16:21 [a]Matt 20:17; Mark 8:31; 9:31; Luke 9:22; 18:31; 24:46; John 2:19   16:22 [1]Grk. *Merciful to you;* meaning "may God be merciful to you in sparing you from having to undergo [some experience]."   16:23 [a]Matt 4:10   [b][Rom 8:7]   16:24 [a]Mark 8:34; Luke 9:23; [Acts 14:22; 2 Cor 4:10–11; 1 Thess 3:3; 2 Tim 3:12]   [b][1 Pet 2:21]   16:25 [a]Luke 17:33; John 12:25   16:26 [a]Luke 12:20–21   [b]Ps 49:7–8   16:27 [a]Matt 26:64; Mark 8:38; Luke 9:26   [b][Dan 7:10]; Zech 14:5   [c]Job 34:11; Ps 62:12; Prov 24:12; Rom 2:6; 2 Cor 5:10; 1 Pet 1:17; Rev 2:23   [1][Pss 28:4; 62:12 (Prov 24:12)]   16:28 [a]Mark 9:1; Luke 9:27; Acts 7:55–56; Rev 19:11   [1]Grk. *will not taste.*   17:1 [a]Matt 17:1–8; Mark 9:2–8; Luke 9:28–36   17:4 [1]Maj. wss *let us make.*

for you, one for Moses, and one for Elijah." [5a]While he was still speaking, a bright cloud overshadowed them, and a voice from the cloud said,[1] "[b]This is my one dear Son,[2] [c]in whom I take great delight. [d]Listen to him!" [6]When the disciples heard this, they were overwhelmed with fear [a]and threw themselves down with their faces to the ground. [7]But Jesus came and [a]touched them. "Get up," he said. "Do not be afraid." [8]When they looked up, all they saw was Jesus alone.

[9]As they were coming down from the mountain, Jesus commanded them, "Do not tell anyone about the vision until the Son of Man is raised from the dead." [10]The disciples asked him, "[a]Why then do the experts in the law say that Elijah must come first?" [11]He answered, "Elijah does indeed come first and will [a]restore all things. [12]And I tell you that Elijah has already come. Yet they did not recognize him, [a]but [b]did to him whatever [c]they wanted. In the same way, the Son of Man will suffer at their hands." [13a]Then the disciples understood that he was speaking to them about John the Baptist.

The Disciples' Failure to Heal

[14]When they came to the crowd, [a]a man came to him, knelt before him, [15]and said, "Lord, have mercy on my son because he has seizures[1] and suffers terribly, for he often falls into the fire and into the water. [16]I brought him to your disciples, but they were not able to heal him." [17]Jesus answered, "You unbelieving and [a]perverse generation! How much longer must I be with you? How much longer must I endure you? Bring him here to me." [18]Then Jesus [a]rebuked the demon and it came out of him, and the boy was healed from that moment. [19]Then the disciples came to Jesus privately and said, "Why couldn't we cast it out?" [20]He told them, "It was because of your little faith. I tell you the truth, [a]if you have faith the size of a mustard seed, you will say to this mountain, 'Move from here to there,' and it will move; nothing will be impossible for you."[1]

Second Prediction of Jesus' Death and Resurrection

[22a]When they gathered together in Galilee, Jesus told them, "The Son of Man is going to be betrayed into the hands of men. [23]They will kill him, and on the third day he will be raised." And they became greatly [a]distressed.

The Temple Tax

[24]After they arrived in Capernaum, the collectors of the temple tax came to Peter and said, "Your teacher pays the double drachma tax, doesn't [a]he?" [25]He said, "Yes." When Peter came into the house, Jesus spoke to him first, "What do you think, Simon? From whom do earthly kings collect tolls or taxes—from their sons or from [a]foreigners?" [26]After he said, "From foreigners," Jesus said to him, "Then the sons are free. [27]But so that we don't offend them, go to the lake and throw out a hook. Take the first fish that comes up, and when you open its mouth, you will find a four-drachma coin. Take that and give it to them for me and you."

Questions about the Greatest

18 At [a]that time the disciples came to Jesus saying, "Who is the greatest in the kingdom of heaven?" [2]He called a [a]child, had him stand among them, [3]and said, "I tell you the truth, [a]unless you turn around and become like little children, you will never[1] enter the kingdom of heaven! [4]Whoever [a]then humbles himself like this little child is the greatest in the kingdom of heaven. [5]And [a]whoever welcomes a child like this in my name welcomes me.

[6]"[a]But if anyone causes one of these little ones who believe in me to sin, it would be better for him to have a huge millstone hung around his neck and to be drowned in the open sea.[1] [7]Woe to the world because

17:5 [a]2 Pet 1:17　[b]Ps 2:7; Matt 3:17; Mark 1:11; Luke 1:35; 3:22; [John 12:28–30]　[c]Isa 42:1; Matt 3:17; 12:18; 2 Pet 1:17　[d][Deut 18:15, 19; Acts 3:22–23]　[1]Grk. behold, a voice from the cloud, saying.　[2]Grk. my beloved Son.　17:6 [a]2 Pet 1:18　17:7 [a]Dan 8:18　17:10 [a]Mal 4:5; Matt 11:14; 16:14; Mark 9:11　17:11 [a][Mal 4:6]; Luke 1:17　17:12 [a]Matt 11:14; Mark 9:12–13　[b]Matt 14:3, 10　[c]Matt 16:21　17:13 [a]Matt 11:14　17:14 [a]Matt 17:14–19; Mark 9:14–28; Luke 9:37–42　17:15 [1]Grk. he is moonstruck; generally regarded as a seizure disorder such as epilepsy.　17:17 [a]Deut 32:5; Phil 2:15　17:18 [a]Luke 4:41　17:20 [a]Matt 21:21; Mark 11:23; Luke 17:6; [1 Cor 12:9]　[1]Some MSS add v. 21: But this kind does not go out except by prayer and fasting.　17:22 [a]Matt 16:21; 26:57; Mark 8:31; Luke 9:22, 44; John 18:12　17:23 [a]Matt 26:22; 27:50; Luke 23:46; 24:46; John 16:6; 19:30; Acts 10:40　17:24 [a]Mark 9:33　17:25 [a][Isa 60:10–17]　18:1 [a]Mark 9:33–37; Luke 9:46–48; 22:24–27　18:2 [a]Matt 19:14; Mark 10:14; Luke 18:14–17　18:3 [a]Ps 131:2; Matt 19:14; Mark 10:15; Luke 18:16; [1 Cor 14:20; 1 Pet 2:2]　[1]A very strong Grk. negative.　18:4 [a][Matt 20:27; 23:11]　18:5 [a][Matt 10:42]; Luke 9:48　18:6 [a]Mark 9:42; Luke 17:2; [1 Cor 8:12]　[1]As opposed to a stretch of water near a coastline.

of stumbling blocks! It is necessary that [a]stumbling blocks come, but [b]woe to the person through whom they come. 8[a]If your hand or your foot causes you to sin, cut it off and throw it away. It is better for you to enter life crippled or lame than to have two hands or two feet and be thrown into eternal fire. 9And if your eye causes you to sin, tear it out and throw it away. It is better for you to enter into life with one eye than to have two eyes and be thrown into fiery hell.

The Parable of the Lost Sheep

10"See that you do not disdain one of these little ones. For I tell you that [a]their angels in heaven always [b]see the face of my Father in heaven.[1] 12[a]What do you think? If someone owns a hundred sheep and one of them goes astray, will he not leave the ninety-nine on the mountains and go look for the one that went astray? 13And if he finds it, I tell you the truth, he will rejoice more over it than over the ninety-nine that did not go astray. 14In the same way, your Father in heaven is not [a]willing that one of these little ones be lost.

Restoring Christian Relationships

15[a]"If your brother[1] sins,[2] go and show him his fault when the two of you are alone. If he listens to [b]you, you have regained your brother. 16But if he does not listen, take one or two others with you, so that [a]*at the testimony of two or three witnesses every matter may be established.*[1] 17If he refuses to listen to them, tell it to the church. If he refuses to listen to the church, treat him like a [a]Gentile[1] or a tax collector.

18"I tell you the truth, [a]whatever you bind on earth will have been bound in heaven, and whatever you release on earth will have been released in heaven. 19[a]Again, I tell you the truth, if two of you on earth agree about whatever you ask, my Father in heaven will do [b]it for you. 20For where two or three are [a]assembled in my name, I am there among them."

21Then Peter came to him and said, "Lord, how many times must I forgive my brother who sins against me? As many as seven times?" 22Jesus said to him, "Not seven times, I tell you, but seventy-seven times!

The Parable of the Unforgiving Slave

23"For this reason, the kingdom of heaven is like a king who wanted to settle accounts with his slaves. 24As he began settling his accounts, a man who owed 10,000 talents was brought to him. 25Because he was not able to repay it, the lord ordered him to be sold, along with his wife, children, and whatever he possessed, and repayment to be made. 26Then the slave threw himself to the ground[1] before him, saying,[2] 'Be patient with me, and I will repay you everything.' 27The lord had compassion on that slave and released him, and forgave him the debt. 28After he went out, that same slave found one of his fellow slaves who owed him 100 silver coins. So he grabbed him by the throat and started to choke him, saying, 'Pay back what you owe me!' 29Then his fellow slave threw himself down and begged him, 'Be patient with me, and I will repay you.' 30But he refused. Instead, he went out and threw him in prison until he repaid the debt. 31When his fellow slaves saw what had happened, they were very upset and went and told their lord everything that had taken place. 32Then his lord called the first slave and said to him, 'Evil slave! I forgave you [a]all that debt because you begged me! 33Should you not have shown mercy to your fellow slave, just as I showed it to you?' 34And in anger his lord turned him over to the prison guards to torture him until he repaid all he owed. 35[a]So also my heavenly Father will do to you, if each of you does not forgive your brother from your heart."

Questions about Divorce

19 Now [a]when Jesus finished these sayings, he left Galilee and went to the region of Judea beyond the Jordan River. 2Large crowds followed him, [a]and he healed them there.

18:7 [a]Luke 17:1; [1 Cor 11:19]; 1 Tim 4:1 [b]Matt 26:24; 27:4-5 18:8 [a]Matt 5:29-30; Mark 9:43, 45 18:10 [a][Ps 34:7]; Zech 13:7; [Heb 1:14] [b]Esth 1:14; Luke 1:19; Acts 12:15; [Rev 8:2] [1]Some mss add v. 11: *For the Son of Man came to save the lost.* 18:12 [a]Matt 18:12-14; Luke 15:4-7 18:14 [a][1 Tim 2:4] 18:15 [a]Lev 19:17; [Luke 17:3-4; Gal 6:1]; 2 Thess 3:15; [Jas 5:19] [b][Jas 5:20]; 1 Pet 3:1 [1]Can mean "fellow believer, fellow Christian," whether male or female. [2]‡ Some wss add *against you.* 18:16 [a]Deut 17:6; 19:15; John 8:17; 2 Cor 13:1; 1 Tim 5:19; Heb 10:28 [1]Deut 19:15 18:17 [a]Rom 16:17; 1 Cor 5:9; [2 Thess 3:6, 14; 2 John 10] [1]Or *a pagan.* 18:18 [a]Matt 16:19; [John 20:22-23; 1 Cor 5:4] 18:19 [a][1 Cor 1:10] [b][1 John 3:22; 5:14] 18:20 [a]Acts 20:7; 1 Cor 14:26 18:26 [1]Grk. *falling therefore the slave bowed down to the ground*; the redundancy signals desperation. [2]Maj. mss add *Lord.* 18:32 [a]Luke 7:41-43 18:35 [a]Prov 21:13; Matt 6:12; Mark 11:26; Jas 2:13 19:1 [a]Matt 19:1-9; Mark 10:1-12; John 10:40 19:2 [a]Matt 12:15

[3]Then some Pharisees came to him in order to test him. They asked, "Is it lawful[1] to divorce a wife for any cause?" [4]He answered, "Have you not read that from the beginning the Creator *made them male and female,*[1] [5]and said, '[a]*For this reason a man will leave his* [b]*father and mother and will be united with his wife, and the two will become one flesh*'?[1] [6]So they are no longer two, but one flesh. Therefore what God has joined together, let no one separate." [7]They said to him, "[a]Why then did Moses command us *to give a certificate of dismissal and to divorce her*?"[1,2] [8]Jesus[1] said to them, "Moses permitted you to divorce your [a]wives because of your [b]hard hearts, but from the beginning it was not this way. [9]Now I say to you that whoever divorces his wife, except for immorality, [a]and marries another commits adultery." [10]The[1] disciples said to him, "[a]If this is the case of a husband with a wife, it is better not to marry!" [11]He said to them, "Not [a]everyone can accept this statement, except those to whom it has been given. [12]For [a]there are some eunuchs who were that way from birth, and some who were made eunuchs[1] by others, and some who became eunuchs for the sake of the kingdom of heaven. The one who is able to accept this should accept it."

Jesus and Little Children

[13][a]Then little children were brought to him for him to lay his hands on them and pray. But the disciples scolded those who brought them. [14]But Jesus said, "Let the little children come to me and do not try to stop them, for the kingdom [a]of heaven belongs to such as these." [15]And he placed his hands on them and went on his way.

The Rich Young Man

[16][a]Now someone came up to him and said, "Teacher, what [b]good thing must I do to gain eternal life?" [17]He said to him, "Why do you ask me about what is [a]good? There is only one who is good. But if you want to enter into life, [b]keep the commandments." [18]"Which ones?" he asked. Jesus replied, "*Do not murder, do not commit adultery, do not steal, do not give false testimony,* [19][a]*honor* [b]*your father and mother,*[1] and *love your neighbor as yourself.*"[2] [20]The young man said to him, "I have wholeheartedly [a]obeyed all these laws. What do I still lack?" [21]Jesus said to him, "If you wish to be perfect, [a]go sell your possessions and give the money to the poor, and you will have treasure in heaven. Then come, follow me." [22]But when the young man heard this he went away sorrowful, for he was very rich.

[23]Then Jesus said to his disciples, "[a]I tell you the truth, it will be hard for a rich person to enter the kingdom of heaven! [24]Again I say, it is easier for a camel[1] to go through the eye of a needle than for a rich person to enter into the kingdom of God." [25]The disciples were greatly astonished when they heard this and said, "Then who can be saved?" [26]Jesus looked at them and replied, "This is impossible [a]for mere humans, but for God all things are possible." [27]Then Peter said to him, "Look, [a]we have left everything to follow you! What then will there be for us?" [28]Jesus said to them, "I tell [a]you the truth: In the age when all things are renewed, when the Son of Man sits on his glorious throne, you who have followed me will also sit on 12 thrones, judging the 12 tribes of Israel. [29][a]And whoever has left houses or brothers or sisters or father or mother or children or fields for my sake will receive a hundred times as much and will inherit eternal life. [30][a]But many who are first will be last, and the last first.

Workers in the Vineyard

20 "For the kingdom of heaven is like a landowner who went out early in the morning to hire workers for his vineyard.

19:3 [1]‡ Maj. mss add *for a man, for someone, for a husband.* Mark 10:5–9; Eph 5:31 [b][1 Cor 6:16; 7:2] [1]Gen 2:24 19:4 [a]Gen 1:27; 5:2; [Mal 2:15] [1]Gen 1:27; 5:2 19:5 [a]Gen 2:24; Mark 10:5–9; Eph 5:31 19:7 [a]Deut 24:1–4; Matt 5:31 [1]Deut 24:1 [2]‡ Some wss omit *her.* 19:8 [a]Mal 2:16 [b]Heb 3:15 [1]Many wss omit *Jesus.* 19:9 [a][Matt 5:32]; Mark 10:11; Luke 16:18; 1 Cor 7:10 19:10 [a][Prov 21:19] [1]‡ Sig. wss and mss *His.* 19:11 [a][1 Cor 7:2, 7, 9, 17] 19:12 [a][1 Cor 7:32] [1]The verb occurs twice in the verse and refers to castration; "became eunuchs" is most likely figurative for maintaining a life of celibacy. 19:13 [a]Matt 20:31; Mark 10:13; Luke 18:15 19:14 [a]Matt 18:3–4; Mark 10:15; Luke 18:17; [1 Cor 14:20; 1 Pet 2:2] 19:16 [a]Matt 19:16–29; Mark 10:17–30; Luke 18:18–30 [b]Luke 10:25 19:17 [a]Ps 25:8; 34:8; Nah 1:7; [Rom 2:4] [b]Lev 18:5; Deut 4:40; 6:17; 7:11; 11:22; 28:9; Neh 9:29; Ezek 20:21; [Gal 3:10] 19:19 [a]Exod 20:12–16; Deut 5:16–20; Matt 15:4 [b]Lev 19:18; Matt 22:39; [Rom 13:9; Gal 5:14; Jas 2:8] [1]Exod 20:12–16; Deut 5:16–20 [2]Lev 19:18 19:20 [a][Phil 3:6–7] 19:21 [a]Matt 6:20; Luke 12:33; Acts 2:45; 4:34–35; 1 Tim 6:18–19 19:23 [a][Matt 13:22]; Mark 10:24; 1 Cor 1:26; [1 Tim 6:9] 19:24 [1]A few wss *rope.* 19:26 [a]Gen 18:14; Num 11:23; Job 42:2; Isa 59:1; Jer 32:17; Zech 8:6; Luke 1:37 19:27 [a]Deut 33:9; Matt 4:20; Luke 5:11 19:28 [a]Matt 20:21; Luke 22:28–30; [1 Cor 6:2; Rev 2:26] 19:29 [a][Matt 6:33]; Mark 10:29–30; Luke 18:29–30 19:30 [a][Matt 20:16; 21:31–32]; Mark 10:31; Luke 13:30

[2] And after agreeing with the workers for the standard wage,[1] he sent them into his vineyard. [3] When it was about nine o'clock in the morning, he went out again and saw others standing around in the marketplace without work. [4] He said to them, 'You go into the vineyard too, and I will give you whatever is right.' [5] So they went. When he went out again about noon and three o'clock that afternoon, he did the same thing. [6] And about five o'clock that afternoon he went out and found others standing around, and said to them, 'Why are you standing here all day without work?' [7] They said to him, 'Because no one hired us.' He said to them, 'You go and work in the vineyard too.' [8] When it was evening the owner of the vineyard said to his manager, 'Call the workers and pay them their wages starting with the last hired until the first.' [9] When those hired about five o'clock came, each received a full day's pay. [10] And when those hired first came, they thought they would receive more. But each one also received the standard wage. [11] When they received it, they began to complain against the landowner, [12] saying, 'These last fellows worked one hour, and you have made them equal to us who bore the hardship and burning heat of the day.' [13] And the landowner replied to one of them, 'Friend, I am not treating you unfairly. Didn't you agree with me to work for the standard wage? [14] Take what is yours and go. I want to give to this last man the same as I gave to you. [15] Am I not[1] permitted to do what I want with what belongs to me? [a]Or [b]are you envious because I am generous?' [16][a]So the last will be first, and the first last."

Third Prediction of Jesus' Death and Resurrection

[17] As Jesus was going up to Jerusalem, he took the twelve[1] aside privately [a]and said to them on the way, [18] "Look, we are going up to Jerusalem, and the Son of Man will [a]be handed over to the chief priests and the experts in the law. They will condemn him to death, [19][a]and will turn him over to the Gentiles to be [b]mocked and flogged [c]severely[1] and [d]crucified. Yet on the third day, he will be [e]raised."

A Request for James and John

[20][a]Then the mother of the sons of [b]Zebedee came to him with her sons, and kneeling down she asked him for a favor. [21] He said to her, "What do you want?" She replied, "Permit these two sons of mine to sit, one at your right hand and one at your left, in your kingdom." [22] Jesus answered, "You don't know what you are asking![1] Are you able to drink [a]the cup I am about to drink?"[2] [b]They said to him, "We are able." [23] He told them, "[a]You will drink my cup,[1] but to sit at my right and at my left is not mine to give. Rather, it is for those for whom it has been prepared by my Father."

[24][a]Now when the other 10 heard this, they were angry with the two brothers. [25] But Jesus called them and said, "You know that the rulers of the Gentiles lord it over them, and those in high positions use their authority over them. [26] It must not be this way among you! Instead [a]whoever wants to be great among you must be your servant, [27][a]and whoever wants to be first among you must be your slave—[28][a]just as the [b]Son of Man did not come to be served [c]but [d]to serve, and to give his life as a ransom [e]for many."

Two Blind Men Healed

[29][a]As they were leaving Jericho, a large crowd followed them. [30][a]Two blind men were sitting by the road. When they heard that Jesus was passing by, they shouted, "Have mercy on us, Lord, [b]Son of David!" [31] The crowd [a]scolded them to get them

to be quiet. But they shouted even more loudly, "Lord, have mercy on us,[1] Son of David!" [32]Jesus stopped, called them, and said, "What do you want me to do for you?" [33]They said to him, "Lord, let our eyes be opened." [34]Moved with [a]compassion, Jesus touched their eyes. Immediately they received their sight and followed him.

The Triumphal Entry

21 Now [a]when [b]they approached Jerusalem and came to Bethphage, at the Mount of Olives, Jesus sent two disciples, [2]telling them, "Go to the village ahead of you. Right away you will find a donkey tied there, and a colt with her. Untie them and bring them to me. [3]If anyone says anything to you, you are to say, 'The Lord needs them,' and he will send them at once." [4]This took place to fulfill what was spoken by the prophet:

[5] "[a]*Tell the people of Zion,*[1]
'*Look, your king is coming to you,*
unassuming and seated on a donkey,
and on a colt, the foal of a donkey.'"[2]

[6a]So the disciples went and did as Jesus had instructed them. [7]They brought the donkey and the colt and [a]placed their cloaks on them, and he sat on them. [8]A very large crowd spread their cloaks on the road. [a]Others cut branches from the trees and spread them on the road. [9]The crowds that went ahead of him and those following kept shouting, "*Hosanna*[1] to the Son of David! [a]*Blessed is the one who comes in the name of the Lord!*[2] *Hosanna* in the highest!" [10]As he entered Jerusalem the whole city was thrown into [a]an uproar, saying, "Who is this?" [11]And [a]the crowds were saying, "This is the prophet Jesus, from Nazareth in Galilee."

Cleansing the Temple

[12a]Then Jesus entered the temple area and drove out all those who were selling and buying in the temple courts and turned over the tables of the [b]money changers and the chairs of those selling doves. [13]And he said to them, "It is written, '[a]*My house will be called a house of prayer,*'[1] but you are turning it into a [b]*den of robbers!*"[2]

[14]The blind and lame came to him in the temple courts, and he healed them. [15]But when the chief priests and the experts in the law saw the wonderful things he did and heard the children crying out in the temple courts, "Hosanna to the [a]Son of David," they became indignant [16]and said to him, "Do you hear what they are saying?" Jesus said to them, "Yes. Have you never read, '*Out [a]of the mouths of children and nursing infants you have prepared praise for yourself*'?"[1] [17]And leaving them, he went [a]out of the city to Bethany and spent the night there.

The Withered Fig Tree

[18a]Now early in the morning, as he returned to the city, he was hungry. [19]After noticing a fig tree by the road he went to it, but found nothing on it except leaves. He said to it, "Never again will there be fruit from you!" [a]And the fig tree withered at once. [20a]When the disciples saw it they were amazed, saying, "How did the fig tree wither so quickly?" [21]Jesus answered them, "I tell you the truth, [a]if you have faith and [b]do not doubt, not only will you do what was done to the fig tree, [c]but even if you say to this mountain, 'Be lifted up and thrown into the sea,' it will happen. [22]And [a]whatever you ask in prayer, if you believe, you will receive."

The Authority of Jesus

[23a]Now after Jesus entered the temple courts, the chief priests and elders of the people came up to him as he was teaching and [b]said, "By what authority are you doing these things, and who gave you this authority?" [24]Jesus answered them, "I will also ask you one question. If you answer me then I will also tell you by what authority I do these things. [25]Where did John's [a]baptism

20:31[1]‡ Maj. MSS *Have mercy on us, Lord.* 20:34[a]Matt 9:36; 14:14; 15:32; 18:27 21:1[a]Mark 11:1–10; Luke 19:29–38 [b][Zech 14:4] 21:5[a]Isa 62:11; Zech 9:9; John 12:15 [1]Grk. *Tell the daughter of Zion*; an idiom for the inhabitants of Jerusalem. [2]Zech 9:9 21:6[a]Mark 11:4 21:7[a]2 Kgs 9:13 21:8[a]Lev 23:40; John 12:13 21:9[a]Ps 118:26; Matt 23:39 [1]Heb. *O Lord, save*; an expression of praise on the order of "Hail to the king." [2]Ps 118:25–26 21:10[a]John 2:13, 15 21:11[a][Deut 18:15, 18]; Matt 2:23; 16:14; Luke 4:16–29; John 6:14; 7:40; 9:17; [Acts 3:22–23] 21:12[a]Mal 3:1; Mark 11:15–18; Luke 19:45–47; John 2:13–16 [b]Deut 14:25 21:13[a]Isa 56:7 [b]Jer 7:11 [1]Isa 56:7 [2]Jer 7:11 21:15[a]Matt 1:1; John 7:42 21:16[a]Ps 8:2; Matt 11:25 [1]Ps 8:2 21:17[a]Matt 26:6; Mark 11:1, 11, 12; 14:3; Luke 19:29; 24:50; John 11:1, 18; 12:1 21:18[a]Mark 11:12–14, 20–24 21:19[a]Mark 11:13 21:20[a]Mark 11:20 21:21[a]Matt 17:20 [b]Jas 1:6 [c]1 Cor 13:2 21:22[a]Matt 7:7–11; Mark 11:24; Luke 11:9; [John 15:7; Jas 5:16; 1 John 3:22; 5:14] 21:23[a]Mark 11:27–33; Luke 20:1–8 [b]Exod 2:14; Acts 4:7; 7:27 21:25[a][John 1:29–34]

come from? From heaven or from people?" They discussed this among themselves, saying, "If we say, 'From heaven,' he will say, 'Then why did you not believe him?' [26]But if we say, 'From people,' we [a]fear the crowd, [b]for they all consider John to be a prophet." [27]So they answered Jesus, "We don't know." Then he said to them, "Neither will I tell you by what authority I am doing these things.

The Parable of the Two Sons

[28]"What do you think? A man had two sons. He went to the first and said, 'Son, go and work in the [a]vineyard today.' [29]The boy answered, 'I will not.' But later he had a change of heart[1] and went. [30]The father went to the other son and said the same thing. This boy answered, 'I will, sir,' but did not go. [31]Which of the two did his father's will?" They said, "The first."[1] Jesus said to them, "I tell you the [a]truth, tax collectors and prostitutes will go ahead of you into the kingdom of God! [32]For [a]John came to you in the way of righteousness, and you did not believe him. [b]But the tax collectors and prostitutes did believe. Although you saw this, you did not later change your minds and believe him.

The Parable of the Tenants

[33]"Listen to another parable: There was a landowner[1][a]who planted a vineyard. He put a fence around it, dug a pit for its winepress, and built a watchtower. Then he leased it to tenant farmers and went on a [b]journey. [34]When the harvest time was near, he sent his slaves to the tenants to collect his portion of the crop. [35]But the tenants seized his slaves, beat one, killed another, [a]and stoned another. [36]Again he sent other slaves, more than the first, and they treated them the same way. [37]Finally he sent his [a]son to them, saying, 'They will respect my son.' [38]But when the tenants saw the son, they said to themselves, '[a]This is the heir. [b]Come, let's kill him and get his inheritance!' [39][a]So they

seized him, threw him out of the vineyard, and killed him. [40]Now when the owner of the vineyard comes, what will he do to those tenants?" [41]They said to him, "[a]He will utterly destroy those evil men! [b]Then he will lease the vineyard to other tenants who will give him his portion at the harvest."

[42]Jesus said to [a]them, "Have you never read in the scriptures:

***"'The stone the builders rejected has
become the cornerstone.[1]
This is from the Lord, and it is
marvelous in our eyes'?[2]***

[43]"For this reason I tell you that [a]the kingdom of God will be taken from you and given to a people who will produce its fruit. [44]The one [a]who falls on this stone will be broken to pieces, and the one on whom [b]it falls will be crushed."[1] [45]When the chief priests and the Pharisees heard his parables, they realized that he was speaking about them. [46]They wanted to arrest him, but they were [a]afraid of [b]the crowds because the crowds regarded him as a prophet.

The Parable of the Wedding Banquet

22 Jesus spoke to them again in parables, saying: [2]"The kingdom of heaven can be compared to a king who gave a wedding banquet for his son. [3]He sent his slaves to summon those who had been invited to the banquet, but they would not come. [4]Again he sent other slaves, saying, 'Tell those who have been invited, "Look! The feast I have prepared for you is ready. [a]My oxen and fattened cattle have been slaughtered, and everything is ready. Come to the wedding banquet."' [5]But they were indifferent and went away, one to his farm, another to his business. [6]The rest seized his slaves, insolently mistreated them, and killed them. [7]The king was furious! He sent [a]his soldiers, and they put those murderers to death[1]and set their city on fire. [8]Then he said to his

---

21:26 [a]Matt 14:5; 21:46; Luke 20:6   [b]Matt 14:5; Mark 6:20   21:28 [a]Matt 20:1; 21:33   21:29 [1]Grk. *to change one's mind about something, with the probable implication of regret* (and v. 32).   21:31 [a]Luke 7:29, 37–50   [1]The MSS evidence provides a difficult textual problem depicting three differing responses of the sons. For a discussion of vv. 29–31, see *NET Bible, Full Notes Edition.*   21:32 [a]Luke 3:1–12; 7:29   [b]Luke 3:12–13   21:33 [a]Ps 80:9; Mark 12:1–12; Luke 20:9–19   [b]Matt 25:14   [1]The owner and manager of a household.   21:35 [a]2 Chr 24:21; 36:16; [Matt 23:34, 37; Acts 7:52; 1 Thess 2:15]; Heb 11:36–37   21:37 [a][John 3:16]   21:38 [a][Ps 2:8; Heb 1:2]   [b][Ps 2:2]; John 11:53; Acts 4:27   21:39 [a][Matt 26:50]; Mark 14:46; Luke 22:54; John 18:12; [Acts 2:23]   21:41 [a]Luke 20:16   [b][Matt 8:11; Acts 13:46; Rom 9; 10]   21:42 [a]Ps 118:22–23; Isa 28:16; Mark 12:10; Luke 20:17; Acts 4:11; [Rom 9:33]; Eph 2:20; [1 Pet 2:6–7]   [1]Or *capstone, keystone.*   [2]Ps 118:22–23   21:43 [a][Matt 8:12]; Acts 13:46   21:44 [a]Isa 8:14–15; Zech 12:3; Luke 20:18; [Rom 9:33]; 1 Pet 2:8   [b][Isa 60:12; Dan 2:44]   [1]A few wss omit v. 44.   21:46 [a]Matt 21:26; Mark 11:18, 32   [b]Matt 21:11; Luke 7:16; John 7:40   22:4 [a]Prov 9:2   22:7 [a][Dan 9:26]   [1]Grk. *he sent his soldiers, destroyed those murderers.*

slaves, 'The wedding is ready, but the ones who had been invited were not [a]worthy. [9]So go into the main streets and invite everyone you find to the wedding banquet.' [10]And those slaves went out into the streets and [a]gathered all they found, both bad and good, and the wedding hall was filled with guests. [11]But when the king came in to see the wedding guests, he saw a man there [a]who was not wearing wedding clothes. [12]And he said to him, 'Friend, how did you get in here without wedding clothes?' But he had nothing to [a]say. [13]Then the king said to his attendants, 'Tie him up hand and foot and throw him [a]into the outer darkness,[1] where there will be weeping and gnashing of teeth!' [14a]For many are called, but few are chosen."

Paying Taxes to Caesar

[15a]Then the Pharisees went out and planned together to entrap him with his own words. [16]They sent to him their disciples along with the [a]Herodians, saying, "Teacher, we know that you are truthful and teach the way of God in accordance with the truth. You do not court anyone's favor because you show no partiality. [17]Tell us then, what do you think? Is it right to pay taxes to Caesar or not?"

[18]But Jesus realized their evil intentions and said, "Hypocrites! Why are you testing me? [19]Show me the coin used for the tax." So they brought him a denarius.[1] [20]Jesus said to them, "Whose image is this, and whose inscription?" [21]They replied, "Caesar's." He said to them, "[a]Then give to [b]Caesar the things that are Caesar's, and to [c]God the things that are God's." [22]Now when they heard this they were stunned, and they left him and went away.

Marriage and the Resurrection

[23]The same day Sadducees (who say [a]there is no resurrection) came to him and asked him, [24]"Teacher, [a]Moses said, '*If a man dies without having children, his brother must marry the widow and father children for his brother.*'[1] [25]Now there were seven brothers among us. The first one married and died, and since he had no children he left his wife to his brother. [26]The second did the same, and the third, down to the seventh. [27]Last of all, the woman died. [28]In the resurrection, therefore, whose wife of the seven will she be? For they all had married her." [29]Jesus answered them, "You are deceived because you don't know the scriptures or the power of God. [30]For in the resurrection they neither marry nor are given in marriage, but [a]are like angels[1] in heaven. [31]Now as for the resurrection of the dead, have you not read what was spoken to you by God, [32a]*I am the God of Abraham, the God of Isaac, and the God of Jacob*'?[1] He is not the God of the dead but of the living!" [33]When [a]the crowds heard this, they were amazed at his teaching.

The Greatest Commandment

[34a]Now when the Pharisees heard that he had silenced the Sadducees, they assembled together.[1] [35]And one of them, [a]an expert in religious law,[1] asked him a question to test him: [36]"Teacher, which commandment in the law is the greatest?" [37]Jesus said to him, "'*Love the Lord [a]your God with all your heart, with all your soul, and with all your mind.*'[1] [38]This is the first and greatest commandment. [39]The second is like it: '*Love [a]your neighbor as yourself.*'[1] [40]All the law and the prophets depend [a]on these two commandments."

The Messiah: David's Son and Lord

[41a]While the Pharisees were assembled, Jesus asked them a question: [42]"What do you think about the Christ? Whose [a]son is he?" They said, "The son of David." [43]He said to them, "How then does David by the Spirit call him 'Lord,' saying,

[44] "'*The Lord said to my lord,
"Sit at my right hand,
until I put your enemies under your feet"*'?[1]

22:8 [a] Matt 10:11   22:10 [a] Matt 13:38, 47, 48; [Acts 28:28]   22:11 [a] [2 Cor 5:3; Eph 4:24; Col 3:10, 12; Rev 3:4; 16:15; 19:8]   22:12 [a] [Rom 3:19]   22:13 [a] Matt 8:12; 25:30; Luke 13:28   [1] Associated with Tartarus, the underworld.   22:14 [a] Matt 20:16   22:15 [a] Mark 12:13–17; Luke 20:20–26   22:16 [a] Mark 3:6; 8:15; 12:13   22:19 [1] Or *silver coin*; "denarius" is used because not all coins carried the image of Caesar.   22:21 [a] Matt 17:25   [b] [Rom 13:1–7; 1 Pet 2:13–15]   [c] [1 Cor 3:23; 6:19–20; 12:27]   22:23 [a] Mark 12:18–27; Luke 20:27–40   22:24 [a] Deut 25:5   [1] Deut 25:5   22:30 [a] [1 John 3:2]   [1] Maj. wss add *of God.*   22:32 [a] Gen 17:7; 26:24; 28:21; Exod 3:6, 15; Mark 12:26; Luke 20:37; Acts 7:32; [Heb 11:16]   [1] Exod 3:6   22:33 [a] Matt 7:28   22:34 [a] Mark 12:28–31; Luke 10:25–37   [1] Grk. *for the same.*   22:35 [a] Luke 7:30; 10:25; 11:45–46, 52; 14:3; Titus 3:13   [1] Trad. *a lawyer*; an expert in the interpretation of the Mosaic law.   22:37 [a] Deut 6:5; 10:12; 30:6   [1] Deut 6:5   22:39 [a] Lev 19:18; Matt 19:19; Mark 12:31; Luke 10:27; [Rom 13:9; Gal 5:14; Jas 2:8]   [1] Lev 19:18   22:40 [a] [Matt 7:12; Rom 13:10; 1 Tim 1:5]   22:41 [a] Mark 12:35–37; Luke 20:41–44   22:42 [a] Matt 1:1; 21:9   22:44 [1] Ps 110:1

⁴⁵If David then calls him 'Lord,' how can he be his son?" ⁴⁶No one was able to answer him ᵃa word, and from that day on ᵇno one dared to question him any longer.

Seven Woes

23 Then Jesus said to the crowds and to his disciples, ²"The experts in ᵃthe law and the Pharisees sit on Moses' seat. ³Therefore pay attention to what ᵃthey tell you and do it. But do not do what they do, for they do not practice what they teach. ⁴They tie up heavy loads, hard to carry, and put them on men's shoulders, ᵃbut they themselves are not willing even to lift a finger to move them. ⁵They do all their deeds to ᵃbe seen by people, for they make their phylacteries wide and their tassels[1] long. ⁶They love ᵃthe place of honor at banquets and the best seats in the synagogues ⁷and elaborate greetings in the marketplaces and to have people call them 'Rabbi.' ⁸ᵃBut you are not to be called 'Rabbi,' for you have one Teacher and you are all brothers. ⁹And call no one your 'father' on earth, ᵃfor you have one Father, who is in heaven. ¹⁰Nor are you to be called 'teacher,' for you have one Teacher, the Christ. ¹¹The greatest among you will be your servant. ¹²ᵃAnd whoever exalts himself will be humbled, and whoever humbles himself will be exalted.

¹³"But ᵃwoe to you, experts in the law and you Pharisees, hypocrites![1] You keep locking people out of the kingdom of heaven! For you neither enter nor permit those trying to enter to go in.[2]

¹⁵"Woe to you, experts in the law and you Pharisees, hypocrites! You cross land and sea to make one convert, and when you get one, you make him twice as much a child of hell[1] as yourselves!

¹⁶"Woe to you, ᵃblind guides, ᵇwho say, 'Whoever swears by the temple is bound by nothing. But whoever swears by the gold of the temple is bound by the oath.' ¹⁷Blind fools! Which is greater, the gold ᵃor the temple that makes the gold sacred? ¹⁸And, 'Whoever swears by the altar is bound by nothing. But if anyone swears by the gift on it he is bound by the oath.' ¹⁹You are blind! For which is greater, the gift ᵃor the altar that makes the gift sacred? ²⁰So whoever swears by the altar swears by it and by everything on it. ²¹And whoever swears by the temple swears by it and the one who dwells in it. ²²And ᵃwhoever swears by heaven swears by the throne of God and the one who sits on it.

²³"Woe to you, experts in the law and you Pharisees, hypocrites! You give ᵃa tenth of mint, dill, and cumin, yet you neglect what is more important in the law—justice, mercy, and faithfulness! You[1] should have done these things without neglecting the others. ²⁴Blind guides! You strain out a gnat yet swallow a camel!

²⁵"Woe to you, experts in the law and you Pharisees, hypocrites! You clean the outside of the cup and the dish, but inside they are full of greed and self-indulgence. ²⁶Blind Pharisee! First clean the inside of the cup,[1] so that the outside may become clean too!

²⁷"Woe to you, experts in the law and you Pharisees, hypocrites! You are like whitewashed tombs that look beautiful on the outside but inside are full of the bones of the dead and of everything unclean. ²⁸In the same way, on the outside you look righteous to people, but inside you are full of hypocrisy and lawlessness.

²⁹"ᵃWoe to you, experts in the law and you Pharisees, hypocrites! You build tombs for the prophets and decorate the graves of the righteous. ³⁰And you say, 'If we had lived in the days of our ancestors, we would not have participated with them in shedding the blood of the prophets.' ³¹By saying this ᵃyou testify against yourselves that you are descendants of those who murdered the prophets. ³²Fill ᵃup then the measure of your ancestors! ³³You snakes, you ᵃoffspring of vipers! How will you escape being condemned to hell?

22:46 ᵃLuke 14:6   ᵇMark 12:34; Luke 20:40   23:2 ᵃDeut 33:3; Ezra 7:6, 25; Neh 8:4, 8; [Mal 2:7]; Mark 12:38; Luke 20:45   23:3 ᵃ[Rom 2:19]   23:4 ᵃ[Matt 11:29–30]; Luke 11:46; Acts 15:10; Rom 2:17–24; [Gal 5:1; 6:13; Col 2:16–17]   23:5 ᵃ[Matt 6:1–6, 16–18]   [1]Could refer to the outer fringe of the garment.   23:6 ᵃMark 12:38–39; Luke 11:43; 20:46; 3 John 9   23:8 ᵃ[2 Cor 1:24; Jas 3:1; 1 Pet 5:3]   23:9 ᵃ[Mal 1:6]; Matt 5:16, 48; 6:1, 9, 14, 26, 32; 7:11   23:12 ᵃJob 22:29; Prov 15:33; 29:23; Luke 14:11; 18:14; Jas 4:6; 1 Pet 5:5   23:13 ᵃLuke 11:52   [1]Grk. *Woe to you … because you … .*   [2]Some MSS add v. 14: *Woe to you experts in the law and you Pharisees, hypocrites! You devour widows' property, and as a show you pray long prayers! Therefore you will receive a more severe punishment.*   23:15 [1]Grk. *a son of Gehenna, a person who belongs to hell.*   23:16 ᵃMatt 15:14; 23:24   ᵇ[Matt 5:33–34]   23:17 ᵃExod 30:29   23:19 ᵃExod 29:37   23:22 ᵃPs 11:4; Isa 66:1; Matt 5:34; Acts 7:49   23:23 ᵃ[1 Sam 15:22; Hos 6:6; Mic 6:8]; Matt 9:13; 12:7   [1]‡ Many WSS *But you.*   23:26 [1]Sig. WSS add *and the dish.*   23:29 ᵃLuke 11:47–48   23:31 ᵃMatt 23:34, 37; [Acts 7:51–52]; 1 Thess 2:15   23:32 ᵃGen 15:16; [1 Thess 2:16]   23:33 ᵃMatt 3:7; 12:34; Luke 3:7

[34]"For this reason I am sending you prophets and wise men and experts in [a]the law, [b]some of whom you will kill and crucify, and [c]some you will flog in your synagogues and pursue from town to town, [35]so [a]that on you will come all the righteous blood shed on earth, [b]from [c]the blood of righteous Abel to the blood of Zechariah son of Barachiah, whom you murdered between the temple and the altar. [36]I tell you the truth, this generation will be held responsible for all these things!

Judgment on Israel

[37]"O Jerusalem, Jerusalem, [a]you who kill the prophets [b]and stone those who are sent to you! How often [c]I have longed to gather your children together as a hen gathers her chicks [d]under her wings, but you would have none of it! [38]Look, your house is left to you desolate! [39]For I tell you, you will not see me from now until you say, '**Blessed** [a]*is the one who comes in the name of the Lord!*'"[1]

The Destruction of the Temple

24 Now as [a]Jesus was going out of the temple courts and walking away, his disciples came to show him the temple buildings. [2]And he said to them, "Do you see all these things? I tell you the truth, [a]not one stone will be left on another. All will be torn down!"

Signs of the End of the Age

[3]As [a]he was sitting on the Mount of Olives, his disciples came to him privately and said, "[b]Tell us, when will these things happen? And what will be the sign of your coming and of the end of the age?" [4]Jesus answered them, "Watch out that no one misleads you. [5]For [a]many will come in my name, saying, 'I am the Christ,'[1] [b]and they will mislead many. [6]You will hear of [a]wars and rumors of wars. Make sure that you are not alarmed, for this must happen, but the end is still to come. [7]For [a]nation will rise up in arms against nation, and kingdom against kingdom. And there will be [b]famines and earthquakes[1] in various places. [8]All these things are the beginning of birth pains.

Persecution of Disciples

[9]"[a]Then they will hand you over to be persecuted and will kill you. You will be hated by all the nations[1] because of my name. [10]Then many will be led into sin,[1] and they will betray one another and hate one another. [11]And [a]many false prophets will appear and [b]deceive many, [12]and because lawlessness will increase so much, the love of many will grow [a]cold. [13a]But the person who endures to the end will be saved. [14]And this [a]gospel of the kingdom [b]will be preached throughout the whole inhabited earth as a testimony to all the nations, and then the end will come.

The Abomination of Desolation

[15]"So when you see [a]the [b]abomination of desolation[1]—spoken about by Daniel the prophet—standing in the holy place" (let the reader understand), [16]"then those in Judea must flee to the mountains. [17]The one on the roof must not come down to take anything out of his house, [18]and the one in the field must not turn back to get his cloak. [19a]Woe to those who are pregnant and to those who are nursing their babies in those days! [20]Pray that your flight may not be in winter or on a Sabbath. [21]For [a]then there will be great suffering[1] unlike anything that has happened from the beginning of the world until now, or ever will happen. [22]And if those days had not been cut short, no one would be saved. [a]But for the sake of the elect those days will be cut short. [23a]Then if anyone says to you, 'Look, here is the Christ!' or 'There he is!' do not believe him. [24]For [a]false messiahs and false

23:34 [a] Matt 21:34–35; Luke 11:49 [b] John 16:2; Acts 7:54–60; 22:19 [c] Matt 10:17; Acts 5:40; 2 Cor 11:24–25 **23:35** [a] Rev 18:24 [b] Gen 4:8; Heb 11:4; 1 John 3:12 [c] 2 Chr 24:20–21 **23:37** [a] Luke 13:34–35 [b] 2 Chr 24:20–21; 36:15–16; Neh 9:26; Matt 21:35–36 [c] Deut 32:11–12; Matt 11:28–30 [d] Ps 17:8; 91:4; Isa 49:5 **23:39** [a] Ps 118:26; Matt 21:9 [1] Ps 118:26 **24:1** [a] Mark 13:1; Luke 21:5–36 **24:2** [a] 1 Kgs 9:7; Mic 3:12; Luke 19:44 **24:3** [a] Mark 13:3 [b] [Matt 24:27, 37, 39; Luke 17:20–37; 1 Thess 5:1–3] **24:5** [a] Jer 14:14; John 5:43; Acts 5:36; [1 John 2:18; 4:3] [b] Matt 24:11 [1] Or *Messiah*; both "Christ" (Grk.) and "Messiah" (Heb., Aram.) mean "one who has been anointed." **24:6** [a] [Rev 6:2–4] **24:7** [a] 2 Chr 15:6; Isa 19:2; Hag 2:22; Zech 14:13 [b] Acts 11:28; Rev 6:5–6 [1] Maj. wss *famines and plagues and earthquakes.* **24:9** [a] Matt 10:17; Luke 21:12; [John 16:2]; Acts 4:2–3; Rev 2:10 [1] Or *the Gentiles.* **24:10** [1] Or *will fall away*; perhaps apostasy. **24:11** [a] Acts 20:29; 2 Pet 2:1; Rev 13:11; 19:20 [b] [1 Tim 4:1] **24:12** [a] [2 Thess 2:3; 2 Tim 3:1–3] **24:13** [a] Matt 10:22; Mark 13:13 **24:14** [a] Matt 4:23 [b] Rom 10:18; Col 1:6, 23 **24:15** [a] Mark 13:14; Luke 21:20; [John 11:48]; Acts 6:13; 21:28 [b] Dan 9:27; 11:31; 12:11 [1] [Dan 9:27] **24:19** [a] Luke 23:29 **24:21** [a] Dan 9:26 [1] Trad. *great tribulation.* **24:22** [a] Isa 65:8–9; [Zech 14:2] **24:23** [a] Mark 13:21; Luke 17:23 **24:24** [a] Deut 13:1; John 4:48; [2 Thess 2:9]; Rev 13:13

prophets will appear and perform great signs and wonders to deceive, [b]if possible, even the elect. [25]Remember,[1] I have told you ahead of time. [26]So then, if someone says to you, 'Look, he is in the wilderness,' do not go out, or 'Look, he is in the inner rooms,' do not believe him. [27a]For just like the lightning comes from the east and flashes to the west, so the coming of the Son of Man will be. [28a]Wherever the corpse is, there the vultures[1] will gather.

The Arrival of the Son of Man

[29] [a]Immediately after [b]the suffering of those days, *the sun will be darkened, and the moon will not give its light; the stars will fall from heaven, and the powers of heaven will be shaken.*[1] [30a]Then the sign of the Son of Man will appear in heaven, [b]and all the tribes of the earth will mourn. They will see *the Son of Man arriving on the clouds of heaven*[1] with power and great glory. [31a]And he will send his angels with a loud trumpet blast, and they will gather his elect from the four winds, from one end of heaven to the other.

The Parable of the Fig Tree

[32]"Learn [a]this parable from the fig tree: Whenever its branch becomes tender and puts out its leaves, you know that summer is near. [33]So also you, when you see all these things, know[1] [a]that he is near, right at the door. [34]I tell you the truth, [a]this generation will not pass away until all these things take place. [35a]Heaven and earth will pass away, but my words will never pass away.

Be Ready!

[36]"[a]But as for that day and hour no one knows it—not even the angels in heaven[1]—except the Father alone. [37]For just like the days of Noah were, so the coming of the Son of Man will be. [38a]For in those days before the flood, people were eating and drinking, marrying and giving in marriage,

until the day Noah entered the ark. [39]And they knew nothing until the flood came and took them all away. It will be the same at the coming of the Son of Man. [40a]Then there will be two men in the field; one will be taken and one left. [41]There will be two women grinding grain with a mill;[1] one will be taken and one left.

[42]"Therefore stay [a]alert because you do not know on what day[1] your Lord will come. [43a]But understand this: If the owner of the house had known at what time of night the thief was coming, he would have been alert and would not have let his house be broken into. [44a]Therefore you also must be ready because the Son of Man will come at an hour when you do not expect him.

The Faithful and Wise Slave

[45]"[a]Who then is the faithful and wise slave, whom the master has put in charge of his household, to give the other slaves their food at the proper time? [46a]Blessed is that slave whom the master finds at work when he comes. [47]I tell you [a]the truth, the master will put him in charge of all his possessions. [48]But if that evil slave should say to himself, 'My master [a]is staying away a long time,' [49]and he begins to beat his fellow slaves and to eat and drink with drunkards, [50]then the master of that slave will come on a day when he does [a]not expect him and at an hour he does not foresee, [51]and will cut him in two,[1] and assign him a place with the hypocrites, where [a]there will be weeping and gnashing of teeth.

The Parable of the 10 Virgins

25 "At that time [a]the kingdom of heaven will be like 10 virgins who took their lamps and went out to meet the bridegroom. [2a]Five of the virgins were foolish, and five were wise. [3]When the foolish ones took their lamps, they did not take extra olive oil with them. [4]But the wise ones took

24:24 [b] [John 6:37; Rom 8:28; 2 Tim 2:19]   24:25 [1] Or *Pay attention!*; Grk. *Behold.*   24:27 [a] Luke 17:24   24:28 [a] Job 39:30; Ezek 39:17; Hab 1:8; Luke 17:37   [1] Or *eagles.*   24:29 [a] [Dan 7:11]   [b] Isa 13:10; 24:23; Ezek 32:7; Joel 2:10, 31; 3:15; Amos 5:20; 8:9; Zeph 1:15; Matt 24:29–35; Acts 2:20; Rev 6:12–17; 8:12   [1] [Isa 13:10; 34:4 LXX; Joel 2:10]   24:30 [a] [Dan 7:13–14; Matt 16:27; 24:3, 37, 39]   [b] Zech 12:12   [1] [Dan 7:13]   24:31 [a] Exod 19:16; Deut 30:4; Isa 27:13; Zech 9:14; [1 Cor 15:52; 1 Thess 4:16]; Heb 12:19; Rev 8:2; 11:15   24:32 [a] Luke 21:29   24:33 [a] [Jas 5:9; Rev 3:20]   [1] *know* can be indicative or imperative.   24:34 [a] [Matt 10:23; 16:28; 23:36]   24:35 [a] Ps 102:25–26; Isa 51:6; Mark 13:31; Luke 21:33; [1 Pet 1:23–25; 2 Pet 3:10]   24:36 [a] Mark 13:32; Acts 1:7; 1 Thess 5:2; 2 Pet 3:10   [1] ‡ Sig. wss add *nor the Son.*   24:38 [a] [Gen 6:3–5]; Luke 17:26; [1 Pet 3:20]   24:40 [a] Luke 17:34   24:41 [1] A hand mill normally operated by two women.   24:42 [a] Matt 25:13; Luke 21:36; 1 Thess 5:6   [1] Maj. later MSS *hour.*   24:43 [a] Luke 12:39; 1 Thess 5:2; Rev 3:3   24:44 [a] Luke 12:35–40; [1 Thess 5:6]   24:45 [a] Luke 12:42–46; [Acts 20:28]   24:46 [a] Rev 16:15   24:47 [a] Matt 25:21, 23; Luke 22:29   24:48 [a] [2 Pet 3:4–9]   24:50 [a] Mark 13:32   24:51 [a] Matt 8:12; 25:30   [1] If taken lit., this servant is dismembered, but it could be hyperbole.   25:1 [a] [Eph 5:29–30; Rev 19:7; 21:2, 9]   25:2 [a] Matt 13:47; 22:10

flasks of olive oil with their lamps. [5]When [a]the bridegroom was delayed a long time, they all became drowsy and fell asleep. [6]But [a]at midnight there was a shout, 'Look, the bridegroom is here! Come out to meet him.' [7]Then all the virgins woke up and [a]trimmed their lamps. [8]The foolish ones said to the wise, 'Give us some of your oil because our lamps are going out.' [9]'No,' they replied. 'There won't be enough for you and for us. Go instead to those who sell oil and buy some for yourselves.' [10]But while [a]they had gone to buy it, the bridegroom arrived, and those who were ready went inside with him to the wedding banquet. Then the door was shut. [11]Later, the other virgins came too, saying, '[a]Lord, lord! Let us in!' [12]But he [a]replied, 'I tell you the truth, I do not know you!' [13]Therefore stay [a]alert because you do not [b]know the day or the hour.[1]

The Parable of the Talents

[14]"[a]For it is [b]like a man going on a journey, who summoned his slaves and entrusted his property to them. [15]To one he gave five talents, [a]to another two, and to another one, each according to his ability. Then he went on his journey. [16]The one who had received five talents went off right away and put his money to work and gained five more. [17]In the same way, the one who had two gained two more. [18]But the one who had received one talent went out and dug a hole in the ground and hid his master's money in it. [19]After a long time, the master of those slaves came and settled his accounts with them. [20]The one who had received the five talents came and brought five more, saying, 'Sir, you entrusted me with five talents. See, I have gained five more.' [21]His master answered, 'Well done, good and [a]faithful slave! You have been [b]faithful in a few things. I will put you in charge of many things. Enter into [c]the joy of your master.' [22]The one with the two talents also came and said, 'Sir, you entrusted two talents to me. See, I have gained two more.' [23]His master answered,

'Well [a]done, good and faithful slave! You have been faithful with a few things. I will put you in charge of many things. Enter into [b]the joy of your master.' [24]Then the one who had received the one talent came and said, 'Sir, I knew that you were a hard man, harvesting where you did not sow, and gathering where you did not scatter seed, [25]so I was afraid, and I went and hid your talent in the ground. See, you have what is yours.' [26]But his master answered, '[a]Evil and lazy slave! So you knew that I harvest where I didn't sow and gather where I didn't scatter? [27]Then you should have deposited my money with the bankers, and on my return I would have received my money back with interest! [28]Therefore take the talent from him and give it to the one who has 10. [29][a]For the one who has will be given more, and he will have more than enough. But the one who does not have, even what he has will be taken from him. [30]And throw that worthless slave [a]into the outer darkness, where [b]there will be weeping and [c]gnashing of teeth.'

The Judgment

[31]"[a]When the Son of Man comes in his glory and all the angels with him, then he will sit on his glorious throne. [32][a]All the nations will be assembled before him, and he will separate people one from another like a [b]shepherd separates the sheep from the goats. [33]He will put the [a]sheep on his right and the goats on his left. [34]Then the king will say to those on his right, 'Come, you who are blessed by my Father, [a]inherit the kingdom [b]prepared for you from the foundation of the world. [35][a]For [b]I was hungry and you gave me food, I was thirsty and you gave me something to drink, I was a stranger and you invited me in, [36]I was [a]naked and you gave me [b]clothing, I was sick and you took care of me, I was in prison and you visited me.' [37]Then the righteous will answer him, 'Lord, when did we see you hungry and feed you, or thirsty and give you something to

25:5 [a]1 Thess 5:6   25:6 [a][Matt 24:31; 1 Thess 4:16]   25:7 [a]Luke 12:35   25:10 [a][Matt 7:21]; Luke 13:25   25:11 [a][Matt 7:21–23; Luke 13:25–30]   25:12 [a][Ps 5:5; Hab 1:13; John 9:31]   25:13 [a]Mark 13:35; [Luke 21:36]; 1 Thess 5:6   [b]Matt 24:36, 42   [1]Maj. later MSS add *in which the Son of Man is coming.*   25:14 [a]Luke 19:12–27   [b]Matt 21:33   25:15 [a][Rom 12:6; 1 Cor 12:7, 11, 29; Eph 4:11]   25:21 [a][Luke 16:10; 1 Cor 4:2; 2 Tim 4:7–8]   [b][Matt 24:47; 25:34, 46; Luke 12:44; 22:29–30; Rev 3:21; 21:7]   [c][2 Tim 2:12; Heb 12:2; 1 Pet 1:8]   25:23 [a]Matt 24:45, 47; 25:21   [b][Ps 16:11; John 15:10–11]   25:26 [a]Matt 18:32; Luke 19:22   25:29 [a]Matt 13:12; Mark 4:25; Luke 8:18; [John 15:2]   25:30 [a]Matt 8:12; 22:13; [Luke 13:28]   [b]Matt 7:23; 8:12; 24:51   [c]Ps 112:10   25:31 [a][Zech 14:5]; Matt 16:27; Mark 8:38; Acts 1:11; [1 Thess 4:16]; 2 Thess 1:7; [Jude 14]; Rev 1:7   25:32 [a][Rom 14:10; 2 Cor 5:10; Rev 20:12]   [b]Ezek 20:38   25:33 [a]Ps 79:13; 100:3; [John 10:11, 27, 28]   25:34 [a][Rom 8:17; 1 Pet 1:4, 9; Rev 21:7]   [b]Matt 20:23; Mark 10:40; 1 Cor 2:9; Heb 11:16   25:35 [a]Isa 58:7; Ezek 18:7, 16; [Jas 1:27; 2:15–16]   [b]Job 31:32; [Heb 13:2]; 3 John 5   25:36 [a]Isa 58:7; Ezek 18:7, 16; [Jas 2:15–16]   [b]2 Tim 1:16

drink? [38]When did we see you a stranger and invite you in, or naked and clothe you? [39]When did we see you sick or in prison and visit you?' [40]And the king will answer them, 'I tell you the truth, just [a]as you did it for one of the least of these brothers or sisters of mine, you did it for me.'

[41]"Then he will say to those on his left, '[a]Depart from me, you accursed, [b]into [c]the eternal fire that has been prepared for the devil and his angels! [42]For I was hungry and you gave me nothing to eat, I was thirsty and you gave me nothing to drink. [43]I was a stranger and you did not receive me as a guest, naked and you did not clothe me, sick and in prison and you did not visit me.' [44]Then they too will answer, 'Lord, when did we see you hungry or thirsty or a stranger or naked or sick or in prison, and did not give you whatever you needed?' [45]Then he will answer them, 'I tell you the truth, just [a]as you did not do it for one of the least of these, you did not do it for me.' [46]And [a]these will depart into eternal punishment, but the righteous into eternal life."

The Plot against Jesus

26 When Jesus had finished saying all these things, he told his disciples, [2]"[a]You know that after two days the Passover is coming, and the Son of Man will be handed over to be crucified." [3][a]Then the chief priests and the elders of the people met together in the palace of the high priest, who was named Caiaphas. [4]They [a]planned to arrest Jesus by stealth and kill him. [5]But they said, "Not during the feast, so that there won't be a riot among the [a]people."

Jesus' Anointing

[6]Now while Jesus was in [a]Bethany at the house of Simon the leper, [7]a woman came to him with an alabaster jar of expensive perfumed oil,[1] and she poured it on his head as he was at the table. [8][a]When the disciples saw this, they became indignant and said, "Why this waste? [9]It could have been sold at a high price and the money given to the poor!" [10]When Jesus learned of this, he said to them, "Why are you bothering this woman? She has done a good service for me. [11][a]For you will always have the poor with you, but you will not always have [b]me![1] [12]When she poured this oil on my body, she did it to prepare me for [a]burial. [13]I tell you the truth, wherever this gospel is proclaimed in the whole world, what she has done will also be told in memory of her."

The Plan to Betray Jesus

[14][a]Then one of the twelve, the one named [b]Judas Iscariot, went to the chief priests [15]and said, "[a]What will you give me to betray him into your hands?" So they set out 30 silver coins for him. [16]From that time on, Judas began looking for an opportunity to betray him.

The Passover

[17][a]Now on the first day of the Feast of Unleavened Bread the disciples came to Jesus and said, "Where do you want us to prepare for you to eat the Passover?" [18]He said, "Go into the city to a certain man and tell him, 'The Teacher says, "[a]My time is near. I will observe the Passover with my disciples at your house."'" [19]So the disciples did as Jesus had instructed them, and they prepared the Passover. [20]When it was evening, [a]he took his place at the table with the twelve.[1] [21]And while they were eating he said, "I tell you the truth, one of you will [a]betray me." [22]They became greatly distressed and each one began to say to him, "Surely not I, Lord?" [23]He answered, "[a]The one who has dipped his hand into the bowl with me will betray me. [24]The Son of Man will go [a]as it is written about him, but [b]woe to that man by whom the Son of Man is betrayed! [c]It would be better for him if he had never been born." [25]Then Judas, the one who would betray him, said, "Surely not I, Rabbi?" Jesus replied, "You have said it yourself."

25:40 [a] Prov 14:31; Matt 10:42; Mark 9:41; Heb 6:10   25:41 [a] Ps 6:8; Matt 7:23; Luke 13:27   [b] Matt 13:40, 42   [c] [2 Pet 2:4]; Jude 6   25:45 [a] Prov 14:31; Zech 2:8; Acts 9:5   25:46 [a] [Dan 12:2; John 5:29; Acts 24:15; Rom 2:7]   26:2 [a] Matt 27:35; Mark 14:1–2; Luke 22:1–2; John 13:1; 19:18   26:3 [a] Ps 2:2; John 11:47; Acts 4:25   26:4 [a] John 11:47; Acts 4:25–28   26:5 [a] Matt 21:26   26:6 [a] Matt 8:2; Mark 14:3–9; Luke 7:37–39; John 11:1–2; 12:1–8   26:7 [1] Or *myrrh*.   26:8 [a] John 12:4   26:11 [a] [Deut 15:11; Mark 14:7]; John 12:8   [b] [Matt 18:20; 28:20; John 13:33; 14:19; 16:5, 28; 17:11]   [1] An emphatic Grk. construction.   26:12 [a] Matt 27:60; Luke 23:53; John 19:38–42   26:14 [a] Mark 14:10–11; Luke 22:3–6; John 13:2, 30   [b] Matt 10:4   26:15 [a] Exod 21:32; Zech 11:12; Matt 27:3   26:17 [a] Exod 12:6, 18–20   26:18 [a] Luke 9:51; John 12:23; 13:1; 17:1   26:20 [a] Mark 14:17–21; Luke 22:14; John 13:21   [1] Many wss *the twelve disciples, his twelve disciples.*   26:21 [a] Matt 26:46; Mark 14:42; Luke 22:21–23; John 6:70–71; 13:21   26:23 [a] Ps 41:9; Luke 22:21; John 13:18   26:24 [a] Ps 22; Dan 9:26; Mark 9:12; Luke 24:25–26, 46; Acts 17:2–3; 26:22–23; 1 Cor 15:3   [b] Matt 27:3–5; Luke 17:1; Acts 1:16–20   [c] John 17:12; Acts 1:25

The Lord's Supper

26 [a]While they were eating, [b]Jesus took bread, and after giving thanks he broke it, gave it to his disciples, and said, "Take, eat, [c]this is my body." 27And after taking the cup and giving thanks, he gave it to them, saying, "[a]Drink from it, all of you, 28for [a]this is my blood, the blood [b]of the covenant,[1] that is poured out [c]for many for the forgiveness of sins. 29I tell you, from now on [a]I will not drink of this fruit of the vine [b]until that day when I drink it new with you in my Father's kingdom." 30After singing [a]a hymn, they went out to the Mount of Olives.

The Prediction of Peter's Denial

31Then Jesus said to them, "This night you will [a]all fall away [b]because of me, for [c]it is written:

> "[a]*I will strike the shepherd,*
> *and the sheep of the flock will be*
> *scattered.*'[1]

32But after [a]I am raised, I will go ahead of you into Galilee." 33Peter said to him, "If they all fall away because of you, I will never fall away!" 34Jesus said to him, "I tell you the [a]truth, on this night, before the rooster crows, you will deny me three times." 35Peter said to him, "Even if I must die with you, I will never deny you." And all the disciples said the same thing.

Gethsemane

36[a]Then Jesus went with them to a place called Gethsemane, and he said to the disciples, "Sit here while I go over there and pray." 37He took with him Peter and [a]the two sons of Zebedee, and he became anguished and distressed. 38Then he said to them, "My soul is deeply grieved, even to the point of death. Remain here and stay awake with [a]me." 39Going a little farther, he threw himself down with his face to the ground and [a]prayed, "My Father, if [b]possible, [c]let this cup pass from me! Yet [d]not what I will, but what you will." 40Then he came to the disciples and found them sleeping. He said to Peter, "So, couldn't you stay awake with me for one hour? 41Stay [a]awake and pray that you will not fall into temptation. [b]The spirit is willing, but the flesh is weak." 42He went away a second time and prayed, "My Father, if this cup cannot be taken away unless I drink it, your will must be done." 43He came again and found them sleeping; they could not keep their eyes open. 44So leaving them again, he went away and prayed for the third time, saying the same thing once more. 45Then he came to the disciples and said to them, "Are you still sleeping and resting? Look, the hour is approaching, and the Son of Man is [a]betrayed into the hands of sinners. 46Get up, let us go. Look! My betrayer is approaching!"

Betrayal and Arrest

47While he was still speaking, Judas,[1] one of the twelve, arrived. With him was a large crowd armed with swords and clubs, sent by the chief priests and elders of the people. 48(Now the betrayer had given them a sign, saying, "The one I kiss is the man. Arrest him!") 49Immediately he went up to Jesus [a]and said, "Greetings, Rabbi," and kissed him. 50Jesus said to him, "[a]Friend, do what you are here to do." Then they came and took hold of Jesus and arrested him. 51But [a]one of those with Jesus grabbed[1] his sword, drew it out, and struck the high priest's slave, cutting off his ear. 52Then Jesus said to him, "Put your sword back in its place! [a]For all who take hold of the sword will die by the sword. 53Or do you think that I cannot call on my Father and that he would send me [a]more than 12 legions of angels right now? 54How then would the scriptures [a]that say it must happen this way be fulfilled?" 55At that moment Jesus said to the crowd, "Have you come out with swords and clubs to arrest me like you would an outlaw?[1] Day after day I sat teaching in the temple courts, yet you did not arrest me. 56But this

26:26 [a] Mark 14:22–25; Luke 22:17–20 [b] 1 Cor 11:23–25 [c] [1 Pet 2:24] 26:27 [a] Mark 14:23 26:28 [a] [Exod 24:8; Lev 17:11; Heb 9:20] [b] Jer 31:31 [c] Matt 20:28; [Rom 5:15; Heb 9:22] [1] Maj. wss *new covenant.* 26:29 [a] Mark 14:25; Luke 22:18 [b] Acts 10:41 26:30 [a] Mark 14:26–31; Luke 22:31–34 26:31 [a] Matt 26:56; Mark 14:27; John 16:32 [b] [Matt 11:6] [c] Zech 13:7 [1] Zech 13:7 26:32 [a] Matt 28:7, 10, 16; Mark 14:28; 16:7; John 21:1 26:34 [a] Matt 26:74–75; Mark 14:30; Luke 22:34; John 13:38 26:36 [a] Mark 14:32–35; Luke 22:39–40; John 18:1 26:37 [a] Matt 4:21; 17:1; Mark 5:37 26:38 [a] John 12:27 26:39 [a] Mark 14:36; Luke 22:42; [Heb 5:7–9] [b] John 12:27 [c] Matt 20:22 [d] Ps 40:8; Isa 50:5; John 5:30; 6:38; Phil 2:8 26:41 [a] Mark 13:33; 14:38; Luke 22:40, 46; [Eph 6:18] [b] Ps 103:14–16; [Rom 7:15; 8:23; Gal 5:17] 26:45 [a] Matt 17:22–23; 20:18–19 26:47 [1] Grk. *behold, Judas.* 26:49 [a] 2 Sam 20:9; [Prov 27:6] 26:50 [a] Ps 41:9; 55:13 26:51 [a] Mark 14:47; Luke 22:50; John 18:10 [1] Grk. *extending his hand, drew out his sword, and struck.* 26:52 [a] Gen 9:6; Rev 13:10 26:53 [a] 2 Kgs 6:17; Dan 7:10 26:54 [a] Isa 50:6; 53:2–11; Luke 24:25–27, 44–46; John 19:28; Acts 13:29; 17:3; 26:23 26:55 [1] Or *a revolutionary.*

has happened so that the [a]scriptures of the prophets would be fulfilled." Then [b]all the disciples left him and fled.

Condemned by the Sanhedrin

[57]Now the ones who had arrested Jesus led him to Caiaphas, the high priest, in whose house the experts in the law [a]and the elders had gathered. [58]But [a]Peter was following him from a distance, all the way to the high priest's courtyard. After going in, he sat with the guards to see the outcome. [59]The chief priests and the whole Sanhedrin were trying to find [a]false testimony against Jesus so that they could put him to death. [60]But they did not find anything, though [a]many false witnesses came forward. Finally [b]two came forward [61]and declared, "[a]This man said, 'I am able to destroy the temple of God and rebuild it in three days.'" [62]So the high priest stood up [a]and said to him, "Have you no answer? What is this that they are testifying against you?" [63]But [a]Jesus was [b]silent. The high priest said to him, "I charge you under oath by the living God, tell us if you are the Christ,[1] the Son of God." [64]Jesus said to him, "You have said it yourself. But I tell you, from now [a]on you will see the Son of Man [b]*sitting at the right hand*[1] of the Power and *coming on the clouds of heaven.*"[2] [65a]Then the high priest tore his clothes and declared, "He has blasphemed! Why do we still need witnesses? Now you have heard the [b]blasphemy! [66]What is your verdict?" [a]They answered, "He is guilty and deserves death." [67a]Then they spat in his face and struck him with their fists. And some slapped him, [68]saying, "[a]Prophesy for us, you Christ! Who hit you?"

Peter's Denials

[69a]Now Peter was sitting outside in the courtyard. A slave girl came to him and said, "You also were with Jesus the Galilean." [70]But he denied it in front of them all: "I don't know what you're talking about!" [71]When he went out to the gateway, another slave girl saw him and said to the people there, "This man was with Jesus the Nazarene." [72]He denied it again with an oath, "I do not know the man!" [73]After a little while, those standing there came up to Peter and said, "You really are one of them too—even your [a]accent gives you away!" [74]At that [a]he began to curse, and he swore with an oath, "I do not know the man!" At that moment a rooster crowed. [75]Then Peter remembered what Jesus had said: "[a]Before the rooster crows, you will deny me three times." And he went outside and wept bitterly.

Jesus Brought before Pilate

27 When it was early in the morning, [a]all the chief priests and the elders of the people plotted against Jesus to execute him. [2]They tied him up, led him away, and [a]handed him over to Pilate[1] the governor.

Judas' Suicide

[3]Now when Judas, who had betrayed him, saw that Jesus had been condemned, [a]he regretted what he had done and returned the 30 silver coins to the chief priests and the elders, [4]saying, "I have sinned by betraying innocent blood!" But they said, "What is that to us? You take care of it yourself!" [5]So Judas threw the silver coins into the temple and [a]left. Then he went out and hanged himself. [6]The chief priests took the silver and said, "It is not lawful to put this into the temple treasury, since it is blood money." [7]After consulting together they bought the Potter's Field with it, as a burial place for foreigners. [8]For this reason that field has been called [a]the "Field of Blood" to this day. [9]Then what was spoken by Jeremiah[1] the prophet was fulfilled: "*They took the 30 silver coins, the price of the one whose price had been set by the people of Israel,*[2] [10]*and they* [a]*gave them for the potter's field, as the Lord commanded me.*"[1]

26:56 [a] Lam 4:20   [b] Zech 13:7; Matt 26:31; Mark 14:27; John 18:15   26:57 [a] Matt 17:22; Mark 14:53–65; Luke 22:54; John 18:12, 19–24   26:58 [a] John 18:15–16   26:59 [a] Exod 20:16; Ps 35:11   26:60 [a] Ps 27:12; 35:11; Mark 14:55; Acts 6:13   [b] Deut 19:15   26:61 [a] Matt 27:40; Mark 14:58; 15:29; John 2:19; Acts 6:14   26:62 [a] Mark 14:60   26:63 [a] Ps 38:13–14; Isa 53:7; Matt 27:12, 14; Acts 8:32   [b] Lev 5:1; 1 Sam 14:24, 26; Luke 22:67–71   [1] Or *Messiah*; both "Christ" (Grk.) and "Messiah" (Heb., Aram.) mean "one who has been anointed."   26:64 [a] Dan 7:13; Matt 16:27; 24:30; 25:31; Luke 21:27; [John 1:51; Rom 14:10; 1 Thess 4:16]; Rev 1:7   [b] Ps 110:1; [Acts 7:55]   [1] [Ps 110:1]   [2] [Dan 7:13]   26:65 [a] 2 Kgs 18:37   [b] John 10:30–36   26:66 [a] Lev 24:16; Matt 20:18; John 19:7   26:67 [a] Job 16:10; Isa 50:6; 53:3; Lam 3:30; Matt 27:30   26:68 [a] Mark 14:65; Luke 22:64   26:69 [a] Mark 14:66–72; Luke 22:55–62; John 18:16–18, 25–27   26:73 [a] Mark 14:70; Luke 22:59; John 18:26   26:74 [a] Matt 26:34; Mark 14:71; Luke 22:34; John 13:38   26:75 [a] Matt 26:34; Luke 22:61; John 13:38   27:1 [a] Ps 2:2; Mark 15:1; Luke 22:66; 23:1; John 18:28   27:2 [a] Matt 20:19; Luke 18:32; Acts 3:13   [1] Maj. mss *Pontius Pilate.*   27:3 [a] Matt 26:14   27:5 [2] 2 Sam 17:23; Matt 18:7; 26:24; John 17:12; Acts 1:18   27:8 [a] Acts 1:19   27:9 [1] Some wss *Zechariah, Isaiah* or omit *Jeremiah.*   [2] Grk. *the sons of Israel.*   27:10 [a] Jer 32:6–9; Zech 11:12–13   [1] [Jer 18:2–6; 19:1–13; 32:6–15; Zech 11:12–13]

Jesus and Pilate

[11]Then Jesus stood before the governor, [a]and the governor asked him, "Are you the king of the Jews?" Jesus said, "You say so." [12]But [a]when he was accused by the chief priests and the elders, he did not respond. [13]Then Pilate said to him, "[a]Don't you hear how many charges they are bringing against you?" [14]But he did not answer even one accusation, so that the governor was quite amazed.

[15a]During the feast the governor was accustomed to release one prisoner to the crowd, whomever they wanted. [16]At that time they had in custody a notorious prisoner named Jesus[1] Barabbas. [17]So after they had assembled, Pilate said to them, "Whom do you want me to release for you, Jesus[1] Barabbas or Jesus who is called the Christ?" [18](For he knew that they had handed him over because of [a]envy.) [19]As he was sitting on the judgment seat, his wife sent a message to him: "Have nothing to do with that innocent man; I have suffered greatly as a result of a dream[1] about him today." [20a]But the chief priests and the elders persuaded the crowds to ask for Barabbas and to have Jesus killed. [21]The governor asked them, "Which of the two do you want me to release for you?" And they said, "[a]Barabbas!" [22]Pilate said to them, "Then what should I do with Jesus who is called the Christ?" They all said, "Crucify him!"[1] [23]He asked, "[a]Why? What wrong has he done?" But they shouted more insistently, "Crucify him!"

Jesus Is Condemned and Mocked

[24]When Pilate saw that he could do nothing, but that instead a riot was starting, he [a]took some water, washed his hands before the crowd and said, "I am innocent of this man's blood. You take care of it yourselves!" [25]In reply all the people said, "Let [a]his blood be on us and on our children!" [26]Then [a]he released Barabbas for them. But after he had Jesus flogged, he handed him over to be crucified. [27a]Then the governor's soldiers took Jesus into the governor's residence and gathered the whole cohort around him. [28]They [a]stripped him and [b]put a scarlet robe around him, [29a]and after braiding a crown of thorns, they put it on his head. They put a staff in his right hand, and kneeling down before him, they mocked him: "Hail, king of the Jews!"[1] [30]They spat on him and took [a]the staff and struck him repeatedly on the head. [31]When they had mocked him, they stripped him of the robe [a]and put his own clothes back on him. Then they led him away to crucify him.

The Crucifixion

[32a]As [b]they were going out, they found a man from Cyrene named Simon, whom they forced to carry his cross. [33]They came to [a]a place called Golgotha[1] (which means "Place of the Skull") [34]and offered Jesus wine mixed with gall to drink. But after tasting it, [a]he would not drink it. [35a]When [b]they had crucified him, *they divided his clothes by throwing dice.*[1,2] [36]Then they sat [a]down and kept guard over him there. [37]Above his head they [a]put the charge against him, which read: "This is Jesus, the king of the Jews." [38a]Then two outlaws were crucified with him, one on his right and one on his left. [39]Those who passed by defamed him, shaking their heads [40]and saying, "[a]You who can destroy the temple and rebuild it in three days, save yourself! [b]If you are God's Son, come down[1] from the cross!" [41]In the same way even the chief priests—together with the experts in the law and elders[1]—were mocking him: [42]"He [a]saved others, but he cannot save himself! He is the king of Israel! If he comes down now from the cross, we will believe in him! [43]*He trusts in God—let God, if [a]he wants to, deliver*

27:11 [a]Mark 15:2–5; Luke 23:2–3; John 18:29–38   27:12 [a]Ps 38:13–14; Matt 26:63; John 19:9   27:13 [a]Matt 26:62; John 19:10   27:15 [a]Mark 15:6–15; Luke 23:18–25; John 18:39—19:16   27:16 [1]Many MSS omit *Jesus.*   27:17 [1]Many MSS omit *Jesus.*   27:18 [a]Matt 21:38; [John 15:22–25]   27:19 [1]Or *greatly in a dream.*   27:20 [a]Mark 15:11; Luke 23:18; John 18:40; Acts 3:14   27:21 [a]Acts 3:14   27:22 [1]Grk. *Him—be crucified!*   27:23 [a]Acts 3:13   27:24 [a]Deut 21:6–8   27:25 [a]Deut 19:10; Josh 2:19; 2 Sam 1:16; 1 Kgs 2:32; Acts 5:28   27:26 [a][Isa 50:6; 53:5]; Matt 20:19; Mark 15:15; Luke 23:16, 24, 25; John 19:1, 16   27:27 [a]Mark 15:16–20; John 19:2   27:28 [a]Mark 15:17; John 19:2   [b]Luke 23:11   27:29 [a]Ps 69:19; Isa 53:3; Matt 20:19; Mark 10:34; Luke 18:32   [1]Or *Long live the King of the Jews!*   27:30 [a]Isa 50:6; 52:14; Mic 5:1; Matt 26:67; Mark 10:34; 14:65; 15:19   27:31 [a]Isa 53:7; Matt 20:19   27:32 [a]1 Kgs 21:13; Acts 7:58; Heb 13:12   [b]Mark 15:21; Luke 23:26; John 19:17   27:33 [a]Mark 15:22–32; Luke 23:33–43; John 19:17   [1]Aram.; See John 19:17.   27:34 [a]Ps 69:21; Matt 27:48   27:35 [a]Mark 15:24; Luke 23:34; John 19:24   [b]Ps 22:18   [1][Ps 22:18]   [2]Grk. *by throwing the lot.*   27:36 [a]Ps 22:17; Matt 27:54   27:37 [a]Mark 15:26; Luke 23:38; John 19:19   27:38 [a]Isa 53:9, 12; Mark 15:27; Luke 23:32–33; John 19:18   27:40 [a]Matt 26:61; John 2:19   [b]Matt 26:63   [1]‡ Many sig. MSS add *then.*   27:41 [1]This structure preserves the emphasis of *the chief priests* as the primary subject of the sentence.   27:42 [a][Matt 18:11; John 3:14–15]   27:43 [a]Ps 22:8

him now because he said, 'I am God's Son'!"[1] [44]The robbers who were crucified with him [a]also spoke abusively to him.

Jesus' Death

[45][a]Now from noon until three, darkness came over all the land. [46]At about three o'clock [a]Jesus shouted with a loud voice, "*Eli, Eli, lema sabachthani?*" that is, "[b]*My God, my God, why have you forsaken me?*"[1] [47]When some of the bystanders heard it, they said, "This man is calling for Elijah." [48]Immediately one of them ran and got a sponge, [a]filled it with sour wine, put it on a stick, and gave it to him to drink. [49]But the rest said, "Leave him alone! Let's see if Elijah will come to save him."[1] [50]Then Jesus cried [a]out again with a loud voice and gave [b]up his spirit. [51]Just [a]then the temple curtain[1] was torn in two, from top to bottom. The earth shook and the rocks were split apart. [52]And tombs were opened, and the bodies of many saints who had died[1] were raised. [53](They came out of the tombs after his resurrection and went into the holy city and appeared to many people.) [54][a]Now when the centurion and those with him who were guarding Jesus saw the earthquake and what took place, they were extremely terrified and said, "[b]Truly this one was God's Son!" [55]Many women [a]who had followed Jesus from Galilee and given him support were also there, watching from a distance. [56][a]Among them were Mary Magdalene, Mary the mother of James and Joseph, and the mother of the sons of Zebedee.

Jesus' Burial

[57]Now [a]when it was evening, there came a rich man from Arimathea, named Joseph, who was also a disciple of Jesus. [58]He went to Pilate and asked for the body of Jesus. Then Pilate ordered that it be given to him. [59]Joseph took the body, wrapped it in a clean linen cloth, [60]and [a]placed it in his own new tomb that he had cut in the rock.[1] Then he rolled a great stone across the entrance of the tomb and went away. [61](Now Mary Magdalene and the other Mary were sitting there, opposite the tomb.)

The Guard at the Tomb

[62]The next day (which is after the day of preparation) the chief priests and the Pharisees assembled before Pilate [63]and said, "Sir, we remember that while that deceiver was still alive he said, '[a]After three days I will rise again.' [64]So give orders to secure the tomb until the third day. Otherwise his disciples may come and steal his body and say to the people, 'He has been raised from the dead,' and the last deception will be worse than the first." [65]Pilate said to them, "Take a guard of soldiers. Go and make it as secure as you can." [66]So they went with the soldiers of the guard and made the tomb secure by [a]sealing the stone.

The Resurrection

28 Now [a]after the Sabbath, at dawn on the first day of the week, Mary Magdalene [b]and the other Mary went to look at the tomb. [2]Suddenly there was [a]a severe earthquake, for an angel of the Lord descending from heaven came and rolled away the stone and sat on it. [3][a]His appearance was like lightning, and his clothes were white as snow. [4]The guards were shaken and became like dead [a]men because they were so afraid of him. [5]But the angel said to the women, "Do not be afraid; I know that you are looking for Jesus, who was crucified. [6]He is not here, for he has been raised, just [a]as he said. Come and see the place where he[1] was lying. [7]Then go quickly and tell his disciples, '[a]He has been raised from the dead. He is going ahead of you into Galilee. You will see him there.' Listen, I have told you!"

27:43 [1][Ps 22:8]   27:44 [a]Mark 15:32; Luke 23:39–43   27:45 [a]Amos 8:9; Mark 15:33–41; Luke 23:44–49   27:46 [a][Heb 5:7] [b]Ps 22:1 [1]Ps 22:1   27:48 [a]Ps 69:21; Mark 15:36; Luke 23:36; John 19:29   27:49 [1]Early and sig. wss add *And another soldier took a spear and pierced him in the side, and water and blood flowed out.*   27:50 [a]Mark 15:37; Luke 23:46; John 19:30 [b]Dan 9:26; Zech 11:10–11; Matt 17:23; [John 10:18; 1 Cor 15:3]   27:51 [a]Exod 26:31; 2 Chr 3:14; Zech 11:10; Mark 15:38; Luke 23:45; Heb 9:3 [1]Either the curtain separating the Holy of Holies from the Holy Place or the one at the entrance of the temple court.   27:52 [1]Grk. *sleep*; often used as a euphemism for the death of a believer.   27:54 [a]Mark 15:39; Luke 23:47 [b]Matt 14:33   27:55 [a]Mark 15:41; Luke 8:2–3   27:56 [a]Matt 28:1; Mark 15:40, 47; 16:9; Luke 8:2; John 19:25; 20:1, 18   27:57 [a]Mark 15:42–47; Luke 23:50–56; John 19:38–42   27:60 [a]Isa 53:9; Matt 26:12 [1]I.e., cut or carved into an outcropping of natural rock, resulting in a cave-like structure.   27:63 [a]Matt 16:21; 17:23; 20:19; 26:61; Mark 8:31; 10:34; Luke 9:22; 13:33; 24:6–7; John 2:19   27:66 [a]Dan 6:17   28:1 [a]Mark 16:1–8; Luke 24:1–10; John 20:1–8 [b]Matt 27:56, 61   28:2 [a]Mark 16:5; Luke 24:4; John 20:12   28:3 [a]Dan 7:9; 10:6; Mark 9:3; John 20:12; Acts 1:10   28:4 [a]Rev 1:17   28:6 [a]Hos 6:2; Ps 16:10; 49:15; Matt 12:40; 16:21; 17:23; 20:19 [1]Some wss *the Lord, the body of the Lord, Jesus.*   28:7 [a]Matt 26:32; 28:10, 16; Mark 16:7

[8]So they left the tomb quickly, with fear and great joy, and ran to tell his disciples. [9]But [a]Jesus met them, saying, "Greetings!" They came to him, held on to his feet and worshiped him. [10]Then Jesus said to them, "Do not be afraid. Go and tell [a]my brothers to go to Galilee. They will see me there."

The Guards' Report

[11]While they were going, some of the guards went into the city and told the chief priests everything that had happened. [12]After they had assembled with the elders and formed a plan, they gave a large sum of money to the soldiers, [13]telling them, "You are to say, 'His disciples came at night and stole his body while we were asleep.' [14]If this matter is heard before the governor, we will satisfy him and keep you out of trouble." [15]So they took the money and did as they were instructed. And this story is told among the Jews to this day.[1]

The Great Commission

[16]So the 11 disciples went to Galilee to the mountain Jesus had designated. [17]When they saw him, they worshiped him, but some [a]doubted.[1] [18]Then Jesus came up and said to them, "[a]All authority in heaven and on earth has been given to me. [19]Therefore [a]go[1] and [b]make disciples of all nations, baptizing them in the name of the Father and the Son and the Holy Spirit,[2] [20][a]teaching them to obey everything I have commanded you. And remember, I am [b]with you always, to the end of the age."[1]

28:9 [a]Mark 16:9; John 20:14   **28:10** [a]Ps 22:22; John 20:17; Rom 8:29; [Heb 2:11]   **28:15** [1]‡ Some early and sig. wss *today/ this day*.   **28:17** [a]John 20:24–29   [1]Or *they doubted*; meaning all the disciples doubted.   **28:18** [a][Dan 7:13–14]; Matt 11:27; Luke 1:32; 10:22; John 3:35; Acts 2:36; Rom 14:9; 1 Cor 15:27; [Eph 1:10, 21]; Phil 2:9–10; [Heb 1:2]; 1 Pet 3:22   **28:19** [a]Mark 16:15   [b]Isa 52:10; Luke 24:47; [Acts 2:38–39]; Rom 10:18; Col 1:23   [1]*go . . . baptizing . . . teaching* modify *make disciples*.   [2]There is no ms support to doubt this trinitarian reading.   **28:20** [a][Acts 2:42]   [b][Acts 4:31; 18:10; 23:11]   [1]Maj. mss add *amen*.

MARK

The message of Mark's Gospel is captured in a single verse: "For even the Son of Man did not come to be served but to serve, and to give his life as a ransom for many" (10:45). Chapter by chapter, the book reveals the dual focus of Christ's life: service and sacrifice. Mark portrays Jesus as a Servant on the move, instantly responsive to the will of the Father. By preaching, teaching, and healing, he ministers to the needs of others even to the point of death. After the resurrection, he commissions his followers to continue his work in his power—servants following in the steps of the perfect Servant. The ancient title for this gospel was *Kata Markon*, "According to Mark." The author is best known by his Latin name *Marcus*, but in Jewish circles he was called by his Hebrew name *John*. Acts 12:12, 25 refer to him as "John Mark."

The Ministry of John the Baptist

1 The [a]beginning of [b]the gospel of Jesus Christ,[1] the Son of God.[2] [2]As it is written in the prophet Isaiah,[1]

> *"Look, I am sending my messenger*
> *ahead of you,*
> *who will prepare your way,*[2]
> [3] *the voice of one shouting in* [a]*the*
> *wilderness,*
> *'Prepare the way for the Lord,*
> *make his paths straight.'"*[1]

[4]In the wilderness [a]John the baptizer[1] began preaching a baptism of repentance for the forgiveness of sins. [5]People from the whole Judean countryside [a]and all of Jerusalem were going out to him, and he was baptizing them in the Jordan River as they confessed their sins. [6]John wore a [a]garment made of camel's hair with a leather belt around his waist, and he ate locusts and wild honey. [7]He proclaimed, "One more powerful than I am is coming after me; I am not worthy to bend down and untie [a]the strap of his sandals. [8a]I baptize you [b]with water, but he will baptize you with the Holy Spirit."

The Baptism and Temptation of Jesus

[9a]Now in those days Jesus came from Nazareth in Galilee and was baptized by John in the Jordan River. [10a]And just as Jesus was coming up out of the water, he saw the heavens splitting apart and the Spirit [b]descending on him like a dove. [11]And a voice came from heaven: "[a]You are my one dear Son;[1] in you I take great delight." [12]The Spirit [a]immediately drove him into the wilderness. [13]He was in the wilderness 40 days, enduring temptations from Satan. He was with wild animals, [a]and angels were ministering to his needs.

Preaching in Galilee and the Call of the Disciples

[14a]Now after John was imprisoned, Jesus went into Galilee and [b]proclaimed the gospel[1] of God. [15]He said, "[a]The time is fulfilled and [b]the kingdom of God is near. Repent and believe the gospel!" [16]As he went along the Sea of Galilee, he saw Simon [a]and Andrew, Simon's brother, casting a net into the sea (for they were fishermen). [17]Jesus said to them, "Follow me, and I will turn you into [a]fishers of people!" [18a]They left their

1:1[a] Matt 1:1; 3:1; Luke 3:22 [b] Ps 2:7; Matt 14:33; Luke 1:35 [1] Either the gospel that Jesus brings (or proclaims) or the gospel about Jesus Christ. [2] A few wss omit *Son of God*; some also omit *Jesus Christ*. 1:2[1] Maj. MSS *in the prophets*. [2] Mal 3:1 (Exod 23:20) 1:3[a] Isa 40:3; Matt 3:3; Luke 3:4; John 1:23 [1] Isa 40:3 1:4[a] Mal 4:6; Matt 3:1; Luke 3:3 [1] Mark uses "the Baptist" only in 6:25 and 8:28. 1:5[a] Matt 3:5 1:6[a] Matt 3:4 1:7[a] Matt 3:11; John 1:27; Acts 13:25 1:8[a] Acts 1:5; 11:16 [b] Isa 44:3; John 20:22; [Acts 2:4; 10:45–46; 1 Cor 12:13] 1:9[a] Matt 3:13–17; Luke 3:21–22 1:10[a] Ezek 1:1; Matt 3:16; John 1:32 [b] Isa 11:2; 61:1; Acts 10:38 1:11[a] [Ps 2:7]; Isa 42:1; Matt 3:17; 12:18; Mark 9:7; Luke 3:22 [1] Grk. *my beloved Son, my Son, the beloved one*. 1:12[a] Matt 4:1–11; Luke 4:1–13 1:13[a] Matt 4:10–11 1:14[a] Matt 4:12 [b] Matt 4:23 [1] Maj. wss *of the kingdom of God*. 1:15[a] Dan 9:25; [Gal 4:4; Eph 1:10; 1 Tim 2:6]; Titus 1:3 [b] Matt 3:2; 4:17; [Acts 20:21] 1:16[a] Matt 4:18–22; Luke 5:2–11; John 1:40–42 1:17[a] Matt 13:47–48 1:18[a] Matt 19:27; [Luke 14:26]

nets immediately and followed him. [19]Going on a little farther, he saw James, the son of Zebedee, and John his brother in their boat mending nets. [20]Immediately he called them, and they left their father Zebedee in the boat with the hired men and followed him.

Jesus' Authority

[21a]Then they went to Capernaum. When the Sabbath came, Jesus went into the [b]synagogue and began to teach. [22a]The people there were amazed by his teaching because he taught them like one who had authority, not like the experts in the law.[1] [23]Just then there was a man in their synagogue with an [a]unclean spirit, and he cried out, [24]"[a]Leave us alone, Jesus the Nazarene! Have you come to destroy us? I [b]know who you are—the [c]Holy One of God!" [25]But Jesus [a]rebuked him: "Silence! Come out of him!" [26]After throwing him into convulsions, the unclean spirit cried out with [a]a loud voice and came out of him. [27]They were all amazed so that they asked each other, "What is this? A new teaching with authority! He even commands the unclean spirits and they obey him." [28]So the [a]news about him spread quickly throughout all the region around Galilee.

Healings at Simon's House

[29a]Now as soon as they left the synagogue, they entered Simon and Andrew's house, with James and John. [30]Simon's mother-in-law was lying down, sick with a fever, so they spoke to Jesus at once about her. [31]He came and raised her up by gently taking her hand. Then the fever left her and she began to serve them. [32]When it [a]was evening, after sunset, they brought to him all who were sick and demon-possessed. [33]The whole town gathered by the door. [34]So he healed many who were sick with various diseases and drove out many demons. But he would not permit the demons to speak because they knew him.[1]

Praying and Preaching

[35]Then Jesus got up early [a]in the morning when it was still very dark, departed, and went out to a deserted place, and there he spent time in [b]prayer. [36]Simon and his companions searched for him. [37]When they found him, they said, "[a]Everyone [b]is looking for you." [38]He replied, "[a]Let us go elsewhere, [b]into the surrounding villages, so that I can preach there too. For that is what I came out here to do." [39]So he went into all of Galilee preaching in their synagogues [a]and casting [b]out demons.

Cleansing a Leper

[40a]Now a leper came to him and fell to his knees, asking for help. "If you are willing, you can make me clean," he said. [41]Moved with indignation,[1] Jesus stretched out his hand and touched him, saying, "[a]I am willing. Be clean!" [42]The leprosy left him [a]at once, and he was clean. [43]Immediately Jesus sent the man away with a very strong warning. [44]He told him, "See that you do not say anything to anyone, but go, show yourself to a priest, and bring the offering that Moses commanded for your cleansing, as a testimony to them."[1] [45a]But as the man went out he began to announce it publicly [b]and spread the story widely, so that Jesus was no longer able to enter any town openly but stayed outside in remote places. Still they kept coming to him from everywhere.

Healing and Forgiving a Paralytic

2 Now after some days, [a]when he returned to Capernaum, the news spread that he was at home. [2]So many gathered that there was no longer any room, not even by the door, and he preached the word to them. [3]Some people came bringing to him a [a]paralytic, carried by four of them. [4]When they were not able to bring him in because of the crowd, they removed the roof above Jesus. Then, after tearing it out, they lowered the stretcher the paralytic was lying on. [5]When Jesus saw their faith, he said to the paralytic,

---

1:21 [a]Matt 4:13; Luke 4:31–37   [b]Ps 22:22; Matt 4:23; Luke 4:16; 13:10   1:22 [a]Matt 7:28–29; 13:54   [1]Or the scribes.   1:23 [a][Matt 12:43]; Mark 5:2; 7:25; Luke 4:33   1:24 [a]Matt 8:28–29; Mark 5:7–8; Luke 8:28   [b]Mark 3:11; Luke 4:41; Jas 2:19   [c]Ps 16:10   1:25 [a][Luke 4:39]   1:26 [a]Mark 9:20   1:28 [a]Matt 4:24; 9:31   1:29 [a]Matt 8:14–15; Luke 4:38–39   1:32 [a]Matt 8:16–17; Luke 4:40–41   1:34 [1]Some mss add to be the Christ.   1:35 [a]Luke 4:42–43   [b]Matt 26:39, 44; Mark 6:46; Luke 5:16; 6:12; 9:28–29; Heb 5:7   1:37 [a]Matt 4:25; John 3:26; 12:19   [b][Heb 11:6]   1:38 [a]Luke 4:43   [b][Isa 61:1–2; Mark 10:45; John 16:28; 17:4, 8]   1:39 [a]Ps 22:22; Matt 4:23; 9:35; Mark 1:21; 3:1; Luke 4:44   [b]Mark 5:8, 13; 7:29–30   1:40 [a]Matt 8:2–4; Luke 5:12–14   1:41 [a]Luke 7:13   [1]Maj. mss compassion.   1:42 [a]Matt 15:28; Mark 5:29   1:44 [1]Or as an indictment against them, as proof to the people.   1:45 [a]Matt 28:15; Luke 5:15   [b]Mark 2:2, 13; 3:7; Luke 5:17; John 6:2   2:1 [a]Matt 9:1   2:3 [a]Matt 4:24; 8:6; Acts 8:7; 9:33

"Son, your sins are forgiven." [6]Now some of the experts in the law were sitting there, turning these things over in their minds: [7]"Why does this man speak this way? He is blaspheming! [a]Who can forgive sins but God alone?" [8]Now immediately, when Jesus realized in his spirit that they were contemplating such thoughts, he said to them, "Why are you thinking such things in your hearts? [9][a]Which is easier, to say to the paralytic, 'Your sins are forgiven,' or to say, 'Stand up, take your stretcher, and walk'? [10]But so that you may know that the Son of Man has authority on earth to forgive sins,"—he said to the paralytic—[11]"I tell you, stand up, take your stretcher, and go home." [12]And immediately the man stood up, took his stretcher, and went out in front of them all. They were all amazed and [a]glorified God, saying, "We have never seen anything like this!"

The Call of Levi; Eating with Sinners

[13]Jesus went out again by the sea. The whole crowd came to him, [a]and he taught them. [14][a]As he went along, he saw Levi, the son of Alphaeus, sitting at the tax booth.[1] [b]"Follow me," he said to him. And he got up and [c]followed him. [15]As Jesus was having a meal in Levi's home, many tax collectors [a]and sinners were eating with Jesus and his disciples, for there were many who followed him. [16]When the experts in the law and the Pharisees saw that he was eating with sinners and tax collectors, they said to his disciples, "Why does he eat with tax collectors and sinners?" [17]When Jesus heard this he said to them, "[a]Those who are healthy don't need a physician, but those who are sick do. I have not come to call the righteous, but sinners."

The Superiority of the New

[18]Now John's disciples and [a]the Pharisees were fasting. So they came to Jesus and said, "Why do the disciples of John and the disciples of the Pharisees fast, but your disciples don't fast?" [19]Jesus said to them, "The wedding guests cannot fast while the bridegroom is with them, can they?[1] As long as they have the bridegroom with them they do not fast. [20]But the days are coming when the bridegroom will be [a]taken from them, and at that time they will fast. [21]No one sews a patch of unshrunk cloth on an old garment; otherwise, the patch pulls away from it, the new from the old, and the tear becomes worse. [22]And no one pours new wine into old wineskins; otherwise, the wine will burst the skins, and both the wine and the skins will be destroyed. Instead new wine is poured into new wineskins."

Lord of the Sabbath

[23]Jesus was going through the grain fields on a Sabbath, [a]and his disciples began [b]to pick some heads of wheat as they made their way. [24]So the Pharisees said to him, "Look, why are they doing what is [a]against the law on the Sabbath?" [25]He said to them, "Have you never read [a]what David did when he was in need and he and his companions were hungry—[26]how he entered the house of God when Abiathar was high priest and ate the sacred bread, [a]which is against the law for any but the priests to eat, and also gave it to his companions?" [27]Then he said to them, "The [a]Sabbath was made for people, not people for the Sabbath. [28]For this reason [a]the Son of Man is lord[1] even of the Sabbath."

Healing a Withered Hand

3 Then Jesus entered [a]the synagogue again, and a man was there who had a withered hand. [2]They [a]watched Jesus closely to see if he would [b]heal him on the Sabbath, so that they could accuse him. [3]So he said to the man who had the withered hand, "Stand up among all these people." [4]Then he said to them, "Is it lawful to do good on the Sabbath, or evil, to save a life or destroy it?" But they were silent. [5]After looking around at them in anger, grieved by the [a]hardness of their hearts, he said to the man, "Stretch out your hand." He stretched it out, and his hand was restored. [6]So [a]the Pharisees went out immediately and began plotting with [b]the Herodians, as to how they could assassinate[1] him.

2:7 [a] Job 14:4; Isa 43:25; Dan 9:9   **2:9** [a] Matt 9:5   **2:12** [a] Matt 15:31; [Phil 2:11]   **2:13** [a] Matt 9:9   **2:14** [a] Matt 9:9–13; Luke 5:27–32   [b] Matt 4:19; 8:22; 19:21; John 1:43; 12:26; 21:22   [c] Luke 18:28   [1] Or *tax office.*   **2:15** [a] Matt 9:10   **2:17** [a] Matt 9:12–13; 18:11; Luke 5:31–32; 19:10   **2:18** [a] Matt 9:14–17; Luke 5:33–38   **2:19** [1] A rhetorical question expecting a negative answer.   **2:20** [a] Acts 1:9; 13:2–3; 14:23   **2:23** [a] Matt 12:1–8; Luke 6:1–5   [b] Deut 23:25   **2:24** [a] Exod 20:10; 31:15   **2:25** [a] 1 Sam 21:1–6   **2:26** [a] Exod 29:32–33; Lev 24:5–9   **2:27** [a] Gen 2:3; Exod 23:12; Deut 5:14; Neh 9:14; Ezek 20:12   **2:28** [a] Matt 12:8   [1] An emphatic Grk. construction.   **3:1** [a] Matt 12:9–14; Luke 6:6–11   **3:2** [a] [Ps 37:32]; Luke 14:1; 20:20   [b] Luke 13:14   **3:5** [a] Zech 7:12   **3:6** [a] Ps 2:2; Mark 12:13   [b] Matt 22:16   [1] Grk. *destroy.*

Crowds by the Sea

[7]Then Jesus went away with his disciples to the sea, [a]and a great multitude from Galilee followed him. And from Judea, [8]Jerusalem, Idumea, beyond the Jordan River, and around Tyre and Sidon a great multitude came to him when they heard about the [a]things he had done. [9]Because of the crowd, he told his disciples to have a small boat ready for him so the crowd would not press toward him. [10]For he had healed [a]many, so that all who were afflicted with diseases pressed toward him in order to [b]touch him. [11][a]And whenever the unclean spirits saw him, they fell down before him and cried out, "[b]You are the Son of God." [12]But [a]he sternly ordered them not to make him known.

Appointing the 12 Apostles

[13]Now Jesus went up the mountain [a]and called for those he wanted, and they came to him. [14]He appointed 12[1] so that they would be with him and he could send them to preach [15]and to have authority to cast out demons. [16][1]To Simon he gave the name Peter; [17]to James and his brother John, the sons of Zebedee, he gave the name Boanerges (that is, "sons of thunder"); [18]and Andrew, Philip, Bartholomew, Matthew, Thomas, James the son of Alphaeus, Thaddaeus,[1] Simon the Zealot,[2] [19]and Judas Iscariot, who betrayed him.

Jesus and Beelzebul

[20]Now Jesus went home, and a crowd gathered [a]so that they were not able to eat. [21]When his family[1] heard this they went out to restrain him, [a]for they said, "He is out of his mind." [22]The experts in [a]the law who came down from Jerusalem said, "He is possessed by Beelzebul," and, "By the [b]ruler of demons he casts out demons!" [23][a]So he called them and spoke to them in parables: "How can Satan cast out Satan? [24]If a kingdom is divided against itself, that kingdom will not be able to stand.

[25]If a house is divided against itself, that house will not be able to stand. [26]And if Satan rises against himself and is divided, he is not able to stand and his end has come. [27]But no [a]one is able to enter a strong man's house and steal his property unless he first ties up the strong man. Then he can thoroughly plunder his house. [28]I tell you the [a]truth, people will be forgiven for all sins, even all the blasphemies they utter. [29]But whoever blasphemes against the Holy Spirit will never be forgiven, but is guilty of an eternal sin" [30](because they [a]said, "He has an unclean spirit").

Jesus' True Family

[31][a]Then Jesus' mother and his brothers came. Standing outside, they sent word to him, to summon him. [32]A crowd was sitting around him and they said to him, "Look, your mother and your brothers[1] are outside looking for you." [33]He answered them and said, "Who are my mother and my brothers?" [34]And looking at those who were sitting around him in a circle, he said, "Here are my mother and my brothers! [35]For whoever does the [a]will of God is my brother and sister and mother."

The Parable of the Sower

4 [a]Again he began to teach by the lake. Such a large crowd gathered around him that he got into a boat on the lake and sat there while the whole crowd was on the shore by the lake. [2]He taught them many things in parables, [a]and in his teaching said to them: [3]"Listen! A sower went out to sow. [4]And as he sowed, some seed fell along the path, and the birds came and devoured it. [5]Other seed fell on rocky ground where it did not have much soil. It sprang up at once because the soil was not deep. [6]When the sun came up it was scorched, and because it did not have sufficient root, it withered. [7]Other seed fell among the thorns, and they grew up and choked it, and it did not produce grain. [8]But other seed fell on good soil

---

3:7 [a]Matt 4:25; Luke 6:17 3:8 [a]Mark 5:19 3:10 [a]Mark 5:29, 34; Luke 7:21 [b]Matt 9:21; 14:36; Mark 6:56; 8:22 3:11 [a]Mark 1:23–24; Luke 4:41 [b]Matt 8:29; 14:33; Mark 1:1; 5:7; Luke 8:28 3:12 [a]Matt 12:16; Mark 1:25, 34 3:13 [a]Matt 10:1; Mark 6:7; Luke 9:1 3:14 [1]Some mss add *whom he named apostles.* 3:16 [1]Some sig. mss add *he appointed twelve.* 3:18 [1]Some wss *Lebbaeus.* [2]Grk. *the Cananean*; derived from the Aram. term for "enthusiast, zealot" with no relation to the geographical Cana or Canaan. 3:20 [a]Mark 6:31 3:21 [a]John 7:5; 10:20; Acts 26:24; [2 Cor 5:13] [1]Some wss *the scribes and others heard about him.* 3:22 [a]Matt 9:34; 10:25; Luke 11:15; John 7:20; 8:48, 52; 10:20 [b][John 12:31; 14:30; 16:11; Eph 2:2] 3:23 [a]Matt 12:25–29; Luke 11:17–22 3:27 [a][Isa 49:24–25]; Matt 12:29 3:28 [a]Matt 12:31–32; Luke 12:10; [1 John 5:16] 3:30 [a]Matt 9:34; John 7:20; 8:48, 52; 10:20 3:31 [a]Matt 12:46–50; Luke 8:19–21 3:32 [1]‡ Many mss add *and your sisters.* 3:35 [a]Eph 6:6; Heb 10:36; 1 Pet 4:2; [1 John 2:17] 4:1 [a]Matt 13:1–15; Luke 8:4–10 4:2 [a]Mark 12:38

and produced grain, sprouting and growing; some yielded thirty times as much, some sixty, and some a hundred times." [9]And he said, "Whoever has ears to hear had better listen!"[1]

The Purpose of Parables

[10,a]When he was alone, those around him with the twelve asked him about the parables. [11]He said to them, "The secret of the kingdom of God has been given[1] to you. But to [a]those outside, everything is in parables,

[12] "so that *although they [a]look they may look but not see,*
and although they hear they may hear but not understand,
so they may not repent and be forgiven."[1]

[13]He said to them, "Don't you understand this parable? Then how will you understand any parable? [14]The sower sows [a]the word. [15]These are the ones on the path where the word is sown: Whenever they hear, immediately Satan comes and snatches the word that was sown in them. [16]These are the ones sown on rocky ground: As soon as they hear the word, they receive it with joy. [17]But they have no root in themselves and do not endure. Then, when trouble or persecution comes because of the word, immediately they fall away. [18]Others are the ones sown among thorns: They are those who hear the word, [19]but worldly [a]cares, [b]the seductiveness of wealth, and the desire for other things come in and choke the word, and it produces nothing. [20]But these are the ones sown on good soil: They hear the word and receive [a]it and bear fruit, one thirty times as much, one sixty, and one a hundred."

The Parable of the Lamp

[21]He [a]also said to them, "A lamp isn't brought to be put under a basket[1] or under a bed, is it? Isn't it to be placed on a lampstand? [22,a]For nothing is hidden except to be revealed, and nothing concealed except to be brought to light. [23,a]If anyone has ears to hear, he had better listen!" [24]And he said to them, "Take care about what you hear. The measure you use will be the measure you receive, and more will be added to you. [25,a]For whoever has will be given more, but whoever does not have, even what he has will be taken from him."

The Parable of the Growing Seed

[26]He also said, "[a]The kingdom of God is like someone who spreads seed on the ground. [27]He goes to sleep and gets up, night and day, and the seed sprouts and [a]grows, though he does not know how. [28]By itself the soil produces a crop, first the stalk, then the head, then the full grain in the head. [29]And [a]when the grain is ripe, he sends in the sickle because the harvest has come."

The Parable of the Mustard Seed

[30]He also asked, "[a]To what can we compare the kingdom of God, or what parable can we use to present it? [31]It is like a mustard seed that when sown in the ground, even though it is the smallest of all the seeds in the ground—[32]when it is sown, it grows up,[1] becomes the greatest of all garden plants, and grows large branches so that the wild birds can nest in its shade."

The Use of Parables

[33,a]So with many parables like these, he spoke the word to them, as they were able to hear. [34]He did not speak to [a]them without a parable. But privately he explained everything to his own disciples.

Stilling of a Storm

[35,a]On that day, when evening came, Jesus said to his disciples, "Let's go across to the other side of the lake." [36]So after leaving the crowd, they took him along, just as he was, in the boat,[1] and other boats were with him. [37]Now a great windstorm developed and the waves were breaking into the boat, so that

4:9 [1]Trad. *let him hear.*   4:10 [a]Matt 13:10; Luke 8:9   4:11 [a][1 Cor 5:12–13; Col 4:5; 1 Thess 4:12; 1 Tim 3:7]   [1]A "divine passive," with God understood as the actor.   4:12 [a]Isa 6:9–10; 43:8; Jer 5:21; Ezek 12:2; Matt 13:14; Luke 8:10; John 12:40; Rom 11:8   [1]Isa 6:9–10   4:14 [a]Matt 13:18–23; Luke 8:11–15   4:19 [a]Luke 21:34   [b]Prov 23:5; Eccl 5:13; Luke 18:24; 1 Tim 6:9–10, 17   4:20 [a][John 15:2, 5; Rom 7:4]   4:21 [a]Matt 5:15; Luke 8:16; 11:33   [1]Or *a bowl.*   4:22 [a]Eccl 12:14; Matt 10:26–27; Luke 12:3; [1 Cor 4:5]   4:23 [a]Matt 11:15; 13:9, 43; Mark 4:9; Luke 8:8; 14:35; Rev 3:6, 13, 22; 13:9   4:25 [a]Matt 13:12; 25:29; Luke 8:18; 19:26   4:26 [a][Matt 13:24–30, 36–43]; Luke 8:1   4:27 [a][2 Cor 3:18; 2 Pet 3:18]   4:29 [a][Matt 13:30, 39]; Rev 14:15   4:30 [a]Matt 13:31–32; Luke 13:18–19; [Acts 2:41; 4:4; 5:14; 19:20]   4:32 [1]Grk. *As a mustard seed, which when sown in the earth, being the smallest of all the seeds in the earth, and when it is sown, it grows up.*   4:33 [a]Matt 13:34–35; [John 16:12]   4:34 [a]Luke 24:27, 45   4:35 [a]Matt 8:18, 23–27; Luke 8:22, 25   4:36 [1]Or *along in the boat in which he was already sitting.*

the boat was nearly swamped. [38]But he was in the stern, sleeping on a cushion. They woke him up and said to him, "[a]Teacher, [b]don't you care that we are about to die?" [39]So he got up and [a]rebuked[1] the wind, and said to the sea, "Be [b]quiet! Calm down!" Then the wind stopped, and it was dead calm. [40]And he said to them, "Why are you cowardly? Do you still not have faith?" [41]They were overwhelmed by fear and said to one another, "Who then is this? Even the wind and sea obey him!"

Healing of a Demoniac

5 So [a]they came to the other side of the lake, to the region of the Gerasenes.[1] [2]Just as Jesus was getting out of the boat, a man with an [a]unclean spirit came from the tombs and met him. [3]He lived among the tombs, and no one could bind him anymore, not even with a chain. [4]For his hands and feet had often been bound with chains and shackles,[1] but he had torn the chains apart and broken the shackles in pieces. No one was strong enough to subdue him. [5]Each night and every day among the tombs and in the mountains, he would cry out and cut himself with stones. [6]When he saw Jesus from a distance, he ran and bowed down before him. [7]Then he cried out with a loud voice, "Leave me alone, Jesus, Son of the Most High God! I [a]implore you by God—do not torment me!" [8](For Jesus had said to him, "Come [a]out of that man, you unclean spirit!") [9]Jesus asked him, "What is your name?" And he said, "My name is Legion, for we are many." [10]He begged Jesus repeatedly not to send them out of the region. [11]There on the hillside, a great herd of [a]pigs was feeding. [12]And the demonic spirits begged him, "Send us into the pigs. Let us enter them." [13]Jesus gave them permission. So the unclean spirits came out and went into the pigs. Then the herd rushed down the steep slope into the lake, and about 2,000 were drowned in the lake.

[14]Now the herdsmen ran off and spread the news in the town and countryside, and the people went out to see what had happened. [15]They came to Jesus and saw the demon-possessed [a]man [b]sitting there, [c]clothed, and in his right mind—the one who had the "Legion"—and they were afraid. [16]Those who had seen what had happened to the demon-possessed man reported it, and they also told about the pigs. [17]Then [a]they began to beg Jesus to leave their region. [18]As [a]he was getting into the boat the man who had been demon-possessed asked if he could go[1] with him. [19]But Jesus did not permit him to do so. Instead, he said to him, "Go to your home and to your people and tell them what the Lord has done for you, that he had mercy on you." [20]So he went away and began to [a]proclaim in the Decapolis what Jesus had done for him, and all were [b]amazed.

Restoration and Healing

[21]When Jesus had crossed again in a boat to the other side, a large crowd gathered around him, [a]and he was by the sea. [22]Then one of the synagogue leaders,[1] named Jairus,[2] came up, [a]and when he saw Jesus, he fell at his feet. [23]He asked him urgently, "My little daughter is near death. Come and [a]lay your hands on her so that she may be healed and live." [24]Jesus went with him, and a large crowd followed and pressed around him.

[25]Now a woman [a]was there who had been suffering from a hemorrhage for 12 years. [26]She had endured a great deal under the care of many doctors and had spent all that she had. Yet instead of getting better, she grew worse. [27]When she heard about Jesus, she came up behind him in the crowd and [a]touched his cloak, [28]for she kept saying, "If only I touch his clothes, I will be healed." [29]At once the bleeding stopped, and she felt in her body that she was healed of her disease. [30]Jesus knew at once that [a]power had gone out from him. He turned around in the crowd and said, "Who touched my clothes?" [31]His disciples said to him, "You see the crowd pressing against you and you say, 'Who touched me?'" [32]But he looked

4:38 [a][Matt 23:8–10] [b]Ps 44:23   **4:39** [a]Mark 9:25; Luke 4:39 [b]Ps 65:7; 89:9; 93:4; 104:6–7; Matt 8:26; Luke 8:24 [1]Or *commanded.*   **5:1** [a]Matt 8:28–34; Luke 8:26–37 [1]Maj. later MSS *Gadarenes*; some MSS *Gergesenes.*   **5:2** [a]Mark 1:23; 7:25; [Rev 16:13–14]   **5:4** [1]Or *fetters*; chains for the feet.   **5:7** [a]Matt 26:63; Mark 1:24; Acts 19:13   **5:8** [a]Mark 1:25; 9:25; [Acts 16:18]   **5:11** [a]Lev 11:7–8; Deut 14:8; Luke 15:15–16   **5:15** [a]Matt 4:24; 8:16; Mark 1:32 [b]Luke 10:39 [c][Isa 61:10]   **5:17** [a]Matt 8:34; Acts 16:39   **5:18** [a]Luke 8:38–39 [1]Grk. *be.*   **5:20** [a]Exod 15:2; Ps 66:16 [b]Matt 9:8, 33; John 5:20; 7:21; Acts 3:12; 4:13   **5:21** [a]Matt 9:1; Luke 8:40   **5:22** [a]Matt 9:18–26; Luke 8:41–56; Acts 13:15 [1]The president of a synagogue. [2]Some MSS omit *named Jairus.*   **5:23** [a]Matt 8:15; Mark 6:5; 7:32; 8:23, 25; 16:18; Luke 4:40; Acts 9:17; 28:8   **5:25** [a]Lev 15:19, 25; Matt 9:20   **5:27** [a]Matt 14:35–36; Mark 3:10; 6:56   **5:30** [a]Luke 6:19; 8:46

around to see who had done it. ³³Then the woman, with ^afear and trembling, knowing what had happened to her, came and fell down before him and told him the whole truth. ³⁴He said to her, "Daughter, ^ayour faith has made you well.[1] ^bGo in peace, and be healed of your disease."

^{35a}While he was still speaking, people came from the synagogue leader's house saying, "Your daughter has died. Why trouble the teacher any longer?" ³⁶But Jesus, paying no attention to what was said, told the synagogue leader, "Do not be afraid; just ^abelieve." ³⁷He did not let anyone follow him except Peter, James, and John, the brother of James. ³⁸They came to the house of the synagogue leader where he saw noisy confusion and people ^aweeping and wailing loudly. ³⁹When he entered he said to them, "Why are you distressed and weeping? The child is not dead but ^aasleep!" ⁴⁰And they began making fun of him. ^aBut he forced them all outside,[1] and he took the child's father and mother and his own companions and went into the room where the child was. ⁴¹Then, gently taking the child by the hand, he said to her, "*Talitha koum,*" which means, "Little girl, I say to you, get up." ⁴²The girl got up at once and began to walk around (she was twelve years old). They were completely ^aastonished at this. ⁴³He strictly ordered that no one should know about this, and told ^athem to give her something to eat.

Rejection at Nazareth

⁶ Now Jesus left that place and came to his hometown, and his disciples followed him. ²When the Sabbath came, he began to teach in the synagogue. Many who heard him were ^aastonished, saying, "^bWhere did he get these ideas? And what is this wisdom that has been given to him? What are these miracles that are done through his hands? ³Isn't this the carpenter, the son[1] of Mary and ^abrother of James, Joses, Judas, and Simon? And aren't his sisters here with us?" And so they took offense at

him. ⁴Then Jesus ^asaid to them, "A prophet is not without honor except in his hometown, and among his relatives, and in his own house." ^{5a}He was not able to do a miracle there, except to lay his hands on a few sick people and heal them. ⁶And ^ahe was amazed because of their unbelief. ^bThen he went around among the villages and taught.

Sending out the 12 Apostles

⁷Jesus called the twelve ^aand began to send them out ^btwo by two. He gave them authority over the unclean spirits. ⁸He instructed them to take nothing for the journey except a staff—no bread, no bag, no money in their belts—⁹and ^ato put on sandals but not to wear two tunics.[1] ¹⁰He said to them, "Wherever you enter ^aa house, stay there until you leave the area. ¹¹If ^aa place will not welcome you or listen to you, as you go out from there, ^bshake the dust off your feet as a testimony against them." ¹²So they went out and preached that all should repent. ¹³They cast out many demons ^aand anointed many sick people with olive oil and healed them.

The Death of John the Baptist

^{14a}Now King Herod heard this, for Jesus' name had become known. Some were saying, "John the baptizer has been raised from the dead, and because of this, miraculous powers are at work in him." ^{15a}Others said, "He is Elijah." Others said, "He is a prophet, like one of the prophets from the past." ^{16a}But when Herod heard this, he said, "John, whom I beheaded, has been raised!" ¹⁷For Herod himself had sent men, arrested John, and bound him in prison on account of Herodias, his brother Philip's wife, because Herod had married her. ¹⁸For John had repeatedly told Herod, "^aIt is not lawful for you to have your brother's wife." ¹⁹So Herodias nursed a grudge against him and wanted to kill him. But she could not ²⁰because Herod stood in ^aawe of John and protected him, since he knew that John was a

5:33 ^a[Ps 89:7]   **5:34** ^aMatt 9:22; Mark 10:52; Acts 14:9   ^b1 Sam 1:17; 20:42; 2 Kgs 5:19; Luke 7:50; 8:48; Acts 16:36; [Jas 2:16]   ¹Or *has delivered you*; Grk. *has saved you.*   **5:35** ^aLuke 8:49   **5:36** ^a[Mark 9:23; John 11:40]   **5:38** ^aMark 16:10; Acts 9:39   **5:39** ^aJohn 11:4, 11   **5:40** ^aActs 9:40   ¹Or *threw them all outside.*   **5:42** ^aMark 1:27; 7:37   **5:43** ^a[Matt 8:4; 12:16–19; 17:9]; Mark 3:12   **6:2** ^aMatt 7:28; Luke 4:32; Acts 4:13   ^bJohn 6:42   **6:3** ^aMatt 12:46; Gal 1:19   ¹Sev. MSS *the son of the carpenter.*   **6:4** ^aMatt 13:57; Luke 4:24; John 4:44   **6:5** ^aGen 19:22; 32:25; Matt 13:58; [Mark 9:23]   **6:6** ^aIsa 59:16; Matt 17:17, 20; [Heb 3:18–19; 4:2]   ^bMatt 9:35; Luke 13:22; Acts 10:38; Eph 2:17   **6:7** ^aMatt 10:1; 28:19–20; Mark 3:13–14; Luke 9:1   ^b[Eccl 4:9–10]   **6:9** ^a[Eph 6:15]   ¹Or *shirts.*   **6:10** ^aMatt 10:11; Luke 9:4; 10:7–8   **6:11** ^aMatt 10:14; Luke 10:10   ^bActs 13:51; 18:6   **6:13** ^a[Jas 5:14]   **6:14** ^aMatt 14:1–12; Mark 6:14–16; Luke 9:7–9   **6:15** ^aMatt 16:14; Mark 8:28; Luke 9:19   **6:16** ^aMatt 14:2; Luke 3:19   **6:18** ^aLev 18:16; 20:21   **6:20** ^aMatt 14:5; 21:26

righteous and holy man. When Herod heard him, he was thoroughly baffled,[1,2] and yet he liked to listen to John.

21 But a suitable day[1] came, when Herod gave a banquet on his birthday for his court officials, military commanders, [a]and leaders of Galilee. 22 When his daughter Herodias[1] came in and danced, she pleased Herod and his dinner guests. The king said to the girl, "Ask me for whatever you want and I will give it to you." 23 He swore to her,[1] "[a]Whatever you ask I will give you, up to half my kingdom." 24 So she went out and said to her mother, "What should I ask for?" Her mother said, "The head of John the baptizer." 25 Immediately she hurried back to the king and made her request: "I want the head of John the Baptist on a platter immediately." 26 Although it grieved the king deeply, he did not want to reject her request because of his oath [a]and his guests. 27 So the king sent an executioner at once to bring John's head, and he went and beheaded John in prison. 28 He brought his head on a platter and gave it to the girl, and the girl gave it to her mother. 29 When John's disciples heard this, they came and [a]took his body and placed it in a tomb.

The Feeding of the 5,000

30 [a]Then the apostles gathered around Jesus and told him everything they had done and taught. 31 He said to them, "Come with me privately to an isolated place [a]and rest a while" (for many were coming and going, and [b]there was no time to eat). 32 [a]So they went away by themselves in a boat to some remote place. 33 But many saw them leaving and [a]recognized them, and they hurried on foot from all the towns and arrived there ahead of them.[1] 34 As Jesus came ashore he saw the large crowd, [a]and he had compassion on them because they were like [b]sheep without a [c]shepherd. So he taught them many things.

35 [a]When it was already late, his disciples came to him and said, "This is an isolated place[1] and it is already very late. 36 Send them away so that they can go into the surrounding countryside and villages and buy something for themselves to eat." 37 But he answered them, "You[1] give them something to eat." And they said, "Should we go and buy bread for 200 silver coins and give it to them to eat?" 38 He said to them, "How many loaves do you have? Go and see." When they found out, they said, "[a]Five—and two fish." 39 Then he [a]directed them all to sit down in groups on the green grass. 40 So they reclined in groups of hundreds and fifties. 41 He took the five loaves and the two fish, and looking [a]up to heaven, he gave [b]thanks and broke the loaves. He gave them to his[1] disciples to serve the people, and he divided the two fish among them all. 42 They all ate and were satisfied, 43 and they picked up the broken pieces and fish that were left over, 12 baskets full. 44 Now there were 5,000 men[1] who ate the bread.[2]

Walking on Water

45 [a]Immediately Jesus made his disciples get into the boat and go on ahead to the other side, to Bethsaida, while he dispersed the crowd. 46 After saying goodbye to them, he [a]went to the mountain to pray. 47 When evening came, the boat was in the middle of the sea and he was alone on the land. 48 He saw them straining at the oars because the wind was against them. As the night was ending,[1] he came to them walking on the sea, for he [a]wanted to pass by them. 49 When they saw him walking on the water they thought he was a [a]ghost. They cried out, 50 for they all saw him and were terrified. But immediately he spoke to them: "Have courage! It is I. Do not [a]be [b]afraid." 51 Then he went up with them into the boat, and the wind [a]ceased. They were completely [b]astonished, 52 because [a]they did not understand about the loaves, but their [b]hearts were hardened.

6:20 [1] Maj. MSS *he did.* [2] Or *terribly disturbed.* 6:21 [a] Matt 14:6 [1] Grk. *a day of opportunity.* 6:22 [1] The MS evidence presents a textual problem concerning whether this is the daughter named Herodias or the daughter of Herodias. For a discussion of this issue, see *NET Bible, Full Notes Edition.* 6:23 [a] Esth 5:3, 6, 7:2 [1] ‡ Some WSS add *insistently.* 6:26 [a] Matt 14:9 6:29 [a] 1 Kgs 13:29–30; Matt 27:58–61; Acts 8:2 6:30 [a] Luke 9:10 6:31 [a] Matt 14:13 [b] Mark 3:20 6:32 [a] Matt 14:13–21; Luke 9:10–17; John 6:5–13 6:33 [a] [Col 1:6] [1] Some MSS *with them.* 6:34 [a] Matt 9:36; 14:14; [Heb 5:2] [b] Num 27:17; 1 Kgs 22:17; 2 Chr 18:16; Zech 10:2 [c] [Isa 48:17; 61:1–3]; Luke 9:11 6:35 [a] Matt 14:15; Luke 9:12 [1] Or *a desert.* 6:37 [1] An emphatic Grk. construction. 6:38 [a] Matt 14:17; Luke 9:13; John 6:9 6:39 [a] Matt 15:35; Mark 8:6 6:41 [a] John 11:41–42 [b] 1 Sam 9:13; Matt 15:36; 26:26; Mark 8:7; Luke 24:30 [1] ‡ Some MSS omit *his.* 6:44 [1] Plus women and children (see Matt 14:21). [2] Many MSS omit *the bread.* 6:45 [a] Matt 14:22–32; John 6:15–21 6:46 [a] Mark 1:35; Luke 5:16 6:48 [a] Luke 24:28 [1] Grk. *about the fourth watch of the night*; 3:00–6:00 a.m. 6:49 [a] Matt 14:26; Luke 24:37 6:50 [a] Matt 9:2; John 16:33 [b] Isa 41:10 6:51 [a] Ps 107:29 [b] Mark 1:27; 2:12; 5:42; 7:37 6:52 [a] Matt 16:9–11; Mark 8:17–18 [b] Isa 63:17; Mark 3:5; 16:14

Healing the Sick

[53a]After they had crossed over, they came to land at Gennesaret and anchored there. [54]As they got out of the boat, people immediately recognized Jesus. [55]They ran through that whole region and began to bring the sick on mats to wherever he was rumored to be. [56]And wherever [a]he would go—into villages, towns, or countryside—they would place the sick in the marketplaces, and would ask him if they could just touch the [b]edge of his cloak, and all who touched it were healed.

Breaking Human Traditions

7 Now [a]the Pharisees and some of the experts in the law who came from Jerusalem gathered around him. [2]And they saw that some of Jesus' disciples ate their bread with unclean hands, that is, [a]unwashed. [3](For the Pharisees and all the Jews do not eat unless they perform a ritual washing,[1] holding fast to the [a]tradition of the elders. [4]And when they come from the marketplace, they do not eat unless they wash. They hold fast to many other traditions: the washing of cups, pots, kettles, and dining couches.)[1] [5]The Pharisees and [a]the experts in the law asked him, "Why do your disciples not live according to the tradition of the elders, but eat with unwashed hands?" [6]He said to them, "Isaiah prophesied correctly about you [a]hypocrites, as it is written:

"[b]*This people honors me with their lips,*
but their hearts[1] *are far from me.*
[7] *They worship me in vain,*
teaching as doctrine the
commandments of men.'[1]

[8]Having no regard for the command of God, you hold fast to human tradition."[1] [9]He also said to them, "[a]You neatly reject the commandment of God in order to set up[1] your tradition. [10]For Moses said, '[a]*Honor your* [b]*father and your mother,*'[1] and, '*Whoever insults his father or mother must be put to death.*'[2] [11]But you say that if anyone tells his father or mother, '[a]Whatever help you would have received from me is *corban*' (that is, a gift for God), [12]then you no longer permit him to do anything for his father or mother. [13]Thus you nullify the word of God by your tradition that you have handed down. And you do many things like this."

[14]Then [a]he called the crowd again and said to them, "Listen to me, everyone, and [b]understand. [15]There is nothing outside of a person that can [a]defile him by going into him. Rather, it is what comes out of a person that defiles him."[1]

[17]Now [a]when Jesus had left the crowd and entered the house, his disciples asked him about the parable. [18]He said to them, "[a]Are you so foolish? Don't you understand that whatever goes into a person from outside cannot defile him? [19]For it does not enter his heart but his stomach, and then goes out into the sewer." (This means all foods are clean.) [20]He said, "[a]What comes out of a person defiles him. [21a]For from within, out of the human heart, [b]come evil ideas, sexual [c]immorality, theft, murder, [22]adultery, [a]greed, evil, [b]deceit, [c]debauchery, envy, [d]slander, [e]pride, and folly. [23]All these evils come from within and defile a person."

A Syrophoenician Woman's Faith

[24a]After Jesus left there, he went to the region of Tyre.[1] When he went into a house, he did not want anyone to know, but he was not able to escape [b]notice. [25]Instead, a woman whose young daughter had an unclean spirit immediately heard about him and came and [a]fell at his feet. [26]The woman was a Greek, of Syrophoenician origin. She asked him to cast the demon out of her daughter. [27]He said to her, "Let the children be satisfied first, for it is not right to take the children's bread and to throw it to the dogs." [28]She answered, "Yes, Lord, but even the dogs under the table eat the children's crumbs." [29]Then he said to her, "Because

6:53 [a]Matt 14:34–36; John 6:24–25   6:56 [a]Matt 9:20; Mark 5:27–28; [Acts 19:12]   [b]Num 15:38–39   7:1 [a]Matt 15:1–20   7:2 [a]Matt 15:20   7:3 [a]Mark 7:5, 8, 9, 13; Gal 1:14; 1 Pet 1:18   [1]Grk. *except they wash the hands with a fist.*   7:4 [1]Sev. sig. wss omit *and dining couches.*   7:5 [a]Matt 15:2   7:6 [a]Matt 23:13–29   [b]Isa 29:13   [1]A collective sing.   7:7 [1]Isa 29:13   7:8 [1]Maj. MSS add *the washing of pots and cups, and you do many other similar things.*   7:9 [a]Prov 1:25; Isa 24:5; Jer 7:23–24   [1]Maj. MSS keep.   7:10 [a]Exod 20:12; Deut 5:16; Matt 15:4   [b]Exod 21:17; Lev 20:9; Prov 20:20   [1]Exod 20:12; Deut 5:16   [2]Exod 20:17; Lev 20:9   7:11 [a]Matt 15:5; 23:18   7:14 [a]Matt 15:10   [b]Matt 16:9, 11, 12   7:15 [a]Isa 59:3; [Heb 12:15]   [1]Some MSS add v. 16: *Let anyone with ears to hear, listen.*   7:17 [a]Matt 15:15   7:18 [a][Isa 28:9–11; 1 Cor 3:2; Heb 5:11–14]   7:20 [a]Ps 39:1; [Matt 12:34–37; Jas 3:6]   7:21 [a]Gen 6:5; 8:21; Prov 6:18; Jer 17:9; Matt 15:19   [b][Gal 5:19–21]   [c]1 Thess 4:3   7:22 [a]Luke 12:15   [b]Rom 1:28–29   [c]1 Pet 4:3   [d]Rev 2:9   [e]1 John 2:16   7:24 [a]Matt 15:21   [b]Mark 2:1–2   [1]Maj. MSS add *and Sidon.*   7:25 [a]Mark 5:22; John 11:32; Rev 1:17

you said this, you may go. The demon has left your daughter." [30] She went home and found the child lying on the bed, and the demon gone.

Healing a Deaf Mute

[31] Then Jesus went out [a] again from the region of Tyre and came through Sidon to the Sea of Galilee in the region of the Decapolis. [32] They brought to him a deaf man who had difficulty speaking, and [a] they asked him to place his hands on him. [33] After Jesus took him aside privately, away from [a] the crowd, he put his fingers in the man's ears, and after spitting, he touched his tongue. [34] Then he looked [a] up to [b] heaven and said with a sigh, "*Ephphatha*" (that is, "Be opened"). [35] And [a] immediately the man's ears were opened, his tongue loosened, and he spoke plainly. [36] Jesus ordered [a] them not to tell anyone. But as much as he ordered them not to do this, they proclaimed it all the more. [37] People were completely [a] astounded and said, "He has done everything well. He even [b] makes the deaf hear and the mute speak."

The Feeding of the 4,000

8 In those days [a] there was another large crowd with nothing to eat. So Jesus called his disciples and said to them, [2] "I have [a] compassion on the crowd because they have already been here with me three days, and they have nothing to eat. [3] If I send them home hungry, they will faint on the way, and some of them have come from a great distance." [4] His disciples answered him, "Where can someone get enough bread in this desolate place to satisfy these people?" [5] He asked [a] them, "How many loaves do you have?" They replied, "Seven." [6] Then he directed the crowd to sit down on the ground. After he took the seven loaves and gave thanks, he broke them and began giving them to the disciples to serve. So they served the crowd. [7] They also had [a] a few small fish. After giving thanks for these, he told them to serve these as well. [8] Everyone ate and was satisfied, and they picked up the broken pieces left over, seven baskets full. [9] There were about 4,000 who ate. Then he dismissed them. [10] Immediately he got into [a] a boat with his disciples and went to the district of Dalmanutha.

The Demand for a Sign

[11a] Then the Pharisees came and began to argue with Jesus, asking for[1] a sign from heaven to test him. [12] Sighing [a] deeply in his spirit he said, "Why does this generation look for a sign? I tell you the truth, [b] no sign will be given to this generation." [13] Then he left them, got back into the boat, and went to the other side.

The Yeast of the Pharisees and Herod

[14a] Now they had forgotten to take bread, except for one loaf they had with them in the boat. [15] And Jesus ordered them, "Watch out! Beware of the yeast of the Pharisees [a] and the yeast of Herod!" [16] So they began to discuss with one another about having no bread. [17] When he learned of this, Jesus said to them, "Why are you arguing[1] about having no bread? [a] Do you still not see or understand? Have your hearts been hardened? [18] Though you have eyes, don't you see? And though you have ears, can't you hear? Don't you remember? [19a] When I broke the five loaves for the 5,000, how many baskets full of pieces did you pick up?" They replied, "Twelve." [20] "[a] When I broke the seven loaves for the 4,000, how many baskets full of pieces did you pick up?" They replied,[1] "Seven." [21] Then he said to them, "Do [a] you still not understand?"

A Two-Stage Healing

[22] Then they came to Bethsaida. They brought a blind [a] man [b] to Jesus and asked him to touch him. [23] He took [a] the blind man by the hand and brought him outside of the village. Then he spit on his eyes, placed his hands on his eyes and asked, "Do you see anything?" [24] Regaining his sight he said, "I see people, but they look like trees walking." [25] Then Jesus placed his hands on the man's eyes again. And he opened his eyes, his sight was restored, and he saw everything

7:31 [a] Matt 15:29; Mark 15:37; Luke 23:46; 24:46; Acts 10:40; 1 Cor 15:4   **7:32** [a] Matt 9:32; Luke 11:14   **7:33** [a] Mark 8:23; John 9:6   **7:34** [a] Mark 6:41; John 11:41; 17:1   [b] John 11:33, 38   **7:35** [a] Isa 35:5–6   **7:36** [a] Mark 5:43   **7:37** [a] Mark 6:51; 10:26   [b] Matt 12:22   **8:1** [a] Matt 15:32–39; Mark 6:34–44; Luke 9:12   **8:2** [a] Matt 9:36; 14:14; Mark 1:41; 6:34   **8:5** [a] Matt 15:34; Mark 6:38; John 6:9   **8:7** [a] Matt 14:19; Mark 6:41   **8:10** [a] Matt 15:39   **8:11** [a] Matt 12:38; 16:1; Luke 11:16; John 2:18; 6:30; 1 Cor 1:22   [1] Grk. *seeking from him.*   **8:12** [a] Mark 7:34   [b] Matt 12:39   **8:14** [a] Matt 16:5   **8:15** [a] Matt 16:6; Luke 12:1   **8:17** [a] Mark 6:52; 16:14   [1] Or *discussing.*   **8:19** [a] Matt 14:20; Mark 6:43; Luke 9:17; John 6:13   **8:20** [a] Matt 15:37   [1] ‡ Some MSS add *to him.*   **8:21** [a] [Mark 6:52]   **8:22** [a] Matt 9:27; John 9:1   [b] Luke 18:15   **8:23** [a] Mark 7:33

clearly. [26]Jesus sent him home, saying, "Do not [a]even go into the village."[1]

Peter's Confession

[27]Then Jesus [a]and his disciples went to the villages of Caesarea Philippi. On the way he asked his disciples, "Who do people say that I am?" [28]They said, "[a]John the Baptist, others say [b]Elijah, and still others, one of the prophets." [29]He asked them, "But who do you say that I am?" Peter answered him, "[a]You are the Christ." [30a]Then he warned them not to tell anyone about him.

First Prediction of Jesus' Death and Resurrection

[31]Then Jesus began to teach [a]them that the Son of Man must suffer many things and be [b]rejected by the elders, chief priests, and experts in the law, and be [c]killed, and after three days rise again. [32]He spoke openly about this. So Peter took him aside and began to rebuke him. [33]But after turning and looking at his disciples, he [a]rebuked Peter and said, "Get behind me, Satan. You are not setting your mind on God's interests, but on man's."

Following Jesus

[34]Then Jesus called the crowd, along with his disciples, and said to them, "If anyone wants to become my follower, he must deny himself, take up his cross, and follow me. [35]For [a]whoever wants to save his life[1] will lose it, but whoever loses his life because of me and because of the gospel[2] will save it. [36]For what benefit is it for a person to gain the whole world, yet forfeit his life? [37]What can a person give in exchange for his life? [38a]For if anyone [b]is ashamed of me and my words in this adulterous and sinful generation, the Son of Man will also be ashamed of him when he comes in the glory of his Father with the holy angels."[1]And he said to

9 them, "I tell you the [a]truth, [b]there are some standing here who will not experience[1] death before they see the kingdom of God come with power."

The Transfiguration

[2]Six days later Jesus took with him Peter, James, [a]and John and led them alone up a high mountain privately. And he was transfigured before them, [3]and his clothes became radiantly [a]white, more so than any launderer in the world could bleach them. [4]Then Elijah appeared before them along with Moses, and they were talking with Jesus. [5]So Peter said to Jesus, "Rabbi, it is good for us to be here. Let us make three shelters[1]—one for you, one for Moses, and one for Elijah." [6](For they were afraid, and he did not know what to say.) [7]Then a [a]cloud overshadowed them, and a voice came from the cloud, "This is [b]my one dear Son.[1] [c]Listen to him!" [8]Suddenly when they looked around, they saw no one with them any more except Jesus.

[9a]As they were coming down from the mountain, he gave them orders not to tell anyone what they had seen until after the Son of Man had risen from the dead. [10]They kept this statement to themselves, discussing [a]what this rising from the dead meant. [11]Then they asked him, "Why do the experts in the law say [a]that Elijah must come first?" [12]He said to them, "Elijah does indeed come first, and restores all things. And [a]why is it written that the Son of Man must suffer many things and [b]be despised? [13]But I tell you that [a]Elijah has certainly come, and they did to him whatever they wanted, just as it is written about him."

The Disciples' Failure to Heal

[14]When they came to the disciples, they saw a large crowd around them [a]and experts in the law arguing with them. [15]When the whole crowd saw him, they were amazed and ran at once and greeted him. [16]He asked them, "What are you arguing about with them?" [17]A [a]member of the crowd said to

8:26 [a] Matt 8:4; Mark 5:43; 7:36   [1] Some MSS *Go to your house, and do not tell anyone, not even in the village, Go to your house, and if you go into the village, do not tell anyone.*   8:27 [a] Matt 16:13–16; Luke 9:18–20   8:28 [a] Matt 14:2   [b] Mark 6:14–15; Luke 9:7–8   8:29 [a] John 1:41; 4:42; 6:69; 11:27; Acts 2:36; 8:37; 9:20   8:30 [a] Matt 8:4; 16:20; Luke 9:21   8:31 [a] [Isa 53:3–11]; Matt 16:21; 20:19; Luke 18:31–33; 1 Pet 1:11   [b] Mark 10:33   [c] Mark 9:31; 10:34   8:33 [a] Mark 16:14; [Rev 3:19]   8:35 [a] Matt 10:39; Luke 17:33; John 12:25   [1] Grk. *soul*; throughout vv. 35–37.   [2] Or *for my sake and for the gospel*; *because of* repeated for clarity.   8:38 [a] Matt 10:33; Luke 9:26; 12:9   [b] Rom 1:16; 2 Tim 1:8–9; 2:12   9:1 [a] Matt 16:28; Mark 13:26; Luke 9:27; Acts 7:55–56; Rev 20:4   [b] [Matt 24:30]   [1] Grk. *will not taste.*   9:2 [a] Matt 17:1–8; Luke 9:28–36   9:3 [a] Dan 7:9; Matt 28:3   9:5 [1] Or *booths, dwellings.*   9:7 [a] Exod 40:34; 1 Kgs 8:10; Acts 1:9; Rev 1:7   [b] Ps 2:7; [Isa 42:1]; Matt 3:17; Mark 1:11; Luke 1:35; 3:22; 2 Pet 1:17   [c] Acts 3:22   [1] Grk. *my beloved Son, my Son, the beloved one.*   9:9 [a] Matt 17:9–13; Mark 16:6; Luke 24:6–7, 46   9:10 [a] John 2:19–22   9:11 [a] Mal 4:5; Matt 17:10   9:12 [a] Ps 22:6; Isa 53:3; Dan 9:26   [b] Luke 23:11; Phil 2:7   9:13 [a] Mal 4:5; Matt 11:14; 17:12; Luke 1:17   9:14 [a] Matt 17:14–19; Luke 9:37–42   9:17 [a] Matt 17:14; Luke 9:38

him, "Teacher, I brought you my son, who is possessed by a spirit that makes him mute. [18] Whenever it seizes him, it throws him down, and he foams at the mouth, grinds his teeth, and becomes rigid. I asked your disciples to cast it out, but they were not able to do so." [19] He answered them, "You [a] unbelieving generation! How much longer must I be with you? How much longer must I endure you? Bring him to me." [20] So they brought the boy to him. [a] When the spirit saw him, it immediately threw the boy into a convulsion. He fell on the ground and rolled around, foaming at the mouth. [21] Jesus asked his father, "How long has this been happening to him?" And he said, "From childhood. [22] It has often thrown him into fire or water to destroy him. But if you are able to do anything, have compassion on us and help us." [23] Then Jesus said to him, "'[a] If you are able?'[1] All things are possible for the one who believes." [24] Immediately the father of the boy cried out and said, "I believe; [a] help my unbelief!"

[25] Now when Jesus saw that a crowd was quickly gathering, he [a] rebuked[1] the unclean spirit, saying to it, "Mute and deaf spirit, I command you, come out of him and never enter him again." [26] It shrieked, threw him into terrible convulsions, and came out. The boy looked so much like a corpse that many said, "He is dead!" [27] But Jesus gently took his hand and raised him to his feet, and he stood up.

[28a] Then, after he went into the house, his disciples asked him privately, "Why couldn't we cast it out?" [29] He told them, "This kind can come out only by [a] prayer."[1]

Second Prediction of Jesus' Death and Resurrection

[30] They went out from there and passed through Galilee. But Jesus did not want anyone to know, [31a] for he was teaching his disciples and telling them, "The Son of Man will be betrayed into the hands of men. They will [b] kill him, and after three days he will [c] rise." [32] But they [a] did not understand this statement and were afraid to ask him.

Questions about the Greatest

[33a] Then they came to Capernaum. After Jesus was inside the house he asked them, "What were you discussing on the way?" [34] But they were silent, for on the way they had [a] argued with one another about who was the [b] greatest. [35] After he sat down, he called the twelve and said to them, "[a] If anyone wants to be first, he must be last of all and servant of all." [36] He took a little child and had him stand among [a] them. Taking him in his arms, he said to them, [37] "Whoever welcomes one of these little children in my name welcomes me, and [a] whoever welcomes me does not welcome me but the one who sent me."

On Jesus' Side

[38a] John said to him, "Teacher, we saw someone casting out demons in your name, and we tried to stop him because he was not following us." [39] But Jesus said, "Do not stop him [a] because no one who does a miracle in my name will be able soon afterward to say anything bad about me. [40] For whoever is not against us is for us. [41a] For I tell you the truth, whoever gives you a cup of water because you bear Christ's name will never lose his reward.

[42] "If anyone causes one of these little ones who believe in me to sin, it would be better for him to have a huge millstone[1] tied around his neck [a] and to be thrown into the sea. [43a] If your hand causes you to sin, cut it off! It is better for you to enter into life crippled than to have two hands and go into hell, to the unquenchable fire.[1] [45] If your foot causes you to sin, cut it off! It is better to enter life lame than to have two feet and be thrown into hell.[1] [47] If your eye causes you to sin, tear it out! It is better to enter into the kingdom of God with one eye than to have two eyes and be thrown into hell, [48] where [a] their worm never dies

9:19 [a] John 4:48   9:20 [a] Mark 1:26; Luke 9:42   9:23 [a] Matt 17:20; Mark 11:23; Luke 17:6; John 11:40   [1] Maj. MSS add *to believe.*
9:24 [a] Luke 17:5   9:25 [a] Mark 1:25   [1] Or *commanded.*   9:28 [a] Matt 17:19   9:29 [a] [Jas 5:16]   [1] Maj. WSS add *and fasting.*
9:31 [a] Matt 17:22; Luke 9:44   [b] Matt 16:21; 27:50; Luke 18:33; 23:46; Acts 2:23   [c] Matt 20:19; Luke 24:46; Acts 10:40; 1 Cor 15:4
9:32 [a] Luke 2:50; 18:34; John 12:16   9:33 [a] Matt 18:1–5; Mark 14:53, 64; Luke 9:46–48; 22:24; John 18:12; 19:7   9:34 [a] [Prov 13:10]; Mark 15:20, 31   [b] Matt 18:4; [Mark 9:50]; 14:65; 15:15, 37; Luke 22:24; 23:46; 24:46   9:35 [a] Matt 20:26–27; 23:11; Mark 10:43–44; Luke 22:26–27   9:36 [a] Mark 10:13–16   9:37 [a] Matt 10:40; Luke 10:16; John 13:20   9:38 [a] Num 11:27–29; Luke 9:49   9:39 [a] 1 Cor 12:3   9:41 [a] Matt 10:42   9:42 [a] Matt 18:6; Luke 17:1–2; [1 Cor 8:12]   [1] Grk. *the millstone of a donkey*; a large flat stone turned to grind grain.   9:43 [a] [Deut 13:6]; Matt 5:29–30; 18:8–9   [1] Maj. later MSS add v. 44: *where their worm never dies and the fire is never quenched.*   9:45 [1] Maj. later MSS add v. 46: *where their worm never dies and the fire is never quenched.*   9:48 [a] Isa 66:24

and the [b]fire is never quenched. [49]Everyone will be [a]salted with fire.[1] [50a]Salt is good, but if it loses its saltiness, how can you make it salty again? [b]Have salt in yourselves, and be at peace with each other."

Divorce

10 Then Jesus left that place and went to [a]the region of Judea and[1] beyond the Jordan River. Again crowds gathered to him, and again, as was his custom, he taught them. [2]Then some Pharisees[1] came, and to test him [a]they asked, "Is it lawful for a man to divorce his wife?" [3]He answered them, "What did Moses command you?" [4]They said, "[a]Moses permitted a man *to write a certificate of dismissal and to divorce* her."[1] [5]But Jesus said to them, "He wrote this commandment for you because of your hard hearts. [6]But from the beginning of creation *he*[1] [a]*made them male and female.*[2] [7a]*For this reason a man will leave his father and mother,*[1] [8]*and the two will become one flesh.*[1] So they are no longer two, but one flesh. [9]Therefore what God has joined together, let no one separate."

[10]In the house once again, the disciples asked him about this. [11]So he told them, "[a]Whoever divorces his wife and marries another commits adultery against her. [12]And if she divorces her husband and marries another, she commits adultery."

Jesus and Little Children

[13]Now people were bringing little children to him for him to touch, but [a]the disciples scolded those who brought them.[1] [14]But when Jesus saw this, he was indignant and said to them, "Let the little children come to me and do not try to stop them, for the kingdom [a]of God belongs to such as these. [15]I tell you the truth, [a]whoever does not receive the kingdom of God like a child will never[1] enter it." [16]After he took the children in his arms, he placed his hands on them and blessed them.

The Rich Man

[17a]Now as Jesus was starting out on his way, someone ran up to him, fell on his knees, and said, "Good teacher, what must I [b]do to inherit eternal life?" [18]Jesus said to him, "Why do you call me good? No one is good except [a]God alone. [19]You know the commandments: '[a]*Do not murder, do not commit adultery, do not steal, do not give false testimony,* do not defraud, *honor your father and mother.*'[1] [20]The man said to him, "Teacher, I have wholeheartedly [a]obeyed all these laws since my youth." [21]As Jesus looked at him, he felt love for him and said, "You lack one thing. Go, [a]sell whatever you have and give the money to the poor, and you will have [b]treasure in heaven. Then come, follow me." [22]But at this statement, the man looked sad and went away sorrowful, for he was very rich.

[23a]Then Jesus looked around and said to his disciples, "How hard it is for the rich to enter the kingdom of God!" [24]The disciples were astonished at these words. But again Jesus said to them, "Children, how hard it is[1] to enter the kingdom of God! [25]It is easier for a camel[1] to go through the eye of a needle than for a [a]rich person to enter the kingdom of God." [26]They were even more astonished and said to one another, "Then who can be saved?" [27]Jesus looked at them and replied, "This is impossible [a]for mere humans, but not for God; all things are possible for God."

[28a]Peter began to speak to him, "Look, we have left everything to follow you!" [29]Jesus said, "I tell you the truth, there is no one who has left home or brothers or sisters or mother or father or children or fields for my sake and for the sake of the gospel [30a]who will not receive in this age a hundred times as much—homes, brothers, sisters, mothers, children, fields, all with [b]persecutions—and in the age to come, eternal life. [31a]But many who are first will be last, and the last first."

9:48 [b]Jer 7:20; [Rev 21:8]   **9:49** [a][Matt 3:11]   [1]Maj. MSS add *and every sacrifice will be salted with salt.*   **9:50** [a]Matt 5:13; Luke 14:34   [b][Eph 4:29]; Col 4:6   **10:1** [a]Matt 19:1–9; John 10:40; 11:7   [1]Some WSS omit *and.*   **10:2** [a]Matt 19:3   [1]Some WSS omit *then some Pharisees came.*   **10:4** [a]Deut 24:1–4; Matt 5:31; 19:7   [1][Deut 24:1]   **10:6** [a]Gen 1:27; 5:2   [1]Maj. MSS *God.* [2]Gen 1:27; 5:2   **10:7** [a]Gen 2:24; [1 Cor 6:16]; Eph 5:31   [1]‡ Maj. MSS add *and will be united with his wife.*   **10:8** [1]Gen 2:24   **10:11** [a]Exod 20:14; [Matt 5:32; 19:9]; Luke 16:18; [Rom 7:3]; 1 Cor 7:10–11   **10:13** [a]Matt 19:13–15; Luke 18:15–17   [1]Some WSS omit *those who brought them.*   **10:14** [a][1 Cor 14:20; 1 Pet 2:2]   **10:15** [a]Matt 18:3–4; 19:14; Luke 18:17   [1]A very strong Grk. negative.   **10:17** [a]Matt 19:16–30; Luke 18:18–30   [b]John 6:28; Acts 2:37   **10:18** [a]1 Sam 2:2   **10:19** [a]Exod 20:12–16; Deut 5:16–20; [Rom 13:9; Jas 2:10–11]   [1]Exod 20:12–16; Deut 5:16–20; [24:14]   **10:20** [a]Phil 3:6   **10:21** [a][Luke 12:33; 16:9]   [b]Matt 6:19–20; 19:21   **10:23** [a]Matt 19:23; [Mark 4:19]; Luke 18:24   **10:24** [1]Maj. MSS add *for those who trust in riches.*   **10:25** [a][Matt 13:22; 19:24]   [1]A few WSS *rope.*   **10:27** [a]Job 42:2; Jer 32:17; Matt 19:26; Luke 1:37   **10:28** [a]Matt 19:27; Luke 18:28   **10:30** [a]2 Chr 25:9; Luke 18:29–30   [b]1 Thess 3:3; 2 Tim 3:12; [1 Pet 4:12–13]   **10:31** [a]Matt 19:30; 20:16; Luke 13:30

Third Prediction of Jesus' Death and Resurrection

32 They were on the way, going up to Jerusalem. Jesus was going ahead of them, and they were amazed, [a] but those who followed were afraid. [b] He took the twelve aside again and began to tell them what was going to happen to him. 33 "Look, we are going up to Jerusalem, and the Son of Man will be handed over to the chief priests and experts in the law. They will condemn him to death and will turn him over to the Gentiles. 34 They will mock him, spit on him, flog [1] him severely, and kill him. Yet after three days,[2] he will rise again."

The Request of James and John

35 [a] Then James and John, the sons of Zebedee, came to him and said, "Teacher, we want you to do for us whatever we ask." 36 He said to them, "What do you want me to do for you?" 37 They said to him, "Permit one of us to sit at your right hand and the other at your left in your glory." 38 But Jesus said to them, "You don't know what you are asking! Are you able to drink the [a] cup I drink or be baptized with the [b] baptism I experience?" 39 They said to him, "We are able." Then Jesus said to them, "[a] You will drink the cup I drink, and you will be baptized with the baptism I experience, 40 but to sit at my right [a] or at my left is not mine to give. It is for those for whom it has been prepared."

41 Now when the other 10 heard this, they became angry with James [a] and John. 42 Jesus called them and said to them, "[a] You know that those who are recognized as rulers of the Gentiles lord it over them, and those in high positions use their authority over them. 43 [a] But it is not this way among you. Instead whoever wants to be great among you must be your servant, 44 and whoever wants to be first among you must be the slave [1] of all. 45 For even [a] the Son of Man did not come [b] to be served but to serve, and to give his life as a ransom for many."

Healing Blind Bartimaeus

46 They came to Jericho. As Jesus [a] and his disciples and a large crowd were leaving Jericho, Bartimaeus the son of Timaeus, a blind beggar, was sitting by the road. 47 When he heard that it was Jesus the Nazarene, he began to shout, "Jesus, [a] Son of David, [b] have mercy on me!" 48 Many scolded [1] him to get him to be quiet, but he shouted all the more, "Son of David, have mercy on me!" 49 Jesus stopped and said, "Call him." So they called the blind man and said to him, "Have courage! Get up! He is calling you." 50 He threw off his cloak, jumped up, and came to Jesus. 51 Then Jesus said to him, "What do you want me to do for you?" The blind man replied, "Rabbi, let me see again."[1] 52 Jesus said to him, "Go, [a] your faith has healed you." Immediately he regained his sight and followed him on the road.

The Triumphal Entry

11 Now [a] as they approached Jerusalem, near Bethphage and Bethany, at the Mount of Olives, Jesus sent two of his disciples 2 and said to them, "Go to the village ahead of you. As soon as you enter it, you will find a colt tied there that has never been ridden. Untie it and bring it here. 3 If anyone says to you, 'Why are you doing this?' say, 'The Lord needs it and will send it back here soon.'" 4 So they went and found a colt tied at a door, outside in the street, and untied it. 5 Some people standing there said to them, "What are you doing, untying that colt?" 6 They replied as Jesus had told them, and the bystanders let them go. 7 Then they brought the colt to Jesus, threw their cloaks [1] on it, and he sat on it. 8 Many spread their cloaks on the road [a] and others spread branches they had cut in the fields. 9 Both those who went ahead and those who followed kept shouting, "*Hosanna!*[1] [a] *Blessed is the one who comes in the name of the Lord!*[2] 10 Blessed is the coming kingdom of our father David! [a] Hosanna in the highest!" 11 Then Jesus entered Jerusalem and went to

10:32 [a] Matt 20:17–19; Luke 18:31–33 [b] Mark 8:31; 9:31; Luke 9:22; 18:31 10:34 [1] Trad. *scourge him*; to beat severely with a whip. [2] Maj. MSS, esp. later ones, *on the third day*. 10:35 [a] [Jas 4:3] 10:38 [a] Matt 26:39, 42; Mark 14:36; Luke 22:42; John 18:11 [b] Luke 12:50 10:39 [a] Matt 10:17–18, 21, 22; 24:9; John 16:33; Acts 12:2; Rev 1:9 10:40 [a] [Matt 25:34; John 17:2, 6, 24; Rom 8:30; Heb 11:16] 10:41 [a] Matt 20:24 10:42 [a] Luke 22:25 10:43 [a] Matt 20:26, 28; Mark 9:35; Luke 9:48 10:44 [1] Grk. *servant*. 10:45 [a] Luke 22:27; John 13:14; [Phil 2:7–8] [b] Matt 20:28; [2 Cor 5:21; 1 Tim 2:5–6; Titus 2:14] 10:46 [a] Matt 20:29–34; Luke 18:35–43 10:47 [a] Jer 23:5; Matt 22:42; Rom 1:3–4; Rev 22:16 [b] Matt 15:22; Luke 17:13 10:48 [1] Or *rebuked*. 10:51 [1] Grk. *that I may see again*. 10:52 [a] Matt 9:22; Mark 5:34 11:1 [a] Matt 21:1–9; Luke 19:29; John 2:13 11:7 [1] Grk. *garments*; their outer cloaks. 11:8 [a] Matt 21:8 11:9 [a] Ps 118:25–26; Matt 21:9 [1] Heb. *O Lord, save*; an expression of praise on the order of "Hail to the king." [2] Ps 119:25–26 11:10 [a] Ps 148:1

the temple. [a]And after looking around at everything, he went out to Bethany with the twelve since it was already late.

Cursing of the Fig Tree

[12][a]Now the next day, as they went out from Bethany, he was hungry. [13]After noticing in the distance [a]a fig tree with leaves, he went to see if he could find any fruit on it. When he came to it he found nothing but leaves, for it was not the season for figs. [14]He said to it, "May no one ever eat fruit from you again." And his disciples heard it.

Cleansing the Temple

[15]Then they came to Jerusalem. Jesus entered the temple area and began to drive out those who were selling [a]and buying in the temple courts. He turned over the tables of the money changers and the chairs of those selling [b]doves, [16]and he would not permit anyone to carry merchandise[1] through the temple courts. [17]Then he began to teach them and said, "Is it not written: '[a]*My house will be called a house of prayer for all nations*'?[1] But you have turned it into a [b]*den of robbers*!"[2] [18]The chief priests and [a]the experts in the law heard it, and they considered how they could assassinate him, for they feared him because the [b]whole crowd was amazed by his teaching. [19]When evening came, Jesus and his disciples went out of the city.

The Withered Fig Tree

[20][a]In the morning as they passed by, they saw the fig tree withered from the roots. [21]Peter remembered and said to him, "Rabbi, look! The fig tree you cursed has withered." [22]Jesus said to them, "Have faith in God. [23]I tell you the [a]truth, if someone says to this mountain, 'Be lifted up and thrown into the sea,' and does not doubt in his heart but believes that what he says will happen, it will be done for him. [24]For this reason I tell you, [a]whatever you pray and ask for, believe that you have received it, and it will be yours. [25]Whenever you stand praying, [a]if you have anything against anyone, forgive

him, so that your Father in heaven will[1] also forgive you your sins."[2]

The Authority of Jesus

[27]They came again to Jerusalem. While Jesus was walking in the temple courts, the chief priests, the experts in the law, [a]and the elders came up to him [28]and said, "By what [a]authority are you doing these things? Or who gave you this authority to do these things?" [29]Jesus said to them, "I will ask you one question. Answer me and I will tell you by what authority I do these things: [30]John's [a]baptism—was it from heaven or from people? Answer me." [31]They discussed with one another, saying, "If we say, 'From heaven,' he will say, 'Then why did you not believe him?' [32]But if we say, 'From people...'" (they feared the crowd, for they [a]all considered John to be truly a prophet). [33]So they answered Jesus, "We don't know." Then Jesus said to them, "Neither will I tell you by what authority I am doing these things."

The Parable of the Tenants

12 Then [a]he began to speak to them in parables: "A man planted a vineyard. He put a fence around it, dug a pit for its winepress, and built a watchtower. Then he leased it to tenant farmers and went on a journey. [2]At harvest time he sent a slave to the tenants to collect from them his portion of the crop. [3]But those tenants seized his slave, beat him, and sent him away empty-handed. [4]So he sent another slave to them again. This one they struck on the head and treated outrageously. [5]He sent another, and that one they killed. This happened to many others, some of whom were [a]beaten, others killed. [6]He had one left, his one dear son. Finally he sent him to them, saying, 'They will respect my son.' [7]But those tenants said to one another, 'This is the heir. Come, let's kill him and the inheritance will be ours!' [8]So they seized him, [a]killed him, and threw his body out of the vineyard. [9]What then will the owner of the vineyard do? He will come and destroy those tenants and give

11:11 [a]Matt 21:12   **11:12** [a]Matt 21:18–22   **11:13** [a]Matt 21:19   **11:15** [a]Mal 3:1; Matt 21:12–16; Luke 19:45–47; John 2:13–16   [b]Lev 14:22   **11:16** [1]Or *things*.   **11:17** [a]Isa 56:7   [b]Jer 7:11   [1]Isa 56:7   [2]Jer 7:11   **11:18** [a]Ps 2:2; Matt 21:45–46; Luke 19:47   [b]Matt 7:28; Mark 1:22; 6:2; Luke 4:32   **11:20** [a]Matt 21:19–22   **11:23** [a]Matt 17:20; 21:21; Luke 17:6   **11:24** [a]Matt 7:7; Luke 11:9; [John 14:13; 15:7; 16:24; Jas 1:5–6]   **11:25** [a]Matt 6:14; 18:23–35; Eph 4:32; [Col 3:13]   [1]Trad. *may*.   [2]Maj. later MSS add v. 26: *But if you do not forgive, neither will your Father in heaven forgive your sins.*   **11:27** [a]Matt 21:23–27; Luke 20:1–8   **11:28** [a]John 5:27   **11:30** [a][Mark 1:4–5, 8]; Luke 7:29–30   **11:32** [a]Matt 3:5; 14:5; Mark 6:20   **12:1** [a]Matt 21:33–46; Luke 20:9–19   **12:5** [a]2 Chr 36:16   **12:8** [a][Acts 2:23]

the vineyard to others. [10]Have you not read this scripture:

> "'[a]*The stone the builders rejected has become the cornerstone.*[1]
> [11] *This is from the Lord, and it is marvelous in our eyes'*?"[1]

[12]Now they wanted to arrest him ([a]but they feared the crowd), because they realized that he told this parable against them. So they left him and went away.

Paying Taxes to Caesar

[13a]Then they sent some of the Pharisees and Herodians to trap him with his own words. [14]When they came they said to him, "Teacher, we know that you are truthful and do not court anyone's favor because you show no partiality but teach the [a]way of God in accordance with the truth. Is it right[1] to pay taxes[2] to Caesar or not? Should we pay or shouldn't we?" [15]But he saw through their [a]hypocrisy and said to them, "Why are you testing me? Bring me a denarius[1] and let me look at it." [16]So they brought one, and he said to them, "Whose image is this, and whose inscription?" They replied, "Caesar's." [17]Then Jesus said to them, "Give to Caesar the things that are Caesar's, and to [a]God the things that are God's." And they were utterly amazed at him.

Marriage and the Resurrection

[18a]Sadducees ([b]who say there is no resurrection) also came to him and asked him, [19]"Teacher, [a]Moses wrote for us: '*If a man's brother dies and leaves a wife but no children, that man must marry the widow and father children for his brother.*'[1] [20]There were seven brothers. The first one married, and when he died he had no children. [21]The second married her and died without any children, and likewise the third. [22]None of the seven had children. Finally, the woman died too. [23]In the resurrection, when they rise again,[1] whose wife will she be? For all seven had

married her." [24]Jesus said to them, "Aren't you deceived[1] for this reason because you don't know the scriptures or the power of God? [25]For when they rise from the dead, they neither marry nor [a]are given in marriage, but are like angels in heaven. [26]Now as for the dead being [a]raised, have you not read in the book of Moses, in the passage about the bush, how God said to him, '[b]*I am the God of Abraham, the God of Isaac, and the God of Jacob*'?[1] [27]He is not the God of the dead but of the living. You are badly mistaken!"

The Greatest Commandment

[28]Now one of [a]the experts in the law came and heard them debating. When he saw that Jesus answered them well, he asked him, "Which commandment is the most important of all?" [29]Jesus answered, "The most important is: '[a]*Listen, Israel, the Lord our God, the Lord is one.* [30a]*Love the Lord your God with all your heart, with all your soul, with all your mind, and with all your strength.*'[1] [31]The second is: '*Love [a]your neighbor as yourself.*'[1] There is no other commandment greater than [b]these." [32]The expert in the law said to him, "That is true, Teacher; you are right to say that *he is one,* [a]*and there is no one else besides him.*[1] [33]And *to love him with all your heart, with all your mind, and with all your strength*[1] and *to love your neighbor as yourself*[2] [a]is more important than all burnt offerings and sacrifices." [34]When Jesus saw that he had answered thoughtfully, he said to him, "You are not far from the kingdom of God." [a]Then no one dared any longer to question him.

The Messiah: David's Son and Lord

[35]While Jesus was teaching in [a]the temple courts, he said, "How is it that the experts in the law say that the Christ is David's son? [36]David himself, [a]by [b]the Holy Spirit, said,

> "'*The Lord said to my lord,*
> *"Sit at my right hand,*
> *until I put your enemies under your feet."*'[1]

12:10 [a]Ps 118:22–23 [1]Or *capstone, keystone.* 12:11 [1]Ps 118:22–23 12:12 [a]Matt 21:45–46; Mark 11:18; John 7:25, 30, 44 12:13 [a]Matt 22:15–22; Luke 20:20–26 12:14 [a]Acts 18:26 [1]Or *lawful;* in accordance with God's divine law. [2]A poll tax paid by each adult male to the Roman government. 12:15 [a]Matt 23:28; Luke 12:1 [1]Or *silver coin; denarius* is used because not all coins carried the image of Caesar. 12:17 [a][Eccl 5:4–5] 12:18 [a]Matt 22:23–33; Luke 20:27–38 [b]Acts 23:8 12:19 [a]Deut 25:5 [1]Deut 25:5 12:23 [1]Sig. wss omit *when they rise again.* 12:24 [1]Or *mistaken.* 12:25 [a][1 Cor 15:42, 49, 52] 12:26 [a][John 5:25, 28, 29]; Acts 26:8; Rom 4:17; [Rev 20:12–13] [b]Exod 3:6, 15 [1]Exod 3:6 12:28 [a]Matt 22:34–40; Luke 10:25–28; 20:39 12:29 [a]Deut 6:4–5; Isa 44:8; 45:22; 46:9; 1 Cor 8:6 12:30 [a][Deut 10:12; 30:6]; Luke 10:27 [1]Deut 6:4–5; Josh 22:5 LXX 12:31 [a]Lev 19:18; Matt 22:39; Gal 5:14; Jas 2:8 [b][Rom 13:9] [1]Lev 19:18 12:32 [a]Deut 4:39; Isa 45:6, 14; 46:9; [John 1:14, 17; 14:6] [1]Deut 4:35 12:33 [a][1 Sam 15:22; Hos 6:6; Mic 6:6–8; Matt 9:13; 12:7] [1]Deut 6:5 [2]Lev 19:18 12:34 [a]Matt 22:46 12:35 [a]Matt 22:41–46; Luke 20:41–44 12:36 [a]2 Sam 23:2 [b]Ps 110:1 [1]Ps 110:1

[37]If David himself calls him 'Lord,' how can he be his [a]son?" And the large crowd was listening to him with delight.

Warnings about Experts in the Law

[38][a]In his teaching Jesus also said, "Watch [b]out for the experts in the law. They like walking around in long robes and elaborate greetings in the marketplaces, [39]and the [a]best seats in the synagogues and the places of honor at banquets. [40][a]They devour widows' property,[1] and as a show make long prayers. These men will receive a more severe punishment."

The Widow's Offering

[41][a]Then he[1] sat down opposite the offering box,[2] and watched the crowd putting coins [b]into it. Many rich people were throwing in large amounts. [42]And a poor widow came and put in two small copper coins, worth less than a penny. [43]He called his disciples and said to them, "I tell you the truth, [a]this poor widow has put more into the offering box than all the others. [44]For they all gave out of their wealth. But she, out of [a]her poverty, put in what she had to live on, everything she had."

The Destruction of the Temple

13 Now [a]as Jesus was going out of the temple courts, one of his disciples said to him, "Teacher, look at these tremendous stones and buildings!" [2]Jesus said to him, "Do you see these great buildings? [a]Not one stone will be left on another. All will be torn down!"

Signs of the End of the Age

[3]So while he was sitting on the Mount of Olives opposite the temple, [a]Peter, [b]James, [c]John, and [d]Andrew asked him privately, [4]"[a]Tell us, when will these things happen? And what will be the sign that all these things are about to take place?" [5]Jesus began to say to them, "Watch out that no one misleads you. [6]Many will come in my name, saying, 'I am he,' and they will mislead many. [7]When you hear of wars and rumors of wars, do not be alarmed. These things must happen, but the end is still to come. [8]For nation will rise up in arms against nation, and [a]kingdom against kingdom. There will be earthquakes in various places, and there will be famines. [b]These are but the beginning of birth pains.

Persecution of Disciples

[9]"You must watch [a]out for yourselves. You will be handed over to councils and beaten in the synagogues. You will stand before governors and kings because of me, as a witness to them. [10]First [a]the gospel must be preached to all nations. [11]When they arrest you and hand you over for trial, do not worry about what to speak. [a]But say whatever is given you at that time, for it is not you speaking, [b]but the Holy Spirit. [12][a]Brother will hand over brother to death, and a father his child. Children will rise against parents and have them put to death. [13][a]You will be hated by everyone because of my name. But [b]the one who endures to the end will be saved.

The Abomination of Desolation

[14]"But when you see *the abomination of* [a]*desolation*[1] standing where it[2] should not be" (let the reader understand), "then those [b]in Judea must flee to the mountains. [15]The one on the roof must not come down or go inside to take anything out of his house. [16]The one in the field must not turn back to get his cloak. [17][a]Woe to those who are pregnant and to those who are nursing their babies in those days! [18]Pray that it may not be in winter. [19][a]For in those days there will be suffering unlike anything that has happened from the beginning of the creation that God created until now, or ever will happen. [20]And if the Lord had not cut short those days, no one would be saved. But because of the elect, whom he chose, he has cut them short. [21][a]Then if anyone says to you, 'Look, here is the Christ!' or 'Look, there he is!' do not believe him. [22]For false messiahs and false prophets will appear and perform signs and [a]wonders to deceive,

12:37 [a] [Acts 2:29–31]   12:38 [a] Mark 4:2   [b] Matt 23:1–7; Luke 20:45–47   12:39 [a] Luke 14:7   12:40 [a] Matt 23:14   [1] Grk. *houses, households.*   12:41 [a] Luke 21:1–4   [b] 2 Kgs 12:9   [1] Maj. MSS *Jesus.*   [2] Or *treasury.*   12:43 [a] [2 Cor 8:12]   12:44 [a] Deut 24:6; [1 John 3:17]   13:1 [a] Matt 24:1; Luke 21:5–36   13:2 [a] Luke 19:44   13:3 [a] Matt 16:18; Mark 1:16   [b] Mark 1:19   [c] Mark 1:19   [d] John 1:40   13:4 [a] Matt 24:3; Luke 21:7   13:8 [a] Hag 2:22   [b] Matt 24:8   13:9 [a] Matt 10:17–18; 24:9; Acts 12:4; [Rev 2:10]   13:10 [a] Matt 24:14   13:11 [a] Matt 10:19–22; Luke 12:11; 21:12–17   [b] Acts 2:4; 4:8, 31   13:12 [a] Mic 7:6; Matt 10:21; 24:10; Luke 21:16   13:13 [a] Matt 24:9; Luke 21:17; John 15:21   [b] Dan 12:12; Matt 10:22; 24:13; [Rev 2:10]   13:14 [a] Matt 24:15   [b] Dan 9:27; 11:31; 12:11   [1] [Dan 9:27]   [2] Or perhaps *he.*   13:17 [a] Luke 21:23   13:19 [a] Dan 9:26; 12:1; Joel 2:2; Matt 24:21; Mark 10:6   13:21 [a] Matt 24:23; Luke 17:23; 21:8   13:22 [a] Deut 13:1–3; Rev 13:13–14

if possible, the elect. [23] Be careful! I have told you everything ahead of time.

The Arrival of the Son of Man

[24] "[a] But in those days, after that suffering, *the sun will be darkened and the moon will not give its light;* [25] *the stars will be falling from heaven, and the powers in the heavens will be* [a] *shaken.*[1] [26][a] Then everyone will see *the Son of Man arriving in the clouds*[1] with great power and glory. [27] Then he will send angels and they will gather his elect from the four winds, from the ends of the earth to the ends of heaven.

The Parable of the Fig Tree

[28] "Learn this parable from the fig tree: Whenever its branch becomes tender and puts out its leaves, you [a] know that summer is near. [29] So also you, when you see these things happening, know that he is near, right at the door. [30] I tell you the truth, this generation will not pass away until all these things take place. [31] Heaven and earth will pass away, but [a] my words will never pass away.

Be Ready!

[32] "But as for that day or hour no [a] one knows it—neither the angels in heaven, nor the Son—except the [b] Father. [33] Watch [a] out! Stay alert![1] For you do not know when the time will come. [34][a] It is like a man going on a journey. He left his house and put his slaves in [b] charge, assigning to each his work, and commanded the doorkeeper to stay alert. [35] Stay [a] alert, then, because you do not know when the owner of the house will return— whether during evening, at midnight, when the rooster crows, or at dawn—[36] or else he might find you asleep when he returns suddenly. [37] What I say to you I say to everyone: Stay alert!"

The Plot against Jesus

14 [a] Two days before [b] the Passover and the Feast of Unleavened Bread, the chief priests and the experts in the law were trying to find a way to arrest Jesus by stealth and kill him. [2] For they said, "Not during the feast, so there won't be a riot among the people."

Jesus' Anointing

[3] Now while Jesus was in Bethany at the house of Simon the leper, reclining at the table, [a] a woman came with an alabaster jar of costly aromatic oil from pure nard. After breaking open the jar, she poured it on his head. [4] But some who were present indignantly said to one another, "Why this waste of expensive ointment? [5] It could have been sold for more than 300 silver [a] coins[1] and the money given to the poor!" So they spoke [b] angrily to her. [6] But Jesus said, "Leave her alone. Why are you bothering her? She has done a good service for me. [7][a] For you will always have the poor with you, and you can do good for them whenever you want. [b] But you will not always have me![1] [8] She did what she could. She anointed my body beforehand for burial. [9] I tell you the truth, wherever the gospel is [a] proclaimed in the whole world, what she has done will also be told in memory of her."

The Plan to Betray Jesus

[10][a] Then Judas Iscariot, one of the twelve, went to the chief priests to betray Jesus into their hands. [11] When they heard this, they were delighted and promised to give him money. So Judas began looking for an opportunity to betray him.

The Passover

[12][a] Now on the first day of the Feast of Unleavened Bread, when the Passover lamb is sacrificed, Jesus' disciples said to him, "Where do you want us to prepare for you to eat the Passover?" [13] He sent two of his disciples and told them, "Go into the city, and a man carrying a jar of water will meet you. Follow him. [14] Wherever he enters, tell the owner of the house, 'The Teacher says, "Where is my guest room where I may eat

13:24 [a] Zeph 1:15; Matt 24:29   **13:25** [a] Isa 13:10; 34:4; Heb 12:26; Rev 6:13   [1] [Isa 13:10; 34:4 LXX; Joel 2:10]   **13:26** [a] [Dan 7:13–14; Matt 16:27; 24:30]; Mark 14:62; Acts 1:11; [1 Thess 4:16; 2 Thess 1:7, 10]; Rev 1:7   [1] [Dan 7:13]   **13:28** [a] Matt 24:32; Luke 21:29   **13:31** [a] Isa 40:8; [2 Pet 3:7, 10, 12]   **13:32** [a] Matt 25:13   [b] Matt 24:36; Acts 1:7   **13:33** [a] Matt 24:42; 25:13; Luke 12:40; 21:34; [Rom 13:11]; 1 Thess 5:6; 1 Pet 4:7   [1] Maj. wss add *and pray.*   **13:34** [a] Matt 24:45; 25:14   [b] [Matt 16:19]   **13:35** [a] Matt 24:42, 44   **14:1** [a] Matt 26:2–5; Luke 22:1–2; John 11:55; 13:1   [b] Exod 12:1–27; Mark 14:12   **14:3** [a] Matt 26:6; Luke 7:37; John 12:1, 3   **14:5** [a] Matt 18:28; Mark 12:15   [b] Matt 20:11; John 6:61   [1] Grk. *three hundred denarii*; the denarius was a silver coin worth about a day's wage for a laborer; this would be about one year's pay.   **14:7** [a] Deut 15:11; Matt 26:11; John 12:8   [b] [John 7:33; 8:21; 14:2, 12; 16:10, 17, 28]   [1] An emphatic Grk. construction.   **14:9** [a] Matt 28:19–20; Mark 16:15; Luke 24:47   **14:10** [a] Ps 41:9; 55:12–14; Matt 10:2–4   **14:12** [a] Exod 12:8; Matt 26:17–19; Luke 22:7-13

the Passover with my disciples?'" [15]He will show you a large room upstairs, furnished and ready. Make preparations for us there." [16]So the disciples left, went into the city, and found things just as he had told them, and they prepared the Passover.

[17]Then, when it was [a]evening, he came to the house with the twelve. [18]While they were at the table eating, Jesus said, "I tell you the truth, [a]one of you eating with me will betray me." [19]They were distressed, and one by one said to him, "Surely not I?" [20]He said to them, "It is one of the twelve, one who dips his hand with me into the bowl. [21]For [a]the Son of Man will go as it is written about him, but woe to that man by whom the Son of Man is betrayed! It would be better for him if he had never been born."

The Lord's Supper

[22]While they were eating, he took bread, [a]and after giving thanks he broke it, gave it to them, and said, "Take it. This is my [b]body." [23]And after taking the cup and giving thanks, he gave it to them, and they all drank from it. [24]He said to them, "This is my blood, the blood of the covenant,[1] that is poured out for many. [25]I tell you the truth, I will no longer drink of the fruit of the vine until that day when I drink it new in the kingdom of God." [26]After singing [a]a hymn, they went out to the Mount of Olives.

The Prediction of Peter's Denial

[27][a]Then Jesus said to them, "You will all fall away, for it is written,

> **'I will strike the shepherd,**
> **and the sheep [b]will be scattered.'[1]**

[28]But [a]after I am raised, I will go ahead of you into Galilee." [29][a]Peter said to him, "Even if they all fall away, I will not!" [30]Jesus said to him, "I tell you the truth, today—this very night—before a rooster crows twice, you will deny me three times." [31]But Peter insisted emphatically, "Even if I must die with you, I will never deny you." And all of them said the same thing.

Gethsemane

[32][a]Then they went to a place called Gethsemane, and Jesus said to his disciples, "Sit here while I pray." [33]He [a]took Peter, James, and John with him, and became very troubled and distressed. [34]He said to them, "[a]My soul is deeply grieved, even to the point of death. Remain here and stay alert." [35]Going a little farther, he threw himself to the ground and prayed that if it were possible the hour would pass from him. [36]He said, "[a]Abba,[1] Father, all [b]things are possible for you. Take this cup away from me. [c]Yet not what I will, but what you will." [37]Then he came and found them sleeping, and said to Peter, "Simon, are you sleeping? Couldn't you stay awake for one hour? [38]Stay [a]awake and pray that you will not fall into temptation. [b]The spirit is willing, but the flesh is weak." [39]He went away again and prayed the same thing. [40]When he came again he found them sleeping; they could not keep their eyes open. And they did not know what to tell him. [41]He came a third time and said to [a]them, "Are you still sleeping and resting?[1] Enough of that![2] The hour has come. Look, the Son of Man is betrayed into the hands of sinners. [42]Get [a]up, let us go. Look! My betrayer is approaching!"

Betrayal and Arrest

[43]Right away, while Jesus was still speaking, Judas, one of the twelve, arrived. With him came a crowd armed with swords [a]and clubs, sent by the chief priests and experts in the law and elders. [44](Now the betrayer had given them a sign, saying, "The one I [a]kiss is the man. Arrest him and lead him away under guard.") [45]When Judas arrived, he went up to Jesus immediately and said, "Rabbi!" and kissed him. [46]Then they took hold of him and arrested him. [47]One of the bystanders drew his sword and struck the high priest's slave, cutting off his ear. [48]Jesus said to them, "Have you come with swords

14:17 [a]Matt 26:20–24; Luke 22:14, 21–23   **14:18** [a]Ps 41:9; Matt 26:46; Mark 14:42; John 6:70–71; 13:18   **14:21** [a]Matt 26:24; Luke 22:22; Acts 1:16–20   **14:22** [a]Matt 26:26–29; Luke 22:17–20; 1 Cor 11:23–25   [b][1 Pet 2:24]   **14:24** [1]Maj. MSS *new covenant.*   **14:26** [a]Matt 26:30   **14:27** [a]Matt 26:31–35; Mark 14:50; John 16:32   [b][Isa 53:5, 10]; Zech 13:7   [1]Zech 13:7   **14:28** [a]Matt 28:16; Mark 16:7; John 21:1   **14:29** [a]Matt 26:33–34; Luke 22:33–34; John 13:37–38   **14:32** [a]Matt 26:36–46; Luke 22:40–46; John 18:1   **14:33** [a]Mark 5:37; 9:2; 13:3   **14:34** [a]Isa 53:3–4; Matt 26:38; John 12:27   **14:36** [a]Rom 8:15; Gal 4:6   [b][Heb 5:7]   [c]Isa 50:5; John 5:30; 6:38   [1]Aram. *my father.*   **14:38** [a]Luke 21:36   [b][Rom 7:18, 21–24; Gal 5:17]   **14:41** [a]John 13:1; 17:1   [1]Or *Sleep on, and get your rest.*   [2]A few wss add *It is the end.*   **14:42** [a]Matt 26:46; Mark 14:18; Luke 9:44; John 13:21; 18:1–2   **14:43** [a]Ps 3:1; Matt 26:47–56; Luke 22:47–53; John 18:3–11   **14:44** [a][Prov 27:6]

[a]and clubs to arrest me like you would an outlaw? [49]Day after day I was with you, [a]teaching in [b]the temple courts, yet you did not arrest me. But this has happened so that the scriptures would be fulfilled." [50a]Then all the disciples left him and fled. [51]A young man was following him, wearing only a linen cloth. They tried to arrest him, [52]but he ran off naked, leaving his linen cloth behind.

Condemned by the Sanhedrin

[53]Then they led Jesus to the high priest, [a]and all the chief priests and elders and experts in the law came [b]together. [54]And [a]Peter had followed him from a distance, up to the high priest's courtyard. He was sitting with the guards and warming himself by the fire. [55a]The chief priests and the whole Sanhedrin were looking for evidence against Jesus so that they could put him to death, but they did not find anything. [56]Many gave [a]false testimony against him, but their testimony did not agree. [57]Some stood up and gave this false testimony against him: [58]"We heard him say, '[a]I will destroy this temple made with hands and in three days build another not made with hands.'" [59]Yet even on this point their testimony did not agree. [60]Then the high priest stood up before them [a]and asked Jesus, "Have you no answer? What is this that they are testifying against you?" [61]But [a]he was silent and did not answer. [b]Again the high priest questioned him, "Are you the Christ, the Son of the Blessed One?" [62]"I am," said Jesus, "[a]and you will see *the Son of Man sitting at the right hand*[1] of the Power and *coming with the clouds of heaven*."[2] [63]Then the high priest tore his clothes and said, "Why do we still need witnesses? [64]You have heard the [a]blasphemy! What is your verdict?" They all condemned him as deserving [b]death. [65]Then some began to spit [a]on him, and to blindfold him, and to strike him with their fists, saying, "Prophesy!" The guards also took him and beat him.

Peter's Denials

[66a]Now while Peter was below in the courtyard, one of the high priest's slave girls came by. [67]When she saw Peter warming himself, she looked directly at him and said, "You also were with that Nazarene, [a]Jesus." [68]But he denied it: "I don't even understand what you're talking about!"[1] Then he went out to the gateway, and a rooster crowed.[2] [69]When the slave girl saw him, she began again to say to the [a]bystanders, "This man is one of them." [70]But he denied it again. [a]A short time later the bystanders again said to Peter, "You must be one of them [b]because you are also a Galilean." [71]Then he began to curse, and he swore with an oath, "I do not know this man you are talking about!" [72]Immediately [a]a rooster crowed a second time. Then Peter remembered what Jesus had said to him: "Before a rooster crows twice, you will deny me three times." And he broke down and wept.

Jesus Brought before Pilate

15 Early [a]in the morning, after forming a plan, the chief priests with the elders and the experts in the law and the whole Sanhedrin tied Jesus up, led him away, and [b]handed him over to Pilate. [2]So Pilate asked him, "Are you [a]the king of the Jews?" He replied, "You say so." [3]Then the chief priests began to accuse him repeatedly. [4a]So Pilate asked him again, "Have you nothing to say? See how many charges they are bringing against you!" [5a]But Jesus made no further reply, so that Pilate was amazed.

Jesus and Barabbas

[6a]During the feast it was customary to release one prisoner to the people, whomever they requested. [7]A man named Barabbas was imprisoned with rebels who had

14:48 [a] Matt 26:55; Luke 22:52   14:49 [a] Matt 21:23   [b] Ps 22:6; Isa 53:7; Luke 22:37; 24:44   14:50 [a] Ps 88:8; Zech 13:7; Matt 26:31; Mark 14:27   14:53 [a] Matt 26:57–68; Mark 10:33; Luke 22:54; John 18:12–13, 19–24   [b] Mark 15:1   14:54 [a] John 18:15   14:55 [a] Matt 26:59   14:56 [a] Exod 20:16; Ps 27:12; 35:11; Prov 6:16–19; 19:5   14:58 [a] Matt 26:61; Mark 15:29; John 2:19; [2 Cor 5:1]   14:60 [a] Matt 26:62; Mark 15:3–5   14:61 [a] Isa 53:7; John 19:9; Acts 8:32; [1 Pet 2:23]   [b] Matt 26:63; Luke 22:67–71   14:62 [a] Matt 24:30; 26:64; Luke 22:69   [1] [Ps 110:1]   [2] [Dan 7:13]   14:64 [a] John 10:33, 36   [b] Matt 20:18; Mark 10:33; John 19:7   14:65 [a] Job 16:10; Isa 50:6; 52:14; Lam 3:30; Mark 10:34; Luke 18:32   14:66 [a] Matt 26:58, 69–75; Luke 22:55–62; John 18:16–18, 25–27   14:67 [a] Mark 10:47; John 1:45; Acts 10:38   14:68 [1] Grk. *I do not know or understand what you are saying.*   [2] Sev. sig. wss omit *and a rooster crowed.*   14:69 [a] Matt 26:71; Luke 22:58; John 18:25   14:70 [a] Matt 26:73; Luke 22:59; John 18:26   [b] Acts 2:7   14:72 [a] Matt 26:75; Mark 14:30; Luke 22:34; John 13:38   15:1 [a] Ps 2:2; Matt 27:1; Luke 22:66; 23:1; John 18:28; Acts 3:13; 4:26   [b] Luke 18:32; Acts 3:13   15:2 [a] Matt 27:11–14; Luke 23:2–3; John 18:29–38   15:4 [a] Matt 27:13   15:5 [a] Ps 38:13–14; Isa 53:7; John 19:9   15:6 [a] Matt 27:15–26; Luke 23:18–25; John 18:39–19:16

committed murder during an insurrection. [8]Then the crowd came up and began to ask Pilate to release a prisoner for them, as was his custom. [9]So Pilate asked them, "Do you want me to release the king of the Jews for you?" [10](For he knew that the chief priests had handed him over because of envy.) [11]But [a]the chief priests stirred up the crowd to have him release Barabbas instead. [12]So Pilate spoke to them again, "Then what do you want me to do[1] with the one you call [a]king of the Jews?" [13]They shouted back, "Crucify him!" [14]Pilate asked them, "Why? [a]What has he done wrong?" But they shouted more insistently, "Crucify him!" [15a]Because he wanted to satisfy the crowd, Pilate released Barabbas for them. Then, after he had Jesus flogged, he handed him over to be [b]crucified.

Jesus Is Mocked

[16]So [a]the soldiers led him into the palace (that is, the governor's residence) and called together the whole cohort. [17]They put a purple cloak on him and after braiding a crown of thorns, they put it on him. [18]They began to salute him: "Hail, king of the Jews!" [19]Again and again they [a]struck him on the head with a staff and spit on him. Then they knelt down and paid homage to him. [20]When they had finished [a]mocking him, they stripped him of the purple cloak and put his own clothes back on him. Then they led him away to crucify him.

The Crucifixion

[21]The soldiers forced a passerby to carry his cross, Simon of Cyrene, who was coming in from the country (he was the father of Alexander [a]and Rufus). [22]They brought Jesus to [a]a place called Golgotha (which is translated, "Place of the Skull"). [23]They offered him wine mixed with myrrh, but [a]he did not take it. [24]Then [a]they crucified him and *divided his clothes, throwing dice*[1,2]

for them, to decide what each would take. [25]It was nine o'clock in the morning when they crucified him. [26]The inscription of [a]the charge against him read, "The king of the Jews." [27]And they crucified two outlaws [a]with him, one on his right and one on his left.[1] [29]Those who passed by defamed him, [a]shaking their heads and saying, "Aha! [b]You who can destroy the temple and rebuild it in three days, [30]save yourself and come down from the cross!" [31]In the same way even the chief priests—together with the experts in the law—were [a]mocking him among themselves: "He saved [b]others, but he cannot save himself! [32]Let the Christ, the king of Israel, come down from the cross now, that we may see and believe!" [a]Those who were crucified with him also spoke abusively to him.

Jesus' Death

[33]Now [a]when it was noon, darkness came over the whole land until three in the afternoon. [34]Around three o'clock Jesus cried out with a loud voice, "*Eloi, Eloi, lema sabachthani?*" which means, "[a]***My God, my God, why have you forsaken me?***"[1] [35]When some of the bystanders heard it they said, "Listen, he is calling for Elijah!" [36]Then [a]someone ran, filled a sponge with sour wine, put it on a stick, and gave it to him to drink, saying, "Leave him alone! Let's see if Elijah will come to take him down!" [37]But Jesus cried out with [a]a loud voice and breathed his last. [38]And [a]the temple curtain[1] was torn in two, from top to bottom. [39]Now [a]when the centurion, who stood in front of him, saw how he died,[1] he said, "Truly this man was God's Son!" [40]There were also women, watching from a distance. Among them were Mary Magdalene, and Mary [a]the mother of James the younger and of Joses, and Salome. [41]When he was in Galilee, they had [a]followed him and given him support. Many other women who had come up with him to Jerusalem were there too.

15:11 [a] Matt 27:20; Acts 3:14   **15:12** [a] Ps 2:6; [Isa 9:7]; Jer 23:5; 33:15; Mic 5:2   [1] Sev. sig. wss *What should I do?*   **15:14** [a] Isa 53:9; John 8:46; 1 Pet 2:21–23   **15:15** [a] Isa 50:6; Matt 27:26; Mark 10:34; John 19:1, 16   [b] [Isa 53:8]   **15:16** [a] Matt 27:27–31   **15:19** [a] [Isa 50:6; 52:14; 53:5]; Mic 5:1; Mark 14:65   **15:20** [a] Ps 35:16; 69:19; Isa 53:3; Matt 20:19; Mark 10:34; Luke 22:63; 23:11   **15:21** [a] Matt 27:32; Luke 23:26   **15:22** [a] Matt 27:33–44; Luke 23:33–43; John 19:17–24; Heb 13:12   **15:23** [a] Ps 69:21; Matt 27:34   **15:24** [a] Ps 22:18; Luke 23:34; John 19:23   [1] [Ps 22:18]   [2] Grk. *by throwing the lot.*   **15:26** [a] Matt 27:37; John 19:19   **15:27** [a] Isa 53:9, 12; Matt 27:38; Luke 22:37   [1] Maj. later mss add v. 28: *And the scripture was fulfilled that says, "He was counted with the lawless ones."*   **15:29** [a] Ps 109:25   [b] Mark 14:58; John 2:19–21   **15:31** [a] Luke 18:32   [b] Luke 7:14–15; John 11:43–44   **15:32** [a] Matt 27:44; Luke 23:39   **15:33** [a] Amos 8:9; Matt 27:45–56; Luke 23:44–49   **15:34** [a] Ps 22:1; Matt 27:46   [1] Ps 22:1   **15:36** [a] Matt 27:48; John 19:29   **15:37** [a] Dan 9:26; Zech 11:10–11; Matt 27:50; Mark 8:31; Luke 23:46; John 19:30   **15:38** [a] Exod 26:31–33; Matt 27:51; Luke 23:45   [1] Either the curtain separating the Holy of Holies from the Holy Place or the one at the entrance of the temple court.   **15:39** [a] Matt 27:54; Luke 23:47   [1] Grk. *the way he breathed his last, the way he expired, that he thus breathed no more.*   **15:40** [a] Matt 27:55; Luke 23:49; John 19:25   **15:41** [a] Luke 8:2–3

Jesus' Burial

42 Now when evening had [a]already come, since it was the day of preparation (that is, the day before the Sabbath), 43 Joseph of Arimathea, [a]a highly regarded member of the council,[1] who was himself looking forward to the kingdom of God, went boldly to Pilate and asked for the body of Jesus. 44 Pilate was surprised that he was already dead. He called the centurion and asked him if he had been dead for some time. 45 When Pilate was informed by the centurion, he gave the body to Joseph. 46 After Joseph bought a linen cloth and took down the body, he wrapped it in the linen and placed it in a tomb cut out of the rock. [a]Then he rolled a stone across the entrance of the tomb. 47 Mary Magdalene and Mary the mother of Joses saw where the body was placed.

The Resurrection

16 When the Sabbath was over, Mary Magdalene, Mary the mother of James, and Salome [a]bought aromatic spices so that they might go and anoint him. 2 And [a]very early on the first day of the week, at sunrise, they went to the tomb. 3 They had been asking each other, "Who will roll away the stone for us from the entrance to the tomb?" 4 But when they looked up, they saw that the stone, which was very large, had been rolled back. 5 Then as they went into the tomb, they saw a young man dressed in a white robe sitting on the right side; [a]and they were alarmed. 6 [a]But he said to them, "Do not be alarmed. You are looking for Jesus the Nazarene, who was crucified. He has been raised!" He is not here. Look, there is the place where they laid him. 7 But go, tell his disciples, even Peter, that he is going ahead of you into Galilee. You will see him there, just [a]as he told you." 8 Then they went out and ran from the tomb, for terror [a]and bewilderment had seized them. And they said nothing to anyone, because they were afraid.

The Longer Ending of Mark[1]

9 [[Early on the first day of the week, after he arose, he appeared first to Mary Magdalene, from whom he had driven [a]out seven demons. 10 [a]She went out and told those who were with him, while they were mourning and weeping. 11 And when they heard that he was alive [a]and had been seen by her, they did not believe.

12 After this he appeared in a different form [a]to two of them while they were on their way to the country. 13 They went back and told the rest, but they did not believe them. 14 [a]Then he appeared to the Eleven themselves, while they were eating, and he rebuked them for their unbelief and hardness of heart because they did not believe those who had seen him resurrected. 15 He said to them, "Go into all the world [a]and preach the gospel to every creature. 16 [a]The one who believes and is baptized will be saved, [b]but the one who does not believe will be condemned. 17 These [a]signs will accompany those who believe: [b]In my name [c]they will drive out demons; they will speak in new languages; 18 they will pick up snakes with their hands, and whatever poison [a]they drink will not harm them; [b]they will place their hands on the sick and they will be well." 19 [a]After the Lord Jesus had spoken to them, he was taken [b]up into heaven and sat [c]down at the right hand of God. 20 They went out and proclaimed everywhere, while the Lord worked with them [a]and confirmed the word through the accompanying signs.]]

15:42 [a]Matt 27:57–61; Luke 23:50–56; John 19:38–42   **15:43** [a]Matt 27:57; Luke 2:25, 38; 23:51; John 19:38   [1]Grk. *a councillor;* a member of the Sanhedrin.   **15:46** [a]Isa 53:9; Matt 27:59–60; Luke 23:53; John 19:40   **16:1** [a]Luke 23:56; John 19:39   **16:2** [a]Luke 24:1; John 20:1   **16:5** [a]Luke 24:3; John 20:11–12   **16:6** [a]Ps 16:10; 49:15; Hos 6:2; Matt 28:6; Mark 9:31; Luke 24:6   [1]A "divine passive," with God understood as the actor.   **16:7** [a]Matt 26:32; 28:16–17; Mark 14:28   **16:8** [a]Matt 28:8   **16:9** [a]Luke 8:2   [1]Mark ends at v. 8 in some MSS, including two of the most respected ones. Other MSS supply a shorter ending: *They reported briefly to those around Peter all that they had been commanded. After these things Jesus himself sent out through them, from the east to the west, the holy and imperishable preaching of eternal salvation. Amen.* Some MSS supply both endings. For a discussion on this matter, see *NET Bible, Full Notes Edition.*   **16:10** [a]Luke 24:10   **16:11** [a]Matt 28:17; Luke 24:11, 41; John 20:25   **16:12** [a]Luke 24:13–35   **16:14** [a]Luke 24:36; John 20:19, 26; 1 Cor 15:5   **16:15** [a]Matt 28:19; [John 15:16; Acts 1:8]; Col 1:6   **16:16** [a][John 3:18, 36; Acts 2:38; 16:30–31; Rom 10:8–10]   [b][John 12:48]   **16:17** [a]Acts 5:12   [b]Mark 9:38; Luke 10:17; Acts 5:16; 8:7; 16:18; 19:12   [c][Acts 2:4; 1 Cor 12:10]   **16:18** [a][Luke 10:19]; Acts 28:3–6   [b][Acts 5:15]; Jas 5:14   **16:19** [a]Acts 1:2–3   [b]Ps 68:18; Luke 9:51; 24:51; John 6:62; 20:17; Acts 1:2, 9–11; [1 Tim 3:16; Rev 4:2]   [c][Ps 110:1]; Luke 22:69; [Acts 7:55]; 1 Pet 3:22   **16:20** [a]Acts 5:12; [1 Cor 2:4–5; Heb 2:4]

LUKE

Luke, a physician, writes with the compassion and warmth of a family doctor as he carefully documents the perfect humanity of the Son of Man, Jesus Christ. Luke emphasizes Jesus' ancestry, birth, and early life before moving carefully and chronologically through his earthly ministry. Belief and opposition develop side by side. Those who believe are challenged to count the cost of discipleship. Those who oppose will not be satisfied until the Son of Man hangs lifeless on a cross. But the resurrection ensures that his purpose will be fulfilled: "To seek and to save the lost" (19:10). *Kata Loukan*, "According to Luke," is the ancient title that was added to this gospel at a very early date. The Greek name *Luke* appears only three times in the New Testament (Col 4:14; 2 Tim 4:11; Phlm v. 24).

Explanatory Preface

1 Now many have undertaken to compile an account of the [a]things that have been fulfilled among us, [2]like the accounts passed [a]on to us by those who were [b]eyewitnesses and servants of the word [c]from the beginning.[1] [3]So it seemed good to me as well, because I have followed all things carefully from the beginning, to write an orderly account for you, [a]most excellent Theophilus, [4]so [a]that you may know for certain[1] the things you were taught.[2]

Birth Announcement of John the Baptist

[5]During the reign of Herod [a]king of Judea, there lived a priest named Zechariah who belonged [b]to the priestly division of [c]Abijah, and he had a [d]wife named Elizabeth, who was a descendant of Aaron. [6]They were both righteous in the sight of God, following[1] all the commandments and ordinances of the Lord blamelessly. [7]But they did not have a child because Elizabeth was barren, and they were both very old.

[8]Now while Zechariah was serving as priest before God when his division was on duty, [9]he was chosen by lot, according [a]to the custom of the priesthood, to enter the Holy Place[1] of the Lord and burn incense. [10a]Now the whole crowd of people were praying outside at the hour of the incense offering. [11]An angel of [a]the Lord, standing on the right side of the altar of incense, appeared to him. [12]And Zechariah, visibly shaken [a]when he saw the angel, was seized with fear. [13]But the angel said to him, "Do not be afraid, Zechariah, for [a]your prayer has been heard, and your wife Elizabeth will bear you a son; you will name him John. [14]Joy and gladness will come to you, and [a]many will rejoice at his birth, [15]for he will be [a]great in the sight of the Lord. He must never drink wine or strong drink, and he will be filled with the Holy Spirit, [b]even before his birth.[1] [16]He will turn many of the people of Israel to the Lord their God. [17]And [a]he will go as forerunner before the Lord in the spirit and power of Elijah, to turn the hearts of the fathers back to their children and the disobedient to the wisdom of the just, to make ready for the Lord a people prepared for him."

[18]Zechariah said to the angel, "[a]How can

1:1 [a] John 20:31   **1:2** [a] Acts 1:3; 10:39; Heb 2:3; 1 Pet 5:1; 2 Pet 1:16; 1 John 1:1   [b] Acts 1:2   [c] Mark 1:1; John 15:27; Acts 1:21–22   [1] Grk. *those who from the beginning were eyewitnesses*; emphasizes they were with Jesus from the start.   **1:3** [a] Acts 1:1   **1:4** [a] [John 20:31]   [1] Or *know the truth about, know the certainty of*.   [2] Or *you heard about*; either information or instruction, likely the latter, meaning Theophilus was probably a believer.   **1:5** [a] Matt 2:1   [b] 1 Chr 24:1, 10   [c] Neh 12:4   [d] Lev 21:13–14   **1:6** [1] Grk. *walking in*; an idiom for lifestyle.   **1:9** [a] Exod 30:7–8; 1 Chr 23:13; 2 Chr 29:11   [1] Or *temple*.   **1:10** [a] Lev 16:17   **1:11** [a] Exod 30:1   **1:12** [a] Judg 6:22; Dan 10:8; Luke 2:9; Acts 10:4; Rev 1:17   **1:13** [a] Luke 1:57, 60, 63   **1:14** [a] Luke 1:58   **1:15** [a] [Luke 7:24–28]   [b] Jer 1:5; Gal 1:15   [1] Grk. *even from his mother's womb*; the idiom may refer to the point of birth but Luke 1:41 suggests it refers to a time before birth.   **1:17** [a] Mal 4:5–6; Matt 3:2; 11:14; Mark 1:4; 9:12   **1:18** [a] Gen 17:17

I be sure of this? For I am an old man, and my wife is old as well." [19]The angel answered him, "I am [a]Gabriel, who stands [b]in the presence of God, and I was sent to speak to you and to bring you this good news. [20]And now because [a]you did not believe my words, which will be fulfilled in their time, you will be silent, unable to speak, until the day these things take place."

[21]Now the people were waiting for Zechariah, and they began to wonder why he was delayed in the Holy Place. [22]When he came out, he was not able to speak to them. They realized that he had seen a vision in the Holy Place because he was making signs to them and remained unable to speak. [23]When his time of service was over, [a]he went to his home.

[24]After some time his wife Elizabeth became pregnant, and for five months she kept herself in seclusion. She said, [25]"This is what the Lord has done for me at the time when he has been gracious to me, to [a]take away my disgrace among people."

Birth Announcement of Jesus the Messiah

[26]In the sixth month of Elizabeth's pregnancy, the angel Gabriel was sent by God to a town of Galilee called Nazareth, [27]to a virgin [a]engaged to a man whose name was Joseph, a descendant of David, and the virgin's name was Mary. [28]The angel came to her and said, "[a]Greetings, favored one,[1] [b]the Lord is with you!"[2] [29]But[1] [a]she was greatly troubled by his words and began to wonder about the meaning of this greeting. [30]So the angel said to her, "Do not be afraid, Mary, for you have found [a]favor with God! [31]Listen: You will become pregnant [a]and give birth to [b]a son, and you will name him Jesus. [32]He will be great [a]and will be called [b]the Son of the Most High, and the Lord God will give him the [c]throne of his [d]father David. [33]He will reign over the house of Jacob forever, [a]and his kingdom will never end." [34]Mary said to the angel, "How will this be, since I have not been intimate with a man?" [35]The angel replied, "[a]The Holy Spirit will come upon you, and [b]the power of the Most High will overshadow you. Therefore the child to be born[1] will be holy; he will be called the Son of God.

[36]"And look, your relative[1] Elizabeth has also become pregnant with a son in her old age—although she was called barren, she is now in her sixth month! [37]For nothing[1] will be impossible [a]with God." [38]So Mary said, "Yes, I am a servant of the Lord; let this happen to me according to your word." Then the angel departed from her.

Mary and Elizabeth

[39]In those days Mary got up and went hurriedly into the hill country, [a]to a town of Judah, [40]and entered Zechariah's house and greeted Elizabeth. [41]When Elizabeth heard Mary's greeting, the baby leaped in her womb, and Elizabeth was [a]filled with the Holy Spirit. [42]She exclaimed with a loud voice, "[a]Blessed are you among women, and blessed is the child in your womb! [43]And who am I that the mother of my Lord should come and visit me? [44]For the instant the sound of your greeting reached my ears, the baby in my womb leaped for joy. [45]And [a]blessed is she who believed that what was spoken to her by the Lord would be fulfilled."

Mary's Hymn of Praise

[46]And Mary[1] said,

"[a]My soul exalts the Lord,
[47] and my spirit has begun to [a]rejoice in
  [b]God my Savior,
[48] because [a]he has looked upon the
  humble state of his servant.
  For from now on [b]all generations will
  call me blessed,
[49] because he who is mighty [a]has done
  great things for me, and [b]holy is
  his name;

1:19 [a]Dan 8:16; [Matt 18:10]; Heb 1:4   [b]Luke 2:10   1:20 [a]Ezek 3:26; 24:27   1:23 [a]2 Kgs 11:5; 1 Chr 9:25   1:25 [a]Gen 30:23; Isa 4:1; 54:1, 4   1:27 [a]Matt 1:18; Luke 2:4–5   1:28 [a]Dan 9:23   [b]Judg 6:12   [1]Grk. *Oh one who is favored*; points to a recipient of God's grace, not a bestower of it.   [2]Maj. MSS add *blessed are you among women.*   1:29 [a]Luke 1:12   [1]Maj. MSS *when [she] saw [the angel].*   1:30 [a]Luke 2:52   1:31 [a]Isa 7:14; Matt 1:21, 25; Gal 4:4   [b]Luke 2:21; [Phil 2:9–11]   1:32 [a]Matt 3:17; 17:5; Mark 5:7; Luke 1:35, 76; 6:35; Acts 7:48   [b]2 Sam 7:12–13, 16; Ps 132:11; [Isa 9:6–7; 16:5; Jer 23:5]   [c]2 Sam 7:14–17; Acts 2:33; 7:55   [d]Matt 1:1   1:33 [a][Dan 2:44; Obad 21; Mic 4:7]; John 12:34; [Heb 1:8]; 2 Pet 1:11   1:35 [a]Matt 1:20   [b]Ps 2:7; Matt 3:17; 14:33; 17:5; Mark 1:1; John 1:34; 20:31; Acts 8:37; [Rom 1:1–4; Heb 1:2, 8]   [1]Some MSS add *by you.*   1:36 [1]Or *cousin;* the term is not necessarily this specific.   1:37 [a]Gen 18:14; Jer 32:17; Matt 19:26; Mark 10:27; Rom 4:21   [1]An emphatic Grk. construction.   1:39 [a]Josh 21:9   1:41 [a]Acts 6:3   1:42 [a]Judg 5:24   1:45 [a]John 20:29   1:46 [a]1 Sam 2:1–10; Ps 34:2–3; Hab 3:18   [1]Some WSS *Elizabeth.*   1:47 [a]Ps 35:9; Hab 3:18   [b]1 Tim 1:1; 2:3; Titus 1:3; 2:10; 3:4; Jude 25   1:48 [a]1 Sam 1:11; Ps 138:6   [b]Luke 11:27   1:49 [a]Ps 71:19; 126:2–3   [b]Ps 111:9; Rev 4:8

[50] from generation to generation [a]he is merciful to those who fear him.

[51] He has demonstrated power with his arm; [a]he has scattered those whose pride wells up from [b]the sheer arrogance of their hearts.

[52] He has brought down [a]the mighty from their thrones, and has lifted up those of lowly position;

[53] he has [a]filled the hungry with good things, and has sent the rich away empty.

[54] He has helped his [a]servant Israel, [b]remembering his mercy,

[55] [a]as he promised[1] to our [b]ancestors, to Abraham and to his [c]descendants forever."

[56]So Mary stayed with Elizabeth about three months and then returned to her home.

The Birth of John

[57]Now the time came for Elizabeth to have her baby, and she gave birth to a son. [58]Her neighbors and relatives heard that the Lord had shown great mercy to her, and they rejoiced[1] [a]with her.

[59a]On the eighth day they came to circumcise the child, and they wanted to name him Zechariah after his father. [60]But his mother replied, "[a]No! He must be named John." [61]They said to her, "But none of your relatives bears this name." [62]So they made signs to the baby's father, inquiring what he wanted to name his son. [63]He asked for a writing tablet and wrote, "His name is John." And they were all amazed. [64]Immediately Zechariah's mouth was opened and his tongue released, and he spoke, blessing God. [65]All their neighbors were filled with fear, and throughout the entire hill country of Judea all these things were talked about. [66]All who heard these things [a]kept [b]them in their hearts,[1] saying, "What then will this child be?" For the Lord's hand was indeed with him.

Zechariah's Praise and Prediction

[67]Then his father Zechariah [a]was filled with the Holy Spirit and prophesied,

[68] "[a]Blessed be [b]the Lord God of Israel, because he has come to help and has redeemed his people.

[69] For he has raised up [a]a horn of salvation for us in the house of his servant David,

[70] [a]as he spoke through the mouth of his holy prophets [b]from long ago,

[71] that we should be saved from our enemies and from the hand of all who hate us.

[72] He has done this [a]to show mercy to our ancestors,[1] and to remember his holy covenant—

[73] the oath that [a]he swore to our ancestor Abraham.

This oath grants

[74] that we, being rescued from the hand of our[1] enemies, may [a]serve him without fear,

[75] [a]in holiness and righteousness before him for as long as we live.

[76] And you, child, will be called the [a]prophet[1] of the Most High. For [b]you will go before[2] the Lord to prepare his ways,

[77] to give his people [a]knowledge of salvation through the forgiveness of their sins.

[78] Because of our God's tender mercy, the dawn will break upon us from on high

[79] to give light [a]to those who sit in darkness and in the shadow of death, to [b]guide our feet into the way of peace."

[80]And [a]the child kept growing and becoming strong in spirit, and he [b]was in the wilderness until the day he was revealed to Israel.

1:50 [a]Gen 17:7; Exod 20:6; 34:6–7; Ps 103:17   1:51 [a]Ps 98:1; 118:15; Isa 40:10   [b]Ps 33:10; [1 Pet 5:5]   1:52 [a]1 Sam 2:7–8   1:53 [a][Matt 5:6]   1:54 [a]Isa 41:8   [b]Ps 98:3; [Jer 31:3]   1:55 [a]Gen 17:19; Ps 132:11; [Gal 3:16]   [b][Rom 11:28]   [c]Gen 17:7   [1]Grk. as he spoke.   1:58 [a][Rom 12:15]   [1]Or they began to rejoice.   1:59 [a]Gen 17:12; Lev 12:3; Luke 2:21; Phil 3:5   1:60 [a]Luke 1:13, 63   1:66 [a]Luke 2:19   [b]Gen 39:2; Acts 11:21   [1]Or kept them in mind, thought about; the context is clearly emotive, suggesting more than merely thinking or reasoning.   1:67 [a]Joel 2:28   1:68 [a]1 Kgs 1:48; Ps 106:48   [b]Exod 3:16   1:69 [a]2 Sam 22:3; Ps 132:17; Ezek 29:21   1:70 [a]Jer 23:5; Rom 1:2   [b]Acts 3:21   1:72 [a]Lev 26:42   [1]Or our forefathers; Grk. our fathers.   1:73 [a]Gen 12:3; 22:16–18; [Heb 6:13]   1:74 [a][Rom 6:18; Heb 9:14]   [1]Many sig. mss omit our.   1:75 [a]Jer 32:39; [Eph 4:24; 2 Thess 2:13]   1:76 [a]Matt 3:3; 11:9; Mark 3:2–3; Luke 3:4; John 1:23   [b]Isa 40:3; Mal 3:1; Matt 11:10   [1]Or a prophet.   [2]Maj. mss before the face of the Lord.   1:77 [a][Jer 31:34; Mark 1:4]; Luke 3:3   1:79 [a]Isa 9:2; Matt 4:16; [Acts 26:18; 2 Cor 4:6; Eph 5:14]   [b][John 10:4; 14:27; 16:33]   1:80 [a]Luke 2:40   [b]Matt 3:1

The Census and the Birth of Jesus

2 Now in those days a decree went out from Caesar[1] Augustus to register all the empire[2] for taxes. [2][a]This was the first registration, taken when Quirinius was governor of Syria. [3]Everyone went to his own town to be registered. [4]So Joseph also went up from [a]the town of Nazareth in Galilee to Judea, to the city of David called Bethlehem, [b]because he was of the house and family line of David. [5]He went to be registered with Mary, who was promised in marriage to [a]him,[1] and who was expecting a child. [6]While they were there, the time came for her to deliver her child. [7]And [a]she gave birth to her firstborn son and wrapped him in strips of cloth and laid him in a manger,[1] because there was no place for them in the inn.[2]

The Shepherds' Visit

[8]Now there were shepherds nearby living out in the field, keeping guard over their flock at night. [9]An angel of the Lord appeared to them, [a]and the glory of the Lord shone around them, and they were absolutely terrified.[1] [10]But the angel said to them, "[a]Do not be afraid! Listen carefully, for I proclaim to you good news [b]that brings great joy to all the people: [11][a]Today your [b]Savior is born in the city of David. He is Christ the Lord. [12]This will be a sign for you: You will find a baby wrapped in strips of cloth and lying in a manger." [13]Suddenly a vast, heavenly army appeared with the angel, praising God [a]and saying,

[14] "[a]Glory to God in the highest,
and on earth [b]peace among people
with whom he is [c]pleased!"[1]

[15]When the angels left them and went back to heaven, the shepherds said to one another, "Let us go over to Bethlehem and see this thing that has taken place, that the Lord has made known to us." [16]So they hurried off and located Mary and Joseph, and found the baby lying in a manger. [17]When they saw him, they related what they had been told about this child, [18]and all who heard it were astonished[1] at what the shepherds said. [19][a]But Mary treasured up all these words, pondering in her heart what they might mean. [20]So the shepherds returned, glorifying and [a]praising God for all they had heard and seen; everything was just as they had been told.

[21][a]At the end of eight days, when he was circumcised, he was named [b]Jesus, the name given by the angel [c]before he was conceived in the womb.

Jesus' Presentation at the Temple

[22]Now when [a]the time came for their[1] purification according to the law of Moses, Joseph and Mary brought Jesus up to Jerusalem to present him to the Lord [23](just [a]as it is written in the law of the Lord, "[b]Every firstborn male will be set apart to the Lord"[1]), [24]and to offer [a]a sacrifice according to what is specified in the law of the Lord, *a pair of doves or two young pigeons*.[1]

The Prophecy of Simeon

[25]Now there was a man in Jerusalem named Simeon who was righteous and devout, looking [a]for the restoration of Israel, and the Holy Spirit was upon him. [26]It had been revealed to him by the Holy Spirit that he would not die before he had [a]seen the Lord's Christ. [27]So Simeon, directed [a]by the Spirit,[1] came into the temple courts, and when the parents brought in the child Jesus to do for him what was customary according to the law, [28]Simeon took him in his arms and blessed God, saying,

[29] "[a]Now, according to your word,
Sovereign Lord, permit your
servant[1] to depart in peace.

2:1 [1]Or *from the emperor*; "Caesar" is a title for the Roman emperor.   [2]Grk. *the whole* (inhabited) *world*; i.e., the Roman Empire.   2:2 [a]Dan 9:25; Acts 5:37   2:4 [a]1 Sam 16:1; Mic 5:2   [b]Matt 1:16   2:5 [a][Matt 1:18]   [1]Trad. *Mary, his betrothed*.   2:7 [a]Matt 1:25; Luke 1:31   [1]Or *a feeding trough*.   [2]Refers to a variety of places for lodging.   2:9 [a]Luke 1:12   [1]Grk. *they feared a great fear*; an idiom of intensity.   2:10 [a]Luke 1:13, 30   [b]Gen 12:3; Isa 49:6; [Matt 28:19; Mark 1:15; Col 1:23]   2:11 [a]Isa 9:6   [b]Matt 1:21; John 4:42; [Acts 5:31]   2:13 [a]Gen 28:12; Ps 103:20; 148:2; Dan 7:10; [Heb 1:14]; Rev 5:11   2:14 [a]Matt 21:9; Luke 19:38; Eph 1:6   [b]Isa 57:19; [Rom 5:1]; Eph 2:17; [Col 1:20]   [c][John 3:16; Eph 2:4, 7; 2 Thess 2:16; 1 John 4:9]   [1]Maj. wss *good will among people*.   2:18 [1]Grk. *marveled*; a mixture of amazement and pondering.   2:19 [a]Gen 37:11; Luke 1:66   2:20 [a]Luke 19:37   2:21 [a]Gen 17:12; Lev 12:3   [b][Matt 1:21]   [c]Luke 1:31   2:22 [a]Lev 12:2–8   [1]Some MSS *her*.   2:23 [a]Exod 13:12; 22:29; Lev 27:26; Deut 18:4; Neh 10:36   [b]Exod 13:2, 12, 15; Num 3:13; 8:17   [1][Exod 13:2, 12, 15]   2:24 [a]Lev 12:2, 8   [1]Lev 12:8; 5:11 LXX   2:25 [a]Isa 40:1; Mark 15:43; Luke 2:38; 23:51   2:26 [a]Ps 89:48; [John 8:51; Heb 11:5]   2:27 [a]Matt 4:1   [1]Grk. *So in the Spirit, So by the Spirit*.   2:29 [a]Gen 46:30; [Phil 1:23]   [1]Grk. *slave*; translated as "servant" in an honorific sense for one specially chosen and appointed to carry out the Lord's tasks.

30 For my eyes [a]have seen your
   salvation
31 that you have prepared in the
   presence of all peoples:
32 a light,
   for [a]revelation to the Gentiles
   and for glory to your people Israel."

33 So the child's father[1] and mother were amazed at what was said about him. 34 Then Simeon blessed them and said to his mother Mary, "Listen carefully: This child is destined to be the cause of the [a]falling [b]and rising of many in Israel and to be a sign that will be rejected. 35 Indeed, [a]as a result of him the thoughts of many hearts will be revealed—and a sword will pierce your own soul as well!"

The Testimony of Anna

36 There was also a prophetess, Anna the daughter of Phanuel, of the tribe of [a]Asher. She was very old,[1] having been married to her husband for seven years until his death. 37 She had lived as a widow since then for eighty-four years. She never left the temple, worshiping with fasting and prayer [a]night and day. 38 At that moment, she came up to them and began to give thanks to God and to speak about the child to all who were waiting [a]for the redemption of Jerusalem.[1]

39 So when Joseph and Mary had performed everything according to the law of the Lord, they returned to Galilee, to their own town of Nazareth. 40[a]And the child grew and became strong,[1] filled with wisdom, and the favor of God was upon him.

Jesus in the Temple

41 Now Jesus' parents went to [a]Jerusalem [b]every year for the Feast of the Passover. 42 When he was twelve years old, they went up[1] according to [a]custom. 43 But [a]when the feast was over, as they were returning home, the boy Jesus stayed behind in Jerusalem. His parents[1] did not know it, 44 but (because

they assumed that he was in their group of travelers) they went a day's journey. Then they began to look for him among their relatives and acquaintances. 45 When they did not find him, they returned to Jerusalem to look for him. 46 After three days they found him in the temple courts, sitting among the teachers, listening to them and asking them questions. 47 And [a]all who heard Jesus were astonished at his understanding and his answers. 48 When his parents saw him, they were overwhelmed. His mother said to him, "Child, why have you treated[1] us like this? Look, your father and I have been looking for you anxiously." 49 But he replied, "Why were you looking for me? Didn't you know that I must be [a]in [b]my Father's house?"[1] 50 Yet his [a]parents did not understand the remark he made to them. 51 Then he went down with them and came to Nazareth, and was obedient to them. But his mother [a]kept all these things in her heart.

52 And Jesus [a]increased[1] in wisdom and in stature [b]and in favor with God and with people.

The Ministry of John the Baptist

3 In the fifteenth year of the reign of Tiberius Caesar,[1] when [a]Pontius Pilate was governor of Judea, and Herod was tetrarch of Galilee, and his brother Philip was tetrarch of the region of Iturea and Trachonitis, and Lysanias was tetrarch of Abilene, 2 during the high priesthood of [a]Annas and Caiaphas, the word of God came to [b]John the son of Zechariah in the wilderness. 3 He went into all the region around the Jordan River, preaching [a]a baptism of repentance [b]for the forgiveness of sins.

4 As it is written in [a]the book of the words of the prophet Isaiah,

*"The voice of one shouting in the
   wilderness:*
'*Prepare the way for the Lord,
   make[1] his paths straight.*

2:30 [a]Ps 119:166, 174; [Isa 52:10; Luke 3:6]   2:32 [a]Isa 9:2; 42:6; 49:6; 60:1–3; Matt 4:16; Acts 10:45; 13:47; 28:28; [Rom 9:24; Gal 3:14]   2:33 [1]Maj. mss *Joseph.*   2:34 [a]Isa 8:14; Hos 14:9; Matt 21:44; [Rom 9:32]; 1 Cor 1:23; [2 Cor 2:16; 1 Pet 2:7–8]   [b]Matt 28:12–15; Acts 4:2; 17:32; 28:22; [1 Pet 2:12; 4:14]   2:35 [a]Ps 42:10; John 19:25   2:36 [a]Josh 19:24   [1]Grk. *she was very old in her many days.*   2:37 [a]Acts 26:7; 1 Tim 5:5   2:38 [a]Lam 3:25–26; Mark 15:43; Luke 24:21   [1]Some mss *Israel.*   2:40 [a]Luke 1:80; 2:52; [1 Cor 1:24, 30]   [1]Maj. mss add *in spirit.*   2:41 [a]John 4:20   [b]Exod 23:15, 17; 34:23; Deut 16:1, 16; Luke 22:15   2:42 [a]Exod 23:14–15   [1]Maj. mss add *to Jerusalem.*   2:43 [a]Exod 12:15   [1]Maj. mss [both] *Joseph and his mother.*   2:47 [a]Matt 7:28; 13:54; 22:33; Mark 1:22; 6:2; 11:18; Luke 4:32; John 7:15   2:48 [1]Or *Child, why did you do this to us?*   2:49 [a]John 9:4   [b][Mark 1:22; Luke 4:22, 32; John 4:34; 5:17, 36]   [1]Or *I must be about my Father's business.*   2:50 [a]Mark 9:32; Luke 9:45; 18:34; John 7:15, 46   2:51 [a]Dan 7:28   2:52 [a][Isa 11:2–3; Col 2:2–3]   [b]1 Sam 2:26; [Prov 3:1–4]   [1]Or *kept increasing.*   3:1 [a]Matt 27:2   [1]Or *Emperor Tiberius*; "Caesar" is a title for the Roman emperor.   3:2 [a]John 11:49; 18:13; Acts 4:6   [b]Luke 1:13   3:3 [a]Matt 3:1; Mark 1:4   [b]Luke 1:77   3:4 [a]Isa 40:3–5; Matt 3:3; Mark 1:3   [1]Probably an allusion to repentance.

5 *Every valley will be filled,*
    and every mountain and hill will be
        brought low,
    and the crooked will be made straight,
    and the rough ways will be made
        smooth,
6 *and [a]all humanity will see the*
        salvation of God."[1]

7 So John said to the crowds that came out to be baptized by him, "You [a]offspring of vipers! Who warned you to flee from the coming wrath? [8]Therefore produce fruit that [a]proves your repentance, and don't begin to say[1] to yourselves, 'We have Abraham as our father.' For I tell you that God can raise up children for Abraham from these stones! [9]Even now the ax is laid at the root of the trees, and [a]every tree that does not produce good fruit will be cut down and thrown into the fire."

10 So the crowds were asking him, "[a]What then should we do?" [11]John answered [a]them, "The person who has two tunics must share with the person who has none, and the person who has food must do likewise." [12]Tax collectors also came to be baptized, and they said to him, "Teacher, what should we do?" [13]He told them, "[a]Collect no more than you are required to." [14]Then some soldiers also asked him, "And as for us—what should we do?" He told them, "Take money from no one by violence [a]or by false accusation, and be content with your pay."

15 While the people were filled with anticipation and they all wondered whether perhaps John could be the Christ, [16]John answered them all, "[a]I [b]baptize you with water,[1] but one more powerful than I am is coming—I am not worthy to untie the strap of his sandals. He will baptize you with the Holy Spirit and fire. [17]His winnowing fork is in his hand to clean out his threshing floor and to [a]gather the wheat into his storehouse, but the chaff he will burn up with inextinguishable fire."

18 And in this way, with many other exhortations, John proclaimed good news to the people. [19a]But when John rebuked Herod the tetrarch because of Herodias, his brother's wife,[1] and because of all the evil deeds that he had done, [20]Herod added this to them all: He locked up John in prison.

The Baptism of Jesus

21 Now when all the people were baptized, Jesus also was baptized. And while he was praying, the heavens opened, [22]and the Holy Spirit descended on him in bodily form like a dove. And a voice came from heaven, "You are my one dear Son;[1] in you I take great delight."[2]

The Genealogy of Jesus

23 So Jesus, when he began his ministry, was [a]about thirty years old. [b]He was the son (as was supposed) of Joseph, the son of Heli, [24]the son of Matthat, the son of Levi, the son of Melchi, the son of Jannai, the son of Joseph, [25]the son of Mattathias, the son of Amos, the son of Nahum, the son of Esli, the son of Naggai, [26]the son of Maath, the son of Mattathias, the son of Semein, the son of Josech, the son of Joda, [27]the son of Joanan, the son of Rhesa, the son of [a]Zerubbabel, the son of Shealtiel, the son of Neri, [28]the son of Melchi, the son of Addi, the son of Cosam, the son of Elmadam, the son of Er, [29]the son of Joshua, the son of Eliezer, the son of Jorim, the son of Matthat, the son of Levi, [30]the son of Simeon, the son of Judah, the son of Joseph, the son of Jonam, the son of Eliakim, [31]the son of Melea, the son of Menna, the son of Mattatha, the son of [a]Nathan, [b]the son of David, [32]the son of Jesse, [a]the son of Obed, the son of Boaz, the son of Sala,[1] the son of Nahshon, [33]the son of Amminadab, the son of Admin, the son of Arni, the son of Hezron, the son of Perez, the son of Judah, [34]the son of Jacob, [a]the son of Isaac, the son of Abraham, the son of Terah, the son of Nahor, [35]the son of Serug, the son of Reu, the son of Peleg, the son of Eber, the son of Shelah, [36]the son of Cainan,[1] [a]the son of [b]Arphaxad, [c]the son of Shem, the son of Noah, the son of Lamech,

---

3:6 [a]Ps 98:2; Isa 52:10; Luke 2:10; [Rom 10:8–18] [1]Isa 40:3–5   **3:7** [a]Matt 3:7; 12:34; 23:33   **3:8** [a][2 Cor 7:9–11] [1]I.e., "do not even begin to think this."   **3:9** [a]Matt 7:19; Luke 13:6–9   **3:10** [a]Luke 3:12, 14; [Acts 2:37–38; 16:30–31]   **3:11** [a]Luke 11:41; 2 Cor 8:14; Jas 2:15–16; [1 John 3:17; 4:20]   **3:13** [a]Luke 19:8   **3:14** [a]Exod 20:16; 23:1; Lev 19:11   **3:16** [a]Matt 3:11–12; Mark 1:7–8 [b]John 7:39; 20:22; Acts 2:1–4 [1]Some mss add *for repentance.*   **3:17** [a]Mic 4:12; Matt 13:24–30   **3:19** [a]Matt 14:3; Mark 6:17 [1]Several mss *the wife of his brother Philip.*   **3:22** [1]Grk. *my beloved Son, my Son, the beloved* [one]. [2]A few wss *You are my Son; today I have fathered you* (a quote of Ps 2:7).   **3:23** [a][Num 4:3, 35, 39, 43, 47] [b]Matt 13:55; John 6:42   **3:27** [a]Ezra 2:2; 3:8   **3:31** [a]Zech 12:12 [b]2 Sam 5:14; 7:12; 1 Chr 3:5; 17:11; Isa 9:7; Jer 23:5   **3:32** [a]Ruth 4:18–22; 1 Chr 2:10–12; Isa 11:1, 10 [1]Maj. mss *Salmon.*   **3:34** [a]Gen 11:24, 26–30; 12:3; Num 24:17; 1 Chr 1:24–27   **3:36** [a]Gen 11:12 [b]Gen 10:22, 24; 11:10–13; 1 Chr 1:17–18 [c]Gen 5:6–32; 9:27; 11:10 [1]Some mss omit *Cainan.*

[37]the son of Methuselah, the son of Enoch, the son of Jared, the son of Mahalalel, the son of Kenan, [38]the son of Enosh, [a]the son of Seth, the son of Adam, the son of God.

The Temptation of Jesus

4 Then [a]Jesus, full of the Holy Spirit, returned from the Jordan River and [b]was led by the Spirit in[1] the wilderness, [2]where for forty days he endured temptations[1] from the devil. He ate nothing [a]during those days, and when they were completed, he was famished. [3]The devil said to him, "If[1] you are [a]the Son of God, command this stone to become bread." [4]Jesus answered him, "It is written, '[a]*Man*[1] *does not live by bread alone.*'"[2,3]

[5]Then the devil led him up[1] to a high place and showed him in a flash all the kingdoms of the world. [6]And he said to him, "To you [a]I will grant this whole realm—and the glory that goes along with it, for it has been relinquished to me, and I can give it to anyone I wish. [7]So then, if you will worship[1] me, all this will be yours." [8]Jesus answered him,[1] "It is written, '[a]*You are to worship the Lord your God and serve* only *him.*'"[2]

[9a]Then the devil brought him to Jerusalem, had him stand on the highest point of the temple, and said to him, "If you are the Son of God, throw yourself down from here, [10]for it is written, '[a]*He will command his angels concerning you, to protect you,*'[1] [11]and '[a]*with their hands they will lift you up, so that you will not strike your foot against a stone.*'"[1] [12]Jesus answered him, "It is said, '[a]*You are not to put the Lord your God to the test.*'"[1] [13]So when the devil had completed every temptation, he departed from him [a]until a more opportune time.

The Beginning of Jesus' Ministry in Galilee

[14a]Then Jesus, [b]in the power of the Spirit, returned to [c]Galilee, and [d]news about him spread throughout the surrounding countryside. [15]He began to [a]teach [b]in their synagogues and was praised[1] by all.

Rejection at Nazareth

[16]Now Jesus came to [a]Nazareth, [b]where he had been brought up, and went into the synagogue on the Sabbath day, as was his custom. He stood up to read, [17]and the scroll of the prophet Isaiah was given to him. He unrolled[1] the scroll and found the place where it was written,

[18] "*The Spirit of [a]the Lord is upon me,*
because he has anointed me to
proclaim good news to the poor.
He has [b]sent me[1] to proclaim release to
the captives
and the regaining of sight to the blind,
to set free those who are oppressed,
[19] *to proclaim the year of the Lord's*
favor."[1]

[20]Then he rolled up the scroll, gave it back to the attendant, and sat down. The eyes of everyone in the synagogue were fixed on him. [21]Then he began to tell them, "Today this scripture has been [a]fulfilled even as you heard it being read." [22]All were speaking well of him, and were [a]amazed at the gracious words coming out of [b]his mouth. They said, "Isn't this Joseph's son?" [23]Jesus said to them, "No doubt you will quote to me the proverb, 'Physician, heal yourself!' and say, 'What we have heard that you did in [a]Capernaum, do here in [b]your hometown too.'" [24]And he added, "I tell you the truth, no [a]prophet is acceptable in his hometown. [25]But in truth I tell you, there were [a]many widows in Israel in Elijah's days, when the sky was shut up three and a half years and there was a great famine over all the land. [26]Yet Elijah was sent to none of them, but only to a woman who was a widow at Zarephath in Sidon. [27a]And there were many lepers in Israel in the time of the prophet

---

3:38 [a]Gen 5:1–2   **4:1** [a][Isa 11:2; 61:1]; Matt 4:1–11; Mark 1:12–13   [b]Ezek 3:12; Luke 2:27   [1]Maj. MSS *into.*   **4:2** [a]Exod 34:28; 1 Kgs 19:8   [1]Grk. *in the desert, for forty days being tempted.*   **4:3** [a]Mark 3:11; John 20:31   [1]I.e., "If (and let's assume that you are) the Son of God."   **4:4** [a]Deut 8:3   [1]Or *a person*; used generically for humanity. "Man" is used because Jesus' response seems to emphasize his dependence on God as a man.   [2]Deut 8:3   [3]Maj. MSS add *but by every word from God.*   **4:5** [1]Maj. MSS *to a high mountain.*   **4:6** [a][John 12:31; 14:30; Rev 13:2, 7]   **4:7** [1]Or *will prostrate yourself in worship before.*   **4:8** [a]Deut 6:13; 10:20; Matt 4:10   [1]Maj. MSS add *Get behind me, Satan!*   [2]Deut 6:13   **4:9** [a]Matt 4:5–7   **4:10** [a]Ps 91:11   [1]Ps 91:11   **4:11** [a]Ps 91:12   [1]Ps 91:12   **4:12** [a]Deut 6:16   [1]Deut 6:16   **4:13** [a][John 14:30; Heb 4:15; Jas 4:7]   **4:14** [a]Matt 4:12   [b]John 4:43   [c]Acts 10:37   [d]Matt 4:24   **4:15** [a]Ps 22:22; Matt 4:23   [b]Isa 52:13   [1]Grk. *being glorified.*   **4:16** [a]Matt 2:23; 13:54; Mark 6:1   [b]Mark 1:21; John 18:20; Acts 13:14–16; 17:2   **4:17** [1]Grk. *opening*; but a scroll of this period would be unrolled.   **4:18** [a]Isa 49:8–9; 61:1–2; Matt 11:5; 12:18; John 3:34   [b][Dan 9:24]   [1]Maj. MSS add *to heal the brokenhearted.*   **4:19** [1]Isa 61:1–2a (Isa 58:6)   **4:21** [a]Matt 1:22–23; Acts 13:29   **4:22** [a][Ps 45:2]; Matt 13:54; Mark 6:2; Luke 2:47; [John 1:14, 17]   [b]John 6:42   **4:23** [a]Matt 4:13; 11:23   [b]Matt 13:54; Mark 6:1   **4:24** [a]Matt 13:57; Mark 6:4; John 4:44   **4:25** [a]1 Kgs 17:9; Jas 5:17   **4:27** [a]2 Kgs 5:1–14

Elisha, yet none of them was cleansed except Naaman the Syrian." [28]When they heard this, all the people in the synagogue were [a]filled with rage. [29]They got up, forced him out of the town, [a]and brought him to the brow of the hill on which their town was built, so that they could throw him down the cliff. [30]But he [a]passed through the crowd and went on his way.[1]

Ministry in Capernaum

[31]So [a]he went down to Capernaum, a town in Galilee, and on the Sabbath he began to teach the people. [32]They were [a]amazed at his teaching [b]because he spoke with authority.

[33][a]Now in the synagogue there was a man who had the spirit of an unclean[1] demon, and he cried out with a loud voice, [34]"Ha! Leave us alone, Jesus the Nazarene! Have you come to destroy us? [a]I know who you are—[b]the Holy One of God." [35]But Jesus rebuked him: "Silence! Come out of him!" Then, after the demon threw the man down in their midst, he came out of him without hurting him. [36]They were all amazed and began to say to one another, "What's happening here? For with authority and power he commands the unclean spirits, and they come out!" [37]So the news about him spread into all areas of the region.

[38]After Jesus left the synagogue, he entered Simon's house. [a]Now Simon's mother-in-law was suffering from [b]a high fever, and they asked Jesus to help her. [39]So he stood over her, [a]commanded[1] the fever, and it left her. Immediately she got up and began to serve them.

[40]As the sun was setting, all those who had any relatives sick with various diseases brought them to Jesus. [a]He placed his hands on every one of them and healed them. [41][a]Demons also came out of many, crying out, "[b]You are the Son of God!"[1] But he [c]rebuked them and would not allow them to speak because they knew that he was the Christ.

[42][a]The next morning Jesus departed and went to a deserted place. Yet the crowds were seeking him, and they came to him and tried to keep him from leaving them. [43]But Jesus said to them, "I must proclaim the good [a]news of the kingdom of God to the other towns too, for that is what I was sent to do." [44][a]So he continued to preach in the synagogues of Judea.[1]

The Call of the Disciples

5 Now Jesus was standing by the Lake of Gennesaret, and the crowd was pressing around him to [a]hear the word of God. [2]He saw two boats by the lake, but the fishermen had gotten out of them and were washing their nets. [3]He got into one of the boats, which was Simon's, and asked him to put out a little way from the shore. Then Jesus sat [a]down and taught the crowds from the boat. [4]When he had finished speaking, he said to Simon, "Put [a]out into the deep water and lower[1] your nets for a catch." [5]Simon answered, "Master, we worked hard all night and caught [a]nothing! But [b]at your word I will lower[1] the nets." [6]When they had done this, they caught so many fish that their nets started to tear. [7]So they motioned to their partners in the other boat to come and help them. And they came and filled both boats, so that they were about to sink. [8]But when Simon Peter saw it, he fell down at Jesus' knees, saying, "Go [a]away from me, Lord, for I am a sinful man!" [9]For Peter and all who were with him were [a]astonished at the catch of fish that they had taken, [10]and so were James and John, Zebedee's sons, who were Simon's business partners. Then Jesus said to Simon, "Do not be afraid; [a]from now on you will be catching people!" [11]So when [a]they had brought their boats to shore, they left everything and followed him.

Healing a Leper

[12]While Jesus was in one of the towns, [a]a man came[1] to him who was covered with [b]leprosy. When he saw Jesus, he bowed down with his face to the ground and

4:28 [a]Luke 6:11   4:29 [a]Luke 17:25; John 8:37; 10:31   4:30 [a]John 8:59; 10:39   [1]Suggests divine direction, perhaps that Jesus is on a journey, a theme present later in Luke.   4:31 [a]Isa 9:1; Matt 4:13; Mark 1:21   4:32 [a]Matt 7:28–29   [b]Luke 4:36; [John 6:63; 7:46; 8:26, 28, 38, 47; 12:49–50]   4:33 [a]Mark 1:23   [1]Grk. *having an unclean, demonic spirit*; i.e., an evil spirit. 4:34 [a]Luke 4:41   [b]Ps 16:10; Isa 49:7; Dan 9:24; Luke 1:35   4:38 [a]Matt 8:14–15; Mark 1:29–31   [b]Mark 5:23   4:39 [a]Luke 8:24 [1]Or *rebuked*.   4:40 [a]Matt 8:16–17; Mark 1:32–34   4:41 [a]Mark 1:34; 3:11; Acts 8:7   [b]Mark 8:29   [c]Mark 1:25, 34; 3:11; Luke 4:34–35   [1]Maj. MSS *the Christ the Son of God*.   4:42 [a]Mark 1:35–38; Luke 9:10   4:43 [a]Mark 1:14; [John 9:4]   4:44 [a]Matt 4:23; 9:35; Mark 1:39   [1]Maj. MSS add *of Galilee, of the Jews*.   5:1 [a]Acts 13:44   5:3 [a]John 8:2   5:4 [a]John 21:6   [1]Or *let down*; the Grk. verb is pl., commanding all in the boat, not just Peter.   5:5 [a]John 21:3   [b]Ps 33:9   [1]Or *let down*.   5:8 [a]2 Sam 6:9; 1 Kgs 17:18   5:9 [a]Mark 5:42; 10:24, 26   5:10 [a]Matt 4:19; Mark 1:17   5:11 [a]Matt 4:20; 19:27; [Mark 1:18; 8:34–35; Luke 9:59–62]; John 12:26   5:12 [a]Matt 8:2–4; Mark 1:40–44   [b]Lev 13:14   [1]Grk. *towns, behold, a man covered with leprosy*.

begged him, "Lord, if you are willing, you can make me clean." [13]So he stretched out his hand and touched him, saying, "I am willing. Be clean!" And [a]immediately the leprosy left him. [14]Then he ordered the man to tell no one, but commanded him, "Go and show yourself to a priest, [a]and bring the offering for your cleansing, as Moses commanded, as a testimony to them." [15]But [a]the news about him spread even more, and [b]large crowds were gathering together to hear him and to be healed of their illnesses. [16a]Yet Jesus himself frequently withdrew to the wilderness and [b]prayed.

Healing and Forgiving a Paralytic

[17]Now on one of those days, while he was teaching, there were Pharisees and teachers of the law sitting nearby (who had come from every village of Galilee and Judea and from Jerusalem), and the power of the Lord was with him[1] to heal. [18]Just then some men showed up, carrying a paralyzed man on a stretcher. They were trying to bring him in [a]and place him before Jesus. [19]But since they found no way to carry him in because of the crowd, they went up on the roof and let him down on the stretcher through the roof tiles right in front [a]of Jesus. [20]When Jesus saw their faith, he said, "Friend, your sins are forgiven."[1] [21]Then the experts in the law [a]and the Pharisees began to think to themselves, "[b]Who is this man who is uttering blasphemies? Who can forgive sins but God alone?" [22]When Jesus [a]perceived their hostile thoughts, he said to them, "Why are you raising objections[1] within yourselves? [23]Which is easier, to say, 'Your sins are forgiven,' or to say, 'Stand up and walk'? [24]But so that you may know that the Son of Man has [a]authority on earth to forgive sins"—he said to the paralyzed man—"I tell you, stand up, take your stretcher and go home." [25]Immediately he stood up before them, picked up the stretcher he had been lying on, and went home, [a]glorifying God. [26]Then astonishment seized them all, and they [a]glorified God. They were filled with awe,[1] saying, "We have seen incredible[2] things today."

The Call of Levi; Eating with Sinners

[27a]After this, Jesus went out and saw a tax collector named Levi sitting at the tax booth. "[b]Follow me," he said to him. [28]And he got up and [a]followed him, leaving everything behind.

[29a]Then Levi gave a great banquet in his house for Jesus, and [b]there was a large crowd of tax collectors and others sitting at the table with them. [30]But the Pharisees and their experts in the law complained[1] to his disciples, saying, "[a]Why do you eat and drink with tax collectors and sinners?" [31]Jesus answered them, "Those who are well don't need a physician, but those who are sick do. [32]I have not come to call the [a]righteous, but sinners to repentance."

The Superiority of the New

[33]Then they said to him, "John's[1] disciples frequently fast and pray, and so do the disciples of the Pharisees, but yours continue to eat and drink."[2] [34]So Jesus said to them, "You cannot make the wedding guests fast while the [a]bridegroom is with them, can you? [35]But those days are coming, and when the bridegroom is taken from them, at that time they will fast." [36]He also told them a parable: "No one tears a patch from a new garment and sews it on an old garment. If [a]he does, he will have torn[1] the new, and the piece from the new will not match the old. [37]And no one pours new wine into old wineskins. If he does, the new wine will burst the skins and will be spilled, and the skins will be destroyed. [38]Instead new wine must be poured into new wineskins.[1] [39]1No[2] one after drinking old wine wants the new, for he says, 'The old is good enough.'"[3]

Lord of the Sabbath

6 Jesus was going through the grain fields on a Sabbath,[1] and his disciples picked some heads of wheat, rubbed them in their

5:13 [a] Matt 20:34; Luke 8:44; John 5:9   **5:14** [a] Matt 8:4; Luke 17:14   **5:15** [a] Mark 1:45   [b] Matt 4:25; Mark 3:7; John 6:2   **5:16** [a] Luke 9:10   [b] Matt 14:23; Mark 1:35; Luke 6:12; 9:18; 11:1   **5:17** [1] Maj. MSS *the power of the Lord was present to heal them.*   **5:18** [a] Matt 9:2–8; Mark 2:3–12   **5:19** [a] Matt 15:30   **5:20** [1] Grk. *Man, your sins are forgiven you.*   **5:21** [a] Matt 9:3; 26:65; Mark 2:6–7; John 10:33   [b] Ps 32:5; 130:4; Isa 43:25   **5:22** [a] Luke 9:47; John 2:25   [1] Grk. *you reason.*   **5:24** [a] Mark 2:11; 5:41; Luke 7:14   **5:25** [a] Luke 17:15, 18; Acts 3:8   **5:26** [a] Luke 1:65; 7:16   [1] Grk. *fear; but mixed with wonder.*   [2] Or *remarkable; unusual and awe inspiring.*   **5:27** [a] Matt 9:9–17; Mark 2:13–22   [b] [Mark 8:34]; Luke 9:59; John 12:26; 21:19, 22   **5:28** [a] Matt 4:22; 19:27; Mark 10:28   **5:29** [a] Matt 9:9–10; Mark 2:15   [b] Luke 15:1   **5:30** [a] Matt 11:19; Luke 15:2; Acts 23:9   [1] Or *grumbled.*   **5:32** [a] Matt 9:13; 1 Tim 1:15   **5:33** [1] Maj. MSS *Why do John's . . . ?*   [2] Grk. *but yours are eating and drinking.*   **5:34** [a] John 3:29   **5:36** [a] Matt 9:16–17; Mark 2:21–22   [1] Grk. *he tears.*   **5:38** [1] Maj. MSS *and both will be preserved.*   **5:39** [1] Some MSS omit v. 39.   [2] ‡ Maj. MSS add *and.*   [3] Maj. MSS *better.*   **6:1** [1] Maj. later MSS *a second-first Sabbath.*

hands, and ate them. [2]But some of the Pharisees said, "Why are you doing [a]what is against the law on the Sabbath?" [3]Jesus answered them, "Haven't you read [a]what David did when he and his companions were hungry—[4]how he entered the house of God, took and ate the sacred bread, [a]which is not lawful for any to eat but the priests alone, and[1] gave it to his companions?"[2] [5]Then he said to them, "The Son of Man is lord[1] of the Sabbath."

Healing a Withered Hand

[6]On another Sabbath, Jesus entered the synagogue and was teaching. [a]Now a man was there whose right hand was withered. [7]The experts in the law and the Pharisees watched Jesus closely to see if he would [a]heal [b]on the Sabbath, so that they could find a reason to accuse him. [8]But he [a]knew their thoughts, and said to the man who had the withered hand, "Get up and stand here." So he rose and stood there. [9]Then Jesus said to them, "[a]I ask you, is it lawful to do good on the Sabbath or to do evil, to save a life or to destroy it?" [10]After looking around at them all, he said to the man, "Stretch out your hand." The man did so, and his hand was restored. [11]But they were filled with mindless rage and began debating with one another what they would do[1] to Jesus.

Choosing the 12 Apostles

[12]Now it was during this time that Jesus went out to the mountain to pray, and he spent all night in [a]prayer to God. [13]When morning came, he called his disciples [a]and chose [b]12 of them, whom he also named apostles: [14]Simon ([a]whom he named Peter), and his brother Andrew; and James, John, Philip, Bartholomew, [15]Matthew, Thomas, James the son of Alphaeus, Simon who was called the Zealot, [16]Judas [a]the son of James, and [b]Judas Iscariot, who became a traitor.

The Sermon on the Plain

[17]Then he came down with them and stood on a level place.[1] [a]And a large number of his disciples had gathered along with a vast multitude from all over Judea, from Jerusalem, and from the seacoast of Tyre and Sidon. They came to hear him and to be healed of their diseases, [18]and those who suffered from[1] unclean spirits were cured. [19]The whole crowd was [a]trying [b]to touch him because [c]power was coming out from him and healing them all. [20]Then he looked up[1] at his disciples and said:

"[a]Blessed are you who are poor, for
   the kingdom of God belongs to you.
[21] [a]Blessed are you who hunger now,
   for you will be [b]satisfied.
[c]Blessed are you who weep now, for
   you will [d]laugh.
[22] [a]Blessed are you when people hate
   you, and when they [b]exclude you
   and insult you and reject you
   as evil on account of the Son of
   Man! [23][a]Rejoice [b]in that day, and
   jump for joy because your reward
   is great in heaven. For their
   ancestors did the same things to
   the prophets.
[24] [a]But woe to you [b]who are rich, for
   [c]you have received your comfort
   already.
[25] [a]Woe to you who are well satisfied
   with food now, for you will be
   hungry.
Woe to you[1] who laugh now, for you
   will mourn and [b]weep.
[26] [a]Woe to you[1] when all people speak
   well of you, for their ancestors
   did the same things to the false
   prophets.

[27]"[a]But I say to you who are listening: Love your enemies, do good to those who

---

6:2 [a]Exod 20:10   6:3 [a]1 Sam 21:6   6:4 [a]Lev 24:9   [1]Maj. mss add *also*.   [2]One ms adds *On the same day, as he saw someone working on the Sabbath he said, "Man, if you know what you are doing, you are blessed, but if you do not know, you are cursed and a violator of the law."*   6:5 [1]An emphatic Grk. construction.   6:6 [a]Matt 12:9–14; Mark 3:1–6; Luke 13:14; 14:3; John 9:16   6:7 [a]Luke 13:14; 14:1–6   [b]Luke 20:20   6:8 [a]Matt 9:4; John 2:24–25   6:9 [a]John 7:23   6:11 [1]Grk. *might do*.   6:12 [a]Matt 14:23; Mark 1:35; Luke 5:16; 9:18; 11:1   6:13 [a]John 6:70   [b]Matt 10:1   6:14 [a]John 1:42   6:16 [a]Jude 1   [b]Luke 22:3–6   6:17 [a]Matt 4:25; Mark 3:7–8   [1]Or *on a plateau*.   6:18 [1]Or *were oppressed by, were troubled with*.   6:19 [a]Matt 9:21; 14:36; Mark 3:10   [b]Mark 5:27–28; Luke 8:44–47   [c]Mark 5:30; Luke 8:46   6:20 [a]Matt 5:3–12; [11:5]; Luke 6:20–23; [Jas 2:5]   [1]Grk. *lifting up his eyes*.   6:21 [a]Isa 55:1; 65:13; Matt 5:6   [b][Rev 7:16]   [c][Isa 61:3; Rev 7:17]   [d]Ps 126:5   6:22 [a]Matt 5:11; 1 Pet 2:19; 3:14; 4:14   [b][John 16:2]   6:23 [a]Matt 5:12; Acts 5:41; [Col 1:24]; Jas 1:2   [b]Acts 7:51   6:24 [a]Amos 6:1; Luke 12:21; Jas 5:1–6   [b]Luke 12:21   [c]Matt 6:2, 5, 16; Luke 16:25   6:25 [a][Prov 14:13]   [b]Jas 4:9   [1]Sev. wss omit *to you*.   6:26 [a][John 15:19; 1 John 4:5]   [1]Sev. wss omit *to you*.   6:27 [a]Exod 23:4; Prov 25:21; Matt 5:44; Rom 12:20

hate you, [28a]bless those who curse you, [b]pray for those who mistreat you. [29a]To the person who strikes you on the cheek, offer the other as well, [b]and from the person who takes away your coat, do not withhold your tunic either. [30a]Give to everyone who asks you, and do not ask for your possessions back from the person who takes them away. [31a]Treat others in the same way that you would want them to treat you.

[32]"If you love those who love you, what credit is that to you? For [a]even sinners love those who love them. [33]And[1] if you do good to those who do good to you, what credit is that to you? Even[2] sinners do the same. [34a]And if you lend to those from whom you hope to be repaid,[1] what credit is that to you? Even sinners lend to sinners, so that they may be repaid in full. [35]But [a]love your enemies, and [b]do good, and [c]lend, expecting nothing back. Then [d]your reward will be great, and you will be sons of the Most High, because he is kind to ungrateful and evil people. [36a]Be merciful, just as your Father is merciful.

Do not Judge Others

[37]"Do not [a]judge, and you will not be judged; do not condemn, and you will not be condemned; [b]forgive, and you will be forgiven. [38a]Give, and it will be given to you: A good measure, pressed down, shaken together, running over, will be poured into your [b]lap. For the measure you use will be the measure you receive."

[39]He also told them a parable: "Someone who is blind [a]cannot lead another who is blind, can he? Won't they both fall into a pit? [40]A disciple is not [a]greater than his teacher, but everyone when fully trained will be like his teacher. [41]Why do you see the speck in your brother's eye, [a]but fail to see the beam of wood in your own? [42]How can you say to your brother, 'Brother, let me remove the speck from your eye,' while you yourself don't see the beam in your own? You hypocrite! First remove the beam from your own eye, and then you can see clearly to remove the speck from your brother's eye.

[43]"[a]For no good tree bears bad[1] fruit, nor again[2] does a bad tree bear good fruit, [44]for [a]each tree is known by its own fruit. For figs are not gathered from thorns, nor are grapes picked from brambles. [45]The good person out of the good [a]treasury [b]of his heart produces good, and the evil person out of his evil treasury produces evil, for his mouth speaks from what fills his heart.

[46]"[a]Why do you call me 'Lord, Lord,'[1] and don't do what I tell you?

[47]"Everyone [a]who comes to me and listens to my words and puts them into practice—I will show you what he is like: [48]He is like a man building a house, who dug down deep and laid the foundation on bedrock. When a flood came, the river burst against that house but could not shake it because it had been well built.[1] [49]But the person who hears and does not put my words into practice is like a man who built a house on the ground without a foundation. When the river burst against that house, it collapsed immediately and was utterly destroyed!"

Healing the Centurion's Slave

7 After Jesus had finished teaching all this to the people, he [a]entered Capernaum. [2]A centurion there had a slave who was highly regarded,[1] but who was sick and at the point of death. [3]When the centurion heard about Jesus, he sent some Jewish elders to him, asking him to come and heal his slave. [4]When they came to Jesus, they urged him earnestly, "He is worthy[1] to have you do this for him [5]because he loves our nation[1] and even built our synagogue." [6]So Jesus went with them. When he was not far from the house, the centurion sent friends to say to him, "Lord, do not trouble yourself, for I am not worthy to have you come under my roof! [7]That is why I did not presume to come to you. Instead, [a]say the word, and my servant must be healed.[1] [8]For I too am

6:28 [a] Rom 12:14   [b] Luke 23:24; Acts 7:60   6:29 [a] Matt 5:39–42   [b] [1 Cor 6:7]   6:30 [a] Deut 15:7–8; Prov 3:27; 21:26; Matt 5:42   6:31 [a] Matt 7:12   6:32 [a] Matt 5:46   6:33 [1] ‡ Sev. sig. MSS for.   [2] Maj. MSS even for.   6:34 [a] Matt 5:42   [1] Grk. to receive.   6:35 [a] [Rom 13:10]   [b] Heb 13:16   [c] Lev 25:35–37; Ps 37:26   [d] Matt 5:46   6:36 [a] Matt 5:48; Eph 4:32   6:37 [a] Matt 7:1–5; Rom 14:4; [1 Cor 4:5]   [b] Matt 18:21–35   6:38 [a] [Prov 19:17; 28:27]   [b] Ps 79:12; Isa 65:6–7; Jer 32:18   6:39 [a] Matt 15:14; 23:16; Rom 2:19   6:40 [a] Matt 10:24; [John 13:16; 15:20]   6:41 [a] Matt 7:3   6:43 [a] Matt 7:16–18, 20   [1] Grk. rotten, diseased.   [2] Maj. MSS omit again.   6:44 [a] Matt 12:33   6:45 [a] Matt 12:35   [b] Prov 15:2, 28; 16:23; 18:21; Matt 12:34   6:46 [a] Mal 1:6; Matt 7:21; 25:11; Luke 13:25   [1] An emphatic Grk. construction.   6:47 [a] Matt 7:24–27; [John 14:21]; Jas 1:22–25   6:48 [1] Maj. MSS because he built [it] on the rock.   7:1 [a] Matt 8:5–13   7:2 [1] Or highly valued.   7:4 [1] An emphatic Grk. construction.   7:5 [1] Or people.   7:7 [a] Ps 33:9; 107:20   [1] Maj. MSS will be healed.

a man set under [a]authority, with soldiers under me. I say to this one, 'Go!' and he goes, and to another, 'Come!' and he comes, and to my slave, 'Do this!' and he does it." [9]When Jesus heard this, he was amazed[1] at him. He turned and said to the crowd that followed him, "I tell you, not even in Israel have I found such faith!" [10]So when those who had been sent returned to the house, they found the slave[1] well.

Raising a Widow's Son

[11]Soon afterward[1] Jesus went to a town called Nain, and his disciples and a large crowd went with him. [12]As he approached the town gate, a man who had died was being carried out, the only son of his mother (who was a widow), and a large crowd from the town was with her. [13]When the Lord saw her, he had [a]compassion for her and said to her, "[b]Do not weep." [14]Then he came up and touched the bier, and those who carried it stood still. He said, "Young man, I say to you, get [a]up!" [15]So the dead man [a]sat up and began to speak, and Jesus [b]gave him back to his mother. [16][a]Fear seized them all, and they began to [b]glorify God, [c]saying, "A great prophet has appeared among us!" and "[d]God has come to help[1] his people!" [17]This report about Jesus circulated throughout Judea and all the surrounding country.

Jesus and John the Baptist

[18]John's disciples informed him about all these things. [a]So John called two of his disciples [19]and sent [a]them to Jesus[1] to ask, "Are you the one who is to come, or should we look for another?" [20]When the men came to Jesus, they said, "John the Baptist has sent us to you to ask, 'Are you the one who is to come, or should we look for another?'" [21]At that very time Jesus cured many people of diseases, sicknesses, and evil spirits, and granted sight to many who were blind. [22][a]So he answered them, "Go tell John what you have seen and heard: The blind [b]see, the lame [c]walk, lepers are [d]cleansed, the deaf [e]hear, [f]the dead are raised, the poor have good news proclaimed to them. [23]Blessed is anyone who takes no offense at me."

[24][a]When John's messengers had gone, Jesus began to speak to the crowds about John: "What did you go out into the wilderness to see? A reed shaken by the wind?[1] [25]What did you go out to see? A man dressed in soft clothing? Look, those who wear soft clothing and live in luxury are in the royal palaces! [26]What did you go out to see? A prophet? Yes, I tell you, and more than a prophet. [27]This is the one about whom it is written, '**Look, I am sending my messenger ahead of you, who will prepare your way before you.**'[1] [28]I tell you, among those born of women no one is [a]greater than John.[1] Yet the one who is least in the kingdom of God is greater than he is." [29](Now all the people who heard this, even the tax collectors, acknowledged God's justice because they had been baptized with John's baptism. [30]However, [a]the Pharisees and the experts in religious law rejected God's purpose for themselves because they had not been baptized by John.)

[31]"To what then should I compare the people of this generation, and what are they like? [32]They are like children sitting in the marketplace and calling out to one another,

"'We played the flute for you, yet you did not dance;
we wailed in mourning, yet you did not weep.'

[33]For [a]John [b]the Baptist has come eating no bread and drinking no wine, and you say, 'He has a demon!' [34]The Son of Man has come [a]eating and drinking, and you say, 'Look at him, a glutton and a drunk, a friend of tax collectors and sinners!' [35][a]But wisdom is vindicated by all her children."

Jesus' Anointing

[36]Now one of [a]the Pharisees asked Jesus to have dinner with him, so he went into the Pharisee's house and took his place at the table. [37]Then when a woman of

7:8[a][Mark 13:34] **7:9**[1]Or *pleased with him and amazed.* **7:10**[1]Maj. MSS *the sick slave.* **7:11**[1]Sev. MSS *next day.* **7:13**[a]Lam 3:32; John 11:35; [Heb 4:15] [b]Luke 8:52 **7:14**[a]Mark 5:41; Luke 8:54; John 11:43; Acts 9:40; [Rom 4:17] **7:15**[a]Matt 11:5; Luke 8:55; John 11:44 [b]1 Kgs 17:23; 2 Kgs 4:36 **7:16**[a]Luke 1:65 [b]Luke 5:26 [c]Luke 24:19; John 4:19; 6:14; 9:17 [d]Luke 1:68 [1]Grk. *visited.* **7:18**[a]Matt 11:2–19 **7:19**[a][Mic 5:2; Zech 9:9; Mal 3:1–3] [1]‡ Some sig. wss *to the Lord.* **7:22**[a]Matt 11:4 [b]John 9:7 [c]Matt 15:31 [d]Luke 17:12–14 [e]Mark 7:37 [f][Isa 61:1–3; Luke 4:18] **7:24**[a]Matt 11:7 [1]Either figurative of someone who is easily blown over or literal of the wilderness vegetation blowing in the wind. **7:27**[1]Mal 3:1 (Exod 23:20) **7:28**[a][Luke 1:15] [1]Some MSS *John the Baptist, the prophet John the Baptist.* **7:30**[a]Acts 20:27 **7:33**[a]Matt 3:1 [b][Matt 3:4]; Luke 1:15 **7:34**[a]Luke 15:2 **7:35**[a]Matt 11:19 **7:36**[a]Matt 26:6; Mark 14:3; John 11:2

that town, who was a sinner, learned that Jesus was dining at the Pharisee's house, she brought an alabaster jar of perfumed oil. [38]As she stood behind him at his feet, weeping, she began to wet his feet with her tears. She wiped them with her hair, kissed them, and anointed them with the perfumed oil. [39]Now when the Pharisee who had invited him saw this, he said to himself, "If this [a]man were a prophet,[1] he would know who and what kind of woman this is who is touching him, that she is a sinner." [40]So Jesus answered him, "Simon, I have something to say to you." He replied, "Say it, Teacher." [41]"A certain creditor had two debtors; one owed him 500 silver [a]coins, and the other 50. [42]When they could not pay, he canceled[1] the debts of both. Now which of them will love him more?" [43]Simon answered, "I suppose the one who had the bigger debt canceled." Jesus said to him, "You have judged rightly." [44]Then, turning toward the woman, he said to Simon, "Do you see this woman? I entered your house. You gave me no [a]water for my feet, but she has wet my feet with her tears and wiped them with her hair. [45]You gave me no [a]kiss of greeting, but from the time I entered she has not stopped kissing my feet. [46a]You did not anoint my head with oil, but she has anointed my feet with perfumed oil. [47]Therefore I tell you, [a]her sins, which were many, are forgiven, thus she loved much;[1] but the one who is forgiven little loves little." [48]Then Jesus said to her, "[a]Your sins are forgiven." [49]But those who were at the table with him began to say among themselves, "[a]Who is this, who even forgives sins?" [50]He said to the woman, "[a]Your faith has saved you; go in peace."

Jesus' Ministry and the Help of Women

8 Sometime afterward[1] he went on through towns and villages, preaching and proclaiming the good news of the kingdom of God. The twelve were with him, [2]and also [a]some women who had been healed of evil spirits and disabilities:[1] Mary (called Magdalene), from whom seven demons had gone [b]out, [3]and Joanna the wife of Cuza (Herod's household manager),[1] Susanna, and many others who provided for them[2] out of their own resources.

The Parable of the Sower

[4]While [a]a large crowd was gathering and people were coming to Jesus from one town after another, he spoke to them in a parable: [5]"A sower went out to sow his seed. And as he sowed, some fell along the path and was trampled on, and the wild birds devoured it. [6]Other seed fell on rock, and when it came up, it withered because it had no moisture. [7]Other seed fell among the thorns, and they grew up with it and choked it. [8]But [a]other seed fell on good soil and grew, and it produced a hundred times as much grain." As he said this, he called out, "The one who has ears to hear had better listen!"[1]

[9a]Then his disciples asked him what this parable meant. [10]He said, "You have been given the opportunity to know the secrets of the kingdom of God, but for others they are in parables, so that *although they [a]see they may not see, and although they hear they may not understand.*[1]

[11]"[a]Now the parable means this: The seed is the [b]word of God. [12]Those along the path are the ones who have heard; then the devil comes and takes away the word from their hearts, so that they may not believe and be saved. [13]Those on the rock are the ones who receive the word with joy when they hear it, but they have no root. They believe for a while, but in a time of testing[1] fall away. [14]As for the seed that fell among thorns, these are the ones who hear, but as they go on their way they are choked by the worries and [a]riches and pleasures of life, and their fruit does not mature. [15]But as for the seed that landed on good soil, these are the ones who, after hearing the word, cling to it with an honest and good heart, and bear fruit with steadfast [a]endurance.

Showing the Light

16 "No [a]one lights a lamp and then covers it with a jar or puts it under a bed, but puts it on a lampstand so that those who come in can see the [b]light. 17[a]For nothing is hidden that will not be [b]revealed, and nothing concealed that will not be made known and brought to light. 18 So listen carefully, [a]for whoever has will be given more, but whoever does not [b]have, even what he thinks he has will be taken from him."

Jesus' True Family

19 Now Jesus' mother and his brothers came to him, but they could not get near him because of [a]the crowd. 20 So he was told, "Your mother and your brothers are standing outside, wanting to see you." 21 But he replied to them, "My mother and my brothers are those who hear the word of God and do it."

Stilling of a Storm

22[a]One day Jesus got into a boat with his disciples and said to them, "Let's go across to the other side of the lake." So they set out, 23 and as they sailed he fell asleep. Now a violent windstorm came down on the lake, and the boat[1] started filling up with water, and they were in danger. 24 They came and woke him, saying, "Master, Master,[1] we are about to die!" So he got up and rebuked[2] the wind and the raging waves; they died down, and it was calm. 25 Then he said to them, "[a]Where is your faith?" But they were afraid and amazed, saying to one another, "[b]Who then is this? He commands even the winds and the water, and they obey him!"

Healing of a Demoniac

26 So they sailed over to [a]the region of the Gerasenes,[1] which is opposite Galilee. 27 As Jesus stepped ashore, a certain man from the town met him who was possessed by demons. For a long time this man had worn no clothes and had not lived in a house, but among the tombs. 28 When he saw Jesus, he cried [a]out, fell down before him, and shouted with [b]a loud voice, "Leave me alone,[1] Jesus, Son of the Most High God! I beg [c]you, do not torment me!" 29 For Jesus had started commanding[1] the evil spirit to come out of the man. (For it had seized him many times, so he would be bound with chains and shackles and kept under guard. But he would break the restraints and be driven by the demon into deserted places.) 30 Jesus then asked him, "What is your name?" He said, "Legion," because many demons had entered him. 31 And they began to beg him not to order them to depart [a]into the abyss.[1] 32 Now a large herd of [a]pigs was feeding there on the hillside, and the demonic spirits begged Jesus to let them go into them. He gave them permission. 33 So the demons came out of the man and went into the pigs, and the herd of pigs rushed down the steep slope into the lake and drowned. 34 When the herdsmen saw what had happened, they ran off and spread the news[1] in the town and countryside. 35 So the people went out to see what had happened, and they came to Jesus. They found the man from whom the demons had gone out, [a]sitting at Jesus' [b]feet, clothed and in his [c]right mind, and they were afraid. 36 Those who had seen it told them how the man who had been demon-possessed had been healed. 37[a]Then all the people of the Gerasenes[1] and the surrounding region [b]asked Jesus to [c]leave them alone, for they were seized with great [d]fear. So he got into the boat and left. 38 The man from whom [a]the demons had gone out begged to go with him, but Jesus sent him away, saying, 39 "Return to your home, and declare what God has done for you." So he went away, proclaiming throughout the whole town what Jesus had done for him.

Restoration and Healing

40 Now when Jesus returned, the crowd welcomed him because they were all

8:16 [a] Matt 5:15; Mark 4:21; Luke 11:33   [b] Matt 5:14   8:17 [a] Matt 10:26; Luke 12:2; [1 Cor 4:5]   [b] [Eccl 12:14; 2 Cor 5:10]   8:18 [a] Matt 25:29   [b] Matt 13:12   8:19 [a] Ps 69:8; Matt 12:46–50; Mark 3:31–35   8:22 [a] Matt 8:23–27; Mark 4:36–41   8:23 [1] Grk. they were being swamped.   8:24 [1] Shows great emotion.   [2] Or commanded.   8:25 [a] Luke 9:41   [b] Luke 4:36; 5:26   8:26 [a] Matt 8:28–34; Mark 5:1–17   [1] Maj. MSS Gadarenes; a few MSS Gergesenes.   8:28 [a] Mark 1:26; 9:26   [b] Mark 1:23–24   [c] Luke 4:41   [1] Grk. What to me and to you?; an idiom for "What have I to do with you that you should do this to me?" or "That is your business, how am I involved?"   8:29 [1] ‡ Early MSS he commanded.   8:31 [a] Rom 10:7; [Rev 20:1, 3]   [1] The place where the dead await the judgment.   8:32 [a] Lev 11:7; Deut 14:8   8:34 [1] Or reported it.   8:35 [a] [Matt 11:28]   [b] Matt 28:9; Mark 7:25; Luke 10:39; 17:16; John 11:32   [c] [2 Tim 1:7]   8:37 [a] Matt 8:34   [b] Mark 1:24; Luke 4:34   [c] Job 21:14; Acts 16:39   [d] Luke 5:26   [1] Maj. MSS Gadarenes; a few MSS Gergesenes.   8:38 [a] Mark 5:18–20

waiting for him. [41]Then [a]a man named Jairus, who was a leader[1] of the synagogue, came up. Falling at Jesus' feet, he pleaded with him to come to his house, [42]because he had an only daughter, about twelve years old, and she [a]was dying.[1]

As Jesus was on his way, the crowds pressed around him. [43a]Now a woman was there who had been suffering from a [b]hemorrhage for twelve years[1] but could not be healed by anyone. [44]She came up behind Jesus and [a]touched the edge of his cloak,[1] and at once the bleeding stopped. [45]Then Jesus asked, "Who was it who touched me?" When they all denied it, Peter[1] said, "Master, the crowds are surrounding you and pressing against you!" [46]But Jesus said, "Someone touched me, for I know that [a]power has gone out from me." [47]When the woman saw that she could not escape notice, she came trembling and fell down before him. In the presence of all the people, she explained why she had touched him and how she had been immediately healed. [48]Then he said to her, "Daughter, [a]your faith has made you well.[1] [b]Go in peace."

[49a]While he was still speaking, someone from the synagogue leader's[1] house came and said, "Your daughter is dead; do not trouble the teacher any longer." [50]But when Jesus heard this, he told him, "Do not be afraid; just believe, and she will be healed." [51]Now when he came to the house, Jesus did not let anyone go in with him except Peter, John, and James, and the child's father and mother. [52]Now they were all wailing and mourning for her, but he said, "Stop your weeping; she is not dead [a]but asleep!" [53]And they began making fun of him because they knew that she was dead. [54]But Jesus gently took her by the hand and said, "Child, get [a]up." [55]Her spirit returned, and she got up immediately. Then he told them to give her something to eat. [56]Her parents were [a]astonished, but he ordered them to tell no one what had happened.

The Sending of the 12 Apostles

9 After Jesus called [a]the twelve[1] together, he [b]gave them power and authority over all demons and to cure diseases, [2]and [a]he sent them out to proclaim the kingdom of God and to heal the sick. [3]He said to them, "Take nothing for your journey—no staff, no bag, no bread, no money, [a]and do not take an extra tunic. [4a]Whatever house you enter, stay there until you leave the area. [5a]Wherever they do not receive you, as you leave that town, [b]shake the dust off your feet as a testimony against them." [6a]Then they departed and went throughout the villages, proclaiming the good news and healing people everywhere.

Herod's Confusion about Jesus

[7a]Now Herod the tetrarch heard about everything that was happening, and he was thoroughly perplexed because some people were saying that John had been raised from the dead, [8]while others were saying that Elijah had appeared, and still others that one of the prophets of long ago had risen. [9]Herod said, "I had John[1] beheaded, but who is this about whom I hear such things?" [a]So Herod wanted to learn about Jesus.[2]

The Feeding of the 5,000

[10]When the apostles returned, they told Jesus everything they had done. [a]Then [b]he took them with him and they withdrew privately to a town[1] called Bethsaida. [11]But when the crowds found out, they followed him. He welcomed them, spoke to them about the kingdom of God, and cured those who needed healing. [12]Now the day began to draw to a close, [a]so the twelve came and said to Jesus, "Send the crowd away, so they can go into the surrounding villages and countryside and find lodging and food because we are in an isolated place." [13]But he said to them, "You[1] give them something to eat." They replied, "We have no more than five loaves and two fish—unless we go and

---

8:41 [a] Matt 9:18–26; Mark 5:22–43 [1] The main elder at the synagogue in charge of organizing the services. 8:42 [a] Luke 7:2 [1] Or *she was beginning to die, was approaching death.* 8:43 [a] Matt 9:20 [b] Luke 15:19–22 [1] ‡ Maj. MSS add *having spent all her money on doctors.* 8:44 [a] Mark 6:56; Luke 5:13 [1] Grk. *garment.* 8:45 [1] Maj. MSS add *and those together with him.* 8:46 [a] Mark 5:30; Luke 6:19 8:48 [a] Mark 5:34; Luke 7:50 [b] John 8:11 [1] Or *has delivered you;* referring only to the woman's healing. 8:49 [a] Mark 5:35 [1] The official in charge of the synagogue, or the president of a synagogue. 8:52 [a] [John 11:11, 13] 8:54 [a] Luke 7:14; John 11:43 8:56 [a] Matt 8:4; 9:30; Mark 5:43 9:1 [a] Matt 10:1–2; Mark 3:13; 6:7 [b] Mark 16:17–18; [John 14:12] [1] Some MSS add *apostles, his disciples.* 9:2 [a] Matt 10:7–8; Mark 6:12; Luke 10:1, 9 9:3 [a] Matt 10:9–15; Mark 6:8–11; Luke 10:4–12; 22:35 9:4 [a] Matt 10:11; Mark 6:10 9:5 [a] Matt 10:14 [b] Luke 10:11; Acts 13:51 9:6 [a] Mark 6:12; Luke 8:1 9:7 [a] Matt 14:1–2; Mark 6:14 9:9 [a] Luke 23:8 [1] Grk. *John I beheaded;* an emphatic Grk. construction. [2] Grk. *was seeking to see him.* 9:10 [a] Mark 6:30 [b] Matt 14:13 [1] Many MSS *to a deserted place, to a deserted place of a town called Bethsaida.* 9:12 [a] Matt 14:15; Mark 6:35; John 6:1, 5 9:13 [1] An emphatic Grk. construction.

buy food for all these people." [14](Now about 5,000 men[1] were there.) Then he said to his disciples, "Have them sit down in groups of about fifty each." [15]So they did as Jesus directed, and the people all sat down.

[16]Then he took the five loaves and the two fish, and looking up to heaven he gave [a]thanks and broke them. He gave them to the disciples to set before the crowd. [17]They all ate and were satisfied, and what was left over was picked up—12 baskets of broken pieces.

Peter's Confession

[18]Once when Jesus was praying by himself [a]and his disciples were nearby, he asked them, "Who do the crowds say that I am?" [19]They answered, "[a]John the Baptist; others say Elijah; and still others that one of the prophets of long ago has risen." [20]Then he said to them, "But who do you say that I am?" [a]Peter answered, "The Christ[1] of God." [21]But he forcefully [a]commanded[1] them not to tell this to anyone, [22]saying, "[a]The Son of Man must suffer many things and be rejected by the elders, chief priests, and experts in the law, and be killed, and on the third day be raised."

A Call to Discipleship

[23a]Then he said to them all, "If anyone wants to become my follower, he must deny[1] himself, take up his cross daily, and follow me. [24a]For whoever wants to save his life[1] will lose it, but whoever loses his life because of me will save it. [25a]For what does it benefit a person if he gains the whole world but loses or forfeits himself? [26a]For whoever is [b]ashamed of me and my words, the Son of Man will be ashamed of that person[1] when he comes in his glory and in the glory of the Father and of the holy angels. [27a]But I tell you most certainly, there are some standing here who will not[1] experience[2] death before they see the kingdom of God."

The Transfiguration

[28a]Now about eight days after these sayings, Jesus took with him Peter, John, and James, and went up the mountain to pray. [29]As he was praying, the appearance of his face was transformed, and his clothes became very bright, a brilliant white.[1] [30]Then two men, [a]Moses and [b]Elijah, began talking with him. [31]They appeared in glorious splendor and spoke about his departure that he was about to carry out at Jerusalem. [32]Now Peter and those with him [a]were quite sleepy, but as they became fully awake, they saw his glory and the two men standing with him. [33]Then as the men were starting to leave, Peter said to Jesus, "Master, it is good for us to be here. Let us make three shelters,[1] one for you and one for Moses and one for Elijah"—not knowing what he was saying. [34]As he was saying this, a [a]cloud came and overshadowed them, and they were afraid as they entered the cloud. [35]Then a voice came from the cloud, saying, "[a]This is my Son, my Chosen One.[1,2] [b]Listen to him!" [36]After the voice had spoken, Jesus was found alone. [a]So they kept silent and told no one at that time anything of what they had seen.

Healing a Boy with an Unclean Spirit

[37a]Now on the next day, when they had come down from the mountain, a large crowd met him. [38]Then a man from the crowd cried out, "Teacher, I beg you to look at my son—he is my only child! [39]A spirit seizes him, and he suddenly screams; it throws him into convulsions and causes him to foam at the mouth. It hardly ever leaves him alone, torturing[1] him severely. [40]I begged your disciples to cast it out, but they could not do so." [41]Jesus answered, "You unbelieving and perverse generation! How much longer must I be with you and endure you? Bring your son here." [42]As the boy was

9:14 [1]The actual count is larger, as women and children were not included.   **9:16** [a]Luke 22:19; 24:30   **9:18** [a]Matt 16:13–16; Mark 8:27–29   **9:19** [a]Matt 14:2   **9:20** [a]Matt 16:16; John 6:68–69   [1]Or *Messiah*; both "Christ" (Grk.) and "Messiah" (Heb., Aram.) mean "one who has been anointed."   **9:21** [a]Matt 8:4; 16:20; Mark 8:30   [1]An emphatic Grk. construction.   **9:22** [a]Matt 16:21; 17:22; Luke 18:31–33; 23:46; 24:46   **9:23** [a]Matt 10:38; 16:24; Mark 8:34; Luke 14:27   [1]Trad. *let him deny*.   **9:24** [a]Matt 10:39; Luke 17:33; [John 12:25]   [1]Grk. *his soul*; either earthly/physical life or inner/transcendent life.   **9:25** [a]Matt 16:26; Mark 8:36; [Luke 16:19–31]; Acts 1:18, 25   **9:26** [a][Rom 1:16]   [b]Matt 10:33; Mark 8:38; Luke 12:9; 2 Tim 2:12   [1]An emphatic Grk. construction.   **9:27** [a]Matt 16:28; Mark 9:1; Acts 7:55–56; Rev 20:4   [1]The strongest possible Grk. negative.   [2]Grk. *will not taste*; not sampling a small amount but coming to know something.   **9:28** [a]Matt 17:1–8; Mark 9:2–8   **9:29** [1]Or *became bright as a flash of lightning*.   **9:30** [a]Heb 11:23–29   [b]2 Kgs 2:1–11   **9:32** [a]Dan 8:18; 10:9; Matt 26:40, 43; Mark 14:40   **9:33** [1]Or *booths, dwellings*; i.e., temporary booths used in the Feast of Tabernacles.   **9:34** [a]Exod 13:21; Acts 1:9   **9:35** [a]Ps 2:7; [Isa 42:1; Matt 3:17; 12:18]; Mark 1:11; Luke 3:22   [b]Acts 3:22   [1]Maj. MSS *the one I love, the one I love, in whom I am well pleased*.   [2]Grk. *the One who has been chosen*.   **9:36** [a]Matt 17:9; Mark 9:9   **9:37** [a]Matt 17:14–18; Mark 9:14–27   **9:39** [1]Or *bruising, crushing*.

approaching, the demon threw him to the ground and shook him with convulsions. But Jesus rebuked the unclean spirit, healed the boy, and gave him back to his father. [43]Then they were all astonished at the mighty power of God.

Another Prediction of Jesus' Suffering

But while the entire crowd was amazed at everything Jesus[1] was doing, he said to his disciples, [44]"[a]Take these words to heart,[1] for the Son of Man is going to be betrayed into the hands of men." [45a]But they did not understand this statement; its meaning had been concealed from them, so that they could not grasp it. Yet they were afraid to ask him about this statement.

Concerning the Greatest

[46]Now an argument started among [a]the disciples as to which of them might be the greatest. [47]But when Jesus [a]discerned their innermost thoughts, he took a child, had him stand by his side, [48]and said to them, "[a]Whoever welcomes this child in my name welcomes me, and [b]whoever [c]welcomes me welcomes the one who sent me, [d]for the one who is least among you all is the one who is great."[1]

On the Right Side

[49a]John answered, "Master, we saw someone casting out demons in your name, and we tried to stop[1] him because he is not a disciple along with us." [50]But Jesus said to him, "Do not stop him, for whoever is not against you is for you."

Rejection in Samaria

[51]Now when the days drew near[1] for [a]him to be taken up, Jesus set out resolutely[2] to go to Jerusalem. [52]He sent messengers on ahead of him. As they went along, they entered a Samaritan village to make things ready in advance for him, [53]but [a]the villagers refused to welcome him because he was determined to go to Jerusalem. [54]Now when his disciples [a]James and John saw this, they said, "Lord, do you want us *to call fire to come down from heaven and consume them?*"[1,2] [55]But Jesus turned and rebuked them,[1] [56]and [a]they went on to another village.

Challenging Professed Followers

[57a]As they were walking[1] along the road, someone said to him, "I will follow you wherever you go."[2] [58]Jesus said to him, "Foxes have dens and the birds in the sky have nests, but the Son of Man [a]has no place to lay his head." [59]Jesus said to another, "Follow me." [a]But he replied, "Lord, first let me go and bury my father." [60]But Jesus said to him, "Let the dead bury their own dead, but as for you, go and proclaim the kingdom of God." [61]Yet another [a]said, "I will follow you, Lord, but first let me say goodbye to my family." [62]Jesus said to him, "No one who puts his hand to the plow and looks back is [a]fit for the kingdom of God."

The Mission of the Seventy-Two

10 After this the Lord appointed seventy-two[1] others and [a]sent them on ahead of him two by two into every town and place where he himself was about to go. [2]He said to [a]them, "The harvest is plentiful, but the workers are few. Therefore [b]ask the Lord of the harvest to send out workers into his harvest. [3]Go! I am sending you out like lambs surrounded by wolves. [4]Do not [a]carry a money bag, a traveler's bag, or sandals, and [b]greet no one on the road. [5a]Whenever you enter a house, first say, 'May peace be on this house!' [6]And if a peace-loving person[1] is there, your peace will remain on him, but if not, it will return to you. [7a]Stay in that same house, [b]eating and drinking what [c]they give you, for the worker deserves his pay. Do not move around from house to house. [8]Whenever you enter a town

9:43 [1]Many MSS omit *Jesus.*   **9:44** [a] Matt 17:22; Mark 10:33; 14:53; Luke 22:54; John 18:12   [1]Grk. *Place these words into your ears*; meaning either do not forget these words or listen carefully to these words.   **9:45** [a] Mark 9:32; Luke 2:50; 18:34   **9:46** [a] Matt 18:1–5; Mark 9:33–37; Luke 22:24   **9:47** [a] Matt 9:4; John 2:24–25   **9:48** [a] Matt 18:5   [b] Matt 10:40; Mark 9:37; John 12:44   [c] John 13:20   [d] [Matt 23:11–12]; 1 Cor 15:9; Eph 3:8   [1]Grk. *among you all, this one is great.*   **9:49** [a] Mark 9:38–40   [1]Maj. MSS *we forbade him.*   **9:51** [a] Isa 50:7; Mark 16:19; Acts 1:2   [1]Grk. *the days were being fulfilled.*   [2]Grk. *he set his face*; an idiom of a firm, unshakable resolve to do something.   **9:53** [a] John 4:4, 9   **9:54** [a] Mark 3:17   [1][2 Kgs 1:10, 12, 14]   [2]Maj. MSS add *as also Elijah did.*   **9:55** [1]Many MSS add *and he said, "You do not know what sort of spirit you are of, for the Son of Man did not come to destroy people's lives, but to save* [them]."   **9:56** [a] Luke 19:10; John 3:17; 12:47   **9:57** [a] Matt 8:19–22   [1]Grk. *going.*   [2]Maj. MSS add *Lord.*   **9:58** [a] Luke 2:7; 8:23   **9:59** [a] Matt 8:21–22   **9:61** [a] 1 Kgs 19:20   **9:62** [a] 2 Tim 4:10   **10:1** [a] Matt 10:1; Mark 6:7   [1]Sev. WSS *seventy.*   **10:2** [a] Matt 9:37–38; John 4:35   [b] [1 Cor 3:9]; 2 Thess 3:1   **10:4** [a] Matt 10:9–14; Mark 6:8–11; Luke 9:3–5   [b] 2 Kgs 4:29   **10:5** [a] 1 Sam 25:6; Matt 10:12   **10:6** [1]Grk. *a son of peace.*   **10:7** [a] Matt 10:11   [b] 1 Cor 10:27   [c] [Matt 10:10]; 1 Cor 9:4–8; 1 Tim 5:18

and the people welcome you, eat what is set before you. [9]Heal the sick in that town [a]and say to [b]them, 'The kingdom of God has come upon[1] you!' [10]But whenever you enter a town and the people do not welcome you, go into its streets and say, [11]'Even [a]the dust of your town that clings to our feet we wipe off against you. Nevertheless know this: The kingdom of God has come.' [12]I tell you, [a]it will be more bearable on that day for Sodom[1] than for that town!

[13]"[a]Woe to you, Chorazin! Woe to you, Bethsaida! [b]For if the miracles done in you had been done in Tyre and Sidon, they would have repented long ago, sitting in sackcloth and ashes. [14]But it will be more bearable for Tyre and Sidon in the judgment than for you! [15a]And you, Capernaum, will you be [b]exalted to heaven? No, you [c]will be thrown down to Hades!

[16]"The one who listens[1] to you listens to me, and [a]the one who rejects you rejects me, and [b]the one who rejects me rejects [c]the one who sent me."

[17]Then [a]the seventy-two[1] returned with joy, saying, "Lord, even the demons submit to us in your name!" [18]So he [a]said to them, "I saw Satan fall like lightning from heaven. [19]Look, [a]I have given you authority to tread on snakes and scorpions and on the full force of the enemy, and nothing will hurt you. [20]Nevertheless, do not rejoice that the spirits submit to [a]you, but rejoice that your names stand written in heaven."

[21]On that same occasion Jesus rejoiced [a]in the Holy Spirit and said, "I praise you, Father, Lord of heaven and earth, because you have hidden these things from the wise and intelligent and revealed them to little children. Yes, Father, for this was your gracious will.[1] [22]All [a]things have been given to me by my Father. [b]No one knows who the Son is except the Father, or who the Father is except the Son and anyone to whom the Son decides to reveal him."

[23]Then Jesus turned to his disciples and said privately, "[a]Blessed are the eyes that see what you see! [24]For I tell you [a]that many prophets and kings longed to see what you see but did not see it, and to hear what you hear but did not hear it."

The Parable of the Good Samaritan

[25]Now an expert in religious law[1] stood up to test Jesus, saying, "[a]Teacher, what must I do to inherit eternal life?" [26]He said to him, "What is written in the law? How do you understand it?" [27]The expert answered, "*Love the Lord [a]your God with all [b]your heart, with all your soul, with all your strength, and with all your mind,*[1] and *love your neighbor as yourself.*"[2] [28]Jesus said to him, "[a]You have answered correctly; do this, and you will live."

[29]But the expert, wanting to [a]justify himself, said to Jesus, "And who is my neighbor?" [30]Jesus replied, "A man was going down from Jerusalem to Jericho, and fell into the hands of robbers, who stripped him, beat him up, and went off, leaving him half dead. [31]Now by chance a priest was going down that road, but [a]when he saw the injured man, he passed by on the other side. [32]So too a Levite, when he came up to the place and saw him, passed by on the other side. [33]But a [a]Samaritan who was traveling came to where the injured man was, and when he saw him, he felt [b]compassion for him. [34]He went up to him and bandaged his wounds, pouring olive oil and wine on them. Then he put him on his own animal, brought him to an inn, and took care of him. [35]The next day he took out two silver [a]coins and gave them to the innkeeper, saying, 'Take care of him, and whatever else you spend, I will repay you when I come back this way.' [36]Which of these three do you think became a neighbor to the man who fell into the hands of the robbers?" [37]The expert in religious law said, "The one who showed mercy to him." So Jesus said to him, "[a]Go and do the same."

10:9 [a] Mark 3:15 [b] Matt 3:2; 10:7; Luke 10:11 [1] Or *come near to you*; suggesting the approach (but not arrival) of the kingdom. **10:11** [a] Matt 10:14; Mark 6:11; Luke 9:5; Acts 13:51 **10:12** [a] Gen 19:24–28; Lam 4:6; Matt 10:15; 11:24; Mark 6:11 [1] An emphatic Grk. construction. **10:13** [a] Matt 11:21–23 [b] Ezek 3:6 **10:15** [a] Matt 11:23 [b] Gen 11:4; Deut 1:28; Isa 14:13–15; Jer 51:53 [c] Ezek 26:20 **10:16** [a] Matt 10:40; Mark 9:37; John 13:20; Gal 4:14 [b] [John 12:48]; 1 Thess 4:8 [c] John 5:23 [1] Grk. *hears you.* **10:17** [a] Luke 10:1 [1] Sev. wss *seventy.* **10:18** [a] John 12:31; Rev 9:1; 12:8–9 **10:19** [a] Ps 91:13; Mark 16:18; Acts 28:5 **10:20** [a] [Exod 32:32–33]; Ps 69:28; Isa 4:3; Dan 12:1; Phil 4:3; Heb 12:23; Rev 13:8 **10:21** [a] Matt 11:25–27 [1] Grk. *for* (to do) *thus was well pleasing before you.* **10:22** [a] Matt 28:18; John 3:35; 5:27; 17:2 [b] [John 1:18; 6:44, 46] **10:23** [a] Matt 13:16–17 **10:24** [a] 1 Pet 1:10–11 **10:25** [a] Matt 19:16–19; 22:35 [1] Trad. *a lawyer*; an expert in the interpretation of the Mosaic law. **10:27** [a] Deut 6:5 [b] Lev 19:18; Matt 19:19 [1] Deut 6:5 [2] Lev 19:18 **10:28** [a] Lev 18:5; Neh 9:29; Ezek 20:11, 13, 21; Matt 19:17; Rom 10:5 **10:29** [a] Luke 16:15 **10:31** [a] Ps 38:11 **10:33** [a] John 4:9 [b] Luke 15:20 **10:35** [a] Matt 20:2 **10:37** [a] Prov 14:21; [Matt 9:13; 12:7]

Jesus and Martha

[38]Now as they went on their way, Jesus entered a certain village where a woman named [a]Martha welcomed him as a guest.[1] [39]She had a sister named Mary, [a]who [b]sat[1] at the Lord's feet and listened to what he said. [40]But Martha was distracted with all the preparations she had to make, so she came up to him and said, "Lord, don't you care[1] that my sister has left me to do all the work alone? Tell her to help me." [41]But the Lord[1] answered her, "Martha, Martha, you are worried and troubled about many things, [42]but one [a]thing[1] is needed. Mary has chosen the best[2] part; it will not be taken away from her."

Instructions on Prayer

11 Now Jesus was praying in a certain place. When he stopped, one of his disciples said to him, "Lord, teach us to pray, just as John taught his disciples." [2]So he said to them, "When you pray, say:

"'Father,[1] may [a]your name be
honored;
may your kingdom come.[2]
[3] Give us each day our daily bread,[1]
[4] and [a]forgive us our sins,
for we also forgive everyone who sins
against us.
And do not lead us into temptation.'"[1]

[5]Then he said to them, "Suppose one of you has a friend, and you go to him at midnight and say to him, 'Friend, lend me three loaves of bread, [6]because a friend of mine has stopped here while on a journey, and I have nothing to set before him.' [7]Then he will reply from inside, 'Do not bother me. The door is already shut, and my children and I are in bed. I cannot get up and give you anything.' [8]I tell you, even [a]though the man inside will not get up and give him anything because he is his friend, yet because of the first man's sheer persistence he will get up and give him whatever he needs.

[9]"[a]So I tell you: Ask, and it will be given to you; [b]seek, and you will find; knock, and the door will be opened for you. [10]For everyone who asks receives, and the one who seeks finds, and to the one who knocks, the door will be opened. [11]What father among you, [a]if your son asks for[1] a fish, will give him a snake instead of a fish? [12]Or if he asks for an egg, will give him a scorpion? [13]If you then, although you are evil, know how to give [a]good gifts to your children, how much more will the heavenly Father give the Holy Spirit to those who ask him!"

Jesus and Beelzebul

[14]Now he was casting out a demon that was mute.[1] When the demon had gone out, the man who had been mute began to speak, [a]and the crowds were amazed. [15]But some of [a]them said, "By the power of Beelzebul, the ruler of demons, he casts out demons!" [16]Others, to test him, began asking [a]for a sign from heaven. [17][a]But [b]Jesus, realizing their thoughts, said to them, "Every kingdom divided against itself is destroyed, and a divided household falls.[1] [18]So if Satan too is divided against himself, how will his kingdom stand? I ask you this because you claim that I cast out demons by Beelzebul. [19]Now if I cast out demons by Beelzebul, by whom do your sons cast them out? Therefore they will be your judges. [20]But if I cast out demons [a]by the finger of God, then the kingdom of God has already overtaken[1] you. [21][a]When a strong man, fully armed, guards his own palace, his possessions are safe. [22]But [a]when a stronger man attacks and conquers him, he takes away the first man's armor on which the man relied and divides up his plunder. [23]Whoever is not with me is against me, and whoever does not [a]gather with me scatters.

Response to Jesus' Work

[24]"[a]When an unclean spirit goes out of a person, it passes through waterless places

10:38 [a]John 11:1; 12:2–3 [1]Maj. mss *into the house, into her house.* 10:39 [a][1 Cor 7:32–40] [b]Luke 8:35; Acts 22:3 [1]The Grk. construction makes it clear that Mary took the initiative in sitting by Jesus. 10:40 [1]A rhetorical question expecting a positive answer. 10:41 [1]Maj. mss *Jesus.* 10:42 [a][Ps 27:4; John 6:27] [1]Some mss *few things are needed—or only one.* [2]Or *better,* Grk. *good.* 11:2 [a]Matt 6:9–13 [1]Maj. mss add *our [Father] in heaven.* [2]Maj. mss *may your will be done on earth as [it is] in heaven.* 11:3 [1]Or *Give us bread each day for the coming day, Give us each day the bread we need for today.* 11:4 [a][Eph 4:32] [1]Maj. mss add *but deliver us from the evil one.* 11:8 [a][Luke 18:1–5] 11:9 [a]Ps 50:14–15; Jer 33:3; [Matt 7:7; 21:22; Mark 11:24; John 15:7; Jas 1:5–6; 1 John 3:22; 5:14–15] [b]Isa 55:6 11:11 [a]Matt 7:9 [1]Maj. mss add *bread, does not give him a stone instead, or.* 11:13 [a]Jas 1:17 11:14 [a]Matt 9:32–34; 12:22, 24 [1]Grk. *a demon [and it was] mute.* 11:15 [a]Matt 9:34; 12:24 11:16 [a]Matt 12:38; 16:1; Mark 8:11 11:17 [a]Matt 12:25–29; Mark 3:23–27 [b]Matt 9:4; John 2:25 [1]Grk. *and house falls on house;* like "a house of cards." 11:20 [a]Exod 8:19 [1]Or *has come near to you.* 11:21 [a]Matt 12:29; Mark 3:27 11:22 [a][Isa 53:12; Col 2:15] 11:23 [a]Matt 12:30; Mark 9:40 11:24 [a]Matt 12:43–45; Mark 1:27; 3:11; 5:13; Acts 5:16; 8:7

looking for rest but not finding any. Then[1] it says, 'I will return to the home I left.' [25]When it returns, it finds the house swept clean and put in order. [26]Then it goes and brings seven [a]other spirits more evil than itself, and they go in and live there, so the last state of that person is worse than the first."

[27]As he said these things, a woman in the crowd spoke out to him, "[a]Blessed is the womb that bore you and the breasts at which you nursed!" [28]But he replied, "Blessed rather are those who hear the word of God and obey it!"

The Sign of Jonah

[29]As the crowds were increasing, Jesus began to say, "This generation is [a]a wicked generation; it looks for a [b]sign, but no sign will be given to it except the sign of Jonah. [30]For just as [a]Jonah became a sign to the people of Nineveh, so the Son of Man will be a sign to this generation.[1] [31]The queen of [a]the South will rise up [b]at the judgment with the people[1] of this generation and condemn them, because she came from the ends of the earth to hear the wisdom of Solomon—and now, something greater than Solomon is here! [32]The people of Nineveh will stand up at [a]the judgment with this generation and condemn it, because they repented when Jonah preached to them— and now, something greater than Jonah is here!

Internal Light

[33]"No [a]one after lighting a lamp puts it in a hidden place or under a [b]basket,[1] but on a lampstand, so that those who come in can see the light. [34]Your eye is [a]the lamp of your body. When your eye is healthy, your whole body is full of light, but when it is diseased, your body is full of darkness. [35]Therefore see to it that the light in you is not darkness. [36]If then your whole body is full of light, with no part in the dark, it will be as full of light as when the light of a lamp shines on you."

Rebuking the Pharisees and Experts in the Law

[37]As he spoke, a Pharisee invited Jesus to have a meal with him, so he went in and took his place at the table. [38]The Pharisee was astonished [a]when he saw that Jesus did not first wash his hands before the meal. [39]But the Lord said to him, "Now you Pharisees clean the outside of the cup and the plate, [a]but inside [b]you are full of greed and wickedness. [40]You fools! Didn't [a]the one who made the outside make the inside as well?[1] [41a]But give from your heart to those in need,[1] and then everything will be clean for you.

[42]"[a]But woe to you Pharisees! You give a tenth of your mint, rue, and every herb, yet you [b]neglect justice and [c]love for God! But you should have done these things without neglecting the others. [43a]Woe to you Pharisees! You love the best seats[1] in the synagogues and elaborate greetings in the marketplaces! [44a]Woe to you!]1 You are like unmarked graves, and people walk over them without realizing it!"

[45]One of the experts in religious law answered him, "Teacher, when you say these things, you insult us too." [46]But Jesus replied, "Woe to you experts in religious law as well! You load people down with burdens difficult to bear, yet you yourselves refuse to touch the burdens with even one of your fingers! [47a]Woe to you! You build the tombs of the prophets whom your ancestors killed. [48]So you testify that you approve of the deeds of your ancestors because they killed the prophets and you build their tombs![1] [49]For [a]this reason also the wisdom of God said, 'I will send them prophets and apostles, some of whom they will kill and persecute,' [50]so that this generation may be held accountable for the blood of all the prophets that has been shed since the beginning of the world, [51a]from the blood of Abel to the blood of Zechariah, who was killed between the altar and the sanctuary. Yes, I tell you, it will be charged against this

generation. [52][a]Woe to you experts in religious law! You have taken away the key to knowledge! You did not go in yourselves, and you hindered those who were going in."

[53]When he went out from there, the experts in the law and the Pharisees began to oppose him bitterly and to ask him hostile questions about many things, [54]plotting against[1] him to catch[2] him [a]in something he might say.

Fear God, not People

12 Meanwhile, when many thousands of [a]the crowd had gathered so that they were trampling on one another, Jesus began to speak first to his disciples, "Be [b]on your guard against the yeast of the Pharisees, which is hypocrisy. [2][a]Nothing is hidden that will not be revealed, and nothing is secret that will not be made known. [3]So then whatever you have said in the dark will be heard in the light, and what you have whispered in private rooms will be proclaimed from the housetops.[1]

[4]"[a]I tell you, [b]my friends, do not be afraid of those who kill the body, and after that have nothing more they can do. [5]But I will warn you whom you should [a]fear: Fear the one who, after the killing, has authority to throw you into hell. Yes, I tell you, fear him! [6]Aren't five sparrows sold for two pennies? Yet [a]not one of them is forgotten before God. [7]In fact, even the hairs on your head are all numbered. Do not be afraid; you are more valuable than many sparrows.

[8]"I tell you, whoever acknowledges me before men, the Son of Man will [a]also acknowledge [b]before God's angels. [9]But the one who [a]denies me before men will be denied before God's angels. [10]And [a]everyone who speaks a word against the Son of Man will be forgiven, but the person who blasphemes against the Holy Spirit will not be forgiven. [11][a]But when they bring you before the synagogues, the rulers, and the authorities, do not worry about how you should make your defense or what you should say,

[12]for the Holy Spirit will [a]teach you at that moment[1] what you must say."

The Parable of the Rich Landowner

[13]Then someone from the crowd said to him, "Teacher, tell my brother to divide the inheritance with me." [14]But Jesus said to him, "[a]Man, who made me a judge or arbitrator between you two?" [15]Then he said to them, "Watch out and guard yourself from all types of greed[1] because one's life does not consist in the abundance of his possessions." [16]He then told them a parable: "The land of a certain rich man produced an abundant crop, [17]so he thought to himself, 'What should I do, for I have nowhere to store my crops?' [18]Then he said, 'I will do this: I will tear down my barns and build bigger ones, and there I will store all my grain and my goods. [19]And I will say to [a]myself, "You have plenty of goods stored up for many years; relax, [b]eat, drink, celebrate!"' [20]But God said to him, 'You fool! This very night [a]your life[1] will be demanded back from you, [b]but who will get what you have prepared for yourself?' [21]So it is with the one who stores up riches for himself, [a]but is not rich toward God."

Exhortation not to Worry

[22]Then Jesus said to his[1] disciples, "Therefore I tell you, [a]do not worry about your[2] life, what you will eat, or about your[3] body, what you will wear. [23]For there is more to life than food, and more to the body than clothing. [24]Consider the ravens: They do not sow or reap, they have no storeroom or barn, yet [a]God feeds them. How much more valuable are you than the birds! [25]And which of you by worrying can add an hour to his life?[1] [26]So if you cannot do such a very little thing as this, why do you worry about the rest? [27]Consider how the flowers[1] grow; they do not work or spin. Yet I tell you, not even [a]Solomon in all his glory was clothed like one of these! [28]And if this is how God clothes the wild grass, which is here today

11:52 [a]Matt 23:13   **11:54** [a]Mark 12:13   [1]Grk. *lying in ambush against.*   [2]A hunting term.   **12:1** [a]Matt 16:6; Mark 8:15   [b]Matt 16:12; Luke 11:39   **12:2** [a]Matt 10:26; Mark 4:22; Luke 8:17; [1 Cor 4:5]   **12:3** [1]An idiom for proclaiming something publicly.   **12:4** [a]Isa 51:7–8, 12, 13; Jer 1:8; Matt 10:28   [b][John 15:13–15]   **12:5** [a]Ps 119:120   **12:6** [a]Matt 6:26   **12:8** [a]1 Sam 2:30; Matt 10:32; [Mark 8:38; Rom 10:9; 2 Tim 2:12; 1 John 2:23]   [b]Ps 119:46   **12:9** [a]Matt 10:33; [Mark 8:38; 2 Tim 2:12]   **12:10** [a][Matt 12:31–32; Mark 3:28; 1 John 5:16]   **12:11** [a]Matt 6:25; 10:19; Mark 13:11   **12:12** [a][John 14:26]   [1]Grk. *in that very hour;* an idiom.   **12:14** [a][John 18:36]   **12:15** [1]Or *avarice, covetousness.*   **12:19** [a]Eccl 11:9; 1 Cor 15:32; Jas 5:5   [b][Eccl 2:24; 3:13; 5:18; 8:15]   **12:20** [a]Job 27:8; Ps 52:7; [Jas 4:14]   [b]Ps 39:6; Jer 17:11   [1]Grk. *your soul.*   **12:21** [a][Matt 6:20; Luke 12:33; 1 Tim 6:18–19; Jas 2:5; 5:1–5]   **12:22** [a]Matt 6:25–33   [1]Some early MSS omit *his.*   [2]Sev. sig. WSS omit *your.*   [3]Sev. sig. WSS omit *your.*   **12:24** [a]Job 38:41; Ps 147:9   **12:25** [1]Or *a cubit to his height.*   **12:27** [a]1 Kgs 10:4–7; 2 Chr 9:3–6   [1]Trad. *lilies.*

and tomorrow is tossed into the fire to heat the oven, how much more will he clothe you, you people of [a]little faith! [29]So do not be overly concerned about what you will eat and what you will drink, and do not worry about such things. [30]For all the nations of the world pursue these things, and your Father [a]knows that you need them. [31][a]Instead, pursue his[1] kingdom, and these things will be given to you as well.

[32]"Do not be afraid, [a]little flock, for your Father is well pleased to give you the kingdom. [33][a]Sell your possessions and give to the [b]poor. [c]Provide yourselves purses that do not wear out—a treasure in heaven that never decreases, where no thief approaches and no moth destroys. [34]For where your treasure is, there your heart will be also.

Call to Faithful Stewardship

[35]"[a]Get dressed for service[1] and keep [b]your lamps burning; [36]be like people waiting for their master to come back from the wedding celebration, so that when he comes and knocks, they can immediately open the door for him. [37][a]Blessed are those slaves whom their master finds alert[1] when he returns! I tell you the truth, he will dress himself to serve, have them take their place at the table, and will come and wait on them! [38]Even if he comes in the second or third watch of the night and finds them alert, blessed are those slaves! [39][a]But understand this: If the owner of the house had known at what hour the thief was coming, he would not have let[1] his house be broken into. [40]You also must be ready because [a]the Son of Man will come at an hour when you do not expect him."

[41]Then Peter said, "Lord, are you telling this parable for us or for everyone?" [42]The Lord replied, "[a]Who then is the faithful and wise manager, whom the master puts in charge of his household servants, to give them their allowance of food at the proper time? [43]Blessed is that slave whom his master finds at work[1] when he returns. [44]I tell you the [a]truth, the master will put him in charge of all his possessions. [45][a]But if that slave should say to himself, 'My master is delayed in returning,' and he begins to beat the other slaves, both men and women, and to eat, drink, and get drunk, [46]then the master of that slave will come on a [a]day when he does not expect him and at an hour he does not foresee, and will cut him in two,[1] and assign him a place with the unfaithful.[2] [47][a]That servant who [b]knew his master's will but did not get ready or do what his master asked will receive a severe beating. [48][a]But the one who did not know his master's will and did things worthy of punishment will receive a light beating. From everyone who has been given much, much will be required, and from the one who has been entrusted with much, even more will be asked.

Not Peace, but Division

[49]"I have come to [a]bring fire on the earth—and how I wish it were already kindled! [50]I have a [a]baptism to undergo, and how distressed I am until it is [b]finished! [51][a]Do you think I have come to bring peace on earth? No, I tell you, [b]but rather division! [52][a]For from now on there will be five in one household divided, three against two and two against three. [53]They will be divided, [a]father against son and son against father, mother against daughter and daughter against mother, mother-in-law against her daughter-in-law and daughter-in-law against mother-in-law."

Reading the Signs

[54]Jesus also said to the crowds, "[a]When you see a cloud rising in the west, you say at once, 'A rainstorm is coming,' and it does. [55]And when you see the south [a]wind blowing, you say, 'There will be scorching heat,' and there is. [56]You hypocrites! You know how to interpret the appearance of

12:28 [a]Matt 6:30; 8:26; 14:31; 16:8   12:30 [a]Matt 6:31–32   12:31 [a]Matt 6:33   [1]Maj. MSS *kingdom of God*.   12:32 [a][Dan 7:18, 27]; Zech 13:7; [Matt 11:25–26; Luke 22:29–30]   12:33 [a]Matt 19:21; Acts 2:45; 4:34   [b]Luke 11:41   [c]Matt 6:20; Luke 16:9; [1 Tim 6:19]   12:35 [a][Eph 6:14; 1 Pet 1:13]   [b][Matt 25:1–13]   [1]Grk. *Let your loins be girded*; tucking the ends of the outer garment into the belt to shorten it in preparation for activities like running.   12:37 [a]Matt 24:46   [1]Or *watching*.   12:39 [a]Matt 24:43; 1 Thess 5:2; [2 Pet 3:10]; Rev 3:3; 16:15   [1]Maj. MSS *he would have watched and not let*.   12:40 [a]Matt 24:44; 25:13; Mark 13:33; [Luke 21:34, 36]; 1 Thess 5:6; [2 Pet 3:12]   12:42 [a]Matt 24:45–46; 25:21; [1 Cor 4:2]   12:43 [1]I.e., doing what he is supposed to be doing.   12:44 [a]Matt 24:47; 25:21; [Rev 3:21]   12:45 [a]Matt 24:48; 2 Pet 3:3–4   12:46 [a]1 Thess 5:3   [1]If taken lit., this servant is dismembered, but it could be hyperbole.   [2]Or *unbelieving*.   12:47 [a]Num 15:30; Deut 25:2; [John 9:41; 15:22; Acts 17:30]   [b][Jas 4:17]   12:48 [a][Lev 5:17]; Num 15:29; [1 Tim 1:13]   12:49 [a]Luke 12:51   12:50 [a]Matt 20:18, 22, 23; Mark 10:38   [b]John 12:27; 19:30   12:51 [a]Matt 10:34–36   [b]Mic 7:6; John 7:43; 9:16; 10:19; Acts 14:4   12:52 [a]Matt 10:35; Mark 13:12   12:53 [a]Matt 10:21, 36   12:54 [a]Matt 16:2–3   12:55 [a]Job 37:17

the earth and the sky, but how can you not know how[1] to interpret the present time?

Clear the Debts

57"And why don't you judge for yourselves what is right? 58aAs you are going with your accuser before the magistrate, make an effort to settle with him bon the way, so that he will not drag you before the judge, and the judge hand you over to the officer, and the officer throw you into prison. 59I tell you, you will never get out of there until you have paid the very last cent!"

A Call to Repent

13 Now there were some present on that occasion who told him about the Galileans whose blood Pilate had mixed with their sacrifices. 2He answered them, "Do you think these Galileans were worse sinners than all the other Galileans because they suffered these things? 3No, I tell you! But unless you repent, you will all perish as well! 4Or those eighteen who were killed when the tower in Siloam fell on them, do you think they were worse offenders than all the others who live in Jerusalem? 5No, I tell you! But unless you repent you will all perish as well!"[1]

Warning to Israel to Bear Fruit

6Then Jesus told this aparable: "A man had a fig tree planted in his vineyard, and he came looking for fruit on it and found none. 7So he said to the worker who tended the vineyard, 'For three years now, I have come looking for fruit on this fig tree, and each time I inspect it I find none. Cut[1] it down! Why should it continue to deplete the soil?' 8But the worker answered him, 'Sir, leave it alone this year too, until I dig around it and put fertilizer on it. 9Then if it bears fruit next year, very well, but if not, you can acut it down.'"

Healing on the Sabbath

10Now he was teaching in one of the synagogues on the Sabbath, 11and a woman was there who had been disabled by a spirit[1] for eighteen years. She was bent over and could not straighten herself up completely. 12When Jesus saw her, he called her to him and said, "Woman, you are freed from your ainfirmity." 13Then he placed his hands on her, aand immediately she straightened up and praised God. 14But the president of the synagogue, indignant because Jesus had ahealed on bthe Sabbath, said to the crowd, "There are six days on which work should be done! So come and be healed on those days, and cnot on the Sabbath day." 15Then the Lord answered him, "You hypocrites! aDoes not each of you on the Sabbath untie his ox or his donkey from its stall and lead it to water? 16Then shouldn't this woman, a daughter of Abraham whom Satan bound for eighteen long years, abe released from this imprisonment[1] on the Sabbath day?" 17When he said this, all his adversaries were humiliated, but the entire crowd was rejoicing at all the wonderful things he was adoing.

On the Kingdom of God

18Thus Jesus asked, "What is athe kingdom of God like? To what should I compare it? 19It is like a mustard seed that a man took and sowed in his garden. It grew and became a tree, and the wild birds nested in its branches."

20Again he said, "To what should I compare the kingdom of God? 21It is like yeast that a woman took and mixed with three ameasures of flour until all the dough had risen."

The Narrow Door

22Then Jesus traveled throughout towns aand villages, teaching and making his way toward Jerusalem. 23Someone asked him, "Lord, will only a afew be saved?" So he said to them, 24"Exert every aeffort to enter through the narrow door because bmany, I tell you, will try to enter and will not be able to. 25aOnce the head of the house gets up and bshuts the door, then you will stand outside and start to knock on the door and beg him, 'cLord, let us din!' But he will

---

12:56 [1] Maj. mss *but how do you not interpret the present time.* **12:58** a Prov 25:8; Matt 5:25–26 b [Ps 32:6; Isa 55:6] **13:5** [1] Or *similarly.* **13:6** a Isa 5:2; Matt 21:19 **13:7** [1] ‡ Sev. wss *therefore.* **13:9** a [John 15:2] **13:11** [1] Grk. *a woman having a spirit of weakness, a spirit of infirmity.* **13:12** a Luke 7:21; 8:2 **13:13** a Mark 16:18; Acts 9:17 **13:14** a [Luke 6:6–11; 14:1–6]; John 5:16 b Exod 20:9; 23:12 c Matt 12:10; Mark 3:2; Luke 6:7; 14:3 **13:15** a [Matt 7:5; 23:13]; Luke 14:5 **13:16** a Luke 19:9 [1] Or *bondage;* Grk. *bond.* **13:17** a Mark 5:19–20 **13:18** a Matt 13:31–32; Mark 4:30–32 **13:21** a Matt 13:33 **13:22** a Matt 9:35; Mark 6:6 **13:23** a [Matt 7:14; 20:16] **13:24** a [Matt 7:13] b [John 7:34; 8:21; 13:33; Rom 9:31] **13:25** a [Ps 32:6]; Isa 55:6 b Matt 25:10; Rev 22:11 c Luke 6:46 d Matt 7:23; 25:12

answer you, 'I don't know where you come from.' [26]Then you will begin to say, 'We ate and drank in your presence, and you taught in our streets.' [27][a]But he will reply,[1] 'I don't know where you come from! Go [b]away from me, all you evildoers!' [28][a]There will be weeping and gnashing of teeth [b]when you see Abraham, Isaac, Jacob, and all the prophets in the kingdom of God but you yourselves thrown out. [29]Then people will come from east and west, and from north and south, and take their places at the banquet table in the kingdom of God. [30]But indeed, some are last who will be first, [a]and some are first who will be last."

Going to Jerusalem

[31]At that time, some Pharisees came up and said to Jesus, "Get away from here because Herod wants to kill you." [32]But he [a]said to them, "Go and tell that fox, 'Look, I am casting out demons and performing healings today and tomorrow, and on the third day I will complete my work. [33]Nevertheless I must go on my way today and tomorrow and the next day, because it is impossible that a prophet should be killed outside Jerusalem.' [34]O Jerusalem, Jerusalem, [a]you who kill the prophets and stone those who are sent to you! How often I have longed to gather your children together as a hen gathers her chicks under her wings, but you would have none of it! [35]Look, [a]your house is forsaken! And I tell you, you will not see me until you say, '[b]*Blessed is the one who comes in the name of the Lord!*'"[1]

Healing Again on the Sabbath

14 Now one Sabbath when Jesus went to dine at the house of a leader[1] of the Pharisees, they were watching him closely. [2]There right in front of him was a man whose body was swollen with fluid. [3]So Jesus asked the experts in religious law and the [a]Pharisees, "Is it lawful to heal on the Sabbath or not?" [4]But they remained silent. So Jesus took hold of the man, healed him, and sent him away. [5]Then he said to them,

"[a]Which of you, if you have a son[1] or an ox that has fallen into a well on a Sabbath day, will not immediately pull him out?" [6]But they could not reply to this.

On Seeking Seats of Honor

[7]Then when Jesus noticed how the guests chose the places of honor,[1] he told them a parable. He said to them, [8]"When you are invited by someone to a wedding feast, do not take the place of honor because a person more distinguished than you may have been invited by your host. [9]So the host who invited both of you will come and say to you, 'Give this man your place.' Then, ashamed,[1] you will begin to move to the least important place. [10][a]But when you are invited, go and take the least important place, so that when your host approaches he will say to you, 'Friend, move up here to a better place.' Then you will be honored in the presence of all who share the meal with you. [11][a]For everyone who exalts himself will be humbled, but the one who humbles himself will be exalted."

[12]He said also to the man who had invited him, "When you host a dinner or a banquet, don't invite your friends or your brothers or your relatives or rich neighbors so you can be invited by them in return and get repaid. [13]But when you host an elaborate meal, invite [a]the poor, the crippled, the lame, and the blind. [14]Then you will be [a]blessed because they cannot repay you, for you will be repaid at the resurrection of the righteous."

The Parable of the Great Banquet

[15]When one of those at the meal with Jesus heard this, he said to him, "[a]Blessed is everyone who will feast in the kingdom of God!" [16][a]But Jesus said to him, "A man once gave a great banquet and invited many guests. [17]At the time for the banquet he [a]sent his slave to tell those who had been invited, 'Come, because everything is now ready.' [18]But one after another they all began to make excuses. The first said to

13:27 [a][Matt 7:23; 25:41] [b]Ps 6:8; [Matt 25:41]; Titus 1:16 [1]Maj. MSS *he will say, 'I say to you', he will say.* **13:28** [a]Matt 8:12; 13:42; 24:51 [b]Matt 8:11 **13:30** [a][Matt 19:30; 20:16]; Mark 10:31 **13:32** [a]Luke 24:46; Acts 10:40; 1 Cor 15:4; [Heb 2:10; 5:9; 7:28] **13:34** [a]Matt 23:37–39; 2 Chr 24:20–21; 36:15–16 **13:35** [a]Lev 26:31–32; Ps 69:25; Isa 1:7; Jer 22:5; Dan 9:27; Mic 3:12 [b]Ps 118:26; Matt 21:9; Mark 11:10; Luke 19:38; John 12:13 [1]Ps 118:26 **14:1** [1]Grk. *a ruler of the Pharisees*; probably a synagogue official. **14:3** [a]Matt 12:10 **14:5** [a][Exod 23:5; Deut 22:4]; Luke 13:15 [1]Some MSS *donkey.* **14:7** [1]Or *the best places*; closest to the host. **14:9** [1]Or *then in disgrace.* **14:10** [a]Prov 25:6–7 **14:11** [a]Job 22:29; Ps 18:27; Prov 29:23; Matt 23:12; Luke 18:14; Jas 4:6; [1 Pet 5:5] **14:13** [a]Neh 8:10, 12 **14:14** [a][Matt 25:34–40] **14:15** [a]Rev 19:9 **14:16** [a]Matt 22:2–14 **14:17** [a]Prov 9:2, 5

him, 'I have bought a field, and I must go out and see it. Please excuse me.' [19] Another said, 'I have bought five yoke of oxen, and I am going out to examine them. Please excuse me.' [20] Another said, 'I just got married, and I cannot come.' [21] So the slave came back and reported this to his master. Then the master of the household was furious and said to his slave, 'Go out quickly to the streets and alleys of the city, and bring in the poor, the crippled, the blind, and the lame.' [22] Then the slave said, 'Sir, what you instructed has been done, and there is still room.' [23] So the master said to his slave, 'Go out to the highways and country roads and urge[1] people to come in, so that my house will be filled. [24] For I tell you, not one of those individuals who were invited will taste my banquet!'"

Counting the Cost

[25] Now large crowds were accompanying Jesus, and turning to them he said, [26] "If anyone comes to me and does not hate[1] his own father and mother, and [a]wife [b]and children, and brothers and sisters, and [c]even his own life,[2] he cannot be my disciple. [27][a]Whoever does not carry his own cross and follow me cannot be my disciple. [28] For [a]which of you, wanting to build a tower, doesn't sit down first and compute the cost to see if he has enough money to complete it? [29] Otherwise, when he has laid a foundation and is not able to finish the tower, all who see it will begin to make fun of him. [30] They will say, 'This man began to build and was not able to finish!' [31] Or what king, going out to confront another king in battle, will not sit down first and determine whether he is able with 10,000 to oppose[1] the one coming against him with 20,000? [32] If he cannot succeed, he will send a representative while the other is still a long way off and ask for terms of peace. [33] In the same way therefore not one of you can be my disciple if he [a]does not renounce all his own possessions.

[34] "[a]Salt is good, but if salt loses its flavor, how can its flavor be restored? [35] It is of no value for the soil or for the manure pile; it is to be thrown out. The one who has ears to hear had better listen!"[1]

The Parable of the Lost Sheep and Coin

15 Now [a]all the tax collectors and sinners were coming to hear him. [2] But the Pharisees [a]and the experts in the law were complaining, "This man welcomes sinners and eats with them."

[3] So Jesus told them this parable: [4] "Which one of you, if he has [a]a hundred sheep and loses one of them, would not leave the ninety-nine in the open pasture[1] and go look for the one that is lost until he finds it? [5] Then when he has found it, he places it on his shoulders, rejoicing. [6] Returning home, he calls together his friends and neighbors, telling them, 'Rejoice [a]with me because [b]I have found my sheep that was lost.' [7] I tell you, in the same way there will be more joy in heaven over one sinner who repents [a]than over ninety-nine righteous people who have no [b]need to repent.

[8] "Or what woman, if she has ten silver coins and loses one of them, does not light a lamp, sweep the house, and search thoroughly until she finds it? [9] Then when she has found it, she calls together her friends and neighbors, saying, 'Rejoice with me, for I have found the coin that I had lost.' [10] In the same way, I tell you, there is joy in the presence of God's angels over one sinner who repents."

The Parable of the Compassionate Father

[11] Then Jesus said, "A man had two sons. [12] The younger of them said to [a]his father, 'Father, give me the share of the estate that will belong to me.' So he divided his assets between them. [13] After a few days, the younger son gathered together all he had and left on a journey to a distant country, and there he squandered his wealth with a wild lifestyle. [14] Then after he had spent everything, a severe famine took place in that country, and he began to be in need. [15] So he went and worked for one of the citizens of that country, who sent him to his fields to feed pigs. [16] He was longing to eat the carob pods the pigs were eating, but no one gave him anything. [17] But when he came to his senses, he said, 'How many of my father's hired workers have food enough to spare, but here I am

---

14:23 [1] Trad. *force, compel.*   **14:26** [a] Deut 13:6; 33:9; Matt 10:37   [b] Rom 9:13   [c] Rev 12:11   [1] This figurative use is relative: God is to be loved more than family or self.   [2] Grk. *his own soul.*   **14:27** [a] Matt 16:24; Mark 8:34; Luke 9:23; [2 Tim 3:12]
14:28 [a] Prov 24:27   **14:31** [1] Or *to meet in battle, to face in battle.*   **14:33** [a] Matt 19:27   **14:34** [a] Matt 5:13; [Mark 9:50]
14:35 [1] Trad. *let him hear.*   **15:1** [a] [Matt 9:10–13]   **15:2** [a] Acts 11:3; Gal 2:12   **15:4** [a] Matt 18:12–14; 1 Pet 2:25   [1] Or *desert.*
15:6 [a] [Rom 12:15]   [b] [Luke 19:10; 1 Pet 2:10, 25]   **15:7** [a] [Luke 5:32]   [b] [Mark 2:17]   **15:12** [a] Mark 12:44

dying from hunger! [18] I [a]will get up and go to my father and say to him, "Father, I have sinned against heaven and against you. [19] I am no longer worthy to be called your son; treat me[1] like one of your hired workers."' [20] So [a]he got up and went to his father. But while he was still a long way from home his father saw him, and his heart went out to him;[1] he ran and hugged his son and kissed him. [21] Then his son said to him, 'Father, I have sinned against heaven [a]and against you; I am no longer worthy to be called your son.' [22] But the father said to his slaves, 'Hurry! Bring the best robe, and put it on him! Put a ring on his finger and sandals on his feet! [23] Bring the fattened calf[1] and kill it! Let us eat and celebrate, [24a]because this son of mine was dead, and is alive again—he was lost and is found!' So they began to celebrate.

[25] "Now his older son was in the field. As he came and approached the house, he heard music and dancing. [26] So he called one of the slaves and asked what was happening. [27] The slave replied, 'Your brother has returned, and your father has killed the fattened calf because he got his son back safe and sound.' [28] But the older son became angry and refused to go in. His father came out and appealed to him, [29] but he answered his father, 'Look! These many years I have worked like a slave for you, and I never disobeyed your commands. Yet you never gave me even a goat so that I could celebrate with my friends! [30] But when this son of yours came back, who has devoured your assets with prostitutes, you killed the fattened calf for him!' [31] Then the father said to him, 'Son, you are always with me, and everything that belongs to me is yours. [32] It was appropriate to celebrate and be glad, [a]for your brother was dead, and is alive; he was lost and is found.'"

The Parable of the Clever Steward

16 Jesus also said to the disciples, "There was a rich man who was informed of accusations[1] that his manager was wasting[2] his assets. [2] So he called the manager in and said to him, 'What is this I hear about you? Turn in the [a]account of your administration, because you can no longer be my manager.' [3] Then the manager said to himself, 'What should I do, since my master is taking my position away from me? I'm not strong enough to dig,[1] and I'm too ashamed to beg. [4] I know what to do so that when I am put out of management, people will welcome me into their homes.' [5] So he contacted his master's debtors one by one. He asked the first, 'How much do you owe my master?' [6] The man replied, '100 measures of olive oil.' The manager said to him, 'Take your bill, sit down quickly, and write 50.' [7] Then he said to another, 'And how much do you owe?' The second man replied, '100 measures of wheat.' The manager said to him, 'Take your bill, and write 80.' [8] The master commended [a]the dishonest manager because he acted shrewdly. For the people of this world are more shrewd in dealing with their contemporaries than the people[1] of light. [9] And I tell you, [a]make friends for yourselves by how you use worldly wealth,[1] so that when it runs out, you will be welcomed into the eternal homes.

[10] "The one who is faithful in a very little is also faithful in much, and [a]the one who is dishonest in a very little is also dishonest in much. [11] If then you haven't been trustworthy in handling worldly wealth, who will entrust you with the true riches? [12] And if you haven't been trustworthy with someone else's property, who will give you your [a]own? [13a]No servant can serve two masters, for either he will hate the one and love the other, or he will be devoted to the one and despise the other. You cannot serve God and money."

More Warnings about the Pharisees

[14] The Pharisees ([a]who loved money) heard all this and ridiculed him. [15] But Jesus said to them, "You are the ones who [a]justify yourselves [b]in men's eyes,[1] but [c]God knows your hearts. For [d]what is highly prized[2] among men is utterly detestable in God's sight.

15:18 [a] Exod 9:27; 10:16; Num 22:34; Josh 7:20; 1 Sam 15:24, 30; 26:21; 2 Sam 12:13; 24:10, 17; Ps 51:4; Matt 27:4   15:19 [1] Or *make me*; a sign of total humility.   15:20 [a] [Jer 3:12]; Matt 9:36; [Acts 2:39; Eph 2:13, 17]   [1] Or *felt great affection for him, felt great pity for him.*   15:21 [a] Ps 51:4   15:23 [1] Or *the prize calf.*   15:24 [a] Matt 8:22; Luke 9:60; 15:32; Rom 11:15; [Eph 2:1, 5; 5:14; Col 2:13; 1 Tim 5:6]   15:32 [a] Luke 15:24   16:1 [1] Not formal legal charges, but reports from friends, acquaintances, etc.   [2] Or *squandering.*   16:2 [a] [Rom 14:12; 2 Cor 5:10; 1 Pet 4:5–6]   16:3 [1] Labor performed by the uneducated; an insulting job for a manager.   16:8 [a] [John 12:36; Eph 5:8]; 1 Thess 5:5   [1] Grk. *sons*; "sons of light" is a reference to the righteous.   16:9 [a] Dan 4:27; [Matt 6:19; 19:21]; Luke 11:41; [1 Tim 6:17–19]   [1] Grk. *unrighteous mammon.*   16:10 [a] Matt 25:21; Luke 19:17   16:12 [a] [1 Pet 1:3–4]   16:13 [a] Matt 6:24; Gal 1:10   16:14 [a] Matt 23:14   16:15 [a] Luke 10:29   [b] [Matt 6:2, 5, 16]   [c] 1 Chr 28:9; 2 Chr 6:30; Ps 7:9; Prov 15:11; Jer 17:10   [d] 1 Sam 16:7; Ps 10:3; Prov 6:16–19; 16:5   [1] Grk. *before men.*   [2] Or *exalted*; the pride that often comes with money and position.

[16]"The law and [a]the prophets were in force until John; since then, the good news of the kingdom of God has been proclaimed, and everyone is urged to enter it.[1] [17]But it is easier for heaven [a]and earth to pass away than for one tiny stroke of a letter[1] in the law to become void.

[18]"Everyone [a]who divorces his wife and marries someone else commits adultery, and the one who marries a woman divorced from her husband commits adultery.

The Rich Man and Lazarus

[19]"There was a rich man who dressed in purple and fine linen and who feasted sumptuously[1] every day. [20]But at his gate lay a poor man named Lazarus whose body was covered with sores, [21]who longed to eat what fell from the rich man's table. In addition, the dogs[1] came and licked his sores.

[22]"Now the poor man died and was carried by the angels to [a]Abraham's side.[1] The rich man also died and was buried. [23]And in Hades, as he was in torment, he looked up and saw Abraham far off with Lazarus at his side. [24]So he called out, 'Father Abraham, have mercy on me, and send Lazarus to dip the tip of his finger in water and [a]cool my tongue because I [b]am in anguish in this fire.' [25]But Abraham said, 'Child, [a]remember that in your lifetime you received your good things and Lazarus likewise bad things, but now he is comforted here and you are in anguish. [26]Besides all this, a great chasm has been fixed between us, so that those who want to cross over from here to you cannot do so, and no one can cross from there to us.' [27]So the rich man said, 'Then I beg you, father—send Lazarus to my father's house [28](for I have five brothers) to warn them so that they don't come into this place of torment.' [29]But Abraham said, '[a]They have Moses and the prophets; they must respond to them.' [30]Then the rich man said, 'No, father Abraham, but if someone from the dead goes to them, they will repent.' [31]He replied to him, '[a]If they do not respond to Moses and the prophets, they will [b]not be convinced even if someone rises from the dead.'"

Sin, Forgiveness, Faith, and Service

17 Jesus said to his disciples, "Stumbling blocks are sure to come, but [a]woe to the one through whom they come! [2]It would be better for him to have a millstone tied around his neck and be thrown into the sea than for him to cause one of these little ones to sin.[1] [3]Watch yourselves! [a]If your brother[1] sins, [b]rebuke him. If he repents, forgive him. [4]Even if he sins against you seven times in a day, and seven times returns to you saying, 'I repent,' you must forgive him."

[5]The apostles said to the Lord, "Increase our faith!" [6][a]So the Lord replied, "If you had faith the size of a mustard seed, you could say to this black mulberry tree, 'Be pulled out by the roots and planted in the sea,'[1] and it would obey you.

[7]"Would any one of you say to your slave who comes in from the field after plowing or shepherding sheep, 'Come at once and sit down for a meal'? [8]Won't the master instead say to him, 'Get my dinner ready, [a]and make yourself ready[1] to serve me while I eat and drink. Then you may eat and drink'? [9]He won't thank the slave because he did what he was told, will he?[1] [10]So you too, when you have done everything you were commanded to do, should say, 'We are slaves [a]undeserving of special praise; we have only done what was our duty.'"

The Grateful Leper

[11]Now [a]on the way to Jerusalem, Jesus was passing along between Samaria and Galilee. [12]As he was entering a village, ten men with leprosy met him. [a]They stood at a distance, [13]raised their voices and said, "Jesus, Master, have mercy on us." [14]When he saw them he said, "[a]Go and show yourselves to the

16:16 [a] Matt 3:1–12; 4:17; 11:12–13; Luke 7:29 [1] Or *is forcing his way into it.* **16:17** [a] Ps 102:26–27; Isa 40:8; 51:6; Matt 5:18; 1 Pet 1:25 [1] Or *one small part of a letter.* **16:18** [a] Matt 5:32; 19:9; Mark 10:11; 1 Cor 7:10–11 **16:19** [1] Or *celebrated with ostentation*; i.e., with showing off. **16:21** [1] Wild dogs, not house pets. **16:22** [a] Matt 8:11 [1] Grk. *to Abraham's bosom*; heaven. **16:24** [a] Zech 14:12 [b] [Isa 66:24; Mark 9:42–48] **16:25** [a] Job 21:13; Luke 6:24; Jas 5:5 **16:29** [a] Isa 8:20; 34:16; [John 5:39, 45]; Acts 15:21; 17:11; [2 Tim 3:15] **16:31** [a] [John 5:46] [b] John 12:10–11 **17:1** [a] Matt 18:6–7; 26:24; Mark 9:42; [2 Thess 1:6]; Jude 11 **17:2** [1] Or *to stumble.* **17:3** [a] [Matt 18:15, 21] [b] Lev 19:17; [Prov 17:10; Gal 6:1; Jas 5:19–20] [1] I.e., a fellow believer or Christian, whether male or female. **17:6** [a] Matt 17:20; 21:21; [Mark 9:23; 11:23]; Luke 13:19 [1] A "divine passive," with God understood as the actor. **17:8** [a] [Luke 12:37] [1] Grk. *and gird yourself*; i.e., with an apron or towel, in preparation for service. **17:9** [1] A rhetorical question expecting a negative answer. **17:10** [a] Job 22:3; 35:7; Ps 16:2; Matt 25:30; Rom 3:12; 11:35; [1 Cor 9:16–17]; Phlm 11 **17:11** [a] Luke 9:51–52; John 4:4 **17:12** [a] Lev 13:46; Num 5:2 **17:14** [a] Lev 13:1–59; 14:1–32; Matt 8:4; Luke 5:14

priests." And as they went along, they were cleansed. [15]Then one of them, when he saw he was healed, turned back, [a]praising God with a loud voice. [16]He fell with his face to the ground at Jesus' feet and thanked him. (Now he was a [a]Samaritan.) [17]Then Jesus said, "Were not ten cleansed? Where are the other nine? [18]Was no one found to turn back and give praise to God except this foreigner?" [19]Then he said to the man, "Get up [a]and go your way. Your faith has made you well."

The Coming of the Kingdom

[20]Now at one point[1] the Pharisees asked Jesus when the kingdom of God was coming, so he answered, "The kingdom of God is not coming with signs to be observed, [21a]nor will they say, 'Look, here it is!' or '[b]There!' For indeed, the kingdom of God is in your midst."[1]

The Coming of the Son of Man

[22]Then [a]he said to the disciples, "The days are coming when you will desire to see one of the days of the Son of Man, and you will not see it. [23a]Then people will say to you, 'Look, there he is!' or 'Look, here he is!' Do not go out or chase after them. [24a]For just like the lightning flashes and lights up the sky from one side to the other, so will the Son of Man be in his day.[1] [25a]But first he must suffer many things and be [b]rejected by this generation. [26a]Just as it [b]was in the [c]days of [d]Noah, so too it will be in the days of the Son of Man. [27]People were eating, they were drinking, they were marrying, they were being given in marriage—right up to the [a]day Noah entered the ark. Then the flood came and [b]destroyed them all. [28a]Likewise, just as it was in the days of Lot, people were eating, drinking, buying, selling, planting, building; [29]but on [a]the day Lot went out from Sodom, fire and sulfur rained down from heaven and destroyed them all. [30]It will be the same on the day the Son of Man [a]is revealed. [31]On that day, anyone [a]who is on the roof, with his goods in the house,

must not come down to take them away, and likewise the person in the field must not turn back. [32a]Remember Lot's wife! [33]Whoever tries to keep his life will lose it, but [a]whoever loses his life will preserve it. [34]I tell you, [a]in that night there will be two people in one bed; one will be taken and the other left. [35]There will be [a]two women grinding grain together; one will be taken and the other left."[1]

[37]Then the disciples said to him, "[a]Where, Lord?" He replied to them, "Where the dead body is, there the vultures[1] will gather."

Prayer and the Parable of the Persistent Widow

18 Then Jesus told them a parable to show them they should [a]always pray and not lose heart. [2]He said, "In a certain city there was a judge who neither feared God nor respected people. [3]There was also a widow in that city who kept coming to him and saying, 'Give me justice against my adversary.' [4]For a while he refused, but later on he said to himself, 'Though I neither fear God nor have regard for people, [5a]yet because this widow keeps on bothering me, I will give her justice, or in the end she will wear me out by her unending pleas.'"[1] [6]And the Lord said, "Listen to what the unrighteous judge says! [7]Won't God give justice to his chosen ones, who cry out to him day and night?[1] Will he delay long to help them? [8]I tell you, he will give them justice speedily. Nevertheless, when the Son of Man comes, will he find faith on earth?"

The Parable of the Pharisee and Tax Collector

[9]Jesus also told this parable to some [a]who were confident that they were righteous and looked down on everyone else. [10]"Two men went up to the temple to pray, one a Pharisee and the other a tax collector. [11]The Pharisee [a]stood and prayed about himself like this: '[b]God, I thank you that I am not like other people: extortionists, unrighteous people,

17:15 [a]Luke 5:25; 18:43   17:16 [a]2 Kgs 17:24; Luke 9:52–53; John 4:9   17:19 [a]Matt 9:22; Mark 5:34; 10:52; Luke 7:50; 8:48; 18:42   17:20 [1]at one point is supplied.   17:21 [a]Luke 17:23   [b][Rom 14:17]   [1]Or in your grasp.   17:22 [a]Matt 9:15; Mark 2:20; Luke 5:35; [John 17:12]   17:23 [a]Matt 24:23; Mark 13:21; [Luke 21:8]   17:24 [a]Matt 24:27   [1]Some sig. mss omit in his day.   17:25 [a]Matt 26:67; 27:29–31; Mark 8:31; 9:31; 10:33   [b]Luke 9:22   17:26 [a]Matt 24:37–39   [b][Gen 6:5–7]   [c][Gen 6:8–13]   [d]1 Pet 3:20   17:27 [a]Gen 7:1–16   [b]Gen 7:19–23   17:28 [a]Gen 19   17:29 [a]Gen 19:16, 24, 29; 2 Pet 2:6–7   17:30 [a][Matt 16:27]; 1 Cor 1:7; [Col 3:4; 2 Thess 1:7]; 1 Pet 1:7; 4:13; 1 John 2:28   17:31 [a]Matt 24:17–18; Mark 13:15   17:32 [a]Gen 19:26   17:33 [a]Matt 10:39; 16:25; Mark 8:35; Luke 9:24; John 12:25   17:34 [a]Matt 24:40–41; [1 Thess 4:17]   17:35 [a]Matt 24:40–41   [1]Sev. mss add v. 36: There will be two in the field; one will be taken and the other left.   17:37 [a]Job 39:30; Matt 24:28   [1]Grk. eagles, vultures.   18:1 [a]Luke 11:5–10; Rom 12:12; [Eph 6:18]; Col 4:2; 1 Thess 5:17   18:5 [a]Luke 11:8   [1]Grk. by her continual coming.   18:7 [1]An emphatic Grk. construction.   18:9 [a]Prov 30:12; Luke 10:29; 16:15   18:11 [a]Ps 135:2   [b]Isa 1:15; 58:2; Rev 3:17

adulterers—or even like this tax collector. [12]I fast twice a week; I give a tenth of everything I get.' [13]The tax collector, however, stood far off and would not even look up[1] to heaven, but beat his breast and said, 'God, be merciful to me, sinner that I am!' [14]I tell you that this man went down to his home justified rather than the Pharisee. [a]For everyone who exalts himself will be humbled, but he who humbles himself will be exalted."

Jesus and Little Children

[15]Now people were even bringing their babies to him for him to touch.[1] [a]But when the disciples saw it, they began to scold those who brought them. [16]But Jesus called for the children, saying, "Let the little children come to me and do not try to stop them, for the kingdom [a]of God belongs to such as these. [17]I tell you the [a]truth, whoever does not receive the kingdom of God like a child will never[1] enter it."

The Wealthy Ruler

[18a]Now a certain leader asked him, "Good teacher, what must I do to inherit eternal life?" [19]Jesus said to him, "Why do you call me good? No one is good except God [a]alone. [20]You know the commandments: '[a]*Do not commit adultery, do not murder, do not steal, do not give false testimony,* [b]*honor your father and mother.*'"[1] [21]The man replied, "I have wholeheartedly obeyed all [a]these laws since my youth." [22]When Jesus heard this, he said to him, "One thing you still lack. [a]Sell all that you have and give the money to the poor, and you will have treasure in heaven. Then come, follow me." [23]But when the man heard this, he became very sad, for he was extremely wealthy. [24]When Jesus noticed this,[1] he said, "[a]How hard it is for the rich to enter the kingdom of God! [25]In fact, it is easier for a camel to go through the eye of a needle than for a rich person to enter the kingdom of God." [26]Those who heard this said, "Then who can be saved?" [27]He replied, "What is impossible for mere humans[1] is possible for God." [28a]And Peter said, "Look, we have left everything we own to follow you! [29]Then Jesus said to them, "I tell you [a]the truth, there is no one who has left home or wife or brothers or parents or children for the sake of God's kingdom [30a]who will [b]not receive many times more in this age—and in the age to come, eternal life."

Another Prediction of Jesus' Passion

[31a]Then Jesus took the twelve aside and said to them, "Look, we are going up to Jerusalem, and everything [b]that is written about the Son of Man by the prophets will be accomplished. [32]For [a]he will be handed over to the Gentiles; he will be mocked, mistreated, and spat on. [33]They will flog him severely[1] and kill him. Yet on the third day he will rise again." [34a]But the twelve understood none of these things. This saying was hidden from them, and they did not grasp what Jesus meant.

Healing a Blind Man

[35]As Jesus approached Jericho, a blind man was sitting by [a]the road begging. [36]When he heard a crowd going by, he asked what was going on. [37]They told him, "Jesus the Nazarene is passing by." [38]So he called out, "Jesus, [a]Son of David, have mercy on me!" [39]And those who were in front scolded him to get him to be quiet, but he shouted even more, "Son of David, have mercy on me!" [40]So Jesus stopped and ordered the beggar to be brought to him. When the man came near, Jesus asked him, [41]"What do you want me to do for you?" He replied, "Lord, let me see again."[1] [42]Jesus said to him, "Receive your sight; [a]your faith has healed you." [43]And immediately he regained his sight and followed Jesus, [a]praising God. When all the people saw it, they too gave praise to God.

Jesus and Zacchaeus

19 Jesus entered [a]Jericho and was passing through it. [2]Now a man named Zacchaeus was there; he was a chief tax

18:13 [1] Grk. *even lift up his eyes.*   18:14 [a] Job 22:29; Matt 23:12; Luke 14:11; [Jas 4:6; 1 Pet 5:5]   18:15 [a] Matt 19:13–15; Mark 10:13–16   [1] Grk. *so that he would touch them;* to convey a blessing.   18:16 [a] Matt 18:3; 1 Cor 14:20; 1 Pet 2:2   18:17 [a] Matt 18:3; 19:14; Mark 10:15   [1] A very strong Grk. negation.   18:18 [a] Matt 19:16–29; Mark 10:17–30   18:19 [a] Ps 86:5; 119:68   18:20 [a] Exod 20:12–16; Deut 5:16–20; Mark 10:19; Rom 13:9   [b] Eph 6:2; Col 3:20   [1] Exod 20:12–16; Deut 5:16–20   18:21 [a] Phil 3:6   18:22 [a] Matt 6:19–20; 19:21; [1 Tim 6:19]   18:24 [a] Prov 11:28; Matt 19:23; Mark 10:23   [1] ‡ Maj. MSS [When Jesus saw him] *becoming sad.*   18:27 [1] Grk. *men;* used generically, referring to both men and women, contrasting mortals and God.   18:28 [a] Matt 19:27   18:29 [a] Deut 33:9   18:30 [a] Job 42:10   18:31 [a] Matt 16:21; 17:22; 20:17; Mark 10:32; Luke 9:51   [b] Ps 22; [Isa 53]   18:32 [a] Matt 26:67; 27:2, 29, 41; Mark 14:65; 15:1, 19, 20, 31; Luke 23:1; John 18:28; Acts 3:13   18:33 [1] Trad. *scourge.*   18:34 [a] Mark 9:32; Luke 2:50; 9:45; [John 10:6; 12:16]   18:35 [a] Matt 20:29–34; Mark 10:46–52   18:38 [a] Matt 9:27   18:41 [1] Grk. *Lord, that I may see* [again].   18:42 [a] Luke 17:19   18:43 [a] Luke 5:26; Acts 4:21; 11:18   19:1 [a] Josh 6:26; 1 Kgs 16:34

collector and was rich. [3]He was trying to get a look at Jesus, but being a short man he could not [a]see over the crowd. [4]So he ran on ahead and climbed up into a sycamore tree to see him because Jesus was going to pass that way. [5]And when Jesus came to that place, he looked up[1] and said to him, "Zacchaeus, come down quickly because I must stay at your house today." [6]So he came down quickly and welcomed Jesus joyfully. [7]And [a]when the people saw it, they all complained, "He has gone in to be the guest of a man who is a sinner." [8]But Zacchaeus stopped and said to the Lord, "Look, Lord, half of my possessions I now give to the [a]poor, and [b]if[1] I have cheated anyone of anything, I am paying back four times as much!" [9]Then Jesus said to him, "Today salvation has come to this household because [a]he too is [b]a son of Abraham! [10][a]For the Son of Man came to seek and to save the lost."

The Parable of the Ten Minas

[11]While the people were listening to these things, Jesus proceeded to tell a parable because he was near to Jerusalem, and because [a]they thought that the kingdom of God was going to[1] appear immediately. [12][a]Therefore he said, "A nobleman went to a distant country to receive for himself a kingdom and then return. [13]And he summoned ten of his slaves, gave them ten minas, and said to them, 'Do business with these until I come back.' [14][a]But his citizens hated him and sent a delegation after him, saying, 'We do not want this man to be king over us!' [15]When he returned after receiving the kingdom, he summoned these slaves to whom he had given the money. He wanted to know how much they had earned by trading. [16]So the first one came before him and said, 'Sir,[1] your mina has made ten minas more.' [17]And the king said to him, 'Well [a]done, good slave! Because you have been [b]faithful in a very small matter, you will have authority over ten cities.' [18]Then the second one came and said, 'Sir, your mina has made five minas.' [19]So the king said to him, 'And you are to be over five cities.' [20]Then another slave came and said, 'Sir, here is your mina that I put away for safekeeping in a piece of cloth. [21][a]For I was afraid of you because you are a severe man. You withdraw what you did not deposit[1] and reap what you did not sow.' [22]The king said to him, 'I will judge you [a]by [b]your own words, you wicked slave! So you knew, did you, that I was a severe man, withdrawing what I didn't deposit and reaping what I didn't sow? [23]Why then didn't you put my money in the bank, so that when I returned I could have collected it with interest?' [24]And he said to his attendants, 'Take the mina from him, and give it to the one who has ten.' [25]But they said to him, 'Sir, he has ten minas already!'[1] [26]'I tell you [a]that everyone who has will be given more, but from the one who does not have, even what he has will be taken away. [27]But as for these enemies of mine who did not want me to be their king, bring them here and slaughter them in front of me!'"

The Triumphal Entry

[28]After Jesus had said this, [a]he continued on ahead, going up to Jerusalem. [29]Now when he approached Bethphage [a]and [b]Bethany, at the place called the Mount of [c]Olives, he sent two of the disciples, [30]telling them, "Go to the village ahead of you. When you enter it, you will find a colt tied there that has never been ridden. Untie it and bring it here. [31]If anyone asks you, 'Why are you untying it?' just say, 'The Lord needs it.'" [32]So those who were sent ahead found it exactly [a]as he had told them. [33]As they were untying the colt, its owners asked them, "Why are you untying that colt?" [34]They replied, "The Lord needs it." [35]Then they brought it to Jesus, threw their cloaks[1] on the colt, [a]and had Jesus get on it. [36]As he rode along, they spread their cloaks on the road. [37]As he approached the road leading down from the Mount of Olives, the whole crowd of his disciples began to [a]rejoice and praise God with a loud voice for all the mighty works[1] they had seen: [38]"[a]***Blessed is the king***

19:3 [a]John 12:21   **19:5** [1]Maj. MSS add *saw him.*   **19:7** [a]Matt 9:11; Luke 5:30; 15:2   **19:8** [a][Ps 41:1]   [b]Exod 22:1; Lev 6:5; Num 5:7; 1 Sam 12:3; 2 Sam 12:6   [1]A statement of reality; Zacchaeus virtually confessed fraud.   **19:9** [a]Luke 3:8; 13:16; [Rom 4:16; Gal 3:7]   [b][Luke 13:16]   **19:10** [a]Matt 18:11; [Luke 5:32; Rom 5:8]   **19:11** [a]Acts 1:6   [1]Or perhaps *must appear immediately.*   **19:12** [a]Matt 25:14–30; Mark 13:34   **19:14** [a][John 1:11]   **19:16** [1]Or *Lord, Master.*   **19:17** [a]Matt 25:21, 23   [b]Luke 16:10   **19:21** [a]Matt 25:24   [1]I.e., depositing money with a banker to earn interest.   **19:22** [a]2 Sam 1:16; Job 15:6; [Matt 12:37]   [b]Matt 25:26   **19:25** [1]A few MSS omit v. 25.   **19:26** [a]Matt 13:12; 25:29; Mark 4:25; Luke 8:18   **19:28** [a]Mark 10:32   **19:29** [a]Matt 21:1; Mark 11:1   [b]Matt 26:6; John 12:1   [c]John 8:1; Acts 1:12   **19:32** [a]Luke 22:13   **19:35** [a]2 Kgs 9:13; Matt 21:7; Mark 11:7   [1]Grk. *garments.*   **19:37** [a]Luke 13:17; 18:43   [1]Or *works of power, miracles.*   **19:38** [a]Ps 118:26; Luke 13:35

who comes in the name of the Lord![1] [b]Peace in heaven and glory in the highest!" [39]But some of the Pharisees in the crowd said to him, "Teacher, rebuke your disciples." [40]He answered, "I tell you, if [a]they keep silent, the very stones will cry out!"

Jesus Weeps for Jerusalem under Judgment

[41]Now when Jesus approached and saw the city, he [a]wept over it, [42]saying, "If [a]you had only known on this day, even you, the things that [b]make for [c]peace! But now they are hidden from your eyes. [43]For the days will come upon you when your enemies will [a]build an embankment against you and surround you and close in on you from every side. [44]They will demolish you—you [a]and your children within your walls—and [b]they will not leave within you one stone on top of another [c]because you did not recognize the time of your visitation from God."

Cleansing the Temple

[45a]Then Jesus entered the temple courts[1] and began to drive out those who were selling things there, [46]saying to them, "It is written, '[a]*My house will be a house of prayer,*'[1] but you have turned it into *a* [b]*den of robbers!*"[2]

[47]Jesus [a]was teaching daily in [b]the temple courts. The chief priests and the experts in the law and the prominent leaders among the people were seeking to assassinate him, [48]but they could not find a way to do it, for all the people hung on his [a]words.

The Authority of Jesus

20 Now one day, as Jesus was teaching the people in the temple courts and proclaiming the gospel, the chief priests and the experts in the law [a]with the elders came up [2]and said to him, "Tell us: [a]By what authority are you doing these things? Or who is it who gave you this authority?" [3]He answered them, "I will also ask you a question, and you tell me: [4]John's [a]baptism—was it from heaven or from people?" [5]So they discussed it with one another, saying, "If we say, 'From heaven,' he will say, 'Why did you not believe him?' [6]But if we say, 'From people,' all the people will stone us [a]because they are convinced that John was a prophet." [7]So they replied that they did not know where it came from. [8]Then Jesus said to them, "Neither will I tell you by whose authority I do these things."

The Parable of the Tenants

[9]Then he [a]began to tell the people this parable: "A man[1] planted a vineyard, leased it to tenant farmers, and went on a journey for a long time. [10]When harvest time came, he [a]sent a slave to the tenants so that they would give[1] him his portion of the crop. However, the tenants beat his slave and sent him away empty-handed. [11]So he sent another slave. They beat this one too, treated him outrageously, and sent him away empty-handed. [12]So he sent still a third. They even wounded this one and threw him out. [13]Then the owner of the vineyard said, 'What should I do? I will send my one dear son;[1] perhaps they will respect him.' [14]But when the tenants saw him, they said to one another, 'This is the [a]heir; [b]let's kill him so the inheritance will be [c]ours!' [15]So they threw him out of the vineyard and [a]killed him. What then will the owner of the vineyard do to them? [16]He will come and destroy those tenants and give the vineyard to [a]others." When the people heard this, they said, "May this never happen!" [17]But Jesus looked straight at [a]them and said, "Then what is the meaning of that which is written: '*The stone the builders rejected has become the cornerstone*'?[1,2] [18]Everyone who falls on this stone will be broken to [a]pieces, and the one [b]on whom it falls will be crushed." [19]Then the experts in the law and the chief priests wanted to arrest him that very hour because they realized he had told this parable against them. But they were afraid of the people.

19:38 [b]Luke 2:14; [Eph 2:14] [1]Ps 118:26   **19:40** [a]Hab 2:11   **19:41** [a]Isa 53:3; John 11:35   **19:42** [a]Ps 95:7–8; Heb 3:13 [b][Luke 1:77–79; Acts 10:36] [c][Rom 5:1]   **19:43** [a]Isa 29:3–4; Jer 6:3, 6; Luke 21:20   **19:44** [a]1 Kgs 9:7–8; Mic 3:12 [b]Matt 24:2; Mark 13:2; Luke 21:6 [c][Dan 9:24; Luke 1:68, 78; 1 Pet 2:12]   **19:45** [a]Mal 3:1; Matt 21:12–13; Mark 11:11, 15–17; John 2:13–16 [1]Grk. *the temple*; also in v. 47.   **19:46** [a]Isa 56:7 [b]Jer 7:11 [1]Isa 56:7 [2]Jer 7:11   **19:47** [a]Luke 21:37; 22:53 [b]Mark 11:18; Luke 20:19; John 7:19; 8:37   **19:48** [a]Luke 21:38   **20:1** [a]Matt 21:23–27; Mark 11:27–33   **20:2** [a]Acts 4:7; 7:27   **20:4** [a]John 1:26, 31   **20:6** [a]Matt 14:5; 21:26; Mark 6:20; Luke 7:24–30   **20:9** [a]Ps 80:8; Matt 21:33–46; Mark 12:1–12 [1]‡ Some wss *a certain man.*   **20:10** [a]2 Kgs 17:13–14; 2 Chr 36:15–16; [Acts 7:52; 1 Thess 2:15] [1]Maj. wss *they might give.*   **20:13** [1]Grk. *my beloved son.*   **20:14** [a][Heb 1:1–3] [b]Matt 27:21–23 [c]John 11:47–48   **20:15** [a]Luke 23:33; Acts 2:22–23; 3:15   **20:16** [a][John 1:11–13]; Rom 11:1, 11; 1 Cor 6:15; Gal 2:17; 3:21; 6:14   **20:17** [a]Ps 118:22; Matt 21:42; 1 Pet 2:7–8 [1]Ps 118:22–23 [2]Or *capstone, keystone.*   **20:18** [a]Isa 8:14–15 [b][Dan 2:34–35, 44, 45]; Matt 21:44

Paying Taxes to Caesar

[20]Then they watched him carefully and sent spies who pretended to be sincere. They wanted to take advantage of what he might say so that they could deliver him up to the authority [a]and jurisdiction of the governor. [21]Thus they asked him, "[a]Teacher, we know that you speak and teach correctly, and show no partiality, but teach the way of God in accordance with the truth. [22]Is it right[1] for us to pay the tribute tax[2] to Caesar[3] or not?" [23]But Jesus perceived their deceit and said to them, [24]"Show me a denarius.[1] Whose image and inscription are on it?" They said, "Caesar's." [25]So he said to them, "Then [a]give to Caesar the things that are Caesar's, and to God the things that are God's." [26]Thus they were unable in the presence of the people to trap him with his own words. And stunned by his answer, they fell silent.

Marriage and the Resurrection

[27][a]Now some Sadducees ([b]who contend that there is no resurrection) came to him. [28]They asked him, "Teacher, Moses wrote for us that *if a man's brother dies leaving a wife but no children, that man must marry the widow and father children for his brother.*[1] [29]Now there were seven brothers. The first one married a woman and died without children. [30]The second[1] [31]and then the third married her, and in this same way all seven died, leaving no children. [32]Finally the woman died too. [33]In the resurrection, therefore, whose wife will the woman be? For all seven had married her."

[34]So Jesus said to them, "The people of this age marry and are given in marriage. [35]But those who are regarded as [a]worthy to share in that age and in the resurrection from the dead neither marry nor are given in marriage. [36]In fact, [a]they can no longer die because they [b]are equal to angels and are sons of God, since they are[1] sons of the resurrection. [37]But even Moses revealed that [a]the dead are raised in the passage about the bush, where he calls the Lord *the God of Abraham and the God of Isaac and the God of Jacob.*[1] [38]Now he is not God of the dead, but of the living, for [a]all live before him." [39]Then some of the experts in the law answered, "Teacher, you have spoken well!" [40]For they did not dare any longer to ask him anything.

The Messiah: David's Son and Lord

[41]But he said to them, "[a]How is it that they say that the Christ[1] is David's son? [42]For David himself says in [a]the book of Psalms,

> *'The Lord said to my lord,*
> *"Sit at my right hand,*
> [43] *until I make your enemies a footstool*
>   *for your feet."'[1]*

[44]If David then calls him 'Lord,' [a]how can he be his son?"[1]

Jesus Warns the Disciples against Pride

[45]As all [a]the people were listening, Jesus said to his disciples, [46]"[a]Beware[1] of the experts in the law. They like walking around in long robes, and they [b]love elaborate greetings in the marketplaces and the best seats in the synagogues and the places of honor at banquets. [47][a]They devour widows' property, and as a [b]show make long prayers. They will receive a more severe punishment."

The Widow's Offering

21 Jesus looked up [a]and saw the rich putting their gifts into the offering box.[1] [2]He also saw a [a]poor widow put in two small copper [b]coins. [3]He said, "I tell you the truth, this poor widow has put in more than all of them. [4]For they [a]all offered their gifts out of their wealth. But she, out of her poverty, put in everything she had to live on."[1]

The Signs of the End of the Age

[5]Now while some were speaking about the temple, how it was adorned with beautiful stones [a]and offerings, Jesus said, [6]"As

---

20:20 [a] Matt 22:15   20:21 [a] Matt 22:16; Mark 12:14   20:22 [1] Or *lawful*; i.e., in accordance with God's divine law.   [2] A poll tax.   [3] Or *to the emperor*; "Caesar" is a title for the Roman emperor.   20:24 [1] Or *silver coin*; "denarius" is used because not all coins carried the image of Caesar.   20:25 [a] Matt 17:24–27; Rom 13:7; [1 Pet 2:13–17]   20:27 [a] Matt 22:23–33; Mark 12:18–27 [b] Acts 23:6, 8   20:28 [1] Deut 25:5   20:30 [1] Maj. MSS add *took the wife and this one died childless.*   20:35 [a] Phil 3:11   20:36 [a] [1 Cor 15:42, 49, 52; 1 John 3:2]   [b] Rom 8:23   [1] Grk. *sons of God, being.*   20:37 [a] Exod 3:1–6, 15; Acts 7:30–32 [1] Exod 3:6   20:38 [a] [Rom 6:10–11; 14:8–9; Heb 11:16]   20:41 [a] Matt 22:41–46; Mark 12:35–37 [1] Or *Messiah*; both "Christ" (Grk.) and "Messiah" (Heb., Aram.) mean "one who has been anointed."   20:42 [a] Ps 110:1; Acts 2:34–35   20:43 [1] Ps 110:1 20:44 [a] Acts 13:22–23; Rom 1:3; 9:4–5 [1] Grk. *David thus calls him 'Lord.' So how is he his son?*   20:45 [a] Matt 23:1–7; Mark 12:38–40   20:46 [a] Matt 23:5   [b] Luke 11:43; 14:7   [1] Or *Be on guard against.*   20:47 [a] Matt 23:14   [b] [Matt 6:5–6] 21:1 [a] Mark 12:41–44   [1] Or *treasury.*   21:2 [a] [2 Cor 6:10]   [b] Mark 12:42   21:4 [a] [2 Cor 8:12]   [1] Or *put in her entire livelihood.*   21:5 [a] Matt 24:1; Mark 13:1

for these things that you are gazing at, the days will come when [a]not one stone will be left on another. All will be torn down!" [7]So they asked him, "Teacher, when will these things happen? And what will be the sign that these things are about to take place?" [8]He said, "Watch [a]out that you are not misled. For many will come in my name, saying, 'I am he,' and, 'The time is near.' Do not follow them! [9]And when you hear of [a]wars and rebellions, do not be afraid.[1] For these things must happen first, but the end will not come at once."

Persecution of Disciples

[10][a]Then he said to them, "Nation will rise up in arms against nation, and kingdom against kingdom. [11]There will be great [a]earthquakes, and famines and plagues in various places, and there will be terrifying sights and great signs from heaven. [12][a]But before all this, they will seize you and persecute you, handing you over to the synagogues and [b]prisons. [c]You will be brought [d]before kings and governors because of my name. [13]This will be a time for you to serve as [a]witnesses. [14][a]Therefore be resolved[1] not to rehearse ahead of time how to make your defense. [15]For I will give you the words along with the wisdom [a]that none of your adversaries will be able to withstand or contradict. [16]You will be betrayed even by parents, brothers, relatives, and friends, and they will have some of [a]you put to death. [17]You will be hated by everyone because of my name. [18][a]Yet not a hair of your head will perish. [19]By your endurance you will gain your lives.

The Desolation of Jerusalem

[20]"[a]But when you see Jerusalem surrounded by armies, then know that its[1] desolation has come near. [21]Then those who are in Judea must flee to the mountains. Those who are inside the city must depart. Those who are out in the country must not

enter it, [22]because these are days of vengeance, to fulfill [a]all that is written. [23][a]Woe to those who are pregnant and to those who are nursing their babies in those days! For there will be great distress on the earth and wrath against this people. [24]They will fall by the edge of the sword and be led away as captives among all nations. Jerusalem will be trampled down by the Gentiles [a]until the times of the Gentiles are fulfilled.

The Arrival of the Son of Man

[25]"[a]And there will be signs in the sun and moon and stars, and on the earth nations will be in distress, anxious over the roaring of the sea and the surging waves. [26]People will be fainting from fear and from the expectation of what is coming on the world, [a]for *the powers of the heavens will be shaken.*[1] [27]Then they will see *the Son of Man* [a]*arriving in a cloud*[1] with power and great glory. [28]But when these things begin to happen, stand up and raise [a]your heads because your redemption is drawing near."

The Parable of the Fig Tree

[29][a]Then he told them a parable: "Look at the fig tree and all the other trees. [30]When they sprout leaves, you see for yourselves and know that summer is now near. [31]So also you, when you see these things happening, know that the kingdom of God is near. [32]I tell you the truth, this generation will not pass away until all these things take place. [33][a]Heaven and earth will pass away, but my [b]words will never pass away.

Be Ready!

[34]"But [a]be on your guard so that your hearts are not weighed down with dissipation and drunkenness and the [b]worries of this life, and that day close down upon you suddenly like a trap. [35]For [a]it will overtake all who live on the face of the whole earth. [36]But stay [a]alert at all times, [b]praying that you may have strength [c]to escape all these

21:6 [a]Isa 64:10–11; Lam 2:6–9; Mic 3:12; Luke 19:41–44   21:8 [a]Matt 24:4; Mark 13:5; Eph 5:6; 2 Thess 2:3; [1 John 4:1]
21:9 [a]Rev 6:4   [1]Not the usual term for fear, but rather, a deep sense of terror and emotional distress.   21:10 [a]Matt 24:7
21:11 [a]Rev 6:12   21:12 [a]Mark 13:9; John 16:2; [Rev 2:10]   [b]Acts 4:3; 5:18; 12:4; 16:24   [c]Acts 25:23   [d]1 Pet 2:13   21:13 [a][Phil
1:12–14, 28; 2 Thess 1:5]   21:14 [a]Matt 10:19; Mark 13:11; Luke 12:11   [1]Grk. *determine in your hearts.*   21:15 [a]Acts 6:10
21:16 [a]Mic 7:6; Mark 13:12   21:18 [a]Matt 10:30; Luke 12:7   21:20 [a]Matt 24:15; Mark 13:14   [1]Grk. *her.*   21:22 [a]Isa 63:4; [Dan
9:24–27]; Hos 9:7; [Zech 11:1]   21:23 [a]Matt 24:19   21:24 [a][Dan 9:27; 12:7]   21:25 [a]Isa 13:9–10, 13; Matt 24:29; Mark 13:24;
[2 Pet 3:10–12]   21:26 [a]Matt 24:29   [1][Isa 34:4]   21:27 [a]Dan 7:13; [Matt 16:27; 24:30; 26:64]; Mark 13:26; Rev 1:7; 14:14
[1][Dan 7:13]   21:28 [a][Rom 8:19, 23]   21:29 [a]Matt 24:32; Mark 13:28   21:33 [a]Isa 51:6; Matt 24:35; Heb 1:10–11; [2 Pet 3:7,
10, 12]   [b]Isa 40:8; Luke 16:17; 1 Pet 1:24–25   21:34 [a]Matt 24:42–44; Mark 4:19; Luke 12:40, 45; Rom 13:13; 1 Thess 5:6;
1 Pet 4:7   [b]Luke 8:14   21:35 [a]1 Thess 5:2; [2 Pet 3:10]; Rev 3:3; 16:15   21:36 [a]Matt 24:42; 25:13; Mark 13:33;
Luke 12:40   [b]Luke 18:1; [Eph 6:18]; Col 4:2; 1 Thess 5:17   [c]Ps 1:5; [Eph 6:13]

things that must happen, and to stand before the Son of Man."

[37]So every day Jesus was teaching in the temple courts, [a]but [b]at night he went and stayed on the Mount of Olives. [38]And all the people came to him early in the morning to listen to him in the temple courts.[1]

Judas' Decision to Betray Jesus

22 Now [a]the Feast of Unleavened Bread, which is called the Passover, was approaching. [2]The chief priests and [a]the experts in the law were trying to find some way to execute[1] Jesus, for they were afraid of the people.

[3]Then Satan entered Judas, the one called Iscariot, who was one of the [b]twelve. [4]He went away and discussed with the chief priests and officers of the temple guard how he might betray Jesus, handing him over to them. [5]They were delighted and [a]arranged to give him money. [6]So Judas agreed and began looking for an opportunity to [a]betray Jesus when no crowd was present.[1]

The Passover

[7a]Then the day for the feast of Unleavened Bread came, on which the Passover lamb had to be sacrificed. [8]Jesus sent Peter and John, saying, "Go and prepare the Passover for us to eat." [9]They said to him, "Where do you want us to prepare it?" [10]He said to them, "Listen, when you have entered the city, a man carrying a jar of water will meet you. Follow him into the house that he enters, [11]and tell the owner of the house, 'The Teacher says to you, "Where is the guest room where I may eat the Passover with my disciples?"' [12]Then he will show you a large furnished room upstairs. Make preparations there." [13]So they went and found [a]things just as he had told them, and they prepared the Passover.

The Lord's Supper

[14]Now [a]when the hour came, Jesus took his place at the table and the apostles joined him. [15]And he said to them, "I have earnestly desired to eat this Passover with you before I suffer. [16]For I tell you, I will not eat it again [a]until it is fulfilled in the kingdom of God." [17]Then he took a cup, and after giving thanks he said, "Take this and divide it among yourselves. [18]For [a]I tell you that from now on I will not drink of the fruit[1] of the vine until the kingdom of God comes." [19]Then he took bread, and after giving thanks he broke it [a]and gave it to them, saying, "This is my [b]body[1] which is given for you. [c]Do this in remembrance of me." [20]And in the same way he took the cup after they had eaten, saying, "[a]This cup that is poured out for you is the new covenant in my blood.

A Final Discourse

[21]"[a]But look, the hand of the one who betrays me is with me on the table. [22a]For the Son of Man is to go just [b]as it has been determined, but woe to that man by whom he is betrayed!" [23a]So they began to question one another as to which of them it could possibly be who would do this.

[24a]A dispute also started among them over which of them was to be regarded as the greatest.[1] [25]So Jesus said to them, "The kings of the Gentiles lord it over them, [a]and those in authority over them are called 'benefactors.' [26a]Not so with you; instead [b]the one who is greatest among you must become like the youngest, and the leader like the one who serves. [27a]For who is greater, the one who is seated at the table, or the one who serves? Is it not the one who is seated at the table? But [b]I am among you as one who serves.

[28]"You are the ones who have remained with me in [a]my trials. [29]Thus [a]I grant to you a kingdom, just as my Father granted to me, [30]that [a]you may eat [b]and drink at my table in my kingdom, and you will sit on thrones judging the 12 tribes of Israel.

[31]"Simon,[1] Simon, pay attention! [a]Satan has demanded to have you all, to [b]sift you

---

21:37 [a] John 8:1–2   [b] Luke 22:39   21:38 [1] Some MSS place 7:53–8:11 here.   22:1 [a] Matt 26:2–5; Mark 14:1–2   22:2 [a] Ps 2:2; John 11:47; Acts 4:27   [1] Grk. *to get rid of by execution*; often through legal or quasi-legal procedures.   22:3 [a] Matt 26:14–16; Mark 14:10–11; John 13:2, 27   [b] Matt 10:2–4   22:5 [a] Zech 11:12   22:6 [a] Ps 41:9   [1] Grk. *apart from the crowd.*   22:7 [a] Matt 26:17–19; Mark 14:12–16   22:13 [a] Luke 19:32   22:14 [a] Matt 26:20; Mark 14:17   22:16 [a] Luke 14:15; [Acts 10:41; Rev 19:9]   22:18 [a] Matt 26:29; Mark 14:25   [1] Grk. *the produce*; a figurative expression for wine.   22:19 [a] Matt 26:26; Mark 14:22   [b] [1 Pet 2:24]   [c] 1 Cor 11:23–26   [1] Some sig. MSS omit the words from this point to the end of v. 20.   22:20 [a] 1 Cor 10:16   22:21 [a] Ps 41:9; Matt 26:21, 23; Mark 14:18; Luke 22:48; John 13:21, 26, 27   22:22 [a] Matt 26:24   [b] John 17:12; Acts 2:23   22:23 [a] Matt 26:22; John 13:22, 25   22:24 [a] Mark 9:34; Luke 9:46–48   [1] Grk. *greater.*   22:25 [a] [Matt 20:25–28]; Mark 10:42–45   22:26 [a] Matt 20:26; [1 Pet 5:3]   [b] Luke 9:48   22:27 [a] [Luke 12:37]   [b] Matt 20:28; John 13:13–14; Phil 2:7   22:28 [a] [Heb 2:18; 4:15]   22:29 [a] Matt 24:47   22:30 [a] [Matt 8:11; Rev 19:9]   [b] Ps 49:14; [Matt 19:28; 1 Cor 6:2; Rev 3:21]   22:31 [a] 1 Pet 5:8   [b] Amos 9:9   [1] Maj. MSS begin this verse with *and the Lord said.*

like wheat, [32]but [a]I have prayed for you, Simon, that your faith may not fail. When you have turned back, [b]strengthen your brothers." [33]But Peter said to him, "Lord, I am ready to go with you both to prison and to death!" [34]Jesus replied, "I tell you, Peter, [a]the rooster will not crow today until you have denied three times that you know me."

[35]Then Jesus said to them, "When I sent you out with no money bag, [a]or traveler's bag, or sandals, you didn't lack anything, did you?" They replied, "Nothing." [36]He said to them, "But now, the one who has a money bag must take it, and likewise a traveler's bag too. And the one who has no sword must sell his cloak and buy one. [37]For I tell you that this scripture must be fulfilled in me, [a]***And he was counted with the transgressors.***[1] For what is written about me is being fulfilled." [38]So they said, "Look, Lord, here are two swords." Then he told them, "It is enough."

On the Mount of Olives

[39]Then Jesus went [a]out and made his way, as [b]he customarily did, to the Mount of Olives, and the disciples followed him. [40]When [a]he came to the place, he said to them, "Pray that you will not fall into temptation." [41]He went away from them about a stone's throw, knelt down, [a]and prayed, [42]"Father, if you are willing, take this cup away from me. Yet [a]not my will but yours be done." [[43]Then [a]an angel from heaven appeared to him and strengthened him. [44a]And in his anguish he prayed more earnestly, and his sweat was like drops of blood falling to the ground.][1] [45]When he got up from prayer, he came to the disciples and found them sleeping, exhausted from grief. [46]So he said to them, "Why are you sleeping? Get up and [a]pray that you will not fall into temptation!"

Betrayal and Arrest

[47]While he was still speaking, suddenly a crowd appeared, and the man named [a]Judas, one of the twelve, was leading them. He walked up to Jesus to kiss him.[1] [48]But Jesus said to him, "Judas, would you betray the Son of Man with a [a]kiss?" [49]When those who were around him saw what was about to happen, they said, "Lord, should we use our swords?" [50]Then [a]one of them struck the high priest's slave, cutting off his right ear. [51]But Jesus said, "Enough of this!" And he touched the man's ear and healed him. [52a]Then Jesus said to the chief priests, the officers of the temple guard, and the elders who had come out to get him, "Have you come out with swords and clubs like you would against an [b]outlaw?[1] [53]Day after day when I was with you in the temple [a]courts, you did not arrest me. But this is your [b]hour, and that of the power of darkness!"

Jesus' Condemnation and Peter's Denials

[54]Then they arrested Jesus, led him away, and brought him into the high priest's house. [a]But Peter was following at a distance. [55a]When they had made a fire in the middle of the courtyard and sat down together, Peter sat down among them. [56]Then a slave girl, seeing him as he sat in the firelight, stared at him and said, "This man was with him too!" [57]But Peter denied it: "Woman, I don't know him!" [58]Then a little later someone else saw him and said, "You are one of them [a]too." But Peter said, "Man, I am not!" [59]And after about an hour still another insisted, "Certainly this man was with him because he [a]too is a [b]Galilean." [60]But Peter said, "Man, I don't know what you're talking about!" At that moment, while he was still speaking, a rooster crowed. [61]Then the Lord turned and looked straight at [a]Peter, and Peter remembered the word of the Lord,[1] how he had said to him, "[b]Before a rooster crows today, you will deny me three times." [62]And he went outside and wept bitterly.

[63a]Now the men who were holding Jesus under guard began to mock him and [b]beat

22:32 [a] [John 17:9, 11, 15]   [b] John 21:15–17; Acts 1:15; 2:14; 2 Pet 1:10–15   22:34 [a] Matt 26:33–35; Mark 14:29–31; Luke 22:61; John 13:37–38   22:35 [a] Matt 10:9; Mark 6:8; Luke 9:3; 10:4   22:37 [a] Isa 53:12; Matt 27:38; Mark 15:28; Luke 22:32   [1] Isa 53:12   22:39 [a] Matt 26:36; John 18:1   [b] Luke 21:37   22:40 [a] Matt 26:36–46; Mark 14:32–42   22:41 [a] Matt 26:39; Mark 14:35; [Luke 18:11–14]   22:42 [a] Isa 50:5; John 4:34; 5:30; 6:38; 8:29   22:43 [a] Matt 4:11   22:44 [a] John 12:27; [Heb 5:7]   [1] Sev. sig. MSS lack vv. 43–44. Because of the serious doubts as to these verses' authenticity, they have been set in brackets.   22:46 [a] 1 Chr 16:11; Luke 22:40; [Eph 6:18]; 1 Thess 5:17   22:47 [a] Ps 41:9; Matt 20:18; Luke 9:44; 22:21; Acts 1:16–17   [1] Many MSS add *for this is the sign he gave to them: Whoever I kiss is* [the one].   22:48 [a] [Prov 27:6]   22:50 [a] Matt 26:51   22:52 [a] Matt 26:55   [b] Luke 23:32   [1] Or *a revolutionary*.   22:53 [a] Luke 19:47–48   [b] [John 12:27]   22:54 [a] Matt 26:58; Mark 14:54; John 18:15   22:55 [a] Matt 26:69–75; Mark 14:66–72; John 18:15, 17, 18   22:58 [a] Matt 26:71; Mark 14:69; John 18:25   22:59 [a] Matt 26:73; Mark 14:70; John 18:26   [b] Acts 1:11; 2:7   22:61 [a] Matt 26:75; Mark 14:72   [b] Matt 26:34, 75; Mark 14:30; Luke 22:34; John 13:38   [1] I.e., a divine prophetic utterance.   22:63 [a] Ps 69:1, 4, 7–9; Matt 26:67–68; Mark 14:65; John 18:22   [b] Job 16:10; Isa 50:6; Lam 3:30

him. [64]They blindfolded him and asked him repeatedly, "Prophesy! Who hit you?" [65]They also said many other things against him, reviling[1] him.

[66a]When day came, [b]the council of the elders of the people gathered together, both the chief priests and the experts in the law. Then they led Jesus away to their council [67]and said, "[a]If you are the Christ, tell us." But he said to them, "If I tell you, you will not believe, [68]and if I ask you, you will not[1] answer. [69a]But from now on *the Son of Man will be seated at the right hand*[1] of the power of God." [70]So they all said, "Are [a]you the Son of God, then?" He answered them, "You say that I am." [71a]Then they said, "Why do we need further testimony? We have heard it ourselves from his own lips!"

Jesus Brought before Pilate

23 Then [a]the whole group of them rose up and brought Jesus before [b]Pilate. [2]They began to [a]accuse him, saying, "We found this man [b]subverting our nation, [c]forbidding us to pay the tribute tax to Caesar and claiming [d]that he himself is Christ, a king." [3]So Pilate asked Jesus, "Are you the king of the Jews?" [a]He replied, "You say so." [4]Then [a]Pilate said to the chief priests and the crowds, "I find no basis for an accusation against this man." [5]But they persisted[1] in saying, "He incites the people by teaching throughout all Judea. It started in [a]Galilee and ended up here!"

Jesus Brought before Herod

[6]Now when Pilate heard this, he asked whether the man was a Galilean. [7]When he learned that he was from [a]Herod's jurisdiction, he sent him over to Herod, who also happened to be in Jerusalem at that time. [8]When [a]Herod saw Jesus, [b]he was very glad, for he had long desired to see him because he had heard about him and was hoping to see him perform some miraculous sign.

[9]So Herod questioned him at considerable length; Jesus gave him [a]no answer. [10]The chief priests and the experts in the law were there, vehemently accusing him. [11]Even Herod with his soldiers treated him with contempt and mocked him. [a]Then, dressing him in elegant clothes, Herod sent him back to Pilate. [12]That very day Herod and [a]Pilate became friends with each other, for prior to this they had been enemies.[1]

Jesus Brought before the Crowd

[13a]Then Pilate called together the chief priests, the leaders, and the people, [14]and said to them, "[a]You brought me this man as one who was misleading the people. When [b]I examined him before you, I did not find this man guilty[1] of anything you accused him of doing. [15]Neither did Herod, for he sent him back to us. Look, he has done nothing deserving death. [16]I [a]will therefore have him flogged[1] and release him."[2]

[18]But [a]they all shouted out together, "Take this man away! Release Barabbas for us!" [19](This was a man who had been thrown into prison for an insurrection started in the city, and for murder.) [20]Pilate addressed them once again because he wanted to release Jesus. [21]But they kept on shouting, "Crucify, crucify him!" [22]A third time he said to them, "Why? What wrong has he done? I have found him guilty of no crime deserving death. I will therefore flog him and release him." [23]But they were insistent, demanding with loud shouts that he be crucified. And their shouts prevailed. [24]So [a]Pilate decided that their demand should be granted. [25]He released the man they asked for, who had been thrown in prison for insurrection and murder. [a]But he handed Jesus over[1] to their will.

The Crucifixion

[26a]As they led him away, they seized Simon of Cyrene, who was coming in from the

---

22:65 [1]Or *insulting.*   **22:66** [a]Matt 27:1; Mark 15:1   [b]Ps 2:2; Acts 4:26   **22:67** [a]Matt 26:63–66; Mark 14:61–63; Luke 22:67–71; John 18:19–21   **22:68** [1]The strongest possible Grk. negation.   **22:69** [a][Ps 110:1; Matt 26:64; Mark 14:62; 16:19]; Acts 2:33; 7:55; Eph 1:20; Col 3:1; Heb 1:3; 8:1   [1][Ps 110:1]   **22:70** [a]Matt 26:64; 27:11; Mark 14:62; Luke 1:35   **22:71** [a]Matt 26:65; Mark 14:63; John 19:7   **23:1** [a]Matt 27:2; Mark 15:1; Luke 18:32; John 18:28   [b]Luke 3:1; 13:1   **23:2** [a]Acts 24:2   [b]Acts 17:7   [c]Matt 17:27; Mark 12:17   [d]John 19:12   **23:3** [a]Matt 27:11; 1 Tim 6:13   **23:4** [a]Matt 27:19; [1 Pet 2:22]   **23:5** [a]John 7:41   [1]Or *were adamant.*   **23:7** [a]Matt 14:1; Mark 6:14; Luke 3:1; 9:7; 13:31   **23:8** [a]Luke 9:9   [b]Matt 14:1; Mark 6:14   **23:9** [a]Isa 53:7; Matt 27:12, 14; Mark 15:5; John 19:9   **23:11** [a]Isa 53:3   **23:12** [a]Acts 4:26–27   [1]Grk. *at enmity with each other.*   **23:13** [a]Matt 27:23; Mark 15:14; John 18:38   **23:14** [a]Luke 23:1–2   [b]Luke 23:4   [1]Grk. *nothing did I find in this man by way of cause*; an emphatic Grk. construction.   **23:16** [a]Matt 27:26; Mark 15:15; Luke 23:22; John 19:1; Acts 16:37   [1]Or *scourged.*   [2]Some wss add v. 17: (*Now he was obligated to release one individual for them at the feast.*)   **23:18** [a]Isa 53:3; Acts 3:13–15   **23:24** [a]Matt 27:26; Mark 15:15; John 19:16   **23:25** [a]Isa 53:8   [1]Or *delivered up.*   **23:26** [a]Matt 27:32; Mark 15:21; John 19:17

country. They placed the cross on his back and made him carry it behind Jesus. [27]A great number of the people followed him, among them women who were mourning and wailing for him. [28]But Jesus turned to them and said, "Daughters of Jerusalem, do not weep for me, but weep for yourselves and for your children. [29a]For this is certain: The days are coming when they will say, 'Blessed are the barren, the wombs that never bore children, and the breasts that never nursed!' [30]Then they will begin *to say to the mountains, 'Fall on us!' and to the hills, 'Cover us!'*[1] [31a]For if such things are done when the wood is green, what will happen when it is dry?"

[32a]Two other criminals[1] were also led away to be executed with him. [33]So [a]when they came to the place that is called "The Skull," they crucified him there, along with the criminals, one on his right and one on his left. [34][But Jesus said, "Father, [a]forgive them, for [b]they don't know what [c]they are doing."][1] Then *they threw dice*[2] *to divide his clothes.*[3] [35]The people also stood [a]there watching, but the [b]leaders ridiculed him, saying, "He saved others. Let him save himself if he is the Christ of God, his chosen one!" [36]The soldiers also mocked him, coming up and offering him [a]sour wine, [37]and saying, "If you are the king of the Jews, save yourself!" [38]There was also [a]an inscription over him, "This is the king of the Jews."

[39]One of [a]the criminals who was hanging there railed at him, saying, "Aren't[1] you the Christ? Save yourself and us!" [40]But the other rebuked him, saying, "Don't[1] you fear God, since you are under the same sentence of condemnation? [41]And we rightly so, for we are getting what we deserve for what we did, but this man has done [a]nothing wrong."

[42]Then he said, "Jesus, remember me when you come in[1] your kingdom." [43]And Jesus said to him, "I tell you the truth, today you will be with me in [a]paradise."

[44]It was now about noon, [a]and darkness came over the whole land until three in the afternoon, [45]because [a]the sun's light failed.[1] The temple curtain[2] was torn in two. [46]Then Jesus, calling out with a loud voice, said, "Father, [a]*into your hands* [b]*I commit my spirit!*"[1] And after he said this he breathed his last.

[47a]Now when the centurion saw what had happened, he praised God and said, "Certainly this man was innocent!"[1] [48]And all the crowds that had assembled for this spectacle, when they saw what had taken place, returned home beating their breasts. [49a]And all those who knew Jesus stood at a distance, and the women who had followed him from Galilee saw these things.

Jesus' Burial

[50a]Now there was a man named Joseph who was a member of the council, a good and righteous man. [51](He had not consented[1] to their plan and action.) He was from the Judean town of Arimathea, and was looking forward to the kingdom of God. [52]He went to Pilate and asked for the body of Jesus. [53a]Then he took it down, wrapped it in a linen cloth, and placed it in a tomb cut out of the rock,[1] where no one had yet been buried.[2] [54]It was [a]the day of preparation, and the Sabbath was beginning.[1] [55]The women [a]who had accompanied Jesus from Galilee followed, and [b]they saw the tomb and how his body was laid in it. [56]Then they returned and [a]prepared aromatic spices and perfumes.

On the Sabbath they rested according [b]to the commandment.

23:29 [a]Matt 24:19; Luke 21:23   **23:30** [a]Isa 2:19; Hos 10:8; Rev 6:16–17; 9:6   [1][Hos 10:8]   **23:31** [a][Prov 11:31; Jer 25:29]; Ezek 20:47; 21:3–4; 1 Pet 4:17   **23:32** [a]Isa 53:9, 12; Matt 27:38; Mark 15:27; John 19:18   [1]Some mss *others, two criminals.*
23:33 [a]Ps 22:16–18; Matt 27:33–44; Mark 15:22–32; John 19:17–24   **23:34** [a]Ps 109:4; [Matt 5:44]; Acts 7:60; 1 Cor 4:12   [b]Acts 3:17   [c]Ps 22:18; Matt 27:35; Mark 15:24; John 19:23   [1]Many sig. mss omit v. 34a. For this reason, it has been set in brackets.   [2]Grk. *cast lots.*   [3][Ps 22:18]   **23:35** [a]Ps 22:17; [Zech 12:10]   [b]Ps 22:8; Matt 27:39; Mark 15:29   **23:36** [a]Ps 69:21   **23:38** [a]Matt 27:37; Mark 15:26; John 19:19   **23:39** [a]Matt 27:44; Mark 15:32   [1]Maj. mss *If you are.*   **23:40** [1]A rhetorical question expecting a positive answer.   **23:41** [a][2 Cor 5:21; Heb 7:26; 1 Pet 2:21–24]   **23:42** [1]‡ Some mss *into.*
23:43 [a][2 Cor 12:4; Eph 4:8–10; Rev 2:7]   **23:44** [a]Amos 8:9; Matt 27:45–56; Mark 15:33–41   **23:45** [a]Exod 26:31–33; Zech 11:10; Matt 27:51; Mark 15:38; [Heb 9:3; 10:19–20]   [1]Maj. mss *the sun was darkened.*   [2]Either the curtain separating the Holy of Holies from the Holy Place or the one at the entrance of the temple court.   **23:46** [a]Ps 31:5; 1 Pet 2:23   [b]Dan 9:26; Zech 11:10–11; Matt 27:50; Mark 15:37; Luke 9:22; 18:33; John 19:30   [1]Ps 31:5   **23:47** [a]Matt 27:54; Mark 15:39   [1]Or *righteous.*   **23:49** [a]Ps 38:11; Matt 27:55; Mark 15:40; John 16:20–22; 19:25   **23:50** [a]Matt 27:57–61; Mark 15:42–47; John 19:38–42   **23:51** [1]Sev. mss *was not consenting.*   **23:53** [a]Isa 53:9; Matt 27:59; Mark 15:46   [1]Cut or carved into an outcropping of natural rock, resulting in a cave-like structure.   [2]Some wss add *And after he* [Jesus] *was laid* [in the tomb], *he* [Joseph of Arimathea] *put a stone over the tomb which scarcely twenty men could roll.*   **23:54** [a]Matt 27:62; Mark 15:42   [1]Or *dawning*; but the Jewish Sabbath begins at 6 p.m.   **23:55** [a]Luke 8:2   [b]Mark 15:47   **23:56** [a]Mark 16:1; Luke 24:1   [b]Exod 20:10; Deut 5:14

The Resurrection

24 Now [a]on the first day of the week, at early dawn, the women went to the tomb, [b]taking the aromatic spices they had prepared. [2a]They found that the stone had been rolled away from the tomb, [3]but when they went in, they did not find [a]the body of the Lord Jesus.[1] [4]While they were perplexed about this, suddenly two men stood beside them in dazzling attire. [5]The women were terribly frightened[1] and bowed their faces to the ground, but the men said to them, "Why do you look for the living among the dead? [6]He is not here, but has been raised![1,2] [a]Remember how he told you, while he was still in Galilee, [7]that the Son of Man must be [a]delivered into the hands of sinful men,[1] and be crucified, and on the third day rise again." [8]Then [a]the women remembered his words, [9]and when they returned from the tomb, they told all these things to the eleven [a]and to all the rest. [10]Now it was Mary Magdalene, [a]Joanna, Mary the mother of James, and the other women with them who told these things to the apostles. [11]But these words seemed like pure nonsense to them, [a]and they did not believe them. [12a]But Peter got up and ran to the tomb. He bent down and saw only the strips of linen cloth; then he went home, wondering what had happened.[1]

Jesus Walks the Road to Emmaus

[13a]Now that very day two of them were on their way to a village called Emmaus, about seven miles from Jerusalem. [14]They were talking to each other about all the things that had happened. [15]While they were talking and debating these things, [a]Jesus himself approached and began to accompany them [16](but [a]their eyes were kept from recognizing him). [17]Then he said to them, "What are these matters you are discussing so intently as you walk along?" And they stood still, looking sad. [18]Then one of them, named Cleopas, answered him, "Are you the only visitor to Jerusalem [a]who doesn't know the things that have happened there in these days?" [19]He said to them, "What things?" "The things concerning Jesus the Nazarene," they replied, "a man [a]who, with his [b]powerful deeds and words, proved to be a prophet before God and all the people; [20a]and how our chief priests and leaders handed him over to be condemned to death, and crucified him. [21]But we had hoped [a]that he was the one who was going to redeem Israel. Not only this, but it is now the third day since these things happened. [22]Furthermore, [a]some women of our group amazed us. They were at the tomb early this morning, [23]and when they did not find his body, they came back and said they had seen a vision of angels, who said he was alive. [24]Then [a]some of those who were with us went to the tomb and found it just as the women had said, but they did not see him."[1] [25]So he said to them, "You foolish people—how slow of heart to believe all that the prophets have spoken! [26]Wasn't it [a]necessary for the Christ to suffer these things and enter into his [b]glory?" [27]Then beginning with [a]Moses and [b]all the prophets, he interpreted to them the things written about[1] himself in all the scriptures.

[28]So they approached the village where they were going. [a]He acted as though he wanted to go farther, [29]but [a]they urged him, "[b]Stay with us because it is getting toward evening and the day is almost done." So he went in to stay with them.

[30]When he had taken [a]his place at the table with them, he took the bread, blessed and broke it, and gave it to them. [31]At this point their eyes were opened and they recognized him. Then he vanished out of their sight. [32]They said to each other, "Didn't our hearts[1] burn within us[2] while he was speaking with us on the road, while

24:1 [a]Matt 28:1–8; Mark 16:1–8; John 20:1–8 [b]Luke 23:56 **24:2** [a]Matt 28:2; Mark 16:4 **24:3** [a]Mark 16:5 [1]A few mss *the body, the body of Jesus.* **24:5** [1]Or *They were extremely afraid.* **24:6** [a]Matt 16:21; Mark 8:31; Luke 9:22 [1]A few mss omit *he is not here, but has been raised.* [2]A "divine passive," with God understood as the actor. **24:7** [a]Hos 6:1–2; Luke 9:44; 11:29–30; 18:31–33 [1]The individuals primarily responsible for the death of Jesus would have been males. **24:8** [a]Luke 9:22, 44; John 2:19–22 **24:9** [a]Matt 28:8; Mark 16:10 **24:10** [a]Luke 8:3 **24:11** [a]Luke 24:25 **24:12** [a]John 20:3–6 [1]A few mss omit v. 12. **24:13** [a]Mark 16:12 **24:15** [a][Matt 18:20] **24:16** [a]John 20:14; 21:4 **24:18** [a]John 19:25 **24:19** [a]Matt 21:11; Luke 7:16; John 3:2; Acts 2:22 [b]Acts 7:22 **24:20** [a]Luke 23:1; Acts 13:27–28 **24:21** [a]Luke 1:68; 2:38; [Acts 1:6] **24:22** [a]Matt 28:8; Mark 16:10; Luke 24:9–10 **24:24** [a]Luke 24:12 [1]An emphatic Grk. construction. **24:26** [a]Acts 17:2–3; [Heb 2:9–10] [b][1 Pet 1:10–12] **24:27** [a][Gen 3:15; 12:3; Num 21:9; Deut 18:15]; John 5:46 [b][Ps 16:9–10; 22; 132:11; Isa 7:14; 9:6; Jer 23:5; 33:14–15; Ezek 34:23; 37:25; Dan 9:24]; Mic 7:20; [Mal 3:1; 4:2]; John 1:45; 5:39; [Rom 1:1–6] [1]Or *regarding, concerning.* **24:28** [a]Gen 32:26; 42:7; Mark 6:48 **24:29** [a]Gen 19:2–3; Acts 16:15 [b][John 14:23] **24:30** [a]Matt 14:19; Mark 8:6; Luke 9:16 **24:32** [1]Grk. *heart*; a collective sing. [2]‡ Some mss omit *within us.*

he was explaining the scriptures to us?" [33]So they got up that very hour and returned to Jerusalem. They found the eleven and those with them gathered together [34]and saying, "The Lord [a]has really risen and has appeared to Simon!" [35]Then they told what had happened on the road, and how they recognized him when he broke the bread.

Jesus Makes a Final Appearance

[36a]While they were saying these things, Jesus himself stood among them and said to them, "Peace be with you."[1] [37]But they were [a]startled and terrified, thinking they saw a ghost. [38]Then he said to them, "Why are you frightened, and why do doubts arise in your hearts? [39]Look at my hands and my feet; it's me! [a]Touch me and see; a [b]ghost does not have flesh and bones like you see I have." [40]When he had said this, he showed them his hands and his feet.[1] [41]And while they still could not believe it (because [a]of their joy) and were amazed, he said to them, "Do you [b]have anything here to eat?" [42]So they gave him a piece of broiled fish, [43a]and he took it and ate it in front of them.

Jesus' Final Commission

[44]Then he said to them, "[a]These are my words that I spoke to you while I was still with you, that everything written about me in the law of Moses and the prophets and the psalms must be fulfilled." [45]Then [a]he opened their minds so they could understand the scriptures, [46]and said to them, "[a]Thus it stands written that the Christ would suffer and would rise from the dead on the third day, [47]and repentance for the [a]forgiveness of sins would be proclaimed in his name [b]to all nations, beginning from Jerusalem. [48a]You are witnesses of these things. [49a]And look, I am sending you what my Father promised. But stay in the city until you have been clothed with power from on high."

Jesus' Departure

[50]Then Jesus led them out as far [a]as Bethany, and lifting up his hands, he blessed them. [51a]Now during the blessing he departed and was taken up into heaven.[1] [52]So they worshiped[1] him [a]and returned to Jerusalem with great joy, [53]and were continually [a]in the temple courts blessing[1] God.[2]

24:34 [a]1 Cor 15:5   24:36 [a]Mark 16:14; John 20:19; 1 Cor 15:5   [1]Some MSS omit *and said to them, "Peace be with you."*   24:37 [a]Matt 14:26; Mark 6:49   24:39 [a]John 20:20, 27; 1 John 1:1   [b][1 Cor 15:50]   24:40 [1]Some MSS omit v. 40.   24:41 [a]Gen 45:26   [b]John 21:5   24:43 [a]Acts 10:39–41   24:44 [a]Matt 16:21; 17:22; 20:18; Mark 8:31; Luke 9:22; 18:31   24:45 [a]Acts 16:14; 1 John 5:20   24:46 [a]Ps 22; Hos 6:2; Luke 11:29–30; Acts 17:3   24:47 [a]Dan 9:24; Acts 5:31; 10:43; 13:38; 26:18   [b][Ps 22:27; Jer 31:34; Mic 4:2]   24:48 [a][Acts 1:8]; 1 Pet 5:1   24:49 [a]Isa 44:3; Joel 2:28; Acts 2:4   24:50 [a]Matt 21:17; Acts 1:12   24:51 [a]Ps 68:18; 110:1; Mark 16:19; Acts 1:9–11   [1]Some MSS omit *and was taken up into heaven.*   24:52 [a]Matt 28:9   [1]Some MSS omit *worshiped him and.*   24:53 [a]Acts 2:46   [1]Some MSS *praising.*   [2]Maj. MSS add *Amen.*

JOHN

Just as a coin has two sides, so Jesus Christ has two natures. Luke presents Christ in his humanity as the Son of Man; John portrays him in his deity as the Son of God. John's purpose is crystal clear: To set forth Christ in his deity in order to spark believing faith in his readers. John's gospel is topical, not primarily chronological, and it revolves around seven miracles and seven "I am" statements of Christ. Following an extended eyewitness description of the Upper Room meal and Discourse, John records events leading up to the resurrection, the final climactic proof that Jesus is who he claims to be—the Son of God. The title of the Fourth Gospel follows the same format as the titles of the synoptic Gospels: *Kata Ioannen,* "According to John." As with the others, the word "Gospel" was added later. *Ioannes* is derived from the Hebrew name *Johanan,* "Yahweh Has Been Gracious."

The Prologue to the Gospel

1 In the beginning [a]was the [b]Word, and the Word was [c]with [d]God, and the Word was fully God.[1] [2]The [a]Word was with God in the beginning. [3a]All things were created by him, and apart from him not one thing was created that has been created.[1] [4a]*In him was life,*[1] and the life was the light of mankind. [5]And [a]the light shines on in the darkness, but the darkness has not mastered it.[1]

[6]A [a]man came, sent from God, whose name was John. [7]He came as a [a]witness to testify about the light, so that everyone might [b]believe through him. [8]He himself was not the [a]light, but he came to testify about the light. [9a]The true light, who gives light to everyone, was coming into the world. [10]He was in [a]the world, and the world was created by him, but the world did not recognize him. [11a]He came to what was his own, but his own people did not receive him. [12]But to all who have received him—those who believe in his name—he [a]has given the right to become God's children—[13a]children not born by human parents or by human desire or a husband's decision, but by God.

[14a]Now the Word [b]became [c]flesh[1] and took up residence[2] among us. [d]We saw his glory—the glory of the one and only,[3] [e]full of grace and truth, who came from the Father. [15a]John testified about him and shouted out, "This one was [b]the one about whom I said, 'He who comes after me is greater than I am, [c]because he existed before me.'" [16]For we have all received from his [a]fullness one gracious gift after another.[1] [17]For [a]the law was given through Moses, but [b]grace and [c]truth came about through Jesus Christ. [18]No one has ever seen God. The only one,[1] himself God, who is in closest fellowship with the Father, has made God [a]known.

1:1 [a]Gen 1:1; [Col 1:17]; 1 John 1:1 [b][John 1:14]; Rev 19:13 [c][John 17:5; 1 John 1:2] [d][1 John 5:20] [1]Or *and what God was the Word was*; for a discussion of this phrase and translating "God" or "a god" see *NET Bible, Full Notes Edition.* 1:2 [a]Gen 1:1 1:3 [a]Ps 33:6; [Eph 3:9; Col 1:16–17; Heb 1:2] [1]Many later mss place *that has been created* with v. 4, loosely translated there as *What has come into being in him was life.* For an explanation of this complicated issue, see *NET Bible, Full Notes Edition.* 1:4 [a][1 John 5:11] [1][Ps 36:9] 1:5 [a][John 3:19] [1]Or *comprehended it, overcome it.* 1:6 [a]Mal 3:1; Matt 3:1–17; Mark 1:1–11; Luke 3:1–22 1:7 [a]John 3:25–36; 5:33–35 [b][John 3:16] 1:8 [a]Isa 9:2; 49:6 1:9 [a]Isa 49:6 1:10 [a]Acts 13:27; 1 Cor 8:6; Col 1:16; Heb 1:2 1:11 [a]Isa 53:3; [Luke 19:14] 1:12 [a][John 11:52]; Gal 3:26 1:13 [a][John 3:5]; Jas 1:18; [1 Pet 1:23; 1 John 2:29; 3:9] 1:14 [a]Matt 1:16; Rev 19:13 [b]Rom 1:3; Gal 4:4; Phil 2:7; 1 Tim 3:16; Heb 2:14; 1 John 1:1; 4:2; 2 John 7 [c]Heb 2:11 [d]Isa 40:5; 2 Pet 1:16–18 [e][John 8:32; 14:6; 18:37]; Col 1:19 [1]In humility and weakness without overtones of sinfulness. [2]Grk. *and tabernacled.* [3]Or *of the unique one;* trad. *only begotten.* 1:15 [a]Mal 3:1; John 3:32 [b][Matt 3:11] [c][Col 1:17] 1:16 [a][Eph 1:23; 3:19; 4:13; Col 1:19; 2:9] [1]Grk. *for from his fullness we have all received, and grace upon grace.* 1:17 [a][Exod 20:1] [b]John 1:14; [Rom 5:21; 6:14] [c][John 8:32; 14:6; 18:37] 1:18 [a]Exod 33:20; Matt 11:27; 1 Tim 6:16 [1]Maj. mss, esp. later ones, *the only son.* For an explanation of this complicated phrase, see *NET Bible, Full Notes Edition.*

The Testimony of John the Baptist

[19]Now this was John's testimony when [a]the Jewish leaders[1] sent[2] priests and Levites from Jerusalem to ask him, "Who are you?" [20]He confessed—[a]he did not deny but confessed—"I am not the Christ!" [21]So [a]they asked him, "Then who are you? Are you Elijah?" He said, "I am not!" "Are you the Prophet?" He answered, "No!" [22]Then they said to him, "Who are you? Tell us so that we can give an answer to those who sent us. What do you say about yourself?"

[23]John [a]said, "I am [b]*the voice of one shouting in the wilderness, 'Make straight the way for the Lord,'*[1] as the prophet Isaiah said." [24](Now they had been sent from the Pharisees.) [25]So they asked John, "Why then are you baptizing if you are not the Christ, nor Elijah, nor the Prophet?"

[26]John answered them, "[a]I baptize with water. Among you stands one whom you do not recognize, [27]who is coming after me. [a]I am not worthy to untie the strap of his sandal!" [28]These things happened [a]in Bethany[1] across the Jordan River where John was baptizing.

[29]On [a]the next day John saw Jesus coming toward him and said, "Look, the Lamb of God [b]who takes away the sin of the world! [30]This is the one about whom I said, 'After me comes a man who is greater than I am, because he existed before me.' [31]I did not recognize him, but I came baptizing with water so that [a]he could be revealed to Israel."

[32]Then John testified, "I saw the Spirit descending like a dove from heaven, [a]and it remained on him. [33]And I did not recognize him, but the one who sent me to baptize with water said to me, 'The one on whom you see the Spirit descending and remaining—[a]this is the one who baptizes with the Holy Spirit.' [34]I have both seen and testified that this man is the Chosen One of God."[1]

[35]Again the next day John was standing there with two of his disciples. [36]Gazing at Jesus as he walked by, he said, "Look, the Lamb of God!" [37]When John's two disciples heard him say this, they [a]followed Jesus. [38]Jesus turned around and saw them following and said to them, "What do you want?" So they said to him, "Rabbi" (which is translated Teacher), "where are you staying?" [39]Jesus answered, "Come and you will see." So they came and saw where he was staying, and they stayed with him that day. Now it was about four o'clock in the afternoon.[1]

Andrew's Declaration

[40][a]Andrew, the brother of Simon Peter, was one of the two disciples who heard what John said and followed Jesus. [41]He first[1] found his own brother Simon and told him, "We have found the Messiah!" (which is translated Christ). [42]Andrew brought Simon to Jesus. Jesus looked at him and said, "[a]You are Simon, the son of John.[1] You will be called Cephas" (which is translated Peter).

The Calling of More Disciples

[43]On the next day Jesus wanted to set out for Galilee. He found [a]Philip and said to him, "Follow me." [44](Now [a]Philip was from Bethsaida, the town of Andrew and Peter.) [45]Philip found [a]Nathanael and told him, "We have found the one [b]Moses wrote about in the law, and the [c]prophets also wrote about—Jesus [d]of Nazareth, the [e]son of Joseph." [46]Nathanael replied, "[a]Can anything good come out of Nazareth?" Philip replied, "Come and see."

[47]Jesus saw [a]Nathanael coming toward him and exclaimed, "Look, a true Israelite *in whom there is no deceit!*"[1] [48]Nathanael asked him, "How do you know me?" Jesus replied, "Before Philip called you, when you were under the fig tree, I saw you." [49]Nathanael answered him, "Rabbi, [a]you are [b]the Son of God; you are the king of Israel!" [50]Jesus said to him, "Because I told you that I saw you under the fig tree, do you believe? You will see greater things than these." [51]He

1:19 [a] John 5:33 [1] Or *the Jewish authorities.* [2] ‡ Sev. sig. wss *to him* here or after "Levites." 1:20 [a] Luke 3:15; John 3:28; Acts 13:25 1:21 [a] Deut 18:15, 18; Matt 21:11; John 6:14; 7:40 1:23 [a] Matt 3:3 [b] Isa 40:3; Mal 3:1 [1] Isa 40:3 1:26 [a] Matt 3:11; [Mark 1:8; Luke 3:16; Acts 1:5] 1:27 [a] [John 3:31]; Acts 19:4; [Col 1:17] 1:28 [a] Judg 7:24 [1] Many wss *Bethabara.* 1:29 [a] [Exod 12:3]; Acts 8:32; [1 Pet 1:19]; Rev 5:6–14 [b] [Isa 53:11; 1 Cor 15:3; Gal 1:4; 1 Pet 2:24; 1 John 2:2; Rev 1:5] 1:31 [a] Mal 3:1; Matt 3:6 1:32 [a] Isa 42:1; 61:1; Matt 3:16; Mark 1:10; Luke 3:22 1:33 [a] Matt 3:11; Mark 1:8; Luke 3:16; Acts 1:5 1:34 [1] ‡ Maj. wss *this is the Son of God.* 1:37 [a] Matt 4:20, 22 1:39 [1] Grk. *about the tenth hour.* 1:40 [a] Matt 4:18; Mark 1:29; 13:3; John 6:8; 12:22 1:41 [1] Maj. wss grammatically suggest Andrew was first to proselytize another, rather than just first proselytizing Peter. 1:42 [a] Matt 16:18 [1] Maj. mss *of Jonah.* 1:43 [a] Matt 10:3; John 6:5; 12:21–22; 14:8–9 1:44 [a] John 12:21 1:45 [a] John 21:2 [b] [Gen 3:15; Deut 18:18]; Luke 24:27 [c] [Isa 4:2; 7:14; 9:6; Mic 5:2; Zech 6:12]; Luke 24:27 [d] [Matt 2:23]; Luke 2:4 [e] Luke 3:23 1:46 [a] John 7:41–42, 52 1:47 [a] Ps 32:2; 73:1 [1] [Ps 32:2] 1:49 [a] Ps 2:7; Matt 14:33; Luke 1:35 [b] Matt 21:5

continued, "I tell all of you the solemn truth—you will see heaven opened and the angels of God ascending and descending on the Son of Man."

Turning Water into Wine

2 Now on the third day there was a [a]wedding at [b]Cana in Galilee. Jesus' [c]mother was there, [2]and Jesus and his disciples were also invited to the wedding. [3]When the wine ran out, Jesus' mother said to him, "They have no wine left." [4]Jesus replied, "[a]Woman, [b]why are you saying this to me?[1] [c]My time[2] has not yet come." [5]His mother told the servants, "Whatever he tells you, do it." [6]Now there were six stone water jars there [a]for Jewish ceremonial washing, each holding 20 or 30 gallons. [7]Jesus told the servants, "Fill the water jars with water." So they filled them up to the very top. [8]Then he told them, "Now draw some out and take it to the head steward,"[1] and they did. [9]When [a]the head steward tasted the water that had been turned to wine, not knowing where it came from (though the servants who had drawn the water knew), he called the bridegroom [10]and said to him, "Everyone serves the good wine first, and then the cheaper wine when the guests are drunk. You have kept the good wine until now!" [11]Jesus did this as the [a]first of his miraculous signs, in Cana of Galilee. In this way he revealed his glory, [b]and his disciples believed in him.

Cleansing the Temple

[12]After this he went down to [a]Capernaum with [b]his mother and brothers and his disciples, and they stayed there a few days. [13a]Now the Jewish Feast of Passover[1] was near, so Jesus went up to Jerusalem.

[14]He found in the temple courts those who were selling oxen [a]and sheep and doves, and the money changers sitting at tables. [15]So he made a whip of cords[1] and drove them all out of the temple courts, with the sheep and the oxen. He scattered the coins of the money changers and overturned their tables. [16]To those who sold the doves he said, "Take these things away from here! Do not make [a]my Father's house a marketplace!" [17]His disciples remembered that it was written, "[a]***Zeal for your house will devour me.***"[1]

[18]So then the Jewish leaders responded, "[a]What sign can you show us, since you are doing these things?" [19]Jesus replied, "[a]Destroy this temple and in three days I will raise it up again." [20]Then the Jewish leaders said to him, "This temple has been under construction for 46 years, and are you going to raise it up in three days?" [21]But Jesus was speaking [a]about the temple of his body. [22]So after he was raised from the dead, [a]his disciples remembered that he had said this, and they believed the scripture and the saying that Jesus had spoken.

Jesus at the Passover Feast

[23]Now while Jesus was in Jerusalem at the Feast of the Passover, many people believed in his name because they saw the miraculous [a]signs he was doing. [24]But Jesus would not entrust himself to them because he [a]knew all people. [25]He did not need anyone to testify about man, for [a]he knew what was in man.

Conversation with Nicodemus

3 Now a certain man, a Pharisee named Nicodemus, who was a member of the Jewish ruling council,[1] [2a]came to Jesus at night and said to him, "Rabbi, we [b]know that you are a teacher who has come from [c]God. For no one could perform the miraculous signs that you do unless God is with him." [3]Jesus replied, "I tell you the solemn truth, [a]unless a person is born from above,[1] he cannot see the kingdom of God." [4]Nicodemus said to him, "How can a man be born when he is old? He cannot enter his mother's womb and be born a second time, can he?"

2:1[a] [Heb 13:4] [b] John 4:46 [c] John 19:25   **2:4**[a] John 19:26   [b] 2 Sam 16:10   [c] John 7:6, 8, 30; 8:20   [1] Grk. *Woman, what to me and to you?*; an idiom probably implying disengagement rather than hostility. [2] Grk. *my hour*; the time of Jesus' crucifixion and return to the Father.   **2:6**[a] Matt 15:2; [Mark 7:3; Luke 11:39]; John 3:25   **2:8**[1] Or *the master of ceremonies.*   **2:9**[a] John 4:46   **2:11**[a] John 4:54   [b] [John 1:14]   **2:12**[a] Matt 4:13; John 4:46   [b] Matt 12:46; 13:55   **2:13**[a] Exod 12:14; Deut 16:1–6; John 5:1; 6:4; 11:55   [1] Grk. *the Passover of the Jews*; the first of at least three (possibly four) Passovers mentioned in the Gospel.   **2:14**[a] Mal 3:1; Matt 21:12; Mark 11:15, 17; Luke 19:45   **2:15**[1] Sev. wss *like a* [whip].   **2:16**[a] Luke 2:49   **2:17**[a] Ps 69:9   [1] Ps 69:9   **2:18**[a] Matt 12:38; John 6:30   **2:19**[a] Matt 26:61; 27:40; [Mark 14:58; 15:29]; Luke 24:46; Acts 6:14; 10:40; 1 Cor 15:4   **2:21**[a] [1 Cor 3:16; 6:19; 2 Cor 6:16; Col 2:9; Heb 8:2]   **2:22**[a] Luke 24:8; John 2:17; 12:16; 14:26   **2:23**[a] [John 5:36; Acts 2:22]   **2:24**[a] Matt 9:4; John 16:30; Rev 2:23   **2:25**[a][1] 1 Sam 16:7; 1 Chr 28:9; Matt 9:4; [Mark 2:8]; John 6:64; 16:30; Acts 1:24; Rev 2:23   **3:1**[1] Grk. *a ruler of the Jews*; a member of the Sanhedrin.   **3:2**[a] John 7:50; 19:39   [b] John 9:16, 33; Acts 2:22   [c] [Acts 10:38]   **3:3**[a] [John 1:13; Gal 6:15; Titus 3:5; Jas 1:18; 1 Pet 1:23; 1 John 3:9]   [1] Or *again.*

[5] Jesus answered, "I tell you the solemn truth,[a] unless a person is born of water and spirit,[1] he cannot enter the kingdom of God. [6] What is born of the [a] flesh is flesh, and what is born of the Spirit is spirit. [7] Do not be amazed that I said to you, 'You must all be born from above.' [8] The wind blows wherever it will, and you hear [a] the sound it makes, but do not know where it comes from and where it is going. So it is with everyone who is born of the Spirit."

[9] Nicodemus replied, "[a] How can these things be?" [10] Jesus answered, "Are you the teacher of Israel and yet you don't understand these things? [11] I tell you the [a] solemn truth, we speak about what we know and testify about what we have seen, but [b] you people do not accept our testimony. [12] If I have told you people about earthly things and you don't believe, how will you believe if I tell you about heavenly things? [13] No [a] one has ascended into heaven except the one who descended from heaven—the Son of Man.[1] [14a] Just as Moses *lifted up the serpent in the wilderness*,[1] so [b] must the Son of Man be lifted up, [15] so that everyone who [a] believes in him may [b] have eternal life."

[16a] For this is the way God loved the world: He gave his one and only[1] [b] Son, so that everyone who believes in him will not perish but have eternal life. [17a] For God did not send his Son into the world to condemn the world, but that the world should be saved through him. [18] The one who believes in him is not condemned. [a] The one who does not believe has been condemned already, because he has not believed in the name of the one and only Son of God. [19] Now this is the basis for judging: [a] that the light has come into the world and people loved the darkness rather than the light because their deeds were evil. [20] For [a] everyone who does evil deeds hates the light and does not come to the light, so that their deeds will not be exposed. [21] But the one who practices the truth comes to the light, so that it may be plainly evident that his deeds have been [a] done in God.

Further Testimony about Jesus by John the Baptist

[22] After this, Jesus [a] and his disciples came into Judean territory, and there he spent time with them and was baptizing. [23] John was also baptizing at Aenon near [a] Salim because water was plentiful there, [b] and people were coming to him and being baptized. [24] (For [a] John had not yet been thrown into prison.)

[25] Now a dispute came about between some of John's disciples and a certain Jew[1] concerning ceremonial washing. [26] So they came [a] to John and said to him, "Rabbi, the one who was with you on the other side of the Jordan River, about whom you testified—see, he is baptizing, and everyone is flocking to him!"

[27] John replied, "No one [a] can receive anything unless it has been given to him from heaven. [28] You yourselves can testify that I said, '[a] I am not the [b] Christ,' but rather, 'I have been sent before him.' [29] The one who has [a] the bride is [b] the bridegroom. The friend of the bridegroom, who stands by and listens for him, rejoices greatly when he hears the bridegroom's voice. This then is my joy, and it is complete. [30a] He must become more important while I become less important."

[31] The one who comes from above is superior to all. [a] The one who [b] is from [c] the earth belongs to [d] the earth and speaks about earthly things. The one who comes from heaven is superior to all.[1] [32] He testifies about [a] what he has seen and heard, but no one accepts his testimony. [33] The one who [a] has accepted his testimony has confirmed clearly that God is truthful. [34a] For the one whom God has sent speaks the words of God, for he does not give the

3:5 [a] Mark 16:16; [Acts 2:38] [1] Or *born of water and wind.* 3:6 [a] John 1:13; 1 Cor 15:50 3:8 [a] Ps 135:7; Eccl 11:5; Ezek 37:9; 1 Cor 2:11 3:9 [a] John 6:52, 60 3:11 [a] [Matt 11:27] [b] John 3:32; 8:14 3:13 [a] Deut 30:12; Prov 30:4; Acts 2:34; Rom 10:6; 1 Cor 15:47; Eph 4:9 [1] Maj. wss add *the one who is in heaven.* 3:14 [a] Num 21:9 [b] Matt 27:35; Mark 15:24; Luke 23:33; John 8:28; 12:34; 19:18 [1] [Num 21:5–9] 3:15 [a] John 6:47 [b] John 3:36 3:16 [a] Rom 5:8; Eph 2:4; 2 Thess 2:16; [1 John 4:9–10; Rev 1:5] [b] [Isa 9:6] [1] Trad. *only begotten.* 3:17 [a] Matt 1:21; Luke 9:56; 1 John 4:14 3:18 [a] John 5:24; 6:40, 47; 20:31; Rom 8:1 3:19 [a] [John 1:4, 9–11] 3:20 [a] Job 24:13; Eph 5:11, 13 3:21 [a] [John 15:4–5]; 1 Cor 15:10 3:22 [a] John 4:1–2 3:23 [a] 1 Sam 9:4 [b] Matt 3:5–6 3:24 [a] Matt 4:12; 14:3; Mark 6:17; Luke 3:20 3:25 [1] Some MSS *Judeans*; i.e., representatives of Jewish authorities. 3:26 [a] John 1:7, 15, 27, 34 3:27 [a] [Rom 12:5–8]; 1 Cor 3:5–6; 4:7; Heb 5:4; [Jas 1:17; 1 Pet 4:10–11] 3:28 [a] John 1:19–27 [b] Mal 3:1; Mark 1:2; [Luke 1:17] 3:29 [a] Matt 22:2; [2 Cor 11:2; Eph 5:25, 27]; Rev 21:9 [b] Song 5:1 3:30 [a] [Isa 9:7] 3:31 [a] John 3:13; 8:23 [b] Matt 28:18; John 1:15, 27; 13:13; Rom 9:5; [Col 1:17–18] [c] 1 Cor 15:47 [d] John 6:33; 1 Cor 15:47; Eph 1:21; Phil 2:9 [1] Some wss omit *is superior to all.* 3:32 [a] Isa 53:1, 3; John 3:11; 15:15 3:33 [a] Rom 3:4; 1 John 5:10 3:34 [a] Deut 18:18; John 7:16

Spirit [b]sparingly.[1] [35]The [a]Father loves the Son and has placed all things under his authority. [36]The one who believes in [a]the Son has eternal life. The one who rejects[1] the Son will not see life, but God's [b]wrath remains on him.

Departure from Judea

4 Now when Jesus[1] knew that the Pharisees had heard that he was winning and [a]baptizing more disciples than John [2](although Jesus himself was not baptizing, but his disciples were), [3]he left Judea and set out once more for Galilee.

Conversation with a Samaritan Woman

[4]But he had to pass through Samaria. [5]Now he came to a Samaritan town called Sychar, near the plot of land that [a]Jacob had [b]given to his son Joseph. [6]Jacob's well was there, so Jesus, since he was tired from the journey, sat right down beside the well. It was about noon.

[7]A Samaritan woman came to draw water. Jesus said to her, "Give me some water to drink." [8](For his disciples had gone off into the town to buy supplies.) [9]So the Samaritan woman said to him, "How can you—a [a]Jew—ask me, a Samaritan woman, for water to drink?" (For Jews use nothing in common with [b]Samaritans.)

[10]Jesus answered her, "If you had known the [a]gift of God and who it is who said to you, 'Give me some water to drink,' you would have asked him, and he would have given you [b]living water." [11]"Sir,"[1] the woman[2] said to him, "you have no bucket and the well is deep; where then do you get this living water? [12]Surely you're not greater than our ancestor Jacob, are you? For he gave us this well and drank from it himself, along with his sons and his livestock."

[13]Jesus replied, "Everyone who drinks some of this water will be thirsty again. [14]But [a]whoever drinks some of the water that [b]I will give him will never be thirsty again,[1] but the water that I will give him will become in him a fountain[2] of water springing up to eternal life." [15a]The woman said to him, "Sir, give me this water, so that I will not be thirsty or have to come here to draw water." [16]He[1] said to her, "Go call your husband and come back here." [17]The woman replied, "I have no husband." Jesus said to her, "Right you are when you said, 'I have no husband,'[1] [18]for you have had five husbands, and the man you are living with now is not your husband. This you said truthfully!"

[19]The woman [a]said to him, "Sir, I see that you are a prophet. [20]Our fathers worshiped on [a]this mountain, and you people say that the place where people must worship is in [b]Jerusalem." [21]Jesus said to her, "Believe me, woman, a time is coming [a]when you will worship the Father neither on this mountain nor in Jerusalem. [22]You people worship [a]what you do not know. We worship what we know because [b]salvation is from the Jews. [23]But a time is coming—and now is here—when the true worshipers will [a]worship the Father in [b]spirit [c]and truth, for the Father seeks such people to be his worshipers. [24a]God is spirit, and the people who worship him must worship in spirit and truth." [25]The woman said to him, "[a]I know that Messiah is coming" ([b]the one called Christ); "whenever he comes, he will tell us everything." [26]Jesus said to her, "[a]I, the one speaking to you, am he."

The Disciples Return

[27]Now at that very moment his disciples came back. They were shocked because he was speaking with a woman. However, no one said, "What do you want?" or "Why are you speaking with her?" [28]Then the woman left her water jar, went off into the town and said to the people, [29]"Come, see a man [a]who told me everything I ever did. Surely he can't be the Messiah, can he?" [30]So they left the town and began coming to him.

3:34[b] John 1:16 [1]Grk. *for not by measure does he give the Spirit*; the Spirit rests upon Jesus without measure. 3:35[a] Matt 11:27; Luke 10:22; John 5:20; [Heb 2:8] 3:36[a] John 3:16–17; 6:47; Rom 1:17; 1 John 5:10 [b] Rom 1:18; Eph 5:6; 1 Thess 1:10 [1]Or *refuses to believe, disobeys*. 4:1[a] John 3:22, 26; 1 Cor 1:17 [1]Sev. sig. wss *Lord*. 4:5[a] Gen 33:19; Josh 24:32 [b] Gen 48:22; Josh 4:12 4:9[a] Acts 10:28 [b] 2 Kgs 17:24; Matt 10:5–6; Luke 9:52; 10:33; 17:16; John 8:48 4:10[a] [Rom 5:15] [b] Isa 12:3; 44:3; Jer 2:13; Zech 13:1; 14:8; John 7:38 4:11[1]Or *Lord*; there is probably a gradual transition from "sir" to "Lord" as the woman's respect for Jesus grows. [2]‡ Some wss omit *the woman*. 4:14[a] [John 6:35, 58] [b] John 7:37–38 [1]Grk. *will never be thirsty forever*, an emphatic Grk. construction. [2]Or *well*. 4:15[a] John 6:34–35; 17:2–3; [Rom 6:23; 1 John 5:20] 4:16[1]Maj. wss *Jesus*. 4:17[1]An emphatic Grk. construction. 4:19[a] Matt 21:11; Luke 7:16, 39; 24:19; John 6:14; 7:40; 9:17 4:20[a] Gen 12:6–8; 33:18, 20; Judg 9:7 [b] Deut 12:5, 11; 1 Kgs 9:3; 2 Chr 7:12; Ps 122:1–9 4:21[a] [Mal 1:11]; 1 Tim 2:8 4:22[a] [2 Kgs 17:28–41] [b] [Isa 2:3; Luke 24:47; Rom 3:1; 9:4–5] 4:23[a] Matt 18:20; [Heb 13:10–14] [b] Phil 3:3 [c] [John 1:17] 4:24[a] 2 Cor 3:17 4:25[a] Deut 18:15 [b] John 4:29, 39 4:26[a] Dan 9:25; Matt 26:63–64; Mark 14:61–62 4:29[a] John 4:25

Workers for the Harvest

[31] Meanwhile the disciples were urging him, "Rabbi, eat something." [32] But he said to them, "I have food to eat that you know nothing about." [33] So the disciples began to say to one another, "No one brought him anything to eat, did they?" [34] Jesus said to them, "[a] My food is to do the will of the one who sent me and to [b] complete his work. [35] Don't you say, '[a] There are four more months and then comes the harvest?' I tell you, look up and see [b] that the fields are already white for harvest! [36] The one who reaps receives pay [a] and gathers fruit for eternal life, so that the one who sows [b] and the one who reaps can rejoice together. [37] For in this instance the saying is true, 'One sows and [a] another reaps.' [38] I sent you to reap what you did not work for; [a] others have labored and you have entered into their labor."

The Samaritans Respond

[39] Now many Samaritans from that town believed in him because [a] of the report of the woman who testified, "He told me everything I ever did." [40] So when the Samaritans came to him, they began asking him to stay with them. He stayed there two days, [41] and because of his [a] word many more[1] believed. [42] They said to the woman, "No longer do [a] we believe because of your words, for we have heard for ourselves, and we know that this one really is the Savior of the world."

Onward to Galilee

[43] After the two days he departed from there to Galilee. [44] (For [a] Jesus himself had testified that a prophet has no honor in his own country.) [45] So when he came to Galilee, the Galileans welcomed him because they had seen all the things he had done [a] in Jerusalem at the feast ([b] for they themselves had gone to the feast).

Healing the Royal Official's Son

[46] Now he came again to Cana in Galilee [a] where he had made the water wine. In Capernaum there was a certain royal official[1] whose son was sick. [47] When he heard that Jesus had come back from Judea to Galilee, he went to him and begged him to come down and heal his son, who was about to die. [48] So Jesus said to him, "[a] Unless you people see signs and wonders you will never believe!" [49] "Sir," the official said to him, "come down before my child dies." [50] Jesus told him, "Go home; your son will live." The man believed the word that Jesus spoke to him, and set off for home.

[51] While he was on his way down, his slaves[1] met him and told him that his son was going to live. [52] So he asked them the time when his condition began to improve, and they told him, "Yesterday at one o'clock in the afternoon the fever left him." [53] Then the father realized that it was the very time Jesus had said to him, "Your son will live," and he himself believed along with his entire household. [54] Jesus did this as his second miraculous sign when he returned from Judea to Galilee.

Healing a Paralytic at the Pool of Bethesda

5 After [a] this there was a Jewish feast,[1] and Jesus went [b] up to Jerusalem. [2] Now there is in Jerusalem [a] by the Sheep Gate a pool called *Bethzatha*[1] in Aramaic, which has five covered walkways. [3] A great number of sick, blind, lame, and paralyzed people were lying in these walkways.[1] [5] Now a man was there who had been disabled for 38 years. [6] When Jesus saw him lying there and when he realized that the man had been disabled a long time already, he said to him, "Do you want to become well?" [7] The sick man answered him, "Sir,[1] I have no one to put me into the pool when the water is stirred up. While I am trying to get into the water, someone else goes down there before me." [8] Jesus said to him, "Stand [a] up! Pick up your mat[1] and walk." [9] Immediately the man was healed, and he picked up his mat and started walking. (Now [a] that day was a Sabbath.)

4:34 [a] Ps 40:7–8; Heb 10:9   [b] Job 23:12; [John 6:38; 17:4; 19:30]   4:35 [a] Gen 8:22   [b] Matt 9:37; Luke 10:2   4:36 [a] Dan 12:3; Rom 6:22   [b] 1 Thess 2:19   4:37 [a] 1 Cor 3:5–9   4:38 [a] Jer 44:4; [1 Pet 1:12]   4:39 [a] John 4:29   4:41 [a] Luke 4:32; [John 6:63]   [1] Or *and they believed much more.*   4:42 [a] John 17:8; 1 John 4:14   4:44 [a] Matt 13:57; Mark 6:4; Luke 4:24   4:45 [a] John 2:13, 23; 3:2   [b] Deut 16:16   4:46 [a] John 2:1, 11   [1] Or *nobleman*; almost certainly a servant of Herod.   4:48 [a] John 6:30; Rom 15:19; 1 Cor 1:22; 2 Cor 12:12; [2 Thess 2:9]; Heb 2:4   4:51 [1] Trad. *servants*; the word does not bear the connotation of a free individual serving another.   5:1 [a] Lev 23:2; Deut 16:16   [b] John 2:13   [1] Some MSS *a feast, the feast.*   5:2 [a] Neh 3:1, 32; 12:39   [1] Some MSS *Bethsaida, Belzetha, Bethesda.*   5:3 [1] Maj. MSS add the following to v. 3: *waiting for the moving of the water.*   5:4 *For an angel of the Lord went down and stirred up the water at certain times. Whoever first stepped in after the stirring of the water was healed from whatever disease which he suffered.*   5:7 [1] Or *Lord.*   5:8 [a] Matt 9:6; Mark 2:11; Luke 5:24   [1] Or *pallet, cot, stretcher.*   5:9 [a] John 9:14

[10] So the Jewish leaders said to the man who had been healed, "[a]It is the Sabbath, and you are not permitted to carry your mat." [11]But he answered them, "The man who made me well said to me, 'Pick up your mat and walk.'" [12]They asked him, "Who is the man who said to you, 'Pick up your mat[1] and walk'?" [13]But the man who had been [a]healed did not know who it was, for Jesus had slipped out, since there was a crowd in that place.

[14]After this Jesus found him at the temple and said to him, "Look, you have become well. Don't [a]sin any more, lest anything worse happen to you." [15]The man went away and informed the Jewish leaders that Jesus was the one who had made him well.

Responding to Jewish Leaders

[16]Now because Jesus was doing these things on the Sabbath, the Jewish leaders began [a]persecuting him. [17]So he[1] told them, "[a]My Father is working until now, and I too am working." [18]For this reason the Jewish leaders were [a]trying even harder to kill him because not only was he breaking the Sabbath, but he was also calling God his own Father, thus [b]making himself equal with God. [19]So Jesus answered [a]them, "I tell you the solemn truth, the Son can do nothing on his own initiative, but only what he sees the Father doing. For whatever the Father does, the Son does likewise. [20]For [a]the Father loves the Son and [b]shows him everything he does, and will show him greater deeds than these, so that you will be amazed. [21]For just as the Father raises the dead [a]and gives them life, so also the Son gives life to whomever he wishes. [22]Furthermore, the Father does not judge anyone, but [a]has assigned all judgment to the Son, [23]so that all people will honor [a]the Son just as they honor the Father. The one who does not honor the Son does not honor the Father who sent him.

[24]"I tell you [a]the solemn truth, the one who hears[1] my message and believes the one who sent me has eternal life and will not be condemned, [b]but has crossed over from death to life. [25]I tell you [a]the solemn truth, a time is coming—and is now here—when the dead will hear the voice of the Son of God, and those who hear will live. [26]For just [a]as the Father has [b]life in himself, thus he has granted the Son to have life in himself, [27]and he [a]has granted the Son authority to execute judgment [b]because he is the Son of Man.

[28]"Do not be amazed at this because a time is coming when all who are in the tombs will [a]hear his voice [29a]and will come out—the ones who have done what is good to the resurrection resulting in life, and the ones who have done what is evil to the resurrection resulting in condemnation. [30a]I can do nothing on my own initiative. Just as I hear, I judge, and my judgment is just because I do not seek my own will, but the will of the one who sent me.

More Testimony about Jesus

[31]"[a]If I testify about myself, my testimony is not true. [32]There is another who testifies about me, and I know [a]the testimony he testifies about me is true. [33]You have sent to John, [a]and he has testified to the truth. [34](I do not accept human testimony, but I say this so that you may be saved.) [35]He was a lamp that was burning and [a]shining, and [b]you wanted to rejoice greatly for a short time in his light.

[36]"But [a]I have a testimony greater than that from John. For [b]the [c]deeds that the Father has assigned me to complete—the deeds I am now doing—testify about me that the Father has sent me. [37]And the Father who sent me [a]has himself testified about me. You people have never heard his voice [b]nor seen his form at any time, [38]nor do you have his word residing in you because you do not believe the one whom he sent. [39]You study the scriptures thoroughly[1] because [a]you think in them you possess eternal life, and it is [b]these same

5:10 [a]Exod 20:10; Neh 13:19; Jer 17:21–22; Matt 12:2; Mark 2:24; Luke 6:2   5:12 [1]Maj. MSS omit *your mat*.   5:13 [a]Luke 13:14; 22:51   5:14 [a]Matt 12:45; [Mark 2:5]; John 8:11   5:16 [a]Luke 4:29; John 8:37; 10:39   5:17 [a][John 9:4; 17:4]   [1‡] Maj. MSS *Jesus*.   5:18 [a]John 7:1, 19   [b]John 10:30; Phil 2:6   5:19 [a]Matt 26:39; John 5:30; 6:38; 8:28; 12:49; 14:10   5:20 [a]Matt 3:17; John 3:35; 2 Pet 1:17   [b][Matt 11:27]   5:21 [a]Luke 7:14; 8:54; [John 11:25]   5:22 [a]Matt 11:27; 28:18; [John 3:35; 17:2; Acts 17:31; 1 Pet 4:5]   5:23 [a]Luke 10:16; 1 John 2:23   5:24 [a]John 3:16, 18; 6:47   [b][1 John 3:14]   [1]Or *obeys*.   5:25 [a][Eph 2:1, 5; Col 2:13]   5:26 [a]Ps 36:9   [b][John 1:4; 14:6]; 1 Cor 15:45   5:27 [a]John 9:39; [Acts 10:42; 17:31]   [b]Dan 7:13   5:28 [a][1 Thess 4:15–17]   5:29 [a]Isa 26:19; [1 Cor 15:52]   5:30 [a]John 5:19   5:31 [a]John 8:14; Rev 3:14   5:32 [a][Matt 3:17; John 8:18; 1 John 5:6]   5:33 [a][John 1:15, 19, 27, 32]   5:35 [a]2 Sam 21:17; 2 Pet 1:19   [b]Matt 13:20; Mark 6:20   5:36 [a]1 John 5:9   [b]John 3:2; 10:25; 17:4   [c]John 9:16; 10:38   5:37 [a]Matt 3:17; John 6:27; 8:18   [b]Deut 4:12; John 1:18; 1 Tim 1:17; 1 John 4:12   5:39 [a]Isa 8:20; 34:16; Luke 16:29; Acts 17:11   [b]Deut 18:15, 18; Luke 24:27   [1]Or *Study the scriptures thoroughly*; an imperative.

scriptures that testify about me, [40a]but you are not willing to come to me so that you may have life.

[41]"I do not accept [a]praise from people, [42]but I know you, that you do not have the love of God within you. [43]I have come in my Father's name, and you do not accept me. If someone else comes in his own name, you will accept him. [44a]How can you believe, if you accept praise from one [b]another and don't seek the praise that comes from the only God?[1]

[45]"Do not suppose that I will accuse you before [a]the Father. The one who accuses you is Moses, in whom you have placed your hope. [46]If you believed Moses, you would believe me [a]because he wrote about me. [47]But if you [a]do not believe what Moses wrote, how will you believe my words?"

The Feeding of the 5,000

6 After [a]this[1] Jesus went away to the other side of the Sea of Galilee (also called the Sea of [b]Tiberias). [2]A large crowd was following him because they were observing the miraculous signs he was performing on the [a]sick. [3]So Jesus went on up the mountainside and sat down there with his disciples. [4]([a]Now the Jewish Feast of the Passover was near.) [5a]Then Jesus, when he looked up and saw that a large crowd was coming to him, said to [b]Philip, "Where can we buy bread so that these people may eat?" [6](Now Jesus said this to test him, for he knew what he was going to do.) [7]Philip replied, "200 silver coins worth[1] of bread would not be enough for them, for each one to get a little." [8]One of Jesus' disciples, [a]Andrew, Simon Peter's brother, said to him, [9]"Here is a boy who has five barley loaves and two fish, [a]but what good are these for so many people?"

[10]Jesus said, "Have the people sit down." (Now there was a lot of grass in that place.) So the men[1] sat down, about 5,000 in number. [11]Then Jesus took the loaves, and when he had given thanks, he distributed the bread to those who were seated. He then did the same with the fish, as much as they wanted. [12]When they were all satisfied, Jesus said to his disciples, "Gather up the broken pieces that are left over, so that nothing is wasted." [13]So they gathered them up and filled 12 baskets with broken pieces from the five barley loaves left over by the people who had eaten.

[14]Now when [a]the people saw the miraculous sign that Jesus performed, they began to say to one another, "This is certainly the Prophet who is to come into the world."[1] [15]Then Jesus, because he knew they were going to come and seize him by force to make him [a]king, withdrew again up the mountainside alone.

Walking on Water

[16a]Now when evening came, his disciples went down to the lake, [17]got into a boat, and started to cross the lake to Capernaum. (It had already become dark, and Jesus had not yet come to them.) [18]By now a strong wind was blowing and the sea was getting rough. [19]Then, when they had rowed about three or four miles, they caught sight of Jesus walking on the lake, approaching the boat, and they were [a]frightened. [20]But he said to them, "[a]It is I. Do not be afraid." [21]Then they wanted to take him into the boat, and immediately the boat came to the land where they had been heading.

[22]The next day the crowd that remained on the other side of the lake realized that only one small boat[1] had been there, and that Jesus had not boarded it with his disciples, but that his disciples had gone away alone. [23]Other boats from Tiberias came to shore near the place where they had eaten the bread after the Lord had given thanks.[1] [24]So when the crowd realized that neither Jesus nor his disciples were there, they got into the boats and came to Capernaum looking [a]for Jesus.

Jesus' Discourse about the Bread of Life

[25]When they found him on the other side of the lake, they said to him, "Rabbi, when did you get here?" [26]Jesus replied, "I tell you

5:40 [a][John 1:11; 3:19]   5:41 [a]John 5:44; 7:18; 1 Thess 2:6   5:44 [a]John 12:43   [b][Rom 2:29]   [1]Sev. sig. wss omit *God*.
5:45 [a]Rom 2:12   5:46 [a][Gen 3:15]; Deut 18:15, 18; John 1:45; Acts 26:22   5:47 [a]Luke 16:29, 31   6:1 [a]Matt 14:13; Mark 6:32;
Luke 9:10, 12   [b]John 6:23; 21:1   [1]A vague temporal reference.   6:2 [a]Matt 4:23; 8:16; 9:35; 14:36; 15:30; 19:2   6:4 [a]Lev
23:5, 7; Deut 16:1; John 2:13   6:5 [a]Matt 14:14; Mark 6:35; Luke 9:12   [b]John 1:43   6:7 [1]Grk. *200 denarii*; about eight
months' pay.   6:8 [a]John 1:40   6:9 [a]2 Kgs 4:43   6:10 [1]The number, 5,000, probably included only adult males.
6:14 [a]Gen 49:10; Deut 18:15, 18; John 1:21; 7:40; Acts 3:22; 7:37   [1][Deut 18:15]   6:15 [a][John 18:36]   6:16 [a]Matt
14:23; Mark 6:47   6:19 [a]Matt 17:6   6:20 [a]Isa 43:1–2   6:22 [1]Maj. wss *one which his disciples had entered*.
6:23 [1]A few wss omit *after the Lord had given thanks*.   6:24 [a]Mark 1:37; Luke 4:42

the solemn truth, you are looking for me not because you saw miraculous signs, but because you ate all the loaves of bread you wanted. [27][a]Do not work [b]for the food that disappears,[1] but for the food that remains to eternal life—the food which the Son of Man will give to you. [c]For God the Father has put his seal of approval on him."

[28]So then they said to him, "What must we do to accomplish the deeds God requires?" [29]Jesus replied, "[a]This is the deed God requires—to believe in the one whom he sent." [30]So they said to him, "Then [a]what miraculous sign will you perform, so that we may see it and believe you? What will you do? [31][a]Our ancestors ate [b]the manna in the wilderness, just as it is written, '*He gave them bread from heaven to eat.*'[1]

[32]Then Jesus told them, "I tell you the solemn truth, it is not Moses who has given you the bread from heaven, but [a]my Father is giving you the true bread from heaven. [33]For the bread of God is the one who comes down from heaven and gives life to the world." [34]So they said to him, "Sir,[1] give us this bread all [a]the time!"

[35]Jesus said to them, "[a]I am [b]the bread of life. The one who comes to me will never go hungry, and the one who believes in me [c]will never be thirsty. [36][a]But I told you that you have seen me[1] and still [b]do not believe. [37][a]Everyone whom [b]the Father gives me will come to me, and the one who comes to me I will never send away. [38]For I have come down from heaven [a]not to do my own will [b]but the will of the one who sent me. [39]Now this is the will of the one who sent me—[a]that I should not lose one person of every one he has given me, but raise them all up[1] at the last day. [40]For this is the will of my Father—[a]for everyone who looks on the Son and believes in him to have eternal life, and I will raise him up at the last day."

[41]Then the Jews who were hostile to Jesus[1] began complaining about him because he said, "I am the bread that came down from heaven," [42]and they said, "[a]Isn't this Jesus the son of Joseph, whose father and mother we know? How can he now say, 'I have come down from heaven'?" [43]Jesus replied, "Do not complain about me to one another. [44][a]No one can come to me unless the Father who sent me [b]draws him,[1] and I will raise him up at the last day. [45]It is written in the prophets, '[a]*And they will all be taught by God.*'[1] Everyone who hears and learns from [b]the Father comes to me. [46]([a]Not that anyone has seen the Father [b]except the one who is from God—he has seen the Father.) [47]I tell you [a]the solemn truth, the one who believes[1] has eternal life. [48][a]I am the bread of life. [49][a]Your ancestors ate the manna in the wilderness, and they died. [50][a]This is the bread that has come down from heaven, so that a person may eat from it and not die. [51]I am the living bread that came down from heaven. If anyone eats from this bread he will live forever. The bread that [a]I will give for [b]the life of the world is my flesh."

[52]Then the Jews who were hostile to Jesus[1] began to [a]argue with one another, "How can this man give us his flesh to eat?" [53]Jesus said to them, "I tell [a]you the solemn truth, unless you eat the flesh of the Son of Man and drink his blood, you have no life in yourselves. [54]The one [a]who eats[1] my flesh and drinks my blood has eternal life, and I will raise him up on the last day. [55]For my flesh is true food, and my blood is true drink. [56]The one who eats my flesh and drinks my blood [a]resides in me, and I in him. [57]Just as the living Father sent me, and I live because of the Father, so the one who consumes me will live because of me. [58][a]This is the bread that came down from heaven; it is not [b]like the bread your ancestors ate, but then later died. The one who eats this bread will live forever."

6:27 [a] Matt 6:19 [b] John 4:14; [Eph 2:8–9] [c] Ps 2:7; Isa 42:1; Matt 3:17; 17:5; Mark 1:11; 9:7; Luke 3:22; 9:35; John 5:37; Acts 2:22; 2 Pet 1:17 [1] Or *perishes*; the temporary nature of this food. **6:29** [a] 1 Thess 1:3; Jas 2:22; [1 John 3:23]; Rev 2:26 **6:30** [a] Matt 12:38; 16:1; Mark 8:11; 1 Cor 1:22 **6:31** [a] Exod 16:15; Num 11:7; 1 Cor 10:3 [b] Exod 16:4, 15; Neh 9:15; Ps 78:24 [1] Ps 78:24 (ref. Exod 16:4–36) **6:32** [a] John 3:13, 16 **6:34** [a] John 4:15 [1] Or *Lord*; it is not clear that the crowd is acknowledging Jesus as Lord. **6:35** [a] John 6:48, 58 [b] John 4:14; 7:37; Rev 7:16 [c] Isa 55:1–2 **6:36** [a] John 6:26, 64; 15:24 [b] John 10:26 [1] A few MSS omit *me*. **6:37** [a] John 6:45 [b] [Matt 24:24; John 10:28–29]; 2 Tim 2:19; 1 John 2:19 **6:38** [a] Matt 26:39; John 5:30 [b] John 4:34 **6:39** [a] John 10:28; 17:12; 18:9 [1] Or *resurrect them all, make them all live again.* **6:40** [a] John 3:15–16; 4:14; 6:27, 47, 54 **6:41** [1] Grk. *Then the Jews.* **6:42** [a] Matt 13:55; Mark 6:3; Luke 4:22 **6:44** [a] Song 1:4 [b] [Eph 2:8–9; Phil 1:29; 2:12–13] [1] Or *attracts him, pulls him.* **6:45** [a] Isa 54:13; Jer 31:34; Mic 4:2; [Heb 8:10] [b] John 6:37 [1] Isa 54:13 **6:46** [a] John 1:18 [b] Matt 11:27; [Luke 10:22]; John 7:29 **6:47** [a] [John 3:16, 18] [1] Maj. wss add *in me.* **6:48** [a] John 6:33, 35; [Gal 2:20; Col 3:3–4] **6:49** [a] John 6:31, 58 **6:50** [a] John 6:51, 58 **6:51** [a] John 3:13 [b] Heb 10:5 **6:52** [a] John 7:43; 9:16; 10:19 [1] Grk. *Then the Jews began to argue.* **6:53** [a] Matt 26:26 **6:54** [a] John 4:14; 6:27, 40 [1] Or *who chews.* **6:56** [a] [1 John 3:24; 4:15–16] **6:58** [a] John 6:49–51 [b] Exod 16:14–35

Many Followers Depart

⁵⁹Jesus said these things while he was teaching in the synagogue in Capernaum. ⁶⁰ᵃThen many of his disciples, when they heard these things, said, "This is a difficult saying! Who can understand it?"¹ ⁶¹When Jesus was aware that his disciples were complaining about this, he said to them, "Does this cause you to be offended?¹ ⁶²Then ᵃwhat if you see the Son of Man ascending where he was before? ⁶³The ᵃSpirit is the one who gives life; human ᵇnature is of no help! The ᶜwords that I have spoken to you are spirit and are life. ⁶⁴But ᵃthere are some of you who do not believe." (For ᵇJesus had already known from the beginning who those were who did not believe, and who it was who would betray him.) ⁶⁵So Jesus added, "Because of ᵃthis I told you that no one can come to me unless the Father has allowed him to come."

Peter's Confession

⁶⁶After this many ᵃof his disciples quit following him and did not accompany him any longer. ⁶⁷So Jesus said to the twelve, "You don't want to go away too, do you?" ⁶⁸Simon Peter answered him, "Lord, to whom would we go? You have ᵃthe words of eternal life. ⁶⁹We have come to believe ᵃand to know that you are the Holy One of God!"¹ ⁷⁰Jesus replied, "ᵃDidn't I choose you, the twelve, ᵇand yet one of you is the devil?"¹ ⁷¹(Now he said this about ᵃJudas son of Simon Iscariot, for Judas, one of the twelve, was going to ᵇbetray him.)

The Feast of Shelters

7 After this Jesus traveled throughout Galilee. He stayed out of Judea ᵃbecause the Jewish leaders wanted to kill him. ²ᵃNow the Jewish Feast of Shelters¹ was near. ³So ᵃJesus' brothers advised him, "Leave here and go to Judea so your disciples may see your miracles that you are performing. ⁴For no one who seeks to make a reputation for himself does anything in secret. If you are doing these things, show yourself to the world." ⁵(For not ᵃeven his own ᵇbrothers believed in him.)

⁶So Jesus replied, "ᵃMy time has not yet arrived, but you are ready at any opportunity! ⁷ᵃThe world cannot hate you, but it hates me ᵇbecause I am testifying about it that its deeds are evil. ⁸You go up to the feast yourselves. I am not going up to this feast¹ ᵃbecause my time² has not yet fully arrived."³ ⁹When he had said this, he remained in Galilee.

¹⁰But when his brothers had gone up to the feast, then Jesus himself also went up, not openly but in secret. ¹¹So ᵃthe Jewish leaders were looking for him at the feast, asking, "Where is he?" ¹²There was a lot of grumbling about him among ᵃthe crowds. ᵇSome were saying, "He is a good man," but others, "He deceives the common people." ¹³However, no one spoke openly about him ᵃfor fear of the Jewish leaders.

Teaching in the Temple

¹⁴When the feast was half over, Jesus went up to the temple courts and began to ᵃteach. ¹⁵Then the Jewish leaders were astonished ᵃand said, "How does this man know so much when he has never had formal instruction?"¹ ¹⁶So Jesus replied, "ᵃMy teaching is not from me, but from the one who sent me. ¹⁷ᵃIf anyone wants to do God's will, he will know about my teaching, whether it is from God or whether I speak from my own authority. ¹⁸The person who speaks on his own authority desires to receive honor for himself; ᵃthe one who ᵇdesires the honor of the one who sent him is a man of integrity, and there is ᶜno unrighteousness

---

6:60 ᵃ Matt 11:6; John 6:66   ¹ Or *obey it*; Grk. *hear it.*   6:61 ¹ Or *Does this cause you to no longer believe?*; Grk. *cause you to stumble.*   6:62 ᵃ Mark 16:19; John 3:13; Acts 1:9; 2:32–33; Eph 4:8   6:63 ᵃ Gen 2:7; 2 Cor 3:6   ᵇ John 3:6   ᶜ [John 6:68; 14:24]   6:64 ᵃ John 6:36   ᵇ John 2:24–25; 13:11   6:65 ᵃ John 6:37, 44, 45   6:66 ᵃ Luke 9:62; John 6:60   6:68 ᵃ Acts 5:20   6:69 ᵃ Matt 16:16; Mark 8:29; Luke 9:20; John 1:49; 11:27   ¹ Some wss *the Christ; the Christ, the Son of God; the Son of God; the Christ, the Son of the living God; the Christ, the holy one of God.*   6:70 ᵃ Luke 6:13   ᵇ [John 13:27]   ¹ Or *a devil*; for a discussion on why "the" was used instead of "a," see *NET Bible, Full Notes Edition.*   6:71 ᵃ John 12:4; 13:2, 26   ᵇ Matt 26:14–16   7:1 ᵃ Matt 21:38; 26:4; John 5:18; 7:19, 25; 8:37, 40   7:2 ᵃ Lev 23:34; Deut 16:13–15; Neh 8:14, 18; Zech 14:16–19   ¹ Or *Feast of Tabernacles, Feast of Booths.*   7:3 ᵃ Matt 12:46; Mark 3:21; John 7:5, 10; Acts 1:14   7:5 ᵃ Ps 69:8; Mic 7:6   ᵇ Matt 12:46; 13:55; Mark 3:21; John 7:3, 10   7:6 ᵃ John 2:4; 8:20   7:7 ᵃ [John 15:19]   ᵇ John 3:19   7:8 ᵃ John 8:20   ¹ Maj. ᴍss *not yet.*   ² A reference to the time of his return to the Father.   ³ Or *my time has not yet come to an end*; a possible hint of Jesus' death at Jerusalem.   7:11 ᵃ John 11:56   7:12 ᵃ John 9:16; 10:19   ᵇ Matt 21:46; Luke 7:16; John 6:14; 7:40   7:13 ᵃ [John 9:22; 12:42; 19:38]   7:14 ᵃ Ps 22:22; Matt 4:23; 5:2; 7:29; Mark 6:34; Luke 4:15; 5:3; John 8:2   7:15 ᵃ Matt 13:54; Mark 6:2; [Luke 4:22]; Acts 2:7   ¹ I.e., Jesus was not the disciple of a particular rabbi.   7:16 ᵃ Deut 18:15, 18, 19; John 3:11   7:17 ᵃ Ps 25:9, 14; Prov 3:32; Dan 12:10; John 3:21; 8:43   7:18 ᵃ John 5:41   ᵇ John 8:50   ᶜ John 8:46; [2 Cor 5:21; Heb 4:15; 7:26; 1 Pet 1:19; 2:22]

in him. [19a]Hasn't Moses given you the law? Yet not one of you keeps the law! [b]Why do you want to kill me?"

[20]The crowd answered, "[a]You're possessed by a demon! Who is trying to kill you?" [21]Jesus replied, "I performed one miracle and you are all amazed. [22]However, because [a]Moses gave you the practice of circumcision (not that it came from Moses, [b]but from the forefathers), you circumcise a male child on the Sabbath. [23]But [a]if a male child is circumcised on the Sabbath so that the law of Moses is not broken, why are you angry with me because I made a man completely well on the Sabbath? [24a]Do not judge according to external appearance, but judge with proper judgment."

Questions about Jesus' Identity

[25]Then some of the residents of Jerusalem began to say, "Isn't this the man they are trying to [a]kill? [26]Yet here he is, speaking publicly, and they are saying nothing to him. [a]Do the ruling authorities really know that this man is the Christ? [27]But [a]we know where this man comes from. Whenever the Christ comes, no one will know where he comes from."

[28]Then Jesus, while teaching in the temple courts, cried out, "[a]You both know me and know where [b]I come from! And I have not come on my own initiative, but the one who sent me [c]is true. You do not know [d]him, [29]but [a]I know him because I have come from him and he sent me."

[30]So then [a]they tried to seize Jesus, but [b]no one laid a hand on him because his time had not yet come. [31]Yet [a]many of the crowd believed in him and said, "Whenever the Christ comes, he won't perform more miraculous signs than this man did, will he?"

[32]The Pharisees heard the crowd murmuring these things about Jesus, so the chief priests and the Pharisees sent officers to arrest him. [33]Then Jesus [a]said, "I will be with you for only a little while longer, and then I am [b]going to the one who sent me. [34]You [a]will look for me but will not find me, and where I am you [b]cannot come."

[35]Then [a]the Jewish leaders said to one another, "Where is he going to go that we cannot find him? He is not going to go to the Jewish people dispersed among the Greeks and teach the Greeks, is he? [36]What did he mean by saying, 'You will look for me but will not find me, and where I am you cannot come'?"

Teaching about the Spirit

[37a]On the last day of the feast, the greatest day, Jesus stood up and shouted out, "[b]If anyone is thirsty, let him come to me, and [38]let [a]the one who believes in me drink.[1] Just as the scripture says, '[b]*From within him will flow rivers of living water.*'"[2] [39]([a]Now he said this about the Spirit, whom those who believed in him were going to receive, for the Spirit had not yet been given[1] because Jesus was not yet [b]glorified.)

Differing Opinions about Jesus

[40]When [a]they heard these words, some of the crowd began to say, "This really is the Prophet!" [41]Others said, "This is [a]the Christ!" But still others said, "No, for the Christ doesn't come from Galilee, does he? [42]Don't the scriptures say that the Christ is [a]*a descendant*[1] *of David*[2] and *comes from Bethlehem,*[3] the village [b]where David lived?" [43]So [a]there was a division in the crowd because of Jesus. [44a]Some of them were wanting to seize him, but no one laid a hand on him.

Lack of Belief

[45]Then the officers returned to the chief priests and Pharisees, who said to them, "Why didn't you bring him back with you?" [46]The officers replied, "[a]No one ever spoke like this man!" [47]Then the Pharisees answered, "You haven't been deceived too, have you? [48]None of the members of the

7:19 [a]Exod 24:3; Deut 33:4; Acts 7:38   [b]Matt 12:14   7:20 [a]John 8:48, 52   7:22 [a]Lev 12:3   [b]Gen 17:9–14; Acts 7:8   7:23 [a]John 5:8–9, 16   7:24 [a]Deut 1:16; Prov 24:23; John 8:15; Jas 2:1   7:25 [a]Matt 21:38; 26:4; Luke 22:2; John 5:18; 8:37, 40   7:26 [a]John 7:48   7:27 [a]Matt 13:55; Mark 6:3; Luke 4:22   7:28 [a]John 8:14   [b]John 5:43   [c]Rom 3:4   [d]John 1:18; 8:55   7:29 [a]Matt 11:27; John 8:55; 17:25   7:30 [a]Mark 11:18   [b]Matt 21:46; John 7:32, 44; 8:20; 10:39   7:31 [a]Matt 12:23   7:33 [a]John 13:33   [b][Mark 16:19; Luke 24:51; Acts 1:9; Heb 9:24; 1 Pet 3:22]   7:34 [a]Hos 5:6   [b][Matt 5:20; 1 Cor 6:9; 15:50; Rev 21:27]   7:35 [a]Ps 147:2; [Isa 11:12; 56:8; Zeph 3:10]; Jas 1:1; 1 Pet 1:1   7:37 [a]Lev 23:36; Num 29:35; Neh 8:18   [b][Isa 55:1]   7:38 [a]Deut 18:15   [b]Isa 12:3; 43:20; 44:3; 55:1; [John 6:35]; Rev 21:6; 22:17   [1]For a discussion of the meaning of this figurative statement, see *NET Bible, Full Notes Edition*.   [2]Isa 44:3; 55:1; 58:11; Zech 14:8   7:39 [a]Isa 44:3; [Joel 2:28]; John 1:33   [b]John 12:16; 13:31; 17:5   [1]Grk. *for the Spirit was not yet*; i.e., the era of the Holy Spirit had not arrived.   7:40 [a]Deut 18:15, 18   7:41 [a]John 4:42; 6:69   7:42 [a]Ps 132:11; Jer 23:5; Mic 5:2; Matt 2:5; [Luke 2:4]   [b]1 Sam 16:1, 4   [1]Grk. *is from the seed.*   [2][Ps 89:4]   [3][Mic 5:2]   7:43 [a]John 7:12   7:44 [a]John 7:30   7:46 [a]Matt 13:54, 56; Luke 4:22

ruling council or the Pharisees have believed in him, have they? [49]But this rabble who do not know the law are accursed!"

[50]Nicodemus, who had gone to Jesus before and who was one of [a]the rulers, said, [51]"Our law [a]doesn't condemn a man unless it first hears from him and learns what he is doing, does it?" [52]They replied, "You aren't from Galilee too, are you? Investigate carefully and you will see that [a]no prophet[1,2] comes from Galilee!"

A Woman Caught in Adultery[1]

[53][[And each one departed to his own house. [1]But Jesus went to the Mount of Olives. [2]Early in the morning he came to the temple courts again. All the people came to him, and he sat down and began to [a]teach them. [3]The experts in the law and the Pharisees brought a woman who had been caught committing adultery. They made her stand in front of them [4]and said to Jesus, "Teacher, this woman was caught in the very act of [a]adultery. [5a]In the law *Moses commanded us to stone to death*[1] such women. What then do you say?" [6](Now they were asking this in an attempt to trap him, so that they could bring charges against him.) Jesus bent down and wrote on the ground with his finger.[1] [7]When [a]they persisted in asking him, he stood up straight and replied, "Whoever among you is guiltless may be the first to throw a stone at her." [8]Then he bent over again and wrote on the ground.

[9]Now when they heard this, they began to drift away one at a time, starting with the older ones, until Jesus was left alone with the woman standing before him. [10]Jesus stood up straight and said to her, "Woman, where are they? Did no one condemn you?" [11]She replied, "No one, Lord." And Jesus said, "I do not condemn you [a]either. Go, and from now on do not [b]sin any more."]][1]

Jesus as the Light of the World

[12]Then Jesus spoke out again, "[a]I am the light of the world! The one who [b]follows me will never[1] walk in darkness but will have the light of life." [13]So the Pharisees objected, "[a]You testify about yourself; your testimony is not true!" [14]Jesus answered, "Even if I testify about myself, my testimony is true because I know where I came from and where I am going. But [a]you people do not know where I came from or where I am going. [15a]You people judge by outward appearances; [b]I do not judge anyone. [16]But [a]if I judge, my evaluation is accurate because I am not alone when I judge, but I and the Father who sent me do so together. [17]It is [a]written in your law that *the testimony of two men is true*.[1] [18]I testify about myself and [a]the Father who sent me testifies about me."

[19]Then they began asking him, "Who is [a]your father?" Jesus answered, "You do not know either me or my Father. [b]If you knew me you would know my Father too." [20](Jesus spoke [a]these words near the offering box while he was teaching in the temple courts. [b]No one seized him because [c]his time[1] had not yet come.)

Where Jesus Came from and Where He Is Going

[21]Then Jesus said to them again,[1] "I am going away, and [a]you [b]will look for me but will die in your sin. Where I am going you cannot come." [22]So the Jewish leaders began to say, "Perhaps he is going to kill himself because he says, 'Where I am going you cannot come.'" [23]Jesus replied, "[a]You people are from below; I am from above. [b]You people are from this world; I am not from this world. [24]Thus I told you that you will die in your sins. [a]For unless you believe that I am he, you will die in your sins."

[25]So they said to him, "Who are you?" Jesus replied, "What I [a]have told you from

7:50 [a]John 3:1–2; 19:39   **7:51** [a]Deut 1:16–17; 19:15   **7:52** [a][Isa 9:1–2]; Matt 4:15   [1]An early sig. MS *the prophet*.   [2]Either overlooking Jonah, who had been from Gath Hepher in Galilee, or meaning that "the" prophet would not come from Galilee.   **7:53** [1]This entire section, 7:53–8:11, is omitted in the earliest and best MSS and is almost certainly not original. For this reason, it has been set in brackets. For an explanation, see *NET Bible, Full Notes Edition*.   **8:2** [a]John 8:20; 18:20   **8:4** [a]Exod 20:14; [Matt 5:27; 19:9; Rom 7:3]   **8:5** [a]Lev 20:10; Deut 22:22–24   [1][Lev 20:10; Deut 22:22–24]   **8:6** [1]Or possibly *Jesus bent down and wrote an accusation on the ground with his finger*.   **8:7** [a]Deut 17:7; [Rom 2:1]   **8:11** [a][Luke 9:56; 12:14; John 3:17]   [b][John 5:14]   [1]This entire section, 7:53–8:11, is omitted in the earliest and best MSS and is almost certainly not original. For this reason, it has been set in brackets. For an explanation, see *NET Bible, Full Notes Edition*.   **8:12** [a]Isa 9:2; Mal 4:2; John 1:4; 9:5; 12:35; [2 Tim 1:10]   [b]1 Thess 5:5   [1]An emphatic Grk. construction.   **8:13** [a]John 5:31   **8:14** [a]John 7:28; 9:29   **8:15** [a]1 Sam 16:7; John 7:24   [b][John 3:17; 12:47; 18:36]   **8:16** [a]John 16:32   **8:17** [a]Deut 17:6; 19:15; Matt 18:16; 2 Cor 13:1; Heb 10:28   [1][Deut 17:6]   **8:18** [a]John 5:37; 1 John 5:9   **8:19** [a]John 16:3   [b]John 14:7   **8:20** [a]Mark 12:41, 43; Luke 21:1   [b]John 2:4; 7:30   [c]John 7:8   [1]Grk. *his hour*.   **8:21** [a]John 7:34; 13:33   [b]John 8:24   [1]After a break in events of unclear duration.   **8:23** [a]John 3:31   [b]John 15:19; 17:16; 1 John 4:5   **8:24** [a][Mark 16:16]   **8:25** [a]John 4:26

the beginning. 26 I have many things to say and to judge about you, but [a]the Father who sent me [b]is truthful, and the things I have heard from him I speak to the world." 27 (They did not understand that he was telling them about his Father.)

28 Then Jesus said, "When you lift [a]up the Son of Man, [b]then you will know [c]that I am he, and I do nothing on my own initiative, but I speak [d]just what the Father taught me. 29 And [a]the one who sent me is with me. [b]He has not left me alone[1] [c]because I always do those things that please him." 30 While he was saying these things, many [a]people believed in him.

Abraham's Children and the Devil's Children

31 Then Jesus said to those Judeans who had believed him, "If you [a]continue to follow my teaching, you are really my disciples 32 and you will know the [a]truth, and [b]the truth will set you free." 33 "We are descendants[1] of Abraham," they replied, "and have never been anyone's slaves! How can you say, 'You will become free'?" 34 Jesus answered them, "I tell you the solemn truth, everyone [a]who practices[1] sin is a slave of sin. 35 The [a]slave does not remain in the family[1] forever, but the son remains forever. 36 So if [a]the son sets you free, you will be really free. 37 I know that [a]you are Abraham's descendants. But you want to kill me because my teaching makes no progress among you. 38 [a]I am telling you the things I have seen while with the[1] Father; as for you, practice the things you have heard from the[2] Father!"

39 They answered him, "[a]Abraham is our father!" Jesus replied, "[b]If you are[1] Abraham's children, you would be doing[2] the deeds of Abraham. 40 [a]But now you are trying to kill me, a man [b]who has told you the truth I heard from God. Abraham did not

do this! 41 You people are doing the deeds of your father."

Then[1] they said to Jesus, "[a]We were not born as a result of immorality! We have only one Father, God himself." 42 Jesus replied, "[a]If God were your Father, you would love me, for [b]I have come from God and am now here. I have [c]not come on my own initiative, but he sent me. 43 [a]Why don't you understand what I am saying? It is because you cannot accept my teaching. 44 [a]You people are from[1] your father the devil, and you want to do what your father [b]desires. He was a murderer from the beginning, and [c]does not uphold the truth[2] because there is no truth in him. Whenever he lies, he speaks according to his own nature because he is a liar and the father of lies. 45 But because I am telling you the truth, you do not believe me. 46 Who among you can prove me guilty[1] of any sin? If I am telling you the truth, why don't you believe me? 47 [a]The one who belongs to God listens and responds to God's words. You don't listen and respond[1] because you don't belong to God."

48 The Judeans replied, "Aren't we correct in saying that you are a Samaritan and are possessed [a]by a demon?" 49 Jesus answered, "I am not possessed by a demon, but I honor my Father—and yet [a]you dishonor me. 50 [a]I am not trying to get praise for myself. There is one who demands it, and he also judges. 51 I tell you the solemn truth, [a]if anyone obeys my teaching, he will never see death."[1]

52 Then[1] the Judeans[2] responded, "Now we know you're possessed [a]by a demon! Both [b]Abraham and the prophets died, and yet you say, 'If anyone obeys my teaching, he will never experience death.' 53 You aren't greater than our father Abraham who died, are you? And the prophets died too! [a]Who do you claim to be?" 54 Jesus replied, "[a]If [b]I glorify myself, my glory is worthless. The one who glorifies me is my Father, about

8:26 [a] John 7:28 [b] John 3:32; 15:15   8:28 [a] Matt 27:35; Mark 15:24; Luke 23:33; John 3:14; 12:32; 19:18 [b] [Rom 1:4] [c] John 5:19, 30 [d] Deut 18:15, 18, 19; John 3:11   8:29 [a] John 14:10 [b] John 8:16; 16:32 [c] John 4:34; 5:30; 6:38 [1] I.e., "he has not abandoned me."   8:30 [a] John 7:31; 10:42; 11:45   8:31 [a] [John 14:15, 23]   8:32 [a] [John 1:14, 17; 14:6] [b] [Rom 6:14, 18, 22; Jas 1:25; 2:12]   8:33 [1] Grk. We are the seed.   8:34 [a] Prov 5:22; Rom 6:16; 2 Pet 2:19 [1] Or who commits, who sins.   8:35 [a] Gen 21:10; Gal 4:30 [1] Or household.   8:36 [a] [Rom 8:2; 2 Cor 3:17]; Gal 5:1   8:37 [a] John 7:19   8:38 [a] [John 3:32; 5:19–30; 14:10, 24] [1] Maj. MSS my. [2] Maj. MSS your.   8:39 [a] Matt 3:9; John 8:37 [b] [Rom 2:28; Gal 3:7, 29] [1] Maj. MSS you were. [2] Some sig. MSS then do.   8:40 [a] John 8:37 [b] John 8:26 [1] An emphatic Grk. construction.   8:41 [a] Deut 32:6; Isa 63:16; Mal 1:6 [1] ‡ Sig. WSS omit Then.   8:42 [a] 1 John 5:1 [b] John 16:27; 17:8, 25 [c] John 5:43; Gal 4:4   8:43 [a] [John 7:17]   8:44 [a] Matt 13:38; 1 John 3:8 [b] 1 John 2:16–17 [c] [1 John 3:8–10, 15] [1] Or You are of your father the devil, You belong to your father, the devil. [2] Grk. he does not stand in the truth.   8:46 [1] Or can convict me.   8:47 [a] Luke 8:15; John 10:26; 1 John 4:6 [1] Grk. you do not hear.   8:48 [a] John 7:20; 10:20   8:49 [a] John 5:41   8:50 [a] John 5:41; 7:18; [Phil 2:6–8]   8:51 [a] John 5:24; 11:26 [1] Grk. he will never see death forever, an emphatic Grk. construction.   8:52 [a] John 7:20; 10:20 [b] Zech 1:5; Heb 11:13 [1] ‡ Sig. WSS omit Then. [2] Grk. the Jews.   8:53 [a] John 10:33; 19:7   8:54 [a] John 5:31–32 [b] John 5:41; Acts 3:13

whom you people say, 'He is our God.' [55]Yet [a]you do not know him, but I know him. If I were to say that I do not know him, I would be a liar like you. But I do know him, and I [b]obey his teaching. [56]Your father Abraham was [a]overjoyed[1] to see my day, [b]and he saw it and was glad."[2]

[57]Then the Judeans replied, "You are not yet fifty years old! Have you seen Abraham?" [58]Jesus said to them, "I tell you the solemn truth, [a]before Abraham came into existence,[1] [b]I am!" [59]Then [a]they picked up stones to throw at him, but Jesus was hidden from them[1] and went out from the temple area.[2]

Healing a Man Born Blind

9 Now as Jesus was passing by,[1] he saw a man who had been blind from birth. [2]His disciples asked him, "Rabbi, [a]who committed the sin that caused him to be born blind, this man or his parents?" [3]Jesus answered, "Neither this man nor his parents sinned, [a]but he was born blind so that the acts of God may be revealed through what happens to him. [4]We must perform the deeds of the one who sent [a]me as long as it is [b]daytime. Night is coming when no one can work. [5]As long as [a]I am in the world, I am the light of the world." [6]Having said this, [a]he spat on the ground and made some mud with the saliva. He smeared the mud on the blind man's eyes [7]and said to him, "Go wash [a]in [b]the pool of Siloam"[1] (which is translated "sent"). So the blind man went away and washed, and came back seeing.

[8]Then the neighbors and the people who had seen him previously as a beggar began saying, "Is this not the man who used to sit and beg?" [9]Some people said, "This is the man!" while others said, "No, but he looks like him." The man himself kept insisting, "I am the one!" [10]So they asked him, "How then were you made to see?" [11]He replied, "The [a]man called Jesus made mud, smeared it on my eyes and told me, 'Go to Siloam and wash.' So I went and washed, and was able to see." [12]They said to him, "Where is that man?" He replied, "I don't know."

The Pharisees' Reaction to the Healing

[13]They brought the man who used to be blind to the Pharisees. [14](Now the day on which Jesus made the mud and caused him to see was a Sabbath.) [15]So the Pharisees asked him again how he had gained his sight. He replied, "He put mud on my eyes and I washed, and now I am able to see." [16]Then some of the Pharisees began to say, "This man is not from God because he does not observe the Sabbath." But others said, "[a]How can a man who is a sinner perform such miraculous signs?" Thus [b]there was a division among them. [17]So again [a]they asked the man who used to be blind, "What do you say about him, since he caused you to see?" "He is a prophet," the man replied.

[18]Now the Jewish religious leaders refused to believe that he had really been blind and had gained his sight until at last they summoned the parents of the man who had become able to see. [19]They asked the parents, "Is this your son, whom you say was born blind? Then how does he now see?" [20]So his parents replied, "We know that this is our son and that he was born blind. [21]But we do not know how he is now able to see, nor do we know who caused him to see. Ask him, he is a mature adult. He will speak for himself." [22](His parents said these things because [a]they were afraid of the Jewish religious leaders. For the Jewish leaders had already agreed that anyone who confessed Jesus to be the Christ[1] [b]would be put out of the synagogue. [23]For this reason his parents said, "He is a mature adult, ask him.")

[24]Then they summoned the man who used to be blind a second time and said to him, "[a]Promise before God to tell the truth.[1] [b]We know that this man is a sinner." [25]He replied, "I do not know whether he is a sinner. I do know one thing—that although I was blind, now I can see." [26]Then they said

8:55 [a]John 7:28–29 [b][John 15:10]   8:56 [a]Luke 10:24 [b]Matt 13:17; Heb 11:13 [1]Or *rejoiced greatly.* [2]Perhaps Abraham finding the ram that replaced his son Isaac on the altar of sacrifice—an occasion of certain rejoicing.   8:58 [a]Mic 5:2; John 17:5; Heb 7:3; Rev 22:13 [b]Exod 3:14; Isa 43:13; John 17:5, 24; Col 1:17; Rev 1:8 [1]Grk. *before Abraham was.*   8:59 [a]John 10:31; 11:8 [1]*from them* is supplied; Jesus' opponents were unable to find him at that moment, not that he turned invisible. [2]Maj. later MSS add *passing through their midst, he went away in this manner.*   9:1 [1]Or *going along.* These words convey only the vaguest indication of the circumstances.   9:2 [a]Luke 13:2; John 9:34; Acts 28:4   9:3 [a]John 11:4   9:4 [a][John 4:34; 5:19, 36; 17:4] [b]John 11:9–10; 12:35; Gal 6:10   9:5 [a][John 1:5, 9; 3:19; 8:12; 12:35, 46]   9:6 [a]Mark 7:33; 8:23   9:7 [a]Neh 3:15; Isa 8:6; Luke 13:4; John 9:11 [b]2 Kgs 5:14 [1]Heb. *shiloah.*   9:11 [a]John 9:6–7   9:16 [a]John 3:2; 9:33 [b]John 7:12, 43; 10:19   9:17 [a][John 4:19; 6:14]   9:22 [a]John 7:13; 12:42; 19:38; Acts 5:13 [b]John 16:2 [1]Or *the Messiah*; both "Christ" (Grk.) and "Messiah" (Heb., Aram.) mean "one who has been anointed."   9:24 [a]Josh 7:19; 1 Sam 6:5; Ezra 10:11; Rev 11:13 [b]John 9:16 [1]Grk. *Give glory to God*; an idiom used in placing someone under oath to tell the truth.

to him, "What did he do to you? How did he cause you to see?" [27] He answered, "I told you already and you didn't listen. Why do you want to hear it again? You people don't want to become his disciples too, do you?"

[28] They heaped insults[1] on him, saying, "You are his disciple! We are disciples of Moses! [29] We know that God has [a]spoken to [b]Moses! [c]We do not know where this man comes from!" [30] The man replied, "This is a remarkable thing that you don't know where he comes from, yet he caused me to see! [31] We know that [a]God doesn't listen to sinners, but if anyone is devout and does his will, God listens to him. [32] Never before[1] has anyone heard of someone causing a man born blind to see. [33a] If this man were not from God, he could do nothing." [34] They replied, "[a]You were born completely in sinfulness,[1] and yet you presume to teach us?" So they threw him out.

The Man's Response to Jesus

[35] Jesus heard that they had thrown him out, so he [a]found the man and said to him, "Do you [b]believe in [c]the Son of Man?"[1] [36] The man replied, "And who is he, sir, that I may believe in him?" [37] Jesus told him, "You have seen him; he is the one speaking [a]with you." [[38] He said, "Lord, I believe," and he [a]worshiped him. [39] Jesus said,][1] "[a]For judgment I have come into this world, so [b]that those who do not see may gain their sight, and the ones who see may become blind."

[40] Some of the Pharisees who were with him heard this [a]and asked him, "We are not blind too, are we?" [41] Jesus replied, "[a]If you were blind, you would not be guilty of sin, but now because you claim that you can see, your guilt remains.

Jesus as the Good Shepherd

10 "I tell you the solemn truth, the one who does not enter the sheepfold by the door, but climbs in some other way, is a thief and a robber. [2] The one who enters by the door is the shepherd of the sheep. [3] The doorkeeper opens the door for him, and the sheep hear his voice. He calls his own sheep by [a]name and leads them out. [4] When he has brought all his own sheep out, he goes ahead of them, and the sheep follow him because they recognize his voice. [5] They will never follow a [a]stranger, but will run away from him because they do not recognize the stranger's voice." [6] Jesus told them this parable, but they did not understand what he was saying to them.

[7] So Jesus said again, "I tell you the solemn truth, I am the door for the sheep. [8] All who came before me were thieves and robbers, but the sheep did not listen to them. [9a] I am the door. If anyone enters through me, he will be saved, and will come in and go out,[1] and find pasture. [10] The thief comes only to steal and kill and destroy; I have come so that they may have life, and may have it abundantly.

[11] "[a]I am the good[1] shepherd. The good shepherd lays down his life[2] for the sheep. [12] The hired hand, who is not a shepherd and does not own sheep, sees the wolf coming and [a]abandons the sheep and runs away.[1] So the wolf attacks the sheep and scatters them. [13] Because he is a hired hand and is not concerned about the sheep, he runs away.[1]

[14] "I am the good shepherd. [a]I know my own and my own know me—[15] just [a]as the Father knows me and I know the Father—[b]and I lay down my life[1] for the sheep. [16] I have [a]other sheep that do not come from this sheepfold. I must bring them too, [b]and they will listen to my voice, so that there will be one flock and one shepherd. [17] This is why the Father [a]loves me—[b]because I lay down my life, so that I may take it back again. [18] No one takes it away from me, but I lay it down of my own free will.[1] I [a]have the authority

---

9:28 [1] Grk. *to insult strongly, slander.*   **9:29** [a] Exod 19:19–20; 33:11; 34:29; Num 12:6–8 [b] [John 5:45–47] [c] John 7:27–28; 8:14   **9:31** [a] Job 27:9; 35:12; Ps 18:41; Prov 1:28; 15:29; 28:9; Isa 1:15; Jer 11:11; 14:12; Ezek 8:18; Mic 3:4; Zech 7:13; [Jas 5:16]   **9:32** [1] Or *Never from the beginning of time*; Grk. *From eternity.*   **9:33** [a] John 3:2; 9:16   **9:34** [a] Ps 51:5; John 9:2 [1] Or *From birth you have been evil.*   **9:35** [a] John 5:14 [b] John 1:7; 16:31 [c] Matt 14:33; 16:16; Mark 1:1; John 10:36; 1 John 5:13 [1] Maj. wss of God.   **9:37** [a] John 4:26   **9:38** [a] Matt 8:2   **9:39** [a] [John 3:17; 5:22, 27; 12:47] [b] Matt 13:13; 15:14 [1] ‡ Some early and sig. wss omit *He said, 'Lord, I believe,' and he worshiped him. Jesus said,* (vv. 38–39a). For this reason, it has been set in brackets.   **9:40** [a] [Rom 2:19]   **9:41** [a] John 15:22, 24   **10:3** [a] John 20:16   **10:5** [a] [2 Cor 11:13–15]   **10:9** [a] [John 14:6; Eph 2:18] [1] In some places, an idiom for living in relationship to a community.   **10:11** [a] Gen 49:24; Isa 40:11; Ezek 34:23; [Heb 13:20]; 1 Pet 2:25; 5:4; Rev 7:17 [1] Or *model.* [2] Or *The good shepherd dies willingly.*   **10:12** [a] Zech 11:16–17 [1] Or *flees.*   **10:13** [1] Sev. sig. mss omit *he runs away.*   **10:14** [a] Isa 40:11; Nah 1:7; Zech 13:7; John 6:64; 2 Tim 2:19   **10:15** [a] Matt 11:27 [b] Matt 27:50; Mark 15:37; Luke 23:46; [John 15:13; 19:30]; 1 John 3:16 [1] Or *I die willingly.*   **10:16** [a] Isa 42:6; 56:8; Acts 10:45; 11:18; 13:46 [b] Ezek 37:22; John 11:52; 17:20; Eph 2:13–18; 1 Pet 2:25   **10:17** [a] John 5:20 [b] [Isa 53:7–8, 12; Heb 2:9]   **10:18** [a] Matt 26:53; [John 2:19; 5:26] [1] Or *of my own accord.*

to lay it down, and I have the authority to take it back again. [b]This commandment I received from my Father."

[19]Another sharp division took place among [a]the Jewish people because of these words. [20]Many of [a]them were saying, "He is possessed by a demon and has lost his mind![1] Why do you listen to him?" [21]Others said, "These are not the words of someone possessed by [a]a demon. A demon cannot [b]cause the blind to see, can it?"

Jesus at the Feast of Dedication

[22]Then came the feast of the Dedication[1] in Jerusalem. [23]It was winter, and Jesus was walking [a]in the temple area in Solomon's Portico. [24]The Jewish leaders surrounded him and asked, "How long will you keep us in suspense?[1] If you are the Christ, tell us plainly." [25]Jesus replied, "I told you and you do not believe. [a]The deeds I do in my Father's name testify about me. [26]But [a]you refuse to believe because you are not my sheep. [27a]My sheep listen to my voice, and I know them, and they follow me. [28]I give them eternal life, and they will never perish; no one will snatch them from my hand. [29a]My Father, who has given them to me, is greater than all,[1] and no one can snatch them from my Father's hand. [30]The Father and [a]I are one."[1]

[31]The Jewish leaders picked up rocks again to stone him to death. [32]Jesus said to them, "I have shown you many good deeds from the Father. For which one of them are you going to stone me?" [33]The Jewish leaders replied, "We are not going to stone you for a good deed but for [a]blasphemy because you, a man, are [b]claiming to be God."

[34]Jesus answered, "Is it not written in your law, '[a]*I said, you are gods*'?[1] [35]If those people [a]to whom the word of God came were called 'gods' (and the scripture [b]cannot be broken), [36]do you say about the one [a]whom the Father set apart[1] and [b]sent into the world, 'You are blaspheming,' [c]because I said, 'I am [d]the Son of God'? [37a]If I do not perform the deeds of my Father, do not

believe me. [38]But if I do them, even if you do not [a]believe me, believe the deeds, so [b]that you may come to know and understand that I am in the Father and the Father is in me." [39]Then[1] they attempted again to seize him, but [a]he escaped their clutches.

[40]Jesus went back across the Jordan River again to the place [a]where John had been baptizing at an earlier time, and he stayed there. [41]Many came to him and began to say, "John performed no miraculous sign, [a]but everything John said about this man was true!" [42]And many believed in Jesus there.

The Death of Lazarus

11 Now a certain man named Lazarus was sick. He was from Bethany, the village where [a]Mary and her sister Martha lived. [2](Now [a]it was Mary who anointed the Lord with perfumed oil and wiped his feet dry with her hair, whose brother Lazarus was sick.) [3]So the sisters sent a message to Jesus, "Lord, look, the one you love is sick." [4]When Jesus heard this, he said, "This sickness will not lead to death, but to God's glory, so that the Son of God may be glorified through it." [5](Now Jesus loved Martha and her sister and Lazarus.)

[6]So [a]when he heard that Lazarus was sick, he remained in the place where he was for two more days. [7]Then after this, he said to his disciples, "Let us go to Judea again." [8]The disciples replied, "Rabbi, the Jewish leaders were just now trying to [a]stone you to death! Are you going there again?" [9]Jesus replied, "Are there not 12 hours in a day? [a]If anyone walks around in the daytime, he does not stumble because he sees the [b]light of this world. [10]But [a]if anyone walks around at night, he stumbles because the light is not in him."

[11]After he said this, he added, "Our friend Lazarus has fallen [a]asleep. But I am going there to awaken him." [12]Then the disciples replied, "Lord, if he has fallen asleep, he will recover." [13](Now Jesus had been talking about his death, but they thought he had been talking about real sleep.)[1]

10:18 [b][John 6:38; 14:31; 17:4; Acts 2:24, 32]   10:19 [a]John 7:43; 9:16   10:20 [a]John 7:20   [1]Or *is insane.*   10:21 [Exod 4:11]   [b]John 9:6–7, 32, 33   10:22 [1]Hanukkah or the Festival of Lights.   10:23 [a]Acts 3:11; 5:12   10:24 [1]Grk. *How long will you take away our life?*   10:25 [a]John 5:36; 10:38   10:26 [John 8:47]   10:27 [a]John 10:4, 14   10:29 [a]John 14:28   [1]Or *is superior to all.*   10:30 [a]John 17:11, 21–24   [1]A significant assertion in Grk., not that Jesus and the Father are one person, but one "thing," having unity of essence.   10:33 [a]Matt 9:3   [b]John 5:18   10:34 [a]Ps 82:6   [1]Ps 82:6   10:35 [a]Matt 5:17–18   [b]1 Pet 1:25   10:36 [a]John 6:27   [b]John 3:17   [c]John 5:17–18   [d]Luke 1:35   [1]Or *dedicated.*   10:37 [a]John 10:25; 15:24   10:38 [a]John 5:36   [b]John 14:10–11   10:39 [a]John 7:30, 44   [1]Some MSS *now, and.*   10:40 [a]John 1:28   10:41 [a][John 1:29, 36; 3:28–36; 5:33]   11:1 [a]Luke 10:38–39; John 11:5, 19   11:2 [a]Matt 26:7   11:6 [a]John 10:40   11:8 [a]John 8:59; 10:31   11:9 [a]Luke 13:33; John 9:4; 12:35   [b]Isa 9:2   11:10 [a]John 12:35   11:11 [a]Deut 31:16; [Dan 12:2]; Matt 9:24; Acts 7:60; [1 Cor 15:18, 51]   11:13 [1]Grk. *the sleep of slumber.*

[14]Then Jesus told them plainly, "Lazarus has died, [15]and I am glad for your sake that I was not there, so that you may believe. But let us go to him." [16]So [a]Thomas (called Didymus) said to his fellow disciples, "Let us go too, so that we may die with him."

Speaking with Martha and Mary

[17]When Jesus arrived, he found that Lazarus had been in the tomb four days already. [18](Now Bethany was less than two miles from Jerusalem, [19]so many of the Jewish people of the region had come to Martha and Mary to console them over the loss of their brother.) [20]So when Martha heard that Jesus was coming, she went out to meet him, but Mary was sitting in the house. [21]Martha said to Jesus, "Lord, if you had been here, my brother would not have died. [22]But even now I know that [a]whatever you ask from God, God will grant you."

[23]Jesus replied, "Your brother will come back to life again." [24]Martha [a]said, "I know that he will come back to life again in the resurrection at the last day." [25]Jesus said to her, "I am [a]the resurrection and [b]the life. The one who believes in me will live even if he [c]dies, [26]and the one who lives and believes in me will never die. Do you believe this?" [27]She replied, "Yes, Lord, [a]I believe that you are the Christ, the Son of God who comes into the world."

[28]And when she had said this, Martha went and called her sister Mary, saying privately, "The Teacher is here and is asking for you." [29]So when Mary heard this, she got up quickly and went to him. [30](Now Jesus had not yet entered the village, but was still in the place where Martha had come out to meet him.) [31a]Then the people who were with Mary in the house consoling her saw her get up quickly and go out. They followed her because they thought she was going to the tomb to weep there.

[32]Now when Mary came to the place where Jesus was and saw him, she [a]fell at his feet and said to him, "[b]Lord, if you had been here, my brother would not have died." [33]When Jesus saw her weeping, and the people who had come with her weeping, he was intensely moved in spirit and greatly distressed. [34]He asked, "Where have you laid him?" They replied, "Lord, come and see." [35a]Jesus wept. [36]Thus the people who had come to mourn said, "Look how much he loved him!" [37]But some of them said, "This is the man [a]who caused the blind man to see! Couldn't he have done something to keep Lazarus from dying?"

Lazarus Raised from the Dead

[38]Jesus, intensely moved again, came to the tomb. (Now it was a cave, and a [a]stone was placed across it.) [39]Jesus said, "Take away the stone." Martha, the sister of the deceased, replied, "Lord, by this time the body will have a bad smell because he has been buried four days." [40]Jesus responded, "Didn't I tell you that if you believe, you would [a]see the glory of God?" [41]So they took away the stone. Jesus looked upward and said, "Father, I thank you that you have listened to me. [42]I knew that you always listen to me, but I said this for the sake [a]of the crowd standing around here, that they may believe that you sent me." [43]When he had said this, he shouted in a loud voice, "Lazarus, come out!" [44]The one who had died came out, his feet and hands tied up with strips of [a]cloth, and a cloth wrapped around [b]his face. Jesus said to them, "Unwrap him and let him go."

The Response of the Jewish Leaders

[45]Then many of the people, who had come with Mary [a]and had seen the things Jesus did, believed in him. [46]But some of them went to the Pharisees and [a]reported to them what Jesus had done. [47]So [a]the chief priests and the Pharisees called the council together and said, "[b]What are we doing? For this man is performing many miraculous signs. [48]If we allow him to go on in this way, everyone will believe in him, and the Romans will come and take away our sanctuary and our nation." [49]Then one of them, [a]Caiaphas, who was high priest that year, said, "You know nothing at all! [50]You do [a]not realize that it is more to your advantage to have one man

11:16 [a] Matt 10:3; Mark 3:18; Luke 6:15; John 14:5; 20:26–28; Acts 1:13   11:22 [a] [John 9:31; 11:41]   11:24 [a] [Luke 14:14; John 5:29]   11:25 [a] John 5:21; 6:39–40, 44; [Rev 1:18]   [b] John 3:16, 36; 1 John 5:10   [c] 1 Cor 15:22; [Heb 9:27]   11:27 [a] Matt 16:16; Luke 2:11; John 4:42; 6:14, 69   11:31 [a] John 11:19, 33   11:32 [a] Mark 5:22; 7:25; Rev 1:17   [b] John 11:21   11:35 [a] Luke 19:41   11:37 [a] John 9:6–7   11:38 [a] Matt 27:60, 66; Mark 15:46; Luke 24:2; John 20:1   11:40 [a] [John 11:4, 23]   11:42 [a] John 12:30; 17:21   11:44 [a] John 19:40   [b] John 20:7   11:45 [a] John 2:23; 10:42; 12:11, 18   11:46 [a] John 5:15   11:47 [a] Ps 2:2; Matt 26:3; Mark 14:1; Luke 22:2   [b] John 12:19; Acts 4:16   11:49 [a] Matt 26:3; Luke 3:2; John 18:14; Acts 4:6   11:50 [a] John 18:14

die for the people than for the whole nation to perish." [51](Now he did not say this on his own, but because he was high priest that year, he prophesied that Jesus was going to die for the Jewish nation, [52]and [a]not for the Jewish nation only, but [b]to gather together into one the children of God who are scattered.) [53]So from that day they planned together to kill him.

[54]Thus Jesus no longer went around publicly among [a]the Judeans, but went away from there to the region near the wilderness, to a town called [b]Ephraim, and stayed there with his disciples. [55]Now the Jewish Feast of Passover was near, [a]and many people went up to Jerusalem from the rural areas before the Passover to [b]cleanse themselves ritually. [56]Thus they were looking for Jesus, and saying to one another as they stood in [a]the temple courts, "What do you think? That he won't come to the feast?" [57](Now the chief priests and the Pharisees had given orders that anyone who knew where Jesus was should report it, so that they could [a]arrest him.)

Jesus' Anointing

12 Then, six days before the Passover, Jesus came to Bethany, [a]where Lazarus lived, whom he had raised from the dead. [2]So they prepared a dinner for Jesus [a]there. Martha was serving, and Lazarus was among those present at the table with him. [3]Then [a]Mary took three quarters of [b]a pound of expensive aromatic oil from pure nard and anointed the feet of Jesus. She then wiped his feet dry with her hair. (Now the house was filled with the fragrance of the perfumed oil.) [4]But [a]Judas Iscariot, one of his disciples (the one who was going to betray him) said, [5]"Why wasn't this oil sold for 300 silver coins and the money given to the poor?" [6](Now Judas said this not because he was concerned about the poor, but because he was a thief. As [a]keeper of the money box, he used to steal what was put into it.) [7]So Jesus said, "Leave her alone. She has kept it for the day of my burial. [8]For you will always have [a]the poor with you, but you will not always have me!"[1,2]

[9]Now a large crowd of Judeans learned that Jesus was there, and so they came not only because of him but also to see Lazarus [a]whom he had raised from the dead. [10a]So the chief priests planned to kill Lazarus too, [11a]for on account of him many of the Jewish people from Jerusalem were going away and believing in Jesus.

The Triumphal Entry

[12]The next day [a]the large crowd that had come to the feast heard that Jesus was coming to Jerusalem. [13]So they took branches of palm trees and went out to meet him. They began to shout, "*Hosanna!* [a]*Blessed is the one who comes in the name of the Lord!*[1] Blessed is the king of Israel!" [14]Jesus found a young donkey [a]and sat on it, just as it is written, [15]"*Do not be [a]afraid, people of Zion; look, your king is coming, seated on a donkey's colt!*"[1] [16]([a]His disciples did not understand these things when they first happened, [b]but when Jesus was glorified, [c]then they remembered that these things were written about him and that these things had happened to him.)

[17]So the crowd who had been with him when he called Lazarus out of the tomb and raised him from the dead were continuing to testify about it. [18]Because they had heard that Jesus had [a]performed this miraculous sign, the crowd went out to meet him. [19]Thus the Pharisees said to one another, "[a]You see that you can do nothing. Look, the world has run off after him!"

Seekers

[20]Now some Greeks [a]were among those [b]who had gone up to worship at the feast. [21]So these approached Philip, [a]who was from Bethsaida in Galilee, and requested, "Sir, we would like to see Jesus." [22]Philip went and told Andrew, and they both went and told Jesus. [23]Jesus replied, "[a]The time has come

11:52 [a]Isa 49:6; Acts 10:45; 11:18; 13:46; [1 John 2:2] [b]Ps 22:27; John 10:16; [Eph 2:14–17] **11:54** [a]John 4:1, 3; 7:1 [b]2 Chr 13:19 **11:55** [a]Matt 26:1; Mark 14:1; Luke 22:1; John 2:13; 5:1; 6:4 [b]Num 9:10, 13; 31:19–20; 2 Chr 30:17; Luke 2:22 **11:56** [a]John 7:11 **11:57** [a]Matt 26:14–16 **12:1** [a]Matt 21:17; John 11:1, 43 **12:2** [a]Matt 26:6; Mark 14:3; Luke 10:38–41 **12:3** [a]Luke 10:38–39; John 11:2 [b]Song 1:12 **12:4** [a]John 13:26 **12:6** [a]John 13:29 **12:8** [a]Deut 15:11; Matt 26:11; Mark 14:7; John 17:11 [1]A few wss omit v. 8. [2]An emphatic Grk. construction. **12:9** [a]John 11:43–44 **12:10** [a]Luke 16:31 **12:11** [a]John 11:45; 12:18 **12:12** [a]Matt 21:4–9; Mark 11:7–10; Luke 19:35–38 **12:13** [a]Ps 118:25–26 [1]Ps 118:25–26 **12:14** [a]Matt 21:7 **12:15** [a]Isa 40:9; Zech 9:9 [1]Zech 9:9 **12:16** [a]Luke 18:34 [b]John 7:39; 12:23 [c][John 14:26] **12:18** [a]John 12:11 **12:19** [a]John 11:47–48 **12:20** [a]Mark 7:26; Acts 17:4 [b]1 Kgs 8:41–42; Acts 8:27 **12:21** [a]John 1:43–44; 14:8–11 **12:23** [a]Matt 26:18, 45; John 13:32; Acts 3:13

for the Son of Man to be glorified. [24] I tell you the solemn truth, [a] unless a kernel of wheat falls into the ground and dies, it remains by itself alone. But if it dies, it produces much grain. [25] The one who loves his life destroys it, and [a] the one who hates his life in this world guards it for eternal life. [26] If anyone wants to serve me, he must [a] follow me, and [b] where I am, my servant will be too. If anyone serves me, the Father will honor him.

[27] "[a] Now my soul is greatly distressed. And what should I say? 'Father, deliver me from this hour'? No, [b] but for this very reason I have come to this hour. [28] Father, glorify your name." [a] Then a voice came from heaven, "I have glorified it, and I will glorify it again." [29] The crowd that stood there and heard the voice said that it had thundered. Others said that an angel had spoken to him. [30] Jesus said, "[a] This voice has not come for my benefit but for yours. [31] Now is [a] the judgment of this world; now the ruler of this world will be driven out. [32] And I, [a] when I am lifted up from the earth, will draw all [b] people to myself." [33] (Now he said [a] this to indicate clearly what kind of death he was going to die.)

[34] Then the crowd responded, "[a] We have heard from the law that *the Christ will remain forever.*[1] How can you say, 'The Son of Man must be lifted up'? Who is this Son of Man?" [35] Jesus replied, "[a] The light is with you for a little while longer. [b] Walk while you have [c] the light, so that the darkness may not overtake you. The one who walks in the darkness does not know where he is going. [36] While you have the light, believe in the light, so that you may become [a] sons of light." When Jesus had said these things, he went away and hid himself from them.

The Outcome of Jesus' Public Ministry Foretold

[37] Although Jesus had performed so many miraculous [a] signs before them, they still refused to believe in him, [38] so that the word of the prophet Isaiah would be fulfilled. He said, "[a] ***Lord, who has believed our message,***

and to whom has the arm of the Lord been revealed?"[1] [39] For this reason they could not believe because again Isaiah said,

[40] "***He has blinded*** [a] ***their eyes***
and hardened their heart,
so that they would not see with their eyes
and understand with their heart,
and turn to me, and I would heal them."[1]

[41] Isaiah said [a] these things because he saw Christ's glory and spoke about him.

[42] Nevertheless, even among the rulers many believed in him, but [a] because of the Pharisees they would not confess Jesus to be the Christ, so that they would not be put out of the synagogue. [43] [a] For they loved praise from men more than praise from God.

Jesus' Final Public Words

[44] But Jesus shouted out, "[a] The one who [b] believes in me does not believe in me, [c] but in the one who sent me, [45] and [a] the one who sees me sees the one who sent me. [46] [a] I have come as a light into the world, so that everyone who believes in me should not remain in darkness. [47] If anyone hears my words and does not obey them, [a] I do not judge [b] him. For I have not come to judge the world, but to save the world. [48] The one who rejects me and does not accept my words has a judge; [a] the word I have spoken will judge him at [b] the last day. [49] For [a] I have not spoken from my own authority, but the Father himself who sent me has commanded me [b] what I should say and what I should speak. [50] And I know that his commandment is eternal life. Thus the things I [a] say, I say just as the Father has told me."

Washing the Disciples' Feet

13 Just [a] before the Passover Feast, Jesus knew that [b] his time[1] had come to depart from this world to the Father. Having [c] loved his own who were in the world, he

---

12:24 [a] [Rom 14:9]; 1 Cor 15:36   12:25 [a] Matt 10:39; Mark 8:35; Luke 9:24   12:26 [a] [Matt 16:24]   [b] John 14:3; 17:24; [1 Thess 4:17]   12:27 [a] [Matt 26:38–39]; Mark 14:34; Luke 12:50; John 11:33   [b] Luke 22:53; John 18:37   12:28 [a] Matt 3:17; 17:5; Mark 1:11; 9:7; Luke 3:22; 9:35   12:30 [a] John 11:42   12:31 [a] Matt 12:29; Luke 10:18; [Acts 26:18; 2 Cor 4:4]   12:32 [a] John 3:14; 8:28   [b] [Rom 5:18; Heb 2:9]   12:33 [a] John 18:32; 21:19   12:34 [a] Ps 89:36–37; Isa 9:6–7; Mic 4:7   [1] [Ps 89:35–37]   12:35 [a] [John 1:9; 7:33; 8:12]   [b] Jer 13:16; [Gal 6:10]; Eph 5:8   [c] John 11:10; [1 John 2:9–11]   12:36 [a] Luke 16:8; John 8:12   12:37 [a] John 11:47   12:38 [a] Isa 53:1; Rom 10:16   [1] Isa 53:1   12:40 [a] Isa 6:9–10   [1] Isa 6:10   12:41 [a] Isa 6:1   12:42 [a] John 7:13; 9:22   12:43 [a] John 5:41, 44   12:44 [a] Mark 9:37   [b] [John 3:16, 18, 36; 11:25–26]   [c] [John 5:24]   12:45 [a] [John 14:9]   12:46 [a] John 1:4–5; 8:12; 12:35–36   12:47 [a] John 5:45   [b] John 3:17   12:48 [a] [Luke 10:16]   [b] Deut 18:18–19; [John 5:45; 8:47]   12:49 [a] John 8:38   [b] Deut 18:18   12:50 [a] John 5:19; 8:28   13:1 [a] Matt 26:2   [b] John 12:23; 17:1   [c] John 15:9   [1] Grk. *his hour.*

now loved them to the very end.[2] [2]The evening meal[1] was in progress, and [a]the devil had already put into the heart of Judas Iscariot, Simon's son, that he should betray Jesus. [3]Because Jesus knew [a]that the Father [b]had handed all things over to him, and that he had come from God and [c]was going back to God, [4]he got [a]up from the meal, removed his outer clothes, took a towel and tied it around himself.[1] [5]He poured water into the washbasin and began to wash the disciples' feet and to dry them with the towel he had wrapped around himself.

[6]Then he came to Simon Peter. Peter said to him, "[a]Lord, are you going to wash my feet?" [7]Jesus replied, "You [a]do not understand what I am doing now, [b]but you will understand after these things." [8]Peter said to him, "You will never wash my feet!"[1] Jesus replied, "[a]If I do not wash you, you have no share with me." [9]Simon Peter said to him, "Lord, wash not only my feet but also my hands and my head!" [10]Jesus replied, "The one who has bathed needs only to wash his feet, but is completely clean. And [a]you disciples are clean, but not every one of you." [11](For Jesus knew [a]the one who was going to betray him. For this reason he said, "Not every one of you is clean.")

[12]So when Jesus had washed their feet and put his outer clothing back on, he took his place at the table again and said to them, "Do you understand what I have done for you? [13][a]You call me 'Teacher' and 'Lord,' and do so correctly, for that is what I am. [14][a]If I then, your Lord and Teacher, have washed your feet, [b]you too ought to wash one another's feet. [15]For [a]I have given you an example—you should do just as I have done for you. [16]I tell you the [a]solemn truth, the slave is not greater than his master, nor is the one who is sent as a messenger greater than the one who sent him. [17][a]If you understand these things, you will be blessed if you do them.

The Announcement of Jesus' Betrayal

[18]"What I am saying does not refer to all of you. I know the ones I have chosen. But this is to fulfill the [a]scripture, '[b]*The one who eats my bread has turned against me.*'[1,2] [19]I am telling you this [a]now, before it happens, so that when it happens you may believe that I am he. [20]I tell you the [a]solemn truth, whoever accepts the one I send accepts me, and whoever accepts me accepts the one who sent me."

[21]When [a]he had said [b]these things, Jesus was greatly distressed in spirit, and testified, "I tell you the solemn truth, [c]one of you will betray me." [22]The disciples began to look at one another, worried and perplexed to know which of them he was talking about. [23]One of his disciples, [a]the one Jesus loved, was at the table to the right of Jesus in a place of honor.[1] [24]So Simon Peter gestured to this disciple to ask Jesus who it was he was referring to. [25]Then the disciple whom Jesus loved leaned back against Jesus' chest and asked him, "Lord, who is it?" [26]Jesus replied, "It is the one to whom I will give this piece of bread after I have dipped it in the dish." Then he dipped the piece of bread in the dish and gave it to [a]Judas Iscariot, Simon's son. [27][a]And after Judas took the piece of bread, Satan entered into him. Jesus said to him, "What you are about to do, do quickly." [28](Now none of those present at the table understood why Jesus said this to Judas. [29]Some thought that because [a]Judas had the money box, Jesus was telling him to buy whatever they needed for the feast, or to give something to the poor.) [30]Judas took the piece of bread and went out immediately. (Now it was night.)

The Prediction of Peter's Denial

[31]When Judas had gone out, Jesus said, "[a]Now the Son of Man is glorified, and [b]God is glorified in him. [32]If God is glorified in him,[1] God will also [a]glorify him in himself,

13:1 [2]Or *completely, to the uttermost.* 13:2 [a]Luke 22:3 [1]Or *supper.* 13:3 [a]Matt 11:27; [John 5:20–23; 17:2]; Acts 2:36; 1 Cor 15:27; [Heb 2:8] [b]John 8:42; 16:28 [c]John 17:11; 20:17 13:4 [a][Luke 22:27; Phil 2:7–8] [1]Grk. *taking a towel he girded himself;* i.e., put it around his waist for use in wiping the disciples' feet. 13:6 [a]Matt 3:14 13:7 [a]John 12:16; 16:12 [b]John 13:19 13:8 [a][Ps 51:2, 7; Ezek 36:25; Acts 22:16; 1 Cor 6:11; Eph 5:26; Titus 3:5; Heb 10:22] [1]Grk. *You will never wash my feet forever;* an emphatic Grk. construction. 13:10 [a][John 15:3; Eph 5:26] 13:11 [a]John 6:64; 18:4 13:13 [a]Matt 23:8, 10; Luke 6:46; [1 Cor 8:6; 12:3]; Eph 6:9; [Phil 2:11] 13:14 [a]Luke 22:27 [b][Rom 12:10; Gal 6:1–2; 1 Pet 5:5] 13:15 [a]Matt 11:29; Phil 2:5; [1 Pet 2:21–24]; 1 John 2:6 13:16 [a]Matt 10:24; [Luke 6:40]; John 15:20 13:17 [a]Matt 7:24; Luke 11:28; [Jas 1:25] 13:18 [a]John 15:25; 17:12 [b]Ps 41:9; Matt 26:23 [1]Ps 41:9 [2]Or *has become my enemy;* Grk. *has lifted up his heel against me.* 13:19 [a]John 14:29; 16:4 13:20 [a]Matt 10:40; Mark 9:37; Luke 9:48; 10:16; Gal 4:14 13:21 [a]Matt 26:21; Mark 14:18; Luke 22:21 [b]John 12:27 [c]Ps 41:9; Matt 26:46; Mark 14:42; Luke 22:48; John 6:64; 18:5; Acts 1:17; 1 John 2:19 13:23 [a]John 19:26; 20:2; 21:7, 20 [1]Grk. *was reclining in the bosom (or lap) of Jesus.* 13:26 [a]Matt 10:4; John 6:70–71; 12:4; Acts 1:16 13:27 [a]Luke 22:3 13:29 [a]John 12:6 13:31 [a]John 12:23; Acts 3:13 [b][John 14:13; 17:4; 1 Pet 4:11] 13:32 [a]John 12:23 [1]Sev. early MSS omit *If God is glorified in him.*

and he will glorify him right away. [33]Children, [a]I am still with you for a little while. You will look for me, [b]and just as I said to the Jewish religious leaders, 'Where I am going you cannot come,' now I tell you the same.

[34]"I give you [a]a new commandment—to love one another. Just as I have loved you, you also are to love one another. [35]Everyone will know [a]by this that you are my disciples—if you have love for one another."

[36]Simon Peter said to him, "Lord, where are you going?" Jesus replied, "Where I [a]am going, [b]you cannot follow me now, but you will follow later." [37]Peter said to him, "Lord, why can't I follow you now? I will lay [a]down my life for you!"[1] [38]Jesus answered, "Will you lay down your life for me?[1] I tell you the solemn truth, the rooster will not [a]crow until you have denied me three times!

Jesus' Parting Words to His Disciples

14 "Do [a]not let your hearts be distressed. You believe in God;[1] believe also in me. [2]There are many [a]dwelling places in my Father's house. Otherwise, I would have told you, because[1] I am going away to make ready a place for you. [3]And [a]if I go and make ready a place for you, I will come again and take you to be with me, so that [b]where I am you may be too. [4]And you know the way where I am going."[1]

[5a]Thomas said, "Lord, we don't know where you are going. How can we know the way?" [6]Jesus replied, "I am [a]the way, and [b]the truth, and [c]the life. [d]No one comes to the Father [e]except through me. [7a]If you have known me, you will know my Father too.[1] And from now on you do know him and have seen him."

[8]Philip said, "Lord, show us the Father, and we will be content." [9]Jesus replied, "Have I been with you for so long and yet you have not known me, Philip? [a]The person who has seen me has seen the Father! How can you say, 'Show us the Father'? [10]Do you not believe that [a]I am [b]in the Father, and the Father is in me? The words that I say to you, I do not speak on my own initiative, but the Father residing in me performs his miraculous deeds. [11]Believe me that I am in the Father, and the Father is in me, but [a]if you do not believe me, believe because of the miraculous deeds themselves. [12]I tell you the [a]solemn truth, the person who believes in me will perform the miraculous deeds that I am doing, and will perform greater deeds than these because I am going to the Father. [13a]And I will do whatever you ask in my name, so that the Father may be [b]glorified in the Son. [14]If you ask me anything in my name, I will do it.

Teaching on the Holy Spirit

[15]"[a]If you love me, you will obey my commandments. [16]Then I will ask [a]the Father, and he will give you another Advocate[1] to be with you forever—[17a]the Spirit of truth, [b]whom the world cannot accept because it does not see him or know him. But you know him because he resides with you [c]and will be[1] in you.

[18]"I [a]will not abandon you as orphans;[1] [b]I will come to you. [19]In a little while the world will not see me any longer, but [a]you will see me; [b]because I live, you will live too. [20]You will know at that time that [a]I am in my Father and you are in me and I am in you. [21]The person who has my commandments and obeys [a]them is the one who loves me. The one who loves me will be loved by my Father, and I will love him and will reveal myself to him."

[22]"Lord," [a]Judas (not Judas Iscariot) said, "what has happened that you are going to reveal yourself to us and not to the world?"

13:33 [a]John 12:35; 14:19; 16:16–19 [b]Mark 16:19; [John 7:34; 8:21]; Acts 1:9   **13:34** [a]Lev 19:18; Eph 5:2; 1 Thess 4:9; Jas 2:8; 1 Pet 1:22; 1 John 2:7   **13:35** [a]1 John 2:5   **13:36** [a]John 13:33; 14:2; 16:5 [b]John 21:17; 2 Pet 1:14   **13:37** [a]Matt 26:33–35; Mark 14:29–31; Luke 22:33–34 [1]Or *I will die willingly for you.*   **13:38** [a]Matt 26:74; Mark 14:30; Luke 22:61; John 18:25–27 [1]Or *Will you die willingly for me?*   **14:1** [a][John 14:27; 16:22, 24] [1]Or *Believe in God.*   **14:2** [a]Matt 25:34; John 13:33, 36; Heb 11:16 [1]Maj. MSS omit *because.*   **14:3** [a][Acts 1:11] [b][John 12:26; 1 Thess 4:17]   **14:4** [1]Maj. MSS *You know where I am going, and you know the way.*   **14:5** [a]Matt 10:3; John 11:16; 20:24–29; 21:2   **14:6** [a][John 10:9; Rom 5:2; Eph 2:18; Heb 9:8; 10:19–20] [b][John 1:14, 17; 8:32; 18:37] [c][John 11:25] [d]1 Tim 2:5 [e][John 10:7–9; Acts 4:12]   **14:7** [a]John 8:19 [1]Some MSS *If you had really known me, you would have known my Father.*   **14:9** [a]John 12:45; Col 1:15; Heb 1:3   **14:10** [a]John 10:38; 14:11, 20 [b]Deut 18:18; John 5:19; 14:24   **14:11** [a]John 5:36; 10:38   **14:12** [a]Matt 21:21; Mark 16:17; Luke 10:17   **14:13** [a]Matt 7:7; [Mark 11:24]; Luke 11:9; John 15:16; 16:23–24; [Jas 1:5–7; 1 John 3:22] [b]John 13:31   **14:15** [a]1 John 5:3   **14:16** [a][John 15:26; 20:22]; Acts 2:4, 33; Rom 8:15 [1]Or *Helper, Counselor.*   **14:17** [a][John 15:26; 16:13; 1 John 4:6; 5:7] [b][1 Cor 2:14] [c][1 John 2:27] [1]Some sig. WSS *he is.*   **14:18** [a][Matt 28:20] [b][John 14:3, 28] [1]I.e., leave you helpless.   **14:19** [a]John 16:16, 22 [b][Rom 5:10; 1 Cor 15:20; 2 Cor 4:10]   **14:20** [a]John 10:38; 14:11   **14:21** [a]1 John 2:5   **14:22** [a]Luke 6:16; Acts 1:13

[23]Jesus replied, "If anyone loves me, he will obey my word, [a]and my Father will love him, and we will come to him and take up residence with him.[1] [24]The person who does not love me does not obey my words. And [a]the word you hear is not mine, but the Father's who sent me.

[25]"I have spoken these things while staying with you. [26]But [a]the Advocate,[1] the Holy Spirit, whom the Father will [b]send in my name, will teach you everything and will cause you to remember everything I said to you. [27]"[a]Peace I leave with you; my peace I give to you; I do not give it to you as the world does. Do not let your hearts be distressed or lacking in courage.[1] [28]You heard me [a]say to you, '[b]I am going away and I am coming back to you.' If you loved [c]me, you would be glad that I am going to the Father because the Father is greater than I am. [29]I have told you [a]now before it happens, so that when it happens you may believe. [30]I will not speak with you much longer, [a]for the ruler of this world is coming. He has no [b]power over me, [31]but I am doing [a]just what the Father commanded me, so that the world may know that I love the Father. Get up, let us go from here.

The Vine and the Branches

15 "I am the true vine and my Father is the gardener. [2]He takes away[1] [a]every branch that does not bear fruit in me. He prunes[2] every branch that bears fruit so that it will bear [b]more fruit. [3][a]You are clean already because of the word that I have spoken to you. [4]Remain[1] in me, and I will remain in you. Just as the branch cannot bear fruit by itself, unless it [a]remains in the vine, so neither can you unless you remain in me.

[5]"I am the vine; you are the branches. The one who remains in me—and I in him— bears much [a]fruit because apart from me you can accomplish [b]nothing. [6]If anyone does not remain in me, [a]he is thrown out like a branch and dries up; and such branches are gathered up and thrown into the fire and are burned up. [7]If you [a]remain in me and my words remain in [b]you, ask whatever you want, and it will be done for you. [8]My Father is honored [a]by this, that you bear much fruit [b]and show that you are[1] my disciples.

[9]"Just as the Father has [a]loved me, I have also loved you; remain in my love. [10][a]If you obey my commandments, you will remain in my love, just as I have obeyed my Father's commandments and remain in his love. [11]I have told you these things so [a]that my joy may be in you, and your joy may be complete. [12][a]My [b]commandment is this—to love one another just as I have loved you. [13]No one has [a]greater love than this—that one lays down his life for his friends. [14][a]You are my friends if you do what I command you. [15]I no longer call you slaves [a]because the slave does not understand what his master is doing. But I have called you friends because I have revealed to you everything I heard from my Father. [16][a]You did not choose me, but I chose you and [b]appointed you to go and bear fruit, fruit that remains, so that whatever you ask the Father [c]in my name he will give you. [17]This I command you—to love one another.

The World's Hatred

[18]"[a]If the world hates you, be aware that it hated me first. [19][a]If you belonged to the world, the world would love you as its own. However, [b]because you do not belong to the world, but I chose you out of the world, for this reason the world hates you. [20]Remember [a]what I told you, 'A slave is not greater than his master.' [b]If they persecuted me, they will also persecute you. If they obeyed my word, they will obey yours too. [21]But they will do [a]all these things to you on account

14:23 [a]2 Cor 6:16; Eph 3:17; [1 John 2:24]; Rev 3:20; 21:3 [1]Grk. *and will make our dwelling place with him*; refers equally to men, women, and children.   **14:24** [a]John 5:19   **14:26** [a]Luke 24:49 [b]John 15:26 [1]Or *Helper, Counselor*.   **14:27** [a]Luke 1:79; [John 16:33; 20:19; Phil 4:7]; Col 3:15 [1]Or *distressed or fearful and cowardly*.   **14:28** [a]John 14:3, 18 [b]John 16:16 [c][John 5:18; Phil 2:6]   **14:29** [a]John 13:19   **14:30** [a][John 12:31] [b][John 8:46; 2 Cor 5:21; Heb 4:15; 1 Pet 1:19; 2:22]   **14:31** [a]Isa 50:5; John 10:18; Phil 2:8   **15:2** [a]Matt 15:13 [b][Matt 13:12] [1]Or *He cuts off*. [2]Or *trims*; Grk. *cleanses*.   **15:3** [a][John 13:10; 17:17]; Eph 5:26   **15:4** [a]John 17:23; Eph 3:17; [Col 1:23] [1]Or *Reside*.   **15:5** [a]Hos 14:8; [Gal 5:22–23] [b]2 Cor 3:5   **15:6** [a]Matt 3:10   **15:7** [a]1 John 2:14 [b]John 14:13; 16:23   **15:8** [a]Ps 22:23; [Matt 5:16]; John 13:31; 17:4; [Phil 1:11]; 1 Pet 4:11 [b]John 8:31 [1]Maj. MSS *will become*.   **15:9** [a]John 5:20; 17:26   **15:10** [a]John 14:15   **15:11** [a][John 16:24]; 1 John 1:4   **15:12** [a]John 13:34; 1 John 3:11 [b]Rom 12:9   **15:13** [a]Eph 5:2; 1 John 3:16   **15:14** [a][Matt 12:50; 28:20]; John 14:15, 21; Acts 10:42; 1 John 3:23–24   **15:15** [a]Gen 18:17   **15:16** [a]John 6:70; 13:18; 15:19; 1 John 4:10 [b][Matt 28:19; Mark 16:15; Col 1:6] [c]John 14:13; 16:23–24   **15:18** [a]John 7:7; 1 John 3:13   **15:19** [a]1 John 4:5 [b]John 17:14   **15:20** [a]Matt 10:24; John 13:16 [b]Ezek 3:7   **15:21** [a]Matt 10:22; 24:9; [1 Pet 4:14]; Rev 2:3

of my name because they do not know the one who sent me.[1] [22a]If I had not come and spoken to them, they would not be guilty of sin.[b] But they no longer have any excuse for their sin. [23]The one who hates me hates my [a]Father too. [24]If I had not performed among [a]them the miraculous deeds that no one else did, they would not be guilty of sin. But now they have [b]seen the deeds and have hated both me and my Father.[1] [25]Now this happened to fulfill [a]the word that is written in their law, '*They hated me without reason.*'[1] [26a]When [b]the Advocate[1] comes, whom I will send you from the Father—the Spirit of truth who goes out from the Father—he will testify about me, [27]and [a]you also will testify because [b]you have been with me from the beginning.

16 "I have told you all these things so that you will not fall away. [2]They will put you out of [a]the synagogue, yet [b]a time is coming when the one who kills you will think he is offering service to God. [3]They will do these [a]things because they have not known the Father or me. [4]But I have told you these things so that when their time[1] comes, you will remember that I told you about them.

"I did not tell you these things from the beginning because I was with you. [5]But now I am [a]going to the one who sent me, and not one of you is asking me, 'Where are you going?' [6]Instead your hearts are filled with [a]sadness because I have said these things to you. [7]But I tell you the truth, it is to your advantage that I am going away. For [a]if I do not go away, the Advocate[1] will not come to you, but if I go, I will send him to you. [8]And when he [a]comes, he will prove the world wrong[1] concerning sin and righteousness and judgment— [9a]concerning sin because they do not believe in me; [10a]concerning righteousness[1] [b]because I am going to the Father and you will see me no longer; [11]and [a]concerning judgment because [b]the ruler of this world has been condemned.

[12]"I have many more things to say to you, [a]but you cannot bear them now. [13]But when [a]he, [b]the Spirit of truth, comes, he will guide you into all truth. For he will not speak on his own authority, but will speak whatever he hears and will tell you what is to come.[1] [14a]He will glorify me because he will receive from me what is mine and will tell it to you. [15a]Everything that the Father has is mine; that is why I said the Spirit will receive from me what is mine and will tell it to you. [16]In a [a]little while you will see me no longer; again after [b]a little while, you will see me."

[17]Then some of his disciples said to one another, "What is the meaning of what he is saying, 'In a little while you will not see me; again after a little while, you will see me,' and 'because I am going to the Father'?" [18]So they kept on repeating, "What is the meaning of what he says, 'In a little while'?[1] We do not understand what he is talking about."

[19]Jesus could see that they wanted to ask him about these things, so he said to them, "Are you asking each other about this—that I said, 'In a little while you will not see me; again after a little while, you will see me'? [20]I tell you the solemn truth, you will weep and [a]wail, but the world will rejoice; you will be sad, but your sadness will turn into [b]joy. [21]When [a]a woman gives birth, she has distress because her time has come, but when her child is born, she no longer remembers the suffering because of her joy that a human being has been born into the world. [22]So also [a]you have sorrow now, but *I will see you again, and your hearts will rejoice, and no one will take your joy away from you.*[1] [23]At that time you will ask me nothing. I tell you the [a]solemn truth, whatever you ask the Father in my name he will give you. [24]Until now you have not asked for anything in my name. Ask and you will receive it, so [a]that your joy may be [b]complete.

15:21 [1] I.e., God.   **15:22** [a] John 9:41; 15:24   [b] [Rom 1:20; Jas 4:17]   **15:23** [1] John 2:23   **15:24** [a] John 3:2   [b] John 14:9   [1] Or *But now they have both seen and hated both me and my Father.*   **15:25** [a] Ps 35:19; 69:4; 109:3–5   [1] Pss 35:18; 69:4   **15:26** [a] Luke 24:49; [John 14:17]; Acts 2:4, 33   [b] 1 John 5:6   [1] Or *Helper, Counselor.*   **15:27** [a] Luke 24:48; 1 Pet 5:1; 2 Pet 1:16   [b] Matt 3:14; Luke 1:2; 1 John 1:1   **16:2** [a] John 9:22   [b] Acts 8:1   **16:3** [a] John 8:19; 15:21; Acts 13:27; Rom 10:2   **16:4** [1] Grk. *their hour.*   **16:5** [a] John 7:33; 13:33; 14:28; 17:11   **16:6** [a] Matt 17:23; [John 16:20, 22]   **16:7** [a] Acts 2:33   [1] Or *Helper, Counselor.*   **16:8** [a] Acts 1:8; 2:1–4, 37   [1] Or *will convict the world, will expose the world.*   **16:9** [a] Acts 2:22   **16:10** [a] Acts 2:32   [b] John 5:32   [1] Two questions arise because of this phrase: what is the meaning of "righteousness" and to whom does it pertain? For a discussion on these questions, see *NET Bible, Full Notes Edition.*   **16:11** [a] Acts 26:18   [b] [Luke 10:18]   **16:12** [a] Mark 4:33   **16:13** [a] [John 14:17]   [b] John 14:26; Acts 11:28; Rev 1:19   [1] Grk. *will tell you the things to come.*   **16:14** [a] John 15:26   **16:15** [a] Matt 11:27; John 3:35   **16:16** [a] John 7:33; 12:35; 13:33; 14:19; 19:40–42; 20:19   [b] John 13:3   **16:18** [1] Grk. *A little while.*   **16:20** [a] Mark 16:10; Luke 23:48; 24:17   [b] Luke 24:32, 41   **16:21** [a] Gen 3:16; Isa 13:8; 26:17; 42:14; 1 Thess 5:3   **16:22** [a] Luke 24:41; John 14:1, 27; 20:20; Acts 2:46; 13:52; 1 Pet 1:8   [1] [Isa 66:14 LXX]   **16:23** [a] Matt 7:7; [John 14:13; 15:16]   **16:24** [a] John 17:13   [b] John 15:11

[25]"I have told you these things in obscure figures of speech;[1] a time is coming when I will no longer speak to you in obscure figures, but will tell you [a]plainly about the Father. [26]At that time you will ask in my name, and I do not say that I will ask the Father on your behalf. [27][a]For the Father himself loves you because you [b]have loved me and have believed that I came from God.[1] [28]I came from the Father and entered [a]into the world, but in turn, I am leaving the world and going back to the Father."

[29]His disciples said, "Look, now you are speaking plainly and not in obscure figures of speech! [30]Now we know that [a]you know everything and do not need anyone to ask you anything. Because of this [b]we believe that you have come from God."

[31]Jesus replied, "Do you now believe? [32][a]Look, a time is coming—and has come—when you will be scattered, each [b]one to his own home, and I will be left alone. [c]Yet I am not alone because my Father is with me. [33]I have told you these things so that [a]in me you may have peace. [b]In the world you have trouble and suffering,[1] but take courage—[c]I have conquered the world."[2]

Jesus Prays for the Father to Glorify Him

17 When Jesus had finished saying [a]these things, he looked upward to heaven and said, "Father, the time[1] has come. Glorify your Son, so that your[2] Son may glorify you—[2]just [a]as you have given him authority over all humanity, so that he may give eternal life to everyone you have given him. [3]Now [a]this is eternal life—that [b]they know you, the only true God, and Jesus Christ, [c]whom you sent. [4][a]I glorified you on earth by completing[1] the work you gave me to do. [5]And now, Father, glorify me at your side with the glory [a]I had with you before the world was created.

Jesus Prays for the Disciples

[6]"[a]I have revealed your name to [b]the men you gave me out of the world. They belonged to you, and you gave them to me, and they have obeyed your word. [7]Now they understand that everything you have given me comes from you, [8]because [a]I have given them the words you have given me. They accepted them [b]and really understand that I came from [c]you, and they believed that you sent me. [9]I am [a]praying on behalf of them. I am not praying on behalf of the world, but on behalf of those you have given me because they belong to you. [10]Everything I have belongs to [a]you, and everything you have belongs to me, and I have been glorified by them. [11]I am no longer in the world, [a]but they are in the world, and I am coming to you. Holy Father, [b]keep them safe in your name that you have given me, so that they may be one just [c]as we are one. [12]When I was with them [a]I kept them safe and watched over them in your name that you have given me. Not [b]one of them was lost [c]except the one destined for destruction,[1] so [d]that the scripture could be fulfilled. [13]But now I am coming to you, and I am saying these things in the world, so they may experience my joy completed in themselves. [14]I have given them your word, [a]and the world has hated them because they do not belong to the world, [b]just as I do not belong to the world. [15]I am not asking you to take them out of the world, but [a]that you keep them safe from the evil one.[1] [16]They do not belong to the world just as I do not belong to the world. [17]Set them [a]apart[1] in the truth; [b]your word is truth. [18]Just [a]as you sent me into the world, so I sent them into the world. [19]And I set myself apart [a]on their behalf, so that they too may be truly set apart.

Jesus Prays for Believers Everywhere

[20]"I am not praying only on their behalf, but also on behalf of those who believe in

me through their testimony, [21][a]that they will all be one, just as you, Father, are in me and I am in you. I pray that they will be in us, so that the world will believe that [b]you sent me. [22]The [a]glory you gave to me I have given to them, [b]that they may be one just as we are one—[23]I in them and you in me—that they may be completely one,[1] so [a]that the world will know that you sent me, and you have loved them just as you have loved me. [24]"[a]Father, I want those you have given me to be with me where I am, so that they can see my glory that you gave me [b]because you loved me before the creation of the world. [25]Righteous [a]Father, even if the world does not know you, [b]I know you, and these [c]men know that you sent me. [26]I made known your name to them, [a]and [b]I will continue to make it known, so that the love you have loved me with may be in them, and I may be in them."

Betrayal and Arrest

18 When [a]he had said [b]these things, Jesus went out with his disciples across the Kidron Valley.[1] There was an orchard[2] there, and he and his disciples went into it. [2](Now Judas, the one who betrayed him, knew the place too, [a]because Jesus had met there many times with his disciples.) [3]So Judas obtained a squad of soldiers[1] and some officers of [a]the chief priests and Pharisees. They came to the orchard with lanterns[2] and torches and weapons.

[4]Then Jesus, because he [a]knew everything that was going to happen to him, came and asked them, "Who are you looking for?" [5]They replied, "[a]Jesus the Nazarene." He told them, "I am he." (Now Judas, the one who [b]betrayed him, was standing there with them.) [6]So when Jesus said to them, "I am he," they retreated and fell to the ground. [7]Then Jesus asked them again, "Who are you looking for?" And they said, "Jesus the Nazarene." [8]Jesus replied, "I told you that I am he. If you are looking for me, let these men go." [9]He said this to fulfill the word he had spoken, "I have not lost a single one [a]of those whom you gave me."

[10][a]Then Simon Peter, who had a sword, pulled it out and struck the high priest's slave, cutting off his right ear. (Now the slave's name was Malchus.) [11]But Jesus said to Peter, "Put your sword back into its sheath! Am I not to drink [a]the cup that the Father has given me?"

Jesus before Annas

[12]Then the squad of soldiers[1] with their commanding officer and the officers of the Jewish leaders arrested Jesus and tied him up. [13][a]They brought him first to [b]Annas, for he was the father-in-law of [c]Caiaphas, who was high priest that year. [14]([a]Now it was Caiaphas who had advised the Jewish leaders that it was to their advantage that one man die for the people.)

Peter's First Denial

[15]Simon Peter and another disciple followed them as they brought Jesus to Annas. ([a]Now [b]the other disciple was acquainted with the high priest, and he went with Jesus into the high priest's courtyard.) [16][a]But Peter was left standing outside by the door. So the other disciple who was acquainted with the high priest came out and spoke to the slave girl who watched the door, and brought Peter inside. [17]The girl who was the doorkeeper said to Peter, "You're not one of this man's disciples too, are you?" He replied, "I am [a]not." [18](Now the slaves and the guards[1] were standing around a charcoal fire they had made, warming themselves because it was cold. Peter also was standing with them, warming himself.)

17:21 [a][John 10:16; Rom 12:5; Gal 3:28]; Eph 4:4, 6 [b]John 10:38; 17:11, 23   **17:22** [a]John 14:20; 1 John 1:3 [b][2 Cor 3:18] **17:23** [a][Col 3:14] [1]Or *completely unified.*   **17:24** [a][John 12:26; 14:3; 1 Thess 4:17] [b]Matt 25:34; John 17:5   **17:25** [a]John 15:21 [b]John 7:29; 8:55; 10:15 [c]John 3:17; 17:3, 8, 18, 21, 23   **17:26** [a]Exod 34:5–7; John 17:6 [b]John 15:9; [Eph 3:17–19]   **18:1** [a]Matt 26:30, 36; Mark 14:26, 32; Luke 22:39 [b]2 Sam 15:23; 1 Kgs 2:37; 15:13; 2 Kgs 23:4, 6, 12; 2 Chr 15:16; 29:16; 30:14; Jer 31:40 [1]Grk. *the wadi of the Kidron, the ravine of the Kidron.* [2]Or *a garden.*   **18:2** [a]Luke 21:37; 22:39   **18:3** [a]Matt 26:47–56; Mark 14:43–50; Luke 22:47–53; Acts 1:16 [1]Grk. *a cohort;* normally a force of 600 men, but the entire cohort was not necessarily present. These Roman soldiers must have accompanied the servants of the chief priests and Pharisees. [2]Lamps that had some sort of covering to protect them from wind and rain.   **18:4** [a]John 6:64; 13:1, 3; 19:28   **18:5** [a]Matt 21:11; Mark 1:24; 14:67; 16:6; Luke 18:37; 24:19 [b]Ps 41:9; Matt 20:18; 26:21; John 13:21   **18:9** [a][John 6:39; 17:12]   **18:10** [a]Matt 26:51; Mark 14:47; Luke 22:49–50   **18:11** [a]Matt 20:22; 26:39; Mark 14:36; Luke 22:42   **18:12** [1]Grk. *a cohort;* normally a force of 600 men, but the entire cohort was not necessarily present.   **18:13** [a]Matt 26:57 [b]Luke 3:2; John 18:24; Acts 4:6 [c]Matt 26:3; John 11:49, 51   **18:14** [a]John 11:50   **18:15** [a]Matt 26:58; Mark 14:54; Luke 22:54 [b]John 20:2–5   **18:16** [a]Matt 26:69; Mark 14:66–68; Luke 22:55–57   **18:17** [a]Matt 26:34   **18:18** [1]The guards of the chief priests.

Jesus Questioned by Annas

[19]While this was happening, the high priest questioned Jesus about his disciples and about his teaching. [20]Jesus replied, "[a]I have spoken publicly to the world. I always taught [b]in the synagogues and [c]in the temple courts, where all the Jewish people assemble together. I have said nothing in secret. [21]Why do you ask me? Ask [a]those who heard what I said. They[1] know what I said." [22]When Jesus had said this, one of the high priest's officers who stood nearby [a]struck him on the face and said, "Is that the way you answer the high priest?" [23]Jesus replied, "If I have said something wrong, confirm what is wrong. But if I spoke correctly, why strike me?" [24a]Then Annas sent him, still tied up, to [b]Caiaphas the high priest.

Peter's Second and Third Denials

[25]Meanwhile Simon Peter was standing in [a]the courtyard warming himself. They said to him, "You aren't one of his disciples too, are you?" Peter denied it: "I am not!" [26]One of the high priest's slaves, a relative of the man whose ear Peter had cut off, said, "Did I not see you in the orchard[1] with him?" [27]Then Peter denied it again, and [a]immediately a rooster crowed.

Jesus Brought before Pilate

[28a]Then they brought Jesus from Caiaphas to the Roman governor's residence.[1] (Now it was very early morning.) They did not go into the governor's residence so they would not be ceremonially defiled, [b]but could eat the Passover meal. [29]So [a]Pilate came outside to them and said, "What accusation do you bring against this man?" [30]They replied, "If this man were not a criminal, we would not have handed him over to you."

[31]Pilate told them, "Take him yourselves and pass judgment on him according to your own law!" The Jewish leaders[1] replied, "We cannot legally put anyone to death." [32](This happened [a]to fulfill the word Jesus had spoken when he [b]indicated what kind of death he was going to die.)

Pilate Questions Jesus

[33]So Pilate went back into [a]the governor's residence, summoned Jesus, and asked him, "Are you the king of the Jews?" [34]Jesus replied, "Are you saying this on your own initiative, or have others told you about me?" [35]Pilate answered, "I am not a Jew, am I? Your own people and your chief priests handed you over[1] to me. What have you done?"

[36a]Jesus replied, "[b]My kingdom is not from this world. If my kingdom were from this world, my servants would be fighting to keep me from being handed over to the Jewish authorities. But as it is, my kingdom is not from here." [37]Then Pilate said, "So you are a king!" Jesus replied, "You say that I am a king. For this reason I was born, and for this reason I came into the world—[a]to [b]testify to the truth. Everyone who [c]belongs to the truth [d]listens to my voice." [38]Pilate asked, "What is truth?"

When he had said this he went back outside to the Jewish leaders and announced, "[a]I find no basis for an accusation against him. [39a]But it is your custom that I release one prisoner for you at the Passover. So do you want me to release for you the king of the Jews?" [40a]Then they shouted back, "Not this man, but Barabbas!" ([b]Now Barabbas was a revolutionary.)

Pilate Tries to Release Jesus

19 Then [a]Pilate took Jesus and had him flogged severely.[1] [2]The soldiers braided a crown of thorns and put it on his head, and they clothed him in a purple robe. [3]They came up to him again and again and said, "Hail, king of the Jews!"[1] And they [a]struck him repeatedly in the face.

[4]Again Pilate went out and said to the Jewish leaders, "Look, I am bringing him out to you, so [a]that you may know that I find

18:20 [a] Matt 26:55; Luke 4:15; John 8:26   [b] John 6:59   [c] Mark 14:49; John 7:14, 28   18:21 [a] Mark 12:37   [1] Grk. Look, these know what I said.   18:22 [a] Job 16:10; Isa 50:6; Jer 20:2; Lam 3:30; Acts 23:2   18:24 [a] Matt 26:57; Luke 3:2; Acts 4:6   [b] John 11:49   18:25 [a] Matt 26:71–75; Mark 14:69–72; Luke 22:58–62   18:26 [1] Or garden.   18:27 [a] Matt 26:74; Mark 14:72; Luke 22:60; John 13:38   18:28 [a] Matt 27:2; Mark 15:1; Luke 23:1; Acts 3:13   [b] John 11:55; Acts 10:28; 11:3   [1] Grk. to the praetorium.   18:29 [a] Matt 27:11–14; Mark 15:2–5; Luke 23:2–3   18:31 [1] Grk. the Jews.   18:32 [a] Matt 20:17–19; 26:2; Mark 10:33; Luke 18:32   [b] John 3:14; 8:28; 12:32–33   18:33 [a] Matt 27:11   18:35 [1] Or delivered you over.   18:36 [a] 1 Tim 6:13   [b] [Dan 2:44; 7:14]; Luke 12:14; John 6:15; 8:15   18:37 [a] [Matt 5:17; 20:28; Luke 4:43; 12:49; 19:10; John 3:17; 9:39; 10:10; 12:47]   [b] Isa 55:4; Rev 1:5   [c] [John 14:6]   [d] John 8:47; 10:27; [1 John 3:19; 4:6]   18:38 [a] Isa 53:9; Matt 27:24; Luke 23:4; John 19:4, 6; 1 Pet 2:22–24   18:39 [a] Matt 27:15–26; Mark 15:6–15; Luke 23:18–25   18:40 [a] Isa 53:3; Acts 3:14   [b] Luke 23:19   19:1 [a] Matt 20:19; 27:26; Mark 15:15; Luke 18:33   [1] Or had him flogged.   19:3 [a] Isa 50:6   [1] Or Long live the King of the Jews!   19:4 [a] Isa 53:9; John 18:33, 38; 1 Pet 2:22–24

no reason for an accusation against him." [5]So Jesus came outside, wearing the crown of thorns and the purple robe. Pilate said to them, "Look, here is the man!" [6]When [a]the chief priests and their officers saw him, they shouted out, "Crucify him! Crucify him!" Pilate said, "You take him and crucify him! Certainly I find no reason for an accusation against him!" [7]The Jewish leaders replied, "[a]We have a law, and according to our law [b]he ought to die because he claimed to be the Son of God!"

[8]When Pilate heard what they said, he was more afraid than ever, [9]and he went back into the governor's residence and said to Jesus, "Where do you come from?" [a]But Jesus gave him no answer. [10]So Pilate said, "Do you refuse to speak to me? Don't you know I have the authority[1] to release you and to crucify you?" [11]Jesus replied, "[a]You would have no authority over me at all, unless it was given to you from above. [b]Therefore the one who handed me over to you is guilty of greater sin."

[12]From this point on, Pilate tried to release him. But the Jewish leaders shouted out, "If you release this man, you are no friend of Caesar! [a]Everyone who claims to be a king opposes Caesar!" [13]When Pilate heard these words [a]he brought Jesus outside and sat down on the judgment seat in the place called "The Stone Pavement" (*Gabbatha* in Aramaic). [14](Now [a]it was the day of preparation for the Passover, about noon.)[1] Pilate said to the Jewish leaders, "Look, here is your king!"

[15]Then they shouted out, "Away with him! Away with him! Crucify him!" Pilate asked, "Shall I crucify your king?" The high priests replied, "[a]We have no king except Caesar!" [16a]Then Pilate handed him over to them to be crucified.

The Crucifixion

So they took Jesus, [17a]and carrying his own cross he went [b]out to the place called "The Place of the Skull" (called in Aramaic *Golgotha*). [18]There they crucified him along with [a]two others, one on each side, with Jesus in the middle. [19]Pilate [a]also had a notice written and fastened to the cross, which read: "Jesus the Nazarene, the king of the Jews." [20]Thus many of the Jewish residents of Jerusalem read this notice because the place where Jesus was crucified was near the city, and the notice was written in Aramaic, Latin, and Greek. [21]Then the chief priests of the Jews[1] said to Pilate, "Do not write, 'The king of the Jews,' but rather, 'This man said, I am king of the Jews.'" [22]Pilate answered, "What I have written, I have written."

[23]Now when [a]the soldiers crucified Jesus, they took his clothes and made four shares, one for each soldier, and the tunic[1] remained. (Now the tunic was seamless, woven from top to bottom as a single piece.) [24]So [a]the soldiers said to one another, "Let's not tear it, but throw dice[1] to see who will get it." This took place to fulfill the scripture that says, "***They divided my garments among them, and for my clothing they threw dice.***"[2] So the soldiers did these things.

[25a]Now standing beside Jesus' cross were his mother, his mother's sister, Mary the wife of [b]Clopas, and Mary Magdalene. [26]So when Jesus saw his [a]mother and the disciple whom he loved standing there, he said to his mother, "[b]Woman, look, here is your son!" [27]He then said to his disciple, "Look, here is your mother!" From that very time[1] the disciple took her [a]into his own home.

Jesus' Death

[28]After this Jesus, realizing that by this time everything was completed,[1] said (in order [a]to fulfill the scripture), "I am thirsty!" [29]A jar full of sour wine was there, so [a]they put a sponge soaked in sour wine on a branch of hyssop and lifted it to his mouth. [30]When he had received the sour wine, Jesus said, "[a]It is completed!"[1] Then he bowed his head and gave up his spirit.

19:6 [a]Acts 3:13   19:7 [a]Lev 24:16   [b]Matt 26:63–66; John 5:18; 10:33   19:9 [a]Isa 53:7; Matt 27:12, 14; Luke 23:9   19:10 [1]Or *the power.*   19:11 [a][Luke 22:53]; John 7:30   [b]John 3:27; Rom 13:1   19:12 [a]Luke 23:2; John 18:33; Acts 17:7   19:13 [a]Deut 1:17; 1 Sam 15:24; Prov 29:25; Isa 51:12; Acts 4:19   19:14 [a]Matt 27:62; John 19:31, 42   [1]Grk. *about the sixth hour.*   19:15 [a][Gen 49:10]   19:16 [a]Matt 27:26, 31; Mark 15:15; Luke 23:24   19:17 [a]Matt 27:31, 33; Mark 15:21–22; Luke 23:26, 33   [b]Num 15:36; Heb 13:12   19:18 [a]Ps 22:16–18; Isa 53:12; Matt 20:19; 26:2   19:19 [a]Matt 27:37; Mark 15:26; Luke 23:38   19:21 [1]Or *the Jewish chief priests.*   19:23 [a]Matt 27:35; Mark 15:24; Luke 23:34   [1]Or *shirt;* a long garment worn under the cloak next to the skin.   19:24 [a]Ps 22:18   [1]Grk. *but choose by lot.*   [2]Ps 22:18   19:25 [a]Matt 27:55; Mark 15:40; Luke 2:35; 23:49   [b]Luke 24:18   19:26 [a]John 13:23; 20:2; 21:7, 20, 24   [b]John 2:4   19:27 [a]Luke 18:28; John 1:11; 16:32; Acts 21:6   [1]Grk. *from that very hour.*   19:28 [a]Ps 22:15   [1]Or *finished, accomplished;* Grk. *fulfilled.*   19:29 [a]Ps 69:21; Matt 27:48, 50; Mark 15:36; Luke 23:36   19:30 [a]Dan 9:26; Zech 11:10–11; John 17:4   [1]Or *It is accomplished, It is finished, It is ended.*

[31]Then because it was [a]the day of preparation, so [b]that the bodies should not stay on the crosses on the Sabbath (for that Sabbath was an especially [c]important one), the Jewish leaders asked Pilate to have the victims' legs broken and the bodies taken down. [32]So the soldiers came and broke the legs of the two men who had been crucified with Jesus, first the one and then the other. [33]But when they came to Jesus and saw that he was already dead, they did not break his legs. [34]But one of the soldiers pierced his side with a spear, and [a]blood and water flowed out immediately. [35]And the person who saw it has testified (and his testimony is [a]true, and he knows that he is telling the truth), so that you also may [b]believe. [36]For these things happened so that the scripture would be fulfilled, "[a]*Not a bone of his will be broken.*"[1] [37]And again another scripture says, "[a]*They will look on the one whom they have pierced.*"[1]

Jesus' Burial

[38a]After this, Joseph of Arimathea, a disciple of Jesus (but secretly [b]because he feared the Jewish leaders), asked Pilate if he could remove the body of Jesus. Pilate gave him permission, so he went and took the body away. [39a]Nicodemus, the man who had previously come to Jesus at night, accompanied Joseph, carrying a mixture of [b]myrrh and aloes weighing about 75 pounds. [40]Then they took Jesus' body and [a]wrapped it, with the aromatic spices, in strips of linen cloth according to Jewish burial customs. [41]Now at the place where Jesus was crucified there was a garden,[1] and in the garden was a new tomb where no one had yet been buried. [42]And [a]so, [b]because it was the Jewish day of preparation and the tomb was nearby, they placed Jesus' body there.

The Resurrection

20 Now very early on the [a]first day of the week, while it was still dark, Mary Magdalene came to the tomb and saw that the [b]stone had been moved away from the entrance. [2]So she went running to Simon Peter and the [a]other disciple [b]whom Jesus loved and told them, "They have taken the Lord from the tomb, and we don't know where they have put him!" [3]Then [a]Peter and the other disciple set out to go to the tomb. [4]The two were running together, but the other disciple ran faster than Peter and reached the tomb first. [5]He bent down and saw [a]the strips of linen cloth lying there, but he did not go in. [6]Then Simon Peter, who had been following him, arrived and went right into the tomb. He saw the strips of linen cloth lying there, [7]and [a]the face cloth, which had been around Jesus' head, not lying with the strips of linen cloth but rolled up in a place by itself. [8]Then the [a]other disciple, who had reached the tomb first, came in, and he saw and believed. [9](For they did not yet understand the [a]scripture that Jesus must rise from the dead.)

Jesus' Appearance to Mary Magdalene

[10]So the disciples went back to their homes. [11a]But Mary stood outside the tomb weeping. As she wept, she bent down and looked into the tomb. [12]And she saw two angels in white sitting where Jesus' body had been lying, one at the head and one at the feet. [13]They said to her, "Woman, why are you weeping?" Mary replied, "They have taken my Lord away, and I do not know where they have put him!" [14]When she had said this, she turned around [a]and saw Jesus standing there, but she [b]did not know that it was Jesus.

[15]Jesus said to her, "Woman, why are you weeping? Who are you looking for?" Because she thought he was the gardener, she said to him, "Sir, if you have carried him away, tell me where you have put him, and I will take him." [16]Jesus said to her, "[a]Mary." She turned and said to him in Aramaic, "*Rabboni*" (which means "Teacher"). [17]Jesus replied, "Do not touch me, for I have not yet [a]ascended to [b]my Father. Go to my

19:31 [a]Matt 27:62; Mark 15:42; Luke 23:54 [b]Deut 21:23; Josh 8:29; 10:26 [c]Exod 12:16; Lev 23:6–7   19:34 [a][1 John 5:6, 8]   19:35 [a]John 21:24 [b][John 20:31]   19:36 [a][Exod 12:46; Num 9:12]; Ps 34:20 [1]Exod 12:46; Num 9:12; Ps 34:20   19:37 [a]Ps 22:16–17; Zech 12:10; 13:6; Rev 1:7 [1]Zech 12:10   19:38 [a]Matt 27:57–61; Mark 15:42–47; Luke 23:50–56 [b][John 7:13; 9:22; 12:42]   19:39 [a]John 3:1–2; 7:50 [b]Ps 45:8; Prov 7:17; Song 4:14; Matt 2:11   19:40 [a]Luke 24:12; John 20:5, 7; Acts 5:6   19:41 [1]Or *an orchard.*   19:42 [a]Isa 53:9; Matt 26:12; Mark 14:8 [b]John 19:14, 31   20:1 [a]Matt 28:1–8; Mark 16:1–8; Luke 24:1–10; Acts 20:7; 1 Cor 16:2 [b]Matt 27:60, 66; 28:2; Mark 15:46; 16:4; Luke 24:2; John 11:38   20:2 [a]John 21:23–24 [b]John 13:23; 19:26; 21:7, 20, 24   20:3 [a]Luke 24:12   20:5 [a]John 19:40   20:7 [a]John 11:44   20:8 [a]John 21:23–24   20:9 [a]Ps 16:10; Acts 2:25, 31; 13:34–35   20:11 [a]Mark 16:5   20:14 [a]Matt 28:9; Mark 16:9 [b][Luke 24:16, 31]; John 21:4   20:16 [a]John 10:3   20:17 [a]Mark 16:19; Luke 24:5; Acts 1:9; 2:34–36; Eph 4:8–10; Heb 4:14 [b]Ps 22:22; Matt 18:10; Rom 8:29; Heb 2:11

brothers and tell them, 'ᶜI am ascending to ᵈmy Father and your Father, to my God and your God.'" ¹⁸ᵃMary Magdalene came and informed the disciples, "I have seen the Lord!" And she told them what Jesus had said to her.

Jesus' Appearance to the Disciples

¹⁹On ᵃthe evening of that day, the first day of the week, the disciples had gathered together and locked the doors of the place because they were ᵇafraid of the Jewish leaders. Jesus came and stood among them and said to them, "ᶜPeace be with you." ²⁰When he had said this, he ᵃshowed them his hands and his side. ᵇThen the disciples rejoiced when they saw the Lord. ²¹So Jesus said to them again, "Peace be with you. Just ᵃas the Father has sent me, I also send you." ²²And after he said this, he breathed on them and said, "Receive the Holy Spirit. ²³If you forgive anyone's sins, they are forgiven; ᵃif you retain anyone's sins, they are retained."

The Response of Thomas

²⁴Now Thomas (ᵃcalled Didymus), one of the twelve, was not with them when Jesus came. ²⁵The other disciples told him, "We have seen the Lord!" But he replied, "Unless I see the wounds from the nails in his hands, and put my finger into the wounds from the nails, and put my hand into his side, I will never believe it!"

²⁶Eight days later the disciples were again together in the house, and Thomas was with them. Although the doors were locked, Jesus came and stood among them and said, "Peace be with you!" ²⁷Then he said to Thomas, "ᵃPut your finger here, and examine my hands. Extend your hand and put it into my side. Do not continue in your ᵇunbelief, but believe." ²⁸Thomas replied to him, "My Lord and my God!" ²⁹Jesus said to him, "Have you believed because you have seen me? ᵃBlessed are the people who have not seen and yet have believed."

³⁰Now Jesus performed many other miraculous signs in the presence of theⁱ disciples, which are not recorded in this book. ³¹ᵃBut these are recorded so that ᵇyou may believeⁱ that Jesus ᶜis the Christ,² the Son of God, ᵈand that by believing you may have life in his name.

Jesus' Appearance to the Disciples in Galilee

21 After thisⁱ Jesus revealed himself again to the disciples by the ᵃSea of Tiberias. Now this is how he did so. ²Simon Peter, ᵃThomas (called Didymus), ᵇNathanael (who was from ᶜCana in Galilee), ᵈthe sons of Zebedee, and two other disciples of his were together. ³Simon Peter told them, "I am going fishing." "We will go with you," they replied. They went out and got into the boat, but that night they caught nothing.

⁴When it was already very early morning, Jesus stood on the beach, but the disciples ᵃdid not know that it was Jesus. ⁵So ᵃJesus said to them, "Children, you don't have any fish, do you?" They replied, "No." ⁶He told them, "ᵃThrow your net on the right side of the boat, and you will find some." So they threw the net and were not able to pull it in because of the large number of fish.

⁷Then the disciple whom Jesus loved said to Peter, "It is the Lord!" So Simon Peter, when he heard ᵃthat it was the Lord, tucked in his outer garment (for he had nothing on underneath it),ⁱ and plunged into the sea. ⁸Meanwhile the other disciples came with the boat, dragging the net full of fish, for they were not far from land, only about a hundred yards.

⁹When they got out on the beach, they saw a charcoal fire ready with a fish placed on it, and bread. ¹⁰Jesus said, "Bring some of the fish you have just now caught." ¹¹So Simon Peter went aboard and pulled the net to shore. It was full of large fish, 153, but although there were so many, the net was not torn. ¹²"Come, have breakfast," Jesus said. But none of the disciples dared to ask

20:17ᶜ John 16:28; 17:11   ᵈ Eph 1:17   **20:18**ᵃ Matt 28:10; Luke 24:10, 23   **20:19**ᵃ Mark 16:14; Luke 24:36; John 14:27; 1 Cor 15:5   ᵇ John 9:22; 19:38   ᶜ John 14:27; 16:33; Eph 2:17   **20:20**ᵃ Acts 1:3   ᵇ John 16:20, 22   **20:21**ᵃ [Matt 28:18–20]; John 17:18–19; [2 Tim 2:2]; Heb 3:1   **20:23**ᵃ Matt 16:19; 18:18   **20:24**ᵃ John 11:16   **20:27**ᵃ Ps 22:16; Zech 12:10; 13:6; 1 John 1:1   ᵇ Mark 16:14   **20:29**ᵃ 2 Cor 5:7; 1 Pet 1:8   **20:30**ⁱ ‡ Maj. mss *his.*   **20:31**ᵃ Luke 1:4   ᵇ John 19:35; 1 John 5:13   ᶜ Luke 2:11; 1 John 5:1   ᵈ John 3:15–16; 5:24; [1 Pet 1:8–9]   ¹ ‡ Some mss *may come to believe.*   ² Or *Jesus is the Messiah;* both "Christ" (Grk.) and "Messiah" (Heb., Aram.) mean "one who has been anointed."   **21:1**ᵃ Matt 26:32; Mark 14:28; John 6:1   ¹ An indefinite time reference.   **21:2**ᵃ John 20:24   ᵇ John 1:45–51   ᶜ John 2:1   ᵈ Matt 4:21; Mark 1:19; Luke 5:10   **21:4**ᵃ Luke 24:16; John 20:14   **21:5**ᵃ Luke 24:41   **21:6**ᵃ Luke 5:4, 6, 7   **21:7**ᵃ John 13:23; 20:2   ¹ Grk. *for he was naked;* meaning stripped for work, with his outer clothing removed. Peter was wearing either a loincloth or a loose-fitting tunic.

him, "Who are you?" because they knew it was the Lord. [13]Jesus came and took the bread and gave it to them, and did the same with the fish. [14]This was now [a]the third time Jesus was revealed to the disciples after he was raised from the dead.

Peter's Restoration

[15]Then when they had finished breakfast, Jesus said to Simon Peter, "Simon, son of John,[1] do you love me more than these do?"[2] He replied, "Yes, Lord, you know I love you."[3] Jesus told him, "[a]Feed my lambs." [16]Jesus said a second time, "Simon, son of John, do you love me?" [a]He replied, "Yes, Lord, you know I love you." Jesus told him, "Shepherd my [b]sheep." [17]Jesus said a third time, "Simon, son of John, do you love me?" Peter was distressed that Jesus asked him a third time, "Do you love me?" and said, "Lord, [a]you know everything. You know that I love you." Jesus[1] replied, "Feed my sheep. [18]I tell you the [a]solemn truth, when you were young, you tied your clothes around you and went wherever you wanted, but when you are old, you will stretch out your hands, and others will tie you up and bring you where you do not want to go." [19](Now Jesus said this to indicate clearly [a]by what kind of death Peter

was going to glorify God.) After he said this, Jesus told Peter, "[b]Follow me."

Peter and the Disciple Jesus Loved

[20]Peter turned around and saw the disciple [a]whom Jesus loved following them. (This was the disciple [b]who had leaned back against Jesus' chest at the meal and asked, "Lord, who is the one who is going to betray you?") [21]So when Peter saw him, he asked Jesus, "Lord, what about him?" [22]Jesus replied, "If I want him to live [a]until I come back, what concern is that of yours? You follow me!" [23]So the saying circulated among the brothers and sisters[1] that this disciple was not going to die. But Jesus did not say to him that he was not going to die, but rather, "If I want him to live until I come back, what concern is that of yours?"

A Final Note

[24]This is the disciple who [a]testifies about these things and has written these things, and we know that his testimony is true. [25a]There are many other [b]things that Jesus did. If every one of them were written down, I suppose the whole world would not have room for the books that would be written.[1]

21:14 [a]John 20:19, 26   21:15 [a]Acts 20:28; 1 Tim 4:6; 1 Pet 5:2   [1]Maj. MSS *Jonah*.   [2]Likely the other disciples, meaning "Do you love me more than these other disciples do?"   [3]Most scholars see no significant difference between the two Grk. words for "love" (*agapaō* and *phileō*) in vv. 15–17, viewing it as stylistic variation. This is supported by (1) the author's tendency for stylistic variation, (2) the interchangeability of the terms in both the Grk. NT and OT translations, and (3) Peter's consistent responses regardless of the verb used.   21:16 [a]Matt 2:6; Acts 20:28; Heb 13:20; 1 Pet 2:25; 5:2, 4   [b]Ps 79:13; Matt 10:16; 15:24; 25:33; 26:31   21:17 [a]John 2:24–25; 16:30   [1]‡ Some wss omit *Jesus*.   21:18 [a]John 13:36; Acts 12:3–4   21:19 [a]2 Pet 1:13–14   [b][Matt 4:19; 16:24]; John 21:22   21:20 [a]John 13:23; 20:2   [b]John 13:25   21:22 [a][Matt 16:27–28; 25:31; 1 Cor 4:5; 11:26; Rev 2:25; 3:11; 22:7, 20]   21:23 [1]Grk. *the brothers*; refers to more than just the immediate disciples.   21:24 [a]John 19:35; 3 John 12   21:25 [a]John 20:30   [b]Amos 7:10   [1]Maj. MSS add *amen*.

ACTS

Jesus' last recorded words have come to be known as the Great Commission: "You will be my witnesses in Jerusalem, and in all Judea and Samaria, and to the farthest parts of the earth" (1:8). The Book of Acts written by Luke is the story of the men and women who took that commission seriously and began to spread the news of a risen Savior to the remotest corners of the known world. Each section of the book (chs. 1–7; 8–12; 13–28) focuses on a particular audience, a key personality, and a significant phase in the expansion of the gospel message. As the second volume in a two-part work by Luke, this book probably had no separate title. But all available Greek manuscripts designate it by the title *Praxeis*, "Acts," or by an expanded title like "The Acts of the Apostles." *Praxeis* was commonly used in Greek literature to summarize the accomplishments of outstanding men. While the apostles are mentioned collectively at several points, this book really records the acts of Peter (chs. 1–12) and of Paul (chs. 13–28).

Jesus Ascends to Heaven

1 I wrote the former account, [a]Theophilus, about all that Jesus began to do and teach [2a]until the day he was taken up to heaven, after he [b]had given orders by the Holy Spirit to the apostles he had chosen. [3a]To the same apostles also, after his suffering, he presented himself alive with many convincing proofs. He was seen by them over a forty-day period and spoke about matters concerning the kingdom of God. [4a]While he was with them, he declared, "Do not leave Jerusalem, but wait there for what my Father promised,[1] which you [b]heard about from me. [5a]For John baptized with water, [b]but you will be baptized with the Holy Spirit not many days from now."

[6]So when they had gathered together, they began to ask him, "Lord, is this the time when you are restoring the kingdom to Israel?" [7]He told them, "You are not [a]permitted to [b]know the times or periods that the Father has set by his own authority. [8a]But you will receive power [b]when the Holy Spirit has come upon [c]you, and you will be my witnesses in Jerusalem, and in all Judea and [d]Samaria, and to the farthest [e]parts of the earth." [9]After he had said this, while they were watching, he was lifted up [a]and a cloud hid him from [b]their sight. [10]As they were still staring into the sky while he was going, suddenly two men [a]in white clothing stood near them [11]and said, "Men of Galilee, why do you stand here looking up into the sky? This same Jesus who has been taken up from you into heaven[1] [a]will come back in the same way you saw him go into heaven."

A Replacement for Judas Is Chosen

[12a]Then they returned to Jerusalem from the mountain called the Mount of Olives (which is near Jerusalem, a Sabbath day's journey away). [13]When they had entered Jerusalem, they went [a]to the upstairs room where they were staying. [b]Peter and John, and James, and Andrew, Philip and Thomas, Bartholomew and Matthew, James son of Alphaeus and [c]Simon the Zealot, and [d]Judas son of James were there. [14]All [a]these

---

1:1 [a] Luke 1:3   1:2 [a] Mark 16:19; Acts 1:9, 11, 22   [b] Matt 28:19; Mark 16:15; John 20:21; Acts 10:42   1:3 [a] Matt 28:17; Mark 16:12, 14; Luke 24:34, 36; John 20:19, 26; 21:1, 14; 1 Cor 15:5–7   1:4 [a] Luke 24:49   [b] [John 14:16–17, 26; 15:26]; Acts 2:33   [1] Grk. *for the promise of the Father*; i.e., the promised gift of the Holy Spirit.   1:5 [a] Matt 3:11; Mark 1:8; Luke 3:16; John 1:33; Acts 11:16   [b] [Joel 2:28]   1:7 [a] 1 Thess 5:1   [b] Matt 24:36; Mark 13:32   1:8 [a] [Acts 2:1, 4]   [b] Luke 24:49   [c] Luke 24:48; John 15:27   [d] Acts 8:1, 5, 14   [e] Matt 28:19; Mark 16:15; Rom 10:18; Col 1:23; [Rev 14:6]   1:9 [a] Luke 24:50–51   [b] Ps 68:18; 110:1; Mark 16:19; Luke 23:43; John 20:17; Acts 1:2; [Heb 4:14; 9:24; 1 Pet 3:22]   1:10 [a] Matt 28:3; Mark 16:5; Luke 24:4; John 20:12; Acts 10:3, 30   1:11 [a] Dan 7:13; Mark 13:26; Luke 21:27; [John 14:3]; 2 Thess 1:10; Rev 1:7   [1] Sev. wss omit *into heaven*.   1:12 [a] Luke 24:52   1:13 [a] Mark 14:15; Luke 22:12; Acts 9:37, 39; 20:8   [b] Matt 10:2–4   [c] Luke 6:15   [d] Jude 1   1:14 [a] Acts 2:1, 46

continued [b]together in prayer with one mind, together with the women, along with Mary the mother of Jesus, and [c]his brothers. [15]In those days Peter stood up among the believers (a gathering [a]of about 120 people) and said, [16]"Brothers, the scripture had to be fulfilled that the Holy Spirit foretold through David concerning Judas—[a]who became the guide for those who arrested Jesus—[17]for [a]he was counted as one of us and received a share in [b]this ministry." [18]([a]Now this man Judas acquired a field with [b]the reward of his unjust deed, and falling headfirst he burst open in the middle and all his intestines gushed out. [19]This became known to all who lived in Jerusalem, so that in their own language they called that field *Hakeldama*, that is, "Field of Blood.") [20]"For it is written in the book of Psalms, '[a]*Let his house become deserted,*[1] *and* [b]*let there be no one to live in it,*'[2] and '*Let another take his position of responsibility.*'[3] [21]Thus one of the men who have accompanied us during all the time the Lord Jesus associated with us, [22]beginning from his baptism by John until [a]the day he was taken up from us—one of these must [b]become a witness of his resurrection together with us." [23]So they[1] proposed two candidates: Joseph called [a]Barsabbas (also called Justus) and Matthias. [24]Then they prayed, "Lord, you know the hearts of all. Show us which one of these two you have chosen [25]to assume the task of this service and apostleship from which Judas turned aside [a]to go to his own place." [26]Then they cast lots for them, and the one chosen was Matthias; so he was counted with the eleven apostles.

The Holy Spirit and the Day of Pentecost

2 Now when [a]the day of Pentecost had come, [b]they were all together in one place. [2]Suddenly a sound like a violent wind blowing came from heaven and filled the entire house where they were [a]sitting. [3]And tongues spreading out like a fire[1] appeared to them and came to rest on each one of them. [4]All of them were filled with [a]the Holy Spirit, and they began [b]to speak in other languages[1] as the Spirit enabled them.[2]

[5]Now there were [a]devout Jews[1] from every nation under heaven residing in Jerusalem. [6]When this sound occurred, a [a]crowd gathered and was in confusion[1] because each one heard them speaking in his own language. [7]Completely baffled, they said,[1] "Aren't all these who are speaking [a]Galileans? [8]And how is it that each one of us hears them in our own native language? [9]Parthians, Medes, Elamites, and residents of Mesopotamia, Judea and [a]Cappadocia, Pontus and the province of Asia, [10]Phrygia and Pamphylia, Egypt and the parts of Libya near Cyrene, and visitors from Rome, [11]both Jews and proselytes, Cretans and Arabs—we hear them speaking in our own languages about the great deeds God has done!" [12]All were astounded and greatly confused, saying to one another, "What does this mean?" [13]But others jeered at the speakers, saying, "They are drunk on new wine!"

Peter's Address on the Day of Pentecost

[14]But Peter stood up with the eleven, raised his voice, and addressed them: "You men of Judea and all you who live in Jerusalem, know this and listen carefully to what I say. [15]In spite of what you think, these men are not drunk, [a]for it is only nine o'clock in the morning. [16]But this is what was spoken about through the prophet Joel:

[17]   '[a]*And* in the last days *it will be,*' *God says,*
    '*that I will pour out my Spirit on all people,*
    and your sons and [b]*your daughters will prophesy,*
    and your young men will see visions,
    and your old men will dream dreams.
[18]   *Even on my servants, both men* [a]*and women,*
    I will pour out my Spirit in those days, and they will prophesy.

1:14 [ab] Luke 23:49, 55   [c] Matt 13:55   **1:15** [a] Luke 22:32; Rev 3:4   **1:16** [a] Matt 26:47; Mark 14:43; Luke 22:47; John 18:3   **1:17** [a] Matt 10:4   [b] Acts 1:25   **1:18** [a] Matt 27:3–10   [b] Matt 18:7; 26:14–15, 24; Mark 14:21; Luke 22:22; John 17:12   **1:20** [a] Ps 69:25   [b] Ps 109:8   [1] Or *uninhabited, empty.*   [2] Ps 69:25   [3] Ps 109:8   **1:22** [a] Acts 1:9   [b] Acts 1:8; 2:32   **1:23** [a] Acts 15:22   [1] Some wss *he; i.e.,* Peter.   **1:25** [a] Acts 1:17   **2:1** [a] Lev 23:15; Deut 16:9; Acts 20:16; 1 Cor 16:8   [b] Acts 1:14   **2:2** [a] Acts 4:31   **2:3** [1] Or *And divided tongues as of fire.*   **2:4** [a] Matt 3:11; 5:6; 10:20; Luke 3:16; John 14:16; 16:7–15; Acts 1:5   [b] Mark 16:17; Acts 10:46; 19:6; [1 Cor 12:10, 28, 30; 13:1]   [1] The same Grk. word translated as the "tongues" of fire in v. 3.   [2] Grk. *just as the spirit gave them to utter.*   **2:5** [a] Luke 2:25; Acts 8:2   [1] Grk. *Jews, devout men.*   **2:6** [a] Acts 4:32   [1] Or *was bewildered.*   **2:7** [a] Matt 26:73; Acts 1:11   [1] Grk. *They were astounded and amazed, saying.*   **2:9** [a] 1 Pet 1:1   **2:15** [a] 1 Thess 5:7   **2:17** [a] Isa 44:3; Ezek 11:19; Joel 2:28–32; [Zech 12:10; John 7:38]   [b] Acts 21:9   **2:18** [a] Acts 21:4, 9; 1 Cor 12:10

19 *And [a]I will perform wonders in the sky*
    above
    and miraculous signs on the earth
    below,
    blood and fire and clouds of smoke.
20 *The sun will be changed to darkness*
    and [a]the moon to blood
    before the great and glorious day of
    the Lord comes.
21 *And then everyone [a]who calls on the*
    name of the Lord will be saved.[1]

22 "Men of Israel, listen to these words: Jesus the Nazarene, a man clearly attested to you [a]by God with powerful deeds, wonders, and miraculous signs that God performed among you through him, just as you yourselves know—23 this man, who was handed over by the predetermined plan and foreknowledge of God, [a]you executed by nailing him to a cross at the hands of Gentiles.[1] 24 But God raised [a]him up, having released him from the pains of death because it was not possible for him to be held in its power. 25 For [a]David says about him,

'*I saw the Lord always in front of me,*
    for he is at my right hand so that I will
    not be shaken.
26 *Therefore my heart was glad and my*
    tongue rejoiced;
    my body also will live in hope,
27 *because you will not leave my soul in*
    Hades,[1]
    nor permit your Holy One to
    experience [a]decay.
28 *You have made known to me the paths*
    of life;
    you will make me full of joy with your
    presence.[1]

29 "Brothers, I can speak confidently to you [a]about our forefather David, that he

both died and was buried, and his tomb is with us to this day. 30 So then, because he was a prophet [a]and knew that God *had sworn to him with an oath to seat one of his descendants on his throne,*[1] 31 David by foreseeing this spoke about the resurrection of the Christ,[1] [a]that *he was neither abandoned to Hades,*[2,3] nor did his body *experience decay.*[4] 32 [a]This Jesus God raised up, and we are all witnesses [b]of it. 33 So [a]then, exalted to the right hand of God, and [b]having received the promise of the Holy Spirit from the Father, he has poured [c]out what you both see and hear. 34 For David did not ascend into heaven, but [a]he himself says,

'*The Lord said to my lord,*
    "*Sit at my right hand*
35   *until I make your enemies a footstool*
    for your feet."'[1]

36 Therefore let all the house of Israel know beyond a doubt[1] that God has made this Jesus whom you crucified both Lord and Christ."[2]

The Response to Peter's Address

37 Now when [a]they heard this, they were acutely distressed and said to Peter and the rest of the apostles, "What should we do, brothers?" 38 Peter said to them, "[a]Repent, and each one of you be baptized[1] in the name of Jesus Christ for[2] the forgiveness of your sins, and you will receive the gift of the Holy Spirit.[3] 39 For the promise is for you and your children, and for all who are far away, as many as the Lord our God will call [a]to himself." 40 With many other words he testified and exhorted them saying, "Save yourselves from this perverse generation!" 41 So those who accepted his message were baptized, and that day about 3,000 people were added.

2:19 [a]Joel 2:30   2:20 [a]Isa 13:10; Ezek 32:7; Matt 24:29; Mark 13:24–25; Luke 21:25; Rev 6:12   2:21 [a]Rom 10:13   [1]Joel 2:28–32   2:22 [a]Isa 50:5; John 3:2; 5:6; Acts 10:38   2:23 [a]Acts 5:30   [1]Grk. *at the hands of lawless men;* i.e., non-Jews who live outside the Mosaic law, specifically, a reference to the Roman soldiers who carried out Jesus' crucifixion. 2:24 [a][Rom 8:11; 1 Cor 6:14; 2 Cor 4:14; Eph 1:20; Col 2:12]; 1 Thess 1:10; Heb 13:20   2:25 [a]Ps 16:8–11   2:27 [a]Acts 13:30–37   [1]Or *will not abandon my soul to Hades;* the place of the dead.   2:28 [1]Ps 16:8–11   2:29 [a]Acts 13:36   2:30 [a]2 Sam 7:12; Ps 132:11; Luke 1:32; Rom 1:3; 2 Tim 2:8   [1][2 Sam 7:12–13; Ps 132:11]   2:31 [a]Ps 16:10; Isa 50:8; 53:10   [1]Or *Messiah;* both "Christ" (Grk.) and "Messiah" (Heb., Aram.) mean "one who has been anointed."   [2][Ps 16:10]   [3]Or *abandoned in the world of the dead.*   [4][Ps 16:10]   2:32 [a]Acts 2:24   [b]Acts 1:8; 3:15   2:33 [a]Ps 110:1; Mark 16:19; [Heb 10:12]   [b]Luke 24:49; [John 14:26]   [c]Matt 3:11; 5:6; Luke 3:16; 22:69; John 14:16; 16:7–15; Acts 2:1–11, 17; 10:45; Eph 4:8   2:34 [a]Ps 68:18; 110:1; Matt 22:44; Luke 23:43; John 20:17; 1 Cor 15:25; Eph 1:20; Heb 1:13   2:35 [1]Ps 110:1   2:36 [1]Or *know for certain;* an emphatic Grk. construction.   [2]Or *Messiah;* both "Christ" (Grk.) and "Messiah" (Heb., Aram.) mean "one who has been anointed."   2:37 [a][Zech 12:10]; Luke 3:10, 12, 14; John 16:8   2:38 [a]Luke 24:47   [1]Or *let each of you be baptized.*   [2]The meaning of the prepositional phrase translated as "for" is much debated, with some believing it is causal, while others explain it differently. For a discussion on this problematic phrase, see *NET Bible, Full Notes Edition.*   [3]The gift is the Holy Spirit.   2:39 [a]Joel 2:28, 32

The Fellowship of the Early Believers

[42]They were devoting themselves to the apostles' teaching [a]and to fellowship, to the breaking of bread and to prayer. [43]Reverential awe came over everyone, and [a]many wonders and miraculous signs came about by the apostles. [44]All who believed were together and [a]held everything in common, [45]and they began selling their property and possessions and [a]distributing the proceeds to everyone, as anyone had need. [46a]Every day they continued to gather together by common consent [b]in the temple courts, [c]breaking bread from house to house, sharing their food with glad and humble hearts, [47]praising God and having [a]the good will of all the people. And the Lord was adding to their number every day those who were being saved.

Peter and John Heal a Lame Man at the Temple

3 Now Peter and John were going up [a]to [b]the temple at the time for prayer, at three o'clock in the afternoon. [2]And [a]a man lame[1] from birth was being carried up, who was placed at the temple gate called "the Beautiful Gate" every day so he could beg for money from those going [b]into the temple courts. [3]When he saw Peter and John about to go into the temple courts, he asked them for money. [4]Peter looked directly at him (as did John) and said, "Look at us!" [5]So the lame man paid attention to them, expecting to receive something from them. [6]But Peter said, "I have no silver or gold, but what I do have I give you. [a]In the name of Jesus Christ the Nazarene, stand up and[1] walk!" [7]Then Peter took hold of him by the right hand and raised him up, and at once the man's feet and ankles were made strong. [8]He jumped up, stood and began walking around, and he entered the temple courts with them, walking and [a]leaping and praising God. [9]All the people saw him walking [a]and praising God, [10]and they recognized him as the man who used to [a]sit and ask for donations at the Beautiful Gate of the temple, and they were filled with astonishment and amazement at what had happened to him.

Peter Addresses the Crowd

[11]While the man was hanging on to Peter and John, all the people, completely astounded, ran together to them in the covered walkway called Solomon's Portico. [12]When Peter saw this, he declared to the people, "Men of Israel,[1] why are you amazed at this? Why do you stare at us as if we had made this man walk by our own power or piety? [13]The God of Abraham, Isaac, and Jacob,[1] [a]the God of our forefathers, has [b]glorified his servant Jesus, whom you handed [c]over and [d]rejected in the presence of Pilate after he had decided to release him. [14]But you rejected [a]the Holy [b]and Righteous One and [c]asked that a man who was a murderer be released to you. [15]You killed the Originator[1] of life, [a]whom God raised from the dead. To this fact we are witnesses! [16a]And on the basis of faith in Jesus' name, his very name has made this man—whom you see and know—strong. The faith that is through Jesus has given him this complete health in the presence of you all. [17]And now, brothers, I know [a]you acted in ignorance, as your rulers did too. [18]But the things God foretold long ago [a]through all the prophets—that his Christ would suffer—he has fulfilled in this way. [19]Therefore [a]repent and turn back so that your sins may be wiped out, [20]so that times of refreshing may come from the presence of the Lord, and so that he may send the Messiah appointed[1] for you—that is, Jesus. [21]This [a]one heaven must receive until the time all things are [b]restored,[1] [c]which God declared from times long ago through his holy prophets. [22]Moses said, '[a]*The Lord your God will raise up for you a prophet like me from among your brothers. You must obey him in everything he tells you.*[1] [23]*Every person who does not obey that prophet will be destroyed and thus removed from the people.*'[1]

2:42 [a]Acts 1:14; Rom 12:12; Eph 6:18; Col 4:2; Heb 10:25   2:43 [a]Mark 16:17; Acts 2:22   2:44 [a]Acts 4:32, 34, 37; 5:2   2:45 [a]Isa 58:7   2:46 [a]Acts 1:14   [b]Luke 24:53   [c]Luke 24:30; Acts 2:42; 20:7; [1 Cor 10:16]   2:47 [a]Acts 5:14   3:1 [a]Acts 2:46   [b]Ps 55:17; Matt 27:45; Acts 10:30   3:2 [a]Acts 14:8   [b]John 9:8; Acts 3:10   [1]Or *crippled.*   3:6 [a]Acts 4:10   [1]Some mss omit *stand up and.*   3:8 [a]Isa 35:6   3:9 [a]Acts 4:16, 21   3:10 [a]John 9:8; Acts 3:2 present.   3:13 [a]John 5:30   [b]Isa 49:3; John 7:39; 12:23; 13:31   [c]Matt 27:2   [d]Matt 27:20; Mark 15:11; Luke 23:18; John 18:40; Acts 13:28   [1]‡ Some mss add *God* before "Isaac, and Jacob."   3:14 [a]Ps 16:10; Mark 1:24; Luke 1:35   [b]Acts 7:52; 2 Cor 5:21   [c]John 18:40   3:15 [a]Acts 2:24   [1]Or *Founder, founding Leader.*   3:16 [a]Matt 9:22; Acts 4:10; 14:9   3:17 [a]Luke 23:34; John 16:3; [Acts 13:27; 17:30]; 1 Cor 2:8; 1 Tim 1:13   3:18 [a]Ps 22; Isa 50:6; 53:5; Dan 9:26; Hos 6:1; Zech 13:6; 1 Pet 1:10   3:19 [a][Acts 2:38; 26:20]   3:20 [1]Or *designated in advance.*   3:21 [a]Acts 1:11   [b]Matt 17:11; [Rom 8:21]   [c]Luke 1:70   [1]Grk. *until the times of the restoration of all things.*   3:22 [a]Deut 18:15, 18, 19; Acts 7:37   [1]Deut 18:15   3:23 [1]Lev 23:29; Deut 18:19

[24]And [a]all the prophets, from Samuel and those who followed him, have spoken about and announced these days. [25][a]You are the sons of the prophets and of the covenant that God made with your ancestors, saying to Abraham, '[b]*And in your descendants*[1] *all the nations*[2] *of the earth will be blessed.*'[3] [26]God raised up his servant and sent him [a]first to you, to bless you [b]by turning each one of you from your iniquities."

The Arrest and Trial of Peter and John

4 While Peter and John were speaking to the people, the priests and the commander of the temple guard and the [a]Sadducees came up[1] to them, [2]angry[1] because they were teaching the people and announcing in Jesus the resurrection of the dead. [3]So they seized them and put them in jail until the next day (for it was already evening). [4]But many of those who had listened to the message believed, and the number of the men came to about 5,000.

[5]On the next day, their rulers, elders, and experts in the law came together in Jerusalem. [6][a]Annas the high priest was there, and Caiaphas, John, Alexander, and others who were members of the high priest's family. [7]After making Peter and John stand in their midst, they began to inquire, "[a]By what power or by what name did you do this?" [8][a]Then Peter, filled with the Holy Spirit, replied, "Rulers of the people and elders,[1] [9]if we are being examined today for a good deed done to a sick man—by what means this man was healed—[10]let it be known to all of you and to all the people of Israel [a]that by the name of Jesus Christ[1] the Nazarene [b]whom you crucified, whom God raised from the dead, this man stands before you healthy. [11]This Jesus is *the* [a]*stone that was rejected by* you, *the builders, that has become the cornerstone.*[1] [12]And there is salvation in [a]no one else, for there is no other name under heaven given among people by which we must be saved."

[13]When they saw the boldness of Peter [a]and John, and discovered that they were uneducated and ordinary men, they were amazed and recognized these men had been with Jesus. [14]And because they saw the man who had been healed [a]standing with them, they had nothing to say against this. [15]But when they had ordered them to go outside the council,[1] they began to confer with one another, [16]saying, "[a]What should we do with these men? For it is [b]plain to all who live in Jerusalem that a notable miraculous sign has come about through them, and we cannot deny it. [17]But to keep this matter from spreading any further among the people, let us warn them to speak no more to anyone in this name." [18][a]And they called them in and ordered them not to speak or teach at all in the name of Jesus. [19]But Peter and John replied, "[a]Whether it is right before God to obey you rather than God, you decide, [20][a]for it is impossible[1] for us not to speak about what [b]we have seen and heard." [21]After threatening them further, they released them, for they could not find how to punish them on account [a]of the people, because they were all [b]praising God for [c]what had happened. [22]For the man, on whom this miraculous sign of healing had been performed, was over forty years old.

The Followers of Jesus Pray for Boldness

[23]When [a]they were released, Peter and John went to their fellow believers and reported everything the high priests and the elders had said to them. [24]When they heard this, they raised their voices to God with one mind and said, "Master of all, [a]you who made the heaven, the earth, the sea, and everything that is in them, [25]who said by the Holy Spirit through your servant David our forefather,

'[a]*Why do the nations*[1] *rage,*
and the peoples plot foolish things?

3:24 [a] 2 Sam 7:12; Luke 24:25   3:25 [a] Acts 2:39; [Rom 9:4, 8; Gal 3:26]   [b] Gen 12:3; 18:18; 22:18; 26:4; 28:14   [1]Or *in your offspring*; Grk. *in your seed.*   [2]Or *families.*   [3] Gen 22:18   3:26 [a] Matt 15:24; John 4:22; Acts 13:46; [Rom 1:16; 2:9]   [b] Isa 42:1; Matt 1:21   4:1 [a] Matt 22:23   [1]Or *approached*; often denotes a sudden appearing.   4:2 [1]Or *greatly annoyed, provoked.*
4:6 [a] Luke 3:2; John 11:49; 18:13   4:7 [a] Exod 2:14; Matt 21:23; Acts 7:27   4:8 [a] Luke 12:11–12   [1]Some MSS add *of Israel.*
4:10 [a] Acts 2:22; 3:6, 16   [b] Acts 2:24   [1]Or *Messiah*; both "Christ" (Grk.) and "Messiah" (Heb., Aram.) mean "one who has been anointed."   4:11 [a] Ps 118:22; Isa 28:16; Matt 21:42   [1]Ps 118:22   4:12 [a] Isa 42:1, 6, 7; 53:11; Dan 9:24; [Matt 1:21; John 14:6; Acts 10:43; 1 Tim 2:5–6]   4:13 [a] Matt 11:25; [1 Cor 1:27]   4:14 [a] Acts 3:11   4:15 [1]Or *the Sanhedrin*; the highest legal, legislative, and judicial body among the Jews.   4:16 [a] John 11:47   [b] Acts 3:7–10   4:18 [a] Acts 5:28, 40   4:19 [a] Acts 5:29
4:20 [a] Acts 1:8; 2:32   [b] Acts 22:15; [1 John 1:1, 3]   [1]Grk. *for we are not able not to speak*; an emphatic Grk. construction.   4:21 [a] Matt 21:26; Luke 20:6, 19; 22:2; Acts 5:26   [b] Matt 15:31   [c] Acts 3:7–8   4:23 [a] Acts 2:44–46; 12:12
4:24 [a] Exod 20:11; 2 Kgs 19:15; Neh 9:6; Ps 146:6   4:25 [a] Ps 2:1–2   [1]Or *Gentiles.*

[26] ***The kings of the earth stood together,
and the rulers assembled together,
against the Lord and against his
Christ.***[1]

[27]"For [a]indeed both Herod and Pontius Pilate, with the Gentiles and the people of Israel, assembled together in this city against [b]your holy servant Jesus, [c]whom you anointed, [28a]to do as much as your power and your plan had decided beforehand[1] would happen. [29]And now, Lord, pay attention to their threats, and grant to your servants to speak your message with great courage, [30]while you extend your hand to heal, [a]and to bring about miraculous signs and wonders [b]through the name of [c]your holy servant Jesus." [31]When [a]they had prayed, the place where they were assembled together was shaken, [b]and they were all filled with the Holy Spirit and began to speak the word of God courageously.

Conditions among the Early Believers

[32]The group of those who believed [a]were of one heart and mind, and [b]no one said that any of his possessions was his own, but everything was held in common. [33]With [a]great power the apostles were giving [b]testimony to the resurrection of the Lord Jesus, and [c]great grace was on them all. [34a]For there was no one needy among them because those who were owners of land or houses were selling them and bringing the proceeds from the sales [35a]and placing them at the apostles' feet. The proceeds were distributed to each, as anyone had need. [36]So Joseph, a Levite who was a native of Cyprus, called by the apostles Barnabas (which is translated "son of encouragement"), [37]sold a field that [a]belonged to him and brought the money and placed it at the apostles' feet.

The Judgment on Ananias and Sapphira

5 Now a man named Ananias, together with Sapphira his wife, sold a piece of property. [2]He kept back for himself part of the proceeds with his wife's knowledge; he brought only part of it and placed it at the apostles' feet. [3a]But Peter said, "Ananias, why has [b]Satan filled your heart to lie to the Holy Spirit and keep back for yourself part of the proceeds from the sale of the land? [4]Before it was sold, did it not belong to you? And when it was sold, was the money not at your disposal? How have you thought up this deed in your heart? You have not lied to people but to God!"

[5]When Ananias heard these words he [a]collapsed and died, and great fear gripped all who heard about it. [6]So the young men came, [a]wrapped him up, carried him out, and buried him. [7]After an interval of about three hours, his wife came in, but she did not know what had happened. [8]Peter said to her, "Tell me, were the two of you paid this amount for the land?" Sapphira said, "Yes, that much." [9]Peter then [a]told her, "Why have you agreed together to test the Spirit of the Lord? Look! The feet of those who have buried your husband are at the door, and they will carry you out!" [10]At once she collapsed at his feet and died. [a]So when the young men came in, they found her dead, and they carried her out and buried her beside her husband. [11]Great fear gripped the whole church [a]and all who heard about these things.

The Apostles Perform Miraculous Signs and Wonders

[12]Now many miraculous signs and wonders came about among the people [a]through the [b]hands of the apostles. By common consent[1] they were all meeting together in Solomon's Portico. [13a]None of the rest dared to join them,[1] [b]but the people held them in high honor. [14]More and more believers in the Lord were added to their number, crowds of both men and women. [15]Thus they even carried the sick out into the streets and put them on cots and pallets, so [a]that when Peter came by at least his shadow would fall on some of them. [16]A crowd of people from the towns around Jerusalem also came together, bringing the [a]sick and those troubled by unclean spirits. They were all being healed.

4:26 [1]Ps 2:1–2   **4:27** [a]Matt 26:3; Luke 22:2; 23:1, 8   [b][Luke 1:35]   [c]Luke 4:18; John 10:36   **4:28** [a]Acts 2:23; 3:18   [1]Or *had predestined.*   **4:30** [a]Acts 2:43; 5:12   [b]Acts 3:6, 16   [c]Acts 4:27   **4:31** [a]Matt 5:6; Acts 2:2, 4; 16:26   [b]Acts 4:29   **4:32** [a]Acts 5:12; Rom 15:5–6; 2 Cor 13:11; Phil 1:27; 2:2; 1 Pet 3:8   [b]Acts 2:44   **4:33** [a][Acts 1:8]   [b]Acts 1:22   [c]Rom 6:15   **4:34** [a][Matt 19:21]; Acts 2:45   **4:35** [a]Acts 4:37; 5:2   **4:37** [a]Acts 4:34–35; 5:1–2   **5:3** [a]Num 30:2; Deut 23:21; Eccl 5:4   [b]Matt 4:10; Luke 22:3; John 13:2, 27   **5:5** [a]Ezek 11:13; Acts 5:10–11   **5:6** [a]John 19:40   **5:9** [a]Matt 4:7; Acts 5:3–4   **5:10** [a]Ezek 11:13; Acts 5:5   **5:11** [a]Acts 2:43; 5:5; 19:17   **5:12** [a]Acts 2:43; 4:30; 6:8; 14:3; 15:12; [Rom 15:19]; 2 Cor 12:12; Heb 2:4   [b]Acts 3:11; 4:32   [1]Or *With one mind.*   **5:13** [a]John 9:22   [b]Acts 2:47; 4:21   [1]Or *to associate with them.*   **5:15** [a]Matt 9:21; 14:36; Acts 19:12   **5:16** [a]Mark 16:17–18; [John 14:12]

Further Trouble for the Apostles

[17] Now [a]the high priest rose up, and all those with him (that is, the religious party of the Sadducees), and they were filled with jealousy. [18] They laid hands on the apostles [a]and put them in a public jail. [19] But during the night [a]an angel of the Lord[1] opened the doors of the prison, led them out, and said, [20] "Go and stand in the temple courts and proclaim to the people [a]all the words of this life." [21] When they heard this, they entered the temple courts at daybreak and began teaching.

[a]Now when the high priest and those who were with him arrived, they summoned the Sanhedrin—that is, the whole high council of the Israelites—and sent to the jail to have the apostles brought before them. [22] But the officers[1] who came for them did not find them in the prison, so they returned and reported, [23] "We found the jail locked securely and the guards standing at the doors, but when we opened them, we found no one inside." [24] Now when [a]the commander of the temple guard and the chief priests heard this report, they were greatly puzzled concerning it, wondering what this could be. [25] But someone came and reported to them, "Look! The men you put in prison are standing in the temple courts and teaching the people!" [26] Then the commander of the temple guard went with the officers and brought the apostles without the use of force ([a]for they were afraid of being stoned by the people).

[27] When they had brought them, they stood them before the council, and the high priest questioned them, [28] saying, "We gave[1] you strict orders[2] not to teach in this name. Look, you have filled Jerusalem with your teaching, [a]and you intend to bring this man's [b]blood on us!" [29] But Peter and the apostles replied, "[a]We must obey God rather than people. [30] The God of our [a]forefathers raised up Jesus, whom you seized and killed by [b]hanging him on a tree.[1] [31] God exalted [a]him[1] to his right hand as [b]Leader and [c]Savior, [d]to give repentance to Israel and forgiveness of sins. [32] And [a]we are witnesses of these events, and so is the Holy Spirit [b]whom God has given to those who obey him."

[33] Now when they heard this, they became [a]furious and wanted to execute them. [34] But a Pharisee whose name was [a]Gamaliel, a teacher of the law who was respected by all the people, stood up in the council and ordered the men to be put outside for a short time. [35] Then he said to the council, "Men of Israel, pay close attention to what you are about to do to these men. [36] For sometime ago Theudas rose up, claiming to be somebody, and about 400 men joined him. He was killed, and all who followed him were dispersed and nothing came of it. [37] After him Judas the Galilean arose in the days of the census and incited people to follow him in revolt. He too was killed, and all who followed him were scattered. [38] So in this case I say to you, stay away from these men and leave them alone because if this plan or this undertaking originates with people, it will come to nothing, [39][a]but if it is from God, you will not be able [b]to stop them, or you may even be found fighting against God." He convinced them, [40] and they [a]summoned the apostles [b]and had them beaten. Then they ordered them not to speak in the name of Jesus and released them. [41] So they left the council [a]rejoicing because they had been considered worthy to suffer dishonor for the sake of the name. [42] And every day both [a]in [b]the temple courts and from house to house, they did not stop teaching and proclaiming the good news that Jesus was the Christ.[1]

The Appointment of the First Seven Deacons

6 Now in those days, [a]when the disciples were growing in number, a complaint arose on the part of the Greek-speaking

5:17 [a] Matt 3:7; Acts 4:1–2, 6   **5:18** [a] Luke 21:12; Acts 4:3; 16:37   **5:19** [a] Matt 1:20, 24; 2:13, 19; 28:2; Luke 1:11; 2:9; Acts 12:7; 16:26   [1] Or *the angel of the Lord.*   **5:20** [a] [John 6:63, 68; 17:3; 1 John 5:11]   **5:21** [a] Acts 4:5–6   **5:22** [1] Used for many types of servants: attendants to a king, officers of the Sanhedrin, assistants to magistrates, and Jewish guards in the temple.   **5:24** [a] Luke 22:4; Acts 4:1; 5:26   **5:26** [a] Matt 21:26   **5:28** [a] Acts 2:23, 36   [b] Matt 23:35   [1] ‡ Maj. MSS *Did we not give you . . . ?*   [2] Grk. *We commanded you with a commandment*; an emphatic Semitic idiom.   **5:29** [a] Acts 4:19   **5:30** [a] Acts 3:13, 15   [b] Acts 10:39; 13:29; [Gal 3:13; 1 Pet 2:24]   [1] An idiom for crucifixion.   **5:31** [a] Mark 16:19; [Acts 2:33, 36; Phil 2:9–11]   [b] Acts 3:15; Rev 1:5   [c] Matt 1:21   [d] Luke 24:47; [Eph 1:7; Col 1:14]   [1] Grk. *This one God exalted*; an emphatic Grk. construction.   **5:32** [a] John 15:26–27; Acts 15:28; Rom 8:16; Heb 2:4   [b] Acts 2:4; 10:44   **5:33** [a] Acts 2:37; 7:54   **5:34** [a] Acts 22:3   **5:39** [a] Luke 21:15; 1 Cor 1:25   [b] Acts 7:51; 9:5   **5:40** [a] Acts 4:18   [b] Matt 10:17; Mark 13:9; Acts 16:22–23; 21:32; 2 Cor 11:25   **5:41** [a] Matt 5:10–12; Rom 5:3; 2 Cor 12:10; Heb 10:34; [Jas 1:2; 1 Pet 4:13–16]   **5:42** [a] Acts 2:46   [b] Acts 4:20, 29   [1] Or *Messiah*; both "Christ" (Grk.) and "Messiah" (Heb., Aram.) mean "one who has been anointed."   **6:1** [a] Acts 2:41; 4:4

[b]Jews[1] against the native Hebraic Jews because their widows were being overlooked [c]in the daily distribution of food. [2]So the twelve called the whole group of the disciples together and said, "[a]It is not right for us to neglect the word of God to wait on tables. [3]But carefully [a]select from among you, brothers, seven men who are well-attested, full of the Spirit and of wisdom, whom we may put in charge of this necessary [b]task. [4]But we [a]will devote ourselves to prayer and to the ministry of the word." [5]The [a]proposal pleased the entire group, so they chose Stephen, a man full of faith and of the Holy Spirit, with [b]Philip, Prochorus, Nicanor, Timon, Parmenas, and [c]Nicolas, a Gentile convert to Judaism[1] from Antioch. [6]They stood these men before [a]the apostles, who prayed and placed their hands on them. [7]The word of God continued to spread, [a]the number [b]of disciples in Jerusalem increased greatly, and a large group of priests became obedient to the faith.

Stephen Is Arrested

[8]Now Stephen, full of grace and power, was performing great [a]wonders and miraculous signs among the people. [9]But some men from the Synagogue of the Freedmen (as it was called),[1] both Cyrenians and Alexandrians, as well as some from Cilicia and the province of Asia, stood up and argued with Stephen. [10]Yet [a]they were not able to resist the wisdom and the Spirit with which he spoke. [11a]Then they secretly instigated some men to say, "We have heard this man speaking blasphemous words against Moses and God." [12]They incited the people, the elders, and the experts in the law; then they approached Stephen, seized him, and brought him before the council. [13]They brought forward false witnesses who said, "This man does not stop saying things against this holy place and the law. [14a]For we have heard him saying that Jesus the Nazarene will destroy this place and change the customs that Moses handed down to us." [15]All who were sitting in the council looked intently at Stephen and saw his face was like the face of an angel.

Stephen's Defense before the Council

[7] Then the high priest said, "Are these things true?" [2]So he replied, "[a]Brothers and fathers, listen to me. The [b]God of glory appeared to our forefather Abraham when he was in Mesopotamia, before he settled in [c]Haran, [3]and said to him, '*Go [a]out from your country and from your relatives, and come to the land I will show you.*'[1] [4]Then [a]he went out from the country of the Chaldeans and settled in Haran. After his father [b]died, God made him move to this country where you now live. [5]He did not give any of it to him for an [a]inheritance, not even a foot of ground, yet God promised *to give it to him as his possession, and to his descendants after him,*[1] even though Abraham as yet had no child. [6]But God spoke as follows: '*Your descendants will be foreigners in [a]a foreign country, whose citizens will [b]enslave them and mistreat them for 400 years. [7a]But I will [b]punish the nation they serve as slaves,*' said God, '[c]*and after these things they will come out of there*[1] and *worship*[2] *me in this place.*'[3] [8a]Then God gave Abraham the covenant of circumcision, and so he became the father of Isaac [b]and circumcised him when he was eight days old, [c]and Isaac became the father of [d]Jacob, and Jacob of the 12 patriarchs. [9a]The patriarchs, because they were jealous of Joseph, [b]sold him into Egypt. [c]But God was with him, [10a]and rescued him from all his troubles, and granted him favor and wisdom in the presence of Pharaoh, king of Egypt, who made him ruler over Egypt and over all his household. [11a]Then a famine occurred throughout Egypt and Canaan, causing great suffering, and our ancestors could not find food. [12a]So when Jacob heard that there was grain[1] in Egypt, he sent our ancestors there the first time. [13]On their [a]second

6:1[b] Acts 9:29; 11:20 [c] Acts 4:35; 11:29 [1] Grk. *the Hellenists*; Greek-speaking Jews who may have adopted some aspects of Grk. culture. 6:2[a] Exod 18:17 6:3[a] Deut 1:13; 1 Tim 3:7 [b] Phil 1:1; 1 Tim 3:8–13 6:4[a] Acts 2:42 6:5[a] Acts 6:3; 11:24 [b] Acts 8:5, 26; 21:8 [c] Rev 2:6, 15 [1] Or *a proselyte.* 6:6[a] Num 8:10; 27:18; Deut 34:9; [Mark 5:23; Acts 8:17; 9:17; 13:3; 19:6; 1 Tim 4:14; 2 Tim 1:6]; Heb 6:2 6:7[a] Acts 12:24; Col 1:6 [b] John 12:42 6:8[a] Acts 2:43; 5:12; 8:15; 14:3 6:9[1] Grk. *the so-called Synagogue of the Freedmen*; slaves who had gained their freedom, or their descendants. 6:10[a] Exod 4:12; Isa 54:17; Luke 21:15 6:11[a] 1 Kgs 21:10, 13; Matt 26:59–60 6:14[a] Acts 10:38; 25:8 7:2[a] Acts 22:1 [b] Ps 29:3; 1 Cor 2:8 [c] Gen 11:31–32 7:3[a] Gen 12:1 [1] Gen 12:1 7:4[a] Gen 11:31; 15:7; Heb 11:8–10 [b] Gen 11:32 7:5[a] Gen 12:7; 13:15; 15:3, 18; 17:8; 26:3 [1] [Gen 12:7; 13:15; 15:2, 18; 17:8; 24:7; 48:4] 7:6[a] Gen 15:13–14, 16; 47:11–12 [b] Exod 1:8–14; 12:40–41; Gal 3:17 7:7[a] Gen 15:14 [b] Exod 14:13–31 [c] Exod 3:12; Josh 3:1–17 [1] Gen 15:13–14 [2] Or *and serve*; with religious overtones. [3] [Exod 3:12] 7:8[a] Gen 17:9–14 [b] Gen 21:1–5 [c] Gen 25:21–26 [d] Gen 29:31–30:24; 35:18, 22–26 7:9[a] Gen 37:4, 11, 28; Ps 105:17 [b] Gen 37:28 [c] Gen 39:2, 21, 23 7:10[a] Gen 41:38–44 7:11[a] Gen 41:54; 42:5 7:12[a] Gen 42:1–2 [1] Or possibly *food.* 7:13[a] Gen 45:4, 16

visit Joseph made himself known to his brothers again, and Joseph's family became known to Pharaoh. [14a]So Joseph sent a message and invited his father Jacob and [b]all his relatives to come, seventy-five people in all. [15a]So Jacob went down to Egypt and died there, along [b]with our ancestors, [16]and their bones were later moved to Shechem and placed in [a]the tomb that Abraham had bought for a certain sum of money from [b]the sons of Hamor in Shechem.

[17]"But as [a]the time drew near for God to fulfill [b]the promise he had declared to Abraham, the people increased greatly in number in Egypt, [18]until *another king who did not know about*[1] *Joseph* [a]*ruled*[2] *over Egypt.*[3] [19]This was the one who exploited[1] our people and was cruel to our ancestors, [a]forcing them to abandon their infants so they would die. [20a]At that time Moses [b]was born, and he was beautiful to God. For three months he was brought up in his father's house, [21]and [a]when he had been abandoned, [b]Pharaoh's daughter adopted him and brought him up[1] as her own son. [22]So Moses was trained in all the wisdom of the Egyptians and was [a]powerful in his words and deeds. [23a]But when he was about forty years old, it entered his mind to visit his fellow countrymen the Israelites. [24]When he saw one of them being hurt unfairly, Moses came to his defense and avenged the person who was mistreated by striking down the Egyptian. [25]He thought his own people would understand that God was delivering them through him, but they did not understand. [26]The next day Moses saw two men fighting and tried to make peace between them, saying, 'Men, you are brothers; why are you hurting one another?' [27]But the man who was unfairly hurting his neighbor pushed[1] Moses aside, saying, '[a]*Who made you a ruler and judge over us?* [28]*You don't want to kill me the way you killed the Egyptian yesterday, do you?*'[1]

[29]When [a]the man said this, Moses fled and became a foreigner[1] in the land of Midian, where he became the [b]father of two sons. [30]"After forty years had passed, [a]*an angel appeared to him in the desert of Mount Sinai, in the flame of a burning bush.*'[1] [31]When Moses saw it, he was amazed at the sight, and when he approached to investigate, there came the voice of the Lord, [32]'[a]*I am the God of your forefathers, the God of Abraham, Isaac, and Jacob.*'[1] Moses began to tremble and did not dare to look more closely. [33]*But* [a]*the Lord said to him, 'Take the sandals off your feet, for the place where you are standing is holy ground.*'[1] [34]*I have certainly* [a]*seen the suffering of my people who are in Egypt and have heard their groaning, and I have come down to rescue them. Now come, I will* [b]*send you to Egypt.*'[1] [35]This same Moses they had rejected, saying, '[a]*Who made you a ruler and judge?*'[1] God sent as both ruler and deliverer[2] [b]through the hand of the angel who appeared to him in the bush. [36]This [a]man led them out, [b]performing wonders [c]and miraculous signs in the land of Egypt, at the Red Sea, [d]and in the wilderness for forty years. [37]This is [a]the Moses who said to the Israelites, '*God will raise up for you a prophet like me from among your brothers.*'[1] [38a]This is [b]the man who was in [c]the congregation in the wilderness with the angel who spoke to him at Mount Sinai, and with our ancestors, and he received living [d]oracles to give to you.[1] [39]Our ancestors were [a]unwilling to obey him, but pushed him aside and turned back to Egypt in their hearts, [40a]saying to Aaron, '*Make us gods who will go in front of us, for this Moses, who led us out of the land of Egypt—we do not know what has happened to him!*'[1] [41]At that time they made an idol in the form of a calf, brought a sacrifice to the idol, [a]and began [b]rejoicing in the works of their hands. [42]But [a]God turned away from [b]them and gave them over to worship the host of heaven, as it is written in the book

7:14 [a]Gen 45:9, 27 [b]Gen 46:26–27; Deut 10:22 7:15 [a]Gen 46:1–7 [b]Gen 49:33; Exod 1:6 7:16 [a]Gen 50:13; Exod 13:19; Josh 24:32 [b]Gen 23:16 7:17 [a]Gen 15:13; Exod 2:23–25; Acts 7:6–7 [b]Exod 1:7–9; Ps 105:24–25 7:18 [a]Exod 1:8 [1]Or simply *did not know.* [2]Grk. *arose; i.e., assumed power.* [3]Exod 1:8 7:19 [a]Exod 1:22 [1]Or *took advantage by clever words, persuaded by sweet talk.* 7:20 [a]Exod 2:1–2 [b]Heb 11:23 7:21 [a]Exod 2:3–4 [b]Exod 2:5–10 [1]Or *and reared him.* 7:22 [a]Luke 24:19 7:23 [a]Exod 2:11–12; Heb 11:24–26 7:27 [a]Exod 2:14; Luke 12:14; Acts 7:35 [1]Or *repudiated Moses, rejected Moses.* 7:28 [1]Exod 2:14 7:29 [a]Heb 11:27 [b]Exod 2:15, 21, 22; 4:20; 18:3 [1]Or *resident alien.* 7:30 [a]Exod 3:1–10; Isa 63:9 [1][Exod 3:2] 7:32 [a]Exod 3:6, 15; [Matt 22:32]; Heb 11:16 [1]Exod 3:6 7:33 [a]Exod 3:5, 7, 8, 10 [1]Exod 3:5 7:34 [a]Exod 2:24–25 [b]Ps 105:26 [1]Exod 3:7–8, 10 7:35 [a]Exod 2:14; Acts 7:27 [b]Exod 14:21 [1]Exod 2:14 [2]Or *liberator.* 7:36 [a]Exod 12:41; 33:1; Deut 6:21, 23; Heb 8:9 [b]Exod 7:8–9; Deut 6:22; Ps 105:27; John 4:48 [c]Exod 14:21 [d]Exod 16:1, 35; Num 14:33; Ps 95:8–10; Acts 7:42; 13:18; Heb 3:8 7:37 [a]Deut 18:15, 18, 19; Acts 3:22 [1]Deut 18:15 7:38 [a]Exod 19:3 [b]Isa 63:9; Gal 3:19; Heb 2:2 [c]Exod 21:1; Deut 5:27; John 1:17 [d]Rom 3:2; Heb 5:12; 1 Pet 4:11 [1]‡ Some mss *us.* 7:39 [a]Ps 95:8–11 7:40 [a]Exod 32:1, 23 [1]Exod 32:1, 23 7:41 [a]Exod 32:2–4; Deut 9:16; Ps 106:19 [b]Exod 32:6, 18, 19 7:42 [a]Ps 81:12; [2 Thess 2:11] [b]Deut 4:19; 2 Kgs 21:3

of the prophets: *'It was not to me that you offered slain animals and sacrifices forty years in the wilderness, was it, house of Israel?* [43] *But you took along the tabernacle of Moloch and the star of the[1] god Rephan, the* [a]*images you made to worship, but I will deport you beyond Babylon.'*[2] [44]Our [a]ancestors had the tabernacle of testimony in the wilderness, just as God who spoke to Moses ordered him to make it according to the design he had seen. [45]Our ancestors received possession of it and brought it in with Joshua when they dispossessed the nations [a]that God drove out before our ancestors, until the [b]time of David. [46a]He found favor with God and [b]asked that he could find a dwelling place for the house[1] of Jacob. [47a]But Solomon built a house for him. [48]Yet [a]the Most High does not live in houses made by human hands, as the prophet says,

[49] '[a]*Heaven is my throne,*
  and earth is the footstool for my feet.
  What kind of house will you build for
    me, says the Lord,
  or what is my resting place?
[50] *Did my hand not* [a]*make all these*
    things?'[1]

[51]"You [a]stubborn people, with [b]uncircumcised hearts and ears![1] You are always resisting the Holy Spirit, like your ancestors did! [52a]Which of [b]the prophets did your ancestors not persecute? They killed those who foretold long ago the coming of the Righteous One, whose betrayers and murderers you have now become! [53a]You received the law by decrees given by angels,[1] but you did not obey it."

Stephen Is Killed

[54a]When they heard these things, they became furious and ground their teeth[1] at him. [55]But Stephen, full of the Holy Spirit, looked intently toward heaven and saw the [a]glory of God, and Jesus standing at the right hand of God. [56]"Look!" he [a]said. "I see the heavens opened, and the [b]Son of Man standing at the right hand of God!" [57]But they covered their ears, shouting out with a loud voice, and rushed at him with one intent. [58]When [a]they had driven him out of the city, they began to stone him, and the witnesses laid their cloaks[1] at the feet of a young man named Saul. [59]They continued to stone Stephen while he prayed, "Lord Jesus, [a]receive my spirit!" [60]Then he fell to his knees and cried out with a loud voice, "[a]Lord, do not hold this sin against them!"

8 When he had said this, he died.[1]And Saul agreed completely with killing him.

Saul Begins to Persecute the Church

Now on that day a great[1] persecution began against [a]the church in Jerusalem, and all except the apostles were forced to scatter throughout the regions of Judea and Samaria. [2]Some devout men buried Stephen and [a]made loud lamentation over him.[1] [3]But Saul was trying to destroy[1] [a]the church; entering one house after another, he dragged off both men and women and put them in prison.

Philip Preaches in Samaria

[4]Now [a]those who had been forced to scatter went around proclaiming the good news of the word. [5a]Philip went down to the main city of Samaria and began proclaiming the Christ[1] to them. [6]The crowds were paying attention with one mind to what Philip said, as they heard and saw the miraculous signs he was performing. [7]For [a]unclean spirits, crying with loud shrieks, were coming out of many who were possessed, and many paralyzed and lame people were healed. [8]So there was great joy in that city.

[9]Now in that city was [a]a man named Simon, who had been practicing magic and [b]amazing the people of Samaria, claiming to be someone great. [10]All the people, from the least to the greatest, paid close

7:43 [a]2 Chr 36:11–21; Jer 25:9–12 [1]‡ Maj. mss *your.* [2]Amos 5:25–27 **7:44** [a]Exod 25:40; [Heb 8:5] **7:45** [a]Neh 9:24; Ps 44:2 [b]2 Sam 6:2–15 **7:46** [a]2 Sam 7:1–13; 1 Kgs 8:17 [b]1 Chr 22:7; Ps 132:4–5 [1]Some mss *God.* **7:47** [a]1 Kgs 6:1–38; 8:20–21; 2 Chr 3:1–17 **7:48** [a]1 Kgs 8:27; 2 Chr 2:6; Acts 17:24 **7:49** [a]Isa 66:1–2; Matt 5:34 **7:50** [a]Ps 102:25 [1]Isa 66:1–2 **7:51** [a]Exod 32:9; Isa 6:10 [b]Lev 26:41 [1]Or *You stubborn and obstinate people!* **7:52** [a]2 Chr 36:16; Matt 21:35; 23:35; 1 Thess 2:15 [b]Acts 3:14; 22:14; 1 John 2:1 **7:53** [a]Exod 20:1; Deut 33:2; Acts 7:38; Gal 3:19; Heb 2:2 [1]Trad. *as ordained by angels.* **7:54** [a]Acts 5:33 [1]Or *they gnashed their teeth*; a picture of violent rage. **7:55** [a][Exod 24:17] **7:56** [a]Matt 3:16 [b]Dan 7:13 **7:58** [a]Acts 22:20 [1]Or *outer garments.* **7:59** [a]Ps 31:5 **7:60** [a]Matt 5:44; Luke 23:34 [1]Lit. *sleep*; often a euphemism for the death of a believer. **8:1** [a]John 16:2; Acts 8:4; 11:19 [1]Or *severe.* **8:2** [a]Gen 23:2 [1]Or *mourned greatly for him.* **8:3** [a]Acts 7:58; 1 Cor 15:9; Gal 1:13; Phil 3:6; 1 Tim 1:13 [1]Or *began to harm* [the church] *severely.* **8:4** [a]Matt 10:23 **8:5** [a]Acts 6:5; 8:26, 30 [1]Or *Messiah*; both "Christ" (Grk.) and "Messiah" (Heb., Aram.) mean "one who has been anointed." **8:7** [a]Mark 16:17 **8:9** [a]Acts 8:11; 13:6 [b]Acts 5:36

attention to him, saying, "This man is the power of God that is called 'Great.'" [11]And they paid close attention to him because he had amazed them for a long time with his magic. [12]But when they believed Philip as he was proclaiming the good news [a]about the kingdom of God and the name of Jesus Christ,[1] they began to be baptized, both men and women. [13]Even Simon himself believed, and after he was baptized, he stayed close to Philip constantly, and when he saw the signs and great miracles that were occurring, he was amazed.

[14]Now when the [a]apostles in Jerusalem heard that Samaria had accepted the word of God, they sent Peter and John to them. [15]These two went down and prayed for them so [a]that they would receive the Holy Spirit. [16](For [a]the Spirit had not yet come upon any of [b]them, but they had only been baptized in the name of the Lord Jesus.) [17]Then Peter and John placed their hands on [a]the Samaritans, and they received the Holy Spirit.

[18]Now Simon, when he saw that the Spirit[1] was given through the laying on of the apostles' hands, offered them money, [19]saying, "Give me this power too, so that everyone I place my hands on may receive the Holy Spirit." [20]But Peter said to him, "May [a]your silver perish with you because you thought you could acquire God's gift with money! [21]You have no share or part in this matter because your [a]heart is not right before God! [22]Therefore repent of this wickedness of yours, and pray to the Lord that he may [a]perhaps forgive you for the intent of your heart. [23]For [a]I see that you are bitterly envious and in bondage to sin." [24]But Simon replied, "You [a]pray to the Lord for me so that nothing of what you have said may happen to me."

[25]So after Peter and John had solemnly testified and spoken the word of the Lord, they started back to Jerusalem, proclaiming the good news to many Samaritan villages as they went.

Philip and the Ethiopian Eunuch

[26]Then an angel of the Lord said to [a]Philip, "Get up and go south on the road that goes down from Jerusalem to Gaza." (This is a desert[1] road.) [27]So he got up [a]and went. There he met an Ethiopian eunuch, [b]a court official of Candace, queen of the Ethiopians, who was in charge of all her treasury. He[1] had come to Jerusalem to worship, [28]and was returning home, sitting in his chariot, reading the prophet Isaiah. [29]Then the Spirit said to Philip, "Go over and join this chariot." [30]So Philip ran up to it and heard the man reading the prophet Isaiah. He asked him, "Do you understand what you're reading?" [31]The man replied, "How in the world can I,[1] unless someone guides me?" So he invited Philip to come up and sit with him. [32]Now [a]the passage of scripture the man was reading was this:

> "*He was led like a sheep to slaughter,*
> *and like a lamb before its shearer is silent,*
> [b]*so he did not open his mouth.*
> [33] *In humiliation*[1] [a]*justice was taken*
>   [b]*from him.*
> *Who can describe his posterity?*
> *For his life was taken away*[2] *from the earth.*"[3]

[34]Then the eunuch said to Philip, "Please tell me, who is the prophet saying this about—himself or someone else?" [35]So Philip started speaking, [a]and beginning with this scripture proclaimed the good news about Jesus to him. [36]Now as they were going along the road, they came to some water, and the eunuch said, "Look, there is water! [a]What is to stop me[1] from being baptized?"[2] [38]So he ordered the chariot to stop, and both Philip and the eunuch went down into the water, and Philip baptized him. [39]Now when [a]they came up out of the water, the Spirit of the Lord snatched Philip away, and the eunuch did not see him any more, but went on his way rejoicing.

8:12 [a] Acts 1:3; 8:4   [1] Or *Messiah*; both "Christ" (Grk.) and "Messiah" (Heb., Aram.) mean "one who has been anointed."   **8:14** [a] Acts 5:12, 29, 40   **8:15** [a] Acts 2:38; 19:2   **8:16** [a] Matt 28:19; Acts 2:38   [b] Acts 10:48; 19:5   **8:17** [a] Acts 6:6; 19:6; Heb 6:2   **8:18** [1] Maj. wss *the Holy Spirit.*   **8:20** [a] 2 Kgs 5:16; Isa 55:1; Dan 5:17; [Matt 10:8]   **8:21** [a] Jer 17:9   **8:22** [a] Dan 4:27; 2 Tim 2:25   **8:23** [a] Heb 12:15   **8:24** [a] Gen 20:7, 17; Exod 8:8; Num 21:7; 1 Kgs 13:6; Job 42:8; Jas 5:16   **8:26** [a] Acts 6:5   [1] Or *wilderness.*   **8:27** [a] Ps 68:31; 87:4; Isa 56:3; Zeph 3:10   [b] 1 Kgs 8:41–42; John 12:20   [1] Grk. *who was over all her treasury, who.*   **8:31** [1] Grk. *How am I able, unless.*   **8:32** [a] Isa 53:7–8   [b] Matt 26:62–63; 27:12, 14; John 19:9   **8:33** [a] Luke 23:1–25   [b] Luke 23:33–46   [1] ‡ Maj. later MSS *his humiliation.*   [2] Grk. *is taken away.*   [3] Isa 53:7–8   **8:35** [a] Luke 24:27; Acts 17:2; 18:28; 28:23   **8:36** [a] Acts 10:47; 16:33   [1] Or *What prevents me*; a rhetorical question.   [2] A few later MSS add v. 37: *He said to him, "If you believe with your whole heart, you may." He replied, "I believe that Jesus Christ is the Son of God."*   **8:39** [a] 1 Kgs 18:12; 2 Kgs 2:16; Ezek 3:12, 14; 2 Cor 12:2

[40]Philip, however, found himself at Azotus, and as he passed through the area, he proclaimed the good news to all the towns until he came to [a]Caesarea.

The Conversion of Saul

9 Meanwhile [a]Saul, still breathing out threats to murder[1] the Lord's disciples, went to the high priest [2]and requested [a]letters from him to the synagogues in Damascus, so that if he found any who belonged to the Way, either men or women, he could bring them as prisoners to Jerusalem. [3][a]As he was going along, approaching Damascus, suddenly a light from heaven flashed around him. [4]He fell to the ground and heard a voice saying to him, "Saul, Saul, [a]why are you persecuting me?" [5]So he said, "Who are you, Lord?" He replied, "I am Jesus whom you are persecuting! [6]But stand up and enter the city, and you will be told what you must do." [7](Now [a]the men who were traveling with him stood there speechless[1] because they heard the voice but saw no one.) [8]So Saul got up from the ground, but although his eyes were open, he could see nothing. Leading him by the hand, his companions brought him into Damascus. [9]For three days he could not see, and he neither ate nor drank anything.

[10]Now there was a disciple in Damascus [a]named Ananias. The Lord said to him in a vision, "Ananias," and he replied, "Here I am, Lord." [11]Then the Lord told him, "Get up and go to the street called 'Straight,' and at Judas' house look for a man from Tarsus named Saul. For he is praying, [12]and he has seen in a vision[1] a man named Ananias come in and place his hands on him so that he may see again." [13]But Ananias replied, "Lord, I have heard from many people about this man, [a]how much harm he has done to your saints in Jerusalem, [14]and here he has authority from the chief priests to imprison all [a]who call on your name!" [15]But the Lord said to him, "Go, because this [a]man is my chosen instrument to carry my name before [b]Gentiles and [c]kings and the [d]people of Israel. [16]For [a]I will show him how much he must suffer for the sake of my [b]name." [17]So Ananias departed [a]and entered the house, [b]placed his hands on Saul and said, "Brother Saul, the Lord Jesus, who appeared to you on the road as you came here, has sent me so that you may see again and [c]be filled with the Holy Spirit." [18]Immediately something like scales[1] fell from his eyes, and he could see again. He got up and was baptized, [19]and after taking some food, his strength returned.

For several days [a]he was with the disciples in Damascus, [20]and immediately he began to proclaim Jesus in the synagogues, saying, "This man is the Son of God." [21]All who heard him were amazed and were saying, "[a]Is this not the man who in Jerusalem was ravaging those who call on this name, and who had come here to bring them as prisoners to the chief priests?" [22]But Saul became more and more capable, [a]and was causing consternation[1] among the Jews who lived in Damascus by proving that Jesus is the Christ.[2]

Saul's Escape from Damascus

[23]Now after some days had passed, [a]the Jews plotted together to kill him, [24][a]but Saul learned of their plot against him. They were also watching[1] the city gates day and night so that they could kill him. [25]But his disciples took him at night and [a]let him down through an opening in the wall by lowering him in a basket.

Saul Returns to Jerusalem

[26]When [a]he arrived in Jerusalem, he attempted to associate with the disciples, and they were all afraid of him because they did not believe that he was a disciple. [27][a]But Barnabas took Saul, brought him to the apostles, [b]and related to them how he had seen the Lord on the road, that the Lord had spoken to him, and how in Damascus he had spoken out boldly in the name of Jesus.

8:40 [a]Acts 21:8   9:1 [a]Acts 7:57; 8:1, 3; 26:10–11; Gal 1:13; 1 Tim 1:13   [1]An idiom for "making threats to murder."   9:2 [a]Acts 22:5   9:3 [a]Acts 22:6; 26:12–13; 1 Cor 15:8   9:4 [a][Matt 25:40]   9:7 [a]Dan 10:7; John 12:29; [Acts 22:9; 26:13]   [1]I.e., they were unable to speak because of fear or amazement.   9:10 [a]Acts 22:12   9:12 [1]‡ Sig. MSS omit in a vision.   9:13 [a]Acts 9:1   9:14 [a]Acts 7:59; 9:2, 21; 1 Cor 1:2; 2 Tim 2:22   9:15 [a]Acts 13:2; 22:21; Rom 1:1; 1 Cor 15:10; Gal 1:15; Eph 3:7–8; 1 Tim 2:7; 2 Tim 1:11   [b]Rom 1:5; 11:13; Gal 2:7–8   [c]Acts 25:22–23; 26:1   [d]Acts 21:40; Rom 1:16; 9:1–5   9:16 [a]Acts 20:23; 2 Cor 11:23–28; 12:7–10; Gal 6:17; Phil 1:29–30   [b]2 Cor 4:11   9:17 [a]Acts 22:12–13   [b]Acts 8:17   [c]Acts 2:4; 4:31; 8:17; 13:52   9:18 [1]Suggests a crusty covering that peeled away.   9:19 [a]Acts 26:20   9:21 [a]Acts 8:3; 9:13; Gal 1:13, 23   9:22 [a]Acts 18:28   [1]Or was confounding.   [2]Or Messiah; both "Christ" (Grk.) and "Messiah" (Heb., Aram.) mean "one who has been anointed."   9:23 [a]Acts 23:12; 2 Cor 11:26   9:24 [a]2 Cor 11:32   [1]Or guarding.   9:25 [a]Josh 2:15; 1 Sam 19:12   9:26 [a]Acts 22:17–20; 26:20; Gal 1:17–18   9:27 [a]Acts 4:36; 13:2   [b]Acts 9:20, 22

28 So [a]he was staying with them, associating openly with them in Jerusalem, speaking out boldly in the name of the Lord. 29 He was speaking and debating with the Greek-speaking [a]Jews,[1] [b]but they were trying to kill him. 30 When the brothers found out about this, they brought him down to Caesarea and sent him away to Tarsus.

31 [a]Then the church throughout Judea, Galilee, and Samaria experienced peace and thus was [b]strengthened. Living in the [c]fear of the Lord and in the [d]encouragement of the Holy Spirit, the church increased in [e]numbers.

Peter Heals Aeneas

32 Now as Peter was traveling around from place to [a]place, he also came down to the saints who lived in Lydda. 33 He found there a man named Aeneas who had been confined to a mattress for eight years because he was paralyzed. 34 Peter said to him, "Aeneas, [a]Jesus the Christ[1] heals you. Get up and make your own bed!"[2] And immediately he got up. 35 All those who lived in Lydda and [a]Sharon saw him, and they [b]turned to the Lord.

Peter Raises Dorcas

36 Now in Joppa there was a disciple named Tabitha (which in translation means Dorcas). She was continually doing good deeds and acts [a]of charity. 37 At that time she became sick [a]and died. When they had washed her body, they placed it in an upstairs room. 38 Because Lydda was near Joppa, when the disciples heard that Peter was there, they sent two men to him and urged him, "Come to us without delay." 39 So Peter got up and went with them, and when he arrived they brought him to the upper room. All the widows stood beside him, crying and showing him the tunics[1] and other clothing Dorcas used to make while she was with them. 40 But Peter [a]sent them all outside, knelt [b]down, and prayed. Turning to the body, he [c]said, "Tabitha, get up." Then she opened her eyes, and when she saw Peter, she sat up. 41 He gave her his hand and helped her get up. Then he called the saints and widows and presented her alive. 42 This became known throughout all Joppa, [a]and many believed in the Lord. 43 So Peter stayed many days in Joppa with a man named [a]Simon, a tanner.[1]

Peter Visits Cornelius

10 Now there was a man in [a]Caesarea named Cornelius, a centurion of what was known as the Italian Cohort. 2 He [a]was a devout, [b]God-fearing man, as was all his household; he did many acts of charity for the people and prayed to God regularly. 3 About three o'clock one afternoon[1] [a]he saw clearly in a vision an angel of God who came in and said to him, "Cornelius." 4 Staring at him and becoming greatly afraid, Cornelius replied, "What is it, Lord?" The angel said to him, "Your prayers and your acts of charity have gone up as a memorial before God. 5 Now [a]send men to Joppa and summon a man named Simon, who is called Peter. 6 This man is staying as a guest with a man named [a]Simon, a tanner, whose house is by [b]the sea." 7 When the angel who had spoken to him departed, Cornelius called two of his personal servants and a devout soldier from among those who served him,[1] 8 and when he had explained everything to them, he sent them to Joppa.

9 About noon the next day, while they were on their way and approaching the city, [a]Peter went up on the roof to pray. 10 He became hungry and wanted to eat, but while they were preparing the meal, a trance came over him. 11 He [a]saw heaven opened and an object something like a large sheet descending, being let down to earth by its four corners. 12 In it were all kinds of four-footed animals and reptiles of the earth and wild birds. 13 Then a voice said to him, "Get up, Peter; slaughter and eat!" 14 But Peter said, "Certainly not, Lord, [a]for I have never eaten anything defiled and ritually

9:28 [a] Gal 1:18   9:29 [a] Acts 6:1; 11:20   [b] Acts 9:23; 2 Cor 11:26   [1] Grk. *the Hellenists*; Greek-speaking Jews who may have adopted some aspects of Grk. culture.   9:31 [a] Acts 5:11; 8:1; 16:5   [b] [Eph 4:16, 29]   [c] Ps 34:9   [d] John 14:16   [e] Acts 16:5   9:32 [a] Acts 8:14   9:34 [a] [Acts 3:6, 16; 4:10]   [1] ‡ Sev. wss *Jesus Christ, the Lord Jesus Christ, the Christ.*   [2] Or perhaps *straighten, rearrange.*   9:35 [a] 1 Chr 5:16; 27:29; Isa 33:9; 35:2; 65:10   [b] Acts 11:21; 15:19   9:36 [a] 1 Tim 2:10; Titus 3:8   9:37 [a] Acts 1:13; 9:39   9:39 [1] Or *shirts*; long garments worn under the cloak next to the skin.   9:40 [a] Matt 9:25   [b] Luke 22:41; Acts 7:60   [c] Mark 5:41–42; John 11:43   9:42 [a] John 11:45   9:43 [a] Acts 10:6   [1] Or *with a certain Simon Berseus.*   10:1 [a] Acts 8:40; 23:23   10:2 [a] Acts 8:2; 9:22; 22:12   [b] [Acts 10:22, 35; 13:16, 26]   10:3 [a] Acts 10:30; 11:13   [1] The time for afternoon prayer.   10:5 [a] Acts 11:13–14   10:6 [a] Acts 9:43   [b] Acts 11:14   10:7 [1] Either a soldier from his entire command or from among his personal staff.   10:9 [a] Acts 10:9–32; 11:5–14   10:11 [a] Ezek 1:1; Matt 3:16; Acts 7:56; Rev 4:1; 19:11   10:14 [a] Lev 11:4; 20:25; Deut 14:3, 7; Ezek 4:14

unclean!" [15]The voice spoke to him again, a second time, "[a]What God has made clean, you must not consider[1] ritually unclean!" [16]This happened three times, and immediately the object was taken up into heaven.

[17]Now while Peter was puzzling over[1] what the vision he had seen could signify, the men sent by Cornelius had learned where Simon's house was and approached the gate. [18]They called out to ask if Simon, known as Peter,[1] was staying there as a guest. [19]While Peter was still thinking seriously about[1] [a]the vision, the Spirit said to him, "Look! Three men are looking for you. [20]But get [a]up, go down, and accompany them without hesitation because I have sent them." [21]So Peter went down to the men and said, "Here I am, the person you're looking for. Why have you come?" [22]They said, "Cornelius the centurion, [a]a righteous and God-fearing man, well spoken of by the whole Jewish nation, was directed by a holy angel to summon you to his house and to hear a message from you." [23]So Peter invited them in and entertained them as guests.

On the next day he got up [a]and set out with them, and some of the brothers from Joppa accompanied him. [24]The following day he entered Caesarea. Now Cornelius was waiting anxiously for them and had called together his relatives and close friends. [25]So when Peter came in, Cornelius met him, fell at his feet, and worshiped him. [26]But Peter helped him up, saying, "Stand [a]up. I too am a mere mortal." [27]Peter continued talking with him as he went in, and he found many people gathered together. [28]He said to them, "You know that it is [a]unlawful for a Jew to associate with or visit a Gentile,[1] yet [b]God has shown me that I should call no person defiled or ritually unclean. [29]Therefore when you sent for me, I came without any objection. Now may I ask why you sent for me?" [30]Cornelius replied, "Four [a]days ago at this very hour, at three o'clock in the afternoon, I was praying [b]in my house, and suddenly a man in shining clothing stood before me [31]and said, 'Cornelius, [a]your prayer has been heard and [b]your acts of charity have been remembered before God. [32]Therefore send to Joppa and summon Simon, who is called Peter. This man is staying as a guest in the house of Simon the tanner, by the sea.' [33]Therefore I sent for you at once, and you were kind enough to come. So now we are all here in the presence of God to listen to everything the Lord has commanded you to say to us."

[34]Then Peter started [a]speaking: "I now truly understand that God does not show favoritism in dealing with people, [35]but [a]in every nation the person who fears him and does what is right is [b]welcomed before him. [36]You know the message he sent to the people of Israel, proclaiming the good [a]news of peace through Jesus Christ ([b]he is Lord of all)—[37]you know what happened throughout Judea, beginning from Galilee after the baptism that John announced: [38]with respect to Jesus from Nazareth, that [a]God anointed him with the Holy Spirit and with power. He went [b]around doing good and healing all who were oppressed by the devil [c]because God was with him. [39]We are [a]witnesses of all the things he did both in Judea and in Jerusalem. They [b]killed him by hanging him on a tree,[1] [40]but [a]God raised him up on the third day and caused him to be seen, [41][a]not by all the people, but by us, the witnesses God had already chosen, [b]who ate and drank with him after he rose from the dead. [42]He commanded us to preach to [a]the people and to warn them [b]that he is the one appointed by God as judge [c]of the living and the dead. [43][a]About him [b]all the prophets testify,[1] that everyone who believes in him receives [c]forgiveness of sins through his name."

The Gentiles Receive the Holy Spirit

[44]While Peter was still speaking [a]these words, the Holy Spirit fell on all those who

heard the message. [45a]The circumcised believers who had accompanied Peter were greatly astonished [b]that the gift of the Holy Spirit[1] had been poured out even on the Gentiles, [46]for they heard them speaking in tongues and praising God. Then Peter said, [47]"No one can withhold the water for these people to be baptized, who have received the Holy Spirit just [a]as we did, can he?" [48a]So he gave orders to have them baptized [b]in the name of Jesus Christ. Then they asked him to stay for several days.

Peter Defends His Actions to the Jerusalem Church

11 Now the apostles and the brothers who were throughout Judea heard that the Gentiles too had accepted the word of God.[1] [2]So when Peter went up to Jerusalem, the circumcised believers[1] took issue with him, [3]saying, "[a]You went to[1] uncircumcised men [b]and shared a meal with them." [4]But Peter began and [a]explained it to them point by point, saying, [5]"[a]I was in the city of Joppa praying, and in a trance I saw a vision, an object something like a large sheet descending, being let down from heaven by its four corners, and it came to me. [6]As I stared I looked into it and saw four-footed animals of the earth, wild animals, reptiles, and wild birds. [7]I also heard a voice saying to me, 'Get up, Peter; slaughter and eat!' [8]But I said, 'Certainly not, Lord, for nothing defiled or ritually unclean has ever entered my mouth!' [9]But the voice replied a second time from heaven, 'What God has made clean, you must not consider ritually unclean!' [10]This happened three times, and then everything was pulled up to heaven again. [11]At that very moment, three men sent to me from Caesarea approached the house where we were staying. [12]The Spirit told me to accompany [a]them without hesitation. [b]These six brothers also went with me, and we entered the man's house. [13]He informed us how he had seen [a]an angel standing in his house and saying, 'Send to Joppa and summon Simon, who is called

Peter, [14]who will speak a message to you by which you and your entire household will be saved.' [15]Then [a]as I began to speak, the Holy Spirit fell on them just as he did on us at the beginning. [16]And I remembered the word of the Lord, as he used to say, '[a]John baptized with water, but [b]you will be baptized with the Holy Spirit.' [17]Therefore [a]if God[1] gave them the same gift as he also gave us after believing[2] in the Lord Jesus Christ, [b]who was I to hinder God?" [18]When they heard this, they ceased their objections[1] and praised God, saying, "So [a]then, God has granted the repentance that leads to life even to the Gentiles."

Activity in the Church at Antioch

[19a]Now those who had been scattered because of the persecution that took place over Stephen went as far as Phoenicia, Cyprus, and Antioch, speaking the message to no one but Jews. [20]But [a]there were some men from Cyprus and Cyrene among them who came to Antioch and began to speak to the Greeks too, proclaiming the good news of the Lord Jesus. [21]The hand of [a]the Lord was with them, and a great number who believed [b]turned to the Lord. [22]A report about them came to the attention of the church in Jerusalem, and they sent [a]Barnabas[1] to Antioch. [23]When he came and saw the grace of God, he rejoiced and [a]encouraged them all to remain true to the Lord with devoted hearts, [24]because he was a good man, [a]full of the Holy Spirit [b]and of faith, and a significant number of people were brought to the Lord. [25]Then Barnabas departed for [a]Tarsus to look for Saul, [26]and when he found him, he brought him to Antioch. So for a whole year Barnabas and Saul met with the church and taught a significant number of people. Now it was in Antioch that the disciples were first called Christians.

Famine Relief for Judea

[27]At that time some [a]prophets came down from Jerusalem to Antioch. [28]One of them, named [a]Agabus, got up and predicted by

10:45 [a]Acts 10:23   [b]Isa 42:1, 6; 49:6; Luke 2:32; John 11:52; Acts 11:18   [1]The gift is the Holy Spirit.   10:47 [a]Acts 2:4; 10:44; 11:17; 15:8   10:48 [a]1 Cor 1:14–17   [b]Acts 2:38; 8:16; 19:5   11:1 [1]I.e., the gospel.   11:2 [1]Or *the Jewish Christians.*   11:3 [a]Matt 9:11; Acts 10:28   [b]Gal 2:12   [1]Or *You were a guest in the home of.*   11:4 [a]Luke 1:3   11:5 [a]Acts 10:9   11:12 [a][John 16:13]; Acts 10:19; 15:7   [b]Acts 10:23   11:13 [a]Acts 10:30   11:15 [a]Acts 2:1–4; 15:7–9   11:16 [a]Matt 3:11; Mark 1:8; John 1:26, 33; Acts 1:5; 19:4   [b]Isa 44:3   11:17 [a][Acts 15:8–9]   [b]Acts 10:47   [1]A few wss omit *God.*   [2]Or *when we believed.*   11:18 [a]Isa 42:1, 6; 49:6; Luke 2:32; John 11:52; Rom 10:12–13; 15:9, 16   [1]Or *became silent.*   11:19 [a]Acts 8:1, 4   11:20 [a]Acts 6:1; 9:29   11:21 [a]Luke 1:66; Acts 2:47   [b]Acts 9:35; 14:1   11:22 [a]Acts 4:36; 9:27   [1]‡ Maj. MSS add *to travel.*   11:23 [a]Acts 13:43; 14:22   11:24 [a]Acts 6:5   [b]Acts 5:14; 11:21   11:25 [a]Acts 9:11, 30   11:27 [a]Acts 2:17; 13:1; 15:32; 21:9; 1 Cor 12:28; Eph 4:11   11:28 [a]John 16:13; Acts 21:10

the Spirit that a severe famine was about to come over the whole inhabited world. (This took place during the reign of [b]Claudius.) [29]So the disciples, each in accordance with his financial ability, decided to send [a]relief to the brothers living in Judea. [30a]They did so, sending their financial aid to the elders by Barnabas and Saul.

James Is Killed and Peter Imprisoned

12 About that time King Herod laid hands on some from the church to harm them. [2]He had James, [a]the brother of John, executed with a sword. [3]When [a]he saw that this pleased the Jews, he proceeded to arrest Peter too. (This took place during the feast of Unleavened Bread.) [4]When [a]he had seized him, he put him in prison, handing him over to four squads of soldiers to guard him. Herod planned to bring him out for public trial[1] after the Passover. [5]So Peter was kept in prison, but those in the church were earnestly praying to God for him. [6]On that very night before Herod was going to bring him out for trial, Peter was sleeping between two soldiers, bound with two chains, while guards in front of the door were keeping watch over the prison. [7]Suddenly [a]an angel of the Lord appeared, and a light shone in the prison cell. He struck[1] Peter on the side and woke him up, saying, "Get up quickly!" And the chains fell off Peter's wrists. [8]The angel said to him, "Fasten your belt and put on your sandals." Peter did so. Then the angel said to him, "Put on your cloak and follow me." [9]Peter went out and followed him; he [a]did not realize that what was happening through [b]the angel was real,[1] but thought he was seeing a vision. [10]After they had passed the first and second guards,[1] they came to the iron gate leading into the city. It opened for them by itself,[2] and they went outside and walked down one narrow street, when at once the angel left him. [11]When Peter came to himself, [a]he said, "Now I know for certain that the Lord [b]has sent his angel and rescued me from the hand of Herod and from everything the Jewish people were expecting to happen."

[12]When Peter realized this, [a]he went to the house of Mary, the mother of [b]John Mark, where many people had gathered together and were [c]praying. [13]When he knocked at the door of the outer gate, a slave girl named Rhoda answered. [14]When she recognized Peter's voice, she was so overjoyed she did not open the gate, but ran back in and told them that Peter was standing at the gate. [15]But they said to her, "You've lost your mind!" But she kept insisting that [a]it was Peter, and they kept saying,[1] "It is his angel!" [16]Now Peter continued knocking, and when they opened the door and saw him, they were greatly astonished. [17]He [a]motioned to them with his hand to be quiet and then related[1] how the Lord had brought him out of the prison. He said, "Tell James and the brothers these things," and then he left and went to another place.

[18]At daybreak there was great consternation among the soldiers over what had become of Peter. [19]When Herod had searched for him and did not find him, he questioned the guards and commanded that they be led away to execution. Then Herod went down from Judea to Caesarea and stayed there.

[20]Now Herod was having an angry quarrel with the people of [a]Tyre and Sidon. So they joined together and presented themselves before him. And after convincing Blastus, the king's personal assistant,[1] to help them, they asked for peace[2] because [b]their country's food supply was provided by the king's country. [21]On a day determined in advance, Herod put on his royal robes, sat down on the judgment seat, and made a speech to them. [22]But the crowd began to shout, "The voice of a god, and not of a man!" [23]Immediately an angel of the Lord [a]struck [b]Herod down because he did not give the glory to God, and he was eaten by worms and died. [24]But [a]the word of God kept on increasing and multiplying.

11:28 [b]Acts 18:2   11:29 [a]Rom 15:26; 1 Cor 16:1; 2 Cor 9:1   11:30 [a]Acts 12:25   12:2 [a]Matt 4:21; 20:23   12:3 [a]Exod 12:15; 23:15; Acts 20:6   12:4 [a]John 21:18   [1]Grk. *out to the people.*   12:7 [a]Acts 5:19   [1]A push or a light tap.   12:9 [a]Ps 126:1   [b]Acts 10:3, 17; 11:5   [1]Grk. *what was done through the angel was a reality.*   12:10 [1]Or perhaps *guard posts.*   [2]I.e., it happened without visible cause.   12:11 [a][Ps 34:7]; Dan 3:28; 6:22; [Heb 1:14]   [b]Job 5:19; [Ps 33:18–19; 34:22; 41:2]; 2 Cor 1:10; [2 Pet 2:9]   12:12 [a]Acts 4:23   [b]Acts 13:5, 13; 15:37; 2 Tim 4:11; Phlm 24; 1 Pet 5:13   [c]Acts 12:5   12:15 [a]Gen 48:16; [Matt 18:10]   [1]I.e., a shouting match between the parties.   12:17 [a]Acts 13:16; 19:33; 21:40   [1]‡ Maj. MSS add *to them.*   12:20 [a]Matt 11:21   [b]1 Kgs 5:11; Ezra 3:7; Ezek 27:17   [1]A highly respected person with considerable responsibility for the king's personal affairs.   [2]Or *for a reconciliation.*   12:23 [a]1 Sam 25:38; 2 Sam 24:16–17; 2 Kgs 19:35; Acts 5:19   [b]Ps 115:1   12:24 [a]Isa 55:11; Acts 6:7; 19:20

[25]So [a]Barnabas and Saul returned to[1] Jerusalem when they had [b]completed their mission, bringing along [c]with them [d]John Mark.[2]

The Church at Antioch Commissions Barnabas and Saul

13 Now there were these prophets and teachers [a]in the church at Antioch: [b]Barnabas, Simeon called Niger, [c]Lucius the Cyrenian, Manaen (a close friend of Herod the tetrarch from childhood[1]) and Saul. [2]While they were serving[1] the Lord and fasting, the Holy Spirit said, "Set apart for me Barnabas and Saul for the work [a]to which I have called them." [3]Then, after they had fasted and prayed and placed their hands on them, they sent them off.

Paul and Barnabas Preach in Cyprus

[4]So Barnabas and Saul, sent out by the Holy Spirit, went down to Seleucia, and from there they sailed to [a]Cyprus. [5]When [a]they arrived in Salamis, they began to proclaim the word of God in the Jewish synagogues. (Now they also had [b]John as their assistant.) [6]When they [a]had crossed over the whole island as far as Paphos, they found a magician, a Jewish false prophet named Bar-Jesus, [7]who was with the proconsul Sergius Paulus, an intelligent man. The proconsul summoned Barnabas and Saul and wanted to hear the word of God. [8]But the magician [a]Elymas (for that is the way his name is translated) opposed them, trying to turn the proconsul away from the faith. [9]But Saul (also known as Paul), [a]filled with the Holy Spirit, stared straight at him [10]and said, "[a]You who are full of all deceit and all wrongdoing, you son of the devil, you enemy of all righteousness—will you not stop making crooked the straight paths of the Lord? [11]Now look, [a]the hand of the Lord is against[1] you, and you will be blind, unable to see the sun for a time!" Immediately mistiness and darkness came over him, and he went around seeking people to lead him by the hand. [12]Then when the proconsul saw what had happened, he believed because he was greatly astounded at the teaching about the Lord.

Paul and Barnabas at Pisidian Antioch

[13]Then Paul and his companions put out to sea from Paphos and came to Perga in Pamphylia, but [a]John left them and returned to Jerusalem. [14]Moving on from Perga, they arrived at Pisidian Antioch, and on the Sabbath day they [a]went into the synagogue and sat down. [15a]After the reading from the law and the prophets, the leaders of the synagogue sent them a message, saying, "Brothers, if you have [b]any message of exhortation for the people, speak it." [16]So Paul stood up, gestured with his hand and said,

"Men of Israel, and [a]you Gentiles who fear God,[1] listen: [17]The God of this people Israel [a]chose our ancestors and made the people great[1] [b]during their stay as foreigners[2] in the country of Egypt, and with uplifted arm he [c]led them out of it. [18]For a period of about [a]forty years he put up with them in the wilderness. [19]After he had destroyed [a]seven nations in [b]the land of Canaan, he gave his people their land as an inheritance. [20]All this took about 450 years. After this [a]he gave them judges [b]until the time of Samuel the prophet. [21]Then they asked for [a]a king, and God gave them [b]Saul son of Kish, a man from the tribe of Benjamin, who ruled forty years. [22]After removing him, God raised up David their king. [a]He testified about him: *'I have found David*[1] [b]the son of Jesse *to be a man after my heart,*[2] who [c]will [d]accomplish everything I want him to do.' [23a]From the descendants[1] of this man God brought [b]to [c]Israel a Savior, Jesus, just as he promised. [24]Before Jesus arrived, John had proclaimed [a]a baptism for repentance to all the people

12:25 [a]Acts 11:30 [b]Acts 11:30 [c]Acts 13:5, 13 [d]Acts 12:12; 15:37 [1]Sev. wss *from Jerusalem, from Jerusalem to Antioch.* [2]Grk. *John who was also called Mark.* 13:1 [a]Acts 14:26 [b]Acts 11:22 [c]Rom 16:21 [1]Or *(a foster brother of Herod the tetrarch).* 13:2 [a]Matt 9:38; Acts 14:26; Rom 10:15; Eph 3:7–8; 1 Tim 2:7; 2 Tim 1:11; Heb 5:4 [1]Often describes priestly service in the tabernacle and the temple. 13:4 [a]Acts 4:36 13:5 [a][Acts 13:46] [b]Acts 12:25; 15:37 13:6 [a]Acts 8:9 13:8 [a]Exod 7:11; 2 Tim 3:8 13:9 [a]Acts 2:4; 4:8 13:10 [a]Matt 13:38; John 8:44; [1 John 3:8] 13:11 [a]Exod 9:3; 1 Sam 5:6; Job 19:21; Ps 32:4; Heb 10:31 [1]Grk. *upon*; but in a negative sense. 13:13 [a]Acts 15:38 13:14 [a]Acts 16:13 13:15 [a]Luke 4:16 [b]Heb 13:22 13:16 [a]Acts 10:35 [1]I.e., Gentiles who worshiped Israel's God and often followed Mosaic law but did not undergo circumcision to become full proselytes to Judaism. 13:17 [a]Exod 6:1, 6; 13:14, 16; Deut 7:6–8 [b]Acts 7:17 [c]Exod 14:8 [1]I.e., in number and power. [2]Or *as resident aliens.* 13:18 [a]Exod 16:35; Num 14:34; Acts 7:36 13:19 [a]Deut 7:1 [b]Josh 14:1–2; 19:51; Ps 78:55 13:20 [a]Judg 2:16; 1 Sam 4:18; 7:15 [b]1 Sam 3:20; Acts 3:24 13:21 [a]1 Sam 8:5 [b]1 Sam 10:20–24 13:22 [a]1 Sam 15:23, 26, 28 [b]1 Sam 16:1, 12, 13 [c]Ps 89:20 [d]1 Sam 13:14 [1]Ps 89:20 [2]1 Sam 13:14 13:23 [a]Isa 11:1 [b]Ps 132:11 [c][Matt 1:21] [1]Or *From the offspring*; Grk. *From the seed.* 13:24 [a]Matt 3:1; [Luke 3:3]

of Israel. [25]But while John was completing his mission, he said repeatedly, '[a]What do you think I am? I am not [b]he. But look, one is coming after me. I am not worthy to untie the sandals on his feet!' [26]Brothers, descendants of Abraham's family, and [a]those Gentiles among you who fear God, the message of this salvation has been sent [b]to us. [27]For the people who live in Jerusalem and their rulers did not recognize him, and they fulfilled the sayings of the prophets that are read every Sabbath by condemning him. [28]Though they found no basis for [a]a death sentence, they asked Pilate to have him executed. [29a]When [b]they had accomplished everything that was written about him, they took him down from the cross[1] and placed him in a tomb. [30a]But God raised him from the dead, [31]and for many days [a]he appeared to those who had accompanied him from Galilee to Jerusalem. These are now his witnesses to the people. [32]And we proclaim to you the good news about the promise to our ancestors, [33]that this promise God has fulfilled to us, their children, by raising Jesus, as also it is written in the second psalm, '*You are my Son; today I have fathered* [a]*you.*'[1] [34]But [a]regarding the fact that he has raised Jesus from the dead, never again to be in a state of decay, God has spoken in this way: '*I will give you*[1] *the holy and trustworthy promises made to David.*'[2] [35]Therefore he also says in another psalm, '[a]*You will not permit your Holy One to experience decay.*'[1] [36]For David, after he had served God's purpose in his own generation, died,[1] was buried with his ancestors, and experienced[2] decay, [37]but the one whom God raised up did not experience decay. [38]Therefore let it be known to you, brothers, that [a]through this one forgiveness of sins is proclaimed to you, [39]and [a]by this one everyone who believes is justified from everything from which the law of Moses could not justify you. [40]Watch out, then, that what is spoken about by the prophets does not happen to you:

[41]'*Look, you scoffers;* [a]*be amazed and perish!*
For I am doing a work in your days,
a work you would never believe, even if someone tells you.'"[1]

[42]As Paul and Barnabas were going out, the people were urging them to speak about these things on the next Sabbath. [43]When the meeting of the synagogue had broken up, many of the Jews and God-fearing proselytes followed Paul and Barnabas, who were speaking with them and were [a]persuading [b]them to continue in the grace of God.

[44]On the next Sabbath almost the whole city assembled together to hear the word of the Lord.[1] [45]But when the Jews saw the crowds, they were filled with jealousy, and they began to [a]contradict what Paul was saying by reviling him. [46]Both Paul and Barnabas replied courageously,[1] "[a]It was necessary to speak the word of God to you first. [b]Since you reject it and do not consider yourselves worthy of eternal life, [c]we are turning to the Gentiles. [47]For [a]this is what the Lord has commanded us: '*I have appointed you to be a light for the Gentiles, to bring salvation to the ends of the earth.*'"[1] [48]When the Gentiles heard this, they began to rejoice [a]and praise the word of the Lord, and all who had been appointed for eternal life believed. [49]So the word of the Lord was spreading through the entire region. [50]But the Jews incited the God-fearing women of high social standing and the prominent men of the city, stirred [a]up persecution against Paul and Barnabas, and threw them out of their region. [51a]So after they shook the dust off their feet in protest against them, they went to Iconium. [52]And the disciples [a]were filled [b]with joy and with the Holy Spirit.

Paul and Barnabas at Iconium

14 The same thing happened in Iconium when Paul and Barnabas went into the Jewish synagogue and spoke in such a way that a large group of both Jews and

13:25 [a] Matt 3:11; Mark 1:7; Luke 3:16 [b] John 1:20, 27 13:26 [a] Ps 66:16 [b] Matt 10:6 13:28 [a] Matt 27:22–23; Mark 15:13–14; Luke 23:21–23; John 19:15; Acts 3:14; [2 Cor 5:21; Heb 4:15]; 1 Pet 2:22 13:29 [a] Luke 18:31 [b] Matt 27:57–61; Mark 15:42–47; Luke 23:50–56; John 19:38–42 [1] Grk. *tree*; but frequently figurative for a cross. 13:30 [a] Ps 16:10–11; Hos 6:2; Matt 12:39–40; 28:6 13:31 [a] Matt 28:16; Acts 1:3, 11; 1 Cor 15:5–8 13:33 [a] Ps 2:7; Heb 1:5 [1] Ps 2:7 13:34 [a] Isa 55:3 [1] "You" is pl. [2] Isa 55:3 13:35 [a] Ps 16:10; Acts 2:27 [1] Ps 16:10 13:36 [1] Grk. *sleep*; often a euphemism for the believer's death. [2] Grk. *saw*. 13:38 [a] Jer 31:34 13:39 [a] [Isa 53:11; John 3:16] 13:41 [a] Hab 1:5 [1] Hab 1:5 13:43 [a] Acts 11:23 [b] Titus 2:11; Heb 12:15; 1 Pet 5:12 13:44 [1] Maj. MSS *God*. 13:45 [a] Acts 18:6; 1 Pet 4:4; Jude 10 13:46 [a] Matt 10:6; Acts 3:26; Rom 1:16 [b] Exod 32:10; Deut 32:21; Isa 55:5; Matt 21:43; Rom 10:19 [c] Acts 18:6 [1] Grk. *spoke out courageously*. 13:47 [a] Isa 42:6; 49:6; Luke 2:32 [1] [Isa 42:6; 49:6] 13:48 [a] [Acts 2:47] 13:50 [a] Acts 7:52; 2 Tim 3:11 13:51 [a] Matt 10:14; Mark 6:11; [Luke 9:5] 13:52 [a] Matt 5:12; John 16:22 [b] Acts 2:4; 4:8, 31; 13:9

[a]Greeks believed. [2]But the Jews who refused to believe stirred up the Gentiles and poisoned their minds against the brothers. [3]So they stayed there for a considerable time, speaking out courageously for the Lord, [a]who testified to the message of his grace, granting miraculous signs and [b]wonders to be performed through their hands. [4]But the population of the city was [a]divided; some sided with the Jews, and some with the [b]apostles. [5]When both the Gentiles and the Jews ([a]together with their rulers) made an attempt to mistreat them and stone them, [6]Paul and Barnabas learned about it and [a]fled to the Lycaonian cities of Lystra and Derbe and the surrounding region. [7]There they continued to proclaim the good news.

Paul and Barnabas at Lystra

[8]In Lystra sat [a]a man who could not use his feet,[1] lame from birth,[2] who had never walked. [9]This man was listening to Paul as he was speaking. When Paul stared intently at him and saw he had faith to be healed, [10]he said with a loud voice, "[a]Stand upright on your feet." And the man leaped up and began walking. [11]So when [a]the crowds saw what Paul had done, they shouted in the Lycaonian language, "The gods have come down to us in human form!" [12]They began to call Barnabas Zeus and Paul Hermes, because he was the chief speaker. [13]The priest of the temple of Zeus, located just outside the city, brought bulls and garlands to the city gates; he and the crowds [a]wanted to offer sacrifices to them. [14]But when [a]the apostles Barnabas and Paul heard about it, they tore their clothes and rushed out into the crowd, shouting, [15]"Men, [a]why are you doing these things? [b]We too are men, with human natures[1] just like you! We are proclaiming the good news to you, so that you should turn from [c]these worthless things [d]to the living God, [e]who made the heaven, the earth, the sea, and everything that is in them. [16a]In past generations he allowed all the nations[1] to go their own ways, [17]yet [a]he

did not leave himself without a witness by doing good, by [b]giving you rain from heaven and fruitful seasons, satisfying you with [c]food and your hearts with joy." [18]Even by saying these things, they scarcely persuaded the crowds not to offer sacrifice to them.

[19]But Jews came from Antioch and Iconium, and after winning [a]the crowds over, [b]they stoned Paul and dragged him out of the city, presuming him to be [c]dead. [20]But after the disciples had surrounded him, he got up and went back into the city. On the next day he left with Barnabas for Derbe.

Paul and Barnabas Return to Antioch in Syria

[21]After they had proclaimed the good news in that city [a]and made many disciples, they returned to Lystra, to Iconium, and to Antioch. [22]They strengthened the souls of the disciples and [a]encouraged them to continue in the faith, saying, "[b]We must enter the kingdom of God through many persecutions." [23]When they had [a]appointed elders for them in the various churches, with prayer and fasting they entrusted them to the protection of the Lord in whom they had believed. [24]Then they passed through Pisidia and came into Pamphylia, [25]and when they had spoken the word in Perga, they went down to Attalia. [26]From there they sailed back to Antioch, where they had been commended to the grace of God for the work they had now completed. [27]When [a]they arrived and gathered the church together, they reported all the things God had done with them, and that he had [b]opened a door of faith for the Gentiles. [28]So they spent considerable time with the disciples.

The Jerusalem Council

15 Now some [a]men came down from Judea and began to teach the brothers, "[b]Unless you are circumcised[1] according to the custom of Moses, you cannot be saved." [2]When [a]Paul and Barnabas had a major argument and debate with them, the

14:1 [a]John 7:35; Acts 18:4; Rom 1:14, 16; 1 Cor 1:22   14:3 [a]Mark 16:20; Acts 4:29; 20:32; Heb 2:4   [b]Acts 5:12   14:4 [a]Luke 12:51   [b]Acts 13:2-3   14:5 [a]2 Tim 3:11   14:6 [a]Matt 10:23   14:8 [a]Acts 3:2   [1]Grk. *powerless in his feet.*   [2]Grk. *lame from his mother's womb.*   14:10 [a][Isa 35:6]   14:11 [a]Acts 8:10; 28:6   14:13 [a]Dan 2:46   14:14 [a]Num 14:6; Matt 26:65; Mark 14:63   14:15 [a]Acts 10:26   [b]Jas 5:17   [c]1 Sam 12:21; Jer 8:19; 14:22; Amos 2:4; 1 Cor 8:4   [d]1 Thess 1:9   [e]Gen 1:1; Exod 20:11; Ps 146:6; Acts 4:24; 17:24; Rev 14:7   [1]Grk. *with the same kinds of feelings.*   14:16 [a]Ps 81:12; Mic 4:5; 1 Pet 4:3   [1]Or *all the Gentiles.*   14:17 [a]Acts 17:24-27; Rom 1:19-20   [b]Lev 26:4; Deut 11:14; [Matt 5:45]   [c]Ps 145:16   14:19 [a]Acts 13:45, 50; 14:2-5; 1 Thess 2:14   [b]Acts 14:5; 2 Cor 11:25; 2 Tim 3:11   [c][2 Cor 12:1-4]   14:21 [a]Matt 28:19   14:22 [a]Acts 11:23   [b]Matt 10:38; Luke 22:28; [Rom 8:17; 2 Tim 2:12; 3:12]   14:23 [a]Matt 9:15; Mark 2:20; Luke 5:35; 2 Cor 8:19; Titus 1:5   14:27 [a]Acts 15:4, 12   [b]1 Cor 16:9; 2 Cor 2:12; Col 4:3; Rev 3:8   15:1 [a]Gal 2:12   [b]John 7:22; Acts 15:5; Gal 5:2; Phil 3:2; [Col 2:8, 11, 16]   [1]A few mss add *and walk.*   15:2 [a]Gal 2:1

church appointed Paul and Barnabas and some others from among them to go up to meet with the apostles and elders in Jerusalem about this point of disagreement. [3]So they were sent on their way by the church, and as they passed through both Phoenicia and Samaria, they were relating at [a]length[1] the conversion of the Gentiles and bringing great joy to all the brothers. [4]When they arrived in Jerusalem, they were received by the church and the apostles and the elders, and they reported all the things God had done with them.[1] [5]But some from the religious party of the Pharisees who had believed stood up and said, "It is necessary to circumcise the Gentiles and to order them to observe the law of Moses."

[6]Both the apostles and the elders met together to deliberate about this matter. [7]After there had been much debate, Peter stood up and said to them, "Brothers, you know that some time ago God chose [a]me to preach to the Gentiles so they would hear the message of the gospel and believe. [8]And God, [a]who knows the heart, has testified to them by [b]giving them the Holy Spirit just as he did to us, [9][a]and he made no distinction between them and us, [b]cleansing their hearts by faith. [10]So now why are you putting God to the test[1] [a]by placing on the neck of the disciples a yoke that neither our ancestors nor we have been able to bear? [11]On the contrary, [a]we believe that we are saved through the grace of the Lord Jesus, in the same way as they are."

[12]The whole group kept quiet and listened to Barnabas and Paul while they explained all the miraculous signs and wonders God had [a]done among the Gentiles through them. [13]After they stopped speaking, [a]James replied, "Brothers, listen to me. [14][a]Simeon has explained how God first concerned himself to select[1] from among the Gentiles a people for his name. [15]The words of the prophets agree with this, as it is written,

[16] '[a]*After this I will return,*
and I will rebuild the fallen tent[1] of
    David;
I will rebuild its ruins and restore it,
[17] *so that the rest of humanity[1] may seek*
    the Lord,
namely, all the Gentiles I have called
    to be my own,' says the Lord,[2] who
makes these things [18]*known from*
long ago.[1]

[19]"Therefore [a]I conclude[1] that we should not cause extra difficulty for those among the Gentiles who [b]are turning to God, [20]but that we should [a]write them a letter telling them to abstain [b]from things defiled by idols and [c]from sexual immorality and [d]from what has been strangled and from blood. [21]For Moses has had those who proclaim him [a]in every town from ancient times, because he is read aloud in the synagogues every Sabbath."

[22]Then the apostles and elders, with the whole church, decided to send men chosen from among them, Judas called [a]Barsabbas and Silas, leaders among the brothers, to Antioch with Paul and Barnabas. [23]They sent this letter with them:

From the apostles and elders, your brothers, to the Gentile brothers and sisters[1] in Antioch, Syria, and Cilicia, greetings! [24]Since we have heard that [a]some have gone out from among us with no orders from us and have confused you, [b]upsetting your minds by what they said, [25]we have unanimously[1] decided to choose men to send to you along with our dear friends Barnabas and Paul, [26][a]who have risked their lives for the name of our Lord Jesus Christ.[1] [27]Therefore we are sending Judas and Silas who will tell you these things themselves in person.[1] [28]For it seemed best to the Holy Spirit and to us not to place any greater burden on

15:3 [a] Acts 14:27; 15:4, 12   [1] Grk. *to provide detailed information in a systematic manner.*   15:4 [1] Grk. *They reported all the things God had done with them.*   15:7 [a] Acts 10:20   15:8 [a] 1 Chr 28:9; Acts 1:24   [b] Acts 2:4; 10:44, 47   15:9 [a] Rom 10:12   [b] Acts 10:15, 28   15:10 [a] Matt 23:4; Gal 5:1   [1] I.e., in a negative manner.   15:11 [a] Rom 3:4; 5:15; 2 Cor 13:13; [Eph 2:5–8; Titus 2:11]   15:12 [a] Acts 14:27; 15:3–4   15:13 [a] Acts 12:17   15:14 [a] Acts 15:7; 2 Pet 1:1   [1] Grk. *to take.*   15:16 [a] Amos 9:11–12   [1] Or *dwelling;* or perhaps *royal tent;* referring to David's ruined kingdom.   15:17 [1] Or *so that all other people.*   [2] Amos 9:11–12 LXX   15:18 [1] [Isa 45:21]   15:19 [a] Acts 15:28; 21:25   [b] 1 Thess 1:9   [1] Or *I have decided, I think.*   15:20 [a] Acts 21:25   [b] Gen 35:2; Exod 20:3, 23; Ezek 20:30; [1 Cor 8:1; 10:20, 28]; Rev 2:14   [c] [1 Cor 6:9]; Gal 5:19; Eph 5:3; Col 3:5; 1 Thess 4:3; 1 Pet 4:3   [d] Gen 9:4; Lev 3:17; Deut 12:16; 1 Sam 14:33   15:21 [a] Acts 13:15, 27; 2 Cor 3:14   15:22 [a] Acts 1:23   15:23 [1] Grk. *to the brothers who are from the Gentiles.*   15:24 [a] Acts 15:1; Gal 2:4; 5:12; Titus 1:10–11   [b] Gal 1:7; 5:10   15:25 [1] Grk. *having become of one mind, we have decided.*   15:26 [a] Acts 13:50; 14:19; 1 Cor 15:30; 2 Cor 11:23–26   [1] Or *Messiah;* both "Christ" (Grk.) and "Messiah" (Heb., Aram.) mean "one who has been anointed."   15:27 [1] Grk. *by means of word;* an idiom for a verbal report.

you than these necessary rules: [29]that you abstain from meat [a]that has been sacrificed to idols and [b]from blood and from what has been strangled[1] and from [c]sexual immorality.[2] If you keep yourselves from doing these things, you will do well. Farewell.

[30]So when they were dismissed, they went down to Antioch, and after gathering the entire group together, they delivered the letter. [31]When they read it aloud, the people rejoiced at its encouragement. [32]Both Judas and Silas, who were [a]prophets themselves, [b]encouraged and strengthened the brothers with a long speech. [33]After they had spent some time there, they were sent [a]off in peace by the brothers to those who had sent them.[1] [35]But [a]Paul and Barnabas remained in Antioch, teaching and proclaiming (along with many others) the word of the Lord.

Paul and Barnabas Part Company

[36]After some days Paul said to Barnabas, "Let's return and visit the brothers in every town where we proclaimed the word of the Lord to see how they are doing." [37]Barnabas wanted to bring [a]John called Mark along with them too, [38]but Paul insisted that [a]they should not take along this one who had left them in Pamphylia and had not accompanied them in the work. [39]They had a sharp disagreement, so that they parted company. Barnabas took along Mark and sailed away to [a]Cyprus, [40]but Paul chose Silas and set out, commended to the grace of the Lord by the brothers and sisters. [41]He passed through Syria and Cilicia, [a]strengthening the churches.

Timothy Joins Paul and Silas

16 He also came to [a]Derbe and to Lystra. A disciple [b]named Timothy was [c]there, the son of a Jewish woman who was a believer, but whose father was a Greek. [2]The brothers in Lystra and Iconium spoke well of him. [3]Paul wanted Timothy to accompany him, and he [a]took him and circumcised him because of the Jews who were in those places, for they all knew that his father was Greek. [4]As they went through the towns, they passed on the [a]decrees that had been decided on by the apostles and elders in Jerusalem for the Gentile believers to obey. [5a]So the churches were being strengthened in the faith and were increasing in number every day.

Paul's Vision of the Macedonian Man

[6]They went through the region of Phrygia and [a]Galatia, having been prevented by the Holy Spirit from speaking the message in the province of Asia. [7]When they came to Mysia, they attempted to go into Bithynia, but the Spirit of Jesus did not allow them to do this, [8]so they passed through Mysia and went [a]down to Troas. [9]A vision appeared to Paul during the night: A Macedonian [a]man was standing there urging him, "Come over to Macedonia and help us!" [10]After Paul saw the vision, we attempted immediately [a]to go over to Macedonia, concluding that God had called us to proclaim the good news to them.

Arrival at Philippi

[11]We put out to sea from Troas and sailed a straight course to Samothrace, the next day to Neapolis, [12]and from there to [a]Philippi, which is a leading city of that district[1] of Macedonia, a Roman colony. We stayed in this city for some days. [13]On the Sabbath day we went outside the city gate to the side of the river, where we thought there would be a place of prayer, and we sat down and began to speak to the women who had assembled there. [14]A woman named Lydia, a dealer in purple cloth from the city of [a]Thyatira, a God-fearing woman, listened to us. [b]The Lord opened her heart to respond to what Paul was saying. [15]After [a]she and her household were baptized, she urged us, "If[1] you consider me to be a believer in the Lord,[2] come and stay in my house." And she persuaded us.

15:29 [a]Acts 15:20; 21:25; Rev 2:14, 20 [b]Lev 17:14 [c]1 Cor 5:1; 6:18; 7:2; Col 3:5; 1 Thess 4:3 [1]A few wss omit *and from what has been strangled.* [2]A few wss add *And whatever you do not want to happen to yourselves, do not do to another/others.* **15:32** [a]Acts 11:27; 1 Cor 12:28; Eph 4:11; Rev 18:20 [b]Acts 14:22; 18:23 **15:33** [a]Mark 5:34; Acts 16:36; 1 Cor 16:11; Heb 11:31 [1]A few mss add v. 34: *But Silas decided to stay there.* **15:35** [a]Acts 13:1 **15:37** [a]Acts 12:12, 25; Col 4:10; 2 Tim 4:11; Phlm 24 **15:38** [a]Acts 13:13 **15:39** [a]Acts 4:36; 13:4 **15:41** [a]Acts 16:5 **16:1** [a]Acts 14:6 [b]Acts 19:22; Rom 16:21; 1 Cor 4:17; 16:10; Phil 1:1; 2:19; 1 Thess 3:2; 2 Tim 1:2 [c]2 Tim 1:5; 3:15 **16:3** [a][1 Cor 9:20; Gal 2:3; 5:2] **16:4** [a]Acts 15:19–21 **16:5** [a]Acts 2:47; 15:41 **16:6** [a]Acts 18:23; Gal 1:1–2 **16:8** [a]Acts 16:11; 20:5; 2 Cor 2:12; 2 Tim 4:13 **16:9** [a]Acts 10:30 **16:10** [a]2 Cor 2:13 **16:12** [a]Acts 20:6; Phil 1:1; 1 Thess 2:2 [1]‡ Some mss *in the first district, first of that district.* **16:14** [a]Rev 1:11; 2:18, 24 [b]Luke 24:45 **16:15** [a]Gen 19:3; 33:11; Judg 19:21; Luke 24:29; [Heb 13:2] [1]I.e., "If (and let's assume that it's true) you consider me." [2]Or *faithful to the Lord.*

Paul and Silas Are Thrown into Prison

[16]Now as we were going to the place of prayer, a slave girl met us who [a]had a spirit that enabled her to foretell the future by supernatural means.[1] She brought her owners a [b]great profit by fortune-telling. [17]She followed behind Paul and us and kept crying out, "These men are servants of the Most High God, who are proclaiming to you the way of salvation." [18]She continued to do this for many days. But Paul became [a]greatly annoyed, [b]and turned and said to the spirit, "I command you in the name of Jesus Christ[1] to come out of her!" And it came out of her at once. [19]But [a]when her owners saw their hope of profit was gone, they seized Paul and Silas and [b]dragged them into the marketplace before the authorities. [20]When they had brought them before the magistrates, they said, "These men are throwing our city into confusion. They are Jews [21]and are advocating customs that are not lawful for us to accept or practice, since we are Romans."

[22]The crowd joined the attack against them, [a]and the magistrates tore the clothes off Paul and Silas and ordered them to be beaten with rods. [23]After they had beaten them severely, they threw them into prison and commanded the jailer to guard them securely. [24]Receiving such orders, he threw them in the inner cell and fastened their feet in the stocks.[1]

[25]About midnight Paul and Silas were praying and singing hymns to God, and the rest of the prisoners were listening to them. [26a]Suddenly a great earthquake occurred, so that the foundations of the prison were shaken. Immediately [b]all the doors flew open, and the bonds of all the prisoners came loose. [27]When the jailer woke up and saw the doors of the prison standing open, he drew his sword and was about to kill himself because he assumed the prisoners had escaped. [28]But Paul called out loudly, "Do not harm yourself, for we are all here!" [29]Calling for lights, the jailer rushed in and fell down trembling at the feet of Paul and Silas. [30]Then he brought them outside and asked, "[a]Sirs, what must I do to be saved?" [31]They replied, "[a]Believe in the Lord Jesus[1] and you will be saved, you and your household." [32]Then they spoke the word of the Lord to him, along with all those who were in his house. [33]At that hour of the night he took them and washed their wounds; then he and all his family were baptized right away. [34]The jailer brought [a]them into his house and set food before them, and he rejoiced greatly that he had come to believe in God, together with his entire household. [35]At daybreak the magistrates[1] sent their police officers, saying, "Release those men." [36]The jailer reported these words to Paul, saying, "The magistrates have sent orders to release you. So come out now and go in peace." [37]But Paul said to the police officers, "They had us beaten in public without a proper trial—even though we are Roman [a]citizens—and they threw us in prison. And now they want to send us away secretly? Absolutely not! They themselves must come and escort us out!" [38]The police officers reported these words to the magistrates. They were frightened when they heard Paul and Silas were Roman citizens [39]and came and apologized to them. After they brought them out, they [a]asked them repeatedly to leave the city. [40]When they came out of the prison, they entered Lydia's house, [a]and when they saw the brothers, they encouraged them and then departed.

Paul and Silas at Thessalonica

17 After they traveled through Amphipolis and Apollonia, they came to [a]Thessalonica, where there was a Jewish synagogue. [2]Paul [a]went to the Jews in the synagogue, as he customarily did, and on three Sabbath days he [b]addressed them from the scriptures, [3]explaining and demonstrating [a]that the Christ[1] had to suffer and to rise from the dead, saying, "This Jesus I am proclaiming to you is the Christ."

16:16 [a]Lev 19:31; 20:6, 27; Deut 18:11; 1 Sam 28:3, 7; 2 Kgs 21:6; 1 Chr 10:13; Isa 8:19   [b]Acts 19:24   [1]Or *who had a spirit of divination*; Grk. *who had a spirit of Python*.   **16:18** [a]Mark 1:25, 34   [b]Mark 16:17   [1]Or *Messiah*; both "Christ" (Grk.) and "Messiah" (Heb., Aram.) mean "one who has been anointed."   **16:19** [a]Acts 16:16; 19:25–26   [b]Matt 10:18   **16:22** [a]2 Cor 6:5; 11:23, 25; 1 Thess 2:2   **16:24** [1]Or perhaps a log or wooden column to which prisoners' feet were chained or tied.   **16:26** [a]Acts 4:31   [b]Acts 5:19; 12:7, 10   **16:30** [a]Luke 3:10; Acts 2:37; 9:6; 22:10   **16:31** [a][John 3:16, 36; 6:47; Acts 13:38–39; Rom 10:9–11; 1 John 5:10]   [1]Maj. Mss add *Christ*.   **16:34** [a]Matt 5:4; Luke 5:29; 19:6   **16:35** [1]These were the chief officials of Philippi.   **16:37** [a]Acts 22:25–29   **16:39** [a]Matt 8:34   **16:40** [a]Acts 16:14   **17:1** [a]Acts 17:11, 13; 20:4; 27:2; Phil 4:16; 1 Thess 1:1; 2 Thess 1:1; 2 Tim 4:10   **17:2** [a]Luke 4:16; Acts 9:20; 13:5, 14; 14:1; 16:13; 19:8   [b]1 Thess 2:1–16   **17:3** [a]Luke 24:26, 46; Acts 18:5, 28; Gal 3:1   [1]Or *Messiah*; both "Christ" (Grk.) and "Messiah" (Heb., Aram.) mean "one who has been anointed."

4Some of them were persuaded [a]and joined Paul and [b]Silas, along with a large group of God-fearing Greeks and quite a few prominent women. 5But the Jews became [a]jealous, and gathering together some worthless men from the rabble in the marketplace, they formed a mob and set the city in an uproar. They attacked [b]Jason's house, trying to find Paul and Silas to bring them out to the assembly. 6When they did not find them, they dragged Jason and some of the brothers before the city officials, screaming, "These [a]people who have stirred up trouble throughout the world have come here too, 7and Jason has welcomed them as guests! They are all acting against Caesar's decrees, [a]saying there is another king named Jesus!" 8They caused confusion among the crowd and the city officials who heard these things. 9After the city officials had received bail from Jason and the others, they released them.

Paul and Silas at Berea

10The [a]brothers sent Paul and Silas off to Berea at once, during the night. When they arrived, they went to the Jewish synagogue. 11These Jews were more open-minded than those in Thessalonica, for they eagerly received the message, [a]examining the scriptures carefully every day to see if these things were so. 12Therefore many of them believed, along with quite a few prominent Greek women and men. 13But when the Jews from Thessalonica heard that Paul had also proclaimed the word of God in Berea, they came there too, inciting and disturbing the crowds. 14[a]Then the brothers sent Paul away to the coast at once, but Silas and Timothy remained in Berea. 15Those who accompanied Paul escorted him as far as Athens, and after [a]receiving an order for Silas and Timothy to come to him as soon as possible, they left.

Paul at Athens

16While Paul was waiting for them in Athens, [a]his spirit was greatly upset because he saw the city was full of idols. 17So he was addressing the Jews and the God-fearing Gentiles in the synagogue, and in the marketplace every day those who happened to be there. 18Also some of the Epicurean and Stoic philosophers were conversing with him, and some were asking, "What does this foolish babbler want to say?" Others said, "He seems to be a proclaimer of foreign gods." (They said this because he was proclaiming the good news about [a]Jesus and the resurrection.) 19So they took Paul and brought him to the Areopagus, saying, "May we know what this new teaching is that you are proclaiming? 20For you are bringing some surprising things to our ears, so we want to know what they mean." 21(All the Athenians and the foreigners who lived there used to spend their time in nothing else than telling or listening to something new.)

22So Paul stood before the Areopagus and said, "Men of Athens, I see that you are very religious[1] in all respects. 23For as I went around and observed closely your objects of worship, I even found an altar with this inscription: 'To an unknown god.' Therefore what you worship without knowing it, this I proclaim to you. 24The [a]God who made the world and everything in it, who is [b]Lord of heaven and earth, [c]does not live in temples made by human hands, 25nor is he served by human hands, as if he needed anything, because he himself [a]gives life and breath and everything to everyone. 26From one man [a]he made every nation of the human race to inhabit the entire earth, determining their set times and the fixed limits of the places where they would live, 27[a]so that they would search for God and perhaps grope around for him and find him, [b]though he is not far from each one of us. 28For [a]in him we live and move about and exist, [b]as even some of your own poets have said, 'For we too are his offspring.' 29So since [a]we are God's offspring, we should not think the deity is like gold or silver or stone, an image made by human skill and imagination. 30Therefore, although God has overlooked such times of ignorance, [a]he [b]now commands all people everywhere to repent, 31because

17:4 [a]Acts 28:24   [b]Acts 15:22, 27, 32, 40   17:5 [a]Acts 13:45   [b]Acts 17:6–7, 9; Rom 16:21   17:6 [a][Acts 16:20]   17:7 [a]Luke 23:2; John 19:12; 1 Pet 2:13   17:10 [a]Acts 9:25; 17:14   17:11 [a]Isa 34:16; Luke 16:29; John 5:39   17:14 [a]Matt 10:23   17:15 [a]Acts 18:5   17:16 [a]2 Pet 2:8   17:18 [a]1 Cor 15:12   17:22 [1]Or perhaps *devout, superstitious*; perhaps intended as a backhanded compliment, playing on the ambiguity.   17:24 [a]Isa 42:5; Acts 14:15   [b]Deut 10:14; Ps 115:16; Matt 11:25   [c]1 Kgs 8:27; Acts 7:48–50   17:25 [a]Gen 2:7; Isa 42:5; Dan 5:23   17:26 [a]Deut 32:8; Job 12:23; Dan 4:35   17:27 [a][Rom 1:20]   [b]Deut 4:7; Ps 139:7, 10; Jer 23:23–24; [Acts 14:17]   17:28 [a][Col 1:17; Heb 1:3]   [b]Titus 1:12   17:29 [a]Ps 115:4–7; Isa 40:18–19; Rom 1:23   17:30 [a]Acts 14:16; [Rom 3:25]   [b]Luke 24:47; Acts 26:20; [Titus 2:11–12]; 1 Pet 1:14; 4:3

[a]he has set a day on which he is going to judge the world in righteousness, by a man whom he designated, having provided proof to everyone by [b]raising him from the dead."

[32]Now when they heard about the resurrection from the dead, some began to scoff, but others said, "We will hear you again about this." [33]So Paul left the Areopagus. [34]But some people joined him and believed. Among them were Dionysius, who was a member of the Areopagus, a woman named Damaris, and others with them.

Paul at Corinth

18 After this Paul departed from Athens and went to Corinth. [2]There he found a Jew named [a]Aquila, a native of Pontus, who had recently come from Italy with his wife Priscilla, because Claudius had ordered all the Jews to depart from Rome. Paul approached them, [3a]and because he worked at the same trade, he stayed with them and worked with them (for they were tentmakers by trade). [4]He addressed both Jews [a]and Greeks in the synagogue every Sabbath, attempting to persuade them.

[5]Now [a]when Silas and Timothy arrived from Macedonia, Paul became wholly [b]absorbed with proclaiming the word, testifying to the Jews that Jesus was the Christ. [6]When they opposed him and reviled him, [a]he protested by shaking out his [b]clothes and said to them, "[c]Your blood be on your own heads! [d]I am guiltless! [e]From now on I will go to the Gentiles!" [7]Then Paul left the synagogue and went to the house of a person named Titius Justus, a Gentile who worshiped God, whose house was next door to the synagogue. [8]Crispus, [a]the president of the synagogue, believed in the Lord together with his entire household, and many of the Corinthians who heard about it believed and were baptized. [9]The Lord said to Paul by a vision in [a]the night, "Do not be afraid, but speak and do not be silent [10]because I am with you, and no one will assault you to harm you [a]because I have many people in this city." [11]So he stayed there a year and six months, teaching the word of God among them.

Paul before the Proconsul Gallio

[12]Now while Gallio was proconsul of Achaia, the Jews attacked Paul together and brought him before the judgment seat, [13]saying, "This man is persuading people to worship God in a way contrary to the law!" [14]But just as Paul was about to speak, Gallio said to the Jews, "If it were a matter of some crime or serious piece of villainy, I would have been justified in accepting the complaint of you Jews, [15]but since it concerns points of [a]disagreement about words and names and your own law, settle it yourselves. I will not be a judge of these things!" [16]Then he had them forced away from the judgment seat. [17]So they all seized [a]Sosthenes, the president of the synagogue, and began to beat him in front of the judgment seat. Yet none of these things were of any concern to Gallio.

Paul Returns to Antioch in Syria

[18]Paul, after staying many more days in Corinth, said farewell to [a]the brothers and sailed away to Syria accompanied by Priscilla and Aquila. He had his hair cut off at [b]Cenchrea because he had made a vow. [19]When they reached Ephesus, Paul left Priscilla and Aquila behind there, but he himself went into the synagogue and addressed the Jews. [20]When they asked him to stay longer, he would not consent, [21]but [a]said farewell to them and added, "I will come back to you again if [b]God wills." Then he set sail from Ephesus, [22]and when he arrived at [a]Caesarea, he went up and greeted the church at Jerusalem and then went down to Antioch. [23]After he spent some time there, Paul left and went through the region of [a]Galatia and Phrygia, [b]strengthening all the disciples.

Apollos Begins His Ministry

[24a]Now a Jew named Apollos, a native of Alexandria, arrived in Ephesus. He was an eloquent speaker, well-versed in the scriptures. [25]He had been instructed in the way of the Lord, and with great [a]enthusiasm he spoke and taught accurately the facts about

17:31 [a] Ps 9:8; 96:13; 98:9; John 5:22, 27; Acts 10:42; Rom 2:16   [b] Acts 2:24   18:2 [a] Rom 16:3; 1 Cor 16:19; 2 Tim 4:19
18:3 [a] Acts 20:34; 1 Cor 4:12; 9:14; 2 Cor 11:7; 12:13; 1 Thess 2:9; 4:11; 2 Thess 3:8   18:4 [a] Acts 17:2   18:5 [a] Acts 17:14–15
[b] Acts 18:28   18:6 [a] Acts 13:45   [b] Neh 5:13; Matt 10:14; Acts 13:51   [c] Lev 20:9, 11, 12; 2 Sam 1:16; 1 Kgs 2:33; Ezek 18:13;
33:4, 6, 8; Matt 27:25; Acts 20:26   [d] [Ezek 3:18–19]   [e] Acts 13:46–48; 28:28   18:8 [a] 1 Cor 1:14   18:9 [a] Acts 23:11
18:10 [a] Jer 1:18–19   18:15 [a] Acts 23:29; 25:19   18:17 [a] 1 Cor 1:1   18:18 [a] Num 6:2, 5, 9, 18; Acts 21:24   [b] Rom 16:1
18:21 [a] Acts 19:21; 20:16   [b] 1 Cor 4:19; Heb 6:3; Jas 4:15   18:22 [a] Acts 8:40   18:23 [a] Gal 1:2   [b] Acts 14:22;
15:32, 41   18:24 [a] Acts 19:1; 1 Cor 1:12; 3:4; 16:12; Titus 3:13   18:25 [a] Rom 12:11

Jesus, [b]although he knew only the baptism of John. [26]He began to speak out fearlessly in the synagogue, but when Priscilla and Aquila heard him, they took him aside and explained the way of God to him more accurately. [27]When Apollos wanted to cross over to Achaia, [a]the brothers encouraged him and wrote to the disciples to welcome him. When he arrived, he assisted greatly those who had believed by grace, [28]for he refuted the Jews vigorously in public debate, [a]demonstrating from the scriptures that the Christ was Jesus.

Disciples of John the Baptist at Ephesus

19 While [a]Apollos was in Corinth, Paul went through [b]the inland regions and came to Ephesus. He found some disciples there [2]and said to them, "Did you receive the Holy Spirit when you believed?" They replied, "No, [a]we have not even heard that there is a Holy Spirit." [3]So Paul said, "[a]Into what then were you baptized?" "Into John's baptism," they replied. [4]Paul said, "[a]John baptized with a baptism of repentance, telling the people to believe in the one who was to come after him, that is, in Jesus." [5]When they heard this, they were baptized [a]in the name of the Lord Jesus, [6]and when Paul [a]placed his hands on them, [b]the Holy Spirit came upon them, and they began to speak in tongues and to prophesy. [7](Now there were about 12 men in all.)

Paul Continues to Minister at Ephesus

[8]So Paul entered the synagogue [a]and spoke out fearlessly for three months, addressing[1] and convincing them [b]about the kingdom of God. [9]But [a]when some were stubborn and refused to believe, reviling the Way before the congregation, he left them and took the disciples with him, addressing them every day in the lecture hall[1] [b]of Tyrannus. [10][a]This went on for two years, so that all who lived in the province of Asia, both Jews and Greeks, heard the word of the Lord.

The Seven Sons of Sceva

[11a]God was performing extraordinary miracles by Paul's hands, [12]so [a]that when even handkerchiefs or aprons that had touched his body were brought to the sick, their diseases left them and the evil spirits went out of them. [13a]But some itinerant[1] Jewish exorcists tried to [b]invoke the name of the Lord Jesus over those who were possessed by evil spirits, saying, "I sternly warn you by Jesus whom Paul [c]preaches." [14](Now seven sons of a man named Sceva, a Jewish high priest, were doing this.) [15]But the evil spirit replied to them, "I know about Jesus[1] and I am acquainted with Paul, but who are you?" [16]Then the man who was possessed by the evil spirit jumped on them and beat them all into submission. He prevailed against them so that they fled from that house naked and wounded. [17]This became known to all who lived in Ephesus, both Jews and Greeks; [a]fear came over them all, and the name of the Lord Jesus was praised. [18]Many of those who had believed came forward, [a]confessing and making their deeds known. [19]Large numbers of those who had practiced magic collected their books[1] and burned them up in the presence of everyone. When the value of the books was added up, it was found to total 50,000 silver coins.[2] [20]In this [a]way the word of the Lord continued to grow in power and to prevail.

A Riot in Ephesus

[21a]Now after all these things had taken place, Paul [b]resolved to go to Jerusalem, passing through [c]Macedonia and Achaia. He said, "After [d]I have been there, I must also see Rome." [22]So after sending two of his assistants, [a]Timothy and [b]Erastus, to Macedonia, he himself stayed on for a while in the province of Asia.

[23]At that time [a]a great disturbance took place concerning [b]the Way. [24]For a man named Demetrius, a silversmith who made silver shrines of Artemis, brought a great [a]deal of business to the craftsmen.

18:25 [b][Matt 3:1–11; Mark 1:7–8; Luke 3:16–17; 7:29; John 1:26, 33]; Acts 19:3   18:27 [a]1 Cor 3:6   18:28 [a]Acts 9:22; 17:3; 18:5   19:1 [a]1 Cor 1:12; 3:5–6; Titus 3:13   [b]Acts 18:23   19:2 [a]1 Sam 3:7; Acts 8:16   19:3 [a]Luke 7:29; Acts 18:25   19:4 [a]Matt 3:11; Mark 1:4, 7, 8; Luke 3:16; [John 1:15, 26, 27]; Acts 13:24   19:5 [a]Matt 28:19; Acts 8:12, 16; 10:48   19:6 [a]Acts 6:6; 8:17   [b]Mark 16:17; Acts 2:4; 10:46   19:8 [a]Acts 17:2; 18:4   [b]Acts 1:3; 28:23   [1]Or reasoned, disputed, argued.   19:9 [a]2 Tim 1:15; 2 Pet 2:2; Jude 10   [b]Acts 9:2; 19:23; 22:4; 24:14   [1]A place where teachers and pupils met.   19:10 [a]Acts 19:8; 20:31   19:11 [a]Mark 16:20; Acts 14:3   19:12 [a]2 Kgs 4:29; Acts 5:15   19:13 [a]Matt 12:27; Luke 11:19   [b]Mark 9:38; Luke 9:49   [c]1 Cor 1:23; 2:2   [1]Grk. some Jewish exorcists who traveled about.   19:15 [1]Grk. Jesus I know about; an emphatic Grk. construction.   19:17 [a]Luke 1:65; 7:16; Acts 2:43; 5:5, 11   19:18 [a]Matt 3:6   19:19 [1]Or scrolls.   [2]Equal to 8,300 weeks of wages for the average worker.   19:20 [a]Acts 6:7; 12:24   19:21 [a]Rom 15:25; Gal 2:1   [b]Acts 20:22; 2 Cor 1:16   [c]Acts 20:1; 1 Cor 16:5   [d]Acts 18:21; 23:11; Rom 1:13; 15:22–29   19:22 [a]1 Tim 1:2   [b]Rom 16:23; 2 Tim 4:20   19:23 [a]2 Cor 1:8   [b]Acts 9:2   19:24 [a]Acts 16:16, 19

[25] He gathered these together, along with the workmen in similar trades, and said, "Men, you know that our prosperity[1] comes from this business. [26] And you see and hear that this Paul has persuaded and turned away a large crowd, not only in Ephesus but in practically all of [a] the province of Asia, by saying that gods made by hands are not gods at all. [27] There is danger not only that this business of ours will come into disrepute, but also that the temple of the great goddess Artemis will be regarded as nothing, and she whom all the province of Asia and the world worship will suffer the loss of her greatness."

[28] When they heard this they became enraged and began to shout, "Great is Artemis of the Ephesians!" [29] The city was filled with the uproar, and the crowd rushed to the theater together, dragging with them [a] Gaius and [b] Aristarchus, the Macedonians who were Paul's traveling companions. [30] But when Paul wanted to enter the public assembly, the disciples would not let him. [31] Even some of the provincial authorities[1] who were his friends sent a message to him, urging him not to venture into the theater. [32] So then some were shouting one thing, some another, for the assembly was in confusion, and most of them did not know why they had met together. [33] Some of the crowd concluded it was about [a] Alexander because the Jews had pushed him to the front. Alexander, [b] gesturing with his hand, was wanting to make a defense before the public assembly. [34] But when they recognized that he was a Jew, they all shouted in unison, "Great is Artemis of the Ephesians!" for about two hours. [35] After the city secretary[1] quieted the crowd, he said, "Men of Ephesus, what person is there who does not know that the city of the Ephesians is the keeper of the temple of the great Artemis and of her image that fell from heaven? [36] So because these facts are indisputable, you must keep quiet and not do anything reckless. [37] For you have brought these men here who are neither temple robbers nor blasphemers of our goddess. [38] If then Demetrius and the craftsmen who are with him have a complaint against someone, the courts are open and there are proconsuls; let them bring charges against one another there. [39] But if you want anything in addition, it will have to be settled in a legal assembly.[1] [40] For we are in danger of being charged with rioting today, since there is no cause we can give to explain this disorderly gathering." [41] After he had said this, he dismissed the assembly.

Paul Travels through Macedonia and Greece

20 After the disturbance had ended, Paul sent for the disciples, and after encouraging them and saying farewell, he [a] left to go to Macedonia. [2] After he had gone through those regions and spoken many words of encouragement to the believers there, he came to [a] Greece, [3] where [a] he stayed for three months. Because the Jews had made a plot against him as he was intending to sail for Syria, he decided to return through Macedonia. [4] Paul was accompanied by Sopater son of Pyrrhus from Berea, [a] Aristarchus and Secundus from Thessalonica, [b] Gaius from Derbe, and [c] Timothy, as well as [d] Tychicus and [e] Trophimus from the province of Asia. [5] These had gone on ahead and were waiting for us in [a] Troas. [6] We sailed away from Philippi after [a] the days of Unleavened Bread, and within five days we came to the others [b] in Troas, where we stayed for seven days. [7] On [a] the first day of the week, when we met [b] to break bread, Paul began to speak to the people, and because he intended to leave the next day, he extended his message until midnight. [8] (Now there were many lamps[1] [a] in the upstairs room where we were meeting.) [9] A young man named Eutychus, who was sitting in the window,[1] was sinking into a deep sleep while Paul continued to speak for a long time. Fast asleep, he fell down from the third story and was picked up dead. [10] But Paul went down, [a] threw himself on the young man, put his arms around

19:25 [1] Or possibly *an easy way for us to earn a living.*   19:26 [a] Deut 4:28; Ps 115:4; Isa 44:10–20; Jer 10:3; Acts 17:29; 1 Cor 8:4; 10:19; Rev 9:20   19:29 [a] Acts 20:4; Rom 16:23; 1 Cor 1:14; 3 John 1   [b] Acts 20:4; 27:2; Col 4:10; Phlm 24   19:31 [1] Grk. *Asiarchs*; high-ranking officials of the province of Asia.   19:33 [a] 1 Tim 1:20; 2 Tim 4:14   [b] Acts 12:17   19:35 [1] Or *clerk.*   19:39 [1] Or *in a legal meeting of the citizens*; a meeting that took place three times a year.   20:1 [a] 1 Cor 16:5; 1 Tim 1:3   20:2 [a] Acts 17:15; 18:1   20:3 [a] Acts 9:23; 23:12; 25:3; 2 Cor 11:26   20:4 [a] Acts 19:29; Col 4:10   [b] Acts 19:29   [c] Acts 16:1   [d] Eph 6:21; Col 4:7; 2 Tim 4:12; Titus 3:12   [e] Acts 21:29; 2 Tim 4:20   20:5 [a] 2 Cor 2:12; 2 Tim 4:13   20:6 [a] Exod 12:14–15   [b] Acts 16:8; 2 Cor 2:12; 2 Tim 4:13   20:7 [a] 1 Cor 16:2; Rev 1:10   [b] Acts 2:42, 46; 20:11; 1 Cor 10:16   20:8 [a] Acts 1:13   [1] Or *torch.*   20:9 [1] Probably a simple opening in the wall.   20:10 [a] 1 Kgs 17:21; 2 Kgs 4:34

him, and said, "[b]Do not be distressed, for he is still alive!" [11]Then Paul went back upstairs, and after he had broken bread and eaten, he talked with them a long time, until dawn. Then he left. [12]They took the boy home alive and were greatly comforted.

The Voyage to Miletus

[13]We went on ahead to the ship and put out to sea for Assos, intending to take Paul aboard there, for he had arranged it this way. He himself was intending to go there by land. [14]When he met us in Assos, we took him aboard and went to Mitylene. [15]We set sail from there, and on the following day we arrived off Chios. The next day we approached Samos, and the day after that we arrived at Miletus. [16]For Paul had decided to sail past [a]Ephesus so as not [b]to spend time in [c]the province of Asia, for he was hurrying to arrive in Jerusalem, if possible, by the day of Pentecost. [17]From Miletus he sent a message to Ephesus, telling the elders of the church to come to him.

[18]When they arrived, he said to them, "You yourselves know how I lived the whole time I was with you, [a]from the first day I set foot in the province of Asia, [19]serving the Lord with all humility and with tears, and with the trials that happened to me because [a]of the plots of the Jews. [20]You know that [a]I did not hold back from proclaiming to you anything that would be helpful, and from teaching you publicly and from house to house, [21a]testifying to both Jews and Greeks about [b]repentance toward God and faith in our Lord Jesus.[1] [22]And now, compelled by the Spirit, [a]I am going to Jerusalem without knowing what will happen to me there, [23]except that [a]the Holy Spirit warns me in town after town that imprisonment and persecutions are waiting for me. [24]But I do [a]not consider my life worth anything to myself, so [b]that I may finish my task[1] [c]and the ministry [d]that I received from the Lord Jesus, to testify to the good news of God's grace.

[25]"And now I know that none of you among whom I went around proclaiming the kingdom will see me[1] again. [26]Therefore I declare to you today that I am [a]innocent of the blood of you all. [27]For I did not hold back from announcing to you [a]the whole purpose of God. [28]Watch out [a]for[1] yourselves and for all the flock of which the Holy Spirit [b]has made you overseers, to shepherd the church of God[2] [c]that he obtained [d]with the blood of his own Son.[3] [29]I know that after I am gone [a]fierce wolves[1] will come in among you, not sparing the flock. [30]Even [a]from among your own group men will arise, teaching perversions of the truth[1] to draw the disciples away after them. [31]Therefore be alert, remembering that night and day [a]for three years I did not stop warning each one of you with tears. [32]And now I entrust you [a]to God and [b]to the message of his grace. This message is able to build you up [c]and give you an inheritance among all those who are sanctified. [33]I have desired[1] no one's silver or gold or clothing. [34]You yourselves know [a]that these hands of mine provided for my needs and the needs of those who were with me. [35]By all these things, I have shown you that [a]by working in this way we must help the weak, and remember the words of the Lord Jesus that he himself said, 'It is more blessed to give than to receive.'"

[36]When he had said these things, he knelt down with them all and prayed. [37]They all began to weep loudly, and [a]hugged Paul and kissed him, [38]especially saddened[1] by what he had said, that they were not going to see him again. Then they accompanied him to the ship.

Paul's Journey to Jerusalem

21 After we tore ourselves away from them, we put out to sea, and sailing a straight course, we came to Cos, on the next day to Rhodes, and from there to Patara. [2]We found a ship crossing over to Phoenicia, went aboard, and put out to sea. [3]After we sighted Cyprus and left it behind on our

20:10[b] Matt 9:23–24; Mark 5:39   20:16[a] Acts 18:21; 19:21; 21:4   [b] Acts 24:17   [c] Acts 2:1; 1 Cor 16:8   20:18[a] Acts 18:19; 19:1, 10; 20:4, 16   20:19[a] Acts 20:3   20:20[a] Acts 20:27   20:21[a] Acts 18:5; 19:10   [b] Mark 1:15   [1] Sev. MSS add Christ.   20:22[a] Acts 19:21   20:23[a] Acts 21:4, 11   20:24[a] Acts 21:13   [b] Acts 13:25; 2 Tim 4:7   [c] Acts 1:17   [d] Gal 1:1   [1] Grk. course.   20:25[1] Grk. will see my face.   20:26[a] Acts 18:6; 2 Cor 7:2   20:27[a] Luke 7:30; John 15:15; Eph 1:11   20:28[a] Luke 12:32; John 21:15–17; Acts 20:29; [1 Tim 4:16]; 1 Pet 5:2   [b] 1 Cor 12:28   [c] Eph 1:7, 14; Col 1:14; Titus 2:14; Heb 9:12; [1 Pet 1:19]; Rev 5:9   [d] Heb 9:14   [1] Or Be on your guard for.   [2] Sev. MSS of the Lord; maj. later MSS of the Lord and God.   [3] Or with his own blood; Grk. with the blood of his own.   20:29[a] Ezek 22:27; Matt 7:15   [1] I.e., people like fierce wolves.   20:30[a] 1 Tim 1:20; 2 Tim 1:15   [1] Grk. speaking crooked things.   20:31[a] Acts 19:8, 10; 24:17   20:32[a] Heb 13:9   [b] Acts 9:31   [c] Acts 26:18; Eph 1:14, 18; 5:5; Col 1:12; 3:24; [Heb 9:15; 1 Pet 1:4]   20:33[1] Trad. coveted.   20:34[a] Acts 18:3; 1 Cor 4:12; 1 Thess 2:9; 2 Thess 3:8   20:35[a] Rom 15:1; 1 Cor 9:12; 2 Cor 11:9, 12; Eph 4:28; 1 Thess 4:11; 2 Thess 3:8   20:37[a] Gen 45:14   20:38[1] Or pained.

port side, we sailed on to Syria and put in at Tyre because the ship was to unload its cargo there. [4]After we located the disciples, we stayed there seven days. [a]They repeatedly told Paul through the Spirit not to set foot in Jerusalem. [5]When our time was over, [a]we left and went on our way. All of them, with their wives and children, accompanied us outside of the city. After kneeling down on the beach and praying, [6]we said farewell to one another. Then we went aboard the ship, and they returned to their own [a]homes. [7]We continued the voyage from Tyre and arrived at Ptolemais, and when we had greeted the brothers, we stayed with them for one day. [8]On the next day we left and came to [a]Caesarea, and entered [b]the house of Philip the evangelist, [c]who was one of the seven, and stayed with him. [9](He had four unmarried[1] daughters [a]who prophesied.)

[10]While we remained there for a number of days, a prophet named [a]Agabus came down from Judea. [11]He came to us, took Paul's belt, tied his own hands and feet with it, and said, "The Holy Spirit says this: 'This is the [a]way the Jews in Jerusalem will tie up the man whose belt this is and will hand him over to the Gentiles.'" [12]When we heard this, both we and the local people begged him not to go up to Jerusalem. [13]Then Paul replied, "[a]What are you doing, weeping and breaking my heart? For I am ready not only to be tied up, but even to die in Jerusalem for the name of the Lord Jesus." [14]Because [a]he could not be persuaded, we said no more except, "The Lord's will be done."

[15]After these days we got ready and started up to Jerusalem. [16]Some of the disciples from Caesarea came along with us too, and brought us to the house of Mnason of Cyprus, a disciple from the earliest times, with whom we were to stay. [17][a]When we arrived in Jerusalem, the brothers welcomed us gladly.[1] [18]The next day Paul went in with us to see [a]James, and all the elders were there. [19]When Paul had greeted [a]them, he began to explain in detail what God had done among the Gentiles [b]through his ministry. [20]When

they heard this, they praised God. Then they said to him, "You see, brother, how many thousands of Jews[1] there are who have believed, and they are all ardent [a]observers of the law. [21]They have been informed about you—that you teach all the Jews now living among the Gentiles to abandon Moses, telling them not to circumcise their children or live according to our customs. [22]What then should we do? They will no doubt hear that you have come. [23]So do what we tell you: We have four men who have taken a vow; [24]take them and purify yourself along with them and pay their expenses, so that they may [a]have their heads shaved. Then everyone will know there is nothing in what they have been told about you, but that you yourself live in conformity with[1] the law. [25]But regarding the Gentiles who have believed, [a]we have written a letter, having decided that they should avoid meat that has been sacrificed to idols and blood and what has been strangled and sexual immorality." [26]Then Paul took the men the next day, and after he had purified himself along with them, he [a]went [b]to the temple and gave notice of the completion of the days of purification, when[1] the sacrifice would be offered for each[2] of them. [27]When [a]the seven days were almost over, the Jews from the province of Asia who had seen him in the temple area stirred up the whole crowd and [b]seized him, [28]shouting, "Men of Israel, help! This is the man [a]who teaches everyone everywhere against our people, our law, and this sanctuary! Furthermore he has brought Greeks into the inner courts of the temple[1] and made this holy place ritually unclean!" [29](For they had seen [a]Trophimus the Ephesian in the city with him previously, and they assumed Paul had brought him into the inner temple courts.) [30]The [a]whole city was stirred up, and the people rushed together. They seized Paul and dragged him out of the temple courts,[1] and immediately the doors were shut. [31]While they were [a]trying to kill him, a report was sent up[1] to the commanding officer of the cohort

21:4 [a][Acts 20:23; 21:12]   21:5 [a]Luke 22:41; Acts 9:40; 20:36   21:6 [a]John 1:11   21:8 [a]Acts 8:40; 21:16   [b]Acts 8:5, 26, 40; Eph 4:11; 2 Tim 4:5   [c]Acts 6:5   21:9 [a]Joel 2:28; Acts 2:17   [1]Grk. virgin; the emphasis seems to be that Philip's daughters were not married.   21:10 [a]Acts 11:28   21:11 [a]Acts 20:23; 21:33; 22:25   21:13 [a]Acts 20:24, 37   21:14 [a]Matt 6:10; 26:42; Luke 11:2; 22:42   21:17 [a]Acts 15:4   [1]Or warmly.   21:18 [a]Acts 15:13; Gal 1:19; 2:9   21:19 [a]Acts 15:4, 12; Rom 15:18–19   [b]Acts 1:17; 20:24; 1 Tim 2:7   21:20 [a]Acts 15:1; 22:3; [Rom 10:2]; Gal 1:14   [1]Grk. thousands there are among the Jews.   21:24 [a]Num 6:2, 13, 18; Acts 18:18   [1]Grk. adhere to the keeping of the law.   21:25 [a]Acts 15:19–20, 29   21:26 [a]John 11:55; Acts 21:24; 24:18   [b]Num 6:13; Acts 24:18   [1]Grk. until.   [2]Grk. for each one.   21:27 [a]Acts 20:19; 24:18   [b]Acts 26:21   21:28 [a][Matt 24:15]; Acts 6:13; 24:6   [1]Grk. into the temple.   21:29 [a]Acts 20:4   21:30 [a]2 Kgs 11:15; Acts 16:19; 26:21   [1]Grk. out of the temple.   21:31 [a]2 Cor 11:23   [1]Grk. went up; to the Antonia Fortress, where the Roman garrison was stationed.

that all Jerusalem was in confusion. [32a]He immediately took soldiers and centurions and ran down to the crowd. When they saw the commanding officer and the soldiers, they stopped beating Paul. [33]Then the commanding [a]officer came up and arrested him and [b]ordered him to be tied up with two chains;[1] he then asked who he was and what he had done. [34]But some in the crowd shouted one thing, and others something else, and when the commanding officer was unable to find out the truth because of the disturbance, he ordered Paul to be brought into the barracks. [35]When he came to the steps, Paul had to be carried by the soldiers because of the violence of the mob, [36]for a crowd of people followed them, screaming, "Away [a]with him!" [37]As Paul was about to be brought into the barracks, he said to the commanding officer, "May I say something to you?" The officer replied, "Do you know Greek? [38]Then [a]you're not that Egyptian who started a rebellion and led the 4,000 men of the 'Assassins'[1] into the wilderness sometime ago?" [39]Paul answered, "I am a Jew from Tarsus in Cilicia, a citizen of an important city. Please allow [a]me to speak to the people." [40]When the commanding officer had given him permission, Paul stood on the steps and [a]gestured to the people with his hand. When they had become silent, he addressed[1] them in [b]Aramaic,[2]

Paul's Defense

22 "[a]Brothers and fathers, listen to my defense that I now make to you." [2](When they heard that he was addressing them in [a]Aramaic,[1] they became even quieter.) Then Paul said, [3]"I am a Jew, born [a]in Tarsus in Cilicia, but brought up in this city, educated with strictness[1] [b]under[2] [c]Gamaliel [d]according to the law of our ancestors, and [e]was zealous for God just [f]as all of you are today. [4]I persecuted [a]this Way even to the point of death, tying up both men and women and putting them in prison, [5]as both the high priest and the [a]whole council

of elders can testify about me. [b]From them I also received letters [c]to the brothers in Damascus, and I was on my way to make arrests there and bring the prisoners to Jerusalem to be punished. [6]As [a]I was en route and near Damascus, about noon a very bright light from heaven suddenly flashed around me. [7]Then I fell to the ground and heard a voice saying to me, 'Saul, Saul, why are you persecuting me?' [8]I answered, 'Who are you, Lord?' He said to me, 'I am Jesus the Nazarene, whom you are persecuting.' [9]Those who were with me saw the light, but did not understand the voice of the one who was speaking to me. [10]So I asked, 'What should I do, Lord?' The Lord said to me, 'Get up and go to Damascus; there you will be told about everything that you have been designated to do.' [11]Since I could not see because of the brilliance of that light, I came to Damascus led by the hand of those who were with me. [12]A [a]man named Ananias, [b]a devout man according to the law, well spoken of by all the [c]Jews who live there, [13]came to me and stood beside me and said to me, 'Brother Saul, regain your sight!' And at that very moment I looked up and saw him. [14]Then [a]he said, 'The God of our ancestors [b]has already chosen you to [c]know his will, to [d]see the Righteous One, [e]and to hear a command from his mouth, [15a]because you will be his witness to all people of [b]what you have seen and heard. [16a]And now what are you waiting for? Get up, be baptized, and have your sins washed away, calling [b]on his name.' [17]When [a]I returned to Jerusalem and was praying in the temple, I fell into a trance [18]and [a]saw the Lord saying to me, 'Hurry and get out of Jerusalem quickly because they will not accept your testimony about me.' [19]I replied, 'Lord, they [a]themselves know that I imprisoned and [b]beat those in the various synagogues who believed in you. [20a]And when the blood of your witness Stephen was shed, I myself was standing nearby, [b]approving, and guarding the cloaks of those who were killing him.'

21:32 [a]Acts 23:27; 24:7   **21:33** [a]Acts 24:7   [b]Acts 20:23; 21:11; Eph 6:20; 2 Tim 1:16; 2:9   [1]I.e., something like handcuffs.
21:36 [a]Luke 23:18; John 19:15; Acts 22:22   **21:38** [a]Acts 5:36   [1]Grk. *the Sicarii.*   **21:39** [a]Acts 9:11; 22:3; 2 Cor 11:22; Phil 3:4–6
21:40 [a]Acts 12:17   [b]John 5:2; Acts 22:2   [1]Or *spoke out to*; with a possible emphasis on loudness.   [2]Grk. *in the Hebrew dialect, saying.*   **22:1** [a]Acts 7:2   **22:2** [a]Acts 21:40   [1]Grk. *in the Hebrew language.*   **22:3** [a]Acts 21:39; 2 Cor 11:22   [b]Deut 33:3   [c]Acts 5:34   [d]Acts 23:6; 26:5; Phil 3:6   [e]Acts 21:20; Gal 1:14   [f][Rom 10:2]   [1]Or *with precision.*   [2]Grk. *strictly at the feet of.*   **22:4** [a]Acts 8:3; 26:9–11; Phil 3:6; 1 Tim 1:13   **22:5** [a]Acts 23:14; 24:1; 25:15   [b]Luke 22:66; Acts 4:5; 1 Tim 4:14   [c]Acts 9:2   **22:6** [a]Acts 9:3; 26:12–13   **22:12** [a]Acts 9:17   [b]Acts 10:22   [c]1 Tim 3:7   **22:14** [a]Acts 3:13; 5:30   [b]Acts 9:15; 26:16; Gal 1:15   [c]Acts 3:14; 7:52   [d]Acts 9:17; 26:16; 1 Cor 9:1; 15:8   [e]1 Cor 11:23; Gal 1:12   **22:15** [a]Acts 23:11   [b]Acts 4:20; 26:16   **22:16** [a]Acts 2:38; 1 Cor 6:11; [Eph 5:26]; Heb 10:22   [b]Acts 9:14; Rom 10:13   **22:17** [a]Acts 9:26; 26:20; 2 Cor 12:2   **22:18** [a]Acts 22:14   **22:19** [a]Acts 8:3; 22:4   [b]Matt 10:17; Acts 26:11   **22:20** [a]Acts 7:54–8:1   [b]Luke 11:48

[21]Then he said to me, 'Go, [a]because I will send you far away to the Gentiles.'"

The Roman Commander Questions Paul

[22]The crowd was listening to him until he said this.[1] Then they raised their voices and shouted, "[a]Away with this man from the earth! For [b]he should not be allowed to live!" [23]While they were screaming and throwing off their cloaks and tossing dust in the air, [24]the commanding officer ordered Paul to be brought back into the barracks. He told them to interrogate Paul by beating him with a lash so that he could find out the reason the crowd was shouting at Paul in this way. [25]When they had stretched him out for the lash,[1] Paul said to the centurion standing nearby, "[a]Is it legal for you to lash a man who is a Roman citizen without a proper trial?"[2] [26]When the centurion heard this, he went to the commanding officer and reported it, saying, "What are you about to do? For this man is a Roman citizen." [27]So the commanding officer came and asked Paul, "Tell me, are you a Roman citizen?" He replied, "Yes." [28]The commanding officer answered, "I acquired this citizenship with a large sum of money." "But I was even born a citizen," Paul replied. [29]Then those who were about to interrogate him stayed away[1] from him, and the commanding officer was frightened when he realized that Paul was a Roman citizen and that he had had him tied up.

Paul before the Sanhedrin

[30]The next day, because the commanding officer wanted to know the true reason Paul was being accused by the Jews, he released him and ordered the chief priests and the whole council to assemble. He then brought Paul down and had him stand before them.

23 Paul looked directly at the council[1] and said, "Brothers, [a]I have lived my life with a clear conscience before God to this day." [2]At that the high priest Ananias ordered those standing near Paul [a]to strike[1] him on the mouth. [3]Then Paul said to him, "God is going to strike you, you whitewashed wall! [a]Do you sit there judging me according to the law,[1] and in violation of the law you order me to be struck?" [4]Those standing near him said, "Do you dare insult God's high priest?" [5]Paul [a]replied, "I did not realize, brothers, that he was the high priest, for it is written, '[b]*You must not speak evil about a ruler of your people.*'"[1]

[6]Then when Paul noticed that part of them were Sadducees and the others Pharisees, he shouted out in the council, "Brothers, [a]I am a Pharisee, a son of Pharisees. I am on trial [b]concerning the hope of the resurrection[1] of the dead!" [7]When he said this, an argument began between the Pharisees and the Sadducees, and the assembly was divided. [8]([a]For the Sadducees say there is no resurrection, or angel, or spirit, but the Pharisees acknowledge them all.) [9]There was a great commotion, and some experts in the law from the party of the Pharisees stood up and protested strongly, "[a]We find nothing wrong with this man. What [b]if a spirit or an angel has spoken to him?" [10]When the argument became so great the commanding officer feared that they would tear Paul to pieces, he ordered the detachment to go down, take him away from them by force, and bring him into the barracks.[1]

[11]The following night [a]the Lord stood near Paul and said, "Have courage, for just as you have testified about me in [b]Jerusalem, so you must also testify in [c]Rome."

The Plot to Kill Paul

[12]When morning came, the Jews formed a conspiracy and bound themselves with an oath not to eat or drink anything until they had [a]killed Paul. [13]There were more than forty of them who formed this conspiracy. [14]They went to the chief priests and the [a]elders and said, "We have bound ourselves with a solemn oath not to partake of anything until we have killed Paul. [15]So now you and the council request the commanding officer to bring him down to you,

22:21 [a] Acts 9:15; Rom 1:5; 11:13; Gal 2:7–8; Eph 3:7–8; 1 Tim 2:7; 2 Tim 1:11   22:22 [a] Acts 21:36; 1 Thess 2:16   [b] Acts 25:24   [1] Grk. *until this word.*   22:25 [a] Acts 16:37   [1] Grk. *the thongs.*   [2] Or *a Roman citizen and uncondemned.*   22:29 [1] I.e., they held back from continuing the flogging.   23:1 [a] Acts 24:16; 1 Cor 4:4; 2 Cor 1:12; 4:2; 2 Tim 1:3; Heb 13:18   [1] Grk. *the Sanhedrin.*   23:2 [a] 1 Kgs 22:24; Jer 20:2; John 18:22   [1] Or *hit.*   23:3 [a] Lev 19:35; Deut 25:1–2; John 7:51   [1] The law of Moses.   23:5 [a] Lev 5:17–18   [b] Exod 22:28; Eccl 10:20; 2 Pet 2:10   [1] Exod 22:28   23:6 [a] Acts 26:5; Phil 3:5   [b] Acts 24:15, 21; 26:6; 28:20   [1] I.e., concerning the hope that the dead will be resurrected.   23:8 [a] Matt 22:23; Mark 12:18; Luke 20:27   23:9 [a] Acts 25:25; 26:31   [b] John 12:29; Acts 22:6–7, 17, 18   23:10 [1] Or *the headquarters.*   23:11 [a] Acts 18:9; 27:23–24   [b] Acts 21:18–19; 22:1–21   [c] Acts 28:16–17, 23   23:12 [a] Acts 9:23–24; 25:3; 26:21; 27:42; 1 Thess 2:15   23:14 [a] Acts 4:5, 23; 6:12; 22:5; 24:1; 25:15

as if you were going to determine[1] his case by conducting a more thorough inquiry. We are ready to kill him before he comes near this place."

[16] But when the son of Paul's sister heard about the ambush, he came and entered the barracks[1] and told Paul. [17] Paul called one of the centurions and said, "Take this young man to the commanding officer, for he has something to report to him." [18] So the centurion took him and brought him to the commanding officer and said, "The prisoner Paul called me and asked me to bring this young man to you because he has something to tell you." [19] The commanding officer took him by the hand, withdrew privately, and asked, "What is it that you want to report to me?" [20] He replied, "[a] The Jews have agreed to ask you to bring Paul down to the council tomorrow, as if they were going to inquire more thoroughly about him. [21] So do not let them persuade you to do this because more than forty of them are lying in ambush for him. They have bound themselves with an oath not to eat or drink anything until they have killed him, and now they are ready, waiting for you to agree to their request."[1] [22] Then the commanding officer sent the young man away, directing him, "Tell no one that you have reported these things to me." [23] Then he summoned two of the centurions and said, "Make ready 200 soldiers to go to [a] Caesarea along with 70 horsemen[1] and 200 spearmen[2] by nine o'clock tonight,[3] [24] and provide mounts for Paul to ride so that he may be brought safely to Felix the governor."[1] [25] He wrote a letter that went like this:

[26] Claudius Lysias to His Excellency Governor Felix, greetings. [27a] This man was seized by the Jews and they were about to kill him, when I came up with the detachment and rescued him because I had learned that he was a Roman citizen. [28a] Since I wanted to know what charge they were accusing him of, I brought him down to their council.[1] [29] I found he was accused with reference [a] to controversial questions about their law, [b] but no charge against him deserved death or imprisonment. [30] When I was informed there would be a plot against this man, I sent him to you at once, [a] also ordering his accusers to state their charges against him before you.

[31] So the soldiers, in accordance with their orders, took Paul and brought him to Antipatris during the night. [32] The next day they let the horsemen go on with him, and they returned to the barracks. [33] When the horsemen came to [a] Caesarea and delivered the [b] letter to the governor, they also presented Paul to him. [34] When the governor had read the letter, he asked what province he was from. When he learned that he was from [a] Cilicia, [35] he [a] said, "I will give you a hearing when your accusers arrive too." Then he ordered that Paul be kept under guard in [b] Herod's palace.

The Accusations against Paul

24 After [a] five days the high priest [b] Ananias came down with some elders and an attorney[1] named Tertullus, and they brought formal charges against Paul to the governor. [2] When Paul had been summoned, Tertullus began to accuse him, saying, "We have experienced a lengthy time of peace through your rule, and reforms are being made in this nation through your foresight. [3] Most excellent Felix, we acknowledge this everywhere and in every way with all gratitude. [4] But so that I may not delay you any further, I beg you to hear us briefly with your customary graciousness. [5a] For we have found this man to be a troublemaker, one who stirs up riots among all the Jews throughout the world, and a ringleader of the sect of the Nazarenes. [6a] He even tried to desecrate the temple, so we arrested him.[1] [8a] When you examine him yourself, you will be able to learn from him about all these things we are accusing him of doing." [9] The

---

23:15 [1] Or *decide.*   23:16 [1] Or *the headquarters.*   23:20 [a] Acts 23:12   23:21 [1] Grk. *waiting for your approval, waiting for your agreement.*   23:23 [a] Acts 8:40; 23:33   [1] Or *cavalrymen.*   [2] A military term of uncertain meaning.   [3] Grk. *from the third hour of the night.*   23:24 [1] Grk. *the procurator.*   23:27 [a] Acts 21:30, 33; 24:7   23:28 [a] Acts 22:30   [1] Grk. *their Sanhedrin.*   23:29 [a] Acts 18:15; 25:19   [b] Acts 25:25; 26:31   23:30 [a] Acts 24:8; 25:6   23:33 [a] Acts 8:40   [b] Acts 23:26–30   23:34 [a] Acts 6:9; 21:39   23:35 [a] Acts 24:1, 10; 25:16   [b] Matt 27:27   24:1 [a] Acts 21:27   [b] Acts 23:2, 30, 35; 25:2   [1] A professional advocate.   24:5 [a] Luke 23:2; Acts 6:13; 16:20; 17:6; 21:28; 1 Pet 2:12, 15   24:6 [a] Acts 21:28   [1] Some MSS add *and we wanted to judge him according to our law.* 24:7 *But Lysias the commanding officer came and took him out of our hands with a great deal of violence,* 24:8 *ordering those who accused him to come before you.*   24:8 [a] Acts 23:30

Jews also joined in the verbal attack, claiming that these things were true.

Paul's Defense before Felix

[10]When the governor gestured for him to speak, Paul replied, "Because I know that you have been a judge over this nation for many years, I confidently make my defense. [11]As you can verify for yourself, not more than 12 days ago I went up [a]to Jerusalem to worship. [12]They did not find me arguing with anyone or stirring up [a]a crowd in the temple courts or in the synagogues or throughout the city, [13]nor can they prove to you the things they are accusing me of doing. [14]But I confess this to you, that I worship [a]the [b]God of our ancestors according to [c]the Way (which they call a sect), believing everything that is according to the law and that is written in the prophets. [15]I have a hope [a]in God ([b]a hope that these men themselves accept too) that there is going to be a resurrection of both the righteous and the unrighteous. [16a]This is the reason I do my best to always have a clear conscience toward God and toward people. [17]After several years [a]I came to bring to my people gifts for the poor and to present offerings,[1] [18]which I was doing when they found me [a]in the temple, ritually [b]purified, without a crowd or a disturbance. [19]But there are some Jews from the province of Asia [a]who should be here before you and bring charges, if they have anything against me. [20]Or these men here should tell what crime they found me guilty of when I stood before the council,[1] [21]other than this one thing I shouted out while I stood before them: 'I am on trial before you today [a]concerning the resurrection of the dead.'"

[22]Then Felix, who understood the facts concerning the [a]Way[1] more accurately, adjourned their hearing, saying, "When [b]Lysias the commanding officer comes down, I will decide your case." [23]He ordered the centurion [a]to guard Paul, but to let him have some freedom, and not to prevent any of his friends[1] from meeting his needs.

Paul Speaks Repeatedly to Felix

[24]Some days later, when Felix arrived with his wife Drusilla, who was Jewish, he sent for Paul and heard him speak about [a]faith in Christ Jesus. [25]While Paul was discussing righteousness, self-control,[1] and the coming judgment, Felix became frightened and said, "Go away for now, and when I have an opportunity, I will send for you." [26]At the same time he was also hoping that Paul would give him [a]money, and for this reason he sent for Paul as often as possible and talked[1] with him. [27]After two years had passed, Porcius Festus succeeded Felix, and because he [a]wanted to do the Jews a favor, Felix left Paul in prison.

Paul Appeals to Caesar

25 Now three days after Festus arrived in the province, he went up to Jerusalem from [a]Caesarea. [2]So [a]the chief priests and the most prominent men of the Jews brought formal charges against Paul to him. [3]Requesting him to do them a favor against Paul, they urged Festus to summon him to Jerusalem, planning an ambush to kill him along the way. [4]Then Festus replied that Paul was being kept at Caesarea, and he himself intended to go there shortly. [5]"So," he said, "let your leaders[1] go down there with me, and [a]if this man has done anything wrong, they may bring charges against him."

[6]After Festus had stayed not more than eight or ten days among them, he went down to Caesarea, and the next day he sat on the judgment seat and ordered Paul to be brought. [7]When he arrived, the Jews who had come down from Jerusalem stood around him, bringing many serious charges that they were not able to prove. [8]Paul said in his defense, "I have committed [a]no offense against the Jewish law[1] or against the temple or against Caesar."[2] [9]But Festus, [a]wanting to do the Jews [b]a favor, asked Paul, "Are you willing to go up to Jerusalem and be tried before me there on these

24:11 [a] Acts 21:15, 18, 26, 27; 24:17   24:12 [a] Acts 25:8; 28:17   24:14 [a] Amos 8:14; Acts 9:2; 24:22   [b] 2 Tim 1:3   [c] Acts 26:22; 28:23   24:15 [a] Acts 23:6; 26:6–7; 28:20   [b] [Dan 12:2; John 5:28–29; 11:24]   24:16 [a] Acts 23:1   24:17 [a] Acts 11:29–30; Rom 15:25–28; 1 Cor 16:1–4; 2 Cor 8:1–4; 9:1–2, 12; Gal 2:10   [1] Or sacrifices.   24:18 [a] Acts 21:27; 26:21   [b] Acts 21:26   24:19 [a] [Acts 23:30; 25:16]   24:20 [1] Grk. the Sanhedrin.   24:21 [a] [Acts 23:6; 24:15; 28:20]   24:22 [a] Acts 9:2; 18:26; 19:9, 23; 22:4   [b] Acts 23:26; 24:7   [1] I.e., Christianity.   24:23 [a] Acts 23:16; 27:3; 28:16   [1] Grk. his own; this could also refer to relatives.   24:24 [a] [John 3:15; 5:24; 11:25; 12:46; 20:31; Rom 10:9]   24:25 [1] Grk. and self-control.   24:26 [a] Exod 23:8   [1] Or conferred.   24:27 [a] Exod 23:2; Acts 12:3; 23:35; 25:9, 14   25:1 [a] Acts 8:40; 25:4, 6, 13   25:2 [a] Acts 24:1; 25:15   25:5 [a] Acts 18:14; 25:18   [1] Grk. let those who are influential among you; i.e., the powerful.   25:8 [a] Acts 6:13; 24:12; 28:17   [1] Grk. the law of the Jews.   [2] Or against the emperor; Caesar is a title for the Roman emperor.   25:9 [a] Acts 12:2; 24:27   [b] Acts 25:20

charges?" [10]Paul replied, "I am standing before Caesar's judgment seat, where I should be tried. I have done nothing wrong to the Jews, as you also know very well. [11]If [a]then [b]I am in the wrong and have done anything that deserves death, I am not trying to escape dying, but if not one of their charges against me is true, no one can hand me over to them. I appeal to Caesar!" [12]Then, after conferring with his council, Festus replied, "You have appealed to Caesar; to Caesar you will go!"

Festus Asks King Agrippa for Advice

[13]After several days had passed, King Agrippa and Bernice arrived at Caesarea to pay their respects to Festus. [14]While they were staying [a]there many days, Festus explained Paul's case to the king to get his opinion, saying, "There is a man left here as a prisoner by Felix. [15]When I was in Jerusalem, the chief priests and the elders of the Jews informed me [a]about him, asking for a sentence of condemnation against him. [16]I answered them that it was not the [a]custom of the Romans to hand over anyone before the accused had met his accusers face-to-face and had been given an opportunity to make a defense against the accusation.[1] [17]So after they came back here [a]with me, I did not postpone the case, but the next day I sat on the judgment seat and ordered the man to be brought. [18]When his accusers stood up, they did not charge him with any of the evil deeds I had suspected. [19][a]Rather they had several points of disagreement with him about their own religion and about a man named Jesus who was dead, whom Paul claimed to be alive. [20]Because I was at a loss how I could investigate these matters, I asked if he were willing to go to Jerusalem and be tried there on these charges. [21]But when Paul [a]appealed to be kept in custody for the decision of His Majesty the Emperor, I ordered him to be kept under guard until I could send him to Caesar." [22][a]Agrippa said to Festus, "I would also like to hear the man myself." "Tomorrow," he replied, "you will hear him."

Paul before King Agrippa and Bernice

[23]So the next day Agrippa and Bernice came with great pomp[1] and entered the audience hall, along with the senior military officers and the prominent men of the city. When Festus gave the order, [a]Paul was brought in. [24]Then Festus said, "King Agrippa, and all you who are present here with us, you see this man about whom [a]the entire Jewish populace[1] petitioned me both in Jerusalem and here, shouting loudly that he ought [b]not to live any longer. [25]But I found that [a]he had done nothing that deserved death, [b]and when he appealed to His Majesty the Emperor, I decided to send him. [26]But I have nothing definite to write to my lord about him. Therefore I have brought him before you all, and especially before you, King Agrippa, so that after this preliminary hearing I may have something to write. [27]For it seems unreasonable to me to send a prisoner without clearly indicating the charges against him."

Paul Offers His Defense

26 So Agrippa said to Paul, "You have permission to speak for yourself." Then Paul held out his hand and began his defense:

[2]"Regarding all the things I have been [a]accused of by the Jews, King Agrippa, I consider myself [b]fortunate that I am about to make my defense [c]before you today, [3]because you are especially familiar with all the customs and controversial issues of the Jews. Therefore I ask you to listen to me patiently. [4]Now all the Jews know the way I lived from my youth, spending my life from the beginning among my own people and in Jerusalem. [5]They know because [a]they have known me from time past, if they are willing to testify, that according to the strictest party of our religion, I lived as a Pharisee. [6][a]And now I stand here on trial because of my hope in [b]the promise made by God to our ancestors, [7]a promise that [a]our 12 tribes hope to attain as they earnestly serve God [b]night and day. Concerning this [c]hope the Jews are accusing me, Your Majesty![1] [8]Why

25:11 [a]Acts 18:14; 23:29; 25:25; 26:31 [b]Acts 26:32; 28:19   25:14 [a]Acts 24:27   25:15 [a]Acts 24:1; 25:2–3   25:16 [a]Acts 25:4–5   [1]Or indictment; a legal technical term.   25:17 [a]Matt 27:19; Acts 25:6, 10   25:19 [a]Acts 18:14–15; 23:29   25:21 [a]Acts 25:11–12   25:22 [a]Acts 9:15   25:23 [a]Acts 9:15   [1]Or great pageantry.   25:24 [a]Acts 25:2–3, 7 [b]Acts 21:36; 22:22 [1]Probably a rhetorical hyperbole.   25:25 [a]Acts 23:9, 29; 26:31 [b]Acts 25:11–12   26:2 [a]Acts 21:28; 24:5–6 [b][1 Pet 3:14; 4:14] [c][1 Pet 3:15–16]   26:5 [a][Acts 22:3; 23:6; 24:15, 21]; Phil 3:5   26:6 [a]Acts 23:6 [b][Gen 3:15; 22:18; 26:4; 49:10; Deut 18:15; 2 Sam 7:12; Ps 132:11; Isa 4:2; 7:14; 9:6; 40:10; Jer 23:5; 33:14–16; Ezek 34:23; 37:24; Dan 9:24]; Acts 13:32; Rom 15:8; [Titus 2:13]   26:7 [a]Jas 1:1 [b]Luke 2:37; 1 Thess 3:10; 1 Tim 5:5 [c]Phil 3:11 [1]Grk. O King!

do you people think it is unbelievable that God raises the dead? [9]Of [a]course, I myself was convinced that it was necessary to do many things hostile to the name of [b]Jesus the Nazarene. [10]And that is [a]what I did in Jerusalem: Not only did I lock up many of the saints in prisons by the authority I received [b]from the chief priests, but I also cast my vote[1] against them when they were sentenced to death. [11]I punished them often in all the synagogues and tried to force them to blaspheme. Because I was so furiously enraged[1] at them, I went to persecute them [a]even in foreign cities.

[12]"[a]While doing this very thing, as I was going to Damascus with authority and complete power from the chief priests, [13]about noon along the road, Your Majesty, I saw a light from heaven, brighter than the sun, shining everywhere around me and those traveling with me. [14]When we had all fallen to the ground, I heard a voice saying to me in Aramaic,[1] 'Saul, Saul, why are you persecuting me? You are hurting yourself by kicking against the goads.'[2] [15]So I said, 'Who are you, Lord?' And the Lord replied, 'I am Jesus whom you are persecuting. [16]But get up and stand on your feet, for I have appeared [a]to you for this reason, to designate you in advance as a servant and witness to the things you have seen[1] and to the things in which I will appear to you. [17]I will rescue you from your own people and from the Gentiles, [a]to whom I am sending you [18]to open their eyes so that they turn from darkness [a]to light and from the power of Satan [b]to God, so [c]that they may receive forgiveness of sins [d]and a share among those who are [e]sanctified by faith in me.'

[19]"Therefore, King Agrippa, I was not disobedient to the heavenly vision, [20]but I [a]declared to those in Damascus first, and then to those in Jerusalem and in all Judea, and to the Gentiles, that they should repent and turn to God, performing [b]deeds consistent with repentance. [21]For this reason the Jews, after they seized me while I was in the temple courts,[1] were trying to kill me. [22]I have experienced help from God to this day, and so I stand testifying to both small and great, saying nothing except [a]what the prophets and [b]Moses said was going to happen: [23][a]that the Christ[1] was to suffer and be the first to rise from the dead, to proclaim light both to our people and to the Gentiles."

[24]As Paul was saying these things in his defense, Festus exclaimed loudly, "[a]You have lost your mind, Paul! Your great learning is driving you insane!" [25]But Paul replied, "I have not lost my mind, most excellent Festus, but am speaking true and rational words. [26]For the king [a]knows about these things, and I am speaking freely to him because I cannot believe that any of these things has escaped his notice, for this was not done in a corner.[1] [27]Do you believe the prophets, King Agrippa? I know that you believe." [28]Agrippa said to Paul, "In such a short time are you persuading me to become a Christian?" [29]Paul [a]replied, "I pray to God that whether in a short or a long time not only you but also all those who are listening to me today could become such as I am, except for these chains."

[30]So the king got up, and with him the governor and Bernice and those sitting with them, [31]and as they were leaving they said to one another, "[a]This man is not doing anything deserving death or imprisonment." [32]Agrippa said to Festus, "This man could have been released [a]if he had not appealed to Caesar."

Paul and Company Sail for Rome

27 When [a]it was decided we would sail to Italy, they handed over Paul and some other prisoners to a centurion of the Augustan Cohort[1] named Julius. [2]We went on board a ship from Adramyttium that was about to sail to various ports along the coast of the province of Asia and put out to sea, accompanied by [a]Aristarchus, a Macedonian from Thessalonica. [3]The next day

26:9 [a]John 16:2; 1 Cor 15:9; 1 Tim 1:12–13   [b]Acts 2:22; 10:38   26:10 [a]Acts 8:1–3; 9:13; Gal 1:13   [b]Acts 9:14   [1]Grk. *cast down a pebble against them.*   26:11 [a]Matt 10:17; Acts 22:19   [1]Or *so insanely angry with them.*   26:12 [a]Acts 9:3–8; 22:6–11; 26:12–18   26:14 [1]Grk. *in the Hebrew language.*   [2]Goads are pointed sticks used to direct a draft animal.   26:16 [a]Acts 22:15; Eph 3:6–8   [‡ Some MSS *of the things in which you have seen me.*   26:17 [a]Acts 22:21   26:18 [a]Isa 35:5; 42:7, 16; Luke 1:79; [John 8:12; 2 Cor 4:4]; Eph 1:18; 1 Thess 5:5   [b]2 Cor 6:14; Eph 4:18; 5:8; [Col 1:13]; 1 Pet 2:9   [c]Luke 1:77   [d]Eph 1:11; Col 1:12   [e]Acts 20:32   26:20 [a]Acts 9:19–20, 22; 11:26   [b]Matt 3:8; Luke 3:8   26:21 [1]Grk. *the temple.*   26:22 [a]Luke 24:27; Acts 24:14; 28:23; Rom 3:21   [b]John 5:46   26:23 [a]1 Cor 15:20, 23; Col 1:18; Rev 1:5   [1]Or *Messiah*; both "Christ" (Grk.) and "Messiah" (Heb., Aram.) mean "one who has been anointed."   26:24 [a]2 Kgs 9:11; John 10:20; [1 Cor 1:23; 2:13–14; 4:10]   26:26 [a]Acts 26:3   [1]I.e., a hidden corner.   26:29 [a]1 Cor 7:7   26:31 [a]Acts 23:9, 29; 25:25   26:32 [a]Acts 25:11   27:1 [a]Acts 25:12, 25   [1]An honorary title given to auxiliary troops.   27:2 [a]Acts 19:29

we put in at Sidon, and Julius, [a]treating Paul kindly, allowed him to go to his friends so they could provide him with what he needed. [4]From there we put out to sea and sailed under the lee of Cyprus because the winds were against us. [5]After we had sailed across the open sea[1] off Cilicia and Pamphylia, we put in at Myra in Lycia. [6]There the centurion found [a]a ship from Alexandria sailing for Italy, and he put us aboard it. [7]We sailed slowly for many days and arrived with difficulty off Cnidus. Because the wind prevented us from going any farther, we sailed under the lee of [a]Crete off Salmone. [8]With difficulty we sailed along the coast of Crete and came to a place called Fair Havens that was near the town of Lasea.

Caught in a Violent Storm

[9]Since considerable time had passed and the voyage was now dangerous [a]because the fast was already over, Paul advised them, [10]"Men, I can see the voyage is going to end in disaster and great loss not only of the cargo and the ship, but also of our lives."[1] [11]But the centurion was more convinced by the captain and the ship's owner than by what Paul said. [12]Because the harbor was not suitable to spend the winter in, the majority decided to put out to sea from there. They hoped that somehow they could reach Phoenix, a harbor of Crete facing southwest and northwest, and spend the winter there. [13]When a gentle south wind sprang up, they thought they could carry out their purpose, so they weighed anchor and sailed close along the coast of Crete. [14]Not long after this, a hurricane-force wind called the northeaster blew down from the island. [15]When the ship was caught in it and could not head into the wind, we gave way to it and were driven along. [16]As we ran under the lee of a small island called Cauda, we were able with difficulty to get the ship's boat under control. [17]After the crew had hoisted it aboard, they used supports to undergird the ship. Fearing they would run aground on the Syrtis,[1] they lowered the sea anchor, thus letting themselves be driven along. [18]The next day, because we were violently battered by the storm, they

began throwing the cargo overboard, [19]and on the third day they threw the ship's gear overboard with their own hands. [20]When neither sun nor stars appeared for many days and a violent storm continued to batter us, we finally abandoned all hope of being saved.[1]

[21]Since many of them had no desire to eat, Paul stood up among them and said, "Men, you should have listened to me and not put out to sea from Crete, thus avoiding this damage and loss. [22]And now I advise you to keep up your courage, for there will be no loss of life among you, but only the ship will be lost. [23a]For last night an angel of the God to [b]whom I belong and whom I serve came to me [24]and said, 'Do not be afraid, Paul! You must stand before Caesar, and God has graciously granted you the safety of all who are sailing with you.' [25]Therefore keep up your courage, men, [a]for I have faith in God that it will be just as I have been told. [26]But [a]we must run aground on some island."

[27]When the fourteenth night had come, while we were being driven across the Adriatic Sea, about midnight the sailors suspected they were approaching some land. [28]They took soundings and found the water was twenty fathoms deep; when they had sailed a little farther they took soundings again and found it was fifteen fathoms deep. [29]Because they were afraid that we would run aground on the rocky coast, they threw out four anchors from the stern and wished[1] for day to appear. [30]Then when the sailors tried to escape from the ship and were lowering the ship's boat into the sea, pretending that they were going to put out anchors from the bow, [31]Paul said to the centurion and the soldiers, "Unless these men stay with the ship, you cannot be saved." [32]Then the soldiers cut the ropes of the ship's boat and let it drift away.

[33]As day was about to dawn, Paul urged them all to take some food, saying, "Today is the fourteenth day you have been in suspense and have gone without food; you have eaten nothing. [34]Therefore I urge you to take some food, [a]for this is important for your survival.[1] For not one of you will lose a

---

27:3 [a]Acts 24:23; 28:16   27:5 [1]Grk. *the depths*; the deep area of a sea, far enough from land that it is not protected by the coast.   27:6 [a]Acts 28:11   27:7 [a]Acts 2:11; 27:12, 21; Titus 1:5, 12   27:9 [a]Lev 16:29–31; 23:27–29; Num 29:7   27:10 [1]Grk. *souls.*   27:17 [1]I.e., on the sandbars and shallows of the Syrtis.   27:20 [1]Grk. *finally all hope that we would be saved was abandoned.*   27:23 [a]Acts 18:9; 23:11; 2 Tim 4:17   [b]Dan 6:16; Rom 1:9; 2 Tim 1:3   27:25 [a]Luke 1:45; Rom 4:20–21; 2 Tim 1:12   27:26 [a]Acts 28:1   27:29 [1]Or *pray.*   27:34 [a]1 Kgs 1:52; [Matt 10:30; Luke 12:7; 21:18]   [1]Or *deliverance.*

hair from his head." [35] After he said this, Paul took bread and [a] gave thanks to God in front of them all, broke it, and began to eat. [36] So all of them were encouraged and took food themselves. [37] (We were in all 276[1] [a] persons on the ship.) [38] When they had eaten enough to be satisfied, they lightened the ship by throwing the wheat into the sea.

Paul Is Shipwrecked

[39] When day came, they did not recognize the land, but they noticed a bay with a beach, where they decided to run the ship aground if they could. [40] So they slipped the anchors and left them in the sea, at the same time loosening the linkage that bound the steering oars[1] together. Then they hoisted the foresail to the wind and steered toward the beach. [41] But [a] they encountered a patch of crosscurrents and ran the ship aground; the bow stuck fast and could not be moved, but the stern was being broken up by the force of the waves. [42] Now the soldiers' plan was to kill the prisoners so that none of them would escape by swimming away. [43] But the centurion, wanting to save Paul's life, prevented them from carrying out their plan. He ordered those who could swim to jump overboard first and get to land, [44] and the rest were to follow, some on planks and some on pieces of the ship. And in this way all were brought safely to land.

Paul on Malta

28 After we had safely reached shore, we learned that [a] the island was called Malta. [2] The local [a] inhabitants showed us extraordinary kindness, for they built a fire and welcomed us all because it had started to rain and was cold. [3] When Paul had gathered a bundle of brushwood and was putting it on the fire, a viper came out because of the heat and fastened itself on his hand. [4] When the local people saw the creature hanging from Paul's hand, they said to one another, "No doubt this man is a murderer! Although he has escaped from the sea, Justice herself[1] has not allowed him to live!"

[5] However, Paul shook the creature off into the fire and [a] suffered no harm. [6] But they were expecting that he was going to swell up or suddenly drop dead. So after they had waited a long time and had seen nothing unusual happen to him, they changed their minds and [a] said he was a god. [7] Now in the region around that place were fields belonging to the chief official[1] of the island, named Publius, who welcomed us and entertained us hospitably as guests for three days. [8] The father of Publius lay sick in bed, suffering from fever and dysentery. Paul went in to see him and after [a] praying, placed his hands on him and [b] healed him. [9] After this had happened, many of the people on the island who were sick also came and were healed. [10] They also bestowed many [a] honors, and when we were preparing to sail, they gave us all the supplies we [b] needed.

Paul Finally Reaches Rome

[11] After three months we put out to sea in [a] an Alexandrian ship that had wintered at the island and had the "Heavenly Twins"[1] as its figurehead.[2] [12] We put in at Syracuse and stayed there three days. [13] From there we cast off[1] and arrived at Rhegium, and after one day a south wind sprang up and on the second day we came to Puteoli. [14] There we found some [a] brothers and were invited to stay with them seven days. And in this way we came to Rome. [15] The brothers from there, when they heard about us, came as far as the Forum of Appius and Three Taverns to meet us. When he saw them, Paul thanked God and took courage. [16] When we entered Rome, [a] Paul was allowed to live by himself, with the soldier who was guarding him.

Paul Addresses the Jewish Community in Rome

[17] After three days Paul called the local Jewish leaders together. When they had assembled, he said to them, "Brothers, [a] although [b] I had done nothing against our people or the customs of our ancestors,

27:35 [a] 1 Sam 9:13; Matt 15:36; Mark 8:6; John 6:11; [1 Tim 4:3–4]   27:37 [a] Acts 2:41; 7:14; Rom 13:1; 1 Pet 3:20   [1] A few wss *about seventy-six.*   27:40 [1] Or *rudders.*   27:41 [a] 2 Cor 11:25   28:1 [a] Acts 27:26   28:2 [a] Acts 28:4; Rom 1:14; 1 Cor 14:11; Col 3:11   28:4 [1] I.e., the goddess Justice has not allowed him to live.   28:5 [a] Mark 16:18; Luke 10:19   28:6 [a] Acts 12:22; 14:11   28:7 [1] The chief Roman official.   28:8 [a] Acts 9:40; [Jas 5:14–15]   [b] Matt 9:18; Mark 5:23; 6:5; 7:32; 16:18; Luke 4:40; Acts 19:11–12; [1 Cor 12:9, 28]   28:10 [a] Matt 15:6; 1 Tim 5:17   [b] [Phil 4:19]   28:11 [a] Acts 27:6   [1] Or the *"Twin Gods".*   [2] Or *its emblem.*   28:13 [1] A few early MSS *sailed from place to place.*   28:14 [a] Rom 1:8   28:16 [a] Acts 23:11; 24:25; 27:3   28:17 [a] Acts 23:29; 24:12–13; 26:31   [b] Acts 21:33

from Jerusalem I was handed over as a prisoner to the Romans. [18]When they had heard my case, they wanted to release me because there was no basis for a death sentence[1] against me. [19]But when the Jews objected, [a]I was forced to appeal to Caesar[1]—not that I had some charge to bring against my own people. [20]So for this reason I have asked to see you and speak with you, [a]for I am bound with [b]this chain because of the hope of Israel." [21]They replied, "We have received no letters from Judea about you, nor have any of the brothers come from there and reported or said anything bad about you. [22]But we would like to hear from you what you think, for regarding this sect we know that people everywhere speak against [a]it."

[23]They set a day [a]to meet with him, and they came to him where he was staying[1] in even greater numbers. [b]From morning until evening he explained things to them, testifying about the kingdom of God and trying to convince them about Jesus from both the law of Moses and the prophets. [24a]Some were convinced by what he said, but others refused to believe. [25]So they began to leave, unable to agree among themselves, after Paul made one last statement:

"The Holy Spirit spoke rightly to your ancestors through the prophet Isaiah [26]when he said,

[a]*Go to this people and say,*
"You will keep on hearing, but will
never understand,
and you will keep on looking, but will
never perceive.
[27] *For the heart of this people has*
become dull,[1]
and their ears are hard of hearing,[2]
and they have closed their eyes,
so that they would not see with their
eyes
and hear with their ears
and understand with their heart
and turn, and I would heal them."'[3]

[28]"Therefore be advised that this salvation from God has been sent [a]to the Gentiles; they will listen!"[1]

[30]Paul lived there two whole years in his own rented quarters[1] and welcomed all who came to him, [31a]proclaiming the kingdom of God and teaching about the Lord Jesus Christ[1] with complete boldness and without restriction.

<hr>

28:18 [1]Grk. *no basis for death.*   28:19 [a]Acts 25:11, 21, 25   [1]Or *to the emperor;* Caesar is a title for the Roman emperor.
28:20 [a]Acts 26:6–7   [b]Acts 26:29; Eph 3:1; 4:1; 6:20; 2 Tim 1:8, 16; Phlm 10, 13   28:22 [a]Luke 2:34; Acts 24:5, 14; [1 Pet 2:12; 3:16; 4:14, 16]   28:23 [a]Luke 24:27; [Acts 17:3; 19:8]   [b]Acts 26:6, 22   [1]Or *in his rented quarters.*   28:24 [a]Acts 14:4; 19:9
28:26 [a]Isa 6:9–10; Jer 5:21; Ezek 12:2; Matt 13:14–15; Mark 4:12; Luke 8:10; John 12:40–41; Rom 11:8   28:27 [1]Or *insensitive.*
[2]Grk. *they hear heavily with their ears.*   [3]Isa 6:9–10   28:28 [a]Isa 42:1, 6; 49:6; Matt 21:41; Luke 2:32; Rom 11:11   [1]Some later MSS add v. 29: *When he had said these things, the Jews departed, having a great dispute among themselves.*   28:30 [1]Or perhaps *two whole years at his own expense.*   28:31 [a]Acts 4:31; Eph 6:19   [1]Or *Messiah;* both "Christ" (Grk.) and "Messiah" (Heb., Aram.) mean "one who has been anointed."

ROMANS

Romans, Paul's greatest work, is placed first among his thirteen epistles in the New Testament. While the four Gospels present the words and works of Jesus Christ, Romans explores the significance of his sacrificial death. Using a question-and-answer format, Paul records the most systematic presentation of doctrine in the Bible. Romans is more than a book of theology; it is also a book of practical exhortation. The good news of Jesus Christ is more than facts to be believed; it is also a life to be lived—a life of righteousness befitting the person "justified freely by his grace through the redemption that is in Christ Jesus" (3:24). Although some manuscripts omit "in Rome" in 1:7, 15, the title *Pros Romaious*, "To the Romans," has been associated with the epistle almost from the beginning.

Salutation

1 From Paul, a slave[1] of Christ Jesus,[2] [a]called to be an apostle, set [b]apart for the gospel of God. [2]This [a]gospel he promised beforehand [b]through his prophets in the holy scriptures, [3]concerning his Son who [a]was a descendant of David with reference to the flesh, [4]who was [a]appointed the Son-of-God-in-power according [b]to the Holy Spirit by the resurrection from the dead, Jesus Christ our Lord. [5]Through him [a]we have received grace and our apostleship to bring about the [b]obedience of faith[1] among all the Gentiles on behalf [c]of his name. [6]You also are among them, called to belong to Jesus Christ. [7]To all those loved by God in Rome, [a]called to be saints: [b]Grace and peace to you from God our Father and the Lord Jesus Christ!

Paul's Desire to Visit Rome

[8]First of all, [a]I thank my God through Jesus Christ for all of [b]you, because your faith is proclaimed throughout the whole world. [9]For [a]God, [b]whom [c]I serve in my spirit in the gospel of his Son, is my witness that I continually remember you, [10]and I always ask in my prayers if, perhaps now at last, I may succeed in visiting you according to the will of God. [11]For [a]I long to see you, so that I may impart to you some spiritual gift to strengthen you, [12]that is, that we may be mutually comforted by one [a]another's faith, both yours and mine. [13]I do not want you to be unaware, brothers and sisters,[1] that I often intended to come to you (and [a]was prevented until now), so that I may have some [b]fruit even among you, just as I already have among the rest of the Gentiles. [14]I am a debtor both to the Greeks and to the barbarians, both to the wise and to the foolish. [15]Thus I am eager also to preach the gospel to you who are in Rome.

The Power of the Gospel

[16]For [a]I am not ashamed of the gospel, for [b]it is God's power [c]for salvation to everyone who believes, to the Jew first and also to the Greek. [17]For the righteousness[1] of God is revealed [a]in [b]the gospel from faith to faith, just as it is written, ***The righteous by faith will live.***"[2]

1:1 [a]1 Cor 1:1; 9:1; 15:9; 2 Cor 1:1; 1 Tim 1:11 [b] Acts 9:15; 13:2; [Gal 1:15] [1]Trad. *servant*; the word does not bear the connotation of a free individual serving another. [2]Many sig. MSS *Jesus Christ.* **1:2** [a] Acts 26:6 [b] Gal 3:8 **1:3** [a] 2 Sam 7:12; 1 Chr 17:11; Isa 9:7; Jer 23:5; Gal 4:4 **1:4** [a] Ps 2:7; Acts 9:20; 13:33; Heb 1:2 [b] Ps 16:10; [Heb 9:14] **1:5** [a] Eph 3:8 [b] Acts 6:7; Rom 16:26 [c] Acts 9:15 [1] Grk. *obedience to* [the] *faith, the obedience faith produces* [or requires], *believing obedience, obedience,* [namely] *faith.* **1:7** [a] Acts 9:13; Rom 8:28; 1 Cor 1:2, 24 [b] Num 6:25; 1 Cor 1:3; 2 Cor 1:2; Gal 1:3; Eph 1:2; Phil 1:2; Col 1:2; 1 Thess 1:1; 2 Thess 1:2 **1:8** [a] 1 Cor 1:4; Eph 1:15; Phil 1:3; Col 1:3; 1 Thess 1:2; 2:13 [b] Acts 28:22; Rom 16:19 **1:9** [a] Rom 9:1 [b] Acts 27:23 [c] 1 Thess 3:10 **1:11** [a] Rom 15:29 **1:12** [a] Titus 1:4 **1:13** [a] [1 Thess 2:18] [b] Phil 4:17 [1] Grk. *brothers*; considerable external evidence supports use of the Grk. word as *brothers and sisters* or *fellow Christians.* **1:16** [a] Ps 40:9–10 [b] 1 Cor 1:18, 24 [c] Luke 2:30; Acts 3:26; Rom 2:9 **1:17** [a] Rom 3:21; 9:30; Phil 3:9 [b] Hab 2:4; Gal 3:11; Heb 10:38 [1] The righteous status given to believers, God's act or declaration that makes one righteous, or God's [own] righteousness. [2] Hab 2:4

The Condemnation of the Unrighteous

[18] [a]For the wrath of God is revealed from heaven against all ungodliness and [b]unrighteousness of people who suppress the truth by their unrighteousness, [19]because [a]what can be known about [b]God is plain to them, because God has made it plain to them. [20]For since the creation of the world [a]his invisible attributes—his eternal power and divine nature—have been clearly seen because they are understood through what has been made. So people are without excuse. [21]For although they knew God, they did not glorify him as God or give him thanks, but they [a]became futile in their thoughts, and their senseless hearts were darkened. [22]Although they [a]claimed to be wise, they became fools [23]and exchanged the glory of the [a]immortal [b]God for an image resembling mortal human beings[1] or birds or four-footed animals or reptiles.

[24][a]Therefore God gave them over in the desires of their hearts [b]to impurity, to dishonor their bodies [c]among themselves. [25]They exchanged [a]the truth of God [b]for a lie and worshiped and served the creation rather than the Creator, who is blessed forever! Amen.

[26]For this reason God gave them over to [a]dishonorable passions. For their women exchanged the natural sexual relations for unnatural ones, [27]and likewise the men also abandoned natural relations with women and were inflamed in their passions for one another. Men committed shameless acts with men and received in themselves the due penalty for their error.

[28]And just as they did not see fit to acknowledge God, God gave them over to a depraved mind, to do what should not be done. [29]They are filled with every kind of unrighteousness, wickedness, covetousness, malice. They are rife with envy, murder, strife, deceit, hostility. They are gossips, [30]slanderers, haters of God, insolent, arrogant, boastful, contrivers of all sorts of evil, disobedient to parents, [31]senseless, covenant-breakers, heartless, ruthless. [32]Although they fully [a]know God's righteous decree that those who practice such things deserve to die, they not only do them but also [b]approve of those who practice them.

The Condemnation of the Moralist

2 Therefore you are without [a]excuse, whoever you are, when you judge someone else. [b]For on whatever grounds you judge another, you condemn yourself, because you who judge practice the same things. [2]Now we know that God's judgment is in accordance with truth against those who practice such things. [3]And do you think, whoever you are, when you judge those who practice such things and yet do them yourself, that you will escape God's judgment? [4]Or do you have contempt for [a]the wealth of his kindness, [b]forbearance, and [c]patience, and yet do [d]not know that God's kindness leads you to repentance? [5]But because of [a]your stubbornness[1] and your unrepentant heart, you are storing up wrath for yourselves in the day of wrath, when God's righteous judgment is revealed! [6]He [a]*will reward each one according to his works*:[1] [7]eternal life to those who by perseverance in good works seek glory and honor and immortality, [8]but wrath and anger to those who live in selfish ambition and [a]do not obey the truth but follow unrighteousness. [9]There will be affliction and distress on everyone who does evil, on the Jew [a]first and also the Greek, [10][a]but glory and honor and peace for everyone who does good, for the Jew first and also the Greek. [11]For [a]there is no partiality with God. [12]For all who have sinned apart from the law will also perish apart from the law, and all who have sinned under the law will be judged by the law. [13]For it is [a]not those who hear the law who are righteous before God, but those who do the law will be declared righteous. [14]For whenever the Gentiles, who do not have the law, do by nature the things required by the law, these

1:18 [a][Acts 17:30]   [b]Rom 6:13; 2 Thess 2:10; 2 Pet 2:13; 1 John 5:17   1:19 [a][Acts 14:17; 17:24]   [b][John 1:9]   1:20 [a]Job 12:7–9; Ps 19:1–6; Jer 5:22   1:21 [a]2 Kgs 17:15; Jer 2:5; Eph 4:17   1:22 [a]Jer 10:14; [1 Cor 1:20]   1:23 [a]1 Tim 1:17; 6:15–16   [b]Deut 4:16–18; Ps 106:20; Jer 2:11; Acts 17:29   [1]Grk. *exchanged the glory of the incorruptible God in likeness of an image of corruptible man.* 1:24 [a]Ps 81:12; Acts 7:42; Eph 4:18–19   [b]1 Cor 6:18   [c]Lev 18:22   1:25 [a]1 Thess 1:9   [b]Isa 44:20; Jer 10:14; 13:25; 16:19   1:26 [a]Lev 18:22; Eph 5:12   1:32 [a][Rom 2:2]   [b][Ps 50:18]; Hos 7:3   2:1 [a][Rom 1:20]   [b]2 Sam 12:5–7; [Matt 7:1–5; Luke 6:37]; John 8:9; Rom 14:22   2:4 [a]Rom 9:23; 11:33; [2 Cor 8:2; Eph 1:7, 18; 2:7; Phil 4:19; Col 1:27; 2:2; Titus 3:6]   [b][Rom 3:25]   [c]Exod 34:6; [Rom 9:22; 1 Tim 1:16]; 1 Pet 3:20   [d]Isa 30:18; [2 Pet 3:9, 15]   2:5 [a][Deut 32:34]; Prov 1:18; Jas 5:3   [1]Grk. *hardness.*   2:6 [a][Job 34:11]; Ps 62:12; Prov 24:12; Jer 17:10; [2 Cor 5:10; Rev 20:12–13]   [1]Ps 62:12; Prov 24:12; Matt 16:27   2:8 [a]Job 24:13; [2 Thess 1:8]   2:9 [a]Amos 3:2; Luke 12:47; Acts 3:26; Rom 1:16; 1 Pet 4:17   2:10 [a]Rom 2:7; Heb 2:7; [1 Pet 1:7]   2:11 [a]Deut 10:17; [Job 34:19]; Acts 10:34; [Eph 6:9]   2:13 [a]Matt 7:21–22; John 13:17; [Jas 1:22, 25; 1 John 3:7]

who do not have the law are a law to themselves. [15]They show that the [a]work of the law is written in their hearts, as their [b]conscience bears witness and their conflicting thoughts accuse or else defend them, [16]on the day when God will judge the secrets of human hearts, [a]according to my gospel [b]through Christ Jesus.

The Condemnation of the Jew

[17]But if [a]you call yourself a Jew and [b]rely on the law [c]and boast of your relationship to God[1] [18]and [a]know his will and [b]approve the superior things because you receive instruction from the law, [19]and if you are convinced that you yourself [a]are a guide to the blind, a light to those who are in darkness, [20]an educator of the senseless, a teacher of little children, because you [a]have in the law the essential features of knowledge and of the truth—[21]therefore [a]you who teach someone else, do you not teach yourself? You who preach against stealing, do you steal? [22]You who tell others not to commit adultery, [a]do you commit adultery? You who abhor idols, do you rob temples? [23]You who boast in the law dishonor God by transgressing the law! [24]For just as it is written, "[a]*the name of God is being* [b]*blasphemed among the Gentiles because of you.*"[1]

[25a]For circumcision has its value if you practice the law, but if you break the law, your circumcision has become uncircumcision. [26]Therefore [a]if the uncircumcised man obeys[1] the righteous requirements of the law, will not his uncircumcision be regarded as circumcision? [27]And the physically uncircumcised man, by keeping the law, will [a]judge you to be the transgressor of the law, even though you have the letter and circumcision! [28]For a person is not a Jew who is one outwardly, nor is circumcision something that is outward in [a]the flesh, [29]but someone is a Jew [a]who is one inwardly, and [b]circumcision is of the heart [c]by the Spirit [d]and not by the letter. This person's praise is not from people but from God.

3 Therefore what advantage does the Jew have, or what is the value of circumcision? [2]Actually, there are many advantages. First of all, the Jews were entrusted with the oracles of God.[1] [3]What then? If [a]some were unfaithful, their unfaithfulness [b]will not nullify God's faithfulness, will it? [4a]Absolutely not! Let [b]God be proven true, and [c]every human being shown up as a liar, just as it is written: "*so* [d]*that you will be justified in your words and will prevail when you are judged.*"[1,2]

[5]But [a]if our unrighteousness demonstrates the righteousness of God, what shall we say? The God who inflicts wrath is not unrighteous, is he? (I am speaking in human terms.) [6]Absolutely not! For otherwise [a]how could God judge the world? [7]For if by my lie the truth of God enhances his glory, why am I still actually being judged as a sinner? [8]And why not say, "[a]Let us do evil so that good may come of it"?—as some who slander us allege that we say. (Their condemnation is deserved!)

The Condemnation of the World

[9]What then? Are we better off? Certainly not, for we have already charged that Jews and Greeks alike are all under sin, [10]just as it is written:

"[a]*There is no one righteous, not even
    one;*
[11] *there is no one who understands;
    there is no one who seeks God.*
[12] *All have turned away;
    together they have become
    worthless;
    there is no one who shows kindness,
    not even one.*"[1]
[13] "[a]*Their throats are open graves;
    they deceive with their tongues;*
    [b]*the poison of asps is under their lips.*"[1]
[14] "[a]*Their mouths are full of cursing
    and bitterness.*"[1]
[15] "[a]*Their feet are swift to shed blood;*
[16] *ruin and misery are in their paths,*

2:15 [a]1 Cor 5:1 [b]Acts 24:25 **2:16** [a]Eccl 12:14; [Matt 25:31]; Rev 20:12 [b]John 5:22; Acts 10:42; 17:31; Rom 3:6; 14:10 **2:17** [a][Matt 3:9]; John 8:33 [b]Mic 3:11; John 5:45; Rom 2:23; 9:4 [c]Isa 48:1–2 [1]Grk. *boast in God.* **2:18** [a]Deut 4:8 [b]Phil 1:10 **2:19** [a]Matt 15:14; John 9:34 **2:20** [a][2 Tim 3:5] **2:21** [a]Ps 50:16; Matt 23:3 **2:22** [a]Mal 3:8 **2:24** [a]Ezek 16:27 [b]2 Sam 12:14; Isa 52:5; Ezek 36:22 [1]Isa 52:5 **2:25** [a]Gen 17:10–14; [Gal 5:3] **2:26** [a][Acts 10:34] [1]Or *keeps*; Grk. connotes obedience and preservation of and devotion to. **2:27** [a]Matt 12:41 **2:28** [a][Matt 3:9]; John 8:39; Rom 2:17; 9:6; [Gal 6:15] **2:29** [a][1 Pet 3:4] [b]Phil 3:3; Col 2:11 [c]Deut 30:6; Rom 2:27; 7:6; [2 Cor 3:6] [d]John 5:44; 12:43; [1 Cor 4:5; 2 Cor 10:18]; 1 Thess 2:4 **3:2** [1]I.e., God's promises to the Jews or the entire OT generally. **3:3** [a]Rom 10:16; Heb 4:2 [b]Num 23:19; [2 Tim 2:13] **3:4** [a]Job 40:8 [b][John 3:33] [c]Ps 62:9 [d]Ps 51:4 [1]Ps 51:4 [2]Or *prevail when you judge.* **3:5** [a]Rom 6:19; 1 Cor 9:8; 15:32; Gal 3:15 **3:6** [a][Gen 18:25] **3:8** [a]Rom 5:20 **3:10** [a]Ps 14:1–3; 53:1–3; Eccl 7:20 **3:12** [1]Ps 14:1–3 **3:13** [a]Ps 5:9 [b]Ps 140:3 [1]Pss 5:9; 140:3 **3:14** [a]Ps 10:7 [1]Ps 10:7 **3:15** [a]Prov 1:16; Isa 59:7–8

[17] *and the way of peace they have not known.*"[1]

[18] *"There is no fear of God before their eyes.*"[1]

[19] Now we know that whatever [a]the law says, it says to those who are under the law, so that [b]every mouth may be silenced and the whole world may be held accountable to God. [20] For *no one is declared righteous before him*[1] [a]*by the works of the law,*[2] for through the law comes the knowledge of sin. [21] But now apart from [a]the law the righteousness of God (although it is attested by the law [b]and the prophets) has been disclosed—[22]namely, [a]the righteousness of God through the faithfulness of Jesus Christ[1] for all who believe. For there is no distinction, [23]for [a]all have sinned and fall short of the glory of God. [24]But they are justified[1] freely [a]by his grace [b]through the redemption that is in Christ Jesus. [25]God publicly displayed him at his death [a]as the mercy seat[1] accessible through faith. This was to demonstrate his righteousness because God [b]in his forbearance had passed over [c]the sins previously committed. [26]This was also to demonstrate his righteousness in the present time, so that he would be just and the justifier of the one who lives because of Jesus' faithfulness.[1]

[27a]Where, then, is boasting? It is excluded! By what principle? Of works? No, but by the principle of faith! [28]For we consider [a]that a person is declared righteous by faith apart from the works of the law. [29]Or is God the God of the Jews only? Is he not the God of the Gentiles too? Yes, of the Gentiles too! [30]Since God is one, [a]he will justify the circumcised by faith and the uncircumcised through faith. [31]Do we then nullify the law through faith? Absolutely not! Instead we uphold the law.

The Illustration of Justification

4 What then shall we say that [a]Abraham, our [b]ancestor according to the flesh, has discovered regarding this matter? [2]For if Abraham was declared [a]righteous by works, he has something to boast about—but not before God. [3]For what does the scripture say? "[a]*Abraham believed God, and it was credited to him as righteousness.*"[1] [4]Now [a]to the one who works, his pay is not credited due to grace but due to obligation. [5]But to the one who [a]does not work, but believes in [b]the one who declares the ungodly righteous, his faith is credited as righteousness. [6]So even David himself [a]speaks regarding the blessedness of the man to whom God credits righteousness apart from works:

[7] "[a]*Blessed are those whose lawless deeds are forgiven, and whose sins are covered;*

[8] *blessed is the one against whom the Lord will never count sin.*"[1]

[9]Is this blessedness then for the circumcision or also for the uncircumcision? For we say, "*faith* **was credited to** *Abraham as* **righteousness.**"[1] [10]How then was it credited to him? Was he circumcised at the time, or not? No, he was not circumcised but uncircumcised! [11]And he received the sign of circumcision as a seal of the righteousness that he had by faith while he was still uncircumcised, so that [a]he would become [b]the father of all those who believe but have never been circumcised, that they too could have righteousness credited to them. [12]And he is also the father of the circumcised, who are not only circumcised, but who also walk in the footsteps of the faith that our father [a]Abraham possessed when he was still uncircumcised.

[13]For the promise to Abraham or to his descendants that he would [a]inherit the world was not fulfilled through the law, but through the righteousness that comes by faith. [14]For [a]if they become heirs by the law, faith is empty and the promise is nullified. [15]For [a]the law brings wrath, because where there is no law there is no transgression either. [16]For this [a]reason it is by faith so that it may be by grace, with the result

3:17[1] Isa 59:7–8   **3:18**[1] Ps 36:1   **3:19**[a] John 10:34   [b] Job 5:16; Ps 107:42   **3:20**[a] Ps 143:2; [Acts 13:39; Gal 2:16]   [1] [Ps 143:2] [2] Grk. *because by the works of the law no flesh is justified before him.*   **3:21**[a] Acts 15:11   [b] 1 Pet 1:10   **3:22**[a] Rom 10:12; [Gal 3:28; Col 3:11]   [1] Or *faith in Christ.*   **3:23**[a] Gal 3:22   **3:24**[a] Rom 4:4, 16; [Eph 2:8; Titus 3:5, 7]   [b] [Matt 20:28; Eph 1:7; Col 1:14; 1 Tim 2:6; Heb 9:12, 15; 1 Pet 1:18–19]   [1] Or *declared righteous.*   **3:25**[a] Lev 16:15   [b] Col 1:20   [c] Acts 14:16; 17:30; [Rom 2:4]   [1] Or *place of sanctification.*   **3:26**[1] Or *of the one who has faith in Jesus.*   **3:27**[a] Rom 2:17, 23; [1 Cor 1:29]; Eph 2:9 **3:28**[a] Gal 2:16   **3:30**[a] Rom 10:12; [Gal 3:8, 20]   **4:1**[a] Gen 11:27–25:9; Isa 51:2; [Matt 3:9]; John 8:33   [b] [Luke 3:8]; John 8:53; Jas 2:21   **4:2**[a] Rom 3:20, 27   **4:3**[a] Gen 15:6; Rom 4:9, 22; Gal 3:6; Jas 2:23   [1] Gen 15:6   **4:4**[a] Rom 11:6   **4:5**[a] [Gal 2:16; Eph 2:8–9]   [b] Josh 24:2   **4:6**[a] Ps 32:1–2   **4:7**[a] Ps 32:1–2   **4:8**[1] Ps 32:1–2   **4:9**[1] Gen 15:6   **4:11**[a] Gen 17:10   [b] Luke 19:9; Rom 4:16   **4:12**[a] Rom 4:18–22   **4:13**[a] Gen 17:4–6; 22:17   **4:14**[a] Gal 3:18   **4:15**[a] Rom 3:20   **4:16**[a] [Gal 3:22]

that the promise may be certain to all the descendants—not only to those [b]who are under the law, but also to those who have the faith of Abraham, who is the father of us all [17](as [a]it is written, "*I have made you the father of many nations*").[1] He is our father in the presence of God [b]whom he believed— the God who makes the dead alive and summons the [c]things that do not yet exist as though they already do. [18]Against hope Abraham believed in hope with the result that he became *the father of many nations*[1] according to the pronouncement, "[a]*so will your descendants be.*"[2] [19]Without being weak in faith, [a]he considered[1] his own body as dead[2] (because he was about one hundred years old) [b]and the deadness of Sarah's womb. [20]He did not waver in unbelief about the promise of God but was strengthened in faith, giving glory to God. [21]He was fully convinced that what God promised [a]he was also able to do. [22]So indeed [a]it was credited to Abraham as righteousness.

[23]But the statement [a]*It was credited to him*[1] was not written only for Abraham's sake, [24]but also for our sake, to whom it will be credited, those who believe [a]in the one who raised Jesus our Lord from the dead. [25a]He [b]was given over because of our transgressions and was raised for the sake of our justification.

The Expectation of Justification

5 Therefore, since we have been declared righteous by faith, we have[1] [a]peace with God through our Lord Jesus Christ, [2a]through whom we have also [b]obtained access[1] into this grace in which we stand, and we [c]rejoice in the hope of God's glory. [3]Not only this, but [a]we also rejoice in sufferings, [b]knowing that suffering produces endurance, [4a]and endurance, character, and character, hope. [5a]And hope does not disappoint, [b]because the love of God[1] has been poured out in our hearts through the Holy Spirit who was given to us.

[6]For while we were still helpless, at the right time [a]Christ died for the ungodly. [7](For rarely will anyone die for a righteous person, though for a good person perhaps someone might possibly dare to die.) [8]But [a]God demonstrates his own love for us, in that while we were still sinners, Christ died for us. [9]Much more then, because we have now been declared righteous [a]by his blood, we will be saved through him [b]from God's wrath. [10]For [a]if while [b]we were enemies we were reconciled to God through the death of his Son, how much more, since we have been reconciled, will we be saved [c]by his life? [11]Not only this, but we also [a]rejoice in God through our Lord Jesus Christ, through whom we have now received this reconciliation.

The Amplification of Justification

[12]So then, just as sin entered the world [a]through one man and [b]death through sin, and so death spread to all people because[1] all sinned—[13]for before the law was given, [a]sin was in the world, but there is no accounting for sin when there is no law. [14]Yet death reigned from Adam until Moses even over those who did not sin in the same way that Adam ([a]who is a type of the coming one) transgressed. [15]But the gracious gift is not like the transgression. For if the many died through the transgression of the one man, how much more did the grace of God and the gift by the grace of the one man Jesus Christ multiply [a]to the many! [16]And the gift is not like the one who sinned. For judgment, resulting from the one transgression, led to condemnation, but the gracious gift from the many failures led to justification. [17]For if, by the transgression of the one man, death reigned through the one, how much more will those who receive the abundance of grace and of the gift of righteousness reign in life through the one, Jesus Christ!

[18]Consequently, just as condemnation for all people came through [a]one transgression,

4:16 [b] Isa 51:2   4:17 [a] Gen 17:5   [b] [Rom 8:11]   [c] Rom 9:26   [1] Gen 17:5   4:18 [a] Gen 15:5   [1] Gen 17:5   [2] Gen 15:5   4:19 [a] Gen 17:17   [b] Heb 11:11   [1] Maj. MSS *he did not consider.*   [2] ‡ Maj. MSS add *already.*   4:21 [a] Gen 18:14; [Ps 115:3; Luke 1:37; Heb 11:19]   4:22 [a] Gen 15:6   4:23 [a] Rom 15:4; 1 Cor 10:6   [1] Gen 15:6   4:24 [a] Acts 2:24   4:25 [a] Isa 53:4–5; [Rom 5:6, 8; 8:32; Gal 2:20; Eph 5:2; Heb 9:28]   [b] [Rom 5:18; 1 Cor 15:17; 2 Cor 5:15]   5:1 [a] [Isa 53:5]; Acts 10:36; [Eph 2:14]   [1] Sig. MSS *let us have.*   5:2 [a] [John 10:9; Eph 2:18; 3:12; Heb 10:19; 1 Pet 3:18]   [b] 1 Cor 15:1   [c] Heb 3:6   [1] ‡ Some sig. MSS add *by faith.*   5:3 [a] Matt 5:11–12; [John 16:33; Acts 5:41; 2 Cor 12:9]; Jas 1:2   [b] Jas 1:3   5:4 [a] Phil 2:22; [Jas 1:12]   5:5 [a] Phil 1:20   [b] 2 Cor 1:22; Eph 1:13   [1] Grk. *our love for God, God's love for us,* or both.   5:6 [a] Isa 53:5; [Rom 4:25; 5:8; 8:32; Gal 2:20; Eph 5:2]   5:8 [a] [John 3:16; 15:13; Rom 8:39]   5:9 [a] Eph 2:13; [1 John 1:7]   [b] Rom 1:18; 1 Thess 1:10   5:10 [a] [Rom 8:32]   [b] Rom 11:28; 2 Cor 5:18; [Eph 2:5–6]; Col 1:21   [c] John 14:19   5:11 [a] [Gal 4:9]   5:12 [a] Gen 2:17; 3:6, 19; [Rom 5:15–17; 1 Cor 15:21]   [b] Gen 2:17   [1] Grk. *in whom* [Adam] *all sinned, with the result that all sinned.*   5:13 [a] 1 John 3:4   5:14 [a] [1 Cor 15:21–22]   5:15 [a] [Isa 53:11]   5:18 [a] [1 Cor 15:21, 45]

so too through the one righteous act came righteousness leading to life [b]for all people. [19]For just as through the disobedience of the [a]one man many were constituted sinners, so also through the obedience of one man many will be constituted righteous. [20]Now [a]the law came in so that the transgression may increase, but where sin [b]increased, grace multiplied all the more, [21]so that just as sin reigned in death, so also grace will reign through righteousness to eternal life through Jesus Christ our Lord.

The Believer's Freedom from Sin's Domination

6 What [a]shall we say then? Are we to remain in sin so that grace may increase? [2]Absolutely not! How can we who [a]died to sin still live in it? [3]Or do you not know that as many [a]as [b]were baptized into Christ Jesus were baptized into his death? [4]Therefore we have been [a]buried with him through baptism into death, in order that [b]just as Christ was raised from [c]the dead through the glory of the Father, so we too may live a new life.

[5a]For if we have become united with him in the likeness of his death, we will certainly also be united in the likeness of his resurrection. [6]We know that [a]our old man was crucified with him so that [b]the body of sin would no longer dominate us,[1] so that we would no longer be enslaved to sin. [7](For someone who has died has been freed from sin.)

[8]Now [a]if we died with Christ, we believe that we will also live with him. [9]We know that since [a]Christ has been raised from the dead, he is never going to die again; death no longer has mastery over him. [10]For [a]the death [b]he died, he died to sin once for all, but the life he lives, he lives to God. [11]So you too consider yourselves[1] [a]dead to sin, but [b]alive to God in Christ Jesus.

[12a]Therefore do not let sin reign in your mortal body so that you obey its desires, [13]and do not present your [a]members to sin as instruments to be used for unrighteousness, but [b]present yourselves to God as those who are alive from the dead and your members to God as instruments to be used for righteousness. [14]For [a]sin will have no mastery over you, because you are not under law but under grace.

The Believer's Enslavement to God's Righteousness

[15]What then? Shall we sin [a]because we are not under law but under grace? Absolutely not! [16]Do you not know that if you present yourselves [a]as obedient slaves,[1] you are slaves of the one you obey, either of sin resulting in death, or obedience resulting in righteousness? [17]But thanks be to God [a]that though you were slaves to sin, you obeyed from the heart that pattern of teaching you were entrusted to, [18]and [a]having been freed from sin, you became enslaved to righteousness. [19](I am speaking in human terms because of the weakness of your flesh.)[1] For just as you once presented your members as slaves to impurity and lawlessness leading to more lawlessness, so now present your members as slaves to righteousness leading to sanctification. [20]For when you were [a]slaves of sin, you were free with regard to righteousness.

[21]So [a]what benefit did you [b]then reap from those things that you are now ashamed of? For the end of those things is death. [22]But now, freed from sin and enslaved to God, you have your benefit leading to sanctification, and the end is eternal life. [23]For [a]the payoff of sin is death, but [b]the gift of God is eternal life in Christ Jesus our Lord.

The Believer's Relationship to the Law

7 Or do you not know, brothers and sisters[1] (for I am speaking to those who know the law), that the law is lord over a person as long as he lives? [2]For a married woman is bound by law to her husband as long as [a]he lives, but if her husband dies, she is released from the law of the marriage. [3]So

5:18[b] Matt 1:21; [John 12:32]   5:19[a] Isa 53:11–12; [Phil 2:8]   5:20[a] John 15:22   [b] Luke 7:47; Rom 6:1; 1 Tim 1:14   6:1[a] Rom 3:8; 6:15   6:2[a] [Rom 6:11; 7:4, 6; Gal 2:19; Col 2:20; 3:3]; 1 Pet 2:24   6:3[a] Acts 2:38; 8:16; 19:5; [Gal 3:27]; Col 2:12   [b] [1 Cor 15:29]   6:4[a] Col 2:12   [b] 1 Cor 6:14   [c] John 2:11   6:5[a] 2 Cor 4:10; Phil 3:10; Col 2:12; 3:1   6:6[a] Gal 2:20; 5:24; 6:14   [b] Col 2:11   [1]Grk. *may be rendered ineffective, inoperative or may be destroyed.*   6:8[a] Rom 6:4; 2 Cor 4:10; 2 Tim 2:11   6:9[a] Rev 1:18   6:10[a] Heb 9:27   [b] Luke 20:38   6:11[a] [Rom 6:2; 7:4, 6]   [b] [Gal 2:19; Col 2:20; 3:3]; 1 Pet 2:24   [1]‡ Some MSS add *to be.*   6:12[a] Ps 19:13   6:13[a] Rom 6:16, 19; 7:5; Col 3:5; Jas 4:1   [b] Rom 12:1; 2 Cor 5:14; 1 Pet 2:24; 4:2   6:14[a] [Rom 7:4, 6; 8:2; Gal 5:18]   6:15[a] 1 Cor 9:21   6:16[a] Prov 5:22; [Matt 6:24]; John 8:34; 2 Pet 2:19   [1]Grk. *as slaves for obedience.*   6:17[a] 2 Tim 1:13   6:18[a] John 8:32; Rom 6:22; 8:2; 1 Cor 7:22; Gal 5:1; 1 Pet 2:16   6:19[1] Or *because of your natural limitations.*   6:20[a] John 8:34   6:21[a] Jer 12:13; Ezek 16:63; Rom 7:5   [b] Rom 1:32; Gal 6:8   6:23[a] Gen 2:17   [b] Rom 2:7; 1 Pet 1:4   7:1[1] Grk. *brothers*; considerable external evidence supports use of the Grk. word as *brothers and sisters* or *fellow Christians.*   7:2[a] 1 Cor 7:39

then, [a]if she is joined to another man while her husband is alive, she will be called an adulteress. But if her husband dies, she is free from that law, and if she is joined to another man, she is not an adulteress. [4]So, my brothers and sisters,[1] you also [a]died to the law through the body of Christ, so that you could [b]be joined to another, to the one who was raised from the dead, to bear fruit to God. [5]For when [a]we were in the flesh,[1] the sinful desires, aroused by the law, were active in the members of our body [b]to bear fruit for death. [6]But now we have been released from the law, because we have died to what controlled us, so that we may serve [a]in the new life of the Spirit and not under the old written code.[1]

[7]What shall we say then? [a]Is the law sin? Absolutely not! Certainly, I would not have known sin except through the law. For indeed I would not have known what it means to desire something belonging to someone else if the law had not said, "*Do not covet.*"[1] [8]But [a]sin, seizing the opportunity through the commandment, produced in me all kinds of wrong desires. For apart [b]from the law, sin is dead. [9]And I was once alive apart from the law, but with the coming of the commandment, sin became alive [10]and [a]I died. So I found that the very commandment that was intended to bring life brought death! [11]For sin, seizing the opportunity through the commandment, deceived me and through it I died. [12]So [a]then, the law is holy, and the commandment is holy, righteous, and good.

[13]Did that which is good, then, become death to me? Absolutely not! But sin, so that it would be shown to be sin, produced death in me through what is good, so that through the commandment sin would become utterly sinful. [14]For we know that the law is spiritual—but I am unspiritual, sold into [a]slavery to sin. [15][a]For I don't understand what I am doing. For I do not do what I want—instead, I do what I hate. [16]But if I do what I don't want, I agree that the law is good. [17]But now it is no longer me doing it, but sin that lives in me. [18]For I know that nothing good lives [a]in me, that is, in my flesh. For I want to do the good, but I cannot do it. [19]For I do not do the good I want, but I do the very evil I do not want! [20]Now if I do what I do not want, it is no longer me doing it but sin that lives in me.

[21]So, I find the law that when I want to do good, evil is present with me. [22]For I [a]delight in [b]the law of God in my inner being. [23]But [a]I see a different law in [b]my members waging war against the law of my mind and making me captive to the law of sin that is in my members. [24]Wretched man that I am! Who will rescue me [a]from this body of death? [25]Thanks be[1] to God through Jesus [a]Christ our Lord! So then, I myself serve the law of God with my mind, but with my flesh I serve the law of sin.

The Believer's Relationship to the Holy Spirit

8 There is therefore now no condemnation for those [a]who are in Christ Jesus.[1] [2]For [a]the law of [b]the life-giving Spirit[1] in Christ Jesus has set you[2] free from [c]the law of sin and death. [3]For [a]God achieved [b]what the law could not do because it was weakened through the flesh. By sending his own Son in the likeness of sinful flesh and concerning sin, he condemned sin in the flesh, [4]so that the righteous requirement of the law may be fulfilled in us, who [a]do not walk according to the flesh but according to the Spirit.

[5]For [a]those who live according to [b]the flesh have their outlook shaped by[1] the things of the flesh, but those who live according to the Spirit have their outlook shaped by the things of the Spirit. [6]For the outlook[1] of the flesh is death, but the outlook of the Spirit is life and peace, [7]because [a]the outlook of the flesh is hostile to God, for it does not submit to the law of God,

7:3 [a][Matt 5:32]   7:4 [a]Rom 8:2; Gal 2:19; 5:18; [Col 2:14]   [b]Gal 5:22   [1]Grk. *brothers*; considerable external evidence supports use of the Grk. word as *brothers and sisters* or *fellow Christians*.   7:5 [a]Rom 6:13   [b]Rom 6:21; Gal 5:19; Jas 1:15   [1]I.e., before we were in Christ.   7:6 [a]Rom 2:29; 2 Cor 3:6   [1]Grk. *in the newness of the Spirit and not in the oldness of the letter.*   7:7 [a]Rom 3:20   [1]Exod 20:17; Deut 5:21   7:8 [a]Rom 4:15   [b]1 Cor 15:56   7:10 [a]Lev 18:5; Ezek 20:11, 13, 21; Luke 10:28; Rom 10:5; 2 Cor 3:7; Gal 3:12   7:12 [a]Ps 19:8   7:14 [a]1 Kgs 21:20, 25; 2 Kgs 17:17; Rom 6:16   7:15 [a]Rom 7:19; [Gal 5:17]   7:18 [a][Gen 6:5; 8:21]   7:22 [a]Ps 1:2   [b][2 Cor 4:16; Eph 3:16; 1 Pet 3:4]   7:23 [a]Rom 6:19; [Gal 5:17]; Jas 4:1; 1 Pet 2:11   [b]Rom 6:13, 19   7:24 [a][Rom 8:11; 1 Cor 15:51–52; 1 Thess 4:14–17]   7:25 [a]1 Cor 15:57   [1]‡ Maj. MSS *I give thanks to God.*   8:1 [a]Gal 5:16   [1]Some MSS add *who do not walk according to the flesh* or *but* [who do walk] *according to the Spirit.*   8:2 [a]Rom 6:18, 22   [b][1 Cor 15:45]   [c]Rom 7:24–25   [1]Grk. *for the law of the Spirit of life.*   [2]Maj. MSS *me.*   8:3 [a][2 Cor 5:21; Gal 3:13]   [b]Acts 13:39; [Heb 7:18]   8:4 [a][Rom 6:4; 2 Cor 5:7]; Gal 5:16, 25; Eph 4:1; 5:2, 15; [1 John 1:7; 2:6]   8:5 [a]John 3:6   [b][Gal 5:22–25]   [1]Grk. *think on, are intent on.*   8:6 [1]Or *mindset, way of thinking.*   8:7 [a]Jas 4:4

[b]nor is it able to do so. [8]Those who are in the flesh cannot please God. [9]You, however, are not in[1] the flesh but in the Spirit, if indeed the Spirit of God lives in you. Now if anyone does not have the Spirit of Christ, this person does not belong to him. [10]But if Christ is in you, your body is dead because of sin, but the Spirit is your life[1] because of righteousness. [11]Moreover if [a]the Spirit of the one who raised Jesus from the dead lives in you, the one who raised Christ[1] from the dead will also make your mortal bodies alive through his Spirit who lives in you.[2]

[12]So then, brothers and sisters,[1] we are under obligation, not to [a]the flesh, to live according to the flesh [13](for [a]if you live according to the flesh, you will die), but if by the Spirit you [b]put to death the deeds of the body, you will live. [14]For [a]all who are led by the Spirit of God are the sons of God. [15]For [a]you did not receive the spirit of slavery leading again [b]to fear, but you received the [c]Spirit of adoption,[1] by whom we cry, "[d]*Abba*,[2] Father." [16a]The Spirit himself bears witness to our spirit that we are God's children. [17]And if children, then [a]heirs (namely, heirs of God and also fellow heirs with Christ)—[b]if indeed we suffer with him so we may also be glorified with him.

[18]For I consider that our present sufferings cannot even be compared to [a]the coming glory that will be revealed to us. [19]For [a]the creation eagerly waits for the revelation of the sons of God. [20]For [a]the creation was subjected to futility—not willingly but because of God who subjected it—in hope [21]that the creation itself will also be set free from the bondage of decay into the glorious [a]freedom of God's children. [22]For we know that the whole creation [a]groans and suffers together until now. [23]Not only this, but we ourselves [a]also, who have [b]the firstfruits of the Spirit, groan [c]inwardly as we eagerly await our adoption,[1] the [d]redemption of our bodies. [24]For in [a]hope we were saved. Now hope that is seen is not hope, because who hopes for what he sees? [25]But if we hope for what we do not see, we eagerly wait for it with endurance.

[26]In the same way, the Spirit helps us in our [a]weakness, for we do not know how we should pray, but [b]the Spirit himself intercedes for us with inexpressible groanings. [27]And [a]he who searches our hearts knows the mind of the Spirit, because the Spirit intercedes on behalf of the saints [b]according to God's will. [28]And we know that all things work together[1] for good for those [a]who love God, who are called according to his purpose, [29]because those whom [a]he foreknew he also predestined to be conformed to the image of [b]his Son, [c]that his Son would be the firstborn among many brothers and sisters.[1] [30]And those he predestined, he also [a]called; and those he called, he also [b]justified; and those he justified, he also [c]glorified.

[31]What then shall we say about these things? [a]If God is for us, who can be against us? [32]Indeed, [a]he who did not spare his own Son, but [b]gave him up for us all—how will he not also, along with him, freely give us all things? [33]Who will bring any charge against God's elect? [a]It is God who justifies. [34a]Who is the one who will condemn? Christ[1] is the one who died (and more than that, he was raised), [b]who is at the right hand of God, and [c]who also is interceding for us. [35]Who will separate us from the love of Christ? Will trouble, or distress, or persecution, or famine, or nakedness, or danger, or sword?[1] [36]As it is written, "[a]*For your sake we encounter death all day long; we were considered as sheep to be slaughtered.*"[1] [37a]No, in all these things we have complete victory through

---

8:7 [b]1 Cor 2:14   8:9 [1]Or *are not controlled by.*   8:10 [1]Or *life-giving*; Grk. *the Spirit is life.*   8:11 [a]1 Cor 6:14   [1]Sev. mss *Christ Jesus.*   [2]Maj. mss *because of his Spirit who lives in you.*   8:12 [a][Rom 6:7, 14]   [1]Grk. *brothers*; considerable external evidence supports use of the Grk. word as *brothers and sisters* or *fellow Christians.*   8:13 [a]Gal 6:8   [b]Eph 4:22; [Col 3:5–10]   8:14 [a][Gal 5:18]   8:15 [a][1 Cor 2:12]; Heb 2:15   [b]2 Tim 1:7   [c][Isa 56:5]   [d]Mark 14:36; Gal 4:6   [1]A legal, technical term for adoption as a son with full rights of inheritance.   [2]Aram. *my father.*   8:16 [a]Eph 1:13   8:17 [a]Acts 26:18   [b]Phil 1:29   8:18 [a]2 Cor 4:17; [1 Pet 1:6; 4:13]   8:19 [a][2 Pet 3:13]   8:20 [a]Gen 3:17–19   8:21 [a][2 Cor 3:17]; Gal 5:1, 13   8:22 [a]Jer 12:4, 11   8:23 [a]2 Cor 5:2, 4   [b]2 Cor 5:5; Eph 1:14   [c][Luke 20:36]   [d]Luke 21:28; Eph 1:14; 4:30; [Phil 3:20–21]   [1]A legal, technical term for adoption as a son with full rights of inheritance.   8:24 [a]Rom 4:18; 2 Cor 5:7; Heb 11:1   8:26 [a]Matt 20:22; 2 Cor 12:8   [b]John 14:16; Rom 8:15; Eph 6:18   8:27 [a]1 Chr 28:9   [b]1 John 5:14   8:28 [a]2 Tim 1:9   [1]Some wss add *God* after *work.*   8:29 [a]2 Tim 2:19   [b]Rom 9:23; 1 Cor 2:7; Eph 1:5, 11   [c][Col 1:15, 18]; Heb 1:6   [1]Grk. *brothers*; considerable external evidence supports use of the Grk. word as *brothers and sisters* or *fellow Christians.*   8:30 [a]Rom 8:28; 9:24; 1 Cor 1:9; Gal 1:6, 15; 5:8; Eph 1:11; 3:11; 2 Thess 2:14; [Heb 9:15; 1 Pet 2:9; 3:9]   [b]1 Cor 6:11; [Gal 2:16]   [c]John 17:22; Rom 8:21   8:31 [a]Num 14:9   8:32 [a]Rom 5:6, 10   [b][Rom 4:25]   8:33 [a]Isa 50:8–9; Rev 12:10   8:34 [a]John 3:18   [b]Mark 16:19; Col 3:1; Heb 1:3   [c]Heb 7:25; 9:24   [1]‡ Many mss *Christ Jesus.*   8:35 [1]Here *sword* is a metonymy that includes both threats of violence and acts of violence, even including death (although death is not necessarily the only thing in view here).   8:36 [a]Ps 44:22; Acts 20:24; 1 Cor 4:9; 15:30; [2 Cor 1:9; 4:10; 6:9; 11:23]   [1]Ps 44:22   8:37 [a]John 16:33; 1 Cor 15:57; 2 Cor 2:14; 1 John 5:4

him who loved us! [38]For I am convinced that neither death, nor life, nor angels, nor heavenly [a]rulers, nor things that are present, nor things to come, nor powers, [39]nor height, nor depth, nor anything else in creation will be able to separate us from the love of God in Christ Jesus our Lord.

Israel's Rejection Considered

9 I am [a]telling the truth in Christ (I am not lying!), for my conscience assures me in the Holy Spirit—[2a]I have great sorrow and unceasing anguish in my heart. [3]For [a]I could wish that I myself were accursed—cut off from Christ—for the sake of my people, my fellow countrymen, [4]who are Israelites. [a]To [b]them belong [c]the adoption as sons, [d]the glory, [e]the covenants, [f]the giving of the law, the temple worship, and the promises. [5a]To [b]them belong the patriarchs, and from them, by human descent, came the Christ,[1] who [c]is God over all, blessed forever! Amen.

[6a]It is not as though [b]the word of God had failed. For not all those who are descended from Israel are truly Israel, [7a]nor are all the children Abraham's true descendants; rather "[b]*through Isaac will your descendants be counted.*"[1] [8]This means it is not [a]the children of the flesh who are the children of God; rather, the children of promise are counted as descendants. [9]For this is [a]what the promise declared: "*About a year from now I will return and Sarah will have a son.*"[1] [10]Not only that, but when [a]Rebekah had conceived children by one man, our ancestor Isaac—[11]even before they were born or had done anything good or bad (so that God's purpose in election would stand, not by works but by his calling)—[12]it was said to her, "[a]*The older will serve the younger,*"[1] [13]just as it is written: "[a]*Jacob I loved, but Esau I hated.*"[1]

[14]What shall we say then? [a]Is there injustice with God? Absolutely not! [15]For he says to Moses: "[a]*I will have mercy on whom I have mercy, and I will have compassion on whom I have compassion.*"[1] [16]So then, it does not depend on human desire or exertion, but on God who shows mercy. [17]For [a]the scripture says to Pharaoh: "[b]*For this very purpose I have raised you up, that I may demonstrate my power in you, and that my name may be proclaimed in all the earth.*"[1] [18]So then, God has mercy on whom he chooses to have mercy, and he [a]hardens whom he chooses to harden.

[19]You will say to me then, "Why does he still find fault? For [a]who has ever resisted his will?" [20]But who indeed are you—a mere human being—to talk back to God? *Does what is molded say to the molder, "Why have you made me like this?"*[1] [21]Has the [a]potter no right to make from the same lump of clay [b]one vessel for special use and another for ordinary use? [22]But what if God, willing to demonstrate his wrath and to make known his power, has endured with much patience [a]the objects of wrath [b]prepared for destruction? [23]And what if [a]he is willing to make known the wealth of his glory on the objects of mercy that he has prepared [b]beforehand for glory—[24]even us, whom he has [a]called, [b]not only from the Jews but also from the Gentiles? [25]As he also says [a]in Hosea:

> "*I will call those who were not my
>   people, 'My people,' and I will call
>   her who was unloved, 'My beloved.'*"[1]
> [26] "[a]*And in the very place where it was
>   said to them, 'You are not my
>   people,'
> there they will be called 'sons of the
>   living God.'*"[1]

[27]And Isaiah cries out on behalf of Israel, "[a]*Though [b]the number of the children of Israel are as the sand of the sea, only the remnant will be saved, [28]for the Lord will execute his sentence on the earth completely and quickly.*"[1,2] [29]Just as Isaiah predicted,

> "*If the Lord of Heaven's Armies had
>   not left us descendants,*

8:38 [a] [1 Cor 15:24; Eph 1:21; 1 Pet 3:22]   **9:1** [a] 2 Cor 1:23   **9:2** [a] Rom 10:1   **9:3** [a] Exod 32:32   **9:4** [a] Exod 4:22; [Rom 8:15] [b] 1 Sam 4:21 [c] Gen 17:2; Deut 29:14; Luke 1:72; Acts 3:25 [d] Deut 4:13; Ps 147:19 [e] Heb 9:1, 6 [f] [Acts 2:39; 13:32; Eph 2:12] **9:5** [a] Deut 10:15 [b] [Luke 1:34–35; 3:23] [c] Jer 23:6 [1] Or *Messiah*; both "Christ" (Grk.) and "Messiah" (Heb., Aram.) mean "one who has been anointed." **9:6** [a] Num 23:19 [b] [John 8:39; Gal 6:16] **9:7** [a] [John 8:33, 39; Gal 4:23] [b] Gen 21:12; Heb 11:18 [1] Gen 21:12 **9:8** [a] Gal 4:28 **9:9** [a] Gen 18:10, 14; Heb 11:11 [1] Gen 18:10, 14 **9:10** [a] Gen 25:21 **9:12** [a] Gen 25:23 [1] Gen 25:23 **9:13** [a] Mal 1:2–3 [1] Mal 1:2–3 **9:14** [a] Deut 32:4 **9:15** [a] Exod 33:19 [1] Exod 33:19 **9:17** [a] Gal 3:8 [b] Exod 9:16 [1] Exod 9:16 **9:18** [a] Exod 4:21; Deut 2:30; Josh 11:20; John 12:40; Rom 11:7, 25 **9:19** [a] 2 Chr 20:6; Job 9:12; Dan 4:35 **9:20** [1] Isa 29:16; 45:9 **9:21** [a] Prov 16:4 [b] 2 Tim 2:20 **9:22** [a] [1 Thess 5:9] [b] Prov 16:4; [1 Pet 2:8] **9:23** [a] [Col 1:27] [b] [Rom 8:28–30] **9:24** [a] [Rom 8:28] [b] Isa 42:6–7; 49:6; Luke 2:32; Rom 3:29 **9:25** [a] Hos 2:23; 1 Pet 2:10 [1] Hos 2:23 **9:26** [a] Hos 1:10 [1] Hos 1:10 **9:27** [a] Isa 10:22–23 [b] Rom 11:5 **9:28** [1] [Isa 10:22–23] [2] Some MSS *For he will execute his sentence completely and quickly in righteousness because the Lord will do it quickly on the earth.*

[a]*we would have become like Sodom,*
and we would have resembled
Gomorrah."[1]

Israel's Rejection Culpable

[30]What shall we say then?—[a]that the Gentiles who did not pursue righteousness obtained it, that [b]is, a righteousness that is by faith, [31]but Israel even though [a]pursuing [b]a law of righteousness did not attain it. [32]Why not? Because [a]they pursued it not by faith but (as if it were possible) by works.[1] They stumbled over the stumbling stone, [33]just as it is written,

"Look, I am laying in Zion a stone that
will cause people to stumble
and a rock that will make them fall,
yet the one who believes in him will not
[a]*be put to shame.*"[1]

10 Brothers and sisters,[1] my heart's desire and prayer to God on behalf of my fellow Israelites is for their salvation. [2]For I can testify [a]that they are zealous for God, but their zeal is not in line with the truth. [3]For ignoring the righteousness that comes from [a]God and seeking instead to establish their own [b]righteousness, they did not submit to God's righteousness. [4]For [a]Christ is the end of the law, with the result that there is righteousness for everyone who believes.

[5]For Moses writes about [a]the righteousness that is by the law: "*The one who does these things will live by them.*"[1] [6]But the righteousness that is by faith says: "[a]*Do not say in your heart,*[1] '*Who will ascend into heaven?*'"[2] (that is, to bring Christ down) [7]or "[a]*Who will descend into the abyss?*"[1] (that is, to bring Christ up from the dead). [8]But what does it say? "[a]*The word is near you, in your mouth and in your heart*"[1] (that is, the word of faith that we preach), [9]because [a]if you confess with your mouth that Jesus is Lord and believe in your heart that God raised him from the dead, you will be saved. [10]For with the heart one believes and thus has righteousness and with the mouth one confesses and thus has salvation. [11]For the scripture says, "[a]*Everyone who believes in him will not be put to shame.*"[1] [12]For [a]there is no distinction between [b]the Jew and the Greek, for the same Lord [c]is Lord of all, who richly blesses all who call on him. [13]For everyone [a]who [b]*calls on the name of the Lord will be saved.*[1]

[14]How are they to call on one they have not believed in? And how are they to believe in one they have not heard of? And how are they to hear [a]without someone preaching to them? [15]And [a]how are they to preach unless they are sent? As it is written, "*How timely is the arrival of those who proclaim the good news.*"[1] [16]But not all have obeyed the good news, for Isaiah says, "[a]*Lord, who has believed our report?*"[1] [17]Consequently faith comes from what is heard, and what is heard comes through the preached word of Christ.[1]

[18]But I ask, have they not heard? Yes, they have: [a]*Their voice has gone out to all the earth, and their words to the ends of the world.*[1] [19]But again I ask, didn't Israel understand? First Moses says, "[a]*I will make you jealous by those who are not a nation; with a* [b]*senseless nation I will provoke you to anger.*"[1] [20]And [a]Isaiah is even bold enough to say, "*I was found by those who did not seek me; I became well known to those who did not ask for me.*"[1] [21]But about Israel he says, "[a]*All day long I held out my hands to this disobedient and stubborn people!*"[1]

Israel's Rejection not Complete nor Final

11 So I ask, God [a]has not rejected his people, has he? [b]Absolutely not! For [c]I too am an Israelite, a descendant of Abraham, from the tribe of Benjamin. [2]God has not

9:29 [a] Deut 29:23; Isa 13:19; Jer 49:18; 50:40; Amos 4:11 [1] Isa 1:9   9:30 [a] Rom 4:11 [b] Rom 1:17; 3:21; 10:6; [Gal 2:16; 3:24; Phil 3:9]; Heb 11:7   9:31 [a] [Rom 10:2–4] [b] [Gal 5:4]   9:32 [a] [Luke 2:34; 1 Cor 1:23] [1] Maj. MSS add *of the law.*   9:33 [a] [Ps 118:22]; Isa 8:14; 28:16; [Matt 21:42; 1 Pet 2:6–8] [1] Isa 8:14; 28:16   10:1 [1] Grk. *brothers;* considerable external evidence supports use of the Grk. word as *brothers and sisters* or *fellow Christians.*   10:2 [a] Acts 21:20; Gal 1:14   10:3 [a] [Rom 1:17] [b] [Phil 3:9]   10:4 [a] Matt 5:17; [Rom 7:1–4; Gal 3:24; 4:5]   10:5 [a] Lev 18:5; Neh 9:29; Ezek 20:11, 13, 21; Rom 7:10; Gal 3:12 [1] Lev 18:5   10:6 [a] Deut 30:12–14 [1] Deut 9:4 [2] Deut 30:12   10:7 [a] Deut 30:13 [1] Deut 30:13   10:8 [a] Deut 30:14 [1] Deut 30:14   10:9 [a] Matt 10:32; Luke 12:8; Acts 8:37; Rom 14:9; [1 Cor 12:3]; Phil 2:11   10:11 [a] Isa 28:16; Jer 17:7; Rom 9:33 [1] Isa 28:16   10:12 [a] Acts 15:9; Rom 3:22, 29; Gal 3:28 [b] Acts 10:36; 1 Tim 2:5 [c] Eph 1:7   10:13 [a] Joel 2:32; Acts 2:21 [b] Acts 9:14 [1] Joel 2:32   10:14 [a] Acts 8:31; Titus 1:3   10:15 [a] Isa 52:7; Nah 1:15 [1] Isa 52:7; Nah 1:15   10:16 [a] Isa 53:1; John 12:38 [1] Isa 53:1   10:17 [1] Maj. MSS *God.*   10:18 [a] Ps 19:4; Matt 24:14; Mark 16:15; Rom 1:8; Col 1:6, 23; 1 Thess 1:8 [1] Ps 19:4   10:19 [a] Deut 32:21; Rom 11:11 [b] Titus 3:3 [1] Deut 32:21   10:20 [a] Isa 65:1; Rom 9:30 [1] Isa 65:1   10:21 [a] Isa 65:2 [1] Isa 65:2   11:1 [a] Ps 94:14; Jer 46:28 [b] 1 Sam 12:22; Jer 31:37 [c] 2 Cor 11:22; Phil 3:5

rejected his people whom [a]he foreknew! Do you not know what the scripture says about Elijah, how he pleads with God against Israel? [3]"[a]Lord, *they have killed your prophets; they have demolished your altars; I alone am left, and they are seeking my life!*"[1] [4]But what was the [a]divine response to him? "*I have kept* for myself *7,000 people who have not bent the knee to Baal.*"[1]

[5a]So in the same way at the present time there is a remnant chosen by grace. [6]And [a]if it is by grace, it is no longer by works, otherwise grace would no longer be grace. [7]What then? [a]Israel failed to obtain what it was diligently seeking, but the elect obtained it. The rest were [b]hardened, [8]as it is written,

> "[a]*God gave them a spirit of stupor,*
> [b]*eyes that would not see and ears that*
> *would not hear,*
> *to this very day.*"[1]

[9]And David says,

> "[a]*Let their table become a snare and*
> *trap,*
> *a stumbling block and a retribution*
> *for them;*
> [10] *let their eyes be darkened so that they*
> *may not see,*
> *and make their backs bend*
> *continually.*"[1]

[11]I ask then, they did not stumble into an irrevocable fall, did they? Absolutely not! But by their transgression salvation has come to the Gentiles, to make Israel [a]jealous. [12]Now if their transgression means riches for the world and their defeat means riches for the Gentiles, how much more will their full restoration bring?

[13]Now [a]I am speaking to you Gentiles. Seeing that I am an apostle to the Gentiles, I magnify my ministry, [14]if somehow I could provoke my people to jealousy and [a]save some of them. [15]For if their rejection is the reconciliation of the world, what will their acceptance be [a]but life from the dead? [16]If [a]the first portion[1] of the dough offered is holy, then the whole batch is holy, and if the root is holy, so too are the branches.

[17]Now if [a]some of the branches were broken off, [b]and you, a wild olive shoot, were grafted in among them and participated in the richness of the olive root, [18]do not boast over the branches. But if you boast, remember that you [a]do not support the root, but the root supports you. [19]Then you will say, "The branches were broken off so that I could be grafted in." [20]Granted! They were broken off because of their [a]unbelief, but you stand by faith. Do not be arrogant, but fear! [21]For if God did not spare the natural branches, perhaps he will not spare you. [22]Notice therefore the kindness and harshness of God—harshness toward those who have fallen, but God's kindness toward you, [a]provided [b]you continue in his kindness; otherwise you also will be cut off. [23]And even they —[a]if they do not continue in their unbelief—will be grafted in, for God is able to graft them in again. [24]For if you were cut off from what is by nature a wild olive tree, and grafted, contrary to nature, into a cultivated olive tree, how much more will these natural branches be grafted back into their own olive tree?

[25]For I do not want you to be ignorant of this mystery, brothers and sisters,[1] so that you may not be [a]conceited: A partial [b]hardening has happened to Israel [c]until the full number of the Gentiles has come in. [26]And so all Israel will be saved, as it is written:

> "[a]*The Deliverer will come out of Zion;*
> *he will remove ungodliness from Jacob.*
> [27] *And [a]this is my covenant with them,*[1]
> *when I take away their sins.*"[2]

[28]In regard to the gospel they are enemies for your sake, but in regard to election they are dearly [a]loved for the sake of the fathers. [29]For the gifts and the call of God are [a]irrevocable. [30]Just as you [a]were formerly

11:2 [a][Rom 8:29]   11:3 [a]1 Kgs 19:10, 14   [1]1 Kgs 19:10, 14   11:4 [a]1 Kgs 19:18   [1]1 Kgs 19:18   11:5 [a]2 Kgs 19:4; Rom 9:27   11:6 [a]Rom 4:4   11:7 [a]Rom 9:31   [b]Mark 6:52; Rom 9:18; 11:25; 2 Cor 3:14   11:8 [a]Isa 29:10, 13   [b]Deut 29:3–4; Isa 6:9; Matt 13:13–14; John 12:40; Acts 28:26–27   [1]Deut 29:4; Isa 29:10   11:9 [a]Ps 69:22–23   11:10 [1]Ps 69:22–23   11:11 [a]Deut 32:21; Acts 13:46; Rom 10:19   11:13 [a]Acts 9:15; 22:21; Gal 1:16; 2:7–9; Eph 3:8   11:14 [a]1 Cor 9:22; 1 Tim 4:16; Jas 5:20   11:15 [a][Isa 26:16–19]   11:16 [a]Lev 23:10; [Jas 1:18]   [1]Grk. *firstfruits.*   11:17 [a]Jer 11:16; [John 15:2]   [b]Acts 2:39; [Eph 2:12]   11:18 [a][1 Cor 10:12]   11:20 [a]Heb 3:19   11:22 [a]1 Cor 15:2; Heb 3:6, 14   [b][John 15:2]   11:23 [a][2 Cor 3:16]   11:25 [a]Rom 12:16   [b]2 Cor 3:14   [c]Luke 21:24; John 10:16; Rom 11:12   [1]Grk. *brothers;* considerable external evidence supports use of the Grk. word as *brothers and sisters* or *fellow Christians.*   11:26 [a]Ps 14:7; Isa 59:20–21   11:27 [a]Isa 27:9; Heb 8:12   [1]Isa 59:20–21   [2]Isa 27:9; Jer 31:33–34   11:28 [a]Deut 7:8; 10:15; Rom 9:5   11:29 [a]Num 23:19   11:30 [a][Eph 2:2]

disobedient to God, but have now received mercy due to their disobedience, [31]so they too have now been disobedient in order that, by the mercy shown to you, they too may now[1] receive mercy. [32]For God has consigned all people to disobedience so that he may show mercy to them [a]all.

[33]Oh, the depth of the riches and wisdom and knowledge of God! How unsearchable are his judgments and how unfathomable his ways!

[34] **For who has known the [a]mind of the Lord,**
   or [b]who has been his counselor?[1]
[35] **[a]Or who has first given to God**
   that God needs to repay him?[1]

[36]For [a]from him and through him and [b]to him are all things. To him be glory forever! Amen.

Consecration of the Believer's Life

12 Therefore I [a]exhort you, brothers [b]and sisters,[1] by the mercies of God, to present your bodies as a sacrifice—alive, holy, and pleasing to God—which is your reasonable service. [2]Do not [a]be conformed to this present world, but be transformed by the renewing of your mind, so that you may test and [b]approve what is the will of God—what is good and well-pleasing and perfect.

Conduct in Humility

[3]For [a]by the grace given to me I say to every one of you [b]not [c]to think more highly of yourself than you ought to think, but to think with sober discernment, as God has distributed to each of you a measure of faith. [4]For just [a]as in one body we have many members, and not all the members serve the same function, [5]so [a]we who are many are one body in Christ, and individually we are members who belong to one another. [6]And we have different gifts according to the grace [a]given to us. If the gift

is prophecy, that individual must use it in proportion to his faith. [7]If it is service, [a]he must serve; if it is teaching, he must teach; [8]if it is exhortation, [a]he must exhort; if it is contributing, [b]he must do so with sincerity; if it is leadership, [c]he must do so [d]with diligence; if it is showing mercy, he must do so with cheerfulness.

Conduct in Love

[9][a]Love must be without hypocrisy. [b]Abhor what is evil, cling to what is good. [10][a]Be devoted to one another with mutual love, [b]showing eagerness in honoring one another. [11]Do not lag in zeal, be enthusiastic in spirit, serve the Lord. [12]Rejoice [a]in hope, [b]endure [c]in suffering, persist in prayer. [13][a]Contribute to the needs of the saints, [b]pursue hospitality. [14][a]Bless those who persecute you, bless and do not curse. [15][a]Rejoice with those who rejoice, weep with those who weep. [16]Live in harmony with one another; do not [a]be haughty but associate with the lowly. [b]Do not be conceited. [17]Do not [a]repay anyone evil for evil; consider what is good before all people. [18]If possible, so far as it depends on you, [a]live peaceably with all people. [19]Do not avenge yourselves, dear friends, but give place to God's wrath, for it is written, "[a]*Vengeance is mine, I will repay,*"[1] says the Lord. [20]Rather, [a]*if your enemy is hungry, feed him; if he is thirsty, give him a drink; for in doing this you will be heaping burning coals on his head.*[1] [21]Do not be [a]overcome by evil, but overcome evil with good.

Submission to Civil Government

13 Let every person be [a]subject to the governing authorities. For there is no authority except by God's appointment, and the authorities that exist have been instituted by God. [2]So [a]the person who resists such authority resists the ordinance of God, and those who resist will incur judgment [3](for rulers cause no fear for good conduct but for bad). [a]Do you desire not to fear

11:31 [1]Some MSS *finally.* **11:32** [a]Rom 3:9; [Gal 3:22] **11:34** [a]Isa 40:13; Jer 23:18; 1 Cor 2:16 [b]Job 36:22 [1]Isa 40:13 **11:35** [a]Job 41:11 [1]Job 41:11 **11:36** [a][1 Cor 8:6; 11:12]; Col 1:16; Heb 2:10 [b]Heb 13:21 **12:1** [a]1 Cor 1:10; 2 Cor 10:1–4 [b]Phil 4:18; Heb 10:18, 20 [1]Grk. *brothers*; considerable external evidence supports use of the Grk. word as *brothers and sisters* or *fellow Christians.* **12:2** [a]Eph 4:23; [Titus 3:5] [b][1 Thess 4:3] **12:3** [a]Rom 1:5; 15:15; 1 Cor 3:10; 15:10; Gal 2:9; Eph 3:7 [b]Prov 25:27 [c][Eph 4:7] **12:4** [a]1 Cor 12:12–14; [Eph 4:4, 16] **12:5** [a][1 Cor 10:17]; Gal 3:28 **12:6** [a][John 3:27] **12:7** [a]Eph 4:11 **12:8** [a]Acts 15:32 [b][Matt 6:1–3] [c][Acts 20:28] [d]2 Cor 9:7 **12:9** [a]2 Cor 6:6; 1 Tim 1:5 [b]Ps 34:14 **12:10** [a]John 13:34; 1 Thess 4:9; Heb 13:1; 2 Pet 1:7 [b]Rom 13:7; Phil 2:3; [1 Pet 2:17] **12:12** [a]Luke 10:20 [b]Luke 21:19 [c]Luke 18:1 **12:13** [a]1 Cor 16:1; Heb 13:16; 1 Pet 4:9 [b]Matt 25:35; 1 Tim 3:2 **12:14** [a][Matt 5:44]; Luke 6:28; 1 Cor 4:12 **12:15** [a][1 Cor 12:26] **12:16** [a]Rom 15:5; 2 Cor 13:11; [Phil 2:2; 4:2]; 1 Pet 3:8 [b]Jer 45:5 **12:17** [a][Matt 5:39]; 1 Pet 3:9 **12:18** [a]Heb 12:14 **12:19** [a]Deut 32:35; Ps 94:1; 1 Thess 4:6; Heb 10:30 [1]Deut 32:25 **12:20** [a]2 Kgs 6:22; Prov 25:21–22; [Matt 5:44]; Luke 6:27 [1]Prov 25:21–22 **12:21** [a][Rom 12:1–2] **13:1** [a]Titus 3:1; 1 Pet 2:13 **13:2** [a][Titus 3:1] **13:3** [a]1 Pet 2:14

authority? Do good and you will receive its commendation [4]because it is God's servant for your well-being. But be afraid if you do wrong because government does not bear the sword for nothing. It is God's servant to administer punishment on the person who does wrong. [5]Therefore [a]it is necessary to be in subjection, not only because of the wrath of the authorities [b]but also because of your conscience. [6]For this reason you also pay taxes, for the authorities are God's servants devoted to governing. [7][a]Pay everyone what is owed: taxes to whom taxes are due, revenue to whom revenue is due, respect to whom respect is due, honor to whom honor is due.

Exhortation to Love Neighbors

[8]Owe no one anything, except to love one [a]another, for the one who loves his neighbor has fulfilled the law. [9]For the commandments, *"Do not commit adultery, do not murder, do not steal, do not covet,"*[1] (and if there is any other commandment) are summed up in this, *"Love [a]your neighbor as [b]yourself."*[2] [10][a]Love does no wrong to a neighbor. Therefore love is the fulfillment of the law.

Motivation to Godly Conduct

[11]And do this because we know the time, that it is already the hour for us [a]to awake from sleep, for our salvation is now nearer than when we became believers. [12]The night has advanced toward dawn; the day is near. So [a]then we must lay aside the works of darkness, and put on the weapons of light. [13][a]Let us live decently as in the daytime, [b]not in carousing and drunkenness, [c]not in sexual immorality and sensuality, [d]not in discord and jealousy. [14]Instead, [a]put on the Lord Jesus Christ, and [b]make no provision for the flesh to arouse its desires.

Exhortation to Mutual Forbearance

14 Now [a]receive the one who is weak in the faith, and do not have disputes over differing opinions. [2]One person believes in eating everything, but the weak person eats only vegetables. [3]The one who eats everything must not despise the one who does not, and the one who abstains must not judge the one who eats everything, for God has accepted him. [4][a]Who are you to pass judgment on another's servant? Before his own master he stands or falls. And he will stand, for the Lord[1] is able to make him stand.

[5]One person regards [a]one day holier than other days, and another regards them all alike. Each must be fully convinced in his own mind. [6]The one who [a]observes [b]the day does it for the Lord. The one who eats, eats for the Lord because he gives thanks to God, and the one who abstains from eating abstains for the Lord, and he gives thanks to God. [7]For [a]none of us lives for himself and none dies for himself. [8]If we [a]live, we live for the Lord; if we die, we die for the Lord. Therefore, whether we live or die, we are the Lord's. [9]For this reason Christ died and returned [a]to life, so that he may be the [b]Lord of both the dead and the living.

[10]But you who eat vegetables only—why do you judge your brother or sister? And you who eat everything—why do you despise your brother or sister? For [a]we will all stand before the judgment seat of God. [11]For it is written, *"[a]As I live, says the Lord, every knee will bow to me, and every tongue will give praise to God."*[1] [12]Therefore, [a]each of us will give an account of himself to God.[1]

Exhortation for the Strong not to Destroy the Weak

[13]Therefore we must [a]not pass judgment on one another, but rather determine never to place an obstacle or a trap before a brother or sister.[1] [14]I know and am convinced in the Lord Jesus [a]that there is nothing unclean in itself; still, it is unclean to the one who considers it unclean. [15]For if your brother or sister[1] is distressed because of what you eat, you are no longer walking in

13:5 [a] Eccl 8:2 [b] Acts 24:16; [1 Pet 2:13, 19]   13:7 [a] Matt 22:21; Mark 12:17; Luke 20:25   13:8 [a] [Matt 7:12; 22:39; John 13:34; Rom 13:10; Gal 5:13–14; 1 Tim 1:5; Jas 2:8]   13:9 [a] Exod 20:13–17; Deut 5:17–21; Matt 19:18 [b] Lev 19:18; Mark 12:31; Jas 2:8 [1] Exod 20:13–15, 17; Deut 5:17–19, 21 [2] Lev 19:18   13:10 [a] [Matt 7:12; 22:39–40; John 13:34]; Rom 13:8; Gal 5:14; Jas 2:8   13:11 [a] Mark 13:37; [1 Cor 15:34; Eph 5:14]; 1 Thess 5:6   13:12 [a] Eph 5:11   13:13 [a] Phil 4:8 [b] Prov 23:20 [c] [1 Cor 6:9] [d] Jas 3:14   13:14 [a] Job 29:14; Gal 3:27; [Eph 4:24; Col 3:10, 12] [b] [Gal 5:16]; 1 Pet 2:11   14:1 [a] [Rom 14:2; 15:1; 1 Cor 8:9; 9:22]   14:4 [a] Rom 9:20; Jas 4:11–12 [1] Maj. mss *God*.   14:5 [a] Gal 4:10   14:6 [a] Gal 4:10 [b] Matt 14:19; 15:36; [1 Cor 10:31; 1 Tim 4:3]   14:7 [a] [1 Cor 6:19; Gal 2:20]; 1 Thess 5:10; [1 Pet 4:2]   14:8 [a] 2 Cor 5:14–15   14:9 [a] 2 Cor 5:15 [b] Acts 10:36   14:10 [a] Rom 2:16; 2 Cor 5:10   14:11 [a] Isa 45:23; [Phil 2:10–11] [1] Isa 45:23   14:12 [a] Matt 12:36; 16:27; [Gal 6:5]; 1 Pet 4:5 [1] ‡ Some mss omit *to God*.   14:13 [a] 1 Cor 8:9 [1] Grk. *brother*; considerable external evidence supports use of the Grk. word as *brother or sister* or *fellow Christian*.   14:14 [a] 1 Cor 10:25   14:15 [1] Grk. *brother*; considerable external evidence supports use of the Grk. word as *brother or sister* or *fellow Christian*.

love. [a]Do not destroy by your food someone for whom Christ died. [16][a]Therefore do not let what you consider good be spoken of as evil. [17][a]For the kingdom of God does not consist of food and drink, but righteousness, [b]peace, and joy in the Holy Spirit. [18]For the one who serves [a]Christ in this way is pleasing to God and approved by people.

[19]So then, let us pursue what makes [a]for peace and for building up [b]one another. [20][a]Do not destroy the work of God for the sake of food. For although all [b]things are clean, [c]it is wrong to cause anyone to stumble by what you eat. [21]It is good not to eat [a]meat or drink wine or to do anything that causes your brother to stumble.[1] [22]The faith you have, keep to yourself before God. [a]Blessed is the one who does not judge himself by what he approves. [23]But the man who doubts is condemned if he eats, because he does not do so from faith, and [a]whatever is not from faith is sin.[1]

Exhortation for the Strong to Help the Weak

15 But we who are strong ought to bear with [a]the failings of the weak, and not just please ourselves. [2][a]Let each of us please his neighbor for his good to build him up. [3][a]For even Christ did not please himself, but just as it is written, "[b]*The insults of those who insult you have fallen on me.*"[1] [4]For [a]everything that was written in former times was written for our instruction, so that through endurance and through encouragement of the scriptures we may have hope. [5][a]Now may the God of endurance and comfort give you unity with one another[1] in accordance with Christ Jesus, [6]so that together you may [a]with one voice glorify the God and Father of our Lord Jesus Christ.

Exhortation to Mutual Acceptance

[7][a]Receive one another, then, just [b]as Christ also received you, to God's glory. [8]For I tell you that Christ has become a servant of the circumcised on behalf of God's truth [a]to confirm the promises made to the fathers, [9]and thus the Gentiles glorify God for his mercy. As it is written, "*Because* [a]*of this I will confess you among the Gentiles, and I will sing praises to your name.*"[1] [10]And again it says: "[a]*Rejoice, O Gentiles, with his people.*"[1] [11]And again, "[a]*Praise the Lord all you Gentiles, and let all the peoples praise him.*"[1] [12]And again Isaiah says, "[a]*The root of Jesse will come, and the one who rises to rule over the Gentiles, in him will the Gentiles hope.*"[1] [13]Now may the God of hope fill you with all [a]joy and peace as you believe in him, so that you may abound in hope by the power of the Holy Spirit.

Paul's Motivation for Writing the Letter

[14]But [a]I myself am fully convinced about you, my brothers and sisters,[1] that you yourselves are full of goodness, [b]filled with all knowledge, and able to instruct one another. [15]But I have written more boldly to you on some points so as to remind you, [a]because of the grace given to me by God [16]to be a [a]minister of Christ Jesus to the Gentiles. I serve the gospel of God[1] like a priest, so that the Gentiles may become an acceptable [b]offering, sanctified by the Holy Spirit.

[17]So [a]I boast in Christ Jesus about the things that pertain to God. [18]For I will not dare to speak of anything except [a]what Christ has accomplished through me in order [b]to bring about the obedience of the Gentiles, by word and deed, [19][a]in the power of signs and wonders, in the power of the Spirit of God. So from Jerusalem even as far as Illyricum I have fully preached the gospel of Christ. [20]And in this way I desire to preach where Christ has not been named, so as not to build on another person's foundation, [21]but as it is written: "*Those who were not* [a]*told about him will see, and those who have not heard will understand.*"[1]

14:15 [a] Rom 14:20; 1 Cor 8:11   14:16 [a] [Rom 12:17]   14:17 [a] 1 Cor 8:8   [b] [Rom 8:6]   14:18 [a] 2 Cor 8:21; Phil 4:8; 1 Pet 2:12   14:19 [a] Ps 34:14; Rom 12:18; 1 Cor 7:15; 2 Tim 2:22; Heb 12:14   [b] 1 Cor 14:12; 1 Thess 5:11   14:20 [a] Rom 14:15   [b] Acts 10:15   [c] 1 Cor 8:9–12   14:21 [a] 1 Cor 8:13   [1] Many MSS add *or to be offended or to be made weak.*   14:22 [a] [1 John 3:21]   14:23 [a] Titus 1:15   [1] Some MSS insert 16:25–27 here.   15:1 [a] Rom 14:1; [Gal 6:1–2]; 1 Thess 5:14   15:2 [a] 1 Cor 9:22; 10:24, 33; 2 Cor 13:9   15:3 [a] Matt 26:39; [Phil 2:5–8]   [b] Ps 69:9   [1] Ps 69:9   15:4 [a] Rom 4:23–24; 1 Cor 10:11; 2 Tim 3:16–17   15:5 [a] 1 Cor 1:10; Phil 1:27   [1] Grk. *grant you to think the same among one another.*   15:6 [a] Acts 4:24   15:7 [a] Rom 14:1, 3   [b] Rom 5:2   15:8 [a] [Rom 4:16]; 2 Cor 1:20   15:9 [a] 2 Sam 22:50; Ps 18:49   [1] Ps 18:49   15:10 [a] Deut 32:43   [1] Deut 32:43   15:11 [a] Ps 117:1   [1] Ps 117:1   15:12 [a] Isa 11:1, 10   [1] Isa 11:10   15:13 [a] Rom 12:12; 14:17   15:14 [a] 2 Pet 1:12   [b] 1 Cor 1:5; 8:1, 7, 10   [1] Grk. *brothers*; considerable external evidence supports use of the Grk. word as *brothers and sisters* or *fellow Christians.*   15:15 [a] Rom 1:5; 12:3   15:16 [a] Acts 9:15; Rom 11:13   [b] [Isa 66:20]   [1] Grk. *the gospel which God brings, the gospel about God.*   15:17 [a] Heb 2:17; 5:1   15:18 [a] Acts 15:12; 21:19; 2 Cor 3:5; Gal 2:8   [b] Rom 1:5   15:19 [a] Acts 19:11   15:21 [a] Isa 52:15   [1] Isa 52:15

Paul's Intention of Visiting the Romans

[22]This [a]is the reason I was often hindered from coming to you. [23]But now there is nothing more to keep me in these regions, and I [a]have for many years desired to come to you [24]when I go to Spain. For I hope to visit you when I pass through [a]and that you will help me on my journey there, after I have [b]enjoyed your company for a while.

[25]But now [a]I go to Jerusalem to minister to the saints. [26]For Macedonia and Achaia are pleased to make some contribution for the poor among the saints in Jerusalem. [27]For they were pleased to do this, and indeed they are indebted to the Jerusalem saints. For [a]if [b]the Gentiles have shared in their spiritual things, they are obligated also to minister to them in material things. [28]Therefore after I have completed [a]this and have safely delivered this bounty to them, I will set out for Spain by way of you, [29a]and I know that when I come to you, I will come in the fullness of Christ's blessing.

[30]Now I urge you, brothers and sisters,[1] [a]through our Lord Jesus Christ and through the love of the Spirit, to join fervently with me in prayer to God on my behalf. [31]Pray [a]that I may be rescued from those who are disobedient in Judea and that [b]my ministry in Jerusalem may be acceptable to the saints, [32]so [a]that [b]by God's will I may come to you with joy and [c]be refreshed in your company. [33]Now may [a]the God of peace be with all of you. Amen.[1]

Personal Greetings

16 Now I commend to you our sister Phoebe, who is a servant[1] of the church in [a]Cenchrea, [2]so [a]that you may welcome her [b]in the Lord in a way worthy of the saints and provide her with whatever help she may need from you, for she has been a great help to many, including me.

[3]Greet Prisca and Aquila, my fellow workers in Christ Jesus, [4]who risked their own necks for my life. Not only I, but all the churches of the Gentiles are grateful to them. [5]Also greet [a]the church in [b]their house. Greet my dear friend Epenetus, who was the first convert to Christ in the province of Asia. [6]Greet Mary, who has worked very hard for you. [7]Greet Andronicus and Junia, my compatriots and my fellow prisoners. They are well known to the [a]apostles, and they [b]were in Christ before me. [8]Greet Ampliatus, my dear friend in the Lord. [9]Greet Urbanus, our fellow worker in Christ, and my good friend Stachys. [10]Greet Apelles, who is approved in Christ. Greet those who belong to the household of Aristobulus. [11]Greet Herodion, my compatriot. Greet those in the household of Narcissus who are in the Lord. [12]Greet Tryphena and Tryphosa, laborers in the Lord. Greet my dear friend Persis, who has worked hard in the Lord. [13]Greet Rufus, [a]chosen in the Lord, and his mother who was also a mother to me. [14]Greet Asyncritus, Phlegon, Hermes, Patrobas, Hermas, and the brothers and sisters[1] with them. [15]Greet Philologus and Julia, Nereus and his sister, and Olympas, and all the believers who are with them. [16a]Greet one another with a holy kiss. All the churches of Christ greet you.

[17]Now I urge you, brothers and sisters,[1] to watch out for those [a]who create dissensions and obstacles contrary to the teaching that you learned. [b]Avoid them! [18]For these are [a]the kind who do not serve our Lord Christ, but their own appetites. [b]By their smooth talk and flattery they deceive the minds of the naive. [19a]Your obedience is known to all and thus I rejoice over you. But I want you to be [b]wise in what is good and innocent in what is evil. [20]The God of peace will quickly crush Satan under your feet. [a]The grace of our Lord Jesus be with you.

[21a]Timothy, my fellow worker, greets you; so do [b]Lucius, [c]Jason, and [d]Sosipater, my compatriots. [22]I, Tertius, who am writing this letter, greet you in the Lord. [23a]Gaius,

---

15:22 [a] Rom 1:13; 1 Thess 2:17–18   15:23 [a] Acts 19:21; 23:11; Rom 1:10–11   15:24 [a] Acts 15:3   [b] Rom 1:12   15:25 [a] Acts 19:21   15:27 [a] Rom 11:17   [b] 1 Cor 9:11   15:28 [a] Phil 4:17   15:29 [a] [Rom 1:11]   15:30 [a] Phil 2:1   [1] Grk. *brothers*; considerable external evidence supports use of the Grk. word as *brothers and sisters* or *fellow Christians*.   15:31 [a] 2 Tim 3:11; 4:17   [b] 2 Cor 8:4   15:32 [a] Rom 1:10   [b] Acts 18:21   [c] 1 Cor 16:18   15:33 [a] Rom 16:20; 1 Cor 14:33; 2 Cor 13:11; Phil 4:9; [1 Thess 5:23]; 2 Thess 3:16; Heb 13:20   [1] Some MSS omit *Amen* and insert 16:25–27 here.   16:1 [a] Acts 18:18   [1] Or *deaconess*.   16:2 [a] Phil 2:29   [b] Phil 1:27   16:5 [a] 1 Cor 16:19; Col 4:15; Phlm 2   [b] 1 Cor 16:15   16:7 [a] Acts 1:13, 26   [b] Rom 8:11; 16:3, 9, 10; 2 Cor 5:17; 12:2; Gal 1:22   16:13 [a] 2 John 1   16:14 [1] Grk. *brothers*; considerable external evidence supports use of the Grk. word as *brothers and sisters* or *fellow Christians*.   16:16 [a] 1 Cor 16:20; 2 Cor 13:12; 1 Thess 5:26; 1 Pet 5:14   16:17 [a] [Acts 15:1]   [b] [1 Cor 5:9]   [1] Grk. *brothers*; considerable external evidence supports use of the Grk. word as *brothers and sisters* or *fellow Christians*.   16:18 [a] Phil 3:19   [b] Col 2:4; 2 Pet 2:3   16:19 [a] Rom 1:8   [b] Jer 4:22; Matt 10:16; 1 Cor 14:20   16:20 [a] Rom 15:33   16:21 [a] Acts 16:1; Heb 13:23   [b] Acts 13:1   [c] Acts 17:5   [d] Acts 20:4   16:23 [a] 1 Cor 1:14

who is host to me and to the whole church, greets you. [b]Erastus the city treasurer and our brother Quartus greet you.[1]

[25][1]Now [a]to him who is able to strengthen you [b]according to my gospel and the proclamation of Jesus Christ, [c]according to the revelation of the mystery that had been [d]kept secret for long ages, [26]but [a]now is disclosed, and through the prophetic scriptures has been made known to all the nations, according to the command of the eternal God, to bring about the [b]obedience of faith—[27]to the only wise [a]God, through Jesus Christ, be glory forever! Amen.

16:23 [b] Acts 19:22; 2 Tim 4:20   [1]Maj. MSS add v. 24: *The grace of our Lord Jesus Christ be with all of you. Amen;* some MSS include the verse after v. 27.   16:25 [a] [Eph 3:20; Jude 24]   [b] Rom 2:16   [c] Matt 13:35; Rom 11:25; 1 Cor 2:1, 7; 4:1; Eph 1:9   [d] Col 1:26; 2:2; 4:3; [1 Tim 3:16]   [1] Some MSS place this doxology here after v. 23, after 14:23, or after 15:33.   16:26 [a] Eph 1:9   [b] [Acts 6:7]; Rom 1:5   16:27 [a] Jude 25

1 CORINTHIANS

Corinth, the most important city in Greece during Paul's day, was a bustling hub of worldwide commerce, degraded culture, and idolatrous religion. There Paul founded a church (Acts 18:1–17), and two of his letters are addressed "To the church of God that is in Corinth" (1 Cor 1:2; 2 Cor 1:1). First Corinthians reveals the problems, pressures, and struggles of a church called out of a pagan society. Paul addresses a variety of issues in the lifestyle of the Corinthian church: factions, lawsuits, immorality, questionable practices, abuse of the Lord's Supper, and spiritual gifts. In addition to words of discipline, Paul shares words of counsel in answer to questions raised by the Corinthian believers. The oldest recorded title of this epistle is *Pros Korinthious A*, in effect, the "First to the Corinthians." The *A* was no doubt a later addition to distinguish this book from 2 Corinthians.

Salutation

1 From Paul, [a]called to be an apostle of Christ Jesus[1] [b]by the will of God, and [c]Sosthenes, our brother, [2]to the church of God that is in Corinth, to those who [a]are sanctified in Christ Jesus, and [b]called to be saints, with all those in every place who call on the name of [c]our Lord Jesus Christ, their Lord and ours. [3][a]Grace and peace to you from God our Father and the Lord Jesus Christ!

Thanksgiving

[4]I always thank my God for you because of the grace of God that was [a]given to you in Christ Jesus. [5]For you were made rich [a]in every way in him, in all your speech and in every kind of knowledge—[6]just as [a]the testimony about Christ has been confirmed among you—[7]so that you do not lack any spiritual gift as you [a]wait for the revelation of our Lord Jesus Christ. [8][a]He will also strengthen you to the end, so [b]that you will be blameless on the day of our Lord Jesus Christ. [9][a]God is faithful, by whom you were called into fellowship with his son, Jesus Christ our Lord.

Divisions in the Church

[10]I urge you, brothers and sisters,[1] by the name of our Lord Jesus Christ, [a]to agree together, to end your divisions, and to be united by the same mind and purpose. [11]For members of Chloe's household have made it clear to me, my brothers and sisters,[1] that there are quarrels among you. [12]Now I mean this, that [a]each of you is saying, "I am with Paul," or "I am with [b]Apollos," or "I am with [c]Cephas," or "I am with Christ." [13]Is [a]Christ divided? Paul wasn't crucified for you, was he? Or were you in fact baptized in the name of Paul? [14]I thank God[1] that I did [a]not baptize any of you except [b]Crispus and [c]Gaius, [15]so that no one can say that you were baptized in my name! [16](I also baptized the household of [a]Stephanus. Otherwise, I do not remember whether I baptized anyone else.) [17]For Christ did [a]not send me to baptize, but to preach the gospel—and not with clever speech, so that the cross of Christ would not become useless.

The Message of the Cross

[18]For the message about the cross is [a]foolishness to [b]those [c]who are perishing, but

1:1 [a] Rom 1:1 [b] 2 Cor 1:1 [c] Acts 18:17 [1] Many sig. MSS *Jesus Christ.*   1:2 [a] [Acts 15:9] [b] Rom 1:7; Eph 4:1; 1 Thess 2:12 [c] [1 Cor 8:6]   1:3 [a] Rom 1:7   1:4 [a] Rom 1:8   1:5 [a] [1 Cor 12:8]   1:6 [a] 2 Thess 1:10; 1 Tim 2:6; 2 Tim 1:8; Rev 1:2   1:7 [a] Luke 17:30; Rom 8:19, 23; Phil 3:20; Titus 2:13; [2 Pet 3:12]   1:8 [a] 1 Thess 3:13; 5:23 [b] Phil 1:6; Col 1:22; 2:7   1:9 [a] Deut 7:9; Isa 49:7; 1 Cor 10:13; 2 Cor 1:18; 1 Thess 5:24; 2 Thess 3:3   1:10 [a] 2 Cor 13:11; 1 Pet 3:8   [1] Grk. *brothers*; considerable external evidence supports use of the Grk. word as *brothers and sisters* or *fellow Christians.*   1:11 [1] Grk. *brothers*; considerable external evidence supports use of the Grk. word as *brothers and sisters* or *fellow Christians.*   1:12 [a] Matt 3:8–10; 1 Cor 3:4 [b] Acts 18:24; 1 Cor 3:22 [c] John 1:42; 1 Cor 3:22; 9:5; 15:5   1:13 [a] 2 Cor 11:4   1:14 [a] John 4:2 [b] Acts 18:8 [c] Rom 16:23   [1] Sig. WSS omit *God.*   1:16 [a] 1 Cor 16:15, 17   1:17 [a] [1 Cor 2:1, 4, 13]   1:18 [a] 1 Cor 2:14 [b] 2 Cor 2:15 [c] [1 Cor 15:2]

to us who are being saved it is the [d]power of God. [19]For [a]it is written, *"I will destroy the wisdom of the wise, and I will thwart the cleverness of the intelligent."*[1] [20][a]Where is the wise man? Where is the expert in the Mosaic law? Where is the debater of this age?[b]Has God not made the wisdom of the world foolish? [21]For since in the [a]wisdom of God the world by its wisdom did not know God, God was pleased to save those who believe by the foolishness of preaching. [22]For [a]Jews demand miraculous signs and Greeks ask for wisdom, [23]but we preach about a crucified Christ, a stumbling block [a]to Jews and [b]foolishness to Gentiles. [24]But to those who are called, both Jews and Greeks, Christ is [a]the power of God and [b]the wisdom of God. [25]For the foolishness of God is wiser than human wisdom, and the weakness of God is stronger than human strength.

[26]Think about the circumstances of your call, brothers and sisters.[1] Not many were wise by human standards, not many were powerful, not many were born to [a]a privileged position. [27]But [a]God chose what the world thinks foolish to shame the wise, and God chose what the world thinks weak to shame the strong. [28]God chose what is low and despised in the world, what is regarded as nothing, to set aside what is regarded as something, [29]so that no one can boast in his presence. [30]He is the reason you have a relationship with Christ Jesus, who became for us wisdom from God, and [a]righteousness and sanctification and redemption, [31]so that, as it is written, *"Let [a]the one who boasts, boast in the Lord."*[1]

2 When I came to you, brothers and sisters,[1] I did not come with superior eloquence or wisdom as I proclaimed the testimony[2] of God. [2]For I decided to be concerned about nothing among you [a]except Jesus Christ, and him crucified. [3]And [a]I was with you [b]in weakness and in fear and with much trembling. [4]My conversation and my preaching [a]were not with persuasive words of wisdom, [b]but with a demonstration of the Spirit and of power, [5]so that your faith would not be based on human wisdom but on the [a]power of God.

Wisdom from God

[6]Now we do speak wisdom among the mature, but not a wisdom of this age or of the rulers of this age, who are perishing. [7]Instead we speak the wisdom of God, hidden in a mystery, that God determined before the ages for our glory. [8]None of the rulers of this age understood it. [a]If they had known it, they would not have [b]crucified the Lord of glory. [9]But just as it is written, *"Things that no [a]eye has seen, or ear heard, or mind imagined, are the things God has prepared for those who love him."*[1] [10][a]God has revealed these to us by the Spirit. For the Spirit searches all things, even the deep things of God. [11]For who among men knows the things of a man except the man's [a]spirit within him? So [b]too, no one knows the things of God except the Spirit of God. [12]Now we have not received [a]the spirit of the world, but the Spirit who is from God, so that we may know the things that are freely given to us by God. [13]And we speak about these things, not with words taught us by human wisdom, but with those taught by the Spirit, explaining spiritual things to spiritual people. [14][a]The unbeliever does not receive the things of the Spirit of God, for they are foolishness to him. And he cannot understand them, because they are spiritually discerned. [15]The one who is spiritual discerns all things, yet he himself is understood by no one. [16]For [a]who has known the mind of the Lord, so as to advise him?[1] [b]But we have the mind of Christ.

Immaturity and Self-Deception

3 So, brothers and sisters,[1] I could not speak to you as spiritual people, but instead as people of the flesh, as [a]infants in Christ. [2]I fed you [a]milk, not solid food, [b]for

1:18[d] Rom 1:16; 1 Cor 1:24   1:19[a] Isa 29:14 [1] Isa 29:14   1:20[a] Isa 19:12; 33:18 [b] Job 12:17; Matt 13:22; 1 Cor 2:6, 8; 3:18–19   1:21[a] Dan 2:20; [Rom 11:33]   1:22[a] Matt 12:38; Mark 8:11; John 2:18; 4:48   1:23[a] Isa 8:14; Luke 2:34; John 6:60; Gal 5:11; [1 Pet 2:8] [b] [1 Cor 2:14]   1:24[a] [Rom 1:4] [b] Col 2:3   1:26[a] John 7:48 [1] Grk. *brothers*; considerable external evidence supports use of the Grk. word as *brothers and sisters* or *fellow Christians*.   1:27[a] Ps 8:2; Matt 11:25   1:30[a] Jer 23:5; 33:16; [2 Cor 5:21; Phil 3:9]   1:31[a] Jer 9:23–24; 2 Cor 10:17 [1] Jer 9:24   2:1[1] Grk. *brothers*; considerable external evidence supports use of the Grk. word as *brothers and sisters* or *fellow Christians*.   2[2] ‡ A few sig. MSS *mystery*.   2:2[a] 1 Cor 1:23; Gal 6:14   2:3[a] Acts 18:1 [b] [2 Cor 4:7]   2:4[a] 2 Pet 1:16 [b] Rom 15:19; 1 Cor 4:20   2:5[a] Rom 1:16; 1 Thess 1:5   2:8[a] Luke 23:34 [b] Matt 27:33–50   2:9[a] [Isa 64:4; 65:17] [1] Isa 64:4   2:10[a] Matt 11:25; 13:11; 16:17; [Gal 1:12; Eph 3:3, 5]   2:11[a] Job 32:8; Eccl 12:7; [1 Cor 6:20; Jas 2:26] [b] Rom 11:33   2:12[a] [Rom 8:15]   2:14[a] Matt 16:23   2:16[a] Job 15:8; Isa 40:13; Rom 11:34 [b] [John 15:15] [1] Isa 40:13   3:1[a] 1 Cor 2:6; Eph 4:14; Heb 5:13 [1] Grk. *brothers*; considerable external evidence supports use of the Grk. word as *brothers and sisters* or *fellow Christians*.   3:2[a] Heb 5:12; 1 Pet 2:2 [b] John 16:12

you were not yet ready. In fact, you are still not ready, [3]for you are still influenced by the flesh. For since there is still jealousy and dissension among you, are you not influenced by the flesh and behaving like unregenerate people? [4]For whenever someone says, "I am with Paul," or "I am with Apollos," are you not merely human?

[5]What is Apollos, really? Or what is Paul? [a]Servants through whom you came to believe, and each of us in the ministry the Lord gave us. [6a]I planted, [b]Apollos watered, [c]but God caused it to grow. [7]So [a]neither the one who plants counts for anything, nor the one who waters, but God who causes the growth. [8]The one who plants and the one who waters work as one, [a]but each will receive his reward according to his work. [9]We are coworkers belonging to [a]God. You are God's field, God's building. [10]According [a]to [b]the grace of God given to me, like a skilled master-builder I laid a foundation, but someone else builds on it. And each one must be careful how he builds. [11]For no one can lay any foundation other than what is being laid, [a]which is Jesus Christ. [12]If anyone builds on the foundation with gold, silver, precious stones, wood, hay, or straw, [13]each builder's work [a]will be plainly seen, for the Day will make [b]it clear, because it will be revealed by fire. And the fire will test what kind of work each has done. [14]If what someone has built survives, he will receive a reward. [15]If someone's work is burned up, he will suffer loss. He himself will be saved, but only as through fire.

[16a]Do you not know that you are God's temple and that God's Spirit lives in you? [17]If someone destroys God's temple, God will destroy him. For God's temple is holy, which is what you are.

[18]Guard against self-deception, each of you. If someone among you thinks he is wise in this age, [a]let him become foolish so that he can become wise. [19]For [a]the wisdom of this age is foolishness with God. As it is written, "*He catches the wise in their craftiness.*"[1] [20]And again, "[a]*The Lord knows that the thoughts of the wise are futile.*"[1] [21]So then, no more boasting about mere mortals! For [a]everything belongs to you, [22]whether Paul or Apollos or Cephas or the world or life or death or the present or the future. Everything belongs to you, [23]and [a]you belong to Christ, and Christ belongs to God.

The Apostles' Ministry

4 One should think about us this way—as [a]servants of Christ [b]and stewards of the mysteries of God. [2]Now what is sought in stewards is that one be found faithful. [3]So for me, it is a minor matter that I am judged by you or by any human court. In fact, I do not even judge myself. [4]For I am not aware of anything against myself, but I am not acquitted because of this. The one who judges me is the Lord. [5]So [a]then, do not judge anything before the time. Wait until the Lord comes. He will bring to [b]light the hidden things of darkness and [c]reveal the motives of hearts. [d]Then each will receive recognition from God.

[6]I have applied these things to myself and Apollos because of you, brothers and sisters,[1] so that through us you may learn "not to go beyond what is written," so that none of you will be puffed up in favor of the one against the other. [7]For who concedes you any superiority? [a]What do you have that you did not receive? And if you received it, why do you boast as though you did not? [8]Already [a]you are satisfied! Already you are rich! You have become kings without us! I wish you had become kings so that we could reign with you! [9]For, I think, God has exhibited us apostles last of all, as men condemned to die, because we have become a [a]spectacle to the world, both to angels and to people. [10]We are [a]fools for Christ, but you are wise in Christ! [b]We are weak, but you are strong! You are distinguished, we are dishonored! [11]To the present hour we are hungry and thirsty, poorly clothed, brutally treated, and without a roof over our heads.

3:5 [a]Rom 15:16; 2 Cor 3:3, 6; 4:1; 5:18; 6:4; Eph 3:7; Col 1:25; 1 Tim 1:12   3:6 [a]Acts 18:4; 1 Cor 4:15; 9:1; 15:1; 2 Cor 10:14   [b]Acts 18:24–27; 1 Cor 1:12   [c][2 Cor 3:5]   3:7 [a]2 Cor 12:11; [Gal 6:3]   3:8 [a]Ps 62:12; Rom 2:6   3:9 [a][1 Cor 3:16; Eph 2:20–22]; Col 2:7; Heb 3:3–4; [1 Pet 2:5]   3:10 [a]Rom 1:5   [b]1 Cor 4:15   3:11 [a]Eph 2:20; 1 Pet 2:4   3:13 [a]1 Pet 1:7   [b]Mal 3:1–3; Luke 2:35   3:16 [a]Rom 8:9; 1 Cor 6:19; 2 Cor 6:16; Eph 2:21   3:18 [a]Prov 3:7   3:19 [a]Job 5:13   [1]Job 5:13   3:20 [a]Ps 94:11   [1]Ps 94:11   3:21 [a][2 Cor 4:5]   3:23 [a][Rom 14:8]; 1 Cor 15:23; 2 Cor 10:7; [Gal 3:29]   4:1 [a]Matt 24:45; Rom 13:6; 2 Cor 3:6; Col 1:25   [b]Luke 12:42; 1 Cor 9:17; Titus 1:7; 1 Pet 4:10   4:5 [a]Matt 7:1; Rom 2:1; [Rev 20:12]   [b]Matt 10:26   [c]1 Cor 3:13   [d]Rom 2:29; 1 Cor 3:8; [2 Cor 5:10]   4:6 [1]Grk. *brothers*; considerable external evidence supports use of the Grk. word as *brothers and sisters* or *fellow Christians*.   4:7 [a]John 3:27; Rom 12:3, 6; 1 Pet 4:10   4:8 [a]Rev 3:17   4:9 [a]Heb 10:33   4:10 [a]Acts 17:18; 26:24; 1 Cor 1:18   [b]1 Cor 2:3; 2 Cor 13:9

[12]We do hard work, toiling with our own [a]hands. When we are verbally abused, we respond with a blessing, when persecuted, we endure, [13]when people lie about us, [a]we answer in a friendly manner. We are the world's dirt and scum, even now.

A Father's Warning

[14]I am not writing these things to shame you, but to correct you [a]as my dear children. [15]For though you may have 10,000 guardians [a]in Christ, you do not have many fathers, because I became your father in Christ Jesus through the gospel. [16]I encourage you, then, be imitators of me. [17]For this reason, I have sent [a]Timothy to you, [b]who is my dear and faithful son in the Lord. He will [c]remind you of my ways in Christ,[1] as I [d]teach them everywhere [e]in every church. [18a]Some have become arrogant, as if I were not coming to you. [19a]But I will come to you soon, [b]if the Lord is willing, and I will find out not only the talk of these arrogant people, but also their power. [20]For [a]the kingdom of God is demonstrated not in idle talk but with [b]power. [21]What do you want? [a]Shall I come to you with a rod of discipline or with love and a spirit of gentleness?

Church Discipline

5 It is actually reported that sexual immorality exists among you, the kind of immorality that is not permitted even among the Gentiles, so that someone is cohabiting with his father's [a]wife. [2a]And you are proud! Shouldn't you have been deeply [b]sorrowful instead and removed the one who did this from among you? [3a]For even though I am absent physically, I am present in spirit. And I have already judged the one who did this, just as though I were present. [4]When you gather together in the [a]name of our Lord Jesus,[1] and I am with you in spirit, along [b]with the power of our Lord Jesus, [5]hand this man [a]over to [b]Satan for the destruction of the flesh, so that his spirit may be saved[1] in the day of the Lord.[2]

[6a]Your boasting is not good. Don't you know [b]that a little yeast affects the whole batch of dough? [7]Clean out the old yeast so that you may be a new batch of dough— you are, in fact, without yeast. For [a]Christ, our Passover [b]lamb, has been sacrificed. [8]So then, [a]let us celebrate the festival, [b]not [c]with the old yeast, the yeast of vice and evil, but with the bread without yeast, the bread of sincerity and truth.

[9]I wrote you in my letter [a]not to associate with sexually immoral people. [10]In no way did I mean the immoral people of this world, or the greedy and swindlers and idolaters, since you would then have to go out [a]of the world. [11]But now [a]I am writing to you not to associate with anyone who calls himself a Christian who is sexually immoral, or greedy, or an idolater, or verbally abusive, or a drunkard, or a swindler. Do not [b]even eat with such a person. [12]For what do I have to do with judging those outside? Are you not to judge those inside? [13]But God will judge those outside. [a]*Remove the evil person from among you.*[1]

Lawsuits

6 When any of you has a legal dispute with another, does he dare go to court before the unrighteous rather than before the [a]saints? [2]Or do you not know that [a]the saints will judge the world? And if the world is to be judged by you, are you not competent to settle trivial suits? [3]Do you not know that we will [a]judge angels? Why not ordinary matters! [4]So if you have ordinary lawsuits, do you appoint as judges those who have no standing in the church? [5]I say this to your shame! Is there no one among you wise enough to settle disputes between fellow Christians? [6]Instead, does a Christian sue a Christian, and do this before unbelievers? [7]The fact that you have lawsuits among yourselves demonstrates that you have

4:12 [a]Acts 18:3; 20:34 **4:13** [a]Lam 3:45 **4:14** [a]2 Cor 6:13; 12:14; 1 Thess 2:11; 1 John 2:1; 3 John 4 **4:15** [a]Num 11:12; Acts 18:11; 1 Cor 3:8; Gal 4:19; Phlm 10 **4:17** [a]Acts 19:22; Phil 2:19 [b]1 Cor 4:14; 1 Tim 1:2, 18; 2 Tim 1:2 [c]1 Cor 11:2 [d]1 Cor 7:17; Titus 1:5 [e]1 Cor 14:33 [1]‡ Sev. sig. MSS *Christ Jesus*; some MSS *Lord Jesus*. **4:18** [a]1 Cor 5:2 **4:19** [a]Acts 19:21; 20:2; 1 Cor 11:34; 16:5, 7–9; 2 Cor 1:15 [b]Acts 18:21; Heb 6:3; Jas 4:15 **4:20** [a]1 Thess 1:5 [b]1 Cor 2:4 **4:21** [a]2 Cor 10:2 **5:1** [a]Lev 18:6–8; Deut 22:30; 27:20 **5:2** [a]1 Cor 4:18 [b]2 Cor 7:7–10 **5:3** [a]Col 2:5; 1 Thess 2:17 **5:4** [a][Matt 18:20] [b][Matt 16:19; John 20:23]; 2 Cor 12:9 [1]Some WSS omit *our*; some WSS *Jesus Christ/Christ Jesus.* **5:5** [a]Ps 109:6; Prov 23:14; Luke 22:31; 1 Tim 1:20 [b][Acts 26:18] [1]Or perhaps *turn this man over to Satan for the destruction of your fleshly works, so that your spirit may be saved*; Grk. *for the destruction of the flesh, so that the spirit may be saved.* For a discussion of this difficult verse, see *NET Bible, Full Notes Edition.* [2]Some WSS add *Jesus, Jesus Christ.* **5:6** [a]1 Cor 3:21 [b]Hos 7:4; Matt 16:6, 12; Gal 5:9; 2 Tim 2:17 **5:7** [a]Isa 53:7 [b]John 19:14 **5:8** [a]Exod 12:15 [b]Deut 16:3 [c]Matt 16:6 **5:9** [a]2 Cor 6:14; Eph 5:11; 2 Thess 3:6 **5:10** [a]John 17:15 **5:11** [a]Matt 18:17 [b]Gal 2:12 **5:13** [a]Deut 13:5; 17:7, 12; 19:19; 21:21; 22:21, 24; 24:7; 1 Cor 5:2 [1][Deut 17:7; 19:19; 22:21, 24] **6:1** [a]Dan 7:22; Matt 19:28 **6:2** [a]Ps 49:14 **6:3** [a]2 Pet 2:4

already been defeated. [a]Why not rather be wronged? Why not rather be cheated? [8]But you yourselves wrong and cheat, and you do this to your brothers and sisters!

[9]Do you not know that [a]the unrighteous will not inherit the kingdom of God? Do not be deceived! The sexually immoral, idolaters, adulterers, passive homosexual partners, practicing homosexuals, [10]thieves, the greedy, drunkards, the verbally abusive, and swindlers will not inherit the kingdom of God. [11][a]Some of you once lived this way. [b]But you were washed, you were sanctified, you were justified in the name of the Lord Jesus Christ[1] and by the Spirit of our God.

Flee Sexual Immorality

[12]"All [a]things are lawful for me"—but not everything is beneficial. "All things are lawful for me"—but I will not be controlled by anything. [13]"[a]Food is for the stomach and the stomach is for food, but God will do away with both." The body is not for [b]sexual immorality, but [c]for the Lord, [d]and the Lord for the body. [14]Now [a]God indeed raised the Lord and he will raise us [b]by his power. [15]Do you not know that [a]your bodies are members of Christ? Should I take the members of Christ and make them members of a prostitute? Never! [16]Or do you not know that anyone who is united with a prostitute is one body with her? For it is said, "[a]*The two will become one flesh.*"[1] [17][a]But the one united with the Lord is one spirit with him. [18][a]Flee sexual immorality! "Every sin a person commits is outside of the body"—but the immoral person sins [b]against his own body. [19]Or [a]do you not know that your body is the temple of the Holy Spirit who is in you, whom you have from God, [b]and you are not your own? [20]For [a]you were bought at a price. Therefore glorify God with your body.

Celibacy and Marriage

7 Now [a]with regard to the issues you wrote about: "It is good for a man not to have sexual relations with a woman." [2]But because of immoralities, each man should have relations with his own wife and each woman with her own husband. [3][a]A husband should fulfill his marital responsibility to his wife, and likewise a wife to her husband. [4]It is not the wife who has the rights to her own body, but the husband. In the same way, it is not the husband who has the rights to his own body, but the wife. [5][a]Do not deprive each other, except by mutual agreement for a specified time, so that you may devote yourselves to prayer.[1] Then resume your relationship, so that [b]Satan may not tempt you because of your lack of self-control. [6]I say this as a concession, [a]not as a command. [7]I [a]wish that everyone was as I am. But each has his own gift from God, one this way, another that.

[8]To the unmarried and widows [a]I say that it is best for them to remain as I am. [9]But [a]if they do not have self-control, let them get married. For it is better to marry than to burn with sexual desire.

[10]To the married I give this command—not I, but the [a]Lord—[b]a wife should not divorce a husband [11](but if she does, let her remain unmarried, or be reconciled to her husband), and a husband should not divorce his wife.

[12]To the rest I say—I, not the Lord—if a brother has a wife who is not a believer and she is happy to live with him, he should not divorce her. [13]And if a woman has a husband who is not a believer and he is happy to live with her, she should not divorce him. [14]For the unbelieving husband is sanctified because of the wife, and the unbelieving wife because of her husband.[1] Otherwise [a]your children are unclean, but now they are holy. [15]But if the unbeliever wants a divorce, let it take place. [a]In these circumstances the brother or sister is not bound. God has called you in peace. [16]For how do you know, wife, whether you will [a]bring your husband to salvation? Or how do you know, husband, whether you will bring your wife to salvation?

6:7 [a][Prov 20:22]   6:9 [a]Acts 20:32; [1 Cor 15:50]; Gal 5:21; Eph 5:5; 1 Tim 1:9   6:11 [a][1 Cor 12:2; Col 3:5–7; Titus 3:3–7]   [b]Heb 10:22   [1]Some wss omit *Christ*.   6:12 [a]1 Cor 10:23   6:13 [a]Matt 15:17; [Rom 14:17]; Col 2:22   [b]1 Cor 5:1; Gal 5:19; Eph 5:3; Col 3:5; 1 Thess 4:3   [c]1 Thess 4:3   [d][Eph 5:23]   6:14 [a]Rom 6:5, 8; 2 Cor 4:14   [b]Eph 1:19   6:15 [a]Rom 12:5; 1 Cor 6:13; 12:27; Eph 5:30   6:16 [a]Gen 2:24; Matt 19:5; Mark 10:8; Eph 5:31   [1]Gen 2:24   6:17 [a][John 17:21–23; Rom 8:9–11]; 1 Cor 6:15; [Gal 2:20]; Eph 4:4   6:18 [a]Rom 6:12; 1 Cor 6:9; 2 Cor 12:21; Eph 5:3; Col 3:5; Heb 13:4   [b]Rom 1:24; 1 Thess 4:4   6:19 [a]John 2:21; 1 Cor 3:16; 2 Cor 6:16   [b]Rom 14:7   6:20 [a]Acts 20:28; 1 Cor 7:23; Gal 3:13; 1 Pet 1:18; 2 Pet 2:1; Rev 5:9   7:1 [a]1 Cor 7:8, 26   7:3 [a]Exod 21:10   7:5 [a]Joel 2:16   [b]1 Thess 3:5   [1]Maj. later wss *fasting and prayer*.   7:6 [a]2 Cor 8:8   7:7 [a]Acts 26:29   7:8 [a]1 Cor 7:1, 26   7:9 [a]1 Tim 5:14   7:10 [a]Mark 10:6–10   [b]Mal 2:14; [Matt 5:32]   7:14 [a]Ezra 9:2; Mal 2:15   [1]Grk. *the brother*, later wss *husband*.   7:15 [a]Rom 12:18   7:16 [a]Rom 11:14; 1 Pet 3:1

The Circumstances of Your Calling

[17]Nevertheless, as the Lord has assigned to each one, as God has called each person, [a]so must he live. I give this sort of direction in all the churches. [18]Was anyone called after he had been circumcised? He should not try to undo his circumcision. Was anyone called who is uncircumcised? He should not get circumcised. [19a]Circumcision is nothing and uncircumcision is nothing. Instead, [b]keeping God's commandments is what counts. [20]Let each one remain in that situation in life in which he was called. [21]Were you called as a slave? Do not worry about it. But if indeed you are able to be free, make the most of the opportunity. [22]For [a]the one who was called in the Lord as a slave is the Lord's freedman. In the same way, the one who was called as a free person is [b]Christ's slave. [23a]You were bought with a price. Do not become slaves of men. [24]In whatever situation someone was called, brothers and sisters,[1] let him remain in it with [a]God.

Remaining Unmarried

[25]With regard to the [a]question about people [b]who have never married,[1] I have no command from the Lord, but I give my opinion as one shown mercy by the Lord to be [c]trustworthy. [26]Because of the impending crisis I think it best for you to remain as you are. [27]The one bound to a wife should not seek divorce. The one released from a wife should not seek marriage. [28]But if you marry, you have not sinned. And if a virgin marries, she has not sinned. But those who marry will face difficult circumstances, and I am trying to spare you such problems. [29]And I say [a]this, brothers and sisters:[1] The time is short. So then those who have wives should be as those who have none, [30]those with tears like those not weeping, those who rejoice like those not rejoicing, those who buy like those without possessions, [31]those who use the world as though they were not using it to the [a]full. For [b]the present shape of this world is passing away.

[32]And I want you to be free from concern. An unmarried man is concerned about [a]the things of the Lord, how to please the Lord. [33]But a married man is concerned about the things of the world, how to please his wife, [34]and he is divided. An unmarried woman or a virgin[1] is [a]concerned about the things of the Lord, to be holy both in body and spirit. But a married woman is concerned about the things of the world, how to please her husband. [35]I am saying this for your benefit, not to place a limitation on you, but so that without distraction you may give notable and constant service to the Lord.

[36]If anyone thinks he is acting inappropriately toward his virgin, if she is past the bloom of youth and it seems necessary, he should do what he wishes; he does not sin. Let them marry. [37]But the man who is firm in his commitment, and is under no necessity but has control over his will, and has decided in his own mind to keep his own virgin, does well. [38]So [a]then, the one who marries his own virgin does well, but the one who does not, does better.

[39]A wife is bound [a]as long as her husband is living. But if her husband dies, she is free to marry anyone she wishes ([b]only someone in the Lord). [40]But [a]in my [b]opinion, she will be happier if she remains as she is—and I think that I too have the Spirit of God!

Food Sacrificed to Idols

8 With regard [a]to food sacrificed to idols, we know that "we all have [b]knowledge." [c]Knowledge puffs up, but love builds up. [2a]If someone thinks he knows something, he does not yet know to the degree that he needs to know. [3]But if someone loves God, he is known by God.

[4]With regard then to eating food sacrificed to idols, we know that "[a]an idol in this world is nothing," [b]and that "there is no God but one." [5]If after all there are [a]so-called gods, whether in heaven or on earth (as there are many gods and many lords), [6]yet [a]for us there is one God, the Father, [b]from

7:17 [a]1 Cor 4:17   7:19 [a][Rom 2:27, 29; Gal 3:28; 5:6; 6:15; Col 3:11]   [b][John 15:14]   7:22 [a][John 8:36]; Rom 6:18; Phlm 16   [b][1 Cor 9:21; Gal 5:13]; Eph 6:6; Col 3:24; 1 Pet 2:16   7:23 [a]Lev 25:42; 1 Cor 6:20; 1 Pet 1:18–19; Rev 5:9   7:24 [a][Eph 6:5–8; Col 3:22–24]   [1]Grk. *brothers*; considerable external evidence supports use of the Grk. word as *brothers and sisters* or *fellow Christians*.   7:25 [a]2 Cor 8:8   [b]2 Cor 4:1; 1 Tim 1:13, 16   [c]1 Tim 1:12   [1]Grk. *virgins*.   7:29 [a][Rom 13:11]; 1 Cor 7:31; 1 Pet 4:7; [2 Pet 3:8–9]   [1]Grk. *brothers*; considerable external evidence supports use of the Grk. word as *brothers and sisters* or *fellow Christians*.   7:31 [a]1 Cor 9:18   [b]Ps 39:6; 1 Cor 7:29; Jas 1:10; 4:14; 1 Pet 1:24; 4:7; [1 John 2:17]   7:32 [a]1 Tim 5:5   7:34 [a]Luke 10:40   [1]Sig. MSS *the unmarried woman and the unmarried virgin*; some WSS *the woman and the unmarried virgin*.   7:38 [a]Heb 13:4   7:39 [a]Rom 7:2   [b]2 Cor 6:14   7:40 [a]1 Cor 7:6, 25   [b]1 Thess 4:8   8:1 [a]Acts 15:20; 1 Cor 8:4, 7, 10   [b]Rom 14:14   [c]Rom 14:3   8:2 [a][1 Cor 13:8–12]; Gal 6:3; [1 Tim 6:4]   8:4 [a]Isa 41:24   [b]Deut 4:35, 39; 6:4; 1 Cor 8:6   8:5 [a][John 10:34]   8:6 [a]Mal 2:10; Eph 4:6   [b]Acts 17:28

whom are all things and for whom we live, and [c]one Lord, Jesus Christ, [d]through whom are all things and [e]through whom we live.

[7]But this knowledge is not shared by all. And some, by being accustomed to idols in former times, eat this food as an idol sacrifice, and their conscience, because [a]it is weak, is [b]defiled. [8]Now [a]food will not bring us close to God. We are no worse if we do not eat and no better if we do. [9]But be [a]careful [b]that this liberty of yours does not become a hindrance to the weak. [10]For if someone weak sees you who possess knowledge dining in an idol's temple, will not his conscience be "[a]strengthened" to eat food offered to idols? [11]So [a]by your knowledge the weak brother or sister, for whom Christ died, is destroyed. [12]If you sin against your brothers or sisters[1] in this way and wound their weak conscience, you sin against Christ. [13]For this reason, [a]if food causes my brother or sister to sin, I will never eat meat again, so that I may not cause one of them to sin.

The Rights of an Apostle

9 Am [a]I not free? Am I not an apostle? [b]Have I not seen Jesus our Lord? [c]Are you not my work in the Lord? [2]If I am not an apostle to [a]others, at least I am to you, for you are the confirming sign of my apostleship in the Lord. [3]This is my defense to those who examine me. [4][a]Do we not have the right to financial support? [5]Do we not have [a]the right to the company of a believing wife, like the other apostles and the Lord's brothers and [b]Cephas? [6]Or do only Barnabas and I lack the right not to work? [7]Who ever serves in the army at his own expense? Who [a]plants a vineyard and does not eat its fruit? Who [b]tends a flock and does not consume its milk? [8]Am I saying these things only on the basis of common sense, or does the law not say this as well? [9]For it is written in the law of Moses, "*Do not muzzle an ox while it is treading out the grain.*"[1] God is not concerned here about oxen, is he? [10]Or is [a]he not surely speaking for our benefit? It was written for us, because the one plowing and threshing ought to work in hope of enjoying the harvest. [11a]If we sowed spiritual blessings among you, is it too much to reap material things from you? [12]If others receive this right from you, are we not more deserving?

[a]But we have not made use of this right. Instead we endure everything so that we may not be a hindrance to the gospel of Christ. [13a]Don't you know that those who serve in the temple eat food from the [b]temple, and those who serve at the altar receive a part of the offerings? [14]In [a]the same way the Lord commanded those who proclaim the gospel to receive their living by the gospel. [15]But [a]I have not used any of these rights. And [b]I am not writing these things so that something will be done for me. In fact, it would be better for me to die than—no one will deprive me of my reason for boasting![1] [16]For if I preach the gospel, I have no [a]reason for boasting, because I am compelled to do this. Woe to me if I do not preach the gospel! [17]For [a]if [b]I do this voluntarily, I have a reward. But if I do it unwillingly, I am entrusted with a responsibility. [18]What then is my reward? That [a]when I preach the gospel I [b]may offer the gospel free of charge, and so not make full use of my rights in the gospel.

[19]For since I am [a]free from all [b]I can make myself a slave to all, in order [c]to gain even more people. [20]To the Jews I became like a Jew [a]to gain the Jews. To those under the law I became like one under the law (though I myself am not under the law)[1] to gain those under the law. [21a]To [b]those free from the law I became like one free from the law (though I am [c]not free from God's law but under the law of Christ) to gain those free from the law. [22]To the weak

8:6 [c]John 13:13; 1 Cor 1:2; Eph 4:5; [1 Tim 2:5]   [d]John 1:3; [Col 1:16–17]; Heb 1:2   [e]Rom 5:11; Rev 4:11; 5:9–10   8:7 [a][1 Cor 10:28]   [b]Rom 14:14, 22   8:8 [a][Rom 14:17]   8:9 [a]Gal 5:13   [b]Rom 14:13, 21; 1 Cor 10:28   8:10 [a]1 Cor 10:28   8:11 [a]Rom 14:15, 20   8:12 [1]Grk. *brothers*; considerable external evidence supports use of the Grk. word as *brothers and sisters* or *fellow Christians.*   8:13 [a]Rom 14:21; 1 Cor 10:32; 2 Cor 6:3; 11:29   9:1 [a]Acts 9:15; 2 Cor 12:12   [b]Acts 9:3, 17; 18:9; 22:14, 18; 23:11; 1 Cor 15:8   [c]1 Cor 3:6; 4:15   9:2 [a]2 Cor 12:12   9:4 [a]1 Cor 9:14; [1 Thess 2:6, 9]; 2 Thess 3:8   9:5 [a]Matt 13:55   [b]Matt 8:14; John 1:42   9:7 [a]Deut 20:6; Prov 27:18; 1 Cor 3:6, 8   [b]John 21:15   9:9 [1]Deut 25:4   9:10 [a]2 Tim 2:6   9:11 [a]Rom 15:27; 1 Cor 9:14   9:12 [a][Acts 18:3; 20:33]; 1 Cor 9:15, 18   9:13 [a]Lev 6:16, 26; 7:6, 31   [b]Num 18:8–31; Deut 18:1   9:14 [a]Matt 10:10; Luke 10:7–8; 1 Tim 5:18   9:15 [a]Acts 18:3; 20:33; 1 Cor 9:12, 18   [b]2 Cor 11:10   [1]Maj. wss, esp. later ones, *than that anyone should deprive me of my boasting.*   9:16 [a]Acts 9:15; [Rom 1:14]   9:17 [a]John 4:36; 1 Cor 3:8, 14; 9:18   [b]1 Cor 4:1; Gal 2:7; Eph 3:2; Col 1:25   9:18 [a]1 Cor 10:33   [b]1 Cor 7:31; 9:12   9:19 [a]1 Cor 9:1   [b]2 Cor 4:5; Gal 5:13   [c]Matt 18:15; 1 Pet 3:1   9:20 [a]Acts 16:3; 21:23–26; Rom 11:14   [1]Some wss omit *(though I myself am not under the law).*   9:21 [a][Gal 2:3; 3:2]   [b][Rom 2:12, 14]   [c][1 Cor 7:22; Gal 6:2]

I became weak in order [a]to [b]gain the weak. I have become all things to all people, so [c]that by all means I may save some.

23 I do all these things because of the gospel, so that I can be a participant in it.

24 Do you not know that all the runners in a stadium compete, but only one receives the prize? So [a]run to win. 25 Each competitor must exercise self-control in everything. They do it to receive [a]a perishable crown, but we an imperishable one.

26 So I do [a]not run uncertainly or box like one who hits only air. 27[a]Instead [b]I subdue my body and make it my slave, so that after preaching to others I myself will not be [c]disqualified.

Learning from Israel's Failures

10 For I do not want you to be unaware, [a]brothers and sisters,[1] that our [b]fathers were all under the cloud and all passed through the sea, 2 and all were baptized[1] into Moses in the cloud and in the sea, 3 and all ate the same [a]spiritual food, 4 and all drank the same [a]spiritual drink. For they were all drinking from the spiritual rock that followed them, and the rock was Christ. 5 But God was not pleased with most of them, for they [a]were cut down in the wilderness. 6 These things happened as examples for us, so that we will not crave evil things as [a]they did. 7 So do not be idolaters, as some of them were. As it is written, ***The people sat down to eat [a]and drink and rose up to play.***[1] 8 And let us [a]not be immoral, as [b]some of them were, and 23,000 died [c]in a single day. 9 And let us not put Christ[1] to the test, as [a]some of them did, and [b]were destroyed by snakes. 10 And do not complain, as [a]some of them did, and [b]were killed by [c]the destroying angel. 11 These things happened to them as examples and [a]were written for our instruction, [b]on whom the ends of the ages have come. 12 So [a]let the one who thinks

he is standing be careful that he does not fall. 13 No trial has overtaken you that is not faced by others. And [a]God is faithful: [b]He will not let you be tried beyond what you are able to bear, but with the trial will also provide a way out so that you may be able to endure it.

Avoid Idol Feasts

14 So then, my dear friends, [a]flee from idolatry. 15 I am speaking to thoughtful people. Consider what [a]I say. 16 Is not [a]the cup of blessing that we bless a sharing in [b]the blood of Christ? Is not the bread that we break a sharing in the body of Christ? 17 Because there is one bread, [a]we who are many are one body, for we all share the one bread. 18 Look at the [a]people of [b]Israel. [c]Are not those who eat the sacrifices partners in the altar? 19 Am I saying [a]that idols or food sacrificed to them amount to anything? 20 No, I mean that what the pagans [a]sacrifice is to demons and not to God. I do not want you to be partners with demons. 21 You cannot drink the cup of the Lord and the cup of demons. [a]You cannot take part in [b]the table of the [c]Lord and the table of demons. 22 Or are we trying to [a]provoke the Lord to jealousy? [b]Are we really stronger than he is?

Live to Glorify God

23 "Everything is lawful," but not everything is [a]beneficial. "Everything is lawful," but not everything builds others up. 24 Do not seek your own [a]good, but the good of the other person. 25[a]Eat anything that is sold in the marketplace without questions of conscience, 26 for [a]*the earth and its abundance are the Lord's.*[1] 27 If an unbeliever invites you to dinner and you want to go, [a]eat whatever is served without asking questions of conscience. 28 But if someone says to you, "This is from a sacrifice," do not eat, because [a]of [b]the one who told you and because of

9:22 [a]Rom 14:1; 15:1; 2 Cor 11:29   [b]1 Cor 10:33   [c]Rom 11:14   9:24 [a]Gal 2:2; 2 Tim 4:7; Heb 12:1   9:25 [a]2 Tim 4:8; Jas 1:12; [1 Pet 5:4; Rev 2:10; 3:11]   9:26 [a]2 Tim 2:5   9:27 [a][Rom 8:13]   [b][Rom 6:18]   [c]Jer 6:30; 2 Cor 13:5   10:1 [a]Exod 13:21–22; Ps 105:39   [b]Exod 14:21–22, 29; Neh 9:11; Ps 66:6   [1]Grk. *brothers*; considerable external evidence supports use of the Grk. word as *brothers and sisters* or *fellow Christians.*   10:2 [1]‡ Some wss *baptized* [themselves].   10:3 [a]Exod 16:4, 15, 35; Deut 8:3; Neh 9:15, 20; Ps 78:24; John 6:31   10:4 [a]Exod 17:5–7; Num 20:11; Ps 78:15   10:5 [a]Num 14:29, 37; 26:65; Heb 3:17; Jude 5   10:6 [a]Num 11:4, 34; Ps 106:14   10:7 [a]Exod 32:4; 1 Cor 5:11; 10:14   [1]Exod 32:6   10:8 [a]Rev 2:14   [b]Num 25:1–9   [c]Ps 106:29   10:9 [a]Exod 17:2, 7   [b]Num 21:6–9   [1]Some sig. wss *Lord.*   10:10 [a]Exod 16:2   [b]Num 14:37   [c]Exod 12:23; 2 Sam 24:16; 1 Chr 21:15; Heb 11:28   10:11 [a]Rom 15:4   [b]Phil 4:5   10:12 [a]Rom 11:20   10:13 [a]1 Cor 1:9   [b]Ps 125:3   10:14 [a]2 Cor 6:17   10:15 [a]1 Cor 8:1   10:16 [a]Matt 26:26–28; Mark 14:23; Luke 22:20; 1 Cor 11:25   [b]Matt 26:26; Luke 22:19; Acts 2:42; 1 Cor 11:23   10:17 [a]Rom 12:5; 1 Cor 12:12, 27; Eph 4:4, 16; Col 3:15   10:18 [a]Rom 4:1   [b]Rom 4:12   [c]Lev 3:3; 7:6, 14; Deut 12:17   10:19 [a]1 Cor 8:4   10:20 [a]Lev 17:7   10:21 [a]2 Cor 6:15–16   [b]Deut 32:38   [c][1 Cor 11:23–29]   10:22 [a]Deut 32:21   [b]Ezek 22:14   10:23 [a]1 Cor 6:12   10:24 [a]Phil 2:4   10:25 [a][1 Tim 4:4]   10:26 [a]Exod 19:5; Ps 24:1; 50:12; 1 Tim 4:4   [1]Ps 24:1 [Pss 50:12; 89:11]   10:27 [a]Luke 10:7–8   10:28 [a][1 Cor 8:7, 10, 12]   [b]Deut 10:14; Ps 24:1

conscience[1]—[29]I do not mean yours but the other person's. For [a]why is my freedom being judged by another's conscience? [30]If I partake with thankfulness, why am I blamed [a]for the food that I give thanks for? [31]So whether you eat [a]or drink, or whatever you do, do everything for the glory of God. [32]Do not [a]give offense to Jews or Greeks or to the church of God, [33]just [a]as I also try to please everyone in all things. I do not seek my own benefit, but the benefit of many,

11 so that they may be saved. [1]Be imitators of me, just as [a]I also am of Christ.

Women's Head Coverings

[2]I praise you[1] because you remember me in everything and maintain the traditions just as I passed them on to you. [3]But I want you to know that Christ is [a]the head of every man, and [b]the man is [c]the head of a woman, and God is the head of Christ. [4]Any man who prays or [a]prophesies with his head covered disgraces his head. [5]But any woman who prays or prophesies with her head uncovered disgraces her head, for it is one and the same thing as having a shaved [a]head. [6]For if a woman will not cover her head, she should cut off her hair. But if it is [a]disgraceful for a woman to have her hair cut off or her head shaved, she should cover her head. [7]For a man should not have his [a]head covered, since he is the image and glory of God. But the woman is the glory of the man. [8]For man did not come [a]from woman, but woman from man. [9]Neither was man created for the sake of woman, but woman [a]for man. [10]For this reason a woman should have a symbol of authority on her head, because of the angels. [11]In any case, in the Lord woman is [a]not independent of man, nor is man independent of woman. [12]For just as woman came from man, so man comes through woman. But all things come from God. [13]Judge for yourselves: Is it proper for a woman to pray to God with her head uncovered? [14]Does not nature itself teach you that if a man has long hair, it is a disgrace for him, [15]but if a woman has long

hair, it is her glory? For her hair is given to her for a covering. [16a]If anyone intends to quarrel about this, we have no other practice, [b]nor do the churches of God.

The Lord's Supper

[17]Now in giving the following instruction I do not praise you, because you come together not for the better but for the worse. [18]For [a]in the first place, when you come together as a church I hear there are divisions among you, and in part I believe it. [19]For [a]there must in fact be divisions among you, so [b]that those of you who are approved may be evident. [20]Now when you come together at the same place, you are not really eating the Lord's Supper. [21]For when it is time to eat, everyone proceeds with his own supper. One is hungry and [a]another becomes drunk. [22]Do you not have houses so that you can eat and drink? Or are you trying to show contempt for [a]the church of God by [b]shaming those who have nothing? What should I say to you? Should I praise you? I will not praise you for this!

[23]For [a]I received from the Lord what I also passed on to you, [b]that the Lord Jesus on the night in which he was betrayed took bread, [24]and after he had given thanks he broke it and said, "This is my body, which is for you. Do this in remembrance of me." [25]In the same way, he also took the cup after supper, saying, "This cup is the new covenant in my blood. Do this, every time you drink it, in remembrance of me." [26]For every time you eat this bread and drink the cup, you proclaim the Lord's death until he comes.

[27]For [a]this reason, whoever eats the bread or drinks the cup of the Lord in an unworthy manner will be guilty of the body and blood of the Lord. [28]A person should examine himself first, and in this way [a]let him eat the bread and drink of the cup. [29]For the one who eats and drinks without careful regard for the body eats and drinks judgment against himself. [30]That is why many of you are weak and sick, and quite a few are dead. [31]But [a]if we examined ourselves, we would

10:28[1]Some wss add essentially v. 26 here again.   10:29[a]Rom 14:16; [1 Cor 9:19]   10:30[a]Rom 14:6   10:31[a]Col 3:17; 1 Pet 4:11   10:32[a]Rom 14:13   10:33[a]Rom 15:2; 1 Cor 9:22; [Gal 1:10]   11:1[a]Eph 5:1   11:2[1]Some wss add *brothers*.   11:3[a]Eph 1:22; 4:15; 5:23; Col 1:18; 2:19   [b]Gen 3:16; [Eph 5:23]   [c]John 14:28   11:4[a]1 Cor 12:10   11:5[a]Deut 21:12   11:6[a]Num 5:18   11:7[a]Gen 1:26–27; 5:1; 9:6; Jas 3:9   11:8[a]Gen 2:21–23; 1 Tim 2:13   11:9[a]Gen 2:18   11:11[a][Gal 3:28]   11:16[a]1 Tim 6:4   [b]1 Cor 7:17   11:18[a]1 Cor 1:10–12; 3:3   11:19[a]Matt 18:7; Luke 17:1; 1 Tim 4:1; 2 Pet 2:1   [b][Deut 13:3]; Luke 2:35; 1 John 2:19   11:21[a]2 Pet 2:13; Jude 12   11:22[a]1 Cor 10:32   [b]Jas 2:6   11:23[a]1 Cor 15:3; Gal 1:12; Col 3:24   [b]Matt 26:26–28; Mark 14:22–24; Luke 22:17–20; 1 Cor 10:16   11:27[a][John 6:51]   11:28[a]Matt 26:22; 2 Cor 13:5; Gal 6:4   11:31[a][Ps 32:5; 1 John 1:9]

not be judged. [32]But when [a]we are judged by the Lord, we are disciplined so that we may not be condemned with the world. [33]So then, my brothers and sisters,[1] when you come [a]together to eat, wait for one another. [34]If anyone is hungry, let him eat at home, so that when you assemble it does not lead to judgment. I will give directions about other matters when I come.

Spiritual Gifts

12 With regard [a]to spiritual gifts, brothers and sisters,[1] I do not want you to be uninformed. [2]You know [a]that when you were pagans you were often led astray by [b]speechless idols, however you were led. [3]So I want you to understand that [a]no one speaking by the Spirit of God says, "Jesus is cursed," and no one can say, "Jesus is Lord," except by the Holy Spirit.

[4]Now [a]there are different gifts, but [b]the same Spirit. [5]And [a]there are different ministries, but the same Lord. [6]And there are different results, but the same God [a]who produces all of them in everyone. [7]To each person the manifestation of the Spirit is given for the benefit of all. [8]For one person is given through [a]the Spirit [b]the message of wisdom, and another the message of knowledge according to the same Spirit, [9]to another faith by the same Spirit, and [a]to another [b]gifts of healing by the one Spirit, [10]to another performance of miracles, [a]to another [b]prophecy, and to another [c]discernment of spirits, to another [d]different kinds of tongues, and to another the interpretation of tongues. [11]It is one and the same Spirit, [a]distributing [b]as he decides to each person, who produces all these things.

Different Members in One Body

[12]For just [a]as the body is one and yet has many members, and all the members of the body—though many—are one body, [b]so too is Christ. [13]For [a]in one Spirit we were all baptized into one body. [b]Whether Jews or Greeks or slaves or free, we were all made to drink of the one Spirit. [14]For in fact the body is not a single member, but many. [15]If the foot says, "Since I am not a hand, I am not part of the body," it does not lose its membership in the body because of that. [16]And if the ear says, "Since I am not an eye, I am not part of the body," it does not lose its membership in the body because of that. [17]If the whole body were an eye, what part would do the hearing? If the whole were an ear, what part would exercise the sense of smell? [18]But as a matter of fact, [a]God has placed each of the members in the body [b]just as he decided. [19]If they were all the same member, where would the body be? [20]So now there are many members, but one body. [21]The eye cannot say to the hand, "I do not need you," nor in turn can the head say to the foot, "I do not need you." [22]On the contrary, those members that seem to be weaker are essential, [23]and those members we consider less honorable we clothe with greater honor, and our unpresentable members are clothed with dignity, [24]but our presentable members do not need this. Instead, God has blended together the body, giving greater honor to the lesser member, [25]so that there may be no division in the body, but the members may have mutual concern for one another. [26]If one member suffers, everyone suffers with it. If a[1] member is honored, all rejoice with it.

[27]Now [a]you are Christ's body, and each of you is a [b]member of it. [28]And [a]God has placed in the church first [b]apostles, second [c]prophets, third teachers, then [d]miracles, [e]gifts of healing, [f]helps, gifts of [g]leadership, different kinds of tongues. [29]Not all are apostles, are they? Not all are prophets, are they? Not all are teachers, are they? Not all perform miracles, do they? [30]Not all have gifts of healing, do they? Not all speak in tongues, do they? Not all interpret, do they? [31]But you should be [a]eager for the greater gifts.

And now I will show you a way that is beyond comparison.

11:32 [a]2 Sam 7:14; Ps 94:12; [Heb 12:5–10; Rev 3:19]   11:33 [a]1 Cor 14:26   [1]Grk. *brothers*; considerable external evidence supports use of the Grk. word as *brothers and sisters* or *fellow Christians*.   12:1 [a]1 Cor 12:4; 14:1, 37   [1]Grk. *brothers*; considerable external evidence supports use of the Grk. word as *brothers and sisters* or *fellow Christians*.   12:2 [a]1 Cor 6:11; Eph 2:11; 1 Pet 4:3   [b]Ps 115:5; Isa 46:7; Jer 10:5; Hab 2:18   12:3 [a]Matt 16:17   12:4 [a]Rom 12:3–8; 1 Cor 12:11; Eph 4:4, 11; Heb 2:4   [b]Eph 4:4   12:5 [a]Rom 12:6   12:6 [a]1 Cor 15:28; Eph 1:23; 4:6   12:8 [a]1 Cor 2:6–7; 2 Cor 1:12   [b]Rom 15:14; [1 Cor 2:11, 16]; 2 Cor 8:7   12:9 [a]Matt 17:19; [1 Cor 13:2]; 2 Cor 4:13   [b]Matt 10:1; Mark 3:15; 16:18; Jas 5:14   12:10 [a]Mark 16:17   [b]Rom 12:6   [c]1 John 4:1   [d]Acts 2:4–11   12:11 [a]Rom 12:6; 2 Cor 10:13   [b][John 3:8]   12:12 [a]Rom 12:4–5; 1 Cor 10:17; Eph 4:4   [b][Gal 3:16]   12:13 [a][Rom 6:5]   [b]Rom 3:22; Gal 3:28; [Eph 2:13–18]; Col 3:11   12:18 [a]1 Cor 12:28   [b]Rom 12:3   12:26 [1]‡ Maj. wss *one*.   12:27 [a]Rom 12:5; Eph 1:23; 4:12; 5:23, 30; Col 1:24   [b]Eph 5:30   12:28 [a]Eph 4:11   [b][Eph 2:20; 3:5]   [c]Acts 13:1; Rom 12:6   [d]1 Cor 12:10, 29; Gal 3:5   [e]Mark 16:18; 1 Cor 12:9, 30   [f]Num 11:17   [g]Rom 12:8; 1 Tim 5:17; Heb 13:17, 24   12:31 [a]1 Cor 14:1, 39

The Way of Love

13 If I speak in the tongues of men and of angels, but I do not have love, I am a noisy gong or a clanging cymbal. [2]And if I have [a]prophecy, and know all mysteries and all knowledge, and if I have all faith so [b]that I can remove mountains, but do not have love, I am nothing. [3]If I give away everything I own, and [a]if I give over my body in order to boast,[1] but do not have love, I receive no benefit.

[4a]Love is patient, love is [b]kind, it is not envious. Love [c]does not brag, it is not puffed up. [5]It is not rude, it is not self-serving, it is not easily angered or resentful. [6a]It is not glad about injustice, but [b]rejoices in the truth. [7]It [a]bears all things, believes all things, hopes all things, endures all things. [8]Love never ends. But if there are prophecies, they will be set aside; if there are tongues, they will cease; if there is knowledge, it will be set aside. [9a]For we know in part, and we prophesy in part, [10]but when what is perfect comes, the partial will be set aside. [11]When I was a child, I talked like a child, I thought like a child, I reasoned like a child. But when I became an adult, I set aside childish ways. [12]For [a]now we see in a mirror indirectly, but then we will see [b]face to face. Now I know in part, but then I will know fully, just as I have been fully known. [13]And now these three remain: faith, hope, and love. But the greatest of these is love.

Prophecy and Tongues

14 Pursue love and be [a]eager for the spiritual gifts, [b]especially that you may prophesy. [2]For the one speaking in a tongue does not [a]speak to people but to God, for no one understands; he is speaking mysteries by the Spirit. [3]But the one who prophesies speaks to people for their [a]strengthening, [b]encouragement, and consolation. [4]The one who speaks in a tongue builds himself up, but the one who prophesies builds up the church. [5]I wish you all spoke in tongues, but even more that you would prophesy. The one who prophesies is greater than the one who speaks in tongues, unless he interprets so that the church may be strengthened.

[6]Now, brothers and sisters,[1] if I come to you speaking in tongues, how will I help you unless I speak to you with a [a]revelation or with knowledge or prophecy or teaching? [7]It is similar for lifeless things that make a sound, like a flute or harp. Unless they make a distinction in the notes, how can what is played on the flute or harp be understood? [8]If, for example, the trumpet makes an unclear sound, who will get ready for battle? [9]It is the same for you. If you do not speak clearly with your tongue, how will anyone know what is being said? For you will be speaking into the air. [10]There are probably many kinds of languages in the world, and none is without meaning. [11]If then I do not know the meaning of a language, I will be a foreigner to the speaker and the speaker a foreigner to me. [12]It is the same with you. Since you are eager for manifestations of the Spirit, seek to abound in order to strengthen the church.

[13]So then, one who speaks in a tongue should pray that he may [a]interpret. [14]If[1] I pray in a tongue, my spirit prays, but my mind is unproductive. [15]What should [a]I do? [b]I will pray with my spirit, but I will also pray with my mind. I will sing praises with my spirit, but I will also sing praises with my mind. [16]Otherwise, if you are praising God with your spirit, how can someone without the gift say "Amen" [a]to your thanksgiving, since he does not know what you are saying? [17]For you are certainly giving thanks well, but the other person is not strengthened. [18]I thank God that I speak in tongues more than all of you, [19]but in the church I want to speak five words with my mind to instruct others, rather than ten thousand words in a tongue.

[20]Brothers and sisters,[1] [a]do not [b]be children in your thinking. Instead, be infants in evil, but in your thinking be mature. [21]It is

13:2 [a]Matt 7:22; 1 Cor 12:8–10, 28; 14:1 [b]Matt 17:20; 21:21; Mark 11:23; Luke 17:6   13:3 [a]Matt 6:1–2 [1]Some wss I will burn, I might burn/it might be burned.   13:4 [a]Prov 10:12; 17:9; 1 Thess 5:14; [1 Pet 4:8] [b]Eph 4:32 [c]Gal 5:26   13:6 [a]Ps 10:3; Rom 1:32 [b]2 John 4; 3 John 3   13:7 [a]Rom 15:1; Gal 6:2; 2 Tim 2:24   13:9 [a]1 Cor 8:2; 13:12   13:12 [a][2 Cor 3:18; 5:7]; Phil 3:12; Jas 1:23 [b]Gen 32:30; Num 12:8; Matt 18:10; [1 John 3:2]   14:1 [a]1 Cor 12:31; 14:39 [b]Num 11:25, 29   14:2 [a]Acts 2:4; 10:46   14:3 [a]Rom 14:19; 15:2; 2 Cor 10:8; 12:19; Eph 4:12, 29 [b]1 Tim 4:13; 2 Tim 4:2; Titus 1:9; 2:15; Heb 3:13; 10:25   14:6 [a]1 Cor 14:26; Eph 1:17 [1]Grk. brothers; considerable external evidence supports use of the Grk. word as brothers and sisters or fellow Christians.   14:13 [a]1 Cor 12:10   14:14 [1]‡ Maj. wss, incl. sig. ones, for.   14:15 [a]Eph 5:19; Col 3:16 [b]Ps 47:7   14:16 [a]Deut 27:15–26; 1 Chr 16:36; Neh 5:13; 8:6; Ps 106:48; Jer 11:5; 28:6; 1 Cor 11:24; Rev 5:14; 7:12   14:20 [a]Ps 131:2; [Matt 11:25; 18:3; 19:14]; Rom 16:19; 1 Cor 3:1; Eph 4:14; Heb 5:12–13 [b][Matt 18:3; 1 Pet 2:2] [1]Grk. brothers; considerable external evidence supports use of the Grk. word as brothers and sisters or fellow Christians.

written [a] in the law: "*By people* [b] *with strange tongues and by the lips of strangers I will speak to this people, yet not even in this way will they listen to me,*"[1] says the Lord. [22] So then, tongues are a [a] sign not for believers but for unbelievers. Prophecy, however, is not for unbelievers but for believers. [23] So if the whole church comes together and all speak in tongues, and unbelievers or uninformed people enter, [a] will they not say that you have lost your minds? [24] But if all prophesy, and an unbeliever or uninformed person enters, he will be convicted by all, he will be called to account by all. [25] The secrets of his heart are disclosed, and in this way he will fall down with his face to the ground and worship God, declaring, "God is really among you."

Church Order

[26] What should you do then, brothers and sisters?[1] When you come together, each one [a] has a song, has a lesson, has a revelation, has a tongue, has an interpretation. [b] Let all these things be done for the strengthening of the church. [27] If someone speaks in a tongue, it should be two, or at the most three, one after the other, and someone must interpret. [28] But if there is no interpreter, he should be silent in the church. Let him speak to himself and to God. [29] Two or three prophets should speak and the others should evaluate what is said. [30] And if someone sitting down receives a revelation, the person [b] who is speaking should conclude. [31] For you can all prophesy one after another, so all can learn and be encouraged. [32] Indeed, [a] the spirits of the prophets are subject to the prophets, [33] for God is not characterized by disorder but by peace.

[a] As in all the churches of the saints, [34] the women should be silent in the churches, for they are not permitted to speak. Rather, [a] let them be in submission, as in fact the [b] law says. [35] If they want to find out about something, they should ask their husbands at home, because it is disgraceful for a woman to speak in church.[1] [36] Did the word of God begin with you, or did it come to you alone?

[37a] If anyone considers himself a prophet or spiritual person, he should acknowledge that what I write to you is the Lord's command. [38] If someone does not recognize this, he is not recognized. [39] So then, brothers and sisters,[1,2] be [a] eager to prophesy, and do not forbid anyone from speaking in tongues. [40a] And do everything in a decent and orderly manner.

Christ's Resurrection

15 Now I want to make clear for you, brothers and sisters,[1] the gospel [a] that I preached to you, that you received and [b] on which you stand, [2] and [a] by which [b] you are being saved, if you hold firmly to the message I preached to you—unless you believed in vain. [3] For [a] I passed on to you as of first importance [b] what I also received— that Christ died for our sins according [c] to the scriptures, [4] and that he was buried, and that he was raised on the third day according [a] to the scriptures, [5a] and that he appeared to Cephas, then to the twelve. [6] Then he appeared to more than 500 of the brothers and sisters at one time, most of whom are still alive, though some have fallen asleep. [7] Then he appeared to James, then to all the apostles. [8] Last of all, as though to one born at [a] the wrong time, he appeared to me also. [9] For I am [a] the least of the apostles, unworthy to be called an apostle, because [b] I persecuted the church of God. [10] But [a] by the grace of God I am what I am, and his grace to me has not been in vain. In fact, I worked harder than all of them—[b] yet not I, but the grace of God with me. [11] Whether then it was I or they, this is the way we preach and this is the way you believed.

No Resurrection?

[12] Now if Christ is being preached as raised from the dead, how can some of you

14:21 [a] John 10:34; 1 Cor 14:34   [b] Isa 28:11–12   [1] Isa 28:11–12   14:22 [a] Mark 16:17   14:23 [a] Acts 2:13   14:26 [a] 1 Cor 12:8–10; 14:6   [b] 1 Cor 12:7; [2 Cor 12:19]   [1] Grk. *brothers*; considerable external evidence supports use of the Grk. word as *brothers and sisters* or *fellow Christians*.   14:32 [a] 1 John 4:1   14:33 [a] 1 Cor 11:16   14:34 [a] 1 Tim 2:11; 1 Pet 3:1   [b] Gen 3:16   14:35 [1] Some wss place vv. 34–35 after v. 40.   14:37 [a] 2 Cor 10:7; [1 John 4:6]   14:39 [a] 1 Cor 12:31; 1 Thess 5:20   [1] ‡ Some sig. wss *my brothers and sisters*.   [2] Grk. *brothers*; considerable external evidence supports use of the Grk. word as *brothers and sisters* or *fellow Christians*.   14:40 [a] 1 Cor 14:33   15:1 [a] Rom 2:16; [Gal 1:11]   [b] [Rom 5:2; 11:20; 2 Cor 1:24]   [1] Grk. *brothers*; considerable external evidence supports use of the Grk. word as *brothers and sisters* or *fellow Christians*.   15:2 [a] Rom 1:16; 1 Cor 1:21   [b] Gal 3:4   15:3 [a] 1 Cor 11:2, 23   [b] [Gal 1:12]   [c] Ps 22:15; Isa 53:5–12; Acts 3:18; 1 Pet 1:11   15:4 [a] Gen 1:9–13; 2 Kgs 20:8; Ps 16:9–11; 68:18; 110:1; Isa 53:10; Hos 6:2; Jonah 1:17; 2:10; Matt 12:39–40; Mark 8:31; Luke 11:29–30; 24:26; John 2:19–21; Acts 2:25   15:5 [a] Luke 24:34   15:8 [a] [Acts 9:3–8; 22:6–11; 26:12–18]; 1 Cor 9:1   15:9 [a] 2 Cor 12:11; Eph 3:8; 1 Tim 1:15   [b] Acts 8:3   15:10 [a] Eph 3:7–8   [b] Matt 10:20; Rom 15:18; Gal 2:8; Phil 2:13

say there is no resurrection of the dead? [13]But if there is no resurrection of [a]the dead, then not even Christ has been raised. [14]And if Christ has not been raised, then our preaching is futile and your faith is empty. [15]Also, [a]we are found to be false witnesses about God, because we have testified against God that he raised Christ from the dead, when in reality he did not raise him, if indeed the dead are not raised. [16]For if the dead are not raised, then not even Christ has been raised. [17]And if Christ has not been raised, [a]your faith is useless; you are still in your sins. [18]Furthermore, those who have fallen [a]asleep[1] in Christ have also perished. [19]For [a]if only in this life we have hope in Christ, we should be pitied more than anyone.

[20]But now [a]Christ has been raised from [b]the dead, the firstfruits of those who have fallen asleep. [21]For [a]since death came [b]through a man, the resurrection of the dead also came through a man. [22]For just as in Adam all die, so also in Christ all will [a]be made alive. [23]But [a]each in his own order: Christ, the firstfruits; then when Christ comes, those who belong to him. [24]Then comes [a]the end, when he hands over the kingdom to God the Father, when he has brought to an end all rule and all authority and power. [25]For he must reign [a]until he has put all his enemies under his feet. [26][a]The last enemy to be eliminated is death. [27]For [a]*he has put everything in subjection under his feet.*[1] But when it says "everything" has been put in subjection, it is clear that this does not include the one who put everything in subjection to him. [28][a]And when all things are subjected to him, then [b]the Son himself will be subjected to the one who subjected everything to him, so that God may be all in all.

[29]Otherwise, what will those do who are baptized for the dead? If the dead are not raised at all, then why are they baptized for them? [30][a]Why too are we in danger every hour? [31]Every day [a]I am in danger of death! This is as sure as my boasting in you,[1] which I have in Christ Jesus our Lord. [32]If from a human [a]point of view I fought with wild beasts at Ephesus, what did it benefit me? If the dead are not raised, [b]*let us eat and drink, for tomorrow we die.*[1] [33]Do not be deceived: "[a]Bad company corrupts good morals." [34]Sober [a]up as you should, and stop sinning! [b]For some have no knowledge of God—[c]I say this to your shame!

The Resurrection Body

[35]But someone will say, "[a]How are the dead raised? With what kind of body will they come?" [36]Fool! [a]What you sow will not come to life unless it dies. [37]And what you sow is not the body that is to be, but a bare seed—perhaps of wheat or something else. [38]But God gives it a body just as he planned, and to each of the seeds a body of its own. [39]All flesh is not the same: People have one flesh, animals have another, birds and fish another. [40]And there are heavenly bodies and earthly bodies. The glory of the heavenly body is one sort and the earthly another. [41]There is one glory of the sun, and another glory of the moon and another glory of the stars, for star differs from star in glory.

[42]It is the same [a]with the resurrection of the dead. What is sown is perishable, what is raised is imperishable. [43]It is sown in dishonor, [a]it is raised in glory; it is sown in weakness, it is raised in power; [44]it is sown a natural body, it is raised a spiritual body. If there is a natural body, there is also a spiritual body. [45]So also it is written, "[a]*The first man, Adam, became a living person*";[1] [b]the [c]last Adam became a life-giving spirit. [46]However, the spiritual did not come first, but the natural, and then the spiritual. [47]The first man is from [a]the earth, [b]made of dust; the second man is [c]from heaven. [48]Like the one made of dust, so too are those made of dust, [a]and like the one from heaven, so too those who are heavenly. [49]And just [a]as [b]we have borne the image of the man of

15:13 [a][1 Thess 4:14]   15:15 [a]Acts 2:24   15:17 [a][Rom 4:25]   15:18 [a]Job 14:12; Ps 13:3   [1]Often a euphemism for death when speaking of believers.   15:19 [a]1 Cor 4:9; 2 Tim 3:12   15:20 [a]Acts 2:24; 1 Pet 1:3   [b]Acts 26:23; 1 Cor 15:23; Rev 1:5   15:21 [a]Gen 3:19; Ezek 18:4; Rom 5:12; 6:23; Heb 9:27   [b]John 11:25   15:22 [a][John 5:28–29]   15:23 [a][1 Thess 4:15–17]   15:24 [a][Dan 2:44; 7:14, 27; 2 Pet 1:11]   15:25 [a]Ps 110:1; Matt 22:44   15:26 [a][2 Tim 1:10; Rev 20:14; 21:4]   15:27 [a]Ps 8:6   [1]Ps 8:6   15:28 [a][Phil 3:21]   [b]1 Cor 3:23; 11:3; 12:6   15:30 [a]2 Cor 11:26   15:31 [a]Rom 8:36   [1]‡ Some wss add *brothers.*   15:32 [a]2 Cor 1:8   [b]Eccl 2:24; Isa 22:13; 56:12; Luke 12:19   [1][Isa 22:13; 56:12]   15:33 [a][1 Cor 5:6]   15:34 [a]Rom 13:11; Eph 5:14   [b][1 Thess 4:5]   [c]1 Cor 6:5   15:35 [a]Ezek 37:3   15:36 [a]John 12:24   15:42 [a][Dan 12:3; Matt 13:43]   15:43 [a][Phil 3:21; Col 3:4]   15:45 [a]Gen 2:7   [b][Rom 5:14]   [c]John 5:21; 6:57; [Rom 8:2; Phil 3:21; Col 3:4]   [1]Gen 2:7   15:47 [a]John 3:31   [b]Gen 2:7; 3:19   [c]John 3:13   15:48 [a]Phil 3:20   15:49 [a]Gen 5:3   [b]Rom 8:29; [2 Cor 3:18; Phil 3:21; 1 John 3:2]

dust, let us also bear[1] the image of the man of heaven.

[50] Now this is what I am saying, brothers and sisters:[1] [a]Flesh and blood cannot inherit the kingdom of God, nor does the perishable inherit the imperishable. [51]Listen, I will tell you a mystery: [a]We will not all sleep,[1] [b]but we will all be changed—[52]in a moment, in the blinking of an eye, at the last trumpet. [a]For the trumpet will sound, and the dead will be raised imperishable, and we will be changed. [53]For [a]this perishable body must put on the imperishable, and this mortal body must put on immortality. [54]Now when this perishable puts on the imperishable, and this mortal puts on immortality, then the saying that is written will happen,

> "[a]**Death has been swallowed up in victory.**"[1]
> [55] "**Where, [a]O death, is your victory? Where, O death, is your sting?**"[1]

[56]The sting of death is sin, and [a]the power of sin is the law. [57a]But thanks be to God, who gives us [b]the victory through our Lord Jesus Christ! [58]So [a]then, dear brothers and sisters,[1] be firm. Do not be moved! Always be outstanding in the work of the Lord, knowing [b]that your labor is not in vain in the Lord.

A Collection to Aid Jewish Christians

16 With regard to [a]the collection for the saints, please follow the directions that I gave to the churches of Galatia: [2a]On the first day of the week, each of you should set aside some income and save it to the extent that God has blessed you, so that a collection will not have to be made when I come. [3]Then, when I arrive, I will send those [a]whom you approve with letters of explanation to carry your gift to Jerusalem. [4a]And if it seems advisable that I should go also, they will go with me.

Paul's Plans to Visit

[5]But I will come to you [a]after I have gone through Macedonia—for I will be going through Macedonia—[6]and perhaps I will stay with you, or even spend the winter, so that you can [a]send me on my journey, wherever I go. [7]For I do not want to see you now in passing, since I hope to spend some time with you, [a]if the Lord allows. [8]But I will stay in Ephesus until [a]Pentecost, [9]because [a]a door of great opportunity stands wide open for me, but [b]there are many opponents.

[10]Now [a]if Timothy comes, see that [b]he has nothing to fear among you, for he is doing the Lord's work, as I am too. [11]So [a]then, let no one treat him with contempt. But send him on his way [b]in peace so that he may come to me. For I am expecting him with the brothers.

[12]With regard to our brother [a]Apollos: I strongly encouraged him to visit you with the other brothers, but it was simply not his intention to come now. He will come when he has the opportunity.

Final Challenge and Blessing

[13]Stay [a]alert, stand [b]firm in the faith, show courage, [c]be strong. [14a]Everything you do should be done in love.

[15]Now, [a]brothers and sisters,[1] you know about [b]the household of Stephanus, that as [c]the first converts of Achaia, they devoted themselves to ministry for the saints. I urge you [16]also [a]to submit to people like this, and to everyone who cooperates in the work and labors [b]hard. [17]I was glad about the arrival of Stephanus, Fortunatus, and Achaicus [a]because they have supplied the fellowship with you that I lacked. [18a]For

15:49[1]‡ A few sig. wss *we will bear.*   **15:50** [a] Matt 16:17; [John 3:3, 5] [1]Grk. *brothers;* considerable external evidence supports use of the Grk. word as *brothers and sisters* or *fellow Christians.*   **15:51** [a] [1 Thess 4:15] [b][Phil 3:21] [1]Some wss *we all will sleep, but we will not all be changed; we will not all sleep, but we will not all be changed; we will all rise, but we will not all be changed.*   **15:52** [a] Zech 9:14; Matt 24:31; John 5:25   **15:53** [a] 2 Cor 5:4   **15:54** [a] Isa 25:8; [Rev 20:14] [1]Isa 25:8   **15:55** [a] Hos 13:14 [1]Hos 13:14   **15:56** [a] [Rom 3:20; 4:15; 7:8]   **15:57** [a] [Rom 7:25]; 2 Cor 2:14 [b] Rom 8:37; [Heb 2:14; 1 John 5:4]; Rev 21:4   **15:58** [a] 2 Pet 3:14 [b] [1 Cor 3:8] [1]Grk. *brothers;* considerable external evidence supports use of the Grk. word as *brothers and sisters* or *fellow Christians.*   **16:1** [a] Acts 11:29; Gal 2:10   **16:2** [a] Acts 20:7   **16:3** [a] 2 Cor 3:1; 8:18   **16:4** [a] 2 Cor 8:4, 19   **16:5** [a] Acts 19:21; 2 Cor 1:15–16   **16:6** [a] Acts 15:3; Rom 15:24; 1 Cor 16:11   **16:7** [a] Acts 18:21; Jas 4:15   **16:8** [a] Lev 23:15–22   **16:9** [a] Acts 14:27; 2 Cor 2:12; Col 4:3 [b] Acts 19:9   **16:10** [a] Acts 19:22; 2 Tim 1:2 [b] Phil 2:20; 1 Thess 3:2   **16:11** [a] 1 Tim 4:12; Titus 2:15 [b] Acts 15:33   **16:12** [a] Acts 18:24; 1 Cor 1:12; 3:5   **16:13** [a] Matt 24:42 [b] 1 Cor 15:1; Gal 5:1; Phil 1:27; 4:1; 1 Thess 3:8; 2 Thess 2:15 [c] [Ps 31:24; Eph 3:16; 6:10; Col 1:11]   **16:14** [a] [1 Pet 4:8]   **16:15** [a] 1 Cor 1:16 [b] Rom 16:5 [c] 2 Cor 8:4 [1]Grk. *brothers;* considerable external evidence supports use of the Grk. word as *brothers and sisters* or *fellow Christians.*   **16:16** [a] Eph 5:21; 1 Thess 5:12; Heb 13:17 [b] [Heb 6:10]   **16:17** [a] 2 Cor 11:9; Phil 2:30   **16:18** [a] Col 4:8

they refreshed my spirit and yours. So then, [b]recognize people like this.

[19]The churches in the province of Asia[1] send greetings to you. Aquila and Prisca greet[2] you warmly in the Lord, [a]with the church that meets in their house. [20]All the brothers and sisters[1] send greetings. [a]Greet one another with a holy kiss.

[21a]I, Paul, send this greeting with my own hand.

[22]Let [a]anyone who has no love for the Lord be accursed. Our Lord, come!

[23]The grace of [a]the Lord Jesus be with you.

[24]My love be with all of you in Christ Jesus.[1]

16:18 [b] Phil 2:29   16:19 [a] Rom 16:5   [1]Grk. *the churches of Asia*; Asia Minor.   [2]The sing. form of *greet* is found in several good MSS.   16:20 [a] Rom 16:16   [1]Grk. *brothers*; considerable external evidence supports use of the Grk. word as *brothers and sisters* or *fellow Christians*.   16:21 [a] Rom 16:22; Gal 6:11; Col 4:18; 2 Thess 3:17; Phlm 19   16:22 [a] Jude 14, 15   16:23 [a] Rom 16:20   16:24 [1] Maj. MSS add *amen*.

2 CORINTHIANS

Since Paul's first letter, the Corinthian church had been swayed by false teachers who stirred the people against Paul. They claimed he was fickle, proud, unimpressive in appearance and speech, dishonest, and unqualified as an apostle of Jesus Christ. Paul sent Titus to Corinth to deal with these difficulties, and upon his return he rejoiced to hear of the Corinthians' change of heart. Paul wrote this letter to express his thanksgiving for the repentant majority and to appeal to the rebellious minority to accept his authority. Throughout the book he defends his conduct, character, and calling as an apostle of Jesus Christ. To distinguish this epistle from 1 Corinthians, it was given the title *Pros Korinthious B*, the "Second to the Corinthians." The *A* and *B* were probably later additions to *Pros Korinthious*.

Salutation

1 From Paul, [a]an apostle of Christ Jesus by the will of God, and [b]Timothy our brother, to the church of God that is in Corinth, [c]with all the saints who are in all Achaia. [2][a]Grace and peace to you from God our Father and the Lord Jesus Christ!

Thanksgiving for God's Comfort

[3][a]Blessed is the God and Father of our Lord Jesus Christ, the Father of mercies and God of all comfort, [4]who [a]comforts us in all our troubles[1] so that we may be able to comfort those experiencing any trouble with the comfort with which we ourselves are comforted by God. [5]For just as [a]the sufferings of Christ[1] overflow toward us, so also our comfort through Christ overflows to you. [6]But if we are afflicted, [a]it is for your comfort and salvation; if we are comforted, it is for your comfort that you experience in your patient endurance of the same sufferings that we also suffer. [7]And our hope for you is [a]steadfast because we know that as you share in our sufferings, so also you will share in our comfort. [8]For we do not want you to be unaware, brothers and sisters,[1] regarding the affliction that happened to [a]us in the province of Asia,[2] that we were burdened excessively, beyond our strength, so that we despaired even of living. [9]Indeed we felt as if the sentence of death had been passed against us, so that we would [a]not trust in ourselves but in God who raises the dead. [10]He delivered us from so great a risk of death, and he will deliver us. We have set our hope on [a]him that[1] he will deliver us yet again, [11]as you also join [a]in helping us by prayer, so that many people may give thanks to God on our behalf [b]for the gracious gift given to us through the help of many.

Paul Defends His Changed Plans

[12]For our reason for confidence is this: The testimony of our conscience, that with pure motives[1] and sincerity which are from [a]God—[b]not by human wisdom but by the grace of God—we conducted ourselves in the world, and all the more toward you. [13]For we do not write you anything other than what you can read and also understand. But I hope that you will understand completely [14]just as also you have partly understood us, [a]that we are [b]your source of pride just as you also are ours in the day of the Lord Jesus.[1] [15]And [a]with this confidence

---

1:1 [a] 1 Cor 1:1; Eph 1:1; Col 1:1; 1 Tim 1:1; 2 Tim 1:1 [b] Acts 16:1; 1 Cor 16:10 [c] Phil 1:1; Col 1:2 **1:2** [a] Rom 1:7 **1:3** [a] Eph 1:3; 1 Pet 1:3 **1:4** [a] Isa 51:12; 66:13; 2 Cor 7:6–7, 13 [1] Or *our trials*; trad. *our affliction*. **1:5** [a] [Acts 9:4]; 2 Cor 4:10; Phil 3:10; Col 1:24 [1] I.e., suffering incurred as a consequence of relationship to Christ. **1:6** [a] 2 Cor 4:15; 12:15; Eph 3:1, 13; 2 Tim 2:10 **1:7** [a] [Rom 8:17; 2 Tim 2:12] **1:8** [a] Acts 19:23; 1 Cor 15:32; 16:9 [1] Grk. *brothers*; considerable external evidence supports use of the Grk. word as *brothers and sisters* or *fellow Christians*. [2] Grk. *Asia*; Asia Minor. **1:9** [a] Jer 17:5, 7 **1:10** [a] [2 Pet 2:9] [1] Sev. sig. wss omit *that* or *yet*. **1:11** [a] Rom 15:30; Phil 1:19; Phlm 22 [b] 2 Cor 4:15; 9:11 **1:12** [a] 2 Cor 2:17 [b] [1 Cor 2:4] [1] Some sig. wss *holiness*; some *gentleness, compassion*. **1:14** [a] 2 Cor 5:12 [b] Phil 2:16; 1 Thess 2:19 [1] ‡ Sev. sig. wss *our Lord Jesus*. **1:15** [a] 1 Cor 4:19

I intended to come to you first so [b]that you would get a second opportunity to see us, [16]and through your help to go on [a]into Macedonia and then from Macedonia to come back to you and be helped on our way into Judea by you. [17]Therefore when [a]I was planning to do this, I did not do so without thinking about what I was doing, did I? Or do I make my plans according to mere human standards so that I would be saying both "Yes, yes" and "No, no" at the same time? [18]But as God is [a]faithful, our message to you is not "Yes" and "No." [19]For [a]the Son of God, Jesus Christ, the one who was proclaimed among you by us—by me and [b]Silvanus and [c]Timothy—was not "Yes" and "No," [d]but it has always been "Yes" in him. [20][a]For every one of God's promises are "Yes" in him; therefore also through him the "Amen" is spoken, to the glory we give to God. [21]But it is God who establishes us together with you in Christ and who anointed us, [22]who [a]also sealed us and [b]gave us the Spirit in our hearts as a down payment.[1]

Why Paul Postponed His Visit

[23]Now [a]I appeal to God as my witness, [b]that to spare you I did not come again to Corinth. [24]I do not mean [a]that we rule over your faith, but we are workers with you for your joy, because [b]by faith you stand[1] firm. **2** [1]So[1] I made up my own mind not to pay you another painful visit. [2]For if I make you [a]sad, who would be left to make me glad but the one I caused to be sad? [3]And [a]I wrote this very thing to you, so that when [b]I came I would not have sadness from those who ought to make me rejoice, since I am confident in you all that my joy would be yours. [4]For out of great distress and anguish of heart I wrote to you with many tears, [a]not to make you sad, but to let you know the love that I have especially for you. [5]But [a]if anyone has caused [b]sadness, he has not saddened me alone, but to some extent (not to exaggerate) he has saddened all of you as well. [6]This punishment on such an individual [a]by the majority is enough for him, [7]so [a]that now instead you should rather forgive and comfort him. This will keep him from being overwhelmed by excessive grief to the point of despair.[1] [8]Therefore I urge you to reaffirm your love for him.[1] [9]For this reason also I wrote you: to test you to see if you are [a]obedient in everything. [10]If you forgive anyone for anything, I also forgive him—for indeed what I have forgiven (if I have forgiven anything) I did so for you in the presence of Christ, [11]so that we may not be exploited by Satan (for we are not ignorant of his schemes). [12]Now [a]when I [b]arrived in Troas to proclaim the gospel of Christ, even though the Lord had opened a door of opportunity for me, [13]I had no [a]relief in my spirit, because I did not find my brother Titus there. So I said goodbye to them and set out for Macedonia.

Apostolic Ministry

[14]But thanks be to God who always leads us in triumphal procession[1] in Christ[2] and who makes known through us the fragrance that consists of the knowledge of him in every place. [15]For we are a sweet aroma of Christ to God [a]among those who are being saved and [b]among those who are perishing—[16]to the [a]latter an odor from death to death, but to the former a fragrance from life to life. And [b]who is adequate for these things? [17]For we are not like so many others, hucksters who [a]peddle the word [b]of God for profit, but we are speaking in Christ before God as persons of sincerity, as persons sent from God.

A Living Letter

3 Are [a]we beginning to commend ourselves again? We don't need [b]letters of recommendation to you or from you as some other people do, do we? [2]You [a]yourselves are our letter, written on our hearts, known and read by everyone, [3]revealing that you are a letter of Christ, [a]delivered by us, written not with ink but by the Spirit

1:15 [b] Rom 1:11; 15:29   1:16 [a] Acts 19:21; 1 Cor 16:3–6   1:17 [a] 2 Cor 10:2; 11:18   1:18 [a] 1 John 5:20   1:19 [a] Mark 1:1; Luke 1:35; John 1:34; 20:31; 1 John 5:5, 20   [b] 1 Thess 1:1; 2 Thess 1:1; 1 Pet 5:12   [c] Acts 18:5; 2 Cor 1:1   [d] [Heb 13:8]   1:20 [a] [Rom 15:8–9]   1:22 [a] [Eph 4:30]   [b] Rom 8:16; 2 Cor 5:5; [Eph 1:14]   [1] Or *first installment, pledge, deposit.*   1:23 [a] Rom 1:9; Gal 1:20; Phil 1:8   [b] 1 Cor 4:21; 2 Cor 2:3; 12:20   1:24 [a] 1 Cor 3:5; 2 Cor 4:5; 11:20; [1 Pet 5:3]   [b] Rom 11:20; 1 Cor 15:1   [1] Or *because you stand firm in the faith.*   2:1 [1] Some wss *now.*   2:2 [a] 2 Cor 7:8   2:3 [a] 1 Cor 4:21; 2 Cor 12:21   [b] 2 Cor 8:22; Gal 5:10; 2 Thess 3:4; Phlm 21   2:4 [a] [2 Cor 2:9; 7:8, 12]   2:5 [a] [1 Cor 5:1]   [b] Gal 4:12   2:6 [a] 1 Cor 5:4–5; 2 Cor 7:11; 1 Tim 5:20   2:7 [a] Gal 6:1; Eph 4:32   [1] Grk. *swallowed up with excessive grief.*   2:8 [1] Or *to show that your love for him is real.*   2:9 [a] 2 Cor 7:15; 10:6   2:12 [a] Acts 16:8   [b] 1 Cor 16:9   2:13 [a] 2 Cor 7:6, 13; 8:6; Gal 2:1, 3; 2 Tim 4:10; Titus 1:4   2:14 [1] Or *always causes us to triumph.*   [2] Or *in the Messiah.*   2:15 [a] [1 Cor 1:18]   [b] [2 Cor 4:3]   2:16 [a] Luke 2:34; [John 9:39; 1 Pet 2:7]   [b] [1 Cor 15:10]   2:17 [a] 2 Pet 2:3   [b] 1 Cor 5:8; 2 Cor 1:12; 1 Thess 2:4; 1 Pet 4:11   3:1 [a] 2 Cor 5:12; 10:12, 18; 12:11   [b] Acts 18:27   3:2 [a] 1 Cor 9:2   3:3 [a] 1 Cor 3:5

of the living God, not [b]*on stone tablets*[1] but [c]on tablets of human hearts.

[4]Now we have such confidence in God through Christ. [5][a]Not that we are adequate in ourselves to consider anything as if it were coming from ourselves, but [b]our adequacy is from God, [6]who made us adequate to be [a]servants of a new covenant not based on [b]the letter but on [c]the Spirit, for the letter kills, [d]but the Spirit gives life.

The Greater Glory of the Spirit's Ministry

[7]But if [a]the ministry that produced death—carved in [b]letters *on stone tablets*—came with glory, so [c]that the Israelites could not keep their eyes fixed on the face of Moses because of the glory of his face (a glory which was made ineffective),[1] [8]how much more glorious will [a]the ministry of the Spirit be? [9]For if there was glory in the ministry that produced condemnation, how much more does the ministry that produces righteousness excel in glory! [10]For indeed, what had been glorious now has no glory because of the tremendously greater glory of what replaced it. [11]For if what was made ineffective came with glory, how much more has what remains come in glory! [12]Therefore, since [a]we have such a hope, we behave with great boldness, [13]and not like Moses [a]who used to put a veil over his face to keep [b]the Israelites from staring at the result of the glory that was made ineffective. [14]But [a]their minds were closed. For to this very day, the same veil remains when they hear the old covenant read. It has not been removed because only in Christ is it taken away. [15]But until this very day whenever Moses is read, a veil lies over their minds, [16]but [a]when one turns to [b]the Lord, *the veil is removed*.[1] [17]Now [a]the Lord is the Spirit, and where the Spirit of the Lord is present, there is [b]freedom. [18]And we all, with unveiled faces reflecting [a]the glory of the Lord,[1] [b]are being transformed into the same image from one degree of glory to another, which is from the Lord, who is the Spirit.

Paul's Perseverance in Ministry

4 Therefore, since we have this ministry, just [a]as God has shown us mercy,[1] we [b]do not become discouraged. [2]But we have rejected[1] shameful hidden deeds, not behaving[2] with deceptiveness or distorting the word of God, but by open proclamation of the truth we [a]commend ourselves to everyone's conscience before God. [3]But even if our gospel is veiled, [a]it is veiled only to those who are perishing, [4]among whom [a]the god of this age [b]has blinded [c]the minds of those [d]who do not believe so they would not see the light of the glorious gospel of Christ, who is the image of God. [5][a]For we do not proclaim [b]ourselves, but Jesus Christ as Lord, and ourselves as your slaves[1] for Jesus' sake. [6]For God, [a]who said "*Let light* [b]*shine out of darkness,*"[1] is the one who shined in our hearts to give us the light of the glorious knowledge of God in the face of Christ.[2]

An Eternal Weight of Glory

[7]But we have this treasure in clay jars, so [a]that the extraordinary power belongs to God and does not come from us. [8]We are experiencing [a]trouble on every side, but are not crushed; we are perplexed, but not driven to despair; [9]we are persecuted, but not [a]abandoned; we are knocked down, but not destroyed, [10][a]always carrying around in our body the death of Jesus,[1] so [b]that the life of Jesus may also be made visible in our body. [11]For we who [a]are alive are constantly being handed over to death for Jesus' sake, so that the life of Jesus may also be made visible in our mortal body. [12]As a result, death is at work in us, but life is at work in you. [13]But

3:3 [b]Exod 24:12; 31:18; 32:15; 2 Cor 3:7   [c]Ps 40:8   [1][Exod 24:12; 31:18; 34:1; Deut 9:10–11]   3:5 [a][John 15:5]   [b]1 Cor 15:10   3:6 [a]1 Cor 3:5; Eph 3:7   [b]Jer 31:31; Matt 26:28; Luke 22:20   [c][Rom 3:20]; Gal 3:10   [d]John 6:63; Rom 8:2   3:7 [a]Rom 7:10   [b]Exod 34:1; Deut 10:1   [c]Exod 34:29   [1]Or *was transitory*; trad. *was fading away.*   3:8 [a][Gal 3:5]   3:12 [a]Acts 4:13, 29; 2 Cor 7:4; Eph 6:19   3:13 [a]Exod 34:33–35; 2 Cor 3:7   [b]Rom 10:4; [Gal 3:23]   3:14 [a]Isa 6:10; 29:10; Acts 28:26; Rom 11:7–8; 2 Cor 4:4   3:16 [a]Exod 34:34; Rom 11:23   [b]Isa 25:7   [1][Exod 34:34]   3:17 [a][1 Cor 15:45]   [b]John 8:32; Gal 5:1, 13   3:18 [a][2 Cor 4:4, 6]   [b][Rom 8:29–30]   [1]Or *faces beholding the glory of the Lord as in a mirror.*   4:1 [a]1 Cor 7:25   [b]Luke 18:1; 2 Cor 4:16; Gal 6:9; Eph 3:13; 2 Thess 3:13   [1]Grk. *just as we have been shown mercy*; a "divine passive," with God understood as the actor.   4:2 [a]2 Cor 5:11   [1]Or *have denounced.*   [2]Or *not conducting ourselves*; Grk. *not walking*; an idiom for conduct, way of life, or behavior.   4:3 [a][1 Cor 1:18]; 2 Cor 2:15   4:4 [a]John 12:31; [Eph 6:12]   [b]John 12:40   [c][2 Cor 3:8–9]   [d][John 1:18]; Phil 2:6; Col 1:15; Heb 1:3   4:5 [a]1 Cor 1:13   [b]1 Cor 9:19   [1]Trad. *servants*; the word does not bear the connotation of a free individual serving another.   4:6 [a]Gen 1:3   [b]Isa 9:2; Mal 4:2; Luke 1:78; 2 Pet 1:19   [1][Gen 1:3; Isa 9:2]   [2]‡ Maj. WSS *Jesus Christ*; some sig. WSS *Christ Jesus.*   4:7 [a]Judg 7:2; 1 Cor 2:5   4:8 [a]2 Cor 1:8; 7:5   4:9 [a]Ps 129:2; [Heb 13:5]   4:10 [a]Phil 3:10   [b]Rom 8:17   [1]Or *at all times we live in the constant threat of being killed as Jesus was.*   4:11 [a]Rom 8:36

since we have [a]the same [b]spirit of faith as that shown in what has been written, "*I believed; therefore I spoke*,"[1] we also believe, therefore we also speak. [14]We do so because we know that [a]the one who raised up Jesus[1] will also raise us up with Jesus and will bring us with you into his presence. [15]For all these [a]things are for your sake, so that the [b]grace that is including more and more people may cause thanksgiving to increase to the glory of God. [16]Therefore we [a]do not despair, but even if our physical body is wearing away, our inner person is [b]being renewed day by day. [17]For [a]our momentary, light suffering is producing for us an eternal weight of glory far beyond all comparison [18a]because we are not looking at what can be seen but at what cannot be seen. For what can be seen is temporary, but what cannot be seen is eternal.

Living by Faith, not by Sight

5 For we know that if [a]our earthly house, the tent we live in, is dismantled, we have a building from God, a house [b]not built by human hands, that is eternal in the heavens. [2]For in this earthly house [a]we groan, because we desire to put on our heavenly dwelling, [3]if indeed, after we have put on[1] our heavenly house, we will not be found naked. [4]For we groan while we are in this tent, since we are weighed down, because we do not want to be unclothed, [a]but clothed, so that what is mortal may be swallowed up by life. [5]Now the one who prepared us for this very purpose is God, who gave us the Spirit [a]as a down payment.[1] [6]Therefore we are always full of courage, and we know that as long as we are alive here on earth we are absent from the Lord—[7]for [a]we live by faith, not by sight. [8]Thus [a]we are full of courage and would prefer to be away from the body and at home with the Lord. [9]So then whether we are alive or away, we make it our ambition to please him. [10a]For we must all appear before the judgment seat of Christ, so [b]that each one may be paid

back according to what he has done while in the body, whether good or evil.

The Message of Reconciliation

[11]Therefore, because we know [a]the fear of the Lord,[1] we try to persuade people,[2] but we are well known to God, and I hope we are well known to your consciences too. [12]We are not trying to commend ourselves to you again, but are giving you an opportunity to be proud of us, so that you may be able to [a]answer those who take pride in outward appearance and not in what is in the heart. [13]For [a]if we are out of our minds, it is for God; if we are of sound mind, it is for you. [14]For the love of Christ[1] controls us, since we have concluded this, that Christ died for all; therefore all have died. [15]And he died for all so [a]that those who live should no longer live for themselves but for him who died for them and was raised. [16]So [a]then from now on we acknowledge no one from an outward human point of view.[1] Even though we have known Christ from such a human point of view,[2] now we do not know him in that way any longer. [17]So then, if anyone [a]is in Christ, he is [b]a new creation; what is [c]old has passed away—look, what is [d]new[1] has come! [18]And all these things are from God [a]who reconciled us to himself through Christ and who has given us the ministry of reconciliation. [19]In other words, in Christ [a]God was reconciling the world to himself, not counting people's trespasses against them, and he has given us the message of reconciliation. [20]Therefore we are [a]ambassadors for Christ, as though God were making his plea through us. We plead with you on Christ's behalf, "Be reconciled to God!" [21]God made [a]the one who did not know sin to be sin for us, so that in him we would become [b]the righteousness of God.

God's Suffering Servants

6 Now because we are fellow [a]workers, we also [b]urge you not to receive the grace of God in vain. [2]For he says, "*I heard you at*

4:13 [a]2 Pet 1:1   [b]Ps 116:10   [1]Ps 116:10   4:14 [a][Rom 8:11]   [1]‡ Sev. sig. wss *the Lord Jesus.*   4:15 [a]Col 1:24   [b]1 Cor 9:19; 2 Cor 1:11   4:16 [a]2 Cor 4:1; Gal 6:9   [b][Isa 40:29, 31; Col 3:10]   4:17 [a]Matt 5:12; Rom 8:18; 1 Pet 1:6   4:18 [a]Rom 8:24; [2 Cor 5:7; Heb 11:1, 13]   5:1 [a]Job 4:19; 1 Cor 15:47; 2 Cor 4:7   [b]Mark 14:58; Acts 7:48; Heb 9:11, 24   5:2 [a]Rom 8:23; 2 Cor 5:4   5:3 [1]‡ Some MSS *taken off.*   5:4 [a]1 Cor 15:53   5:5 [a]Rom 8:23; [2 Cor 1:22]; Eph 1:14   [1]Or *first installment, pledge, deposit.*   5:7 [a]Rom 8:24; Heb 11:1   5:8 [a]Phil 1:23   5:10 [a]Matt 16:27; Acts 10:42; Rom 2:16; 14:10, 12   [b]Gal 6:7; Eph 6:8   5:11 [a][Heb 10:31; 12:29; Jude 23]   [1]Or *know what it means to fear the Lord.*   [2]Grk. *men*; used in a generic sense, as both men and women are in view.   5:12 [a]2 Cor 3:1   5:13 [a]Mark 3:21; 2 Cor 11:1, 16; 12:11   5:14 [1]Grk. *our love for Christ, Christ's love for us.*   5:15 [a][Rom 6:11]   5:16 [a]2 Cor 10:3   [1]Grk. *no one according to the flesh.*   [2]Grk. *we have known Christ according to the flesh.*   5:17 [a][John 6:63]   [b][Rom 8:9]   [c]Isa 43:18; 65:17; [Eph 4:24]; Rev 21:4   [d][Rom 6:3–10; Col 3:3]   [1]Maj. MSS add *all things.*   5:18 [a]Rom 5:10; [Eph 2:16; Col 1:20]   5:19 [a][Rom 3:24]   5:20 [a]Mal 2:7; Eph 6:20   5:21 [a]Isa 53:6, 9   [b][Rom 1:17; 3:21]; 1 Cor 1:30   6:1 [a]1 Cor 3:9   [b]2 Cor 5:20

the acceptable time, and [a]*in the day of salvation I helped you.*"[1] Look, now is *the acceptable time;* look, now is *the day of salvation!* [3][a]We do not give anyone an occasion for taking an offense in anything,[1] so that no fault may be found with our ministry. [4]But [a]as God's servants, we have commended ourselves in every way, with great endurance, in persecutions, in difficulties, in distresses, [5][a]in beatings, in imprisonments, in riots, in troubles, in sleepless nights, in hunger, [6]by purity, by knowledge, by patience, by benevolence, by the Holy Spirit, by genuine love, [7][a]by truthful teaching, by [b]the power of God, with weapons of righteousness both for [c]the right hand and for the left, [8]through glory and dishonor, through slander and praise; regarded as impostors, and yet true; [9]as unknown, and [a]yet well-known; [b]as dying and yet—see!—we continue to live; [c]as those who are scourged and yet not executed; [10]as sorrowful, but always rejoicing; as poor, but making many [a]rich; as having nothing, and yet possessing everything.

[11]We have spoken freely to you, Corinthians; [a]our heart has been opened wide to you. [12]Our affection for [a]you is not restricted, but you are restricted in your affections for us. [13]Now as a [a]fair exchange—I speak as to my children—open wide your hearts to us also.

Unequal Partners

[14]Do not become partners with those who [a]do not believe, for [b]what partnership is there between righteousness and lawlessness, or what fellowship does light have with darkness? [15]And what agreement does Christ have with Beliar? Or what does a believer share in common with an unbeliever? [16]And what mutual agreement does the temple of God have with idols? For [a]we are[1] the temple of the [b]living God, just as God said, "*I will live in them and will walk among them, and I will be their God, and they will be my people.*"[2] [17]Therefore "*come* [a]*out from their midst, and be separate,*" says the Lord, "*and touch no unclean thing,*[1] and I will welcome you,*[2] [18]and [a]I will be a father to you, and you will be my [b]sons and daughters,*"[1] says the All-Powerful Lord.

Self-Purification

7 [a]Therefore, since we have these promises, dear friends, let us cleanse ourselves from everything that could defile the body and the spirit, and thus accomplish holiness out of reverence for God. [2]Make room for us in your hearts; [a]we have wronged no one; we have ruined no one; we have exploited no one. [3]I do not say [a]this to condemn you, for I told you before that you are in our hearts so that we die together and live together with you.

A Letter That Caused Sadness

[4]I have [a]great confidence in you; I take [b]great [c]pride on your behalf. I am filled with encouragement; I am overflowing with joy in the midst of all our suffering. [5]For even [a]when [b]we came into Macedonia, our body had no rest at all, but we were troubled in every way—struggles from the [c]outside, fears from within. [6]But [a]God, who encourages [b]the downhearted, encouraged us by the arrival of Titus. [7]We were encouraged not only by his arrival, but also by the encouragement you gave him, as he reported to us your longing, your mourning, your deep concern for me, so that I rejoiced more than ever. [8]For even if I [a]made you sad by my letter, I do not regret having written it (even [b]though I did regret it, for[1] I see that my letter made you sad, though only for a short time). [9]Now I rejoice, not because you were made sad, but because you were made sad to the point of repentance. For you were made sad as God intended, so that you were not harmed in any way by us. [10]For sadness as intended by [a]God produces a repentance that leads to salvation, leaving no regret, [b]but worldly sadness brings about death. [11]For see what this very thing, this sadness as God intended, has produced in you: what

6:2 [a] Isa 49:8 [1] Isa 49:8   6:3 [a] Rom 14:13   [1] Or *not putting an obstacle in the way of anyone, giving no one in anything a cause to sin.*   6:4 [a] 1 Cor 4:1   6:5 [a] 2 Cor 11:23   6:7 [a] 2 Cor 7:14 [b] 1 Cor 2:4 [c] Rom 13:12; 2 Cor 10:4   6:9 [a] 2 Cor 4:2; 5:11 [b] 1 Cor 4:9, 11 [c] Ps 118:18   6:10 [a] 1 Cor 1:5; [2 Cor 8:9]   6:11 [a] Isa 60:5; 2 Cor 7:3   6:12 [a] 2 Cor 12:15   6:13 [a] 1 Cor 4:14   6:14 [a] Deut 7:2–3; 22:10; 1 Cor 5:9 [b] 1 Sam 5:2–3; 1 Kgs 18:21; Eph 5:6–7, 11; 1 John 1:6   6:16 [a] [1 Cor 3:16–17; 6:19]; Eph 2:21; [Heb 3:6] [b] Exod 29:45; Lev 26:12; Jer 31:33; 32:38; Ezek 37:26–27; Zech 8:8 [1] Maj. wss *you are.* [2] Lev 26:12 (Jer 32:38; Ezek 37:27)   6:17 [a] Num 33:51–56; Isa 52:11; Rev 18:4 [1] Isa 52:11 [2] [Ezek 20:41]   6:18 [a] 2 Sam 7:14; Jer 31:1, 9; [Rev 21:7] [b] [John 1:12; Rom 8:14; Gal 4:5–7]; Phil 2:15; 1 John 3:1 [1] [2 Sam 7:14; Isa 43:6]   7:1 [a] [1 John 3:3]   7:2 [a] Acts 20:33   7:3 [a] 2 Cor 6:11–12   7:4 [a] 2 Cor 3:12 [b] 1 Cor 1:4 [c] Phil 2:17; Col 1:24   7:5 [a] Rom 15:26; 2 Cor 2:13 [b] 2 Cor 4:8 [c] Deut 32:25   7:6 [a] Isa 49:13; 2 Cor 1:3–4 [b] 2 Cor 2:13; 7:13   7:8 [a] 2 Cor 2:2 [b] 2 Cor 2:4 [1] A few sig. MSS omit *for.*   7:10 [a] 2 Sam 12:13; Ps 32:10; Matt 26:75 [b] Prov 17:22

eagerness, what [a]defense of yourselves, what indignation, what alarm, what longing, what deep concern, what punishment! In everything you have proved yourselves to be [b]innocent in this matter. [12]So then, even though I wrote to you, it was not on account of the one who did wrong or on account of the one who was wronged, [a]but to reveal to you your eagerness on our behalf before God. [13]Therefore we have been encouraged. And in addition to our own encouragement, we rejoiced even more at the joy of Titus because all of you have refreshed his spirit. [14]For if I have boasted to him about anything concerning you, I have not been embarrassed by you, but just as everything we said to you was true, so our boasting to Titus about you has proved true as well. [15]And his affection for you is much greater when [a]he remembers the obedience of you all, how you welcomed him with fear and trembling. [16]I [a]rejoice because in everything I am fully confident in you.

Completing the Collection for the Saints

8 Now we make known to you, brothers and sisters,[1] the grace of God given to the churches of Macedonia, [2]that during a severe ordeal of suffering, [a]their abundant joy and their extreme poverty have overflowed in the wealth of their generosity. [3]For I testify, they gave according to their means and beyond their means. They did so voluntarily, [4]begging us with great earnestness for [a]the blessing and fellowship of helping the saints. [5]And they did this not just as we had hoped, but they [a]gave themselves first to the Lord and to us by the [b]will of God. [6]Thus [a]we urged Titus that, just as he had previously begun this work, so also he should complete this act of kindness for you. [7]But as [a]you excel in everything—in faith, in speech, in knowledge, and in all eagerness and in the love from us that is in you[1]—make sure [b]that you excel in this act of kindness too. [8]I am not [a]saying this as a command, but I am testing the genuineness of your love by comparison with the eagerness of others. [9]For you know the grace[1] of our Lord Jesus Christ, [a]that although he was rich, he became poor for your sakes, so that you by his poverty could become [b]rich. [10]So here [a]is my opinion on this matter: [b]It is to your advantage, since you made a good start last year both in your giving and your desire to give, [11]to finish what you started, so that just as you wanted to do it eagerly, you can also complete it according to your means. [12]For [a]if the eagerness is present, the gift itself is acceptable according to whatever one has, not according to what he does not have. [13]For I do not say this so there would be relief for others and suffering for you, but as a matter of equality. [14]At the present time, your abundance will meet their need, so that one day their abundance may also meet your need, and thus there may be equality, [15]as it is written: "[a]*The one who gathered much did not have too much, and the one who gathered little did not have too little.*"

The Mission of Titus

[16]But thanks be to God who put in the heart of Titus the same devotion I have for you, [17]because he not only accepted our request, but since he was very eager, he is coming to you of his own accord. [18]And we are sending along with him [a]the brother who is praised by all the churches for his work in spreading the gospel. [19]In addition, this brother has also been [a]chosen by the churches as our traveling companion as we administer this generous gift [b]to the glory of the Lord himself and to show our readiness to help. [20]We did this as a precaution so that no one should blame us in regard to this generous gift we are administering. [21]For we are [a]*concerned about what is right not only before the Lord but also before men.*[1] [22]And we are sending with them our brother whom we have tested many times and found eager in many matters, but who now is much more eager than ever because of the great confidence he has in you. [23]If there is any question about [a]Titus, he is

7:11 [a] Eph 5:11   [b] 2 Cor 2:5–11   7:12 [a] 2 Cor 2:4   7:15 [a] 2 Cor 2:9; Phil 2:12   7:16 [a] 2 Cor 2:3; 8:22; 2 Thess 3:4; Phlm 8, 21   8:1 [1] Grk. *brothers*; considerable external evidence supports use of the Grk. word as *brothers and sisters* or *fellow Christians.*   8:2 [a] Mark 12:44   8:4 [a] Acts 11:29; 24:17; Rom 15:25–26; 1 Cor 16:1, 3, 4; 2 Cor 9:1   8:5 [a] [Rom 12:1–2]   [b] [Eph 6:6]   8:6 [a] 2 Cor 8:17; 12:18   8:7 [a] [1 Cor 1:5; 12:13]   [b] 2 Cor 9:8   [1] Sev. wss *your love for us.*   8:8 [a] 1 Cor 7:6   8:9 [a] Matt 8:20; Luke 9:58; Phil 2:6–7   [b] Rom 9:23; [Eph 1:7; Rev 3:18]   [1] Or *generosity.*   8:10 [a] 1 Cor 7:25, 40   [b] [Prov 19:17; Matt 10:42; 1 Tim 6:18–19; Heb 13:16]   8:12 [a] Mark 12:43–44; Luke 21:3–4; 2 Cor 9:7   8:15 [a] Exod 16:18   [1] Exod 16:18   8:18 [a] 1 Cor 16:3; 2 Cor 12:18   8:19 [a] Acts 14:23; 1 Cor 16:3–4   [b] 2 Cor 4:15   8:21 [a] Rom 12:17; Phil 4:8; 1 Pet 2:12   [1] [Prov 3:4]   8:23 [a] 2 Cor 7:13–14

my partner and fellow worker among you; if there is any question about our brothers, they are [b]messengers of the churches, a glory to Christ. 24Therefore show them openly before the churches the proof of your love and of our [a]pride in you.

Preparing the Gift

9 For it is not necessary for me to write you about this service to [a]the saints 2because I know your eagerness to help. I keep boasting to the Macedonians about this eagerness of yours, that Achaia has been ready to give since last [a]year, and your zeal to participate has stirred up most of them. 3aBut I am sending these brothers so that our boasting about you may not be empty in this case, so that you may be ready just as I kept telling them. 4For if any of the Macedonians should come with me and find that you are not ready to give, we would be humiliated[1] (not to mention you) by this confidence we had in you. 5Therefore I thought it necessary to urge these brothers to go to you in advance and to arrange ahead of time the generous contribution you had promised, so this may be ready as a generous gift and not as something you feel forced to do. 6aMy point is this: The person who sows sparingly will also reap sparingly, and the person who sows generously will also reap generously. 7Each one of you should give just as he has decided in his heart, [a]not reluctantly or under compulsion, because [b]God loves a cheerful giver. 8aAnd God is able to make all grace overflow to you so that because you have enough of everything in every way at all times, you will overflow in every good work. 9Just as it is written, "[a]*He has scattered widely, he has given to the poor; his righteousness remains forever.*"[1] 10Now God who [a]provides seed for the sower and bread for food will provide and multiply your supply of seed and will cause the harvest of your [b]righteousness to grow. 11You will be enriched in every way so that you may be generous on every occasion, [a]which is producing through us

thanksgiving to God, 12because the service of this ministry is not only [a]providing for the needs of the saints but is also overflowing with many thanks to God. 13Through the evidence of this service they will [a]glorify God because of your obedience to your confession in the gospel of Christ and the generosity of your [b]sharing with them and with everyone. 14And in their prayers on your behalf, they long for you because of the extraordinary [a]grace God has shown to you. 15Thanks be to God [a]for his indescribable gift!

Paul's Authority from the Lord

10 Now [a]I, Paul, appeal to you personally by the meekness and gentleness of Christ (I [b]who am meek when present among you, but am full of courage toward you when away!)—2now I ask [a]that when I am present I may not have to be bold with the confidence that (I expect) I will dare to use against some who consider us to be behaving according to human standards. 3For though we live as human beings, we do not wage war according to human standards, 4afor the weapons of our warfare are not human weapons, but are made [b]powerful by God [c]for tearing down strongholds. We tear down arguments 5aand every arrogant obstacle that is raised up against the knowledge of God, and we take every thought captive to make it obey Christ. 6We are [a]also ready to punish every act of disobedience, whenever [b]your obedience is complete. 7You are looking at outward appearances. If anyone is confident that he belongs to Christ, he should reflect on this again: Just as he himself belongs to Christ, so too [a]do [b]we. 8For if I boast somewhat more [a]about our [b]authority that the Lord gave us for building you up and not for tearing you down, I will not be ashamed of doing so. 9I do not want to seem as though I am trying to terrify you with my letters, 10because some say, "[a]His letters are weighty and forceful, but his physical presence is weak and his [b]speech is of no account." 11Let

8:23 [b][John 13:16]; Phil 2:25   8:24 [a]2 Cor 7:4, 14; 9:2   9:1 [a]Acts 11:29; Rom 15:26; 1 Cor 16:1; 2 Cor 8:4; Gal 2:10   9:2 [a]2 Cor 8:10   9:3 [a]2 Cor 8:6, 17   9:4 [1]Or *be disgraced*; Grk. *be put to shame.*   9:6 [a]Prov 11:24; 22:9; Gal 6:7, 9   9:7 [a]Deut 15:7 [b]Deut 15:10; 1 Chr 29:17; [Prov 11:25]; Rom 12:8; [2 Cor 8:12]   9:8 [a][Prov 11:24]   9:9 [a]Ps 112:9   [1]Ps 112:9   9:10 [a]Isa 55:10 [b]Hos 10:12   9:11 [a]2 Cor 1:11   9:12 [a]2 Cor 8:14   9:13 [a][Matt 5:16]   [b][Heb 13:16]   9:14 [a]2 Cor 8:1   9:15 [a][John 3:16; 4:10; Rom 6:23; 8:32; Eph 2:8; Jas 1:17]   10:1 [a]Rom 12:1   [b]1 Thess 2:7   10:2 [a]1 Cor 4:21; 2 Cor 13:2, 10   10:4 [a]Eph 6:13   [b]Acts 7:22   [c]Jer 1:10; [2 Cor 10:8; 13:10]   10:5 [a]1 Cor 1:19   10:6 [a]2 Cor 13:2, 10   [b]2 Cor 7:15   10:7 [a][John 7:24]; 2 Cor 5:12   [b][Rom 14:8]; 1 Cor 3:23   10:8 [a]2 Cor 13:10   [b]2 Cor 7:14   10:10 [a]1 Cor 2:3-4; 2 Cor 12:7; Gal 4:13   [b][1 Cor 1:17]; 2 Cor 11:6

such a person consider this: What we say by letters when we are absent, we also are in actions when we are present.

Paul's Mission

[12a]For we would not dare to classify or compare ourselves with some of those who recommend themselves. But when they measure themselves by themselves and compare themselves with themselves, they are without understanding. [13]But [a]we will not boast beyond certain limits, but will confine our boasting according to the limits of the work to which God has appointed us, that reaches even as far as you. [14a]For we were not overextending ourselves, as though we did not reach as far as you, because we were the first to reach as far as you with the gospel about Christ. [15]Nor do we boast beyond certain limits in the work done [a]by others, but we hope that as your faith continues to grow, our work may be greatly expanded among you according to our limits, [16]so that we may preach the gospel in the regions that lie beyond you, and not boast of work already done in another person's area. [17]But [a]*the one who boasts must boast in the Lord.*[1] [18]For it is [a]not the person who commends himself who is approved, but the [b]person the Lord commends.

Paul and His Opponents

11 I wish that you would be patient with me in a little [a]foolishness, but indeed you are being patient with me! [2]For I am [a]jealous for you [b]with godly jealousy, because I promised you in marriage to one husband, to present you as [c]a pure virgin to Christ. [3]But I am afraid that just as [a]the serpent deceived Eve by his treachery, your minds [b]may be led astray from a sincere and pure[1] devotion to Christ. [4]For if someone comes and proclaims another Jesus different from the one we proclaimed, or if you receive a [a]different spirit than the one you received, or a different gospel than the one you accepted, you put up with it well enough! [5]For [a]I consider myself not at all inferior to those "super-apostles."

[6]And even [a]if [b]I am unskilled in speaking, yet I am certainly not so in knowledge. Indeed, [c]we have made this plain to you in everything in every way. [7]Or did I commit a sin by humbling myself so that you could be exalted, because I proclaimed the gospel of God to you free of [a]charge? [8]I robbed other churches by receiving support from them so that I could serve you! [9]When [a]I was with you and was in need, I was not a burden to anyone, for [b]the brothers who came from Macedonia fully supplied my needs. I kept myself from being a burden to you in any way, and will continue to do so. [10]As the truth of Christ is in me, this [a]boasting of mine will [b]not be stopped in the regions of Achaia. [11]Why? [a]Because I do not love you? God knows I do! [12]And what I am doing I will continue to do, so [a]that I may eliminate any opportunity for those who want a chance to be regarded as our equals in the things they boast about. [13]For such people [a]are false apostles, [b]deceitful workers, disguising themselves as apostles of Christ. [14]And no wonder, for even [a]Satan disguises himself as an angel of light. [15]Therefore it is not surprising his servants also disguise themselves as servants of righteousness, [a]whose end will correspond to their actions.

Paul's Sufferings for Christ

[16]I say again, let no one think that I am a fool. But if you do, then at least accept me as a fool, so that I too may boast a little. [17]What [a]I am saying with this boastful confidence I do not say the way the Lord would. Instead it is, as it were, foolishness. [18]Since many are boasting according to human standards, I too will boast. [19]For [a]since you are so wise, you put up with fools gladly. [20]For you put up with it [a]if someone makes slaves of you, if someone exploits you, if someone takes advantage of you, if someone behaves arrogantly toward you, if someone strikes you in the face. [21](To my [a]disgrace I must say that we were too weak [b]for that!) But whatever anyone else dares to boast about (I am speaking foolishly), I also dare to boast about the same thing. [22]Are they

10:12[a]2 Cor 5:12   **10:13**[a]2 Cor 10:15   **10:14**[a]1 Cor 3:5–6   **10:15**[a]Rom 15:20   **10:17**[a]Isa 65:16; Jer 9:24; 1 Cor 1:31   [1]Jer 9:24   **10:18**[a]Prov 27:2   [b]Rom 2:29; [1 Cor 4:5]   **11:1**[a]Matt 17:17; 2 Cor 11:4, 16, 19   **11:2**[a]Gal 4:17   [b]Hos 2:19; [Eph 5:26]   [c]Col 1:28   **11:3**[a]Gen 3:4, 13; John 8:44; 1 Thess 3:5; 1 Tim 2:14; [Rev 12:9, 15]   [b]Eph 6:24   [1]Maj. MSS omit *and pure.*   **11:4**[a]Gal 1:6–8   **11:5**[a][1 Cor 15:10]; 2 Cor 12:11; Gal 2:6   **11:6**[a][1 Cor 1:17]   [b][1 Cor 12:8; Eph 3:4]   [c][2 Cor 12:12]   **11:7**[a]Acts 18:3; 1 Cor 9:18; 2 Cor 12:13   **11:9**[a]Acts 20:33   [b]Phil 4:10   **11:10**[a]Rom 1:9; 9:1; 2 Cor 1:23; [Gal 2:20]   [b]1 Cor 9:15   **11:11**[a]2 Cor 6:11; 12:15   **11:12**[a]1 Cor 9:12   **11:13**[a]Acts 15:24; Rom 16:18; Gal 1:7; Phil 1:15; 2 Pet 2:1; Rev 2:2   [b]Phil 3:2; Titus 1:10   **11:14**[a]Gal 1:8   **11:15**[a][Phil 3:19]   **11:17**[a]1 Cor 7:6   **11:19**[a]1 Cor 4:10   **11:20**[a]2 Cor 1:24; [Gal 2:4; 4:3, 9; 5:1]   **11:21**[a]2 Cor 10:10   [b]Phil 3:4

[a]Hebrews? So am I. Are they Israelites? So am I. Are they descendants of Abraham? So am I. 23Are they servants of Christ? (I am talking like I am out of my mind!) I am even more so: [a]with much greater labors, [b]with far more imprisonments, [c]with more severe beatings, facing death many times. 24Five times I received from the Jews [a]forty lashes less one. 25Three times I was [a]beaten with a rod. [b]Once I received [c]a stoning. Three times I suffered shipwreck. A night and a day I spent adrift in the open sea. 26I have been on journeys many times, in dangers from rivers, in dangers from robbers, in dangers from my own countrymen, in dangers from Gentiles, in dangers [a]in the city, [b]in dangers in the wilderness, in dangers at sea, in dangers from false brothers, 27[a]in hard work and toil, through many sleepless nights, in hunger and thirst, many times without [b]food, in cold and without enough clothing. 28Apart from other things, there is the daily pressure on me of [a]my anxious concern for all the churches. 29[a]Who is weak, and I am not weak? Who is led into sin, and I do not burn with indignation? 30If [a]I must boast, I will boast about the things that show my weakness. 31The God and [a]Father of the Lord Jesus, [b]who is blessed forever, knows I am not lying. 32[a]In Damascus, the governor under King Aretas was guarding the city of Damascus in order to arrest me, 33but I was let down in a rope-basket through a window in the city wall, and escaped his hands.

Paul's Thorn in the Flesh

12 It is necessary to go on boasting. Though it is not profitable, I will go on to [a]visions and [b]revelations from the Lord. 2I know a man [a]in Christ who fourteen years ago (whether in the body or out of the body I do not know, God knows) [b]was caught up to the third heaven. 3And I know that this man (whether in the body or apart from the body I do not know, God knows) 4was caught up into [a]paradise and heard things too sacred to be put into words, things that a person is not permitted to speak. 5On behalf of such an individual I will [a]boast, but on my own behalf I will not boast, except about my weaknesses. 6For even if I wish to boast, I will not be a fool, for I would be telling the truth, but I refrain from this so that no one may regard me beyond what he sees in me or what he hears from me, 7even because of the extraordinary character of the revelations. Therefore,[1] so that I would not become arrogant, a [a]thorn in the flesh [b]was given to me, a messenger of Satan to trouble me—so that I would not become arrogant. 8I asked the Lord three times [a]about this, that it would depart from me. 9But he [a]said to me, "My grace is enough for you, for my[1] power is made perfect in weakness." So then, I will boast most gladly about my weaknesses, so [b]that the power of Christ may reside in me. 10Therefore [a]I am content with weaknesses, with insults, with troubles, with persecutions and difficulties for the sake of Christ, [b]for whenever I am weak, then I am strong.

The Signs of an Apostle

11I [a]have become a fool. You yourselves forced me to do it, for [b]I should have been commended by you. For [c]I lack nothing in comparison to those "super-apostles," even though I am nothing. 12[a]Indeed, the signs of an apostle were performed among you with great perseverance by signs and [b]wonders and powerful [c]deeds. 13For how were you treated worse than the other churches, except that I myself was not a burden to you? Forgive me this injustice! 14[a]Look, for the [b]third time I am ready to come to you, and I will not be a burden to you, because I do not want your possessions, but you. [c]For children should not have to save up for their parents, but parents for their children. 15Now I will most gladly spend and be spent [a]for your lives! If I love you more, am

11:22 [a] Acts 22:3; Rom 11:1; Phil 3:4–6 11:23 [a] 1 Cor 15:10 [b] Acts 9:16 [c] 1 Cor 15:30 11:24 [a] Deut 25:3 11:25 [a] Acts 16:22–23; 21:32 [b] Acts 14:5, 19 [c] Acts 27:1–44 11:26 [a] Acts 9:23–24; 13:45, 50; 17:5, 13; 1 Thess 2:15 [b] Acts 14:5, 19; 19:23; 27:42 11:27 [a] 1 Cor 4:11; Phil 4:12 [b] Acts 9:9; 13:2–3; 14:23 11:28 [a] Acts 20:18; [Rom 1:14]; 2 Cor 7:12; 12:20; Gal 4:11; 1 Thess 3:10 11:29 [a] [1 Cor 8:9, 13; 9:22] 11:30 [a] [2 Cor 12:5, 9, 10] 11:31 [a] Rom 1:9; Gal 1:20; 1 Thess 2:5 [b] Rom 9:5 11:32 [a] Acts 9:19–25 12:1 [a] Acts 16:9; 18:9; 22:17–18; 23:11; 26:13–15; 27:23 [b] Acts 9:3–6; 1 Cor 14:6; 2 Cor 12:7; [Gal 1:12; 2:2; Eph 3:3–6] 12:2 [a] Rom 16:7; Gal 1:22 [b] Acts 22:17 12:4 [a] Luke 23:43; [Rev 2:7] 12:5 [a] 2 Cor 11:30 12:7 [a] Num 33:55; Ezek 28:24; Hos 2:6; Gal 4:13–14 [b] Job 2:7; Matt 4:10; Luke 13:16; [1 Cor 5:5] [1] Maj. MSS omit Therefore. 12:8 [a] Deut 3:23; Matt 26:44 12:9 [a] 2 Cor 11:30 [b] [1 Pet 4:14] [1] Some WSS omit my. 12:10 [a] [Rom 5:3; 8:35] [b] 2 Cor 13:4 12:11 [a] 2 Cor 5:13; 11:1, 16; 12:6 [b] 1 Cor 15:10; 2 Cor 11:5 [c] 1 Cor 3:7; 13:2; 15:9 12:12 [a] Acts 14:3; Rom 15:18 [b] Acts 15:12 [c] Acts 14:8–10; 16:16–18; 19:11–12; 20:6–12; 28:1–10 12:14 [a] 2 Cor 1:15; 13:1–2 [b] Acts 20:33; [1 Cor 10:24–33] [c] 1 Cor 4:14; Gal 4:19 12:15 [a] John 10:11; Rom 9:3; 2 Cor 1:6; Phil 2:17; Col 1:24; 1 Thess 2:8; [2 Tim 2:10]

I to be loved less? [16]But be that as it may, [a]I have not burdened you. Yet because I was a crafty person, I took you in by deceit! [17]I have not taken advantage of you through anyone I have sent to you, have I? [18]I urged Titus to visit you, and I sent our [a]brother along with him. Titus did not take advantage of you, did he? Did we not conduct ourselves in the same spirit? Did we not behave in the same way? [19a]Have you been thinking all this time[1] that we have been defending ourselves to you? [b]We are speaking in Christ before God, [c]and everything we do, dear friends, is to build you up. [20]For [a]I am afraid that somehow when I come I will not find you what I wish, and you will find me not what you wish. I am afraid that somehow there may be quarreling, jealousy, intense anger, selfish ambition, slander, gossip, arrogance, and disorder. [21]I am afraid that when [a]I come again, my God may humiliate me before you, and I will grieve for many of those [b]who previously sinned and have not repented of the impurity, sexual [c]immorality, and licentiousness that they have practiced.

Paul's Third Visit to Corinth

13 This is [a]the third time I am coming to visit you. [b]*By the testimony of two or three witnesses every matter will be established.*[1] [2]I [a]said before when I was present the second time and now, though absent, I say again to those [b]who [c]sinned previously and to all the rest, that if I come again, I will not spare anyone, [3]since you are demanding proof that Christ is [a]speaking [b]through me. He is not weak toward you but is powerful among you. [4a]For indeed he was crucified by reason of weakness, but he lives because of God's power. For we also are weak in him, but we will live [b]together with him, because of God's [c]power toward you. [5]Put yourselves to the test to see if you are in the faith; examine yourselves! Or do you not recognize regarding yourselves [a]that Jesus Christ is in you—unless, indeed, you fail the [b]test! [6]And I hope that you will realize that we have not failed the test! [7]Now we pray to God that you may not do anything wrong, not so that [a]we may appear to have passed the test, but so that you may do what is right even if we may appear to have failed the test. [8]For we cannot do anything against the truth, but only for the sake of the truth. [9]For we rejoice [a]whenever we are weak, but you are strong. And we pray for this: [b]that you may become fully qualified. [10]Because of this I am writing these things while absent, so that when I arrive I may not have to deal harshly with you by using my authority—[a]the Lord gave [b]it to me for building up, not for tearing down!

Final Exhortations and Greetings

[11]Finally, brothers and sisters,[1] rejoice, set things right, [a]be encouraged, agree with one another, live in peace, [b]and the God of love and peace will be with you. [12a]Greet one another with a holy kiss. All the saints greet you. [13]The grace of [a]the Lord Jesus Christ and [b]the love of God and the fellowship of the Holy Spirit be with you all.[1]

12:16 [a]2 Cor 11:9   **12:18** [a]2 Cor 8:18   **12:19** [a]2 Cor 5:12   [b][Rom 9:1–2]; 2 Cor 11:31   [c]1 Cor 10:33   [1]Some wss *again.*   **12:20** [a]1 Cor 4:21; 2 Cor 13:2, 10   **12:21** [a]2 Cor 2:1, 4   [b]2 Cor 13:2   [c]1 Cor 5:1   **13:1** [a]2 Cor 12:14   [b]Num 35:30, Deut 17:6; 19:15; Matt 18:16; John 8:17; Heb 10:28   [1]Deut 19:15   **13:2** [a]2 Cor 10:2   [b]2 Cor 12:21   [c]2 Cor 1:23; 10:11   **13:3** [a]Matt 10:20; [1 Cor 5:4; 7:40]   [b][1 Cor 9:2]   **13:4** [a]Phil 2:7–8; [1 Pet 3:18]   [b][Rom 1:4; 6:4; 1 Cor 6:14]   [c][2 Cor 10:3–4]   **13:5** [a]Rom 8:10; [Gal 4:19]   [b]1 Cor 9:27   **13:7** [a]2 Cor 6:9   **13:9** [a]1 Cor 4:10   [b]1 Cor 1:10; 2 Cor 13:11; Eph 4:12; [1 Thess 3:10]   **13:10** [a]1 Cor 4:21   [b]1 Cor 5:4; 2 Cor 10:8   **13:11** [a]Rom 12:16, 18   [b]Rom 15:33; Eph 6:23   [1]Grk. *brothers*; considerable external evidence supports use of the Grk. word as *brothers and sisters* or *fellow Christians.*   **13:12** [a]Rom 16:16   **13:13** [a]Rom 16:24   [b]Phil 2:1   [1]Maj. wss add *amen.*

GALATIANS

The Galatians, having launched their Christian voyage by faith, seem content to chart a new course based on works—a course Paul finds disturbing. His letter to the Galatians is a vigorous attack against the gospel of works and a defense of the gospel of faith. Paul begins by setting forth his credentials as an apostle with a message from God: blessing comes from God on the basis of faith, not law. The law declares human beings guilty and imprisons them; faith sets them free to enjoy liberty in Christ. But liberty is not license. Freedom in Christ means freedom to produce the fruits of righteousness through a Spirit-led lifestyle. The book is called *Pros Galatas*, "To the Galatians," and it is the only letter of Paul that is specifically addressed to a number of churches ("To the churches of Galatia," 1:2). The name *Galatians* was given to this Celtic people because they originally lived in Gaul before their migration to Asia Minor.

Salutation

1 From Paul, an apostle (not from men, nor [a]by human agency, but by Jesus Christ and God the Father [b]who raised him from the dead) [2]and all the brothers with me, to the churches of Galatia. [3]Grace and peace to you from God the Father and our[1] Lord Jesus Christ, [4][a]who gave himself for our sins to rescue us [b]from this present evil age according to the will of our God and Father, [5]to whom be glory forever and ever! Amen.

Occasion of the Letter

[6]I am astonished that you are so quickly deserting the one who called you by the grace of Christ[1] and are following a different gospel—[7]not [a]that there really is another gospel, but there are some [b]who are disturbing you and wanting to [c]distort the gospel of Christ. [8]But even if [a]we (or an angel from heaven) should preach[1] a gospel contrary to the one we preached to you, let him be condemned to hell! [9]As we have said before, and now I say again, if any one is preaching to you a gospel [a]contrary to what you received, let him be condemned to hell! [10]Am I now trying to gain the [a]approval of people,[1] or of God? Or am I trying to please people?[2] If I were still trying to please people,[3] I would not be a slave[4] of Christ!

Paul's Vindication of His Apostleship

[11][a]Now I want you to know, brothers and sisters,[1] that the gospel I preached is not of human origin. [12]For [a]I did not receive it or learn it from any human source; instead I received it [b]by a revelation of Jesus Christ. [13]For you have heard of my former way of [a]life in Judaism, how [b]I was savagely persecuting the church of God and trying to destroy it. [14]I was advancing in Judaism beyond many of my contemporaries in my nation, and [a]was extremely zealous [b]for the traditions of my ancestors. [15]But when the one[1] [a]who set me apart from birth and called me by his grace was pleased [16]to reveal his Son in me so that I could preach him among the Gentiles, I did not go [a]to ask [b]advice from any human [c]being, [17]nor did I go up to Jerusalem to see those who

---

1:1[a] Acts 9:6 [b] Acts 2:24   1:3[1]‡ Some wss *God our Father and the Lord Jesus Christ.*   1:4[a] [Matt 20:28] [b] Heb 2:5 1:6[1] Some wss *grace of Jesus Christ, grace of God, grace.*   1:7[a] 2 Cor 11:4 [b] Acts 15:1; Gal 5:10, 12 [c] 2 Cor 2:17   1:8[a] 1 Cor 16:22 [1]‡ Maj. wss add *to you.*   1:9[a] Deut 4:2   1:10[a] 1 Sam 24:7 [1] Grk. *men*; the word can be used in a generic sense of both men and women. [2] Grk. *men*; the word can be used in a generic sense of both men and women. [3] Grk. *men*; the word can be used in a generic sense of both men and women. [4] Trad. *servant*; the word does not bear the connotation of a free individual serving another.   1:11[a] [Rom 2:16]; 1 Cor 15:1 [1] Grk. *brothers*; considerable external evidence supports use of the Grk. word as *brothers and sisters* or *fellow Christians.*   1:12[a] 1 Cor 15:1 [b] [Eph 3:3–5]   1:13[a] Acts 9:1 [b] Acts 8:3; 22:4–5   1:14[a] Acts 26:9; Phil 3:6 [b] Jer 9:14; Matt 15:2; Mark 7:3; [Col 2:8]   1:15[a] Isa 49:1, 5; Jer 1:5; Acts 9:15; Rom 1:1; Gal 1:6 [1]‡ Sev. sig. wss add *God.*   1:16[a] [2 Cor 4:5–7] [b] Acts 9:15; Gal 2:9 [c] Matt 16:17

were apostles before me, but right away I departed to Arabia, and then returned to Damascus.

[18]Then after three years [a]I went up to Jerusalem to visit Cephas and get information from him, and I stayed with him fifteen days. [19]But [a]I saw none of the other apostles except [b]James the Lord's brother. [20]I assure you that, before God, I am not lying about what I am writing to you! [21a]Afterward I went to the regions of Syria and Cilicia. [22]But I was personally unknown to the churches of Judea that are in Christ. [23]They were only [a]hearing, "The one who once [b]persecuted us is now proclaiming the good news of the faith he once tried to destroy." [24]So they [a]glorified God because of me.

Confirmation from the Jerusalem Apostles

2 Then after fourteen years [a]I went up to Jerusalem again with Barnabas, taking Titus along too. [2]I went there because of [a]a [b]revelation and presented to them the gospel that I preach among the Gentiles. But I did so only in a private meeting with the influential people, to make sure that I was not running—or had not run—in vain. [3]Yet not even Titus, who was with me, was compelled to be circumcised, although he was a Greek. [4]Now this matter arose because of the [a]false brothers with false pretenses who slipped in unnoticed to spy on our [b]freedom that we have in Christ Jesus, [c]to make us slaves. [5]But we did not surrender to [a]them even for a moment, in order that the truth of the gospel would remain with you.

[6]But from those [a]who were influential (whatever they were makes no difference to me; [b]God shows no favoritism between people)—those influential leaders [c]added nothing to my message. [7]On the contrary, [a]when they saw that I was entrusted with the gospel to the uncircumcised just as Peter was entrusted with the gospel to the circumcised [8](for he who empowered Peter for his apostleship to the [a]circumcised [b]also empowered me for my apostleship to the Gentiles) [9]and when James, Cephas, and John, who had a reputation as [a]pillars, recognized [b]the grace that had been given to me, they gave to Barnabas and me the right hand of fellowship, agreeing [c]that we would go to the Gentiles and they to the circumcised. [10]They requested only that we remember [a]the poor, the very thing I also was eager to do.

Paul Rebukes Peter

[11a]But when Cephas came to Antioch, I opposed him to his face, because he had clearly done wrong. [12]Until certain people came from James, [a]he had been eating with the Gentiles. But when they arrived, he stopped doing this and separated himself because he was afraid of those who were pro-circumcision. [13]And the rest of the Jews also joined with him in this hypocrisy, so that even Barnabas was led astray with them by their hypocrisy. [14]But when I saw that [a]they were not behaving consistently with the truth of the gospel, I said to Cephas in front [b]of them all, "[c]If you, although you are a Jew, live like a Gentile and not like a Jew, how can you try to force the Gentiles to live like Jews?"

The Justification of Jews and Gentiles

[15a]We are Jews by birth and not Gentile [b]sinners, [16]yet we [a]know that no one is justified by the works of the law but [b]by the faithfulness of Jesus Christ.[1] And we have come to believe in Christ Jesus, so that we may be justified [c]by the faithfulness of Christ[2] and not by the works of the law, because by the works of the law no one will be justified. [17]But if while seeking to be justified in Christ we ourselves have also been found to be [a]sinners, is Christ then one who encourages sin? Absolutely not! [18]But if I build up again those things I once destroyed, I demonstrate that I am one who breaks God's law. [19]For [a]through the law I [b]died to the law so that I may [c]live to God. [20]I have been [a]crucified [b]with Christ, and it

1:18 [a] Acts 9:26   1:19 [a] 1 Cor 9:5   [b] Matt 13:55   1:21 [a] Acts 9:30   1:23 [a] Acts 9:20–21   [b] Acts 8:3   1:24 [a] Acts 11:18   2:1 [a] Acts 15:2   2:2 [a] Acts 15:1–4   [b] [Rom 9:16; 1 Cor 9:24]; Gal 5:7; Phil 2:16; 1 Thess 3:5; 2 Tim 4:7; Heb 12:1   2:4 [a] Acts 15:1, 24; 2 Cor 11:13, 26; Gal 1:7   [b] Gal 3:25; 5:1, 13; [Jas 1:25]   [c] Gal 4:3, 9   2:5 [a] [Gal 1:6; 2:14; 3:1]; Col 1:5   2:6 [a] Gal 2:9; 6:3   [b] Acts 10:34; Rom 2:11   [c] 2 Cor 11:5; 12:11   2:7 [a] Acts 9:15; 13:46; 22:21; Rom 11:13   2:8 [a] 1 Pet 1:1   [b] Acts 9:15   2:9 [a] Matt 16:18   [b] Rom 1:5   [c] Acts 13:3   2:10 [a] Acts 11:30   2:11 [a] Acts 15:35   2:12 [a] [Acts 10:28; 11:2–3]   2:14 [a] Gal 1:6; 2:5; Col 1:5   [b] 1 Tim 5:20   [c] [Acts 10:28]; Gal 2:12   2:15 [a] [Acts 15:10]   [b] Matt 9:11   2:16 [a] Acts 13:38–39; Gal 3:11   [b] Rom 1:17   [c] Ps 143:2; Rom 3:20   [1] Or *faith in Jesus Christ.*   [2] Or *by faith in Christ.*   2:17 [a] [1 John 3:8]   2:19 [a] Rom 8:2   [b] [Rom 6:2, 14; 7:4]; 1 Cor 9:20   [c] [Rom 6:11]   2:20 [a] [Rom 6:6; Gal 5:24; 6:14]   [b] Rom 6:8–11; 2 Cor 5:15; [Eph 2:4–6; Col 3:1–4]

is no longer I [c]who live, but Christ lives in me. So the life I now live in the body, I live because of the faithfulness of the Son of God,[1,2] who loved me and gave himself for me. [21]I do not set aside God's grace, because [a]if righteousness could come through the law, then Christ died for nothing!

Justification by Law or by Faith?

3 You foolish Galatians! Who has cast a spell on you? Before your eyes Jesus Christ was vividly portrayed as crucified! [2]The only thing I want to learn from you is this: Did you receive the Spirit by doing the works of the law[1] [a]or by believing what you heard? [3]Are you so foolish? Although you began with [a]the Spirit, are you now trying to finish by human effort? [4][a]Have you suffered so many things for nothing?— if indeed it was for nothing. [5]Does God then give you the Spirit and work miracles among you by your doing the works of the law[1] or by your believing what you heard?[2]

[6]Just as Abraham [a]*believed God, and it was credited to him as righteousness,*[1] [7]so then, understand that [a]those who believe are the sons of Abraham. [8]And [a]the scripture, foreseeing that God would justify the Gentiles by faith, proclaimed the gospel to Abraham ahead of time, saying, "*All the nations will be blessed* [b]*in you.*"[1] [9]So then those who believe are blessed along with Abraham the believer. [10]For all who rely on doing the works of the law are under a curse because it is written, "[a]*Cursed is everyone who does not keep on doing everything written in the book of the law.*"[1] [11]Now it is clear no one is justified before God by [a]the law because *the righteous one will live by faith.*[1,2] [12]But [a]the law is not based on faith, but [b]*the one who does* the works of the law *will live by them.*[1] [13][a]Christ redeemed us from the curse of the law by becoming a curse for us (because it is written, "[b]*Cursed is everyone who hangs on a tree*")[1] [14]in order [a]that in Christ

Jesus the blessing of Abraham would come to the [b]Gentiles, so that we could receive [c]the promise of the Spirit by faith.

Inheritance Comes from Promises and not Law

[15]Brothers and sisters,[1] I offer an example from everyday life: When a covenant has been ratified, even [a]though it is only a human contract, no one can set it aside or add anything to it. [16]Now the promises were spoken to Abraham [a]and to his descendant.[1] Scripture does not say, "and to the descendants,"[2] referring to many, but "*and to your descendant,*"[3] referring to [b]one, who is [c]Christ. [17]What [a]I am saying is this: The law [b]that came 430 years later does not cancel a covenant previously ratified by God,[1] so as to invalidate the promise. [18]For if [a]the [b]inheritance is based on the law, it is no longer based on the promise, but God graciously gave it to Abraham through the promise.

[19]Why then was the law given? [a]It was added[1] because of transgressions,[2] until the arrival of the [b]descendant[3] to whom the promise had been made. It was [c]administered through angels by an intermediary. [20]Now an intermediary is not for one party alone, [a]but God is one. [21]Is the law therefore opposed to the promises of God?[1] Absolutely not! For if a law had been given that was able to give life, then righteousness would certainly have come by the law. [22]But the scripture imprisoned [a]everything under sin so [b]that the promise could be given— because of the faithfulness[1] of Jesus Christ— to those who believe.

Sons of God Are Heirs of Promise

[23]Now before faith[1] came we were held in custody under the law, being kept as prisoners until the coming faith would be revealed. [24]Thus [a]the law had become our guardian until Christ, so [b]that we could be declared righteous by faith. [25]But now that faith has

2:20 [c]Isa 53:12; Eph 5:2 [1]Some sig. wss of *God and Christ.* [2]Or *live by faith in the Son of God.* 2:21 [a]Heb 7:11 3:2 [a]Rom 10:16–17 [1]Grk. *by* [the] *works of* [the] *law;* i.e., the Mosaic law. 3:3 [a]Heb 7:16 3:4 [a]Heb 10:35 3:5 [1]Grk. *by* [the] *works of* [the] *law.* [2]Grk. *by* [the] *hearing of faith.* 3:6 [a]Gen 15:6 [1]Gen 15:6 3:7 [a]John 8:39 3:8 [a]Rom 9:17 [b]Gen 12:3; 18:18; 22:18; 26:4; 28:14 [1]Gen 12:3; 18:18 3:10 [a]Deut 27:26 [1]Deut 27:26 3:11 [a]Hab 2:4; Rom 1:17; Heb 10:38 [1]Hab 2:4 [2]Or *the one who is righteous by faith will live.* 3:12 [a]Rom 4:4–5 [b]Lev 18:5; Rom 10:5 [1]Lev 18:5 3:13 [a][Rom 8:3] [b]Deut 21:23 [1]Deut 21:23 3:14 [a][Rom 4:1–5, 9, 16; Gal 3:28] [b]Isa 42:1, 6; 49:6; Luke 2:32; Rom 3:29–30 [c]Isa 32:15 3:15 [a]Heb 9:17 [1]Grk. *brothers;* considerable external evidence supports use of the Grk. word as *brothers and sisters* or *fellow Christians.* 3:16 [a]Gen 12:3, 7; 13:15; 24:7 [b]Gen 22:18 [c][1 Cor 12:12] [1]Grk. *his seed.* [2]Grk. *to seeds.* [3]Gen 12:7; 13:15; 17:7; 24:7 3:17 [a]Gen 15:13; Exod 12:40; Acts 7:6 [b][Rom 4:13] [1]Maj. mss add *in Christ.* 3:18 [a][Rom 8:17] [b]Rom 4:14 3:19 [a]John 15:22 [b]Gal 4:4 [c]Acts 7:53 [1]Sev. wss *established.* [2]One ws *traditions, commandments.* [3]Grk. *the seed.* 3:20 [a][Rom 3:29] 3:21 [1]Some sig. wss omit *of God.* 3:22 [a]Rom 11:32 [b]Rom 4:11 [1]Or *by faith in Jesus Christ.* 3:23 [1]Or *the faithfulness* [of Christ] *came.* 3:24 [a]Rom 10:4 [b]Acts 13:39

come, we are no longer under a guardian. [26] For in Christ Jesus you [a] are all sons of God through faith. [27] For all of you who were baptized into Christ [a] have clothed yourselves with Christ. [28] There is neither Jew nor Greek, [a] there is neither slave[1] nor free, [b] there is neither male nor female—for all of you are [c] one in Christ Jesus. [29] And [a] if you belong to Christ, then you are Abraham's [b] descendants,[1] [c] heirs according to the promise.

4 Now I mean that the heir, as long as he is a minor, is no different from a slave, though he is the owner of everything. [2] But he is under guardians and managers until the date set by his father. [3] So also we, when we [a] were minors, were enslaved under the basic forces of the world. [4] But [a] when the appropriate time had come, God sent out his Son, [b] born [c] of a woman, [d] born under the law, [5] [a] to redeem those who were under the law, so [b] that we may be adopted as sons with full rights. [6] And because you are sons, God sent [a] the Spirit of his Son into our hearts, who calls "*Abba!* Father!" [7] So you are no longer a slave but a son, [a] and if you are a son, then you are also an heir through God.[1]

Heirs of Promise Are not to Return to Law

[8] Formerly [a] when [b] you did not know God, you were enslaved to beings that by nature are not gods at all. [9] But now that you have come to know God (or rather to be known by God), [a] how can you turn back again to [b] the weak and worthless basic forces? Do you want to be enslaved to them all over again? [10] [a] You are observing religious days and months and seasons and years. [11] I fear for you that my work for you may have been in vain. [12] I beg [a] you, brothers and sisters,[1] become like me, because I have become like you. You have done me no wrong!

Personal Appeal of Paul

[13] But you know it was because [a] of a physical illness that I first proclaimed the gospel to you, [14] and though my physical condition

put you to the test, you did not despise or reject me. Instead, you welcomed me as [a] though I were an angel of God, as though I were Christ Jesus himself! [15] Where then is your sense of happiness now? For I testify about you that if it were possible, you would have pulled out your eyes and given them to me! [16] So then, have I become your enemy by telling you the truth?

[17] They court you eagerly, but for no good purpose; they want to exclude you, so that you would seek them eagerly. [18] However, it is good to be sought eagerly for a good purpose at all times, and not only when I am present with you. [19] [a] My children—I am again undergoing birth pains until Christ is formed in you! [20] I wish I could be with you now and change my tone of voice, because I am perplexed about you.

An Appeal from Allegory

[21] Tell me, you who want to be under the law, do you not understand the law? [22] For it is written that Abraham had two sons, one by [a] the slave woman and [b] the other by the free woman. [23] But one, the son by the slave woman, [a] was born by natural descent, [b] while the other, the son by the free woman, was born through the promise. [24] These things may be treated as an allegory, for these women represent two covenants. One is from Mount [a] Sinai bearing children for slavery; this is Hagar. [25] Now Hagar represents Mount Sinai in Arabia and corresponds to the present Jerusalem, for she is in slavery with her children. [26] But the [a] Jerusalem above is free, and she is our mother. [27] For it is written:

> "[a] *Rejoice, O barren woman who does not bear children;*
> *break forth and shout, you who have no birth pains,*
> *because the children of the desolate woman are more numerous*
> *than those of the woman who has a husband.*"[1]

3:26 [a] John 1:12   3:27 [a] Rom 10:12; 13:14   3:28 [a] [John 10:16]; Rom 3:22; 10:12; [Eph 2:14]; Col 3:11   [b] [1 Cor 12:13]   [c] John 17:11; [1 Cor 12:13; Eph 2:15–16]   [1] Trad. *servant*; the word does not bear the connotation of a free individual serving another.   3:29 [a] Gen 21:10; Heb 11:18   [b] Rom 4:11; Gal 3:7   [c] Gen 12:3; 18:18; Rom 8:17   [1] Grk. *seed*.   4:3 [a] Gal 4:9; Col 2:8, 20; Heb 5:12; 9:10   4:4 [a] [Gen 49:10]   [b] [John 1:14]; Rom 1:3; 8:3; [Phil 2:7]   [c] Gen 3:15; [Isa 7:14; Matt 1:25]   [d] [Matt 5:17]; Luke 2:21, 27   4:5 [a] [Matt 20:28; Gal 3:13]   [b] [John 1:12]   4:6 [a] [Acts 16:7; Rom 5:5; 8:9, 15, 16; 2 Cor 3:17]   4:7 [a] [Rom 8:16–17]   [1] Some wss *because of God, through Christ, through Jesus Christ, of God through Christ.*   4:8 [a] 1 Cor 1:21; Eph 2:12; 1 Thess 4:5; 2 Thess 1:8   [b] Rom 1:25   4:9 [a] Gal 3:1–3; Col 2:20   [b] Heb 7:18   4:10 [a] Rom 14:5; Col 2:16   4:12 [a] 2 Cor 2:5   [1] Grk. *brothers*; considerable external evidence supports use of the Grk. word as *brothers and sisters* or *fellow Christians.*   4:13 [a] 1 Cor 2:3   4:14 [a] Mal 2:7   4:19 [a] 1 Cor 4:15   4:22 [a] Gen 16:15   [b] Gen 21:2   4:23 [a] Rom 9:7–8; Gal 4:29   [b] Gen 16:15; 17:15–19; 18:10; 21:1; Gal 4:28; Heb 11:11   4:24 [a] Exod 24:6–8; Deut 33:2   4:26 [a] [Isa 2:2]   4:27 [a] Isa 54:1   [1] Isa 54:1

[28]But [a]you,[1] brothers and sisters,[2] are [b]children of the promise like Isaac. [29]But just as at that time [a]the one born by natural descent persecuted the one born according to the Spirit, so it is now. [30]But what does [a]the scripture say? "*Throw [b]out [c]the slave woman and her son, for the son of the slave woman will not share the inheritance with the son*"[1] of the free woman. [31]Therefore, brothers and sisters,[1] we are not children of the slave woman but of the free woman.

Freedom of the Believer

5 For freedom Christ has set us free. Stand [a]firm, then, and do not be subject again to the [b]yoke of slavery. [2]Listen! I, Paul, tell you that [a]if you let yourselves be circumcised, Christ will be of no benefit to you at all! [3]And I testify again to every man who lets himself be circumcised [a]that he is obligated to obey the whole law. [4]You who are trying to be declared righteous by the law have been alienated from Christ; [a]you have fallen away from grace! [5]For through the Spirit, by faith, we wait expectantly [a]for the hope of righteousness. [6]For [a]in Christ Jesus neither circumcision nor uncircumcision carries any weight—the only thing that matters is [b]faith working through love.

[7]You were [a]running well; who prevented you from obeying the truth? [8]This persuasion does not come from the one who calls you! [9]A little [a]yeast makes the whole batch of dough rise! [10]I am confident in the Lord that you will accept no other view. But the one who is confusing you will pay the penalty,[1] whoever he may be. [11]Now, brothers and sisters,[1] if I am still preaching circumcision, [a]why am I still being persecuted? In that case [b]the offense of the cross has been removed. [12]I [a]wish those agitators[1] would go so far as to castrate themselves!

Practice Love

[13]For you were called to [a]freedom, brothers and sisters;[1] only do not use your freedom as an [b]opportunity to indulge your flesh, but [c]through love serve one another. [14]For the [a]whole law can be summed up in a single commandment, namely, "[b]*You must love your neighbor as yourself.*"[1] [15]However, if you continually bite and devour one another, beware that you are not consumed by one another. [16]But I say, [a]live by the Spirit and you will not carry out the desires of the flesh. [17]For [a]the flesh has desires that are opposed to the Spirit, and the Spirit has desires that are opposed to the flesh, for these are in opposition to each other, [b]so that you cannot do what you want. [18]But [a]if you are led by the Spirit, you are not under the law. [19]Now [a]the works of the flesh are obvious: sexual immorality, impurity, depravity, [20]idolatry, sorcery, hostilities, strife, jealousy, outbursts of anger, selfish rivalries, dissensions, factions, [21]envying, murder,[1] drunkenness, carousing, and similar things. I am warning you, as I had warned you before: [a]Those who practice such things will not inherit the kingdom of God!

[22]But [a]the fruit of the Spirit is [b]love, joy, peace, patience, kindness, [c]goodness, [d]faithfulness, [23]gentleness, and self-control. [a]Against such things there is no law. [24]Now those who belong to Christ[1] [a]have crucified the flesh with its passions[2] and desires. [25][a]If we live by the Spirit, let us also behave in accordance with the Spirit. [26][a]Let us not become conceited, provoking one another, being jealous of one another.

Support One Another

6 Brothers and sisters,[1] if a person is discovered in some sin, you who are spiritual restore such a person in a spirit of [a]gentleness. Pay close attention to

4:28 [a]Rom 9:7–8; Gal 3:29 [b]Acts 3:25 [1]Maj. MSS *we*. [2]Grk. *brothers*; considerable external evidence supports use of the Grk. word as *brothers and sisters* or *fellow Christians*. **4:29** [a]Gen 21:9 **4:30** [a][Gal 3:8, 22] [b]Gen 21:10, 12 [c][John 8:35] [1]Gen 21:10 **4:31**[1]Grk. *brothers*; considerable external evidence supports use of the Grk. word as *brothers and sisters* or *fellow Christians*. **5:1** [a]Phil 4:1 [b]Acts 15:10; Gal 2:4 **5:2** [a]Acts 15:1; Gal 5:3, 6, 11 **5:3** [a][Deut 27:26; Rom 2:25; Gal 3:10] **5:4** [a][Rom 9:31] **5:5** [a]Rom 8:24 **5:6** [a][1 Cor 7:19; Gal 6:15; Col 3:11] [b]Col 1:4; 1 Thess 1:3; [Jas 2:18, 20, 22] **5:7** [a]1 Cor 9:24 **5:9** [a]1 Cor 5:6 **5:10** [1]Or *will suffer condemnation*; Grk. *will bear his judgment*. **5:11** [a]1 Cor 15:30 [b]Rom 9:33; [1 Cor 1:23] [1]Grk. *brothers*; considerable external evidence supports use of the Grk. word as *brothers and sisters* or *fellow Christians*. **5:12** [a]Josh 7:25 [1]Grk. *the ones who are upsetting you*. **5:13** [a][Rom 8:2]; 1 Cor 8:9; Gal 5:1 [b]Rom 6:1; 1 Pet 2:16 [c]1 Cor 9:19; Eph 5:21 [1]Grk. *brothers*; considerable external evidence supports use of the Grk. word as *brothers and sisters* or *fellow Christians*. **5:14** [a]Matt 7:12; 22:40; Rom 13:8, 10; Gal 6:2 [b]Lev 19:18; Matt 22:39; Rom 13:9 [1]Lev 19:18 **5:16** [a]Rom 6:12 **5:17** [a]Rom 7:18, 22, 23; 8:5 [b]Rom 7:15 **5:18** [a][Rom 6:14; 7:4; 8:14; 1 Tim 1:9] **5:19** [a]Rom 1:26–31; Eph 5:3, 11; 2 Tim 3:2–4 **5:21** [a]1 Cor 6:9–10 [1]‡ Some MSS omit *murder*. **5:22** [a][John 15:2] [b][Rom 5:1–5; 1 Cor 13:4; Col 3:12–15] [c]Rom 15:14 [d]1 Cor 13:7 **5:23** [a]1 Tim 1:9 **5:24** [a]Rom 6:6; [Gal 2:20; 6:14] [1]‡ Some MSS *Christ Jesus*. [2]I.e., strong physical (esp. sexual) desires. **5:25** [a][Rom 8:4–5] **5:26** [a]Phil 2:3 **6:1** [a]Eph 4:2 [1]Grk. *brothers*; considerable external evidence supports use of the Grk. word as *brothers and sisters* or *fellow Christians*.

yourselves, so that you are not tempted too. [2a]Carry one [b]another's burdens, and in this way you will fulfill the law of Christ. [3]For [a]if anyone thinks [b]he is something when he is nothing, he deceives himself. [4]Let each one examine his own work. Then he can take pride in himself and [a]not compare himself with someone else. [5]For each [a]one will carry his own load.

[6a]Now the one who receives instruction in the word must share all good things with the one who teaches it. [7]Do not be deceived. God will not be made [a]a fool. For a person will reap what he sows, [8]because the person who sows to his own flesh will reap corruption from the flesh, but the one who sows to the Spirit will reap [a]eternal life from the Spirit. [9]So we must not grow weary in doing good, for in due time we will reap, [a]if we do not give up. [10a]So then, whenever we have an opportunity, [b]let us do good to all people, and [c]especially to those who belong to the family of faith.

Final Instructions and Benediction

[11]See what big letters I make as I write to you with my own hand!

[12]Those who want to make a good showing in external matters are trying to force you to be circumcised. They do so [a]only to avoid being persecuted for the cross of Christ. [13]For those who are circumcised do not obey the law themselves, but they want you to be circumcised so that they can boast about your flesh. [14]But may I never boast except in the [a]cross of our Lord Jesus Christ, through which the world has been crucified to me, and [b]I to the world. [15]For[1] neither circumcision nor uncircumcision counts for [a]anything; the only thing that matters is a new creation! [16]And all who will behave in accordance with this rule, peace and mercy be on them, and on the Israel of God.

[17]From now on let no one cause me trouble, for I bear the marks of Jesus on my body. [18]The grace of our Lord Jesus Christ be with your spirit, brothers and sisters.[1] Amen.

6:2 [a] Acts 20:35; Rom 15:1; 1 Thess 5:14   [b] [Jas 2:8]   6:3 [a] Rom 12:3   [b] [2 Cor 3:5; Jas 1:22]   6:4 [a] Luke 18:11   6:5 [a] [Rom 2:6]   6:6 [a] 1 Cor 9:11, 14   6:7 [a] [Rom 2:6]   6:8 [a] [Rom 6:8]   6:9 [a] [Matt 24:13]; Heb 12:3, 5; [Jas 5:7–8]   6:10 [a] Prov 3:27; [John 9:4; 12:35]   [b] Titus 3:8   [c] Rom 12:13   6:12 [a] Gal 5:11; Phil 3:8   6:14 [a] [1 Cor 1:18]   [b] [Gal 2:20]; Col 2:20   6:15 [a] [Rom 2:26, 28]; 1 Cor 7:19; [Gal 5:6]   [1] Some MSS add *in Christ Jesus.*   6:18 [1] Grk. *brothers*; considerable external evidence supports use of the Grk. word as *brothers and sisters* or *fellow Christians.*

EPHESIANS

Ephesians is addressed to a group of believers who are rich beyond measure in Jesus Christ yet living as beggars, and only because they are ignorant of their wealth. Paul begins by describing in chapters 1–3 the contents of the Christian's heavenly "bank account": adoption, acceptance, redemption, forgiveness, wisdom, inheritance, the seal of the Holy Spirit, life, grace, citizenship—in short, every spiritual blessing. In chapters 4–6 the Christian learns a spiritual walk rooted in his spiritual wealth. "For we are his creative work, having been created in Christ Jesus [chs. 1–3] for good works ... so we can do them [chs. 4–6]" (2:10). The traditional title of this epistle is *Pros Ephesious*, "To the Ephesians." Many ancient manuscripts, however, omit *en Epheso*, "in Ephesus," in 1:1. This has led a number of scholars to challenge the traditional view that this message was directed specifically to the Ephesians. They propose that it was a circular letter sent by Paul to the churches of Asia, that Ephesians is really a Christian treatise designed for general use: it involves no controversy and deals with no specific problems in any particular church. Some scholars accept an ancient tradition that Ephesians is Paul's letter to the Laodiceans (Col 4:16), but there is no way to be sure. If Ephesians began as a circular letter, it eventually became associated with Ephesus, the foremost of the Asian churches. Another plausible option is that this epistle was directly addressed to the Ephesians but written in such a way as to make it helpful for all the churches in Asia.

Salutation

1 From Paul, an apostle of Christ Jesus by the will of God, to the saints [in Ephesus],[1] the faithful in Christ Jesus. [2]Grace and peace to you from God our Father and the Lord Jesus Christ!

Spiritual Blessings in Christ

[3a]Blessed is the God and Father of our Lord Jesus Christ, who has blessed us with every spiritual blessing in the heavenly realms in Christ. [4]For [a]he chose us in Christ [b]before the foundation of the world that we should [c]be holy and blameless before him in love. [5a]He did this by predestining us to [b]adoption as his legal heirs[1] through Jesus Christ, according [c]to the pleasure of his will—[6]to [a]the praise of the glory of his grace that he has freely bestowed on us in his dearly loved Son. [7a]In him we have redemption through his blood, the forgiveness of our offenses, according to [b]the riches of his grace [8]that he lavished on us in all wisdom and insight. [9a]He did this when he revealed to us the mystery[1] of his will, according to his good pleasure [b]that he set forth in Christ, [10]toward the administration of [a]the fullness of the times, [b]to head up all [c]things in Christ—the things in heaven and the things on earth. [11a]In Christ we too have been claimed as God's own possession,[1] since we were predestined according to [b]the purpose of him who accomplishes all things according to the counsel of his will [12]so [a]that we, [b]who were the first to set our hope on Christ,[1] would be to the praise of

---

1:1 [1]The earliest and maj. sig. MSS omit *in Ephesus*. For this reason, the phrase is set in brackets. For an explanation of this issue, see *NET Bible, Full Notes Edition*. **1:3** [a]2 Cor 1:3 **1:4** [a]Rom 8:28 [b]1 Pet 1:2 [c]Luke 1:75 **1:5** [a]Acts 13:48; [Rom 8:29] [b]John 1:12 [c][1 Cor 1:21] [1]Grk. *to adoption as sons*; a legal, technical term for adoption as a son with full rights of inheritance. **1:6** [a]Matt 3:17 **1:7** [a][Heb 9:12] [b][Rom 3:24–25] **1:9** [a][Rom 16:25] [b][2 Tim 1:9] [1]Or *secret*; i.e., a divine secret previously undisclosed. **1:10** [a]Gal 4:4 [b]1 Cor 3:22 [c]Eph 3:15; [Phil 2:9; Col 1:16, 20] **1:11** [a]Rom 8:17 [b]Isa 46:10 [1]Or *been appointed a portion of the inheritance*; Grk. *we were appointed by lot* [for an inheritance]. **1:12** [a]2 Thess 2:13 [b]Jas 1:18 [1]Or *the Messiah*.

his glory. [13]And when you heard [a]the word of truth (the gospel of [b]your salvation)—when you believed in Christ—you were marked with the seal of the promised Holy Spirit, [14a]who is the down payment[1] of our inheritance, [b]until [c]the redemption of God's own possession, [d]to the praise of his glory.

Prayer for Wisdom and Revelation

[15]For this reason, because I have heard of your faith in the Lord Jesus and your love[1] for all the saints, [16]I [a]do not cease to give thanks for you when I remember you in my prayers. [17]I pray that [a]the God of our Lord Jesus Christ, the glorious Father, will give you spiritual wisdom and revelation in your growing knowledge of him, [18]—since [a]the eyes of your[1] heart have been enlightened—so that you can know what is [b]the hope of his calling, what is the wealth of his glorious[2] inheritance in the saints, [19]and what is the incomparable greatness of his power toward us who believe, as displayed [a]in the exercise of his immense strength. [20]This power [a]he exercised in Christ when he raised him from the dead and [b]seated him[1] at his right hand in the heavenly realms [21a]far above every [b]rule and authority and power and dominion and every name that is named, not only in this age but also in the one to come. [22]And God *put all things under Christ's feet,*[1] and gave him to [a]the church as head over all things. [23a]Now [b]the church is his body, the fullness of him [c]who fills all in all.

New Life Individually

2 And although [a]you were dead in your offenses and sins, [2a]in which you formerly lived according to this world's present path, according to [b]the ruler of [c]the domain of the air, the ruler of the spirit that is now energizing the sons of disobedience, [3a]among whom all of us also formerly lived out our lives in [b]the cravings of our flesh, indulging the desires of the flesh and the mind, and

[c]were by nature children of wrath even as the rest... [4]But God, being rich in mercy because of his [a]great love with which he loved us, [5a]even though we were dead in offenses, [b]made us alive together with Christ—by grace you are saved!—[6]and he raised us up together with him and seated us together with him [a]in the heavenly realms in Christ Jesus, [7]to demonstrate in the coming ages the surpassing wealth of [a]his grace in kindness toward us in Christ Jesus. [8a]For by grace you are saved [b]through [c]faith,[1] and this is not from yourselves, it is the gift of God; [9]it is not from [a]works, so that no one can [b]boast. [10]For we are [a]his creative work, having been created in Christ Jesus for good works that God prepared beforehand so we can do them.[1]

New Life Corporately

[11]Therefore remember that formerly you, [a]the Gentiles in the flesh—who are called "uncircumcision" by the so-called "circumcision" that is performed on the body by human hands—[12]that you were at that time without the Messiah,[1] alienated from the citizenship of Israel and strangers to the covenants of promise, having no hope and without God in the world. [13]But now in Christ Jesus you who used to be far away have been brought near by the blood of Christ. [14]For he is our peace, the one who made both groups into one and who destroyed the middle wall of partition, the hostility, [15]when he nullified[1] in his flesh the law of commandments in decrees. He did this to create in himself one [a]new man[2] out of two, thus making peace, [16]and to [a]reconcile them both [b]in one body to God through the cross, by which the hostility has been killed. [17]And he came and preached peace to you who were far off and peace to those who were near, [18]so that [a]through him we both have access [b]in one Spirit to the Father. [19]So then you are no longer foreigners

1:13 [a]John 1:17   [b][2 Cor 1:22]   1:14 [a]2 Cor 5:5   [b]Rom 8:23   [c][Acts 20:28]   [d]1 Pet 2:9   [1]Or *first installment, pledge, deposit.*   1:15 [1]Some wss omit *your love.*   1:16 [a]Rom 1:9   1:17 [a]John 20:17; Rom 15:6   1:18 [a]Acts 26:18; 2 Cor 4:6; Heb 6:4   [b]Eph 2:12   [1]‡ Some wss omit *your.*   [2]Grk. *of the glory of his inheritance.*   1:19 [a]Col 2:12   1:20 [a]Acts 2:24   [b]Ps 110:1   [1]Sev. sig. mss *by seating.*   1:21 [a]Isa 9:6–7; Luke 1:32–33; Phil 2:9–10; Rev 19:12   [b][Rom 8:38–39]   1:22 [a]Ps 8:6; 110:1; Matt 28:18; 1 Cor 15:27   [1][Ps 8:6]   1:23 [a]Rom 12:5   [b]Col 2:9   [c][1 Cor 12:6]   2:1 [a]Eph 2:5; Col 2:13   2:2 [a]Col 1:21   [b][John 12:31]; Eph 6:12   [c]Col 3:6   2:3 [a]1 Pet 4:3   [b]Gal 5:16   [c][Ps 51:5]   2:4 [a]John 3:16; 1 John 4:9–10   2:5 [a]Rom 5:6, 8   [b][Rom 6:4–5]   2:6 [a]Eph 1:20   2:7 [a]Titus 3:4   2:8 [a][2 Tim 1:9]   [b]Rom 4:16   [c][John 1:12–13]   [1]Some mss *through the faith.*   2:9 [a]Rom 4:4–5; 11:6   [b]Rom 3:27   2:10 [a]Isa 19:25   [1]Grk. *so that we might walk in them* (or *by them*).   2:11 [a][Rom 2:28; Col 2:11]   2:12 [1]Or *without Christ;* both "Christ" (Grk.) and "Messiah" (Heb., Aram.) mean "one who has been anointed."   2:15 [a]Gal 6:15   [1]Or *rendered inoperative.*   [2]I.e., a new corporate entity united in Christ.   2:16 [a]2 Cor 5:18; [Col 1:20–22]   [b][Rom 6:6]   2:18 [a]John 10:9   [b]1 Cor 12:13; Eph 4:4

and noncitizens, but you are fellow citizens with the saints and members of God's household, [20]because you have been [a]built [b]on the foundation of the [c]apostles and prophets, with Christ Jesus himself as [d]the cornerstone. [21]In him the whole building, being joined together, grows into [a]a holy temple in the Lord, [22][a]in whom you also are being built together into a dwelling [b]place of God in the Spirit.

Paul's Relationship to the Divine Mystery

3 For this reason I, Paul, the prisoner of Christ Jesus[1] for the sake of you Gentiles [2]if indeed you have heard of the stewardship of God's grace that was given to me for you, [3][a]that by revelation [b]the mystery[1] was made known to me, as I wrote before briefly. [4]When reading this, you will be able to understand my insight into the mystery[1] of Christ [5](which was not disclosed to people[1] in former generations as it has now been revealed to his holy apostles and prophets by the Spirit), [6]namely, that through the gospel the Gentiles are fellow heirs, fellow members of the body, and fellow partakers of the promise in Christ Jesus. [7]I became a servant [a]of this gospel [b]according to [c]the gift of God's grace that was given to me by the exercise of his power. [8]To me—less than [a]the least of all the saints—this grace was given, to proclaim to the Gentiles the unfathomable riches of Christ [9]and to enlighten everyone about God's secret plan—the mystery that has been hidden for ages in God who has [a]created all things. [10]The purpose of this enlightenment is that through the church the multifaceted wisdom of God should now be disclosed [a]to [b]the rulers and the authorities in the heavenly realms. [11]This was [a]according to the eternal purpose that he accomplished in Christ Jesus our Lord, [12][a]in whom we have boldness and confident access to God by way of Christ's faithfulness.[1] [13]For this [a]reason I ask you not to lose heart because of what I am suffering for you, [b]which is your glory.

Prayer for Strengthened Love

[14]For this reason I kneel before the [a]Father,[1] [15]from whom every family in heaven and on earth is named. [16]I pray that [a]according [b]to [c]the wealth of his glory he will grant you to be strengthened with power through his Spirit in the inner person, [17]that Christ will dwell in your hearts through faith, so [a]that, because you have been rooted and grounded [b]in love, [18][a]you will be able to comprehend with all the saints [b]what is the breadth and length and height and depth, [19]and thus to know the love of Christ that surpasses knowledge, so that you will be filled up [a]to all the fullness of God.

[20]Now [a]to him who by the power that is working within us is able to do far [b]beyond[1] all that we ask [c]or think, [21]to him be the glory in the church and in Christ Jesus [a]to all generations, forever and ever. Amen.

Live in Unity

4 I, therefore, the prisoner for the Lord, urge you to [a]live worthily of the calling with which you have been called, [2]with all humility and gentleness, with patience, putting up with one another in love, [3]making every effort to keep the unity of the Spirit [a]in the bond of peace. [4]There is one body and one Spirit, just as you too were called to [a]the one hope of your calling, [5][a]one Lord, one faith, one baptism, [6][a]one God and Father of all, who is over all and [b]through all and in all.

[7]But to each one of us grace was given according [a]to the measure of Christ's gift. [8]Therefore it says, "[a]*When he ascended on high he captured captives; he gave gifts to men.*"[1] [9][a]Now what is the meaning of "*he ascended,*" except that he also descended[1] to the lower regions,[2] namely, the earth?

2:20 [a]1 Pet 2:4 [b]Matt 16:18; 1 Cor 3:10–11; Rev 21:14 [c]1 Cor 12:28; Eph 3:5 [d]Ps 118:22; Luke 20:17 **2:21** [a]1 Cor 3:16–17 **2:22** [a]1 Pet 2:5 [b]John 17:23 **3:1** [1]Sev. sig. wss omit *Jesus*. **3:3** [a]Acts 22:17, 21; 26:16 [b][Rom 11:25; 16:25; Eph 3:4, 9; 6:19]; Col 1:26; 4:3 [1]Or *secret*; i.e., a divine secret previously undisclosed. **3:4** [1]Or *secret*; i.e., a divine secret previously undisclosed. **3:5** [1]Grk. *the sons of men*; a Semitic idiom referring to humans. **3:7** [a]Rom 15:16 [b]Rom 1:5 [c]Rom 15:18 **3:8** [a][Col 1:27; 2:2–3] **3:9** [a]John 1:3; Col 1:16; Heb 1:2 **3:10** [a]1 Pet 1:12 [b][1 Tim 3:16] **3:11** [a][Eph 1:4, 11] **3:12** [a]2 Cor 3:4; Heb 4:16; 10:19, 35; [1 John 2:28; 3:21] [1]Or *God through faith in him*. **3:13** [a]Phil 1:14 [b]2 Cor 1:6 **3:14** [a]Eph 1:3 [1]Sev. wss add *of our Lord Jesus Christ*. **3:16** [a][Eph 1:7; 2:4; Phil 4:19] [b]1 Cor 16:13; Phil 4:13; Col 1:11 [c]Rom 7:22 **3:17** [a]John 14:23; Rom 8:9; 2 Cor 13:5; [Eph 2:22] [b]Col 1:23 **3:18** [a]Eph 1:18 [b]Rom 8:39 **3:19** [a]Eph 1:23 **3:20** [a]Rom 16:25 [b]1 Cor 2:9 [c]Col 1:29 [1]Or *infinitely beyond, far more abundantly than*. **3:21** [a]Rom 11:36 **4:1** [a]Eph 2:10; [Col 1:10; 2:6]; 1 Thess 2:12 **4:3** [a]Col 3:14 **4:4** [a]Rom 12:5 **4:5** [a]1 Cor 12:12–13; [Heb 6:6] **4:6** [a]Mal 2:10; 1 Cor 8:6; 12:6 [b]Rom 11:36 **4:7** [a][1 Cor 12:7, 11] **4:8** [a]Ps 68:18; [Col 2:15] [1]Ps 68:18 **4:9** [a]Luke 23:43; John 3:13; 20:17; [1 Pet 3:19–20] [1]Maj. mss *he first descended*. [2]Some wss omit *regions*.

[10]He, the very one [a]who descended, is also the one who ascended above all the heavens, in order [b]to fill all things. [11]And he himself gave some as apostles, some as prophets, some as evangelists, and some as pastors and teachers, [12]to equip the saints [a]for [b]the work of ministry, that is, to build up the body of Christ, [13]until we all attain to the unity of the faith [a]and of the knowledge of the Son of God—[b]a mature person, attaining to the measure of Christ's full stature. [14]So we are no longer to be [a]children, tossed back and forth by waves and carried about by every wind of teaching by the trickery of people who craftily carry out their [b]deceitful schemes. [15]But practicing the truth in love, we will in all things grow up into Christ, who is the [a]head. [16a]From him the whole body grows, fitted and held together through every supporting ligament. As each one does its part, the body builds itself up in love.

Live in Holiness

[17]So I say this, and insist in the Lord, that you no [a]longer live as the Gentiles do, in the futility of their thinking. [18]They are darkened in their understanding, being alienated from the life of God because of the ignorance that is in them due to the [a]hardness of their hearts. [19]Because [a]they are callous, they [b]have given themselves over to indecency for the practice of every kind of impurity with greediness. [20]But you did not learn about Christ like this, [21]if indeed you heard about him and were taught in him, just as the truth is in Jesus. [22]You were taught with reference to your former way of life to lay [a]aside the old man who is being corrupted in accordance with deceitful desires, [23]to [a]be renewed in the spirit of your mind, [24]and to put [a]on the new man who has been created in God's image[1]—in righteousness and holiness that comes from truth.[2]

[25]Therefore, having laid aside falsehood, *each one of you speak the truth with his neighbor*[1] because [a]we are members of one another. [26a]*Be angry and do not sin;*[1] do not let the sun go down on the cause of your anger. [27]Do [a]not give the devil an opportunity. [28]The one who steals must steal no longer; instead he must labor, doing good with his own hands, so that he will have something [a]to share with the one who has need. [29]You must [a]let no unwholesome word come out of your mouth, but only [b]what is beneficial for the building up of the one in need, [c]that it would give grace to those who hear. [30]And [a]do not grieve the Holy Spirit of God, by whom you were sealed for the day of redemption. [31a]You must put away all bitterness, anger, wrath, quarreling, and slanderous talk—indeed all malice. [32]Instead,[1] [a]be kind to one another, compassionate, [b]forgiving one another, just as God in Christ also forgave you.

Live in Love

5 [a]Therefore, be imitators of God as dearly loved [b]children [2]and [a]live in love, just [b]as Christ also loved us[1] and gave himself [c]for us, a sacrificial and fragrant offering to God. [3]But among you there must not be either sexual immorality, [a]impurity of any kind, or [b]greed, as these are not fitting for the saints. [4a]Neither should there be vulgar speech, foolish [b]talk, or coarse jesting—all of [c]which are out of character—but rather [d]thanksgiving. [5]For you can be confident of this one thing: that no person who is immoral, impure, or greedy (such a person is an idolater) has any [a]inheritance in the kingdom of Christ and God.

Live in the Light

[6]Let nobody deceive you with empty words, for because of these things God's wrath comes on the sons of disobedience. [7]Therefore do not be sharers [a]with them, [8]for you were at one time darkness, but now you are [a]light in the Lord. Live like children of light—[9]for [a]the fruit of the light[1] consists in all goodness, righteousness, and

4:10 [a] Acts 1:9 [b] [Acts 2:33; Eph 1:23] **4:12** [a] 1 Cor 14:26 [b] Col 1:24 **4:13** [a] Col 2:2 [b] 1 Cor 14:20; Col 1:28; Heb 5:14 **4:14** [a] 1 Cor 14:20 [b] Rom 16:18 **4:15** [a] Eph 1:22 **4:16** [a] [Rom 12:4]; Col 2:19 **4:17** [a] Eph 2:2; 4:22 **4:18** [a] Rom 1:21 **4:19** [a] 1 Tim 4:2 [b] 1 Pet 4:3 **4:22** [a] Col 3:8 **4:23** [a] [Rom 12:2; Col 3:10] **4:24** [a] [Rom 6:4; 7:6; 12:2; 2 Cor 5:17; Col 3:10] [1] Or *God's likeness*; Grk. *according to God.* [2] Or *holiness which is based on truth, originated from truth.* **4:25** [a] Rom 12:5 [1] Zech 8:16 **4:26** [a] Ps 4:4; 37:8 [1] Ps 4:4 **4:27** [a] [Rom 12:19; Jas 4:7]; 1 Pet 5:9 **4:28** [a] Luke 3:11; 1 Thess 4:12 **4:29** [a] Matt 12:34; Eph 5:4; Col 3:8 [b] 1 Thess 5:11 [c] Col 3:16 **4:30** [a] Isa 7:13 **4:31** [a] Rom 3:14; Col 3:8, 19 **4:32** [a] [Matt 6:14]; 2 Cor 6:10 [b] [Mark 11:25; Luke 6:37] [1] ‡ A few sig. MSS omit *instead.* **5:1** [a] [Matt 5:48]; Luke 6:36; Eph 4:32 [b] 1 Pet 1:14–16 **5:2** [a] 1 Thess 4:9 [b] John 15:9; Gal 1:4; 1 John 3:16 [c] Exod 29:18, 25; 2 Cor 2:14–15 [1] Some sig. WSS *you.* **5:3** [a] Col 3:5–7 [b] [Luke 12:15] **5:4** [a] Matt 12:34–35; Eph 4:29; Col 3:8; Jas 1:21 [b] Titus 3:9 [c] Rom 1:28 [d] Phil 4:6; Col 3:17; [1 Thess 5:18] **5:5** [a] 1 Cor 6:9–10; Col 3:5 **5:7** [a] 1 Tim 5:22 **5:8** [a] 1 Thess 5:5 **5:9** [a] Gal 5:22 [1] Several MSS *Spirit.*

truth—[10]trying to [a]learn what is pleasing to the Lord. [11]Do [a]not participate in the unfruitful deeds of darkness, but rather expose them. [12a]For the things they do in secret are shameful even to mention. [13]But all [a]things being exposed by the light are made visible. [14]For everything made visible is light, and for this reason it says:

"[a]Awake, O sleeper!
  Rise from the dead,
  and Christ will shine on you!"[1]

Live Wisely

[15]Therefore [a]consider carefully how you live—not as unwise but as wise, [16]taking [a]advantage of every opportunity [b]because the days are evil. [17a]For this reason do not be foolish, but be wise by [b]understanding[1] [c]what the Lord's will is. [18]And [a]do not get drunk with wine, which is debauchery, but be filled by the Spirit, [19]speaking to one another [a]in psalms, hymns, and spiritual songs, singing and making [b]music in your hearts to the Lord, [20]always [a]giving thanks to God the Father for all things [b]in the name of our Lord Jesus Christ, [21]and submitting [a]to one another out of reverence for Christ.

Exhortations to Households

[22]Wives, [a]submit[1] to your husbands as to the Lord, [23]because [a]the husband is the head of the wife as also [b]Christ is the head of the church (he himself being the savior of the body). [24]But as the church submits to Christ, so also wives should submit to their husbands [a]in everything. [25a]Husbands, love your wives just as Christ loved the church and [b]gave himself for her [26]to sanctify her by cleansing her [a]with the washing of the water [b]by the word, [27]so [a]that he may present the church to himself as glorious—[b]not having a stain or wrinkle, or any such blemish, but holy and blameless. [28]In the same way husbands ought to love their wives as their own bodies. He who loves his wife loves himself. [29]For no one has ever hated his own body, but he feeds it and takes care of it, just as Christ also does the church, [30]because [a]we are members of his body.[1] [31a]*For this reason a man will leave his father and mother and will be joined to his wife, and the [b]two will become one flesh.*[1] [32]This mystery is great—but I am actually speaking with reference to Christ and the church. [33]Nevertheless, each one of you must also love his own wife as he loves himself, and the wife must [a]respect her husband.

6 Children, [a]obey your parents in the Lord,[1] for this is right. [2a]*Honor your father and mother,*"[1] which is the first commandment accompanied by a promise, namely, [3]*"that it will go well with you and that you will live a long time on the earth."*[1]

[4]Fathers, do not provoke [a]your children to anger, but [b]raise them up in the discipline and instruction of the Lord.

[5a]Slaves, obey your human masters [b]with fear and trembling, [c]in the sincerity of your heart, as to Christ, [6a]not like those who do their work only when someone is watching[1]—as people-pleasers—but as slaves of Christ doing the will of God from the heart. [7]Obey with enthusiasm, as though serving the Lord and not people, [8]because you [a]know that each person, whether slave or free, if he does something good, this will be rewarded by the Lord.

[9]Masters, treat your slaves the same way, giving up the use of threats, because you know that both you and they have the same [a]master in heaven, and [b]there is no favoritism with him.

Exhortations for Spiritual Warfare

[10]Finally, be strengthened in the Lord and in the strength of his power. [11a]Clothe yourselves with the full armor of God, so that you will be able to stand against the schemes of the devil. [12]For our struggle is not against flesh and blood, but against the rulers, against the powers, against the world

5:10 [a][Rom 12:1–2]   5:11 [a]1 Cor 5:9; 2 Cor 6:14   5:12 [a]Rom 1:24   5:13 [a][John 3:20–21]   5:14 [a][Isa 26:19; 60:1; Rom 13:11]   [1]Isa 26:19; 51:17; 52:1; 60:1   5:15 [a]Col 4:5   5:16 [a]Col 4:5   [b]Eccl 11:2   5:17 [a]Col 4:5   [b][Rom 12:2]; Col 1:9   [c]1 Thess 4:3   [1]‡ Some wss *being wise.*   5:18 [a]Prov 20:1; 23:31; Rom 13:13; 1 Cor 5:11; 1 Thess 5:7   5:19 [a]Acts 16:25   [b]Jas 5:13   5:20 [a]Ps 34:1   [b][1 Pet 2:5]   5:21 [a][Phil 2:3]; 1 Pet 5:5   5:22 [a]Eph 5:22–6:9; Col 3:18–4:1; 1 Pet 3:1–6   [1]Some wss omit *submit.*   5:23 [a][1 Cor 11:3]   [b]Col 1:18   5:24 [a]Titus 2:4–5   5:25 [a]Eph 5:28, 33; Col 3:19; [1 Pet 3:7]   [b]Acts 20:28   5:26 [a]John 3:5   [b][John 15:3; 17:17; Rom 10:8; Eph 6:17]   5:27 [a][2 Cor 4:14; 11:2]; Col 1:22   [b]Song 4:7   5:30 [a]Gen 2:23   [1]Maj. wss add *of his flesh and of his bones*; assuming an allusion to Gen 2:23.   5:31 [a]Gen 2:24; Matt 19:5; Mark 10:7   [b][1 Cor 6:16]   [1]Gen 2:24   5:33 [a]1 Pet 3:1, 6   6:1 [a]Prov 6:20; 23:22; Col 3:20   [1]Some mss omit *in the Lord.*   6:2 [a]Exod 20:12; Deut 5:16   [1]Exod 20:12; Deut 5:16   6:3 [1]Exod 20:12; Deut 5:16   6:4 [a]Col 3:21   [b]Gen 18:19; Deut 6:7; 11:19; Ps 78:4; Prov 22:6; 2 Tim 3:15   6:5 [a]Col 3:22; [1 Tim 6:1]; Titus 2:9; 1 Pet 2:18   [b]2 Cor 7:15   [c]1 Chr 29:17   6:6 [a]Col 3:22   [1]Grk. *not according to eye-service.*   6:8 [a]Rom 2:6   6:9 [a]Job 31:13; John 13:13; Col 4:1   [b]Deut 10:17; Acts 10:34; Rom 2:11; Col 3:25   6:11 [a][2 Cor 6:7]

rulers of this darkness, against the spiritual forces of evil [a]in [b]the heavens. [13]For this reason, take up [a]the full armor of God so that you may be able to stand your ground[1] [b]on the evil day, and having done everything, to stand. [14]Stand firm therefore, by fastening the belt of truth around your waist,[1] by putting on the breastplate of righteousness, [15a]by fitting your feet with the preparation that comes from the good news of peace, [16]and in all of this, by taking up [a]the shield of faith with which you can extinguish all the flaming arrows of the evil one. [17]And [a]take [b]*the helmet of salvation*[1] and the sword of the Spirit (which is the word of God). [18]With every prayer and petition, [a]pray at all times [b]in the Spirit, and to this end be alert, with all perseverance and [c]petitions for all the saints. [19]Pray for me also, [a]that I may be given the right words when I begin to speak—that I may confidently make known the mystery of the gospel, [20]for [a]which I am an ambassador in chains. Pray that I may be able to speak boldly as I ought to speak.

Farewell Comments

[21a]Tychicus, my dear brother and [b]faithful servant in the Lord, will make everything known to you, so that you too may know about my circumstances, how I am doing. [22]I have sent [a]him to you for this very purpose, that you may know our circumstances and that he may [b]encourage your hearts.

[23]Peace to the brothers and sisters,[1] and love with faith, from God the Father and the Lord Jesus Christ. [24]Grace be with all those who love our Lord Jesus Christ with an undying love.[1]

6:12 [a] Rom 8:38   [b] Luke 22:53   6:13 [a] [2 Cor 10:4]   [b] Eph 5:16   [1] With the idea of resisting, standing firm, or standing one's ground.   6:14 [1] Grk. *girding your waist with truth.*   6:15 [a] Isa 52:7; Rom 10:15   6:16 [a] 1 John 5:4   6:17 [a] 1 Thess 5:8   [b] Isa 49:2; Hos 6:5; [Heb 4:12]   [1] [Isa 59:17]   6:18 [a] Luke 18:1; Col 1:3; 4:2; 1 Thess 5:17   [b] [Matt 26:41]   [c] Phil 1:4   6:19 [a] Acts 4:29; Col 4:3   6:20 [a] 2 Cor 5:20; Phlm 9   6:21 [a] Acts 20:4; 2 Tim 4:12; Titus 3:12   [b] 1 Cor 4:1–2   6:22 [a] Col 4:8   [b] 2 Cor 1:6   6:23 [1] Grk. *brothers*; considerable external evidence supports use of the Grk. word as *brothers and sisters* or *fellow Christians.*   6:24 [1] Maj. wss add *amen.*

PHILIPPIANS

Paul writes a thank-you note to the believers at Philippi for their help in his hour of need, and he uses the occasion to send along some instruction on Christian unity. His central thought is simple: Only in Christ are real unity and joy possible. With Christ as your model of humility and service, you can enjoy a oneness of purpose, attitude, goal, and labor—a truth that Paul illustrates from his own life and one the Philippians desperately need to hear. Within their own ranks, fellow workers in the Philippian church are at odds, hindering the work in proclaiming new life in Christ. Because of this, Paul exhorts the church to "stand in the Lord … Agree in the Lord … Rejoice in the Lord always … In every situation, through prayer and petition with thanksgiving, tell your requests to God … And the peace of God that surpasses all understanding will guard your hearts and minds in Christ Jesus" (4:1–2, 4, 6–7). This epistle is called *Pros Philippesious*, "To the Philippians." The church at Philippi was the first church Paul founded in Macedonia.

Salutation

1 From Paul and Timothy, slaves[1] of Christ Jesus, to all the saints in Christ Jesus who are in Philippi, with the overseers and [a]deacons. [2]Grace and peace to you from God our Father and the Lord Jesus Christ!

Prayer for the Church

[3]I thank my God every [a]time I remember you. [4]I always pray with joy in my [a]every prayer for all of you [5][a]because of your participation in the gospel from the first day until now. [6]For I [a]am sure of this very thing, that the one who began a good work in you will perfect it until the day of Christ Jesus. [7]For it is right for me to think this about all of you, because I have you in my heart, since both in my imprisonment and in the defense and confirmation of the gospel all of you became partners in God's grace together with me. [8]For God is my witness that I long for all of you with the affection of Christ Jesus. [9]And I pray this, that your love may abound even more and more in knowledge and every kind of insight [10]so that you can decide what is best, and thus be sincere and blameless for the day of Christ, [11]filled with the fruit of righteousness that comes through Jesus Christ [a]to the glory and praise of God.

Ministry as a Prisoner

[12]I want you to know, brothers and sisters,[1] that my situation has actually turned out to advance the gospel: [13]The whole imperial guard and everyone else knows that I am in prison for the sake [a]of Christ, [14]and most of the brothers and sisters,[1] having confidence in the Lord because of my imprisonment, now more than ever dare to speak the word[2] fearlessly.

[15]Some, to be sure, are preaching Christ from envy and rivalry, but others from goodwill. [16]The latter do so from love because they know that I am placed here for the defense of the gospel. [17]The former proclaim Christ from selfish ambition, not sincerely, because they think they can cause trouble for me in my imprisonment. [18]What is the result? Only that in every way, whether in pretense or in truth, Christ is being proclaimed, and in this I rejoice.

Yes, and I will continue to rejoice, [19]for I know that [a]this will turn out for my

---

1:1 [a][1 Tim 3:8–13]   [1]Trad. *servants*; but the word does not connote a free individual serving another person.   1:3 [a]1 Cor 1:4   1:4 [a]Eph 1:16; 1 Thess 1:2   1:5 [a][Rom 12:13]   1:6 [a][John 6:29]   1:11 [a]John 15:8   1:12 [1]Grk. *brothers*; considerable external evidence supports use of the Grk. word as *brothers and sisters* or *fellow Christians*.   1:13 [a]Phil 4:22   1:14 [1]Grk. *brothers*; considerable external evidence supports use of the Grk. word as *brothers and sisters* or *fellow Christians*.   [2]Sev. sig. MSS add *of God*.   1:19 [a]Job 13:16, LXX

deliverance through your prayers and the help of the Spirit of Jesus Christ. [20]My confident hope is that I will in no way be ashamed but that [a]with complete boldness, even now as always, Christ will be exalted in my body, whether I live [b]or die. [21]For to me, living is Christ and dying is gain. [22]Now if I am to go on living in the body, this will mean productive work for me, yet I don't know which I prefer: [23]I feel torn between the two because I have a [a]desire to depart and be with Christ, which is better by [b]far, [24]but it is more vital for your sake that I remain in the body. [25]And since I am sure of this, I know that I will remain and continue with all of you for the sake of your progress and joy in the faith, [26]so that what [a]you can be proud of may increase[1] because of me in Christ Jesus, when I come back to you.

[27]Only conduct yourselves in a manner worthy of the gospel of Christ so that—whether [a]I come and see you or whether I remain absent—I should hear that you are standing firm in one spirit, with one mind, by contending side by [b]side for the faith of the gospel, [28]and by not being intimidated in any way by your opponents. This is a sign of their destruction, but of your salvation—a sign which is from God. [29]For [a]it has been granted to you [b]not only to believe in Christ but also to [c]suffer for him, [30]since you are [a]encountering the same conflict [b]that you saw me face and now hear that I am facing.

Christian Unity and Christ's Humility

2 Therefore, if there is any encouragement in Christ, any comfort provided by love, any fellowship in the Spirit, any [a]affection or mercy, [2a]complete my joy and be of the same mind, [b]by having the same love, being united in spirit, and having [c]one purpose. [3a]Instead of [b]being motivated by selfish ambition[1] or vanity, each of you should, in humility, be moved to treat one another as more important than yourself. [4a]Each of you should be concerned not only about your own interests, but about the interests of [b]others as well.[1] [5a]You should have the same attitude toward one another that Christ Jesus had,[1]

6 who, though he [a]existed in the form of God,
did not regard equality with God as something to be grasped,
7 [a]but emptied himself by taking on the form [b]of a slave,
by looking like other men,
and by sharing [c]in human nature.
8 He humbled himself by [a]becoming [b]obedient to the point of death
—even death on a cross!
9 As a [a]result God highly exalted him and [b]gave him the name
that is above every name,
10 so [a]that at the name of Jesus every knee will bow
—in heaven and on earth and under the earth—
11 and every tongue confess [a]that Jesus Christ is Lord
to the glory of God the Father.

Lights in the World

[12]So then, my dear friends, just [a]as you have always obeyed, not only in my presence but even more in my absence, continue working [b]out your salvation with [c]awe and reverence, [13]for the one bringing forth in you both the desire and the effort—for the sake [a]of his good pleasure—is God. [14]Do everything [a]without grumbling or [b]arguing, [15]so that you may be blameless and pure, children of God without blemish though you live in a crooked and perverse society, in which you shine as [a]lights in the world [16]by holding on to the word of life so that on the day of Christ [a]I [b]will have a reason to

1:20 [a]Eph 6:19–20   [b][Rom 14:8]   1:23 [a][2 Cor 5:2, 8]; 2 Tim 4:6   [b][Ps 16:11]   1:26 [a]2 Cor 1:14   [1]Grk. *your boasting may overflow in Christ Jesus because of me*; or possibly *your boasting in me may overflow in Christ Jesus.*   1:27 [a]1 Cor 1:10; Eph 4:3   [b]Jude 3   1:29 [a][Matt 5:11–12; Acts 5:41; Rom 5:3]   [b]Eph 2:8   [c][2 Tim 3:12]   1:30 [a]Col 1:29; 2:1; 1 Thess 2:2; 1 Tim 6:12; 2 Tim 4:7; Heb 10:32; 12:1   [b]Acts 16:19–40; Phil 1:13; 1 Thess 2:2   2:1 [a]Col 3:12   2:2 [a]John 3:29   [b]Rom 12:16   [c]Phil 4:2   2:3 [a]Gal 5:26; Jas 3:14   [b]Rom 12:10; Eph 5:21   [1]Grk. *not according to selfish ambition*; i.e., "Don't even *think* any thoughts motivated by selfish ambition."   2:4 [a]1 Cor 13:5   [b]Rom 15:1–2   [1]Many wss omit *as well.*   2:5 [a][Matt 11:29]; Rom 15:3   [1]Grk. *Have this attitude in/among yourselves which also* [was] *in Christ Jesus, Have this attitude in/among yourselves which* [you] *also* [have] *in Christ Jesus.*   2:6 [a]2 Cor 4:4   2:7 [a]Ps 22:6   [b]Isa 42:1   [c][John 1:14]; Rom 8:3; Gal 4:4; [Heb 2:17]   2:8 [a]Ps 40:6–8; Matt 26:39; John 10:18; [Rom 5:19]   [b]Heb 5:8   2:9 [a][Matt 28:18]; Heb 2:9   [b]Isa 9:6; Luke 1:32; Eph 1:21   2:10 [a]Isa 45:23; Rom 14:11; Rev 5:13   2:11 [a]John 13:13; [Rom 10:9; 14:9]   2:12 [a]Phil 1:5–6; 4:15   [b]John 6:27, 29; 2 Pet 1:10   [c]Eph 6:5   2:13 [a]Eph 1:5   2:14 [a]1 Cor 10:10; 1 Pet 4:9   [b]Rom 14:1   2:15 [a]Matt 5:15–16   2:16 [a]2 Cor 1:14   [b]Gal 2:2

boast: that I did not run in [c]vain nor labor in vain. [17]But even [a]if I am being poured out like a drink offering on the sacrifice [b]and [c]service of your faith, I am glad and rejoice together with all of you. [18]And in the same way you also should be glad and rejoice together with me.

Models for Ministry

[19]Now I hope in the Lord Jesus to send [a]Timothy to you soon, so that I, too, may be encouraged by hearing news about you. [20]For there is no one here [a]like him who will readily demonstrate his deep concern for you. [21]Others are busy with their own concerns, not those of Jesus Christ. [22]But you know his qualifications [a]that like a son working with his father, he served with me in advancing the gospel. [23]So I hope to send him as soon as I know more about my situation, [24]though I am confident in the Lord that I, too, will be coming to see you soon.

[25]But for now I have considered it necessary to send [a]Epaphroditus to you. For he is my brother, coworker and [b]fellow soldier, [c]and your messenger and minister to me in my need. [26a]Indeed, he greatly missed all of you and was distressed because you heard that he had been ill. [27]In fact he became so ill that he nearly died. But God showed mercy to him—and not to him only, but also to me—so that I would not have grief on top of grief. [28]Therefore I am all the more eager to send him, so that when you see him again you can rejoice and I can be free from anxiety. [29]So welcome him in the Lord with great joy, and honor people like him, [30]since it was because of the work of Christ that he almost died. He risked his life so [a]that he could make up for your inability to serve me.

True and False Righteousness

3 Finally, my brothers and sisters,[1] [a]rejoice in the Lord! To write this again is no trouble to me, and it is a safeguard for you. [2]Beware of the dogs, [a]beware of the [b]evil workers, [c]beware of those who mutilate the flesh! [3]For we are [a]the circumcision, the ones [b]who worship by the Spirit of God,[1] exult in Christ Jesus, and do not rely on human credentials [4]—though mine, too, are significant. If someone thinks he has good reasons to put confidence in human credentials, [a]I have [b]more: [5]I was circumcised on the eighth day, from the people [a]of [b]Israel [c]and the tribe of Benjamin, a Hebrew of Hebrews. I lived according to the law as a Pharisee. [6]In my zeal for God I [a]persecuted the church. According to the righteousness stipulated in the law I was blameless. [7]But these assets I have come to regard as liabilities because of Christ. [8]More than that, I now regard all things as liabilities compared to the far greater value of knowing Christ Jesus my Lord, [a]for whom I have suffered the loss of all things—indeed, I regard them as dung!—that I may gain Christ [9]and be found in him, not because I have my [a]own righteousness derived from the law, but because I have the righteousness [b]that comes by way of Christ's faithfulness—a righteousness from God that is in fact based on Christ's faithfulness. [10]My aim is to know him, to experience the [a]power of his resurrection, to share in his sufferings, and to be like him in his death, [11]and so, somehow, to [a]attain to the resurrection from the dead.

Keep Going Forward

[12]Not that I have already [a]attained this— that is, I have not already been [b]perfected— but I strive to lay hold of that for which Christ Jesus also laid hold of me. [13]Brothers and sisters,[1] I do not consider myself to have attained this. Instead I am single-minded: [a]Forgetting the things that are behind and [b]reaching out for the things that are ahead, [14]with [a]this goal in mind, I strive toward [b]the prize of the upward call of God in Christ Jesus. [15]Therefore let those of us who are "[a]perfect" embrace this point of view. If you think otherwise, [b]God will reveal to you the error of your ways. [16]Nevertheless,

2:16 [c]Isa 49:4; Gal 4:11; 1 Thess 3:5   **2:17** [a]2 Cor 12:15; 2 Tim 4:6   [b]Num 28:6–7; Rom 15:16   [c]2 Cor 7:4   **2:19** [a]Rom 16:21   **2:20** [a]1 Cor 16:10; 2 Tim 3:10   **2:22** [a]1 Cor 4:17   **2:25** [a]Phil 4:18   [b]Phlm 2   [c]John 13:16; 2 Cor 8:23   **2:26** [a]Phil 1:8   **2:30** [a]1 Cor 16:17; Phil 4:10   **3:1** [a]1 Thess 5:16   [1]Grk. *brothers*; considerable external evidence supports use of the Grk. word as *brothers and sisters* or *fellow Christians*.   **3:2** [a]Ps 22:16, 20; Gal 5:15; Rev 22:15   [b]Ps 119:115   [c]Rom 2:28   **3:3** [a]Deut 30:6; Rom 2:28–29; 9:6; [Gal 6:15]   [b]John 4:24; Rom 7:6   [1]Sev. sig. wss *worship God by the Spirit*.   **3:4** [a]2 Cor 5:16; 11:18   [b]2 Cor 11:22–23   **3:5** [a]Rom 11:1   [b]2 Cor 11:22   [c]Acts 23:6   **3:6** [a]Acts 8:3; 22:4–5; 26:9–11   **3:8** [a]Isa 53:11; Jer 9:23; John 17:3; 1 Cor 2:2; [Eph 4:13]   **3:9** [a]Rom 10:3   [b]Rom 1:17   **3:10** [a]Eph 1:19–20   **3:11** [a]Acts 26:6–8; [1 Cor 15:23; Rev 20:5]   **3:12** [a]1 Cor 9:24; [1 Tim 6:12, 19]   [b]Heb 12:23   **3:13** [a]Luke 9:62   [b]Heb 6:1   [1]Grk. *brothers*; considerable external evidence supports use of the Grk. word as *brothers and sisters* or *fellow Christians*.   **3:14** [a]2 Tim 4:7   [b]Heb 3:1   **3:15** [a]Matt 5:48; 1 Cor 2:6   [b]Hos 6:3; Jas 1:5

[a]let us live up to the standard[1] that we have already attained.

[17a]Be imitators of me, brothers and sisters,[1] and watch carefully those who are living this way, just as [b]you have us as an example. [18]For many live, about whom I have often told you, and now, with tears, I tell you that [a]they are the enemies of the cross of Christ. [19a]Their end is destruction, [b]their god is the belly, they exult in their shame, and they think about earthly things. [20]But [a]our citizenship is in heaven—and we also eagerly await a savior [b]from there, the Lord Jesus Christ, [21a]who will transform these humble bodies of ours into the [b]likeness of his glorious body by means [c]of that power by which he is able to [d]subject all things to himself.

Christian Practices

4 So then, my brothers and sisters,[1] dear friends whom I long to [a]see, [b]my joy [c]and crown, stand in the Lord in this way, my dear friends!

[2]I appeal [a]to Euodia and to Syntyche to agree in the Lord. [3]Yes, I say also to you, true companion, help them. They have struggled [a]together in [b]the gospel ministry along with me and Clement and my other coworkers, whose names are in the book of life. [4a]Rejoice in the Lord always. Again I say, rejoice! [5]Let everyone see your gentleness. [a]The Lord is near! [6]Do not [a]be anxious about anything. Instead, in every situation, through prayer and petition with [b]thanksgiving, tell your requests to God. [7]And [a]the peace of God that surpasses all understanding will guard your hearts and minds in Christ Jesus.

[8]Finally, brothers and sisters,[1] whatever is [a]true, whatever is worthy of [b]respect, whatever is [c]just, [d]whatever is pure, whatever is [e]lovely, whatever is commendable, if something is excellent or praiseworthy, think about these things. [9]And what you learned and received and heard and saw in me, do [a]these things. And the God of peace will be with you.

Appreciation for Support

[10]I have great joy in the Lord because now at last [a]you have again expressed your concern for me. (Now I know you were concerned before but had no opportunity to do anything.)[1] [11]I am not saying this because I am in need, for I have learned [a]to be content in any circumstance. [12]I have [a]experienced times of need and times of abundance. In any and every circumstance I have learned the secret of contentment, whether I go satisfied or hungry, have plenty or nothing. [13]I am able to do all things [a]through the one[1] who strengthens me. [14]Nevertheless, [a]you did well to share with me in my trouble.

[15]And as you Philippians know, at the beginning of my gospel ministry, when I left Macedonia, [a]no church shared with me in this matter of giving and receiving except you alone. [16]For even in Thessalonica on more than one occasion you sent something for my need. [17]I do not say this because I am seeking a gift. [a]Rather, I seek the credit that abounds to your account. [18]For I have received everything, and I have plenty. I have all I need because I received from [a]Epaphroditus [b]what you sent—[c]a fragrant offering, an acceptable sacrifice, very pleasing to God. [19]And my God will supply your [a]every need according to his glorious riches in Christ Jesus. [20a]May glory be given to God our Father forever and ever. Amen.

Final Greetings

[21]Give greetings to all the saints in Christ Jesus. The brothers[1] with me here send greetings. [22]All the saints greet you, especially those who belong to Caesar's household. [23]The grace of the Lord Jesus Christ be with your spirit.[1]

3:16 [a]Gal 6:16 [1]Some wss omit *standard* or place it elsewhere in the verse.   3:17 [a][1 Cor 4:16; 11:1]; Phil 4:9 [b]Titus 2:7–8; 1 Pet 5:3 [1]Grk. *brothers*; considerable external evidence supports use of the Grk. word as *brothers and sisters* or *fellow Christians*.   3:18 [a]Gal 1:7   3:19 [a]2 Cor 11:15 [b]1 Tim 6:5   3:20 [a]Eph 2:6, 19; Phil 1:27; [Col 3:1; Heb 12:22] [b]Acts 1:11 3:21 [a][1 Cor 15:43–53] [b]1 John 3:2 [c]Eph 1:19 [d][1 Cor 15:28]   4:1 [a]Phil 1:8 [b]2 Cor 1:14 [c]1 Cor 16:13; Phil 1:27 [1]Grk. *brothers*; considerable external evidence supports use of the Grk. word as *brothers and sisters* or *fellow Christians*.   4:2 [a]Phil 2:2; 3:16   4:3 [a]Rom 16:3 [b]Exod 32:32; Luke 10:20   4:4 [a]Rom 12:12   4:5 [a]1 Cor 16:22; Heb 10:25, 37; [Jas 5:7–9]; Rev 22:7, 20 4:6 [a]Ps 55:22; Matt 6:25; 1 Pet 5:7 [b][1 Thess 5:17–18]   4:7 [a][Isa 26:3; John 14:27]; Phil 4:9; Col 3:15   4:8 [a]Eph 4:25 [b]2 Cor 8:21 [c]Deut 16:20 [d]1 Thess 5:22; Jas 3:17 [e]1 Cor 13:4–7 [1]Grk. *brothers*; considerable external evidence supports use of the Grk. word as *brothers and sisters* or *fellow Christians*.   4:9 [a]Rom 15:33; Heb 13:20   4:10 [a]2 Cor 11:9; Phil 2:30 [1]Grk. *for you were even concerned, but you lacked opportunity*.   4:11 [a]2 Cor 9:8; 1 Tim 6:6, 8; Heb 13:5   4:12 [a]1 Cor 4:11   4:13 [a]John 15:5 [1]Maj. wss *through Christ*.   4:14 [a]Phil 1:7   4:15 [a]2 Cor 11:8–9   4:17 [a]Titus 3:14   4:18 [a]Phil 2:25 [b]Heb 13:16 [c]Rom 12:1; 2 Cor 9:12   4:19 [a]Ps 23:1; 2 Cor 9:8   4:20 [a]Rom 16:27   4:21 [1]Or perhaps *brothers and sisters*; it is more probable that only Paul's traveling companions are in view.   4:23 [1]Maj. wss add *amen*.

COLOSSIANS

If Ephesians can be labeled the epistle portraying the church of Christ, then Colossians must surely reveal the Christ of the church. Ephesians focuses on the body; Colossians focuses on the Head. Like Ephesians, the little Book of Colossians divides neatly in half with the first portion doctrinal (1–2) and the second practical (3–4). Paul's purpose is to show that Christ is preeminent—first and foremost in everything—and the Christian's life should reflect that priority. Because believers are rooted in him, alive in him, hidden in him, and complete in him, it is utterly inconsistent for them to live life without him. Clothed in his love, with his peace ruling in their hearts, they are equipped to make Christ first in every area of life. This epistle became known as *Pros Kolossaeis*, "To the Colossians," because of 1:2. Paul also wanted it to be read in the neighboring church at Laodicea (4:16).

Salutation

1 From Paul, [a]an apostle of Christ Jesus by the will of God, and Timothy our brother, [2]to the saints, the faithful brothers and sisters[1] in Christ, at Colossae. [b]Grace and peace to you from God our Father![2]

Paul's Thanksgiving and Prayer for the Church

[3]We always give thanks to God, the Father of our Lord Jesus Christ, when [a]we pray for you, [4]since we heard about your faith [a]in Christ Jesus and the love that [b]you have for all the saints. [5]Your faith and love have arisen from the hope laid up[1] for you in heaven, [a]which you have heard about in the message of truth, the gospel [6]that [a]has come to you. Just as in the entire world this gospel [b]is bearing fruit and growing, so it has also been bearing fruit and growing among you from [c]the first day you heard it and understood the grace of God in truth. [7]You learned the gospel from [a]Epaphras, our [b]dear fellow slave—a faithful minister of Christ on our[1] behalf—[8]who also told us of your [a]love in the Spirit.

Paul's Prayer for the Growth of the Church

[9a]For this reason we also, from the day we heard about you, have not ceased praying for you and asking God [b]to fill you with [c]the knowledge of his will [d]in all spiritual wisdom and understanding, [10]so [a]that you may live worthily of the Lord and please him in all [b]respects—bearing fruit [c]in every good deed, growing in the [d]knowledge of God, [11]being [a]strengthened with all power according to his glorious might [b]for the display of all patience and steadfastness, [c]joyfully [12]giving thanks to the Father who has qualified you to share [a]in [b]the saints' inheritance in the light. [13]He delivered us from [a]the power of darkness [b]and transferred us to the kingdom of the Son he loves, [14a]in whom we have redemption,[1] the forgiveness of sins.

The Supremacy of Christ

[15] He is [a]the image of [b]the invisible God,
the firstborn[1] over all creation,
[16] for all things [a]in heaven and on
earth were created in him—all

1:1 [a]Eph 1:1   1:2 [a]1 Cor 4:17   [b]Gal 1:3   [1]Grk. *brothers*; considerable external evidence supports use of the Grk. word as *brothers and sisters* or *fellow Christians*.   [2]Maj. wss add *and the Lord Jesus Christ*.   1:3 [a]1 Cor 1:4; Eph 1:16; Phil 1:3   1:4 [a]Eph 1:15   [b][Heb 6:10]   1:5 [a][1 Pet 1:4]   [1]Or *reserved*.   1:6 [a]Matt 24:14   [b]John 15:16   [c]Eph 3:2   1:7 [a]Col 4:12; Phlm 23   [b]1 Cor 4:1–2; 2 Cor 11:23   [1]‡ Some wss *your*.   1:8 [a]Rom 15:30   1:9 [a]Eph 1:15–17   [b]1 Cor 1:5   [c][Rom 12:2]; Eph 5:17   [d]Eph 1:8   1:10 [a]Eph 4:1; Phil 1:27; 1 Thess 2:12   [b]1 Thess 4:1   [c]Heb 13:21   [d]2 Pet 3:18   1:11 [a][Eph 3:16; 6:10]   [b]Eph 4:2   [c][Acts 5:41]; 2 Cor 8:2; [Heb 10:34]   1:12 [a][Eph 5:20]   [b]Eph 1:11   1:13 [a]Eph 6:12   [b]2 Pet 1:11   1:14 [a]Eph 1:7   [1]Sev. wss add *through his blood*.   1:15 [a]2 Cor 4:4; Heb 1:3   [b]Ps 89:27; Rev 3:14   [1]Either a firstborn child or one who is preeminent in rank (the word is used of the Davidic king in Ps 89:27); here, it is used in this latter sense.   1:16 [a]John 1:3; Heb 1:2–3

things, whether visible or invisible, whether thrones or [b]dominions, whether principalities or powers—all things were created [c]through him and for him. [17] He himself is before all things, [a]and all [b]things are held together in him. [18] [a]He is the head of the body, the church, as well as the beginning, the firstborn[1] from the dead, so that he himself may become first in all things. [19] For God was pleased to have all his fullness dwell [a]in the Son [20] and [a]through him to reconcile all [b]things to himself by making peace through the blood of his cross—through him,[1] whether things on earth or things [c]in heaven.

Paul's Goal in Ministry

[21] And you were at one time strangers and enemies in your minds as expressed [a]through your evil deeds, [22] but now he has reconciled you[1] [a]by his physical body through death [b]to present you holy, without blemish, and blameless before him—[23] if [a]indeed you remain in the faith, established and firm, [b]without shifting from the hope of the gospel that you heard. This gospel has also been preached in all creation under heaven, and [c]I, Paul, have become its servant.

[24] Now [a]I rejoice in my sufferings [b]for you, and I fill up in my physical body—for the sake of his body, the church—[c]what is lacking in [d]the sufferings of Christ. [25] I became a servant of [a]the church according to the stewardship from God—given to me for you—in order to complete the word of God, [26] that is, [a]the mystery that has been kept hidden from ages and generations, [b]but has now been revealed to his saints.

[27] God wanted [a]to make known to [b]them the glorious riches of this mystery among the Gentiles, which is [c]Christ in you, [d]the hope of glory. [28] We proclaim him by [a]instructing and teaching all people[1] with all wisdom so [b]that we may present every person mature in Christ. [29] Toward this goal I also labor, struggling according to his power that [a]powerfully works in me.

2 For I want you to know how great a [a]struggle I have for you, and for those in Laodicea, and for those who have not met me face to face. [2] My goal is that their hearts, having been knit together in love, may be encouraged, and that they may have all the riches that assurance brings in their understanding of the knowledge of the mystery of God, namely, Christ,[1] [3][a]in whom are hidden all the treasures of wisdom and knowledge. [4] I say this so that no one will deceive you through arguments[1] that sound reasonable. [5] For [a]though I am absent from [b]you in body, I am present with you in spirit, rejoicing to see your morale and the [c]firmness of your faith in Christ.

Warnings against the Adoption of False Philosophies

[6] Therefore, just [a]as you received Christ Jesus as Lord, continue to live your lives in him, [7][a]rooted and built up in him and firm in your faith just as you were taught, and overflowing with thankfulness. [8] Be careful not to allow anyone to captivate you through an empty, deceitful philosophy that is according to human traditions and [a]the elemental spirits[1] of the world, and not according to Christ. [9] For [a]in him all the fullness of deity lives in bodily form, [10] and you have been filled in him, who is the [a]head over every ruler and authority. [11] In him you also were [a]circumcised—not, however, with a circumcision performed by human hands, but by the [b]removal of the fleshly body, that is, through the circumcision done by Christ.

1:16 [b] [Eph 1:20–21; Col 2:15]   [c] John 1:3; Rom 11:36; 1 Cor 8:6; Heb 2:10   1:17 [a] [John 17:5]   [b] Heb 1:3   1:18 [a] 1 Cor 11:3; Eph 1:22   [1] I.e., Jesus was the first to rise from the dead.   1:19 [a] John 1:16   1:20 [a] Rom 5:1; Eph 2:14   [b] 2 Cor 5:18   [c] Eph 1:10   [1] Sev. wss omit through him.   1:21 [a] Titus 1:15   1:22 [a] 2 Cor 5:18; [Eph 2:14–16]   [b] [Eph 5:27]; Col 1:28   [1] Some wss you were reconciled.   1:23 [a] Eph 3:17; Col 2:7   [b] [John 15:6]; 1 Cor 15:58   [c] Mark 16:15; Acts 2:5; Rom 10:18; Col 1:6   1:24 [a] 2 Cor 7:4   [b] Eph 3:1, 13   [c] [Rom 8:17; 2 Cor 1:5; 12:15]; Phil 2:17   [d] Eph 1:23   1:25 [a] Gal 2:7   1:26 [a] [1 Cor 2:7]   [b] [2 Tim 1:10]   1:27 [a] 2 Cor 2:14   [b] Rom 9:23   [c] [Rom 8:10–11]   [d] 1 Tim 1:1   1:28 [a] Acts 20:20   [b] Eph 5:27   [1] Grk. men; the word can be used in a generic sense of both men and women.   1:29 [a] Eph 3:7   2:1 [a] Phil 1:30; Col 1:29; 4:12; 1 Thess 2:2   2:2 [1] Some wss of God, who is in Christ; of God, the Father of Christ; of the God and Father of Christ; of the God and Father, and of Christ.   2:3 [a] 1 Cor 1:24, 30   2:4 [1] Or persuasive speech, art of persuasion.   2:5 [a] 1 Thess 2:17   [b] 1 Cor 14:40   [c] 1 Pet 5:9   2:6 [a] 1 Thess 4:1   2:7 [a] Eph 2:21   2:8 [a] Gal 1:14   [1] Grk. the material elements which comprise the physical world (unlikely here), the elementary teachings of the world, the elemental spirits of the world (most likely).   2:9 [a] [John 1:14]; Col 1:19   2:10 [a] [Eph 1:20–21; 1 Pet 3:22]   2:11 [a] Deut 10:16   [b] Rom 6:6; 7:24; Gal 5:24; Col 3:5

[12]Having been [a]buried with him in baptism, you also have been raised with him through your [b]faith in the power of God [c]who raised him from the dead. [13]And even though you were dead in your transgressions and in the uncircumcision of your flesh, he nevertheless made you alive with him, having forgiven all your transgressions. [14]He has destroyed what was against us, [a]a certificate of indebtedness expressed in decrees opposed to us. He has taken it away by nailing it to the cross. [15a]Disarming the [b]rulers and authorities, he has made a public disgrace of them, triumphing over them by the cross.

[16]Therefore do not let anyone [a]judge you with respect to food or drink, or in the matter of a feast, new moon, or Sabbath days—[17a]these are only the shadow of the things to come, but the reality is Christ! [18]Let no one who delights in false humility and the worship of angels pass judgment on you. That person goes on at great lengths about what he has supposedly seen, but he is puffed up with empty notions by his fleshly mind. [19]He has not held fast to [a]the head from whom the whole body, supported and knit together through its ligaments and sinews, [b]grows with a growth that is from God.

[20]If you have [a]died with Christ to the elemental spirits[1] of the world, [b]why do you submit to them as though you lived in the world? [21]"Do not handle! [a]Do not taste! Do not touch!" [22]These are all destined to perish with use, founded as they are [a]on human commands and teachings. [23]Even though [a]they have the appearance of wisdom with their self-imposed worship and humility achieved by an unsparing treatment of the body—a wisdom with no true value—they in reality result in fleshly indulgence.

Exhortations to Seek the Things Above

3 Therefore, if you have been [a]raised with Christ, keep seeking the things above, [b]where Christ is, seated at the right hand of God. [2]Keep thinking about things above, not things on the [a]earth, [3a]for you have died [b]and your life is hidden with Christ in God. [4a]When Christ (who is [b]your[1] life) appears, then you too will be revealed in [c]glory with him. [5]So put to [a]death whatever in [b]your nature belongs to the earth: sexual [c]immorality, impurity, shameful passion, evil desire, and greed [d]which is idolatry. [6]Because [a]of [b]these things the wrath of God is coming on the sons of disobedience.[7]You also lived your lives [a]in this way at one time, when you used to live among them. [8a]But now, put off all such things as anger, rage, malice, slander, abusive language from your mouth. [9]Do not lie to one another since you have put off the old man with its practices [10]and have been clothed with the new man that [a]is being renewed in knowledge according [b]to the image of the one who [c]created it. [11]Here there is neither [a]Greek nor Jew, circumcised or uncircumcised, barbarian, Scythian, slave or free, [b]but Christ is all and in all.

Exhortation to Unity and Love

[12]Therefore, [a]as the elect of God, holy and dearly loved, clothe yourselves with a heart of mercy, kindness, humility, gentleness, and patience, [13a]bearing with one another and forgiving one another, if someone happens to have a complaint against anyone else. Just as the Lord has forgiven you, so you also forgive others. [14a]And to all these virtues add love, which is the perfect [b]bond. [15]Let [a]the peace of Christ be in control in your heart ([b]for you were in fact called [c]as one body to this peace), and [d]be thankful. [16]Let the word of Christ[1] dwell [a]in you richly, teaching and exhorting one another with all wisdom, singing psalms, hymns, and spiritual songs, all with grace in your hearts to God. [17]And [a]whatever you do in word or deed, do it all in the name of the Lord Jesus, giving thanks to God the Father through him.

2:12 [a]Rom 6:4 [b]Eph 1:19–20 [c]Acts 2:24   2:14 [a][Eph 2:15–16]; Col 2:20   2:15 [a][Isa 53:12; Heb 2:14] [b]Eph 6:12 2:16 [a]Rom 14:3   2:17 [a]Heb 8:5; 10:1   2:19 [a]Eph 4:15 [b]Eph 1:23; 4:16   2:20 [a]Rom 6:2–5 [b]Gal 4:3, 9 [1]Grk. *the material elements which comprise the physical world* (unlikely here), *the elementary teachings of the world, the elemental spirits of the world* (most likely).   2:21 [a]1 Tim 4:3   2:22 [a]Isa 29:13; Matt 15:9; Titus 1:14   2:23 [a]Rom 13:14; 1 Tim 4:8   3:1 [a]Rom 6:5; Eph 2:6; Col 2:12 [b]Ps 68:18; 110:1; [Rom 8:34]; Eph 1:20   3:2 [a][Matt 6:19–21]   3:3 [a][Rom 6:2; 2 Cor 5:14; Gal 2:20]; Col 2:20 [b][2 Cor 5:7]   3:4 [a][1 John 3:2] [b]John 14:6 [c]1 Cor 15:43 [1]Some MSS *our life*.   3:5 [a][Rom 8:13] [b][Rom 6:13] [c]Eph 5:3 [d]Mark 7:21; 1 Cor 6:9, 18; 2 Cor 12:21; Gal 5:19; Eph 4:19; 5:3, 5   3:6 [a]Rom 1:18; Eph 5:6; Rev 22:15 [b][Eph 2:2] [1]Some sig. WSS omit *on the sons of disobedience*.   3:7 [a]1 Cor 6:11; [Eph 2:2]; Titus 3:3   3:8 [a]Eph 4:22; 1 Pet 2:1   3:10 [a]Rom 12:2; 2 Cor 4:16 [b][Rom 8:29] [c][Eph 2:10]   3:11 [a]Rom 10:12; [1 Cor 12:13]; Gal 3:27–28 [b]Eph 1:23   3:12 [a][1 Pet 1:2]   3:13 [a][Mark 11:25]   3:14 [a]1 Pet 4:8 [b]Eph 4:3   3:15 [a][John 14:27; Phil 4:7] [b]1 Cor 7:15 [c]Eph 4:4 [d][1 Thess 5:18]   3:16 [a]Eph 5:19 [1]Some WSS *word of God, word of the Lord*.   3:17 [a]1 Cor 10:31

Exhortation to Households

18 a Wives, submit to your husbands, b as is fitting in the Lord. 19 a Husbands, love your wives and do not be b embittered against them. 20 a Children, obey your parents b in everything, for this is pleasing in the Lord. 21 a Fathers, do not provoke[1] your children, so they will not become disheartened. 22 Slaves, obey your earthly masters in every respect, not only when they are watching—like those who are strictly people-pleasers—but with a a sincere heart, fearing the Lord. 23 Whatever you are doing, work at it with enthusiasm, as to the Lord a and not for people,[1] 24 because you a know that you will receive your inheritance from the Lord as the reward. Serve the Lord Christ. 25 For a the one who does wrong will be repaid for his wrong, and there are no exceptions.[1]

4 1 a Masters, treat your slaves with justice and fairness, because you know that you also have a master in heaven.

Exhortation to Pray for the Success of Paul's Mission

2 Be a devoted to prayer, keeping alert in it b with thanksgiving. 3 At the same a time pray for us too, that God may b open a door for c the message so that we may proclaim the mystery of Christ, d for which I am in chains.[1] 4 Pray that I may make it known as I should. 5 a Conduct yourselves with b wisdom toward outsiders, making the c most of the opportunities. 6 Let your speech always be gracious, seasoned a with salt, b so c that you may know how you should answer everyone.

Personal Greetings and Instructions

7 a Tychicus, a dear brother, faithful minister, and fellow slave in the Lord, will tell you all the news about me. 8 I sent a him to you for this very purpose that you may know how we are doing and that he may encourage your hearts. 9 I sent him with a Onesimus, the faithful and dear brother, who is one of you. They will tell you about everything here. 10 a Aristarchus, my fellow prisoner, sends you greetings, as does b Mark, the cousin of Barnabas (about whom you received instructions; if he comes to you, welcome him). 11 And Jesus who is called Justus also sends greetings. In terms of Jewish converts,[1] these are the only fellow workers for the kingdom of God, and they have been a comfort to me. 12 a Epaphras, who is one of you and a slave of Christ,[1] greets you. He is always b struggling in prayer on your behalf, so that you may stand c mature and fully assured in all the will of God. 13 For I can testify that he has worked hard for you and for those in Laodicea and Hierapolis. 14 Our dear friend a Luke the physician and b Demas greet you. 15 Give my greetings to a the brothers and sisters[1] who are in Laodicea and to Nympha and the church that meets in her[2] house. 16 And after you have read a this letter, have it read to the church of Laodicea. In turn, read the letter from Laodicea as well. 17 And tell a Archippus, "See to it that you complete b the ministry you received in the Lord."

18 I, Paul, write a this greeting by my own hand. b Remember my chains.[1] Grace be with you.[2]

3:18 a 1 Pet 3:1   b [Col 3:18–4:1; Eph 5:22–6:9]   **3:19** a [Eph 5:25; 1 Pet 3:7]   b Eph 4:31   **3:20** a Eph 6:1   b Eph 5:24   **3:21** a Eph 6:4   1 Or *not cause your children to become resentful.*   **3:22** a Eph 6:5; [1 Tim 6:1]; Titus 2:9; 1 Pet 2:18   **3:23** a [Eccl 9:10]   1 Grk. *men*; the word can be used in a generic sense of both men and women.   **3:24** a Eph 6:8   **3:25** a Rom 2:11   1 Or *partiality*; used to describe unjust or unrighteous favoritism (Rom 2:11; Eph 6:9; Jas 2:1).   **4:1** a Eph 6:9   **4:2** a Luke 18:1   b Col 2:7   **4:3** a Eph 6:19   b 1 Cor 16:9   c Eph 3:3–4; 6:19   d Eph 6:20   1 Or *in prison.*   **4:5** a Eph 5:15   b [Matt 10:16]   c Eph 5:16   **4:6** a Eccl 10:12   b Mark 9:50   c 1 Pet 3:15   **4:7** a Acts 20:4; Eph 6:21; 2 Tim 4:12; Titus 3:12   **4:8** a Eph 6:22   **4:9** a Phlm 10   **4:10** a Acts 19:29; 20:4; 27:2; Phlm 24   b Acts 15:37; 2 Tim 4:11   **4:11** 1 Grk. *those of the circumcision.*   **4:12** a Col 1:7; Phlm 23   b Rom 15:30   c Matt 5:48; 1 Cor 2:6   1 ‡ Some wss add *Jesus.*   **4:14** a 2 Tim 4:11; Phlm 24   b 2 Tim 4:10   **4:15** a Rom 16:5; 1 Cor 16:19   1 Grk. *brothers*; considerable external evidence supports use of the Grk. word as *brothers and sisters* or *fellow Christians.*   2 Some mss *his house, their house.*   **4:16** a 1 Thess 5:27; 2 Thess 3:14   **4:17** a Phlm 2   b 1 Tim 4:6; 2 Tim 4:5   **4:18** a 1 Cor 16:21; 2 Thess 3:17   b Heb 13:3   1 Or *my imprisonment.*   2 Maj. wss add *amen.*

1 THESSALONIANS

P aul has many pleasant memories of the days he spent with the infant Thessalonian church. The people's faith, hope, love, and perseverance in the face of persecution are exemplary. Paul's labors as a spiritual parent to the fledgling church have been richly rewarded, and his affection is visible in every line of his letter. Paul encourages them to excel in their newfound faith, to increase in their love for one another, and to rejoice, pray, and give thanks always. He closes his letter with instruction regarding the return of the Lord, whose advent signifies hope and comfort for believers both living and dead. Because this is the first of Paul's two canonical letters to the church at Thessalonica, it received the title *Pros Thessalonikeis A*, the "First to the Thessalonians."

Salutation

1 From Paul and [a]Silvanus and Timothy, to the church of the [b]Thessalonians in God the Father and the Lord Jesus Christ. Grace and peace to you![1]

Thanksgiving for Response to the Gospel

[2]We thank God always for all of you as [a]we mention you constantly[1] in our prayers, [3]because we recall in the presence of our God and Father [a]your work produced by faith and [b]labor motivated by love and endurance inspired by hope in our Lord Jesus Christ. [4]We know, brothers and sisters[1] loved by God, that he has chosen [a]you,[2] [5]in that [a]our gospel did not come to you merely in words, but in power [b]and in the Holy Spirit [c]and with deep conviction (surely you recall the character we displayed when we came among you to help you).

[6]And [a]you became imitators of us and of the Lord when you received the message [b]with joy that comes from the Holy Spirit, despite great affliction. [7]As a result you became an example[1] to all the believers in Macedonia and in Achaia. [8]For from you the message of the Lord [a]has echoed forth not just [b]in Macedonia and Achaia, but in every place reports of your faith in God have spread, so that we do not need to say anything. [9]For people everywhere report how you welcomed us [a]and how you turned to God from idols to serve the living and true God [10]and [a]to wait for his Son [b]from heaven, whom he raised from the dead, Jesus our deliverer from the coming wrath.

Paul's Ministry in Thessalonica

2 For you yourselves know, brothers and sisters,[1] about our coming to you—it has not proven to be purposeless. [2]But although we suffered earlier and were mistreated in [a]Philippi, as you know, we had the [b]courage in our God to declare to you the gospel of God[1] in spite of much opposition. [3a]For the appeal we make does not come from error or impurity or with deceit, [4]but just as [a]we have been approved by God [b]to be entrusted with the gospel, so we declare it, [c]not to please people but God, [d]who examines our hearts. [5]For we [a]never appeared with flattering speech, as you know, nor with a pretext for greed—[b]God is our witness—[6a]nor

1:1 [a]1 Pet 5:12   [b]Acts 17:1–9   [1]Maj. wss add *from God our Father and the Lord Jesus Christ.*   1:2 [a]Rom 1:8; 2 Thess 1:3   [1]Or *mention you in our prayers because we recall constantly.*   1:3 [a]John 6:29   [b]Rom 16:6   1:4 [a]Col 3:12   [1]Grk. *brothers;* considerable external evidence supports use of the Grk. word as *brothers and sisters* or *fellow Christians.*   [2]Grk. *your election.*   1:5 [a]Mark 16:20   [b]2 Cor 6:6   [c]Heb 2:3   1:6 [a]1 Cor 4:16; 11:1   [b]Acts 5:41; 13:52; 2 Cor 6:10; Gal 5:22   1:7 [1]Maj. MSS examples.   1:8 [a]Rom 10:18   [b]Rom 1:8; 16:19; 2 Cor 2:14; 2 Thess 1:4   1:9 [a]1 Cor 12:2   1:10 [a][Rom 2:7]   [b]Matt 3:7; Rom 5:9   2:1 [1]Grk. *brothers;* considerable external evidence supports use of the Grk. word as *brothers and sisters* or *fellow Christians.*   2:2 [a]Acts 14:5; 16:19–24; Phil 1:30   [b]Acts 17:1–9   [1]Either *the gospel which God brings, the gospel about God,* or both.   2:3 [a]2 Cor 7:2   2:4 [a]1 Cor 7:25   [b]Titus 1:3   [c]Gal 1:10   [d]Prov 17:3   2:5 [a]2 Cor 2:17   [b]Rom 1:9; 1 Thess 2:10   2:6 [a]1 Tim 5:17

to seek glory from people, either from you or from others, [7]although [a]we could have imposed our weight as apostles of Christ; instead we became little children[1] among you. Like a nursing mother caring for her own children, [8]with such affection for you we were happy [a]to share with you not only the gospel of God but also [b]our own lives, because you had become dear to us. [9]For you recall, brothers and sisters,[1] our [a]toil and drudgery: By working night and day so [b]as not to impose a burden on any of you, we preached to you the gospel of God. [10a]You are witnesses, and so is God, [b]as to how holy and righteous and blameless our conduct was toward you who believe. [11]As you know, we treated each one of you as a father treats his own children, [12]exhorting and encouraging you and insisting [a]that you live in a way worthy of God [b]who calls you to his own kingdom and his glory. [13]And so we too [a]constantly thank God that when you [b]received God's message that you heard from us, you accepted it [c]not as a human message, but as it truly is, God's message, which is at [d]work among you who believe. [14]For you became imitators, brothers and sisters,[1] [a]of God's churches in Christ Jesus that are in Judea, because [b]you too suffered the same things from your own countrymen as they in fact did from the Jews, [15a]who killed both [b]the Lord Jesus [c]and the prophets[1] and persecuted us severely. They are displeasing to God and are opposed to all people [16]because they [a]hinder us from speaking [b]to the Gentiles so that they may be saved. Thus they constantly fill up their measure of sins, [c]but wrath[1] has come upon them completely.

Forced Absence from Thessalonica

[17]But when we were separated from you, brothers and sisters,[1] for a short time ([a]in presence, not in affection) we became all the more fervent in our great desire to see you in person. [18]For we wanted to come to you (I, Paul, in fact tried again and again), but [a]Satan thwarted us. [19]For [a]who is our hope or joy or [b]crown to boast of [c]before our Lord Jesus [d]at his coming? Is it not of course you? [20]For you are our glory and joy!

3 So when we could bear it no longer, we decided to stay on in Athens alone. [2]We sent [a]Timothy, our brother and fellow worker for God[1] in the gospel of Christ, to strengthen you and encourage you about your faith, [3]so [a]that no one would be shaken by these afflictions. For you yourselves know that [b]we are destined for this. [4a]For in fact when we were with you, we were telling you in advance that we would suffer affliction, and so it has happened, as you well know. [5]So when I could bear it no longer, I sent to find out about your faith, for fear that the tempter somehow tempted you and [a]our toil had proven useless.

[6a]But now Timothy has come to us from you and given us the good news of your faith and love and that you always think of us with affection and long to see us just [b]as we also long to see you! [7]So in all our distress and affliction, [a]we were reassured about you, brothers and sisters,[1] through your faith. [8]For now we are alive again if you [a]stand firm in the Lord. [9]For how can we thank God enough for you, for all the joy we feel because of you before our God? [10]We pray earnestly night [a]and day to see you in person and make up what may be lacking in your faith.

[11]Now may God our Father himself and our Lord Jesus [a]direct our way to you. [12]And may the Lord cause you to increase and [a]abound in love for one another and for all, just as we do for you, [13]so that [a]your hearts are strengthened in holiness to be blameless before our God and Father at the coming of our Lord Jesus with all his saints.[1]

2:7 [a]1 Cor 2:3 [1]Sev. wss *gentle.*   **2:8** [a]Rom 1:11 [b]2 Cor 12:15; 1 John 3:16   **2:9** [a]Acts 18:3; 20:34–35; 1 Cor 4:12; 2 Thess 3:7–8 [b]2 Cor 12:13 [1]Grk. *brothers*; considerable external evidence supports use of the Grk. word as *brothers and sisters* or *fellow Christians.*   **2:10** [a]2 Cor 1:12; 1 Thess 1:5 [b]2 Cor 7:2   **2:12** [a]Eph 4:1; Col 1:10 [b]Rom 8:28; 1 Cor 1:9; 1 Thess 5:24; 2 Thess 2:14; [2 Tim 1:9]   **2:13** [a]Rom 1:8; 1 Thess 1:2–3 [b]Mark 4:20 [c][Matt 10:20; Gal 4:14] [d][1 Pet 1:23]   **2:14** [a]Gal 1:22 [b]Acts 17:5; 1 Thess 3:4; 2 Thess 1:4 [1]Grk. *brothers*; considerable external evidence supports use of the Grk. word as *brothers and sisters* or *fellow Christians.*   **2:15** [a]Luke 24:20; Acts 2:23 [b]Jer 2:30; Matt 5:12; 23:34–35; Acts 7:52 [c]Esth 3:8 [1]Sev. wss *their own prophets.*   **2:16** [a]Luke 11:52 [b]Gen 15:16; Dan 8:23; Matt 23:32 [c]Matt 24:6 [1]Some mss *the wrath of God.*   **2:17** [a]1 Cor 5:3 [1]Grk. *brothers*; considerable external evidence supports use of the Grk. word as *brothers and sisters* or *fellow Christians.*   **2:18** [a]Rom 1:13; 15:22   **2:19** [a]2 Cor 1:14 [b]Prov 16:31 [c]Jude 24 [d]1 Cor 15:23   **3:2** [a]Rom 16:21 [1]Some wss *and fellow worker, and servant of God, and a servant of God and our fellow worker, and servant and fellow worker for God.*   **3:3** [a]Eph 3:13 [b]John 16:2; Acts 9:16; 14:22; 1 Cor 4:9; 2 Tim 3:12; 1 Pet 2:21   **3:4** [a]Acts 20:24   **3:5** [a]Gal 2:2   **3:6** [a]Acts 18:5 [b]Phil 1:8   **3:7** [a]2 Cor 1:4 [1]Grk. *brothers*; considerable external evidence supports use of the Grk. word as *brothers and sisters* or *fellow Christians.*   **3:8** [a][Eph 6:13–14]; Phil 4:1   **3:10** [a]2 Cor 13:9; Col 4:12   **3:11** [a]Mark 1:3   **3:12** [a]Phil 1:9; 1 Thess 4:1, 10; 2 Thess 1:3   **3:13** [a]2 Thess 2:17 [1]‡ Some sig. and early wss add *amen.*

A Life Pleasing to God

4 Finally then, brothers and sisters,[1] we ask you and urge you in the Lord Jesus, [a]that as you received instruction from [b]us about how you must live and please God (as you are in fact living)[2] that you do so more and more. [2]For you know what commands we gave you through the Lord Jesus. [3]For this is God's will: that [a]you become holy, [b]that you keep away from sexual immorality, [4a]that each of you know how to possess his own body in holiness and honor, [5a]not in lustful passion like the Gentiles who do not know God. [6]In [a]this matter no one should violate the rights of his brother or take advantage of him, because the Lord is the avenger in all these cases, as we also told you earlier and warned you solemnly. [7]For God did not call us to impurity [a]but in holiness. [8]Consequently [a]the one [b]who rejects this is not rejecting human authority but God, who gives his Holy Spirit to you.

[9]Now on the topic of brotherly love you have no need for anyone to write you, for you [a]yourselves are taught by God [b]to love one another. [10]And indeed you are practicing it toward all the brothers and sisters[1] in all of Macedonia. But we urge you, brothers and sisters, to do so more and more, [11]to aspire [a]to lead a quiet life, [b]to attend to your own business, and to work with your own hands, as we commanded you. [12]In this [a]way you will live a decent life before outsiders and not be in need.

The Lord Returns for Believers

[13]Now we do not want you to be uninformed, brothers and sisters,[1] about those who are asleep,[2] so that you will not grieve [a]like the rest [b]who have no hope. [14]For [a]if we believe that Jesus died and rose again, so also we believe that God will bring with him [b]those who have fallen asleep as Christians.

[15]For we tell you this [a]by the word of the Lord, that [b]we who are alive, who are left until the coming of the Lord, will surely not go ahead of those who have fallen asleep. [16]For [a]the Lord himself will come down from heaven with a shout of command, with [b]the voice of the archangel, [c]and with the trumpet of God, and the dead in Christ will rise first. [17a]Then we who are alive, who are left,[1] will be suddenly caught up together with them in the clouds to meet the Lord [b]in the air. And so [c]we will always be with the Lord. [18a]Therefore encourage one another with these words.

The Day of the Lord

5 Now on [a]the topic of times and seasons, brothers and sisters,[1] you have no need for anything to be written to you. [2]For you know quite well that [a]the day of the Lord will come in the same way as a thief in the night. [3]Now when[1] they are saying, "There is peace and security," then [a]sudden destruction comes on them, [b]like labor pains on a pregnant woman, and they will surely not escape. [4a]But you, brothers and sisters,[1] are not in the darkness for the day to overtake you like a thief would. [5]For you all are [a]sons of the light and sons of the day. We are not of the night nor of the darkness. [6]So then we must not sleep as [a]the rest, but must stay alert and sober. [7]For [a]those who sleep, sleep at night, and those who get drunk [b]are drunk at night. [8]But since we are of the day, we must stay sober *by putting [a]on the breastplate*[1] of faith and love and as *a helmet* our hope *for salvation.*[2] [9]For [a]God did not destine us for wrath [b]but for gaining salvation through our Lord Jesus Christ. [10a]He died for us so that whether we are alert or asleep, we will come to life together with him. [11]Therefore encourage one another and build up each other, just as you are in fact doing.

4:1 [a] 1 Cor 15:58 [b] Phil 1:27; Col 1:10 [1] Grk. *brothers*; considerable external evidence supports use of the Grk. word as *brothers and sisters* or *fellow Christians.* [2] Some later wss omit *(as you are in fact living).* **4:3** [a] Eph 5:27 [b] [1 Cor 6:15–20; Col 3:5] **4:4** [a] Rom 6:19 **4:5** [a] Col 3:5 **4:6** [a] 2 Thess 1:8 **4:7** [a] Lev 11:44; [Heb 12:14]; 1 Pet 1:14–16 **4:8** [a] Luke 10:16 [b] 1 Cor 2:10 **4:9** [a] [Jer 31:33–34]; John 6:45; 15:12, 17; [1 John 2:27] [b] Matt 22:39 **4:10** [1] Grk. *brothers*; considerable external evidence supports use of the Grk. word as *brothers and sisters* or *fellow Christians.* **4:11** [a] 2 Thess 3:11; 1 Pet 4:15 [b] Acts 20:35 **4:12** [a] Rom 13:13; Col 4:5; [1 Pet 2:12] **4:13** [a] Lev 19:28 [b] [Eph 2:12] [1] Grk. *brothers*; considerable external evidence supports use of the Grk. word as *brothers and sisters* or *fellow Christians.* [2] Maj. wss *who have fallen asleep.* **4:14** [a] 1 Cor 15:13 [b] 1 Cor 15:20, 23 **4:15** [a] 1 Kgs 13:17; 20:35; 2 Cor 12:1; Gal 1:12 [b] 1 Cor 15:51–52; 1 Thess 5:10 **4:16** [a] [Matt 24:30–31] [b] [1 Cor 15:52] [c] [1 Cor 15:23]; 2 Thess 2:1; Rev 14:13; 20:6 **4:17** [a] [1 Cor 15:51–53]; 1 Thess 5:10 [b] Dan 7:13; Acts 1:9; Rev 11:12 [c] John 14:3; 17:24 [1] Some mss omit [the ones] *who are left.* **4:18** [a] 1 Thess 5:11 **5:1** [a] Matt 24:3 [1] Grk. *brothers*; considerable external evidence supports use of the Grk. word as *brothers and sisters* or *fellow Christians.* **5:2** [a] Luke 21:34; 1 Thess 5:4; [2 Pet 3:10]; Rev 3:3; 16:15 **5:3** [a] Isa 13:6–9 [b] Hos 13:13 [1] ‡ Some wss omit *now;* some wss *for.* **5:4** [a] [Acts 26:18]; Rom 13:12; Eph 5:8; 1 John 2:8 [1] Grk. *brothers*; considerable external evidence supports use of the Grk. word as *brothers and sisters* or *fellow Christians.* **5:5** [a] Eph 5:8 **5:6** [a] Matt 25:5 **5:7** [a] [Luke 21:34] [b] Acts 2:15; 2 Pet 2:13 **5:8** [a] Isa 59:17; Eph 6:14 [1] [Isa 59:17] [2] [Isa 59:17] **5:9** [a] Rom 9:22 [b] [2 Thess 2:13] **5:10** [a] 2 Cor 5:15

Final Instructions

[12] Now we ask you, brothers and sisters,[1] [a]to acknowledge those who labor among you and preside over you in the Lord and admonish you, [13] and to esteem them most highly in love [a]because of their work. Be at peace among yourselves. [14] And we urge you, brothers and sisters,[1] [a]admonish the undisciplined, [b]comfort the discouraged, [c]help the weak, [d]be patient toward all. [15][a]See that no one pays back evil for evil to anyone, but always [b]pursue what is good for one another and for all. [16] Always [a]rejoice, [17] constantly [a]pray, [18] in everything give thanks. For this is God's will for you in Christ Jesus. [19][a]Do not extinguish the Spirit. [20][a]Do not treat prophecies with contempt. [21] But [a]examine all things; [b]hold fast to what is good. [22] Stay away from every form of evil.

Conclusion

[23] Now may [a]the God of peace himself [b]make you completely holy and may your spirit and soul and body [c]be kept entirely blameless at the coming of our Lord Jesus Christ. [24] He who calls you is [a]trustworthy, and he will in fact [b]do this. [25] Brothers and sisters,[1] pray for us too. [26] Greet all the brothers and sisters[1] with a holy kiss. [27] I call on you solemnly in the Lord to have this letter read to all the brothers and sisters.[1,2] [28] The grace of our Lord Jesus Christ be with you.[1]

5:12 [a] 1 Cor 16:18; 1 Tim 5:17; Heb 13:7, 17 [1] Grk. *brothers*; considerable external evidence supports use of the Grk. word as *brothers and sisters* or *fellow Christians.* 5:13 [a] Mark 9:50 5:14 [a] 2 Thess 3:6–7, 11 [b] Heb 12:12 [c] Rom 14:1; 15:1; 1 Cor 8:7 [d] Gal 5:22 [1] Grk. *brothers*; considerable external evidence supports use of the Grk. word as *brothers and sisters* or *fellow Christians.* 5:15 [a] Lev 19:18 [b] Rom 12:9; Gal 6:10; 1 Thess 5:21 5:16 [a] [2 Cor 6:10] 5:17 [a] Eph 6:18 5:19 [a] Eph 4:30 5:20 [a] Acts 13:1; 1 Cor 14:1, 31 5:21 [a] 1 Cor 14:29; 1 John 4:1 [b] Phil 4:8 5:23 [a] Phil 4:9 [b] 1 Thess 3:13 [c] 1 Cor 1:8–9 5:24 [a] [1 Cor 10:13]; 2 Thess 3:3 [b] Phil 1:6 5:25 [1] Grk. *brothers*; considerable external evidence supports use of the Grk. word as *brothers and sisters* or *fellow Christians.* 5:26 [1] Grk. *brothers*; considerable external evidence supports use of the Grk. word as *brothers and sisters* or *fellow Christians.* 5:27 [1] Maj. wss *holy brothers* [and sisters]. [2] Grk. *brothers*; considerable external evidence supports use of the Grk. word as *brothers and sisters* or *fellow Christians.* 5:28 [1] Maj. wss add *amen.*

2 THESSALONIANS

Since Paul's first letter, the seeds of false doctrine have been sown among the Thessalonians, causing them to waver in their faith. Paul removes these destructive seeds and replants the seeds of truth. He begins by commending the believers for their faithfulness in the midst of persecution and encouraging them that present suffering will be repaid with future glory. Therefore expectation can be high. Paul then deals with the central matter of his letter: a misunderstanding spawned by false teachers regarding the coming day of the Lord. Despite reports to the contrary, that day has not yet come, and Paul recounts the events that must first take place. Laboring for the gospel rather than lazy resignation is the proper response. As the second letter in Paul's Thessalonian correspondence, this was entitled *Pros Thessalonikeis B*, the "Second to the Thessalonians."

Salutation

1 From Paul and Silvanus and Timothy, to the church of the Thessalonians in God our Father and the Lord Jesus Christ. [2a]Grace and peace to you from God the[1] Father and the Lord Jesus Christ!

Thanksgiving

[3]We ought to thank God always for you, brothers and sisters,[1] and rightly so, because your faith flourishes more and more and the love of each one of you all for one another is ever greater. [4]As a result [a]we ourselves boast about you in the churches of God [b]for your perseverance and faith [c]in all the persecutions and afflictions you are enduring.

Encouragement in Persecution

[5]This is evidence of God's righteous judgment, to make you worthy of the kingdom of God, [a]for which in fact you are suffering. [6a]For it is right for God to repay with affliction those who afflict you, [7]and to you who are being afflicted to give [a]rest [b]together with us when the Lord Jesus is revealed from heaven with his mighty angels. [8]*With flaming fire he will mete out punishment on those who do not know God*[1] and do not obey the gospel of our Lord Jesus. [9]They will undergo [a]the penalty of eternal destruction, *away* [b]*from the presence of the Lord and from the glory of his strength,*[1] [10]when he comes [a]to be [b]glorified among his saints and admired on that day among all who have believed—and you did in fact believe our testimony. [11]And in this regard we pray for you always, that our God will make you worthy of his calling and fulfill by his power your every desire for goodness and every work of faith, [12a]that the name of our Lord Jesus may be glorified in you, and you in him, according to the grace of our God and the Lord Jesus Christ.

The Day of the Lord

2 Now [a]regarding the arrival of our Lord Jesus Christ [b]and our being gathered to be with him, we ask you, brothers and sisters,[1] [2a]not to be easily shaken from your composure or disturbed by any kind of spirit or message or letter allegedly from us, to the effect that the day of the Lord is already here. [3]Let no one deceive you in any way. For

---

1:2 [a]1 Cor 1:3 [1]‡ Maj. wss *our Father.*   1:3 [1]Grk. *brothers*; considerable external evidence supports use of the Grk. word as *brothers and sisters* or *fellow Christians.*   1:4 [a]2 Cor 7:4; [1 Thess 2:19] [b]1 Thess 1:3 [c]1 Thess 2:14   1:5 [a]1 Thess 2:14   1:6 [a]Rev 6:10   1:7 [a]Rev 14:13 [b][1 Thess 4:16]; Jude 14   1:8 [1][Jer 10:25 (Ps 79:6; Isa 66:15)]   1:9 [a]Phil 3:19; 1 Thess 5:3 [b]Deut 33:2 [1][Isa 2:10, 19, 21]   1:10 [a]Matt 25:31 [b]Isa 49:3; John 17:10; 1 Thess 2:12   1:12 [a][Col 3:17]   2:1 [a]Mark 13:26; [1 Thess 4:15–17] [b]Matt 24:31 [1]Grk. *brothers*; considerable external evidence supports use of the Grk. word as *brothers and sisters* or *fellow Christians.*   2:2 [a]Matt 24:4

that day will not arrive until [a]the rebellion comes and [b]the man of lawlessness[1] is revealed, the son of destruction. [4]He opposes and [a]*exalts himself* [b]*above every* so-called *god* or object of worship, and as a result *he takes his seat*[1] in God's temple, displaying himself as God. [5]Surely you recall that I used to tell you these things while I was still with you. [6]And so you know what holds him back, so that he will be revealed in his own time. [7]For [a]the hidden power of lawlessness is already at work. However, the one who holds him back will do so until he is taken out of the way, [8]and then the lawless one will be revealed, [a]whom the Lord[1] will destroy by the breath of his mouth and wipe out by the manifestation of his arrival. [9]The arrival of the lawless one will be [a]by Satan's working with all kinds of miracles and [b]signs and false wonders, [10]and with every kind of evil deception directed against [a]those who are perishing, because [b]they found no place in their hearts for the truth so as to be saved. [11a]Consequently God sends on them a deluding influence so [b]that they will believe what is false. [12]And so all of them who have not believed the truth but have delighted in evil will be condemned.

Call to Stand Firm

[13]But we ought to thank God always for you, brothers and sisters[1] loved by the Lord, because God [a]chose you [b]from the beginning[2] for salvation [c]through sanctification by the Spirit and faith in the truth. [14]He called you to this salvation through our gospel, so that you may possess [a]the glory of our Lord Jesus Christ. [15]Therefore, brothers and sisters,[1] stand [a]firm and hold on to [b]the traditions that we taught you, whether by speech or by letter. [16]Now may our Lord Jesus Christ himself and God our Father, [a]who loved us and by grace gave us eternal comfort and [b]good hope, [17]encourage your hearts [a]and strengthen you in every good thing you do or say.

Request for Prayer

3 Finally, [a]pray for us, brothers and sisters,[1] that the Lord's message may spread quickly and be honored as in fact it was among you, [2]and [a]that we may be delivered from perverse and evil people. [b]For not all have faith. [3]But [a]the Lord is faithful, and he will strengthen you and [b]protect you from the evil one. [4]And [a]we are confident about you in the Lord that you are both doing—and will do—what we are commanding. [5]Now may [a]the Lord direct your hearts toward the love of God[1] and the endurance of Christ.[2]

Response to the Undisciplined

[6]But we command you, brothers and sisters,[1] in the name of our Lord Jesus Christ, to keep away [a]from any brother who lives an [b]undisciplined life and not according to the tradition they[2] received from us. [7]For you know yourselves how you must imitate us, because we did not behave without discipline among you, [8]and we did not eat anyone's food without paying. Instead, in [a]toil and drudgery we worked night and day in order not to burden any of you. [9]It was not because we do not have that [a]right, but to give ourselves as an example for you to imitate. [10]For even when we were with you, we used to give you this command: "If anyone is not willing to work, neither should he eat." [11]For we hear that some among you are living an undisciplined life, not doing their own work but meddling in the work of [a]others. [12]Now such people we command and urge in the Lord Jesus Christ [a]to work quietly and so provide their own food to eat. [13]But you, brothers and sisters,[1]

2:3 [a] Dan 7:25; 8:25; 11:36; 2 Thess 2:8; Rev 13:5   [b] John 17:12   [1] Maj. wss *of sin*.   2:4 [a] Isa 14:13–14; Ezek 28:2   [b] 1 Cor 8:5   [1] [Isa 14:13–14; Dan 11:36; Ezek 28:2–9]   2:7 [a] 1 John 2:18   2:8 [a] Dan 7:10   [1] ‡ Sev. sig. wss add *Jesus*.   2:9 [a] John 8:41   [b] Deut 13:1   2:10 [a] 2 Cor 2:15   [b] 1 Cor 16:22   2:11 [a] Rom 1:28   [b] 1 Tim 4:1   2:13 [a] 1 Thess 1:4   [b] Eph 1:4   [c] 1 Thess 4:7; [1 Pet 1:2]   [1] Grk. *brothers*; considerable external evidence supports use of the Grk. word as *brothers and sisters* or *fellow Christians*.   [2] ‡ Sev. mss *as a firstfruit*.   2:14 [a] 1 Pet 5:10   2:15 [a] 1 Cor 16:13   [b] Rom 6:17; 1 Cor 11:2; 2 Thess 3:6; Jude 3   [1] Grk. *brothers*; considerable external evidence supports use of the Grk. word as *brothers and sisters* or *fellow Christians*.   2:16 [a] [Rev 1:5]   [b] Titus 3:7; 1 Pet 1:3   2:17 [a] 1 Cor 1:8   3:1 [a] Eph 6:19   [1] Grk. *brothers*; considerable external evidence supports use of the Grk. word as *brothers and sisters* or *fellow Christians*.   3:2 [a] Rom 15:31   [b] Acts 28:24   3:3 [a] 1 Cor 1:9; 1 Thess 5:24   [b] John 17:15   3:4 [a] 2 Cor 7:16   3:5 [a] 1 Chr 29:18   [1] Either *God's love, your love for God*, or both.   [2] Either *Christ's endurance, endurance for Christ*, or both.   3:6 [a] 1 Cor 5:1   [b] 1 Thess 4:11   [1] Grk. *brothers*; considerable external evidence supports use of the Grk. word as *brothers and sisters* or *fellow Christians*.   [2] Sev. wss *you received*.   3:8 [a] 1 Thess 2:9   3:9 [a] 1 Cor 9:4, 6–14   3:11 [a] 1 Tim 5:13; 1 Pet 4:15   3:12 [a] Eph 4:28; 1 Thess 4:11–12   3:13 [1] Grk. *brothers*; considerable external evidence supports use of the Grk. word as *brothers and sisters* or *fellow Christians*.

[a]do not grow weary in doing what is right. [14]But if anyone [a]does not obey our message through this letter, take note of him and do not associate closely with him, so that he may be ashamed. [15a]Yet do not regard him as an enemy, [b]but admonish him as a brother.

Conclusion

[16]Now may [a]the Lord of peace himself give you peace at all times and in every way. The Lord be with you all. [17a]I, Paul, write this greeting with my own hand, which is how I write in every letter. [18a]The grace of our Lord Jesus Christ be with you all.[1]

3:13 [a]2 Cor 4:1; Gal 6:9   **3:14** [a]Matt 18:17   **3:15** [a]Lev 19:17   [b]Titus 3:10   **3:16** [a]John 14:27; Rom 15:33; Phil 4:9   **3:17** [a]1 Cor 16:21   **3:18** [a]Rom 16:20, 24; 1 Thess 5:28   [1]Maj. wss add *amen.*

1 TIMOTHY

Paul, the aged and experienced apostle, writes to the young pastor Timothy who is facing a heavy burden of responsibility in the church at Ephesus. The task is challenging: False doctrine must be erased, public worship safeguarded, and mature leadership developed. In addition to the conduct of the church, Paul talks pointedly about the conduct of the minister. Timothy must be on his guard lest his youthfulness become a liability rather than an asset to the gospel. He must be careful to avoid false teachers and greedy motives and pursue instead righteousness, godliness, faith, love, perseverance, and the gentleness that befits a person of God. The Greek title for this letter is *Pros Timotheon A*, the "First to Timothy." *Timothy* means "Honoring God" or "Honored by God" and probably was given to him by his mother, Eunice.

Salutation

1 From Paul, an apostle of Christ Jesus by the command of God our Savior and of Christ Jesus our hope, [2]to Timothy, my [a]genuine child in the faith. [b]Grace, mercy, and peace from God the Father and Christ Jesus our Lord!

Timothy's Task in Ephesus

[3]As I urged you [a]when I was leaving for Macedonia, stay on in Ephesus to instruct certain people not to spread false teachings, [4][a]nor to occupy themselves with myths and interminable genealogies. Such things promote useless speculations rather than God's redemptive plan[1] that operates by faith. [5]But [a]the aim of our instruction[1] is love that comes [b]from a pure heart, a good conscience, and a sincere faith. [6]Some have strayed from these and turned away to empty discussion. [7]They want to be teachers of the law, but they do not understand what they are saying or the things they insist on so confidently.

[8]But we know that the law is [a]good if someone uses it legitimately, [9]realizing that law is not intended for a righteous person, but for lawless and rebellious people, for the ungodly and sinners, for the unholy and profane, for those who kill their fathers or mothers, for murderers, [10]sexually immoral people, practicing homosexuals, kidnappers, liars, perjurers—in fact, for any who live contrary to sound teaching. [11]This accords with the glorious gospel of the [a]blessed God that was entrusted to me.

[12]I am grateful to the one who has [a]strengthened me, Christ Jesus our Lord, [b]because he considered me faithful in [c]putting me into ministry, [13]even though [a]I was formerly a blasphemer and a persecutor, and an arrogant man. But [b]I was treated with mercy because I acted ignorantly in unbelief, [14][a]and our Lord's grace was abundant, [b]bringing faith and love in Christ Jesus. [15]This saying [a]is trustworthy and deserves full acceptance: "[b]Christ Jesus came into the world to save sinners"—and I am the worst of them! [16]But here is why I was treated with mercy: so that in me as the worst, Christ Jesus could demonstrate his utmost patience, as an example for those who are going to believe in him for eternal life. [17]Now to [a]the eternal King, [b]immortal, [c]invisible, the only[1] God, [d]be honor and glory forever and ever! Amen.

[18]I put this charge before you, Timothy

1:2 [a]Acts 16:1–2; Rom 1:7; 2 Tim 1:2; Titus 1:4 [b]Gal 1:3 1:3 [a]Acts 20:1, 3 1:4 [a]1 Tim 6:3–4, 20; Titus 1:14 [1]A few MSS *God's edification.* 1:5 [a]Rom 13:8–10; Gal 5:14 [b]Eph 6:24 [1]Grk. *the instruction*; i.e., orthodox Christian teaching. 1:8 [a]Rom 7:12, 16 1:11 [a]1 Tim 6:15 1:12 [a]1 Cor 15:10 [b]1 Cor 7:25 [c]Col 1:25 1:13 [a]Acts 8:3; 1 Cor 15:9 [b]John 4:21 1:14 [a]Rom 5:20; 1 Cor 3:10; 2 Cor 4:15; Gal 1:13–16 [b]1 Thess 1:3; 1 Tim 2:15; 4:12; 6:11; 2 Tim 1:13; 2:22; Titus 2:2 1:15 [a]1 Tim 3:1; 4:9; 2 Tim 2:11; Titus 3:8 [b]Isa 53:5; 61:1; Hos 6:1–3; Matt 1:21; 9:13 1:17 [a]Ps 10:16 [b]Rom 1:23 [c]Heb 11:27 [d]1 Chr 29:11 [1]Maj. later wss add *wise.*

my child, in keeping with the prophecies once spoken about you, in order that with such encouragement you may fight the good fight. [19]To do this you must hold firmly to faith and a good conscience, which some have rejected and so have suffered shipwreck in regard to the faith. [20]Among these are [a]Hymenaeus and [b]Alexander, whom I handed over to Satan to be taught not to [c]blaspheme.

Prayer for All People

2 First of all, then, I urge that requests, prayers, intercessions, and thanks be offered on behalf of all people,[1] [2]even [a]for kings and [b]all who are in authority, that we may lead a peaceful and quiet life in all godliness and dignity. [3]Such prayer for all is [a]good and welcomed before God our Savior, [4]since [a]he wants all people[1] to be saved [b]and to come to a knowledge of the truth. [5a]For there is [b]one God and one intermediary between God and humanity, Christ Jesus, himself human, [6a]who gave himself as a ransom for all, revealing God's purpose at his appointed time. [7a]For this I [b]was appointed a preacher and apostle—I am telling the truth;[1] I am not lying—and a teacher of the Gentiles in faith and truth. [8]So I want the men in [a]every place to pray, lifting [b]up holy hands without anger or dispute.

Conduct of Women

[9]Likewise the [a]women are to dress in suitable apparel, with modesty and self-control. Their adornment must not be with braided hair and gold or pearls or expensive clothing, [10a]but with good deeds, as is proper for women who profess reverence for God. [11]A woman must learn quietly with all submissiveness. [12]But [a]I do not allow a woman to teach or exercise authority over a man. She must remain quiet.[1] [13]For Adam was formed first and then Eve. [14]And Adam was not deceived, but the woman, because she was fully deceived, fell into transgression. [15]But she will be delivered through childbearing,[1] if she[2] continues in faith and love and holiness with self-control.

Qualifications for Overseers and Deacons

3 This saying is trustworthy: "If someone aspires to the office of overseer, he desires a good work." [2]The overseer then must be above reproach, the husband of one wife, temperate, self-controlled, respectable, hospitable, an able teacher, [3]not a drunkard, not violent, but gentle, not contentious, free from the love of money. [4]He must manage his own household well and keep his children in control without losing his dignity. [5]But if someone does not know how to manage his own household, how will he care for the church of God? [6]He must not be a recent convert, or he may become arrogant and fall into the punishment that the devil will exact. [7]And he must be well thought of by those outside the faith, so that he may not fall into disgrace and be caught by the devil's [a]trap.

[8]Deacons likewise must be dignified, [a]not two-faced, not given to excessive drinking, not greedy for gain, [9]holding to the mystery of the faith with a clear conscience. [10]And these also must be tested first and then let them serve as deacons if they are found blameless. [11]Likewise also their wives[1] must be dignified, not slanderous, temperate, faithful in every respect. [12]Deacons must be husbands of one wife[1] and good managers of their children and their own households. [13]For those who have served well as deacons [a]gain a good standing for themselves and great boldness in the faith that is in Christ Jesus.

Conduct in God's Church

[14]I hope to come to you soon, but I am writing these instructions to you [15]in case I am delayed to let you know how people ought to conduct themselves in the household of God, because it is the church of the living God, the support and bulwark of the

1:20 [a]2 Tim 2:17–18 [b]2 Tim 4:14 [c]Acts 13:45   2:1 [1]Grk. *all men*; but here generically referring to both men and women.   2:2 [a]Ezra 6:10 [b][Rom 13:1]   2:3 [a]Rom 12:2   2:4 [a]Ezek 18:23, 32; John 3:17; 1 Tim 4:10; Titus 2:11; 2 Pet 3:9 [b][John 17:3]   [1]Grk. *all men*; but here generically referring to both men and women.   2:5 [a]1 Cor 8:6; Gal 3:20 [b][Heb 9:15]   2:6 [a]Mark 10:45   2:7 [a]Eph 3:7–8; 1 Tim 1:11; 2 Tim 1:11 [b][Gal 1:15–16] [1]Maj. MSS add *in Christ*.   2:8 [a]Luke 23:34 [b]Ps 134:2   2:9 [a]1 Pet 3:3   2:10 [a]1 Pet 3:4   2:12 [a]1 Cor 14:34; Titus 2:5 [1]Grk. *but to be in quietness*; either absolute silence or a quiet demeanor.   2:15 [1]Or *But she will be preserved through childbearing*; or *But she will be saved in spite of childbearing*; for an explanation of this difficult verse, see *NET Bible, Full Notes Edition*. [2]Grk. *if they continue*.   3:7 [1]1 Tim 6:9; 2 Tim 2:26   3:8 [a]Ezek 44:21   3:11 [1]Or *also deaconesses*; for an explanation of this term, see *NET Bible, Full Notes Edition*.   3:12 [1]Or *men married only once, devoted solely to their wives*.   3:13 [a]Matt 25:21

truth. [16]And we all agree, our religion contains amazing revelation:

> He[1] was revealed in the flesh,
> [a]vindicated by the Spirit,
> [b]seen by angels,
> [c]proclaimed among Gentiles,
> believed [d]on in the world,
> taken [e]up in glory.

Timothy's Ministry in the Later Times

4 Now the Spirit explicitly says that in the later times some will desert the faith and occupy themselves with deceiving spirits and demonic teachings, [2][a]influenced by the hypocrisy of liars whose consciences are [b]seared. [3]They will prohibit marriage and require abstinence from foods that God created to be received with thanksgiving by those who believe and know the truth. [4]For every creation of God is good, and no food is to be rejected if it is received with thanksgiving. [5]For it is sanctified by God's word and by prayer.

[6]By pointing out such things to the brothers and sisters,[1] you will be a good servant of Christ Jesus, having [a]nourished yourself on the words of the faith and of the good teaching that you have followed. [7]But [a]reject those myths fit only for the godless and gullible, and [b]train yourself for godliness. [8]For "[a]physical exercise has some value, but godliness is valuable in every way. It [b]holds promise for the present life and for the life to come." [9]This saying is trustworthy and deserves full acceptance. [10]In fact this is why we work hard and struggle,[1] because we have set our hope on the living God, [a]who is the Savior of all people,[2] especially of believers.

[11]Command and teach these things. [12]Let no one look down on you because you are young, but set an [a]example for the believers in your speech, conduct, love, faithfulness, and purity. [13]Until I come, give attention to the public reading of scripture, to exhortation, to teaching. [14][a]Do not neglect the spiritual gift you have, given to you and confirmed by prophetic words [b]when the elders laid hands on you. [15]Take pains with

these things; be absorbed in them, so that everyone will see your progress. [16]Be conscientious about how you live and what you teach. Persevere in this, because by doing so you will save both yourself and those who listen to you.

Instructions about Specific Groups

5 Do not address an older man harshly but appeal to him as a father. Speak to younger men as brothers, [2]older women as mothers, and younger women as sisters— with complete purity.

[3]Honor widows who are truly in need. [4]But if a widow has children or grandchildren, they should first learn [a]to fulfill their duty toward their own household and so repay their parents what is owed them. For this is what pleases God. [5]But the widow who is truly in need, and completely on her own, has set her hope on God and continues in her pleas and prayers [a]night and day. [6]But the one who lives for pleasure is dead even while she lives. [7]Reinforce these commands, so that they will be beyond reproach. [8]But if someone does not provide for his own, especially his own family, he has denied the faith [a]and is worse than [b]an unbeliever.

[9]No widow should be put on the list unless she is at least sixty years old, was the wife of one husband,[1] [10]and has a reputation for good works: as one who has raised children,[1] practiced hospitality, washed the feet of the saints, helped those in distress— as one who has exhibited all kinds of good works. [11]But do not accept younger widows on the list, because their passions may lead them away from Christ and they will desire to marry, [12]and so incur judgment for breaking their former pledge. [13]And besides that, going around from house to house they learn to be lazy, and they are not only lazy, but also gossips and busybodies, talking about things they should not. [14]So I want younger women to marry, raise children, and manage a household, in order to give the adversary no opportunity to vilify us. [15]For some have already wandered away to follow Satan. [16]If a believing woman[1] has

3:16 [a] [Matt 3:16; Rom 1:4] [b] Matt 28:2 [c] Acts 10:34; Rom 10:18 [d] Rom 16:26; 2 Cor 1:19; Col 1:6, 23 [e] Luke 24:51 [1]A few wss *God.* 4:2 [a] Matt 7:15 [b] Eph 4:19 4:6 [a] 2 Tim 3:14 [1]Grk. *brothers*; considerable external evidence supports use of the Grk. word as *brothers and sisters* or *fellow Christians.* 4:7 [a] 2 Tim 2:16; Titus 1:14 [b] Heb 5:14 4:8 [a] 1 Cor 8:8 [b] Ps 37:9 4:10 [a] Ps 36:6 [1]Sev. MSS *suffer reproach.* [2]Grk. *men;* referring to both men and women. 4:12 [a] Phil 3:17; Titus 2:7; 1 Pet 5:3 4:14 [a] 2 Tim 1:6 [b] Acts 6:6; 1 Tim 5:22 5:4 [a] Gen 45:10 5:5 [a] Acts 26:7 5:8 [a] Isa 58:7; 2 Cor 12:14 [b] Matt 18:17 5:9 [1]Or *a woman married only once, was devoted solely to her husband.* 5:10 [1]Grk. *if she raised children.* 5:16 [1]Maj. wss *man or woman.*

widows in her family, let her help them. The church should not be burdened so that it may help the widows who are truly in need.

[17]Elders who provide effective leadership must be counted worthy of double honor, especially those who work hard in speaking and teaching. [18]For [a]the scripture says, "**Do not muzzle an ox while it is treading out the grain,**"[1] and, "The worker deserves his pay."[2] [19]Do not accept an accusation against an elder unless it can be confirmed *by two or three witnesses.*[1] [20]Those guilty of sin must be rebuked before all, as a warning to the rest. [21]Before God and Christ Jesus and the elect angels, I solemnly charge you to carry out these commands without [a]prejudice or favoritism of any kind. [22]Do not lay hands on anyone hastily and so [a]identify with the sins of others. Keep yourself pure. [23](Stop drinking just water, but use a little wine for your digestion and your frequent illnesses.) [24]The sins of some people are obvious, going before them into judgment, but for others, they show up later. [25]Similarly good works are also obvious, and the ones that are not cannot remain hidden.

6 Those who are under the yoke as [a]slaves[1] must regard their own masters as deserving of full respect. This will prevent the name of God and Christian teaching from being discredited. [2]But those who have believing masters must not show them less respect[1] because they are brothers. Instead they are to serve all the more, because those who benefit from their service are believers and dearly loved.

Summary of Timothy's Duties

Teach them and exhort them about these things. [3]If someone spreads false teachings and does not agree with [a]sound words (that is, those of our Lord Jesus Christ) [b]and with the teaching that accords with godliness, [4]he is conceited and understands nothing, but has an unhealthy interest in controversies and verbal disputes. This gives rise to envy, dissension, slanders, evil suspicions, [5]and constant bickering by people corrupted in their minds and deprived of the truth, who suppose that godliness[1] is a way of making a profit. [6]Now godliness combined with [a]contentment brings great profit. [7]For we have brought nothing into this world and so we cannot take [a]a single thing out either. [8]But if we have food and shelter, we will be [a]satisfied with that. [9]Those who long to be rich, however, stumble into temptation and a trap and many senseless and harmful desires that plunge people into ruin and destruction. [10]For the love of money is the root of all evils. Some people in reaching for it have strayed from the faith and stabbed themselves with many pains.

[11]But you, as a person dedicated to God, keep away from all that. Instead pursue righteousness, godliness, faithfulness, love, endurance, and gentleness. [12]Compete well for the faith and lay hold of that eternal life you were called for and made your good confession for in the presence of many witnesses. [13]I charge you[1] before God [a]who gives life to all things and Christ Jesus who made his good confession before Pontius Pilate, [14]to obey this command without fault or failure until the appearing of our Lord Jesus Christ [15]—whose appearing the blessed and only Sovereign, the King of kings and Lord of lords, will reveal at the right time. [16]He alone possesses immortality and lives in [a]unapproachable light, [b]whom no human has ever seen or is able to see. To him be honor and eternal power! Amen.

[17]Command those who are rich in this world's goods not to be haughty or to set their hope on [a]riches, which are uncertain, but on God who richly provides us with all things [b]for our enjoyment. [18]Tell them to do good, to be rich in good deeds, to be generous givers, sharing with others. [19]In this way they will save up a [a]treasure for themselves as a firm foundation for the future and so lay hold of what is truly life.

Conclusion

[20]O Timothy, [a]protect what has been entrusted to you. [b]Avoid the profane chatter and absurdities of so-called "knowledge." [21]By professing it, some have strayed from the faith. Grace be with you all.[1]

5:18 [a]Lev 19:13; Deut 24:15; Matt 10:10; Luke 10:7; 1 Cor 9:14 [1]Deut 25:4 [2]Luke 10:7 5:19 [1][Deut 17:6; 19:15] 5:21 [a]Deut 1:17 5:22 [a]Eph 5:6–7; 2 John 11 6:1 [a]Eph 6:5; Titus 2:9; 1 Pet 2:18 [1]Trad. *servants*; but the word does not bear the connotation of a free individual serving another. 6:2 [1]Or *think the less of them*; Grk. *despise them, look down on them.* 6:3 [a]2 Tim 1:13 [b]Titus 1:1 6:5 [1]Maj. wss add *stay away from such things.* 6:6 [a]Phil 4:11; Heb 13:5 6:7 [a]Job 1:21; Ps 49:17; Eccl 5:15 6:8 [a]Prov 30:8–9 6:13 [a]Matt 27:2; John 18:36–37 [1]‡ Some wss omit *you.* 6:16 [a]Dan 2:22 [b]John 6:46 6:17 [a]Jer 9:23; 48:7 [b]Eccl 5:18–19 6:19 [a][Matt 6:20–21; 19:21] 6:20 [a][2 Tim 1:12, 14] [b]Titus 1:14 6:21 [1]Maj. wss add *amen.*

2 TIMOTHY

P rison is the last place from which to expect a letter of encouragement, but that is where Paul's second letter to Timothy originates. He begins by assuring Timothy of his continuing love and prayers and reminds him of his spiritual heritage and responsibilities. Only the one who perseveres, whether as a soldier, athlete, farmer, or minister of Jesus Christ, will reap the reward. Paul warns Timothy that his teaching will come under attack as people desert the truth for ear-tickling words (4:3). But Timothy has Paul's example to guide him and God's Word to fortify him as he faces growing opposition and glowing opportunities in the last days. Paul's last epistle received the title *Pros Timotheon B*, the "Second to Timothy." When Paul's epistles were collected together, the *B* was probably added to distinguish this letter from the first letter he wrote to Timothy.

Salutation

1 From Paul, an apostle of Christ Jesus by the will of God, to further the [a]promise of life in Christ Jesus, [2]to Timothy, my [a]dear child. Grace, mercy, and peace from God the Father and Christ Jesus our Lord!

Thanksgiving and Charge to Timothy

[3]I am thankful to God, whom I have served with a clear conscience as my [a]ancestors did, when I remember you in my prayers as I do constantly night and day. [4]As I remember your tears, I long to see you, so that I may be filled with joy. [5]I recall your sincere faith that was alive first in your [a]grandmother Lois and in [b]your mother Eunice, and I am sure is in you.

[6]Because of this I remind you [a]to rekindle God's gift that you possess through the laying on of my hands. [7]For [a]God did not give us a Spirit of fear [b]but of power and love and self-control. [8]So do not be ashamed of [a]the testimony about our Lord or of me, a prisoner for his [b]sake, but by God's power accept your share of suffering[1] for the gospel. [9]He is the one who saved us and called us with a holy calling, [a]not based [b]on our works but on his own purpose and grace, granted to us in Christ Jesus [c]before time began, [10]but now made visible through the appearing of our Savior Christ Jesus. He [a]has broken the power of death and brought life and immortality to light through the gospel! [11a]For this gospel I was appointed a preacher and apostle and teacher.[1] [12]Because of this, in fact, I suffer as I do. But I am not ashamed [a]because I know the one in whom my faith is set and I am convinced that he is able to protect what has been entrusted to me until that day. [13a]Hold to [b]the standard of [c]sound words that you heard from me and do so with the faith and love that are in Christ Jesus. [14]Protect that good thing entrusted to you, through the Holy Spirit who lives within us.

[15]You know that everyone in the province of Asia deserted me, including Phygelus and Hermogenes. [16]May the Lord grant mercy to the [a]family of Onesiphorus because he often refreshed me and was not ashamed of my imprisonment. [17]But when he arrived in Rome, he eagerly searched for me and found me. [18]May the Lord [a]grant him to find mercy from the Lord [b]on that day! And you know very well all the ways he [c]served me in Ephesus.

Serving Faithfully Despite Hardship

2 So you, [a]my child, [b]be strong in the grace that is in Christ Jesus. [2]And what you heard me say in the presence of many witnesses entrust to faithful people[1] who will

1:1 [a]Titus 1:2   1:2 [a]1 Tim 1:2; 2 Tim 2:1; Titus 1:4   1:3 [a]Acts 24:14   1:5 [a]1 Tim 1:5; 4:6   [b]Acts 16:1   1:6 [a]1 Tim 4:14   1:7 [a]John 14:27; Rom 8:15; 1 John 4:18   [b][Acts 1:8]   1:8 [a]1 Tim 2:6   [b]Eph 3:1; 2 Tim 1:16   [1]Grk. *suffer hardship together.*   1:9 [a][Rom 3:20]; Eph 2:8–9   [b]Rom 8:28   [c]Rom 16:25; Eph 1:4; Titus 1:2   1:10 [a]Eph 1:9   1:11 [a]Acts 9:15   [1]Maj. MSS add *of the Gentiles.*   1:12 [a]1 Pet 4:19   1:13 [a]2 Tim 3:14; Titus 1:9   [b]Rom 2:20; 6:17   [c]1 Tim 6:3   1:16 [a]2 Tim 4:19   1:18 [a]Matt 6:4; Mark 9:41   [b]2 Thess 1:10   [c]Heb 6:10   2:1 [a]1 Tim 1:2   [b]Eph 6:10   2:2 [1]Grk. *faithful men*; but here generically referring to both men and women.

be competent to teach others as well. [3] Take your share of [a]suffering[1] [b]as a good soldier of Christ Jesus. [4] No one in military service gets entangled in matters of everyday life; otherwise he will [a]not please the one who recruited him. [5] Also, [a]if anyone competes as an athlete, he will not be crowned as the winner unless he competes according to the rules. [6] The farmer who works hard ought to have the first share of the crops. [7] Think about what I am saying and the Lord will [a]give you understanding of all this.

[8] Remember Jesus Christ, raised [a]from the dead, [b]a descendant of David; [c]such is my gospel, [9][a]for which I suffer hardship to the point of imprisonment[1] as a criminal, [b]but God's message[2] is not imprisoned![3] [10] So [a]I endure all things for the sake of those chosen by God, [b]that they, too, may obtain salvation in Christ Jesus and its eternal glory. [11] This saying is trustworthy:

[a]If we died with him, we will also live with him.

[12] [a]If we endure, we will also reign with him.

If we deny[1] him, he will also deny us.

[13] If we are unfaithful, he remains faithful, since he [a]cannot deny himself.

Dealing with False Teachers

[14] Remind people of these things and solemnly [a]charge them before the Lord[1] not to wrangle over words. This is of no benefit; it just brings ruin on those who listen. [15] Make every effort to present yourself [a]before God as a proven worker who does not need to be ashamed, teaching the message of truth accurately. [16] But avoid profane chatter because those occupied with it will stray further and further into ungodliness, [17] and their message will spread its infection like gangrene. [a]Hymenaeus and Philetus are in this group. [18] They have strayed from the truth by [a]saying that the resurrection has already occurred, and they are undermining some people's faith. [19] However, God's solid foundation remains standing, bearing this seal: "[a]*The Lord* [b]*knows those who are his,*"[1] and "Everyone who confesses the name of the Lord must turn away from evil."

[20] Now in a wealthy home there are not only gold and silver [a]vessels, but also ones made of wood and of clay, and some are for honorable use, but others for ignoble use. [21] So if someone cleanses himself of such behavior, he will be a vessel for honorable use, set apart, useful for the Master, [a]prepared for every good work. [22] But keep away [a]from youthful passions, and pursue righteousness, faithfulness, love, and peace, in company with others who call on the Lord from a pure heart. [23] But reject foolish and ignorant[1] controversies because you know they breed infighting. [24] And the Lord's [a]slave[1] must not engage in heated disputes but be kind toward all, an apt teacher, [b]patient, [25] correcting opponents [a]with gentleness. Perhaps God will grant them repentance and then knowledge of the truth, [26] and they will come to their senses and [a]escape the devil's trap where they are held captive to do his will.

Ministry in the Last Days

3 But understand this, that [a]in the last days difficult times will come. [2] For people[1] will be lovers of themselves, lovers of money, boastful, arrogant, blasphemers, disobedient to parents, ungrateful, unholy, [3] unloving, irreconcilable, slanderers, without self-control, savage, opposed to what is good, [4][a]treacherous, reckless, conceited, loving pleasure rather than loving God. [5] They will [a]maintain the outward appearance of religion but will have [b]repudiated its power. So avoid people like these. [6] For some [a]of these insinuate themselves into households and captivate weak women who are overwhelmed with sins and led along by various passions. [7] Such women are always seeking instruction, yet never able [a]to arrive at a knowledge of the truth. [8][a]And just as Jannes and Jambres opposed Moses, so these

2:3 [a] 2 Tim 4:5 [b] 1 Cor 9:7; 1 Tim 1:18 [1] Grk. *suffer hardship together.* 2:4 [a] [2 Pet 2:20] 2:5 [a] [1 Cor 9:25] 2:7 [a] Prov 2:6 2:8 [a] Rom 1:3–4 [b] 1 Cor 15:4 [c] Rom 2:16 2:9 [a] Acts 9:16 [b] Acts 28:31; [2 Tim 4:17] [1] Or *chains, bonds.* [2] Or *word.* [3] Or *chained, bound.* 2:10 [a] Eph 3:13 [b] 2 Cor 1:6; 1 Thess 5:9 2:11 [a] Rom 6:5, 8; 1 Thess 5:10 2:12 [a] Matt 10:33; Luke 12:9; 1 Tim 5:8 [1] Or *renounce, disown, repudiate.* 2:13 [a] Num 23:19; Titus 1:2 2:14 [a] 1 Tim 5:21; 6:4; 2 Tim 2:23; Titus 3:9 [1] ‡ Some wss *God, Christ.* 2:15 [a] 1 Tim 4:13; 2 Pet 1:10 2:17 [a] 1 Tim 1:20 2:18 [a] 1 Cor 15:12 2:19 [a] Matt 24:24; [1 Cor 3:11] [b] Num 16:5; [Nah 1:7]; John 10:14, 27 [1] Num 16:5 2:20 [a] Rom 9:21 2:21 [a] 2 Cor 9:8; [Eph 2:10]; 2 Tim 3:17 2:22 [a] 1 Tim 6:11 2:23 [1] Or *uninstructed, silly.* 2:24 [a] Titus 3:2 [b] 1 Tim 3:3; Titus 1:7 [1] Trad. *servant;* but the word does not bear the connotation of a free individual serving another. 2:25 [a] Gal 6:1; Titus 3:2; 1 Pet 3:15 2:26 [a] 1 Tim 3:7 3:1 [a] 1 Tim 4:1; 2 Pet 3:3; 1 John 2:18; Jude 17, 18 3:2 [1] Grk. *men;* but here generically referring to both men and women. 3:4 [a] 2 Pet 2:10 3:5 [a] Titus 1:16 [b] 1 Tim 5:8 3:6 [a] Matt 23:14; Titus 1:11 3:7 [a] 1 Tim 2:4 3:8 [a] Exod 7:11–12, 22; 8:7; 9:11

[b]people—who have warped minds and are [c]disqualified in the faith—also oppose the truth. [9]But they will not go much further, for their foolishness will be obvious to everyone, just [a]like it was with Jannes and Jambres.

Continue in What You Have Learned

[10]You, [a]however, have followed my teaching, my way of life, my purpose, my faith, my patience, my love, my endurance, [11]as well as the persecutions and sufferings that happened to me [a]in Antioch, [b]in Iconium, and [c]in Lystra. I endured these persecutions, and the Lord delivered me [d]from them all. [12]Now in fact [a]all who want to live godly lives in Christ Jesus will be persecuted. [13a]But evil people and charlatans will go from bad to worse, deceiving others and being deceived themselves. [14]You, however, must [a]continue in the things you have learned and are confident about. You know who taught you [15]and how from infancy you have known [a]the holy writings, which are able to give you wisdom for salvation through faith in Christ Jesus. [16a]Every scripture is inspired by God [b]and useful for teaching, for reproof,[1] for correction, and for training in righteousness, [17a]that the person dedicated to God[1] may be capable and equipped for every good work.

Charge to Timothy Repeated

4 I solemnly [a]charge you before God and Christ Jesus, [b]who is going to judge the living and the dead, and by his appearing and his kingdom: [2]Preach the message, be ready whether it is convenient or not, [a]reprove, [b]rebuke, [c]exhort with complete patience and instruction. [3a]For there will be a time when people will not tolerate [b]sound teaching. [c]Instead, following their own desires, they will accumulate teachers for themselves because they have an insatiable curiosity to hear new things. [4]And they will turn away from hearing the truth, but on the other hand they will turn aside to myths. [5]You, however, be self-controlled in all things, [a]endure hardship, do [b]an evangelist's work, fulfill your ministry. [6]For [a]I am already being poured out as an offering, and the time for [b]me to depart is at hand. [7]I have competed well; [a]I have finished the race; I have kept the faith! [8]Finally [a]the crown of righteousness is reserved for me. The Lord, the righteous [b]Judge, will award it to me [c]in that day—and not to me only, but also to all who have set their affection on his appearing.

Travel Plans and Concluding Greetings

[9]Make every effort to come to me soon. [10]For [a]Demas deserted me, since he loved the present age, and he went to Thessalonica. Crescens went to Galatia and Titus to Dalmatia. [11]Only Luke is with me. Get [a]Mark and bring him with you because he is a great help to me in ministry. [12]Now I have sent [a]Tychicus to Ephesus. [13]When you come, bring with you the cloak I left in Troas with Carpas and the scrolls, especially the parchments. [14a]Alexander the coppersmith did me a great deal of harm. *The Lord will repay him in keeping with his deeds.*[1] [15]You be on guard against him too, because he vehemently opposed our words. [16]At my first defense no one appeared in my support; instead they all deserted me—[a]may they not be held accountable for it. [17a]But the Lord stood by me and strengthened me, [b]so that through me the message would be fully proclaimed for all the Gentiles to hear. And so I was delivered from the lion's [c]mouth! [18]The Lord will deliver me from every evil deed [a]and will bring me safely [b]into his heavenly kingdom. To him be glory for ever and ever! Amen.

[19]Greetings to [a]Prisca and Aquila and the family of [b]Onesiphorus. [20a]Erastus stayed in Corinth. [b]Trophimus I left ill in Miletus. [21]Make every effort to come before winter. Greetings to you from Eubulus, Pudens, Linus, Claudia, and all the brothers and sisters.[1] [22]The Lord[1] be with your spirit. Grace be with you.[2]

3:8[b]1 Tim 6:5 [c]Rom 1:28 **3:9**[a]Exod 7:11–12; 8:18; 9:11 **3:10**[a]Phil 2:20, 22; 1 Tim 4:6 **3:11**[a]Acts 13:44–52 [b]Acts 14:1–6, 19 [c]Acts 14:8–20 [d]Ps 34:19 **3:12**[a][Ps 34:19] **3:13**[a]2 Thess 2:11 **3:14**[a]2 Tim 1:13; Titus 1:9 **3:15**[a]Ps 119:97–104; John 5:39 **3:16**[a][2 Pet 1:20] [b]Rom 4:23; 15:4 [1]Or *rebuke, censure.* **3:17**[a]1 Tim 6:11 [1]Grk. *the man of God;* but here in a generic sense, referring to both men and women. **4:1**[a]1 Tim 5:21; 2 Tim 4:1 [b]Acts 10:42 **4:2**[a]Titus 2:15 [b]1 Tim 5:20; Titus 1:13; 2:15 [c]1 Tim 4:13 **4:3**[a]2 Tim 3:1 [b]1 Tim 1:10; 2 Tim 1:13 [c]Isa 30:9–11; Jer 5:30–31; 2 Tim 3:6 **4:5**[a]2 Tim 1:8 [b]Acts 21:8 **4:6**[a]Phil 2:17 [b][Phil 1:23]; 2 Pet 1:14 **4:7**[a]1 Cor 9:24–27; Phil 3:13–14 **4:8**[a][1 Cor 9:25; 2 Tim 2:5]; Jas 1:12 [b]John 5:22 [c]2 Tim 1:12 **4:10**[a]Col 4:14; Phlm 24 **4:11**[a]Acts 12:12, 25; 15:37–39; Col 4:10 **4:12**[a]Acts 20:4; Eph 6:21–22; Col 4:7; Titus 3:12 **4:14**[a]Acts 19:33; 1 Tim 1:20 [1][Ps 28:4] **4:16**[a]Acts 7:60; [1 Cor 13:5] **4:17**[a]Deut 31:6; Acts 23:11 [b]Acts 9:15; Phil 1:12 [c]1 Sam 17:37; Ps 22:21 **4:18**[a]Ps 121:7; [2 Pet 2:9] [b]Rom 11:36; Gal 1:5; Heb 13:21; 2 Pet 3:18 **4:19**[a]Acts 18:2; Rom 16:3 [b]2 Tim 1:16 **4:20**[a]Acts 19:22; Rom 16:23 **4:20**[b]Acts 20:4; 21:29 **4:21**[1]Grk. *brothers;* considerable external evidence supports use of the Grk. word as *brothers and sisters* or *fellow Christians.* **4:22**[1]Some wss *the Lord Jesus, the Lord Jesus Christ.* [2]Maj. wss add *amen.*

TITUS

Titus, a young pastor, faces the unenviable assignment of setting in order the church at Crete. Paul advises him to appoint elders, men of proven spiritual character in their homes and businesses, to oversee the work of the church. But elders are not the only individuals in the church who are required to excel spiritually. Men and women, young and old, all have vital functions to fulfill in the church if they are to be living examples of the doctrine they profess. Throughout his letter to Titus, Paul stresses the necessary, practical working out of salvation in the daily lives of both the elders and the congregation. Good works are desirable and profitable for all believers. This third Pastoral Epistle is simply titled *Pros Titon*, "To Titus." Ironically, this was also the name of the Roman general who destroyed Jerusalem in AD 70 and succeeded his father, Vespasian, as emperor.

Salutation

1 From Paul, a slave[1] of God and apostle of Jesus Christ, to [a]further the faith of God's chosen ones and the knowledge of the truth that is in keeping with godliness, [2]in hope of eternal life, which God, who does [a]not lie, promised before time began. [3]But now in his own time he has made his message evident through the preaching I was entrusted with according to the command of God our Savior. [4]To [a]Titus, my genuine son in a common faith. Grace and peace from God the Father and Christ Jesus our Savior!

Titus' Task on Crete

[5]The reason I left you in Crete was to set in [a]order the remaining matters and to appoint elders in every town, as I directed you. [6]An elder must be blameless, the husband of one wife,[1] with faithful children who cannot be charged with dissipation or rebellion. [7]For the overseer must be blameless as one entrusted with God's work, [a]not arrogant, not prone to anger, not a drunkard, not violent, not greedy for gain. [8]Instead he must be hospitable, devoted to what is good, sensible, upright, devout, and self-controlled. [9]He must hold firmly to the faithful message as it has been taught, so that he will be able to give exhortation in such healthy teaching and correct those who speak against it.

[10]For there are many[1] rebellious people, idle [a]talkers, and deceivers, especially those with Jewish connections,[2] [11]who must be silenced because they mislead whole families by teaching [a]for dishonest gain what ought not to be taught. [12]A certain [a]one of them, in fact, one of their own prophets, said, "Cretans are always liars, evil beasts, lazy gluttons."[13]Such testimony is true. [a]For this reason rebuke them sharply that they may be healthy in the faith [14]and not pay attention to Jewish myths and [a]commands of people who reject the truth. [15]All is pure [a]to those who are pure. But to those who are corrupt and unbelieving, nothing is pure, but both their minds and consciences are corrupted. [16]They profess to [a]know God but with their deeds they deny him, [b]since they are detestable, disobedient, [c]and unfit for any good deed.

Conduct Consistent with Sound Teaching

2 But as for you, communicate the behavior that goes with sound teaching. [2]Older men are to be temperate, dignified, self-controlled, sound in faith, in love, and in endurance. [3]Older women likewise are to

1:1 [a] 2 Tim 2:25 [1] Trad. *servant*; but the word does not bear the connotation of a free individual serving another.
1:2 [a] Num 23:19   1:4 [a] 2 Cor 2:13; 8:23; Gal 2:3; 2 Tim 4:10   1:5 [a] 1 Cor 11:34   1:6 [1] Or *married only once, devoted solely to his wife.*   1:7 [a] Lev 10:9   1:10 [a] Jas 1:26   [1] ‡ Sev. sig. wss *also many.*   [2] Grk. *those of the circumcision.*   1:11 [a] 1 Tim 6:5
1:12 [a] Acts 17:28   1:13 [a] 2 Cor 13:10; 2 Tim 4:2   1:14 [a] Isa 29:13   1:15 [a] Luke 11:41; Rom 14:14, 20; 1 Cor 6:12
1:16 [a] Matt 7:20–23; 25:12; 1 John 2:4   [b] [2 Tim 3:5, 7]   [c] Rom 1:28

exhibit behavior fitting for those who are holy, not slandering, not slaves to excessive drinking, but teaching what is good. [4]In this way they will train the younger women to love their husbands, to love their children, [5]to be self-controlled, pure, fulfilling their duties at [a]home, kind, being [b]subject to their own husbands, so [c]that the message of God may not be discredited. [6]Encourage younger men likewise to be self-controlled, [7]showing yourself to be [a]an example of good works [b]in every way. In your teaching show integrity, dignity, [8]and a sound message that cannot be criticized, so that any opponent will be at a loss because he has nothing evil to say about us. [9a]Slaves[1] are to be subject to their own masters in everything, to do what is wanted and not talk back, [10]not pilfering, but showing all good faith, in order to bring credit to the teaching of God our Savior in everything.

[11]For [a]the grace of God has appeared, bringing salvation to all people.[1] [12]It trains us to reject godless ways and worldly desires and to live self-controlled, upright, and godly lives in the present age, [13]as we wait [a]for the happy fulfillment of our [b]hope in the glorious appearing[1] of our great God and Savior, Jesus Christ. [14a]He gave himself for us to set us free from every kind of lawlessness [b]and to purify for himself a people who are truly [c]his, who are eager to do good. [15]So communicate these things with the sort of [a]exhortation or rebuke that carries full authority. Don't let anyone look down on you.

Conduct Toward Those Outside the Church

3 Remind them [a]to be subject [b]to rulers and authorities, to be obedient, to be ready for every good work. [2]They must not slander anyone, but be peaceable, gentle, showing complete courtesy to all people. [3]For [a]we, too, were once foolish, disobedient, misled, enslaved to various passions and desires, spending our lives in evil and envy, hateful and hating one another. [4]But "when [a]the kindness of [b]God our Savior and his love for mankind appeared, [5]he saved us [a]not by works of righteousness that we have done but on [b]the basis of his mercy, through the washing of the new birth and the renewing of the Holy Spirit, [6a]whom he poured out on us in full measure through Jesus Christ our Savior. [7]And so, since [a]we have been justified by his grace, we become heirs with the confident expectation of eternal life."

Summary of the Letter

[8]This saying [a]is trustworthy, and I want you to insist on such truths, so that those who have placed their faith in God may be intent on engaging in good works. These things are good and beneficial for all people. [9]But [a]avoid foolish controversies, genealogies, quarrels, and fights about the law because they are useless and empty. [10a]Reject a divisive person after one or two warnings. [11]You know that such a person is twisted by sin and is conscious of it himself.

Final Instructions and Greeting

[12]When I send Artemas or [a]Tychicus to you, do your best to come to me at Nicopolis, for I have decided to spend the winter there. [13]Make every effort to help Zenas the lawyer and [a]Apollos on their way; make sure they have what they need. [14]Here is another way that our people can learn to engage in good works to meet pressing needs and so not be unfruitful. [15]Everyone with me greets you. Greet those who love us in the faith. Grace be with you all.[1]

2:5 [a]1 Tim 5:14 [b]1 Cor 14:34; 1 Tim 2:11 [c]Rom 2:24   2:7 [a]Phil 3:17; 1 Tim 4:12 [b]Eph 6:24   2:9 [a]Eph 6:5; 1 Tim 6:1 [1]Trad. *servant*; but the word does not bear the connotation of a free individual serving another.   2:11 [a][Rom 5:15] [1]Grk. *all men*; but here generically referring to both men and women.   2:13 [a]1 Cor 1:7 [b][Col 3:4] [1]Grk. *the blessed hope and glorious appearing*.   2:14 [a]Isa 53:12; Gal 1:4 [b]Ezek 37:23; [Heb 1:3; 9:14; 1 John 1:7] [c]Exod 15:16   2:15 [a]1 Tim 4:13; 5:20; 2 Tim 4:2   3:1 [a][Rom 13:1]; 1 Pet 2:13 [b]Col 1:10   3:3 [a]1 Cor 6:11; 1 Pet 4:3   3:4 [a]Titus 2:11 [b]1 Tim 2:3   3:5 [a][Rom 3:20]; Eph 2:4–9 [b]John 3:3   3:6 [a]Ezek 36:26   3:7 [a][Matt 25:34]; Mark 10:17; [Rom 8:17, 23, 24; Titus 1:2]   3:8 [a]1 Tim 1:15   3:9 [a]1 Tim 1:4; 2 Tim 2:23   3:10 [a]Matt 18:17   3:12 [a]Acts 20:4; Eph 6:21; Col 4:7; 2 Tim 4:12   3:13 [a]Acts 18:24; 1 Cor 16:12   3:15 [1]Maj. wss add *amen*.

PHILEMON

Does Christian love really work, even in situations of extraordinary tension and difficulty? Will it work, for example, between a prominent slave owner and one of his runaway slaves? Paul has no doubt! He writes a postcard to Philemon, his beloved brother and fellow worker, on behalf of Onesimus—a deserter, thief, and formerly worthless slave but now Philemon's brother in Christ. With much tact and tenderness, Paul asks Philemon to receive Onesimus back with the same gentleness with which he would receive Paul himself. Any debt Onesimus owes, Paul promises to make good. Knowing Philemon, Paul is confident that brotherly love and forgiveness will carry the day. Since this letter is addressed to Philemon in verse 1, it becomes known as *Pros Philemona*, "To Philemon." Like 1–2 Timothy and Titus, it is addressed to an individual, but unlike the Pastoral Epistles, Philemon is also addressed to a family and a church (v. 2).

Salutation

[1]From Paul, a [a]prisoner of Christ Jesus, and Timothy our brother, to Philemon, our dear friend and colaborer, [2]to Apphia our sister,[1] to [a]Archippus our fellow soldier, and to the church that meets in your house. [3]Grace and peace to you from God our Father and the Lord Jesus Christ!

Thanks for Philemon's Love and Faith

[4]I always thank my God as [a]I remember you in my prayers, [5]because I [a]hear of your faith in the Lord Jesus and your love for all the saints. [6]I pray that the faith you share [a]with us may deepen your understanding of [b]every blessing[1] that belongs to you[2] in Christ. [7]I have had great joy and encouragement because of your love, for the hearts[1] of the saints have been refreshed through you, brother.

Paul's Request for Onesimus

[8]So, although I have quite a lot of confidence in Christ and could command you to do what is proper, [9]I would rather appeal to you on the basis of love—I, Paul, an old man and even now a prisoner for the sake of Christ Jesus—[10]I am appealing[1] to you concerning my child, whose spiritual father I have become during my imprisonment, that is, [a]Onesimus, [11]who was formerly useless to you, but is now useful to you[1] and me. [12]I have sent[1] him (who is my very heart) back to you. [13]I wanted to keep him with me so that he could serve me in your place during my imprisonment for the sake of the gospel.[1] [14]However,[1] without your consent I did not want to do anything so [a]that your good deed would not be out of compulsion, but from your own willingness. [15]For perhaps it was for this reason that he was separated from you for a little while so that you would have him back eternally, [16]no longer as a slave,[1] but more than a slave, as a dear brother. He is especially so to me, and even more so to you now, both humanly [a]speaking and in the Lord. [17]Therefore if you regard me as a partner, accept him as you would me. [18]Now if he has defrauded you of anything or owes you anything, charge what he owes to me. [19]I, Paul, have written this letter with my own [a]hand: I will repay it. I could also mention that you owe me your very self. [20]Yes, brother, let me have some benefit from you in the Lord. Refresh my heart in Christ. [21]Since [a]I

1 [a] Eph 3:1   2 [a] Col 4:17   [1] Maj. wss *beloved, dear.*   4 [a] Eph 1:16; 1 Thess 1:2; 2 Thess 1:3   5 [a] Eph 1:15; Col 1:4; 1 Thess 3:6   6 [a] Phil 1:9; [Col 1:9; 3:10; Jas 2:14–17]   [b] [1 Thess 5:18]   [1] Grk. *everything good.*   [2] ‡ Some wss *us.*   7 [1] Lit. one's *inward parts*; commonly used figuratively for "heart" as the seat of the emotions.   10 [a] Col 4:9   [1] Or *I am encouraging.*   11 [1] ‡ A few wss *both you.*   12 [1] Sev. wss add *receive, accept* at various places in the verse.   13 [1] Grk. *in the chains of the gospel.*   14 [a] 2 Cor 9:7; 1 Pet 5:2   [1] The Grk. text does not include "however," but it is clearly implied.   16 [a] Eph 6:5; Col 3:22   [1] Trad. *servant;* but the word does not bear the connotation of a free individual serving another.   19 [a] 1 Cor 16:21; Gal 6:11; 2 Thess 3:17   21 [a] 2 Cor 7:16

was confident that you would obey, I wrote to you because I knew that you would do even more than[1] what I am asking you to do. [22]At the same [a]time also, prepare a place for me to stay, for I hope that [b]through your prayers I will be given back to you.

Concluding Greetings

[23a]Epaphras, my fellow prisoner in Christ Jesus, greets you. [24a]Mark, [b]Aristarchus, [c]Demas, and [d]Luke, my colaborers, greet you too. [25]May [a]the grace of the Lord Jesus Christ be with your spirit.[1]

21 [1]Grk. *that you would even go beyond.*   22 [a]Phil 1:25; 2:24   [b]2 Cor 1:11   23 [a]Col 1:7; 4:12   24 [a]Acts 12:12, 25; 15:37–39; Col 4:10   [b]Acts 19:29; 27:2; Col 4:10   [c]Col 4:14; 2 Tim 4:10   [d]2 Tim 4:11   25 [a]2 Tim 4:22   [1]Maj. wss add *amen.*

HEBREWS

Many Jewish believers, having stepped out of Judaism into Christianity, want to reverse their course in order to escape persecution by their countrymen. The writer of Hebrews exhorts them to "move on to maturity" (6:1). His appeal is based on the superiority of Christ over the Judaic system. Christ is better than the angels, for they worship him. He is better than Moses, for he created him. He is better than the Aaronic priesthood, for his sacrifice was once for all time. He is better than the law, for he mediates a better covenant. In short, there is more to be gained in Christ than to be lost in Judaism. Pressing on in Christ produces tested faith, self-discipline, and a visible love seen in good works. Although the King James Version uses the title "The Epistle of Paul the Apostle to the Hebrews," there is no early manuscript evidence to support it. The oldest and most reliable title is simply *Pros Ebraious*, "To Hebrews."

Introduction: God Has Spoken Fully and Finally in His Son

1 After God spoke long ago [a]in various portions[1] and in various ways to our ancestors through the prophets, [2]in these last days he has spoken to us in a son,[1] whom he appointed heir of all things, and through whom he created the world. [3]The [a]Son is the radiance of his glory and the [b]representation of his essence, and he [c]sustains all things by his powerful word,[1] and so [d]when he had accomplished cleansing for sins, he [e]*sat down at the right hand of the Majesty on high*.[2] [4]Thus [a]he became so far better than the angels as he has inherited a name superior to theirs.

The Son Is Superior to Angels

[5]For to which of the angels did God ever say, "*You are my son! Today I have fathered* [a]*you*"?[1] And in another place he says, "[b]*I will be his father and he will be my son*."[2] [6]But when [a]he again brings his firstborn into the world, he says, "[b]*Let all the angels of God worship him!*"[1] [7]And he says of the angels, "*He makes his angels winds and his ministers a flame of fire*,"[1] [8]but of[1] the Son he says,

"[a]*Your throne, O God, is forever and ever,*
and a righteous scepter is the scepter of your kingdom.
[9] *You have loved righteousness and hated lawlessness.*
So God, your God, [a]*has anointed you over your companions with the oil of rejoicing*."[1]

[10]And,

"*You founded the earth in the beginning, Lord,*
and the heavens are the works of [a]*your hands.*
[11] [a]*They will perish, but you continue.*
And they will all grow old like a garment,
[12] *and like a robe you will fold them up*
and like a garment[1] *they will be changed,*
but you are the [a]*same and your years will never run out*."[2]

[13]But to which of the angels has he ever said, "*Sit* [a]*at my right hand until I make your enemies a footstool for your feet*"?[1] [14]Are

---

1:1 [a] Num 12:6, 8; Joel 2:28 [1] Or *many times*.   1:2 [1] The Grk. emphasizes the quality of God's final revelation in the Son. 1:3 [a] John 1:14 [b] 2 Cor 4:4; Col 1:15 [c] Col 1:17 [d] [Heb 7:27] [e] Ps 110:1 [1] Grk. *by the word of his power*. [2] [Ps 110:1]   1:4 [a] Isa 9:6–7; Luke 1:32–33; [Phil 2:9–10]   1:5 [a] Ps 2:7; Acts 13:33; Heb 5:5 [b] 2 Sam 7:14 [1] Ps 2:7 [2] 2 Sam 7:14   1:6 [a] Ps 89:27; [Rom 8:29] [b] Deut 32:43, LXX, DSS; Ps 97:7; 1 Pet 3:22; Rev 5:11–13 [1] Deut 32:43; Ps 97:7   1:7 [1] Ps 104:4   1:8 [a] Ps 45:6–7 [1] Or *to*. 1:9 [a] Isa 61:1, 3 [1] Ps 45:6–7   1:10 [a] Ps 102:25–27   1:11 [a] [Isa 34:4]   1:12 [a] Heb 13:8 [1] Maj. wss omit *like a garment*; it is not in Ps 102:26 (101:27 LXX). [2] Ps 102:25–27   1:13 [a] Ps 110:1; Matt 22:44; Heb 1:3 [1] Ps 110:1

[a]they not all ministering spirits, sent out to serve those who will [b]inherit salvation?

Warning against Drifting Away

2 Therefore we must pay closer attention to what we have heard, so that we do not drift away. [2]For if the message [a]spoken through angels proved to be so firm that [b]every violation or disobedience received its just penalty, [3][a]how will we escape if we neglect such a great salvation? [b]It was first communicated through the Lord and was [c]confirmed to us by those who heard him, [4]while [a]God confirmed their witness with signs and wonders and various miracles and gifts of the Holy Spirit [b]distributed[1] according [c]to his will.

Exposition of Psalm 8: Jesus and the Destiny of Humanity

[5]For [a]he did not put the world to come, about which we are speaking, under the control of angels. [6]Instead someone testified somewhere:

> "[a]*What is man that you think of him*
> *or the son of man that you care for*
> *him?*
> [7] *You made him lower than the angels*
> *for a little while.*
> *You crowned him with glory and*
> *honor.*[1]
> [8] [a]*You put all things under his control.*"[1]

For when he *put all things under his control,* he left nothing outside of his control. At present [b]we do not yet see *all things under his control,*[2] [9]but we see Jesus, [a]who was made *lower than the angels for a little while,*[1] now [b]crowned with glory and honor because he suffered death,[2] so that by God's grace he would experience death on behalf [c]of everyone. [10]For it was fitting for him, [a]for whom and through whom all things exist, in bringing many sons to glory, to make the pioneer of their salvation [b]perfect through sufferings. [11]For [a]indeed [b]he who makes holy and those being made holy all have the same origin, and so he is not ashamed to call them brothers and sisters,[1] [12]saying, "[a]*I will proclaim your name to my brothers; in the midst of the assembly I will praise you.*"[1] [13]Again he says, "[a]I will be confident in him," and again, "[b]*Here I am, with the children God has given me.*"[1] [14]Therefore, since the children share in flesh and blood, [a]he likewise shared in their humanity, so [b]that through [c]death he could destroy[1] the one who holds the power of death (that is, the devil), [15]and set free those who were held in slavery all their lives by their fear of death. [16]For surely his concern is not for angels, but he is concerned for Abraham's descendants. [17]Therefore he had [a]to be [b]made like his brothers and sisters[1] in every respect, so that he could become a merciful and faithful high priest in things relating to God, to make atonement[2] for the sins of the people. [18][a]For since he himself suffered when he was tempted, he is able to help those who are tempted.

Jesus and Moses

3 Therefore, holy brothers and sisters,[1] partners in a heavenly calling, take note of Jesus, the apostle and high priest whom we confess, [2]who is faithful to the one who appointed him, as [a]Moses was also in God's house.[1] [3]For [a]he has come to deserve greater glory than Moses, just as the builder of a house deserves greater honor than the house itself! [4]For every house is built by someone, but [a]the builder of all things is God. [5]Now Moses was *faithful in all God's house*[1] as [a]a [b]servant, [c]to testify to the things that would be spoken. [6]But Christ is [a]faithful as a son over God's house. We are of [b]his house, [c]if in fact we hold firmly[1] to our confidence and the hope we take pride in.

1:14 [a]Ps 103:20; Dan 7:10 [b]Rom 8:17 **2:2** [a]Deut 33:2; Acts 7:53; Gal 3:19 [b]Num 15:30 **2:3** [a]Heb 10:28 [b]Matt 4:17 [c]Mark 16:20; Luke 1:2; 1 John 1:1 **2:4** [a]Mark 16:20 [b]1 Cor 12:4, 7, 11; Eph 4:7 [c]Eph 1:5, 9 [1]Grk. *and distributions of the Holy Spirit.* **2:5** [a][2 Pet 3:13] **2:6** [a]Job 7:17; Ps 8:4–6 **2:7** [1]Sev. early and sig. wss add *You have given him dominion over the works of your hands;* likely to conform to Ps 8:6 (8:7 LXX). **2:8** [a]Matt 28:18 [b]Ps 8:6; 1 Cor 15:25, 27 [1]Ps 8:4–6 [2]Ps 8:6 **2:9** [a]Phil 2:7–9; Heb 1:9 [b]Acts 2:33; 3:13; 1 Pet 1:21 [c]Isa 53:12; [John 3:16] [1]Ps 8:5 [2]Grk. *because of the suffering of death.* **2:10** [a]Col 1:16 [b]Heb 5:8–9; 7:28 **2:11** [a]Heb 10:10 [b]Matt 28:10 [1]Grk. *brothers;* considerable external evidence supports use of the Grk. word as *brothers and sisters* or *fellow Christians.* **2:12** [a]Ps 22:22 [1]Ps 22:22 **2:13** [a]2 Sam 22:3; Isa 8:17 [b]Isa 8:18 [1]Isa 8:17–18 **2:14** [a]John 1:14 [b]Col 2:15 [c][1 Cor 15:54–57]; 2 Tim 1:10 [1]Or *break the power of, reduce to nothing.* **2:17** [a]Phil 2:7; Heb 2:14 [b][Heb 4:15; 5:1–10] [1]Grk. *brothers;* considerable external evidence supports use of the Grk. word as *brothers and sisters* or *fellow Christians.* [2]Or *propitiation.* **2:18** [a][Heb 4:15–16] **3:1** [1]Grk. *brothers;* considerable external evidence supports use of the Grk. word as *brothers and sisters* or *fellow Christians.* **3:2** [a]Exod 40:16; Num 12:7; Heb 3:5 [1]‡ Maj. mss *in all his house.* **3:3** [a]Zech 6:12–13 **3:4** [a][Eph 2:10] **3:5** [a]Exod 40:16; Num 12:7; Heb 3:2 [b]Exod 14:31; Num 12:7 [c]Deut 18:15, 18, 19 [1]Num 12:7 **3:6** [a]Ps 2:7; 110:4; Heb 1:2 [b][1 Cor 3:16]; 1 Tim 3:15 [c][Matt 10:22] [1]Maj. mss *secure until the end.*

Exposition of Psalm 95: Hearing God's Word in Faith

[7]Therefore, as [a]the Holy Spirit says,

> *"Oh, that [b]today you would listen as he speaks!"*[1]
> [8] *Do not harden your hearts as in the rebellion, in the day of testing in the wilderness.*
> [9] *There your fathers tested me and tried me, and they saw my works for forty years.*
> [10] *Therefore, I became provoked at that generation and said, 'Their hearts are always wandering, and they have not known my ways.'*
> [11] *As I swore in my anger, 'They will never enter my rest!'"*[1]

[12]See to it, brothers and sisters,[1] that none of you has an evil, unbelieving heart that forsakes[2] the living God. [13]But exhort one another each day, as long as it is called "Today," that none of you may become hardened by sin's deception. [14]For we have become partners with Christ, if in fact we hold our initial confidence firm until the end. [15]As it says, *"Oh, that [a]today you would listen as he speaks![1] Do not harden your hearts as in the rebellion."*[2] [16a]For which ones heard and rebelled? Was it not all who came out of Egypt under Moses' leadership? [17]And against whom was God provoked for forty years? Was it not those who sinned, [a]*whose dead bodies fell in the wilderness?*[1] [18]And [a]to whom did he swear they would never enter into his rest, except those who were disobedient? [19]So we see that they could not enter because of [a]unbelief.

God's Promised Rest

4 Therefore we must be wary that, while the promise of entering his rest remains open, none of you may seem to have come short of it. [2]For we had good news proclaimed to us just as they did. But the message they heard did them no good, since they did not join in with those who heard it in faith.[1] [3]For we who have believed enter that rest, as he has said, "[a]*As I swore in my anger, 'They will never enter my rest!'"*[1] And yet God's works were accomplished from the foundation of the world. [4]For he has spoken somewhere about the seventh day in this way: "[a]*And God rested on the seventh day from all his works,"*[1] [5]but to repeat [a]the text cited earlier: *"They will never enter my rest!"*[1] [6]Therefore it remains for some to enter it, yet those to whom it was previously proclaimed did not enter because of disobedience. [7]So God again ordains a certain day, "[a]Today," speaking through David after so long a time, as in the words quoted before, *"Oh, that today you would listen as he speaks![1] Do not harden your hearts."*[2] [8]For if Joshua had [a]given them rest, God would not have spoken afterward about another day. [9]Consequently a Sabbath rest remains for the people of God. [10]For the one who enters God's rest has also rested from his works, just as God did from his own works. [11a]Thus we must make every effort to enter that rest, so that no one may fall by following the same pattern of disobedience. [12]For the word of God is [a]living and active and [b]sharper than any [c]double-edged sword, piercing even to the point of dividing soul from spirit, [d]and joints from marrow; it is able to judge the desires and thoughts of the heart. [13a]And no creature is hidden from God, but everything is [b]naked and exposed to the eyes of him to whom we must render an account.

Jesus Our Compassionate High Priest

[14]Therefore since we have a great [a]high priest who has passed through the heavens, Jesus the Son of God, [b]let us hold fast to our confession. [15]For [a]we do not have [b]a high priest incapable of sympathizing with our weaknesses, but one who has been tempted in every way just as we are, [c]yet without sin. [16]Therefore [a]let us confidently approach the throne of grace to receive mercy and find grace whenever we need help.

3:7 [a] Acts 1:16 [b] Ps 95:7–11; Heb 3:15; 4:7 [1] Grk. *today if you hear his voice.* **3:11** [1] Ps 95:7b–11 **3:12** [1] Grk. *brothers;* considerable external evidence supports use of the Grk. word as *brothers and sisters* or *fellow Christians.* [2] Or *deserts, rebels against.* **3:15** [a] Ps 95:7–8 [1] Grk. *today if you hear his voice.* [2] Ps 95:7b–8 **3:16** [a] Num 14:2, 11, 30; Deut 1:35–36, 38 **3:17** [a] Num 14:22–23 [1] [Num 14:29, 32] **3:18** [a] Num 14:30 **3:19** [a] Num 14:1–39; 1 Cor 10:11–12 **4:2** [1] A few MSS *since it [the message] was not combined with faith by those who heard it.* **4:3** [a] Ps 95:11; Heb 3:11 [1] Ps 95:11 **4:4** [a] Gen 2:2; Exod 20:11; 31:17 [1] Gen 2:2 **4:5** [a] Ps 95:11 [1] Ps 95:11 **4:7** [a] Ps 95:7–8 [1] Grk. *today if you hear his voice.* [2] Ps 95:7b–8 **4:8** [a] Josh 22:4 **4:11** [a] 2 Pet 1:10 **4:12** [a] Ps 147:15 [b] Isa 49:2 [c] Eph 6:17; Rev 2:12 [d] [John 12:48]; 1 Cor 14:24–25 **4:13** [a] 2 Chr 16:9; Ps 33:13–15; 90:8 [b] Job 26:6; Prov 15:11 **4:14** [a] Heb 2:17; 7:26 [b] Heb 10:23 **4:15** [a] Isa 53:3–5 [b] Luke 22:28 [c] 2 Cor 5:21; Heb 7:26 **4:16** [a] [Eph 2:18; Heb 10:19, 22]

5 For every high priest [a]is taken from among the people[1] and appointed to represent them before God, to offer both gifts and sacrifices for sins. [2]He is able to deal compassionately with those who are ignorant and erring, since he also is subject to [a]weakness, [3]and for this reason he is obligated to make sin offerings for [a]himself as well as for the people. [4]And no one assumes this honor on his own initiative, but only when called to it by God, as in fact [a]Aaron was. [5][a]So also Christ did not glorify himself in becoming high priest, but the one who glorified him was God, who said to him, "*You are my Son! Today I have fathered [b]you,*"[1] [6]as also in another place God says, "[a]*You are a priest forever in the order of Melchizedek.*"[1] [7]During his earthly life Christ [a]offered both requests and supplications, [b]with loud cries and tears, to the one [c]who was able to save him from death, and he was heard because [d]of his devotion. [8]Although he was a son, he learned [a]obedience through the things he suffered. [9]And by being perfected [a]in this way, he became the source of eternal salvation to all who obey him, [10]and he was designated by God as high priest [a]*in the order of Melchizedek.*[1]

The Need to Move on to Maturity

[11]On this topic [a]we have much to say, and it is difficult to explain, since you have become [b]sluggish in hearing. [12]For though you should in fact be teachers by this time, you need someone to teach you the beginning elements of God's utterances. You have gone back to needing [a]milk, not solid food. [13]For everyone who lives on milk is inexperienced in the [a]message of righteousness because he is an infant. [14]But solid food is for the mature, whose perceptions are trained by practice [a]to discern both good and evil.

6 Therefore we must progress [a]beyond the elementary instructions about Christ and move on to maturity, not laying this foundation again: repentance from [b]dead works and faith in God, [2]teaching about ritual washings, laying on [a]of hands, resurrection [b]of the dead, [c]and eternal judgment. [3]And this is what we intend to do, if God permits. [4]For it is impossible in the case of [a]those who [b]have once been enlightened, tasted the heavenly gift, become partakers of the Holy Spirit, [5]tasted the good word of God and the miracles of the coming age, [6]and then have committed apostasy,[1] to renew them again to repentance, [a]since they are crucifying the Son of God for themselves all over again and holding him up to contempt. [7]For the ground that has soaked up the rain that frequently falls on it and yields useful vegetation for those who tend it [a]receives a blessing from God. [8][a]But if it produces thorns and thistles, it is useless and about to be cursed; its fate is to be burned. [9]But in your case, dear friends, even though we speak like this, we are convinced of better things relating to salvation. [10]For [a]God is not unjust so as to forget [b]your work and the love you have demonstrated for his name, in having [c]served and continuing to serve the saints. [11]But we passionately want each of you to demonstrate the same eagerness [a]for the fulfillment of your hope until the end, [12]so that you may not be sluggish, but imitators of those who through faith and perseverance [a]inherit the promises.

[13]Now [a]when God made his promise to Abraham, since he could swear by no one greater, he swore by himself, [14]saying, "[a]*Surely I will bless you greatly and multiply your descendants abundantly.*"[1,2] [15]And so by persevering, Abraham inherited the [a]promise. [16]For people[1] swear by something greater [a]than themselves, and the oath serves as a confirmation to end all dispute. [17]In [a]the same way God wanted to demonstrate more clearly to [b]the heirs of the promise that his purpose was unchangeable,[1] and so he intervened with an oath, [18]so that we who have found refuge in him may find strong encouragement to hold fast to the hope set before us through two unchangeable things, since it is impossible for God to [a]lie. [19]We have

5:1 [a]Heb 2:17; 8:3 [1]Grk. *from among men*; but shared humanity is understood. **5:2** [a]Heb 7:28 **5:3** [a]Lev 9:7; 16:6; [Heb 7:27; 9:7] **5:4** [a]Exod 28:1; Num 16:40; 1 Chr 23:13 **5:5** [a]John 8:54 [b]Ps 2:7 [1]Ps 2:7 **5:6** [a]Ps 110:4; Heb 7:17 [1]Ps 110:4 **5:7** [a]Matt 26:39, 42, 44; Mark 14:36, 39; Luke 22:41, 44 [b]Ps 22:1 [c]Matt 26:53 [d]Matt 26:39 **5:8** [a]Phil 2:8 **5:9** [a]Heb 2:10 **5:10** [a]Ps 110:4 [1]Ps 110:4 **5:11** [a][John 16:12]; Heb 7:1–22 [b][Matt 13:15] **5:12** [a]1 Cor 3:1–3; 1 Pet 2:2 **5:13** [a]Eph 4:14 **5:14** [a]Isa 7:15; Phil 1:9 **6:1** [a]Heb 5:12 [b][Heb 9:14] **6:2** [a]John 3:25; Acts 19:3–5 [b][Acts 8:17] [c]Acts 24:25 **6:4** [a][John 4:10]; Eph 2:8 [b][Gal 3:2, 5]; Heb 2:4 **6:6** [a]Heb 10:29 [1]Or *have fallen away.* **6:7** [a]Ps 65:10 **6:8** [a]Isa 5:6 **6:10** [a]Rom 3:4 [b]1 Thess 1:3 [c]Rom 15:25; Heb 10:32–34 **6:11** [a]Col 2:2 **6:12** [a]Heb 10:36 **6:13** [a]Gen 22:16–17; Luke 1:73 **6:14** [a]Gen 22:16–17 [1]Gen 22:17 [2]Grk. *in blessing I will bless you and in multiplying I will multiply you*; the Grk. form of a Heb. idiom showing intensity. **6:15** [a]Gen 12:4; 21:5 **6:16** [a]Exod 22:11 [1]Grk. *men*; used generically for men and women. **6:17** [a]Rom 8:17; Heb 11:9 [b]Rom 11:29 [1]Or *immutable*; Grk. *the unchangeableness of his purpose.* **6:18** [a]Num 23:19; 1 Sam 15:29; Titus 1:2

this hope as an anchor for the soul, sure [a]and steadfast, which reaches inside behind the curtain, [20][a]where Jesus our forerunner entered on our behalf, since he became [b]*a priest forever in the order of Melchizedek.*[1]

The Nature of Melchizedek's Priesthood

7 Now this [a]*Melchizedek, king of Salem, priest of the most high God, met Abraham as he was returning from defeating the kings* and *blessed him.*[1] [2]To him also *Abraham apportioned a tithe of everything.*[1] His name first means king of righteousness, then *king of Salem,*[2] that is, king of peace. [3]Without father, without mother, without genealogy, he has neither beginning of days nor end of life but is like the son of God, and he remains a priest for all time. [4]But see how great he must be, if Abraham the patriarch gave him a tithe of his plunder. [5]And [a]those of the sons of Levi who receive the priestly office have authorization according to the law to collect a tithe from the people, that is, from their fellow countrymen, although they, too, are descendants of Abraham. [6]But Melchizedek who does not share their ancestry collected a tithe from Abraham [a]and blessed the one who possessed the promise. [7]Now without dispute the inferior is blessed by the superior, [8]and in one case tithes are received by mortal men, while in the other by him who is affirmed to be alive. [9]And it could be said that Levi himself, who receives tithes, paid a tithe through Abraham. [10]For he was still in his ancestor Abraham's loins when Melchizedek met him.

Jesus and the Priesthood of Melchizedek

[11]So if perfection had in fact been possible through [a]the Levitical priesthood—for on that basis the people received the law—what further need would there have been for another priest to arise, said to be in the order of Melchizedek and not in Aaron's order? [12]For when the priesthood changes, a change in the law must come as well. [13]Yet the one these things are spoken about belongs to a different tribe, and no one from that tribe has ever officiated at the altar. [14]For it is clear that [a]our Lord is descended from [b]Judah, yet Moses said nothing about priests in connection with that tribe. [15]And this is even clearer if another priest arises in the likeness of Melchizedek, [16]who has become a priest not by a legal regulation about physical descent but by the power of an indestructible life. [17]For here is the testimony about him: "[a]*You are a priest forever in the order of Melchizedek.*"[1] [18]On the one hand a former command is set aside because [a]it is weak and useless, [19]for [a]the [b]law made nothing perfect. On the other hand a better hope is introduced, through which [c]we draw near to God. [20]And since this was not done without a sworn affirmation—for the others have become priests without a sworn affirmation, [21]but Jesus did so with a sworn affirmation by [a]the one who said to him, *"The Lord has sworn and will not change his mind, 'You are a priest forever'"*[1]—[22]accordingly Jesus has become the guarantee of a [a]better covenant. [23]And the others who became priests were numerous because death prevented them from continuing in office, [24]but he holds his priesthood permanently since he lives forever. [25]So he is [a]able [b]to save completely those who come to God through him because he always lives to intercede for them. [26]For it is indeed fitting for us to have such a high priest: holy, innocent, undefiled, separate from sinners, [a]and exalted above the heavens. [27]He has no need to do every day what those priests do, to offer sacrifices first for their [a]own sins and then for the sins of the people, since he did this in offering himself once for all. [28]For the law appoints as high priests men subject to weakness, but the word of solemn affirmation that came after the law appoints a son made perfect forever.

The High Priest of a Better Covenant

8 Now the main point of what we are saying is this: We have such a high priest, one [a]who *sat down at the right hand of the throne of the Majesty in heaven,*[1] [2]a minister in [a]the sanctuary and [b]the true tabernacle

6:19 [a]Lev 16:2, 15; Heb 9:3, 7   **6:20** [a][John 14:2; Heb 4:14]   [b]Gen 14:17-19; Ps 110:4; Heb 3:1; 5:10-11   [1]Ps 110:4   **7:1** [a]Gen 14:18-20; Heb 7:6   [1]Gen 14:17-19   **7:2** [1]Gen 14:20   [2]Gen 14:18   **7:5** [a]Num 18:21-26; 2 Chr 31:4   **7:6** [a]Gen 14:19-20   **7:11** [a][Rom 7:7-14]; Gal 2:21; Heb 7:18; 8:7   **7:14** [a]Gen 49:8-10; Num 24:17; Isa 1:1; Mic 5:2; Matt 1:3; 2:6; Rev 5:5   [b]Matt 1:2   **7:17** [a]Ps 110:4; Heb 5:6; 6:20; 7:21   [1]Ps 110:4   **7:18** [a][Rom 8:3]; Gal 3:21; Heb 7:11   **7:19** [a][Acts 13:39]; Rom 3:20; 7:7; Gal 2:16; 3:21; Heb 9:9; 10:1   [b]Heb 6:18-19   [c]Lam 3:57; Rom 5:2; [Eph 2:18]; Heb 4:16; Jas 4:8   **7:21** [a]Ps 110:4; Heb 5:6; 7:17   [1]Ps 110:4   **7:22** [a]Heb 8:6   **7:25** [a]Jude 24   [b]Rom 8:34; 1 Tim 2:5; Heb 9:24; 1 John 2:1   **7:26** [a]Eph 1:20   **7:27** [a]Lev 9:7; 16:6; Heb 5:3   **8:1** [a]Ps 68:18; 110:1; Eph 1:20; Col 3:1; Heb 2:17; 3:1; 10:12   [1][Ps 110:1]   **8:2** [a]Heb 9:8, 12   [b]Heb 9:11, 24

that the Lord, not man, set up. [3]For [a]every high priest is appointed to offer both gifts and sacrifices. So this one, too, had to have something to offer. [4]Now if he were on earth, he would not be a priest, since there are already priests who offer the gifts prescribed by the law. [5]The place where [a]they serve is a sketch[1] and [b]shadow of the heavenly sanctuary, just as Moses was warned by God as he was about to complete the tabernacle. For he says, "[c]*See that you make everything according to the design[2] shown to you on the mountain.*"[3] [6]But now Jesus has obtained a superior ministry, since [a]the covenant that he mediates is also [b]better and is enacted on better promises.

[7]For if that [a]first covenant had been faultless, no one would have looked for a second one.[1] [8]But showing its fault, God says to them,[1]

"Look, the days are coming, says the Lord, when I will complete a new covenant with the house of Israel and with the house of Judah.
[9] *It will not be like the covenant that I made with their fathers, on the day when I took them by the hand to lead them out of Egypt, because they did not continue in my covenant, and I had no regard for them, says the Lord.*
[10] *For this is the covenant that I will establish with the house of Israel after those days, says the [a]Lord. [b]I will put my laws in their minds, and I will inscribe them on their hearts. And I will be their God, and they will be my people.*
[11] *And there will be [a]no need at all for each one to teach his countryman or each one to teach his brother saying, 'Know the [b]Lord,' since they will all know me, from the least to the greatest.*
[12] *For I will be merciful toward their evil deeds, [a]and their sins I will remember no longer.*"[1]

[13]When he speaks of a new covenant, he makes the first obsolete. Now what is [a]growing obsolete and aging is about to disappear.

The Arrangement and Ritual of the Earthly Sanctuary

9 Now [a]the first covenant, in fact, had regulations for worship and its earthly sanctuary. [2]For a tent was prepared, the outer one, which contained the lampstand, the table, and the presentation of the loaves; this is called the Holy Place. [3a]And after the second curtain there was a tent called the holy of holies. [4]It contained the [a]golden altar of incense and [b]the ark of [c]the covenant covered entirely with gold. In this ark were the golden urn containing the manna, [d]Aaron's rod that budded, and [e]the stone tablets of the covenant. [5]And [a]above the ark were the cherubim of glory overshadowing the mercy seat. Now is not the time to speak of these things in detail. [6]So with [a]these things prepared like this, the priests enter continually into the outer tent as they perform their duties. [7]But only the high priest enters [a]once a year into the inner tent, and not without blood that he offers for [b]himself and for the sins of the people committed in ignorance.[1] [8]The Holy Spirit is making clear that [a]the way into the Holy Place had not yet appeared as long as the old tabernacle was standing. [9]This was a symbol for the time then present, when gifts and sacrifices were offered that could not perfect the conscience of the worshiper. [10]They served only for matters of [a]food and drink and [b]various ritual washings; [c]they are external regulations[1] imposed until the new order came.

Christ's Service in the Heavenly Sanctuary

[11]But now Christ has come as [a]the high priest of the good things to come. He passed through the greater and more perfect tent not made with hands, that is, not of this

8:3 [a][Rom 4:25; 5:6, 8; Gal 2:20; Eph 5:2]; Heb 5:1; 8:4   **8:5** [a]Heb 9:23–24   [b]Col 2:17; Heb 10:1   [c]Exod 25:40   [1]Or *prototype, outline.*   [2]Or *type, pattern, model.*   [3]Exod 25:40   **8:6** [a][2 Cor 3:6–8]   [b][Luke 22:20]; Heb 7:22   **8:7** [a]Exod 3:8; 19:5   [1]Grk. *no occasion for a second one would have been sought.*   **8:8** [1]‡ Several wss [in finding fault with] *them,* [he says]; alluding to Israel's failings mentioned in v. 9b.   **8:10** [a]Jer 31:33; Rom 11:27; Heb 10:16   [b]Zech 8:8   **8:11** [a]Isa 54:13; John 6:45; [1 John 2:27]   [b]Jer 31:34   **8:12** [a]Rom 11:27   [1]Jer 31:31–34   **8:13** [a][2 Cor 5:17]; Heb 1:11   **9:1** [a]Exod 25:8; [Heb 8:2; 9:11, 24]   **9:3** [a]Exod 26:31–35; 40:3   **9:4** [a]Lev 16:12   [b]Exod 25:10   [c]Exod 16:33   [d]Num 17:1–10   [e]Exod 25:16; 34:29; Deut 10:2–5   **9:5** [a]Exod 25:17, 20; Lev 16:2; 1 Kgs 8:7   **9:6** [a]Num 18:2–6; 28:3   **9:7** [a]Exod 30:10; Lev 16:34; Heb 10:3   [b]Heb 5:3   [1]Or perhaps *the unintentional sins of the people;* Grk. *the ignorances of the people.*   **9:8** [a][John 14:6; Heb 10:20]   **9:10** [a]Lev 11:2; Col 2:16   [b]Num 19:7   [c]Eph 2:15   [1]Maj. wss *various washings, and external regulations.*   **9:11** [a][Eph 1:3–11]; Heb 10:1

creation, [12] and he entered once for [a] all into the Most Holy Place not [b] by the blood of goats and calves but [c] by his own blood, and so he himself secured eternal redemption. [13] For if [a] the blood of goats and bulls and [b] the ashes of a young cow sprinkled on those who are defiled consecrated them and provided ritual purity, [14] how much more will the blood of Christ, who through the eternal Spirit offered himself without blemish to God, [a] purify our[1] consciences from [b] dead works [c] to worship the living God.

[15] And so [a] he is the mediator of a new covenant, so that [b] those who are called may receive the eternal inheritance he has promised, since he died to set them free from the violations committed under the first covenant. [16] For where there is a will, the death of the one who made it must be proven. [17] For [a] a will takes effect only at death, since it carries no force while the one who made it is alive. [18] So even [a] the first covenant was inaugurated with blood. [19] For [a] when Moses had spoken every command to all the people according to the law, he took the blood of calves and goats [b] with water and scarlet wool and hyssop and sprinkled both the book itself and all the people, [20] and said, "[a]*This is the* [b]*blood of the covenant that God has commanded you to keep.*"[1] [21] And both [a] the tabernacle and all the utensils of worship he likewise sprinkled with blood. [22] Indeed according to the law almost everything was purified with blood, and [a] without the shedding of blood there is no forgiveness. [23] So it was necessary for [a] the sketches[1] of the things in heaven to be purified with these sacrifices, but the heavenly things themselves required better sacrifices than these. [24] For [a] Christ did not enter a sanctuary made with hands—[b] the representation of the true sanctuary—but [c] into heaven itself, and he appears now in God's presence for us. [25] And [a] he did not enter to offer himself again and again, the way the high priest enters the sanctuary year after year with blood that is not his own, [26] for then he would have had to suffer again and again since the foundation of the world. But now he has appeared once for all at the consummation of the ages to put away sin by his sacrifice. [27] [a] And just as people[1] are appointed to die once, [b] and then to face judgment, [28] so also, after [a] Christ was [b] offered once to *bear the sins* [c]*of many,*[1] to those who [d] eagerly await him he will appear a second time, not to bear sin but to bring salvation.

Concluding Exposition: Old and New Sacrifices Contrasted

10 For the law possesses a [a] shadow of the good things to come but not the reality itself, and is therefore completely [b] unable, by the same sacrifices offered continually, year after year, to perfect those who come to worship. [2] For otherwise would they not have ceased to be offered, since the worshipers would have been purified once for all and so have no further consciousness of sin? [3] But in those sacrifices there is a reminder of sins year after year. [4] For [a] it is impossible for the blood of bulls and goats to take away sins. [5] So when he came into the world, he said,

> "[a]*Sacrifice and offering you did not*
> *desire, but a body you prepared*
> *for me.*
> [6] *Whole burnt offerings and*
> *sin-offerings you took no delight in.*
> [7] *Then I said, 'Here I am: I have come—it*
> *is written of me in the scroll of the*
> *book—to do your will, O God.'*"[1]

[8] When he says above, "*Sacrifices and offerings* and *whole burnt offerings and sin-offerings you did not desire nor did you take delight* in them"[1] (which are offered according to the law), [9] then he says, "*Here I am: I have come to do your will.*"[1,2] He does away with the first to establish the second. [10] [a] By his will we have been made holy [b] through the offering of the body of Jesus Christ once for all. [11] And every priest stands day after day [a] serving and offering the same

9:12 [a] Zech 3:9 [b] Heb 10:4 [c] Isa 53:12; Eph 1:7 **9:13** [a] Lev 16:14–15; Heb 9:19; 10:4 [b] Num 19:2 **9:14** [a] 1 John 1:7 [b] Heb 6:1 [c] Luke 1:74 [1] Many wss *your.* **9:15** [a] Rom 3:25 [b] Heb 3:1 **9:17** [a] Gal 3:15 **9:18** [a] Exod 24:6 **9:19** [a] Exod 24:5–6 [b] Lev 14:4, 7; Num 19:6, 18 **9:20** [a] [Matt 26:28] [b] Exod 24:3–8 [1] Exod 24:8 **9:21** [a] Exod 29:12, 36 **9:22** [a] Lev 17:11 **9:23** [a] Heb 8:5 [1] Or *prototypes, outlines*; referring to the earthly sanctuary. **9:24** [a] Heb 6:20 [b] Heb 8:2 [c] Rom 8:34 **9:25** [a] Heb 9:7 **9:27** [a] Gen 3:19; Eccl 3:20 [b] [2 Cor 5:10]; 1 John 4:17 [1] Grk. *men*; used generically for men and women. **9:28** [a] Rom 6:10 [b] Isa 53:12; 1 Pet 2:24 [c] Matt 26:28 [d] 1 Cor 1:7; Titus 2:13 [1] [Isa 53:12] **10:1** [a] Heb 8:5 [b] Heb 7:19; 9:9 **10:4** [a] Mic 6:6–7 **10:5** [a] Ps 40:6–8 **10:7** [1] Ps 40:6–8 LXX **10:8** [1] Ps 40:6 **10:9** [1] Ps 40:8 [2] Maj. mss *God.* **10:10** [a] John 17:19; [Eph 5:26; Heb 2:11; 10:14, 29; 13:12] [b] [Heb 9:12] **10:11** [a] Num 28:3

sacrifices again and again—sacrifices that can never take away sins. [12a]But when this priest had offered one sacrifice for sins for all time, *he sat down* [b]*at the right hand*[1] of God, [13]where he is now waiting [a]*until his enemies are made a footstool for his feet.*[1] [14]For by one offering he has perfected for all time those who are made holy. [15]And the Holy Spirit also witnesses to us, for after saying, [16]"[a]*This is the covenant that I will establish with them after those days, says the Lord. I will put my laws on their hearts and I will inscribe them on their minds,*"[1] [17]then he says, "[a]*Their sins and their lawless deeds I will remember no longer.*"[1] [18]Now where there is forgiveness of these, there is no longer any offering for sin.

Drawing Near to God in Enduring Faith

[19]Therefore, brothers and sisters,[1] since we have [a]confidence to enter [b]the sanctuary by the blood of Jesus, [20]by the fresh and [a]living way that he inaugurated for us through the curtain, that is, through his flesh, [21]and since we have a great priest over the house of God, [22]let us [a]draw near with a sincere heart [b]in the assurance that faith brings, because we have had our hearts sprinkled clean from an evil conscience and our bodies washed in pure water. [23]And let us hold unwaveringly to [a]the hope that we confess, for the one who made the promise is trustworthy. [24]And let us take thought of how to spur one another on to love and good works, [25a]not abandoning our own meetings, as [b]some are in [c]the habit of doing, but encouraging each other, and even more so because you see the day drawing near.

[26]For [a]if we deliberately keep on sinning [b]after receiving the [c]knowledge of the truth, no further sacrifice for sins is left for us, [27]but only a certain fearful expectation of judgment and *a fury*[1,2] of [a]*fire that will consume God's enemies.*[3] [28]Someone who rejected the law of Moses was put to death

without mercy *on the testimony of two or three* [a]*witnesses.*[1] [29]How much greater punishment do you think that person deserves who has contempt for[1] the Son [a]of God, and [b]profanes the blood of the covenant that made him holy, [c]and insults the Spirit of grace? [30]For we know the one who said, "[a]*Vengeance is mine, I will repay,*"[1] and again, "[b]*The Lord will judge his people.*"[2] [31a]It is a terrifying thing to fall into the hands of the living God.

[32]But [a]remember the former days when you endured a harsh conflict of suffering after you were enlightened. [33]At times you were publicly exposed to [a]abuse and afflictions, and at other times [b]you came to share with others who were treated in that way. [34]For [a]in fact you shared the sufferings of those in prison,[1] and you accepted the confiscation of your belongings with [b]joy, because [c]you knew that you certainly had a better and lasting possession. [35]So do not throw away your confidence, [a]because it has great reward. [36a]For [b]you need endurance in order to do God's will and so receive what is promised. [37]For [a]*just a little longer*[1] and [b]*he who is coming will arrive and not delay. [38]But my righteous one will live by faith, and if* [a]*he shrinks back, I take no pleasure in him.*[1] [39]But we are not among those [a]who shrink back and thus perish, but are among those who have [b]faith and preserve their souls.

People Commended for Their Faith

11 Now faith is being sure [a]of what we hope for, being convinced of what we do not see. [2]For by it the people of old received God's commendation. [3]By faith we understand that [a]the worlds were set in order at God's command, so that the visible has its origin in the invisible. [4]By faith [a]Abel offered God a greater sacrifice than Cain, and through his faith he was commended as righteous because God commended him for his offerings. And through his faith he still [b]speaks, though he is dead. [5]By faith

10:12 [a]Col 3:1; Heb 1:3   [b]Ps 110:1   [1][Ps 110:1]   10:13 [a]Ps 110:1; Heb 1:13   [1][Ps 110:1]   10:16 [a]Jer 31:33–34; Heb 8:10   [1]Jer 31:33   10:17 [a]Jer 31:34   [1]Jer 31:34   10:19 [a][Eph 2:18]; Heb 4:16   [b]Heb 9:8, 12   [1]Grk. *brothers*; considerable external evidence supports use of the Grk. word as *brothers and sisters* or *fellow Christians*.   10:20 [a]John 14:6; [Heb 7:24–25]   10:22 [a]Heb 7:19; 10:1   [b]Eph 3:12   10:23 [a]1 Cor 1:9; 10:13; 1 Thess 5:24; Heb 11:11   10:25 [a]Acts 2:42   [b]Rom 13:11   [c]Phil 4:5   10:26 [a]Num 15:30   [b]2 Pet 2:20   [c]Heb 6:6   10:27 [a]Zeph 1:18   [1][Zeph 1:18]   [2]Grk. *zeal*.   [3][Isa 26:11]   10:28 [a]Deut 17:2–6; 19:15; Matt 18:16; Heb 2:2   [1][Deut 17:6]   10:29 [a][Heb 2:3]   [b]1 Cor 11:29   [c][Matt 12:31]   [1]Grk. *tramples under foot*.   10:30 [a]Deut 32:35; Rom 12:19   [b]Deut 32:36   [1]Deut 32:35   [2]Deut 32:36   10:31 [a][Luke 12:5]   10:32 [a]Gal 3:4; Heb 6:9–10   10:33 [a]1 Cor 4:9; Heb 12:4   [b]Phil 1:7   10:34 [a]2 Tim 1:16   [b]Matt 5:12   [c]Matt 6:20   [1]Maj. wss *my imprisonment*.   10:35 [a]Matt 5:12   10:36 [a]Luke 21:19; Heb 12:1   [b][Col 3:24]   10:37 [a]Luke 18:8   [b]Hab 2:3–4; Heb 10:25; Rev 22:20   [1]Isa 26:20   10:38 [a]Hab 2:3–4; Rom 1:17; Gal 3:11   [1]Hab 2:3–4   10:39 [a]2 Pet 2:20   [b]Acts 16:31   11:1 [a]Rom 8:24; [2 Cor 4:18; 5:7]; Heb 11:7, 27   11:3 [a]Gen 1:1; Ps 33:6; [John 1:3]; 2 Pet 3:5   11:4 [a]Gen 4:3–5; Matt 23:35; 1 John 3:12   [b]Gen 4:8–10; Heb 12:24

Enoch was taken up so that he did not see death, [a] and he was not to be found because God took him up. For before his removal he had been commended as having pleased God. [6] Now without faith it is impossible to please him, for the one who approaches God must believe that he exists and that he rewards those who seek him. [7] By faith [a] Noah, when he was warned about things not yet seen, with reverent regard [b] constructed an ark for [c] the deliverance of his family. Through faith he condemned the world and became an heir of the righteousness that comes by faith.

[8] By faith [a] Abraham obeyed when he was called to go out to a place he would later receive as an inheritance, and he went out without understanding where he was going. [9] By faith he lived as a foreigner in the promised land as though it were a foreign country, [a] living in tents with Isaac and Jacob, who were fellow heirs of [b] the same promise. [10] For [a] he was looking forward to the city with firm foundations, [b] whose architect and builder is God. [11] By faith, even though [a] Sarah herself was barren and [b] he was too old, he received the ability to procreate[1] because he regarded the one who had given the promise to be [c] trustworthy. [12] So in fact children were fathered by one man—and this one as good as [a] dead—*like the number of* [b] *stars in the sky and like the innumerable grains of sand on the seashore.*[1] [13] These all died in faith [a] without receiving the things [b] promised, but they saw them [c] in the distance and welcomed them and [d] acknowledged that they were strangers and foreigners on the earth. [14] For those who speak in such a way [a] make it clear that they are seeking a homeland. [15] In fact, if they had been thinking of the land [a] that they had left, they would have had opportunity to return. [16] But as it is, they aspire [a] to a better land, that is, a heavenly one. Therefore, God is not ashamed to be called their God, for he has [b] prepared a city for them. [17] By faith Abraham, [a] when he was tested, offered up Isaac. He had received the promises, yet he was ready to offer up his only son. [18] God had told him, "[a] *Through Isaac descendants will carry on your name,*"[1] [19] and he reasoned that God could even raise him from the dead, and in [a] a sense he received him back from there. [20] By faith also [a] Isaac blessed Jacob and Esau concerning the future. [21] By faith Jacob, as he was dying, [a] blessed each of the sons of Joseph and *worshiped as he leaned on his staff.*[1] [22] By faith [a] Joseph, at the end of his life, mentioned the exodus of the sons of Israel and gave instructions about his burial.

[23] By faith, when [a] Moses was born, his parents hid him for three months because they saw the child was beautiful and they were not afraid of the king's [b] edict. [24] By faith, when he grew up, [a] Moses refused to be called the son of Pharaoh's daughter, [25] choosing rather to be ill-treated with the people of God than to enjoy sin's fleeting pleasure. [26] He regarded abuse suffered for Christ to be greater wealth than [a] the treasures of Egypt, for his eyes were fixed on the [b] reward. [27] By faith [a] he left Egypt without fearing the king's anger, for he persevered as though he could see the one who is invisible. [28] By faith [a] he kept the Passover and the sprinkling of the blood, so that the one who destroyed the firstborn would not touch them. [29] By faith [a] they crossed the Red Sea as if on dry ground, but when the Egyptians tried it, they were swallowed up. [30] By faith [a] the walls of Jericho fell after the people marched around them for seven days. [31] By faith Rahab [a] the prostitute escaped the destruction of the disobedient because [b] she welcomed the spies in peace.

[32] And what more shall I say? For time will fail me if I tell of [a] Gideon, [b] Barak, [c] Samson, [d] Jephthah, of [e] David and [f] Samuel and the prophets. [33] Through faith they conquered kingdoms, administered justice, gained what was promised, [a] shut the mouths of lions, [34] [a] quenched raging fire, escaped the edge of the sword, gained strength in

11:5 [a] Gen 5:21–24   11:7 [a] Gen 6:13–22   [b] 1 Pet 3:20   [c] Rom 3:22   11:8 [a] Gen 12:1–4; Acts 7:2–4   11:9 [a] Gen 12:8; 13:3, 18; 18:1, 9   [b] Heb 6:17   11:10 [a] [Heb 12:22; 13:14]   [b] [Rev 21:10]   11:11 [a] Gen 17:19; 18:11–14; 21:1–2   [b] Luke 1:36   [c] Heb 10:23   [1] Grk. *power to deposit seed, power to conceive seed*; the latter possibly indicating Sarah's faith.   11:12 [a] Rom 4:19   [b] Gen 15:5; 22:17; 32:12   [1] [Gen 22:17 (Gen 15:5)]   11:13 [a] Heb 11:39   [b] Gen 12:7   [c] John 8:56; Heb 11:27   [d] Gen 23:4; 47:9; 1 Chr 29:15; Ps 39:12; Eph 2:19; 1 Pet 1:17; 2:11   11:14 [a] Heb 13:14   11:15 [a] Gen 11:31   11:16 [a] Gen 26:24; 28:13; Exod 3:6, 15; 4:5   [b] [John 14:2]; Heb 11:10; [Rev 21:2]   11:17 [a] Gen 22:1–14; Jas 2:21   11:18 [a] Gen 21:12; Rom 9:7   [1] Gen 21:12   11:19 [a] Rom 4:17   11:20 [a] Gen 27:26–40   11:21 [a] Gen 48:1, 5, 16, 20   [1] Gen 47:31 LXX   11:22 [a] Gen 50:24–25; Exod 13:19   11:23 [a] Exod 2:1–3   [b] Exod 1:16, 22   11:24 [a] Exod 2:11–15   11:26 [a] Heb 13:13   [b] Rom 8:18; 2 Cor 4:17   11:27 [a] Exod 10:28   11:28 [a] Exod 12:21   11:29 [a] Exod 14:22–29; Jude 5   11:30 [a] Josh 6:20   11:31 [a] Josh 2:9; 6:23; Jas 2:25   [b] Josh 2:1   11:32 [a] Judg 6:11; 7:1–25   [b] Judg 4:6–24   [c] Judg 13:24—16:31   [d] Judg 11:1–29; 12:1–7   [e] 1 Sam 16; 17   [f] 1 Sam 7:9–14   11:33 [a] Judg 14:6; 1 Sam 17:34; Dan 6:22   11:34 [a] Dan 3:23–28

weakness, became mighty in battle, put foreign armies to flight, [35] and [a]women received back their dead raised to life. But others were [b]tortured, not accepting release, to obtain resurrection to a better life. [36] And others experienced mocking and flogging, and even chains and imprisonment. [37] They were stoned, sawed apart,[1] murdered with [a]the sword; [b]they went about [c]in sheepskins and goatskins; they were destitute, afflicted, ill-treated [38] (the world was not worthy of them); they wandered [a]in deserts and mountains and caves and openings in the earth. [39] And these all were commended for their faith, yet they did not receive what was promised. [40] For God had provided something better for us, so that they would be [a]made perfect together with us.

The Lord's Discipline

12 Therefore, since we are surrounded by such a great cloud of witnesses, we must get rid of every weight and the sin that clings so closely, and run [a]with endurance the race set out for us, [2] keeping our eyes fixed on Jesus, the pioneer and perfecter of our faith. For the joy set out for him he [a]endured the cross, disregarding its shame, and [b]*has taken his seat at the right hand of the throne* of God. [3][a]Think of him who endured such opposition against himself by sinners, so that you may not grow weary in your souls and give up. [4] You have not yet resisted to the point of bloodshed in [a]your struggle against sin. [5] And have you forgotten the exhortation addressed to you as sons?

> "[a]*My son, do not scorn the Lord's discipline*
> *or give up when he corrects you.*
> [6] *For the Lord disciplines the [a]one he loves and chastises every son he accepts.*"[1]

[7][a]Endure your suffering as discipline; God is treating you as sons. For what [b]son is there that a father does not discipline?

[8] But if you do not experience discipline, something all sons have shared in, then you are illegitimate and are not sons. [9] Besides, we have experienced discipline from our earthly [a]fathers and we respected them; shall we not submit ourselves all the more to the Father of spirits and receive life? [10] For they disciplined us for [a]a little while as seemed good to them, but he does so for our benefit, that we may share his holiness. [11] Now all discipline seems painful at [a]the time, not joyful. But later it produces the fruit of peace and righteousness for those trained by it. [12] Therefore, [a]*strengthen your listless hands and your weak knees,*[1] [13] and *make straight paths for your feet,*[1] so that what is lame may not be put out of joint but be healed.

Do not Reject God's Warning

[14][a]Pursue peace with everyone, and holiness, for [b]without it no one will see the Lord. [15] See to it that no one comes [a]short of the grace of God, that no one be like *a bitter* [b]*root springing up*[1] and causing trouble, and through it many become defiled. [16] And see to it that no one becomes an [a]immoral or godless person like Esau, [b]who *sold his own birthright for a single meal.*[1] [17] For you know that later when he wanted to inherit the blessing, he was [a]rejected, for he found no opportunity for repentance, although he sought the blessing with tears. [18] For you have not come to something that can be touched, to a burning fire and darkness and gloom and a whirlwind [19] and the blast of a trumpet and a voice uttering words such that those who heard [a]begged to hear no more. [20] For they could not bear what was [a]commanded: "*If even an animal touches the mountain, it must be stoned.*"[1] [21] In fact, the scene was so [a]terrifying that Moses said, "*I shudder with fear.*"[1] [22] But you have come to Mount Zion, the city of the living God, the heavenly Jerusalem, and to myriads of angels, to the assembly [23] and congregation of [a]the firstborn, [b]who are enrolled in

11:35 [a]1 Kgs 17:22; 2 Kgs 4:35–37 [b]Acts 22:25   11:37 [a]1 Kgs 21:13; 2 Chr 24:21; Acts 7:58 [b]2 Kgs 1:8; Matt 3:4 [c]1 Kgs 19:13, 19; 2 Kgs 2:8, 13; Zech 13:4 [1]Some wss *they were burned*; Some wss add *they were tempted*; or it replaces "sawed apart." 11:38 [a]1 Kgs 18:4, 13; 19:9   11:40 [a]Heb 5:9   12:1 [a]Rom 12:12; Heb 10:36   12:2 [a]Ps 69:7, 19; Phil 2:8; [Heb 2:9] [b]Ps 110:1 [1][Ps 110:1]   12:3 [a]Matt 10:24   12:4 [a][1 Cor 10:13]   12:5 [a]Job 5:17; Prov 3:11–12   12:6 [a]Ps 94:12; Rev 3:19 [1]Prov 3:11–12   12:7 [a]Deut 8:5; 2 Sam 7:14 [b]Prov 13:24; 19:18; 23:13   12:9 [a][Job 12:10]   12:10 [a]Lev 11:44   12:11 [a]Isa 32:17; 2 Tim 4:8; Jas 3:17–18   12:12 [a]Isa 35:3 [1]Isa 35:3   12:13 [1]Prov 4:26   12:14 [a]Ps 34:14 [b]Matt 5:8; [Heb 9:28]   12:15 [a]2 Cor 6:1; Gal 5:4; Heb 4:1 [b]Deut 29:18 [1][Deut 29:18]   12:16 [a][1 Cor 6:13–18] [b]Gen 25:33 [1][Gen 27:34–41]   12:17 [a]Gen 27:30–40   12:19 [a]Exod 20:18–26; Deut 5:25; 18:16   12:20 [a]Exod 19:12–13 [1]Exod 19:12–13   12:21 [a]Deut 9:19 [1]Deut 9:19   12:23 [a][Jas 1:18] [b]Luke 10:20

heaven, and to God, [c]the judge of all, and to the spirits of the righteous, who have been [d]made perfect, 24and to Jesus, [a]the mediator of a new covenant, and to [b]the sprinkled blood that speaks of something better [c]than Abel's does.

25Take care not to refuse the one who is speaking! For [a]if they did not escape when they refused the one who warned them on earth, how much less shall we, if we reject the one who warns from heaven? 26Then his voice shook the earth, but now he has promised, *"I will once [a]more shake not only the earth but heaven too."*[1] 27Now this phrase *"once more"*[1] indicates the [a]removal of what is shaken, that is, of created things, so that what is unshaken may remain. 28So since we are receiving an unshakable kingdom, let us give thanks, and through this let us offer [a]worship pleasing to God in devotion and awe. 29For [a]our *God is indeed a devouring fire.*[1]

Final Exhortations

13 Brotherly love must continue. 2[a]Do not neglect hospitality because through it [b]some have entertained angels without knowing it. 3[a]Remember those in prison as though you were in prison with them, and those ill-treated as though you, too, felt their torment. 4[a]Marriage must be honored among all and the marriage bed kept undefiled, [b]for God will judge sexually immoral people and adulterers. 5Your conduct must be free from the love of money, and you must be content [a]with what you have, for he has said, *"I will never leave you and I will never abandon you."*[1] 6So we can say with confidence, *"[a]The Lord is my helper, and I will not be afraid. What can people do to me?"*[1] 7Remember your leaders, who spoke God's message to you; reflect on the outcome of their lives and imitate their faith. 8Jesus Christ is [a]the same yesterday and today and forever! 9Do not be carried away by all sorts of strange teachings. For it is good for the heart to be strengthened by grace, not ritual meals, which have never benefited those who participated in them. 10We have an altar that those who serve in the tabernacle have no right to eat from. 11For the bodies of those animals whose blood the high priest brings into the sanctuary as an offering for sin are burned outside the camp. 12Therefore, to sanctify the people by his own blood, Jesus also suffered outside the camp. 13We must go out to [a]him, then, outside the camp, bearing the abuse he experienced. 14For here we have no lasting city, but we seek the city that is to come. 15Through him [a]then let us continually offer up a sacrifice of praise to God, that is, [b]the fruit of our lips, acknowledging his name. 16[a]And do not neglect to do good and to share what you have, for God is pleased [b]with such sacrifices.

17[a]Obey your leaders and submit to [b]them, for they keep watch over your souls and will give an account for their work. Let them do this with joy and not with complaints, for this would be no advantage for you. 18[a]Pray for us, for we are sure that we have a [b]clear conscience and desire to conduct ourselves rightly in every respect. 19I especially ask you to pray that I may be restored to you very soon.

Benediction and Conclusion

20Now may [a]the God of peace [b]who [c]by the blood of the eternal covenant brought back from the dead the great shepherd of the sheep, our Lord Jesus, 21equip you with every good thing to do his will, [a]working in us[1] what is pleasing before him through Jesus Christ, to whom be glory forever.[2] Amen.

22Now I urge you, brothers and sisters,[1] bear with my message of exhortation, for in fact I have written to you briefly. 23You should know that our brother Timothy has been released. If he comes soon, he will be with me when I see you. 24Greetings to all your leaders and all the saints. Those from Italy send you greetings. 25Grace be with you all.[1]

12:23 [c]Gen 18:25; Ps 50:6; 94:2   [d][Phil 3:12]   12:24 [a]1 Tim 2:5; Heb 8:6; 9:15   [b]Exod 24:8   [c]Gen 4:10; Heb 11:4   12:25 [a]Heb 2:2–3   12:26 [a]Hag 2:6   [1]Hag 2:6   12:27 [a][Isa 34:4; 54:10; 65:17; Rom 8:19, 21]; 1 Cor 7:31; Heb 1:10   [1]Hag 2:6   12:28 [a]Heb 13:15, 21   12:29 [a]Exod 24:17   [1]Deut 4:24; 9:3   13:2 [a]Matt 25:35; Rom 12:13   [b]Gen 18:1–22; 19:1   13:3 [a]Matt 25:36; Heb 10:34   13:4 [a]Prov 5:18–19   [b]1 Cor 6:9; Gal 5:19, 21; 1 Thess 4:6   13:5 [a]Gen 28:15; Deut 31:6, 8; Josh 1:5   [1]Deut 31:6, 8   13:6 [a]Ps 27:1; 118:6   [1]Ps 118:6   13:8 [a][John 8:58]; 2 Cor 1:19; Heb 1:12   13:13 [a]1 Pet 4:14   13:15 [a]Eph 5:20   [b]Lev 7:12   13:16 [a]Rom 12:13   [b]2 Cor 9:12; Phil 4:18   13:17 [a]Phil 2:29   [b]Isa 62:6; Ezek 3:17; Acts 20:28   13:18 [a]Eph 6:19   [b]Acts 23:1   13:20 [a]Rom 5:1–2, 10; 15:33   [b]Ps 16:10–11; Hos 6:2; Rom 4:24   [c]Zech 9:11; Heb 10:29   13:21 [a]Phil 2:13   [1]Some MSS *in you.*   [2]‡ Maj. MSS add *and ever.*   13:22 [1]Grk. *brothers*; considerable external evidence supports use of the Grk. word as *brothers and sisters* or *fellow Christians.*   13:25 [1]Maj. WSS add *amen.*

JAMES

Faith without works is dead" (2:26), and a dead faith is worse than none at all. Faith must work; it must produce; it must be visible. Throughout his epistle to Jewish believers, James integrates true faith and everyday practical experience by stressing that true faith must manifest itself in works. Faith endures trials; trials come and go, but a strong faith will face them head-on and develop endurance. Faith understands temptations; it will not allow us to consent to our lust and slide into sin. Faith obeys the Word; it will not merely hear and not do. Faith harbors no prejudice; for James, faith and favoritism cannot coexist. Faith is more than mere words; it is more than knowledge; it is demonstrated by obedience, and it overtly responds to the promises of God. Faith controls the tongue; this small but immensely powerful part of the body must be held in check. Faith gives us the ability to choose wisdom that is heavenly and to shun wisdom that is earthly; it provides us with the ability to resist the devil and humbly draw near to God. Finally, faith waits patiently for the coming of the Lord. Through trouble and trial, it stifles complaining. The name *Iakobos* (James) in 1:1 is the basis for the early title *Iakobou Epistole*, "Epistle of James." *Iakobos* is the Greek form of the Hebrew name Jacob, a Jewish name common in the first century.

Salutation

1 From [a]James, a slave[1] of God and the Lord Jesus Christ, to the 12 tribes dispersed abroad.[2] Greetings!

Joy in Trials

[2] My brothers and sisters,[1] [a]consider it nothing but joy [b]when you fall into all sorts of trials, [3]because you [a]know that the testing of your faith produces endurance. [4]And let endurance have its perfect effect, so that you will be perfect and complete, not deficient in anything. [5]But [a]if anyone is deficient in wisdom, he should ask God, who gives to all generously and [b]without reprimand, and it will be given to him. [6a]But he must ask in faith without doubting, for the one who doubts is like a wave of the sea, blown and tossed around by the wind. [7]For that person must not suppose that he will receive anything from the Lord, [8]since he is [a]a double-minded individual, unstable in all his ways.

[9]Now the believer[1] of humble means should take pride in his high position. [10]But the rich person's pride should be in his humiliation because he will pass away [a]like a wildflower in the meadow. [11]For the sun rises with its heat and dries up the meadow; the petal of the flower falls off and its beauty is lost forever. So also the rich person in the midst of his pursuits will wither away. [12a]Happy is [b]the one[1] [c]who endures testing because when he has proven to be genuine, he will receive the crown of life that God[2] promised to those who love him. [13]Let no one say when he is tempted, "I am tempted by God," for God cannot be tempted by evil, and he himself tempts no one. [14]But each one is tempted when he is

1:1 [a] Acts 12:17   [1] Trad. *servant*; the word does not bear the connotation of a free individual serving another.   [2] Grk. *to the 12 tribes in the Diaspora.*   1:2 [a] Acts 5:41   [b] 1 Pet 1:6   [1] Grk. *brothers*; considerable external evidence supports use of the Grk. word as *brothers and sisters* or *fellow Christians.*   1:3 [a] Rom 5:3–5   1:5 [a] 1 Kgs 3:9; Jas 3:17   [b] Jer 29:12   1:6 [a] [Mark 11:23–24]; Acts 10:20   1:8 [a] Jas 4:8   1:9 [1] Grk. *brother*; the term broadly connotes familial relationships within the family of God.   1:10 [a] Job 14:2   1:12 [a] Job 5:17; Luke 6:22; Heb 10:36; Jas 5:11; [1 Pet 3:14; 4:14]   [b] [1 Cor 9:25]   [c] Matt 10:22   [1] Grk. *man, male*; used generically for someone, i.e., a person.   [2] Maj. MSS *the Lord.*

lured and enticed by his own desires. [15]Then [a]when desire conceives, it gives birth to sin, and when sin is full grown, it gives birth to death. [16]Do not be led astray, my dear brothers and sisters.[1] [17]All generous giving and [a]every perfect gift is from above, coming down from the Father of lights, [b]with whom there is no variation or the slightest hint of change.[1] [18a]By his sovereign plan he gave us birth through the [b]message of truth, [c]that we would be a kind of firstfruits of all he created.

Living out the Message

[19]Understand this, my dear brothers and sisters![1] Let every person be quick to listen, [a]slow to speak, [b]slow to anger. [20]For human[1] anger does not accomplish God's righteousness. [21]So put away all filth and evil excess and humbly welcome the message implanted within you, [a]which is able to save your souls. [22]But [a]be sure you live out the message and do not merely listen to it and so deceive yourselves. [23]For [a]if someone merely listens to the message and does not live it out, he is like someone[1] who gazes at his own face in a mirror. [24]For he gazes at himself and then goes out and immediately forgets what sort of person he was. [25]But [a]the one who peers into the perfect law of liberty and fixes [b]his attention there, and does not become a forgetful listener but one who lives it out—he will be blessed in what he does. [26]If someone thinks he is religious yet [a]does not bridle his tongue, and so deceives his heart, his religion is futile. [27a]Pure and undefiled religion before God the Father is this: [b]to care for orphans [c]and widows in their adversity[1] and to keep oneself unstained by the world.

Prejudice and the Law of Love

2 My [a]brothers and sisters,[1] do not show [b]prejudice[2] if you possess faith[3] in our glorious Lord Jesus Christ. [2]For if someone[1] comes into your assembly[2] wearing a gold ring and fine clothing, and a poor person enters in filthy clothes, [3]do you pay attention to the one who is finely dressed and say, "You sit here in a good place," and to the poor person, "You stand over there," or "Sit on the floor"? [4]If so, have you not made distinctions among yourselves and become judges with evil motives? [5]Listen, my dear brothers and sisters![1] Did not God choose the poor in the world to be [a]rich in faith and heirs of the kingdom [b]that he promised to those who love him? [6]But [a]you have dishonored the poor! Are not the rich oppressing you [b]and dragging you into the courts? [7]Do they not blaspheme the good name of the one you [a]belong to?[1] [8]But if [a]you fulfill the royal law as expressed in this scripture, "**You shall love your neighbor as yourself,**"[1] you are doing well. [9]But if you show prejudice, you are committing sin and are convicted by the law as [a]violators. [10]For the one who obeys the whole law but [a]fails in one point has become guilty of all of it. [11]For he who said, "[a]**Do not commit adultery,**"[1] also said, "[b]**Do not murder.**"[2] Now if you do not commit adultery but do commit murder, you have become a violator of the law. [12]Speak and act as those who will be judged by a law that gives freedom. [13]For [a]judgment is merciless for the one who has shown [b]no [c]mercy. But [d]mercy triumphs over judgment.

Faith and Works Together

[14a]What good is it, my brothers and sisters,[1] if someone claims to have faith but

1:15 [a]Job 15:35; Ps 7:14; Isa 59:4   **1:16** [1]Grk. *brothers*; considerable external evidence supports use of the Grk. word as *brothers and sisters* or *fellow Christians*.   **1:17** [a]John 3:27   [b]Num 23:19   [1]Grk. *variation or shadow of turning*; referring to the motions of heavenly bodies causing variations of light and darkness.   **1:18** [a]John 1:13   [b]2 Cor 6:7; 1 Thess 2:13; 2 Tim 2:15; [1 Pet 1:3, 23]   [c][Eph 1:12–13]; Heb 12:23; Rev 14:4   **1:19** [a]Prov 10:19; 17:27   [b]Prov 14:17; 16:32; Eccl 7:9   [1]Grk. *brothers*; considerable external evidence supports use of the Grk. word as *brothers and sisters* or *fellow Christians*.   **1:20** [1]Grk. *man, male*; used generically for someone, i.e., a person.   **1:21** [a]Acts 13:26   **1:22** [a]Matt 7:21–28; Luke 6:46–49; [Rom 2:13; Jas 1:22–25; 2:14–20]   **1:23** [a]Luke 6:47   [1]Grk. *man, male*; used generically for someone, i.e., a person.   **1:25** [a][John 8:32; Rom 8:2; 2 Cor 3:17]; Gal 2:4; 6:2; Jas 2:12; 1 Pet 2:16   [b]John 13:17   **1:26** [a]Ps 34:13   **1:27** [a]Matt 25:34–36   [b]Isa 1:17   [c][Rom 12:2]   [1]Trad. *affliction*.   **2:1** [a]Acts 7:2; 1 Cor 2:8   [b]Lev 19:15   [1]Grk. *brothers*; considerable external evidence supports use of the Grk. word as *brothers and sisters* or *fellow Christians*.   [2]Or *partiality*.   [3]Grk. *do not have faith with personal prejudice*.   **2:2** [1]Grk. *man, male*; used generically for someone, i.e., a person.   [2]Grk. *synagogue*.   **2:5** [a]Luke 12:21; 1 Tim 6:18; Rev 2:9   [b]Exod 20:6   [1]Grk. *brothers*; considerable external evidence supports use of the Grk. word as *brothers and sisters* or *fellow Christians*.   **2:6** [a]1 Cor 11:22   [b]Acts 13:50   **2:7** [a]Acts 11:26; 1 Pet 4:16   [1]Grk. *that was invoked over you*; referring to their baptism in which they confessed their faith in Christ and were pronounced to be his.   **2:8** [a]Lev 19:18   [1]Lev 19:18   **2:9** [a]Lev 19:15; Deut 1:17   **2:10** [a]Gal 3:10   **2:11** [a]Exod 20:14; Deut 5:18   [b]Exod 20:13; Deut 5:17   [1]Exod 20:14; Deut 5:18   [2]Exod 20:13; Deut 5:17   **2:13** [a]Job 22:6   [b]Prov 21:13; Matt 18:32–35; [Luke 6:37]   [c]Mic 7:18; [Matt 5:7]   [d]Rom 12:8   **2:14** [a]Matt 7:21–23, 26; 21:28–32   [1]Grk. *brothers*; considerable external evidence supports use of the Grk. word as *brothers and sisters* or *fellow Christians*.

does not have works? Can this kind of faith save him? [15a]If a brother or sister[1] is poorly clothed and lacks daily food, [16]and [a]one of you says to them, "Go in peace, keep warm and eat well," but you do not give them what the body needs, what good is it? [17]So also faith, if it does not have works, is dead being by itself. [18]But someone will say, "You have faith and I have works." [a]Show me your faith without works [b]and I will show you faith by my works. [19]You believe that God is one; well and good. Even the demons believe that— and tremble with fear.

[20]But would you like evidence, you empty fellow, that faith without works is useless?[1] [21]Was not Abraham our father justified by works [a]when he offered Isaac his son on the altar? [22]You see [a]that his faith was working together with his [b]works and his faith was perfected by works. [23]And the scripture was fulfilled that says, "*Now [a]Abraham believed God and it was counted to him for righteousness*,"[1] and [b]*he was called God's friend*.[2] [24]You see that a person is justified by works and not by faith alone. [25]And similarly, [a]was not Rahab the prostitute also justified by works when she welcomed the messengers and sent them out by another way? [26]For just as the body without the spirit is dead, so also faith without works is dead.

The Power of the Tongue

3 Not many of you should become teachers, my brothers and sisters,[1] because you [a]know that we will be judged more strictly. [2]For [a]we all stumble in many ways. [b]If someone does not stumble in what he says, [c]he is a perfect individual,[1] able to control the entire body as well. [3]And if [a]we put bits into the mouths of horses to get them to obey us, then we guide their entire bodies. [4]Look at ships too: Though they are so large and driven by harsh winds,

they are steered by a tiny rudder wherever the pilot's inclination directs. [5]So, too, [a]the tongue is a small part of the body, yet it [b]has great pretensions. Think how small a flame sets a huge forest ablaze. [6]And [a]the tongue is a fire! The tongue represents the world of wrongdoing among the parts of our bodies. It [b]pollutes the entire body and sets fire to the course of human existence—and is set on fire by hell.

[7]For every kind of animal, bird, reptile, and sea creature is subdued and has been subdued by humankind. [8]But no human being can subdue the tongue; it is a restless[1] evil, [a]full of deadly poison. [9]With it we bless the Lord[1] and Father, and with it we curse people[2] made [a]in God's image. [10]From the same mouth come blessing and cursing. These things should not be so, my brothers and sisters.[1] [11]A spring does not pour out fresh water and bitter water from the same opening, does it? [12]Can a [a]fig tree produce olives, my brothers and sisters,[1] or a vine produce figs? Neither can a salt water spring produce fresh water.

True Wisdom

[13a]Who is wise and understanding among you? By his good conduct he should show his works done in the gentleness that wisdom brings. [14]But if you have [a]bitter jealousy and selfishness in your hearts, [b]do not boast and tell lies against the truth. [15]Such wisdom does not come from above but [a]is earthly, natural, demonic. [16]For [a]where there is jealousy and selfishness, there is disorder and every evil practice. [17]But [a]the wisdom from above is first pure, then peaceable, gentle, accommodating,[1] full of mercy [b]and good fruit, impartial, and not hypocritical.[2] [18a]And the fruit that consists of righteousness[1] is planted in peace among those who make peace.

2:15 [a]Matt 25:35; Luke 3:11 [1]In the Grk. text, both *brother* and *sister* occur here. **2:16** [a][1 John 3:17–18] **2:18** [a]Col 1:6; 1 Thess 1:3; Heb 6:10 [b][Gal 5:6]; Jas 3:13 **2:20** [1]Maj. MSS *dead*. **2:21** [a]Gen 22:9–10, 12, 16–18 **2:22** [a][John 6:29]; Heb 11:17 [b]John 8:39 **2:23** [a]Gen 15:6; Rom 4:3 [b]2 Chr 20:7; Isa 41:8 [1]Gen 15:6 [2][2 Chr 20:7; Isa 41:8; 51:2] **2:25** [a]Heb 11:31 **3:1** [a]Luke 6:37 [1]Grk. *brothers*; considerable external evidence supports use of the Grk. word as *brothers and sisters* or *fellow Christians*. **3:2** [a]1 Kgs 8:46 [b]Ps 34:13 [c][Matt 12:34–37; Jas 3:2–12] [1]Grk. *man, male*; used generically for someone, i.e., a person. **3:3** [a]Ps 32:9 **3:5** [a]Prov 12:18; 15:2; Jas 1:26 [b]Ps 12:3; 73:8 **3:6** [a]Ps 120:2–3; Prov 16:27 [b][Matt 12:36; 15:11, 18] **3:8** [a]Ps 140:3; Eccl 10:11; Rom 3:13 [1]Maj. MSS *uncontrollable*. **3:9** [a]Gen 1:26; 5:1; 9:6; 1 Cor 11:7 [1]Maj. later MSS *God*. [2]Grk. *men*; used generically for both men and women. **3:10** [1]Grk. *brothers*; considerable external evidence supports use of the Grk. word as *brothers and sisters* or *fellow Christians*. **3:12** [a]Matt 7:16–20 [1]Grk. *brothers*; considerable external evidence supports use of the Grk. word as *brothers and sisters* or *fellow Christians*. **3:13** [a]Gal 6:4 **3:14** [a]Rom 13:13 [b]Rom 2:17 **3:15** [a]Phil 3:19 **3:16** [a]1 Cor 3:3 **3:17** [a]1 Cor 2:6–7 [b]Rom 12:9; 2 Cor 6:6; 1 Pet 1:22 [1]Or *willing to yield, open to persuasion.* [2]Or *sincere.* **3:18** [a]Prov 11:18; Isa 32:17; Hos 10:12; Amos 6:12; [Gal 6:8; Phil 1:11] [1]Grk. *the fruit of righteousness*; meaning righteous living as a fruit produced.

Passions and Pride

4 Where do the conflicts and where do the quarrels among you come from? Is it not from this, from your passions [a]that battle inside you? [2]You desire and you do not have; you murder and envy and you cannot obtain; you quarrel and fight. You do not have because you do not ask; [3a]you ask and do not receive [b]because you ask wrongly, so you can spend it on your passions.

[4]Adulterers, do you not know that [a]friendship with the world means hostility toward God? So [b]whoever decides to be the world's friend makes himself God's enemy. [5]Or do you think [a]the scripture means nothing when it says, "The spirit that God caused[1] to live within us has an envious yearning"? [6]But he gives greater grace. Therefore it says, "[a]**God opposes the proud, but he gives grace to the humble.**"[7]So submit to God. But [a]resist the devil and he will flee from you. [8]Draw near to God and he will [a]draw near to you. [b]Cleanse your hands, you sinners, and [c]make your hearts pure, you double-minded. [9a]Grieve, mourn, and weep. Turn your laughter into mourning and your joy into despair. [10a]Humble yourselves before the Lord and he will exalt you.

[11a]Do not speak against one another, brothers and sisters.[1] He who speaks against a fellow believer[2][b]or judges a fellow believer speaks against the law and judges the law. But if you judge the law, you are not a doer of the law but its judge. [12]But there is only one [a]who is lawgiver and judge—the one who is able to save and destroy. On the other hand, [b]who are you to judge your neighbor?

[13]Come now, you who say, "Today or tomorrow we will go into this or that town and spend a year there and do business and make a profit." [14]You do not know about tomorrow. What is your life like? For you are a puff of smoke that appears for a short time and then vanishes. [15]You ought to say instead, "[a]If the Lord is willing, then we will live and do this or that." [16]But as it is, you boast about your arrogant plans. [a]All such boasting is evil. [17]So whoever knows what is good [a]to do and does not do it is guilty of sin.

Warning to the Rich

5 Come now, you [a]rich! Weep and cry aloud over the miseries that are coming on you. [2]Your [a]riches have rotted and [b]your clothing has become moth-eaten. [3]Your gold and silver have rusted and their rust will be a witness against [a]you. It will consume your flesh like fire. It is in the last days that you have hoarded treasure![1] [4]Look, [a]the pay you have held back from [b]the workers who mowed your fields cries out against you, and the cries of the reapers have reached the ears of the Lord of Heaven's Armies.[1] [5]You have lived indulgently and luxuriously on the earth. You have fattened your hearts in a day of slaughter. [6]You have condemned and murdered the righteous person, although he does not resist you.

Patience in Suffering

[7]So be patient, brothers and sisters,[1] until the Lord's return.[2] Think of how the farmer waits for the precious fruit of the ground and is patient for it until it receives the early and late rains. [8]You also be patient and strengthen your hearts, for the Lord's return is near. [9]Do not grumble against one another, brothers and sisters,[1] so that you may not be judged. See, the judge stands before the gates! [10a]As an example of suffering and [b]patience, brothers and sisters,[1] take the prophets who spoke in the Lord's name. [11]Think of how [a]we regard as blessed those

who have [b]endured. You have heard of Job's endurance and you have seen [c]the Lord's purpose, that [d]*the Lord is full of compassion and mercy.*[1] [12]And above all, my brothers and sisters,[1] [a]do not swear, either by heaven or by earth or by any other oath. But let your "Yes" be yes and your "No" be no, so that you may not fall into judgment.

Prayer for the Sick

[13]Is anyone among you suffering? He should [a]pray. Is anyone in good spirits? He should sing praises. [14]Is anyone among you ill? He should summon the elders of the church, and they should pray for him and [a]anoint him with olive oil in the name of the Lord. [15]And the prayer of faith will save the one who is sick [a]and the Lord will raise him up—and if he has committed sins, he will be forgiven. [16]So confess your sins to one [a]another and pray for one another so that you may be healed. The prayer of a righteous person has great effectiveness.[1] [17]Elijah was a human being like us, and he prayed earnestly that [a]it would not rain and [b]there was no rain on the land for three years and six months! [18]Then he prayed [a]again, and the sky gave rain and the land sprouted with a harvest.

[19]My brothers and sisters,[1] if anyone among you wanders from the truth and someone [a]turns him back, [20]he should know that the one who turns a sinner back from his wandering path [a]will save that person's soul from death and will [b]cover a multitude of sins.

5:11 [b] [Jas 1:12] [c] Job 1:21–22; 2:10 [d] Job 42:10 [1] [Exod 34:6; Neh 9:17; Pss 86:15; 102:13; Joel 2:13; Jonah 4:2] 5:12 [a] Matt 5:34–37 [1] Grk. *brothers*; considerable external evidence supports use of the Grk. word as *brothers and sisters* or *fellow Christians.* 5:13 [a] Ps 50:14–15 5:14 [a] Mark 6:13; 16:18 5:15 [a] Isa 33:24 5:16 [a] Num 11:2 [1] Or *the fervent prayer of a righteous person is very powerful.* 5:17 [a] Acts 14:15 [b] 1 Kgs 17:1; 18:1 5:18 [a] 1 Kgs 18:1, 42 5:19 [a] Matt 18:15; Gal 6:1 [1] Grk. *brothers*; considerable external evidence supports use of the Grk. word as *brothers and sisters* or *fellow Christians.* 5:20 [a] Rom 11:14; 1 Cor 1:21; Jas 1:21 [b] Prov 10:12; [1 Pet 4:8]

1 PETER

Persecution can cause either growth or bitterness in the Christian life. Response determines the result. Peter encourages the Jewish believers struggling amid persecution to conduct themselves courageously for the person and program of Christ. Having been born again to a living hope, they are to imitate the Holy One who has called them. The fruit of that character will be actions rooted in submission: citizens to government, servants to masters, wives to husbands, husbands to wives, and Christians to one another. Only after submission is fully understood does Peter deal with the difficult area of suffering. The Christians are not to "be astonished that a trial by fire is occurring among you, as though something strange were happening to you" (4:12); they are to rejoice as partakers of the suffering of Christ. That response to life is truly the climax of one's submission to the good hand of God. Both their character and their conduct must be above reproach. This epistle begins with the phrase *Petros apostolos Iesou Christou*, "Peter, an apostle of Jesus Christ." This is the basis of the early title *Petrou A*, the "First of Peter."

Salutation

1 From Peter, an apostle [a]of Jesus Christ, to those temporarily residing[1] abroad[2] (in Pontus, Galatia, Cappadocia, the province of Asia, and Bithynia) who are chosen [2a]according to the foreknowledge of God the Father by [b]being [c]set apart by the Spirit for [d]obedience and for [e]sprinkling with Jesus Christ's blood. May [f]grace and peace be yours in full measure!

New Birth to Joy and Holiness

[3a]Blessed be the God and Father of our Lord Jesus Christ! [b]By his great mercy he gave us new birth into [c]a living hope [d]through the resurrection of Jesus Christ from the dead, [4]that is, into an inheritance imperishable, undefiled, and unfading. It is [a]reserved in heaven for you, [5a]who by God's power are protected through faith for a salvation ready to be revealed in the last time. [6]This brings you great joy, although you may have to suffer[1] for a short time [a]in various trials. [7]Such trials show [a]the proven character of your [b]faith,[1] which is much more valuable than gold—gold that is tested by fire, even though it is passing away—and will bring praise and glory and honor when Jesus Christ is revealed. [8]You have not seen [a]him, but you love him. You do not see him now but you believe in him, and so you rejoice with an indescribable and glorious joy, [9]because you are attaining the goal of your faith—the salvation of your souls.

[10]Concerning this salvation, the prophets who predicted the grace that would come to you searched and investigated carefully. [11]They probed into what person or time[1] [a]the Spirit of Christ within them was indicating when he testified beforehand about the sufferings appointed for Christ and his subsequent glory. [12]They were shown that they were serving not themselves but you, in regard to the things now announced to you through those who proclaimed the gospel to you by the Holy Spirit sent from heaven—things [a]angels long to catch a glimpse of.

1:1 [a] John 7:35; Jas 1:1 [1] Or *to those living as resident foreigners, to the exiles.* [2] Grk. *in the Diaspora;* Jews scattered among the Gentiles, but here it is probably metaphorical, used of Gentile Christians spread in the midst of a godless world. 1:2 [a] Eph 1:4 [b] 2 Thess 2:13 [c] [Rom 8:29]; 1 Pet 1:20 [d] Rom 1:5 [e] Isa 52:15; Heb 10:22; 12:24 [f] Rom 1:7 1:3 [a] Eph 1:3 [b] Gal 6:16; Titus 3:5 [c] [John 3:3, 5] [d] 1 Cor 15:20; 1 Pet 3:21 1:4 [a] Col 1:5 1:5 [a] John 10:28; [Phil 4:7] 1:6 [a] Matt 5:12 [1] Grk. *Though now, for a little while if necessary, you may have to suffer.* 1:7 [a] Jas 1:3 [b] Job 23:10 [1] Or *genuineness; or that the proving of your faith . . . may bring praise.* 1:8 [a] 1 John 4:20 1:11 [a] 2 Pet 1:21 [1] Or *time or circumstances.* 1:12 [a] Eph 3:10

[13]Therefore, get your minds ready for action by being fully sober, and set your hope completely on the grace that will be brought to you when Jesus Christ is revealed. [14]Like obedient children, do not comply [a]with the evil urges you used to follow in your ignorance, [15][a]but, like the Holy One who called you, become holy yourselves in all of your conduct, [16]for it is written, "**You shall [a]be holy, because I am holy.**"[1] [17]And if you address as Father the one who impartially judges according to each one's work, live [a]out the time of your temporary residence here[1] in reverence. [18]You know that from your empty way of life inherited from your ancestors you were ransomed—not by perishable things like silver or gold, [19]but by precious blood [a]like that of an unblemished and spotless lamb, namely Christ. [20]He was foreknown before [a]the foundation of the world but was manifested [b]in these last times for your sake. [21]Through him you now trust in God, [a]who raised him from the dead and [b]gave him glory, so that your faith and hope are in God.

[22]You [a]have purified your souls by obeying the truth[1] in order to show sincere mutual [b]love. So love one another earnestly from a pure heart.[2] [23][a]You have been born anew, not from perishable but from imperishable seed, [b]through the living and enduring word of God. [24]For

> [a]**all flesh is like grass**
> **and all its glory like the flower of the grass;**
> **the grass withers and the flower falls off,**
> [25] [a]**but the word of the Lord endures forever.**[1]

And this is the word that was proclaimed to you.

2 So get rid of all evil and all deceit and hypocrisy and envy and all slander. [2]And yearn [a]like newborn infants for pure, spiritual [b]milk,[1] so that by it you may grow up to salvation,[2] [3]if **you have [a]experienced**[1] **the Lord's kindness.**[2]

A Living Stone, a Chosen People

[4]So as you come to him, a living stone [a]rejected by men but chosen and precious in God's sight, [5]you yourselves, as living stones, are built up as a spiritual house to be a holy priesthood and to offer spiritual sacrifices that are acceptable to God through Jesus Christ. [6]For it says in scripture, "**Look, I lay in Zion a stone, a chosen and precious cornerstone, and whoever believes in him will never [a]be put to shame.**"[1] [7]So you who believe see his value, but for those who do not believe, [a]**the stone that the builders rejected has become the cornerstone,**[1] [8]and [a]**a stumbling-stone**[1] **and a rock to trip over.**[2] [b]They stumble because they disobey the word, as they were destined [c]to do. [9]But you are a *chosen race, a royal priesthood, a holy nation, a people of his own,* so that you may *proclaim the virtues*[1] of the one who called you out of [a]*darkness into his marvelous light.* [10][a]You once were *not a people,* but now you are God's people. You were *shown no mercy,*[1] but now you have received mercy.

[11]Dear friends, I urge you as foreigners and exiles to keep away from fleshly desires [a]that do battle against the soul, [12]and [a]maintain good conduct among [b]the non-Christians, so that though they now malign you as wrongdoers, they may see your good deeds and glorify God when he appears.

Submission to Authorities

[13]Be subject to every human institution [a]for the Lord's sake, whether to a king as supreme [14]or to governors as those he commissions to punish wrongdoers and praise

1:14 [a][Rom 12:2]; 1 Pet 4:2   **1:15** [a][2 Cor 7:1]   **1:16** [a]Lev 11:44–45; 19:2; 20:7   [1]Lev 19:2   **1:17** [a]Acts 10:34   [1]Grk. *the time of your sojourn.*   **1:19** [a]Exod 12:5; Isa 53:7   **1:20** [a]Rom 3:25   [b]Gal 4:4   **1:21** [a]Acts 2:24   [b]Acts 2:33   **1:22** [a]Acts 15:9   [b]John 13:34; Rom 12:10; Heb 13:1; 1 Pet 2:17; 3:8   [1]Maj. later MSS *through the Spirit.*   [2]A few MSS *from the heart, from a true heart.*   **1:23** [a]John 1:13   [b]1 Thess 2:13; Jas 1:18   **1:24** [a]Isa 40:6–8; Jas 1:10   **1:25** [a][John 1:1]   [1]Isa 40:6, 8   **2:2** [a][Matt 18:3; 19:14; Mark 10:15; Luke 18:17]; 1 Cor 14:20   [b]1 Cor 3:2   [1]There is a play on words here. The Grk. word for "spiritual" is *logikos.* This is a subtle indication that the nourishment for their growth must be the living and enduring word (Grk. *logos*) of God, through which they were born anew (1:23–25).   [2]Some MSS omit *to salvation.*   **2:3** [a]Ps 34:8; Titus 3:4; Heb 6:5   [1]Grk. *have tasted that the Lord is kind.*   [2]Ps 34:8   **2:4** [a]Ps 118:22   **2:6** [a]Isa 28:16; Rom 9:32–33; 10:11; 1 Pet 2:8   [1]Isa 28:16   **2:7** [a]Ps 118:22; Matt 21:42; Luke 2:34   [1]Ps 118:22   **2:8** [a]Isa 8:14   [b]1 Cor 1:23; Gal 5:11   [c]Rom 9:22   [1]Grk. *a stone of stumbling and a rock of offense*; the latter denotes an obstacle to faith, something that arouses anger and rejection.   [2]Isa 8:14   **2:9** [a]Isa 9:2; 42:16; [Acts 26:18; 2 Cor 4:6]   [1][Exod 19:5–6; 23:22 LXX; Isa 43:20–21; Mal 3:17]   **2:10** [a]Hos 1:9–10; 2:23; Rom 9:25; 10:19   [1]Hos 1:6, 9; 2:23   **2:11** [a][Rom 8:13]; Gal 5:17; Jas 4:1   **2:12** [a]2 Cor 8:21; Phil 2:15; Titus 2:8; 1 Pet 2:15; 3:16   [b]Matt 5:16; 9:8; John 13:31; 1 Pet 4:11, 16   **2:13** [a]Matt 22:21

those who do good. [15]For God wants you to silence the ignorance of foolish people by doing good. [16]Live [a]as free people, not [b]using your freedom as a pretext for evil, but as God's slaves.[1] [17]Honor all people, love the family of believers, fear [a]God, honor the king.

[18][a]Slaves, be subject to your masters with all reverence, not only to those who are good and gentle, but also to those who are perverse. [19]For this finds God's [a]favor, if because of conscience toward God[1,2] someone endures hardships in suffering unjustly. [20]For [a]what credit is it if you sin and are mistreated and endure it? But if you do good and suffer and so endure, this finds favor with God. [21]For [a]to this you were called, since Christ also suffered for you, [b]leaving an example for you to follow in his steps. [22][a]He **committed no** sin **nor was deceit found in his mouth.**[1] [23]When [a]he was maligned, he did not answer back; when he suffered, he threatened no retaliation, but [b]committed himself to God who judges justly. [24][a]He **himself bore our sins**[1] in his body on the tree, [b]that we may cease from sinning and live for righteousness. [c]**By his wounds you were healed.**[2] [25]For [a]you were **going astray like sheep**[1] but now you have turned back [b]to the shepherd and guardian of your souls.

Wives and Husbands

3 In the same way, wives, be [a]subject to your own husbands. Then, even if some are disobedient to [b]the word, they will [c]be won over without a word by the way you live, [2][a]when they see your pure and reverent conduct. [3][a]Let your beauty not be external—the braiding of hair and wearing of gold jewelry or fine clothes—[4]but [a]the inner person of the heart, the lasting beauty of a gentle and tranquil spirit, which is precious in God's sight. [5]For in the same way the holy women who hoped in God long ago adorned themselves by being subject to their husbands, [6]like Sarah who obeyed Abraham,

[a]calling him lord. You become her children when you do what is good and have no fear in doing so.[1] [7][a]Husbands, in the same way, treat your wives with consideration as the weaker partners and show them honor [b]as fellow heirs of the grace of life. In this way nothing will hinder your prayers.

Suffering for Doing Good

[8]Finally, all of you be harmonious, sympathetic, affectionate, compassionate, and humble. [9]Do [a]not return evil for evil or insult for insult, but instead [b]bless others because you were called [c]to inherit a blessing. [10]For

> [a]*the one who wants to love life and*
> *see good days must keep his tongue*
> *from evil and his lips from uttering*
> *deceit.*
> [11] *And he must turn [a]away from evil and*
> *do good;*
> *he must seek peace and pursue it.*
> [12] *For the eyes of the Lord are upon the*
> *righteous [a]and his ears are open to*
> *their prayer.*
> *But the Lord's face is against those*
> *who do evil.*[1]

[13][a]For who is going to harm you if you are devoted to what is good? [14][a]But in fact, if you happen to suffer for doing what is right,[1] you are blessed. [b]**But do not be terrified of them or be shaken.**[2] [15]But set Christ[1] apart[2] as Lord in your hearts and always [a]be ready to give an answer to anyone who asks about the [b]hope you possess. [16]Yet do it with courtesy and respect, [a]keeping a good conscience, so that those who slander your good conduct in Christ may be put to shame when they accuse you. [17]For it is better to suffer for doing good, if God wills it, than for doing evil.

> [18] Because Christ also suffered[1] once for
> sins,
> *the just for the unjust,*[2]

2:16 [a]Rom 6:14, 20, 22; 1 Cor 7:22; [Gal 5:1] [b] Gal 5:13 [1] Trad. *servant*; the word does not bear the connotation of a free individual serving another. **2:17** [a]Prov 24:21 **2:18** [a]Eph 6:5–8 **2:19** [a]Matt 5:10 [1]Some wss *good conscience.* [2]Grk. *conscious(ness) of God*; i.e., an awareness of God and allegiance to him. **2:20** [a]Luke 6:32–34 **2:21** [a]Matt 16:24; 1 Thess 3:3–4 [b][1 John 2:6] **2:22** [a]Isa 53:9; 2 Cor 5:21 [1]Isa 53:9 **2:23** [a]Isa 53:7; Heb 12:3; 1 Pet 3:9 [b]Luke 23:46 **2:24** [a]Isa 53:4, 11; 1 Cor 15:3; [Heb 9:28] [b]Rom 7:6 [c]Isa 53:5 [1]Isa 53:4, 12 [2]Isa 53:5 **2:25** [a]Isa 53:5–6 [b]Isa 40:11; [Ezek 34:23]; Zech 13:7 [1]Isa 53:6 **3:1** [a]Gen 3:16; 1 Cor 14:34; Eph 5:22; Col 3:18 [b]1 Cor 7:16 [c]Matt 18:15 **3:2** [a]1 Pet 2:12; 3:6 **3:3** [a]Isa 3:18; 1 Tim 2:9 **3:4** [a]Rom 2:29 **3:6** [a]Gen 18:12 [1]Grk. *doing good and not fearing any intimidation.* **3:7** [a]1 Cor 7:3; [Eph 5:25]; Col 3:19 [b]1 Cor 12:23 **3:9** [a][Prov 17:13] [b]Matt 5:44 [c]Matt 25:34 **3:10** [a]Ps 34:12–16 **3:11** [a]Ps 37:27 **3:12** [a]John 9:31 [1]Ps 34:12–16 **3:13** [a]Prov 16:7 **3:14** [a]Jas 1:12 [b]Isa 8:12 [1]Grk. *because of righteousness.* [2]Isa 8:12 **3:15** [a]Ps 119:46 [b][Titus 3:7] [1]Maj. later mss *God.* [2]Or *sanctify Christ as Lord.* **3:16** [a]1 Tim 1:5; Heb 13:18; 1 Pet 3:21 **3:18** [1]Some wss *died.* [2][Isa 53:11–12]

to bring you to God,
by being put to death in the flesh
but by being made alive in the spirit.
[19] In it he went and preached to the
spirits in prison,

[20]after they were disobedient long ago when God patiently waited in the days of Noah as an ark was being constructed. In the ark a few, that is eight souls, were delivered through water. [21a]And this prefigured baptism, which now saves you—[b]not the washing off of physical dirt [c]but the pledge[1] of a good conscience to God—through the resurrection of Jesus Christ, [22]who went into heaven and [a]is at the right hand of God with [b]angels and authorities and powers subject to him.

4 So, since Christ suffered[1] in the flesh, you also arm yourselves with the same attitude because the one who has suffered in the flesh has finished with sin, [2]in that he spends the rest of his time on earth concerned about the will of God and not human desires. [3]For the time that has passed was sufficient for you to do what the non-Christians desire. You lived then in debauchery, evil desires, drunkenness, carousing, drinking bouts, and wanton idolatries. [4]So they are astonished[1] when you do not rush with them into the same flood of wickedness, and they vilify you. [5]They will face a reckoning before Jesus Christ who stands ready [a]to judge the living and the dead. [6]Now it was for this very purpose that [a]the gospel was preached to those who are now dead, so that though they were judged in the flesh by human standards they may [b]live spiritually[1] by God's standards.

Service, Suffering, and Judgment

[7]For [a]the culmination of all things is near. So be self-controlled and sober-minded for the sake of prayer. [8]Above all keep your [a]love for one another fervent because *love covers a multitude of sins*.[1] [9a]Show hospitality to one another [b]without complaining.

[10]Just [a]as each one has received a gift, use it to serve one another [b]as good stewards of [c]the varied grace of God. [11a]Whoever speaks, let it be with God's words. Whoever serves, do so with the strength that God supplies, so that [b]in everything God will be glorified through Jesus Christ. To him belong the glory and the power forever and ever. Amen.

[12]Dear friends, do not be astonished[1] that a trial by fire is occurring among you, as though something strange were happening to you. [13]But rejoice in the degree that you have shared in the sufferings of Christ, so that [a]when his glory is revealed you may also rejoice and be glad. [14]If you are insulted for the name of Christ, you are [a]blessed, because the Spirit of glory,[1] who is *the Spirit of God, rests*[2] on you. [15]But let none of you suffer as a murderer or thief or criminal or as a troublemaker. [16]But if you suffer as a Christian, do not be ashamed, but glorify God that you bear such a name. [17]For it is time [a]for judgment to begin, starting with the house of God. And if it starts with us, [b]what will be the fate of those who are disobedient to the gospel of God? [18]And [a]*if the righteous are barely saved, what will become of the ungodly and sinners?*[1] [19]So then let those who suffer according to the will of God [a]entrust their souls to a faithful Creator as they do good.

Leading and Living in God's Flock

5 So as your fellow elder and a [a]witness of Christ's sufferings and as one who shares in the [b]glory that will be revealed, I urge the elders among you: [2]Give a shepherd's [a]care to[1] God's flock among you, exercising oversight[2] [b]not merely as a duty[3] but willingly under God's direction, [c]not for shameful profit but eagerly. [3]And do not lord it over those entrusted to you, but [a]be examples to the flock. [4]Then when [a]the Chief Shepherd appears, you will receive [b]the crown of glory that never fades away.

[5]In the same way, you who are younger, be subject to the elders. And [a]all of you, clothe

3:21 [a] Acts 16:33; Eph 5:26   [b] [Titus 3:5]   [c] [Rom 10:10]   [1] Or *response, answer*.   3:22 [a] Ps 110:1   [b] Rom 8:38; Heb 1:6   4:1 [1] Maj. MSS add *for us, for you*.   4:4 [1] Or *are surprised, are taken aback*.   4:5 [a] Acts 10:42; Rom 14:9; 2 Tim 4:1   4:6 [a] 1 Pet 1:12; 3:19   [b] [Rom 8:9, 13]; Gal 5:25   [1] Grk. *in spirit*.   4:7 [a] Rom 13:11; Heb 9:26; Jas 5:8–9; 1 John 2:18   4:8 [a] [Prov 10:12]; 1 Cor 13:4; Jas 5:20   [1] Prov 10:12   4:9 [a] 1 Tim 3:2; Heb 13:2   [b] 2 Cor 9:7   4:10 [a] Rom 12:6–8   [b] Matt 24:45; 1 Cor 4:1–2   [c] [1 Cor 12:4]   4:11 [a] Eph 4:29   [b] [1 Cor 10:31]; Eph 5:20   4:12 [1] Or *do not be surprised, taken aback*.   4:13 [a] 2 Tim 2:12   4:14 [a] Matt 5:11; Luke 6:22; Acts 5:41   [1] Many MSS add *and of power*.   [2] Isa 11:2   4:17 [a] Isa 10:12   [b] Luke 10:12   4:18 [a] Prov 11:31   [1] Prov 11:21 LXX   4:19 [a] Ps 37:5–7; 2 Tim 1:12   5:1 [a] Matt 26:37   [b] Rom 8:17–18   5:2 [a] John 21:16; Acts 20:28   [b] 1 Cor 9:17   [c] 1 Tim 3:3   [1] Grk. *shepherd, tend, pastor*.   [2] A few sig. early MSS omit *exercising oversight*.   [3] Or *not under compulsion/coercion*.   5:3 [a] Ezek 34:4; Matt 20:25   5:4 [a] Isa 40:11; Zech 13:7; Heb 13:20; 1 Pet 2:25   [b] 2 Tim 4:8   5:5 [a] Rom 12:10; Eph 5:21

yourselves with humility toward one another because [b]God **opposes the proud but** [c]**gives grace to the humble.** [1] [6]And God will exalt you in due time, if you humble yourselves under his mighty hand [7]by casting all your cares on him because he cares for you. [8]Be sober and alert. Your enemy the devil, *like a roaring lion,* [1] is on the prowl looking for someone [2] to devour. [9]Resist him, strong in your faith, because you know that your brothers and sisters [1] throughout the world are enduring the same kinds of suffering. [10]And, after you have suffered for a little while, the God of all grace [a]who called you to his eternal glory in Christ [1] will himself restore, confirm, strengthen, and establish you. [11a]To him belongs the power forever. Amen.

Final Greetings

[12]Through [a]Silvanus, whom I know to be [b]a faithful brother, I have written to you briefly, in order to encourage you and testify that this is the true grace of God. Stand fast in it. [13]The church in Babylon, chosen together with you, greets you, and so does [a]Mark, my son. [14]Greet one another with a loving kiss. Peace to all of you who are in Christ. [1]

5:5 [b] Prov 3:34; Jas 4:6   [c] Isa 57:15   [1] Prov 3:34   5:8 [1] [Ps 22:13]   [2] Some MSS *whom.*   5:9 [1] Grk. *your brotherhood;* used generically in familial terms for the Christian community as a whole. This same word occurs in 2:17, where it is translated as "family of believers."   5:10 [a] 1 Cor 1:9; 1 Thess 2:12   [1] Maj. MSS *Christ Jesus.*   5:11 [a] Rev 1:6   5:12 [a] 2 Cor 1:19; 1 Thess 1:1; 2 Thess 1:1   [b] Acts 20:24   5:13 [a] Acts 12:12, 25; 15:37, 39; Col 4:10; Phlm 24   5:14 [1] Maj. MSS add *amen.*

2 PETER

First Peter deals with problems from the outside; 2 Peter deals with problems from the inside. Peter warns the believers about the false teachers peddling damaging doctrine, urging them to keep close watch on their personal lives. The Christian life demands diligence in pursuing moral excellence, knowledge, self-control, perseverance, godliness, kindness, and selfless love. By contrast, the false teachers are sensual, arrogant, greedy, and covetous. They scoff at the thought of future judgment and live their lives as if the present would be the pattern for the future. Peter reminds them that although God may be long-suffering in sending judgment, ultimately it will come. In view of that fact, believers should live lives of godliness, blamelessness, and steadfastness. The statement of authorship in 1:1 is very clear: "Simeon Peter, a slave and apostle of Jesus Christ." To distinguish this epistle from the first by Peter, it was given the Greek title *Petrou B*, the "Second of Peter."

Salutation

1 From Simeon[1] Peter, a slave[2] and [a]apostle of Jesus Christ, to those who through the righteousness of our God[3] and Savior,[4] Jesus Christ, have been granted a faith just as precious as ours. [2]May [a]grace and peace be lavished on you as you grow in the rich knowledge of God and of Jesus our Lord!

Believers' Salvation and the Work of God

[3]I can pray this because his [a]divine power has bestowed on us everything necessary for life and godliness through the rich knowledge of the one [b]who called us by[1] his own glory and excellence. [4]Through these things he has bestowed on us his precious and most magnificent promises, so that by means [a]of what was promised you may become [b]partakers of the divine nature, after escaping the worldly corruption that is produced by evil desire.[1] [5]For this very reason, [a]make every effort to add to your faith excellence,[1] to excellence, [b]knowledge;

[6]to knowledge, self-control; to self-control, perseverance;[1] to perseverance, godliness; [7][a]to godliness, brotherly affection; to brotherly affection, unselfish love. [8]For if these things are really yours [a]and are continually increasing, they will keep you from becoming ineffective and unproductive in your pursuit of knowing our Lord Jesus Christ more intimately. [9]But concerning the one who lacks such things—he is blind. That is to say, he is [a]nearsighted, since he has forgotten about the cleansing of his past sins. [10]Therefore, brothers and sisters,[1] make every effort [a]to be sure of your calling and election. For by doing this you will never stumble into sin. [11]For thus an entrance into the eternal kingdom of our Lord and Savior, Jesus Christ, will be richly provided for you.

Salvation Based on the Word of God

[12]Therefore, [a]I intend to remind you constantly of these things even [b]though you know them and are well established in the truth that you now have. [13]Indeed, [a]as long

1:1 [a] Gal 2:8 [1]Sev. wss *Simon*. [2]Trad. *servant*; the word does not bear the connotation of a free individual serving another. [3]A few wss *Lord*. [4]"God and Savior" both refer to the same person, Jesus Christ; this is one of the clearest statements in the NT concerning the deity of Christ. For a discussion on this Grk. construction, see *NET Bible, Full Notes Edition*. 1:2 [a]Dan 4:1 1:3 [a]1 Pet 1:5 [b]1 Thess 2:12; 2 Thess 2:14; 1 Pet 5:10 [1]Or *for* [the benefit of] *his own glory and excellence*. 1:4 [a]2 Cor 1:20; 7:1 [b][2 Cor 3:18] [1]Grk. *the corruption in the world* (in/because of) *lust*. 1:5 [a]2 Pet 3:18 [b]2 Pet 1:2 [1]Or *moral excellence, virtue*. 1:6 [1]Or perhaps *steadfastness*. 1:7 [a]Gal 6:10 1:8 [a][John 15:2] 1:9 [a]1 John 2:9–11 1:10 [a]2 Cor 13:5; 1 John 3:19 [1]Grk. *brothers*; considerable external evidence supports use of the Grk. word as *brothers and sisters* or *fellow Christians*. 1:12 [a]Phil 3:1; 1 John 2:21; Jude 5 [b]1 Pet 5:12 1:13 [a][2 Cor 5:1, 4]; 2 Pet 1:14

as I am in this tabernacle,[1] I consider it right [b]to stir you up by way of a reminder, [14]since I [a]know that my tabernacle will soon be removed because [b]our Lord Jesus Christ revealed this to me. [15]Indeed, I will also make every effort that, after my departure, you have a testimony of these things.

[16]For we did not follow cleverly concocted fables when we made known to you the [a]power and [b]return of our Lord Jesus Christ; no, we were [c]eyewitnesses of his grandeur. [17]For he received honor and glory from God the Father, when that voice was conveyed to him by the Majestic Glory: "[a]This is my dear Son, in whom I am delighted." [18]When this voice was conveyed from heaven, we ourselves heard it, for we were with him on [a]the holy mountain. [19]Moreover, we possess the prophetic word as an altogether reliable thing. You do well if you pay attention to this as you would to a [a]light shining in a murky place, [b]until [c]the day dawns and the morning star rises in your [d]hearts. [20]Above all, you do well if you recognize this: [a]No prophecy of scripture ever comes about by the prophet's own imagination, [21]for no [a]prophecy was ever borne of human impulse; [b]rather, men[1] carried along by the Holy Spirit spoke from God.

The False Teachers' Ungodly Lifestyle

2 But [a]false prophets arose among the people, just as there will be false teachers among you. These false teachers will infiltrate your midst[1] with destructive heresies,[2] even to the point of denying the Master who bought them. As a result, they will bring swift destruction on themselves. [2]And many will follow their debauched lifestyles.[1] Because of these false teachers, the way of truth will be slandered.[2] [3]And in their greed they will exploit you with deceptive words. Their condemnation pronounced long ago

is not sitting idly by; their destruction is not asleep.

[4]For if God did not spare the angels who sinned, but threw them into hell and locked them up[1] in chains[2] in utter darkness, to be kept until the judgment, [5]and if he did not spare the ancient world, but did protect Noah, a herald of righteousness, along with seven others, when God brought a flood on an ungodly world, [6]and if he turned to ashes the cities of [a]Sodom and Gomorrah when he condemned them to destruction,[1] having appointed them to serve as an example to future generations of the ungodly, [7]and if he [a]rescued Lot, a righteous man in anguish over the debauched lifestyle of lawless men, [8](for while he lived among them day after day, that righteous man was [a]tormented in his righteous soul by the lawless deeds he saw and heard) [9]—if so, [a]then the Lord knows how to rescue the godly from their trials, and to reserve the unrighteous for punishment at the day of judgment, [10]especially [a]those who indulge their fleshly desires and who despise authority.

Brazen and insolent, [b]they are not afraid to insult the glorious ones, [11]yet even [a]angels, who are much more powerful, do not bring a slanderous judgment against them in the presence of the Lord.[1] [12]But these men,[1] [a]like irrational animals—creatures of instinct, born to be caught and destroyed—do not understand whom they are insulting, and consequently in their destruction they will be destroyed, [13]suffering harm as the wages for their harmful ways. By considering it [a]a pleasure [b]to carouse in broad daylight, [c]they are stains and blemishes, indulging in their deceitful pleasures when [d]they feast together with you. [14]Their eyes, full of adultery, never stop sinning; [a]they entice unstable people. They have trained their hearts for greed, these

1:13 [b] 2 Pet 3:1   [1] Or *tent*; a metaphor for his physical body.   1:14 [a] [2 Cor 5:1; 2 Tim 4:6]   [b] John 13:36; 21:18–19   1:16 [a] [Matt 28:18; Eph 1:19–22]   [b] [1 Pet 5:4]   [c] Matt 17:1–5; Luke 1:2   1:17 [a] Ps 2:7; Isa 42:1; Matt 17:5; Mark 9:7; Luke 1:35; 9:35   1:18 [a] Matt 17:1   1:19 [a] [John 1:4–5, 9]   [b] Prov 4:18   [c] Rev 2:28; 22:16   [d] [2 Cor 4:5–7]   1:20 [a] [Rom 12:6]   1:21 [a] Jer 23:26; [2 Tim 3:16]   [b] 2 Sam 23:2; Luke 1:70; Acts 1:16; 3:18; 1 Pet 1:11   [1] If "prophecy" is the "prophecy of scripture" mentioned in v. 20, then "men" would refer specifically to the human authors of scripture, who (as far as we know) were all men. If, however, "prophecy" refers to oral prophecy as well, then women would be included, since Joel 2:20 specifically mentions "sons and daughters" as having the ability to prophesy, and the NT clearly mentions prophetesses (Luke 2:36; Acts 21:9).   2:1 [a] Matt 24:5, 24; 1 Tim 4:1–2   [1] Grk. *will bring in*; often with the connotation of secretiveness.   [2] Or *destructive opinions, destructive viewpoints*.   2:2 [1] Lit. *licentiousnesses, sensualities, debaucheries*.   [2] Or *blasphemed, reviled, treated with contempt*.   2:4 [1] Grk. *handed them over*.   [2] A few wss *pits*.   2:6 [a] Gen 19:1–26; Jude 7   [1] Sev. sig. wss omit *destruction*.   2:7 [a] Gen 19:16, 29   2:8 [a] Ps 119:139   2:9 [a] Ps 34:15–19; 1 Cor 10:13; Rev 3:10   2:10 [a] Jude 4, 7, 8   [b] Exod 22:28; Jude 8   2:11 [a] Jude 9   [1] Sev. wss omit *in the presence of the Lord*; some wss *from the Lord*.   2:12 [a] Jude 10   [1] The false teachers could be men or women, but in v. 14 they are said to have eyes "full of adultery (Grk. *an adulteress*)." Because this refers to men, here and in v. 17, the false teachers are described as "men."   2:13 [a] Phil 3:19   [b] Rom 13:13   [c] Jude 12   [d] 1 Cor 11:20–21   2:14 [a] Jude 11

cursed children! [15]By forsaking the right path they have gone astray, because they followed the way of [a]Balaam son of Bosor, who loved the wages of unrighteousness, [16]yet was rebuked for his own transgression (a dumb donkey,[1] speaking with a human voice, restrained the prophet's madness).

[17]These [a]men are waterless springs and mists driven by a storm, for whom the utter depths of darkness have been reserved. [18]For by speaking high-sounding but empty words they are able to entice, with fleshly desires and with debauchery, people who have just escaped from those who reside in error. [19]Although these false teachers promise such people freedom, they themselves are enslaved to immorality. [a]For whatever a person succumbs to, to that he is enslaved. [20]For if after they [a]have escaped the filthy things[1] of the world through the rich knowledge of our Lord and Savior Jesus Christ, they [b]again get entangled in them and succumb to them, their last state has become worse for them than their first. [21]For [a]it would have been better for them never to have known the way of righteousness than, having known it, to turn back from the holy commandment that had been delivered to them. [22]They [a]are illustrations of this true proverb: "**A dog returns to its own vomit**,"[1] and "A sow, after washing herself, wallows in the mire."

The False Teachers' Denial of the Lord's Return

3 Dear [a]friends, this is already the second letter I have written you, in which I am trying to stir up your pure mind by way of reminder: [2]I want you to recall both the predictions foretold by the holy prophets [a]and the commandment of the Lord and Savior through your apostles. [3]Above all, understand this: In the last days blatant scoffers will come, being [a]propelled by their own evil urges [4]and saying, "Where is his promised return? For ever since our ancestors died,[1] all things have continued as they were from the beginning of [a]creation." [5]For they deliberately suppress this fact, that [a]by the word of God heavens existed long ago and an earth was [b]formed out of water and by means of water. [6a]Through these things the world existing at that time was destroyed when it was deluged with water. [7]But by [a]the same word the present heavens and earth have been reserved for [b]fire, by being kept for the day of judgment and destruction of the ungodly.

[8]Now, [a]dear friends, do not let this one thing escape your notice, that a single day is like a thousand years with the Lord and a thousand years are like a single day. [9a]The Lord is not slow concerning his promise,[1] as some regard slowness, but [b]is being patient toward you because he does [c]not wish for any to perish but for all to come to repentance. [10]But [a]the day of [b]the Lord will come like a thief; when it comes, the heavens will disappear with a horrific noise, and the celestial bodies will melt away in a blaze, and the earth and every deed done on it will be laid bare.[1] [11]Since all these things are to melt away in this manner, what sort of people must you be, conducting your lives [a]in holiness and godliness, [12]while waiting [a]for and hastening the coming of the day of God? [b]Because of this day, the heavens will be burned up and dissolve, and the celestial bodies will melt [c]away in a blaze! [13]But, according to his promise, we are waiting for[1] [a]new heavens and a [b]new earth, in which righteousness truly resides.

Exhortation to the Faithful

[14]Therefore, dear friends, since you are waiting for these things, strive [a]to be found at peace, without spot or blemish, when you come into his presence. [15]And regard [a]the patience of our Lord as salvation,[1] just as also our dear brother Paul wrote to you,

2:15 [a] Num 22:5, 7; Deut 23:4; Neh 13:2; Jude 11; Rev 2:14   2:16 [1] I.e., mute, silent, or incapable of speech.   2:17 [a] Jude 12, 13   2:19 [a] John 8:34; Rom 6:16   2:20 [a] Matt 12:45   [b] Luke 11:26; [Heb 6:4–6]   [1] Grk. *defilements, contaminations, pollutions*.   2:21 [a] Luke 12:47   2:22 [a] Prov 26:11   [1] Prov 26:11   3:1 [a] 2 Pet 1:13   3:2 [a] Jude 17   3:3 [a] 2 Pet 2:10   3:4 [a] Gen 6:1–7   [1] Lit. *sleep*; often used as a euphemism for the death of a believer.   3:5 [a] Gen 1:6, 9; Heb 11:3   [b] Ps 24:2; 136:6   3:6 [a] Gen 7:11–12, 21–23; Matt 24:37–39; Luke 17:26–27; 2 Pet 2:5   3:7 [a] 2 Pet 3:10, 12   [b] Matt 25:41; [2 Thess 1:8]   3:8 [a] Ps 90:4   3:9 [a] Hab 2:3; Rom 13:11; Heb 10:37   [b] Ps 86:15; Isa 30:18   [c] Ezek 33:11   [1] Or perhaps *the Lord is not delaying* [the fulfillment of] *his promise, the Lord of the promise is not delaying.*   3:10 [a] Matt 24:42–43; Luke 12:39; 1 Thess 5:2; Rev 3:3; 16:15   [b] Gen 1:6–8; Ps 102:25–26; Isa 51:6; Rev 20:11   [1] ‡ The Grk. reading of this phrase, which is by far best supported, is so difficult a reading that many scholars regard it as nonsensical. For a discussion on this difficult textual problem, see *NET Bible, Full Notes Edition.*   3:11 [a] 1 Pet 1:15   3:12 [a] 1 Cor 1:7–8; Titus 2:13–15   [b] Ps 50:3   [c] Isa 24:19; 34:4; Mic 1:4   3:13 [a] Isa 65:17; 66:22   [b] [Rom 8:21]; Rev 21:1   [1] Or possibly *let us wait for.*   3:14 [a] 1 Cor 1:8; 15:58; [1 Thess 3:12–13; 5:23]   3:15 [a] Ps 86:15; Rom 2:4; 1 Pet 3:20   [1] The language here is cryptic. It probably means "regard the patience of our Lord as an opportunity for salvation."

according to the wisdom given to him, [16]speaking of these things in all his [a]letters. Some things in these letters are hard to understand, things the ignorant and unstable twist[1] to their own destruction, as they also do to the [b]rest of the scriptures. [17]Therefore, dear friends, [a]since you have been forewarned, be [b]on your guard that you do not get led astray by the error of these unprincipled men and fall from your firm grasp on the truth. [18a]But grow in the grace and knowledge of our Lord and Savior Jesus Christ. [b]To him be the honor both now and on that eternal day.[1]

3:16 [a] Rom 8:19; 1 Cor 15:24; 1 Thess 4:15; 2 Thess 1:10   [b] 2 Tim 3:16   [1] Or *distort, wrench, torture.*   3:17 [a] Mark 13:23   [b] Eph 4:14   3:18 [a] Eph 4:15   [b] Rom 11:36; 2 Tim 4:18; Rev 1:6   [1] Maj. MSS add *amen.*

1 JOHN

God is light, God is love, and God is life. John is enjoying a delightful fellowship with that God, and he desperately desires that his spiritual children enjoy the same fellowship. God is light: To engage in fellowship with God, we must walk in light and not in darkness. Two major roadblocks that hinder this walk are falling in love with the world and falling for the alluring lies of false teachers. As we walk in the light, we will regularly confess our sins, allowing the blood of Christ to continually cleanse us. God is love: since we are his children, we must walk in love. In fact, John says that if we do not love, we do not know God. Love is more than just words—it is actions; it is giving—not getting. Biblical love is unconditional. Christ's love fulfilled those qualities and when that brand of love characterizes us, we will be free of self-condemnation and experience confidence before God. God is life: Spiritual life begins with spiritual birth, which occurs through faith in Jesus Christ. Faith in Jesus Christ infuses us with God's life—eternal life. Although the apostle John's name is not found in this book, it was given the title *Ioannou A*, the "First of John."

The Prologue to the Letter

1 This is [a]what we proclaim to you: what was from the beginning, what we have heard, what we have [b]seen with our eyes, [c]what we have looked at and [d]our hands have touched (concerning the [e]word of life—[2][a]and the life [b]was revealed, [c]and we have seen and testify and announce to you the eternal life that was [d]with the Father and was revealed to us). [3]What we have seen and heard we announce to you too, so that you may have fellowship[1] [a]with us (and indeed our fellowship is with the Father and with his Son Jesus Christ). [4]Thus we are writing these things so [a]that our[1] joy may be complete.

God Is Light, so We Must Walk in the Light

[5]Now [a]this is the gospel message we have heard from him and announce to you: [b]God is light, and in him there is no darkness at all. [6][a]If we say we have fellowship with him and yet keep on walking in the darkness, we are lying and not practicing[1] the truth. [7]But if we [a]walk in [b]the light as he himself is in the light, we have fellowship with one another and the blood of Jesus his Son cleanses us from all sin. [8]If we say we do not bear the guilt of sin,[1] we are deceiving ourselves and the truth is not in us. [9]But if we [a]confess our sins, he is [b]faithful and righteous, forgiving us our sins and [c]cleansing us from all unrighteousness. [10]If we say we have not sinned, we [a]make him a liar and his word is not in us.

2 [1](My little children, I am writing these things to you so that you may not sin.) But if anyone does sin, [a]we have an advocate[1] with the Father, Jesus Christ the Righteous One, [2]and he [a]himself is the atoning sacrifice[1] for our sins, and not only for our sins but [b]also for the whole world.

Keeping God's Commandments

[3]Now by this we know that we have come to know God: if we keep his commandments. [4]The one who says "I have come to

1:1 [a] [John 1:1]; 1 John 2:13–14 [b] Luke 1:2; John 1:14 [c] 2 Pet 1:16 [d] Luke 24:39; John 20:27 [e] [John 1:1, 4, 14] **1:2** [a] John 1:4; [1 John 3:5, 8; 5:20] [b] Rom 16:26; 1 Tim 3:16 [c] John 21:24 [d] [John 1:1, 18; 16:28] **1:3** [a] John 17:21; 1 Cor 1:9; 1 John 2:24 [1]Or *communion, association.* **1:4** [a] John 15:11; 16:24; 1 Pet 1:8 [1]Sev. sig. MSS *your.* **1:5** [a] John 1:19; 1 John 3:11 [b] [1 Tim 6:16]; Jas 1:17 **1:6** [a] [John 8:12]; 2 Cor 6:14; [1 John 2:9–11] [1]Or *not living according to.* **1:7** [a] Isa 2:5 [b] [1 Cor 6:11] **1:8** [1]Grk. *say we do not have sin.* **1:9** [a] Ps 32:5; Prov 28:13 [b] [Rom 3:24–26] [c] Ps 51:2 **1:10** [a] John 3:33; 1 John 5:10 **2:1** [a] Rom 8:34; 1 Tim 2:5; Heb 7:25; 9:24 [1]Or *Paraclete* (Grk. *paraklētos*); i.e., an intercessor or legal advocate. **2:2** [a] [Rom 3:25]; Heb 2:17; 1 John 4:10 [b] John 1:29 [1]Or *expiation, propitiation, atonement.*

know God" and yet does not keep his commandments is a [a]liar, and the truth is not in such a person. [5]But [a]whoever obeys his word, truly [b]in this person the love of God has been perfected. By this we know that we are in him. [6]The one who says [a]he resides in God [b]ought himself to walk[1] just as Jesus walked.

[7]Dear friends, I am not writing a new commandment to you, but an old commandment which you have had [a]from the beginning. The old commandment is the word that you have already heard. [8]On the other [a]hand, I am writing a new commandment to you, which is true in him and in you, [b]because [c]the darkness is passing away and the true light is already shining. [9]The one who says [a]he is in the light but still hates his fellow Christian[1] is still in the darkness. [10]The one who loves his fellow Christian[1] resides in [a]the light, and [b]there is no cause for stumbling in him. [11]But the one who [a]hates his fellow Christian is in the darkness, [b]walks in the darkness, and does not know where he is going because the darkness has blinded his eyes.

Words of Reassurance

[12]I am writing to [a]you, little children, that your sins have been forgiven because of his name. [13]I am writing to you, fathers, that you have known him who has been [a]from the beginning. I am writing to you, young people, that you have conquered the evil one. [14]I have written to you, children, that you have [a]known the Father. I have written to you, fathers, that you have known him who has been from the beginning. I have written to you, young people, that [b]you are strong, and the word of God resides in you, and you have conquered the evil one.

[15a]Do not love the world or the things in the world. [b]If anyone loves the world, the love of the Father is not in him, [16]because all that is in [a]the world (the desire of the flesh and the desire of the eyes and the arrogance produced by material possessions) is not from the Father, but is from the world. [17]And [a]the world is passing away with all its desires, but the person who does the will of God remains forever.

Warning about False Teachers

[18]Children, [a]it is [b]the last hour, [c]and just as you heard [d]that the antichrist is coming, so now many antichrists have appeared. We know from this that it is the last hour. [19]They went out from us, but [a]they did not really belong to us because [b]if they had belonged [c]to us, they would have remained with us. But they went out from us to demonstrate that all of them do not belong to us. [20]Nevertheless [a]you have an anointing [b]from the Holy One, and [c]you all know.[1] [21]I have not written to you that you do not know the truth, but that you do know it, and that no lie is of the truth. [22a]Who is the liar but the person who denies that [b]Jesus is the Christ?[1] This one is the antichrist: the person who denies the Father and the Son. [23]Everyone [a]who denies the Son does not have the [b]Father [c]either. The person who confesses the Son has the Father also.[1]

[24]As for you, [a]what you have heard from the beginning must remain in [b]you. If what you heard from the beginning remains in you, you also will remain in the Son and in the Father. [25a]Now this is the promise that he himself made to us: eternal life. [26]These things I have written to you about those who are trying to deceive you.

[27]Now as for you, the [a]anointing that [b]you received from him resides in you, and you have no need for anyone to [c]teach you. But as his anointing teaches you about all things, it is true and is not a lie. Just as it has taught you, you reside in him.

2:4 [a]Rom 3:4　2:5 [a]John 14:21, 23　[b][1 John 4:12]　2:6 [a]John 15:4　[b]Matt 11:29; John 13:15; 15:10; 1 Pet 2:21　[1]I.e., ought to behave in the same way Jesus did. "Walking" is a common NT idiom for one's behavior or conduct.　2:7 [a]John 13:34; 1 John 3:11, 23; 4:21; 2 John 5　2:8 [a]John 13:34; 15:12　[b]Rom 13:12; Eph 5:8; 1 Thess 5:4　[c][John 1:9; 8:12; 12:35]　2:9 [a][1 Cor 13:2]; 1 John 3:14　[1]Grk. his brother; the term "brother" means "fellow believer" or "fellow Christian."　2:10 [a][1 John 3:14]　[b]2 Pet 1:10　[1]Grk. his brother; the term "brother" means "fellow believer" or "fellow Christian."　2:11 [a][1 John 2:9; 3:15; 4:20]　[b]John 12:35; 1 John 1:6　2:12 [a][1 Cor 6:11]　2:13 [a]John 1:1; Rev 22:13　2:14 [a][Rom 8:15–17; Gal 4:6]　[b]Eph 6:10　2:15 [a][Rom 12:2]; Gal 1:4; Jas 1:27　[b]Matt 6:24; Jas 4:4　2:16 [a][Eccl 5:10–11]　2:17 [a]1 Cor 7:31; 1 Pet 1:24　2:18 [a]Rom 13:11; 1 Tim 4:1; Heb 1:2; 1 Pet 4:7　[b]2 Thess 2:3　[c]Matt 24:5, 24; 1 John 2:22; 4:3; 2 John 7　[d]1 Tim 4:1　2:19 [a]Deut 13:13　[b]Matt 24:24　[c]1 Cor 11:19　2:20 [a]2 Cor 1:21; Heb 1:9; 1 John 2:27　[b]Acts 3:14　[c]Prov 28:5; [John 16:13]; 1 Cor 2:15–16　[1]Some MSS you know all things.　2:22 [a]2 John 7　[b]1 John 4:3　[1]Or the Messiah.　2:23 [a]John 15:23　[b]John 5:23　[c]1 John 4:15; 5:1; 2 John 9　[1]Some MSS omit The person who confesses the Son has the Father also.　2:24 [a]2 John 5, 6　[b]John 14:23; 1 John 1:3; 2 John 9　2:25 [a]John 3:14–16; 6:40; 17:2–3; 1 John 1:2　2:27 [a][John 14:16; 16:13]; 1 John 2:20　[b][Jer 31:33]　[c][John 14:16; 1 Cor 2:12]; 1 Thess 4:9

Children of God

[28] And now, little children, remain in him, so that when he appears we may have [a]confidence and not shrink away from him in shame when he comes back. [29][a]If you know that he is righteous, you also know that [b]everyone who practices righteousness has been fathered by him.

3 (See [a]what sort of love the Father has given to us: that [b]we should be called God's children—and indeed we are![1] For this reason the world does not know us: [c]Because it did not know him. [2]Dear friends, we are God's children [a]now, and what we will be has not yet been revealed. We know that whenever [b]it is revealed [c]we will be like him because [d]we will see him just as he is. [3][a]And everyone who has this hope focused on him purifies himself, just as Jesus is pure).

[4]Everyone who practices [a]sin also practices lawlessness; indeed, sin is lawlessness. [5]And you know [a]that Jesus was revealed [b]to take away sins, and [c]in him there is no sin. [6]Everyone who resides in him does not sin;[1] everyone who sins has neither seen him nor known him. [7]Little children, let no one deceive you: The one who practices righteousness is righteous, just as Jesus is righteous. [8]The one who practices sin is of [a]the devil because the devil has been sinning from the beginning. For this purpose the Son of God was revealed: [b]to destroy the works of the devil. [9]Everyone who has been [a]fathered by God does not practice sin because [b]God's seed resides in him, and thus he is not able to sin because he has been fathered by God. [10]By this the children of God and the children of the devil are revealed: Everyone who does not practice righteousness—the one who does not love his fellow Christian[1]—is not of God.

God Is Love, so We Must Love One Another

[11]For this is the gospel message that you have heard from the beginning: that we [a]should love one another, [12]not like [a]Cain who was of the evil one and brutally murdered his brother. And why did he murder him? Because his deeds were evil, but his brother's were righteous.

[13]Therefore do not be surprised, [a]brothers and sisters,[1] if the world hates you. [14]We know that we have crossed over from death to life because we love our fellow Christians.[1] The one who does not love remains in death. [15]Everyone [a]who hates his fellow Christian[1] is a murderer, and you [b]know that no murderer has eternal life residing in him. [16]We have come to know love [a]by this: [b]that Jesus laid down his life for us; thus we ought to lay down our lives for our fellow Christians. [17]But [a]whoever has the world's possessions and sees his fellow Christian[1] in need and shuts off his compassion against him, how can the love of God reside in such a person?

[18]Little children, [a]let us not love with word or with tongue but in deed and truth. [19]And by this we will know [a]that we are of the truth and will convince our conscience[1] in his presence, [20]that if our conscience condemns[1] us, [a]that God is greater than our conscience and knows all things. [21]Dear friends, if our conscience does not condemn us, [a]we have confidence in the presence of God, [22]and [a]whatever we ask we receive from him, because we keep his commandments [b]and do the things that are pleasing to him. [23]Now this is his commandment: that we believe in the name of his Son Jesus Christ [a]and love one another, just as he gave us the commandment. [24]And [a]the person who keeps his commandments

---

2:28 [a] Eph 3:12; 1 John 3:21; 4:17; 5:14   2:29 [a] Acts 22:14   [b] John 7:18; 1 John 3:7, 10   3:1 [a] [John 3:16; Eph 2:4–7; 1 John 4:10]   [b] [John 1:12]   [c] John 15:18, 21; 16:3   [1] Some MSS omit *and we are*.   3:2 [a] [Isa 56:5; Rom 8:15–16]   [b] [Rom 8:18–19, 23]   [c] Rom 8:29; 2 Pet 1:4   [d] [Ps 16:11]   3:3 [a] 1 John 4:17   3:4 [a] Rom 4:15; 1 John 5:17   3:5 [a] 1 John 1:2; 3:8   [b] [Isa 53:5–6]; John 1:29; [2 Cor 5:21; Heb 9:26]   [c] [2 Cor 5:21]; 1 John 2:29   3:6 [1] Perhaps with a habitual meaning. For a discussion of this problematic grammatical issue, see *NET Bible, Full Notes Edition*.   3:8 [a] Matt 13:38; John 8:44; 1 John 3:10   [b] Luke 10:18; [Heb 2:14]   3:9 [a] John 1:3; 3:3; [1 John 2:29; 4:7; 5:1, 4, 18]; 3 John 11   [b] 1 Pet 1:23   3:10 [1] Grk. *his brother*; the term "brother" means "fellow believer" or "fellow Christian."   3:11 [a] [John 13:34; 15:12]; 1 John 4:7, 11, 21; 2 John 5   3:12 [a] Gen 4:4, 8   3:13 [a] [John 15:18; 17:14]   [1] Grk. *brothers*; the Grk. word may be used for "brothers and sisters" or "fellow Christians."   3:14 [1] Grk. *our brothers*; the term "brother" means "fellow believer" or "fellow Christian."   3:15 [a] Matt 5:21; John 8:44   [b] [Gal 5:20–21; Rev 21:8]   [1] Grk. *his brother*; the term "brother" means "fellow believer" or "fellow Christian."   3:16 [a] [John 3:16]   [b] John 10:11; 15:13; Gal 2:20   3:17 [a] Deut 15:7   [1] Grk. *his brother*; the term "brother" means "fellow believer" or "fellow Christian."   3:18 [a] Ezek 33:31   3:19 [a] John 18:37   [1] Lit. *heart*; often represents the mind, the will, the emotions, or the conscience.   3:20 [a] [1 Cor 4:4–5]   [1] This word has legal or forensic connotations, and in this context refers to the believer's self-condemnation resulting from a guilty conscience concerning sin.   3:21 [a] [Heb 10:22; 1 John 2:28; 5:14]   3:22 [a] Ps 34:15; [John 15:7]; 1 John 5:14–15   [b] John 8:29; Heb 13:21   3:23 [a] Matt 22:39   3:24 [a] John 14:23

[b]resides in God, and God in him. Now [c]by this we know that God resides in us: by the Spirit he has given us.

Testing the Spirits

4 Dear friends, do not believe every spirit, but [a]test the spirits to determine if they are from God, because [b]many false prophets[1] have gone out into the world. [2]By this you know the Spirit of God: [a]Every spirit that confesses Jesus as the Christ who has come in the flesh is from God, [3]but every spirit that refuses to confess Jesus,[1] that spirit is not from God, and this is the spirit of the antichrist, which you have heard is coming, and now is already in the world.

[4]You are from God, little children, and have conquered [a]them because the one who is in you is greater than the one who is in the world. [5]They are from the world; therefore they speak from the world's perspective and the world listens to [a]them. [6]We are from God; the person who knows God listens to us, but whoever is not from God does not listen to us. [a]By this we know the Spirit of truth and the spirit of deceit.

God Is Love

[7]Dear [a]friends, let us love one another, because love is from God, and everyone who [b]loves has been fathered by God and knows God. [8]The person who does not love does not know God because God is love. [9]By this the love of God[1] is revealed [a]in us: that God has sent his one and only [b]Son into the world so that we may live through him. [10]In this is love: [a]not that we have loved God, but that he loved us and sent his Son [b]to be the atoning sacrifice for our sins. [11]Dear friends, [a]if God so loved us, then we also ought to love one another.[1] [12]No one has seen God at any time. If we love one another, God resides in us, and his love is perfected in us. [13a]By this we know that we reside in God and he in us: in that he has given us of his Spirit. [14]And [a]we have seen and testify that [b]the Father has sent the Son to be the Savior of the world.

[15a]If anyone confesses that Jesus is the Son of God, God resides in him and he in God. [16]And we have come to know and to believe [a]the love that God has [b]in us. God is love, and the one who resides in love resides in God, and God resides in him. [17]By this love is perfected with us, so that [a]we may have confidence in the day of judgment, because just as Jesus is, so also are we in this world. [18]There is no fear in love, but perfect love drives out fear because fear has to do with punishment. The one who fears punishment has not been perfected in love. [19a]We love because he loved us first.

[20a]If anyone says "I love God" and yet hates his fellow Christian,[1] he is a liar because the one who does not love his fellow Christian[2] [b]whom he has seen cannot love God whom he has not seen. [21]And the commandment we have from him is [a]this: that[1] the one who loves God should love his fellow Christian[2] too.

5 [1]Everyone who believes that [a]Jesus is the Christ[1] has been [b]fathered by God, and everyone who loves the father[2] loves the child fathered by him. [2]By this we know that we love the children of God: whenever we love God and obey his commandments. [3a]For this is the love of God: that we keep [b]his commandments. And his commandments do not weigh us down, [4]because [a]everyone who [b]has been fathered by God conquers the world.

Testimony about the Son

This is the conquering power that has conquered the world: our faith. [5]Now who is [a]the person who has conquered the world

3:24 [b]John 14:21; 17:21   [c]John 14:17; Rom 8:9, 14, 16; 1 Thess 4:8; 1 John 4:13   **4:1** [a]1 Cor 14:29   [b]Matt 24:5   [1]I.e., the secessionist opponents.   **4:2** [a][Rom 10:8–10]; 1 Cor 12:3; 1 John 5:1   **4:3** [1]Some wss *Jesus as Lord, Jesus as Christ, the Christ, Christ Jesus, Jesus as the Christ.*   **4:4** [a]John 14:30; 16:11   **4:5** [a]John 3:31   **4:6** [a][1 Cor 2:12–16]   **4:7** [a]1 John 3:10–11, 23   [b]1 Thess 4:9; [1 John 3:14]   **4:9** [a]Rom 5:8   [b]Isa 9:6–7; John 3:16   [1]I.e., God's love for us rather than our love for God, because it describes God's action in sending his Son into the world.   **4:10** [a]Titus 3:5   [b]1 John 2:2   **4:11** [a]Matt 18:33   [1]Reality is assumed for the sake of argument.   **4:12** [a]John 1:18; 1 Tim 6:16; 1 John 4:20   **4:13** [a]John 14:20   **4:14** [a]John 1:14   [b]John 3:17; 4:42; 1 John 2:2   **4:15** [a][Rom 10:9]; 1 John 3:23; 4:2; 5:1, 5   **4:16** [a][1 John 3:24]   [b][John 14:23]   **4:17** [a][Jas 2:13]; 1 John 2:28   **4:19** [a]1 John 4:10   **4:20** [a][1 John 2:4]   [b]1 Pet 1:8; 1 John 4:12   [1]Grk. *his brother;* the term "brother" means "fellow believer" or "fellow Christian."   [2]Grk. *his brother;* the term "brother" means "fellow believer" or "fellow Christian."   **4:21** [a]Lev 19:18; [Matt 5:43–44; 22:39]; John 13:34   [1]Either the purpose of or the result of the commandment mentioned in the first half of the verse, or, more likely, explaining what the commandment consists of.   [2]Grk. *his brother;* the term "brother" means "fellow believer" or "fellow Christian."   **5:1** [a]1 John 2:22; 4:2, 15   [b]John 1:13   [1]Or *the Messiah.*   [2]‡ Maj. wss (should) *also love the.*   **5:3** [a]John 14:15; 2 John 6   [b]Mic 6:8; Matt 11:30; 23:4   **5:4** [a]John 16:33   [b]1 John 2:13; 4:4   **5:5** [a]1 Cor 15:57

except the one who believes that Jesus is the Son of God? [6]Jesus Christ is the one who came [a]by water [b]and blood—not by the water only, but by the water and the blood. And the Spirit is the one who testifies, because the Spirit is the truth. [7]For [a]there are three that testify,[1] [8]the Spirit and [a]the water and the blood, and these three are in agreement.

[9]If we accept [a]the testimony of men, the testimony of God is greater [b]because this is the testimony of God that he has testified concerning his Son. [10](The one who believes in the Son of God [a]has the testimony in himself; the one who does not believe God [b]has made him a liar because he has not believed in the testimony that God has testified concerning his Son.) [11]And this is the testimony: God has given us eternal life, and this life is in his Son. [12]The one who has [a]the Son has this eternal life; the one who does not have the Son of God does not have this eternal life.

Assurance of Eternal Life

[13]I have written these things to you who believe in the name of the Son of God so that you may know that you have eternal life.

[14]And this is the confidence that we have before him: that [a]whenever we ask anything according to his will, he hears us. [15]And if we know that he hears us in regard to whatever we ask, then we know that we have the requests that we have asked from him. [16]If anyone sees his fellow Christian[1] committing a sin not resulting in death, [a]he should ask, and God will grant life to [b]the person who [c]commits a sin not resulting in death. There is a sin resulting in death. I do not say that he should ask about that. [17a]All unrighteousness is sin, but there is sin not resulting in death.

[18]We know that everyone fathered by God does not sin, but God [a]protects the one he has fathered, and the evil one cannot touch him. [19]We know that we are from God, and [a]the whole world lies in the power of the evil one. [20]And we know that the [a]Son of God [b]has come and has given us insight [c]to know him who is true, and we are in him who is true, in his Son Jesus Christ. This [d]one is the true God [e]and eternal life. [21]Little children, guard yourselves from idols.[1]

5:6 [a] John 1:31–34; [Eph 5:26–27] [b] [John 14:17]   5:7 [a] [John 1:1] [1] TR *in heaven, the Father, the Word, and the Holy Spirit, and these three are one.* 5:8 *And there are three that testify on earth.*   5:8 [a] John 15:26   5:9 [a] John 5:34, 37; 8:17–18 [b] [Matt 3:16–17]; John 5:32, 37   5:10 [a] [Rom 8:16]; Gal 4:6; Rev 12:17 [b] John 3:18, 33; 1 John 1:10   5:12 [a] [John 3:15, 36; 6:47; 17:2–3]   5:14 [a] [1 John 2:28; 3:21–22]   5:16 [a] Job 42:8 [b] [Matt 12:31] [c] Jer 7:16; 14:11 [1] Grk. *his brother*; the term "brother" means "fellow believer" or "fellow Christian."   5:17 [a] 1 John 3:4   5:18 [a] Jas 1:27   5:19 [a] John 12:31; 17:15; Gal 1:4   5:20 [a] 1 John 4:2 [b] Luke 24:45 [c] John 17:3; Rev 3:7 [d] Isa 9:6 [e] 1 John 5:11–12   5:21 [1] Maj. later MSS add *amen.*

2 JOHN

L et the one who thinks he is standing be careful that he does not fall" (1 Cor 10:12). These words of the apostle Paul could well stand as a subtitle for John's little epistle. The recipients, a chosen lady and her children, were obviously standing, walking in truth, remaining faithful to the commandments they had received from the Father. John is deeply pleased to be able to commend them, but he takes nothing for granted. Realizing that standing is just one step removed from falling, he doesn't hesitate to issue a reminder: "Love one another" (v. 5). Loving one another, he stresses, is walking according to God's commandments. John indicates, however, that this love must be discerning. It is not a naive, unthinking, open-to-anything-and-anyone kind of love. Biblical love is a matter of choice; it is dangerous and foolish to float through life with undiscerning love. False teachers abound who do not acknowledge Christ as having come in the flesh—it is false charity to open the door to false teaching. We must have fellowship with God. We must have fellowship with Christians. But we must not have fellowship with false teachers. The "elder" of verse 1 has been traditionally identified with the apostle John, resulting in the Greek title *Ioannou B*, the "Second of John."

Introduction and Thanksgiving

[1]From [a]the elder, to an elect lady[1] and her children, whom I love in truth (and not I alone, but also all those who know the truth), [2]because of the truth[1] that resides in us and will be with us forever. [3][a]Grace, mercy, and peace will be with us from God the Father and from[1] Jesus Christ the Son of the Father, in truth and love.

[4]I [a]rejoiced greatly because I have found some of your children living according to the truth, just as the Father commanded us.

Warning against False Teachers

[5]But now I ask you, lady (not as if I were writing [a]a new commandment to you, but the one we have had from the beginning), that we love one another. [6](Now [a]this is love: that we walk according to his commandments.) This is the commandment, just [b]as you have heard from the beginning; thus you should walk in it. [7]For [a]many deceivers have gone out into the world, people [b]who do not confess Jesus as Christ[1] coming in the flesh. This [c]person is the deceiver and the antichrist! [8][a]Watch out, so [b]that you do not lose the things we have worked for, but receive a full reward.

[9]Everyone [a]who goes on ahead and does not remain[1] in the teaching of Christ[2] does not have God. The one who remains in this teaching has both the Father and the Son. [10]If anyone comes to you and [a]does not bring this teaching, do not receive him into your house and do not give him any greeting [11]because the person who gives him a greeting shares in his evil deeds.

Conclusion

[12]Though I [a]have many other things to write to you, I do not want to do so with paper and ink, but I hope to come visit you and speak face to face so [b]that our joy may be complete.

[13][a]The children of your elect sister greet you.[1]

---

1 [a]Col 1:5 [1]This phrase may refer to an individual or to a church (or the church at large). The "elect lady" is probably a particular local church some distance from the author. 2 [1]Some sig. MSS omit *because of the truth*. 3 [a]Rom 1:7; 1 Tim 1:2 [1]Maj. WSS *Lord Jesus Christ*. 4 [a]1 Thess 2:19–20; 3 John 3, 4 5 [a][John 13:34–35; 15:12, 17]; 1 John 3:11; 4:7, 11 6 [a]John 14:15; 1 John 2:5; 5:3 [b]1 John 2:24 7 [a]1 John 2:19; 4:1 [b]1 John 4:2 [c]1 John 2:22 [1]Or *Messiah*. 8 [a]Mark 13:9 [b]Gal 3:4 9 [a]John 7:16; 8:31; 1 John 2:19, 23, 24 [1]Grk. *remain, reside*. [2]Either the teaching about Christ, Christ's own teaching, or both. 10 [a]1 Kgs 13:16; Rom 16:17; 2 Thess 3:6, 14; Titus 3:10 12 [a]3 John 13, 14 [b]John 17:13 13 [a]1 Pet 5:13 [1]Some MSS add *amen*.

3 JOHN

In 3 John the apostle encourages fellowship with Christian believers. Following his expression of love for Gaius, John assures him of his prayers for his health and voices his joy over Gaius's persistent walk in truth and hospitality and support for missionaries who have come to his church. But not everyone in the church feels the same way. Diotrephes's heart is 180 degrees removed from Gaius's heart—he is no longer living in love. Pride has taken precedence in his life. He has refused a letter John has written for the church, fearing that his authority might be superseded by the apostle's. He also has accused John of evil words and refused to accept missionaries. He forbids others to do so and even expels them from the church if they disobey him. John uses this negative example as an opportunity to encourage Gaius to continue his hospitality. Demetrius has a good testimony and may even be one of those turned away by Diotrephes; he is widely known for his good character and his loyalty to the truth. Here he is well commended by John and stands as a positive example for Gaius. The Greek titles of 1–3 John are *Ioannou A, B*, and *G*. The *G* is gamma, the third letter of the Greek alphabet; *Ioannou G* means the "Third of John."

Introduction and Thanksgiving

[1]From the elder, to Gaius my dear brother, [a]whom I love in truth. [2]Dear friend, I pray that all may go well with you and that you may be in good health, just as it is well with your soul. [3]For I [a]rejoiced greatly when the brothers came and testified to your truth, just as you are living according to the truth.

[4]I have no greater [a]joy than this: to hear that [b]my children are living according to the truth.[1]

The Charge to Gaius

[5]Dear friend, you demonstrate faithfulness by whatever you do for the brothers (even though they are strangers). [6]They have testified to your love before the church. You will do well to send them on their way in a manner worthy of God. [7]For they have gone forth on behalf of "The Name," [a]accepting nothing from the pagans. [8]Therefore we ought to support such people so that we become coworkers in cooperation with the truth.

Diotrephes the Troublemaker

[9]I wrote something to the church, but Diotrephes, who loves to be first among them, does not acknowledge us. [10]Therefore, if [a]I come, I will call attention to the deeds he is doing—the bringing of unjustified charges against us with evil words! And not being content with that, he not only refuses to welcome the brothers himself, but hinders the people who want to do so and throws them out of the church! [11]Dear friend, [a]do not imitate what is bad, but what is good. [b]The one who does good is of [c]God; the one who does what is bad has not seen God.

Worthy Demetrius

[12]Demetrius [a]has been testified to by all, even by the truth itself. We also testify to him, [b]and you know that our testimony is true.

Conclusion

[13]I have many [a]things to write to you, but I do not wish to write to you with pen and ink. [14]But I hope to see you right away, and we will speak face to face. [15]Peace be with you. The friends here greet you. Greet the friends there by name.

1 [a]2 John 1   3 [a]2 John 4   4 [a]1 Thess 2:19–20; 2 John 4   [b][1 Cor 4:15]   [1]Grk. *walking in* [the] *truth.*   7 [a]1 Cor 9:12, 15
10 [a]Prov 10:8, 10   11 [a]Ps 34:14; 37:27; Rom 14:19; 1 Thess 5:15; 1 Tim 6:11; 2 Tim 2:22   [b][1 John 2:29; 3:10]   [c][1 John 3:10]
12 [a]Acts 6:3; 1 Tim 3:7   [b]John 19:35; 21:24   13 [a]2 John 12

JUDE

Fight! Contend! Do battle! When apostasy arises, when false teachers emerge, when the truth of God is attacked, it is time to fight for the faith. Only believers who are spiritually fit can answer the summons. At the beginning of his letter Jude focuses on the believers' common salvation but then feels compelled to challenge them to contend for the faith. The danger is real. False teachers have crept into the church and turned God's grace into license to do as they please. Jude reminds such men of God's past dealings with unbelieving Israel, disobedient angels, and wicked Sodom and Gomorrah. In the face of such danger, Christians should not be caught off guard. The challenge is great, but so is the God who is able to keep them from stumbling. The Greek title *Iouda,* "Of Jude," comes from the name *Ioudas,* which appears in verse 1. This name, which can be translated "Jude" or "Judas," was popular in the first century because of Judas Maccabaeus (died 160 BC), a leader of the Jewish resistance against Syria during the Maccabean revolt.

Salutation

[1] From Jude, a slave[1] of Jesus Christ and [a]brother of James, to those who are [b]called, wrapped in the love of God the Father and [c]kept for Jesus Christ. [2] May mercy, [a]peace, and love be lavished on you!

Condemnation of the False Teachers

[3] Dear friends, although I have been eager to write to you [a]about our common salvation, I now feel compelled instead to write to encourage [b]you to contend earnestly for the faith that was once for all entrusted to the saints. [4] For certain men[1] have secretly slipped in among you—men who long ago were marked out for the condemnation I am about to describe—ungodly men who have turned the grace of our God into a license for evil and who deny our only Master[2] and Lord,[3] Jesus Christ.

[5] Now I desire to remind you (even though you have been fully informed of [a]these facts once for all[1]) that Jesus,[2] having saved the people out of the land of Egypt, later destroyed those who did not believe. [6] You also know that the angels who did not keep within their proper domain but abandoned their own place of residence, he has kept in eternal chains in utter darkness, locked up for the judgment of the great Day. [7] So also [a]Sodom and Gomorrah and the neighboring towns, since they indulged in sexual immorality and pursued unnatural desire in a way similar to these angels, are now displayed as an example by suffering the punishment of eternal fire.

[8] [a]Yet these men,[1] as [b]a result of their dreams,[2] defile the flesh, reject authority, and insult the glorious ones. [9] But even when Michael [a]the archangel was arguing with the devil and debating with him concerning Moses' body, he did not dare to bring a slanderous judgment, but said, "May the Lord rebuke you!" [10] [a]But these men do not understand the things they slander, and they are being destroyed by the very things that, like irrational animals, they instinctively comprehend. [11] Woe to them!

1 [a] Acts 1:13 [b] Rom 1:7 [c] John 17:11–12 [1] Trad. *servant*; the word does not bear the connotation of a free individual serving another. 2 [a] 1 Pet 1:2; 2 Pet 1:2 3 [a] Titus 1:4 [b] Phil 1:27 4 [1] Grk. *people*; if Jude is arguing that Peter's prophecy about false teachers has come true, these are most likely men in the original historical and cultural setting. [2] Maj. later wss *Master God.* [3] "Master" and "Lord" refer to the same person. For a discussion on this Grk. construction, see *NET Bible, Full Notes Edition.* 5 [a] Exod 12:51; 1 Cor 10:5–10; Heb 3:16 [1] The textual history of "(. . . once for all) that Jesus, having saved the people" is quite complex, with at least 13 variants. For a discussion on this textual problem, see *NET Bible, Full Notes Edition.* [2] Some wss *the Lord, God, God Christ.* 7 [a] Gen 19:24; 2 Pet 2:6 8 [a] 2 Pet 2:10 [b] Exod 22:28 [1] I.e., the false teachers. [2] Grk. *dreaming*; sometimes used of apocalyptic visions, both of true and false prophets. 9 [a] Zech 3:2 10 [a] 2 Pet 2:12

For they have traveled down Cain's path, and because [a]of greed [b]have abandoned themselves to Balaam's error; hence, they will [c]certainly perish in Korah's rebellion. [12]These men are dangerous reefs[1] at your love feasts,[2] feasting without reverence,[3] feeding only themselves. They are waterless clouds, carried along by the winds; autumn trees without fruit—twice dead, uprooted; [13a]wild sea waves, spewing out the [b]foam of their shame; wayward stars [c]for whom the utter depths of eternal darkness have been reserved.

[14]Now Enoch, the seventh in descent beginning with Adam, even prophesied of them, saying, "Look! The Lord is coming with thousands and thousands of his holy ones, [15]to execute judgment on all, and to convict every person of all their thoroughly ungodly deeds that they have committed, and of all the harsh [a]words that ungodly sinners have spoken against him." [16]These people are grumblers and fault-finders who go wherever their desires lead them, and [a]they give bombastic speeches, [b]enchanting folks for their own gain.

Exhortation to the Faithful

[17a]But you, dear friends—recall the predictions foretold by the apostles of our Lord Jesus Christ. [18]For they said to you, "At [a]the end of time there will come scoffers, propelled by their own ungodly desires."[1] [19]These people are divisive, worldly, devoid of the Spirit. [20]But you, dear friends, by [a]building yourselves up in your most holy faith, by [b]praying in the Holy Spirit, [21]maintain yourselves [a]in the love of God while anticipating[1] the mercy of our Lord Jesus Christ that brings eternal life. [22]And have mercy on those who waver; [23]save [a]others by snatching [b]them out of the fire; have mercy on others, coupled with a fear of God, hating even the clothes stained by the flesh.[1]

Final Blessing

[24a]Now [b]to the one who is able to keep you from falling, and to cause you to stand, rejoicing, without blemish before his glorious presence,[1] [25]to the only God our Savior through Jesus Christ our Lord, be glory, majesty, power, and authority, before all time, and now, and for all eternity. Amen.

11[a] Gen 4:3–8; Heb 11:4; 1 John 3:12 [b] Num 31:16; 2 Pet 2:15; Rev 2:14 [c] Num 16:1–3, 31–35 12[1] Or *blemishes, stains*; the Grk. word was often used of a mere rock, though it normally was associated with a rock along the shore or one jutting out in the water. [2] Sev. wss *deceptions*. [3] Or *fearlessly*. 13[a] Isa 57:20 [b] [Phil 3:19] [c] 2 Pet 2:17; Jude 6 15[a] 1 Sam 2:3 16[a] 2 Pet 2:18 [b] Prov 28:21 17[a] 2 Pet 3:2 18[a] Acts 20:29; [1 Tim 4:1]; 2 Tim 3:1; 4:3; 2 Pet 3:3 [1] 2 Pet 3:3 20[a] Col 2:7; 1 Thess 5:11 [b] [Rom 8:26] 21[a] Titus 2:13; Heb 9:28; 2 Pet 3:12 [1] Or *waiting for*. 23[a] Rom 11:14 [b] [Zech 3:4–5]; Rev 3:4 [1] Grk. *hating even the tunic spotted by the flesh*; "flesh" is metaphorical, referring to the sin nature. 24[a] [Eph 3:20] [b] Col 1:22 [1] Or *in the presence of his glory, before his glory*.

REVELATION

Just as Genesis is the book of beginnings, Revelation is the book of consummation. In it the divine program of redemption is brought to fruition, and the holy name of God is vindicated before all creation. Although there are numerous prophecies in the Gospels and Epistles, Revelation is the only New Testament book that focuses primarily on prophetic events. Its title means "Unveiling" or "Disclosure"; thus the book is an unveiling of the character and program of God. Penned by John during his exile on the island of Patmos, Revelation centers on visions and symbols of the resurrected Christ who alone has authority to judge the earth, to remake it, and to rule it in righteousness. The title of this book in the Greek text is *Apokalypsis Ioannou,* "Revelation of John." It is also known as the Apocalypse, a transliteration of the word *apokalypsis* meaning "Unveiling," "Disclosure," or "Revelation." Thus the book is an unveiling of that which otherwise could not be known. A better title comes from the first verse: *Apokalypsis Iesou Christou,* "Revelation of Jesus Christ." This could be taken as a revelation that came from Christ or as a revelation that is about Christ—both are appropriate. Because of the unified contents of this book, it should not be called Revelations.

The Prologue

1 The revelation of Jesus Christ,[1] [a]which God gave him to show his servants[2] what must happen very soon. [b]He made it clear by sending his angel to his servant[3] John, [2][a]who then testified to [b]everything that he saw concerning the word of God and the testimony about Jesus Christ. [3][a]Blessed is the one who reads the words of this prophecy aloud,[1] and blessed are those who hear and obey the [b]things written in it, because the time is near!

[4]From John, to the seven churches that are in the province of Asia: Grace and peace to you from "he [a]who is,"[1] and [b]who was, [c]and who is still to come, and from the seven spirits who are before his throne, [5]and from Jesus Christ—[a]the faithful [b]witness, the [c]firstborn from among [d]the dead, the ruler over the kings of the earth. To the one [e]who loves us [f]and has set us free[1] from our sins at the cost of his own blood [6]and has [a]appointed us as a kingdom, as priests serving his God and Father—[b]to him be the glory and the power for ever and ever![1] Amen.

[7] (Look! *He is returning with the* [a]*clouds,*[1]
and *every eye will see him,*
even those who pierced him,[2]
and all [b]the tribes on the earth will
mourn because of him.
This will certainly come to pass![3]
Amen.)

[8]"I am the Alpha and the Omega,"[1] says the Lord God—the one who [a]is, and [b]who was, and who is still to come—the [c]All-Powerful![2] [9]I, John, your brother and the one who [a]shares with you in the persecution, [b]kingdom, and endurance that are in Jesus, was

1:1 [a]John 3:32   [b]Rev 22:6   [1]The revelation about Jesus Christ, the revelation from Jesus Christ, or both.   [2]Grk. *slaves*; in a spiritual sense, voluntarily becoming slaves of God or of Jesus Christ.   [3]Grk. *slave*; in a spiritual sense, voluntarily becoming a slave of God or of Jesus Christ.   1:2 [a]1 Cor 1:6   [b]1 John 1:1   1:3 [a]Luke 11:28; Rev 22:7   [b]Jas 5:8; Rev 22:10   [1]*aloud* is supplied; in the original historical setting, reading would usually refer to reading out loud in public.   1:4 [a]Exod 3:14   [b]John 1:1   [c][Isa 11:2]; Zech 3:9; Rev 3:1; 4:5; 5:6   [1]Some wss *from God who is.*   1:5 [a]John 8:14; Prov 14:5   [b]Isa 55:4   [c]Ps 89:27; 1 Cor 15:20; [Col 1:18]   [d]Rev 17:14   [e]John 13:34   [f]Heb 9:14   [1]Some wss *washed.*   1:6 [a]1 Pet 2:5, 9   [b]1 Tim 6:16   [1]Some wss omit *and ever.*   1:7 [a]Matt 24:30   [b]Zech 12:10–14; John 19:37   [1][Dan 7:13]   [2][Zech 12:10]   [3]Grk. *Yes, Amen.*   1:8 [a]Isa 41:4; Rev 21:6; 22:13   [b]Rev 4:8; 11:17   [c]Isa 9:6   [1]Some wss add *the beginning and the end.*   [2]Grk. *the Almighty, All-Powerful, Omnipotent* [One]; only used of God.   1:9 [a]Phil 1:7   [b][Rom 8:17; 2 Tim 2:12]

on the island called Patmos because of the word of God and the testimony about Jesus. [10]I was [a]in [b]the Spirit on the Lord's [c]Day when I heard behind me a loud voice like a trumpet, [11]saying: "Write in a book what you see and send it to the seven churches—to Ephesus, Smyrna, Pergamum, Thyatira, Sardis, Philadelphia, and Laodicea."

[12]I turned to see whose [a]voice was speaking to me, and when I did so, I saw seven golden lampstands, [13a]and in the midst of the lampstands was one *like a son of man*.[1] He was dressed in a robe extending down to his feet, and [b]he [c]wore a wide golden belt around his chest. [14]His head and [a]hair were as white as wool, even as white as snow, and [b]his eyes were like a fiery flame. [15a]His feet were like polished bronze[1] refined[2] in a furnace, and his voice was like the roar of many waters. [16]He [a]held seven stars in his right hand, and a sharp double-edged sword extended [b]out of his mouth. [c]His face shone like the sun shining at full strength. [17a]When I saw him I fell down at his feet as though I were dead, but he placed his right hand on me and said: "Do not be afraid! I am [b]the [c]first and the last, [18]and the one who [a]lives! [b]I was dead, but look, now [c]I am alive—forever and ever—and I hold the keys of death and of Hades! [19]Therefore write what you saw, what is, [a]and what will be after these things. [20]The mystery of the seven stars that you saw in my right hand and the seven golden lampstands is this: The seven stars are [a]the angels[1] of the seven churches, and the seven lampstands are the seven churches.

To the Church in Ephesus

2 "To [a]the angel of the church in Ephesus, write the following:

"This is the solemn pronouncement of the one [b]who has a firm grasp on the seven stars in his right hand—the one who walks among the seven golden lampstands: [2]I know your works as well as your labor and steadfast endurance, and that you cannot tolerate [a]evil. [b]You have even put to the test those [c]who refer to themselves as apostles (but are not), and have discovered that they are false. [3]I am also aware that you have persisted steadfastly, endured much for the sake of my name, and have [a]not grown weary. [4]But I have this against you: You have departed from your first love! [5]Therefore, remember from what high state you have fallen and repent! Do the deeds you did at the first; [a]if not, I will come to you and remove your lampstand from its place—that is, if you do not repent. [6]But you do have this going for you: You hate what the Nicolaitans practice—practices I also hate. [7]The one who has an ear had better [a]hear what the Spirit says [b]to [c]the churches. To the one who conquers,[1] I will permit him to eat from the tree of life that is in the paradise of God.'[2]

To the Church in Smyrna

[8]"To [a]the angel of the church in Smyrna write the following:

"This is the solemn pronouncement of the one who is the first and the last, the one who was dead, but came to life: [9]'I know the distress you are suffering[1] and your poverty (but you are [a]rich). I also know the slander against you by [b]those who call themselves Jews and really are not, [c]but are a synagogue of Satan. [10a]Do not be afraid of the things you are about to suffer. The devil is about to have some of you thrown into prison so you may be tested, and you will experience suffering[1] for ten days. [b]Remain faithful even to [c]the point of death, and I will give you the crown that is life itself. [11]The one who has an ear had better [a]hear what [b]the Spirit says to the churches. The one who conquers[1] will in no way be harmed by the second death.'

To the Church in Pergamum

[12]"To [a]the angel of the church in Pergamum write the following:

1:10 [a] Acts 10:10   [b] Acts 20:7   [c] Rev 4:1   1:12 [a] Exod 25:37; Zech 4:2; Rev 1:20; 2:1   1:13 [a] Rev 2:1   [b] Dan 10:5   [c] Rev 15:6   [1] [Dan 7:13]   1:14 [a] Dan 7:9   [b] Dan 10:6; Rev 2:18; 19:12   1:15 [a] Ezek 1:24; 43:2; Rev 14:2; 19:6   [1] Or *fine brass/bronze*; the emphasis is probably less on its value and more on its lustrous quality.   [2] Or *that has been heated in a furnace until it glows*.   1:16 [a] Rev 1:20; 2:1; 3:1   [b] Isa 49:2; [Heb 4:12]; Rev 2:12, 16; 19:15   [c] Matt 17:2; Acts 26:13; Rev 10:1   1:17 [a] Ezek 1:28   [b] Dan 8:18; 10:10, 12   [c] Isa 41:4; 44:6; 48:12; Rev 2:8; 22:13   1:18 [a] Rom 6:9; Rev 2:8; 10:6; 15:7   [b] Rev 4:9   [c] Ps 68:20   1:19 [a] John 16:13; Rev 4:1   1:20 [a] Exod 25:37; 37:23; Zech 4:2; Matt 5:15; Phil 2:15   [1] Or perhaps *the messengers*.   2:1 [a] Rev 1:16   [b] Rev 1:13   2:2 [a] Ps 1:6   [b] John 6:6; 1 John 4:1   [c] 2 Cor 11:13   2:3 [a] Gal 6:9; Heb 12:3, 5   2:5 [a] Matt 21:41   2:7 [a] Matt 11:15; Rev 2:11, 17; 3:6, 13, 22; 13:9   [b] [Rev 22:2, 14]   [c] [Gen 2:9; 3:22]   [1] Or *who is victorious*; trad. *who overcomes*.   [2] Some wss *my God*.   2:8 [a] Rev 1:8, 17, 18   2:9 [a] Luke 12:21   [b] Rom 2:17   [c] Rev 3:9   [1] Or *know your suffering*; perhaps caused by persecution.   2:10 [a] Matt 10:22   [b] Matt 24:13   [c] Jas 1:12   [1] Or *experience persecution, will be in distress*.   2:11 [a] Rev 13:9   [b] [Rev 20:6, 14; 21:8]   [1] Or *who is victorious*; trad. *who overcomes*.   2:12 [a] Isa 49:2; Rev 1:16; 2:16

"This is the solemn pronouncement of the one who has the sharp double-edged sword: [13]'I know[1] where you live—where Satan's throne is. Yet you continue to cling to my name, and you have not denied your faith in me, even in the days of Antipas, my faithful witness, who was killed in your city where Satan lives. [14]But I have a few things against you: You have some people there who follow the teaching of [a]Balaam, who instructed Balak [b]to put a stumbling block[1] before the people[2] of Israel so they would eat food sacrificed to idols [c]and commit sexual immorality. [15]In the same way, there are also some among you who follow the teaching of the Nicolaitans. [16]Therefore,[1] repent! If not, [a]I will come against you quickly and make war against those people with the sword of my mouth. [17]The one who has an ear had better hear what the Spirit says to the churches. To the one who conquers,[1] I will give him some of the hidden [a]manna, [b]and I will give him a white stone, and on that stone will be written a new name that no one can understand except the one who receives it.'

To the Church in Thyatira

[18]"To the angel of the church in Thyatira write the following:

"This is the solemn pronouncement of the Son of God, the one [a]who has eyes like a fiery flame and whose feet are like polished bronze:[1] [19]'I know your deeds: your love, [a]faith, service, and steadfast endurance.[1] In fact, your more recent deeds are greater than your earlier ones. [20]But I have this against you: You tolerate that woman[1] [a]Jezebel, who calls herself a prophetess, and by her teaching deceives my servants[2] [b]to commit sexual immorality and to eat food sacrificed to idols. [21]I have given her time [a]to repent, but she is not willing to repent of her sexual immorality. [22]Look! I am throwing her onto a bed of violent illness, and those who commit adultery with her into terrible suffering,[1] unless they repent of her deeds. [23]Furthermore, I will strike her followers[1] with a deadly disease, and then all the churches will know that I am the one who [a]searches minds and hearts. I will repay each one of you what your deeds deserve. [24]But to the rest of you [a]in Thyatira, all who do not hold to this teaching (who have not learned the so-called "deep secrets of Satan"), to you I say: I do not put any additional burden on you. [25]However, hold on to [a]what you have until I come. [26]And to the one who conquers[1] and who continues in [a]my deeds until the end, I will give him authority over the nations—

[27] *he will rule[1] [a]them with an iron rod,*
and like clay jars he will break them to pieces,[2]

[28]just as I have received [a]the right to rule from my Father—and I will give him the morning star. [29]The one who has an ear had better hear what the Spirit says to the churches.'

To the Church in Sardis

3 "To the angel of the church in Sardis write the following:

"This is the solemn pronouncement of the one who [a]holds the seven spirits of God and the seven stars: 'I know your deeds, that you have a reputation that you are alive, but in reality you are dead. [2]Wake up then, and strengthen what remains that was about to die, because I have not found your deeds complete in the sight of my God. [3]Therefore, [a]remember what you received and heard, and obey it, and [b]repent. [c]If you do not wake up, I will come [d]like a thief, and you will never know at what hour I will come against you. [4]But you [a]have a few individuals[1] in Sardis who have not [b]stained[2] their clothes, and they will walk with me

---

2:13 [1]Some wss add *your works and.*   2:14 [a]Num 31:16   [b]Num 25; Acts 15:29; [1 Cor 10:20]; Rev 2:20   [c]1 Cor 6:13   [1]Or *who instructed Balak to cause the people of Israel to sin by eating food sacrificed to idols.*   [2]Grk. *sons;* "sons of Israel" is an idiom for the people of Israel as an ethnic entity.   2:16 [a]Isa 11:4; 2 Thess 2:8; Rev 19:15   [1]Some wss omit *Therefore.* 2:17 [a]Exod 16:33–34; [John 6:49, 51]   [b]Isa 56:5; 62:2; 65:15; Rev 3:12   [1]Or *who is victorious;* trad. *who overcomes.*   2:18 [a]Rev 1:14–15   [1]Or *fine brass/bronze;* the emphasis is probably less on its value and more on its lustrous quality.   2:19 [a]Rev 2:2   [1]Or *perseverance.*   2:20 [a]1 Kgs 16:31; 21:25; 2 Kgs 9:7, 22, 30   [b]Exod 34:15   [1]Some mss *your woman.*   [2]Grk. *slaves;* in a spiritual sense, voluntarily becoming slaves of God or of Jesus Christ.   2:21 [a]Rom 2:5; Rev 9:20; 16:9, 11   2:22 [1]Or *into great distress;* not specified as physical or emotional and could involve persecution.   2:23 [a]Ps 7:9; 26:2; 139:1; Jer 11:20; 17:10; Matt 16:27; Luke 16:15; Acts 1:24; Rom 8:27   [1]Grk. *her children.*   2:24 [a]Acts 15:28   2:25 [a]Rev 3:11   2:26 [a][John 6:29]   [1]Or *who is victorious;* trad. *who overcomes.*   2:27 [a]Ps 2:8–9; Rev 12:5; 19:15   [1]Grk. *will shepherd.*   [2]Ps 2:9 (Ps 2:8)   2:28 [a]2 Pet 1:19; Rev 22:16   3:1 [a]Rev 1:4, 16   3:3 [a]1 Tim 6:20   [b]Rev 3:19   [c]Matt 24:42–43; Luke 12:39   [d]1 Thess 5:2; [2 Pet 3:10; Rev 16:15]   3:4 [a]Acts 1:15   [b][Jude 23]   [1]Grk. *a few names.*   [2]Or *soiled.*

dressed [c]in white because they are worthy. [5]The one who conquers[1] will be dressed like them in white clothing,[2] and I will never erase[3] his name from the [a]book of [b]life, but will declare[4] his name before my Father and before his angels. [6]The one who has an ear had better [a]hear what the Spirit says to the churches.'

To the Church in Philadelphia

[7]"To [a]the angel of [b]the church in Philadelphia write [c]the following:

"This is [d]the solemn pronouncement of the Holy One, the True One, who holds the key of David, who opens doors no one can [e]shut, and shuts doors no one can open: [8]'I know your deeds. (Look! [a]I have put in front of you [b]an open door that no one can shut.) I know that you have little strength,[1] but you have obeyed my word and have not denied my name. [9]Listen! I am going to make [a]those people from the synagogue of Satan—who say they are Jews yet are not, but are [b]lying—look, I will make them come and bow down[1] at your feet and acknowledge that I have loved you. [10]Because you have kept my [a]admonition to endure steadfastly,[1] I will also keep you from [b]the hour of testing that is about to come [c]on the whole world to test those who live on the earth. [11]I am [a]coming soon. [b]Hold on to what you have so that no one can take away [c]your crown. [12]The one who conquers[1] I will [a]make a pillar in the temple of my God, and he will never [b]depart from [c]it. I will write on him the name of my God and the name of the city of my God (the [d]new Jerusalem that [e]comes down out of heaven from my God), [f]and my new name as well. [13]The one who has an ear had better [a]hear what the Spirit says to the churches.'

To the Church in Laodicea

[14]"To the angel of the church in Laodicea write the following:

"[a]This is [b]the solemn pronouncement of [c]the Amen, the faithful and true witness, the originator of God's creation: [15]'I know your deeds, that you are [a]neither cold nor hot. I wish you were either cold or hot! [16]So because you are lukewarm, and neither hot nor cold, I am going to vomit you out of my mouth! [17]Because you say, "[a]I am rich and have acquired great wealth, and need nothing," but do not realize that you are wretched, pitiful, poor, blind, and naked, [18]take my advice and [a]buy gold from me refined by fire so you can become rich! Buy from me [b]white clothing so you can be clothed and your shameful nakedness will not be exposed, and buy eye salve to put on your eyes so you can see! [19a]All those I love, I rebuke and [b]discipline. So be earnest and repent! [20]Listen! [a]I am standing at the door and knocking! [b]If anyone hears my [c]voice and opens the door I will come into his home and share a meal with him, and he with me. [21]I [a]will grant the one who conquers[1] permission to sit with me on my throne, just as I, too, conquered[2] and sat down with my Father on his throne. [22]The one who has an ear had better [a]hear what the Spirit says to the churches.'"

The Amazing Scene in Heaven

4 After these things I looked, and there was a door standing [a]open in heaven! And the first voice I had heard speaking to me like a [b]trumpet said: "Come up here so that I can show you what must happen after these things." [2]Immediately [a]I [b]was in the Spirit, and a throne was standing in heaven with someone seated on it! [3]And the one seated on it was [a]like jasper [b]and carnelian in appearance, and a rainbow looking like it was made of emerald encircled the throne. [4]In a circle [a]around the throne were twenty-four other thrones, and seated on those thrones were twenty-four elders. They were [b]dressed in white clothing and had golden

3:4 [c] Rev 4:4; 6:11   3:5 [a] Phil 4:3   [b] Matt 10:32; Luke 12:8   [1] Or *who overcomes.*   [2] Or *white robes.*   [3] Or *will never wipe out.*   [4] *Grk. will confess.*   3:6 [a] Rev 2:7   3:7 [a] Acts 3:14   [b] John 14:6; 1 John 5:20; Rev 3:14; 19:11   [c] Isa 9:7; 22:22; Jer 23:5   [d] [Matt 16:19; Rev 1:18]   [e] Job 12:14   3:8 [a] Rev 3:1   [b] 1 Cor 16:9   [1] Or *little power.*   3:9 [a] Rev 2:9   [b] Isa 45:14; 49:23; 60:14   [1] This Grk. verb normally refers to worship.   3:10 [a] 2 Tim 2:12; 2 Pet 2:9   [b] Luke 2:1   [c] Isa 24:17   [1] Or *to persevere.*   3:11 [a] Phil 4:5   [b] Rev 2:25   [c] [Rev 2:10]   3:12 [a] 1 Kgs 7:21; Jer 1:18; Gal 2:9   [b] Ps 23:6   [c] [Rev 14:1; 22:4]   [d] [Heb 12:22]   [e] Rev 21:2   [f] [Rev 2:17; 22:4]   [1] Or *who is victorious;* trad. *who overcomes.*   3:13 [a] Rev 2:7   3:14 [a] Isa 65:16; 2 Cor 1:20   [b] Rev 1:5; 3:7; 19:11   [c] [Col 1:15]   3:15 [a] Rev 3:1   3:17 [a] Hos 12:8; Zech 11:5; [Matt 5:3]; 1 Cor 4:8   3:18 [a] Isa 55:1; Matt 13:44   [b] 2 Cor 5:3   3:19 [a] Job 5:17   [b] Prov 3:12; [2 Cor 11:32]; Heb 12:6   3:20 [a] Song 5:2   [b] Luke 12:36–37; John 10:3   [c] [John 14:23]   3:21 [a] Matt 19:28; 2 Tim 2:12; [Rev 2:26; 20:4]   [1] Or *who is victorious;* trad. *who overcomes.*   [2] Or *who is victorious;* trad. *who overcomes.*   3:22 [a] Rev 2:7   4:1 [a] Ezek 1:1; Rev 19:11   [b] Rev 1:10   4:2 [a] Rev 1:10   [b] 1 Kgs 22:19; Isa 6:1; Ezek 1:26; Dan 7:9; Rev 3:21; 4:9   4:3 [a] Matt 5:8; Rev 21:11   [b] Gen 9:13–17; Ezek 1:28; Rev 10:1   4:4 [a] Rev 11:16   [b] Rev 3:4–5

crowns on their heads. [5]From the throne came out flashes of [a]lightning and roaring and crashes of thunder. [b]Seven flaming torches, which are [c]the seven spirits of God, were burning in front of the throne, [6]and in front of the throne was something like [a]a sea of glass, like crystal.

In the middle of the throne[1] [b]and around the throne were four living creatures full of eyes in front and in back. [7]The first living creature was like a lion, [a]the second creature like an ox, the third creature had a face like a man's, and the fourth creature looked like an eagle flying. [8]Each one of the four living creatures had [a]six wings and was full of eyes all around and inside. They never rest day or night, saying:

> "[b]**Holy, Holy, Holy is the [c]Lord God,**
> **the All-Powerful,**[1]
> [d]Who was, and who is, and who is still
> to come!"

[9]And whenever the living creatures give glory, honor, and thanks to the one [a]who sits on the throne, who lives forever and ever, [10]the twenty-four elders throw [a]themselves to the ground before the one who sits on the throne and worship the one who lives forever and ever, and they offer their crowns before his throne, saying:

> [11] "You [a]are worthy, our Lord and God,
> to receive glory and honor and power,
> [b]since [c]you created all things,
> and because of your will they existed
> and were created!"[1]

The Opening of the Scroll

5 Then I [a]saw in the right hand of the one who was seated on the throne a scroll written on the front and back and [b]sealed with seven seals. [2]And I saw a powerful angel proclaiming in a loud voice: "[a]Who is worthy to open the scroll and to break its seals?" [3]But no one in heaven or on earth or under the earth was able to open the scroll

or look into it. [4]So I began weeping bitterly because no one was found who was worthy to open the scroll or to look into it. [5]Then one of [a]the elders said to me, "Stop weeping! Look, the Lion of the tribe of [b]Judah, [c]the root of David, has [d]conquered;[1] thus he can open the scroll [e]and its seven seals."

[6]Then I [a]saw standing in the middle of the throne[1] and of the four living creatures, and in the middle of the elders, a Lamb that appeared to have been killed.[2] He had [b]seven horns and seven eyes, which are [c]the seven[3] spirits of God sent out into all the earth. [7]Then he came and took the scroll from the right hand [a]of the one who was seated on the throne, [8]and when [a]he had taken the scroll, the four living creatures and the twenty-four elders threw themselves to the ground before the Lamb. Each of them had a harp and golden bowls full of incense (which are the [b]prayers of the saints). [9]They were singing a new song:

> "You are worthy to take [a]the scroll
> and to open its seals
> because [b]you were killed,[1]
> and [c]at the cost of your own blood
> you [d]have purchased[2] for God
> persons from every tribe, language,
> people, and nation.
> [10] You have appointed them[1] as a
> [a]kingdom and [b]priests to serve our
> God, and they will reign[2] on the
> earth."

[11]Then I looked and heard the voice of many angels in a circle around the throne, as well as the living creatures and the elders. Their number was ten thousand times ten thousand—thousands times thousands—[12]all of whom were singing in a loud voice:

> "Worthy is the lamb who was killed
> to receive power and wealth
> and wisdom and might
> and honor and glory and praise!"

4:5 [a]Gen 49:9–10; Exod 19:16; Rev 8:5; 11:19; 16:18   [b]Exod 37:23   [c]2 Sam 7:12; [Rev 1:4]   **4:6** [a]Exod 38:8; Ezek 1:22; Rev 15:2   [b]Ezek 1:5; Rev 4:8; 5:6; 6:1, 6; 7:11; 14:3; 15:7; 19:4   [1]Perhaps in the middle of the throne area.   **4:7** [a]Ezek 1:10; 10:14   **4:8** [a]Isa 6:2   [b]Isa 6:3   [c]Rev 1:8   [d]Rev 1:4   [1]Isa 6:3   **4:9** [a]Rev 1:18   **4:10** [a]Rev 5:8, 14; 7:11; 11:16; 19:4   **4:11** [a]Rev 1:6; 5:12   [b]Gen 1:1; John 1:3   [c]Col 1:16   [1]One MS omits *and were created*; one MS *having come into being*; one MS *they did not exist*.   **5:1** [a]Ezek 2:9–10   [b]Isa 29:11; Dan 12:4   **5:2** [a]Rev 4:11; 5:9   **5:5** [a]Gen 49:9   [b]Heb 7:14   [c]Isa 11:1, 10; Rom 15:12; Rev 22:16   [d]Rev 3:21   [e]Rev 6:1   [1]Or *who is victorious*; trad. *who overcomes*.   **5:6** [a]Isa 53:7; [John 1:29; 1 Pet 1:19]   [b]Zech 3:9; 4:10   [c]Rev 1:4; 3:1; 4:5   [1]Perhaps in the middle of the throne area.   [2]Or *slaughtered*; trad. *slain*.   [3]Some MSS omit *seven*.   **5:7** [a]Rev 4:2   **5:8** [a]Rev 4:8–10; 19:4   [b]Ps 141:2; Rev 8:3   **5:9** [a]Rev 14:3   [b]Rev 4:11   [c][Heb 9:12; 1 Pet 1:18–19]   [d]John 1:29   [1]Or *slaughtered*; trad. *slain*.   [2]A few WSS *purchased us for God*; a few MSS omit *for God*.   **5:10** [a]Exod 19:6   [b]Isa 61:6   [1]TR *us*.   [2]Some WSS *they are reigning*.

[13]Then I heard [a]every creature—in heaven, on earth, under the earth, in the sea, and all that is in them—singing:

> "To the one seated on the throne and
> to the Lamb
> be [b]praise, honor, glory, and ruling
> power[1] forever and ever!"

[14]And the four living creatures were saying "Amen," and the elders threw themselves to the ground and worshiped.

The Seven Seals

6 I looked on when the Lamb opened one of the seven seals, and [a]I heard [b]one of the four living creatures saying with a thunderous voice, "Come!"[1] [2]So I looked,[1] [a]and [b]here came a white horse! The one who rode it had a bow, [c]and he was given a crown, and as a conqueror he rode out to [d]conquer.

[3]Then when the Lamb opened the second seal, [a]I heard the second living creature saying, "Come!" [4]And [a]another horse, fiery red, came out, and the one who rode it was granted permission to [b]take peace from the earth so that people would butcher[1] one another, and he was given a huge sword.

[5]Then when the Lamb opened the [a]third [b]seal I heard the third living creature saying, "Come!" So I looked,[1] and here came a black horse! The one who rode it had a balance [c]scale in his hand. [6]Then I heard something like a voice from among the four living creatures saying, "A quart of wheat will cost a day's pay,[1] and three quarts of barley will cost a day's pay. But [a]do not damage the olive oil and the wine!"

[7]Then when the Lamb opened the fourth seal [a]I heard the voice of the fourth living creature saying, "Come!" [8][a]So I looked[1] and here came a pale green[2] horse! The name of the one who rode it was Death, and Hades followed right behind. They were given authority over a fourth of the earth, [b]to kill its population with the sword, famine, [c]and disease, and by the wild animals of the earth.

[9]Now when [a]the Lamb opened [b]the fifth seal, I saw under the altar the souls of those who had been violently killed[1] because [c]of [d]the word of God and because of the testimony they had given. [10]They cried out with a loud voice, "[a]How long, Sovereign Master, [b]holy and true, before you judge those who live on the earth and avenge our blood?" [11]Each of them was given a long [a]white robe, and they were told [b]to rest for a little longer, until the full number was reached of both their fellow servants[1] and their brothers who were going to be killed just as they had been.

[12]Then I looked when the Lamb opened the sixth seal, [a]and a huge earthquake took place; [b]the sun became as black as sackcloth made of hair, and the full moon became blood red; [13][a]and the stars in the sky fell to the earth like a fig tree dropping its unripe figs when shaken by a fierce wind. [14]The sky was split apart like a scroll being rolled up, [a]and [b]every mountain and island was moved from its place. [15]Then the [a]kings of the earth, the very important people, the generals, the rich, the powerful, and everyone, slave[1] and free, [b]hid themselves in the caves and among the rocks of the mountains. [16]They said to the mountains [a]and to the rocks, "Fall on us and hide us from the face of the one who is [b]seated on the throne and from the wrath of the Lamb, [17]because the great day of their[1] wrath has come, [a]and who is able to withstand it?"[2]

The Sealing of the 144,000

7 After this I saw four angels standing at the four corners of the earth, holding [a]back the four winds of the earth so no

5:13 [a] Phil 2:10; Rev 5:3   [b] 1 Chr 29:11; Rom 9:5; 1 Tim 6:16; 1 Pet 4:11   [1] Or *dominion*.   6:1 [a] Isa 53:7; [John 1:29; Rev 5:5–7, 12; 13:8]   [b] Rev 4:7   [1] Some wss add *and see*.   6:2 [a] Zech 1:8; 6:3   [b] Ps 45:4–5, LXX   [c] Zech 6:11; Rev 9:7; 14:14; 19:12   [d] Matt 24:5; Rev 3:21   [1] *Some* mss *omit So I looked*.   6:3 [a] Rev 4:7   6:4 [a] Zech 1:8; 6:2   [b] Matt 24:6–7   [1] I.e., a violent death or murder.   6:5 [a] Rev 4:7   [b] Zech 6:2, 6   [c] Matt 24:7   [1] *Some* mss *omit So I looked*.   6:6 [a] Rev 7:3; 9:4   [1] Grk. *a quart of wheat for a denarius*.   6:7 [a] Rev 4:7   6:8 [a] Zech 6:3   [b] Jer 14:12; 15:2; 24:10; 29:17; Ezek 5:12, 17; 14:21; 29:5; Matt 24:9   [c] Lev 26:22   [1] *Some* mss *omit So I looked*.   [2] A sickly pallor, when referring to persons, or the green color of plants.   6:9 [a] Rev 8:3   [b] [Rev 20:4]   [c] Rev 1:2, 9   [d] 2 Tim 1:8   [1] Or *murdered*; i.e., a violent death or murder.   6:10 [a] Ps 13:1–6; Zech 1:12   [b] Rev 3:7   6:11 [a] Rev 3:4–5; 7:9   [b] Heb 11:40   [1] Grk. *slaves*; in a spiritual sense, voluntarily becoming slaves of God or of Jesus Christ.   6:12 [a] Matt 24:7; Rev 8:5; 11:13; 16:18   [b] Isa 13:10; Joel 2:10, 31; 3:15; Matt 24:29; Mark 13:24   6:13 [a] Matt 24:29; Mark 13:25; Rev 8:10; 9:1   6:14 [a] Ps 102:26; Isa 34:4; [2 Pet 3:10]; Rev 20:11; 21:1   [b] Jer 3:23; Rev 16:20   6:15 [a] Ps 2:2–4   [b] Isa 2:10, 19, 21; 24:21; Rev 19:18   [1] In a spiritual sense, voluntarily becoming a slave of God or of Jesus Christ.   6:16 [a] Hos 10:8; Luke 23:29–30; Rev 9:6   [b] Rev 20:11   6:17 [a] Isa 63:4; Jer 30:7; Joel 1:15; 2:1, 11, 31; Zeph 1:14; Rev 16:14   [1] Maj. mss *his*.   [2] The imagery of holding one's ground in a military campaign or an attack.   7:1 [a] Jer 49:36; Dan 7:2; Zech 6:5; Matt 24:31

wind could blow on the earth, on the sea, or on any tree. ²Then I saw another angel ascending from the east, who had the seal of the living God. He shouted out with a loud voice to the four angels who had been given permission to damage the earth and the sea: ³"Do not damage the earth or the sea or the trees until we have put a seal ᵃon the foreheads of the servants[1] of our God." ⁴ᵃNow I heard the number of those who were marked with the seal, 144,000, sealed ᵇfrom all the tribes of the people of Israel:[1]

5 From the tribe of Judah, 12,000 were sealed,
   from the tribe of Reuben, 12,000,
   from the tribe of Gad, 12,000,
6 from the tribe of Asher, 12,000,
   from the tribe of Naphtali, 12,000,
   from the tribe of Manasseh, 12,000,
7 from the tribe of Simeon, 12,000,
   from the tribe of Levi, 12,000,
   from the tribe of Issachar, 12,000,
8 from the tribe of Zebulun, 12,000,
   from the tribe of Joseph, 12,000,
   from the tribe of Benjamin, 12,000 were sealed.

⁹After these things I looked, ᵃand here was an enormous crowd that no one could count, made up of persons ᵇfrom every nation, tribe, people, and language, standing before the throne and before the Lamb ᶜdressed in long white robes, and with palm branches in their hands. ¹⁰They were shouting out in a loud voice,

"ᵃSalvation belongs to our God, ᵇwho is seated on the throne, and to the Lamb!"

¹¹And ᵃall the angels stood there in a circle around the throne and around the elders and the four living creatures, and they threw themselves down with their faces to the ground before the throne and ᵇworshiped God, ¹²ᵃsaying,

"Amen! Praise and glory,
and wisdom and thanksgiving,
and honor and power and strength
be to our God for ever and ever.
Amen!"

¹³Then one of the elders asked me, "These dressed in long ᵃwhite robes—who are they and where have they come from?" ¹⁴So I said to him, "My lord, you know the answer." Then he said to me, "ᵃThese are the ones who have come out of the great tribulation. They have ᵇwashed their robes and made them white in the blood of the Lamb! ¹⁵For this reason they are before the throne of God, and they serve[1] him day and night in his temple, and the one seated on the throne will ᵃshelter them.[2] ¹⁶*They will never go hungry or be thirsty again, and ᵃthe sun will not beat down on ᵇthem, nor any burning heat*,[1] ¹⁷because the Lamb in the middle of the throne ᵃwill shepherd them ᵇand lead them to springs of living water, *and God will wipe away every tear from their eyes*."[1]

The Seventh Seal

8 Now ᵃwhen the Lamb opened the seventh seal there was silence in heaven for about half an hour. ²Then I saw the seven angels who stand before God, ᵃand seven trumpets were given to them. ³Another angel holding a golden censer came and was stationed at ᵃthe altar. A large amount of incense was given to him to offer up, with ᵇthe prayers of all the saints, on the golden altar that is before the throne. ⁴The smoke coming from ᵃthe incense, along with the prayers of the saints, ascended before God from the angel's hand. ⁵Then ᵃthe angel took the censer, filled it with fire from the altar, and threw it on the earth, and there were crashes of thunder, roaring, flashes of ᵇlightning, ᶜand an earthquake. ⁶Now the seven angels holding the seven trumpets prepared to blow them.

⁷The first angel blew his trumpet, ᵃand there was hail and fire mixed with blood,

7:3 ᵃEzek 9:4, 6; Rev 22:4 [1]Grk. *slaves*; in a spiritual sense, voluntarily becoming slaves of God or of Jesus Christ. **7:4** ᵃRev 9:16 ᵇGen 49:1–27 [1]Grk. *the sons of Israel*; normally an idiom for the Israelites as an ethnic entity, however, many scholars understand the expression here to refer to Christians instead. **7:9** ᵃIsa 60:1–5; Rom 11:25 ᵇRev 5:9 ᶜRev 3:5, 18; 4:4; 6:11 **7:10** ᵃPs 3:8; Isa 43:11; Jer 3:23; Hos 13:4; Rev 19:1 ᵇRev 5:13 **7:11** ᵃRev 4:6 ᵇRev 4:11; 5:9, 12, 14; 11:16 **7:12** ᵃRev 5:13–14 **7:13** ᵃRev 7:9 **7:14** ᵃRev 6:9 ᵇIsa 1:18; Zech 3:3–5; [Heb 9:14] **7:15** ᵃIsa 4:5–6; Rev 21:3 [1]Or *worship*; Grk. *latreuō*. [2]Grk. *will spread his tent over them*; i.e., extending protection or shelter. **7:16** ᵃPs 121:5; Isa 49:10 ᵇPs 121:6; Rev 21:4 [1][Isa 49:10] **7:17** ᵃPs 23:1; Matt 2:6; [John 10:11, 14] ᵇIsa 25:8; Matt 5:4; Rev 21:4 [1][Isa 25:8] **8:1** ᵃRev 6:1 **8:2** ᵃ2 Chr 29:25–28 **8:3** ᵃRev 5:8 ᵇExod 30:1; Rev 8:3 **8:4** ᵃPs 141:2; Luke 1:10 **8:5** ᵃExod 19:16; Rev 11:19; 16:18 ᵇRev 4:5 ᶜ2 Sam 22:8; 1 Kgs 19:11; Acts 4:31 **8:7** ᵃExod 9:23; Isa 28:2; Ezek 38:22; Joel 2:30

and it was thrown [b]at the earth so that a third [c]of the earth was burned up, a third of the trees were burned up, and all the green grass was burned up.

[8]Then the second angel blew his trumpet, [a]and something like [b]a great mountain of burning fire was thrown into the sea. A third of the sea [c]became blood, [9a]and a third of the creatures living in the sea died, and a third of the ships were completely destroyed.

[10]Then the third angel blew his trumpet, [a]and a huge star burning like a torch fell from the sky; it landed on a third of the rivers [b]and on the springs of water. [11](Now [a]the [b]name of the star is Wormwood.) So a third of the waters became wormwood,[1] and many people died from these waters because they were poisoned.

[12a]Then the fourth angel blew his trumpet, and a third of the sun was struck, and a third of the moon, and a third of the stars, so that a third of them were darkened. And there was no light for a third of the day and for a third of the night likewise. [13]Then I looked, [a]and I heard an eagle[1] flying directly overhead, proclaiming with a loud voice, "[b]Woe! Woe! Woe to those who live on the earth because of the remaining sounds of the trumpets of the three angels who are about to blow them!"

9 Then the fifth angel blew his trumpet, [a]and I saw a star that had fallen from [b]the sky to the earth, and he was given the key to the shaft of the abyss.[1] [2]He opened the shaft of the abyss and smoke rose out of it like smoke from a giant furnace. The [a]sun and the air were darkened with smoke from the shaft. [3]Then out of the smoke came locusts onto the earth, and they were given power [a]like that of the scorpions of the earth. [4]They were told [a]not to damage [b]the grass of [c]the earth, or any green plant or tree, but only those people[1] who did not have the seal of God on their forehead. [5]The locusts were not given permission to kill

them, [a]but only to torture them for five months, and their torture was like that of a scorpion when it stings a person.[1] [6]In those days [a]people[1] will seek death, but will not be able to find it; they will long to die, but death will flee from them.

[7]Now [a]the locusts looked like horses equipped for battle. [b]On their heads were something like crowns similar to gold, [c]and their faces looked like men's[1] faces. [8]They had hair like women's hair, and [a]their teeth were like lions' teeth. [9]They had breastplates [a]like iron breastplates, and the sound of their wings was like the noise of many horse-drawn chariots charging into battle. [10]They have tails and stingers like scorpions, and their ability to injure people for five months is in their tails. [11]They have as king over [a]them the angel of the abyss, whose name in Hebrew is *Abaddon,* and in Greek, *Apollyon.*

[12]The [a]first woe has passed, but two woes are still coming after these things!

[13]Then the sixth angel blew his trumpet, and I heard a single voice coming from the[1] horns on the [a]golden altar that is before God, [14]saying to the sixth angel, the one holding the trumpet, "Set free the four angels who are bound [a]at the great river Euphrates!" [15]Then the four angels who had been prepared for this hour, day, month, and year were set free to kill a [a]third of humanity. [16]The number of soldiers on horseback was 200,000,000; I heard [a]their number. [17]Now this is what the horses and their riders looked like in my vision: The riders had breastplates that were fiery red, dark blue, [a]and sulfurous yellow in color. The heads of the horses looked like lions' heads, and fire, smoke, and sulfur[1] came out of their mouths. [18]A third of humanity was killed by these three plagues, that is, by the fire, the smoke, and the sulfur that came out of their mouths. [19a]For the power of the horses resides in their mouths and in their tails because their tails are like

8:7 [b] Rev 16:2 [c] Isa 2:13; Rev 9:4, 15–18 **8:8** [a] Jer 51:25; Amos 7:4 [b] Exod 7:17; Rev 11:6; 16:3 [c] Ezek 14:19 **8:9** [a] Rev 16:3 **8:10** [a] Isa 14:12; Rev 6:13; 9:1 [b] Rev 14:7; 16:4 **8:11** [a] Ruth 1:20 [b] Exod 15:23 [1] I.e., terribly bitter; "wormwood" is a particularly bitter herb with medicinal value. **8:12** [a] Isa 13:10; Joel 2:31; Amos 8:9; Matt 24:29; Rev 6:12 **8:13** [a] Rev 14:6; 19:17 [b] Rev 9:12; 11:14; 12:12 [1] Some wss *angel.* **9:1** [a] Luke 10:18; Rev 8:10 [b] Luke 8:31; Rev 9:2, 11; 17:8 [1] I.e., the netherworld; the abode of the dead, the demons, and the Antichrist; the dungeon where the devil is kept. **9:2** [a] Joel 2:2, 10 **9:3** [a] Exod 10:4; Judg 7:12 **9:4** [a] Rev 6:6 [b] Rev 8:7 [c] Exod 12:23; Ezek 9:4; Rev 7:2–3 [1] Grk. *men*; used in a generic sense of both men and women. **9:5** [a] [Rev 9:10; 11:7] [1] Grk. *a man*; used in an individualized sense without being limited to the male gender. **9:6** [a] Job 3:21; 7:15; Isa 2:19; Jer 8:3; Rev 6:16 [1] Grk. *men*; used in a generic sense of both men and women. **9:7** [a] Joel 2:4 [b] Nah 3:17 [c] Dan 7:8 [1] Or *human faces.* **9:8** [a] Joel 1:6 **9:9** [a] Jer 47:3; Joel 2:5–7 **9:11** [a] Eph 2:2 **9:12** [a] Rev 8:13; 11:14 **9:13** [a] Rev 8:3 [1] ‡ Some mss *four horns.* **9:14** [a] Gen 15:18; Deut 1:7; Josh 1:4; Rev 16:12 **9:15** [a] Rev 8:7–9; 9:18 **9:16** [a] Ps 68:17; Dan 7:10 **9:17** [a] 1 Chr 12:8; Isa 5:28–29 [1] Trad. *brimstone.* **9:19** [a] Isa 9:15

snakes, having heads that inflict injuries. [20]The rest of humanity, who had not been killed by these plagues, [a]did not repent of the works of their hands so that they did not stop worshiping [b]demons [c]and idols made of gold, silver, bronze, stone, and wood—idols that cannot see or hear or walk about. [21]Furthermore, they did not repent of their murders, of their magic spells, of their sexual immorality, [a]or of their stealing.

The Angel with the Little Scroll

10 Then I saw another powerful angel descending from heaven, wrapped in a cloud, [a]with a rainbow above [b]his head; [c]his face was like the sun, and his legs were like pillars of fire. [2]He held in his hand a little scroll that was open, [a]and he put his right foot on the sea and his left on the land. [3]Then he shouted in a loud voice like a lion roaring, and when he shouted, the [a]seven thunders sounded their voices. [4]When the seven thunders spoke, I was preparing to write, but just then I heard a voice from heaven say, "Seal [a]up what the seven thunders spoke and do not write it down." [5]Then the angel I saw standing on the sea and on the land [a]raised his right hand to heaven [6]and swore by the one who lives forever and ever, [a]who created heaven and what is in it, and the earth and what is in it, and the sea and what is in it, "There will be no more delay! [7]But [a]in the days when the seventh angel is about to blow his trumpet, the mystery of God is completed, just as he has[1] proclaimed to his servants[2] the prophets." [8]Then the voice I had heard from heaven began to speak to me again, "Go and take the open scroll in the hand of the angel who is standing on the sea and on the land." [9]So I went to the angel and asked him to give me the little scroll. He said to me, "[a]Take the scroll and eat it. It will make your stomach bitter, but it will be as sweet as honey in your mouth." [10]So I took the little scroll from the angel's hand [a]and ate it, and it did taste as sweet as honey in [b]my mouth, but when I had eaten it, my stomach became bitter. [11]Then they told me: "You must prophesy again about many peoples, nations, languages, and kings."

The Fate of the Two Witnesses

11 Then [a]a measuring rod like a staff was given to me, and I was told, "Get [b]up and measure the temple of God, and the altar, and the ones who worship there. [2]But do not measure [a]the outer courtyard of the temple; leave it out [b]because it has been given to the Gentiles, and they will [c]trample on the holy city [d]for forty-two months. [3]And I will grant my two [a]witnesses authority to [b]prophesy for 1,260 days, dressed in sackcloth." [4](These are the [a]two olive trees and the two lampstands that stand before the Lord of the earth.) [5]If anyone wants to harm them, [a]fire comes out of their mouths [b]and completely consumes their enemies. If anyone wants to harm them, they must be killed this way. [6]These two [a]have the power to close up the sky so that it does not rain during the time they are prophesying. They have power to turn the waters to blood and to strike the earth with every kind of plague whenever they want. [7]When they have [a]completed [b]their testimony, the beast that comes up [c]from the abyss [d]will make war on them and conquer[1] them and kill them. [8]Their corpses will lie in [a]the street[1] of the great city that is symbolically called Sodom and Egypt, [b]where their Lord was also crucified. [9]For three [a]and a half days those from every people, tribe, nation, [b]and language will look at their corpses because they will not permit them to be placed in a tomb. [10a]And those who live on the earth will rejoice over them and celebrate, even sending gifts to each other [b]because these two prophets had tormented those who live on the earth. [11]But after three [a]and a half days a breath of life from God entered [b]them, and they stood on their feet, and tremendous

9:20 [a]Deut 31:29 [b]Lev 17:7; Deut 32:17; Ps 106:37; 1 Cor 10:20 [c]Ps 115:4–7; 135:15–17; Dan 5:23   9:21[a]Rev 21:8; 22:15
10:1 [a]Ezek 1:26–28; Rev 4:3 [b]Matt 17:2; Rev 1:16 [c]Rev 1:15   10:2 [a]Ps 95:5; Matt 28:18   10:3 [a]Ps 29:3–9; Rev 4:5; 8:5
10:4 [a]Dan 8:26; 12:4, 9; Rev 22:10   10:5 [a]Exod 6:8; Deut 32:40; Dan 12:7   10:6 [a]Gen 1:1; Exod 20:11; Neh 9:6; Rev 4:11
10:7 [a]Rev 11:15 [1]Not necessarily the OT prophets; perhaps to the martyrs in the church. [2]Grk. *slaves*; in a spiritual sense, voluntarily becoming slaves of God or of Jesus Christ.   10:9 [a]Jer 15:16; Ezek 2:8; 3:1–3   10:10 [a]Ezek 3:3 [b]Ezek 2:10
11:1 [a]Ezek 40:3–42:20; Zech 2:1; Rev 21:15 [b]Num 23:18   11:2 [a]Ezek 40:17, 20 [b]Ps 79:1; Luke 21:24 [c]Dan 8:10 [d]Dan 7:25;
12:7; Rev 12:6; 13:5   11:3 [a]Deut 17:6; Rev 20:4 [b]Rev 19:10   11:4 [a]Ps 52:8; Jer 11:16; Zech 4:2–3, 11, 14   11:5 [a]2 Kgs 1:10–12;
Jer 1:10; 5:14; Ezek 43:3; Hos 6:5; Rev 9:17 [b]Num 16:29   11:6 [a]1 Kgs 17:1; Luke 4:25; [Jas 5:16–17]   11:7 [a]Luke 13:32
[b]Rev 13:1, 11; 17:8 [c]Rev 9:1–2 [d]Dan 7:21; Rev 13:7 [1]Or *be victorious over;* trad, *overcome.*   11:8 [a]Rev 14:8
[b]Heb 13:12 [1]I.e., a major (broad) street.   11:9 [a]Rev 17:15 [b]1 Kgs 13:22; Ps 79:2–3   11:10 [a]Neh 8:10, 12;
Esth 9:19, 22 [b]Rev 16:10   11:11 [a]Rev 11:9 [b]Ezek 37:5, 9, 10

fear seized those who were watching them. [12]Then they[1] heard a loud voice from heaven saying to them: "Come up here!" [a]So the two prophets went up to heaven [b]in [c]a cloud while their enemies stared at them. [13]Just then a major earthquake took place and a tenth of [a]the city collapsed; seven thousand people were killed in the earthquake, [b]and the rest were terrified [c]and gave glory to the God of heaven.

[14]The second woe has come and gone; [a]the third is coming quickly.

The Seventh Trumpet

[15]Then [a]the seventh angel blew his trumpet, [b]and [c]there were loud voices in heaven saying:

> "The kingdom of the world
> has become the kingdom of our Lord
> [d]and of his Christ,[1]
> and he will reign for ever and ever."

[16]Then [a]the twenty-four elders who are seated on their thrones before God threw themselves down with their faces to the ground and [b]worshiped God [17]with these words:

> "We give you thanks, Lord God, the
> All-Powerful,
> the one [a]who is [b]and who was,
> because you have taken your great
> power
> and begun to reign.
> [18] The nations were [a]enraged,
> but your wrath has come,
> and the time has come for the [b]dead
> to be judged,
> and the time has come to give to
> your servants,[1]
> the prophets, their reward,
> as well as to the saints
> and to those who revere your name,
> both small and great,
> and the time has come to destroy
> those who destroy the earth."

[19]Then [a]the temple of God in heaven was opened, and [b]the ark of his covenant was visible within his temple. [c]And there were flashes of lightning, roaring, crashes of thunder, an earthquake, and a great hailstorm.

The Woman, the Child, and the Dragon

12 Then a great sign appeared in heaven: a woman clothed with the sun, and with the moon under her feet, and on her head was a crown of twelve stars. [2]She was pregnant and was [a]screaming in labor pains, struggling to give birth. [3]Then [a]another sign appeared in heaven: a huge red dragon that had seven heads and ten horns, and on its heads were seven diadem crowns. [4]Now the [a]dragon's tail swept away a third [b]of the stars in heaven [c]and hurled them to the earth. Then the dragon stood [d]before the woman who was about to give birth, so [e]that he might devour her child as soon as it was born. [5]So the woman gave birth to a son, a male child, [a]who is going *to rule over all the nations with an iron rod*.[1] Her child was suddenly caught [b]up to God and to his throne, [6]and she fled into [a]the wilderness where a place had been prepared for her by God, so she could be taken care of for 1,260 days.

War in Heaven

[7]Then war broke out in heaven: [a]Michael and his angels fought [b]against the dragon, and the dragon and his angels fought back. [8]But the dragon was not strong enough to prevail, so there was no longer any place left in heaven for him and his angels. [9]So that huge dragon—[a]the ancient serpent, the one called the devil and Satan, [b]who deceives [c]the whole world—was thrown down to the earth, and his angels along with him. [10]Then I heard a loud voice in heaven saying,

> "The salvation and the power
> and the kingdom of our God,
> and the ruling authority of his
> Christ,[1] have [a]now come,

11:12 [a]Isa 14:13 [b]Isa 60:8; Acts 1:9 [c]2 Kgs 2:11–12 [1]The people ("those who were watching them," v. 11) or "the two prophets." 11:13 [a]Rev 6:12; 8:5; 11:19; 16:18 [b]Rev 16:19 [c]Josh 7:19; John 9:24; Rev 14:7; 16:9; 19:7 11:14 [a]Rev 8:13; 9:12 11:15 [a]Rev 8:2; 10:7 [b]Isa 27:13 [c]Rev 12:10 [d]Exod 15:18; Dan 2:44; 7:14, 27; Luke 1:33 [1]Or *Messiah*; both "Christ" (Grk.) and "Messiah" (Heb., Aram.) mean "one who has been anointed." 11:16 [a]Matt 19:28; Rev 4:4 [b]Rev 4:11; 5:9, 12, 14; 7:11 11:17 [a]Rev 16:5 [b]Rev 19:6 11:18 [a]Ps 2:1 [b]Dan 7:10; [Rev 20:12–13] [1]Grk. *slaves*; in a spiritual sense, voluntarily becoming slaves of God or of Jesus Christ. 11:19 [a]Rev 4:1; 15:5, 8 [b]Rev 8:5 [c]Rev 16:21 12:2 [a]Isa 26:17; 66:6–9; Mic 4:9; Gal 4:19 12:3 [a]Rev 13:1; 17:3, 7, 9 12:4 [a]Rev 9:10, 19 [b]Rev 8:7, 12 [c]Dan 8:10 [d]Rev 12:2 [e]Exod 1:16; Matt 2:16 12:5 [a]Ps 2:9; Isa 7:14; 9:6; Rev 2:27; 19:15 [b]Luke 24:51; Acts 1:9–11 [1][Ps 2:9] 12:6 [a]Rev 12:4, 14 12:7 [a]Dan 10:13, 21; 12:1; Jude 9 [b]Rev 20:2 12:9 [a]Luke 10:18; John 12:31 [b]Rev 20:3 [c]Rev 9:1 12:10 [a]Rev 11:15 [1]Or *Messiah*; both "Christ" (Grk.) and "Messiah" (Heb., Aram.) mean "one who has been anointed."

because [b]the accuser of our brothers
and sisters,[2]
the one who accuses them day and
night before our God,
has been thrown down.
11 But [a]they overcame him
by the blood of the Lamb
[b]and by the word of their testimony,
and they did not love their lives so
much that they were afraid to die.
12 Therefore you heavens [a]rejoice, and
all who reside in them!
But [b]woe to the earth and the sea
[c]because the devil has come down to
you!
He is filled with terrible anger,
for he knows that he only has a little
time!"

[13]Now when [a]the dragon realized that he had been thrown down to the earth, he pursued the woman who had given birth to the male child. [14][a]But the woman was given the two wings of a giant eagle [b]so that she could fly out [c]into the wilderness, to the place God prepared for her, where she is taken care of—away from the presence of the serpent—for a time, times, and half a time.[1] [15]Then the serpent [a]spouted water like a river out of his mouth after the woman in an attempt to sweep her away by a flood, [16]but the earth came to her rescue; the ground opened up and swallowed the river that the dragon had spewed from his mouth. [17]So the dragon became enraged at the woman and went away to make war on the rest of her children, those who keep God's commandments and hold to the testimony about Jesus.[1] [18]And the dragon stood[1] on the sand of the seashore.

The Two Beasts

13 Then I [a]saw a beast coming up out of the sea. It [b]had ten horns and seven heads, and on its horns were ten diadem crowns, and on its heads a [c]blasphemous

name.[1] [2]Now the beast that I saw was like a leopard, but its feet were like a bear's, and its mouth was like a lion's mouth. The [a]dragon gave the beast his power, his throne, and great authority to rule. [3]One of the beast's heads [a]appeared to have been killed, but the lethal wound had been healed. And the [b]whole world followed the beast in amazement; [4]they worshiped the dragon because he had given ruling authority to the beast, and they worshiped the beast too, saying: "[a]Who is like the beast?" and "Who is able to make war against him?" [5]The [a]beast was given a mouth speaking proud words and blasphemies, and he was permitted to exercise ruling authority [b]for forty-two months. [6]So the beast opened [a]his mouth to blaspheme against God—to blaspheme both his name and his dwelling place,[1] that is, those who dwell in heaven. [7]The beast was permitted [a]to go to war against the saints and conquer them.[1] He was given ruling [b]authority over every tribe, people, language, and nation, [8]and all those who live on the earth will worship the beast, everyone whose name has [a]not been written [b]since the foundation of the world in the book of life belonging to the Lamb who was killed.[1] [9][a]If anyone has an ear, he had better listen!

10 If anyone is meant for captivity,
into captivity [a]he will go.
If anyone is to be killed by [b]the
sword,[1]
then by the sword he must be killed.

[c]This requires steadfast endurance[2] and faith from the saints.

[11]Then I saw another beast coming [a]up from the earth. He had two horns like a lamb, but was speaking like a dragon. [12]He exercised all the ruling authority of the first beast on his behalf, and made the earth and those who inhabit it worship the first beast, the one [a]whose lethal wound had been healed. [13]He performed momentous

---

12:10 [b] Job 1:9, 11; 2:5; Zech 3:1   [2] Grk. *brothers*; but the Grk. word may be used for "brothers and sisters" or "fellow Christians."   12:11 [a] Rom 16:20   [b] Luke 14:26; [Rev 2:10]   12:12 [a] Ps 96:11; Isa 44:23; Rev 18:20   [b] Rev 8:13   [c] Rev 10:6   12:13 [a] Rev 12:5   12:14 [a] Exod 19:4; Deut 32:11; Isa 40:31   [b] Rev 12:6   [c] Rev 17:3   [1] One sig. MS omits *and half a time.*   12:15 [a] Isa 59:19   12:17 [1] Grk. *the testimony of Jesus; Jesus' testimony* or, more likely, *testimony about Jesus.*   12:18 [1] Maj. MSS *I stood.*   13:1 [a] Dan 7:2, 7   [b] Rev 12:3   [c] Dan 7:8; 11:36; Rev 17:3   [1] ‡ Sev. MSS *names.*   13:2 [a] Rev 12:3, 9; 13:4, 12   13:3 [a] Rev 13:12, 14   [b] Rev 17:8   13:4 [a] Exod 15:11; Isa 46:5; Rev 18:18   13:5 [a] Dan 7:8, 11, 20, 25; 11:36; 2 Thess 2:3   [b] Rev 11:2   13:6 [a] [John 1:14; Col 2:9]   [1] One sig. MS omits *and his dwelling place.*   13:7 [a] Dan 7:21; Rev 11:7   [b] Rev 11:18   [1] Many MSS omit *was permitted to go to war against the saints and conquer them.*   13:8 [a] Exod 32:32; [Rev 20:12–15]   [b] Matt 25:34; Rev 17:8   [1] Or *slaughtered*; trad. *slain.*   13:9 [a] Rev 2:7   13:10 [a] Isa 33:1; Jer 15:2; 43:11   [b] Gen 9:6; Matt 26:52; Rev 11:18   [c] Heb 6:12; Rev 14:12   [1] Many MSS *if anyone will kill with the sword, it is necessary for him to be killed with the sword.*   [2] Or *perseverance.*   13:11 [a] Rev 11:7   13:12 [a] Rev 13:3–4

signs, even making fire come down from [a]heaven to earth in front of people[1] [14]and, [a]by the signs he was permitted to perform on behalf of the beast, [b]he deceived those who live on the earth. He told those who live on the earth to make an image to the beast who had been wounded by the sword, [c]but still lived. [15]The second beast was empowered to give life to the image of the first beast so that it could speak, [a]and could cause all those who did not worship the image of the beast to be killed. [16]He also caused everyone (small and great, rich and poor, free and slave[1]) [a]to obtain a mark on their right hand or on their forehead. [17]Thus no one was allowed to buy or sell things unless [a]he bore the mark of the beast—that is, his name [b]or his number. [18a]This calls for wisdom: Let the one who has [b]insight calculate [c]the beast's number, [d]for it is man's number,[1] and his number is 666.[2]

An Interlude: The Song of the 144,000

14 Then I looked, and here was the [a]Lamb standing [b]on Mount Zion, and with him were 144,000, who had his name and his Father's name [c]written on their foreheads. [2]I also heard a sound coming out of heaven [a]like the sound of many waters and like the sound of loud thunder. Now the sound I heard was like that made by [b]harpists playing their harps, [3]and they were singing a new song before the throne and before the four living creatures and the elders. No one was able to learn the song [a]except the 144,000 who had been redeemed from the earth.

[4]These are the ones who have not defiled themselves with women, [a]for they are virgins. These are the ones [b]who follow the Lamb wherever he goes. These [c]were redeemed from humanity as firstfruits to God and to the Lamb, [5]and no lie was found [a]on their lips; [b]they[1] are blameless.

Three Angels and Three Messages

[6]Then I saw another[1] angel [a]flying directly overhead, and he [b]had an eternal gospel to proclaim [c]to those who live on the earth—to every nation, tribe, language, and people. [7]He declared in a loud voice: "[a]Fear God [b]and give him glory because the hour of his judgment has arrived, and worship the one who made heaven and earth, the sea and the springs of water!"

[8]A second[1] angel followed the first, declaring: "Fallen, fallen is [a]Babylon the great city! [b]She made all the nations drink of the wine of her immoral passion."

[9]A third angel followed the first two, declaring in a loud voice: "[a]If anyone worships the beast and his image, and takes the [b]mark on his forehead or his hand, [10]that person will also drink of the wine of God's anger that has been [a]mixed undiluted in [b]the cup of his wrath, and [c]he will be tortured with [d]fire and sulfur[1] in front of the holy angels and in front of the Lamb. [11]And [a]the smoke from their torture will go up forever and ever, and those who worship the beast and his image will have no rest day or night, along with anyone who receives the mark of his name." [12a]This requires the steadfast endurance of the saints—those who obey God's commandments and hold to their faith in Jesus.[1]

[13]Then I heard a voice from heaven say, "Write this:

'[a]Blessed are the dead,
those [b]who die in the Lord from this
moment on!'"

"Yes," says the Spirit, "[c]so they can rest from their hard work, because their deeds will follow [d]them."

[14]Then I looked, and a white cloud appeared, and seated *on the cloud was one like a son of man!*[1] He had a golden crown on his

---

13:13 [a]Deut 13:1; Matt 24:24; 2 Thess 2:9; Rev 16:14 [1]A generic use of the Grk. "man," referring to both men and women. **13:14** [a]2 Thess 2:9 [b]Rev 12:9 [c]2 Kgs 20:7 **13:15** [a]Rev 16:2 **13:16** [a]Gal 6:17; Rev 7:3; 14:9; 20:4 [1]In a spiritual sense, voluntarily becoming a slave of God or of Jesus Christ. **13:17** [a]Rev 14:9–11 [b]Rev 15:2 **13:18** [a]Rev 17:9 [b][1 Cor 2:14] [c]Rev 15:2 [d]Rev 21:17 [1]Grk. *it is man's number*; the Grk. construction could simply indicate that "666" represents humankind. While an individual is in view, his number may represent all humankind. The counterfeit "perfect man" is less than the perfect (i.e., "777"). [2]A few MSS 616. **14:1** [a]Rev 5:6 [b]Rev 7:4; 14:3 [c]Ezek 9:4; Rev 7:3; 22:4 **14:2** [a]Rev 1:15; 19:6 [b]Rev 5:8 **14:3** [a]Rev 5:9 **14:4** [a][Matt 19:12; 2 Cor 11:2; Eph 5:27] [b]Rev 3:4; 7:17 [c]Rev 5:9 **14:5** [a]Ps 32:2; Zeph 3:13; Mal 2:6; John 1:47; 1 Pet 2:22 [b]Eph 5:27 [1]Sev. MSS *for they are blameless*. **14:6** [a]Rev 8:13 [b]Eph 3:9 [c]Rev 13:7 [1]Maj. MSS omit *another*. **14:7** [a]Rev 11:18 [b]Neh 9:6 **14:8** [a]Isa 21:9; Jer 51:8; Rev 18:2 [b]Jer 51:7; Rev 17:2 [1]Sev. MSS *another, a second angel*; some MSS *another, a second*. **14:9** [a]Rev 13:14–15; 14:11 [b]Rev 13:16 **14:10** [a]Rev 18:6 [b]Rev 16:19 [c]Rev 20:10 [d]Gen 19:24; Ezek 38:22; 2 Thess 1:7; Rev 19:20 [1]Trad. *brimstone*. **14:11** [a]Isa 34:8–10; Rev 18:9, 18; 19:3 **14:12** [a]Rev 12:17 [1]Grk. *faith of Jesus*; either faith in Jesus or faithful to Jesus. **14:13** [a]Eccl 4:1–2 [b]1 Cor 15:18; [1 Thess 4:16] [c]2 Thess 1:7; Heb 4:9–10; Rev 6:11 [d][1 Cor 3:11–15; 15:58] **14:14** [1][Dan 7:13]

head and a sharp sickle in his hand. [15]Then another angel came [a]out of the temple, shouting in a loud voice to the one seated on the cloud, "[b]Use your sickle and start to reap, because the time to reap has come, since the earth's harvest is ripe!" [16]So the one seated on the cloud swung his sickle over the earth, and the earth was reaped. [17]Then another angel came out of the temple in heaven, and he, too, had a sharp sickle. [18]Another angel, [a]who was in charge of the fire, came from the altar and called in a loud voice to the angel who had the sharp sickle, "Use your sharp sickle and gather the clusters of grapes off the vine of the earth, because its grapes are now ripe." [19]So [a]the angel swung his sickle over the earth and gathered the grapes from the vineyard of the earth and tossed them into the great winepress of the wrath of God. [20]Then [a]the winepress was stomped [b]outside the city, and blood poured out of the winepress [c]up to the height of horses' bridles for a distance of almost 200 miles.

The Final Plagues

15 Then [a]I saw another great and astounding sign in heaven: [b]seven angels who have seven final plagues (they are final [c]because in them God's anger is completed).

[2]Then I [a]saw something like a sea of glass [b]mixed with fire, and those who had conquered[1] the beast and his image and the [c]number of his name. They were standing by the sea of glass, [d]holding harps given to them by God. [3]They sang [a]the song of Moses the servant[1] of God and the song of the [b]Lamb:

"[c]Great and astounding are your
   deeds,
Lord God, the All-Powerful!
[d]Just[2] and true are your ways,
King over the nations![3]
[4] [a]Who will not fear you, O Lord,
  and glorify your name, because you
  alone are [b]holy?

[c]All nations will come and worship
  before you
for your righteous acts have been
  revealed."

[5]After [a]these things I looked, and the temple (the tent of the testimony) was opened in heaven, [6]and the seven angels who had the seven plagues came out of the temple, dressed [a]in clean bright linen, wearing wide golden belts around their chests. [7a]Then one of the four living creatures gave the seven angels seven golden bowls filled with the wrath of God [b]who lives forever and ever, [8]and [a]the temple was filled with smoke [b]from God's glory and from his power. Thus no one could enter the temple until the seven plagues from the seven angels were completed.

The Bowls of God's Wrath

16 Then I heard a loud voice from the temple declaring [a]to the seven angels: "Go and pour out on the earth the seven bowls containing God's wrath." [2]So the first angel went and poured out his bowl [a]on the earth. Then ugly and [b]painful sores appeared on the people[1] [c]who had the mark of the beast and [d]who worshiped his image.

[3]Next, the second angel poured out his bowl [a]on the sea, and [b]it turned into blood, like that of a corpse, [c]and every living creature that was in the sea died.

[4]Then the third angel poured out his bowl [a]on the rivers [b]and the springs of water, and they turned into blood. [5]Now I heard the angel of the waters saying:

"[a]You are just[1]—the one [b]who is and
  who was,
the Holy One—because you have
  passed these judgments,
[6] because [a]they poured out the blood
  [b]of your saints [c]and prophets,
so you have given them blood
  to drink. They got what they
  deserved!"

14:15[a]Rev 16:17 [b]Joel 3:13; Mark 4:29; Rev 14:18 **14:18**[a]Rev 16:8 **14:19**[a]Isa 63:2; Rev 19:15 **14:20**[a]Isa 63:3; Lam 1:15; Rev 19:15 [b]Heb 13:12; Rev 11:8 [c]Isa 34:3 **15:1**[a]Rev 12:1, 3 [b]Rev 21:9 [c]Rev 14:10 **15:2**[a]Rev 4:6 [b][Matt 3:11] [c]Rev 13:17 [d]Rev 5:8 [1]Or *had been victorious over*; trad. *had overcome.* **15:3**[a]Exod 15:1–21 [b]Rev 15:3 [c]Deut 32:3–4; Ps 92:5; Rom 11:33 [d]Ps 145:17; Rev 16:7 [1]Grk. *slave*; in a spiritual sense, voluntarily becoming a slave of God or of Jesus Christ. [2]Or *righteous.* [3]Some mss *ages.* **15:4**[a]Exod 15:14 [b]Lev 11:44; 1 Pet 1:16; Rev 4:8 [c]Ps 86:9; Isa 66:23 **15:5**[a]Exod 38:21; Num 1:50; Heb 8:5; Rev 13:6 **15:6**[a]Exod 28:6 **15:7**[a]Rev 4:6 [b]1 Thess 1:9 **15:8**[a]Exod 19:18; 40:34; Lev 16:2; 1 Kgs 8:10; 2 Chr 5:13; Isa 6:4 [b]2 Thess 1:9 **16:1**[a]Rev 15:1 **16:2**[a]Rev 8:7 [b]Exod 9:9–11; Deut 28:35; Rev 16:11 [c]Rev 13:15–17; 14:9 [d]Rev 13:14 [1]Grk. *the men*; a generic use referring to both men and women. **16:3**[a]Rev 8:8; 11:6 [b]Exod 7:17–21 [c]Rev 8:9 **16:4**[a]Rev 8:10 [b]Exod 7:17–20; Ps 78:44; Rev 11:6 **16:5**[a]Rev 15:3–4 [b]Rev 1:4, 8 [1]Or *righteous.* **16:6**[a]Matt 23:34 [b]Rev 11:18 [c]Isa 49:26; Luke 11:49–51

[7]Then I heard the altar reply, "Yes, [a]Lord God, the All-Powerful, your judgments are [b]true and just!"

[8]Then the fourth angel poured out his bowl [a]on the sun, [b]and it was permitted to scorch people[1] with fire. [9]Thus people[1] were scorched by the terrible heat, yet they [a]blasphemed the name of God, who has ruling authority over these plagues, [b]and they would not repent [c]and give him glory.

[10]Then the fifth angel poured out his bowl [a]on the throne of the beast so that darkness covered his kingdom, [b]and people[1] began to bite their tongues because of their pain. [11]They blasphemed the God of heaven because of their sufferings and because of their sores, but nevertheless they still refused to repent of their deeds.

[12]Then the sixth angel poured out his bowl [a]on the great river Euphrates [b]and dried up its water to prepare the way for the kings from the east. [13]Then I saw three unclean [a]spirits that looked like frogs coming out of [b]the mouth of [c]the dragon, out of the mouth of the beast, and out of the mouth of the false prophet. [14]For they are the spirits of the demons [a]performing signs who go out to [b]the kings of [c]the earth to bring them together for the battle that will take place on the great day of God, the All-Powerful.

[15] (Look! I will come like a thief!
Blessed is the one who stays alert
    and does not lose his clothes
    so that he will not have to walk
    around naked and his shameful
    condition [a]be seen.)

[16]Now the spirits gathered the kings [a]and their armies to the place that is called Armageddon[1,2] in Hebrew.

[17]Finally the seventh angel poured out his bowl into the air and a loud voice came out of the temple from the throne, saying: "[a]It is done!" [18]Then [a]there were flashes of lightning, roaring, [b]and crashes of thunder, and there was a tremendous earthquake—an earthquake [c]unequaled since humanity[1] has been on the earth, so tremendous was that earthquake. [19]The great city was split into three parts, and [a]the cities of the nations collapsed. So Babylon the [b]great [c]was remembered before God and was given the cup filled with the wine made of God's furious wrath. [20][a]Every island fled away, and no mountains could be found. [21]And gigantic hailstones, weighing about 100 pounds each, fell from heaven on people,[1] but they blasphemed God because of the plague of hail, since it was so horrendous.

The Great Prostitute and the Beast

17 Then [a]one of the seven angels who had the seven bowls came and spoke to me. "Come," he [b]said, "I will show you [c]the condemnation and punishment of the great prostitute [d]who sits on many waters, [2][a]with whom the kings of the earth committed sexual immorality and the earth's inhabitants got drunk with [b]the wine of her immorality." [3]So he carried me away in the Spirit [a]to a wilderness, and there I saw a woman sitting [b]on a scarlet beast that was full of blasphemous [c]names and had seven heads and ten horns. [4]Now the woman [a]was dressed in purple [b]and scarlet clothing, and adorned with gold, precious stones, and pearls. She [c]held in her hand a golden cup [d]filled with detestable things and unclean things from her sexual immorality.[1] [5]On her forehead was written a name, a [a]mystery: "Babylon the Great, the Mother of prostitutes and of the detestable things of the earth." [6]I saw that [a]the woman was drunk [b]with [c]the blood of the saints and the blood of those who testified to Jesus. I was greatly astounded[1] when I saw her. [7]But the angel said to me, "Why are you astounded? I will

16:7 [a] Rev 15:3 [b] Rev 13:10; 19:2   16:8 [a] Rev 8:12 [b] Rev 9:17–18 [1] Grk. *men*; a generic use referring to both men and women.   16:9 [a] Rev 16:11 [b] Dan 5:22 [c] Rev 11:13 [1] Grk. *men*; a generic use referring to both men and women.   16:10 [a] Rev 13:2 [b] Rev 11:10 [1] Grk. *men*; a generic use referring to both men and women.   16:12 [a] Rev 9:14 [b] Jer 50:38   16:13 [a] 1 John 4:1 [b] Rev 12:3, 9 [c] Rev 13:11, 14; 19:20; 20:10   16:14 [a] 2 Thess 2:9 [b] Luke 2:1 [c] 1 Kgs 22:21–23; Rev 17:14; 19:19; 20:8   16:15 [a] Matt 24:43; Luke 12:39; Rev 3:3, 11   16:16 [a] Rev 19:19 [1] The MSS contain many variations of the spelling of this name. [2] Or *Harmagedon* (a literal transliteration of the Grk.), *Har-Magedon* (Heb. "the Mount of Magedon").   16:17 [a] Rev 10:6; 21:6   16:18 [a] Rev 4:5 [b] Rev 11:13 [c] Dan 12:1; Matt 24:21 [1] Gk. *man*; used generically to refer to the human race.   16:19 [a] Rev 14:8 [b] Rev 17:5, 18 [c] Rev 14:8; 18:5   16:20 [a] Rev 6:14; 20:11   16:21 [1] Grk. *on men*, used in a generic sense to refer to people (the hailstones did not single out adult males, but would have also fallen on women and children).   17:1 [a] Rev 1:1; 21:9 [b] Rev 16:19 [c] Isa 1:21; Jer 2:20; Nah 3:4; Rev 17:5, 15; 19:2 [d] Jer 51:13; Rev 17:15   17:2 [a] Rev 2:22; 18:3, 9 [b] Jer 51:7; Rev 14:8   17:3 [a] Rev 12:6, 14; 21:10 [b] Rev 12:3 [c] Rev 13:1   17:4 [a] Ezek 28:13; Rev 18:12, 16 [b] Dan 11:38 [c] Jer 51:7; Rev 18:6 [d] Rev 14:8 [1] Sev. MSS *sexual immorality on/of the earth.*   17:5 [a] 2 Thess 2:7; Rev 1:20; 17:7   17:6 [a] Rev 18:24 [b] Rev 13:15 [c] Rev 6:9–10 [1] Grk. *I marveled a great marvel.*

interpret for you the mystery of the woman and of the beast with the seven heads and ten horns that carries her. [8]The beast you saw was, and is not, but is about [a]to come up from the abyss and then [b]go to destruction. The [c]inhabitants of the earth—all those [d]whose names have not been written in the book of life since the foundation of the world—[e]will be astounded when they see that the beast was, and is not, but is to come. [9]([a]This requires a mind that has wisdom.) [b]The seven heads are seven mountains the woman sits on. They are also seven kings: [10]five have fallen; one is, and the other has not yet come, but whenever he does come, he must [a]remain for only a brief time. [11]The [a]beast that was, and is not, is himself an eighth king and yet is one of the seven, and is going to destruction. [12]The ten horns that you saw are ten kings who have not yet received a kingdom, but will receive ruling authority as kings with [a]the beast for one hour. [13]These kings have a single intent, and they will give their power and authority to the beast. [14]They will make war with [a]the Lamb, but the Lamb will [b]conquer them, [c]because he is Lord of lords [d]and King of kings, and those accompanying the Lamb are the called, chosen, and faithful."

[15]Then [a]the angel said to me, "The waters you saw (where the prostitute is seated) [b]are peoples, multitudes, nations, and languages. [16]The ten horns that you saw, and the beast—[a]these will hate the prostitute and make her [b]desolate [c]and naked. They will consume her flesh and [d]burn her up with fire. [17a]For God has put into their minds to carry out his purpose by making a decision to give their royal power to the beast [b]until the words of God are fulfilled. [18]As for the woman you saw, she [a]is the great city that has sovereignty over the kings of the earth."

Babylon Is Destroyed

18 [a]After these things I saw another angel, who possessed great authority, coming down out of heaven, [b]and the earth was lit up by his radiance. [2]He shouted with a powerful voice:

"Fallen, fallen, is [a]Babylon the great!
She [b]has become [c]a lair for demons,
a haunt for every unclean spirit,
a haunt for every unclean bird,
a haunt for every unclean and
detested beast.[1]
[3] For all the nations [a]have fallen[1] from
the wine of her immoral passion,
and the kings of the earth have
committed sexual immorality with
her,
[b]and the merchants of the earth have
gotten rich from the power of her
sensual behavior."

[4]Then I heard another voice from heaven saying, "Come [a]out of her, my people, so you will not take part in her sins and so you will not receive her plagues, [5a]because her sins have piled up all the way to heaven and [b]God has remembered her crimes. [6]Repay her the same way she [a]repaid others; pay her back double corresponding to her deeds. [b]In the cup she mixed, [c]mix double the amount for her. [7]As much as she exalted herself and lived [a]in sensual luxury, to this extent give her torment and grief because she said to herself, 'I rule as [b]queen and am no widow; I will never experience grief!' [8]For this reason, she will experience her plagues [a]in a single day: disease, mourning, and famine, and [b]she will be burned down with fire, [c]because the Lord God who judges her is powerful!"

[9]Then [a]the kings of the earth who committed immoral acts with her and lived in sensual luxury with her [b]will weep and wail for her [c]when they see the smoke from the fire that burns her up. [10]They will stand a long way off because they are afraid of her torment, and will say,

"[a]Woe, woe, [b]O great city,
Babylon the powerful city!

17:8 [a]Rev 11:7 [b]Rev 13:10; 17:11 [c]Rev 3:10 [d]Matt 25:34; Rev 13:8 [e]Rev 13:3 17:9 [a]Rev 13:18 [b]Rev 13:1 17:10 [a]Rev 13:5 17:11 [a]Rev 13:3, 12, 14; 17:8 17:12 [a]Dan 7:20 17:14 [a]Rev 16:14; 19:19 [b]Rev 19:20 [c]Deut 10:17; 1 Tim 6:15; Rev 19:16 [d]Jer 50:44 17:15 [a]Isa 8:7; Jer 47:2; Rev 17:1 [b]Rev 13:7 17:16 [a]Jer 50:41 [b]Rev 18:17, 19 [c]Ezek 16:37, 39 [d]Rev 18:8 17:17 [a]2 Thess 2:11 [b]Rev 10:7 17:18 [a]Rev 11:8; 16:19 18:1 [a]Rev 17:1, 7 [b]Ezek 43:2 18:2 [a]Isa 13:19; 21:9; Jer 51:8; Rev 14:8 [b]Isa 13:21; 34:11, 13–15; Jer 50:39; 51:37; Zeph 2:14 [c]Isa 14:23 [1]Some MSS omit *a haunt for every unclean spirit* and/or *a haunt for every unclean bird*; sev. sig. MSS omit *a haunt for every unclean and detested beast.* 18:3 [a]Jer 51:7; Rev 14:8 [b]Isa 47:15 [1]‡ A few MSS *have drunk.* 18:4 [a]Isa 48:20 18:5 [a]Gen 18:20 [b]Rev 16:19 18:6 [a]Ps 137:8; Jer 50:15, 29 [b]Rev 14:10 [c]Rev 16:19 18:7 [a]Ezek 28:2–8 [b]Isa 47:7–8; Zeph 2:15 18:8 [a]Isa 47:9; Jer 50:31; Rev 18:10 [b]Rev 17:16 [c]Jer 50:34; Heb 10:31; Rev 11:17 18:9 [a]Ezek 26:16; 27:35 [b]Jer 50:46; Rev 17:2; 18:3 [c]Rev 19:3 18:10 [a]Isa 21:9 [b]Rev 18:17, 19

For in a single hour your doom[1] has
   come!"

[11]Then [a]the merchants of the earth will
weep and mourn for her because no one
buys their cargo any longer—[12]cargo such
as gold, silver, precious stones, pearls, fine
linen, purple cloth, silk, scarlet cloth, all
sorts of things made of citron wood, all
sorts of objects made of ivory, all sorts of
things made of expensive wood, bronze,
iron [a]and marble, [13]cinnamon, spice, incense, perfumed ointment, frankincense,
wine, olive oil and costly flour, wheat, cattle
and sheep, horses and four-wheeled carriag-
es, slaves and human [a]lives.[1]

[14] (The ripe fruit you greatly desired
   has gone from you,
   and all your luxury and splendor
   have gone from you—
   they will never ever be found again!)

[15]The merchants who sold these things,
who got rich from her, will stand a long way
off because they are afraid of her torment.
They will weep and mourn, [16]saying,

   "Woe, woe, O great city—
   dressed in fine linen, purple and
     scarlet clothing,
   and adorned with gold, precious
     stones, and pearls—
[17] [a]because in a single hour such great
     wealth has been destroyed!"

And [b]every ship's captain, and all who sail
along the coast—seamen, and all who make
their living from the sea, stood a long way
off [18a]and began to shout when they saw the
smoke from the fire that burned her up,
[b]"Who is like the great city?" [19]And [a]they
threw dust on their heads and were shouting with weeping and mourning,

   "Woe, Woe, O great city—
   in which all those who had ships on
     the sea got rich from her wealth—
   [b]because in a single hour she has
     been destroyed!"

[20] ([a]Rejoice over her, O heaven,
   and you saints and apostles and
     prophets,
   for [b]God has pronounced judgment
     against her on your behalf!)

[21]Then one powerful angel picked up [a]a
stone like a huge millstone, threw it into
the sea, and said,

   "With this kind of sudden violent
     force
   Babylon the great city will be thrown
     down,
   and it will never be found again!
[22] And [a]the sound of the harpists,
     musicians,
   flute players, and trumpeters
   will never be heard in you again.
   No craftsman who practices any
     trade
   will ever be found in you again;
   the noise of a mill will never be
     heard in you again.
[23] Even [a]the light from a lamp
   will never shine in you again!
   The voices of the bridegroom [b]and
     his bride
   will never be heard in [c]you again.
   [d]For your merchants were the
     tycoons of the world,
   because all the nations were
     deceived by your magic spells!
[24] The blood of the saints and prophets
     was found [a]in her,
   along with the blood of all those who
     had been killed on the earth."

19 After these [a]things I heard what
sounded like the loud voice of a vast
throng in heaven, saying,

   "Hallelujah! [b]Salvation and glory and
     power belong to our God,
[2] because his judgments are [a]true and
     just.
   For he [b]has judged the great
     prostitute
   who corrupted the earth with her
     sexual immorality,

18:10 [1]Or *judgment, condemnation, punishment.*   **18:11** [a]Ezek 27:27–34   **18:12** [a]Ezek 27:12–22; Rev 17:4   **18:13** [a]1 Chr 5:21;
Ezek 27:13   [1]*Grk. and bodies and souls of men.*   **18:17** [a]Rev 18:10   [b]Isa 23:14   **18:18** [a]Ezek 27:30   [b]Rev 13:4   **18:19** [a]Josh
7:6; Job 2:12; Lam 2:10; Ezek 27:30   [b]Rev 18:8   **18:20** [a]Isa 44:23; 49:13; Jer 51:48; Rev 12:12   [b]Luke 11:49; Rev 19:2
18:21 [a]Rev 12:8; 16:20   **18:22** [a]Eccl 12:4; Jer 7:34; 16:9; 25:10; Rev 14:1–3   **18:23** [a]Jer 25:10   [b]Jer 7:34; 16:9
[c]Isa 23:8; Rev 6:15; 18:3   [d]2 Kgs 9:22   **18:24** [a]Rev 16:6; 17:6   **19:1** [a]Jer 51:48; Rev 11:15; 19:6
[b]Rev 4:11   **19:2** [a]Rev 15:3; 16:7   [b]Deut 32:43; 2 Kgs 9:7; Luke 18:7–8; Rev 6:10

and has avenged the blood of his servants[1] poured out by her own hands!"

[3] Then a second time the crowd shouted, "Hallelujah!" The smoke rises from [a] her forever and ever. [4] The twenty-four elders and [a] the four living creatures threw themselves to the ground and worshiped God, who was seated on the throne, saying: "[b] Amen! Hallelujah!"

[5] Then a voice came from the throne, saying:

"[a] Praise our God
all you his servants,
and all you who fear him,
[b] both the small and the great!"

The Wedding Celebration of the Lamb

[6] Then I heard what sounded like the voice of a vast throng, like the roar of many waters [a] and like loud crashes of thunder. [b] They were shouting:

"Hallelujah!
For the Lord our God,[1] the
All-Powerful,[2] reigns!
[7] Let us rejoice and exult
and give him glory,
because [a] the wedding celebration of
the Lamb has come,
and his bride has made herself ready.
[8] She was permitted [a] to be dressed in
bright, clean, fine linen" ([b] for the
fine linen is the righteous deeds of
the saints).

[9] Then the angel said to me, "Write the following: [a] Blessed are those who are invited to the banquet at the wedding celebration of the Lamb!" He also said to me, "[b] These are the true words of God." [10] So [a] I threw myself down at his feet to worship him, but he said, "Do not [b] do this! I am only a [c] fellow servant[1] with you and your brothers and sisters[2] who hold to [d] the [e] testimony about Jesus. Worship God, for the testimony about Jesus is the spirit of prophecy."

The Son of God Goes to War

[11] Then I saw heaven opened [a] and here [b] came a white horse! The one riding it was called "[c] Faithful" and "True," and [d] with justice[1] he judges and goes to war. [12][a] His eyes are like a fiery flame and there are many diadem crowns on his [b] head. He has a name written that no one knows except himself. [13] He is dressed in clothing dipped[1] in blood, and [a] he is called [b] the Word of God. [14][a] The armies that are in heaven, dressed [b] in white, clean, fine linen, were following him on white horses. [15] From his [a] mouth extends a sharp sword so that with it he can strike the nations. *He will rule*[1] *them with an iron rod,*[2] and [b] he stomps [c] the winepress of the furious wrath of God, the All-Powerful. [16] He has a name written on his clothing and on his thigh: "[a] King of kings and Lord of lords."

[17] Then I saw one angel standing in the sun, and he shouted in a loud voice to all the birds flying high in the sky:

"[a] Come, gather around for the great
banquet of God,
[18] [a] to eat your fill of the flesh of kings,
the flesh of generals,
the flesh of powerful people,
the flesh of horses and those who
ride them,
and the flesh of all people, both free
and slave,[1]
and small and great!"

[19] Then I saw the beast [a] and the kings of the earth and their armies assembled to do battle with the one who rode the horse and with his army. [20] Now the beast was seized, [a] and along with him the false prophet who had performed the signs on

19:2 [1] Grk. *slaves*; in a spiritual sense, voluntarily becoming slaves of God or of Jesus Christ.   19:3 [a] Isa 34:10; Rev 14:11   19:4 [a] Rev 4:4, 6, 10   [b] 1 Chr 16:36   19:5 [a] Ps 134:1   [b] Rev 11:18   19:6 [a] Ezek 1:24; Rev 1:15; 14:2   [b] Rev 11:15   [1] Some MSS *God our Lord*; sev. sig. MSS omit *our*; some MSS omit *Lord*.   [2] Grk. *the Almighty, All-Powerful, Omnipotent* [One]; only used of God.   19:7 [a] [Matt 22:2; 25:10]; Luke 12:36; John 3:29; [2 Cor 11:2]; Eph 5:23, 32; Rev 19:9   19:8 [a] Ps 45:13; Ezek 16:10   [b] Ps 132:9   19:9 [a] Matt 22:2; Luke 14:15   [b] Rev 22:6   19:10 [a] Rev 22:8   [b] Acts 10:26; Rev 22:9   [c] [Heb 1:14]   [d] 1 John 5:10   [e] Luke 24:27; John 5:39   [1] Grk. *fellow slave*; in a spiritual sense, voluntarily becoming a slave of God or of Jesus Christ.   [2] Grk. *brother*, refers to family relationships, but used in a broader sense to connote relationships within the family of God.   19:11 [a] Rev 15:5   [b] Ps 45:3–4; Rev 6:2; 19:19, 21   [c] Rev 3:7, 14   [d] Ps 96:13; Isa 11:4   [1] Or *in righteousness*.   19:12 [a] Dan 10:6; Rev 1:14   [b] Rev 2:17; 19:16   19:13 [a] Isa 63:2–3   [b] [John 1:1, 14]   [1] Sev. MSS *sprinkled*.   19:14 [a] Rev 14:20   [b] Matt 28:3   19:15 [a] Isa 11:4; 2 Thess 2:8; Rev 1:16   [b] Ps 2:8–9   [c] Isa 63:3–6; Rev 14:20   [1] Grk. *will shepherd*.   [2] Ps 2:9   19:16 [a] Dan 2:47   19:17 [a] 1 Sam 17:44; Jer 12:9; Ezek 39:17   19:18 [a] Ezek 39:18–20   [1] In a spiritual sense, voluntarily becoming a slave of God or of Jesus Christ.   19:19 [a] Rev 16:13–16   19:20 [a] Rev 16:13

his behalf—signs by which he deceived [b]those who had received [c]the mark of the beast and those who worshiped his image. Both of them were thrown alive into the lake of fire [d]burning with sulfur.[1] [21]The others [a]were killed by the sword that extended from the mouth of the one who rode the horse, [b]and all the birds gorged themselves with their flesh.

The Thousand-Year Reign

20 Then I saw an angel descending from heaven, [a]holding in his hand the key to the abyss and a huge chain. [2]He seized [a]the dragon—the ancient serpent, who is the devil and Satan—and tied him up for a thousand years. [3]The angel then threw him into the abyss and locked and sealed it [a]so that he could not deceive the nations until the one thousand years were finished. (After these things he must be released for a brief period of time.)

[4]Then I saw [a]thrones and seated on them were those who had been given authority to [b]judge. I also saw [c]the souls of those who had been beheaded because of the testimony about Jesus and because of the word of God. [d]These had not [e]worshiped the beast or his image and had refused to receive his mark on their forehead or hand. They came to [f]life and [g]reigned with Christ for a thousand years. [5](The rest of the dead did not come to life until the thousand years were finished.) This is the first resurrection. [6]Blessed and holy is [a]the one who takes part in the first resurrection. The second death has no power over them, but they will be [b]priests of God [c]and of Christ, and they will reign with him for a thousand years.

Satan's Final Defeat

[7]Now when the thousand years are finished, Satan will be released from his prison [8]and will go out [a]to deceive[1] the nations at the four corners of the earth, [b]Gog and Magog, [c]to bring them together for the battle. They are as numerous as the grains of sand in the sea.[2] [9]They went up on [a]the broad plain of the earth and encircled the camp of the saints and the beloved city, but fire came down from heaven and devoured them completely. [10]And the devil who deceived[1] them was thrown into the lake of fire and sulfur,[2] [a]where the beast and the false prophet are too, and they [b]will be tormented there day and night forever and ever.

The Great White Throne

[11]Then I saw a large white throne and [a]the one who was seated on it; the earth [b]and the heaven fled from his presence, and no place was found for them. [12]And I saw the dead, the [a]great and the small, standing before the throne. Then books were opened, [b]and another [c]book was opened—the book of life. So the dead were judged by what was written in the books, according [d]to their deeds. [13]The sea gave up the dead that were in it, [a]and Death [b]and Hades gave up the dead that were in them, and each one was judged according to his deeds. [14]Then [a]Death and Hades were thrown into the lake of fire. [b]This is the second death—the lake of fire. [15]If anyone's name [a]was not found written in the book of life, that person was thrown into the lake of fire.

A New Heaven and a New Earth

21 Then [a]I saw a new heaven and a new earth, [b]for the first heaven and earth had ceased to exist, and the sea existed no more. [2]And I saw [a]the holy city—the new Jerusalem—descending out of heaven from God, made ready [b]like a bride adorned for her husband. [3]And I heard a loud voice from [a]the throne saying: "Look! The residence[1] of God is among human beings.[2] He will live among them, and they will be his people, and God himself will be with them.[3] [4]He will wipe away every tear from their eyes, [a]and [b]death will not exist any more—[c]or

19:20 [b]Rev 13:8, 12, 13   [c]Isa 30:33; Dan 7:11   [d]Rev 14:10   [1]Trad. *brimstone.*   19:21 [a]Rev 19:15   [b]Rev 19:17–18   20:1 [a]Rev 1:18; 9:1   20:2 [a]Isa 24:22; 2 Pet 2:4; Jude 6   20:3 [a]Rev 12:9; 20:8, 10   20:4 [a]Dan 7:9; Matt 19:28; Luke 22:30   [b]Dan 7:22; [1 Cor 6:2–3]   [c]Rev 6:9   [d]Rev 13:12   [e]Rev 13:15   [f]John 14:19   [g]Rom 8:17; 2 Tim 2:12   20:6 [a][Rev 2:11; 20:14]   [b]Isa 61:6; 1 Pet 2:9; Rev 1:6   [c]Rev 20:4   20:8 [a]Rev 12:9; 20:3, 10   [b]Ezek 38:2; 39:1, 6   [c]Rev 16:14   [1]Or *mislead.*   [2]Grk. *of whom the number of them* [is] *like the sand of the sea.*   20:9 [a]Isa 8:8; Ezek 38:9, 16   20:10 [a]Rev 19:20; 20:14–15   [b]Rev 14:10   [1]Or *misled.*   [2]Trad. *brimstone.*   20:11 [a]2 Pet 3:7; Rev 21:1   [b]Dan 2:35; Rev 12:8   20:12 [a]Rev 19:5   [b]Dan 7:10   [c]Ps 69:28; Dan 12:1; Phil 4:3; Rev 3:5   [d]Jer 17:10; Matt 16:27; Rom 2:6; Rev 2:23; 20:12   20:13 [a]1 Cor 15:26; Rev 1:18; 6:8; 21:4   [b]Matt 16:27; Rev 2:23; 20:12   20:14 [a]1 Cor 15:26; Rev 1:18; 6:8; 21:4   [b]Rev 21:8   20:15 [a]Rev 19:20   21:1 [a]Isa 65:17; 66:22; [2 Pet 3:13]   [b][2 Pet 3:10]; Rev 20:11   21:2 [a]Isa 52:1; [Gal 4:26]; Heb 11:10   [b]Isa 54:5; 2 Cor 11:2   21:3 [a]Lev 26:11; Ezek 43:7; 2 Cor 6:16   [1]Or *dwelling place;* trad. *tabernacle;* lit. *tent.*   [2]Or *people;* Grk. *men;* with a generic use of the term.   [3]‡ Some MSS add [as] *their God.*   21:4 [a]Isa 25:8; Rev 7:17   [b]1 Cor 15:26; Rev 20:14   [c]Isa 35:10; 51:11; 65:19

mourning, or crying, or pain, for the former things have ceased to exist."

5 And [a]the one seated on the throne said: "Look! I am making all things new!" Then he said to me, "Write it down, because [b]these words are reliable and true." 6 He also said to me, "[a]It is done! [b]I am the Alpha and the Omega, the beginning and the end. To the one who is thirsty [c]I will give water free of charge from the spring of the water of life. 7 The one who conquers[1] [a]will inherit these things, and I will be his God and he will be my son. 8[a]But as for [b]the cowards, unbelievers, detestable persons, murderers, the sexually immoral, and those who practice magic spells, idol worshipers, and all those who lie, their place will be in the lake that burns with fire and sulfur.[1] That is the second death."

The New Jerusalem Descends

9 Then one of [a]the seven angels who had [b]the seven bowls full of the seven final plagues came and spoke to me, saying, "Come, I will show you the bride, the wife of the Lamb!" 10 So he took me away [a]in [b]the Spirit to a huge, majestic mountain and showed me the holy city, Jerusalem, descending out of heaven from God. 11 The city [a]possesses the glory of God; its brilliance is like a precious jewel, like a stone of crystal-clear jasper. 12 It has a massive, high wall with [a]twelve gates, with twelve angels at the gates, and the names of the twelve tribes of the nation of Israel are written on the gates. 13 There are [a]three gates on the east side, three gates on the north side, three gates on the south side, and three gates on the west side. 14 The wall of the city has twelve foundations, and [a]on them are the twelve names of the twelve apostles of the Lamb. 15 The angel who spoke to me [a]had a golden measuring rod with which to measure the city and its foundation stones and wall. 16 Now the city is laid out as a square, its length and width the same. He measured the city with the measuring rod at 1,400 miles (its length and width and height are equal). 17 He also measured its wall, 144 cubits[1] according to human measurement, which is also the angel's. 18 The city's wall is made of jasper and the city is pure gold, like transparent glass. 19 The foundations of [a]the city's wall are decorated with every kind of precious stone. The first foundation is jasper, the second sapphire, the third agate, the fourth emerald, 20 the fifth onyx, the sixth carnelian, the seventh chrysolite, the eighth beryl, the ninth topaz, the tenth chrysoprase, the eleventh jacinth, and the twelfth amethyst. 21 And the twelve gates are twelve [a]pearls—each one of the gates is made from just one pearl! [b]The main street[1] of the city is pure gold, like transparent glass.

22 Now I saw no temple in the city, because the Lord God—the All-Powerful—[a]and the Lamb are its temple. 23 The city does not need [a]the sun or the moon to shine on it, because the glory of God lights it up, and its lamp is the Lamb. 24 The nations will walk by its light, [a]and the kings of the earth will bring their grandeur into it. 25[a]Its gates will never be closed during [b]the day (and there will be no night there). 26 They will bring the grandeur [a]and the wealth of the nations into it, 27 but nothing ritually unclean will ever enter into it, nor anyone who does what is detestable[1] or practices falsehood, but only those whose names are written in [a]the Lamb's [b]book of life.

22 Then the [a]angel showed me the river of the water of life—water as clear as crystal—pouring out from the throne of God and of the Lamb, 2 flowing [a]down [b]the middle of the city's main street.[1] On each side of the river is the tree of life producing 12 kinds of fruit, yielding its fruit every month of the year. Its leaves are [c]for the healing of the nations. 3 And [a]there will no longer be any curse, [b]and the throne of God and the Lamb will be in the city. His

21:5 [a] Rev 4:2, 9; 20:11   [b] Rev 19:9; 22:6   21:6 [a] Rev 10:6; 16:17   [b] Rev 1:8; 22:13   [c] Isa 12:3; 55:1; John 4:10; Rev 7:17; 22:17   21:7 [a] Zech 8:8; Heb 8:10   [1] Or *who is victorious*; trad. *who overcomes*.   21:8 [1] 1 Cor 6:9; Gal 5:19; Eph 5:5; 1 Tim 1:9; [Heb 12:14]   [b] Rev 20:14   [1] Trad. *brimstone*.   21:9 [a] Rev 15:1   [b] Rev 19:7; 21:2   21:10 [a] Rev 1:10   [b] Ezek 48   21:11 [a] Isa 60:1; Ezek 43:2; Rev 15:8; 21:23; 22:5   21:12 [a] Ezek 48:31–34   21:13 [a] Ezek 48:31–34   21:14 [a] Matt 16:18; Luke 22:29–30; Gal 2:9; Eph 2:20   21:15 [a] Ezek 40:3; Zech 2:1; Rev 11:1   21:17 [1] The measurement is kept in cubits because of the possible symbolic significance of the number 144 (12 x 12). This is about 216 ft (65 m).   21:19 [a] Exod 28:17–20; Isa 54:11; Ezek 28:13   21:21 [a] Matt 13:45–46   [b] Rev 22:2   [1] I.e., a major (broad) street.   21:22 [a] Matt 24:2; John 4:21, 23   21:23 [a] Isa 24:23; 60:19–20; Rev 21:25; 22:5   21:24 [a] Isa 60:3, 5; 66:12   21:25 [a] Isa 60:11   [b] Isa 60:20; Zech 14:7   21:26 [a] Rev 21:24   21:27 [a] Isa 35:8; Joel 3:17   [b] Phil 4:3   [1] Or *what is abhorrent*; Grk. *who practices abominations*.   22:1 [a] Ps 46:4; Ezek 47:1; [Zech 14:8]   22:2 [a] Ezek 47:12   [b] Gen 2:9; [Rev 2:7; 22:14, 19]   [c] Rev 21:24   [1] I.e., a major (broad) street.   22:3 [a] Zech 14:11   [b] Ezek 48:35

^{c}servants[1] will worship him, [4]and ^{a}they will see ^{b}his face, and his name will be on their foreheads. [5]Night will be no more, and they will not need ^{a}the ^{b}light of a lamp or ^{c}the light of the sun, because the Lord God will shine on them, ^{d}and they will reign forever and ever.

A Final Reminder

[6]Then the angel said to me, "^{a}These words are reliable and true. The Lord, the God of the spirits of the prophets, has ^{b}sent his angel to show his servants[1] what must happen soon."

[7]   (^{a}Look! I am coming soon!
   ^{b}Blessed is the one who keeps the
      words of the prophecy expressed
      in this book.)

[8]I, John, am the one who heard and saw these ^{a}things, and when I heard and saw them, I threw myself down to worship at the feet of the angel who was showing them to me. [9]But he said to me, "Do not ^{a}do this! I am a fellow servant[1] with you and with your brothers the prophets, and with those who obey the words of this book. Worship God!" [10][a]Then he said to me, "Do not seal up the words of the prophecy contained in this book, ^{b}because the time is near. [11]The evildoer must continue to do evil, and the one who is morally filthy must continue to be filthy. The one who is righteous must continue to act righteously, and the one who is holy must continue to be holy."

[12]   (Look! I am coming soon,
      and ^{a}my reward is with me ^{b}to pay
         each one according to what he has
         done!
[13] ^{a}I am the Alpha and the Omega,
      the first and the last,
      the beginning and the end!)

[14][a]Blessed are those who wash their robes so they can have access ^{b}to the tree of life ^{c}and can enter into the city by the gates. [15][a]Outside are the ^{b}dogs and the sorcerers and the sexually immoral, and the murderers, and the idolaters and everyone who loves and practices falsehood![1] [16]"^{a}I, Jesus, have sent my angel to testify to you about these things for the churches. I am the root and the descendant of David, ^{b}the bright morning star!" [17]And the Spirit and ^{a}the bride say, "Come!" ^{b}And let the one who hears say: "Come!" And let the one who is thirsty come; let the one who wants it take the water of life free of charge.

[18]I testify to everyone who hears the words of the prophecy contained in this book: ^{a}If anyone adds to them, God will add to him the plagues described in this book. [19]And if anyone takes away from the words of this book of prophecy, ^{a}God will take away his share in the tree of life[1] and in the holy city that are described in this book.

[20]The one who testifies to these things says, "Yes, I am coming soon!" Amen! Come, Lord Jesus! [21]The grace of the Lord Jesus be with all.[1]

22:3 ^{c}Rev 7:15   [1]Grk. *slaves*; in a spiritual sense, voluntarily becoming slaves of God or of Jesus Christ.   22:4 ^{a}[Ps 17:15; 42:2; Matt 5:8; 1 Cor 13:12; 1 John 3:2] ^{b}Rev 14:1   22:5 ^{a}Isa 60:19; Rev 21:23 ^{b}Rev 7:15 ^{c}Ps 36:9 ^{d}Dan 7:18, 27; Matt 19:28; [Rom 5:17]; 2 Tim 2:12; Rev 20:4   22:6 ^{a}Rev 19:9 ^{b}Rev 1:1   [1]Grk. *slaves*; in a spiritual sense, voluntarily becoming slaves of God or of Jesus Christ.   22:7 ^{a}[Rev 3:11] ^{b}Rev 1:3   22:8 ^{a}Rev 19:10   22:9 ^{a}Rev 19:10   [1]Grk. *fellow slaves*; in a spiritual sense, voluntarily becoming slaves of God or of Jesus Christ.   22:10 ^{a}Dan 8:26; Rev 10:4 ^{b}Rev 1:3   22:12 ^{a}Isa 40:10; 62:11 ^{b}Rev 20:12   22:13 ^{a}Isa 41:4   22:14 ^{a}Dan 12:12; [1 John 3:24] ^{b}[Prov 11:30]; Rev 2:7 ^{c}Rev 21:27   22:15 ^{a}Matt 8:12; 1 Cor 6:9; Gal 5:19; Col 3:6; Rev 21:8 ^{b}Deut 23:18; Matt 7:6; Phil 3:2   [1]Or *lying, deceit.*   22:16 ^{a}2 Sam 7:12; Isa 9:7; Jer 23:5; Rev 5:5 ^{b}Num 24:17; Luke 1:78; 2 Pet 1:19   22:17 ^{a}[Rev 21:2, 9] ^{b}Isa 55:1; Rev 21:6   22:18 ^{a}Deut 4:2; 12:32; Prov 30:6   22:19 ^{a}Exod 32:33   [1]TR *the book of life.*   22:21 [1]Maj. MSS add *amen.*

NET Concordance

This concordance indexes over 7,050 words, phrases, and proper nouns with over 34,900 context lines of definitions and verses in which they are used in the NET. Words and phrases are referenced with Scripture quotations, in which the first letter of the word or phrase, bolded and italicized, stands for the entire word or phrase.

Proper names are defined by descriptive phrases and Scripture references. If a name applies to more than one person, place, or group, the different identities are distinguished by a dash ("—").

A

AARON
Ancestry and family of, Exod 6:16–20, 23
Helper and prophet to Moses, Exod 4:13–31; 7:1–2
Appears before Pharaoh, Exod 5:1–4
Performs miracles, Exod 7:9–10, 19–20
Supports Moses' hands, Exod 17:10–12
Ascends Mt. Sinai; sees God's glory, Exod 19:24; 24:1, 9–10
Judges Israel in Moses' absence, Exod 24:14
Chosen by God as priest, Exod 28:1
Consecrated, Exod 29; Lev 8
Duties prescribed, Exod 30:7–10
Tolerates Israel's idolatry, Exod 32
Priestly ministry begins, Lev 9
Sons offer profane fire; Aaron's humble response, Lev 10
Conspires against Moses, Num 12:1–16
Rebelled against by Korah, Num 16
Intercedes to stop plague, Num 16:45–48
Rod buds to confirm his authority, Num 17:1–10
With Moses, fails at Meribah, Num 20:1–13
Dies; son succeeds him as priest, Num 20:23–29
His priesthood compared:
    with Melchizedek's, Heb 7:11–19
    with Christ's, Heb 9:6–15, 23–28

ABADDON
Angel of the abyss, Rev 9:11

ABANDON
LORD will not *a* his people . . . . 1 Sam 12:22
But let us *a* this practice . . . . Neh 5:10
You did not *a* them . . . . Neh 9:17
did not *a* them in the wilderness . . Neh 9:19
You will not *a* me to Sheol . . . . Ps 16:10
Do not forsake or *a* me . . . . Ps 27:9
he does not *a* the nation . . . . Ps 94:14
and I will never *a* you . . . . Heb 13:5

ABANDONED
why have you *a* me . . . . Ps 22:1
my father and mother *a* me . . . . Ps 27:10
never seen the godly *a* . . . . Ps 37:25
they *a* because of the Israelites . . . . . Isa 17:9
For a short time I *a* you . . . . Isa 54:7
are persecuted, but not *a* . . . . 2 Cor 4:9

ABANDONING
not *a* our own meetings . . . . Heb 10:25

ABANDONS
never *a* his faithful followers . . . . Ps 37:28
a the sheep and runs away . . . . John 10:12

ABATED
The king's rage then *a* . . . . Esth 7:10

ABBA
A, Father, all things are
    possible . . . . Mark 14:36
A, Father . . . . Rom 8:15
who calls "*A* . . . . Gal 4:6

ABDOMEN
His *a* is like polished ivory . . . . Song 5:14

ABEDNEGO
Babylonian name given to Azariah, a Hebrew captive, Dan 1:7
Appointed by Nebuchadnezzar, Dan 2:49
Refuses to serve idols; cast into furnace but delivered, Dan 3:12–30

ABEL
Adam's second son, Gen 4:2
His offering accepted, Gen 4:4
Murdered by Cain, Gen 4:8
His sacrifice offered by faith, Heb 11:4

ABEL BETH MAACAH [or ABEL OF BETH MAACAH]
Captured by Tiglath-Pileser, 2 Kgs 15:29
Refuge of Sheba; saved from destruction, 2 Sam 20:14–22
Seized by Ben Hadad, 1 Kgs 15:20
Also called "Abel of Beth Maacah," 2 Sam 20:14–22

ABEL OF BETH MAACAH
See ABEL BETH MAACAH

ABEL MEHOLAH
A city a few miles east of Jabesh Gilead, Judg 7:22; 1 Kgs 4:12
Elisha's native city, 1 Kgs 19:16

ABEL OF BETH MAACAH
See ABEL BETH MAACAH

ABHOR
and I will not *a* you . . . . Lev 26:11
A what is evil . . . . Rom 12:9

ABHORRED
and have *a* my statutes . . . . Lev 26:43
his altar and *a* his temple . . . . Lam 2:7

ABHORRENCE
to shame and everlasting *a* . . . . Dan 12:2

ABHORRENT
not learn the *a* practices . . . . Deut 18:9
will find the sight *a* . . . . Isa 66:24

ABHORS
LORD *a* dishonest scales . . . . Prov 11:1

ABIATHAR
A priest who escapes Saul at Nob, 1 Sam 22:20–23
Becomes high priest under David, 1 Sam 23:6, 9–12
Remains faithful to David, 2 Sam 15:24–29
Informs David about Ahithophel, 2 Sam 15:34–36
Supports Adonijah's usurpation, 1 Kgs 1:7, 9, 25
Deposed by Solomon, 1 Kgs 2:26–27, 35

ABIEZRITES
Relatives of Gideon; rally to his call, Judg 6:11, 24, 34

ABIGAIL
Wise wife of foolish Nabal, 1 Sam 25:3

ABIGAIL
Appeases David and becomes his wife, 1 Sam 25:14–42
Mother of Kileab, 2 Sam 3:3

ABIHU
Second son of Aaron, Exod 6:23
Offers profane fire and dies, Lev 10:1–7

ABIJAH
Samuel's second son; follows corrupt ways, 1 Sam 8:2–3
—Descendant of Aaron; head of an office of priests, 1 Chr 24:3, 10
Zechariah belongs to division of, Luke 1:5
—Son of Jeroboam I, 1 Kgs 14:1–18
King of Judah, 1 Kgs 14:31
Follows the sins of his father, 1 Kgs 15:1–7
Defeats Jeroboam and takes cities, 2 Chr 13:13–20

ABILENE
A province or tetrarchy of Syria, Luke 3:1

ABILITY
a to make wise judicial decisions . . . . 1 Kgs 3:11
when you have the *a* to help . . . . . . Prov 3:27
each according to his *a* . . . . Matt 25:15

ABIMELECH
King of Gerar; takes Sarah in ignorance, Gen 20:1–18
Makes treaty with Abraham, Gen 21:22–34
—A second king of Gerar; sends Isaac away, Gen 26:1–16
Makes treaty with Isaac, Gen 26:17–33
—Gideon's son by a concubine, Judg 8:31
Conspires to become king, Judg 9

ABINADAB
A man of Kiriath Jearim in whose house the ark was kept, 1 Sam 7:1–2
—The second of Jesse's eight sons, 1 Sam 16:8
Serves in Saul's army, 1 Sam 17:13
—A son of Saul slain at Mt. Gilboa, 1 Sam 31:1–8
Bones of, buried by men of Jabesh, 1 Chr 10:1–12

ABIRAM
Reubenite who conspired against Moses, Num 16:1–50

ABISHAG
A Shunammite employed as David's nurse, 1 Kgs 1:1–4, 15
Witnessed David's choice of Solomon as successor, 1 Kgs 1:15–31
Adonijah slain for desiring to marry her, 1 Kgs 2:13–25

ABISHAI
David's nephew; joins Joab in blood revenge against Abner, 2 Sam 2:18–24
Loyal to David during Absalom's and Sheba's rebellion, 2 Sam 16:9–12; 20:1–6, 10
Rebuked by David, 2 Sam 16:9–12; 19:21–23
His exploits, 2 Sam 21:16–17; 23:18; 1 Chr 18:12–13

ABLE

you are *a* to count them...........Gen 15:5
not *a* to bring this people........Num 14:16
must give as you are *a*.........Deut 16:17
is *a* to make judicial decisions.....1 Kgs 3:9
and who is *a* to deliver ....Isa 63:1
not be *a* to deliver them..........Ezek 7:19
he is *a* to rescue us................Dan 3:17
He is *a* to bring down those.......Dan 4:37
believe that I am *a* to do this.....Matt 9:28
the one who is *a* to destroy.....Matt 10:28
Are you *a* to drink the cup......Matt 20:22
and will not be *a* to.............. Luke 13:24
and was not *a* to finish .... Luke 14:30
will be *a* to withstand ....Luke 21:15
will be *a* to separate us...........Rom 8:39
is *a* to make him stand ....Rom 14:4
who is *a* to strengthen you.......Rom 16:25
beyond what you are *a* to bear...1 Cor 10:13
is *a* to make all grace overflow....2 Cor 9:8
you will be *a* to comprehend.......Eph 3:18
be *a* to stand your ground.........Eph 6:13
I am *a* to do all things ....Phil 4:13
a to protect what has been
   entrusted...................... 2 Tim 1:12
never *a* to arrive at a knowledge ..2 Tim 3:7
a to help those who are tempted.. Heb 2:18
he is *a* to save completely.........Heb 7:25
a to control the entire body..........Jas 3:2
a to keep you from falling...........Jude 1:24
was *a* to open the scroll............Rev 5:3
and who is *a* to withstand..........Rev 6:17

ABNER

Saul's cousin; commander of his army,
  1 Sam 14:50–51
Rebuked by David, 1 Sam 26:5, 14–16
Supports Ish Bosheth; defeated by David's
  men; kills Asahel, 2 Sam 2:8–32
Makes covenant with David, 2 Sam 3:6–21
Killed by Joab; mourned by David,
  2 Sam 3:22–39

ABOLISH

to *a* the law or the prophets.......Matt 5:17

ABOMINATION

be an *a* to the Egyptians...........Exod 8:26
seven things that are an *a*.........Prov 6:16
and the scorner is an *a* ....Prov 24:9
even his prayer is an *a*............Prov 28:9
is an *a* to the righteous..........Prov 29:27
the *a* that causes desolation.......Dan 11:31
the *a* that causes desolation......Dan 12:11
you see the *a* of desolation......Matt 24:15

ABOMINATIONS

great *a* that the people............Ezek 8:6
house of Judah commits these *a*...Ezek 8:17

ABOUND

When words *a*...................Prov 10:19
a in order to strengthen the
   church......................1 Cor 14:12

ABOUNDING

a in loyal love and faithfulness ...Exod 34:6
slow to anger and *a* in mercy......Jonah 4:2

ABOUT

the LORD God moving *a* ....Gen 3:8
I heard you moving *a* .... Gen 3:10
who did not know *a* Joseph......Exod 1:8
the LORD your God walks *a*...... Deut 23:14
what you can *a* the land.............Josh 2:1
queen of Sheba heard *a* Solomon..1 Kgs 10:1
in the ears of those who hear *a*.. 2 Kgs 21:12
he wanders *a*.....................Job 15:23
their little ones dance *a* ....Job 21:11
wander *a* for lack of food...........Job 38:41
As I thought *a* it ....Ps 39:3
also tell *a* your justice ....Ps 71:24
the day the LORD has brought *a*...Ps 118:24
No one cares *a* me ....Ps 142:4
no one is concerned *a* my life ......Ps 142:4
that have not heard *a* me..........Isa 66:19
to bring *a* something new ....Jer 31:22
you will skip *a* like calves...........Mal 4:2

we live and move *a* and exist.....Acts 17:28
teaching *a* the Lord Jesus Christ..Acts 28:31
worldly sadness brings *a* death...2 Cor 7:10

ABOVE

See also BORN FROM ABOVE
more than 20 feet *a* the
   mountains......................Gen 7:20
anything that is in heaven *a* ......Exod 20:4
He reached down from *a* ...... 2 Sam 22:17
look down from his sanctuary *a* ...Ps 102:19
must all be born from *a* ....John 3:7
one who comes from *a* ....John 3:31
I am from *a*......................John 8:23
unless it was given to you from *a*..John 19:11
the name that is *a* every name .....Phil 2:9
keep seeking the things *a* ....Col 3:1
every perfect gift is from *a* ....Jas 1:17

ABRAHAM

Ancestry and family, Gen 11:26–31
Receives God's call; enters Canaan,
  Gen 12:1–6
Promised Canaan by God; pitches tent near
  Bethel, Gen 12:7–8
Deceives Egyptians concerning Sarai,
  Gen 12:11–20
Separates from Lot; inherits Canaan, Gen 13
Rescues Lot from captivity, Gen 14:11–16
Gives a tithe to Melchizedek; refuses spoil,
  Gen 14:18–24
Covenant renewed; promised a son, Gen 15
Takes Hagar as concubine; Ishmael born,
  Gen 16
Name changed from Abram; circumcision
  commanded, Gen 17
Entertains Lord and angels, Gen 18:1–15
Intercedes for Sodom, Gen 18:16–33
Deceives Abimelech concerning Sarah,
  Gen 20
Birth of Isaac, Gen 21:1–7
Sends Hagar and Ishmael away, Gen 21:9–14
Offers Isaac in obedience to God,
  Gen 22:1–19
Finds wife for Isaac, Gen 24
Marries Keturah; fathers other children;
  dies, Gen 25:1–10
Friend of God, 2 Chr 20:7
Justified by faith, Rom 4:1–12
Father of true believers, Rom 4:11–25
In the line of faith, Heb 11:8–10
Eternal home of, in heaven, Luke 16:19–25

A and his son Ishmael .... Gen 17:26
A was walking with them.........Gen 18:16
A journeyed from there .... Gen 20:1
bore *A* a son in his old age.........Gen 21:2
A circumcised him just as God .... Gen 21:4
A was one hundred years old.......Gen 21:5
son whom Hagar had borne to *A*.. Gen 21:9
after these things God tested *A* ....Gen 22:1
Now *A* was old ....Gen 24:1
A had taken another wife..........Gen 25:1
the son of *A* ....Gen 25:19
remembered his covenant with *A*.. Exod 2:24
the land I swore to give to *A*....... Exod 6:8
the land that I swore to give to *A*.. Num 32:11
the promise he made to *A*........1 Chr 16:16
the descendants of your friend *A*..2 Chr 20:7
O children of *A* ....Ps 105:6
the one who delivered *A* ....Isa 29:22
offspring of *A* my friend.............Isa 41:8
the son of *A* ....Matt 1:1
before *A* came into existence..... John 8:58
shall we say that *A*..................Rom 4:1
if *A* was declared righteous.........Rom 4:2
A believed God ....Rom 4:3
have the faith of *A* ....Rom 4:16
the blessing of *A* would come ..... Gal 3:14
the promises were spoken to *A* ....Gal 3:16
it is written that *A* had two sons....Gal 4:22
A apportioned a tithe of
  everything........................Heb 7:2
By faith *A* obeyed.................Heb 11:8
A, when he was tested, offered up
  Isaac............................Heb 11:17

Now *A* believed God................Jas 2:23
like Sarah who obeyed *A*..........1 Pet 3:6

ABRAM

See ABRAHAM

ABROAD

to those temporarily residing *a*......1 Pet 1:1

ABRONAH

Israelite encampment, Num 33:34

ABSALOM

Son of David, 2 Sam 3:3
Kills Amnon for raping Tamar; flees from
  David, 2 Sam 13:20–39
Returns through Joab's intrigue; reconciled
  to David, 2 Sam 14
Attempts to usurp throne, 2 Sam 15:1–18:8
Caught and killed by Joab, 2 Sam 18:9–18
Mourned by David, 2 Sam 18:19–19:8

ABSENT

even though I am *a* physically ......1 Cor 5:3
here on earth we are *a* from the
  Lord............................2 Cor 5:6

ABSOLUTE

a darkness throughout the
  land .... Exod 10:22
Surely the king's authority is *a* ..... Eccl 8:4

ABSOLUTELY

See also ABSOLUTELY NOT
We are *a* terrified of you ....Josh 2:9
I have been *a* loyal................1 Kgs 19:10
I *a* hate them ....Ps 139:22
I *a* despise your festivals ....Amos 5:21

ABSOLUTELY NOT

to send us away secretly? *A* ....Acts 16:37
A! Let God be proven true..........Rom 3:4
A! For otherwise how could ....Rom 3:31
A! How can we who died ....Rom 6:2
under law but under grace? *A* .....Rom 6:15
Is the law sin? *A* ....Rom 7:7
Is there injustice with God? *A* .....Rom 9:14
not rejected his people, has he? *A*..Rom 11:1
an irrevocable fall, did they? *A* ....Rom 11:11
then one who encourages sin? *A* ... Gal 2:17
opposed to the promises of God? *A*...Gal 3:21

ABSORBED

a with proclaiming the word ...... Acts 18:5

ABSTAIN

a from things defiled by idols ....Acts 15:20

ABSURDITIES

Avoid the profane chatter and *a*..1 Tim 6:20

ABUNDANCE

seven years of *a* in the land....... Gen 41:53
In the *a* of your majesty ....Exod 15:7
blessings will come to you in *a* ...Deut 28:2
Scatter abroad the *a* of your
  anger........................Job 40:11
A king's glory is the *a* of people ..Prov 14:28
in the *a* of his possessions........Luke 12:15
times of need and times of *a* ....Phil 4:12

ABUNDANT

a righteousness he does not
  oppress........................Job 37:23
you cause *a* showers to fall.........Ps 68:9
your faithfulness is *a* ....Lam 3:23
a shoot by *a* water................Ezek 17:5
a joy and their extreme poverty...2 Cor 8:2
our Lord's grace was *a*.............1 Tim 1:14

ABUNDANTLY

I will *a* supply what she needs...... Ps 132:15
and may have it *a*................John 10:10

ABUSE

subjected Israel to humiliating *a* .. Isa 43:28
discouraged because of their *a* ....Isa 51:7
bearing the *a* he experienced......Heb 13:13

ABUSIVE

or verbally *a*......................1 Cor 5:11
the verbally *a*....................1 Cor 6:10

ABUSIVELY

also spoke *a* to him..............Mark 15:32

ABYSS
the key to the shaft of the *a* . . . . Rev 9:1
angel then threw him into the *a* . . . Rev 20:3

ACACIA
make an ark of *a* wood . . . . Exod 25:10
make a table of *a* wood . . . . Exod 25:23

ACCEPT
a your burnt sacrifice. . . . . .Ps 20:3
a the proper sacrifices. . . . . .Ps 51:19
I will not *a* them . . . . .Jer 14:12
a our penitential prayer . . . . .Hos 14:2
Should I *a* this from you . . . . Mal 1:13
if you are willing to *a* it . . . . Matt 11:14
I do not *a* praise from people. . . . . . John 5:41
you cannot *a* my teaching . . . . John 8:43
whom the world cannot *a* . . . . John 14:17
But do not *a* younger widows . . . . .1 Tim 5:11

ACCEPTABLE
sacrifice it so that it is *a* . . . . Lev 22:29
now is the *a* time . . . . .2 Cor 6:2
spiritual sacrifices that are *a*. . . . . . .1 Pet 2:5

ACCEPTED
for God has *a* him . . . . .Rom 14:3

ACCEPTS
one who *a* reproof is honored. . . . Prov 13:18
chastises every son he *a* . . . . Heb 12:6

ACCESS
we have also obtained *a* . . . . Rom 5:2
a to God by way of Christ's . . . . Eph 3:12
can have *a* to the tree of life . . . . . . Rev 22:14

ACCIDENTALLY
Anyone who *a* killed someone . . . Deut 4:42

ACCOMMODATING
a, full of mercy and good fruit . . . . . . Jas 3:17

ACCOMPANY
will *a* those who believe . . . . Mark 16:17

ACCOMPLISH
right hand will *a* mighty acts . . . . . . .Ps 45:4
and *a* justice on my behalf. . . . . .Mic 7:9
to *a* the deeds God requires. . . . . . John 6:28
apart from me you can *a* nothing . . John 15:5
does not *a* God's righteousness . . . . .Jas 1:20

ACCOMPLISHED
he *a* justice . . . . Ps 9:16
the LORD's purpose will be *a* . . . . . . Isa 53:10

ACCOMPLISHMENTS
known his *a* among the nations . . .1 Chr 16:8
known his *a* among the nations . . . . Ps 105:1

ACCORDING TO THE FLESH
that Abraham, our ancestor *a* . . . . . .Rom 4:1
walk *a* but according to the Spirit . . .Rom 8:4
For those who live *a* . . . . .Rom 8:5
not to the flesh, to live *a*. . . . . .Rom 8:12
for if you live *a*, you will die . . . . . . .Rom 8:13

ACCORDING TO THE LAW
a of his separation. . . . . .Num 6:21
And let it be done *a* . . . . .Ezra 10:3
a of the Medes and Persians . . . . Dan 6:8
time came for their purification *a* . .Luke 2:22
Mary had performed
   everything *a* . . . . Luke 2:39
Ananias, a devout man *a* . . . . .Acts 22:12
Do you sit there and judge me *a*. . .Acts 23:3
a almost everything was purified. . .Heb 9:22
which are offered *a*. . . . . .Heb 10:8

ACCORDING TO THE WORD OF THE LORD
So Moses numbered them *a* . . . . . .Num 3:16
a, as the LORD had commanded . . .Num 3:51
Moses and Aaron numbered *a* . . . Num 4:37
Moses and Aaron numbered *a* . . . Num 4:41
Moses and Aaron numbered *a* . . .Num 4:45
A they were numbered . . . . .Num 4:49

ACCOUNT
a for every worthless word. . . . . . .Matt 12:36
I wrote the former *a*. . . . . .Acts 1:1
give an *a* of himself to God . . . . . . .Rom 14:12
a of the one who was wronged. . .2 Cor 7:12

and his speech is of no *a*. . . . . .2 Cor 10:10
will give an *a* for their work . . . . . .Heb 13:17

ACCOUNTABLE
Hold them *a* for all their sins . . . . . .Ps 69:27
a for the blood of all the
   prophets. .Luke 11:50
the whole world may be held *a*. . . .Rom 3:19
they not be held *a* for it . . . . .2 Tim 4:16

ACCOUNTING
no *a* for sin when there is no law . .Rom 5:13

ACCOUNTS
Do you not recognize their *a* . . . . . Job 21:29

ACCUMULATE
Beware, those who *a* houses . . . . .Isa 5:8
a for yourselves treasures on
   earth . . . . .Matt 6:19
will *a* teachers for themselves. . . . .2 Tim 4:3

ACCUMULATED
moveable property that he had *a* . .Gen 31:18

ACCURATE
an *a* weight is his delight . . . . .Prov 11:1

ACCURSED
you *a*, into the eternal fire. . . . . . . Matt 25:41
who do not know the law are *a* . . .John 7:49
wish that I myself were *a*. . . . . .Rom 9:3

ACCUSATION
filed an *a* against the inhabitants . . .Ezra 4:6
Hear the LORD's *a* . . . . .Mic 6:2
by violence or by false *a*. . . . . .Luke 3:14
not accept an *a* against an elder . . 1 Tim 5:19

ACCUSE
He does not always *a*. . . . . Ps 103:9
a anyone without legitimate
   cause . . . . Prov 3:30
They began to *a* him. . . . . Luke 23:2
will *a* you before the Father . . . . . .John 5:45
thoughts *a* or else defend them . . .Rom 2:15

ACCUSED
a by the chief priests and the
   elders. . . . . .Matt 27:12

ACCUSER
indictment that my *a* had
   written . . . . Job 31:35
with your *a* while on the way. . . . . Matt 5:25
the *a* of our brothers and sisters . .Rev 12:10

ACCUSERS
My *a* will be covered with
   shame . . . . .Ps 109:29
before the accused had met
   his *a* . . . . .Acts 25:16

ACHAIA
Visited by Paul, Acts 18:1, 12
Apollos preaches in, Acts 18:24–28
Gospel proclaimed throughout,
   1 Thess 1:7–8

ACHAN
Sin of, caused Israel's defeat, Josh 7:1–15
Stoned to death, Josh 7:16–25
Sin of, recalled, Josh 22:20

ACHE
in laughter the heart may *a*. . . . . . Prov 14:13

ACHISH
A king of Gath, 1 Sam 21:10–15
David seeks refuge with, 1 Sam 27:1–12
Forced by Philistine lords to expel David,
   1 Sam 29:1–11
Receives Shimei's servants, 1 Kgs 2:39–40

ACHOR, VALLEY OF [or VALLEY OF DISASTER]
Site of Achan's stoning, Josh 7:24–26
On Judah's boundary, Josh 15:7
Promises concerning, Isa 65:10
Also called "Valley of Disaster,"
   Josh 7:24–26

ACHSAH
A daughter of Caleb, 1 Chr 2:49
Given to Othniel, Josh 15:16–19
Given springs of water, Judg 1:12–15

ACKNOWLEDGE
a the greatness of our God . . . . Deut 32:3
and he did not *a* his own . . . . Deut 33:9
A God's power. . . . . .Ps 68:34
A him in all your ways. . . . . .Prov 3:6
they will *a* the LORD's authority . . . .Isa 19:21
I *a* and glorify you . . . . Dan 2:23
destroyed my people by failing
   to *a*. . . . . Hos 4:6
you must not *a* any God but me. . . .Hos 13:4
they did not see fit to *a* God. . . . . . .Rom 1:28
a that what I write to you. . . . . .1 Cor 14:37
we *a* no one from an outward . . . .2 Cor 5:16

ACQUAINTED
and was *a* with illness . . . . .Isa 53:3

ACQUIRE
and *a* property in it. . . . . Gen 34:10
A it before those sitting here . . . . . . Ruth 4:4
let the discerning *a* guidance . . . . . . Prov 1:5
A truth and do not sell it . . . . Prov 23:23
could *a* God's gift with money. . . . Acts 8:20

ACQUIRED
his possessions that he had *a*. . . . . .Gen 36:6
I have also *a* Ruth the Moabite . . . Ruth 4:10
my wife Michal whom I *a*. . . . . 2 Sam 3:14
a his horses from Egypt . . . . .1 Kgs 10:28
a much wisdom and knowledge. . . .Eccl 1:16
Judas *a* a field with the reward . . . . .Acts 1:18

ACQUITS
one who *a* the guilty. . . . . Prov 17:15

ACQUITTED
owner of the ox will be *a* . . . . Exod 21:28
that I had not previously *a*. . . . . .Joel 3:21

ACROSS
do go *a* the Jordan River. . . . . .Deut 12:10

ACT
Be strong and *a* like men . . . . 1 Sam 4:9
It is time for the LORD to *a* . . . . Ps 119:126
and *a*! Don't delay . . . . Dan 9:19
caught in the very *a* of adultery . . . .John 8:4

ACTED
unfaithful and *a* as treacherously . . .Ps 78:57

ACTION
I will spring into *a* . . . . .Ps 12:5
God springs into *a*. . . . . Ps 68:1

ACTIONS
guilt of our rebellious *a* from us. . . Ps 103:12
and unfaithful in their *a* . . . . .Ps 106:39
I consider my *a* . . . . Ps 119:59
I hate all deceitful *a* . . . . .Ps 119:104
in all his *a* and exhibits love . . . . . . .Ps 145:17

ACTIVE
living and *a* and sharper . . . . Heb 4:12

ACTIVITY
appropriate time for every *a* on
   earth . . . . .Eccl 3:1

ACTS
did great and awesome *a*. . . . . 2 Sam 7:23
God *a* in a faithful manner. . . . . . .2 Sam 22:31
whose rebellious *a* are forgiven . . . . .Ps 32:1
will confess my rebellious *a* . . . . .Ps 32:5
wipe away my rebellious *a* . . . . .Ps 51:1
I am aware of my rebellious *a* . . . . . . .Ps 51:3
awesome *a* of deliverance. . . . . .Ps 65:5
mighty *a* of the Sovereign LORD. . . . .Ps 71:16
and tell about your mighty *a* . . . . . . Ps 145:4
the power of your awesome *a*. . . . . .Ps 145:6
his mighty *a* among the nations . . . . .Isa 12:4
your sinful *a* have alienated you. . . . Isa 59:2
tell of the faithful *a* of the LORD. . . . Isa 63:7
all our so-called righteous *a*. . . . . . . Isa 64:6
unfaithful *a* will bring down
   discipline . . . . .Jer 2:19
seen your disgusting *a* of
   worship. . . . . .Jer 13:27
when rebellious *a* are complete . . . Dan 8:23
shameless *a* with men and
   received . . . . .Rom 1:27

ACTUALLY
a delight in the death of the
   wicked...........................Ezek 18:23

ADAM
Creation of, Gen 1:26–27; 2:7
Given dominion over the earth, Gen 1:28–30
Given a wife, Gen 2:18–25
Temptation, fall, and exile from Eden, Gen 3
Children of, Gen 4:1–2; 5:3–4
Transgression results in sin and death,
   Rom 5:12–14
—Last or second Adam, an appellation of
   Christ, Rom 5:14–15; 1 Cor 15:20–24, 45–48

ADD
not *a* a thing to what I command.. Deut 4:2
not *a* to it or subtract from......Deut 12:32
not *a* to his words .... Prov 30:6
by worrying can *a* even one
   hour........................ Matt 6:27
by worrying can *a* an hour....... Luke 12:25
set it aside or *a* anything to it....... Gal 3:15
every effort to *a* to your faith ......2 Pet 1:5

ADDED
was *a* because of transgressions ... Gal 3:19

ADDING
Lord was *a* to their number ....Acts 2:47

ADDRESS
not *a* an older man harshly.........1 Tim 5:1

ADDRESSED
he *a* them from the scriptures..... Acts 17:2

ADDS
and he *a* no sorrow to it........... Prov 10:22
If anyone *a* to them...............Rev 22:18

ADEQUACY
but our *a* is from God ....2 Cor 3:5

ADEQUATE
Not that we are *a* in ourselves......2 Cor 3:5

ADMINISTER
God's servant to *a* punishment....Rom 13:4

ADMINISTRATION
Turn in the account of your *a*......Luke 16:2
the *a* of the fullness of the times ... Eph 1:10

ADMIRATION
will bring *a* and honor.................Isa 4:2

ADMIRE
a you when you see me restore ..Zeph 3:20

ADMIRED
the leading officials I *a* so much..... Ps 16:3

ADMONISH
a the undisciplined .... 1 Thess 5:14
but *a* him as a brother..........2 Thess 3:15

ADMONITION
kept my *a* to endure steadfastly....Rev 3:10

ADONI-ZEDEK
An Amorite king of Jerusalem, Josh 10:1–5
Defeated and slain by Joshua, Josh 10:6–27

ADONIJAH
David's fourth son, 2 Sam 3:2, 4
Attempts to usurp throne, 1 Kgs 1:5–53
Desires Abishag as wife, 1 Kgs 2:13–18
Executed by Solomon, 1 Kgs 2:19–25

ADONIRAM [or HADORAM]
Official under David, Solomon, and
   Rehoboam, 2 Sam 20:24; 1 Kgs 5:14; 12:18
Stoned by angry Israelites, 1 Kgs 12:18
Also called "Hadoram," 2 Chr 10:18

ADOPTION
but you received the Spirit of *a*....Rom 8:15
as we eagerly await our *a*.... Rom 8:23
us to *a* as his legal heirs .... Eph 1:5

ADORNED
a with beautiful stones and
   offerings.....................Luke 21:5
a themselves by being subject......1 Pet 3:5
ready like a bride *a* for her
   husband ....Rev 21:2

ADORNMENT
a must not be with braided hair ...1 Tim 2:9

ADRIFT
a among the dead ....Ps 88:5

ADULLAM
A town of Canaan, Gen 38:1, 12, 20; Josh 12:7,
   15; 15:20, 35
David seeks refuge in caves of,
   1 Sam 23:13–17

ADULT
he is a mature *a* ....John 9:21
But when I became an *a*.......... 1 Cor 13:11

ADULTERER
both the *a* and the adulteress .... Lev 20:10
eye of the *a* watches for the
   twilight ....Job 24:15

ADULTERERS
a, passive homosexual partners ...1 Cor 6:9
sexually immoral people and *a*.... Heb 13:4
A, do you not know that friendship...Jas 4:4

ADULTERESS
mouth of an *a* is like a deep pit...Prov 22:14

ADULTEROUS
Israel's *a* worship of other gods ......Jer 3:8
evil and *a* generation asks for a
   sign.........................Matt 12:39

ADULTERY
You shall not commit *a*.......... Exod 20:14
You must not commit *a* ....Deut 5:18
commits *a* with a woman......... Prov 6:32
a with their neighbors' wives......Jer 29:23
For they have committed *a*.... Ezek 23:37
they are children conceived in *a*.... Hos 2:4
and continually commits *a* ....Hos 3:1
commit *a*, do not let Judah become
   guilty ....Hos 4:15
committed *a* with her in his
   heart .... Matt 5:28
makes her commit *a*.............. Matt 5:32
do not commit *a*...................Matt 19:18
and marries another commits *a*...Mark 10:11
marries someone else
   commits *a*.................Luke 16:18
who had been caught
   committing *a*................John 8:3
eyes, full of *a*, never stop sinning.. 2 Pet 2:14
commit *a* with her into terrible
   suffering....................... Rev 2:22

ADVANCE
make things ready in *a* for him ...Luke 9:52

ADVANCING
was *a* in Judaism beyond many......Gal 1:14

ADVANTAGE
no *a* for humans over animals......Eccl 3:19
to your *a* that I am going away ....John 16:7
Therefore what *a* does the Jew
   have .... Rom 3:1
taking *a* of every opportunity ......Eph 5:16
violate the rights of his brother
   or take *a*...................1 Thess 4:6
for this would be no *a* for you.....Heb 13:17

ADVERSARIES
The LORD shatters his *a* ....1 Sam 2:10
I will seek vengeance against my *a* ..Isa 1:24
of your *a* will be able to
   withstand.....................Luke 21:15

ADVERSARY
might become our *a* in the
   battle.......................1 Sam 29:4
An opposed Israel ....1 Chr 21:1
that *a* of the Jews...................Esth 8:1
will the *a* hurl insults ....Ps 74:10
Give me justice against my *a* ......Luke 18:3
give the *a* no opportunity to vilify..1 Tim 5:14

ADVERSITY
and a relative is born to help in *a*.. Prov 17:17
but in times of *a* consider this......Eccl 7:14
care for orphans and widows in
   their *a* ....Jas 1:27

ADVICE
not follow the *a* of the wicked......... Ps 1:1
You guide me by your wise *a*.......Ps 73:24
and you neglected all my *a*........Prov 1:25
they did not comply with my *a* ....Prov 1:30

ADVISE
a you as I look you in the eye........Ps 32:8
I *a* you to keep up your
   courage.....................Acts 27:22
so as to *a* him?1 Cor 2:16

ADVISER
and is called Wonderful *A* .... Isa 9:6
no one who serves as an *a*......... Isa 41:28

ADVISERS
imprison his officials and to teach
   his *a*........................Ps 105:22

ADVOCATE
my *a* is on high .... Job 16:19
father to the fatherless and an *a* ....Ps 68:5
another *A* to be with you
   forever ....John 14:16
When the *A* comes ....John 15:26
we have an *a* with the Father......1 John 2:1

AENON
A place near Salim where John the Baptist
   baptized, John 3:22–23

AFFECTION
with the *a* of Christ Jesus............Phil 1:8
any *a* or mercy ....Phil 2:1
godliness, brotherly *a*; to
   brotherly *a* ....2 Pet 1:7

AFFIRMATION
this was not done without a
   sworn *a*........................Heb 7:20

AFFLICT
predisposed to *a* or to grieve
   people.........................Lam 3:33

AFFLICTED
Why have you *a* your servant .....Num 11:11
Before I was *a* I used to stray off .. Ps 119:67
All the days of the *a* are bad...... Prov 15:15
he will not be *a* by calamity ......Prov 19:23
and *a* for something he had done .. Isa 53:4
He was treated harshly and *a*........Isa 53:7
the most *a* of all the flock .... Zech 11:7
and to you who are being *a*...... 2 Thess 1:7
they were destitute, *a*, ill-treated..Heb 11:37

AFFLICTION
surely seen the *a* of my people.... Exod 3:7
obligation that would bring *a*.... Num 30:13
as symbolic of *a* ....Deut 16:3
the days of my *a* confront me .....Job 30:27
held captive by the cords of *a* ......Job 36:8
on my *a* because my enemy boasts .. Lam 1:9
despite great *a* ....1 Thess 1:6
that we would suffer *a* ....1 Thess 3:4
repay with *a* those who afflict
   you ....2 Thess 1:6

AFFLICTIONS
no one would be shaken by
   these *a* ....1 Thess 3:3
persecutions and *a* you are
   enduring.....................2 Thess 1:4

AFRAID
See also DO NOT BE AFRAID
and I was *a* because I was naked .. Gen 3:10
Do not be *a*.....................Gen 26:24
surrounding cities were *a* of God.. Gen 35:5
Do not be *a* to go down to Egypt..Gen 46:3
because he was *a* to look at God .. Exod 3:6
Do not be *a* or discouraged........Deut 1:21
do not be *a* of them ....Deut 20:1
Do not be *a* or discouraged........Deut 31:8
a to submit to the Babylonian
   officials..................... 2 Kgs 25:24
David was *a* of God that day and
   said.........................1 Chr 13:12
I am not *a* of the multitude of
   people.......................... Ps 3:6
I am *a* of no one ....Ps 27:1

a when a man becomes rich........Ps 49:16
When I am *a*..........................Ps 56:3
more *a* of disobeying your
    instructions....................Ps 119:161
Don't be *a* of what scares them .....Isa 8:12
do not be *a* of Assyria.............Isa 10:24
Don't be *a*..........................Isa 41:10
Don't be *a*...........................Isa 43:1
Don't be *a*...........................Isa 44:8
Don't be *a* of the insults of men ....Isa 51:7
Why are you *a* of mortal men ......Isa 51:12
Don't be *a*..........................Isa 54:4
not be *a* of those to whom I send
    you...................................Jer 1:8
Don't be *a*.........................Dan 10:19
so *a* that each cried out to his own
    god...............................Jonah 1:5
Do not be *a*.......................Matt 14:27
Do not be *a*.......................Mark 5:36
Do not be *a*........................Luke 1:13
Do not be *a*........................Luke 1:30
do not be *a* of those who kill the
    body.............................Luke 12:4
Do not be *a*......................Luke 12:32
for they were *a* of the people ....Luke 22:2
Do not be *a*.......................Acts 27:24
But be *a* if you do wrong ....Rom 13:4
a of the things you are about to
    suffer.............................Rev 2:10

AFTER
a that he will release you...........Exod 11:1
and chase *a* dry chaff..............Job 13:25
he looks *a* the lowly ....Ps 138:6
a rainbow in the clouds *a* the rain.. Ezek 1:28
what will happen *a* these things... Dan 12:8
Do not go out or chase *a* them ...Luke 17:23

AGAG
A king of Amalek in Balaam's prophecy,
    Num 24:7
—Amalekite king spared by Saul, but slain
    by Samuel, 1 Sam 15:8–9, 20–24, 32–33

AGAIN
and is alive *a*..................... Luke 15:24
to renew them *a* to repentance .... Heb 6:6
to offer himself *a* and *a* ....Heb 9:25

AGAINST
See also SINNED AGAINST THE LORD;
    SINNED AGAINST YOU
will set my face *a* that man........ Lev 20:3
those who rebel *a* the light........Job 24:13
and rebelled *a* the Most High ......Ps 78:17
whoever provokes him sins *a*
    himself .... Prov 20:2
come to set a man *a* his father .. Matt 10:35
kingdom divided *a* itself is
    destroyed ....Matt 12:25
Whoever is not with me is *a* me .. Matt 12:30
a the Spirit will not be forgiven... Matt 12:31
because the wind was *a* it .... Matt 14:24
nation will rise up in arms *a*
    nation ....Matt 24:7
have sinned *a* heaven and *a* you..Luke 15:18
eats my bread has turned *a* me... John 13:18
a the Lord and *a* his Christ ....Acts 4:26
everyone everywhere *a* our
    people.........................Acts 21:28
A hope Abraham believed in
    hope...........................Rom 4:18
our struggle is not *a* flesh and
    blood.............................Eph 6:12
Do not speak *a* one another.........Jas 4:11
But I have this *a* you...............Rev 2:20

AGATE
the third *a* ....Rev 21:19

AGE
See also AGE TO COME
eyes were failing because of his *a*..Gen 48:10
come to your grave in a full *a*.....Job 5:26
in the *a* to come................Mark 10:30
The people of this *a* marry ......Luke 20:34
wisdom of this *a* is foolishness ....1 Cor 3:19
since he loved the present *a*......2 Tim 4:10
and the miracles of the coming *a*... Heb 6:5

AGE TO COME
either in this age or in the *a* .....Matt 12:32
and in the *a* eternal life..........Mark 10:30
and in the *a* eternal life......... Luke 18:30

AGED
wisdom found among the *a* ....Job 12:12
It is not the *a* who are wise.........Job 32:9

AGES
determined before the *a* for our
    glory..............................1 Cor 2:7
at the consummation of the *a*.....Heb 9:26

AGILITY
He gives me the *a* of a deer .... Ps 18:33
He gives me the *a* of a deer ....Hab 3:19

AGING
what is growing obsolete and *a* ... Heb 8:13

AGO
of his holy prophets from long *a* ..Luke 1:70
killed those who foretold long *a*...Acts 7:52
spoke long *a* in various portions .... Heb 1:1

AGONY
when they cried out in *a*...........Judg 2:18
will tremble and writhe in *a* ....Jer 51:29

AGREE
We *a*! Praise the LORD........... 1 Chr 16:36
We *a*! Praise the LORD........... Ps 106:48
if two of you on earth *a* ....Matt 18:19
but their testimony did not *a*....Mark 14:56
And we all *a* ....1 Tim 3:16

AGREED
the people and their leaders had *a*..Jer 34:10

AGREEMENT
with Sheol we have made an *a* .....Isa 28:15
come to the king of the north to
    make an *a* ....Dan 11:6
Reach *a* quickly with your
    accuser .... Matt 5:25
what *a* does Christ have with
    Beliar..........................2 Cor 6:15
what mutual *a* does the temple ..2 Cor 6:16

AHAB
A wicked king of Israel, 1 Kgs 16:29
Marries Jezebel; promotes Baal worship,
    1 Kgs 16:31–33; 18:17–46
Denounced by Elijah, 1 Kgs 17:1
Wars against Ben Hadad, 1 Kgs 20:1–43
Covets Naboth's vineyard, 1 Kgs 21:1–16
Death predicted; repentance delays
    judgment, 1 Kgs 21:17–29
Goes to war in spite of Micaiah's warning;
    killed in battle, 1 Kgs 22:1–37
Prophecy concerning, fulfilled, 1 Kgs 22:38
—Lying prophet, Jer 29:21–23

AHASUERUS
The father of Darius the Mede, Dan 9:1
—Persian king, probably Xerxes I,
    486–465 BC, Ezra 4:6; Esth 1:1
Makes Esther queen, Esth 2:16–17
Orders Jews annihilated, by Haman's advice,
    Esth 3:8–15
Reverses decree at Esther's request,
    Esth 7–8
Exalts Mordecai, Esth 10:1–3

AHAZ
King of Judah; pursues idolatry; submits to
    Assyrian rule; desecrates the temple,
    2 Kgs 16
Defeated by Syria and Israel, 2 Chr 28:5–15
Comforted by Isaiah; refuses to ask a sign,
    Isa 7:1–17

AHAZIAH
King of Israel; son of Ahab and Jezebel;
    worships Baal, 1 Kgs 22:51–53
Falls through lattice; calls on Baal Zebub;
    dies according to Elijah's word,
    2 Kgs 1:2–18
—King of Judah; Ahab's son-in-law; reigns
    wickedly, 2 Kgs 8:25–29; 2 Chr 22:1–6
Killed by Jehu, 2 Kgs 9:27–29; 2 Chr 22:7–9

AHEAD
Go to the village *a* of you..........Matt 21:2
will surely not go *a* of those.... 1 Thess 4:15
who goes on *a* and does not
    remain......................... 2 John 1:9

AHIJAH
A prophet of Shiloh who foretells division
    of Solomon's kingdom, 1 Kgs 11:29–39
Foretells elimination of Jeroboam's line,
    1 Kgs 14:1–18
A writer of prophecy, 2 Chr 9:29

AHIKAM
Sent in Josiah's mission to Huldah,
    2 Kgs 22:12–14
Protects Jeremiah, Jer 26:24
The father of Gedaliah, governor under
    Nebuchadnezzar, 2 Kgs 25:22; Jer 39:14

AHIMAAZ
A son of Zadok the high priest, 1 Chr 6:8–9
Warns David of Absalom's plans,
    2 Sam 15:27, 36
First to tell David of Absalom's defeat,
    2 Sam 18:19–30

AHIMELECH
High priest in Saul's reign; helps David,
    1 Sam 21:1–9
Betrayed and killed by Doeg; son Abiathar
    escapes, 1 Sam 22:9–20
David writes concerning, Ps 52:title

AHINOAM
Wife of David, 1 Sam 25:43; 27:3; 30:5, 18
Mother of Amnon, 2 Sam 3:2

AHITHOPHEL
David's counselor, 2 Sam 15:12
Joins Absalom's insurrection; counsels him,
    2 Sam 15:31; 16:20–23
His counsel rejected; commits suicide,
    2 Sam 17:1–23

AI
Israel defeated at, Josh 7:2–5
Israel destroys completely, Josh 8:1–28

AIJALON
Amorites not driven from, Judg 1:35
Miracle there, Josh 10:12–13
City of refuge, 1 Chr 6:66–69
Fortified by Rehoboam, 2 Chr 11:5, 10
Captured by Philistines, 2 Chr 28:18

AIM
the *a* of our instruction is love......1 Tim 1:5

AIR
and the birds of the *a*.............. Gen 1:26
like one who hits only *a* ....1 Cor 9:26
you will be speaking into the *a* ... 1 Cor 14:9
the ruler of the domain of the *a*..... Eph 2:2
to meet the Lord in the *a*....... 1 Thess 4:17
poured out his bowl into the *a* .... Rev 16:17

ALABASTER
brought an *a* jar of perfumed oil.. Luke 7:37

ALARM
a all the people whom you
    encounter ....Exod 23:27
Its appearance caused *a*...........Dan 2:31
Sound the *a* in Beth Aven .... Hos 5:8

ALARMED
King Herod heard this he was *a* ....Matt 2:3

ALERT
stay *a* because you do not know..Matt 24:42
he would have been *a* ....Matt 24:43
Stay *a*, then......................Mark 13:35
master finds *a* when he returns ..Luke 12:37
But stay *a* at all times .... Luke 21:36
Stay *a*, stand firm in the faith.....1 Cor 16:13
keeping *a* in it with thanksgiving ....Col 4:2
that whether we are *a* or asleep ..1 Thess 5:10
Be sober and *a* ....1 Pet 5:8
Blessed is the one who stays *a* .... Rev 16:15

ALERTED
Then Saul *a* all the land saying ...1 Sam 13:3

ALEXANDER
A member of the high-priestly family,
  Acts 4:6
—A Jew in Ephesus, Acts 19:33–34
—An apostate condemned by Paul,
  1 Tim 1:19–20

ALEXANDRIA
Men of, persecute Stephen, Acts 6:9
Paul sails in ship of, Acts 27:6

ALGUM
and *a* trees from Lebanon........2 Chr 2:8

ALIENATED
who have *a* themselves from me..Ezek 14:5
have been *a* from Christ............Gal 5:4
a from the citizenship of Israel.....Eph 2:12
being *a* from the life of God.......Eph 4:18

ALIKE
another regards them all *a* ....Rom 14:5

ALIVE
went down *a* into the pit .... Num 16:33
are still *a* to this very day.......... Deut 4:4
May they go down *a* into Sheol .... Ps 55:15
my people who are still *a*...........Jer 23:3
they heard that he was *a* ....Mark 16:11
a with many convincing proofs......Acts 1:3
but *a* to God in Christ Jesus .... Rom 6:11
once *a* apart from the law..........Rom 7:9
sin became *a* ....Rom 7:9
a, holy, and pleasing to God .... Rom 12:1
most of whom are still *a*..........1 Cor 15:6
in Christ all will be made *a* ...... 1 Cor 15:22
nevertheless made you *a* with him .. Col 2:13
that we who are *a* .... 1 Thess 4:15
while the one who made it is *a* .... Heb 9:17
but by being made *a* in the spirit . .1 Pet 3:18
now I am *a* .... Rev 1:18
a reputation that you are *a*....... Rev 3:1
thrown *a* into the lake of fire..... Rev 19:20

ALL
See also ALL THE DAYS OF HIS LIFE; ALL
  THE EARTH; ALL THE SAINTS; WITH
  ALL YOUR HEART
curse them at *a* nor bless them ..Num 23:25
A I see are sick and wounded........Jer 6:7
he died to sin once for *a*.......... Rom 6:10
I have *a* I need.....................Phil 4:18
offering himself once for *a* .... Heb 7:27
and he entered once for *a*........ Heb 9:12

ALL THE DAYS OF HIS LIFE
dedicate him to the LORD *a*........1 Sam 1:11
a he is dedicated to the LORD ....1 Sam 1:28
So Samuel led Israel *a*............1 Sam 7:15

ALL THE EARTH
over the cattle, and over *a*........ Gen 1:26
there is no one like me in *a*....... Exod 9:14
Sing to the LORD, *a* ....1 Chr 16:23
A worships you and sings praises....Ps 66:4
one of bronze, will rule in *a* .... Dan 2:39
before the LORD of *a* .... Zech 6:5

ALL THE SAINTS
and your love for *a* .... Eph 1:15
less than the least of *a*............Eph 3:8
be able to comprehend with *a*....... Eph 3:18
perseverance and petitions for *a* .. Eph 6:18
the love that you have for *a* .... Col 1:4
with prayers of *a* ....Rev 8:3

ALL-POWERFUL
who is still to come—the *A* ...... Rev 1:8
the *A*, Who was................... Rev 4:8
the *A*, your judgments are true.... Rev 16:7
the *A*, reigns.......................Rev 19:6
God, the *A*.........................Rev 19:15

ALLEGIANCE
shifted his *a* to other gods.........1 Kgs 11:4
those who swear *a* to the LORD ....Zeph 1:5

ALLEGORY
things may be treated as an *a* ......Gal 4:24

ALLIANCE
a to fight against Joshua and Israel..Josh 9:2

ALLIES
All your *a* have abandoned you.... Jer 30:14

ALLOTMENT
For the LORD's *a* is his people .... Deut 32:9

ALLOW
will not *a* your faithful follower .... Ps 16:10
and *a* to live in your palace courts...Ps 65:4
the Spirit of Jesus did not *a* them...Acts 16:7
I do not *a* woman to teach........1 Tim 2:12

ALLOWED
a to go into the LORD's temple ..... Jer 36:5
unless the Father has *a* him ...... John 6:65
he *a* all the nations to go .... Acts 14:16

ALLOWS
if the Lord *a* ....1 Cor 16:7

ALLURE
in the future I will *a* her ....Hos 2:14

ALMIGHTY
and to Jacob as God *A* .... Exod 6:3
does the *A* pervert what is right..... Job 8:3
find out the perfection of the *A* .....Job 11:7
drink of the anger of the *A* ....Job 21:20
will delight yourself in the *A*......Job 22:26
the breath of the *A* gives me life ...Job 33:4

ALMOND
the *a* blossoms grow white........Eccl 12:5

ALMOST
my feet *a* slipped...................Ps 73:2
a everything was purified.........Heb 9:22

ALOES
a, and cassia........................Ps 45:8
a, and cinnamon....................Prov 7:17
a mixture of myrrh and *a*.........John 19:39

ALONE
for I am *a* and oppressed...........Ps 25:16
city once full of people now sits all *a* .. Lam 1:1
the one that lives *a* in a thicket.....Mic 7:14

ALONG
walking *a* with the great throng .....Ps 42:4
and the grasshopper drags itself *a*.. Eccl 12:5
letting themselves be driven *a* ... Acts 27:17
and led *a* by various passions......2 Tim 3:6

ALOUD
and read it *a* to the people .... Exod 24:7

ALPHA
I am the *A* and the Omega........... Rev 1:8
I am the *A* and the Omega.........Rev 22:13

ALTAR
Noah built an *a* to the LORD ....Gen 8:20
Abram built an *a* there ....Gen 12:7
built an *a* to the LORD ....Gen 13:18
Abraham built the *a* there.........Gen 22:9
Isaac built an *a* there ....Gen 26:25
Make an *a* there to God ....Gen 35:1
Moses built an *a*...................Exod 17:15
make for me an *a* made of earth..Exod 20:24
two sides of the *a* when
  carrying it .... Exod 27:7
the incense *a* of acacia wood.... Exod 37:25
remain on the hearth on the *a*......Lev 6:9
on the *a* to make atonement ....Lev 17:11
was the dedication for the *a*...... Num 7:84
you must build an *a* there .... Deut 27:5
Joshua built an *a* for the LORD.....Josh 8:30
an impressive *a*...................Josh 22:10
and Gadites named the *a*.........Josh 22:34
Baal *a* and cut down the nearby...Judg 6:25
and built an *a* there.............. Judg 21:4
built an *a* to the LORD there .....1 Sam 7:17
Saul built an *a* for the LORD ....1 Sam 14:35
build an *a* for the LORD.........2 Sam 24:18
built an *a* for the LORD there ...2 Sam 24:25
offered sacrifices on the *a*.......1 Kgs 12:33
He cried out against the *a*.........1 Kgs 13:2
a for Baal in the temple of Baal ..1 Kgs 16:32
He repaired the *a* of the LORD...1 Kgs 18:30
Uriah the priest built an *a* ....2 Kgs 16:11
David built there an *a* to the
  LORD ....1 Chr 21:26

He made a bronze *a*.............. 2 Chr 4:1
the gold *a*, the tables ....2 Chr 4:19
He repaired the *a* of the LORD.... 2 Chr 15:8
He erected the *a* of the LORD.....2 Chr 33:16
started to build the *a* of the God ...Ezra 3:2
Then I will go to the *a* of God ....Ps 43:4
taken from the *a* with tongs........ Isa 6:6
will be an *a* for the LORD ....Isa 19:19
The Lord rejected his *a* ....Lam 2:7
the *a* was in front of the temple ..Ezek 40:47
You cover the *a* of the LORD........Mal 2:13
if you bring your gift to the *a*.... Matt 5:23
swears by the *a* is bound by
  nothing...................... Matt 23:18
found an *a* with this inscription...Acts 17:23
and those who serve at the *a*......1 Cor 9:13
the sacrifices partners in the *a* ...1 Cor 10:18
We have an *a* that those who
  serve ....Heb 13:10
he offered Isaac his son on the *a* ....Jas 2:21
I saw under the *a* the souls....... Rev 6:9
and was stationed at the *a*.......Rev 8:3
the golden *a* that is before God ....Rev 9:13
came from the *a* and called ....Rev 14:18

ALTARS
eliminated his high places and a.. 2 Kgs 18:22
the LORD's high places and *a* ....2 Chr 32:12
protect her young near your *a* ......Ps 84:3
point on the horns of their *a* .... Jer 17:1
Your *a* will be ruined .... Ezek 6:4
has built many *a* for sin offerings...Hos 8:11
their *a* will be like stones.......... Hos 12:11
I will destroy Bethel's *a*..........Amos 3:14
they have demolished your *a*..... Rom 11:3

ALWAYS
you will *a* have the poor..........Matt 26:11
I am with you *a*...................Matt 28:20
you are *a* with me ....Luke 15:31
a pray and not lose heart..........Luke 18:1
A be outstanding in the work.... 1 Cor 15:58
Rejoice in the Lord *a* .... Phil 4:4
we will *a* be with the Lord...... 1 Thess 4:17
a be ready to give an answer ......1 Pet 3:15

AM
See also HERE I AM; I AM WITH YOU
said to Moses, "I *A* that I *A* ....Exod 3:14
I *a* the first and I *a* the last.......... Isa 44:6
in my name, I *a* there............. Matt 18:20
I *a* the bread of life ....John 6:35
I *a* the light of the world..........John 8:14
I *a* from above....................John 8:23
came into existence, I *a*...........John 8:58
I *a* the door......................John 10:9
I *a* the good shepherd ....John 10:11
I *a* the resurrection and the ......John 11:25
I *a* the way, and the truth.........John 14:6
grace of God I *a* what I *a* ....1 Cor 15:10

AMALEK
Grandson of Esau, Gen 36:11–12
A chief of Edom, Gen 36:16
First among nations, Num 24:20

AMALEKITES
Destruction predicted, Exod 17:14;
  Deut 25:17–19
Defeated by Israel, Exod 17:8–13;
  Judg 7:12–25; 1 Sam 14:47–48; 28:7–9;
  1 Chr 4:42–43
Overcome Israel, Num 14:39–45; Judg 3:13

AMASA
Commands Absalom's rebels, 2 Sam 17:25
Made David's commander, 2 Sam 19:13
Treacherously killed by Joab, 2 Sam 20:9–12
Death avenged, 1 Kgs 2:28–34

AMASSING
he gives the task of *a* wealth ...... Eccl 2:26

AMAZED
in the LORD's temple, she was *a* ..2 Chr 9:4
and are *a* at his rebuke.............Job 26:11
Be *a* at this ....Jer 2:12
crowds were *a* by his teaching ... Matt 7:28
Jesus heard this he was *a*......... Matt 8:10

The crowds were *a* and said . . . . . . Matt 9:33
All the crowds were *a* and said . . . Matt 12:23
so that the governor was quite *a* . . . Matt 27:14
he was *a* because of their unbelief . . Mark 6:6
so that Pilate was *a* . . . . Mark 15:5
were *a* at what was said about
   him . . . . Luke 2:33
some women of our
   group *a* us . . . . Luke 24:22
it (because of their joy) and
   were *a* . . . . Luke 24:41
not be *a* that I said to you . . . . John 3:7
Do not be *a* at this . . . . John 5:28
why are you *a* at this . . . . Acts 3:12
that were occurring, he was *a* . . . . . Acts 8:13

AMAZEMENT
world followed the beast in *a* . . . . . . Rev 13:3

AMAZIAH
King of Judah; kills his father's
   assassinators, 2 Kgs 14:1–6; 2 Chr 25:1–4
Hires troops from Israel; is rebuked by
   a man of God; sends troops home,
   2 Chr 25:5–10
Defeats Edomites; worships their gods,
   2 Chr 25:11–16
Wars with Israel, 2 Kgs 14:8–14;
   2 Chr 25:17–24
Killed by conspirators, 2 Chr 25:25–28

AMAZING
We consider it *a* . . . . Ps 118:23
your deeds are awesome and *a* . . . . Ps 139:14
our religion contains *a* revelation . . 1 Tim 3:16

AMBASSADOR
for which I am an *a* in chains . . . . . . Eph 6:20

AMBASSADORS
Therefore we are *a* for Christ . . . . 2 Cor 5:20

AMBITION
motivated by selfish *a* or vanity . . . . . Phil 2:3

AMBUSH
Set an *a* behind the city . . . . Josh 8:2
So Israel hid men in *a* . . . . Judg 20:29
waiting in *a* to take my life . . . . . . 1 Sam 24:11
wicked set an *a* for the godly . . . . Ps 37:32
Paul's sister heard about the *a* . . . Acts 23:16
planning an *a* to kill him . . . . Acts 25:3

AMBUSHED
and *a* the surprised army . . . . Judg 8:11

AMEN
the woman must say, "A amen . . . Num 5:22
all the people will say, 'A . . . . Deut 27:15
say "A" to your thanksgiving . . . . . 1 Cor 14:16
through him the "A" is spoken . . . 2 Cor 1:20
solemn pronouncement of the A . . . Rev 3:14
four living creatures were saying "A . . Rev 5:14
A! Come, Lord Jesus . . . . Rev 22:20

AMENDS
and how can I make *a* . . . . 2 Sam 21:3

AMETHYST
a jacinth, an agate, and an *a* . . . . . Exod 28:19
and the twelfth *a* . . . . Rev 21:20

AMMON
A nation fathered by Lot, Gen 19:36, 38

AMMONITES
Excluded from assembly for hostility to
   Israel, Deut 23:3–6
Propose cruel treaty; conquered by Saul,
   1 Sam 11:1–3, 11
Abuse David's ambassadors; conquered by
   his army, 2 Sam 10:1–14
Harass postexilic Jews, Neh 4:3, 7–8
Defeated by Israel and Judah, Judg 11:4–33;
   2 Chr 20:1–25; 27:5–6
Prophecies concerning, Ps 83:1–18;
   Jer 25:9–21; Ezek 25:1–7; Amos 1:13–15;
   Zeph 2:9–11

AMNON
A son of David, 2 Sam 3:2
Rapes his half sister, 2 Sam 13:1–18
Killed by Absalom, 2 Sam 13:19–29

AMON
King of Judah, 2 Kgs 21:18–19
Follows evil, 2 Chr 33:22–23
Killed by conspiracy, 2 Kgs 21:23–24
—A governor of Samaria, 1 Kgs 22:10, 26

AMONG
I am there *a* them . . . . Matt 18:20

AMORITES
Defeated by Joshua, Josh 10:1–43
Not driven out of Canaan, Judg 1:34–36
Put to forced labor under Solomon,
   1 Kgs 9:20–21

AMOS
A prophet of Israel, Amos 1:1
Pronounces judgment against nations,
   Amos 1:1–3, 15
Denounces Israel's sins, Amos 4:1–7:9
Condemns Amaziah, the priest of Bethel,
   Amos 7:10–17
Predicts Israel's downfall, Amos 9:1–10
Foretells great blessings, Amos 9:11–15

AMPHIPOLIS
A city in Macedonia visited by Paul, Acts 17:1

AMRAM
Son of Kohath, Num 3:17–19
The father of Aaron, Moses, and Miriam,
   Exod 6:18–20; 1 Chr 6:3

AMULETS
sashes, sachets, *a* . . . . Isa 3:20

ANANIAS
Disciple at Jerusalem; slain for lying to God,
   Acts 5:1–11
—A Christian disciple at Damascus,
   Acts 9:10–19; 22:12–16
—A Jewish high priest, Acts 23:1–5

ANATHOTH
A Levitical city in Benjamin, Josh 21:18
Jeremiah's birthplace; he buys property
   there, Jer 1:1; 32:6–15
To be invaded by Assyria, Isa 10:30

ANCESTORS
promised to give to your *a* . . . . Deut 1:8
the God of your *a* . . . . Deut 1:11
In you our *a* trusted . . . . Ps 22:4
just as all my *a* were . . . . Ps 39:12
our *a* have told us what you did . . . . . Ps 44:1
our *a* to make his deeds known . . . . . Ps 78:5
in the sight of their *a* . . . . Ps 78:12
We have sinned like our *a* . . . . Ps 106:6
your *a* as a lasting possession . . . . Jer 7:7
and the iniquities of our *a* . . . . Dan 9:16
for their *a* did the same things . . . Luke 6:26
Our *a* ate the manna . . . . John 6:31
and was cruel to our *a* . . . . Acts 7:19
a yoke that neither our *a* nor we . . Acts 15:10
clear conscience as my *a* did . . . . . . 2 Tim 1:3

ANCHOR
this hope as an *a* for the soul . . . . . . Heb 6:19

ANCIENT
Remember the *a* days . . . . Deut 32:7
Do not move an *a* boundary stone . . Isa 37:26
until the A of Days arrived . . . . Dan 7:22

ANDREW
A disciple of John the Baptist, then of
   Christ, Matt 4:18–19; John 1:40–42
Among the Twelve, Matt 10:2
Mentioned, Mark 13:3–4; John 6:8–9;
   12:20–22; Acts 1:13

ANEW
You have been born *a* . . . . 1 Pet 1:23

ANGEL
See also ANGEL OF GOD; ANGEL OF THE
   LORD
a of the Lord found Hagar . . . . Gen 16:7
the *a* who has protected me . . . . . . Gen 48:16
going to send an *a* before you . . . Exod 23:20
donkey saw the *a* of the Lord . . . Num 22:23
that it was the *a* of the Lord . . . . . . Judg 6:22
Manoah said to the *a* of the Lord . . . Judg 13:17

as reliable as the *a* of God . . . . 1 Sam 29:9
mounted a winged *a* and flew . . . 2 Sam 22:11
When the *a* extended his hand . . 2 Sam 24:16
the *a* of the Lord went out . . . . . . 2 Kgs 19:35
mounted a winged *a* and flew . . . . . . Ps 18:10
struggled with an *a* and prevailed . . Hos 12:4
as he stood there before the *a* . . . . . Zech 3:3
like the *a* of the Lord before
   them . . . . Zech 12:8
an *a* of the Lord appeared . . . . Matt 1:20
an *a* of the Lord descending . . . . . . Matt 28:2
An *a* of the Lord . . . . Luke 1:11
An *a* of the Lord appeared to
   them . . . . Luke 2:9
Then an *a* from heaven
   appeared . . . . Luke 22:43
that an *a* had spoken to him . . . . . . John 12:29
an *a* of the Lord opened the
   doors . . . . Acts 5:19
the *a* who appeared to him . . . . Acts 7:35
an *a* of the Lord struck Herod . . . . Acts 12:23
or *a*, or spirit . . . . Acts 23:8
a spirit or an *a* has spoken . . . . Acts 23:9
last night an *a* of the God . . . . Acts 27:23
killed by the destroying *a* . . . . 1 Cor 10:10
Satan disguises himself as an *a* . . . 2 Cor 11:14
an *a* from heaven . . . . Gal 1:8
a proclaiming in a loud voice . . . . Rev 5:2
king over them the *a* of the abyss . . Rev 9:11
one *a* standing in the sun . . . . Rev 19:17
have sent my *a* to testify . . . . Rev 22:16

ANGEL OF GOD
The *a* called to Hagar . . . . Gen 21:17
In the dream the *a* said to me . . . . . Gen 31:11
The *a*, who was going before . . . . Exod 14:19
you are as reliable as the *a* . . . . . . 1 Sam 29:9
saw clearly in a vision an *a* . . . . Acts 10:3
as though I were an *a* . . . . Gal 4:14

ANGEL OF THE LORD
The *a* found Hagar near . . . . Gen 16:7
The *a* called to Abraham . . . . Gen 22:15
The *a* appeared to him in a flame . . Exod 3:2
And the donkey saw the *a* . . . . . . Num 22:23
The *a* went up from Gilgal . . . . Judg 2:1
The *a* appeared and said . . . . Judg 6:12
The *a* appeared to the woman . . . . . Judg 13:3
the *a* was near the threshing . . . 2 Sam 24:16
But the *a* told Elijah . . . . 2 Kgs 1:3
the *a* went out and killed . . . . 2 Kgs 19:35
the *a* will destroy throughout . . . . 1 Chr 21:12
The *a* camps around . . . . Ps 34:7
As the *a* chases them . . . . Ps 35:6
riders then agreed with the *a* . . . . . Zech 1:11
high priest standing before the *a* . . . Zech 3:1
like the *a* before them . . . . Zech 12:8
an *a* appeared to him . . . . Matt 1:20
an *a* descending from heaven . . . . Matt 28:2
An *a*, standing on the right . . . . Luke 1:11
an *a* opened the doors . . . . Acts 5:19
Then an *a* said to Philip . . . . Acts 8:26
Suddenly an *a* appeared . . . . Acts 12:7
an *a* struck Herod down . . . . Acts 12:23

ANGELS
and attributes folly to his *a* . . . . Job 4:18
order his *a* to protect you . . . . Ps 91:11
Praise him, all his *a* . . . . Ps 148:2
command his *a* concerning you . . . Matt 4:6
A will come and separate . . . . Matt 13:49
a in heaven always see the face . . Matt 18:10
but are like *a* in heaven . . . . Matt 22:30
even the *a* in heaven . . . . Matt 24:36
and all the *a* with him . . . . Matt 25:31
more than 12 legions of *a* . . . . Matt 26:53
joy in the presence of God's *a* . . . Luke 15:10
carried by the *a* to Abraham's
   side . . . . Luke 16:22
equal to *a* and are sons of God . . Luke 20:36
And she saw two *a* in white . . . . . . John 20:12
not know that we will judge *a* . . . . . 1 Cor 6:3
because of the *a* . . . . 1 Cor 11:10
false humility and the worship of *a* . . Col 2:18
from heaven with his mighty *a* . . 2 Thess 1:7
vindicated by the Spirit, seen by *a* . . 1 Tim 3:16
became so far better than the *a* . . . . Heb 1:4

surely his concern is not for *a* ..... Heb 2:16
and to myriads of *a* .... Heb 12:22
entertained *a* without knowing. ....Heb 13:2
a long to catch a glimpse .... 1 Pet 1:12
did not spare the *a* who sinned.... 2 Pet 2:4
a who did not keep within.......... Jude 1:6
a fought against the dragon .... Rev 12:7

ANGER
See also SLOW TO ANGER
Cursed be their *a* .... Gen 49:7
so that the fierce *a* of the LORD .. Num 25:4
relent from his intense *a* .... Deut 13:17
heated display of *a* all about. ....Deut 29:24
and *a* slays the silly one .... Job 5:2
his *a* lasts only a brief moment...... Ps 30:5
turned on us in your *a* .... Ps 60:1
your raging *a* overtake them ...... Ps 69:24
can withstand your intense *a*....... Ps 76:7
He often holds back his *a*.......... Ps 78:38
He sent his *a* in full force .... Ps 78:50
Your *a* overwhelms me............. Ps 88:16
Will your *a* continue to burn ...... Ps 89:46
fathom the intensity of your *a*...... Ps 90:11
So I made a vow in my *a*............. Ps 95:11
in the day he unleashes his *a* ...... Ps 110:5
with great *a* bears the penalty.... Prov 19:19
for *a* resides in the lap of fools ..... Eccl 7:9
his *a* does not subside .... Isa 5:25
your *a* subsided .... Isa 12:1
left in a stupor by the LORD's *a* .. Isa 51:20
In a burst of *a* I rejected you........ Isa 54:8
I struck you down in my *a*.......... Isa 60:10
my raging *a* drove me on........... Isa 63:5
with *a* at what they had done....... Jer 15:17
to bring great *a* and wrath......... Jer 36:7
will release my *a* against you....... Ezek 7:3
No one can resist his fierce *a*....... Nah 1:6
looking around at them in *a*...... Mark 3:5
intense *a*, selfish ambition....... 2 Cor 12:20
on the cause of your *a*............. Eph 4:26
a, wrath, quarreling................. Eph 4:31
lifting up holy hands without *a*.... 1 Tim 2:8
not prone to *a*...................... Titus 1:7
As I swore in my *a*.................. Heb 3:11
without fearing the king's *a* ...... Heb 11:27
human *a* does not accomplish...... Jas 1:20
He is filled with terrible *a* .... Rev 12:12
in them God's *a* is completed....... Rev 15:1

ANGER OF THE LORD
The *a* flared up against Israel..... Num 25:3
Then the *a* will erupt against ...... Deut 7:4
the *a* of Heaven's Armies........... Isa 9:19
The *a* will not turn back........... Jer 30:24
your lives from the fierce *a*........ Jer 51:45

ANGERED
it is not easily *a* or resentful....... 1 Cor 13:5

ANGRILY
Then he *a* speaks to them .... Ps 2:5
a cudgel with which I *a* punish....... Isa 10:5

ANGRY
Why are you *a*...................... Gen 4:6
May the Lord not be *a*............. Gen 18:30
became very *a*...................... Job 32:2
Otherwise he will be *a*.............. Ps 2:12
he is *a* throughout the day .... Ps 7:11
Will you stay *a* forever .... Ps 79:5
a throughout future generations .... Ps 85:5
you are *a* with your chosen king ... Ps 89:38
one against whom the LORD is *a* .. Prov 22:14
not make friends with an *a*
    person....................... Prov 22:24
gossiping tongue brings forth
    an *a*...................... Prov 25:23
An *a* person stirs up dissension.. Prov 29:22
the people with whom I was *a*....... Isa 10:6
I am not *a*......................... Isa 27:4
LORD is *a* at all the nations .... Isa 34:2
I was *a* at my people................ Isa 47:6
hostile forever or perpetually *a* .... Isa 57:16
a because of their sinful greed ..... Isa 57:17
will not always be *a* with me .... Jer 3:5
prayers to Baal have made me *a* ..Hos 7:16
Are you really so very *a* .... Jonah 4:4

Who does not stay *a* forever .... Mic 7:18
very *a* with your ancestors .... Zech 1:2
anyone who is *a* with a brother... Matt 5:22
they were *a* with the two
    brothers.................... Matt 20:24
Be *a* and do not sin .... Eph 4:26

ANGUISH
the queen was overcome with *a*.... Esth 4:4
Distress and *a* terrify him .... Job 15:24
continually suffer such painful *a*.... Jer 15:18
because I am in *a* in this fire..... Luke 16:24
in his *a* he prayed more
    earnestly .... Luke 22:44
great distress and *a* of heart....... 2 Cor 2:4
a righteous man in *a*............... 2 Pet 2:7

ANIMAL
of every kind of clean *a*............. Gen 7:2
say that a wild *a* ate him..........Gen 37:20
One who beats an *a* .... Lev 24:18
I was as senseless as an *a*.......... Ps 73:22
cares for the life of his *a*.......... Prov 12:10
put him on his own *a* .... Luke 10:34
even an *a* touches the mountain.. Heb 12:20

ANIMALS
They are like *a* that perish.......... Ps 49:12
fattened *a* as burnt sacrifices........ Ps 66:15
He gives food to the *a*........... Ps 147:9
and wild *a* will live there.......... Isa 34:11
four-footed *a* and reptiles .... Acts 10:12
or four-footed *a* or reptiles........ Rom 1:23
like irrational *a* .... Jude 1:10

ANNA
Aged prophet, Luke 2:36–38

ANNAS
A Jewish high priest, Luke 3:2
Christ appeared before, John 18:12–24
Peter and John appeared before, Acts 4:6

ANNIHILATED
kings of Assyria have *a* all lands.. 2 Kgs 19:11

ANNOUNCE
I will *a* the LORD's decree............. Ps 2:7
to *a* the year when the LORD .... Isa 61:2
A to the surrounding nations........ Jer 4:16
see delusion and *a* lying omens ... Ezek 13:9
prominent men *a* what they wish ... Mic 7:3
he began to *a* it publicly .... Mark 1:45
seen and heard we *a* to you too ... 1 John 1:3

ANNOUNCED
spoken about and *a* these days.... Acts 3:24
after the baptism that John *a* ..... Acts 10:37

ANNOUNCES
a messenger who *a* peace .... Isa 52:7
one who *a* it may read it........... Hab 2:2

ANNOUNCING
a in Jesus the resurrection......... Acts 4:2

ANOINT
a them and ordain them........ Exod 28:41
not *a* yourself with olive oil .....Deut 28:40
You will *a* for me the one.........1 Sam 16:3
Don't *a* yourself with oil.......... 2 Sam 14:2
and to *a* a Most Holy Place........ Dan 9:24
a your head and wash your face... Matt 6:17
so that they might go and *a* him... Mark 16:1
pray for him and *a* him .... Jas 5:14

ANOINTED
See also LORD'S ANOINTED
priest who is *a* and ordained ......Lev 16:32
to destroy the LORD's *a*............ 2 Sam 1:14
he cursed the LORD's *a* .... 2 Sam 19:21
These are the two *a* ones......... Zech 4:14
a my body beforehand for burial.. Mark 14:8
has *a* me to proclaim good news.. Luke 4:18
has *a* my feet with perfumed oil.. Luke 7:46
it was Mary who *a* the Lord......John 11:2
holy servant Jesus, whom you *a*.... Acts 4:27
with you in Christ and who *a* us ... 2 Cor 1:21

ANOINTING
He made the sacred *a* oil........Exod 37:29
have an *a* from the Holy One.... 1 John 2:20
the *a* that you received from him... 1 John 2:27

ANOTHER
See also LOVE ONE ANOTHER
not offer false testimony
    against *a*.................... Deut 5:20
Speak the truth, each of you, to
    one *a* .... Zech 8:16
who call out to one *a*............. Matt 11:16
One sows and *a* reaps............John 4:37
you also are to love one *a* ...... John 13:34
he will give you *a* Advocate ...... John 14:16
Let *a* take his position............. Acts 1:20

ANOTHER'S
mutually comforted by one *a* faith .. Rom 1:12

ANSWER
a him one time in a thousand .... Job 9:3
and I will *a* .... Job 13:22
a me, O God who vindicates me...... Ps 4:1
and he will *a* your prayers........... Ps 37:4
quickly *a* me....................... Ps 102:2
faithfulness and justice, *a* me........ Ps 143:1
has joy in giving an appropriate *a*.. Prov 15:23
who gives an *a* before he listens... Prov 18:13
the one who gives an honest *a* .. Prov 24:26
not *a* a fool according to his folly.. Prov 26:4
How have I wearied you? *A* me...... Mic 6:3
be able to *a* those who take
    pride....................... 2 Cor 5:12
know how you should *a* everyone ...Col 4:6
always be ready to give an *a*....... 1 Pet 3:15

ANSWERED
God *a* Manoah's prayer............. Judg 13:9

ANSWERS
but a rich man *a* harshly..........Prov 18:23

ANT
Go to the *a* .... Prov 6:6

ANTICHRIST
you heard that the *a* is coming ...1 John 2:18
This one is the *a* .... 1 John 2:22
and this is the spirit of the *a*...... 1 John 4:3
person is the deceiver and the *a*... 2 John 1:7

ANTICIPATE
My eyes *a* the nighttime hours ... Ps 119:148

ANTICIPATION
the people were filled with *a* ......Luke 3:15

ANTIOCH
—In Syria:
First Gentile church established, Acts 11:19–21
Disciples first called "Christians" in, Acts 11:26
Church commissions Paul, Acts 13:1–4;
    15:35–41
Church troubled by Judaizers, Acts 15:1–4;
    Gal 2:11–21
—In Pisidia:
Paul visits; Jews reject the gospel, Acts 13:14,
    42–51

ANTIPATRIS
A city between Jerusalem and Caesarea,
    Acts 23:31

ANXIETY
A in a person's heart weighs......Prov 12:25
will eat their bread with *a* .... Ezek 12:19
and I can be free from *a* .... Phil 2:28

ANXIOUS
LORD will give you an *a* heart.... Deut 28:65
dispelled for those who were *a*....... Isa 9:1
Do not be *a* about anything .... Phil 4:6

ANY
turned back to me with *a* sincerity .. Jer 3:10
there are not *a* of them remaining .. Jer 49:1

ANYONE
I did not tell *a* what my God....... Neh 2:12
Do not repay *a* evil for evil .... Rom 12:17

ANYTHING
but you could not see *a*...........Deut 4:12
rather than doing *a* you please.....Isa 58:13
not aware of *a* against myself ..... 1 Cor 4:4
Do not be anxious about *a* .... Phil 4:6
not deficient in *a* .... Jas 1:4

APART

See also SET APART
Set *a* to me every firstborn male .. Exod 13:2
I set *a* for myself all the firstborn .. Num 3:13
the one whom the Father set *a*..John 10:36
set *a* for the gospel of God..........Rom 1:1
by faith *a* from the works of the
   law .... Rom 3:28
The sky was split *a* like a scroll.....Rev 6:14

APHEK

A town in the Plain of Sharon, Josh 12:18
Site of Philistine camp, 1 Sam 4:1; 29:1
—A city in Jezreel, 1 Kgs 20:26–30
Syria's defeat prophesied here, 2 Kgs 13:14–19

APOLLONIA

A town between Amphipolis and
   Thessalonica, Acts 17:1

APOLLOS

An Alexandrian Jew; instructed by Aquila and
   Priscilla and sent to Achaia, Acts 18:24–28
Referred to as having ministered in Corinth,
   1 Cor 1:12; 3:4, 22; 4:6; 16:12

APOLLYON

Angel of the abyss, Rev 9:11

APOSTASY

and then have committed *a* .... Heb 6:6

APOSTLE

called to be an *a*......................Rom 1:1
I am an *a* to the Gentiles ....Rom 11:13
Am I not an *a*.......................1 Cor 9:1
the signs of an *a* were performed..2 Cor 12:12
I was appointed a preacher and *a*..1 Tim 2:7
a and high priest whom we confess..Heb 3:1

APOSTLES

See also TWELVE APOSTLES
these are the names of the 12 *a*....Matt 10:2
whom he also named *a*...........Luke 6:13
God has exhibited us *a* last of all .. 1 Cor 4:9
For I am the least of the *a* ....1 Cor 15:9
For such people are false *a* ....2 Cor 11:13
none of the other *a* except James ...Gal 1:19
And he himself gave some as *a*.....Eph 4:11
who refer to themselves as *a*........Rev 2:2
and you saints and *a* and
   prophets................... Rev 18:20

APOSTLESHIP

a from which Judas turned aside .. Acts 1:25
have received grace and our *a* .... Rom 1:5
confirming sign of my *a* ....1 Cor 9:2
empowered Peter for his *a* ....Gal 2:8

APPALLED

Many are *a* when they see me........Ps 71:7

APPEAL

I *a* to Caesar .... Acts 25:11
but *a* to him as a father............1 Tim 5:1
rather *a* to you on the basis of
   love............................. Phlm 1:9

APPEAR

to one place and let dry ground *a* ...Gen 1:9
will *a* before the Sovereign
   LORD ....Exod 23:17
when all Israel comes to *a*........ Deut 31:11
Why do you *a* to be depressed ..... Neh 2:2
to go and *a* in God's presence ....Ps 42:2
splendor will again *a* in our land.....Ps 85:9
false prophets will *a* and
   perform........................Matt 24:24
kingdom of God was going to *a* .. Luke 19:11
all *a* before the judgment seat.....2 Cor 5:10
he will *a* a second time ....Heb 9:28

APPEARANCE

impressed by his *a* or his height ..1 Sam 16:7
wisdom brightens his *a* and softens.. Eccl 8:1
His *a* is like Lebanon.............Song 5:15
no special *a* that we should want....Isa 53:2
Now their *a* is darker than soot ....Lam 4:8
judge correctly the *a* of the sky....Matt 16:3
His *a* was like lightning...........Matt 28:3
the *a* of his face was
   transformed................Luke 9:29

not judge according to external *a* .. John 7:24
who take pride in outward *a* .....2 Cor 5:12
they have the *a* of wisdom ....Col 2:23
maintain the outward *a* of
   religion.........................2 Tim 3:5

APPEARANCES

You people judge by outward *a* ...John 8:15
You are looking at outward *a*.....2 Cor 10:7

APPEARED

See also LORD APPEARED TO
and they *a* before God.............Josh 24:1
side of the altar of incense, *a*.......Luke 1:11
They *a* in glorious splendor........Luke 9:31
For the grace of God has *a* ....Titus 2:11
But now he has *a* once for all......Heb 9:26

APPEARING

the *a* of our Lord Jesus Christ ....1 Tim 6:14
the *a* of our Savior Christ Jesus...2 Tim 1:10
and by his *a* and his kingdom......2 Tim 4:1
set their affection on his *a*........ 2 Tim 4:8
glorious *a* of our great God.......Titus 2:13

APPEARS

can keep standing when he *a*........Mal 3:2
a, then you too will be revealed .....Col 3:4
and glorify God when he *a* ....1 Pet 2:12
Then when the Chief Shepherd *a* ...1 Pet 5:4
when he *a* we may have
   confidence....................1 John 2:28

APPEASED

love and truth iniquity is *a*.........Prov 16:6

APPETITE

and satisfy the *a* of the lions.......Job 38:39
if you possess a large *a* ....Prov 23:2
whose *a* is satisfied loathes honey..Prov 27:7

APPLE

Like an *a* tree among the trees.... Song 2:3

APPLES

Like *a* of gold in settings of silver .. Prov 25:11
refresh me with *a*.................. Song 2:5

APPLY

and *a* it for your own good ....Job 5:27

APPOINT

and *a* each man to his service .... Num 4:19
now *a* over us a king to lead us....1 Sam 8:5
and to *a* elders in every town.......Titus 1:5

APPOINTED

See also APPOINTED FEASTS; APPOINTED
   TIME
a Joseph overseer of his
   household......................Gen 39:4
and *a* me as leader over .... 2 Sam 6:21
a you to be a prophet to the nations ...Jer 1:5
I have *a* you a watchman ....Ezek 3:17
was *a* the Son-of-God-in-power ....Rom 1:4
just as people are *a* to die once....Heb 9:27
and has *a* us as a kingdom...........Rev 1:6

APPOINTED FEASTS

sheep of Jerusalem during her *a*...Ezek 36:38
all the *a* of the house of Israel....Ezek 45:17
before the LORD at the *a* .... Ezek 46:9
At the festivals and at the *a* .....Ezek 46:11

APPOINTED TIME

observe the Passover at its *a* ...... Num 9:2
until the completion of the *a* ...2 Sam 24:15
the vision pertains to the *a* .... Dan 8:19
there is still an end at the *a* ....Dan 11:27
God's purpose at his *a*.............1 Tim 2:6

APPOINTS

LORD *a* as rulers over you ....Jer 13:21

APPORTIONED

Abraham *a* a tithe of everything.... Heb 7:2

APPRECIATE

failed to *a* your miraculous deeds ..Ps 106:7

APPRECIATION

expressed his *a* to all the
   Levites.....................2 Chr 30:22

APPROACH

is to *a* any close relative...........Lev 18:6
all people *a* you ....Ps 65:2

APPROACHING

wicked *a* and entering the temple.. Eccl 8:10

APPROPRIATE

which you have announced is *a* .. 2 Kgs 20:19
a for the king to provide............Esth 3:8
Luxury is not *a* for a fool ....Prov 19:10
But when the *a* time had come......Gal 4:4

APPROVAL

trying to gain the *a* of people....... Gal 1:10

APPROVE

those who *a* of their philosophy....Ps 49:13
a of those who practice them .....Rom 1:32
and *a* the superior things..........Rom 2:18
test and *a* what is the will of God..Rom 12:2

APPROVED

an *a* stone .... Isa 28:16
pleasing to God and *a* by people...Rom 14:18
just as we have been *a* by God ..1 Thess 2:4

APRONS

or *a* that had touched his body ... Acts 19:12

AQUILA

Paul's host in Corinth, Acts 18:2–3
Travels to Syria and Ephesus with Paul,
   Acts 18:18–19
Instructs Apollos, Acts 18:24–26
Esteemed by Paul, Rom 16:3–4

AR

A chief Moabite city, Num 21:15
On Israel's route, Deut 2:18
Destroyed by Sihon, Num 21:28
Destroyed by God, Isa 15:1

ARABIA

Pays tribute to Solomon, 1 Kgs 10:14–15
Plunders Jerusalem, 2 Chr 21:16–17
Defeated by Uzziah, 2 Chr 26:1, 7
Denounced by prophets, Isa 21:13–17

ARAM NAHARAIM

See MESOPOTAMIA

ARAMEANS

Abraham's kindred, Gen 22:20–23; 25:20
Hostile to Israel, 2 Sam 8:11–13; 10:6–19;
   1 Kgs 20:1–34; 22:1–38; 2 Kgs 6:8–7:7
Defeated by Assyria, 2 Kgs 16:9
Destruction of, foretold, Isa 17:1–3
Gospel preached to, Acts 15:23, 41

ARARAT

Site of ark's landing, Gen 8:4
Assassins flee to, 2 Kgs 19:37; Isa 37:38

ARAUNAH [or ORNAN]

A Jebusite, 2 Sam 24:15–25
His threshing floor bought by David,
   2 Sam 24:18–25
   becomes site of temple, 2 Chr 3:1
Also called "Ornan," 1 Chr 21:18–28

ARBITER

Nor is there an *a* between us ....Job 9:33

ARBITRATOR

judge or *a* between you two......Luke 12:14

ARCHANGEL

with the voice of the *a*..........1 Thess 4:16
Michael the *a* was arguing.......... Jude 1:9

ARCHELAUS

Son of Herod the Great, Matt 2:22

ARCHITECT

whose *a* and builder is God........Heb 11:10

AREOPAGUS

Paul preaches at, Acts 17:18–34

ARGUE

a a case with your neighbor ...... Prov 25:9

ARGUED

They *a* vehemently with him ...... Judg 8:1

ARGUES

One who *a* with his Creator .... Isa 45:9

ARGUING

Why are you *a* among yourselves ..Matt 16:8
Michael the archangel was *a* .... Jude 1:9

ARGUMENT
Present your *a* . . . . Isa 41:21
had a major *a* and debate . . . . Acts 15:2
a began between the Pharisees . . . Acts 23:7

ARGUMENTS
and fill my mouth with *a* . . . . Job 23:4
always starting *a* and quarrels . . . . . . Jer 15:10

ARIEL
Ezra's friend, Ezra 8:15–17
—Name applied to Jerusalem, Isa 29:1–2, 7

ARISE
A! Shine! For your light arrives . . . . . . Isa 60:1

ARISEN
a greater than John the Baptist . . . . Matt 11:11

ARISTARCHUS
A Macedonian Christian, Acts 19:29
Accompanies Paul, Acts 20:1, 4
Imprisoned with Paul, Col 4:10

ARK
an *a* of cypress wood . . . . Gen 6:14
bring into the *a* two of every kind . . Gen 6:19
a came to rest on one of the
   mountains . . . . Gen 8:4
the atonement lid on top of
   the *a* . . . . Exod 25:21
Bezalel made the *a* of acacia
   wood . . . . Exod 37:1
the atonement lid that is on the *a* . . Lev 16:2
and placed the tablets into the *a* . . Deut 10:5
Go in front of the *a* of the Lord . . . . Josh 4:5
Pick up the *a* of the covenant . . . . . . Josh 6:6
take with us the *a* of the covenant . . 1 Sam 4:3
The *a* of God was taken . . . . 1 Sam 4:11
that the *a* of God was captured . . . 1 Sam 4:19
Philistines had captured the *a* . . . . . 1 Sam 5:1
the *a* stayed at Kiriath Jearim . . . . . . 1 Sam 7:2
grabbed hold of the *a* of God . . . . . 2 Sam 6:6
They brought the *a* of the Lord . . 2 Sam 6:17
in the *a* except the two stone
   tablets . . . . 1 Kgs 8:9
his hand to take hold of the *a* . . . . . 1 Chr 13:9
Place the holy *a* in the temple . . . . 2 Chr 35:3
golden altar of incense and the *a* . . . Heb 9:4
a for the deliverance of his family . . Heb 11:7
as an *a* was being constructed . . . . 1 Pet 3:20
the *a* of his covenant was visible . . . Rev 11:19

ARM
redeem you with an outstretched *a* . . Exod 6:6
have an *a* as powerful as God's . . . . . Job 40:9
the *a* of the wicked and evil . . . . Ps 10:15
Your *a* is powerful . . . . Ps 89:13
mighty *a* accomplish deliverance . . . . Ps 98:1
I *a* you for battle . . . . Isa 45:5
demonstrated power with his *a* . . . Luke 1:51
with uplifted *a* he led them out . . . Acts 13:17
a yourselves with the same attitude . . 1 Pet 4:1

ARMAGEDDON
Possible site of final battle, Rev 16:16
See also MEGIDDO

ARMED
fully *a*, guards his own palace . . . . Luke 11:21

ARMIES
See also LORD GOD OF HEAVEN'S ARMIES;
   LORD OF HEAVEN'S ARMIES
name of the Lord of
   Heaven's *A* . . . . 1 Sam 17:45
as the Lord of Heaven's *A* lives . . 1 Kgs 18:15
Can his *a* be numbered . . . . Job 25:3
The Lord of Heaven's *A* . . . . Ps 46:7
do not go into battle with our *a* . . . Ps 60:10
as awe-inspiring as bannered *a* . . . . Song 6:4
of the Lord of Heaven's *A* . . . . Isa 39:5
the Lord of Heaven's *A* . . . . Isa 47:4
see Jerusalem surrounded by *a* . . Luke 21:20
Lord of Heaven's *A* had not left . . . Rom 9:29
ears of the Lord of Heaven's *A* . . . . . Jas 5:4
The *a* that are in heaven . . . . Rev 19:14
and their *a* assembled to do battle . . Rev 19:19

ARMOR
his desire for justice like body *a* . . . Isa 59:17

Put on the *a* . . . . Jer 46:4
with the full *a* of God . . . . Eph 6:11

ARMS
underneath you are his eternal *a* . . Deut 33:27
he took the children in his *a* . . . . . Mark 10:16
Simeon took him in his *a* and . . . . . Luke 2:28

ARMY
I can charge against an *a* . . . . 2 Sam 22:30
No king is delivered by his vast *a* . . . Ps 33:16
an extremely great *a* . . . . Ezek 37:10
heavenly *a* appeared with the
   angel . . . . Luke 2:13
serves in the *a* at his own expense . . 1 Cor 9:7

ARNON
Boundary between Moab and Ammon,
   Num 21:13, 26
Border of Reuben, Deut 3:12, 16
Ammonites reminded of, Judg 11:18–26

AROER
A town in east Jordan; rebuilt by Gadites,
   Num 32:34; Deut 2:36
Assigned to Reuben, Deut 3:12
Ruled by Amorites, Josh 12:2; 13:9–10, 16

AROMA
Lord smelled the soothing *a* . . . . . . Gen 8:21
For we are a sweet *a* of Christ . . . . 2 Cor 2:15

AROSE
until you *a* . . . . Judg 5:7
David *a* and fled from Saul . . . . . . 1 Sam 21:10
she *a* and stood before the king . . . . Esth 8:4
I *a* to open for my beloved . . . . Song 5:5

AROUND
They jumped *a* on the altar . . . . . . 1 Kgs 18:26
the beasts of the forest prowl *a* . . Ps 104:20
ropes of death tightened *a* me . . . . Ps 116:3
He built a hedge *a* it . . . . Isa 5:2
walking *a* in the midst of the fire . . Dan 3:25
unless you turn *a* and become . . . . Matt 18:3
standing *a* in the marketplace . . . . Matt 20:3
glory of the Lord shone *a* them . . . Luke 2:9
the crowd was pressing *a* him . . . . . . Luke 5:1
If anyone walks *a* in the daytime . . John 11:9
and a cloth wrapped *a* his face . . . John 11:44
Jesus no longer went *a* publicly . . John 11:54
grope *a* for him and find him . . . . . Acts 17:27
going *a* from house to house . . . . . 1 Tim 5:13

ARPHAXAD
A son of Shem, Gen 10:22, 24
Born two years after the flood, Gen 11:10–13
An ancestor of Christ, Luke 3:36

ARRANGED
Philistines *a* their forces to fight . . 1 Sam 4:2
they *a* their battle lines to fight . . 1 Sam 17:2
she also has *a* her table . . . . Prov 9:2
and *a* to give him money . . . . Luke 22:5

ARREST
with swords and clubs to *a* me . . Matt 26:55
a you and hand you over for trial . . Mark 13:11
he proceeded to *a* Peter too . . . . . . Acts 12:3

ARRESTED
For Herod had *a* John . . . . Matt 14:3

ARRIVAL
is the *a* of those who proclaim . . . Rom 10:15

ARRIVES
the dawn *a* and the shadows flee . . Song 2:17

ARRIVING
Son of Man *a* in the clouds . . . . . . Mark 13:26

ARROGANCE
A is their necklace . . . . Ps 73:6
Lord confirms this oath by the *a* . . Amos 8:7
from the sheer *a* of their hearts . . . Luke 1:51
a produced by material
   possessions . . . . 1 John 2:16

ARROGANT
Do not let *a* men overtake me . . . . Ps 36:11
haughty demeanor and an *a* . . . . . . Ps 101:5
I hate *a* pride and the evil way . . . . Prov 8:13
The Lord abhors every *a* person . . Prov 16:5
A proud and *a* person . . . . Prov 21:24

my boasting, *a* ones . . . . Isa 13:3
He will have an *a* attitude . . . . Dan 8:25
Some have become *a* . . . . 1 Cor 4:18
so that I would not become *a* . . . . 2 Cor 12:7
or he may become *a* and fall . . . . . . 1 Tim 3:6
a, blasphemers, disobedient . . . . . . 2 Tim 3:2

ARROGANTLY
back in full the one who acts *a* . . . . . Ps 31:23

ARROW
This *a* symbolizes the victory . . . . . 2 Kgs 13:17
the *a* that flies by day . . . . Ps 91:5
club or a sword or a sharp *a* . . . . . . Prov 25:18
made me the target for his *a* . . . . . . Lam 3:12

ARROWS
He shot *a* and scattered them . . 2 Sam 22:15
A do not make it flee . . . . Job 41:28
put their *a* on the strings . . . . Ps 11:2
For your *a* pierce me . . . . Ps 38:2
There he shattered the *a* . . . . Ps 76:3
are like *a* in a warrior's hand . . . . . . Ps 127:4
equip yourselves with flaming *a* . . . Isa 50:11
a will send you to your grave . . . . . . Jer 5:16
Their tongues are like deadly *a* . . . . . Jer 9:8
He shot his *a* into my heart . . . . Lam 3:13
you commission your *a* . . . . Hab 3:9
extinguish all the flaming *a* . . . . Eph 6:16

ARTAXERXES
Artaxerxes I, king of Persia (465–425 BC),
   authorizes Ezra's mission to Jerusalem,
   Ezra 7:1–28
Temporarily halts rebuilding program at
   Jerusalem, Ezra 4:7–23
Authorizes Nehemiah's mission, Neh 2:1–10
Permits Nehemiah to return, Neh 13:6

ARTEMIS
Worship of at Ephesus creates uproar,
   Acts 19:23–41

ARTISTIC
a designs for work with gold . . . . . . Exod 31:4

ARTS
those skilled in magical *a* . . . . Isa 3:3

AS IT IS WRITTEN
Just *a* in the law of Moses . . . . Dan 9:13
The Son of Man will go *a* . . . . Matt 26:24
A in the prophet Isaiah . . . . Mark 1:2
about you hypocrites, *a* . . . . Mark 7:6
just *a* about him . . . . Mark 9:13
manna in the wilderness, just *a* . . . John 6:31
from faith to faith, just *a* . . . . Rom 1:17
all Israel will be saved, *a* . . . . Rom 11:26
not please himself, but just *a* . . . . . . Rom 15:3

ASA
Third king of Judah; restores true worship,
   1 Kgs 15:8–15; 2 Chr 14–15
Hires Ben Hadad against Baasha; rebuked
   by a prophet, 1 Kgs 15:16–22; 2 Chr 16:1–10
Diseased, seeks physicians rather than the
   Lord, 2 Chr 16:12
Death and burial, 2 Chr 16:13–14

ASAHEL
David's nephew; captain in his army; noted
   for valor, 2 Sam 2:18; 23:24; 1 Chr 2:16;
   27:7
Killed by Abner, 2 Sam 2:19–23
Avenged by Joab, 2 Sam 3:27, 30

ASAPH
A Levite choir leader under David and
   Solomon, 1 Chr 15:16–19; 16:1–7; 2 Chr 5:6,
   12
Twelve psalms assigned to, 2 Chr 29:30;
   Pss 50; 73–83

ASCEND
a the mountain of the Lord . . . . Ps 24:3
You *a* on high . . . . Ps 68:18
If I were to *a* to heaven . . . . Ps 139:8

ASCENDED
Who has *a* into heaven . . . . Prov 30:4
No one has *a* into heaven . . . . John 3:13
When he *a* on high he captured . . . . Eph 4:8
one who *a* above all the heavens . . Eph 4:10

ASCENDING
angels of God *a* and descending....John 1:51
if you see the Son of Man *a* ......John 6:62

ASCRIBE
I will *a* righteousness...............Job 36:3

ASENATH
Daughter of Potiphera and wife of Joseph,
   Gen 41:45
Mother of Manasseh and Ephraim,
   Gen 41:50–52; 46:20

ASHAMED
I am *a* and embarrassed............Ezra 9:6
harm me be turned back and *a*......Ps 35:4
harm me be turned back and *a*.....Ps 40:14
Let none who seek you be *a*........Ps 69:6
my life be embarrassed and *a*.......Ps 70:2
All who worship idols are *a*..........Ps 97:7
a because we have been insulted.. Jer 51:51
anyone is *a* of me and my words.. Mark 8:38
For I am not *a* of the gospel.......Rom 1:16
is that I will in no way be *a*.........Phil 1:20
not *a* to be called their God.......Heb 11:16
do not be *a*.....................1 Pet 4:16

ASHDOD [or AZOTUS]
One of five Philistine cities, Josh 13:3
Seat of Dagon worship, 1 Sam 5:1–8
Opposes Nehemiah, Neh 4:7
Women of, marry Jews, Neh 13:23–24
A city which Philip visited, Acts 8:40
Also called "Azotus," Acts 8:40

ASHER
Jacob's second son by Zilpah, Gen 30:12–13
Goes to Egypt with Jacob, Gen 46:8, 17
Blessed by Jacob, Gen 49:20
—Tribe of:
Census of, Num 1:41; 26:47
Slow to fight against Canaanites,
   Judg 1:31–32; 5:17
Among Gideon's army, Judg 6:35; 7:23
A godly remnant among, 2 Chr 30:11

ASHERAH; ASHERAHS
The female counterpart of Baal, Judg 3:7;
   1 Kgs 18:19
Image of, erected by Manasseh in the
   temple, 2 Kgs 21:7
Vessels of, destroyed by Josiah, 2 Kgs 23:4
—Asherah Poles, idols used in the worship
   of Asherah, Exod 34:13; Deut 12:3; 16:21;
   1 Kgs 16:32–33; 2 Kgs 23:6–7

ASHES
Your maxims are proverbs of *a*.....Job 13:12
come to resemble dust and *a*......Job 30:19
For I eat *a* as if they were bread....Ps 102:9
He feeds on *a*.....................Isa 44:20
and sat on *a*.....................Jonah 3:6
sitting in sackcloth and *a*.........Luke 10:13
and the *a* of a young cow..........Heb 9:13

ASHKELON
One of five Philistine cities, Josh 13:3;
   Jer 47:5, 7
Captured by Judah, Judg 1:18
Men of, killed by Samson, Judg 14:19–20
Repossessed by Philistines, 1 Sam 6:17;
   2 Sam 1:20
Doom of, pronounced by the prophets,
   Jer 47:5, 7; Amos 1:8; Zeph 2:4, 7; Zech 9:5

ASHTAROTH
A city in Bashan; residence of King Og,
   Deut 1:4; Josh 12:4
Captured by Israel, Josh 9:10
—A general designation of the Canaanite
   female deities, 1 Sam 7:3–4; 31:10

ASHTORETH; ASHTORETHS
A mother-goddess worshiped by the
   Philistines, 1 Sam 31:10
Israel ensnared by, Judg 2:13; 10:6
Worshiped by Solomon, 1 Kgs 11:5, 33
Destroyed by Josiah, 2 Kgs 23:13

ASHURBANIPAL
Called "the great and noble," Ezra 4:10

ASIA
Paul forbidden to preach in, Acts 16:6
Paul's later ministry in, Acts 19:1–26
Seven churches of, Rev 1:4, 11

ASIDE
See also TURN ASIDE
to his way and have not turned *a*...Job 23:11
The wicked turn *a* from birth........Ps 58:3
turned *a* and gone their own way ...Jer 5:23
to set *a* what is regarded as.......1 Cor 1:28
they will be set *a*...................1 Cor 13:8
set *a* some income and save it.....1 Cor 16:2
I do not set *a* God's grace.........Gal 2:21
a former command is set *a*........ Heb 7:18

ASK
When your children *a* someday ....Josh 4:6
when I *a* for just one more sign ...Judg 6:39
You do not *a* for burnt sacrifices ... Ps 40:6
A for a confirming sign..............Isa 7:11
They will *a* the way to Zion.........Jer 50:5
A the LORD for rain in the season..Zech 10:1
a the Lord of the harvest.........Matt 9:38
whatever you *a* in prayer........Matt 21:22
A, and it will be given to you......Luke 11:9
whatever you *a* from God........John 11:22
a me anything in my name.......John 14:14
Then I will *a* the Father...........John 14:16
you will *a* me nothing...........John 16:23
will *a* the Father on your behalf ..John 16:26
should *a* their husbands at home ..1 Cor 14:35
to do far beyond all that we *a*.....Eph 3:20
he should *a* God.....................Jas 1:5
a in faith without doubting...........Jas 1:6
not have because you do not *a*.......Jas 4:2
in regard to whatever we *a*........1 John 5:15
I do not say that he should *a*.....1 John 5:16

ASKED
So she *a* the LORD.................Gen 25:22
Then Jacob *a*.....................Gen 32:29
The Israelites *a* the LORD........Judg 20:27
So David *a* the LORD.............1 Sam 23:2
I have *a* the LORD for one thing......Ps 27:4
a him to place his hands on him..Mark 7:32
I *a* the Lord three times about
   this......................2 Cor 12:8

ASKING
am not *a* you to take them out ...John 17:15

ASKS
For everyone who *a* receives......Matt 7:8
if his son *a* for bread..............Matt 7:9
if your son *a* for a fish............Luke 11:11

ASLEEP
were plundered; they "fell *a*.........Ps 76:5
lives to an end and they "fall *a*.......Ps 90:5
and was sound *a*...................Jonah 1:5
But he was *a*.....................Matt 8:24
the girl is not dead but *a*.........Matt 9:24
or else he might find you *a*......Mark 13:36
Our friend Lazarus has fallen *a*....John 11:11
though some have fallen *a*........1 Cor 15:6
those who have fallen *a*......... 1 Thess 4:14
ahead of those who have
   fallen *a*..................... 1 Thess 4:15
their destruction is not *a*..........2 Pet 2:3

ASPIRE
they *a* to a better land............Heb 11:16

ASPIRES
a to the office of overseer.........1 Tim 3:1

ASSAULT
no one will *a* you to harm you....Acts 18:10

ASSEMBLE
look, the kings *a*....................Ps 48:4
A my covenant people...............Ps 50:5
A and come.......................Ezek 39:17

ASSEMBLED
and they *a* the entire community..Num 1:18
Israelite community *a* at Shiloh ....Josh 18:1
a the army that was with him ....2 Sam 18:1
of this same month the Israelites *a*..Neh 9:1
the Jews who were in Susa *a* ......Esth 9:18
nations will be *a* before him.....Matt 25:32

ASSEMBLIES
at new moon festivals and *a*......1 Chr 23:31

ASSEMBLY
to kill this whole *a* with hunger ...Exod 16:3
complete rest, a holy *a*...........Lev 23:3
by loud horn blasts, a holy *a*...... Lev 23:24
nor can sinners join the *a*...........Ps 1:5
middle of the *a* I will praise.........Ps 22:22
God stands in the *a* of El............Ps 82:1
faithfulness in the angelic *a*.......Ps 89:5
honored in the great angelic *a*.....Ps 89:7
all his heavenly *a*...................Ps 148:2
proclaim a sacred *a*...............Joel 1:14
proclaim a sacred *a*...............Joel 2:15
defense before the public *a* ......Acts 19:33
midst of the *a* I will praise you .... Heb 2:12
into your *a* wearing a gold ring.......Jas 2:2

ASSETS
his manager was wasting his *a* ....Luke 16:1
these *a* I have come to regard.......Phil 3:7

ASSHUR
One of the sons of Shem; progenitor of the
   Assyrians, Gen 10:22; 1 Chr 1:17
—The chief god of the Assyrians; seen in
   names like Ashurbanipal (Osnapper),
   Ezra 4:10
—A city in Assyria or the nation of Assyria:
   see ASSYRIA

ASSIGNED
land that Moses *a* to you east......Josh 1:14
he *a* Israel their tribal portions....Josh 11:23
as the Lord has *a* to each one .....1 Cor 7:17

ASSISTANT
the king's personal *a*.............Acts 12:20

ASSOCIATE
a with men who are unfaithful.......Ps 50:18
they *a* with thieves..................Isa 1:23
against the man who is my *a* ......Zech 13:7

ASSOCIATES
who *a* with the wise grows wise..Prov 13:20

ASSOS
A seaport of Mysia in Asia to which Paul
   walked, Acts 20:13

ASSURANCE
have all the riches that *a* brings .....Col 2:2
with a sincere heart in the *a*......Heb 10:22

ASSURED
a that the evil person will not .....Prov 11:21

ASSYRIA [or ASSHUR]
Founded by Nimrod, Gen 10:8–12; Mic 5:6
Agent of God's purposes, Isa 7:17–20; 10:5–6
Attacks and finally conquers Israel,
   2 Kgs 15:19–20, 29; 17:3–41
Invades and threatens Judah, 2 Kgs 18:13–37
Hezekiah prays for help against; army
   miraculously slain, 2 Kgs 19:1–35
Prophecies concerning, Num 24:22–24;
   Isa 10:12–19; 14:24–25; 19:23–25; Hos 10:6;
   11:5; Nah 3:1–19
Also called "Asshur," Num 24:22, 24

ASTONISHED
do not be *a* by the matter...........Eccl 5:8
They were *a* and said...........Matt 13:54
disciples were *a* at these words..Mark 10:24
all who heard Jesus were *a*.......Luke 2:47
were *a* at the catch of fish.........Luke 5:9
Her parents were *a*...............Luke 8:56
accompanied Peter were
   greatly *a*.......................Acts 10:45
they were greatly *a*...............Acts 12:16
a that you are so quickly deserting.. Gal 1:6
a when you do not rush with them.. 1 Pet 4:4
a that a trial by fire is occurring ...1 Pet 4:12

ASTONISHING
Her demise was *a* ....Lam 1:9

ASTONISHMENT
filled with *a* and amazement.......Acts 3:10

ASTOUNDED
he was greatly *a* at the teaching... Acts 13:12
I was greatly *a* when I saw her......Rev 17:6

ASTOUNDING
Great and *a* are your deeds......... Rev 15:3

ASTRAY
We have sinned and gone *a* ......2 Chr 6:37
These people desire to go *a* ....Ps 95:10
who goes *a* is an abomination.....Prov 3:32
They truly love to go *a* ....Jer 14:10
were loyal, led them *a*............Amos 2:4
sheep and one of them goes *a*....Matt 18:12
your minds may be led *a* ....2 Cor 11:3
Do not be led *a*......................Jas 1:16
you were going *a* like sheep......1 Pet 2:25

ASTROLOGERS
a, sorcerers, and wise men .... Dan 2:2
loudly to summon the *a*........... Dan 5:7

AT THE RIGHT HAND
he stands *a* of the needy .... Ps 109:31
the Son of Man sitting *a*........Matt 26:64
into heaven and sat down *a* ..... Mark 16:19
and Jesus standing *a* of God.......Acts 7:55
who is *a* of God.................... Rom 8:34
he sat down *a* of the Majesty........Heb 1:3
who sat down *a* of the throne......Heb 8:1
and is *a* of God with angels......1 Pet 3:22

ATE
she took some of its fruit and *a* .... Gen 3:6
brought it to him, and he *a* it.....Gen 27:25
a all of it just before you arrived ..Gen 27:33
say that a wild animal *a* him......Gen 37:20
cows *a* the seven fine-looking..... Gen 41:4
the Israelites *a* manna 40 years .. Exod 16:35
you got up and *a* food...........2 Sam 12:21
a the food of the mighty ones......Ps 78:25
a it, and it was sweet like honey....Ezek 3:3
They all *a* and were satisfied .... Matt 14:20
They all *a* and were satisfied .....Matt 15:37
and he *a* locusts and wild honey... Mark 1:6
high priest and *a* the sacred
   bread.........................Mark 2:26
They all *a* and were satisfied .....Mark 6:42
Everyone *a* and was satisfied .....Mark 8:8
They all *a* and were satisfied ......Luke 9:17
a the manna in the wilderness..... John 6:31
and all *a* the same spiritual food .. 1 Cor 10:3
from the angel's hand and *a* it.....Rev 10:10

ATHALIAH
Daughter of Ahab and Jezebel, 2 Kgs 8:18,
   26; 2 Chr 22:2–3
Kills royal children; usurps throne,
   2 Kgs 11:1–3; 2 Chr 22:10–11
Killed in priestly uprising, 2 Kgs 11:4–16;
   2 Chr 23:1–21

ATHENS
Paul preaches in, Acts 17:15–34
Paul resides in, 1 Thess 3:1

ATONEMENT
Aaron is to make *a* on its horns..Exod 30:10
for on this day *a* is to be made ....Lev 16:30
to make *a* for your lives ....Lev 17:11
it is a day of *a* to make *a*.......... Lev 23:28
sin offerings to make *a* ....Neh 10:33
make *a* for all you have done.....Ezek 16:63
make *a* for the sins of the people ..Heb 2:17

ATROCITY
committed such an unthinkable *a*..Judg 20:6

ATTACHED
Ephraim has *a* himself to idols ....Hos 4:17

ATTACK
So they got ready to *a* the city...1 Kgs 20:12
trumpets to signal the *a* .... 2 Chr 13:12
who anticipate my defeat *a* me......Ps 56:2
they *a* me for no reason...........Ps 109:3
I will *a* you.......................Isa 1:25
king of the south will *a* him ......Dan 11:40

ATTACKED
Jonathan *a* the Philistine outpost...1 Sam 13:3
They *a* Ziklag and burned it ... 1 Sam 30:1
prefer that we be *a* by the LORD..2 Sam 24:14
Since my youth they have often *a* ...Ps 129:1
he was being punished, *a* by God... Isa 53:4

I *a* them and angrily rejected.......Isa 57:17
They *a* Jason's house .... Acts 17:5

ATTACKERS
who defend the city from *a*........ Isa 28:6

ATTACKS
the angel of the LORD *a* them ....Ps 35:5
wolf *a* the sheep and scatters ....John 10:12

ATTAIN
a to the resurrection from the dead.. Phil 3:11

ATTALIA
A seaport of Pamphylia from which Paul
   sailed to Antioch, Acts 14:25

ATTEND
to *a* to your own business ....1 Thess 4:11

ATTENDANT
and the flaming fire his *a*...........Ps 104:4

ATTENDANTS
Then the king said to his *a*.......Matt 22:13

ATTENTION
God paid *a* to Leah .... Gen 30:17
close *a* to my commandments ... Deut 11:13
Pay *a* to my cry for help ....Ps 17:1
The LORD pays *a* to the godly ......Ps 34:15
May the Lord pay *a* to me ....Ps 40:17
Pay *a* to my plea for mercy.........Ps 86:6
Pay *a* to my cry for help.............Ps 88:2
but no one was paying *a*...........Prov 1:24
pay *a* to my words.................Prov 4:20
we will not need to pay *a*.........Jer 18:18
pay *a*, and act....................... Dan 9:19
pay *a* to their threats...............Acts 4:29
give *a* to the public reading.......1 Tim 4:13
do you pay *a* to the one who ....Jas 2:3

ATTESTED
a man clearly *a* to you by God.....Acts 2:22
a by the law and the prophets.....Rom 3:21

ATTIRE
Worship the LORD in holy *a* ..... 1 Chr 16:29
let them bring royal *a* ....Esth 6:8
is this one wearing royal *a*...........Isa 63:1

ATTITUDE
your *a* be wrong toward your .....Deut 15:9
demeanor and an arrogant *a* .... Ps 101:5
you have a willing *a* and obey ..... Isa 1:19

ATTRACTIVE
was *a* to the eye.................... Gen 3:6
among them an *a* woman .... Deut 21:11
Now this woman was very *a*......2 Sam 11:2
She was a very *a* woman .... 2 Sam 14:27
for she was very *a* ....Esth 1:11
young woman was very *a* ....Esth 2:7
and moral knowledge will be *a*....Prov 2:10

ATTRIBUTES
of the world his invisible *a*.........Rom 1:20

AUCTION
and *a* off your friend ....Job 6:27

AUTHORITIES
synagogues, the rulers, and the *a* ..Luke 12:11
be subject to the governing *a* ..... Rom 13:1
for the *a* are God's servants ....Rom 13:6
the *a* in the heavenly realms ......Eph 3:10
Disarming the rulers and *a* .... Col 2:15
to be subject to rulers and *a*........Titus 3:1
with angels and *a* and powers.....1 Pet 3:22

AUTHORITY
be placed under the *a* of Hegai.....Esth 2:8
wrote with full *a* to confirm ....Esth 9:29
placed everything under their *a* ......Ps 8:6
has *a* over human kingdoms ....Dan 4:17
For his *a* is an everlasting *a*.......Dan 4:34
taught them like one who had *a*.. Matt 7:29
For I too am a man under *a*....... Matt 8:9
has *a* on earth to forgive sins...... Matt 9:6
who had given such *a* to men ..... Matt 9:8
gave them *a* over unclean spirits ..Matt 10:1
high positions use their *a*........Matt 20:25
All *a* in heaven and on earth..... Matt 28:18
has *a* on earth to forgive sins.....Mark 2:10
and to have *a* to cast out demons...Mark 3:15

what *a* are you doing these
   things...................... Mark 11:28
because he spoke with *a* .... Luke 4:32
has *a* on earth to forgive sins..... Luke 5:24
power and *a* over all demons.......Luke 9:1
and he has granted the Son *a*..... John 5:27
I have the *a* to lay it down ....John 10:18
given him *a* over all humanity .... John 17:2
I have the *a* to release you....... John 19:10
You would have no *a* over me..... John 19:11
the Father has set by his own *a*..... Acts 1:7
no *a* except by God's appointment.. Rom 13:1
have a symbol of *a* on her head .. 1 Cor 11:10
end all rule and all *a* and power .. 1 Cor 15:24
above every rule and *a* and power.. Eph 1:21
the head over every ruler and *a* .... Col 2:10
kings and all who are in *a*.........1 Tim 2:2
teach or exercise *a* over a man .. 1 Tim 2:12
or rebuke that carries full *a* ....Titus 2:15
reject *a*, and insult the glorious..... Jude 1:8
and *a*, before all time.............Jude 1:25
give him *a* over the nations........ Rev 2:26
will receive ruling *a* as kings.......Rev 17:12

AUTHORIZATION
have *a* according to the law .... Heb 7:5

AUTHORIZED
reserved for those *a* to use it....... Isa 35:8

AUTUMN
is he who gives us the *a* rains....... Jer 5:24
a trees without fruit...............Jude 1:12

AVENGE
he will *a* his servants' blood .....Deut 32:43
your God comes to *a* .... Isa 35:4
Do not *a* yourselves ....Rom 12:19
live on the earth and *a* our blood .. Rev 6:10

AVENGER
The *a* of blood himself must kill .. Num 35:19
because the Lord is the *a*........1 Thess 4:6

AVOID
But *a* foolish controversies .... Titus 3:9

AWAIT
as we eagerly *a* our adoption..... Rom 8:23
we also eagerly *a* a savior ....Phil 3:20
to those who eagerly *a* him ....Heb 9:28

AWAKE
I *a* you will reveal yourself..........Ps 17:15
I stay *a*; I am like a solitary bird.....Ps 102:7
A, O stringed instrument...........Ps 108:2
A, O north wind .... Song 4:16
sleep in the dusty ground will *a* ....Dan 12:2
Stay *a* and pray................... Matt 26:41
Couldn't you stay *a* for one
   hour..........................Mark 14:37
Stay *a* and pray.................Mark 14:38
the hour for us to *a* from sleep....Rom 13:11
A, O sleeper ....Eph 5:14

AWARE
a that just as a parent disciplines.. Deut 8:5
ever *a* of your faithfulness...........Ps 26:3

AWAY
Will you really sweep *a* the godly ..Gen 18:23
But God does not take *a* life.... 2 Sam 14:14
and turn *a* from their sin ....1 Kgs 8:35
Should a man like me run *a* ....Neh 6:11
one who feared God and turned *a*.... Job 1:1
as water wears *a* stones........... Job 14:19
Turn *a* from us......................Job 21:14
drive *a* my honor like the wind .... Job 30:15
Do not remain far *a* from me........Ps 22:11
who see me in the street run *a*..... Ps 31:11
Turn *a* from evil and do what is
   right.................................Ps 34:14
not take your Holy Spirit *a* ....Ps 51:11
He has taken *a* my strength ....Ps 102:23
I am fading *a* like a shadow........Ps 109:23
I stay *a* from every evil path ......Ps 119:101
the treacherous will be torn *a* .... Prov 2:22
fear the LORD and turn *a* from evil.. Prov 3:7
A gentle response turns *a* anger... Prov 15:1
A time to throw *a* stones...........Eccl 3:5
come *a* with me .... Song 2:10

like a shoot that is thrown *a*........Isa 14:19
the stars in the sky will fade *a*......Isa 34:4
riches stashed *a* in secret places....Isa 45:3
He was led *a* after an unjust trial...Isa 53:8
driven *a*, and unconsoled..........Isa 54:11
your sons come from far *a* ....Isa 60:4
has taken *a* all that our ancestors .. Jer 3:24
turned *a* from you many times......Jer 14:7
cannot keep from running *a*........Jer 14:10
Put *a* violence and destruction ... Ezek 45:9
take *a* every last one of them ......Hos 9:12
immediately he falls *a*..........Matt 13:21
Heaven and earth will pass *a*....Matt 24:35
will all fall *a* because of me......Matt 26:31
If they all fall *a* because of you .. Matt 26:33
immediately they fall *a*...........Mark 4:17
Heaven and earth will pass *a*....Mark 13:31
You will all fall *a*..................Mark 14:27
Who will roll *a* the stone .... Mark 16:3
has sent the rich *a* empty..........Luke 1:53
who takes *a* the sin of the world ..John 1:29
You don't want to go *a* too ....John 6:67
I am going *a* ....John 8:21
going *a* to make ready a place.....John 14:2
He takes *a* every branch..........John 15:2
A with him......................John 19:15
and for all who are far *a*..........Acts 2:39
A with him......................Acts 21:36
have your sins washed *a*........Acts 22:16
but God will do *a* with both ....1 Cor 6:13
only in Christ is it taken *a* ....2 Cor 3:14
you have fallen *a* from grace ....Gal 5:4
far *a* have been brought near.......Eph 2:13
keep *a* from all that ....1 Tim 6:11
so that we do not drift *a*.............Heb 2:1
that can never take *a* sins ....Heb 10:11
of his pursuits will wither *a*...........Jas 1:11
put *a* all filth and evil excess.......... Jas 1:21
even though it is passing *a* ....1 Pet 1:7
turn *a* from evil and do good......1 Pet 3:11
crown of glory that never fades *a* .. 1 Pet 5:4
the celestial bodies will melt *a* ... 2 Pet 3:10
the darkness is passing *a*.........1 John 2:8
And the world is passing *a*........1 John 2:17
and not shrink *a* from him.......1 John 2:28
He will wipe *a* every tear...........Rev 21:4
takes *a* from the words...........Rev 22:19

AWE
who live in the world stand in *a* .....Ps 33:8
should tremble in *a* before me ..... Jer 5:22
salvation with *a* and reverence .....Phil 2:12

AWE-INSPIRING
For the Lord Most High is *a*.........Ps 47:2

AWESOME
What an *a* place this is............ Gen 28:17
is a great and *a* God ....Deut 7:21
and *a* God who is unbiased.......Deut 10:17
fear this glorious and *a* name ...Deut 28:58
God's angel—he was very *a*........Judg 13:6
he is more *a* than all gods .... 1 Chr 16:25
by doing great and *a* deeds.......1 Chr 17:21
great and *a* God ....Neh 1:5
Remember the great and *a* Lord .. Neh 4:14
the great, powerful, and *a* God ....Neh 9:32
around God is *a* majesty...........Job 37:22
performing *a* acts of deliverance ....Ps 65:5
How *a* are your deeds...............Ps 66:3
acts on behalf of people are *a* ....Ps 66:5
You are *a*! Yes, you ....Ps 76:7
of the earth regard him as *a* ....Ps 76:12
more *a* than all who surround him .. Ps 89:7
he is more *a* than all gods ....Ps 96:4
praise your great and *a* name .....Ps 99:3
His name is holy and *a*.............Ps 111:9
your deeds are *a* and amazing..... Ps 139:14
proclaim the power of your *a* ......Ps 145:6
absolute power and *a* strength....Isa 40:26
When you performed *a* deeds...... Isa 64:3
Their rims were high and *a*........Ezek 1:18
great and *a* God who is faithful.....Dan 9:4

AWESOMELY
glittering *a* like ice................Ezek 1:22

AWESTRUCK
living in the remotest areas are *a*....Ps 65:8

AWFUL
and an *a* injustice..................Eccl 2:21

AWL
pierce his ear with an *a*...........Exod 21:6
take an *a* and pierce a hole ....Deut 15:17

AWOKE
a from his drunken stupor ....Gen 9:24
I *a*, for the Lord protects me.......... Ps 3:5
then the Lord *a* from his sleep .....Ps 78:65
When Joseph *a* from sleep ....Matt 1:24

AX
he raises the *a* to cut the tree .....Deut 19:5
He took an *a* in his hand.......... Judg 9:48
a head dropped into the water ....2 Kgs 6:5
an *a* exalt itself over the one ....Isa 10:15
now the *a* is laid at the root ......Matt 3:10

AXHEAD
iron *a* is blunt and a workman.... Eccl 10:10

AZARIAH
A prophet who encourages King Asa,
    2 Chr 15:1–8
—Son of King Jehoshaphat, 2 Chr 21:2
—King of Judah, 2 Kgs 15:1
—A high priest who rebukes King Uzziah,
    2 Chr 26:16–20
—Chief priest in the time of Hezekiah,
    2 Chr 31:9–10
—The Hebrew name of Abednego, Dan 1:7

AZEKAH
Camp of Goliath, 1 Sam 17:1, 4, 17
Besieged by Nebuchadnezzar, Jer 34:7

AZMAVETH
A village near Jerusalem, Neh 12:29

AZOTUS
See ASHDOD

B

BAAL; BAALS
Deities of Canaanite polytheism,
    Judg 10:10–14
The male god of the Phoenicians and
    Canaanites, 2 Kgs 23:5
Nature of the worship of, 1 Kgs 18:26, 28;
    19:18; Ps 106:28; Jer 7:9; 19:5; Hos 9:10;
    13:1–2
Worshiped by Israelites, Num 25:1–5;
    Judg 2:11–14; 3:7; 6:28–32; 1 Kgs 16:31–32;
    2 Kgs 21:3; Jer 11:13; Hos 2:8
Ahaz makes images to, 2 Chr 28:1–4
Overthrown by Elijah, 1 Kgs 18:17–40
    by Josiah, 2 Kgs 23:4–5
Denounced by prophets, Jer 19:4–6;
    Ezek 16:1–2, 20–21
Historic retrospect, Rom 11:4

BAAL OF PEOR
See BAAL PEOR

BAAL PEOR [or BAAL OF PEOR]
A Moabite god; worshiped by Israelites,
    Num 25:1–9
Also called "Baal of Peor," Ps 106:28

BAAL PERAZIM
See MOUNT PERAZIM

BAAL ZEBUB [or BEELZEBUL]
A Philistine god at Ekron, 2 Kgs 1:2
Ahaziah inquires of, 2 Kgs 1:2, 6, 16
Jesus accused of serving, Matt 10:25; 12:24–27
Also called "Beelzebul," Matt 10:25; 12:24

BAALAH
See KIRIATH JEARIM

BAANAH
A murderer of Ish Bosheth, 2 Sam 4:1–12

BAASHA
Usurps throne of Israel; his evil reign; wars
    with Judah, 1 Kgs 15:16—16:7

BABBLER
this foolish *b* want to say ....Acts 17:18

BABBLING
senseless *b*, a syllable here ....Isa 28:10

BABEL, TOWER OF
A huge brick structure intended to magnify
    man and preserve the unity of the race,
    Gen 11:1–4
Objectives of, thwarted by God, Gen 11:5–9

BABIES
mouths of children and nursing *b* ....Ps 8:2
even bringing their *b* to him......Luke 18:15

BABY
I realized it was not my *b*..........1 Kgs 3:21
but the *b* will lack wisdom.........Hos 13:13
b in my womb leaped for joy ......Luke 1:44
a *b* wrapped in strips of cloth......Luke 2:12

BABYLON
Built by Nimrod; Tower of Babel,
    Gen 10:8–10; 11:1–9
Descriptions of, Isa 13:19; 14:4; Jer 51:44;
    Dan 4:30
Jews carried captive to, 2 Kgs 25:1–21;
    2 Chr 36:5–21
Inhabitants of, described, Isa 47:1, 9–13;
    Jer 50:35–38; Dan 5:1–3
Prophecies concerning, Isa 13:1–22;
    Jer 21:1–7; 25:9–12; 27:5–8; 29:10;
    Jer 50:1–46; Dan 2:31–38; 7:2–4
The prophetic city, Rev 14:8; 16:19; 17:1–18:24

BACK
you not kept *b* a blessing.........Gen 27:36
Turn *b* from your evil ways ...... 2 Kgs 17:13
the shadow go *b* 10 steps .... 2 Kgs 20:11
they turned *b* to the Lord God... 2 Chr 15:4
The wicked are turned *b*............. Ps 9:17
Pay them *b* for their evil deeds......Ps 28:4
but he pays *b* in full.................. Ps 31:23
turned *b* and longed for God ....Ps 78:34
Pay *b* our neighbors in full..........Ps 79:12
Turn *b* toward us ....Ps 90:13
you will see the wicked paid *b*.......Ps 91:8
the Jordan River turned *b*...........Ps 114:3
I will pay *b* evil....................Prov 20:22
my *b* to those who attacked........Isa 50:6
hold *b* your tender compassion ....Isa 63:15
how can you still hold *b* ....Isa 64:12
the Lord paying *b* his enemies .....Isa 66:6
want to come *b*.......................Jer 4:1
good be paid *b* with evil ....Jer 18:20
Let us come *b* to you ....Jer 31:18
he pays *b* in full.....................Jer 51:56
I will go *b* to my husband...........Hos 2:7
Still you did not come *b* to me.... Amos 4:6
had been rolled *b*.................Mark 16:4
hand to the plow and looks *b*.....Luke 9:62
paying *b* four times as much ......Luke 19:8
leaned *b* against Jesus' chest ......John 13:25
Therefore repent and turn *b*.......Acts 3:19
He kept *b* for himself part..........Acts 5:2
so that each one may be paid *b*...2 Cor 5:10
no one pays *b* evil for evil ...... 1 Thess 5:15
him (who is my very heart) *b*......Phlm 1:12
who shrink *b* and thus perish.....Heb 10:39
women received *b* their dead......Heb 11:35
and someone turns him *b* ....Jas 5:19
have turned *b* to the shepherd ...1 Pet 2:25
written on the front and *b*...........Rev 5:1

BACKS
and a rod for the *b* of fools .... Prov 26:3

BACKSLIDER
The *b* will be paid back ....Prov 14:14

BACKWARD
Eli fell *b* from his chair............1 Sam 4:18

BAD
The *b*, thin cows ate the seven..... Gen 41:4
good for *b* or bad for good ....Lev 27:10
He does not fear *b* news..........Ps 112:7
b tooth or a foot out of joint......Prov 25:19
It is incurably *b* ....Jer 17:9
in Egypt are like those *b* figs........Jer 24:8
but the *b* tree bears bad fruit......Matt 7:17

For no good tree bears *b* fruit .... Luke 6:43
had done anything good or *b*...... Rom 9:11
fear for good conduct but for *b*.... Rom 13:3
B company corrupts good
   morals.........................1 Cor 15:33
do not imitate what is *b* .... 3 John 1:11

BAFFLED
Completely *b*, they said............ Acts 2:7

BAG
was each man's *b* of money ......Gen 42:35
would be sealed up in a *b*.........Job 14:17
no *b* for the journey .... Matt 10:10

BAGS
with holes in their money *b* ....Hag 1:6

BAIT
trap on the ground if there is no *b* .. Amos 3:5

BAKE
take choice wheat flour and *b* ......Lev 24:5

BAKED
b cakes of bread without yeast .. Exod 12:39
she kneaded it and *b* bread.....1 Sam 28:24

BAKER
royal *b* offended their master ..... Gen 40:1

BAKERS
They are all like *b*................... Hos 7:4

BAKERS'
every day from the *b* street ....Jer 37:21

BAKES
he kindles a fire and *b* bread ...... Isa 44:15

BALAAM
Sent by Balak to curse Israel, Num 22:5-7;
   Josh 24:9
Hindered by talking donkey, Num 22:22-35;
   2 Pet 2:16
Curse becomes a blessing, Deut 23:4-5;
   Josh 24:10
Prophecies of, Num 23:7-10, 18-24; 24:3-9,
   15-24
NT references to, 2 Pet 2:15-16; Jude 1:11;
   Rev 2:14

BALAK
A Moabite king, Num 22:4
Hires Balaam to curse Israel, Num 22-24

BALANCES
You must have honest *b*...........Lev 19:36
weighed on the *b* and found....... Dan 5:27

BALD
Priests must not have a *b*.......... Lev 21:5
their heads will be shaved *b*.......Ezek 7:18

BALDY
b! Go on up......................2 Kgs 2:23

BALM
little *b* and a little honey...........Gen 43:11

BANDAGE
but he will *b* our wounds ....Hos 6:1

BANDAGED
have not been cleansed or *b*..........Isa 1:6
He went up to him and *b* ....Luke 10:34

BANDIT
your poverty will come like a *b*.. Prov 24:34

BANDS
will be raided by marauding *b*....Gen 49:19
hooks of the posts and their *b*... Exod 27:10
who sew *b* on all their wrists ..... Ezek 13:18

BANISH
B emotional stress from...........Eccl 11:10

BANISHED
back the one he has *b* ....2 Sam 14:13

BANK
you put my money in the *b*...... Luke 19:23

BANKERS
deposited my money with the *b*.. Matt 25:27

BANKS
and along the *b* of the Jordan.... Num 13:29
when it was overflowing its *b*.....1 Chr 12:15

trees on the *b* of the river .... Ezek 47:7
coming from between the *b*....... Dan 8:16

BANQUET
the king prepared a large *b*........ Esth 2:18
to the *b* that I have prepared .... Esth 5:4
brought me into the *b* hall........ Song 2:4
queen mother then entered the *b* .. Dan 5:10
who had been invited to the *b*.... Matt 22:3
you find to the wedding *b* .... Matt 22:9
with him to the wedding *b*...... Matt 25:10
A man once gave a great *b* ...... Luke 14:16
gather around for the great *b* ..... Rev 19:17

BANQUETS
religious *b* where they sprawl .... Amos 6:7
and the places of honor at *b*.....Luke 20:46

BAPTISM
and Sadducees coming to his *b*....Matt 3:7
Where did John's *b* come from ...Matt 21:25
began preaching a *b* of repentance.. Mark 1:4
baptized with the *b* I experience ..Mark 10:38
John's *b*—was it from heaven .... Mark 11:30
preaching a *b* of repentance........Luke 3:3
I have a *b* to undergo .... Luke 12:50
John's *b*—was it from heaven .....Luke 20:4
beginning from his *b* by John ...... Acts 1:22
after the *b* that John announced.. Acts 10:37
proclaimed a *b* for repentance ...Acts 13:24
he knew only the *b* of John ....Acts 18:25
Into John's *b*," they replied........ Acts 19:3
baptized with a *b* of repentance... Acts 19:4
with him through *b* into death..... Rom 6:4
one Lord, one faith, one *b* ....Eph 4:5
been buried with him in *b* .... Col 2:12
And this prefigured *b*..............1 Pet 3:21

BAPTIZE
I *b* you with water .... Matt 3:11
I *b* you with water .... Mark 1:8
I *b* you with water ....Luke 3:16
who sent me to *b* with water .... John 1:33
I thank God that I did not *b* any ...1 Cor 1:14
For Christ did not send me to *b* ...1 Cor 1:17

BAPTIZED
from Galilee to John to be *b* ....Matt 3:13
I need to be *b* by you ....Matt 3:14
After Jesus was *b* ....Matt 3:16
was *b* by John in the Jordan........ Mark 1:9
or be *b* with the baptism ....Mark 10:38
you will be *b* with the baptism...Mark 10:39
believes and is *b* will be saved... Mark 16:16
crowds that came out to be *b* ......Luke 3:7
Tax collectors also came to be *b*...Luke 3:12
when all the people were *b*........Luke 3:21
because they had not been *b* ..... Luke 7:30
For John *b* with water .... Acts 1:5
be *b* in the name of Jesus Christ ...Acts 2:38
who accepted his message were *b*.. Acts 2:41
they began to be *b*................. Acts 8:12
and after he was *b*................. Acts 8:13
b in the name of the Lord Jesus.... Acts 8:16
What is to stop me from being *b*.. Acts 8:36
and Philip *b* him ....Acts 8:38
He got up and was *b*.............. Acts 9:18
water for these people to be *b* ...Acts 10:47
b in the name of Jesus Christ .....Acts 10:48
John *b* with water..................Acts 11:16
she and her household were *b*.... Acts 16:15
he and all his family were *b*...... Acts 16:33
about it believed and were *b* ...... Acts 18:8
Into what then were you *b* .... Acts 19:3
b, and have your sins washed.....Acts 22:16
as were *b* into Christ Jesus.........Rom 6:3
b the household of Stephanus......1 Cor 1:16
and all were *b* into Moses .... 1 Cor 10:2
we were all *b* into one body ......1 Cor 12:13
who are *b* for the dead .... 1 Cor 15:29
of you who were *b* into Christ......Gal 3:27

BAPTIZER
John the *b* began preaching .... Mark 1:4

BAPTIZING
was *b* them in the Jordan River.... Matt 3:6
b them in the name of........... Matt 28:19
was *b* them in the Jordan River.... Mark 1:5

b if you are not the Christ ....John 1:25
Jordan River where John was *b* ....John 1:28
but I came *b* with water ....John 1:31
spent time with them and was *b*...John 3:22
John was also *b* at Aenon........John 3:23
b, and everyone is flocking ....John 3:26
winning and *b* more disciples....... John 4:1
although Jesus himself was not *b*...John 4:2
John had been *b* at an earlier
   time .... John 10:40

BAR-JESUS [or ELYMAS]
A Jewish false prophet, Acts 13:6-12
Also called "Elymas" in Arabic, Acts 13:8

BARABBAS
A murderer released instead of Jesus,
   Matt 27:16-26; Acts 3:14-15

BARAK
Defeats Jabin, Judg 4:1-24
A man of faith, Heb 11:32

BARBARIAN
b, Scythian, slave or free.............Col 3:11

BARBARIANS
both to the Greeks and to the *b* ... Rom 1:14

BAREFOOT
in undergarments and *b*............ Isa 20:2

BARGAIN
Will partners *b* for it................ Job 41:6

BARLEY
b, vines, fig trees.................... Deut 8:8
I saw a stale cake of *b* bread....... Judg 7:13
beginning of the *b* harvest......... Ruth 1:22
boy who has five *b* loaves ....John 6:9
of *b* will cost a day's pay............ Rev 6:6

BARN
gather the wheat into my *b*...... Matt 13:30
they have no storeroom or *b* .... Luke 12:24

BARNABAS
A disciple from Cyprus; gives property,
   Acts 4:36-37
Supports Paul, Acts 9:27
Ministers in Antioch, Acts 11:22-30
Travels with Paul, Acts 12:25; 13-15
Breaks with Paul over John Mark,
   Acts 15:36-39

BARNS
b will be filled completely ....Prov 3:10
or gather into *b*.................... Matt 6:26
tear down my *b* and build ....Luke 12:18

BARREN
But Sarai was *b*.....................Gen 11:30
the *b* woman of the family ....Ps 113:9
I was bereaved and *b* .... Isa 49:21
Blessed are the *b* ....Luke 23:29
b woman who does not bear
   children ....Gal 4:27

BARRIER
permanent *b* that it can never cross ..Jer 5:22

BARS
and I broke the *b* of your yoke ....Lev 26:13
makes the *b* of your gates strong .. Ps 147:13
and iron *b* I will hack through ...... Isa 45:2
when I break the *b* of their yoke ..Ezek 34:27

BARSABBAS
Nominated to replace Judas, Acts 1:23
Sent to Antioch, Acts 15:22

BARTHOLOMEW [or NATHANAEL]
One of the Twelve, Matt 10:3; Acts 1:13
Also called "Nathanael," John 1:45-46

BARTIMAEUS
Blind beggar healed by Jesus, Mark 10:46-52

BARUCH
Son of Neriah, Jer 32:12-13
Jeremiah's faithful friend and scribe,
   Jer 36:4-32

BARZILLAI
Supplies David with food, 2 Sam 17:27-29
Age restrains him from following David,
   2 Sam 19:31-39

BASHAN
Conquered by Israel, Num 21:33–35
Assigned to Manasseh, Deut 3:13
Conquered by Hazael, king of Syria,
  2 Kgs 10:32–33

BASIN
to make a large bronze *b* . . . . Exod 30:18
full like the sacrificial *b* . . . . Zech 9:15

BASINS
He also made 10 bronze *b* . . . . 1 Kgs 7:38

BASIS
with food on a regular *b* . . . . Ps 104:27

BASKET
top *b* there were baked goods . . . . Gen 40:17
she took a papyrus *b* for him . . . . . . Exod 2:3
priest will then take the *b* . . . . Deut 26:4
Your *b* and your mixing bowl . . . . Deut 28:5
Your *b* and your mixing bowl . . . . Deut 28:17
b had very good-looking figs . . . . Jer 24:2
A *b* of summer fruit . . . . Amos 8:2
b between the earth and the sky . . Zech 5:9
lamp and put it under a *b* . . . . Matt 5:15
a hidden place or under a *b* . . . . . . Luke 11:33

BASKETS
b of white bread on my head . . . . . Gen 40:16
LORD showed me two *b* of figs . . . . . Jer 24:1
pieces left over, 12 *b* full . . . . . Matt 14:20
pieces left over, seven *b* full . . . . . Matt 15:37

BATHE
will *b* their feet in the blood of . . . . . Ps 58:10

BATHED
The one who has *b* needs only . . . John 13:10

BATHSHEBA
Wife of Uriah, taken by David, 2 Sam 11
Her first child dies, 2 Sam 12:14–19
Bears Solomon, 2 Sam 12:24
Secures throne for Solomon, 1 Kgs 1:15–31
Deceived by Adonijah, 1 Kgs 2:13–25

BATS
caves where rodents and *b* live . . . . Isa 2:20

BATTLE
land of Egypt prepared for *b* . . . . . . Exod 13:18
you will arm yourselves for *b* . . . . Num 32:20
For the *b* is the LORD's . . . . 1 Sam 17:47
He trains my hands for *b* . . . . 2 Sam 22:35
cried out to God during the *b* . . . . . 1 Chr 5:20
for the day of war and *b* . . . . Job 38:23
You give me strength for *b* . . . . Ps 18:39
is prepared for the day of *b* . . . . . . Prov 21:31
the *b* is not always won by . . . . Eccl 9:11
and from the severity of the *b* . . . . . Isa 21:15
The noise of *b* can be heard . . . . . . Jer 50:22
to confront another king in *b* . . . . Luke 14:31
who will get ready for *b* . . . . 1 Cor 14:8
became mighty in *b* . . . . Heb 11:34
fleshly desires that do *b* . . . . 1 Pet 2:11
to bring them together for the *b* . . Rev 16:14

BATTLEMENT
will build on her a *b* of silver . . . . . Song 8:9

BATTLES
and lead us and fight our *b* . . . . . . 1 Sam 8:20
to help us and fight our *b* . . . . 2 Chr 32:8

BDELLIUM
its color like the color of *b* . . . . Num 11:7

BE FRUITFUL AND MULTIPLY
B and fill the water in the seas . . . . . Gen 1:22
B! Fill the earth and subdue it . . . . . Gen 1:28
increase and *b* on the earth . . . . Gen 8:17
B and fill the earth . . . . Gen 9:1
b, increase abundantly . . . . Gen 9:7
I am the Sovereign God. *B* . . . . Gen 35:11

BEAM
and put it on a carrying *b* . . . . Num 4:10
spear was like a weaver's *b* . . . . . . 1 Sam 17:7
the *b* from your own eye . . . . Matt 7:5

BEAMS
and cedar *b* above the pillars . . . . . 1 Kgs 7:2
timber for *b* for the gates . . . . Neh 2:8

the *b* of the upper rooms . . . . Ps 104:3
b of our bedroom chamber . . . . Song 1:17

BEAR
See also BEAR FRUIT
whom Sarah will *b* to you . . . . Gen 17:21
to *b* the ephod before me . . . . 1 Sam 2:28
from the lion and the *b* . . . . 1 Sam 17:37
who can *b* a crushed spirit . . . . Prov 18:14
like a *b* robbed of her cubs . . . . Hos 13:8
ran from a lion only to meet a *b* . . Amos 5:19
is not able to *b* bad fruit . . . . Matt 7:18
For my yoke is easy to *b* . . . . Matt 11:30
because you *b* Christ's name . . . . . Mark 9:41
wife Elizabeth will *b* you a son . . . . . Luke 1:13
branch that does not *b* fruit . . . . . . John 15:2
does not *b* the sword for nothing . . . Rom 13:4
b with the failings of the weak . . . . . Rom 15:1
b the marks of Jesus on my body . . . Gal 6:17
once to *b* the sins of many . . . . Heb 9:28

BEAR FRUIT
take root in the ground and *b* . . . . . Isa 37:31
planted to grow branches, *b* . . . . . Ezek 17:8
the word and receive it and *b* . . . . Mark 4:20
b with steadfast endurance . . . . . . Luke 8:15
every branch that does not *b* . . . . . John 15:2
the branch cannot *b* by itself . . . . . John 15:4
from the dead, to *b* to God . . . . Rom 7:4
members of our body to *b* . . . . Rom 7:5

BEAR'S
but its feet were like a *b* . . . . Rev 13:2

BEARABLE
more *b* for the region of Sodom . . Matt 10:15

BEARD
or ruin the corners of your *b* . . . . . Lev 19:27
Joab took hold of Amasa's *b* . . . . . 2 Sam 20:9
which flows down the *b* . . . . Ps 133:2
to those who tore out my *b* . . . . Isa 50:6

BEARING
b with one another and forgiving . . . Col 3:13
b the abuse he experienced . . . . . . Heb 13:13

BEARS
prunes every branch that *b* fruit . . John 15:2
It *b* all things, believes all things . . . 1 Cor 13:7

BEAST
a *b* coming up out of the sea . . . . . . Rev 13:1
b coming up from the earth . . . . . . Rev 13:11
Now the *b* was seized . . . . Rev 19:20

BEASTS
should we be regarded as *b* . . . . Job 18:3
I fought with wild *b* at Ephesus . . . 1 Cor 15:32

BEAT
They will *b* their swords into . . . . Isa 2:4
with which the LORD will *b* . . . . Isa 30:32
but *b* his breast and said . . . . Luke 18:13

BEATEN
handed over to councils and *b* . . . . Mark 13:9
Three times I was *b* with a rod . . . 2 Cor 11:25

BEATING
will receive a severe *b* . . . . Luke 12:47

BEATINGS
B and wounds cleanse away
  evil . . . . Prov 20:30

BEAUTIFUL
daughters of humankind were *b* . . . Gen 6:2
know that you are a *b* woman . . . . Gen 12:11
that the woman was very *b* . . . . . . Gen 12:14
young woman was very *b* . . . . Gen 24:16
because she is very *b* . . . . Gen 26:7
lovely figure and *b* appearance . . . Gen 29:17
She was both wise and *b* . . . . 1 Sam 25:3
had a *b* sister named Tamar . . . . . . 2 Sam 13:1
as *b* as Job's daughters . . . . Job 42:15
the most *b* of all places . . . . Ps 50:2
ring in a pig's snout is a *b* . . . . Prov 11:22
Oh, how *b* you are . . . . Song 1:15
O most *b* of women . . . . Song 5:9
O most *b* among women . . . . Song 6:1
you are as *b* as Tirzah . . . . Song 6:4
How *b* are your sandaled feet . . . . . Song 7:1

How *b* you are . . . . Song 7:6
of food and *b* clothes . . . . Isa 23:18
the most *b* piece of property . . . . Jer 3:19
and a *b* crown on your head . . . . . Ezek 16:12
You became extremely *b* . . . . Ezek 16:13
and *b* crowns on their heads . . . . . Ezek 23:42
I am perfectly *b* . . . . Ezek 27:3
b with its many branches . . . . Ezek 31:9
he will enter the *b* land . . . . Dan 11:41
that look *b* on the outside . . . . . . Matt 23:27
it was adorned with *b* stones . . . . . Luke 21:5
called "the *B* Gate" every day . . . . . Acts 3:2
at the *B* Gate of the temple . . . . . . Acts 3:10
they saw the child was *b* . . . . Heb 11:23

BEAUTIFULLY
God has made everything fit *b* . . . . . Eccl 3:11

BEAUTIFY
to *b* my palace . . . . Isa 60:13

BEAUTY
for glory and for *b* . . . . Exod 28:2
The *b* of Israel lies slain . . . . 2 Sam 1:19
people and the officials her *b* . . . . . Esth 1:11
will be attracted by your *b* . . . . Ps 45:11
lust in your heart for her *b* . . . . Prov 6:25
Charm is deceitful and *b* is . . . . . . Prov 31:30
prisoner's brand will replace *b* . . . . . Isa 3:24
called 'the perfection of *b* . . . . Lam 2:15
and you disgraced your *b* . . . . Ezek 16:25
and perfect in *b* . . . . Ezek 28:12
of God could rival its *b* . . . . Ezek 31:8
and its *b* is lost forever . . . . Jas 1:11
b of a gentle and tranquil . . . . 1 Pet 3:4

BECAME
and the man *b* a living being . . . . Gen 2:7
and *b* extremely strong . . . . Exod 1:7
He *b* hungry and wanted to eat . . . Acts 10:10
b your father in Christ Jesus . . . . . . 1 Cor 4:15
To the Jews I *b* like a Jew . . . . 1 Cor 9:20

BECAUSE
b I long for you . . . . Ps 143:8
governors and kings *b* of me . . . . . Matt 10:18

BECOME
May he *b* famous in Israel . . . . Ruth 4:14
day I have *b* your father . . . . Ps 2:7
b as hardheaded as a rock . . . . Jer 5:3
I have *b* compassionate . . . . Zech 1:16
Listen: You will *b* pregnant . . . . Luke 1:31
wants to *b* my follower . . . . Luke 9:23
what will *b* of the ungodly . . . . 1 Pet 4:18

BECOMING
David was *b* steadily stronger . . . . . 2 Sam 3:1

BED
I spread out my *b* in darkness . . . . . . Job 17:13
I remember you on my *b* . . . . Ps 63:6
foliage is our canopied *b* . . . . Song 1:16
For the *b* is too short . . . . Isa 28:20
elevated hill you prepare your *b* . . . . Isa 57:7
will be two people in one *b* . . . . Luke 17:34
the marriage *b* kept undefiled . . . . . Heb 13:4

BEDROOM
was resting on his bed in his *b* . . . . 2 Sam 4:7
Bring the cakes into the *b* . . . . 2 Sam 13:10
come out from his *b* and . . . . Joel 2:16

BEDS
shout for joy upon their *b* . . . . Ps 149:5
they rest on their *b* . . . . Isa 57:2
lie around on *b* decorated . . . . Amos 6:4

BEELZEBUL
See BAAL ZEBUB

BEER
who get up early to drink *b* . . . . Isa 5:11
blessings of wine and *b* . . . . Mic 2:11

BEER LAHAI ROI
Angel meets Hagar there, Gen 16:7–14
Isaac dwells in, Gen 24:62

BEER SHEBA [or SHIBAH]
Name given to a well and town,
  Gen 26:31–33

God appears there to Hagar, Gen 21:14–19
  to Isaac, Gen 26:23–25
  to Jacob, Gen 46:1–5
  to Elijah, 1 Kgs 19:3–7
Oaths sworn there by Abraham,
  Gen 21:31–33
  by Isaac, Gen 26:26–33
Also called "Shibah," Gen 26:33

BEES
b from the land of Assyria..........Isa 7:18

BEFORE
b when you were cupbearer......Gen 40:13
we die *b* your very eyes..........Gen 47:15
show me as holy *b* the Israelites...Num 20:12
and doing what is right *b* him.....Deut 13:18
Israelites did evil *b* the LORD.......Judg 2:11
should tremble in awe *b* me........Jer 5:22
Be silent *b* the Sovereign LORD.....Zeph 1:7
trembling and fell down *b*........Luke 8:47
who are righteous *b* God........Rom 2:13
righteous *b* him by the works....Rom 3:20
going *b* them into judgment.....1 Tim 5:24

BEFOREHAND
he has prepared *b* for glory......Rom 9:23
works that God prepared *b*......Eph 2:10
testified *b* about the sufferings.....1 Pet 1:11

BEG
and I'm too ashamed to *b*........Luke 16:3
man who used to sit and *b*........John 9:8
I *b* you, brothers and sisters........Gal 4:12

BEGAN
people *b* to worship the LORD.....Gen 4:26
an argument *b* between the.......Acts 23:7
you *b* with the Spirit..................Gal 3:3
the one who *b* a good work.........Phil 1:6

BEGGED
I *b* the Lord for mercy................Ps 30:8
Then the demons *b* him..........Matt 8:31
b him to leave their region.......Matt 8:34
threw himself down and *b*......Matt 18:29
who heard *b* to hear no more.....Heb 12:19

BEGINNING
In the *b* God created................Gen 1:1
b with the firstborn................Gen 43:33
Your *b* will seem so small...........Job 8:7
b to the end of their lives..........Eccl 3:11
not read that from the *b*.........Matt 19:4
In the *b* was the Word...............John 1:1
was a murderer from the *b*.......John 8:44
been with me from the *b*........John 15:27
as well as the *b*......................Col 1:18
to teach you the *b* elements.......Heb 5:12
neither *b* of days nor end of........Heb 7:3
the *b* and the end..................Rev 21:6

BEGINNINGS
dares make light of small *b*.......Zech 4:10

BEHALF
words to speak on God's *b*........Job 36:2
plead with you on Christ's *b*.....2 Cor 5:20

BEHAVE
you hate all who *b* wickedly.........Ps 5:5

BEHAVING
not *b* with deceptiveness..........2 Cor 4:2
b according to human standards...2 Cor 10:2

BEHAVIOR
will die because of your *b*...........Ps 2:12
b of the Lord is not right.........Ezek 33:17
from her sexually immoral *b*.......Hos 2:2
dearly love their shameful *b*.......Hos 4:18
are to exhibit *b* fitting for..........Titus 2:3
the power of her sensual *b*.........Rev 18:3

BEHEADED
had John *b* in the prison..........Matt 14:10
b because of the testimony........Rev 20:4

BEHEMOTH
Described, Job 40:15–24

BEHIND
Jesus stayed *b* in Jerusalem........Luke 2:43
She followed *b* Paul and us.......Acts 16:17

BEING
the man became a living *b*..........Gen 2:7
human *b* who is permanently....Lev 27:29
whole mind, your whole *b*.........Deut 6:5
You really are *b* kind to me........Ruth 2:13
and with your entire *b*..........1 Chr 22:19
heart and my entire *b* shout.........Ps 84:2
Now they come into *b*............Isa 48:7
ask advice from any human *b*.......Gal 1:16
human *b* can subdue the tongue.....Jas 3:8

BEINGS
less than the heavenly *b*..............Ps 8:5
beside each of the four *b*.........Ezek 1:15
though we live as human *b*.......2 Cor 10:3

BEL [or MARDUK]
Patron god of Babylon, Isa 46:1; Jer 50:2;
  51:44
Also called "Marduk," Jer 50:2

BELIEVE
And if they do not *b* me.............Exod 4:1
how long will they not *b* in me.....Num 14:11
I did not *b* these things until.......1 Kgs 10:7
would I be if I did not *b*.............Ps 27:13
naive person will *b* anything.......Prov 14:15
you will not *b* even though..........Hab 1:5
one of these little ones who *b*....Matt 18:6
if you *b*, you will receive........Matt 21:22
Then why did you not *b* him.....Matt 21:25
we will *b* in him..................Matt 27:42
Repent and *b* the gospel..........Mark 1:15
Do not be afraid; just *b*.........Mark 5:36
I *b*; help my unbelief............Mark 9:24
these little ones who *b* in me.....Mark 9:42
b that you have received it......Mark 11:24
that we may see and *b*........Mark 15:32
not *b* those who had seen him..Mark 16:14
They *b* for a while..................Luke 8:13
just *b*, and she will be healed....Luke 8:50
you will not *b*..................Luke 22:67
slow of heart to *b* all.............Luke 24:25
everyone might *b* through him.....John 1:7
who *b* in his name..................John 1:12
earthly things and you don't *b*......John 3:12
do we *b* because of your words....John 4:42
do not *b* the one whom he sent..John 5:38
that we may see it and *b* you....John 6:30
have come to *b* and to know.....John 6:69
For unless you *b* that I am he.....John 8:24
Do you *b* in the Son of Man.......John 9:35
But you refuse to *b*.................John 10:26
even if you do not *b* me.........John 10:38
I *b* that you are the Christ........John 11:27
they may *b* that you sent me.....John 11:42
they still refused to *b* in him......John 12:37
you may *b* that I am he...........John 13:19
You *b* in God........................John 14:1
B me that I am in the Father......John 14:11
we *b* that you have come........John 16:30
world will *b* that you sent me....John 17:21
so that you also may *b*...........John 19:35
I will never *b* it...................John 20:25
recorded so that you may *b*.....John 20:31
the Jews who refused to *b*........Acts 14:2
message of the gospel and *b*.....Acts 15:7
B in the Lord Jesus..............Acts 16:31
b in the one who was to come.....Acts 19:4
b that any of these things.......Acts 26:26
Do you *b* the prophets..........Acts 26:27
of Jesus Christ for all who *b*......Rom 3:22
the father of all those who *b*......Rom 4:11
b in your heart that God raised....Rom 10:9
b in one they have not heard of..Rom 10:14
b by the foolishness of preaching..1 Cor 1:21
partners with those who do
  not *b*........................2 Cor 6:14
who *b* are the sons of Abraham....Gal 3:7
to those who *b*....................Gal 3:22
to *b* in Christ but also to suffer....Phil 1:29
if we *b* that Jesus died and rose..1 Thess 4:14
they will *b* what is false..........2 Thess 2:11
must *b* that he exists.............Heb 11:6
You *b* that God is one..............Jas 2:19
So you who *b* see his value........1 Pet 2:7

b in the name of his Son Jesus...1 John 3:23
do not *b* every spirit...............1 John 4:1
b the love that God has in us.....1 John 4:16
b in the name of the Son of God...1 John 5:13

BELIEVED
Abram *b* the LORD................Gen 15:6
and the people *b*...................Exod 4:31
have *b* what we just heard..........Isa 53:1
people of Nineveh *b* in God.......Jonah 3:5
b that what was spoken to her....Luke 1:45
and they *b* the scripture........John 2:22
not *b* in the name of the one.....John 3:18
Samaritans from that town *b*.....John 4:39
If you *b* Moses....................John 5:46
not even his own brothers *b*........John 7:5
things Jesus did, *b* in him........John 11:45
who has *b* our message..........John 12:38
and he saw and *b*.................John 20:8
b because you have seen me....John 20:29
had listened to the message *b*.....Acts 4:4
b were of one heart and mind.....Acts 4:32
appointed for eternal life *b*....Acts 13:48
the Holy Spirit when you *b*.....Acts 19:2
Abraham *b* God....................Rom 4:3
call on one they have not *b* in....Rom 10:14
you *b* in vain.....................1 Cor 15:2
I *b*; therefore I spoke.............2 Cor 4:13
Just as Abraham *b* God.............Gal 3:6
b on in the world.................1 Tim 3:16

BELIEVER
If you consider me to be a *b*......Acts 16:15
has a wife who is not a *b*..........1 Cor 7:12
along with Abraham the *b*..........Gal 3:9

BELIEVERS
than when we became *b*...........Rom 13:11
all people, especially of *b*.........1 Tim 4:10
set an example for the *b*.........1 Tim 4:12
are *b* and dearly loved............1 Tim 6:2
love the family of *b*..............1 Pet 2:17

BELIEVES
See also ONE WHO BELIEVES
possible for the one who *b*.......Mark 9:23
not doubt in his heart but *b*......Mark 11:23
one who *b* and is baptized........Mark 16:16
who *b* in him will not perish.......John 3:16
who *b* in the Son has eternal life..John 3:36
who hears my message and *b*....John 5:24
b in me will never be thirsty.......John 6:35
looks on the Son and *b* in him....John 6:40
the one who *b* has eternal life....John 6:47
let the one who *b* in me drink....John 7:38
one who *b* in me will live.........John 11:25
one who *b* in me does not *b*.....John 12:44
b in him receives forgiveness.....Acts 10:43
everyone who *b* is justified.......Acts 13:39
salvation to everyone who *b*......Rom 1:16
righteousness for everyone
  who *b*........................Rom 10:4
For with the heart one *b*..........Rom 10:10
b all things, hopes all things.......1 Cor 13:7
who *b* that Jesus is the Christ......1 John 5:1
b that Jesus is the Son of God....1 John 5:5
one who *b* in the Son of God....1 John 5:10

BELIEVING
that by *b* you may have life.......John 20:31
or by *b* what you heard..............Gal 3:2
those who have *b* masters.........1 Tim 6:2

BELLIES
our *b* pressed to the ground........Ps 44:25

BELLOWING
from Jerusalem he comes *b*.......Amos 1:2

BELLY
On your *b* you will crawl..........Gen 3:14
Your *b* is a mound of wheat.......Song 7:2
was in the *b* of the huge fish.....Matt 12:40
their god is the *b*..................Phil 3:19

BELONG
Don't interpretations *b* to God....Gen 40:8
b to the LORD your God.........Deut 10:14
secret things *b* to the LORD......Deut 29:29

and awesome might *b* to God ......Job 25:2
b the glory and the power forever.. 1 Pet 4:11

BELONGS
sacrifice which *b* to the LORD......Lev 7:20
For our shield *b* to the LORD.......Ps 89:18
the flock that *b* to you.............Mic 7:14
b to a different tribe...............Heb 7:13
Salvation *b* to our God............Rev 7:10

BELOVED
b of the LORD will live safely.....Deut 33:12
My *b* is like a fragrant pouch ......Song 1:13
is your *b* better than others ....Song 5:9
Where has your *b* gone............Song 6:1
leaning on her *b* ....Song 8:5
camp of the saints and the *b* city .. Rev 20:9

BELOW
You people are from *b*............John 8:23

BELSHAZZAR
King of Babylon; Daniel interprets his
    dream, Dan 5

BELT
camel's hair with a leather *b*....... Matt 3:4
took Paul's *b*, tied his hands ....Acts 21:11

BELTESHAZZAR
Daniel's Babylonian name, Dan 1:7

BELTS
and traded *b* to the merchants ...Prov 31:24
wide golden *b* around their chests .. Rev 15:6

BEN AMMI
Son of Lot; father of the Ammonites,
    Gen 19:38

BEN HADAD
Ben Hadad I, king of Damascus; hired by
    Asa, king of Judah, to attack Baasha, king
    of Israel, 1 Kgs 15:18–21
—Ben Hadad II, king of Damascus; makes
    war on Ahab, king of Israel, 1 Kgs 20
Falls in siege against Samaria,
    2 Kgs 6:24–33; 7:6–20
Killed by Hazael, 2 Kgs 8:7–15
—Ben Hadad III, king of Damascus; loses all
    Israelite conquests made by Hazael, his
    father, 2 Kgs 13:3–25

BEN ONI
Rachel's name for Benjamin, Gen 35:16–18

BENAIAH
The son of Jehoiada; a mighty man,
    2 Sam 23:20–23
Faithful to David, 2 Sam 15:18; 20:23
Escorts Solomon to the throne,
    1 Kgs 1:38–40
Executes Adonijah, Joab, and Shimei,
    1 Kgs 2:25, 29–34, 46
—A Pirathonite; another of David's mighty
    men, 2 Sam 23:30
Divisional commander, 1 Chr 27:14

BEND
I will *b* Judah as my bow...........Zech 9:13

BENDS
LORD's shout *b* the large trees.......Ps 29:9

BENEFACTORS
authority over them are
    called '*b* ....Luke 22:25

BENEFICIAL
not everything is *b*................1 Cor 6:12
are good and *b* for all people......Titus 3:8

BENEFIT
What *b* do people get from..........Eccl 1:3
For what does it *b* a person...... Matt 16:26
For what *b* is it for a person......Mark 8:36
For what does it *b* a person......Luke 9:25
So what *b* did you then reap......Rom 6:21
b leading to sanctification .... Rom 6:22
I do not seek my own *b*..........1 Cor 10:33
Christ will be of no *b* to you ....Gal 5:2
This is of no *b*.....................2 Tim 2:14
but he does so for our *b*........ Heb 12:10

BENEVOLENCE
by *b*, by the Holy Spirit ....2 Cor 6:6

BENJAMIN
Jacob's youngest son, Gen 35:16–20
Taken to Egypt against Jacob's wishes,
    Gen 42–45
Jacob's prophecy concerning, Gen 49:27
—Tribe of:
Families of, Num 26:38–41
Territory allotted to, Josh 18:11–28
Attacked by remaining tribes for condoning
    sin of Gibeah, Judg 20:12–48
Wives provided for remnant of, Judg 21:1–23
Tribe of Saul, 1 Sam 9:1–2
    of Paul, Phil 3:5

BENT
is *b* cannot be straightened......... Eccl 1:15
make straight what he has *b*.......Eccl 7:13
have not *b* the knee to Baal .... Rom 11:4

BEREA
A city of Macedonia; visited by Paul,
    Acts 17:10–15

BEREAVE
you *b* them of their children......Ezek 36:12

BERNICE
Sister of Herod Agrippa II, Acts 25:13, 23
Hears Paul's defense, Acts 26:1–30

BERRY
and the caper *b* shrivels up.........Eccl 12:5

BERYL
a ruby, a topaz, and a *b*.......... Exod 28:17
of gems, your gates out of *b*.......Isa 54:12
and *b*; your settings and mounts.. Ezek 28:13
the eighth *b*, the ninth topaz ..... Rev 21:20

BESIDE
slept *b* him until morning.........Ruth 3:14

BESIEGED
and attacked and *b* Samaria ..... 2 Kgs 6:24
marched to Jerusalem and *b*....2 Kgs 24:10
she is a *b* city ....Isa 1:8

BESIEGING
Babylon were *b* Jerusalem...........Jer 32:2

BEST
b for a person during his life........Eccl 6:12
very *b* oils on themselves......... Amos 6:6
b seats in the synagogues .... Matt 23:6
b seats in the synagogues ....Mark 12:39
Bring the *b* robe .... Luke 15:22
you can decide what is *b*........... Phil 1:10

BESTOW
B on us your deliverance ....Ps 85:7
LORD will *b* his good blessings...... Ps 85:12

BESTOWED
have *b* wisdom and power......... Dan 2:23
Daniel to high position and *b*......Dan 2:48
grace that he has freely *b* on us ..... Eph 1:6

BETH HORON
Twin towns of Ephraim, Josh 16:3, 5
Fortified by Solomon, 2 Chr 8:3–5
Prominent in battles, Josh 10:10–14;
    1 Sam 13:18

BETH MILLO
Scene of Joash's death, 2 Kgs 12:20–21

BETH PEOR
Town near Pisgah, Deut 3:29
Moses buried near, Deut 34:6
Assigned to Reubenites, Josh 13:15, 20

BETH SHAN [or BETH SHEAN]
A town in Issachar, Josh 17:11–16
Saul's corpse hung up at, 1 Sam 31:10–13;
    2 Sam 21:12–14
Also called "Beth Shean," Josh 17:11–16

BETH SHEAN
See BETH SHAN

BETH SHEMESH
Ark brought to, 1 Sam 6:12–19
Joash defeats Amaziah at, 2 Kgs 14:11
Taken by Philistines, 2 Chr 28:18

BETHANY
A town on the Mt. of Olives, Luke 19:29
Home of Lazarus, John 11:1
Home of Simon, the leper, Matt 26:6
Jesus visits there, Mark 11:1, 11–12
Scene of the ascension, Luke 24:50–51

BETHANY BEYOND THE JORDAN
A place beyond the Jordan where John
    baptized, John 1:28

BETHEL
Abram settles near, Gen 12:7–8
Site of Abram's altar, Gen 13:3–4
Site of Jacob's vision of the ladder,
    Gen 28:10–19
Jacob returns to, Gen 35:1–15
Samuel judges there, 1 Sam 7:15–16
Site of worship and sacrifice, 1 Sam 10:3
Center of idolatry, 1 Kgs 12:28–33
Josiah destroys altars of, 2 Kgs 23:4, 15–20
Denounced by prophets, 1 Kgs 13:1–10;
    Amos 7:10–13; Jer 48:13; Hos 10:15

BETHLEHEM [or EPHRATH; EPHRATHAH]
Originally called "Ephrath," Gen 35:16
Rachel buried there, Gen 35:19
Home of Naomi and Boaz, Ruth 1:1, 19;
    4:9–11
Home of David, 1 Sam 16:1–18
Predicted place of Messiah's birth, Mic 5:2
Christ born there, Matt 2:1; Luke 2:4–7;
    John 7:42
Children of, killed by Herod, Matt 2:16–18
Also called "Ephrath," Gen 35:16
Also called "Ephrathah," Mic 5:2

BETHPHAGE
Village near Bethany, Mark 11:1
Near Mt. of Olives, Matt 21:1

BETHSAIDA
A city of Galilee, Mark 6:45
Home of Andrew, Peter, and Philip,
    John 1:44; 12:21
Blind man healed there, Mark 8:22–23
More than 5,000 fed nearby, Luke 9:10–17
Unbelief of, denounced, Matt 11:21;
    Luke 10:13

BETHZATHA
Jerusalem pool, John 5:2–4

BETRAY
b the one who tries to escape ....Isa 16:3
Indeed, wine will *b* the proud....... Hab 2:5
Why do we *b* one another ....Mal 2:10
one of you will *b* me............. Matt 26:21
b the Son of Man with a kiss.....Luke 22:48
one who is going to *b* you ....John 21:20

BETRAYED
your own family have *b* you........Jer 12:6
Son of Man is going to be *b* ......Matt 17:22
on the night in which he was *b* ...1 Cor 11:23

BETRAYER
My *b* is approaching.............Matt 26:46

BETTER
obedience is *b* than sacrifice.....1 Sam 15:22
b to take shelter in the LORD .... Ps 118:8
B is little with the fear of .... Prov 15:16
B is a dry crust of bread .... Prov 17:1
B is a poor person who walks ..... Prov 19:1
b to live in the wilderness .... Prov 21:19
is *b* than a brother far away ......Prov 27:10
B is one handful with some......... Eccl 4:6
Two people are *b* than one .... Eccl 4:9
b than an old and foolish king ......Eccl 4:13
old days *b* than these days .... Eccl 7:10
their appearance was *b* and .... Dan 1:15
it is *b* to marry than to burn .... 1 Cor 7:9
which is *b* by far ....Phil 1:23
so far *b* than the angels............Heb 1:4
that speaks of something *b*.......Heb 12:24

BEWARE
B, those who call evil good .... Isa 5:20
B of the dogs ....Phil 3:2

BEWILDERED
but the one with a *b* mind ....Prov 12:8

BEWILDERMENT
terror and *b* had seized them.....Mark 16:8

BEYOND
with things that are *b* me............Ps 131:1
it was *b* my grasp..................Eccl 7:23
not to go *b* what is written ....1 Cor 4:6
glory far *b* all comparison ....2 Cor 4:17
means and *b* their means..........2 Cor 8:3
advancing in Judaism *b* many.......Gal 1:14
far *b* all that we ask or think.......Eph 3:20

BEZALEL
Hur's grandson, 1 Chr 2:20
Tabernacle builder, Exod 31:1-11; 35:30-35

BEZER
A city of refuge in the territory of Reuben,
    Deut 4:43; John 20:8

BICKERING
constant *b* by people corrupted ...1 Tim 6:5

BIER
came up and touched the *b*.........Luke 7:14

BIG
His appetite is as *b* as Sheol's........ Hab 2:5

BILDAD
One of Job's friends, Job 2:11
Makes three speeches, Job 8:1-22; 18:1-21;
    25:1-6

BILHAH
Rachel's maid, Gen 29:29
The mother of Dan and Naphtali,
    Gen 30:1-8
Commits incest with Reuben, Gen 35:22

BILLOWS
b and waves overwhelm me.........Ps 42:7

BIND
b the wild ox to a furrow ....Job 39:10
b them around your neck...........Prov 3:3
B them on your heart ....Prov 6:21
B them on your forearm............Prov 7:3
and *b* themselves to the LORD......Jer 50:5
Whatever you *b* on earth.........Matt 16:19

BINDING
was a *b* ordinance for Israel ....1 Sam 30:25

BIRD
with the blood of the *b* ....Lev 14:52
play with it, like a *b*................Job 41:5
Flee to a mountain like a *b* .... Ps 11:1
like a solitary *b* on a roof ....Ps 102:7
like a *b* from a hunter's snare.......Ps 124:7
like a *b* hurrying into a trap........Prov 7:23
for a *b* might report ....Eccl 10:20
Ephraim will be like a *b*............. Hos 9:11
a haunt for every unclean *b* ....Rev 18:2

BIRDS
b will eat your flesh from you ....Gen 40:19
Even the *b* find a home there........Ps 84:3
where the *b* make nests ....Ps 104:17
like *b* that are caught in a snare ....Eccl 9:12
kinds of wild *b* will settle in it...... Isa 34:11
Look at the *b* in the sky...........Matt 6:26
and the *b* in the sky have nests...Matt 8:20

BIRTH
See also NEW BIRTH
pregnant and gave *b* to Cain.........Gen 4:1
not given *b* to any children ....Gen 16:1
who gives *b* to it..................Job 38:29
better than the day of one's *b* ....Eccl 7:1
who is straining to give *b*...........Isa 13:8
LORD summoned me from *b* ....Isa 49:1
one who has not given *b*............Isa 54:1
b of Jesus Christ happened ....Matt 1:18
conceive and give *b* to a son.......Matt 1:23
and many will rejoice at his *b*......Luke 1:14
even before his *b*..................Luke 1:15
who had been blind from *b*.........John 9:1
Jews by *b* and not Gentile ....Gal 2:15
the washing of the new *b* and ..... Titus 3:5

it gives *b* to sin, and when sin........ Jas 1:15
the woman gave *b* to a son.........Rev 12:5

BIRTHDAY
it was Pharaoh's *b* ....Gen 40:20
gave a banquet on his *b* ....Mark 6:21

BIRTHRIGHT
First sell me your *b*...............Gen 25:31
So Esau despised his *b*............Gen 25:34
who sold his own *b* for a..........Heb 12:16

BIT
and they *b* the people ....Num 21:6

BITE
If the snake should *b* before....... Eccl 10:11
b and devour one another..........Gal 5:15

BITHYNIA
The Spirit keeps Paul from, Acts 16:7
Peter writes to Christians of, 1 Pet 1:1

BITS
smash the large house to *b*.......Amos 6:11
b into the mouths of horses ....Jas 3:3

BITTER
with very great and *b* sorrow.....Gen 50:10
their lives *b* by hard service ......Exod 1:14
b into sweet and sweet into *b* ...... Isa 5:20
like a *b* root springing up ....Heb 12:15
But if you have *b* jealousy ....Jas 3:14
It will make your stomach *b*........Rev 10:9

BITTERLY
Then Hezekiah wept *b*........... 2 Kgs 20:3
to those who are *b* distressed .....Prov 31:6
he went outside and wept *b*.....Matt 26:75

BITTERNESS
another man dies in *b* of soul...... Job 21:25
The heart knows its own *b* ....Prov 14:10
The Israelites turn justice into *b*...Amos 5:7

BLACK
hair is curly—*b* like a raven ....Song 5:11
to make one hair white or *b*...... Matt 5:36
and here came a *b* horse ....Rev 6:5
sun became as *b* as sackcloth ......Rev 6:12

BLACKSMITH
A *b* could not be found ....1 Sam 13:19
A *b* works with his tool .... Isa 44:12

BLADE
handle went in after the *b*.........Judg 3:22

BLAME
so that no one should *b* us .... 2 Cor 8:20

BLAMED
why am I *b* for the food.........1 Cor 10:30

BLAMELESS
b among his contemporaries ....Gen 6:9
Walk before me and be *b*...........Gen 17:1
b before the LORD your God......Deut 18:13
he rewarded my *b* behavior ....2 Sam 22:21
I was *b* before him..............2 Sam 22:24
that man was *b* and upright ....Job 1:1
a *b* and upright man................Job 1:8
although I am *b*....................Job 9:20
b man is a laughingstock ....Job 12:4
that you make your ways *b*........Job 22:3
he rewarded my *b* behavior ....Ps 18:20
I will be *b* and innocent.............Ps 19:13
one whose deeds are *b*............Ps 24:4
those whose actions are *b*.........Ps 119:1
The righteousness of the *b* ....Prov 11:5
who are *b* in their ways...........Prov 11:20
b will inherit what is good .... Prov 28:10
You were *b* in your behavior......Ezek 28:15
you will be *b* on the day ....1 Cor 1:8
that we should be holy and *b*.......Eph 1:4
but holy and *b*,...................Eph 5:27
be sincere and *b* for the day ....Phil 1:10
so that you may be *b* and pure .....Phil 2:15
stipulated in the law I was *b*........Phil 3:6
b our conduct was toward you ...1 Thess 2:10
b before our God and Father ...1 Thess 3:13
and body be kept entirely *b* ....1 Thess 5:23
as deacons if they are found *b*....1 Tim 3:10

An elder must be *b* ....Titus 1:6
For the overseer must be *b*.........Titus 1:7
on their lips; they are *b*............Rev 14:5

BLANKET
and she put a *b* over him ....Judg 4:18

BLASPHEME
enemy *b* your name forever........Ps 74:10
and tried to force them to *b* ......Acts 26:11
to Satan to be taught not to *b* ....1 Tim 1:20
Do they not *b* the good name ....Jas 2:7
beast opened his mouth to *b* ....Rev 13:6
b both his name and his ....Rev 13:6

BLASPHEMED
and declared, "He has *b* ......Matt 26:65
the name of God is being *b*....... Rom 2:24
yet they *b* the name of God ....Rev 16:9

BLASPHEMER
formerly a *b* and a persecutor .....1 Tim 1:13

BLASPHEMERS
b, disobedient to parents ....2 Tim 3:2

BLASPHEMES
foolish nation *b* your name......... Ps 74:18
b against the Holy Spirit........Mark 3:29
b against the Holy Spirit..........Luke 12:10

BLASPHEMIES
this man who is uttering *b*.........Luke 5:21
speaking proud words and *b* ....Rev 13:5

BLASPHEMING
This man is *b* .... Matt 9:3

BLASPHEMOUS
that was full of *b* names............Rev 17:3

BLASPHEMY
forgiven for every sin and *b* ......Matt 12:31
You have heard the *b*...........Mark 14:64
for a good deed but for *b*........John 10:33

BLAST
and by the *b* of his anger ....Job 4:9

BLAZE
will melt away in a *b*...............2 Pet 3:12

BLEACH
launderer in the world could *b* ....Mark 9:3

BLEEDING
At once the *b* stopped............Mark 5:29
and at once the *b* stopped........Luke 8:44

BLEMISH
There is no *b* in you ....Song 4:7
without *b*, and blameless.......... Col 1:22
offered himself without *b* ....Heb 9:14
without spot or *b*................. 2 Pet 3:14
without *b* before his glorious..... Jude 1:24

BLESS
See also BLESS THE LORD
and I will *b* you ....Gen 12:2
I will *b* those who *b* you ....Gen 12:3
I will indeed *b* you..............Gen 22:17
I will *b* you and multiply..........Gen 26:24
I may *b* you before I die ....Gen 27:4
B me too, my father ....Gen 27:34
unless you *b* me ....Gen 32:26
b your bread and your water ....Exod 23:25
LORD *b* you and protect you......Num 6:24
whoever you *b* is blessed.........Num 22:6
tribes must stand to *b* .... Deut 27:12
had no desire to *b* anyone ....Ps 109:17
takes notice of us; he will *b*.........Ps 115:12
He will *b* his loyal followers ....Ps 115:13
from today on I will *b* you ....Hag 2:19
b those who curse you ....Luke 6:28
B those who persecute you........Rom 12:14
Surely I will *b* you greatly.........Heb 6:14
we *b* the Lord and Father.............Jas 3:9

BLESS THE LORD
Stand up and *b* your God...........Neh 9:5
With it we *b* and Father..............Jas 3:9

BLESSED
See also BLESSED BE THE LORD
God *b* them and said ....Gen 1:22

God *b* the seventh day.............. Gen 2:3
God *b* Noah and his sons ....Gen 9:1
those who bless you be *b*.........Gen 27:29
you arrived, and I *b* him ....Gen 27:33
the LORD *b* the Sabbath day ......Exod 20:11
that whoever you bless is *b*.......Num 22:6
has *b*, and I cannot reverse it ....Num 23:20
B is the one who blesses you.....Num 24:9
You will be *b* in the city..........Deut 28:3
The LORD *b* Obed-Edom..........2 Sam 6:11
b the work of his hands............Job 1:10
b is the one who does not .... Ps 1:1
b is the one whose wrongdoing .....Ps 32:2
b is the nation whose God........ Ps 33:12
b is the one who treats ....Ps 41:1
b are those who promote ....Ps 106:3
the name of the LORD be *b*........Ps 118:26
b is the man who fills...............Ps 127:5
who fears the LORD will be *b* .....Ps 128:4
b are the people who..............Ps 144:15
B is the one who has found.........Prov 3:13
is kind to the needy is *b* ....Prov 14:21
b is the one who trusts .... Prov 16:20
who keeps the law, *b* is he.......Prov 29:18
have risen and called her *b* ......Prov 31:28
All nations will call you *b*..........Mal 3:12
B are the poor in spirit ....Matt 5:3
B are those who mourn ....Matt 5:4
B are the meek....................Matt 5:5
B are those who hunger...........Matt 5:6
B are the merciful ....Matt 5:7
B are the pure in heart ....Matt 5:8
B are the peacemakers ....Matt 5:9
B are those who are persecuted.. Matt 5:10
B are you when people insult...... Matt 5:11
b is anyone who takes no offense.. Matt 11:6
eyes are *b* because they see .....Matt 13:16
B is the one who comes ....Matt 21:9
you who are *b* by my Father.....Matt 25:34
B is the one who comes ....Luke 13:35
will be *b* if you do them ....John 13:17
B are the people who have ......John 20:29
It is more *b* to give than ....Acts 20:35
who is *b* forever ....Rom 1:25
who is God over all, *b* forever ......Rom 9:5
B is the one who does not ....Rom 14:22
to the extent that God has *b*.......1 Cor 16:2
B is the God and Father ....2 Cor 1:3
those who believe are *b* ....Gal 3:9
B is the God and Father ....Eph 1:3
glorious gospel of the *b* God ...... 1 Tim 1:11
inferior is *b* by the superior........ Heb 7:7
will be *b* in what he does ....Jas 1:25
B is the one who reads ....Rev 1:3
B are the dead....................Rev 14:13
B is the one who stays alert ....Rev 16:15
B are those who are invited ....Rev 19:9
B and holy is the one ....Rev 20:6
B is the one who keeps............Rev 22:7
B are those who wash ....Rev 22:14

BLESSED BE THE LORD
B who has delivered you .... Exod 18:10
B God of our fathers...............Ezra 7:27
B, for I am rich....................Zech 11:5
B God of Israel ....Luke 1:68

BLESSES
richly *b* all who call on him ....Rom 10:12

BLESSING
you will exemplify divine *b* ....Gen 12:2
the *b* he gave to Abraham ....Gen 28:4
I will command my *b* for you.....Lev 25:21
today a *b* and a curse............Deut 11:26
LORD will decree *b* for you ....Deut 28:8
life and death, *b* and curse....... Deut 30:19
up above all *b* and praise ....Neh 9:5
the *b* of the dying man ....Job 29:13
experience the LORD's *b*............Ps 129:8
The *b* from the LORD .... Prov 10:22
and my *b* on your children..........Isa 44:3
regions around my hill into a *b* .. Ezek 34:26
and leave *b* in his wake ....Joel 2:14
save you and you will be a *b*......Zech 8:13

and pour out *b* for you ....Mal 3:10
in the fullness of Christ's *b* ....Rom 15:29
we respond with a *b*.................1 Cor 4:12
the cup of *b* that we bless ....1 Cor 10:16
Christ Jesus the *b* of Abraham...... Gal 3:14
blessed us with every spiritual *b*..... Eph 1:3
those who tend it receives a *b*...... Heb 6:7
when he wanted to inherit the *b*... Heb 12:17
mouth come *b* and cursing ....Jas 3:10

BLESSINGS
including the *b* and the curses.....Josh 8:34
pronounce *b* with their mouths .....Ps 62:4
pronounce *b* on him all day long ... Ps 72:15
B are on the head of the
    righteous ....Prov 10:6

BLEW
and *b* them into the Red Sea ..... Exod 10:19
and *b* the horns as the ark ....Josh 6:8
The first angel *b* his trumpet ....Rev 8:7

BLIGHT
I destroyed your crops with *b* .... Amos 4:9
products of your labor with *b* ....Hag 2:17

BLIND
bribes *b* the eyes of the wise .....Deut 16:19
I was eyes for the *b* and ....Job 29:15
You are totally *b*...................Isa 29:9
to open *b* eyes, to release .... Isa 42:7
b along an unfamiliar way .... Isa 42:16
out the people who are *b*......... Isa 43:8
All their watchmen are *b* .... Isa 56:10
offer *b* animals as a sacrifice........Mal 1:8
The *b* see, the lame walk .... Matt 11:5
They are *b* guides.................Matt 15:14
the regaining of sight to the *b* .... Luke 4:18
We are not *b* too ....John 9:40
pitiful, poor, *b*, and naked...........Rev 3:17

BLINDED
May their eyes be *b*..................Ps 69:23
b their eyes and hardened.........John 12:40
the god of this age has *b*...........2 Cor 4:4
the darkness has *b* his eyes.......1 John 2:11

BLINDFOLD
spit on him, and to *b* him ....Mark 14:65

BLINDLY
wander *b* through the streets ....Lam 4:14

BLOCK
See also STUMBLING BLOCK
sheep at the slaughtering *b*........ Ps 44:22
You are a stumbling *b* to me......Matt 16:23
a stumbling *b* to Jews..............1 Cor 1:23

BLOCKS
because of stumbling *b*.............Matt 18:7
Stumbling *b* are sure to come ....Luke 17:1

BLOOD
See also FIELD OF BLOOD; FLESH AND
    BLOOD; INNOCENT BLOOD
your brother's *b* is crying out...... Gen 4:10
with its life (that is, its *b*) in it....... Gen 9:4
Whoever sheds human *b*.......... Gen 9:6
and dipped the tunic in the *b* .....Gen 37:31
you are a bridegroom of *b*........Exod 4:25
the Nile was turned to *b*..........Exod 7:20
The *b* will be a sign for you ......Exod 12:13
took the *b* and splashed it ....Exod 24:8
of every living thing is in the *b*......Lev 17:11
for the life of all flesh is its *b* ..... Lev 17:14
do not cover my *b* ....Job 16:18
your hands are covered with *b* ..... Isa 1:15
will display the *b* shed on it........Isa 26:21
helplessly in your *b*..............Ezek 16:6
the moon to the color of *b* ....Joel 2:31
the righteous *b* shed on earth ... Matt 23:35
for this is my *b*...................Matt 26:28
sinned by betraying innocent *b*... Matt 27:4
called the "Field of *B*" to this ..... Matt 27:8
I am innocent of this man's *b* ... Matt 27:24
Let his *b* be on us and on our.... Matt 27:25
is the new covenant in my *b*.....Luke 22:20
his sweat was like drops of *b*.....Luke 22:44
eats my flesh and drinks my *b*.... John 6:54

Hakeldama, that is, "Field of *B* .....Acts 1:19
to darkness and the moon to *b*... Acts 2:20
with the *b* of his own Son .... Acts 20:28
declared righteous by his *b*........Rom 5:9
sharing in the *b* of Christ ....1 Cor 10:16
Flesh and *b* cannot inherit....... 1 Cor 15:50
redemption through his *b* .... Eph 1:7
brought near by the *b* of Christ.....Eph 2:13
is not against flesh and *b*.......... Eph 6:12
making peace through the *b*........Col 1:20
not by the *b* of goats and calves... Heb 9:12
This is the *b* of the covenant.......Heb 9:20
everything was purified with *b* ....Heb 9:22
to enter the sanctuary by the *b*... Heb 10:19
sprinkling with Jesus Christ's *b* ..... 1 Pet 1:2
but by precious *b* like that of ...... 1 Pet 1:19
b of Jesus his Son cleanses us ..... 1 John 1:7
Spirit and the water and the *b*.... 1 John 5:8
at the cost of his own *b*.............. Rev 1:5
at the cost of your own *b*...........Rev 5:9
the full moon became *b* red ....Rev 6:12
white in the *b* of the Lamb ....Rev 7:14
A third of the sea became *b* .... Rev 8:8
they overcame him by the *b*.......Rev 12:11
drunk with the *b* of the saints ......Rev 17:6
dressed in clothing dipped in *b* .... Rev 19:13

BLOODSHED
accountable for the *b*..............Deut 21:8
for you are a man of *b*......... 2 Sam 16:8
resisted to the point of *b* .... Heb 12:4

BLOOM
for our vineyard is in *b* ....Song 2:15
rejoice and *b* like a lily...............Isa 35:1

BLOSSOM
Israel will *b* and grow branches...... Isa 27:6

BLOSSOMED
b and give off their fragrance......Song 2:13

BLOSSOMS
is like a cluster of henna *b*.........Song 1:14
B have appeared in the land ......Song 2:12

BLOT
would *b* out Israel's memory ....2 Kgs 14:27

BLOW
you must *b* with your trumpets .. Num 10:10
while the priests *b* the horns ....Josh 6:4
are with me *b* our trumpets ....Judg 7:18
B on my garden so that...........Song 4:16
B the trumpet in Zion ....Joel 2:1
LORD will *b* the trumpet and...... Zech 9:14

BLOWING
sound like a violent wind *b* ....Acts 2:2

BLOWN
b and tossed around by.................Jas 1:6

BLOWS
but when the hot wind *b* ....Ps 103:16
the wind sent by the LORD *b*........Isa 40:7
The wind *b* wherever it will.........John 3:8

BLUE
b, purple, scarlet, fine linen.......Exod 25:4
to make pomegranates of *b* .....Exod 28:33
the entrance of the tent of *b* ....Exod 36:37
they must spread a *b* cloth .... Num 4:7
put a *b* thread on the tassel ..... Num 15:38
He made the curtain out of *b*..... 2 Chr 3:14
in *b* and white royal attire ....Esth 8:15
dark *b*, and sulfurous yellow........Rev 9:17

BLUSH
do not even know how to *b*........Jer 6:15

BOANERGES
Surname of James and John, Mark 3:17

BOAST
should not *b* like one who is......1 Kgs 20:11
B about his holy name.............1 Chr 16:10
I will *b* in the LORD ....Ps 34:2
In God we *b* all day long.............Ps 44:8
b of your relationship to God......Rom 2:17
not *b* of work already done.......2 Cor 10:16
so that I too may *b* a little ....2 Cor 11:16

so that no one can *b*.................Eph 2:9
do not *b* and tell lies.................Jas 3:14

BOASTFUL
b, contrivers of all sorts of evil ....Rom 1:30
b, arrogant, blasphemers.........2 Tim 3:2

BOASTING
is *b*? It is excluded.................Rom 3:27
Your *b* is not good.................1 Cor 5:6
deprive me of my reason for *b* ....1 Cor 9:15
All such *b* is evil ....Jas 4:16

BOASTS
and the tongue that *b* .... Ps 12:3
one who *b* of a gift not given .....Prov 25:14
one who *b*, boast in the Lord ......1 Cor 1:31
who *b* must boast in the Lord ... 2 Cor 10:17

BOAT
a *b* with their father Zebedee.....Matt 4:21
getting into a *b* he crossed ....Matt 9:1
the disciples get into the *b* .... Matt 14:22
again in a *b* to the other side ..... Mark 5:21
away by themselves in a *b*.....Mark 6:32
b was in the middle of the sea....Mark 6:47
One day Jesus got into a *b*........Luke 8:22
wanted to take him into the *b* .....John 6:21

BOATS
They glide by like reed *b*...........Job 9:26

BOAZ
A wealthy Bethlehemite, Ruth 2:1, 4–18
Husband of Ruth, Ruth 4:10–13
Ancestor of Christ, Matt 1:5
—Along with Yakin, one of the two pillars in
   front of Solomon's temple, 1 Kgs 7:21

BODIES
whole valley where dead *b* .... Jer 31:40
hearts of stone from their *b* ...... Ezek 11:19
the redemption of our *b*.......... Rom 8:23
present your *b* as a sacrifice....... Rom 12:1
your *b* are members of Christ .....1 Cor 6:15
are heavenly and earthly *b* ....1 Cor 15:40
love their wives as their own *b* .... Eph 5:28
among the parts of our *b*..........Jas 3:6
the celestial *b* will melt away ..... 2 Pet 3:10

BODILY
on him in *b* form like a dove...... Luke 3:22

BODY
was his *b* lying on the road ...... 1 Kgs 13:24
his *b* well nourished.................Job 21:24
my whole *b* wasted away.............Ps 32:3
will bring healing to your *b*.......Prov 3:8
and healing to one's entire *b* .... Prov 4:22
study is exhausting to the *b* ......Eccl 12:12
b became damp with the dew ..... Dan 4:33
The eye is the lamp of the *b* ......Matt 6:22
who kill the *b* but cannot kill .... Matt 10:28
Take, eat, this is my *b*............Matt 26:26
and asked for the *b* of Jesus ..... Matt 27:58
about the temple of his *b*........John 2:21
nor did his *b* experience decay .... Acts 2:31
rescue me from this *b* of death... Rom 7:24
one *b* we have many members ... Rom 12:4
b is not for sexual immorality .....1 Cor 6:13
commits is outside of the *b*........1 Cor 6:18
know that your *b* is the temple... 1 Cor 6:19
glorify God with your *b*...........1 Cor 6:20
Instead I subdue my *b* and........1 Cor 9:27
we who are many are one *b* ......1 Cor 10:17
This is my *b*, which is for you .....1 Cor 11:24
be guilty of the *b* and blood ......1 Cor 11:27
the *b* is one and yet has many ....1 Cor 12:12
were all baptized into one *b* ....1 Cor 12:13
the *b* is not a single member ....1 Cor 12:14
Now you are Christ's *b* ....1 Cor 12:27
over my *b* in order to boast ......1 Cor 13:3
it is sown a natural *b* ....1 Cor 15:44
this perishable *b* must put on ....1 Cor 15:53
and this mortal *b* must put on....1 Cor 15:53
physical *b* is wearing away........2 Cor 4:16
could defile the *b* and the spirit ... 2 Cor 7:1
the life I now live in the *b*..........Gal 2:20
reconcile them both in one *b*.......Eph 2:16
has ever hated his own *b* .... Eph 5:29

Christ will be exalted in my *b*.......Phil 1:20
his physical *b* through death........ Col 1:22
the removal of the fleshly *b* ....Col 2:11
unsparing treatment of the *b*.......Col 2:23
called as one *b* to this peace........ Col 3:15
how to possess his own *b* ....1 Thess 4:4
but a *b* you prepared for me.......Heb 10:5
the offering of the *b* of Jesus ...... Heb 10:10
the *b* without the spirit is dead ..... Jas 2:26
tongue is a small part of the *b*........Jas 3:5
bore our sins in his *b* on the tree .. 1 Pet 2:24

BOLD
person has put on a *b* face........Prov 21:29

BOLDNESS
b and without restriction ....Acts 28:31
have *b* and confident access........Eph 3:12
but that with complete *b* ....Phil 1:20
and great *b* in the faith ....1 Tim 3:13

BOLT
a two-pronged lightning *b* ....Hab 3:4

BOLTS
lightning *b* lit up the world ....Ps 77:18
lightning *b* light up the world........Ps 97:4

BOND
into the *b* of the covenant .... Ezek 20:37
of the Spirit in the *b* of peace........Eph 4:3
which is the perfect *b*............. Col 3:14

BONDAGE
Those delivered from *b*............. Isa 35:9
those delivered from *b* .... Isa 51:10

BONE
This one at last is *b* of my bones... Gen 2:23
Not a *b* of his will be broken......John 19:36

BONES
carry my *b* up from this place ....Gen 50:25
which made all my *b* shake......... Job 4:14
My *b* stick to my skin and ....Job 19:20
Its *b* are tubes of bronze............Job 40:18
I can count all my *b*............... Ps 22:17
and my *b* become brittle .... Ps 31:10
b were not hidden from you....... Ps 139:15
or how the *b* form in the womb .... Eccl 11:5
fractured *b* and heals their ....Isa 30:26
Prophesy over these *b*............ Ezek 37:4
and the *b* came together ....Ezek 37:7
b are all the house of Israel....... Ezek 37:11
full of the *b* of the dead.......... Matt 23:27

BOOK
See also BOOK OF LIFE; BOOK OF THE LAW
read from the *b* of God's law ...... Neh 8:8
is written in a dependable *b* ....Dan 10:21
are found written in the *b* .... Dan 12:1
written in the *b* of the law ....Gal 3:10
and sprinkled both the *b* .... Heb 9:19
written in the Lamb's *b* of life .....Rev 21:27
prophecy contained in this *b* ......Rev 22:18
the words of this *b* of prophecy .. Rev 22:19

BOOK OF LIFE
whose names are in the *b* ....Phil 4:3
erase his name from the *b*..........Rev 3:5
the *b* belonging to the Lamb ....Rev 13:8
not been written in the *b* ....Rev 17:8
book was opened—the *b*.......... Rev 20:12
not found written in the *b* .... Rev 20:15
are written in the Lamb's *b* ....Rev 21:27

BOOK OF THE LAW
to bring the *b* of Moses.............Neh 8:1
were eager to hear the *b* .... Neh 8:3
Ezra read in the *b* of God ....Neh 8:18
read from the *b* of the Lord........ Neh 9:3
everything written in the *b* ....Gal 3:10

BOOKS
to the making of many *b* ....Eccl 12:12
not have room for the *b*...........John 21:25
collected their *b* and burned ..... Acts 19:19
Then *b* were opened.............. Rev 20:12

BOOTH
Matthew sitting at the tax *b* .... Matt 9:9
Levi sitting at the tax *b* ....Luke 5:27

BORDER
He restored the *b* of Israel.......2 Kgs 14:25
dedicated to the Lord at its *b* ......Isa 19:19

BORDERS
before you and enlarge your *b* ..Exod 34:24

BORE
Who *b* these children for me ...... Isa 49:21
b the hardship and burning heat .. Matt 20:12
b our sins in his body on the tree .. 1 Pet 2:24

BORN
See also BORN FROM ABOVE
b you must throw into the river ...Exod 1:22
but people are *b* to trouble.......... Job 5:7
Man, *b* of woman, lives..............Job 14:1
This one was *b* there ....Ps 87:4
yet to be *b* will praise the Lord ... Ps 102:18
A time to be *b* .... Eccl 3:2
For a child has been *b* to us.......... Isa 9:6
nation be *b* in a single moment..... Isa 66:8
by whom Jesus was *b*............. Matt 1:16
Today your Savior is *b*............. Luke 2:11
a person is *b* from above ....John 3:3
What is *b* of the flesh is flesh .....John 3:6
For this reason I was *b*............John 18:37
to one *b* at the wrong time ....1 Cor 15:8
was *b* by natural descent ....Gal 4:23

BORN FROM ABOVE
unless a person is *b*................John 3:3
You must all be *b* ....John 3:7

BORNE
b the image of the man of dust.. 1 Cor 15:49
was ever *b* of human impulse .....2 Pet 1:21

BORROW
Evil men *b*, but do not repay........ Ps 37:21

BORROWER
the *b* is servant to the lender......Prov 22:7
the *b* as well as the lender......... Isa 24:2

BOTTOM
down to the *b* like a stone.........Exod 15:5
from top to *b* ....Matt 27:51
from top to *b* ....Mark 15:38

BOUGH
Joseph is a fruitful *b* ....Gen 49:22

BOUGHT
belong to the one who *b* it .... Lev 25:28
David *b* the threshing floor.... 2 Sam 24:16
She considered a field and *b* it.... Prov 31:16
So I *b* the field at Anathoth....... Jer 32:9
will again be *b* with silver......... Jer 32:44
sold all that he had and *b*........ Matt 13:44
sold everything he had and *b*.... Matt 13:46
For you were *b* at a price ....1 Cor 6:20
denying the Master who *b*..........2 Pet 2:1

BOUND
and *b* him in bronze chains........ Judg 16:21
You are *b* for judgment..............Mal 3:9
will have been *b* in heaven........Matt 16:19
for I am *b* with this chain ....Acts 28:20
married woman is *b* by law.........Rom 7:2
one *b* to a wife should not........ 1 Cor 7:27

BOUNDARIES
You must set *b* for the people ....Exod 19:12
set your *b* from the Red Sea......Exod 23:31
he extends the *b* of nations........Job 12:23

BOUNDARY
You set up a *b* for them.............Ps 104:9

BOUNDING
b over the hills.....................Song 2:8

BOUTS
carousing, drinking *b*, and.........1 Pet 4:3

BOW
and nations *b* down to you ....Gen 27:29
brothers really come and *b*.......Gen 37:10
But his *b* will remain steady .....Gen 49:24
must not *b* down to their gods ..Exod 23:24
should be taught "The *B*.........2 Sam 1:18
my *b* ever new in my hand ....Job 29:20
For I do not trust in my *b*...........Ps 44:6

He shatters the *b* and breaks . . . . . . .Ps 46:9
unreliable as a malfunctioning *b*. . . .Ps 78:57
let us *b* down and worship. . . . . .Ps 95:6
Surely every knee will *b* to me . . . . Isa 45:23
them by the warrior's *b*. . . . . .Hos 1:7
every knee will *b* to me. . . . . Rom 14:11
of Jesus every knee will *b*. . . . . .Phil 2:10
The one who rode it had a *b*. . . . . . . .Rev 6:2

BOWED
See also BOWED DOWN
surrounded my sheaf and *b* . . . . . . .Gen 37:7
not *b* their knees to Baal . . . . .1 Kgs 19:18

BOWED DOWN
Abram *b* with his face . . . . .Gen 17:3
Then I *b* and worshiped. . . . . .Gen 24:48
Surrounded my sheaf and *b* . . . . . . Gen 37:7
Joseph's brothers came and *b* . . . .Gen 42:6
people *b* low to the ground. . . . . . Exod 12:27
He worshiped and *b* to Baal . . . . .1 Kgs 22:53
He *b* to all the stars in the sky . . . . 2 Kgs 21:3
they *b* and worshiped the **Lord** . . . . . Neh 8:6
I *b* in sorrow .Ps 35:14
they *b* and worshiped him . . . . Matt 2:11
he *b* with his face . . . . .Luke 5:12

BOWL
or the golden *b* is broken. . . . . .Eccl 12:6
poured out his *b* on the earth . . . . . .Rev 16:2

BOWLS
its shovels, its tossing *b* . . . . Exod 27:3
was not used for silver *b* . . . . 2 Kgs 12:13
the meat forks, *b*, and jars . . . . 1 Chr 28:17
drink wine from sacrificial *b* . . . . . Amos 6:6
and golden *b* full of incense . . . . .Rev 5:8
seven *b* containing God's wrath . . . . Rev 16:1
b full of the seven final plagues. . . . .Rev 21:9

BOWS
b of warriors are shattered . . . . .1 Sam 2:4

BOX
put more into the offering *b* . . . . .Mark 12:43
their gifts into the offering *b* . . . . . .Luke 21:1
Judas had the money *b* . . . . .John 13:29
b like one who hits only air . . . . . . .1 Cor 9:26

BOY
and then gave the *b* a drink. . . . . . . .Gen 21:19
Do not harm the *b*. . . . . Gen 22:12
The *b* isn't there . . . . .Gen 37:30
Don't sin against the *b*. . . . . .Gen 42:22
and the *b* is not with us. . . . . Gen 44:30
The *b* Samuel was serving . . . . .1 Sam 2:11
the *b* Samuel was growing up . . .1 Sam 2:26
Now the *b* Samuel continued. . . . . .1 Sam 3:1
She named the *b* Ichabod . . . . .1 Sam 4:21
a ruddy and handsome *b* . . . . .1 Sam 17:42
spread his body out over the *b* . . .2 Kgs 4:34
the *b* Jesus stayed behind. . . . . Luke 2:43
b who has five barley loaves. . . . . . .John 6:9

BOY'S
the *b* breath returned to him . . . . 1 Kgs 17:22

BOYS
full of *b* and girls playing . . . . Zech 8:5

BOZRAH
City of Edom, Gen 36:33
Destruction of, foretold, Amos 1:12
Figurative of Messiah's victory, Isa 63:1

BRACELET
the *b* which was on his arm. . . . . . .2 Sam 1:10

BRACELETS
wrist *b* weighing ten shekels . . . . .Gen 24:22
armlets, *b*, signet rings . . . . Num 31:50
sisters put *b* on their wrists. . . . . . Ezek 23:42

BRAG
Love does not *b* . . . . .1 Cor 13:4

BRAIDED
not be with *b* hair and gold . . . . . . .1 Tim 2:9

BRAIDS
weave the seven *b* of my hair. . . . . Judg 16:13

BRAMBLES
nor are grapes picked from *b*. . . .Luke 6:44

BRANCH
blossoms are to be on one *b* . . . . Exod 25:33
his hand and cut off a tree *b* . . . . . . Judg 9:48
raise up for them a righteous *b*. . . . .Jer 23:5
take one *b* and write on it . . . . .Ezek 37:16
introduce my servant, the *B* . . . . Zech 3:8
is the man whose name is *B* . . . . . .Zech 6:12
its *b* becomes tender and. . . . . . . .Matt 24:32
He takes away every *b*. . . . . .John 15:2
Just as the *b* cannot bear fruit . . . .John 15:4
thrown out like a *b* and dries . . . . . .John 15:6

BRANCHES
and his *b* will not flourish. . . . . .Job 15:32
the highest cedars by its *b*. . . . . .Ps 80:10
b reached the Mediterranean . . . . . Ps 80:11
is ready to cut off the *b*. . . . . .Isa 10:33
b will be good for nothing . . . . .Jer 11:16
wild birds nested in its *b*. . . . . .Luke 13:19
I am the vine; you are the *b*. . . . . . . .John 15:5
so too are the *b*. . . . . Rom 11:16
if some of the *b* were broken. . . . . .Rom 11:17

BRASH
The woman called Folly is *b* . . . . . . .Prov 9:13

BRAVE
you are very strong and *b* . . . . .Josh 1:7
He is a *b* warrior and . . . . .1 Sam 16:18
Be strong and *b*. . . . . .2 Chr 32:7

BRAVEHEARTED
The *b* were plundered . . . . .Ps 76:5

BRAWLS
arguments, *b*, and fistfights. . . . . Isa 58:4

BRAZEN
B and insolent . . . . 2 Pet 2:10

BREACHES
Repair its *b* . . . . .Ps 60:2

BREAD
See also FEAST OF UNLEAVENED BREAD;
   UNLEAVENED BREAD
brought out *b* and wine. . . . . .Gen 14:18
to rain *b* from heaven . . . . Exod 16:4
the Feast of Unleavened *B*. . . . . . . Exod 23:15
cannot live by *b* alone . . . . Deut 8:3
for there was no *b* there. . . . . .1 Sam 21:6
a land of *b* and vineyards . . . . .2 Kgs 18:32
ate my morsel of *b* myself. . . . . .Job 31:17
as if they were eating *b* . . . . Ps 14:4
Indeed they have eaten *b* . . . . .Prov 4:17
Better is a dry crust of *b* . . . . Prov 17:1
B gained by deceit. . . . . .Prov 20:17
my allotted portion of *b* . . . . .Prov 30:8
give me my *b* and my water . . . . Hos 2:5
like a ruined cake of *b* . . . . .Hos 7:8
b eaten while in mourning. . . . . .Hos 9:4
these stones to become *b* . . . . Matt 4:3
Man does not live by *b* alone . . . . . . Matt 4:4
Give us today our daily *b* . . . . Matt 6:11
Jesus took *b*, and after giving . . . .Matt 26:26
no *b*, no bag, no money. . . . . .Mark 6:8
the Feast of Unleavened *B*. . . . . .Mark 14:1
lend me three loaves of *b*. . . . . Luke 11:5
the loaves of *b* you wanted . . . . John 6:26
given you the *b* from heaven . . . . . .John 6:32
I am the *b* of life . . . . .John 6:48
I will give this piece of *b* . . . . .John 13:26
Is not the *b* that we break . . . . .1 Cor 10:16
which he was betrayed took *b*. . . .1 Cor 11:23
For every time you eat this *b* . . . . .1 Cor 11:26

BREADTH
the *b* and length and height . . . . .Eph 3:18

BREAK
you must not *b* a bone of it. . . . . . . Exod 12:46
Lord *b* through against them . . . Exod 19:22
B off the gold earrings. . . . . Exod 32:2
and will *b* their bones. . . . . .Num 24:8
I will never *b* my covenant. . . . . Judg 2:1
b the teeth in their mouths. . . . . .Ps 58:6
they *b* my rules and do not. . . . . . . .Ps 89:31
I will not *b* my covenant . . . . .Ps 89:34
they *b* your law. . . . . .Ps 119:126
crushed reed he will not *b*. . . . . Isa 42:3

b every burdensome yoke. . . . . Isa 58:6
Do not *b* it . . . . .Jer 14:21
B up the unplowed ground . . . . .Hos 10:12
where thieves *b* in and steal . . . . . . .Matt 6:19
He will not *b* a bruised reed . . . . . Matt 12:20
they did not *b* his legs . . . . .John 19:33
when we met to *b* bread. . . . . .Acts 20:7
not the bread that we *b* . . . . .1 Cor 10:16

BREAKING
the *b* of bread and to prayer. . . . . . .Acts 2:42
b bread from house to house. . . . . .Acts 2:46
weeping and *b* my heart. . . . . .Acts 21:13

BREAKS
and *b* his covenant. . . . . .Deut 17:2
he *b* his solemn promises . . . . .Ps 55:20
b one of the least of these. . . . . . . .Matt 5:19

BREASTPIECE
a *b*, an ephod, a robe, a fitted. . . . .Exod 28:4

BREASTPLATE
on the *b* of righteousness . . . . .Eph 6:14

BREASTS
blessings of the *b* and womb . . . . .Gen 49:25
feel secure on my mother's *b*. . . . . . .Ps 22:9
her *b* satisfy you at all times. . . . . . .Prov 5:19
Your two *b* are like two fawns. . . . .Song 4:5
satisfying *b* and be nourished . . . . . .Isa 66:11
and the *b* at which you nursed . . .Luke 11:27
returned home beating their *b* . .Luke 23:48

BREATH
See also BREATH OF LIFE
the powerful *b* from his nose. . .2 Sam 22:16
By the *b* of God they perish . . . . .Job 4:9
a *b* of air passes by my face. . . . . Job 4:15
b from God is in my nostrils . . . . . . .Job 27:3
b of the Almighty gives me life . . . . .Job 33:4
you take away their life's *b* . . . . Ps 104:29
you send your life-giving *b* . . . . Ps 104:30
that has *b* praise the **Lord**. . . . . .Ps 150:6
both have the same *b*. . . . . .Eccl 3:19
the life's *b* returns to God . . . . .Eccl 12:7
Though the *b* of tyrants . . . . Isa 25:4
one who gives *b* to the people. . . . . .Isa 42:5
about to infuse *b* into you . . . . .Ezek 37:5
in his control your very *b* . . . . Dan 5:23
gives life and *b* and everything . . .Acts 17:25
destroy by the *b* of his mouth . . .2 Thess 2:8

BREATH OF LIFE
breathed into his nostrils the *b* . . . . Gen 2:7
creatures that have the *b*. . . . . .Gen 6:17
creatures that have the *b*. . . . . .Gen 7:15
had the *b* in its nostrils died . . . . . . Gen 7:22
a *b* from God entered them . . . . .Rev 11:11

BREATHE
he could no longer *b*. . . . . .1 Kgs 17:17
and *b* on these corpses . . . . Ezek 37:9

BREATHED
and *b* into his nostrils. . . . . Gen 2:7
he *b* on them and said . . . . .John 20:22

BREATHES
he *b* on it, and the water flows . . . . Ps 147:18

BREED
you know they *b* infighting . . . . . . .2 Tim 2:23

BREVITY
my mortality and the *b* of life . . . . . . .Ps 39:4

BRIBE
You must not accept a *b*. . . . . Exod 23:8
Do not take a *b* . . . . .Deut 16:19
let a large *b* turn you aside . . . . .Job 36:18
to do wrong or offer a *b* . . . . .Ps 26:10
a *b* corrupts the heart . . . . .Eccl 7:7

BRIBERY
All of them love *b* . . . . Isa 1:23

BRIBES
tents of those who accept *b* . . . . . . .Job 15:34
whoever hates *b* will live . . . . .Prov 15:27
the innocent, you take *b*. . . . . .Amos 5:12

BRICK
and burn incense on *b* altars . . . . . . Isa 65:3

BRICKS
let's make *b* and bake them . . . . Gen 11:3
to the people for making *b* . . . . Exod 5:7
the same quota of *b* . . . . Exod 5:8
produce your quota of *b*. . . . . Exod 5:18
The *b* have fallen . . . . Isa 9:10
mud *b* to strengthen your walls . . . Nah 3:14

BRIDE
b stands at your right hand. . . . . Ps 45:9
my *b*! How much better is . . . . Song 4:10
put them on as if you were a *b* . . . . Isa 49:18
has the *b* is the bridegroom . . . . . . John 3:29
I will show you the *b*. . . . . Rev 21:9
And the Spirit and the *b* say . . . . . . Rev 22:17

BRIDEGROOM
Surely you are a *b* of blood . . . . Exod 4:25
b when he wears a turban . . . . Isa 61:10
As a *b* rejoices over a bride . . . . Isa 62:5
and went out to meet the *b* . . . . . . Matt 25:1
who has the bride is the *b* . . . . John 3:29

BRIDLE
they are controlled by a *b* . . . . Ps 32:9

BRIEF
elation of the wicked is *b*. . . . . Job 20:5

BRIERS
b and thorns surround you . . . . Ezek 2:6
suffer from the sharp *b*. . . . . Ezek 28:24

BRIGHT
If even the moon is not *b* . . . . Job 25:5
and the night is as *b* as day . . . . Ps 139:12
is like the *b* morning light . . . . Prov 4:18
b look brings joy to the heart. . . . . Prov 15:30
b as the sun. . . . . Song 6:10
kings to your *b* light . . . . Isa 60:3

BRIGHTER
b and *b* until full day. . . . . Prov 4:18
ones were *b* than snow . . . . Lam 4:7
b than the sun . . . . Acts 26:13

BRIGHTLY
her vindication shines *b* . . . . Isa 62:1

BRIGHTNESS
From the *b* in front of him. . . . . . 2 Sam 22:13
He is like the *b* after rain . . . . 2 Sam 23:4

BRIMSTONE
down burning coals and *b*. . . . . Ps 11:6
hailstones, fire, and *b* . . . . Ezek 38:22

BRING
ravens to *b* you food there . . . . 1 Kgs 17:4
Let them *b* us two bulls . . . . 1 Kgs 18:23
Why *b* calamity on yourself . . . . . 2 Kgs 14:10
my lips would *b* you relief. . . . . Job 16:5
proud man and *b* him low . . . . Job 40:11
For you *b* him rich blessings. . . . . Ps 21:3
b them back from the depths. . . . . . Ps 68:22
You *b* their lives to an end. . . . . Ps 90:5
king *b* me into his bedroom . . . . . . Song 1:4
b a baby to the birth opening. . . . . . Isa 66:9
B the best robe. . . . . Luke 15:22
will tie you up and *b* you . . . . John 21:18
to *b* this man's blood on us . . . . . . Acts 5:28
came to *b* to my people gifts . . . . . Acts 24:17
Who will *b* any charge. . . . . Rom 8:33
to *b* Christ down. . . . . Rom 10:6
to *b* Christ up from the dead . . . . . . Rom 10:7
Now food will not *b* us close . . . . . 1 Cor 8:8
God will *b* with him those . . . . . . 1 Thess 4:14
and will *b* me safely . . . . 2 Tim 4:18

BRINGING
I am *b* my deliverance near. . . . . Isa 46:13

BRINGS
Whoever *b* a fool into the world . . Prov 17:21

BROAD
to carouse in *b* daylight. . . . . 2 Pet 2:13

BROCADE
in a *b* trimmed with gold . . . . Ps 45:13

BROKE
and *b* them to pieces . . . . Exod 32:19
gave thanks and *b* the loaves. . . . Matt 14:19

and *b* the legs of the two men. . . . John 19:32
given thanks he *b* it and said . . . . 1 Cor 11:24

BROKEN
like a *b* jar . . . . Ps 31:12
and their bows will be *b* . . . . Ps 37:15
painful heart the spirit is *b*. . . . . . Prov 15:13
All Israel has *b* your law . . . . Dan 9:11
they have *b* God's laws . . . . Zeph 3:4
the scripture cannot be. . . . . John 10:35
He has *b* the power of death . . . . . 2 Tim 1:10

BROKENHEARTED
He heals the *b* and bandages . . . . . . Ps 147:3
to help the *b*. Isa 61:1

BRONZE
So Moses made a *b* snake . . . . Num 21:9
sky above your heads will be *b* . . . Deut 28:23
demolished the *b* serpent . . . . 2 Kgs 18:4
Or is my flesh made of *b* . . . . Job 6:12
and *b* as rotten wood. . . . . Job 41:27
For he shattered the *b* gates. . . . . . Ps 107:16
Instead of *b*, I will bring. . . . . Isa 60:17
iron pillar, and a *b* wall . . . . Jer 1:18
a fortified wall of *b* . . . . Jer 15:20
third kingdom, one of *b* . . . . Dan 2:39
I will give you *b* hooves. . . . . Mic 4:13
two mountains of *b*. . . . . Zech 6:1
polished *b* refined in a furnace . . . . Rev 1:15

BROOKS
good land, a land of *b*, springs. . . . . Deut 8:7

BROTHER
Where is your *b* Abel. . . . . Gen 4:9
I would for a friend or my *b* . . . . Ps 35:14
You plot against your *b*. . . . . Ps 50:20
chased his *b* with a sword . . . . Amos 1:11
Esau was Jacob's *b*. . . . . Mal 1:2
B will hand over *b* to death. . . . . . Matt 10:21
times must I forgive my *b* . . . . Matt 18:21
b to divide the inheritance. . . . . . . Luke 12:13
Your *b* will come back to life . . . . . John 11:23
the weak *b* or sister . . . . 1 Cor 8:11
than a slave, as a dear *b* . . . . Phlm 1:16
and brutally murdered his *b*. . . . . . 1 John 3:12
your *b* and the one who shares. . . . . . Rev 1:9

BROTHER'S
see the speck in your *b* eye. . . . . Matt 7:3

BROTHER-IN-LAW
fulfill the duty of a *b* to her. . . . . . . Gen 38:8

BROTHERHOOD
failed to observe a treaty of *b*. . . . . Amos 1:9
to annul the covenant of *b*. . . . . . . Zech 11:14

BROTHERLY
B love must continue. . . . . Heb 13:1

BROTHERS
He will live away from his *b* . . . . . . Gen 16:12
My *b* have been as treacherous . . . . Job 6:15
own *b* treat me like a stranger. . . . . . Ps 69:8
when *b* truly live in unity . . . . Ps 133:1
and you are all *b*. . . . . Matt 23:8
tell my *b* to go to Galilee . . . . Matt 28:10
Who are my mother and my *b*. . . . Mark 3:33
My mother and my *b* are those. . . . Luke 8:21
not even his own *b* believed. . . . . . . John 7:5
B, the scripture had to be. . . . . Acts 1:16
six *b* also went with me . . . . Acts 11:12
in dangers from false *b* . . . . 2 Cor 11:26
false *b* with false pretenses. . . . . Gal 2:4
refuses to welcome the *b*. . . . . 3 John 1:10
with your *b* the prophets. . . . . Rev 22:9

BROUGHT
b stones and put them in a pile . . . Gen 31:46
they *b* the one who cursed . . . . . . Lev 24:23
b the east wind through the sky. . . . Ps 78:26
Holy One of Israel has *b* it . . . . Isa 41:20
people were *b* to the Lord. . . . . . . Acts 11:24

BROW
sweat of your *b* you will eat . . . . . . Gen 3:19

BRUISED
They beat me; they *b* me . . . . Song 5:7
He will not break a *b* reed . . . . . . Matt 12:20

BRUISES
by inflicting them with *b*. . . . . Ps 89:32

BRUTAL
will hand you over to *b* men . . . . . Ezek 21:31

BRUTISH
I am more *b* than any other . . . . . . Prov 30:2

BUCKET
are like a drop in a *b*. . . . . Isa 40:15
no *b* and the well is deep . . . . John 4:11

BUD
a *b* will sprout from his roots. . . . . . . Isa 11:1
When the fig tree does not *b* . . . . . . Hab 3:17

BUILD
b ourselves a city and a tower . . . . . Gen 11:4
fine cities you did not *b*. . . . . Deut 6:10
must *b* the altar of the LORD . . . . . Deut 27:6
Then *b* an altar for the LORD . . . . . Judg 6:26
b for him a lasting dynasty . . . . . . 1 Sam 2:35
really intend to *b* a house. . . . . 2 Sam 7:5
strong desire to *b* a temple. . . . . . . 1 Kgs 8:17
LORD will *b* a dynastic house . . . . 1 Chr 17:10
the one who will *b* my temple. . . . 1 Chr 28:6
who can really *b* a temple . . . . 2 Chr 2:6
to *b* the temple of the LORD. . . . . . . Ezra 1:5
the LORD does not *b* a house. . . . . . Ps 127:1
afterward *b* your house . . . . Prov 24:27
and a time to *b* up . . . . Eccl 3:3
b a level road through . . . . Isa 40:3
the house you will *b* for me . . . . Isa 66:1
There I will *b* them up . . . . Jer 24:6
b Zion through bloody crimes. . . . . . Mic 3:10
once again *b* the ruined places . . . . . Mal 1:4
to *b* and was not able to finish. . . Luke 14:30
What kind of house will you *b*. . . . . Acts 7:49
message is able to *b* you up . . . . . Acts 20:32
for his good to *b* him up. . . . . Rom 15:2
b on another person's
   foundation. . . . . Rom 15:20

BUILDER
whose architect and *b* is God. . . . . . Heb 11:10

BUILDERS
The stone that the *b* discarded . . . . Ps 118:22
The stone the *b* rejected. . . . . Matt 21:42
The stone the *b* rejected. . . . . Mark 12:10
The stone the *b* rejected. . . . . Luke 20:17
that was rejected by you, the *b* . . . . Acts 4:11
the stone that the *b* rejected . . . . . 1 Pet 2:7

BUILDING
You are God's field, God's *b* . . . . 1 Cor 3:9
we have a *b* from God. . . . . 2 Cor 5:1
for *b* you up and not for tearing . . 2 Cor 10:8
In him the whole *b* . . . . Eph 2:21
by *b* yourselves up. . . . . Jude 1:20

BUILDS
but someone else *b* on it . . . . 1 Cor 3:10
not everything *b* others up . . . . . . 1 Cor 10:23
speaks in a tongue *b* himself . . . . . 1 Cor 14:4
the body *b* itself up in love . . . . Eph 4:16

BUILT
Wisdom has *b* her house . . . . Prov 9:1
woman has *b* her household . . . . . . Prov 14:1
I *b* houses for myself . . . . Eccl 2:4
I have *b* for a royal residence . . . . . Dan 4:30
a wise man who *b* his house. . . . . . Matt 7:24
a foolish man who *b* his house . . . Matt 7:26
what someone has *b* survives . . . . . 1 Cor 3:14
have been *b* on the foundation . . . . Eph 2:20
every house is *b* by someone. . . . . . . Heb 3:4

BULL
take a *b* from your household . . . . . . Ps 50:9

BULLS
The blood of *b*. . . . . Isa 1:11
the blood of goats and *b*. . . . . Heb 9:13

BULWARK
the support and *b* of the truth. . . . 1 Tim 3:15

BURDEN
lay the *b* of this entire people . . . . Num 11:11
Have I become a *b* to you. . . . . Job 7:20
Throw your *b* upon the LORD. . . . . . . Ps 55:22

a *b* that I am tired of carrying .... Isa 1:14
LORD will remove their *b* .... Isa 10:27
to place any greater *b* on you ..... Acts 15:28
I myself was not a *b* to you ...... 2 Cor 12:13
to impose a *b* on any of you ..... 1 Thess 2:9
not put any additional *b* on you .... Rev 2:24

BURDENED
Yet you *b* me with your sins .... Isa 43:24
all you who are weary and *b* ...... Matt 11:28
that we were *b* excessively .... 2 Cor 1:8
I have not *b* you .... 2 Cor 12:16
The church should not be *b* .... 1 Tim 5:16

BURDENS
Carry one another's *b* .... Gal 6:2

BURDENSOME
God has given people a *b* task ..... Eccl 1:13

BURIAL
cave that was in it as a *b* site ..... Gen 23:20
at the *b* of your ancestors .... Jer 34:5
she did it to prepare me for *b* ... Matt 26:12
my body beforehand for *b* .... Mark 14:8
kept it for the day of my *b* .... John 12:7
gave instructions about his *b* ...... Heb 11:22

BURIED
there I will be *b* .... Ruth 1:17
took the body and *b* it .... Matt 14:12
man also died and was *b* .... Luke 16:22
b with him through baptism .... Rom 6:4
and that he was *b* .... 1 Cor 15:4
been *b* with him in baptism ...... Col 2:12

BURN
my anger can *b* against them .... Exod 32:10
and *b* their chariots .... Josh 11:6
both will *b* together .... Isa 1:31
Didn't our hearts *b* within us .... Luke 24:32
and *b* her up with fire .... Rev 17:16

BURNED
when he *b* with anger .... Lam 1:12
I, the LORD, have *b* it .... Ezek 20:48
its fate is to be *b* .... Heb 6:8
are *b* outside the camp .... Heb 13:11

BURNING
b in my heart and soul .... Jer 20:9
heaping *b* coals on his head ..... Rom 12:20
to a *b* fire and darkness .... Heb 12:18
great mountain of *b* fire .... Rev 8:8
a huge star *b* like a torch .... Rev 8:10

BURNT
offered *b* offerings on the altar .... Gen 8:20
the lamb for the *b* offering .... Gen 22:7
with sacrifices and *b* offerings ... Exod 10:25
a *b* offering and sacrifices .... Exod 18:12
the altar for the *b* offering .... Exod 40:6
a *b* offering from the herd .... Lev 1:3
offered *b* sacrifices to the LORD ... Josh 8:31
as a *b* sacrifice on the wood ..... Judg 6:26
make a *b* sacrifice to the LORD ... Judg 13:16
b offering and the grain offering .. Judg 13:23
offer up 1,000 *b* sacrifices .... 1 Kgs 3:4
Solomon offered *b* offerings ..... 1 Kgs 9:25
could offer *b* offerings on it .... Ezra 3:2
you do not desire a *b* sacrifice .... Ps 51:16
cannot accept the *b* offerings .... Jer 6:20
built to offer up *b* offerings ...... Ezek 43:18
offer me *b* and grain offerings ... Amos 5:22

BURST
new wineskins ready to *b* .... Job 32:19
with doors when it *b* forth .... Job 38:8
new wine will *b* the skins .... Luke 5:37

BURY
You may *b* your dead .... Gen 23:6
and there is no one to *b* them ...... Ps 79:3
to *b* him with criminals .... Isa 53:9
first go and *b* my father .... Matt 8:21
the dead *b* their own dead .... Matt 8:22

BUSH
flame of fire from within a *b* ...... Exod 3:2
who resided in the burning *b* .... Deut 33:16
who appeared to him in the *b* .... Acts 7:35

BUSINESS
and conducts his *b* honestly .... Ps 112:5
another to his *b* .... Matt 22:5
deal of *b* to the craftsmen .... Acts 19:24
do *b* and make a profit .... Jas 4:13

BUSYBODIES
but also gossips and *b* .... 1 Tim 5:13

BUT I SAY TO YOU
B that anyone who is angry .... Matt 5:22
B that whoever looks at .... Matt 5:28
B, do not take oaths .... Matt 5:34
B, do not resist .... Matt 5:39
B, love your enemy .... Matt 5:44
B who are listening .... Luke 6:27

BUTTER
steps were bathed with *b* .... Job 29:6
words are as smooth as *b* .... Ps 55:21
churning of milk produces *b* ..... Prov 30:33

BUY
b from you the threshing floor .. 2 Sam 24:21
no money, come! *B* and eat .... Isa 55:1
B that field with silver .... Jer 32:25
b food for all these people .... Luke 9:13
to *b* whatever they needed .... John 13:29
those who *b* like those .... 1 Cor 7:30
take my advice and *b* gold .... Rev 3:18
was allowed to *b* or sell .... Rev 13:17

BUYER
It's worthless!" says the *b* .... Prov 20:14
the seller as well as the *b* .... Isa 24:2

BUYS
no one *b* their cargo any longer ... Rev 18:11

BYWORD
He has made me a *b* to people ..... Job 17:6

C

CAESAR
—Augustus Caesar (31 BC–AD 14):
Decree of brings Joseph and Mary to
    Bethlehem, Luke 2:1
—Tiberius Caesar (AD 14–37):
Christ's ministry dated by, Luke 3:1–23
Tribute paid to, Matt 22:17–21
Jews side with, John 19:12
—Claudius Caesar (AD 41–54):
Famine in time of, Acts 11:28
Banished Jews from Rome, Acts 18:2
—Nero Caesar (AD 54–68):
Paul appealed to, Acts 25:8–12
Christian converts in household of, Phil 4:22
Paul tried before, 2 Tim 4:16–18
Called Augustus, Acts 25:21

CAESAREA
Roman capital of Palestine, Acts 12:19; 23:33
Paul escorted to, Acts 23:23–33
Paul imprisoned at; appeals to Caesar,
    Acts 25:4, 8–13
Peter preaches at, Acts 10:34–43
Paul preaches at, Acts 9:26–30; 18:22; 21:8

CAESAREA PHILIPPI
A city in northern Palestine; scene of
    Peter's great confession, Matt 16:13–20
Probable site of the transfiguration,
    Matt 17:1–3

CAGE
Like a *c* filled with the birds .... Jer 5:27

CAIAPHAS
Son-in-law of Annas; high priest, John 18:13
Makes prophecy, John 11:49–52
Jesus appears before, John 18:23–24
Apostles appear before, Acts 4:1–22

CAIN
Adam's first son, Gen 4:1
His offering rejected, Gen 4:2–7; Heb 11:4
Murders Abel; is exiled; settles in Nod,
    Gen 4:8–17
A type of evil, Jude 1:11

CAKES
Sustain me with raisin *c* .... Song 2:5
love to offer raisin *c* to idols .... Hos 3:1

CALAMITIES
He will deliver you from six *c* .... Job 5:19

CALAMITY
because I experience no *c* .... Ps 10:6
the wicked are filled with *c* .... Prov 12:21

CALCULATED
who has *c* the cost in his mind ..... Prov 23:7

CALEB
Sent as spy; gives good report; rewarded,
    Num 13:2, 6, 27, 30; 14:5–9, 24–38
Inherits Hebron, Josh 14:6–15
Conquers his territory with Othniel's help,
    Josh 15:13–19

CALF
and made a molten *c* .... Exod 32:4
made an image of a *c* at Horeb .... Ps 106:19
like a *c* untrained to the yoke .... Jer 31:18
Bring the fattened *c* and kill it .... Luke 15:23

CALL
I will *c* on the LORD so that ...... 1 Sam 12:17
C the men of Judah together .... 2 Sam 20:4
To you, O people, I *c* out .... Prov 8:4
I *c* you by name .... Isa 43:1
c to him while he is nearby .... Isa 55:6
C on me in prayer .... Jer 33:3
They will *c* on my name .... Zech 13:9
not come to *c* the righteous .... Matt 9:13
Why do you *c* me good .... Mark 10:18
God will *c* to himself .... Acts 2:39
c those who were not my people .. Rom 9:25
How are they to *c* on one .... Rom 10:14
the *c* of God are irrevocable ...... Rom 11:29
the circumstances of your *c* ...... 1 Cor 1:26
God did not *c* us to impurity ..... 1 Thess 4:7

CALLED
God *c* the light "day" and .... Gen 1:5
The LORD again *c* .... 1 Sam 3:6
and is *c* Wonderful Adviser .... Isa 9:6
you have been *c* our Protector ..... Isa 63:16
I *c* my Son out of Egypt .... Matt 2:15
He came to a town *c* Nazareth ... Matt 2:23
c according to his purpose .... Rom 8:28
he predestined, he also *c* .... Rom 8:30
God has *c* you in peace .... 1 Cor 7:15
who *c* you out of darkness .... 1 Pet 2:9
knowledge of the one who *c* .... 2 Pet 1:3
we should be *c* God's children ..... 1 John 3:1

CALLING
turned their glorious *c* .... Hos 4:7
to live worthily of the *c* .... Eph 4:1
to the one hope of your *c* .... Eph 4:4
called us with a holy *c* .... 2 Tim 1:9
partners in a heavenly *c* .... Heb 3:1
be sure of your *c* and election ..... 2 Pet 1:10

CALLOUSED
are *c*; they speak arrogantly .... Ps 17:10

CALLS
If David himself *c* him 'Lord ..... Mark 12:37
He *c* his own sheep by name ...... John 10:3
c on the name of the Lord .... Rom 10:13

CALM
for a *c* response can undo .... Eccl 10:4
Make sure you stay *c* .... Isa 7:4
and will *c* its turbulence .... Zech 10:11
and it was dead *c* .... Matt 8:26

CALMED
You *c* the raging seas .... Ps 65:7
I have *c* and quieted myself .... Ps 131:2

CALMLY
if you *c* trusted in me .... Isa 30:15

CALVE
cows *c* and do not miscarry .... Job 21:10

CALVES
he made two golden *c* .... 1 Kgs 12:28
like *c* released from the stall .... Mal 4:2

not by the blood of goats and *c*.... Heb 9:12
took the blood of *c* and goats ..... Heb 9:19

CAME
Spirit of the LORD *c* upon me...... Ezek 11:5
When the Sabbath *c*.............. Mark 6:2
the time *c* for her to deliver ...... Luke 2:6

CAMEL
a *c* to go through the eye of ..... Matt 19:24
out a gnat yet swallow a *c*....... Matt 23:24

CAMEL'S
a garment made of *c* hair......... Mark 1:6

CAMP
This is the *c* of God .... Gen 32:2
going before the *c* of Israel.......Exod 14:19
also suffered outside the *c* ....Heb 13:12
outside the *c*....................Heb 13:13

CAN
who *c* really build a temple........2 Chr 2:6
God *c* raise up children .... Matt 3:9

CANA
A village of upper Galilee; home of
    Nathanael, John 21:2
Site of Christ's first miracle, John 2:1–11
Healing at, John 4:46–54

CANAAN
A son of Ham, Gen 10:6
Cursed by Noah, Gen 9:20–25
—Promised Land, Gen 12:5
Boundaries of, Gen 10:19
God's promises concerning, given to
    Abraham, Gen 12:1–3
    to Isaac, Gen 26:2–3
    to Jacob, Gen 28:10–13
    to Israel, Exod 3:8
Conquest of, announced, Gen 15:7–21
    preceded by spying expedition,
        Num 13:1–33
    delayed by unbelief, Num 14:1–35
    accomplished by the Lord, Josh 23:1–16
    achieved only in part, Judg 1:21, 27–36

CANAANITES
Israelites commanded to:
    drive them out; not serve their gods,
        Exod 23:23–33
    shun their abominations, Lev 18:24–30
    not make covenants or intermarry with
        them, Deut 7:1–3

CANCEL
does not *c* a covenant previously... Gal 3:17

CANCELED
who had the bigger debt *c*........ Luke 7:43

CANE
sweet-smelling *c* imported .... Jer 6:20

CAPABLE
is *c* of helping or defeating ....2 Chr 25:8
The LORD is *c* of giving you ....2 Chr 25:9
c of entering the king's royal ....Dan 1:4
may be *c* and equipped............2 Tim 3:17

CAPACITY
the *c* to be his spokesman.......... Isa 50:4

CAPERNAUM
Simon Peter's home, Mark 1:21, 29
Christ performs healings there, Matt 8:5–17;
    9:1–8; Mark 1:21–28; John 4:46–54
    preaches there, Mark 9:33–50;
        John 6:24–71
    uses as headquarters, Matt 4:13–17
    pronounces judgment upon,
        Matt 11:23–24

CAPPADOCIA
Jews from, at Pentecost, Acts 2:1, 9
Christians of, addressed by Peter, 1 Pet 1:1

CAPSTONE
bring forth the temple *c* .... Zech 4:7

CAPTAIN
and the *c* of the guard .... Gen 39:1
the *c* of the royal guard......... 2 Kgs 25:11

CAPTIVATE
to allow anyone to *c* you ....Col 2:8

CAPTIVATED
be *c* by her love always............Prov 5:19

CAPTIVE
Get up, *c* Jerusalem................. Isa 52:2

CAPTIVES
you have taken many *c*............Ps 68:18
as *c* among all nations ....Luke 21:24
on high he captured *c*.............. Eph 4:8

CAPTIVITY
God will reverse your *c*...........Deut 30:3
If anyone is meant for *c* ....Rev 13:10

CAPTURED
on high he *c* captives .... Eph 4:8

CAPTURES
better than one who *c* a city......Prov 16:32

CARE
was sick and you took *c* of me... Matt 25:36
and took *c* of him................. Luke 10:34
don't you *c* that my sister.......Luke 10:40
he feeds it and takes *c* of it .... Eph 5:29
how will he *c* for the church.......1 Tim 3:5
son of man that you *c* for him ...... Heb 2:6
a shepherd's *c* to God's flock ....1 Pet 5:2

CARED
but who even *c* .... Isa 53:8

CAREFREE
and enjoyed *c* ease .... Ezek 16:49

CAREFUL
Be *c* what you do when you go ......Eccl 5:1
be *c* that he does not fall ....1 Cor 10:12
Be *c* not to allow anyone ....Col 2:8

CAREFULLY
For if you *c* observe all ....Deut 11:22
c obey all that is written.............Josh 1:8
You must *c* obey at all times..... 2 Kgs 17:37
c plot against your people...........Ps 83:3
or *c* measured the sky .... Isa 40:12
Let us *c* examine our ways ...... Lam 3:40
You will listen *c* yet............... Matt 13:14
Investigate *c* and you will see......John 7:52
consider *c* how you live............Eph 5:15
c those who are living .... Phil 3:17
searched and investigated *c* ....1 Pet 1:10

CARES
casting all your *c* on him...........1 Pet 5:7
because he *c* for you................1 Pet 5:7

CARGO
in ships and carried *c*.............Ps 107:23

CARING
nursing mother *c* for her own ... 1 Thess 2:7

CARMEL
City of Judah, Josh 15:55
Site of Saul's victory, 1 Sam 15:12
—A mountain of Palestine: *see* MOUNT
    CARMEL

CAROUSING
c, and similar things .... Gal 5:21
c, drinking bouts....................1 Pet 4:3

CARPENTER
A *c* takes measurements ....Isa 44:13
Isn't this the *c*....................Mark 6:3

CARPET
lay out the *c* .... Isa 21:5

CARRIED
he *c* our pain...................... Isa 53:4
for he *c* their sins .... Isa 53:11
weaknesses and *c* our diseases....Matt 8:17
So he *c* me away in the Spirit.......Rev 17:3

CARRIES
uncircumcision *c* any weight ....Gal 5:6

CARRY
c me out of Egypt and bury.......Gen 47:30
and you will *c* my bones up.......Exod 13:19
did not *c* out his fierce anger ... 1 Sam 28:18

need to *c* the tabernacle..........1 Chr 23:26
I will *c* you........................ Isa 46:4
I will *c* it out .... Isa 46:11
who *c* the LORD's holy items........ Isa 52:11
not worthy to *c* his sandals .... Matt 3:11
a passerby to *c* his cross..........Mark 15:21
Do not *c* a money bag .... Luke 10:4
not *c* his own cross and follow .. Luke 14:27
not permitted to *c* your mat.......John 5:10
C one another's burdens .... Gal 6:2

CARRYING
you saw him *c* you along .... Deut 1:31
c his bag of seed....................Ps 126:6
They were *c* grain offerings........Jer 41:5
and a man *c* a jar of water ..... Mark 14:13
and *c* his own cross.............. John 19:17
always *c* around in our body......2 Cor 4:10

CART
the ark of the LORD on the *c*......1 Sam 6:11
the ark of God on a new *c* .... 2 Sam 6:3
who pull sin as with *c* ropes ....Isa 5:18
like a *c* loaded down with grain...Amos 2:13

CARVED
make for yourself a *c* image ......Exod 20:4
use it to make a *c* image........... Judg 17:3
worshiped Micah's *c* image .... Judg 18:31
He *c* cherubim.....................1 Kgs 6:35

CASE
to God I would set forth my *c* .... Job 5:8
Will you argue the *c* for God........ Job 13:8
I have prepared my *c* .... Job 13:18
lay out my *c* before him .... Job 23:4
first to state his *c* seems right .... Prov 18:17
Present your *c* before the hills....... Mic 6:1
Festus explained Paul's *c* ....Acts 25:14

CASSIA
with myrrh, aloes, and *c* ....Ps 45:8

CAST
See also CAST OUT DEMONS
They *c* lots to determine ....1 Chr 25:8
was *c* before Haman................ Esth 3:7
He had *c* pur (that is the lot ....Esth 9:24
the people *c* off restraint.........Prov 29:18
let's *c* lots to find out .... Jonah 1:7
c out demons in your name ...... Matt 7:22
so they could *c* them out ....Matt 10:1
do your sons *c* them out.........Matt 12:27
How can Satan *c* out Satan ......Mark 3:23
do your sons *c* them out......... Luke 11:19

CAST OUT DEMONS
and *c* in your name .... Matt 7:22
raise the dead, cleanse lepers, *c* .. Matt 10:8
He does not *c* except by .... Matt 12:24
to have authority to *c*............. Mark 3:15
Now if I *c* by Beelzebul .... Luke 11:19

CASTING
See also CASTING OUT DEMONS
Andrew his brother, *c* a net........Matt 4:18
by *c* all your cares on him ....1 Pet 5:7

CASTING OUT DEMONS
in their synagogues and *c*........ Mark 1:39
saw someone *c* in your name.....Mark 9:38
saw someone *c* in your name.....Luke 9:49
am *c* and performing healings....Luke 13:32

CASTS
one who *c* spells.................. Deut 18:11
So if Satan *c* out Satan........... Matt 12:26

CATCH
waiting to *c* the oppressed ....Ps 10:9
and lower your nets for a *c*........ Luke 5:4
to *c* him in something ....Luke 11:54

CATCHERS
like bird *c* hiding in ambush .... Jer 5:26

CATCHES
it *c* the scent of battle .... Job 39:25
He *c* the wise in their ....1 Cor 3:19

CATCHING
you will be *c* people .... Luke 5:10

CATTLE
of the *c* after their kinds . . . . Gen 6:20
plunder its goods and *c*. . . . . Josh 8:2
allow their *c* to decrease . . . . Ps 107:38
there are no *c* in the stalls . . . . Hab 3:17

CAUGHT
a ram *c* in the bushes. . . . . Gen 22:13
When Isaac *c* the scent . . . . Gen 27:27
have been *c* by the words . . . . Prov 6:2
that *c* all kinds of fish. . . . . Matt 13:47
but that night they *c* nothing . . . . . . John 21:3

CAUSE
reaches out to *c* such change . . . . . . Ezra 6:12
who hate me without *c* . . . . Ps 35:19
publicly defend your just *c* . . . . Ps 37:6
those who hate me without *c*. . . . . . . Ps 38:19
day long they *c* me trouble . . . . Ps 56:5
He upheld the *c* of the poor . . . . Jer 22:16
then he will defend my *c* . . . . Mic 7:9
c one of these little ones to sin . . . . Luke 17:2
demon cannot *c* the blind to see . . John 10:21

CAUSED
Lord God had not *c* it to rain. . . . . Gen 2:5
the Lord God *c* the man. . . . . Gen 2:21
made the mud and *c* him to see . . . John 9:14
but God *c* it to grow . . . . 1 Cor 3:6

CAUSES
c one of these little ones . . . . Mark 9:42

CAUTIOUS
the one who is always *c* . . . . Prov 28:14

CAVE
in a *c* with his two daughters . . . . . Gen 19:30
field and the *c* that is in it. . . . . Gen 23:11
him in the *c* of Machpelah. . . . . Gen 25:9
and hid in the *c* at Makkedah . . . . . Josh 10:16
escaped to the *c* of Adullam . . . . . . 1 Sam 22:1
a *c*, and a stone was placed . . . . John 11:38

CAVES
So the army hid in *c* . . . . 1 Sam 13:6
and hid them in two *c* . . . . 1 Kgs 18:4
deserts and mountains and *c* . . . . . . Heb 11:38

CEASE
day and night will not *c*. . . . . Gen 8:22
wicked *c* from turmoil. . . . . Job 3:17
the grinders begin to *c*. . . . . Eccl 12:3
are tongues, they will *c* . . . . 1 Cor 13:8
I do not *c* to give thanks . . . . Eph 1:16
that we may *c* from sinning. . . . . . . 1 Pet 2:24

CEASED
and he *c* on the seventh day . . . . Gen 2:2
have not *c* praying for you. . . . . Col 1:9

CEASES
Lord's loyal kindness never *c* . . . . . Lam 3:22

CEDAR
in a palace made from *c* . . . . 2 Sam 7:2
high like a *c* in Lebanon. . . . . Ps 92:12
panels it with *c*. . . . . Jer 22:14
a *c* in Lebanon . . . . Ezek 31:3

CEDARS
Lord's shout breaks the *c*. . . . . Ps 29:5
c of Lebanon that he planted . . . . . Ps 104:16
c are the beams of our bedroom . . Song 1:17

CELEBRATE
c it as a pilgrim festival . . . . Lev 23:41
and everything in them *c* . . . . 1 Chr 16:32
to Jerusalem to *c* the dedication. . Neh 12:27
how long will the wicked *c* . . . . Ps 94:3
I will *c* my deliverance. . . . . Ps 116:13
They *c* deliverance. . . . . Ps 118:15
gives them reason to *c* . . . . Isa 57:19
c your sacred festivals. . . . . Nah 1:15
appropriate to *c* and be glad. . . . . Luke 15:32

CELEBRATING
when you are a *c* a festival . . . . Isa 30:29

CELEBRATION
house of Obed-Edom with *c* . . . . . 1 Chr 15:25
the wedding *c* of the Lamb . . . . Rev 19:7

CELEBRATIONS
c disappear from the earth . . . . Isa 24:11

CENCHREA
A harbor of Corinth, Acts 18:18
Home of Phoebe, Rom 16:1

CENSER
each with a *c* in his hand. . . . . Ezek 8:11
Then the angel took the *c* . . . . Rev 8:5

CENSUS
you take a *c* of the Israelites . . . . . Exod 30:12
a *c* of the entire Israelite. . . . . Num 1:2
c his father David had taken . . . . . . 2 Chr 2:17
arose in the days of the *c*. . . . . Acts 5:37

CENTURION
c came to him asking for help . . . . . Matt 8:5
Now when the *c* . . . . Mark 15:39
A *c* there had a slave. . . . . Luke 7:2
Now when the *c* saw . . . . Luke 23:47
Cornelius the *c* . . . . Acts 10:22
said to the *c* standing nearby . . . . Acts 22:25
a *c* of the Augustan Cohort. . . . . Acts 27:1

CEPHAS
See PETER

CEREMONY
does this *c* mean to you . . . . Exod 12:26

CERTAIN
be *c* to tithe all the produce . . . . . Deut 14:22
may know for *c* the things. . . . . Luke 1:4
a *c* royal official whose son . . . . John 4:46
God again ordains a *c* day . . . . Heb 4:7
only a *c* fearful expectation. . . . . . . Heb 10:27

CERTAINLY
c a man cannot rescue . . . . Ps 49:7
The Lord will *c* exclude me . . . . Isa 56:3
I will *c* gather all of you. . . . . Mic 2:12
will *c* not allow the wicked . . . . Nah 1:3
would *c* have come by the law . . . . Gal 3:21

CERTAINTY
will have no *c* of surviving . . . . Deut 28:66

CERTIFICATE
your mother's divorce *c* . . . . Isa 50:1
c of dismissal and to divorce . . . . . Mark 10:4
c of indebtedness expressed . . . . . . Col 2:14

CHAFF
like *c* swept away by. . . . . Job 21:18
are like wind-driven *c*. . . . . Ps 1:4
be like wind-driven *c* . . . . Ps 35:5
you give birth to *c* . . . . Isa 33:11
scatter your people like *c*. . . . . Jer 13:24
disappears like windblown *c*. . . . . . Zeph 2:2
arrogant evildoers will be *c*. . . . . Mal 4:1
but the *c* he will burn up. . . . . Matt 3:12

CHAIN
key to the abyss and a huge *c* . . . . . Rev 20:1

CHAINS
with palm trees and *c*. . . . . 2 Chr 3:5
bind their enemies' kings in *c*. . . . . . Ps 149:8
down with heavy prison *c* . . . . Lam 3:7
the *c* fell off Peter's wrists. . . . . Acts 12:7
except for these *c* . . . . Acts 26:29
Remember my *c*. . . . . Col 4:18
in *c* in utter darkness . . . . 2 Pet 2:4

CHAIR
bed, table, *c*, and lamp. . . . . 2 Kgs 4:10
made a sedan *c* for himself . . . . Song 3:9

CHALDEA
Originally, the southern portion of
   Babylonia, Gen 11:31
Applied later to all Babylonia, Dan 3:8
Abram came from, Gen 11:28-31

CHALDEANS
Attack Job, Job 1:17
Nebuchadnezzar, king of, 2 Kgs 24:1
Jerusalem defeated by, 2 Kgs 25:1-21
Babylon, "the most admired of," Isa 13:19
Predicted captivity of Jews among,
   Jer 25:1-26
God's agent, Hab 1:6

CHALLENGE
c him with difficult questions. . . . . 1 Kgs 10:1
those who *c* God escape. . . . . Mal 3:15

CHALLENGED
They willfully *c* God by asking . . . . . Ps 78:18
again *c* God and offended . . . . Ps 78:41
ancestors *c* my authority . . . . Ps 95:9

CHAMBERS
bring me into his bedroom *c* . . . . . Song 1:4

CHAMPION
a *c* came out from the camp. . . . . . 1 Sam 17:4

CHAMPIONS
those who are *c* at drinking. . . . . Isa 5:22

CHANCE
and *c* may overcome them . . . . Eccl 9:11

CHANGE
that he should *c* his mind. . . . . Num 23:19
will *c* his plans concerning. . . . . . . Deut 32:36
you *c* his appearance . . . . Job 14:20
These men *c* night into day. . . . . . . Job 17:12
and who can *c* him. . . . . Job 23:13
refuse to *c*, and do not fear . . . . Ps 55:19
c the way you have been . . . . Jer 7:3
c the color of his skin. . . . . Jer 13:23
wicked *c* his behavior and live . . . . Ezek 33:11
c times established by law . . . . Dan 7:25
and *c* my tone of voice . . . . Gal 4:20
and will not *c* his mind. . . . . Heb 7:21
or the slightest hint of *c* . . . . Jas 1:17

CHANGED
and *c* my wages ten times . . . . Gen 31:7
c his clothes . . . . Gen 41:14
God *c* his inmost person. . . . . 1 Sam 10:9
Has a nation ever *c* its gods. . . . . Jer 2:11
which cannot be *c* . . . . Dan 6:8
which cannot be *c* . . . . Dan 6:12
sun will be *c* to darkness . . . . Acts 2:20
but we will all be *c*. . . . . 1 Cor 15:51
like a garment they will be *c*. . . . . . . Heb 1:12

CHANGERS
the money *c* sitting at tables. . . . . . John 2:14

CHANGES
He *c* times and seasons. . . . . Dan 2:21
For when the priesthood *c*. . . . . Heb 7:12

CHANT
they will *c* it . . . . Ezek 32:16

CHAOS
currents of *c* overwhelmed me . . . . . Ps 18:4

CHARACTER
can find a wife of noble *c* . . . . Prov 31:10
endurance, *c*, and *c*, hope. . . . . Rom 5:4
of the extraordinary *c* . . . . 2 Cor 12:7

CHARCOAL
Like *c* is to burning coals . . . . Prov 26:21

CHARGE
obeyed me and kept my *c* . . . . Gen 26:5
do not *c* him interest . . . . Exod 22:25
obey my *c* not to practice . . . . Lev 18:30
not *c* interest on a loan . . . . Deut 23:19
was in *c* of transport. . . . . 1 Chr 15:22
c God with moral impropriety . . . . . . Job 1:22
they put the *c* against him . . . . Matt 27:37
any *c* against God's elect . . . . Rom 8:33
offer the gospel free of *c* . . . . 1 Cor 9:18
gospel of God to you free of *c*. . . . . 2 Cor 11:7
I put this *c* before you . . . . 1 Tim 1:18
c you before God who gives life . . 1 Tim 6:13
c what he owes to me . . . . Phlm 1:18
the water of life free of *c* . . . . Rev 22:17

CHARGES
bring *c* against the nations. . . . . Jer 25:31
bringing many serious *c* . . . . Acts 25:7

CHARIOT
fiery *c* pulled by fiery horses . . . . . 2 Kgs 2:11
He makes the clouds his *c* . . . . Ps 104:3
Go over and join this *c*. . . . . Acts 8:29

CHARIOTEERS
David killed 700 Aramean *c* . . . . 2 Sam 10:18

CHARIOTS
jammed the wheels of their *c*. . . . . Exod 14:25
trust in *c* and others in horses. . . . . . Ps 20:7
God has countless *c* . . . . Ps 68:17

CHARLATANS
But evil people and *c* will go......2 Tim 3:13

CHARM
C is deceitful and beauty is.......Prov 31:30

CHARMED
should bite before it is *c*...........Eccl 10:11
snakes that cannot be *c*..............Jer 8:17

CHASE
can one man *c* a thousand.......Deut 32:30
arrogantly *c* the oppressed..........Ps 10:2
Rescue me from those who *c*.......Ps 142:6

CHASES
but whoever *c* daydreams.........Prov 12:11

CHASING
c the wind...........................Eccl 1:14

CHASM
a great *c* has been fixed.........Luke 16:26

CHASTISES
and *c* every son he accepts........Heb 12:6

CHATTER
the profane *c* and absurdities.....1 Tim 6:20

CHEAT
The businessmen love to *c*........Hos 12:7

CHEATED
Why not rather be *c*...............1 Cor 6:7

CHEEK
c to the one who hits him........Lam 3:30
strikes you on the right *c*.........Matt 5:39

CHEEKS
Your *c* are beautiful................Song 1:10
His *c* are like garden beds........Song 5:13

CHEER
and let your heart *c* you...........Eccl 11:9

CHEERFUL
joyful heart makes the face *c*.....Prov 15:13
A *c* heart brings good healing....Prov 17:22
because God loves a *c* giver.......2 Cor 9:7

CHEERFULNESS
he must do so with *c*..............Rom 12:8

CHEESE
milk and curdle me like *c*..........Job 10:10

CHEMOSH
The god of the Moabites, Num 21:29
Children sacrificed to, 2 Kgs 3:26–27
Solomon builds altars to, 1 Kgs 11:7
Josiah destroys altars of, 2 Kgs 23:13

CHERUB
Make one *c* on one end.........Exod 25:19
one *c* on one end and one *c*.......Exod 37:8
second *c* also had a wingspan....1 Kgs 6:25
with an anointed guardian *c*.....Ezek 28:14

CHERUBIM
are to make two *c* of gold.......Exod 25:18
it is to be made with *c*...........Exod 26:31
sits enthroned between the *c*.....2 Sam 6:2
made two *c* of olive wood.......1 Kgs 6:23
the *c* in the inner sanctuary.......1 Kgs 6:27
ornamental lions, bulls, and *c*.....1 Kgs 7:29
He engraved ornamental *c*.......1 Kgs 7:36
under the wings of the *c*.......1 Kgs 8:6
sit enthroned above the *c*..........Ps 80:1
who is enthroned on the *c*.........Isa 37:16
wheelwork underneath the *c*.....Ezek 10:2
c and decorative palm trees.....Ezek 41:18
above the ark were the *c*.........Heb 9:5

CHERUBIM'S
The *c* wings extended over.......2 Chr 5:8

CHEST
put in a *c* beside it the gold.......1 Sam 6:8
along with the *c*.................1 Sam 6:11
a *c* and drilled a hole in its lid....2 Kgs 12:9
the *c* to the royal accountant....2 Chr 24:11
man hold fire against his *c*.......Prov 6:27
are these wounds on your *c*.......Zech 13:6
leaned back against Jesus' *c*......John 13:25

CHEW
do not *c* the cud are unclean......Lev 11:26

CHICKS
gathers her *c* under her wings...Matt 23:37
gathers her *c* under her wings...Luke 13:34

CHIEF
when the *C* Shepherd appears......1 Pet 5:4

CHILD
gave her the *c*....................Gen 21:14
saw that he was a healthy *c*.......Exod 2:2
When the *c* grew older...........Exod 2:10
for the *c* will be dedicated.........Judg 13:5
Cut the living *c* in two............1 Kgs 3:25
like a weaned *c* with its mother.....Ps 131:2
wise *c* makes a father rejoice......Prov 10:1
foolish *c* is a grief to his father....Prov 17:25
Train a *c* in the way..............Prov 22:6
Discipline your *c*.................Prov 29:17
c knows how to reject evil...........Isa 7:16
For a *c* has been born to us..........Isa 9:6
as a small *c* leads them along.......Isa 11:6
my firstborn *c* as payment........Mic 6:7
when seeking a *c* from God........Mal 2:15
twice as much a *c* of hell.........Matt 23:15
a little *c* and had him stand......Mark 9:36
the kingdom of God like a *c*.....Mark 10:15
blessed is the *c* in your womb.....Luke 1:42
What then will this *c* be..........Luke 1:66
And the *c* kept growing...........Luke 1:80
When I was a *c*...................1 Cor 13:11
to you concerning my *c*............Phlm 1:10
given birth to the male *c*..........Rev 12:13

CHILDBEARING
will be delivered through *c*.......1 Tim 2:15

CHILDHOOD
And he said, "From *c*..............Mark 9:21

CHILDISH
I set aside *c* ways.................1 Cor 13:11

CHILDLESS
since I continue to be *c*...........Gen 15:2
as though he were *c*...............Jer 22:30

CHILDREN
See also LITTLE CHILDREN
she could not give Jacob *c*.........Gen 30:1
belongs to us and to our *c*........Gen 31:16
allowed me to see your *c* too......Gen 48:11
of fathers by dealing with *c*.......Exod 34:7
not enabled her to have *c*........1 Sam 1:5
mouths of *c* and nursing babies......Ps 8:2
He blesses your *c* within you......Ps 147:13
the glory of *c* is their parents......Prov 17:6
blessed are his *c* after him........Prov 20:7
Her *c* have risen and called her...Prov 31:28
and my blessing on your *c*.........Isa 44:3
Your *c* hurry back.................Isa 49:17
c will be followers of the LORD.....Isa 54:13
c who are not disloyal.............Isa 63:8
For my people, my dear *c*..........Jer 14:17
They will not bear *c*...............Hos 9:11
and their *c* to return to me........Mal 4:6
C will rise against parents.......Matt 10:21
revealed them to little *c*.........Matt 11:25
and become like little *c*..........Matt 18:3
little *c* were brought to him.......Matt 19:13
Let the little *c* come to me........Matt 19:14
mouths of *c* and nursing infants..Matt 21:16
and father *c* for his brother......Matt 22:24
None of the seven had *c*.........Mark 12:22
the right to become God's *c*.......John 1:12
If you are Abraham's *c*............John 8:39
a teacher of little *c*..............Rom 2:20
that we are God's *c*...............Rom 8:16
to correct you as my dear *c*.......1 Cor 4:14
do not be *c* in your thinking.....1 Cor 14:20
c should not have to save up....2 Cor 12:14
were by nature *c* of wrath...........Eph 2:3
we are no longer to be *c*.........Eph 4:14
Live like *c* of light...............Eph 5:8
c of God without blemish..........Phil 2:15
You become her *c* when you.......1 Pet 3:6

we are God's *c* now................1 John 3:2
that we love the *c* of God.........1 John 5:2
to hear that my *c* are living.......3 John 1:4

CHILDREN'S
c teeth have grown numb..........Jer 31:29
not right to take the *c* bread.....Matt 15:26
eat the *c* crumbs.................Mark 7:28

CHIRP
from the magicians who *c*...........Isa 8:19

CHOICE
As with *c* meat you satisfy..........Ps 63:5
knowledge rather than *c* gold.....Prov 8:10
c as its cedars...................Song 5:15

CHOIR
second *c* was proceeding.........Neh 12:38

CHOIRS
The *c* sang loudly................Neh 12:42

CHOKE
come in and *c* the word..........Mark 4:19

CHOKED
they grew up and *c* them..........Matt 13:7
c by the worries and riches.......Luke 8:14

CHOOSE
Therefore *c* life..................Deut 30:19
I *c* the path of faithfulness.......Ps 119:30
do not *c* any of his ways..........Prov 3:31
reject evil and *c* what is right......Isa 7:15
he will again *c* Israel.............Isa 14:1
You did not *c* me.................John 15:16
God *c* the poor in the world.........Jas 2:5

CHOSE
your mother's womb, I *c* you........Jer 1:5
yet I *c* Jacob.....................Mal 1:2
c me to preach to the Gentiles....Acts 15:7
c what the world thinks foolish....1 Cor 1:27
For he *c* us in Christ..............Eph 1:4
God *c* you from the beginning..2 Thess 2:13

CHOSEN
See also LORD'S CHOSEN ONE
has *c* you to be his people........Deut 14:2
LORD your God has *c* them.......Deut 21:5
you have *c* this son of Jesse......1 Sam 20:30
God's *c* ones....................1 Chr 16:13
But now I have *c* Jerusalem......2 Chr 6:6
the people whom he has *c*........Ps 33:12
A good name is to be *c*..........Prov 22:1
given orders to my *c* soldiers......Isa 13:3
my servant whom I have *c*.........Isa 43:10
because the LORD has *c* me.........Isa 61:1
Mary has *c* the best part........Luke 10:42
I know the ones I have *c*..........John 13:18
and the one was Matthias.........Acts 1:26
c you to know his will............Acts 22:14
a *c* and precious cornerstone.......1 Pet 2:6
But you are a *c* race..............1 Pet 2:9

CHRIST
Preexistence of, Ps 2:7; John 8:58;
   Col 1:15–18
Birth of, from a virgin, Isa 7:14; Matt 1:18–25
Deity of, Isa 9:6; John 1:1, 14, 18; 20:28–29;
   Rom 9:5; Heb 1:8
Humanity of, Gen 3:15; Matt 22:45;
   Luke 3:38; John 1:14; 1 Cor 15:45–47;
   Gal 4:4; Phil 2:5–11; 1 Tim 2:5
Character of:
   eternal, John 1:1–2, 15
   forgiving, Luke 23:34
   gentle, Matt 11:29
   guileless, 1 Pet 2:22
   holy, Luke 1:35
   humble, Phil 2:8
   innocent, Matt 27:4
   just, Zech 9:9
   merciful, Heb 2:17
   omnipotent, Matt 28:18
   omnipresent, Matt 18:20
   omniscient, Col 2:3
   righteous, Isa 53:11
   sinless, 2 Cor 5:21
   spotless, 1 Pet 1:19

Mission of:
  complete revelation, Heb 1:1
  destroy Satan's works, Heb 2:14;
    1 John 3:8
  do God's will, John 6:38
  fulfill the OT, Matt 5:17
  give life, John 10:10, 28
  save sinners, Luke 19:10
Worshiped by:
  all, Phil 2:10–11
  angels, Heb 1:6
  demons, Mark 5:2, 6
  disciples, Luke 24:52
  men, John 9:38
  OT saints, Josh 5:13–15
  saints in glory, Rev 7:9–10
OT types of:
  Abel, Heb 12:24
  Adam, Rom 5:14
  bronze serpent, John 3:14
  manna, John 6:32
  Moses, Deut 18:15
  Passover, 1 Cor 5:7
See JESUS

See also ANTICHRIST; LORD JESUS
  CHRIST; LOVE OF CHRIST; YOU ARE
  THE CHRIST

the genealogy of Jesus *C* .... Matt 1:1
who is called *C* .... Matt 1:16
You are the *C*.......................Matt 16:16
do you think about the *C* .... Matt 22:42
tell us if you are the *C* .... Matt 26:63
of the gospel of Jesus *C*............ Mark 1:1
You are the *C*...................... Mark 8:29
Are you the *C*..................... Mark 14:61
He is *C* the Lord .... Luke 2:11
The *C* of God ....Luke 9:20
claiming that he himself is *C*...... Luke 23:2
is translated *C*...................... John 1:41
that the *C* will remain forever ....John 12:34
believe that Jesus is the *C* ....John 20:31
you crucified both Lord and *C*....Acts 2:36
good news that Jesus was the *C*...Acts 5:42
by proving that Jesus is the *C*.....Acts 9:22
Jesus the *C* heals you...............Acts 9:34
the *C* had to suffer and to rise..... Acts 17:3
that the *C* was Jesus ....Acts 18:28
that the *C* was to suffer .... Acts 26:23
faithfulness of Jesus *C*............ Rom 3:22
through our Lord Jesus *C*.......... Rom 5:1
C died for the ungodly..............Rom 5:6
through our Lord Jesus *C*.......... Rom 5:11
life through the one, Jesus *C*....... Rom 5:17
as *C* was raised from the dead..... Rom 6:4
eternal life in *C* Jesus .... Rom 6:23
through the body of *C*...............Rom 7:4
for those who are in *C* Jesus........ Rom 8:1
does not have the Spirit of *C* ...... Rom 8:9
and also fellow heirs with *C* .... Rom 8:17
C is the one who died .... Rom 8:34
by human descent, came the *C*.....Rom 9:5
For *C* is the end of the law........Rom 10:4
are many are one body in *C* .... Rom 12:5
put on the Lord Jesus *C*........... Rom 13:14
C died and returned to life ....Rom 14:9
C did not please himself...........Rom 15:3
just as *C* also received you.........Rom 15:7
do not serve our Lord *C*.......... Rom 16:18
who are sanctified in *C* Jesus .... 1 Cor 1:2
Is *C* divided.......................1 Cor 1:13
C did not send me to baptize...... 1 Cor 1:17
we preach about a crucified *C*......1 Cor 1:23
have a relationship with *C*........ 1 Cor 1:30
among you except Jesus *C*......... 1 Cor 2:2
which is Jesus *C*....................1 Cor 3:11
and you belong to *C*.............. 1 Cor 3:23
We are fools for *C*................. 1 Cor 4:10
For *C*, our Passover lamb......... 1 Cor 5:7
your bodies are members of *C* ....1 Cor 6:15
C, through whom are all things.... 1 Cor 8:6
you sin against *C* .... 1 Cor 8:12
and the rock was *C*............... 1 Cor 10:4

just as I also am of *C*................1 Cor 11:1
C is the head of every man .... 1 Cor 11:3
C died for our sins................. 1 Cor 15:3
if *C* has not been raised........... 1 Cor 15:14
in *C* all will be made alive......... 1 Cor 15:22
own order: *C*, the firstfruits ......1 Cor 15:23
through our Lord Jesus *C*......... 1 Cor 15:57
the sufferings of *C* overflow....... 2 Cor 1:5
in triumphal procession in *C*...... 2 Cor 2:14
that you are a letter of *C* .... 2 Cor 3:3
only in *C* is it taken away .... 2 Cor 3:14
of the glorious gospel of *C* ....2 Cor 4:4
before the judgment seat of *C*....2 Cor 5:10
if anyone is in *C*................... 2 Cor 5:17
what agreement does *C* have..... 2 Cor 6:15
meekness and gentleness of *C* .. 2 Cor 10:1
confident that he belongs to *C* ...2 Cor 10:7
as a pure virgin to *C* .... 2 Cor 11:2
to distort the gospel of *C*............Gal 1:7
freedom that we have in *C* .... Gal 2:4
seeking to be justified in *C* .... Gal 2:17
I have been crucified with *C*........Gal 2:20
referring to one, who is *C* .... Gal 3:16
in *C* Jesus you are all sons .... Gal 3:26
And if you belong to *C*.............. Gal 3:29
until *C* is formed in you............. Gal 4:19
For freedom *C* has set us free .....Gal 5:1
have been alienated from *C*........ Gal 5:4
the cross of our Lord Jesus *C*...... Gal 6:14
Father of our Lord Jesus *C*......... Eph 1:3
to head up all things in *C* .... Eph 1:10
This power he exercised in *C*.....Eph 1:20
made us alive together with *C*......Eph 2:5
C Jesus himself as the
  cornerstone .... Eph 2:20
the unfathomable riches of *C*........Eph 3:8
C will dwell in your hearts..........Eph 3:17
in all things grow up into *C*.........Eph 4:15
as God in *C* also forgave you ...... Eph 4:32
and *C* will shine on you.............Eph 5:14
C is the head of the church........ Eph 5:23
just as *C* loved the church .... Eph 5:25
C is being proclaimed .... Phil 1:18
living is *C* and dying is gain......... Phil 1:21
desire to depart and be with *C* ..... Phil 1:23
worthy of the gospel of *C* .... Phil 1:27
toward one another that *C* ....Phil 2:5
confess that Jesus *C* is Lord........ Phil 2:11
regard as liabilities because of *C* ....Phil 3:7
the enemies of the cross of *C* ...... Phil 3:18
his glorious riches in *C* Jesus ....Phil 4:19
heard about your faith in *C*........ Col 1:4
which is *C* in you .... Col 1:27
every person mature in *C* .... Col 1:28
mystery of God, namely, *C* .... Col 2:2
just as you received *C* Jesus .... Col 2:6
but the reality is *C*................. Col 2:17
if you have been raised with *C*........Col 3:1
your life is hidden with *C*........... Col 3:3
C (who is your life) appears ....Col 3:4
but *C* is all and in all.................Col 3:11
word of *C* dwell in you richly .... Col 3:16
the dead in *C* will rise first....... 1 Thess 4:16
through our Lord Jesus *C*....... 1 Thess 5:9
and the Lord Jesus *C*........... 2 Thess 1:2
arrival of our Lord Jesus *C* ...... 2 Thess 2:1
tglory of our Lord Jesus *C* ......2 Thess 2:14
C Jesus our Lord.................... 1 Tim 1:12
C Jesus came into the world....... 1 Tim 1:15
C Jesus could demonstrate .... 1 Tim 1:16
C Jesus, himself human............ 1 Tim 2:5
in *C* Jesus before time began ...... 2 Tim 1:9
as a good soldier of *C* Jesus........ 2 Tim 2:3
obtain salvation in *C* Jesus........ 2 Tim 2:10
want to live godly lives in *C*........ 2 Tim 3:12
salvation through faith in *C*........ 2 Tim 3:15
charge you before God and *C* ...... 2 Tim 4:1
God and Savior, Jesus *C*............Titus 2:13
But *C* is faithful as a son............ Heb 3:6
become partners with *C*........... Heb 3:14
C did not glorify himself........... Heb 5:5
instructions about *C* and ....Heb 6:1
C has come as the high priest ......Heb 9:11
more will the blood of *C*........... Heb 9:14

C did not enter a sanctuary........Heb 9:24
after *C* was offered once ....Heb 9:28
of Jesus *C* once for all .... Heb 10:10
Jesus *C* is the same yesterday ..... Heb 13:8
the Spirit of *C* within them .... 1 Pet 1:11
and spotless lamb, namely *C* .... 1 Pet 1:19
since *C* also suffered for you .... 1 Pet 2:21
C also suffered once for sins .... 1 Pet 3:18
the resurrection of Jesus *C* .... 1 Pet 3:21
shared in the sufferings of *C*....... 1 Pet 4:13
insulted for the name of *C*........ 1 Pet 4:14
a slave and apostle of Jesus *C* ...... 2 Pet 1:1
return of our Lord Jesus *C*..........2 Pet 1:16
Jesus *C* the Righteous One .... 1 John 2:1
denies that Jesus is the *C* .... 1 John 2:22
the name of his Son Jesus *C* ..... 1 John 3:23
confesses Jesus as the *C* .... 1 John 4:2
believes that Jesus is the *C* .... 1 John 5:1
in his Son Jesus *C*................. 1 John 5:20
not remain in the teaching of *C*... 2 John 1:9
Master and Lord, Jesus *C*......... Jude 1:4
The revelation of Jesus *C*...........Rev 1:1
and from Jesus *C* .... Rev 1:5
of our Lord and of his *C* ....Rev 11:15
the ruling authority of his *C* ....Rev 12:10
and reigned with *C* .... Rev 20:4
be priests of God and of *C*........ Rev 20:6

CHRIST'S
Now you are *C* body.............. 1 Cor 12:27
measure of *C* full stature ....Eph 4:13
sprinkling with Jesus *C* blood....... 1 Pet 1:2

CHRISTIAN
persuading me to become a *C* ... Acts 26:28
does a *C* sue a Christian .... 1 Cor 6:6
But if you suffer as a *C* .... 1 Pet 4:16
one who loves his fellow *C* .... 1 John 2:10
who hates his fellow *C*............ 1 John 3:15
fellow *C* committing a sin .... 1 John 5:16

CHRISTIANS
disciples were first called *C*....... Acts 11:26
disputes between fellow *C* .... 1 Cor 6:5
we love our fellow *C*............. 1 John 3:14
our lives for our fellow *C* .... 1 John 3:16

CHRYSOLITE
a *c*, an onyx, and a jasper ....Exod 28:20
a *c*, an onyx, and a jasper .... Exod 39:13
like rods of gold set with *c*........ Song 5:14
the *c*, onyx, and jasper ....Ezek 28:13
the seventh *c*, the eighth .... Rev 21:20

CHRYSOPRASE
the tenth *c*, the eleventh......... Rev 21:20

CHURCH
on this rock I will build my *c*......Matt 16:18
tell it to the *c* ....Matt 18:17
contempt for the *c* of God.........1 Cor 11:22
I persecuted the *c* of God......... 1 Cor 15:9
gave him to the *c* as head...........Eph 1:22
the *c* the multifaceted wisdom .....Eph 3:10
just as Christ loved the *c*........... Eph 5:25
may present the *c* to himself ...... Eph 5:27
as Christ also does the *c*........... Eph 5:29
no *c* shared with me...............Phil 4:15
the sake of his body, the *c* .... Col 1:24
it is the *c* of the living God........ 1 Tim 3:15
c should not be burdened .... 1 Tim 5:16
angel of the *c* in Ephesus .... Rev 2:1

CHURCHES
elders for them in the various *c* .. Acts 14:23
strengthening the *c*............... Acts 15:41
All the *c* of Christ greet you ......Rom 16:16
of God's *c* in Christ Jesus .... 1 Thess 2:14
seven *c* that are in the province ..... Rev 1:4
the angels of the seven *c* ....Rev 1:20
about these things for the *c* ....Rev 22:16

CHURNED
I listened and my stomach *c*........Hab 3:16

CHURNING
the *c* of milk produces butter.... Prov 30:33

CHURNS
For this reason my stomach *c* .... Isa 21:3

CILICIA
Paul's homeland, Acts 21:39
Students from, argued with Stephen,
   Acts 6:9
Paul labors in, Gal 1:21

CINNAMON
pounds—of sweet-smelling *c* ....Exod 30:23
and *c* with every kind of spice .... Song 4:14
c, spice, incense, perfumed .... Rev 18:13

CIRCULATING
For the report that I hear *c* ...... 1 Sam 2:24

CIRCUMCISE
necessary to *c* the Gentiles .... Acts 15:5

CIRCUMCISED
male among you must be *c* ....Gen 17:10
were *c* on the very same day ..... Gen 17:26
c him just as God had
   commanded.................... Gen 21:4
at the city gate was *c* ....Gen 34:24
all his males must be *c* .... Exod 12:48
the men who left were *c*............. Josh 5:5
really *c* in the LORD's sight.......... Jer 9:26
c him when he was eight days ......Acts 7:8
he will justify the *c* by faith .... Rom 3:30
Was he *c* at the time. .... Rom 4:10
become a servant of the *c* ....Rom 15:8
if you let yourselves be *c* .... Gal 5:2
I was *c* on the eighth day ....Phil 3:5
In him you also were *c*.............. Col 2:11

CIRCUMCISION
Abraham the covenant of *c*......... Acts 7:8
c something that is outward...... Rom 2:28
and *c* is of the heart .... Rom 2:29
C is nothing and .... 1 Cor 7:19
neither *c* nor uncircumcision .... Gal 5:6
For we are the *c* ....Phil 3:3
c performed by human hands .... Col 2:11

CIRCUMSTANCES
marry will face difficult *c* .... 1 Cor 7:28

CISTERN
drink water from his own *c* ..... 2 Kgs 18:31
Drink water from your own *c* ...... Prov 5:15
wheel is broken at the *c* ....Eccl 12:6

CISTERNS
throw him into one of the *c* ......Gen 37:20
have dug *c* for themselves........... Jer 2:13
They go to the *c* ....Jer 14:3

CITADEL
barred gates of a fortified *c*....... Prov 18:19

CITIES
So he overthrew those *c*.......... Gen 19:25
reestablish the ruined *c*.............Isa 61:4
Your chosen *c* have become....... Isa 64:10
Your *c* will become ruins .... Jer 4:7
c of the nations collapsed .... Rev 16:19

CITIZEN
are you a Roman *c*.................Acts 22:27
that he was a Roman *c*............Acts 23:27

CITIZENS
himself above his fellow *c* .... Deut 17:20
O *c* of Zion.........................Isa 12:6
But his *c* hated him...............Luke 19:14
are fellow *c* with the saints ....Eph 2:19

CITIZENSHIP
acquired this *c* with a large sum..Acts 22:28
But our *c* is in heaven.............. Phil 3:20

CITY
See also CITY OF DAVID; HOLY CITY
Cain was building a *c* ....Gen 4:17
bring joy to the *c* of God.............Ps 46:4
LORD's *c* is in the holy hills.......... Ps 87:1
they found no road to a *c*...........Ps 107:4
Jerusalem is a *c* designed...........Ps 122:3
If the LORD does not guard a *c*.......Ps 127:1
the gates opening into the *c*.......Prov 8:3
c has become a prostitute .... Isa 1:21
c where we hold religious .... Isa 33:20
they live in the holy *c* .... Isa 48:2

The *c* once full of people ....Lam 1:1
this enormous *c* ....Jonah 4:11
the once-proud *c* will end up ..... Zeph 2:15
the *c* filled with oppressors.........Zeph 3:1
c located on a hill cannot be......Matt 5:14
he has prepared a *c* for them......Heb 11:16
the *c* of the living God .... Heb 12:22
here we have no lasting *c*..........Heb 13:14
will trample on the holy *c* .... Rev 11:2
fallen is Babylon the great *c* .....Rev 14:8
and the beloved *c*.................. Rev 20:9
And I saw the holy *c* ....Rev 21:2
and the *c* is pure gold............. Rev 21:18
The *c* does not need the sun.......Rev 21:23
enter into the *c* by the gates.......Rev 22:14

CITY OF DAVID
of Zion (that is, the *C* .... 2 Sam 5:7
to be with him in the *C* ....2 Sam 6:10
and was buried int the *C*.......... 1 Kgs 2:10
LORD's covenant from the *C*........1 Kgs 8:1
covenant entered the *C*. .... 1 Chr 15:29
fortified terrace of the *C*.........2 Chr 32:5
to the west side of the *C*........ 2 Chr 32:30
that go down from the *C* ....Neh 3:15
directly up the steps of the *C*..... Neh 12:37
breaks in the walls of the *C*....... Isa 22:9
to the *C* called Bethlehem ...... Luke 2:4
your Savior is born in the *C*........ Luke 2:11

CLAIMED
Although they *c* to be wise .... Rom 1:22

CLAN
against that man and his *c*...... Lev 20:5
message is for the entire *c*........ Amos 3:1

CLANGING
a noisy gong or a *c* cymbal ....1 Cor 13:1

CLANS
the God of all the *c* of Israel .... Jer 31:1
from all the *c* of the earth ....Amos 3:2

CLAP
c your hands........................Ps 47:1
Let the rivers *c* their hands ....Ps 98:8
trees in the field will *c*..............Isa 55:12
and *c* your hands together........Ezek 21:14

CLAPS
c its hands at him in derision ......Job 27:23

CLAUDIUS LYSIAS
Roman commander who protected Paul,
   Acts 24:22–24, 26

CLAY
who live in houses of *c* .... Job 4:19
have made me as with the *c*........Job 10:9
defenses are defenses of *c*..........Job 13:12
have been molded from *c* ....Job 33:6
The earth takes shape like *c*......Job 38:14
I beat them underfoot like *c* ....Ps 18:42
he realizes we are made of *c* ..... Ps 103:14
the potter be regarded as *c*....... Isa 29:16
c should not say to the potter ...... Isa 45:9
We are the *c*....................... Isa 64:8
like the *c* in this potter's hand .... Jer 18:6
and buy a *c* jar from a potter .... Jer 19:1
partly of iron and partly of *c* ...... Dan 2:33
from the same lump of *c* ....Rom 9:21
have this treasure in *c* jars ....2 Cor 4:7
ones made of wood and of *c*..... 2 Tim 2:20

CLEAN
of every kind of *c* animal .... Gen 7:2
to a ceremonially *c* place ....Lev 4:12
c from her flow of blood...........Lev 15:28
priest is to pronounce him *c*........Lev 13:23
priest is to pronounce him *c*.......Lev 13:34
I have kept my heart *c* ....Prov 20:9
be *c* from all your impurities ..... Ezek 36:25
made *c*, and refined. ,...........Dan 12:10
will *c* out his threshing floor.......Matt 3:12
you can make me *c* .... Matt 8:2
swept *c*, and put in order .... Matt 12:44
You *c* the outside of the cup.... Matt 23:25
First *c* the inside of the cup..... Matt 23:26
wrapped it in a *c* linen cloth ..... Matt 27:59

means all foods are *c*............ Mark 7:19
everything will be *c* for you....... Luke 11:41
but is completely *c* ....John 13:10
Not every one of you is *c*...........John 13:11
You are *c* already because.........John 15:3
What God has made *c*...........Acts 10:15
For although all things are *c*.....Rom 14:20
had our hearts sprinkled *c*.......Heb 10:22
dressed in bright, *c*, fine linen ......Rev 19:8

CLEANNESS
through the *c* of your hands......Job 22:30

CLEANSE
Therefore, *c* your hearts..........Deut 10:16
God will also *c* your heart ....Deut 30:6
C me of my sin .... Ps 51:2
C me with hyssop .... Ps 51:7
Wash! *C* yourselves.................. Isa 1:16
c lepers, cast out demons......... Matt 10:8
c ourselves from everything....... 2 Cor 7:1
C your hands .... Jas 4:8

CLEANSED
one being *c* must then wash......Lev 14:8
be *c* from your uncleanness ......Ezek 24:13
Immediately his leprosy was *c*..... Matt 8:3
lepers are *c*....................... Matt 11:5
they were *c*.......................Luke 17:14
Were not ten *c*....................Luke 17:17

CLEANSES
c himself of such behavior........2 Tim 2:21
blood of Jesus his Son *c* us.........1 John 1:7

CLEANSING
c until the time of the end........Dan 11:35
c their hearts by faith.............Acts 15:9
to sanctify her by *c* her .... Eph 5:26
forgiving us our sins and *c* us......1 John 1:9

CLEAR
done this with a *c* conscience......Gen 20:5
c a way for the LORD................. Isa 40:3
it is *c* no one is justified.............Gal 3:11
the faith with a *c* conscience....... 1 Tim 3:9
served with a *c* conscience .... 2 Tim 1:3
For it is *c* that our Lord............ Heb 7:14
The Holy Spirit is making *c* .... Heb 9:8
as *c* as crystal.......................Rev 22:1

CLEARLY
see *c* to remove the speck..........Matt 7:5
confirmed *c* that God is truthful...John 3:33
he saw *c* in a vision an angel.......Acts 10:3

CLEFTS
home in the *c* of the rocks......... Jer 49:16

CLEVER
not with *c* speech.................. 1 Cor 1:17

CLIFF
like the shade of a large *c*...........Isa 32:2

CLIFFS
in the safety of the rocky *c* .... Obad 1:3

CLIMBS
but *c* in some other way........... John 10:1

CLING
c to what is good ....Rom 12:9

CLOAK
the *c* that had fallen off Elijah ....2 Kgs 2:14
I spread my *c* over you ....Ezek 16:8
touched the edge of his *c*.........Matt 9:20
He threw off his *c*.................Mark 10:50

CLOAKS
spread their *c* on the road ....Luke 19:36
witnesses laid their *c* at the feet...Acts 7:58
and throwing off their *c* ....Acts 22:23

CLODS
the *c* of the torrent valley ....Job 21:33

CLOSE
my *c* friend whom I trusted......... Ps 41:9

CLOSED
floodgates of heaven were *c*........Gen 8:2
matters are *c* and sealed.......... Dan 12:9
and they have *c* their eyes.......Acts 28:27

CLOSELY
and the sin that clings so c .... Heb 12:1

CLOSER
Come c so I can touch you .... Gen 27:21
we must pay c attention .... Heb 2:1

CLOSEST
All my c friends detest me .... Job 19:19

CLOTH
unshrunk c on an old garment .... Matt 9:16
wrapped it in a clean linen c .... Matt 27:59
saw the strips of linen c .... John 20:5
a dealer in purple c .... Acts 16:14

CLOTHE
and c them with tunics .... Exod 40:14
c its neck with a mane .... Job 39:19
c yourself with glory and honor ... Job 40:10
honorable we c with greater ...... 1 Cor 12:23

CLOTHED
and c them .... Gen 3:21
You c me with skin and flesh .... Job 10:11
and the hills are c with joy .... Ps 65:12
meadows are c with sheep .... Ps 65:13
priests be c with integrity .... Ps 132:9
were c with scarlet .... Prov 31:21
and he will be c in splendor .... Zech 6:13
was c like one of these .... Matt 6:29
c, and in his right mind .... Mark 5:15
brother or sister is poorly c .... Jas 2:15
white clothing so you can be c ...... Rev 3:18
a woman c with the sun .... Rev 12:1

CLOTHES
See also TORE HIS CLOTHES
she removed her widow's c .... Gen 38:14
and put on her widow's c .... Gen 38:19
and dressed in worn-out c .... Josh 9:5
c and sandals have worn out ...... Josh 9:13
and my own c abhor me .... Job 9:31
They are dividing up my c .... Ps 22:18
like c you will remove them .... Ps 102:26
Let your c always be white .... Eccl 9:8
and stained all my c .... Isa 63:3
Remove his filthy c .... Zech 3:4
how God c the wild grass .... Matt 6:30
was not wearing wedding c .... Matt 22:11
divided his c by throwing dice ... Matt 27:35
and his c were white as snow ..... Matt 28:3
his c became radiantly white ...... Mark 9:3
his c became very bright .... Luke 9:29
removed his outer c .... John 13:4
poor person enters in filthy c .... Jas 2:2
gold jewelry or fine c .... 1 Pet 3:3
even the c stained by the flesh .... Jude 1:23

CLOTHING
Your c did not wear out .... Deut 8:4
the lambs will be for your c ...... Prov 27:26
c was strong and splendid .... Prov 31:25
who wear foreign styles of c .... Zeph 1:8
and will dress you in fine c .... Zech 3:4
and more to the body than c ..... Matt 6:25
Why do you worry about c .... Matt 6:28
who come to you in sheep's c ..... Matt 7:15
A man dressed in soft c .... Matt 11:8
and for my c they threw dice .... John 19:24
two men in white c stood near .... Acts 1:10
other c Dorcas used to make ...... Acts 9:39
man in shining c stood before .... Acts 10:30
in cold and without enough c ..... 2 Cor 11:27
gold ring and fine c .... Jas 2:2
c has become moth-eaten .... Jas 5:2
like them in white c .... Rev 3:5
in c dipped in blood .... Rev 19:13

CLOUD
in a pillar of c to lead them .... Exod 13:21
the c covered the mountain ...... Exod 24:15
the pillar of c would descend ..... Exod 33:9
the c over the atonement lid .... Lev 16:2
the c of incense will cover .... Lev 16:13
a c filled the LORD's temple .... 1 Kgs 8:10
a c filled the LORD's temple .... 2 Chr 5:13
guided them with a pillar of c ..... Neh 9:12

The pillar of c did not stop .... Neh 9:19
He led them with a c by day .... Ps 78:14
to them from a pillar of c .... Ps 99:7
c of mist in the heat of harvest ..... Isa 18:4
who float along like a c .... Isa 60:8
bright c overshadowed them ...... Matt 17:5
c came and overshadowed .... Luke 9:34
Son of Man arriving in a c .... Luke 21:27
a c hid him from their sight .... Acts 1:9
fathers were all under the c .... 1 Cor 10:1
by such a great c of witnesses ...... Heb 12:1
went up to heaven in a c .... Rev 11:12

CLOUDS
place my rainbow in the c .... Gen 9:13
When the rainbow is in the c ...... Gen 9:16
in thick rain c .... 2 Sam 22:12
in which there are no c .... 2 Sam 23:4
spread out the c .... Job 37:18
The c poured down rain .... Ps 77:17
O fire and hail, snow and c .... Ps 148:8
so that the c drip down dew ...... Prov 3:20
like the c of the spring rain .... Prov 16:15
observes the c will not reap .... Eccl 11:4
stacked up into the c .... Jer 51:9
rainbow in the c after the rain ..... Ezek 1:28
arriving on the c of heaven ...... Matt 24:30
in the c to meet the Lord .... 1 Thess 4:17
They are waterless c .... Jude 1:12
He is returning with the c .... Rev 1:7

CLUB
broken the c of the wicked .... Isa 14:5
Babylon, you are my war c .... Jer 51:20

CLUMSILY
strong young men c stumble ...... Isa 40:30

CLUSTER
is like a c of henna blossoms ...... Song 1:14

CNIDUS
City of Asia Minor on Paul's voyage,
  Acts 27:7

COAL
In his hand was a hot c .... Isa 6:6

COALS
burning c and brimstone .... Ps 11:6
He hurled down fiery c .... Ps 18:8
rain down fiery c upon them ...... Ps 140:10
Can a man walk on hot c .... Prov 6:28
heap c of fire on his head .... Prov 25:22
There are no c to warm them ...... Isa 47:14
heaping burning c on his head ... Rom 12:20

COARSE
foolish talk, or c jesting .... Eph 5:4

COASTLANDS
Let the many c rejoice .... Ps 97:1
c were your customers .... Ezek 27:15
All the inhabitants of the c ...... Ezek 27:35

COAT
Her prophets c their messages .. Ezek 22:28
let him have your c also .... Matt 5:40

COATED
wall you c with whitewash .... Ezek 13:14

CODE
not under the old written c .... Rom 7:6

COERCED
you c me into being a prophet ...... Jer 20:7

COFFIN
his body was placed in a c .... Gen 50:26

COHORT
the whole c around him .... Matt 27:27

COIN
A toss of a c ends disputes .... Prov 18:18

COINS
set out 30 silver c for him .... Matt 26:15
the crowd putting c into it .... Mark 12:41
ten silver c and loses one .... Luke 15:8
put in two small copper c .... Luke 21:2

COLD
and harvest, c and heat .... Gen 8:22

the c wind he sends .... Ps 147:17
Like the c of snow .... Prov 25:13
c water to a weary person .... Prov 25:25
love of many will grow c .... Matt 24:12
you are neither c nor hot .... Rev 3:15

COLLAPSE
I c in the dirt .... Ps 119:25

COLLAPSED
against that house, and it c .... Matt 7:27
heard these words he c .... Acts 5:5

COLLATERAL
one of you is seizing the c .... Neh 5:7

COLLECTED
I could have c it with interest .... Luke 19:23

COLLECTION
regard to the c for the saints ...... 1 Cor 16:1

COLOGNES
of your c is delightful .... Song 1:3

COLOR
its c like the c of bdellium .... Num 11:7

COLOSSAE
A city in Asia Minor, Col 1:2
Evangelized by Epaphras, Col 1:7
Not visited by Paul, Col 2:1
Paul writes against errors of, Col 2:16–23

COLT
and his c to the choicest vine ...... Gen 49:11
on a c, the foal of a donkey .... Matt 21:5
threw their cloaks on the c ...... Luke 19:35

COLUMNS
and c of smoke .... Joel 2:30

COME
See also AGE TO COME
does it c from .... Job 28:20
our God c and not be silent .... Ps 50:3
c with me from Lebanon .... Song 4:8
c to the water .... Isa 55:1
Your dynasty will c to an end ...... Nah 1:14
may your kingdom c .... Matt 6:10
Are you the one who is to c .... Matt 11:3
C to me, all you who are weary ... Matt 11:28
out of the heart c evil ideas ...... Matt 15:19
For many will c in my name ...... Matt 24:5
human heart, c evil ideas .... Mark 7:21
The kingdom of God has c .... Luke 10:9
I have c in my Father's name ..... John 5:43
not c on my own initiative .... John 7:28
let him c to me .... John 7:37
for I have c from God .... John 8:42
c as a light into the world .... John 12:46
I will c to you .... John 14:18
not c and spoken to them .... John 15:22
fierce wolves will c in among .... Acts 20:29
Our Lord, c .... 1 Cor 16:22
same mouth c blessing and .... Jas 3:10
does not c from above .... Jas 3:15
I will c into his home .... Rev 3:20
let the one who is thirsty c .... Rev 22:17

COMES
your God c to avenge .... Isa 35:4
your deliverer c .... Isa 62:11
is this who c from Edom .... Isa 63:1
your fruitfulness c from me .... Hos 14:8
to another 'Come!' and he c .... Matt 8:9
thief c only to steal and kill ...... John 10:10
the Lord's death until he c .... 1 Cor 11:26
then when Christ c .... 1 Cor 15:23
Then c the end .... 1 Cor 15:24

COMFORT
This one will bring us c .... Gen 5:29
Turn and c me .... Ps 71:21
When will you c me .... Ps 119:82
C, c my people .... Isa 40:1
I will provide c to them .... Isa 57:18
She has no one to c her .... Lam 1:2
there was no one to c her .... Lam 1:9
the LORD will c Zion .... Zech 1:17
received your c already .... Luke 6:24
of mercies and God of all c .... 2 Cor 1:3

so also our *c* through Christ . . . . 2 Cor 1:5
any *c* provided by love. . . . . Phil 2:1
by grace gave us eternal *c* . . . . . . 2 Thess 2:16

COMFORTED
was *c* after his mother's death. . . Gen 24:67
So David *c* his wife Bathsheba . . 2 Sam 12:24
I refused to be *c* . . . . Ps 77:2
and refusing to be *c* . . . . Jer 31:15
she did not want to be *c* . . . . Matt 2:18
for they will be *c*. . . . . Matt 5:4
but now he is *c* here . . . . Luke 16:25
and were greatly *c* . . . . Acts 20:12
we ourselves are *c* by God. . . . . 2 Cor 1:4

COMFORTERS
What miserable *c* are you all . . . . . . Job 16:2
for *c*, but find none . . . . Ps 69:20

COMFORTING
but no one was *c* them . . . . Eccl 4:1

COMFORTS
was like one who *c* mourners . . . . Job 29:25
what *c* me in my trouble. . . . . Ps 119:50
who *c* us in all our troubles . . . . 2 Cor 1:4

COMING
For indeed the day is *c*. . . . . Mal 4:1
but the one *c* after me. . . . . Matt 3:11
and *c* to rest on him . . . . Matt 3:16
will be the sign of your *c* . . . . Matt 24:3
more powerful than I am is *c* . . . . . Luke 3:16
I am *c* soon . . . . Rev 3:11
Look! I am *c* soon. . . . . Rev 22:7
I am *c* soon . . . . Rev 22:20

COMMAND
so that he may *c* his children . . . . . . Gen 18:19
speak everything I *c* you . . . . Exod 7:2
not add a thing to what I *c* . . . . Deut 4:2
you must *c* your children . . . . Deut 32:46
disobeyed the *c* . . . . Josh 22:20
general in *c* of the army . . . . 1 Sam 17:55
for he gave the *c*. . . . . Ps 148:5
Tell them everything I *c* you . . . . Jer 26:2
c these stones to become . . . . Matt 4:3
He will *c* his angels . . . . Matt 4:6
He will *c* his angels . . . . Luke 4:10
if you do what I *c* you. . . . . John 15:14
This I *c* you . . . . John 15:17
as a concession, not as a *c* . . . . 1 Cor 7:6
I am not saying this as a *c* . . . . 2 Cor 8:8
with a shout of *c*. . . . . 1 Thess 4:16
C those who are rich . . . . 1 Tim 6:17
Moses had spoken every *c* . . . . Heb 9:19

COMMANDED
See also LORD COMMANDED
the LORD God *c* the man. . . . . Gen 2:16
did all that the LORD *c* him . . . . Gen 7:5
did just as the LORD *c* them. . . . . . . Exod 7:6
words that the LORD had *c* . . . . Exod 19:7
he *c* them all that the LORD. . . . . . Exod 34:32
The LORD *c* us to obey. . . . . Deut 6:24
David did just as the LORD *c* . . . . . 2 Sam 5:25
they carefully obey all I *c* . . . . 2 Kgs 21:8
carefully obey all I *c* them . . . . 2 Chr 33:8
ever in your life *c* the morning . . . . Job 38:12
He *c* our ancestors to make . . . . . . , . Ps 78:5
exactly as I *c* you . . . . Jer 11:4
to obey everything I have *c*. . . . . Matt 28:20
doing just what the Father *c* . . . . . John 14:31
the same way the Lord *c* . . . . 1 Cor 9:14
could not bear what was *c* . . . . Heb 12:20
just as the Father *c* us . . . . 2 John 1:4

COMMANDER
the *c* of his army. . . . . Gen 21:22
the *c* of the LORD's army . . . . Josh 5:14
the *c* of the army . . . . 1 Kgs 1:19
Rehum the *c* and Shimshai . . . . Ezra 4:8
It has no *c* . . . . Prov 6:7
our *c*, the LORD . . . . Isa 33:22

COMMANDING
do everything I am *c* you . . . . Deut 12:32
I am *c* you to make sure . . . . Deut 15:11
What I am *c* you today. . . . . Deut 30:16
and will do—what we are *c* . . . . . . 2 Thess 3:4

COMMANDMENT
transgressing the *c* of the LORD . . Num 14:41
Teacher, which *c* in the law . . . . . . Matt 22:36
This is the first and greatest *c* . . . Matt 22:38
He wrote this *c* for you . . . . Mark 10:5
no other *c* greater than these. . . . Mark 12:31
they rested according to the *c*. . . . Luke 23:56
c I received from my Father . . . . . . John 10:18
I know that his *c* is eternal life. . . John 12:50
I give you a new *c*. . . . . John 13:34
My *c* is this John 15:12
with the coming of the *c*. . . . . Rom 7:9
so that through the *c* . . . . Rom 7:13
c accompanied by a promise . . . . Eph 6:2
to turn back from the holy *c* . . . . . . 2 Pet 2:21
the *c* of the Lord and Savior . . . . 2 Pet 3:2
not writing a new *c* to you. . . . . 1 John 2:7
Now this is his *c* . . . . 1 John 3:23
as if I were writing a new *c* . . . . 2 John 1:5

COMMANDMENTS
who love me and keep my *c* . . . . . . Exod 20:6
tablets with the law and the *c* . . . Exod 24:12
of the covenant, the Ten *C*. . . . . . . Exod 34:28
You must be sure to do my *c* . . . . . . Lev 22:31
remember all the *c* of the LORD . . Num 15:39
you to keep, the Ten *C*. . . . . Deut 4:13
choose me and keep my *c* . . . . Deut 5:10
if we carefully keep all these *c* . . . Deut 6:25
love him and keep his *c* . . . . Deut 7:9
keep carefully all these *c* . . . . Deut 8:1
Ten *C*, which he had spoken . . . . . . Deut 10:4
and *c* at all times . . . . Deut 11:1
all the *c* I am giving you . . . . Deut 11:8
if you take to heart the *c* . . . . Deut 11:27
careful to observe all his *c* . . . . Deut 28:1
and keep his *c* and statutes . . . . . . Deut 30:10
c, regulations, and laws . . . . 1 Kgs 2:3
instructions and obey the *c*. . . . . . . 1 Kgs 8:58
his rules and obeying his *c*. . . . . 1 Kgs 8:61
who love him and obey his *c* . . . . Neh 1:5
you issued *c* . . . . Neh 9:14
but let your heart keep my *c* . . . . . . Prov 3:1
For the *c* are like a lamp . . . . Prov 6:23
Fear God and keep his *c* . . . . Eccl 12:13
If only you had obeyed my *c*. . . . . . . Isa 48:18
who love him and keep his *c*. . . . . . . Dan 9:4
by turning away from your *c* . . . . . . Dan 9:5
you have ignored my *c* . . . . Mal 3:7
as doctrines the *c* of men. . . . . Matt 15:9
to enter into life, keep the *c* . . . . . . Matt 19:17
depend on these two *c* . . . . Matt 22:40
You know the *c*. . . . . Mark 10:19
following all the *c* and . . . . Luke 1:6
You know the *c* . . . . Luke 18:20
who has my *c* and obeys. . . . . John 14:21
If you obey my *c*. . . . . John 15:10
c, "Do not commit adultery. . . . . Rom 13:9
keeping God's *c* is what counts . . . 1 Cor 7:19
the law of *c* in decrees. . . . . Eph 2:15
if we keep his *c* . . . . 1 John 2:3
because we keep his *c* . . . . 1 John 3:22
keeps his *c* resides in God . . . . 1 John 3:24
love God and obey his *c* . . . . 1 John 5:2
we walk according to his *c* . . . . 2 John 1:6
those who keep God's *c* . . . . Rev 12:17
who obey God's *c*. . . . . Rev 14:12

COMMANDS
obey the *c* and instructions. . . . . . . Josh 22:5
committed to obeying my *c* . . . . . . 1 Chr 28:7
willing to obey your *c*. . . . . 1 Chr 29:19
to observe his law and *c* . . . . 2 Chr 14:4
The LORD's *c* are pure . . . . Ps 19:8
and they will obey his *c*. . . . . Ps 78:7
only Israel would keep my *c*. . . . . . . Ps 81:13
who are careful to obey his *c* . . . . . Ps 103:18
great delight in keeping his *c* . . . . . Ps 112:1
Do not hide your *c* from me. . . . . . . Ps 119:19
I will find delight in your *c* . . . . Ps 119:47
consider your *c* to be reliable. . . . . . Ps 119:66
All your *c* are reliable. . . . . Ps 119:86
but your *c* are beyond full . . . . Ps 119:96
I love your *c* more than gold. . . . . . Ps 119:127
store up my *c* inside yourself . . . . . . Prov 2:1
my *c* bring a reward . . . . Mic 2:7

one of the least of these *c* . . . . Matt 5:19
He even *c* the unclean spirits . . . . . Mark 1:27
now *c* all people everywhere . . . . . Acts 17:30
on human *c* and teachings. . . . . Col 2:22

COMMEMORATE
c the daughter of Jephthah . . . . . . Judg 11:40

COMMEND
beginning to *c* ourselves. . . . . 2 Cor 3:1
we *c* ourselves to everyone's . . . . . 2 Cor 4:2

COMMENDABLE
whose behavior he finds *c*. . . . . Ps 37:23
whatever is *c* . . . . Phil 4:8

COMMENDATION
and you will receive its *c*. . . . . Rom 13:3

COMMENDED
master *c* the dishonest manager . . Luke 16:8
had been *c* to the grace of God . . Acts 14:26
through his faith he was *c* . . . . Heb 11:4
been *c* as having pleased God . . . . . Heb 11:5

COMMENDS
not the person who *c* himself. . . . 2 Cor 10:18

COMMISSION
officially *c* you . . . . Isa 42:6

COMMISSIONED
he *c* me when my mother . . . . Isa 49:1

COMMIT
You shall not *c* adultery . . . . Exod 20:14
You must not *c* adultery. . . . . Deut 5:18
C yourself to the LORD . . . . Ps 22:8
C your works to the LORD . . . . Prov 16:3
I will *c* myself to you forever . . . . . . Hos 2:19
into your hands I *c* my spirit. . . . . Luke 23:46
Do not *c* adultery. . . . . Jas 2:11
and *c* sexual immorality . . . . Rev 2:14

COMMITMENT
and his lasting *c* to them. . . . . 2 Chr 9:8

COMMITS
When a person *c* a trespass. . . . . Lev 5:15
He *c* godless deeds . . . . Isa 32:6
marries another *c* adultery . . . . Matt 19:9
sin a person *c* is outside . . . . 1 Cor 6:18
c a sin not resulting in death. . . . . . 1 John 5:16

COMMITTED
Are you as *c* to me. . . . . 2 Kgs 10:15
c themselves to doing evil . . . . 2 Kgs 17:17
c to following the LORD. . . . . 2 Chr 17:6
were not really *c* to him . . . . Ps 78:37
wholeheartedly *c* to you. . . . . Ps 86:11
fully *c* to your statutes. . . . . Ps 119:80
have *c* a double wrong. . . . . Jer 2:13
Jerusalem *c* terrible sin . . . . Lam 1:8
I have *c* no offense. . . . . Acts 25:8
He *c* no sin nor was deceit. . . . . 1 Pet 2:22
but *c* himself to God. . . . . 1 Pet 2:23

COMMITTING
his fellow Christian *c* a sin . . . . 1 John 5:16

COMMON
whole earth had a *c* language. . . . . . Gen 11:1
and held everything in *c*. . . . . Acts 2:44
share in *c* with an unbeliever . . . . . 2 Cor 6:15
my genuine son in a *c* faith . . . . Titus 1:4
to you about our *c* salvation . . . . . . Jude 1:3

COMMOTION
the *c* made by the nations . . . . Ps 65:7
enemies are making a *c* . . . . Ps 83:2
those who make a *c* . . . . Isa 17:12
There was a great *c*. . . . . Acts 23:9

COMPANION
I will make a *c* for him . . . . Gen 2:18
been my faithful *c* . . . . Jer 3:4
true *c*, help them . . . . Phil 4:3

COMPANIONS
c who harm one another . . . . Prov 18:24
anointed you over your *c*. . . . . Heb 1:9

COMPANY
end up in the *c* of the departed. . . Prov 21:16
so that they parted *c* . . . . Acts 15:39

to the *c* of a believing wife......... 1 Cor 9:5
Bad *c* corrupts good morals ...... 1 Cor 15:33

COMPARE

can *c* to the LORD.......................Ps 89:6
you desire can *c* with her .... Prov 3:15
To whom can you *c*.................... Isa 46:5
should I *c* this generation........ Matt 11:16
should I *c* the kingdom of God .. Luke 13:20
dare to classify or *c* ourselves ... 2 Cor 10:12

COMPARED

desirable things cannot be *c*....... Prov 8:11
be *c* to the coming glory..........Rom 8:18

COMPARISON

a way that is beyond *c*............1 Cor 12:31

COMPASSION

Due to your great *c*.................. Neh 9:19
All day long they show *c*............Ps 37:26
Because of your great *c*..............Ps 51:1
and has *c* on his servants .... Ps 135:14
has *c* on all he has made............Ps 145:9
withhold *c* from the child........ Isa 49:15
he then has *c* on us .... Lam 3:32
he had *c* on his people.............Joel 2:18
show brotherhood and *c* .... Zech 7:9
he had *c* on them.................. Matt 9:36
and he had *c* on them ....Matt 14:14
I have *c* on the crowd.............Matt 15:32
The lord had *c* on that slave .....Matt 18:27
Moved with *c*....................Matt 20:34
and he had *c* on them ....Mark 6:34
I have *c* on the crowd.............Mark 8:2
have *c* on whom I have *c*........Rom 9:15
that the Lord is full of *c*..............Jas 5:11
and shuts off his *c* against him.... 1 John 3:17

COMPASSIONATE

the *c* and gracious God .... Exod 34:6
Yet he is *c*..........................Ps 78:38
are a *c* and merciful God ....Ps 86:15
The LORD is merciful and *c* ....Ps 145:8
our God is *c* and forgiving .... Dan 9:9
for he is merciful and *c*..........Joel 2:13
Perhaps he will be *c*...............Joel 2:14
c, forgiving one another .... Eph 4:32
c, and humble ....1 Pet 3:8

COMPASSIONATELY

He is able to deal *c* .... Heb 5:2

COMPASSIONS

his *c* never end ....Lam 3:22
All my tender *c* are aroused .... Hos 11:8

COMPELLED

c by the Spirit.................... Acts 20:22
was *c* to be circumcised .... Gal 2:3
I now feel *c* instead to write ....Jude 1:3

COMPENSATION

This is *c* for you.................. Gen 20:16
He will not consider any *c* .... Prov 6:35
even if you multiply the *c*........ Prov 6:35

COMPETE

be able to *c* with horses ....Jer 12:5
c well for the faith................1 Tim 6:12

COMPETED

I have *c* well ....2 Tim 4:7

COMPETES

he *c* according to the rules ....2 Tim 2:5

COMPETITOR

c must exercise self-control ......1 Cor 9:25

COMPLACENT

You *c* women........................ Isa 32:9

COMPLAIN

should any living person *c*........Lam 3:39
And do not *c*....................1 Cor 10:10

COMPLAINED

You *c* among yourselves...............Deut 1:27

COMPLAINT

Even today my *c* is still bitter ....Job 23:2
Carefully consider my *c*................Ps 5:1
someone happens to have a *c* ...... Col 3:13

COMPLAINTS

has contentions? Who has *c*...... Prov 23:29
with joy and not with *c* ....Heb 13:17

COMPLETE

it is one *c* in knowledge.............Job 36:4
third day I will *c* my work........Luke 13:32
has enough money to *c* it........ Luke 14:28
then is my joy, and it is *c*...........John 3:29
the Father has assigned me to *c*...John 5:36
and your joy may be *c*.............John 15:11
should *c* this act of kindness.......2 Cor 8:6
c it according to your means .....2 Cor 8:11
c my joy and be of the same.........Phil 2:2
you will be perfect and *c* ....Jas 1:4
so that our joy may be *c*...........1 John 1:4

COMPLETED

the LORD's temple was *c*........2 Chr 8:16
city is built and its walls are *c*...... Ezra 4:13
When those days were *c*..........Esth 1:5
that her punishment is *c*............ Isa 40:2
devil had *c* every temptation .....Luke 4:13
my joy *c* in themselves .... John 17:13
by this time everything was *c*.... John 19:28
Jesus said, "It is *c*.................John 19:30
they had *c* their mission ....Acts 12:25
for the work they had now *c*......Acts 14:26
in them God's anger is *c*........ Rev 15:1

COMPLETELY

waters *c* inundated the earth ...... Gen 7:19
that person must be *c* cut off..... Num 15:31
will be *c* liable ....Ezra 7:26
Do not *c* abandon me............. Ps 119:8
your barns will be filled *c*........Prov 3:10
You keep *c* safe the people .... Isa 26:3
forgotten me and *c* disregarded .. Ezek 23:35
I made a man *c* well ....John 7:23
were born *c* in sinfulness .... John 9:34
but is *c* clean......................John 13:10
they may be *c* one ....John 17:23
agreed *c* with killing him .... Acts 8:1
wrath has come upon them *c*... 1 Thess 2:16
himself make you *c* holy...... 1 Thess 5:23
save *c* those who come........... Heb 7:25
set your hope *c* on the grace ......1 Pet 1:13

COMPLETING

by *c* the work you gave me ....John 17:4

COMPREHEND

because you cannot *c* it............ Judg 13:18
able to *c* with all the saints ....Eph 3:18

COMPRESSES

and one who *c* his lips .... Prov 16:30

COMPULSION

not reluctantly or under *c* ....2 Cor 9:7

CONCEAL

Almighty's mind I will not *c*.........Job 27:11
glory of God to *c* a matter .... Prov 25:2

CONCEALED

and *c* the body in the sand........Exod 2:12

CONCEITED

Let us not become *c*.................Gal 5:26

CONCEIVE

young woman is about to *c*......... Isa 7:14
virgin will *c* and give birth ....Matt 1:23

CONCEIVED

the moment my mother *c* me ...... Ps 51:5

CONCEIVES

Then when desire *c*................. Jas 1:15

CONCERN

are not your primary *c*............. Ps 40:6
or *c* myself with things .... Ps 131:1
want you to be free from *c* .... 1 Cor 7:32
members may have mutual *c*.... 1 Cor 12:25
anxious *c* for all the churches ... 2 Cor 11:28
again expressed your *c* for me..... Phil 4:10

CONCERNED

and I am *c* about my sins .... Ps 38:18
I was *c* for my holy reputation.... Ezek 36:21
not be more *c* about Nineveh..... Jonah 4:11

I am very much *c* for Zion .... Zech 8:2
and is not *c* about the sheep......John 10:13
he was *c* about the poor...........John 12:6
how God first *c* himself.......... Acts 15:14
c about the things of the Lord .... 1 Cor 7:32
God is not *c* here about oxen...... 1 Cor 9:9
we are *c* about what is right ...... 2 Cor 8:21
Each of you should be *c* .... Phil 2:4

CONCERNING

speak *c* the welfare of Pharaoh....Gen 41:16

CONCERNS

and know my *c* .... Ps 139:23

CONCESSION

I say this as a *c*................... 1 Cor 7:6

CONCLUSION

I have reached this *c*..............Eccl 12:13

CONCLUSIONS

I jumped to *c* and said .... Ps 31:22

CONCUBINE

his father's *c*.....................Gen 35:22
His *c*, who lived in Shechem ...... Judg 8:31
acquired a *c* from Bethlehem......Judg 19:1
Now Saul had a *c* named .... 2 Sam 3:7
Abraham's *c*, gave birth...........1 Chr 1:32

CONCUBINES

married more *c* and wives........ 2 Sam 5:13
Sleep with your father's *c*.......2 Sam 16:21
royal wives and 300 *c* ....1 Kgs 11:3
who was overseeing the *c* .... Esth 2:14
sixty queens, and eighty *c* .... Song 6:8

CONDEMN

Do not *c* me .... Job 10:2
c them, O God .... Ps 5:10
Who dares to *c* me .... Isa 50:9
They will *c* him to death .... Matt 20:18
do not *c*, and you will not be...... Luke 6:37
into the world to *c* the world ......John 3:17
Did no one *c* you ....John 8:10
I do not *c* you either .... John 8:11
you *c* yourself .... Rom 2:1
Who is the one who will *c* .... Rom 8:34
I do not say this to *c* you. .... 2 Cor 7:3
if our conscience does not *c* ......1 John 3:21

CONDEMNATION

the resurrection resulting in *c* .....John 5:29
Their *c* is deserved ....Rom 3:8
no *c* for those who are in Christ ....Rom 8:1
the ministry that produced *c* .....2 Cor 3:9
c pronounced long ago .... 2 Pet 2:3
were marked out for the *c*.......... Jude 1:4

CONDEMNED

by your words you will be *c* ......Matt 12:37
you escape being *c* to hell .... Matt 23:33
and you will not be *c* .... Luke 6:37
who believes in him is not *c* ......John 3:18
eternal life and will not be *c*......John 5:24
ruler of this world has been *c* .....John 16:11
he *c* sin in the flesh ....Rom 8:3
who doubts is *c* if he eats........Rom 14:23
Through faith he *c* the world .... Heb 11:7
when he *c* them to destruction.... 2 Pet 2:6

CONDEMNS

that if our conscience *c* us.......1 John 3:20

CONDONE

c the use of rigged scales.......... Mic 6:11

CONDUCT

c my business with integrity........Ps 101:2
The Lord's *c* is unjust ....Ezek 18:25
how people ought to *c*............ 1 Tim 3:15
desire to *c* ourselves rightly ....Heb 13:18
By his good *c* he should show ...... Jas 3:13

CONDUCTS

who *c* himself in integrity..........Prov 10:9

CONDUIT

at the *c* of the upper pool .... 2 Kgs 18:17
of the *c* of the upper pool .... Isa 7:3
at the *c* of the upper pool .... Isa 36:2

CONFER
began to *c* with one another....... Acts 4:15

CONFERRING
after *c* with his council........... Acts 25:12

CONFESS
I will *c* my rebellious acts............ Ps 32:5
c that you have done wrong........ Jer 3:13
if you *c* with your mouth .... Rom 10:9
and high priest whom we *c*.......... Heb 3:1
c your sins to one another........... Jas 5:16
But if we *c* our sins .... 1 John 1:9

CONFESSED
Then I *c* my sin .... Ps 32:5
He *c*—he did not deny .... John 1:20
who *c* Jesus to be the Christ .... John 9:22

CONFESSES
c them and forsakes them........ Prov 28:13
and with the mouth one *c*........ Rom 10:10
who *c* the name of the Lord .... 2 Tim 2:19
c the Son has the Father also .... 1 John 2:23
spirit that *c* Jesus as the Christ.... 1 John 4:2
c that Jesus is the Son of God..... 1 John 4:15

CONFESSING
standing and *c* their sins .... Neh 9:2
c my sin and the sin of my........ Dan 9:20

CONFESSION
your *c* in the gospel of Christ..... 2 Cor 9:13
and made your good *c*........ 1 Tim 6:12
good *c* before Pontius Pilate...... 1 Tim 6:13
let us hold fast to our *c* .... Heb 4:14

CONFIDENCE
not have *c* in the LORD........... Deut 1:32
will be the source of your *c*....... Prov 3:26
your *c* may be in the LORD....... Prov 22:19
Now we have such *c* in God .... 2 Cor 3:4
having *c* in the Lord .... Phil 1:14
we hold firmly to our *c* .... Heb 3:6
c to enter the sanctuary .... Heb 10:19
do not throw away your *c* ...... Heb 10:35
So we can say with *c*............... Heb 13:6
have *c* and not shrink away...... 1 John 2:28
have *c* in the day of judgment ...1 John 4:17
the *c* that we have before him.... 1 John 5:14

CONFIDENT
war is imminent, I remain *c*........... Ps 27:3
Be strong and *c*................. Ps 27:14
He is *c*; he trusts in the LORD .... Ps 112:7
can be as *c* as a lion........... Prov 28:1
since I am *c* in you all .... 2 Cor 2:3
c that he belongs to Christ....... 2 Cor 10:7
c about you in the Lord.......... 2 Thess 3:4
I will be *c* in him .... Heb 2:13

CONFIDENTLY
let us *c* approach the throne....... Heb 4:16

CONFIRM
will *c* my covenant with you....... Gen 6:18
Then I will *c* my covenant ....Gen 17:2
C to your servant your .... Ps 119:38
to *c* the promises made ....Rom 15:8
c, strengthen, and establish........ 1 Pet 5:10

CONFIRMATION
defense and *c* of the gospel .... Phil 1:7
as a *c* to end all dispute........... Heb 6:16

CONFIRMED
and *c* the word through .... Mark 16:20
c to us by those who heard......... Heb 2:3

CONFISCATION
c of your belongings with joy..... Heb 10:34

CONFLICT
encountering the same *c* .... Phil 1:30

CONFLICTS
c and where do the quarrels.......... Jas 4:1

CONFORMED
to be *c* to the image of his Son ... Rom 8:29
not be *c* to this present world ..... Rom 12:2

CONFORMITY
live in *c* with the law.............. Acts 21:24

CONFRONT
Distress and hardship *c* me....... Ps 119:143

CONFRONTED
c me in my day of calamity ..... 2 Sam 22:19

CONFUSE
go down and *c* their language ...... Gen 11:7

CONFUSED
there the LORD *c* the language...... Gen 11:9
wandering around *c* in the land.... Exod 14:3

CONFUSING
is *c* you will pay the penalty .... Gal 5:10

CONFUSION
and *c* of mind.................... Deut 28:28
strike every horse with *c*....... Zech 12:4
for the assembly was in *c*........ Acts 19:32

CONGREGATION
the man who was in the *c* .... Acts 7:38
and *c* of the firstborn............. Heb 12:23

CONIAH
See JEHOIACHIN

CONNECTIONS
especially those with Jewish *c* ..... Titus 1:10

CONQUER
not *c* the land by their swords....... Ps 44:3
By God's power we will *c*........... Ps 60:12
Who will *c* our evil deeds.......... Mic 7:19
but the Lamb will *c* them........ Rev 17:14

CONQUERED
of land remains to be *c*............ Josh 13:1
have *c* the world................. John 16:33
Through faith they *c* kingdoms ....Heb 11:33
that you have *c* the evil one ...... 1 John 2:13
have *c* them because the one..... 1 John 4:4
person who has *c* the world .... 1 John 5:5
c; thus he can open the scroll........ Rev 5:5
had *c* the beast and his image ...... Rev 15:2

CONQUEROR
O *c* of the nations................... Isa 14:12
as a *c* he rode out to conquer........ Rev 6:2

CONQUERS
The LORD's right hand .... Ps 118:15
fathered by God *c* the world...... 1 John 5:4
To the one who *c*................... Rev 2:7
c will in no way be harmed .... Rev 2:11
To the one who *c*................... Rev 2:17
one who *c* will be dressed .... Rev 3:5
will grant the one who *c*........... Rev 3:21
c will inherit these things........... Rev 21:7

CONSCIENCE
have a clear *c* toward God........ Acts 24:16
as their *c* bears witness............ Rom 2:15
c assures me in the Holy Spirit ..... Rom 9:1
but also because of your *c*........ Rom 13:5
and their *c*, because it is weak..... 1 Cor 8:7
without questions of *c*........... 1 Cor 10:25
being judged by another's *c* ..... 1 Cor 10:29
to everyone's *c* before God........ 2 Cor 4:2
of the faith with a clear *c* .... 1 Tim 3:9
sprinkled clean from an evil *c* .... Heb 10:22
keeping a good *c* .... 1 Pet 3:16
that if our *c* condemns us........ 1 John 3:20

CONSCIENCES
of liars whose *c* are seared .... 1 Tim 4:2
minds and *c* are corrupted.......... Titus 1:15
purify our *c* from dead works ..... Heb 9:14

CONSECRATE
Ritually *c* yourselves................. Josh 3:5

CONSECRATED
have *c* this temple you built .... 1 Kgs 9:3
have chosen and *c* this temple.... 2 Chr 7:16
about things *c* to the LORD .... 2 Chr 35:3

CONSENT
try to entice you, do not *c* .... Prov 1:10
gather together by common *c*..... Acts 2:46

CONSENTED
He had not *c* to their plan .... Luke 23:51

CONSEQUENCES
not consider the *c* of her sin........ Lam 1:9

CONSIDER
teach us to *c* our mortality .... Ps 90:12
We *c* it amazing .... Ps 118:23
I *c* my actions and follow .... Ps 119:59
c carefully what is before you .... Prov 23:1
Next, I decided to *c* wisdom........ Eccl 2:12
C the work of God.................. Eccl 7:13
they all *c* John to be a prophet... Matt 21:26
C the ravens..................... Luke 12:24
to *c* anything as if it were........... 2 Cor 3:5
c it nothing but joy .... Jas 1:2

CONSIDERED
who remains silent is *c* wise ..... Prov 17:28
She *c* a field and bought it........ Prov 31:16
and we *c* him insignificant........... Isa 53:3
c as sheep to be slaughtered ..... Rom 8:36
because he *c* me faithful.......... 1 Tim 1:12

CONSIGNED
c all people to disobedience ...... Rom 11:32

CONSIST
one's life does not *c* in............ Luke 12:15

CONSISTENTLY
they were not behaving *c*........... Gal 2:14

CONSOLATION
encouragement, and *c*........... 1 Cor 14:3

CONSOLATIONS
Are God's *c* too trivial for you .... Job 15:11

CONSOLE
stood by him to *c* him .... Gen 37:35
sympathy for him and to *c* him...... Job 2:11
May your loyal love *c* me .... Ps 119:76
Certainly the LORD will *c* Zion ..... Isa 51:3
to *c* all who mourn .... Isa 61:2
to Martha and Mary to *c* them ...John 11:19

CONSOLED
he *c* them and spoke kindly ...... Gen 50:21

CONSOLES
For the LORD *c* his people .... Isa 49:13
I, I am the one who *c* you........... Isa 51:12
As a mother *c* a child .... Isa 66:13

CONSTANTLY
And so we too *c* thank God..... 1 Thess 2:13
c pray....................... 1 Thess 5:17

CONSTELLATIONS
the *c* of the southern sky .... Job 9:9

CONSTERNATION
causing *c* among the Jews .... Acts 9:22

CONSTRAINS
the spirit within me *c* me.......... Job 32:18

CONSUME
this intense fire will *c* us.......... Deut 5:25

CONSUMED
but it was not being *c*.............. Exod 3:2
c thirty cors of finely milled ...... 1 Kgs 4:22
It *c* the offering.................. 1 Kgs 18:38
Yes, we are *c* by your anger........ Ps 90:7
are not *c* by one another .... Gal 5:15

CONSUMES
the one who *c* me will live........ John 6:57

CONSUMING
C fire goes ahead of him............. Ps 50:3
and a *c* flame of fire .... Isa 29:6

CONSUMMATION
once for all at the *c* of the ages .... Heb 9:26

CONTAIN
large enough to *c* two seahs..... 1 Kgs 18:32
highest heavens cannot *c* him ..... 2 Chr 2:6

CONTAINER
and correct measuring *c*......... Deut 25:15
opened a goatskin *c* of milk .... Judg 4:19
Put my tears in your leather *c*..... Ps 56:8

CONTEMPORARIES
he was blameless among his *c*...... Gen 6:9
shrewd in dealing with their *c* .....Luke 16:8

CONTEMPT
He pours *c* on noblemen . . . . .Job 12:21
he holds fools up to public *c* . . . . . . .Prov 3:35
c shows up with him . . . . .Prov 18:3
do you have *c* for the wealth . . . . . .Rom 2:4
to show *c* for the church . . . . .1 Cor 11:22
who has *c* for the Son of God . . . . .Heb 10:29

CONTENDED
So the people *c* with Moses . . . . . . .Exod 17:2

CONTENDING
tell me why you are *c* with me . . . . . .Job 10:2

CONTENDS
c with God on behalf of man . . . . . . .Job 16:21

CONTENT
and be *c* with your pay . . . . .Luke 3:14
to be *c* in any circumstance . . . . Phil 4:11
be *c* with what you have . . . . .Heb 13:5

CONTENTED
They left happy and *c* . . . . .2 Chr 7:10

CONTENTION
With pride comes only *c* . . . . .Prov 13:10
Drive out the scorner and *c* . . . . . . Prov 22:10

CONTENTIOUS
not *c*, free from the love of . . . . .1 Tim 3:3

CONTENTMENT
I have learned the secret of *c* . . . . . .Phil 4:12
godliness combined with *c* . . . . .1 Tim 6:6

CONTINUAL
a cheerful heart has a *c* feast . . . . Prov 15:15

CONTINUALLY
enables you to live *c* in the
   land . . . . .Deut 30:20
May they *c* shout for joy . . . . .Ps 5:11
you will *c* shelter each one . . . . Ps 12:7
I *c* look to the Lord for help . . . . .Ps 25:15
my mouth will *c* praise him . . . . .Ps 34:1
love and faithfulness *c* protect . . . . . Ps 40:11
the Lord *c* shows loyal love . . . . Ps 103:17
so that I might observe it *c* . . . . Ps 119:33
Then I will keep your law *c* . . . . Ps 119:44
I will praise your name *c* . . . . .Ps 145:1
c suffer such painful anguish . . . . Jer 15:18
I *c* think about this . . . . .Lam 3:20
let us *c* offer up a sacrifice . . . . . . .Heb 13:15

CONTINUE
your kingdom will not *c* . . . . .1 Sam 13:14
you *c* to follow my teaching . . . . . .John 8:31
to *c* in the grace of God . . . . .Acts 13:43
provided you *c* in his kindness . . . .Rom 11:22
they did not *c* in my covenant . . . . . .Heb 8:9
Brotherly love must *c* . . . . .Heb 13:1

CONTINUED
His Influence *c* to grow . . . . .Gen 26:13
Every day they *c* to gather . . . . .Acts 2:46
Now Peter *c* knocking . . . . .Acts 12:16
all things have *c* as they were . . . . . . 2 Pet 3:4

CONTINUES
c in faith and love and holiness . . . 1 Tim 2:15

CONTRACTIONS
Before her *c* begin . . . . Isa 66:7

CONTRARY
in a way *c* to the law . . . . Acts 18:13
c to nature . . . . .Rom 11:24
who live *c* to sound teaching . . . . . .1 Tim 1:10

CONTRIBUTE
wants to *c* to the Lord today . . . . .1 Chr 29:5
With pure motives I *c* all this . . . . 1 Chr 29:17
C to the needs of the saints . . . . Rom 12:13

CONTRIBUTION
to make some *c* for the poor . . . . .Rom 15:26
generous *c* you had promised . . . . .2 Cor 9:5

CONTRITE
favor to the humble and *c* . . . . .Isa 66:2

CONTROL
will want to *c* your husband . . . . Gen 3:16
do not allow such sins to *c* me . . . . . .Ps 19:13

CONTROLS
and one who *c* his temper . . . . .Prov 16:32
For the love of Christ *c* us . . . . .2 Cor 5:14

who cannot *c* his temper . . . . Prov 25:28
peace of Christ be in *c* . . . . Col 3:15
and keep his children in *c* . . . . .1 Tim 3:4
able to *c* the entire body . . . . .Jas 3:2

CONTROVERSIES
an unhealthy interest in *c* . . . . .1 Tim 6:4
reject foolish and ignorant *c* . . . . . .2 Tim 2:23
But avoid foolish *c* . . . . Titus 3:9

CONTROVERSY
of *c* in your villages . . . . .Deut 17:8

CONVENED
c in Jerusalem Israel's elders . . . . . . .1 Kgs 8:1

CONVENIENT
ready whether it is *c* or not . . . . .2 Tim 4:2

CONVERSION
at length the *c* of the Gentiles . . . . . Acts 15:3

CONVERT
land and sea to make one *c* . . . . . .Matt 23:15
He must not be a recent *c* . . . . .1 Tim 3:6

CONVICT
and to *c* every person . . . . .Jude 1:15

CONVICTED
he will be *c* by all . . . . .1 Cor 14:24
are *c* by the law as violators . . . . .Jas 2:9

CONVICTION
Holy Spirit and with deep *c* . . . . . .1 Thess 1:5

CONVINCE
and will *c* our conscience . . . . .1 John 3:19

CONVINCED
not be *c* even if someone rises . . .Luke 16:31
be fully *c* in his own mind . . . . .Rom 14:5
am fully *c* about you . . . . .Rom 15:14
c that he is able to protect . . . . 2 Tim 1:12
being *c* of what we do not see . . . . . . Heb 11:1

CONVOCATION
first day there will be a holy *c* . . .Exod 12:16

COO
we *c* mournfully like doves . . . . Isa 59:11

COOKED
women *c* their own children . . . . . . .Lam 4:10

COOL
in water and *c* my tongue . . . . Luke 16:24

COPPER
whose hills you can mine *c* . . . . Deut 8:9
or *c* in your belts . . . . Matt 10:9

COPPERSMITH
Alexander the *c* . . . . .2 Tim 4:14

CORALS
bodies more ruddy than *c* . . . . .Lam 4:7

CORBAN
have received from me is *c* . . . . .Mark 7:11

CORD
God has untied my tent *c* . . . . .Job 30:11
a three-stranded *c* is not . . . . .Eccl 4:12
before the silver *c* is removed . . . . . . .Eccl 12:6

CORDS
who pull evil along using *c* . . . . .Isa 5:18
I drew them with leather *c* . . . . Hos 11:4
So he made a whip of *c* . . . . .John 2:15

CORIANDER
was like *c* seed and was white . . . .Exod 16:31
the manna was like *c* seed . . . . .Num 11:7

CORINTH
Paul labors at, Acts 18:1–18
Site of church, 1 Cor 1:2
Visited by Apollos, Acts 19:1

CORNELIUS
A religious Gentile, Acts 10:1–48

CORNER
in Jerusalem at the *C* Gate . . . . .2 Chr 26:9
to live on a *c* of the housetop . . . . . .Prov 21:9

be left with just a *c* of a bed . . . . . .Amos 3:12
for this was not done in a *c* . . . . . .Acts 26:26

CORNERS
its four horns on its four *c* . . . . Exod 27:2
on the *c* of their garments . . . . Num 15:38
down to earth by its four *c* . . . . . . .Acts 10:11
at the four *c* of the earth . . . . Rev 7:1

CORNERSTONE
or who laid its *c* . . . . .Job 38:6
discarded has become the *c* . . . . . . Ps 118:22
precious *c* for the foundation . . . . . . Isa 28:16
rejected has become the *c* . . . . Matt 21:42
that has become the *c* . . . . .Acts 4:11
a chosen and precious *c* . . . . .1 Pet 2:6
rejected has become the *c* . . . . .1 Pet 2:7

CORPSE
as if you were a mangled *c* . . . . .Isa 14:19
Wherever the *c* is . . . . .Matt 24:28

CORPSES
like *c* lying in the grave . . . . .Ps 88:5

CORRECT
accurate and *c* stone weight . . . . . Deut 25:15
strike me in love and *c* me . . . . .Ps 141:5
to *c* you as my dear children . . . . . . 1 Cor 4:14
c those who speak against it . . . . .Titus 1:9

CORRECTION
And he reveals this for *c* . . . . .Job 36:10
did not respond to such *c* . . . . Jer 2:30
for *c*, and for training . . . . .2 Tim 3:16

CORRECTLY
to judge *c* the appearance . . . . .Matt 16:3
You have answered *c* . . . . .Luke 10:28

CORRECTS
blessed is the man whom God *c* . . . . .Job 5:17
or give up when he *c* you . . . . .Heb 12:5

CORRESPONDS
a companion for him who *c* . . . . Gen 2:18

CORRUPT
who is abominable and *c* . . . . .Job 15:16
they are all morally *c* . . . . .Ps 14:3
they are all morally *c* . . . . .Ps 53:3
who are *c* and unbelieving . . . . .Titus 1:15

CORRUPTED
the old man who is being *c* . . . . .Eph 4:22
great prostitute who *c* the earth . . . .Rev 19:2

CORRUPTION
draws near to the place of *c* . . . . . . .Job 33:22
will reap *c* from the flesh . . . . .Gal 6:8
after escaping the worldly *c* . . . . .2 Pet 1:4

COST
sit down first and compute
   the *c* . . . . .Luke 14:28

COSTLY
alabaster jar of *c* aromatic oil . . . . . Mark 14:3

COUCH
got on my *c* . . . . .Gen 49:4
It is Solomon's portable *c* . . . . Song 3:7

COULD
that he *c* not defeat Jacob . . . . .Gen 32:25
She did what she *c* . . . . .Mark 14:8
that God *c* even raise him . . . . .Heb 11:19
crowd that no one *c* count . . . . .Rev 7:9

COUNCIL
be brought before the *c* . . . . Matt 5:22
regarded member of the *c* . . . . . .Mark 15:43
members of the ruling *c* . . . . .John 7:48
called the *c* together . . . . .John 11:47

COUNCILS
You will be handed over to *c* . . . . . Mark 13:9

COUNSEL
c and understanding are his . . . . .Job 12:13
c of the wicked is far from me . . . . . .Job 21:16
Who is this who darkens *c* . . . . .Job 38:2
stuffed full of their own *c* . . . . Prov 1:31
C in a person's heart . . . . .Prov 20:5
Plans are established by *c* . . . . .Prov 20:18
according to the *c* of his will . . . . .Eph 1:11

COUNSELOR
or who has been his *c* ....Rom 11:34

COUNSELORS
success in the abundance of *c* .....Prov 11:14
c not give her any good advice ..... Jer 49:7

COUNT
able to *c* the dust of the earth .....Gen 13:16
David to *c* how many warriors.....1 Chr 21:1
started to *c* the men but.........1 Chr 27:24
Surely now you *c* my steps ....Job 14:16
by wisdom can *c* the clouds ....Job 38:37
I can *c* all my bones..................Ps 22:17

COUNTED
more days than can even be *c*.......Jer 2:32
was *c* with the transgressors ....Luke 22:37
was *c* with the eleven apostles ....Acts 1:26
was *c* to him for righteousness ....Jas 2:23

COUNTENANCE
LORD lift up his *c* upon you ....Num 6:26

COUNTRY
Go out from your *c*..................Gen 12:1
must go instead to my *c*...........Gen 24:4
let us pass through your *c*........Num 20:17
lived in the *c* of the Philistines...1 Sam 27:11
another route to their own *c* .....Matt 2:12
on a journey to a distant *c*.....Luke 15:13
as though it were a foreign *c* ....Heb 11:9

COUNTRYMAN
each one to teach his *c* ....Heb 8:11

COUNTRYMEN
my people, my fellow *c*.............Rom 9:3

COUNTRYSIDE
surrounding *c* and villages........Mark 6:36

COUNTS
He *c* the number of the stars ....Ps 147:4

COURAGE
See also HAVE COURAGE
we lost our *c*.......................Josh 2:11
But I am full of the *c*................Mic 3:8
Have *c*, son ....Matt 9:2
be distressed or lacking in *c* .....John 14:27
Paul thanked God and took *c*.....Acts 28:15
show *c*, be strong.................1 Cor 16:13
we are always full of *c*.............2 Cor 5:6

COURAGEOUS
Be strong and *c*...................Deut 31:6

COURSE
In the *c* of time she gave birth....1 Sam 1:20
it enjoys running its *c*..............Ps 19:5
to the *c* of human existence ....Jas 3:6

COURT
to the king in the inner *c*...........Esth 4:11
a cloud filled the inner *c*..........Ezek 10:3
brought me to the outer *c*.......Ezek 40:17
You do not *c* anyone's favor ..... Matt 22:16
by you or by any human *c* ....1 Cor 4:3
They *c* you eagerly ....Gal 4:17

COURTESY
complete *c* to all people...........Titus 3:2

COURTS
to live in your palace *c*.............Ps 65:4
in the *c* of the LORD's temple........Ps 84:2
they grow in the *c* of our God ......Ps 92:13
and his *c* with praise................Ps 100:4
will drink the wine in the *c* ....Isa 62:9
found him in the temple *c*.......Luke 2:46
consent in the temple *c*...........Acts 2:46

COURTYARD
make the *c* of the tabernacle .....Exod 27:9
He made the *c* of the priests.......2 Chr 4:9
in the *c* of the guardhouse.........Jer 32:2

COVENANT
See also NEW COVENANT
will confirm my *c* with you ....Gen 6:18
now confirm my *c* with you........Gen 9:9
LORD made a *c* with Abram.......Gen 15:18
my *c* between me and you.....Gen 17:2

this is my *c* with you................Gen 17:4
listen to me and keep my *c*........Exod 19:5
He took the Book of the *C*........Exod 24:7
generations as a perpetual *c*.....Exod 31:16
It is a *c* of salt forever............Num 18:19
he revealed to you the *c*........Deut 4:13
These are the words of the *c* ....Deut 29:1
never break my *c* with you .... Judg 2:1
So Jonathan made a *c*...........1 Sam 20:16
two of them had made a *c*......1 Sam 23:18
the ark containing the *c* ....1 Kgs 8:21
words of the scroll of the *c*......2 Kgs 23:2
words of the scroll of the *c* .....2 Chr 34:30
who keeps his loving *c*...............Neh 1:5
I made a *c* with my eyes ....Job 31:1
my *c* with him is secure............Ps 89:28
keep my *c* and the rules............Ps 132:12
has ignored her marriage *c*........Prov 2:17
and make you a *c* mediator........Isa 42:6
make a permanent *c* with them ....Isa 61:8
Hear the terms of the *c* I made ...... Jer 11:2
make a new *c* with the people......Jer 31:31
I made a *c* with your ancestors .....Jer 34:13
make a *c* of peace with them ....Ezek 37:26
will confirm a *c* with many.........Dan 9:27
At Adam they broke the *c* ....Hos 6:7
cut it in two to annul my *c*........Zech 11:10
and the messenger of the *c*........Mal 3:1
the blood of the *c*................Matt 26:28
the blood of the *c*................Mark 14:24
is the new *c* in my blood.......Luke 22:20
is the new *c* in my blood..........1 Cor 11:25
to be servants of a new *c*..........2 Cor 3:6
a *c* previously ratified by God....... Gal 3:17
c that he mediates is also better....Heb 8:6
first *c* had been faultless............Heb 8:7
When he speaks of a new *c*........ Heb 8:13
he is the mediator of a new *c*.......Heb 9:15
the mediator of a new *c* ....Heb 12:24
by the blood of the eternal *c* ......Heb 13:20

COVENANT-BREAKERS
senseless, *c*, heartless, ruthless.... Rom 1:31

COVENANTAL
c loyalty to your servants.........1 Kgs 8:23
c loyalty to your servants.........2 Chr 6:14

COVENANTS
the *c*, the giving of the law......... Rom 9:4
these women represent two *c*.....Gal 4:24

COVER
and will *c* you with my hand.....Exod 33:22
and to *c* a person's pride...........Job 33:17
spread out a cloud for a *c*........Ps 105:39
waters completely *c* the sea.........Isa 11:9
will no longer *c* up its slain ....Isa 26:21
I can *c* it with sackcloth.............Isa 50:3
and to the hills, '*C* us ....Luke 23:30
and will *c* a multitude of sins ....Jas 5:20

COVERED
The depths have *c* them ....Exod 15:5
if I have *c* my transgressions......Job 31:33
removed my sackcloth and *c* ...... Ps 30:11
the wings of the dove are *c* ....Ps 68:13
but the sea *c* their enemies.........Ps 78:53
two wings they *c* their faces.........Isa 6:2
should not have his head *c* ....1 Cor 11:7

COVERING
hair is given to her for a *c*.....1 Cor 11:15

COVERINGS
and made *c* for themselves......... Gen 3:7
she had made *c* for herself ....Prov 31:22

COVERS
He *c* himself with light............Ps 104:2
love *c* a multitude of sins..........1 Pet 4:8

COVET
shall not *c* your neighbor's ......Exod 20:17

COW
and the ashes of a young *c* ....Heb 9:13

COWARDLY
Why are you *c*.....................Matt 8:26

COWARDS
But as for the *c* ....Rev 21:8

COWORKERS
We are *c* belonging to God .... 1 Cor 3:9

COWS
fat *c* were coming up out..........Gen 41:2
bad-looking *c* ate up...............Gen 41:20
Get two *c* that have calves........1 Sam 6:7
you *c* of Bashan who live ....Amos 4:1

CRAFTINESS
catches the wise in their own *c*..... Job 5:13

CRAFTSMAN
c encourages the metalsmith........Isa 41:7
Look, I create the *c* ....Isa 54:16

CRAFTSMEN
and the Valley of the *C* ....Neh 11:35
of business to the *c*................Acts 19:24

CRAFTY
Jonadab was a very *c* man ....2 Sam 13:3
frustrates the plans of the *c* .... Job 5:12

CRAGS
places of the mountain *c* ....Song 2:14

CRAMPED
This place is too *c* for us............Isa 49:20

CRAMPS
c and pain seize hold ....Isa 13:8

CRANE
c recognize the normal times........Jer 8:7

CRASH
when its waves *c* and foam ....Ps 46:3

CRAVE
nor should you *c* his house ....Deut 5:21

CRAVED
people that *c* different food ......Num 11:34

CRAVES
the sluggard *c* but gets nothing....Prov 13:4

CREATE
C for me a pure heart................Ps 51:10
LORD will *c* over all Mount Zion ......Isa 4:5
I, the LORD, *c* it....................Isa 45:8
Look, I *c* the craftsman ....Isa 54:16
I am ready to *c* new heavens ....Isa 65:17
Did not one God *c* us ....Mal 2:10
to *c* in himself one new man........Eph 2:15

CREATED
God *c* the heavens and the earth ....Gen 1:1
God *c* the great sea creatures ......Gen 1:21
God *c* humankind in his own ....Gen 1:27
and the earth when they were *c*....Gen 2:4
When God *c* humankind..............Gen 5:1
whom I have *c*......................Gen 6:7
the day God *c* humankind ....Deut 4:32
you *c* the cycle of summer ....Ps 74:17
You *c* the north and the south......Ps 89:12
life-giving breath, they are *c*......Ps 104:30
LORD *c* me as the beginning ......Prov 8:22
c all these heavenly lights ....Isa 40:26
the one who *c* the sky ....Isa 42:5
the one who *c* you...................Isa 43:1
the one who *c* the sky ....Isa 45:18
the place where you were *c* .....Ezek 21:30
On the day you were *c*...........Ezek 28:13
creation that God *c* until now....Mark 13:19
All things were *c* by him ....John 1:3
man *c* for the sake of woman......1 Cor 11:9
having been *c* in Christ Jesus ......Eph 2:10
in God who has *c* all things ....Eph 3:9
who has been *c* in God's image....Eph 4:24
and on earth were *c* in him ....Col 1:16
foods that God *c* to be received ...1 Tim 4:3
a kind of firstfruits of all he *c*.......Jas 1:18
since you *c* all things.................Rev 4:11
who *c* heaven and what is in it......Rev 10:6

CREATES
forms light and *c* darkness ....Isa 45:7

CREATION
from the beginning of *c*...........Mark 10:6
from the beginning of the *c*......Mark 13:19

before the *c* of the world . . . . John 17:24
For since the *c* of the world . . . . Rom 1:20
the *c* was subjected to futility . . . . Rom 8:20
the whole *c* groans and suffers . . . Rom 8:22
anything else in *c* will be able . . . . . Rom 8:39
he is a new *c* . . . . 2 Cor 5:17
that matters is a new *c* . . . . Gal 6:15
the firstborn over all *c* . . . . Col 1:15
For every *c* of God is good . . . . 1 Tim 4:4
not of this *c* . . . . Heb 9:11
from the beginning of *c* . . . . 2 Pet 3:4
the originator of God's *c* . . . . Rev 3:14

CREATOR
C of heaven and earth . . . . Gen 14:19
Is he not your father, your *C* . . . . . . Deut 32:6
C, who gives songs in the night . . . . Job 35:10
kneel before the Lord, our *C* . . . . . . Ps 95:6
the *C* of heaven and earth . . . . Ps 115:15
Lord is the *C* of them both . . . . Prov 22:2
So remember your *C* . . . . Eccl 12:1
men will trust in their *C* . . . . Isa 17:7
the *C* of the whole earth . . . . Isa 40:28
One who argues with his *C* . . . . Isa 45:9
the creation rather than the *C* . . . . . Rom 1:25
entrust their souls to a faithful *C* . . 1 Pet 4:19

CREATURE
See also LIVING CREATURE
and every living *c* with you . . . . Gen 9:12
long for the *c* you have made . . . . Job 14:15
preach the gospel to every *c* . . . . . Mark 16:15
no *c* is hidden from God . . . . Heb 4:13
Then I heard every *c* . . . . Rev 5:13
every living *c* that was in the sea . . . Rev 16:3

CREATURES
See also LIVING CREATURES
God created the great sea *c* . . . . Gen 1:21
c on the earth were sinful . . . . Gen 6:12
were four living *c* full of eyes . . . . Rev 4:6

CREDENTIALS
and do not rely on human *c* . . . . Phil 3:3

CREDIT
what *c* is that to you . . . . Luke 6:32
I seek the *c* that abounds . . . . Phil 4:17
For what *c* is it if you sin . . . . 1 Pet 2:20

CREDITED
Lord *c* it as righteousness to him . . Gen 15:6
This was *c* to Phinehas . . . . Ps 106:31
his pay is not *c* due to grace . . . . Rom 4:4
his faith is *c* as righteousness . . . . . . Rom 4:5
have righteousness *c* to them . . . . . Rom 4:11
the statement it was *c* to him . . . . . Rom 4:23
was *c* to him as righteousness . . . . Gal 3:6

CREDITOR
c must remit what he has loaned . . Deut 15:2
the *c* is coming to take away . . . . 2 Kgs 4:1
Repay your *c* . . . . 2 Kgs 4:7
May the *c* seize all he owns . . . . Ps 109:11
A certain *c* had two debtors . . . . Luke 7:41

CREDITS
to whom God *c* righteousness . . . . . Rom 4:6

CREEPING
c things, and wild animals . . . . Gen 1:24
figure of *c* thing and beast . . . . Ezek 8:10

CRETE
Paul visits, Acts 27:7–21
Titus dispatched to, Titus 1:5
Inhabitants of, evil and lazy, Titus 1:12

CREVICES
into the *c* of the rocky cliffs . . . . Isa 2:21
and in the *c* of the cliffs . . . . Isa 7:19

CRIED
So she *c* and refused to eat . . . . 1 Sam 1:7
To you they *c* out . . . . Ps 22:5
from the belly of Sheol I *c* out . . . . . Jonah 2:2
starting to sink, he *c* out . . . . Matt 14:30

CRIES
will be no terrified *c* in our city . . . . Ps 144:14
of trumpet blasts and battle *c* . . . . . Zeph 1:16
with loud *c* and tears . . . . Heb 5:7

CRIMES
build Zion through bloody *c* . . . . Mic 3:10

CRIMINAL
point of imprisonment as a *c* . . . . . . 2 Tim 2:9
as a murderer or thief or *c* . . . . 1 Pet 4:15

CRIMINALS
Two other *c* were also led
  away . . . . Luke 23:32

CRIMSON
purple, *c*, and white fabrics . . . . 2 Chr 3:14

CRIPPLED
for you to enter into life *c* . . . . Mark 9:43
the poor, the *c*, the blind . . . . Luke 14:21

CR SPUS
Chief ruler of synagogue of Corinth,
  Acts 18:8
Baptized by Paul, 1 Cor 1:14

CRITICIZED
You have *c* me sharply . . . . Mal 3:13
How have we *c* you . . . . Mal 3:13

CROOKED
whose paths are morally *c* . . . . Prov 2:15
the *c* will be made straight . . . . Luke 3:5
making *c* the straight paths . . . . Acts 13:10
live in a *c* and perverse society . . . . . Phil 2:15

CROP
By itself the soil produces a *c* . . . . . Mark 4:28
produced an abundant *c* . . . . Luke 12:16

CROPS
make it produce and yield *c* . . . . Isa 55:10
eat up your *c* and your food . . . . Jer 5:17
You will plant *c* . . . . Mic 6:15

CROSS
I would never *c* the Jordan . . . . Deut 4:21
take up his *c* and follow me . . . . . Matt 10:38
take up his *c*, and follow me . . . . . Matt 16:24
You *c* land and sea . . . . Matt 23:15
they forced to carry his *c* . . . . Matt 27:32
come down from the *c* . . . . Matt 27:40
take up his *c*, and follow me . . . . . Mark 8:34
take up his *c* daily . . . . Luke 9:23
carry his own *c* and follow me . . . Luke 14:27
carrying his own *c* he went out . . . John 19:17
so that the *c* of Christ . . . . 1 Cor 1:17
that case the offense of the *c* . . . . . . Gal 5:11
persecuted for the *c* of Christ . . . . . . Gal 6:12
never boast except in the *c* . . . . Gal 6:14
body to God through the *c* . . . . Eph 2:16
even death on a *c* . . . . Phil 2:8
the enemies of the *c* of Christ . . . . . Phil 3:18
through the blood of his *c* . . . . Col 1:20
by nailing it to the *c* . . . . Col 2:14
he endured the *c* . . . . Heb 12:2

CROSSED
By faith they *c* the Red Sea . . . . Heb 11:29

CROSSROADS
You are standing at the *c* . . . . Jer 6:16

CROUCHING
sin is *c* at the door . . . . Gen 4:7

CROW
the rooster will not *c* today . . . . . . Luke 22:34

CROWD
You must not follow a *c* . . . . Exod 23:2
walk together among the *c* . . . . Ps 55:14
When the *c* saw this . . . . Matt 9:8
I have compassion on the *c* . . . . Matt 15:32
After instructing the *c* to sit . . . . . Matt 15:35
a large *c* followed them . . . . Matt 20:29
c was trying to touch him . . . . Luke 6:19
c that no one could count . . . . Rev 7:9

CROWDS
C, great *c* are in the Valley . . . . Joel 3:14
the *c* were amazed and said . . . . . Matt 12:23
things in parables to the *c* . . . . Matt 13:34
he instructed the *c* to sit . . . . Matt 14:19
taught the *c* from the boat . . . . Luke 5:3
the *c* are surrounding you . . . . Luke 8:45
persuaded the *c* not to offer . . . . . . Acts 14:18

CROWN
place a golden *c* on his head . . . . Ps 21:3
c the year with your good . . . . Ps 65:11
thrown his *c* to the ground . . . . Ps 89:39
and his *c* will shine . . . . Ps 132:18
c of the wise is their riches . . . . Prov 14:24
Gray hair is like a *c* of glory . . . . Prov 16:31
c of Ephraim's drunkards . . . . Isa 28:1
c and a splendid diadem . . . . Isa 28:5
c has fallen from our head . . . . Lam 5:16
after braiding a *c* of thorns . . . . . . Matt 27:29
wearing the *c* of thorns . . . . John 19:5
to receive a perishable *c* . . . . 1 Cor 9:25
long to see, my joy and *c* . . . . Phil 4:1
our hope or joy or *c* . . . . 1 Thess 2:19
c of righteousness is reserved . . . . 2 Tim 4:8
he will receive the *c* of life . . . . Jas 1:12
you will receive the *c* of glory . . . . . . 1 Pet 5:4
I will give you the *c* that is life . . . . . Rev 2:10
no one can take away your *c* . . . . Rev 3:11
He had a golden *c* on his head . . . . . Rev 14:14

CROWNED
You *c* mankind with honor . . . . Ps 8:5
will be *c* with knowledge . . . . Prov 14:18
c him with glory and honor . . . . Heb 2:7

CROWNS
had golden *c* on their heads . . . . Rev 4:4
heads were seven diadem *c* . . . . Rev 12:3
its horns were ten diadem *c* . . . . Rev 13:1
many diadem *c* on his head . . . . Rev 19:12

CRUCIBLE
The *c* is for refining silver . . . . Prov 17:3

CRUCIFIED
and flogged severely and *c* . . . . Matt 20:19
will be handed over to be *c* . . . . Matt 26:2
two outlaws were *c* with him . . . . Matt 27:38
looking for Jesus, who was *c* . . . . . Matt 28:5
he handed him over to be *c* . . . . . . Mark 15:15
when they *c* him . . . . Mark 15:25
Jesus the Nazarene, who was *c* . . . Mark 16:6
they *c* him there . . . . Luke 23:33
hands of sinful men, and be *c* . . . . . Luke 24:7
condemned to death, and *c* . . . . . . Luke 24:20
him over to them to be *c* . . . . John 19:16
the place where Jesus was *c* . . . . . . John 19:41
the Nazarene whom you *c* . . . . Acts 4:10
our old man was *c* with him . . . . Rom 6:6
Paul wasn't *c* for you . . . . 1 Cor 1:13
we preach about a *c* Christ . . . . 1 Cor 1:23
except Jesus Christ, and him *c* . . . . . 1 Cor 2:2
not have *c* the Lord of glory . . . . 1 Cor 2:8
was *c* by reason of weakness . . . . . 2 Cor 13:4
I have been *c* with Christ . . . . Gal 2:20
was vividly portrayed as *c* . . . . Gal 3:1
to Christ have *c* the flesh . . . . Gal 5:24
the world has been *c* to me . . . . Gal 6:14
where their Lord was also *c* . . . . Rev 11:8

CRUCIFY
of whom you will kill and *c* . . . . . . Matt 23:34
They all said, "*C* him . . . . Matt 27:22
They shouted back, "*C* him . . . . Mark 15:13
kept on shouting "*C*, *c* him . . . . Luke 23:21
to release you and to *c* you . . . . John 19:10
Away with him! *C* him . . . . John 19:15

CRUCIFYING
since they are *c* the Son of God . . . . Heb 6:6

CRUEL
for it was *c* . . . . Gen 49:7
C rulers are not your allies . . . . Ps 94:20
acts of the wicked are *c* . . . . Prov 12:10

CRUMBLE
mountains will *c* beneath him . . . . . . Mic 1:4

CRUMBS
the table eat the children's *c* . . . . . . Mark 7:28

CRUSH
torment me and *c* me . . . . Job 19:2
that a foot might *c* them . . . . Job 39:15
Lord desired to *c* him . . . . Isa 53:10
they *c* and destroy . . . . Isa 59:7
you *c* the needy . . . . Amos 4:1
will quickly *c* Satan under . . . . Rom 16:20

CRUSHED
who are c like a moth.........Job 4:19
helpers of Rahab lie c.........Job 9:13
you c the people living there.......Ps 44:2
a c spirit dries up the bones....Prov 17:22
but who can bear a c spirit......Prov 18:14
A reed he will not break........Isa 42:4
He will not grow dim or be c......Isa 42:4
c because of our sins..........Isa 53:5
my dear people are being c......Jer 8:21
c under judgment...............Hos 5:11
but are not c..................2 Cor 4:8

CRY
and their desperate c..........Exod 2:23
c out because of the excess.....Job 35:9
Surely it is an empty c.........Job 35:13
will scurry at the battle c.....Isa 30:17
A voice says, "C out..........Isa 40:6
Do not raise a c of prayer......Jer 7:16
and must c earnestly to God.....Jonah 3:8
who c out to him day and night..Luke 18:7

CRYING
saw the child—a boy, c........Exod 2:6
you c and why won't you eat....1 Sam 1:8
Then the prophet started c......2 Kgs 8:11
c and mourning for several days..Neh 1:4
or mourning, or c, or pain......Rev 21:4

CRYSTAL
gold nor c can be compared......Job 28:17
like a sea of glass, like c......Rev 4:6

CRYSTAL-CLEAR
like a stone of c jasper........Rev 21:11

CUBS
like a bear robbed of her c.....Hos 13:8

CUCUMBERS
the c, the melons, the leeks....Num 11:5

CUD
chew the c and have divided.....Lev 11:4
that chew the c or those that...Deut 14:7

CULMINATION
For the c of all things is near...1 Pet 4:7

CULTIVATE
was no man to c the ground......Gen 2:5

CULTIVATED
while Cain c the ground.........Gen 4:12
They c fields and planted.......Ps 107:37

CUNNING
the c is brought to a quick end...Job 5:13

CUP
my c is completely full.........Ps 23:5
a c full of foaming wine........Ps 75:8
Take this c the LORD passed to you..Isa 51:17
The c of wine.................Jer 25:15
a c that brings dizziness.......Hab 2:16
gives only a c of cold water....Zech 12:2
You will drink my c............Matt 10:42
First clean the inside of the c..Matt 20:23
taking this c and giving thanks..Matt 23:26
let this c pass from me.........Matt 26:27
whoever gives you a c of water...Matt 26:39
clean the outside of the c......Mark 9:41
in the same way he took the c...Luke 11:39
take this c away from me........Luke 22:20
cannot drink the c of the Lord...Luke 22:42
he also took the c after supper..1 Cor 10:21
undiluted c of his wrath........1 Cor 11:25
the c filled with the wine......Rev 14:10
held in her hand a golden c.....Rev 16:19
Rev 17:4

CURDS
then took some c and milk.......Gen 18:8
she served him c................Judg 5:25

CURE
want to c your waywardness......Jer 3:22
all demons and to c diseases....Luke 9:1

CURIOSITY
they have an insatiable c.......2 Tim 4:3

CURRENT
the ocean c engulfed me.........Jonah 2:3

CURRENTS
c of chaos overwhelmed me.......Ps 18:4

CURSE
will never again c the ground...Gen 8:21
treats you lightly I must c.....Gen 12:3
c against you will fall on me...Gen 27:13
not blaspheme God or c..........Exod 22:28
You must not c a deaf person....Lev 19:14
come and c this nation for me...Num 22:6
changed the c to a blessing.....Deut 23:5
stand for the c on Mount Ebal...Deut 27:13
had hired Balaam to c them......Neh 13:2
C God, and die.................Job 2:9
They c, but you will bless......Ps 109:28
LORD's c is on the household....Prov 3:33
so a c without cause...........Prov 26:2
a king even in your thoughts....Eccl 10:20
So a treaty c devours the earth...Isa 24:6
I will put a c on people........Isa 48:10
A c on anyone who is lax........Jer 17:5
This is a c traveling..........Zech 5:3
were a c to the nations........Zech 8:13
bless those who c you..........Luke 6:28
bless and do not c.............Rom 12:14
are under a c..................Gal 3:10
redeemed us from the c.........Gal 3:13
c people made in God's image....Jas 3:9
there will no longer be any c...Rev 22:3

CURSED
c are you above all the cattle...Gen 3:14
exposed on a tree is c by God...Deut 21:23
will be considered c............Isa 65:20
of those who have been c.......Jer 42:18
Jesus is c....................1 Cor 12:3
C is everyone who hangs.........Gal 3:13
useless and about to be c.......Heb 6:8

CURSES
anyone c his father or mother...Lev 20:9
will write these c on a scroll...Num 5:23
both the blessings and the c....Deut 30:1
because the LORD has said.......2 Sam 16:10
but inwardly they utter c.......Ps 62:4
c his father and his mother.....Prov 20:20
an example to be used in c......Jer 24:9

CURSING
For his sons were c God........1 Sam 3:13
There is only c................Hos 4:2

CURTAIN
length of each c is to be 42 feet..Exod 26:2
hang this c under the clasps....Exod 26:33
out the skies like a tent c.....Ps 104:2
the temple c was torn in two....Matt 27:51
reaches inside behind the c.....Heb 6:19

CUSH
Ham's oldest son, 1 Chr 1:8-10

CUSHAN RISHATHAIM
Mesopotamian king; oppresses Israel,
Judg 3:8
Othniel delivers Israel from, Judg 3:9-10

CUSHION
tears saturate the c beneath me...Ps 6:6

CUSTOM
according to the c of Moses......Acts 15:1

CUSTOMER
The c should not rejoice........Ezek 7:12

CUT
You must never c his hair.......Judg 13:5
My hair has never been c........Judg 16:17
C the living child in two.......1 Kgs 3:25
umbilical cord was not c........Ezek 16:4
watching as a stone was c......Dan 2:34
c it off and throw it away......Matt 5:30
and will c him in two..........Matt 24:51
man whose ear Peter had c off...John 18:26

CYMBAL
a noisy gong or a clanging c....1 Cor 13:1

CYPRUS [or KITTIM]
Mentioned in prophecies, Num 24:24;
Isa 23:1-12; Jer 2:10
Christians preach to Jews of, Acts 11:19-20
Paul and Barnabas visit, Acts 13:4-13; 15:39
Also called "Kittim," Num 24:24; Dan 11:30

CYRENE
A Greek colonial city in North Africa; home
of Simon the cross-bearer, Matt 27:32
Synagogue of, Acts 6:9
Christians from, become missionaries,
Acts 11:20

CYRUS
King of Persia, referred to as God's
anointed, Isa 44:28-45:1

D

DAGON
The national god of the Philistines, Judg 16:23
Falls before ark, 1 Sam 5:1-5

DAILY
Three times d he was kneeling.....Dan 6:10
Give us today our d bread........Matt 6:11
take up his cross d.............Luke 9:23

DALMATIA
A region east of the Adriatic Sea; Titus
departs for, 2 Tim 4:10

DAMAGE
d the olive oil and the wine.....Rev 6:6
Do not d the earth or the sea....Rev 7:3

DAMAGING
to find any such d evidence......Dan 6:4

DAMASCUS
Capital of Syria; captured by David; ruled by
enemy kings, 2 Sam 8:5-6; 1 Kgs 11:23-24;
15:18
Elisha's prophecy in, 2 Kgs 8:7-15
Taken by Assyrians, 2 Kgs 16:9
Prophecy concerning, Isa 8:3-4
Paul converted on road to; first preaches
there, Acts 9:1-22 escapes from,
2 Cor 11:32-33 revisits, Gal 1:17

DAMP
body became d with the dew......Dan 4:33

DAN
Jacob's son by Bilhah, Gen 30:5-6
Prophecy concerning, Gen 49:16-17
—Tribe of:
Numbered, Num 1:38-39
Blessed, Deut 33:22
Receive their inheritance, Josh 19:40-47,
Fall into idolatry, Judg 18:1-31
—Town, northern boundary of Israel,
Judg 20:1
Leshem captured by Danites; renamed Dan,
Josh 19:47
Center of idolatry, 1 Kgs 12:28-30
Destroyed by Ben Hadad, 1 Kgs 15:20

DANCE
and a time to d...............Eccl 3:4
yet you did not d..............Matt 11:17

DANCED
the daughter of Herodias d......Matt 14:6

DANCING
and saw the calf and the d......Exod 32:19
was d with all his strength.....2 Sam 6:14
turned my lament into d........Ps 30:11
praise his name with d.........Ps 149:3
our d is turned to mourning.....Lam 5:15
he heard music and d...........Luke 15:25

DANGER
rescued me from every d........1 Kgs 1:29
I fear no d....................Ps 23:4
shelter in the day of d........Ps 27:5
walk in the midst of d.........Ps 138:7
A shrewd person saw d..........Prov 22:3
or nakedness, or d, or sword....Rom 8:35
are we in d every hour........1 Cor 15:30

DANGEROUS
like a dark and d land to you...Jer 2:31

DANGERS

The godly face many *d* .... Ps 34:19
innumerable *d* surround me .... Ps 40:12
in *d* from rivers .... 2 Cor 11:26

DANIEL

Taken to Babylon; refuses
    Nebuchadnezzar's foods, Dan 1
Interprets dreams; honored by king, Dan 2
Interprets handwriting on wall; honored by
    Belshazzar, Dan 5:10–29
Appointed to high office; conspired against
    and thrown to lions, Dan 6:1–23
Visions of four beasts, ram, and goat,
    Dan 7–8
Intercedes for Israel, Dan 9:1–19
Further visions, Dan 9:20–12:13

DARE

might possibly *d* to die .... Rom 5:7
does he *d* go to court .... 1 Cor 6:1
d to speak the word .... Phil 1:14

DARES

anyone else *d* to boast about ..... 2 Cor 11:21

DARIUS

Darius the Mede, son of Ahasuerus; made
    king of the Chaldeans, Dan 9:1
Succeeds Belshazzar, Dan 5:30–31
Co-ruler with Cyrus, Dan 6:28
—Darius Hystaspis (522–486 BC), king of all
    Persia; temple work dated by his reign,
    Ezra 4:5, 24
Confirms Cyrus's royal edict, Ezra 6:1–14
—Darius the Persian (423–404 BC); priestly
    records kept during his reign, Neh 12:22

DARK

ground became *d* with them ..... Exod 10:15
skin has turned *d* on me .... Job 30:30
darkness is not too *d* for you ...... Ps 139:12
I am *d* but lovely .... Song 1:5
it will grow *d* .... Mic 3:6
What I say to you in the *d* .... Matt 10:27
while it was still *d* .... John 20:1

DARKENED

their minds are spiritually *d* .... Isa 8:20
are *d* in their understanding .... Eph 4:18

DARKEST

walk through the *d* valley .... Ps 23:4

DARKNESS

light "day" and the *d* "night .... Gen 1:5
The Lord illumines the *d* .... 2 Sam 22:29
said that he lives in thick *d* .... 1 Kgs 8:12
judge through such deep *d* .... Job 22:13
They sat in utter *d* .... Ps 107:10
even the *d* is not too dark .... Ps 139:12
The people walking in *d* .... Isa 9:2
turn the *d* in front of them .... Isa 42:16
I can clothe the sky in *d* .... Isa 50:3
d covers the earth .... Isa 60:2
reside in deepest *d* .... Lam 3:6
can turn the *d* into morning ...... Amos 5:8
whole body will be full of *d* .... Matt 6:23
thrown out into the outer *d* ...... Matt 8:12
and that of the power of *d* .... Luke 22:53
and people loved the *d* .... John 3:19
the *d* may not overtake you ...... John 12:35
for you were at one time *d* .... Eph 5:8
the world rulers of this *d* .... Eph 6:12
from the power of *d* and .... Col 1:13
not of the night nor of the *d* .... 1 Thess 5:5
who called you out of *d* .... 1 Pet 2:9
depths of *d* have been reserved ... 2 Pet 2:17
in him there is no *d* at all .... 1 John 1:5
yet keep on walking in the *d* ...... 1 John 1:6
because the *d* is passing away ..... 1 John 2:8
eternal *d* have been reserved ...... Jude 1:13

DARNEL

then the *d* also appeared .... Matt 13:26

DARTING

and its fruit will be a *d* adder ...... Isa 14:29

DASHED

infants will be *d* to the ground ..... Hos 13:16

DATHAN

Joins Korah's rebellion, Num 16:1–35
Swallowed up by the earth, Ps 106:17

DAUGHTER

I am the *d* of Bethuel .... Gen 24:24
Leah's *d* whom she bore .... Gen 34:1
Jochebed, *d* of Levi .... Num 26:59
d hurrying out to meet him .... Judg 11:34
Rejoice greatly, *d* of Zion .... Zech 9:9
My *d* has just died .... Matt 9:18
he said, "Have courage, *d* .... Matt 9:22
a *d* of Abraham whom Satan ..... Luke 13:16
called the son of Pharaoh's *d* ...... Heb 11:24

DAUGHTER-IN-LAW

Judah said to his *d* Tamar .... Gen 38:11
by her Moabite *d* Ruth .... Ruth 1:22
obscenely defiles his *d* .... Ezek 22:11
and a *d* her mother-in-law .... Mic 7:6
d against her mother-in-law ..... Matt 10:35

DAUGHTERS

he had other sons and *d* .... Gen 5:4
d of humankind were beautiful ..... Gen 6:2
Lot's *d* became pregnant .... Gen 19:36
for your two *d* and 6 years .... Gen 31:41
Then the *d* of Zelophehad .... Num 27:1
to give them our *d* as wives .... Judg 21:7
Go back home, my *d* .... Ruth 1:11
O *d* of Israel .... 2 Sam 1:24
king's virgin *d* used to wear ..... 2 Sam 13:18
were as beautiful as Job's *d* .... Job 42:15
The leech has two *d* .... Prov 30:15
Many *d* have done valiantly ...... Prov 31:29
her *d* will go into captivity .... Ezek 30:18
sons and *d* will prophesy .... Joel 2:28
D of Jerusalem .... Luke 23:28
sons and your *d* will prophesy ..... Acts 2:17
unmarried *d* who prophesied ...... Acts 21:9
you will be my sons and *d* .... 2 Cor 6:18

DAVID

Anointed by Samuel, 1 Sam 16:1–13
Becomes royal harpist, 1 Sam 16:14–23
Defeats Goliath, 1 Sam 17
Makes covenant with Jonathan, 1 Sam 18:1–4
Honored by Saul; loved by the people; Saul
    becomes jealous, 1 Sam 18:5–16
Wins Michal as wife, 1 Sam 18:17–30
Flees from Saul, 1 Sam 19–20; 21:10–22:5;
    23:14–29
Eats the holy bread, 1 Sam 21:1–6;
    Matt 12:3–4
Saves Keilah from Philistines, 1 Sam 23:1–13
Twice spares Saul's life, 1 Sam 24:1–22;
    26:1–25
Anger at Nabal appeased by Abigail;
    marries her, 1 Sam 25:2–42
Allies with the Philistines, 1 Sam 27:1–28:2
    rejected by them, 1 Sam 29
Avenges destruction of Ziklag, 1 Sam 30
Mourns death of Saul and Jonathan, 2 Sam 1
Anointed king of Judah, 2 Sam 2:1–7
War with Saul's house; Abner defects to
    David, 2 Sam 3:1, 6–21
Mourns Abner's death, 2 Sam 3:28–39
Punishes Ish Bosheth's murderers, 2 Sam 4
Anointed king of all Israel, 2 Sam 5:1–5
Conquers Jerusalem; makes it his capital,
    2 Sam 5:6–16
Defeats Philistines, 2 Sam 5:17–25
Brings ark to Jerusalem, 2 Sam 6
Receives eternal covenant, 2 Sam 7
Further conquests, 2 Sam 8; 10
Shows kindness to Mephibosheth, 2 Sam 9
Commits adultery and murder, 2 Sam 11
Rebuked by Nathan; repents, 2 Sam 12:1–23;
    Ps 32; 51
Absalom's rebellion, 2 Sam 15–18
Mourns Absalom's death, 2 Sam 18:33–19:8
Shows himself merciful, 2 Sam 19:18–39
Sheba's rebellion, 2 Sam 19:40–20:22
Avenges the Gibeonites, 2 Sam 21:1–14
Song of deliverance, 2 Sam 22
Sins by numbering the people, 2 Sam 24:1–17

Buys threshing floor to build altar,
    2 Sam 24:18–25
Secures Solomon's succession, 1 Kgs 1:5–53
Instructions to Solomon, 1 Kgs 2:1–11
Last words, 2 Sam 23:1–7
Inspired by Spirit, Matt 22:43
As prophet, Acts 2:29–34
Faith of, Heb 11:32–34

See also CITY OF DAVID; HOUSE OF
    DAVID; SON OF DAVID; THRONE OF
    DAVID

Jesse was the father of *D* .... Ruth 4:22
Send me your son *D* .... 1 Sam 16:19
D prevailed over the Philistine . 1 Sam 17:50
D was playing the lyre .... 1 Sam 18:10
all Israel and Judah lived *D* ...... 1 Sam 18:16
D chanted this lament .... 2 Sam 1:17
D, wearing a linen ephod .... 2 Sam 6:14
King *D* leaping and dancing ..... 2 Sam 6:16
D defeated the Philistines .... 2 Sam 8:1
D reigned over all Israel .... 2 Sam 8:15
D had done upset the Lord ..... 2 Sam 11:27
D has made Solomon king .... 1 Kgs 1:43
D reigned over Israel forty .... 1 Kgs 2:11
this one be the Son of *D* .... Matt 12:23
How then does *D* by the Spirit .. Matt 22:43
D did not ascend into heaven ...... Acts 2:34
who holds the key of *D* .... Rev 3:7

DAWN

are like the red glow of *d* .... Job 41:18
on the wings of the *d* .... Ps 139:9
d arrives and the shadows flee .... Song 4:6
this who appears like the *d* .... Song 6:10
son of the *d* .... Isa 14:12
as the appearance of the *d* .... Hos 6:3
forth like the light of the *d* .... Hos 6:5
the rooster crows, or at *d* .... Mark 13:35
the *d* will break upon us .... Luke 1:78
day of the week, at early *d* .... Luke 24:1

DAY

See also DAY OF THE LORD; LAST DAY;
    THIRD DAY

the light "*d*" and the darkness .... Gen 1:5
God blessed the seventh *d* .... Gen 2:3
at the breezy time of the *d* .... Gen 3:8
seventeenth *d* of the month .... Gen 7:11
d and night will not cease .... Gen 8:22
because on this very *d* .... Exod 12:17
gather the amount for each *d* ...... Exod 16:4
the sixth *d* they will prepare .... Exod 16:5
people rested on the seventh *d* .. Exod 16:30
Remember the Sabbath *d* .... Exod 20:8
eaten on the *d* of your sacrifice ..... Lev 19:6
is the *D* of Atonement .... Lev 23:27
It is a solemn assembly *d* .... Lev 23:36
clothes on the seventh *d* .... Num 31:24
and in a cloud by *d* .... Deut 1:33
the *d* of their disaster is near .... Deut 32:35
memorize it *d* and night .... Josh 1:8
the *d* after the Passover .... Josh 5:11
a *d* like it before or since .... Josh 10:14
So on the *d* of the battle .... 1 Sam 13:22
So the victory of that *d* .... 2 Sam 19:2
This is a *d* to celebrate .... 2 Kgs 7:9
This is a *d* of distress .... 2 Kgs 19:3
inside a cistern on a snowy *d* ..... 1 Chr 11:22
from the *d* the foundation .... 2 Chr 8:16
for this *d* is holy .... Neh 8:11
making it a *d* for banqueting ...... Esth 9:18
and cursed the *d* he was born .... Job 3:1
for the *d* of war and battle .... Job 38:23
d I have become your father .... Ps 2:7
D after *d* it speaks out .... Ps 19:2
shelter in the *d* of danger .... Ps 27:5
blessings on him all *d* long .... Ps 72:15
one *d* in your temple courts .... Ps 84:10
shadow at the end of the *d* .... Ps 109:23
is the *d* the Lord has brought ..... Ps 118:24
sun will not harm you by *d* .... Ps 121:6
the night is as bright as *d* .... Ps 139:12
and brighter until full *d* .... Prov 4:18
off a garment on a cold *d* .... Prov 25:20

what a *d* may bring forth...........Prov 27:1
I could cry *d* and night................Jer 9:1
made a covenant with the *d*......Jer 33:20
Look, the *d*! Look, it is coming....Ezek 7:10
battle on the *d* of the LORD........Ezek 13:5
from the *d* you were created.....Ezek 28:15
on the *d* of your fall.............Ezek 32:10
You stumble *d* and night...........Hos 4:5
be a *d* of dreadful darkness.........Joel 2:2
the *d* of the LORD is awesome......Joel 2:11
a *d* of disaster will come...........Amos 6:3
a worm at dawn the next *d*.........Jonah 4:7
and died the next *d*...............Jonah 4:10
for the LORD's *d* of judgment......Zeph 1:7
It will happen in one *d*............Zech 14:7
endure the *d* of his coming.........Mal 3:2
on the *d* of judgment.............Matt 10:15
until that *d* when I drink it
  new.............................Matt 26:29
seven times in a *d*................Luke 17:4
and on the third *d* rise again......Luke 24:7
and glorious *d* of the Lord........Acts 2:20
one *d* holier than other days......Rom 14:5
for the *D* will make it clear.......1 Cor 3:13
he was raised on the third *d*.......1 Cor 15:4
Every *d* I am in danger............1 Cor 15:31
night and a *d* I spent adrift.......2 Cor 11:25
circumcised on the eighth *d*.........Phil 3:5
the *d* of the Lord will come......1 Thess 5:2
of the light and sons of the *d*....1 Thess 5:5
God again ordains a certain *d*.......Heb 4:7
every priest stands *d* after.......Heb 10:11
a single *d* is like a thousand.......2 Pet 3:8
place on the great *d* of God........Rev 16:14

DAY OF THE LORD

strong in battle on the *d*........Ezek 13:5
the day is near, the *d*............Ezek 30:3
For the *d* is near...................Joel 1:15
before the *d* comes...............Joel 2:31
to those who wish for the *d*......Amos 5:18
For the *d* is approaching..........Obad 1:15
the great and terrible *d*...........Mal 4:5
the great and glorious *d*..........Acts 2:20
may be saved in the *d*............1 Cor 5:5
also are ours in the *d* Jesus......2 Cor 1:14
the *d* will come like a thief........2 Pet 3:10

DAYS

See also ALL THE DAYS OF HIS LIFE;
  LAST DAYS

seasons and *d* and years.........Gen 1:14
seven *d* I will cause it to rain....Gen 7:4
among you who is eight *d* old.....Gen 17:12
seven *d* you must eat bread.....Exod 12:15
Six *d* you will gather it...........Exod 16:26
giving you food for two *d*........Exod 16:29
For six *d* you may labor..........Exod 20:9
a gift to the LORD for seven *d*......Lev 23:8
that your *d* may be extended.....Deut 5:16
d are swifter than a weaver's.......Job 7:6
for my *d* are a vapor...............Job 7:16
lives but a few *d*..................Job 14:1
will pursue me all my *d*............Ps 23:6
The *d* of our lives add up..........Ps 90:10
For my *d* go up in smoke...........Ps 102:3
I recall the old *d*.................Ps 143:5
from her younger *d*...............Prov 2:17
not harm all the *d* of her life......Prov 31:12
old *d* better than these *d*.........Eccl 7:10
in the *d* of your youth.............Eccl 12:1
and tested them for 10 *d*..........Dan 1:14
he fasted 40 and 40 nights.......Matt 4:2
But the *d* are coming.............Matt 9:15
d had not been cut short........Matt 24:22
had not cut short those *d*.......Mark 13:20
But those *d* are coming...........Luke 5:35
to raise it up in three *d*..........John 2:20
he has been buried four *d*.......John 11:39
and on three Sabbath *d*..........Acts 17:2
You are observing religious *d*......Gal 4:10
new moon, or Sabbath *d*..........Col 2:16
to love life and see good *d*........1 Pet 3:10
In the last *d* blatant scoffers.......2 Pet 3:3
to prophesy for 1,260 *d*...........Rev 11:3

DAYTIME

sent me as long as it is *d*.........John 9:4

DAZZLING

My beloved is *d* and ruddy.......Song 5:10
stood beside them in *d* attire.....Luke 24:4

DEACONS

with the overseers and *d*...........Phil 1:1
D likewise must be dignified.......1 Tim 3:8
D must be husbands of one
  wife............................1 Tim 3:12

DEAD

See also RAISED FROM THE DEAD;
  RAISED HIM FROM THE DEAD

We are all *d*.....................Exod 12:33
between the *d* and the living....Num 16:48
amazing things for the *d*..........Ps 88:10
who have been *d* for ages.........Ps 143:3
the *d* do not know anything.......Eccl 9:5
Your *d* will come back to life......Isa 26:19
by consulting the *d*..............Jer 27:9
let the *d* bury their own *d*.......Matt 8:22
the *d* are raised...................Matt 11:5
God of the *d* but of the living....Matt 22:32
this son of mine was *d*............Luke 15:24
the *d* will hear the voice..........John 5:25
Christ was raised from the *d*......Rom 6:4
consider yourselves *d* to sin......Rom 6:11
apart from the law, sin is *d*........Rom 7:8
of both the *d* and the living........Rom 14:9
and quite a few are *d*............1 Cor 11:30
preached as raised from the *d*....1 Cor 15:12
who are baptized for the *d*.......1 Cor 15:29
you were *d* in your offenses.........Eph 2:1
the *d* in Christ will rise first......1 Thess 4:16
is *d* even while she lives..........1 Tim 5:6
body without the spirit is *d*........Jas 2:26
of the *d* did not come to life.....Rev 20:5
And I saw the *d*...................Rev 20:12

DEAD SEA [or SALT SEA]

Large army attacks Jehoshaphat from,
  2 Chr 20:1–2
Also called the "Salt Sea," Gen 14:3

DEADLY

full of *d* poison......................Jas 3:8

DEADNESS

and the *d* of Sarah's womb.......Rom 4:19

DEAF

makes a person mute or *d*........Exod 4:11
the *d* will be able to hear.........Isa 29:18
d ears will hear...................Isa 35:5
my messenger is truly *d*..........Isa 42:19
those who are *d*..................Isa 43:8
and act as if they were *d*.........Mic 7:16
the *d* hear, the dead are raised....Matt 11:5

DEAL

she did a great *d* of praying........1 Sam 1:12

DEALING

fathers by *d* with children.........Exod 20:5

DEAR

See also ONE DEAR SON

I hear my *d* people crying out.......Jer 8:19
my *d* children.....................Jer 14:17
This is my one *d* Son..............Matt 3:17
you had become *d* to us..........1 Thess 2:8
as a *d* brother....................Phlm 1:16
This is my *d* Son..................2 Pet 1:17
our *d* brother Paul wrote.........2 Pet 3:15

DEARLY

d love their shameful behavior....Hos 4:18

DEATH

See also SECOND DEATH

me die the *d* of the upright......Num 23:10
d will be able to separate me......Ruth 1:17
down to the barred gates of *d*.....Job 17:16
you are bringing me to *d*.........Job 30:23
you in the realm of *d*.............Ps 6:5
you deliver my life from *d*.........Ps 56:13
without experiencing *d*...........Ps 89:48
and condemn to *d* the innocent....Ps 94:21

she has set her house by *d*........Prov 2:18
all who hate me love *d*............Prov 8:36
D and life are in the power.......Prov 18:21
you will deliver him from *d*.......Prov 23:14
D and Destruction are never....Prov 27:20
swallow up *d* permanently.........Isa 25:8
no delight in the *d* of anyone....Ezek 18:32
Will I redeem them from *d*........Hos 13:14
who will not experience *d*.......Matt 16:28
crossed over from *d* to life.......John 5:24
he will never see *d*...............John 8:51
displayed him at his *d*............Rom 3:25
Yet *d* reigned from Adam..........Rom 5:14
just as sin reigned in *d*...........Rom 5:21
d no longer has mastery..........Rom 6:9
For the payoff of sin is *d*.........Rom 6:23
our body to bear fruit for *d*.......Rom 7:5
we encounter *d* all day long......Rom 8:36
you proclaim the Lord's *d*........1 Cor 11:26
since *d* came through a man......1 Cor 15:21
Every day I am in danger of *d*...1 Cor 15:31
D has been swallowed up.......1 Cor 15:54
The sting of *d* is sin..............1 Cor 15:56
the latter an odor from *d* to *d*....2 Cor 2:16
in our body the *d* of Jesus........2 Cor 4:10
d is at work in us..................2 Cor 4:12
sadness brings about *d*............2 Cor 7:10
obedient to the point of *d*........Phil 2:8
because he suffered *d*............Heb 2:9
through *d* he could destroy........Heb 2:14
so that he did not see *d*...........Heb 11:5
it gives birth to *d*................Jas 1:15
by being put to *d* in the flesh......1 Pet 3:18
a sin not resulting in *d*............1 John 5:16
faithful even to the point of *d*......Rev 2:10
The second *d* has no power.......Rev 20:6
and *d* will not exist any more......Rev 21:4
That is the second *d*...............Rev 21:8

DEBATE

Let's *d*! You, prove to me..........Isa 43:26

DEBATER

Where is the *d* of this age........1 Cor 1:20

DEBATING

arguing with the devil and *d*........Jude 1:9

DEBAUCHED

anguish over the *d* lifestyle........2 Pet 2:7

DEBAUCHERY

deceit, *d*, envy, slander...........Mark 7:22
You lived then in *d*...............1 Pet 4:3

DEBIR [or KIRIATH SEPHER]

City of Judah; captured by Joshua,
  Josh 10:38–39
Recaptured by Othniel, Josh 15:15–17;
  Judg 1:11–13
Also called "Kiriath Sepher," Josh 15:15–17;
  Judg 1:11–13

DEBORAH

A prophet and judge, Judg 4:4–14
Composed song of triumph, Judg 5:1–31

DEBT

and forgave him the *d*...........Matt 18:27

DEBTOR

I am a *d* both to the Greeks.......Rom 1:14

DEBTORS

have forgiven our *d*..............Matt 6:12
he contacted his master's *d*......Luke 16:5

DEBTS

declare a cancellation of *d*.......Deut 15:1
time of the cancellation of *d*....Deut 31:10
and forgive us our *d*.............Matt 6:12
he canceled the *d* of both........Luke 7:42

DECAPOLIS

Multitudes from follow Jesus, Matt 4:25
Jesus heals demon-possessed, preaches in,
  Mark 5:20

DECAY

raised up did not experience *d*...Acts 13:37
set free from the bondage of *d*....Rom 8:21

DECEIT
in whose spirit there is no *d* ....Ps 32:2
I hate and despise *d* ....Ps 119:163
D is in the heart .... Prov 12:20
seize the kingdom through *d* ...... Dan 11:21
in whom there is no *d* ....John 1:47
You who are full of all *d* ....Acts 13:10
committed no sin nor was *d* ...... 1 Pet 2:22
Spirit of truth and the spirit of *d* .. 1 John 4:6

DECEITFUL
a perverse and *d* generation...... Deut 32:5
do not associate with *d* men........Ps 26:4
Deliver me from *d* and evil .... Ps 43:1
Violent and *d* people ....Ps 55:23
D people will not live .... Ps 101:7
Therefore I hate all *d* actions ......Ps 119:104
counsels of the wicked are *d* ......Prov 12:5
human mind is more *d* ....Jer 17:9
they are *d* men ....Zeph 3:4
d workers, disguising themselves 2 Cor 11:13
d philosophy that is according....... Col 2:8

DECEITFULLY
nor had he spoken *d* .... Isa 53:9
many will unite with them *d* ......Dan 11:34

DECEIVE
Who will *d* Ahab.................1 Kgs 22:20
I will never *d* David ....Ps 89:35
warn you not to *d* yourselves........Jer 37:9
prophets will appear and *d* ....Matt 24:11
great signs and wonders to *d* ....Matt 24:24
d you with empty words.............Eph 5:6
listen to it and so *d* yourselves .....Jas 1:22
let no one *d* you ....1 John 3:7
will go out to *d* the nations........ Rev 20:8

DECEIVED
they *d* him with their words ....Ps 78:36
his *d* mind misleads him...........Isa 44:20
made a fool by being *d* ....Ezek 14:9
You haven't been *d* too ....John 7:47
d me and through it I died .... Rom 7:11
Do not be *d*.......................1 Cor 6:9
serpent *d* Eve by his treachery ....2 Cor 11:3
Do not be *d*.........................Gal 6:7
And Adam was not *d* .... 1 Tim 2:14
others and being *d* themselves ... 2 Tim 3:13
all the nations were *d*..............Rev 18:23
And the devil who *d* them .... Rev 20:10

DECEIVER
The *d* deceives.....................Isa 21:2
that *d* was still alive he said ......Matt 27:63

DECEIVERS
D deceive, *d* thoroughly deceive... Isa 24:16
For many *d* have gone out........2 John 1:7

DECEIVES
and so *d* his heart..................Jas 1:26
who *d* the whole world............Rev 12:9

DECEIVING
with *d* spirits and demonic ....1 Tim 4:1
d others and being deceived...... 2 Tim 3:13
we are *d* ourselves................1 John 1:8

DECENT
in a *d* and orderly manner ....1 Cor 14:40
you will live a *d* life .... 1 Thess 4:12

DECENTLY
Let us live *d* as in the daytime .... Rom 13:13

DECEPTION
is left of your answers but *d*........Job 21:34
They hold fast to their *d*............Jer 8:5
become hardened by sin's *d* ....Heb 3:13

DECEPTIVE
evil words or use *d* speech ....Ps 34:13
people are *d* and unreliable ....Ps 119:118
exploit you with *d* words .... 2 Pet 2:3

DECEPTIVELY
become satisfied and act *d* ....Prov 30:9

DECEPTIVENESS
with *d* or distorting the word......2 Cor 4:2

DECIDE
that you can *d* what is best .... Phil 1:10

DECIDED
So we *d* to build this altar ....Josh 22:26
d to frustrate the sound advice .. 2 Sam 17:14
d to be concerned about nothing... 1 Cor 2:2
just as he has *d* in his heart........2 Cor 9:7

DECIDES
whom the Son *d* to reveal him ... Matt 11:27

DECISION
into the breastpiece of *d*.........Exod 28:30
Make a just *d* on my behalf.......... Ps 17:2
their every *d* is from the LORD....Prov 16:33
crowds are in the Valley of *D* ......Joel 3:14

DECISIONS
ability to make wise judicial *d* .....1 Kgs 3:11
legal *d* will be made fairly ....Ps 99:4

DECLARATION
with a public *d* of praise ....Jonah 2:9

DECLARE
Would you *d* me guilty ....Job 40:8
heavens *d* the glory of God...........Ps 19:1
d your name to my countrymen...Ps 22:22
d what he has done for me ....Ps 66:16

DECLARED
God has *d* one principle ....Ps 62:11
d a fast and put on sackcloth ......Jonah 3:5

DECORATE
d the graves of the righteous.... Matt 23:29

DECREASES
treasure in heaven that never *d* .. Luke 12:33

DECREE
LORD will *d* blessing for you ......Deut 28:8
continually his covenant *d* ......1 Chr 16:15
King Cyrus enacted a *d* .... Ezra 5:13
I will announce the LORD's *d*.......... Ps 2:7
He issued the *d*......................Ps 33:9
D Jacob's deliverance ....Ps 44:4
D that your loyal love ....Ps 61:7
remembers his covenantal *d* ....Ps 105:8
a *d* that will not be revoked ....Ps 148:6
when he gave the sea his *d* .... Prov 8:29
d of our God is forever reliable..... Isa 40:8
For I will issue a *d* ....Isa 51:4
to *d* the release of the captives ....Isa 61:1
is by the *d* of the sentinels..........Dan 4:17
d of the king and his nobles ......Jonah 3:7
d went out from Caesar Augustus .. Luke 2:1
know God's righteous *d* ....Rom 1:32

DECREED
d a blessing will be available........ Ps 133:3
to carry out the *d* destruction ..... Isa 10:23
long ago exactly as you *d* .....Isa 25:1

DECREES
For the LORD's *d* are just.............Ps 33:4
the LORD *d* his loyal love ....Ps 42:8
they stand firm by your *d*..........Ps 119:91
make just *d* for the nations.........Isa 42:1
law of commandments in *d*.........Eph 2:15
expressed in *d* opposed to us....... Col 2:14

DEDICATED
anything permanently *d* .... Lev 27:28
built a new house and not *d* ......Deut 20:5

DEDICATION
See also FEAST OF THE DEDICATION
the *d* of this temple of God........ Ezra 6:17
feast of the *D* in Jerusalem ......John 10:22

DEED
God will evaluate every *d*.........Eccl 12:14
absolutely extraordinary *d* .... Isa 29:14
copies of the *d* of purchase........ Jer 32:11
not turn from his wicked *d* ....Ezek 3:19
This is the *d* God requires .... John 6:29
whatever you do in word or *d* ...... Col 3:17
good *d* would not be out of.......Phlm 1:14
tongue but in *d* and truth.........1 John 3:18

DEEDS
rival your works and mighty *d*.... Deut 3:24
all the great *d* of the LORD......... Deut 11:7
will perform miraculous *d* ....Josh 3:5

tell of the LORD's victorious *d* ......Judg 5:11
repaid me for my godly *d* .... 2 Sam 22:21
about your praiseworthy *d* ...... 1 Chr 16:35
May the evil *d* of the wicked......... Ps 7:9
tell about all your amazing *d* .... Ps 9:1
he rewards godly *d* ....Ps 11:7
compassionate and faithful *d*.......Ps 25:6
your amazing *d* experienced ....Ps 88:12
about the LORD's faithful *d* .... Ps 89:1
heavens praise your amazing *d*......Ps 89:5
are your earlier faithful *d*............Ps 89:49
who punished their sinful *d*.........Ps 99:8
Do not forget all his kind *d* .... Ps 103:2
his *d* to the Israelites .... Ps 103:7
The LORD's *d* are great .... Ps 111:2
amazing *d* all by himself...........Ps 136:4
a witness against their evil *d*........Ps 141:5
I will declare your great *d* ....Ps 145:6
person according to his *d*........Prov 24:12
weighed down by evil *d* .... Isa 1:4
blots out your rebellious *d* ....Isa 43:25
complacent in your evil *d* ....Isa 47:10
because of our rebellious *d*..........Isa 53:5
had committed no violent *d* .... Isa 53:9
my *d* are not like your *d* .... Isa 55:8
people with their rebellious *d* ......Isa 58:1
of our many rebellious *d* ....Isa 59:12
I hate their *d* and thoughts .... Isa 66:18
pours out wicked *d* ....Jer 6:7
things and you do mighty *d*.........Jer 32:19
miracles and amazing *d* ....Jer 32:21
with all her abominable *d* .... Ezek 22:2
for all his *d* are right...............Dan 4:37
oppressive *d* occurring in it....... Amos 3:9
powerful *d* in your name ....Matt 7:22
of the *d* of your ancestors ....Luke 11:48
his powerful *d* and words....... Luke 24:19
because their *d* were evil..........John 3:19
does evil *d* hates the light .... John 3:20
show him greater *d* than these ... John 5:20
doing the *d* of your father ....John 8:41
d I do in my Father's name ......John 10:25
perform the miraculous *d* ....John 14:12
powerful in his words and *d* ......Acts 7:22
put to death the *d* of the body.....Rom 8:13
rejected shameful hidden *d*.......2 Cor 4:2
the unfruitful *d* of darkness .... Eph 5:11
but with their *d* they deny him ....Titus 1:16
merciful toward their evil *d*........ Heb 8:12
shares in his evil *d* .... 2 John 1:11
their *d* will follow them.............Rev 14:13
refused to repent of their *d*........Rev 16:11
the righteous *d* of the saints........Rev 19:8
according to their *d*...............Rev 20:12

DEEP
the man to fall into a *d* sleep ......Gen 2:21
able to see through *d* darkness.... Isa 29:18
Like a monster from the *d*..........Jer 51:34
The great *d* shouts out .... Hab 3:10
because the soil was not *d*........Matt 13:5

DEEPER
It is *d* than Sheol...................Job 11:8

DEEPLY
a strong urge to sleep *d* ....Isa 29:10
Sighing *d* in his spirit ....Mark 8:12

DEER
gives me the agility of a *d* .... Ps 18:33
As a *d* longs for streams............. Ps 42:1
the lame will leap like a *d*.......... Isa 35:6
gives me the agility of a *d* ....Hab 3:19

DEFAMED
Those who passed by *d* him ..... Matt 27:39

DEFEAT
men are adequate to *d* Ai........... Josh 7:3

DEFEATED
were his allies came and *d* .... Gen 14:5
who *d* the Midianites..............Gen 36:35
Israel was *d*........................1 Sam 4:10
So the Philistines were *d* ....1 Sam 7:13
Later David *d* the Philistines........2 Sam 8:1
again invaded and *d* Judah........2 Chr 28:17

DEFEND
surely *d* my ways to his face........Job 13:15
and violence he will *d* them ....Ps 72:14
D the cause of the poor ....Ps 82:3
D the rights of the widow ....Isa 1:17

DEFENDED
For you *d* my just cause ....Ps 9:4

DEFENDING
have been *d* ourselves to you.... 2 Cor 12:19

DEFENSE
incapable of arguing his *d* ....Ps 38:14
how you should make your *d*..... Luke 12:11
what *d* of yourselves ....2 Cor 7:11
At my first *d* no one appeared....2 Tim 4:16

DEFENSELESS
who is as delicate and *d* ....Jer 6:2

DEFENSES
Consider its *d*........................Ps 48:13

DEFERRED
Hope *d* makes the heart sick ..... Prov 13:12

DEFICIENT
not *d* in anything ....Jas 1:4
But if anyone is *d* in wisdom..........Jas 1:5

DEFIED
and *d* God Most High..............Ps 78:56

DEFILE
and these things *d* a person ......Matt 15:18
d the body and the spirit .... 2 Cor 7:1
d the flesh .... Jude 1:8

DEFILED
I declared them to be *d*.........Ezek 20:26
not be ceremonially *d* ....John 18:28
have never eaten anything *d* ..... Acts 10:14
I should call no person *d* ....Acts 10:28
because it is weak, is *d* .... 1 Cor 8:7

DEFILES
d a person is not what goes into.. Matt 15:11

DEFINITELY
nations will *d* be destroyed........ Isa 60:12

DEFRAUD
They *d* people of their homes ....Mic 2:2

DEFRAUDED
if he has *d* you of anything ....Phlm 1:18

DEITY
not think the *d* is like gold........Acts 17:29
all the fullness of *d* lives.............Col 2:9

DELAIAH
Son of Shemaiah; urges Jehoiakim not to
   burn Jeremiah's scroll, Jer 36:12, 25

DELAY
not *d* when the matter is ....Eccl 8:3
coming will arrive and not *d*...... Heb 10:37

DELAYED
It will not be *d* any longer ....Ezek 12:25

DELIBERATELY
For if we *d* keep on sinning.......Heb 10:26
For they *d* suppress this fact....... 2 Pet 3:5

DELICACIES
I will not eat their *d*................ Ps 141:4
Do not crave that ruler's *d*........Prov 23:3
daily ration from his royal *d* ....Dan 1:5

DELICATE
will no longer be called *d*............Isa 47:1

DELIGHT
then you will *d* yourself ....Job 22:26
he find *d* in the Almighty ....Job 27:10
you always give me sheer *d* ....Ps 16:11
bring greater *d* than honey ....Ps 19:10
you will take *d* in the LORD ....Ps 37:4
I find *d* in your statutes...............Ps 119:16
for I *d* to walk in it..................Ps 119:35
For I find *d* in your law..............Ps 119:77
I find *d* in your law.................Ps 119:174
who *d* in doing evil ....Prov 2:14
let's *d* ourselves with love's........Prov 7:18

and I was his *d* day by day .... Prov 8:30
an accurate weight is his *d*.........Prov 11:1
who deal truthfully are his *d*....Prov 12:22
We will rejoice and *d* in you ......Song 1:4
I *d* to sit in his shade............. Song 2:3
take *d* in obeying the LORD......... Isa 11:3
will take *d* in the Holy One .... Isa 29:19
the LORD will take *d* in you .... Isa 62:4
are the children I take *d* in.........Jer 31:20
take *d* in doing good to them......Jer 32:41
object in which their eyes *d* .....Ezek 24:25
For I *d* in faithfulness................ Hos 6:6
in him I take great *d* ....Matt 3:17
For I *d* in the law of God...........Rom 7:22

DELIGHTED
Just as the LORD *d* to do good ...Deut 28:63
in whom I am *d*.....................2 Pet 1:17

DELIGHTFUL
sought to find *d* words ....Eccl 12:10
How *d* it is to see approaching ......Isa 52:7

DELIGHTS
for he *d* in him.....................Ps 22:8
the son in whom he *d* ....Prov 3:12
with your *d* ....Song 7:6
but *d* in showing loyal love ....Mic 7:18
who *d* in false humility ....Col 2:18

DELILAH
Deceives Samson, Judg 16:4–22

DELIVER
I have come down to *d* them ...... Exod 3:8
you will use me to *d* Israel.........Judg 6:37
will *d* you from six calamities..... Job 5:19
who can *d* out of your hand ...... Job 10:7
God will not *d* him................. Ps 3:2
D me because of your ....Ps 6:4
D me from all who chase me...........Ps 7:1
Let the LORD *d* him ....Ps 22:8
D your people ....Ps 28:9
you *d* us from our enemies..........Ps 44:7
you *d* my life from death ....Ps 56:13
and *d* me from my enemies ....Ps 57:3
Listen to me. *D* me .... Ps 71:2
will *d* the children of the poor ......Ps 72:4
D me, so that I can keep...........Ps 119:146
is more than willing to *d*............Ps 130:7
d Israel from all their sins ....Ps 130:8
to *d* you from the adulterous......Prov 2:16
retribution he comes to *d* you......Isa 35:4
The LORD is about to *d* me ....Isa 38:20
Is my hand too weak to *d* you ......Isa 50:2
For I am ready to *d* you.............Isa 56:1
hand is not too weak to *d* you.......Isa 59:1
and who is able to *d* ....Isa 63:1
false belief that will not *d* you ....Jer 7:8
d them from the power of Sheol .. Hos 13:14
he is a warrior who can *d*.........Zeph 3:17
but *d* us from the evil one ....Matt 6:13
d him now because he said ...... Matt 27:43
d me from this hour ....John 12:27
d me from every evil deed........2 Tim 4:18

DELIVERANCE
rejoice because of your *d*............Ps 9:14
experience the joy of your *d*........Ps 51:12
will soon experience his *d* ....Ps 85:9
d and peace greet each other........Ps 85:10
D goes before him ....Ps 85:13
wicked have no chance for *d* .....Ps 119:155
I hope for your *d*...................Ps 119:166
The LORD's *d* ....Isa 26:1
walls, '*D*,' and your gates ....Isa 60:18
and her *d* burns like a torch ....Isa 62:1
brought about a great *d* ....Jer 51:10

DELIVERED
unless their Rock had *d* them ...Deut 32:30
are a people *d* by the LORD ......Deut 33:29
rejected the God who *d* them ......Ps 106:21
those *d* by the LORD speak out ....Ps 107:2
Support me so that I will be *d* ......Ps 119:117
walks blamelessly will be *d* ....Prov 28:18
Turn to me so you can be *d*.......Isa 45:22
and still we have not been *d*........Jer 8:20

who have been *d* will go up........Obad 1:21
He *d* us from so great a risk ...... 2 Cor 1:10
will be *d* through childbearing.... 1 Tim 2:15
were *d* through water ....1 Pet 3:20

DELIVERER
raised up a *d* for the Israelites ......Judg 3:9
he raised up a *d* for them ....Judg 3:15
ridge, my stronghold, my *d*.......2 Sam 22:2
LORD provided a *d* for Israel....... 2 Kgs 13:5
he is our *d* and shield...............Ps 33:20
You are my helper and my *d*........Ps 40:17
Look, God is my *d* ....Ps 54:4
God Most High was their *d*........Ps 78:35
O God our *d* ....Ps 85:4
He is their *d* and protector ....Ps 115:9
he has become my *d*................Ps 118:14
Our *d* is the LORD...................Ps 124:8
my refuge and my *d* ....Ps 144:2
send them a *d* and defender........Isa 19:20
Holy One of Israel, your *d* .... Isa 43:3
the LORD is a powerful *d* ....Isa 45:24
I, the LORD, am your *D*..............Isa 60:16
He became their *d*..................Isa 63:8
God sent as both ruler and *d*......Acts 7:35
The *D* will come out of Zion......Rom 11:26
our *d* from the coming wrath....1 Thess 1:10

DELIVERERS
you provided them with *d* ....Neh 9:27

DELIVERS
The God who *d* me is exalted...2 Sam 22:47
He always *d* me.................2 Sam 23:5
The LORD *d* ....Ps 3:8
you are the God who *d* me ....Ps 25:5
d those who are discouraged.......Ps 34:18
he is the one who *d* me............. Ps 62:1
Our God is a God who *d*...........Ps 68:20
a God who vindicates and *d* ....Isa 45:21
because of the God who *d* me......Hab 3:18

DELIVERY
observe at the *d* ....Exod 1:16

DELUDING
sends on them a *d* influence.... 2 Thess 2:11

DEMAND
For Jews *d* miraculous signs ....1 Cor 1:22

DEMANDING
The work is *d* and extensive....... Neh 4:19
the work was *d* on this people..... Neh 5:18

DEMANDS
reveals his covenantal *d* to .... Ps 25:14

DEMAS
Follows Paul, Col 4:14
Forsakes Paul, 2 Tim 4:10

DEMEANOR
anyone who has a haughty *d* .... Ps 101:5

DEMETRIUS
A silversmith at Ephesus, Acts 19:24–31
—A believer of character, 3 John 1:12

DEMON
After the *d* was cast out .... Matt 9:33
He has a *d* .... Matt 11:18
Then Jesus rebuked the *d*.........Matt 17:18
cast the *d* out of her daughter....Mark 7:26
had the spirit of an unclean *d*..... Luke 4:33
He has a *d* .... Luke 7:33
by the *d* into deserted places..... Luke 8:29
the *d* threw him to the ground ... Luke 9:42
casting out a *d* that was mute .... Luke 11:14
You're possessed by a *d* .... John 7:20
and are possessed by a *d* .... John 8:48
He is possessed by a *d*............ John 10:20

DEMON-POSSESSED
many *d* people were brought......Matt 8:16
was *d* and unable to speak .... Matt 9:32
My daughter is horribly *d*........Matt 15:22
all who were sick and *d*........... Mark 1:32
had been *d* had been healed...... Luke 8:36

DEMONIC
spirits and *d* teachings.............1 Tim 4:1
but is earthly, natural, *d* ....Jas 3:15

DEMONS
See also CAST OUT DEMONS; CASTING
   OUT DEMONS
They sacrificed to *d*................Deut 32:17
their sons and daughters to *d* .....Ps 106:37
and those possessed by *d* ....Matt 4:24
and cast out *d* in your name......Matt 7:22
Then the *d* begged him...........Matt 8:31
ruler of *d* he casts out demons ... Matt 9:34
cleanse lepers, cast out *d*........ Matt 10:8
cast out *d* except by the power.. Matt 12:24
diseases and drove out many *d*... Mark 1:34
have authority to cast out *d* ...... Mark 3:15
cast out many *d* and anointed .... Mark 6:13
casting out *d* in your name.......Mark 9:38
he had driven out seven *d* .... Mark 16:9
name they will drive out *d*...... Mark 16:17
D also came out of many.........Luke 4:41
whom seven *d* had gone out ...... Luke 8:2
many *d* had entered him .... Luke 8:30
and authority over all *d*...........Luke 9:1
casting out *d* in your name ...... Luke 9:49
even the *d* submit to us ....Luke 10:17
the ruler of *d* ....Luke 11:15
I am casting out *d* ....Luke 13:32
of the Lord and the cup of *d*......1 Cor 10:21
Even the *d* believe that ....Jas 2:19
stop worshiping *d* and idols .... Rev 9:20
of the *d* performing signs........Rev 16:14
She has become a lair for *d*........Rev 18:2

DEMONSTRATE
was to *d* his righteousness .... Rom 3:25
readily *d* his deep concern......... Phil 2:20

DEMONSTRATES
But God *d* his own love for us ......Rom 5:8

DEMONSTRATION
a *d* of the Spirit and of power ..... 1 Cor 2:4

DEMORALIZING
For he is *d* the soldiers .... Jer 38:4

DEN
and thrown into a *d* of lions .... Dan 6:16
turning it into a *d* of robbers .... Matt 21:13

DENARIUS
So they brought him a *d*........ Matt 22:19

DENIED
have *d* what the Lord says ....Jer 5:12
will be *d* before God's angels......Luke 12:9
Then Peter *d* it again ....John 18:27
he has *d* the faith and is worse ....1 Tim 5:8
have not *d* your faith in me........Rev 2:13
and have not *d* my name ....Rev 3:8

DENIES
whoever *d* me before people.... Matt 10:33
who *d* that Jesus is the Christ....1 John 2:22

DENOUNCE
and nations will *d* him ....Prov 24:24

DENOUNCES
d his neighbor lacks sense.........Prov 11:12

DENS
withdraw and sleep in their *d*......Ps 104:22
Foxes have *d*......................Matt 8:20

DENSE
to come to you in a *d* cloud....... Exod 19:9

DENY
you if you *d* your God ....Josh 24:27
d him also before my Father..... Matt 10:33
he must *d* himself .... Matt 16:24
you will *d* me three times ....Matt 26:34
did not *d* but confessed...........John 1:20
since he cannot *d* himself........2 Tim 2:13
with their deeds they *d* him .... Titus 1:16
d our only Master and Lord .... Jude 1:4

DENYING
to the point of *d* the Master ....2 Pet 2:1

DEPART
scepter will not *d* from Judah.....Gen 49:10
D from me, you accursed........ Matt 25:41
time for me to *d* is at hand .... 2 Tim 4:6

DEPARTED
d and was taken up into heaven.. Luke 24:51

DEPARTS
Their life's breath *d*.................Ps 146:4

DEPEND
d on the Holy One of Israel..........Isa 17:7
the law and the prophets *d* on...Matt 22:40

DEPENDABLE
what is written in a *d* book ....Dan 10:21

DEPENDENT
been *d* on you since birth...........Ps 22:10

DEPORTATION
David to the *d* to Babylon .... Matt 1:17

DEPRESSED
d because of the daughters.......Gen 27:46
Why do you appear to be *d*...... Neh 2:2

DEPRIVE
Do not completely *d* me........... Ps 119:43
Do not *d* each other ....1 Cor 7:5
one will *d* me of my reason.......1 Cor 9:15

DEPRIVED
sins have *d* you of my bounty ...... Jer 5:25
their minds and *d* of the truth .....1 Tim 6:5

DEPRIVING
d a righteous man of justice ....Prov 18:5
and *d* myself of pleasure ....Eccl 4:8

DEPTH
nor *d*, nor anything else .... Rom 8:39
Oh, the *d* of the riches............ Rom 11:33
length and height and *d* ....Eph 3:18

DEPTHS
The *d* have covered them..........Exod 15:5
d of the sea were exposed...........Ps 18:15
my life from the *d* of Sheol ....Ps 86:13
then dropped into the *d* ....Ps 107:26
our sins into the *d* of the sea ....Mic 7:19
utter *d* of eternal darkness ....Jude 1:13

DERBE
Paul visits, Acts 14:6, 20
Paul meets Timothy at, Acts 16:1

DERISIVE
whose *d* speech you do not ....Isa 33:19

DESCENDANT
you have not given me a *d*..........Gen 15:3
a righteous *d* of David ....Jer 33:15
to Abraham and to his *d*............Gal 3:16
the root and the *d* of David........Rev 22:16

DESCENDANTS
your *d* will be counted..............Gen 21:12
the *d* the Lord gives you............Ruth 4:12
d like the grass of the earth ....Job 5:25
All you *d* of Jacob.................Ps 22:23
their *d* inherit the land...............Ps 25:13
and is faithful to their *d*............ Ps 103:17
but the *d* of the righteous ....Prov 11:21
d of Israel will be vindicated........Isa 45:25
will see *d* and enjoy long life....... Isa 53:10
We are *d* of Abraham................John 8:33
so will your *d* be...................Rom 4:18
had not left us *d* .... Rom 9:29
then you are Abraham's *d* ....Gal 3:29

DESCENDANTS OF ANAK
A race of giants; very strong, Num 13:28–33;
   Deut 2:10–11, 21
Defeated:
   by Joshua, Josh 10:36–39; 11:21
   by Caleb, Josh 14:6–15

DESCENDED
the Lord had *d* on it in fire ....Exod 19:18
he also *d* to the lower regions ...... Eph 4:9
He, the very one who *d*........... Eph 4:10

DESCENDING
I saw the Spirit *d* like a dove....... John 1:32
and *d* on the Son of Man ....John 1:51
d out of heaven from God ....Rev 21:10

DESCRIBE
no one can bear to *d* it..............Eccl 1:8
Who can *d* his posterity ....Acts 8:33

DESCRIBED
d in the law scroll of Moses .... Josh 8:31
the plagues *d* in this book ....Rev 22:18

DESECRATE
they *d* your dwelling place...........Ps 74:7
He even tried to *d* the temple .....Acts 24:6

DESECRATED
holy things and *d* my Sabbaths ... Ezek 22:8

DESERT
wilderness and *d* be happy ....Isa 35:1
land of *d* and deep darkness..........Jer 2:6
times some will *d* the faith ....1 Tim 4:1

DESERTED
he *d* the God who made him .....Deut 32:15
those who have been *d*..............Ps 68:6
For Demas *d* me...................2 Tim 4:10
instead they all *d* me ....2 Tim 4:16

DESERTING
you are so quickly *d* the one......... Gal 1:6

DESERTS
wandered in *d* and mountains.....Heb 11:38

DESERVE
what we *d* for what we did ...... Luke 23:41

DESERVES
Give him the honor he *d*.............Ps 66:2
The worker *d* his pay .... 1 Tim 5:18

DESERVING
has done nothing *d* of death.....Deut 22:26

DESIGN
to them the *d* of the temple ......Ezek 43:11
according to the *d* shown...........Heb 8:5

DESIGNATED
by a man whom he *d* ....Acts 17:31

DESIGNER
are the work of an artistic *d* ...... Exod 26:1
the work of an artistic *d* ....Exod 36:8
the work of an artistic *d* ....Exod 39:3

DESIRABLE
was *d* for making one wise ....Gen 3:6
is *d* for a person is to show ....Prov 19:22
he is totally *d* ....Song 5:16

DESIRE
Whom does all Israel *d* ....1 Sam 9:20
will rule over all that you *d* ...... 2 Sam 3:21
and brings all I *d* to fruition......2 Sam 23:5
for you to have a strong *d* .... 1 Kgs 8:18
and I *d* to argue my case..........Job 13:3
they *d* other gods.................. Ps 16:4
You grant him his heart's *d* ...... Ps 21:2
this is what I *d* ....Ps 27:4
those who *d* my vindication ....Ps 35:27
d integrity in the inner man .... Ps 51:6
you do not *d* a burnt sacrifice ....Ps 51:16
there is no one I *d* but you..........Ps 73:25
d of the wicked will perish..........Ps 112:10
you *d* can compare with her....... Prov 3:15
righteous *d* will be granted...... Prov 10:24
The *d* of the righteous............. Prov 11:23
do not *d* to be with them ....Prov 24:1
We *d* your fame and reputation .... Isa 26:8
I *d* people to do these things .... Jer 9:24
they *d* and seize the houses ....Mic 2:2
looks at a woman to *d* her........ Matt 5:28
the *d* for other things come ...... Mark 4:19
or by human *d* or a husband's ......John 1:13
known what it means to *d*.........Rom 7:7
on human *d* or exertion ....Rom 9:16
heart's *d* and prayer to God ....Rom 10:1
d to put on our heavenly ....2 Cor 5:2
I have a *d* to depart..................Phil 1:23
both the *d* and the effort ....Phil 2:13
evil *d*, and greed which is..........Col 3:5
your every *d* for goodness........2 Thess 1:11
and offering you did not *d* .... Heb 10:5
d to conduct ourselves rightly .....Heb 13:18
Then when *d* conceives..............Jas 1:15
You *d* and you do not have ....Jas 4:2
d of the flesh and the *d* of ....1 John 2:16

DESIRED
led them to the harbor they *d* .....Ps 107:30
the LORD *d* to crush him........... Isa 53:10
earnestly *d* to eat this Passover .. Luke 22:15
I have *d* no one's silver .... Acts 20:33

DESIRES
living thing with the food it *d* ...... Ps 145:16
be ensnared by their own *d* .... Prov 11:6
sluggard *d* will kill him........... Prov 21:25
lacks nothing that his heart *d* .... Eccl 6:2
and he *d* me .... Song 7:10
you satisfy your selfish *d* .... Isa 58:3
one whose *d* are not upright .... Hab 2:4
to do what your father *d* .... John 8:44
all kinds of wrong *d* ....Rom 7:8
for the flesh to arouse its *d* ...... Rom 13:14
not carry out the *d* of the flesh ..... Gal 5:16
with its passions and *d* ....Gal 5:24
d of the flesh and the mind..........Eph 2:3
many senseless and harmful *d* ....1 Tim 6:9
following their own *d*. ....2 Tim 4:3
godless ways and worldly *d* .... Titus 2:12
to judge the *d* and thoughts .... Heb 4:12
and enticed by his own *d* .... Jas 1:14
keep away from fleshly *d* .... 1 Pet 2:11
by their own ungodly *d*............Jude 1:18

DESOLATE
two kings you fear will be *d* ....Isa 7:16
will no longer be called "D .... Isa 62:4
your house is left to you *d* .... Matt 23:38

DESOLATION
you see the abomination of *d*.... Matt 24:15
know that its *d* has come near... Luke 21:20

DESPAIR
To the one in *d* .... Job 6:14
mocks at the *d* of the innocent .....Job 9:23
and *d* runs before it ....Job 41:22
I call out to you in my *d* .... Ps 61:2
d about all the fruit of my labor ... Eccl 2:20

DESPAIRED
So he *d* of life and said........... Jonah 4:8
so that we *d* even of living......... 2 Cor 1:8

DESPERATE
I have fought a *d* struggle ....Gen 30:8

DESPERATELY
d want to be in the courts ....Ps 84:2
d long to know your regulations... Ps 119:20

DESPISE
will this people *d* me .... Num 14:11
who *d* me will be cursed......... 1 Sam 2:30
I *d* my life......................... Job 9:21
Therefore I *d* myself............... Job 42:6
people insult me and *d* me .... Ps 22:6
You *d* all who stray .... Ps 119:118
People do not *d* a thief .... Prov 6:30
and do not *d* your mother .... Prov 23:22
I absolutely *d* your festivals ......Amos 5:21
I *d* Jacob's arrogance............. Amos 6:8
devoted to the one and *d* the
    other .... Matt 6:24
desires and who *d* authority...... 2 Pet 2:10

DESPISED
was pregnant, she *d* Sarai .... Gen 16:4
So Esau *d* his birthright...........Gen 25:34
because you have *d* the LORD ....Num 11:20
dancing before the LORD, she *d* ..2 Sam 6:16
d the people who belonged ...... Ps 106:40
but fools have *d* wisdom .... Prov 1:7
a bewildered mind will be *d* .... Prov 12:8
a poor man's wisdom is *d*....... Eccl 9:16
the offer would be utterly *d* ...... Song 8:7
was *d* and rejected by people.......Isa 53:3
You have *d* my holy things....... Ezek 22:8
suffer many things and be *d*...... Mark 9:12
what is low and *d* in the world....1 Cor 1:28

DESPISES
The one who *d* instruction........ Prov 13:13
one who *d* his neighbor sins...... Prov 14:21
a foolish person *d* his mother ... Prov 15:20
one who *d* his ways will die....... Prov 19:16

and *d* obeying a mother ....Prov 30:17
The sword *d* every tree............Ezek 21:10

DESTINATION
swiftly his order reaches its *d* ..... Ps 147:15

DESTINE
God did not *d* us for wrath ......1 Thess 5:9

DESTINED
d to be the cause of the falling ... Luke 2:34

DESTINY
You determine my *d*..................Ps 31:15
This is the *d* of fools..............Ps 49:13
do not control their own *d* ....Jer 10:23

DESTITUTE
responds to the prayer of the *d* ... Ps 102:17

DESTROY
I might *d* you on the way .... Exod 33:3
the Midianites, and *d* them ...... Num 25:17
I *d* those who hate me............2 Sam 22:41
they *d* the land ....Job 12:15
to use all the words that *d*..........Ps 52:4
I will *d* all the wicked people .... Ps 101:8
will no longer injure or *d* .... Isa 11:9
d Babylonia just as I did Sodom ...Jer 50:40
I will *d* you.......................Hos 13:9
moth and devouring insect *d*......Matt 6:19
d both soul and body in hell.... Matt 10:28
I am able to *d* the temple....... Matt 26:61
You who can *d* the temple.......Matt 27:40
to save a life or *d* it ....Mark 3:4
d this temple made with hands..Mark 14:58
to save a life or to *d* it .... Luke 6:9
D this temple and in three days ...John 2:19
only to steal and kill and *d*........John 10:10
Saul was trying to *d* the church..... Acts 8:3
Do not *d* the work of God .... Rom 14:20
I will *d* the wisdom of the wise ....1 Cor 1:19
d by the breath of his mouth ....2 Thess 2:8
one who is able to save and *d* ......Jas 4:12
to *d* the works of the devil........ 1 John 3:8

DESTROYED
the LORD *d* every living thing...... Gen 7:23
until the wicked are *d* .... Ps 94:13
d by the counsel of the wicked .... Prov 11:11
Woe to me! I am *d*...............Isa 6:5
be *d* by God just as Sodom ...... Isa 13:19
Edom will be *d* like Sodom .... Jer 49:18
Lord, like an enemy, *d* Israel.......Lam 2:5
You have *d* my people.............. Hos 4:6
They have *d* my vines..............Joel 1:7
crops of the fields have been *d* .....Joel 1:10
I *d* your crops with blight......... Amos 4:9
the majestic trees have been *d* ....Zech 11:2
collapsed—it was utterly *d*....... Matt 7:27
and the skins will be *d*........... Luke 5:37
and was utterly *d*...............Luke 6:49
for whom Christ died, is *d* ....1 Cor 8:11
He has *d* what was against us....... Col 2:14
born to be caught and *d* .... 2 Pet 2:12
in a single hour she has been *d*....Rev 18:19

DESTROYER
the *d* so he might devastate .... Isa 54:16
destruction from the Divine *D* ......Joel 1:15

DESTROYING
will keep me from *d* them .... Jer 13:14

DESTROYS
but he *d* all the wicked ....Ps 145:20
is a brother to one who *d*..........Prov 18:9
If someone *d* God's temple........1 Cor 3:17

DESTRUCTION
afraid of the *d* when it comes....... Job 5:21
the place of *d* lies uncovered....Job 26:6
way of the wicked ends in *d* ....Ps 1:6
Let *d* take them by surprise .... Ps 35:8
but it is *d* to evildoers ....Prov 10:29
Pride goes before *d*............. Prov 16:18
Before *d* the heart of a person.... Prov 18:12
console me concerning the *d* ...... Isa 22:4
city doomed to *d* .... Jer 4:30
You are doomed to *d* ....Jer 13:27

except the one destined for *d* .... John 17:12
objects of wrath prepared for *d* .. Rom 9:22
to Satan for the *d* of the flesh ..... 1 Cor 5:5
This is a sign of their *d*.............Phil 1:28
Their end is *d*......................Phil 3:19
then sudden *d* comes on them ..1 Thess 5:3
the penalty of eternal *d*.........2 Thess 1:9
the son of *d*.....................2 Thess 2:3
judgment and *d* of the ungodly.... 2 Pet 3:7
twist to their own *d* .... 2 Pet 3:16

DESTRUCTIVE
You are *d* like water ....Gen 49:4
and from the *d* plague.............. Ps 91:3
infiltrate your midst with *d* ....2 Pet 2:1

DETERIORATED
nor have your sandals *d*......... Deut 29:5

DETERMINE
You *d* my destiny ....Ps 31:15

DETERMINED
Since man's days are *d*.............. Job 14:5
I am *d*, O God..................... Ps 57:7
Seventy weeks have been *d* ....Dan 9:24
d before the ages for our glory .... 1 Cor 2:7

DETERMINING
d their set times and the fixed.... Acts 17:26

DETESTABLE
I consider your incense *d* .... Isa 1:13
is utterly *d* in God's sight ....Luke 16:15
since they are *d*................... Titus 1:16

DETESTED
they *d* me as well.................. Zech 11:8

DEVASTATE
LORD is ready to *d* the earth........Isa 24:1

DEVASTATED
D, I continued to sit there ....Ezra 9:4

DEVASTATION
who brings *d* to the earth ....Ps 46:8
sounds of destruction and *d*....... Isa 60:18

DEVELOPED
a great storm *d* on the sea........Matt 8:24
a great windstorm *d*..............Mark 4:37

DEVIATE
I do not *d* from them .... Ps 17:5

DEVIL
Titles of:
    Abaddon, Apollyon, angel of the abyss,
      Rev 9:11
    accuser, Rev 12:10
    ancient serpent, Rev 20:2
    Beelzebul, ruler of demons, Matt 12:24
    Beliar, 2 Cor 6:15
    enemy, 1 Pet 5:8
    evil one, Matt 6:13
    god of this age, 2 Cor 4:4
    murderer, liar, father of lies, John 8:44
    ruler of the domain of the air, Eph 2:2
    ruler of this world, John 14:30
    Satan, Luke 10:18
    serpent, Gen 3:4
Origin of, in heaven, Isa 14:12–20; Rev 12:7–9
Power of and activities of:
    tempted Eve, Gen 3:1
    tempted David, 1 Chr 21:1
    accused and tormented Job, Job 1:6–2:10
    opposed Joshua the high priest, Zech 3:1
    tempted Jesus, Matt 4:1–11; Mark 3:22–28;
      Luke 22:31
    entered Judas at betrayal, Luke 22:3;
      John 13:27
    deceives and ensnares, 2 Cor 11:3–15;
      1 Tim 3:6–7; Rev 20:7–8
    works in evildoers, Acts 13:8–10; Eph 2:2
    accuses believers before God, Rev 12:10
Believers must resist, 2 Cor 2:10–11;
    Eph 6:11–16; Jas 4:7; 1 Pet 5:8–9;
    1 John 2:13
His defeat by Christ, Gen 3:15; Rev 12:10–12;
    20:7–10
See SATAN

to be tempted by the *d* ....Matt 4:1
enemy who sows them is the *d*...Matt 13:39
for the *d* and his angels..........Matt 25:41
temptations from the *d*...............Luke 4:2
the *d* comes and takes away.......Luke 8:12
and yet one of you is the *d*........John 6:70
are from your father the *d*........John 8:44
d had already put into the heart...John 13:2
who were oppressed by the *d*...Acts 10:38
you son of the *d*...................Acts 13:10
not give the *d* an opportunity......Eph 4:27
against the schemes of the *d*.......Eph 6:11
punishment that the *d* will exact..1 Tim 3:6
power of death (that is, the *d*......Heb 2:14
resist the *d* and he will flee...........Jas 4:7
Your enemy the *d*..................1 Pet 5:8
who practices sin is of the *d*.....1 John 3:8
arguing with the *d* and debating....Jude 1:9
d is about to have some of you.....Rev 2:10
the one called the *d* and Satan.....Rev 12:9
because the *d* has come down.....Rev 12:12
who is the *d* and Satan...........Rev 20:2
And the *d* who deceived them....Rev 20:10

DEVIL'S
and escape the *d* trap............2 Tim 2:26

DEVIOUS
and who are *d* in their ways.......Prov 2:15
keep *d* talk far from your lips......Prov 4:24

DEVISING
countries *d* plots that will fail..........Ps 2:1

DEVOID
are a nation *d* of wisdom.......Deut 32:28

DEVOTE
will *d* to the LORD the spoils........Mic 4:13
we will *d* ourselves to prayer.......Acts 6:4

DEVOTED
d in Israel will be yours...........Num 18:14
Because he is *d* to me..............Ps 91:14
how *d* you were to me...............Jer 2:2
be *d* to the one and despise......Matt 6:24
true to the Lord with *d* hearts....Acts 11:23
Be *d* to prayer.......................Col 4:2

DEVOTING
They were *d* themselves...........Acts 2:42

DEVOTION
show you the same kind of *d*.......Ruth 1:8
and with wholehearted *d*........2 Kgs 20:3
my *d* will not be removed.........Isa 54:10
he was heard because of his *d*.....Heb 5:7

DEVOUR
Dogs will *d* Jezebel................2 Kgs 9:10
they *d* their rulers.....................Hos 7:7
You *d* my people's flesh.............Mic 3:3
if you continually bite and *d*.......Gal 5:15
looking for someone to *d*..........1 Pet 5:8
so that he might *d* her child........Rev 12:4

DEVOURED
you will be *d* by the sword.........Isa 1:20
the birds came and *d* them........Matt 13:4
came down from heaven and *d*....Rev 20:9

DEVOURING
d fire on the top of the mountain..Exod 24:17
who goes before you is a *d* fire....Deut 9:3
Locusts kept *d* your orchards......Amos 4:9
our God is indeed a *d* fire.........Heb 12:29

DEVOURS
So a treaty curse *d* the earth.......Isa 24:6

DEVOUT
who was righteous and *d*.........Luke 2:25
anyone is *d* and does his will......John 9:31
Some *d* men buried Stephen.......Acts 8:2
servants and a *d* soldier..........Acts 10:7

DEW
God give you the *d* of the sky....Gen 27:28
its heavens rain down *d*.........Deut 33:28
the *d* of your youth................Ps 110:3
favor is like *d* on the grass........Prov 19:12
drenched with the morning *d*.....Isa 26:19

as quickly as dawn's *d*...............Hos 6:4
be like the *d* the LORD sends........Mic 5:7

DIADEM
put the holy *d* on the turban......Exod 29:6

DIAMOND
It is inscribed with a *d* point.........Jer 17:1

DIBON
Amorite town, Num 21:30
Taken by Israel, Num 32:2–5
Destruction of, foretold, Jer 48:18, 22

DICE
The *d* are thrown into the lap....Prov 16:33
throwing *d* for them............Mark 15:24

DID
d not know his master's will.....Luke 12:48
he *d* many acts of charity..........Acts 10:2

DIE
eat from it you will surely *d*........Gen 2:17
or else you will *d*...................Gen 3:3
in the land of Egypt will *d*........Exod 11:5
today I am about to *d*...........Josh 23:14
Wherever you *d*....................Ruth 1:17
I am about to *d*...................1 Kgs 2:2
Curse God, and *d*...................Job 2:9
or else I will *d*.......................Ps 13:3
sees that even wise people *d*......Ps 49:10
May those who did this *d*........Ps 80:16
make them *d* in the wilderness...Ps 106:26
make their descendants *d*.........Ps 106:27
I will not *d*.........................Ps 118:17
On that day their plans *d*........Ps 146:4
will *d* because there was no......Prov 5:23
but fools *d* for lack of sense......Prov 10:21
one who hates reproof will *d*.....Prov 15:10
he will not *d*......................Prov 23:13
and a time to *d*....................Eccl 3:2
you might *d* before your time......Eccl 7:17
for tomorrow we *d*.................Isa 22:13
that eat them will not *d*.........Isa 66:24
person will *d* for his own sins......Jer 31:30
Those who *d* by the sword........Lam 4:9
he will *d* for his iniquity...........Ezek 3:19
The one who sins will *d*.........Ezek 18:4
you must certainly *d*...........Ezek 33:8
so that we might not *d*..........Jonah 1:6
We are about to *d*.............Matt 8:25
Even if I must *d* with you........Matt 26:35
take hold of the sword will *d*....Matt 26:52
they can no longer *d*.............Luke 20:36
may eat from it and not *d*........John 6:50
that you will *d* in your sins........John 8:24
that Jesus was going to *d*........John 11:51
ought to *d* because he claimed....John 19:7
d for a righteous person...........Rom 5:7
to the flesh, you will *d*............Rom 8:13
if we *d* we *d* for the Lord........Rom 14:8
as men condemned to *d*........1 Cor 4:9
For just as in Adam all *d*........1 Cor 15:22
people are appointed to *d* once...Heb 9:27
those who *d* in the Lord..........Rev 14:13

DIED
that moved on the earth *d*.........Gen 7:21
If only we had *d* by the hand......Exod 16:3
and *d* in the flames..............1 Kgs 16:18
Hadad *d*.........................1 Chr 1:51
d because he was unfaithful......1 Chr 10:13
poor man *d* and was carried....Luke 16:22
these words he collapsed and *d*....Acts 5:5
she collapsed at his feet and *d*....Acts 5:10
Christ *d* for the ungodly...........Rom 5:6
Christ *d* for us.....................Rom 5:8
has *d* has been freed from sin.....Rom 6:7
Now if we *d* with Christ...........Rom 6:8
deceived me and through it I *d*....Rom 7:11
For this reason Christ *d*...........Rom 14:9
for whom Christ *d*...............1 Cor 8:11
Christ *d* for our sins.............1 Cor 15:3
that Christ *d* for all..............2 Cor 5:14
And he *d* for all..................2 Cor 5:15
through the law I *d* to the law......Gal 2:19
If you have *d* with Christ..........Col 2:20

have *d* and your life is hidden.......Col 3:3
that Jesus *d* and rose again.....1 Thess 4:14
He *d* for us so that...............1 Thess 5:10
If we *d* with him...................2 Tim 2:11
These all *d* in faith................Heb 11:13
ever since our ancestors *d*........2 Pet 3:4

DIES
If a man *d*, will he live again.......Job 14:14
When a wicked person *d*.........Prov 11:7
the wise man *d*....................Eccl 2:16
will live even if he *d*.............John 11:25
falls into the ground and *d*....John 12:24
but if her husband *d*.............Rom 7:2
and none *d* for himself..........Rom 14:7
not come to life unless it *d*......1 Cor 15:36

DIFFERENCE
will teach my people the *d*......Ezek 44:23
they were makes no *d* to me.......Gal 2:6

DIFFERENT
because he had a *d* spirit.......Num 14:24
they were *d* from one another......Dan 7:3
And we have *d* gifts..............Rom 12:6
Now there are *d* gifts............1 Cor 12:4
And there are *d* ministries......1 Cor 12:5
And there are *d* results.........1 Cor 12:6
to another *d* kinds of tongues....1 Cor 12:10
or if you receive a *d* spirit.........2 Cor 11:4
and are following a *d* gospel........Gal 1:6

DIFFERS
for star *d* from star in glory.......1 Cor 15:41

DIFFICULT
is not too *d* for you...............Deut 30:11
How *d* it is for me.................Ps 139:17
seem to be *d* in the opinion......Zech 8:6
narrow is the gate and *d* the way...Matt 7:14
This is a *d* saying..................John 6:60
last days *d* times will come........2 Tim 3:1

DIFFICULTY
since I speak with *d*..............Exod 6:12
Since I speak with *d*..............Exod 6:30

DIG
cisterns you did not *d*...........Deut 6:11
arrogant *d* pits to trap me........Ps 119:85
d into the wall....................Ezek 8:8
I'm not strong enough to *d*.......Luke 16:3

DIGESTION
use a little wine for your *d*........1 Tim 5:23

DIGNIFIED
their wives must be *d*............1 Tim 3:11
temperate, *d*, self-controlled......Titus 2:2

DIGNITARIES
are the *d* of the earth...............Isa 23:8

DIGNITY
members are clothed with *d*.....1 Cor 12:23
in control without losing his *d*.....1 Tim 3:4

DILIGENCE
he must do so with *d*.............Rom 12:8

DILIGENT
The *d* person will rule............Prov 12:24
but the desire of the *d*............Prov 13:4
is *d* in disciplining him............Prov 13:24

DILIGENTLY
who seek me *d* will find me.......Prov 8:17
works *d* becomes wealthy.........Prov 10:4

DILL
a tenth of mint, *d*, and cumin....Matt 23:23

DIM
eyes grow *d* from suffering...........Ps 6:7
through the windows grow *d*.......Eccl 12:3
d wick he will not extinguish.......Isa 42:3

DINAH
Daughter of Leah, Gen 30:20–21
Defiled by Shechem, Gen 34:1–24
Avenged by brothers, Gen 34:25–31

DINING
d in an idol's temple...............1 Cor 8:10

DINNER
an unbeliever invites you to *d* . . . 1 Cor 10:27

DIOTREPHES
Unruly church member, 3 John 1:9–10

DIP
and *d* them in the blood . . . . Lev 14:51
d it in the water . . . . Num 19:18
may he *d* his foot in olive oil . . . . . Deut 33:24
D your bread in the vinegar . . . . . . .Ruth 2:14
d the tip of his finger in water . . . Luke 16:24

DIPPED
and *d* the tunic in the blood . . . . . . .Gen 37:31
he *d* his finger in the blood . . . . .Lev 9:9
d in the Jordan seven times . . . . 2 Kgs 5:14
after I have *d* it in the dish . . . . John 13:26
dressed in clothing *d* in blood . . . . . Rev 19:13

DIRECT
may the Lord *d* your hearts . . . . .2 Thess 3:5

DIRECTION
In what *d* does light reside . . . . .Job 38:19
news that comes from every *d* . . . . .Ps 31:13

DIRECTIONS
From whom does he receive *d* . . . . Isa 40:14
please follow the *d* that I gave . . . . .1 Cor 16:1

DIRT
are the world's *d* and scum . . . . .1 Cor 4:13
the washing off of physical *d* . . . . . .1 Pet 3:21

DISABLED
d by a spirit for eighteen years . . . Luke 13:11
who had been *d* for 38 years . . . . . . .John 5:5

DISAPPEAR
you *d* from this good land . . . . Josh 23:13
Let them *d* like water . . . . .Ps 58:7
the clouds *d* after the rain . . . . .Eccl 12:2
what remains of Judah will *d* . . . . . . Jer 40:15

DISAPPEARED
For the godly have *d* . . . . .Ps 12:1
d as quickly as a fire . . . . .Ps 118:12
men have *d* from the land . . . . .Mic 7:2

DISAPPEARS
As water *d* from the sea . . . . .Job 14:11
days like a shadow that *d* . . . . .Ps 144:4
even the memory of them *d* . . . . Eccl 9:5
not work for the food that *d* . . . . . .John 6:27

DISAPPOINTED
otherwise you might be *d* . . . . .Eccl 7:16

DISARMING
D the rulers and authorities . . . . Col 2:15

DISARMS
and *d* the powerful . . . . .Job 12:21

DISASTER
death and *d* on the other . . . . Deut 30:15
for the day of their *d* is near . . . . . Deut 32:35
So I am ready to bring *d* . . . . 1 Kgs 14:10
will laugh when *d* strikes . . . . .Prov 1:26
his *d* will come suddenly . . . . .Prov 6:15
preparing to bring *d* on you . . . . . . .Jer 18:11
to bring a *d* on this place . . . . .Jer 19:3
prophesied war, *d*, and plagues . . . . .Jer 28:8
demolished and brought *d* . . . . .Jer 31:28
the *d* I am ready to bring . . . . .Jer 51:64
D after *d* will come . . . . Ezek 7:26
If *d* overtakes a city . . . . .Amos 3:6
You no longer need to fear *d* . . . . .Zeph 3:15
voyage is going to end in *d* . . . . . . .Acts 27:10

DISASTER, VALLEY OF
See ACHOR, VALLEY OF

DISCARDED
stone that the builders *d* . . . . Ps 118:22

DISCERN
Am I able to *d* good and bad . . . . 2 Sam 19:35
shrewd person is to *d* his way . . . . .Prov 14:8
one who evaluates hearts *d* it . . . .Prov 24:12
Let him *d* these things . . . . .Hos 14:9
to *d* both good and evil . . . . .Heb 5:14

DISCERNED
they are spiritually *d* . . . . .1 Cor 2:14

DISCERNING
let the *d* acquire guidance . . . . Prov 1:5
All of them are clear to the *d* . . . . . .Prov 8:9
but a *d* person keeps silent . . . . .Prov 11:12
The *d* mind seeks knowledge . . . . . Prov 15:14
who is wise in heart is called *d* . . . Prov 16:21
d person acquires knowledge . . . . Prov 18:15
a *d* poor person can evaluate . . . . . Prov 28:11

DISCERNMENT
wisdom and very great *d* . . . . .1 Kgs 4:29
Now give me wisdom and *d* . . . . . 2 Chr 1:10
son who has *d* and insight . . . . 2 Chr 2:12
takes away the *d* of elders . . . . .Job 12:20
proper *d* and understanding . . . . . . .Ps 119:66
is the beginning of *d* . . . . Prov 1:7
wisdom for the one who has *d* . . .Prov 10:23
but to think with sober *d* . . . . .Rom 12:3
and to another *d* of spirits . . . . .1 Cor 12:10

DISCERNS
who is spiritual *d* all things . . . . .1 Cor 2:15

DISCIPLE
d is not greater than his teacher . .Matt 10:24
little ones in the name of a *d* . . . . Matt 10:42
he is not a *d* along with us . . . . .Luke 9:49
he cannot be my *d* . . . . Luke 14:26
and the *d* whom he loved . . . . .John 19:26
Then the *d* whom Jesus loved . . . . . John 21:7
saw the *d* whom Jesus loved . . . . . .John 21:20

DISCIPLES
See also TWELVE DISCIPLES
Then John's *d* came to Jesus . . . . . . .Matt 9:14
Jesus called his twelve *d* . . . . .Matt 10:1
your *d* disobey the tradition . . . . . . .Matt 15:2
all the *d* left him and fled . . . . .Matt 26:56
go and make *d* of all nations . . . . . Matt 28:19
Jesus went away with his *d* . . . . Mark 3:7
his *d* and chose 12 of them . . . . .Luke 6:13
and his *d* believed in him . . . . .John 2:11
many of his *d* quit following . . . . . . John 6:66
you are really my *d* . . . . .John 8:31
want to become his *d* too . . . . .John 9:27
We are *d* of Moses . . . . .John 9:28
His *d* did not understand . . . . .John 12:16
by this that you are my *d* . . . . .John 13:35
and show that you are my *d* . . . . . . .John 15:8
Then the *d* rejoiced . . . . .John 20:20
when the *d* were growing . . . . Acts 6:1
d were first called Christians . . . . . Acts 11:26
strengthened the souls of the *d* . .Acts 14:22
strengthening all the *d* . . . . .Acts 18:23

DISCIPLINE
will also *d* you seven times . . . . Lev 26:28
despise the *d* of the Almighty . . . . . .Job 5:17
severely *d* people for their sins . . . . .Ps 39:11
die because there was no *d* . . . . . . .Prov 5:23
who loves *d* loves knowledge . . . . . Prov 12:1
A fool rejects his father's *d* . . . . . . .Prov 15:5
Severe *d* is for the one . . . . .Prov 15:10
D your child . . . . .Prov 19:18
the rod of *d* will drive it . . . . .Prov 22:15
not withhold *d* from a child . . . . . .Prov 23:13
D your child . . . . .Prov 29:17
because of your *d* . . . . Isa 26:16
I will indeed *d* you . . . . .Jer 30:11
I will *d* them when I hear . . . . .Hos 7:12
I will *d* them . . . . .Hos 10:10
d and instruction of the Lord . . . . . . Eph 6:4
Endure your suffering as *d* . . . . .Heb 12:7
But if you do not experience *d* . . . . Heb 12:8
d from our earthly fathers . . . . .Heb 12:9
Now all *d* seems painful . . . . .Heb 12:11
I rebuke and *d* . . . . .Rev 3:19

DISCIPLINED
who lacks sense will be *d* . . . . .Prov 10:13
You *d* us, and we learned . . . . .Jer 31:18
they *d* us for a little while . . . . Heb 12:10

DISCIPLINES
just as a parent *d* his child . . . . Deut 8:5
who *d* the nations not punish . . . . . . .Ps 94:10
the Lord *d* those he loves . . . . .Prov 3:12
the Lord *d* the one he loves . . . . Heb 12:6

DISCIPLINING
loves his child is diligent in *d* . . . . .Prov 13:24

DISCLOSED
but now is *d* . . . . Rom 16:26
secrets of his heart are *d* . . . . 1 Cor 14:25

DISCORD
and a person who spreads *d* . . . . . . .Prov 6:19
not in *d* and jealousy . . . . Rom 13:13

DISCOURAGED
Do not be afraid or *d* . . . . Deut 1:21
Don't let anyone be *d* . . . . .1 Sam 17:32
he delivers those who are *d* . . . . . . .Ps 34:18
also with the *d* and humiliated . . . . .Isa 57:15
comfort the *d* . . . . 1 Thess 5:14

DISCOVER
and *d* in those records . . . . .Ezra 4:15

DISCOVERED
I have *d* David . . . . Ps 89:20
This alone have I *d* . . . . Eccl 7:29
if a person is *d* in some sin . . . . Gal 6:1

DISCREDITED
Christian teaching from being *d* . . . .1 Tim 6:1

DISCRETION
D will protect you . . . . Prov 2:11
and I find knowledge and *d* . . . . . . .Prov 8:12
woman who rejects *d* . . . . .Prov 11:22

DISCRIMINATE
They must not *d* in judgment . . . . . . Deut 1:17

DISCUSSED
and *d* with the chief priests . . . . . . .Luke 22:4

DISCUSSING
Paul was *d* righteousness . . . . .Acts 24:25

DISCUSSION
and turned away to empty *d* . . . . . . .1 Tim 1:6

DISDAIN
You made us an object of *d* . . . . .Ps 44:13
Do not treat with *d* the place . . . . . . .Jer 14:21
not *d* one of these little ones . . . . .Matt 18:10

DISEASE
for dealing with infectious *d* . . . . . . .Lev 14:57
cure him of his skin *d* . . . . .2 Kgs 5:3
the men with a skin *d* . . . . .2 Kgs 7:8
Asa developed a foot *d* . . . . 2 Chr 16:12
d appeared on his forehead . . . . .2 Chr 26:19
was a skin *d* on his forehead . . . . 2 Chr 26:20
afflicted by a skin *d* and
   banned . . . . .2 Chr 26:21
or the *d* that ravages at noon . . . . . . .Ps 91:6
then struck them with a *d* . . . . .Ps 106:15
For Samaria's *d* is incurable . . . . .Mic 1:9

DISEASED
But if your eye is *d* . . . . Matt 6:23

DISEASES
who heals all your *d* . . . . .Ps 103:3
and carried our *d* . . . . .Matt 8:17
sick with various *d* . . . . .Luke 4:40
over all demons and to cure *d* . . . . .Luke 9:1
their *d* left them . . . . .Acts 19:12

DISFIGURED
d he no longer looked like a man . . .Isa 52:14

DISGRACE
taken away the *d* of Egypt . . . . .Josh 5:9
and plead my *d* against me . . . . Job 19:5
will act in shameful *d* . . . . .Prov 13:5
but sin is a *d* to any people . . . . .Prov 14:34
the *d* of your abandonment . . . . Isa 54:4
calling into a shameful *d* . . . . Hos 4:7
he did not want to *d* her . . . . .Matt 1:19
take away my *d* among people . . . .Luke 1:25
it is a *d* for him . . . . .1 Cor 11:14
has made a public *d* of them . . . . . . Col 2:15
he may not fall into *d* . . . . .1 Tim 3:7

DISGRACED
because Shechem had *d* Israel . . . . . Gen 34:7

DISGRACEFUL
because it is *d* for a woman . . . . . . .1 Cor 14:35

DISGRACES
his head covered *d* his head . . . . . . .1 Cor 11:4

DISGUISES
hates others *d* it with his lips . . . . Prov 26:24
d himself as an angel of light . . . . .2 Cor 11:14

DISGUISING
d themselves as apostles . . . . .2 Cor 11:13

DISGUST
Lord laughs in *d* at them. . . . . Ps 37:13
laugh in *d* at them . . . . .Ps 59:8

DISGUSTED
I was continually *d*. . . . . .Ps 95:10
she became *d* with them . . . . .Ezek 23:17

DISGUSTING
who takes care of sheep is *d*. . . . .Gen 46:34
not to do this *d* thing I hate. . . . . . . .Jer 44:4

DISH
plunged his hand into the *d* . . . . . .Prov 19:24

DISHEARTENED
have *d* the righteous person. . . . . .Ezek 13:22
so they will not become *d* . . . . Col 3:21

DISHEVEL
not *d* the hair of your heads. . . . . . .Lev 10:6

DISHONEST
See also DISHONEST GAIN
consort with those who are *d* . . . . . .Ps 26:4
even consider doing what is *d* . . . . . Ps 101:3
commended the *d* manager . . . . . . .Luke 16:8
one who is *d* in a very little . . . . . .Luke 16:10

DISHONEST GAIN
all of them are greedy for *d* . . . . .Jer 6:13
all of them are greedy for *d* . . . . .Jer 8:10
the *d* you have hoarded away . . . . .Mic 6:10
by teaching for *d* . . . . .Titus 1:11

DISHONESTLY
they made money *d* . . . . .1 Sam 8:3

DISHONOR
to *d* the pride that comes. . . . . Isa 23:9
yet you *d* me . . . . John 8:49
considered worthy to suffer *d* . . . . . Acts 5:41
to *d* their bodies. . . . . .Rom 1:24
It is sown in *d*. . . . . .1 Cor 15:43
through glory and *d* . . . . .2 Cor 6:8

DISHONORABLE
gave them over to *d* passions . . . . .Rom 1:26

DISHONORED
leave me lying *d* in the dust . . . . Ps 7:5
are distinguished, we are *d* . . . . 1 Cor 4:10
But you have *d* the poor. . . . . .Jas 2:6

DISLIKE
made our neighbors *d* us . . . . Ps 80:6

DISLOCATED
socket of Jacob's hip was *d* . . . . . . .Gen 32:25
all my bones are *d*. . . . . Ps 22:14

DISLOYAL
people that has been *d* to him. . . . . . .Jer 9:2

DISMANTLED
the tent we live in, is *d*. . . . . 2 Cor 5:1

DISMAY
I am overwhelmed with *d* . . . . .Jer 8:21

DISMISSAL
to write a certificate of *d* . . . . .Mark 10:4

DISOBEDIENCE
but look what he got—*d* . . . . .Isa 5:7
through the *d* of the one man . . . . .Rom 5:19
now energizing the sons of *d* . . . . . .Eph 2:2
or *d* received its just penalty . . . . . . Heb 2:2

DISOBEDIENT
they grew *d* and rebelled. . . . . .Neh 9:26
and the *d* to the wisdom. . . . . .Luke 1:17
this *d* and stubborn people. . . . . . .Rom 10:21
you were formerly *d* to God. . . . . . .Rom 11:30
blasphemers, *d* to parents. . . . . . . .2 Tim 3:2
we too were once foolish, *d* . . . . Titus 3:3
if some are *d* to the word. . . . . 1 Pet 3:1
after they were *d* long ago . . . . . . .1 Pet 3:20

DISOBEY
did not *d* his orders. . . . . .Ps 105:28
d the tradition of the elders . . . . . . .Matt 15:2
because they *d* the word . . . . .1 Pet 2:8

DISOBEYED
But you have *d* me. . . . . .Judg 2:2
I never *d* your commands . . . . Luke 15:29

DISORDER
God is not characterized by *d* . . . 1 Cor 14:33
is *d* and every evil practice . . . . .Jas 3:16

DISORDERLY
to explain this *d* gathering. . . . . . . .Acts 19:40

DISOWN
then that place will *d* him. . . . . Job 8:18

DISPERSE
d them throughout the lands. . . .Ezek 20:23

DISPERSED
what direction is lightning *d*. . . . . .Job 38:24
caused my people to be *d* . . . . .Jer 23:2
people *d* among the Greeks . . . . . . .John 7:35

DISPLACED
are removed and the hills *d* . . . . Isa 54:10

DISPLAY
you *d* your power against me. . . . . . Job 10:16
the outward *d* of his power. . . . . .Hab 3:4

DISPLAYS
the sky *d* his handiwork . . . . .Ps 19:1

DISPLEASED
Judah's firstborn, *d* the LORD . . . . . . .1 Chr 2:3
because you are *d* with them. . . . . . .Ps 80:16
lest the LORD see it, and be *d*. . . . .Prov 24:18
I am greatly *d* with the nations . . . . Zech 1:15

DISPLEASES
you chose to do what *d* me. . . . . .Isa 65:12

DISPUTE
A *d* also started among them. . . . Luke 22:24
without anger or *d*. . . . . .1 Tim 2:8

DISPUTES
A toss of a coin ends *d*. . . . . .Prov 18:18
d between many distant nations. . . .Mic 4:3
must not engage in heated *d* . . . . 2 Tim 2:24

DISQUALIFIED
I myself will not be *d* . . . . .1 Cor 9:27

DISREGARDING
endured the cross, *d* its shame . . . . .Heb 12:2

DISSENSION
quick-tempered person stirs
  up *d* . . . . .Prov 15:18
d, slanders, evil suspicions. . . . . .1 Tim 6:4

DISSENSIONS
for those who create *d* . . . . .Rom 16:17
selfish rivalries, *d*, factions. . . . . .Gal 5:20

DISSIPATION
not weighed down with *d*. . . . . . . Luke 21:34
be charged with *d* or rebellion. . . . . .Titus 1:6

DISSOLVE
will be burned up and *d* . . . . .2 Pet 3:12

DISTANCE
and worship from a *d*. . . . . Exod 24:1
but they saw them in the *d*. . . . . Heb 11:13

DISTANT
See also DISTANT LAND
emerges from the *d* horizon. . . . . Ps 19:6

DISTANT LAND
your exiles are in the most *d* . . . . .Deut 30:4
We have come from a *d*. . . . . .Josh 9:6
come from the *d* of Babylon. . . . .2 Kgs 20:14
so is good news from a *d* . . . . .Prov 25:25
they will flee to a *d* . . . . Isa 17:13
are coming from a *d*. . . . . .Jer 4:16

DISTINCTION
no *d* between them and us . . . . Acts 15:9
For there is no *d*. . . . . Rom 3:22
For there is no *d*. . . . . .Rom 10:12

DISTINGUISH
will *d* between the livestock. . . . . . . .Exod 9:4

DISTORT
to *d* the gospel of Christ. . . . . .Gal 1:7

DISTORTING
or *d* the word of God . . . . .2 Cor 4:2

DISTRACTED
But Martha was *d*. . . . . .Luke 10:40

DISTRAUGHT
Give them a *d* heart . . . . .Lam 3:65

DISTRESS
in my time of *d* .Gen 35:3
your *d* when all these things. . . . . . .Deut 4:30
This is a day of *d*. . . . . 2 Kgs 19:3
from the mouth of *d*. . . . . .Job 36:16
Deliver me from my *d* . . . . Ps 25:17
rescue Israel from all their *d*. . . . . . .Ps 25:22
for I am in *d* . . . . Ps 31:9
you protect me from *d* . . . . Ps 32:7
painful *d* and suffering . . . . .Ps 107:39
In my *d* I cried out to the LORD. . . . . .Ps 118:5
in *d* they looked for you . . . . Isa 26:16
The Lord will give you *d* . . . . Isa 30:20
Deliver us when *d* comes. . . . . Isa 33:2
a time of *d* unlike any other . . . . .Dan 12:1
nations will be in *d* . . . . Luke 21:25
There will be affliction and *d* . . . . . . .Rom 2:9
trouble, or, *d*, or persecution. . . . . . Rom 8:35
helped those in *d* . . . . .1 Tim 5:10

DISTRESSED
you are aware of how *d* I am . . . . .Ps 31:7
And they became greatly *d*. . . . . . .Matt 17:23
became very troubled and *d*. . . . . Mark 14:33
how *d* I am until it is finished. . . . Luke 12:50
d that Jesus asked him. . . . . John 21:17

DISTRESSES
and *d* will overcome them. . . . . . . .Deut 31:17

DISTRIBUTED
The proceeds were *d* to each. . . . . . Acts 4:35

DISTRIBUTING
d the proceeds to everyone . . . . . . .Acts 2:45

DISTURBANCE
that time a great *d* took place . . . .Acts 19:23
After the *d* had ended . . . . .Acts 20:1

DISTURBED
and my mind are deeply *d*. . . . . Jer 23:9
or *d* by any kind of spirit. . . . . .2 Thess 2:2

DISTURBING
there are some who are *d* you. . . . . . .Gal 1:7

DIVIDE
brother to *d* the inheritance . . . . . .Luke 12:13
and *d* it among yourselves. . . . . . . .Luke 22:17
threw dice to *d* his clothes. . . . . . . .Luke 23:34

DIVIDED
and the water was *d*. . . . . .Exod 14:21
or those that have *d* hooves. . . . . . .Deut 14:7
again be *d* into two kingdoms . . . Ezek 37:22
kingdom is *d* and given over. . . . . . .Dan 5:28
Every kingdom *d* against itself. . . .Matt 12:25
Every kingdom *d* against itself. . . . Luke 11:17
be five in one household *d*. . . . . . . Luke 12:52
he *d* his assets between them . . . .Luke 15:12
They *d* my garments. . . . . .John 19:24
Is Christ *d*. . . . . .1 Cor 1:13

DIVIDENDS
and he does not lack the *d*. . . . . .Prov 31:11

DIVIDING
point of *d* soul from spirit . . . . Heb 4:12

DIVINATION
either *d* or soothsaying. . . . . .Lev 19:26
rebellion is like the sin of *d* . . . . . .1 Sam 15:23
to predict the future by *d*. . . . . Jer 27:9

DIVINE
opened and I saw a *d* vision . . . . . . .Ezek 1:1
his *d* power has bestowed. . . . . .2 Pet 1:3

DIVINERS
or *d* can possibly disclose it . . . . . . .Dan 2:27

DIVISION
So there was a *d* in the crowd . . . . .John 7:43
there may be no *d* in the body. . . 1 Cor 12:25

DIVISIONS
one of the *d* of the nighttime....... Ps 90:4
to end your *d* ....1 Cor 1:10
I hear there are *d* among you. .... 1 Cor 11:18
must in fact be *d* among you ..... 1 Cor 11:19

DIVISIVE
Reject a *d* person after one........ Titus 3:10
These people are *d* ....Jude 1:19

DIVORCE
never *d* her as long as he lives... Deut 22:19
he may draw up a *d* document ....Deut 24:1
your mother's *d* certificate ....Isa 50:1
and gave her *d* papers ....Jer 3:8
I hate *d* ....Mal 2:16
he intended to *d* her privately ..... Matt 1:19
lawful to *d* a wife for any cause. ...Matt 19:3
husband should not *d* his wife..... 1 Cor 7:11
if the unbeliever wants a *d* ....1 Cor 7:15
to a wife should not seek *d* ....1 Cor 7:27

DIVORCED
a wife *d* from her husband ....Lev 21:7
not marry a widow, a *d* woman....Lev 21:14
daughter is a widow or *d* ....Lev 22:13
vow of a widow or of a *d*
   woman ....Num 30:9
her first husband who *d* her ......Deut 24:4
who marries a woman *d*..........Luke 16:18

DIVORCEE
not marry a widow or a *d*........Ezek 44:22

DIVORCES
If a man *d* his wife ....Jer 3:1
Whoever *d* his wife ....Matt 5:31
that everyone who *d* his wife..... Matt 5:32
that whoever *d* his wife...........Matt 19:9
Whoever *d* his wife and ....Mark 10:11
Everyone who *d* his wife and .....Luke 16:18

DIZZINESS
d to all the surrounding nations...Zech 12:2

DIZZY
I'm very *d*..........................2 Sam 1:9

DO
See also DO NOT BE AFRAID; DO NOT
   FEAR
Don't *d* this wicked thing ....Judg 19:23
d to your loyal followers............Ps 119:132
is encouraged to *d* evil.............Eccl 8:11
those who love to *d* wrong ....Isa 29:20
I the LORD will quickly *d* this ......Isa 60:22
d one evil thing after another ....Jer 9:3
D what is just and right..............Jer 22:3
d something in your lifetime ....Hab 1:5
themselves and *d* not endure..... Mark 4:17
d this, and you will live ....Luke 10:28
Son can *d* nothing on his own .....John 5:19
what must I *d* to be saved ....Acts 16:30
but those who *d* the law ....Rom 2:13
d evil so that good may come ....Rom 3:8
but I cannot *d* it....................Rom 7:18
For I *d* not do the good I want.....Rom 7:19
I *d* the very evil I do not want......Rom 7:19
or whatever you *d*................1 Cor 10:31
when I was planning to *d* this......2 Cor 1:17
so we can *d* them...................Eph 2:10
whatever you *d* in word or deed.... Col 3:17
every good thing you *d* or say ..2 Thess 2:17
who are eager to *d* good .... Titus 2:14
And *d* not neglect to do good ......Heb 13:16
we will live and *d* this or that........Jas 4:15
d not let this one thing escape..... 2 Pet 3:8

DO NOT BE AFRAID
D, for I am with you ....Gen 26:24
D or discouraged .... Deut 1:21
who outnumber you, *d* .... Deut 20:1
You are safe! D ....Judg 6:23
D of sudden disaster ....Prov 3:25
D of those to whom I send ....Jer 1:8
D to submit to the Babylonians ....Jer 40:9
D! Instead, be strong ....Zech 8:13
d to take Mary as your wife ......Matt 1:20
Have courage! It is I. D............Matt 14:27

Get up," he said. "D................Matt 17:7
angel said to the women, "D......Matt 28:5
D; just believe ....Mark 5:36
D, Zechariah, for your prayer...... Luke 1:13
D, Mary, for you have found.......Luke 1:30
angel said to them, "D............ Luke 2:10
Jesus said to Simon, "D........... Luke 5:10
d of those who kill the body......Luke 12:4
D, but speak and do not .... Acts 18:9
D, Paul! You must stand .... Acts 27:24
D, I am the first and the last........ Rev 1:17

DO NOT FEAR
D, for God has come............. Exod 20:20
D and tremble or be..............Deut 20:3
we *d* when the earth shakes........Ps 46:2
Be strong! D .... Isa 35:4
D them or be terrified..............Ezek 3:9
D, my land. Rejoice ....Joel 2:21
D, because I made a promise .... Hag 2:5
in this way show they *d* me.........Mal 3:15

DOCUMENT
he may draw up a divorce *d* ....Deut 24:1

DOE
Naphtali is a free running *d*....... Gen 49:21

DOEG
An Edomite; chief of Saul's herdsmen,
   1 Sam 21:7
Betrays David, 1 Sam 22:9–10
Kills 85 priests, 1 Sam 22:18–19

DOES
the blind person *d* in darkness ..Deut 28:29
The LORD *d* what is fair.............Ps 103:6
in whatever he *d* he succeeds .....Prov 17:8
in himself and *d* not endure ......Matt 13:21
everyone who *d* evil deeds ....John 3:20
God *d* not show favoritism ....Acts 10:34
fears him and *d* what is right .....Acts 10:35
on the person who *d* wrong ....Rom 13:4
D God then give you the Spirit....... Gal 3:5

DOG
Am I a *d* ....1 Sam 17:43
a *d* that returns to its vomit .... Prov 26:11
live *d* is better than a dead lion ... Eccl 9:4
I will howl like a wild *d* .... Mic 1:8
A *d* returns to its own vomit......2 Pet 2:22

DOGS
You must throw it to the *d* ...... Exod 22:31
D will eat the members............1 Kgs 14:11
D will devour Jezebel..............2 Kgs 9:10
they growl like *d* and prowl ....Ps 59:6
The *d* have big appetites............Isa 56:11
Do not give what is holy to *d* ..... Matt 7:6
but even the *d* eat the crumbs....Matt 15:27
d came and licked his sores ......Luke 16:21
are the *d* and the sorcerers........Rev 22:15

DOING
I hate *d* evil......................... Ps 101:3
stop *d* the evil things ....Jer 35:15
don't understand what I am *d* .....Rom 7:15
does not keep on *d* everything ..... Gal 3:10
not *d* their own work........... 2 Thess 3:11
d this you will never stumble......2 Pet 1:10

DOMAIN
to the ruler of the *d* of the air ......Eph 2:2

DOMINATE
but he will *d* you................... Gen 3:16

DOMINION
have *d* and exalt yourself.........1 Chr 29:11
D and awesome might belong......Job 25:2

DON'T
you *d* know the scriptures........ Matt 22:29

DONE
one who has *d* this evil thing ....2 Sam 3:39
sinned and *d* this evil thing .....2 Sam 24:17
discerned all that God has *d*........Eccl 8:17
have seen the wrong *d* to me......Lam 3:59
Well *d*, good and faithful slave....Matt 25:21
signs and wonders God had *d* .... Acts 15:12
to do what should not be *d*........Rom 1:28

DONKEY
He will be a wild *d* of a man ....Gen 16:12
d saw the angel of the LORD.....Num 22:23
Does the wild *d* bray.................Job 6:5
d recognizes where its owner ....Isa 1:3
humble and riding on a *d*.......... Zech 9:9
and riding on a young *d* .... Zech 9:9
unassuming and seated on a *d*....Matt 21:5
Jesus found a young *d* ....John 12:14
d, speaking with a human voice .. 2 Pet 2:16

DONKEY'S
when a wild *d* colt is born .... Job 11:12

DONKEYS
the wild *d* quench their thirst...... Ps 104:11
teams of horses, riders on *d*.........Isa 21:7
Wild *d* stand on the hilltops ....Jer 14:6

DOOM
single hour your *d* has come ......Rev 18:10

DOOR
sin is crouching at the *d* .... Gen 4:7
a *d* that turns on its hinges ....Prov 26:14
I am the *d* for the sheep ....John 10:7
a *d* of great opportunity...........1 Cor 16:9
opened a *d* of opportunity......... 2 Cor 2:12
that God may open a *d* .... Col 4:3
an open *d* that no one can shut......Rev 3:8
standing at the *d* and knocking.... Rev 3:20
there was a *d* standing open.........Rev 4:1

DOORFRAME
and top of the *d* of the houses.....Exod 12:7

DOORFRAMES
Inscribe them on the *d* .... Deut 6:9

DOORKEEPER
The *d* opens the door for him .....John 10:3

DOORS
Rise up, you eternal *d* ....Ps 24:7
watching at my *d* day by day ..... Prov 8:34
the *d* along the street are shut .....Eccl 12:4
would close the temple *d*...........Mal 1:10

DOORWAY
Your instructions are a *d* .... Ps 119:130

DOORWAYS
at the entrance of the *d* ....Prov 8:3

DOR
City captured by Joshua and assigned to
   Manasseh, Josh 12:23; 17:11; Judg 1:27

DORCAS
See TABITHA

DOTHAN
Ancient town where Joseph was sold,
   Gen 37:14–25
Elisha strikes Syrians at, 2 Kgs 6:8–23

DOUBLE
May I receive a *d* portion ....2 Kgs 2:9
LORD has made her pay *d* ....Isa 40:2
be counted worthy of *d* honor.... 1 Tim 5:17
d corresponding to her deeds .....Rev 18:6

DOUBLE-MINDED
since he is a *d* individual..............Jas 1:8
make your hearts pure, you *d* .... Jas 4:8

DOUBT
life will hang in *d* before you ....Deut 28:66
why did you *d* ....Matt 14:31
and does not *d* in his heart ......Mark 11:23
No *d* this man is a murderer.......Acts 28:4

DOUBTING
must ask in faith without *d*........... Jas 1:6

DOUBTS
why do *d* arise in your hearts....Luke 24:38
who *d* is like a wave of the sea ...... Jas 1:6

DOUGH
d before the yeast was added ... Exod 12:34
you may be a new batch of *d* ....1 Cor 5:7

DOVE
d could not find a resting place..... Gen 8:9
I wish I had wings like a *d*...........Ps 55:6

not hand the life of your *d*..........Ps 74:19
I coo like a *d*..........Isa 38:14
Ephraim has been like a *d*..........Hos 7:11
descending like a *d* and..........Matt 3:16

DOVES
we coo mournfully like *d*..........Isa 59:11
as serpents and innocent as *d*....Matt 10:16
the chairs of those selling *d*......Matt 21:12
pair of *d* or two young pigeons...Luke 2:24

DOWN
See also BOWED DOWN
going up and coming *d* it........Gen 28:12
Write *d* these words..........Exod 34:27
struck them *d* and defeated......Judg 15:8
and strike *d* the Amalekites......1 Sam 15:3
struck *d* both the lion and......1 Sam 17:36
Saul has struck *d* his thousands..1 Sam 18:7
and bent *d* over him..........2 Kgs 4:35
For you write *d* bitter things......Job 13:26
we will trample *d* our foes..........Ps 44:5
wealth will not follow him *d*.......Ps 49:17
He bends *d* to look at the sky......Ps 113:6
remembered us when we were *d*..Ps 136:23
will hunt *d* a violent man..........Ps 140:11
Like a city that is broken *d*......Prov 25:28
weighed *d* by evil deeds..............Isa 1:4
Moab will be trampled *d*..........Isa 25:10
he brings *d* an elevated town.......Isa 26:5
get back up when they fall *d*.......Jer 8:4
Drink until you fall *d*..............Jer 25:27
I will rain *d* on him..........Ezek 38:22
Even if they could dig *d*..........Amos 9:2
lying in rubble and settle *d*......Amos 9:14
so that the sea will calm *d*.......Jonah 1:12
they will be trampled *d*..........Mic 7:10
angrily trample *d* the nations.......Hab 3:12
cut *d* and thrown into the fire....Matt 3:10
bowed *d* before him and said.....Matt 15:25
and kneeling *d* before him......Matt 27:29
comes *d* now from the cross....Matt 27:42
to the sea, "Be quiet! Calm *d*......Mark 4:39
come *d* from the cross now....Mark 15:32
sat *d* at the right hand of God...Mark 16:19
pressed *d*, shaken together......Luke 6:38
who dug *d* deep and laid..........Luke 6:48
I will tear *d* my barns..........Luke 12:18
fire and sulfur rained *d*..........Luke 17:29
looked *d* on everyone else........Luke 18:9
Jerusalem will be trampled *d*....Luke 21:24
not weighed *d* with dissipation..Luke 21:34
I have come *d* from heaven.......John 6:38
good shepherd lays *d* his life.....John 10:11
Will you lay *d* your life for me...John 13:38
by striking *d* the Egyptian..........Acts 7:24
since we are weighed *d*..........2 Cor 5:4
Lord himself will come *d*.......1 Thess 4:16
Let no one look *d* on you.......1 Tim 4:12
who sat *d* at the right hand..........Heb 8:1
that Jesus laid *d* his life for us.....1 John 3:16
come and bow *d* at your feet........Rev 3:9
sun will not beat *d* on them.......Rev 7:16
thrown *d* to the earth..............Rev 12:9

DOWNCAST
why is your expression *d*..........Gen 4:6
then he will save the *d*..........Job 22:29

DOWNFALL
their own schemes be their *d*........Ps 5:10
for your sin has been your *d*........Hos 14:1

DOWNHEARTED
who encourages the *d*..........2 Cor 7:6

DOWNTRODDEN
right decisions for the *d*..........Isa 11:4
O my *d* people..........Isa 21:10

DRAGNET
he catches them in his *d*..........Hab 1:15

DRAGON
red *d* that had seven heads.........Rev 12:3
angels fought against the *d*......Rev 12:7
they worshiped the *d*..........Rev 13:4
He seized the *d*..........Rev 20:2

DRANK
I *d* them in..........Jer 15:16
and they all *d* from it..........Mark 14:23
who ate and *d* with him..........Acts 10:41
all *d* the same spiritual drink.....1 Cor 10:4

DRAW
to the well to *d* more water.....Gen 24:20
I will *d* lots for you here..........Josh 18:6
Evil men *d* their swords..........Ps 37:14
and the years *d* near when........Eccl 12:1
D me after you..........Song 1:4
Joyfully you will *d* water..........Isa 12:3
Now *d* some out and take it.......John 2:8
will *d* all people to myself........John 12:32
us *d* near with a sincere heart...Heb 10:22
D near to God and he will *d* near....Jas 4:8

DRAWS
the Father who sent me *d* him....John 6:44

DREAD
the people of the earth with *d*....Deut 2:25

DREADED
very thing I *d* has happened........Job 3:25

DREAM
Joseph had a *d*..........Gen 37:5
I will speak with him in a *d*........Num 12:6
Like a *d* he flies away..........Job 20:8
like a *d* after one wakes up........Ps 73:20
It will be like a *d*..........Isa 29:7
prophet who has had a *d*..........Jer 23:28
the *d* and its interpretation........Dan 4:19
appeared to Joseph in a *d*........Matt 2:13
as a result of a *d* about him.....Matt 27:19
your old men will *d* dreams........Acts 2:17

DREAMING
we thought we were *d*..............Ps 126:1
but my mind was *d*..............Song 5:2
hungry man *d* that he is eating.....Isa 29:8

DREAMS
We both had *d*..........Gen 40:8
thoughts of the *d* in the night......Job 4:13
Just as *d* come when..........Eccl 5:3
as there is futility in many *d*........Eccl 5:7
Nebuchadnezzar had many *d*.......Dan 2:1
elderly will have prophetic *d*......Joel 2:28
as a result of their *d*..............Jude 1:8

DREGS
to settle undisturbed on its *d*.......Jer 48:11

DRENCH
night long I *d* my bed in tears.........Ps 6:6
I will *d* the land..........Ezek 32:6

DRENCHED
Their land is *d* with blood..........Isa 34:7

DRESSED
boy was *d* in a linen ephod.......1 Sam 2:18
d in bright red..........Isa 63:1
d you in embroidered clothing...Ezek 16:10
A man *d* in soft clothing..........Matt 11:8
the woman was *d* in purple..........Rev 17:4

DREW
I *d* him from the water..........Exod 2:10

DRINK
What can we *d*..........Exod 15:24
Do not *d* wine or strong *d*..........Lev 10:9
d of the anger of the Almighty....Job 21:20
they give me vinegar to *d*..........Ps 69:21
D water from your own cistern....Prov 5:15
and strong *d* is a brawler..........Prov 20:1
lest they *d* and forget..............Prov 31:5
Give strong *d* to the one..........Prov 31:6
d and forget their poverty..........Prov 31:7
d your wine with a happy heart....Eccl 9:7
You will *d* the milk of nations......Isa 60:16
my servants will *d*..............Isa 65:13
will *d* its fill from their blood........Jer 46:10
you must *d* water by measure....Ezek 4:11
Bring us more to *d*..........Amos 4:1
you gave me nothing to *d*........Matt 25:42
I will not *d* of this fruit..........Matt 26:29

wine mixed with gall to *d*........Matt 27:34
Give me some water to *d*..........John 4:7
not to eat meat or *d* wine......Rom 14:21
every time you *d* it..............1 Cor 11:25
made to *d* of the one Spirit.......1 Cor 12:13
all the nations *d* of the wine..........Rev 14:8

DRINKING
those who are champions at *d*......Isa 5:22
Stop *d* just water..................1 Tim 5:23
not slaves to excessive *d*..........Titus 2:3

DRINKS
who *d* some of this water..........John 4:13
eats my flesh and *d* my blood....John 6:54
and *d* without careful regard....1 Cor 11:29

DRIP
adulterous woman *d* honey........Prov 5:3
Your lips *d* sweetness..........Song 4:11
will *d* with sweet wine..............Joel 3:18

DRIPPED
my hands *d* with myrrh..........Song 5:5

DRIPPING
wife is like a constant *d*..........Prov 19:13
lilies *d* with drops of myrrh..........Song 5:13

DRIVE
I will *d* them out before you.....Exod 23:30
must *d* out all the inhabitants...Num 33:52
so you *d* them away..................Ps 68:2
rod of discipline will *d* it far......Prov 22:15
I will *d* you out of my sight..........Jer 7:15
I will *d* them out of my land.......Hos 9:15
and began to *d* out those........Mark 11:15

DRIVEN
will be *d* from human society......Dan 4:25

DRIVES
perfect love *d* out fear..............1 John 4:18

DROP
and made him *d* his prey..........Job 29:17
drink it to its very last *d*..........Ps 75:8
nations are like a *d* in a bucket....Isa 40:15

DROSS
Remove the *d* from the silver....Prov 25:4
too much *d* to be removed.........Jer 6:29

DROUGHT
be concerned in a year of *d*........Jer 17:8
I have called for a *d*..................Hag 1:11

DROVE
When he *d* the man out..........Gen 3:24
d out all those who were selling..Matt 21:12
d them all out of the temple......John 2:15

DROWSINESS
and *d* clothes them with rags.....Prov 23:21

DROWSY
all became *d* and fell asleep......Matt 25:5

DRUDGERY
our toil and *d*....................1 Thess 2:9

DRUM
took a hand *d* in her hand.......Exod 15:20

DRUNK
got *d* and uncovered himself......Gen 9:21
have *d* my wine and my milk.......Song 5:1
will stagger around like a *d*........Isa 24:20
who is *d*, but not from wine........Isa 51:21
I made them *d* in my rage..........Isa 63:6
I am like a *d* person..................Jer 23:9
a glutton and a *d*..................Luke 7:34
when the guests are *d*..........John 2:10
these men are not *d*..............Acts 2:15
and another becomes *d*..........1 Cor 11:21
And do not get *d* with wine..........Eph 5:18
who get *d* are *d* at night......1 Thess 5:7
d with the wine of her immorality..Rev 17:2
twoman was *d* with the blood......Rev 17:6

DRUNKARD
gone up into the hand of a *d*......Prov 26:9
or verbally abusive, or a *d*..........1 Cor 5:11
not a *d*, not violent, but gentle.....1 Tim 3:3

DRUNKENNESS
be overcome by *d* and sorrow... Ezek 23:33
with dissipation and *d* .... Luke 21:34
not in carousing and *d* .... Rom 13:13
d, carousing, and similar things..... Gal 5:21
d, carousing, drinking bouts ....1 Pet 4:3

DRUSILLA
Wife of Felix; hears Paul, Acts 24:24–25

DRY
fleece was *d* and the ground...... Judg 6:40
and I make the *d* tree sprout ....Ezek 17:24
I will *d* up the waterways .... Ezek 30:12
what will happen when it is *d*....Luke 23:31
and to *d* them with the towel...... John 13:5

DUE
for in *d* time we will reap............Gal 6:9
God will exalt you in *d* time ....1 Pet 5:6

DUG
legal proof that I *d* this well ...... Gen 21:30
d back in the days of his father ... Gen 26:15
in my tomb that I *d* for myself.....Gen 50:5
They have *d* a pit for me......... Ps 57:6
So I went to Perath and *d* up .... Jer 13:7
d a pit for its winepress...........Matt 21:33

DULL
but his eye was not *d*............. Deut 34:7
of this people has become *d*...... Matt 13:15
of this people has become *d*......Acts 28:27

DUMBFOUNDED
I sat *d* among them there...........Ezek 3:15

DUNG
I regard them as *d* ....Phil 3:8

DUST
for you are *d*........................ Gen 3:19
your descendants like the *d* ....Gen 13:16
I am but *d* and ashes.............. Gen 18:27
Who can count the *d* of Jacob ... Num 23:10
and throw your gold in the *d* ......Job 22:24
and I repent in *d* and ashes.........Job 42:6
the *d* of the grave praise you ....Ps 30:9
make mankind return to the *d* ......Ps 90:3
feel compassion for the *d*...........Ps 102:14
both come from the *d* .... Eccl 3:20
regarded as *d* on the scales........ Isa 40:15
will lick the *d* like a snake .... Mic 7:17
shake the *d* off your feet ....Matt 10:14
the image of the man of *d*........1 Cor 15:49

DUTY
the *d* of a brother-in-law .... Deut 25:5
only done what was our *d* ....Luke 17:10

DWELL
d in an exalted and holy place ......Isa 57:15
Christ will *d* in your hearts ....Eph 3:17
all his fullness *d* in the Son ....Col 1:19
word of Christ *d* in you richly...... Col 3:16

DWELLING
to put on our heavenly *d* ....2 Cor 5:2

DYING
the legal rights of all the *d*........Prov 31:8
I am not trying to escape *d* .... Acts 25:11
living is Christ and *d* is gain........ Phil 1:21
as he was *d*........................ Heb 11:21

E

EACH
and *e* of us found his money...... Gen 43:21
E of you must turn .... Jer 25:5
their wings touched *e* other .... Ezek 1:9
E had four faces ....Ezek 10:21

EAGER
and be *e* for the spiritual gifts .....1 Cor 14:1
you are *e* for manifestations.......1 Cor 14:12
and found *e* in many matters .....2 Cor 8:22
who are *e* to do good............. Titus 2:14

EAGERLY
they *e* received the message.......Acts 17:11
just as you wanted to do it *e*.......2 Cor 8:11
it is good to be sought *e* .... Gal 4:18

EAGERNESS
e in honoring one another........Rom 12:10
what *e*, what defense ....2 Cor 7:11
but to reveal to you your *e* ...... 2 Cor 7:12
comparison with the *e* of.........2 Cor 8:8

EAGLE
Like an *e* that stirs up its nest..... Deut 32:11
like an *e* that swoops down........Job 9:26
fly off into the sky like an *e*.......Prov 23:5
the way of an *e* in the sky........ Prov 30:19
and also the face of an *e*.......... Ezek 1:10
creature looked like an *e* ....Rev 4:7
the two wings of a giant *e* .... Rev 12:14

EAGLES
move more swiftly than *e* ....Jer 4:13
your home where the *e* nest....... Jer 49:16

EAGLES'
rise up as if they had *e* wings ...... Isa 40:31

EAR
will pierce his *e* with an awl ....Exod 21:6
Does not the *e* test words .... Job 12:11
cutting off his right *e*.............John 18:10
no eye has seen, or *e* heard........ 1 Cor 2:9
And if the *e* says ....1 Cor 12:16
who has an *e* had better hear.......Rev 2:7

EARLIER
are your *e* faithful deeds........... Ps 89:49

EARLY
those that had ripened *e*........... Jer 24:2
And very *e* on the first day ...... Mark 16:2
at the tomb *e* this morning ......Luke 24:22

EARNEST
So be *e* and repent ....Rev 3:19

EARNESTLY
and *e* vowed to offer lavish........Jonah 1:16
e desired to eat this Passover ... Luke 22:15
his anguish he prayed more *e* ...Luke 22:44
prayed *e* that it would not rain ......Jas 5:17
So love one another *e* ....1 Pet 1:22
to contend *e* for the faith...........Jude 1:3

EARS
See also EARS TO HEAR
one who shuts his *e* to the cry.... Prov 21:13
Do not speak in the *e* of a fool.... Prov 23:9
e deaf and their eyes blind..........Isa 6:10
who has *e* had better listen....... Matt 11:15
hear with their *e* and understand..Matt 13:15
his *e* are open to their prayer......1 Pet 3:12

EARS TO HEAR
and *e*, but do not hear ....Ezek 12:2
has *e* had better listen.............Mark 4:9
has *e*, he had better listen ....Mark 4:23
who has *e* had better listen....... Luke 8:8
who has *e* had better listen....... Luke 14:35

EARTH
See also ALL THE EARTH; HEAVEN AND
    EARTH
Now the *e* was without shape ....Gen 1:2
had yet grown on the *e*............ Gen 2:5
e was ruined in the sight of God....Gen 6:11
a wind to blow over the *e*............Gen 8:1
and multiply and fill the *e* ....Gen 9:1
the whole *e* was populated .... Gen 9:19
that the *e* belongs to the LORD ...Exod 9:29
the *e* swallowed them ....Exod 15:12
What if the *e* swallows us too ... Num 16:34
in heaven above, on *e* below...... Deut 5:8
and the *e* beneath you iron ...... Deut 28:23
heavens and the *e* to witness ... Deut 31:28
the *e* shook, the heavens poured ...Judg 5:4
foundations of the *e* belong ....1 Sam 2:8
the *e* was divided.................1 Chr 1:19
Sing to the LORD, all the *e* .... 1 Chr 16:23
for he comes to judge the *e* ......1 Chr 16:33
humanity have hard service on *e* .....Job 7:1
he suspends the *e* on nothing ......Job 26:7
I laid the foundation of the *e* ....Job 38:4
owns the *e* and all it contains..... Ps 24:1
over the rulers of the *e*.............Ps 47:9
You visit the *e* and give it rain ......Ps 65:9

the *e* shakes .... Ps 99:1
majesty extends over the *e*........ Ps 148:13
laid the foundation of the *e*....... Prov 3:19
three things the *e* has trembled .. Prov 30:21
but the *e* remains the same..........Eccl 1:4
in heaven and you are on *e*....... Eccl 5:2
for the downtrodden of the *e* .... Isa 11:4
a treaty curse devours the *e*....... Isa 24:6
the sky and to found the *e*....... Isa 51:16
the sky is higher than the *e*....... Isa 55:9
and the *e* is my footstool............Isa 66:1
new heavens and the new *e* ....Isa 66:22
up between the *e* and sky ....Ezek 8:3
and the *e* radiated his glory..... Ezek 43:2
in the heavens and on the *e* ...... Dan 6:27
e dark in the middle of the day ... Amos 8:9
majesty will fill the *e*............... Hab 2:14
The whole *e* is speechless ....Hab 2:20
for they will inherit the *e* ....Matt 5:5
until heaven and *e* pass away......Matt 5:18
may your will be done on *e*....... Matt 6:10
for yourselves treasures on *e*.....Matt 6:19
whatever you bind on *e*............Matt 18:18
the tribes of the *e* will mourn....Matt 24:30
authority in heaven and on *e* .... Matt 28:18
Heaven and *e* will pass away .....Mark 13:31
and on *e* peace among people...Luke 2:14
authority on *e* to forgive sins ..... Luke 5:24
will he find faith on *e* ....Luke 18:8
e is the footstool for my feet ......Acts 7:49
long as we are alive here on *e* .....2 Cor 5:6
Then his voice shook the *e* .... Heb 12:26
spends the rest of his time on *e* ...1 Pet 4:2
the present heavens and *e*......... 2 Pet 3:7
new heavens and a new *e* ....2 Pet 3:13
tribes on the *e* will mourn .... Rev 1:7
Do not damage the *e* ....Rev 7:3
thrown down to the *e* ....Rev 12:9
but the *e* came to her rescue ......Rev 12:16
all those who live on the *e*..........Rev 13:8
swung his sickle over the *e*.........Rev 14:16
e was lit up by his radiance ....Rev 18:1
the *e* and the heaven fled..........Rev 20:11
a new heaven and a new *e*.........Rev 21:1

EARTHLY
heavenly bodies and *e* bodies ...1 Cor 15:40
we know that if our *e* house ...... 2 Cor 5:1
discipline from our *e* fathers ...... Heb 12:9
not come from above but is *e* ....Jas 3:15

EARTHQUAKE
windstorm there was an *e*.........1 Kgs 19:11
flee as you fled from the *e*........Zech 14:5
there was a severe *e*.............. Matt 28:2
a great *e* occurred ....Acts 16:26
and a huge *e* took place ....Rev 6:12
there was a tremendous *e*.........Rev 16:18

EARTHQUAKES
will be *e* in various places......... Mark 13:8

EASE
and the careless *e* of fools......... Prov 1:32
at *e* from the dread of harm .... Prov 1:33
those who live in *e* in Zion.........Amos 6:1

EASIER
Which is *e* ....Mark 2:9
is *e* for a camel to go through ...Mark 10:25
it is *e* for heaven and earth .... Luke 16:17

EAST
planted an orchard in the *e*......... Gen 2:8
LORD brought an *e* wind...........Exod 10:13
assigned to you *e* of the Jordan ...Josh 1:14
e winds scattered over the earth...Job 38:24
those living in the *e* and west.......Ps 65:8
From the *e* I will bring your.......... Isa 43:5
will recognize from *e* to west....... Isa 45:6
wise men from the *E* came.........Matt 2:1
will come from the *e* and west ... Matt 8:11
will come from *e* and west ...... Luke 13:29
way for the kings from the *e*....... Rev 16:12

EAT
You may freely *e* fruit ....Gen 2:16
Did you *e* from the tree............. Gen 3:11
and dust you will *e*................ Gen 3:14
You must not *e* from it ....Gen 3:17

will *e* the grain of the field......... Gen 3:18
You may *e* any moving thing .... Gen 9:3
and *e* some of my wild game ..... Gen 27:19
and invited his relatives to *e*...... Gen 31:54
This is how you are to *e* it .... Exod 12:11
by no means *e* the blood ....Deut 12:23
e only what is sufficient ....Prov 25:16
to *e* too much honey .... Prov 25:27
Go, *e* your food with joy............ Eccl 9:7
leaders will have nothing to *e* ....Isa 5:13
He will *e* sour milk and honey ....Isa 7:15
you will *e* what grows wild ....Isa 37:30
like an ox, will *e* straw .... Isa 65:25
those who *e* the flesh of pigs ....Isa 66:17
e what you see in front of you..... Ezek 3:1
I gave you no food to *e* .... Amos 4:6
They *e* lambs from the flock..... Amos 6:4
what you will *e* or drink .... Matt 6:25
even the dogs *e* the crumbs .....Matt 15:27
for you to *e* the Passover........Matt 26:17
where I may *e* the Passover ..... Mark 14:14
what you will *e* .... Luke 12:22
longing to *e* the carob pods ......Luke 15:16
who longed to *e* what fell........Luke 16:21
I have food to *e*...................John 4:32
this man give us his flesh to *e* ....John 6:52
slaughter and *e*..................Acts 10:13
oath not to *e* or drink anything... Acts 23:21
It is good not to *e* meat........... Rom 14:21
I will never *e* meat again..........1 Cor 8:13
e whatever is served............. 1 Cor 10:27
neither should he *e*............2 Thess 3:10
have no right to *e* from ....Heb 13:10
Take the scroll and *e* it ....Rev 10:9

EATEN
e on the day of your sacrifice.......Lev 19:6
e my honeycomb and my honey....Song 5:1
are so bad they cannot be *e* .... Jer 24:8
have *e* the fruit of deception ......Hos 10:13

EATING
No foreigner may share in *e* it... Exod 12:43
sinning against the LORD by *e* ...1 Sam 14:33
Job's sons and daughters were *e*..... Job 1:13
as if they were *e* bread ....Ps 53:4
he spent the night without *e*....... Dan 6:18
John came neither *e* nor .... Matt 11:18
people were *e* and drinking......Matt 24:38
while they were *e* he said........ Matt 26:21
that he was *e* with sinners........ Mark 2:16
While they were *e*...............Mark 14:22
e and drinking what they give ....Luke 10:7

EATS
welcomes sinners and *e*...........Luke 15:2
The one who *e* my flesh ....John 6:54
The one who *e* this bread........ John 6:58
The one who *e* everything........Rom 14:3
The one who *e*.....................Rom 14:6
For the one who *e* and drinks ....1 Cor 11:29

EBAL, MOUNT
See MOUNT EBAL

EBED MELECH
Ethiopian court official; rescues Jeremiah,
    Jer 38:7–13
Promised divine protection, Jer 39:15–18

EBENEZER
Site of Israel's defeat, 1 Sam 4:1–10
Ark transferred from, 1 Sam 5:1
Site of memorial stone, 1 Sam 7:10, 12

EBER
Great-grandson of Shem, Gen 10:21–24;
    1 Chr 1:25
Progenitor of the:
    Hebrews, Gen 11:16–26
    Arabians and Arameans, Gen 10:25–30
Ancestor of Christ, Luke 3:35

ECSTATIC
the God who gives me *e* joy ....Ps 43:4

EDEN
First home of humanity, Gen 2:8–15
Zion becomes like, Isa 51:3
Called the "garden of God," Ezek 28:13

EDGE
cows at the *e* of the river...........Gen 41:3
reeds along the *e* of the Nile........ Exod 2:3
cut off an *e* of Saul's robe........1 Sam 24:4
touched the *e* of his cloak ....Matt 9:20
only touch the *e* of his cloak..... Matt 14:36

EDICT
let a royal *e* go forth from him .....Esth 1:19
for a royal *e* to be issued .... Dan 6:7

EDOM
Name given to Esau, Gen 25:30
—Land of Esau, Gen 32:3
People of, cursed, Isa 34:5–6
Horites of, dispossessed by Esau's
    descendants, Deut 2:12
Desolation of, Ezek 35:15
Also called "Seir," Gen 32:3
Also called "Idumea" by Greeks and
    Romans, Mark 3:8

EDOMITES
Descendants of Esau, Gen 36:9
Refuse passage to Israel, Num 20:18–20
Hostile to Israel, Gen 27:40; 1 Sam 14:47;
    2 Chr 20:10; Ps 137:7
Prophecies concerning, Gen 27:37;
    Isa 34:5–17; Ezek 25:12–14; 35:5–7;
    Amos 9:11–12

EDREI
Capital of Bashan, Deut 3:10
Site of Og's defeat, Num 21:33–35

EDUCATED
e and having keen insight............Dan 1:4

EFFECT
a will takes *e* only at death .... Heb 9:17

EFFECTIVE
who provide *e* leadership......... 1 Tim 5:17

EFFECTIVENESS
righteous person has great *e* ....Jas 5:16

EFFORT
makes an *e* to take hold of you..... Isa 64:7
Exert every *e* to enter through .. Luke 13:24
every *e* to keep the unity...........Eph 4:3
every *e* to come to me soon...... 2 Tim 4:9
every *e* to enter that rest...........Heb 4:11

EGG
any taste in the white of an *e*........Job 6:6
Or if he asks for an *e* .... Luke 11:12

EGLON
City of Judah, Josh 15:39

EGYPT
Abram visits, Gen 12:10
Joseph sold into, Gen 37:28, 36
    becomes leader in, Gen 39:1–4
Hebrews move to, Gen 46:5–7
    persecuted in, Exod 1:15–22
Plagues on, Exod 7–11
Israel leaves, Exod 12:31–33
Army of, perishes, Exod 14:26–28
Prophecies concerning, Gen 15:13;
    Isa 19:18–25; Ezek 29:14–15; 30:24–25;
    Matt 2:15

EHUD
Son of Gera, Judg 3:15
Slays Eglon, Judg 3:16–26

EIGHT
son Isaac was *e* days old........... Gen 21:4
He had *e* sons ....1 Sam 17:12
Josiah was *e* years old .... 2 Kgs 22:1
At the end of *e* days ....Luke 2:21
e days after these sayings ....Luke 9:28
to a mattress for *e* years...........Acts 9:33
that is *e* souls.................... 1 Pet 3:20

EIGHTH
and you may sow the *e* year...... Lev 25:22
On the *e* day they came ....Luke 1:59

EIGHTY
Now Moses was *e* years old .... Exod 7:7
I am now *e* years old............ 2 Sam 19:35
and *e* other brave priests........2 Chr 26:17

EKRON
Philistine city, Josh 13:3
Captured by Judah, Judg 1:18
Assigned to Dan, Josh 19:40, 43
Ark sent to, 1 Sam 5:10
Denounced by the prophets, Jer 25:9, 20

EL
E, God, the LORD has spoken ....Ps 50:1

EL BETHEL
Site of Jacob's altar, Gen 35:6–7

ELAH
King of Israel, 1 Kgs 16:6, 8–10

ELAMITES
Descendants of Shem, Gen 10:22
Destruction of, Jer 49:34–39
In Persian Empire, Ezra 4:9
Jews from, at Pentecost, Acts 2:9

ELAT
Seaport on Red Sea, 1 Kgs 9:26
Built by Azariah, 2 Kgs 14:21–22
Captured by Syrians, 2 Kgs 16:6

ELATION
the *e* of the wicked is brief ....Job 20:5

ELDER
an accusation against an *e*........ 1 Tim 5:19
From the *e*, to an elect lady........2 John 1:1
From the *e*, to Gaius............... 3 John 1:1

ELDERLY
are like a crown to the *e*...........Prov 17:6

ELDERS
See also TWENTY-FOUR ELDERS
seventy of the *e* of Israel .... Exod 24:1
He summoned Israel's *e*........... Josh 24:1
along with counsel from the *e*.... Ezek 7:26
disobey the tradition of the *e*......Matt 15:2
things at the hands of the *e*.......Matt 16:21
all the chief priests and the *e*......Matt 27:1
and be rejected by the *e*..........Luke 9:22
and the *e* who had come out ....Luke 22:52
e, and the experts in the law....... Acts 6:12
When they had appointed *e* ......Acts 14:23
the apostles and the *e* met .... Acts 15:6
telling the *e* of the church ....Acts 20:17
and the whole council of *e*........Acts 22:5
when the *e* laid hands on you..... 1 Tim 4:14
E who provide effective .... 1 Tim 5:17
to appoint *e* in every town..........Titus 1:5
summon the *e* of the church ....Jas 5:14
I urge the *e* among you............. 1 Pet 5:1
thrones were twenty-four *e* .... Rev 4:4
the twenty-four *e* throw...........Rev 4:10
the twenty-four *e* threw ....Rev 5:8

ELEAZAR
Son of Aaron; succeeds him as high priest,
    Exod 6:23, 25; 28:1; Lev 10:6–7; Num 3:32;
    20:25–28; Josh 14:1; 24:33

ELECT
and they will gather his *e*........ Matt 24:31
but the *e* obtained it................ Rom 11:7
children of your *e* sister greet ....2 John 1:13

ELECTION
to *e* they are dearly loved ....Rom 11:28
be sure of your calling and *e*.......2 Pet 1:10

ELEMENTS
beginning *e* of God's utterances ... Heb 5:12

ELEVATED
you are *e* high above all gods........Ps 97:9
Every valley must be *e*.............Isa 40:4
Then the king *e* Daniel.............Dan 2:48

ELEVEN
his *e* sons and crossed the ford...Gen 32:22
and *e* stars were bowing down ....Gen 37:9
They found the *e* and those .....Luke 24:33
counted with the *e* apostles ....Acts 1:26

ELI
Officiates in Shiloh, 1 Sam 1:3
Blesses Hannah, 1 Sam 1:12–19
Becomes Samuel's guardian, 1 Sam 1:20–28

Samuel ministers before, 1 Sam 2:11
Sons of, 1 Sam 2:12–17
    rebukes, 1 Sam 2:22–25
Rebuked by a man of God, 1 Sam 2:27–36
Instructs Samuel, 1 Sam 3:1–18
Death of, 1 Sam 4:15–18

ELIAB [or ELIHU]
Brother of David, 1 Sam 16:5–13
Fights in Saul's army, 1 Sam 17:13
Discounts David's worth, 1 Sam 17:28–29
Also called "Elihu," 1 Chr 27:18

ELIAKIM
Son of Hilkiah, 2 Kgs 18:18
Confers with Assyria's chief adviser,
    Isa 36:4, 11–22
Sent to Isaiah, Isa 37:2–5
Becomes type of the Messiah, Isa 22:20–25
—Son of King Josiah: *see* JEHOIAKIM

ELIASHIB
High priest, Neh 12:10
Rebuilds Sheep Gate, Neh 3:1, 20–21
Allies with foreigners, Neh 13:4–5, 28

ELIHU
David's brother: *see* ELIAB
—One who reproved Job and his friends,
    Job 32:2, 4–6

ELIJAH
Denounces Ahab; goes into hiding; fed by
    ravens, 1 Kgs 17:1–7
Dwells with widow; performs miracles for
    her, 1 Kgs 17:8–24
Sends message to Ahab; overthrows
    prophets of Baal, 1 Kgs 18:1–40
Brings rain, 1 Kgs 18:41–45
Flees from Jezebel; fed by angels,
    1 Kgs 19:1–8
Receives revelation from God, 1 Kgs 19:9–18
Condemns Ahab, 1 Kgs 21:15–29
Condemns Ahaziah; fire consumes troops
    sent against him, 2 Kgs 1:1–16
Taken up to heaven, 2 Kgs 2:1–15
Appears with Christ in transfiguration,
    Matt 17:1–4
Type of John the Baptist, Mal 4:5–6;
    Luke 1:17

ELIMELECH
Naomi's husband, Ruth 1:1–3; 2:1, 3; 4:3–9

ELIPHAZ
One of Job's friends, Job 2:11
Rebukes Job, Job 4:1, 5
Is forgiven, Job 42:7–9

ELISHA
Chosen as Elijah's successor; follows him,
    1 Kgs 19:16–21
Witnesses Elijah's translation; receives his
    prophetic spirit and cloak, 2 Kgs 2:1–18
Performs miracles, 2 Kgs 2:19–25; 4:1–6:23
Prophesies victory over Moab; fulfilled,
    2 Kgs 3:11–27
Prophesies end of siege; fulfilled, 2 Kgs 7
Prophesies death of Ben Hadad,
    2 Kgs 8:7–15
Sends servant to anoint Jehu, 2 Kgs 9:1–3
Last words and death; miracle performed
    by his bones, 2 Kgs 13:14–21

ELIZABETH
Barren wife of Zacharias, Luke 1:5–7
Conceives a son, Luke 1:13, 24–25
Salutation to Mary, Luke 1:36–45
Mother of John the Baptist, Luke 1:57–60

ELIZAPHAN
Chief of Kohathites, Num 3:30
Heads family, 1 Chr 15:5, 8
Family consecrated, 2 Chr 29:12–16

ELKANAH
Father of Samuel, 1 Sam 1:1–23
—Son of Korah, Exod 6:24
Escapes judgment, Num 26:11

ELNATHAN
Father of Nehushta, 2 Kgs 24:8
Goes to Egypt, Jer 26:22
Entreats with king, Jer 36:25

ELOQUENT
I am not an *e* man . . . . Exod 4:10
He was an *e* speaker . . . . Acts 18:24

ELSE
joy no one *e* can share . . . . Prov 14:10

ELYMAS
See BAR-JESUS

EMACIATED
will make his healthy ones *e* . . . . Isa 10:16

EMBALM
physicians in his service to *e* . . . . Gen 50:2

EMBANKMENT
your enemies will build an *e* . . . . . Luke 19:43

EMBARRASSMENT
captivity, plunder and *e* . . . . Ezra 9:7

EMBITTERED
and do not be *e* against them . . . . Col 3:19

EMBRACE
e the bosom of a different . . . . Prov 5:20
a time to *e*, and a time to . . . . Eccl 3:5

EMBRACED
They *e* other gods . . . . 1 Kgs 9:9

EMBRACES
and his right hand *e* me . . . . Song 2:6

EMERALD
turquoise, a sapphire, and an *e* . . Exod 28:18
and *e*, the chrysolite . . . . Ezek 28:13
the third agate, the fourth *e* . . . . . . Rev 21:19

EMMANUEL
and they will name him *E* . . . . Matt 1:23

EMMAUS
Town near Jerusalem, Luke 24:13–18

EMPOWERED
child grew and the LORD *e* him . . . Judg 13:24
who *e* Peter for his apostleship . . . . . . Gal 2:8
second beast was *e* to give life . . . . Rev 13:15

EMPTIED
e himself by taking on the form . . . . . Phil 2:7

EMPTINESS
pull evil along using cords of *e* . . . . . . Isa 5:18

EMPTY
earth was without shape and *e* . . . . . . Gen 1:2
the cistern was *e* . . . . Gen 37:24
them all trumpets and *e* jars . . . . Judg 7:16
since they are *e* . . . . 1 Sam 12:21
an *e* man will become wise . . . . Job 11:12
it finds the house *e* . . . . Matt 12:44
and has sent the rich away *e* . . . . Luke 1:53
e and the promise is nullified . . . . . . Rom 4:14
deceive you with *e* words . . . . Eph 5:6
they are useless and *e* . . . . Titus 3:9

EMPTY-HANDED
certainly have sent me away *e* . . . . . Gen 31:42
one may appear before me *e* . . . . Exod 23:15
one will appear before me *e* . . . . . Exod 34:20
not go to your mother-in-law *e* . . . . Ruth 3:17
and sent him away *e* . . . . Mark 12:3

EN GEDI
Assigned to Judah, Josh 15:62–63
David's hiding place, 1 Sam 23:29
Noted for vineyards, Song 1:14

EN HAKKORE
Miraculous spring, Judg 15:14–19

EN ROGEL
Fountain outside Jerusalem, 2 Sam 17:17
Seat of Adonijah's plot, 1 Kgs 1:5–9

ENABLED
The LORD *e* her to conceive . . . . Ruth 4:13
had not *e* her to have children . . . . . 1 Sam 1:5
languages as the Spirit *e* them . . . . . Acts 2:4

ENACT
those who *e* unjust policies . . . . Isa 10:1

ENACTED
and is *e* on better promises . . . . Heb 8:6

ENCHANTING
e folks for their own gain . . . . Jude 1:16

ENCOURAGE
and *e* and strengthen him . . . . Deut 3:28
will *e* you and provide for you . . . . . Ruth 4:15
commissioned me to *e* the poor . . . . Isa 61:1
e fathers and their children . . . . Mal 4:6
e you, then, be imitators of me . . . 1 Cor 4:16
and that he may *e* your hearts . . . . . Eph 6:22
and that he may *e* your hearts . . . . . . Col 4:8
to strengthen you and *e* you . . . . . . 1 Thess 3:2
Therefore *e* one another . . . . 1 Thess 4:18
Therefore *e* one another . . . . 1 Thess 5:11
e your hearts and strengthen . . . 2 Thess 2:17
E younger men likewise . . . . Titus 2:6

ENCOURAGED
He *e* him through God . . . . 1 Sam 23:16
Oded the prophet, he was *e* . . . . . . 2 Chr 15:8
LORD energized and *e* Zerubbabel . . Hag 1:14
e and strengthened the brothers . . Acts 15:32
so all can learn and be *e* . . . . 1 Cor 14:31
I strongly *e* him to visit you . . . . 1 Cor 16:12
together in love, may be *e* . . . . Col 2:2

ENCOURAGEMENT
is translated "son of *e* . . . . Acts 4:36
and in the *e* of the Holy Spirit . . . . . Acts 9:31
the people rejoiced at its *e* . . . . Acts 15:31
and through *e* of the scriptures . . . . Rom 15:4
if there is any *e* in Christ . . . . Phil 2:1
may find strong *e* to hold fast . . . . . Heb 6:18

ENCOURAGES
who *e* the downhearted . . . . 2 Cor 7:6

ENCOURAGING
but an *e* word brings him joy . . . . . Prov 12:25

END
At the *e* of 40 days . . . . Gen 8:6
one cherub on one *e* . . . . Exod 25:19
the *e* of the 40 days and nights . . . . Deut 9:11
At the *e* of every seven years . . . . . . Deut 15:1
Man puts an *e* to the darkness . . . . . Job 28:3
an *e* to the vindictive enemy . . . . Ps 8:2
one *e* of the sky to the other . . . . Ps 19:6
years do not come to an *e* . . . . Ps 102:27
e is the way that leads to death . . . Prov 14:12
will not be blessed in the *e* . . . . Prov 20:21
There is no *e* to all the people . . . . . Eccl 4:16
The *e* of a matter is better . . . . Eccl 7:8
the *e* from the beginning . . . . Isa 46:10
his compassions never *e* . . . . Lam 3:22
Our *e* drew near . . . . Lam 4:18
pertains to the time of the *e* . . . . . . Dan 8:17
until the time of the *e* . . . . Dan 11:35
e has come for my people . . . . Amos 8:2
harvest is the *e* of the age . . . . Matt 13:39
but the *e* is still to come . . . . Matt 24:6
to the *e* of the age . . . . Matt 28:20
his kingdom will never *e* . . . . Luke 1:33
loved them to the very *e* . . . . John 13:1
the *e* of those things is death . . . . . Rom 6:21
For Christ is the *e* of the law . . . . . . Rom 10:4
confidence firm until the *e* . . . . Heb 3:14
in my deeds until the *e* . . . . Rev 2:26
the beginning and the *e* . . . . Rev 22:13

ENDOR
Town of Manasseh which was the home
    of the witch whom Saul consulted,
    Josh 17:11; 1 Sam 28:1–10; Ps 83:9–10

ENDOWED
God *e* them with knowledge . . . . Dan 1:17

ENDS
the cherubim on the two *e* . . . . Exod 25:19
judgment to the *e* of the earth . . . 1 Sam 2:10
he looks to the *e* of the earth . . . . . Job 28:24
e of the earth see our God . . . . Ps 98:3
established all the *e* of the earth . . . Prov 30:4
came from the *e* of the earth . . . . . Matt 12:42

salvation to the *e* of the earth .... Acts 13:47
words to the *e* of the world.......Rom 10:18
Love never *e*.......................1 Cor 13:8

ENDURANCE
and bear fruit with steadfast *e*.....Luke 8:15
e you will gain your lives ....Luke 21:19
that suffering produces *e*...........Rom 5:3
the God of *e* and comfort..........Rom 15:5
labor motivated by love and *e*....1 Thess 1:3
love, *e*, and gentleness............1 Tim 6:11
my patience, my love, my *e*.......2 Tim 3:10
e in order to do God's will........Heb 10:36
run with the race set out..........Heb 12:1
testing of your faith produces *e* ......Jas 1:3
let *e* have its perfect effect..........Jas 1:4
You have heard of Job's *e*...........Jas 5:11
and *e* that are in Jesus ....Rev 1:9
requires steadfast *e* and faith......Rev 13:10

ENDURE
punishment is too great to *e*...... Gen 4:13
to fear the LORD are right and *e* ...... Ps 19:9
e the insults of those who insult.....Ps 69:9
May his fame *e* .... Ps 72:17
You *e* through all generations .....Ps 102:24
the splendor of the LORD *e*........ Ps 104:31
your instructions *e* .... Ps 119:89
them so they would *e* ....Ps 148:6
who tells the truth will *e*.......... Prov 12:19
of the LORD's temple will *e* ....Isa 2:2
your heart or can your hands.. Ezek 22:14
much longer must I *e* you .... Matt 17:17
in hope, *e* in suffering............. Rom 12:12
when persecuted, we *e* ....1 Cor 4:12
so that you may be able to *e*.....1 Cor 10:13
So I *e* all things ....2 Tim 2:10
E your suffering as discipline ....Heb 12:7
sin and are mistreated and *e* .....1 Pet 2:20

ENDURED
I have *e* chastisement.............Job 34:31
you have *e* the insults .... Ezek 36:6
She had *e* a great deal ....Mark 5:26
I *e* these persecutions .... 2 Tim 3:11
him who *e* such opposition.........Heb 12:3
as blessed those who have *e*........ Jas 5:11

ENDURES
See also HIS LOYAL LOVE ENDURES
certainly his loyal love *e*.......... 2 Chr 5:13
certainly his loyal love *e* ....2 Chr 7:3
His loyal love *e* ....Ps 100:5
his integrity *e*...................Ps 112:3
the LORD's faithfulness *e* ....Ps 117:2
and his loyal love *e* ....Ps 118:1
Your justice *e*....................Ps 119:142
your name *e* ....Ps 135:13
for his loyal love *e*.................Ps 136:1
he *e* forever ....Dan 6:26
who *e* to the end will be saved .. Matt 10:22
hopes all things, *e* all things ....1 Cor 13:7
Happy is the one who *e* testing......Jas 1:12
the word of the Lord *e* forever ....1 Pet 1:25

ENDURING
an *e* protector .... Isa 26:4
living and *e* word of God .... 1 Pet 1:23

ENEMIES
See also LOVE YOUR ENEMIES
will be an enemy to your *e* ......Exod 23:22
May your *e* be scattered........ Num 10:35
I brought you to curse my *e* ...... Num 23:11
cause your *e* who attack you ..... Deut 28:7
has driven out *e* before you .... Deut 33:27
from the hands of our *e* ....1 Sam 12:10
defeated all your *e* before you... 2 Sam 7:9
I was delivered from my *e*.......2 Sam 22:4
LORD, how numerous are my *e*.......Ps 3:1
All my *e* will turn back..........Ps 6:10
I was delivered from my *e* .... Ps 18:3
He delivers me from my *e*........Ps 18:48
in plain sight of my *e* ....Ps 23:5
my *e* triumphantly rejoice ....Ps 25:2
my adversaries and *e* attack........Ps 27:2
who are my *e* for no reason .... Ps 38:19

His *e* scatter .... Ps 68:1
and his *e* will lick the dust ....Ps 72:9
you scattered your *e*.................Ps 89:10
I will crush his *e* before him ....Ps 89:23
I make your *e* your footstool ....Ps 110:1
make me wiser than my *e* .... Ps 119:98
snatched us away from our *e*......Ps 136:24
they have become my *e* ....Ps 139:22
Certainly my *e* chase me ....Ps 143:3
reconciles his *e* to himself ....Prov 16:7
man's *e* are his own family ....Mic 7:6
My *e*, do not gloat over me ....Mic 7:8
drive his *e* into darkness.............Nah 1:8
man's *e* will be the members .... Matt 10:36
should be saved from our *e* .... Luke 1:71
until I make your *e* a footstool ..Luke 20:43
For if while we were *e* ....Rom 5:10
they are *e* for your sake ....Rom 11:28
put all his *e* under his feet .... 1 Cor 15:25
at one time strangers and *e* ....Col 1:21
until his *e* are made a footstool....Heb 10:13
fire that will consume God's *e*....Heb 10:27
completely consumes their *e*....... Rev 11:5

ENEMY
I will be an *e* to your enemies ...Exod 23:22
God has delivered your *e*........1 Sam 26:8
and regard me as your *e*...........Job 13:24
he regards me as his *e*..............Job 33:10
or helped his lawless *e* ....Ps 7:4
put an end to the vindictive *e* ....Ps 8:2
my *e* does not triumph over me.....Ps 41:11
it is not an *e* who insults me........Ps 55:12
that protects me from the *e*........ Ps 61:3
If your *e* is hungry ....Prov 25:21
kisses of an *e* are excessive....... Prov 27:6
attacked you like an *e* would ...... Jer 30:14
e grabbed all her valuables .... Lam 1:10
neighbor' and 'hate your *e*........Matt 5:43
love your *e* and pray for those..... Matt 5:44
and the *e* who sows them ....Matt 13:39
and on the full force of the *e* ....Luke 10:19
Rather, if your *e* is hungry .... Rom 12:20
last *e* to be eliminated is death . 1 Cor 15:26
your *e* by telling you the truth.......Gal 4:16
Yet do not regard him as an *e* .. 2 Thess 3:15
makes himself God's *e*..............Jas 4:4
Your *e* the devil.....................1 Pet 5:8

ENERGIZED
You made me bold and *e* me .... Ps 138:3

ENERGIZING
e the sons of disobedience ....Eph 2:2

ENERGY
with the same *e* I had then ....Josh 14:11
he gives renewed *e* ....Isa 40:29

ENGAGED
a virgin who is not *e* ....Exod 22:16
man came across the *e* woman.. Deut 22:25
You will be *e* to a woman........Deut 28:30
mother Mary was *e* to Joseph .... Matt 1:18
to a virgin *e* to a man ....Luke 1:27

ENGRAVE
onyx stones and *e* on them ....Exod 28:9
about to *e* an inscription on it ..... Zech 3:9

ENGULF
punishment is about to *e* you...... Isa 10:22

ENGULFED
The waves of death *e* me ....2 Sam 22:5
The waves of death *e* me ....Ps 18:4
the ocean current *e* me............Jonah 2:3

ENJOY
and *e* life.......................Eccl 8:15
E fine food......................... Isa 55:2
to *e* sin's fleeting pleasure ....Heb 11:25

ENJOYMENT
I recommend the *e* of life...........Eccl 8:15
with all things for our *e*............ 1 Tim 6:17

ENLIGHTENED
those who have once been *e* ...... Heb 6:4
of suffering after you were *e* .....Heb 10:32

ENOCH
Father of Methuselah, Gen 5:21
Walks with God, Gen 5:22
Taken up to heaven, Gen 5:24
Prophecy of, cited, Jude 1:14–15

ENOUGH
four that have never said, "*E*.....Prov 30:15
Today has *e* trouble of its own.... Matt 6:34
sleeping and resting? *E* of that .. Mark 14:41
workers have food *e* to spare..... Luke 15:17
by the majority is *e* for him........2 Cor 2:6
you have *e* of everything ....2 Cor 9:8

ENRAGED
I was so furiously *e* at them ...... Acts 26:11
The nations were *e* .... Rev 11:18
So the dragon became *e*.......... Rev 12:17

ENRICHED
A generous person will be *e* ...... Prov 11:25
You will be *e* in every way ....2 Cor 9:11

ENROLL
E this man in the register..........Jer 22:30

ENROLLED
who are *e* in heaven .... Heb 12:23

ENSLAVED
would no longer be *e* to sin....... Rom 6:6
freed from sin and *e* to God ...... Rom 6:22
are *e* to immorality................ 2 Pet 2:19

ENSNARED
The evil person is *e*............... Prov 12:13
and will be *e* and captured...........Isa 8:15

ENTANGLED
military service gets *e* in matters .. 2 Tim 2:4

ENTER
never *e* into the resting place........Ps 95:11
E his gates with thanksgiving.......Ps 100:4
uprightly *e* a place of peace ....Isa 57:2
Jonah began to *e* the city ....Jonah 3:4
you will never *e* the kingdom.....Matt 5:20
E through the narrow gate ....Matt 7:13
e into the kingdom of heaven ....Matt 7:21
Whenever you *e* a town or ...... Matt 10:11
to *e* into life with one eye.........Matt 18:9
than for a rich person to *e* .... Matt 19:24
E into the joy of your master .....Matt 25:21
able to *e* a strong man's house ...Mark 3:27
like a child will never *e* it .... Mark 10:15
hard it is to *e* the kingdom.......Mark 10:24
Whatever house you *e*............ Luke 9:4
to *e* through the narrow door ... Luke 13:24
cannot *e* his mother's womb ....John 3:4
cannot *e* the kingdom of God ......John 3:5
e the sheepfold by the door ......John 10:1
who have believed *e* that rest ...... Heb 4:3
confidence to *e* the sanctuary .... Heb 10:19
no one could *e* the temple.......Rev 15:8
can *e* into the city by the gates ....Rev 22:14

ENTERED
until the day Noah *e* the ark.....Matt 24:38
afraid as they *e* the cloud.........Luke 9:34
up to the day Noah *e* the ark ...Luke 17:27
Then Satan *e* Judas ....Luke 22:3
just as sin *e* the world ....Rom 5:12
Jesus our forerunner *e*............Heb 6:20
and he *e* once for all............... Heb 9:12

ENTERS
If anyone *e* through me..........John 10:9
For the one who *e* God's rest......Heb 4:10

ENTERTAINED
invited them in and *e* them ....Acts 10:23

ENTHRONED
e over the engulfing waters........Ps 29:10

ENTHUSIASM
rouse his strength and *e*.........Dan 11:25
and with great *e* he spoke ....Acts 18:25

ENTHUSIASTIC
people were *e* in their work ....Neh 4:6
be *e* in spirit ....Rom 12:11

ENTICE
they *e* unstable people ....2 Pet 2:14
words they are able to *e*..........2 Pet 2:18

ENTICED
lured and *e* by his own desires.......Jas 1:14

ENTICING
smooth talk she was *e* him ....Prov 7:21

ENTIRE
across the face of the *e* earth.......Gen 11:4
splendor fills the *e* earth..........Isa 6:3
mercy on the *e* house of Israel .. Ezek 39:25
able to control the *e* body ....Jas 3:2
It pollutes the *e* body................Jas 3:6

ENTIRELY
allow you to go *e* unpunished .....Jer 46:28

ENTRANCE
stand at the *e* to the temple........Ps 84:10
stone across the *e* of the tomb ..Matt 27:60
an *e* into the eternal kingdom ..... 2 Pet 1:11

ENTRAP
who seek my life try to *e* me ....Ps 38:12
of every size to *e* people's lives...Ezek 13:18
to *e* him with his own words......Matt 22:15

ENTRUST
will *e* you with the true riches .... Luke 16:11
But Jesus would not *e* himself .....John 2:24
And now I *e* you to God ....Acts 20:32
e to faithful people who will.......2 Tim 2:2
e their souls to a faithful Creator ..1 Pet 4:19

ENTRUSTED
I am *e* with a responsibility ....1 Cor 9:17
to be *e* with the gospel ....1 Thess 2:4
protect what has been *e* to you...1 Tim 6:20
protect what has been *e* to me ... 2 Tim 1:12
was once for all *e* to the saints .....Jude 1:3

ENVIED
For I *e* those who are proud .... Ps 73:3
as what they hated and *e* ....Eccl 9:6

ENVIOUS
you *e* because I am generous.... Matt 20:15
it is not *e*............................1 Cor 13:4

ENVOY
but a faithful *e* brings healing..... Prov 13:17

ENVY
Why do you look with *e* ....Ps 68:16
Do not *e* a violent man ....Prov 3:31
e is rottenness to the bones ..... Prov 14:30
Do not let your heart *e* sinners ...Prov 23:17
Do not *e* evil people ....Prov 24:1
handed him over because of *e*... Matt 27:18
They are rife with *e*................Rom 1:29
preaching Christ from *e* and........ Phil 1:15
spending our lives in evil and *e*.... Titus 3:3
murder and *e* and you cannot ....Jas 4:2
hypocrisy and *e* and all slander.....1 Pet 2:1

ENVYING
e, murder, drunkenness .... Gal 5:21

EPAPHRAS
Leader of the Colossian church, Col 1:7–8
Suffers as a prisoner in Rome, Phlm 1:23

EPAPHRODITUS
Messenger from Philippi, Phil 2:25–27
Brings a gift to Paul, Phil 4:18

EPHES DAMMIM [or PAS DAMMIM]
Philistine encampment, 1 Sam 17:1
Also called "Pas Dammim," 1 Chr 11:13

EPHESUS
Paul visits, Acts 18:18–21
Miracles done here, Acts 19:11–21
Demetrius stirs up riot in, Acts 19:24–29
Elders of, addressed by Paul at Miletus,
    Acts 20:17–38
Letter sent to, Eph 1:1
Site of one of the seven churches, Rev 1:11
Letter to, Rev 2:1–7

EPHOD
other gems to be set in the *e* ..... Exod 25:7
a breastpiece, an *e*, a robe ....Exod 28:4

He made the *e* of gold...........Exod 39:2
Next he put the *e* on him...........Lev 8:7
used all this to make an *e*..........Judg 8:27
an *e* and some personal idols...... Judg 17:5
boy was dressed in a linen *e*......1 Sam 2:18
Ahijah was carrying an *e*..........1 Sam 14:3
Bring the *e*.................... 1 Sam 23:9
Bring me the *e*...................1 Sam 30:7
wearing a linen *e* ....2 Sam 6:14

EPHRAIM
Joseph's younger son, Gen 41:52
Obtains Jacob's blessing, Gen 48:8–20
—Tribe of:
Predictions concerning, Gen 48:20
Territory assigned to, Josh 16:1–10
Assist Deborah, Judg 5:14–15
    Gideon, Judg 7:24–25
Quarrel with Gideon, Judg 8:1–3
    with Jephthah, Judg 12:1–4
Leading tribe of kingdom of Israel,
    Isa 7:2–17
Provoke God by sin, Hos 12:7–14
Many of, join Judah, 2 Chr 15:8–9
Captivity of, predicted, Hos 9:3–17
Messiah promised to, Zech 9:9–13

EPHRATH
See BETHLEHEM

EPHRATHAH
See BETHLEHEM

EPHRON
Hittite who sold Machpelah to Abraham,
    Gen 23:8–20

EPICUREAN
Sect of pleasure-loving philosophers,
    Acts 17:18

EQUAL
you have made them *e* to us..... Matt 20:12
e to angels and are sons
    of God.........................Luke 20:36
making himself *e* with God........John 5:18

EQUALITY
and thus there may be *e*..........2 Cor 8:14
did not regard *e* with God ....Phil 2:6

EQUALLY
share *e* in what we steal .... Prov 1:14

EQUIP
e you with every good thing.......Heb 13:21

EQUITABLY
and your oppressed ones *e*..........Ps 72:2

EQUITY
e and justice are the foundation .....Ps 97:2
righteousness, justice, and *e*........ Prov 1:3

ER
Son of Judah, Gen 38:1–7; 46:12

ERASTUS
Paul's friend at Ephesus, Acts 19:21–22;
    2 Tim 4:20
Treasurer of Corinth, Rom 16:23

ERROR
the due penalty for their *e*........Rom 1:27
e of these unprincipled men.......2 Pet 3:17
themselves to Balaam's *e*..........Jude 1:11

ERRORS
Who can know all his *e*..............Ps 19:12

ESARHADDON
Son of Sennacherib; king of Assyria
    (681–669 BC), 2 Kgs 19:36–37

ESAU
Isaac's favorite son, Gen 25:25–28
Sells his birthright, Gen 25:29–34
Deprived of blessing; seeks to kill Jacob,
    Gen 27
Reconciled to Jacob, Gen 33:1–17
Descendants of, Gen 36

ESCAPE
E to the mountains or ....Gen 19:17
let even one of them *e*..........1 Kgs 18:40

and *e* eludes them .... Job 11:20
I will *e* to a distant place............Ps 55:7
do not let them *e*.................Ps 56:7
will not *e* punishment ....Prov 19:5
How can we *e* now .... Isa 20:6
the one doing these things *e*...... Ezek 17:15
e being condemned to hell ...... Matt 23:33
you may have strength to *e*...... Luke 21:36
you will *e* God's judgment..........Rom 2:3
and they will surely not *e*....... 1 Thess 5:3
and *e* the devil's trap .... 2 Tim 2:26
will we *e* if we neglect such......... Heb 2:3
did not *e* when they refused ...... Heb 12:25

ESCAPED
I alone *e* to tell you ....Job 1:15
e alive with only the skin of........Job 19:20
We *e* with our lives ....Ps 124:7
they have *e* the filthy things ......2 Pet 2:20

ESCAPES
for nothing *e* them ....Joel 2:3

ESCAPING
after *e* the worldly corruption ......2 Pet 1:4

ESHBAAL
Son of Saul, 1 Chr 8:33

ESHCOL
Valley near Hebron, Num 13:22–27;
    Deut 1:24

ESPECIALLY
must be *e* magnificent............1 Chr 22:5

ESSENCE
Can you discover the *e* of God.......Job 11:7
and the representation of his *e* ......Heb 1:3

ESSENTIAL
that seem to be weaker are *e*.... 1 Cor 12:22

ESTABLISH
E your work outside .... Prov 24:27
I will *e* a lasting covenant........ Ezek 16:60
to *e* their own righteousness ......Rom 10:3
away with the first to *e* the .... Heb 10:9

ESTABLISHED
instructions which the LORD *e*.... Lev 26:46
He has made you and *e* you ...... Deut 32:6
The world is *e* ....1 Chr 16:30
securely *e* and will not fear..........Job 11:15
e it upon the ocean currents.........Ps 24:2
He *e* a rule in Jacob ....Ps 78:5
his sanctuary is firmly *e* ....Ps 96:6
earlier times you *e* the earth ......Ps 102:25
has *e* his throne in heaven......... Ps 103:19
that all your ways may be *e*...... Prov 4:26
When he *e* the heavens........... Prov 8:27
when he *e* the clouds above ...... Prov 8:28
and your plans will be *e* ....Prov 16:3
through understanding it is *e*..... Prov 24:3
a trustworthy king will be *e* ....Isa 16:5
by his wisdom *e* the world..........Jer 10:12
every matter may be *e* ....Matt 18:16

ESTABLISHES
it is God who *e* us together........2 Cor 1:21

ESTEEM
E her highly and she will exalt......Prov 4:8
to *e* them most highly in love... 1 Thess 5:13

ESTHER [or HADASSAH]
Selected for harem, Esth 2:7–16
Chosen to be queen, Esth 2:17–18
Agrees to intercede for her people, Esth 4
Invites king to banquet, Esth 5:1–8
Denounces Haman; obtains reversal of
    decree, Esth 7:1–8:8
Establishes Purim, Esth 9:29–32
Also called "Hadassah," her Jewish name,
    Esth 2:7

ESTIMATION
Do not be wise in your own *e*.......Prov 3:7

ETAM
Rock where Samson took refuge,
    Judg 15:8–19

ETERNAL
See also ETERNAL LIFE

underneath you are his *e* arms .. Deut 33:27
of the LORD's *e* love for Israel .... 1 Kgs 10:9
LORD sits enthroned as the *e* king ..Ps 29:10
You are an *e* priest..................Ps 110:4
kingdom is an *e* kingdom.......... Ps 145:13
man goes to his *e* home ....Eccl 12:5
and be thrown into *e* fire ....Matt 18:8
thing must I do to gain *e* life......Matt 19:16
and will inherit *e* life............. Matt 19:29
will depart into *e* punishment ...Matt 25:46
must I do to inherit *e* life .... Mark 10:17
in the age to come, *e* life........Mark 10:30
in him may have *e* life .... John 3:15
not perish but have *e* life .... John 3:16
water springing up to *e* life........John 4:14
gathers fruit for *e* life................John 4:36
has *e* life and will not be...........John 5:24
think in them you possess *e* life ...John 5:39
the food that remains to *e* life ....John 6:27
believes in him to have *e* life .....John 6:40
one who believes has *e* life ....John 6:47
drinks my blood has *e* life .... John 6:54
You have the words of *e* life ...... John 6:68
I give them *e* life...................John 10:28
so that he may give *e* life .... John 17:2
Now this is *e* life....................John 17:3
yourselves worthy of *e* life ......Acts 13:46
e life to those who by..............Rom 2:7
to *e* life through Jesus Christ ......Rom 5:21
and the end is *e* life................ Rom 6:22
but the gift of God is *e* life........ Rom 6:23
an *e* weight of glory .... 2 Cor 4:17
but what cannot be seen is *e* .....2 Cor 4:18
that is *e* in the heavens .... 2 Cor 5:1
reap *e* life from the Spirit............Gal 6:8
the penalty of *e* destruction ..... 2 Thess 1:9
Now to the *e* King ....1 Tim 1:17
lay hold of that *e* life............. 1 Tim 6:12
in hope of *e* life.....................Titus 1:2
confident expectation of *e* life..... Titus 3:7
and *e* judgment......................Heb 6:2
himself secured *e* redemption.... Heb 9:12
announce to you the *e* life.........1 John 1:2
he himself made to us: *e* life.....1 John 2:25
has *e* life residing in him..........1 John 3:15
God has given us *e* life............. 1 John 5:11
know that you have *e* life...........1 John 5:13
one is the true God and *e* life....1 John 5:20
in *e* chains in utter darkness........ Jude 1:6
that brings *e* life ....Jude 1:21

ETERNAL LIFE
blessing will be available—*e* .... Ps 133:3
thing must I do to gain *e*...........Matt 19:16
the righteous into *e*..............Matt 25:46
and the age to come, *e* ....Mark 10:30
must I do to inherit *e* ....Luke 10:25
will not perish but have *e*........John 3:16
and gathers fruit for *e* .... John 4:36
think in them you possess *e*.......John 5:39
You have the words of *e* ....John 6:68
guards it for *e*......................John 12:25
Now this is *e*.......................John 17:3
been appointed for *e* believed....Acts 13:48
e to those who by ....Rom 2:7
to *e* through Jesus Christ ....Rom 5:21
the gift of God is *e*................ Rom 6:23
and lay hold of that *e*............. 1 Tim 6:12
in hope of *e*, which God ....Titus 1:2
and announce to you the *e* ....1 John 1:2
he himself made to us: *e*......... 1 John 2:25
no murderer has *e* residing........1 John 3:15
God has given us *e*................. 1 John 5:11
Lord Jesus Christ that brings *e*.....Jude 1:21

ETERNITY
From *e* I have been fashioned .... Prov 8:23

ETHAM
Israel's encampment, Exod 13:20

ETHIOPIA
Hostile to Israel and Judah, 2 Chr 12:2–3;
    14:9–15; Isa 43:3; Dan 11:43
Prophecies against, Isa 20:1–6; Ezek 30:4–9

ETHIOPIANS
Philip preaches to court official of Candace,
    queen of, Acts 8:26–40
Skin of, unchangeable, Jer 13:23

EUNICE
Mother of Timothy, 2 Tim 1:5

EUNUCH
e who oversees the women .... Esth 2:3
There he met an Ethiopian *e*.......Acts 8:27

EUNUCHS
seven *e* who attended him......... Esth 1:10
e in the palace of the king .... Isa 39:7
e who were that way from birth ..Matt 19:12

EUPHRATES
River of Eden, Gen 2:14
Boundary of Promised Land, Gen 15:18;
    1 Kgs 4:21, 24
Scene of battle, Jer 46:2, 6, 10
Angels bound there, Rev 9:14

EUTYCHUS
Sleeps during Paul's sermon, Acts 20:9
Restored to life, Acts 20:12

EVALUATE
E my inner thoughts and ....Ps 26:2

EVALUATED
You have carefully *e* me ....Ps 17:3

EVALUATES
but the LORD *e* the motives........Prov 16:2

EVALUATION
my *e* is accurate ....John 8:16

EVANGELIST
the house of Philip the *e*...........Acts 21:8

EVANGELIST'S
do an *e* work.....................2 Tim 4:5

EVANGELISTS
some as *e*, and some as pastors .... Eph 4:11

EVEN
E in laughter the heart may ache.. Prov 14:13
E a young man is known..........Prov 20:11
e to the point of denying ....2 Pet 2:1

EVENING
There was *e*.........................Gen 1:5
In the *e* the quail came up ....Exod 16:13
must sacrifice it in the *e* ....Deut 16:6
was time for the *e* offering ..... 1 Kgs 18:36
They return in the *e* ....Ps 59:6
hands like the *e* offering............Ps 141:2
not stop working until the *e* ....Eccl 11:6
When *e* comes you say ....Matt 16:2
When *e* came.....................Mark 6:47
during *e*, at midnight .... Mark 13:35
it is getting toward *e*.............Luke 24:29

EVER
being innocent, *e* perished...........Job 4:7
or *e* will happen .... Matt 24:21
no one *e* eat fruit from you......Mark 11:14
No one has *e* seen God .... John 1:18
told me everything I *e* did .... John 4:29
No one *e* spoke like this man..... John 7:46
has *e* hated his own body.......... Eph 5:29
of the angels has he *e* said.......... Heb 1:13
he will reign for *e* and ever ....Rev 11:15

EVERLASTING
The *e* God is a refuge............Deut 33:27
and lead me in the *e* way ....Ps 139:24
E Father, Prince of Peace .... Isa 9:6
the land of Babylon an *e* ruin ......Jer 25:12
have loved you with an *e* love ....Jer 31:3
some to *e* life......................Dan 12:2

EVERY
and we will cancel *e* loan ....Neh 10:31
one who forms *e* human heart ..... Ps 33:15
to *e* one of you not to think ....Rom 12:3
Then I heard *e* creature.............Rev 5:13

EVERYONE
and *e* will be hostile to him........Gen 16:12
e will faint, and every knee ....Ezek 21:7

e who is born of the Spirit..........John 3:8
E who belongs to the truth ....John 18:37

EVERYTHING
I realize that *e* has its limits........Ps 119:96
E will be all right.....................Jer 6:14

EVERYWHERE
for the wicked seem to be *e* .... Ps 12:8

EVIDENCE
Show me *e* of your favor ....Ps 86:17
Tie up the scroll as legal *e*..........Isa 8:16

EVIL
See also EVIL ONE; TREE OF THE
    KNOWLEDGE OF GOOD AND EVIL

knowledge of good and *e*........... Gen 2:9
knowing good and *e*................ Gen 3:5
minds was only *e* all the time....... Gen 6:5
how could I do such a great *e*......Gen 39:9
have you repaid good with *e*......Gen 44:4
not follow a crowd in doing *e*..... Exod 23:2
must purge *e* from among you ....Deut 13:5
and an *e* spirit from the LORD ...1 Sam 16:14
Then an *e* spirit from the LORD ...1 Sam 19:9
From *e* people *e* proceeds .....1 Sam 24:13
firmly committed to doing *e*..... 1 Kgs 21:25
turn from their *e* practices ....Neh 9:35
and turned away from *e*.............Job 1:1
in seven no *e* will touch you ....Job 5:19
when he sees *e*......................Job 11:11
They sin and commit *e* deeds.........Ps 14:1
E people self-destruct ....Ps 34:21
he does not reject what is *e* ....Ps 36:4
Turn away from *e*...................Ps 37:27
You love justice and hate *e* ....Ps 45:7
done what is *e* in your sight .... Ps 51:4
You love *e* more than good..........Ps 52:3
For *e* is in their dwelling place......Ps 55:15
who love the LORD, hate *e*..........Ps 97:10
I will not permit *e*...................Ps 101:4
we have done *e*....................Ps 106:6
I stay away from every *e* path .....Ps 119:101
and turn away from *e*................Prov 3:7
fear of the LORD is to hate *e* ....Prov 8:13
but the one who searches for *e*... Prov 11:27
watch on those who are *e* ....Prov 15:3
is to turn away from *e* ....Prov 16:17
pays attention to *e* counsel........Prov 17:4
the one who repays *e* for good ... Prov 17:13
hearts of all people are full of *e* .... Eccl 9:3
who call *e* good and good *e*........ Isa 5:20
Your *e* is removed ....Isa 6:7
For *e* burned like a fire ....Isa 9:18
godly disappear because of *e*........Isa 57:1
purify your hearts from *e*...........Jer 4:14
regrets the *e* he has done...........Jer 8:6
Seek good and not *e*..............Amos 5:14
turn from their *e* way of living....Jonah 3:8
from your *e* wickedness............Zech 1:4
who practice *e* are successful.......Mal 3:15
rise on the *e* and the good........Matt 5:45
although you are *e*................. Matt 7:11
respond with *e* in your hearts ..... Matt 9:4
the *e* person brings *e* things ......Matt 12:35
An *e* and adulterous generation .. Matt 12:39
separate the *e* from the
    righteous.....................Matt 13:49
or *e*, to save a life or destroy it ....Mark 3:4
human heart, come *e* ideas.......Mark 7:21
greed, *e*, deceit, debauchery......Mark 7:22
out of his *e* treasury produces *e* .. Luke 6:45
although you are *e*................Luke 11:13
the *e* spirits went out of them ....Acts 19:12
You must not speak *e*..............Acts 23:5
I do the very *e* I do not want.......Rom 7:19
e is present with me................Rom 7:21
Abhor what is *e*....................Rom 12:9
Do not repay anyone *e* for *e* ......Rom 12:17
Do not be overcome by *e*......... Rom 12:21
good be spoken of as *e* ....Rom 14:16
good and innocent in what is *e* ...Rom 16:19
be infants in *e* ....1 Cor 14:20
whether good or *e*.................2 Cor 5:10
from this present *e* age..............Gal 1:4

forces of *e* in the heavens . . . . .Eph 6:12
stand your ground on the *e* day . . . .Eph 6:13
away from every form of *e* . . . . .1 Thess 5:22
but have delighted in *e* . . . . .2 Thess 2:12
spending our lives in e . . . . Titus 3:3
that none of you has an *e* . . . . .Heb 3:12
God cannot be tempted by *e* . . . . Jas 1:13
put away all filth and *e* excess . . . . Jas 1:21
get rid of all *e* and all deceit . . . . .1 Pet 2:1
freedom as a pretext for *e* . . . . .1 Pet 2:16
must keep his tongue from *e* . . . . . .1 Pet 3:10
is against those who do *e* . . . . .1 Pet 3:12

EVIL MERODACH
Babylonian king (562–560 BC),
  2 Kgs 25:27-30

EVIL ONE
More than this is from the *e* . . . . . . Matt 5:37
but deliver us from the *e* . . . . .Matt 6:13
keep them safe from the *e* . . . . John 17:15
and protect you from the *e* . . . . . .2 Thess 3:3

EVILDOER
God says this to the *e* . . . . .Ps 50:16
do not resist the *e* . . . . Matt 5:39
e must continue to do evil . . . . Rev 22:11

EVILDOERS
and all the *e* glisten . . . . .Ps 92:7
all the *e* boast . . . . .Ps 94:4
the arrogant *e* will be chaff . . . . Mal 4:1
Go away from me, all you *e* . . . . . .Luke 13:27

EVILS
love of money is the root of all *e* . .1 Tim 6:10

EXACTLY
e three years Moab's splendor . . . . . .Isa 16:14

EXAGGERATE
e he has saddened all of you . . . . . . .2 Cor 2:5

EXALT
and I will *e* him .Exod 15:2
Why then do you *e* yourselves . . . . .Num 16:3
e the power of his anointed one . .1 Sam 2:10
E the one who rides on . . . . .Ps 68:4
them *e* him in the assembly . . . . . . .Ps 107:32
her highly and she will *e* you . . . . . .Prov 4:8
I will *e* you in praise . . . . .Isa 25:1
E the lowly . . . . .Ezek 21:26
the Lord and he will *e* you . . . . .Jas 4:10
God will *e* you in due time . . . . .1 Pet 5:6

EXALTED
who delivers me is *e* as king . . . .2 Sam 22:47
They are *e* for a little while . . . . . . .Job 24:24
Indeed, God is *e* in his power . . . . . .Job 36:22
he thunders with an *e* voice . . . . .Job 37:4
who delivers me is *e* as king . . . . . . .Ps 18:46
I will be *e* over the nations . . . . .Ps 46:10
for you have *e* your promise . . . . . . .Ps 138:2
Though the LORD is *e* . . . . .Ps 138:6
for his name alone is *e* . . . . .Ps 148:13
A city is *e* by the blessing . . . . .Prov 11:11
LORD alone will be *e* in that day . . . . . Isa 2:11
The LORD is *e* . . . . .Isa 33:5
what the high and *e* one says . . . . . .Isa 57:15
bring low the *e* . . . . .Ezek 21:26
humbles himself will be *e* . . . . . . .Matt 23:12
God *e* him to his right hand . . . . Acts 5:31
Christ will be *e* in my body . . . . .Phil 1:20
As a result God highly *e* him . . . . . . .Phil 2:9

EXALTS
brings one down and *e* another . . . . . Ps 75:7
he *e* the oppressed . . . . .Ps 149:4
Righteousness *e* a nation . . . . .Prov 14:34
My soul *e* the Lord . . . . .Luke 1:46
e himself will be humbled . . . . Luke 14:11
He opposes and *e* himself . . . . . . .2 Thess 2:4

EXAMINE
e inner thoughts and motives . . . . .Ps 7:9
his eyes *e* all people . . . . .Ps 11:4
E me, O LORD . . . . .Ps 26:2
you *e* me and know me . . . . .Ps 139:1
e people's hearts and minds . . . . . . .Jer 11:20
person should *e* himself first . . . . .1 Cor 11:28

are in the faith; *e* yourselves . . . . . .2 Cor 13:5
Let each one *e* his own work . . . . .Gal 6:4
But *e* all things . . . . .1 Thess 5:21

EXAMINES
for the LORD *e* all minds . . . . .1 Chr 28:9

EXAMINING
e the scriptures carefully . . . . .Acts 17:11

EXAMPLE
For I have given you an *e* . . . . John 13:15
just as you have us as an *e* . . . . Phil 3:17
became an *e* to all the believers . .1 Thess 1:7
as an *e* for you to imitate . . . . .2 Thess 3:9
but set an *e* for the believers . . . . .1 Tim 4:12
leaving an *e* for you to follow . . . . .1 Pet 2:21
as an *e* to future generations . . . . . .2 Pet 2:6
are now displayed as an *e* . . . . .Jude 1:7

EXAMPLES
things happened to them as *e* . . . . .1 Cor 10:11
but be *e* to the flock . . . . .1 Pet 5:3

EXCELLENCE
by his own glory and *e* . . . . .2 Pet 1:3
effort to add to your faith *e* . . . . .2 Pet 1:5

EXCELLENCY
with majesty and *e* . . . . .Job 40:10

EXCELLENT
for I will speak *e* things . . . . .Prov 8:6
most *e* Festus .Acts 26:25
something is *e* or praiseworthy . . . . . Phil 4:8

EXCESSIVE
the kisses of an enemy are *e* . . . . . . .Prov 27:6

EXCHANGE
a person give in *e* for his life . . . . . Matt 16:26

EXCHANGED
e the glory of the immortal God . . .Rom 1:23
They *e* the truth of God . . . . .Rom 1:25
e the natural sexual relations . . . . . .Rom 1:26

EXCLUDE
when they *e* you and insult you . . . Luke 6:22
they want to *e* you . . . . .Gal 4:17

EXCREMENT
the Lord will wash the *e* . . . . Isa 4:4

EXCUSE
looking for an *e* to fight me . . . . .2 Kgs 5:7
have any *e* for their sin . . . . John 15:22
So people are without *e* . . . . .Rom 1:20
Therefore you are without *e* . . . . . . .Rom 2:1

EXCUSES
they all began to make *e* . . . . .Luke 14:18

EXECUTE
he did not *e* their sons . . . . .2 Chr 25:4
provides the ability to *e* plans . . . . . .Isa 11:2
the Son authority to *e* judgment . . .John 5:27

EXECUTED
They *e* his miraculous signs . . . . . . .Ps 105:27

EXERCISE
E true judgment and show . . . . .Zech 7:9
the *e* of his immense strength . . . . . .Eph 1:19
physical *e* has some value . . . . .1 Tim 4:8
permitted to *e* ruling authority . . . . .Rev 13:5

EXERCISED
This power he *e* in Christ . . . . .Eph 1:20

EXERTION
depend on human desire or *e* . . . . .Rom 9:16

EXHAUSTED
security for the one who is *e* . . . . . .Isa 28:12

EXHAUSTING
much study is *e* to the body . . . . . . .Eccl 12:12

EXHIBITED
has *e* all kinds of good works . . . .1 Tim 5:10

EXHORT
Therefore I *e* you . . . . Rom 12:1
if it is exhortation, he must *e* . . . . . .Rom 12:8
and *e* them about these things . . . .1 Tim 6:2
e with complete patience . . . . .2 Tim 4:2
But *e* one another each day . . . . . . .Heb 3:13

EXHORTATION
message of *e* for the people . . . . . .Acts 13:15
to *e*, to teaching . . . . .1 Tim 4:13
he will be able to give *e* . . . . .Titus 1:9
with the sort of *e* or rebuke . . . . . .Titus 2:15
bear with my message of *e* . . . . . . .Heb 13:22

EXHORTED
the angel of the LORD *e* Joshua . . . .Zech 3:6

EXHORTING
teaching and *e* one another . . . . .Col 3:16

EXILE
an *e* from your own country . . . . .2 Sam 15:19
Judah has departed into *e* . . . . .Lam 1:3
he will not prolong your *e* . . . . .Lam 4:22
now be the first to go into *e* . . . . . . Amos 6:7

EXIST
to my God as long as I *e* . . . . .Ps 104:33
we live and move about and *e* . . . .Acts 17:28
the things that do not yet *e* . . . . . . .Rom 4:17
former things have ceased to *e* . . . .Rev 21:4

EXISTED
he *e* in the form of God . . . . .Phil 2:6
they *e* and were created . . . . .Rev 4:11

EXISTENCE
and they came into *e* . . . . .Ps 148:5
fire to the course of human *e* . . . . .Jas 3:6

EXOTIC
plants and plant *e* vines . . . . .Isa 17:10

EXPANSE
God made the *e* and separated . . . . . .Gen 1:7
brightness of the heavenly *e* . . . . . . .Dan 12:3

EXPECT
when you do not *e* him . . . . .Luke 12:40

EXPECTATION
a certain fearful *e* of judgment . . . Heb 10:27

EXPECTED
when I *e* light . . . . Job 30:26
You *e* a large harvest . . . . .Hag 1:9

EXPECTING
e to receive something . . . . .Acts 3:5

EXPENDED
I have *e* my energy . . . . .Isa 49:4

EXPENSIVE
gold or pearls or *e* clothing . . . . .1 Tim 2:9

EXPERIENCE
They *e* his favor .Ps 25:13
may *e* sorrow during the night . . . . . .Ps 30:5
e the joy of your deliverance . . . . .Ps 51:12
his command will not *e* harm . . . . Eccl 8:5
here who will not *e* death . . . . Mark 9:1
e death on behalf of everyone . . . . . .Heb 2:9

EXPERIENCED
had not *e* the earlier battles . . . . .Judg 3:2
I have *e* times of need . . . . .Phil 4:12
have *e* the Lord's kindness . . . . .1 Pet 2:3

EXPIRE
e as I came out of the womb . . . . . . .Job 3:11

EXPERTS IN THE LAW
the chief priests and *e* . . . . Matt 2:4
that of the *e* and the Pharisees . . .Matt 5:20
Then Pharisees and *e* came . . . . .Matt 15:1
do the *e* say that Elijah . . . . .Matt 17:10
But woe to you, *e* . . . . .Matt 23:13
Woe to you, *e* and . . . . .Matt 23:15
Woe to you, *e* . . . . Matt 23:23
Woe to you, *e* . . . . Matt 23:25
Woe to you, *e* . . . . Matt 23:27
Woe to you, *e* . . . . Matt 23:29
had authority, not like the *e* . . . . . . Mark 1:22
The Pharisees and *e* asked . . . . Mark 7:5
and *e* arguing with them . . . . Mark 9:14
and the *e* heard it . . . . .Mark 11:18
Watch out for the *e* . . . . .Mark 12:38
and their *e* complained . . . . .Luke 5:30

EXPLAIN
e to me how I have been . . . . .Job 6:24
E this parable to us . . . . Matt 15:15

EXPLAINED

But privately he *e* everything.....Mark 4:34
aside and *e* the way of God.......Acts 18:26

EXPLAINING

while he was *e* the scriptures....Luke 24:32

EXPLICITLY

Now the Spirit *e* says..............1 Tim 4:1

EXPLOIT

Do not *e* a poor person.......... Prov 22:22
e or mistreat resident foreigners ....Jer 22:3
and those who *e* workers............Mal 3:5
in their greed they will *e* you ...... 2 Pet 2:3

EXPLOITED

we may not be *e* by Satan ....2 Cor 2:11
we have *e* no one...................2 Cor 7:2

EXPLOITS

Come and witness God's *e*...........Ps 66:5

EXPOSE

not *e* your father's nakedness ...... Lev 18:7
Strip off your clothes and *e*......... Isa 32:11

EXPOSED

one who is left *e* on a tree.......Deut 21:23
so that its foundation is *e*.........Ezek 13:14
that their deeds will not be *e*..... John 3:20
e by the light are made visible......Eph 5:13
is naked and *e* to the eyes .... Heb 4:13
you were publicly *e* to abuse ..... Heb 10:33

EXPRESS

messengers to *e* his sympathy... 2 Sam 10:3

EXPRESSED

you have again *e* your concern .... Phil 4:10

EXTEND

E your loyal love.....................Ps 36:10
ready to *e* to her prosperity .... Isa 66:12

EXTENDED

so that your days may be *e*........Deut 5:16
e his message until midnight ......Acts 20:7
sword that *e* from the mouth....... Rev 19:21

EXTERNAL

Let your beauty not be *e* ....1 Pet 3:3

EXTINGUISH

that no one will be able to *e*.........Jer 4:4
or *e* a smoldering wick .... Matt 12:20
can *e* all the flaming arrows ....Eph 6:16
Do not *e* the Spirit............... 1 Thess 5:19

EXTINGUISHED

they were *e*........................Isa 43:17

EXTRAORDINARY

your deeds are *e*....................Ps 77:13
a Spirit that gives *e* wisdom .... Isa 11:2
an *e* spirit.........................Dan 5:12
the *e* power belongs to God.......2 Cor 4:7

EXTREME

in my state of *e* weariness......... Dan 9:21

EYE

e for *e*, tooth for tooth.......... Exod 21:24
she put on some *e* liner.......... 2 Kgs 9:30
but now my *e* has seen you........Job 42:5
protect the pupil of your *e*........... Ps 17:8
forms the human *e* not see..........Ps 94:9
who winks his *e* causes trouble...Prov 10:10
that hears and the *e* that sees ... Prov 20:12
The *e* that mocks at a father......Prov 30:17
The *e* is never satisfied ....Eccl 1:8
e has seen any God besides you .... Isa 64:4
touches the pupil of his *e*.......... Zech 2:8
your right *e* causes you to sin ..... Matt 5:29
An *e* for an *e* and a tooth .... Matt 5:38
The *e* is the lamp of the body..... Matt 6:22
the speck in your brother's *e*.......Matt 7:3
e is the lamp of your body........Luke 11:34
Things that no *e* has seen........... 1 Cor 2:9
Since I am not an *e* ....1 Cor 12:16
If the whole body were an *e* ......1 Cor 12:17
in the blinking of an *e*............. 1 Cor 15:52
and every *e* will see him.............. Rev 1:7

EYELIDS

or slumber to your *e*................Prov 6:4

EYES

your *e* will open .... Gen 3:5
Now Israel's *e* were failing........Gen 48:10
perceptive *e*, or discerning .... Deut 29:4
and thorns that blind your *e*...... Josh 23:13
open his *e* so he can see.......... 2 Kgs 6:17
God has enlightened our *e* ....Ezra 9:8
Do you have *e* of flesh..............Job 10:4
whom my own *e* will behold.......Job 19:27
I was *e* for the blind and..........Job 29:15
e gaze intently from a distance ....Job 39:29
e look for some unfortunate ....Ps 10:8
His *e* watch ....Ps 11:4
my *e* grow tired from looking ....Ps 69:3
see it with your very own *e*.........Ps 91:8
e, but cannot see ....Ps 115:5
Open my *e* so I can truly see ....Ps 119:18
as the *e* of servants look.......... Ps 123:2
I will not allow my *e* to sleep ....Ps 132:4
Your *e* saw me......................Ps 139:16
your *e* look directly in front .... Prov 4:25
haughty *e*, a lying tongue........Prov 6:17
e of the LORD are in every place ...Prov 15:3
e of a fool run to the ends ....Prov 17:24
Who has dullness of the *e* .... Prov 23:29
e of a person are never satisfied.. Prov 27:20
content with what the *e* can see.... Eccl 6:9
Your *e* are like doves .... Song 1:15
My *e* have seen the king..............Isa 6:5
ears deaf and their *e* blind............Isa 6:10
e of the blind will be able to see ... Isa 29:18
Open your *e* ....Isa 37:17
my *e* grow tired from looking ......Isa 38:14
see with their very own *e*.......... Isa 52:8
who have *e* but do not discern ......Jer 5:21
my *e* will overflow with tears....... Jer 13:17
were full of *e* all around .... Ezek 1:18
were full of *e* all around ....Ezek 10:12
They have *e* to see..................Ezek 12:2
horn that had *e* and a mouth ...... Dan 7:20
conspicuous horn between its *e*.... Dan 8:5
His *e* were like blazing torches ... Dan 10:6
And their *e* were opened........Matt 9:30
e are blessed because they see.. Matt 13:16
e and be thrown into fiery hell ....Matt 18:9
could not keep their *e* open ..... Matt 26:43
two *e* and be thrown into hell ....Mark 9:47
and it is marvelous in our *e*.......Mark 12:11
mud on my *e* and I washed ....John 9:15
and they have closed their *e*......Acts 28:27
e that would not see................ Rom 11:8
have pulled out your *e* .... Gal 4:15
since the *e* of your heart............ Eph 1:18
what we have seen with our *e*..... 1 John 1:1
and the desire of the *e*............1 John 2:16
his *e* were like a fiery flame .... Rev 1:14
put on your *e* so you can see ......Rev 3:18
four living creatures full of *e* ...... Rev 4:6
had seven horns and seven *e*.......Rev 5:6
away every tear from their *e* ....Rev 21:4

EYEWITNESSES

by those who were *e* ....Luke 1:2
we were *e* of his grandeur.........2 Pet 1:16

EZEKIEL

Sent to rebellious Israel, Ezek 2–3
Prophesies by symbolic action:
   siege of Jerusalem, Ezek 4
   destruction of Jerusalem, Ezek 5
   captivity of Judah, Ezek 12:1–20
   destruction of the temple, Ezek 24:15–27
Visions of:
   God's glory, Ezek 1:4–28
   abominations, Ezek 8:5–18
   valley of dry bones, Ezek 37:1–14
   messianic times, Ezek 40–48
   river of life, Ezek 47:1–5
Parables, allegories, dirges of, Ezek 15–17;
   19; 23–24

EZION GEBER

Town on the Red Sea, 1 Kgs 9:26
Israelite encampment, Num 33:35
Seaport of Israel's navy, 1 Kgs 22:48

EZRA

Scribe, priest, and reformer of postexilic
   times; commissioned by Artaxerxes,
   Ezra 7
Returns with exiles to Jerusalem, Ezra 8
Institutes reforms, Ezra 9
Reads the Law, Neh 8
Assists in dedication of wall, Neh 12:27–43

F

FABLES

not follow cleverly concocted *f*....2 Pet 1:16

FACE

See also FACE TO FACE
I have seen God *f* to *f*.............Gen 32:30
you will not see my *f* again......Gen 44:23
Joseph hugged his father's *f* ...... Gen 50:1
would speak to Moses *f* to *f*......Exod 33:11
that the skin of his *f* shone ......Exod 34:29
he would put a veil on his *f* ......Exod 34:33
LORD make his *f* to shine .... Num 6:25
and hide my *f* from them......... Deut 31:17
he covered his *f* with his robe ....1 Kgs 19:13
He turned his *f* to the wall....... 2 Kgs 20:2
no doubt curse you to your *f* .... Job 1:11
will lift up your *f* toward God......Job 22:26
the light of my *f* to darken........Job 29:24
he sees God's *f* with rejoicing......Job 33:26
I am innocent I will see your *f* ....Ps 17:15
the *f* is reflected as a *f*...........Prov 27:19
away the tears from every *f* .... Isa 25:8
I have made your *f* adamant........Ezek 3:8
ruler on the side of his *f* .... Mic 5:1
His *f* shone like the sun........... Matt 17:2
of his *f* was transformed.......... Luke 9:29
f was like the *f* of an angel....... Acts 6:15
but then we will see *f* to *f*........1 Cor 13:12
eyes fixed on the *f* of Moses.......2 Cor 3:7
if someone strikes you in the *f* .. 2 Cor 11:20
I opposed him to his *f* ....Gal 2:11
gazes at his own *f* in a mirror.......Jas 1:23
Lord's *f* is against those.............1 Pet 3:12
They will *f* a reckoning ....1 Pet 4:5
His *f* shone like the sun............. Rev 1:16
creature had a *f* like a man's.........Rev 4:7
and they will see his *f*.............. Rev 22:4

FACE TO FACE

I have seen God *f*...................Gen 32:30
would speak to Moses *f* ....Exod 33:11
With him I will speak *f*...............Num 12:8
The LORD spoke *f* with you....... Deut 5:4
who knew the LORD *f*.......... Deut 34:10
into judgement with you *f*......Ezek 20:35
but then we will see *f*..............1 Cor 13:12

FACED

the gate that *f* toward the east ....Ezek 43:1

FACES

do not let your *f* be ashamed........Ps 34:5
people hid their *f* from him..........Isa 53:3
do their *f* turn so deathly pale ..... Jer 30:6
each had four *f* and four wings .....Ezek 1:6
All their *f* turn pale with fright......Joel 2:6
they make their *f* unattractive....Matt 6:16
f reflecting the glory..............2 Cor 3:18
down with their *f* to the ground .... Rev 7:11

FACTIONS

selfish rivalries, dissensions, *f* ....Gal 5:20

FADING

My strength is *f*....................Ps 143:7

FAIL

He will not *f* you or abandon ......Deut 31:6
will not *f* to have a successor...... 1 Kgs 2:4
will never *f* to have a successor...1 Kgs 8:25
will not *f* to have a successor..... 2 Chr 7:18
But the eyes of the wicked *f*........ Job 11:20
At dawn he appears without *f*..... Zeph 3:5
that your faith may not *f* .... Luke 22:32
For time will *f* me..................Heb 11:32

FAILED

My kinsmen have *f* me .... Job 19:14
I have not *f* to tell about........... Ps 40:10
Has his promise *f* forever........... Ps 77:8

FAILS

strength *f* me because of my sin.... Ps 31:10
so my strength *f* me .... Ps 40:12
and every vision *f*................. Ezek 12:22
f in one point has become guilty .... Jas 2:10

FAILURES

Today I recall my *f*................. Gen 41:9

FAINT

the souls of those who are *f*........ Jer 31:25
children and infants *f*............... Lam 2:11
They *f* like a wounded warrior...... Lam 2:12

FAINTED

they *f* from exhaustion .... Ps 107:5

FAINTING

People will be *f* from fear .... Luke 21:26

FAIR

his breath the skies became *f*...... Job 26:13
The LORD is both kind and *f*......... Ps 25:8
and everything he does is *f*.......... Ps 33:4
LORD, you have always been *f*....... Jer 12:1
It will be *f* weather .... Matt 16:2

FAIR HAVENS

Harbor of Crete at which Paul landed,
   Acts 27:8

FAIRLY

judge your fellow citizen *f*......... Lev 19:15
He will treat the poor *f*............. Isa 11:4

FAIRNESS

your *f* like the deepest sea.......... Ps 36:6
The heavens declare his *f*.......... Ps 50:6
f resided in her .... Isa 1:21
f the plumb line .... Isa 28:17
F will produce peace................ Isa 32:17
slaves with justice and *f*............ Col 4:1

FAITH

he has no *f* in his life................ Job 24:22
people who maintain their *f*........ Isa 26:3
of the flock who kept *f* with me ... Zech 11:11
you people of little *f*................ Matt 6:30
not found such *f* in anyone .... Matt 8:10
Your *f* has made you well.......... Matt 9:22
You of little *f* .... Matt 14:31
your *f* is great...................... Matt 15:28
f the size of a mustard seed ..... Matt 17:20
Do you still not have *f*............ Mark 4:40
Have *f* in God...................... Mark 11:22
in Israel have I found such *f* .... Luke 7:9
you people of little *f*.............. Luke 12:28
Increase our *f*.....................Luke 17:5
will he find *f* on earth............. Luke 18:8
basis of *f* in Jesus' name .... Acts 3:16
full of *f* and of the Holy Spirit....... Acts 6:5
full of the Holy Spirit and of *f*..... Acts 11:24
saw he had *f* to be healed .... Acts 14:9
being strengthened in the *f*....... Acts 16:5
who are sanctified by *f* in me..... Acts 26:18
bring about the obedience of *f* .... Rom 1:5
because your *f* is proclaimed ...... Rom 1:8
in the gospel from *f* to *f* .... Rom 1:17
is declared righteous by *f*......... Rom 3:28
f is credited as righteousness....... Rom 4:5
that he had by *f* while he was...... Rom 4:11
f is empty and the promise .... Rom 4:14
For this reason it is by *f*........... Rom 4:16
Without being weak in *f*........... Rom 4:19
been declared righteous by *f*....... Rom 5:1
righteousness that is by *f* says..... Rom 10:6
the word of *f* that we preach..... Rom 10:8
f comes from what is heard ...... Rom 10:17
but you stand by *f* .... Rom 11:20
to each of you a measure of *f*...... Rom 12:3
use it in proportion to his *f*....... Rom 12:6
The *f* you have.....................Rom 14:22
he does not do so from *f*........ Rom 14:23
f would not be based on human... 1 Cor 2:5
f so that I can remove mountains ..1 Cor 13:2

f, hope, and love................... 1 Cor 13:13
is futile and your *f* is empty....... 1 Cor 15:14
stand firm in the *f* .... 1 Cor 16:13
for we live by *f*..................... 2 Cor 5:7
as your *f* continues to grow ..... 2 Cor 10:15
the *f* he once tried to destroy....... Gal 1:23
righteous one will live by *f* .... Gal 3:11
But the law is not based on *f* ...... Gal 3:12
promise of the Spirit by *f*......... Gal 3:14
before *f* came we were held....... Gal 3:23
But now that *f* has come......... Gal 3:25
is *f* working through love........... Gal 5:6
belong to the family of *f*........... Gal 6:10
you are saved through *f*........... Eph 2:8
one *f*, one baptism................. Eph 4:5
attain to the unity of the *f*......... Eph 4:13
by taking up the shield of *f*....... Eph 6:16
for the *f* of the gospel .... Phil 1:27
and firm in your *f*................... Col 2:7
your work produced by *f*......... 1 Thess 1:3
putting on the breastplate of *f*... 1 Thess 5:8
and every work of *f*.............. 2 Thess 1:11
by the Spirit and *f* in the truth .. 2 Thess 2:13
For not all have *f* .... 2 Thess 3:2
my genuine child in the *f*........... 1 Tim 1:2
plan that operates by *f* .... 1 Tim 1:4
you must hold firmly to *f*.......... 1 Tim 1:19
if she continues in *f* and love .... 1 Tim 2:15
holding to the mystery of the *f*.... 1 Tim 3:9
the *f* that is in Christ Jesus......... 1 Tim 3:13
he has denied the *f*................. 1 Tim 5:8
Compete well for the *f* .... 1 Tim 6:12
I have kept the *f* .... 2 Tim 4:7
genuine son in a common *f*......... Titus 1:4
self-controlled, sound in *f* .... Titus 2:2
but showing all good *f*............. Titus 2:10
with those who heard it in *f* .... Heb 4:2
from dead works and *f* in God...... Heb 6:1
through *f* and perseverance .... Heb 6:12
in the assurance that *f* brings..... Heb 10:22
righteous one will live by *f* ...... Heb 10:38
f is being sure of what we hope ... Heb 11:1
without *f* it is impossible .... Heb 11:6
These all died in *f*.................. Heb 11:13
were commended for their *f* ...... Heb 11:39
pioneer and perfecter of our *f*..... Heb 12:2
and imitate their *f*.................. Heb 13:7
of your *f* produces endurance .... Jas 1:3
ask in *f* without doubting .... Jas 1:6
if someone claims to have *f*........ Jas 2:14
You have *f* and I have works....... Jas 2:18
that *f* without works is useless ..... Jas 2:20
justified by works and not by *f* ..... Jas 2:24
And the prayer of *f* will save........ Jas 5:15
the proven character of your *f*...... 1 Pet 1:7
attaining the goal of your *f*........ 1 Pet 1:9
strong in your *f*..................... 1 Pet 5:9
to add to your *f* excellence .... 2 Pet 1:5
up in your most holy *f*............. Jude 1:20
your love, *f*, service................. Rev 2:19
steadfast endurance and *f*......... Rev 13:10
and hold to their *f* in Jesus........ Rev 14:12

FAITHFUL

he is *f* in all my house .... Num 12:7
who remained *f* to the LORD....... Deut 4:4
the *f* God who keeps covenant .... Deut 7:9
raise up for myself a *f* priest..... 1 Sam 2:35
good and right and *f*.............. 2 Chr 31:20
his heart was *f* toward you .... Neh 9:8
to be loyal to one who is *f*.......... Ps 18:25
true God acts in a *f* manner .... Ps 18:30
Because you are *f* to me............ Ps 25:7
not committed and *f* to God........ Ps 78:8
he is *f* through all generations...... Ps 100:5
f witness tells what is right .... Prov 12:17
exhibit *f* covenant love .... Prov 14:22
but a *f* person.................... Prov 20:6
f person will have an
   abundance.................... Prov 28:20
because of the *f* LORD .... Isa 49:7
I have continued to be *f* to you .... Jer 31:3
LORD be a true and *f* witness ...... Jer 42:5
he remains *f* to the Holy One...... Hos 11:12
Who then is the *f* and wise ...... Matt 24:45

good and *f* slave .... Matt 25:23
Who then is the *f* and wise ...... Luke 12:42
one who is *f* in a very little .... Luke 16:10
f, by whom you were called .... 1 Cor 1:9
stewards is that one be found *f*.... 1 Cor 4:2
my dear and *f* son in the Lord ..... 1 Cor 4:17
And God is *f*..................... 1 Cor 10:13
But as God is *f*................... 2 Cor 1:18
and *f* servant in the Lord .... Eph 6:21
f brothers and sisters in Christ ...... Col 1:2
because he considered me *f*....... 1 Tim 1:12
f in every respect.................. 1 Tim 3:11
entrust to *f* people .... 2 Tim 2:2
a merciful and *f* high priest........ Heb 2:17
f to the one who appointed......... Heb 3:2
Moses was *f* in all God's house .... Heb 3:5
he is *f* and righteous.............. 1 John 1:9
f even to the point of death .... Rev 2:10

FAITHFULLY

serve him *f* with all your heart ..1 Sam 12:24
they *f* consecrated themselves .. 2 Chr 31:18
I have served you *f* .... Isa 38:3

FAITHFULNESS

and showing covenant *f* ....Exod 20:6
But I trust in your *f*................ Ps 13:5
he demonstrated his amazing *f*......Ps 31:21
your *f* to the clouds............... Ps 36:5
love and *f* continually protect ..... Ps 40:11
F grows from the ground.......... Ps 85:11
I will proclaim your *f* .... Ps 89:1
in the skies you set up your *f*........ Ps 89:2
Your *f* surrounds you............... Ps 89:8
f is like a shield or a protective ...... Ps 91:4
and your *f* during the night......... Ps 92:2
and his *f* endures forever........... Ps 111:3
and the LORD's *f* endures.......... Ps 117:2
your *f* to all generations........... Ps 119:90
Because of your *f* and justice...... Ps 143:1
your *f* is abundant .... Lam 3:23
there is neither *f* nor loyalty......... Hos 4:1
For your *f* is as fleeting .... Hos 6:4
For I delight in *f*.................... Hos 6:6
love *f*, and to live obediently........ Mic 6:8
will live because of his *f* .... Hab 2:4
will not nullify God's *f*.............. Rom 3:3
through the *f* of Jesus Christ....... Rom 3:22
but by the *f* of Jesus Christ .... Gal 2:16
of the *f* of the Son of God .... Gal 2:20
patience, kindness, goodness, *f*.... Gal 5:22
conduct, love, *f*, and purity .... 1 Tim 4:12
godliness, *f*, love, endurance....... 1 Tim 6:11

FALL

man to *f* into a deep sleep.......... Gen 2:21
they stumble and *f* .... Ps 27:2
a thousand may *f* beside you .... Ps 91:7
wicked *f* into their own nets....... Ps 141:10
The LORD supports all who *f* ...... Ps 145:14
f through their own wickedness... Prov 11:5
who trusts in his riches will *f*...... Prov 11:28
and a haughty spirit before a *f*.... Prov 16:18
righteous person will *f* seven......Prov 24:16
one who digs a pit will *f* into it... Prov 26:27
For if they *f*....................... Eccl 4:10
You will stumble and *f*............ Jer 50:32
suddenly Babylonia will *f*........... Jer 51:8
both will *f* into a pit.............. Matt 15:14
dogs eat the crumbs that *f* ....Matt 15:27
the stars will *f* from heaven .....Matt 24:29
you will not *f* into temptation ... Matt 26:41
I saw Satan *f* like lightning........ Luke 10:18
f by the edge of the sword........ Luke 21:24
shadow would *f* on some......... Acts 5:15
f short of the glory of God........ Rom 3:23
a rock that will make them *f*...... Rom 9:33
stumble into an irrevocable *f*...... Rom 11:11
be careful that he does not *f*...... 1 Cor 10:12
and *f* into the punishment......... 1 Tim 3:6
f into the hands of the living God. Heb 10:31
F on us and hide us................Rev 6:16

FALLEN

fire of God has *f* from heaven .... Job 1:16
how you have *f* from the sky .... Isa 14:12
Babylon has *f*.....................Isa 21:9

who insult you have *f* on me........Rom 15:3
f from the sky to the earth..........Rev 9:1
F, f is Babylon the great city........Rev 14:8

FALLING
cause of the *f* and rising of many..Luke 2:34
drops of blood *f* to the ground..Luke 22:44
who is able to keep you from *f*....Jude 1:24

FALLS
there is no guidance a nation *f*.....Prov 11:14
not rejoice when your enemy *f*...Prov 24:17
like a leaf withers and *f*...........Isa 34:4
not one of them *f* to the ground..Matt 10:29
The one who *f* on this stone...Matt 21:44
and a divided household *f*........Luke 11:17
wheat *f* into the ground and dies..John 12:24
his own master he stands or *f*.....Rom 14:4

FALSE
See also FALSE PROPHETS; FALSE
    WITNESS
You shall not give *f* testimony...Exod 20:16
You must not offer *f* testimony...Deut 5:20
a *f* witness who pours out lies.....Prov 6:19
those who bear *f* testimony........Isa 29:21
your confidence in the *f* belief........Jer 7:4
taking *f* oaths and making empty..Hos 10:4
Do not favor a *f* oath.............Zech 8:17
do not give *f* testimony.............Matt 19:18
f messiahs and *f* prophets.......Matt 24:24
many *f* witnesses came forward..Matt 26:60
f messiahs and *f* prophets.......Mark 13:22
to be *f* witnesses about God......1 Cor 15:15
in dangers from *f* brothers......2 Cor 11:26
f brothers with *f* pretenses..........Gal 2:4
no one who delights in *f* humility...Col 2:18
and signs and *f* wonders.........2 Thess 2:9
discovered that they are *f*..........Rev 2:2
of the mouth of the *f* prophet.....Rev 16:13

FALSE PROPHETS
Watch out for *f*.....................Matt 7:15
And many *f* will appear..........Matt 24:11
false messiahs and *f* will appear..Matt 24:24
false messiahs and *f* will appear..Mark 13:22
did the same things to the *f*......Luke 6:26
But *f* arose among the people......2 Pet 2:1
because many *f* have gone out....1 John 4:1

FALSE WITNESS
If a *f* testifies against.............Deut 19:16
a *f* who pours out lies..............Prov 6:19
but a *f* speaks deceit..............Prov 12:17
but a *f* breathes out lies...........Prov 14:5
A *f* will not go unpunished.........Prov 19:5
A *f* will not go unpunished.........Prov 19:9
against his neighbor as a *f*........Prov 25:18

FALSEHOOD
If I have walked in *f*................Job 31:5
Remove *f* and lies far from me...Prov 30:8
Therefore, having laid aside *f*......Eph 4:25
is detestable or practices *f*......Rev 21:27

FALSELY
and denies it and swears *f*.........Lev 6:3
swears *f* will suffer the same fate..Zech 5:3
about you *f* on account of me.....Matt 5:11

FAME
This city will bring me *f*............Jer 33:9
f spread among the nations......Ezek 16:14

FAMILIAR
and do not seek *f* spirits...........Lev 19:31
spirits of the dead and *f* spirits....Lev 20:6
especially *f* with all the customs...Acts 26:3

FAMILIES
so that all the *f* of the earth.......Gen 12:3
And so all the *f* of the earth......Gen 28:14
cared for his *f* like a flock..........Ps 107:41
the two *f* of Israel and Judah.......Jer 33:24
because they mislead whole *f*.....Titus 1:11

FAMILY
and they become one *f*...........Gen 2:24
and my *f* will worship the LORD..Josh 24:15
symbolizes the special chosen *f*.....Isa 6:13
the clan of the *f* of Nathan.......Zech 12:12

Joseph's *f* became known..........Acts 7:13
descendants of Abraham's *f*......Acts 13:26
he and all his *f* were baptized.....Acts 16:33
who belong to the *f* of faith........Gal 6:10
f in heaven and on earth............Eph 3:15
mercy to the *f* of Onesiphorus....2 Tim 1:16
for the deliverance of his *f*.........Heb 11:7

FAMINE
There was a *f* in the land.........Gen 12:10
There was a *f* in the land.........Gen 26:1
seven years of *f* will occur........Gen 41:30
the *f* was severe in the land......Gen 43:1
a *f* will overtake the land..........2 Kgs 8:1
In time of *f* he will redeem you.....Job 5:20
sustaining them during times of *f*.. Ps 33:19
called down a *f* upon the earth....Ps 105:16
f and sword.......................Isa 51:19
destructive arrows of *f*............Ezek 5:16
a severe *f* took place..........Luke 15:14
f occurred throughout Egypt.......Acts 7:11
or *f*, or nakedness.................Rom 8:35

FAMINES
there will be *f* and earthquakes...Matt 24:7

FAMOUS
heroes of old, the *f* men........Gen 6:4
became *f* throughout the land.....Josh 6:27

FAR
put my relatives *f* from me.........Job 19:13
Those *f* from you die...............Ps 73:27
As *f* as the eastern horizon is......Ps 103:12
The LORD is *f* from the wicked...Prov 15:29
Those both near and *f* from you.. Ezek 22:5
but their hearts are *f* from me.....Matt 15:8
he is not *f* from each one of us...Acts 17:27

FAREWELL
encouraging them and saying *f*....Acts 20:1

FARMER
The *f* who works hard.............2 Tim 2:6
Think of how the *f* waits..............Jas 5:7

FARMERS
Then he leased it to tenant *f*.....Matt 21:33
Then he leased it to tenant *f*......Mark 12:1
leased it to tenant *f*................Luke 20:9

FASHIONED
He *f* two bronze pillars.............1 Kgs 7:15

FAST
and *f* on my behalf................Esth 4:16
don't you notice when we *f*........Isa 58:3
Even if they *f*.....................Jer 14:12
to *f* in the LORD's temple...........Jer 36:6
Announce a holy *f*..................Joel 1:14
f runners will not save their lives..Amos 2:15
declared a *f* and put on sackcloth.. Jonah 3:5
When you *f*......................Matt 6:16
we and the Pharisees *f* often......Matt 9:14
wedding guests cannot *f*.........Mark 2:19
you hold *f* to human tradition.....Mark 7:8
I *f* twice a week...................Luke 18:12
let us hold *f* to our confession...Heb 4:14
Stand *f* in it......................1 Pet 5:12

FASTED
then they *f* for seven days.......1 Sam 31:13
prayed to God for the child and *f*..2 Sam 12:16
So we *f* and prayed to our God....Ezra 8:23
When you *f* and lamented.........Zech 7:5
he *f* 40 days and 40 nights........Matt 4:2
after they had *f* and prayed.......Acts 13:3

FASTENED
the peg *f* into a solid place.........Isa 22:25

FASTING
I continued *f* and praying...........Neh 1:4
this really the kind of *f* I want......Isa 58:5
with *f*, weeping, and mourning.....Joel 2:12
to others when you are *f*.........Matt 6:18
worshiping with *f* and prayer.....Luke 2:37

FAT
cows ate up the seven *f* cows.....Gen 41:20
the *f* belongs to the LORD..........Lev 3:16
Eglon was a very *f* man............Judg 3:17

FATE
what will be the *f* of those.........1 Pet 4:17

FATHER
See also FATHER IN HEAVEN; GOD THE
    FATHER; HEAVENLY FATHER
a man leaves his *f* and mother.....Gen 2:24
Ham, the *f* of Canaan............Gen 9:22
the *f* of a multitude of nations......Gen 17:4
Come, let's make our *f* drunk.....Gen 19:32
the blessing his *f* had given........Gen 27:41
the *f* of the Edomites.............Gen 36:43
saw that their *f* loved him more...Gen 37:4
So Joseph's *f* wept for him........Gen 37:35
Is your *f* still alive................Gen 43:7
tell my *f* about all my honor......Gen 45:13
Get your *f* and your households..Gen 45:18
the God of your *f*.................Gen 46:3
and went up to meet his *f*........Gen 46:29
Joseph went up to bury his *f*......Gen 50:7
Honor your *f* and your mother..Exod 20:12
Honor your *f* and your mother....Deut 5:16
no attention to his *f* or mother...Deut 21:18
Now he became the *f* of Jesse.....Ruth 4:17
I am a lot harsher than my *f*......1 Kgs 12:10
and I will become his *f*............1 Chr 22:10
and I will become his *f*...........1 Chr 28:6
You are my *f*.....................Job 17:14
I was a *f* to the needy............Job 29:16
if my *f* and mother abandoned.....Ps 27:10
He is a *f* to the fatherless...........Ps 68:5
As a *f* has compassion..............Ps 103:13
When I was a son to my *f*..........Prov 4:3
guard the commands of your *f*...Prov 6:20
wise child makes a *f* rejoice.......Prov 10:1
wise child brings joy to his *f*.....Prov 15:20
and the *f* of a fool has no joy......Prov 17:21
foolish child is a grief to his *f*......Prov 17:25
who curses his *f* and his mother..Prov 20:20
The *f* of a righteous person......Prov 23:24
loves wisdom brings joy to his *f*.. Prov 29:3
Everlasting *F*, Prince of Peace........Isa 9:6
The *f* of your nation sinned........Isa 43:27
For you are our *f*..................Isa 63:16
You are my *f*.........................Jer 3:4
because I am Israel's *f*.............Jer 31:9
A son naturally honors his *f*.........Mal 1:6
Do we not all have one *f*..........Mal 2:10
your *F*, who sees in secret........Matt 6:4
heavenly *F* will also forgive........Matt 6:14
your *F* will not forgive you........Matt 6:15
and your heavenly *F* knows......Matt 6:32
F in heaven give good gifts........Matt 7:11
loves *f* or mother more...........Matt 10:37
handed over to me by my *F*......Matt 11:27
Honor your *f* and mother........Matt 15:4
always see the face of my *F*......Matt 18:10
man will leave his *f* and mother...Matt 19:5
call no one your '*f* on earth......Matt 23:9
you who are blessed by my *F*....Matt 25:34
F, if this cup cannot be taken....Matt 26:42
F and the Son and the Holy Spirit...Matt 28:19
he comes in the glory of his *F*....Mark 8:38
man will leave his *f* and mother..Mark 10:7
nor the Son—except the *F*.......Mark 13:32
F, all things are possible.........Mark 14:36
f and I have been looking.........Luke 2:48
just as your *F* is merciful..........Luke 6:36
first let me go and bury my *f*......Luke 9:59
been given to me by my *F*.......Luke 10:22
What *f* among you.................Luke 11:11
more will the heavenly *F* give....Luke 11:13
f against son and son against *f*...Luke 12:53
not hate his own *f* and mother..Luke 14:26
go to my *f* and say to him........Luke 15:18
f—send Lazarus to my father's
    house................Luke 16:27
F, if you are willing..............Luke 22:42
F, forgive them...................Luke 23:34
who came from the *F*............John 1:14
The *F* loves the Son..............John 3:35
the *F* in spirit and truth...........John 4:23
My *F* is working until now........John 5:17
what he sees the *F* doing.........John 5:19
as the *F* raises the dead...........John 5:21

the *F* does not judge anyone ......John 5:22
just as they honor the *F* ....John 5:23
Everyone whom the *F* gives me ...John 6:37
Not that anyone has seen the *F* ..John 6:46
I testify about myself and the *F*....John 8:18
I speak just what the *F* taught ...John 8:28
are doing the deeds of your *f*.....John 8:41
are from your *f* the devil ....John 8:44
The *F* and I are one ....John 10:30
I am in the *F* and the *F* is in me...John 10:38
F, I thank you that you have ....John 11:41
F, glorify your name ....John 12:28
show us the *F*......................John 14:8
has seen me has seen the *F*........John 14:9
not believe that I am in the *F*.......John 14:10
because I am going to the *F* ......John 14:12
Then I will ask the *F* ....John 14:16
loves me will be loved by my *F*...John 14:21
glad that I am going to the *F*......John 14:28
and my *F* is the gardener..........John 15:1
you ask the *F* in my name ....John 15:16
you ask the *F* in my name ....John 16:23
I came from the *F* ....John 16:28
F, glorify me at your side ....John 17:5
I have not yet ascended to my *F*..John 20:17
of the Holy Spirit from the *F* ......Acts 2:33
the *F* of all those who believe......Rom 4:11
made you the *f* of many nations...Rom 4:17
by whom we cry, "Abba, *F*".....Rom 8:15
and *F* of our Lord Jesus Christ....Rom 15:6
and *F* of our Lord Jesus Christ .....2 Cor 1:3
and I will be a *f* to you ....2 Cor 6:18
access in one Spirit to the *F* ....Eph 2:18
I kneel before the *F*.................Eph 3:14
one God and *F* of all ....Eph 4:6
man will leave his *f* and mother ....Eph 5:31
glory be given to God our *F* ....Phil 4:20
as a *f* treats his own children ....1 Thess 2:11
but appeal to him as a *f*...........1 Tim 5:1
his *f* and he will be my son ....Heb 1:5
Without *f*, without mother ....Heb 7:3
that a *f* does not discipline ....Heb 12:7
down from the *F* of lights ....Jas 1:17
we bless the Lord and *F* ....Jas 3:9
And if you address as *F*............1 Pet 1:17
have an advocate with the *F*.......1 John 2:1
the love of the *F* is not in him ....1 John 2:15
sort of love the *F* has given........1 John 3:1
that the *F* has sent the Son ....1 John 4:14
declare his name before my *F*.......Rev 3:5

FATHER IN HEAVEN

and give honor to your *F* ....Matt 5:16
you may be like your *F* ....Matt 5:45
have no reward with your *F* ....Matt 6:1
Our *F*, may your name be ....Matt 6:9
will your *F* give good gifts ....Matt 7:11
who does the will of my *F* ....Matt 7:21
acknowledge before my *F* ....Matt 10:32
deny him also before my *F* ....Matt 10:33
does the will of my *F* ....Matt 12:50
reveal this to you, but my *F*.......Matt 16:17
always see the face of my *F* ......Matt 18:10
your *F* is not willing ....Matt 18:14
ask, my *F* will do it for you ....Matt 18:19
your *F* will also forgive ....Mark 11:25

FATHER'S

f attitude toward me has changed.. Gen 31:5
Joseph hugged his *f* face...........Gen 50:1
along with his *f* family ....Gen 50:22
I will praise him, my *f* God........Exod 15:2
to a *f* instruction....................Prov 4:1
wise son accepts his *f* discipline ...Prov 13:1
will not die for his *f* iniquity ......Ezek 18:17
will not suffer for his *f* iniquity ..Ezek 18:20
with you in my *F* kingdom.......Matt 26:29
I must be in my *F* house ....Luke 2:49
many of my *f* hired workers .....Luke 15:17
my *F* house a marketplace ......John 2:16
The deeds I do in my *F* name....John 10:25
dwelling places in my *F* house ...John 14:2
but the *F* who sent me ....John 14:24
cohabiting with his *f* wife........1 Cor 5:1

FATHERED

who loves has been *f* by God ..... 1 John 4:7
is the Christ has been *f* by God ....1 John 5:1
everyone *f* by God does not sin ..1 John 5:18

FATHERLESS

and your children will be *f*.......Exod 22:24
you deliver the *f* ....Ps 10:14
You defend the *f* and oppressed....Ps 10:18
He is a father to the *f* ....Ps 68:5
May his children be *f* ....Ps 109:9
He lifts up the *f* and the widow.....Ps 146:9
or take over the fields of the *f*....Prov 23:10

FATHERS

Bury me with my *f*................Gen 49:29
he swore to your *f* to give you.....Exod 13:5
to the transgression of *f*........Exod 20:5
for the sin of the *f* who reject...... Deut 5:9
be the LORD God of our *f*..........Ezra 7:27
whoever *f* a wise child...........Prov 23:24
generation who curse their *f* .....Prov 30:11
if a man *f* a hundred children...... Eccl 6:3
The *f* eat sour grape ....Ezek 18:2
when your *f* made me angry......Zech 8:14
f worshiped on this mountain ...John 4:20
you do not have many *f*.........1 Cor 4:15
our *f* were all under the cloud.....1 Cor 10:1
F, do not provoke your children .... Eph 6:4
F, do not provoke your children .... Col 3:21
There your *f* tested me .... Heb 3:9

FATTENED

father has killed the *f* calf ....Luke 15:27
You have *f* your hearts ....Jas 5:5

FAULT

f could your ancestors have ....Jer 2:5
go and show him his *f* ....Matt 18:15
Why does he still find *f*.............Rom 9:19
obey this command without *f* ....1 Tim 6:14

FAULT-FINDERS

people are grumblers and *f*.........Jude 1:16

FAULTLESS

that first covenant had been *f*...... Heb 8:7

FAVOR

But Noah found *f*...................Gen 6:8
So Joseph found *f*.................Gen 39:4
You gave me life and *f*............Job 10:12
you show *f* to your people............ Ps 3:8
protect them in your good *f*......... Ps 5:12
would experience the LORD's *f* ... Ps 27:13
his good *f* restores one's life..........Ps 30:5
How great is your *f* ....Ps 31:19
Because you *f* Zion ....Ps 51:18
never again show me his *f*...........Ps 77:7
LORD bestows *f* and honor ...... Ps 84:11
God extend his *f* to us ....Ps 90:17
you show *f* to your people...........Ps 106:4
find *f* and good understanding .....Prov 3:4
and received *f* from the LORD .... Prov 8:35
person obtains *f* from the
    LORD ....Prov 12:2
Keen insight wins *f* ....Prov 13:15
shows *f* to the needy ....Prov 14:31
and his *f* is like the clouds ....Prov 16:15
but his *f* is like dew ....Prov 19:12
f more than silver or gold ....Prov 22:1
of a wise person win him *f*.........Eccl 10:12
I decide to show my *f*...............Isa 49:8
my *f* and have compassion ....Isa 60:10
when the LORD will show his *f*.......Isa 61:2
and seek the LORD's *f*..............Jer 26:19
you have found *f* with God ....Luke 1:30
the *f* of God was upon him ....Luke 2:40
wisdom and in stature and in *f* ...Luke 2:52
the year of the Lord's *f*............Luke 4:19
granted him *f* and wisdom.........Acts 7:10
wanted to do the Jews a *f*.........Acts 24:27
For this finds God's *f*..............1 Pet 2:19
this finds *f* with God ....1 Pet 2:20

FAVORABLY

f to your servant's prayer...........1 Kgs 8:28
The LORD responded *f*..........2 Chr 30:20

FAVORED

be praised because he *f* you ....2 Chr 9:8
f one, the Lord is with you.........Luke 1:28

FAVORITISM

God shows no *f* between people ....Gal 2:6
without prejudice or *f* ....1 Tim 5:21

FEAR

See also DO NOT FEAR; FEAR THE LORD
F not, Abram ....Gen 15:1
for I *f* God ....Gen 42:18
saw it they trembled with *f*......Exod 20:18
and *f* my sanctuary ....Lev 19:30
do not *f* the people of the land ... Num 14:9
will do to all the people you *f*.....Deut 7:19
refuse to *f* this glorious..........Deut 28:58
Then *f* overwhelmed those ......1 Sam 14:15
houses are safe and without *f* ...... Job 21:9
laughs at *f* and is not dismayed....Job 39:22
I *f* no danger........................Ps 23:4
I *f* no one .... Ps 27:1
against me, I do not *f* .... Ps 27:3
Let the whole earth *f* the LORD......Ps 33:8
F the LORD........................Ps 34:9
He does not *f* God ....Ps 36:1
that do not normally cause *f* .....Ps 53:5
F and panic overpower me ....Ps 55:5
your enemies cower in *f*..........Ps 66:3
People will *f* you....................Ps 72:5
you will not be filled with *f* .... Prov 3:24
f of people becomes a snare...... Prov 29:25
so that men will *f* him ....Eccl 3:14
F God and keep his ....Eccl 12:13
I will trust in him and not *f*.........Isa 12:2
You should *f* me ....Jer 5:22
of the land shake with *f*............Joel 2:1
f the one who is able to destroy.. Matt 10:28
with *f* and trembling...............Mark 5:33
may serve him without *f*............Luke 1:74
F seized them all ....Luke 7:16
People will be fainting from *f*.... Luke 21:26
Don't you *f* God ....Luke 23:40
of slavery leading again to *f* ....Rom 8:15
we know the *f* of the Lord.........2 Cor 5:11
not give us a Spirit of *f* ....2 Tim 1:7
by their *f* of death .... Heb 2:15
tremble with *f* ....Jas 2:19
f God, honor the king..............1 Pet 2:17
do what is good and have no *f*......1 Pet 3:6
There is no *f* in love ....1 John 4:18
F God and give him glory..........Rev 14:7
and all you who *f* him..............Rev 19:5

FEAR OF THE LORD

The *f*—that is wisdom..............Job 28:28
The *f* is to hate evil ....Prov 8:13
f one has strong confidence ......Prov 14:26
f is like a life-giving fountain......Prov 14:27
Better is a little with the *f* .... Prov 15:16
f provides wise instruction ....Prov 15:33
Living in the *f*......................Acts 9:31
because we know the *f*............2 Cor 5:11

FEAR THE LORD

you do not yet *f* God ....Exod 9:30
thus learn about and *f*...........Deut 31:12
f and serve him faithfully ....1 Sam 12:24
Let the whole earth *f*..............Ps 33:8
f and turn away from evil..........Prov 3:7
since we did not *f*..................Hos 10:3

FEARED

But the midwives *f* God ....Exod 1:17
they *f* the LORD...................Exod 14:31
and *f* God more than many do...... Neh 7:2
f God nor respected people ....Luke 18:2

FEARFUL

f in praises.........................Exod 15:11

FEARING

f the LORD one avoids evil.........Prov 16:6
f the Lord.........................Col 3:22
without *f* the king's anger ....Heb 11:27

FEARS

f God and turns away from evil......Job 1:8
Is it for nothing that Job *f* God........Job 1:9

he delivered me from all my *f* ....Ps 34:4
his uprightness *f* the LORD.........Prov 14:2
A woman who *f* the LORD ....Prov 31:30
who *f* him and does what is right..Acts 10:35
The one who *f* punishment.......1 John 4:18

FEAST
See also FEAST OF HARVEST; FEAST OF
   INGATHERING; FEAST OF SHELTERS;
   FEAST OF THE DEDICATION; FEAST
   OF UNLEAVENED BREAD; FEAST OF
   WEEKS
He prepared a *f* for them...........Gen 19:3
the *F* of Unleavened Bread ....Exod 12:17
you must make a pilgrim *f*....... Exod 23:14
observe the *F* of Harvest .... Exod 23:16
observe the *F* of Weeks ....Exod 34:22
from the *F* of Passover ....Exod 34:25
is the *F* of Shelters................ Lev 23:34
You prepare a *f* before me...........Ps 23:5
go to a funeral than a *f* .... Eccl 7:2
As if it were a *f* day ....Lam 2:2
The *f* I have prepared for you..... Matt 22:4
Not during the *f* .... Mark 14:2
for the *F* of the Passover ....Luke 2:41
someone to a wedding *f*..........Luke 14:8
F of the Passover was near ....John 6:4
When the *f* was half over ....John 7:14
On the last day of the *f* ....John 7:37
Just before the Passover *F*..........John 13:1
or in the matter of a *f*............. Col 2:16

FEAST OF HARVEST
are also to observe the *F* .... Exod 23:16

FEAST OF INGATHERING
the *F* at the end of the year...... Exod 23:16
the *F* at the end of the year......Exod 34:22

FEAST OF SHELTERS
of this seventh month is the *F*.... Lev 23:34
You must celebrate the *F*.........Deut 16:13
Feast of Weeks, and the *F* ....Deut 16:16
cancellation of debts, at the *F* ....Deut 31:10
They observed the *F*................Ezra 3:4
and to observe the *F* ....Zech 14:16
Now the Jewish *F* was near ....John 7:2

FEAST OF THE DEDICATION
Then came the *f* in Jerusalem.....John 10:22

FEAST OF UNLEAVENED BREAD
So you will keep the *F*.............Exod 12:17
You are to observe the *F* .... Exod 23:15
You must keep the *F* ....Exod 34:18
in Jerusalem to observe the *F* ...2 Chr 30:13
They observed the *F*................Ezra 6:22
Now on the first day of the *F*...Matt 26:17
before the Passover and the *F*....Mark 14:1
F, which is called Passover ....Luke 22:1

FEAST OF WEEKS
You must observe the *F* ....Exod 34:22
to the LORD during your *F*.......Num 28:26
you are to celebrate the *F*........Deut 16:10

FEASTING
a house full of *f* with strife......... Prov 17:1

FEASTS
See also APPOINTED FEASTS
F are made for laughter ....Eccl 10:19
dangerous reefs at your love *f*......Jude 1:12

FEATURES
have in the law the essential *f* ....Rom 2:20

FED
bodies are strong and well *f*.........Ps 73:4
f themselves and did not feed ..... Ezek 34:8
he was *f* grass like oxen ....Dan 5:21
I *f* you milk ....1 Cor 3:2

FEED
you will *f* with joy................Isa 66:11
I myself will *f* my sheep ....Ezek 34:15
F my lambs......................John 21:15
F my sheep.....................John 21:17
f him; if he is thirsty ....Rom 12:20

FEEDING
f you with unfamiliar manna. ...... Deut 8:3

FEEDS
teaching of the righteous *f* ....Prov 10:21
Ephraim continually *f*..............Hos 12:1
your heavenly Father *f* them .....Matt 6:26
but he *f* it and takes care of it ..... Eph 5:29

FEELINGS
and my *f* were stirred for him ..... Song 5:4

FEET
See also UNDER HIS FEET
Take your sandals off your *f*....... Exod 3:5
linen, 150 *f* long for one side......Exod 27:9
your sandals from your *f* ....Josh 5:15
But both his *f* were crippled .... 2 Sam 9:13
covered and his *f* were bare ....2 Sam 15:30
my *f* do not slip..................2 Sam 22:37
for the blind and *f* for the lame....Job 29:15
they pin my hands and *f*...........Ps 22:16
their *f* do not slip ....Ps 37:31
He placed my *f* on a rock...........Ps 40:2
does not allow our *f* to slip ....Ps 66:9
my *f* almost slipped ....Ps 73:2
my *f* almost slid out ....Ps 73:2
and my *f* from stumbling ....Ps 116:8
Our *f* are standing ....Ps 122:2
Her *f* go down to death............Prov 5:5
f that are swift to run to evil.......Prov 6:18
soles of your *f* to your head ....Isa 1:6
with two they covered their *f*........Isa 6:2
take your sandals off your *f* ....Isa 20:2
will lick the dirt on your *f* .... Isa 49:23
f of a messenger who announces....Isa 52:7
its *f* were partly of iron .... Dan 2:33
his arms and *f* had the gleam .... Dan 10:6
billow like dust under his *f* ....Nah 1:3
On that day his *f* will stand .... Zech 14:4
shake the dust off your *f* ....Matt 10:14
to have two hands or two *f*.......Matt 18:8
he fell at his *f*....................Mark 5:22
and came and fell at his *f*.........Mark 7:25
lame than to have two *f* ....Mark 9:45
she stood behind him at his *f*..... Luke 7:38
sitting at Jesus' *f* ....Luke 8:35
who sat at the Lord's *f*...........Luke 10:39
and sandals on his *f*.............Luke 15:22
Look at my hands and my *f*.....Luke 24:39
began to wash the disciples' *f* ..... John 13:5
have washed your *f*................John 13:14
at the head and one at the *f* .....John 20:12
f and ankles were made strong.....Acts 3:7
placing them at the apostles' *f*.....Acts 4:35
Take the sandals off your *f* ....Acts 7:33
tied his own hands and *f*..........Acts 21:11
Their *f* are swift to shed blood ....Rom 3:15
in subjection under his *f*..........1 Cor 15:27
put all things under Christ's *f*.......Eph 1:22
fitting your *f* with the preparation..Eph 6:15
make straight paths for your *f*.....Heb 12:13
I fell down at his *f* .... Rev 1:17
I threw myself down at his *f*.......Rev 19:10

FELIX
Governor of Judea; letter addressed to,
   Acts 23:24–30
Paul's defense before, Acts 24:1–27

FELL
Saul took his sword and *f* on it ...1 Sam 31:4
Saul took the sword and *f* on it... 1 Chr 10:4
words *f* on them drop by drop ....Job 29:22
f into the furnace of blazing fire ... Dan 3:23
some seeds *f* along the path......Matt 13:4
But other seeds *f* on good soil.....Matt 13:8
he *f* at his feet ....Mark 5:22
and as they sailed he *f* asleep..... Luke 8:23
when the tower in Siloam *f*........Luke 13:4
f from the rich man's table ....Luke 16:21
f at his feet and said to him.......John 11:32
Then he *f* to his knees ....Acts 7:60
the Holy Spirit *f* on all those......Acts 10:44
he *f* down from the third story ... Acts 20:9
By faith the walls of Jericho *f*......Heb 11:30
stars in the sky *f* to the earth......Rev 6:13
like a torch *f* from the sky ....Rev 8:10

FELLING
As one of them was *f* a tree ....2 Kgs 6:5

FELLOW
found one of his *f* slaves......... Matt 18:28
he begins to beat his *f* slaves ....Matt 24:49
he is my partner and *f* worker....2 Cor 8:23
but you are *f* citizens ....Eph 2:19
the Gentiles are *f* heirs ....Eph 3:6
these are the only *f* workers........Col 4:11
I am only a *f* servant with you ......Rev 19:10

FELLOWSHIP
in closest *f* with the Father .... John 1:18
the apostles' teaching and to *f*.....Acts 2:42
called into *f* with his son............1 Cor 1:9
f does light have with darkness...2 Cor 6:14
and me the right hand of *f*..........Gal 2:9
any *f* in the Spirit ....Phil 2:1
that you may have *f* with us ....1 John 1:3
If we say we have *f* with him.......1 John 1:6
we have *f* with one another ....1 John 1:7

FELT
David *f* guilty after.............2 Sam 24:10

FEMALE
male and *f* he created them ....Gen 1:27
from all flesh, male and *f* ....Gen 6:19
and *f*, came into the ark .... Gen 7:9
for the male or the *f* child .... Lev 12:7
Creator made them male and *f*....Matt 19:4
there is neither male nor *f*.........Gal 3:28

FENCE
leaning wall or an unstable *f* ....Ps 62:3
soon *f* her in with thorns .... Hos 2:6
He put a *f* around it...............Mark 12:1

FERTILE
if I have been given *f* fields .... Ps 16:6
I brought you into a *f* land...........Jer 2:7

FERVENT
your love for one another *f*.........1 Pet 4:8

FESTIVAL
must keep a *f* to the LORD... Num 29:12
Josiah observed a Passover *f* ..... 2 Chr 35:1
full moon when our *f* begins .... Ps 81:3
when you are celebrating a *f* ......Isa 30:29

FESTIVALS
such as on your appointed *f* .... Num 10:10
I will turn your *f* into funerals ... Amos 8:10

FESTUS
Governor of Judea, Acts 24:27
Paul's defense made to, Acts 25:1–22

FEVER
consumption and *f* ....Lev 26:16
my body is hot with *f* ....Job 30:30
sick with a *f*......................Matt 8:14
Then the *f* left her ....Mark 1:31
commanded the *f*.................. Luke 4:39
suffering from *f* and dysentery ....Acts 28:8

FEW
years of my life have been *f* ....Gen 47:9
lives but a *f* days...................Job 14:1
May his days be *f* ....Ps 109:8
let your words be *f* ....Eccl 5:2
and there are *f* who find it.........Matt 7:14
but the workers are *f*............. Matt 9:37
will only a *f* be saved ....Luke 13:23
In the ark a *f*......................1 Pet 3:20

FIELD
See also FIELD OF BLOOD; POTTER'S
   FIELD
the living creatures of the *f*........Gen 2:20
like the scent of an open *f*........Gen 27:27
Like a flower in the *f*...............Ps 103:15
passed by the *f* of a sluggard ....Prov 24:30
considered a *f* and bought it......Prov 31:16
or a shelter in a cucumber *f* ....Isa 1:8
accumulate *f* after *f*.................Isa 5:8
are like the flowers in the *f*.........Isa 40:6
trees in the *f* will clap...............Isa 55:12
Buy that *f* with silver ....Jer 32:25
thrown out into the open *f* ....Ezek 16:5
Zion will be plowed up like a *f*.....Mic 3:12
how the flowers of the *f* grow ....Matt 6:28
The *f* is the world..................Matt 13:38

hidden in a *f* .... Matt 13:44
one in the *f* must not turn back .. Matt 24:18
f has been called the "F of Blood .. Matt 27:8
I have bought a *f* .... Luke 14:18
You are God's *f* .... 1 Cor 3:9

FIELD OF BLOOD [or HAKELDAMA]
A field bought as a cemetery for Judas'
    burial, Matt 27:1–10
Predicted in the OT, Zech 11:12–13
Also called "Hakeldama," Acts 1:19

FIELDS
gathered grain in the *f* .... Ruth 2:3
We are putting up our *f* .... Neh 5:3
and sends water on the *f* .... Job 5:10
f and everything in them .... Ps 96:12
take over the *f* of the fatherless .. Prov 23:10
and the *f* yield no crops .... Hab 3:17
Jesus went through the grain *f* ..... Matt 12:1
or children or *f* for my sake ..... Matt 19:29
was going through the grain *f* ...... Luke 6:1
f are already white for harvest ... John 4:35

FIERCE
The *f* anger of the LORD .... Jer 4:8
relent and turn from his *f* anger .. Jonah 3:9

FIERY
there was a *f* appearance .... Num 9:15
he gave a *f* law to them .... Deut 33:2
suddenly a *f* chariot .... 2 Kgs 2:11
burn them up like a *f* furnace .... Ps 21:9
says 'Fool' will be sent to *f* .... Matt 5:22
his eyes were like a *f* flame .... Rev 1:14
f red, came out .... Rev 6:4

FIFTEEN
and I stayed with him *f* days .... Gal 1:18

FIFTH
there was morning, a *f* day .... Gen 1:23
the Lamb opened the *f* seal .... Rev 6:9
the *f* angel poured out his bowl ... Rev 16:10

FIFTY
sit down in groups of about *f* ..... Luke 9:14
You are not yet *f* years old .... John 8:57

FIG
they sewed *f* leaves together .... Gen 3:7
f trees, and pomegranates .... Deut 8:8
of their vines and *f* trees .... 1 Kgs 4:25
like an early *f* before harvest ...... Isa 28:4
f withers and falls from a tree ..... Isa 34:4
the *f* tree and the vine yield .... Joel 2:22
When the *f* tree does not bud ...... Hab 3:17
noticing a *f* tree by the road ...... Matt 21:19
parable from the *f* tree .... Matt 24:32
looking for fruit on this *f* tree ..... Luke 13:7
f tree and all the other trees ..... Luke 21:29
I saw you under the *f* tree .... John 1:50

FIGHT
The LORD will *f* for you .... Exod 14:14
Must you *f* Baal's battles .... Judg 6:31
Act like men and *f* .... 1 Sam 4:9
Our God will *f* for us .... Neh 4:20
F for me against an ungodly .... Ps 43:1
you may *f* the good *f* .... 1 Tim 1:18
you quarrel and *f* .... Jas 4:2

FIGHTING
servants would be *f* to keep ...... John 18:36

FIGHTS
the LORD your God *f* for you ..... Josh 23:10
f the battles of the LORD .... 1 Sam 25:28

FIGMENT
this is a *f* of your imagination .... Neh 6:8

FIGS
The fig tree has ripened its *f* ...... Song 2:13
showed me two baskets of *f* .... Jer 24:1
from thorns or *f* from thistles ..... Matt 7:16
f are not gathered from thorns ... Luke 6:44
or a vine produce *f* .... Jas 3:12
fig tree dropping its unripe *f* ...... Rev 6:13

FILL
F the earth and subdue it .... Gen 1:28
and multiply and *f* the earth .... Gen 9:1

to *f* their bags with grain .... Gen 42:25
F four water jars and pour .... 1 Kgs 18:33
f your mouth with laughter .... Job 8:21
f my mouth with arguments .... Job 23:4
splendor *f* the whole earth .... Ps 72:19
that I may *f* their treasuries .... Prov 8:21
I will *f* this temple with glory .... Hag 2:7
F the water jars with water .... John 2:7
f you with all joy and peace .... Rom 15:13
in order to *f* all things .... Eph 4:10

FILLED
See also FILLED WITH THE HOLY SPIRIT
to the spring, *f* her jug .... Gen 24:16
and the glory of the LORD *f* .... Exod 40:34
earth will be *f* with the glory ..... Num 14:21
the LORD's glory *f* his temple ...... 1 Kgs 8:11
and they are *f* with food .... Ps 104:28
barns will be *f* completely .... Prov 3:10
f with wisdom .... Luke 2:40
They were *f* with awe............... Luke 5:26
they *f* them up to the very top ..... John 2:7
f 12 baskets with broken pieces.... John 6:13
your hearts are *f* with sadness..... John 16:6
were *f* with the Holy Spirit .... Acts 2:4
has Satan *f* your heart to lie .... Acts 5:3
They are *f* with every kind .... Rom 1:29
f with all knowledge .... Rom 15:14
but be *f* by the Spirit .... Eph 5:18
f with the fruit of righteousness .... Phil 1:11
and you have been *f* in him .... Col 2:10

FILLED WITH THE HOLY SPIRIT
be *f*, even before his birth .... Luke 1:15
and Elizabeth was *f* .... Luke 1:41
his father Zechariah was *f* .... Luke 1:67
All of them were *f* .... Acts 2:4
Then Peter, *f*, replied .... Acts 4:8
and they were all *f* .... Acts 4:31
you may see again and be *f* .... Acts 9:17
Saul (also known as Paul), *f* .... Acts 13:9

FILLS
who *f* his quiver with them .... Ps 127:5
splendor *f* the entire earth .... Isa 6:3
speaks from what *f* the heart.... Matt 12:34

FILTH
put away all *f* and evil excess .... Jas 1:21

FILTHINESS
end to the other with their *f* .... Ezra 9:11

FILTHY
Joshua was dressed in *f* clothes.... Zech 3:3
poor person enters in *f* clothes....... Jas 2:2
the one who is morally *f* .... Rev 22:11

FINAL
the time of *f* punishment .... Ezek 21:25

FIND
If I *f* in the city of Sodom .... Gen 18:26
but did not *f* the idols .... Gen 31:35
Can we *f* a man like Joseph .... Gen 41:38
wherever you can *f* it .... Exod 5:11
continue to *f* favor in your sight .. Exod 33:13
that your sin will *f* you out .... Num 32:23
you will *f* him .... Deut 4:29
Run, find the *f* the arrows ...... 1 Sam 20:36
Can you *f* out the perfection........ Job 11:7
I knew where I might *f* him .... Job 23:3
but they will not *f* me .... Prov 1:28
are life to those who *f* them .... Prov 4:22
seek me diligently will *f* me .... Prov 8:17
wisely in a matter will *f* success .. Prov 16:20
can *f* a wife of noble character ... Prov 31:10
and *f* enjoyment in all his toil....... Eccl 3:13
you *f* to do with your hands .... Eccl 9:10
If you *f* my beloved .... Song 5:8
you will *f* me available to you....... Jer 29:13
not *f* among the entire group .... Dan 1:19
were trying to *f* some pretext ...... Dan 6:4
When you *f* him .... Matt 2:8
seek and you will *f* .... Matt 7:7
and there are few who *f* it .... Matt 7:14
you will *f* a four-drachma coin.... Matt 17:27
you will *f* a colt tied there .... Mark 11:2

or else he might *f* you asleep .... Mark 13:36
You will *f* a baby wrapped .... Luke 2:12
and you will *f* .... Luke 11:9
you will *f* a colt tied there .... Luke 19:30
I *f* no basis for an accusation ..... Luke 23:4
look for me but will not *f* me ...... John 7:34
did not *f* them in the prison .... Acts 5:22
I *f* the law that when I want....... Rom 7:21
to receive mercy and *f* grace ...... Heb 4:16
but will not be able to *f* it .... Rev 9:6

FINDING
looking for rest but not *f* any .... Luke 11:24

FINDS
like one who *f* much plunder ..... Ps 119:162
one who *f* me has found life ..... Prov 8:35
and the one who seeks *f* .... Matt 7:8
Whoever *f* his life will lose it .... Matt 10:39
it *f* the house empty............. Matt 12:44
f at work when he comes........ Matt 24:46
and the one who seeks *f* .... Luke 11:10
search thoroughly until she *f* it .... Luke 15:8

FINE
thin cows ate the seven *f* .... Gen 41:4
a covering of *f* leather .... Exod 26:14
I grind them as *f* as the dust.... 2 Sam 22:43
f timber and precious gems ...... 2 Chr 9:10
and an ornament of *f* gold........ Prov 25:12
clothing was *f* linen and purple... Prov 31:22
wearing a gold ring and *f* clothing.... Jas 2:2
dressed in bright, clean, *f* linen ..... Rev 19:8

FINGER
written by the *f* of God .... Exod 31:18
written by the very *f* of God ...... Deut 9:10
not willing even to lift a *f* .... Matt 23:4
cast out demons by the *f* of God.. Luke 11:20
to dip the tip of his *f* in water.... Luke 16:24
wrote on the ground with his *f* ..... John 8:6
Put your *f* here .... John 20:27

FINGERS
which your *f* made.................... Ps 8:3
and points with his *f*............... Prov 6:13
their own *f* have fashioned .... Isa 2:8
pointing *f* and speaking sinfully .... Isa 58:9
the *f* of a human hand appeared.... Dan 5:5
he put his *f* in the man's ears ..... Mark 7:33

FINISH
f my task and the ministry........ Acts 20:24

FINISHED
seventh day God *f* the work .... Gen 2:2
Moses *f* writing on a scroll ...... Deut 31:24
So they *f* dividing up the land...... Josh 19:51
f constructing the LORD's temple .. 1 Kgs 7:51
Jesus *f* saying these things........ Matt 7:28
I have *f* the race .... 2 Tim 4:7
the one thousand years were *f* .... Rev 20:3

FIRE
LORD rained down sulfur and *f* ... Gen 19:24
flame of *f* from within a bush...... Exod 3:2
nor the pillar of *f* by night .... Exod 13:22
LORD had descended on it in *f*....Exod 19:18
and burned it in the *f*............. Exod 32:20
but *f* would be on it at night..... Exod 40:38
took his *f* pan and put *f* in it .... Lev 10:1
and the *f* died out................. Num 11:2
speak from the middle of the *f* ... Deut 5:24
The god who responds with *f* .... 1 Kgs 18:24
Then *f* from the LORD fell .... 1 Kgs 18:38
there was a *f* .... 1 Kgs 19:12
we passed through *f* and water..... Ps 66:12
They set your sanctuary on *f* ...... Ps 74:7
F goes before him .... Ps 97:3
the flaming *f* his attendant .... Ps 104:4
O *f* and hail .... Ps 148:8
For evil burned like a *f*............... Isa 9:18
the one whose *f* is in Zion .... Isa 31:9
When you walk through the *f* ...... Isa 43:2
a *f* that keeps burning all day....... Isa 65:5
like a flaming *f* against you.......... Jer 4:4
their sons and daughters by *f*........ Jer 7:31
was something like *f*................ Ezek 8:2

spoken in the *f* of my zeal .... Ezek 36:5
of a furnace of blazing *f* .... Dan 3:6
from the furnace of blazing *f* ....Dan 3:17
around in the midst of the *f* .... Dan 3:25
physically unharmed by the *f* .... Dan 3:27
he will break out like .... Amos 5:6
summoning a shower of *f* .... Amos 7:4
stick snatched from the *f* .... Zech 3:2
he will be like a refiner's *f* .... Mal 3:2
with the Holy Spirit and *f* .... Matt 3:11
burn up with inextinguishable *f* ... Matt 3:12
into the *f* to heat the oven .... Matt 6:30
for he often falls into the *f* .... Matt 17:15
eternal *f* that has been prepared .. Matt 25:41
come to bring *f* on the earth .... Luke 12:49
I am in anguish in this *f* .... Luke 16:24
tongues spreading out like a *f* ..... Acts 2:3
shook the creature off into the *f* .. Acts 28:5
With flaming *f* he will mete out .. 2 Thess 1:8
and his ministers a flame of *f* ...... Heb 1:7
to a burning *f* and darkness .... Heb 12:18
God is indeed a devouring *f* ...... Heb 12:29
And the tongue is a *f* .... Jas 3:6
be astonished that a trial by *f* ..... 1 Pet 4:12
the punishment of eternal *f* .... Jude 1:7
but *f* came down from heaven ..... Rev 20:9
were thrown into the lake of *f* .... Rev 20:14

FIREBRANDS
who shoots *f* and deadly arrows .. Prov 26:18

FIRM
and it stood *f* .... Ps 33:9
brothers and sisters, be *f* .... 1 Cor 15:58
stand *f* in the faith .... 1 Cor 16:13
because by faith you stand *f* ...... 2 Cor 1:24
Stand *f*, then .... Gal 5:1
Stand *f* therefore .... Eph 6:14
established and *f* .... Col 1:23
and *f* in your faith .... Col 2:7
if you stand *f* in the Lord .... 1 Thess 3:8
proved to be so *f* .... Heb 2:2
hold our initial confidence *f* .... Heb 3:14

FIRMLY
if you hold *f* to the message .... 1 Cor 15:2

FIRMNESS
the *f* of your faith in Christ .... Col 2:5

FIRS
f, and cypresses grow together ..... Isa 41:19

FIRST
marking the *f* day .... Gen 1:5
f of the firstfruits of your soil .... Exod 23:19
Give the *f* woman .... 1 Kgs 3:27
The *f* to state his case .... Prov 18:17
I am the *f* and I am the last .... Isa 44:6
F go and be reconciled .... Matt 5:24
F remove the beam .... Matt 7:5
he *f* ties up the strong man ...... Matt 12:29
is worse than the *f* .... Matt 12:45
many who are *f* will be last ...... Matt 19:30
and whoever wants to be *f* ..... Matt 20:27
f and greatest commandment ... Matt 22:38
f the stalk .... Mark 4:28
say that Elijah must come *f* .... Mark 9:11
and whoever wants to be *f* ...... Mark 10:44
F the gospel must be preached .. Mark 13:10
Early on the *f* day of the week .... Mark 16:9
f let me go and bury my father ... Luke 9:59
f he must suffer many things .... Luke 17:25
He *f* found his own brother .... John 1:41
the *f* of his miraculous signs ...... John 2:11
may be the *f* to throw a stone ..... John 8:7
disciples were *f* called Christians .. Acts 11:26
the Jew *f* and also the Greek .... Rom 2:9
Or who has *f* given to God .... Rom 11:35
in the church *f* apostles .... 1 Cor 12:28
The *f* man .... 1 Cor 15:45
the *f* to set our hope on Christ .... Eph 1:12
which is the *f* commandment .... Eph 6:2
may become *f* in all things .... Col 1:18
the dead in Christ will rise *f* .... 1 Thess 4:16
F of all, then, I urge .... 1 Tim 2:1
For Adam was formed *f* .... 1 Tim 2:13
f learn to fulfill their duty .... 1 Tim 5:4

f covenant had been faultless .... Heb 8:7
wisdom from above is *f* pure .... Jas 3:17
We love because he loved us *f* ... 1 John 4:19
who loves to be *f* among them ... 3 John 1:9
I am the *f* and the last .... Rev 1:17
have departed from your *f* love .... Rev 2:4
The *f* angel blew his trumpet .... Rev 8:7
This is the *f* resurrection .... Rev 20:5
for the *f* heaven and earth .... Rev 21:1

FIRST AND THE LAST
Do not be afraid! I am the *f* .... Rev 1:17
the *f*, the one who was dead .... Rev 2:8
the Alpha and Omega, the *f* ...... Rev 22:13

FIRSTBORN
I am Esau, your *f* .... Gen 27:19
Israel is my son, my *f* .... Exod 4:22
attacked all the *f* in the land .... Exod 12:29
Reuben was the *f* of Israel .... Num 26:5
struck down all the *f* in Egypt ...... Ps 78:51
like the bitter cry for a *f* .... Zech 12:10
she gave birth to her *f* son .... Luke 2:7
that his Son would be the *f* ...... Rom 8:29
the *f* over all creation .... Col 1:15
the *f* from the dead .... Col 1:18
the *f* from among the dead .... Rev 1:5

FIRSTFRUITS
the *f* of our land and the *f* .... Neh 10:35
from the *f* of all your crops .... Prov 3:9
who have the *f* of the Spirit ...... Rom 8:23
f of those who have fallen asleep .. 1 Cor 15:20
the *f*; then when Christ comes .... 1 Cor 15:23
a kind of *f* of all he created .... Jas 1:18
as *f* to God and to the Lamb .... Rev 14:4

FISH
Rule over the *f* of the sea .... Gen 1:28
Like *f* that are caught .... Eccl 9:12
a huge *f* to swallow Jonah .... Jonah 1:17
made people like *f* in the sea ...... Hab 1:14
Or if he asks for a *f* .... Matt 7:10
in the belly of the huge *f* .... Matt 12:40
only five loaves and two *f* .... Matt 14:17
you don't have any *f* .... John 21:5
and did the same with the *f* ...... John 21:13

FISHERMEN
The *f* will mourn and lament .... Isa 19:8
will catch these people like *f* .... Jer 16:16

FISHERS
I will turn you into *f* of people ..... Matt 4:19

FISHHOOK
who cast a *f* into the river .... Isa 19:8

FIT
is *f* for the kingdom of God .... Luke 9:62

FITTED
f and held together .... Eph 4:16

FITTING
so honor is not *f* for a fool .... Prov 26:1
as is *f* in the Lord .... Col 3:18
For it is indeed *f* for us .... Heb 7:26

FITTINGS
are in flashing metal *f* .... Nah 2:3

FIVE
bring the *f* kings out of the cave .. Josh 10:22
picked out *f* smooth stones .... 1 Sam 17:40
F of the virgins were foolish ...... Matt 25:2
To one he gave *f* talents .... Matt 25:15
f sparrows sold for two pennies ... Luke 12:6
I have bought *f* yoke of oxen ...... Luke 14:19
for you have had *f* husbands ...... John 4:18
to speak *f* words with my mind .... 1 Cor 14:19

FIXED
chasm has been *f* between us ... Luke 16:26
eyes *f* on the face of Moses .... 2 Cor 3:7
his eyes were *f* on the reward ..... Heb 11:26

FIXES
and *f* his attention there .... Jas 1:25

FLAG
like a signal *f* for the nations .... Isa 11:10
lift a signal *f* for the nations .... Isa 11:12

Lift a signal *f* for the nations .... Isa 62:10
Raise a signal *f* that tells people ..... Jer 4:6

FLAGS
they set up their battle *f* .... Ps 74:4
battle *f* throughout the lands ...... Jer 51:27

FLAME
the *f* of a whirling sword .... Gen 3:24
LORD appeared to him in a *f* ...... Exod 3:2
a *f* will wither his shoots .... Job 15:30
Holy One will become a *f* ...... Isa 10:17
and a consuming *f* of fire .... Isa 29:6
a *f* blazes behind them .... Joel 2:3
and his ministers a *f* of fire .... Heb 1:7
his eyes were like a fiery *f* .... Rev 1:14

FLAMES
dry grass disintegrates in the *f* ..... Isa 5:24
the *f* will not harm you .... Isa 43:2
stick snatched from the *f* .... Amos 4:11

FLAMING
firepot with a *f* torch passed .... Gen 15:17
LORD's shout strikes with *f* fire ...... Ps 29:7
and the *f* fire his attendant ...... Ps 104:4
extinguish all the *f* arrows .... Eph 6:16
With *f* fire he will mete out ...... 2 Thess 1:8

FLASH
and showed him in a *f* .... Luke 4:5

FLATTERING
and a *f* mouth works ruin .... Prov 26:28
never appeared with *f* speech ... 1 Thess 2:5

FLATTERS
The one who *f* his neighbor .... Prov 29:5

FLATTERY
smooth talk and *f* they deceive ... Rom 16:18

FLAVOR
But if salt loses its *f* .... Matt 5:13

FLAW
who has a physical *f* .... Lev 21:17

FLAWLESS
a *f* ram from the flock .... Lev 6:6
My teaching is *f* .... Job 11:4

FLED
So Moses *f* from Pharaoh .... Exod 2:15
they *f* from the men of Ai .... Josh 7:4
The sea looked and *f* .... Ps 114:3
The wicked person *f* .... Prov 28:1

FLEE
may those who hate you *f* .... Num 10:35
Where can I *f* to escape .... Ps 139:7
and the shadows *f* .... Song 2:17
and *f* to Egypt .... Matt 2:13
those in Judea must *f* .... Matt 24:16
F sexual immorality .... 1 Cor 6:18
and he will *f* from you .... Jas 4:7

FLEECE
a wool *f* on the threshing floor .... Judg 6:37

FLEES
he *f* headlong from its power ...... Job 27:22

FLEETING
the few days of his *f* life .... Eccl 6:12

FLESH
See also ACCORDING TO THE FLESH
bone of my bones and *f* of my *f* ... Gen 2:23
yet in my *f* I will see God .... Job 19:26
my *f* yearns for you .... Ps 63:1
that they were made of *f* .... Ps 78:39
and give you a heart of *f* .... Ezek 36:26
the two will become one *f* .... Matt 19:5
but the *f* is weak .... Matt 26:41
the two will become one *f* ...... Mark 10:8
but the *f* is weak .... Mark 14:38
Now the Word became *f* .... John 1:14
What is born of the *f* is *f* .... John 3:6
life of the world is my *f* .... John 6:51
eat the *f* of the Son of Man .... John 6:53
The one who eats my *f* and ...... John 6:54
For my *f* is true food .... John 6:55
For when we were in the *f* .... Rom 7:5
lives in me, that is, in my *f* .... Rom 7:18

with my *f* I serve the law .... Rom 7:25
who live according to the *f* ....Rom 8:5
the outlook of the *f* is death .... Rom 8:6
the outlook of the *f* is hostile.......Rom 8:7
are in the *f* cannot please God..... Rom 8:8
not in the *f* but in the Spirit....... Rom 8:9
if you live according to the *f* ....Rom 8:13
make no provision for the *f* ....Rom 13:14
are still influenced by the *f* ....1 Cor 3:3
for the destruction of the *f* .... 1 Cor 5:5
The two will become one *f* ...... 1 Cor 6:16
All *f* is not the same .... 1 Cor 15:39
carry out the desires of the *f* ...... Gal 5:16
f has desires that are opposed...... Gal 5:17
have crucified the *f* ....Gal 5:24
person who sows to his own *f* ....Gal 6:8
they can boast about your *f* ...... Gal 6:13
the two will become one *f* ....Eph 5:31
of those who mutilate the *f* ....Phil 3:2
He was revealed in the *f* ....1 Tim 3:16
through his *f* ....Heb 10:20
since Christ suffered in the *f* ....1 Pet 4:1
desire of the *f* and the desire .....1 John 2:16
who has come in the *f* ....1 John 4:2
defile the *f* ....Jude 1:8

FLESH AND BLOOD
You are indeed my own *f* ....Gen 29:14
My own son, my very own *f* ....2 Sam 16:11
turn your back on your own *f* ...... Isa 58:7
because *f* did not reveal this......Matt 16:17
F cannot inherit the kingdom....1 Cor 15:50
our struggle is not against *f* ....Eph 6:12
since the children share in *f* .... Heb 2:14

FLESHLY
to keep away from *f* desires .... 1 Pet 2:11

FLIES
to send swarms of *f* on you........Exod 8:21
the arrow that *f* by day .... Ps 91:5
like swarms of stinging *f*...........Jer 46:20

FLIGHT
your *f* may not be in winter......Matt 24:20
put foreign armies to *f*.............Heb 11:34

FLINT
water flow from a *f* rock...........Deut 8:15
of their horses are hard as *f* .... Isa 5:28

FLIRT
and *f* with their eyes................Isa 3:16

FLOAT
and made the ax head *f*...........2 Kgs 6:6

FLOCK
some of the firstborn of his *f* ..... Gen 4:4
Go to the *f* and get me two........Gen 27:9
made the rest of the *f* face ......Gen 30:40
Moses was shepherding the *f*.......Exod 3:1
through the wilderness like a *f* .....Ps 78:52
follow the tracks of my *f* ....Song 1:8
Like a shepherd he tends his *f*......Isa 40:11
with the shepherd of his *f* ....Isa 63:11
Shepherd the *f* set aside............Zech 11:4
that the *f* may be scattered........Zech 13:7
sheep of the *f* will be scattered...Matt 26:31
guard over their *f* at night .... Luke 2:8
Do not be afraid, little *f*........Luke 12:32
so that there will be one *f* ....John 10:16
yourselves and for all the *f* ......Acts 20:28
not sparing the *f*....................Acts 20:29
Who tends a *f* and does not .... 1 Cor 9:7
a shepherd's care to God's *f* ....1 Pet 5:2
but be examples to the *f*...........1 Pet 5:3

FLOCKS
walk among all your *f* ....Gen 30:32
care of the rest of Laban's *f*.......Gen 30:36
little children and their *f*.........Gen 50:8
take your *f* and your herds ...... Exod 12:32
army spared the best of the *f*....1 Sam 15:15
wander around beside the *f*.......Song 1:7
lion among the *f* of sheep ....Mic 5:8

FLOG
F a scorner ....Prov 19:25
and *f* you in their synagogues ....Matt 10:17

f him severely ....Mark 10:34
f him and release him ....Luke 23:22

FLOOD
will the waters become a *f*........ Gen 9:15
over the earth after the *f*........Gen 10:32
the *f* came.................... Matt 7:25
those days before the *f*........Matt 24:38
When a *f* came ....Luke 6:48
a *f* on an ungodly world .... 2 Pet 2:5

FLOODS
like a stream that *f* its banks....... Isa 66:12

FLOODWATERS
the *f* engulfed the earth .... Gen 7:10

FLOOR
went down to the threshing *f*..... Ruth 3:6
woman visited the threshing *f*.....Ruth 3:14
David bought the threshing *f*.. 2 Sam 24:24
for the Lord on the threshing *f*...1 Chr 21:18
will clean out his threshing *f*......Matt 3:12
to clean out his threshing *f* ....Luke 3:17
or "Sit on the *f*......................Jas 2:3

FLOUR
a handful of *f* in a jar...............1 Kgs 17:12
The jar of *f* was never empty .....1 Kgs 17:16
Get some *f*.......................2 Kgs 4:41

FLOURISH
During his days the godly will *f*....Ps 72:7
the tent of the upright will *f*.......Prov 14:11

FLOW
will *f* rivers of living water........John 7:38

FLOWER
He grows up like a *f* .... Job 14:2
a *f* in the field it flourishes.........Ps 103:15
am a meadow *f* from Sharon ....Song 2:1
The withering *f* ....Isa 28:4
like the *f* of the grass..............1 Pet 1:24

FLOWERS
shaped like almond *f* ....Exod 25:33
are like the *f* in the field ....Isa 40:6
the *f* wither........................Isa 40:7
Consider how the *f* grow ....Luke 12:27

FLOWING
a land *f* with milk and honey ...... Deut 6:3
wisdom is like a *f* brook ....Prov 18:4

FLOWS
and the water *f*....................Ps 147:18

FLUTE
who play the harp and the *f* .... Gen 4:21
stringed instruments and the *f* .....Ps 150:4
sound of the horn, *f*, zither ....Dan 3:5
and saw the *f* players.............Matt 9:23
We played the *f* for you .... Luke 7:32

FLY
let birds *f* above the earth .... Gen 1:20
I would *f* away and settle ....Ps 55:6
pass quickly and we *f* away........Ps 90:10
f off into the sky like an eagle .....Prov 23:5
dead *f* makes the perfumer's ....Eccl 10:1

FLYING
bird or like a *f* swallow .... Prov 26:2

FOAL
the *f* of a female donkey........... Zech 9:9
the *f* of a donkey ....Matt 21:5

FOES
you make my *f* kneel .... 2 Sam 22:40
will trample down our *f* ....Ps 44:5

FOLD
like a robe you will *f* them up...... Heb 1:12

FOLDING
little *f* of the hands to relax........Prov 6:10
little *f* of the hands to relax....... Prov 24:33

FOLLOW
f the Lord your God.............1 Sam 12:14
Lord is the true God, then *f* him ..1 Kgs 18:21
you were determined to *f* God ... 2 Chr 19:3
not *f* the advice of the wicked ....Ps 1:1
my actions and *f* your rules........ Ps 119:59

fears God will *f* both warnings......Eccl 7:18
F the impulses of your heart ....Eccl 11:9
who *f* in David's succession.........Jer 17:25
nations *f* their respective gods .....Mic 4:5
F me, and I will turn you..........Matt 4:19
I will *f* you wherever you go ....Matt 8:19
F me, and let the dead bury ......Matt 8:22
F me," he said to him ....Matt 9:9
take up his cross and *f* me.......Matt 10:38
take up his cross, and *f* me ......Matt 16:24
Then come, *f* me..................Mark 10:21
have left everything to *f* you.....Mark 10:28
I will *f* you wherever you go ...... Luke 9:57
Jesus said to another, "*F* me ......Luke 9:59
Then come, *f* me..................Luke 18:22
F him into the house ....Luke 22:10
and the sheep *f* him ....John 10:4
They will never *f* a stranger ....John 10:5
he must *f* me ....John 12:26
Put on your cloak and *f* me........ Acts 12:8
used to *f* in your ignorance ....1 Pet 1:14
an example for you to *f*........... 1 Pet 2:21
are the ones who *f* the Lamb ......Rev 14:4
their deeds will *f* them ....Rev 14:13

FOLLOWED
their nets immediately and *f* .....Matt 4:20
large crowds *f* him..................Matt 8:1
Many women who had *f* Jesus... Matt 27:55
and *f* him on the road ....Mark 10:52
from the spiritual rock that *f* .....1 Cor 10:4
have *f* my teaching ....2 Tim 3:10
they *f* the way of Balaam .... 2 Pet 2:15

FOLLOWER
anyone wants to become my *f*....Mark 8:34

FOLLOWERS
Your loyal *f* trust in you .... Ps 9:10
You loyal *f* of the Lord ....Ps 22:23
The Lord shows his faithful *f*.......Ps 25:12
loyal *f* receive his guidance.........Ps 25:14
every one of your faithful *f*.........Ps 32:6
Lord takes notice of his loyal *f*..... Ps 33:18
camps around the Lord's loyal *f* ....Ps 34:7
never abandons his faithful *f*.......Ps 37:28
the lives of his faithful *f*............Ps 97:10
compassion on his faithful *f* ...... Ps 103:13
He will bless his loyal *f* ....Ps 115:13
the lives of his faithful *f*...........Ps 116:15
Let the loyal *f* of the Lord say...... Ps 118:4
Your loyal *f* will be glad............Ps 119:74
every one of the Lord's loyal *f* ......Ps 128:1
takes delight in his faithful *f*........Ps 147:11

FOLLOWING
if you turn away from *f* him ..... Num 32:15
back today from *f* the Lord ......Josh 22:16
turned from *f* the Lord..........2 Chr 25:27
was *f* him from a distance ....Matt 26:58
because he was not *f* us...........Mark 9:38
and saw them *f* and said...........John 1:38
disciple whom Jesus loved *f* .....John 21:20

FOLLOWS
The one who *f* me will never ......John 8:12

FOLLY
foolish people proclaim *f*.........Prov 12:23
F is a joy to one who............Prov 15:21
but *f* leads to the discipline.......Prov 16:22
person's *f* subverts his way.......Prov 19:3
F is bound up in the heart.......Prov 22:15
there is *f* in their hearts............Eccl 9:3

FONDLED
f her virgin breasts ....Ezek 23:8

FOOD
They will be yours for *f*........... Gen 1:29
of your brow you will eat *f* ....Gen 3:19
giving them *f* and clothing........Deut 10:18
I have no *f* ....1 Kgs 17:12
so that his life loathes *f*...........Job 33:20
and supplies *f* in abundance.......Job 36:31
young lions sometimes lack *f*.......Ps 34:10
and refrained from eating *f*........Ps 35:13
They are filled with *f*.............Ps 36:8
to give us *f* in the wilderness ....Ps 78:19

But can he also give us *f*	Ps 78:20
produce *f* from the ground	Ps 104:14
work so hard for your *f*	Ps 127:2
give her poor all the *f* they need	Ps 132:15
To the one who gives *f*	Ps 136:25
and *f* obtained in secret	Prov 9:17
Abundant *f* may come	Prov 13:23
righteous has enough *f*	Prov 13:25
prepare their *f* in the summer	Prov 30:25
provided *f* for her household	Prov 31:15
Go, eat your *f* with joy	Eccl 9:7
f and a constant supply of water	Isa 33:16
Enjoy fine *f*	Isa 55:2
I want you to share your *f*	Isa 58:7
risk of our lives we get our *f*	Lam 5:9
f you eat will be eight ounces	Ezek 4:10
I ate no choice *f*	Dan 10:3
lacked *f* everywhere you lived	Amos 4:6
there may be *f* in my temple	Mal 3:10
give the other slaves their *f*	Matt 24:45
hungry and you gave me *f*	Matt 25:35
and the person who has *f*	Luke 3:11
there is more to life than *f*	Luke 12:23
give them their allowance of *f*	Luke 12:42
I have *f* to eat	John 4:32
My *f* is to do the will	John 4:34
work for the *f* that disappears	John 6:27
sharing their *f* with glad	Acts 2:46
satisfying you with *f*	Acts 14:17
Do not destroy by your *f*	Rom 14:15
F is for the stomach	1 Cor 6:13
f causes my brother or sister	1 Cor 8:13
all ate the same spiritual *f*	1 Cor 10:3
and bread for *f*	2 Cor 9:10
we did not eat anyone's *f*	2 Thess 3:8
provide their own *f* to eat	2 Thess 3:12
But if we have *f* and shelter	1 Tim 6:8
not solid *f*	Heb 5:12
But solid *f* is for the mature	Heb 5:14
poorly clothed and lacks daily *f*	Jas 2:15

FOODS

require abstinence from *f*	1 Tim 4:3

FOOL

Abner have died like a *f*	2 Sam 3:33
scheme is enjoyable to a *f*	Prov 10:23
and the *f* will be a servant	Prov 11:29
The way of a *f* is right in his	Prov 12:15
but a *f* displays his folly	Prov 13:16
f rejects his father's discipline	Prov 15:5
than a hundred blows on a *f*	Prov 17:10
Wisdom is unattainable for a *f*	Prov 24:7
a *f* according to his folly	Prov 26:4
The fate of the *f* will happen	Eccl 2:15
yet a *f* keeps on babbling	Eccl 10:14
whoever says 'F' will be sent	Matt 5:22
You *f*! This very night	Luke 12:20
I have become a *f*	2 Cor 12:11
God will not be made a *f*	Gal 6:7

FOOLISH

a *f* person devours all he has	Prov 21:20
A *f* scheme is sin	Prov 24:9
because my people are *f*	Jer 4:22
are you still so *f*	Matt 15:16
both to the wise and to the *f*	Rom 1:14
the wisdom of the world *f*	1 Cor 1:20
the world thinks *f* to shame	1 Cor 1:27
f so that he can become wise	1 Cor 3:18
You *f* Galatians	Gal 3:1
For this reason do not be *f*	Eph 5:17
f and ignorant controversies	2 Tim 2:23
were once *f*	Titus 3:3
But avoid *f* controversies	Titus 3:9

FOOLISHLY

have behaved *f* and have made	1 Sam 26:21
am speaking *f*	2 Cor 11:21

FOOLISHNESS

message about the cross is *f*	1 Cor 1:18
For the *f* of God is wiser	1 Cor 1:25
wisdom of this age is *f* with God	1 Cor 3:19

FOOLS

F say to themselves	Ps 14:1
but *f* have despised wisdom	Prov 1:7

the folly of *f* is deception	Prov 14:8
F mock at reparation	Prov 14:9
God takes no pleasure in *f*	Eccl 5:4
F are placed in many positions	Eccl 10:6
Blind *f*! Which is greater	Matt 23:17
they became *f*	Rom 1:22
We are *f* for Christ	1 Cor 4:10

FOOT

every place you set *f*	Josh 1:3
soon as they set *f* on dry land	Josh 4:18
he not allow your *f* to slip	Ps 121:3
strike your *f* against a stone	Matt 4:6
or your *f* causes you to sin	Matt 18:8
strike your *f* against a stone	Luke 4:11
If the *f* says	1 Cor 12:15

FOOTING

and gave me secure *f*	Ps 40:2

FOOTPRINTS

but left no *f*	Ps 77:19

FOOTSTEPS

f have strayed from the way	Job 31:7

FOOTSTOOL

Worship before his *f*	Ps 99:5
I make your enemies your *f*	Ps 110:1
and the earth is my *f*	Isa 66:1
by earth because it is his *f*	Matt 5:35
and earth is the *f* for my feet	Acts 7:49

FORBID

not *f* anyone from speaking	1 Cor 14:39

FORBIDDEN

just as he has *f* you	Deut 4:23

FORBIDDING

f wilderness that you saw	Deut 1:19

FORCE

will come upon you in full *f*	Deut 28:15
and on the full *f* of the enemy	Luke 10:19
seize him by *f* to make him king	John 6:15
tried to *f* them to blaspheme	Acts 26:11
can you try to *f* the Gentiles	Gal 2:14
since it carries no *f*	Heb 9:17

FORCED

they *f* to carry his cross	Matt 27:32
f him out of the town	Luke 4:29

FORCES

with armed *f* against Jerusalem	Neh 4:8
anyone *f* you to go one mile	Matt 5:41
weak and worthless basic *f*	Gal 4:9

FOREARM

Bind them on your *f*	Prov 7:3

FOREHEAD

them as symbols on your *f*	Deut 6:8
the seal of God on their *f*	Rev 9:4
receive his mark on their *f*	Rev 20:4

FOREHEADS

hard to match their *f*	Ezek 3:8
and put a mark on the *f*	Ezek 9:4

FOREIGN

See also FOREIGN GODS

resident foreigner in a *f* land	Exod 2:22
Now put aside the *f* gods	Josh 24:23
fell in love with many *f* women	1 Kgs 11:1
by marrying *f* women	Ezra 10:2
by marrying *f* wives	Neh 13:27
left a *f* nation behind	Ps 114:1
song to the LORD in a *f* land	Ps 137:4
because I love those *f* gods	Jer 2:25
put *f* armies to flight	Heb 11:34

FOREIGN GODS

Get rid of the *f*	Gen 35:2
themselves with the *f*	Deut 31:16
Now put aside the *f*	Josh 24:23
They threw away the *f*	Judg 10:16
He removed the *f*	2 Chr 33:15
because I love those *f*	Jer 2:25
rejected me and served *f*	Jer 5:19
to be a proclaimer of *f*	Acts 17:18

FOREIGNER

a resident *f* in a foreign land	Exod 2:22
must not wrong a resident *f*	Exod 22:21

you lived as a *f* in his land	Deut 23:7
even though I am a *f*	Ruth 2:10
I am a *f* in their eyes	Job 19:15
LORD protects the resident *f*	Ps 146:9
like a resident *f* in the land	Jer 14:8
refuse to help the resident *f*	Mal 3:5
praise to God except this *f*	Luke 17:18
Moses fled and became a *f*	Acts 7:29
I will be a *f* to the speaker	1 Cor 14:11
By faith he lived as a *f*	Heb 11:9

FOREIGNERS

and who loves resident *f*	Deut 10:18
For we are resident *f*	1 Chr 29:15
of *f* who speak lies	Ps 144:11
Plenty of *f* are around	Isa 2:6
F will rebuild your walls	Isa 60:10
F will take care of your sheep	Isa 61:5
F are consuming	Hos 7:9
the Athenians and the *f*	Acts 17:21
no longer *f* and noncitizens	Eph 2:19
strangers and *f* on the earth	Heb 11:13
I urge you as *f* and exiles	1 Pet 2:11

FOREKNEW

whom he *f* he also predestined	Rom 8:29
rejected his people whom he *f*	Rom 11:2

FOREKNOWLEDGE

predetermined plan and *f* of God	Acts 2:23
according to the *f* of God	1 Pet 1:2

FOREKNOWN

He was *f* before the foundation	1 Pet 1:20

FORERUNNER

Jesus our *f* entered on our behalf	Heb 6:20

FORESEE

at an hour he does not *f*	Matt 24:50
at an hour he does not *f*	Luke 12:46

FORESEEING

f that God would justify	Gal 3:8

FORESKINS

circumcise the flesh of your *f*	Gen 17:11
except 100 Philistine *f*	1 Sam 18:25

FOREST

every wild animal in the *f*	Ps 50:10
small a flame sets a huge *f*	Jas 3:5

FORESTS

strips the leaves from the *f*	Ps 29:9

FOREVER

and eat, and live *f*	Gen 3:22
This is my name *f*	Exod 3:15
LORD will reign *f* and ever	Exod 15:18
and they will inherit it *f*	Exod 32:13
to us and our descendants *f*	Deut 29:29
I do not want to live *f*	Job 7:16
Do not reject us *f*	Ps 44:23
and will endure *f*	Ps 125:1
will be my resting place *f*	Ps 132:14
live praise his holy name *f*	Ps 145:21
who remains *f* faithful	Ps 146:5
The LORD rules *f*	Ps 146:10
tells the truth will endure *f*	Prov 12:19
for riches do not last *f*	Prov 27:24
decree of our God is *f* reliable	Isa 40:8
the one who rules *f*	Isa 57:15
the Lord will not reject us *f*	Lam 3:31
name of God be praised *f*	Dan 2:20
possession of the kingdom *f*	Dan 7:18
will be like the stars *f*	Dan 12:3
follow the LORD our God *f*	Mic 4:5
who eats this bread will live *f*	John 6:58
that the Christ will remain *f*	John 12:34
Advocate to be with you *f*	John 14:16
his righteousness remains *f*	2 Cor 9:9
who is blessed *f*	2 Cor 11:31
to whom be glory *f* and ever	Gal 1:5
f and ever	Eph 3:21
given to God our Father *f*	Phil 4:20
is *f* and ever	Heb 1:8
f in the order of Melchizedek	Heb 5:6
f in the order of Melchizedek	Heb 6:20
appoints a son made perfect *f*	Heb 7:28
same yesterday and today and *f*	Heb 13:8

word of the Lord endures *f* ....1 Pet 1:25
and ruling power *f* and ever ....Rev 5:13
they will reign *f* and ever .... Rev 22:5

FOREVERMORE
The LORD deserves praise *f* .... Ps 89:52
name be praised now and *f* ....Ps 113:2

FORFEIT
f the mercy that could be theirs .. Jonah 2:8

FORFEITS
gains the whole world but *f* ..... Matt 16:26

FORGAVE
And then you *f* my sins .... Ps 32:5
you *f* all their sin.....................Ps 85:2
and *f* him the debt................Matt 18:27
I *f* you all that debt .... Matt 18:32
as God in Christ also *f* you......... Eph 4:32

FORGED
No weapon *f* to be used ....Isa 54:17

FORGET
God has made me *f*................Gen 41:51
that you do not *f* the covenant ... Deut 4:23
for he cannot *f* the covenant ......Deut 4:31
be careful not to *f* the LORD ....Deut 6:12
the destiny of all who *f* God .... Job 8:13
will not *f* the works of God..........Ps 78:7
I do not *f* your instructions.........Ps 119:16
If I *f* you .... Ps 137:5
do not *f* my teaching .... Prov 3:1
I will not *f* you .... Isa 44:21
Can a woman *f* her baby........... Isa 49:15
Why do you *f* the LORD........... Isa 51:13
Does a young woman *f*............Jer 2:32
unjust so as to *f* your work .... Heb 6:10

FORGETFUL
does not become a *f* listener ....Jas 1:25

FORGETS
goes out and immediately *f*.........Jas 1:24

FORGETTING
F the things that are behind .... Phil 3:13

FORGIVE
f my sin this time only............Exod 10:17
if you will *f* their sin ....Exod 32:32
LORD will be unwilling to *f*.......Deut 29:20
f their sin ....1 Kgs 8:39
f their sin .... 2 Chr 7:14
f my sin, because it is great..........Ps 25:11
But you are willing to *f* ....Ps 130:4
for he will freely *f* them ....Isa 55:7
For I will *f* their sin ....Jer 31:34
I will *f* all their sins ....Jer 33:8
O Lord, *f* Dan 9:19
and *f* us our debts ....Matt 6:12
For if you *f* others their sins ......Matt 6:14
But if you do not *f* others..........Matt 6:15
many times must I *f* my
    brother........................Matt 18:21
f your brother from your heart... Matt 18:35
Who can *f* sins but God alone ..... Mark 2:7
f him, so that your Father........ Mark 11:25
has authority on earth to *f* sins... Luke 5:24
f, and you will be forgiven .... Luke 6:37
and *f* us our sins...................Luke 11:4
If he repents, *f* him ....Luke 17:3
you must *f* him ....Luke 17:4
f them, for they don't know .... Luke 23:34
If you *f* anyone's sins ....John 20:23
that he may perhaps *f* you........Acts 8:22
rather *f* and comfort him ....2 Cor 2:7
If you *f* anyone for anything ......2 Cor 2:10
F me this injustice .... 2 Cor 12:13

FORGIVEN
whose rebellious acts are *f*.......... Ps 32:1
your sin is *f*.......................Isa 6:7
this sin will not be *f*.............Isa 22:14
Jacob's sin will be *f*.............. Isa 27:9
will never be *f* ....Mark 3:29
may not repent and be *f*........ Mark 4:12
are *f*, thus she loved much........ Luke 7:47
indeed what I have *f*............2 Cor 2:10
f all your transgressions .... Col 2:13

he will be *f*............................Jas 5:15
that your sins have been *f*........1 John 2:12

FORGIVENESS
But you are a God of *f*............ Neh 9:17
repentance for the *f* of sins........ Mark 1:4
for the *f* of your sins..............Acts 2:38
f of sins is proclaimed ....Acts 13:38
they may receive *f* of sins ....Acts 26:18
the *f* of our offenses............... Eph 1:7
the *f* of sins ....Col 1:14
where there is *f* of these..........Heb 10:18

FORGIVES
the one who *f* all your sins ....Ps 103:3
Who *f* sin and pardons ....Mic 7:18
who even *f* sins...................Luke 7:49

FORGIVING
you are kind and *f* ....Ps 86:5
God is compassionate and *f* ...... Dan 9:9
f one another......................Eph 4:32
and *f* one another ....Col 3:13
f us our sins and cleansing........1 John 1:9

FORGO
LORD will *f* destroying you..........Jer 26:13

FORGOT
not remember Joseph—he *f* him ..Gen 40:23
They *f* the LORD their God..........Judg 3:7
They *f* what he had done ....Ps 78:11
quickly *f* what he had done....... Ps 106:13

FORGOTTEN
The LORD has *f* me .... Isa 49:14
I have *f* what happiness is .... Lam 3:17
not one of them is *f* before God ...Luke 12:6
And have you *f* the exhortation ....Heb 12:5
he has *f* about the cleansing.......2 Pet 1:9

FORK
stands at the *f* in the road .... Ezek 21:21
His winnowing *f* is in his hand .....Matt 3:12

FORM
he will see the *f* of the LORD.......Num 12:8
he had no stately *f* or majesty ....Isa 53:2
on him in bodily *f* like a dove ..... Luke 3:22
heard his voice nor seen his *f*......John 5:37
he existed in the *f* of God...........Phil 2:6
by taking on the *f* of a slave ....Phil 2:7
fullness of deity lives in bodily *f* .....Col 2:9
Stay away from every *f* of evil .. 1 Thess 5:22

FORMED
The LORD God *f* the man .... Gen 2:7
His hands *f* the dry land ....Ps 95:5
No god was *f* before me...........Isa 43:10
people whom I *f* for myself........Isa 43:21
f you in your mother's womb........Jer 1:5
until Christ is *f* in you..............Gal 4:19
Adam was *f* first and then Eve.... 1 Tim 2:13

FORMER
the *f* prophets called out ....Zech 1:4
through the *f* prophets ....Zech 7:12
I wrote the *f* account ....Acts 1:1
heard of my *f* way of life.............Gal 1:13
to your *f* way of life................. Eph 4:22

FORMERLY
early and the late rains as *f*.........Joel 2:23
who was *f* useless to you .... Phlm 1:11

FORMIDABLE
appearance was more *f*...........Dan 7:20

FORMS
one who *f* every human heart ...... Ps 33:15
Who *f* a god and casts an idol ..... Isa 44:10
I am the one who *f* light ....Isa 45:7
who *f* the human spirit ....Zech 12:1

FORSAKE
Do not *f* or abandon me............Ps 27:9
and do not *f* the teaching.......... Prov 1:8

FORSAKEN
why have you *f* me ....Matt 27:46

FORSAKES
confesses them and *f* them.......Prov 28:13
heart that *f* the living God ....Heb 3:12

FORSAKING
By *f* the right path .... 2 Pet 2:15

FORTH
and bring *f* words..................Job 8:10
Ride *f* for the sake of ....Ps 45:4
it will sway back and *f*............Isa 24:20
river of fire was streaming *f* .... Dan 7:10
break *f* and shout..................Gal 4:27
that he set *f* in Christ ....Eph 1:9
for the one bringing *f* in you.......Phil 2:13

FORTIFIED
will lead me into the *f* city.......... Ps 60:9

FORTIFY
F the walls of Jerusalem ....Ps 51:18

FORTRESS
on a rocky crag and a *f* ....Job 39:28
the *f* of foreigners .... Isa 25:2

FORTRESSES
God is in its *f* ....Ps 48:3
in the *f* of Ashdod .... Amos 3:9

FORTUNATE
Leah said, "How *f*.................Gen 30:11

FORTUNE
Making a *f* by a lying tongue.......Prov 21:6
We hoped for good *f* ....Jer 8:15

FORTUNE-TELLING
a great profit by *f*................. Acts 16:16

FORTY
When Isaac was *f* years old.......Gen 25:20
When Esau was *f* years old ......Gen 26:34
I was *f* years old when Moses ..... Josh 14:7
the land had rest for *f* years .... Judg 5:31
where for *f* days he endured....... Luke 4:2
he was about *f* years old...........Acts 7:23
After *f* years had passed...........Acts 7:30
were more than *f* of them ....Acts 23:13
because more than *f* of them.....Acts 23:21
received from the Jews *f* lashes.. 2 Cor 11:24
they saw my works for *f* years...... Heb 3:9
was God provoked for *f* years ......Heb 3:17

FORUM OF APPIUS
A town about 40 miles south of Rome
    where Christians came to meet Paul,
    Acts 28:15

FORWARD
from this time *f*.....................Isa 26:4
must look *f* to the Sabbath ....Isa 58:13
looking *f* to the kingdom ....Mark 15:43
looking *f* to the kingdom ....Luke 23:51

FOUGHT
have *f* a desperate struggle........Gen 30:8
the LORD *f* for Israel ....Josh 10:14
angels *f* against the dragon.........Rev 12:7

FOUL-SMELLING
that produces rotten, *f* grapes.......Jer 2:21

FOUND
corresponded to him was *f*........Gen 2:20
can it be *f*...........................Job 28:12
the one who has *f* wisdom......... Prov 3:13
one who has *f* a good wife........Prov 18:22
I have not *f* ....Eccl 7:28
when I *f* my beloved............... Song 3:4
where security can be *f*............Isa 28:12
is nowhere to be *f* in it............. Jer 7:28
f them to be ten times better...... Dan 1:20
and *f* to be lacking.................. Dan 5:27
and *f* Daniel praying................Dan 6:11
not *f* such faith in anyone......... Matt 8:10
he *f* a pearl of great value .... Matt 13:46
f nothing on it except leaves......Matt 21:19
and *f* them sleeping ....Matt 26:40
you have *f* favor with God........Luke 1:30
After three days they *f* him....... Luke 2:46
looking for fruit on it and *f*
    none..........................Luke 13:6
was lost and is *f* .... Luke 15:24
f that the stone had been rolled .. Luke 24:2
He first *f* his own brother......... John 1:41

We *f* the jail locked securely......Acts 5:23
f an altar with this inscription ....Acts 17:23
f that the very commandment.....Rom 7:10
is that one be *f* faithful ....1 Cor 4:2
and be *f* in him ....Phil 3:9
if they are *f* blameless...........1 Tim 3:10
strive to be *f* at peace.............2 Pet 3:14
name was not *f* written...........Rev 20:15

FOUNDATION
when I laid the *f* of the earth ......Job 38:4
For he set its *f* upon the seas.......Ps 24:2
are the *f* of your throne ....Ps 89:14
LORD laid the *f* of the earth........Prov 3:19
righteous are an everlasting *f* ...Prov 10:25
and laid the *f* on bedrock........Luke 6:48
on the ground without a *f*.......Luke 6:49
master-builder I laid a *f*..........1 Cor 3:10
For no one can lay any *f*..........1 Cor 3:11
before the *f* of the world ....Eph 1:4
God's solid *f* remains standing....2 Tim 2:19
not laying this *f* again...............Heb 6:1
since the *f* of the world...........Rev 13:8

FOUNDATIONS
when he lays its *f*..................Josh 6:26
When the *f* are destroyed ....Ps 11:3
established the earth on its *f*.......Ps 104:5
will reestablish the ancient *f*.......Isa 58:12
f of the prison were shaken ......Acts 16:26
The *f* of the city's wall ....Rev 21:19

FOUNTAIN
May your *f* be blessed.............Prov 5:18
and the *f* of wisdom ....Prov 18:4
a *f* of water springing up..........John 4:14

FOUNTAINS
f of the great deep burst open......Gen 7:11

FOUR
it divides into *f* headstreams ......Gen 2:10
of the cherubim had *f* faces ......Ezek 10:14
Each had *f* faces ....Ezek 10:21
But I see *f* men ....Dan 3:25
Then *f* large beasts came up........Dan 7:3
there arose *f* others stands........Dan 8:22
These are the *f* spirits ....Zech 6:5
had been in the tomb *f* days.......John 11:17
down to earth by its *f* corners.....Acts 10:11
He had *f* unmarried daughters ....Acts 21:9
f living creatures full of eyes........Rev 4:6
with a loud voice to the *f* angels.....Rev 7:2

FOWLER
a bird from the trap of the *f*........Prov 6:5

FOX
If even a *f* were to climb up.........Neh 4:3
Go and tell that *f* ....Luke 13:32

FOXES
Catch the *f* for us...................Song 2:15
F have dens and the birds ....Luke 9:58

FRAGRANCE
f of your garments is like the *f*....Song 4:11
with the *f* of the perfumed oil .....John 12:3

FRAGRANT
like a *f* billow of myrrh and........Song 3:6
sacrificial and *f* offering to God......Eph 5:2

FRAIL
mercy on me, LORD, for I am *f*........Ps 6:2

FRANKINCENSE
pour olive oil on it and put *f*.........Lev 2:1
fragrant billow of myrrh and *f*.....Song 3:6
gifts of gold, *f*, and myrrh..........Matt 2:11
perfumed ointment, *f*, wine ....Rev 18:13

FREE
the slave is *f* from his master........Job 3:19
to set *f* the oppressed ....Isa 58:6
You will become *f* ....John 8:33
So if the son sets you *f*.............John 8:36
has set you *f* from the law.........Rom 8:2
not *f*? Am I not an apostle..........1 Cor 9:1
there is neither slave nor *f*...........Gal 3:28
But the Jerusalem above is *f*........Gal 4:26
For freedom Christ has set us *f*.....Gal 5:1

whether slave or *f* ....Eph 6:8
Set *f* the four angels................Rev 9:14
rich and poor, *f* and slave..........Rev 13:16

FREED
you are *f* from your infirmity.....Luke 13:12
has died has been *f* from sin.......Rom 6:7
and having been *f* from sin ....Rom 6:18
f from sin and enslaved to God... Rom 6:22

FREEDMAN
as a slave is the Lord's *f*...........1 Cor 7:22

FREEDOM
glorious *f* of God's children........Rom 8:21
For why is my *f* being judged....1 Cor 10:29
is present, there is *f* ....2 Cor 3:17
For *f* Christ has set us free..........Gal 5:1
For you were called to *f* ....Gal 5:13
using your *f* as a pretext for evil...1 Pet 2:16

FREEING
and the *f* of prisoners................Isa 61:1

FREELY
may *f* eat fruit from every tree ....Gen 2:16
praise flow *f* from my lips ....Ps 119:171
Drink *f*, O lovers...................Song 5:1
and love them *f*...................Hos 14:4
F you received....................Matt 10:8
f give us all things ....Rom 8:32
the things that are *f* given ....1 Cor 2:12
We have spoken *f* to you ....2 Cor 6:11

FRESH
glory will always be *f* in me........Job 29:20
They are *f* every morning........Lam 3:23
salt water spring produce *f*..........Jas 3:12

FRIEND
way a person speaks to a *f*........Exod 33:11
to the descendants of your *f*......2 Chr 20:7
My intercessor is my *f*.............Job 16:20
would for a *f* or my brother ....Ps 35:14
close *f* in whom I confided..........Ps 55:13
a *f* to all your loyal followers ......Ps 119:63
A *f* loves at all times..............Prov 17:17
Do not forsake your *f*.............Prov 27:10
f of tax collectors and sinners ....Matt 11:19
Suppose one of you has a *f*........Luke 11:5
Our *f* Lazarus has fallen asleep....John 11:11
you are no *f* of Caesar ....John 19:12
Our dear *f* Luke the physician ......Col 4:14
our dear *f* and colaborer............Phlm 1:1
and he was called God's *f*........Jas 2:23

FRIENDS
and hate your *f* ....2 Sam 19:6
my *f* have forgotten me ....Job 19:14
snare for that group of *f*...........Ps 69:22
All my so-called *f*..................Jer 20:10
lays down his life for his *f* ....John 15:13
You are my *f* if you do ....John 15:14
But I have called you *f*...........John 15:15
not to prevent any of his *f*.......Acts 24:23
Dear *f*, let us love one another ... 1 John 4:7
Dear *f*, if God so loved us.........1 John 4:11

FRIENDSHIP
intimate *f* was experienced.........Job 29:4
that *f* with the world.................Jas 4:4

FRIGHT
they were overcome with *f*.........Dan 10:7

FRIGHTENED
saw a dream that *f* me badly ....Dan 4:5

FRO
they will stagger to and *f*..........Jer 25:16

FROGS
plague all your territory with *f* ....Exod 8:2
spirits that looked like *f* ....Rev 16:13

FRONTLETS
and for *f* on your forehead ....Exod 13:16

FRUIT
See also BEAR FRUIT
and showed the *f* of the land ....Num 13:26
yields its *f* at the proper time.........Ps 1:3
f is better than the purest gold ....Prov 8:19

The *f* of the righteous ....Prov 11:30
from the *f* of his words ....Prov 12:14
and his *f* is sweet to my taste...... Song 2:3
root in the ground and bear *f*.......Isa 37:31
f that proves your repentance..... Matt 3:8
that does not produce good *f*.....Matt 3:10
recognize them by their *f*..........Matt 7:16
every good tree bears good *f*......Matt 7:17
not drink of this *f* of the vine ....Matt 26:29
and their *f* does not mature ......Luke 8:14
he came looking for *f* on it ....Luke 13:6
Then if it bears *f* next year........Luke 13:9
branch that does not bear *f*........John 15:2
that you bear much *f*...............John 15:8
to go and bear *f* ....John 15:16
to bear *f* to God ....Rom 7:4
But the *f* of the Spirit is love........Gal 5:22
for the *f* of the light................Eph 5:9
with the *f* of righteousness.........Phil 1:11
f in every good deed................Col 1:10
later it produces the *f* of peace ....Heb 12:11
the *f* of our lips ....Heb 13:15
full of mercy and good *f*.............Jas 3:17
f that consists of righteousness .....Jas 3:18
farmer waits for the precious *f*.......Jas 5:7
autumn trees without *f*.............Jude 1:12
producing twelve kinds of *f*........Rev 22:2

FRUITFUL
See also BE FRUITFUL AND MULTIPLY
Be *f* and multiply and fill ....Gen 1:22
Joseph is a *f* bough ....Gen 49:22
They rejected the *f* land ....Ps 106:24
Your wife will be like a *f* vine ....Ps 128:3
rain from heaven and *f* seasons .. Acts 14:17

FRUITFULNESS
your *f* comes from me............. Hos 14:8

FRUSTRATE
Why do you *f* the intent ....Num 32:7
F their plans.......................Ps 55:9
and who can possibly *f* it ....Isa 14:27

FRUSTRATED
Do not be angry and *f* ....Ps 37:8

FRUSTRATION
great wisdom comes great *f*........Eccl 1:18

FUEL
people became *f* for the fire.........Isa 9:19
It is thrown in the fire for *f* ....Ezek 15:4

FUGITIVES
Hide the *f*..........................Isa 16:3
Moabite *f* live among you ....Isa 16:4
will be *f* among the nations.........Hos 9:17

FULFILL
for us to *f* all righteousness........Matt 3:15
abolish these things but to *f*.......Matt 5:17
But this is to *f* the scripture ......John 13:18
you will *f* the law of Christ..........Gal 6:2
f by his power your every
　desire.......................2 Thess 1:11
first learn to *f* their duty...........1 Tim 5:4
f your ministry.....................2 Tim 4:5
But if you *f* the royal law ....Jas 2:8

FULFILLED
today I have *f* my vows ....Prov 7:14
A desire *f* will be sweet...........Prov 13:19
and is *f* as I intend ....Isa 55:11
through the prophet would be *f*...Matt 1:22
it must happen this way be *f*.....Matt 26:54
The time is *f* and the kingdom.....Mark 1:15
to her by the Lord would be *f* .....Luke 1:45
this scripture has been *f*..........Luke 4:21
times of the Gentiles are *f*....... Luke 21:24
this scripture must be *f* in me ...Luke 22:37
and the psalms must be *f*........Luke 24:44
the scripture had to be *f*...........Acts 1:16
requirement of the law may be *f*...Rom 8:4
loves his neighbor has *f* the law ...Rom 13:8
until the words of God are *f* ....Rev 17:17

FULFILLING
f their duties at home ....Titus 2:5

FULFILLMENT
love is the *f* of the law .... Rom 13:10
the happy *f* of our hope .... Titus 2:13
for the *f* of your hope. .... Heb 6:11

FULL
did not set for about a *f* day ...... Josh 10:13
I left here *f*. .... Ruth 1:21
They ate until they were *f* .... Neh 9:25
For I am *f* of words .... Job 32:18
but the sea is not *f*. .... Eccl 1:7
punish them in *f* for their sins ...... Jer 16:18
people will be filled to the *f* .... Jer 31:14
and it was *f* of bones .... Ezek 37:1
But I am *f* of the courage .... Mic 3:8
whole body will be *f* of light ...... Matt 6:22
f of the Holy Spirit. .... Luke 4:1
f of grace and truth. .... John 1:14
f of faith and of the Holy Spirit ..... Acts 6:5
but receive a *f* reward .... 2 John 1:8

FULLNESS
have all received from his *f*. .... John 1:16
of the *f* of the times .... Eph 1:10
filled up to all the *f* of God. .... Eph 3:19
in him all the *f* of deity lives .... Col 2:9

FULLY
my time has not yet *f* arrived. ...... John 7:8
He was *f* convinced. .... Rom 4:21
I have *f* preached the gospel. ...... Rom 15:19
message would be *f* proclaimed. .. 2 Tim 4:17

FUN
makes *f* of you. .... Isa 37:22
they began making *f* of him ...... Matt 9:24

FUNCTION
members serve the same *f* .... Rom 12:4

FUNERAL
better to go to a *f* than a feast. ...... Eccl 7:2

FURIOUS
The Lord was *f* with Israel .... Judg 2:14
With *f* anger I will carry out .... Mic 5:15
they became *f* and. .... Acts 5:33
winepress of the *f* wrath of God... Rev 19:15

FURNACE
that iron-smelting *f*. .... Deut 4:20
burn them up like a fiery *f*. .... Ps 21:9
purified you in the *f* of misery ..... Isa 48:10
midst of a *f* of blazing fire .... Dan 3:6
burning like a *f* .... Mal 4:1
throw them into the fiery *f* ...... Matt 13:42
like smoke from a giant *f*. .... Rev 9:2

FURNISHED
f and ready .... Mark 14:15

FURNISHINGS
and the pattern of all its *f*. .... Exod 25:9
all its *f* and over everything. .... Num 1:50

FURROWS
You saturate its *f*. .... Ps 65:10

FURY
in *f*, and in wrath. .... Jer 21:5
my spirit full of *f*. .... Ezek 3:14
in anger and raging *f*. .... Ezek 5:15
judgment and a *f* of fire .... Heb 10:27

FUTILE
console me with your *f* words ..... Job 21:34
F! *F*!" laments the Teacher. .... Eccl 1:2
This continual longing is *f* .... Eccl 6:9
thoughts of the wise are *f* .... 1 Cor 3:20
his religion is *f*. .... Jas 1:26

FUTILITY
made to inherit months of *f* .... Job 7:3
creation was subjected to *f*. ...... Rom 8:20

FUTURE
in the *f* and forevermore .... 1 Chr 16:36
since your *f* will flourish .... Job 8:7
you make my *f* secure .... Ps 16:5
who promotes peace has a *f*. .... Ps 37:37
the wicked have no *f*. .... Ps 37:38
give you a *f* filled with hope .... Jer 29:11
happen to your people in *f* days.. Dan 10:14
The *f* splendor of this temple. .... Hag 2:9

G

GAAL
Son of Ebed; vilifies Abimelech,
    Judg 9:26–41

GAASH, MOUNT
See MOUNT GAASH

GABBATHA
Place of Pilate's court, John 19:13

GABRIEL
Messenger archangel; interprets Daniel's
    vision, Dan 8:16–27
Reveals the prophecy of 70 weeks,
    Dan 9:21–27
Announces:
    John's birth, Luke 1:11–22
    Christ's birth, Luke 1:26–38
Stands in God's presence, Luke 1:19

GAD
Son of Jacob by Zilpah, Gen 30:10–11
Blessed by Jacob, Gen 49:19
—Tribe of:
Census of, Num 1:24–25
Territory of, Num 32:20–36
Captivity of, 1 Chr 5:26
Later references to, Rev 7:5
—Prophet in David's reign, 1 Sam 22:5
Message of, to David, 2 Sam 24:10–16

GADARENES
Healing of demon-possessed in territory of,
    Matt 8:28–34

GAIN
See also DISHONEST GAIN
so you may *g* lasting fame....... 2 Sam 7:26
also hear and *g* instruction .... Prov 1:5
of all who *g* profit unjustly .... Prov 1:19
and her *g* is better than gold ...... Prov 3:14
that you may *g* discernment....... Prov 4:1
The one who is greedy for *g*...... Prov 15:27
the one who hates unjust *g*....... Prov 28:16
dishonest *g* you have hoarded...... Mic 6:10
builds his house by unjust *g* .... Hab 2:9
you will *g* your lives .... Luke 21:19
in order to *g* even more people .. 1 Cor 9:19
living is Christ and dying is *g* .... Phil 1:21
I may *g* Christ. .... Phil 3:8
g a good standing for
    themselves .... 1 Tim 3:13
not greedy for *g* .... Titus 1:7
by teaching for dishonest *g*........ Titus 1:11
folks for their own *g*. .... Jude 1:16

GAINED
Wealth *g* quickly will dwindle ..... Prov 13:11
Bread *g* by deceit tastes sweet .. Prov 20:17
An inheritance *g* easily .... Prov 20:21
nothing *g* from them on earth. ..... Eccl 2:11
money to work and *g* five more.. Matt 25:16
one who had two *g* two more .... Matt 25:17
I have *g* five more .... Matt 25:20
g what was promised. .... Heb 11:33

GAINING
g salvation through our Lord .... 1 Thess 5:9

GAINS
g the whole world but forfeits... Matt 16:26

GAIUS
Companion of Paul, Acts 19:29
—Convert at Derbe, Acts 20:4
—Paul's host at Corinth, Rom 16:23;
    1 Cor 1:14

GALATIA
Paul visits, Acts 16:6; 18:23
Paul writes to Christians in, Gal 1:1
Paul writes to Christians in, 1 Pet 1:1

GALE
the strong wind and the *g* .... Ps 55:8

GALILEANS
Speech of, Mark 14:70
Faith of, John 4:45
Pilate's cruelty toward, Luke 13:1–2

GALILEE [or KINNERETH; GENNESARET]
Prophecies concerning, Deut 33:18–23;
    Isa 9:1–2
Dialect of, distinctive, Matt 26:73
Herod's jurisdiction over, Luke 3:1
Christ's contacts with, Matt 2:22; 4:12–25;
    26:32; 27:55; John 4:1, 3
Also called, "Kinnereth," 1 Kgs 15:20
Also called "Gennesaret," Matt 14:34

**GALILEE, SEA OF [or KINNERETH; LAKE
    OF GENNESARET; SEA OF TIBERIAS]**
Scene of many events in Christ's life,
    Mark 7:31
Also called "Kinnereth," Num 34:11
Also called "Lake of Gennesaret," Luke 5:1
Also called "Sea of Tiberias," John 6:1

GALL
offered Jesus wine mixed with *g*.. Matt 27:34

GALLIO
Roman proconsul of Achaia, dismisses
    charges against Paul, Acts 18:12–17

GALLONS
holding twenty or thirty *g* .... John 2:6

GALLOWS
conspirators hanged on a *g*. ...... Esth 2:23
were hanged on the *g* .... Esth 9:25

GAMALIEL
Famous Jewish teacher, Acts 22:3
Respected by people, Acts 5:34–39

GAMBLE
you would *g* for the fatherless...... Job 6:27

GAME
he had a taste for fresh *g* .... Gen 25:28
Bring me some wild *g* .... Gen 27:7

GANG
g of evil men crowd around me .... Ps 22:16

GANGRENE
will spread its infection like *g*...... 2 Tim 2:17

GANGS
g rob people out in the streets ...... Hos 7:1

GAP
repair the wall and stand in the *g*.. Ezek 22:30

GARDEN
You are a locked *g*. .... Song 4:12
will be like a well-watered *g*........ Isa 58:11
the *g* of God. .... Ezek 28:13
was crucified there was a *g*........ John 19:41

GARDENER
and my Father is the *g*. .... John 15:1
she thought he was the *g*. .... John 20:15

GARDENS
I designed royal *g* and parks. .... Eccl 2:5
Plant *g* and eat .... Jer 29:5

GARLAND
like an elegant *g* on your head ..... Prov 1:9

GARLANDS
bulls and *g* to the city gates ...... Acts 14:13

GARLIC
the leeks, the onions, and the *g*.... Num 11:5

GARMENT
took the *g* and placed it .... Gen 9:23
like a hairy *g*. .... Gen 25:25
grabbed him by his outer *g*. ...... Gen 39:12
she laid his outer *g* beside her.... Gen 39:16
like a *g* eaten by moths. .... Job 13:28
with light as if it were a *g*. .... Ps 104:2
who takes off a *g* on a cold day.. Prov 25:20
g dragged through blood. .... Isa 9:5
a *g* symbolizing praise. .... Isa 61:3
unshrunk cloth on an old *g*. ...... Mark 2:21
will all grow old like a *g* .... Heb 1:11

GARMENTS
Lord God made *g* from skin .... Gen 3:21
You, whose *g* are hot. .... Job 37:17
are rolling dice for my *g*. .... Ps 22:18
made linen *g* then sold them ..... Prov 31:24

not just your *g*.......................Joel 2:13
divided my *g* among them........John 19:24

GATE
Boaz went up to the village *g*......Ruth 4:1
people who were at the *g* ....Ruth 4:11
This is the LORD's *g*................Ps 118:20
is well known in the city *g*........Prov 31:23
Enter through the narrow *g* ....Matt 7:13
is the *g* and difficult the way......Matt 7:14
in Jerusalem by the Sheep *G*.......John 5:2
at the temple *g* called ....Acts 3:2
she did not open the *g*............Acts 12:14

GATES
its *g* have been burned down.......Neh 1:3
fall on the *g* of Jerusalem..........Neh 13:19
down to the barred *g* of death......Job 17:16
Look up, you *g*.....................Ps 24:7
The LORD loves the *g* of Zion........Ps 87:2
Enter his *g* with thanksgiving......Ps 100:4
the *g* of the just king's temple......Ps 118:19
works praise her in the city *g*.....Prov 31:31
Come through the *g*................Isa 62:10
the *g* of the netherworld ....Jonah 2:6
g of Hades will not overpower ...Matt 16:18
the judge stands before the *g* ....Jas 5:9
high wall with twelve *g*............Rev 21:12
the twelve *g* are twelve pearls......Rev 21:21
Its *g* will never be closed ....Rev 21:25

GATEWAY
Lot was sitting in the city's *g* ....Gen 19:1

GATH
Philistine city, 1 Sam 6:17
Ark carried to, 1 Sam 5:8
David takes refuge in, 1 Sam 21:10–15
    second flight to, 1 Sam 27:3–12
Captured by David, 1 Chr 18:1
Destruction of, prophetic, Amos 6:1–3
Name becomes proverbial, Mic 1:10

GATH HEPHER
Birthplace of Jonah, 2 Kgs 14:25

GATHER
went to *g* the plunder ....2 Chr 20:25
and a time to *g* stones..............Eccl 3:5
g Israel's dispersed people ....Isa 11:12
g those forces back inside..........Jer 21:4
and will *g* his wheat ....Matt 3:12
or *g* into barns....................Matt 6:26
and *g* where I didn't scatter ....Matt 25:26
and they will *g* his elect..........Mark 13:27
whoever does not *g* with me .....Luke 11:23
have longed to *g* your children ...Luke 13:34

GATHERED
had *g* what he could eat ....Exod 16:18
g around me because of............Ezra 9:4
and *g* from foreign lands ....Ps 107:3
g at the harvest what it will eat.....Prov 6:8
Grapes are not *g* from thorns ....Matt 7:16
and *g* the church together........Acts 14:27
had *g* a bundle of brushwood .....Acts 28:3
The one who *g* much..............2 Cor 8:15
and our being *g* to be with him .. 2 Thess 2:1
Now the spirits *g* the kings ....Rev 16:16

GATHERING
there was a widow *g* wood ....1 Kgs 17:10
I am a couple of sticks..........1 Kgs 17:12
g where you did not scatter .....Matt 25:24
to explain this disorderly *g*......Acts 19:40

GATHERS
and *g* the exiles of Israel............Ps 147:2
who *g* crops in the summer.......Prov 10:5
one who *g* it little by little.......Prov 13:11
g it for someone who is gracious ..Prov 28:8
the one who *g* the dispersed ....Isa 56:8
as a hen *g* her chicks ....Matt 23:37

GAUGE
measured the waters with a *g* ....Job 28:25

GAVE
See also GAVE HIMSELF
g some of it to her husband........Gen 3:6

The woman whom you *g* me ....Gen 3:12
Abram *g* Melchizedek a tenth ....Gen 14:20
g Hagar, her Egyptian servant ......Gen 16:3
and then *g* the boy a drink.........Gen 21:19
she *g* him a drink..................Gen 24:18
g Esau some bread and lentil
    stew..........................Gen 25:34
the land God *g* to Abraham........Gen 28:4
Joseph *g* orders to fill their bags...Gen 42:25
g Moses two tablets of testimony..Exod 31:18
So they *g* it to me.................Exod 32:24
stone tablets and *g* them to me .. Deut 5:22
they *g* a loud battle cry...........Josh 6:20
So he *g* her both the upper.......Josh 15:19
clothes and *g* them to the men...Judg 14:19
so I *g* her to your best man........Judg 15:2
she doubled over and *g* birth.....1 Sam 4:19
robe he was wearing and *g* it......1 Sam 18:4
Saul then *g* him his daughter ....1 Sam 18:27
So the priest *g* him holy bread ...1 Sam 21:6
and *g* him provisions ....1 Sam 22:10
God *g* Solomon wisdom..........1 Kgs 4:29
g the king 120 talents of gold....1 Kgs 10:10
David *g* to his son Solomon ......1 Chr 28:11
Hilkiah *g* the scroll to Shaphan ..2 Chr 34:15
g him a written copy of the law.....Esth 4:8
and *g* it to Mordecai.................Esth 8:2
and *g* me secure footing. ....Ps 40:2
returns to God who *g* it............Eccl 12:7
who *g* you birth..................Isa 51:2
g Daniel the name Belteshazzar.....Dan 1:7
g them a diet of vegetables.........Dan 1:16
and *g* him gifts of gold............. Matt 2:11
and *g* them authority..............Matt 10:1
and who *g* you this authority .....Matt 21:23
hungry and you *g* me food ......Matt 25:35
naked and you *g* me clothing....Matt 25:36
he *g* it to them..................Matt 26:27
on a platter and *g* it to the girl....Mark 6:28
he *g* the body to Joseph ....Mark 15:45
Jesus *g* him back to his mother....Luke 7:15
You *g* me no water for my feet... Luke 7:44
and *g* them to the innkeeper .... Luke 10:35
but no one *g* him anything ....Luke 15:16
they too *g* praise to God.........Luke 18:43
He *g* his one and only Son........John 3:16
The glory you *g* to me............John 17:22
Therefore God *g* them over ....Rom 1:24
g us the Spirit in our hearts.......2 Cor 1:22
g themselves first to the Lord .....2 Cor 8:5
God graciously *g* it to Abraham ... Gal 3:18
g him to the church as head.......Eph 1:22
he *g* gifts to men .... Eph 4:8
he himself *g* some as apostles......Eph 4:11
and the sky *g* rain ....Jas 5:18
great mercy he *g* us new birth......1 Pet 1:3
from the dead and *g* him glory .... 1 Pet 1:21
as he *g* us the commandment ... 1 John 3:23
God *g* him to show his servants ......Rev 1:1
g the seven angels seven golden ...Rev 15:7

GAVE HIMSELF
who *g* for our sins ....Gal 1:14
who loved me and *g* for me ....Gal 2:20
Christ also *g* lived us and *g*...........Eph 5:2
loved the church and *g*............. Eph 5:25
who *g* as a ransom for all............1 Tim 2:6
He *g* for us to set us free .... Titus 2:14

GAZA
Philistine city, Josh 13:3
Samson removes the gates of, Judg 16:1–3
Samson taken there as prisoner; his
    revenge, Judg 16:21–31
Sin of, condemned, Amos 1:6–7
Philip journeys to, Acts 8:26

GAZAM
What the *g*-locust left ....Joel 1:4
and the *g*-locust ....Joel 2:25

GAZE
let your *g* look straight before.... Prov 4:25

GEBA
Levite city in Benjamin, Josh 18:24; 21:17
Rebuilt by Asa, 1 Kgs 15:22

GEDALIAH
Made governor of Judah, 2 Kgs 25:22–26
Befriends Jeremiah, Jer 40:5–6
Murdered by Ishmael, Jer 41:2, 18

GEHAZI
Elisha's servant; seeks reward from
    Naaman, 2 Kgs 5:20–24
Afflicted with leprosy, 2 Kgs 5:25–27
Relates Elisha's deeds to Jehoram,
    2 Kgs 8:4–6

GEMS
make your pinnacles out of *g*.......Isa 54:12

GENEALOGIES
according to their *g*...............Gen 10:32
with myths and interminable *g*....1 Tim 1:4

GENEALOGY
record of the *g* of Jesus Christ...... Matt 1:1
father, without mother, without *g* .. Heb 7:3

GENERAL
The *g* of his army was Sisera ....Judg 4:2

GENERATION
See also THIS GENERATION
godly among this *g* ....Gen 7:1
my memorial from *g* to *g*.........Exod 3:15
to the third and fourth *g*..........Exod 34:7
that *g* that had done wickedly....Num 32:13
a perverse and deceitful *g*.........Deut 32:5
That entire *g* passed away.........Judg 2:10
their children to the fourth *g* ....Job 42:16
A whole *g* will serve him .... Ps 22:30
We will tell the next *g* ....Ps 78:4
so that the next *g*....................Ps 78:6
a stubborn and rebellious *g* ....Ps 78:8
One *g* will praise your deeds ....Ps 145:4
does a crown last from *g* to *g* ... Prov 27:24
is a *g* who curse their fathers.....Prov 30:11
g who are pure in their own......Prov 30:12
A *g* comes and a *g* goes.............Eccl 1:4
G after *g* it will be a wasteland .... Isa 34:10
You people of this *g* ....Jer 2:31
from one *g* to the next .... Dan 4:3
from one *g* to the next ....Dan 4:34
their children the following *g*........Joel 1:3
it was said to an older *g* ....Matt 5:21
should I compare this *g*........... Matt 11:16
evil and adulterous *g* asks........Matt 12:39
this *g* will not pass away.........Matt 24:34
You unbelieving *g* ....Mark 9:19
from *g* to *g* he is merciful......... Luke 1:50
g may be held accountable.......Luke 11:50
this *g* will not pass away.........Luke 21:32
from this perverse *g*...............Acts 2:40
provoked at that *g*................. Heb 3:10

GENERATIONS
covenant for all subsequent *g* .....Gen 9:12
your *g* every male among you.....Gen 17:12
to the third and fourth *g*..........Exod 20:5
until the third and fourth *g* ....Num 14:18
to a thousand *g*................... Deut 7:9
for the sins of earlier *g* ....Ps 79:8
We will tell coming *g* ....Ps 79:13
to future *g* I will proclaim ....Ps 89:1
our protector through all *g*.........Ps 90:1
he is faithful through all *g* ....Ps 100:5
he made to a thousand *g* ....Ps 105:8
your faithfulness to all *g*...........Ps 119:90
all *g* will call me blessed...........Luke 1:48
to people in former *g*...............Eph 3:5
kept hidden from ages and *g* ....Col 1:26

GENEROSITY
in the wealth of their *g* ....2 Cor 8:2

GENEROUS
for God has been *g* to me ....Gen 33:11
A *g* person will be enriched ......Prov 11:25
A *g* person will be blessed........ Prov 22:9
g giving and every perfect gift....... Jas 1:17

GENEROUSLY
well for the one who *g* lends ....Ps 112:5
and the person who sows *g* ....2 Cor 9:6
who gives to all *g*....................Jas 1:5

GENNESARET
See GALILEE

GENNESARET, LAKE OF
See GALILEE, SEA OF

GENTILE
a road that leads to G regions .....Matt 10:5
like a G or a tax collector........Matt 18:17

GENTILES
babble repetitiously like the G .... Matt 6:7
for revelation to the G............ Luke 2:32
trampled down by the G .... Luke 21:24
to carry my name before G........ Acts 9:15
poured out even on the G ....Acts 10:45
you to be a light for the G ....Acts 13:47
Jews and the God-fearing G ....Acts 17:17
blasphemed among the G .... Rom 2:24
he not the God of the G too ...... Rom 3:29
permitted even among the G.......1 Cor 5:1
in dangers from G .... 2 Cor 11:26
had been eating with the G.........Gal 2:12
of this mystery among the G .... Col 1:27
a teacher of the G in faith ....1 Tim 2:7

GENTLE
g response turns away anger ...... Prov 15:1
I am g and humble in heart.......Matt 11:29
g, showing complete courtesy .... Titus 3:2
g, accommodating, full of mercy .... Jas 3:17
to those who are good and g .....1 Pet 2:18
beauty of a g and tranquil spirit ....1 Pet 3:4

GENTLENESS
with love and a spirit of g..........1 Cor 4:21
g, and self-control ....Gal 5:23
with all humility and g.............. Eph 4:2
Let everyone see your g............Phil 4:5
love, endurance, and g............1 Tim 6:11
correcting opponents with g .... 2 Tim 2:25
in the g that wisdom brings ....Jas 3:13

GENUINE
by the Holy Spirit, by g love ....2 Cor 6:6
when he has proven to be g ....Jas 1:12

GENUINENESS
I am testing the g of your love.....2 Cor 8:8

GERAR
Town of Philistia, Gen 10:19
Visited by Abraham, Gen 20:1–18
    by Isaac, Gen 26:1–17
Abimelech, king of, Gen 26:1, 26

GERIZIM, MOUNT
See MOUNT GERIZIM

GERSHOM
Son of Moses, Exod 2:21–22
Circumcised, Exod 4:25
Founder of Levite family, 1 Chr 23:14–16

GESHUR
Inhabitants of, not expelled by Israel,
    Josh 13:13
Talmai, king of, grandfather of Absalom,
    2 Sam 3:3
Absalom flees to, 2 Sam 13:37–38

GET
I g no pleasure from your ....Amos 5:21
kill him and g his inheritance.... Matt 21:38
give a tenth of everything I g ....Luke 18:12
g your minds ready for action .....1 Pet 1:13

GETHSEMANE
Garden near Jerusalem, Matt 26:30, 36
Often visited by Christ, Luke 22:39
Scene of Christ's agony and betrayal,
    Matt 26:36–56; John 18:1–12

GETS
He g trees from the forest......... Isa 44:14

GEZER
Canaanite city, Josh 10:33
Inhabitants not expelled, Josh 16:10
Given as dowry of Pharaoh's daughter,
    1 Kgs 9:15–17

GHOST
they thought he was a g .... Mark 6:49
thinking they saw a g ....Luke 24:37
a g does not have flesh ....Luke 24:39

GHOSTS
go through life as mere g...........Ps 39:6

GIBBERISH
they will hear meaningless g ...... Isa 28:10
will sound like meaningless g .....Isa 28:13

GIBEAH
Town of Benjamin; known for wickedness,
    Judg 19:12–30
Destruction of, Judg 20:1–48
Saul's birthplace, 1 Sam 10:26
    political capital, 1 Sam 15:34
Wickedness of, long remembered, Hos 9:9

GIBEON
Sun stands still at, Josh 10:12
Location of tabernacle, 1 Chr 16:39
Joab struck Amasa at, 2 Sam 20:8–10
Joab killed at, 1 Kgs 2:28–34
Site of Solomon's sacrifice and dream,
    1 Kgs 3:5–15

GIBEONITES
Trick Joshua into making treaty; subjected
    to forced labor, Josh 9:3–27
Rescued by Joshua, Josh 10
Massacred by Saul; avenged by David,
    2 Sam 21:1–9

GIDEON [or JERUB BAAL]
Called by an angel, Judg 6:11–24
Destroys Baal's altar, Judg 6:25–32
Fleece confirms call from God,
    Judg 6:36–40
Miraculous victory over the Midianites,
    Judg 7
Takes revenge on Succoth and Penuel,
    Judg 8:4–21
Refuses kingship; makes an ephod,
    Judg 8:22–28
Fathers 71 sons; dies, Judg 8:29–35
Also called "Jerub Baal," Judg 7:1

GIFT
person's g makes room for him .. Prov 18:16
g given in secret subdues anger .. Prov 21:14
these things are a g from God......Eccl 3:13
if you bring your g to the altar.... Matt 5:23
so that your g may be in secret.... Matt 6:4
anyone swears by the g on it .... Matt 23:18
the g or the altar .... Matt 23:19
a g for God ....Mark 7:11
you had known the g of God .....John 4:10
receive the g of the Holy Spirit ....Acts 2:38
acquire God's g with money ...... Acts 8:20
that the g of the Holy Spirit ......Acts 10:45
if God gave them the same g ......Acts 11:17
impart to you some spiritual g .....Rom 1:11
the gracious g is not like...........Rom 5:15
and of the g of righteousness......Rom 5:17
the g of God is eternal life........ Rom 6:23
each has his own g from God.......1 Cor 7:7
can someone without the g ......1 Cor 14:16
it is the g of God....................Eph 2:8
because I am seeking a g ....Phil 4:17
neglect the spiritual g you have .. 1 Tim 4:14
remind you to rekindle God's g....2 Tim 1:6
tasted the heavenly g............... Heb 6:4
as each one has received a g......1 Pet 4:10

GIFTS
all your g you must offer up..... Num 18:29
friend of the person who gives g ..Prov 19:6
to give good g to your children.... Matt 7:11
putting their g into the offering ... Luke 21:1
And we have different g...........Rom 12:6
With regard to spiritual g..........1 Cor 12:1
Now there are different g ....1 Cor 12:4
be eager for the spiritual g ....1 Cor 14:1
he gave g to men .... Eph 4:8

GIHON
River of Eden, Gen 2:13
—Spring outside Jerusalem, 1 Kgs 1:33–45
Source of water supply, 2 Chr 32:30

GILBOA
Range of limestone hills in Issachar,
    1 Sam 28:4
Scene of Saul's death, 1 Sam 31:1–9
Under David's curse, 2 Sam 1:17, 21

GILBOA, MOUNT
See MOUNT GILBOA

GILEAD
Plain east of the Jordan; taken from the
    Amorites and assigned to Gad, Reuben,
    and Manasseh, Num 21:21–31; 32:33–40;
    Deut 3:12–13; Josh 13:24–31
Ish Bosheth rules over, 2 Sam 2:8–9
David takes refuge in, 2 Sam 17:21–26
Conquered by Hazael, 2 Kgs 10:32–33
Balm of, figurative of national healing,
    Jer 8:22

GILEAD, MOUNT
See MOUNT GILEAD

GILGAL
Site of memorial stones, circumcision,
    first Passover in the Promised Land,
    Josh 4:19–5:12
Site of Gibeonite covenant, Josh 9:3–15
One location on Samuel's circuit,
    1 Sam 7:15–16
Saul made king and later rejected,
    1 Sam 11:15; 13:4–15
Denounced for idolatry, Hos 9:15

GIRGASHITES
Descendants of Canaan, Gen 10:15–16
Land of, given to Abraham's descendants,
    Gen 15:18, 21
Delivered to Israel, Josh 24:11

GIRLS
her slave g moan like doves .... Nah 2:7

GITTITES
600 follow David, 2 Sam 15:18–23

GIVE
LORD g me yet another son......Gen 30:24
You shall not g false testimony .. Exod 20:16
The land will g its fruit.............Lev 25:19
whole army g a loud battle cry ..... Josh 6:5
G your hearts to the LORD.........1 Sam 7:3
You g me strength for battle .. 2 Sam 22:40
g you a wise and discerning ....1 Kgs 3:12
G your household instructions ...2 Kgs 20:1
G thanks to the LORD..............1 Chr 16:8
g me wisdom and discernment... 2 Chr 1:10
g praise to the LORD God.........Ezra 10:11
G sincere homage .... Ps 2:12
He will surely g me shelter .... Ps 27:5
G him the honor he deserves........Ps 66:2
g him the honor he deserves .... Ps 67:7
will g you an eternal dynasty ....Ps 89:4
G him thanks ....Ps 100:4
G me understanding............... Ps 119:34
G me a desire for your rules....... Ps 119:36
precepts g me discernment ...... Ps 119:104
G me insight ....Ps 119:125
G me insight so that I can live .... Ps 119:144
G me insight by your word ...... Ps 119:169
g her poor all the food........... Ps 132:15
do not g Jerusalem priority......... Ps 137:6
G me your heart.................. Prov 23:26
G the oppressed reason .... Isa 1:17
you g them great joy ....Isa 9:3
your decrees can g men life ....Isa 38:16
and g you a title of respect ....Isa 45:4
G to the one who asks you .... Matt 5:42
G us today our daily bread .... Matt 6:11
and g the money to the poor .....Matt 19:21
g him his portion at the harvest ..Matt 21:41
Then g to Caesar the things ......Matt 22:21
I can g it to anyone I wish .... Luke 4:6
will g him a scorpion .... Luke 11:12

and *g* the money to the poor .... Luke 18:22
I *g* them eternal life .... John 10:28
I *g* you a new commandment..... John 13:34
my peace I *g* to you............. John 14:27
but what I do have I *g* you.......... Acts 3:6
him as God or *g* him thanks ...... Rom 1:21
freely *g* us all things .... Rom 8:32
g offense to Jews or Greeks ..... 1 Cor 10:32
not *g* the devil an opportunity..... Eph 4:27
g grace to those who hear......... Eph 4:29
did not *g* us a Spirit of fear .... 2 Tim 1:7
are able to *g* you wisdom.......... 2 Tim 3:15
always be ready to *g* an answer ... 1 Pet 3:15
and I will *g* you the crown ....Rev 2:10
g him some of the hidden manna .. Rev 2:17
I will *g* him the morning star ...... Rev 2:28
to *g* me the little scroll ....Rev 10:9
I will *g* water free of charge ....Rev 21:6

GIVEN
so he has *g* a blessing to you .... Exod 32:29
the good land he has *g* you....... Deut 8:10
the LORD has *g* me the request...1 Sam 1:27
the LORD has *g* Israel a victory ...1 Sam 11:13
It shall be *g* to you.................. Esth 5:6
one who boasts of a gift not *g*....Prov 25:14
you have *g* your sisters reason ..Ezek 16:52
these things will be *g* to you...... Matt 6:33
Ask and it will be *g* to you.......... Matt 7:7
whoever has will be *g* more ..... Matt 13:12
one who has will be *g* more ..... Matt 25:29
who has been *g* much .... Luke 12:48
my body which is *g* for you...... Luke 22:19
has *g* the right to become ....John 1:12
the law was *g* through Moses ......John 1:17
person of every one he has *g*..... John 6:39
the Spirit had not yet been *g* ......John 7:39
that you have *g* me............... John 17:12
things that are freely *g* to us.....1 Cor 2:12
to each one of us grace was *g* ......Eph 4:7
I may be *g* the right words..........Eph 6:19
sort of love the Father has *g*.......1 John 3:1
was *g* a long white robe .... Rev 6:11
g permission to damage the earth...Rev 7:2

GIVER
because God loves a cheerful *g*....2 Cor 9:7

GIVERS
to be generous *g* .... 1 Tim 6:18

GIVES
he *g* a revelation to people .... Job 33:16
one true God *g* me strength......... Ps 18:32
The one who *g* an answer .... Prov 18:13
The one who *g* to the poor ...... Prov 28:27
God *g* wisdom...................... Eccl 2:26
Wisdom *g* a wise person ....Eccl 7:19
g the thirsty nothing to drink....... Isa 32:6
g all this to those who fear him..... Isa 33:6
or *g* him instruction .... Isa 40:13
He *g* me the agility of a deer ......Hab 3:19
and *g* life to the world.............John 6:33
Father *g* me will come to me .....John 6:37
who *g* to all generously................ Jas 1:5
But he *g* greater grace............... Jas 4:6

GIVING
the apostles were *g* testimony ....Acts 4:33
by *g* you rain from heaven........ Acts 14:17
generous *g* and every perfect gift ... Jas 1:17

GLAD
wine that makes people *g* .... Ps 104:15
was *g* because they said to me ......Ps 122:1
Rejoice and be *g*................... Matt 5:12
to celebrate and be *g*............Luke 15:32
and he saw it and was *g* .... John 8:56
you would be *g* that I am going..John 14:28
with *g* and humble hearts ....Acts 2:46
you may also rejoice and be *g* .....1 Pet 4:13

GLASS
was something like a sea of *g* ...... Rev 4:6
like transparent *g*.................. Rev 21:21

GLEAMED
the wheels *g* like jasper............Ezek 10:9

GLISTENS
In the morning it *g* and sprouts..... Ps 90:6

GLITTERING
g awesomely like ice.............. Ezek 1:22

GLOOM
fire and darkness and *g*...........Heb 12:18

GLORIFIED
because Jesus was not yet *g* ....John 7:39
but when Jesus was *g*............. John 12:16
I *g* you on earth..................... John 17:4
has *g* his servant Jesus............. Acts 3:13
and those he justified, he also *g* .. Rom 8:30
in everything God will be *g* .... 1 Pet 4:11

GLORIFY
I acknowledge and *g* you .... Dan 2:23
If I *g* myself...................... John 8:54
Father, *g* your name ....John 12:28
He will *g* me..................... John 16:14
g me at your side .... John 17:5
Peter was going to *g* God......... John 21:19
they did not *g* him as God .... Rom 1:21
g God with your body ....1 Cor 6:20
Christ did not *g* himself........... Heb 5:5
g God that you bear such a name ..1 Pet 4:16

GLORIFYING
praising and *g* the LORD ....Ezra 3:11

GLORIOUS
g, and sovereign over all..........1 Chr 29:11
His *g* name deserves praise .... Ps 72:19
His work is majestic and *g*........... Ps 111:3
light of the *g* gospel of Christ......2 Cor 4:4
the church to himself as *g* .... Eph 5:27
the likeness of his *g* body...........Phil 3:21
according to his *g* riches............Phil 4:19
g appearing of our great God.....Titus 2:13
not afraid to insult the *g* ones .... 2 Pet 2:10

GLORY
See also GLORY OF GOD; GLORY OF THE
  LORD
Show me your *g*.................. Exod 33:18
earth will be filled with the *g* .....Num 14:21
The *g* has departed from Israel...1 Sam 4:21
my *g* and the one who restores ...... Ps 3:3
Gray hair is like a crown of *g* ..... Prov 16:31
The *g* of young men ....Prov 20:29
It is the *g* of God to conceal ...... Prov 25:2
not share my *g* with anyone .... Isa 42:8
Then the *g* of the LORD arose .... Ezek 10:4
the source of *g* in her midst .... Zech 2:5
Solomon in all his *g* was clothed . Matt 6:29
in the *g* of his Father.............Matt 16:27
with power and great *g*.........Matt 24:30
G to God in the highest..........Luke 2:14
We saw his *g* .... John 1:14
In this way he revealed his *g*........John 2:11
with the *g* I had with you .... John 17:5
The *g* you gave to me............. John 17:22
he did not give the *g* to God...... Acts 12:23
g and honor and immortality.......Rom 2:7
giving *g* to God .... Rom 4:20
the *g*, the covenants .... Rom 9:4
make known the wealth of his *g*.. Rom 9:23
be *g* forever ....Rom 16:27
he is the image and *g* of God ...... 1 Cor 11:7
with *g*, so that the Israelites .... 2 Cor 3:7
now has no *g* .... 2 Cor 3:10
an eternal weight of *g* .... 2 Cor 4:17
be revealed in *g* with him........... Col 3:4
For you are our *g* and joy.......1 Thess 2:20
crowned him with *g* and honor..... Heb 2:7
in bringing many sons to *g* .... Heb 2:10
its *g* like the flower of the grass ...1 Pet 1:24
belong the *g* and the power .... 1 Pet 4:11
because the Spirit of *g*.............1 Pet 4:14
receive *g* and honor and power .... Rev 4:11

GLORY OF GOD
The heavens declare the *g*...........Ps 19:1
you would see the *g* ....John 11:40
toward heaven and saw the *g* .....Acts 7:55
sinned and fall short of the *g* .....Rom 3:23

do everything for the *g*............1 Cor 10:31
he is the image and *g*.............. 1 Cor 11:7
to increase to the *g*................ 2 Cor 4:15
Jesus Christ is Lord to the *g* .... Phil 2:11
The city possesses the *g*.........Rev 21:11
because the *g* lights it up.........Rev 21:23

GLORY OF THE LORD
the *g* appeared in the cloud ..... Exod 16:10
The *g* resided on Mount Sinai ... Exod 24:16
the *g* filled the tabernacle ....Exod 40:35
that the *g* may appear to you........Lev 9:6
g appeared to all the Israelites ...Num 14:10
g appeared to the whole......... Num 16:9
and the *g* appeared.............. Num 16:42
and the *g* appeared to them......Num 20:6
it looked like the *g*................Ezek 1:28
and the *g* was standing there.....Ezek 3:23
the *g* arose from the cherub..... Ezek 10:4
The *g* came into the temple ...... Ezek 43:4
I noticed the *g* filling.............. Ezek 44:4
the *g* shone around them.......... Luke 2:9
faces reflecting the *g* .... 2 Cor 3:18

GLUTTON
a *g* and a drunk.................... Luke 7:34

GLUTTONS
and *g* become impoverished .....Prov 23:21
companion of *g* brings shame .... Prov 28:7
always liars, evil beasts, lazy *g*..... Titus 1:12

GNASHING
will be weeping and *g* of teeth.....Matt 8:12

GNATS
g throughout all the land .... Exod 8:16
g invaded their whole territory.... Ps 105:31

GO
Let me *g*..........................Gen 32:26
presence does not *g* with us..... Exod 33:15
For wherever you *g*................. Ruth 1:16
If I *g* to the east....................Job 23:8
liars *g* astray as soon .... Ps 58:3
can I *g* to escape your Spirit........ Ps 139:7
G to the ant.........................Prov 6:6
Both *g* to the same place.......... Eccl 3:20
to *g* to a funeral than a feast .... Eccl 7:2
follow you wherever you *g* ....Matt 8:19
do not *g* out .... Matt 24:26
G into all the world and preach.. Mark 16:15
I say to this one, '*G* .... Luke 7:8
to whom would we *g*............. John 6:68
let these men *g*....................John 18:8

GOAL
attaining the *g* of your faith ....1 Pet 1:9

GOAT
a lamb or young *g* ....Exod 12:21

GOATS
Do I drink the blood of *g* ....Ps 50:13
separates the sheep from the *g* .. Matt 25:32
not by the blood of *g* and calves... Heb 9:12
of bulls and *g* to take away sins ... Heb 10:4

GOD
Names of:
  eternal King, 1 Tim 1:17
  everlasting God, Deut 33:27
  Father of lights, Jas 1:17
  God of heaven, Jonah 1:9
  God of Heaven's Armies, Ps 80:7
  heavenly Father, Matt 6:26
  Holy One of Israel, Isa 43:3
  I AM, Exod 3:14
  Jealous, Exod 34:14
  living God, Josh 3:10
  LORD God, Gen 2:4
  mighty God, Isa 10:21
  Most High God, Gen 14:18–22
  only Sovereign, 1 Tim 6:15
  Sovereign LORD, Gen 15:2, 8
  Sovereign LORD of Heaven's Armies,
    Isa 1:24
Manifestations of:
  angel of, Gen 16:7–13
  face of, Gen 32:30

form of, Num 12:6–8
glory of, Exod 40:34–35
name of, Exod 34:5–7
voice of, Deut 5:22–26
Nature of:
one, Deut 6:4
personal, John 17:1–3
spirit, John 4:24
trinitarian, 2 Cor 13:14
Attributes of:
eternal, Isa 57:15
foreknowing, Isa 48:3, 5
holy, Rev 4:8
impartial, 1 Pet 1:17
incomparable, 2 Sam 7:22
infinite, 1 Kgs 8:27
inscrutable, Isa 40:28
invisible, John 1:18
just, Ps 89:14
longsuffering, Exod 34:6–7
love, 1 John 4:8, 16
mercy, Lam 3:22–23
omnipotent, Jer 32:17, 27
omnipresent, Ps 139:7–12
omniscient, 1 John 3:20
truth, Ps 117:2
unchangeable, Num 23:19
unequaled, Isa 40:13–25
unsearchable, Rom 11:33–34
vengeance, Deut 32:34–41
wise, Acts 15:18
wrath, Deut 32:22

See also ANGEL OF GOD; GLORY OF GOD;
GOD THE FATHER; HAND OF GOD;
HOUSE OF GOD; KINGDOM OF GOD;
LORD GOD OF HEAVEN'S ARMIES;
LORD GOD OF ISRAEL; LOVE OF GOD;
LOVE THE LORD YOUR GOD; MAN OF
GOD; PEOPLE OF GOD; POWER OF
GOD; RIGHTEOUSNESS OF GOD; SON
OF GOD; SONS OF GOD; SPIRIT OF
GOD; THINGS OF GOD; THRONE OF
GOD; WILL OF GOD; WORD OF GOD;
WRATH OF GOD

In the beginning *G* created . . . . Gen 1:1
by the Most High *G*. . . . . .Gen 14:19
I will be their *G* .Gen 17:8
I have seen *G* face to face . . . . . . .Gen 32:30
I am the *G* of your father . . . . Exod 3:6
the *G* of Israel . . . . .Exod 5:1
This is my *G* . . . . .Exod 15:2
and may *G* be with you . . . . .Exod 18:19
I, the LORD, am your *G* . . . . .Exod 20:2
G is not a man . . . . Num 23:19
your *G* is a consuming fire . . . . .Deut 4:24
for the LORD your *G* . . . . .Deut 7:21
your *G* will become my *G* . . . . Ruth 1:16
will realize that Israel has a *G* . . .1 Sam 17:46
There is no *G* besides you . . . . .2 Sam 7:22
who is *G* besides the LORD . . . . .2 Sam 22:32
If the LORD is the true *G*. . . . . .1 Kgs 18:21
our *G* is greater than all gods. . . . . .2 Chr 2:5
G is greater than a human. . . . . .Job 33:12
Indeed, *G* is mighty . . . . .Job 36:5
Yes, *G* is great . . . . .Job 36:26
you have been my *G* . . . . .Ps 22:10
Where is your *G* .Ps 42:3
G is our strong refuge . . . . .Ps 46:1
G lives within it. .Ps 46:5
G is king of the whole earth . . . . .Ps 47:7
El, *G*, the LORD has spoken . . . . .Ps 50:1
I am *G*, your *G* . . . . .Ps 50:7
O *G*. Renew a resolute spirit. . . . . Ps 51:10
Our *G* is a *G* who delivers . . . . Ps 68:20
G, your deeds are extraordinary. . . . Ps 77:13
O *G* of Heaven's Armies . . . . .Ps 80:7
You alone are *G* .Ps 86:10
Praise the LORD our G. . . . . .Ps 99:9
our *G* is compassionate. . . . . .Ps 116:5
Give thanks to the *G* of heaven. . . .Ps 136:26
to bring up a matter before *G* . . . . . Eccl 5:2
Mighty *G*, Everlasting Father . . . . Isa 9:6

Look, *G* is my deliverer. . . . . .Isa 12:2
here is our *G*. . . . . .Isa 25:9
Here is your *G*. .Isa 40:9
Is there any *G* but me . . . . .Isa 44:8
Your *G* reigns. .Isa 52:7
attacked by *G*. .Isa 53:4
I will be their *G* . . . . .Jer 31:33
Who is a *G* like you . . . . .Mic 7:18
which means "*G* with us . . . . .Matt 1:23
to rejoice in *G* my Savior . . . . .Luke 1:47
and the Word was with *G*. . . . . .John 1:1
cannot enter the kingdom of *G*. . . . .John 3:5
is the way *G* loved the world . . . . . .John 3:16
that *G* is truthful. . . . . .John 3:33
G is spirit . . . . .John 4:24
My Lord and my *G*. . . . . .John 20:28
To an unknown *g* . . . . .Acts 17:23
Let *G* be proven true . . . . .Rom 3:4
If *G* is for us . . . . .Rom 8:31
G is faithful. . . . . .1 Cor 1:9
yet for us there is one *G*. . . . . .1 Cor 8:6
G will supply your every need. . . . . . .Phil 4:19
Every scripture is inspired by *G* . . .2 Tim 3:16
as Moses was warned by *G*. . . . . .Heb 8:5
And I will be their *G* . . . . .Heb 8:10
G is indeed a devouring fire . . . . . .Heb 12:29
G is greater than our conscience. .1 John 3:20
not love does not know *G* . . . . .1 John 4:8
No one has seen *G* at any time . . .1 John 4:12
a pillar in the temple of my *G* . . . . . .Rev 3:12
gave glory to the *G* of heaven . . . . .Rev 11:13
residence of *G* is among human . . . .Rev 21:3
be his *G* and he will be my son . . . . .Rev 21:7

GOD THE FATHER

For *G* has put his seal. . . . . .John 6:27
he hands over the kingdom to *G*. . 1 Cor 15:24
and *G* who raised him . . . . .Gal 1:1
Grace and peace to you from *G* . . . . .Gal 1:3
always giving thanks to *G* . . . . .Eph 5:20
from *G* and the Lord Jesus. . . . . .Eph 6:23
is Lord to the glory of *G*. . . . . .Phil 2:11
giving thanks to *G* . . . . .Col 3:17
in *G* and the Lord Jesus Christ . . . . 1 Thess 1:1
and peace to you from *G* . . . . .2 Thess 1:2
and peace from *G* . . . . .1 Tim 1:2
and peace from *G* . . . . .2 Tim 1:2
and peace from *G* . . . . .Titus 1:4
undefiled religion before *G*. . . . . .Jas 1:27
to the foreknowledge of *G* . . . . .1 Pet 1:2
and glory from *G* . . . . .2 Pet 1:17
will be with us from *G* . . . . .2 John 1:3
wrapped in the love of *G* . . . . .Jude 1:1

GOD-FEARING

G proselytes followed Paul. . . . . . . .Acts 13:43

GODDESS

worshiped the Sidonian *g* . . . . .1 Kgs 11:5

GODLESS

the hope of the *g* perishes. . . . . .Job 8:13
joy of the *g* lasts but a moment . . .Job 20:5
what hope does the *g* have . . . . .Job 27:8
The *g* at heart nourish anger . . . . . .Job 36:13
for the whole nation was *g* . . . . .Isa 9:17
prophets and priests are *g*. . . . . .Jer 23:11
fit only for the *g* and gullible . . . . . .1 Tim 4:7

GODLINESS

but *g* is valuable in every way . . . . .1 Tim 4:8
g combined with contentment . . . .1 Tim 6:6
necessary for life and *g*. . . . . .2 Pet 1:3
to perseverance, *g*. . . . . .2 Pet 1:6

GODLY

Noah was a *g* man . . . . Gen 6:9
really sweep away the *g* . . . . .Gen 18:23
kill the *g* with the wicked . . . . .Gen 18:25
LORD guards the way of the *g* . . . . .Ps 1:6
LORD shows the *g* special favor. . . . . . .Ps 4:3
Certainly you reward the *g* . . . . .Ps 5:12
what can the g accomplish . . . . .Ps 11:3
to slaughter those who are *g* . . . . . .Ps 37:14
but the LORD sustains the *g* . . . . .Ps 37:17
but the *g* show compassion . . . . .Ps 37:21
never seen the *g* abandoned . . . . . . .Ps 37:25
The *g* speak wise words . . . . .Ps 37:30

The *g* will rule over them. . . . . .Ps 49:14
the *g* will be blessed. . . . . .Ps 112:2
a light shines for the *g*. . . . . .Ps 112:4
The LORD loves the *g* . . . . .Ps 146:8
The *g* perish . . . . .Isa 57:1
All your people will be *g*. . . . . .Isa 60:21
there are no *g* men left . . . . .Mic 7:2
and *g* lives in the present age. . . . .Titus 2:12
Lord knows how to rescue the *g* . .2 Pet 2:9

GODS

See also FOREIGN GODS

These are your *g*. . . . . Exod 32:4
is God of *g* and LORD of lords . . . .Deut 10:17
in the midst of the *g* . . . . .Ps 82:1
You are *g* . . . . .Ps 82:6
as a prostitute to many *g* . . . . .Jer 3:1
and have trusted in false *g*. . . . . .Jer 13:25
g have spoken wickedness . . . . . . .Zech 10:2
came were called '*g* . . . . .John 10:35
The *g* have come down to us . . . . . .Acts 14:11

GOES

behavior that *g* with sound. . . . . .Titus 2:1

GOG

Prince of Meshech and Tubal, Ezek 38:2–3
—Leader of the final battle, Rev 20:8–15

GOING

Where I am *g* you cannot come . . .John 8:21
because I am *g* to the Father . . . . .John 14:12

GOLAN

City of refuge, Josh 20:8, 21:27

GOLD

The *g* of that land is pure. . . . . .Gen 2:12
an atonement lid of pure *g* . . . . . . Exod 25:17
a *g* bell and a pomegranate. . . . . .Exod 28:34
accumulate much silver and *g* . . . .Deut 17:17
five *g* sores and five *g* mice. . . . . . . 1 Sam 6:4
in *g* or said to pure *g* . . . . .Job 31:24
are of greater value than *g* . . . . .Ps 19:10
apples of *g* in settings of silver . . .Prov 25:11
The silver and *g* will be mine . . . . . . .Hag 2:8
I have no silver or *g*. . . . . .Acts 3:6
braided hair and *g* or pearls . . . . . . .1 Tim 2:9
a *g* ring and fine clothing . . . . .Jas 2:2
Your *g* and silver have rusted. . . . . . . .Jas 5:3
is much more valuable than *g* . . . . . .1 Pet 1:7
perishable things like silver or *g*. . .1 Pet 1:18
main street of the city is pure *g* . . .Rev 21:21

GOLDEN

g calves remained in Bethel . . . . .2 Kgs 10:29
or the *g* bowl is broken. . . . . .Eccl 12:6
and the seven *g* lampstands . . . . . . .Rev 1:20
and *g* bowls full of incense . . . . .Rev 5:8
from the horns on the *g* altar. . . . . . .Rev 9:13
She held in her hand a *g* cup . . . . . .Rev 17:4

GOLGOTHA [or PLACE OF THE SKULL, THE SKULL]

Christ crucified there, Matt 27:33;
Mark 15:22; John 19:17
Also called "Place of the Skull," Matt 27:33;
Mark 15:22; John 19:17
Also called "The Skull," Luke 23:33

GOLIATH

Giant of Gath, 1 Sam 17:4
Killed by David, 1 Sam 17:50
—Brother of above; killed by Elhanan,
2 Sam 21:19

GOMER

Son of Japheth, Gen 10:2–3; 1 Chr 1:5–6
Northern nation, Ezek 38:6
—Unfaithful wife of Hosea, Hos 1:2–3
Purchased by and restored to Hosea,
Hos 3:1–5

GOMORRAH

With Sodom, defeated by Kedorlaomer; Lot
captured, Gen 14:8–12
Destroyed by God, Gen 19:23–29
Later references to, Isa 1:10; Amos 4:11;
Matt 10:15
See also SODOM AND GOMORRAH

GONE
Harvest time has come and *g* . . . . Jer 8:20
am *g* fierce wolves will come . . . . Acts 20:29
and have *g* without food . . . . Acts 27:33

GONG
noisy *g* or a clanging cymbal . . . . . . 1 Cor 13:1

GOOD
See also GOOD WORKS; LORD IS GOOD;
   TREE OF THE KNOWLEDGE OF GOOD
   AND EVIL
God saw that it was *g* . . . . Gen 1:10
God intended it for a *g* purpose . . Gen 50:20
LORD has promised *g* things . . . . . Num 10:29
for the *g* of his people . . . . Esth 10:3
receive what is *g* from God . . . . Job 2:10
Who can show us anything *g* . . . . Ps 4:6
Certainly God is *g* to Israel . . . . Ps 73:1
and those who are *g* . . . . Prov 15:3
cheerful heart brings *g* healing . . . Prov 17:22
messenger who brings *g* news . . . . . Isa 52:7
The LORD then addressed *g* . . . . Zech 1:13
able to say anything *g* . . . . Matt 12:34
The *g* person brings *g* things . . . . . Matt 12:35
what *g* thing must I do . . . . Matt 19:16
ask me about what is *g* . . . . Matt 19:17
She has done a *g* service . . . . Matt 26:10
for I proclaim to you *g* news . . . . . Luke 2:10
love your enemies, and do *g* . . . . . Luke 6:35
the seed that landed on *g* soil . . . . . Luke 8:15
g come out of Nazareth . . . . John 1:46
He went around doing *g* . . . . Acts 10:38
because he was a *g* man . . . . Acts 11:24
without a witness by doing *g* . . . . Acts 14:17
that nothing *g* lives in me . . . . Rom 7:18
but overcome evil with *g* . . . . Rom 12:21
fruit in every *g* deed . . . . Col 1:10
we know that the law is *g* . . . . 1 Tim 1:8
you may fight the *g* fight . . . . 1 Tim 1:18
Such prayer for all is *g* . . . . 1 Tim 2:3
he desires a *g* work . . . . 1 Tim 3:1
suffering as a *g* soldier . . . . 2 Tim 2:3
prepared for every *g* work . . . . 2 Tim 2:21
tasted the *g* word of God . . . . Heb 6:5
not blaspheme the *g* name . . . . Jas 2:7
What *g* is it . . . . Jas 2:14
and maintain *g* conduct . . . . 1 Pet 2:12
to love life and see *g* days . . . . 1 Pet 3:10
better to suffer for doing *g* . . . . 1 Pet 3:17
serve one another as *g* stewards . . 1 Pet 4:10

GOOD WORKS
who by perseverance in *g* . . . . Rom 2:7
created in Christ Jesus for *g* . . . . Eph 2:10
has a reputation for *g* . . . . 1 Tim 5:10
Similarly *g* are also obvious . . . . . . 1 Tim 5:25
example of *g* in every way . . . . Titus 2:7
be intent on engaging in *g* . . . . Titus 3:8
can learn to engage in *g* . . . . Titus 3:14
another on to love and *g* . . . . Heb 10:24

GOODNESS
all my *g* pass before your face . . . Exod 33:19
Surely your *g* and faithfulness . . . . . . Ps 23:6
kindness, *g*, faithfulness . . . . Gal 5:22

GOODS
Bless, O LORD, his *g* . . . . Deut 33:11
You have plenty of *g* stored up . . . Luke 12:19

GOSHEN
District of Egypt where Israel lived; the best
   of the land, Gen 45:10; 46:28–29; 47:1–11

GOSPEL
See also PREACH THE GOSPEL
beginning of the *g* of Jesus Christ . . Mark 1:1
Repent and believe the *g* . . . . Mark 1:15
First the *g* must be preached . . . . Mark 13:10
set apart for the *g* of God . . . . Rom 1:1
I am not ashamed of the *g* . . . . Rom 1:16
those who proclaim the *g* . . . . 1 Cor 9:14
For if I preach the *g* . . . . 1 Cor 9:16
But even if our *g* is veiled . . . . 2 Cor 4:3
are following a different *g* . . . . Gal 1:6
g of your salvation . . . . Eph 1:13
known the mystery of the *g* . . . . Eph 6:19

shifting from the hope of the *g* . . . . . Col 1:23
an eternal *g* to proclaim . . . . Rev 14:6

GOSSIP
be protected from malicious *g* . . . . . Job 5:21
g, arrogance, and disorder . . . . 2 Cor 12:20

GOSSIPING
and a *g* tongue brings forth . . . . . . Prov 25:23

GOSSIPS
They are *g* . . . . Rom 1:29
but also *g* and busybodies . . . . 1 Tim 5:13

GOT
Finally the LORD *g* very angry . . . 2 Chr 36:16

GOTTEN
g rich at our father's expense . . . . . . Gen 31:1

GRAB
G your small shield and . . . . Ps 35:2

GRABBED
I *g* the two tablets . . . . Deut 9:17
with Jesus *g* his sword . . . . Matt 26:51

GRACE
a spirit of *g* and supplication . . . . Zech 12:10
but *g* and truth came about . . . . . . John 1:17
and great *g* was on them all . . . . . . Acts 4:33
G and peace to you . . . . Rom 1:7
receive the abundance of *g* . . . . Rom 5:17
And if it is by *g* . . . . Rom 11:6
g of our Lord Jesus be with you . . Rom 16:20
the *g* of our Lord Jesus Christ . . . . . 2 Cor 8:9
My *g* is enough for you . . . . 2 Cor 12:9
you have fallen away from *g* . . . . Gal 5:4
according to the riches of his *g* . . . . . Eph 1:7
For by *g* you are saved . . . . Eph 2:8
the stewardship of God's *g* . . . . Eph 3:2
to each one of us *g* was given . . . . . Eph 4:7
G be with all those who love . . . . . Eph 6:24
G and peace to you . . . . 1 Thess 1:1
according to the *g* of our God . . 2 Thess 1:12
by *g* gave us eternal comfort . . 2 Thess 2:16
in the *g* that is in Christ Jesus . . . . . 2 Tim 2:1
For the *g* of God has appeared . . . . Titus 2:11
have been justified by his *g* . . . . Titus 3:7
G be with you all . . . . Titus 3:15
and insults the Spirit of *g* . . . . Heb 10:29
But he gives greater *g* . . . . Jas 4:6
the *g* that would come . . . . 1 Pet 1:10
as fellow heirs of the *g* of life . . . . . 1 Pet 3:7
that this is the true *g* of God . . . . . . 1 Pet 5:12
grow in the *g* and knowledge . . . . . 2 Pet 3:18

GRACIOUS
May God be *g* to you . . . . Gen 43:29
be *g* to whom I will be *g* . . . . Exod 33:19
if God is *g* to him and says . . . . Job 33:24
a *g* and compassionate God . . . . Jonah 4:2
that he might be *g* to us . . . . Mal 1:9
were amazed at the *g* words . . . . . Luke 4:22

GRAFT
for God is able to *g* them in . . . . . . Rom 11:23

GRAIN
to buy *g* because the famine . . . . . Gen 41:57
Israel's sons came to buy *g* . . . . Gen 42:5
your ox when it is treading *g* . . . . . Deut 25:4
you provide *g* for the people . . . . Ps 65:9
there be an abundance of *g* . . . . Ps 72:16
carrying his sheaves of *g* . . . . Ps 126:6
of the one who gathers the *g* . . . . . Ps 129:7
curse the one who withholds *g* . . . Prov 11:26
Send your *g* overseas . . . . Eccl 11:1
and harvest *g* in abundance . . . . . . Hos 14:7
so we can open up the *g* bins . . . . . Amos 8:5
mix in some chaff with the *g* . . . . Amos 8:6
gathered them like stalks of *g* . . . . . Mic 4:12
G will make the young men . . . . . . Zech 9:17
two women grinding *g* . . . . Matt 24:41
while it is treading out the *g* . . . . . . 1 Cor 9:9
while it is treading out the *g* . . . . . . 1 Tim 5:18

GRANARIES
and *g* have been torn down . . . . Joel 1:17

GRANDCHILDREN
and that you might see your *g* . . . . . Ps 128:6
leaves an inheritance for his *g* . . . . Prov 13:22

GRANDEUR
we were eyewitnesses of his *g* . . . . 2 Pet 1:16

GRANT
the LORD *g* all your requests . . . . Ps 20:5
g us success . . . . Ps 118:25
I will *g* the one who conquers . . . . . . Rev 3:21

GRANTED
LORD has *g* me success . . . . Gen 24:56
He *g* him favor . . . . Gen 39:21
and *g* sight to many . . . . Luke 7:21
he has *g* the Son authority . . . . John 5:27
have been *g* a faith . . . . 2 Pet 1:1

GRANTS
The LORD *g* success . . . . Ps 37:23

GRAPES
his robes in the blood of *g* . . . . Gen 49:11
Their *g* contain venom . . . . Deut 32:32
for it to produce edible *g* . . . . Isa 5:2
has stomped on *g* in a vat . . . . Isa 63:2
stomped *g* in the winepress . . . . Isa 63:3
discovered in a cluster of *g* . . . . Isa 65:8
will be no *g* on their vines . . . . Jer 8:13
The fathers eat sour *g* . . . . Ezek 18:2
G are not gathered from thorns . . . Matt 7:16
because its *g* are now ripe . . . . Rev 14:18

GRAPEVINE
Each will sit under his own *g* . . . . . . Mic 4:4

GRASP
from your firm *g* on the truth . . . . . 2 Pet 3:17

GRASPED
with God as something to be *g* . . . . . Phil 2:6

GRASS
as rain drops upon the *g* . . . . Deut 32:2
your descendants like the *g* . . . . Job 5:25
they are like the *g* that sprouts . . . . . Ps 90:5
A person's life is like *g* . . . . Ps 103:15
The *g* dries up . . . . Isa 40:7
how God clothes the wild *g* . . . . . . Matt 6:30
crowds to sit down on the *g* . . . . . Matt 14:19
For all flesh is like *g* . . . . 1 Pet 1:24

GRASSHOPPERS
its inhabitants are like *g* . . . . Isa 40:22

GRATITUDE
and in every way with all *g* . . . . . . Acts 24:3

GRAVE
one who goes down to the *g* . . . . Job 7:9
hope for the *g* to be my home . . . . . Job 17:13
their throats like an open *g* . . . . Ps 5:9
descending into the *g* . . . . Ps 28:1
Her house is the way to the *g* . . . . . Prov 7:27
nor wisdom in the *g* . . . . Eccl 9:10

GRAVES
there are no *g* in Egypt . . . . Exod 14:11
You are like unmarked *g* . . . . Luke 11:44
Their throats are open *g* . . . . Rom 3:13

GRAY
bring down my *g* hair in sorrow . . Gen 42:38
splendor of old men is *g* hair . . . . Prov 20:29

GRAY-HAIRED
the infant and the *g* man . . . . Deut 32:25

GRAZE
cow and a bear will *g* together . . . . . Isa 11:7

GREAT
God made two *g* lights . . . . Gen 1:16
make you into a *g* nation . . . . Gen 12:2
reward you in *g* abundance . . . . Gen 15:1
there was a *g* cry in Egypt . . . . Exod 12:30
out of Egypt with his *g* power . . . . Deut 4:37
brought this *g* calamity on us . . . . . 1 Sam 6:9
For the LORD is *g* . . . . 1 Chr 16:25
I will build a *g* temple . . . . 2 Chr 2:5
g and unsearchable things . . . . Job 5:9
He is *g* in power . . . . Job 37:23
because of your *g* faithfulness . . . . Ps 5:7
offer praise in the *g* assembly . . . . . Ps 22:25
because of your *g* loyal love . . . . Ps 69:13
Use your *g* strength . . . . Ps 79:11
and show *g* faithfulness . . . . Ps 86:5

g loyal love and faithfulness........Ps 86:15
How *g* are your works...............Ps 92:5
demonstrates *g* loyal love..........Ps 103:8
LORD has accomplished *g* things .. Ps 126:2
and imparts *g* wisdom.............Isa 28:29
because of his *g* strength...........Isa 63:1
for *g* things for yourself ....Jer 45:5
and concerned a *g* war ....Dan 10:1
LORD's *g* day of judgment ....Zeph 1:14
He takes *g* delight in you.........Zeph 3:17
be called *g* in the kingdom ....Matt 5:19
found a pearl of *g* value .... Matt 13:46
whoever wants to be *g* ....Matt 20:26
a *g* windstorm developed ....Mark 4:37
before the *g* and glorious day .... Acts 2:20
was performing *g* wonders........Acts 6:8
claiming to be someone *g*.........Acts 8:9
G is Artemis of the Ephesians ....Acts 19:28
I have *g* sorrow....................Rom 9:2
g opportunity stands wide open...1 Cor 16:9
because of his *g* love .... Eph 2:4
This mystery is *g* .... Eph 5:32
with contentment brings *g* profit...1 Tim 6:6
of our *g* God and Savior ....Titus 2:13
yet it has *g* pretensions...........Jas 3:5
By his *g* mercy he gave us .... 1 Pet 1:3
Babylon the *G* .... Rev 17:5
the *g* and the small .... Rev 20:12

GREATER
will be *g* than you ....Gen 41:40
the LORD is *g* than all the gods ... Exod 18:11
arisen *g* than John the Baptist .....Matt 11:11
something *g* than the temple......Matt 12:6
something *g* than Jonah ....Matt 12:41
something *g* than Solomon...... Matt 12:42
You will see *g* things...............John 1:50
not *g* than our ancestor Jacob .....John 4:12
slave is not *g* than his master.....John 13:16
No one has *g* love than this.......John 15:13
slave is not *g* than his master.....John 15:20
we clothe with *g* honor...........1 Cor 12:23
should be eager for the *g* gifts...1 Cor 12:31
The one who prophesies is *g* ......1 Cor 14:5
g glory of what replaced it........2 Cor 3:10
with much *g* labors..............2 Cor 11:23
he could swear by no one *g* .... Heb 6:13
God is *g* than our conscience....1 John 3:20
the testimony of God is *g*......... 1 John 5:9

GREATEST
like this little child is the *g*........Matt 18:4
first and *g* commandment.......Matt 22:38
was to be regarded as the *g* .....Luke 22:24
But the *g* of these is love ....1 Cor 13:13

GREATLY
g increase your labor pains........ Gen 3:16
g multiply your descendants ..... Gen 16:10
I love them *g* ....Ps 119:167
They became *g* distressed.......Matt 26:22

GREATNESS
after night it reveals his *g* .... Ps 19:2
No one can fathom his *g* ....Ps 145:3
incomparable *g* of his power .... Eph 1:19

GREECE
Paul preaches in, Acts 17:16–31
Daniel's vision of, Dan 8:21

GREED
full of *g* and self-indulgence.....Matt 23:25
full of *g* and wickedness........Luke 11:39
guard yourself from all types
   of *g*.........................Luke 12:15
impurity of any kind, or *g*........Eph 5:3
trained their hearts for *g* .... 2 Pet 2:14

GREEDINESS
every kind of impurity with *g*.......Eph 4:19

GREEDY
g person stirs up dissension ..... Prov 28:25
thieves, the *g* ....1 Cor 6:10

GREEK
in Aramaic, Latin, and *G* ....John 19:20
the Jew first and also to the *G* .....Rom 1:16

although he was a *G* .... Gal 2:3
There is neither Jew nor *G*.........Gal 3:28

GREEK-SPEAKING JEWS
Widows overlooked, Acts 6:1
Hostile to Paul, Acts 9:29
Gospel preached to, Acts 11:20

GREEKS
Natives of Greece, Joel 3:6; Acts 16:1
Spiritual state of, Rom 10:12
Some believe, Acts 14:1

GREEN
and under every *g* tree ....2 Kgs 17:10
and here came a pale *g* horse ...... Rev 6:8

GREET
deliverance and peace *g*...........Ps 85:10
if you only *g* your brothers .... Matt 5:47

GREETED
and *g* Elizabeth .... Luke 1:40

GREETINGS
brothers and sisters send *g*......1 Cor 16:20

GREW
My frustration *g*....................Ps 39:2
but it *g* to be very great .... Dan 8:9
and they *g* up and choked it.......Mark 4:7
child *g* and became strong ......Luke 2:40

GRIEF
only my *g* could be weighed.........Job 6:2
I collapse from *g*...................Ps 119:28
the end of joy may be *g* ....Prov 14:13
because I am overcome with *g* .....Isa 38:15
I experience is trouble and *g* ......Jer 20:18
will turn their *g* into gladness ...... Jer 31:13
exhausted from *g*.................Luke 22:45
would not have *g* on top of *g*....... Phil 2:27

GRIEVE
Who will *g* over you ....Jer 15:5
Do not *g* for him....................Jer 22:10
Her virgins *g*........................ Lam 1:4
to afflict or to *g* people...........Lam 3:33
As for those who *g* .... Zeph 3:18
And do not *g* the Holy Spirit....... Eph 4:30
g like the rest who have no
   hope......................... 1 Thess 4:13
G, mourn, and weep .... Jas 4:9

GRIEVED
not my soul *g* for the poor ....Job 30:25
Although it *g* the king ....Matt 14:9
My soul is deeply *g*.............Matt 26:38
g by the hardness of their
   hearts .... Mark 3:5

GRIEVES
What my eyes see *g* me .... Lam 3:51

GRIND
and *g* the faces of the poor..........Isa 3:15

GRINDERS
and the *g* begin to cease............Eccl 12:3

GRIP
will *g* you like that of a woman..... Jer 13:21

GRIPS
Is this why pain *g* you................Mic 4:9

GROAN
From the city the dying *g*.........Job 24:12
I am exhausted as I *g*................Ps 6:6
I will remember God while I *g* .....Ps 77:3
end of your life you will *g* ....Prov 5:11
those who like to celebrate *g*...... Isa 24:7
g inwardly as we eagerly await ... Rom 8:23
g while we are in this tent ....2 Cor 5:4

GROANING
God heard their *g*.................Exod 2:24
my *g* is not hidden from you ....Ps 38:9

GROANINGS
with inexpressible *g* .... Rom 8:26

GROPE
They *g* about in darkness..........Job 12:25
we *g* like those who cannot see ... Isa 59:10

GROUND
and let dry *g* appear ....Gen 1:9
the *g* is cursed because of you......Gen 3:17
you are standing is holy *g* .... Exod 3:5
he struck the dust of the *g* ....Exod 8:17
will destroy the watered *g*....... Deut 29:19
lay face down on the *g* ....Josh 7:6
trembled and the *g* shook.......1 Sam 14:15
purified in a furnace on the *g*........ Ps 12:6
You cleared the *g* for it .... Ps 80:9
pour water on the parched *g* .... Isa 44:3
Break up your unplowed *g* ....Jer 4:3
the *g* will respond to the grain .... Hos 2:22
and the *g* its yield................Zech 8:12
seed that when sown in the *g* .... Mark 4:31

GROUNDED
have been rooted and *g* in love..... Eph 3:17

GROUPS
in *g* of about fifty each .... Luke 9:14

GROW
g in the courts of our God..........Ps 92:13
to *g* in power and to prevail ......Acts 19:20
will all *g* old like a garment......... Heb 1:11
g in the grace and knowledge .... 2 Pet 3:18

GROWN
they have *g* fat and sleek ....Jer 5:28
and when sin is full *g* .... Jas 1:15

GROWS
hail struck everything that *g*......Exod 9:25
every tree that *g* for you........Exod 10:5
Faithfulness *g* from the ground......Ps 85:11
g into a holy temple in the Lord....Eph 2:21

GROWTH
with a *g* that is from God........... Col 2:19

GRUMBLED
They *g* in their tents...............Ps 106:25

GRUMBLERS
people are *g* and fault-finders ......Jude 1:16

GRUMBLING
without *g* or arguing................Phil 2:14

GUARANTEE
G the welfare of your servant .....Ps 119:122
the *g* of a better covenant.........Heb 7:22

GUARD
g the way to the tree of life........Gen 3:24
stationed a *g* to protect .... Neh 4:9
If the LORD does not *g* a city........Ps 127:1
g them within your heart..........Prov 4:21
G your heart with all vigilance.... Prov 4:23
God of Israel is your rear *g* ....Isa 52:12
LORD of Heaven's Armies will *g* ...Zech 9:15
whole imperial *g* and everyone..... Phil 1:13
will *g* your hearts and minds ....Phil 4:7
g yourselves from idols...........1 John 5:21

GUARDIAN
Am I my brother's *g* ....Gen 4:9
the law had become our *g*..........Gal 3:24
we are no longer under a *g*........Gal 3:25
shepherd and *g* of your souls......1 Pet 2:25

GUARDIANS
may have 10,000 *g* in Christ.......1 Cor 4:15
he is under *g* and managers ....Gal 4:2

GUARDING
who were *g* the gates.............. Neh 11:19
By *g* it according to................Ps 119:9
was *g* the city of Damascus......2 Cor 11:32

GUARDS
one who *g* his words *g* his life ..... Prov 13:3
g his way safeguards his life ...... Prov 16:17
The *g* were shaken ....Matt 28:4
g also took him and beat him....Mark 14:65

GUEST
who may be a *g* in your home........Ps 15:1

GUESTS
g chose the places of honor ....Luke 14:7

GUIDANCE
your servant finds moral *g* ....Ps 19:11
loyal followers receive his *g* ....Ps 25:14

there is no *g* a nation falls ....Prov 11:14
there is no more *g* available ....Lam 2:9
not want the LORD's help or *g* .....Zeph 1:6

GUIDE
g me today .... Gen 24:12
and you could be our *g* ....Num 10:31
G me into your truth ....Ps 25:5
there your hand would *g* me ......Ps 139:10
I will *g* them down paths ....Isa 42:16
to *g* our feet into the way ....Luke 1:79
he will *g* you into all truth ....John 16:13
g for those who arrested Jesus ....Acts 1:16
yourself are a *g* to the blind ......Rom 2:19

GUIDES
He *g* us ....Ps 48:14
blind *g*, who say .... Matt 23:16
unless someone *g* me ....Acts 8:31

GUIDING
The LORD alone was *g* him ...... Deut 32:12

GUILT
our *g* extends to the heavens.......Ezra 9:6
our *g* has been great................Ezra 9:7
my *g* is not hidden from you ....Ps 69:5

GUILTLESS
the LORD will not hold *g*..........Exod 20:7
Whoever among you is *g*..........John 8:7
I am *g*.............................Acts 18:6

GUILTY
but condemn the *g* ....Deut 25:1
David felt *g* ....2 Sam 24:10
you know that I am not *g*..........Job 10:7
The one who says to the *g*.......Prov 24:24
and yet are not *g* ....Matt 12:5
what crime they found me *g* of . Acts 24:20
has become *g* of all of it............Jas 2:10

GUMS
my tongue sticks to my *g*...........Ps 22:15

H

HABAKKUK
Prophet in Judah just prior to Babylonian
    invasion, Hab 1:1
Prayer of, in praise of God, Hab 3:1–19

HABIT
as some are in the *h* of doing.....Heb 10:25

HADADEZER
King of Zobah, 2 Sam 8:3–13
Defeated by David, 2 Sam 10:6–19

HADASSAH
See ESTHER

HADES
you will be thrown down to *H*....Matt 11:23
gates of *H* will not overpower....Matt 16:18
in *H*, as he was in torment....... Luke 16:23
will not leave my soul in *H*........Acts 2:27
the keys of death and of *H* .... Rev 1:18
Death and *H* were thrown....... Rev 20:14

HADORAM
See ADONIRAM

HAGAR
Sarah's servant; bears Ishmael to Abraham,
    Gen 16
Abraham sends her away; God comforts
    her, Gen 21:9–21
Paul explains symbolic meaning of,
    Gal 4:22–31

HAGGAI
Postexilic prophet; contemporary of
    Zechariah, Ezra 5:1–2; 6:14; Hag 1:1

HAGGITH
One of David's wives, 2 Sam 3:4
Mother of Adonijah, 1 Kgs 1:5

HAIL
very severe *h* to rain down .... Exod 9:18
or seen the armory of the *h* ....Job 38:22
came *h* and fiery coals.............Ps 18:12
h will sweep away ....Isa 28:17

HAILSTONES
He throws his *h* like crumbs....... Ps 147:17
And gigantic *h* .... Rev 16:21

HAIR
will bring down my gray *h*........Gen 42:38
His *h* began to grow back........Judg 16:22
His *h* will never be cut.............1 Sam 1:11
to weigh the *h* of his head ......2 Sam 14:26
it makes the *h* of my flesh ....Job 4:15
Gray *h* is like a crown of glory.... Prov 16:31
splendor of old men is gray *h* ...Prov 20:29
Your *h* is like a flock of ....Song 4:1
His *h* is curly......................Song 5:11
even when you have gray *h*......... Isa 46:4
until his *h* became long............Dan 4:33
His head is filled with gray *h*........ Hos 7:9
to make one *h* white or black .... Matt 5:36
garment made of camel's *h* ...... Mark 1:6
a *h* of your head will perish......Luke 21:18
wiped his feet dry with her *h* ....John 11:2
He had his *h* cut off.............. Acts 18:18
will lose a *h* from his head.......Acts 27:34
but if a woman has long *h* .... 1 Cor 11:15
must not be with braided *h*........1 Tim 2:9
braiding of *h* and wearing ....1 Pet 3:3
His head and *h* were as white ...... Rev 1:14
black as sackcloth made of *h* ......Rev 6:12
They had *h* like women's *h* .... Rev 9:8

HAIRS
outnumber the *h* of my head.......Ps 40:12
h on your head are numbered... Matt 10:30

HAIRY
like a *h* garment ....Gen 25:25
He was a *h* man................... 2 Kgs 1:8
the *h* garment of a prophet ....Zech 13:4

HAKELDAMA
See FIELD OF BLOOD

HAKILAH
Hill in the wilderness of Ziph where David
    hid, 1 Sam 23:19–26

HAKKOZ
Descendant of Aaron, 1 Chr 24:1, 10
Descendants of, kept from priesthood,
    Neh 7:63–64

HALF
and placed each *h* opposite........Gen 15:10
h of it in the morning.............. Lev 6:20
and the *h* of Manasseh left ....Josh 22:9
H the people supported Tibni ....1 Kgs 16:21
for as much as *h* the kingdom ...... Esth 5:6
up to *h* my kingdom..............Mark 6:23
shut up three and a *h* years....... Luke 4:25
h of my possessions ....Luke 19:8
and *h* a time ....Rev 12:14

HALL
in the lecture *h* of Tyrannus ....Acts 19:9

HALLELUJAH
the crowd shouted, "*H*..............Rev 19:3

HALT
should the work come to a *h* .... Neh 6:3

HAM
Noah's youngest son, Gen 5:32
Enters ark, Gen 7:7
His immoral behavior merits Noah's curse,
    Gen 9:22–25
Father of descendants of repopulated
    earth, Gen 10:6–20

HAMAN
Plots to destroy Jews, Esth 3:3–15
Invited to Esther's banquet, Esth 5:1–14
Forced to honor Mordecai, Esth 6:5–14
Hanged on his own gallows, Esth 7:1–10

HAMATH
Israel's northern boundary, Num 34:8;
    1 Kgs 8:65; Ezek 47:16–20
Conquered, 2 Kgs 18:34; Jer 49:23
Israelites exiled there, Isa 11:11

HAMMER
like a *h* that breaks a rock ....Jer 23:29
how that '*h*' has been broken......Jer 50:23

HAMOR
Sells land to Jacob, Gen 33:18–20; Acts 7:16
Killed by Jacob's sons, Gen 34:1–31

HAMSTRUNG
for pleasure they have *h* oxen.....Gen 49:6

HANANI
Father of Jehu the prophet, 1 Kgs 16:1, 7
Rebukes Asa; confined to prison,
    2 Chr 16:7–10
—Nehemiah's brother; brings news
    concerning the Jews, Neh 1:2
Becomes a governor of Jerusalem, Neh 7:2

HANANIAH
False prophet who contradicts Jeremiah,
    Jer 28:1–17
—Hebrew name of Shadrach, Dan 1:6–7, 11
See SHADRACH

HAND
See also AT THE RIGHT HAND; HAND OF
    GOD; HAND OF THE LORD; HIS RIGHT
    HAND; MY RIGHT HAND; STRETCH OUT
    MY HAND; STRETCHED OUT HIS HAND
stretch out his *h* and take also..... Gen 3:22
Put your *h* under my thigh ....Gen 24:2
he put Ephraim on his right *h*.....Gen 48:13
What is that in your *h* ....Exod 4:2
took the staff of God in his *h* .....Exod 4:20
tooth for tooth, *h* for *h* ....Exod 21:24
his *h* on the head of the bull.......Lev 4:4
Is the LORD's *h* shortened ....Num 11:23
I will *h* him over to you..............Judg 4:7
from the *h* of this Philistine......1 Sam 17:37
good *h* of our God was on us......Ezra 8:18
let loose his *h* and kill me ....Job 6:9
stretches out his *h* against God.... Job 15:25
your own right *h* can save you.....Job 40:14
your right *h* supports me...........Ps 18:35
My *h* will support him...............Ps 89:21
Sit down at my right *h*...............Ps 110:1
Long life is in her right *h*..........Prov 3:16
heart is in the *h* of the LORD....... Prov 21:1
His left *h* is under my head ....Song 8:3
Yes, my *h* founded the earth........Isa 48:13
the LORD's *h* is not too weak ....Isa 59:1
and a measuring stick in his *h* .... Ezek 40:3
fingers of a human *h* appeared ..... Dan 5:5
Then a *h* touched me .... Dan 10:10
your right *h* causes you to sin .... Matt 5:30
do not let your left *h* know .... Matt 6:3
If your *h* causes you to sin........Mark 9:43
at the right *h* of the Power ......Mark 14:62
from the *h* of our enemies.........Luke 1:74
Because he is a hired *h* ....John 10:13
Sit at my right *h* ....Acts 2:34
standing at the right *h* of God .....Acts 7:55
who is at the right *h* of God ...... Rom 8:34
h this man over to Satan........... 1 Cor 5:5
Since I am not a *h*..................1 Cor 12:15
this greeting with my own *h*......1 Cor 16:21
the right *h* of fellowship ....Gal 2:9
I write to you with my own *h*........Gal 6:11
seated at the right *h* of God ....Col 3:1
h until I make your enemies........Heb 1:13
who sat down at the right *h* ....Heb 8:1
sat down at the right *h* of God.... Heb 10:12
held seven stars in his right *h*...... Rev 1:16
the seven stars in his right *h*........ Rev 2:1
his mark on their forehead or *h* ...Rev 20:4

HAND OF GOD
for the *h* has struck me............Job 19:21
as their works, are in the *h*.........Eccl 9:1
sat down at the right *h* ....Mark 16:19
exalted to the right *h* ....Acts 2:33
Jesus standing at the right *h* ......Acts 7:55
standing at the right *h*.............Acts 7:56
who is at the right *h* ....Rom 8:34
seated at the right *h*...................Col 3:1
he sat down at the right *h* .... Heb 10:12
and is at the right *h*................1 Pet 3:22

HAND OF THE LORD
only we had died by the *h* ....Exod 16:3
the very *h* that eliminated.........Deut 2:15

The *h* was against the ....1 Sam 7:13
the *h* will be against both........1 Sam 12:15
the *h* his God was on him..........Ezra 7:6
gained strength as the *h* ....Ezra 7:28
that the *h* has done this ....Job 12:9
king's heart is in the *h* .... Prov 21:1
majestic crown in the *h*............ Isa 62:3
the *h* rested powerfully..........Ezek 3:14
The *h* was on me ....Ezek 37:1
The *h* was with them ....Acts 11:21
the *h* is against you................Acts 13:11

HANDED
h it over to the construction.....2 Chr 34:10

HANDIWORK
the sky displays his *h* ....Ps 19:1
the skies are your *h*................Ps 102:25

HANDKERCHIEFS
h or aprons that had touched..... Acts 19:12

HANDS
but the *h* are Esau's..............Gen 27:22
the *h* of Moses became heavy....Exod 17:12
Moses had placed his *h* on him... Deut 34:9
I took my life into my own *h*.....1 Sam 28:21
but his *h* also heal .... Job 5:18
make my *h* clean with lye ....Job 9:30
Your *h* have shaped me.............Job 10:8
they pin my *h* and feet............ Ps 22:16
will lift you up in their *h* ....Ps 91:12
His *h* formed the dry land ....Ps 95:5
She extended her *h* to the spool ..Prov 31:19
you find to do with your *h*......... Eccl 9:10
takes matters into his own *h* ......Isa 59:16
In my *h*, you, O nation ....Jer 18:6
to have the form of human *h* .....Ezek 10:8
and clap your *h* together ....Ezek 21:14
but not by human *h* ....Dan 2:34
set me on my *h* and knees........ Dan 10:10
The *h* of Zerubbabel................Zech 4:9
or lame than to have two *h*.......Matt 18:8
pick up snakes with their *h* ...... Mark 16:18
and fell into the *h* of robbers ....Luke 10:30
into your *h* I commit my spirit...Luke 23:46
Look at my *h* and my feet ....Luke 24:39
but also my *h* and my head.......John 13:9
wounds from the nails in his *h*... John 20:25
in houses made by human *h*......Acts 7:48
these *h* of mine provided........Acts 20:34
placed his *h* on him and healed... Acts 28:8
house not built by human *h* ...... 2 Cor 5:1
doing good with his own *h* .... Eph 4:28
performed by human *h*.............Col 2:11
lifting up holy *h*.................1 Tim 2:8
when the elders laid *h* on you ....1 Tim 4:14
not lay *h* on anyone hastily.......1 Tim 5:22
the laying on of my *h* ....2 Tim 1:6
laying on of *h*.....................Heb 6:2
perfect tent not made with *h*......Heb 9:11
fall into the *h* of the living God ...Heb 10:31
Cleanse your *h*.......................Jas 4:8
and our *h* have touched ....1 John 1:1

HANDSOME
no man as *h* as Absalom.........2 Sam 14:25
You are the most *h* of all men ....Ps 45:2

HANG
will *h* from this peg.................Isa 22:24

HANGED
he went out and *h* himself........Matt 27:5

HANGS
everyone who *h* on a tree ....Gal 3:13

HANNAH
Barren wife of Elkanah; prays for a son,
  1 Sam 1:1–18
Bears Samuel and dedicates him to the
  Lord, 1 Sam 1:19–28
Magnifies God, 1 Sam 2:1–10

HANUN
King of Ammon; disgraces David's
  ambassadors and is defeated by him,
  2 Sam 10:1–14

HAPPEN
will *h* to you in future days .... Gen 49:1
Let them tell us what will *h*........Isa 41:22
determine what will *h* to them ....Jer 10:23
h to your people in future days... Dan 10:14

HAPPENED
For these things *h* so that ....John 19:36

HAPPENS
if some accident *h* to him.........Gen 42:4

HAPPIER
You make me *h* than those .... Ps 4:7

HAPPINESS
a day for banqueting and *h* .... Esth 9:17
he will bring you *h*.................Prov 29:17
h and joy will overwhelm them......Isa 51:11
as *h* fills their hearts................ Isa 65:14

HAPPY
are truly *h* ....2 Chr 9:7
who take shelter in you be *h* ....Ps 5:11
I will be *h* and rejoice in you...........Ps 9:2
my heart rejoices and I am *h* .... Ps 16:9
Let the earth be *h* .... Ps 97:1
We will be *h* and rejoice in it........Ps 118:24
you will be *h*.......................Isa 66:14
h because of the God...............Hab 3:18
Be *h* and boast................... Zeph 3:14
and she is *h* to live with him.......1 Cor 7:12

HARAN
Abraham's younger brother, Gen 11:26–31
—City of Mesopotamia, Gen 11:31
Abraham leaves, Gen 12:4–5
Jacob dwells at, Gen 29:4–35

HARASSED
he *h* the oppressed and needy.....Ps 109:16

HARBOR
led them to the *h* they desired ....Ps 107:30

HARBORED
If I had *h* sin in my heart............Ps 66:18

HARD
discouragement and *h* labor....... Exod 6:9
Pharaoh's heart is *h* ....Exod 7:14
Its heart is *h* as rock...............Job 41:24
people experience *h* times ....Ps 60:3
h to carry.......................Matt 23:4
knew that you were a *h* man ....Matt 25:24
we worked *h* all night .... Luke 5:5
are *h* to understand .... 2 Pet 3:16

HARDEN
But I will *h* his heart ....Exod 4:21
Do not *h* your hearts .... Heb 3:8

HARDENED
But Pharaoh *h* his heart ....Exod 8:32
but their hearts were *h* ....Mark 6:52
and *h* their heart.................John 12:40
The rest were *h*..................... Rom 11:7
become *h* by sin's deception.......Heb 3:13

HARDENS
but whoever *h* his heart ....Prov 28:14
and he *h* whom he chooses........Rom 9:18

HARDER
h to reach than a strong city......Prov 18:19
made your forehead *h* than flint....Ezek 3:9

HARDEST
olive oil from the *h* of rocks ......Deut 32:13

HARDSHIP
Distress and *h* confront me....... Ps 119:143
for which I suffer *h* ....2 Tim 2:9
endure *h*, do an evangelist's work...2 Tim 4:5

HARDSHIPS
all the *h* we have experienced ... Num 20:14

HAREM
h of beautiful concubines........... Eccl 2:8

HARM
you meant to *h* me .... Gen 50:20
Saul was planning to *h* him ...... 1 Sam 23:9
Don't *h* my prophets .... 1 Chr 16:22

they intended to do me *h*........... Neh 6:2
who were seeking their *h*..........Esth 9:2
or do *h* to others .... Ps 15:3
hate me and want to *h* me........Ps 35:19
May those who plan to *h* me ....Ps 35:4
From *h* and violence................. Ps 72:14
No *h* will overtake you .... Ps 91:10
Don't *h* my prophets ....Ps 105:15
sun will not *h* you by day...........Ps 121:6
will protect you from all *h*..........Ps 121:7
at ease from the dread of *h*....... Prov 1:33
misses me brings *h* to himself.... Prov 8:36
companions who *h* one another ..Prov 18:24
not *h* all the days of her life ...... Prov 31:12
other people to their *h* .... Eccl 8:9
and does not seek to *h* others ....Isa 33:15
I will not cause you any *h*..........Jer 25:6
not to *h* you .... Jer 29:11
Why will you do such great *h*....... Jer 44:7
poison they drink will not *h* ..... Mark 16:18
from the church to *h* them ....Acts 12:1
Do not *h* yourself.................Acts 16:28

HARMED
but I am not *h* .... Prov 23:35
be *h* by the second death........... Rev 2:11

HARMONY
Live in *h* with one another........Rom 12:16

HAROD
Spring near Gideon's camp, Judg 7:1

HARP
who play the *h* and the flute....... Gen 4:21
thanks to the Lord with the *h*......Ps 33:2
accompanied by a *h* ....Ps 98:5
with the lyre and the *h* ....Ps 150:3
h, pipes, and all kinds.............. Dan 3:10
had a *h* and golden bowls ....Rev 5:8

HARPS
by cymbals, *h*, and lyres .... Neh 12:27
in her midst we hang our *h*.........Ps 137:2
by harpists playing their *h*.......Rev 14:2
h given to them by God ....Rev 15:2

HARSH
but a *h* word stirs up wrath......... Prov 15:1
and driven by *h* winds ....Jas 3:4

HARSHLY
king responded to the people *h* ..1 Kgs 12:13
He was treated *h* and afflicted.......Isa 53:7
not have to deal *h* with you..... 2 Cor 13:10

HARSHNESS
but with force and *h* .... Ezek 34:4
the kindness and *h* of God....... Rom 11:22

HARVEST
See also FEAST OF HARVEST
planting time and *h*.................Gen 8:22
the beginning of the barley *h*.... 2 Sam 21:9
joy when they reap the *h* ....Ps 126:5
the one who sleeps during *h* ......Prov 10:5
cloud of mist in the heat of *h*......Isa 18:4
but will *h* weeds .... Jer 12:13
plant and *h* grain in abundance....Hos 14:7
for the *h* is ripe ....Joel 3:13
but will not *h* them ....Mic 6:15
The *h* is plentiful.................. Matt 9:37
ask the Lord of the *h* .... Matt 9:38
I *h* where I didn't sow...........Matt 25:26
because the *h* has come..........Mark 4:29
The *h* is plentiful................. Luke 10:2
months and then comes the *h*....John 4:35
work in hope of enjoying the *h* ... 1 Cor 9:10
h of your righteousness to grow..2 Cor 9:10
since the earth's *h* is ripe .... Rev 14:15

HARVESTED
be cut down and *h* will come.......Jer 51:33

HARVESTERS
in your presence as *h* rejoice ....Isa 9:3

HASTE
You are to eat it in *h*................Exod 12:11

HASTENING
h the coming of the day of God....2 Pet 3:12

HASTENS
stingy person *h* after riches ..... Prov 28:22

HASTILY
acts *h* makes poor choices......... Prov 19:2
not lay hands on anyone *h*........1 Tim 5:22

HASTY
someone who is *h* in his words.. Prov 29:20
or *h* in your heart................. Eccl 5:2

HATE
You must not *h* your brother ...... Lev 19:17
h all who behave wickedly........... Ps 5:5
who *h* the godly are punished ...... Ps 34:21
who *h* the LORD cower in fear ....Ps 81:15
You who love the LORD, *h* evil ......Ps 97:10
I *h* all deceitful actions............ Ps 119:104
h people with divided loyalties .... Ps 119:113
I *h* and despise deceit.............. Ps 119:163
and my lips *h* wickedness ....Prov 8:7
and a time to *h* .... Eccl 3:8
and *h* robbery and sin .... Isa 61:8
H what is wrong..................... Amos 5:15
yet you *h* what is good .... Mic 3:2
for either he will *h* the one .... Matt 6:24
I do what I *h* .... Rom 7:15
h what the Nicolaitans practice......Rev 2:6
will *h* the prostitute .... Rev 17:16

HATED
So Esau *h* Jacob.................... Gen 27:41
they *h* moral knowledge........... Prov 1:29
you will be *h* by everyone ...... Matt 10:22
h both me and my Father.........John 15:24
They *h* me without reason........John 15:25
and the world has *h* them .... John 17:14
but Esau I *h*....................... Rom 9:13
has ever *h* his own body........... Eph 5:29
and *h* lawlessness ....Heb 1:9

HATEFUL
h and hating one another.......... Titus 3:3

HATERS
slanderers, *h* of God ....Rom 1:30

HATES
six things that the LORD *h* ....Prov 6:16
and the one who *h* his life ....John 12:25
If the world *h* you .... John 15:18
who *h* his fellow Christian .... 1 John 2:11

HATING
h even the clothes stained......... Jude 1:23

HAUGHTY
nor do I have a *h* look .... Ps 131:1
and a *h* spirit before a fall .... Prov 16:18
not to be *h* or to set their hope... 1 Tim 6:17

HAUNT
a *h* for every unclean spirit ....Rev 18:2

HAURAN
District southeast of Mt. Hermon,
    Ezek 47:16

HAVE COURAGE
H, son! Your sins are forgiven ..... Matt 9:2
H, daughter! Your faith ....Matt 9:22
H! It is I. Do not be afraid........Matt 14:27
H! It is I. Do not be afraid .... Mark 6:50
H! Get Up! He is calling.........Mark 10:49
H, for just as you have............Acts 23:11

HAVE MERCY
H on me and respond .... Ps 4:1
toward me and *h* on me .... Ps 25:16
H on me, O God .... Ps 51:1
For it is time to *h* on her........... Ps 102:13
h on the entire house of Israel... Ezek 39:25
H on us, Son of David............. Matt 9:27
H on me, Lord ....Matt 15:22
Lord, *h* on my son .... Matt 17:15
H on us, Lord ....Matt 20:30
Son of David, *h* on me ....Mark 10:47
Father Abraham, *h* on me ...... Luke 16:24
Jesus, Master, *h* on us......... Luke 17:13
Son of David, *h* on me .... Luke 18:38
I will *h* on whom I *h* ....Rom 9:15

HAVEN
will live by the *h* of the sea .... Gen 49:13

HAY
precious stones, wood, *h* ....1 Cor 3:12

HAZAEL
Anointed king of Syria by Elijah,
    1 Kgs 19:15–17
Elisha predicts his taking the throne,
    2 Kgs 8:7–15
Oppresses Israel, 2 Kgs 8:28–29; 10:32–33;
    12:17–18; 13:3–7, 22

HAZAR ENAN
Village of north Palestine, Num 34:9–10

HAZEROTH
Scene of sedition of Miriam and Aaron,
    Num 11:35—12:16

HAZOR
Royal Canaanite city destroyed by Joshua,
    Josh 11:1–13
Rebuilt and assigned to Naphtali, Josh 19:32,
    36
Army of, defeated by Deborah and Barak,
    Judg 4:1–24

HEAD
he will strike your *h* ....Gen 3:15
of white bread on my *h*............Gen 40:16
bowed down at the *h* of his bed .. Gen 47:31
Put your right hand on his *h*......Gen 48:18
had a bronze helmet on his *h*.....1 Sam 17:5
he cut off his *h* with it ....1 Sam 17:51
crown of their king from his *h*.. 2 Sam 12:30
Tamar put ashes on her *h* ......2 Sam 13:19
clothes torn and dirt on his *h*... 2 Sam 15:32
said to his father, "My *h*! My *h*....2 Kgs 4:19
place a golden crown on his *h* .... Ps 21:3
You refresh my *h* with oil.......... Ps 23:5
outnumber the hairs of my *h*.......Ps 40:12
like fine oil poured on the *h* .... Ps 133:2
my *h* not refuse choice oil ....Ps 141:5
heap coals of fire on his *h* .... Prov 25:22
My *h* is drenched with dew........ Song 5:2
Your *h* has a massive wound .... Isa 1:5
Do not take an oath by your *h*.... Matt 5:36
anoint your *h* and wash...........Matt 6:17
Give me the *h* of John ....Matt 14:8
first the stalk, then the *h* ....Mark 4:28
she poured it on his *h* .... Mark 14:3
did not anoint my *h* with oil ..... Luke 7:46
has no place to lay his *h* .... Luke 9:58
Then he bowed his *h* ....John 19:30
heaping burning coals on his *h* .. Rom 12:20
prophesies with his *h* covered.....1 Cor 11:4
prophesies with her *h* uncovered .. 1 Cor 11:5
as having a shaved *h*................1 Cor 11:5
gave him to the church as *h* ....Eph 1:22
because the husband is the *h*...... Eph 5:23
h and hair were as white as........ Rev 1:14
had a golden crown on his *h*.......Rev 14:14
many diadem crowns on his *h*....Rev 19:12

HEADBANDS
I will tear off your *h* .... Ezek 13:21

HEADS
mock me and shake their *h*.......... Ps 22:7
men to ride over our *h* ....Ps 66:12
They walk with their *h* high.......... Isa 3:16
bowing their *h* like a reed .... Isa 58:5
will shave their *h* in mourning..... Jer 48:37
shaking their *h*.................... Matt 27:39
without a roof over our *h*..........1 Cor 4:11
had seven *h* and ten horns .... Rev 12:3

HEAL
I smash and I *h* .... Deut 32:39
I will *h* you...................... 2 Kgs 20:5
H me, LORD....................... Ps 6:2
H me, for I have sinned.............. Ps 41:4
and a time to *h* ....Eccl 3:3
Who can *h* you .... Lam 2:13
but he will *h* us ....Hos 6:1
he will *h* us in a little while .... Hos 6:2
whenever I want to *h* Israel.......... Hos 7:1
and *h* every kind of disease........Matt 10:1

H the sick......................... Matt 10:8
lawful to *h* on the Sabbath ....Matt 12:10
and I would *h* them................ Matt 13:15
they were not able to *h* him ......Matt 17:16
Physician, *h* yourself.............. Luke 4:23

HEALED
not wash in them and be *h* .... 2 Kgs 5:12
have *h* him from his illness .... Ps 41:3
an assuring word and *h* them..... Ps 107:20
they might repent and be *h*....... Isa 6:10
of his wounds we have been *h*......Isa 53:5
and he *h* them .... Matt 4:24
and my servant will be *h* .... Matt 8:8
and *h* all who were sick............Matt 8:16
and he *h* them .... Matt 15:30
and to be *h* of their diseases......Luke 6:17
demon-possessed had been *h*....Luke 8:36
rebuked the unclean spirit, *h*.....Luke 9:42
touched the man's ear and *h* .... Luke 22:51
They were all being *h*............Acts 5:16
saw he had faith to be *h*............Acts 14:9
be put out of joint but be *h*.......Heb 12:13
so that you may be *h* ....Jas 5:16
By his wounds you were *h*........ 1 Pet 2:24
the lethal wound had been *h* ....Rev 13:3

HEALING
This will bring *h* to your body ......Prov 3:8
and *h* to one's entire body........ Prov 4:22
words of the wise bring *h* ....Prov 12:18
and *h* to the bones................Prov 16:24
cheerful heart brings good *h* .....Prov 17:22
will rise with *h* wings .... Mal 4:2
and *h* every kind of disease....... Matt 4:23
went around doing good and *h*....Acts 10:38
and to another gifts of *h*..........1 Cor 12:9
Not all have gifts of *h* .... 1 Cor 12:30
are for the *h* of the nations ..... Rev 22:2

HEALINGS
h today and tomorrow ....Luke 13:32

HEALS
who *h* all your diseases.............. Ps 103:3
He *h* the brokenhearted........... Ps 147:3
that *h* is like a life-giving tree......Prov 15:4
and *h* their severe wound ....Isa 30:26
Jesus the Christ *h* you ....Acts 9:34

HEALTH
people not been restored to *h*...... Jer 8:22
Yes, I will restore you to *h* .... Jer 30:17
has given him this complete *h*..... Acts 3:16
and that you may be in good *h* ....3 John 1:2

HEALTHIER
h than all the young men........... Dan 1:15

HEALTHY
saw that he was a *h* child .... Exod 2:2
are *h* don't need a physician.......Matt 9:12
that they may be *h* in the faith.....Titus 1:13

HEAP
will *h* coals of fire on his head ... Prov 25:22

HEAR
See also EARS TO HEAR
I will surely *h* their cry........... Exod 22:23
H, O Israel........................... Deut 6:4
and the sound of cattle that I *h* . 1 Sam 15:14
H from inside your heavenly .....1 Kgs 8:30
You *h* prayers...................... Ps 65:2
makes the human ear not *h* ....Ps 94:9
deaf ears will *h* .... Isa 35:5
Do you not *h* .... Isa 40:21
deaf *h*, the dead are raised .... Matt 11:5
although they *h* they do not *h*....Matt 13:13
although they *h* they may *h* ..... Mark 4:12
Take care about what you *h* .....Mark 4:24
you have ears, can't you *h* .... Mark 8:18
you *h* the sound it makes........John 3:8
it is not those who *h* the law ..... Rom 2:13
And how are they to *h*...........Rom 10:14
give grace to those who *h* .... Eph 4:29
curiosity to *h* new things ....2 Tim 4:3
are those who *h* and obey .... Rev 1:3
better *h* what the Spirit says........Rev 2:7

HEARD
man and his wife *h* the sound ...... Gen 3:8
I have *h* their cry .... Exod 3:7
h speech but you could not see....Deut 4:12
However, God *h* ....Ps 66:19
words of the wise are *h* in quiet ....Eccl 9:17
You have *h*; now look............. Isa 48:6
have believed what we just *h*.......Isa 53:1
no one has *h* or perceived..........Isa 64:4
has ever *h* of such a thing ....Isa 66:8
I have indeed *h* the people ....Jer 31:18
many words they will be *h*......... Matt 6:7
have they not *h*....................Rom 10:18
no eye has seen, or ear *h* .... 1 Cor 2:9
and *h* things too sacred............2 Cor 12:4
or by believing what you *h* .... Gal 3:2
And what you *h* me say...........2 Tim 2:2
attention to what we have *h*........Heb 2:1
But the message they *h* .... Heb 4:2
was *h* because of his devotion..... Heb 5:7
what we have *h*................... 1 John 1:1
I *h* behind me a loud voice......... Rev 1:10

HEARING
was read aloud in the *h*............. Neh 13:1
what part would do the *h*.........1 Cor 12:17
have become sluggish in *h*......... Heb 5:11

HEARS
godly cry out and the LORD *h*....... Ps 34:17
he *h* your cry of despair .... Isa 30:19
If anyone *h* my words ....John 12:47
And let the one who *h* say.........Rev 22:17

HEART
See also WITH ALL YOUR HEART
whose *h* stirred him .... Exod 36:2
seek him with all your *h* ....Deut 4:29
take to *h* the commandments ....Deut 11:27
will also cleanse your *h*..........Deut 30:6
was intense searching of *h* ....Judg 5:16
My *h* has rejoiced in the LORD..... 1 Sam 2:1
but the LORD looks at the *h* ......1 Sam 16:7
My *h* grows faint within me ......Job 19:27
God has made my *h* faint.........Job 23:16
My *h* is in turmoil unceasingly.....Job 30:27
Who has put wisdom in the *h* ....Job 38:36
h is stirred by a beautiful song....... Ps 45:1
and make me lose *h* .... Ps 69:20
h and my entire being shout.........Ps 84:2
with my whole *h*....................Ps 111:1
With all my *h* I seek you .... Ps 119:10
In my *h* I store up your words ...... Ps 119:11
my *h* is not proud.................. Ps 131:1
joyful *h* makes the face cheerful.. Prov 15:13
h is in the hand of the LORD .... Prov 21:1
are fervent lips with an evil *h*.... Prov 26:23
person's *h* reflects the person....Prov 27:19
trusts in his own *h* is a fool ...... Prov 28:26
h of the wise is in the house....... Eccl 7:4
your whole *h* is sick .... Isa 1:5
So my *h* constantly sighs ....Isa 16:11
I will give them one *h*............. Ezek 11:19
fashion yourselves a new *h*....... Ezek 18:31
those uncircumcised in *h*........ Ezek 44:7
Blessed are the pure in *h* .... Matt 5:8
there your *h* will be also...........Matt 6:21
out of the *h* come evil ideas .... Matt 15:19
he had a change of *h* and went .. Matt 21:29
and does not doubt in his *h*.....Mark 11:23
were of one *h* and mind ....Acts 4:32
Satan filled your *h* to lie .... Acts 5:3
your *h* is not right before God..... Acts 8:21
and circumcision is of the *h* ...... Rom 2:29
and believe in your *h* ....Rom 10:9
For with the *h* one believes......Rom 10:10
in the sincerity of your *h* .... Eph 6:5
yourselves with a *h* of mercy .... Col 3:12
be in control in your *h*............. Col 3:15
Refresh my *h* in Christ........... Phlm 1:20

HEARTLESS
covenant-breakers, *h*, ruthless..... Rom 1:31

HEARTS
all who had willing *h*............. Exod 35:22
Therefore, cleanse your *h* ....Deut 10:16

h of those who seek the LORD......Ps 105:3
Didn't our *h* burn within us......Luke 24:32
not let your *h* be distressed .... John 14:1
cleansing their *h* by faith ....Acts 15:9
will guard your *h* and minds.........Phil 4:7
Their *h* are always wandering ..... Heb 3:10

HEAT
cold and *h*, summer and winter....Gen 8:22
a shade from the *h* .... Isa 25:4

HEAVED
The earth *h* and shook............ Ps 18:7

HEAVEN
See also FATHER IN HEAVEN; HEAVEN AND
  EARTH; KINGDOM OF HEAVEN; LORD
  GOD OF HEAVEN'S ARMIES; LORD OF
  HEAVEN'S ARMIES
Creator of *h* and earth.............Gen 14:19
called to him from *h*...............Gen 22:11
This is the gate of *h*...............Gen 28:17
going to rain bread from *h* ....Exod 16:4
From *h* he spoke to you ....Deut 4:36
LORD took Elijah up to *h*.......... 2 Kgs 2:1
highest *h* cannot contain you...... 2 Chr 6:18
The one enthroned in *h*............. Ps 2:4
the LORD's throne is in *h*............Ps 11:4
The LORD looks down from *h* ....Ps 14:2
Whom do I have in *h* but you.......Ps 73:25
they stand secure in *h* ....Ps 119:89
God is in *h* and you are on earth.... Eccl 5:2
come to understand that *h* rules ..Dan 4:26
if they could climb up to *h*........ Amos 9:2
These are the four spirits of *h* ..... Zech 6:5
Repent, for the kingdom of *h*.......Matt 3:2
give honor to your Father in *h*.....Matt 5:16
Our Father in *h* .... Matt 6:9
on earth as it is in *h*............... Matt 6:10
the stars will fall from *h* ....Matt 24:29
H and earth will pass away ......Matt 24:35
a sign from *h* to test him ....Mark 8:11
but are like angels in *h* ....Mark 12:25
coming with the clouds of *h*....Mark 14:62
Satan fall like lightning from *h* ...Luke 10:18
your names stand written in *h*...Luke 10:20
there will be more joy in *h*........Luke 15:7
I have sinned against *h* and ......Luke 15:18
descending like a dove from *h*.... John 1:32
see *h* opened and the angels ....John 1:51
No one has ascended into *h* .... John 3:13
given you the bread from *h*........John 6:32
Then a voice came from *h*.......John 12:28
being let down from *h*............Acts 11:5
bear the image of the man of *h*.. 1 Cor 15:49
every family in *h* and on earth......Eph 3:15
hope laid up for you in *h* ....Col 1:5
there was silence in *h*.............. Rev 8:1
a great sign appeared in *h* .... Rev 12:1
saw a new *h* and a new earth....... Rev 21:1

HEAVEN AND EARTH
God, Creator of *h*...................Gen 14:19
I invoke *h* as witnesses .... Deut 30:19
servants of God of *h*..............Ezra 5:11
the Creator of *h* ....Ps 121:2
the Creator of *h* .... Ps 134:3
the one who made *h*..............Ps 146:6
fixed laws governing *h*............. Jer 33:25
until *h* pass away ....Matt 5:18
H will pass away ....Matt 24:35
praise you, Father, Lord of *h*.....Luke 10:21
who is Lord of *h* .... Acts 17:24
the one who made *h*............... Rev 14:7
first *h* had ceased to exist .... Rev 21:1

HEAVENLY
See also HEAVENLY FATHER
all the *h* assembly standing...... 1 Kgs 22:19
h army appeared with the angel...Luke 2:13
h bodies and earthly bodies .....1 Cor 15:40
so too those who are *h* .... 1 Cor 15:48
tasted the *h* gift................... Heb 6:4
the *h* Jerusalem................... Heb 12:22

HEAVENLY FATHER
perfect, as your *h* is perfect ......Matt 5:48
your *h* will also forgive you........Matt 6:14

yet your *h* feeds them ....Matt 6:26
your *h* knows that you need...... Matt 6:32
plant that my *h* did not plant..... Matt 15:13
So also my *h* will do to you.......Matt 18:35
the *h* give the Holy Spirit.........Luke 11:13

HEAVENS
The *h*—indeed the highest *h* ......Deut 10:14
but the LORD made the *h*......... 1 Chr 16:26
until the *h* are no more...........Job 14:12
h declare the glory of God.............Ps 19:1
The *h* declare his fairness..........Ps 50:6
The *h* belong to you .... Ps 89:11
When he established the *h* .... Prov 8:27
create new *h* and a new earth ......Isa 65:17
The *h* are my throne................Isa 66:1
h above could be measured ....Jer 31:37
h opened and he saw the Spirit....Matt 3:16
the *h* opened ....Luke 3:21
spiritual forces of evil in the *h*......Eph 6:12
h are the works of your hands......Heb 1:10
the *h* will disappear.............. 2 Pet 3:10

HEAVY
the sound of a *h* rainstorm ....1 Kgs 18:41
from the *h* downpour .... Isa 4:6

HEBREW
the *H* women are not like .... Exod 1:19

HEBREW
Term applied to:
  Abram, Gen 14:13
  Israelites, 1 Sam 4:6, 9
  Jews, Acts 6:1
  Paul, Phil 3:5

HEBRON [or KIRIATH ARBA]
Abram, Isaac, and Jacob dwell there,
  Gen 13:18; 23:2–20; 35:27
Visited by spies, Num 13:21–22
Defeated by Joshua, Josh 10:1–37
Caleb's inheritance, Josh 14:12–15
David's original capital; sons born there,
  2 Sam 2:1–3, 11; 3:2–5
Site of Absalom's rebellion, 2 Sam 15:7–10
Also called "Kiriath Arba," Gen 23:2

HEDGED
and whom God has *h* in .... Job 3:23

HEED
See also TAKE HEED
to *h* Samuel's warning............1 Sam 8:19
Take *h*, do not turn to evil .... Job 36:21
will not take *h* of the sheep....... Zech 11:16

HEEDS
h reproof shows good sense....... Prov 15:5

HEEL
and you will strike his *h* ....Gen 3:15
his hand clutching Esau's *h* ....Gen 25:26

HEIFER
a red *h* without blemish ....Num 19:2
had not plowed with my *h*....... Judg 14:18
rebelled like a stubborn *h* .... Hos 4:16

HEIGHT
nor *h*, nor depth, nor anything.... Rom 8:39
and length and *h* and depth ....Eph 3:18

HEIR
This man will not be your *h* .... Gen 15:4
Now I mean that the *h*.............. Gal 4:1
you are also an *h* through God ......Gal 4:7
he appointed *h* of all things.........Heb 1:2
an *h* of the righteousness...........Heb 11:7

HEIRS
And if children, then *h*............Rom 8:17
and also fellow *h* with Christ ......Rom 8:17
to adoption as his legal *h* .... Eph 1:5
the Gentiles are fellow *h* ....Eph 3:6
and *h* of the kingdom................Jas 2:5
fellow *h* of the grace of life.........1 Pet 3:7

HELAM
Place between Damascus and Hamath
  where David defeated Syrians,
  2 Sam 10:16–19

HELD
who *h* the words of the God........Ezra 9:4
with your head *h* so high ....Ps 75:5
You *h* my eyelids open ....Ps 77:4
h by the cords of his own sin .....Prov 5:22

HELL
will be sent to fiery *h* ....Matt 5:22
and be thrown into fiery *h*........Matt 18:9
escape being condemned to *h*... Matt 23:33
authority to throw you into *h*......Luke 12:5
let him be condemned to *h*.........Gal 1:8
is set on fire by *h* ....Jas 3:6

HELMET
is like a *h* on his head..............Isa 59:17
And take the *h* of salvation ....Eph 6:17
as a *h* our hope for salvation ....1 Thess 5:8

HELP
but there is no one to *h* them ..2 Sam 22:42
and your request for *h*.............. 1 Kgs 9:3
my power to *h* myself nothing .....Job 6:13
the poor who cried out for *h* ......Job 29:12
send you *h* from his temple ....Ps 20:2
Give us *h* against the enemy........Ps 60:11
hurry and *h* me.......................Ps 71:12
Ask him for *h*........................Isa 12:4
a nation that cannot *h* them........Isa 30:5
day of deliverance I will *h* ....Isa 49:8
but they will not *h* you ....Isa 57:12
to *h* the brokenhearted...............Isa 61:1
man is not seeking to *h*..............Jer 38:4
to *h* the resident foreigner ....Mal 3:5
h my unbelief.....................Mark 9:24
because he has come to *h* ....Luke 1:68
God has come to *h* his people .....Luke 7:16
Tell her to *h* me...................Luke 10:40
human nature is of no *h*...........John 6:63
we must *h* the weak............Acts 20:35
she has been a great *h* to many....Rom 16:2
I know your eagerness to *h*........2 Cor 9:2
h the weak.....................1 Thess 5:14
let her *h* them ....1 Tim 5:16
because he is a great *h* to me..... 2 Tim 4:11
find grace whenever we need *h* ... Heb 4:16

HELPED
Up to here the Lord has *h* us.....1 Sam 7:12
but the Lord *h* me ....2 Sam 22:19
If the Lord had not *h* me..........Ps 94:17
and no one *h* them up ....Ps 107:12
but the Lord *h* me ....Ps 118:13
h by keeping his requirements ....Mal 3:14
He has *h* his servant Israel........Luke 1:54

HELPER
truly our *h* in times of trouble.......Ps 46:1
The Lord is my *h*....................Heb 13:6

HELPLESS
they were bewildered and *h*......Matt 9:36
For while we were still *h*............Rom 5:6

HELPS
Spirit *h* us in our weakness ....Rom 8:26
h, gifts of leadership.............1 Cor 12:28

HEMAN
Composer of a psalm, Ps 88:title

HEN
as a *h* gathers her chicks ....Matt 23:37
as a *h* gathers her chicks ....Luke 13:34

HENNA
choice fruits: *h* with nard.........Song 4:13

HERALD
on a high mountain, O *h* Zion.......Isa 40:9
A *h* is running on the mountains ...Nah 1:15
a *h* of righteousness...............2 Pet 2:5

HERBS
without yeast and with bitter *h*....Exod 12:8
without yeast and with bitter *h*....Num 9:11

HERD
Then Abraham ran to the *h*........Gen 18:7
a burnt offering from the *h* .... Lev 1:3
send us into the *h* of pigs.........Matt 8:31

HERDS
All the tithe of *h* or flocks ....Lev 27:32

HERDSMEN
h ran off and spread the news.... Mark 5:14

HERE
See also HERE I AM
H I am, send me ....Isa 6:8
H is your God.......................Isa 40:9
been *h* with me three days ....Matt 15:32
all *h* in the presence of God ......Acts 10:33

HERE I AM
H!" Abraham replied................Gen 22:1
H!" Esau replied ....Gen 27:1
H! I replied .... Gen 31:11
He replied, "*H* ....Gen 46:2
And Moses said, "*H* .... Exod 3:4
and he replied, "*H* ....1 Sam 3:4
H. Bring a charge against ....1 Sam 12:3
I answered, "*H*, send me ....Isa 6:8
and he will reply, '*H* ....Isa 58:9
I said, '*H*! *H*!' to a nation ....Isa 65:1
and he replied, "*H*, Lord ....Acts 9:10

HERESIES
with destructive *h* ....2 Pet 2:1

HERMES
Paul acclaimed as, Acts 14:12

HERMON, MOUNT
See MOUNT HERMON

HEROD
—Herod the Great, procurator of Judea
   (37–4 BC), Luke 1:5
Inquires about Jesus' birth, Matt 2:3–8
Slays children of Bethlehem, Matt 2:12–18
—Herod Antipas, the tetrarch, ruler of
   Galilee and Perea (4 BC–AD 39), Luke 3:1
Imprisons John the Baptist, Luke 3:18–21
Has John the Baptist beheaded, Matt 14:1–12
Disturbed about Jesus, Luke 9:7–9
Jesus sent to him, Luke 23:7–11
—Herod Agrippa I (AD 37–44), Acts 12:1, 19
Kills James, Acts 12:1–2
Imprisons Peter, Acts 12:3–11, 19
Slain by an angel, Acts 12:20–23
—Herod Agrippa II (AD 53–70);
   called Agrippa and King Agrippa,
   Acts 25:22–24, 26
Festus tells him about Paul, Acts 25:13–27
Paul makes a defense before, Acts 26:1–32

HERODIANS
Join Pharisees against Jesus, Mark 3:6
Seek to trap Jesus, Matt 22:15–22
Jesus warns against, Mark 8:15

HERODIAS
Granddaughter of Herod the Great; plots
   John's death, Matt 14:3–12
Married her uncle, Mark 6:17–18

HERONS
evergreens in which the *h* live.....Ps 104:17

HESHBON
Ancient Moabite city; taken by Moses,
   Num 21:23–34
Assigned to Reubenites, Num 32:1–37
Prophecies concerning, Isa 15:1–4; 16:8–14;
   Jer 48:2, 34–35

HETH
Son of Canaan, Gen 10:15
Abraham buys field from sons of,
   Gen 23:3–20
Esau marries daughters of, Gen 27:46

HEZEKIAH
Righteous king of Judah; reforms temple
   and worship, 2 Chr 29–31
Wars with Assyria; prayer for deliverance is
   answered, 2 Kgs 18:7–19:37
His sickness and recovery; thanks-giving,
   2 Kgs 20:1–11; Isa 38:9–22
Boasts to Babylonian ambassadors,
   2 Kgs 20:12–19
Death, 2 Kgs 20:20–21

HID
I was naked, so I *h*.................Gen 3:10
she *h* him for three months ....Exod 2:2
because she *h* the messengers ....Josh 6:25
So David *h* in the field ....1 Sam 20:24
people *h* their faces from him .....Isa 53:3
and *h* his master's money in it... Matt 25:18
h themselves in the caves ....Rev 6:15

HIDDEN
kept the matter *h* from me ....2 Kgs 4:27
So he was *h* from Athaliah........2 Kgs 11:2
it has been *h* from the eyes........Job 28:21
my guilt is not *h* from you..........Ps 69:5
open rebuke than *h* love...........Prov 27:5
I will give you *h* treasures .... Isa 45:3
you are a God who keeps *h*........Isa 45:15
in some *h* place....................Isa 45:19
is *h* that will not be revealed .... Matt 10:26
announce what has been *h* ....Matt 13:35
is *h* that will not be revealed ......Luke 8:17
but Jesus was *h* from them .... John 8:59
h in a mystery ....1 Cor 2:7
give him some of the *h* manna .....Rev 2:17

HIDE
H out in the Kerith Valley..........1 Kgs 17:3
H me in the shadow ....Ps 17:8
You *h* them with you ....Ps 31:20
will find no place to *h*...............Amos 2:14
Fall on us and *h* us.................Rev 6:16

HIDEOUT
is to be a *h* for robbers ....Jer 7:11

HIDING
You are my *h* place ....Ps 32:7

HIEL
Native of Bethel; rebuilds Jericho,
   1 Kgs 16:34
Fulfills Joshua's curse, Josh 6:26

HIGH
See also HIGH PLACE; HIGH PLACES; HIGH
   PRIEST; MOST HIGH
the priest of the Most *H* God......Gen 14:18
Is not God on *h* in heaven........Job 22:12
Lord Most *H* is awe-inspiring ....Ps 47:2
will be set on *h* ....Prov 29:25
lifted *h*, and greatly exalted ....Isa 52:13
the *h* and exalted one says ....Isa 57:15
the Most *H* has authority...........Dan 4:17
were to soar *h* like an eagle ....Obad 1:4
privately up a *h* mountain ....Matt 17:1
and the power of the Most *H*......Luke 1:35
a merciful and faithful *h* priest .....Heb 2:17

HIGH PLACE
making a sacrifice at the *h*........1 Sam 9:12
coming down from the *h*........1 Sam 10:5
built a *h* for the detestable .... 1 Kgs 11:7
at the *h* made by Jeroboam......2 Kgs 23:15
at that *h* and crushed them......2 Kgs 23:15
What is this *h* you go to ....Ezek 20:29
it is called "*H*" to this day........Ezek 20:29

HIGH PLACES
I will destroy your *h* .... Lev 26:30
and demolish their *h* ....Num 33:52
lies slain on your *h*................2 Sam 1:19
offering sacrifices at the *h* .... 1 Kgs 3:2
He built temples on the *h* ....1 Kgs 12:31
The *h* were not eliminated ....1 Kgs 15:14
He eliminated the *h* ....2 Kgs 18:4
to offer sacrifices on the *h*......2 Kgs 23:5
removed the *h* and the incense... 2 Chr 14:5
demolished all the *h* and altars...2 Chr 31:1
who eliminated the Lord's *h* ....2 Chr 32:12
Judah and Jerusalem of the *h* ....2 Chr 34:3
went up to the *h* to lament........Isa 15:2
and I will destroy your *h*...........Ezek 6:3
made for yourself decorated *h* ...Ezek 16:16
The *h* of the "House of ....Hos 10:8

HIGH PRIEST
The *h*—who is greater than ....Lev 21:10
in the palace of the *h* ....Matt 26:3
when Abiathar was *h* ....Mark 2:26

and struck the *h*'s slave..........Mark 14:47
who was *h* that year..............John 11:49
was acquainted with the *h*........John 18:15
into the *h*'s courtyard............John 18:15
Annas the *h* was there.............Acts 4:6
members of the *h*'s family.........Acts 4:6
went to the *h*....................Acts 9:1
the *h* Ananias ordered those ......Acts 23:2
a merciful and faithful *h*...........Heb 2:17
since we have a great *h*...........Heb 4:14
a *h* incapable of sympathizing.....Heb 4:15
h in the order of Melchizedek.....Heb 5:10
We have such a *h*..................Heb 8:1
only the *h* enters once a year.......Heb 9:7

HIGH-SOUNDING
speaking *h* but empty words ......2 Pet 2:18

HIGHER
It is *h* than the heavens.............Job 11:8

HIGHEST
the *h* heavens.....................Deut 10:14
Hosanna in the *h* ....Matt 21:9
Glory to God in the *h*.............Luke 2:14
and glory in the *h*................Luke 19:38

HIGHLY
As a result God *h* exalted him ....Phil 2:9

HIGHWAY
path of the upright is like a *h*.....Prov 15:19

HILKIAH
Shallum's son, 1 Chr 6:13
High priest in Josiah's reign, 2 Chr 34:9–22
Oversees temple work, 2 Kgs 22:4–7
Finds the scroll of the law, 2 Kgs 22:8–14
Aids in reformation, 2 Kgs 23:4

HILL
on Zion, my holy *h*...................Ps 2:6
on a *h* cannot be hidden...........Matt 5:14
and *h* will be brought low ....Luke 3:5
to the brow of the *h*..............Luke 4:29

HILLS
things of the age-old *h*...........Gen 49:26
one of *h* and valleys ....Deut 11:11
For the *h* bring it food............Job 40:20
as you descend from the *h* ....Ps 76:4
I look up toward the *h*.............Ps 121:1
before the *h* ....Prov 8:25

HILLSIDE
feeding there on the *h*............Luke 8:32

HINDER
who was I to *h* God...............Acts 11:17
they *h* us from speaking........ 1 Thess 2:16
nothing will *h* your prayers.........1 Pet 3:7

HINNOM, VALLEY OF BEN
Place near Jerusalem used for human
    sacrifice, 2 Kgs 23:10; 2 Chr 28:3;
    Jer 7:31–32; 19:1–15

HINT
or the slightest *h* of change..........Jas 1:17

HIP
he struck the socket of his *h*......Gen 32:25

HIRAM
King of Tyre; provided materials for David's
    palace and Solomon's temple, 2 Sam 5:11;
    1 Kgs 5:1–12; 9:10–14, 26–28; 10:11; 1 Chr 14:1

HIRE
to *h* workers for his vineyard.....Matt 20:1

HIRED
h workers will be depressed........Isa 19:10
those *h* about five o'clock ....Matt 20:9
father's *h* workers have food .....Luke 15:17

HIS LOYAL LOVE ENDURES
for he is good and *h*............1 Chr 16:34
he is good; certainly *h* ....2 Chr 5:13
thanks to the LORD, for *h*........2 Chr 20:21
for he is good, and *h*..............Ps 106:1
for he is good, and *h*..............Ps 107:1
for he is good, and *h*..............Ps 118:1
for he is good, for *h*.............Ps 136:1

HIS RIGHT HAND
he put Ephraim on *h*.............Gen 48:13
H and his mighty arm..............Ps 98:1
and *h* embraces me...............Song 2:6
The LORD swears an oath by *h*......Isa 62:8
He withdrew *h* as the enemy.......Lam 2:3
Satan standing at *h* to accuse.....Zech 3:1
They put a staff in *h*.........Matt 27:29
God exalted him to *h*.............Acts 5:31
and seated him at *h*.................Eph 1:20
He held seven stars in *h* .... Rev 1:16
on the seven stars in *h*.............Rev 2:1
raised *h* to heaven.................Rev 10:5

HIT
and *h* a pregnant woman........ Exod 21:22

HITS
box like one who *h* only air.......1 Cor 9:26

HITTITES
One of seven Canaanite nations, Deut 7:1
Israelites intermarry with, Judg 3:5–6;
    1 Kgs 11:1; Ezra 9:1–2

HIVITES
One of seven Canaanite nations, Deut 7:1
Esau intermarries with, Gen 36:2
Gibeonites belong to, Josh 9:3, 7

HOLD
we are to *h* a pilgrim feast........ Exod 10:9
grabbed *h* of the horns ....1 Kgs 1:50
to take *h* of the ark.................1 Chr 13:9
God won't *h* me accountable ......Ps 10:4
will not *h* me accountable ....Ps 10:13
Do not *h* against me the sins ....Ps 25:7
H them accountable.................Ps 69:27
right hand would grab *h* of me ....Ps 139:10
who takes *h* of your right hand......Isa 41:13
that cannot even *h* water...........Jer 2:13
and forceful people lay *h* of it ....Matt 11:12
do not *h* this sin against them ....Acts 7:60
if you *h* firmly to the message.....1 Cor 15:2
H on to what you have ....Rev 3:11

HOLDING
you will be *h* a son................2 Kgs 4:16
and *h* him up to contempt..........Heb 6:6

HOLDS
h fools up to public contempt .....Prov 3:35
the one who *h* him back.........2 Thess 2:7

HOLE
and dug a *h* in the ground .... Matt 25:18

HOLES
and into *h* in the ground.............Isa 2:19

HOLIER
for I am *h* than you .... Isa 65:5

HOLINESS
in *h*, fearful in praises............. Exod 15:11
H to the LORD ....Exod 28:36
I have vowed by my own *h* ....Ps 89:35
H aptly adorns your house ....Ps 93:5
will be called the Way of *H* .... Isa 35:8
accomplish *h* out of reverence ....2 Cor 7:1
not call us to impurity but in *h* ..1 Thess 4:7
that we may share his *h* ....Heb 12:10
conducting your lives in *h* ....2 Pet 3:11

HOLLOW
he hid me in the *h* of his hand ...... Isa 49:2

HOLY
See also FILLED WITH THE HOLY SPIRIT;
    HOLY CITY; HOLY NAME; HOLY ONE
    OF ISRAEL; HOLY PLACE; HOLY SPIRIT;
    MOST HOLY PLACE
are standing is *h* ground............ Exod 3:5
a *h* Sabbath to the LORD........... Exod 16:23
kingdom of priests and a *h* .... Exod 19:6
Sabbath day to set it apart as *h*...Exod 20:8
put the *h* diadem on the turban ..Exod 29:6
Then the altar will be most *h* ....Exod 29:37
between the *h* and the common...Lev 10:10
You must be *h* because I.............Lev 19:2
for the priest is *h* to his God........Lev 21:7

the whole community is *h*.........Num 16:3
No one is *h* like the LORD..........1 Sam 2:2
the priest gave him *h* bread ......1 Sam 21:6
Worship the LORD in *h* attire ....1 Chr 16:29
that the *h* race has become........Ezra 9:2
This day is *h* to the LORD ....Neh 8:9
of the *h* ones will you turn..........Job 5:1
The LORD is in his *h* temple........Ps 11:4
Who may live on your *h* hill ....Ps 15:1
God sits on his *h* throne ....Ps 47:8
city of our God, his *h* hill ....Ps 48:1
H, h, h is the LORD ....Isa 6:3
the *H* One of Israel ....Isa 10:20
They will honor the *H* One ....Isa 29:23
the *H* One of Israel ....Isa 41:14
H People, the Ones Protected .....Isa 62:12
both sides of the *h* allotment.... Ezek 48:21
to be a spirit of the *h* gods..........Dan 4:9
Announce a *h* fast ....Joel 2:15
name of your *h* servant Jesus.....Acts 4:30
h and trustworthy promises.......Acts 13:34
of the dough offered is *h* ...... Rom 11:16
h, and pleasing to God.............Rom 12:1
Greet one another with a *h*......Rom 16:16
we should be *h* and blameless........Eph 1:4
that you become *h* ....1 Thess 4:3
lifting up *h* hands without ....1 Tim 2:8
and called us with a *h* calling ......2 Tim 1:9
indeed he who makes *h* ....Heb 2:11
we have been made *h* .... Heb 10:10
become *h* yourselves.............1 Pet 1:15
You shall be *h* ....1 Pet 1:16
house to be a *h* priesthood.........1 Pet 2:5
a *h* nation.......................1 Pet 2:9
H, H, H is the Lord God........... Rev 4:8
because you alone are *h*..........Rev 15:4
is *h* must continue to be *h* ...... Rev 22:11

HOLY CITY
to settle Jerusalem, the *h*....... Neh 11:1
total of the Levites in the *h*...... Neh 11:18
Indeed, they live in the *h* ...... Isa 48:2
O Jerusalem, *h*....................Isa 52:1
your people and your *h*...........Dan 9:24
devil took him to the *h* .... Matt 4:5
and went into the *h*..............Matt 27:53
they will trample on the *h*.........Rev 11:2
And I saw the *h*...................Rev 21:2
and showed me the *h*.............Rev 21:10
tree of life and in the *h* ....Rev 22:19

HOLY NAME
and profaned my *h*................Lev 20:3
Boast about his *h*................1 Chr 16:10
you to honor your *h* ....1 Chr 29:16
give thanks to his *h* ....Ps 30:4
for we trust in his *h*...............Ps 33:21
Give thanks to his *h* ....Ps 97:12
is within me, praise his *h* ....Ps 103:1
Boast about his *h*.................Ps 105:3
give thanks to your *h*.............Ps 106:47
all who live praise his *h*............Ps 145:21
my *h* will not be profaned.......Ezek 20:39
I will be zealous for my *h*........Ezek 39:25

HOLY ONE OF ISRAEL
so arrogantly? At the *H*..........2 Kgs 19:22
accompanied by a harp, O *H*........Ps 71:22
our king to the *H* ....Ps 89:18
and rejected the *H*..................Isa 1:4
rely on the LORD, the *H*...........Isa 10:20
for the *H* acts mightily..............Isa 12:6
LORD, your Protector, the *H* ......Isa 41:14
the *H* who has chosen you ....Isa 49:7
proudly defied me, the *H*.........Jer 50:29

HOLY PLACE
between the *H* and the Most *H*..Exod 26:33
when he goes into the *H*........Exod 28:29
and sweet incense for the *H* ......Exod 31:11
H inside the special curtain.......Lev 16:2
that would be the Most *H* ....1 Kgs 6:16
of the meeting tent and the *H* ...1 Chr 23:32
in the Most *H* under the wings ....2 Chr 5:7
secure position in his *h*............Ezra 9:8

This is the Most *H* ....Ezek 41:4
standing in the *h*................ Matt 24:15
he was delayed in the *H* ....Luke 1:21
saying things against this *h* ....Acts 6:13
made this *h* ritually unclean ......Acts 21:28
once for all into the Most *H* ....Heb 9:12

HOLY SPIRIT
Affirmed as divine:
    called God, Acts 5:3–4
    Creator, Gen 1:2
    eternal, Heb 9:14
    joined with the Father and the Son,
        Matt 28:19; 2 Cor 13:14
    new creation, John 3:3, 8
    omnipotent, Luke 1:35
    omnipresent, Ps 139:7–13
    omniscient, 1 Cor 2:10–11
    sin against, unforgiveable, Matt 12:31–32
    sovereign, 1 Cor 12:6, 11
Work of:
    anoints, 1 John 2:20, 27
    baptizes, Acts 2:17–41
    bears fruit, Gal 5:22–23
    bears witness, Rom 8:16; Heb 10:15
    comforts, Acts 9:31
    empowers, Mic 3:8
    gives discernment, 1 Cor 2:10–16;
        1 John 4:1–6
    gives joy, Rom 14:17
    gives gifts, 1 Cor 12:3–11
    guides, John 16:13
    helps, John 14:16–26
    illuminates the mind, 1 Cor 2:12–13;
        Eph 1:16 17
    indwells, Rom 8:11
    regenerates, John 3:3, 5
    reveals things of God, Isa 40:13–14;
        1 Cor 2:10, 13
    role in Christ's ministry, Matt 3:16;
        12:28; Luke 1:35; 4:1, 17–18; Rom 1:4;
        1 Tim 3:16; Heb 9:14
    sanctifies, Rom 15:16; 2 Thess 2:13
    speaks in Scripture, Acts 1:16–17; 28:25;
        2 Tim 3:16
Promised, Joel 2:28–32
Received by disciples, Acts 2:1–21
Received by Gentiles, Acts 10:45
Persons filled by:
    Barnabas, Acts 11:22, 24
    Bezalel, Exod 31:2
    certain disciples, Acts 13:52
    Elizabeth, Luke 1:41
    Jesus, Luke 4:1
    John the Baptist, Luke 1:15, 60
    Paul, Acts 13:9
    Pentecost Christians, Acts 2:1–4
    Peter, Acts 4:8
    seven men, Acts 6:3–5
    Stephen, Acts 7:55
    Zacharias, Luke 1:67

Also see FILLED WITH THE HOLY SPIRIT
not take your *h* away from me ......Ps 51:11
rebelled and offended his *h* ....Isa 63:10
to be pregnant through the *H* .....Matt 1:18
baptize you with the *H* and fire.... Matt 3:11
speaks against the *H*..............Matt 12:32
Father and the Son and the *H* ... Matt 28:19
blasphemes against the *H* ....Mark 3:29
David himself, by the *H*.........Mark 12:36
not you speaking, but the *H* .....Mark 13:11
he will be filled with the *H*........Luke 1:15
was filled with the *H*...............Luke 1:41
was filled with the *H*...............Luke 1:67
revealed to him by the *H* ....Luke 2:26
and the *H* descended on him ..... Luke 3:22
Then Jesus, full of the *H*............Luke 4:1
for the *H* will teach you..........Luke 12:12
But the Advocate, the *H*..........John 14:26
and said, "Receive the *H*.........John 20:22
baptized with the *H* ....Acts 1:5
when the *H* has come upon you .... Acts 1:8
were filled with the *H* ....Acts 2:4

received the promise of the *H* .....Acts 2:33
receive the gift of the *H* ....Acts 2:38
Peter, filled with the *H*..............Acts 4:8
they were filled with the *H* ....Acts 4:31
filled your heart to lie to the *H* .....Acts 5:3
are always resisting the *H* ....Acts 7:51
would receive the *H* ....Acts 8:15
and be filled with the *H*............Acts 9:17
the encouragement of the *H* ......Acts 9:31
the *H* fell on all those...........Acts 10:44
full of the *H* and of faith ....Acts 11:24
the *H* said, "Set apart for me ...... Acts 13:2
with joy and with the *H*...........Acts 13:52
by giving them the *H* ....Acts 15:8
it seemed best to the *H*...........Acts 15:28
prevented by the *H*................Acts 16:6
except that the *H* warns me ..... Acts 20:23
the *H* has made you overseers .. Acts 20:28
The *H* says this ....Acts 21:11
conscience assures me in the *H* ....Rom 9:1
peace, and joy in the *H* ....Rom 14:17
sanctified by the *H* ....Rom 15:16
body is the temple of the *H* ...... 1 Cor 6:19
body is the temple of the *H* ......1 Cor 12:3
benevolence, by the *H*.............2 Cor 6:6
and the fellowship of the *H*......2 Cor 13:13
the seal of the promised *H* .... Eph 1:13
do not grieve the *H* of God ....Eph 4:30
the *H* who lives within us .... 2 Tim 1:14
and the renewing of the *H*.........Titus 3:5
miracles and gifts of the *H* ....Heb 2:4
become partakers of the *H* ....Heb 6:4
carried along by the *H*............2 Pet 1:21
by praying in the *H* ....Jude 1:20

HOME
that your *h* will be secure ....Job 5:24
he will hide me in his *h* ....Ps 27:5
a permanent guest in your *h* .... Ps 61:4
Even the birds find a *h* there........Ps 84:3
man goes to his eternal *h*.........Eccl 12:5
Go to your *h* and to your people .. Mark 5:19
there is no one who has left *h* ...Mark 10:29
take your stretcher and go *h* ..... Luke 5:24
took her into his own *h*...........John 19:27
let him eat at *h* ....1 Cor 11:34
should ask their husbands at *h* .. 1 Cor 14:35
and at *h* with the Lord.............2 Cor 5:8
Now in a wealthy *h* there are.... 2 Tim 2:20

HOMELESS
You will be a *h* wanderer .... Gen 4:12

HOMES
men of Israel back to their *h* ....Judg 7:8
God settles in their own *h* ....Ps 68:6
deliver the *h* of Judah first.........Zech 12:7
welcomed into the eternal *h* .....Luke 16:9

HOMETOWN
without honor except in his *h* ....Matt 13:57
without honor except in his *h* .....Mark 6:4

HOMOSEXUALS
partners, practicing *h*..............1 Cor 6:9
practicing *h*, kidnappers ....1 Tim 1:10

HONEST
we are *h* men......................Gen 42:11
back to him an *h* report ....Josh 14:7
weigh me with *h* scales............Job 6:25
with an *h* and good heart.........Luke 8:15

HONESTLY
and speaks *h*...................... Ps 15:2
the one who speaks *h* ....Isa 45:19

HONESTY
h stumbles in the city square.......Isa 59:14

HONEY
See also MILK AND HONEY
that flows with milk and *h* ....Num 16:13
What is sweeter than *h* ....Judg 14:18
tasted just a little of this *h* ..... 1 Sam 14:29
bring greater delight than *h* ...... Ps 19:10
satisfy your appetite with *h*........ Ps 81:16
sweeter in my mouth than *h* .... Ps 119:103
Eat *h*, my child....................Prov 24:13

not good to eat too much *h* ..... Prov 25:27
of locusts and wild *h*.............. Matt 3:4
as sweet as *h* in my mouth ....Rev 10:10

HONEYCOMB
sweetest honey from a *h* ....Ps 19:10
Pleasant words are like a *h* ....Prov 16:24
lips drip sweetness like the *h*......Song 4:11

HONOR
H your father and your mother.. Exod 20:12
and *h* so that you will be ....1 Kgs 3:13
whom the king wishes to *h*.......Esth 6:6
yourself with glory and *h*..........Job 40:10
Give him the *h* he deserves........Ps 66:2
rescue him and bring him *h* ....Ps 91:15
I will focus on your *h* ....Ps 145:5
H the LORD from your wealth ......Prov 3:9
The wise inherit *h* ....Prov 3:35
before *h* comes humility..........Prov 15:33
is an *h* for a person to cease...... Prov 20:3
so *h* is not fitting for a fool ....Prov 26:1
has a lowly spirit will gain *h* ..... Prov 29:23
they will *h* my name...............Isa 29:23
h to your Father in heaven ....Matt 5:16
A prophet is not without *h* ....Matt 13:57
H your father and mother ....Matt 15:4
They love the place of *h* .... Matt 23:6
that all people will *h* the Son .....John 5:23
but I *h* my Father ....John 8:49
the Father will *h* him ....John 12:26
right of Jesus in a place of *h* ......John 13:23
h to whom honor is due ....Rom 13:7
and *h* people like him............. Phil 2:29
own body in holiness and *h*.......1 Thess 4:4
be *h* and glory forever..............1 Tim 1:17
counted worthy of double *h*.......1 Tim 5:17
And no one assumes this *h* ....Heb 5:4
H all people.......................1 Pet 2:17
For he received *h* and glory ......2 Pet 1:17
h, and thanks to the one............ Rev 4:9

HONORABLE
fool will no longer be called *h* ....Isa 32:5
members we consider less *h* ....1 Cor 12:23

HONORED
I cause my name to be *h*........Exod 20:24
of all the people I will be *h* ....Lev 10:3
h in the great angelic assembly......Ps 89:7
may your name be *h*.............. Matt 6:9
My Father is *h* by this..............John 15:8
Marriage must be *h* .... Heb 13:4

HONORS
h the LORD's loyal followers .... Ps 15:4
made to the one who *h* you .... Ps 119:38
A son naturally *h* his father.......... Mal 1:6
people *h* me with their lips ....Mark 7:6

HOOFBEATS
the *h* of the enemies' horses ....Jer 47:3

HOOKS
their spears into pruning *h* ....Mic 4:3

HOOVES
and have divided *h*..................Lev 11:4
I will give you bronze *h*............Mic 4:13

HOPE
h that I could get married .... Ruth 1:12
come to an end without *h* ....Job 7:6
I will *h* in him ....Job 13:15
so you destroy man's *h* ....Job 14:19
h for the grave to be my home ....Job 17:13
where then is my *h* ....Job 17:15
uproots my *h* like an uprooted .... Job 19:10
You are my only *h* ....Ps 39:7
he is the one who gives me *h*........Ps 62:5
For you are my *h* ....Ps 71:5
I find in your word...............Ps 119:147
h in the LORD ....Ps 130:7
and your *h* will not be cut off.....Prov 23:18
more *h* for a fool than for him....Prov 26:12
is among the living has *h* ....Eccl 9:4
into an 'Opportunity for *H*...........Hos 2:15
you prisoners, with *h* ....Zech 9:12
in his name the Gentiles will *h*....Matt 12:21

I have a *h* in God......................Acts 24:15
Against *h* Abraham believed.......Rom 4:18
rejoice in the *h* of God's glory ......Rom 5:2
And *h* does not disappoint..........Rom 5:5
For in *h* we were saved..........Rom 8:24
we *h* for what we do not see .....Rom 8:25
three remain: faith, *h*, and love ...1 Cor 13:13
in this life we have *h* in Christ ....1 Cor 15:19
what is the *h* of his calling..........Eph 1:18
to the one *h* of your calling.........Eph 4:4
h laid up for you in heaven..........Col 1:5
the *h* of glory ....Col 1:27
who is our *h* or joy or crown ...1 Thess 2:19
like the rest who have no *h*.....1 Thess 4:13
as a helmet our *h* for salvation ..1 Thess 5:8
and of Christ Jesus our *h*.............1 Tim 1:1
in *h* of eternal life....................Titus 1:2
our *h* in the glorious appearing....Titus 2:13
hold fast to the *h* set before us ....Heb 6:18
a better *h* is introduced............Heb 7:19
new birth into a living *h* ....1 Pet 1:3
asks about the *h* you possess......1 Pet 3:15
has this *h* focused on him ....1 John 3:3

HOPED
But when I *h* for good ....Job 30:26
We *h* for good fortune................Jer 8:15
the holy women who *h* in God .....1 Pet 3:5

HOPES
the *h* of the oppressed ....Ps 9:18
been the object of Israel's *h* ....Jer 14:8

HOPHNI
Wicked son of Eli. 1 Sam 1:3; 2:12–17, 22–25
Prophecy against, 1 Sam 2:27–36; 3:11–14
Carries ark into battle; killed, 1 Sam 4:1–11

HOR, MOUNT
See MOUNT HOR

HORDE
bury Gog and all his *h* ....Ezek 39:11

HOREB
God appears to Moses at, Exod 3:1–22
Water flows from, Exod 17:6
Elijah lodged here 40 days, 1 Kgs 19:8–9

HOREB, MOUNT
See MOUNT HOREB

HORITES
Inhabitants of Mt. Seir, Gen 36:20
Defeated by Kedorlaomer, Gen 14:5–6
Driven out by Esau's descendants,
   Gen 36:20–29; Deut 2:12, 22

HORIZON
the eastern *h* is from the west.....Ps 103:12
when he marked out the *h* ....Prov 8:27
one who sits on the earth's *h*......Isa 40:22
Praise him from the *h* ....Isa 42:10

HORMAH
Destroyed by Israel, Num 21:1–3

HORN
When the ram's *h* sounds.........Exod 19:13
and buried my *h* in the dust ....Job 16:15
the *h* that saves me...................Ps 18:2
Sound the ram's *h* on the day ....Ps 81:3
goat had a conspicuous *h*...........Dan 8:5
raised up a *h* of salvation ....Luke 1:69

HORNS
priests carry seven rams' *h*.........Josh 6:4
amid the blaring of ram's *h*...........Ps 47:5

HORRIBLE
committed the same *h* sins.......2 Kgs 21:2
Something *h* and shocking ....Jer 5:30

HORRIFIED
were *h* by the sight of you.........Isa 52:14

HORROR
will become an occasion of *h*....Deut 28:37
a cup of *h* and desolation........Ezek 23:33
you have become a *h* ....Ezek 27:36

HORSE
h and its rider he has thrown.......Exod 15:1
Do you give the *h* its strength .....Job 39:19

A *h* disappoints those ....Ps 33:17
with the strength of a *h*..........Ps 147:10
A *h* is prepared for the day ....Prov 21:31
and here came a white *h* ....Rev 6:2
and here came a black *h*...........Rev 6:5
and here came a pale green *h* ......Rev 6:8
and here came a white *h* ....Rev 19:11

HORSEBACK
I have seen slaves on *h* ....Eccl 10:7

HORSEMEN
on horseback with some *h* .....1 Kgs 20:20

HORSES
of his chariot *h* delayed............Judg 5:28
chariots and *h* were kept ....1 Kgs 9:19
His *h* move more swiftly............Jer 4:13
Can *h* run on rocky cliffs........Amos 6:12
Their *h* gallop........................Hab 1:8
put bits into the mouths of *h* ....Jas 3:3

HOSANNA
H to the Son of David..............Matt 21:9

HOSEA
Son of Beeri, prophet of the northern
   kingdom, Hos 1:1

HOSHEA
Original name of Joshua, the son of Nun,
   Deut 32:44; Num 13:8, 16
See JOSHUA
—Israel's last king; usurps throne,
   2 Kgs 15:30
Reigns wickedly; Israel taken to Assyria
   during his reign, 2 Kgs 17:1–23

HOSPITABLE
h, an able teacher...................1 Tim 3:2

HOSPITALITY
practiced *h*, washed the feet.......1 Tim 5:10
Do not neglect *h*....................Heb 13:2
Show *h* to one another ....1 Pet 4:9

HOSTED
Samson *h* a party there..........Judg 14:10

HOSTILE
of the flesh is *h* to God ....Rom 8:7

HOSTILITY
h between you and the woman.....Gen 3:15
God sent a spirit to stir up *h*.......Judg 9:23
murder, strife, deceit, *h*...........Rom 1:29
by which the *h* has been killed......Eph 2:16
means *h* toward God ....Jas 4:4

HOT
until the *h* anger of our God......Ezra 10:14
you are neither cold nor *h*..........Rev 3:15

HOUR
worrying can add even one *h*.....Matt 6:27
that day and *h* no one knows....Matt 24:36
h when you do not expect him ..Matt 24:44
the *h* is approaching.............Matt 26:45
But this is your *h* ....Luke 22:53
deliver me from this *h*...........John 12:27
know at what *h* I will come.........Rev 3:3
keep you from the *h* of testing .....Rev 3:10

HOURS
there not twelve *h* in a day ....John 11:9

HOUSE
See also HOUSE OF DAVID; HOUSE OF
   GOD; HOUSE OF THE LORD
for you his good treasure *h*......Deut 28:12
the good things of your *h*............Ps 65:4
For she has set her *h* by death.....Prov 2:18
A *h* and wealth are inherited .....Prov 19:14
By wisdom a *h* is built ....Prov 24:3
who keep watch over the *h*.......Eccl 12:3
man who built his *h* on rock......Matt 7:24
the winds beat against that *h*.....Matt 7:25
the winds beat against that *h*.....Matt 7:27
when Jesus entered Peter's *h*.....Matt 8:14
Jesus entered the leader's *h* .....Matt 9:23
lost sheep of the *h* of Israel.......Matt 10:6
And if the *h* is worthy............Matt 10:13

or *h* divided against itself........Matt 12:25
enter a strong man's *h*...........Matt 12:29
h will be called a *h* of prayer......Matt 21:13
your *h* is left to you desolate ....Matt 23:38
at the *h* of Simon the leper.......Matt 26:6
h will be called a *h* of prayer......Mark 11:17
and entered Zechariah's *h*........Luke 1:40
who built a *h* on the ground......Luke 6:49
Whatever *h* you enter ....Luke 9:4
so that my *h* will be filled........Luke 14:23
sweep the *h* ....Luke 15:8
my Father's *h* a marketplace ......John 2:16
Zeal for your *h* will devour me ....John 2:17
h was filled with the fragrance ....John 12:3
places in my Father's *h* ....John 14:2
breaking bread from *h* to *h*.......Acts 2:46
I was praying in my *h*.............Acts 10:30
in the *h* of Simon the tanner......Acts 10:32
publicly and from *h* to *h*.........Acts 20:20
greet the church in their *h*........Rom 16:5
we know that if our earthly *h*......2 Cor 5:1
For in this earthly *h* we groan .....2 Cor 5:2
church that meets in your *h*........Phlm 1:2
of a *h* deserves greater honor ...... Heb 3:3
every *h* is built by someone .... Heb 3:4
faithful as a son over God's *h*....... Heb 3:6
great priest over the *h* of God.... Heb 10:21
are built up as a spiritual *h* ....1 Pet 2:5
starting with the *h* of God ....1 Pet 4:17
do not receive him into your *h* .. 2 John 1:10

HOUSE OF DAVID
a covenant with the *h*............1 Sam 20:16
house of Saul and the *h*...........2 Sam 3:1
house of Saul and the *h*..........2 Sam 3:6
They passed the *h* ....Neh 12:37
on the thrones of the *h*............Ps 122:5
I will place the key to the *h*.......Isa 22:22

HOUSE OF GOD
nothing else than the *h*........... Gen 28:17
sacred stone will be the *h* ....Gen 28:22
and lest the *h* be rebuilt ....Ezra 5:15
a time to meet in the *h*............Neh 6:10
olive tree in the *h*...................Ps 52:9
the *h* in Jerusalem ....Dan 5:3
he entered the *h* and ate ....Matt 12:4
how he entered the *h*..............Mark 2:26
how he entered the *h*.............. Luke 6:4
a great priest over the *h*.......... Heb 10:21
starting with the *h*..................1 Pet 4:17

HOUSE OF THE LORD
you must bring to the *h* ....Exod 23:19
you must bring to the *h* ....Exod 34:26
went to the *h* and worshiped ...2 Sam 12:20
at the founding of the *h* ....Zech 8:9
be a Canaanite in the *h*..........Zech 14:21

HOUSEHOLD
and your father's *h* ....Gen 12:1
over the ways of her *h*...........Prov 31:27
Give instructions to your *h* ....Isa 38:1
will be the members of his *h* ....Matt 10:36
salvation has come to this *h*.......Luke 19:9
she and her *h* were baptized .....Acts 16:15
you and your *h* ....Acts 16:31
baptized the *h* of Stephanus.......1 Cor 1:16
know about the *h* of Stephanus ..1 Cor 16:15
who belong to Caesar's *h*.......... Phil 4:22
must manage his own *h* well ......1 Tim 3:4
and manage a *h*....................1 Tim 5:14

HOUSEHOLDS
he made *h* for them ....Exod 1:21
insinuate themselves into *h* ....2 Tim 3:6

HOUSES
h are safe and without fear.........Job 21:9
filled their *h* with good things .....Job 22:18
those who accumulate *h* ....Isa 5:8
entered into our fortified *h*..........Jer 9:21
And whoever has left *h*........... Matt 19:29
Do you not have *h*.................1 Cor 11:22

HOUSETOP
to live on a corner of the *h* ....Prov 25:24

HOUSETOPS
proclaim from the *h* . . . . Matt 10:27
will be proclaimed from the *h* . . . . . Luke 12:3

HOW
to know *h* to do all the work . . . . . . Exod 36:1
who knows *h* to play the lyre . . . . 1 Sam 16:16
every day *h* he delivers . . . . 1 Chr 16:23
h you want me to live . . . . Ps 27:11
h you deliver your people . . . . Ps 67:2
know *h* to reject evil . . . . Isa 7:15
do not even know *h* to blush . . . . Jer 6:15
H will this be . . . . Luke 1:34
H long will you keep us . . . . John 10:24
and *h* you turned to God . . . . 1 Thess 1:9

HUGGED
h his neck . . . . Gen 33:4
Joseph *h* his father's face . . . . Gen 50:1

HULDAH
Wife of Shullam, 2 Kgs 22:14
Foretells Jerusalem's ruin, 2 Kgs 22:15–17;
   2 Chr 34:22–25
Exempts Josiah from trouble,
   2 Kgs 22:18–20

HUMAN
h spirit is like the lamp . . . . Prov 20:27
not by *h* agency . . . . Dan 8:25
that a *h* being has been born . . . . . John 16:21
by *h* wisdom but by the grace . . . . . 2 Cor 1:12
according to *h* traditions . . . . Col 2:8

HUMANITY
all *h* will see the salvation . . . . Luke 3:6
authority over all *h* . . . . John 17:2
rest of *h* may seek the Lord . . . . . . Acts 15:17
between God and *h* . . . . 1 Tim 2:5
set free to kill a third of *h* . . . . Rev 9:15
The rest of *h* . . . . Rev 9:20

HUMANKIND
Let us make *h* in our image . . . . Gen 1:26
and named them "*h* . . . . Gen 5:2
saw that the daughters of *h* . . . . Gen 6:2
I will wipe *h* . . . . Gen 6:7
curse the ground because of *h* . . . . Gen 8:21

HUMANS
The Egyptians are mere *h* . . . . Isa 31:3
This is impossible for mere *h* . . . Mark 10:27

HUMBLE
the man Moses was very *h* . . . . Num 12:3
he show the *h* what is right . . . . Ps 25:9
when we *h* ourselves . . . . Isa 58:3
people merely *h* themselves . . . . Isa 58:5
I show special favor to the *h* . . . . . . Isa 66:2
Strive to be *h* . . . . Zeph 2:3
I am gentle and *h* in heart . . . . Matt 11:29
transform these *h* bodies . . . . Phil 3:21
but he gives grace to the *h* . . . . Jas 4:6
H yourselves before the Lord . . . . . . Jas 4:10
compassionate, and *h* . . . . 1 Pet 3:8
but gives grace to the *h* . . . . 1 Pet 5:5
if you *h* yourselves . . . . 1 Pet 5:6

HUMBLED
h himself before the God . . . . 2 Chr 33:12
He *h* himself by becoming . . . . Phil 2:8

HUMBLES
he *h* and he exalts . . . . 1 Sam 2:7

HUMBLING
he might, by *h* you, test you . . . . . . Deut 8:2

HUMILIATE
and in so doing *h* all Israel . . . . . . 1 Sam 11:2
I will *h* David's descendants . . . . . 1 Kgs 11:39
I will *h* his enemies . . . . Ps 132:18
He will *h* three kings . . . . Dan 7:24

HUMILIATED
how you can be subdued and *h* . . . . Judg 16:6
be *h* and absolutely terrified . . . . Ps 6:10
Please do not let me be *h* . . . . Ps 25:2
who rely on you will be *h* . . . . Ps 25:3
May all who hate Zion be *h* . . . . Ps 129:5
with the discouraged and *h* . . . . Isa 57:15
but we are *h* this day . . . . Dan 9:7

HUMILIATION
For I suffer *h* for your sake . . . . Ps 69:7
and *h*, as when a baby is ready . . . . . Isa 37:3
pass by in nakedness and *h* . . . . Mic 1:11
we will not be overtaken by *h* . . . . . . Mic 2:6
In *h* justice was taken . . . . Acts 8:33
pride should be in his *h* . . . . Jas 1:10

HUMILITY
for *h* and fearing the LORD . . . . Prov 22:4
serving the Lord with all *h* . . . . Acts 20:19
with all *h* and gentleness . . . . Eph 4:2
one who delights in false *h* . . . . Col 2:18
h, gentleness, and patience . . . . Col 3:12
clothe yourselves with *h* . . . . 1 Pet 5:5

HUNDRED
some a *h* times as much . . . . Matt 13:8

HUNGER
who *h* he has filled with food . . . . . . Ps 107:9
due to a fever from *h* . . . . Lam 5:10
h and thirst for righteousness . . . . . Matt 5:6
in sleepless nights, in *h* . . . . 2 Cor 6:5

HUNGRY
Calamity is *h* for him . . . . Job 18:12
from the *h* you withheld food . . . . . . Job 22:7
sometimes lack food and are *h* . . . . . Ps 34:10
and gives food to the *h* . . . . Ps 146:7
h mouth every bitter thing . . . . Prov 27:7
They will not be *h* or thirsty . . . . Isa 49:10
You must actively help the *h* . . . . . . Isa 58:10
I was *h* and you gave me food . . . Matt 25:35
did we see you *h* and feed you . . Matt 25:37
for you will be *h* . . . . Luke 6:25
comes to me will never go *h* . . . . . . John 6:35
To the present hour we are *h* . . . . . 1 Cor 4:11
h and another becomes drunk . . . . 1 Cor 11:21
If anyone is *h* . . . . 1 Cor 11:34
whether I go satisfied or *h* . . . . Phil 4:12
will never go *h* or be thirsty . . . . Rev 7:16

HUNTED
Our enemies *h* us down . . . . Lam 4:18

HUNTER
a mighty *h* before the LORD . . . . Gen 10:9
Esau became a skilled *h* . . . . Gen 25:27
from the snare of the *h* . . . . Ps 91:3

HUR
Man of Judah; of Caleb's house,
   1 Chr 2:18–20
Supports Moses' hands, Exod 17:10–12
Aids Aaron, Exod 24:14

HURAM
Master craftsman of Solomon's temple,
   1 Kgs 7:13–40, 45; 2 Chr 2:13–14

HURL
h all our sins into the depths . . . . . . Mic 7:19

HUSBAND
also gave some of it to her *h* . . . . Gen 3:6
will want to control your *h* . . . . Gen 3:16
that her *h* Uriah was dead . . . . 2 Sam 11:26
h is well known in the city . . . . Prov 31:23
h is the one who made you . . . . Isa 54:5
though I was like a faithful *h* . . . . . . Jer 31:32
h'; you will never again call me . . . Hos 2:16
I have no *h* . . . . John 4:17
each woman with her own *h* . . . . . . 1 Cor 7:2
unbelieving *h* is sanctified . . . . 1 Cor 7:14
will bring your *h* to salvation . . . . . . 1 Cor 7:16
you in marriage to one *h* . . . . 2 Cor 11:2
because the *h* is the head . . . . Eph 5:23
the *h* of one wife . . . . 1 Tim 3:2
like a bride adorned for her *h* . . . . . . Rev 21:2

HUSBAND'S
Her *h* heart has trusted her . . . . Prov 31:11

HUSBANDS
for you have had five *h* . . . . John 4:18
should ask their *h* at home . . . . . . 1 Cor 14:35
H, love your wives . . . . Eph 5:25
H, love your wives . . . . Col 3:19
Deacons must be *h* of one wife . . . 1 Tim 3:12

younger women to love their *h* . . . . Titus 2:4
be subject to your own *h* . . . . 1 Pet 3:1

HUSHAI
Arkite; David's friend, 2 Sam 15:32–37
Feigns sympathy with Absalom,
   2 Sam 16:16–19
Defeats Ahithophel's advice, 2 Sam 17:5–23

HUT
a *h* that a watchman has made . . . . Job 27:18
a *h* in a vineyard or a shelter . . . . Isa 1:8

HYMENAEUS
False teacher excommunicated by Paul,
   1 Tim 1:19–20

HYMN
After singing a *h* . . . . Matt 26:30

HYMNS
h to the LORD God of Israel . . . . 1 Chr 16:4
praying and singing *h* to God . . . . . Acts 16:25
h, and spiritual songs . . . . Eph 5:19

HYPOCRISY
are full of *h* and lawlessness . . . . . Matt 23:28
of the Pharisees, which is *h* . . . . Luke 12:1
Love must be without *h* . . . . Rom 12:9
led astray with them by their *h* . . . . Gal 2:13
all evil and all deceit and *h* . . . . 1 Pet 2:1

HYPOCRITE
harsh condemnation for the *h* . . . . . Mal 1:14

HYPOCRITES
do not be like the *h* . . . . Matt 6:5
H! Why are you testing me . . . . . . Matt 22:18
h! You keep locking people out . . . Matt 23:13

HYPOCRITICAL
impartial, and not *h* . . . . Jas 3:17

HYSSOP
Cleanse me with *h* . . . . Ps 51:7
sour wine on a branch of *h* . . . . John 19:29

I

I AM WITH YOU
Do not be afraid, for *I* . . . . Gen 26:24
I! I will protect you . . . . Gen 28:15
they will know that *I* . . . . Josh 3:7
Do not be afraid, for *I* . . . . Isa 41:10
pass through the waters, *I* . . . . Isa 43:2
Do not be afraid, for *I* . . . . Isa 43:5
Jacob, my servant, for *I* . . . . Jer 46:28
I," decrees the LORD . . . . Hag 1:13
For *I*," decrees the LORD . . . . Hag 2:4
And remember, *I* always . . . . Matt 28:20
I, and no one will assault you . . . . . Acts 18:10
and *I* in spirit . . . . 1 Cor 5:4

I TELL YOU THE TRUTH
I, until heaven and earth . . . . Matt 5:18
I, they have their reward . . . . Matt 6:2
I, I have not found such faith . . . . . . Matt 8:10
I, among those born of women . . . . Matt 11:11
I, there are some standing . . . . Matt 16:28
I, if you have the faith . . . . Matt 17:20
I, whatever you bind on earth . . . . Matt 18:18
I, it will be hard for a rich . . . . Matt 19:23
I, not one stone will be left . . . . Matt 24:2
I, just as you did it for . . . . Matt 25:40
I, one of you will betray me . . . . . . Matt 26:21
I, people will be forgiven . . . . Mark 3:28
I, no sign will be given . . . . Mark 8:12
I, there is no one who has left . . . Mark 10:29
I, the poor widow has put . . . . Mark 12:43
I, wherever the gospel is . . . . Mark 14:9
I, I will no longer drink . . . . Mark 14:25
I, no prophet is acceptable . . . . Luke 4:24
I, today you will be with me . . . . . Luke 23:43

I WILL BE WITH YOU
Then *I* and will bless you . . . . Gen 26:3
and to your relatives. *I* . . . . Gen 31:3
I, and this will be the sign . . . . Exod 3:12
have promised them, and *I* . . . . . . Deut 31:23
As I was with Moses, so *I* . . . . Josh 1:5
LORD said to him, "Ah, but *I* . . . . . . Judg 6:16

Then *I* and establish for you ......1 Kgs 11:38
for *I* to protect you .... Jer 1:8
for *I* to rescue you................. Jer 1:19
For *I* to rescue you .... Jer 15:20
that *I* and will rescue you........... Jer 30:11
I to save you and to rescue .... Jer 42:11
I for only a little while .... John 7:33

IBZAN
Judge of Israel; father of 60 children,
    Judg 12:8–9

ICE
They are dark because of *i* .... Job 6:16
glittering awesomely like *i* .... Ezek 1:22

ICHABOD
Son of Phinehas, 1 Sam 4:19–22

ICONIUM
City of Asia Minor; visited by Paul, Acts 13:51
Many converts in, Acts 14:1–6

IDDO
Leader of Jews at Casiphia, Ezra 8:17–20
—Seer whose writings are cited, 2 Chr 9:29

IDEAS
foolish behavior and *i* .... Eccl 1:17
out of the heart come evil *i* .... Matt 15:19

IDLE
For this is no *i* word for you ..... Deut 32:47
the *i* person will go hungry .... Prov 19:15
of *i* hands the house leaks........ Eccl 10:18
i talkers, and deceivers .... Titus 1:10

IDLENESS
she would not eat the bread of *i*.. Prov 31:27

IDOL
offers incense also praises an *i* .... Isa 66:3
Instruction from a wooden *i*........ Jer 10:8
he has rejected your calf *i* .... Hos 8:5

IDOLATER
immoral, or greedy, or an *i* .... 1 Cor 5:11
a person is an *i* .... Eph 5:5

IDOLATERS
sexually immoral, *i*, adulterers .... 1 Cor 6:9
the *i* and everyone who loves ..... Rev 22:15

IDOLATRIES
and wanton *i* .... 1 Pet 4:3

IDOLATRY
for a spirit of *i* is in them .... Hos 5:4
flee from *i* .... 1 Cor 10:14
i, sorcery, hostilities .... Gal 5:20
and greed which is *i* .... Col 3:5

IDOLS
Rachel stole the household *i* ......Gen 31:19
personal *i*, disgusting images... 2 Kgs 23:24
i are made of silver and gold ......Ps 115:4
Their land is full of worthless *i* ......Isa 2:8
disgusting *i* out of my sight......... Jer 4:1
because of those *i* they fear .... Jer 50:38
get rid of the detestable *i*........ Ezek 20:7
They consult their wooden *i*........Hos 4:12
to pursue worthless *i*............. Hos 5:11
who worship worthless *i* ....Jonah 2:8
abstain from things defiled by *i*...Acts 15:20
You who abhor *i*............. Rom 2:22
eating food sacrificed to *i*.......... 1 Cor 8:4
by being accustomed to *i*.......... 1 Cor 8:7
i or food sacrificed to them........ 1 Cor 10:19
guard yourselves from *i* ....1 John 5:21
demons and *i* made of gold........ Rev 9:20

IDUMEA
See EDOM

IGNITES
when his anger quickly *i*............. Ps 2:12

IGNORANCE
placed *i* in the human heart .... Eccl 3:11
sins inadvertently or through *i* ..Ezek 45:20
I know you acted in *i* .... Acts 3:17
overlooked such times of *i* ....Acts 17:30
sins of the people committed in *i*... Heb 9:7
silence the *i* of foolish people .....1 Pet 2:15

IGNORANT
I was *i* and lacked insight...........Ps 73:22
you *i* people ....Ps 94:8
to be *i* of this mystery .... Rom 11:25
foolish and *i* controversies ......2 Tim 2:23
those who are *i* and erring......... Heb 5:2
things the *i* and unstable twist.... 2 Pet 3:16

IGNORANTLY
because I acted *i* in unbelief ....1 Tim 1:13

IGNORE
will not *i* those who hate him..... Deut 7:10
if you *i* the LORD your God ...... Deut 28:15
did not *i* any of the commands .... Josh 11:15
of all the nations that *i* God ...... Ps 9:17
Why do you *i* me ....Ps 42:9
not *i* my appeal for mercy .... Ps 55:1
not *i* me in my time of trouble......Ps 102:2
When you *i* them .... Ps 104:29

IGNORED
needy are not permanently *i* .... Ps 9:18
has *i* her marriage covenant ....Prov 2:17
caused you to be *i* and belittled .... Mal 2:9

IGNORING
For *i* the righteousness ....Rom 10:3

IJON
Town of Naphtali; captured by Ben Hadad,
    1 Kgs 15:20
Captured by Tiglath-Pileser, 2 Kgs 15:29

ILL
and the child became very *i* .....2 Sam 12:15
Trophimus I left *i* in Miletus ......2 Tim 4:20

ILL-TREATED
to be *i* with the people of God.....Heb 11:25
and those *i* as though you ....Heb 13:3

ILLEGITIMATE
because they bore *i* children ....Hos 5:7
you are *i* and are not sons .... Heb 12:8

ILLNESS
no *i* will come near your home ...... Ps 91:10
and was acquainted with *i* ....Isa 53:3
because of a physical *i*.............. Gal 4:13

ILLNESSES
who suffered with various *i*....... Matt 4:24
digestion and your frequent *i*.....1 Tim 5:23

ILLUMINATES
God *i* the darkness around me .....Ps 18:28

ILLUMINATING
nor did the pillar of fire stop *i* ..... Neh 9:19

ILLYRICUM
Paul preaches in, Rom 15:19

IMAGE
us make humankind in our *i* ...... Gen 1:26
an *i* in the form of any kind....... Deut 4:16
Whose *i* is this.................... Matt 22:20
he is the *i* and glory of God........ 1 Cor 11:7
is the *i* of the invisible God .... Col 1:15
curse people made in God's *i*........ Jas 3:9
worships the beast and his *i* ....Rev 14:9
those who worshiped his *i*...... Rev 19:20

IMAGES
smash their *i*..................... Exod 34:13
chamber of his idolatrous *i*.......Ezek 8:12

IMAGINATION
it is like a high wall in his *i*.........Prov 18:11
by the prophet's own *i*............ 2 Pet 1:20

IMAGINED
seen, or ear heard, or mind *i*........ 1 Cor 2:9

IMITATE
and *i* their faith ....Heb 13:7

IMITATORS
Be *i* of me .... Phil 3:17
i of those who through faith....... Heb 6:12

IMMANUEL
will name him *I* ....Isa 7:14

IMMEASURABLE
and he will bring *i* prosperity........Isa 9:7

IMMEDIATELY
i drove him into the wilderness....Mark 1:12
left their nets *i* and followed ......Mark 1:18
i Satan comes and snatches ...... Mark 4:15
I Zechariah's mouth was opened .Luke 1:64
I an angel of the Lord struck...... Acts 12:23
and then goes out and *i* forgets .....Jas 1:24
I I was in the Spirit..................Rev 4:2

IMMORAL
that no person who is *i*.............Eph 5:5
becomes an *i* or godless person ...Heb 12:16
of the wine of her *i* passion........Rev 14:8
the sexually *i* ....Rev 21:8

IMMORALITY
except for *i* .... Matt 5:32
except for *i* ....Matt 19:9
not born as a result of *i*...........John 8:41
and from sexual *i* ....Acts 15:29
not in sexual *i* and sensuality .... Rom 13:13
sexual *i* exists among you ....1 Cor 5:1
Flee sexual *i* .... 1 Cor 6:18
sexual *i*, impurity .... Gal 5:19
keep away from sexual *i*........1 Thess 4:3
since they indulged in sexual *i*......Jude 1:7
to repent of her sexual *i*...........Rev 2:21

IMMORTAL
the glory of the *i* God............. Rom 1:23
i, invisible, the only God ....1 Tim 1:17

IMMORTALITY
seek glory and honor and *i*.........Rom 2:7
mortal body must put on *i* .....1 Cor 15:53
He alone possesses *i* and lives.... 1 Tim 6:16
and brought life and *i*............ 2 Tim 1:10

IMPART
to *i* understanding to you......... Dan 9:22
i to you some spiritual gift.........Rom 1:11

IMPARTIAL
i, and not hypocritical ....Jas 3:17

IMPARTS
i knowledge to human beings ......Ps 94:10

IMPENDING
Because of the *i* crisis ....1 Cor 7:26

IMPERISHABLE
what is raised is *i*................ 1 Cor 15:42
the perishable inherit the *i* ......1 Cor 15:50
and the dead will be raised *i*..... 1 Cor 15:52
body must put on the *i* ....1 Cor 15:53
into an inheritance *i* ....1 Pet 1:4
perishable but from *i* seed.........1 Pet 1:23

IMPLANTED
welcome the message *i* within .... Jas 1:21

IMPLORE
to *i* him by prayer and requests .... Dan 9:3

IMPORTANCE
as if it is of no *i* .... Mal 1:7

IMPORTANT
you neglect what is more *i* ......Matt 23:23
more *i* while I become less *i* ...... John 3:30

IMPOSSIBLE
Is anything *i* for the LORD.........Gen 18:14
nothing will be *i* for you ...... Matt 17:20
This is *i* for mere humans....... Matt 19:26
This is *i* for mere humans.......Mark 10:27
For nothing will be *i* with God ..... Luke 1:37
What is *i* for mere humans ...... Luke 18:27
For it is *i* in the case .... Heb 6:4
since it is *i* for God to lie........... Heb 6:18
it is *i* for the blood of bulls .... Heb 10:4
without faith it is *i* to please .... Heb 11:6

IMPOVERISHED
lest you become *i*.................Prov 20:13

IMPRISONED
The LORD releases the *i* .... Ps 146:7
heard that John had been *i* ....Matt 4:12
Now after John was *i* ....Mark 1:14
scripture *i* everything under sin ....Gal 3:22
but God's message is not *i* .....2 Tim 2:9

IMPRISONMENT
in your place during my *i*..........Phlm 1:13
and even chains and *i*.............Heb 11:36

IMPRISONMENTS
In beatings, in *i*, in riots...........2 Cor 6:5
with far more *i*....................2 Cor 11:23

IMPROPRIETY
he charge God with moral *i*.........Job 1:22

IMPURE
yourselves against anything *i*.....Deut 23:9
who is immoral, *i*, or greedy.........Eph 5:5

IMPURITIES
will be clean from all your *i*......Ezek 36:25

IMPURITY
Israelites apart from their *i*........ Lev 15:31
cleanse them from sin and *i*.......Zech 13:1
the desires of their hearts to *i*.....Rom 1:24
your members as slaves to *i*.......Rom 6:19
sexual immorality, *i*, depravity......Gal 5:19
immorality, *i*, shameful passion......Col 3:5
not call us to *i* but in holiness ...1 Thess 4:7

IN MY NAME
words that prophet speaks *i*......Deut 18:19
presumes to speak anything *i* ... Deut 18:20
claim to be prophesying *i*........Jer 14:15
person who swears falsely *i* .... Zech 5:4
offerings will be offered *i*...........Mal 1:11
welcomes a child like this *i*.......Matt 18:5
two or three are assembled *i*.... Matt 18:20
For many will come *i*.............Matt 24:5
one who does a miracle *i*........Mark 9:39
I they will drive out demons..... Mark 16:17
whatever you ask *i* ....John 14:13
whom the Father will send *i*......John 14:26
whatever you ask the Father *i*....John 15:16
At that time you will ask *i* ......John 16:26
that you were baptized *i*..........1 Cor 1:15

IN THE WORLD
Everyone *i* wanted to visit.......1 Kgs 10:24
all who live *i* stand in awe ....Ps 33:8
who live *i* learn about justice....... Isa 26:9
He was *i*, and the world...........John 1:10
As long as I am *i*...................John 9:5
loved his own who were *i* ....John 13:1
I you have trouble.................John 16:33
I am no longer *i*....................John 17:11
I am saying these things *i*...... John 17:13
law was given, sin was *i*...........Rom 5:13
low and despised *i*................1 Cor 1:28
we conducted ourselves *i*..........2 Cor 1:12
and without God *i* ....Eph 2:12
you shine as lights *i*.............Phil 2:15
as though you lived *i* ....Col 2:20
believed on *i*, taken up ....1 Tim 3:16
love the world or the things *i*.....1 John 2:15
greater than the one who is *i*.....1 John 4:4

INABILITY
for your *i* to serve me ....Phil 2:30

INAUGURATED
first covenant was *i* with blood.... Heb 9:18

INCANTATIONS
and those who know *i*.................Isa 3:3

INCENSE
anointing oil and for fragrant *i*....Exod 25:6
Aaron is to burn sweet *i*.........Exod 30:7
he is to burn *i* on it ....Exod 30:8
oil and the pure fragrant *i* ....Exod 37:29
then put the *i* on the fire .... Lev 16:13
take his censer, put *i* in it ....Num 16:17
burned *i* on the high places........1 Kgs 3:3
accept my prayer like *i* ....Ps 141:2
I consider your *i* detestable......... Isa 1:13
olive oil and my *i* to them ......Ezek 16:18
I and pure offerings ....Mal 1:11
of the Lord and burn *i*.............Luke 1:9
right side of the altar of *i* ....Luke 1:11
the golden altar of *i* ....Heb 9:4
and golden bowls full of *i*.........Rev 5:8
smoke coming from the *i*.......... Rev 8:4
i, perfumed ointment..............Rev 18:13

INCHES
leaving 18 *i* from the top............ Gen 6:16

INCLINATION
Every *i* of the thoughts .... Gen 6:5
though the *i* of their minds .... Gen 8:21

INCLINATIONS
who follow the stubborn *i*..........Jer 23:17

INCOME
abundant *i* without justice.........Prov 16:8

INCOMPARABLE
the *i* greatness of his power .... Eph 1:19

INCREASE
May he *i* your numbers.............Ps 115:14
When the wicked *i*................Prov 29:16
for ways to *i* your wealth ....Jer 22:17
and knowledge will *i*.............. Dan 12:4
I our faith........................Luke 17:5
that the transgression may *i*...... Rom 5:20
in sin so that grace may *i*........ Rom 6:1
to *i* to the glory of God .... 2 Cor 4:15
may *i* because of me...............Phil 1:26

INCREASED
As the waters *i*......................Gen 7:17
And Jesus *i* in wisdom .... Luke 2:52
of disciples in Jerusalem *i*...........Acts 6:7

INCREASES
If wealth *i*.........................Ps 62:10
whoever *i* his knowledge ....Eccl 1:18
someone's prosperity *i* ....Eccl 5:11

INCREASING
his wealth by *i* interest .... Prov 28:8
the word of God kept on *i*.........Acts 12:24
and are continually *i*................2 Pet 1:8

INCURABLE
My wound is *i* ....Job 34:6
Your injuries are *i*..................Jer 30:12
that your pain is *i*..................Jer 30:15

INDEBTED
are *i* to the Jerusalem saints......Rom 15:27

INDECENCY
given themselves over to *i*.........Eph 4:19

INDECISION
going to be paralyzed by *i*........1 Kgs 18:21

INDEED
you *i* obey the Lord your God.....Deut 28:1
I, the signs of an apostle......... 2 Cor 12:12

INDEFINITELY
not remain in humankind *i* .... Gen 6:3

INDESCRIBABLE
with an *i* and glorious joy...........1 Pet 1:8

INDESTRUCTIBLE
by the power of an *i* life .... Heb 7:16

INDIA
Eastern limit of Persian Empire, Esth 1:1

INDICATING
was *i* when he testified ....1 Pet 1:11

INDIFFERENT
but the *i* will refuse................Ezek 3:27

INDIGNANT
they became *i* and said ....Matt 26:8
he was *i* and said to them .... Mark 10:14

INDIGNATION
No one can withstand his *i* ....Nah 1:6

INDIRECTLY
For now we see in a mirror *i*......1 Cor 13:12

INDISPUTABLE
So because these facts are *i* ......Acts 19:36

INDIVIDUALLY
and *i* we are members.............Rom 12:5

INDULGE
who *i* their fleshly desires .... 2 Pet 2:10

INDULGENCE
in reality result in fleshly *i*...........Col 2:23

INDULGENTLY
have lived *i* and luxuriously...........Jas 5:5

INEFFECTIVE
becoming *i* and unproductive ......2 Pet 1:8

INEXPERIENCED
and impart wisdom to the *i*......... Ps 19:7
who lives on milk is *i* ....Heb 5:13

INEXPRESSIBLE
for us with *i* groanings............. Rom 8:26

INEXTINGUISHABLE
he will burn up with *i* fire..........Matt 3:12
he will burn up with *i* fire..........Luke 3:17

INFANCY
how from *i* you have known......2 Tim 3:15

INFANT
because he is an *i*...................Heb 5:13

INFANTS
i who have never seen the light .... Job 3:16
of children and nursing *i*..........Matt 21:16
as *i* in Christ ....1 Cor 3:1
yearn like newborn *i* for pure ......1 Pet 2:2

INFERIOR
will arise, one *i* to yours .... Dan 2:39
and sacrifices something *i* .... Mal 1:14
I consider myself not at all *i* ....2 Cor 11:5

INFLAME
i your lusts among the oaks ....Isa 57:5

INFLAMED
princes become *i* with wine ....Hos 7:5

INFLICT
I will *i* horror on you................Lev 26:16

INFLUENCE
its powerful *i* has been broken .....Jer 48:17

INFORM
and you will *i* me ....Job 40:7

INGATHERING
See also FEAST OF INGATHERING
Feast of *I* at the end of the year ..Exod 34:22

INHABIT
wicked will not *i* the land........ Prov 10:30

INHABITABLE
who makes the streets *i* again......Isa 58:12

INHABITANTS
carefully at all the earth's *i* ....Ps 33:14
all you *i* of the world................Ps 49:1

INHABITED
She will be *i* ....Isa 44:26
he formed it to be *i*................ Isa 45:18

INHERIT
to *i* the sins of my youth...........Job 13:26
their descendants *i* the land .... Ps 25:13
The wise *i* honor....................Prov 3:35
who love me to *i* wealth...........Prov 8:21
blameless will *i* what is good .... Prov 28:10
i the kingdom prepared for you.. Matt 25:34
must I do to *i* eternal life .... Mark 10:17
will not *i* the kingdom of God ..... 1 Cor 6:9
you were called to *i* a blessing......1 Pet 3:9
will *i* these things...................Rev 21:7

INHERITANCE
will have no *i* in their land .... Num 18:20
they possess a permanent *i*........ Ps 37:18
i gained easily in the beginning.. Prov 20:21
the *i* of Jacob's descendants ....Jer 10:16
i is turned over to strangers........Lam 5:2
people Israel who are my *i* ....Joel 3:2
give any of it to him for an *i* ....Acts 7:5
and give you an *i*..................Acts 20:32
if the *i* is based on the law..........Gal 3:18
you to share in the saints' *i*.........Col 1:12
he would later receive as an *i*.......Heb 11:8
into an *i* imperishable ....1 Pet 1:4

INHERITED
The naive have *i* folly............Prov 14:18
as he has *i* a name superior.........Heb 1:4
Abraham *i* the promise............ Heb 6:15

INIQUITIES
and they make up for their *i* ......Lev 26:41
How many are my *i* and sins....... Job 13:23

INIQUITY
has not looked on *i* in Jacob ..... Num 23:21
and *i* shuts its mouth .... Job 5:16
who sows *i* will reap trouble...... Prov 22:8

INJURE
They will no longer *i* or destroy ..... Isa 11:9

INJURED
He has *i* us.........................Hos 6:1

INJURES
his tongue *i* and destroys............ Ps 10:7

INJUSTICE
but it is swept away by *i* ....Prov 13:23
Is there *i* with God..................Rom 9:14
Forgive me this *i*................. 2 Cor 12:13

INK
written not with *i*.................2 Cor 3:3
to do so with paper and *i* ....2 John 1:12

INN
no place for them in the *i*..........Luke 2:7
brought him to an *i* .... Luke 10:34

INNER
you go into an *i* room to hide....2 Chr 18:24
Man's *i* thoughts.....................Ps 64:6
the law of God in my *i* being...... Rom 7:22
but the *i* person of the heart ....1 Pet 3:4

INNOCENT
See also INNOCENT BLOOD
conscience and with *i* hands........Gen 20:5
the one who struck him is *i*.......Exod 21:19
not kill the *i* and the righteous ... Exod 23:7
they shall exonerate the *i*........Deut 25:1
takes a bribe to kill an *i* person.. Deut 27:25
You are more *i* than I ....1 Sam 24:17
more *i* and morally upright....... 1 Kgs 2:32
bribes to testify against the *i* .... Ps 15:5
I was *i* before him .... Ps 18:23
Tell the *i* it will go well...............Isa 3:10
I was found to be *i* before him..... Dan 6:22
They sold the *i* for silver.......... Amos 2:6
not have condemned the *i*........ Matt 12:7
sinned by betraying *i* blood....... Matt 27:4
I am *i* of this man's blood........ Matt 27:24
Certainly this man was *i* ...... Luke 23:47
I am *i* of the blood of you all..... Acts 20:26
holy, *i*, undefiled, separate........ Heb 7:26

INNOCENT BLOOD
You must not shed *i* ....Deut 19:10
the guilt of shedding *i* ....Deut 19:13
purge the guilt of *i*.................Deut 21:9
would you sin against *i* ....1 Sam 19:5
having poured out *i*............1 Sam 25:31
They shed *i* ....Ps 106:38
and hands that shed *i*............Prov 6:17
wicked lie in wait to shed *i* ....Prov 12:6
eager to do evil, to shed *i*......... Isa 59:7
in whose land they shed *i*..........Joel 3:19
hold us guilty of shedding *i*........ Jonah 1:14
sinned by betraying *i* .... Matt 27:4

INNUMERABLE
like the *i* grains of sand............ Heb 11:12

INQUIRE
whenever someone went to *i*..... 1 Sam 9:9
I may go to her and *i* of her...... 1 Sam 28:7
i more thoroughly about him.... Acts 23:20

INSANE
he pretended to be *i*............. 1 Sam 21:13

INSCRIBE
I will *i* them on their hearts....... Heb 8:10
I will *i* them on their minds....... Heb 10:16

INSCRIBED
i your name on my palms .... Isa 49:16

INSCRIPTION
and wrote on it an *i*...............Exod 39:30
and whose *i*.....................Matt 22:20

(column 2)
i of the charge against him ......Mark 15:26
found an altar with this *i*......... Acts 17:23

INSECT
moth and devouring *i* destroy.....Matt 6:19

INSECTS
swarms of biting *i* against them ....Ps 78:45

INSIGHT
acquire good moral *i* .... Ps 111:10
Keen *i* wins favor .... Prov 13:15
I is like a life-giving fountain......Prov 16:22
in all wisdom and *i*................. Eph 1:8
has come and has given us *i* .....1 John 5:20
the one who has *i* calculate........ Rev 13:18

INSIGNIFICANT
the nations are *i* before him .... Isa 40:17
despised *i* Jacob, men of Israel...... Isa 41:14
i among the clans of Judah ....Mic 5:2

INSINUATE
i themselves into households......2 Tim 3:6

INSIST
I want you to *i* on such truths ..... Titus 3:8

INSOLENT
i, arrogant, boastful................Rom 1:30

INSPIRED
i man is viewed as a madman ...... Hos 9:7

INSPIRING
You are awe-*i*......................Ps 68:35

INSTANT
I may consume them in an *i* ......Num 16:21

INSTINCTS
motherly *i* were awakened ....1 Kgs 3:26

INSTITUTION
Be subject to every human *i*.......1 Pet 2:13

INSTRUCT
I will *i* you in the way ....1 Sam 12:23
imparted your good Spirit to *i*.....Neh 9:20
I will *i* and teach you.................Ps 32:8
blessed is the one whom you *i* .....Ps 94:12
everything I *i* you to say .... Jer 1:17
and able to *i* one another......... Rom 15:14

INSTRUCTED
Joseph *i* the physicians ....Gen 50:2
king had *i* all his supervisors........ Esth 1:8
Look, you have *i* many................Job 4:3
been *i* in the way of the Lord .....Acts 18:25

INSTRUCTING
We proclaim him by *i*............... Col 1:28

INSTRUCTION
according to the LORD's *i* .... Exod 17:1
hate *i* and reject my words ....Ps 50:17
wise also hear and gain *i*........... Prov 1:5
despised wisdom and moral *i* ...... Prov 1:7
I hereby give you good *i* ....Prov 4:2
Hold on to *i*.......................Prov 4:13
i is like a light.................... Prov 6:23
Listen to my *i* so that ....Prov 8:33
Give *i* to a wise person ....Prov 9:9
If you stop listening to *i* ....Prov 19:27
Apply your heart to *i* ....Prov 23:12
be the center for moral *i* ....Isa 2:3
I from a wooden idol ....Jer 10:8
he has never had formal *i* ....John 7:15
you receive *i* from the law........Rom 2:18
was written for our *i*.............Rom 15:4
and were written for our *i*........1 Cor 10:11
discipline and *i* of the Lord .... Eph 6:4

INSTRUCTIONS
The wise person accepts *i* ....Prov 10:8

INSTRUMENT
of a ten-stringed *i* .... Ps 33:2
O stringed *i* and harp.................Ps 57:8
and the ten-stringed *i* .... Ps 81:2
a ten-stringed *i* and a lyre .... Ps 92:3
Awake, O stringed *i* and harp......Ps 108:2
by a ten-stringed *i* .... Ps 144:9
this man is my chosen *i*............. Acts 9:15

(column 3)
INSTRUMENTS
playing various stringed *i*.........2 Sam 6:5
they were to play various *i* ....1 Chr 15:16
sound of stringed *i* and
    trumpets .... 2 Chr 20:28
praise him with stringed *i* ....Ps 150:4
LORD with his *i* of judgment.........Isa 13:5
your members to sin as *i* ....Rom 6:13

INSULT
or *i* his neighbor..................... Ps 15:3
are you when people *i* you .... Matt 5:11
you *i* us too.......................Luke 11:45
you dare *i* God's high priest ....Acts 23:4
The insults of those who *i* you.....Rom 15:3

INSULTED
the poor has *i* his Creator .... Prov 14:31
are *i* for the name of Christ........1 Pet 4:14

INSULTS
it is not an enemy who *i* me .... Ps 55:12
Their *i* are painful.................... Ps 69:20
hide my face from *i* and spitting.... Isa 50:6
Don't be afraid of the *i* of men ......Isa 51:7
how I have put up with their *i* ...... Jer 15:15
Whoever *i* his father or mother .. Mark 7:10
with *i*, with troubles .... 2 Cor 12:10
and *i* the Spirit of grace...........Heb 10:29

INTEGRITY
worship him with *i* and loyalty ...Josh 24:14
rewards each man for his *i* ....1 Sam 26:23
serve me with *i* and sincerity ....1 Kgs 9:4
he still holds firmly to his *i* .... Job 2:3
then God will discover my *i*.........Job 31:6
people of *i* have vanished..........Ps 12:1
May *i* and godliness protect ....Ps 25:21
for I have *i*.............................Ps 26:1
protects those who have *i*...........Ps 31:23
note of the one who has *i* ....Ps 37:37
uphold me because of my *i*.........Ps 41:12
you desire *i* in the inner man .... Ps 51:6
from those who have *i*.............Ps 84:11
for those who live with *i*...........Prov 2:7
those with *i* will remain in it........Prov 2:21
who conducts himself in *i* ....Prov 10:9
The *i* of the upright guides .... Prov 11:3
poor person who walks in his *i* .... Prov 19:1
righteous person behaves in *i* .... Prov 20:7
poor person who walks in his *i* ... Prov 28:6
but the person of *i* will live .... Hab 2:4
walked with me in peace and *i*...... Mal 2:6
who sent him is a man of *i*.........John 7:18
In your teaching show *i*........... Titus 2:7

INTELLIGENT
things from the wise and *i*........ Matt 11:25
Sergius Paulus, an *i* man........... Acts 13:7

INTENDED
Just as I have *i* .... Isa 14:24

INTENSE
there was *i* heart searching........Judg 5:15
acknowledge their *i* pain ....2 Chr 6:29

INTENSIFIED
my anxiety *i*.........................Ps 39:3

INTENT
when he brings it with evil *i* ......Prov 21:27
i on engaging in good works....... Titus 3:8

INTENTIONS
The *i* of the heart................. Prov 16:1

INTENTLY
looked *i* toward heaven ....Acts 7:55

INTERCEDE
who can *i* for him................1 Sam 2:25
he always lives to *i* for them....... Heb 7:25

INTERCEDED
i with him and turned back........Ps 106:23

INTERCEDES
but the Spirit himself *i* for us ..... Rom 8:26

INTERCESSOR
My *i* is my friend ....Job 16:20

INTEREST
do not charge him *i* ....Exod 22:25
Do not take *i* or profit .... Lev 25:36
He does not charge *i* .... Ps 15:5
I could have collected it with *i* ... Luke 19:23
an unhealthy *i* in controversies ....1 Tim 6:4

INTERESTED
nor are they *i* in gold .... Isa 13:17

INTERMARRY
and *i* with these abominable....... Ezra 9:14

INTERMEDIARY
through angels by an *i* .... Gal 3:19
i between God and humanity......1 Tim 2:5

INTERMINABLE
with myths and *i* genealogies.......1 Tim 1:4

INTERPRET
no one could *i* them for him....... Gen 41:8
Not all *i*, do they...................1 Cor 12:30
should pray that he may *i* ....1 Cor 14:13
and someone must *i*............. 1 Cor 14:27

INTERPRETATION
disclose the dream and its *i* .... Dan 2:6
to another the *i* of tongues.......1 Cor 12:10
has a tongue, has an *i*............ 1 Cor 14:26

INTERPRETATIONS
Don't *i* belong to God..............Gen 40:8
you are able to provide *i*.......... Dan 5:16

INTERPRETED
i to them the things written ..... Luke 24:27

INTERVENED
and *i* on behalf of the rebels........Isa 53:12
and so he *i* with an oath .... Heb 6:17

INTERVENES
he is shocked that no one *i*........Isa 59:16

INTERVENTION
your *i* watched over my spirit ..... Job 10:12

INTIMIDATED
they be *i* by human beings......... Deut 1:17
by not being *i* in any way ....Phil 1:28

INTO
them breaking *i* your homes .... Jer 2:34
i morning and daylight *i* night .... Amos 5:8
you fall *i* all sorts of trials............. Jas 1:2
to open the scroll or look *i* it ....Rev 5:3

INTOXICATING
you have made us drink *i* wine ......Ps 60:3

INTRODUCED
and *i* them to Pharaoh.............Gen 47:2

INVADERS
being destroyed by foreign *i*.......... Isa 1:7

INVALIDATE
so as to *i* the promise............... Gal 3:17

INVENT
they *i* musical instruments .... Amos 6:5

INVENTORS
you, however, are *i* of lies........... Job 13:4

INVESTIGATE
Send out men to *i* the land ....Num 13:2
will thoroughly *i* the matter ......Deut 19:18

INVISIBLE
He is the image of the *i* God.........Col 1:15
immortal, *i*, the only God...........1 Tim 1:17
visible has its origin in the *i*.........Heb 11:3
he could see the one who is *i*......Heb 11:27

INVITE
Then *i* Jesse to the sacrifice.......1 Sam 16:3
did not *i* Nathan the prophet......1 Kgs 1:10
and *i* everyone you find ....Matt 22:9
see you a stranger and *i* you in .. Matt 25:38

INVITED
Absalom *i* all the king's sons ... 2 Sam 13:23
and has *i* all the king's sons......1 Kgs 1:19
Queen Esther *i* only me ....Esth 5:12
who had been *i* to the banquet... Matt 22:3
was a stranger and you *i* me in .. Matt 25:35

Pharisee who had *i* him........... Luke 7:39
to the man who had *i* him ....Luke 14:12
were also *i* to the wedding ....John 2:2
So Peter *i* them in ....Acts 10:23
i to stay with them seven days ...Acts 28:14

INVOKES
No one *i* your name .... Isa 64:7

INWARDLY
but *i* are voracious wolves........Matt 7:15
is a Jew who is one *i*............. Rom 2:29

IRON
and make your sky like *i*..........Lev 26:19
sarcophagus was made of *i*........ Deut 3:11
place an *i* yoke on your neck ....Deut 28:48
saws, *i* picks, and *i* axes.........2 Sam 12:31
It regards *i* as straw................ Job 41:27
As *i* sharpens *i*....................Prov 27:17
Your neck muscles are like *i*........ Isa 48:4
Its legs were of *i*................... Dan 2:33
all the nations with an *i* rod ....Rev 12:5

IRRECONCILABLE
unloving, *i*, slanderers ....2 Tim 3:3

IRRESISTIBLY
Solomon was *i* attracted...........1 Kgs 11:2

IRREVOCABLE
gifts and the call of God are *i*.....Rom 11:29

ISAAC
Promised heir of the covenant, Gen 17:16–21
Born and circumcised, Gen 21:1–7
Abraham told to sacrifice as a test,
    Gen 22:1–19
Marries Rebekah, Gen 24:62–67
Prays for children; prefers Esau,
    Gen 25:21–28
Dealings with Abimelech, king of Gerar,
    Gen 26:1–31
Mistakenly blesses Jacob, Gen 27:1–28:5
Dies in his old age, Gen 35:28–29
NT references to, Luke 3:34; Gal 4:21–31;
    Heb 11:9, 20

ISAIAH
Prophet during reigns of Uzziah, Jotham,
    Ahaz, and Hezekiah, Isa 1:1
Responds to prophetic call, Isa 6:1–13
Prophesies to Hezekiah, 2 Kgs 19–20
Writes Uzziah's biography, 2 Chr 26:22
    Hezekiah's biography, 2 Chr 32:32
Quoted in NT, Matt 1:22–23; 3:3; 8:17;
    12:17–21; Luke 4:17–19; Acts 13:34;
    Rom 9:27, 29; 10:16, 20–21; 11:26–27; 15:12;
    1 Pet 2:22

ISCARIOT, JUDAS
Listed among the Twelve, Mark 3:14, 19;
    Luke 6:16
Criticizes Mary, John 12:3–6
Identified as betrayer, John 13:21–30
Takes money to betray Christ,
    Matt 26:14–16
Betrays Christ with a kiss, Mark 14:43–45
Regretful and commits suicide,
    Matt 27:3–10
His place filled, Acts 1:15–26

ISH BOSHETH
One of Saul's sons; made king, 2 Sam 2:8–10
Offends Abner, 2 Sam 3:7–11
Slain; his assassins executed, 2 Sam 4:1–12

ISHMAEL
Abram's son by Hagar, Gen 16:3–4, 11–16
Circumcised, Gen 17:25
Scoffs at Isaac's feast; exiled with his
    mother, Gen 21:8–21
His sons; his death, Gen 25:12–18
—Son of Nethaniah; kills Gedaliah,
    2 Kgs 25:22–26

ISHMAELITES
Settle at Havilah, Gen 25:17–18
Joseph sold to, Gen 37:25–28
Sell Joseph to Potiphar, Gen 39:1

ISLAND
must run aground on some *i* .... Acts 27:26
the chief official of the *i* ....Acts 28:7
mountain and *i* was moved........Rev 6:14
Every *i* fled away .... Rev 16:20

ISOLATED
in a boat to an *i* place............Matt 14:13

ISRAEL
Used to refer to:
    Jacob, Gen 32:28: *see* JACOB
    Jacob's descendants, Gen 49:16, 28: *see*
        ISRAELITES
    restored nation after exile, Ezra 9:1
    ten northern tribes (in contrast to
        Judah), 1 Sam 11:8
    true church, Gal 6:16

See also HOLY ONE OF ISRAEL; LORD GOD
    OF ISRAEL

but *I*, because you have fought ...Gen 32:28
Hear, O *I*: The LORD is our God .... Deut 6:4
sent the pieces throughout *I*......Judg 19:29
I wish the deliverance of *I* .... Ps 14:7
rescue *I* from all their distress......Ps 25:22
Certainly God is good to *I* ....Ps 73:1
I, if only you would obey me......... Ps 81:8
When *I* left Egypt.................... Ps 114:1
Let *I* say, "Yes, his loyal love ....Ps 118:2
O *I*, hope in the LORD................Ps 130:7
Let *I* rejoice in their Creator ....Ps 149:2
will shepherd my people *I* .... Matt 2:6
such faith in anyone in *I* .... Matt 8:10
lost sheep of the house of *I*,...... Matt 10:6
judging the twelve tribes of *I* .... Matt 19:28
He is the king of *I*................. Matt 27:42
He has helped his servant *I*........Luke 1:54
the day he was revealed to *I*...... Luke 1:80
Are you the teacher of *I* ....John 3:10
restoring the kingdom to *I*.......... Acts 1:6
God brought to *I* a Savior......... Acts 13:23
because of the hope of *I*......... Acts 28:20
descended from *I* are truly *I* .... Rom 9:6
And so all *I* will be saved ....Rom 11:26
Look at the people of *I* ....1 Cor 10:18
and on the *I* of God................. Gal 6:16
from the people of *I* ....Phil 3:5
covenant with the house of *I* .... Heb 8:8
the tribes of the people of *I* ....Rev 7:4
tribes of the nation of *I* .... Rev 21:12

ISRAELITES
Afflicted in Egypt, Exod 1:12–22
Escape from Egypt, Exod 12:29–42, 50;
    13:17–22
Receive law at Sinai, Exod 19
Idolatry and rebellion of, Exod 32;
    Num 13–14
Wander in the wilderness, Num 14:26–39
Cross Jordan; conquer Canaan, Josh 4; 12
Ruled by judges, Judg 2
Saul chosen as king, 1 Sam 10
Kingdom divided, 1 Kgs 12
Northern kingdom carried captive,
    2 Kgs 17
Southern kingdom carried captive,
    2 Kgs 24
70 years in exile, 2 Chr 36:20–21
Return after exile, Ezra 1:1–5
Nation rejects Christ, Matt 27:20–27
Nation destroyed, Luke 21:20–24

circumcise the *I* once again.........Josh 5:2
I moved among all the *I* ....2 Sam 7:7

ISSACHAR
Jacob's fifth son, Gen 30:17–18
—Tribe of:
Genealogy of, 1 Chr 7:1–5
Prophecy concerning, Gen 49:14–15
Census at Sinai, Num 1:28–29
Inheritance of, Josh 19:17–23

ISSUED
So Darius the king *i* orders .... Ezra 6:1

IT IS WRITTEN
Indeed, *i* down in the Scroll . . . . . . 2 Sam 1:18
temporary shelters, as *i* . . . . Neh 8:15
Just as *i* in the law of Moses . . . . Dan 9:13
for *i* this way by the prophet . . . . . . Matt 2:5
I, 'Man does not live by bread . . . . Matt 4:4
For *i*, 'He will command angels . . . . Matt 4:6
again *i*: 'You are not to put . . . . Matt 4:7
For *i*: 'You are to worship . . . . Matt 4:10
This is the one about whom *i* . . . . . Matt 11:10
I, "My house will be called . . . . Matt 21:13
fall away because of me, for *i* . . . . Matt 26:31
i in the prophets . . . . John 6:45
For *i* in the book of Psalms . . . . Acts 1:20
for *i*, 'You must not speak . . . . Acts 23:5
for *i*, 'You shall be holy . . . . 1 Pet 1:16

ITALIAN
was known as the *I* Cohort . . . . Acts 10:1

ITALY
Jews expelled from, Acts 18:2
Paul sails for, Acts 27:1, 6
Christians in, Acts 28:14

ITEMS
these *i* for the LORD's temple . . . . . 1 Kgs 7:48
and all the holy *i* in the tent . . . . 2 Chr 5:5

ITHAMAR
Youngest son of Aaron, Exod 6:23
Consecrated as priest, Exod 28:1
Duty entrusted to, Exod 38:21
Jurisdiction over Gershonites and
    Merarites, Num 4:21–33

ITINERANT
But some *i* Jewish exorcists . . . . . . Acts 19:13

ITUREA
Region ruled by Herod Philip, Luke 3:1

IVORY
large throne decorated with *i* . . . . 1 Kgs 10:18
is like a tower made of *i* . . . . Song 7:4
beds decorated with *i* . . . . Amos 6:4

J

JABBOK
River entering the Jordan about 20 miles
    north of the Dead Sea, Num 21:24
Scene of Jacob's conflict, Gen 32:22–32
Boundary marker, Deut 3:16

JABESH GILEAD
Consigned to destruction, Judg 21:8–15
Saul defeats the Ammonites at, 1 Sam 11:1–11
Citizens of, rescue Saul's body,
    1 Sam 31:11–13
David thanks citizens of, 2 Sam 2:4–7

JABIN
Canaanite king of Hazor; leads confederacy
    against Joshua, Josh 11:1–14
—Another king of Hazor; oppresses
    Israelites, Judg 4:2
Defeated by Deborah and Barak,
    Judg 4:3–24
Immortalized in poetry, Judg 5:1–31

JACINTH
the third row, a *j*, an agate . . . . Exod 28:19
eleventh *j*, and the twelfth . . . . Rev 21:20

JACKALS
went and captured 300 *j* . . . . Judg 15:4
J will settle there . . . . Isa 34:13

JACOB [or ISRAEL]
Son of Isaac and Rebekah; Rebekah's
    favorite, Gen 25:21–28
Obtains birthright, Gen 25:29–34
Obtains blessing meant for Esau; flees,
    Gen 27:1–28:5
Sees vision of ladder, Gen 28:10–22
Serves Laban for Rachel and Leah,
    Gen 29:1–30
Fathers children, Gen 29:31–30:24
Flees from, makes covenant with Laban,
    Gen 30:25–31:55

Makes peace with Esau, Gen 32:1–21; 33:1–17
Wrestles with God, Gen 32:22–32
Returns to Bethel; renamed Israel,
    Gen 35:1–15
Shows preference for Joseph, Gen 37:3
Mourns Joseph's disappearance,
    Gen 37:32–35
Sends sons to Egypt for food, Gen 42:1–5
Reluctantly allows Benjamin to go,
    Gen 43:1–15
Moves his household to Egypt, Gen 45:25–
    47:12
Blesses his sons and grandsons; dies,
    Gen 48–49
Buried in Canaan, Gen 50:1–14
Also called "Israel," Gen 32:28

JACOB'S WELL
Christ teaches a Samaritan woman at,
    John 4:5–26

JAEL
Wife of Heber the Kenite; kills Sisera,
    Judg 4:17–22
Praised by Deborah, Judg 5:24–27

JAIL
and put them in a public *j* . . . . Acts 5:18

JAILER
When the *j* woke up . . . . Acts 16:27

JAIR
Manassite warrior; conquers towns in
    Gilead, Num 32:41; Deut 3:14
—Eighth judge of Israel, Judg 10:3–5

JAIRUS
Ruler of the synagogue; Jesus raises his
    daughter, Mark 5:22–24, 35–43

JAMES
Son of Zebedee, called as disciple,
    Matt 4:21–22; Luke 5:10–11
One of the Twelve, Matt 10:2; Mark 3:17
Zealous for the Lord, Luke 9:52–54
Ambitious for honor, Mark 10:35–45
Witnesses transfiguration, Matt 17:1–9
Martyred by Herod Agrippa, Acts 12:2
—Son of Alphaeus; one of the Twelve,
    Matt 10:3–4
Called "the younger," Mark 15:40
—Jesus' half brother, Matt 13:55–56; Gal 1:19
Becomes leader of Jerusalem Council and
    Jerusalem church, Acts 15:13–22; Gal 2:9
Author of an epistle, Jas 1:1

JANNES AND JAMBRES
Two Egyptian magicians; oppose Moses,
    Exod 7:11–22; 2 Tim 3:8

JANOAH
Town of Naphtali, 2 Kgs 15:29

JAPHETH
One of Noah's three sons, Gen 5:32
Receives blessing, Gen 9:20–27
His descendants occupy Asia Minor and
    Europe, Gen 10:2–5

JAR
Take a *j* and put in it . . . . Exod 16:33
smash them like a potter's *j* . . . . Ps 2:9
wine *j* is made to be filled . . . . Jer 13:12
out from one *j* to another . . . . Jer 48:11
to him with an alabaster *j* . . . . Matt 26:7
came with an alabaster *j* . . . . Mark 14:3
brought an alabaster *j* . . . . Luke 7:37
a man carrying a *j* of water . . . . . . Luke 22:10

JARED
Father of Enoch, Gen 5:15–20
Ancestor of Noah, 1 Chr 1:2
Ancestor of Christ, Luke 3:37

JARS
all trumpets and empty *j* . . . . Judg 7:16
Fill four water *j* and pour . . . . 1 Kgs 18:33
meat forks, bowls, and *j* . . . . 1 Chr 28:17
Fill the water *j* with water . . . . John 2:7
like clay *j* he will break them . . . . . . Rev 2:27

JASON
Welcomes Paul at Thessalonica, Acts 17:5–9
Described as Paul's compatriot, Rom 16:21

JASPER
a chrysolite, an onyx, and a *j* . . . . Exod 28:20
Of coral and *j* no mention . . . . Job 28:18
was like gleaming *j* . . . . Ezek 1:16
the wheels gleamed like *j* . . . . Ezek 10:9
onyx, and *j*, the sapphire . . . . Ezek 28:13
His body resembled yellow *j* . . . . . . Dan 10:6
like a stone of crystal-clear *j* . . . . . . Rev 21:11

JAVAN
Son of Japheth, Gen 10:2, 4
Descendants of, to receive good news,
    Isa 66:19–20

JAW
I would grab it by its *j* . . . . 1 Sam 17:35
or pierce its *j* with a hook . . . . Job 41:2
all my enemies on the *j* . . . . Ps 3:7

JAWBONE
to see a solid *j* of a donkey . . . . Judg 15:15

JAWS
j to those who tore out my beard . . Isa 50:6
I will put hooks in your *j* . . . . Ezek 29:4
put hooks into your *j* . . . . Ezek 38:4

JEALOUS
LORD, your God, am a *j* God . . . . . . Exod 20:5
whose name is *J* . . . . Exod 34:14
if *j* feelings come over him . . . . Num 5:14
he is a *j* God . . . . Deut 4:24
because they were *j* of Joseph . . . . . Acts 7:9
For I am *j* for you . . . . 2 Cor 11:2

JEALOUSY
j kindles a husband's rage . . . . Prov 6:34
have spoken in my *j* . . . . Ezek 5:13
not in discord and *j* . . . . Rom 13:13
still *j* and dissension . . . . 1 Cor 3:3
to provoke the Lord to *j* . . . . 1 Cor 10:22
jealous for you with godly *j* . . . . 2 Cor 11:2
there is *j* and selfishness . . . . Jas 3:16

JEBUS
Canaanite name of Jerusalem before
    captured by David, 1 Chr 11:4–8

JEBUSITES
Descendants of Canaan, Gen 15:18–21;
    Num 13:29
Defeated by Joshua, Josh 11:1–12
Not driven from Jerusalem; later conquered
    by David, Judg 1:21; 2 Sam 5:6–8
Put to forced labor under Solomon,
    1 Kgs 9:20–21

JECONIAH
See JEHOIACHIN

JEDIDIAH
Name given to Solomon by Nathan,
    2 Sam 12:24–25

JEDUTHUN
Levite musician appointed by David,
    1 Chr 16:41–42
Heads a family of musicians, 2 Chr 5:12
Name appears in psalm titles, Ps 39; 62; 77

JEGAR SAHADUTHA
Name given by Laban to memorial stones,
    Gen 31:46–47

JEHOAHAZ
Son and successor of Jehu, king of Israel,
    2 Kgs 10:35
Seeks the Lord in defeat, 2 Kgs 13:2–9
—Son and successor of Josiah, king of Judah,
    2 Kgs 23:30–34
Also called "Shallum," 1 Chr 3:15
—Also called "Ahaziah," youngest son of
    King Joram, 2 Chr 21:17

JEHOASH
Son of Ahaziah: *see* JOASH

JEHOIACHIN [or JECONIAH]
Son of Jehoiakim; next to the last king of
    Judah, 2 Kgs 24:8

JESHURUN
Poetic name of endearment for Israel,
Deut 32:15

JESSE
Grandson of Ruth and Boaz, Ruth 4:17–22
Father of David, 1 Sam 16:1–13
Mentioned in prophecy, Isa 11:1, 10

JESTING
foolish talk, or coarse *j* ....Eph 5:4

JESUS
Preexistence of, Ps 2:7; John 8:58;
    Col 1:15–18
Birth of, from a virgin, Isa 7:14; Matt 1:18–25
Deity of, Isa 9:6; John 1:1, 14, 18; 20:28–29;
    Rom 9:5; Heb 1:8
Humanity of, Gen 3:15; Matt 22:45;
    Luke 3:38; John 1:14; 1 Cor 15:45–47;
    Gal 4:4; Phil 2:5–11; 1 Tim 2:5
Character of:
    eternal, John 1:1–2, 15
    forgiving, Luke 23:34
    gentle, Matt 11:29
    guileless, 1 Pet 2:22
    holy, Luke 1:35
    humble, Phil 2:8
    innocent, Matt 27:4
    just, Zech 9:9
    merciful, Heb 2:17
    omnipotent, Matt 28:18
    omnipresent, Matt 18:20
    omniscient, Col 2:3
    righteous, Isa 53:11
    sinless, 2 Cor 5:21
    spotless, 1 Pet 1:19
Mission of:
    complete revelation, Heb 1:1
    destroy Satan's works, Heb 2:14;
        1 John 3:8
    do God's will, John 6:38
    fulfill the OT, Matt 5:17
    give life, John 10:10, 28
    save sinners, Luke 19:10
Worshiped by:
    all, Phil 2:10–11
    angels, Heb 1:6
    demons, Mark 5:2, 6
    disciples, Luke 24:52
    men, John 9:38
    OT saints, Josh 5:13–15
    saints in glory, Rev 7:9–10
OT types of:
    Abel, Heb 12:24
    Adam, Rom 5:14
    bronze serpent, John 3:14
    manna, John 6:32
    Moses, Deut 18:15
    Passover, 1 Cor 5:7
See CHRIST

See also LORD JESUS CHRIST

birth of *J* Christ happened.........Matt 1:18
and you will name him *J*...........Matt 1:21
Then *J* was led by the Spirit........Matt 4:1
J sent out these twelve.............Matt 10:5
J said to him, "Friend............Matt 26:50
and to have *J* killed...............Matt 27:20
J the Nazarene.....................Mark 1:24
J went away with his disciples.....Mark 3:7
But *J* said, "Do not stop him......Mark 9:39
Then *J* entered Jerusalem.........Mark 11:11
after he had *J* flogged............Mark 15:15
And *J* increased in wisdom........Luke 2:52
Then *J* asked, "Who was it........Luke 8:45
But *J* rebuked the unclean spirit..Luke 9:42
J said to him, "Foxes have........Luke 9:58
was trying to get a look at *J*......Luke 19:3
walked up to *J* to kiss him.......Luke 22:47
J himself stood among them ....Luke 24:36
came about through *J* Christ.......John 1:17
J said to him, "Stand up............John 5:8
Then *J*, when he looked up........John 6:5
sight of *J* walking on the lake......John 6:19

J bent down and wrote.............John 8:6
J wept.............................John 11:35
and anointed the feet of *J*.........John 12:3
place where *J* was crucified......John 19:20
many other things that *J* did......John 21:25
This *J* God raised up................Acts 2:32
name of your holy servant *J*....Acts 4:30
he began to proclaim *J*...........Acts 9:20
believing in the Lord *J* Christ......Acts 11:17
as were baptized into Christ *J*......Rom 6:3
life-giving Spirit in Christ *J*..........Rom 8:2
with your mouth that *J* is Lord.....Rom 10:9
nothing among you except *J*.......1 Cor 2:2
heavenly realms in Christ *J*..........Eph 2:6
name of *J* every knee will bow......Phil 2:10
and urge you in the Lord *J*.........1 Thess 4:1
but we see *J*........................Heb 2:9
J the Son of God....................Heb 4:14
keeping our eyes fixed on *J*.......Heb 12:2
J Christ the Righteous One.......1 John 2:1
that *J* is the Son of God............1 John 5:5
The revelation of *J* Christ.............Rev 1:1
Amen! Come, Lord *J*..............Rev 22:20

JETHER
Gideon's oldest son, Judg 8:20–21

JETHRO [or REUEL]
Priest of Midian; becomes Moses' father-in-
    law, Exod 2:16–22
Blesses Moses' departure, Exod 4:18
Visits and counsels Moses, Exod 18
Also called "Reuel," Num 10:29

JEW
How can you—a *J*—ask me..........John 4:9
I am not a *J* ....John 18:35
recognized that he was a *J*........Acts 19:34
I am a *J*, born in Tarsus ....Acts 22:3
J first and also to the Greek ....Rom 1:16
the *J* first and also the Greek ......Rom 2:9
For a person is not a *J* ....Rom 2:28
advantage does the *J* have..........Rom 3:1
between the *J* and the Greek .....Rom 10:12
although you are a *J*................Gal 2:14
like a Gentile and not like a *J* ......Gal 2:14
There is neither *J* nor Greek.......Gal 3:28
there is neither Greek nor *J*.........Col 3:11

JEWELRY
wear all of them like *j* ....Isa 49:18
so that you could wear *j*..........Ezek 16:7
I adorned you with *j*..............Ezek 16:11

JEWELS
is lovely with strings of *j*...........Song 1:10
of your thighs are like *j*.............Song 7:1
forget to put on her *j*...............Jer 2:32

JEWISH
happened to be a *J* man ....Esth 2:5
you have begun to fall is *J* ....Esth 6:13
J men whom you appointed ....Dan 3:12
for *J* ceremonial washing..........John 2:6
the *J* people were expecting.......Acts 12:11
in the *J* synagogues................Acts 13:5
some itinerant *J* exorcists ....Acts 19:13
pay attention to *J* myths..........Titus 1:14

JEWS
Jesus born King of the, Matt 2:2
Salvation comes through the, John 4:22;
    Acts 11:19; Rom 1:16; 2:9–10
Reject Christ, Matt 27:21–25
Reject the gospel, Acts 13:42–46

See also GREEK-SPEAKING JEWS; KING OF
    THE JEWS

Let the governor of the *J* ....Ezra 6:7
What are these feeble *J* doing ......Neh 4:2
against their fellow *J*................Neh 5:1
But the *J* who were in Susa ....Esth 9:18
Letters were sent to all the *J*.......Esth 9:30
one who is born king of the *J*......Matt 2:2
Are you the king of the *J*..........Matt 27:11
salvation is from the *J*.............John 4:22
the king of the *J* ....John 19:19

Now there were devout *J*..........Acts 2:5
consternation among the *J* ....Acts 9:22
the *J* incited the God-fearing .....Acts 13:50
he refuted the *J* vigorously ....Acts 18:28
is God the God of the *J* only ......Rom 3:29
a stumbling block to *J*.............1 Cor 1:23
To the *J* I became like a Jew.......1 Cor 9:20
J or Greeks or slaves or free......1 Cor 12:13
I received from the *J*.............. 2 Cor 11:24
those who call themselves *J*........Rev 2:9
say they are *J* yet are not ....Rev 3:9

JEZEBEL
Ahab's idolatrous wife, 1 Kgs 16:31
Her abominable acts, 1 Kgs 18:4, 13; 19:1–2;
    21:1–16
Death prophesied; prophecy fulfilled,
    1 Kgs 21:23; 2 Kgs 9:7, 30–37
—Type of paganism in the church, Rev 2:20

JEZREEL
Ahab's capital, 1 Kgs 18:45; 21:1
Ahab's family destroyed at, 1 Kgs 21:23;
    2 Kgs 9:30–37; 10:1–11

JOAB
David's nephew; commands his army,
    2 Sam 2:10–32; 8:16; 10:1–14; 11:1, 14–25;
    20:1–23
Kills Abner, 2 Sam 3:26–27
Intercedes for Absalom, 2 Sam 14:1–33
Remains loyal to David; kills Absalom,
    2 Sam 18:1–5, 9–17
Demoted; kills Amasa, 2 Sam 19:13; 20:8–10
Opposes census, 2 Sam 24:1–9; 1 Chr 21:1–6
Supports Adonijah, 1 Kgs 1:7
Solomon orders his death in obedience to
    David's command, 1 Kgs 2:1–6, 28–34

JOANNA
Wife of Cuza, Herod's steward, Luke 8:1–3
With others, heralds Christ's resurrection,
    Luke 23:55–56

JOASH
Son of Ahaziah; saved from Athaliah's
    massacre and crowned by Jehoiada,
    2 Kgs 11:1–12
Repairs the temple, 2 Kgs 12:1–16
Turns away from the Lord and is killed,
    2 Chr 24:17–25
Also called "Jehoash," 2 Kgs 11:21
—Wicked king of Israel; son of Jehoahaz,
    2 Kgs 13:10–25
Defeats Amaziah in battle, 2 Kgs 14:8–15;
    2 Chr 25:17–24

JOB
May another take his *j*..............Ps 109:8

JOB
Model of righteousness, Job 1:1–5
His faith tested, Job 1:6—2:10
Debates with his three friends; complains
    to God, Job 3–33
Elihu intervenes, Job 34–37
God's answer, Job 38–41
Humbles himself and repents, Job 42:1–6
Restored to prosperity, Job 42:10–17

JOCHEBED
Daughter of Levi; mother of Miriam, Aaron,
    and Moses, Exod 6:20

JOEL
Preexilic prophet, Joel 1:1
Quoted in NT, Acts 2:16

JOGBEHAH
Town in Gilead, Judg 8:11

JOHANAN
Military leader of Judah; warns Gedaliah of
    Ishmael's plot, Jer 40:13–16
Avenges Gedaliah; takes the people to
    Egypt, Jer 41:11–18

JOHN
The apostle, son of Zebedee; called as
    disciple, Matt 4:21–22; Luke 5:1–11
One of the Twelve, Matt 10:2

JUDAS
One of the Twelve: *see* THADDAEUS
—Judas Barsabbas, a chief deputy,
　Acts 15:22–32
—Betrayer of Christ: *see* ISCARIOT, JUDAS
—Half brother of Christ: *see* JUDE

JUDE [or JUDAS]
Half brother of Christ, Matt 13:55
Does not believe in Christ, John 7:5
Becomes Christ's disciple, Acts 1:14
Writes an epistle, Jude 1:1
Also called "Judas," Matt 13:55

JUDEA
both in *J* and in Jerusalem ....Acts 10:39

JUDEA
Christ born in, Matt 2:1, 5–6
Hostile toward Christ, John 7:1
Gospel preached in, Acts 8:1, 4
Churches established in, Acts 9:31

JUDEAN
to keep a fellow *J* enslaved .... Jer 34:9

JUDEANS
I am afraid of the *J*...................Jer 38:19
carried into exile 745 *J* ....Jer 52:30
Then Jesus said to those *J* ....John 8:31

JUDGE
LORD *j* between you and me....... Gen 16:5
Dan will *j* his people ....Gen 49:16
you a ruler and a *j* over us........ Exod 2:14
Moses sat to *j* the people........Exod 18:13
The LORD will *j* his people .... Deut 32:36
for he comes to *j* the earth ......1 Chr 16:33
O *j* of the earth ....Ps 94:2
For he comes to *j* the earth........Ps 96:13
For he comes to *j* the earth........Ps 98:9
j in righteousness...................Prov 31:9
hand you over to the *j* .... Matt 5:25
Do not *j* so that.....................Matt 7:1
made me a *j* or arbitrator........Luke 12:14
a *j* who neither feared God ......Luke 18:2
the Father does not *j* anyone ......John 5:22
I *j*, and my judgment is just....... John 5:30
Do not *j* according to external....John 7:24
You people *j* by outward ....John 8:15
I do not *j* him.....................John 12:47
when you *j* those who practice .....Rom 2:1
how could God *j* the world ......Rom 3:6
one who does not *j* himself.......Rom 14:22
the saints will *j* the world....... 1 Cor 6:2
know that we will *j* angels ....1 Cor 6:3
J for yourselves................... 1 Cor 11:13
do not let anyone *j* you............. Col 2:16
to *j* the living and the dead ....2 Tim 4:1
the righteous *J*..................... 2 Tim 4:8
to *j* the desires and thoughts ...... Heb 4:12
the *j* of all.........................Heb 12:23
will *j* sexually immoral people..... Heb 13:4
one who is lawgiver and *j*...........Jas 4:12
the *j* stands before the gates ....Jas 5:9
to *j* the living and the dead ....1 Pet 4:5
before you *j* those who live........Rev 6:10
had been given authority to *j* ......Rev 20:4

JUDGED
They *j* the people................ Exod 18:26
so that you will not be *j*............Matt 7:1
You have *j* rightly..................Luke 7:43
will be *j* by the law.................Rom 2:12
will prevail when you are *j*........Rom 3:4
the world is to be *j* by you.......1 Cor 6:2
when we are *j* by the Lord........1 Cor 11:32
those who will be *j* by a law ......Jas 2:12
we will be *j* more strictly ....Jas 3:1
so that you may not be *j*...........Jas 5:9
So the dead were *j*............... Rev 20:12

JUDGES
During the time of the *j* .... Ruth 1:1
He told the *j*................... 2 Chr 19:6
He *j* the world fairly ....Ps 9:8
a God who *j* in the earth............Ps 58:11
For the LORD *j* all humanity .... Isa 66:16
one who *j* me is the Lord .... 1 Cor 4:4

the one who impartially *j*...........1 Pet 1:17
to God who *j* justly ....1 Pet 2:23

JUDGING
Now this is the basis for *j*.........John 3:19

JUDGMENT
must not discriminate in *j* .... Deut 1:17
should go to court for *j*...........Deut 25:1
Praised be your good *j*............ 1 Sam 25:33
your angry *j* upon men ....Ps 76:10
midst of the gods he renders *j*....... Ps 82:1
and execute *j* on the earth...........Ps 82:8
wicked receive is *j* ....Prov 10:16
who knows the ruinous *j* ....Prov 24:22
the dreadful *j* of the LORD ....Isa 2:10
The Lord decreed *j* on Jacob.........Isa 9:8
What will you do on *j* day ....Isa 10:3
angry *j* to his adversaries ....Isa 59:18
I will bring down *j* on you..........Jer 2:35
am calling down *j* on them ....Jer 4:12
will pass *j* on all humankind ....Jer 25:31
and *j* was rendered ....Dan 7:22
time of *j* is about to arrive..........Hos 9:7
Exercise true *j* ....Zech 7:9
I will send *j* on you................Mal 2:2
will be subjected to *j* ....Matt 5:21
on the day of *j* than for you.......Matt 11:22
will rise up at the *j* ....Matt 12:42
and my *j* is just ....John 5:30
but judge with proper *j*............John 7:24
For *j* I have come ....John 9:39
Now is the *j* of this world.........John 12:31
For *j*, resulting from ....Rom 5:16
stand before the *j* seat of God....Rom 14:10
not pass *j* on one another ....Rom 14:13
eats and drinks *j*....................1 Cor 11:29
before the *j* seat of Christ ....2 Cor 5:10
and so incur *j* .... 1 Tim 5:12
going before them into *j*............1 Tim 5:24
and then to face *j*...................Heb 9:27
For *j* is merciless...................Jas 2:13
For it is time for *j* to begin.........1 Pet 4:17
a slanderous *j* against them ....2 Pet 2:11
confidence in the day of *j*.........1 John 4:17
for the *j* of the great Day ....Jude 1:6
the hour of his *j* has arrived ....Rev 14:7

JUDGMENTS
experienced the *j* of the LORD ..... Deut 11:2
You provided them with just *j* ..... Neh 9:13
The *j* given by the LORD .... Ps 19:9
Terrifying *j* make their demise...... Ps 73:19
How unsearchable are his *j*...... Rom 11:33
because his *j* are true and just....Rev 19:2

JUG
with her water *j* on ....Gen 24:15
the spear and the *j* of water ....1 Sam 26:12

JULIUS
Roman centurion assigned to guard Paul,
　Acts 27:1–44

JUMPING
King David *j* and celebrating..... 1 Chr 15:29

JUST
by doing what is right and *j*........Gen 18:19
j as the LORD commanded........Num 26:4
for all his ways are *j* ....Deut 32:4
LORD, consider my *j* cause...........Ps 17:1
is *j* and never unfair .... Ps 92:15
remember one who is *j*.............Ps 112:6
The LORD is *j* in all his actions ..... Ps 145:17
the LORD is a *j* God .... Isa 30:18
and do what is *j* and right .... Ezek 45:9
and his ways are *j*................Dan 4:37
he would be *j* and the justifier ... Rom 3:26
j as you too were called .... Eph 4:4
love your wives *j* as Christ........ Eph 5:25
whatever is *j*......................Phil 4:8
received its *j* penalty................Heb 2:2
J and true are your ways............Rev 15:3
your judgments are true and *j*......Rev 16:7

JUSTICE
so as to pervert *j* ....Exod 23:2
and perverted *j* ....1 Sam 8:3

guaranteed *j* for all his people... 2 Sam 8:15
Does God pervert *j* ....Job 8:3
but he gives *j* to the poor..........Job 36:6
I will tell others about your *j* ....Ps 35:28
great assembly about your *j*....... Ps 40:9
You love *j* and hate evil...............Ps 45:7
execute *j* among the nations ....Ps 67:4
Equity and *j* are the foundation.....Ps 89:14
and are vindicated by your *j* ....Ps 89:16
executes *j* for all the oppressed ....Ps 103:6
Your *j* endures.....................Ps 119:142
abundant income without *j*........Prov 16:8
Evil people do not understand *j* .. Prov 28:5
J will be like a belt ....Isa 11:5
they do not learn about *j* ....Isa 26:10
make *j* the measuring line...........Isa 28:17
No one is concerned about *j*........Isa 59:4
J is driven back ....Isa 59:14
his desire for *j* drives him on ....Isa 59:16
desire for *j* like body armor ....Isa 59:17
love *j* and hate robbery and sin......Isa 61:8
LORD has provided us with *j* .... Jer 23:6
LORD has provided us with *j*.......Jer 33:16
and by their standard of *j*.........Ezek 7:27
by maintaining love and *j*...........Hos 12:6
Israelites turn *j* into bitterness ....Amos 5:7
He wants you to carry out *j*.........Mic 6:8
Where is the God of *j*...............Mal 2:17
will proclaim *j* to the nations .....Matt 12:18
neglect *j* and love for God ....Luke 11:42
In humiliation *j* was taken ....Acts 8:33

JUSTIFICATION
raised for the sake of our *j* .... Rom 4:25
many failures led to *j* ....Rom 5:16

JUSTIFIED
by your words you will be *j*.......Matt 12:37
went down to his home *j* ....Luke 18:14
everyone who believes is *j*........Acts 13:39
you will be *j* in your words ....Rom 3:4
they are *j* freely by his grace...... Rom 3:24
and those he called, he also *j* ..... Rom 8:30
were *j* in the name of the Lord .....1 Cor 6:11
is *j* by the works of the law .... Gal 2:16
is *j* before God by the law ....Gal 3:11
j by works and not by faith alone... Jas 2:24
j by works when she welcomed .... Jas 2:25

JUSTIFIER
he would be just and the *j* .... Rom 3:26

JUSTIFIES
It is God who *j*.....................Rom 8:33

JUSTIFY
wanting to *j* himself ....Luke 10:29
are the ones who *j* yourselves ....Luke 16:15
he will *j* the circumcised..........Rom 3:30
would *j* the Gentiles by faith........Gal 3:8

JUSTLY
to God who judges *j*...............1 Pet 2:23

JUSTUS
Surname of Joseph, a disciple, Acts 1:23
—Man of Corinth; befriends Paul, Acts 18:7
—Fellow worker of Paul, also called Jesus,
　Col 4:11

K

KADESH
Spies sent from, Num 13:3, 26
Moses strikes rock at, Num 20:1–13
Boundary in the new Israel, Ezek 47:19

KADESH BARNEA
Boundary of Promised Land, Num 34:1–4
Limit of Joshua's military campaign,
　Josh 10:41

KARNAIM
Conquered region, Amos 6:13

KEBAR
River in Babylonia, Ezek 1:3
Site of Ezekiel's visions, Ezek 10:15, 20

KEDESH
Town in south Judah, Josh 15:23
—Levite city in Issachar, 1 Chr 6:72

KEDESH NAPHTALI
City of refuge, Josh 21:27, 32
Home of Barak, Judg 4:6

KEDORLAOMER
A king of Elam; invaded Canaan, Gen 14:1–16

KEEN
and having *k* insight . . . . .Dan 1:4

KEEP
So you will *k* the Feast. . . . . .Exod 12:17
K me from harm. . . . . 1 Chr 4:10
Israel would *k* my commands . . . . . . .Ps 81:13
to *k* your just regulations. . . . . Ps 119:106
a time to *k* silent. . . . . .Eccl 3:7
k the poor from getting fair . . . . .Isa 10:2
k the commandments . . . . Matt 19:17
tries to *k* his life will lose it . . . . . . .Luke 17:33
k them safe in your name . . . . .John 17:11
to *k* the unity of the Spirit . . . . .Eph 4:3
K yourself pure. . . . . .1 Tim 5:22
and to *k* oneself unstained . . . . .Jas 1:27
must *k* his tongue from evil . . . . . . .1 Pet 3:10
if we *k* his commandments. . . . . .1 John 2:3
we *k* his commandments. . . . . .1 John 3:22
the angels who did not *k* within . . . . Jude 1:6
is able to *k* you from falling . . . . . . .Jude 1:24
also *k* you from the hour . . . . .Rev 3:10

KEEPER
me the *k* of the vineyard . . . . .Song 1:6

KEEPING
by *k* one hand on the work . . . . Neh 4:17
with no intention of *k* them . . . . .Ps 24:4
helped by *k* his requirements. . . . . . .Mal 3:14
k our eyes fixed on Jesus . . . . .Heb 12:2

KEEPS
who *k* covenant faithfully. . . . . Deut 7:9
who *k* covenant fidelity. . . . . .Neh 9:32
The one who *k* the law . . . . Prov 28:7
Yet not one of you *k* the law. . . . . . .John 7:19

KEILAH
Town of Judah; rescued from Philistines by
    David, 1 Sam 23:1–5
Prepares to betray David; he escapes,
    1 Sam 23:6–13

KENITES
Canaanite tribe whose land is promised to
    Abraham's seed, Gen 15:19
Subjects of Balaam's prophecy,
    Num 24:20–22
Settle with Judahites, Judg 1:16
Spared by Saul in war with Amalekites,
    1 Sam 15:6

KEPT
waters *k* receding steadily. . . . . Gen 8:3
must be *k* burning on it. . . . . .Lev 6:9
You have *k* your word . . . . 2 Chr 6:15
I have *k* my motives pure. . . . . .Ps 73:13
k the charge of my sanctuary. . . . Ezek 44:15
k them safe and watched over. . . . . John 17:12
have *k* for myself 7,000 people. . . . . Rom 11:4
been *k* secret for long ages. . . . . . .Rom 16:25
be *k* entirely blameless. . . . . .1 Thess 5:23
I have *k* the faith. . . . . .2 Tim 4:7
to be *k* until the judgment. . . . . 2 Pet 2:4
you have *k* my admonition . . . . .Rev 3:10

KERITH VALLEY
God hides Elijah here and the ravens feed
    him, 1 Kgs 17:3–6

KERNEL
unless a *k* of wheat falls . . . . .John 12:24

KETTLES
k, and dining couches. . . . . .Mark 7:4

KETURAH
Abraham's second wife, Gen 25:1
Sons of:
    listed, Gen 25:1–2
    given gifts and sent away, Gen 25:6

KEY
I will place the *k* to the house . . . . . Isa 22:22
away the *k* to knowledge. . . . . .Luke 11:52

who holds the *k* of David . . . . .Rev 3:7
in his hand the *k* to the abyss. . . . . . .Rev 20:1

KEYS
k of the kingdom of heaven . . . . . .Matt 16:19
the *k* of death and of Hades . . . . Rev 1:18

KIBROTH HATTAAVAH
Burial site of Israelites slain by God,
    Num 11:33–35

KIDNAPPERS
k, liars, perjurers. . . . . .1 Tim 1:10

KIDNAPS
k someone and sells him . . . . .Exod 21:16

KIDNEYS
Without pity he pierces my *k*. . . . . . .Job 16:13

KIDRON
Valley near Jerusalem; crossed by David
    and Christ, 2 Sam 15:23; John 18:1
Idols dumped there, 2 Chr 29:16

KILION
Elimelech's son, Ruth 1:2
Orpah's deceased husband, Ruth 1:4–5
Boaz redeems his estate, Ruth 4:9

KILL
whoever finds me will *k* me . . . . Gen 4:14
k the godly with the wicked . . . . . . Gen 18:25
and *k* the Passover animals. . . . . . .Exod 12:21
I *k* and give life . . . . Deut 32:39
Can I *k* or restore life . . . . .2 Kgs 5:7
only you would *k* the wicked . . . . . .Ps 139:19
a time to *k*, and a time to heal . . . . . .Eccl 3:3
those men who want to *k* you. . . . . .Jer 38:16
I will certainly *k* you . . . . Hos 6:5
you who *k* the prophets . . . . Matt 23:37
they will *k* and persecute. . . . . .Luke 11:49
afraid of those who *k* the body . . . .Luke 12:4
Why do you want to *k* me . . . . .John 7:19
to steal and *k* and destroy. . . . . . . .John 10:10
and was about to *k* himself. . . . . . .Acts 16:27
k its population with the sword . . . . Rev 6:8

KILLED
his brother Abel and *k* him . . . . .Gen 4:8
have a *k* man for wounding me. . . .Gen 4:23
the LORD *k* all the firstborn. . . . . . .Exod 13:15
we are *k* all day long. . . . . .Ps 44:22
k in the middle of the streets. . . . . .Prov 22:13
dear people who have been *k* . . . . . .Jer 9:1
k and on the third day be raised. .Matt 16:21
and to have Jesus *k*. . . . . .Matt 27:20
k when the tower in Siloam fell . . .Luke 13:4
You *k* the Originator of life . . . . Acts 3:15
whom you seized and *k* . . . . .Acts 5:30
who *k* both the Lord Jesus. . . . . 1 Thess 2:15
who was *k* in your city. . . . . .Rev 2:13
Worthy is the lamb who was *k* . . . . .Rev 5:12
appeared to have been *k* . . . . .Rev 13:3

KILLS
LORD both *k* and gives life. . . . . .1 Sam 2:6
for the letter *k*. . . . . .2 Cor 3:6

KIND
You really are being *k* to me. . . . . . .Ruth 2:13
The LORD is both *k* and fair. . . . . .Ps 25:8
May your *k* presence lead me . . . . .Ps 143:10
and *k* speech increases . . . . .Prov 16:21
This *k* can come out only . . . . .Mark 9:29
k to ungrateful and evil people . . . Luke 6:35
Love is patient, love is *k* . . . . .1 Cor 13:4
Instead, be *k* to one another. . . . . . . Eph 4:32

KINDLED
the anger of the LORD was *k*. . . . . . . Num 11:10
how I wish it were already *k*. . . . . .Luke 12:49

KINDLY
treating Paul *k*. . . . . .Acts 27:3

KINDNESS
the LORD show you true *k* . . . . 2 Sam 2:6
for all his acts of *k* to me . . . . .Ps 116:12
the *k* and harshness of God . . . . . . Rom 11:22
k, goodness, faithfulness . . . . .Gal 5:22
when the *k* of God our Savior . . . . . Titus 3:4
experienced the Lord's *k* . . . . .1 Pet 2:3

KINDS
Of the birds after their *k*. . . . . .Gen 6:20
different *k* of your animals . . . . Lev 19:19
different *k* of tongues . . . . .1 Cor 12:28

KING
See also KING OF THE JEWS
Melchizedek *k* of Salem . . . . .Gen 14:18
In those days Israel had no *k* . . . . . .Judg 17:6
Give us a *k* to lead us. . . . . 1 Sam 8:6
Long live the *k*. . . . . 1 Sam 10:24
stands his chosen *k*. . . . . .1 Sam 16:6
they anointed David as *k* . . . . 2 Sam 2:4
we are loyal to the *k*. . . . . Ezra 4:14
have installed my *k* on Zion . . . . Ps 2:6
LORD will deliver his chosen *k* . . . . . .Ps 20:6
The LORD will deliver the *k*. . . . . .Ps 20:9
sit as *k* receiving the praises. . . . . . . .Ps 22:3
For the LORD is *k* and rules . . . . .Ps 22:28
the majestic *k* will enter. . . . . .Ps 24:7
k is delivered by his vast army. . . . . .Ps 33:16
reigned as *k* from long ago . . . . .Ps 55:19
grant the *k* the ability. . . . . Ps 72:1
But God has been my *k*. . . . . Ps 74:12
out of prison to become *k* . . . . .Eccl 4:14
when your *k* is childish . . . . .Eccl 10:16
the year of *K* Uzziah's death. . . . . .Isa 6:1
a *k* will promote fairness . . . . .Isa 32:1
commander, the LORD, our *k* . . . . . .Isa 33:22
her divine *K* no longer there. . . . . . . .Jer 8:19
God and the everlasting *K*. . . . . .Jer 10:10
that I am about to bring *K* . . . . Ezek 26:7
granted you a *k* in my anger. . . . . . . Hos 13:11
the LORD will reign as *K* . . . . .Obad 1:21
sitting as *k* on his throne . . . . .Zech 6:13
The LORD will then be *k* . . . . Zech 14:9
who is born *k* of the Jews. . . . . .Matt 2:2
the *k* of the Jews. . . . . .Matt 27:37
want this man to be *k* over us . . . . .Luke 19:14
by force to make him *k* . . . . .John 6:15
here is your *k*. . . . . .John 19:14
is another *k* named Jesus . . . . Acts 17:7
Now to the eternal *K* . . . . .1 Tim 1:17
K of kings and Lord of lords . . . . . . 1 Tim 6:15
k of Salem . . . . .Heb 7:1
honor the *k*. . . . . .1 Pet 2:17
K of kings and Lord of lords . . . . . .Rev 19:16

KING OF THE JEWS
the one who is born *k* . . . . .Matt 2:2
Are you the *k*. . . . . .Matt 27:11
This is Jesus, the *k* . . . . Matt 27:37
you want to release the *k*. . . . . Mark 15:9
salute him: "Hail *k*. . . . . .Mark 15:18
you are the *k*, save yourself . . . . . Luke 23:37
This man said, I am *k* . . . . .John 19:21

KING'S
can the *k* successor do . . . . .Eccl 2:12

KINGDOM
See also KINGDOM OF GOD; KINGDOM
    OF HEAVEN
k of priests and a holy nation. . . . . Exod 19:6
LORD has torn the *k* of Israel . . . .1 Sam 15:28
mankind and the animal *k*. . . . . .Ps 36:6
scepter of your *k* is a scepter. . . . . . .Ps 45:6
his *k* extends over everything . . . . .Ps 103:19
Your *k* is an eternal *k* . . . . .Ps 145:13
will raise up an everlasting *k* . . . . . .Dan 2:44
k is divided and given over . . . . .Dan 5:28
His *k* will not be destroyed. . . . . .Dan 7:14
the *k* of heaven has suffered . . . . . Matt 11:12
are the people of the *k* . . . . .Matt 13:38
they will gather from his *k* . . . . . . .Matt 13:41
up to half my *k* . . . . .Mark 6:23
Blessed is the coming *k*. . . . . .Mark 11:10
and *k* against *k* . . . . Mark 13:8
and his *k* will never end . . . . .Luke 1:33
k of God has come upon you . . . . . .Luke 10:9
may your *k* come . . . . .Luke 11:2
Every *k* divided against itself . . . . . Luke 11:17
pleased to give you the *k*. . . . . .Luke 12:32
k of God belongs to such . . . . .Luke 18:16
and *k* against *k* . . . . .Luke 21:10
drink at my table in my *k*. . . . . .Luke 22:30

when you come in your *k*........Luke 23:42
he cannot enter the *k* of God.......John 3:5
My *k* is not from this world.......John 18:36
around proclaiming the *k*........Acts 20:25
when he hands over the *k*.......1 Cor 15:24
has any inheritance in the *k*.........Eph 5:5
who calls you to his own *k*......1 Thess 2:12
scepter is the scepter of your *k*......Heb 1:8
are receiving an unshakable *k*......Heb 12:28
an entrance into the eternal *k*.....2 Pet 1:11
and has appointed us as a *k*........Rev 1:6
The *k* of the world...................Rev 11:15

KINGDOM OF GOD

the *k* has already overtaken.....Matt 12:28
rich person to enter into the *k*...Matt 19:24
ahead of you into the *k*..........Matt 21:31
the *k* will be taken from you.....Matt 21:43
fulfilled and the *k* is near.........Mark 1:15
The secret of the *k*.................Mark 4:11
what can we compare the *k*.....Mark 4:30
death before they see the *k*.......Mark 9:1
enter into the *k* with one eye.....Mark 9:47
for the *k* belongs to such........Mark 10:14
for the rich to enter the *k*......Mark 10:23
You are not far from the *k*.....Mark 12:34
I drink it new in the *k*..........Mark 14:25
looking forward to the *k*........Mark 15:43
the good news of the *k*..........Luke 4:43
for the *k* belongs to you.........Luke 6:20
who is least in the *k*...............Luke 7:28
to proclaim the *k* and to heal......Luke 9:2
and all the prophets in the *k*.....Luke 13:28
who will feast in the *k*...........Luke 14:15
the good news of the *k*.........Luke 16:16
The *k* is not coming with signs..Luke 17:20
indeed, the *k* is in your midst.....Luke 17:21
the *k* was going to appear.......Luke 19:11
know that the *k* is near.........Luke 21:31
he cannot see the *k*..............John 3:3
matters concerning the *k*..........Acts 1:3
We must enter the *k*.............Acts 14:22
testifying about the *k*...........Acts 28:23
k does not consist of food.......Rom 14:17
For the *k* is demonstrated........1 Cor 4:20
will not inherit the *k*...............1 Cor 6:9
cannot inherit the *k*.............1 Cor 15:50
will not inherit the *k*................Gal 5:21
fellow workers for the *k*...........Col 4:11
make you worthy of the *k*.......2 Thess 1:5

KINGDOM OF HEAVEN

Repent for the *k* is near...........Matt 3:2
for the *k* belongs to them........Matt 5:10
you will never enter the *k*......Matt 5:20
will enter into the *k*...............Matt 7:21
and Jacob in the *k*.................Matt 8:11
The *k* is near.......................Matt 10:7
who is least in the *k*...............Matt 11:11
know the secrets of the *k*.........Matt 13:11
The *k* is like a mustard seed......Matt 13:31
The *k* is like yeast.................Matt 13:33
The *k* is like a treasure...........Matt 13:44
the *k* is like a net................Matt 13:47
give you the keys of the *k*......Matt 16:19
Who is the greatest in the *k*.....Matt 18:1
will never enter the *k*.............Matt 18:3
is the greatest in the *k*..........Matt 18:4
the *k* is like a king...............Matt 18:23
for the *k* belongs to such........Matt 19:14
rich person to enter the *k*.......Matt 19:23
the *k* is like a landowner.........Matt 20:1
The *k* can be compared to.......Matt 22:2
locking people out of the *k*.......Matt 23:13
the *k* will be like ten virgins......Matt 25:1

KINGDOMS

k are overthrown...................Ps 46:6
the one who made *k* tremble.......Isa 14:16
has authority over human *k*.......Dan 4:17
all the *k* of the world.............Matt 4:8

KINGS

k of the earth form a united.........Ps 2:2
All *k* will bow down to him..........Ps 72:11
the *k* of the earth regard him.......Ps 76:12

k reign, and by me..................Prov 8:15
take his position before *k*.......Prov 22:29
hearts of *k* are unsearchable......Prov 25:3
ways to that which ruins *k*.........Prov 31:3
It is not for *k*......................Prov 31:4
K will be your children's...........Isa 49:23
k without my consent.............Hos 8:4
before governors and *k*..........Matt 10:18
prophets and *k* longed to see....Luke 10:24
have become *k* without us.........1 Cor 4:8
for the *k* from the east.............Rev 16:12
eat your fill of the flesh of *k*.......Rev 19:18

KINNERETH

Region: *see* GALILEE
—Sea: *see* GALILEE, SEA OF

KIR HARESETH

Fortified city of Moab, 2 Kgs 3:25; Isa 15:1;
  16:7

KIRIATH ARBA

See HEBRON

KIRIATH JEARIM [or BAALAH]

Gibeonite town, Josh 9:17
Ark taken from, 1 Chr 13:5
Also called "Baalah," Josh 15:9

KIRIATH SEPHER

See DEBIR

KISH

Benjamite of Gibeah; father of King Saul,
  1 Sam 9:1–3

KISHON

River of north Palestine; Sisera's army
  swept away by, Judg 4:7, 13
Elijah executes prophets of Baal at,
  1 Kgs 18:40

KISS

how I wish you would *k* me........Song 1:2
The one I *k* is the man...........Mark 14:44
gave me no *k* of greeting.........Luke 7:45
walked up to Jesus to *k* him.....Luke 22:47
one another with a holy *k*........Rom 16:16
one another with a holy *k*.......2 Cor 13:12
and sisters with a holy *k*........1 Thess 5:26
one another with a loving *k*.......1 Pet 5:14

KISSED

Then they *k* each other..........1 Sam 20:41
Greetings, Rabbi," and *k* him....Matt 26:49
his feet with her hair, *k* them.....Luke 7:38

KISSERS

to the calf idol are calf *k*...........Hos 13:2

KITTIM

Descendants of Javan, Gen 10:4
—Hebrew name for Cyprus: *see* CYPRUS

KNEE

every *k* will bow to me.............Isa 45:23
have not bent the *k* to Baal........Rom 11:4
every *k* will bow to me...........Rom 14:11
name of Jesus every *k* will bow.....Phil 2:10

KNEEL

make my foes *k* before me........Ps 18:39
I *k* before the Father...............Eph 3:14

KNEES

steady the *k* that shake.............Isa 35:3
you will play on her *k*............Isa 66:12
and your weak *k*...................Heb 12:12

KNEW

and they *k* they were naked........Gen 3:7
I never *k* you.......................Matt 7:23
And all those who *k* Jesus......Luke 23:49
for he *k* what was in man.........John 2:25
because he *k* everything.........John 18:4
you *k* that you certainly had......Heb 10:34

KNIFE

the fire and the *k* in his hand......Gen 22:6
he took a *k*......................Judg 19:29
and put a *k* to your throat.......Prov 23:2

KNIT

and *k* me together.................Job 10:11

KNOCK

who plan to *k* me over.............Ps 140:4
k and the door will be opened......Matt 7:7

KNOCKING

standing at the door and *k*......Rev 3:20

KNOTS

my stomach is in *k*................Lam 1:20
my stomach is in *k*................Lam 2:11

KNOW

you will *k* that I am the LORD......Exod 6:7
but you have not let me *k*.......Exod 33:12
that I may *k* you...............Exod 33:13
And *k* that your sin..............Num 32:23
Samuel did not yet *k* the LORD....1 Sam 3:7
k for sure that you will..........1 Kgs 2:42
I *k* that there is no God..........2 Kgs 5:15
I *k* that my Redeemer lives......Job 19:25
What does God *k*..................Job 22:13
Who can *k* all his errors........Ps 19:12
You cause those who *k* me......Ps 88:8
and *k* my concerns.................Ps 139:23
and does not *k* that poverty......Prov 28:22
those who *k* incantations.............Isa 3:3
I *k* where you live................Isa 37:28
my people will *k* my name......Isa 52:6
you did not previously *k*..........Isa 55:5
language you will not *k*.............Jer 5:15
that they understand and *k* me.....Jer 9:24
and relatives to *k* me...............Jer 31:34
you will *k* that I am the LORD......Ezek 6:13
will *k* that I am the LORD.........Ezek 17:24
will *k* that the house of Israel....Ezek 39:23
I wanted to *k* the meaning..........Dan 7:19
You ought to *k* what is just.........Mic 3:1
You *k* how to judge correctly....Matt 16:3
you *k* that summer is near......Matt 24:32
you do not *k* on what day.......Matt 24:42
I do not *k* the man...............Matt 26:72
I do not *k* the man...............Matt 26:74
You *k* the commandments......Mark 10:19
don't *k* what you are asking.....Mark 10:38
I *k* that power has gone out......Luke 8:46
k how to give good gifts.........Luke 11:13
I *k* what to do.....................Luke 16:4
k that its desolation has come...Luke 21:20
we speak about what we *k*.......John 3:11
worship what you do not *k*......John 4:22
come to believe and to *k*........John 6:69
not *k* either me or my Father......John 8:19
I *k* that you are Abraham's........John 8:37
We *k* that God doesn't listen......John 9:31
I *k* my own and my own *k* me....John 10:14
and I *k* them.....................John 10:27
I *k* the ones I have chosen......John 13:18
we *k* that you *k* everything.....John 16:30
if the world does not *k* you......John 17:25
you *k* I love you...................John 21:15
not permitted to *k* the times.....Acts 1:7
I *k* about Jesus...................Acts 19:15
k that all things work together...Rom 8:28
by its wisdom did not *k* God.......1 Cor 1:21
For we *k* in part...................1 Cor 13:9
k that the one who raised......2 Cor 4:14
k that as long as we are alive.....2 Cor 5:6
who did not *k* sin to be sin.......2 Cor 5:21
I *k* a man in Christ..............2 Cor 12:2
when you did not *k* God........Gal 4:8
thus to *k* the love of Christ........Eph 3:19
My aim is to *k* him................Phil 3:10
k that you also have a master.......Col 4:1
k how to possess his own body..1 Thess 4:4
you *k* what holds him back......2 Thess 2:6
I *k* the one in whom my faith......2 Tim 1:12
k that the testing of your faith.......Jas 1:3
k that your brothers and sisters....1 Pet 5:9
k that we have come to *k* God....1 John 2:3
I have come to *k* God............1 John 2:4
and you all *k*......................1 John 2:20
have come to *k* love by this......1 John 3:16
will *k* that we are of the truth....1 John 3:19
we *k* that God resides in us......1 John 3:24
We *k* that we are from God......1 John 5:19
I *k* your works.....................Rev 2:2

KNOWING
k good and evil .... Gen 3:5
k good and evil .... Gen 3:22
k that suffering produces.......... Rom 5:3
k that your labor is not in vain... 1 Cor 15:58
entertained angels without *k* it..... Heb 13:2

KNOWLEDGE
See also TREE OF THE KNOWLEDGE OF
 GOOD AND EVIL
tree of the *k* of good and evil....... Gen 2:9
k, and in all kinds of work ....Exod 35:31
yesterday and do not have *k*.........Job 8:9
Can anyone teach God *k*............Job 21:22
it is one complete in *k*..............Job 36:4
k is beyond my comprehension .... Ps 139:6
By his *k* the primordial sea .... Prov 3:20
k rather than choice gold..........Prov 8:10
who are wise store up *k* ....Prov 10:14
shrewd person conceals *k*.......Prov 12:23
to have zeal without *k*.............Prov 19:2
by *k* its rooms are filled ....Prov 24:4
man of *k* makes his strength ..... Prov 24:5
the benefit of wisdom and *k*........ Eccl 1:17
whoever increases his *k* ....Eccl 1:18
the advantage of *k* is this...........Eccl 7:12
nor *k* nor wisdom in the grave .... Eccl 9:10
come to those with the most *k*..... Eccl 9:11
and *k* will increase................. Dan 12:4
have taken away the key to *k*.....Luke 11:52
proceeds with his wife's *k* ....Acts 5:2
the essential features of *k*........ Rom 2:20
through the law comes the *k* ..... Rom 3:20
we know that "we all have *k*........1 Cor 8:1
and another the message of *k*....1 Cor 12:8
know all mysteries and all *k*.......1 Cor 13:2
if there is *k* ....1 Cor 13:8
fragrance that consists of the *k*... 2 Cor 2:14
light of the glorious *k* of God......2 Cor 4:6
by *k*, by patience...................2 Cor 6:6
raised up against the *k* of God.... 2 Cor 10:5
love of Christ that surpasses *k*..... Eph 3:19
fill you with the *k* of his will .... Col 1:9
treasures of wisdom and *k* .... Col 2:3
absurdities of so-called "*k*........1 Tim 6:20
and then *k* of the truth .... 2 Tim 2:25
excellence, to excellence, *k*........2 Pet 1:5
grow in the grace and *k* .... 2 Pet 3:18

KNOWN
See also WELL KNOWN
each tree is *k* by its own fruit.....Luke 6:44
way of peace they have not *k*......Rom 3:17
I would not have *k* sin ....Rom 7:7
has *k* the mind of the Lord .... Rom 11:34
k through us the fragrance ....2 Cor 2:14
rather to be *k* by God.............Gal 4:9
you have *k* the holy writings......2 Tim 3:15

KNOWS
for God *k* that when you eat........ Gen 3:5
for the LORD is a God who *k*......1 Sam 2:3
k a person's secret thoughts........Ps 44:21
He *k* what is in the darkness....... Dan 2:22
Who *k*? Perhaps God might ......Jonah 3:9
your Father *k* what you need...... Matt 6:8
that day and hour no one *k* it.....Matt 24:36
No one *k* who the Son is......... Luke 10:22
but God *k* your hearts............. Luke 16:15
k the mind of the Spirit........... Rom 8:27
k the things of a man ....1 Cor 2:11
The Lord *k* that the thoughts....1 Cor 3:20
The Lord *k* those who are his.....2 Tim 2:19
So whoever *k* what is good.......... Jas 4:17
than our conscience and *k*.......1 John 3:20

KOHATH
Second son of Levi, Gen 46:8, 11
Brother of Jochebed, mother of Aaron and
 Moses, Exod 6:16–20

KOHATHITES
Numbered, Num 3:27–28
Duties assigned to, Num 4:15–20
Leaders of temple music, 1 Chr 6:31–38;
 2 Chr 20:19

KORAH
Leads rebellion against Moses and Aaron;
 supernaturally destroyed, Num 16:1–35
Sons of, not destroyed, Num 26:9–11

KOUM
Talitha *k*," which means .... Mark 5:41

L

LABAN
Son of Bethuel; brother of Rebekah; father
 of Leah and Rachel, Gen 24:15, 24, 29;
 29:16
Agrees to Rebekah's marriage to Isaac,
 Gen 24:50–51
Entertains Jacob, Gen 29:1–14
Substitutes Leah for Rachel, Gen 29:15–30
Agrees to division of cattle; grows resentful
 of Jacob, Gen 30:25—31:2
Pursues Jacob and makes covenant with
 him, Gen 31:21–55

LABOR
and observed their hard *l*.......... Exod 2:11
groaned because of the slave *l* ... Exod 2:23
For six days you may *l*............Exod 20:9
a man acquire from all his *l*........ Eccl 2:22
we are all the product of your *l*..... Isa 64:8
Before she goes into *l* .... Isa 66:7
does not pay them for their *l*.......Jer 22:13
you have entered into their *l* ..... John 4:38
that your *l* is not in vain .... 1 Cor 15:58
instead he must *l* .... Eph 4:28
work produced by faith and *l*.....1 Thess 1:3
your works as well as your *l*........ Rev 2:2

LABORER'S
l appetite has labored for him ....Prov 16:26

LABORS
with much greater *l* ....2 Cor 11:23

LACHISH
Defeated by Joshua, Josh 10:3–33
Taken by Sennacherib, 2 Kgs 18:13–17;
 Isa 36:1–2; 37:8

LACK
to perish for *l* of clothing..........Job 31:19
I *l* nothing .... Ps 23:1
but fools die for *l* of sense........Prov 10:21
gives to the poor will not *l*....... Prov 28:27
will never *l* a male descendant .....Jer 35:19
What do I still *l*............... Matt 19:20
You *l* one thing .... Mark 10:21
you didn't *l* anything............. Luke 22:35
your *l* of self-control...............1 Cor 7:5

LACKED
who gathered little *l* nothing .... Exod 16:18

LACKING
and found to be *l* .... Dan 5:27

LACKS
denounces his neighbor *l* sense ...Prov 11:12
a great oppressor *l* wisdom.......Prov 28:16
poorly clothed and *l* daily food......Jas 2:15
the one who *l* such things ....2 Pet 1:9

LADIES
The wisest of her *l* answer.........Judg 5:29
noble *l* of Persia and Media.........Esth 1:18

LADY
to an elect *l* and her children ......2 John 1:1

LAG
Do not *l* in zeal ....Rom 12:11

LAID
went and *l* the foundations........ Ezra 5:16
Jerusalem and *l* it under siege .... Dan 1:1
l the foundations of this temple ... Zech 4:9
ax is *l* at the root of the trees......Matt 3:10
the place where they *l* him .... Mark 16:6
and *l* him in a manger ....Luke 2:7
l the foundation on bedrock......Luke 6:48
Where have you *l* him ....John 11:34
master-builder I *l* a foundation ... 1 Cor 3:10

LAIR
I will return again to my *l*...........Hos 5:15

LAISH [or LESHEM]
Taken by Danites, Judg 18:7, 14, 27
Also called "Leshem," Josh 19:47; Judg 18:29

LAKE
by the *L* of Gennesaret ....Luke 5:1
to the other side of the *l*..........Luke 8:22
l of fire burning with sulfur....... Rev 19:20

LAMB
is the *l* for the burnt offering ...... Gen 22:7
must take a *l* for themselves ......Exod 12:3
he took the poor man's *l* .... 2 Sam 12:4
sacrificed the Passover *l*.......... Ezra 6:20
A wolf will reside with a *l*............ Isa 11:6
l led to the slaughtering block....... Isa 53:7
wolf and a *l* will graze together.... Isa 65:25
Passover *l* had to be sacrificed ... Luke 22:7
the *L* of God who takes away...... John 1:29
a *l* before its shearer is silent ......Acts 8:32
our Passover *l* ....1 Cor 5:7
unblemished and spotless *l*...... 1 Pet 1:19
a *L* that appeared...................Rev 5:6
Worthy is the *l* who was killed......Rev 5:12
by the blood of the *L*.............Rev 12:11
belonging to the *L* ....Rev 13:8
wedding celebration of the *L* ....Rev 19:9
the wife of the *L* ....Rev 21:9

LAMB'S
written in the *L* book of life ....Rev 21:27

LAMBS
slaughtered the Passover *l* ......2 Chr 30:17
like *l*, O hills .... Ps 114:6
gathers up the *l* with his arm ......Isa 40:11
like *l* surrounded by wolves .....Luke 10:3
Feed my *l* ....John 21:15

LAME
the *l* will drag off plunder .... Isa 33:23
the *l* will leap like a deer............ Isa 35:6
when you offer the *l* and sick....... Mal 1:8
The blind see, the *l* walk....... Matt 11:5
And a man *l* from birth .... Acts 3:2
not use his feet, *l* from birth........ Acts 14:8
so that what is *l*................... Heb 12:13

LAMECH
Son of Methushael, of Cain's race,
 Gen 4:17–18
—Son of Methuselah; father of Noah,
 Gen 5:25–31

LAMENT
David chanted this *l* over Saul ....2 Sam 1:17
the following *l* for Abner .... 2 Sam 3:33
you turned my *l* into dancing....... Ps 30:11
noontime I will *l* and moan .... Ps 55:17
I pour out my *l* before him .... Ps 142:2
in Daughter Judah mourn and *l*..... Lam 2:5
They will *l* for him ....Zech 12:10

LAMENTATION
On that day the *l* in Jerusalem .... Zech 12:11
and made loud *l* over him ....Acts 8:2

LAMP
Indeed, you are my *l*.............2 Sam 22:29
Yes, the *l* of the wicked............. Job 18:5
l of the wicked extinguished.......Job 21:17
Indeed, you light my *l* ....Ps 18:28
Your word is a *l* to walk by .... Ps 119:105
the *l* of the wicked goes out ....Prov 13:9
his *l* will be extinguished ....Prov 20:20
light a *l* and put it under ....Matt 5:15
The eye is the *l* of the body....... Matt 6:22
lights a *l* and then covers it....... Luke 8:16
the light of a *l* shines on you...... Luke 11:36
does not light a *l*..................Luke 15:8
l that was burning and shining.....John 5:35
a *l* will never shine in you..........Rev 18:23
and its *l* is the Lamb ....Rev 21:23
will not need the light of a *l* .... Rev 22:5

LAMPS
He made its seven *l* ....Exod 37:23
through Jerusalem with *l* ....Zeph 1:12
woke up and trimmed their *l* ..... Matt 25:7

LAMPSTAND
three branches of the *l* ....Exod 25:32
under a basket but on a *l* ....Matt 5:15
which contained the *l* ....Heb 9:2
remove your *l* from its place ....Rev 2:5

LAND
See also DISTANT LAND; LAND OF THE
    LIVING
God called the dry ground "*l* ....Gen 1:10
and lived in the *l* of Nod ....Gen 4:16
to the *l* that I will show you. ....Gen 12:1
descendants I will give this *l* ....Gen 12:7
There was a famine in the *l* ....Gen 12:10
Is not the whole *l* before you ....Gen 13:9
and walk throughout the *l* ....Gen 13:17
your descendants I give this *l* ....Gen 15:18
Now leave this *l* immediately ....Gen 31:13
give you the best *l* in Egypt ....Gen 45:18
may live in the *l* of Goshen ....Gen 46:34
foreigner in a foreign *l* ....Exod 2:22
to bring them up from that *l* ....Exod 3:8
to the *l* of the Canaanites. ....Exod 3:17
to give them the *l* of Canaan. ......Exod 6:4
pass through the *l* of Egypt ....Exod 12:12
he made the sea into dry *l* ....Exod 14:21
the *l* has become unclean ....Lev 18:25
The *l* must not be sold. ....Lev 25:23
I will grant peace in the *l* ....Lev 26:6
Any tithe of the *l* ....Lev 27:30
to investigate the *l* of Canaan. .....Num 13:17
the evil report about the *l* ....Num 14:37
l is subdued before the LORD ....Num 32:22
the good *l* that he promised ......Deut 6:18
a *l* of wheat, barley, vines. ....Deut 8:8
bless you in the *l* he is giving ....Deut 28:8
Lead these people into the *l* ....Josh 1:2
begin the conquest of the *l* ....Josh 1:11
here tonight to spy on the *l* ....Josh 2:2
Joshua conquered the whole *l* .....Josh 11:23
the *l* among the Israelites ....Josh 18:10
assigned *l* included Zorah ....Josh 19:41
they finished dividing up the *l* .....Josh 19:51
The *l* had rest for 40 years ....Judg 8:28
to return to the *l* of Judah ....Ruth 1:7
is selling the portion of *l*. ....Ruth 4:3
and magicians from the *l* ....1 Sam 28:9
in the plot of *l* at Jezreel ....2 Kgs 9:37
received a beautiful tract of *l* .....Ps 16:6
favor in the *l* of the living. ....Ps 27:13
Settle in the *l* and maintain. ....Ps 37:3
picked out for us a special *l* ....Ps 47:4
He turned the sea into dry *l* ....Ps 66:6
in the *l* of oblivion ....Ps 88:12
l was polluted by bloodshed. ....Ps 106:38
a dry *l* into springs of water ....Ps 107:35
thirsts for you in a parched *l* ......Ps 143:6
is good news from a distant *l* .... Prov 25:25
have appeared in the *l* ....Song 2:12
the produce of the *l* ....Isa 4:2
you will see a wide *l* ....Isa 33:17
to a *l* just like your own. ....Isa 36:17
rejoice over the *l* they receive .....Isa 61:7
your *l* will no longer be called .....Isa 62:4
I brought you into a fertile *l* ......Jer 2:7
trample all over my chosen *l* ......Jer 12:10
O *L*, *l*, *l* of Judah. ....Jer 22:29
tree in the middle of the *l* ....Dan 4:10
in the *l* of Judah. ....Matt 2:6
those who were owners of *l* ......Acts 4:34
proceeds from the sale of the *l* ....Acts 5:3
the sea and his left on the *l* .....Rev 10:2

LAND OF THE LIVING
cannot be found in the *l* ....Job 28:13
the LORD's favor in the *l* ....Ps 27:13
uproot you from the *l* ....Ps 52:5
serve the LORD in the *l* ....Ps 116:9
my security in the *l* ....Ps 142:5
longer see the LORD in the *l* ....Isa 38:11

was cut off from the *l* ....Isa 53:8
or stand in the *l*. ....Ezek 26:20

LANDS
scatter them among foreign *l* .....Ps 106:27

LANGUAGE
whole earth had a common *l* .... Gen 11:1
go down and confuse their *l* ....Gen 11:7
whose *l* you do not comprehend ...Isa 33:19
them speaking in his own *l* ....Acts 2:6
abusive *l* from your mouth ....Col 3:8
nation, tribe, *l*, and people. ....Rev 14:6

LANGUAGES
according to their *l* ....Gen 10:20
they will speak in new *l*. ....Mark 16:17
them speaking in our own *l*. ....Acts 2:11
many kinds of *l* in the world. ......1 Cor 14:10
peoples, nations, *l*, and kings ..... Rev 10:11

LANGUISHES
has dried up; the fig tree *l* ....Joel 1:12

LAODICEA
Paul's concern for, Col 2:1; 4:12–16
Site of one of the seven churches, Rev 1:11
Letter to, Rev 3:14–22

LARGE
I will build myself a *l* palace ....Jer 22:14
and a *l* crowd followed ....Mark 5:24
the *l* crowd was listening ....Mark 12:37
Then I saw a *l* white throne. ....Rev 20:11

LASH
Is it legal for you to *l* a man. ....Acts 22:25

LAST
See also FIRST AND THE LAST; LAST DAY;
    LAST DAYS
You will not *l* long there ....Deut 4:26
that as the *l* he will stand. ....Job 19:25
am the first and I am the *l*. ....Isa 44:6
So the *l* will be first. ....Matt 20:16
and breathed his *l* ....Mark 15:37
some are *l* who will be first. ......Luke 13:30
On the *l* day of the feast. ....John 7:37
And in the *l* days it will be ....Acts 2:17
The *l* enemy to be eliminated ... 1 Cor 15:26
at the *l* trumpet ....1 Cor 15:52
in these *l* days he has spoken. ....Heb 1:2
Children, it is the *l* hour. ....1 John 2:18

LAST DAY
but raise them up at the *l*. ....John 6:39
in the resurrection at the *l*. ....John 11:24
will judge him at the *l* ....John 12:48

LAST DAYS
And in the *l* it will be. ....Acts 2:17
l difficult times will come. ....2 Tim 3:1
in these *l* he has spoken ....Heb 1:2
the *l* that you have hoarded ....Jas 5:3
l blatant scoffers will come. ....2 Pet 3:3

LASTING
to Israel as a *l* promise ....Ps 105:10
I will give you *l* peace. ....Jer 14:13
had a better and *l* possession. .....Heb 10:34
For here we have no *l* city ....Heb 13:14

LATE
to rise early, come home *l* ....Ps 127:2

LATER
but you will follow *l* ....John 13:36
the *l* times some will desert ....1 Tim 4:1
they show up *l* ....1 Tim 5:24

LATIN
in Aramaic, *L*, and Greek ....John 19:20

LATTICE
through my window *l*. ....Prov 7:6
peering through the *l*. ....Song 2:9

LAUGH
Why did Sarah *l* and say ....Gen 18:13
God has made me *l*. ....Gen 21:6
and a time to *l* ....Eccl 3:4
mock kings and *l* at rulers ....Hab 1:10
Woe to you who *l* now ....Luke 6:25

LAUGHED
At that time we *l* loudly ....Ps 126:2
and she *l* at the time to come. .....Prov 31:25

LAUGHING
At whom are you *l*. ....Isa 57:4

LAUGHINGSTOCK
I am a *l* to my friends. ....Job 12:4
I have become a constant *l* ....Jer 20:7

LAUGHS
it *l* at the rattling of the lance. ......Job 41:29
in heaven *l* in disgust ....Ps 2:4

LAUGHTER
Turn your *l* into mourning. ....Jas 4:9

LAUNDERER
than any *l* in the world. ....Mark 9:3

LAVISHED
and love be *l* on you ....Jude 1:2

LAW
See also ACCORDING TO THE LAW; BOOK
    OF THE LAW; EXPERTS IN THE LAW;
    LAW AND PROPHETS; LAW OF MOSES;
    LAW OF THE LORD; UNDER THE LAW;
    WORKS OF THE LAW
a duplicate of the *l*. ....Josh 8:32
The *l* of the LORD is perfect. ....Ps 19:7
The *l* of their God controls .... Ps 37:31
condemned in a court of *l* ....Ps 37:33
but I find delight in your *l*. ....Ps 119:70
The *l* you have revealed ....Ps 119:72
For I find delight in your *l*. ....Ps 119:77
O how I love your *l* ....Ps 119:97
and your *l* is reliable. ....Ps 119:142
but the one who keeps the *l*. ......Prov 29:18
who are aware of my *l*. ....Isa 51:7
not reject the *l* of their God ....Isa 58:2
your companion and wife by *l* ....Mal 2:14
have come to abolish the *l*. ....Matt 5:17
fulfills the *l* and the prophets. ......Matt 7:12
not like their experts in the *l* ..... Matt 7:29
Then an expert in the *l* came .....Matt 8:19
prophets and the *l* prophesied. ....Matt 11:13
are doing what is against the *l*. ....Matt 12:2
All the *l* and the prophets ....Matt 22:40
expert in the *l* said to him ....Mark 12:32
the experts in the *l* ....Mark 12:38
and the experts in the *l*. ....Mark 14:1
the experts in religious *l* ....Luke 7:30
you experts in religious *l* ....Luke 11:46
tiny stroke of a letter in the *l*. ....Luke 16:17
l was given through Moses ....John 1:17
Our *l* doesn't condemn a man .....John 7:51
a teacher of the *l* who was. ....Acts 5:34
all ardent observers of the *l* .....Acts 21:20
devout man according to the *l*. ....Acts 22:12
judging me according to the *l*. .....Acts 23:3
by the works of the *l* ....Rom 3:20
For the *l* brings wrath ....Rom 4:15
for before the *l* was given ....Rom 5:13
because you are not under *l*. ......Rom 6:14
you also died to the *l*. ....Rom 7:4
Is the *l* sin. ....Rom 7:7
we know that the *l* is spiritual .....Rom 7:14
But I see a different *l* ....Rom 7:23
the *l* of the life-giving Spirit ....Rom 8:2
what the *l* could not do. ....Rom 8:3
is the expert in the Mosaic *l*. ...... 1 Cor 1:20
To those free from the *l* ....1 Cor 9:21
and the power of sin is the *l*. ......1 Cor 15:56
I am one who breaks God's *l* ......Gal 2:18
through the *l* I died to the *l* ....Gal 2:19
by doing the works of the *l* ....Gal 3:2
held in custody under the *l* ....Gal 3:23
l had become our guardian. ....Gal 3:24
born under the *l*. ....Gal 4:4
the whole *l* can be summed up .....Gal 5:14
you will fulfill the *l* of Christ. ....Gal 6:2
I lived according to the *l* ....Phil 3:5
want to be teachers of the *l* ....1 Tim 1:7
realizing that *l* is not intended. .....1 Tim 1:9
and fights about the *l*. ....Titus 3:9

into the perfect *l* of liberty ....Jas 1:25
But if you fulfill the royal *l* ....Jas 2:8

LAW AND THE PROPHETS
for this fulfills the *l* ....Matt 7:12
All the *l* depend on these.......Matt 22:40
The *l* were in force.................Luke 16:16
After reading from the *l* ....Acts 13:15
it is attested by the *l*..............Rom 3:21

LAW OF MOSES
and laws as written in the *l* ....1 Kgs 2:3
recorded in the scroll of the *l*....2 Kgs 14:6
outlined in the *l*.................2 Chr 30:16
who was skilled in the *l*..........Ezra 7:6
to bring the book of the *l*...........Neh 8:1
threatened in the *l*................Dan 9:11
could not obey the *l*.............Zech 7:12
according to the *l*................Luke 2:22
written about me in the *l*.....Luke 24:44
so that the *l* is not broken.........John 7:23
the *l* could not justify you ....Acts 13:39
order them to observe the *l*......Acts 15:5
Someone who rejected the *l*.....Heb 10:28

LAW OF THE LORD
the *l* may be in your mouth.......Exod 13:9
wholeheartedly obey the *l*....2 Kgs 10:31
you may obey the *l* ....1 Chr 22:12
Israel rejected the *l*..............2 Chr 12:1
might be obedient to the *l*.......2 Chr 31:4
to the study of the *l* ....Ezra 7:10
The *l* is perfect ....Ps 19:7
who obey the *l*.....................Ps 119:1
they have rejected the *l* ....Isa 5:24
We are wise! We have the *l*.........Jer 8:8
just as it is written in the *l* ....Luke 2:23
everything according to the *l*.....Luke 2:39

LAWBREAKERS
Go away from me, you *l* ....Matt 7:23

LAWFUL
All things are *l* for me ....1 Cor 6:12

LAWGIVER
only one who is *l* and judge.........Jas 4:12

LAWLESS
the *l* deeds he saw and heard......2 Pet 2:8

LAWLESSNESS
and the man of *l* is revealed .....2 Thess 2:3
For the hidden power of *l* ....2 Thess 2:7
set us free from every kind of *l*... Titus 2:14
loved righteousness and hated *l*.....Heb 1:9
practices sin also practices *l*......1 John 3:4

LAWS
know the *l* of the heavens ....Job 38:33
have established the fixed *l*........Jer 33:25

LAY
has no place to *l* his head.........Matt 8:20
l it down of my own free will .....John 10:18
not *l* hands on anyone hastily ....1 Tim 5:22
I *l* in Zion a stone ....1 Pet 2:6

LAYING
the *l* on of the apostles' hands.....Acts 8:18
through the *l* on of my hands......2 Tim 1:6
not *l* this foundation again...........Heb 6:1
l on of hands.......................Heb 6:2

LAYS
l the beams of the upper rooms....Ps 104:3
l the foundations of the earth .....Zech 12:1

LAZARUS
Beggar described in a parable,
    Luke 16:20–25
—Brother of Mary and Martha; raised from
    the dead, John 11:1–44
Attends a supper, John 12:1–2
Jews seek to kill, John 12:9–11

LAZINESS
L brings on a deep sleep.........Prov 19:15
Because of *l* the roof caves in ....Eccl 10:18

LAZY
one who is *l* becomes poor.......Prov 10:4
Evil and *l* slave.................Matt 25:26

they learn to be *l* ....1 Tim 5:13
liars, evil beasts, *l* gluttons.........Titus 1:12

LEAD
to *l* them in the way ....Exod 13:21
They sank like *l*.................Exod 15:10
you will *l* me into a wide.............Ps 4:1
l me along a level path ....Ps 27:11
you *l* me and guide me ....Ps 31:3
L me up to a rocky summit.........Ps 61:2
l Egypt astray in all she does ....Isa 19:14
and *l* in the furnace.............Ezek 22:18
and *l* for your products..........Ezek 27:12
and placed the *l* cover on top......Zech 5:8
do not *l* us into temptation.......Matt 6:13
who is blind cannot *l* ....Luke 6:39
do not *l* us into temptation.......Luke 11:4
seeking people to *l* him...........Acts 13:11
to aspire to *l* a quiet life ....1 Thess 4:11
l a peaceful and quiet life ....1 Tim 2:2
their passions may *l* them away ...1 Tim 5:11
to *l* them out of Egypt ....Heb 8:9
and *l* them to springs..............Rev 7:17

LEADER
the LORD has chosen you as *l*.....1 Sam 10:1
to make you *l* of my people ......2 Sam 7:8
God is with us as our *l* ....2 Chr 13:12
your wise *l* been destroyed.........Mic 4:9
right hand as *L* and Savior ....Acts 5:31

LEADERS
The LORD raised up *l* ....Judg 2:16
LORD raised up *l* for them ....Judg 2:18
the place where the *l* preside......Ps 107:32
l and the highly respected ....Isa 9:15
the earth's *l* insignificant ....Isa 40:23
give you *l* who will be faithful ....Jer 3:15
l who are ruling over his people .....Jer 23:2
The Jewish *l* picked up rocks .....John 10:31
l among the brothers.............Acts 15:22
Remember your *l*...................Heb 13:7

LEADING
l to more lawlessness..............Rom 6:19

LEADS
he *l* me to refreshing water..........Ps 23:2
He *l* me down the right paths ....Ps 23:3
as a small child *l* them along ....Isa 11:6
blind *l* another who is blind ......Matt 15:14
sheep by name and *l* them out ....John 10:3
kindness *l* you to repentance.......Rom 2:4
to God who always *l* us ....2 Cor 2:14

LEAF
plucked olive *l* in its beak...........Gen 8:11
to torment a windblown *l* ....Job 13:25

LEAH
Laban's eldest daughter; given to Jacob
    deceitfully, Gen 29:16–27
Unloved by Jacob, but bears children,
    Gen 29:30–35; 30:16–21

LEAN
The *l*, bad-looking cows ....Gen 41:20

LEAP
the lame will *l* like a deer...........Isa 35:6

LEAPED
the baby *l* in her womb...........Luke 1:41

LEAPING
l and dancing before the LORD ..2 Sam 6:16
killed by the *l* flames ....Dan 3:22
walking and *l* and praising.........Acts 3:8

LEARN
l to fear the LORD your God ......Deut 31:13
during the night *l* reflect and ....Ps 16:7
so that I might *l* your statutes ......Ps 119:71
l wisdom and moral instruction ....Prov 1:2
lest you *l* his ways ....Prov 22:25
L to do what is right ....Isa 1:17
yoke on you and *l* from me........Matt 11:29
For I did not receive it or *l* it.........Gal 1:12
did not *l* about Christ like this .....Eph 4:20
A woman must *l* quietly ....1 Tim 2:11

can *l* to engage in good works.....Titus 3:14
No one was able to *l* the song .....Rev 14:3

LEARNED
When he *l* of this ....Mark 8:17
l obedience through the things......Heb 5:8
l the so-called "deep secrets"........Rev 2:24

LEARNING
great *l* is driving you insane ..... Acts 26:24

LEARNS
Everyone who hears and *l*........John 6:45

LEAST
in no way *l* among the rulers ...... Matt 2:6
one of the *l* of these commands...Matt 5:19
For I am the *l* of the apostles ......1 Cor 15:9

LEATHER
a *l* belt tied around his waist.......2 Kgs 1:8
put fine *l* sandals on your feet....Ezek 16:10
I drew them with *l* cords...........Hos 11:4
with a *l* belt around his waist......Mark 1:6

LEAVE
not let mercy and truth *l* you.......Prov 3:3
the earth and *l* it in ruins ....Isa 24:1
I will never *l* you.....................Heb 13:5

LEAVES
a man *l* his father and mother .....Gen 2:24
so they sewed fig *l* together ....Gen 3:7
while my strength *l* me.............Ps 77:3
My strength *l* me ....Ps 143:4
who *l* the husband................Prov 2:17
Its *l* are always green ....Jer 17:8
found nothing on it except *l* ......Matt 21:19
Its *l* are for the healing ....Rev 22:2

LEBANON
Part of Israel's inheritance, Josh 13:5–7
Not completely conquered, Judg 3:1–3
Source of materials for temple, 1 Kgs 5:2–18;
    Ezra 3:7
Mentioned in prophecy, Isa 10:34; 29:17;
    35:2; Ezek 17:3; Hos 14:5–7

LEBONAH
Town north of Shiloh, Judg 21:19

LED
l you through the wilderness .....Deut 29:5
empowered him and he *l* Israel....Judg 3:10
So Samuel *l* Israel...............1 Sam 7:15
He *l* them on a level road..........Ps 107:7
lamb *l* to the slaughtering block.....Isa 53:7
you will be *l* along in peace........Isa 55:12
and *l* my people Israel astray.......Jer 23:13
they have *l* my people astray.....Ezek 13:10
Jesus was *l* by the Spirit ....Matt 4:1
they *l* him away to crucify him ..Mark 15:20
Then the devil *l* him up.............Luke 4:5
was *l* like a sheep to slaughter.....Acts 8:32
For all who are *l* by the Spirit......Rom 8:14
But if you are *l* by the Spirit ....Gal 5:18

LEFT
Abraham *l* to his son Isaac.........Gen 25:5
from the time you *l* the land.......Deut 9:7
When the servant had *l*.........1 Sam 20:41
have *l* in Israel 7,000 followers ...1 Kgs 19:18
lie on your *l* side...................Ezek 4:4
If ten men are *l* in one house ..... Amos 6:9
people who are *l* will plunder .....Zeph 2:9
do not let your *l* hand know.......Matt 6:3
have *l* everything to follow you...Matt 19:27
And whoever has *l* houses.......Matt 19:29
all the disciples *l* him and fled ...Matt 26:56
sit at my right or at my *l* ......Mark 10:40
the right hand and for the *l*......2 Cor 6:7
l until the coming of the Lord ...1 Thess 4:15
By faith he *l* Egypt.................Heb 11:27

LEGION
My name is *L* ....Mark 5:9
L," because many demons........Luke 8:30

LEGIONS
more than twelve *l* of angels ....Matt 26:53

LEGITIMATE
He is *l* and victorious .... Zech 9:9

LEGS
Like *l* dangle uselessly........... Prov 26:7
His *l* are like pillars of marble .....Song 5:15
they did not break his *l* ....John 19:33

LEHI
Samson kills Philistines at, Judg 15:9–19

LEMUEL
King taught by his mother, Prov 31:1–31

LEND
l money to any of my people ....Exod 22:25
l him whatever he needs ....Deut 15:8
they show compassion and *l*........Ps 37:26
L your aid and come................ Joel 3:11
And if you *l* to those.............. Luke 6:34
l me three loaves of bread........ Luke 11:5

LENDER
borrower is servant to the *l* ......Prov 22:7
the borrower as well as the *l* .... Isa 24:2

LENDING
are *l* them money and grain .... Neh 5:10

LENDS
who is gracious to the poor *l* ..... Prov 19:17

LENGTH
l of years should make wisdom..... Job 32:7
its *l* and width the same .... Rev 21:16

LEOPARD
and a *l* will lie down .... Isa 11:6
Can a *l* remove its spots ....Jer 13:23

LEPER
expel from the camp every *l* ...... Num 5:2
a *l* approached and bowed .... Matt 8:2
at the house of Simon the *l*....... Mark 14:3

LEPERS
cleanse *l*, cast out demons........ Matt 10:8
there were many *l* in Israel .... Luke 4:27

LEPROSY
immediately the *l* left him........Luke 5:13
ten men with *l* met him...........Luke 17:12

LEPROUS
l like snow...................... Exod 4:6
l like snow.....................Num 12:10

LESHEM
See LAISH

LESSEN
L the demands your father ....1 Kgs 12:9

LET
L there be light ....Gen 1:3
L me go there ....Gen 19:20
then *l* my brother Amnon go... 2 Sam 13:26
L the little children come........Matt 19:14
He will not *l* you be tried ....1 Cor 10:13

LETHAL
the *l* wound had been healed....... Rev 13:3

LETTER
the smallest *l* or stroke of a *l*......Matt 5:18
they delivered the *l*................Acts 15:30
by the Spirit and not by the *l* ..... Rom 2:29
You yourselves are our *l*............ 2 Cor 3:2
that you are a *l* of Christ........... 2 Cor 3:3
covenant not based on the *l*....... 2 Cor 3:6
if I made you sad by my *l* .... 2 Cor 7:8
message or *l* allegedly from us ..2 Thess 2:2
whether by speech or by *l* ..... 2 Thess 2:15
our message through this *l* ..... 2 Thess 3:14
is how I write in every *l* .... 2 Thess 3:17

LETTERS
need *l* of recommendation .... 2 Cor 3:1
His *l* are weighty and forceful ...2 Cor 10:10
See what big *l* I make..............Gal 6:11
of these things in all his *l* .... 2 Pet 3:16

LEVEL
He led them on a *l* road ....Ps 107:7
lead me into a *l* land...............Ps 143:10
The way of the righteous is *l* ....Isa 26:7

LEVI
Third son of Jacob and Leah, Gen 29:34
Avenges rape of Dinah, Gen 34:25–31
Jacob's prophecy concerning, Gen 49:5–7
Ancestor of Moses and Aaron, Exod 6:16–27
—One of the Twelve: *see* MATTHEW

LEVIATHAN
Can you pull in *L* with a hook.......Job 41:1

LEVITE
your brother Aaron the *L*......... Exod 4:14
So too a *L*, when he came up .... Luke 10:32
L who was a native of Cyprus......Acts 4:36

LEVITES
and will cleanse the *L*................Mal 3:3

LEVITES
Rewarded for dedication, Exod 32:26–29
Appointed over tabernacle, Num 1:47–54
Substituted for Israel's firstborn,
    Num 3:12–45
Consecrated to the Lord's service,
    Num 8:5–26
Cities assigned to, Num 35:2–8; Josh 14:3–4;
    1 Chr 6:54–81
Organized for temple service, 1 Chr 9:14–34;
    23:1–26:28

LEVITICAL
through the *L* priesthood........... Heb 7:11

LEWDNESS
and become full of *l* ....Lev 19:29
so there is no *l* in your midst .....Lev 20:14

LIABILITIES
I now regard all things as *l*..........Phil 3:8

LIAR
l listens to a malicious tongue.....Prov 17:4
he is a *l* and the father of lies ..... John 8:44
human being shown up as a *l*.......Rom 3:4
we make him a *l*...................1 John 1:10
Who is the *l* but the person...... 1 John 2:22
he is a *l* because the one who ...1 John 4:20
God has made him a *l* .... 1 John 5:10

LIARS
You destroy *l* .... Ps 5:6
All men are *l*...................... Ps 116:11
the offspring of *l*.................. Isa 57:4
by the hypocrisy of *l*..............1 Tim 4:2
Cretans are always *l*..............Titus 1:12

LIBERTY
into the perfect law of *l*..............Jas 1:25

LIBNAH
Canaanite city, captured by Joshua,
    Josh 10:29–30
Given to Aaron's descendants, Josh 21:13

LIBYA
Mentioned in prophecy, Ezek 30:5;
    Dan 11:43
Jews from, present at Pentecost, Acts 2:1–10

LID
an atonement *l* of pure gold..... Exod 25:17

LIE
that he should *l*................... Num 23:19
Go back and *l* down ....1 Sam 3:9
I will *l* down in the dust............. Job 7:21
People *l* to one another .... Ps 12:2
who does not *l*.....................Ps 24:4
and a leopard will *l* down........... Isa 11:6
they swear to is really a *l* ....Jer 5:2
you *l* in the name of the LORD.....Zech 13:3
Satan filled your heart to *l*.........Acts 5:3
Do not *l* to one another ....Col 3:9
who does not *l*....................Titus 1:2
and that no *l* is of the truth ....1 John 2:21
no *l* was found on their lips......Rev 14:5
and all those who *l* ....Rev 21:8

LIED
not *l* to people but to God........Acts 5:4

LIES
you must not tell *l*................Lev 19:11
and gives birth to harmful *l* ....Ps 7:14

l in ambush in a hidden place........Ps 10:9
mouths of those who speak *l*........Ps 63:11
smear my reputation with *l*........Ps 119:69
LORD abhors a person who *l*....Prov 12:22
the one who spouts out *l*........Prov 19:5
she *l* in wait like a robber........Prov 23:28
prophets are prophesying *l*........Jer 14:14
They are prophesying *l* to you......Jer 29:9
who are prophesying *l* to you ......Jer 29:21
will trade *l* with one another ......Dan 11:27
do not boast and tell *l*..............Jas 3:14
l in the power of the evil one.....1 John 5:19

LIFE
See also ALL THE DAYS OF HIS LIFE; BOOK
    OF LIFE; BREATH OF LIFE; ETERNAL
    LIFE; TREE OF LIFE; WATER OF LIFE
into his nostrils the breath of *l* ..... Gen 2:7
the tree of *l* and the tree of......... Gen 2:9
the breath of *l* in its nostrils ...... Gen 7:22
then you will give a *l* for a *l* ...... Exod 21:23
you know the *l* of a foreigner...... Exod 23:9
for the *l* of every living thing .... Lev 17:11
set before you today *l* and....... Deut 30:15
I kill and give *l* .... Deut 32:39
as much as he did his own *l*....... 1 Sam 18:1
You gave me *l* and favor........... Job 10:12
is the *l* of every creature.......... Job 12:10
when God takes away his *l* .... Job 27:8
enlightened with the light of *l* .....Job 33:30
Whoever lives a blameless *l* ...... Ps 15:2
my *l* is safe .... Ps 16:9
and preserves one's *l*.............. Ps 19:7
and give insight for *l*............... Ps 19:8
Into your hand I entrust my *l*........ Ps 31:5
love to live a long, happy *l*........ Ps 34:12
might serve God as I enjoy *l* ..... Ps 56:13
will be available—eternal *l* ...... Ps 133:3
is concerned about my *l* .... Ps 142:4
will they reach the paths of *l* ......Prov 2:19
She is like a tree of *l*.................Prov 3:18
will become *l* for your soul .....Prov 3:22
does it destroys his own *l*......... Prov 6:32
who finds me has found *l*........ Prov 8:35
Fearing the LORD prolongs *l*......Prov 10:27
cares for the *l* of his animal.......Prov 12:10
The path of *l* is upward ....Prov 15:24
preserves the *l* of its owner ....Eccl 7:12
Enjoy *l* with your beloved wife ..... Eccl 9:9
and the prime of *l* are fleeting..... Eccl 11:10
One will result in *l*.................Jer 21:8
You will escape with your *l*........Jer 39:18
do not worry about your *l* ...... Matt 6:25
can add even one hour to his *l*.... Matt 6:27
world but forfeits his *l*........... Matt 16:26
one's *l* does not consist..........Luke 12:15
there is more to *l* than food .....Luke 12:23
can add an hour to his *l*........ Luke 12:25
In him was *l*....................... John 1:4
raises the dead and gives them *l* ... John 5:21
as the Father has *l* in himself ......John 5:26
Spirit is the one who gives *l* ......John 6:63
but will have the light of *l* ....John 8:12
lay down my *l* for the sheep...... John 10:15
I am the resurrection and the *l* ... John 11:25
you lay down your *l* for me......John 13:38
in the new *l* of the Spirit ....Rom 7:6
remain in that situation in *l*.......1 Cor 7:20
so that the *l* of Jesus..............2 Cor 4:10
the *l* I now live in the body ....Gal 2:20
your *l* is hidden with Christ.......... Col 3:3
to aspire to lead a quiet *l* ....1 Thess 4:11
God who gives *l* to all things....1 Tim 6:13
and receive *l*...................... Heb 12:9
What is your *l* like ....Jas 4:14
from your empty way of *l* ...... 1 Pet 1:18
necessary for *l* and godliness.......2 Pet 1:3
and the *l* was revealed............1 John 1:2
God has given us eternal *l*........1 John 5:11
has the Son has this eternal *l*.....1 John 5:12
was empowered to give *l* .... Rev 13:15
They came to *l* and reigned....... Rev 20:4
of the dead did not come to *l*...... Rev 20:5
written in the Lamb's book of *l*....Rev 21:27

have access to the tree of *l* . . . . Rev 22:14
the water of *l* free of charge . . . . Rev 22:17
away his share in the tree of *l* . . . . Rev 22:19

LIFE-GIVING
fear of the LORD is like a *l* . . . . Prov 14:27

LIFEBLOOD
For your *l l* I will surely exact . . . . Gen 9:5

LIFESPAN
Take note of my brief *l* . . . . Ps 89:47

LIFESTYLE
and maintained a pure *l* . . . . Ps 73:13
wicked need to abandon their *l* . . . . . Isa 55:7
an end to her adulterous *l* . . . . Hos 2:2

LIFESTYLES
will follow their debauched *l* . . . . . . 2 Pet 2:2

LIFT
LORD *l* up his countenance . . . . Num 6:26
I will *l* up my hands . . . . Ps 63:4
L a signal flag for the nations . . . . . . Isa 62:10

LIFTED
they *l* the ark and raised it . . . . Gen 7:17
for you *l* me up . . . . Ps 30:1
he *l* them up and carried them . . . . . Isa 63:9

LIFTS
The LORD *l* up the oppressed . . . . Ps 147:6

LIGAMENT
through every supporting *l* . . . . Eph 4:16

LIGAMENTS
through its *l* and sinews . . . . Col 2:19

LIGHT
Let there be *l* . . . . Gen 1:3
God called the *l* "day . . . . Gen 1:5
Israelites had *l* in the places . . . . . Exod 10:23
a pillar of fire to give them *l* . . . . . Exod 13:21
oil of pressed olives for the *l* . . . . Exod 27:20
is like the *l* of morning . . . . 2 Sam 23:4
l will shine on your ways . . . . Job 22:28
the wicked the *l* is withheld . . . . Job 38:15
In what direction does *l* reside . . . . . Job 38:19
Indeed, you *l* my lamp . . . . Ps 18:28
LORD is my *l* and my salvation . . . . Ps 27:1
Reveal your *l* and your . . . . Ps 43:3
The godly bask in the *l* . . . . Ps 97:11
and a *l* to illumine my path . . . . Ps 119:105
The *l* of the righteous shines . . . . . . Prov 13:9
The LORD gives *l* to the eyes . . . . . . Prov 29:13
L is sweet . . . . Eccl 11:7
walk in the LORD's guiding *l* . . . . Isa 2:5
will turn the *l* into darkness . . . . Isa 5:30
The *l* of the full moon . . . . Isa 30:26
darkness in front of them into *l* . . . Isa 42:16
Then your *l* will shine . . . . Isa 58:8
For your *l* arrives . . . . Isa 60:1
Nations come to your *l* . . . . Isa 60:3
your permanent source of *l* . . . . Isa 60:20
fixed the sun to give *l* by day . . . . . . Jer 31:35
gloomy blackness, not bright *l* . . Amos 5:20
have seen a great *l* . . . . Matt 4:16
You are the *l* of the world . . . . Matt 5:14
let your *l* shine before people . . . . . Matt 5:16
whole body will be full of *l* . . . . Matt 6:22
the moon will not give its *l* . . . . . . Matt 24:29
the *l* in you is not darkness . . . . Luke 11:35
than the people of *l* . . . . Luke 16:8
the life was the *l* of mankind . . . . . . John 1:4
The true *l*, who gives *l* . . . . John 1:9
the *l* has come into the world . . . . . John 3:19
does evil deeds hates the *l* . . . . John 3:20
practices the truth comes to
    the *l* . . . . John 3:21
I am the *l* of the world . . . . John 8:12
While you have the *l* . . . . John 12:36
come as a *l* into the world . . . . John 12:46
bring to *l* the hidden things . . . . 1 Cor 4:5
Let *l* shine out of darkness . . . . 2 Cor 4:6
but now you are *l* in the Lord . . . . . . Eph 5:8
you all are sons of the *l* . . . . 1 Thess 5:5
to *l* through the gospel . . . . 2 Tim 1:10
into his marvelous *l* . . . . 1 Pet 2:9

a *l* shining in a murky place . . . . 2 Pet 1:19
God is *l* . . . . 1 John 1:5
But if we walk in the *l* . . . . 1 John 1:7
one who says he is in the *l* . . . . 1 John 2:9
And there was no *l* . . . . Rev 8:12
Even the *l* from a lamp . . . . Rev 18:23
will not need the *l* of a lamp . . . . . . Rev 22:5

LIGHTNING
thunder and *l* and a dense cloud . . Exod 19:16
there was *l* in their land . . . . Ps 105:32
like the *l* comes from the east . . . Matt 24:27
His appearance was like *l* . . . . Matt 28:3
Satan fall like *l* from heaven . . . . . Luke 10:18
came out flashes of *l* . . . . Rev 4:5

LIGHTS
Let there be *l* in the expanse . . . . . . Gen 1:14
one who made the great *l* . . . . Ps 136:7
shine as *l* in the world . . . . Phil 2:15
down from the Father of *l* . . . . Jas 1:17
the glory of God *l* it up . . . . Rev 21:23

LIKE
Who is *l* you . . . . Exod 15:11
it is you, a man *l* me . . . . Ps 55:13
the nations that *l* to do battle . . . . . Ps 68:30
L a lily among the thorns . . . . Song 2:2
gleamed *l* polished bronze . . . . Ezek 1:7
human natures just *l* you . . . . Acts 14:15
by looking *l* other men . . . . Phil 2:7
there is no one here *l* him . . . . Phil 2:20
made *l* his brothers and sisters . . . . Heb 2:17
Elijah was a human being *l* us . . . . . . Jas 5:17

LIKED
Saul's son Jonathan *l* David . . . . . . 1 Sam 19:1

LIKEN
To what image can you *l* him . . . . . . Isa 40:18

LIKENESS
in our image, after our *l* . . . . Gen 1:26
l of anything that is in heaven . . . . Exod 20:4
with him in the *l* of his death . . . . . . Rom 6:5
own Son in the *l* of sinful flesh . . . . . Rom 8:3
into the *l* of his glorious body . . . . . Phil 3:21

LILIES
pillars were shaped like *l* . . . . 1 Kgs 7:22
l dripping with drops of myrrh . . . Song 5:13
he grazes among the *l* . . . . Song 6:3

LILY
a *l* from the valleys . . . . Song 2:1
Like a *l* among the thorns . . . . Song 2:2
rejoice and bloom like a *l* . . . . Isa 35:1
he will blossom like a *l* . . . . Hos 14:5

LIMESTONE
of the altars like crushed *l* . . . . Isa 27:9

LIMIT
Do you *l* wisdom to yourself . . . . Job 15:8
he imposed a *l* for the rain . . . . Job 28:26

LIMITS
that everything has its *l* . . . . Ps 119:96

LIMP
All their hands will hang *l* . . . . Ezek 7:17

LINE
house and family *l* of David . . . . Luke 2:4

LINEN
clothed him with fine *l* clothes . . . Gen 41:42
They made tunics of fine *l* . . . . Exod 39:27
priest must put on his *l* robe . . . . . . Lev 6:10
He must put on a holy *l* tunic . . . . . . Lev 16:4
and take off the *l* garments . . . . Lev 16:23
boy was dressed in a *l* ephod . . . . . 1 Sam 2:18
David was wrapped in a *l* robe . . . . 1 Chr 15:27
clothing was fine *l* and purple . . . . Prov 31:22
Go and buy some *l* shorts . . . . Jer 13:1
called to the man dressed in *l* . . . . Ezek 9:3
the man clothed in *l* . . . . Dan 12:7
wrapped it in a clean *l* cloth . . . . . Matt 27:59
he wrapped it in the *l* . . . . Mark 15:46
dressed in purple and fine *l* . . . . . Luke 16:19
in strips of *l* cloth . . . . John 19:40
saw the strips of *l* cloth lying . . . . . John 20:5

dressed in fine *l* . . . . Rev 18:16
dressed in bright, clean, fine *l* . . . . Rev 19:8

LINGER
Those who *l* over wine . . . . Prov 23:30

LION
and he tore the *l* in two . . . . Judg 14:6
a *l* or bear would come . . . . 1 Sam 17:34
one who is *l*-hearted . . . . 2 Sam 17:10
and the *l* standing beside it . . . . . . 1 Kgs 13:28
went down and killed a *l* . . . . 1 Chr 11:22
you hunt me as a fierce *l* . . . . Job 10:16
A *l*, like an ox . . . . Isa 11:7
the face of a *l* on the right . . . . Ezek 1:10
the third that of a *l* . . . . Ezek 10:14
I will be like a *l* to Ephraim . . . . Hos 5:14
like a roaring *l* . . . . 1 Pet 5:8
living creature was like a *l* . . . . Rev 4:7
the *L* of the tribe of Judah . . . . Rev 5:5

LION'S
You are a *l* cub . . . . Gen 49:9
a *l* face toward the palm tree . . . . Ezek 41:19

LIONS
were twelve statues of *l* . . . . 1 Kgs 10:20
I am surrounded by *l* . . . . Ps 57:4
be thrown into a den of *l* . . . . Dan 6:7
shut the mouths of *l* . . . . Heb 11:33

LIONS'
of the horses looked like *l* . . . . Rev 9:17

LIPS
scroll must not leave your *l* . . . . Josh 1:8
LORD cut off all flattering *l* . . . . Ps 12:3
May lying *l* be silenced . . . . Ps 31:18
my *l* are contaminated by sin . . . . Isa 6:5
For with mocking *l* . . . . Isa 28:11
may offer the praise of our *l* . . . . . . Hos 14:2
people honors me with their *l* . . . . Mark 7:6
poison of asps is under their *l* . . . . . Rom 3:13
and by the *l* of strangers . . . . 1 Cor 14:21
the fruit of our *l* . . . . Heb 13:15
and his *l* from uttering deceit . . . . . 1 Pet 3:10
no lie was found on their *l* . . . . Rev 14:5

LISTED
their names be *l* with the godly . . . . Ps 69:28

LISTEN
L to this dream I had . . . . Gen 37:6
Now *l* to me . . . . Exod 18:19
speak to us and we will *l* . . . . Exod 20:19
you must *l* to him . . . . Deut 18:15
God refused to *l* to Balaam . . . . Deut 23:5
l from your heavenly dwelling . . . . 1 Kgs 8:43
Don't *l* to Hezekiah . . . . 2 Kgs 18:32
L to me! Hear what I say . . . . Ps 17:6
L to me. Quickly deliver me . . . . Ps 31:2
l attentively to my sayings . . . . Prov 4:20
and *l* to the words of the wise . . . . Prov 22:17
near to *l* rather than to offer . . . . Eccl 5:1
L, O heavens . . . . Isa 1:2
L continually, but don't . . . . Isa 6:9
l to what I have done . . . . Isa 33:13
Come near, you nations, and *l* . . . . . Isa 34:1
L, your watchmen shout . . . . Isa 52:8
L carefully to me . . . . Isa 55:2
I spoke and you did not *l* . . . . Isa 65:12
Who would *l* if I spoke . . . . Jer 6:10
L attentively, my God . . . . Dan 9:18
But if he does not *l* . . . . Matt 18:16
If he refuses to *l* to them . . . . Matt 18:17
L! A sower went out to sow . . . . Mark 4:3
that God doesn't *l* to sinners . . . . . . John 9:31
Why do you *l* to him . . . . John 10:20
My sheep *l* to my voice . . . . John 10:27
you Gentiles who fear God, *l* . . . . . Acts 13:16
Let every person be quick to *l* . . . . . Jas 1:19
and do not merely *l* to it . . . . Jas 1:22
he had better *l* . . . . Rev 13:9

LISTENED
LORD *l* to the voice of Israel . . . . . . Num 21:3
he *l* to me this time as well . . . . . . Deut 9:19
You have not *l* to me . . . . Jer 25:7
who had *l* to the message . . . . Acts 4:4
you should have *l* to me . . . . Acts 27:21

LISTENER
does not become a forgetful *l* ....Jas 1:25

LISTENING
for your servant is *l*. ....1 Sam 3:9

LISTENS
But the one who *l* to me. ....Prov 1:33
one who *l* to advice is wise ....Prov 12:15
The one who *l* to you *l* to me .....Luke 10:16
to the truth *l* to my voice ....John 18:37
merely *l* to the message. ....Jas 1:23
who knows God *l* to us ....1 John 4:6

LISTLESS
strengthen your *l* hands ....Heb 12:12

LITIGATION
Do not go out hastily to *l* ....Prov 25:8

LITTLE
See also LITTLE CHILDREN
one who gathers it *l* by *l*. ....Prov 13:11
the *l* foxes, that ruin ....Song 2:15
We have a *l* sister. ....Song 8:8
but instead there was *l* ....Hag 1:9
I was a *l* displeased with them. .....Zech 1:15
You of *l* faith. ....Matt 14:31
who is forgiven *l* loves *l*. ....Luke 7:47
Let the *l* children come to me ....Luke 18:16
the one who gathered *l*. ....2 Cor 8:15
l yeast makes the whole batch ......Gal 5:9
than the angels for a *l* while .... Heb 2:7
For just a *l* longer. ....Heb 10:37
L children, guard yourselves. .....1 John 5:21
to give me the *l* scroll ....Rev 10:9
that he only has a *l* time. ....Rev 12:12

LITTLE CHILDREN
turn around and become like *l* ....Matt 18:3
Then *l* were brought to him ......Matt 19:13
welcomes one of these *l*. ....Mark 9:37
Let the *l* come to me ....Mark 10:14
My *l*, I am writing. ....1 John 2:1
I am writing to you, *l* ....1 John 2:12
And now, *l*, remain in him ....1 John 2:28
L, let no one deceive you ....1 John 3:7
You are a gift from God, *l*. ....1 John 4:4
L, guard yourselves from idols ...1 John 5:21

LIVE
and eat, and *l* forever. ....Gen 3:22
anyone who does so will *l* ....Lev 18:5
cannot *l* by bread alone ....Deut 8:3
I do not want to *l* forever. ....Job 7:16
Who may *l* on your holy hill ....Ps 15:1
the way they should *l*. ....Ps 25:12
l in the tents of the wicked ....Ps 84:10
so that we might *l* wisely. ....Ps 90:12
in which the herons *l*. ....Ps 104:17
in the house where I *l*. ....Ps 119:54
all who *l* praise his holy name .....Ps 145:21
It is better to *l* on a corner. ....Prov 25:24
who will *l* in a secure place ....Isa 33:16
where the nomads of Kedar *l*. ....Isa 42:11
he will certainly *l* ....Ezek 3:21
and let it *l* with the animals. ....Dan 4:15
Seek me so you can *l* ....Amos 5:4
l because of his faithfulness ....Hab 2:4
Man does not *l* by bread alone ...... Matt 4:4
and they go in and *l* there. ....Matt 12:45
and I *l* because of the Father. ....John 6:57
because I *l*, you will *l* too ....John 14:19
him to *l* until I come back ....John 21:22
and all you who *l* in Jerusalem. .....Acts 2:14
in him we *l* and move about ......Acts 17:28
so we too may *l* a new life ....Rom 6:4
who *l* according to the flesh ....Rom 8:5
l peaceably with all people ....Rom 12:18
us *l* decently as in the daytime ... Rom 13:13
for we *l* by faith. ....2 Cor 5:7
we continue to *l*. ....2 Cor 6:9
I will *l* in them and will walk ....2 Cor 6:16
l like a Gentile and not like ....Gal 2:14
and it is no longer I who *l*. ....Gal 2:20
righteous one will *l* by faith. ....Gal 3:11
l by the Spirit and you will. ....Gal 5:16
If we *l* by the Spirit ....Gal 5:25

and *l* in love ....Eph 5:2
L like children of light ....Eph 5:8
so that you may *l* worthily. ....Col 1:10
continue to *l* your lives in him ......Col 2:6
you used to *l* among them. ....Col 3:7
how you must *l* and please
    God. ....1 Thess 4:1
all who want to *l* godly lives ......2 Tim 3:12
righteous one will *l* by faith. ......Heb 10:38
L as free people ....1 Pet 2:16
they may *l* spiritually ....1 Pet 4:6
I know where you *l*. ....Rev 2:13
He will *l* among them. ....Rev 21:3

LIVED
who *l* in a way that is morally ...... Isa 65:2
I *l* as a Pharisee. ....Acts 26:5
in which you formerly *l*. ....Eph 2:2

LIVES
a nation that *l* alone ....Num 23:9
I know that my Redeemer *l*. ....Job 19:25
Whoever *l* a blameless life. .... Ps 15:2
the LORD God *l* there ....Ps 68:18
l of the needy he will save .... Ps 72:13
He *l* in Salem ....Ps 76:2
The days of our *l* add up. ....Ps 90:10
l in the shelter of the Most High. ......Ps 91:1
They will escape with their *l*. ....Jer 21:9
Indeed! All *l* are mine. ....Ezek 18:4
you will gain your *l* ....Luke 21:19
who have risked their *l* ....Acts 15:26
but the life he *l* ....Rom 6:10
but sin that *l* in me ....Rom 7:17
the Spirit of God *l* in you ....Rom 8:9
Jesus from the dead *l* in you. .....Rom 8:11
For none of us *l* for himself. ....Rom 14:7
that God's Spirit *l* in you. ....1 Cor 3:16
he *l* because of God's power. ......2 Cor 13:4
but Christ *l* in me ....Gal 2:20
all the fullness of deity *l* ....Col 2:9
all who want to live godly *l* ......2 Tim 3:12
since he *l* forever ....Heb 7:24
we ought to lay down our *l*. ......1 John 3:16
and the one who *l* ....Rev 1:18
slaves and human *l* ....Rev 18:13

LIVESTOCK
I also possessed more *l*. ....Eccl 2:7

LIVING
See also LAND OF THE LIVING; LIVING
    CREATURE; LIVING CREATURES
and the man became a *l* being. ..... Gen 2:7
principle for wise *l*. ....Ps 111:10
the *l* should take this to heart ...... Eccl 7:2
the *l* know that they will die. ....Eccl 9:5
should any *l* person complain .....Lam 3:39
God of the dead but of the *l* .....Matt 22:32
look for the *l* among the dead. ...Luke 24:5
am the *l* bread that came down. ...John 6:51
will flow rivers of *l* water. ....John 7:38
L in the fear of the Lord ....Acts 9:31
as judge of the *l* and the dead ....Acts 10:42
l is Christ and dying is gain .... Phil 1:21
those who are *l* this way. ....Phil 3:17
it is the church of the *l* God. .... 1 Tim 3:15
to judge the *l* and the dead ....2 Tim 4:1
the word of God is *l* and active .... Heb 4:12
fall into the hands of the *l* God ....Heb 10:31
l in tents with Isaac and Jacob ......Heb 11:9
a *l* stone rejected by men. ....1 Pet 2:4
to judge the *l* and the dead ....1 Pet 4:5
children *l* according to the truth. .. 2 John 1:4
and the four *l* creatures ....Rev 7:11

LIVING CREATURE
every *l* of the earth ....Gen 9:10
from the eyes of every *l*. ....Job 28:21
Every *l* that swarms ....Ezek 47:9
The first *l* was like a lion. ....Rev 4:7
I heard the second *l* saying. ....Rev 6:3
l that was in the sea died ....Rev 16:3

LIVING CREATURES
with swarms of *l*. ....Gen 1:20
the *l* that move in the water. ....Lev 11:46

These were the *l* that I saw ......Ezek 10:20
around the throne were four *l* ...... Rev 4:6
four *l* were saying "Amen. ....Rev 5:14
before the four *l* and the elders ....Rev 14:3
four *l* gave the seven angels. ....Rev 15:7
the four *l* threw themselves ....Rev 19:4

LIZARD
l you can catch with the hand ...Prov 30:28

LO-AMMI
Symbolic name of Hosea's son, Hos 1:8–9

LO-RUHAMAH
Symbolic name of Hosea's daughter, Hos 1:6

LOAD
and my *l* is not hard to carry .....Matt 11:30
l people down with burdens. .....Luke 11:46
each one will carry his own *l* ....Gal 6:5

LOADED
l their grain on their donkeys. .....Gen 42:26
She *l* them on donkeys ....1 Sam 25:18

LOADS
They tie up heavy *l* ....Matt 23:4

LOAF
except for one *l* they had. ....Mark 8:14

LOATHE
I *l* it; I do not want ....Job 7:16
They will *l* themselves. ....Ezek 6:9

LOATHED
I *l* life because what happens ....Eccl 2:17
I *l* all the fruit of my effort. ....Eccl 2:18

LOATHES
so that his life *l* food. ....Job 33:20

LOAVES
only five *l* and two fish ....Matt 14:17
took the seven *l* and the fish ....Matt 15:36

LOCAL
think that I am some *l* deity .... Jer 23:23

LOCKED
Although the doors were *l*. ....John 20:26

LOCKING
You keep *l* people out ....Matt 23:13

LOCKS
adversary *l* his eyes on me .... Job 16:9

LOCUSTS
the valley like a swarm of *l* ....Judg 7:12
He ordered *l* to come. ....Ps 105:34
l have no king. ....Prov 30:27
consisted of *l* and wild honey. ...... Matt 3:4
and he ate *l* and wild honey .... Mark 1:6
out of the smoke came *l*. ....Rev 9:3

LOFTY
I have built a *l* temple for you ......2 Chr 6:2
generation whose eyes are so *l*. ...Prov 30:13

LOGS
these two stubs of smoking *l*. ......Isa 7:4

LONG
The ark is to be 450 feet *l* .... Gen 6:15
L live the king ....1 Sam 10:24
she was wearing a *l* robe ....2 Sam 13:18
would grant me what I *l* for ....Job 6:8
and *l* to travel the roads ....Ps 84:5
l for your deliverance. ....Ps 119:81
I *l* for your deliverance. ....Ps 119:174
provide a *l* and full life. ....Prov 3:2
L life is in her right hand. ....Prov 3:16
walking around in *l* robes. ....Mark 12:38
as a show make *l* prayers. ....Luke 20:47
we encounter death all day *l* ..... Rom 8:36
that I *l* for all of you ....Phil 1:8
angels *l* to catch a glimpse .... 1 Pet 1:12
How *l*, Sovereign Master ....Rev 6:10

LONGS
As a deer *l* for streams of water. .....Ps 42:1

LOOK
L from the place. ....Gen 13:14
Don't *l* behind you. ....Gen 19:17
When I *l* up at the heavens ....Ps 8:3

I continually *l* to the LORD . . . . Ps 25:15
as I *l* you in the eye . . . . Ps 32:8
L to him and be radiant. . . . . Ps 34:5
I *l* up toward the hills . . . . Ps 121:1
L, this young woman is about . . . . Isa 7:14
will I to him for guidance . . . . Isa 11:10
L at Zion, the city . . . . Isa 33:20
L at the rock from which . . . . Isa 51:1
must *l* forward to the Sabbath. . . . . . Isa 58:13
to *l* on you with displeasure . . . . Jer 3:12
I know you *l* for faithfulness. . . . . Jer 5:3
I will *l* after their welfare . . . . Jer 24:6
L at the nations. . . . . Hab 1:5
so that they will *l* to me . . . . Zech 12:10
L at the birds in the sky. . . . . Matt 6:26
you *l* righteous to people . . . . Matt 23:28
L, there he is. . . . . Luke 17:23
would not even *l* up to heaven . . . Luke 18:13
L at the fig tree . . . . Luke 21:29
L!" he said . . . . Acts 7:56

LOOKED
he no longer *l* like a man . . . . Isa 52:14
I *l* for a man from among them. . Ezek 22:30
saw that you *l* malnourished . . . . Dan 1:10
he has *l* upon the humble state. . . Luke 1:48
turned and *l* straight at Peter. . . . Luke 22:61

LOOKING
grow tired from *l* for my God. . . . . . . Ps 69:3
Are you *l* for great things. . . . . Jer 45:5
l for a message from the LORD . . . Amos 8:12

LOOKS
God *l* down from heaven . . . . Ps 53:2
the one who *l* to me for help . . . . . . Isa 57:13
l at a woman to desire her. . . . . Matt 5:28
his hand to the plow and *l* back . . Luke 9:62

LOOM
into the fabric on the *l*. . . . . Judg 16:14
from the *l* he cuts me off . . . . Isa 38:12

LOOSE
shake *l* from its foundation. . . . . Isa 13:13
of all the prisoners came *l*. . . . . Acts 16:26

LOOSENED
his tongue *l*, and he spoke. . . . . Mark 7:35

LOOTED
and *l* their storehouses. . . . . Isa 10:13
people are *l* and plundered . . . . Isa 42:22

LOOTERS
handed Israel over to the *l*. . . . . Isa 42:24

LORD
See also ACCORDING TO THE WORD
OF THE LORD; ANGEL OF THE LORD;
ANGER OF THE LORD; BLESS THE
LORD; BLESSED BE THE LORD; DAY
OF THE LORD; FEAR OF THE LORD;
FEAR THE LORD; GLORY OF THE LORD;
HAND OF THE LORD; HOUSE OF THE
LORD; LAW OF THE LORD; LORD
APPEARED TO; LORD COMMANDED;
LORD GOD OF HEAVEN'S ARMIES;
LORD GOD OF ISRAEL; LORD HAS
SPOKEN; LORD IS GOOD; LORD JESUS
CHRIST; LORD OF HEAVEN'S ARMIES;
LORD OF LORDS; LORD WAS WITH
HIM; LORD'S ANOINTED; LORD'S
CHOSEN ONE; LOVE THE LORD YOUR
GOD; PRAISE THE LORD; REJOICE IN
THE LORD; SEEK THE LORD; SERVE
THE LORD; SINNED AGAINST THE
LORD; SPIRIT OF THE LORD; VOICE OF
THE LORD; VOW TO THE LORD; WAY
OF THE LORD; WORD OF THE LORD;
WRATH OF THE LORD
L is my strength and my song . . . . . Exod 15:2
The *L* is a warrior. . . . . Exod 15:3
The *L* is our God. . . . . Deut 6:4
offensive to the *L* your God . . . . Deut 17:1
The *L* was furious with Israel . . . . . . Judg 10:7
for your *l* Saul is dead . . . . 2 Sam 2:7
the *L* is the only genuine God . . . . 1 Kgs 8:60
If the *L* is the true God . . . . 1 Kgs 18:21

You alone are the *L*. . . . . Neh 9:6
The *L* of Heaven's Armies . . . . Ps 24:10
our shield belongs to the *L* . . . . Ps 89:18
let us sing for joy to the *L* . . . . Ps 95:1
For the *L* is a great God. . . . . Ps 95:3
The *L* is merciful and fair . . . . Ps 116:5
the *L* surrounds his people . . . . Ps 125:2
The *L* is just. Ps 129:4
The *L* is near all who cry out . . . . . Ps 145:18
L is ready to show you mercy . . . . . Isa 30:18
L has provided us with justice . . . . . Jer 23:6
L has accomplished great things. . . . Joel 2:21
The *L* will then be king . . . . Zech 14:9
put the *L* your God to the test. . . . . Matt 4:7
worship the *L* your God . . . . Matt 4:10
is *l* even of the Sabbath. . . . . Mark 2:28
He is Christ the *L* . . . . Luke 2:11
Why do you call me '*L*. . . . . Luke 6:46
The *L* has really risen. . . . . Luke 24:34
call me 'Teacher' and '*L*. . . . . John 13:13
he is *L* of all. . . . . Acts 10:36
Who are you, *L*?' And the *L*. . . . . . Acts 26:15
that Jesus is *L* and believe . . . . Rom 10:9
for the same *L* is *L* of all . . . . Rom 10:12
Jesus is *L*. . . . . 1 Cor 12:3
Now the *L* is the Spirit. . . . . 2 Cor 3:17
confess that Jesus Christ is *L* . . . . . . Phil 2:11
And do not *l* it over those . . . . 1 Pet 5:3
For the *L* our God . . . . Rev 19:6

LORD APPEARED TO
The *L* Abram and said . . . . Gen 12:7
the *L* him and said . . . . Gen 17:1
The *L* Abraham by the oaks . . . . Gen 18:1
glory of the *L* all the people . . . . Lev 9:23
the glory of the *L* them. . . . . Num 20:6
the *L* Solomon in a dream . . . . 1 Kgs 3:5
the *L* Solomon a second time. . . . . . 1 Kgs 9:2

LORD COMMANDED
Noah did all that the *L*. . . . . Gen 7:15
did exactly as the *L* . . . . Exod 12:50
Just as the *L* Moses . . . . Exod 16:34
This is what the *L* to give . . . . Lev 7:36
commandments which the *L* . . . . . Lev 27:34
all that the *L* Moses . . . . Num 2:34
just as the *L* Moses . . . . Num 15:36
Moses did as the *L* him . . . . Num 27:22
the statutes that the *L* Moses . . . . . Num 30:16
The *L* us to obey all. . . . . Deut 6:24
have not obeyed what the *L* . . . . . 1 Sam 13:14
David did just as the *L* . . . . 2 Sam 5:25
The *L* the enemy . . . . Jer 5:10
the *L* the fish . . . . Jonah 2:10
for the potter's field, as the *L*. . . . Matt 27:10
the *L* those who proclaim . . . . 1 Cor 9:14

LORD GOD OF HEAVEN'S ARMIES
for the *L* was with him. . . . . 2 Sam 5:10
absolutely loyal to the *L*. . . . . 1 Kgs 19:10
O *L*, restore us. . . . . Ps 80:19
O *L*, hear my prayer . . . . Ps 84:8
I belong to you, O *L*. . . . . Jer 15:16
The *L* is his name. . . . . Amos 4:13

LORD GOD OF ISRAEL
My son, honor the *L* . . . . Josh 7:19
built an altar for the *L* . . . . Josh 8:30
them in the name of the *L*. . . . . Josh 9:19
for the *L* fought for Israel. . . . . Josh 10:42
their inheritance is the *L*. . . . . Josh 13:33
and submit to the *L*. . . . . Josh 24:23
I will sing to the *L*. . . . . Judg 5:3
Why, O *L* has this happened . . . . . . Judg 21:3
repaid fully by the *L* . . . . Ruth 2:12
O *L*, respond with Urim. . . . . 1 Sam 14:41
O *L*, your servant has clearly . . . 1 Sam 23:10
This is what the *L* has said. . . . . . . 2 Sam 12:7
The *L* is worthy of praise . . . . 1 Kgs 8:15
a temple to honor the *L* . . . . 1 Kgs 8:17
These sins angered the *L* . . . . 1 Kgs 15:30
prayed before the LORD: "*L*. . . . . . . 2 Kgs 19:15
and bring the ark of the *L* . . . . 1 Chr 15:12
to build a temple for the *L*. . . . . 1 Chr 22:6
L has given his people rest . . . . 1 Chr 23:25
determined to worship the *L* . . . . . 2 Chr 11:16

they turned back to the *L* . . . . 2 Chr 15:4
Passover celebration for the *L* . . . . . 2 Chr 30:1
build the temple of the *L* . . . . Ezra 1:3
the land to seek the *L* . . . . Ezra 6:21
The *L* deserves praise . . . . Ps 41:13
Blessed be the *L* . . . . Luke 1:68

LORD HAS SPOKEN
and obey all that the *L* . . . . Exod 24:7
all the statutes that the *L* . . . . Lev 10:11
commandments that the *L* . . . . Num 15:22
El, God, the *L* . . . . Ps 50:1
Know for certain that the *L*. . . . . Isa 1:20
Sovereign *L* to me clearly . . . . Isa 50:5
not be arrogant! For the *L*. . . . . Jer 13:15

LORD IS GOOD
Taste and see that the *L* . . . . Ps 34:8
For the *L*. His loyal love. . . . . Ps 100:5
Praise the LORD for the *L* . . . . Ps 135:3
The *L* to all, and has . . . . Ps 145:9
the *L* and his unfailing love . . . . Jer 33:11
The *L* to those who trust . . . . Lam 3:25
The *L*—indeed, he is . . . . Nah 1:7

LORD JESUS CHRIST
after believing in the *L*. . . . . Acts 11:17
for the name of our *L*. . . . . Acts 15:26
with God through our *L* . . . . Rom 5:1
in God through our *L* . . . . Rom 5:11
put on the *L* . . . . Rom 13:14
for the revelation of our *L* . . . . 1 Cor 1:7
blameless on the day of our *L* . . . . . 1 Cor 1:8
victory through our *L*. . . . . 1 Cor 15:57
know the grace of our *L* . . . . 2 Cor 8:9
except in the cross of our *l* . . . . Gal 6:14
in the name of our *L*. . . . . Eph 5:20
a savior from there, the *L*. . . . . Phil 3:20
salvation through our *L*. . . . . 1 Thess 5:9
at the coming of our *L* . . . . 1 Thess 5:23
the arrival of our *L* . . . . 2 Thess 2:1
faith in our glorious *L*. . . . . Jas 2:1
our *L* more intimately . . . . 2 Pet 1:8
our *L* revealed this to me. . . . . 2 Pet 1:14
by the apostles of our *L* . . . . Jude 1:17

LORD OF HEAVEN'S ARMIES
and to sacrifice to the *L* . . . . 1 Sam 1:3
O *L*, if you would truly look. . . . . . . 1 Sam 1:11
ark of the covenant of the *L* . . . . . . 1 Sam 4:4
in the name of the *L* . . . . 1 Sam 17:45
The *L* is God over Israel . . . . 2 Sam 7:26
The zeal of the *L* will . . . . 2 Kgs 19:31
for the *L* was with him. . . . . 1 Chr 11:9
this majestic king? The *L* . . . . Ps 24:10
The *L* is on our side. . . . . Ps 46:7
place where you live, O *L* . . . . Ps 84:1
If the *L* had not left us . . . . Isa 1:9
the *L* has planned a day . . . . Isa 2:12
Is the vineyard of the *L* . . . . Isa 5:7
Holy, holy, holy is the *L* . . . . Isa 6:3
the authority of the *L*. . . . . Isa 8:13
The zeal of the *L*. . . . . Isa 9:7
of the anger of the *L*. . . . . Isa 9:19
of the fury of the *L* . . . . Isa 13:13
for the *L* will rule . . . . Isa 24:23
the *L* will become a. . . . . Isa 28:5
O *L*, O God of Israel . . . . Isa 37:16
their Protector, the *L* . . . . Isa 44:6
one who made you—the *L* . . . . Isa 54:5
O *L*, you test and prove. . . . . Jer 20:12
God, the living God, the *L* . . . . Jer 23:36
pray earnestly to the *L* . . . . Jer 27:18
His name is the *L* . . . . Jer 31:35
Give thanks to the *L* . . . . Jer 33:11
forsaken by their God, the *L*. . . . . . . Jer 51:5
The *L* has solemnly sworn. . . . . Jer 51:14
harassed the people of the *L* . . . . . . Zeph 2:10
temple of their God, the *L* . . . . Hag 1:14
So the *L* has said. . . . . Hag 2:7
The *L* says, 'Turn to me . . . . Zech 1:3
O *L*, how long before you. . . . . Zech 1:12
know that the *L* has sent me . . . . . . Zech 2:9
but by my Spirit,' says the *L* . . . . . . Zech 4:6
the *L* poured out great wrath. . . . . . Zech 7:12
mountain of the *L* . . . . Zech 8:3

seek the *L* and to ask his favor ... Zech 8:22
The *L* will guard them ....Zech 9:15
to worship the King, the *L* ....Zech 14:16
am a great king," says the *L*........ Mal 1:14
he is the messenger of the *L*.........Mal 2:7
will return to you," says the *L* ....Mal 3:7

LORD OF LORDS
God of gods and *L* ....Deut 10:17
Give thanks to the *L* ....Ps 136:3
the King of kings and *L* .... 1 Tim 6:15
he is the *L* and King of kings....... Rev 17:14
King of kings and *L* ....Rev 19:16

LORD WAS WITH HIM
master observed that the *L*....... Gen 39:3
Joseph's care because the *L*.....Gen 39:23
continued to grow, and the *L*...1 Sam 3:19
success in all he did, for the *L* ...1 Sam 18:14
The *L*; he succeeded in all .... 2 Kgs 18:7
earlier times, and the *L*...........1 Chr 9:20
the power of the *L* to heal.........Luke 5:17

LORD'S ANOINTED
your hand to destroy the *L* ....2 Sam 1:14
I have put the *L* to death ....2 Sam 1:16
After all, he cursed the *L* ....2 Sam 19:21
the *L* king—was caught .... Lam 4:20

LORD'S CHOSEN ONE
to my lord, who is the *L* ....1 Sam 24:6
my lord, for he is the *L* ....1 Sam 24:10
extend his hand against the *L* .. 1 Sam 26:9
my hand against the *L* ....1 Sam 26:11
protected your lord, the *L* ...... 1 Sam 26:16
extend my hand against the *L* .1 Sam 26:23
Saul, who was the *L* .... 2 Sam 21:6

LORDS
See also LORD OF LORDS
are many gods and many *l*.........1 Cor 8:5
Lord of *l* and King of kings........ Rev 17:14

LOSE
to *l* one of your members .... Matt 5:29
wants to save his life will *l* it..... Matt 16:25
l the things we have worked for .. 2 John 1:8
and does not *l* his clothes .... Rev 16:15

LOSES
human heart *l* its courage ....Isa 13:7
But if salt *l* its flavor ....Matt 5:13
has ten silver coins and *l* one .....Luke 15:8
l his life will preserve it...........Luke 17:33

LOSS
he will suffer *l* ....1 Cor 3:15

LOST
to give something up as *l* .... Eccl 3:6
wealth was *l* through bad luck......Eccl 5:14
Gold has *l* its luster................. Lam 4:1
one of these little ones be *l*.......Matt 18:14
go look for the one that is *l*.......Luke 15:4
found my sheep that was *l*........Luke 15:6
found the coin that I had *l*........Luke 15:9
by a demon and has *l* his mind .. John 10:20
Not one of them was *l*............ John 17:12
I have not *l* a single one ....John 18:9
I have not *l* my mind............. Acts 26:25

LOT
land must be divided by *l*........Num 26:55
the *l* God allots the wicked ....Job 20:29

LOT
Abram's nephew; accompanies him,
 Gen 11:27–12:5; 13:1
Separates from Abram, Gen 13:5–12
Rescued by Abram, Gen 14:12–16
Saved from Sodom for his hospitality,
 Gen 19:1–29
Tricked into committing incest,
 Gen 19:30–38

LOTS
Then they cast *l* for them..........Acts 1:26

LOT'S WIFE
Disobedient, becomes pillar of salt,
 Gen 19:26
Event to be remembered, Luke 17:32

LOUD
You must sound *l* horn blasts.......Lev 25:9
whole army give a *l* battle cry ......Josh 6:5
Praise him with *l* cymbals ....Ps 150:5
Jesus shouted with a *l* voice .....Matt 27:46
a *l* voice like a trumpet ....Rev 1:10

LOUDLY
but I screamed *l* .... Gen 39:14
He wept *l* ....Gen 45:2
All the land was weeping *l*...... 2 Sam 15:23
and I praised the LORD God ....2 Chr 20:19
l proclaim what he has done.......Ps 107:22
laughed *l* and shouted for joy ......Ps 126:2

LOVE
See also HIS LOYAL LOVE ENDURES; LOVE
 OF CHRIST; LOVE OF GOD; LOVE ONE
 ANOTHER; LOVE THE LORD YOUR
 GOD; LOVE YOUR ENEMIES; LOVE
 YOUR NEIGHBORS; LOYAL LOVE
abounding in loyal *l* ....Exod 34:6
l your neighbor as yourself .... Lev 19:18
and abounding in loyal *l* ....Num 14:18
must *l* the LORD your God........ Deut 6:5
l was more special to me .... 2 Sam 1:26
the LORD's eternal *l* for Israel..... 1 Kgs 10:9
and his loyal *l* endures............. 1 Chr 16:34
and unfailing in your loyal *l* .... Neh 9:17
will you *l* what is worthless...........Ps 4:2
L the LORD...........................Ps 31:23
Would you *l* to live a long .... Ps 34:12
your loyal *l* and faithfulness ....Ps 40:10
You *l* justice and hate evil.......... Ps 45:7
God's loyal *l* protects me .... Ps 52:1
trust in God's loyal *l* ....Ps 52:8
May God send his loyal *l* ....Ps 57:3
They *l* to use deceit................Ps 62:4
demonstrate loyal *l*................Ps 62:12
experiencing your loyal *l* ....Ps 63:3
Has his loyal *l* disappeared ....Ps 77:8
Loyal *l* and faithfulness ....Ps 85:10
l is permanently established.........Ps 89:2
Loyal *l* and faithfulness ....Ps 89:14
to proclaim your loyal *l*...........Ps 92:2
His loyal *l* endures..................Ps 100:5
crowns you with his loyal *l* ....Ps 103:4
l extends beyond the sky ....Ps 108:4
For his loyal *l* towers over us........Ps 117:2
your loyal *l* fills the earth ....Ps 119:64
O how I *l* your law .... Ps 119:97
Those who *l* your law............. Ps 119:165
the LORD exhibits loyal *l*...........Ps 130:7
demonstrates great loyal *l*.........Ps 145:8
protects all those who *l* him.......Ps 145:20
but *l* covers all transgressions ....Prov 10:12
those who *l* the rich are many... Prov 14:20
A time to *l* .... Eccl 3:8
or arouse *l* until it pleases .... Song 3:5
there I will give you my *l* ....Song 7:12
For *l* is as strong as death .... Song 8:6
Surging waters cannot quench *l*... Song 8:7
I will sing to my *l* ....Isa 5:1
show unfailing *l* to thousands ...... Jer 32:18
you had reached the age for *l* .....Ezek 16:8
steadfast *l* and tender ....Hos 2:19
and *l* them freely ....Hos 14:4
to *l* faithfulness.....................Mic 6:8
l your enemy and pray..............Matt 5:44
For if you *l* those who *l* you.......Matt 5:46
which of them will *l* him more.... Luke 7:42
have the *l* of God within you......John 5:42
you have *l* for one another ....John 13:35
If you *l* me......................John 14:15
l one another just as I have........John 15:12
No one has greater *l* than this ... John 15:13
do you *l* me more than these.....John 21:15
do you *l* me......................John 21:16
l of God has been poured out.......Rom 5:5
L must be without hypocrisy .....Rom 12:9
to one another with mutual *l*.....Rom 12:10
except to *l* one another............Rom 13:8
L does no wrong to a neighbor ...Rom 13:10
but *l* builds up ....1 Cor 8:1

L is patient.....................1 Cor 13:4
L never ends.....................1 Cor 13:8
But the greatest of these is *l* ......1 Cor 13:13
For the *l* of Christ controls us ....2 Cor 5:14
and the God of *l* and peace.......2 Cor 13:11
the fruit of the Spirit is *l*............Gal 5:22
rooted and grounded in *l*........ Eph 3:17
body builds itself up in *l* ....Eph 4:16
Husbands, *l* your wives ....Eph 5:25
with an undying *l* ....Eph 6:24
any comfort provided by *l*...........Phil 2:1
been knit together in *l*...............Col 2:2
Husbands, *l* your wives ....Col 3:19
the breastplate of faith and *l* .....1 Thess 5:8
the aim of our instruction is *l*.......1 Tim 1:5
if she continues in faith and *l* ..... 1 Tim 2:15
l, faithfulness, and purity .... 1 Tim 4:12
For the *l* of money is the root ....1 Tim 6:10
women to *l* their husbands .... Titus 2:4
Brotherly *l* must continue ....Heb 13:1
but you *l* him ....1 Pet 1:8
l the family of believers.............1 Pet 2:17
l covers a multitude of sins ....1 Pet 4:8
brotherly affection, unselfish *l* ......2 Pet 1:7
Do not *l* the world................1 John 2:15
we *l* our fellow Christians ....1 John 3:14
have come to know *l* by this......1 John 3:16
how can the *l* of God reside ......1 John 3:17
The person who does not *l* ......1 John 4:8
In this is *l* .... 1 John 4:10
If we *l* one another ....1 John 4:12
By this *l* is perfected with us......1 John 4:17
There is no fear in *l* ....1 John 4:18
We *l* because he loved us first....1 John 4:19
For this is the *l* of God............1 John 5:3
wrapped in the *l* of God ....Jude 1:1
and *l* be lavished on you .... Jude 1:2
have departed from your first *l* .....Rev 2:4
your *l*, faith, service.................Rev 2:19
and they did not *l* their lives........Rev 12:11

LOVE OF CHRIST
will separate us from the *l*........ Rom 8:35
For the *l* controls us ....2 Cor 5:14
l that surpasses knowledge.........Eph 3:19

LOVE OF GOD
do not have the *l* within you........John 5:2
the *l* has been poured out ....Rom 5:5
to separate us from the *l* .... Rom 8:39
and the *l* and the fellowship ......2 Cor 13:13
your hearts toward the *l*..........2 Thess 3:5
the *l* has been perfected...........1 John 2:5
how can the *l* reside ....1 John 3:17
the *l* is revealed in us .... 1 John 4:9
For this is the *l*....................1 John 5:3
wrapped in the *l*....................Jude 1:1
maintain yourselves in the *l* ....Jude 1:21

LOVE ONE ANOTHER
a new commandment—to *l*........John 13:34
to *l* just as I have loved you.......John 15:12
This I command you—to *l*........John 15:17
no one anything, except to *l* ......Rom 13:8
are taught by God to *l* ....1 Thess 4:9
So *l* earnestly from a pure.........1 Pet 1:22
that we should *l* ....1 John 3:11
and *l*, just as he gave us.......... 1 John 3:23
Dear friends, let us *l* .... 1 John 4:7
then we ought to *l* ....1 John 4:11
If we *l*, God resides in us.........1 John 4:12
the beginning), that we *l*..........2 John 1:5

LOVE THE LORD YOUR GOD
l with your whole mind............. Deut 6:5
l and do what he requires ....Deut 11:1
you today is to *l* .... Deut 30:16
L, follow all his instructions ....Josh 22:5
Jesus said to him, "*L* .... Matt 22:37
L with all your heart.............Mark 12:30
The expert answered, "*L*........ Luke 10:27

LOVE YOUR ENEMIES
You seem to *l* and hate ....2 Sam 19:6
L, do good to those who hate .... Luke 6:27
l, and do good, and lend .... Luke 6:35

LOVE YOUR NEIGHBOR

but you must *l* as yourself . . . . Lev 19:18
said, '*L*' and 'hate your enemy . . . . Matt 5:43
and mother, and *l* as yourself . . . . . Matt 19:19
summed up in this, "*L* . . . . Rom 13:9
namely, "You must *l* . . . . Gal 5:14
You shall *l* . . . . Jas 2:8

LOVED

a person will be *l* or hated . . . . Eccl 9:1
thus she *l* much . . . . Luke 7:47
the way God *l* the world . . . . John 3:16
Look how much he *l* him . . . . John 11:36
the one Jesus *l* . . . . John 13:23
Just as the Father has *l* me . . . . John 15:9
l them just as you have *l* me . . . . . . John 17:23
Jacob I *l*, but Esau I hated . . . . Rom 9:13
l for the sake of the fathers . . . . Rom 11:28
l me and gave himself for me . . . . . . Gal 2:20
on us in his dearly *l* Son . . . . Eph 1:6
Therefore, be imitators of God as
    dearly *l* children . . . . Eph 5:1
just as Christ *l* the church . . . . Eph 5:25
You have *l* righteousness . . . . Heb 1:9
not that we have *l* God . . . . 1 John 4:10

LOVELY

l is the place where you live . . . . Ps 84:1
I am dark but *l* . . . . Song 1:5
whatever is pure, whatever is *l* . . . . . Phil 4:8

LOVEMAKING

let's drink deeply of *l* . . . . Prov 7:18
l is more delightful than wine . . . . . . Song 1:2

LOVER

My *l* is mine and I am his . . . . Song 2:16

LOVERS

I will seek out my *l* . . . . Hos 2:5
has hired prostitutes as *l* . . . . Hos 8:9
people will be *l* of themselves . . . . . 2 Tim 3:2

LOVES

provides for those whom he *l* . . . . . . Ps 127:2
A friend *l* at all times . . . . Prov 17:17
l father or mother more . . . . Matt 10:37
one who *l* his life destroys it . . . . . . John 12:25
is the one who *l* me . . . . John 14:21
If anyone *l* me . . . . John 14:23
because God *l* a cheerful giver . . . . 2 Cor 9:7
He who *l* his wife *l* himself . . . . Eph 5:28
to the kingdom of the Son he *l* . . . . . Col 1:13
If anyone *l* the world . . . . 1 John 2:15
that the one who *l* God . . . . 1 John 4:21
who *l* the father *l* the child . . . . 1 John 5:1
who *l* us and has set us free . . . . Rev 1:5

LOVESICK

Tell him that I am *l* . . . . Song 5:8

LOVING

she met with his *l* approval . . . . Esth 2:17
with *l* instruction on her tongue . . Prov 31:26
Greet one another with a *l* kiss . . . . 1 Pet 5:14

LOVINGLY

and he looked at me *l* . . . . Song 2:4

LOW

approached and bowed *l* . . . . Matt 8:2
and hill will be brought *l* . . . . Luke 3:5

LOWER

made him *l* than the angels . . . . Heb 2:7

LOWEST

The *l* of slaves he will be . . . . Gen 9:25

LOWLIEST

even the *l* of human beings . . . . Dan 4:17

LOWLY

he looks after the *l* . . . . Ps 138:6
It is better to be *l* in spirit . . . . Prov 16:19

LOYAL

See also HIS LOYAL LOVE ENDURES;
    LOYAL LOVE
and remain *l* to him . . . . Deut 13:4
to obey him and be *l* to him . . . . . Deut 30:20
remained *l* to the LORD my God . . . Josh 14:8
he did not remain *l* to the LORD . . . 1 Kgs 11:6

all you who are *l* to God . . . . Ps 66:16
Protect me, for I am *l* . . . . Ps 86:2
they are not really *l* to me . . . . Isa 29:13

LOYAL LOVE

See also HIS LOYAL LOVE ENDURES
keeping *l* for thousands . . . . Exod 34:7
he is good and his *l* endures . . . . . 1 Chr 16:34
your *l* reaches to the sky . . . . Ps 36:5
His *l* endures . . . . Ps 100:5
Yes, his *l* endures . . . . Ps 118:2
delights in showing *l* . . . . Mic 7:18

LOYALTIES

I hate people with divided *l* . . . . Ps 119:113

LOYALTY

worship him with integrity and *l* . . Josh 24:14
each man for his integrity and *l* . . 1 Sam 26:23
I will sing about *l* and justice . . . . Ps 101:1

LUD

A people descended from Shem, 1 Chr 1:17

LUKE

"The beloved physician," Col 4:14
Paul's last companion, 2 Tim 4:11
Author of third Gospel, Luke:title

LUKEWARM

So because you are *l* . . . . Rev 3:16

LUMP

make from the same *l* of clay . . . . . . Rom 9:21

LURED

when he is *l* and enticed . . . . Jas 1:14

LUSH

He takes me to *l* pastures . . . . Ps 23:2

LUST

not *l* in your heart for her beauty . . Prov 6:25

LUXURIOUS

the *l* palaces comes the music . . . . . . Ps 45:8

LUXURIOUSLY

have lived indulgently and *l* . . . . Jas 5:5

LUXURY

L is not appropriate for a fool . . . . Prov 19:10
live in *l* are in the royal palaces . . . Luke 7:25

LYCAONIA

District of Asia Minor where Paul preached,
    Acts 14:6, 11

LYCIA

Province of Asia Minor visited by Paul,
    Acts 21:1–2; 27:5–6

LYDDA

Aeneas healed at, Acts 9:32–35

LYDIA

Woman of Thyatira; Paul's first European
    convert, Acts 16:14–15, 40
—District of Asia Minor containing Ephesus,
    Smyrna, Thyatira, and Sardis, Rev 1:11

LYING

Dagon was *l* on the ground . . . . 1 Sam 5:3
placed a *l* spirit in the mouths . . . 1 Kgs 22:23
haughty eyes, a *l* tongue . . . . Prov 6:17
A *l* witness will perish . . . . Prov 21:28
If a *l* windbag should come . . . . Mic 2:11
a paralytic *l* on a stretcher . . . . Matt 9:2
strips of cloth and *l* in a manger . . . Luke 2:12
found the baby *l* in a manger . . . . . . Luke 2:16
saw the strips of linen cloth *l* . . . . . John 20:5

LYRE

who knows how to play the *l* . . . . 1 Sam 16:16
David was playing the *l* . . . . 1 Sam 18:10
ten-stringed instrument and a *l* . . . . . Ps 92:3
praise him with the *l* and . . . . Ps 150:3

LYRES

Azaziah were to play the *l* . . . . 1 Chr 15:21

LYSIAS, CLAUDIUS

See CLAUDIUS LYSIAS

LYSTRA

Paul visits; is worshiped by people of and
    stoned by Jews, Acts 14:6–20
Home of Timothy, Acts 16:1–2

M

MAACAH

Small Syrian kingdom near Mt. Hermon,
    Deut 3:14
Not possessed by Israel, Josh 13:13
—David's wife; mother of Absalom,
    2 Sam 3:3
—Wife of Rehoboam; mother of King
    Abijah, 2 Chr 11:18–21
Makes idol; is deposed as queen mother,
    1 Kgs 15:13

MACEDONIA

Paul preaches in, Acts 16:9—17:14
Paul's troubles in, 2 Cor 7:5
Churches of, generous, Rom 15:26;
    2 Cor 8:1–5

MACHIR [or MAKIR]

Manasseh's only son, Gen 50:23
Founder of the family of Machirites,
    Num 26:29
Also called "Makir," Gen 50:23

MACHPELAH

Field containing a cave; bought by
    Abraham, Gen 23:9–18
Sarah and Abraham buried here, Gen 23:19;
    25:9–10
Isaac, Rebekah, Leah, and Jacob buried
    here, Gen 49:29–31

MAD

so they have all gone *m* . . . . Jer 51:7

MADE

God *m* two great lights . . . . Gen 1:16
God saw all that he had *m* . . . . Gen 1:31
the seventh day and *m* it holy . . . . . . Gen 2:3
The LORD God *m* garments . . . . Gen 3:21
It is I who *m* Abram rich . . . . Gen 14:23
LORD *m* a covenant with Abram . . . Gen 15:18
had *m* his journey successful . . . . . Gen 24:21
and he *m* a special tunic . . . . Gen 37:3
m everything he was doing . . . . Gen 39:3
m himself known to his
    brothers . . . . Gen 45:1
They *m* their lives bitter . . . . Exod 1:14
he *m* the sea into dry land . . . . Exod 14:21
and *m* a molten calf . . . . Exod 32:4
He *m* an atonement lid . . . . Exod 37:6
So Moses *m* a bronze snake . . . . Num 21:9
m him jealous with other gods . . Deut 32:16
m the sky sink as he
    descended . . . . 2 Sam 22:10
David has *m* Solomon king . . . . 1 Kgs 1:43
their sins have *m* me angry . . . . 1 Kgs 16:2
He *m* the Most Holy Place . . . . 2 Chr 3:8
David *m* for giving thanks . . . . 2 Chr 7:6
not *m* a hedge around him . . . . Job 1:10
have shaped me and *m* me . . . . Job 10:8
have *m* me as with the clay . . . . Job 10:9
has *m* me a byword to people . . . . . . Job 17:6
which your fingers *m* . . . . Ps 8:3
You *m* them a little less . . . . Ps 8:5
and *m* me feel secure . . . . Ps 22:9
m us and we belong to him . . . . Ps 100:3
He *m* cursing a way of life . . . . Ps 109:18
you *m* my mind and heart . . . . Ps 139:13
God has *m* everything fit . . . . Eccl 3:11
Feasts are *m* for laughter . . . . Eccl 10:19
m me weary with your evil . . . . Isa 43:24
I *m* the earth . . . . Isa 45:12
once restitution is *m* . . . . Isa 53:10
husband is the one who *m* you . . . . . Isa 54:5
My hand *m* them . . . . Isa 66:2
by his power *m* the earth . . . . Jer 10:12
But Daniel *m* up his mind . . . . Dan 1:8
m a promise to your ancestors . . . . . Hag 2:5
Your faith has *m* you well . . . . Matt 9:22
he *m* them male and female . . . . . . Mark 10:6
destroy this temple *m* with
    hands . . . . Mark 14:58
the crooked will be *m* straight . . . . . Luke 3:5
has *m* God known . . . . John 1:18
m this holy place ritually . . . . Acts 21:28

m the wisdom of the world....... 1 Cor 1:20
in Christ all will be *m* alive....... 1 Cor 15:22
m the one who did not know sin .. 2 Cor 5:21
power is *m* perfect in weakness .. 2 Cor 12:9
m us alive together with Christ......Eph 2:5
nevertheless *m* you alive .... Col 2:13
m your good confession for ...... 1 Tim 6:12
who *m* his good confession....... 1 Tim 6:13
m him lower than the angels .... Heb 2:7
one who *m* it must be proven ..... Heb 9:16
enemies are *m* a footstool........Heb 10:13
by being *m* alive in the spirit.......1 Pet 3:18
m them white in the blood .... Rev 7:14
one who *m* heaven and earth.......Rev 14:7

MADMAN
inspired man is viewed as a *m*...... Hos 9:7

MADMEN
Her people act like *m*.............. Jer 50:38

MAGADAN
City of Galilee, Matt 15:39

MAGDALENE
See MARY

MAGGOTS
m that eat them will not die .... Isa 66:24

MAGIC
or by practicing *m* .... Jer 27:9
those who had practiced *m*....... Acts 19:19

MAGICIAN
But the *m* Elymas.................. Acts 13:8

MAGICIANS
does not respond to the *m* ....Ps 58:5
the *m* who chirp and mutter........Isa 8:19

MAGNIFICENT
how *m* is your reputation.............. Ps 8:1
princess looks absolutely *m* .... Ps 45:13
O LORD my God, you are *m*........ Ps 104:1

MAGNIFIED
The LORD greatly *m* Solomon ...1 Chr 29:25
May the LORD be *m* .... Mal 1:5

MAGNIFY
M the LORD with me .... Ps 34:3
I will *m* my great name .... Ezek 36:23
I will exalt and *m* myself........ Ezek 38:23
He will exalt and *m* himself........Dan 11:36

MAGOG
People among Japheth's descendants,
   Gen 10:2
Associated with Gog, Ezek 38:2
Representatives of final enemies, Rev 20:8

MAHANAIM
Name given by Jacob to a sacred site,
   Gen 32:2
Becomes Ish Bosheth's capital,
   2 Sam 2:8–29
David flees to, during Absalom's rebellion,
   2 Sam 17:24, 27

MAHER SHALAL HASH BAZ
Symbolic name of Isaiah's second son;
   prophetic of the fall of Damascus and
   Samaria, Isa 8:1–4

MAHLON
Husband of Ruth; without child, Ruth 1:2–5

MAIDENS
O *m* of Jerusalem..................Song 1:5

MAINTAIN
I *m* a pure lifestyle..............Ps 26:6
and *m* your integrity.................Ps 37:3
and *m* the traditions........... 1 Cor 11:2
m yourselves in the love...Jude 1:21

MAINTAINED
and *m* a pure lifestyle........... Ps 73:13
yet I *m* my objectivity .... Eccl 2:9

MAINTAINING
by *m* love and justice..............Hos 12:6

MAJESTIC
m in holiness, fearful in praises... Exod 15:11

M splendor emanates from
   him .... 1 Chr 16:27
Who is this *m* king................Ps 24:8
the LORD's shout is *m*..............Ps 29:4
M splendor emanates from him.....Ps 96:6
His work is *m* and glorious ...... Ps 111:3
on your honor and *m* splendor ....Ps 145:5
the Just One is *m* ....Isa 24:16
from your holy, *m* palace..........Isa 63:15
to him by the *M* Glory............2 Pet 1:17

MAJESTY
In the abundance of your *m* ....Exod 15:7
and by reason of his *m* .... Job 31:23
around God is awesome *m* ....Job 37:22
reveal your *m* in the heavens......... Ps 8:1
He is robed in *m*...................... Ps 93:1
he had no stately form or *m*........Isa 53:2
She and her daughters had *m* ... Ezek 16:49
was like you in *m* and loftiness ... Ezek 31:18
I will display my *m*...............Ezek 39:21
at the right hand of the *M*.........Heb 1:3
m, power, and authority ....Jude 1:25

MAKE
m humankind in our image........ Gen 1:26
so that we may *m* a name ....Gen 11:4
m you into a great nation.........Gen 12:2
m you the father of a multitude ...Gen 17:5
m for yourself a carved image....Exod 20:4
m from you a great nation....... Exod 32:10
not *m* yourselves detestable....... Lev 11:43
will *m* the land desolate .... Lev 26:32
and *m* your abdomen swell....... Num 5:22
The LORD *m* his face to shine..... Num 6:25
M a poisonous snake...............Num 21:8
m for yourself a wooden ark ...... Deut 10:1
m his dynasty permanent ....2 Sam 7:13
and *m* a just decision .... 1 Kgs 8:32
to *m* one final meal................1 Kgs 17:12
first *m* me a small cake...........1 Kgs 17:13
and *m* a just decision ....2 Chr 6:23
and *m* my hands clean..............Job 9:30
terror would not *m* me afraid ......Job 9:34
m me safe and secure ....Ps 4:8
God of Jacob *m* you secure ....Ps 20:1
M me understand your ways........Ps 25:4
will *m* insightful observations ....Ps 78:2
you *m* unjust legal decisions........Ps 82:2
M me wholeheartedly.............. Ps 86:11
you *m* all people so mortal ...... Ps 89:47
m them successful.................. Ps 90:17
There I will *m* David strong........Ps 132:17
wisdom to *m* the heavens .... Ps 136:5
he will *m* your paths straight ....Prov 3:6
M the path for your feet level .... Prov 4:26
When you *m* a vow to God ....Eccl 5:4
M haste, my beloved .... Song 8:14
m the front of their heads bald......Isa 3:17
M the hearts of these people........Isa 6:10
M it known that he is unique ......Isa 12:4
m human beings more scarce ...... Isa 13:12
I will *m* them happy .... Isa 56:7
I will *m* a lasting covenant.........Jer 32:40
m the children who follow.........Jer 33:22
m known to me its
   interpretation ....Dan 5:15
you *m* the poor pay taxes .... Amos 5:11
to *m* the ship lighter...............Jonah 1:5
Why would a craftsman *m* it ...... Hab 2:18
they *m* their faces unattractive....Matt 6:16
cross land and sea to *m* one.....Matt 23:15
Let us *m* three shelters............Mark 9:5
how can you *m* it salty again ..... Mark 9:50
M preparations for us there .... Mark 14:15
Do not *m* my Father's house ......John 2:16
I will *m* you jealous ....Rom 10:19
to *m* Israel jealous................Rom 11:11
m no provision for the flesh ...... Rom 13:14
able to *m* all grace overflow......2 Cor 9:8
to *m* us slaves ....Gal 2:4
m known the mystery .... Eph 6:19
may *m* it known as I should .... Col 4:4
m you completely holy ....1 Thess 5:23
I *m* your enemies a footstool.......Heb 1:13

and *m* your hearts pure .... Jas 4:8
m him a liar and his word is ......1 John 1:10
It will *m* your stomach bitter ....Rev 10:9

MAKER
Israel has forgotten his *M* .... Hos 8:14

MAKES
He *m* nations great ....Job 12:23
He *m* firm commitments .... Ps 15:4
m the winds his messengers........Ps 104:4
wise child *m* a father rejoice.......Prov 10:1
Hope deferred *m* the heart sick .. Prov 13:12
m herself praiseworthy...........Prov 31:30
and a rampart, *m* it secure ....Isa 26:1
man *m* honorable plans .... Isa 32:8
while he *m* himself available .... Isa 55:6
he *m* the lightning flash .... Jer 51:16
temple that *m* the gold sacred ...Matt 23:17
He even *m* the deaf hear .... Mark 7:37
my teaching *m* no progress.......John 8:37
God who *m* the dead alive........Rom 4:17
m himself God's enemy .... Jas 4:4

MAKING
humbled you by *m* you hungry .... Deut 8:3
and from *m* business deals ....Isa 58:13
and *m* me captive to the law ......Rom 7:23
and *m* music in your hearts........Eph 5:19
I am *m* all things new...............Rev 21:5

MAKIR
See MACHIR

MAKKEDAH
Canaanite town assigned to Judah,
   Josh 15:20, 41

MALACHI
Prophet and writer, Mal 1:1

MALCHUS
Servant of the high priest, John 18:10

MALE
created them *m* and female .... Gen 5:2
m and female, came into .... Gen 7:9
every *m* among you ....Gen 17:12
apart to me every firstborn *m*.....Exod 13:2
for the *m* or the female child .... Lev 12:7
sexual relations with a *m*..........Lev 18:22
Exterminate every *m* ....Judg 21:11
on *m* and female servants ....Joel 2:29
made them *m* and female ....Matt 19:4
there is neither *m* nor female ......Gal 3:28

MALICE
wickedness, covetousness, *m*......Rom 1:29
slanderous talk—indeed all *m* ......Eph 4:31
m, slander, abusive language ....Col 3:8

MALICIOUS
be protected from *m* gossip .... Job 5:21

MALIGNED
When he was *m* ....1 Pet 2:23

MALKI-SHUA
Son of King Saul, 1 Sam 14:49
Killed at Gilboa, 1 Sam 31:2

MALTA
Site of Paul's shipwreck, Acts 28:1–8

MAMRE
Town or district near Hebron, Gen 23:19
Abram dwells by the oaks of, Gen 13:18

MAN
See also MAN OF GOD; NEW MAN; OLD
   MAN; RIGHTEOUS MAN; SON OF MAN;
   WISE MAN
m leaves his father and mother ...Gen 2:24
m and his wife were both naked...Gen 2:25
Can a son be born to a *m*.......Gen 17:17
Then a *m* wrestled with him......Gen 32:24
We are all the sons of one *m* ......Gen 42:11
God is not a *m*................... Num 23:19
m of yours that I do not cut off...1 Sam 2:33
You are that *m*.................... 2 Sam 12:7
Be strong and become a *m* .... 1 Kgs 2:2
and like a hired *m* .... Job 7:2
not reject a blameless *m* ....Job 8:20

empty *m* will become wise ....Job 11:12
Were you the first *m* ever born......Job 15:7
righteous *m* holds to his way.......Job 17:9
not find a wise *m* among you......Job 17:10
that the evil *m* is spared...........Job 21:30
an innocent *m* will inherit ....Job 27:17
the wicked *m* reject God ....Ps 10:13
This oppressed *m* cried out.........Ps 34:6
desire integrity in the inner *m* ....Ps 51:6
Even a young *m* is known........Prov 20:11
grab hold of one *m* at that time ......Isa 4:1
honorable *m* makes honorable......Isa 32:8
But if you warn the wicked *m* ....Ezek 33:9
Son of *m*, can these bones........Ezek 37:3
When Israel was a young *m* ....Hos 11:1
O *m*, what is good...............Mic 6:8
M does not live by bread .... Matt 4:4
to him a demon-possessed *m* ....Matt 12:22
m will leave his father and.......Matt 19:5
I want to give to this last *m*......Matt 20:14
the coming of the Son of *M* .....Matt 24:27
to a certain *m* and tell him.......Matt 26:18
saw the demon-possessed *m*.....Mark 5:15
young *m* was following him .....Mark 14:51
A *m* had a fig tree planted........Luke 13:6
A *m* had two sons ....Luke 15:11
a rich *m* who dressed in purple...Luke 16:19
a poor *m* named Lazarus.......Luke 16:20
Now a *m* named Zacchaeus......Luke 19:2
a *m* be born when he is old........John 3:4
He is a good *m*..................John 7:12
have one *m* die for the people....John 11:50
here is the *m* ....John 19:5
very name has made this *m* ....Acts 3:16
m full of faith and of the Holy ......Acts 6:5
physically uncircumcised *m* ...... Rom 2:27
Where is the wise *m*.............. 1 Cor 1:20
But a married *m* is concerned .... 1 Cor 7:33
m did not come from woman .....1 Cor 11:8
since death came through a *m*....1 Cor 15:21
been clothed with the new *m*....... Col 3:10
not address an older *m* harshly....1 Tim 5:1
old *m* and even now a prisoner.... Phlm 1:9

MAN OF GOD

the blessing Moses the *m* ....Deut 33:1
and me to Moses, the *m*...........Josh 14:6
Then a *m* came to Eli .... 1 Sam 2:27
there is a *m* in this town...........1 Sam 9:6
descendants of Moses the *m* ....1 Chr 23:14
David the *m* had ordered.........2 Chr 8:14
in the law of Moses, the *m*.......2 Chr 30:16
in the law of Moses the *m* ....Ezra 3:2
specified by David the *m* ....Neh 12:24
A prayer of Moses, the *m*............Ps 90:1

MAN'S

must not desire another *m* wife ...Deut 5:21
M inner thoughts....................Ps 64:6
enter a strong *m* house..........Matt 12:29
to enter a strong *m* house........Mark 3:27
fell from the rich *m* table........Luke 16:21
mud on the blind *m* eyes ....John 9:6
for it is *m* number .... Rev 13:18

MAN-MADE

consists of nothing but *m* ritual ....Isa 29:13

MANAGE

must *m* his own household well...1 Tim 3:4

MANAGER

is the faithful and wise *m*........ Luke 12:42
commended the dishonest *m* .....Luke 16:8

MANAGERS

and good *m* of their children ..... 1 Tim 3:12

MANASSEH

Joseph's firstborn son, Gen 41:50–51
Adopted by Jacob, Gen 48:5–6
Loses his birthright to Ephraim,
    Gen 48:13–20
—Tribe of:
Numbered, Num 1:34–35
Half-tribe of, settle east of Jordan,
    Num 32:33–42; Deut 3:12–15
Help Joshua against Canaanites, Josh 1:12–18

Land assigned to western half-tribe,
    Josh 17:1–13
Eastern half-tribe builds altar, Josh 22:9–34
Some of, help David, 1 Chr 12:19–31
—Wicked king of Judah; son of Hezekiah,
    2 Kgs 21:1–18; 2 Chr 33:1–9
Captured and taken to Babylon; repents
    and is restored, 2 Chr 33:10–13
Removes idols and altars, 2 Chr 33:14–20

MANGER

and laid him in a *m* ....Luke 2:7
found the baby lying in a *m*........Luke 2:16

MANIFESTATION

the *m* of the Spirit is given.........1 Cor 12:7

MANIFESTED

but was *m* in these last times......1 Pet 1:20

MANKIND

is *m* that you make so much.........Job 7:17
the life was the light of *m* ....John 1:4

MANNA

Israelites ate *m* forty years ......Exod 16:35
the *m* was like coriander seed..... Num 11:7
feeding you with unfamiliar *m*..... Deut 8:3
The *m* stopped appearing ....Josh 5:12
You did not withhold your *m*.....Neh 9:20
rained down *m* for them to eat.....Ps 78:24
Our ancestors ate the *m*...........John 6:31
golden urn containing the *m* ....Heb 9:4
give him some of the hidden *m*.....Rev 2:17

MANNER

in an impressive and fitting *m* ....Ps 45:2
we answer in a friendly *m* ....1 Cor 4:13
in an unworthy *m* will be guilty...1 Cor 11:27
in a decent and orderly *m* ....1 Cor 14:40
are to melt away in this *m*.........2 Pet 3:11

MANOAH

Danite; father of Samson, Judg 13:1–25

MANY

also have available *m* workers... 1 Chr 22:15
m women spread the good news... Ps 68:11
How *m* living things .... Ps 104:24
your days will be *m*................. Prov 9:11
just as *m* were horrified ....Isa 52:14
the LORD will kill *m*...............Isa 66:16
he did *m* acts of charity...........Acts 10:2
through *m* sleepless nights.......2 Cor 11:27

MAON

Village in Judah, Josh 15:55
David stays at, 1 Sam 23:24–25
Nabal's house here, 1 Sam 25:2

MARA

Name chosen by Naomi, Ruth 1:20

MARAH

First Israelite camp after passing through
    the Red Sea, Num 33:8–9

MARCH

who were ready to *m*........... 1 Chr 12:38
m through the wastelands...........Ps 68:7
m on the earth's mountaintops...... Mic 1:3

MARCHES

m on the heights of the earth ....Amos 4:13

MARDUK

See BEL

MARK

LORD put a special *m* on Cain...... Gen 4:15
then you would not *m* my sin ..... Job 14:16
the moon to *m* the months........Ps 104:19
obtain a *m* on their right hand.....Rev 13:16
receives the *m* of his name ....Rev 14:11

MARK (JOHN)

Son of Mary of Jerusalem; travels with
    Barnabas and Saul, Acts 12:12, 25
Leaves Paul at Perga, Acts 13:13
Barnabas and Paul separate because of
    him, Acts 15:37–40
Later approved by Paul, Col 4:10; 2 Tim 4:11
Companion of Peter, 1 Pet 5:13
Author of the second Gospel, Mark 1:1

MARKERS

those who move boundary *m* ..... Hos 5:10

MARKETPLACE

my Father's house a *m* ....John 2:16
anything that is sold in the *m*.... 1 Cor 10:25

MARRIAGE

alliance by *m* with Pharaoh.........1 Kgs 3:1
marry nor are given in *m* ....Matt 22:30
they were being given in *m*.......Luke 17:27
marry and are given in *m*........Luke 20:34
They will prohibit *m*............... 1 Tim 4:3
M must be honored among all .... Heb 13:4

MARRIED

he *m* Pharaoh's daughter...........1 Kgs 3:1
David *m* more wives...............1 Chr 14:3
woman who becomes *m* ..... Prov 30:23
The first one *m* and died........ Matt 22:25
I just got *m* ....Luke 14:20
For a *m* woman is bound ....Rom 7:2
people who have never *m* .... 1 Cor 7:25

MARRIES

young man *m* a young woman ..... Isa 62:5
m another commits adultery ......Matt 19:9
And if a virgin *m*.................. 1 Cor 7:28

MARROW

and joints from *m* .... Heb 4:12

MARRY

and someone else *m* her ....Deut 20:7
M your servant .... Ruth 3:9
if he agrees to *m* you ....Ruth 3:13
it is better not to *m*................Matt 19:10
they neither *m* nor are given ....Matt 22:30
The people of this age *m* ....Luke 20:34
is better to *m* than to burn .... 1 Cor 7:9
I want younger women to *m* ..... 1 Tim 5:14

MARRYING

m and giving in marriage ....Matt 24:38
they were *m* ....Luke 17:27

MARTHA

Sister of Mary and Lazarus; loved by Jesus,
    John 11:1–5
Affirms her faith, John 11:19–28
Offers hospitality to Jesus, Luke 10:38;
    John 12:1–2
Gently rebuked by Christ, Luke 10:39–42

MARVELOUS

Your rules are *m*................... Ps 119:129
out of darkness into his *m* light.....1 Pet 2:9

MARY

Mother of Christ, Matt 1:16
Visited by angel, Luke 1:26–38
Visits Elizabeth and offers praise,
    Luke 1:39–56
Gives birth to Jesus, Luke 2:6–20
Flees to Egypt, Matt 2:13–18
Visits Jerusalem with Jesus, Luke 2:41–52
Entrusted to John's care, John 19:25–27
—Mother of James and Joseph; present at
    crucifixion and burial, Matt 27:55–61
Sees the risen Lord; informs disciples,
    Matt 28:1–10
—Magdalene; delivered from seven demons;
    supports Christ's ministry, Luke 8:2–3
Present at crucifixion and burial,
    Matt 27:55–61
First to see the risen Lord, Mark 16:1–10;
    John 20:1–18
—Sister of Martha and Lazarus; loved by
    Jesus, John 11:1–5
Grieves for Lazarus, John 11:19–20, 28–33
Anoints Jesus, Matt 26:6–13; John 12:1–8
Commended by Jesus, Luke 10:38–42
—Mark's mother, Acts 12:12–17

MASSAH AND MERIBAH

The Lord provides water for Israel here,
    Exod 17:1–7

MASSAH

See also MASSAH AND MERIBAH
at *M* in the wilderness..............Ps 95:8

MASTER

of his *m* Abraham ....Gen 24:9
If she does not please her *m*......Exod 21:8
my *m* were in the presence........2 Kgs 5:3
my *m*! It was borrowed...........2 Kgs 6:5
look to the hand of their *m*...... Ps 123:2
he will be *m* over all the fruit......Eccl 2:19
for I am your true *m*................Jer 3:14
never again call me, 'My *m*........Hos 2:16
and the slave like his *m*........ Matt 10:25
whom the *m* finds at work ......Matt 24:46
M, M, we are about to die ....Luke 8:24
M, it is good for us to be here .... Luke 9:33
the *m* of that slave will come.... Luke 12:46
m commended the dishonest .....Luke 16:8
M, have mercy on us .... Luke 17:13
slave is not greater than his *m*.... John 13:16
slave is not greater than his *m*....John 15:20
useful for the *M* ....2 Tim 2:21
deny our only *M* and Lord..........Jude 1:4

MASTER-BUILDER

a skilled *m* I laid a foundation .... 1 Cor 3:10

MASTERED

but the darkness has not *m* it ...... John 1:5

MASTERS

slave *m* had set over them........Exod 5:14
refreshes the heart of his *m* ......Prov 25:13
m other than you have ruled us ....Isa 26:13
No servant can serve two......Luke 16:13
M, treat your slaves the same ...... Eph 6:9
M, treat your slaves with justice..... Col 4:1
those who have believing *m*........1 Tim 6:2
to be subject to their own *m* ...... Titus 2:9

MATCH

a vase of gold *m* its worth ....Job 28:17

MATING

male goats *m* with the flock.......Gen 31:10

MATTANIAH

King Zedekiah's original name, 2 Kgs 24:17

MATTER

If the *m* being adjudicated.........Deut 1:17
one who deals wisely in a *m*..... Prov 16:20

MATTERS

Why not ordinary *m*...............1 Cor 6:3
good showing in external *m*........Gal 6:12
entangled in *m* of everyday life....2 Tim 2:4
set in order the remaining *m* ....Titus 1:5

MATTHEW [or LEVI]

Becomes Christ's follower, Matt 9:9
One of the Twelve, Matt 10:2–3
Author of the first Gospel, Matt:title
Also called "Levi," the son of Alphaeus,
    Mark 2:14

MATTHIAS

Chosen by lot to replace Judas, Acts 1:15–26

MATURE

and their fruit does not *m* .... Luke 8:14
speak wisdom among the *m*....... 1 Cor 2:6
but in your thinking be *m*........1 Cor 14:20
present every person *m* ....Col 1:28
But solid food is for the *m*......... Heb 5:14

MATURITY

and move on to *m*.................Heb 6:1

MEADOW

like a wildflower in the *m*...........Jas 1:10

MEAL

Better a *m* of vegetables .... Prov 15:17
has prepared a sacrificial *m* ....Zeph 1:7
invited Jesus to have a *m* ....Luke 11:37
when you host an elaborate *m* ...Luke 14:13
but could eat the Passover *m*.....John 18:28
and shared a *m* with them......Acts 11:3
birthright for a single *m* ....Heb 12:16
and share a *m* with him............Rev 3:20

MEAN

does this ceremony *m* to you.... Exod 12:26
we want to know what they *m* ...Acts 17:20

MEANING

This is its *m*......................Gen 40:12
not know the *m* of a language.... 1 Cor 14:11

MEANS

does not have sufficient *m* .... Lev 14:21
by no *m* clearing the guilty ....Num 14:18
have not done so by honest *m*.......Jer 9:3
which *m* "God with us [..........Matt 1:23
which *m,* "Little girl.............. Mark 5:41
which *m,* "My God.............. Mark 15:34
the future by supernatural *m*..... Acts 16:16
by all *m* I may save some........1 Cor 9:22
to their *m* and beyond their *m*.....2 Cor 8:3
the believer of humble *m*.............Jas 1:9

MEANT

you *m* to harm me................. Gen 50:20
asked him what this parable *m*.... Luke 8:9

MEASURE

you reveal your anger in full *m*....Ps 76:10
the smaller-than-standard *m* ....Mic 6:10
and the *m* you use...................Matt 7:2
A good *m*, pressed down ....Luke 6:38
For the *m* you use ....Luke 6:38
to each of you a *m* of faith........Rom 12:3
But when they *m* themselves.... 2 Cor 10:12
the *m* of Christ's full stature.........Eph 4:13
Get up and *m* the temple of God ....Rev 11:1

MEASURED

Who has *m* out the waters .... Isa 40:12
if the heavens above could be *m* ...Jer 31:37
can be neither *m* nor numbered....Hos 1:10
He also *m* its wall.................. Rev 21:17

MEASURES

Diverse weights and diverse *m* .. Prov 20:10

MEASURING

I will make justice the *m* line ....Isa 28:17
the man's hand was a *m* stick.....Ezek 40:5
with a *m* line in his hand...........Zech 2:1
Then a *m* rod like a staff............Rev 11:1

MEAT

the LORD gives you *m* to eat.... Exod 16:8
m was still between their teeth...Num 11:33
both the raw and cooked *m* ....Ps 58:9
he provide *m* for his people ....Ps 78:20
He rained down *m* on them ....Ps 78:27
not to eat *m* or drink wine........Rom 14:21
I will never eat *m* again............1 Cor 8:13

MEDEBA

Moabite town assigned to Judah,
    Num 21:29–30; Josh 13:9, 16

MEDES; MEDIA

Part of Medo-Persian Empire, Esth 1:19
Israel deported to, 2 Kgs 17:6
Babylon falls to, Dan 5:30–31
Daniel rises high in kingdom of, Dan 6:1–28
Cyrus, king of, allows Jews to return,
    2 Chr 36:22–23
Agents in Babylon's fall, Isa 13:17–19

MEDIATES

covenant that he *m* is also better... Heb 8:6

MEDIATOR

the *m* of a new covenant .... Heb 12:24

MEDICINE

no matter how much *m* you use.... Jer 46:11

MEDITATE

M as you lie in bed ....Ps 4:4
I will *m* on your precepts...........Ps 119:15
All day long I *m* on it .... Ps 119:97

MEDITATES

he *m* on his commands.................Ps 1:2

MEDITATION

and hinder *m* before God.......... Job 15:4

MEDITERRANEAN SEA [or SEA OF THE
    PHILISTINES; WESTERN SEA]

Border of Promised Land, Deut 11:24;
    Josh 1:4

Also called the "Sea of the Philistines,"
    Exod 23:31
Also called the "western sea," Zech 14:8

MEDIUM

Find me a woman who is a *m*.... 1 Sam 28:7

MEEK

a humble and *m* group ....Zeph 3:12
Blessed are the *m* ....Matt 5:5
who am *m* when present......... 2 Cor 10:1

MEEKNESS

m and gentleness of Christ .... 2 Cor 10:1

MEET

to *m* them and bowed low......... Gen 18:2
Loyal love and faithfulness *m*.....Ps 85:10
prepare to *m* your God ....Amos 4:12
went out to *m* the bridegroom ....Matt 25:1
Come out to *m* him............... Matt 25:6
carrying a jar of water will *m* .... Luke 22:10
she went out to *m* him ....John 11:20
to *m* the Lord in the air......... 1 Thess 4:17

MEETING

In the tent of *m* outside .... Exod 27:21

MEETINGS

not abandoning our own *m*....... Heb 10:25

MEGIDDO

City of Canaan; scene of battles,
    Judg 5:19–21; 2 Kgs 23:29–30
Fortified by Solomon, 1 Kgs 9:15
Possible site of Armageddon, Rev 16:16

MELCHIZEDEK

Priest and king of Salem, Gen 14:18–20
Type of Christ's eternal priesthood,
    Heb 7:1–22

MELT

The mountains *m* like wax...........Ps 97:5

MEMBER

the body is not a single *m* ....1 Cor 12:14
If they were all the same *m*.......1 Cor 12:19
greater honor to the lesser *m* ... 1 Cor 12:24
If one *m* suffers...................1 Cor 12:26

MEMBERS

m of the prophetic guild...........2 Kgs 2:3
better to lose one of your *m*...... Matt 5:29
do not present your *m* to sin ......Rom 6:13
in one body we have many *m*......Rom 12:4
your bodies are *m* of Christ.......1 Cor 6:15
So now there are many *m* ....1 Cor 12:20
we are *m* of one another .... Eph 4:25

MEMORIAL

this is my *m* from generation......Exod 3:15
This day will become a *m*.........Exod 12:14
and a *m* on your forehead.........Exod 13:9
gone up as a *m* before God........Acts 10:4

MEMORIES

I have fond *m* of you.................Jer 2:2

MEMORIZE

You must *m* it day and night........Josh 1:8

MEMORY

His *m* perishes from the earth......Job 18:17
cut off the *m* of his children .....Ps 109:15
The *m* of the righteous ....Prov 10:7
will also be told in *m* of her...... Matt 26:13
will also be told in *m* of her....... Mark 14:9

MEMPHIS

Ancient capital of Egypt, Hos 9:6
Prophesied against by Isaiah, Isa 19:13
Jews flee to, Jer 44:1
Denounced by the prophets, Jer 46:19

MEN

See also WISE MEN
we are honest *m*....................Gen 42:11
two Hebrew *m* fighting............Exod 2:13
Send out *m* to investigate ....Num 13:2
and the *m* of the city ....Judg 6:27
the advice of the older *m*........ 2 Chr 10:13
God abandons me to evil *m* ....Job 16:11
Wicked *m*...........................Job 34:18

in the footsteps of violent *m* .... Ps 17:4
Protect me from the wicked *m* ...... Ps 17:9
wicked *m* seem to succeed .... Ps 37:1
Wicked *m* will be wiped out .... Ps 37:9
Evil *m* will soon disappear.......... Ps 37:10
What can mere *m* do to me .... Ps 56:4
You receive tribute from *m*........ Ps 68:18
away from me, you evil *m* ...... Ps 119:115
to flog honorable *m* is wrong.....Prov 17:26
stand in the place of great *m* .... Prov 25:6
so that *m* will fear him.............Eccl 3:14
beloved among the young *m* ...... Song 2:3
Proud *m* will be brought low .... Isa 2:11
malicious young *m* will rule ....Isa 3:4
have raced on foot against *m*........Jer 12:5
The leading *m* of the cities ....Jer 14:3
But I see four *m* .... Dan 3:25
demon-possessed *m* coming ..... Matt 8:28
they loved praise from *m*.........John 12:43
your young *m* will see visions .... Acts 2:17
both *m* and women................. Acts 2:18
likewise the *m* also abandoned....Rom 1:27
If I speak in the tongues of *m*......1 Cor 13:1
a living stone rejected by *m* ....1 Pet 2:4

MENAHEM
Cruel king of Israel, 2 Kgs 15:14–18

MENORAH
I see a *m* of pure gold .... Zech 4:2

MENSTRUATION
is to be in her *m* seven days .... Lev 15:19
she lies on during her *m*...........Lev 15:20

MENTIONED
m the exodus of the sons..........Heb 11:22

MEPHIBOSHETH
Son of King Saul, 2 Sam 21:8
—Grandson of King Saul; crippled son of
    Jonathan, 2 Sam 4:4–6
Sought out and honored by David,
    2 Sam 9:1–13
Accused by Ziba, 2 Sam 16:1–4
Later explains himself to David,
    2 Sam 19:24–30
Spared by David, 2 Sam 21:7
Also called "Meribbaal," 1 Chr 8:34

MERAB
King Saul's eldest daughter, 1 Sam 14:49
Saul promises her to David, but gives her to
    Adriel, 1 Sam 18:17–19

MERARI
Third son of Levi, Gen 46:11
—Descendants of, called Merarites:
Duties in the tabernacle, Num 3:35–37
Cities assigned to, Josh 21:7, 34–40
Duties in the temple, 1 Chr 26:10–19
Assist Ezra after Exile, Ezra 8:18–19

MERCHANDISE
perceived that her *m* was good... Prov 31:18

MERCHANTS
the Midianite *m* passed by........Gen 37:28
your *m* more than the stars ....Nah 3:16
your *m* were the tycoons..........Rev 18:23

MERCIES
by the *m* of God .... Rom 12:1
the Father of *m* and .... 2 Cor 1:3

MERCIFUL
for he is a *m* God ....Deut 4:31
Blessed are the *m* ....Matt 5:7
he is *m* to those who fear him.... Luke 1:50
Be *m*, just as your Father is ....Luke 6:36
be *m* to me ....Luke 18:13
be *m* toward their evil deeds ...... Heb 8:12

MERCY
See also HAVE MERCY; MERCY SEAT
m to whom I will show *m*........ Exod 33:19
have *m* on you.................... Deut 13:17
for his *m* is great ....2 Sam 24:14
be shown *m* by their captors ... 2 Chr 30:9
has heard my appeal for *m*.........Ps 6:9
Hear my plea for *m*................Ps 28:2

not ignore my appeal for *m* .... Ps 55:1
Listen to my appeal for *m* .... Ps 119:170
attention to my plea for *m* ....Ps 130:2
not let *m* and truth leave you.......Prov 3:3
If the wicked are shown *m* .... Isa 26:10
In his love and *m* he protected .... Isa 63:9
They are cruel and show no *m* .... Jer 6:23
I will not show any pity, *m*.........Jer 13:14
and abounding in *m* ....Jonah 4:2
once again have *m* on us .... Mic 7:19
I want *m* and not sacrifice ....Matt 9:13
Should you not have shown *m* ...Matt 18:33
have *m* on whom I have *m*.........Rom 9:15
but on God who shows *m* ....Rom 9:16
he may show *m* to them all....... Rom 11:32
as one shown *m* by the Lord......1 Cor 7:25
just as God has shown us *m* .... 2 Cor 4:1
in *m* because of his great love ...... Eph 2:4
yourselves with a heart of *m* ...... Col 3:12
But I was treated with *m* ....1 Tim 1:13
to find *m* from the Lord .... 2 Tim 1:18
but on the basis of his *m* .... Titus 3:5
to receive *m* and find grace........ Heb 4:16
the one who has shown no *m* ......Jas 2:13
is full of compassion and *m*.......... Jas 5:11
the *m* of our Lord Jesus Christ......Jude 1:21

MERCY SEAT
him at his death as the *m*......... Rom 3:25
glory overshadowing the *m* .... Heb 9:5

MERIBBAAL
See MEPHIBOSHETH

MERODACH BALADAN
Sends ambassadors to Hezekiah, Isa 39:1–8
A king of Babylon, 2 Kgs 20:12–19

MEROM
Lake on Jordan, Josh 11:5, 7

MEROZ
Town cursed for failing to help the Lord,
    Judg 5:23

MERRYMAKING
is in the house of *m*................. Eccl 7:4

MESH
and he wanders into a *m* .... Job 18:8

MESHACH
Babylonian name given to Mishael, Dan 1:7
Advanced to high position, Dan 2:49
Remains faithful in testing, Dan 3:13–30

MESHECH
Son of Japheth, Gen 10:2
His descendants, mentioned in prophecy,
    Ezek 27:13; 32:26; 38:2–3

MESOPOTAMIA [or ARAM NAHARAIM;
    PADDAN ARAM]
Home of Abraham's relatives, Gen 24:4,
    10, 15
Israel enslaved to, Judg 3:8–10
Jews from, present at Pentecost, Acts 2:9
Also called "Aram Naharaim," Gen 24:10
Also called "Paddan Aram," Gen 25:20

MESSAGE
a *m* by the hand of a fool .... Prov 26:6
heard a *m* from the LORD.......... Jer 49:14
a *m* was revealed to Daniel........Dan 10:1
the *m* that I tell you ....Jonah 3:2
m about the cross is foolishness...1 Cor 1:18
the *m* of wisdom ....1 Cor 12:8
But the *m* they heard.............. Heb 4:2
welcome the *m* implanted.......... Jas 1:21
Now this is the gospel *m* ....1 John 1:5

MESSAGES
m to us about what is right........ Isa 30:10

MESSENGER
Jezebel sent a *m* to Elijah..........1 Kgs 19:2
and a *m* came to Job...............Job 1:14
so is a faithful *m*..................Prov 25:13
a *m* who announces peace..........Isa 52:7
m sent from his very presence ..... Isa 63:9
I am about to send my *m*........... Mal 3:1
sending my *m* ahead of you ...... Matt 11:10

the one who is sent as a *m* .... John 13:16
a *m* of Satan to trouble me....... 2 Cor 12:7

MESSENGERS
that sends *m* by sea ....Isa 18:2
m sent to make peace weep........Isa 33:7

MESSIAH
We have found the *M* .... John 1:41
at that time without the *M* ....Eph 2:12

MESSIAHS
false *m* and false prophets.......Matt 24:24

MET
the angels of God *m* him ....Gen 32:1
without having *m*...................Amos 3:3
ten men with leprosy *m* him......Luke 17:12
Cornelius *m* him...................Acts 10:25
a slave girl *m* us ....Acts 16:16
m Abraham as he was returning.....Heb 7:1

METAL
will purify your *m* with flux..........Isa 1:25

METHODS
They use deceitful *m* .... Isa 59:8

METHUSELAH
Oldest man on record at 969 years old,
    Gen 5:27

MICAH
Prophet, contemporary of Isaiah, Isa 1:1;
    Mic 1:1

MICAIAH
Prophet who predicts Ahab's death,
    1 Kgs 22:8–28
—Contemporary of Jeremiah, Jer 36:11–13

MICE
five gold sores and five gold *m* ... 1 Sam 6:4

MICHAEL
Leading prince, Dan 10:13, 21
Disputes with Satan, Jude 1:9
Fights the dragon, Rev 12:7–9

MICHAL
Daughter of King Saul, 1 Sam 14:49
Loves and marries David, 1 Sam 18:20–28
Saves David from Saul, 1 Sam 19:9–17
Given to Paltiel, 1 Sam 25:44
David demands her from Abner,
    2 Sam 3:13–16
Ridicules David; becomes barren,
    2 Sam 6:16–23

MICMASH
Site of battle with Philistines, 1 Sam 13:5,
    11, 16, 23
Scene of Jonathan's victory, 1 Sam 14:1–16

MIDDLE
sanctuary will be in the *m* of it ... Ezek 48:8
boat was in the *m* of the sea......Mark 6:47
with Jesus in the *m* ....John 19:18
the *m* wall of partition..............Eph 2:14

MIDIAN
Son of Abraham by Keturah, Gen 25:1–4
—Region in the Arabian desert occupied by
    the Midianites, Gen 25:6; Exod 2:15

MIDIANITES
Descendants of Abraham by Keturah,
    Gen 25:1–2
Moses flees to, Exod 2:15
Join Moab in cursing Israel, Num 22:4–7
Intermarriage with incurs God's wrath,
    Num 25:1–18
Defeated by Israel, Num 31:1–10
Oppress Israel; defeated by Gideon,
    Judg 6–7

MIDST
that I am in the *m* of Israel ....Joel 2:27

MIGDOL
Israelite encampment, Exod 14:2
Place Jews flee to in Egypt, Jer 44:1

MIGHT
You possess strength and *m*..... 1 Chr 29:12
Dominion and awesome *m*.........Job 25:2

not saved by his great *m*............ Ps 33:16
do it with all your *m* .... Eccl 9:10
that wisdom is better than *m* ...... Eccl 9:16
the *m* of earthly kingdoms .... Hag 2:22
according to his glorious *m*.......... Col 1:11

MIGHTILY
Holy One of Israel acts *m*............ Isa 12:6

MIGHTY
were the *m* heroes of old........... Gen 6:4
He was a *m* hunter .... Gen 10:9
out of there with a *m* hand .... Exod 13:3
How the *m* have fallen............. 2 Sam 1:19
wise in heart and *m* in strength...... Job 9:4
even all your *m* efforts .... Job 36:19
LORD who is strong and *m*.......... Ps 24:8
and the *m* waves of the sea.......... Ps 93:4
recount the LORD's *m* acts.......... Ps 106:2
Praise him for his *m* acts .... Ps 150:2
M God, Everlasting Father........... Isa 9:6
will rule there as our *m* king........ Isa 33:21
m power and great strength........ Jer 21:5
and you do *m* deeds .... Jer 32:19
all the *m* waves you sent .... Jonah 2:3
the *m* soldiers are dressed .... Nah 2:3
who is *m* has done great things.... Luke 1:49
He has brought down the *m*....... Luke 1:52
from heaven with his *m* angels .. 2 Thess 1:7

MILCOM
Ammonite god worshiped by Solomon,
  1 Kgs 11:5
Altar of, destroyed by Josiah, 2 Kgs 23:12–13

MILETUS
Paul meets Ephesian elders here,
  Acts 20:15–38
Paul leaves Trophimus here, 2 Tim 4:20

MILITARY
his great power and *m* ability....2 Kgs 17:36

MILK
See also MILK AND HONEY
flowing with *m* and honey......... Exod 3:8
and she gave him *m* .... Judg 5:25
you not pour me out like *m* .... Job 10:10
and *m* are under your tongue ..... Song 4:11
Buy wine and *m* .... Isa 55:1
whiter than *m* .... Lam 4:7
the hills will flow with *m* .... Joel 3:18
gone back to needing *m*............. Heb 5:12
everyone who lives on *m*........... Heb 5:13
for pure, spiritual *m* .... 1 Pet 2:2

MILK AND HONEY
a land flowing with *m*.............. Exod 3:8
is indeed flowing with *m* .... Num 13:27
have a land flowing with *m*........ Deut 6:3
a land rich in *m*..................... Josh 5:6
a land flowing with *m*............... Jer 11:5
a land flowing with *m*............. Ezek 20:6

MILL
sound of the grinding *m*........... Eccl 12:4
grinding grain with a *m*.......... Matt 24:41

MILLSTONE
huge *m* hung around his neck..... Matt 18:6
a stone like a huge *m*............. Rev 18:21

MIND
and confusion of *m*..............Deut 28:28
and put out of *m* the God........ Deut 32:18
she was speaking in her *m*........ 1 Sam 1:13
a wise and discerning *m*.......... 1 Kgs 3:12
I will take control of his *m*....... 2 Kgs 19:7
calculated the cost in his *m*...... Prov 23:7
human *m* is more deceitful........ Jer 17:9
and will no longer call to *m*....... Jer 31:34
visions of my *m*..................... Dan 4:5
and with all your *m*............... Matt 22:37
and in his right *m*.................. Mark 5:15
with all your *m* .... Mark 12:33
were of one heart and *m*.......... Acts 4:32
the law of God with my *m*........ Rom 7:25
knows the *m* of the Spirit........ Rom 8:27
has known the *m* of the Lord..... Rom 11:34
by the renewing of your *m*....... Rom 12:2

fully convinced in his own *m* ......Rom 14:5
has known the *m* of the Lord...... 1 Cor 2:16
I will also pray with my *m* .... 1 Cor 14:15
speak five words with my *m*...... 1 Cor 14:19
talking like I am out of my *m* .... 2 Cor 11:23
with this goal in *m*................. Phil 3:14
to stir up your pure *m*............. 2 Pet 3:1

MINDS
of their *m* was only evil............. Gen 6:5
Lest the people change their *m*.. Exod 13:17
examine people's hearts and *m*... Jer 11:20
Then he opened their *m*........... Luke 24:45
upsetting your *m* by .... Acts 15:24
that you have lost your *m* .... 1 Cor 14:23
I will put my laws in their *m* .... Heb 8:10
get your *m* ready for action .... 1 Pet 1:13
who searches *m* and hearts .... Rev 2:23

MINISTER
a *m* in the sanctuary................ Heb 8:2

MINISTERING
Many thousands were *m* .... Dan 7:10
angels came and began *m* .... Matt 4:11
Are they not all *m* spirits .... Heb 1:14

MINISTRIES
And there are different *m* .... 1 Cor 12:5

MINISTRY
I magnify my *m*.................... Rom 11:13
if the *m* that produced death..... 2 Cor 3:7
since we have this *m*................ 2 Cor 4:1
the *m* of reconciliation .... 2 Cor 5:18
for the work of *m*.................. Eph 4:12
m you received in the Lord .... Col 4:17
fulfill your *m*....................... 2 Tim 4:5
Jesus has obtained a superior *m*.... Heb 8:6

MINT
You give a tenth of *m*............ Matt 23:23

MIRACLE
Pharaoh says to you, 'Do a *m*...... Exod 7:9
who does a *m* in my name....... Mark 9:39

MIRACLES
performing extraordinary *m*.......Acts 19:11
to another performance of *m* .... 1 Cor 12:10
Not all perform *m* .... 1 Cor 12:29
with all kinds of *m* and signs .... 2 Thess 2:9
and wonders and various *m* .... Heb 2:4
and the *m* of the coming age .... Heb 6:5

MIRIAM
Sister of Aaron and Moses, Num 26:59
Chosen by God; a prophet, Exod 15:20
Punished for rebellion, Num 12:1–16
Buried at Kadesh, Num 20:1

MISERABLE
How *m* I am .... Ps 120:5

MISERIES
over the *m* that are coming........... Jas 5:1

MISERY
remember their *m* no more .... Prov 31:7
by its owner to his own *m*......... Eccl 5:13

MISFORTUNE
is fruitless and a grave *m* .... Eccl 6:2

MISHNEH
in Jerusalem in the *M* district....2 Kgs 22:14

MISLEAD
your leaders *m* you................. Isa 3:12
prophets who *m* my people .... Mic 3:5

MISLEADS
Watch out that no one *m* you .... Matt 24:4

MISLED
Watch out that you are not *m* .....Luke 21:8

MISSED
he greatly *m* all of you............. Phil 2:26

MISSES
But the one who *m* me .... Prov 8:36

MISSING
is *m* cannot be supplied .... Eccl 1:15
of these creatures will be *m* ...... Isa 34:16

MIST
of *m* in the heat of harvest .... Isa 18:4
as fleeting as the morning *m* .... Hos 6:4

MISTAKE
It was a *m* .... Eccl 5:6
You are making a fatal *m*......... Jer 42:20

MISTREAT
and to *m* his servants............. Ps 105:25
and *m* them for 400 years......... Acts 7:6

MISTREATED
Egyptians *m* and oppressed us ... Deut 26:6
deal with those who *m* you....... Zeph 3:19
insolently *m* them .... Matt 22:6
be mocked, *m*, and spat on ...... Luke 18:32
and were *m* in Philippi............ 1 Thess 2:2
you sin and are *m* and endure .... 1 Pet 2:20

MISUSES
who *m* the name of the LORD .....Lev 24:16

MITYLENE
Visited by Paul, Acts 20:13–15

MIXED
m with three measures of flour .. Luke 13:21

MIZPAH
Site of covenant between Jacob and Laban,
  Gen 31:44–53
—Town of Benjamin; outraged Israelites
  gather here, Josh 18:21, 26; Judg 20:1, 3
Samuel gathers Israel, 1 Sam 7:5–16; 10:17–25
Residence of Gedaliah, 2 Kgs 25:23, 25

MOAB
Son of Lot, Gen 19:33–37
—Country of the Moabites, Deut 1:5

MOABITES
Descendants of Lot, Gen 19:36–37
Join Midian in cursing Israel, Num 22:4
Excluded from Israel, Deut 23:3–6
Kindred of Ruth, Ruth 1:4
Subdued by Israel, 1 Sam 14:47; 2 Sam 8:2;
  2 Kgs 3:4–27
Women of, lead Solomon astray, 1 Kgs 11:1–8
Prophecies concerning, Isa 11:14; 15:1–9;
  Jer 48:1–47; Amos 2:1–3

MOAN
the people who *m* and groan ...... Ezek 9:4

MOANS
So my heart *m* for Moab .... Jer 48:36

MOB
I hate the *m* of evil men .... Ps 26:5
they formed a *m* and set .... Acts 17:5

MOCK
They *m* and say evil things .... Ps 73:8
m when what you dread comes ... Prov 1:26
Fools *m* at reparation............... Prov 14:9
and nations will *m* all of you........ Mic 6:16
m kings and laugh at rulers......... Hab 1:10

MOCKED
At noon Elijah *m* them............ 1 Kgs 18:27
to be *m* and flogged severely.... Matt 20:19
they *m* him: "Hail, king of the.... Matt 27:29

MOCKER
Whoever corrects a *m*............. Prov 9:7
Wine is a *m* and strong drink...... Prov 20:1

MOCKING
m lips and a foreign tongue .... Isa 28:11
experienced *m* and flogging....... Heb 11:36

MOCKS
The one who *m* the poor .... Prov 17:5

MODESTY
with *m* and self-control........... 1 Tim 2:9

MOISTURE
the wilderness glisten with *m* ...... Ps 65:12

MOLDED
what is *m* say to the molder...... Rom 9:20

MOLECH
Human sacrifice made to, Lev 18:21;
  2 Kgs 23:10

MOMENT
In a *m* they die......................Job 34:20
his anger lasts only a brief *m*........Ps 30:5
nation be born in a single *m*........Isa 66:8
a *m*, in the blinking of an eye.....1 Cor 15:52

MOMENTARILY
of anger I rejected you *m*.............Isa 54:8

MOMENTARY
For our *m*, light suffering.........2 Cor 4:17

MONEY
return each man's *m* to his
   sack............................Gen 42:25
in trouble or owed someone *m*..1 Sam 22:2
interest when he lends his *m*.........Ps 15:5
one who generously lends *m*........Ps 112:5
the point of a fool having *m*......Prov 17:16
The one who loves *m*...............Eccl 5:10
but *m* is the answer.................Eccl 10:19
will not be redeemed for *m*..........Isa 52:3
You who have no *m*...................Isa 55:1
I have not lent *m* to anyone........Jer 15:10
extort *m* from your neighbors....Ezek 22:12
You cannot serve God and *m*....Matt 6:24
the tables of the *m* changers....Matt 21:12
and hid his master's *m* in it......Matt 25:18
and promised to give him *m*......Mark 14:11
Do not carry a *m* bag..............Luke 10:4
sent you out with no *m* bag.....Luke 22:35
As keeper of the *m* box............John 12:6
with a large sum of *m*............Acts 22:28
free from the love of *m*............1 Tim 3:3
love of *m* is the root of all evils...1 Tim 6:10
be free from the love of *m*.........Heb 13:5

MONSTER
Did you not wound the sea *m*.......Isa 51:9
great *m* lying in the midst........Ezek 29:3

MONTH
day of the seventh *m*................Gen 8:4
This *m* is to be your beginning....Exod 12:2
will bear fruit every *m*............Ezek 47:12
In the sixth *m* of Elizabeth's.......Luke 1:26
she is now in her sixth *m*..........Luke 1:36
yielding its fruit every *m*............Rev 22:2

MONTHS
she hid him for three *m*............Exod 2:2
with Elizabeth about three *m*......Luke 1:56
days and *m* and seasons............Gal 4:10
to torture them for five *m*..........Rev 9:5
authority for forty-two *m*..........Rev 13:5

MONUMENT
they will be a *m* to the LORD........Isa 55:13

MOON
the *m*, and eleven stars............Gen 37:9
and the *m* stood motionless.......Josh 10:13
and see the *m* and the stars..........Ps 8:3
as the *m* remains in the sky.........Ps 72:7
the *m* to mark the months........Ps 104:19
or the *m* by night...................Ps 121:6
Beautiful as the *m*.................Song 6:10
sun and the *m* grow dark...........Joel 2:10
the *m* to the color of blood.........Joel 2:31
The sun and *m* are darkened.......Joel 3:15
The sun and *m* stand still..........Hab 3:11
the *m* will not give its light......Mark 13:24
the sun and *m* and stars.........Luke 21:25
new *m*, or Sabbath days.............Col 2:16
the full *m* became blood red.......Rev 6:12
not need the sun or the *m*........Rev 21:23

MORALE
rejoicing to see your *m*.............Col 2:5

MORALITY
m is not even able to enter........Isa 59:14

MORDECAI
Esther's guardian; advises her, Esth 2:5-20
Reveals plot to kill the king, Esth 2:21-23
Refuses homage to Haman, Esth 3:1-6
Honored by the king, Esth 6:1-12
Exalted highly, Esth 8:15; 9:4
Institutes feast of Purim, Esth 9:20-31

MORE
m so than any launderer..........Mark 9:3
that it is *m* to your advantage....John 11:50
be pitied *m* than anyone..........1 Cor 15:19
that you do so *m* and *m*.........1 Thess 4:1

MORESHETH GATH
Birthplace of Micah the prophet, Mic 1:14

MORIAH, MOUNT
See MOUNT MORIAH

MORNING
and there was *m*......................Gen 1:5
must leave nothing until *m*.......Exod 12:10
So they gathered it each *m*.......Exod 16:21
Be prepared in the *m*.............Exod 34:2
she slept beside him until *m*......Ruth 3:14
in the *m* you will hear me............Ps 5:3
but joy arrives in the *m*...........Ps 30:5
m, and noontime I will lament......Ps 55:17
in the *m* my prayer confronts......Ps 88:13
your loyal love in the *m*............Ps 92:2
They are fresh every *m*............Lam 3:23
and in the *m*......................Matt 16:3
It was nine o'clock in the *m*......Mark 15:25
the *m* star rises in your hearts.....2 Pet 1:19
the bright *m* star...................Rev 22:16

MORTAL
do you make all people so *m*......Ps 89:47
let sin reign in your *m* body.......Rom 6:12
also make your *m* bodies alive....Rom 8:11
is *m* may be swallowed up.........2 Cor 5:4
tithes are received by *m* men.......Heb 7:8

MORTALITY
my *m* and the brevity of life.........Ps 39:4
So teach us to consider our *m*......Ps 90:12

MORTALS
Yet you will die like *m*.................Ps 82:7
boasting about mere *m*............1 Cor 3:21

MOSES
Born; hidden by mother; adopted by
   Pharaoh's daughter, Exod 2:1-10
Kills Egyptian and flees to Midian,
   Exod 2:11-22
Receives call from God, Exod 3:1-4:17
Returns to Israelites in Egypt, Exod 4:18-31
Wins Israel's deliverance with plagues,
   Exod 5:1-6:13; 6:28-11:10; 12:29-42
Leads Israel out of Egypt and through the
   Red Sea, Exod 13:17-14:31
His song of praise, Exod 15:1-18
Provides miraculously for the people,
   Exod 15:22-17:7
Appoints judges, Exod 18
Receives the law on Mount Sinai,
   Exod 19-23
Receives instructions for tabernacle,
   Exod 25-31
Intercedes for Israel's sin, Exod 32
Recommissioned and encouraged,
   Exod 33-34
Further instructions and building of the
   tabernacle, Exod 35-40
Consecrates Aaron, Lev 8:1-36
Takes census, Num 1:1-54
Resumes journey to Canaan, Num 10:11-36
Complains; 70 elders appointed,
   Num 11:1-35
Intercedes for people when they refuse to
   enter Canaan, Num 14:11-25
Puts down Korah's rebellion, Num 16
Sins in anger, Num 20:1-13
Makes bronze serpent, Num 21:4-9
Travels toward Canaan, Num 21:10-20
Takes second census, Num 26
Commissions Joshua as his successor,
   Num 27:12-23
Receives further laws, Num 28-30
Commands conquest of Midian, Num 31
Final instructions, Num 32-36
Forbidden to enter Promised Land,
   Deut 3:23-28
Gives farewell messages, Deut 32-33

Sees Promised Land; dies, Deut 34:1-7
Is mourned and extolled, Deut 34:8-12
Appears with Christ at transfiguration,
   Matt 17:1-3
See LAW OF MOSES
She named him *M*.................Exod 2:10
So *M* fled from Pharaoh............Exod 2:15
And *M* said, "Here I am.............Exod 3:4
LORD became angry with *M*......Exod 4:14
And *M* and Aaron did so............Exod 7:6
So *M* extended his staff...........Exod 10:13
M stretched out his hand.........Exod 14:21
people murmured against *M*....Exod 15:24
Whenever *M* would raise.........Exod 17:11
M wrote down all the words.....Exod 24:4
M said, "Show me your glory....Exod 33:18
the skin of *M'* face shone........Exod 34:35
M an Elijah also appeared.........Matt 17:3
Why then did *M* command us.....Matt 19:7
not read in the book of *M*.......Mark 12:26
law was given through *M*...........John 1:17
Just as *M* lifted up the serpent...John 3:14
death reigned from Adam until *M*..Rom 5:14
as *M* was also in God's house.......Heb 3:2
They sang the song of *M*...........Rev 15:3

MOST
See also MOST HIGH; MOST HOLY PLACE
the *m* beautiful of all places.........Ps 50:2
up in your *m* holy faith.............Jude 1:20

MOST HIGH
Blessed be Abram by the *M*.......Gen 14:19
the knowledge of the *M*.........Num 24:16
the *M* shouted loudly.........2 Sam 22:14
will sing praises to you, O *M*........Ps 9:2
because of the *M*'s faithfulness......Ps 21:7
the LORD *M* is awe-inspiring.........Ps 47:2
I cry out for help to God *M*.........Ps 57:2
that God *M* was their deliverer.....Ps 78:35
all of you are sons of the *M*.........Ps 82:6
lives in the shelter of the *M*.........Ps 91:1
the instructions of the *M*...........Ps 107:11
will make myself like the *M*........Isa 14:14
not from the mouth of the *M*.....Lam 3:38
servants of the *m* God.............Dan 3:26
that the *M* has authority.........Dan 4:17
The holy ones of the *M*...........Dan 7:18
Son of the *M* God.................Mark 5:7
the *M* does not live in houses.....Acts 7:48
are servants of the *M* God........Acts 16:17
priest of the *m* God...............Heb 7:1

MOST HOLY PLACE
the Holy Place and the *M*........Exod 26:33
he is to purify the *M*...............Lev 16:33
that would be the *M*...............1 Kgs 6:16
He made the *M*.....................2 Chr 3:8
said to me, "This is the *M*.........Ezek 41:4
entered once for all into the *M*.....Heb 9:12

MOTH
a *m* will eat away at them..........Isa 50:9
where *m* and devouring insect....Matt 6:19

MOTHER
she was the *m* of all the living......Gen 3:20
Honor your father and your *m*..Exod 20:12
Honor your father and your *m*....Deut 5:16
family a happy *m* of children........Ps 113:9
foolish child is a grief to his *m*.....Prov 10:1
the special daughter of her *m*.....Song 6:9
Like *m*, like daughter.............Ezek 16:44
saw the child with Mary his *m*.....Matt 2:11
loves father or *m* more..........Matt 10:37
will leave his father and *m*........Matt 19:5
are my *m* and my brothers.......Mark 3:33
father and *m* were amazed........Luke 2:33
his *m* kept all these things.........Luke 2:51
the only son of his *m*..............Luke 7:12
m against daughter................Luke 12:53
not hate his own father and *m*...Luke 14:26
here is your *m*.....................John 19:27
and she is our *m*....................Gal 4:26
without *m*, without genealogy......Heb 7:3
the *M* of prostitutes................Rev 17:5

MOTHER'S
should return to your *m* home .....Ruth 1:8
I came from my *m* womb............Job 1:21
feel secure on my *m* breasts........Ps 22:9
pulled me from my *m* womb .... Ps 71:6
making my pregnant *m* womb .....Jer 20:17

MOTHER-IN-LAW
Now Simon's *m* was suffering ....Luke 4:38

MOTIONLESS
and the moon stood *m* .... Josh 10:13

MOTIVE
and understands every *m*.........1 Chr 28:9

MOTIVES
you understand my *m* .... Ps 139:2
but the Lord evaluates the *m* .....Prov 16:2
with pure *m* and sincerity ....2 Cor 1:12

MOUNT CARMEL
Scene of Elijah's triumph, 1 Kgs 18:19–45
Elisha journeys to, 2 Kgs 2:25
Shunammite woman comes to Elisha at,
   2 Kgs 4:25

MOUNT EBAL
Mountain in Samaria, Deut 27:12–13
Cursed by God, Deut 11:29
Stones of the Law erected upon,
   Deut 27:1–8; Josh 8:30–35

MOUNT GAASH
Mount of Ephraim, Judg 2:9
Joshua buried near, Josh 24:30

MOUNT GERIZIM
Mount of blessing, Deut 11:29; 27:12
Jotham speaks to people of Shechem here,
   Judg 9:7
Samaritans' sacred mountain, John 4:20–21

MOUNT GILBOA
Men of Israel slain at, 1 Sam 31:1
Saul and his sons slain at, 1 Sam 31:8

MOUNT GILEAD
Gideon divides the people for battle at,
   Judg 7:3

MOUNT HERMON [or SIRION; SENIR]
Highest mountain (9,166 ft.) in Syria,
   Josh 12:1
Also called "Sirion" and "Senir," Deut 3:8–9

MOUNT HOR
Mountain of Edom; Lord speaks to Moses
   and Aaron on, Num 20:23
Aaron dies on, Num 20:25–28

MOUNT HOREB
Sons of Israel stripped of ornaments at,
   Exod 33:6
The mountain of God, Exod 3:1
See also MOUNT SINAI

MOUNT MORIAH
Place where Abraham offered Isaac,
   Gen 22:2
Elevation where Solomon built the temple,
   1 Chr 3:1

MOUNT NEBO
Place where Moses viewed the Promised
   Land, Deut 32:49
Moses dies here, Deut 32:49; 34:1, 5

MOUNT OF OLIVES
David flees to, 2 Sam 15:30
Prophecy concerning, Zech 14:4
Christ's triumphal entry from, Matt 21:1
Prophetic discourse delivered from,
   Matt 24:3
Christ's ascension from, Acts 1:9–12

MOUNT PERAZIM [or BAAL PERAZIM]
Site of David's victory over the Philistines,
   2 Sam 5:18–20
Also called "Baal Perazim," 2 Sam 5:20

MOUNT SINAI
Lord descends upon, in fire, Exod 19:18
Lord calls Moses to the top of,
   Exod 19:20

The glory of the Lord rests on, for six days,
   Exod 24:16

MOUNT TABOR
Deborah sends Barak there to defeat
   Canaanites, Judg 4:6–14

MOUNT ZION [or MOUNT SIYON]
Survivors shall go out from, 2 Kgs 19:31
Also called "Mount Siyon," Deut 4:48

MOUNTAIN
In the *m* of the Lord .... Gen 22:14
and came to the *m* of God.......... Exod 3:1
to go up on the *m* nor touch......Exod 19:12
and a dense cloud on the *m* ......Exod 19:16
when he went up the *m* .... Exod 24:18
a *m* falls away and crumbles...... Job 14:18
m of Bashan is a towering *m* ...... Ps 68:15
the *m* peaks belong to him ....Ps 95:4
let us go up to the Lord's *m*..........Isa 2:3
and every *m* and hill leveled........Isa 40:4
became a large *m*................. Dan 2:35
alarm signal on my holy *m* ....Joel 2:1
you great *m* .... Zech 4:7
took him to a very high *m* .... Matt 4:8
he went up the *m*................. Matt 5:1
you will say to this *m* .... Matt 17:20
coming down from the *m* ....Mark 9:9
if someone says to this *m* ....Mark 11:23
m and hill will be brought low.....Luke 3:5
fathers worshiped on this *m*........John 4:20
were with him on the holy *m* ......2 Pet 1:18
every *m* and island was moved.....Rev 6:14
to a huge, majestic *m*..............Rev 21:10

MOUNTAINS
tops of the *m* became visible .... Gen 8:5
He who removes *m* suddenly........Job 9:5
the *m* tumble into the depths ....Ps 46:2
m will bring news of peace ....Ps 72:3
the *m* came into existence..........Ps 90:2
The *m* melt like wax................Ps 97:5
The *m* skipped like rams ....Ps 114:4
As the *m* surround Jerusalem ......Ps 125:2
O *m*, give a joyful shout ....Isa 44:23
see approaching over the *m*........Isa 52:7
Even if the *m* are removed .... Isa 54:10
the *m* trembled before you......... Isa 64:3
The *m* will topple................Ezek 38:20
whose home is high in the *m* ...... Obad 1:3
in Judea must flee to the *m* ...... Matt 24:16
among the tombs and in the *m*....Mark 5:5
they will begin to say to the *m* ..Luke 23:30
faith so that I can remove *m*.......1 Cor 13:2
wandered in deserts and *m*.......Heb 11:38
and no *m* could be found......... Rev 16:20

MOURN
are to *m* the burning ....Lev 10:6
and *m* my virginity................Judg 11:37
a time to *m* .... Eccl 3:4
Her gates will *m* and lament........ Isa 3:26
to console all who *m* ....Isa 61:2
those who *m* for the dead ....Jer 16:7
People will not *m* for him ....Jer 22:18
Blessed are those who *m*.......... Matt 5:4
wedding guests cannot *m* ....Matt 9:15
Grieve, *m*, and weep .... Jas 4:9
will *m* because of him .... Rev 1:7

MOURNING
them *m* at the threshing floor .....Gen 50:11
as if I were *m* for my mother ...... Ps 35:14
all day long I walk around *m*.......Ps 38:6
instead of *m* ....Isa 61:3
over you with intense *m*..........Ezek 27:31
we wailed in *m* ....Matt 11:17
Turn your laughter into *m*.......... Jas 4:9
shouting with weeping and *m* .....Rev 18:19
or *m*, or crying, or pain ....Rev 21:4

MOUTH
Who gave a *m* to man ....Exod 4:11
and put the words in his *m* ....Exod 4:15
and the earth opened its *m*...... Num 16:32
opened the *m* of the donkey ....Num 22:28
comes from the Lord's *m* .... Deut 8:3

in your *m* and in your mind...... Deut 30:14
m will continually praise him .... Ps 34:1
Then my *m* will praise you ....Ps 51:15
and every sinner shuts his *m* .....Ps 107:42
The *m* of an adulteress ....Prov 22:14
a flattering *m* works ruin........ Prov 26:28
opened her *m* with wisdom ......Prov 31:26
He touched my *m* with it.............Isa 6:7
bit into the *m* of the nations.......Isa 30:28
he did not even open his *m*.........Isa 53:7
I have placed in your *m*............Isa 59:21
and touched my *m* and said ....Jer 1:9
sweet like honey in my *m* ....Ezek 3:3
a *m* speaking arrogant things....... Dan 7:8
that comes from the *m* of God .... Matt 4:4
is not what goes into the *m*....... Matt 15:11
causes him to foam at the *m* .....Luke 9:39
so he did not open his *m* ....Acts 8:32
in your *m* and in your heart ......Rom 10:8
if you confess with your *m* ....Rom 10:9
and with the *m* one confesses ....Rom 10:10
word come out of your *m* .... Eph 4:29
the same *m* come blessing ....Jas 3:10
to vomit you out of my *m* ....Rev 3:16
as sweet as honey in your *m*.......Rev 10:9

MOUTHS
From the *m* of children................ Ps 8:2
They open their *m* to devour ...... Ps 22:13
their food was still in their *m* ...... Ps 78:30
They have *m*.......................Ps 115:5
and closed the lions' *m* ....Dan 6:22
Out of the *m* of children..........Matt 21:16

MOVE
mountain will *m* northward ...... Zech 14:4
M from here to there............ Matt 17:20
to lift a finger to *m* them .... Matt 23:4

MOVED
it cannot be *m* ....Ps 46:5
righteous will never be *m* .... Prov 10:30
he was intensely *m* in spirit....... John 11:33
Jesus, intensely *m* again .... John 11:38
Do not be *m* .... 1 Cor 15:58

MOVING
but the Spirit of God was *m* ....Gen 1:2

MUCH
I have become *m* wiser ....Eccl 1:16
and *m* study is exhausting.........Eccl 12:12
How *m* better is your love........ Song 4:10
lawlessness will increase so *m*... Matt 24:12
a hundred times as *m*............Mark 10:30
who has been given *m*........... Luke 12:48
M more then ....Rom 5:9

MUD
out of the slimy *m*..................Ps 40:2
made some *m* with the saliva.......John 9:6

MULTIFACETED
the *m* wisdom of God ....Eph 3:10

MULTIPLIED
the more they *m* and spread ......Exod 1:12

MULTIPLY
See also BE FRUITFUL AND MULTIPLY
Be fruitful and *m* and fill............Gen 1:22
greatly *m* your descendants ...... Gen 16:10
greatly *m* your descendants ...... Gen 22:17
will greatly *m* your children ......Deut 28:11
their troubles *m* .... Ps 16:4
and *m* your supply of seed ....2 Cor 9:10

MULTIPLYING
kept on increasing and *m*.........Acts 12:24

MULTITUDE
love covers a *m* of sins ....1 Pet 4:8

MURDER
You shall not *m*.................. Exod 20:13
Rescue me from the guilt of *m* ......Ps 51:14
You *m*. You commit adultery ....Jer 7:9
because the land is full of *m*.......Ezek 7:23
the land is full of *m*................ Ezek 9:9
Do not *m* ....Matt 5:21
m, adultery, sexual immorality ...Matt 15:19

who had committed *m* .... Mark 15:7
breathing out threats to *m* .... Acts 9:1
m, strife, deceit .... Rom 1:29
envying, *m*, drunkenness .... Gal 5:21
you *m* and envy .... Jas 4:2

MURDERED
of those who *m* the prophets ..... Matt 23:31
and brutally *m* his brother .... 1 John 3:12

MURDERER
was a *m* from the beginning ...... John 8:44
man who was a *m* be released ..... Acts 3:14
none of you suffer as a *m* .... 1 Pet 4:15
hates his fellow Christian is a *m* .. 1 John 3:15

MURDERERS
but now only *m* .... Isa 1:21
their fathers or mothers, for *m* ..... 1 Tim 1:9
m, the sexually immoral .... Rev 21:8

MURDERS
whoever *m* will be subjected ..... Matt 5:21
they did not repent of their *m* ...... Rev 9:21

MURKY
a light shining in a *m* place .... 2 Pet 1:19

MUSIC
Make *m* to him .... 1 Chr 16:9
with joy and *m* .... 2 Chr 23:18
and the sound of *m* .... Ps 98:5
he heard *m* and dancing .... Luke 15:25
and making *m* in your hearts .... Eph 5:19

MUSICAL
who had the *m* instruments .... 2 Chr 7:6

MUSICIANS
stringed instruments for the *m* ... 1 Kgs 10:12
Levites carrying the ark, the *m* ... 1 Chr 15:27
stringed instruments for the *m* ... 2 Chr 9:11
the *m* with various instruments . 2 Chr 23:13

MUST
You *m* keep carefully .... Deut 8:1
he *m* repay seven times over ...... Prov 6:31
say that Elijah *m* come first .... Matt 17:10
the Son of Man *m* suffer .... Mark 8:31
These things *m* happen .... Mark 13:7
the gospel *m* be preached .... Mark 13:10
I *m* be in my Father's house ...... Luke 2:49
You *m* all be born from above ...... John 3:7
He *m* become more important ... John 3:30
m worship in spirit and truth ..... John 4:24
We *m* perform the deeds .... John 9:4
Jesus *m* rise from the dead .... John 20:9
by which we *m* be saved .... Acts 4:12
how much he *m* suffer .... Acts 9:16
you *m* not consider ritually .... Acts 10:15
m put on the imperishable .... 1 Cor 15:53
If I *m* boast .... 2 Cor 11:30
then *m* be above reproach .... 1 Tim 3:2
likewise *m* be dignified .... 1 Tim 3:8
m not engage in heated .... 2 Tim 2:24
who made it *m* be proven .... Heb 9:16
m believe that he exists .... Heb 11:6
what sort of people *m* you be ..... 2 Pet 3:11
what *m* happen very soon .... Rev 1:1
these things he *m* be released ..... Rev 20:3
what *m* happen soon .... Rev 22:6

MUSTARD
have faith the size of a *m* seed .. Matt 17:20

MUSTER
to *m* the Israelite army .... 2 Sam 24:4

MUSTERING
m a large army .... Dan 11:10

MUTE
or who makes a person *m* .... Exod 4:11
like a *m* who cannot speak .... Ps 38:13
the *m* tongue will shout .... Isa 35:6
had been *m* began to speak ...... Matt 9:33
by a spirit that makes him *m* ..... Mark 9:17
M and deaf spirit .... Mark 9:25
a demon that was *m* .... Luke 11:14

MUZZLE
You must not *m* your ox .... Deut 25:4
Do not *m* an ox .... 1 Tim 5:18

MY RIGHT HAND
because he is at *m* .... Ps 16:8
you hold *m* .... Ps 73:23
Sit down at *m* until .... Ps 110:1
may *m* be crippled .... Ps 137:5
m spread out the sky .... Isa 48:13
said to my lord, "Sit at *m* .... Matt 22:44
for he is at *m* .... Acts 2:25
Sit at *m* until I make .... Heb 1:13
stars that you saw in *m* .... Rev 1:20

MYRA
Paul changes ships here, Acts 27:5–6

MYRIADS
and to *m* of angels .... Heb 12:22

MYRRH
have perfumed my bed with *m* .... Prov 7:17
my hands dripped with *m* .... Song 5:5
gold, frankincense, and *m* .... Matt 2:11
him wine mixed with *m* .... Mark 15:23

MYSIA
Paul and Silas pass through here,
    Acts 16:7–8

MYSTERIES
who reveals *m* .... Dan 2:28
know all *m* and all knowledge ..... 1 Cor 13:2
he is speaking *m* by the Spirit ..... 1 Cor 14:2

MYSTERY
hidden in a *m* .... 1 Cor 2:7
Listen, I will tell you a *m* .... 1 Cor 15:51
revealed to us the *m* of his will ...... Eph 1:9
This *m* is great .... Eph 5:32
m that has been kept hidden .... Col 1:26

MYTHS
to occupy themselves with *m* ..... 1 Tim 1:4
they will turn aside to *m* .... 2 Tim 4:4

N

NAAMAN
Captain in the Syrian army, 2 Kgs 5:1–11
Healed of his leprosy, 2 Kgs 5:14–17
Referred to by Christ, Luke 4:27

NABAL
Refuses David's request, 1 Sam 25:2–12
Escapes David's wrath; struck down by the
    Lord, 1 Sam 25:13–39

NABOTH
Murdered for his vineyard by King Ahab,
    1 Kgs 21:1–16
His murder avenged, 1 Kgs 21:17–25

NADAB
Eldest of Aaron's four sons, Exod 6:23
Takes part in affirming covenant, Exod 24:1,
    9–12
Becomes priest, Exod 28:1
Consumed by fire, Lev 10:1–7
—King of Israel, 1 Kgs 14:20
Killed by Baasha, 1 Kgs 15:25–31

NAHASH
King of Ammon; makes impossible
    demands, 1 Sam 11:1–15

NAHOR
Grandfather of Abraham, Gen 11:24–26
—Son of Terah, brother of Abraham,
    Gen 11:27

NAHUM
Prophet to Judah concerning Nineveh,
    Nah 1:1

NAILING
executed by *n* him to a cross ...... Acts 2:23
it away by *n* it to the cross .... Col 2:14

NAIN
Village south of Nazareth; Jesus raises
    widow's son here, Luke 7:11–17

NAIOTH
Prophets' school in Ramah, 1 Sam 19:18–19,
    22–23

NAIVE
deceive the minds of the *n* .... Rom 16:18

NAKED
man and his wife were both *n* ..... Gen 2:25
and they knew they were *n* .... Gen 3:7
Who told you that you were *n* ...... Gen 3:11
N I came from .... Job 1:21
underworld is *n* before God .... Job 26:6
n and you gave me clothing ..... Matt 25:36
but he ran off *n* .... Mark 14:52
we will not be found *n* .... 2 Cor 5:3
everything is *n* and exposed .... Heb 4:13
poor, blind, and *n* .... Rev 3:17

NAKEDNESS
saw his father's *n* .... Gen 9:22
she is your father's *n* .... Lev 18:8
n, and poverty you will serve .... Deut 28:48
or *n*, or danger .... Rom 8:35
n will not be exposed .... Rev 3:18

NAME
See also HOLY NAME; IN MY NAME
that was its *n* .... Gen 2:19
and I will make your *n* great .... Gen 12:2
will your *n* be Abram .... Gen 17:5
Sarah will be her *n* .... Gen 17:15
Your *n* is Jacob .... Gen 35:10
This is my *n* forever .... Exod 3:15
that my *n* may be declared .... Exod 9:16
the LORD is his *n* .... Exod 15:3
Israel called its *n* "manna .... Exod 16:31
not take the *n* of the LORD .... Exod 20:7
whose *n* is Jealous .... Exod 34:14
glorious and awesome *n* .... Deut 28:58
he has no *n* in the land .... Job 18:17
Let us praise his *n* together .... Ps 34:3
n their lands after themselves ...... Ps 49:11
in your *n* I will lift up .... Ps 63:4
Sing praises to his *n* .... Ps 68:4
His glorious *n* deserves praise ...... Ps 72:19
Praise his *n* .... Ps 100:4
but to your *n* bring honor .... Ps 115:1
and give thanks to your *n* .... Ps 138:2
n of the LORD is like a strong ..... Prov 18:10
A good *n* is to be chosen .... Prov 22:1
What is his *n* .... Prov 30:4
but we praise your *n* alone .... Isa 26:13
That is my *n* .... Isa 42:8
will be called by a new *n* .... Isa 62:2
No one invokes your *n* .... Isa 64:7
and made a *n* for yourself .... Dan 9:15
They will call on my *n* .... Zech 13:9
my *n* will be great among .... Mal 1:11
for you who respect my *n* .... Mal 4:2
and you will *n* him Jesus .... Matt 1:21
may your *n* be honored .... Matt 6:9
didn't we prophesy in your *n* ..... Matt 7:22
because of my *n* .... Matt 10:22
prophet in the *n* of a prophet ..... Matt 10:41
in his *n* the Gentiles will hope .... Matt 12:21
are assembled in my *n* .... Matt 18:20
For many will come in my *n* ...... Matt 24:5
What is your *n* .... Mark 5:9
in my *n* welcomes me .... Mark 9:37
In my *n* they will drive out .... Mark 16:17
you will *n* him John .... Luke 1:13
to a man whose *n* was Joseph ..... Luke 1:27
and you will *n* him Jesus .... Luke 1:31
and holy is his *n* .... Luke 1:49
His *n* is John .... Luke 1:63
who believe in his *n* .... John 1:12
I have come in my Father's *n* ..... John 5:43
He calls his own sheep by *n* ...... John 10:3
whatever you ask in my *n* .... John 14:13
the Father will send in my *n* ..... John 14:26
keep them safe in your *n* .... John 17:11
calls on the *n* of the Lord .... Acts 2:21
the basis of faith in Jesus' *n* .... Acts 3:16
for there is no other *n* .... Acts 4:12
for the sake of the *n* .... Acts 5:41
baptized in the *n* of Jesus .... Acts 10:48
who calls on the *n* of the Lord .... Rom 10:13
and every *n* that is named .... Eph 1:21

the *n* that is above every *n* ....Phil 2:9
so that at the *n* of Jesus..............Phil 2:10
all in the *n* of the Lord Jesus........ Col 3:17
inherited a *n* superior to theirs......Heb 1:4
acknowledging his *n*..................Heb 13:15
not blaspheme the good *n*............Jas 2:7
in the *n* of the Lord...................Jas 5:14
insulted for the *n* of Christ ...1 Pet 4:14
been forgiven because of his *n* ...1 John 2:12
in the *n* of the Son of God ....1 John 5:13
you continue to cling to my *n* .....Rev 2:13
and have not denied my *n*.........Rev 3:8
his *n* or his number................. Rev 13:17
his *n* and his Father's *n* ....Rev 14:1
and glorify your *n* ....Rev 15:4
a *n* written that no one knows.....Rev 19:12

NAMED
So the man *n* all the animals ......Gen 2:20
The man *n* his wife Eve.............Gen 3:20
whom he *n* Enosh ....Gen 4:26
May my name be *n* in them ......Gen 48:16
She *n* him Moses ....Exod 2:10
feet of a young man *n* Saul........Acts 7:58
and every name that is *n* ....Eph 1:21

NAMES
he *n* all of them.....................Ps 147:4
the *n* of the twelve apostles ....Matt 10:2
that your *n* stand written.........Luke 10:20
whose *n* are in the book of life ......Phil 4:3
whose *n* have not been written.....Rev 17:8
and the *n* of the twelve tribes .....Rev 21:12
twelve *n* of the twelve apostles....Rev 21:14

NAOMI
Widow of Elimelech, Ruth 1:1–3
Returns to Bethlehem with Ruth,
    Ruth 1:14–19
Asks to be called Mara, Ruth 1:20
Arranges Ruth's marriage to Boaz, Ruth 3–4

NAPHTALI
Son of Jacob by Bilhah, Gen 30:1–8
Receives Jacob's blessing, Gen 49:21, 28
—Tribe of:
Numbered, Num 1:42–43
Territory assigned to, Josh 19:32–39
Joins Gideon's army, Judg 7:23
Attacked by Ben Hadad and Tiglath-Pileser,
    1 Kgs 15:20; 2 Kgs 15:29
Prophecy of great light in; fulfilled in
    Christ's ministry, Isa 9:1–7; Matt 4:12–16

NARD
henna with *n* ....Song 4:13
costly aromatic oil from pure *n*... Mark 14:3

NARROW
Enter through the *n* gate ....Matt 7:13

NATHAN
Son of David, 2 Sam 5:14
Mary's lineage traced through, Zech 12:12
—Prophet under David and Solomon,
    1 Chr 29:29
Reveals God's plan to David, 2 Sam 7:2–29
Rebukes David's sin, 2 Sam 12:1–15
Reveals Adonijah's plot, 1 Kgs 1:10–46

NATHANAEL
See BARTHOLOMEW

NATION
will make you into a great *n*........Gen 12:2
slaughter an innocent *n* ....Gen 20:4
kingdom of priests and a holy *n* .. Exod 19:6
the *n* whose God is the LORD........Ps 33:12
could be your very own *n* ....Ps 74:2
not done so with any other *n* ...Ps 147:20
Righteousness exalts a *n* ....Prov 14:34
so a righteous *n* can enter.........Isa 26:2
The father of your *n* sinned........Isa 43:27
will become a large *n*...............Isa 60:22
n that did not invoke my name.....Isa 65:1
n be born in a single moment ....Isa 66:8
Has a *n* ever changed its gods ......Jer 2:11
make them one *n* in the land ... Ezek 37:22

whole *n* is guilty ....Mal 3:9
For *n* will rise up in arms ....Matt 24:7
because he loves our *n* ....Luke 7:5
N will rise up in arms..............Luke 21:10
than for the whole *n* to perish....John 11:50
by those who are not a *n* ....Rom 10:19
a royal priesthood, a holy *n*.......1 Pet 2:9
people, language, and *n* ....Rev 13:7

NATION'S
from the *n* beginning...............Dan 12:1

NATIONS
the *n* were separated..............Gen 10:5
Two *n* are in your womb.........Gen 25:23
be reckoned among the *n* ....Num 23:9
you will lend to many *n*......... Deut 28:12
will scatter you among all *n* .....Deut 28:64
O *n*, with his people ....Deut 32:43
thanks, O LORD, before the *n*...2 Sam 22:50
accomplishments among the *n*....1 Chr 16:8
Why do the *n* rebel ....Ps 2:1
and I will give you the *n* ....Ps 2:8
The LORD judges the *n*. ....Ps 7:8
Let all the *n* worship you ....Ps 22:27
I will be exalted over the *n* ....Ps 46:10
All you *n*, clap your hands ....Ps 47:1
Let the *n* thank you.................Ps 67:5
all *n* will serve him ....Ps 72:11
May all *n* consider him ....Ps 72:17
n will respect the reputation ......Ps 102:15
LORD is exalted over all the *n*........Ps 113:4
Why should the *n* say................Ps 115:2
Praise the LORD, all you *n* ....Ps 117:1
and all you *n*.......................Ps 148:11
judge disputes between *n* ....Isa 2:4
N will look to him ....Isa 11:10
All the *n* are insignificant ....Isa 40:17
and a light to the *n* ....Isa 42:6
you will summon *n* ....Isa 55:5
where all *n* may pray ....Isa 56:7
N come to your light ....Isa 60:3
will enjoy the wealth of *n*.........Isa 61:6
N will see your vindication ....Isa 62:2
the riches of *n* will flow...........Isa 66:12
O King of all *n* ....Jer 10:7
an object of scorn to the *n*........Ezek 22:4
all the *n* subject to my rule........Amos 9:12
between many distant *n*..........Mic 4:3
will live among the *n* ....Mic 5:8
n to give me acceptable praise ....Zeph 3:9
I will also shake up all the *n* ....Hag 2:7
Many *n* will join themselves.......Zech 2:11
will announce peace to the *n* .....Zech 9:10
I scatter them among the *n*.......Zech 10:9
a heavy burden for all the *n* ......Zech 12:3
For I will gather all the *n*.........Zech 14:2
will be great among the *n* ....Mal 1:11
and make disciples of all *n*.......Matt 28:19
in his name to all *n* ....Luke 24:47
your descendants all the *n*........Acts 3:25
became the father of many *n*.......Rom 4:18
the *n* will be blessed in you........Gal 3:8
going to rule over all the *n* ....Rev 12:5
For all the *n* have fallen..........Rev 18:3
are for the healing of the *n* ....Rev 22:2

NATURAL
the *n* sexual relations..............Rom 1:26
abandoned *n* relations............Rom 1:27
did not spare the *n* branches ......Rom 11:21
it is sown a *n* body...............1 Cor 15:44
did not come first, but the *n*.....1 Cor 15:46
but is earthly, *n*, demonic............Jas 3:15

NATURE
human *n* is of no help ....John 6:63
eternal power and divine *n*........Rom 1:20
do by *n* the things required........Rom 2:14
Does not *n* itself teach you ....1 Cor 11:14
were by *n* children of wrath ....Eph 2:3
partakers of the divine *n* ....2 Pet 1:4

NAZARENE
Jesus to be called, Matt 2:23
Descriptive of Jesus' followers, Acts 24:5

NAZARETH
Town in Galilee; considered obscure,
    John 1:46
City of Jesus' parents, Matt 2:23
Early home of Jesus, Luke 2:39–51
Jesus rejected by, Luke 4:16–30

NEAPOLIS
Seaport of Philippi, Acts 16:11

NEAR
nation has a god so *n* to them .....Deut 4:7
For the thing is very *n* you.......Deut 30:14
The LORD is *n* all who cry out......Ps 145:18
they want to be *n* God..............Isa 58:2
the kingdom of heaven is *n*........Matt 3:2
know that he is *n* ....Matt 24:33
the kingdom of God is *n*..........Luke 21:31
The word is *n* you ....Rom 10:8
peace to those who were *n*........Eph 2:17
The Lord is *n* ....Phil 4:5
you see the day drawing *n*........Heb 10:25
for the Lord's return is *n*...........Jas 5:8
because the time is *n*...............Rev 1:3

NEARBY
call to him while he is *n* .... Isa 55:6
Now there were shepherds *n*...... Luke 2:8

NEARER
for our salvation is now *n*..........Rom 13:11

NEARS
For my life *n* its end in pain......... Ps 31:10

NEBO
Babylonian god, Isa 46:1
—Summit of Pisgah; *see* MOUNT NEBO

NEBUCHADNEZZAR
Monarch of the Neo-Babylonian Empire
    (605–562 BC); carries Jews captive to
    Babylon, Dan 1:1–3
Crushes Jehoiachin's revolt, 2 Kgs 24:10–17
Destroys Jerusalem; captures Zedekiah,
    Jer 39:5–8
Prophecies concerning, Isa 14:4–27;
    Jer 21:7–10; 25:8–9; 27:4–11; 32:28–36;
    43:10–13; Ezek 26:7–12

NEBUZARADAN
Nebuchadnezzar's captain at siege of
    Jerusalem, 2 Kgs 25:8–20
Protects Jeremiah, Jer 39:11–14

NECESSARY
n that stumbling blocks come.....Matt 18:7
n to speak the word of God ......Acts 13:46
n to circumcise the Gentiles.......Acts 15:5
n for the sketches of the things ...Heb 9:23

NECK
and the smooth part of his *n* .....Gen 27:16
he hugged his *n* and wept ....Gen 46:29
bind them around your *n*.........Prov 3:3
and grace around your *n* ....Prov 3:22
The one who stiffens his *n*........Prov 29:1
Your *n* is like a tower..............Song 7:4
and their yoke from your *n*........Isa 10:27
Your *n* muscles are like iron........Isa 48:4
millstone hung around his *n*.......Matt 18:6

NECKS
risked their own *n* for my life......Rom 16:4

NEED
your *n* like an armed robber......Prov 24:34
your Father knows what you *n* .... Matt 6:8
healthy don't *n* a physician ....Matt 9:12
David did when he was in *n*.......Mark 2:25
from your heart to those in *n*.....Luke 11:41
and he began to be in *n*...........Luke 15:14
do we *n* further testimony.......Luke 22:71
as anyone had *n* ....Acts 2:45
as anyone had *n* ....Acts 4:35
I do not *n* you......................1 Cor 12:21
abundance will meet their *n*......2 Cor 8:14
and minister to me in my *n*.......Phil 2:25
have experienced times of *n*.......Phil 4:12
you sent something for my *n*.......Phil 4:16
God will supply your every *n*.......Phil 4:19

does not *n* to be ashamed . . . . .2 Tim 2:15
find grace whenever we *n* help . . . . Heb 4:16
you *n* someone to teach you . . . . . . Heb 5:12
no *n* for anyone to teach you . . . . 1 John 2:27
sees his fellow Christian in *n* . . . . .1 John 3:17
does not *n* the sun or the moon . . .Rev 21:23

NEEDLE
go through the eye of a *n* . . . . Luke 18:25

NEEDS
abundantly supply what she *n* . . . . Ps 132:15
The Lord *n* them. . . . . .Matt 21:3
The Lord *n* it. . . . . .Mark 11:3
provided for my *n* . . . . Acts 20:34

NEEDY
turn the *n* from the pathway . . . . . . .Job 24:4
that he hears the cry of the *n* . . . . . .Job 34:28
n are not permanently ignored . . . . . . Ps 9:18
For the LORD listens to the *n* . . . . . .Ps 69:33
For he will rescue the *n*. . . . . .Ps 72:12
Yet he protected the *n*. . . . . .Ps 107:41
at the right hand of the *n* . . . . .Ps 109:31
generously gives to the *n* . . . . .Ps 112:9
and lifts up the *n* . . . . .Ps 113:7
shows favor to the *n*. . . . . Prov 14:31
extended her hands to the *n* . . . . .Prov 31:20
the *n* will rest securely . . . . Isa 14:30
a protector for the *n*. . . . . Isa 25:4
the *n* for a pair of sandals . . . . Amos 2:6
was no one *n* among them . . . . . . .Acts 4:34

NEGLECT
you *n* what is more important . . . Matt 23:23
Do not *n* the spiritual gift. . . . . . . .1 Tim 4:14
if we *n* such a great salvation . . . . Heb 2:3
Do not *n* hospitality . . . . .Heb 13:2
And do not *n* to do good . . . . .Heb 13:16

NEGLIGENCE
guilty of no *n* or corruption. . . . . Dan 6:4

NEHEMIAH
Jewish cupbearer to King Artaxerxes; prays
   for restoration of Jerusalem, Neh 1:4–11
King commissions him to rebuild walls,
   Neh 2:1–8
Overcomes opposition and accomplishes
   rebuilding, Neh 4–6
Appointed governor, Neh 5:14
Participates with Ezra in restored worship,
   Neh 8–10
Registers the people and the priests and
   Levites, Neh 11:1–12:26
Dedicates the wall, Neh 12:27–43
Returns to Jerusalem after absence and
   institutes reforms, Neh 13:4–31

NEIGHBOR
See also LOVE YOUR NEIGHBOR
to request from his or her *n* . . . . . .Exod 11:2
false testimony against your *n* . . .Exod 20:16
do take the garment of your *n* . . .Exod 22:26
must love your *n* as yourself . . . . . . Lev 19:18
who slanders his *n* in secret . . . . . . Ps 101:5
Do not say to your *n* . . . . Prov 3:28
one who despises his *n* sins . . . . . .Prov 14:21
be a witness against your *n* . . . . . .Prov 24:28
a *n* nearby is better . . . . Prov 27:10
who force your *n* to drink wine . . . .Hab 2:15
Love your *n* . . . . .Matt 5:43
Love your *n* as yourself. . . . . .Matt 22:39
And who is my *n*. . . . . Luke 10:29
became a *n* to the man . . . . Luke 10:36
Love your *n* as yourself. . . . . Rom 13:9
must love your *n* as yourself . . . . . . Gal 5:14

NEIGHBOR'S
shall not covet your *n* house . . . .Exod 20:17
encroach on your *n* property . . . .Deut 19:14
who sleeps with his *n* wife. . . . . . . Prov 6:29

NEIGHBORS
Go and ask all your *n* . . . . 2 Kgs 4:3
who talk so friendly to their *n* . . . . .Ps 28:3
my *n* stand far away . . . . .Ps 38:11
an object of disdain to our *n* . . . . . .Ps 44:13
Pay back our *n* in full . . . . .Ps 79:12

and *n* to keep their distance . . . . .Ps 88:18
their *n* and relatives to know . . . . . .Jer 31:34
or your relatives or rich *n* . . . . .Luke 14:12
Then the *n* and the people. . . . . .John 9:8

NEIGHING
Its proud *n* is terrifying . . . . Job 39:20

NEST
an eagle that stirs up its *n* . . . . Deut 32:11
and builds its *n* on high . . . . .Job 39:27
bird that wanders from its *n* . . . . . . Prov 27:8
over the *n* of a serpent . . . . Isa 11:8
make your *n* among the stars . . . . . Obad 1:4
build his *n* way up high . . . . Hab 2:9
come and *n* in its branches . . . . . .Matt 13:32

NET
and encircled me with his *n* . . . . .Job 19:6
from the enemy's *n*. . . . . Ps 25:15
but they hid a *n* to catch me. . . . . . . .Ps 35:7
have prepared a *n* to trap me. . . . . . .Ps 57:6
hauls them in with his throw *n* . . . . Hab 1:15
casting a *n* into the sea . . . . .Matt 4:18
a *n* that was cast into the sea . . . .Matt 13:47
Throw your *n* on the right side . . . .John 21:6
and pulled the *n* to shore. . . . . .John 21:11

NETS
wicked fall into their own *n* . . . . . . Ps 141:10
They left their *n* immediately. . . . .Matt 4:20
and lower your *n* for a catch. . . . . . . Luke 5:4
at your word I will lower the *n* . . . . Luke 5:5

NETTLES
firs will grow in place of *n* . . . . Isa 55:13

NEVER
My hair has *n* been cut . . . . Judg 16:17
he will *n* lose his reward. . . . . .Matt 10:42
comes to me will *n* go hungry . . . . .John 6:35
and believes in me will *n* die. . . . . . John 11:26
Love *n* ends. .1 Cor 13:8
that can *n* take away sins . . . . .Heb 10:11
I will *n* leave you. . . . . .Heb 13:5
will *n* be put to shame. . . . . 1 Pet 2:6

NEW
See also NEW BIRTH; NEW COVENANT;
   NEW MAN
Then a *n* king. . . . . .Exod 1:8
does something entirely *n* . . . . Num 16:30
God chose *n* leaders. . . . . .Judg 5:8
with two brand *n* ropes. . . . . Judg 15:13
the ark of God on a *n* cart . . . . 2 Sam 6:3
reason to sing a *n* song . . . . .Ps 40:3
Sing to the LORD a *n* song . . . . Ps 96:1
will overflow with *n* wine . . . . .Prov 3:10
is nothing truly *n* on earth. . . . . Eccl 1:9
am about to do something *n* . . . . . . Isa 43:19
will be called by a *n* name . . . . Isa 62:2
create *n* heavens and a *n* earth . . . Isa 65:17
I will make a *n* covenant. . . . . Jer 31:31
I will give you a *n* heart. . . . . .Ezek 36:26
And no one pours *n* wine . . . . .Matt 9:17
placed it in his own *n* tomb. . . . . .Matt 27:60
they will speak in *n* languages . . . Mark 16:17
I give you a *n* commandment. . . . .John 13:34
or listening to something *n* . . . . . . .Acts 17:21
so we too may live a *n* life . . . . Rom 6:4
he is a *n* creation . . . . 2 Cor 5:17
I will complete a *n* covenant. . . . . . . Heb 8:8
the mediator of a *n* covenant . . . . . Heb 9:15
for *n* heavens and a *n* earth. . . . . . 2 Pet 3:13
writing a *n* commandment . . . . 1 John 2:8
will be written a *n* name. . . . . .Rev 2:17
n Jerusalem that comes down . . . . . .Rev 3:12
They were singing a *n* song. . . . . . . .Rev 5:9
saw a *n* heaven and a *n* earth. . . . . Rev 21:1
I am making all things *n* . . . . Rev 21:5

NEW BIRTH
the washing of the *n* and . . . . .Titus 3:5
gave us *n* into a living hope. . . . . 1 Pet 1:3

NEW COVENANT
when I will make a *n*. . . . . Jer 31:31
is the *n* in my blood . . . . .Luke 22:20
cup is the *n* in my blood . . . . .1 Cor 11:25

to be servants of a *n*. . . . . 2 Cor 3:6
when I will complete a *n*. . . . . Heb 8:8
he is the mediator of a *n*. . . . . Heb 9:15
Jesus, the mediator of a *n*. . . . . .Heb 12:24

NEW MAN
create in himself one *n* . . . . Eph 2:15
and to put on the *n* . . . . Eph 4:24
have been clothed with the *n*. . . . . . Col 3:10

NEWBORN
the doe abandons her *n* fawn. . . . . . .Jer 14:5

NEWLY
When a man is *n* married. . . . . Deut 24:5

NEWS
spread the *n* in the streets. . . . . . . 2 Sam 1:20
women spread the good *n*. . . . . Ps 68:11
He does not fear bad *n* . . . . .Ps 112:7
and good *n* gives health . . . . .Prov 15:30
is good *n* from a distant land . . . . Prov 25:25
and *n* about him spread . . . . Luke 4:14
proclaim good *n* to the poor. . . . . . Luke 4:18
proclaiming the good *n*. . . . . Luke 9:6
proclaiming the good *n*. . . . . .Acts 5:42
proclaiming the good *n*. . . . . .Acts 8:4
proclaiming the good *n* . . . . .Acts 17:18
testify to the good *n*. . . . . .Acts 20:24
proclaiming the good *n*. . . . . Gal 1:23
the good *n* of your faith . . . . 1 Thess 3:6

NICANOR
One of the seven servants in the early
   church, Acts 6:1–5

NICE
seized a *n* robe from Babylon . . . . . Josh 7:21

NICODEMUS
Pharisee; converses with Jesus, John 3:1–12
Protests unfairness of Christ's trial,
   John 7:50–52
Brings gifts to anoint Christ's body,
   John 19:39–40

NICOLAITANS
Group teaching moral laxity, Rev 2:6–15

NICOLAS
One of the seven servants in the early
   church, Acts 6:1–5

NIGHT
light "day" and the darkness "*n* . . . . . .Gen 1:5
and day and *n* will not cease. . . . . . Gen 8:22
that *n* they made their father. . . . . Gen 19:33
was a *n* of vigil for the LORD. . . . . Exod 12:42
nor the pillar of fire by *n* . . . . .Exod 13:22
a strong east wind all that *n* . . . . . .Exod 14:21
God came to Balaam that *n* . . . . .Num 22:20
must memorize it day and *n*. . . . . . . Josh 1:8
And the *n* stretches on . . . . Job 7:4
who gives songs in the *n*. . . . . .Job 35:10
on his commands day and *n* . . . . .Ps 1:2
during the *n* I reflect and learn . . . . . .Ps 16:7
n after *n* it reveals his greatness. . . . . Ps 19:2
experience sorrow during the *n* . . . . .Ps 30:5
not fear the terrors of the *n* . . . . .Ps 91:5
your faithfulness during the *n*. . . . . . .Ps 92:2
moon and stars to rule by *n* . . . . . . .Ps 136:9
and the *n* is as bright as day . . . . . . Ps 139:12
she rose while it was still *n* . . . . . . .Prov 31:15
what is left of the *n*. . . . . .Isa 21:11
I look for you during the *n*. . . . . Isa 26:9
and his mother during the *n* . . . . . .Matt 2:14
guard over their flock at *n* . . . . .Luke 2:8
and he spent all *n* in prayer. . . . . . .Luke 6:12
came to Jesus at *n* and said. . . . . .John 3:2
N is coming when no one. . . . . .John 9:4
previously come to Jesus at *n*. . . . . .John 19:39
On that very *n*. . . . . Acts 12:6
For last *n* an angel of the God . . . .Acts 27:23
n has advanced toward dawn. . . . . .Rom 13:12
same way as a thief in the *n* . . . . . .1 Thess 5:2
not of the *n* nor of the darkness. .1 Thess 5:5
They never rest day or *n*. . . . . Rev 4:8
who accuses them day and *n* . . . . . .Rev 12:10
there will be no *n* there. . . . . .Rev 21:25
N will be no more . . . . Rev 22:5

NIGHTS
for forty days and forty *n*........... Gen 7:4
forty days and forty *n* .... Exod 24:18
fasted forty days and forty *n* ...... Matt 4:2
for three days and three *n* .... Matt 12:40
in sleepless *n* .... 2 Cor 6:5
through many sleepless *n* .... 2 Cor 11:27

NILE
Hebrew children drowned in, Exod 1:22
Moses hidden in, Exod 2:3–10
Water of, turned to blood, Exod 7:14–21
Mentioned in prophecies, Isa 19:5–8; 23:3;
    27:12; Jer 46:7–9; Amos 9:5

NIMROD
Ham's grandson, Gen 10:6–12

NINE
n o'clock in the morning........... Matt 20:3
Where are the other *n* .... Luke 17:17

NINETY-NINE
leave the *n* on the mountains..... Matt 18:12

NINEVEH
Capital of Assyria, 2 Kgs 19:36
Jonah preaches to; people repent,
    Jonah 3:1–10; Matt 12:41
Prophecy against, Nah 2:13–3:19;
    Zeph 2:13–15

NO
I gave you *n* food to eat .... Amos 4:6
I receive *n* benefit .... 1 Cor 13:3
n prophecy was ever borne........ 2 Pet 1:21

NOAH
Son of Lamech, Gen 5:28–32
Finds favor with God; commissioned to
    build the ark, Gen 6:8–22
Fills ark and survives flood, Gen 7
Leaves ark; builds altar; receives God's
    promise, Gen 8
God's covenant with, Gen 9:1–17
Blesses and curses his sons; dies,
    Gen 9:18–29

NOB
City of priests; David flees to, 1 Sam 21:1–9
Priests of, killed by Saul, 1 Sam 22:9–23

NOBILITY
your king is the son of *n*........... Eccl 10:17

NOBLE
to one of the king's *n* officials ...... Esth 6:9
A *n* wife is the crown .... Prov 12:4

NOBLEMAN'S
Where now is the *n* house........ Job 21:28

NOBLES
the voices of the *n* fell silent....... Job 29:10

NOBODY
N will be able to resist you .... Deut 11:25

NOD
Place (east of Eden) of Cain's exile,
    Gen 4:16–17

NOISE
When Joshua heard the *n*........ Exod 32:17
a loud *n* on the mountains.......... Isa 13:4
king of Egypt is just a big *n* .... Jer 46:17
disappear with a horrific *n*........ 2 Pet 3:10

NOISY
away from me your *n* songs ..... Amos 5:23

NONCITIZENS
no longer foreigners and *n* .... Eph 2:19

NONEXISTENT
their accomplishments are *n* .... Isa 41:29

NORTH
I will say to the *n* .... Isa 43:6
from the land of the *n* .... Jer 16:15
from the remote parts of the *n*... Ezek 38:6
from the remote parts of the *n*...Ezek 38:15
and from *n* and south .... Luke 13:29

NOSTRILS
and breathed into his *n* .... Gen 2:7
breath from God is in my *n*........ Job 27:3
life's breath is in their *n*........... Isa 2:22

NOTABLE
give *n* and constant service....... 1 Cor 7:35

NOTE
takes *n* of all their actions .... Ps 33:15
take *n* of Jesus...................... Heb 3:1

NOTES
make a distinction in the *n* .... 1 Cor 14:7

NOTHING
and reduce my words to *n*........ Job 24:25
will inherit *n* .... Prov 11:29
and yet has *n* .... Prov 13:7
All who form idols are *n* .... Isa 44:9
having accomplished *n* .... Isa 55:11
and it produces *n* .... Mark 4:19
can do *n* on my own initiative .... John 5:30
you can accomplish *n*............. John 15:5
it will come to *n* .... Acts 5:38
but do not have love, I am *n*....... 1 Cor 13:2
then Christ died for *n*.............. Gal 2:21
have plenty or *n*.................... Phil 4:12
brought *n* into this world.......... 1 Tim 6:7
accepting *n* from the pagans ..... 3 John 1:7

NOTICE
that you should *n* them............... Ps 8:4
Look, the LORD takes *n*.............. Ps 33:18
down from heaven and take *n*...... Ps 80:14
your god might take *n* of us........ Jonah 1:6
Pilate also had a *n* written........ John 19:19

NOTORIOUS
had in custody a *n* prisoner...... Matt 27:16

NOURISH
something that will not *n* you ...... Isa 55:2

NOURISHED
having *n* yourself on the words.... 1 Tim 4:6

NOW
Swear an oath to me *n* .... Gen 25:33

NOWHERE
I have *n* to run...................... Ps 142:4

NULLIFIED
You have *n* the word of God......Matt 15:6
and the promise is *n*.............. Rom 4:14
when he *n* in his flesh .... Eph 2:15

NULLIFIES
he *n* the plans of the peoples....... Ps 33:10

NULLIFY
Thus you *n* the word of God...... Mark 7:13
n the law through faith .... Rom 3:31

NUMBER
will fulfill the *n* of your days..... Exod 23:26
marvelous things without *n* .... Job 5:9
He counts the *n* of the stars .... Ps 147:4
about 5,000 in *n*................... John 6:10
because of the large *n* of fish..... John 21:6
and a great *n* who believed....... Acts 11:21
increasing in *n* every day .... Acts 16:5
until the full *n* of the Gentiles .... Rom 11:25
the *n* of stars in the sky........... Heb 11:12
calculate the beast's *n*............. Rev 13:18

NUMBERED
guilty after he had *n* the army ..2 Sam 24:10
and was *n* with the rebels .... Isa 53:12
has *n* your kingdom's days .... Dan 5:26
the hairs on your head are *n*..... Matt 10:30

NUMBERS
the church increased in *n*.......... Acts 9:31

NUMEROUS
n as the very stars of the sky ...... Deut 1:10
great, powerful, and *n* people .... Deut 26:5
as *n* as the grains of sand.......... Job 29:18
When the righteous become *n* .... Prov 29:2

NURSE
and serve as his *n*................... 1 Kgs 1:2

O

OAKS
and went to live by the *o* ....Gen 13:18
among the *o* and under every .... Isa 57:5
be called *o* of righteousness......... Isa 61:3
Howl, *o* of Bashan .... Zech 11:2

OATH
two of them swore an *o*...........Gen 21:31
the army was afraid of the *o*.... 1 Sam 14:26
Judah was happy about the *o*.... 2 Chr 15:15
and an *o* to adhere to the law .... Neh 10:29
swore an *o* to the Powerful One.... Ps 132:2
you took an *o* before God .... Eccl 8:2
I solemnly make this *o* .... Isa 45:23
makes an *o* in the earth ....Isa 65:16
I swore on *o* to your ancestors ...... Jer 11:5
because of his *o* ....Matt 14:9
He denied it again with an *o*..... Matt 26:72
and he swore with an *o*........... Matt 26:74
the *o* that he swore............... Luke 1:73
bound themselves with an *o*...... Acts 23:12
or by earth or by any other *o*........ Jas 5:12

OATHS
who takes *o* in his name............. Ps 63:11

OBADIAH
King Ahab's steward, 1 Kgs 18:3–16
—Prophet of Judah, Obad 1:1

OBED
Son of Boaz and Ruth, Ruth 4:17–22

OBED-EDOM
Philistine from Gath; ark of the Lord left in
    his house, 2 Sam 6:10–12; 1 Chr 13:13–14

OBEDIENCE
o is better than sacrifice......... 1 Sam 15:22
to bring about the *o* of faith .... Rom 1:5
the *o* of the Gentiles............... Rom 15:18
Your *o* is known to all .... Rom 16:19
your *o* to your confession .... 2 Cor 9:13
learned *o* through the things .... Heb 5:8
set apart by the Spirit for *o*....... 1 Pet 1:2

OBEDIENT
priests became *o* to the faith........ Acts 6:7
present yourselves as *o* slaves..... Rom 6:16
o to the point of death.............. Phil 2:8
Like *o* children.................... 1 Pet 1:14

OBEY
that I should *o* him .... Exod 5:2
o all that the LORD has spoken ... Exod 24:7
to the LORD your God and *o* him .. Deut 4:30
If you indeed *o* the LORD .... Deut 28:1
if you *o* the LORD your God..... Deut 30:10
the LORD our God and *o* him .... Josh 24:24
and *o* all my commandments...... 1 Kgs 6:12
o the God of your father.......... 1 Chr 28:9
by giving me the desire to *o* ....Ps 51:12
carry out his decrees and *o*....... Ps 103:20
determined to *o* your statutes..... Ps 119:112
have a willing attitude and *o*...... Isa 1:19
O me. If you do...................... Jer 7:23
O me and carry out the terms....... Jer 11:4
You must make sure to *o* me...... Jer 17:24
We will *o* what the LORD .... Jer 42:6
will serve him and *o* him .... Dan 7:27
reward for those who *o* them ...... Mic 2:7
o the voice of the LORD........... Zech 6:15
the winds and the sea *o* him...... Matt 8:27
teaching them to *o* everything ..Matt 28:20
unclean spirits and they *o* him.... Mark 1:27
you will *o* my commandments ... John 14:15
If you *o* my commandments...... John 15:10
must *o* God rather than people....Acts 5:29
and do not *o* the truth.............Rom 2:8
thought captive to make it *o* ..... 2 Cor 10:5
obligated to *o* the whole law .... Gal 5:3
Slaves, *o* your human masters....Eph 6:5
Children, *o* your parents...........Col 3:20
Slaves, *o* your earthly masters......Col 3:22
and do not *o* the gospel .... 2 Thess 1:8
confident that you would *o*........ Phlm 1:21
eternal salvation to all who *o*....... Heb 5:9

O your leaders and submit ....Heb 13:17
to get them to *o* us ....Jas 3:3
are those who hear and *o* ....Rev 1:3
with those who *o* the words.......Rev 22:9

OBEYED
because Abraham *o* me ....Gen 26:5
Their ancestors had *o* ....Judg 2:17
have *o* the LORD's commands ..2 Sam 22:22
have not *o* the LORD our God.......Jer 3:25
nation that has not *o* the LORD .....Jer 7:28
wholeheartedly *o* all these laws.. Matt 19:20
wholeheartedly *o* all these laws...Mark 10:20
If they *o* my word..................John 15:20
you *o* from the heart ....Rom 6:17
not all have *o* the good news .....Rom 10:16
By faith Abraham *o* ....Heb 11:8
like Sarah who *o* Abraham ....1 Pet 3:6

OBEYING
and despises *o* a mother...........Prov 30:17
purified your souls by *o* the truth ..1 Pet 1:22

OBEYS
one who *o* commandments ......Prov 19:16

OBJECTS
the *o* of wrath prepared ....Rom 9:22

OBLIGATED
he is *o* to obey the whole law........Gal 5:3

OBLIGATION
due to grace but due to *o* ....Rom 4:4

OBLIVION
deliverance in the land of *o*........Ps 88:12

OBSERVATIONS
make insightful *o* about the past ....Ps 78:2

OBSERVE
you must *o* your Sabbath..........Lev 23:32
and *o* all the words of this law....Deut 17:19
have them *o* the fourteenth ....Esth 9:21
O the upright.......................Ps 37:37
carefully *o* me when I travel........Ps 139:3
and let your eyes *o* my ways .... Prov 23:26
You must *o* the Sabbath............Isa 58:13
they failed to *o* a treaty...........Amos 1:9

OBSERVED
Josiah *o* a Passover festival .... 2 Chr 35:1
not coming with signs to be *o* ... Luke 17:20

OBSERVERS
they are all ardent *o* of the law ...Acts 21:20

OBSERVES
The one who *o* the day ....Rom 14:6

OBSERVING
by *o* the Sabbath throughout.....Exod 31:16

OBSOLETE
he makes the first *o* ....Heb 8:13

OBSTACLE
because their wealth was the *o*....Ezek 7:19
not be an *o* leading to iniquity... Ezek 18:30
determine never to place an *o*....Rom 14:13

OBSTACLES
remove the *o* in the way..............Ps 5:8

OBSTINATE
had made him *o* and stubborn....Deut 2:30

OBTAIN
to *o* resurrection to a better life...Heb 11:35
and envy and you cannot *o*..........Jas 4:2

OBVIOUS
good works are also *o*............1 Tim 5:25

OCCUPY
nor to *o* themselves with myths....1 Tim 1:4
o themselves with deceiving........1 Tim 4:1

OCCURRED
resurrection has already *o*........2 Tim 2:18

OCEAN
the deep *o* surrounded me ....Jonah 2:5

OCEANS
he puts the *o* in storehouses ....Ps 33:7
When there were no deep *o*...... Prov 8:24

ODDS
continued to be at *o* with David...1 Sam 18:29

ODED
Prophet of Samaria, 2 Chr 28:9–15

ODIOUS
that rebellious and *o* city ....Ezra 4:12

ODOR
an *o* from death to death........2 Cor 2:16

OF THE WORLD
them to all the people *o* .... Deut 4:19
regions *o* were uncovered ......2 Sam 22:16
all you inhabitants *o* ....Ps 49:1
or the top soil *o* ....Prov 8:26
fill the surface *o* with cities ....Isa 14:21
all the kingdoms *o* horrified........Jer 15:4
hidden from the foundation *o* ...Matt 13:35
the beginning *o* until now ...... Matt 24:21
nations *o* pursue these things ... Luke 12:30
who takes away the sin *o*..........John 1:29
this one really is the Savior *o* ..... John 4:42
give for the life *o* is my flesh.......John 6:51
I am the light *o* ....John 8:12
rejection is the reconciliation *o*....Rom 11:15
have not received the spirit *o*......1 Cor 2:12
concerned about the things *o* .... 1 Cor 7:33
under the basic forces *o*.............Gal 4:3
before the foundation *o* ....Eph 1:4
and the elemental spirits *o* ....Col 2:8
escaped the filthy things *o*........2 Pet 2:20
the Son to be the Savior *o* ......1 John 4:14
since the foundation *o* ....Rev 17:8

OF THIS WORLD
from the murderers *o* ....Ps 17:14
people *o* are more shrewd ....Luke 16:8
because he sees the light *o*........ John 11:9
for the ruler *o* is coming..........John 14:30
the immoral people *o* .... 1 Cor 5:10
shape *o* is passing away ....1 Cor 7:31

OFF
See also PUT OFF
tear *o* his yoke from your neck..Gen 27:40
you may pluck *o* the kernels..... Deut 23:25
and its leaves never fall *o*...............Ps 1:3
slacked *o* in the day of trouble .. Prov 24:10
Strip *o* your clothes ....Isa 32:11
Shake *o* the dirt ....Isa 52:2
led *o* all the Judean remnant ....Jer 43:5
headed *o* to Tarshish ....Jonah 1:3
those far *o* into a mighty nation.....Mic 4:7
hurried *o* and located Mary ......Luke 2:16
saw Abraham far *o* .... Luke 16:23
chains fell *o* Peter's wrists......... Acts 12:7
He had his hair cut *o*............. Acts 18:18
the petal of the flower falls *o*.........Jas 1:11
withers and the flower falls *o*......1 Pet 1:24
and shuts *o* his compassion ......1 John 3:17

OFFEND
But so that we don't *o* them......Matt 17:27

OFFENDED
and he was highly *o* .... Gen 6:6
and *o* the Holy One of Israel........Ps 78:41
A relative *o* is harder to reach ....Prov 18:19
rebelled and *o* his Holy Spirit......Isa 63:10
Does this cause you to be *o* ....John 6:61

OFFENSE
who forgives an *o* seeks love ......Prov 17:9
And so they took *o* at him........Matt 13:57
not give *o* to Jews or Greeks.....1 Cor 10:32
that case the *o* of the cross..........Gal 5:11

OFFENSES
My *o* would be sealed up..........Job 14:17
punish your sin and reveal your *o*.. Lam 4:22
the forgiveness of our *o* ....Eph 1:7
were dead in your *o* and sins ....Eph 2:1

OFFER
O him up there as a burnt.........Gen 22:2
must not *o* strange incense.......Exod 30:9
and *o* a burnt offering ....Job 42:8
will *o* sacrifices in his dwelling.......Ps 27:6

They *o* only superficial help ....Jer 6:14
For when you *o* blind animals ....Mal 1:8
o the other as well.................Luke 6:29
o the gospel free of charge .... 1 Cor 9:18
o sacrifices first for their own ..... Heb 7:27
and to *o* spiritual sacrifices ....1 Pet 2:5
and they *o* their crowns ....Rev 4:10

OFFERED
Then Jacob *o* a sacrifice........... Gen 31:54
men who *o* incense.............. Num 16:35
voluntarily *o* to the LORD...........Ezra 3:5
o Jesus wine mixed with gall..... Matt 27:34
o them money....................Acts 8:18
to eat food *o* to idols .... 1 Cor 8:10
o himself without blemish....... Heb 9:14
after Christ was *o* once ....Heb 9:28
same sacrifices *o* continually ......Heb 10:1
are *o* according to the law ....Heb 10:8
had *o* one sacrifice for sins .... Heb 10:12
By faith Abel *o* God a greater.......Heb 11:4

OFFERING
but with Cain and his *o* ....Gen 4:5
He poured out a drink *o* .... Gen 35:14
a freewill *o* to the LORD ....Exod 35:29
presents an *o* to the LORD .... Lev 1:2
his *o* is a burnt *o* from the herd...... Lev 1:3
for a sin *o*.........................Lev 4:32
you must present a grain *o*........Lev 6:21
This is the law of the sin *o*..........Lev 6:25
be eaten on the day of his *o* .... Lev 7:15
is a Passover *o* to the LORD.......Lev 23:5
offer the ram as a peace *o*........Num 6:17
Have no respect for their *o*.......Num 16:15
Bring me the burnt *o* ....1 Sam 13:9
the grain *o* and the incense........ Neh 13:9
Present to God a thank *o*..........Ps 50:14
presents a thank *o* honors me..... Ps 50:23
I will present a thank *o* to you.......Ps 116:17
no longer accept an *o* from you .... Mal 1:10
will offer the LORD a proper *o*.......Mal 3:3
bring the *o* for your cleansing .....Luke 5:14
he is *o* service to God..............John 16:2
and fragrant *o* to God ....Eph 5:2
poured out like a drink *o* ....Phil 2:17
fragrant *o*, an acceptable ....Phil 4:18
being poured out as an *o* .... 2 Tim 4:6
and *o* you did not desire...........Heb 10:5
o of the body of Jesus Christ....... Heb 10:10
For by one *o* he has perfected.... Heb 10:14
there is no longer any *o* for sin ... Heb 10:18

OFFERINGS
offered burnt *o* on the altar ....Gen 8:20
LORD take pleasure in burnt *o*...1 Sam 15:22
bring sacrifices and thank *o* .....2 Chr 29:31
he take notice of all your *o*..........Ps 20:3
Receiving sacrifices and *o* .... Ps 40:6
Let them present thank *o* ....Ps 107:22
the freewill *o* of my praise........Ps 119:108
bring any more meaningless *o* ...... Isa 1:13
make *o* at her places of worship... Jer 48:35
feed on the sin *o* of my people ..... Hos 4:8
brings grain *o* or drink *o*.............Joel 1:9
Whole burnt *o* and sin-*o*...........Heb 10:6

OFFICE
restored me to my *o*...............Gen 41:13

OFFICER
sent up to the commanding *o* .....Acts 21:31

OFFICERS
o of the army were sitting.........2 Kgs 9:5
Your *o* are slumbering..............Nah 3:18
The *o* replied .... John 7:46
chief priests and their *o* saw.......John 19:6

OFFICIAL
a court *o* in the royal palace........Jer 38:7

OFFICIALS
appoint *o* throughout the land ... Gen 41:34
appoint judges and court *o* ....Ezra 7:25
authority to imprison his *o* ....Ps 105:22
I will make youths their *o* ....Isa 3:4
o will promote justice ....Isa 32:1

was in charge of his court o ....Dan 1:3
o and judges take bribes.............Mic 7:3

OFFSPRING
See also OFFSPRING OF VIPERS
The o of the wicked ....Isa 14:20
will pour my Spirit on your o.......Isa 44:3
O of vipers.................... Matt 12:34
For we too are his o ....Acts 17:28
So since we are God's o ....Acts 17:29

OFFSPRING OF VIPERS
You o! Who warned you...........Matt 3:7
O! How are you able............. Matt 12:34
You snakes, you o ....Matt 23:33
You o! Who warned you...........Luke 3:7

OFTEN
How o I have longed to gather ...Luke 13:34

OG
Amorite king of Bashan, Deut 3:1–13
Defeated and killed by Israel, Num 21:32–35

OHOLAH
Symbolic name of Samaria, Ezek 23:4–5, 36

OIL
o for the light.....................Exod 25:6
to be my sacred anointing o .....Exod 30:31
And take the anointing o ....Exod 40:9
poured some of the anointing o....Lev 8:12
going to stop producing my o .....Judg 9:9
and a little olive o in a jug ....1 Kgs 17:12
and the jug of o never ran out....1 Kgs 17:16
the olive o stopped flowing........2 Kgs 4:6
the olive o to the storerooms .....Neh 13:12
streams of olive o ....Job 29:6
You refresh my head with o ....Ps 23:5
I am covered with fresh o ....Ps 92:10
o to make their faces shine........Ps 104:15
fine o poured on the head..........Ps 133:2
my head not refuse choice o ....Ps 141:5
o symbolizing joy..................Isa 61:3
anointed you with fragrant o.....Ezek 16:9
with fresh wine and olive o........Joel 2:24
ten thousand streams of olive o....Mic 6:7
take extra olive o with them...... Matt 25:3
flasks of olive o with their lamps ..Matt 25:4
Give us some of your o ....Matt 25:8
jar of expensive perfumed o...... Matt 26:7
jar of costly aromatic o ....Mark 14:3
not anoint my head with o........Luke 7:46
olive o and wine on them........Luke 10:34
Why wasn't this o sold.............John 12:5
and anoint him with olive o.......Jas 5:14
do not damage the olive o..........Rev 6:6

OINTMENT
O and incense make the heart.....Prov 27:9
is still medicinal o available........Jer 8:22

OLD
See also OLD MAN
After Noah was 500 years o.......Gen 5:32
Abram was ninety-nine years o.....Gen 17:1
o and full of days ....Job 42:17
I was once young, now I am o.....Ps 37:25
Do not reject me in my o age........Ps 71:9
bear fruit even when they are o....Ps 92:14
and when he is o..................Prov 22:6
Why were the o days better ....Eccl 7:10
both new and o....................Song 7:13
or an o man die before his time ...Isa 65:20
new wine into o wineskins........Matt 9:17
and they were both very o........Luke 1:7
and my wife is o as well ....Luke 1:18
When he was twelve years o ......Luke 2:42
a man be born when he is o........John 3:4
You are not yet fifty years o........John 8:57
but when you are o................John 21:18
your o men will dream dreams ....Acts 2:17
that our o man was crucified.......Rom 6:6
hear the o covenant read ....2 Cor 3:14
what is o has passed away........2 Cor 5:17
you have put off the o man........Col 3:9
For by it the people of o............Heb 11:2

OLD MAN
will not be an o in your house ....1 Sam 2:31
or an o die before his time.........Isa 65:20
For I am an o ....Luke 1:18
our o was crucified with him ...... Rom 6:6
to lay aside the o ....Eph 4:22
you have putt of the o ....Col 3:9

OLDER
the o will serve the younger.......Gen 25:23
her o son Esau's best clothes .....Gen 27:15
men far o than your father ....Job 15:10
Now his o son was in the field... Luke 15:25
starting with the o ones ....John 8:9
O men are to be temperate ....Titus 2:2
O women likewise..................Titus 2:3

OLIVE
was a freshly plucked o leaf ....Gen 8:11
and o groves you did not plant ....Deut 6:11
of o trees and honey...............Deut 8:8
a land of o oil and honey ....2 Kgs 18:32
I am like a flourishing o tree........Ps 52:8
children will be like o branches..... Ps 128:3
and o tree have not produced .....Hag 2:19
in the richness of the o root.......Rom 11:17
what is by nature a wild o tree ...Rom 11:24

OLIVES, MOUNT OF
See MOUNT OF OLIVES

OMENS
no longer be able to read the o......Mic 3:6
her prophets read o for pay .... Mic 3:11

OMRI
Made king of Israel by army, 1 Kgs 16:16,
    21–22
Builds Samaria; reigns wickedly,
    1 Kgs 16:23–27

ONAN
Second son of Judah; slain for failure to give
    his brother an heir, Gen 38:8–10

ONCE
delivered o and for all ....Isa 45:17
And the fig tree withered at o ....Matt 21:19
and at o the bleeding stopped....Luke 8:44
Therefore I sent for you at o......Acts 10:33
o alive apart from the law ....Rom 7:9
O I received a stoning ....2 Cor 11:25
people are appointed to die o .....Heb 9:27
after Christ was offered o ....Heb 9:28
You o were not a people..........1 Pet 2:10
Christ also suffered o for sins .....1 Pet 3:18

ONE
See also EVIL ONE; HOLY ONE OF ISRAEL;
    LORD'S CHOSEN ONE; LOVE ONE
    ANOTHER; ONE DEAR SON; ONE WHO
    BELIEVES
and they become o family..........Gen 2:24
desirable for making o wise ....Gen 3:6
the tenth o will be holy.............Lev 27:32
the LORD is o ....Deut 6:4
around the city o time..............Josh 6:14
I ask for just o more sign ....Judg 6:39
the Sovereign O has treated.......Ruth 1:20
May the o who took notice........Ruth 2:19
were standing on o hill ....1 Sam 17:3
half to o and half to the other ...1 Kgs 3:25
o of all the faithful promises......1 Kgs 8:56
No o was able to stand ....Esth 9:2
o who feared God and turned ....Job 1:1
certainly he is the strong o ....Job 9:19
How blessed is the o ....Ps 1:1
LORD grants success to the o......Ps 37:23
the o who trusts in the LORD ....Ps 40:4
does what is right, not even o ....Ps 53:3
offended the Holy O of Israel......Ps 78:41
to the o whom you raised up ....Ps 80:17
covenant with my chosen o ......Ps 89:3
shadow of the Sovereign O..........Ps 91:1
How blessed is every o ....Ps 128:1
the o who has found wisdom......Prov 3:13
O person is generous.............Prov 11:24
but the o who lies ....Prov 12:19

though no o was pursuing.........Prov 28:1
Two people are better than o...... Eccl 4:9
My beautiful o......................Song 2:10
will grab hold of o man.............Isa 4:1
power of the Sovereign O ....Isa 13:6
no o can close it ....Isa 22:22
will be gathered up o by o.........Isa 27:12
deceitful o is as good as dead ......Isa 33:1
o in whom I take pleasure...........Isa 42:1
my chosen o........................Isa 45:4
the Powerful O of Jacob............Isa 49:26
barren o who has not given birth....Isa 54:1
O afflicted o........................Isa 54:11
every o of you......................Jer 18:11
The first o was like a lion...........Dan 7:4
I heard a holy o speaking..........Dan 8:13
until an anointed o ....Dan 9:25
remains faithful to the Holy O..... Hos 11:12
Do we not all have o father.........Mal 2:10
deliver us from the evil o...........Matt 6:13
causes o of these little ones ......Matt 18:6
the two will become o flesh ....Matt 19:5
no o would be saved...............Matt 24:22
day and hour no o knows it......Matt 24:36
awake with me for o hour ......Matt 26:40
o of these little children ....Mark 9:37
Permit o of us to sit ....Mark 10:37
You must be o of them ....Mark 14:70
The voice of o shouting............ Luke 3:4
No o lights a lamp ....Luke 8:16
over o sinner who repents........Luke 15:10
The first o married a woman ....Luke 20:29
Did no o condemn you ....John 8:10
The Father and I are o ....John 10:30
love o another.....................John 13:34
they may be o just as we are o ....John 17:11
keep them safe from the evil o ...John 17:15
Holy O to experience decay ....Acts 2:27
the Holy and Righteous O .... Acts 3:14
There is no o righteous...........Rom 3:10
For no o is declared righteous.... Rom 3:20
blessed is the o against whom..... Rom 4:8
Owe no o anything ....Rom 13:8
no o can boast in his presence.....1 Cor 1:29
is that o be found faithful.......... 1 Cor 4:2
but we an imperishable o.........1 Cor 9:25
no o will be justified ....Gal 2:16
all of you are o in Christ Jesus .....Gal 3:28
through love serve o another.......Gal 5:13
Carry o another's burdens.........Gal 6:2
o new man out of two..............Eph 2:15
There is o body and o Spirit ....Eph 4:4
o Lord, o faith, o baptism ....Eph 4:5
o God and Father of all ....Eph 4:6
flaming arrows of the evil o ....Eph 6:16
lawless o will be revealed ....2 Thess 2:8
o God and o intermediary ....1 Tim 2:5
the husband of o wife ....1 Tim 3:2
Let no o look down on you ....1 Tim 4:12
a heavenly o........................Heb 11:16
But each o is tempted ....Jas 1:14
So love o another earnestly ....1 Pet 1:22
Show hospitality to o another......1 Pet 4:9
Jesus Christ the Righteous O ......1 John 2:1
you have conquered the evil o....1 John 2:14
the evil o cannot touch him ......1 John 5:18
lies in the power of the evil o.....1 John 5:19
I will repay each o of you......... Rev 2:23
pronouncement of the Holy O ....Rev 3:7
opened o of the seven seals ....Rev 6:1
was o like a son of man............Rev 14:14

ONE DEAR SON
o; in him I take great delight........Matt 3:17
o, in whom I take great delight ....Matt 17:5
o; in you I take great delight........Mark 1:11
This is my o. Listen to him.........Mark 9:7
o; in you I take great delight.......Luke 3:22

ONE WHO BELIEVES
things are possible for the o......Mark 9:23
The o and is baptized............ Mark 16:16
o in him is not condemned ....John 3:18
The o in the Son has eternal.......John 3:36

o in me will never be thirsty......John 6:35
the *o* has eternal life........John 6:47
let the *o* in me drink........John 7:38
The *o* in me will live ....John 11:25
yet the *o* in him will not ....Rom 9:33
o that Jesus is the Son of God .....1 John 5:5
The *o* in the Son of God ....1 John 5:10

ONES
with ten thousand holy *o*........Deut 33:2
He watches over his holy *o*........1 Sam 2:9
Don't touch my anointed *o*......1 Chr 16:22
places no trust in his holy *o*........Job 15:15
your oppressed *o* equitably ....Ps 72:2
protect the way of his pious *o*......Prov 2:8
and my chosen *o* will enjoy........Isa 65:22
wage war against the holy *o*........Dan 7:21
He will harass the holy *o*.........Dan 7:25
water to one of these little *o*.... Matt 10:42
relations for unnatural *o* ....Rom 1:26
and insult the glorious *o*..........Jude 1:8

ONESIMUS
Slave of Philemon converted by Paul in
   Rome, Phlm 1:10–17
With Tychicus, carries Paul's letters to
   Colossae and to Philemon, Col 4:7–9

ONESIPHORUS
Ephesian Christian commended for his
   service, 2 Tim 1:16–18

ONLY
glory of the one and *o*............John 1:14

ONWARD
upon David from that day *o* .....1 Sam 16:13
eye on David from that day *o*.....1 Sam 18:9

ONYX
the fifth, *o*, the sixth carnelian ....Rev 21:20

OPEN
your eyes will *o*........Gen 3:5
The altar will split *o* ....1 Kgs 13:3
o his eyes so he can see ....2 Kgs 6:17
o their eyes........2 Kgs 6:20
if only he would *o* his lips..........Job 11:5
You broke *o* the spring ....Ps 74:15
you *o* your hand................Ps 104:28
O my eyes so I can truly see........Ps 119:18
Better is *o* rebuke ....Prov 27:5
O your mouth on behalf..........Prov 31:8
and *o* wounds ....Isa 1:6
to *o* doors before him..........Isa 45:1
he did not even *o* his mouth........Isa 53:7
I will *o* my mouth in parables....Matt 13:35
After breaking *o* the jar..........Mark 14:3
falling headfirst he burst *o* ....Acts 1:18
she did not *o* the gate ....Acts 12:14
put in front of you an *o* door ....Rev 3:8
Who is worthy to *o* the scroll........Rev 5:2

OPEN-MINDED
Jews were more *o* than those......Acts 17:11

OPENED
and the earth *o* its mouth ....Num 16:32
o the mouth of the donkey......Num 22:28
The Lord *o* the servant's eyes....2 Kgs 6:17
Ezra *o* the book in plain view.......Neh 8:5
heavens *o* and I saw a divine........Ezek 1:1
upper room *o* toward Jerusalem ..Dan 6:10
knock and the door will be *o* ....Matt 7:7
let our eyes be *o*..................Matt 20:33
the man's ears were *o*..........Mark 7:35
At this point their eyes were *o*...Luke 24:31
Then he *o* their minds..........Luke 24:45
o the doors of the prison ....Acts 5:19
I see the heavens *o* ....Acts 7:56
Lamb *o* one of the seven seals......Rev 6:1
He *o* the shaft of the abyss........Rev 9:2
Then I saw heaven *o*..............Rev 19:11
Then books were *o* ....Rev 20:12

OPENING
Protect the *o* of my lips ....Ps 141:3
who is always *o* his mouth .... Prov 20:19

OPENINGS
and caves and *o* in the earth........Heb 11:38

OPENLY
I am ready to vindicate you *o*........Isa 56:1
not *o* but in secret..................John 7:10

OPENS
When he *o* the door ....Isa 22:22
doorkeeper *o* the door for him....John 10:3
who *o* doors no one can shut........Rev 3:7
hears my voice and *o* the door ....Rev 3:20

OPHEL
Hill, southeast of Jerusalem, Neh 3:15–27
Fortified by Manasseh, 2 Chr 27:3
Residence of Nethinim, Neh 3:26

OPHIR
Region famous for gold, 1 Chr 29:4

OPHRAH
Town in Manasseh; home of Gideon,
   Judg 6:11, 15
Site of Gideon's burial, Judg 8:32

OPINION
of a fool is right in his own *o* .....Prov 12:15
lest he be wise in his own *o*.......Prov 26:5
who are pure in their own *o*......Prov 30:12
give my *o* as one shown mercy...1 Cor 7:25
So here is my *o* on this matter....2 Cor 8:10

OPPONENTS
but there are many *o*..............1 Cor 16:9
in any way by your *o*................Phil 1:28

OPPORTUNITY
while there is a window of *o*..........Ps 32:6
looking for an *o* to betray him... Matt 26:16
and when I have an *o* ....Acts 24:25
given an *o* to make a defense.....Acts 25:16
o through the commandment......Rom 7:8
you would get a second *o* ....2 Cor 1:15
giving you an *o* to be proud ......2 Cor 5:12
so that I may eliminate any *o*....2 Cor 11:12
freedom as an *o* to indulge........Gal 5:13
whenever we have an *o* ....Gal 6:10
but had no *o* to do anything ....Phil 4:10
the adversary no *o* to vilify us ....1 Tim 5:14
they would have had *o* to return ..Heb 11:15

OPPOSE
stood in the road to *o* him.......Num 22:22
I will *o* your adversary............Isa 49:25

OPPOSED
I *o* him to his face.................Gal 2:11
o to the promises of God..........Gal 3:21
expressed in decrees *o* to us ....Col 2:14
and are *o* to all people..........1 Thess 2:15
Jannes and Jambres *o* Moses ......2 Tim 3:8
he vehemently *o* our words ......2 Tim 4:15

OPPOSES
He *o* and exalts himself..........2 Thess 2:4
God *o* the proud....................Jas 4:6
because God *o* the proud..........1 Pet 5:5

OPPOSING
was *o* me for twenty-one days ....Dan 10:13

OPPOSITE
o the lampstand .... Dan 5:5
sitting there, *o* the tomb........Matt 27:61
sat down *o* the offering box ..... Mark 12:41
which is *o* Galilee................Luke 8:26

OPPOSITION
these are in *o* to each other ....Gal 5:17
endured such *o* against himself ....Heb 12:3

OPPRESS
to *o* them with hard labor ....Exod 1:11
a resident foreigner nor *o* him.... Exod 22:21
You must not *o* your neighbor...... Lev 19:13
is to *o* his fellow citizen............Lev 25:17
Is it good for you to *o* ....Job 10:3
righteousness he does not *o*......Job 37:23
o the nation that belongs to you ....Ps 94:5
He let no one *o* them..............Ps 105:14
you *o* your workers.................Isa 58:3

OPPRESSED
will no longer *o* my people ....Ezek 45:8
You must not *o* the widow ....Zech 7:10

OPPRESSED
Whom have I *o*..................1 Sam 12:3
For he has *o* the poor.............Job 20:19
heard the request of the *o*........Ps 10:17
defend the fatherless and *o* ....Ps 10:18
Let the *o* eat and be filled ....Ps 22:26
let the *o* hear and rejoice...........Ps 34:2
You rescue the *o*..................Ps 35:10
the *o* will possess the land.........Ps 37:11
bring down the *o* and needy........Ps 37:14
I am *o* and needy ....Ps 40:17
You sustain the *o* ....Ps 68:10
o and poor praise your name.......Ps 74:21
executes justice for all the *o*........Ps 103:6
defends the cause of the *o* ......Ps 140:12
The Lord lifts up the *o*............Ps 147:6
the *o* among his people..........Isa 14:32
o and the poor look for water .....Isa 41:17
help the hungry and feed the *o*....Isa 58:10
For he rescues the *o*..............Jer 20:13
to set free those who are *o*....... Luke 4:18
and healing all who were *o*.......Acts 10:38

OPPRESSES
The one who *o* the poor..........Prov 14:31
The one who *o* the poor..........Prov 22:16
poor person who *o* the weak..... Prov 28:3

OPPRESSING
Are not the rich *o* you ....Jas 2:6

OPPRESSION
because of the excess of *o*..........Job 35:9
in what you can gain by *o*..........Ps 62:10
the *o* that continually occurs ......Eccl 4:1
o can turn a wise person into.......Eccl 7:7

OPPRESSIVE
Deliver me from *o* men........... Ps 119:134

OPPRESSOR
do not hear the voice of the *o* ....Job 3:18
who is a great *o* lacks wisdom....Prov 28:16
at the anger of the *o*..............Isa 51:13
against them anymore as an *o*.....Zech 9:8

OPPRESSORS
Do not abandon me to my *o*......Ps 119:121
from the power of their *o* ....Eccl 4:1
to the Lord because of *o*..........Isa 19:20

OPTION
exercise my redemption *o*......... Ruth 4:6

ORACLE
they offer an *o* of peace ....Mic 3:5

ORACLES
Seek *o* at the pits used ....Isa 8:19
they will receive no divine *o*........Mic 3:7
received living *o* to give to you ....Acts 7:38
entrusted with the *o* of God........Rom 3:2

ORCHARD
The Lord God planted an *o* ....Gen 2:8
There was an *o* there.............John 18:1

ORDAINED
you have *o* praise...................Ps 8:2
o that his covenant be observed.....Ps 111:9

ORDER
arguments in *o* before me..........Job 33:5
For he will *o* his angels ....Ps 91:11
in *o* to cleanse the land..........Ezek 39:12
and put in *o*..................... Matt 12:44
o me to come to you .... Matt 14:28
swept clean and put in *o*.........Luke 11:25
But each in his own *o*.............1 Cor 15:23
in the *o* of Melchizedek ....Heb 5:6
until the new *o* came ....Heb 9:10
set in *o* at God's command ....Heb 11:3

ORDERED
I *o* your ancestors ....2 Kgs 17:13
Nathan the prophet had *o* ...... 2 Chr 29:25

ORDERING
fixed *o* of the heavenly lights........Jer 31:36

ORDERS
o as to what you are to do.........Ezra 6:8
obeyed the *o* of your ancestor......Jer 35:18
with no *o* from us ....Acts 15:24

ORDINANCE
This is the *o* of the Passover..... Exod 12:43
This is to be a lasting *o* ....Exod 27:21
by a perpetual *o*.................Exod 29:9
be to you for an eternal *o* ,.......Num 10:8
resists the *o* of God...............Rom 13:2

ORDINARY
If an *o* individual sins ....Lev 4:27
uneducated and *o* men ....Acts 4:13

ORIGINATOR
You killed the *O* of life............Acts 3:15
the *o* of God's creation ....Rev 3:14

ORION
Brilliant constellation, Job 9:9

ORNAMENT
and an *o* of fine gold..............Prov 25:12

ORNAMENTS
cheeks are beautiful with *o*........Song 1:10

ORNAN
See ARAUNAH

ORPAH
Ruth's sister-in-law, Ruth 1:4, 14

ORPHAN
justly treats the *o* and widow.....Deut 10:18
to vote against the *o*...............Job 31:21
not take up the cause of the *o*.......Isa 1:23
show compassion to *O* Israel.......Hos 14:3
the *o*, the resident foreigner...... Zech 7:10

ORPHANS
and loot what belongs to *o*..........Isa 10:2
We have become fatherless *o* ......Lam 5:3
I will not abandon you as *o*.......John 14:18
to care for *o* and widows ....Jas 1:27

OSTRICHES
O will live there ....Isa 13:21
like *o* in the wilderness..............Lam 4:3

OTHERS
Your land will be given to *o*.......Amos 7:17
For if you forgive *o* their sins .....Matt 6:14
meddling in the work of *o*...... 2 Thess 3:11
sharing with *o* ....1 Tim 6:18
along with seven *o* .... 2 Pet 2:5

OTHNIEL
Son of Kenaz, Caleb's youngest brother,
      Judg 1:13
Captures Kiriath Sepher; receives Caleb's
      daughter as wife, Josh 15:15–17
First judge of Israel, Judg 3:9–11

OUGHT
people *o* to conduct
      themselves ....1 Tim 3:15

OUTCAST
you have been called an *o*.........Jer 30:17

OUTCASTS
and assemble the *o*.................Mic 4:6

OUTCRY
o against this place is so great.....Gen 19:13

OUTLAWS
they crucified two *o* with him ... Mark 15:27

OUTLOOK
the *o* of the flesh is hostile ....Rom 8:7

OUTSIDE
the *o* may become clean too ....Matt 23:26
that look beautiful on the *o* .....Matt 23:27
Pharisees clean the *o* of the cup.. Luke 11:39
go out to him, then, *o* the camp ...Heb 13:13
O are the dogs and the sorcerers. Rev 22:15

OUTSIDERS
with wisdom toward *o*..............Col 4:5

OUTSTANDING
be *o* in the work of the Lord..... 1 Cor 15:58

OUTWARD
look on the *o* appearance ....1 Sam 16:7
are looking at *o* appearances..... 2 Cor 10:7

OUTWARDLY
is not a Jew who is one *o* .... Rom 2:28

OUTWEIGH
little folly can *o* much wisdom......Eccl 10:1

OVER
greater light to rule *o* the day ......Gen 1:16
you must give *o* to the LORD .....Exod 13:12
I am handing *o* to you ....Josh 1:3
is ready to hand *o* to you...........Josh 1:11
when God watched *o* me..........Job 29:2
I can jump *o* a wall...............Ps 18:29
thrown *o* the side of a cliff..........Ps 141:6
Watching *o* the ways ....Prov 31:27
Seraphs stood *o* him..................Isa 6:2
wings out *o* your entire land........ Isa 8:8
her time of warfare is *o*.............Isa 40:2
and the summer is *o*..............Jer 8:20
when the seventy years are *o*......Jer 25:12
he no longer watches *o* them..... Lam 4:16
have been handed *o* to me .... Matt 11:27
and turned *o* the tables...........Matt 21:12
Brother will hand *o* brother .....Mark 13:12
bent *o* and could not straighten .. Luke 13:11
When the feast was half *o*........John 7:14
Then he bent *o* again ....John 8:8
He was given *o* .... Rom 4:25
when he hands *o* the kingdom ... 1 Cor 15:24
o all and through all and in all ...... Eph 4:6
mercy triumphs *o* judgment.........Jas 2:13
and a rock to trip *o*................1 Pet 2:8
crossed *o* from death to life ......1 John 3:14

OVERCAME
But they *o* him by the blood........Rev 12:11

OVERCOME
fear of the Jews had *o* them .... Esth 8:17
crown of those *o* with wine.........Isa 28:1
they will not be able to *o* you........ Jer 1:19
Do not be *o* by evil ....Rom 12:21

OVERCONFIDENT
fool throws off restraint and is *o*.. Prov 14:16

OVEREXTENDING
For we were not *o* ourselves ....2 Cor 10:14

OVERFLOW
vats will *o* with new wine..........Prov 3:10
floodwaters cannot *o* it............Song 8:7
the vats *o* with fresh wine ....Joel 2:24

OVERFLOWING
They will be like an *o* stream .... Jer 47:2
and *o* with thankfulness.............Col 2:7

OVERJOYED
will be *o* because of my God........Isa 61:10
Abraham was *o* to see my day.... John 8:56

OVERLOOK
I will no longer *o* their sin .... Amos 7:8

OVERLOOKED
their widows were being *o* .... Acts 6:1

OVERPOWER
Don't let the current *o* me..........Ps 69:15
gates of Hades will not *o* it ......Matt 16:18

OVERPOWERED
The water would have *o* us.........Ps 124:4

OVERSEAS
Send your grain *o*...................Eccl 11:1

OVERSEER
no commander, *o*, or ruler.........Prov 6:7
will make prosperity your *o* ..... Isa 60:17
aspires to the office of *o*...........1 Tim 3:1
For the *o* must be blameless ......Titus 1:7

OVERSEERS
Holy Spirit has made you *o*....... Acts 20:28

OVERSHADOW
of the Most High will *o* you.......Luke 1:35

OVERSIGHT
exercising *o* not merely as a duty...1 Pet 5:2

OVERTAKE
this disaster will *o* me ....Gen 19:19
or else he will quickly *o* us.......2 Sam 15:14
No harm will *o* you .... Ps 91:10
the darkness may not *o* you......John 12:35
to *o* you like a thief would.......1 Thess 5:4

OVERTAKEN
No trial has *o* you.................1 Cor 10:13

OVERTAKING
pursuing and *o* you..............Deut 28:45

OVERTHREW
So he *o* those cities................ Gen 19:25
I *o* some of you....................Amos 4:11

OVERTHROW
you must completely *o* them....Exod 23:24
I will *o* royal thrones...............Hag 2:22
but I will *o* ....Mal 1:4

OVERTHROWN
The wicked are *o* and perish...... Prov 12:7
which was *o* in a moment ....Lam 4:6
Nineveh will be *o*...................Jonah 3:4

OVERTHROWS
and *o* the potentates ....Job 12:19
he *o* them in the night.............Job 34:25

OVERTURNED
and *o* their tables...................John 2:15

OVERWHELM
eyes away from me—they *o* me ... Song 6:5
happiness and joy will *o* them..... Isa 35:10
they will not *o* you...................Isa 43:2

OVERWHELMED
waters completely *o* the earth..... Gen 7:18
the currents of chaos *o* me..........Ps 18:4
they were *o*......................Luke 2:48
women who are *o* with sins ......2 Tim 3:6

OVERWHELMING
But with an *o* flood...................Nah 1:8

OVERWHELMS
but the LORD's faithfulness *o*........Ps 32:10

OWE
much do you *o* my master.........Luke 16:5
O no one anything..................Rom 13:8
you *o* me your very self ....Phlm 1:19

OWED
a man who *o* 10,000 talents ..... Matt 18:24
who *o* him 100 silver coins ...... Matt 18:28
until he repaid all he *o*........... Matt 18:34
one *o* him 500 silver coins........Luke 7:41
Pay everyone what is *o*............Rom 13:7

OWL
and screech like an *o* ....Mic 1:8

OWN
humankind in his *o* image ....Gen 1:27
a dream with its *o* meaning........Gen 41:11
as much as he did his *o* life ....1 Sam 18:1
Israel your very *o* people........2 Sam 7:24
each to his *o* city....................Ezra 2:1
reproach on their *o* head ....Neh 4:4
the wise in their *o* craftiness........ Job 5:13
rely on your *o* understanding.......Prov 3:5
be wise in your *o* estimation.......Prov 3:7
is right in his *o* opinion ....Prov 12:15
seem right in his *o* opinion ....Prov 16:2
with a thief is his *o* enemy.......Prov 29:24
the product of their *o* hands..........Isa 2:8
you may eat from his *o* vine........Isa 36:16
inclinations of their *o* hearts........Jer 9:14
man's enemies are his *o* family ......Mic 7:6
the beam of wood in your *o* ....Matt 7:3
let the dead bury their *o* dead.... Matt 8:22
He came to what was his *o*........John 1:11
Having loved his *o*.................John 13:1
world would love you as its *o*..... John 15:19
took her into his *o* home ....John 19:27
speaking in his *o* language..........Acts 2:6
by our *o* power or piety ....Acts 3:12
God demonstrates his *o* love ....Rom 5:8
who did not spare his *o* Son ...... Rom 8:32

and you are not your *o* .... 1 Cor 6:19
each has his *o* gift from God........1 Cor 7:7
their wives as their *o* bodies....... Eph 5:28
are busy with their *o* concerns .....Phil 2:21
manage his *o* household well......1 Tim 3:4
but by his *o* blood .... Heb 9:12
gazes at his *o* face in a mirror ......Jas 1:23
a people of his *o*...................1 Pet 2:9
by the prophet's *o* imagination... 2 Pet 1:20
their *o* place of residence........... Jude 1:6
at the cost of his *o* blood .... Rev 1:5

OWNERS
who were *o* of land or houses .....Acts 4:34
brought her *o* a great profit ...... Acts 16:16

OX
You must not muzzle your *o* ..... Deut 25:4
Is the wild *o* willing................Job 39:9
Can you bind the wild *o* ....Job 39:10
and Sirion like a young *o* ....Ps 29:6
like that of a wild *o* ....Ps 92:10
than a fattened *o* where .... Prov 15:17
An *o* recognizes its owner ....Isa 1:3
the face of an *o* on the left........ Ezek 1:10
untie his *o* or his donkey ....Luke 13:15
Do not muzzle an *o*................. 1 Cor 9:9
the second creature like an *o*........Rev 4:7

P

PADDAN ARAM
See MESOPOTAMIA

PAGAN
very memory of the *p* priests.......Zeph 1:4

PAGANS
accepting nothing from the *p*......3 John 1:7

PAID
They *p* 600 silver pieces...........2 Chr 1:17
you have *p* the very last cent.... Luke 12:59
p a tithe through Abraham .... Heb 7:9

PAIN
with *p* you will give birth .... Gen 3:16
p when I gave birth to him.........1 Chr 4:9
acknowledge their intense *p*......2 Chr 6:29
my *p* is not relieved .... Job 16:6
often does God apportion *p*........Job 21:17
because you notice my *p* ....Ps 31:7
and I am in constant *p*.............. Ps 38:17
and my insides felt sharp *p*........ Ps 73:21
his work produces *p*.................Eccl 2:23
put away *p* from your body........Eccl 11:10
day of disease and incurable *p*....Isa 17:11
will lie down in a place of *p*...... Isa 50:11
one who experienced *p*..............Isa 53:3
that your *p* is incurable.............Jer 30:15
or mourning, or crying, or *p*........Rev 21:4

PAINFUL
have been few and *p*................Gen 47:9
bound in *p* iron chains............Ps 107:10
discipline seems *p* at the time.....Heb 12:11

PAINS
greatly increase your labor *p* ..... Gen 3:16
are the beginning of birth *p* ......Matt 24:8
from the *p* of death.................Acts 2:24
like labor *p* on a pregnant .... 1 Thess 5:3
themselves with many *p*..........1 Tim 6:10

PAINTS
and *p* its rooms red.................Jer 22:14

PAIRS
P of all creatures ....Gen 7:15

PALACE
was taken to the royal *p*...........Esth 2:8
of high rank in the king's *p* ....Esth 9:4
and enter the royal *p* ....Ps 45:15
the king departed to his *p* .... Dan 6:18
in the *p* of the high priest........ Matt 26:3
guards his own *p* .... Luke 11:21

PALACES
luxurious *p* comes the music ....Ps 45:8
He destroyed all her *p*..............Lam 2:5

PALE
their faces turn so deathly *p*........ Jer 30:6
their faces turn *p* with fright........Joel 2:6

PALLET
followed behind the funeral *p* ....2 Sam 3:31

PALM
and seventy *p* trees............. Exod 15:27
p trees, and flowers in bloom.....1 Kgs 6:29
Your stature is like a *p* tree....... Song 7:7
they took branches of *p* trees .... John 12:13
with *p* branches in their hands ......Rev 7:9

PALMS
inscribed your name on my *p*...... Isa 49:16

PALTIEL
Man to whom Saul gives Michal, David's
   wife, in marriage, 1 Sam 25:44; 2 Sam 3:15

PAMPERED
be called delicate and *p*..............Isa 47:1

PAMPERS
If someone *p* his servant ....Prov 29:21

PAMPHYLIA
People from, at Pentecost, Acts 2:10
Paul visits; John Mark returns home from,
   Acts 13:13; 15:38
Paul preaches in cities of, Acts 14:24–25

PAN
took his fire *p* and put fire in it ..... Lev 10:1

PANIC
When you ignore them, they *p* ... Ps 104:29
p grips the godless ....Isa 33:14
Tell those who *p*..................... Isa 35:4

PANICKED
the Benjaminites *p*................Judg 20:41

PANT
and *p* for breath like jackals ....Jer 14:6

PAPERS
and gave her divorce *p* ....Jer 3:8

PAPHOS
Paul blinds Elymas at, Acts 13:6–13

PAPYRUS
she took a *p* basket for him .... Exod 2:3

PARABLE
tell a *p* to the house of Israel ......Ezek 17:2
Learn this *p* from the fig tree....Matt 24:32
Don't you understand this *p* ......Mark 4:13
he told this *p* against them ...... Mark 12:12
are you telling this *p* for us ....Luke 12:41

PARABLES
spoke in *p* through the prophets ..Hos 12:10
spoke all these things in *p*.......Matt 13:34
but for others they are in *p*......Luke 8:10

PARADISE
today you will be with me in *p*...Luke 23:43
was caught up into *p* ....2 Cor 12:4
that is in the *p* of God ....Rev 2:7

PARALYTIC
then he said to the *p*............... Matt 9:6
stretcher the *p* was lying on.......Mark 2:4

PARALYZED
Your hands must not be *p* .... Zeph 3:16
servant is lying at home *p* .... Matt 8:6
and *p* people were lying...........John 5:3
many *p* and lame people ....Acts 8:7

PARAN
Residence of exiled Ishmael, Gen 21:21
Israelites camp in, Num 10:12
Headquarters of spies, Num 13:3, 26
Site of David's refuge, 1 Sam 25:1

PARCHED
in a dry and *p* land................... Ps 63:1
My heart is *p* and withered.........Ps 102:4
soul thirsts for you in a *p* land......Ps 143:6
their tongues are *p* from thirst .....Isa 41:17

PARCHMENTS
especially the *p*..................2 Tim 4:13

PARDON
not *p* your transgressions .... Exod 23:21
not *p* my transgression............. Job 7:21

PARDONED
whose sin is *p*...................... Ps 32:1

PARENTS
the glory of children is their *p* .....Prov 17:6
The *p* have eaten sour grapes ......Jer 31:29
Children will rise against *p* ....Matt 10:21
Jesus' *p* went to Jerusalem.........Luke 2:41
or brothers or *p* or children ..... Luke 18:29
children not born by human *p*.....John 1:13
this man or his *p*.....................John 9:2
disobedient to *p* ....Rom 1:30
not have to save up for their *p*... 2 Cor 12:14
obey your *p* in everything ....Col 3:20
disobedient to *p* ....2 Tim 3:2

PARMENAS
One of the seven servants in the early
   church, Acts 6:1–5

PART
he took *p* of the man's side.........Gen 2:21
in the habitable *p* of his earth .....Prov 8:31
they no longer have a *p*............. Eccl 9:6
Mary has chosen the best *p* ..... Luke 10:42
he brought only *p* of it.............. Acts 5:2
no share or *p* in this matter .... Acts 8:21
For we know in *p* ....1 Cor 13:9

PARTIAL
A *p* hardening has happened ..... Rom 11:25

PARTIALITY
You must neither show *p*......... Lev 19:15
It is terrible to show *p* ....Prov 18:5
and are showing *p*................. Mal 2:9
because you show no *p*.......... Matt 22:16
and show no *p*................... Luke 20:21
For there is no *p* with God........ Rom 2:11

PARTICIPATE
not *p* in the unfruitful deeds........ Eph 5:11

PARTICIPATION
of your *p* in the gospel.............. Phil 1:5

PARTITION
destroyed the middle wall of *p* .....Eph 2:14

PARTNER
if you regard me as a *p* .... Phlm 1:17

PARTNERS
passive homosexual *p*.............. 1 Cor 6:9
those who eat the sacrifices *p* ....1 Cor 10:18
want you to be *p* with
   demons.......................1 Cor 10:20
became *p* in God's grace............ Phil 1:7
have become *p* with Christ .... Heb 3:14
weaker *p* and show them honor....1 Pet 3:7

PARTNERSHIP
for what *p* is there.................2 Cor 6:14

PARTRIDGE
for a *p* in the hill country ....1 Sam 26:20

PARTS
to the farthest *p* of the earth .... Acts 1:8

PARTY
religious *p* of the Sadducees....... Acts 5:17
the strictest *p* of our religion ......Acts 26:5

PAS DAMMIM
See EPHES DAMMIM

PASHHUR
Official opposing Jeremiah, Jer 21:1; 38:1–13
—Priest who puts Jeremiah in jail,
   Jer 20:1–6

PASS
see the blood I will *p* over you.....Exod 12:13
years of our lives *p* quickly .... Ps 90:9
When you *p* through the waters.... Isa 43:2
In this way I will *p* sentence .... Jer 1:16
p under the shepherd's staff......Ezek 20:37
seven periods of time will *p* .... Dan 4:32
let this cup *p* from me.............Matt 26:39

PASSED
My days have *p* ....Job 17:11
The winter has *p*. ....Song 2:11
p over the sins previously .... Rom 3:25
what is old has *p* away............. 2 Cor 5:17
For the time that has *p* ....1 Pet 4:3

PASSERBY
forced a *p* to carry his cross ..... Mark 15:21

PASSING
Jesus the Nazarene is *p* by........Luke 18:37

PASSION
p is as unrelenting as Sheol........Song 8:6
and your life's *p*..................Ezek 24:21
shameful *p*, evil desire.............. Col 3:5
in lustful *p* like the Gentiles .....1 Thess 4:5
the wine of her immoral *p*.........Rev 14:8

PASSIONS
them over to dishonorable *p* ......Rom 1:26
keep away from youthful *p*...... 2 Tim 2:22
your *p* that battle inside you..........Jas 4:1
so you can spend it on your *p* ....Jas 4:3

PASSOVER
It is the LORD's *P*. .... Exod 12:11
sacrifice from the Feast of *P*.....Exod 34:25
Israelites are to observe the *P*..... Num 9:2
to keep the *P* to the LORD .... Num 9:14
celebrated the *P* in the evening ... Josh 5:10
such a *P* of the LORD ....2 Kgs 23:23
decided to observe the *P*........2 Chr 30:2
you will celebrate the *P* ....Ezek 45:21
I will observe the *P*............. Matt 26:18
where I may eat the *P* .... Mark 14:14
Jewish Feast of *P* was near ....John 2:13
Jewish Feast of the *P* was near .....John 6:4
Jewish Feast of *P* was near .... John 11:55
Then, six days before the *P*........John 12:1
day of preparation for the *P*......John 19:14
By faith he kept the *P* ....Heb 11:28

PAST
observations about the *p*...........Ps 78:2
In *p* generations he allowed ...... Acts 14:16

PASTORS
and some as *p* and teachers .... Eph 4:11

PASTURE
against the sheep of your *p*.......... Ps 74:1
we are the people of his *p*...........Ps 95:7
In a good *p* I will feed them...... Ezek 34:14
come in and go out, and find *p*....John 10:9

PASTURES
He takes me to lush *p* ....Ps 23:2

PATARA
Port of Lycia where Paul changes ships,
   Acts 21:1–2

PATH
You widen my *p* ....2 Sam 22:37
hidden *p* no bird of prey knows ....Job 28:7
You lead me in the *p* of life ....Ps 16:11
lead me along a level *p* ....Ps 27:11
choose the *p* of faithfulness ....Ps 119:30
bent on traveling a sinful *p* ....Ps 125:5
But the *p* of the righteous ....Prov 4:18
not know the *p* of the wind....... Eccl 11:5
the *p* of the righteous .... Isa 26:7
make a *p* through the depths.......Isa 51:10
they do not alter their *p*.............Joel 2:7
traveled down Cain's *p* ....Jude 1:11

PATHROS
Described as a lowly kingdom,
   Ezek 29:14–16
Refuge for dispersed Jews, Jer 44:1–15
Jews to be regathered from, Isa 11:11

PATHS
He leads me down the right *p* ....Ps 23:3
Teach me your *p*....................Ps 25:4
and all her *p* are peaceful..........Prov 3:17
p they have never traveled .... Isa 42:16
make his *p* straight ....Matt 3:3
ruin and misery are in their *p*......Rom 3:16
make straight *p* for your feet......Heb 12:13

PATHWAY
he knows the *p* that I take.........Job 23:10
p through the surging waters.......Isa 43:16

PATIENCE
love, joy, peace, *p*, kindness.........Gal 5:22
humility and gentleness, with *p* .... Eph 4:2
could demonstrate his utmost *p*...1 Tim 1:16
an example of suffering and *p*......Jas 5:10
And regard the *p* of our Lord.....2 Pet 3:15

PATIENT
You are *p* and demonstrate..........Ps 86:15
he is *p* and demonstrates...........Ps 103:8
Be *p* with me .... Matt 18:26
Love is *p*, love is kind..............1 Cor 13:4
be *p* toward all .... 1 Thess 5:14

PATIENTLY
Wait *p* for the LORD ....Ps 37:7
I will wait *p* for the LORD ....Isa 8:17
those who wait *p* for me........... Isa 49:23
good to wait *p* for deliverance....Lam 3:26
not fulfilled right away, wait *p* ...... Hab 2:3
when God *p* waited............... 1 Pet 3:20

PATMOS
John, banished here, receives the
   Revelation, Rev 1:9

PATRIARCHS
and Jacob of the twelve *p*...........Acts 7:8
To them belong the *p*..............Rom 9:5

PATTERN
after the *p* of Melchizedek .... Ps 110:4

PAUL [or SAUL]
Roman citizen from Tarsus; studied under
   Gamaliel, Acts 22:3, 25–28
Persecutes the church, Acts 7:58; 8:1, 3;
   9:1–2
Converted on road to Damascus,
   Acts 9:3–19
Preaches in Damascus; escapes to
   Jerusalem and then to Tarsus,
   Acts 9:20–30
Ministers in Antioch; sent to Jerusalem,
   Acts 11:25–30
First missionary journey, Acts 13–14
Speaks for Gentiles at Jerusalem Council,
   Acts 15:1–5, 12
Second missionary journey, Acts 15:36–
   18:22
Third missionary journey, Acts 18:23–21:14
Arrested in Jerusalem; defense before
   Roman authorities, Acts 21:15–26:32
Sent to Rome, Acts 27:1–28:31
His epistles, Rom; 1 and 2 Cor; Gal; Eph;
   Phil; Col; 1 and 2 Thess; 1 and 2 Tim;
   Titus; Philem
Also called "Saul," Acts 7:58

PAULUS, SERGIUS
Roman proconsul of Cyprus, Acts 13:4, 7

PAVEMENT
like a *p* made of sapphire.........Exod 24:10
the place called "The Stone *P* .... John 19:13

PAWS
It *p* the ground in the valley .... Job 39:21

PAY
get revenge and *p* them back.... Deut 32:35
he does not *p* attention..............Ps 10:11
P them back for their evil ....Ps 28:4
p close attention....................Prov 5:1
do not have enough to *p*......... Prov 22:27
Why *p* money for something ...... Isa 55:2
but will *p* them back................Isa 65:6
nor *p* attention to me................Jer 7:26
I want to see you *p* them back......Jer 11:20
Is it right to *p* taxes to Caesar ....Matt 22:17
Is it right to *p* taxes to Caesar ... Mark 12:14
and be content with your *p*........Luke 3:14
for the worker deserves his *p* ....Luke 10:7
p is not credited due to grace ..... Rom 4:4
The worker deserves his *p*........ 1 Tim 5:18
we must *p* closer attention..........Heb 2:1
the *p* you have held back ....Jas 5:4

will cost a day's *p*.................. Rev 6:6
to *p* each one according ....Rev 22:12

PAYMENT
in our hearts as a down *p*........2 Cor 1:22
the Spirit as a down *p* ....2 Cor 5:5
the down *p* of our inheritance...... Eph 1:14

PAYOFF
For the *p* of sin is death........... Rom 6:23

PAYOFFS
and look for *p* ....Isa 1:23

PEACE
These men are at *p* with us........ Gen 34:21
I will grant *p* in the land .... Lev 26:6
and give you *p*....................Num 6:26
made *p* with Israel and lived........Josh 10:1
Do you come in *p*.................1 Sam 16:4
Do you come in *p*..................1 Kgs 2:13
be asleep and then at *p*.............Job 3:13
wild animals will be at *p*............Job 5:23
a time of *p* marauders attack......Job 15:21
I was in *p*, and he has shattered ....Job 16:12
Strive for *p* and promote it ....Ps 34:14
will make *p* with his people...........Ps 85:8
I am committed to *p*................Ps 120:7
Pray for the *p* of Jerusalem ....Ps 122:6
be *p* inside your defenses............Ps 122:7
May Israel experience *p*.............Ps 125:5
and a time for *p* ....Eccl 3:8
Everlasting Father, Prince of *P*....... Isa 9:6
which will lie down there in *p* ....Isa 17:2
They are unfamiliar with *p*..........Isa 59:8
that lives in *p* and security.........Jer 49:31
They will seek *p* .... Ezek 7:25
P and prosperity...................Dan 4:1
He will give us *p*...................Mic 5:5
in this place I will give *p* .... Hag 2:9
will announce *p* to the nations ... Zech 9:10
let your *p* come on it ....Matt 10:13
come to bring *p* to the earth .... Matt 10:34
and on earth *p* among people ....Luke 2:14
the things that make for *p* ...... Luke 19:42
P I leave with you..................John 14:27
so that in me you may have *p* ....John 16:33
Grace and *p* to you .... Rom 1:7
we have *p* with God .... Rom 5:1
of the Spirit is life and *p* .... Rom 8:6
God of *p* will quickly crush ...... Rom 16:20
God has called you in *p*............1 Cor 7:15
agree with one another,
   live in *p* ....2 Cor 13:11
p, patience, kindness ....Gal 5:22
For he is our *p* ....Eph 2:14
in the bond of *p* ....Eph 4:3
from the good news of *p*...........Eph 6:15
And the *p* of God ....Phil 4:7
making *p* through the blood........Col 1:20
Let the *p* of Christ .... Col 3:15
Be at *p* among yourselves ...... 1 Thess 5:13
faithfulness, love, and *p*......... 2 Tim 2:22
king of Salem, that is, king of *p*..... Heb 7:2
Pursue *p* with everyone ....Heb 12:14
in *p* among those who make *p*.......Jas 3:18
May grace and *p* be lavished ....2 Pet 1:2
to take *p* from the earth........... Rev 6:4

PEACE-LOVING
And if a *p* person is there.........Luke 10:6

PEACE-OFFERING
from the *p* sacrifice..................Lev 3:9

PEACEABLE
then *p*, gentle, accommodating......Jas 3:17

PEACEABLY
live *p* with all people ....Rom 12:18

PEACEFUL
will live in *p* settlements............Isa 32:18
may lead a *p* and quiet life......... 1 Tim 2:2

PEACEFULLY
I will lie down and sleep *p* ....Ps 4:8

PEACEMAKERS
Blessed are the *p* ....Matt 5:9

PEARL
he found a *p* of great value . . . . . . Matt 13:46
PEARLS
p and lapis lazuli are also there . . . . .Gen 2:12
price of wisdom is more than *p*. . . .Job 28:18
or throw your *p* before pigs . . . . Matt 7:6
braided hair and gold or *p* . . . . 1 Tim 2:9
twelve gates are twelve *p*. . . . . Rev 21:21
PEG
took a tent *p* in one hand. . . . . .Judg 4:21
like a *p* into a solid place . . . . Isa 22:23
PEKAH
Son of Remaliah; usurps Israel's throne,
   2 Kgs 15:25–28
Forms alliance with Rezin of Syria against
   Ahaz, Isa 7:1–9
Alliance defeated; captives returned,
   2 Kgs 16:5–9
Territory of, overrun by Tiglath-Pileser,
   2 Kgs 15:29
Assassinated by Hoshea, 2 Kgs 15:30
PEKAHIAH
Son of Menahem; king of Israel,
   2 Kgs 15:22–26
Assassinated by Pekah, 2 Kgs 15:23–25
PEN
to write to you with *p* and ink . . . .3 John 1:13
PENKNIFE
cut them off with a *p* . . . . Jer 36:23
PENNY
until you have paid the last *p* . . . . Matt 5:26
two sparrows sold for a *p* . . . . Matt 10:29
PENTECOST
when the day of *P* had come . . . . Acts 2:1
by the day of *P* . . . . .Acts 20:16
I will stay in Ephesus until *P* . . . . . . 1 Cor 16:8
PENUEL
Place east of Jordan; site of Jacob's
   wrestling with angel, Gen 32:24–31
Inhabitants of, slain by Gideon, Judg 8:8–9,
   17
PEOPLE
See also PEOPLE OF GOD
city of Sodom fifty godly *p* . . . . Gen 18:26
take you to myself for a *p* . . . . Exod 6:7
So all the skilled *p* . . . . Exod 36:4
For you are a *p* holy . . . . Deut 7:6
to be some poor *p* in the land . . . . Deut 15:11
are a *p* delivered by the LORD . . . Deut 33:29
p will become my people. . . . . Ruth 1:16
not view things the way *p* do . . . . .1 Sam 16:7
were upright *p* ever destroyed . . . . . .Job 4:7
evil *p* cannot dwell with you. . . . . Ps 5:4
Arrogant *p* cannot stand. . . . . Ps 5:5
when *p* promote evil . . . . Ps 12:8
As for God's chosen *p* . . . . Ps 16:3
p insult me and despise me. . . . . .Ps 22:6
the *p* of the earth acknowledge . . . .Ps 22:27
Evil *p* self-destruct. . . . . Ps 34:21
Pay attention, all you *p* . . . . Ps 49:2
Assemble my covenant *p* . . . . .Ps 50:5
and all *p* will fear . . . . .Ps 64:9
to fall on your chosen *p* . . . . Ps 68:9
not despise his captive *p* . . . . .Ps 69:33
blessed are the *p* who worship . . . . .Ps 89:15
we are his *p*. . . . . Ps 100:3
I will favor the honest *p* . . . . Ps 101:6
What can *p* do to me . . . . Ps 118:6
are the *p* who experience. . . . . Ps 144:15
Let the *p* of Zion delight. . . . . .Ps 149:2
Bad *p* have bowed before . . . . .Prov 14:19
his position before obscure *p*. . . . Prov 22:29
Do not envy evil *p* . . . . .Prov 24:1
what is profitable for *p* to do . . . . . .Eccl 2:3
gather Israel's dispersed *p*. . . . . .Isa 11:12
Blessed be my *p*. . . . . .Isa 19:25
For these are rebellious *p* . . . . Isa 30:9
all *p* will see it at the same time . . . . Isa 40:5
All *p* are like grass. . . . . Isa 40:6
was despised and rejected by *p*. . . . .Isa 53:3

Prepare the way for the *p* . . . . Isa 62:10
p continually and blatantly . . . . Isa 65:3
Powerful *p* should not boast . . . . Jer 9:23
religion of these *p* is worthless . . . . . .Jer 10:3
dishonest *p* have such easy lives . . . . Jer 12:1
on those *p* who trust in me. . . . . Jer 17:7
caused my *p* to be dispersed . . . . Jer 23:2
those of my *p* who are still alive. . . . . Jer 23:3
and they will be my *p*. . . . . Jer 24:7
you dear poor *p* of Egypt . . . . Jer 46:11
are not any *p* of the nation . . . . .Jer 49:1
they will become my *p* . . . . Ezek 37:23
Name him 'Not My *P*' . . . . Hos 1:9
the number of the *p* of Israel. . . . . . . Hos 1:10
deal with the *p* and priests . . . . Hos 4:9
my Spirit on all kinds of *p* . . . . Joel 2:28
I will bring back my *p*. . . . . .Amos 9:14
all you humble *p* of the land. . . . . . . Zeph 2:3
all *p* everywhere. . . . . .Zech 2:13
will turn you into fishers of *p*. . . . . . .Matt 4:19
let your light shine before *p* . . . . . .Matt 5:16
acknowledges me before *p* . . . . . . Matt 10:32
and forceful *p* lay hold of it. . . . . . . Matt 11:12
p will be forgiven for every sin . . . Matt 12:31
p will give an account. . . . . .Matt 12:36
prophets and righteous *p*. . . . . Matt 13:17
p will be forgiven for all sins. . . . . . .Mark 3:28
Who do *p* say that I am. . . . . Mark 8:27
a *p* prepared for him. . . . . Luke 1:17
and on earth peace among *p* . . . . . .Luke 2:14
when all *p* speak well of you. . . . . . . Luke 6:26
kind to ungrateful and evil *p*. . . . . . . Luke 6:35
over ninety-nine righteous *p*. . . . . . .Luke 15:7
unrighteous *p*, adulterers. . . . . Luke 18:11
as Jesus was teaching the *p*. . . . . Luke 20:1
it from heaven or from *p* . . . . .Luke 20:4
Unless you *p* see signs. . . . . John 4:48
All the *p* came to him. . . . . .John 8:2
to have one man die for the *p* . . . . . John 11:50
Do not be afraid, *p* of Zion . . . . John 12:15
pour out my Spirit on all *p*. . . . . Acts 2:17
the good will of all the *p*. . . . . .Acts 2:47
not lied to *p* but to God . . . . .Acts 5:4
came about among the *p* . . . . Acts 5:12
afraid of being stoned by the *p* . . . .Acts 5:26
miraculous signs among the *p*. . . . . . Acts 6:8
the *p* increased greatly . . . . Acts 7:17
seen the suffering of my *p*. . . . . Acts 7:34
amazing the *p* of Samaria . . . . Acts 8:9
favoritism in dealing with *p*. . . . . . Acts 10:34
a significant number of *p* . . . . Acts 11:24
from among the Gentiles a *p* . . . . Acts 15:14
all *p* everywhere to repent . . . . Acts 17:30
heart of this *p* has become dull. . .Acts 28:27
call those who were not
   my *p*. . . . . Rom 9:25
disobedient and stubborn *p* . . . . . .Rom 10:21
God has not rejected his *p*. . . . . Rom 11:2
what is good before all *p* . . . . .Rom 12:17
speak to you as spiritual *p*. . . . . .1 Cor 3:1
with sexually immoral *p*. . . . . 1 Cor 5:9
not speak to *p* but to God . . . . .1 Cor 14:2
and they will be my *p* . . . . 2 Cor 6:16
with the influential *p* . . . . Gal 2:2
serving the Lord and not *p* . . . . Eph 6:7
for lawless and rebellious *p* . . . . 1 Tim 1:9
there are many rebellious *p* . . . . Titus 1:10
to purify for himself a *p* . . . . Titus 2:14
and they will be my *p*. . . . . Heb 8:10
The Lord will judge his *p* . . . . Heb 10:30
a *p* of his own. . . . . 1 Pet 2:9
You once were not a *p*. . . . . 1 Pet 2:10
every tribe, language, *p* . . . . Rev 5:9
In those days *p* will seek death . . . . . Rev 9:6
nation, tribe, language, and *p*. . . . . . .Rev 14:6
permitted to scorch *p* with fire . . . . .Rev 16:8
and they will be his *p* . . . . Rev 21:3
PEOPLE OF GOD
rest remains for the *p* . . . . Heb 4:9
to be ill-treated with the *p*. . . . . Heb 11:25
PEOPLES
p serve you and nations bow . . . . . .Gen 27:29
from the other *p* to be mine. . . . . . .Lev 20:26

PEOR
Mountain of Moab opposite Jericho,
   Num 23:28
Israel's camp seen from, Num 24:2
—Moabite god called Baal Peor, Num 25:3,
   5, 18
Israelites punished for worship of,
   Num 31:16
Also called "Baal of Peor," Ps 106:28
PERAZIM, MOUNT
See MOUNT PERAZIM
PERCEIVE
yet I do not *p* him. . . . . .Job 23:8
not *p* what he is bringing about . . . . . Isa 5:12
Look continually, but don't *p* . . . . Isa 6:9
PERCEIVED
no one has heard or *p* . . . . Isa 64:4
Jesus *p* their hostile thoughts. . . . . Luke 5:22
PERCEPTIONS
whose *p* are trained by practice . . . Heb 5:14
PEREZ
One of Judah's twin sons by Tamar,
   Gen 38:24–30
PERFECT
Your lamb must be *p* . . . . .Exod 12:5
his work is *p* . . . . Deut 32:4
The law of the LORD is *p*. . . . . Ps 19:7
be *p*, as your heavenly Father . . . . Matt 5:48
If you wish to be *p* . . . . Matt 19:21
good and well-pleasing and *p*. . . . . .Rom 12:2
but when what is *p* comes. . . . . .1 Cor 13:10
power is made *p* in weakness . . . .2 Cor 12:9
a good work in you will *p* it. . . . . .Phil 1:6
let those of us who are "*p* . . . . .Phil 3:15
for the law made nothing *p*. . . . . Heb 7:19
appoints a son made *p* forever . . . . Heb 7:28
the greater and more *p* tent. . . . . Heb 9:11
who have been made *p*. . . . . Heb 12:23
let endurance have its *p* effect. . . . . . . Jas 1:4
and every *p* gift is from above . . . . . . Jas 1:17
he is a *p* individual. . . . . Jas 3:2
but *p* love drives out fear. . . . . .1 John 4:18
PERFECTED
I have not already been *p*. . . . . .Phil 3:12
the love of God has been *p* . . . . .1 John 2:5
PERFECTION
You were the sealer of *p*. . . . . Ezek 28:12
PERFORM
and *p* great signs and wonders . .Matt 24:24
p signs and wonders to deceive . .Mark 13:22
miraculous sign will you *p*. . . . . John 6:30
PERFORMED
They *p* the service of their God. . . Neh 12:45
John *p* no miraculous sign . . . . .John 10:41
PERFUMER'S
dead fly makes the *p* ointment . . . . .Eccl 10:1
PERGA
Visited by Paul, Acts 13:13–14; 14:25
PERGAMUM
Site of one of the seven churches, Rev 1:11
Letter to, Rev 2:12–17
PERIOD
marital relations during her *p* . . . . .Ezek 18:6
PERIODS
to know the times or *p* . . . . .Acts 1:7
PERISH
We *p*, we all *p*. . . . . .Num 17:12
If I *p*, I *p* . . . . Esth 4:16
all flesh would *p* together . . . . .Job 34:15
They are like animals that *p* . . . . .Ps 49:12
who spouts out lies will *p*. . . . . Prov 19:9
Together they will *p* . . . . Isa 31:3
The godly *p*. . . . . Isa 57:1
you will all *p* as well . . . . .Luke 13:3
will not *p* but have eternal life. . . . . John 3:16
and they will never *p* . . . . John 10:28
than for the whole nation to *p*. . . . John 11:50
May your silver *p* with you . . . . .Acts 8:20

will also *p* apart from the law .....Rom 2:12
are all destined to *p* with use.......Col 2:22
They will *p*............................ Heb 1:11
who shrink back and thus *p* ......Heb 10:39
does not wish for any to *p*.........2 Pet 3:9

PERISHABLE
do it to receive a *p* crown.........1 Cor 9:25
What is sown is *p*................. 1 Cor 15:42
the *p* inherit the imperishable... 1 Cor 15:50
by *p* things like silver or gold...... 1 Pet 1:18

PERISHED
Who, being innocent, ever *p*.........Job 4:7
our hope has *p* ....Ezek 37:11

PERISHES
mighty lion *p* for lack of prey........Job 4:11

PERISHING
veiled only to those who are *p* ....2 Cor 4:3
against those who are *p* ....2 Thess 2:10

PERIZZITES
One of seven Canaanite nations, Deut 7:1
Possessed Palestine in Abraham's time,
    Gen 13:7
Jacob's fear of, Gen 34:30
Many of, slain by Judah, Judg 1:4–5

PERMANENT
Your throne, O God, is *p*..............Ps 45:6
But the deliverance I give is *p* ....Isa 51:6
will be your *p* source of light ...... Isa 60:19

PERMANENTLY
and *p* desolate....................... Zeph 2:9

PERMIT
neither enter nor *p* those trying ..Matt 23:13
p your Holy One to experience....Acts 2:27

PERMITS
what we intend to do, if God *p* ..... Heb 6:3

PERPETUAL
as a *p* covenant between me ....Gen 17:7
So this will be a *p* ordinance......Num 19:21

PERPLEXED
worried and *p* to know ....John 13:22
p, but not driven to despair........2 Cor 4:8
because I am *p* about you .... Gal 4:20

PERSECUTE
people insult you and *p* you .... Matt 5:11
Bless those who *p* you............ Rom 12:14

PERSECUTED
they *p* the prophets before you ...Matt 5:12
If they *p* me.....................John 15:20
because I *p* the church of God.....1 Cor 15:9
we are *p*, but not abandoned ......2 Cor 4:9
The one who once *p* us............. Gal 1:23
why am I still being *p*.............Gal 5:11

PERSECUTING
those who have been *p* me........ Jer 15:15

PERSECUTION
when trouble or *p* comes......... Matt 13:21
on that day a great *p* began .... Acts 8:1

PERSECUTIONS
with *p*—and in the age to
    come ....Mark 10:30
through many *p* ....Acts 14:22
in *p*, in difficulties.................2 Cor 6:4
with *p* and difficulties........... 2 Cor 12:10
as well as the *p* and sufferings.... 2 Tim 3:11

PERSECUTOR
formerly a blasphemer and a *p*....1 Tim 1:13

PERSEVERANCE
with all *p* and petitions ....Eph 6:18
and *p* inherit the promises........ Heb 6:12
self-control, *p*; to *p*, godliness ......2 Pet 1:6

PERSEVERED
he *p* as though he could see ....Heb 11:27

PERSEVERING
And so by *p*...................... Heb 6:15

PERSIST
p in prayer...................... Rom 12:12

PERSISTENCE
the first man's sheer *p*............. Luke 11:8

PERSON
no uncircumcised *p* may eat..... Exod 12:48
God changed his inmost *p*........1 Sam 10:9
How you have saved the *p*.........Job 26:2
to do with a perverse *p*............. Ps 101:4
whoever reproves a wicked *p* ......Prov 9:7
A righteous *p* was delivered....... Prov 11:8
wicked *p* earns deceitful wages....Prov 11:18
evil *p* will not be unpunished ......Prov 11:21
One *p* is generous .... Prov 11:24
A good *p* obtains favor ....Prov 12:2
righteous *p* cares for the life......Prov 12:10
The wicked *p* has desired......... Prov 12:12
The righteous *p* is cautious.......Prov 12:26
lazy *p* does not roast his prey ....Prov 12:27
was easy for a discerning *p* ....Prov 14:6
The wisdom of the shrewd *p* ......Prov 14:8
naive *p* will believe anything..... Prov 14:15
the shrewd *p* discerns his steps .. Prov 14:15
A wise *p* is cautious............... Prov 14:16
A poor *p* will be disliked......... Prov 14:20
A *p* plans his course ....Prov 16:9
a way that seems right to a *p*....Prov 16:25
truly wise *p* restrains his words ..Prov 17:27
the righteous *p* runs to it ....Prov 18:10
discerning *p* acquires knowledge ..Prov 18:15
A poor *p* makes supplications ....Prov 18:23
p who walks in his integrity........ Prov 19:1
and the idle *p* will go hungry ..... Prov 19:15
The steps of a *p* are ordained....Prov 20:24
A shrewd *p* saw danger............Prov 22:3
A generous *p* will be blessed ..... Prov 22:9
the words of the treacherous *p*...Prov 22:12
The wicked *p* fled..................Prov 28:1
righteous *p* can be as confident ...Prov 28:1
poor *p* who walks in his integrity..Prov 28:6
righteous *p* cares for the legal.... Prov 29:7
a righteous *p* dies prematurely .....Eccl 7:15
wise *p* knows the proper time...... Eccl 8:5
But if the wicked *p* turns .... Ezek 18:21
When a wicked *p* turns...........Ezek 18:27
Can a *p* rob God ....Mal 3:8
Whoever receives a righteous *p* ..Matt 10:41
good *p* brings good things out....Matt 12:35
defiles a *p* is not what goes into .. Matt 15:11
from within and defile a *p*........Mark 7:23
for a *p* to gain the whole world...Mark 8:36
if a peace-loving *p* is there........ Luke 10:6
anyone die for a righteous *p*........Rom 5:7
though for a good *p* perhaps ....Rom 5:7
One *p* regards one day holier......Rom 14:5
Do not even eat with such a *p* .....1 Cor 5:11
p is given through the Spirit.......1 Cor 12:8
himself a prophet or spiritual *p*.. 1 Cor 14:37
our inner *p* is being renewed .....2 Cor 4:16
Yet because I was a crafty *p* ..... 2 Cor 12:16
For a *p* will reap what he sows ...... Gal 6:7
that no *p* who is immoral............Eph 5:5
to see you in *p*................... 1 Thess 3:10
that the *p* dedicated to God ......2 Tim 3:17
that such a *p* is twisted by sin ..... Titus 3:11
immoral or godless *p* like Esau....Heb 12:16
p in the midst of his pursuits ....Jas 1:11
forgets what sort of *p* he was.......Jas 1:24
and to the poor *p*..................Jas 2:3
and murdered the righteous *p*.......Jas 5:6
The prayer of a righteous *p*.......Jas 5:16
but the inner *p* of the heart........1 Pet 3:4
For whatever a *p* succumbs to.... 2 Pet 2:19

PERSON'S
p ways are pleasing to the LORD...Prov 16:7
A *p* gift makes room for him .....Prov 18:16
A *p* pride will bring him low ..... Prov 29:23
build on another *p* foundation... Rom 15:20
But the rich *p* pride should be.......Jas 1:10

PERSONS
detestable *p*, murderers............Rev 21:8

PERSUADE
not let them *p* you to do this .....Acts 23:21
we try to *p* people ....2 Cor 5:11

PERSUADED
patience a ruler can be *p* ....Prov 25:15

PERSUADING
p me to become a Christian ..... Acts 26:28

PERSUASIVE
not with *p* words of wisdom....... 1 Cor 2:4

PERSUASIVELY
We speak *p* .... Ps 12:4

PERVERSE
what you are doing is *p*...........Num 22:32
p person spreads dissension......Prov 16:28
but whoever is *p* in his ways......Prov 28:18
from this *p* generation............ Acts 2:40
but also to those who are *p* ....1 Pet 2:18

PERVERSELY
behaves *p* will be found out ......Prov 10:9

PERVERT
not *p* justice or show favor ....Deut 16:19
and *p* all that is right.................Mic 3:9

PESTILENCE
p will march right behind him ...... Hab 3:5

PETER [or SIMON]
Surname "Son of Jonah," Matt 16:17
Fisherman; called to discipleship,
    Matt 4:18–20; John 1:40–42
Called as apostle, Matt 10:2–4
Walks on water, Matt 14:28–33
Confesses Christ's deity, Matt 16:13–19
Rebuked by Christ, Matt 16:21–23
Witnesses transfiguration, Matt 17:1–8;
    2 Pet 1:16–18
Denies Christ three times, Matt 26:69–75
Commissioned to feed Christ's sheep,
    John 21:15–17
Leads disciples, Acts 1:15–26
Preaches at Pentecost, Acts 2:1–41
Performs miracles, Acts 3:1–11; 5:14–16;
    9:32–43
Called to minister to Gentiles, Acts 10
Defends his visit to Gentiles, Acts 11:1–18
Imprisoned and delivered, Acts 12:3–19
Speaks at Jerusalem Council, Acts 15:7–14
Writes epistles, 1 Pet 1:1; 2 Pet 1:1
Also called "Simon," Matt 4:18

PETITION
With every prayer and *p*...........Eph 6:18
prayer and *p* with thanksgiving..... Phil 4:6

PHARAOH
Kings of Egypt, contemporaries of:
    Abraham, Gen 12:15–20
    Joseph, Gen 40–41
    Moses in youth, Exod 1:8–11
    the Exodus, Exod 5–14
    Solomon, 1 Kgs 3:1; 11:17–20
Other Pharaohs, 1 Kgs 14:25–26; 2 Kgs 17:4;
    18:21; 19:9; 23:29; Jer 44:30

PHARISEE
Blind *P*! First clean the inside....Matt 23:26
the *P* who had invited him........ Luke 7:39
P invited Jesus to have a meal ....Luke 11:37
P and the other a tax collector ...Luke 18:10
a *P* named Nicodemus...............John 3:1
P whose name was Gamaliel......Acts 5:34
I lived as a *P* ....Acts 26:5
according to the law as a *P* ....Phil 3:5

PHARISEES
he saw many *P* and Sadducees .....Matt 3:7
When the *P* saw this.................Matt 9:11
do we and the *P* fast often.........Matt 9:14
But the *P* said..................... Matt 9:34
But when the *P* saw this...........Matt 12:2
when the *P* heard this saying .....Matt 15:12
yeast of the *P* and Sadducees......Matt 16:6
Then some *P* came to him.........Matt 19:3
and the *P* heard his parables .... Matt 21:45
the *P* went out and planned .....Matt 22:15
P heard that he had silenced .... Matt 22:34
the *P* assembled before Pilate... Matt 27:62
the *P* came and began to argue....Mark 8:11

were *P* and teachers of the law....Luke 5:17
P and the experts in religious .... Luke 7:30
P clean the outside of the cup.... Luke 11:39
But woe to you *P* .... Luke 11:42
against the yeast of the *P*......... Luke 12:1
P came up and said to Jesus...... Luke 13:31
in religious law and the *P*.........Luke 14:3
P and the experts in the law.......Luke 15:2
The *P* (who loved money ....Luke 16:14
at one point the *P* asked Jesus... Luke 17:20
P heard the crowd murmuring ....John 7:32
So the *P* objected.................John 8:13
So the *P* asked him again..........John 9:15
went to the *P* and reported....... John 11:46
the chief priests and the *P*........ John 11:57
but because of the *P* they ....John 12:42
the religious party of the *P*........ Acts 15:5
Sadducees and the others *P*.......Acts 23:6

PHILADELPHIA
Site of one of the seven churches, Rev 1:11
Letter to, Rev 3:7–13

PHILEMON
Christian at Colossae to whom Paul writes,
    Phlm 1:1
Paul appeals to him to receive Onesimus,
    Phlm 1:9–21

PHILETUS
False teacher, 2 Tim 2:17–18

PHILIP
Son of Herod the Great, Matt 14:3
—One of the Twelve, Matt 10:3
Brings Nathanael to Christ, John 1:43–48
Tested by Christ, John 6:5–7
Introduces Greeks to Christ, John 12:20–22
Gently rebuked by Christ, John 14:8–12
—One of the seven servants in the early
    church, Acts 6:1–5
Called an evangelist, Acts 21:8
Preaches in Samaria, Acts 8:5–13
Leads the Ethiopian eunuch to Christ,
    Acts 8:26–40

PHILIPPI
City of Macedonia (named after Philip of
    Macedon); visited by Paul, Acts 16:12;
    20:6
Paul writes letter to church of, Phil 1:1

PHILISTIA
The land of the Philistines, Gen 21:32, 34;
    Josh 13:2; Ps 60:8

PHILISTINES
Not attacked by Joshua, Josh 13:1–3
Left to test Israel, Judg 3:1–4
God delivers Israel to, as punishment,
    Judg 10:6–7
Israel delivered from, by Samson, Judg 13–16
Capture, then return the ark of the Lord,
    1 Sam 4–6
Wars and dealings with Saul and David,
    1 Sam 13:15–14:23; 17:1–52; 18:25–27;
    21:10–15; 27:1–28:6; 29:1–11; 31:1–13;
    2 Sam 5:17–25
Originally on the island of Crete, Jer 47:4
Prophecies concerning, Isa 9:11–12;
    Jer 25:15–20; 47:1–7; Ezek 25:15–17;
    Zeph 2:4–6

PHILISTINES, SEA OF
See MEDITERRANEAN SEA

PHILOSOPHERS
the Epicurean and Stoic *p* .... Acts 17:18

PHILOSOPHY
deceitful *p* that is according ....Col 2:8

PHINEHAS
Aaron's grandson; executes God's
    judgment, Num 25:1–18; Ps 106:30–31
Settles dispute over memorial altar,
    Josh 22:11–32
—Younger son of Eli; abuses his office,
    1 Sam 1:3; 2:12–17, 22–36
Killed by Philistines, 1 Sam 4:11, 17

PHOENICIA
Mediterranean coastal region including the
    cities of Ptolemais, Tyre, Zarephath, and
    Sidon; evangelized by early Christians,
    Acts 11:19
Jesus preaches here, Matt 15:21

PHRYGIA
Jews from, at Pentecost, Acts 2:1, 10
Visited twice by Paul, Acts 16:6

PHYLACTERIES
p wide and their tassels long ..... Matt 23:5

PHYSICAL
but his *p* presence is weak.......2 Cor 10:10
reconciled you by his *p* body .... Col 1:22
p exercise has some value.........1 Tim 4:8

PHYSICIAN
There is still a *p* there .... Jer 8:22
who are healthy don't need a *p*....Matt 9:12
Our dear friend Luke the *p* .... Col 4:14

PHYSICIANS
all of you are worthless *p*........... Job 13:4

PI HAHIROTH
Israel camps there before crossing the Red
    Sea, Exod 14:2, 9; Num 33:7–8

PICK
to *p* some heads of wheat ....Mark 2:23

PICKED
disciples *p* some heads of wheat ...Luke 6:1

PIECE
one hammered *p* of pure gold...Exod 25:36
or a *p* of an ear ....Amos 3:12
gave him a *p* of broiled fish.....Luke 24:42
top to bottom as a single *p* ......John 19:23

PIECES
thirty *p* of silver .... Zech 11:12
the broken *p* left over .... Matt 14:20
this stone will be broken to *p*.... Matt 21:44
baskets of broken *p* ....Luke 9:17
twelve baskets with broken *p* .....John 6:13
he will break them to *p*........... Rev 2:27

PIERCE
will *p* his ear with an awl ....Exod 21:6
a sword will *p* your own soul ..... Luke 2:35

PIERCED
the one they have *p* ....Zech 12:10
soldiers *p* his side with a spear ...John 19:34
even those who *p* him .... Rev 1:7

PIERCING
p even to the point of dividing..... Heb 4:12

PIETY
But you even break off *p* .... Job 15:4

PIG
The *p* is unclean to you.............Lev 11:7

PIG'S
Like a gold ring in a *p* snout ...... Prov 11:22

PIGS
those who eat the flesh of *p*........Isa 66:17
or throw your pearls before *p* ..... Matt 7:6
came out and went into the *p* .... Matt 8:32
carob pods the *p* were eating.....Luke 15:16

PILATE, PONTIUS
Governor of Judea (AD 26–36), Luke 3:1
Questions Jesus and delivers him to Jews,
    Matt 27:2, 11–26; John 18:28–19:16

PILE
or for the manure *p* .... Luke 14:35

PILES
He *p* up the water of the sea .... Ps 33:7

PILLAR
was turned into a *p* of salt........ Gen 19:26
by day in a *p* of cloud.............Exod 13:21
the *p* on each doorpost...........1 Kgs 6:31
king standing by the *p* ....2 Kgs 11:14
a sacred *p* on a high place ....Isa 6:13
as well as a sacred *p*................Isa 19:19
I will make a *p* in the temple ......Rev 3:12

PILLARS
stand between two *p* ....Judg 16:25
He fashioned two bronze *p*........1 Kgs 7:15
broke the two bronze *p* ....2 Kgs 25:13
I make its *p* secure .... Ps 75:3
has carved out its seven *p* ....Prov 9:1
the tops of the support *p* .... Amos 9:1
who had a reputation as *p*..........Gal 2:9
his legs were like *p* of fire ....Rev 10:1

PILOT'S
wherever the *p* inclination...........Jas 3:4

PIONEER
p and perfecter of our faith.........Heb 12:2

PISGAH
Mountain in Moab where Balaam offers
    sacrifice, Num 23:14
Moses views Promised Land from,
    Deut 3:27
Site of Moses' death, Deut 34:1–7

PISHON
One of Eden's four rivers, Gen 2:10–11

PISIDIA
Twice visited by Paul, Acts 13:13–14; 14:24

PIT
faithful follower to see the *P* .... Ps 16:10
delivers your life from the *P*........Ps 103:4
is like a deep *p*....................Prov 22:14
a prostitute is like a deep *p* ......Prov 23:27
fall into his own *p* .... Prov 28:10
in the *p* of my stomach..............Jer 4:19
They shut me up in a *p* ....Lam 3:53
those who descend to the *P* ......Ezek 31:16
brought me up from the *P*........Jonah 2:6
from the waterless *p* .... Zech 9:11
fell into a *p* on the Sabbath....... Matt 12:11
both will fall into a *p*..............Matt 15:14

PITCH
cover it with *p* inside and out...... Gen 6:14

PITCHER
the *p* is shattered at the well ....Eccl 12:6

PITFALL
panic and *p* have come upon us ...Lam 3:47

PITHOM
Egyptian city built by Hebrew slaves,
    Exod 1:11

PITS
arrogant dig *p* to trap me.......... Ps 119:85

PITY
you must not *p* them..............Deut 7:16
or *p* for the young ....Deut 28:50
and have *p* on you................. Deut 30:3
Have *p* on me......................Job 19:21
take *p* on the poor and needy ...... Ps 72:13
Have *p* on your servants............Ps 90:13
Have *p*, O Lord....................Joel 2:17

PLACE
See also HIGH PLACE; HOLY PLACE; MOST
    HOLY PLACE

not find a resting *p* for its feet...... Gen 8:9
to your holy dwelling *p*...........Exod 15:13
Mankind does not know its *p*......Job 28:13
meeting *p* for all the living.........Job 30:23
which you set in *p* .... Ps 8:3
lies in ambush in a hidden *p* ....Ps 10:9
and settle in a safe *p*.................Ps 55:6
rules from his holy dwelling *p* ....Ps 68:5
fruitful land into a barren *p*........Ps 107:34
Let us go to his dwelling *p* ....Ps 132:7
the mountains were set in *p*....... Prov 8:25
Both go to the same *p*............. Eccl 3:20
up from the washing *p* ....Song 4:2
It will not take *p* ....Isa 7:7
burial *p* is already prepared ....Isa 30:33
My dwelling *p* is removed ....Isa 38:12
dwelling *p* will be with them ..... Ezek 37:27
in his holy dwelling *p* ....Zech 2:13
until everything takes *p* ....Matt 5:18
see the *p* where he was lying.....Matt 28:6
was no *p* for them in the inn.......Luke 2:7

go and take the least important *p* . .Luke 14:10
to make ready a *p* for you . . . . .John 14:2
aside to go to his own *p* . . . . Acts 1:25
everyone I *p* my hands on . . . . Acts 8:19
built together into a dwelling *p* . . . . Eph 2:22

PLACED
and *p* him on the altar . . . . Gen 22:9
p the staff on the child's face . . . . . 2 Kgs 4:31
could be *p* as a footstool . . . . 1 Chr 28:2
p ignorance in the human heart . . . . Eccl 3:11
and *p* it at the apostles' feet . . . . . . Acts 4:37
p his hands on him and healed . . . Acts 28:8

PLACES
See also HIGH PLACES
you put them in slippery *p* . . . . Ps 73:18
he *p* it on his shoulders . . . . Luke 15:5
dwelling *p* in my Father's house . . . John 14:2

PLAGUE
I will bring one more *p* . . . . .Exod 11:1
with a very great *p* . . . . Num 11:33
Those that died in the *p* . . . . Num 25:9
three days of *p* in your land . . . . 2 Sam 24:13
and from the destructive *p* . . . . Ps 91:3
p that stalks in the darkness . . . . Ps 91:6
and the *p* subsided . . . . Ps 106:30
will be the nature of the *p* . . . . Zech 14:12
Then I will stop the *p* . . . . Mal 3:11
because of the *p* of hail . . . . Rev 16:21

PLAGUES
all my *p* on your very self . . . . Exod 9:14
bring on your *p* . . . . Hos 13:14
add to him the *p* described . . . . Rev 22:18

PLAIN
fight him in the *P* of Megiddo . . . 2 Chr 35:22
known about God is *p* to them . . . . Rom 1:19

PLAINLY
I *p* revealed myself . . . . 1 Sam 2:27
If you are the Christ, tell us *p* . . . . John 10:24
now you are speaking *p* . . . . John 16:29

PLAN
the *p* that you were shown . . . . . . .Exod 26:30
who *p* ways to harm me . . . . Ps 140:2
This is the *p* I have devised . . . . Isa 14:26
You *p* great things . . . . Jer 32:19
Do not *p* evil in your hearts . . . . .Zech 8:17
by the predetermined *p* . . . . Acts 2:23
rather than God's redemptive *p* . . . .1 Tim 1:4

PLANNED
LORD of Heaven's Armies *p* it . . . . Isa 23:9
p to arrest Jesus by stealth . . . . Matt 26:4
chief priests *p* to kill Lazarus . . . . . John 12:10

PLANNING
They spend all their time *p* . . . . .Ps 62:4
work nor *p* nor knowledge . . . . Eccl 9:10
not know what the LORD is *p* . . . . . . Mic 4:12

PLANS
may he bring all your *p* to pass . . . . . .Ps 20:4
nullifies the *p* of the peoples . . . . . Ps 33:10
he *p* ways to sin . . . . Ps 36:4
p to harm the ones you cherish . . . . Ps 83:3
Your *p* are very intricate . . . . Ps 92:5
On that day their *p* die . . . . Ps 146:4
a heart that devises wicked *p* . . . . . Prov 6:18
and your *p* will be established . . . . . Prov 16:3
A person *p* his course . . . . Prov 16:9
P are established by counsel . . . . Prov 20:18
and sinful people their *p* . . . . .Isa 55:7
my *p* are not like your *p* . . . . Isa 55:8
He reveals his *p* to men . . . . .Amos 4:13

PLANT
give every green *p* for food . . . . Gen 1:30
began to *p* a vineyard . . . . .Gen 9:20
describing every kind of *p* . . . . 1 Kgs 4:33
Can the papyrus *p* grow tall . . . . Job 8:11
who shed tears as they *p* . . . . Ps 126:5
time to *p*, and a time to uproot . . . . . Eccl 3:2
they will *p* vineyards and eat . . . . . .Isa 65:21
justice into a poisonous *p* . . . . .Amos 6:12
LORD God appointed a little *p* . . . . Jonah 4:6
p that my heavenly Father . . . . .Matt 15:13

PLANTED
The LORD God *p* an orchard . . . . Gen 2:8
Abraham *p* a tamarisk tree . . . . Gen 21:33
a tree *p* by flowing streams . . . . .Ps 1:3
the root your right hand *p* . . . . .Ps 80:15
and *p* a vine . . . . Isa 5:2
Indeed, they are barely *p* . . . . Isa 40:24
land that had never been *p* . . . . .Jer 2:2
I *p* you in the land . . . . Jer 2:21
like a tree *p* near a stream . . . . Jer 17:8
You have *p* much . . . . Hag 1:6
and *p* in the sea . . . . .Luke 17:6
I *p*, Apollos watered . . . . 1 Cor 3:6
is *p* in peace among those . . . . .Jas 3:18

PLANTER
and provide seed for the *p* . . . . Isa 55:10

PLANTING
prepare for them a healthy *p* . . . .Ezek 34:29

PLANTS
p yielding seeds and . . . . Gen 1:11
as short-lived as *p* in the field . . .2 Kgs 19:26
and wither away like *p* . . . . .Ps 37:2
Then our sons will be like *p* . . . . . . Ps 144:12
who *p* counts for anything . . . . .1 Cor 3:7

PLATFORM
stood on a towering wooden *p* . . . . . Neh 8:4

PLATTER
of John the Baptist here on a *p* . . . .Matt 14:8

PLAY
and they rose up to *p* . . . . Exod 32:6
P skillfully as you shout . . . . Ps 33:3
p over the hole of a snake . . . . Isa 11:8
P it well, *p* lots of songs . . . . .Isa 23:16
and drink and rose up to *p* . . . . 1 Cor 10:7

PLAYED
We *p* the flute for you . . . . .Matt 11:17

PLAYERS
flute *p*, and trumpeters . . . . .Rev 18:22

PLAZAS
she shouts loudly in the *p* . . . . .Prov 1:20

PLEA
he has heard my *p* for mercy . . . . Ps 28:6
making his *p* through us . . . . 2 Cor 5:20

PLEADED
he *p* with him to come . . . . .Luke 8:41

PLEAS
continues in her *p* and prayers . . . . 1 Tim 5:5

PLEASANT
How good and how *p* it is . . . . Ps 133:1
for they are *p* . . . . Ps 141:6
Her ways are very *p* . . . . Prov 3:17
but *p* words are pure . . . . Prov 15:26
P words are like a honeycomb . . .Prov 16:24

PLEASANTNESS
calling one "*P*" and the other . . . . . . Zech 11:7

PLEASE
p sleep with my servant . . . . Gen 16:2
live wherever you *p* . . . . Gen 20:15
P forgive the sin of . . . . Gen 50:17
Now *p* forgive my sin . . . . .1 Sam 15:25
p honor me before the elders . . 1 Sam 15:30
P let my sister Tamar . . . . 2 Sam 13:5
P, LORD, deliver . . . . Ps 118:25
do those things that *p* him . . . . John 8:29
are in the flesh cannot *p* God . . . . . . Rom 8:8
Let each of us *p* his neighbor . . . . . Rom 15:2
how to *p* the Lord . . . . 1 Cor 7:32
how to *p* his wife . . . . 1 Cor 7:33
how to *p* her husband . . . . 1 Cor 7:34
Or am I trying to *p* people . . . . Gal 1:10
it is impossible to *p* him . . . . Heb 11:6

PLEASED
the LORD was *p* with Abel . . . . Gen 4:4
because he was *p* with me . . . . 2 Sam 22:20
because he was *p* with me . . . . Ps 18:19
Will he be *p* with you . . . . Mal 1:8
I am not *p* with you . . . . Mal 1:10

danced before them and
   p Herod . . . . .Matt 14:6
for your Father is well *p* . . . . .Luke 12:32
was not *p* with most of them . . . . . 1 Cor 10:5
called me by his grace was *p* . . . . Gal 1:15
commended as having *p* God . . . . . . Heb 11:5

PLEASES
I want to do what *p* you . . . . Ps 40:8
He does whatever he *p* . . . . .Ps 115:3
He does whatever he *p* . . . . Ps 135:6
Teach me to do what *p* you . . . . Ps 143:10
man who *p* God escapes her . . . . . . Eccl 7:26
or arouse love until it *p* . . . . Song 2:7

PLEASING
as a *p* aroma to me . . . . Num 28:2
ways are *p* to the LORD . . . . Prov 16:7
learn what is *p* to the Lord . . . . .Eph 5:10
very *p* to God . . . . Phil 4:18
for this is *p* in the Lord . . . . .Col 3:20
offer worship *p* to God . . . . Heb 12:28
what is *p* before him . . . . .Heb 13:21

PLEASURE
I am worn out will I have *p* . . . . .Gen 18:12
LORD take *p* in burnt offerings . .1 Sam 15:22
he finds *p* in obeying . . . . Ps 1:2
The one who loves *p* . . . . Prov 21:17
I will try self-indulgent *p* . . . . .Eccl 2:1
For God takes no *p* in fools . . . . Eccl 5:4
according to the *p* of his will . . . . Eph 1:5
the sake of his good *p* . . . . Phil 2:13
one who lives for *p* is dead . . . . .1 Tim 5:6
I take no *p* in him . . . . Heb 10:38
to enjoy sin's fleeting *p* . . . . .Heb 11:25

PLEASURES
worries and riches and *p* of life . . . Luke 8:14

PLEDGE
Will you give me a *p* . . . . Gen 38:17
if you have made a *p* . . . . Prov 6:1
strikes hands in *p* and puts up . . . .Prov 17:18
one who strikes hands in *p* . . . . . . Prov 22:26

PLEIADES
Part of God's creation, Job 9:9; Amos 5:8

PLENTIFUL
was attractive and its fruit *p* . . . . . . Dan 4:21
The harvest is *p* . . . . .Matt 9:37

PLENTY
will have *p* of food . . . . .Prov 12:11
of the diligent lead only to *p* . . . . . . Prov 21:5

PLOT
Evil men *p* against the godly . . . . Ps 37:12
disguise a well-conceived *p* . . . . Ps 64:6
p evil against your neighbor . . . . . . Prov 3:29
you *p* against the LORD . . . . Nah 1:9
should anyone secretly *p* evil . . . . . Zech 7:10
p of land that Jacob had given . . . . . John 4:5
but Saul learned of their *p* . . . . .Acts 9:24

PLOTS
p evil with perverse thoughts . . . . . .Prov 6:14

PLOW
The sluggard will not *p* . . . . Prov 20:4
Can one *p* the sea with oxen . . . . . .Amos 6:12
hand to the *p* and looks back . . . .Luke 9:62

PLOWED
Zion will become a *p* field . . . . Jer 26:18
But you have *p* wickedness . . . . . . .Hos 10:13

PLOWING
the one *p* and threshing . . . . 1 Cor 9:10

PLOWMAN
p will catch up to the reaper . . . . . .Amos 9:13

PLOWSHARES
to sharpen *p* and cutting . . . . 1 Sam 13:21
will beat their swords into *p* . . . . .Isa 2:4
Beat your *p* into swords . . . . .Joel 3:10
beat their swords into *p* . . . . .Mic 4:3

PLUCK
all who pass by *p* its fruit . . . . .Ps 80:12

PLUNDER
you will p Egypt .... Exod 3:22
like one who finds much p........ Ps 119:162
when they divide up the p............ Isa 9:3
P the silver .... Nah 2:9
divided as p in your midst .... Zech 14:1

PLUNDERED
The bravehearted were p........... Ps 76:5
these people are looted and p .... Isa 42:22

PLUNGE
that p people into ruin. .... 1 Tim 6:9

POETS
of your own p have said .... Acts 17:28

POINT
on the highest p of the temple .... Luke 4:9
obedient to the p of death. .... Phil 2:8
to the p of imprisonment. .... 2 Tim 2:9
main p of what we are saying. ...... Heb 8:1
fails in one p has become guilty ..... Jas 2:10

POISON
They put bitter p into my food ..... Ps 69:21
which is a bitter p. .... Lam 3:19
p they drink will not harm. ...... Mark 16:18
p of asps is under their lips .... Rom 3:13
full of deadly p .... Jas 3:8

POISONED
and p their minds against. .... Acts 14:2

POMEGRANATE
to be a gold bell and a p .... Exod 28:34
the p, date, and apple. .... Joel 1:12

POMEGRANATES
You are to make p of blue .... Exod 28:33
some of the p and the figs. ...... Num 13:23
grain, or figs, or vines, or p .... Num 20:5
p, of olive trees and honey .... Deut 8:8

POMP
came with great p and entered ... Acts 25:23

PONDERING
p in her heart. .... Luke 2:19

PONTUS
Jews from, at Pentecost, Acts 2:5, 9
Home of Aquila, Acts 18:2
Christians of, addressed by Peter, 1 Pet 1:1

POOL
a desert into a p of water. .... Ps 107:35
a rock into a p of water. .... Ps 114:8
wilderness into a p of water .... Isa 41:18
a p called Bethzatha. .... John 5:2
Go wash in the p of Siloam .... John 9:7

POOLS
covers it with p of water. .... Ps 84:6
eyes are the p in Heshbon .... Song 7:4

POOR
and the p are not to pay less .... Exod 30:15
show partiality to the p. ...... Lev 19:15
are needy and p in your land ..... Deut 15:11
whether rich or p. .... Ruth 3:10
raises the p from the ash heap .... 1 Sam 2:8
a p and lightly esteemed man ... 1 Sam 18:23
one rich and the other p. .... 2 Sam 12:1
some of the p of the land. ...... 2 Kgs 25:12
and providing for the p. .... Esth 9:22
Thus the p have hope. .... Job 5:16
For he has oppressed the p. ...... Job 20:19
the p who cried out for help. ...... Job 29:12
my soul grieved for the p. .... Job 30:25
one who treats the p properly. ...... Ps 41:1
Defend the cause of the p. .... Ps 82:3
He raises the p from the dirt .... Ps 113:7
her p all the food they need ...... Ps 132:15
and vindicates the p .... Ps 140:12
one who is lazy becomes p .... Prov 10:4
another pretends to be p .... Prov 13:7
The one who mocks the p .... Prov 17:5
to the cry of the p .... Prov 21:13
rich and the p are met together .. Prov 22:2
A p person who oppresses .... Prov 28:3
for the legal rights of the p .... Prov 29:7

Or lest I become p and steal. ...... Prov 30:9
to devour the p from the earth. . Prov 30:14
the cause of the p and needy ...... Prov 31:9
opened her hand to the p. .... Prov 31:20
a p but wise man lived. .... Eccl 9:15
p from getting fair treatment. .... Isa 10:2
He will treat the p fairly .... Isa 11:4
you are a protector for the p .... Isa 25:4
to encourage the p .... Isa 61:1
p people who owned nothing ..... Jer 39:10
did not help the p and needy .... Ezek 16:49
wronged the p and needy .... Ezek 22:29
by showing mercy to the p .... Dan 4:27
you make the p pay taxes .... Amos 5:11
resident foreigner, or the p .... Zech 7:10
Blessed are the p in spirit. .... Matt 5:3
and the p have good news. .... Matt 11:5
and give the money to the p. ...... Matt 19:21
always have the p with you. ...... Matt 26:11
a p widow came and put in ...... Mark 12:42
proclaim good news to the p .... Luke 4:18
Blessed are you who are p. ...... Luke 6:20
the p have good news .... Luke 7:22
and give to the p. .... Luke 12:33
invite the p .... Luke 14:13
I now give to the p. .... Luke 19:8
some contribution for the p ...... Rom 15:26
as p, but making many rich .... 2 Cor 6:10
he became p for your sakes ...... 2 Cor 8:9
he has given to the p .... 2 Cor 9:9
only that we remember the p ...... Gal 2:10
p in the world to be rich in faith ...... Jas 2:5
p, blind, and naked .... Rev 3:17
small and great, rich and p .... Rev 13:16

POORLY
p clothed, brutally treated. .... 1 Cor 4:11

POPLAR
fresh-cut branches from p. ...... Gen 30:37

POPLARS
On the p in her midst. .... Ps 137:2

POPULATED
the whole earth was p. .... Gen 9:19

PORCIUS FESTUS
Paul stands trial before, Acts 25:1–22

PORTENTS
I will produce p. .... Joel 2:30

PORTICO
walkway called Solomon's P. ...... Acts 3:11

PORTION
because it is your allotted p .... Lev 10:13
of the first p of your harvest. ...... Lev 23:10
more than my allotted p. .... Job 23:12
a p to her female servants .... Prov 31:15
a p with the multitudes. .... Isa 53:12
My p is the LORD .... Lam 3:24
first p of the dough offered. ...... Rom 11:16

PORTIONS
various p and in various ways .... Heb 1:1

PORTRAYED
was vividly p as crucified .... Gal 3:1

POSITION
in a p to contribute this much ... 1 Chr 29:14
lifted up those of lowly p. .... Luke 1:52
were born to a privileged p. ...... 1 Cor 1:26
should take pride in his high p. ...... Jas 1:9

POSITIONS
took their p against Gibeah. ...... Judg 20:30

POSSESS
the land you are about to p. ..... Deut 28:21
the land you are about to p. ..... Deut 28:63
p the land that you had sworn. .... Neh 9:15
to enter in order to p. .... Neh 9:23
The godly will p the land .... Ps 37:29
you want me to p wisdom. .... Ps 51:6
live in them and p Zion. .... Ps 69:35
know how to p his own body .... 1 Thess 4:4

POSSESSING
and yet p everything. .... 2 Cor 6:10

POSSESSION
after you as a permanent p. .... Gen 17:8
I will give it to you as a p .... Exod 6:8
Jacob is his special p. .... Deut 32:9
Israel to be his special p. .... Ps 135:4
as your most prized p .... Prov 7:2
to take p of it for yourself .... Jer 32:8
to give it to him as his p .... Acts 7:5
claimed as God's own p .... Eph 1:11
redemption of God's own p .... Eph 1:14
had a better and lasting p .... Heb 10:34

POSSESSIONS
but personal p are precious ...... Prov 12:27
offer all his p to buy love .... Song 8:7
who buy like those without p. ..... 1 Cor 7:30
produced by material p. .... 1 John 2:16
But whoever has the world's p ... 1 John 3:17

POSSIBLE
if p, let this cup pass from me ... Matt 26:39
All things are p for the one .... Mark 9:23
If p, so far as it depends on you. ... Rom 12:18
testify about you that if it were p. ... Gal 4:15

POSTERITY
Who can describe his p. .... Acts 8:33

POT
from a boiling p over burning ..... Job 41:20
clay into another kind of p. .... Jer 18:4
the city is a cooking p .... Ezek 11:3

POTENTATES
p decree righteousness. .... Prov 8:15

POTIPHAR
High Egyptian officer, Gen 39:1
Puts Joseph in jail, Gen 39:20

POTIPHERA
Egyptian priest of On (Heliopolis),
   Gen 41:45–50
Father of Asenath, Joseph's wife, Gen 46:20

POTS
when we sat by the p of meat ..... Exod 16:3
They also took the p. .... Jer 52:18
treated like broken clay p .... Lam 4:2
p, kettles, and dining couches ..... Mark 7:4

POTTER
See also POTTER'S FIELD
the p be regarded as clay. .... Isa 29:16
and you are our p. .... Isa 64:8
Has the p no right to make .... Rom 9:21

POTTERY
take holy water in a p jar .... Num 5:17
broken p to scrape himself .... Job 2:8
is as dry as a piece of p .... Ps 22:15
the p say about the potter .... Isa 29:16
like broken pieces of fine p ...... Jer 25:34

POTTER'S FIELD
Judas's money used for purchase of,
   Matt 27:7–8

POUCH
is like a fragrant p of myrrh .... Song 1:13

POUND
took three quarters of a p .... John 12:3

POUNDING
My heart is p inside me. .... Lam 1:20

POUNDS
weighing about seventy-five p. ... John 19:39

POUR
P out your hearts before him. ...... Ps 62:8
P out your anger on the nations. .... Ps 79:6
p water on the parched ground. ..... Isa 44:3
I will p out my Spirit. .... Joel 2:28
I will p out on the kingship .... Zech 12:10
and p out blessing for you. .... Mal 3:10
p out my Spirit on all people ...... Acts 2:17
p out my Spirit in those days ...... Acts 2:18
Go and p out on the earth .... Rev 16:1

POURED
fury will be p out on this land ...... Jer 7:20
is p out like volcanic fire. .... Nah 1:6

she *p* it on his head . . . . Mark 14:3
the love of God has been *p* out . . . . . Rom 5:5
p out on us in full measure . . . . Titus 3:6

POVERTY
p you will serve your enemies . . . Deut 28:48
are brought to ruin by their *p* . . . . Prov 10:15
and comes to *p* . . . . Prov 11:24
ends up in *p* and shame . . . . Prov 13:18
only brings *p* . . . . Prov 14:23
do not give me *p* or riches . . . . Prov 30:8
out of her *p* . . . . Luke 21:4
joy and their extreme *p* . . . . 2 Cor 8:2
by his *p* could become rich . . . . 2 Cor 8:9
you are suffering and your *p* . . . . Rev 2:9

POWER
See also POWER OF GOD
came to *p* over Egypt . . . . Exod 1:8
was majestic in *p* . . . . Exod 15:6
with great strength and *p* . . . . Deut 9:29
tremendous strength and *p* . . . . . . Deut 26:8
So now we are in your *p* . . . . Josh 9:25
With God are wisdom and *p* . . . . Job 12:13
the thunder of his *p* . . . . Job 26:14
Because of your great *p* . . . . Ps 66:3
the people *p* and strength . . . . Ps 68:35
the *p* of your awesome acts . . . . Ps 145:6
hope based on *p* has perished . . . . . Prov 11:7
are in the *p* of the tongue . . . . Prov 18:21
no one has *p* over the wind . . . . Eccl 8:8
military *p* establishes his rule . . . . . . Isa 40:10
his absolute *p* and awesome . . . . Isa 40:26
for the revelation of my *p* . . . . Isa 51:5
is not in their *p* to determine . . . . . . Jer 10:23
slow to anger but great in *p* . . . . Nah 1:3
Not by strength and not by *p* . . . . . . Zech 4:6
the scriptures or the *p* of God . . . Matt 22:29
that *p* had gone out from him . . . . Mark 5:30
the scriptures or the *p* of God . . . Mark 12:24
demonstrated *p* with his arm . . . . . . Luke 1:51
in the *p* of the Spirit . . . . Luke 4:14
p of the Lord was with him . . . . Luke 5:17
because *p* was coming out . . . . Luke 6:19
that *p* has gone out from me . . . . . Luke 8:46
he gave them *p* and authority . . . . . . Luke 9:1
and that of the *p* of darkness . . . Luke 22:53
clothed with *p* from on high . . . . . Luke 24:49
But you will receive *p* . . . . Acts 1:8
by our own *p* or piety . . . . Acts 3:12
full of grace and *p* . . . . Acts 6:8
This man is the *p* of God . . . . Acts 8:10
Give me this *p* too . . . . Acts 8:19
with the Holy Spirit and with *p* . . . Acts 10:38
to grow in *p* and to prevail . . . . Acts 19:20
from the *p* of Satan to God . . . . Acts 26:18
for it is God's *p* for salvation . . . . Rom 1:16
eternal *p* and divine nature . . . . Rom 1:20
demonstrate my *p* in you . . . . Rom 9:17
by the *p* of the Holy Spirit . . . . Rom 15:13
in the *p* of signs and wonders . . . . Rom 15:19
being saved it is the *p* of God . . . . . . 1 Cor 1:18
Christ is the *p* of God . . . . 1 Cor 1:24
of the Spirit and of *p* . . . . 1 Cor 2:4
wisdom but on the *p* of God . . . . 1 Cor 2:5
not in idle talk but with *p* . . . . 1 Cor 4:20
all rule and all authority and *p* . . . . 1 Cor 15:24
it is raised in *p* . . . . 1 Cor 15:43
extraordinary *p* belongs to God . . . 2 Cor 4:7
by the *p* of God . . . . 2 Cor 6:7
p is made perfect in weakness . . . . 2 Cor 12:9
but he lives because of God's *p* . . . 2 Cor 13:4
greatness of his *p* toward us . . . . Eph 1:19
authority and *p* and dominion . . . . . Eph 1:21
by the exercise of his *p* . . . . Eph 3:7
the *p* that is working within us . . . . Eph 3:20
and in the strength of his *p* . . . . Eph 6:10
the *p* of his resurrection . . . . Phil 3:10
from the *p* of darkness . . . . Col 1:13
your faith in the *p* of God . . . . Col 2:12
in *p* and in the Holy Spirit . . . . 1 Thess 1:5
by his *p* your every desire . . . . 2 Thess 1:11
a Spirit of fear but of *p* . . . . 2 Tim 1:7
by God's *p* accept your share . . . . . . 2 Tim 1:8
but will have repudiated its *p* . . . . . . 2 Tim 3:5

the one who holds the *p* of death . . Heb 2:14
the *p* of an indestructible life . . . . . . Heb 7:16
who by God's *p* are protected . . . . . . 1 Pet 1:5
his divine *p* has bestowed on us . . . . 2 Pet 1:3
we made known to you the *p* . . . . . . 2 Pet 1:16
This is the conquering *p* . . . . 1 John 5:4
p, and authority . . . . Jude 1:25
receive glory and honor and *p* . . . . . Rev 4:11
and ruling *p* forever and ever . . . . . . Rev 5:13
and honor and *p* and strength . . . . . Rev 7:12
have gotten rich from the *p* . . . . Rev 18:3
Salvation and glory and *p* . . . . Rev 19:1
The second death has no *p* . . . . Rev 20:6

POWER OF GOD
teach you about the *p* . . . . Job 27:11
the Scriptures or the *p* . . . . Matt 22:29
at the right hand of the *p* . . . . Luke 22:69
This man is the *p* . . . . Acts 8:10
are being saved it is the *p* . . . . 1 Cor 1:18
Christ is the *p* . . . . 1 Cor 1:24
human wisdom but on the *p* . . . . 1 Cor 2:5
truthful teaching, by the *p* . . . . 2 Cor 6:7
through your faith in the *p* . . . . Col 2:12

POWERFUL
for they are too *p* for me . . . . Num 22:6
The Lord's shout is *p* . . . . Ps 29:4
p will be like a thread of yarn . . . . Isa 1:31
the Lord is a *p* deliverer . . . . Isa 45:24
have become *p* in the land . . . . Jer 9:3
one coming after me is more *p* . . . . Matt 3:11
not many were *p* . . . . 1 Cor 1:26
but are made *p* by God . . . . 2 Cor 10:4
all things by his *p* word . . . . Heb 1:3
who are much more *p* . . . . 2 Pet 2:11
Lord God who judges her is *p* . . . . . . Rev 18:8
Babylon the *p* city . . . . Rev 18:10

POWERFULLY
his power that *p* works in me . . . . Col 1:29

POWERLESS
How you have helped the *p* . . . . Job 26:2

POWERS
the *p* of heaven will be shaken . . Matt 24:29
nor things to come, nor *p* . . . . Rom 8:38
against the rulers, against the *p* . . . . Eph 6:12
whether principalities or *p* . . . . Col 1:16
authorities and *p* subject to him . . . 1 Pet 3:22

PRACTICE
judge those who *p* such things . . . . . Rom 2:3
we have no other *p* . . . . 1 Cor 11:16
Those who *p* such things . . . . Gal 5:21
perceptions are trained by *p* . . . . Heb 5:14
who does not *p* righteousness . . . 1 John 3:10
hate what the Nicolaitans *p* . . . . Rev 2:6

PRACTICED
p divination and omen reading . . 2 Kgs 17:17
of those who had *p* magic . . . . Acts 19:19
licentiousness that they have *p* . . 2 Cor 12:21

PRACTICES
they enjoy these disgusting *p* . . . . . . Isa 66:3
who *p* sin is a slave of sin . . . . John 8:34
put off the old man with its *p* . . . . . . Col 3:9
everyone who *p* righteousness . . 1 John 2:29
p sin also practices lawlessness . . 1 John 3:4
who loves and *p* falsehood . . . . Rev 22:15

PRACTICING
who had been *p* magic . . . . Acts 8:9

PRAISE
See also PRAISE THE LORD
This time I will *p* the Lord . . . . Gen 29:35
your brothers will *p* you . . . . Gen 49:8
and I will *p* him . . . . Exod 15:2
He is the one you should *p* . . . . . . Deut 10:21
and you will receive *p* . . . . Deut 26:19
and give him *p* . . . . Josh 7:19
who is worthy of *p* . . . . 2 Sam 22:4
and certainly worthy of *p* . . . . 1 Chr 16:25
P the Lord . . . . 1 Chr 16:36
p the Lord with the instruments . . 1 Chr 23:5
thanks and *p* to the Lord . . . . 1 Chr 23:30
giving thanks and *p* to the Lord . . . 1 Chr 25:3

and *p* your majestic name . . . . 1 Chr 29:13
and *p* his majestic splendor . . . . . . 2 Chr 20:21
they began to shout and *p* . . . . 2 Chr 20:22
told the Levites to *p* the Lord . . 2 Chr 29:30
and offer *p* in the gates . . . . 2 Chr 31:2
stood to *p* the Lord . . . . Ezra 3:10
above all blessing and *p* . . . . Neh 9:5
songs of *p* and thanks to God . . . . Neh 12:46
You are the reason I offer *p* . . . . Ps 22:25
I will *p* you . . . . Ps 30:1
morally upright to offer him *p* . . . . . . Ps 33:1
I will *p* the Lord at all times . . . . Ps 34:1
mouth will continually *p* him . . . . Ps 34:1
Let us *p* his name together . . . . Ps 34:3
and *p* you all day long . . . . Ps 35:28
nations will *p* you forever . . . . Ps 45:17
I will *p* you while I live . . . . Ps 63:4
P awaits you . . . . Ps 65:1
Shout out *p* to God . . . . Ps 66:1
heavens and the earth *p* him . . . . . . Ps 69:34
I *p* you continually . . . . Ps 71:6
and *p* you continually . . . . Ps 84:4
heavens *p* your amazing deeds . . . . . Ps 89:5
P the Lord our God . . . . Ps 99:5
and his courts with *p* . . . . Ps 100:4
P the Lord . . . . Ps 103:1
O God whom I *p* . . . . Ps 109:1
Lord's name is deserving of *p* . . . . . Ps 113:3
and I will *p* you . . . . Ps 118:28
Seven times a day I *p* you . . . . Ps 119:164
great and certainly worthy of *p* . . . . . Ps 145:3
My mouth will *p* the Lord . . . . Ps 145:21
P the Lord . . . . Ps 148:1
P him with loud cymbals . . . . Ps 150:5
that has breath *p* the Lord . . . . Ps 150:6
Let another *p* you . . . . Prov 27:2
and let her works *p* her . . . . Prov 31:31
we will *p* your love . . . . Song 1:4
but we *p* your name alone . . . . Isa 26:13
and your gates, '*P* . . . . Isa 60:18
a garment symbolizing *p* . . . . Isa 61:3
for you give me reason to *p* . . . . Jer 17:14
and *p* before them for the joy . . . . . . Jer 33:9
p and exalt and glorify . . . . Dan 4:37
will *p* the name of the Lord . . . . Joel 2:26
nations to give me acceptable *p* . . . Zeph 3:9
so that people will *p* them . . . . Matt 6:2
I *p* you, Father, Lord of heaven . . . Matt 11:25
have prepared *p* for yourself . . . . . Matt 21:16
they too gave *p* to God . . . . Luke 18:43
and *p* God with a loud voice . . . . . . Luke 19:37
I do not accept *p* from people . . . . . John 5:41
not trying to get *p* for myself . . . . . John 8:50
For they loved *p* from men . . . . John 12:43
person's *p* is not from people . . . . . Rom 2:29
tongue will give *p* to God . . . . Rom 14:11
P the Lord all you Gentiles . . . . Rom 15:11
p you because you remember . . . . . 1 Cor 11:2
Should I *p* you . . . . 1 Cor 11:22
the *p* of the glory of his grace . . . . . . Eph 1:6
would be to the *p* of his glory . . . . . . Eph 1:12
to the *p* of his glory . . . . Eph 1:14
to the glory and *p* of God . . . . Phil 1:11
of the assembly I will *p* you . . . . Heb 2:12
offer up a sacrifice of *p* to God . . . . Heb 13:15
and *p* those who do good . . . . 1 Pet 2:14
and honor and glory and *p* . . . . Rev 5:12
P our God all you his servants . . . . . Rev 19:5

PRAISE THE LORD
This time I will *p* . . . . Gen 29:35
eat your fill and then *p* . . . . Deut 8:10
We agree! *P* . . . . 1 Chr 16:36
their cymbals, stood to *p* . . . . Ezra 3:10
those who seek his help *p* . . . . Ps 22:26
people yet to be born will *p* . . . . . . Ps 102:18
P, O my soul. *P* . . . . Ps 104:35
P. Give thanks to the Lord . . . . Ps 106:1
The dead do not *p* . . . . Ps 115:17
P, all you nations . . . . Ps 117:1
I will *p* as long as I live . . . . Ps 146:2
P. *P* from the sky . . . . Ps 148:1
that has breath *p*! *P*! . . . . Ps 150:6
P! Ask him for help . . . . Isa 12:4

will eat it, and will *p* .... Isa 62:9
Sing to the LORD! *P* .... Jer 20:13
P all you Gentiles .... Rom 15:11

PRAISED
they loudly *p* the LORD .... 2 Chr 5:13
a loud shout as they *p* the LORD .... Ezra 3:11
and they *p* the LORD .... Neh 5:13
May the LORD be *p* .... Ps 35:27
May the LORD be *p* .... Ps 40:16
person will be *p* in accordance .... Prov 12:8
her husband also has *p* her .... Prov 31:28
where our ancestors *p* you .... Isa 64:11
and I *p* and glorified the one ...... Dan 4:34
and they *p* the God of Israel ...... Matt 15:31
name of the Lord Jesus was *p* .... Acts 19:17
who is *p* by all the churches ..... 2 Cor 8:18

PRAISES
majestic in holiness, fearful in *p* .. Exod 15:11
I will sing *p* to the LORD .... Ps 13:6
receiving the *p* of Israel .... Ps 22:3
I will sing *p* to you .... Ps 71:22
shout out *p* to our Protector .... Ps 95:1
Shout out *p* to the LORD .... Ps 100:1
I will sing *p* .... Ps 101:1
good to sing *p* to our God .... Ps 147:1
and singing *p* to the LORD .... Isa 60:6
I will sing *p* with my spirit .... 1 Cor 14:15
He should sing *p* .... Jas 5:13

PRAISEWORTHY
if something is excellent or *p* .... Phil 4:8

PRAISING
and priests were *p* the LORD ..... 2 Chr 30:21
p and glorifying the LORD .... Ezra 3:11
p God and saying .... Luke 2:13
glorifying and *p* God .... Luke 2:20
p God and having the good will .... Acts 2:47
walking and leaping and *p* God ..... Acts 3:8

PRAY
P to the LORD that he would ...... Num 21:7
by ceasing to *p* for you .... 1 Sam 12:23
should *p* to you while there is .... Ps 32:6
but I continue to *p* .... Ps 109:4
bow down to you and *p* to you .... Isa 45:14
You who *p* to the LORD .... Isa 62:6
p for those who persecute you ... Matt 5:44
Whenever you *p* .... Matt 6:5
But whenever you *p* .... Matt 6:6
When you *p*, do not babble .... Matt 6:7
So *p* this way .... Matt 6:9
the mountain by himself to *p* .... Matt 14:23
lay his hands on them and *p* ..... Matt 19:13
while I go over there and *p* ...... Matt 26:36
Stay awake and *p* .... Matt 26:41
he went to the mountain to *p* ... Mark 6:46
whatever you *p* and ask for ...... Mark 11:24
Sit here while I *p* .... Mark 14:32
Stay awake and *p* .... Mark 14:38
went out to the mountain to *p* .... Luke 6:12
p for those who mistreat you ..... Luke 6:28
and went up the mountain to *p* ... Luke 9:28
always *p* and not lose heart .... Luke 18:1
went up to the temple to *p* ...... Luke 18:10
P that you will not fall into ...... Luke 22:40
Get up and *p* that you will not ... Luke 22:46
and *p* to the Lord that he .... Acts 8:22
You *p* to the Lord for me .... Acts 8:24
Peter went up on the roof to *p* .... Acts 10:9
do not know how we should *p* .... Rom 8:26
Is it proper for a woman to *p* ..... 1 Cor 11:13
should *p* that he may interpret ... 1 Cor 14:13
If I *p* in a tongue .... 1 Cor 14:14
I will *p* with my spirit .... 1 Cor 14:15
Now we *p* to God that you ...... 2 Cor 13:7
And we *p* for this .... 2 Cor 13:9
p at all times in the Spirit .... Eph 6:18
I always *p* with joy .... Phil 1:4
And I *p* this .... Phil 1:9
constantly *p* .... 1 Thess 5:17
p for us too .... 1 Thess 5:25
we *p* for you always .... 2 Thess 1:11
Finally, *p* for us .... 2 Thess 3:1

men in every place to *p* .... 1 Tim 2:8
P for us .... Heb 13:18
He should *p* .... Jas 5:13
and *p* for one another .... Jas 5:16
I *p* that all may go well .... 3 John 1:2

PRAYED
Abraham *p* to God .... Gen 20:17
So Moses *p* for the people .... Num 21:7
Manoah *p* to the LORD .... Judg 13:8
For this boy I *p* .... 1 Sam 1:27
Hezekiah *p* before the LORD ..... 2 Kgs 19:15
we fasted and *p* to our God .... Ezra 8:23
Jonah *p* to the LORD his God ...... Jonah 2:1
He *p* to the LORD and said .... Jonah 4:2
to the wilderness and *p* .... Luke 5:16
The Pharisee stood and *p* .... Luke 18:11
And in his anguish he *p* more .... Luke 22:44
p earnestly that it would not rain .... Jas 5:17

PRAYER
The LORD answered Elijah's *p* .. 1 Kgs 17:22
who led in thanksgiving and *p* ..... Neh 11:17
and my *p* is pure .... Job 16:17
a *p* to the God of my life .... Ps 42:8
Listen to my *p* .... Ps 88:2
to the *p* of the destitute .... Ps 102:17
the *p* of the upright pleases .... Prov 15:8
hears the *p* of the righteous ..... Prov 15:29
times daily he offers his *p* .... Dan 6:13
accept the *p* and requests .... Dan 9:17
And whatever you ask in *p* ...... Matt 21:22
kind can come out only by *p* .... Mark 9:29
will be called a house of *p* ...... Mark 11:17
worshiping with fasting and *p* ... Luke 2:37
he spent all night in *p* to God ..... Luke 6:12
My house will be a house of *p* ... Luke 19:46
these continued together in *p* ..... Acts 1:14
the breaking of bread and to *p* .... Acts 2:42
to the temple at the time for *p* ..... Acts 3:1
we will devote ourselves to *p* ..... Acts 6:4
your *p* has been heard .... Acts 10:31
there would be a place of *p* ...... Acts 16:13
were going to the place of *p* ..... Acts 16:16
heart's desire and *p* to God ...... Rom 10:1
persist in *p* .... Rom 12:12
join fervently with me in *p* ...... Rom 15:30
may devote yourselves to *p* ...... 1 Cor 7:5
With every *p* and petition .... Eph 6:18
in my every *p* for all of you .... Phil 1:4
through *p* and petition .... Phil 4:6
Be devoted to *p* .... Col 4:2
is always struggling in *p* .... Col 4:12
by God's word and by *p* .... 1 Tim 4:5
And the *p* of faith will save .... Jas 5:15
his ears are open to their *p* .... 1 Pet 3:12
sober-minded for the sake of *p* .... 1 Pet 4:7

PRAYERS
God responded to their *p* .... 2 Sam 21:14
their *p* for help and vindicate ..... 1 Kgs 8:45
to the *p* offered in this place ...... 2 Chr 7:15
may my *p* go unanswered .... Ps 35:13
and he will answer your *p* .... Ps 37:4
when you offer your many *p* ...... Isa 1:15
was kneeling and offering *p* ...... Dan 6:10
and as a show make long *p* ...... Luke 20:47
p and your acts of charity .... Acts 10:4
through your *p* and the help .... Phil 1:19
p, intercessions, and thanks ..... 1 Tim 2:1
her pleas and *p* night and day ..... 1 Tim 5:5
as I remember you in my *p* .... Phlm 1:4
nothing will hinder your *p* .... 1 Pet 3:7
are the *p* of the saints .... Rev 5:8

PRAYING
for I am *p* to you .... Ps 5:2
found Daniel *p* and asking .... Dan 6:11
yes, while I was still *p* .... Dan 9:21
Whenever you stand *p* .... Mark 11:25
Jesus was *p* in a certain place .... Luke 11:1
I am *p* on behalf of them .... John 17:9
am not *p* only on their behalf .... John 17:20
were *p* and singing hymns .... Acts 16:25
have not ceased *p* for you .... Col 1:9
by *p* in the Holy Spirit .... Jude 1:20

PRAYS
woman who *p* or prophesies ...... 1 Cor 11:5
my spirit *p* .... 1 Cor 14:14

PREACH
See also PREACH THE GOSPEL
Jesus began to *p* this message ..... Matt 4:17
p the gospel to every creature ... Mark 16:15
eager also to *p* the gospel .... Rom 1:15
the word of faith that we *p* .... Rom 10:8
And how are they to *p* .... Rom 10:15
And in this way I desire to *p* ..... Rom 15:20
we *p* about a crucified Christ ...... 1 Cor 1:23
this is the way we *p* .... 1 Cor 15:11
p him among the Gentiles .... Gal 1:16
the gospel that I *p* .... Gal 2:2
P the message .... 2 Tim 4:2

PREACH THE GOSPEL
into all the world and *p* .... Mark 16:15
to *p* to you who are in Rome ...... Rom 1:15
not send me to baptize, but to *p* ... 1 Cor 1:17
Woe to me if I do not *p* .... 1 Cor 9:16
Then when I *p* I may offer .... 1 Cor 9:18
that we may *p* in the regions .... 2 Cor 10:16

PREACHED
repented when Jonah *p* to them .. Matt 12:41
and *p* that all should repent ...... Mark 6:12
gospel must be *p* to all nations .. Mark 13:10
contrary to the one we *p* to you ..... Gal 1:8
This gospel has also been *p* .... Col 1:23
and *p* to the spirits in prison ...... 1 Pet 3:19

PREACHER
was appointed a *p* and apostle .... 1 Tim 2:7
was appointed a *p* and apostle .... 2 Tim 1:11

PREACHES
by Jesus whom Paul *p* .... Acts 19:13

PREACHING
p a baptism of repentance .... Mark 1:4
p and proclaiming .... Luke 8:1
without someone *p* to them ...... Rom 10:14
My conversation and my *p* .... 1 Cor 2:4
so that after *p* to others .... 1 Cor 9:27
then our *p* is futile .... 1 Cor 15:14
is *p* to you a gospel contrary .... Gal 1:9
p Christ from envy and rivalry ..... Phil 1:15
the *p* I was entrusted with .... Titus 1:3

PRECEPTS
The LORD's *p* are fair .... Ps 19:8
all his *p* are reliable .... Ps 111:7
that your *p* be carefully kept ...... Ps 119:4
Look, I long for your *p* .... Ps 119:40
But I meditate on your *p* .... Ps 119:78
for I observe your *p* .... Ps 119:100
See how I love your *p* .... Ps 119:159

PRECIOUS
and held a *p* stone .... 2 Sam 12:30
She is more *p* than rubies .... Prov 3:15
of *p* and pleasing treasures .... Prov 24:4
set in place as a *p* cornerstone .... Isa 28:16
Since you are *p* and special .... Isa 43:4
The *p* sons of Zion .... Lam 4:2
How *p* and fair .... Zech 9:17
silver, *p* stones, wood, hay .... 1 Cor 3:12
for the *p* fruit of the ground .... Jas 5:7
but by *p* blood like that of .... 1 Pet 1:19
chosen and *p* in God's sight .... 1 Pet 2:4
a chosen and *p* cornerstone .... 1 Pet 2:6
which is *p* in God's sight .... 1 Pet 3:4
a faith just as *p* as ours .... 2 Pet 1:1
his *p* and most magnificent .... 2 Pet 1:4

PREDESTINED
he also *p* to be conformed .... Rom 8:29
p according to the purpose .... Eph 1:11

PREDESTINING
He did this by *p* us to adoption ..... Eph 1:5

PREFER
yet I don't know which I *p* .... Phil 1:22

PREFERABLE
that wisdom is *p* to folly .... Eccl 2:13

PREFIGURED
And this *p* baptism . . . . .1 Pet 3:21

PREGNANCY
they will not enjoy *p*. . . . . Hos 9:11

PREGNANT
as a result she has become *p* . . . . .Gen 38:24
be *p* through the Holy Spirit. . . . . . . Matt 1:18
Woe to those who are *p*. . . . . Matt 24:19
labor pains on a *p* woman . . . . . . .1 Thess 5:3

PREJUDICE
without *p* or favoritism. . . . . 1 Tim 5:21
But if you show *p*. . . . . .Jas 2:9

PREMEDITATION
if he does not do it with *p* . . . . .Exod 21:13

PREPARATION
the day of *p* for the Passover . . . . .John 19:14
fitting your feet with the *p*. . . . . .Eph 6:15

PREPARE
P your supplies .Josh 1:11
the banquet that I will *p* . . . . Esth 5:8
the wicked *p* their bows . . . . .Ps 11:2
You *p* a feast before me . . . . Ps 23:5
their swords and *p* their bows . . . . . . Ps 37:14
p its food in the summer . . . . .Prov 6:8
p their food in the summer . . . . . . Prov 30:25
that you *p* is straight. . . . . Isa 26:7
P the way for the people . . . . Isa 62:10
P the way for the Lord. . . . . .Matt 3:3
p for you to eat the Passover . . . . .Matt 26:17
P the way for the Lord. . . . . .Mark 1:3
p the Passover for us to eat . . . . . . Luke 22:8

PREPARED
into the place that I have *p* . . . . . .Exod 23:20
and all their bows are *p*. . . . . Isa 5:28
Belshazzar *p* a great banquet. . . . . . .Dan 5:1
LORD has *p* a sacrificial meal . . . . . . .Zeph 1:7
it has been *p* by my Father . . . . . .Matt 20:23
p for the devil and his angels . . . . Matt 25:41
you have *p* in the presence . . . . . . .Luke 2:31
has *p* for those who love him. . . . . . 1 Cor 2:9
p us for this very purpose . . . . .2 Cor 5:5
p for every good work. . . . . .2 Tim 2:21
for he has *p* a city for them. . . . . . . Heb 11:16

PREPARES
Who *p* prey for the raven. . . . . .Job 38:41

PRESCRIBED
to what is *p* in the law . . . . .1 Chr 16:40
when I *p* its limits. . . . . .Job 38:10

PRESENCE
out from the *p* of the LORD. . . . . Gen 4:16
My *p* will go with you. . . . . Exod 33:14
honor the *p* of an elder. . . . . .Lev 19:32
Seek his *p* continually . . . . 1 Chr 16:11
why I am terrified in his *p* . . . . .Job 23:15
absolute joy in your *p* . . . . .Ps 16:11
upright will live in your *p*. . . . . .Ps 140:13
May your kind *p* lead me . . . . .Ps 143:10
will shake at my *p* . . . . .Ezek 38:20
who stands in the *p* of God . . . . .Luke 1:19
We ate and drank in your *p*. . . . . . Luke 13:26
unable in the *p* of the people . . . .Luke 20:26
full of joy with your *p*. . . . . .Acts 2:28
is our father in the *p* of God . . . . . . .Rom 4:17
no one can boast in his *p* . . . . .1 Cor 1:29
for you in the *p* of Christ . . . . .2 Cor 2:10
but his physical *p* is weak. . . . . . . .2 Cor 10:10
not only in my *p* but. . . . . .Phil 2:12
for in the *p* of many witnesses. . . . 1 Tim 6:12
appears now in God's *p* for us . . . . .Heb 9:24
blemish before his glorious *p*. . . . . .Jude 1:24

PRESENT
I will *p* my case to you. . . . . Ps 5:3
I will *p* a thank offering. . . . . .Ps 116:17
then come and *p* your gift. . . . . . . .Matt 5:24
do not *p* your members to sin . . . . .Rom 6:13
evil is *p* with me . . . . .Rom 7:21
I consider that our *p* sufferings. . . .Rom 8:18
nor things that are *p*. . . . . .Rom 8:38
p your bodies as a sacrifice . . . . Rom 12:1

or death or the *p* or the future . . .1 Cor 3:22
I am *p* in spirit . . . . .1 Cor 5:3
For if the eagerness is *p* . . . . .2 Cor 8:12
am meek when *p* among you. . . . . 2 Cor 10:1
to *p* you as a pure virgin . . . . .2 Cor 11:2
only when I am *p* with you . . . . .Gal 4:18
may *p* the church to himself. . . . . . . Eph 5:27
through death to *p* you holy. . . . . . . Col 1:22
every effort to *p* yourself. . . . . .2 Tim 2:15
and godly lives in the *p* age. . . . . . .Titus 2:12

PRESENTED
p strange fire before the LORD . . . . .Lev 10:1
Then they *p* the Israelites. . . . . .Num 13:32
p me with the two stone tablets. . .Deut 9:11
edict was to be *p* as law . . . . .Esth 3:14
edict was to be *p* as law . . . . .Esth 8:13
he *p* himself alive. . . . . .Acts 1:3
they also *p* Paul to him . . . . .Acts 23:33
p your members as slaves . . . . .Rom 6:19

PRESENTING
p my request before the LORD. . . . .Dan 9:20

PRESENTS
Whoever *p* a thank offering . . . . . . Ps 50:23

PRESERVE
sent me ahead of you to *p* life . . . . .Gen 45:5
sent me ahead of you to *p* you . . . .Gen 45:7
only *p* his life . . . . .Job 2:6
p mankind and the animal. . . . . .Ps 36:6
he will *p* his life. . . . . .Ezek 18:27
whoever loses his life will *p* it . . . .Luke 17:33

PRESERVED
to be *p* for a sign to the rebels. . . .Num 17:10

PRESERVES
is perfect and *p* one's life . . . . Ps 19:7

PRESSED
p toward him in order to touch. . . .Mark 3:10

PRETENDED
he *p* to be insane . . . . .1 Sam 21:13
she has only *p* to do so . . . . .Jer 3:10

PRETEXT
your freedom as a *p* for evil . . . . . .1 Pet 2:16

PREVAIL
don't let men *p* against you. . . . . . .2 Chr 14:11
peace will *p* as long. . . . . .Ps 72:7
For justice will *p* . . . . .Ps 94:15
but he will not continue to *p* . . . . . Dan 11:12
to grow in power and to *p*. . . . . . . .Acts 19:20
will *p* when you are judged. . . . . . . .Rom 3:4

PREVAILED
then Israel *p* . . . . Exod 17:11
struggled with an angel and *p* . . . . .Hos 12:4

PREVAILS
own strength that one *p*. . . . . .1 Sam 2:9

PREVENT
Nothing can *p* the LORD . . . . .1 Sam 14:6

PREVENTED
been *p* by the Holy Spirit . . . . .Acts 16:6
was *p* until now. . . . . Rom 1:13
p you from obeying the truth. . . . . . .Gal 5:7

PREY
drop his *p* from his teeth . . . . .Job 29:17
where you killed your *p* . . . . .Ps 76:4
hand us over as *p* to their teeth . . . .Ps 124:6
they will no longer be *p* . . . . .Ezek 34:22
if he has not cornered his *p*. . . . . . .Amos 3:4

PRICE
its *p* be weighed out in silver . . . . . .Job 28:15
pay God an adequate ransom *p* . . . . .Ps 49:7
the ransom *p* for a human life. . . . . .Ps 49:8
For you were bought at a *p*. . . . . . .1 Cor 6:20
You were bought with a *p* . . . . .1 Cor 7:23

PRIDE
arrogant *p* and the evil way. . . . . . .Prov 8:13
With *p* comes only contention. . . .Prov 13:10
P goes before destruction . . . . .Prov 16:18
person's *p* will bring him low . . . .Prov 29:23
patience is better than *p*. . . . . .Eccl 7:8

an end to the *p* of the insolent. . . . . .Isa 13:11
your heart will swell with *p*. . . . . . . .Isa 60:5
Jerusalem the *p* of the earth. . . . . . .Isa 62:7
source of your confident *p* . . . . . .Ezek 24:21
down those who live in *p*. . . . . .Dan 4:37
and his spirit filled with *p*. . . . . .Dan 5:20
envy, slander, *p*, and folly. . . . . . . .Mark 7:22
we are your source of *p*. . . . . .2 Cor 1:14
I take great *p* on your behalf . . . . . . .2 Cor 7:4
and the hope we take *p* in . . . . .Heb 3:6

PRIEST
See also HIGH PRIEST
the *p* of the Most High God . . . . . . .Gen 14:18
The *p* who succeeds him . . . . .Exod 29:30
the *p* must offer all of it . . . . Lev 1:9
and the *p* must arrange them . . . . . .Lev 1:12
the *p* is to make atonement . . . . . . .Lev 19:22
for the *p* is holy to his God . . . . Lev 21:7
Eleazar the *p* spoke with them . . . Num 26:3
by Moses and Eleazar the *p* . . . . .Num 26:63
that Eleazar the *p*. . . . . .Josh 19:51
When Phinehas the *p*. . . . . Josh 22:30
while the *p* was standing . . . . Judg 18:17
the time Eli the *p* was sitting . . . . . .1 Sam 1:9
raise up for myself a faithful *p*. . . 1 Sam 2:35
the *p* of the LORD in Shiloh . . . . . . .1 Sam 14:3
While Saul spoke to the *p* . . . . .1 Sam 14:19
replied to Ahimelech the *p* . . . . . . .1 Sam 21:2
the *p* gave him holy bread . . . . .1 Sam 21:6
Uriah the *p* built an altar . . . . .2 Kgs 16:11
the *p* sent out the officers . . . . . . .2 Chr 23:14
the *p* found the law scroll . . . . . . .2 Chr 34:14
was a *p* who could consult. . . . . Neh 7:65
You are an eternal *p*. . . . . .Ps 110:4
there will be a *p* with him . . . . .Zech 6:13
lips of a *p* should preserve. . . . . .Mal 2:7
show yourself to the *p*. . . . . Matt 8:4
to Caiaphas, the high *p* . . . . .Matt 26:57
the high *p* stood up and said. . . . .Matt 26:62
they led Jesus to the high *p* . . . . . .Mark 14:53
Annas the high *p* was there. . . . . . . .Acts 4:6
a merciful and faithful high *p*. . . . . .Heb 2:17
the apostle and high *p*. . . . . .Heb 3:1
since we have a great high *p*. . . . . . Heb 4:14
p incapable of sympathizing. . . . . . .Heb 4:15
You are a *p* forever . . . . .Heb 5:6
You are a *p* forever . . . . .Heb 7:21
We have such a high *p*. . . . . .Heb 8:1
he would not be a *p* . . . . .Heb 8:4
the high *p* enters once a year. . . . . . .Heb 9:7
Christ has come as the high *p* . . . . .Heb 9:11

PRIEST'S
and struck the high *p* slave . . . . . . .John 18:10

PRIESTHOOD
anointing will make them a *p*. . . . Exod 40:15
they have defiled the *p* . . . . Neh 13:29
during the high *p* of Annas . . . . .Luke 3:2
For when the *p* changes . . . . .Heb 7:12
he holds his *p* permanently. . . . . . . .Heb 7:24
to be a holy *p* and to offer. . . . . .1 Pet 2:5
a royal *p*, a holy nation . . . . .1 Pet 2:9

PRIESTLY
gave to Ezra the *p* scribe . . . . .Ezra 7:11

PRIESTS
will be to me a kingdom of *p* . . . . .Exod 19:6
they may minister as my *p* . . . . . . .Exod 28:41
p, must present the blood. . . . . Lev 1:5
p, must put fire on the altar . . . . Lev 1:7
Instruct the *p* carrying the ark. . . . .Josh 4:16
summoned the *p* and instructed. . . .Josh 6:6
had killed the *p* of the LORD . . . . .1 Sam 22:21
He eliminated the pagan *p*. . . . . . . .2 Kgs 23:5
the *p* Benaiah and Jahaziel. . . . . . . .1 Chr 16:6
with the *p* and the Levites . . . . Ezra 1:5
or the *p* or the nobles or . . . . Neh 2:16
Their *p* fell by the sword. . . . . .Ps 78:64
and Aaron were among his *p* . . . . . . .Ps 99:6
p be clothed with integrity . . . . .Ps 132:9
I will protect her *p*. . . . . .Ps 132:16
p and prophets stagger. . . . . .Isa 28:7
will be called, 'the LORD's *p*. . . . . . . .Isa 61:6

bronze utensils used by the *p* ......Jer 52:18
and the iniquities of her *p* ....Lam 4:13
Her *p* abuse my law ....Ezek 22:26
and the *p* will scatter salt........Ezek 43:24
Hear this, you *p*....................Hos 5:1
p, those who serve the LORD ....Joel 1:9
p proclaim rulings for profit........ Mic 3:11
the *p* in the temple desecrate .....Matt 12:5
p and the experts in the law......Matt 21:15
went to the chief *p* ....Matt 26:14
to the chief *p* and the elders.....Matt 27:3
the chief *p* stirred up the crowd ..Mark 15:11
show yourselves to the *p*.........Luke 17:14
Then Jesus said to the chief *p*....Luke 22:52
Then Pilate said to the chief *p*....Luke 23:4
chief *p* planned to kill Lazarus....John 12:10
do every day what those *p* do .....Heb 7:27
the law appoints as high *p*.........Heb 7:28
p serving his God and Father ....Rev 1:6
will be *p* of God and of Christ .....Rev 20:6

PRINCE

Everlasting Father, *P* of Peace .... Isa 9:6
rise up against the *P* of princes....Dan 8:25
an anointed one, a *p* arrives ....Dan 9:25
in battle with the *p* of Persia......Dan 10:20
except Michael your *p*.............Dan 10:21
many days without a king or *p* ..... Hos 3:4

PRINCES

who shows no partiality to *p* ......Job 34:19
that he might seat him with *p* ......Ps 113:8
in the LORD than to trust in *p*....... Ps 118:9
you *p* and all you leaders ....Ps 148:11
your *p* feast in the morning........Eccl 10:16
your *p* feast at the proper time....Eccl 10:17

PRINCESSES

P are among your honored..........Ps 45:9
p will nurse your children ....Isa 49:23

PRINCIPALITIES

whether *p* or powers ....Col 1:16

PRINCIPLE

God has declared one *p* ....Ps 62:11
fundamental *p* for wise living.......Ps 111:10
It is excluded! By what *p*...........Rom 3:27

PRINCIPLED

will no longer be called *p*...........Isa 32:5

PRINCIPLES

the *p* of agriculture ....Isa 28:26

PRISCA

See PRISCILLA

PRISCILLA [or PRISCA]

Wife of Aquila, Acts 18:1–3
With Aquila, instructs Apollos, Acts 18:26
Mentioned by Paul, Rom 16:3; 1 Cor 16:19;
    2 Tim 4:19
Also called "Prisca," Rom 16:3; 1 Cor 16:19;
    2 Tim 4:19

PRISON

and threw him into the *p* ....Gen 39:20
Free me from *p*......................Ps 142:7
Now when John heard in *p* .... Matt 11:2
had John beheaded in the *p*.......Matt 14:10
I was in *p* and you visited me ....Matt 25:36
or in *p* and visit you...............Matt 25:39
or naked or sick or in *p*.........Matt 25:44
Lord opened the doors of the *p* ...Acts 5:19
did not find them in the *p* ....Acts 5:22
So Peter was kept in *p*.............Acts 12:5
of the *p* were shaken ....Acts 16:26
doors of the *p* standing open......Acts 16:27
Remember those in *p* ....Heb 13:3
preached to the spirits in *p* ......1 Pet 3:19
Satan will be released from his *p* .. Rev 20:7

PRISONER

p named Jesus Barabbas.........Matt 27:16
customary to release one *p*.......Mark 15:6
the *p* of Christ Jesus ....Eph 3:1
the *p* for the Lord...................Eph 4:1
a *p* for his sake ....2 Tim 1:8
a *p* of Christ Jesus ....Phlm 1:1

PRISONERS

There the *p* relax together ....Job 3:18
to release *p* from dungeons ....Isa 42:7
you *p*, with hope..................Zech 9:12
rest of the *p* were listening ......Acts 16:25
compatriots and my fellow *p*.....Rom 16:7

PRISONS

over to the synagogues and *p* ....Luke 21:12

PRIVATELY

he intended to divorce her *p* ......Matt 1:19
the disciples came to Jesus *p*.....Matt 17:19
and Andrew asked him *p* ....Mark 13:3
they withdrew *p* to a town .... Luke 9:10

PRIZE

but only one receives the *p*.......1 Cor 9:24
I strive toward the *p*..................Phil 3:14

PRIZED

what is highly *p* among men..Luke 16:15

PROBE

p into people's minds................Jer 17:10

PROBLEMS

For past *p* will be forgotten.........Isa 65:16

PROCEEDS

for himself part of the *p* ....Acts 5:2
part of the *p* from the sale.........Acts 5:3

PROCESSIONS

They see your *p* ....Ps 68:24

PROCHORUS

One of the seven servants in the early
    church, Acts 6:1–5

PROCLAIM

and I will *p* the LORD by name... Exod 33:19
I will *p* the name of the LORD..... Deut 32:3
I will *p* your justice ....Ps 71:16
I will *p* your faithfulness.............. Ps 89:1
So they *p* that the LORD .... Ps 92:15
and *p* to it the message............Jonah 3:2
p from the housetops .... Matt 10:27
go and *p* the kingdom of God ....Luke 9:60
we *p* to you the good news.......Acts 13:32
this I *p* to you......................Acts 17:23
those who *p* the good news ......Rom 10:15
you *p* the Lord's death............1 Cor 11:26
For we do not *p* ourselves ....2 Cor 4:5
p your name to my brothers....... Heb 2:12
so that you may *p* the virtues.......1 Pet 2:9

PROCLAIMED

gospel is *p* in the whole world....Mark 14:9
went out and *p* everywhere .....Mark 16:20
have good news *p* to them .... Luke 7:22
will be *p* from the housetops......Luke 12:3
would be *p* in his name...........Luke 24:47
forgiveness of sins is *p* to you .... Acts 13:38
had also *p* the word of God........Acts 17:13
Christ is being *p* ....Phil 1:18
the message would be fully *p*.....2 Tim 4:17
we had good news *p* to us..........Heb 4:2

PROCLAIMER

to be a *p* of foreign gods.......... Acts 17:18

PROCLAIMING

the LORD is *p* against you..........Amos 3:1
p throughout the whole town ....Luke 8:39
and began *p* the Christ to them ....Acts 8:5

PROCLAIMS

comes and *p* another Jesus ....2 Cor 11:4

PROCLAMATION

and the *p* of Jesus Christ..........Rom 16:25
but by open *p* of the truth.........2 Cor 4:2

PROCONSUL

turn the *p* away from the faith.....Acts 13:8
while Gallio was *p* of Achaia......Acts 18:12

PRODS

words of the sages are like *p* ......Eccl 12:11

PRODUCE

as well as the *p* of your soil.......Deut 28:4

PRODUCED

fell on good soil and *p* grain.......Matt 13:8
p in me all kinds of wrong...........Rom 7:8
p death in me through what.......Rom 7:13
as God intended, has *p* in you .....2 Cor 7:11

PRODUCES

the churning of milk *p* butter.... Prov 30:33
spring that continually *p* water ..... Isa 58:11
it *p* much grain ....John 12:24
that suffering *p* endurance ....Rom 5:3
same God who *p* all of them......1 Cor 12:6
later it *p* the fruit of peace.......... Heb 12:11
testing of your faith *p* endurance..... Jas 1:3

PRODUCT

we are all the *p* of your labor....... Isa 64:8

PROFANE

between the holy and the *p* ..... Ezek 22:26

PROFANED

Judah has *p* the holy things......... Mal 2:11

PROFANES

p the blood of the covenant ......Heb 10:29

PROFANING

But you are *p* it by saying........... Mal 1:12

PROFESS

who *p* reverence for God.........1 Tim 2:10
They *p* to know God...............Titus 1:16

PROFESSION

I was not a prophet by *p*.........Amos 7:14

PROFIT

It does not *p* a man...............Job 34:9
What will it *p* you.................Job 35:3
p is there in taking my life...........Ps 30:9
dishonest *p* you have made.......Ezek 22:13
they can get dishonest *p*.........Ezek 22:27
priests proclaim rulings for *p*...... Mic 3:11
brought her owners a great *p* .... Acts 16:16
saw their hope of *p* was gone .... Acts 16:19
is a way of making a *p* ....1 Tim 6:5
contentment brings great *p* ....1 Tim 6:6
do business and make a *p* ....Jas 4:13
not for shameful *p* but eagerly .....1 Pet 5:2

PROFITABLE

that even a wise man is *p*...........Job 22:2
Though it is not *p*...................2 Cor 12:1

PROFOUND

I will share my *p* thoughts ....Ps 49:3

PROGRESS

The evening meal was in *p* .... John 13:2
that everyone will see your *p*...... 1 Tim 4:15

PROHIBIT

They will *p* marriage................1 Tim 4:3

PROLONG

nor will they *p* their days ....Eccl 8:13

PROLONGS

Fearing the LORD *p* life ....Prov 10:27

PROMINENT

will be more *p* than other hills....... Mic 4:1
and quite a few *p* women.......... Acts 17:4

PROMISE

his faithfulness to the *p*........... Deut 7:8
must I make you solemnly *p*.....1 Kgs 22:16
the LORD's *p* is reliable ....Ps 18:30
Has his *p* failed forever.............Ps 77:8
nor be unfaithful to my *p*..........Ps 89:33
the sacred *p* he made..............Ps 105:42
for your *p* revives me.............. Ps 119:50
The LORD made a reliable *p* ....Ps 132:11
p that I make does not return ......Isa 55:11
the *p* of the Holy Spirit............Acts 2:33
p is for you and your children .....Acts 2:39
to fulfill the *p* he had declared..... Acts 7:17
hope in the *p* made by God........Acts 26:6
and the *p* is nullified ....Rom 4:14
that the *p* may be certain.........Rom 4:16
unbelief about the *p* of God ......Rom 4:20
this is what the *p* declared......... Rom 9:9
so as to invalidate the *p* .... Gal 3:17

no longer based on the *p* .... Gal 3:18
heirs according to the *p* .... Gal 3:29
children of the *p* like Isaac......... Gal 4:28
accompanied by a *p* .... Eph 6:2
It holds *p* for the present life ...... 1 Tim 4:8
p of entering his rest remains ....Heb 4:1
Abraham inherited the *p* .... Heb 6:15
to the heirs of the *p* .... Heb 6:17
the one who had given the *p* ....Heb 11:11
p such people freedom........... 2 Pet 2:19
not slow concerning his *p* .... 2 Pet 3:9
the *p* that he himself made...... 1 John 2:25

PROMISED
his people secure just as he *p* .... 1 Kgs 8:56
I will surely do what I have *p* ......Jonah 2:9
sending you what my
    Father *p* ....Luke 24:49
for what my Father *p* .... Acts 1:4
God *p* he was also able to do ......Rom 4:21
because I *p* you in marriage ....2 Cor 11:2
without receiving the things *p*..... Heb 11:13
did not receive what was *p* ....Heb 11:39

PROMISES
I will fulfill my *p* ....Ps 22:25
do not go back on my *p* ....Mal 3:6
of God's *p* are "Yes" in him ....2 Cor 1:20
the *p* were spoken to Abraham..... Gal 3:16
and perseverance inherit the *p* .... Heb 6:12
and most magnificent *p* ....2 Pet 1:4

PROMOTE
when people *p* evil .... Ps 12:8
P justice. Give the oppressed........ Isa 1:17
P justice at the city gate ....Amos 5:15

PROMOTED
Nebuchadnezzar *p* Shadrach......Dan 3:30

PROMOTES
He *p* equity and justice .... Ps 33:5

PRONOUNCE
could not *p* the word correctly .... Judg 12:6
They *p* the guilty innocent..........Isa 5:23

PROOFS
alive with many convincing *p*.......Acts 1:3

PROPER
Do whatever is *p* and good .... Deut 6:18
Is it *p* for a woman to pray .... 1 Cor 11:13
is *p* for women who profess...... 1 Tim 2:10

PROPERTY
encroach on your neighbor's *p* ...Deut 19:14
of the earth as your personal *p*....... Ps 2:8
I prepare my own special *p*........ Mal 3:17
man's house and steal his *p*...... Matt 12:29
and they began selling their *p* .....Acts 2:45
sold a piece of *p* .... Acts 5:1

PROPHECIES
Do not treat *p* with contempt ..1 Thess 5:20

PROPHECY
If the gift is *p* ....Rom 12:6
of miracles, to another *p* ....1 Cor 12:10
And if I have *p* ....1 Cor 13:2
P, however, is not for............. 1 Cor 14:22
no *p* was ever borne of human ....2 Pet 1:21
about Jesus is the spirit of *p* ....Rev 19:10
the words of this book of *p*........Rev 22:19

PROPHESIED
they *p*, but did not do so again ...Num 11:25
yet they *p* anyway ....Jer 23:21
prophet *p* peace and prosperity .... Jer 28:9
all the prophets and the law *p*.....Matt 11:13
unmarried daughters who *p*....... Acts 21:9

PROPHESIES
Any man who prays or *p* ....1 Cor 11:4
any woman who prays or *p*.......1 Cor 11:5
who *p* builds up the church....... 1 Cor 14:4

PROPHESY
The prophets *p* lies..................Jer 5:31
and continually *p* lies ....Jer 23:14
sons and daughters will *p* ....Joel 2:28
Who can refuse to *p*...............Amos 3:8

didn't we *p* in your name .... Matt 7:22
saying, "*P* for us, you Christ .....Matt 26:68
with their fists, saying, "*P*.......Mark 14:65
sons and your daughters will *p* .... Acts 2:17
and we *p* in part ....1 Cor 13:9
especially that you may.........1 Cor 14:1
even more that you would.......1 Cor 14:5
you can all *p* one after another ...1 Cor 14:31
be eager to *p* ....1 Cor 14:39

PROPHESYING
When Saul had finished *p*........1 Sam 10:13

PROPHET
brother Aaron will be your *p* ....Exod 7:1
God will raise up for you a *p*.....Deut 18:15
No *p* ever again arose in Israel .. Deut 34:10
only *p* of the LORD who is left ... 1 Kgs 18:22
you to be a *p* to the nations .... Jer 1:5
As for the *p*, if he is made a........Ezek 14:9
The *p* is considered a fool .... Hos 9:7
I was not a *p* by profession ....Amos 7:14
I will send you Elijah the *p*.......... Mal 4:5
receives a *p* in the name of a *p* ...Matt 10:41
except the sign of the *p* Jonah ....Matt 12:39
A *p* is not without honor..........Matt 13:57
p is acceptable in his hometown.. Luke 4:24
a *p* should be killed outside ......Luke 13:33
proved to be a *p* before God..... Luke 24:19
Are you the *P*......................John 1:21
certainly the *P* who is to come ....John 6:14
that no *p* comes from Galilee......John 7:52
p named Agabus came down..... Acts 21:10
along with him the false *p* .... Rev 19:20

PROPHETESS
Miriam the *p*..................... Exod 15:20
a *p*, wife of Lappidoth ....Judg 4:4
There was also a *p*..................Luke 2:36

PROPHETIC
p scriptures has been made
    known........................ Rom 16:26
we possess the *p* word ....2 Pet 1:19

PROPHETS
See also FALSE PROPHETS; LAW AND THE
    PROPHETS
all the LORD's people were *p* .....Num 11:29
Is even Saul among the *p*........1 Sam 10:12
in the mouths of all his *p*.......1 Kgs 22:22
Now a wife of one of the *p* ..... 2 Kgs 4:1
there are no longer any *p*...........Ps 74:9
the *p* who prophesied to you.......Jer 37:19
will come against her false *p* ......Jer 50:36
prophesy against the *p* of Israel ...Ezek 13:2
Her *p* are proud .... Zeph 3:4
to abolish the law or the *p*........Matt 5:17
this fulfills the law and the *p* .....Matt 7:12
Jeremiah or one of the *p*.........Matt 16:14
You build tombs for the *p* ....Matt 23:29
sending you *p* and wise men ....Matt 23:34
who kill the *p* and stone those... Matt 23:37
And many false *p* will appear...Matt 24:11
They have Moses and the *p*..... Luke 16:29
You are the sons of the *p*.........Acts 3:25
of the *p* did your ancestors ....Acts 7:52
About him all the *p* testify........Acts 10:43
Do you believe the *p*..............Acts 26:27
his *p* in the holy scriptures .... Rom 1:2
attested by the law and the *p*......Rom 3:21
Lord, they have killed your *p* ...... Rom 11:3
of the *p* are subject to the *p* ..... 1 Cor 14:32
some as apostles, some as *p*........ Eph 4:11
take the *p* who spoke................Jas 5:10
the *p* who predicted the grace..... 1 Pet 1:10
false *p* arose among the people ....2 Pet 2:1
many false *p* have gone out ....1 John 4:1
the blood of your saints and *p*.....Rev 16:6
The blood of the saints and *p* .... Rev 18:24
and with your brothers the *p*...... Rev 22:9

PROPORTION
must use it in *p* to his faith ....Rom 12:6

PROPOSED
So they *p* two candidates.......... Acts 1:23

PROSPER
you will *p* and be successful ....Josh 1:8
May those who love her *p*..........Ps 122:6
his transgressions will not *p*......Prov 28:13
who trusts in the LORD will *p*.... Prov 28:25

PROSPERED
this Daniel *p* during the reign......Dan 6:28

PROSPERING
continued building and *p* ....Ezra 6:14

PROSPERITY
must not seek peace and *p* .... Deut 23:6
they live out their days in *p*........Job 36:11
observed the *p* of the wicked........ Ps 73:3
p causes them to do wrong......... Ps 73:7
see the *p* of your chosen ones......Ps 106:5
When someone's *p* increases....... Eccl 5:11
In times of *p* be joyful ....Eccl 7:14
lasting peace and *p* in this land .....Jer 14:13
In a time of *p* ....Dan 11:24
p comes from this business....... Acts 19:25

PROSTITUTE
his daughters *p* themselves...... Exod 34:16
must never be a sacred *p*.........Deut 23:17
house of a *p* named Rahab ....Josh 2:1
for a *p* is like a deep pit.......... Prov 23:27
Go marry a *p* who will bear..........Hos 1:2
anyone who is united with a *p*.... 1 Cor 6:16
By faith Rahab the *p* escaped....... Heb 11:31
punishment of the great *p*.......... Rev 17:1

PROSTITUTES
tax collectors and *p* will go .... Matt 21:31
Mother of *p* and of the detestable.. Rev 17:5

PROSTITUTION
your wicked *p* to other gods..........Jer 3:2
she took her *p* so lightly..............Jer 3:9
your shameless *p* to ....Jer 13:27
in *p* while she was mine .... Ezek 23:5
put away their spiritual *p* ....Ezek 43:9
For you have engaged in *p*...........Hos 5:3

PROTECT
I will *p* you wherever you go ..... Gen 28:15
P me and deliver me .... Ps 25:20
you *p* me from distress ....Ps 32:7
LORD will *p* you from all harm.......Ps 121:7
LORD will *p* you in all you do ....Ps 121:8
I will *p* her priests .... Ps 132:16
to *p* the way of his pious ones......Prov 2:8
Discretion will *p* you............... Prov 2:11
the words of the wise *p* them .... Prov 14:3
He will *p* and deliver it............... Isa 31:5
angels concerning you, to *p* ...... Luke 4:10
strengthen you and *p* you ....2 Thess 3:3
p what has been entrusted ....1 Tim 6:20

PROTECTED
he continually *p* him.............. Deut 32:10
He continually *p* us ....Josh 24:17
The LORD *p* David wherever......2 Sam 8:6
stood in awe of John and *p* ...... Mark 6:20
are *p* through faith revealed........ 1 Pet 1:5

PROTECTION
whom you have sought *p*.........Ruth 2:12
shelter in the *p* of your wings .... Ps 61:4
I run to you for *p* ....Ps 143:9
For wisdom provides *p* ....Eccl 7:12

PROTECTIVE
p shield and your exalted sword..Deut 33:29

PROTECTOR
Who is a *p* besides our God ....2 Sam 22:32
My *P* is praiseworthy...........2 Sam 22:47
LORD God is our sovereign *p* ...... Ps 84:11
He is their deliverer and *p*........Ps 115:9
May your *P* not sleep................Ps 121:3
The LORD is your *p* ....Ps 121:5
for their *P* is strong............... Prov 23:11
For you are a *p* for the poor .... Isa 25:4
your *P*, the Holy One of Israel...... Isa 41:14
A *p* comes to Zion .... Isa 59:20
you have been called our *P*........Isa 63:16

PROTECTS
he *p* him all the time ....Deut 33:12
for the LORD *p* me.....................Ps 3:5
The LORD *p* my life ....Ps 27:1
LORD strengthens and *p* me.........Ps 28:7
p those who have integrity ....Ps 31:23
he *p* them in times of trouble......Ps 37:39
but God always *p* my heart........Ps 73:26
He *p* the lives of his faithful ....Ps 97:10
The LORD *p* the untrained ....Ps 116:6
LORD *p* the resident foreigner ......Ps 146:9
wise person's good sense *p* him ...Eccl 10:2
he *p* those who seek refuge ....Nah 1:7
God *p* the one he has fathered ...1 John 5:18

PROUD
but you watch the *p* ....2 Sam 22:28
your *p* waves will be confined .....Job 38:11
those who have a *p* look............Ps 18:27
not seek help from the *p* ....Ps 40:4
For I envied those who are *p* ....Ps 73:3
my heart is not *p* ....Ps 131:1
from far away humbles the *p*.......Ps 138:6
tears down the house of the *p*....Prov 15:25
the *p* will be brought low............Isa 5:15
Indeed, wine will betray the *p* ......Hab 2:5
God opposes the *p* ....Jas 4:6
God opposes the *p* ....1 Pet 5:5

PROUDLY
they *p* threaten violence.............Ps 73:8
for what he has *p* planned..........Isa 10:12

PROVE
But what does your reproof *p* ......Job 6:25
you test and *p* the righteous.......Jer 20:12
can *p* me guilty of any sin ....John 8:46
he will *p* the world wrong ....John 16:8

PROVEN
before God as a *p* worker ....2 Tim 2:15

PROVERB
a *p*, and an object of ridicule.....Deut 28:37
p dangles in the mouth of fools .. Prov 26:7
p has gone up into the mouth ....Prov 26:9
Recite a *p* to this rebellious.......Ezek 24:3
are illustrations of this true *p*.....2 Pet 2:22

PROVERBS
He composed 3,000 *p* ....1 Kgs 4:32
The *p* of Solomon ....Prov 1:1
These also are *p* of Solomon ......Prov 25:1
evaluated and arranged many *p*....Eccl 12:9

PROVIDE
God will *p* for himself the lamb....Gen 22:8
Will he *p* meat for his people......Ps 78:20
prosperity that I will *p* for it ....Jer 33:9
will also *p* a way out...............1 Cor 10:13
does not *p* for his own.............1 Tim 5:8
who *p* effective leadership .... 1 Tim 5:17

PROVIDED
He *p* honey for him.................Deut 32:13
p her with her cosmetics ....Esth 2:9
asked for would be *p* for her ......Esth 2:13
and *p* food for her household ....Prov 31:15
hands of mine *p* for my needs...Acts 20:34
God had *p* something better .....Heb 11:40

PROVIDES
God who *p* seed for the sower ...2 Cor 9:10
God who richly *p* us with all......1 Tim 6:17

PROVISION
and make no p for the flesh ......Rom 13:14

PROVISIONS
for the worker deserves his *p* ... Matt 10:10

PROVOKE
you continued to *p* the LORD .....Deut 9:22
who *p* God are confident ....Job 12:6
Fathers, do not *p* your children..... Eph 6:4
Fathers, do not *p* your children..... Col 3:21

PROVOKED
not let yourself be quickly *p*........Eccl 7:9
I became *p* at that generation .....Heb 3:10
was God *p* for forty years..........Heb 3:17

PROVOKES
whoever *p* him sins................ Prov 20:2

PROVOKING
p one another ....Gal 5:26

PROWL
on the *p* looking for someone ......1 Pet 5:8

PRUDENCE
have dwelt with *p*...................Prov 8:12

PRUDENT
but the *p* conceals dishonor ...... Prov 12:16
but a *p* wife is from the LORD......Prov 19:14

PRUNES
p every branch that bears fruit .... John 15:2

PSALM
is written in the second *p*......... Acts 13:33

PSALMS
speaking to one another in *p* ....Eph 5:19
singing *p*, hymns, and spiritual ..... Col 3:16

PTOLEMAIS
Seaport city south of Tyre; Paul lands at,
    Acts 21:7

PUBLIC
They had us beaten in *p* ....Acts 16:37

PUBLICLY
Jesus no longer went around *p* ... John 11:54

PUBLIUS
Roman official; entertains Paul, Acts 28:7–8

PUFFED
it is not *p* up ....1 Cor 13:4

PUL
King of Assyria: *see* TIGLATH-PILESER
—Country and people in Africa, Isa 66:19

PULL
those who *p* evil along................Isa 5:18

PULLED
p me from the surging water .... Ps 18:16

PUNISH
But on the day that I *p*...........Exod 32:34
then seize the man and *p* him ... Deut 22:18
May the LORD *p* him...............1 Kgs 2:32
say that his anger does not *p* ......Job 35:15
Please do not *p* me for sins..........Ps 19:12
for what they do. P them ....Ps 28:4
the LORD does not *p*..................Ps 32:2
terrible to *p* a righteous
    person........................Prov 17:26
I will *p* the world for its evil ....Isa 13:11
for me to *p* your people............Jer 2:30
even when you *p* these people ......Jer 5:3
I will surely *p* them ....Jer 5:9
to ruin when I *p* them ....Jer 8:12
the time comes to *p* them.........Jer 10:15
So I will *p* you for the evil..........Jer 23:2
p all who try to oppress them .....Jer 30:20
p them both for their ways ....Hos 4:9
commissions to *p* wrongdoers ....1 Pet 2:14

PUNISHED
p because of our brother.........Gen 42:21
p you with ordinary whips........1 Kgs 12:11
and am *p* every morning ....Ps 73:14
we thought he was being *p* ....Isa 53:4
tried to devour them were *p* ....Jer 2:3
much longer without being *p*......Hos 8:5
I *p* them often in all................Acts 26:11

PUNISHES
For the LORD is a God who *p* ....Jer 51:56

PUNISHMENT
My *p* is too great to endure........ Gen 4:13
endured *p* that made us well ......Isa 53:5
The *p* of my people exceeds........Lam 4:6
your *p* will come to an end ....Lam 4:22
will depart into eternal *p* ....Matt 25:46
This *p* on such an individual ....2 Cor 2:6
flaming fire he will mete out *p* ..2 Thess 1:8
much greater *p* do you think ....Heb 10:29
for *p* at the day of judgment.......2 Pet 2:9

PUNON
Israelite camp, Num 33:42–43

PUPIL
like the *p* of his eye...............Deut 32:10
touches the *p* of his eye .... Zech 2:8

PURCHASE
cannot be measured out for *p*.....Job 28:16

PURCHASED
I *p* male and female slaves.......... Eccl 2:7
of your own blood you have *p*.......Rev 5:9

PURE
an atonement lid of *p* gold ...... Exod 25:17
and with *p* motives ....2 Chr 19:9
they all were ceremonially *p*...... Ezra 6:20
a *p* and upright man................Job 2:3
a man *p* before his Creator ....Job 4:17
if you become *p* and upright........Job 8:6
and I am *p* in your sight ....Job 11:4
is man that he should be *p* ......Job 15:14
if even the heavens are not *p*......Job 15:15
and the stars are not *p*..............Job 25:5
with hyssop and I will be *p* .... Ps 51:7
Create for me a *p* heart..............Ps 51:10
to those whose motives are *p* ....Ps 73:1
and maintained a *p* lifestyle .... Ps 73:13
young person maintain a *p* life ..... Ps 119:9
but pleasant words are *p* ....Prov 15:26
I am *p* from my sin ....Prov 20:9
but as for the *p* ....Prov 21:8
are *p* in their own opinion.........Prov 30:12
p gold loses value ....Lam 4:1
will sprinkle you with *p* water ... Ezek 36:25
Blessed are the *p* in heart ....Matt 5:8
as a *p* virgin to Christ ....2 Cor 11:2
you may be blameless and *p* ....Phil 2:15
whatever is *p* ....Phil 4:8
Keep yourself *p*....................1 Tim 5:22
All is *p* to those who are *p*....... Titus 1:15
to be self-controlled, *p* .... Titus 2:5
bodies washed in *p* water........Heb 10:22
P and undefiled religion ....Jas 1:27
wisdom from above is first *p* ....Jas 3:17
like newborn infants for *p*..........1 Pet 2:2
your *p* and reverent conduct ....1 Pet 3:2
just as Jesus is *p* ....1 John 3:3

PURGE
must *p* evil from among you ......Deut 17:7
p Israel of wickedness............Judg 20:13
will *p* them like straw blown ....Jer 15:7

PURIFICATION
for use in the water of *p*.......... Num 19:9
purified with the water of *p* ......Num 31:23

PURIFIED
I have *p* this water.................2 Kgs 2:21
as silver *p* in a furnace.............. Ps 12:6
was *p* with blood ....Heb 9:22
You have *p* your souls ....1 Pet 1:22

PURIFIER
like a refiner and *p* of silver..........Mal 3:3

PURIFIES
hope focused on him *p* himself....1 John 3:3

PURIFY
You are to *p* the altar.............Exod 29:36
the Israelites and *p* them .... Num 8:6
p your hearts from evil ....Jer 4:14
They will *p* the altar ....Ezek 43:22
p our consciences ....Heb 9:14

PURIM
these days are known as *P* ....Esth 9:26

PURITY
by *p*, by knowledge.................2 Cor 6:6
love, faithfulness, and *p*............ 1 Tim 4:12
and provided ritual *p* .... Heb 9:13

PURPLE
rich man who dressed in *p*........Luke 16:19
they clothed him in a *p* robe.......John 19:2

PURPOSE

called according to his *p* .... Rom 8:28
according to the eternal *p* .... Eph 3:11
way of life, my *p*, my faith .... 2 Tim 3:10
that his *p* was unchangeable....... Heb 6:17
For this *p* the Son of God........ 1 John 3:8
to carry out his *p* .... Rev 17:17

PURPOSES

for worthless *p* .... Deut 5:11
and carried out your *p* for us .... Ps 40:5

PURSUE

Five of you will *p* a hundred .... Lev 26:8
You must *p* justice alone .... Deut 16:20
and two *p* ten thousand .... Deut 32:30
do you *p* me like God does .... Job 19:22
and faithfulness will *p* me .... Ps 23:6
those who *p* righteousness........ Prov 15:9
unconverted *p* these things...... Matt 6:32
who did not *p* righteousness ..... Rom 9:30
P love and be eager .... 1 Cor 14:1
but always *p* what is good ...... 1 Thess 5:15
Instead *p* righteousness .... 1 Tim 6:11
and *p* righteousness .... 2 Tim 2:22
P peace with everyone .... Heb 12:14
he must seek peace and *p* it....... 1 Pet 3:11

PURSUED

I am *p* without reason .... Ps 119:86
All who *p* her overtook her........ Lam 1:3

PURSUES

Calamity *p* sinners................ Prov 13:21

PURSUING

though no one was *p* ....Prov 28:1
p a law of righteousness...........Rom 9:31

PUT

See also PUT OFF; PUT ON
She *p* the child in it .... Exod 2:3
p the LORD your God to the
     test.............................. Deut 6:16
P men in ambush................... Jer 51:12
p the Lord your God to the
     test............................. Matt 4:7
p your enemies under your
     feet.........................Matt 22:44
tell me where you have *p*
     him.........................John 20:15
p my finger into the wounds .... John 20:25
p on the Lord Jesus Christ .... Rom 13:14
let us not *p* Christ to the test ..... 1 Cor 10:9
p all things under his control .... Heb 2:8

PUT OFF

p all such things as anger............ Col 3:8
you have *p* the old man............... Col 3:9

PUT ON

tore his clothes, *p* sackcloth......Gen 37:34
priest must *p* his linen robe ....Lev 6:10
p garments for mourning........ 2 Sam 14:2
I *p* righteousness .... Job 29:14
P your cloak and follow me .... Acts 12:8
and *p* the weapons of light ...... Rom 13:12
p the Lord Jesus Christ .... Rom 13:14
body must *p* immortality......... 1 Cor 15:53
to *p* our heavenly dwelling .... 2 Cor 5:2
have *p* our heavenly house .... 2 Cor 5:3
and to *p* the new man .... Eph 4:24
widow should be *p* the list......... 1 Tim 5:9
buy eye salve to *p* your eyes....... Rev 3:18

PUTEOLI

Seaport of Italy, Acts 28:13

PUTTING

Stop *p* your confidence.............. Jer 7:4

Q

QUAIL

and brought *q* from the sea .... Num 11:31
and he sent *q* .... Ps 105:40

QUAKE

You made the earth *q* .... Ps 60:2
The people of the earth will *q* ..... Jer 49:21

QUAKES

The earth *q* before them ....Joel 2:10

QUALIFIED

that you may become fully *q* ..... 2 Cor 13:9
to the Father who has *q* you........ Col 1:12

QUARREL

loves a *q* loves transgression ..... Prov 17:19
He will not *q* or cry out............ Matt 12:19
anyone intends to *q* about this ... 1 Cor 11:16
you *q* and fight .... Jas 4:2

QUARRELING

no *q* between me and you.........Gen 13:8

QUARRELS

but every fool *q* .... Prov 20:3
starting arguments and *q*...........Jer 15:10
q, and fights about the law .... Titus 3:9
the *q* among you come from .... Jas 4:1

QUARRELSOME

in company with a *q* wife........ Prov 25:24

QUARTERS

in his own rented *q*.............. Acts 28:30

QUEEN

Q Vashti also gave a banquet....... Esth 1:9
rule forever as permanent *q*....... Isa 47:7
called the Q of Heaven............. Jer 44:17
The *q* of the South will rise...... Matt 12:42
q of the Ethiopians ....Acts 8:27
I rule as *q* and am no widow.......Rev 18:7

QUEENS

There may be sixty *q* .... Song 6:8

QUENCH

Surging waters cannot *q* love.... Song 8:7

QUENCHED

q raging fire ....Heb 11:34

QUESTIONS

challenge him with difficult *q*......1 Kgs 10:1
and asking them *q*................. Luke 2:46
without *q* of conscience .... 1 Cor 10:25

QUICK

every person be *q* to listen .... Jas 1:19

QUICK-TEMPERED

A *q* person stirs up dissension.... Prov 15:18

QUICKLY

q crossed the Euphrates River.....Gen 31:21
They have *q* turned aside......... Exod 32:8
Q deliver me .... Ps 31:2
how *q* my life will pass ....Ps 39:4
they pass *q* and we fly away....... Ps 90:10
q answer me...................... Ps 102:2
q forgot what he had done .... Ps 106:13
not let yourself be *q* provoked ..... Eccl 7:9
they come *q* and swiftly .... Isa 5:26
Reach agreement *q*................ Matt 5:25
down *q* because I must stay ......Luke 19:5
What you are about to do, do *q*... John 13:27
on the earth completely and *q*.... Rom 9:28

QUIET

I will give Israel peace and *q* ...... 1 Chr 22:9
lying down and would be *q*........Job 3:13
But if God is *q* ....Job 34:29
The whole earth rests and is *q*.......Isa 14:7
I kept *q* and held back .... Isa 42:14
of Jerusalem I will not be *q*........ Isa 62:1
everything is at rest and *q*.......Zech 1:11
scolded him to get him to
     be *q*.........................Mark 10:48
may lead a peaceful and *q* life ..... 1 Tim 2:2

QUIETED

I have calmed and *q* myself.........Ps 131:2
the city secretary *q* the crowd.... Acts 19:35

QUIETLY

to work *q* and so provide.......2 Thess 3:12
A woman must learn *q* .... 1 Tim 2:11

QUIVER

On it the *q* rattles.................Job 39:23
who fills his *q* with them .... Ps 127:5
he hid me in his *q*................. Isa 49:2

R

RABBAH

Capital of Ammon, Amos 1:14
Besieged by Joab; defeated and enslaved by
     David, 2 Sam 12:26–31
Destruction of, foretold, Jer 49:2–3

RABBI

to have people call them 'R....... Matt 23:7
you are not to be called 'R........ Matt 23:8

RABBONI

said to him in Aramaic, "R...... John 20:16

RACE

importance is the human *r* .... Ps 8:4
The *r* is not always won .... Eccl 9:11
I have finished the *r* ....2 Tim 4:7
run with endurance the *r*........... Heb 12:1
But you are a chosen *r*..............1 Pet 2:9

RACHEL

Laban's younger daughter; Jacob's favorite
     wife, Gen 29:28–30
Supports her husband's position,
     Gen 31:14–16
Mother of Joseph and Benjamin,
     Gen 30:22–25
Prophecy concerning; quoted, Jer 31:15;
     Matt 2:18

RADIANCE

The Son is the *r* of his glory ....Heb 1:3

RADIANT

Look to him and be *r*.................Ps 34:5

RADIANTLY

his clothes became *r* white .... Mark 9:3

RAFTERS

r and boards made of cedar .... 1 Kgs 6:9
He overlaid the temple's *r*.......... 2 Chr 3:7
the wooden *r* will answer back ..... Hab 2:11

RAG

a menstrual *r* in your sight .... Isa 64:6

RAGE

He sent fury, *r*, and trouble........ Ps 78:49
long will your *r* burn like fire ....Ps 79:5
R takes hold of me .... Ps 119:53
I will exhaust my *r* on them .... Ezek 5:13
fully vent my *r* against them....... Ezek 6:12
I will pour out my *r* on them...... Hos 5:10
Why do the nations *r*..............Acts 4:25

RAGES

his heart *r* against the LORD .... Prov 19:3

RAGING

Like a *r* storm it will rage...........Jer 23:19

RAGS

drowsiness clothes them with *r* .. Prov 23:21

RAHAB

Prostitute in Jericho; helps Joshua's spies,
     Josh 2:1–21
Spared in battle, Josh 6:17–25
Mentioned in the NT, Matt 1:5; Heb 11:31;
     Jas 2:25
—Used figuratively of Egypt, Ps 87:4

RAIN

not caused it to *r* on the earth...... Gen 2:5
And the *r* fell on the earth..........Gen 7:12
going to *r* bread from heaven .... Exod 16:4
I will send *r* for your land........ Deut 11:14
teaching will drop like the *r* ...... Deut 32:2
there will be no dew or *r* .... 1 Kgs 17:1
he gives *r* on the earth.............. Job 5:10
provides the earth with *r* .... Ps 147:8
snow in summer or *r* in harvest ...Prov 26:1
like a driving *r* without food ...... Prov 28:3
clouds disappear after the *r*........Eccl 12:2
like the *r* on the grass ....Mic 5:7
they will get no *r* ....Zech 14:17
sends *r* on the righteous and .... Matt 5:45
The *r* fell, the flood came......... Matt 7:25
by giving you *r* from heaven....... Acts 14:17
ground that has soaked up the *r*.... Heb 6:7

Column 1

that it would not *r*....................Jas 5:17
and the sky gave *r*....................Jas 5:18

RAINBOW
I will place my *r* in the clouds...... Gen 9:13
appearance of a *r* in the clouds....Ezek 1:28
and a *r* looking like it was............Rev 4:3

RAINED
r down manna for them to eat .....Ps 78:24

RAINS
and to the torrential *r*.................Job 37:6
the winter *r* are over and gone ... Song 2:11
why the *r* have been withheld.........Jer 3:3
the autumn *r* and the spring *r* ......Jer 5:24
the early *r* as vindication ....Joel 2:23
receives the early and late *r* ....Jas 5:7

RAINSTORM
sound of a heavy *r* can be heard..1 Kgs 18:41
a shelter from the *r*.................Isa 25:4

RAISE
a battle cry or *r* your voices ....Josh 6:10
in three days I will *r* it up ....John 2:19
will *r* him up at the last day....... John 6:40
will also *r* us up with Jesus........2 Cor 4:14
and the Lord will *r* him up ....Jas 5:15

RAISED
See also RAISED FROM THE DEAD; RAISED
   HIM FROM THE DEAD
The LORD *r* up leaders.............Judg 2:16
many others *r* their voice.......... Ezra 3:12
I *r* children, I brought them up........ Isa 1:2
and on the third day be *r* ....Matt 16:21
he will be *r*........................ Matt 20:19
He has been *r* from the dead ..... Matt 28:7
But God *r* him up....................Acts 2:24
Christ was *r* from the dead .... Rom 6:4
who *r* Jesus from the dead........ Rom 8:11
and more than that, he was *r*.... Rom 8:34
Now God indeed *r* the Lord ..... 1 Cor 6:14
that he was *r* on the third day .....1 Cor 15:4
not even Christ has been *r*........1 Cor 15:13
that he *r* Christ from the dead....1 Cor 15:15
And if Christ has not been *r* ......1 Cor 15:17
Christ has been *r* from the dead..1 Cor 15:20
How are the dead *r*...............1 Cor 15:35
dead will be *r* imperishable...... 1 Cor 15:52
he *r* us up together with him ....Eph 2:6
if you have been *r* with Christ ....Col 3:1

RAISED FROM THE DEAD
the Baptist. He has been *r*.........Matt 14:2
until the Son of Man is *r*...........Matt 17:9
So after he was *r*....................John 2:22
Lazarus whom he had *r*............John 12:9
the disciples after he was *r*.......John 21:14
of life, whom God *r*................Acts 3:15
just as Christ was *r* .... Rom 6:4
that since Christ has been *r*........ Rom 6:9
Christ is being preached as *r*......1 Cor 15:12
now Christ has been *r* ....1 Cor 15:20
Remember Jesus Christ, *r* ....2 Tim 2:8

RAISED HIM FROM THE DEAD
out of the tomb and *r*.............John 12:17
But God *r*.........................Acts 13:30
in your heart that God *r* ....Rom 10:9
God the Father who *r*................Gal 1:1
he *r* and seated him ....Eph 1:20
the power of God who *r*............Col 2:12
who *r* and gave him glory ....1 Pet 1:21

RAISES
He *r* the poor from the dirt...........Ps 113:7
just as the Father *r* the dead.......John 5:21
but in God who *r* the dead........ 2 Cor 1:9

RAM
I looked up and saw a *r*............Dan 8:3

RAMAH
Fortress built, 1 Kgs 15:17–22
Samuel's headquarters, 1 Sam 7:15, 17
David flees to, 1 Sam 19:18–23

RAMESES
Treasure city built by Hebrew slaves, Exod 1:11

Column 2

RAMOTH GILEAD [or RAMOTH IN GILEAD]
City of refuge east of Jordan, Deut 4:43;
   Josh 20:8; 1 Chr 6:80
Site of Ahab's fatal conflict with Syrians,
   1 Kgs 22:1–39
Also called "Ramoth in Gilead," Deut 4:43

RAMOTH IN GILEAD
See RAMOTH GILEAD

RAMPART
that stood against its outer *r* ...2 Sam 20:15
like walls and a *r*......................Isa 26:1
Guard the *r*..........................Nah 2:1
her *r* was the sea .... Nah 3:8

RAMS
with the smell of sacrificial *r*........Ps 66:15
blood of young *r* and goats .... Isa 34:6
r of Nebaioth will be available...... Isa 60:7

RAN
but the other disciple *r* faster..... John 20:4

RANKS
the one who leads out their *r*......Isa 40:26

RANSOM
from the hand of tyrants *r* me......Job 6:23
The *r* of a person's life.............Prov 13:8
to give his life as a *r* for
   many ....Mark 10:45
who gave himself as a *r* for all ....1 Tim 2:6

RANSOMED
those whom the LORD has *r* .... Isa 35:10
from your ancestors you were *r*... 1 Pet 1:18

RAPED
They *r* women in Zion ....Lam 5:11

RAPIDLY
it is approaching very *r*............Zeph 1:14

RARE
message from the LORD was *r*.....1 Sam 3:1

RASH
Do not be *r* with your mouth....... Eccl 5:2

RASHLY
and he spoke *r*.....................Ps 106:33

RATIFIED
a covenant previously *r*............. Gal 3:17

RATION
king assigned them a daily *r*.........Dan 1:5

RATIONAL
am speaking true and *r* words... Acts 26:25

RAVEN
and sent out a *r*...................... Gen 8:7
Who prepares prey for the *r*........ Job 38:41
hair is curly—black like a *r*.........Song 5:11

RAVENS
the young *r* when they chirp........Ps 147:9
Consider the *r* ....Luke 12:24

RAZOR
no *r* may be used on his head ..... Num 6:5
it is as effective as a sharp *r* ....Ps 52:2
the Lord will use a *r* ....Isa 7:20

REACH
and salvation does not *r* us ....Isa 59:9

REACHED
that you had *r* the age for love ...Ezek 16:8
until the full number was *r* ....Rev 6:11

REACHES
r inside behind the curtain......... Heb 6:19

REACHING
with its top *r* to the heavens...... Gen 28:12
and *r* out for the things...........Phil 3:13

REACTION
I fear the *r* of their enemies .....Deut 32:27

READ
R this," he responds ....Isa 29:11
if you are able to *r* this writing..... Dan 5:16
you never *r* in the scriptures..... Matt 21:42
He stood up to *r*....................Luke 4:16

Column 3

known and *r* by everyone..........2 Cor 3:2
whenever Moses is *r*..............2 Cor 3:15
after you have *r* this letter.........Col 4:16

READER
let the *r* understand .... Mark 13:14

READING
the man *r* the prophet Isaiah ..... Acts 8:30
to the public *r* of scripture........ 1 Tim 4:13

READS
r the words of this prophecy .... Rev 1:3

READY
the hand of a man standing *r*...... Lev 16:21
those who were *r* went inside ... Matt 25:10
but did not get *r* or do...........Luke 12:47
I am *r* to go with you both.......Luke 22:33
to make *r* a place for you..........John 14:2
find that you are not *r* to give .....2 Cor 9:4
are also *r* to punish every act.....2 Cor 10:6
r whether it is convenient or not .. 2 Tim 4:2
always be *r* to give an answer .....1 Pet 3:15
made *r* like a bride adorned ....Rev 21:2

REAFFIRM
urge you to *r* your love for him....2 Cor 2:8

REALITY
before God's decree becomes *r* ... Zeph 2:2
but not the *r* itself ....Heb 10:1

REALIZE
but I did not *r* it...................Gen 28:16
So *r* that the LORD your God ...... Deut 7:9
will *r* that Israel has a God.......1 Sam 17:46

REALIZED
and all Israel *r* on that day....... 2 Sam 3:37
my father David, be *r*.............1 Kgs 8:26
to my father David be *r*............ 2 Chr 1:9
Jesus *r* their evil intentions ...... Matt 22:18
when Jesus *r* in his spirit..........Mark 2:8

REALLY
God does not *r* live on the earth..1 Kgs 8:27
the ruling authorities *r* know ......John 7:26
This *r* is the Prophet...............John 7:40
God is *r* among you................1 Cor 14:25

REALM
I will grant this whole *r*............Luke 4:6

REALMS
blessing in the heavenly *r*............Eph 1:3
in the heavenly *r* in Christ ....Eph 2:6
authorities in the heavenly *r*........Eph 3:10

REAP
observes the clouds will not *r* ......Eccl 11:4
so they will *r* the whirlwind.......... Hos 8:7
r unfailing love......................Hos 10:12
or *r*, or gather into barns ....Matt 6:26
too much to *r* material things .....1 Cor 9:11
a person will *r* what he sows ....Gal 6:7
for in due time we will *r* ....Gal 6:9
Use your sickle and start to *r*......Rev 14:15

REAPED
you have *r* injustice.................Hos 10:13
and the earth was *r*................Rev 14:16

REAPER
plowman will catch up to the *r* ...Amos 9:13

REAPER'S
which cannot fill the *r* hand ....Ps 129:7

REAPERS
At harvest time I will tell the *r*... Matt 13:30
and the *r* are angels ....Matt 13:39

REAPING
and *r* what I didn't sow ....Luke 19:22

REAPS
One sows and another *r*..........John 4:37

REASON
his mind does not *r* this way........Isa 10:7
who gives them *r* to celebrate......Isa 57:19
They hated me without *r* ....John 15:25
I have no *r* for boasting........... 1 Cor 9:16
For this very *r*, make every ....2 Pet 1:5

REASONED
I *r* like a child . . . . 1 Cor 13:11

REASSURE
your rod and your staff *r* me . . . . Ps 23:4

REBEKAH
Great-niece of Abraham, Gen 22:20–23
Becomes Isaac's wife, Gen 24:15–67
Mother of Esau and Jacob, Gen 25:21–28
Encourages Jacob to deceive Isaac, then to
flee, Gen 27:1–29, 42–46

REBEL
do not *r* against him . . . . Exod 23:21
do not *r* against the LORD . . . . Num 14:9
Why do the nations *r* . . . . Ps 2:1
Why do you continue to *r* . . . . Isa 1:5
But if you refuse and *r* . . . . Isa 1:20
were labeled a *r* from birth . . . . Isa 48:8
Go to Bethel and *r* . . . . Amos 4:4

REBELLED
they grew disobedient and *r* . . . . . . Neh 9:26
they *r* and did not obey . . . . Neh 9:29
for they have *r* against you . . . . Ps 5:10
How often they *r* against him . . . . . . Ps 78:40
but they have *r* against me . . . . Isa 1:2
you have so blatantly *r* against . . . . . . Isa 31:6
your spokesmen *r* against me . . . . . Isa 43:27
Your rulers *r* against me . . . . Jer 2:8
nations who have *r* against me . . . . Ezek 2:3
we have *r* by turning away . . . . Dan 9:5
the more they *r* against me . . . . Hos 4:7
For which ones heard and *r* . . . . Heb 3:16

REBELLING
Are you *r* against the king . . . . Neh 2:19

REBELLION
not forgive your *r* or your sins . . . . Josh 24:19
r is like the sin of divination . . . . . 1 Sam 15:23
and innocent of blatant *r* . . . . Ps 19:13
from all my sins of *r* . . . . Ps 39:8
of those who persist in *r* . . . . Ps 68:21
punish their *r* by beating them . . . . . Ps 89:32
An evil person seeks only *r* . . . . Prov 17:11
because of the *r* of his own . . . . Isa 53:8
counseled *r* against the LORD . . . . . . Jer 28:16
and the destructive act of *r* . . . . Dan 8:13
child as payment for my *r* . . . . Mic 6:7
and pardons the *r* of those . . . . Mic 7:18
not arrive until the *r* comes . . . . . . 2 Thess 2:3
charged with dissipation or *r* . . . . . . Titus 1:6
harden your hearts as in the *r* . . . . . . Heb 3:8
certainly perish in Korah's *r* . . . . Jude 1:11

REBELLIOUS
acted like fools in their *r* ways . . . . . Ps 107:17
All *r* sinners will be shattered . . . . Isa 1:28
all day long to my *r* people . . . . Isa 65:2
have stubborn and *r* hearts . . . . Jer 5:23

REBELLIOUSNESS
not be ashamed of all your *r* . . . . . . Zeph 3:11

REBELS
Sinful *r* are totally destroyed . . . . . . Ps 37:38
teach *r* your merciful ways . . . . Ps 51:13
r should not exalt themselves . . . . Ps 66:7
But sinful *r* live in the desert . . . . Ps 68:6
and do not associate with *r* . . . . Prov 24:21
and was numbered with the *r* . . . . . Isa 53:12
are the most stubborn of *r* . . . . Jer 6:28
all their rulers are *r* . . . . Hos 9:15

REBUILD
so that I can *r* it . . . . Neh 2:5
Let's *r* the wall of Jerusalem . . . . Neh 2:17
will *r* the perpetual ruins . . . . Isa 61:4
will *r* the fallen tent of David . . . . . Acts 15:16

REBUILDING
We are *r* the temple . . . . Ezra 5:11
heard that we were *r* the wall . . . . . . Neh 4:1

REBUILDS
The LORD *r* Jerusalem . . . . Ps 147:2

REBUILT
let the house of God be *r* . . . . Ezra 5:15
heard that I had *r* the wall . . . . Neh 6:1
and the ruins will be *r* . . . . Ezek 36:33

REBUKE
He would certainly *r* you . . . . Job 13:10
and are amazed at his *r* . . . . Job 26:11
You should respond to my *r* . . . . . . Prov 1:23
and do not loathe his *r* . . . . Prov 3:11
one who rejects *r* goes astray . . . . Prov 10:17
r makes a greater impression . . . . . Prov 17:10
is open *r* than hidden love . . . . Prov 27:5
a *r* from those who are wise . . . . Eccl 7:5
If your brother sins, *r* him . . . . Luke 17:3
r your disciples . . . . Luke 19:39
For this reason *r* them sharply . . . . Titus 1:13
May the Lord *r* you . . . . Jude 1:9
I *r* and discipline . . . . Rev 3:19

REBUKED
he got up and *r* the winds . . . . Matt 8:26
he *r* them for their unbelief . . . . . Mark 16:14
Those guilty of sin must be *r* . . . . . 1 Tim 5:20
r for his own transgression . . . . 2 Pet 2:16

REBUKES
and *r* of discipline are like . . . . Prov 6:23

RECAB
Assassin of Ish Bosheth, 2 Sam 4:2, 6

RECALL
R the miraculous deeds . . . . 1 Chr 16:12
Your mind will *r* the terror . . . . Isa 33:18

RECEDED
over the earth and the waters *r* . . . . Gen 8:1

RECEIVE
if you believe, you will *r* . . . . Matt 21:22
you did not *r* me as a guest . . . . . . Matt 25:43
his own people did not *r* him . . . . . . John 1:11
Ask and you will *r* it . . . . John 16:24
R the Holy Spirit . . . . John 20:22
Lord Jesus, *r* my spirit . . . . Acts 7:59
Did you *r* the Holy Spirit . . . . Acts 19:2
Now *r* the one who is weak . . . . Rom 14:1
to *r* their living by the gospel . . . . . 1 Cor 9:14
to *r* the grace of God in vain . . . . . . 2 Cor 6:1
Did you *r* the Spirit by doing . . . . . . Gal 3:2
will *r* anything from the Lord . . . . . . Jas 1:7
we ask we *r* from him . . . . 1 John 3:22

RECEIVED
and *r* favor from the LORD . . . . Prov 8:35
Some that I *r* in the house . . . . Zech 13:6
Freely you *r*, freely give . . . . Matt 10:8
have *r* your comfort already . . . . . . Luke 6:24
you *r* your good things . . . . Luke 16:25
But to all who have *r* him . . . . John 1:12
and *r* a share in this ministry . . . . . Acts 1:17
For I *r* from the Lord . . . . 1 Cor 11:23
Five times I *r* from the Jews . . . . . 2 Cor 11:24
as you *r* Christ Jesus as Lord . . . . Col 2:6
the tradition they *r* from us . . . . . . 2 Thess 3:6
r God's commendation . . . . Heb 11:2
he *r* the ability to procreate . . . . . . Heb 11:11
He had *r* the promises . . . . Heb 11:17
Just as each one has *r* a gift . . . . 1 Pet 4:10
For he *r* honor and glory . . . . 2 Pet 1:17
had *r* the mark of the beast . . . . Rev 19:20

RECEIVES
Whoever *r* you *r* me . . . . Matt 10:40
and immediately *r* it with joy . . . . Matt 13:20
For everyone who asks *r* . . . . Luke 11:10
but only one *r* the prize . . . . 1 Cor 9:24
who *r* tithes, paid a tithe . . . . Heb 7:9

RECEIVING
r the knowledge of the truth . . . . . Heb 10:26
are *r* an unshakable kingdom . . . . . Heb 12:28

RECENT
your more *r* deeds are greater . . . . . Rev 2:19

RECHAB
Father of Jehonadab, founder of the
Rechabites, 2 Kgs 10:15–23
Related to the Kenites, 1 Chr 2:55

RECHABITES
Kenite clan fathered by Rechab, committed
to nomadic life, Jer 35:1–19

RECKLESS
and not do anything *r* . . . . Acts 19:36

RECKLESSLY
Jehu son of Nimshi; he
drives *r* . . . . 2 Kgs 9:20

RECOGNITION
each will receive *r* from God . . . . . . 1 Cor 4:5

RECOGNIZE
Stop your striving and *r* . . . . Ps 46:10
will *r* that I am the LORD . . . . Isa 49:26
and Israel does not *r* us . . . . Isa 63:16
but the world did not *r* him . . . . John 1:10
If someone does not *r* this . . . . 1 Cor 14:38

RECOGNIZED
holy God's authority will be *r* . . . . . . Isa 5:16
r the grace that had been given . . . . . Gal 2:9

RECOMMEND
of those who *r* themselves . . . . 2 Cor 10:12

RECOMPENSE
the *r* that the wicked receive . . . . . Prov 10:16

RECONCILE
R yourself with God . . . . Job 22:21
to *r* them both in one body . . . . Eph 2:16
to *r* all things to himself . . . . Col 1:20

RECONCILED
go and be *r* to your brother . . . . . . Matt 5:24
enemies we were *r* to God . . . . Rom 5:10
Be *r* to God . . . . 2 Cor 5:20

RECONCILIATION
we have now received this *r* . . . . Rom 5:11
rejection is the *r* of the world . . . . . Rom 11:15
given us the message of *r* . . . . 2 Cor 5:19

RECONCILING
was *r* the world to himself . . . . 2 Cor 5:19

RECORDED
days ordained for me were *r* . . . . . . Ps 139:16

RECORDS
may initiate a search of the *r* . . . . . . Ezra 4:15

RECOUNT
but they are too numerous to *r* . . . . Ps 40:5

RECOVER
Will I *r* from this sickness . . . . 2 Kgs 8:8

RECOVERY
that we are beyond *r* . . . . Jer 14:19

RED
tie this *r* rope in the window . . . . . . Josh 2:18
stained you like the color *r* . . . . Isa 1:18
Why are your clothes *r* . . . . Isa 63:2
because the sky is *r* . . . . Matt 16:2
r dragon that had seven heads . . . . . Rev 12:3

RED SEA
Divided for Israelites, Exod 14:15–31
Boundary of Promised Land, Exod 23:31

REDDISH
The first came out *r* all over . . . . . . Gen 25:25

REDEEM
the firstborn sons you must *r* . . . . . Num 18:15
he will *r* you from death . . . . Job 5:20
Will I *r* them from death . . . . Hos 13:14
one who was going to *r* Israel . . . Luke 24:21
r those who were under the law . . . . Gal 4:5

REDEEMED
the people whom you have *r* . . . . . Exod 15:13
you will not be *r* for money . . . . Isa 52:3
and has *r* his people . . . . Luke 1:68
Christ *r* us from the curse . . . . Gal 3:13
These were *r* from humanity . . . . . . Rev 14:4

REDEEMER
I know that my *R* lives . . . . Job 19:25

REDEMPTION
waiting for the *r* of Jerusalem . . . . Luke 2:38
because your *r* is drawing near . . Luke 21:28
the *r* that is in Christ Jesus . . . . Rom 3:24
the *r* of our bodies . . . . Rom 8:23
and sanctification and *r* . . . . 1 Cor 1:30
we have *r* through his blood . . . . Eph 1:7
were sealed for the day of *r* . . . . Eph 4:30
he himself secured eternal *r* . . . . . . Heb 9:12

REED
crushed *r* he will not break.........Isa 42:3
A *r* shaken by the wind............Matt 11:7
He will not break a bruised *r* ....Matt 12:20

REEDS
Can *r* flourish without water........Job 8:11
against the wild beast of the *r*.....Ps 68:30
did not buy me aromatic *r*........Isa 43:24

REEFS
These men are dangerous *r* ....Jude 1:12

REESTABLISH
I will *r* honest judges ....Isa 1:26
they will *r* the ruined cities ....Isa 61:4

REFINE
r them like gold and silver...........Mal 3:3

REFINED
and a place where gold is *r* ....Job 28:1
where it is thoroughly *r*............Ps 12:6
you purified us like *r* silver ....Ps 66:10
Look, I have *r* you..................Isa 48:10
refine them like silver is *r*.........Zech 13:9
polished bronze *r* in a furnace......Rev 1:15
buy gold from me *r* by fire.........Rev 3:18

REFINER
like a *r* and purifier of silver ....Mal 3:3

REFINER'S
For he will be like a *r* fire ....Mal 3:2

REFLECTION
sober *r* is good for the heart........Eccl 7:3

REFRAIN
I will not *r* my mouth ....Job 7:11

REFRESH
bit of food so that you may *r* ......Gen 18:5
You *r* my head with oil...............Ps 23:5
R my heart in Christ...............Phlm 1:20

REFRESHED
and be *r* in your company ....Rom 15:32
they *r* my spirit and yours ....1 Cor 16:18
all of you have *r* his spirit.........2 Cor 7:13
because he often *r* me............2 Tim 1:16

REFRESHES
he *r* the heart of his masters .....Prov 25:13

REFUGE
must select six towns of *r* ....Num 35:6
The everlasting God is a *r* ....Deut 33:27
horn that saves me, and my *r*........Ps 18:2
God is our strong *r* ....Ps 46:1
my *r* and my deliverer ....Ps 144:2
shield for those who take *r* ......Prov 30:5
and a *r* from a rainstorm ....Isa 32:2
the LORD is a *r* for his people......Joel 3:16
he protects those who seek *r*.......Nah 1:7
we who have found *r* in him.......Heb 6:18

REFUSE
if you *r* to release my people .....Exod 10:4
May my head not *r* choice oil........Ps 141:5
But if you *r* and rebel................Isa 1:20
They *r* to pay attention to me ....Jer 9:6
wicked people *r* to obey............Jer 13:10
because they *r* to repent ....Hos 11:5
the stars *r* to shine................Joel 2:10
to *r* the one who is speaking......Heb 12:25

REFUSED
stubbornly *r* to release us ....Exod 13:15
r to obey and did not recall........Neh 9:17
But Queen Vashti *r* to come......Esth 1:12
I have *r* to touch such things.........Job 6:7
I *r* to be comforted ....Ps 77:2

REFUTE
God will *r* him ....Job 32:13

REGAIN
Jeroboam did not *r* power ....2 Chr 13:20

REGAINED
you have *r* your brother ....Matt 18:15

REGARD
let not God on high *r* it ....Job 3:4

REGARDED
are *r* as dust on the scales ....Isa 40:15
had a slave who was highly *r* ......Luke 7:2

REGARDS
One person *r* one day holier.......Rom 14:5

REGION
foreigner in the *r* of Moab.......... Ruth 1:1
to the *r* of the Gerasenes.......... Mark 5:1

REGIONS
for the dark *r* of the earth ....Ps 74:20
subterranean *r* of the earth........Isa 44:23
he leads them through dry *r*....... Isa 48:21
also descended to the lower *r* ...... Eph 4:9

REGISTERED
went to his own town to be *r*......Luke 2:3

REGISTRATION
This was the first *r*................. Luke 2:2

REGRETS
r the evil he has done................Jer 8:6

REGRETTED
LORD *r* that he had made ....Gen 6:6
he *r* what he had done............Matt 27:3

REGULAR
it is to be a *r* incense offering.....Exod 30:8

REGULATIONS
and *r* given through Moses ....2 Chr 33:8
your *r* are good....................Ps 119:39
have not carried out my *r*..........Ezek 5:7
they did not observe my *r*........Ezek 20:24
they are external *r* imposed ....Heb 9:10

REHOBOAM
Son and successor of Solomon; refuses
  reform, 1 Kgs 11:43–12:15
Ten tribes revolt against, 1 Kgs 12:16–24
Reigns over Judah 17 years, 1 Kgs 14:21–31;
  2 Chr 11:5–23
Apostasizes, then repents, 2 Chr 12:1–16

REHOBOTH
Name of a well dug by Isaac, Gen 26:22

REIGN
LORD will *r* forever and ever......Exod 15:18
May he *r* forever before God .... Ps 61:7
But you, O LORD, *r* forever...........Ps 92:8
The LORD will *r* over them...........Mic 4:7
will *r* over the house of Jacob......Luke 1:33
let sin *r* in your mortal body.......Rom 6:12
r until he has put all his
  enemies ....1 Cor 15:25
and they will *r* on the earth........Rev 5:10
he will *r* for ever and ever ....Rev 11:15
r with him for a thousand years ...Rev 20:6

REIGNED
death *r* from Adam until Moses ...Rom 5:14
death *r* through the one ....Rom 5:17
so that just as sin *r* in death ......Rom 5:21
came to life and *r* with Christ......Rev 20:4

REIGNS
he *r* in a just manner...................Ps 9:7
God *r* over the nations...............Ps 47:8
The LORD *r* .... Ps 93:1
Your God *r*.........................Isa 52:7
the All-Powerful, *r*.................Rev 19:6

REINSTITUTED
of the LORD's temple was *r* ..... 2 Chr 29:35

REJECT
r my statutes and abhor my ......Lev 26:15
but if you *r* him ....2 Chr 15:2
will not *r* you if you return.......2 Chr 30:9
does the wicked man *r* God ....Ps 10:13
Do not *r* me ....Ps 27:9
you who *r* God.....................Ps 50:22
If his sons *r* my law................Ps 89:30
but I do not *r* your precepts ....Ps 119:87

help him know how to *r* evil.........Isa 7:15
sins have caused him to *r* you ......Isa 59:2
neatly *r* the commandment ....Mark 7:9
But *r* foolish and ignorant ....2 Tim 2:23
It trains us to *r* godless ways ......Titus 2:12
R a divisive person after one ..... Titus 3:10

REJECTED
If we had *r* our God.................Ps 44:20
and *r* the instructions.............Ps 107:11
r the gently flowing waters ....Isa 8:6
You have *r* this message...........Isa 30:12
despised and *r* by people ....Isa 53:3
They have *r* me......................Jer 2:13
who have *r* the covenant ....Dan 11:32
has *r* what is morally good ....Hos 8:3
and *r* Esau ....Mal 1:3
The stone the builders *r*.........Matt 21:42
and be *r* by this generation ....Luke 17:25
r the Holy and Righteous One .....Acts 3:14
This same Moses they had *r*.......Acts 7:35
have *r* shameful hidden deeds.....2 Cor 4:2
and no food is to be *r*.............1 Tim 4:4
a living stone *r* by men ....1 Pet 2:4
the stone that the builders *r*........1 Pet 2:7

REJECTS
curses and *r* the LORD .... Ps 10:3
but the one who *r* rebuke ....Prov 10:17
woman who *r* discretion.......... Prov 11:22
he *r* all sound judgment .... Prov 18:1
and the one who *r* you *r* me ......Luke 10:16
r this is not rejecting human......1 Thess 4:8

REJOICE
See also REJOICE IN THE LORD
Also, in the time when you *r*..... Num 10:10
May your loyal followers *r*........2 Chr 6:41
then I would *r* ....Job 6:10
I made the widow's heart *r* ....Job 29:13
may Jacob *r*......................... Ps 14:7
triumphantly *r* over me..............Ps 25:2
R in the LORD and be happy.........Ps 32:11
Then I will *r* in the LORD ....Ps 35:9
those who *r* in my troubles.........Ps 35:26
r when they see vengeance........Ps 58:10
under your wings I *r*.................Ps 63:7
But the king will *r* in God.............Ps 63:11
they *r* before God ....Ps 68:3
r in your name all day long ....Ps 89:16
Let the sky *r*........................ Ps 96:11
I will *r* in the LORD.................Ps 104:34
they *r*, and every sinner shuts .....Ps 107:42
they *r* in perverse evil ....Prov 2:14
you *r* in the wife you married......Prov 5:18
R, young man.......................Eccl 11:9
We will *r* and delight in you ....Song 1:4
I will greatly *r* in the LORD ....Isa 61:10
my servants will *r*..................Isa 65:13
r as if they had drunk wine .... Zech 10:7
he will *r* more over it .... Matt 18:13
spirit has begun to *r* in God........Luke 1:47
do not *r* that the spirits submit ..Luke 10:20
but the world will *r*...............John 16:20
and your hearts will *r*............John 16:22
R with those who *r* ....Rom 12:15
who ought to make me *r* ....2 Cor 2:3
and in this I *r*......................Phil 1:18
R in the Lord always................Phil 4:4
Always *r* .... 1 Thess 5:16
you *r* with an indescribable.........1 Pet 1:8
r and exult and give him glory......Rev 19:7

REJOICE IN THE LORD
R and be happy......................Ps 32:11
You godly ones, *r*....................Ps 97:12
downtrodden will again *r*.......... Isa 29:19
You will *r* .... Isa 41:16
I will greatly *r*......................Isa 61:10
my brothers and sisters, *r* ....Phil 3:1
R always. Again I say .... Phil 4:4

REJOICED
as he *r* over your ancestors.......Deut 30:9
My heart has *r* in the LORD........1 Sam 2:1
Jesus *r* in the Holy Spirit...........Luke 10:21

REJOICES
my heart *r* and I am happy .... Ps 16:9
a bridegroom *r* over a bride .... Isa 62:5
but *r* in the truth.................1 Cor 13:6

REJOICING
r in the habitable part .... Prov 8:31
but went on his way *r*...............Acts 8:39
but always *r* ....2 Cor 6:10
with the oil of *r*.....................Heb 1:9
to cause you to stand, *r*...........Jude 1:24

REKINDLE
I remind you to *r* God's gift........2 Tim 1:6

RELATIONS
not have marital *r* with her ....Matt 1:25
also abandoned natural *r*..........Rom 1:27

RELATIVE
a *r* is born to help in adversity .... Prov 17:17
A *r* offended is harder to reach... Prov 18:19
entitled as my closest *r* to buy,......Jer 32:7

RELATIVES
not even trust any of his *r*...........Jer 9:4

RELAX
He went out to *r* in the field ......Gen 24:63

RELEASE
must proclaim a *r* in the land......Lev 25:10
to decree the *r* of captives........... Isa 61:1
and whatever you *r* on earth .....Matt 16:19
do you want me to *r* for you......Matt 27:17
customary to *r* one prisoner...... Mark 15:6
to proclaim *r* to the captives...... Luke 4:18
I have the authority to *r* you......John 19:10
not accepting *r* ....Heb 11:35

RELEASED
compassion on that slave and *r*...Matt 18:27
Then he *r* Barabbas for them.... Matt 27:26
be *r* from this imprisonment ..... Luke 13:16
r him from the pains of death .....Acts 2:24
she is *r* from the law.................Rom 7:2
we have been *r* from the law ......Rom 7:6
Satan will be *r* from his prison..... Rev 20:7

RELEASES
The Lord *r* the imprisoned.........Ps 146:7

RELENT
and I will not *r* or turn back......... Jer 4:28

RELENTED
Then the Lord *r* over the evil ... Exod 32:14
the Lord watched and *r*...........1 Chr 21:15
r concerning the judgment ....Jonah 3:10

RELIABILITY
about your *r* and deliverance.......Ps 40:10

RELIABLE
a *r* God who is never unjust ...... Deut 32:4
Lord's words are absolutely *r*...... Ps 12:6
You prove to be *r*....................Ps 18:26
are *r* and impart wisdom .... Ps 19:7
all his precepts are *r*.................Ps 111:7
All your commands are *r* ....Ps 119:86
are just and absolutely *r*...........Ps 119:138
and your law is *r*....................Ps 119:142
and all your commands are *r* ......Ps 119:151
Your instructions are totally *r* .... Ps 119:160
these words are *r* and true ....Rev 21:5

RELIED
I *r* completely on the Lord...........Ps 40:1

RELIEF
Pharaoh saw that there was *r*.....Exod 8:15
and has given us a little *r*...........Ezra 9:8
so that I may find *r* ....Job 32:20
We hoped for a time of *r* ....Jer 8:15

RELIGION
with him about their own *r*........Acts 25:19
r contains amazing revelation .... 1 Tim 3:16
the outward appearance of *r* ......2 Tim 3:5
his *r* is futile ....Jas 1:26
Pure and undefiled *r* before God ....Jas 1:27

RELIGIOUS
I see that you are very *r* ....Acts 17:22
You are observing *r* days ....Gal 4:10
If someone thinks he is *r* ....Jas 1:26

RELUCTANTLY
not *r* or under compulsion........2 Cor 9:7

RELY
r on your own understanding.......Prov 3:5
and *r* on his God.................. Isa 50:10
You *r* on your swords........... Ezek 33:26
Do not *r* on a friend ....Mic 7:5
do not *r* on human credentials ......Phil 3:3

REMAIN
Will you *r* angry ....Ps 85:5
she does not *r* at home........... Prov 7:11
R here and stay awake ....Matt 26:38
slave does not *r* in the family......John 8:35
R in me, and I will *r* in you......John 15:4
r in me and my words *r* in you.....John 15:7
r in my love........................John 15:9
Are we to *r* in sin ....Rom 6:1
And now these three *r*............1 Cor 13:13
that I *r* in the body.................Phil 1:24
if indeed you *r* in the faith .... Col 1:23

REMAINED
and it *r* on him....................John 1:32
they would have *r* with us ....1 John 2:19

REMAINS
burn with fire whatever *r*........Exod 12:10
turned aside to see the lion's *r*.... Judg 14:8
who *r* forever faithful...............Ps 146:6
the food that *r* to eternal life .....John 6:27
your guilt *r* ....John 9:41
The one who *r* in me.................John 15:5
fruit that *r* ....John 15:16
Sabbath rest *r* for the people...... Heb 4:9
does the will of God *r* forever ....1 John 2:17
and strengthen what *r*...............Rev 3:2

REMEMBER
But *r* me when it goes well ....Gen 40:14
R the Sabbath day to set it
   apart.........................Exod 20:8
R that you were a slave........... Deut 15:15
O Sovereign Lord, *r* me ....Judg 16:28
R your covenant promises..........Ps 74:20
I will *r* God while I groan .... Ps 77:3
I will *r* the song I once sang....... Ps 77:6
I *r* your ancient regulations........Ps 119:52
I *r* your name during the night..... Ps 119:55
and weep when we *r* Zion ....Ps 137:1
So *r* your Creator ....Eccl 12:1
Don't *r* these earlier events........Isa 43:18
r to show us mercy .... Hab 3:2
Don't you *r* the five loaves........Matt 16:9
and to *r* his holy covenant.........Luke 1:72
R Lot's wife.......................Luke 17:32
r me when you come .... Luke 23:42
r the words of the Lord Jesus.... Acts 20:35
that I continually *r* you ....Rom 1:9
only that we *r* the poor.............Gal 2:10
R my chains ....Col 4:18
R Jesus Christ....................2 Tim 2:8
their sins I will *r* no longer.......... Heb 8:12
But *r* the former days.............Heb 10:32
R your leaders....................Heb 13:7
r from what high state................Rev 2:5

REMEMBERED
God *r* Noah and all the wild ....Gen 8:1
God *r* his covenant ....Exod 2:24
To the one who *r* us ....Ps 136:23
people *r* the ancient times......... Isa 63:11
Peter *r* what Jesus had said ......Matt 26:75
And I *r* the word of the Lord......Acts 11:16

REMEMBERS
r you in the realm of death ....Ps 6:5
always *r* his covenantal decree .....Ps 105:8
No one *r* the former events ....Eccl 1:11

REMEMBRANCE
Do this in *r* of me.................Luke 22:19
Do this in *r* of me.................1 Cor 11:24

REMIND
R me of what happened...........Isa 43:26
I intend to *r* you constantly........2 Pet 1:12
Now I desire to *r* you .... Jude 1:5

REMINDER
permanent *r* that will remain.......Isa 55:13
is a *r* of sins year after year........ Heb 10:3
your pure mind by way of *r*.........2 Pet 3:1

REMINDERS
are *r* and object lessons ....Isa 8:18

REMNANT
For a *r* will leave Jerusalem .... 2 Kgs 19:31
with no survivor or *r*...............Ezra 9:14
A *r* will come back.................Isa 10:21
Judean *r* who have come ....Jer 44:28
the *r* will be those ....Joel 2:32
be different now to this *r*.........Zech 8:11
there is a *r* chosen by grace .... Rom 11:5

REMOVE
r Israel from this good land.......1 Kgs 14:15
I will *r* you from my land .... 2 Chr 7:20
and *r* you from your home ....Ps 52:5
like clothes you will *r* them.........Ps 102:26
R falsehood and lies............... Prov 30:8
I will *r* all your slag ....Isa 1:25
R your veil...........................Isa 47:2
I will *r* the heart of stone ....Ezek 36:26
will *r* the iniquity of this land ...... Zech 3:9
r the speck from your eye ....Luke 6:42
to you and *r* your lampstand ....Rev 2:5

REMOVED
r the male cultic prostitutes ......1 Kgs 15:12
Even if the mountains are *r*....... Isa 54:10
they *r* the roof above Jesus ....Mark 2:4
r his outer clothes ....John 13:4
offense of the cross has been *r*......Gal 5:11

REMOVES
He who *r* mountains suddenly........Job 9:5

RENDER
they will *r* a verdict.................Deut 17:9
I will *r* it filthy to them........... Ezek 7:20
we must *r* an account............. Heb 4:13

RENEW
R a resolute spirit within me .... Ps 51:10

RENEWED
youth is *r* like an eagle's............Ps 103:5
he gives *r* energy ....Isa 40:29
Lord's help find *r* strength ...... Isa 40:31
the age when all things are *r* .... Matt 19:28
our inner person is being *r* ....2 Cor 4:16
be *r* in the spirit of your mind ..... Eph 4:23
that is being *r* in knowledge .... Col 3:10

RENEWING
by the *r* of your mind..............Rom 12:2
and the *r* of the Holy Spirit .... Titus 3:5

RENOUNCE
not *r* all his own possessions .....Luke 14:33

RENTED
in his own *r* quarters ....Acts 28:30

REPAID
God has *r* me for what I did .... Judg 1:7
he has *r* my good with evil.......1 Sam 25:21

REPAIRS
r on the temple of your God......2 Chr 24:5

REPARATION
Fools mock at *r*....................Prov 14:9

REPAY
will *r* them as they deserve........ Deut 7:10
Is this how you *r* the Lord........ Deut 32:6
R your creditor ....2 Kgs 4:7
They *r* me evil for the good........ Ps 35:12
They *r* me evil for good.............Ps 109:5
How can I *r* the Lord...............Ps 116:12
I will *r* them because of...............Isa 61:8
I will *r* them for their deeds .... Hos 4:9
and I will *r* you everything........ Matt 18:26
will *r* you when I come back..... Luke 10:35
because they cannot *r* you........Luke 14:14
Do not *r* anyone evil for evil........Rom 12:17
Vengeance is mine, I will *r*........Rom 12:19
r their parents what is owed.......1 Tim 5:4
I will *r* it...........................Phlm 1:19
R her the same way she repaid.....Rev 18:6

REPAYS
r him for what he has done........Job 21:31
r you for what you dished out......Ps 137:8
the one who *r* evil for good......Prov 17:13

REPEAT
I *r*, be strong and brave............Josh 1:9
In our time *r* those deeds..........Hab 3:2

REPEATS
but whoever *r* a matter............Prov 17:9

REPENT
and I *r* in dust and ashes...........Job 42:6
and *r* of your ways...................Ps 4:4
because they refuse to *r*...........Hos 11:5
Return to the LORD and *r*.........Hos 14:2
R, for the kingdom of heaven......Matt 3:2
R and believe the gospel.........Mark 1:15
But unless you *r*...................Luke 13:3
who have no need to *r*...........Luke 15:7
R, and each one of you..........Acts 2:38
Therefore *r* and turn back........Acts 3:19
all people everywhere to *r*.......Acts 17:30
state you have fallen and *r*..........Rev 2:5
So be earnest and *r*.................Rev 3:19

REPENTANCE
fruit that proves your *r*...........Matt 3:8
baptize you with water, for *r*......Matt 3:11
preaching a baptism of *r*...........Mark 1:4
granted the *r* that leads to life.....Acts 11:18
God's kindness leads you to *r*......Rom 2:4
a *r* that leads to salvation.........2 Cor 7:10
Perhaps God will grant them *r*...2 Tim 2:25
r from dead works..............Heb 6:1
to renew them again to *r*..........Heb 6:6
he found no opportunity for *r*.....Heb 12:17
but for all to come to *r*..........2 Pet 3:9

REPENTANT
and *r* heart you will not reject.......Ps 51:17

REPENTED
No king before or after *r*.........2 Kgs 23:25
turned away from you we *r*.........Jer 31:19
they *r* when Jonah preached.....Matt 12:41

REPETITIOUSLY
not babble *r* like the Gentiles......Matt 6:7

REPHAIM
Valley near Jerusalem, 2 Sam 23:13–14
Scene of Philistine defeats, 2 Sam 5:18–22

REPHIDIM
Israelite camp, Num 33:12–15
Moses strikes rock at, Exod 17:1–7
Amalek defeated at, Exod 17:8–16

REPLENISH
you *r* the surface of the ground...Ps 104:30

REPORT
You must not give a false *r*.......Exod 23:1
the *r* that I hear circulating......1 Sam 2:24
So a *r* about him spread..........Matt 4:24
who has believed our *r*..........Rom 10:16

REPRESENTATION
r of the true sanctuary.............Heb 9:24

REPRIMAND
to all generously and without *r*.......Jas 1:5

REPROACH
so that this *r* will not continue......Neh 2:17
my conscience will not *r* me........Job 27:6
and with shame comes a *r*.........Prov 18:3
overseer then must be above *r*....1 Tim 3:2

REPROBATE
He despises a *r*.....................Ps 15:4

REPROOF
the one who hates *r* is stupid......Prov 12:1
The person who hears the *r*......Prov 15:31
useful for teaching, for *r*..........2 Tim 3:16

REPROVE
Do not *r* a mocker..................Prov 9:8

REPROVES
whoever *r* a wicked person........Prov 9:7
The one who *r* another..........Prov 28:23

REPUDIATED
You have *r* your covenant.........Ps 89:39
but will have *r* its power...........2 Tim 3:5

REPUTATION
how magnificent is your *r*...........Ps 8:1
the majesty of the LORD's *r*........Ps 29:2
in Israel his *r* is great................Ps 76:1
for the sake of his *r*..............Ps 106:8
your *r*, O LORD, lasts...............Ps 135:13
you have a *r* that you are alive......Rev 3:1

REQUEST
grant the *r* that you have asked ..1 Sam 1:17
What is your *r*.....................Esth 5:6
heard the *r* of the oppressed.......Ps 10:17
you do not refuse his *r*.............Ps 21:2
He granted their *r*.................Ps 106:15
to make your *r* known to him.....Jer 42:9

REQUESTS
May the LORD grant all your *r*.......Ps 20:5
implore him by prayer and *r*........Dan 9:3
tell your *r* to God...................Phil 4:6
both *r* and supplications...........Heb 5:7
we know that we have the *r*.....1 John 5:15

REQUIRE
the LORD your God *r* of you......Deut 10:12

REQUIRED
given much, much will be *r*......Luke 12:48

REQUIREMENT
according to the *r* for each day.....Ezra 3:4
observing the festival is a *r*.........Ps 81:4

REQUIREMENTS
so he can teach us his *r*..............Isa 2:3
been helped by keeping his *r*.......Mal 3:14
obeys the righteous *r* of the
   law...........................Rom 2:26

RESCUE
The LORD will *r* us..............2 Kgs 18:32
R me from their destructive........Ps 35:17
But God will *r* my life..............Ps 49:15
r him and bring him honor.........Ps 91:15
wickedness cannot *r* the wicked....Eccl 8:8
and I will *r* your children............Isa 49:25
Do I lack the power to *r* you......Isa 50:2
to *r* you and deliver you...........Jer 15:20
r me from those who persecute....Jer 17:14
r your people......................Jer 31:7
one who will *r* them is strong.....Jer 50:34
no one will be able to *r* them......Hos 5:14
to *r* the godly from their trials.....2 Pet 2:9

RESCUED
for I *r* the poor who cried out.....Job 29:12
and *r* them from the power.......Ps 106:10

RESCUES
ignore the God who *r* you..........Isa 17:10
For he *r* the oppressed............Jer 20:13

RESENTFUL
it is not easily angered or *r*........1 Cor 13:5

RESERVE
I *r* for the time of trouble..........Job 38:23
and to *r* the unrighteous..........2 Pet 2:9

RESERVED
It is *r* in heaven for you............1 Pet 1:4

RESIDE
In what direction does light *r*......Job 38:19
love of God *r* in such a person....1 John 3:17
we know that we *r* in God.......1 John 4:13

RESIDED
The glory of the LORD *r*.........Exod 24:16

RESIDENCE
his place of *r* know him............Job 7:10
could come to his place of *r*......Job 23:3
becomes their permanent *r*.......Ps 49:11
and his *r* will be majestic..........Isa 11:10
and took up *r* among us..........John 1:14
and take up *r* with him..........John 14:23
the time of your temporary *r*......1 Pet 1:17
abandoned their own place of *r*....Jude 1:6
The *r* of God is among human......Rev 21:3

RESIDENT
I am a foreign *r*....................Gen 23:4
No *r* of Zion will say...............Isa 33:24

RESIDES
r in the protective shadow.........Ps 91:1
in which righteousness truly *r*....2 Pet 3:13
because God's seed *r* in him......1 John 3:9

RESIDING
do you have his word *r* in you....John 5:38
but the Father *r* in me...........John 14:10
has eternal life *r* in him..........1 John 3:15

RESIST
Nobody will be able to *r* you.....Deut 7:24
do not *r* the evildoer..............Matt 5:39
were not able to *r* the wisdom.....Acts 6:10
But *r* the devil and he will flee........Jas 4:7
R him, strong in your faith..........1 Pet 5:9

RESISTED
has *r* him and remained safe........Job 9:4
For who has ever *r* his will.........Rom 9:19
have not yet *r* to the point.........Heb 12:4

RESISTING
are always *r* the Holy Spirit........Acts 7:51

RESOLUTELY
set out *r* to go to Jerusalem.......Luke 9:51

RESOLVED
that reason I am steadfastly *r*.......Isa 50:7
be *r* not to rehearse ahead.......Luke 21:14
Paul *r* to go to Jerusalem.........Acts 19:21

RESPECT
and I will *r* him....................Job 42:8
He is the one you must *r*..........Isa 8:13
you who *r* his word...............Isa 66:5
to show no *r* for me................Jer 2:19
fill their hearts and minds with *r*..Jer 32:40
whole earth admire and *r* them ..Zeph 3:19
where is my *r*......................Mal 1:6
But for you who *r* my name.......Mal 4:2
They will *r* my son...............Matt 21:37
r to whom respect is due..........Rom 13:7
whatever is worthy of *r*...........Phil 4:8

RESPECTABLE
r, hospitable, an able teacher.......1 Tim 3:2

RESPECTED
He is highly *r*.....................1 Sam 9:6
feared God nor *r* people..........Luke 18:2
teacher of the law who was *r*......Acts 5:34
earthly fathers and we *r* them......Heb 12:9

RESPECTS
and please him in all *r*..............Col 1:10

RESPOND
If you do not *r* to me...............Ps 28:1
does no one *r* when I call..........Isa 50:2
You don't listen and *r*.............John 8:47

RESPONDED
and the LORD *r* favorably.........2 Kgs 13:4

RESPONDS
r to the prayer of the destitute ....Ps 102:17

RESPONSE
A gentle *r* turns away anger........Prov 15:1

RESPONSIBILITY
He shoulders *r* and is called.........Isa 9:6
another take his position of *r*......Acts 1:20
I am entrusted with a *r*...........1 Cor 9:17

REST
is a Sabbath of complete *r*........Exod 31:15
you will have no *r*.................Deut 28:65
there be a place of peaceful *r*.....Deut 28:65
and the weary are at *r*............Job 3:17
one handful with some *r*...........Eccl 4:6
LORD's Spirit will *r* on him...........Isa 11:2
deprived of the *r* of my years......Isa 38:10
is the place where I will *r*..........Isa 66:1
you will find *r* for your souls........Jer 6:16
stay there and *r*...................Jer 47:6
and I will give you *r*..............Matt 11:28
you will find *r* for your souls.....Matt 11:29
to give *r* together with us........2 Thess 1:7

They will never enter my *r* ....Heb 3:11
a Sabbath *r* remains ....Heb 4:9
every effort to enter that *r* ....Heb 4:11
They never *r* day or night.......... Rev 4:8
told to *r* for a little longer .... Rev 6:11
can *r* from their hard work .... Rev 14:13
r of the dead did not come .... Rev 20:5

RESTED
When the Spirit *r* on them.......Num 11:25
And God *r* on the seventh day......Heb 4:4

RESTING
Are you still sleeping and *r* .....Matt 26:45

RESTITUTION
once *r* is made.....................Isa 53:10

RESTORATION
your *r* will quickly arrive............ Isa 58:8
looking for the *r* of Israel.........Luke 2:25

RESTORE
and *r* them to this place .... Jer 27:22
Yes, I will *r* you to health ....Jer 30:17
will *r* us in a very short time........ Hos 6:2
and *r* it to what it was like .... Amos 9:11
and will *r* all things ....Matt 17:11
are spiritual *r* such a person .... Gal 6:1

RESTORED
r like the rest of his skin ....Exod 4:7
his flesh is *r* like a youth's ....Job 33:25
the LORD *r* what Job had lost ......Job 42:10
and his hand was *r*.................Mark 3:5
until the time all things are *r* ......Acts 3:21
to pray that I may be *r* to you .....Heb 13:19

RESTORES
God *r* to him his righteousness....Job 33:26
He *r* my strength ....Ps 23:3

RESTORING
are *r* the kingdom to Israel ....Acts 1:6

RESTRAIN
God does not *r* his anger ....Job 9:13
power over the wind to *r* it ....Eccl 8:8

RESTRAINS
one who *r* his words is wise ......Prov 10:19

RESTRAINT
r toward our iniquities..............Ezra 9:13
people throw off all *r*..............Job 30:11

RESTRICTION
boldness and without *r*...........Acts 28:31

RESTS
Wisdom *r* in the heart ....Prov 14:33
The whole earth *r* and is quiet.......Isa 14:7

RESURRECTION
say there is no *r* ....Matt 22:23
In the *r*, therefore, whose wife...Matt 22:28
out of the tombs after his *r*......Matt 27:53
In the *r*, when they rise ....Mark 12:23
repaid at the *r* of the righteous...Luke 14:14
since they are sons of the *r*......Luke 20:36
to the *r* resulting in life ....John 5:29
I am the *r* and the life..............John 11:25
witness of his *r* together........Acts 1:22
news about Jesus and the *r*......Acts 17:18
about the *r* from the dead........Acts 17:32
there is going to be a *r*...........Acts 24:15
united in the likeness of his *r*......Rom 6:5
say there is no *r* of the dead......1 Cor 15:12
experience the power of his *r* ......Phil 3:10
that the *r* has already occurred...2 Tim 2:18
to obtain *r* to a better life.........Heb 11:35
the *r* of Jesus Christ................1 Pet 3:21
This is the first *r* .... Rev 20:5

RETAIN
if you *r* anyone's sins ....John 20:23

RETREATED
they *r* and fell to the ground.......John 18:6

RETRIBUTION
The time of *r* is imminent.......... Hos 9:7

RETURN
not *r* to their foolish ways .....Ps 85:8
they *r* to the ground................Ps 146:4

None who go in to her will *r*.......Prov 2:19
naked will he *r* as he came ....Eccl 5:15
many days you will get a *r*..........Eccl 11:1
They should *r* to the LORD..........Isa 55:7
promise that I make does not *r*.....Isa 55:11
will wholeheartedly *r* to me ....Jer 24:7
so that we may *r* to you ....Lam 5:21
R! Turn from your idols..........Ezek 14:6
But you must *r* to your God ......Hos 12:6
r to me with all your heart.......Joel 2:12
R to the stronghold...............Zech 9:12
R to me, and I will *r* to you ....Mal 3:7
and their children to *r* to me ......Mal 4:6
I will *r* to the home I left......... Matt 12:44
it will *r* to you....................Luke 10:6
Do not *r* evil for evil ....1 Pet 3:9
and *r* of our Lord Jesus Christ ....2 Pet 1:16
Where is his promised *r* ....2 Pet 3:4

RETURNS
Like a dog that *r* to its vomit .....Prov 26:11
A dog *r* to its own vomit..........2 Pet 2:22

REUBEN
Jacob's eldest son, Gen 29:31–32
Lies with Bilhah; loses preeminence,
  Gen 35:22; 49:3–4
Plots to save Joseph, Gen 37:21–30
Offers sons as pledge for Benjamin,
  Gen 42:37
—Tribe of:
Numbered, Num 1:20–21; 26:5–11
Settle east of Jordan, Num 32:1–42
Join in war against Canaanites, Josh 1:12–18
Erect memorial altar, Josh 22:10–34

REUEL
See JETHRO

REVEAL
The heavens *r* his iniquity ....Job 20:27
you will *r* yourself to me.............Ps 17:15
I will *r* my power to deliver........Ps 50:23
r your anger in full measure........Ps 76:10
whom the Son decides to *r* him ..Matt 11:27
flesh and blood did not *r* this.....Matt 16:17
love him and will *r* myself ....John 14:21
are going to *r* yourself to us ......John 14:22
to *r* his Son in me...................Gal 1:16
God will *r* to you the error.........Phil 3:15

REVEALED
those that are *r* belong to us ....Deut 29:29
God has *r* himself in Judah........... Ps 76:1
splendor of the LORD will be *r*......Isa 40:5
the mystery was *r* to Daniel .... Dan 2:19
nothing is hidden except to be *r*..Mark 4:22
is hidden that will not be *r*........Luke 12:2
on the day the Son of Man is *r*... Luke 17:30
Moses *r* that the dead are
  raised.........................Luke 20:37
In this way he *r* his glory.........John 2:11
I have *r* your name to the men ....John 17:6
After this Jesus *r* himself again ....John 21:1
wrath of God is *r* from heaven..... Rom 1:18
God's righteous judgment is *r* ......Rom 2:5
glory that will be *r* to us ....Rom 8:18
has *r* these to us by the Spirit..... 1 Cor 2:10
been *r* to his holy apostles...........Eph 3:5
has now been *r* to his saints ....Col 1:26
Lord Jesus is *r* from heaven.... 2 Thess 1:7
then the lawless one will be *r*....2 Thess 2:8
He was *r* in the flesh.............. 1 Tim 3:16
ready to be *r* in the last time ....1 Pet 1:5
when Jesus Christ is *r*...............1 Pet 1:7
so that when his glory is *r*.........1 Pet 4:13
and the life was *r* ....1 John 1:2
we will be has not yet been *r* ......1 John 3:2
the Son of God was *r*............. 1 John 3:8
the love of God is *r* in us.........1 John 4:9

REVEALER
r of mysteries.......................Dan 2:29
and *r* of mysteries ....Dan 2:47

REVEALING
and *r* your sins.....................Ezek 21:24
without first *r* his plan.............Amos 3:7

REVEALS
r the deep things of darkness......Job 12:22
rebuilds Zion and *r* his splendor...Ps 102:16
goes about gossiping *r* secrets...Prov 20:19
The LORD *r* his royal power........Isa 52:10
he *r* deep and hidden things.......Dan 2:22

REVEL
those who *r* and celebrate...........Isa 5:14

REVELATION
for *r* to the Gentiles .... Luke 2:32
for the *r* of the sons of God.......Rom 8:19
the *r* of our Lord Jesus Christ.......1 Cor 1:7
a song, has a lesson, has a *r*......1 Cor 14:26
by a *r* of Jesus Christ................Gal 1:12
I went there because of a *r* ....Gal 2:2
spiritual wisdom and *r*............. Eph 1:17
r the mystery was made known .....Eph 3:3
our religion contains amazing *r*... 1 Tim 3:16
The *r* of Jesus Christ ....Rev 1:1

REVELATIONS
visions and *r* from the Lord.......2 Cor 12:1

REVENGE
I will get *r* and pay them back ... Deut 32:35
For the one who takes *r* .... Ps 9:12
show mercy when he takes *r*..... Prov 6:34
LORD has planned a day of *r*........ Isa 34:8
prevail over him and get our *r*.....Jer 20:10

REVERBERATES
quakes before them; the sky *r*......Joel 2:10

REVERE
Then they will learn to *r* me ...... Deut 4:10
must *r* the LORD your God........Deut 6:13
the LORD your God and *r* only.....Deut 13:4
Everyone should *r* you..............Jer 10:7

REVERENCE
holiness out of *r* for God .... 2 Cor 7:1
one another out of *r* for Christ .....Eph 5:21
your salvation with awe and *r* ......Phil 2:12

REVERENT
see your pure and *r* conduct........1 Pet 3:2

REVIVE
R me, or else I will die ....Ps 13:3
r me once again ....Ps 71:20
Will you not *r* us once more.........Ps 85:6
R me with your word..............Ps 119:25

REVIVES
for your promise *r* me..............Ps 119:50

REVOKE
promise on oath and will not *r* ..... Ps 110:4

REVOLT
and those who *r* against me .....Ezek 20:38
r are knee-deep in slaughter........ Hos 5:2

REVOLTED
r against me to this very day ....Ezek 2:3

REVOLUTIONARY
Barabbas was a *r* .... John 18:40

REWARD
will *r* you in great abundance.......Gen 15:1
obey them receive a rich *r*...........Ps 19:11
you grant me the *r*................... Ps 61:5
r that the righteous receive.......Prov 10:16
reaps a genuine *r* ....Prov 11:18
and the LORD will *r* you.......... Prov 25:22
was my *r* for all my effort ....Eccl 2:10
because that is their *r* ....Eccl 3:22
for this is their *r* ....Eccl 5:18
his *r* is with him....................Isa 40:10
your *r* is great in heaven...........Matt 5:12
r with your Father in heaven........Matt 6:1
they have their *r*.................. Matt 6:2
will receive a prophet's *r* ....Matt 10:41
he will never lose his *r*............ Matt 10:42
Then your *r* will be great .... Luke 6:35
He will *r* each one according.......Rom 2:6
his *r* according to his work .... 1 Cor 3:8
his eyes were fixed on the *r* ....Heb 11:26
but receive a full *r* .... 2 John 1:8
and my *r* is with me ....Rev 22:12

REWARDED

The most *r* of women ....Judg 5:24
he *r* my blameless behavior .... 2 Sam 22:21
LORD *r* me for my godly deeds..2 Sam 22:25
godly people are *r* by the LORD......Ps 24:5
the godly are *r*......................Ps 58:11
in a land where right is *r*...........Isa 26:10

REWARDS

but prosperity *r* the righteous.... Prov 13:21
give your *r* to someone else........Dan 5:17
that he *r* those who seek him.......Heb 11:6

REZIN

King of Damascus; joins Pekah against
    Ahaz, 2 Kgs 15:37
Confederacy of, inspires Isaiah's great
    messianic prophecy, Isa 7:1—9:12

REZON

Son of Eliada; establishes Syrian kingdom,
    1 Kgs 11:23-25

RHEGIUM

City in Italy where Paul visits, Acts 28:13

RHODA

Servant girl, Acts 12:13-16

RHODES

Island off coast of Asia Minor which Paul
    passes, Acts 21:1

RIBLAH

Headquarters of:
    Pharaoh Necho, 2 Kgs 23:31-35
    Nebuchadnezzar, 2 Kgs 25:6, 20-21
Zedekiah blinded here, Jer 39:5-7

RICH

R people from Tyre will seek........Ps 45:12
afraid when a man becomes *r*.......Ps 49:16
one who pretends to be *r*.........Prov 13:7
those who love the *r* are many .. Prov 14:20
The *r* and the poor are met....... Prov 22:2
The *r* rule over the poor..........Prov 22:7
A *r* person is wise in his own ..... Prov 28:11
and do not curse the *r*............Eccl 10:20
it will be hard for a *r* person.....Matt 19:23
for he was very *r*.................Mark 10:22
hard it is for the *r* to enter......Mark 10:23
But woe to you who are *r*........Luke 6:24
were made *r* in every way ....1 Cor 1:5
Already you are *r*...................1 Cor 4:8
that although he was *r*............2 Cor 8:9
Those who long to be *r*............1 Tim 6:9
poor in the world to be *r* in faith .....Jas 2:5
r and have acquired great wealth...Rev 3:17

RICHES

command about the city's *r* ....Josh 7:1
house contains wealth and *r*.........Ps 112:3
her left hand are *r* and honor......Prov 3:16
R and honor are with me..........Prov 8:18
who trusts in his *r* will fall .... Prov 11:28
crown of the wise is their *r*.......Prov 14:24
is *r* and honor and life .... Prov 22:4
for *r* do not last forever .... Prov 27:24
things you do and in your *r*.........Jer 48:7
who stores up *r* for himself.......Luke 12:21
the unfathomable *r* of Christ ....Eph 3:8
or to set their hope on *r*..........1 Tim 6:17
Your *r* have rotted....................Jas 5:2

RICHLY

word of Christ dwell in you *r* .... Col 3:16
r provides us with all things ...... 1 Tim 6:17

RICHNESS

in the *r* of the olive root ....Rom 11:17

RID

must get *r* of every weight ....Heb 12:1

RIDDLE

I will give you a *r*...................Judg 14:12

RIDDLES

sayings of the wise and their *r*......Prov 1:6

RIDE

and make me *r* on it ....Job 30:22
men to *r* over our heads..............Ps 66:12

RIDER

horse and its *r* he has thrown...... Exod 15:1
she laughs at the horse and its *r*...Job 39:18

RIDES

LORD *r* on a swift-moving cloud ..... Isa 19:1

RIDGE

The LORD is my high *r*............2 Sam 22:2
For you are my high *r*.................Ps 31:3

RIDICULE

object of *r* among the nations ......Ps 44:14
will make them an object of *r* ...... Jer 24:9
an object of horror and *r*...........Jer 49:13

RIFFRAFF

r will challenge those who...........Isa 3:5

RIGHT

See also AT THE RIGHT HAND; HIS RIGHT
    HAND; MY RIGHT HAND
that if you do what is *r*..............Gen 4:7
then I'll go to the *r*..................Gen 13:9
who had led me on the *r* path ....Gen 24:48
the tip of the *r* ear of his sons ...Exod 29:20
put it on Aaron's *r* earlobe.........Lev 8:23
go the *r* of the firstborn ....Deut 21:17
what he considered to be *r*.......Judg 21:25
Almighty pervert what is *r*...........Job 8:3
I know that I am *r*..................Job 13:18
so that you might be *r*.............Job 40:8
none of them does what is *r*..........Ps 14:1
are *r* when you condemn me........ Ps 51:4
and do what is *r* all the time........Ps 106:3
Sit down at my *r* hand ....Ps 110:1
a way that seems *r* to a person ... Prov 14:12
ways seem *r* in his own opinion ...Prov 16:2
ways seem *r* in his own opinion ...Prov 21:2
Learn to do what is *r* ....Isa 1:17
prove to me that you are *r*.......... Isa 43:26
from doing what is *r*...............Isa 46:12
and do what is *r* ....Jer 35:15
until he comes to whom is the *r*..Ezek 21:27
give you the *r* to be heard ....Ezek 29:21
by doing what is *r*..................Dan 4:27
sanctuary will be put *r* again....... Dan 8:14
For the ways of the LORD are *r* .....Hos 14:9
not know how to do what is *r* ....Amos 3:10
and pervert all that is *r* ....Mic 3:9
Strive to do what is *r* .... Zeph 2:3
your *r* eye causes you to sin ...... Matt 5:29
strikes you on the *r* cheek....... Matt 5:39
will give you whatever is *r* ...... Matt 20:4
Is it *r* to pay taxes to Caesar .....Matt 22:17
Sit at my *r* hand...................Matt 22:44
will put the sheep on his *r*....... Matt 25:33
and in his *r* mind................... Mark 5:15
clothed and in his *r* mind .... Luke 8:35
judge for yourselves what is *r* ....Luke 12:57
the *r* to become God's children.....John 1:12
It is not *r* for us to neglect..........Acts 6:2
Jesus standing at the *r* hand ....Acts 7:55
your heart is not *r* before God.....Acts 8:21
Has the potter no *r* ....Rom 9:21
the *r* to financial support .... 1 Cor 9:4
are concerned about what is *r*....2 Cor 8:21
for this is *r*............................Eph 6:1
sat down at the *r* hand of God.... Heb 10:12
have no *r* to eat from...............Heb 13:10
to suffer for doing what is *r* ....1 Pet 3:14
the seven stars in his *r* hand........ Rev 2:1
Then I saw in the *r* hand.............Rev 5:1
obtain a mark on their *r* hand ..... Rev 13:16

RIGHTEOUS

See also RIGHTEOUS MAN
not kill the innocent and the *r*.... Exod 23:7
that he should be *r* ....Job 15:14
The *r* see their destruction ....Job 22:19
the innocent secure, O *r* God.........Ps 7:9
to guard the paths of the *r*..........Prov 2:8
But the path of the *r*..............Prov 4:18
satisfies the appetite of the *r*......Prov 10:3
speech of the *r* is a fountain ...... Prov 10:11
reward that the *r* receive is life ...Prov 10:16
The hope of the *r* is joy .... Prov 10:28

but the descendants of the *r*.......Prov 11:21
but the *r* will flourish ,............. Prov 11:28
r are recompensed on earth.......Prov 11:31
In the house of the *r* is.............Prov 15:6
he hears the prayer of the *r* ......Prov 15:29
brings joy to the *r* .... Prov 21:15
When the *r* become numerous ... Prov 29:2
So do not be excessively *r*..........Eccl 7:16
there is not one truly *r* person.....Eccl 7:20
the *r* and the wicked.............. Eccl 9:2
Open the gates so a *r* nation...... Isa 26:2
The way of the *r* is level .... Isa 26:7
a *r* descendant of David ....Jer 33:15
in her midst the blood of the *r*.....Lam 4:13
You are *r*............................Dan 9:7
was a *r* man........................Matt 1:19
I did not come to call the *r*........Matt 9:13
Then the *r* will shine..............Matt 13:43
all the *r* blood shed on earth .... Matt 23:35
both *r* in the sight of God............Luke 1:6
at the resurrection of the *r*........Luke 14:14
confident that they were *r*.........Luke 18:9
both the *r* and the unrighteous...Acts 24:15
The *r* by faith will live.............. Rom 1:17
There is no one *r* ....Rom 3:10
For no one is declared *r* .... Rom 3:20
have been declared *r* by faith.......Rom 5:1
to be declared *r* by the law ....Gal 5:4
how holy and *r* and blameless..1 Thess 2:10
he was commended as *r*............Heb 11:4
and to the spirits of the *r* .... Heb 12:23
And if the *r* are barely saved.......1 Pet 4:18
he is faithful and *r* ....1 John 1:9
one who is *r* must continue........ Rev 22:11

RIGHTEOUS MAN

But the *r* holds to his way .... Job 17:9
he stores up a *r* will wear........... Job 27:17
depriving the *r* of justice...........Prov 18:5
But if a *r* turns away .... Ezek 18:24
her husband to be, was a *r*........ Matt 1:19
of the council, a good and *r*......Luke 23:50
that *r* was tormented.............. 2 Pet 2:8

RIGHTEOUSNESS

See also RIGHTEOUSNESS OF GOD
LORD credited it as *r* to him .... Gen 15:6
Because of my own *r* .... Deut 9:4
I will maintain my *r*..................Job 27:6
I put on *r* and it clothed me........Job 29:14
to my Creator I will ascribe *r* ....Job 36:3
shout for joy because of your *r*......Ps 51:14
but *r* delivers from death ....Prov 10:2
The *r* of the blameless............. Prov 11:5
r of the upright will deliver .... Prov 11:6
True *r* leads to life.................Prov 11:19
In the path of *r* there is life ....Prov 12:28
R guards the one who lives........Prov 13:6
R exalts a nation.................Prov 14:34
it is attained in the path of *r* ...... Prov 16:31
The one who pursues *r*........... Prov 21:21
will denounce your so-called *r*.....Isa 57:12
They will be called oaks of *r*.........Isa 61:3
the place where *r* dwells,...........Jer 31:23
be judged according to his *r* .....Ezek 18:20
to bring in perpetual *r*..............Dan 9:24
those bringing many to *r* ....Dan 12:3
Sow *r* for yourselves...............Hos 10:12
it is right for us to fulfill all *r*.....Matt 3:15
unless your *r* goes beyond........Matt 5:20
display your *r* merely to be seen ...Matt 6:1
came to you in the way of *r*.......Matt 21:32
in holiness and *r* before him.......Luke 1:75
For the *r* of God is revealed .... Rom 1:17
namely, the *r* of God............. Rom 3:22
seal of the *r* that he had by faith... Rom 4:11
was credited to Abraham as *r* .... Rom 4:22
and of the gift of *r* reign in life..... Rom 5:17
the one righteous act came *r*......Rom 5:18
grace will reign through *r*.......... Rom 5:21
Spirit is your life because of *r*..... Rom 8:10
did not pursue *r* obtained it ...... Rom 9:30
a law of *r* did not attain it.......... Rom 9:31
the *r* that comes from God........Rom 10:3
we would become the *r* of God... 2 Cor 5:21

the harvest of your *r* to grow.....2 Cor 9:10
if *r* could come through the law .... Gal 2:21
and it was credited to him as *r*.......Gal 3:6
putting on the breastplate of *r* .....Eph 6:14
not because I have my own *r*.......Phil 3:9
Instead pursue *r*....................1 Tim 6:11
he saved us not by works of *r*.....Titus 3:5
of the *r* that comes by faith.........Heb 11:7
does not accomplish God's *r*.........Jas 1:20
the fruit that consists of *r*..........Jas 3:18
a herald of *r* ....2 Pet 2:5
in which *r* truly resides ....2 Pet 3:13
everyone who practices *r*.......1 John 2:29
who practices *r* is righteous ....1 John 3:7
who does not practice *r* ....1 John 3:10

RIGHTEOUSNESS OF GOD
For the *r* is revealed .... Rom 1:17
demonstrates the *r*...................Rom 3:5
apart from the law the *r*..........Rom 3:21
r through the faithfulness .... Rom 3:22
we would become the *r* .... 2 Cor 5:21

RIGHTLY
r the young women adore you .....Song 1:4
And we *r* so.......................Luke 23:41
desire to conduct ourselves *r*......Heb 13:18

RIGHTS
or her marital *r*....................Exod 21:10
has the *r* to her own body ....1 Cor 7:4
violate the *r* of his brother........1 Thess 4:6

RING
the king removed his signet *r*......Esth 3:10
Like a gold *r* in a pig's snout ....Prov 11:22
who hears about it *r*.................Jer 19:3
king sealed it with his signet *r*......Dan 6:17
a gold *r* and fine clothing ....Jas 2:2

RINGLEADER
r of the sect of the Nazarenes.....Acts 24:5

RIOT
won't be a *r* among the people ... Mark 14:2

RIOTS
stirs up *r* among all the Jews.......Acts 24:5

RIP
will *r* me to shreds like a lion..........Ps 7:2

RIPPED
he *r* his clothes and said ....Judg 11:35

RISE
It is vain for you to *r* early ....Ps 127:2
the sun of vindication will *r*........ Mal 4:2
sun to *r* on the evil and the good...Matt 5:45
on the third day he will *r* again ...Luke 18:33
Christ had to suffer and to *r*....... Acts 17:3
be the first to *r* from the dead... Acts 26:23
R from the dead.....................Eph 5:14
the dead in Christ will *r* first ...., 1 Thess 4:16

RISEN
until all the dough had *r*..........Matt 13:33
The Lord has really *r*..............Luke 24:34

RISES
if someone *r* from the dead ......Luke 16:31

RISING
this *r* from the dead meant.......Mark 9:10
of the falling and *r* of many.......Luke 2:34

RIVALRY
from envy and *r* ....Phil 1:15

RIVER
If the *r* rages......................Job 40:23
to drink from the *r* ....Ps 36:8
passed through the *r* on foot........Ps 66:6
overwhelms like a flooding *r* ......Isa 30:28
that will flow like a *r*...............Isa 66:12
baptizing them in the Jordan *R* .... Mark 1:5
like a *r* out of his mouth ....Rev 12:15
the angel showed me the *r*.........Rev 22:1

RIVER'S
The *r* channels bring joy...........Ps 46:4

RIVERS
searched the sources of the *r*.......Job 28:11
By the *r* of Babylon................Ps 137:1

R and wide streams will flow.......Isa 33:21
will flow *r* of living water ....John 7:38
in dangers from *r*................. 2 Cor 11:26

RIZPAH
Saul's concubine taken by Abner,
   2 Sam 3:6–8
Sons of, killed, 2 Sam 21:8–9
Grief-stricken, cares for corpses,
   2 Sam 21:10–14

ROAD
in a wasteland with no *r* .... Ps 107:40
are like the *r* leading to life .... Prov 6:23
build a level *r* through the rift ......Isa 40:3
who made a *r* through the sea......Isa 43:16
will make a *r* in the wilderness ....Isa 43:19
he had seen the Lord on the *r* .....Acts 9:27

ROADS
the *r* that lead to your temple ....Ps 84:5
His are ancient *r*.....................Hab 3:6

ROADWAY
Build it—Build the *r*................Isa 62:10

ROADWAYS
I will construct my *r*................Isa 49:11

ROAR
the waves *r*...........................Ps 93:3
The lions *r* for prey ....Ps 104:21
wrath is like the *r* of a lion........Prov 19:12
Lord will *r* from the heights.......Jer 25:30
He will *r* like a lion.................Hos 11:10
Does a lion *r* in the woods........ Amos 3:4

ROARING
Like a *r* lion or a roving bear......Prov 28:15
They sound like the *r* sea...........Jer 6:23
The Lord comes *r* out of Zion.....Amos 1:2
anxious over the *r* of the sea .... Luke 21:25
like a *r* lion........................1 Pet 5:8
in a loud voice like a lion *r*..........Rev 10:3

ROARS
The Lord *r* from Zion ....Joel 3:16

ROB
Can a person *r* God..................Mal 3:8
do you *r* temples .... Rom 2:22

ROBBED
All who pass by have *r* him ....Ps 89:41
who tries to avoid evil is *r* ....Isa 59:15
Because you *r* many countries...... Hab 2:8
I *r* other churches by receiving ....2 Cor 11:8

ROBBER
is a thief and a *r*.....................John 10:1

ROBBERS
is to be a hideout for *r*...............Jer 7:11
are turning it into a den of *r* ......Matt 21:13
and fell into the hands of *r* ......Luke 10:30
before me were thieves and *r* .....John 10:8
who are neither temple *r*........Acts 19:37
in dangers from *r*................. 2 Cor 11:26

ROBBERY
in what you can gain by *r*...........Ps 62:10
love justice and hate *r* and sin.......Isa 61:8

ROBE
the *r* of the ephod ....Exod 29:5
seized a nice *r* from Babylon ......Josh 7:21
cut off an edge of Saul's *r*........1 Sam 24:4
tore the long *r* she was
   wearing.......................2 Sam 13:19
David was wrapped in a
   linen *r* ....1 Chr 15:27
was like a *r* and a turban..........Job 29:14
garment will replace a fine *r*.......Isa 3:24
hem of his *r* filled the temple......Isa 6:1
a *r* symbolizing vindication.........Isa 61:10
Bring the best *r*...................Luke 15:22
they clothed him in a purple *r*......John 19:2
like a *r* you will fold them up ....Heb 1:12
was given a long white *r*...........Rev 6:11

ROBED
He is *r* in majesty ....Ps 93:1
are *r* in splendor and majesty.......Ps 104:1

ROBES
cut the lower part of their *r* off... 2 Sam 10:4
In embroidered *r* she is escorted ...Ps 45:14
like walking around in long *r* ....Luke 20:46
dressed in long white *r* ....Rev 7:9

ROBS
The one who *r* his father ....Prov 19:26

ROCK
there on the *r* in Horeb.............Exod 17:6
will put you in a cleft in the *r* ....Exod 33:22
struck the *r* twice with his staff...Num 20:11
forgot the *R* who fathered you .. Deut 32:18
our enemies' *r* is not like our *R*...Deut 32:31
Fire flared up from the *r*...........Judg 6:21
There is no *r* like our God ....1 Sam 2:2
and as a *r* will be removed......... Job 14:18
Its heart is hard as *r* ....Job 41:24
turned a *r* into a pool of water...... Ps 114:8
r from which you were chiseled ..... Isa 51:1
that breaks a *r* in pieces ....Jer 23:29
man who built his house on *r*..... Matt 7:24
on this *r* I will build my church ...Matt 16:18
Other seed fell on *r*............... Luke 8:6
in a tomb cut out of the *r*........ Luke 23:53
a *r* that will make them fall....... Rom 9:33
drinking from the spiritual *r*...... 1 Cor 10:4
a stumbling-stone and a *r* ....1 Pet 2:8

ROCKS
and the *r* were split apart.........Matt 27:51
to the mountains and to the *r* ......Rev 6:16

ROD
which passes under the *r*..........Lev 27:32
correct him with the *r* of men ... 2 Sam 7:14
your *r* and your staff reassure.......Ps 23:4
r and reproof impart wisdom.....Prov 29:15
with a *r* of discipline................1 Cor 4:21
Aaron's *r* that budded ....Heb 9:4
will rule them with an iron *r*....... Rev 2:27
measuring *r* like a staff...............Rev 11:1
will rule them with an iron *r*.......Rev 19:15
with the measuring *r* ....Rev 21:16

RODE
with the one who *r* the horse......Rev 19:19

ROLLING
are *r* dice for my garments ....Ps 22:18

ROME
Jews expelled from, Acts 18:2
Paul:
    writes to Christians of, Rom 1:7
    desires to go to, Acts 19:21
    comes to, Acts 28:14
    imprisoned in, Acts 28:16

ROOF
and walked around on the *r* ......2 Sam 11:2
their tongues stuck to the *r*........Job 29:10
May my tongue stick to the *r*.......Ps 137:6
removed the *r* above Jesus ....Mark 2:4
up on the *r* and let him down......Luke 5:19
Peter went up on the *r* to pray ....Acts 10:9

ROOFTOPS
as short-lived as grass on the *r* ....Isa 37:27

ROOM
See also UPPER ROOM
he went to his *r* and wept there ..Gen 43:30
upper *r* all by himself..............Judg 3:20
will not be enough *r* for them ... Zech 10:10
and there is still *r*.................Luke 14:22
would not have *r* for the books...John 21:25
they went to the upstairs *r* ....Acts 1:13

ROOMS
Make *r* in the ark ....Gen 6:14
while adding its upper *r*............Jer 22:13
he is in the inner *r*.................Matt 24:26

ROOSTER
Before the *r* crows...............Matt 26:75

ROOT
no *r* producing poisonous ....Deut 29:18
have seen the fool taking *r* ....Job 5:3
At that time a *r* from Jesse.........Isa 11:10

r in the ground and bear fruit.........Isa 37:31
they did not have sufficient r......Matt 13:6
and if the r is holy ....Rom 11:16
love of money is the r ....1 Tim 6:10
that no one be like a bitter r.......Heb 12:15
r and the descendant of David.....Rev 22:16

ROOTED
been r and grounded in love........Eph 3:17
r and built up in him.................Col 2:7

ROOTS
Although its r may grow old........Job 14:8
for its r went down deep ....Ezek 31:7
send down his r like a cedar........Hos 14:5
fig tree withered from the r .....Mark 11:20

ROPE
tie this red r in the window........Josh 2:18

ROPE-BASKET
but I was let down in a r.........2 Cor 11:33

ROPES
The r of Sheol tightened.........2 Sam 22:6
The r of death tightened............Ps 116:3
he cut the r of the wicked ....Ps 129:4

ROSE
after he r from the dead..........Acts 10:41
that Jesus died and r again........1 Thess 4:14

ROTTED
riches have r and your clothing.......Jas 5:2

ROTTENNESS
is like r in his bones..................Prov 12:4

ROUGH
r terrain will become a level........Isa 40:4

ROUNDS
and on its r it returns.................Eccl 1:6

ROUSES
It r the spirits of the dead............Isa 14:9

ROWERS
r have brought you into surging .. Ezek 27:26

ROYAL
your servant settle in the r city ...1 Sam 27:5
as a r palace for himself .... 2 Chr 2:1
the entire r line of Judah.........2 Chr 22:10
So he placed the r high turban..... Esth 2:17
from his r splendor..................Isa 2:10
on my entire r mountain .... Isa 11:9
a r turban in the hand .... Isa 62:3
for a r edict to be issued............Dan 6:7
But if you fulfill the r law ....Jas 2:8
a r priesthood ....1 Pet 2:9

RUBBLE
made the city into a heap of r ...... Isa 25:2

RUBIES
She is more precious than r .... Prov 3:15
For wisdom is better than r........ Prov 8:11
her value is far more than r.......Prov 31:10

RUDDY
Now he was r....................1 Sam 16:12
My beloved is dazzling and r ..... Song 5:10

RUDE
It is not r, it is not self-serving .....1 Cor 13:5

RUIN
or r the corners of your beard.....Lev 19:27
you bring them down to r..........Ps 73:18
foolishness will come to r ....Prov 10:8
a flattering mouth works r ...... Prov 26:28
r the highly exalted position.........Jer 13:9
concerned over the r of Joseph... Amos 6:6
plunge people into r................1 Tim 6:9
brings r on those who listen ......2 Tim 2:14

RUINED
earth was r in the sight of God .....Gen 6:11
and indeed it was r ....Gen 6:12
income of the wicked will be r.....Prov 15:6
we have r no one ....2 Cor 7:2

RUINS
cities are in r and unpopulated ...... Isa 6:11
will rebuild the perpetual r ....Isa 61:4

it will lie in r forever ....Jer 49:13
my temple remains in r...............Hag 1:9
will rebuild its r and restore it .... Acts 15:16

RULE
so they may r over the fish .... Gen 1:26
A king will r over us ....1 Sam 12:12
godless man should not r..........Job 34:30
you appoint them to r over............Ps 8:6
He established a r in Jacob........Ps 78:5
You r over the proud sea ....Ps 89:9
R in the midst of your enemies......Ps 110:2
acts wisely will r over an heir.......Prov 17:2
will r over Israel on my behalf......Mic 5:2
an end all r and all authority..... 1 Cor 15:24
far above every r and authority..... Eph 1:21
he will r them with an iron rod .... Rev 2:27
and great authority to r.............Rev 13:2
I r as queen and am no widow......Rev 18:7
He will r them with an iron rod....Rev 19:15

RULED
masters other than you have r us... Isa 26:13

RULER
Who made you a r and a judge ... Exod 2:14
he is faithful to his chosen r .... 2 Sam 22:51
lack of subjects is the ruin of a r .. Prov 14:28
you sit down to eat with a r.......Prov 23:1
a wicked r over a poor people....Prov 28:15
If a r listens to lies ....Prov 29:12
is r over human kingdoms.........Dan 4:32
the r of demons .... Matt 12:24
r of this world will be driven...... John 12:31
the r of this world has been ....John 16:11
made you a r and judge over us ...Acts 7:27
not speak evil about a r.............Acts 23:5
the r of the domain of the air........Eph 2:2
head over every r and authority ....Col 2:10

RULERS
r collaborate against the LORD ....Ps 2:2
Though r plot and slander me ..... Ps 119:23
one who reduces r to nothing .....Isa 40:23
I will install r over them .... Jer 23:4
her r are as hungry as wolves...... Zeph 3:3
the r of the Gentiles lord it over.. Matt 20:25
nor heavenly r................... Rom 8:38
for r cause no fear for good .... Rom 13:3
the r of this age understood it..... 1 Cor 2:8
but against the r....................Eph 6:12
Disarming the r and authorities .... Col 2:15
be subject to r and authorities......Titus 3:1

RULES
one who r fairly among men ....2 Sam 23:3
obeying my r and regulations......1 Kgs 3:14
But the LORD r forever ....Ps 9:7
The LORD r forever ....Ps 10:16
and I do not reject his r ....Ps 18:22
know that God r over Jacob ....Ps 59:13
He r by his power forever ....Ps 66:7
are those who observe his r.........Ps 119:2
for I observe your r.................Ps 119:22
keep the r you have revealed........Ps 119:88
for I meditate on your r..............Ps 119:99
Therefore I love your r ....Ps 119:119
Your r are marvelous ....Ps 119:129
on you than these necessary r....Acts 15:28
competes according to the r........2 Tim 2:5

RULINGS
priests proclaim r for profit......... Mic 3:11

RUMOR
and one r after another.............Ezek 7:26

RUMORS
hear of wars and r of wars........Matt 24:6
hear of wars and r of wars........ Mark 13:7

RUN
I r along the path of your .... Ps 119:32
they r without growing weary ..... Isa 40:31
So I do not r uncertainly...........1 Cor 9:26
that I did not r in vain..............Phil 2:16
and r with endurance the race.....Heb 12:1

RUNNER
My days are swifter than a r........Job 9:25
One r after another will come ......Jer 51:31

RUNNING
A herald is r on the mountains ..... Nah 1:15
The two were r together ....John 20:4
to make sure that I was not r........Gal 2:2
You were r well....................Gal 5:7

RUSHING
For he comes like a r stream ....Isa 59:19

RUSTED
Your gold and silver have r..........Jas 5:3

RUTH
Moabite, Ruth 1:4
Follows Naomi, Ruth 1:6–18
Marries Boaz, Ruth 4:9–13
Ancestor of Christ, Ruth 4:13, 21–22

RUTHLESS
covenant-breakers, heartless, r.... Rom 1:31

S

SABBATH
a holy S to the LORD.............Exod 16:23
Remember the S day to set it ....Exod 20:8
So you must keep the S ....Exod 31:14
S of complete rest to the LORD... Exod 35:2
must be a S of complete rest ....Lev 23:3
must observe a S to the LORD .....Lev 25:2
Be careful to observe the S day ...Deut 5:12
gates of Jerusalem on the S day .... Jer 17:21
through the grain fields on a S .... Matt 12:1
The S was made for people.......Mark 2:27
is lord even of the S ....Mark 2:28
lawful to do good on the S ....Mark 3:4
lawful to do good on the S .... Luke 6:9
It is the S, and you are not.........John 5:10
not only was he breaking the S....John 5:18
circumcise a male child on
    the S....................John 7:22
aloud in the synagogues
    every S ....Acts 15:21

SABBATHS
Surely you must keep my S ....Exod 31:13
You must keep my S..............Lev 26:2
S, and convocations .... Isa 1:13
I also gave them my S ....Ezek 20:12

SACKCLOTH
I have sewed s on my skin.........Job 16:15
you removed my s................... Ps 30:11
remove the s from your waist ......Isa 20:2
with fasting, s, and ashes .... Dan 9:3
declared a fast and put on s ....Jonah 3:5
repented long ago in s............ Matt 11:21

SACRED
make this into a s anointing
    oil ....Exod 30:25
proclaim a s assembly ....Joel 1:14
too s to be put into words........ 2 Cor 12:4

SACRIFICE
offering is a peace-offering s .... Lev 3:1
law of the peace-offering s ....Lev 7:11
must s the Passover animal ....Deut 16:2
to worship and to s to the LORD...1 Sam 1:3
scorning my s and my offering .. 1 Sam 2:29
to s to the LORD our God .... 1 Sam 15:15
s God desires is a humble spirit .....Ps 51:17
acceptable to the LORD than s.....Prov 21:3
person's s is an abomination......Prov 21:27
than to offer a s like fools ....Eccl 5:1
LORD is holding a s in Bozrah....... Isa 34:6
orders to offer s and incense ......Dan 2:46
not simply in s......................Hos 6:6
I promise to offer a s to you ......Jonah 2:9
you offer blind animals as a s........Mal 1:8
I want mercy and not s ....Matt 9:13
I want mercy and not s ....Matt 12:7
to present your bodies as a s ...... Rom 12:1
This is from a s ....1 Cor 10:28
an acceptable s ....Phil 4:18
to put away sin by his s...........Heb 9:26
one s for sins for all time ....Heb 10:12
no further s for sins is left........Heb 10:26

a greater *s* than Cain................Heb 11:4
offer up a *s* of praise to God.......Heb 13:15
is the atoning *s* for our sins....... 1 John 2:2
to be the atoning *s* for our sins.. 1 John 4:10

SACRIFICED
They *s* their sons and daughters...Ps 106:37
They *s* to the Baal idols............ Hos 11:2
our Passover lamb, has been *s*......1 Cor 5:7
they would eat food *s* to idols......Rev 2:14

SACRIFICES
s to a god other than the LORD...Exod 22:20
your *s*, your tithes ....Deut 12:6
offered burnt *s* to the LORD .... Josh 8:31
and offered burnt *s* and peace..2 Sam 24:25
Receiving *s* and offerings........... Ps 40:6
to me are your many *s*................Isa 1:11
I have had my fill of burnt *s* ....Isa 1:11
will present *s* and offerings.........Isa 19:21
the one who *s* a lamb............. Isa 66:3
pleasure from the *s* they offer.....Jer 6:20
offerings, *s*, grain offerings ....Jer 17:26
than all burnt offerings and *s*.... Mark 12:33
offer *s* first for their own sins...... Heb 7:27
to be purified with these *s*.........Heb 9:23
God is pleased with such *s*.........Heb 13:16
spiritual *s* that are acceptable ......1 Pet 2:5

SACRIFICIAL
They offer up *s* gifts to me ....Hos 8:13
s and fragrant offering to God.......Eph 5:2

SACRIFICING
That is why I am *s* to the LORD ...Exod 13:15
But ever since we stopped *s*.......Jer 44:18

SAD
they stood still, looking *s*........ Luke 24:17
you will be *s*......................John 16:20
For if I make you *s*.................2 Cor 2:2
not because you were made *s*.....2 Cor 7:9

SADDUCEES
Rejected by John, Matt 3:7
Test Jesus, Matt 16:1–12
Silenced by Jesus, Matt 22:23–34
Disturbed by teaching of resurrection,
    Acts 4:1–2
Oppose apostles, Acts 5:17–40

SADNESS
your hearts are filled with *s* ....John 16:6
For *s* as intended by God ....2 Cor 7:10

SAFE
my life is *s* ....Ps 16:9
got his son back *s* and sound ....Luke 15:27

SAFEGUARDS
who guards his way *s* his life ..... Prov 16:17

SAFELY
If you really do return *s*.........2 Chr 18:27
He guided them *s* along ....Ps 78:53
all were brought *s* to land .... Acts 27:44

SAFETY
His children are far from *s*...........Job 5:4
and will take your rest in *s*.........Job 11:18
the *s* they so desperately desire..... Ps 12:5
will find *s* under his wings...........Ps 91:4
as well as *s* and protection .... Isa 4:6
he will find *s* in the rocky...........Isa 33:16

SAGES
words of the *s* are like prods ...... Eccl 12:11

SAID
The man did just as Joseph *s*...... Gen 43:17
blessing you just as he *s* ....Deut 1:11
Then David *s* to Abishai ....2 Sam 16:11
issued a proclamation and *s*.......Jonah 3:7
He *s* to her......................Matt 20:21
at what the shepherds *s*..........Luke 2:18
they *s*, "Lord....................Luke 9:54
His disciples *s*.....................John 16:29

SAINTS
See also ALL THE SAINTS
and called to be *s*.................1 Cor 1:2
than the least of all the *s* ....Eph 3:8

our Lord Jesus with all his *s*......1 Thess 3:13
to be glorified among his *s* .....2 Thess 1:10
once for all entrusted to the *s* ......Jude 1:3
blood of your *s* and prophets.......Rev 16:6
encircled the camp of the *s*........Rev 20:9

SAKE
the *s* of my servant Abraham.....Gen 26:24
and to Egypt for Israel's *s*........ Exod 18:8
for the *s* of Jonathan...............2 Sam 9:1
for your father David's *s*..........1 Kgs 11:12
for the *s* of his reputation ....Ps 23:3
For the *s* of your reputation ....Ps 25:11
the *s* of your own reputation ....Ps 31:3
s of your glorious reputation ....Ps 79:9
for the *s* of his reputation ....Ps 106:8
for the *s* of your reputation........Ps 109:21
for the *s* of your reputation........Ps 143:11
with their insults for your *s*.........Jer 15:15
the *s* of the kingdom of heaven...Matt 19:12
or children or fields for my *s* .... Matt 19:29
But for the *s* of the elect.........Matt 24:22
for the *s* of God's kingdom ......Luke 18:29
for the *s* of my name ....Acts 9:16
much for the *s* of my name.........Rev 2:3

SAKES
he became poor for your *s* ....2 Cor 8:9

SALAMIS
Paul preaches here, Acts 13:4–5

SALE
s of a house which is his ....Lev 25:33

SALEM
Jerusalem's original name, Gen 14:18
Used poetically, Ps 76:2

SALIM
Place near Aenon, John 3:23

SALOME
One of the ministering women,
    Mark 15:40–41
Visits empty tomb, Mark 16:1
—Herodias's daughter (not named in the
    Bible), Matt 14:6–11

SALT
was turned into a pillar of *s*....... Gen 19:26
of your grain offerings with *s*....... Lev 2:13
It is a covenant of *s* forever.......Num 18:19
leveled the city and spread *s* ......Judg 9:45
not rubbed down with *s* ....Ezek 16:4
You are the *s* of the earth..........Matt 5:13
S is good, but if it loses .... Mark 9:50
seasoned with *s* ....Col 4:6

SALT SEA
See DEAD SEA

SALTED
Everyone will be *s* with fire...... Mark 9:49

SALTY
how can it be made *s* again........Matt 5:13

SALVATION
and see the *s* of the LORD ....Exod 14:13
The LORD is my light and my *s*....... Ps 27:1
all day long proclaim your *s* ....Ps 71:15
he has raised up a horn of *s* ......Luke 1:69
my eyes have seen your *s* ....Luke 2:30
Today *s* has come to this ....Luke 19:9
because *s* is from the Jews.........John 4:22
And there is *s* in no one else...... Acts 4:12
bring *s* to the ends of the earth... Acts 13:47
for *s* to everyone who believes.... Rom 1:16
fellow Israelites is for their *s* ...... Rom 10:1
one confesses and thus has *s*.....Rom 10:10
s has come to the Gentiles ....Rom 11:11
for our *s* is now nearer ....Rom 13:11
in the day of *s* I helped you........2 Cor 6:2
And take the helmet of *s* ....Eph 6:17
continue working out your *s*.......Phil 2:12
gaining *s* through our Lord ......1 Thess 5:9
for *s* through sanctification......2 Thess 2:13
may obtain *s* in Christ Jesus ......2 Tim 2:10
bringing *s* to all people ....Titus 2:11
if we neglect such a great *s*.........Heb 2:3

make the pioneer of their *s*........ Heb 2:10
Concerning this *s* ....1 Pet 1:10
S belongs to our God...............Rev 7:10
S and glory and power ....Rev 19:1

SAMARIA
Capital of Israel, 1 Kgs 16:24–29
Besieged by Ben Hadad, 1 Kgs 20:1–21
Besieged again; miraculously delivered,
    2 Kgs 6:24–7:20
Inhabitants deported by Assyria; re-
    populated with foreigners, 2 Kgs 17:5–6,
    24–41
—District of Palestine in Christ's time,
    Luke 17:11–19
Disciples forbidden to preach in, Matt 10:5
Gospel preached there after the ascension,
    Acts 1:8; 9:31; 15:3

SAMARITAN
But a *S* who was traveling .... Luke 10:33
So the *S* woman said to him........John 4:9

SAMARITANS
People of mixed heredity, 2 Kgs 17:24–41
Christ preaches to, John 4:5–42
Parable of "the good Samaritan,"
    Luke 10:30–37
Converts among, Acts 8:5–25

SAMOS
Paul visits, Acts 20:15

SAMSON
Birth predicted and accomplished,
    Judg 13:2–25
Marries Philistine; avenges betrayal, Judg 14
Defeats Philistines singlehandedly, Judg 15
Betrayed by Delilah; loses strength,
    Judg 16:4–22
Destroys many in his death, Judg 16:23–31

SAMUEL
Born in answer to prayer; dedicated to God,
    1 Sam 1:1–28
Receives revelation; recognized as prophet,
    1 Sam 3:1–21
Judges Israel, 1 Sam 7:15–17
Warns Israel against a king, 1 Sam 8:10–18
Anoints Saul, 1 Sam 9:15–10:1
Rebukes Saul, 1 Sam 15:10–35
Anoints David, 1 Sam 16:1–13
Death of, 1 Sam 25:1

SANBALLAT
Influential Samaritan; attempts to thwart
    Nehemiah's plans, Neh 2:10; 4:7–8; 6:1–14

SANCTIFICATION
and righteousness and *s* and ..... 1 Cor 1:30
through *s* by the Spirit..........2 Thess 2:13

SANCTIFIED
and *s* the people..................Exod 19:14
s in the midst of the Israelites .... Lev 22:32
s by the Holy Spirit ....Rom 15:16
those who are *s* in Christ Jesus .....1 Cor 1:2
you were washed, you were *s* .....1 Cor 6:11
the unbelieving husband is *s*......1 Cor 7:14
For it is *s* by God's word and.......1 Tim 4:5

SANCTIFY
send for them and *s* them............Job 1:5
know that I, the LORD, *s* Israel... Ezek 37:28
to *s* her by cleansing her...........Eph 5:26

SANCTUARY
Let them make for me a *s* ....Exod 25:8
God has spoken in his *s*.......... Ps 60:6
They set your *s* on fire...............Ps 74:7
He will become a *s* ....Isa 8:14
I have been a little *s* for them..... Ezek 11:16
favor to your devastated *s*..........Dan 9:17
for worship and its earthly *s*.........Heb 9:1
brings into the *s* as an offering .... Heb 13:11

SAND
your descendants like the *s*....... Gen 32:12
heavier than the *s* of the sea........ Job 6:3
outnumber the grains of *s*....... Ps 139:18
as the *s* on the seashore.......... Isa 10:22

its waves toss up mud and *s*.......Isa 57:20
the innumerable grains of *s*.......Heb 11:12

SANDAL
remove his *s* from his foot.......Deut 25:9
and he removed his *s*.............Ruth 4:8

SANDALED
How beautiful are your *s* feet.......Song 7:1

SANDALS
Take your *s* off your feet ....Exod 3:5
am not worthy to carry his *s*.......Matt 3:11
and untie the strap of his *s* ....Mark 1:7
a traveler's bag, or *s* ....Luke 10:4
your belt and put on your *s*.......Acts 12:8

SANDS
the *s* that are on the seashore.....Jer 33:22

SANG
Moses and the Israelites *s* ....Exod 15:1
singers *s* and the trumpeters ... 2 Chr 29:28
The choirs *s* loudly ....Neh 12:42
the morning stars *s* in chorus......Job 38:7
they *s* praises to him ....Ps 106:12
They *s* the song of Moses ....Rev 15:3

SANHEDRIN
chief priests and the whole *S*....Matt 26:59
they summoned the *S*.............Acts 5:21

SAPPHIRA
Wife of Ananias; struck dead for lying,
    Acts 5:1–11

SAPPHIRE
a *s*, and an emerald..............Exod 28:18
the second *s*, the third agate.......Rev 21:19

SAPPHIRES
a place whose stones are *s* ....Job 28:6

SARAH [or SARAI]
Barren wife of Abram, Gen 11:29–31
Represented as Abram's sister, Gen 12:10–20
Gives Abram her maid, Gen 16:1–3
Receives promise of a son, Gen 17:15–21
Gives birth to Isaac, Gen 21:1–8
Also called "Sarai," Gen 17:15

SARAI
See SARAH

SARCOPHAGUS
that his *s* was made of iron........Deut 3:11

SARDIS
Site of one of the seven churches, Rev 1:11
Letter to, Rev 3:1–6

SASH
fitted tunic, a turban, and a *s* .....Exod 28:4

SASHES
wrapped *s* around them............Lev 8:13

SAT
he *s* down at the right hand ....Heb 1:3

SATAN
Titles of:
    Abaddon, Apollyon, angel of the abyss,
        Rev 9:11
    accuser, Rev 12:10
    ancient serpent, Rev 20:2
    Beelzebul, ruler of demons, Matt 12:24
    Beliar, 2 Cor 6:15
    devil, Matt 4:1
    enemy, 1 Pet 5:8
    evil one, Matt 6:13
    god of this age, 2 Cor 4:4
    murderer, liar, father of lies, John 8:44
    ruler of the domain of the air, Eph 2:2
    ruler of this world, John 14:30
    serpent, Gen 3:4
Origin of, in heaven, Isa 14:12–20; Rev 12:7–9
Power and activities of:
    tempted Eve, Gen 3:1
    tempted David, 1 Chr 21:1
    accused and tormented Job, Job 1:6–2:10
    opposed Joshua the high priest, Zech 3:1
    tempted Jesus, Matt 4:1–11; Mark 3:22–28;
        Luke 22:31

entered Judas at betrayal, Luke 22:3;
    John 13:27
deceives and ensnares, 2 Cor 11:3–15;
    1 Tim 3:6–7; Rev 20:7–8
works in evildoers, Acts 13:8–10; Eph 2:2
accuses believers before God, Rev 12:10
Believers must resist, 2 Cor 2:10–11;
    Eph 6:11–16; Jas 4:7; 1 Pet 5:8–9;
    1 John 2:13
His defeat by Christ, Gen 3:15; Rev 12:10–12;
    20:7–10
See DEVIL

S also arrived among them...........Job 1:6
The LORD said to *S* ....Zech 3:2
Jesus said to him, "Go away, *S* .... Matt 4:10
said to Peter, "Get behind me, *S*..Matt 16:23
enduring temptations from *S*......Mark 1:13
How can *S* cast out *S* ....Mark 3:23
I saw *S* fall like lightning..........Luke 10:18
Then *S* entered Judas...............Luke 22:3
S has demanded to have you all .. Luke 22:31
has *S* filled your heart to lie ....Acts 5:3
quickly crush *S* under your feet.. Rom 16:20
hand this man over to *S* ....1 Cor 5:5
for even *S* disguises himself ......2 Cor 11:14
messenger of *S* to trouble me.... 2 Cor 12:7
whom I handed over to *S*.........1 Tim 1:20
but are a synagogue of *S* ....Rev 2:9
so-called "deep secrets of *S* ....Rev 2:24
one called the devil and *S* ....Rev 12:9
S will be released from ....Rev 20:7

SATAN'S
one will be by *S* working ....2 Thess 2:9
you live—where *S* throne is.........Rev 2:13

SATISFIED
you will be *s* with bread ....Exod 16:12
heard this explanation, he was *s*.. Lev 10:20
If only we had been *s* to live........Josh 7:7
For he has *s* those who thirst........Ps 107:9
his stomach will be *s* ....Prov 27:7
appetite is *s* loathes honey ....Prov 27:7
will be *s* with food.................Prov 28:19
I become *s* and act deceptively ... Prov 30:9
three things that will never
    be *s*............................Prov 30:15
will never be *s* with money .... Eccl 5:10
but were not *s* ....Isa 9:20
will be *s* when he understands ..... Isa 53:11
until its appetite is *s* ....Jer 46:10
and yet you were still not *s*...... Ezek 16:28
he is never *s* ....Hab 2:5
for they will be *s*...................Matt 5:6
They all ate and were *s* ....Matt 14:20
Let the children be *s* first ....Mark 7:27
Already you are *s*..................1 Cor 4:8
whether I go *s* or hungry ....Phil 4:12
we will be *s* with that..............1 Tim 6:8

SATISFIES
s your life with good things.........Ps 103:5
He *s* the desire....................Ps 145:19
s the appetite of the righteous ....Prov 10:3

SATISFY
S us in the morning...............Ps 90:14
I will *s* him with long life..........Ps 91:16
enough food to *s* his appetite.....Prov 13:25
on something that will not *s*........Isa 55:2
I will fully *s* the needs ....Jer 31:25
to *s* so great a crowd ....Matt 15:33

SAUL
Becomes first king of Israel, 1 Sam 9–11
Sacrifices unlawfully, 1 Sam 13:1–14
Wars with Philistines, 1 Sam 13:15–14:52
Disregards the Lord's command; rejected
    by God, 1 Sam 15
Suffers from distressing spirits,
    1 Sam 16:14–23
Becomes jealous of David; attempts to kill
    him, 1 Sam 18:5–19:22
Pursues David; twice spared by him,
    1 Sam 22–24; 26
Consults medium, 1 Sam 28:7–25

Defeated, commits suicide; buried, 1 Sam 31
—of Tarsus, apostle to the Gentiles: *see*
    PAUL

SAVE
then he will *s* the downcast.......Job 22:29
lives of the needy he will *s*.........Ps 72:13
champion who cannot *s* anyone.....Jer 14:9
he may *s* you in all your cities .....Hos 13:10
Assyria cannot *s* us ....Hos 14:3
will *s* his people from their sins ... Matt 1:21
woke him up saying, "Lord, *s* us .. Matt 8:25
wants to *s* his life will lose it..... Matt 16:25
it in three days, *s* yourself ....Matt 27:40
to *s* a life or destroy it ....Mark 3:4
wants to *s* his life will lose it.....Mark 8:35
s yourself and come down.......Mark 15:30
to *s* a life or to destroy it ....Luke 6:9
wants to *s* his life will lose it.....Luke 9:24
S yourself and us ....Luke 23:39
but to *s* the world ....John 12:47
S yourselves from this........... Acts 2:40
and *s* some of them .... Rom 11:14
pleased to *s* those who believe ....1 Cor 1:21
that by all means I may *s* some...1 Cor 9:22
set aside some income and *s* it ....1 Cor 16:2
into the world to *s* sinners.........1 Tim 1:15
you will *s* both yourself and ......1 Tim 4:16
was able to *s* him from death...... Heb 5:7
which is able to *s* your souls ......Jas 1:21
Can this kind of faith *s* him ....Jas 2:14
who is able to *s* and destroy........Jas 4:12
will *s* that person's soul.............Jas 5:20

SAVED
See also WILL BE SAVED
So the LORD *s* Israel ....Exod 14:30
will be *s* from your enemies...... Num 10:9
You *s* me from death ....Ps 116:16
You have *s* them....................Jer 14:8
Then who can be *s*..............Matt 19:25
endures to the end will be *s* ..... Matt 24:13
He *s* others ....Matt 27:42
Then who can be *s*...............Mark 10:26
endures to the end will be *s* ......Mark 13:13
no one would be *s*................Mark 13:20
He *s* others ....Mark 15:31
and is baptized will be *s* .... Mark 16:16
should be *s* from our enemies..... Luke 1:71
Your faith has *s* you ....Luke 7:50
He *s* others ....Luke 23:35
world should be *s* through him.... John 3:17
he will be *s* ....John 10:9
name of the Lord will be *s*........Acts 2:21
you cannot be *s*....................Acts 15:1
what must I do to be *s*.............Acts 16:30
For in hope we were *s* .... Rom 8:24
And so all Israel will be *s* .... Rom 11:26
so that his spirit may be *s* .... 1 Cor 5:5
so that they may be *s*..............1 Cor 10:33
by which you are being *s* ....1 Cor 15:2
among those who are being *s* ....2 Cor 2:15
by grace you are *s* through faith.....Eph 2:8
hearts for the truth so as to
    be *s*............................2 Thess 2:10
he wants all people to be *s* ....1 Tim 2:4
he *s* us not by works.............. Titus 3:5

SAVES
sword or spear that the LORD *s*..1 Sam 17:47
So he *s* from the sword.............Job 5:15
the horn that *s* me .... Ps 18:2
which now *s* you....................1 Pet 3:21

SAVING
by *s* their lives from death..........Ps 33:19
my God for his *s* intervention ...... Ps 42:11

SAVIOR
Except for me there is no *S*........Hos 13:4
begun to rejoice in God my *S*.....Luke 1:47
S is born in the city of David.......Luke 2:11
one really is the *S* of the world ... John 4:42
his right hand as Leader and *S*..... Acts 5:31
brought to Israel a *S*............. Acts 13:23
himself being the *s* of the body.... Eph 5:23
by the command of God our *S* .....1 Tim 1:1

who is the *S* of all people.........1 Tim 4:10
appearing of our *S* Christ Jesus...2 Tim 1:10
of our great God and *S* ....Titus 2:13
the kindness of God our *S*........ Titus 3:4
to be the *S* of the world ....1 John 4:14
to the only God our *S*.............Jude 1:25

SAW
A shrewd person *s* danger.........Prov 22:3
I *s* the Lord always in front ....Acts 2:25

SAY
See also BUT I SAY TO YOU
I will *s* nothing sinful ....Ps 17:3
Certainly they *s* such things .... Isa 8:20
These people *s* they are loyal......Isa 29:13
But I *s* to you that anyone .... Matt 5:22
how to speak or what to *s*.......Matt 10:19
But who do you *s* that I am......Matt 16:15
But he had nothing to *s*.......... Matt 22:12
The words that I *s* to you ....John 14:10
every good thing you do or *s* ...2 Thess 2:17
this topic we have much to *s* .... Heb 5:11
If we *s* we do not bear the guilt....1 John 1:8

SAYING
This is a difficult *s*...............John 6:60
you understand what I am *s* ......John 8:43
This *s* is trustworthy..............1 Tim 1:15

SAYINGS
my *s* will drip like the dew........ Deut 32:2

SAYS
that I am the one who *s* .... Isa 52:6
not stumble in what he *s* ....Jas 3:2

SCALE
they *s* walls like soldiers............Joel 2:7
had a balance *s* in his hand ....Rev 6:5

SCALES
him weigh me with honest *s*........Job 31:6
or the hills on *s*....................Isa 40:12
they use dishonest *s*................Hos 12:7
like *s* fell from his eyes ....Acts 9:18

SCARLET
blue, purple, *s*, fine linen........Exod 25:4
household were clothed with *s*... Prov 31:21
Your lips are like a *s* thread........ Song 4:3
as easy to see as the color *s* .... Isa 1:18
and put a *s* robe around him.....Matt 27:28
a woman sitting on a *s* beast .... Rev 17:3

SCATTER
I will *s* you among the nations.... Lev 26:33
His enemies *s*.......................... Ps 68:1
I will *s* to the four winds..........Jer 49:32
and gather where I didn't *s* ......Matt 25:26

SCATTERED
Otherwise we will be *s* ....Gen 11:4
All the evildoers are *s* ....Ps 92:9
people to be destroyed and *s*.......Jer 23:1
one who *s* Israel will regather ......Jer 31:10
people of Israel are like *s* sheep ...Jer 50:17
sheep of the flock will be *s* ....Matt 26:31
and the sheep will be *s* ....Mark 14:27
you will be *s*.......................John 16:32

SCATTERS
God *s* the nations................... Ps 68:30
does not gather with me *s* ....Matt 12:30

SCEPTER
s will not depart from Judah......Gen 49:10
and a *s* will rise out of Israel..... Num 24:17
king extends to him the gold *s* .....Esth 4:11
will break them with an iron *s*.......Ps 2:9
s of your kingdom is a *s* of....Ps 45:6
Judah my royal *s*.....................Ps 60:7
s is the *s* of your kingdom ....Heb 1:8

SCHEME
wicked *s* is enjoyable to a fool....Prov 10:23

SCHEMERS
Beware wicked *s*.....................Mic 2:1

SCHEMES
man who carries out wicked *s*.......Ps 37:7
they have sought many evil *s* ......Eccl 7:29

harbor up wicked *s* within you ......Jer 4:14
we are not ignorant of his *s*........2 Cor 2:11
stand against the *s* of the devil ..... Eph 6:11

SCOFFER
a *s* has never listened to rebuke... Prov 13:1

SCOFFERS
or sit in the assembly of *s* ....Ps 1:1
With arrogant *s* he is scornful .....Prov 3:34
last days blatant *s* will come........ 2 Pet 3:3
end of time there will come *s*......Jude 1:18

SCORCHED
sun came out, they were *s*.......Matt 13:6
were *s* by the terrible heat ....Rev 16:9

SCORCHING
and his slander is like a *s* fire .....Prov 16:27

SCORN
they have struck my cheek in *s*.... Job 16:10
do not *s* the Lord's discipline ....Heb 12:5

SCORNER
The *s* sought wisdom..............Prov 14:6
s is an abomination to people .... Prov 24:9

SCORNFUL
S people inflame a city .... Prov 29:8

SCORPION
will give him a *s*....................Luke 11:12

SCORPION ASCENT
An ascent on the south of the Dead Sea,
   Num 34:4
One border of Judah, Josh 15:3

SCORPIONS
and you live among *s*...............Ezek 2:6
to tread on snakes and *s*.........Luke 10:19
have tails and stingers like *s*........Rev 9:10

SCOUNDREL
A wicked *s* digs up evil.............Prov 16:27

SCRIBE
He was a *s* who was skilled.........Ezra 7:6
the stylus of an experienced *s*....... Ps 45:1
Where is the *s* ....Isa 33:18
and gave it to the *s* Baruch .... Jer 36:32

SCRIBES
Levites were *s*, officials ....2 Chr 34:13
royal *s* were summoned.......... Esth 3:12

SCRIPTURE
Today this *s* has been fulfilled .....Luke 4:21
the *s* cannot be broken............John 10:35
This took place to fulfill the *s*.....John 19:24
Now the passage of *s*..............Acts 8:32
For what does the *s* say............Rom 4:3
But the *s* imprisoned everything ...Gal 3:22
Every *s* is inspired by God ....2 Tim 3:16
you think the *s* means nothing ......Jas 4:5
prophecy of *s* ever comes about .. 2 Pet 1:20

SCRIPTURES
the *s* or the power of God ......Matt 22:29
so that the *s* would be fulfilled ..Mark 14:49
well-versed in the *s*...............Acts 18:24
they also do to the rest of the *s* .. 2 Pet 3:16

SCROLL
that they were written on a *s*......Job 19:23
written in the *s* pertains to me ......Ps 40:7
inscribe it on a *s* so that .... Isa 30:8
read the *s* of the LORD..............Isa 34:16
I am about to tell you in a *s*........ Jer 30:2
in a *s* all the LORD's words ....Jer 36:4
after the king had burned the *s*.... Jer 36:27
eat this *s*...........................Ezek 3:1
and there was a flying *s*...........Zech 5:1
A *s* was prepared before him.......Mal 3:16
in the *s* of the book...............Heb 10:7
s written on the front and back..... Rev 5:1
was able to open the *s*..............Rev 5:3
sky was split apart like a *s*.........Rev 6:14

SCRUTINIZED
You have *s* my inner motives........Ps 17:3

SCUM
You make us like filthy *s*...........Lam 3:45
We are the world's dirt and *s*.......1 Cor 4:13

SEA
he has thrown into the *s*...........Exod 15:4
depths of the *s* shook with fear..... Ps 77:16
Over here is the deep, wide *s*......Ps 104:25
Some traveled on the *s* in ships ...Ps 107:23
when he gave the *s* his decree....Prov 8:29
a mere shout I can dry up the *s*..... Isa 50:2
the faraway lands along the *s*.......Jer 31:10
just as the waters fill up the *s*...... Hab 2:14
the winds and the *s* obey him .... Matt 8:27
I spent adrift in the open *s*....... 2 Cor 11:25
something like a *s* of glass......... Rev 4:6
something like a *s* of glass.........Rev 15:2
and the *s* existed no more.......... Rev 21:1

SEAL
a cylinder *s* over your heart .... Song 8:6
put his *s* of approval on him......John 6:27
as a *s* of the righteousness .... Rom 4:11
bearing this *s* ....2 Tim 2:19
Lamb opened the second *s*..........Rev 6:3
Lamb opened the seventh *s* ....Rev 8:1

SEALED
offenses would be *s* up in a bag ....Job 14:17
these matters are closed and *s* .... Dan 12:9
also *s* us and gave us the Spirit ... 2 Cor 1:22
s for the day of redemption .... Eph 4:30
s from all the tribes................Rev 7:4

SEALER
You were the *s* of perfection .... Ezek 28:12

SEALS
and sealed with seven *s* ....Rev 5:1

SEAMLESS
the tunic was *s*....................John 19:23

SEARCH
glory of a king to *s* out a matter.. Prov 25:2
a time to *s*, and a time to give ...... Eccl 3:6

SEARCHED
s and investigated carefully........ 1 Pet 1:10

SEARCHES
And he who *s* our hearts .... Rom 8:27
For the Spirit *s* all things.......... 1 Cor 2:10
one who *s* minds and hearts....... Rev 2:23

SEASON
Threshing *s* will extend.............Lev 26:5

SEASONS
indicate *s* and days and years.......Gen 1:14
He changes times and *s*.............Dan 2:21
and months and *s* and years.......Gal 4:10
on the topic of times and *s* ....1 Thess 5:1

SEAT
See also MERCY SEAT
he might *s* him with princes ....Ps 113:8
the Pharisees sit on Moses' *s* ..... Matt 23:2
mercy *s* accessible through faith.. Rom 3:25
before the judgment *s* of Christ ..2 Cor 5:10
overshadowing the mercy *s* .... Heb 9:5

SEATED
unassuming and *s* on a donkey ....Matt 21:5
s on a donkey's colt................John 12:15
and *s* him at his right hand ....Eph 1:20
s at the right hand of God ....Col 3:1
And the one *s* on it ....Rev 4:3
and *s* on those thrones .... Rev 4:4
the prostitute is *s*................. Rev 17:15

SEATS
the best *s* in the synagogues...... Matt 23:6
the best *s* in the synagogues......Luke 11:43

SECLUSION
she kept herself in *s* ....Luke 1:24

SECOND
See also SECOND DEATH
there was morning, a *s* day.........Gen 1:8
The *s* is like it....................Matt 22:39
the *s* man is from heaven......... 1 Cor 15:47
And after the *s* curtain............. Heb 9:3
he will appear a *s* time............Heb 9:28
the *s* creature like an ox.............Rev 4:7
the *s* angel blew his trumpet .... Rev 8:8

SECOND DEATH
no way harmed by the *s* .... Rev 2:11
The *s* has no power .... Rev 20:6
is the *s*—the lake of fire .... Rev 20:14
That is the *s* .... Rev 21:8

SECRET
when I was made in *s* .... Ps 139:15
like a prostitute and with *s*
   intent .... Prov 7:10
reveal the *s* of another person .... Prov 25:9
I have not spoken in *s* .... Isa 45:19
and pray to your Father in *s* .... Matt 6:6
s that will not be made known .. Matt 10:26
The *s* of the kingdom of God ..... Mark 4:11
I have said nothing in *s* .... John 18:20
had been kept *s* for long ages .... Rom 16:25
things they do in *s* are shameful .... Eph 5:12

SECRETARY
the city *s* quieted the crowd ...... Acts 19:35

SECRETLY
s because he feared the Jewish ... John 19:38

SECRETS
reveal to you the *s* of wisdom .... Job 11:6
slandering others reveals *s* .... Prov 11:13
do not share *s* .... Mic 7:5
to know the *s* of the kingdom .... Matt 13:11
judge the *s* of human hearts .... Rom 2:16
The *s* of his heart are disclosed .. 1 Cor 14:25

SECURE
He is *s* at all times .... Ps 10:5
and made me feel *s* .... Ps 22:9
you made me *s* .... Ps 30:7
he wants his servant to be *s* .... Ps 35:27
even those who seem *s* .... Ps 39:5
my covenant with him is *s* .... Ps 89:28
Your throne has been *s* .... Ps 93:2
I will be *s* .... Ps 119:45
they stand *s* in heaven .... Ps 119:89
love your law are completely *s* ... Ps 119:165
He will *s* their release .... Jer 31:11
So give orders to *s* the tomb .... Matt 27:64

SECURED
he himself *s* eternal redemption ... Heb 9:12

SECURELY
the needy will rest *s* .... Isa 14:30
who lives *s* .... Isa 47:8
I will allow them to live *s* .... Hos 2:18

SECURITY
whose *s* is a spider's web .... Job 8:14
Who else will put up *s* for me ...... Job 17:3
let them rest in a feeling of *s* ...... Job 24:23
You are my *s* .... Job 31:24
The Lord is my source of *s* .... Ps 119:57
peace and result in lasting *s* .... Isa 32:17
nation that lives in peace and *s* ..... Jer 49:31
There is peace and *s* .... 1 Thess 5:3

SEDUCTIVENESS
the *s* of wealth choke the word ... Matt 13:22

SEE
You cannot *s* my face .... Exod 33:20
to *s* if you have it within you .... Deut 8:2
s which way you should go .... Josh 3:4
yet in my flesh I will *s* God .... Job 19:26
May your servants *s* your work ..... Ps 90:16
to *s* if it is worthwhile .... Eccl 2:1
man can *s* where he is going .... Eccl 2:14
for a person to *s* the sun .... Eccl 11:7
as easy to *s* as the color scarlet ..... Isa 1:18
they might *s* with their eyes .... Isa 6:10
he will *s* descendants .... Isa 53:10
will *s* that I make a distinction ...... Mal 3:18
for they will *s* God .... Matt 5:8
that people will *s* them fasting .... Matt 6:16
Why do you *s* the speck .... Matt 7:3
but fail to *s* the beam .... Matt 7:3
Although they *s* they do not *s* .... Matt 13:13
You will *s* greater things .... John 1:50
was overjoyed to *s* my day .... John 8:56
and was able to *s* .... John 9:11
causing a man born blind to *s* .... John 9:32

we would like to *s* Jesus .... John 12:21
world will not *s* me any longer ... John 14:19
so that they can *s* my glory ...... John 17:24
For three days he could not *s* .... Acts 9:9
But *s* how great he must be .... Heb 7:4
s your pure and reverent
   conduct .... 1 Pet 3:2
we will *s* him just as he is .... 1 John 3:2
and they will *s* his face .... Rev 22:4

SEED
who plant *s* by all the banks .... Isa 32:20
of heaven is like a mustard *s* ..... Matt 13:31
and the good *s* are the people .... Matt 13:38
The *s* is the word of God .... Luke 8:11
but from imperishable *s* .... 1 Pet 1:23
because God's *s* resides in him ... 1 John 3:9

SEEDS
do not cast *s* among thorns .... Jer 4:3
each of the *s* a body of its own .. 1 Cor 15:38

SEEK
See also SEEK THE LORD
if you *s* the Lord your God .... Deut 4:29
s to please me .... 2 Chr 7:14
for like you we *s* your God .... Ezra 4:2
and many will *s* your favor .... Job 11:19
With all my heart I *s* you .... Ps 119:10
and those who *s* me diligently ..... Prov 8:17
for people to *s* their own glory .. Prov 25:27
S me in vain .... Isa 45:19
They *s* me day after day .... Isa 58:2
who sent you to *s* my help .... Jer 37:7
will *s* the lost and bring back .... Ezek 34:16
Let us *s* to know the Lord .... Hos 6:3
S me so you can live .... Amos 5:4
and people should *s* instruction .... Mal 2:7
s and you will find .... Matt 7:7
came to *s* and to save the lost .... Luke 19:10
because I do not *s* my own will ... John 5:30
s glory and honor and .... Rom 2:7
Do not *s* your own good .... 1 Cor 10:24
we *s* the city that is to come ...... Heb 13:14

SEEK THE LORD
But if you *s* your God .... Deut 4:29
hearts of those who *s* rejoice ..... 1 Chr 16:10
s your God wholeheartedly ...... 1 Chr 22:19
his disease, he did not *s* .... 2 Chr 16:12
the land to *s* God of Israel .... Ezra 6:21
who *s* lack no good thing .... Ps 34:10
S and the strength he gives .... Ps 105:4
who *s* understand it all .... Prov 28:5
pursue godliness, who *s* .... Isa 51:1
S while he makes himself .... Isa 55:6
will turn and *s* their God .... Hos 3:5
S so you can live .... Amos 5:6
the rest of humanity may *s* .... Acts 15:17

SEEKING
keep *s* the things above .... Col 3:1

SEEKS
and the one who *s* finds .... Matt 7:8
for the Father *s* such people .... John 4:23
there is no one who *s* God .... Rom 3:11

SEEMS
a way that *s* right to a person ..... Prov 14:12

SEEN
I have *s* God face to face .... Gen 32:30
I have *s* all this .... Eccl 8:9
Have you *s* my beloved .... Song 3:3
Who has ever *s* this .... Isa 66:8
so that there is no one to be *s* ..... Zech 1:21
We have *s* incredible things ...... Luke 5:26
No one has ever *s* God .... John 1:18
heard his voice nor *s* his form ..... John 5:37
I have *s* while with the Father ..... John 8:38
who has *s* me has *s* the Father ..... John 14:9
what we have *s* and heard .... Acts 4:20
and caused him to be *s* .... Acts 10:40
Have I not *s* Jesus our Lord .... 1 Cor 9:1
can be *s* but at what cannot
   be *s* .... 2 Cor 4:18
whom no human has ever *s* ...... 1 Tim 6:16
what we have *s* with our eyes ..... 1 John 1:1

SEES
You are the God who *s* me .... Gen 16:13
he *s* all people .... Ps 33:13
s his fellow Christian in need ..... 1 John 3:17
anyone *s* his fellow Christian ..... 1 John 5:16

SEIR
See EDOM

SEIZE
anguish will *s* the inhabitants ..... Exod 15:14
trembling will *s* the leaders .... Exod 15:15
hiding place and *s* the city .... Josh 8:7
pointed it saying, "*S* him .... 1 Kgs 13:4
and *s* the houses they want .... Mic 2:2

SEIZED
You have *s* me .... Job 16:8
it had *s* him many times .... Luke 8:29
they *s* Paul and Silas .... Acts 16:19
s me while I was in the temple ... Acts 26:21
He *s* the dragon .... Rev 20:2

SELECTED
has *s* and brought from Egypt .... Deut 4:20
for I have *s* a king for myself ..... 1 Sam 16:1

SELF-CONFIDENCE
In my *s* I said .... Ps 30:6

SELF-CONTROL
s and not in drunkenness .... Eccl 10:17
s, and the coming judgment ...... Acts 24:25
because of your lack of *s* .... 1 Cor 7:5
But if they do not have *s* .... 1 Cor 7:9
must exercise *s* in everything .... 1 Cor 9:25
gentleness, and *s* .... Gal 5:23
with modesty and *s* .... 1 Tim 2:9
and love and holiness with *s* ..... 1 Tim 2:15
but of power and love and *s* ..... 2 Tim 1:7
slanderers, without *s*, savage ..... 2 Tim 3:3
knowledge, *s*; to *s*, perseverance ... 2 Pet 1:6

SELF-CONTROLLED
be *s* in all things .... 2 Tim 4:5
upright, devout, and *s* .... Titus 1:8
be *s*, pure, fulfilling their duties .... Titus 2:5
worldly desires and to live *s* ...... Titus 2:12
So be *s* and sober-minded .... 1 Pet 4:7

SELFISH
s ambition, slander .... 2 Cor 12:20
s rivalries, dissensions .... Gal 5:20
motivated by *s* ambition .... Phil 2:3

SELFISHNESS
where there is jealousy and *s* .... Jas 3:16

SELL
First *s* me your birthright .... Gen 25:31
s whatever you have and give ... Mark 10:21
must *s* his cloak and buy one .... Luke 22:36
was allowed to buy or *s* things .... Rev 13:17

SELLING
s, planting, building .... Luke 17:28
and they began *s* their property ... Acts 2:45

SEND
May God *s* his loyal love .... Ps 57:3
Quickly *s* your compassion .... Ps 79:8
Whom will I *s* .... Isa 6:8
he will *s* them a deliverer .... Isa 19:20
I did not *s* those prophets .... Jer 23:21
Son of Man will *s* his angels ...... Matt 13:41
S the crowds away .... Matt 14:15
And he will *s* his angels .... Matt 24:31
S us into the pigs .... Mark 5:12
began to *s* them out two by two .... Mark 6:7
S them away so that they can .... Mark 6:36
s them prophets and apostles .... Luke 11:49
and *s* Lazarus to dip the tip ...... Luke 16:24
For God did not *s* his Son .... John 3:17
to me I will never *s* away .... John 6:37
the Father will *s* in my name ..... John 14:26
I also *s* you .... John 20:21
do well to *s* them on their way ... 3 John 1:6

SENDING
am *s* you to Jesse in Bethlehem .. 1 Sam 16:1
I am *s* you out like sheep .... Matt 10:16
I am *s* you out like lambs .... Luke 10:3

s you what my Father
promised ....Luke 24:49
By *s* his own Son....................Rom 8:3

SENDS
s rain on the righteous and .... Matt 5:45

SENIR
See MOUNT HERMON

SENNACHERIB
Assyrian king (705–681 BC); son and
successor of Sargon II, 2 Kgs 18:13
Death of, by assassination, 2 Kgs 19:36–37

SENSE
adultery with a woman lacks *s* ... Prov 6:32
chases daydreams lacks *s* ......Prov 12:11
heeds reproof shows good *s* ......Prov 15:5
The one who lacks *s* .... Prov 17:18
who respond with good *s* ....Prov 26:16
like children who have no *s* .... Jer 4:22

SENSELESS
their *s* hearts were darkened ...... Rom 1:21
s, covenant-breakers, heartless.... Rom 1:31

SENSITIVE
You displayed a *s* spirit ....2 Kgs 22:19

SENT
and *s* the dove out again........... Gen 8:12
I AM has *s* me to you ....Exod 3:14
Moses *s* to investigate the land...Num 13:16
one the LORD *s* to anoint you..... 1 Sam 15:1
the Sovereign LORD has *s* me...... Isa 48:16
that I *s* this commandment......... Mal 2:4
receives the one who *s* me ......Matt 10:40
but the one who *s* me ....Mark 9:37
At harvest time he *s* a slave ..... Mark 12:2
has *s* me to proclaim release ..... Luke 4:18
John the Baptist has *s* us to you .. Luke 7:20
welcomes the one who *s* me .....Luke 9:48
rejects the one who *s* me........Luke 10:16
A man came, *s* from God .... John 1:6
the will of the one who *s* me ...... John 6:38
the Father who *s* me testifies......John 8:18
as you *s* me into the world .... John 17:18
Just as the Father has *s* me ......John 20:21
they to preach unless they
are *s*.......................Rom 10:15
the Holy Spirit *s* from heaven ..... 1 Pet 1:12
that he loved us and *s* his Son .. 1 John 4:10
has *s* his angel to show .... Rev 22:6

SENTENCE
will execute his *s* on the earth.... Rom 9:28

SENTRIES
angelic *s* who used the flame...... Gen 3:24

SEPARATE
he must *s* himself from wine ...... Num 6:3
will be able to *s* me from you...... Ruth 1:17
S yourselves from the local.......Ezra 10:11
let no one *s*.......................Matt 19:6
s us from the love of Christ....... Rom 8:35
s from sinners .... Heb 7:26

SEPARATED
in their deaths were they *s* ...... 2 Sam 1:23
poor person is *s* from his friend ...Prov 19:4

SEPARATES
repeats a matter *s* close friends ...Prov 17:9

SERAPHS
S stood over him ....Isa 6:2

SERGIUS PAULUS
Roman proconsul of Cyprus, converted by
Paul, Acts 13:7–12

SERIOUS
have committed a very *s* sin.....Exod 32:30

SERPENT
Now the *s* was shrewder ....Gen 3:1
The *s* tricked me....................Gen 3:13
like a deaf *s* that does not hear.....Ps 58:4
underfoot a young lion and a *s* ......Ps 91:13
Their tongues wound like a *s*.......Ps 140:3
Just as Moses lifted up the *s* ......John 3:14
ancient *s*, the one called the devil ..Rev 12:9

SERPENT'S
will grow out of the *s* root......... Isa 14:29

SERPENTS
the venom of *s* within him........Job 20:14
wise as *s* and innocent as doves ..Matt 10:16

SERVANT
replied, "I am Ruth, your *s* .... Ruth 3:9
He said to his *s* ....1 Sam 20:36
please accept a gift from your *s* .. 2 Kgs 5:15
the prophet's *s* ....2 Kgs 8:4
a *s* longing for the evening .... Job 7:2
Deliver this son of your female *s* ...Ps 86:16
Be kind to your *s* ....Ps 119:17
will be a *s* to the wise person..... Prov 11:29
A *s* who acts wisely................Prov 17:2
s cannot be corrected by words ..Prov 29:19
My *s* is truly blind .... Isa 42:19
is my *s* whom I have chosen......Matt 12:18
great among you must be
your *s*......................Matt 20:26
he must be last of all and *s*
of all...........................Mark 9:35
great among you must be
your *s*......................Mark 10:43
I am a *s* of the Lord................Luke 1:38
the humble state of his *s* ....Luke 1:48
s who knew his master's will .... Luke 12:47
my *s* will be too..................John 12:26
against your holy *s* Jesus..........Acts 4:27
a *s* and witness to the things .....Acts 26:16
it is God's *s* for your well-being....Rom 13:4
that Christ has become a *s* ...... Rom 15:8
be a good *s* of Christ Jesus......1 Tim 4:6

SERVANTS
the Israelites are my *s* .... Lev 25:42
as all his *s* and priests ....2 Kgs 10:19
If God puts no trust in his *s*.......Job 4:18
for all things are your *s*............Ps 119:91
She has sent out her female *s* ......Prov 9:3
s of our God ....Isa 61:6
in charge of his household *s* ..... Luke 12:42
my *s* would be fighting ....John 18:36
s of Christ and stewards............1 Cor 4:1
But as God's *s* ....2 Cor 6:4
Are they *s* of Christ...............2 Cor 11:23

SERVE
See also SERVE THE LORD
in order that they may *s* me ......Exod 8:1
he must *s* with you ....Lev 25:40
s him, and take oaths..............Deut 6:13
I will *s* the LORD ....Ps 116:9
lack a male descendant to *s* me ...Jer 35:19
No one can *s* two masters .... Matt 6:24
I myself *s* the law of God .... Rom 7:25
enthusiastic in spirit, *s* the Lord ...Rom 12:11
but through love *s* one another..... Gal 5:13
and they *s* him day and night ....Rev 7:15

SERVE THE LORD
so that they may *s* their God ..... Exod 10:7
Go, *s* as you have requested......Exod 12:31
You must *s* your God............Exod 23:25
S with all your heart............. 1 Sam 12:20
to *s* God of Israel ....2 Chr 33:16
S in fear. Repent in terror ....Ps 2:11
s in the land of the living .... Ps 116:9
who *s*, are in mourning..............Joel 1:9
those who *s* weep ....Joel 2:17
enthusiastic in spirit, *s*............Rom 12:11
Lord as the reward. *S* Christ........Col 3:24

SERVED
s foreign gods in your own land .....Jer 5:19
not come to be *s* but to serve ...Matt 20:28
not come to be *s* but to serve ...Mark 10:45
worshiped and *s* the creation......Rom 1:25

SERVES
If anyone *s* me....................John 12:26
Whoever *s*, do so with............ 1 Pet 4:11

SERVICE
performed the *s* of their God.... Neh 12:45
commissions him for *s*..............Isa 41:2
of entering the king's royal *s* ....Dan 1:4

Get dressed for *s* ....Luke 12:35
think he is offering *s* to God.......John 16:2
is your reasonable *s* .... Rom 12:1
one in military *s* gets entangled ...2 Tim 2:4
s, and steadfast endurance ....Rev 2:19

SERVING
boy Samuel was *s* the LORD ......1 Sam 2:11
While they were *s* the Lord........ Acts 13:2
s the Lord with all humility ......Acts 20:19
as though *s* the Lord................Eph 6:7

SET
See also SET APART
and *s* it apart as holy ....Exod 20:11
I have *s* before you today life.... Deut 30:15
you have *s* his limit .... Job 14:5
On what were its bases *s* ....Job 38:6
I am about to *s* your stones.........Isa 54:11
I *s* you apart ....Jer 1:5
must *s* the Sabbath day apart.......Jer 17:24
is *s* on their own advantage...... Ezek 33:31
and the truth will *s* you free ....John 8:32
S them apart in the truth......... John 17:17
And I *s* myself apart .... John 17:19
who *s* me apart from birth ....Gal 1:15
no one can *s* it aside .... Gal 3:15
the first to *s* our hope on Christ .... Eph 1:12
the one in whom my faith is *s* .... 2 Tim 1:12
to *s* us free from every kind ...... Titus 2:14

SET APART
lambs that you have *s* .... Gen 21:29
S to me every firstborn male ......Exod 13:2
the LORD *s* the tribe of Levi....... Deut 10:8
it must be *s* for the LORD .... Josh 6:17
Israel was *s* to the LORD ....Jer 2:3
s as the holy allotment .... Ezek 45:6
the Father and sent into ....John 10:36
they too many be truly *s*.......... John 17:19

SETH
Third son of Adam, Gen 4:25
In Christ's ancestry, Luke 3:38

SETTING
s your mind on God's interests ...Matt 16:23

SETTLE
S in the land and maintain........... Ps 37:3

SETTLED
and *s* in the Gerar Valley .... Gen 26:17
and *s* his accounts with them.... Matt 25:19

SETTLEMENTS
people will live in peaceful *s*........Isa 32:18

SETTLER
a temporary *s* ....Gen 23:4

SETTLERS
temporary *s*, with me............. Lev 25:23
foreigners and temporary *s* ..... 1 Chr 29:15

SEVEN
cows ate up the *s* fat cows........Gen 41:20
s priests carrying the *s* rams' ......Josh 6:13
The child sneezed *s* times ....2 Kgs 4:35
Joash was *s* years old .... 2 Chr 24:1
S times a day I praise you .... Ps 119:164
righteous person will fall *s* times .Prov 24:16
there are *s* abominations .... Prov 26:25
S women will grab hold ....Isa 4:1
for the *s* days of the festival ......Ezek 45:21
let *s* periods of time go by......... Dan 4:16
will be a period of *s* weeks .... Dan 9:25
took the *s* loaves and the fish.....Matt 15:36
As many as *s* times ....Matt 18:21
whose wife of the *s* will she be .. Matt 22:28
from whom *s* demons had gone.... Luke 8:2
it goes and brings *s* other spirits.. Luke 11:26
s men who are well-attested ....Acts 6:3
to the *s* churches ....Rev 1:4
I saw *s* golden lampstands........ Rev 1:12
The mystery of the *s* stars........Rev 1:20
has firm grasp on the *s* stars....... Rev 2:1
s spirits of God and the *s* stars....... Rev 3:1
S flaming torches....................Rev 4:5
and sealed with *s* seals .... Rev 5:1
Then I saw the *s* angels..............Rev 8:2

s thunders sounded their voices....Rev 10:3
s thousand people were killed......Rev 11:13
red dragon that had *s* heads........Rev 12:3
It had ten horns and *s* heads........Rev 13:1
s angels who have *s* final plagues...Rev 15:1
s angels who had the *s* bowls........Rev 17:1
s angels who had the *s* bowls........Rev 21:9

SEVENTH
the *s* day God finished the work....Gen 2:2
seventeenth day of the *s* month....Gen 8:4
and on the *s* day there will be ....Exod 12:16
but on the *s* day ....Exod 16:26
the Lamb opened the *s* seal ....Rev 8:1
in the days when the *s* angel.......Rev 10:7
the *s* angel blew his trumpet ....Rev 11:15
the *s* angel poured out his bowl ...Rev 16:17
sixth carnelian, the *s* chrysolite...Rev 21:20

SEVENTY
s weeks have been determined ...Dan 9:24
Then the *s* returned with joy .....Luke 10:17

SEVERE
Our wound is *s* ....Jer 10:19
because you are a *s* man.........Luke 19:21

SEVERELY
You *s* discipline people ....Ps 39:11
The LORD *s* punished me ....Ps 118:18

SEVERITY
because of the *s* of the siege ....Deut 28:53

SEWS
s a patch of unshrunk cloth....... Mark 2:21

SEXUAL
and from *s* immorality............Acts 15:20
that *s* immorality exists ....1 Cor 5:1
body is not for *s* immorality ....1 Cor 6:13
Flee *s* immorality ....1 Cor 6:18
keep away from *s* immorality ...1 Thess 4:3
and commit *s* immorality............Rev 2:14
repent of her *s* immorality ....Rev 2:21

SEXUALLY
associate with *s* immoral people ..1 Cor 5:9
the *s* immoral....................Rev 21:8

SHACKLES
tear off the *s* they've put on us ...... Ps 2:3
The *s* hurt his feet ....Ps 105:18
and their nobles in iron *s* ....Ps 149:8

SHADE
I delight to sit in his *s* .... Song 2:3
to provide *s* from the heat........... Isa 4:6
safety in Egypt's protective *s* .... Isa 30:2
wild birds can nest in its *s* ....Mark 4:32

SHADOW
and the deepest *s* claim it ....Job 3:5
darkness and the deepest *s*........Job 10:21
he flees like a *s* ....Job 14:2
my whole frame is but a *s* ....Job 17:7
Hide me in the *s* of your wings ......Ps 17:8
days like a *s* that disappears........Ps 144:4
for they pass away like a *s*.........Eccl 6:12
and putting on eye *s*...............Jer 4:30
the *s* of the things to come ....Col 2:17
a *s* of the good things to come .....Heb 10:1

SHADOWS
the dawn arrives and the *s* flee....Song 2:17

SHADRACH
Hananiah's Babylonian name, Dan 1:3, 7
Cast into the fiery furnace, Dan 3:1–28

SHAFT
the key to the *s* of the abyss........Rev 9:1

SHAKE
Make them *s* violently..............Ps 69:23
steady the knees that *s*.............Isa 35:3
the nations *s* at your presence.....Isa 64:2
so the thresholds *s*...............Amos 9:1
I will *s* the family of Israel ....Amos 9:9
mountains see you, they *s*........ Hab 3:10
again *s* the sky and the earth ...... Hag 2:6
s the dust off your feet ....Matt 10:14
s the dust off your feet ....Mark 6:11

but could not *s* it ....Luke 6:48
once more *s* not only the earth... Heb 12:26

SHAKEN
lives like this will never be *s* .... Ps 15:5
I will not be *s* ....Ps 16:8
For he will never be *s*..............Ps 112:6
and he was visibly *s*............... Dan 5:9
A reed *s* by the wind............... Matt 11:7
powers of heaven will be *s* ......Matt 24:29
The guards were *s* ....Matt 28:4
powers in the heavens will
   be *s*........................... Mark 13:25
were assembled together
   was *s* .... Acts 4:31
foundations of the prison
   were *s* ....Acts 16:26
easily *s* from your composure ...2 Thess 2:2

SHAKES
who *s* the earth out of its place......Job 9:6
LORD's shout *s* the wilderness.......Ps 29:8
the earth *s*..........................Ps 68:8
He *s* the nations ....Isa 30:28
the earth *s*.........................Jer 10:10
taunts her and *s* his fist........... Zeph 2:15

SHAKING
and saw that they were *s* ....Jer 4:24
drink your water with
   anxious *s* ....Ezek 12:18

SHALLUM
See JEHOAHAZ

SHALMANESER
Assyrian king, 2 Kgs 17:3

SHAME
God has taken away my *s*.........Gen 30:23
to *s* and humiliate myself........2 Sam 6:22
try to turn my honor into *s*...........Ps 4:2
May they die in *s* .... Ps 83:17
Spare me *s* and humiliation........ Ps 119:22
and with *s* comes a reproach ......Prov 18:3
All who leave you will suffer *s*......Jer 17:13
lasting *s* and lasting disgrace ......Jer 23:40
Israel will be put to *s* ....Hos 10:6
will never again be put to *s*.......Joel 2:26
Yet the unjust know no *s* ....Zeph 3:5
will not be put to *s*................ Rom 9:33
thinks foolish to *s* the wise ....1 Cor 1:27
I say this to your *s* ....1 Cor 6:5
they exult in their *s*.................Phil 3:19
disregarding its *s* ....Heb 12:2
put to *s* when they accuse you ....1 Pet 3:16

SHAMEFUL
sleeps during harvest is a *s* son....Prov 10:5
in secret are *s* even to mention.....Eph 5:12

SHAMGAR
Judge of Israel; strikes down 600
   Philistines, Judg 3:31

SHAMMAH
Son of Jesse, 1 Sam 16:9
Also called "Shimea," 1 Chr 2:13
—One of David's mighty men, 2 Sam 23:11
Also called "Shammoth the Harorite,"
   1 Chr 11:27

SHAMMOTH THE HARORITE
One of David's men: *see* SHAMMAH

SHAPE
earth was without *s* and empty......Gen 1:2
s of this world is passing away.....1 Cor 7:31

SHAPHAN
Scribe under Josiah, 2 Kgs 22:3–14

SHARD
one who is like a mere *s*........... Isa 45:9

SHARE
with its joy no one else can *s* .....Prov 14:10
to *s* the spoils with the proud ....Prov 16:19
s your food with the hungry .... Isa 58:7
give me the *s* of the estate ......Luke 15:12
as worthy to *s* in that age........Luke 20:35
you have no *s* with me............John 13:8

for we all *s* the one bread ....1 Cor 10:17
that as you *s* in our sufferings ..... 2 Cor 1:7
must *s* all good things ....Gal 6:6
he will have something to *s*........ Eph 4:28
to *s* in his sufferings ....Phil 3:10
to *s* in the saints' inheritance ....Col 1:12
you came to *s* with others .... Heb 10:33
not neglect to do good and to *s* ...Heb 13:16
away his *s* in the tree of life........Rev 22:19

SHARED
have *s* in their spiritual things ....Rom 15:27

SHARES
Whoever *s* with a thief ....Prov 29:24
Everyone *s* the same fate.......... Eccl 9:2
and made four *s* ....John 19:23
and as one who *s* in the glory.......1 Pet 5:1
s with you in the persecution........Rev 1:9

SHARING
a *s* in the blood of Christ ....1 Cor 10:16
generosity of your *s* with them... 2 Cor 9:13

SHARON
Coastal plain between Joppa and Mt.
   Carmel, 1 Chr 27:29
Famed for roses, Song 2:1
Inhabitants of, turn to the Lord, Acts 9:35

SHARP
it is as effective as a *s* razor..........Ps 52:2
s as a two-edged sword ....Prov 5:4
you like a *s* threshing sledge........ Isa 41:15
my mouth like a *s* sword ....Isa 49:2
take a *s* sword and use it ....Ezek 5:1
and a *s* double-edged sword........ Rev 1:16
has the *s* double-edged sword......Rev 2:12
and a *s* sickle in his hand ....Rev 14:14

SHARPEN
s their tongues like swords ....Ps 64:3
a workman does not *s* its edge ... Eccl 10:10

SHATTERED
and he has *s* me ....Job 16:12

SHAVE
must *s* his consecrated head ..... Num 6:18
s off the seven braids of his hair.. Judg 16:19
to *s* the hair off the head ....Isa 7:20
will *s* their heads in mourning .....Jer 48:37

SHAVED
s off half of each one's beard....2 Sam 10:4
they may have their heads *s*......Acts 21:24

SHEALTIEL
Son of King Jeconiah (Jehoiachin) and
   father of Zerubbabel, 1Chr 3:17

SHEAR JASHUB
Symbolic name given to Isaiah's son, Isa 7:3

SHEATH
Return it to its *s* ....Ezek 21:30
Put your sword back into its *s* .....John 18:11

SHEBA
Land of, occupied by Sabeans, famous
   traders, Job 1:15; Ps 72:10
Queen of, visits Solomon; marvels at his
   wisdom, 1 Kgs 10:1–13
Mentioned by Christ, Matt 12:42

SHEBNA
Treasurer under Hezekiah, Isa 22:15
Demoted to position of scribe, 2 Kgs 19:2
Man of pride and luxury, replaced by
   Eliakim, Isa 22:19–21

SHECHEM
Son of Hamor; rapes Dinah, Jacob's
   daughter, Gen 34:1–31
—Ancient city of Ephraim, Gen 33:18
Joshua's farewell address delivered at,
   Josh 24:1–25
Supports Abimelech; destroyed, Judg 9
Rebuilt by Jeroboam I, 1 Kgs 12:25

SHED
They *s* innocent blood.............Ps 106:38
Do not *s* any more tears...........Jer 31:16
has been *s* since the beginning ...Luke 11:50

of your witness Stephen was *s* .. Acts 22:20
Their feet are swift to *s* blood . . . . Rom 3:15

SHEDDING
without the *s* of blood there is . . . . Heb 9:22

SHEEP
like *s* that have no shepherd. . . . . 2 Chr 18:16
us over like *s* to be eaten . . . . Ps 44:11
like *s* at the slaughtering block . . . . Ps 44:22
meadows are clothed with *s* . . . . Ps 65:13
your people like a flock of *s* . . . . Ps 77:20
the *s* of your pasture . . . . Ps 79:13
lead Joseph like a flock of *s* . . . . Ps 80:1
the *s* he owns . . . . Ps 95:7
the *s* of his pasture . . . . Ps 100:3
for his families like a flock of *s* . . Ps 107:41
have wandered off like a lost *s* . . . Ps 119:176
had wandered off like *s* . . . . Isa 53:6
a *s* silent before her shearers . . . . Isa 53:7
away like *s* to be slaughtered . . . . Jer 12:3
shepherds watch over their *s* . . . . Jer 23:1
the young *s*, and the calves . . . . Jer 31:12
My people have been lost *s* . . . . Jer 50:6
but you do not feed the *s* . . . . Ezek 34:3
My *s* wandered over all. . . . . Ezek 34:6
I myself will search for my *s* . . . . . Ezek 34:11
between one *s* and another. . . . . . Ezek 34:17
my *s*, the *s* of my pasture . . . . Ezek 34:31
lion among the flocks of *s* . . . . Mic 5:8
the *s* disappear from the pen . . . . . . Hab 3:17
like *s* without a shepherd. . . . . Matt 9:36
the lost *s* of the house of Israel. . . Matt 10:6
like *s* surrounded by wolves . . . . . Matt 10:16
lost *s* of the house of Israel. . . . . . Matt 15:24
If someone owns a hundred *s* . . . Matt 18:12
separates the *s* from the goats . . Matt 25:32
He will put the *s* on his right . . . . Matt 25:33
were like *s* without a shepherd. . . Mark 6:34
and the *s* will be scattered. . . . . . Mark 14:27
has a hundred *s* and loses one. . . . . Luke 15:4
after plowing or shepherding *s* . . . Luke 17:7
is the shepherd of the *s* . . . . John 10:2
and the *s* hear his voice. . . . . John 10:3
have other *s* that do not come. . . . John 10:16
because you are not my *s* . . . . John 10:26
Shepherd my *s*. . . . . John 21:16
Feed my *s*. John 21:17
was led like a *s* to slaughter . . . . Acts 8:32
as *s* to be slaughtered . . . . Rom 8:36
the great shepherd of the *s* . . . . . . Heb 13:20
you were going astray like *s* . . . . . 1 Pet 2:25

SHEEPFOLD
that do not come from this *s* . . . . . John 10:16

SHEEPFOLDS
you lie down among the *s* . . . . Ps 68:13

SHEET
like a large *s* descending. . . . . Acts 10:11

SHELTER
rocky summit where I take *s* . . . . 2 Sam 22:3
shield to all who take *s* in him . . 2 Sam 22:31
who take *s* in you be happy. . . . . Ps 5:11
S them so that those who . . . . Ps 5:11
though the LORD is their *s* . . . . Ps 14:6
rocky summit where I take *s* . . . . Ps 18:2
shield to all who take *s* in him . . . . . Ps 18:30
give me *s* in the day of danger . . . . . . Ps 27:5
you conceal them in a *s*. . . . . Ps 31:20
the one who takes *s* in him . . . . Ps 34:8
For in you I have taken *s* . . . . Ps 57:1
God is our *s*. . . . . Ps 62:8
I have taken *s*. Ps 71:1
but you are my secure *s* . . . . Ps 71:7
He will *s* you with his wings . . . . Ps 91:4
and my God will *s* me . . . . Ps 94:22
better to take *s* in the LORD . . . . Ps 118:8
You are my *s*. Ps 142:5
a *s* from the rainstorm. . . . . Isa 25:4

SHELTERS
See also FEAST OF SHELTERS
is the Feast of *S* for seven days . . . Lev 23:34
You must live in temporary *s* . . . . . Lev 23:42
the Feast of *S* for seven days . . . . . Deut 16:13

should live in temporary *s* . . . . Neh 8:14
you are the God who *s* me. . . . . Ps 43:2
I will make three *s* . . . . Matt 17:4
Jewish Feast of *S* was near. . . . . John 7:2

SHEM
Oldest son of Noah, Gen 5:32
Escapes the flood, Gen 7:13
Receives a blessing, Gen 9:23, 26
Ancestor of Semitic people, Gen 10:22–32

SHEMAIAH
Prophet of Judah, 1 Kgs 12:22–24
Explains Shishak's invasion as divine
    punishment, 2 Chr 12:5–8
Records Rehoboam's reign, 2 Chr 12:15

SHEMER
Sells Omri the hill on which Samaria is
    built, 1 Kgs 16:23–24

SHEOL
are turned back and sent to *S* . . . . Ps 9:17
will not abandon me to *S* . . . . Ps 16:10
you pulled me up from *S* . . . . Ps 30:3
my life from the power of *S* . . . . Ps 55:15
the snares of *S* confronted me . . . . . Ps 116:3
S below is stirred up about you . . . . Isa 14:9
S does not give you thanks . . . . Isa 38:18
them from the power of *S*. . . . . Hos 13:14
from the belly of *S* I cried out . . . . . Jonah 2:2

SHEPHERD
the God who has been my *s* . . . . . . Gen 48:15
You will *s* my people Israel . . . . 2 Sam 5:2
The LORD is my *s* . . . . Ps 23:1
with death as their *s* . . . . Ps 49:14
and made him the *s* of Jacob . . . . . . Ps 78:71
Like a *s* he tends his flock . . . . Isa 40:11
the one I appointed as *s* . . . . Isa 44:28
scattered because they had
    no *s*. . . . . Ezek 34:5
I will set one *s* over them. . . . . Ezek 34:23
s salvages from the lion's
    mouth . . . . Amos 3:12
Woe to the worthless *s* who. . . . . . Zech 11:17
I will strike the *s* . . . . Matt 26:31
I am the good *s* . . . . John 10:11
S my sheep . . . . John 21:16
to *s* the church of God. . . . . Acts 20:28
the great *s* of the sheep . . . . Heb 13:20
when the Chief *S* appears . . . . 1 Pet 5:4
will *s* them and lead them . . . . Rev 7:17

SHEPHERDS
s who have no understanding . . . . . . Isa 56:11
like *s* watch over their sheep . . . . Jer 23:1
Their *s* have allowed them . . . . Jer 50:6
s did not search for my flock . . . . . Ezek 34:8
Now there were *s* nearby. . . . . Luke 2:8

SHESHBAZZAR
Prince of Judah, Ezra 1:8, 11

SHETHAR-BOZENAI
Official of Persia, Ezra 5:3, 6

SHIBAH
See BEER SHEBA

SHIELD
s and the one who will reward. . . . . Gen 15:1
s the ark with the special curtain . . Exod 40:3
protective *s* and your exalted. . . . Deut 33:29
the *s* of warriors was defiled . . . . . 2 Sam 1:21
my *s*, the horn that saves me . . . . 2 Sam 22:3
s to all who take shelter in him . 2 Sam 22:31
I will *s* this city and rescue it. . . . . 2 Kgs 19:34
are a *s* that protects me . . . . Ps 3:3
Like a *s* you protect them . . . . Ps 5:12
my *s*, the horn that saves me . . . . Ps 18:2
s to all who take shelter in him. . . . . Ps 18:30
You give me your protective *s* . . . . . Ps 18:35
he is our deliverer and *s* . . . . Ps 33:20
His faithfulness is like a *s* . . . . Ps 91:4
are my hiding place and my *s* . . . . . Ps 119:114
by taking up the *s* of faith . . . . Eph 6:16

SHIELDS
large *s* of hammered gold . . . . 2 Chr 9:15

SHIHOR
Name given to the Nile, Isa 23:3
Israel's southwestern border, Josh 13:3

SHILOH
Center of worship, Judg 18:31
Headquarters for division of Promised
    Land, Josh 18:1, 10
Benjamites seize women of, Judg 21:19–23
Ark of the covenant taken from,
    1 Sam 4:3–11
Punishment given to, Jer 7:12–15

SHIMEA
Son of Jesse: *see* SHAMMAH

SHIMEI
Benjamite; insults David, 2 Sam 16:5–13
Pardoned, but confined, 2 Sam 19:16–23
Breaks agreement; executed by Solomon,
    1 Kgs 2:39–46

SHIMSHAI
Scribe opposing the Jews, Ezra 4:8–24

SHINAR
Tower built at, Gen 11:2–9

SHINE
LORD make his face to *s* upon
    you . . . . Num 6:25
and the moon does not *s* . . . . Isa 13:10
Arise! *S*! For your light arrives . . . . . . Isa 60:1
wise will *s* like the brightness . . . . . . Dan 12:3
let your light *s* before people . . . . . Matt 5:16
righteous will *s* like the sun . . . . . . Matt 13:43
you *s* as lights in the world . . . . Phil 2:15
the sun or the moon to *s* on it . . . . . Rev 21:23

SHINES
light *s* on those who live in . . . . Isa 9:2
splendor of the LORD *s* on you . . . . . Isa 60:1
but the LORD *s* on you . . . . Isa 60:2
the light *s* on in the darkness . . . . John 1:5

SHINING
to a light *s* in a murky place . . . . 2 Pet 1:19
and the true light is already *s* . . . . . 1 John 2:8
His face shone like the sun *s* . . . . Rev 1:16

SHINY
all you *s* stars . . . . Ps 148:3

SHIP
the way of a *s* in the sea . . . . Prov 30:19
merchant *s* heading to Tarshish . . . Jonah 1:3
We found a *s* crossing over . . . . Acts 21:2
and some on pieces of the *s* . . . . . Acts 27:44

SHIPHRAH
Hebrew midwife, Exod 1:15

SHIPS
Some traveled on the sea in *s* . . . . . Ps 107:23
She was like the merchant *s* . . . . . . Prov 31:14
for all the impressive *s* . . . . Isa 2:16
Look at *s* too . . . . Jas 3:4

SHIPWRECK
suffered *s* in regard to the faith . . . . 1 Tim 1:19

SIRION
See MOUNT HERMON

SHITTIM
Spies sent from, Josh 2:1
Israel's last camp before crossing the
    Jordan, Josh 3:1

SHOCKED
who passes by it will be *s* . . . . 1 Kgs 9:8
I am absolutely *s*. . . . . Ps 143:4

SHOCKING
horrible and *s* is going on. . . . . Jer 5:30

SHONE
that the skin of Moses' face *s*. . . . . Exod 34:35
His face *s* like the sun. . . . . Matt 17:2
and a light *s* in the prison cell . . . . . Acts 12:7

SHOOK
the whole mountain *s* violently . . . Exod 19:18
the earth *s*, the heavens poured . . . . Judg 5:4
so loudly that the ground *s* . . . . 1 Sam 4:5
The earth heaved and *s*. . . . . 2 Sam 22:8

The earth heaved and *s*............. Ps 18:7
The earth trembled and *s*.......... Ps 77:18
Is this the man who *s* the earth..... Isa 14:16
you *s* your head in contempt...... Jer 48:27
They sneered and *s* their heads.... Lam 2:15
earth *s* and the rocks were split .. Matt 27:51
they *s* the dust off their feet.......Acts 13:51

SHOOT
But God will *s* at them............. Ps 64:7
s will grow out of Jesse's root .... Isa 11:1

SHOOTS
its *s* spread over its garden......... Job 8:16
put forth *s* like a new plant......... Job 14:9
both the *s* and stalk in one day ..... Isa 9:14
His young *s* will grow............. Hos 14:6

SHORE
put out a little way from the *s* .... Luke 5:3

SHORT
You have cut *s* his youth........... Ps 89:45
those days had not been cut *s* .. Matt 24:22
Lord had not cut *s* those days ... Mark 13:20
being a *s* man he could not see.... Luke 19:3
and fall *s* of the glory of God ...... Rom 3:23
comes *s* of the grace of God....... Heb 12:15

SHORTENED
life span of the wicked will be *s* .. Prov 10:27

SHORTS
Go and buy some linen *s* .... Jer 13:1

SHOULD
You *s* have done these things.... Matt 23:23
do not know how we *s* pray ...... Rom 8:26
talking about things they *s* not ... 1 Tim 5:13

SHOULDERS
He *s* responsibility.................. Isa 9:6

SHOUT
the sea and everything in it *s* ... 1 Chr 16:32
they began to *s* and praise...... 2 Chr 20:22
S for joy, all you who are .... Ps 32:11
Play skillfully as you *s* out .... Ps 33:3
s for joy and rejoice................. Ps 35:27
God gives a *s* .... Ps 46:6
S out to God in celebration.......... Ps 47:1
S for joy to God..................... Ps 81:1
Break out in a joyful *s* and sing..... Ps 98:4
Your *s* made the waters retreat..... Ps 104:7
will enter Zion with a happy *s* ..... Isa 35:10
will enter Zion with a happy *s* ...... Isa 51:11
But at midnight there was a *s* ..... Matt 25:6

SHOUTED
enemy *s* in the LORD's temple ..... Lam 2:7

SHOUTING
of one *s* in the wilderness .... Matt 3:3
But they kept on *s*................. Luke 23:21

SHOUTS
demanding with loud *s* .... Luke 23:23

SHOW
to the land that I will *s* you .... Gen 12:1
did he *s* his loving favor .... Deut 10:15
children who *s* no loyalty....... Deut 32:20
May God *s* us his favor .... Ps 67:1
s us your loyal love .... Ps 85:7
May no one *s* him kindness........ Ps 109:12
no longer *s* their embarrassment.. Isa 29:22
I will *s* them abundant peace .... Jer 33:6
and *s* brotherhood................. Zech 7:9
to *s* them a sign from heaven...... Matt 16:1
go and *s* him his fault............ Matt 18:15
because you *s* no partiality ...... Matt 22:16
S me the coin used for the tax... Matt 22:19
s yourself to the world .... John 7:4
s us the Father..................... John 14:8
S us the Father..................... John 14:9
And now I will *s* you a way....... 1 Cor 12:31
S me your faith without works ..... Jas 2:18
I can *s* you what must happen....... Rev 4:1

SHOWED
with Joseph and *s* him kindness .. Gen 39:21
and the LORD *s* him a tree .... Exod 15:25
and *s* him all the kingdoms .... Matt 4:8

s him in a flash all the kingdoms... Luke 4:5
s them his hands and his feet....Luke 24:40
s them his hands and his side....John 20:20
and *s* me the holy city .... Rev 21:10

SHOWERS
With rain *s* you soften its soil....... Ps 65:10
you cause abundant *s* to fall........ Ps 68:9
Do the skies themselves send *s*... Jer 14:22
and *s* deliverance on you .... Hos 10:12

SHOWN
you have *s* me great kindness .....Gen 19:19
all the faithful love you have *s*.... Gen 32:10
have *s* loyalty and integrity .... Judg 9:16
I have *s* you many good deeds... John 10:32

SHOWS
LORD *s* the godly special favor........ Ps 4:3
he *s* his enemies his power .... Isa 42:13
and *s* him everything he does .... John 5:20
God *s* no favoritism.................. Gal 2:6

SHREWD
s person conceals knowledge..... Prov 12:23

SHREWDLY
because he acted *s* .... Luke 16:8

SHREWDNESS
impart *s* to the morally naive....... Prov 1:4

SHRINES
who made silver *s* of Artemis..... Acts 19:24

SHROUDED
He *s* himself in darkness............. Ps 18:11
You *s* yourself with a cloud....... Lam 3:44

SHRUB
went and sat down under a *s* ..... 1 Kgs 19:4

SHUNAMMITE
Abishag, David's nurse, 1 Kgs 1:3, 15
—Woman who cared for Elisha, 2 Kgs 4:8–12

SHUNEM
Town of Issachar, Josh 19:18

SHUR
Wilderness in south Palestine, Gen 16:7
Israel went from Red Sea to, Exod 15:22
Hagar fled here, Gen 16:7

SHUT
S her out from the camp .... Num 12:14
He has *s* your eyes............... Isa 29:10
s the mouths of lions .... Heb 11:33
open door that no one can *s* .... Rev 3:8

SHUTS
s his ears to the cry of the poor .. Prov 21:13
and *s* doors no one can open .... Rev 3:7

SHUTTING
s the door behind him .... Gen 19:6

SIBLINGS
he has no children nor *s*............. Eccl 4:8

SICK
and pretend to be *s*............... 2 Sam 13:5
My whole body is *s*................. Ps 38:3
your whole heart is *s* .... Isa 1:5
I am *s* at heart .... Jer 8:18
How *s* is your heart.............. Ezek 16:30
was *s* and you took care of me .. Matt 25:36
A great number of *s* .... John 5:3
the one you love is *s*............... John 11:3
many of you are weak and *s*......1 Cor 11:30
will save the one who is *s*........... Jas 5:15

SICKLE
Rush forth with the *s* .... Joel 3:13
Use your *s* and start to reap ...... Rev 14:15

SICKNESS
Will I recover from this *s* ....2 Kgs 8:8
sustains him through *s* .... Prov 18:14
every kind of disease and *s*....... Matt 4:23
every kind of disease and *s*....... Matt 9:35
This *s* will not lead to death ...... John 11:4

SIDE
along the east *s* of Assyria......... Gen 2:14
on the eastern *s* of the orchard.... Gen 3:24

with two rings on one *s*.......... Exod 25:12
foot and a half on the one *s* ..... Exod 26:13
For the south *s* there are to be ... Exod 27:9
He tears me down on every *s*...... Job 19:10
The LORD is on my *s*................. Ps 118:6
on the other *s* of the sea........... Ps 139:9
for your part lie on your left *s* ..... Ezek 4:4
on each *s* of the east gate .... Ezek 40:10
sitting on the right *s* .... Mark 16:5
he passed by on the other *s* ......Luke 10:31
by the angels to Abraham's *s* .... Luke 16:22
pierced his *s* with a spear......... John 19:34
them his hands and his *s* .... John 20:20
and put my hand into his *s* ...... John 20:25
Throw your net on the right *s* ..... John 21:6

SIDON
Canaanite city; inhabitants not expelled,
   Judg 1:31
Hostile relations with Israel, Judg 10:12;
   Isa 23:12; Joel 3:4–6
Jesus preaches to, Matt 15:21; Luke 6:17
See also TYRE AND SIDON

SIFT
to *s* you like wheat ....Luke 22:31

SIGH
our lives pass quickly, like a *s*....... Ps 90:9

SIGHING
my *s* comes in place of my food ....Job 3:24

SIGHS
my heart constantly *s* for Moab .... Isa 16:11

SIGHT
turn aside to see this amazing *s* ... Exod 3:3
considered stupid in your *s*......... Job 18:3
you make me an appalling *s* ....Ps 88:8
let them escape from your *s*....... Prov 3:21
Immediately he regained his *s*...Mark 10:52
utterly detestable in God's *s*.....Luke 16:15
he was amazed at the *s*............ Acts 7:31
we live by faith, not by *s*........... 2 Cor 5:7
which is precious in God's *s* ....1 Pet 3:4

SIGHTS
and there will be terrifying *s*...... Luke 21:11

SIGN
will give you a confirming *s*.......... Isa 7:14
we want to see a *s* from you..... Matt 12:38
generation asks for a *s*............ Matt 12:39
will be the *s* of your coming ...... Matt 24:3
to be a *s* that will be rejected..... Luke 2:34
perform some miraculous *s* ...... Luke 23:8
as his second miraculous *s* .... John 4:54
that a notable miraculous *s*........ Acts 4:16
s of my apostleship................. 1 Cor 9:2
This is a *s* of their destruction ...... Phil 1:28
a great *s* appeared in heaven .... Rev 12:1

SIGNAL
the *s* from the rams' horns .... Josh 6:5

SIGNALS
s with his feet...................... Prov 6:13

SIGNS
See also SIGNS AND WONDERS
let them be *s* to indicate seasons... Gen 1:14
They executed his miraculous *s* ...Ps 105:27
How great are his *s*................ Dan 4:3
evaluate the *s* of the times .... Matt 16:3
through the accompanying *s* ....Mark 16:20
the first of his miraculous *s*........ John 2:11
perform the miraculous *s* .... John 3:2
you saw miraculous *s*............. John 6:26
perform such miraculous *s* .... John 9:16
performing many miraculous *s*... John 11:47
many other miraculous *s* .... John 20:30
Jews demand miraculous *s* ....1 Cor 1:22
of the demons performing *s*......Rev 16:14

SIGNS AND WONDERS
with great awe-inspiring *s* .... Deut 26:8
to tell you about the *s* .... Dan 4:2
appear and perform great *s* ..... Matt 24:24
Unless you people see *s* .... John 4:48
bring about miraculous *s* .... Acts 4:30

granting miraculous *s* .... Acts 14:3
in the power of *s* .... Rom 15:19
great perseverance by *s* .... 2 Cor 12:12
confirmed their witness with *s* ..... Heb 2:4

SIHON
Amorite king; defeated by Israel,
    Num 21:21–32
Territory of, assigned to Reuben and Gad,
    Num 32:1–38

SILAS [or SILVANUS]
Leader in Jerusalem church; sent to
    Antioch, Acts 15:22–35
Travels with Paul, Acts 15:40–41
Jailed and released, Acts 16:25–40
Mentioned in epistles, 2 Cor 1:19; 1 Thess 1:1;
    2 Thess 1:1; 1 Pet 5:12
Also called "Silvanus," 1 Thess 1:1

SILENCE
have dwelt in the *s* of death .... Ps 94:17
s the ignorance of foolish........... 1 Pet 2:15
there was *s* in heaven................. Rev 8:1

SILENCED
that every mouth may be *s* .... Rom 3:19

SILENT
and I, for my part, will be *s* .... Job 6:24
you would keep completely *s*........ Job 13:5
will sing to you and not be *s*........ Ps 30:12
I was stone *s*......................... Ps 39:2
our God come and not be *s*.......... Ps 50:3
The earth was afraid and *s*.......... Ps 76:8
and the waves grew *s*.............. Ps 107:29
a sheep *s* before her shearers ...... Isa 53:7
I will not keep *s*..................... Isa 65:6
s before the Sovereign LORD .... Zeph 1:7
But Jesus was *s* .... Matt 26:63
you will be *s*, unable to speak ... Luke 1:20
by his answer, they fell *s*........ Luke 20:26
a lamb before its shearer is *s* ..... Acts 8:32
should be *s* in the churches...... 1 Cor 14:34

SILENTLY
Sit *s*! Go to a hiding place........... Isa 47:5

SILK
and covered you with *s*........... Ezek 16:10

SILOAM
Tower of, falls and kills 18 people, Luke 13:4
Blind man washes in pool of, John 9:1–11

SILVANUS
See SILAS

SILVER
and the choicest *s* for you .... Job 22:25
If he piles up *s* like dust............. Job 27:16
as *s* purified in a furnace............. Ps 12:6
purified us like refined *s*........... Ps 66:10
is more profitable than *s* .... Prov 3:14
is more desirable than *s* .... Prov 16:16
The crucible is for refining *s* ...... Prov 17:3
Your *s* has become scum .... Isa 1:22
are regarded as 'rejected *s*......... Jer 6:30
eager to trade *s* for the poor ..... Amos 8:6
May your *s* perish with you....... Acts 8:20

SIMEON
Son of Jacob by Leah, Gen 29:32–33
Avenges his sister's dishonor, Gen 34:25–31
Held hostage by Joseph, Gen 42:18–20, 24
Rebuked by Jacob, Gen 49:5–7
—Tribe of:
Numbered, Num 1:23; 26:12–14
Receive inheritance, Josh 19:1–9
Fight Canaanites with Judah, Judg 1:1–3,
    17–20
—Devout man; blesses infant Jesus,
    Luke 2:25–35

SIMON
Simon Peter: *see* PETER
—One of the Twelve; called "the Zealot,"
    Matt 10:4
—One of Jesus' half brothers, Matt 13:55
—Pharisee, Luke 7:36–40
—Man of Cyrene, bears Jesus' cross,
    Matt 27:32

—Sorcerer, Acts 8:9–24
—Tanner in Joppa, Acts 9:43

SIMPLETONS
will you *s* love naiveté .... Prov 1:22

SIN
s is crouching at the door........... Gen 4:7
and their *s* so blatant.............. Gen 18:20
s did I commit against you......... Gen 20:9
committed a very serious *s*...... Exod 32:30
the *s* they have committed .... Lev 4:14
his *s* that he has committed .... Lev 5:6
is the law of the *s* offering........... Lev 6:25
bear responsibility for their *s*..... Lev 20:20
bear responsibility for his *s*....... Lev 24:15
any *s* that people commit .... Num 5:6
If you *s* unintentionally .... Num 15:22
but he died for his own *s* .... Num 27:3
all the *s* you had committed...... Deut 9:18
trespass or *s* that he commits ....Deut 19:15
s against the LORD your God .... Deut 20:18
a *s* punishable by death.......... Deut 21:22
be put to death for his own *s*.... Deut 24:16
forgive the *s* of your servant....1 Sam 25:28
forgive the *s* of your people ......1 Kgs 8:34
your people will *s* against you....1 Kgs 8:46
This caused Israel to *s* .... 1 Kgs 12:30
and encouraged Israel to *s*....... 1 Kgs 15:26
angered me and made Israel *s*... 1 Kgs 21:22
put to death only for his own *s* ...2 Kgs 14:6
has encouraged Judah to *s*...... 2 Kgs 21:11
forgive the *s* of your people ......2 Chr 6:25
forgive their *s*, and heal.......... 2 Chr 7:14
executed only for his own *s* ......2 Chr 25:4
and do not wipe out their *s*......... Neh 4:5
In all this Job did not *s*.............. Job 1:22
In all this Job did not *s*............. Job 2:10
and inquire about my *s*............ Job 10:6
he adds transgression to his *s* ..... Job 34:37
Tremble with fear and do not *s*........ Ps 4:4
forgive my *s*, because it is great .....Ps 25:11
whose *s* is pardoned.................. Ps 32:1
Then I confessed my *s*............... Ps 32:5
because of my *s* .... Ps 38:3
I do not *s* with my tongue .... Ps 39:1
Cleanse me of my *s*.................. Ps 51:2
am forever conscious of my *s* .... Ps 51:3
I was guilty of *s* from birth .... Ps 51:5
I had harbored *s* in my heart ....Ps 66:18
so I might not *s* against you .... Ps 119:11
Do not let any *s* dominate me.....Ps 119:133
s is a disgrace to any people...... Prov 14:34
I am pure from my *s*............... Prov 20:9
let your mouth cause you to *s* ...... Eccl 5:6
lips are contaminated by *s*.......... Isa 6:5
your *s* is forgiven .... Isa 6:7
s of all of us to attack him .... Isa 53:6
he lifted up the *s* of many .... Isa 53:12
I have not committed any *s*.......... Jer 2:35
What *s* have we done............... Jer 16:10
he will die for his *s*................. Ezek 3:20
to bring *s* to completion........... Dan 9:24
Even now they persist in *s*........... Hos 13:2
Who forgives *s* and pardons....... Mic 7:18
who are entrenched in their *s* .... Zeph 1:12
your right eye causes you to *s* .... Matt 5:29
for every *s* and blasphemy ...... Matt 12:31
who believe in me to *s*............. Matt 18:6
Then many will be led into *s* .... Matt 24:10
If your hand causes you to *s*......Mark 9:43
takes away the *s* of the world ..... John 1:29
Don't *s* any more .... John 5:14
now on do not *s* any more......... John 8:11
but will die in your *s*............... John 8:21
who practices *s* is a slave of *s*.... John 8:34
can prove me guilty of any *s* ...... John 8:46
s that caused him to be born
    blind............................. John 9:2
you would not be guilty of *s*...... John 9:41
the world wrong concerning *s*..... John 16:8
alike are all under *s*................. Rom 3:9
comes the knowledge of *s*........ Rom 3:20
the Lord will never count *s*........ Rom 4:8
just as *s* entered the world ....Rom 5:12

s was in the world .... Rom 5:13
but where *s* increased .... Rom 5:20
Are we to remain in *s*................. Rom 6:1
so that the body of *s*................. Rom 6:6
he died to *s* once for all........... Rom 6:10
For *s* will have no mastery........Rom 6:14
s because we are not under law ...Rom 6:15
though you were slaves to *s*.......Rom 6:17
freed from *s* and enslaved to ..... Rom 6:22
For the payoff of *s* is death ...... Rom 6:23
Is the law *s*.......................... Rom 7:7
s became alive....................... Rom 7:9
but *s* that lives in me .... Rom 7:17
from the law of *s* and death ....Rom 8:2
your body is dead because of *s*... Rom 8:10
Every *s* a person commits .... 1 Cor 6:18
If you *s* against your brothers .....1 Cor 8:12
The sting of death is *s* .... 1 Cor 15:56
not know *s* to be *s* for us .... 2 Cor 5:21
Who is led into *s*................. 2 Cor 11:29
is discovered in some *s*............... Gal 6:1
just as we are, yet without *s*....... Heb 4:15
no longer any offering for *s* ...... Heb 10:18
it gives birth to *s*.................... Jas 1:15
you are committing *s*................ Jas 2:9
does not do it is guilty of *s*......... Jas 4:17
For what credit is it if you *s*....... 1 Pet 2:20
committed no *s* nor was deceit... 1 Pet 2:22
has finished with *s*.................. 1 Pet 4:1
cleanses us from all *s*............. 1 John 1:7
do not bear the guilt of *s* .... 1 John 1:8
so that you may not *s*............. 1 John 2:1
Everyone who practices *s* .... 1 John 3:4
The one who practices *s*.......... 1 John 3:8
does not practice *s* .... 1 John 3:9
a *s* not resulting in death .... 1 John 5:16
All unrighteousness is *s* .... 1 John 5:17

SINAI, MOUNT
Used allegorically by Paul, Gal 4:24–25
—Physical mountain: *See* MOUNT SINAI

SINCE
s the foundation of the world .....Heb 9:26

SINCERE
I will give you *s* thanks............. Ps 119:7
from a *s* and pure devotion........ 2 Cor 11:3
and thus be *s* and blameless........ Phil 1:10
a *s* heart, fearing the Lord .... Col 3:22
good conscience, and a *s* faith ...... 1 Tim 1:5
let us draw near with a *s* heart ... Heb 10:22
to show *s* mutual love .... 1 Pet 1:22

SINCERITY
he must do so with *s*.............. Rom 12:8
the bread of *s* and truth .... 1 Cor 5:8
with pure motives and *s*......... 2 Cor 1:12
before God as persons of *s* ...... 2 Cor 2:17
in the *s* of your heart .... Eph 6:5

SINEWS
through its ligaments and *s*......... Col 2:19

SINFUL
those *s* Amalekites .... 1 Sam 15:18
repudiate their *s* practices .... 2 Chr 7:14
They speak *s* words................. Ps 59:12
Beware *s* nation .... Isa 1:4
and *s* people their plans .... Isa 55:7
adulterous and *s* generation......Mark 8:38
for I am a *s* man .... Luke 5:8
into the hands of *s* men .... Luke 24:7
sin would become utterly *s*........ Rom 7:13
in the likeness of *s* flesh .... Rom 8:3

SING
S to the LORD..................... Exod 15:21
wake up, *s* a song.................. Judg 5:12
I will *s* praises to you .... 2 Sam 22:50
S to the LORD. .... 1 Chr 16:23
S praises to the LORD............. Ps 9:11
S to him a new song............... Ps 33:3
will then *s* my insightful song .... Ps 49:4
shout joyfully, yes, they *s*........ Ps 65:13
S praises about the majesty .... Ps 66:2
I will *s* continually .... Ps 89:1
S to the LORD a new song .... Ps 98:1

will *s* about loyalty and justice........Ps 101:1
s to the LORD as long as I live......Ps 104:33
S praises to his name.......... Ps 135:3
S for us a song about Zion......... Ps 137:3
them *s* about the LORD's deeds..... Ps 138:5
S to the LORD a new song .... Ps 149:1
S to the LORD............Isa 12:5
S to the LORD a brand new song... Isa 42:10
s as she did when she was young ...Hos 2:15
S out and be happy............... Zech 2:10
He should *s* praises...................Jas 5:13

SINGERS
the *s* sang and the trumpeters .. 2 Chr 29:28
S walk in front...................... Ps 68:25
acquired male *s* and female *s*....... Eccl 2:8

SINGING
Enter his presence with joyful *s* ....Ps 100:2
for pruning and *s* has come........Song 2:12
and *s* praises to the LORD........... Isa 60:6
s and making music ....Eph 5:19
s psalms, hymns.................... Col 3:16
They were *s* a new song ....Rev 5:9
and they were *s* a new song ....Rev 14:3

SINGLE
the body is not a *s* member ......1 Cor 12:14

SINGLE-MINDED
Instead I am *s*......................Phil 3:13

SINGS
That person *s* to others............Job 33:27

SINK
I *s* into the deep mire.................Ps 69:2
the sky *s* and come down...........Ps 144:5
And starting to *s*................ Matt 14:30

SINNED
See also SINNED AGAINST THE LORD;
   SINNED AGAINST YOU
he *s* again: both he and his ....Exod 9:34
for we have *s* ....Num 14:40
who *s* at the cost of their lives... Num 16:38
will have *s* against the LORD..... Num 32:23
will be regarded as having *s* ....Deut 15:9
We have *s* .... Judg 10:15
I have *s* ....1 Sam 26:21
Perhaps my children have *s*............Job 1:5
If I have *s*—what have I done........Job 7:20
for I have *s* against you.............. Ps 41:4
you above all—I have *s*............... Ps 51:4
Our forefathers *s* and are dead..... Lam 5:7
we have *s*! We have done........... Dan 9:5
s since the time of Gibeah .... Hos 10:9
s by betraying innocent blood.... Matt 27:4
I have *s* against heaven and.....Luke 15:18
who have *s* apart from the law ....Rom 2:12
for all have *s* and fall short ....Rom 3:23
you have not *s*................... 1 Cor 7:28
not spare the angels who *s*... 2 Pet 2:4
If we say we have not *s* ....1 John 1:10

SINNED AGAINST THE LORD
s your God and against you...... Exod 10:16
you had indeed *s* your God...... Deut 9:16
I have *s* God of Israel ....Josh 7:20
confessed there, "We have *s*......1 Sam 7:6
to Nathan, "I have *s*..............2 Sam 12:13
For we have *s* our God.............. Jer 3:25
You have *s*...................... Jer 44:23
for they have *s*................... Zeph 1:17

SINNED AGAINST YOU
We have *s*. We abandoned........Judg 10:10
Even though I have not *s* ....1 Sam 24:11
by an enemy because they *s*...... 1 Kgs 8:33
because your people *s*..........2 Chr 6:26
Heal me, for I have *s*................ Ps 41:4
We have indeed *s*............... Jer 14:20
for we have *s*................... Dan 9:11

SINNER
so the grave snatches up the *s*.....Job 24:19
a *s* the moment my mother ....Ps 51:5
how much more the wicked *s* .....Prov 11:31
wickedness overthrows the *s*...... Prov 13:6
the wealth of a *s* is stored up .....Prov 13:22

but to the *s* ....Eccl 2:26
but the *s* is captured by her ....Eccl 7:26
though a *s* might commit..........Eccl 8:12
also happens to the *s*.............. Eccl 9:2
but one *s* can destroy much .... Eccl 9:18
who was a *s*......................Luke 7:37
over one *s* who repents...........Luke 15:7
be merciful to me, *s* that I am ....Luke 18:13
How can a man who is a *s* ....John 9:16
We know that this man is a *s* .....John 9:24

SINNERS
See also TAX COLLECTORS AND SINNERS
a brood of *s*...................... Num 32:14
stand in the pathway with *s* .... Ps 1:1
nor can *s* join the assembly............Ps 1:5
teaches *s* the right way to live ....Ps 25:8
Do not sweep me away with *s*.......Ps 26:9
s disappear from the earth ....Ps 104:35
if *s* try to entice you .... Prov 1:10
Calamity pursues *s* .... Prov 13:21
Do not let your heart envy *s*......Prov 23:17
Woe to the wicked *s*................. Isa 3:11
S are afraid in Zion ....Isa 33:14
All the *s* among my people ...... Amos 9:10
tax collectors and *s* came......... Matt 9:10
to call the righteous, but *s*.........Matt 9:13
friend of tax collectors and *s* .....Matt 11:19
is betrayed into the hands of *s*...Matt 26:45
tax collectors and *s* were eating... Mark 2:15
is betrayed into the hands of *s*... Mark 14:41
but *s* to repentance................ Luke 5:32
s love those who love them ...... Luke 6:32
friend of tax collectors and *s* .....Luke 7:34
these Galileans were worse *s*.....Luke 13:2
welcomes *s* and eats with them ...Luke 15:2
that God doesn't listen to *s*........John 9:31
in that while we were still *s*........Rom 5:8
many were constituted *s* ....Rom 5:19
for the ungodly and *s*.............. 1 Tim 1:9
came into the world to save *s* .....1 Tim 1:15
separate from *s*.................... Heb 7:26
against himself by *s*................Heb 12:3
become of the ungodly and *s*......1 Pet 4:18
that ungodly *s* have spoken ....Jude 1:15

SINNING
if we deliberately keep on *s* ......Heb 10:26
never stop *s*, they entice........... 2 Pet 2:14
has been *s* from the beginning ... 1 John 3:8

SINS
When a person *s* by straying ....Lev 4:2
If the high priest *s* ....Lev 4:3
s by straying unintentionally .... Lev 5:15
when only one man *s*............. Num 16:22
s which Jeroboam committed ....1 Kgs 14:16
many are my iniquities and *s* ...... Job 13:23
from committing flagrant *s*..........Ps 19:13
against me the *s* of my youth........ Ps 25:7
Forgive all my *s*.................... Ps 25:18
My *s* overtake me .... Ps 40:12
Hide your face from my *s*........... Ps 51:9
you are aware of my foolish *s* ....Ps 69:5
Forgive our *s* for the sake ....Ps 79:9
You are aware of our *s*............... Ps 90:8
one who forgives all your *s* ....Ps 103:3
were to keep track of *s* ....Ps 130:3
despises his neighbor *s* ....Prov 14:21
does good and never *s*............. Eccl 7:20
crushed because of our *s*............Isa 53:5
for he carried their *s*................Isa 53:11
s have caused him to reject you .... Isa 59:2
Your *s* have deprived you........... Jer 5:25
for the *s* you have committed ...... Jer 17:3
s are bound around my neck ......Lam 1:14
The one who *s* will die............Ezek 18:4
Throw away all your *s*............Ezek 18:31
save his people from their *s* ....Matt 1:21
as they confessed their *s* .... Matt 3:6
For if you forgive others their *s*....Matt 6:14
authority on earth to forgive *s*..... Matt 9:6
If your brother *s*..................Matt 18:15
for the forgiveness of *s*..........Matt 26:28
for the forgiveness of *s* .... Mark 1:4

can forgive *s* but God alone .... Mark 2:7
will also forgive you your *s*...... Mark 11:25
for the forgiveness of *s*............. Luke 3:3
authority on earth to forgive *s*.... Luke 5:24
forgive everyone who *s*........... Luke 11:4
If your brother *s*...................Luke 17:3
that you will die in your *s*......... John 8:24
when I take away their *s*.......... Rom 11:27
Christ died for our *s* ....1 Cor 15:3
you are still in your *s* ....1 Cor 15:17
who gave himself for our *s* .... Gal 1:4
the forgiveness of *s*................Col 1:14
s of some people are obvious ....1 Tim 5:24
accomplished cleansing for *s*.......Heb 1:3
to bear the *s* of many..............Heb 9:28
one sacrifice for *s* for all time..... Heb 10:12
confess your *s* to one another ....Jas 5:16
will cover a multitude of *s*.........Jas 5:20
himself bore our *s* in his body .... 1 Pet 2:24
But if we confess our *s* ....1 John 1:9
atoning sacrifice for our *s* .... 1 John 2:2
your *s* have been forgiven.........1 John 2:12
was revealed to take away *s*.......1 John 3:5
who *s* has neither seen him....... 1 John 3:6
the atoning sacrifice for our *s* ... 1 John 4:10
you will not take part in her *s* ......Rev 18:4

SISERA
Canaanite commander of Jabin's army; slain
by Jael, Judg 4:2–22

SISTER
So tell them you are my *s* ....Gen 12:13
She is my *s* .... Gen 26:7
a beautiful *s* named Tamar ......2 Sam 13:1
My mother,' or 'My *s* ....Job 17:14
my *s*, my bride..................... Song 4:10
We have a little *s* .... Song 8:8
Her *s*, unfaithful Judah.................Jer 3:7
Your older *s* was Samaria........ Ezek 16:46
my brother and *s* and mother ... Matt 12:50
s has left me to do all the work.. Luke 10:40
Jesus loved Martha and her *s*......John 11:5
do you judge your brother or *s*...Rom 14:10
commend to you our *s* Phoebe.... Rom 16:1
the brother or *s* is not bound......1 Cor 7:15

SISTERS
the least of these brothers or *s*..Matt 25:40
among many brothers and *s*...... Rom 8:29
sin against your brothers or *s* .....1 Cor 8:12
the brothers and *s* at one time ....1 Cor 15:6
brothers and *s* with a holy kiss ..1 Thess 5:26
made like his brothers and *s*.......Heb 2:17
know that your brothers and *s* .....1 Pet 5:9
accuser of our brothers and *s* .....Rev 12:10

SIT
he will *s* on my throne............. 1 Kgs 1:13
who *s* at the city gate gossip........Ps 69:12
Do not *s* in judgment............... Ps 143:2
S in the dirt......................Isa 47:1
the people who *s* in darkness.....Matt 4:16
to *s* at my right and at my left ...Matt 20:23
Pharisees *s* on Moses' seat .... Matt 23:2
of us to *s* at your right hand .....Mark 10:37
S at my right hand................Mark 12:36
to those who *s* in darkness........Luke 1:79
S at my right hand until .... Heb 1:13
You *s* here in a good place............Jas 2:3
to *s* with me on my throne ....Rev 3:21

SITS
God *s* on his holy throne ....Ps 47:8
who *s* on the earth's horizon ......Isa 40:22
to the one who *s* on the throne..... Rev 4:9
who *s* on many waters.............. Rev 17:1

SITTING
Eli the priest was *s* in his chair......1 Sam 1:9
I saw the LORD *s* on his throne .. 1 Kgs 22:19
I saw the LORD *s* on his throne .. 2 Chr 18:18
Why are we just *s* here ....Jer 8:14
Now Peter was *s* outside ....Matt 26:69
Son of Man *s* at the right hand .. Mark 14:62
she saw two angels in white *s* ....John 20:12
a woman *s* on a scarlet beast.......Rev 17:3

SIX
S days you will gather it . . . . Exod 16:26
For *s* days you may labor . . . . Exod 20:9

SIYON, MOUNT
See MOUNT ZION

SIZE
I may know the *s* of the army . . . . 2 Sam 24:2

SKETCH
is a *s* and shadow . . . . Heb 8:5

SKETCHES
the *s* of the things in heaven . . . . Heb 9:23

SKIES
the *s* thundered . . . . Ps 77:17
who in the *s* can compare . . . . Ps 89:6
throne will endure like the *s* . . . . Ps 89:37
the *s* are high above the earth . . . . . . Ps 103:11

SKILL
My own ability and *s* . . . . Deut 8:17
He had the *s* and knowledge . . . . . . 1 Kgs 7:14
he led them with *s* . . . . Ps 78:72
Your work lacks *s* . . . . Isa 45:9
with knowledge and *s* . . . . Dan 1:17

SKILLED
Esau became a *s* hunter . . . . Gen 25:27
Every woman who was *s* . . . . Exod 35:25
and every *s* person . . . . Exod 36:1
seen a person *s* in his work . . . . . . Prov 22:29
They are *s* at doing evil . . . . Jer 4:22
those who are the most *s* at it . . . . . . Jer 9:17
who are *s* in destruction . . . . Ezek 21:31

SKILLFUL
I considered all the *s* work . . . . Eccl 4:4

SKIN
made garments from *s* . . . . Gen 3:21
that the *s* of his face shone . . . . . . Exod 34:29
everything that is made of *s* . . . . . Num 31:20
answered the LORD, "*S* for *s* . . . . Job 2:4
sewed sackcloth on my *s* . . . . Job 16:15
My bones stick to my *s* . . . . Job 19:20
bones protrude from my *s* . . . . Ps 102:5
change the color of his *s* . . . . Jer 13:23
Our *s* is as hot as an oven . . . . Lam 5:10
You flay my people's *s* . . . . Mic 3:2

SKINS
put the *s* of the young goats . . . . . . Gen 27:16

SKIP
He makes them *s* like a calf . . . . Ps 29:6

SKULL, THE
See GOLGOTHA

SKULL, PLACE OF THE
See GOLGOTHA

SKY
God called the expanse "*s* . . . . Gen 1:8
numerous as the stars in the *s* . . . . . Gen 26:4
God give you the dew of the *s* . . . Gen 27:28
blessings from the *s* above . . . . Gen 49:25
extended his staff toward the *s* . . . Exod 9:23
and make your *s* like iron . . . . Lev 26:19
harvest produced by the *s* . . . . Deut 33:13
foundations of the *s* trembled . . . 2 Sam 22:8
if the *s* and the highest heaven . . . 1 Kgs 8:27
fire come down from the *s* . . . . 2 Kgs 1:12
rain by opening holes in the *s* . . . . 2 Kgs 7:2
the *s* displays his handiwork . . . . Ps 19:1
sun and moon remain in the *s* . . . . . . Ps 72:5
praise him in the *s* . . . . Ps 150:1
from looking up to the *s* . . . . Isa 38:14
the *s* is higher than the earth . . . . . . Isa 55:9
and birds of the *s* live . . . . Dan 2:38
fair weather because the *s* is red . . Matt 16:2
the birds in the *s* have nests . . . . . . Luke 9:58
the number of stars in the *s* . . . . . . Heb 11:12
and the *s* gave rain . . . . Jas 5:18
The *s* was split apart . . . . Rev 6:14

SLACKERS
for they are *s* . . . . Exod 5:8

SLAG
the wicked of the earth like *s* . . . . . Ps 119:119
house of Israel has become *s* . . . . Ezek 22:18

SLAIN
The beauty of Israel lies *s* . . . . 2 Sam 1:19
all those she has *s* are many . . . . . . Prov 7:26
Your *s* were not cut down . . . . Isa 22:2
will no longer cover up its *s* . . . . Isa 26:21

SLANDER
you *s* your own brother . . . . Ps 50:20
and the one who spreads *s* . . . . . . Prov 10:18
not *s* a servant to his master . . . . Prov 30:10
theft, false testimony, *s* . . . . Matt 15:19
hypocrisy and envy and all *s* . . . . . . 1 Pet 2:1
who *s* your good conduct . . . . 1 Pet 3:16

SLANDERED
my name is constantly *s* . . . . Isa 52:5

SLANDERER
You must not go about as a *s* . . . . . . Lev 19:16

SLANDERERS
s, haters of God, insolent . . . . Rom 1:30
s, without self-control . . . . 2 Tim 3:3

SLANDERING
For those who are holy, not *s* . . . . . . Titus 2:3

SLANDEROUS
they are safe from *s* attacks . . . . Ps 31:20
be dignified, not *s*, temperate . . . . . 1 Tim 3:11

SLANDERS
dissension, *s*, evil suspicions . . . . 1 Tim 6:4

SLAPS
s his hand and says to him . . . . Dan 4:35

SLAUGHTER
really *s* an innocent nation . . . . Gen 20:4
that valley the Valley of *S* . . . . Jer 7:32
lamb ready to be led to the *s* . . . . . . Jer 11:19
the flock set aside for *s* . . . . Zech 11:4
and *s* them in front of me . . . . Luke 19:27
He was led like a sheep to *s* . . . . . . Acts 8:32
Get up, Peter; *s* and eat . . . . Acts 10:13

SLAUGHTERED
sword has *s* heavenly powers . . . . . . Isa 34:5
You *s* your prophets . . . . Jer 2:30
considered as sheep to be *s* . . . . . . Rom 8:36

SLAUGHTERING
Like a lamb led to the *s* block . . . . . . Isa 53:7

SLAVE
were a *s* in the land of Egypt . . . . . Deut 15:15
Israel is not a *s* . . . . Jer 2:14
and a *s* respects his master . . . . Mal 1:6
nor a *s* greater than his master . . Matt 10:24
good and faithful *s* . . . . Matt 25:21
Evil and lazy *s* . . . . Matt 25:26
s into the outer darkness . . . . Matt 25:30
you must be the *s* of all . . . . Mark 10:44
At harvest time he sent a *s* . . . . Mark 12:2
and to my *s* . . . . Luke 7:8
have worked like a *s* for you . . . . . Luke 15:29
who practices sin is a *s* of sin . . . . . John 8:34
s is not greater than his master . . John 15:20
struck the high priest's *s* . . . . John 18:10
a *s* of Christ Jesus . . . . Rom 1:1
Were you called as a *s* . . . . 1 Cor 7:21
I would not be a *s* of Christ . . . . Gal 1:10
there is neither *s* nor free . . . . Gal 3:28
are no longer a *s* but a son . . . . Gal 4:7
barbarian, Scythian, *s* or free . . . . . . Col 3:11
is one of you and a *s* of Christ . . . . . Col 4:12
a *s* of God and apostle . . . . Titus 1:1
a *s* of God and the Lord . . . . Jas 1:1
a *s* and apostle of Jesus . . . . 2 Pet 1:1
a *s* of Jesus Christ . . . . Jude 1:1

SLAVERY
from the land of *s* . . . . Exod 13:14
sold into *s* to sin . . . . Rom 7:14
did not receive the spirit of *s* . . . . . Rom 8:15
bearing children for *s* . . . . Gal 4:24
subject again to the yoke of *s* . . . . . . Gal 5:1
those who were held in *s* . . . . Heb 2:15

SLAVES
We are now my lord's *s* . . . . Gen 44:16
I have seen *s* on horseback . . . . Eccl 10:7
free their male and female *s* . . . . . . Jer 34:10

S rule over us . . . . Lam 5:8
Again he sent other *s* . . . . Matt 21:36
s whom their master finds alert . . Luke 12:37
We are *s* undeserving . . . . Luke 17:10
I no longer call you *s* . . . . John 15:15
that though you were *s* to sin . . . . . . Rom 6:17
s to impurity and lawlessness . . . . . Rom 6:19
Do not become *s* of men . . . . 1 Cor 7:23
Jews or Greeks or *s* or free . . . . 1 Cor 12:13
as your *s* for Jesus' sake . . . . 2 Cor 4:5
S, obey your human masters . . . . Eph 6:5
but as *s* of Christ . . . . Eph 6:6
s of Christ Jesus . . . . Phil 1:1
S, obey your earthly masters . . . . . . Col 3:22
treat your *s* with justice . . . . Col 4:1
S are to be subject to their own . . . Titus 2:9
but as God's *s* . . . . 1 Pet 2:16
s and human lives . . . . Rev 18:13

SLEEP
the man to fall into a deep *s* . . . . Gen 2:21
made him go to *s* on her lap . . . . . . Judg 16:19
when a deep *s* falls on men . . . . Job 4:13
as they *s* in their beds . . . . Job 33:15
Why do you *s* . . . . Ps 44:23
May your Protector not *s* . . . . Ps 121:3
Israel's Protector does not *s* . . . . Ps 121:4
even when they *s* . . . . Ps 127:2
I will not allow my eyes to *s* . . . . Ps 132:4
your *s* will be pleasant . . . . Prov 3:24
s unless they cause harm . . . . Prov 4:16
A little *s*, a little slumber . . . . Prov 6:10
Do not love *s* . . . . Prov 20:13
A little *s*, *s* little slumber . . . . Prov 24:33
s of the laborer is pleasant . . . . Eccl 5:12
He was unable to *s* . . . . Dan 6:18
was sinking into a deep *s* . . . . Acts 20:9
hour for us to awake from *s* . . . . . . Rom 13:11
We will not all *s* . . . . 1 Cor 15:51
we must not *s* as the rest . . . . 1 Thess 5:6

SLEEPER
O *s*! Rise from the dead . . . . Eph 5:14

SLEEPING
is *s* and needs to be awakened . . 1 Kgs 18:27
But while everyone was *s* . . . . Matt 13:25
Are you still *s* and resting . . . . Matt 26:45
Why are you *s* . . . . Luke 22:46
was *s* between two soldiers . . . . Acts 12:6

SLEEPS
the one who *s* during harvest . . . . . . Prov 10:5

SLEEPY
those with him were quite *s* . . . . . . Luke 9:32

SLEPT
I rested and *s* . . . . Ps 3:5

SLING
took his *s* in hand . . . . 1 Sam 17:40
Like tying a stone in a *s* . . . . Prov 26:8

SLIPPERY
May their path be dark and *s* . . . . Ps 35:6
you put them in *s* places . . . . Ps 73:18
will be dark and *s* . . . . Jer 23:12

SLIPS
at the time their foot *s* . . . . Deut 32:35

SLOPE
their tongues like a steep *s* . . . . Ps 5:9
herd rushed down the steep *s* . . . . Matt 8:32

SLOTHFUL
s will be put to forced labor . . . . . . Prov 12:24

SLOW
See also SLOW TO ANGER
s of speech and *s* of tongue . . . . . . Exod 4:10
understanding is *s* to anger . . . . Prov 14:29
The LORD is *s* to anger . . . . Nah 1:3
s of heart to believe . . . . Luke 24:25
s to speak, *s* to anger . . . . Jas 1:19
not *s* concerning his promise . . . . . . 2 Pet 3:9

SLOW TO ANGER
and gracious God, *s* . . . . Exod 34:6
The LORD is *s* . . . . Num 14:18
who is *s* calms a quarrel . . . . Prov 15:18

and compassionate, *s*.................Joel 2:13
s and abounding in mercy.........Jonah 4:2
The LORD is *s*...........................Nah 1:3
slow to speak, *s*.......................Jas 1:19

SLOWLY
I will walk *s* all my years.............Isa 38:15

SLUGGARD
you *s*, will you lie there..............Prov 6:9
The appetite of the *s* craves.......Prov 13:4
The *s* has plunged his hand.......Prov 19:24
I passed by the field of a *s*........Prov 24:30
s is wiser in his own opinion......Prov 26:16

SLUGGISH
you have become *s* in hearing......Heb 5:11

SLURP
will *s* it up and drink it................Ps 75:8

SMALL
make you *s* among nations.........Jer 49:15
make light of *s* beginnings........Zech 4:10
faithful in a very *s* matter.........Luke 19:17
tongue is a *s* part of the body.......Jas 3:5
the great and the *s*................Rev 20:12

SMART
is *s* keeps quiet in such a time....Amos 5:13

SMASH
I *s* and I heal........................Deut 32:39
They *s* me into the ground.........Ps 143:3

SMASHED
she *s* his head....................Judg 5:26

SMEAR
s my reputation with lies.........Ps 119:69

SMEARED
s the mud on the blind man's........John 9:6

SMELL
are infected and starting to *s*........Ps 38:5
the body will have a bad *s*........John 11:39

SMILE
S upon us, LORD.......................Ps 4:6
S on your servant....................Ps 31:16
May he *s* on us......................Ps 67:1
S on your servant...................Ps 119:135

SMOKE
he saw the *s* rising up............Gen 19:28
s is driven away by the wind........Ps 68:2
For my days go up in *s*.............Ps 102:3
like a wineskin dried up in *s*......Ps 119:83
like a column of *s*.................Song 3:6
its *s* will ascend continually......Isa 34:10
the sky will dissipate like *s*.........Isa 51:6
blood and fire and clouds of *s*.....Acts 2:19
For you are a puff of *s*.............Jas 4:14
and *s* rose out of it..................Rev 9:2
filled with *s* from God's glory.......Rev 15:8
The *s* rises from her forever........Rev 19:3

SMOKING
by these two stubs of *s* logs.........Isa 7:4

SMOLDERING
or extinguish a *s* wick............Matt 12:20

SMOOTH
rough ways will be made *s*.........Luke 3:5

SMOOTH-SKINNED
to a nation of tall, *s* people..........Isa 18:2

SMYRNA
Site of one of the seven churches, Rev 1:11
Letter to, Rev 2:8-11

SNAIL
be like a *s* that melts away..........Ps 58:8

SNAKE
Make a poisonous *s*..............Num 21:8
venom is like that of a *s*.............Ps 58:4
will subdue a lion and a *s*...........Ps 91:13
the way of a *s* on a rock.......Prov 30:19
If the *s* should bite...............Eccl 10:11
play over the hole of a *s*............Isa 11:8
the eggs of a poisonous *s*..........Isa 59:5
will give him a *s*..................Matt 7:10

SNAKES
authority to tread on *s*..............Luke 10:19

SNAKES'
Their wine is *s* poison...........Deut 32:33

SNARE
it will surely be a *s* to you.......Exod 23:33
It became a *s* to Gideon..........Judg 8:27
she may become a *s* to him.....1 Sam 18:21
like a bird from a hunter's *s*.......Ps 124:7
like birds that are caught in a *s*....Eccl 9:12
s are ready to overtake you.........Isa 24:17
like an antelope in a *s*..............Isa 51:20

SNARES
the *s* of death trapped me...........Ps 18:5

SNATCH
will *s* them from my hand.......John 10:28

SNATCHED
The fatherless child is *s*............Job 24:9
the Spirit of the Lord *s* Philip......Acts 8:39

SNATCHES
comes and *s* what was sown.......Matt 13:19

SNOOZE
and love to *s*.......................Isa 56:10

SNOW
See also WHITE AS SNOW
heat snatch up the melted *s*.......Job 24:19
For to the *s* he says..................Job 37:6
entered the storehouse of the *s*...Job 38:22
and I will be whiter than *s*...........Ps 51:7
He sends the *s* that is white........Ps 147:16
Like *s* in summer...................Prov 26:1
you can become white like *s*........Isa 1:18
His attire was white like *s*..........Dan 7:9
his clothes were white as *s*.......Matt 28:3
even as white as *s*..................Rev 1:14

SOAKED
They are *s* by mountain rains.......Job 24:8

SOAP
use as much *s* as you want.........Jer 2:22

SOBER
we must stay *s*...................1 Thess 5:8

SOBER-MINDED
So be self-controlled and *s*.........1 Pet 4:7

SOCKET
he struck the *s* of his hip..........Gen 32:25
arm be broken off at the *s*........Job 31:22

SOCOH
Town in Judah where David kills Goliath,
Josh 15:1, 35; 1 Sam 17:1, 49

SODA
or like vinegar poured on *s*......Prov 25:20

SODOM
Lot chooses to live there, Gen 13:10-13
Plundered by Kedorlaomer, Gen 14:8-24
Abraham intercedes for, Gen 18:16-33
Destroyed by God, Gen 19:1-29
Cited as example of sin and destruction,
Deut 29:23; 32:32; Isa 1:9-10; 3:9;
Jer 23:14; 49:18; Lam 4:6; Ezek 16:46-63;
Matt 11:23-24; 2 Pet 2:6; Jude 1:7
See also SODOM AND GOMORRAH

SODOM AND GOMORRAH
When the kings of *S* fled.........Gen 14:10
outcry against *S* is so great......Gen 18:20
rained sulfur and fire on *S*......Gen 19:24
the destruction of *S*.............Deut 29:23
Babylonia just as I did *S*..........Jer 50:40
the way God overthrew *S*.......Amos 4:11
bearable for the region of *S*.....Matt 10:15
to ashes the cities of *S*..........2 Pet 2:6
S and the neighboring towns.....Jude 1:7

SOFT
a *s* tongue can break a bone......Prov 25:15

SOFTER
His words seem *s* than oil.........Ps 55:21

SOIL
formed the man from the *s*.........Gen 2:7
and the produce of your *s*.......Deut 28:51
or the top *s* of the world..........Prov 8:26
other seeds fell on good *s*........Matt 13:8

SOLD
and *s* his birthright to Jacob......Gen 25:33
For we have been *s*................Esth 7:4
s your people for a pittance........Ps 44:12
Joseph was *s* as a servant.........Ps 105:17
They *s* the innocent for silver......Amos 2:6
he went out and *s* everything....Matt 13:46
Eat anything that is *s*...........1 Cor 10:25

SOLDIER
as a good *s* of Christ Jesus.........2 Tim 2:3

SOLDIERS
Why will your *s* be defeated.......Jer 46:15
He sent his *s*......................Matt 22:7
a large sum of money to the *s*...Matt 28:12
The *s* also mocked him..........Luke 23:36
Then the squad of *s*.............John 18:12
s braided a crown of thorns.......John 19:2
The number of *s* on horseback.....Rev 9:16

SOLEMNLY
The man *s* warned us............Gen 43:3
For I *s* warned your ancestors........Jer 11:7

SOLID
breadth of the waters freeze *s*.....Job 37:10
like a peg into a *s* place...........Isa 22:23
I fed you milk, not *s* food..........1 Cor 3:2
God's *s* foundation remains......2 Tim 2:19
needing milk, not *s* food..........Heb 5:12

SOLOMON
David's son by Bathsheba, 2 Sam 12:24
Becomes king, 1 Kgs 1:5-53
Receives and carries out David's
instructions, 1 Kgs 2
Prays for and demonstrates wisdom,
1 Kgs 3:3-28; 4:29-34
Builds and dedicates temple; builds palace,
1 Kgs 5-8
Lord appears to, 1 Kgs 9:1-9
His fame and glory, 1 Kgs 9:10-10:29
Falls into idolatry; warned by God,
1 Kgs 11:1-13
Adversaries arise, 1 Kgs 11:14-40
Death of, 1 Kgs 11:41-43
Writings credited to him, Ps 72; 127; Prov 1:1;
10:1; 25:1; Eccl 1:1; Song 1:1

SOLUTION
Who knows the *s* to a problem......Eccl 8:1

SOLVE
They could not *s* the riddle.......Judg 14:14

SOME
S of the prophets were visiting...2 Kgs 4:38
There will be *s* left behind..........Isa 17:6
in *s* hidden place..................Isa 45:19

SOMEBODY
claiming to be *s*....................Acts 5:36

SOMEONE
if *s* makes slaves of you..........2 Cor 11:20

SOMETHING
I have *s* to say to you.............Luke 7:40
he is *s* when he is nothing..........Gal 6:3

SON
See also ONE DEAR SON; SON OF DAVID;
SON OF GOD; SON OF MAN
wife is going to bear you a *s*......Gen 17:19
bore Abraham a *s* in his old age....Gen 21:2
Take your *s*—your only *s*........Gen 22:2
prepared to slaughter his *s*.......Gen 22:10
he called his older *s* Esau........Gen 27:1
I am your firstborn *s*.............Gen 27:32
and gave birth to a *s*.............Gen 29:32
My *s* Joseph is still alive........Gen 45:28
When she bore a *s*.................Exod 2:22
A *s* has been born to Naomi......Ruth 4:17
Send me your *s* David...........1 Sam 16:19
Later she gave birth to a *s*.....2 Sam 12:24

The king is grieved over his *s* .... 2 Sam 19:2
he told Solomon his *s* .... 1 Kgs 2:1
and took my *s* from my side ...... 1 Kgs 3:20
My *s*, I really wanted to build ..... 1 Chr 22:7
David gave to his *s* Solomon....... 1 Chr 28:11
You are my *s*........................... Ps 2:7
him to be my firstborn *s*............ Ps 89:27
When I was a *s* to my father .... Prov 4:3
O my *s*, O *s* of my womb .... Prov 31:2
and will give birth to a *s*............ Isa 7:14
a *s* has been given to us .... Isa 9:6
s of the dawn .... Isa 14:12
summoned my *s* out of Egypt .... Hos 11:1
A *s* naturally honors his father ...... Mal 1:6
She will give birth to a *s* .... Matt 1:21
This is my one dear *S*.............. Matt 3:17
knows the *S* except the Father ... Matt 11:27
Isn't this the carpenter's *s* .... Matt 13:55
the *S* of the living God............. Matt 16:16
For the *S* of Man will come..... Matt 16:27
Finally he sent his *s* to them..... Matt 21:37
Whose *s* is he........................ Matt 22:42
how can he be his *s*.............. Matt 22:45
coming of the *S* of Man will be .. Matt 24:37
I am God's *S* .... Matt 27:43
the *S* of God .... Mark 1:1
the *S* of Man has authority .... Mark 2:10
This is my one dear *S*.............. Mark 9:7
his one dear *s*..................... Mark 12:6
Truly this man was God's *S*...... Mark 15:39
called the *S* of the Most High...... Luke 1:32
You are my one dear *S* .... Luke 3:22
You are the *S* of God .... Luke 4:41
the *S* of Man has authority .... Luke 5:24
The *S* of Man is lord of .... Luke 6:5
the only *s* of his mother .... Luke 7:12
The *S* of Man has come........... Luke 7:34
father against *s* and *s* against.... Luke 12:53
worthy to be called your *s*....... Luke 15:19
he ran and hugged his *s* .... Luke 15:20
he too is a *s* of Abraham......... Luke 19:9
I will send my one dear *s* .... Luke 20:13
Are you the *S* of God .... Luke 22:70
He gave his one and only *S*........ John 3:16
For God did not send his *S* ..... John 3:17
The Father loves the *S*............. John 3:35
S can do nothing on his own ..... John 5:19
For the Father loves the *S* .... John 5:20
looks on the *S* and believes....... John 6:40
but the *s* remains forever....... John 8:35
So if the *s* sets you free......... John 8:36
S of Man must be lifted up ...... John 12:34
here is your *s* .... John 19:26
translated "*s* of encouragement ... Acts 4:36
in the gospel of his *S* .... Rom 1:9
By sending his own *S*............ Rom 8:3
who did not spare his own *S*...... Rom 8:32
the *S* himself will be subjected .. 1 Cor 15:28
God sent out his *S*................. Gal 4:4
no longer a slave but a *s*......... Gal 4:7
You are my *s*........................ Heb 1:5
as a *s* over God's house............ Heb 3:6
Although he was a *s* .... Heb 5:8
the *s* of Pharaoh's daughter .... Heb 11:24
This is my dear *S* .... 2 Pet 1:17
and the blood of Jesus his *S* ...... 1 John 1:7
Everyone who denies the *S*...... 1 John 2:23
he loved us and sent his *S*........ 1 John 4:10
that Jesus is the *S* of God......... 1 John 4:15
who believes in the *S* of God .... 1 John 5:10
has the *S* has this eternal life..... 1 John 5:12
the woman gave birth to a *s*....... Rev 12:5

SON OF DAVID
Solomon *s* solidified his .... 2 Chr 1:1
The proverbs of Solomon, *s*....... Prov 1:1
words of the Teacher, the *s*......... Eccl 1:1
of Jesus Christ, the *s*.............. Matt 1:1
Joseph, *s*, do not be afraid .... Matt 1:20
Have mercy on us, *S*............ Matt 9:27
Could this one be the *S*....... Matt 12:23
Have mercy on me, Lord, *S*....... Matt 15:22
Hosanna to the *S*................. Matt 21:9
They said, "The *s* .... Matt 22:42

Jesus, *S*, have mercy on me...... Mark 10:47
the son of Nathan, the *s*.......... Luke 3:31
Jesus, *S*, have mercy on me...... Luke 18:39

SON OF GOD
If you are the *S* .... Matt 4:3
S, leave us alone.................. Matt 8:29
Truly you are the *S* .... Matt 14:33
if you are the Christ, the *S*..... Matt 26:63
gospel of Jesus Christ, the *S* ...... Mark 1:1
he will be called the *S*........... Luke 1:35
the son of Adam, the *s*......... Luke 3:38
Rabbi, you are the *S* .... John 1:49
name of the one and only *S* ...... John 3:18
will hear the voice of the *S* .... John 5:25
because I said, 'I am the *S* .... John 10:36
that the *S* may be glorified .... John 11:4
S who comes into the world...... John 11:27
he claimed to be the *S*........... John 19:7
Jesus is the Christ, the *S*....... John 20:31
This man is the *S* .... Acts 9:20
the *S*, who loved me............ Gal 2:20
of the knowledge of the *S* ...... Eph 4:13
the heavens, Jesus the *S* .... Heb 4:14
are crucifying the *S*.............. Heb 6:6
but is like the *s* .... Heb 7:3
has contempt for the *S* .... Heb 10:29
purpose the *S* was revealed ..... 1 John 3:8
that Jesus is the *S*................ 1 John 5:5
pronouncement of the *S* .... Rev 2:18

SON OF JONAH
See PETER

SON OF MAN
S, stand on your feet .... Ezek 2:1
S, eat what you see................ Ezek 3:1
one like a *s* was approaching ...... Dan 7:13
but the *S* has no place .... Matt 8:20
that the *S* has authority .... Matt 9:6
before the *S* comes............... Matt 10:23
The *S* came eating and .... Matt 11:19
the *S* is lord of the Sabbath........ Matt 12:8
speaks a word against the *S* .... Matt 12:32
so the *S* will be in the heart ..... Matt 12:40
good seed is the *S*............... Matt 13:37
do people say that the *S* is........ Matt 16:13
S coming in his kingdom .... Matt 16:28
until the *S* is raised from .... Matt 17:9
S is going to be betrayed......... Matt 17:22
S sits on his glorious throne ...... Matt 19:28
the *S* will be handed over........ Matt 20:18
S did not come to be served.... Matt 20:28
the coming of the *S* will be ...... Matt 24:27
the *S* will be handed over....... Matt 26:2
The *S* will go as it is written ..... Matt 26:24
S must suffer many things........ Mark 8:31
the *S* will also be ashamed .... Mark 8:38
the *S* will also acknowledge ...... Luke 12:8
see one of the days of the *S* ..... Luke 17:22
For the *S* came to seek .... Luke 19:10
to stand before the *S* .... Luke 21:36
you betray the *S* with a kiss .... Luke 22:48
and descending on the *S* ...... John 1:51
from heaven—the *S*............ John 3:13
because he is the *S* .... John 5:27
food which the *S* will give .... John 6:27
eat the flesh of the *S* .... John 6:53
When you lift up the *S*.......... John 8:28
for the *S* to be glorified........... John 12:23
Now the *S* is glorified............. John 13:31
the *S* standing at the right....... Acts 7:56
or the *s* that you care for him ...... Heb 2:6
was one like a *s*.................. Rev 1:13
cloud was one like a *s* .... Rev 14:14

SONG
LORD is my strength and my *s*..... Exod 15:2
Then Israel sang this *s*........... Num 21:17
Sing to him a new *s*............. Ps 33:3
me reason to sing a new *s*....... Ps 40:3
by night he gives me a *s*......... Ps 42:8
will then sing my insightful *s* .... Ps 49:4
Sing to the LORD a new *s* .... Ps 96:1
Sing for us a *s* about Zion....... Ps 137:3
I will sing a new *s* to you........... Ps 144:9

Sing to the LORD a new *s*........... Ps 149:1
Most Excellent Love *S*.............. Song 1:1
s to my lover about his vineyard....... Isa 5:1
they break into *s*..................... Isa 14:7
Sing to the LORD a brand new *s* ... Isa 42:10
their mocking *s* all day long .... Lam 3:14
you are like a sensual *s*......... Ezek 33:32
will sing this taunt *s* to you .... Mic 2:4
each one has a *s* .... 1 Cor 14:26
They were singing a new *s*.......... Rev 5:9
they were singing a new *s* .... Rev 14:3
They sang the *s* of Moses.......... Rev 15:3

SONGS
Israel's beloved singer of *s*...... 2 Sam 23:1
s accompanied by cymbals .... Neh 12:27
who gives *s* in the night........... Job 35:10
drunkards mock me in their *s* ...... Ps 69:12
Your statutes have been my *s* ..... Ps 119:54
captors ask us to compose *s*........ Ps 137:3
who sings *s* to a heavy heart.... Prov 25:20
and all their *s* grow faint.......... Eccl 12:4
the object of their mocking *s*..... Lam 3:63
away from me your noisy *s*...... Amos 5:23
psalms, hymns, and spiritual *s*...... Eph 5:19

SONS
See also SONS OF GOD
Jacob had twelve *s*................ Gen 35:22
the *s* of Eli were wicked men ..... 1 Sam 2:12
These were the *s* of David......... 1 Chr 3:1
If his *s* are honored................. Job 14:21
s will carry on the dynasty.......... Ps 45:16
of you are *s* of the Most High........ Ps 82:6
Yes, *s* are a gift from the LORD...... Ps 127:3
I and the *s* whom the LORD......... Isa 8:18
your *s* come from far away .... Isa 60:4
For none of his *s* will succeed ..... Jer 22:30
The precious *s* of Zion.............. Lam 4:2
fathers will eat their *s* .... Ezek 5:10
Then the *s* are free .... Matt 17:26
A man had two *s*................. Matt 21:28
will be *s* of the Most High .... Luke 6:35
you may become *s* of light........ John 12:36
You are the *s* of the prophets....... Acts 3:25
belong the adoption as *s* .... Rom 9:4
called '*s* of the living God......... Rom 9:26
will be my *s* and daughters ...... 2 Cor 6:18
believe are the *s* of Abraham........ Gal 3:7
that we may be adopted as *s* .... Gal 4:5
And because you are *s*.............. Gal 4:6
s of the light and *s* of the day.... 1 Thess 5:5
in bringing many *s* to glory........ Heb 2:10
addressed to you as *s*.............. Heb 12:5
are illegitimate and are not *s* ...... Heb 12:8

SONS OF GOD
the *s* saw that the daughters .... Gen 6:2
when the *s* came to present.......... Job 1:6
and all the *s* shouted for joy........ Job 38:7
equal to angels are the *s*........ Luke 20:36
Spirit of God are the *s* .... Rom 8:14
the revelation of the *s* .... Rom 8:19
you ae all *s* through faith .... Gal 3:26

SOON
I am coming *s*....................... Rev 3:11

SOOTHING
offering to the LORD, a *s* aroma . Exod 29:18
a gift of a *s* aroma to the LORD ...... Lev 1:9

SORCERER
omen reader, a soothsayer, a *s* ... Deut 18:10

SORCERERS
Outside are the dogs and the *s* .... Rev 22:15

SORCERESS
You must not allow a *s* to live ... Exod 22:18

SORCERY
idolatry, *s*, hostilities................ Gal 5:20

SORES
body was covered with *s* .... Luke 16:20

SORROW
with very great and bitter *s*....... Gen 50:10
confronted with trouble and *s*...... Ps 116:3
and he adds no *s* to it............ Prov 10:22

s is better than laughter.............Eccl 7:3
your time of *s* will be over.........Isa 60:20
cry out as *s* fills your hearts ....Isa 65:14
great *s* and unceasing anguish......Rom 9:2

SORROWFUL
heard this he went away *s* ....Matt 19:22
looked sad and went away *s*.....Mark 10:22
you have been deeply *s*...........1 Cor 5:2

SORRY
But who feels *s* for you.............Isa 51:19

SORTS
you fall into all *s* of trials ....Jas 1:2

SOSTHENES
Ruler of the synagogue at Corinth,
    Acts 18:17
—Paul's Christian brother, 1 Cor 1:1

SOUGHT
Moses *s* the favor of the LORD....Exod 32:11
I *s* the LORD's help...................Ps 34:4
S After, City Not Abandoned ....Isa 62:12
or *s* the lost.......................Ezek 34:4
Now what is *s* in stewards..........1 Cor 4:2
he *s* the blessing with tears........Heb 12:17

SOUL
O my *s*, do not come into..........Gen 49:6
speak in the bitterness of my *s*......Job 10:1
are you depressed, O my *s* ....Ps 42:5
but cannot kill the *s* ....Matt 10:28
with all your *s* ....Matt 22:37
My *s* exalts the Lord................Luke 1:46
sword will pierce your own *s* .....Luke 2:35
Now my *s* is greatly distressed ...John 12:27
will not leave my *s* in Hades ......Acts 2:27
your spirit and *s* and body......1 Thess 5:23
save that person's *s* from death ....Jas 5:20
that do battle against the *s* ....1 Pet 2:11
tormented in his righteous *s*.......2 Pet 2:8
just as it is well with your *s*.......3 John 1:2

SOULS
the one who wins *s* is wise ....Prov 11:30
you will find rest for your *s*......Matt 11:29
have faith and preserve their *s* ...Heb 10:39
which is able to save your *s*..........Jas 1:21
salvation of your *s*..................1 Pet 1:9
I also saw the *s* of those ....Rev 20:4

SOUND
then what is this *s* of sheep......1 Sam 15:14
to hear the *s* of chariots ....2 Kgs 7:6
Asaph was to *s* the cymbals ....1 Chr 16:5
my flute for the *s* of weeping......Job 30:31
the *s* of the surging water ....Ps 93:4
the *s* of the grinding mill ....Eccl 12:4
The *s* of weeping or cries...........Isa 65:19
s of battle comes from the city .....Isa 66:6
A *s* is heard in Ramah..............Jer 31:15
a *s* of crying in bitter grief ....Jer 31:15
I heard the *s* of their wings ....Ezek 1:24
s of the living beings' wings ....Ezek 3:13
s was like that of rushing water .. Ezek 43:2
s the alarm signal....................Joel 2:1
There will be a bitter *s*...............Zeph 1:14
For the trumpet will *s* ....1 Cor 15:52
live contrary to *s* teaching.........1 Tim 1:10
does not agree with *s* words.......1 Tim 6:3
Hold to the standard of *s* words.. 2 Tim 1:13
and the *s* of their wings.............Rev 9:9
a *s* coming out of heaven..........Rev 14:2

SOUNDS
Terrifying *s* fill his ears.............Job 15:21
will be *s* of joy and gladness........Jer 33:11

SOURCE
the *s* of eternal salvation ....Heb 5:9

SOUTH
in the arid *s* are replenished ....Ps 126:4
and to the *s*.......................Isa 43:6
Then the king of the *s* ....Dan 11:5
queen of the *S* will rise up.......Matt 12:42

SOVEREIGN
I am the *S* God.....................Gen 17:1
May the *S* God bless you ....Gen 28:3

LORD God is our *s* protector........Ps 84:11
s authority of the LORD his God .....Mic 5:4
the blessed and only *S*...........1 Tim 6:15

SOW
who *s* trouble reap the same ....Job 4:8
let me *s* and let another eat ....Job 31:8
watches the wind will not *s*.........Eccl 11:4
They *s* the wind.....................Hos 8:7
S righteousness for yourselves ....Hos 10:12
harvesting where you did not *s*..Matt 25:24
They do not *s* or reap...........Luke 12:24
you *s* will not come to life ....1 Cor 15:36

SOWED
an enemy came and *s* darnel ....Matt 13:25
The one who *s* the good seed ....Matt 13:37
If we *s* spiritual blessings ....1 Cor 9:11

SOWER
A *s* went out to sow ....Matt 13:3
A *s* went out to sow ....Mark 4:3
The *s* sows the word................Mark 4:14
A *s* went out to sow his seed .....Luke 8:5

SOWN
they are barely *s*....................Isa 40:24
where the word is *s*...............Mark 4:15
It is *s* in dishonor ....1 Cor 15:43

SOWS
the one who *s* righteousness......Prov 11:18
One *s* and another reaps..........John 4:37
The person who *s* sparingly ....2 Cor 9:6
a person will reap what he *s*........Gal 6:7

SPACIOUS
gate is wide and the way is *s*......Matt 7:13

SPAN
and my life *s* is nothing ....Ps 39:5

SPARE
S him from going down ....Job 33:24
But I will *s* some of you............Ezek 6:8
for you to *s* you....................Ezek 16:5
I will *s* them as a man.............Mal 3:17
he who did not *s* his own Son .... Rom 8:32
if God did not *s* the natural........Rom 11:21
trying to *s* you such problems....1 Cor 7:28
if God did not *s* the angels........2 Pet 2:4

SPARED
s from the kings of Assyria ...... 2 Chr 30:6

SPARES
who *s* his rod hates his child......Prov 13:24

SPARINGLY
he does not give the Spirit *s* ....John 3:34

SPARK
their deeds like a *s*................. Isa 1:31

SPARKLES
when it *s* in the cup................Prov 23:31

SPARKLING
precious stones of a crown *s* ..... Zech 9:16

SPARKS
as surely as the *s* fly upward.........Job 5:7

SPARROWS
more valuable than many *s*.......Matt 10:31

SPAT
s on him and took the staff ......Matt 27:30

SPEAK
will *s* for you to the people ....Exod 4:16
since I *s* with difficulty........... Exod 6:12
but you may only *s* the word ....Num 22:35
God can *s* to human beings........Deut 5:24
and *s* of them as you sit ....Deut 6:7
But if only God would *s*...........Job 11:5
s wickedly on God's behalf ....Job 13:7
Look, I waited for you to *s*.........Job 32:11
I will *s* comprehensively ....Job 36:3
it *s* to you with tender words ....Job 41:3
sure you don't *s* evil words ....Ps 34:13
s in an impressive and ....Ps 45:2
Do not *s* in the ears of a fool .....Prov 23:9
mind will *s* perverse things ......Prov 23:33
on behalf of those unable to *s* .....Prov 31:8

and a time to *s*.......................Eccl 3:7
he will *s* to these people............Isa 28:11
s as his messenger anymore........Jer 20:9
and *s* tenderly to her ....Hos 2:14
S the truth, each of you ....Zech 8:16
when all people *s* well of you.....Luke 6:26
we *s* about what we know..........John 3:11
not *s* with you much longer ......John 14:30
will not *s* on his own authority ...John 16:13
began to *s* in other languages ......Acts 2:4
Not all *s* in tongues..............1 Cor 12:30
If I *s* in the tongues of men ....1 Cor 13:1
to *s* five words with my mind.....1 Cor 14:19
a person is not permitted to *s* ....2 Cor 12:4
S and act as those who will..........Jas 2:12

SPEAKING
s kind words to them..............1 Kgs 12:7
while they are still *s* ....Isa 65:24
For it is not you *s* ....Matt 10:20
he was *s* with us on the road ......Luke 24:32
the one *s* to you ....John 4:26
by the Holy Spirit from *s* ....Acts 16:6
even if I am unskilled in *s*..........2 Cor 11:6
that Christ is *s* through me ....2 Cor 13:3

SPEAKS
the way a person *s* to a friend ....Exod 33:11
For God *s*, the first time ....Job 33:14
but the one who *s* foolishness.....Prov 10:8
but the one who *s* perversion ....Prov 10:31
despise anyone who *s* honestly.. Amos 5:10
has sent *s* the words of God.......John 3:34
s according to his own nature ....John 8:44
than the one who *s* in tongues....1 Cor 14:5
If someone *s* in a tongue ....1 Cor 14:27
And through his faith he still *s*......Heb 11:4
blood that *s* of something better.. Heb 12:24
who *s* against a fellow believer ......Jas 4:11

SPEAR
pierced his side with a *s* ....John 19:34

SPEARS
whose teeth are *s* and arrows ....Ps 57:4
and their *s* into pruning hooks........Isa 2:4
are armed with bows and *s*......... Jer 6:23
your pruning hooks into *s*..........Joel 3:10

SPECIAL
he made a *s* tunic for him.......... Gen 37:3
you will be my *s* possession ....Exod 19:5
for a *s* votive offering...............Lev 22:21
you to be his *s* people ....Deut 26:18
Your love was more *s* to me.....2 Sam 1:26
Israel to be his *s* possession ....Ps 135:4

SPECK
see the *s* in your brother's eye......Matt 7:3

SPECTACLE
I will make you a public *s*...........Nah 3:6
have become a *s* to the world .....1 Cor 4:9

SPECULATIONS
Such things promote useless *s* .....1 Tim 1:4

SPEECH
There is no actual *s* or word......... Ps 19:3
foolish *s* leads to imminent.......Prov 10:14
S that heals is like a life-giving.....Prov 15:4
Excessive *s* is not becoming ....Prov 17:7
deceitful in *s* falls into trouble....Prov 17:20
speak in eloquent figures of *s* ...Ezek 20:49
not with clever *s* ....1 Cor 1:17
and his *s* is of no account........2 Cor 10:10
Let your *s* always be gracious ....Col 4:6

SPEECHLESS
but the wicked are made *s*.......1 Sam 2:9

SPELL
there is no *s* against Jacob ....Num 23:23
Who has cast a *s* on you..............Gal 3:1

SPEND
I did not *s* my time...................Jer 15:17
and whatever else you *s*.........Luke 10:35
most gladly *s* and be spent ......2 Cor 12:15
you can *s* it on your passions........Jas 4:3

SPENDING
s my life from the beginning.......Acts 26:4

SPENT
after he had *s* everything . . . . Luke 15:14

SPICES
s for the anointing oil . . . . Exod 25:6
a very large quantity of *s* . . . . 1 Kgs 10:10
that its fragrant *s* may send out . . Song 4:16
will replace the smell of *s* . . . . Isa 3:24
Salome bought aromatic *s* . . . . Mark 16:1
aromatic *s* they had prepared . . . . . Luke 24:1
with the aromatic *s* . . . . John 19:40

SPIES
You are *s*; you have come to . . . . . . Gen 42:9
s went and brought out Rahab . . . Josh 6:23
s who pretended to be sincere . . Luke 20:20

SPIN
they do not work or *s*. . . . . Matt 6:28

SPINDLE
and her hands grasped the *s* . . . . . . Prov 31:19

SPIRIT
See also FILLED WITH THE HOLY SPIRIT;
    HOLY SPIRIT; SPIRIT OF GOD; SPIRIT
    OF THE LORD; SPIRIT OF TRUTH;
    UNCLEAN SPIRIT
My *S* will not remain . . . . Gen 6:3
filled with the *s* of wisdom . . . . Exod 28:3
everyone whose *s* was willing . . . Exod 35:21
familiar *s* must be put to death . . . Lev 20:27
part of the *S* that is on you . . . . Num 11:17
And the *S* rested on them . . . . Num 11:26
LORD would put his *S* on them . . . Num 11:29
because he had a different *s* . . . . . Num 14:24
a man in whom is the *S* . . . . Num 27:18
God sent a *s* to stir up hostility . . . . Judg 9:23
double portion of the
    prophetic *s* . . . . 2 Kgs 2:9
Then a *s* stepped forward . . . . 2 Chr 18:20
You imparted your good *S* . . . . Neh 9:20
admonished them by your *S* . . . . . . Neh 9:30
intervention watched over my *s* . . . Job 10:12
And whose *s* has come forth . . . . . . Job 26:4
Do not take your Holy *S* away . . . . . Ps 51:11
Yes, my *s* was bitter . . . . Ps 73:21
The human *s* is like the lamp . . . . Prov 20:27
the human *s* ascends upward . . . . . Eccl 3:21
my *s* within me seeks you . . . . Isa 26:9
will sound like a *s* speaking . . . . Isa 29:4
horses are made of flesh, not *s* . . . . Isa 31:3
and his own *S* gathers them . . . . . . Isa 34:16
I have placed my *S* on him . . . . Isa 42:1
accompanied by his *S*. . . . . Isa 48:16
man's *s* would grow faint . . . . Isa 57:16
who follow their own *s* . . . . Ezek 13:3
a new heart and a new *s* . . . . Ezek 18:31
I will put my *S* within you . . . . Ezek 36:27
there is a *s* of the holy gods . . . . Dan 4:8
an extraordinary *s* . . . . Dan 5:12
forms the human *s* within . . . . Zech 12:1
pregnant through the Holy *S* . . . . . Matt 1:18
Blessed are the poor in *s* . . . . Matt 5:3
I will put my *S* on him . . . . Matt 12:18
S descending on him like a dove . . Mark 1:10
The *S* immediately drove him . . . . . Mark 1:12
The *s* is willing . . . . Mark 14:38
in the *s* and power of Elijah . . . . Luke 1:17
in the power of the *s* . . . . Luke 4:14
When an unclean *s* goes out . . . . . Luke 11:24
blasphemes against the Holy *S* . . Luke 12:10
into your hands I commit my *s* . . Luke 23:46
S descending like a dove . . . . John 1:32
person is born of water and *s* . . . . . John 3:5
God is *s*. . . . . John 4:24
S is the one who gives life . . . . John 6:63
he was intensely moved in *s* . . . . . John 11:33
was greatly distressed in *s* . . . . John 13:21
were filled with the Holy *S* . . . . Acts 2:4
a *s* or an angel has spoken . . . . Acts 23:9
according to the Holy *S*. . . . . Rom 1:4
whom I serve in my *s* . . . . Rom 1:9
who live according to the *S*. . . . . . . Rom 8:5
outlook of the *S* is life and . . . . Rom 8:6
not in the flesh but in the *S* . . . . Rom 8:9

The *S* himself bears witness . . . . . . Rom 8:16
knows the mind of the *S*. . . . . Rom 8:27
revealed these to us by the *S* . . . 1 Cor 2:10
but the same *S* . . . . 1 Cor 12:4
my *s* prays . . . . 1 Cor 14:14
on the letter but on the *S*. . . . . 2 Cor 3:6
Now the Lord is the *S* . . . . 2 Cor 3:17
we have the same *s* of faith . . . . . . 2 Cor 4:13
you began with the *S* . . . . Gal 3:3
God sent the *S* of his Son . . . . Gal 4:6
live by the *S* and you will not . . . . . Gal 5:16
But if you are led by the *S* . . . . Gal 5:18
But the fruit of the *S* is love . . . . . . Gal 5:22
If we live by the *S*. . . . . Gal 5:25
the one who sows to the *S* . . . . Gal 6:8
seal of the promised Holy *S* . . . . . . Eph 1:13
to keep the unity of the *S* . . . . Eph 4:3
is one body and one *S* . . . . Eph 4:4
are standing firm in one *s* . . . . Phil 1:27
being united in *s* . . . . Phil 2:2
I am present with you in *s* . . . . Col 2:5
Do not extinguish the *S* . . . . 1 Thess 5:19
your *s* and soul and body . . . . 1 Thess 5:23
through sanctification by
    the *S* . . . . 2 Thess 2:13
vindicated by the *S* . . . . 1 Tim 3:16
the *S* explicitly says that . . . . 1 Tim 4:1
did not give us a *S* of fear . . . . 2 Tim 1:7
point of dividing soul from *s* . . . . . Heb 4:12
through the eternal *S* offered . . . . . Heb 9:14
body without the *s* is dead . . . . Jas 2:26
The *s* that God caused to live . . . . . . Jas 4:5
the *S* of Christ within them . . . . 1 Pet 1:11
by being made alive in the *s* . . . . . . 1 Pet 3:18
by the *S* he has given us . . . . 1 John 3:24
do not believe every *s* . . . . 1 John 4:1
he has given us of his *S* . . . . 1 John 4:13
the *S* is the one who testifies . . . . . 1 John 5:6
devoid of the *S* . . . . Jude 1:19
in the *S* on the Lord's Day . . . . Rev 1:10
the *S* says to the churches . . . . Rev 2:7
Immediately I was in the *S* . . . . Rev 4:2
And the *S* and the bride say . . . . . . Rev 22:17

SPIRIT OF GOD
S was moving over the surface . . . . . Gen 1:2
one in whom the *S* is present . . . . . Gen 41:38
filled him with the *S* in skill . . . . . . Exod 31:3
and the *S* came upon him . . . . Num 24:2
Then the *S* rushed upon Saul . . . 1 Sam 10:10
the *S* came upon Saul's . . . . 1 Sam 19:20
The *S* has made me . . . . Job 33:4
was given to me by the *S* . . . . Ezek 11:24
the *S* descending like a dove . . . . . Matt 3:16
cast out demons by the *S* . . . . Matt 12:28
if indeed the *S* lives in you . . . . Rom 8:9
in the power of the *S* . . . . Rom 15:19
receive the things of the *S* . . . . 1 Cor 2:14
I too have the *S*. . . . . 1 Cor 7:40
no one speaking by the *S* . . . . 1 Cor 12:3
ones who worship by the *S* . . . . Phil 3:3
this you know by the *S* . . . . 1 John 4:2

SPIRIT OF THE LORD
the *S* will rush upon you . . . . 1 Sam 10:6
The *S* rushed upon David . . . . 1 Sam 16:13
the *S* had turned away . . . . 1 Sam 16:14
so the *S* granted them rest . . . . Isa 63:14
S came upon me and said . . . . Ezek 11:5
The *S* is upon me . . . . Luke 4:18
agreed together to test the *S* . . . . . Acts 5:9
the *S* snatched Philip away . . . . . . Acts 8:39
and where the *S* is present . . . . 2 Cor 3:17

SPIRIT OF TRUTH
the *S*, whom the world . . . . John 14:17
the *S* who goes out . . . . John 15:26
when he, the *S*, comes . . . . John 16:13
By this we know the *S* . . . . 1 John 4:6

SPIRITS
See also UNCLEAN SPIRITS
the God of the *s* of all people . . . . Num 16:22
to conjure up underworld *s* . . . . Isa 8:19
authority over unclean *s* . . . . Matt 10:1
to another discernment of *s* . . . . . 1 Cor 12:10

to the elemental *s* of the world . . . . Col 2:20
themselves with deceiving *s* . . . . . 1 Tim 4:1
Are they not all ministering *s* . . . . . Heb 1:14
Father of *s* and receive life . . . . Heb 12:9
Is anyone in good *s* . . . . Jas 5:13
preached to the *s* in prison . . . . . . 1 Pet 3:19
but test the *s* to determine . . . . . . 1 John 4:1

SPIRITUAL
we know that the law is *s* . . . . Rom 7:14
who is *s* discerns all things . . . . . . 1 Cor 2:15
the *s* did not come first . . . . 1 Cor 15:46
who are *s* restore such a person . . . . Gal 6:1
will give you *s* wisdom . . . . Eph 1:17
are built up as a *s* house . . . . 1 Pet 2:5

SPIRITUALLY
because they are *s* discerned . . . . . 1 Cor 2:14

SPIT
Then he *s* on his eyes . . . . Mark 8:23
They will mock him, *s* on him . . . Mark 10:34
Then some began to *s* on him . . . Mark 14:65

SPITTING
my face from insults and *s* . . . . Isa 50:6
and after *s*, he touched his . . . . Mark 7:33

SPLENDOR
where your *s* is revealed . . . . Ps 26:8
gaze at the *s* of the LORD . . . . Ps 27:4
witnessed your power and *s* . . . . . . Ps 63:2
Majestic *s* emanates from him . . . . . Ps 96:6
on your honor and majestic *s* . . . . . Ps 145:5
the *s* of your kingdom . . . . Ps 145:11
the *s* of old men is gray hair . . . . . Prov 20:29
Your *s* has been brought down . . . . Isa 14:11
its beautiful *s* . . . . Isa 28:1
You will see a king in his *s* . . . . Isa 33:17
his *s* appears over you . . . . Isa 60:2
Daughter Zion's *s* has departed . . . . Lam 1:6
and they will defile your *s* . . . . Ezek 28:7
and he will be clothed in *s* . . . . Zech 6:13

SPLINTERED
that *s* reed staff . . . . Isa 36:6

SPLIT
that was under them *s* open . . . . . Num 16:31
You *s* the sea before them . . . . Neh 9:11
Mount of Olives will be *s* . . . . Zech 14:4
great city was *s* into three parts . . Rev 16:19

SPOILS
Can *s* be taken from a warrior . . . . . Isa 49:24

SPOKE
God *s* to Moses and said . . . . Exod 6:2
I *s* and they did not listen . . . . Isa 66:4
who respected the LORD *s* . . . . Mal 3:16
No one ever *s* like this man . . . . . . John 7:46
After God *s* long ago . . . . Heb 1:1
by the Holy Spirit *s* from God . . . . 2 Pet 1:21
When the seven thunders *s* . . . . . . Rev 10:4

SPOKEN
See also LORD HAS SPOKEN
you have *s* in my hearing . . . . Num 14:28
I have not *s* in secret . . . . Isa 45:19
all that the prophets have *s* . . . . . Luke 24:25
know that God has *s* to Moses . . . John 9:29
and *s* the word of the Lord . . . . . . Acts 8:25

SPOKESMAN
me the capacity to be his *s* . . . . Isa 50:4
I commission you as my *s* . . . . Isa 51:16

SPONGE
one of them ran and got a *s* . . . . . Matt 27:48

SPOT
Priests must not have a bald *s* . . . . . Lev 21:5

SPOTLESS
an unblemished and *s* lamb . . . . . . 1 Pet 1:19

SPREAD
and *s* my hands to the LORD . . . . . . Ezra 9:5
evil men *s* a net by the path . . . . . . Ps 140:5
word of God continued to *s* . . . . . . Acts 6:7
message will *s* its infection . . . . . . 2 Tim 2:17

SPREADING
word of the Lord was *s* . . . . Acts 13:49

SPREADS
he alone *s* out the heavens .... Job 9:8
he *s* the frost that is white .... Ps 147:16
s it out like a pitched tent .... Isa 40:22
who *s* seed on the ground .... Mark 4:26

SPRING
muddied *s* and a polluted well... Prov 25:26
you are an enclosed *s* .... Song 4:12
his *s* will dry up .... Hos 13:15
s does not pour out fresh water ..... Jas 3:11
from the *s* of the water of life ...... Rev 21:6

SPRINGING
be like a bitter root *s* up .... Heb 12:15

SPRINGS
gone to the *s* that fill the sea ...... Job 38:16
He turns *s* into streams .... Ps 104:10
your *s* be dispersed outside .... Prov 5:16
no *s* overflowing with water ...... Prov 8:24
from the *s* of deliverance .... Isa 12:3
the parched ground *s* of water ...... Isa 35:7
and the arid land into *s* .... Isa 41:18
These men are waterless *s* .... 2 Pet 2:17
lead them to *s* of living water .... Rev 7:17

SPRINKLE
I will *s* you with pure water ...... Ezek 36:25

SPRINKLED
s both the book itself and .... Heb 9:19
to the *s* blood that speaks .... Heb 12:24

SPRINKLING
s with Jesus Christ's blood .... 1 Pet 1:2

SPROUT
it will *s* again .... Job 14:7

SPROUTS
and the seed *s* and grows .... Mark 4:27

SPUR
to *s* one another on to love .... Heb 10:24

SPURNED
just as I *s* Israel .... 2 Kgs 23:27
they have *s* the commands .... Isa 5:24

SPY
Joshua sent to *s* on Jericho .... Josh 6:25
s out the land and explore it .... Judg 18:2
who slipped in unnoticed to *s* .... Gal 2:4

SQUANDERED
s his wealth with a wild lifestyle .. Luke 15:13

SQUARE
spend the night in the town *s* ...... Gen 19:2
and sat down in the town *s* ...... Judg 19:15
secured my seat in the public *s* .... Job 29:7
Now the city is laid out as a *s* ...... Rev 21:16

SQUARES
throughout the streets and *s* ...... Song 3:2

SQUEEZE
You *s* me in from behind .... Ps 139:5

STABILITY
you give me *s* and prosperity .... Ps 16:5
and gives me *s* .... Ps 73:26
your constant source of *s* .... Isa 33:6

STABLE
it will remain *s* .... Ps 89:37

STADIUM
all the runners in a *s* compete .... 1 Cor 9:24

STAFF
took the *s* of God in his hand ..... Exod 4:20
Each man threw down his *s* .... Exod 7:12
and your *s* in your hand .... Exod 12:11
struck the rock twice with his *s*.. Num 20:11
he beat his donkey with a *s* .... Num 22:27
rod and your *s* reassure me .... Ps 23:4
pass under the shepherd's *s* ..... Ezek 20:37
they were a reed *s* .... Ezek 29:6
I took my *s* "Pleasantness .... Zech 11:10
for the journey except a *s* .... Mark 6:8
struck him on the head with a *s*.. Mark 15:19
worshiped as he leaned on his *s*... Heb 11:21

STAG
is like a gazelle or a young *s* ...... Song 2:9

STAGE
at flood *s* all during harvest .... Josh 3:15

STAGGER
makes them *s* like drunkards ...... Job 12:25

STAIN
having a *s* or wrinkle .... Eph 5:27

STAINED
your hands are *s* with blood .... Isa 59:3
even the clothes *s* by the flesh .... Jude 1:23
who have not *s* their clothes .... Rev 3:4

STAINS
they are *s* and blemishes .... 2 Pet 2:13

STAIRWAY
saw a *s* erected on the earth ...... Gen 28:12

STAKES
its *s* will never be pulled up .... Isa 33:20

STALLS
there are no cattle in the *s* .... Hab 3:17

STAND
S firm and see the salvation ...... Exod 14:13
is able to *s* before the LORD ..... 1 Sam 6:20
Each *s* had four bronze wheels .. 1 Kgs 7:30
no one can *s* against you .... 2 Chr 20:6
are unable to *s* here outside ...... Ezra 10:13
he will *s* upon the earth .... Job 19:25
s in the pathway with sinners .... Ps 1:1
do you *s* far off .... Ps 10:1
in the world *s* in awe of him .... Ps 33:8
LORD's decisions *s* forever .... Ps 33:11
Who will *s* up for me .... Ps 94:16
an accuser *s* at his right side .... Ps 109:6
and *s* in the gap before me ...... Ezek 22:30
But it will *s* forever .... Dan 2:44
animal was able to *s* before it ...... Dan 8:4
will *s* on the Mount of Olives .... Zech 14:4
divided against itself will *s* .... Matt 12:25
kingdom will not be able to *s* .... Mark 3:24
how will his kingdom *s* .... Luke 11:18
why do you *s* here looking up ...... Acts 1:11
into this grace in which we *s* .... Rom 5:2
may be able to *s* your ground ...... Eph 6:13
s in the Lord in this way .... Phil 4:1
if you *s* firm in the Lord .... 1 Thess 3:8
and to cause you to *s* .... Jude 1:24

STANDARD
For by the *s* you judge .... Matt 7:2
Hold to the *s* of sound words ..... 2 Tim 1:13

STANDING
you are *s* is holy ground .... Exod 3:5
is a person of humble *s* .... Prov 12:9
You are *s* at the crossroads .... Jer 6:16
I saw the Lord *s* by the altar .... Amos 9:1
s before the angel of the LORD ..... Zech 3:1
can keep *s* when he appears .... Mal 3:2
to pray while *s* in synagogues ..... Matt 6:5
s here who will not experience ... Mark 9:1
with the woman *s* before him ...... John 8:9
you are *s* is holy ground .... Acts 7:33
Son of Man *s* at the right hand .... Acts 7:56
who have no *s* in the church .... 1 Cor 6:4
who thinks he is *s* be careful ..... 1 Cor 10:12
solid foundation remains *s* ...... 2 Tim 2:19
I am *s* at the door and knocking ... Rev 3:20
I saw one angel *s* in the sun ...... Rev 19:17

STANDS
made ten bronze movable *s* ...... 1 Kgs 7:27
movable *s* with their ten
   basins .... 1 Kgs 7:43
and the movable *s* .... 2 Kgs 25:16
Among you *s* one whom .... John 1:26
his own master he *s* or falls .... Rom 14:4
great opportunity *s* wide open .... 1 Cor 16:9
the judge *s* before the gates .... Jas 5:9

STAR
s will march forth out of Jacob .. Num 24:17
we saw his *s* when it rose .... Matt 2:2
will give him the morning *s* .... Rev 2:28
a huge *s* burning like a torch .... Rev 8:10
the bright morning *s* .... Rev 22:16

STARS
He made the *s* also .... Gen 1:16
as countless as the *s* in the sky ... Gen 22:17
eleven *s* were bowing down .... Gen 37:9
the *s* are not pure .... Job 25:5
the morning *s* sang in chorus .... Job 38:7
and see the moon and the *s* .... Ps 8:3
moon and *s* to rule by night .... Ps 136:9
all you shiny *s* .... Ps 148:3
s withhold their brightness .... Joel 3:15
s will be falling from heaven ..... Mark 13:25
and another glory of the *s* .... 1 Cor 15:41
the number of *s* in the sky .... Heb 11:12
wayward *s* for whom .... Jude 1:13
held seven *s* in his right hand ...... Rev 1:16
was a crown of twelve *s* .... Rev 12:1

STARTLE
so now he will *s* many nations ...... Isa 52:15

STARTLED
But they were *s* and terrified ..... Luke 24:37

STARVATION
die in battle or of *s* or disease .... Jer 21:9
will bring war, *s*, and disease ...... Jer 24:10
and he is sure to die of *s* .... Jer 38:9

STARVED
I am so *s* my knees shake .... Ps 109:24

STATE
and *s* my case against you .... Ps 50:21
so the last *s* of that person ...... Matt 12:45
the humble *s* of his servant ...... Luke 1:48
their last *s* has become worse .... 2 Pet 2:20

STATEMENT
Not everyone can accept this *s* ... Matt 19:11

STATUE
had a golden *s* made .... Dan 3:1

STATURE
increased in wisdom and in *s* ..... Luke 2:52
the measure of Christ's full *s* .... Eph 4:13

STATUTE
This is a perpetual *s* .... Lev 3:17
This is a perpetual *s* .... Lev 23:14

STATUTES
you must not walk in their *s* .... Lev 18:3
keep my *s* and my regulations ...... Lev 18:5
Teach me your *s* .... Ps 119:12
Your *s* have been my songs .... Ps 119:54
focus on your *s* continually .... Ps 119:117
my regulations and my *s* .... Ezek 5:6
did not follow my *s* .... Ezek 20:21

STAY
S until you have weaned him ...... 1 Sam 1:23
and they do not *s* on its paths ..... Job 24:13
I *s* away from every evil path ..... Ps 119:101
They may not *s* here any longer ... Lam 4:15
I must *s* at your house today ...... Luke 19:5

STAYED
So Mary *s* with Elizabeth .... Luke 1:56

STEADFAST
anchor for the soul, sure and *s* .... Heb 6:19

STEADFASTLY
that reason I am *s* resolved .... Isa 50:7
my admonition to endure *s* .... Rev 3:10

STEADFASTNESS
display of all patience and *s* .... Col 1:11

STEADY
and so his hands were *s* .... Exod 17:12
s the knees that shake .... Isa 35:3

STEAL
You shall not *s* .... Exod 20:15
You *s*. You murder .... Jer 7:9
prophets who *s* messages .... Jer 23:30
thieves break in and *s* .... Matt 6:19
house and *s* his property .... Matt 12:29
may come and *s* his body .... Matt 27:64
not commit adultery, do
   not *s* .... Mark 10:19
thief comes only to *s* and kill .... John 10:10

STEALING
You who preach against *s* ....Rom 2:21

STEALS
whoever *s* will be removed........Zech 5:3
who *s* must steal no longer........Eph 4:28

STEALTH
planned to arrest Jesus by *s* ......Matt 26:4
arrest Jesus by *s* and kill him ......Mark 14:1

STEEP
water dumped down a *s* slope.......Mic 1:4

STENCH
putrid *s* will replace the smell ...... Isa 3:24

STEP
one *s* between me and death....1 Sam 20:3
they watch my every *s*..............Ps 56:6

STEPHEN
One of the seven servants in the early
   church, Acts 6:1–5
Falsely accused by Jews; gives defense,
   Acts 6:9–7:53
Becomes first Christian martyr,
   Acts 7:54–60

STEPS
ahead ten *s* or to go back ten *s* .. 2 Kgs 20:9
feet have followed his *s* closely.....Job 23:11
see my ways and count all my *s* .... Job 31:4
he observes all a person's *s*........Job 34:21
Direct my *s* by your word..........Ps 119:133
your *s* will not be hampered.......Prov 4:12
but the LORD directs his *s*.......Prov 16:9
s of a person are ordained......Prov 20:24
spreads a net for his *s* .... Prov 29:5
the shadow go back ten *s*...........Isa 38:8
for you to follow in his *s*...........1 Pet 2:21

STEWARD
When the head *s* tasted ....John 2:9

STEWARDS
and *s* of the mysteries of God ......1 Cor 4:1
as good *s* of the varied grace ......1 Pet 4:10

STEWARDSHIP
heard of the *s* of God's grace........Eph 3:2

STICK
With only my walking *s*...........Gen 32:10
man's hand was a measuring *s* ... Ezek 40:5
s snatched from the flames.......Amos 4:11
s snatched from the fire...........Zech 3:2
put it on a *s*......................Mark 15:36

STICKS
who *s* closer than a brother ......Prov 18:24
The *s* you write on...............Ezek 37:20

STIFF-NECKED
what a *s* people they are..........Exod 32:9

STILL
when the earth is *s* .... Job 37:17
s have to contend with you........Ps 139:18

STILLBORN
I not buried like a *s* infant .... Job 3:16
Let them be like *s* babies ....Ps 58:8
A *s* child is better off .... Eccl 6:3

STING
whips that really *s* your flesh.....1 Kgs 12:11

STINGS
like a snake and *s* like a viper.... Prov 23:32
a scorpion when it *s* a person........Rev 9:5

STINGY
not eat the food of a *s* person .... Prov 23:6
s person hastens after riches .... Prov 28:22

STINK
because you have made us *s* ......Exod 5:21

STIRRED
heart is *s* by a beautiful song .... Ps 45:1

STOCK
grow out of Jesse's root *s*...........Isa 11:1
special vine of the very best *s* ......Jer 2:21

STOCKS
And you put my feet in the *s* ...... Job 13:27
Then he put him in the *s*...........Jer 20:2
put any such person in the *s*.......Jer 29:26

STOIC
Epicurean and *S* philosophers.... Acts 17:18

STOLE
Rachel *s* the household idols ......Gen 31:19
s his body while we were asleep.. Matt 28:13

STOLEN
must return whatever he had *s*......Lev 6:4
S waters are sweet ....Prov 9:17
You have *s* my heart..............Song 4:9

STOMACH
Jonah was in the *s* of the fish ..... Jonah 1:17
into the mouth enters the *s* ...... Matt 15:17
not enter his heart but his *s* ...... Mark 7:19
Food is for the *s* and the *s* is.......1 Cor 6:13

STOMACHS
their *s* are like the place .... Ps 5:9

STOMP
your feet may *s* in their blood......Ps 68:23

STOMPED
The Lord has *s* like grapes.........Lam 1:15
winepress was *s* outside the city .. Rev 14:20

STOMPING
those *s* juice from the grapes......Jer 25:30

STOMPS
and he *s* the winepress ....Rev 19:15

STONE
you anointed the sacred *s* ....Gen 31:13
Jacob set up a sacred *s* pillar...... Gen 35:14
down to the bottom like a *s* ......Exod 15:5
this *s* will be a witness against....Josh 24:27
I was *s* silent........................Ps 39:2
s that the builders discarded ...... Ps 118:22
move an ancient boundary *s*.....Prov 22:28
s is heavy and sand is weighty.....Prov 27:3
I am laying a *s* in Zion .... Isa 28:16
I will remove the hearts of *s*...... Ezek 11:19
I will remove the heart of *s*...... Ezek 36:26
watching as a *s* was cut out........Dan 2:34
he who says to speechless *s* .... Hab 2:19
will give him a *s*.................... Matt 7:9
one who falls on this *s*........... Matt 21:44
tomb secure by sealing the *s* ....Matt 27:66
The *s* the builders rejected ...... Luke 20:17
be the first to throw a *s* at her......John 8:7
are you going to *s* me ....John 10:32
now trying to *s* you to death....... John 11:8
They continued to *s* Stephen ......Acts 7:59
not on *s* tablets but on tablets.....2 Cor 3:3
a living *s* rejected by men...........1 Pet 2:4
and I will give him a white *s* ......Rev 2:17
powerful angel picked up a *s* .....Rev 18:21
like a *s* of crystal-clear jasper......Rev 21:11
with every kind of precious *s* ......Rev 21:19

STONE-HARD
an iron chisel on their *s* hearts ......Jer 17:1

STONED
They were *s* ....Heb 11:37

STONES
This pile of *s* is a witness ....Gen 31:48
picked out five smooth *s* ....1 Sam 17:40
settings of antimony and other *s*..1 Chr 29:2
made of valuable *s* of alabaster..... Esth 1:6
about to set your *s* in antimony .... Isa 54:11
the smooth *s* of the stream........ Isa 57:6
the *s* in the walls will cry out ....Hab 2:11
for Abraham from these *s* .... Matt 3:9
these *s* to become bread .... Matt 4:3
tremendous *s* and buildings ......Mark 13:1
you yourselves, as living *s* ....1 Pet 2:5

STONING
Once I received a *s*................ 2 Cor 11:25

STOOD
The king *s* by the pillar ....2 Kgs 23:3

STOP
That's enough! *S* now...........2 Sam 24:16
S opposing God ....2 Chr 35:21
Please *s* wounding me..............Ps 39:10
you *s* listening to instruction .....Prov 19:27
from my sight. *S* sinning............. Isa 1:16
I will *s* the flow of wine...........Jer 48:33
from my eyes and will not *s* ......Lam 3:49
and do not try to *s* them..........Matt 19:14
Do not *s* him because no one.....Mark 9:39
you will not be able to *s* them .....Acts 5:39
not *s* teaching and
   proclaiming..........................Acts 5:42
is to *s* me from being baptized ....Acts 8:36

STOPPED
and they *s* building the city.........Gen 11:8
and the sea *s* raging .... Jonah 1:15
At once the bleeding *s*...........Mark 5:29
she has not *s* kissing my feet .....Luke 7:45
and at once the bleeding *s*.......Luke 8:44

STORE
who are wise *s* up knowledge ....Prov 10:14
I have nowhere to *s* my crops ....Luke 12:17

STORED
is *s* up for the righteous ....Prov 13:22

STOREHOUSE
you entered the *s* of the snow.....Job 38:22
The seed is still in the *s*............Hag 2:19

STOREHOUSES
Is it not sealed up in my *s*........Deut 32:34

STORES
He *s* up effective counsel...........Prov 2:7

STORK
the *s* knows when it is time..........Jer 8:7

STORM
He calmed the *s* ....Ps 107:29
strikes you like a devastating *s* ....Prov 1:27
mighty *s* of military destruction ... Jer 25:32
you will come like a *s*............. Ezek 38:9
whirlwind and the raging *s* ....Nah 1:3
a great *s* developed on the sea ... Matt 8:24

STRAIGHT
can make *s* what he has bent.......Eccl 7:13
Their legs were *s* ....Ezek 1:7
make his paths *s*...................Mark 1:3
make his paths *s*................... Luke 3:4
Make *s* the way for the Lord.......John 1:23
and go to the street called '*S* ......Acts 9:11
make *s* paths for your feet........Heb 12:13

STRAIN
s out a gnat yet swallow a
   camel........................Matt 23:24

STRAINING
woman who is *s* to give birth........Isa 13:8

STRANGE
presented *s* fire before the LORD ... Lev 10:1
to perform his task, his *s* task ......Isa 28:21

STRANGER
he pretended to be a *s* to them....Gen 42:7
s had to spend the night outside... Job 31:32
own brothers treat me like a *s*.......Ps 69:8
has put up security for a *s*.........Prov 11:15
was a *s* and you invited me in.... Matt 25:35
They will never follow a *s*.........John 10:5

STRANGERS
will be *s* in a foreign country ......Gen 15:13
May *s* loot his property............ Ps 109:11
s to the covenants of promise......Eph 2:12
were at one time *s* and
   enemies..............................Col 1:21
they were *s* and foreigners .... Heb 11:13
though they are *s*.................3 John 1:5

STRANGLING
I would prefer *s* and death..........Job 7:15

STRAP
S your sword to your thigh..........Ps 45:3
and untie the *s* of his sandals.......Mark 1:7

STRAPS
leather cords, with *s* of hide .... Hos 11:4

STRAW
no longer give *s* to the people ..... Exod 5:7
are they like *s* before the wind ..... Job 21:18
A lion, like an ox, will eat *s*. .... Isa 11:7
You conceive *s*, you give birth ...... Isa 33:11
like windblown *s* with his bow ..... Isa 41:2
like *s* that the fire burns up .... Isa 47:14
stones, wood, hay, or *s* .... 1 Cor 3:12

STRAY
to *s* from your commands .... Ps 119:10
who *s* from your commands .... Ps 119:21
fools will not *s* into it .... Isa 35:8
will *s* further and further .... 2 Tim 2:16

STRAYED
have *s* from the faith .... 1 Tim 6:10
They have *s* from the truth .... 2 Tim 2:18

STREAM
five smooth stones from the *s*. .. 1 Sam 17:40
as treacherous as a seasonal *s* ...... Job 6:15
One deep *s* calls out to another ..... Ps 42:7
From the *s* along the road .... Ps 110:7
Tears *s* down from my eyes .... Ps 119:136
All the nations will *s* to it .... Isa 2:2
a *s* flowing with brimstone .... Isa 30:33
For he comes like a rushing *s* ...... Isa 59:19
like a *s* that floods its banks .... Isa 66:12
People will *s* to it .... Mic 4:1

STREAMS
As a deer longs for *s* of water .... Ps 42:1
God's *s* are full of water .... Ps 65:9
caused *s* to flow from the rock ..... Ps 78:16
He turned *s* into a desert .... Ps 107:33
just as the *s* in the arid south .... Ps 126:4
All the *s* flow into the sea. .... Eccl 1:7
cause *s* to flow on the dry land ..... Isa 44:3
I can turn *s* into a desert............. Isa 50:2

STREET
and the dangers in the *s* .... Eccl 12:5
synagogues and on *s* corners ...... Matt 6:5
go to the *s* called 'Straight .... Acts 9:11
main *s* of the city is pure gold ..... Rev 21:21
middle of the city's main *s* .... Rev 22:2

STREETS
not publicize himself in the *s* .... Isa 42:2
go into the main *s* and invite ..... Matt 22:9
and you taught us in our *s* .... Luke 13:26
quickly to the *s* and alleys .... Luke 14:21

STRENGTH
to show you my *s*. .... Exod 9:16
out of Egypt by your *s* .... Deut 9:26
a man is judged by his *s* .... Judg 8:21
not by one's own *s*. .... 1 Sam 2:9
You give me *s* for battle .... 2 Sam 22:40
to the LORD splendor and *s*. ... 1 Chr 16:28
has with him mere human *s* ...... 2 Chr 32:8
Is my *s* like that of stones .... Job 6:12
rely on it because its *s* is great...... Job 39:11
my source of *s*. .... Ps 18:1
He restores my *s* .... Ps 23:3
The LORD gives his people *s* .... Ps 29:11
gives the people power and *s*...... Ps 68:35
you give them splendor and *s* ..... Ps 89:17
makes his *s* stronger .... Prov 24:5
absolute power and awesome *s* ... Isa 40:26
Clothe yourself with *s* .... Isa 52:1
you give me *s* and protect me ..... Jer 16:19
Not by *s* and not by power .... Zech 4:6
the exercise of his immense *s* ...... Eph 1:19
and in the *s* of his power .... Eph 6:10
and from the glory of his *s* ...... 2 Thess 1:9
gained *s* in weakness .... Heb 11:34
with the *s* that God supplies .... 1 Pet 4:11
I know that you have little *s* .... Rev 3:8
and honor and power and *s* .... Rev 7:12

STRENGTHEN
S the hands that have gone limp .... Isa 35:3
to *s* those who mourn in Zion ...... Isa 61:3
I will *s* them by my power .... Zech 10:12

turned back, *s* your brothers .... Luke 22:32
to him who is able to *s* you ...... Rom 16:25
He will also *s* you to the end .... 1 Cor 1:8
and *s* you in every good thing .. 2 Thess 2:17
he will *s* you and protect you .... 2 Thess 3:3
Therefore, *s* your listless
    hands .... Heb 12:12
be patient and *s* your hearts......... Jas 5:8
and *s* what remains................. Rev 3:2

STRENGTHENED
You have not *s* the weak......... Ezek 34:4
s the souls of the disciples........ Acts 14:22
but was *s* in faith .... Rom 4:20
grant you to be *s* with power ...... Eph 3:16
Finally, be *s* in the Lord .... Eph 6:10
your hearts are *s* in holiness..... 1 Thess 3:13
grateful to the one who has *s*...... 1 Tim 1:12
Lord stood by me and *s* me....... 2 Tim 4:17
for the heart to be *s* by grace...... Heb 13:9

STRENGTHENING
speaks to people for their *s*........ 1 Cor 14:3
done for the *s* of the church ..... 1 Cor 14:26

STRENGTHENS
The LORD *s* his people .... Ps 28:8
through the one who *s* me .... Phil 4:13

STRESS
woman under a great deal of *s* ... 1 Sam 1:15
emotional *s* from your mind...... Eccl 11:10

STRETCH
See also STRETCH OUT MY HAND
you will *s* out your hands .... John 21:18

STRETCH OUT MY HAND
I will *s* against them .... Ezek 6:14
I will *s* against him................. Ezek 14:9
and I *s* against it .... Ezek 14:13
I will *s* against Edom............. Ezek 25:13
to *s* against the Philistines........ Ezek 25:16
I will *s* against you................. Ezek 35:3

STRETCHED
See also STRETCHES OUT HIS HAND
He *s* out over the boy............. 1 Kgs 17:21
who *s* out the sky.................. Isa 51:13
s it out and it was restored .... Matt 12:13

STRETCHED OUT HIS HAND
He *s*, took the dove................. Gen 8:9
Moses *s* toward the sea .... Exod 14:21
The LORD *s* over the sea............ Isa 23:11
cherubim *s* toward the fire .... Ezek 10:7
He *s* and touched him .... Matt 8:3
Jesus *s* and touched him .... Mark 1:41
So he *s* and touched him .... Luke 5:13

STRETCHER
take your *s*, and go home.......... Matt 9:6

STRETCHES
he *s* out his hand against God ..... Job 15:25

STRIFE
The lips of a fool enter into *s* ...... Prov 18:6
for a person to cease from *s* ...... Prov 20:3
s, jealousy, outbursts of anger ...... Gal 5:20

STRIKE
he will *s* your head .... Gen 3:15
S these people with blindness .... 2 Kgs 6:18
s all my enemies on the jaw .... Ps 3:7
May the godly *s* me in love.......... Ps 141:5
If you *s* him with the rod .... Prov 23:14
s the leader of the wicked .... Hab 3:13
S the shepherd that the flock..... Zech 13:7
and *s* the earth with judgment...... Mal 4:6
not *s* your foot against a stone .... Matt 4:6
I will *s* the shepherd.............. Matt 26:31
I will *s* the shepherd.............. Mark 14:27
if I spoke correctly, why *s* me..... John 18:23
s the earth with every kind .... Rev 11:6

STRIKES
he *s*, but his hands also heal........ Job 5:18
God *s* the heads of his enemies...... Ps 68:21
person who *s* you on the cheek .. Luke 6:29
if someone *s* you in the face .... 2 Cor 11:20

STRINGED
to you with a *s* instrument.......... Ps 71:22
sound of your *s* instruments........ Isa 14:11
music of your *s* instruments..... Amos 5:23

STRIP
I will *s* her naked and expose........ Hos 2:3

STRIVE
I *s* to lay hold of that................. Phil 3:12
I *s* toward the prize.................. Phil 3:14
s to be found at peace........... 2 Pet 3:14

STRONG
for compelled by my *s* hand........ Exod 6:1
Be *s* and courageous............. Deut 31:6
sure you are very *s* and brave .... Josh 1:7
Step on the necks of the *s* .... Judg 5:21
Be *s* and act like men .... 1 Sam 4:9
so be *s* and act decisively......... Ezra 10:4
LORD who is *s* and mighty .... Ps 24:8
God is our *s* refuge .... Ps 46:1
from the *s* wind and the gale .... Ps 55:8
a *s* tower that protects me .... Ps 61:3
I have heard: God is *s*............... Ps 62:11
arm is powerful, your hand *s* .... Ps 89:13
one has *s* confidence .... Prov 14:26
of the LORD is like a *s* tower ..... Prov 18:10
for their Protector is *s*............ Prov 23:11
A wise warrior is *s*............... Prov 24:5
clothing was *s* and splendid ...... Prov 31:25
attention to your *s* protector .... Isa 17:10
We have a *s* city................... Isa 26:1
he makes it with his *s* arm......... Isa 44:12
Its boughs were *s*................. Ezek 19:11
one *s* like iron .... Dan 2:40
But when he saw the *s* wind..... Matt 14:30
When a *s* man .... Luke 11:21
who are *s* ought to bear with...... Rom 15:1
but you are *s*..................... 1 Cor 4:10
then I am *s*...................... 2 Cor 12:10
but you are *s*..................... 2 Cor 13:9
s in your faith................... 1 Pet 5:9
that you are *s*................... 1 John 2:14
the dragon was not *s* enough....... Rev 12:8

STRONGER
weakness of God is *s* than .... 1 Cor 1:25

STRONGEST
was the *s* among his brothers ..... 1 Chr 5:2

STRONGHOLD
my *s*, my deliverer................ 2 Sam 22:1
a *s* where I can be safe.............. Ps 31:2
my shelter and my *s*................ Ps 91:2
way of the LORD is like a *s* ...... Prov 10:29

STRONGHOLDS
possess the *s* of their enemies... Gen 24:60

STRUCK
s the rock twice with his staff .... Num 20:11
and they *s* them down............... Josh 11:8
for the hand of God has *s* me...... Job 19:21
he *s* a rock and water flowed ...... Ps 78:20
I *s* you down in my anger.......... Isa 60:10
s it and broke off its two horns..... Dan 8:7
s all the products of your labor..... Hag 2:17
and *s* him with their fists .... Matt 26:67
s him repeatedly on the head.... Matt 27:30
s him on the head with a staff ... Mark 15:19
s him repeatedly in the face .... John 19:3

STRUGGLE
a desperate *s* with my sister....... Gen 30:8
how great a *s* I have for you.......... Col 2:1

STRUGGLES
s from the outside, fears from..... 2 Cor 7:5

STRUGGLING
s to give birth...................... Rev 12:2

STUBBORN
person has a *s*, rebellious son .... Deut 21:18
don't be *s* like your fathers .... 2 Chr 30:8
Do not be *s* like they were........ Ps 95:8
because I know how *s* you are..... Isa 48:4
You *s* people....................... Acts 7:51

STUBBORNNESS
ignore the *s*......................Deut 9:27
about your rebellion and *s*.......Deut 31:27
STUDENT
teacher as well as *s*...............1 Chr 25:8
STUDY
You *s* the scriptures thoroughly ..John 5:39
STUMBLE
For I am about to *s* ....Ps 38:17
nothing causes them to *s*.........Ps 119:165
and you will not *s*.................Prov 3:23
do not know what they *s* over.....Prov 4:19
None tire or *s*.....................Isa 5:27
and a rock that makes one *s*........Isa 8:14
Many will *s* over the stone........Isa 8:15
the one who helps will *s*..........Isa 31:3
we *s* at noontime as if it were .....Isa 59:10
the wilderness they did not *s*.......Isa 63:13
Do it before you *s* into distress.....Jer 13:16
not *s* because he sees the light ....John 11:9
stone that will cause
   people to *s* ....Rom 9:33
not *s* into an irrevocable fall.......Rom 11:11
s into temptation and a trap........1 Tim 6:9
For we all *s* in many ways ....Jas 3:2
STUMBLED
who *s* have taken on strength .....1 Sam 2:4
none of his tribes *s*................Ps 105:37
they have *s* and fallen in defeat.....Jer 46:6
STUMBLING
See also STUMBLING BLOCK
s block in front of a blind person ..Lev 19:14
from tears and my feet from *s*......Ps 116:8
They stumbled over the *s* stone .. Rom 9:32
s block to Jews and foolishness..1 Cor 1:23
there is no cause for *s* in him .... 1 John 2:10
STUMBLING BLOCK
s in front of a blind person ....Lev 19:14
You are a *s* to me.................Matt 16:23
a *s* and a retribution for them .... Rom 11:9
a *s* to Jews and foolishness to .....1 Cor 1:23
to put a *s* before the people ....Rev 2:14
STUNNED
they heard this they were *s*......Matt 22:22
STUPID
and considered *s* in your sight.......Job 18:3
the one who hates reproof is *s* .... Prov 12:1
STUPOR
awoke from his drunken *s*.........Gen 9:24
STUTTERS
the tongue that *s* will speak ....Isa 32:4
STYLUS
the *s* of an experienced scribe.......Ps 45:1
words on it with an ordinary *s*........Isa 8:1
SUBDUE
You will *s* a lion and a snake.........Ps 91:13
s my body and make it my slave. .1 Cor 9:27
human being can *s* the tongue.......Jas 3:8
SUBDUED
Though they had *s* the land........Josh 18:1
He *s* nations beneath us ....Ps 47:3
SUBDUES
A gift given in secret *s* anger .....Prov 21:14
SUBJECT
s to the governing authorities ..... Rom 13:1
able to *s* all things to himself ....Phil 3:21
being *s* to their own husbands.... Titus 2:5
to be *s* to rulers and authorities ....Titus 3:1
Be *s* to every human institution ...1 Pet 2:13
be *s* to your own husbands.........1 Pet 3:1
authorities and powers *s* to him...1 Pet 3:22
be *s* to the elders ....1 Pet 5:5
SUBJECTED
the creation was *s* to futility......Rom 8:20
when all things are *s* to him .....1 Cor 15:28
SUBJECTS
unless they became my *s*...........Isa 27:5

SUBMISSIVENESS
must learn quietly with all *s* ....1 Tim 2:11
SUBMIT
Return to your mistress and *s* ..... Gen 16:9
s to the LORD God of Israel ......Josh 24:23
S to the LORD and come to his .. 2 Chr 30:8
they *s* to me ....Ps 18:44
does not *s* to the law of God.......Rom 8:7
Wives, *s* to your husbands........Eph 5:22
why do you *s* to them ....Col 2:20
Wives, *s* to your husbands........Col 3:18
not *s* ourselves all the more ...... Heb 12:9
So *s* to God..........................Jas 4:7
SUBVERTED
s the words of the treacherous ...Prov 22:12
SUBVERTING
found this man *s* our nation ...... Luke 23:2
SUBVERTS
s the words of the righteous...... Exod 23:8
SUCCEED
It will not *s*.......................Num 14:41
will not *s* in anything you do.....Deut 28:29
God caused him to *s*...............2 Chr 26:5
Look, my servant will *s*.............Isa 52:13
to be used against you will *s*......Isa 54:17
SUCCEEDED
he *s* in all his endeavors ....2 Kgs 18:7
Hezekiah *s* in all that he did .... 2 Chr 32:30
SUCCEEDS
in whatever he does he *s* ....Prov 17:8
SUCCESS
The LORD grants *s* to the one.......Ps 37:23
has the advantage of giving *s* .... Eccl 10:10
to the ground and enjoyed *s*....... Dan 8:12
SUCCESSFUL
s and lived in the household.......Gen 39:2
was *s* and all Israel was loyal ....1 Chr 29:23
Why are wicked people *s*............Jer 12:1
SUCCESSFULLY
and *s* reinstituted service........2 Chr 31:21
SUCCUMB
entangled in them and *s*.........2 Pet 2:20
SUDDENLY
will *s* come to his temple............ Mal 3:1
S a vast, heavenly army.............Luke 2:13
down upon you *s* like a trap ..... Luke 21:34
SUE
if someone wants to *s* you........Matt 5:40
SUFFER
has caused me to *s* ....Ruth 1:21
and *s* in broad daylight ....Ps 13:2
Son of Man must *s* many things .. Mark 8:31
Son of Man must *s* many things .. Mark 9:12
Son of Man must *s* many things .. Luke 9:22
he must *s* many things............Luke 17:25
for the Christ to *s* these things ..Luke 24:26
Christ would *s* and would rise ...Luke 24:46
his Christ would *s*..................Acts 3:18
how much he must *s* ....Acts 9:16
Christ had to *s* and to rise ....Acts 17:3
that the Christ was to *s*........... Acts 26:23
indeed we *s* with him..............Rom 8:17
but also to *s* for him.................Phil 1:29
do good and *s* and so endure.....1 Pet 2:20
to *s* for doing what is right ....1 Pet 3:14
is better to *s* for doing good.......1 Pet 3:17
none of you *s* as a murderer.......1 Pet 4:15
s according to the will of God .....1 Pet 4:19
the things you are about to *s* ......Rev 2:10
SUFFERED
Israel *s* greatly.....................Judg 10:9
Having *s*, he will reflect.............Isa 53:11
Through all that they *s* ....Isa 63:9
have a *s* crushing blow ....Jer 14:17
s greatly as a result of a dream...Matt 27:19
who *s* from unclean spirits ....Luke 6:18
s so many things for nothing ....Gal 3:4
I have *s* the loss of all things........Phil 3:8

and honor because he *s* death...... Heb 2:9
s when he was tempted .... Heb 2:18
through the things he *s*............. Heb 5:8
regarded abuse *s* for Christ........Heb 11:26
Jesus also *s* outside the camp......Heb 13:12
since Christ also *s* for you ....1 Pet 2:21
when he *s*, he threatened no ......1 Pet 2:23
Christ also *s* once for sins ....1 Pet 3:18
since Christ *s* in the flesh...........1 Pet 4:1
you have *s* for a little while.......1 Pet 5:10
SUFFERING
fruitful in the land of my *s*.......Gen 41:52
look on the *s* of your servant......1 Sam 1:11
LORD saw Israel's intense *s* ......2 Kgs 14:26
days of *s* take hold of me...........Job 30:16
see one who inflicts pain and *s* ..... Ps 10:14
rescue me from my *s* ....Ps 25:17
See my pain and *s* ....Ps 25:18
I am oppressed and *s*..............Ps 69:29
I am *s* terribly....................Ps 119:107
has added sorrow to my *s*.........Jer 45:3
be great *s* unlike anything .... Matt 24:21
she no longer remembers the *s* .. John 16:21
you have trouble and *s*............John 16:33
after his *s*, he presented himself.....Acts 1:3
seen the *s* of my people ....Acts 7:34
endure in *s*, persist in prayer .....Rom 12:12
light *s* is producing for us......... 2 Cor 4:17
joy in the midst of all our *s* .... 2 Cor 7:4
relief for others and *s* for you .... 2 Cor 8:13
of what I am *s* for you ....Eph 3:13
endured a harsh conflict of *s* .....Heb 10:32
an example of *s* and patience........Jas 5:10
Is anyone among you *s* ....Jas 5:13
s the punishment of eternal fire....Jude 1:7
will experience *s* for ten days.......Rev 2:10
adultery with her into terrible *s* ... Rev 2:22
SUFFERINGS
but we also rejoice in *s* ....Rom 5:3
s cannot even be compared ....Rom 8:18
the same *s* that we also suffer...... 2 Cor 1:6
is lacking in the *s* of Christ........ Col 1:24
as the persecutions and *s*......... 2 Tim 3:11
salvation perfect through *s* ....Heb 2:10
the *s* appointed for Christ ....1 Pet 1:11
SUFFERS
who *s* will soon be released ....Isa 51:14
and *s* from depression..............Isa 54:6
If one member *s*.................1 Cor 12:26
SUITABLE
are to dress in *s* apparel ....1 Tim 2:9
SUKKOTH
Place east of the Jordan, Judg 8:4–5
Jacob's residence here, Gen 33:17
—Israel's first camp, Exod 12:37
SULFUR
LORD rained down *s* and fire......Gen 19:24
burning *s* is scattered...............Job 18:15
s came out of their mouths........Rev 9:17
into the lake of fire and *s* ....Rev 20:10
SULLEN
not look *s* like the hypocrites......Matt 6:16
SUMMER
cold and heat, *s* and winter.........Gen 8:22
in the intense heat of *s* ....Ps 32:4
the cycle of *s* and winter............Ps 74:17
you know that *s* is near.............Matt 24:32
SUMMIT
rocky *s* where I take shelter ..... 2 Sam 22:3
on an inaccessible rocky *s* ....Ps 27:5
Lead me up to a rocky *s* ....Ps 61:2
SUMMITS
will be like the abandoned *s*........Isa 17:9
SUMMON
s the elders of the church ....Jas 5:14
SUMMONED
The LORD *s* me from birth...........Isa 49:1
After many days you will be *s* .... Ezek 38:8
and I *s* my son out of Egypt.........Hos 11:1

SUMPTUOUSLY
and who feasted *s* every day ..... Luke 16:19
SUN
The *s* stood still and the moon ... Josh 10:13
like the rising *s* at its brightest..... Judg 5:31
a well-watered plant in the *s* .... Job 8:16
he has pitched a tent for the *s*....... Ps 19:4
The *s* will not harm you by day .....Ps 121:6
the *s* to rule by day .... Ps 136:8
for a person to see the *s*........... Eccl 11:7
s and the light of the moon........ Eccl 12:2
bright as the *s* .... Song 6:10
s will no longer supply light .... Isa 60:19
will seem as if the *s* had set......... Jer 15:9
fixed the *s* to give light .... Jer 31:35
s and the moon grow dark......... Joel 2:10
s will set on these prophets .... Mic 3:6
The *s* and moon stand still.......... Hab 3:11
s to rise on the evil and.......... Matt 5:45
There is one glory of the *s*........ 1 Cor 15:41
do not let the *s* go down........... Eph 4:26
s became as black as sackcloth..... Rev 6:12
s will not beat down on them....... Rev 7:16
city does not need the *s* or .... Rev 21:23
SUN'S
will be like the *s* glare .... Isa 30:26
because the *s* light failed .... Luke 23:45
SUNLIGHT
s will be turned to darkness .... Joel 2:31
SUNRISE
your light will shine like the *s*...... Isa 58:8
SUPERIOR
not come with *s* eloquence......... 1 Cor 2:1
inherited a name *s* to theirs .... Heb 1:4
SUPERNATURAL
who gives *s* guidance .... Isa 28:29
SUPPER
not really eating the Lord's *S* ...1 Cor 11:20
he also took the cup after *s*....... 1 Cor 11:25
SUPPLICATION
make your *s* to the Almighty .... Job 8:5
SUPPLICATIONS
it make numerous *s* to you .... Job 41:3
offered both requests and *s* .... Heb 5:7
SUPPLIED
s the cedars and evergreens...... 1 Kgs 5:10
s the people with 30,000 lambs .. 2 Chr 35:7
SUPPLY
you will *s* the food I need.......... 1 Kgs 5:9
my God will *s* your every need .... Phil 4:19
SUPPORT
let no one *s* him .... Prov 28:17
Here is my servant whom I *s* .... Isa 42:1
there was no one offering *s* .... Isa 63:5
the *s* and bulwark of the truth.... 1 Tim 3:15
SUPPORTED
s and knit together .... Col 2:19
SUPPORTING
through every *s* ligament........... Eph 4:16
SUPPORTS
The Lord *s* all who fall .... Ps 145:14
SUPPOSE
who *s* that godliness is a way...... 1 Tim 6:5
s that he will receive anything........ Jas 1:7
SUPPOSEDLY
about what he has *s* seen............ Col 2:18
SUPREME
whether to a king as *s* .... 1 Pet 2:13
SURE
you must be *s* to keep them....... Lev 25:18
must be *s* to open your hand ...... Deut 15:8
s you pull out ears of grain .... Ruth 2:16
am *s* that the Lord will deliver .....Ps 20:6
Stumbling blocks are *s* to come ... Luke 17:1
faith is being *s* of what we hope .... Heb 11:1
s that we have a clear conscience..Heb 13:18
s of your calling and election .....2 Pet 1:10

SURELY
But God will *s* come to you...... Gen 50:24
s wipe out the remembrance.....Exod 17:14
SURFACE
over the *s* of the watery deep ....Gen 1:2
SURGING
But the wicked are like a *s* sea..... Isa 57:20
SURPASSES
love of Christ that *s* knowledge..... Eph 3:19
SURPASSING
praise him for his *s* greatness...... Ps 150:2
the *s* wealth of his grace............. Eph 2:7
SURPRISED
and ambushed the *s* army .... Judg 8:11
Therefore do not be *s* .... 1 John 3:13
SURROUND
You must *s* the king .... 2 Kgs 11:8
SURROUNDED
All the nations *s* me .... Ps 118:10
evil deeds have now *s* them .... Hos 7:2
s by such a great cloud of.......... Heb 12:1
SURVIVE
of them I have allowed to *s*....... Jer 50:20
SURVIVED
God face to face and have *s* ...... Gen 32:30
no one escaped or *s* .... Lam 2:22
SURVIVES
If what someone has built *s* ...... 1 Cor 3:14
SURVIVORS
had not left us a few *s* .... Isa 1:9
SUSA
Residence of Persian monarchs, Esth 1:2
SUSANNA
Believing woman ministering to Christ,
    Luke 8:2–3
SUSPENDS
he *s* the earth on nothing.......... Job 26:7
SUSPENSE
you have been in *s* and .... Acts 27:33
SUSPICIONS
dissension, slanders, evil *s*......... 1 Tim 6:4
SUSTAIN
S me by giving me the desire.......Ps 51:12
You *s* the oppressed.................Ps 68:10
S me as you promised ....Ps 119:116
S me with raisin cakes............. Song 2:5
SUSTAINED
For forty years you *s* them .... Neh 9:21
They are *s* as they travel along ......Ps 84:7
SUSTAINS
but the Lord *s* the godly .... Ps 37:17
spirit *s* him through sickness ..... Prov 18:14
s his rage against his enemies ...... Nah 1:2
s all things by his powerful word ....Heb 1:3
SWADDLING
and thick darkness its *s* band.....Job 38:9
SWALLOW
fluttering bird or like a flying *s* ... Prov 26:2
Like a *s* or a thrush I chirp......... Isa 38:14
Lord sent a huge fish to *s*
    Jonah .... Jonah 1:17
strain out a gnat yet *s* a camel... Matt 23:24
SWALLOWED
the earth *s* them................... Exod 15:12
monster from the deep he *s* me.... Jer 51:34
SWAY
tops of the mountains may it *s* ..... Ps 72:16
SWAYS
like a reed that *s* in the water..... 1 Kgs 14:15
SWEAR
I solemnly *s* by my own name ..... Gen 22:16
he could *s* by no one greater ...... Heb 6:13
do not *s*, either by heaven .... Jas 5:12

SWEARS
Whoever *s* by the altar .... Matt 23:18
SWEAT
By the *s* of your brow.............. Gen 3:19
his *s* was like drops of blood.....Luke 22:44
SWEEP
Do not *s* me away with sinners .....Ps 26:9
he will *s* it away along with ....Ps 58:9
SWEET
to stop producing my *s* figs........ Judg 9:11
If evil is *s* in his mouth.......... Job 20:12
clods of the torrent valley are *s* ... Job 21:33
and his fruit is *s* to my taste ...... Song 2:3
for your voice is *s*................ Song 2:14
His mouth is very *s*............... Song 5:16
was *s* like honey in my mouth ...... Ezek 3:3
as *s* as honey in your mouth........Rev 10:9
SWEETER
What is *s* than honey .... Judg 14:18
are *s* in my mouth than honey.... Ps 119:103
SWEETNESS
likewise the *s* of one's friend ..... Prov 27:9
SWELL
and your abdomen *s*............... Num 5:21
and their feet did not *s* .... Neh 9:21
SWEPT
and his army will be *s* away........ Dan 11:26
waves you sent *s* over me .... Jonah 2:3
SWERVE
Do not *s* from it to the right......... Josh 1:7
SWIFTLY
s his order reaches .... Ps 147:15
SWINDLERS
s will not inherit the kingdom .... 1 Cor 6:10
SWORD
See also TWO-EDGED SWORD
the flame of a whirling *s*........... Gen 3:24
Use your *s* to rescue me............. Ps 17:13
and I do not prevail by my *s* .... Ps 44:6
Assyria will fall by a *s*............... Isa 31:8
my *s* has slaughtered heavenly ..... Isa 34:5
Lord's *s* is dripping with blood..... Isa 34:6
The *s* is outside................... Ezek 7:15
A *s*, a *s* is sharpened .... Ezek 21:9
A *s*, a *s* drawn for slaughter....... Ezek 21:28
the warrior's bow and *s*........... Hos 2:18
my people will die by the *s* ...... Amos 9:10
Awake, *s*, against my shepherd ....Zech 13:7
not come to bring peace but a *s*.. Matt 10:34
Put your *s* back in its place ...... Matt 26:52
a *s* will pierce your own soul ..... Luke 2:35
not bear the *s* for nothing .... Rom 13:4
and the *s* of the Spirit............... Eph 6:17
than any double-edged *s* .... Heb 4:12
a sharp double-edged *s*............. Rev 1:16
his mouth extends a sharp *s*....... Rev 19:15
SWORDS
it was not by your *s* or bows...... Josh 24:12
not conquer the land by their *s*...... Ps 44:3
but they are really like sharp *s*...... Ps 55:21
whose tongues are sharp *s* .... Ps 57:4
beat their *s* into plowshares......... Isa 2:4
chasing after them with *s*............ Jer 9:16
beat their *s* into plowshares......... Mic 4:3
here are two *s* .... Luke 22:38
SWORE
As I *s* in my anger............... Heb 3:11
and *s* by the one who lives.....Rev 10:6
SWORN
Lord has *s* and will not change ..... Heb 7:21
SWUNG
So the angel *s* his sickle .... Rev 14:19
SYCHAR
Town of Samaria; Jesus talks to woman at
    well here, John 4:5–39
SYLLABLE
babbling, a *s* here, a *s* there........ Isa 28:10

SYMBOL
all of you are a *s* .... Zech 3:8
a *s* for the time then present .... Heb 9:9
SYMBOLS
as *s* on your forehead............. Deut 6:8
SYMPATHETIC
the court officials *s* to Daniel .... Dan 1:9
s, affectionate, compassionate...... 1 Pet 3:8
SYMPATHIZING
a high priest incapable of *s* .... Heb 4:15
SYMPATHY
I look for *s* .... Ps 69:20
SYNAGOGUE
into the *s* on the Sabbath day..... Luke 4:16
who was a leader of the *s*......... Luke 8:41
meeting of the *s* had broken up .. Acts 13:43
in the *s* every Sabbath .... Acts 18:4
but are a *s* of Satan .... Rev 2:9
SYRACUSE
City visited by Paul, Acts 28:12
SYROPHOENICIAN
Daughter of, freed of demon, Mark 7:25–31

T

TABERAH
Israelite camp; fire destroys many there,
     Num 11:1–3
TABERNACLE
pattern of the *t* and the............ Exod 25:9
The *t* itself you are to make ...... Exod 26:1
took along the *t* of Moloch .... Acts 7:43
and the true *t* that the Lord .... Heb 8:2
as long as I am in this *t* .... 2 Pet 1:13
my *t* will soon be removed .... 2 Pet 1:14
TABITHA [or DORCAS]
Disciple at Joppa; raised to life,
     Acts 9:36–42
Also called "Dorcas," Acts 9:36
TABLE
to make a *t* of acacia wood ...... Exod 25:23
their dining *t* become a trap .... Ps 69:22
on his head as he was at the *t* .... Matt 26:7
but even the dogs under the *t*....Mark 7:28
their *t* become a snare and trap ... Rom 11:9
t of the Lord and the *t* of demons.. 1 Cor 10:21
TABLES
the *t* are covered with vomit .... Isa 28:8
the *t* of the money changers ..... Matt 21:12
the word of God to wait on *t* .... Acts 6:2
TABLET
write them on the *t* of your heart .. Prov 3:3
TABLETS
I will give you the stone *t*........ Exod 24:12
Cut out two *t* of stone .... Exod 34:1
He wrote on the *t* the words ....Exod 34:28
with the two *t* of the
     testimony .... Exod 34:29
writing them on two stone *t*....... Deut 4:13
stone *t* but on *t* of human hearts .. 2 Cor 3:3
the stone *t* of the covenant........ Heb 9:4
TABOR, MOUNT
See MOUNT TABOR
TADMOR
Trading center near Damascus, 2 Chr 8:4
TAHPANHES
City of Egypt; refuge of fleeing Jews,
     Jer 2:16; 44:1; Ezek 30:18
TAIL
and grab it by the *t* .... Exod 4:4
you the head and not the *t* ...... Deut 28:13
It makes its *t* stiff like a cedar ..... Job 40:17
dragon's *t* swept away a third ...... Rev 12:4
TAILS
jackals in pairs by their *t*........... Judg 15:4
t and stingers like scorpions........ Rev 9:10
because their *t* are like snakes ..... Rev 9:19

TAKE
See also TAKE HEED
must *t* with you seven pairs .... Gen 7:2
T your son—your only son......... Gen 22:2
I will *t* you to myself.............. Exod 6:7
not *t* the name of the Lord...... Exod 20:7
Now *t* off your ornaments....... Exod 33:5
Then I will *t* away my hand ...... Exod 33:23
and *t* us for your inheritance .... Exod 34:9
You must not *t* vengeance......... Lev 19:18
t oaths using only his name ...... Deut 6:13
come up to *t* Samson prisoner ... Judg 15:10
We will only *t* you prisoner....... Judg 15:13
not *t* his eyes off the righteous..... Job 36:7
the Lord would *t* me in .... Ps 27:10
not *t* your Holy Spirit away.......... Ps 51:11
In you I *t* shelter.................... Ps 141:8
in order to *t* revenge .... Ps 149:7
will *t* his position before kings... Prov 22:29
to sue you and *t* your tunic .... Matt 5:40
Do not *t* gold .... Matt 10:9
T my yoke on you .... Matt 11:29
t up his cross .... Matt 16:24
T what is yours and go .... Matt 20:14
T, eat, this is my body .... Matt 26:26
T it. This is my body ....Mark 14:22
T this cup away from me ....Mark 14:36
and *t* the least important place... Luke 14:10
so that I may *t* it back again ...... John 10:17
and *t* you to be with me .... John 14:3
we *t* every thought captive .... 2 Cor 10:5
we cannot *t* a single thing out ..... 1 Tim 6:7
T your share of suffering .... 2 Tim 2:3
t my advice and buy gold........... Rev 3:18
TAKE HEED
T to yourselves not to go up...... Exod 19:12
T because of him ....Exod 23:31
T; do not turn to evil................ Job 36:21
will not *t* of the sheep .... Zech 11:16
TAKEN
part he had *t* out of the man ...... Gen 2:22
for she was *t* out of man........... Gen 2:23
for out of it you were *t* .... Gen 3:19
you have *t* us away to die......... Exod 14:11
you have *t* many captives........Ps 68:18
you have *t* refuge in the Lord ...... Ps 91:9
will be *t* from you and given..... Matt 21:43
one will be *t* and one left .... Matt 24:40
he has will be *t* from him.........Mark 4:25
only in Christ is it *t* away .... 2 Cor 3:14
until he is *t* out of the way.......2 Thess 2:7
TAKES
who *t* his name in vain............. Exod 20:7
Lord *t* delight in his faithful........ Ps 147:11
Lord *t* delight in his people .... Ps 149:4
Lord *t* his position to judge......... Isa 3:13
He *t* great delight in you..........Zeph 3:17
who *t* no offense at me............ Matt 11:6
he *t* his seat in God's temple ....2 Thess 2:4
TAKING
by *t* the wife of Uriah............ 2 Sam 12:10
profit is there in *t* my life .... Ps 30:9
t the cup and giving thanks..... Matt 26:27
by *t* on the form of a slave.......... Phil 2:7
TALENT
and hid your *t* in the ground..... Matt 25:25
TALENTS
a man who owed 10,000 *t* .... Matt 18:24
To one he gave five *t* ....Matt 25:15
TALITHA
T koum," which means .... Mark 5:41
TALK
Does he argue with useless *t* ...Job 15:3
foolish *t*, or coarse jesting ....Eph 5:4
TALKATIVE
this *t* man be vindicated.............Job 11:2
TALKED
I *t* like a child .... 1 Cor 13:11
TALKER
you deceptive *t* .... Ps 120:3

TALKERS
idle *t*, and deceivers .... Titus 1:10
TALKING
but merely *t* about it .... Prov 14:23
TALL
and *t* as the Anakites .... Deut 2:10
to a nation of *t*......................Isa 18:2
you grew *t* and came of age .... Ezek 16:7
TAMAR
Wife of Er and mother of Perez and Zerah,
     Gen 38:6–30
—Absalom's sister, 2 Sam 13:1–32
TAMBOURINE
accompaniment of *t* and harp ...... Job 21:12
with the *t* and with dancing .... Ps 150:4
TAMBOURINES
dancing to the rhythm of *t* .... Judg 11:34
happy sound of the *t* stops .... Isa 24:8
TANNER
a man named Simon, a *t*........... Acts 9:43
TAPROOT
But leave its *t* in the ground .... Dan 4:15
TARGET
have you set me as your *t* ....Job 7:20
made me the *t* for his arrow....... Lam 3:12
TARSHISH
City at a great distance from Palestine,
     Jonah 1:3
Ships of, noted in commerce, Ps 48:7
TARSUS
Paul's birthplace, Acts 21:39
Paul sent to, Acts 9:30
Visited by Barnabas, Acts 11:25
TASK
given people a burdensome *t*....... Eccl 1:13
to perform his *t*.....................Isa 28:21
TASSELS
to make *t* for themselves........ Num 15:38
You shall make yourselves *t*..... Deut 22:12
and their *t* long................... Matt 23:5
TASTE
T and see that the Lord is good.....Ps 34:8
and his fruit is sweet to my *t* ...... Song 2:3
invited will *t* my banquet .... Luke 14:24
Do not *t*! Do not touch .... Col 2:21
TASTED
it *t* like wafers with honey........Exod 16:31
It *t* like fresh olive oil .... Num 11:8
t the heavenly gift .... Heb 6:4
t the good word of God .... Heb 6:5
TASTELESS
that is *t* be eaten without salt ....Job 6:6
TASTING
But after *t* it .... Matt 27:34
TATTENAI
Persian governor opposing the Jews,
     Ezra 5:3, 6
TAUGHT
have *t* me since I was young........Ps 71:17
He *t* them many things............Mark 4:2
So he *t* them many things ....Mark 6:34
and you *t* in our streets......... Luke 13:26
And they will all be *t* by God ..... John 6:45
just what the Father *t* me........ John 8:28
he spoke and *t* accurately .... Acts 18:25
words *t* us by human wisdom ..... 1 Cor 2:13
heard about him and were *t*.......Eph 4:21
just as you were *t*................... Col 2:7
the traditions that we *t* you ....2 Thess 2:15
TAUNT
All who see me *t* me.............. Ps 22:7
who live on our borders *t*.......... Ps 44:13
those who *t* will vanish .... Isa 29:20
TAUNTS
The Lord *t* them .... Ps 2:4

TAX
See also TAX COLLECTOR; TAX
    COLLECTORS AND SINNERS
the *t* authorized by Moses........2 Chr 24:6
the *t* collectors do the same......Matt 5:46
the collectors of the temple *t*....Matt 17:24
t collectors and prostitutes.......Matt 21:31
me the coin used for the *t*.......Matt 22:19
to pay the tribute *t* to Caesar.....Luke 23:2

TAX COLLECTOR
See also TAX COLLECTORS AND SINNERS
Thomas and Matthew the *t*.......Matt 10:3
treat him like a Gentile or a *t*....Matt 18:17
and saw a *t* named Levi..........Luke 5:27
a Pharisee and the other a *t*....Luke 18:10
he was a chief *t* and was rich......Luke 19:2

TAX COLLECTORS AND SINNERS
t came and ate with Jesus........Matt 9:10
and a drunk, a friend of *t*.......Matt 11:19
Why does he eat with *t*..........Mark 2:16
t were coming to hear him........Luke 15:1

TAXES
earthly kings collect tolls or *t*.....Matt 17:25
Is it right to pay *t* to Caesar.......Matt 22:17
t to whom *t* are due..............Rom 13:7

TEACH
ordinances I am about to *t* you.....Deut 4:1
instead *t* them to your children...Deut 4:9
must *t* them to your children......Deut 6:7
will *t* Jacob your ordinances.....Deut 33:10
Can anyone *t* God knowledge......Job 21:22
t you about the power of God......Job 27:11
t me what I cannot see...........Job 34:32
T me your paths.....................Ps 25:4
T me how you want me to live......Ps 27:11
t you what it means to fear.........Ps 34:11
t rebels your merciful ways.........Ps 51:13
t us to consider our mortality......Ps 90:12
T me your statutes.................Ps 119:12
he can *t* us his requirements.........Isa 2:3
Who is the LORD trying to *t*........Isa 28:9
t it have used their writings.......Jer 8:8
need to *t* their neighbors..........Jer 31:34
the synagogue and began to *t*.....Mark 1:21
t us to pray......................Luke 11:1
for the Holy Spirit will *t* you......Luke 12:12
will *t* you everything..............John 14:26
orders not to *t* in this name......Acts 5:28
you who *t* someone else..........Rom 2:21
if it is teaching, he must *t*.........Rom 12:7
Does not nature itself *t* you......1 Cor 11:14
to *t* or exercise authority.........1 Tim 2:12
Command and *t* these things......1 Tim 4:11
T them and exhort them..........1 Tim 6:2
no need for anyone to *t* you.....1 John 2:27

TEACHER
The words of the *T*..................Eccl 1:1
T, we know that you are
    truthful........................Matt 22:16
for you have one *T*...............Matt 23:8
T, don't you care................Mark 4:38
Good *t*, what must I do..........Mark 10:17
a *t* who has come from God........John 3:2
T, this woman was caught........John 8:4
The *T* is here and is asking........John 11:28
You call me '*T*' and 'Lord.........John 13:13
a *t* of little children..............Rom 2:20
a *t* of the Gentiles in faith..........1 Tim 2:7

TEACHERS
more insight than all my *t*.........Ps 119:99
your *t* will no longer be hidden...Isa 30:20
third *t*, then miracles...........1 Cor 12:28
and some as pastors and *t*.........Eph 4:11
should in fact be *t* by this time....Heb 5:12
of you should become *t*.............Jas 3:1
there will be false *t* among you.....2 Pet 2:1

TEACHES
that is why he *t* sinners............Ps 25:8
and *t* others to do so.............Matt 5:19
But as his anointing *t* you........1 John 2:27

TEACHING
My *t* is flawless....................Job 11:4
t of the righteous feeds many....Prov 10:21
responsible for *t* my law.............Jer 2:8
against the *t* of the Pharisees.....Matt 16:12
t them to obey everything.......Matt 28:20
were amazed by his *t*............Mark 1:22
A new *t* with authority..........Mark 1:27
t as doctrine the commandments...Mark 7:7
My *t* is not from me...............John 7:16
if anyone obeys my *t*..............John 8:51
because they were *t* the people....Acts 4:2
filled Jerusalem with your *t*........Acts 5:28
did not stop *t* and proclaiming....Acts 5:42
pattern of *t* you were entrusted...Rom 6:17
knowledge or prophecy or *t*......1 Cor 14:6
carried about by every wind of *t*...Eph 4:14
t all people with all wisdom.........Col 1:28
who live contrary to sound *t*......1 Tim 1:10
t the message of truth
    accurately.....................2 Tim 2:15
have followed my *t*................2 Tim 3:10
inspired by God and useful for *t*..2 Tim 3:16
people will not tolerate sound *t*...2 Tim 4:3
by *t* for dishonest gain..............Titus 1:11
In your *t* show integrity............Titus 2:7
to bring credit to the *t* of God....Titus 2:10
not remain in the *t* of Christ......2 John 1:9

TEACHINGS
on human commands and *t*........Col 2:22
deceiving spirits and demonic *t*....1 Tim 4:1
away by all sorts of strange *t*......Heb 13:9

TEAR
You who *t* yourself to pieces.......Job 18:4
I myself will *t* them to pieces.......Hos 5:14
T your hearts.....................Joel 2:13
and *t* you to pieces...............Matt 7:6
He will wipe away every *t*.........Rev 21:4

TEARS
I have seen your *t*................2 Kgs 20:5
my *t* saturate the cushion............Ps 6:6
have given them *t* as food..........Ps 80:5
and mix my drink with my *t*.......Ps 102:9
I will saturate you with my *t*........Isa 16:9
wipe away the *t* from every face....Isa 25:8
until *t* stream from our own eyes...Jer 9:18
shedding *t* of contrition.............Jer 31:9
back with *t* of repentance..........Jer 50:4
my eyes flow with *t*...............Lam 1:16
to wet his feet with her *t*.........Luke 7:38
warning each one of you with *t*...Acts 20:31
As I remember your *t*.............2 Tim 1:4
with loud cries and *t*................Heb 5:7
he sought the blessing with *t*......Heb 12:17

TEETH
and his *t* white from milk.........Gen 49:12
with only the skin of my *t*.........Job 19:20
will break the *t* of the wicked.........Ps 3:7
Like vinegar to the *t*.............Prov 10:26
weeping and gnashing of *t*........Matt 8:12

TEKOA
Home of a wise woman, 2 Sam 14:2, 4, 9
Home of Amos, Amos 1:1

TELL
See also I TELL YOU THE TRUTH
no one could *t* me its meaning...Gen 41:24
should *t* the one who sent me..2 Sam 24:13
T the nations about his splendor..1 Chr 16:24
to *t* the great assembly............Ps 40:10
you can *t* the next generation......Ps 48:13
Let them *t* us what will happen.....Isa 41:22
I will *t* of the faithful acts..........Isa 63:7
and say whatever I *t* you............Jer 1:7
the message that I *t* you..........Jonah 3:2
attention to what they *t* you......Matt 23:3
he will *t* us everything............John 4:25
and will *t* it to you..............John 16:14
t your requests to God...........Phil 4:6

TELLING
t you the things I have seen......John 8:38

TEMAN
Tribe in northeast Edom, Gen 36:34
Judgment pronounced against, Amos 1:12
God appears from, Hab 3:3

TEMPERATE
t, self-controlled, respectable......1 Tim 3:2
Older men are to be *t*.............Titus 2:2

TEMPLE
Solomon finished building the *t*..1 Kgs 6:14
and will build a *t* for the LORD....2 Chr 2:12
strong desire to build a *t*.........2 Chr 6:7
LORD's splendor filled the *t*........2 Chr 7:1
The LORD is in his holy *t*...........Ps 11:4
and contemplate in his *t*............Ps 27:4
great throng to the *t* of God.........Ps 42:4
the precincts of God's *t*............Ps 73:17
to the *t* of the God of Jacob.........Isa 2:3
the *t* was filled with smoke..........Isa 6:4
make them happy in the *t*.........Isa 56:7
The *t* of the LORD is here.............Jer 7:4
He destroyed his *t* as if it...........Lam 2:6
his altar and abhorred his *t*.........Lam 2:7
will suddenly come to his *t*........Mal 3:1
greater than the *t* is here.........Matt 12:6
between the *t* and the altar.......Matt 23:35
the *t* curtain was torn in two.....Matt 27:51
Destroy this *t* and in three days...John 2:19
speaking about the *t* of his body..John 2:21
at the Beautiful Gate of the *t*......Acts 3:10
know that you are God's *t*.........1 Cor 3:16
know that your body is the *t*.....1 Cor 6:19
grows into a holy *t* in the Lord.....Eph 2:21
he takes his seat in God's *t*.......2 Thess 2:4
Then the *t* of God in heaven.......Rev 11:19
Now I saw no *t* in the city..........Rev 21:22

TEMPORARILY
For I have lived *t* in Meshech.......Ps 120:5
people went to live *t* in Egypt......Isa 52:4

TEMPORARY
For what can be seen is *t*.........2 Cor 4:18

TEMPT
so that Satan may not *t* you........1 Cor 7:5

TEMPTATION
And do not lead us into *t*..........Matt 6:13
pray that you will not fall into *t*..Matt 26:41
And do not lead us into *t*..........Luke 11:4
stumble into *t* and a trap..........1 Tim 6:9

TEMPTATIONS
enduring *t* from Satan.............Mark 1:13
he endured *t* from the devil.......Luke 4:2

TEMPTED
so that you are not *t* too............Gal 6:1
suffered when he was *t*............Heb 2:18
t in every way just as we are.......Heb 4:15
Let no one say when he is *t*..........Jas 1:13
t when he is lured and enticed.......Jas 1:14

TEMPTER
The *t* came and said to him........Matt 4:3

TEN
the *T* Commandments............Exod 34:28
t men with leprosy met him......Luke 17:12
had seven heads and *t* horns.......Rev 12:3
had *t* horns and seven heads........Rev 13:1
t horns that you saw are *t* kings...Rev 17:12

TENDER
Leah's eyes were *t*...............Gen 29:17
hold back your *t* compassion.......Isa 63:15
Because of our God's *t* mercy.....Luke 1:78

TENDERHEARTED
The hands of *t* women.............Lam 4:10

TENDERLY
and speak *t* to her.................Hos 2:14

TENDING
LORD took me from *t* flocks......Amos 7:15

TENDRILS
he will prune the *t*...................Isa 18:5

TENDS
Who *t* a flock and does not........1 Cor 9:7

TENT

Moses took the *t* and pitched it .. Exod 33:7
did not leave the *t* . . . . Exod 33:11
cloud covered the *t* of meeting. . . Exod 40:34
messengers who ran to the *t* . . . . . . Josh 7:22
a *t* that stays put. . . . . Isa 33:20
from me as a shepherd's *t*. . . . . Isa 38:12
Make your *t* larger . . . . Isa 54:2
rebuild the fallen *t* of David . . . . . . Acts 15:16
the *t* we live in. . . . . 2 Cor 5:1
the greater and more perfect *t* . . . . . Heb 9:11
t of the testimony . . . . Rev 15:5

TENTH

Abram gave Melchizedek a *t* . . . . . Gen 14:20
I will surely give you back a *t* . . . . . Gen 28:22
to the LORD a *t* of the tithe . . . . . Num 18:26
They brought a *t* of everything . . . 2 Chr 31:5
along with a *t* of the produce. . . . . Neh 10:37
will bring up a *t* of the tithes . . . . . Neh 10:38
You give a *t* of mint. . . . . Matt 23:23

TENTMAKERS

they were *t* by trade. . . . . Acts 18:3

TENTS

live in *t* and keep livestock . . . . Gen 4:20
How beautiful are your *t* . . . . Num 24:5
the *t* of robbers are peaceful . . . . . . Job 12:6
than live in the *t* of the wicked . . . . .Ps 84:10
deliverance in the *t* of the godly. . . .Ps 118:15
resided among the *t* of Kedar . . . . . .Ps 120:5
But our *t* have been destroyed . . . . Jer 10:20

TERAH

Father of Abram, Gen 11:26
Idolater, Josh 24:2
Dies in Haran, Gen 11:25–32

TERMS

I am speaking in human *t*. . . . . Rom 6:19

TERRAIN

rough *t* will become a level. . . . . Isa 40:4

TERRIBLE

the great and *t* day of the LORD . . . . Mal 4:5

TERRIBLY

This displeased Jonah *t* . . . . Jonah 4:1

TERRIFIED

bird of the sky will be *t* of you. . . . . . Gen 9:2
Do not be *t* of them . . . . .Deut 1:29
why I am *t* in his presence. . . . . Job 23:15
the Almighty has *t* me. . . . . Job 23:16
They are absolutely *t* . . . . Ps 14:5
you rejected me and I was *t* . . . . . . .Ps 30:7
we are *t* by your wrath . . . . .Ps 90:7
t of what will happen to you. . . . . . . Jer 20:4
they were *t* and said. . . . . Matt 14:26
they were extremely *t* and said. . Matt 27:54

TERRIFIES

and *t* them in his rage . . . . Ps 2:5

TERRIFY

and to *t* them when they hear . . . . Deut 2:25
dreams and *t* me with visions . . . . . . Job 7:14
no fear of me should *t* you . . . . Job 33:7
when he rises up to *t* the earth. . . . . . Isa 2:19
The LORD will *t* them. . . . . Zeph 2:11
come to *t* Judah's enemies. . . . . Zech 1:21

TERRIFYING

to sleep without anyone *t* you. . . . Lev 26:6
is awesome and very *t*. . . . . Joel 2:11
a *t* thing to fall into the hands . . . .Heb 10:31
scene was so *t* that Moses said . . . .Heb 12:21

TERRITORY

to plague all your *t* with frogs . . . . . Exod 8:2
to bring locusts into your *t* . . . . Exod 10:4
He brings peace to your *t*. . . . . Ps 147:14

TERROR

and great *t* overwhelmed him . . . . .Gen 15:12
and *t* will do so inside . . . . Deut 32:25
you see a *t* and are afraid. . . . . Job 6:21
calamity from God was a *t*. . . . . Job 31:23
but instead we experience *t*. . . . . . . .Jer 8:15
will cause anguish and *t* to fall. . . . . .Jer 15:8
The *t* you inspire in others. . . . . Jer 49:16

TERRORS

God's sudden *t* are arrayed. . . . . .Job 6:4
T frighten him on all sides. . . . . .Job 18:11
marched off to the king of *t* . . . . . . Job 18:14
T overwhelm him like a flood . . . Job 27:20
need not fear the *t* of the night. . . . . Ps 91:5

TERTULLUS

Orator who accuses Paul, Acts 24:1–8

TEST

Why do you *t* the LORD. . . . . Exod 17:2
for God has come to *t* you. . . . . Exod 20:20
he could use them to *t* Israel . . . . Judg 3:1
T me, and know my concerns . . . . .Ps 139:23
want to put the LORD to a *t*. . . . . Isa 7:12
fires of affliction and *t* them. . . . . .Jer 9:7
will *t* them like gold is tested. . . . . Zech 13:9
T me in this matter. . . . . Mal 3:10
came to him in order to *t* him . . . . .Matt 19:3
Now Jesus said this to *t* him . . . . . . .John 6:6
to *t* the Spirit of the Lord. . . . . Acts 5:9
are you putting God to the *t*. . . . . . Acts 15:10
fire will *t* what kind of work . . . . . .1 Cor 3:13
you fail the *t*. . . . . 2 Cor 13:5
appear to have failed the *t*. . . . . 2 Cor 13:7
but *t* the spirits to determine. . . . . .1 John 4:1
t those who live on the earth . . . . . .Rev 3:10

TESTED

God *t* Abraham. . . . . .Gen 22:1
t you at the waters of Meribah . . . . . .Ps 81:7
and *t* them for ten days. . . . . Dan 1:14
And these also must be *t* first . . . . .1 Tim 3:10
your fathers *t* me and tried me. . . . . Heb 3:9
that is *t* by fire. . . . . .1 Pet 1:7

TESTIFIED

has himself *t* about me . . . . .John 5:37
the person who saw it has *t* . . . . . .John 19:35
t to the message of his grace . . . . . . Acts 14:3
have *t* about me in Jerusalem . . . .Acts 23:11
he has *t* concerning his Son . . . . . . 1 John 5:9
came and *t* to your truth . . . . .3 John 1:3
t to everything that he saw. . . . . Rev 1:2
blood of those who *t* to Jesus. . . . . .Rev 17:6

TESTIFIES

He *t* about what he has seen . . . . . .John 3:32
is another who *t* about me . . . . .John 5:32

TESTIFY

your own lips *t* against you. . . . . Job 15:6
and our sins *t* against us. . . . . .Isa 59:12
be quick to *t* against those . . . . Mal 3:5
and *t* about what we have seen. . . . .John 3:11
If I *t* about myself. . . . . .John 5:31
scriptures that *t* about me. . . . . .John 5:39
to *t* to the good news. . . . . Acts 20:24
and *t* that this is the true grace. . . . .1 Pet 5:12
t that the Father has sent
    the Son. . . . . .1 John 4:14
For there are three that *t*. . . . . .1 John 5:7
have sent my angel to *t* to you . . . .Rev 22:16

TESTIMONY

gave Moses two tablets of *t*. . . . . . .Exod 31:18
the *t* of two or three witnesses. . . .Deut 17:6
it gives reliable *t* about . . . . Hab 2:3
the *t* of two or three witnesses. . .Matt 18:16
as a *t* to all the nations . . . . Matt 24:14
dust off your feet as a *t* against. . . .Mark 6:11
Now this was John's *t*. . . . . .John 1:19
you people do not accept our *t*. . . . .John 3:11
but no one accepts his *t*. . . . . .John 3:32
The one who has accepted his *t* . . .John 3:33
But I have a *t* greater than that. . . . .John 5:36
that the *t* of two men is true . . . . . . .John 8:17
we know that his *t* is true. . . . . .John 21:24
as I proclaimed the *t* of God. . . . . . .1 Cor 2:1
you have a *t* of these things . . . . . . .2 Pet 1:15
If we accept the *t* of men . . . . 1 John 5:9
Son of God has the *t* in himself. . . 1 John 5:10
And this is the *t*. . . . . 1 John 5:11
because of the *t* they had given . . . . Rev 6:9
and by the word of their *t*. . . . . .Rev 12:11
who hold to the *t* about Jesus . . . . .Rev 19:10
because of the *t* about Jesus. . . . . . . Rev 20:4

TESTING

because of their *t* the LORD. . . . . . .Exod 17:7
LORD your God will be *t* you. . . . . .Deut 13:3
Why are you *t* me . . . . Matt 22:18
but in a time of *t* fall away. . . . . Luke 8:13
the day of *t* in the wilderness. . . . . . Heb 3:8
the *t* of your faith produces. . . . . Jas 1:3
Happy is the one who endures *t*. . . . Jas 1:12
keep you from the hour of *t*. . . . . . . Rev 3:10

TESTS

likewise the LORD *t* hearts. . . . . Prov 17:3

TETRARCH

and Herod was *t* of Galilee . . . . Luke 3:1
Now Herod the *t* heard about . . . . . Luke 9:7
close friend of Herod the *t* . . . . Acts 13:1

THADDAEUS [or JUDAS]

One of the Twelve, Mark 3:18; Luke 6:13, 16
Offers a question, John 14:22
Also called, "Judas," Luke 6:16

THAN

he loves more *t* the other . . . . Deut 21:15
is not greater *t* his teacher . . . . . . Matt 10:24

THANK

bring sacrifices and *t* offerings . .2 Chr 29:31
t the LORD with all my heart. . . . . Ps 9:1
Let the nations *t* you . . . . Ps 67:3
It is fitting to *t* the LORD. . . . . Ps 92:1
Let them present *t* offerings. . . . . . .Ps 107:22
He won't *t* the slave . . . . .Luke 17:9
I *t* you that I am not like other. . . . Luke 18:11
I *t* my God through Jesus Christ . . . .Rom 1:8
so we too constantly *t* God. . . . . . 1 Thess 2:13
how can we *t* God enough. . . . . . . .1 Thess 3:9

THANKED

ground at Jesus' feet and *t* him . . .Luke 17:16

THANKS

Give *t* to the LORD. . . . . 1 Chr 16:34
and gave *t* to the LORD . . . . 2 Chr 7:3
for giving *t* to the LORD. . . . . 2 Chr 7:6
In Sheol who gives you *t*. . . . . Ps 6:5
to give you *t* . . . . Ps 26:7
We give *t* to you. . . . . Ps 75:1
Give *t* to the LORD. . . . . Ps 107:1
Give *t* to the LORD. . . . . .Ps 136:1
your works will give *t* to you . . . . . .Ps 145:10
and after giving *t* he broke it . . . . Matt 26:26
taking the cup and giving *t* . . . . . . Matt 26:27
and began to give *t* to God . . . . Luke 2:38
and when he had given *t*. . . . . John 6:11
because he gives *t* to God . . . . .Rom 14:6
and after he had given *t* . . . . .1 Cor 11:24
But *t* be to God. . . . . .1 Cor 15:57
T be to God for his indescribable. . .2 Cor 9:15
giving *t* to God the Father . . . . Eph 5:20
in everything give *t* . . . . 1 Thess 5:18
let us give *t*. . . . . Heb 12:28
We give you *t*. . . . . .Rev 11:17

THANKSGIVING

enter his presence with *t* . . . . .Ps 95:2
Enter his gates with *t*. . . . . .Ps 100:4
prayer and petition with *t* . . . . Phil 4:6
keeping alert in it with *t*. . . . . Col 4:2
to be received with *t*. . . . . .1 Tim 4:3
and wisdom and *t* . . . . Rev 7:12

THEATER

crowd rushed to the *t* together. . .Acts 19:29

THEBES

Nineveh compared to, Nah 3:8

THEOPHILUS

Luke addresses his writings to, Luke 1:3;
    Acts 1:1

THESSALONICA

Paul preaches in, Acts 17:1–13
Paul writes letters to churches of, 1 Thess 1:1

THICK

a *t* swarm of flies came into . . . . . .Exod 8:24
and yet dark with a *t* cloud . . . . . . .Deut 4:11
in *t* rain clouds. . . . . .2 Sam 22:12
T clouds are a veil for him . . . . .Job 22:14

t darkness its swaddling band ......Job 38:9
in *t* rain clouds............................Ps 18:11

THICKETS
because the *t* of the Jordan.......Zech 11:3

THIEF
When you see a *t*....................Ps 50:18
not despise a *t* when he steals....Prov 6:30
shares with a *t* is his own enemy..Prov 29:24
as a *t* has to suffer dishonor.......Jer 2:26
through the windows like a *t*.......Joel 2:9
time of night the *t* was coming ..Matt 24:43
where no *t* approaches...........Luke 12:33
is a *t* and a robber..................John 10:1
but because he was a *t*.............John 12:6
of the Lord will come like a *t*.....2 Pet 3:10
I will come like a *t*..................Rev 3:3
Look! I will come like a *t*..........Rev 16:15

THIEVES
they associate with *t*................Isa 1:23
and where *t* break in and steal ....Matt 6:19
before me were *t* and robbers.....John 10:8

THIGH
Put your hand under my *t*........Gen 24:2
The right *t* you must give.........Lev 7:32
LORD makes your *t* fall away .....Num 5:21
Strap your sword to your *t*........Ps 45:3
the *t* and the shoulder...........Ezek 24:4

THIN
t cows were coming up............Gen 41:3

THING
for it is a fearful *t*..................Exod 34:10
For the *t* is very near you........Deut 30:14
such a disgraceful *t* in Israel.......Josh 7:15
Who can make a clean *t*..........Job 14:4
I will again do an amazing *t*........Isa 29:14
You lack one *t*....................Mark 10:21
but one *t* is needed.............Luke 10:42
One *t* you still lack.............Luke 18:22
This is a remarkable *t*..............John 9:30
as an altogether reliable *t* ....2 Pet 1:19
this one *t* escape your notice ......2 Pet 3:8

THINGS
See also THINGS OF GOD
great and awesome *t*.............Deut 10:21
secret *t* belong to the LORD .....Deut 29:29
marvelous *t* without number.......Job 5:9
day long they say deceitful *t*.......Ps 38:12
you have done amazing *t*...........Ps 40:5
the God who does amazing *t*.......Ps 77:14
the earth is full of the living *t*....Ps 104:24
who gives food to all living *t*....Ps 136:25
desirable *t* cannot be compared...Prov 8:11
quick temper will do foolish *t* ....Prov 14:17
t that will never be satisfied......Prov 30:15
wisdom in the scheme of *t* ....Eccl 7:25
For a fool speaks disgraceful *t*......Isa 32:6
misleading *t* about the LORD ....Isa 32:6
done so many unfaithful *t*...........Jer 5:6
no limit to the evil *t* they do......Jer 5:28
because of the disgraceful *t*........Jer 31:19
wicked *t* that have been done ......Jer 44:9
kept all these *t* in her heart.......Luke 2:51
We have seen incredible *t*.......Luke 5:26
you received your good *t*........Luke 16:25
the *t* written about himself.....Luke 24:27
if I tell you about heavenly *t*......John 3:12
some surprising *t* to our ears.....Acts 17:20
and approve the superior *t*........Rom 2:18
bring to light the hidden *t*.........1 Cor 4:5
must share all good *t*...............Gal 6:6
they think about earthly *t*........Phil 3:19
we are convinced of better *t*.......Heb 6:9
the heavenly *t* themselves........Heb 9:23
the filthy *t* of the world............2 Pet 2:20
filled with detestable *t*............Rev 17:4
the detestable *t* of the earth......Rev 17:5
for the former *t* have ceased .....Rev 21:4

THINGS OF GOD
all things, even the deep *t*........1 Cor 2:10
the *t* except the Spirit of God .....1 Cor 2:11

THINK
did you *t* you were doing ....Gen 44:15
Don't *t* badly of me..............2 Sam 19:19
Do not *t* that I have come ....Matt 5:17
t that by their many words ....Matt 6:7
T about how the flowers ....Matt 6:28
Do you *t* I have come.............Luke 12:51
because you *t* in them............John 5:39
In spite of what you *t*..............Acts 2:15
to *t* more highly of yourself ....Rom 12:3
One should *t* about us this way....1 Cor 4:1
I *t* that I too have the Spirit.......1 Cor 7:40
let no one *t* that I am a fool......2 Cor 11:16
beyond all that we ask or *t* ....Eph 3:20
t about these things ....Phil 4:8
T of him who endured..............Heb 12:3

THINKING
do not be children in your *t* .....1 Cor 14:20
t about what I was doing ....2 Cor 1:17
Keep *t* about things above...........Col 3:2

THINKS
is so arrogant he always *t* ....Ps 10:4
a son *t* his father is a fool............Mic 7:6
even what he *t* he has ....Luke 8:18
t he is wise in this age ....1 Cor 3:18
t he knows something ....1 Cor 8:2
the one who *t* he is standing.....1 Cor 10:12
if anyone *t* he is something.........Gal 6:3
If someone *t* he is religious.........Jas 1:26

THIRD
See also THIRD DAY
there was morning, a *t* day ....Gen 1:13
the *t* that of a lion ....Ezek 10:14
Then a *t* kingdom...................Dan 2:39
and on the *t* day be raised........Matt 16:21
and on the *t* day be raised........Luke 9:22
on the *t* day he will rise again ...Luke 18:33
and on the *t* day rise again ....Luke 24:7
rise from the dead on the *t* day..Luke 24:46
was caught up to the *t* heaven....2 Cor 12:2
t creature had a face like a man's...Rev 4:7
the Lamb opened the *t* seal ....Rev 6:5
a *t* of the earth was burned up .....Rev 8:7
the *t* is coming quickly............Rev 11:14
t angel poured out his bowl ....Rev 16:4

THIRD DAY
and there was morning, a *t*.........Gen 1:13
t the LORD will come down.......Exod 19:11
burned up in the fire on the *t*.......Lev 7:17
what is left over until the *t* ....Lev 19:6
sprinkle the unclean on the *t*.....Num 19:19
Return to me on the *t* ....2 Chr 10:12
and on the *t* be raised ....Matt 16:21
on the *t* he will be raised ....Matt 17:23
on the *t*, he will be raised........Matt 20:19
secure the tomb until the *t*.....Matt 27:64
and on the *t* be raised ....Luke 9:22
t I will complete my work ....Luke 13:32
on the *t* he will rise again........Luke 18:33
and on the *t* rise again............Luke 24:7
it is now the *t* since..............Luke 24:21
from the dead on the *t* ....Luke 24:46
God raised him up on the *t*......Acts 10:40
that he was raised on the *t* ....1 Cor 15:4

THIRST
for them in their time of *t* ....Neh 9:15
I *t* for God ....Ps 42:2
he has satisfied those who *t*........Ps 107:9
tongues are parched from *t* ....Isa 41:17
and *t* for righteousness............Matt 5:6

THIRSTY
David was *t* and said.............2 Sam 23:15
and if he is *t*........................Prov 25:21
It will be like a *t* man ....Isa 29:8
gives the *t* nothing to drink........Isa 32:6
but you will be *t*....................Isa 65:13
in a dry and *t* land ....Ezek 19:13
but remained *t* ....Amos 4:8
I was *t* and you gave me ....Matt 25:35
see you hungry or *t* or a stranger..Matt 25:44
will never be *t* again...............John 4:14

believes in me will never be *t*......John 6:35
If anyone is *t*........................John 7:37
fulfill the scripture), "I am *t*......John 19:28
if he is *t*, give him a drink........Rom 12:20
hour we are hungry and *t* ....1 Cor 4:11
never go hungry or be *t* again ......Rev 7:16
one who is *t* I will give water ....Rev 21:6
And let the one who is *t* come.....Rev 22:17

THIRTY
from *t* years old and upward .... Num 4:3
was about *t* years old.............Luke 3:23

THIS
See also THIS GENERATION
Nothing like *t* has happened......Judg 19:30

THIS GENERATION
consider you godly among *t*........Gen 7:1
what should I compare *t*........ Matt 11:16
at the judgment of *t* ....Matt 12:41
t will be held responsible........Matt 23:36
t will not pass away.............Matt 24:34
Why does *t* look for a sign.......Mark 8:12
will be a sign to *t* ....Luke 11:30
will be charged against *t*.........Luke 11:51
and be rejected by *t* ....Luke 17:25
t will not pass away until ....Luke 21:32

THISTLES
make them like dead *t*.............Ps 83:13
from thorns or figs from *t* ....Matt 7:16

THOMAS
Apostle of Christ, Matt 10:3
Ready to die with Christ, John 11:16
Doubts Christ's resurrection, John 20:24–29

THORN
a *t* has gone up into the hand.....Prov 26:9
The best of them is like a *t* ....Mic 7:4
t in the flesh was given to me ....2 Cor 12:7

THORNBUSH
their godly are like a *t* ....Mic 7:4

THORNBUSHES
will grow in place of *t*..............Isa 55:13

THORNS
It will produce *t* and thistles....... Gen 3:18
then let *t* sprout up in place ....Job 31:40
T and snares are in the path......Prov 22:5
t under a cooking pot..............Eccl 7:6
Like a lily among the *t*............Song 2:2
t and briers will grow there...........Isa 5:6
do not cast seeds among *t*...........Jer 4:3
from *t* or figs from thistles........Matt 7:16
Other seeds fell among the *t* ......Matt 13:7
after braiding a crown of *t*.......Matt 27:29
are the ones sown among *t*.......Mark 4:18
wearing the crown of *t*............John 19:5

THOUGHT
you *t* I was exactly like you.........Ps 50:21
I *t* to myself.........................Eccl 1:16
so he *t* to himself.................Luke 12:17
t you could acquire God's gift ....Acts 8:20
but *t* he was seeing a vision ....Acts 12:9
I *t* like a child ....1 Cor 13:11
and we take every *t* captive ......2 Cor 10:5
t of how to spur one another.....Heb 10:24

THOUGHTFULLY
saw that he had answered *t* .....Mark 12:34

THOUGHTS
every motive of one's *t*...........1 Chr 28:9
examine inner *t* and motives ....Ps 7:9
words and my *t* be acceptable...... Ps 19:14
he knows a person's secret *t*........Ps 44:21
I will share my profound *t*..........Ps 49:3
We would share personal *t*.........Ps 55:14
LORD knows that peoples' *t* ....Ps 94:11
May my *t* be pleasing to him ......Ps 104:31
and probe my *t*...................Ps 139:23
would pour out my *t* to you ......Prov 1:23
When Jesus perceived their *t* ......Matt 9:4
discerned their innermost *t* ......Luke 9:47
they became futile in their *t*.......Rom 1:21
knows that the *t* of the wise......1 Cor 3:20

THOUSAND

a single day is like a *t* years........ 2 Pet 3:8
tied him up for a *t* years .... Rev 20:2

THOUSANDS

provided out of the *t* of Israel ..... Num 31:5

THREAD

the midwife took a scarlet *t* ...... Gen 38:28

THREATENED

the judgment solemnly *t* .... Dan 9:11
he *t* no retaliation .... 1 Pet 2:23

THREATS

pay attention to their *t* .... Acts 4:29
still breathing out *t* to murder...... Acts 9:1
giving up the use of *t* .... Eph 6:9

THREE

the vine there were *t* branches ...Gen 40:10
were *t* baskets of white bread .... Gen 40:16
she hid him for *t* months .... Exod 2:2
T times in the year............. Exod 23:14
At *t* times in the year .... Exod 34:23
At the end of every *t* years ..... Deut 14:28
T times a year all your males ..... Deut 16:16
out over the boy *t* times........ 1 Kgs 17:21
He struck the ground *t* times.... 2 Kgs 13:18
t years of famine .... 1 Chr 21:12
When Job's *t* friends heard .... Job 2:11
Wasn't it *t* men that we tied up.... Dan 3:24
T times daily he offers his .... Dan 6:13
and before which *t* others fell ..... Dan 7:20
T more kings will arise .... Dan 11:2
has committed *t* crimes .... Amos 1:3
for *t* days and *t* nights .... Matt 12:40
I will make *t* shelters ....Matt 17:4
where two or *t* are assembled... Matt 18:20
you will deny me *t* times ...... Matt 26:34
temple and rebuild it in *t* days...Matt 27:40
After *t* days I will rise again...... Matt 27:63
and after *t* days rise again .... Mark 8:31
you will deny me *t* times .... Mark 14:30
temple and rebuild it in *t* days... Mark 15:29
For *t* days he could not see........ Acts 9:9
spoke out fearlessly for *t* months .. Acts 19:8
And now these *t* remain.......... 1 Cor 13:13
For there are *t* that testify......... 1 John 5:7
was killed by these *t* plagues ...... Rev 9:18
Then I saw *t* unclean spirits........ Rev 16:13

THRESH

certainly does not *t* it forever ..... Isa 28:28
You will *t* the mountains .... Isa 41:15
Get up and *t* .... Mic 4:13

THRESHING

a wool fleece on the *t* floor........ Judg 6:37
she went down to the *t* floor ...... Ruth 3:6
So David bought the *t* floor.... 2 Sam 24:24
he will clean out his *t* floor .... Matt 3:12

THRESHOLD

with her hands on the *t*........... Judg 19:27
off and were lying at the *t*......... 1 Sam 5:4
rested to the *t* of the temple .... Ezek 9:3

THREW

Each man *t* down his staff .... Exod 7:12
He *t* stones at David............. 2 Sam 16:6
and they *t* dust into the air .... Job 2:12
I *t* myself face down............... Ezek 1:28
we tied up and *t* into the fire ...... Dan 3:24
picked Jonah up and *t* him........ Jonah 1:15
went out and *t* him in prison ...... Matt 18:30
So Judas *t* the silver coins .... Matt 27:5
t their cloaks on the colt........ Luke 19:35
they *t* dice to divide his clothes.. Luke 23:34
they *t* them into prison........... Acts 16:23
t it into the sea .... Rev 18:21
t themselves to the ground....... Rev 19:4
angel then *t* him into the abyss.... Rev 20:3

THROAT

and put a knife to your *t*.......... Prov 23:2

THROATS

their *t* like an open grave........... Ps 5:9
Their *t* are open graves........... Rom 3:13

THRONE

See also THRONE OF DAVID; THRONE
   OF GOD

I saw the LORD sitting on his *t*.... 1 Kgs 22:19
the LORD's *t* is in heaven.............. Ps 11:4
Your *t*, O God...................... Ps 45:6
has established his *t* in heaven .... Ps 103:19
his *t* is upheld by loyal love...... Prov 20:28
seated on a high, elevated *t* .... Isa 6:1
bestow honor on my *t* room ...... Isa 60:13
The heavens are my *t*.............. Isa 66:1
will be called the LORD's *t* .... Jer 3:17
where your glorious *t* sits .... Jer 14:21
seated on your glorious *t*.......... Jer 17:12
sitting as king on his *t* .... Zech 6:13
because it is the *t* of God .... Matt 5:34
the *t* of his father David .... Luke 1:32
Your *t*, O God...................... Heb 1:8
approach the *t* of grace .... Heb 4:16
where Satan's *t* is................. Rev 2:13
to sit with me on my *t* .... Rev 3:21
Then I saw a large white *t* .... Rev 20:11

THRONE OF DAVID

to establish the *t* over Israel..... 2 Sam 3:10
succeed in occupying the *t* .... Jer 22:30
line will occupy the *t* .... Jer 36:30

THRONE OF GOD

because it is the *t*................. Matt 5:34
by heaven swears by the *t*....... Matt 23:22
at the right hand of the *t* .... Heb 12:2
they are before the *t*.............. Rev 7:15
pouring out from the *t* ....Rev 22:1
and the *t* and the Lamb........... Rev 22:3

THRONES

the leaders sit there on *t* .... Ps 122:5
t were set up .... Dan 7:9
will also sit on twelve *t* .... Matt 19:28
down the mighty from their *t* .....Luke 1:52
whether *t* or dominions ....Col 1:16
were twenty-four other *t*.......... Rev 4:4

THRONG

walking along with the great *t*.......Ps 42:4
loud voice of a vast *t* in heaven..... Rev 19:1

THROUGH

Walk *t* its fortresses .... Ps 48:13
and all passed *t* the sea........... 1 Cor 10:1
who has passed *t* the heavens..... Heb 4:14

THROUGHOUT

his plans abide *t* the ages........... Ps 33:11

THROW

T him into this cistern .... Gen 37:22
Take your staff and *t* it down...... Exod 7:9
T her down......................... 2 Kgs 9:33
T your burden upon the LORD...... Ps 55:22
and a time to *t* away............... Eccl 3:6
the LORD will *t* you far away....... Isa 22:17
T to the potter that exorbitant ... Zech 11:13
t yourself down.................... Matt 4:6
if you *t* yourself to the ground..... Matt 4:9
tear it out and *t* it away.......... Matt 5:29
and *t* it to the dogs .... Matt 15:26
authority to *t* you into hell .... Luke 12:5
be the first to *t* a stone at her ...... John 8:7
T your net on the right side .... John 21:6

THROWING

divided his clothes by *t* dice ..... Matt 27:35
After *t* him into convulsions...... Mark 1:26

THROWN

its rider he has *t* into the sea ..... Exod 15:1
his army he has *t* into the sea .... Exod 15:4
t his crown to the ground .... Ps 89:39
The dice are *t* into the lap .....Prov 16:33
and *t* into a den of lions .... Dan 6:16
cut down and *t* into the fire ..... Matt 3:10
and to be *t* into the sea........... Mark 9:42
cut down and *t* into the fire ...... Luke 3:9
he is *t* out like a branch........... John 15:6
was *t* into the lake of fire ...... Rev 20:15

THROWS

t me into the hands of wicked...... Job 16:11

THRUSH

Like a swallow or a *t* I chirp .... Isa 38:14

THUMMIM

put the Urim and the *T*.......... Exod 28:30
Your *T* and Urim belong.......... Deut 33:8
consult the Urim and *T*.......... Ezra 2:63
consult the Urim and *T*.......... Neh 7:65

THUNDER

understand the *t* of his power ..... Job 26:14
that is, "sons of *t*................. Mark 3:17
and like the sound of loud *t* .... Rev 14:2
and like loud crashes of *t*.......... Rev 19:6

THUNDERCLOUD

I answered you from a dark *t*........ Ps 81:7

THUNDERED

The LORD *t* from the sky........ 2 Sam 22:14
The LORD *t* in the sky............. Ps 18:13

THUNDERING

seeing the *t* and the lightning.... Exod 20:18

THUNDEROUS

Your *t* voice was heard .... Ps 77:18
at the sound of your *t* voice .... Ps 104:7

THUNDERS

God *t* with his voice .... Job 37:5
the majestic God *t*.................. Ps 29:3
He *t* loudly........................ Ps 68:33

THWART

know what it means to *t* me..... Num 14:34

THYATIRA

Residence of Lydia, Acts 16:14
Site of one of the seven churches, Rev 1:11
Letter to, Rev 2:18–24

TIBERIAS, SEA OF

See GALILEE, SEA OF

TIE

should *t* them as a reminder ...... Deut 6:8
t this red rope in the window....... Josh 2:18
you *t* the bands of the Pleiades.... Job 38:31
T the offering with ropes .... Ps 118:27
T him up hand and foot..........Matt 22:13

TIED

t the red rope in the window ...... Josh 2:21
towel and *t* it around himself...... John 13:4
t your clothes around you .... John 21:18
t his own hands and feet .... Acts 21:11
t him up for a thousand years ..... Rev 20:2

TIGHTLY

but Ruth clung *t* to her .... Ruth 1:14

TIGLATH-PILESER [or PUL]

Powerful Assyrian king who invades
   Samaria, 2 Kgs 15:29
Also called, "Pul," 2 Kgs 15:19

TIGRIS

Hebrew name of the river Tigris, Gen 2:14;
   Dan 10:4

TIMBER

With the *t* the king made steps....2 Chr 9:11

TIME

See also APPOINTED TIME; TIME OF
   TROUBLE

at the breezy *t* of the day........... Gen 3:8
minds was only evil all the *t*........ Gen 6:5
the appointed *t* of the month.... Exod 34:18
give you your rains in their *t*....... Lev 26:4
offering at its appointed *t* .... Num 9:13
This *t* I am justified.............. Judg 15:3
yields its fruit at the proper *t*........ Ps 1:3
In my *t* of trouble I cry out .... Ps 86:7
at evening *t* it withers .... Ps 90:6
lived for a *t* in the land of Ham ... Ps 105:23
and a word at the right *t*........ Prov 15:23
there is an appointed *t* .... Eccl 3:1
appropriate *t* for every activity...... Eccl 3:1
A *t* to be born .... Eccl 3:2
and still live a long *t*................ Eccl 8:12
for *t* and chance may overcome .... Eccl 9:11
At that *t* the crops given............. Isa 4:2
at the same *t* you fast .... Isa 58:3

When the right *t* comes ....Isa 60:22
Harvest *t* has come and gone.......Jer 8:20
a *t* of trouble and distress ....Jer 15:11
let seven periods of *t* go by.,.......Dan 4:16
At that *t* Michael ....Dan 12:1
t for rebuilding the LORD's temple...Hag 1:2
will be given to you at that *t*......Matt 10:19
their food at the proper *t*.......Matt 24:45
My *t* is near......................Matt 26:18
and prayed for the third *t*.......Matt 26:44
He came a third *t* and said.....Mark 14:41
a rooster crowed a second *t*....Mark 14:72
the *t* came for her to deliver.......Luke 2:6
but in a *t* of testing fall away ......Luke 8:13
t of your visitation from God ....Luke 19:44
not to rehearse ahead of *t*....Luke 21:14
My *t* has not yet come............John 2:4
and be born a second *t* ....John 3:4
But a *t* is coming...................John 4:23
My *t* has not yet arrived.........John 7:6
t has come for the Son of Man ...John 12:23
a *t* is coming when I will.........John 16:25
the *t* has come....................John 17:1
Jesus said a second *t*.............John 21:16
Jesus said a third *t*.............John 21:17
For every *t* you eat this bread ....1 Cor 11:26
for in due *t* we will reap ....Gal 6:9
will be revealed in his own *t*.....2 Thess 2:6
in Christ Jesus before it began .....2 Tim 1:9
because the *t* is near ....Rev 1:3
that he only has a little *t*........Rev 12:12
for a *t*, times, and half a *t*.........Rev 12:14

TIME OF TROUBLE
During his *t* King Ahaz...........2 Chr 28:22
which I reserve for the *t*........Jonah 38:23
In my *t* I sought the Lord ....Ps 77:2
In my *t* I cry out to you ....Ps 86:7
Do not ignore me in my *t*...........Ps 102:2
an unfaithful person at the *t*......Prov 25:19
upon you in a *t* and distress ....Jer 15:11
what a terrible *t* it is...............Jer 30:7

TIMELY
How *t* is the arrival ....Rom 10:15

TIMES
Three *t* in the year you must ....Exod 23:14
are the LORD's appointed *t* ....Lev 23:4
marched around it seven *t*.........Josh 6:15
wash seven *t* in the Jordan........2 Kgs 5:10
understood the *t* and knew.......1 Chr 12:32
Why are *t* not appointed ....Job 24:1
I will praise the LORD at all *t*.........Ps 34:1
be ashamed when hard *t* come ..... Ps 37:19
protects them in *t* of trouble ......Ps 37:39
Trust in him at all *t* ....Ps 62:8
Seven *t* a day I praise you ....Ps 119:164
rejoicing before him at all *t*.......Prov 8:30
A friend loves at all *t* ....Prov 17:17
person will fall seven *t*...........Prov 24:16
glare will be seven *t* brighter ......Isa 30:26
our Protector from ancient *t*.......Isa 63:16
found them to be ten *t* better .....Dan 1:20
heat the furnace seven *t* hotter....Dan 3:19
to change *t* established by law ....Dan 7:25
In those *t* many will oppose ......Dan 11:14
evaluate the signs of the *t*........Matt 16:3
Not seven *t*, I tell you............Matt 18:22
a hundred *t* as much grain.........Luke 8:8
sins against you seven *t* ....Luke 17:4
t of the Gentiles are fulfilled.....Luke 21:24
you will deny me three *t*..........Luke 22:61
to know the *t* or periods............Acts 1:7
This happened three *t*............Acts 10:16
their set *t* and the fixed limits ....Acts 17:26
last days difficult *t* will come ......2 Tim 3:1

TIMON
One of the seven servants in the early
   church, Acts 6:1–5

TIMOTHY
Paul's companion, Acts 16:1–3; 18:5; 20:4–5;
   2 Cor 1:19; Phil 1:1; 2 Tim 4:9, 21
Ministers independently, Acts 17:14–15;
   19:22; 1 Cor 4:17; Phil 2:19, 23;
   1 Thess 3:1–6; 1 Tim 1:1–3; 4:14

TIN
do you see, Amos?" I said, "T.....Amos 7:8

TINGLE
both of his ears will *t*.............1 Sam 3:11

TIP
put it on the *t* of the right ear ...Exod 29:20
dip the *t* of his finger in water ...Luke 16:24

TIRE
None *t* or stumble................Isa 5:27

TIRED
He does not get *t* or weary ....Isa 40:28
strength to those who are *t* ....Isa 40:29
Even youths get *t* and weary ......Isa 40:30
they walk without getting *t*........Isa 40:31
you must travel, you get *t* ....Isa 57:10
I am *t* of trying to hold it in ....Jer 6:11

TIRESOME
All this monotony is *t*................Eccl 1:8
How *t* it is ....Mal 1:13

TIRZAH
Seat of Jeroboam's rule, 1 Kgs 14:17
Capital of Israel until Omri's reign,
   1 Kgs 16:6–23

TITHE
If a man redeems part of his *t*.....Lev 27:31
the *t* that I have given you.......Num 18:26
your villages your *t* of grain ......Deut 12:17
t all the produce of your seed ...Deut 14:22
bring all the *t* of your produce ...Deut 14:28
brought the *t* of the grain ....Neh 13:12
the entire *t* into the storehouse ....Mal 3:10

TITHES
of all your *t* that you receive..... Num 18:28
contributions, firstfruits, and *t*....Neh 12:44
along with the *t* of the grain........Neh 13:5
t are received by mortal men....... Heb 7:8
who receives *t*......................Heb 7:9

TITHING
you finish *t* all your income...... Deut 26:12

TITLES
know how to give honorary *t*......Job 32:22

TITUS
Ministers in Crete, Titus 1:4–5
Paul's representative in Corinth,
   2 Cor 7:6–7, 13–14; 8:6–23

TOBIAH
Ammonite servant; ridicules the Jews,
   Neh 2:10

TODAY
you want to bake, bake *t* ....Exod 16:23
consecrated *t* for the LORD......Exod 32:29
t the LORD is going to appear........Lev 9:4
T you are going to cross.........Deut 2:18
as witnesses against you *t* ....Deut 4:26
I am commanding you *t* ....Deut 6:6
God is making with you *t*........Deut 29:12
T I have taken away ....Josh 5:9
by turning back *t* from ....Josh 22:16
You are witnesses *t*...............Ruth 4:10
When you leave me *t*.............1 Sam 10:2
t you have rejected your God....1 Sam 10:19
For *t* the LORD has given Israel ...1 Sam 11:13
Give us *t* our daily bread ....Matt 6:11
here *t* and tomorrow is tossed ...Matt 6:30
go and work in the vineyard *t* ...Matt 21:28
T your Savior is born ....Luke 2:11
T this scripture has been ....Luke 4:21
here *t* and tomorrow is tossed .. Luke 12:28
T salvation has come ....Luke 19:9
t you will be with me in..........Luke 23:43
T I have fathered you..............Heb 1:5
that *t* you would listen ....Heb 3:7
same yesterday and *t* and ....Heb 13:8

TOGARMAH
Northern country inhabited by descendants
   of Gomer, Gen 10:3
Supplied horses to Tyrians and soldiers to
   the army of Gog, Ezek 27:14; 38:6

TOGETHER
bound *t* in close friendship ....1 Sam 18:1
gathered *t* the descendants........1 Chr 15:4
made in secret and sewed *t* ....Ps 139:15
rich and the poor are met *t*.......Prov 22:2
Shout out loudly, 'Gather *t* ....Jer 4:5
met *t* in the palace................Matt 26:3
and experts in the law came *t* ...Mark 14:53
shaken *t*, running over.........Luke 6:38
these continued *t* in prayer.........Acts 1:14
where they were assembled *t* .. Acts 4:31
many people had gathered *t* ......Acts 12:12
t in the name of our Lord...........1 Cor 5:4
God has blended *t* the body .....1 Cor 12:24
I am glad and rejoice *t*..............Phil 2:17
all things are held *t* in him............Col 1:17
having been knit *t* in love............Col 2:2

TOIL
in painful *t* you will eat ....Gen 3:17
there is no end to all his *t*...........Eccl 4:8

TOILING
For whom am I *t*....................Eccl 4:8

TOLD
the LORD my God *t* me to do ...... Deut 4:5
I have *t* the great assembly.........Ps 40:9
what I *t* you the LORD said..........Jer 36:6
I have *t* you.......................Matt 28:7
had *t* this parable against them.. Luke 20:19
see a man who *t* me everything .. John 4:29
a man who has *t* you the truth ....John 8:40
I would have *t* you.................John 14:2
t you now before it happens......John 14:29

TOLERATE
t anyone who has a haughty........Ps 101:5

TOMB
sitting there, opposite the *t*.......Matt 27:61
his body and placed it in a *t*.......Mark 6:29
the linen and placed it in a *t* .....Mark 15:46
been rolled away from the *t*......Luke 24:2
Lazarus had been in the *t*.........John 11:17
he called Lazarus out of the *t*.... John 11:43
in the garden was a new *t* ....John 19:41
Mary Magdalene came to the *t*....John 20:1

TOMBS
You are like whitewashed *t*.....Matt 23:27
You build *t* for the prophets.....Matt 23:29
And *t* were opened ....Matt 27:52
You build the *t* of the prophets...Luke 11:47
are in the *t* will hear his voice ....John 5:28

TOMORROW
Sanctify yourselves for *t*........Num 11:18
consecrate yourselves for *t*.....Josh 7:13
Do not boast about *t* ....Prov 27:1
for *t* we die ....Isa 22:13
T will be just like today.............Isa 56:12
and *t* is tossed into the fire ....Matt 6:30
do not worry about *t* ....Matt 6:34
today and *t* and the next day .....Luke 13:33
for *t* we die ....1 Cor 15:32
You do not know about *t*...........Jas 4:14

TONGUE
slow of speech and slow of *t* .....Exod 4:10
and he hides it under his *t*........Job 20:12
and the *t* that boasts ....Ps 12:3
sure I do not sin with my *t*..........Ps 39:1
Then my *t* will shout for joy ....Ps 51:14
May my *t* stick to the roof.........Ps 137:6
my *t* does not frame a word ....Ps 139:4
t of the wise treats knowledge ....Prov 15:2
guards his mouth and his *t* ....Prov 21:23
and a soft *t* can break a bone....Prov 25:15
one who flatters with the *t* ....Prov 28:23
loving instruction on her *t*........Prov 31:26
mocking lips and a foreign *t*......Isa 28:11
every *t* will solemnly affirm ....Isa 45:23
his *t* loosened, and he spoke .....Mark 7:35
was opened and his *t* released.....Luke 1:64
cool my *t* because I am...........Luke 16:24
and every *t* will give praise ....Rom 14:11
For the one speaking in a *t* ....1 Cor 14:2

every *t* confess that Jesus..........Phil 2:11
yet does not bridle his *t*...........Jas 1:26
t is a small part of the body.........Jas 3:5
And the *t* is a fire................Jas 3:6
human being can subdue the *t*.....Jas 3:8
not love with word or with *t*......1 John 3:18

TONGUES
whose *t* are sharp swords.........Ps 57:4
t spreading out like a fire.........Acts 2:3
and they began to speak in *t*.....Acts 19:6
in the *t* of men and of angels.....1 Cor 13:1
t are a sign not for believers.....1 Cor 14:22

TOOK
he *t* part of the man's side.........Gen 2:21
He then *t* some of every kind.....Gen 8:20
And Abram *t* his wife Sarai........Gen 12:5
wife *t* notice of Joseph and........Gen 39:7
Then Moses *t* his wife and sons..Exod 4:20
So they *t* soot from a furnace....Exod 9:10
Moses *t* the bones of Joseph.....Exod 13:19
Moses *t* the redemption money..Num 3:49
and he *t* some of the Spirit.......Num 11:25
So Israel *t* all these cities........Num 21:25
They *t* all the plunder.............Num 31:11
I *t* it, melted it down..............Deut 9:21
t hold of the two middle pillars...Judg 16:29
So Tamar *t* the cakes...........2 Sam 13:10
the Ancient of Days *t* his seat.......Dan 7:9
t the child and his mother.........Matt 2:14
the devil *t* him to the holy city.....Matt 4:5
He *t* our weaknesses.............Matt 8:17
He *t* the five loaves.............Matt 14:19
he *t* the seven loaves............Matt 15:36
So Peter *t* him aside.............Matt 16:22
ten virgins who *t* their lamps.....Matt 25:1
So Peter *t* him aside.............Mark 8:32
He *t* a little child................Mark 9:36
guards also *t* him and beat
  him.......................Mark 14:65
Then he *t* a cup.................Luke 22:17
he *t* his place at the table........John 13:12
sin-offerings you *t* no delight......Heb 10:6

TOOLS
and shaped all kinds of *t*...........Gen 4:22

TOOTH
eye for eye, *t* for *t*...............Exod 21:24
eye for eye, *t* for *t*...............Lev 24:20
eye for eye, a *t* for a *t*...........Deut 19:21
a bad *t* or a foot out of joint......Prov 25:19
eye for an eye and a *t* for a *t*......Matt 5:38

TOP
tower with its *t* in the heavens.....Gen 11:4
fire on the *t* of the mountain....Exod 24:17
atonement lid on *t* of the ark....Exod 25:21
torn in two, from *t* to bottom...Matt 27:51
torn in two, from *t* to bottom...Mark 15:38

TOPHETH
T in the Valley of Ben Hinnom.......Jer 7:31
I will make it like *T*..............Jer 19:12
just like this place, *T*.............Jer 19:13

TORCH
a flaming *t* passed between.......Gen 15:17
a burning *t* among sheaves........Zech 12:6

TORCHES
lit the *t* and set the jackals loose..Judg 15:5
His eyes were like blazing *t*........Dan 10:6
Seven flaming *t*.................Rev 4:5

TORE
See also TORE HIS CLOTHES
stood up and *t* his garments......2 Sam 13:31
and it into twelve pieces.........1 Kgs 11:30
and it *t* him up and killed him...1 Kgs 13:26
Then Job got up and *t* his robe.....Job 1:20
Each of them *t* his robes..........Job 2:12

TORE HIS CLOTHES
Joseph was not in it! He *t*.......Gen 37:29
Jacob *t*, put on sackcloth.........Gen 37:34
Joshua *t*; he and the leaders........Josh 7:6
he *t*, put on sackcloth...........1 Kgs 21:27
read the letter, he *t*..............2 Kgs 5:7

of the law scroll, he *t*...........2 Kgs 22:11
words of the law, he *t*..........2 Chr 34:19
high priest *t* and declared.......Matt 26:65
high priest *t* and said...........Mark 14:63

TORMENT
How long will you *t* me............Job 19:2
You *t* the innocent...............Amos 5:12
to *t* us before the time..........Matt 8:29
as he was in it...................Luke 16:23
don't come into this place of *t*....Luke 16:28

TORMENTED
will be *t* there day and night......Rev 20:10

TORMENTING
evil spirit from God is *t* you.....1 Sam 16:15

TORN
has surely been *t* to pieces.......Gen 37:33
The LORD has *t* the kingdom....1 Sam 15:28
my paths and *t* me to pieces........Lam 3:11
He himself has *t* us to pieces........Hos 6:1
the temple curtain was *t* in two..Matt 27:51
the temple curtain was *t* in two..Mark 15:38
I feel *t* between the two............Phil 1:23

TORRENTIAL
might of a driving, *t* rainstorm......Isa 28:2

TORTURE
to *t* them for five months...........Rev 9:5
And the smoke from their *t*.......Rev 14:11

TORTURED
But others were *t*..................Heb 11:35
will be *t* with fire and sulfur.......Rev 14:10

TOTAL
How vast is their sum *t*...........Ps 139:17

TOTALLY
they never *t* conquered them.....Judg 1:28

TOUCH
and you must not *t* it............Gen 3:3
on the mountain nor *t* its edge...Exod 19:12
you must not *t* their carcasses......Lev 11:8
in seven no evil will *t* you...........Job 5:19
Don't *t* anything unclean..........Isa 52:11
If only I *t* his cloak................Matt 9:21
only *t* the edge of his cloak......Matt 14:36
If only I *t* his clothes.............Mark 5:28
and asked him to *t* him..........Mark 8:22
babies to him for him to *t*.......Luke 18:15
T me and see...................Luke 24:39
and *t* no unclean thing............2 Cor 6:17
handle! Do not taste! Do not *t*.....Col 2:21
the evil one cannot *t* him........1 John 5:18

TOUCHED
anyone or *t* any of the dead......Num 31:19
men whose hearts God had *t*...1 Sam 10:26
t my mouth with it and said........Isa 6:7
out his hand and *t* my mouth........Jer 1:9
he *t* me and stood me upright.....Dan 8:18
Who *t* my clothes................Mark 5:30
he came up and *t* the bier........Luke 7:14
Who was it who *t* me.............Luke 8:45
to something that can be *t*.......Heb 12:18
and our hands have *t*............1 John 1:1

TOUCHES
is a person who *t* anything.........Lev 5:2
who *t* their carcass..............Lev 11:24
who *t* them will be unclean........Lev 15:27
who *t* anything made unclean......Lev 22:4
he *t* the mountains.............Ps 104:32
t you *t* the pupil of his eye........Zech 2:8

TOWARD
no longer be hostile *t* Ephraim......Isa 11:13

TOWEL
a *t* and tied it around himself......John 13:4

TOWER
a *t* with its top in the heavens......Gen 11:4
to see the city and the *t*...........Gen 11:5
a strong *t* that protects me.........Ps 61:3
neck is like a *t* made of ivory......Song 7:4
when the *t* in Siloam fell......Luke 13:4
wanting to build a *t*..............Luke 14:28

TOWN
came to a *t* called Nazareth......Matt 2:23

TOWNS
t surrounding all these cities......Josh 17:11
or their surrounding *t*............Judg 1:27
the *t* of Judah are happy...........Ps 48:11

TRACE
Not a *t* of them could be found....Dan 2:35

TRADE
eager to *t* silver for the poor.....Amos 8:6

TRADERS
whose *t* are the dignitaries.........Isa 23:8
and planted it in a city of *t*........Ezek 17:4

TRADITION
disobey the *t* of the elders.........Matt 15:2
on account of your *t*.............Matt 15:6
fast to the *t* of the elders.........Mark 7:3
to the *t* they received from us...2 Thess 3:6

TRADITIONS
for the *t* of my ancestors...........Gal 1:14
according to human *t*...............Col 2:8
to the *t* that we taught you...2 Thess 2:15

TRAIN
T a child in the way..............Prov 22:6
they will no longer *t* for war........Isa 2:4
and *t* yourself for godliness.......1 Tim 4:7

TRAINED
but everyone when fully *t*......Luke 6:40
whose perceptions are *t*.......Heb 5:14
righteousness for those *t* by it.....Heb 12:11

TRAINING
and for *t* in righteousness........2 Tim 3:16

TRAINS
It *t* us to reject godless ways......Titus 2:12

TRAITOR
but if he is found to be a *t*.........1 Kgs 1:52
who became a *t*..................Luke 6:16

TRAMPLE
will *t* underfoot a young lion........Ps 91:13
t on the dirt-covered heads.......Amos 2:7
You will *t* on the wicked............Mal 4:3
will *t* them under their feet........Matt 7:6
they will *t* on the holy city.........Rev 11:2

TRAMPLED
I *t* them down in my rage...........Isa 63:3

TRAMPLING
animals *t* on my courtyards.........Isa 1:12

TRANCE
t with my face to the ground......Dan 8:18
a *t* came over him.................Acts 10:10
and in a *t* I saw a vision.............Acts 11:5

TRANQUIL
A *t* spirit revives the body........Prov 14:30
beauty of a gentle and *t* spirit.....1 Pet 3:4

TRANSFERRED
and *t* us to the kingdom.............Col 1:13

TRANSFIGURED
And he was *t* before them........Matt 17:2

TRANSFORMED
appearance of his face was *t*......Luke 9:29
t by the renewing of your mind....Rom 12:2
being *t* into the same image......2 Cor 3:18

TRANSGRESS
person will *t* over the smallest...Prov 28:21

TRANSGRESSING
now *t* the commandment.......Num 14:41
dishonor God by *t* the law........Rom 2:23

TRANSGRESSION
responding to the *t* of fathers....Exod 20:5
forgiving iniquity and *t* and sin...Exod 34:7
Show me my *t* and my sin.........Job 13:23
I am pure, without *t*................Job 33:9
although I am without *t*.............Job 34:6
For he adds *t* to his sin.............Job 34:37
and that he does not know *t*......Job 35:15
who loves a quarrel loves *t*.......Prov 17:19

In the *t* of an evil person.......... Prov 29:6
person is abounding in *t*......... Prov 29:22
is no law there is no *t* either.......Rom 4:15
gracious gift is not like the *t*......Rom 5:15
by the *t* of the one man......... Rom 5:17
fully deceived, fell into *t*.......... 1 Tim 2:14

TRANSGRESSIONS
for he will not pardon your *t* .... Exod 23:21
have covered my *t* as men do ..... Job 31:33
but love covers all *t*............... Prov 10:12
Israel for their covenant *t* ....Amos 3:14
given over because of our *t*....... Rom 4:25
It was added because of *t*........... Gal 3:19
you were dead in your *t* .... Col 2:13

TRANSGRESSOR
judge you to be the *t* of the law .. Rom 2:27

TRANSGRESSORS
he was counted with the *t* .... Luke 22:37

TRANSJORDANIAN
of Israel in the *T* wilderness .... Deut 1:1

TRANSLATED
Which is *t*, "Place of the Skull.... Mark 15:22
which is *t* Christ .... John 1:41
which is is *t* Peter.................John 1:42

TRAP
dining table become a *t*............ Ps 69:22
will become a *t* and a snare..........Isa 8:14
bird swoop down into a *t*.........Amos 3:5
to *t* him with his own words......Mark 12:13
to *t* him with his own words......Luke 20:26
table become a snare and *t*....... Rom 11:9
to place an obstacle or a *t* .... Rom 14:13
stumble into temptation and a *t*...1 Tim 6:9
and escape the devil's *t*.......... 2 Tim 2:26

TRAPPED
the snares of death *t* me............. Ps 18:5
all of them are *t* in pits .... Isa 42:22

TRAPS
They set *t* for me .... Ps 140:5
the *t* the evildoers have set......... Ps 141:9
yet *t* are laid for him................ Hos 9:8

TRAVEL
observe me when I *t*............... Ps 139:3

TRAVELER
have you become like a *t* .... Jer 14:8

TRAVELERS
places *t* have long forgotten........Job 28:4
there are no *t*..................... Isa 33:8

TREACHEROUS
no mercy on any *t* evildoers..........Ps 59:5
and the *t* will be torn away .... Prov 2:22
but the *t* will be ensnared .... Prov 11:6
of the *t* ends in destruction....... Prov 13:15
t, reckless, conceited ....2 Tim 3:4

TREACHEROUSLY
to act *t* against the LORD .... Num 31:16
must not act *t* against justice.....Prov 16:10

TREACHERY
serpent deceived Eve by his *t*......2 Cor 11:3

TREAD
authority to *t* on snakes ....Luke 10:19

TREASON
committed *t* against the LORD...... Hos 5:7

TREASURE
search for it like hidden *t*...........Prov 2:4
There is desirable *t* and.......... Prov 21:20
For where your *t* is ....Matt 6:21
kingdom of heaven is like a *t* .... Matt 13:44
who brings out of his *t* ....Matt 13:52
you will have *t* in heaven .... Matt 19:21
you will have *t* in heaven .... Mark 10:21
t in heaven that never decreases...Luke 12:33
For where your *t* is .... Luke 12:34
you will have *t* in heaven .... Luke 18:22
But we have this *t* in clay jars.....2 Cor 4:7
save up a *t* for themselves........1 Tim 6:19
that you have hoarded *t* ....Jas 5:3

TREASURED
have *t* the words of his mouth...... Job 23:12

TREASURER
Erastus the city *t* and............. Rom 16:23

TREASURES
the hidden *t* of the shores .... Deut 33:19
for it more than for hidden *t* ...... Job 3:21
T gained by wickedness ....Prov 10:2
I will give you hidden *t* .... Isa 45:3
for yourselves *t* on earth ....Matt 6:19
t of wisdom and knowledge........ Col 2:3
wealth than the *t* of Egypt.........Heb 11:26

TREASURIES
and that I may fill their *t*...........Prov 8:21

TREASURY
good things out of his good *t*.....Matt 12:35

TREAT
and he did *t* Abram well...........Gen 12:16
Should he *t* our sister............ Gen 34:31
Oppressors *t* my people cruelly .....Isa 3:12
and *t* the LORD's holy day...........Isa 58:13
You must *t* one another fairly ....Jer 7:5
t others as you would want........Matt 7:12
t me like one of your hired .... Luke 15:19
no one *t* him with contempt...... 1 Cor 16:11
t one another as more important....Phil 2:3
not *t* prophecies with
     contempt...................1 Thess 5:20

TREATED
has *t* me very harshly.............. Ruth 1:20
for you *t* my life with value ......1 Sam 26:21
have they been *t* with olive oil........Isa 1:6

TREATING
I am not *t* you unfairly .... Matt 20:13

TREATS
but the one who *t* you lightly.......Gen 12:3
justly *t* the orphan and widow....Deut 10:18
one who *t* the poor properly ....Ps 41:1
tongue of the wise *t* knowledge ...Prov 15:2

TREATY
made a peace *t* with them .... Josh 9:15
I want to make a *t* with you ......1 Kgs 15:19
I want to make a *t* with you .....1 Kgs 20:34
I want to make a *t* with you ...... 2 Chr 16:3

TREE
See also TREE OF LIFE; TREE OF THE
     KNOWLEDGE OF GOOD AND EVIL
you must not eat from the *t*........Gen 2:17
Did you eat from the *t*...........Gen 3:11
the land as far as the oak *t* .... Gen 12:6
Abraham planted a tamarisk *t*.... Gen 21:33
of the Oak *T* of the Diviners ...... Judg 9:37
from his own vine and fig *t*...... 2 Kgs 18:31
But there is hope for a *t* .... Job 14:7
t planted by flowing streams ....Ps 1:3
like a green *t* grows .... Ps 37:35
The godly grow like a palm *t* .... Ps 92:12
whether a *t* falls to the south....... Eccl 11:3
an apple *t* among the trees .... Song 2:3
I see a branch of an almond *t*.........Jer 1:11
called you a thriving olive *t*.........Jer 11:16
like a *t* planted near a stream ....Jer 17:8
The *t* that you saw that grew......Dan 4:20
the fig *t* languishes .... Joel 1:12
every good *t* bears good fruit .... Matt 7:17
Make a *t* good and its fruit ......Matt 12:33
noticing a fig *t* by the road........Matt 21:19
they saw the fig *t* withered ...... Mark 11:20
fig *t* you cursed has withered.....Mark 11:21
t is known by its own fruit.......Luke 6:44
climbed up into a sycamore *t*.....Luke 19:4
is by nature a wild olive *t*.........Rom 11:24
everyone who hangs on a *t*......... Gal 3:13
our sins in his body on the *t*...... 1 Pet 2:24
fig *t* dropping its unripe figs ....Rev 6:13

TREE OF LIFE
t and the tree of knowledge .... Gen 2:9
take also from the *t* and eat .... Gen 3:22
to guard the way to the *t*......... Gen 3:24

She is a like a *t*...................... Prov 3:18
longing fulfilled is like a *t*........ Prov 13:12
permit him to eat from the *t* ....Rev 2:7
the *t* producing twelve kinds .... Rev 22:2
can have access to the *t* .... Rev 22:14
take away his share in the *t*.........Rev 22:19

TREE OF THE KNOWLEDGE OF GOOD AND EVIL
the tree of life and the *t* were ...... Gen 2:9
you must not eat from the *t*.......Gen 2:17

TREES
LORD God made all kinds of *t*...... Gen 2:9
the *t* of the field will produce...... Lev 26:4
you must not chop down its *t* ... Deut 20:19
t were determined to go out......Judg 9:8
all the *t* said to the thornbush .....Judg 9:14
t of the forest shout with joy ....Ps 96:12
The *t* of the LORD receive..........Ps 104:16
planted all kinds of fruit *t*........... Eccl 2:5
one of the large sacred *t*..........Isa 6:13
olive *t* grow in the wilderness ....Isa 41:19
all the *t* in the field will clap ....Isa 55:12
my people will live as long as *t* .... Isa 65:22
and animals, on *t* and crops ....Jer 7:20
All the *t* of the field will know ....Ezek 17:24
all the *t* of Eden, in the garden.....Ezek 31:9
decorative palm *t* were carved .. Ezek 41:20
when the olive *t* do not produce....Hab 3:17
but they look like *t* walking.......Mark 8:24
they took branches of palm *t*..... John 12:13
autumn *t* without fruit.............Jude 1:12
the earth or the sea or the *t* ....Rev 7:3
third of the *t* were burned up........Rev 8:7
These are the two olive *t* .... Rev 11:4

TREMBLE
T before him, all the earth....... 1 Chr 16:30
The dead *t*—those beneath ....Job 26:5
T before him, all the earth...........Ps 96:9
The nations *t* .... Ps 99:1
T O earth, before the Lord..........Ps 114:7
the whole land to *t* with fear ....Jer 8:16
The nations will *t* in awe.............Jer 33:9
Hearts faint, knees *t* .... Nah 2:10

TREMBLED
three things the earth has *t*.......Prov 30:21

TREMBLES
the earth sees and *t* .... Ps 97:4
My body *t* because I fear you..... Ps 119:120

TREMBLING
t will seize the leaders of Moab ..Exod 15:15
and in fear and with much *t* ...... 1 Cor 2:3
welcomed him with fear and *t*.... 2 Cor 7:15
human masters with fear and *t*.....Eph 6:5

TRENCH
Around the altar he made a *t*.... 1 Kgs 18:32

TRESPASS
a person commits a *t* and sins...... Lev 5:15
a person sins and commits a *t*.......Lev 6:2

TRESPASSES
not counting people's *t* against...2 Cor 5:19

TRIAL
was led away after an unjust *t* ...... Isa 53:8
I am on *t* before you today .... Acts 24:21
No *t* has overtaken you.......... 1 Cor 10:13
that a *t* by fire is occurring .... 1 Pet 4:12

TRIALS
remained with me in my *t*.......Luke 22:28
you fall into all sorts of *t* .... Jas 1:2

TRIBE
is to be a man from each *t*..........Num 1:4
t of Levi you must not number ... Num 1:49
not allow the *t* of the families .... Num 4:18
to the war, 1,000 from every *t*.....Num 31:6
one leader from every *t* .... Num 34:18
cut off an entire *t* from Israel...... Judg 21:6
about belongs to a different *t* ......Heb 7:13
the Lion of the *t* of Judah ....Rev 5:5
for God persons from every *t* .... Rev 5:9
ruling authority over every *t* .... Rev 13:7

TRIBES
See also TWELVE TRIBES
These are the twelve *t* of Israel...Gen 49:28
The *t* go up there.....................Ps 122:4
to reestablish the *t* of Jacob.........Isa 49:6
the *t* of your inheritance............Isa 63:17
our twelve *t* hope to attain......Acts 26:7
the twelve *t* dispersed abroad.........Jas 1:1

TRIBULATION
have come out of the great *t*......Rev 7:14

TRIBUTE
You receive *t* from men............Ps 68:18
kings bring *t* to you................Ps 68:29
and Seba will bring *t*................Ps 72:10
t and were a source of shame....Zeph 3:18

TRICK
Why did you *t* us by saying........Josh 9:22
your ability to oppress and *t*.......Isa 30:12

TRICKED
The serpent *t* me....................Gen 3:13
Why have you *t* me...............Gen 29:25

TRICKERY
the *t* of people who craftily........Eph 4:14

TRICKING
But Jehu was *t* them.............2 Kgs 10:19

TRIED
I *t* to understand....................Eccl 7:25
will not let you be *t* beyond......1 Cor 10:13

TRIES
everyone who *t* to accuse you......Isa 54:17

TRIGON
flute, zither, *t*, harp, pipes..........Dan 3:15

TRIMMED
woke up and *t* their lamps........Matt 25:7

TRIP
for a moment or has taken a *t*...1 Kgs 18:27
a stone that makes a person *t*.......Isa 8:14

TRIPS
Even if he *t*, he will not fall.........Ps 37:24

TRIUMPHED
for he has *t* gloriously.............Exod 15:1

TRIUMPHING
t over them by the cross............Col 2:15

TROAS
Paul receives vision at, Acts 16:8–11

TROOPS
I defy Israel's *t* this day..........1 Sam 17:10

TROUBLE
See also TIME OF TROUBLE
saw that they were in *t*...........Exod 5:19
then do not let me see my *t*......Num 11:15
from all your *t* and distress......1 Sam 10:19
but people are born to *t*.............Job 5:7
For you will forget your *t*...........Job 11:16
and they are full of *t*................Job 14:1
root of the *t* is found in him.......Job 19:28
when I hoped for good, *t* came...Job 30:26
I reserve for the time of *t*.........Job 38:23
provides safety in times of *t*.........Ps 9:9
t is near and I have no one..........Ps 22:11
protects them in times of *t*.........Ps 37:39
I take shelter until *t* passes..........Ps 57:1
for I am in *t*......................Ps 69:17
immune to the *t* common............Ps 73:5
marred by *t* and oppression......Ps 90:10
be with him when he is in *t*.........Ps 91:15
protect him from times of *t*........Ps 94:13
what comforts me in my *t*........Ps 119:50
distressing *t* comes on you........Prov 1:27
person was delivered out of *t*.....Prov 11:8
slacked off in the day of *t*......Prov 24:10
person at the time of *t*.........Prov 25:19
them when they were in *t*........Jer 14:8
for safety when I am in *t*.........Jer 16:19
I experience is *t* and grief......Jer 20:18
Today has enough *t* of its own....Matt 6:34
when *t* or persecution comes.....Matt 13:21

when *t* or persecution comes.....Mark 4:17
do not *t* yourself...................Luke 7:6
Will *t*, or distress.................Rom 8:35
experiencing *t* on every side.......2 Cor 4:8
a messenger of Satan to *t* me....2 Cor 12:7

TROUBLED
worried and *t* about many.......Luke 10:41

TROUBLES
their *t* multiply.....................Ps 16:4
For my life is filled with *t*............Ps 88:3
The one who *t* his family.........Prov 11:29
greedy for gain *t* his household...Prov 15:27
tongue keeps his life from *t*......Prov 21:23
rescued him from all his *t*.........Acts 7:10
who comforts us in all our *t*.......2 Cor 1:4

TROUBLING
it was *t* to me.....................Ps 73:16

TROUGH
the night at your feeding *t*.........Job 39:9

TROUSERS
nor were their *t* damaged.........Dan 3:27

TRUE
your words prove to be *t*........2 Sam 7:28
not sought the one *t* God.........2 Chr 15:3
t laws, and good statutes.........Neh 9:13
investigated this, so it is *t*.........Job 5:27
show you *t* and reliable words....Prov 22:21
The LORD is the only *t* God........Jer 10:10
be a *t* and faithful witness..........Jer 42:5
know whose word proves *t*........Jer 44:28
promotes *t* justice between........Ezek 18:8
Exercise *t* judgment...............Zech 7:9
He taught what was *t*..............Mal 2:6
The *t* light, who gives light.........John 1:9
a *t* Israelite in whom...............John 1:47
he testifies about me is *t*..........John 5:32
is giving you the *t* bread..........John 6:32
but the one who sent me is *t*.....John 7:28
testimony of two men is *t*.........John 8:17
said about this man was *t*........John 10:41
I am the *t* vine.....................John 15:1
the only *t* God....................John 17:3
speaking *t* and rational words...Acts 26:25
Let God be proven *t*..............Rom 3:4
is *t*, whatever is worthy............Phil 4:8
representation of the *t* sanctuary..Heb 9:24
which is *t* in him and in you.......1 John 2:8
to know him who is *t*............1 John 5:20
Just and *t* are your ways..........Rev 15:3
his judgments are *t* and just......Rev 19:2
These are the *t* words of God......Rev 19:9
called "Faithful" and "*T*.........Rev 19:11
these words are reliable and *t*......Rev 21:5

TRULY
T you are the Son of God........Matt 14:33
T this one was God's Son........Matt 27:54
T this man was God's Son.......Mark 15:39
they too may be *t* set apart.......John 17:19
a people who are *t* his............Titus 2:14
t in this person the love of God....1 John 2:5

TRUMPET
you will hear a *t* being blown........Isa 18:3
the *t* throughout the land...........Jer 4:5
LORD will blow the *t*............Zech 9:14
do not blow a *t* before you........Matt 6:2
the *t* makes an unclear sound....1 Cor 14:8
blinking of an eye, at the last *t*...1 Cor 15:52
and with the *t* of God...........1 Thess 4:16
a loud voice like a *t*................Rev 1:10
the one holding the *t*.............Rev 9:14

TRUMPETS
took supplies and their *t*............Judg 7:8
t and the blaring of the ram's.......Ps 98:6
seven *t* were given to them......Rev 8:2
remaining sounds of the *t*.......Rev 8:13

TRUST
T in the LORD your God........2 Chr 20:20
places no *t* in his holy ones.........Job 15:15
sacrifices and *t* in the LORD...........Ps 4:5
I constantly *t* in the LORD.............Ps 16:8

But I *t* in you........................Ps 31:14
for we *t* in his holy name..........Ps 33:21
T in the LORD and do.............Ps 37:3
T in him, and he will act............Ps 37:5
t in God's loyal love................Ps 52:8
All the ends of the earth *t*.........Ps 65:5
did not *t* him to do amazing......Ps 78:32
my God in whom I *t*..............Ps 91:2
in the LORD than to *t* in people....Ps 118:8
T in the LORD with all your heart...Prov 3:5
stronghold in which they *t*......Prov 21:22
I will *t* in him and not fear........Isa 12:2
men will *t* in their Creator........Isa 17:7
T in the LORD from this time....Isa 26:4
t in the name of the LORD.........Isa 50:10
those people who *t* in me..........Jer 17:7
because you *t* in me...............Jer 39:18
Yet they claim to *t* the LORD........Mic 3:11

TRUSTED
He *t* in the LORD God of Israel....2 Kgs 18:5
because they *t* in him..............1 Chr 5:20
He *t* in his great wealth............Ps 52:7
t in you since I was young..........Ps 71:5
if you calmly *t* in me..............Isa 30:15

TRUSTING
We are *t* in the LORD our God...2 Kgs 18:22
We are *t* in the LORD our God......Isa 36:7
temple that you are *t* to protect.....Jer 7:14

TRUSTS
overwhelms the one who *t*.........Ps 32:10
blessed is the one who *t*.........Prov 16:20
t in the LORD will prosper.......Prov 28:25
t in his own heart is a fool.......Prov 28:26
but whoever *t* in the LORD.......Prov 29:25
He *t* in God.....................Matt 27:43

TRUSTWORTHY
are *t* and absolutely just.............Ps 19:9
who is *t* conceals a matter........Prov 11:13
t and guilty of no negligence.......Dan 6:4
t in handling worldly wealth......Luke 16:11
t with someone else's property...Luke 16:12
He who calls you is *t*...........1 Thess 5:24
t and deserves full acceptance....1 Tim 1:15
who made the promise is *t*.......Heb 10:23
given the promise to be *t*..........Heb 11:11

TRUTH
See also I TELL YOU THE TRUTH; SPIRIT
  OF TRUTH
to tell me only the *t*.............2 Chr 18:15
in *t*, my words are not false.........Job 36:4
Guide me into your *t*................Ps 25:5
tells the *t* will endure forever.....Prov 12:19
love and *t* iniquity is appeased.....Prov 16:6
It hurled *t* to the ground...........Dan 8:12
Speak the *t*, each of you.........Zech 8:16
so love *t* and peace..............Zech 8:19
I tell you the *t*..................Luke 12:44
but grace and *t* came about........John 1:17
must worship in spirit and *t*.......John 4:24
and you will know the *t*...........John 8:32
Promise before God to tell the *t*..John 9:24
the way, and the *t*, and the life.....John 14:6
the Spirit of *t*....................John 16:13
Set them apart in the *t*..........John 17:17
What is *t*.......................John 18:38
who suppress the *t*...............Rom 1:18
the bread of sincerity and *t*........1 Cor 5:8
but rejoices in the *t*.............1 Cor 13:6
But practicing the *t* in love........Eph 4:15
each one of you speak the *t*.......Eph 4:25
fastening the belt of *t*.............Eph 6:14
about in the message of *t*.........Col 1:5
place in their hearts for the *t*...2 Thess 2:10
am telling the *t*..................1 Tim 2:7
and then knowledge of the *t*....2 Tim 2:25
arrive at a knowledge of the *t*.....2 Tim 3:7
are well established in the *t*........2 Pet 1:12
the way of *t* will be slandered.....2 Pet 2:2
with tongue but in deed and *t*....1 John 3:18
know that we are of the *t*........1 John 3:19
By this we know the Spirit of *t*...1 John 4:6

because the Spirit is the *t*........ 1 John 5:6
came and testified to your *t*.......3 John 1:3

TRUTHFUL
deprive me of a *t* testimony .... Ps 119:43
A *t* witness does not lie........... Prov 14:5
A *t* witness rescues lives.........Prov 14:25
Jerusalem will be called "*t* city..... Zech 8:3
we know that you are *t*.......... Matt 22:16

TRUTHFULLY
those who deal *t* are his delight ..Prov 12:22

TUBAL
Son of Japheth, Gen 10:2
–Tribe associated with Javan and Meshech,
   Isa 66:19; Ezek 27:13
In Gog's army, Ezek 38:2–3
Punishment of, Ezek 32:26–27

TUBAL-CAIN
Son of Lamech, Gen 4:19–22

TUBES
Its bones are *t* of bronze ....Job 40:18

TUMORS
boils of Egypt and with *t*.........Deut 28:27

TUNIC
he made a special *t* for him........ Gen 37:3
to sue you and take your *t*........Matt 5:40
do not withhold your *t* either..... Luke 6:29
and the *t* remained ....John 19:23

TUNICS
but not to wear two *t*..............Mark 6:9
The person who has two *t*........ Luke 3:11
crying and showing him the *t*......Acts 9:39

TURBAN
was like a robe and a *t*.............Job 29:14
by giving them a *t* ....Isa 61:3
t in the hand of your God........... Isa 62:3
Tear off the *t* ....Ezek 21:26

TURMOIL
caused them to be in great *t*....... 2 Chr 15:6
the wicked cease from *t*.............Job 3:17
t has come upon me...............Job 3:26
But when you cause *t*............. Hab 3:2

TURN
See also TURN ASIDE
T from your burning anger ...... Exod 32:12
Do not *t* to idols ....Lev 19:4
who can *t* him back.................Job 9:12
do not *t* to evil.....................Job 36:21
acknowledge the LORD and *t*........Ps 22:27
T toward me and have mercy ......Ps 25:16
T and comfort me ....Ps 71:21
we will not *t* away from you.......Ps 80:18
T toward me and have mercy ......Ps 86:16
not *t* aside from your law...........Ps 119:51
not *t* to the right or to the left.... Prov 4:27
t yourself away from evil .... Prov 4:27
not let your heart *t* aside ....Prov 7:25
each will *t* toward home............Isa 13:14
T to me so you can be .... Isa 45:22
t your back on your own flesh...... Isa 58:7
t from your wicked ways .... Jer 25:5
t from all your wickedness ...... Ezek 18:30
t toward Gog .... Ezek 38:2
their faces *t* pale with fright ....Joel 2:6
must *t* from their evil way........Jonah 3:8
T to me,' says the LORD............. Zech 1:3
T now from your evil ....Zech 1:4
t you into fishers of people........Matt 4:19
t the other to him as well........ Matt 5:39
to *t* the hearts of the fathers ..... Luke 1:17
your sadness will *t* into joy ....John 16:20
t from these worthless things .... Acts 14:15
they *t* from darkness to light .....Acts 26:18
should repent and *t* to God......Acts 26:20
to *t* the waters to blood .... Rev 11:6

TURN ASIDE
t to see this amazing sight....... Exod 3:3
not *t* to the right or the left....... Deut 2:27
don't *t* from the LORD ....1 Sam 12:20
t from following the LORD......2 Chr 34:33

Caravans *t* from their routes .... Job 6:18
The wicked *t* from birth.............Ps 58:3
Yet I do not *t* from your law ....Ps 119:51
let your heart *t* to her ways ....Prov 7:25
they will *t* to myths.............. 2 Tim 4:4

TURNED
in the Nile was *t* to blood.........Exod 7:20
t them over to their enemies ....Judg 2:14
t away from the LORD's dwelling..2 Chr 29:6
whom I love have *t* against me .... Job 19:19
be *t* back and ashamed.............Ps 40:14
has *t* against me ....Ps 41:9
t back and ashamed.................Ps 70:2
I have *t* into skin and bones ...... Ps 109:24
has not *t* away from us .... Jer 4:8
have *t* their glorious calling......... Hos 4:7
sunlight will be *t* to darkness.......Joel 2:31
t from their evil way of living....Jonah 3:10
water that had been *t* to wine.......John 2:9
eats my bread has *t* against me... John 13:18
and they *t* to the Lord ....Acts 9:35
who believed *t* to the Lord ....Acts 11:21
how you *t* to God from idols .....1 Thess 1:9

TURNING
are *t* it into a den of robbers...... Matt 21:13
Then, *t* toward the woman .... Luke 7:44
Gentiles who are *t* to God .... Acts 15:19

TURNS
t away his ear from hearing ...... Prov 28:9
t from his righteousness.......... Ezek 3:20
person *t* from all the sin .... Ezek 18:21
person *t* from the wickedness....Ezek 18:27
but he *t* from his sin ....Ezek 33:14
the wicked *t* from his sin ....Ezek 33:19
but no one *t* back................. Nah 2:8
the one who *t* a sinner back........Jas 5:20

TURQUOISE
they exchanged *t* ....Ezek 27:16

TURTLEDOVE
the voice of the *t* is heard ....Song 2:12

TURTLEDOVES
present his offering from the *t* ..... Lev 1:14

TWELVE
See also TWELVE APOSTLES; TWELVE
   DISCIPLES; TWELVE TRIBES
Jacob had *t* sons ....Gen 35:22
These are the *t* tribes of Israel....Gen 49:28
t, corresponding to the number..Exod 39:14
with the *t* leaders of Israel........ Num 1:44
Manasseh was *t* years old ....2 Kgs 21:1
Jesus called his *t* disciples ....Matt 10:1
When he was *t* years old .... Luke 2:42
a hemorrhage for *t* years .... Luke 8:43
Didn't I choose you, the *t*.........John 6:70
her head was a crown of *t* stars .... Rev 12:1
the *t* gates are twelve pearls ...... Rev 21:21

TWELVE APOSTLES
these are the names of the *t*.......Matt 10:2
the twelve names of the *t* ....Rev 21:14

TWELVE DISCIPLES
Jesus called his *t* and gave them...Matt 10:1
finished instructing his *t*...........Matt 11:1

TWELVE TRIBES
These are the *t* of Israel ....Gen 49:28
according to the *t* of Israel ....Exod 24:4
name according to the *t* ....Exod 28:21
corresponding to one of the *t* ... Exod 39:14
the land to the *t* of Israel ....Ezek 47:13
judging the *t* of Israel ....Matt 19:28
judging the *t* of Israel............Luke 22:30
a promise that our *t* hope ....Acts 26:7
to the *t* dispersed abroad.............Jas 1:1
and the names of the *t* ....Rev 21:12

TWENTY-FOUR ELDERS
on those thrones were *t*.......... Rev 4:4
the *t* throw themselves............Rev 4:10
and the *t* threw themselves ....Rev 5:8
the *t* who are seated...............Rev 11:16
The *t* and the four living............Rev 19:4

TWICE
struck the rock *t* with his staff....Num 20:11
a rooster crows *t* ....Mark 14:30
Before a rooster crows *t*.........Mark 14:72

TWIG
sprouted up like a *t* before God .....Isa 53:2

TWILIGHT
at *t*, is a Passover offering ....Lev 23:5

TWINS
there were *t* in her womb ....Gen 25:24
there were *t* in her womb ....Gen 38:27
t of a gazelle...................... Song 7:3
Heavenly *T*" as its figurehead..... Acts 28:11

TWIST
the ignorant and unstable *t*....... 2 Pet 3:16

TWISTED
this vine *t* its roots toward him....Ezek 17:7

TWO
God made *t* great lights ....Gen 1:16
t of every kind of unclean animal... Gen 7:2
T nations are in your womb ......Gen 25:23
Take a young bull and *t* rams.... Exod 29:1
Moses *t* tablets of testimony .....Exod 31:18
hooves are completely split in *t* .....Lev 11:3
she must take *t* turtledoves ....Lev 12:8
the *t* tablets of the covenant ......Deut 9:15
and carved out *t* stone tablets.... Deut 10:3
of *t* or three witnesses...........Deut 19:15
hold of the *t* middle pillars ....Judg 16:29
divided the Red Sea in *t* .... Ps 136:13
T people are better than one ...... Eccl 4:9
With *t* wings they covered........... Isa 6:2
and saw a ram with *t* horns........ Dan 8:3
that you saw with the *t* horns .....Dan 8:20
watched as *t* others stood there....Dan 12:5
go with him *t* ....Matt 5:41
only five loaves and *t* fish........ Matt 14:17
take one or *t* others with you.....Matt 18:16
where *t* or three are assembled . Matt 18:20
the *t* will become one flesh........Matt 19:5
A man had *t* sons .... Matt 21:28
gave five talents, to another *t* ....Matt 25:15
Then *t* outlaws were crucified... Matt 27:38
temple curtain was torn in *t*...Matt 27:51
they said, "Five—and *t* fish........Mark 6:38
the *t* will become one flesh.......Mark 10:8
put in *t* small copper coins ......Mark 12:42
crucified *t* outlaws with him..... Mark 15:27
temple curtain was torn in *t*.....Mark 15:38
doves or *t* young pigeons......... Luke 2:24
than five loaves and *t* fish ....Luke 9:13
A man had *t* sons .... Luke 15:11
servant can serve *t* masters ......Luke 16:13
put in *t* small copper coins ......Luke 21:2
T other criminals were also ..... Luke 23:32
temple curtain was torn in *t*.....Luke 23:45
t of them were on their way..... Luke 24:13
five barley loaves and *t* fish.........John 6:9
women represent *t* covenants......Gal 4:24
one new man out of *t*...............Eph 2:15
the *t* will become one flesh........Eph 5:31
by *t* or three witnesses ....1 Tim 5:19
grant my *t* witnesses authority ..... Rev 11:3
He had *t* horns like a lamb..........Rev 13:11

TWO-EDGED SWORD
and a *t* in their hands ....Ps 149:6
sharp as a *t* ....Prov 5:4

TYCHICUS
Paul's companion, Acts 20:1, 4
Paul's messenger, Eph 6:21–22; Col 4:7–9;
   2 Tim 4:12

TYPE
is a *t* of the coming one............Rom 5:14

TYRANTS
from the hand of *t* ransom me .....Job 6:23
bring down the arrogance of *t*.......Isa 13:11

TYRE
City of Phoenicia noted for its commerce,
   Josh 19:29; 2 Sam 5:11; Jer 25:22
See also TYRE AND SIDON

TYRE AND SIDON
help that remains for *T* . . . . Jer 47:4
doing these things to me, *T*. . . . . Joel 3:4
had been done in *T* . . . . Matt 11:21
Jesus went to the region of *T* . . . . Matt 15:21
will be more bearable for *T*. . . . . . Luke 10:14
quarrel with the people of *T* . . . . . Acts 12:20

U

ULAI
Scene of Daniel's visions, Dan 8:2–16

ULCER
Job with a malignant *u*. . . . . Job 2:7

ULTIMATE
the *u* joy of being forgiven. . . . . Ps 51:8

UNABLE
do wrong and are *u* to repent . . . . Jer 9:5

UNATTAINABLE
Wisdom is *u* for a fool . . . . Prov 24:7

UNAWARE
I do not want you to be *u* . . . . Rom 1:13

UNBELIEF
there because of their *u* . . . . Matt 13:58
I believe; help my *u*. . . . . Mark 9:24
he rebuked them for their *u* . . . . . Mark 16:14
Do not continue in your *u* . . . . . . John 20:27
He did not waver in *u*. . . . . Rom 4:20
I acted ignorantly in *u* . . . . 1 Tim 1:13
could not enter because of *u* . . . . . . Heb 3:19

UNBELIEVABLE
u that God raises the dead. . . . . Acts 26:8

UNBELIEVER
u does not receive the things . . . . . 1 Cor 2:14
But if the *u* wants a divorce. . . . . . . 1 Cor 7:15
share in common with an *u*. . . . . . . 2 Cor 6:15
and is worse than an *u*. . . . . 1 Tim 5:8

UNBELIEVERS
not for believers but for *u* . . . . 1 Cor 14:22
u or uninformed people enter . . . 1 Cor 14:23
u, detestable persons. . . . . Rev 21:8

UNBELIEVING
You *u* and perverse generation . . . Matt 17:17
You *u* generation . . . . Mark 9:19
the *u* husband is sanctified . . . . 1 Cor 7:14
those who are corrupt and *u* . . . . . . Titus 1:15
u heart that forsakes . . . . Heb 3:12

UNBLEMISHED
that of an *u* and spotless lamb. . . . . 1 Pet 1:19

UNCEASING
down nations with *u* blows . . . . Isa 14:6
and *u* anguish in my heart . . . . Rom 9:2

UNCHANGEABLE
through two *u* things . . . . Heb 6:18

UNCIRCUMCISED
u hearts become humbled. . . . . Lev 26:41
For who is this *u* Philistine. . . . . . . 1 Sam 17:26
those in heart and in flesh. . . . . Ezek 44:7
with *u* hearts and ears. . . . . Acts 7:51
and the *u* through faith . . . . Rom 3:30
with the gospel to the *u* . . . . Gal 2:7
circumcised or *u*. . . . . Col 3:11

UNCIRCUMCISION
circumcision has become *u* . . . . Rom 2:25
circumcision or also for the *u* . . . . . Rom 4:9
Circumcision is nothing and *u* . . . . 1 Cor 7:19
called "*u*" by the so-called . . . . Eph 2:11

UNCLEAN
See also UNCLEAN SPIRIT; UNCLEAN
  SPIRITS
two of every kind of *u* animal . . . . . . Gen 7:2
anything ceremonially *u*. . . . . Lev 5:2
anything ceremonially *u*. . . . . Lev 7:19
person touches anything *u* . . . . Lev 7:21
between the *u* and the clean . . . . . . Lev 10:10
they are *u* to you . . . . Lev 11:8
will be *u* until the evening . . . . Lev 11:24
uncircumcised and *u* pagans . . . . Isa 52:1

Don't touch anything *u* . . . . Isa 52:11
We are all like one who is *u* . . . . Isa 64:6
the dead and of everything *u* . . . . Matt 23:27
even commands the *u* spirits . . . . . Mark 1:27
he commands the *u* spirits . . . . Luke 4:36
no person defiled or ritually *u* . . . Acts 10:28
there is nothing *u* in itself . . . . Rom 14:14
Otherwise your children are *u*. . . . 1 Cor 7:14
and touch no *u* thing . . . . 2 Cor 6:17
a haunt for every *u* spirit . . . . Rev 18:2

UNCLEAN SPIRIT
and the *u* from the land . . . . Zech 13:2
When an *u* goes out . . . . Matt 12:43
their synagogue with an *u* . . . . Mark 1:23
the *u* cried out with a loud . . . . Mark 1:26
He has an *u* . . . . Mark 3:30
a man with an *u* came from . . . . Mark 5:2
young daughter had an *u* . . . . Mark 7:25
he rebuked the *u* . . . . Mark 9:25
Jesus rebuked the *u* . . . . Luke 9:42
When an *u* goes out . . . . Luke 11:24
a haunt for every *u* . . . . Rev 18:2

UNCLEAN SPIRITS
gave them authority over *u* . . . . Matt 10:1
He even commands the *u* . . . . Mark 1:27
whenever the *u* saw him . . . . Mark 3:11
the *u* came out and went . . . . Mark 5:13
suffered from *u* were cured . . . . Luke 6:18
and those troubled by *u* . . . . Acts 5:16
u crying with loud shrieks . . . . Acts 8:7
Then I saw three *u* . . . . Rev 16:13

UNCLEANNESS
while that person's *u* persists . . . . . Lev 7:20
from her menstrual *u*. . . . . 2 Sam 11:4
will save you from all your *u* . . . . Ezek 36:29

UNCLOTHED
we do not want to be *u* . . . . 2 Cor 5:4

UNCONDITIONAL
an *u* covenantal promise . . . . Isa 55:3

UNCONVERTED
For the *u* pursue these things . . . . Matt 6:32

UNCOVER
he will *u* the woman's head. . . . . . . Num 5:18
I will *u* their hiding places . . . . Jer 49:10

UNCOVERED
and *u* himself inside his tent. . . . . . . Gen 9:21
u by the LORD's battle cry . . . . . . 2 Sam 22:16
prophesies with her head *u*. . . . . . . 1 Cor 11:5
pray to God with her head *u* . . . . . 1 Cor 11:13

UNCOVERING
by *u* your transgressions . . . . Ezek 21:24

UNCOVERS
woman and *u* her nakedness . . . . . Lev 20:18

UNDEFILED
and the marriage bed kept *u* . . . . . Heb 13:4
Pure and *u* religion before God . . . . Jas 1:27
imperishable, *u*, and unfading . . . . . 1 Pet 1:4

UNDER HIS FEET
U there was something like . . . . . Exod 24:10
a thick cloud was *u* . . . . 2 Sam 22:10
a thick cloud was *u* . . . . Ps 18:9
clouds billow like dust *u*. . . . . Nah 1:3
put all his enemies *u*. . . . . 1 Cor 15:25
everything in subjection *u* . . . . 1 Cor 15:27

UNDER THE LAW
all who have sinned *u*. . . . . Rom 2:12
to those who are *u* . . . . Rom 3:19
I became like one *u*. . . . . 1 Cor 9:20
born of a woman, born *u* . . . . Gal 4:4
you who want to be *u* . . . . Gal 4:21
you are not *u* . . . . Gal 5:18

UNDERGARMENTS
has walked around in *u*. . . . . Isa 20:3

UNDERMINING
they are *u* some people's faith. . . . 2 Tim 2:18

UNDERSTAND
won't be able to *u* each other . . . . . Gen 11:7
can *u* the thunder of his power . . . Job 26:14

that makes them *u* . . . . Job 32:8
u the spreading of the clouds. . . . . Job 36:29
when will you ever *u* . . . . Ps 94:8
u what your precepts mean . . . . . . Ps 119:27
will *u* how to fear the LORD. . . . . . . Prov 2:5
u righteousness and justice. . . . . Prov 2:9
Evil people do not *u* justice . . . . . . Prov 28:5
my people do not *u*. . . . . Isa 1:3
but don't *u*. . . . . Isa 6:9
They do not comprehend or *u*. . . . Isa 44:18
Who can *u* it. Jer 17:9
I am anxious to *u* the dream. . . . . . . Dan 2:3
king may *u* the interpretation . . . . Dan 2:30
to *u* and to humble yourself. . . . . . Dan 10:12
None of the wicked will *u* . . . . Dan 12:10
they do not *u* his strategy . . . . Mic 4:12
carefully yet will never *u* . . . . Matt 13:14
u with their hearts and turn . . . . . Matt 13:15
they may hear but not *u* . . . . Mark 4:12
they hear they may not *u*. . . . . Luke 8:10
don't you *u* what I am saying . . . . . John 8:43
and *u* with their heart . . . . John 12:40
do not *u* what I am doing now. . . . . John 13:7
If you *u* these things . . . . John 13:17
Do you *u* what you're reading . . . . Acts 8:30
u that God does not show . . . . Acts 10:34
u with their heart and turn . . . . . . Acts 28:27
I don't *u* what I am doing . . . . Rom 7:15
who have not heard will *u* . . . . Rom 15:21
And he cannot *u* them. . . . . 1 Cor 2:14
in these letters are hard to *u* . . . . . 2 Pet 3:16

UNDERSTANDING
in skill, in *u*, in knowledge . . . . Exod 31:3
has not given you an *u* mind. . . . . . Deut 29:4
breadth of his *u* was as infinite . . . 1 Kgs 4:29
counsel and *u* are his . . . . Job 12:13
leaders of the earth of their *u* . . . . Job 12:24
Where is the place of *u* . . . . Job 28:12
to turn away from evil is *u*. . . . . Job 28:28
If you have *u*. Job 34:16
great things beyond our *u* . . . . Job 37:5
or has imparted *u* to the mind. . . . Job 38:36
and did not impart *u* to her. . . . . . . Job 39:17
I have declared without *u*. . . . . Job 42:3
u so that I might observe . . . . Ps 119:34
proper discernment and *u* . . . . Ps 119:66
me *u* so that I might learn . . . . Ps 119:73
by turning your heart to *u* . . . . Prov 2:2
u will guard you . . . . Prov 2:11
do not rely on your own *u* . . . . Prov 3:5
established the heavens by *u* . . . . . . Prov 3:19
To those who lack *u* . . . . Prov 9:4
and proceed in the way of *u* . . . . . . Prov 9:6
the Holy One is *u* . . . . Prov 9:10
u was easy for a discerning. . . . . Prov 14:6
with great *u* is slow to anger . . . . . Prov 14:29
has *u* follows an upright course . . Prov 15:21
listens to reproof acquires *u*. . . . . . Prov 15:32
to acquire *u* is more desirable. . . . . Prov 16:16
A fool takes no pleasure in *u* . . . . . . Prov 18:2
who acquires *u* loves himself. . . . . . Prov 19:8
who preserves *u* will prosper. . . . . . Prov 19:8
wisdom, and discipline, and *u*. . . . Prov 23:23
For these people lack *u*. . . . . Isa 27:11
And by his *u* . . . . Jer 10:12
with wisdom and *u* . . . . Jer 23:5
by his *u*, he spread out. . . . . Jer 51:15
that lacks *u* will come to ruin. . . . . . Hos 4:14
They are darkened in their *u* . . . . . . Eph 4:18
peace of God that surpasses all *u*. . . Phil 4:7
all spiritual wisdom and *u* . . . . Col 1:9
the Lord will give you *u*. . . . . 2 Tim 2:7
without *u* where he was going. . . . . Heb 11:8
Who is wise and *u* among you. . . . . Jas 3:13

UNDERSTANDS
God *u* the way to it . . . . Job 28:23
when he *u* what he has done . . . . . . Isa 53:11
there is no one who *u* . . . . Rom 3:11

UNDERSTOOD
saw the Israelites, and God *u* . . . . . Exod 2:25
my ears have heard and *u* it . . . . Job 13:1
u the destiny of the wicked. . . . . Ps 73:17
Have you not *u* from the time. . . . . Isa 40:21

Have you *u* all these things .... Matt 13:51
u the facts concerning the Way .. Acts 24:22
u through what has been made .... Rom 1:20

UNDESERVING
are slaves *u* of special praise ..... Luke 17:10

UNDESIRABLE
you *u* nation .... Zeph 2:1

UNDISCIPLINED
admonish the *u* .... 1 Thess 5:14
brother who lives an *u* life .... 2 Thess 3:6

UNDO
response can *u* great offenses ..... Eccl 10:4

UNEDUCATED
they were *u* and ordinary men .... Acts 4:13

UNENDING
U joy will crown them .... Isa 35:10

UNFADING
imperishable, undefiled, and *u* ...... 1 Pet 1:4

UNFAIR
is just and never *u* .... Ps 92:15

UNFAITHFUL
they were *u* to the God .... 1 Chr 5:25
he was *u* to the LORD .... 1 Chr 10:13
they were *u* to the LORD .... 2 Chr 12:2
who were *u* to the LORD God ..... 2 Chr 30:7
We have been *u* to our God ...... Ezra 10:2
thereby being *u* to our God .... Neh 13:27
But still her *u* sister Judah .... Jer 3:8
But, you have been *u* to me .... Jer 3:20
land is full of people *u* to him ..... Jer 23:10
for they were *u* to me .... Ezek 39:23
and do not be *u* .... Mal 2:16
assign him a place with the *u* ..... Luke 12:46
If we are *u*, he remains faithful ... 2 Tim 2:13

UNFAITHFULLY
because they have acted *u* .... Ezek 15:8

UNFAITHFULNESS
to Babylon because of their *u* ...... 1 Chr 9:1

UNFRUITFUL
in the *u* deeds of darkness .... Eph 5:11
pressing needs and so not be *u* .... Titus 3:14

UNFULFILLED
to the family of Israel was left *u* .. Josh 21:45

UNGODLINESS
the reason that *u* has spread .... Jer 23:15
all *u* and unrighteousness .... Rom 1:18
he will remove *u* from Jacob ...... Rom 11:26

UNGODLY
against an *u* nation .... Ps 43:1
who declares the *u* righteous ...... Rom 4:5
Christ died for the *u* .... Rom 5:6
and destruction of the *u* .... 2 Pet 3:7
that *u* sinners have spoken .... Jude 1:15

UNGRATEFUL
disobedient to parents, *u*, unholy .. 2 Tim 3:2

UNHARMED
were physically *u* by the fire .... Dan 3:27

UNHOLY
for the *u* and profane .... 1 Tim 1:9

UNINFORMED
I do not want you to be *u* .... 1 Cor 12:1

UNINHABITED
it will be *u* for forty years .... Ezek 29:11

UNINTELLIGIBLE
sent to a people of *u* speech ...... Ezek 3:5

UNINTENTIONAL
because it was *u* and .... Num 15:25

UNINTENTIONALLY
person sins by straying *u* .... Lev 4:2
you sin *u* and do not observe .... Num 15:22

UNIQUE
Make it known that he is *u* .... Isa 12:4

UNISON
and will worship him in *u* .... Zeph 3:9

UNIT
must appoint *u* commanders ..... Deut 20:9

UNITE
God moved the people to *u* ..... 2 Chr 30:12

UNITED
But the one *u* with the Lord ...... 1 Cor 6:17

UNITES
and *u* with his wife .... Gen 2:24

UNITY
brothers truly live in *u* .... Ps 133:1
give you *u* with one another ...... Rom 15:5
to keep the *u* of the Spirit .... Eph 4:3
attain to the *u* of the faith .... Eph 4:13

UNIVERSAL
there will be *u* submission .... Isa 11:9

UNJUST
a reliable God who is never *u* ..... Deut 32:4
you make *u* legal decisions .... Ps 82:2
The Lord's conduct is *u* .... Ezek 18:25
The Lord's conduct is *u* .... Ezek 18:29
Yet the *u* know no shame .... Zeph 3:5
For God is not *u* .... Heb 6:10
the just for the *u* .... 1 Pet 3:18

UNJUSTLY
right is rewarded, they act *u* ...... Isa 26:10
hardships in suffering *u* .... 1 Pet 2:19

UNKNOWN
To an *u* god .... Acts 17:23
personally *u* to the churches .... Gal 1:22

UNLAWFUL
know that it is *u* for a Jew .... Acts 10:28

UNLEAVENED BREAD
See also FEAST OF UNLEAVENED BREAD
you will keep the Feast of *U* ...... Exod 12:17
including *u* and roasted grain ...... Josh 5:11
the meat and *u* on this rock ...... Judg 6:20
to observe the Feast of *U* .... 2 Chr 30:13
They observed the Feast of *U* ..... Ezra 6:22
the first day of the Feast of *U* .... Matt 26:17
Now the Feast of *U* .... Luke 22:1
place during the feast of *U* .... Acts 12:3

UNLOVED
LORD saw that Leah was *u* .... Gen 29:31
under an *u* woman who .... Prov 30:23

UNMARRIED
and their virgins remained *u* .... Ps 78:63
To the *u* and widows I say .... 1 Cor 7:8
An *u* woman or a virgin .... 1 Cor 7:34

UNPRODUCTIVE
but my mind is *u* .... 1 Cor 14:14

UNPUNISHED
the evil person will not be *u* ...... Prov 11:21
A false witness will not go *u* ...... Prov 19:9
to gain riches will not go *u* ...... Prov 28:20
do you think you will go *u* .... Jer 49:12

UNQUENCHABLE
and go into hell, to the *u* fire .... Mark 9:43

UNQUENCHED
is still weak and his thirst *u* .... Isa 29:8

UNREPENTANT
stubbornness and your *u* heart .... Rom 2:5

UNRIGHTEOUS
rain on the righteous and the *u* ... Matt 5:45
both the righteous and the *u* ..... Acts 24:15
the *u* will not inherit the .... 1 Cor 6:9

UNRIGHTEOUSNESS
and there is no *u* in him .... John 7:18
against all ungodliness and *u* ...... Rom 1:18
obey the truth but follow *u* .... Rom 2:8
instruments to be used for *u* ...... Rom 6:13
and cleansing us from all *u* .... 1 John 1:9
All *u* is sin .... 1 John 5:17

UNROLLED
He *u* it before me .... Ezek 2:10
u the scroll and found the place ... Luke 4:17

UNSEARCHABLE
He does great and *u* things .... Job 5:9
so the hearts of kings are *u* .... Prov 25:3
How *u* are his judgments .... Rom 11:33

UNSHAKABLE
are receiving an *u* kingdom .... Heb 12:28

UNSHRUNK
No one sews a patch of *u* cloth .... Matt 9:16

UNSKILLED
even if I am *u* in speaking .... 2 Cor 11:6

UNSTABLE
u in all his ways .... Jas 1:8
they entice *u* people .... 2 Pet 2:14

UNSTAINED
keep oneself *u* by the world .... Jas 1:27

UNTRAINED
The LORD protects the *u* .... Ps 116:6
They give insight to the *u* .... Ps 119:130

UNVEILED
u faces reflecting the glory .... 2 Cor 3:18

UNWASHED
it is not eating with *u* hands ..... Matt 15:20
but eat with *u* hands .... Mark 7:5

UNWAVERINGLY
let us hold *u* to the hope .... Heb 10:23

UNWHOLESOME
u word come out of your mouth .. Eph 4:29

UNWISE
as *u* but as wise .... Eph 5:15

UNWORTHY
Indeed, I am completely *u* .... Job 40:4
u to be called an apostle .... 1 Cor 15:9

UNWRAP
U him and let him go .... John 11:44

UP
closed *u* the place with flesh .... Gen 2:21
or when she got *u* .... Gen 19:35
Next he tied *u* his son Isaac .... Gen 22:9
Abraham looked *u* and saw ...... Gen 22:13
going *u* and coming down it ...... Gen 28:12
Jacob woke *u* and thought .... Gen 28:16
Suddenly my sheaf rose *u* .... Gen 37:7
does the bush not burn *u* .... Exod 3:3
Aaron's staff swallowed *u* .... Exod 7:12
When Aaron sets *u* the lamps .... Exod 30:8
Your strength will be used *u* ...... Lev 26:20
rest and make *u* its Sabbaths .... Lev 26:34
Deborah got *u* and went .... Judg 4:9
and get dressed *u* .... Ruth 3:3
But the boy Samuel grew *u* .... 1 Sam 2:21
So Samuel got *u* and went .... 1 Sam 3:6
Solomon would offer *u* .... 1 Kgs 3:4
and to raise *u* its ruins .... Ezra 9:9
I got *u* during the night .... Neh 2:12
lifted *u* above all blessing .... Neh 9:5
but it does not hold *u* .... Job 8:15
Who shut *u* the sea with doors .... Job 38:8
Rise *u*, O LORD .... Ps 21:13
my prayers do not let *u* .... Ps 22:2
are dividing *u* my clothes .... Ps 22:18
u to his holy dwelling place .... Ps 24:3
He piles *u* the water of the sea ...... Ps 33:7
Rise *u* and help us .... Ps 44:26
Rise *u* above the sky .... Ps 57:5
who speak lies will be shut *u* .... Ps 63:11
of the house divides *u* the loot ..... Ps 68:12
my heart I store *u* your words ...... Ps 119:11
lifts *u* all who are bent over .... Ps 146:8
He lifts *u* the fatherless .... Ps 146:9
and store *u* my commands .... Prov 2:1
Who has bound *u* the waters ..... Prov 30:4
bring *u* a matter before God .... Eccl 5:2
go *u* to the LORD's mountain .... Isa 2:3
Go *u* into the rocky cliffs .... Isa 2:10
Tie *u* the scroll as legal .... Isa 8:16
I will climb *u* to the sky .... Isa 14:13
I will set *u* my throne .... Isa 14:13
The earth dries *u* and withers ...... Isa 24:4

he dreams *u* evil plans................Isa 32:7
Now I will rise *u* ....Isa 33:10
sky will roll *u* like a scroll........... Isa 34:4
The grass dries *u* ....Isa 40:7
he gathers *u* the lambs ....Isa 40:11
rise *u* as if they had eagles' .... Isa 40:31
and hills wither *u* ....Isa 42:15
But he lifted *u* our illnesses......... Isa 53:4
he lifted *u* the sin of many.........Isa 53:12
to cheer *u* the humiliated..........Isa 57:15
climb *u* among the rocks .... Jer 4:29
when I will raise *u* for them ....Jer 23:5
LORD has raised *u* prophets ......Jer 29:15
will take *u* the tambourine ....Jer 31:4
I will dry *u* their sea ....Jer 51:36
rounded *u* all my mighty ones......Lam 1:15
Let us lift *u* our hearts.............Lam 3:41
three men that we tied *u* ....Dan 3:24
and giving *u* their bodies ....Dan 3:28
u and rushed to the lions' den ..... Dan 6:19
you should seal *u* the vision ....Dan 8:26
I got *u* and again carried out....... Dan 8:27
punishment is being stored *u*......Hos 13:12
I will make *u* for the years........ Joel 2:25
a stream that never dries *u*...... Amos 5:24
if they could climb *u* to heaven... Amos 9:2
the little plant so that it dried *u* ...Jonah 4:7
Zion will be plowed *u*..............Mic 3:12
also shake *u* all the nations......... Hag 2:7
You turn *u* your nose at it .... Mal 1:13
raise *u* children for Abraham ...... Matt 3:9
she got *u* and began to serve.....Matt 8:15
got *u* and rebuked the winds .....Matt 8:26
does not take *u* his cross ....Matt 10:38
he first ties *u* the strong man....Matt 12:29
will stand *u* at the judgment......Matt 12:41
picked *u* the broken pieces ......Matt 14:20
Be lifted *u* and thrown............Matt 21:21
of the people came *u* to him....Matt 21:23
They tie *u* heavy loads............Matt 23:4
Then all the virgins woke *u*.......Matt 25:7
and gave *u* his spirit ....Matt 27:50
when it is sown, it grows *u* ......Mark 4:32
got *u* and rebuked the wind .....Mark 4:39
take *u* his cross....................Mark 8:34
u from the sheer arrogance ..... Luke 1:51
Mary treasured *u* all these words..Luke 2:19
Then he rolled *u* the scroll........Luke 4:20
he looked *u* at his disciples......Luke 6:20
take *u* his cross daily ....Luke 9:23
she straightened *u* and ....Luke 13:13
will get *u* and go to my father ....Luke 15:18
looked *u* and saw Abraham......Luke 16:23
climbed *u* into a sycamore tree....Luke 19:4
with the elders came *u* ....Luke 20:1
and lifting *u* his hands ....Luke 24:50
and was taken *u* into heaven .... Luke 24:51
as Moses lifted *u* the serpent......John 3:14
springing *u* to eternal life..........John 4:14
look *u* and see that the fields.....John 4:35
Gather *u* the broken pieces.......John 6:12
his feet and hands tied *u*......John 11:44
I am lifted *u* from the earth......John 12:32
Son of Man must be lifted *u*......John 12:34
and take *u* residence with him...John 14:23
out like a branch and dries *u* ..... John 15:6
and gave *u* his spirit ....John 19:30
lifted *u* and a cloud hid him........ Acts 1:9
He got *u* and was baptized ....Acts 9:18
leaped *u* and began walking ..... Acts 14:10
are summed *u* in this ....Rom 13:9
someone's work is burned *u*.......1 Cor 3:15
Knowledge puffs *u* ....1 Cor 8:1
but love builds *u*..................1 Cor 8:1
Sober *u* as you should .... 1 Cor 15:34
Death has been swallowed *u* .... 1 Cor 15:54
raised *u* against the knowledge..2 Cor 10:5
gave it to me for building *u* ...... 2 Cor 13:10
But if I build *u* again .... Gal 2:18
whole law can be summed *u* .... Gal 5:14
if we do not give *u*.................Gal 6:9
to head *u* all things in Christ........Eph 1:10
filled *u* to all the fullness ....Eph 3:19

all things grow *u* into Christ........Eph 4:15
take *u* the full armor of God........Eph 6:13
by taking *u* the shield of faith.......Eph 6:16
so that he could make *u* ....Phil 2:30
let us live *u* to the standard........Phil 3:16
rooted and built *u* in him ....Col 2:7
fill *u* their measure of sins......1 Thess 2:16
and build *u* each other...........1 Thess 5:11
lifting *u* holy hands ....1 Tim 2:8
taken *u* in glory....................1 Tim 3:16
that has soaked *u* the rain ....Heb 6:7
By faith Enoch was taken *u*.........Heb 11:5
weary in your souls and give *u* .....Heb 12:3
give *u* when he corrects you.......Heb 12:5
offer *u* a sacrifice of praise ....Heb 13:15
and dries *u* the meadow.............Jas 1:11
are built *u* as a spiritual house......1 Pet 2:5
Wake *u* then.......................Rev 3:2
third of the trees were burned *u* ....Rev 8:7
the power to close *u* the sky ...... Rev 11:6
Come *u* here.......................Rev 11:12
was suddenly caught *u* to God.....Rev 12:5
and dried *u* its water...............Rev 16:12
earth was lit *u* by his radiance ...... Rev 18:1
because her sins have piled *u*........Rev 18:5
The sea gave *u* the dead .... Rev 20:13
Do not seal *u* the words ....Rev 22:10

UPENDED

I will not be *u*........................Ps 62:2

UPHELD

He *u* the cause of the poor ....Jer 22:16

UPHOLD

u you with my victorious right......Isa 41:10

UPHOLDS

your right hand *u* me...............Ps 63:8

UPPER ROOM

he closed the doors of the *u*........Judg 3:23
carried him to the *u* ....1 Kgs 17:19
u and furnish it with a bed........2 Kgs 4:10
windows in his *u* opened ....Dan 6:10
brought him to the *u* ....Acts 9:39

UPRIGHT

She is more *u* than I am ....Gen 38:26
Let me die the death of the *u*.... Num 23:10
he is fair and *u* ....Deut 32:4
man was blameless and *u* ....Job 1:1
a blameless and *u* man ....Job 1:8
leave the *u* paths to walk ....Prov 2:13
the *u* will reside in the land.......Prov 2:21
is like a stronghold for the *u*..... Prov 10:29
integrity of the *u* guides them ..... Prov 11:3
The righteousness of the *u* ....Prov 11:6
tent of the *u* will flourish ....Prov 14:11
prayer of the *u* pleases him........Prov 15:8
path of the *u* is like a highway ....Prov 15:19
follows an *u* course...............Prov 15:21
one who leads the *u* astray ...... Prov 28:10
God made humankind *u*...........Eccl 7:29
one whose desires are not *u*........Hab 2:4
self-controlled, *u*, and godly ......Titus 2:12

UPRIGHTLY

The one who lives *u* ....Isa 33:15

UPRIGHTNESS

what constitutes his *u*.............Job 33:23
The one who walks in his *u*.........Prov 14:2

UPROAR

and the city is in an *u* ....1 Kgs 1:45
people making such an *u* ....Isa 17:12
these people make an *u* ....Isa 17:13
city was filled with the *u*...........Acts 19:29

UPROOT

you may *u* the wheat ....Matt 13:29

UPROOTED

So the LORD has *u* them ....Deut 29:28
without fruit—twice dead, *u* ....Jude 1:12

UPROOTS

u my hope like an uprooted tree ..Job 19:10

UPSET

Jacob was very afraid and *u*........ Gen 32:7

David was very *u* ....1 Sam 30:6
Why are you *u*......................Ps 42:5
I am so *u* and distressed.............Ps 55:2
was *u* for a brief time..............Dan 4:19
his spirit was greatly *u*...........Acts 17:16

UPSTAIRS

will show you a large room *u*.... Mark 14:15

UPWARD

as surely as the sparks fly *u* .... Job 5:7
path of life is *u* for the wise.......Prov 15:24
looked *u* to heaven and said.......John 17:1

UR OF THE CHALDEANS

City of Abram's early life, Gen 11:28–31; 15:7
Located in Mesopotamia by Stephen,
   Acts 7:2, 4

URGE

a strong *u* to sleep deeply .... Isa 29:10
and *u* people to come in......... Luke 14:23
I *u* you to reaffirm your love.......2 Cor 2:8
u you to live worthily ....Eph 4:1
command and *u* in the Lord ....2 Thess 3:12
I *u* that requests ....1 Tim 2:1
I *u* you as foreigners and exiles.... 1 Pet 2:11

URGED

they *u* him earnestly...............Luke 7:4

URGES

do not comply with the evil *u* ..... 1 Pet 1:14

URGING

Stop *u* me to abandon you ....Ruth 1:16
the disciples were *u* him...........John 4:31
people were *u* them to speak.....Acts 13:42

URIAH

Hittite; one of David's warriors, 2 Sam 23:39
Husband of Bathsheba; condemned to
   death by David, 2 Sam 11:1–27
—High priest in Ahaz's time, 2 Kgs 16:10–16
—Prophet in Jeremiah's time, Jer 26:20–23

URIM

put the *U* and the Thummim ....Exod 28:30
by the decision of the *U* .... Num 27:21
Your Thummim and *U*...........Deut 33:8
consult the *U* and Thummim ......Ezra 2:63
consult the *U* and Thummim ......Neh 7:65

URINE

their knees will be wet with *u* .....Ezek 7:17

URN

golden *u* containing the manna..... Heb 9:4

US

which means "God with *u* ....Matt 1:23
is not against *u* is for *u*.......... Mark 9:40
If God is for *u*......................Rom 8:31
They went out from *u* ....1 John 2:19

USE

u of the name of the LORD......... Deut 5:11
Nations will not *u* weapons.........Mic 4:3
and the measure you *u* ....Matt 7:2
high positions *u* their authority..Mark 10:42
one vessel for special *u*...........Rom 9:21
those who *u* the world ....1 Cor 7:31
only do not *u* your freedom ....Gal 5:13
all destined to perish with *u*........Col 2:22
but *u* a little wine.................1 Tim 5:23
some are for honorable *u* .... 2 Tim 2:20
but others for ignoble *u* ....2 Tim 2:20
U your sickle and start to reap ....Rev 14:15

USED

have *u* their writings.................Jer 8:8
you who *u* to be far away...........Eph 2:13

USEFUL

will it be *u* for anything............Ezek 15:4
u for the Master .... 2 Tim 2:21
inspired by God and *u* for ....2 Tim 3:16

USELESS

your faith is *u*....................1 Cor 15:17
who was formerly *u* to you........ Phlm 1:11
because it is weak and *u*............Heb 7:18

USES

if someone *u* it legitimately ....1 Tim 1:8

UTTER
my lips will *u* knowledge .... Job 33:3

UTTERANCES
beginning elements of God's *u* .... Heb 5:12

UTTERED
by the words you have *u*. .... Prov 6:2

UTTERLY
offer would be *u* despised .... Song 8:7
unless you have *u* rejected us ..... Lam 5:22

UZZAH
Son of Abinadab, struck down for touching
 the ark of the covenant, 2 Sam 6:3–11

UZZIAH
King of Judah, called Azariah, 2 Kgs 14:21;
 15:1–7
Reigns righteously, 2 Chr 26:1–15
Usurps priestly function; stricken with
 leprosy, 2 Chr 26:16–21
Life of, written by Isaiah, 2 Chr 26:22–23

V

VAIN
name of the LORD your God in *v* .. Exod 20:7
while you look on in *v* all day .... Deut 28:32
those who build it work in *v* .... Ps 127:1
I have worked in *v* .... Isa 49:4
and they worship me in *v* .... Matt 15:9
They worship me In *v* .... Mark 7:7
you believed in *v* .... 1 Cor 15:2
your labor is not in *v* .... 1 Cor 15:58
did not run in *v* nor labor in *v* ..... Phil 2:16

VALIANTLY
but Israel will act *v* .... Num 24:18
Many daughters have done *v* .... Prov 31:29

VALIDATE
and *v* his choice of Jerusalem ...... Zech 1:17

VALLEY
the arid rift *v* provides food .... Job 24:5
walk through the darkest *v* .... Ps 23:4
they pass through the Baca V .... Ps 84:6
look for the blossoms of the *v* ..... Song 6:11
let the arid rift *v* rejoice .... Isa 35:1
Every *v* must be elevated .... Isa 40:4
rugged landscape a wide *v* .... Isa 40:4
her arid rift *v* like the garden .... Isa 51:3
in the midst of the *v* .... Ezek 37:1
are in the V of Decision .... Joel 3:14
Every *v* will be filled .... Luke 3:5
across the Kidron V .... John 18:1

VALLEYS
and not a god of the *v* .... 1 Kgs 20:28
a lily from the *v* .... Song 2:1
and the *v* will split apart .... Mic 1:4

VALUABLE
was made of large *v* stones .... 1 Kgs 7:10
you more *v* than they are .... Matt 6:26
more *v* than many sparrows ..... Matt 10:31
more *v* is a person than a sheep .. Matt 12:12
more *v* than many sparrows ...... Luke 12:7
more *v* are you than the birds ... Luke 12:24
is much more *v* than gold .... 1 Pet 1:7

VALUE
are of greater *v* than gold .... Ps 19:10
her *v* is far more than rubies ..... Prov 31:10
he found a pearl of great *v* ...... Matt 13:46
v of the books was added up ..... Acts 19:19
what is the *v* of circumcision .... Rom 3:1
far greater *v* of knowing Christ ..... Phil 3:8
wisdom with no true *v*. .... Col 2:23
physical exercise has some *v* ..... 1 Tim 4:8

VALUES
LORD *v* the lives of his faithful ..... Ps 116:15

VANISH
they *v* from their place .... Job 6:17

VANISHED
Then he *v* out of their sight ...... Luke 24:31

VANITY
by selfish ambition or *v* .... Phil 2:3

VAPOR
are nothing but *v* .... Ps 39:5
Surely all people are a mere *v* ...... Ps 39:11
People are like a *v* .... Ps 144:4

VARIATION
with whom there is no *v* .... Jas 1:17

VARIED
of the *v* grace of God .... 1 Pet 4:10

VARIOUS
and earthquakes in *v* places ...... Matt 24:7
who were sick with *v* diseases .... Mark 1:34
and led along by *v* passions .... 2 Tim 3:6
in *v* portions and in *v* ways .... Heb 1:1

VASHTI
Queen of Ahasuerus, deposed and
 divorced, Esth 1:9–22

VAST
How *v* is their sum total .... Ps 139:17
Suddenly a *v*, heavenly army ...... Luke 2:13

VAULT
and forth in the *v* of heaven .... Job 22:14

VEGETABLES
meal of *v* where there is love ..... Prov 15:17
providing us with some *v* to eat .... Dan 1:12
the weak person eats only *v* .... Rom 14:2

VEGETATION
they ate all the *v* of the ground ... Exod 10:15
plants in the field, or green *v* .... 2 Kgs 19:26
plants in the field or green *v* .... Isa 37:27

VEIL
took her *v* and covered herself ... Gen 24:65
he would put a *v* on his face ..... Exod 34:33
your forehead behind your *v* ...... Song 6:7
used to put a *v* over his face ...... 2 Cor 3:13
the same *v* remains .... 2 Cor 3:14
the *v* is removed .... 2 Cor 3:16

VEILED
But even if our gospel is *v* .... 2 Cor 4:3

VENGEANCE
not take *v* or bear a grudge .... Lev 19:18
puts on the garments of *v* .... Isa 59:17
when our God will seek *v* .... Isa 61:2
take out your *v* on her .... Jer 50:15
because these are days of *v* ..... Luke 21:22
V is mine, I will repay .... Rom 12:19
V is mine, I will repay .... Heb 10:30

VENOM
Their grapes contain *v* .... Deut 32:32
it becomes the *v* of serpents ..... Job 20:14
viper's *v* is behind their lips .... Ps 140:3

VENOMOUS
So the LORD sent *v* snakes .... Num 21:6

VERDICT
The divine *v* is in the words .... Prov 16:10

VERSED
well *v* in all kinds of wisdom .... Dan 1:4

VERY
When Joshua was *v* old .... Josh 13:1
I am *v* old .... Josh 23:2
King David was *v* old .... 1 Kgs 1:1
took him to a *v* high mountain .... Matt 4:8
and it is already *v* late .... Mark 6:35
for he was *v* rich .... Mark 10:22
She was *v* old .... Luke 2:36
to you for this *v* purpose .... Eph 6:22

VESSEL
one *v* for special use .... Rom 9:21

VEXATION
v by a fool is more burdensome ... Prov 27:3

VICTIM
v of his own destructive plans .... Ps 7:16

VICTORIES
gives his king magnificent *v* .... Ps 18:50

VICTORIOUS
your right hand *v* .... Ps 89:13
with my *v* right hand .... Isa 41:10
He is legitimate and *v* .... Zech 9:9

VICTORY
the LORD gave them a great *v* .. 2 Sam 23:12
will shout for joy over your *v* .... Ps 20:5
The LORD's right hand gives *v* ...... Ps 118:16
but the *v* is from the LORD .... Prov 21:31
spoils of *v* with the powerful .... Isa 53:12
have complete *v* through him .... Rom 8:37
has been swallowed up in *v* ..... 1 Cor 15:54
Where, O death, is your *v* .... 1 Cor 15:55
v through our Lord Jesus Christ .. 1 Cor 15:57

VIEW
an outward human point of *v* ..... 2 Cor 5:16

VIGIL
was a night of *v* for the LORD .... Exod 12:42

VIGILANCE
Guard your heart with all *v* .... Prov 4:23

VILLAGE
Do not even go into the *v* .... Mark 8:26
the *v* where David lived .... John 7:42

VILLAGES
can go into the *v* and buy food ... Matt 14:15
Samaritan *v* as they went .... Acts 8:25

VINDICATE
prayers for help and *v* them ...... 1 Kgs 8:45
V me, O LORD .... Ps 26:1
V me by your justice .... Ps 35:24
V me, O God .... Ps 43:1
V me by your power .... Ps 54:1
V the oppressed and suffering .... Ps 82:3
so that he may *v* you .... Prov 20:22

VINDICATED
God has *v* me .... Gen 30:6
v by the God who delivers .... Ps 24:5
his loyal followers will be *v* .... Ps 149:9
will be *v* by the LORD .... Isa 45:25
wisdom is *v* by all her children ... Luke 7:35
v by the Spirit .... 1 Tim 3:16

VINDICATES
one true God completely *v* me .. 2 Sam 22:48
O God who *v* me .... Ps 4:1
to the LORD when he *v* me .... Ps 13:6
For the LORD *v* his people .... Ps 135:14
v the oppressed .... Ps 146:7

VINDICATION
But the *v* I provide .... Isa 51:8
until her *v* shines brightly .... Isa 62:1

VINDICTIVE
put an end to the *v* enemy .... Ps 8:2

VINE
there was a *v* in front of me .... Gen 40:9
Binding his foal to the *v* .... Gen 49:11
v is from the stock of Sodom .... Deut 32:32
You uprooted a *v* from Egypt .... Ps 80:8
special *v* of the very best stock ..... Jer 2:21
thoroughly gleaned from a *v* .... Jer 6:9
a fertile *v* that yielded fruit .... Hos 10:1
the *v* will produce its fruit .... Zech 8:12
not drink of this fruit of the *v* .... Matt 26:29
drink of the fruit of the *v* .... Mark 14:25
I am the true *v* and my Father ..... John 15:1
unless it remains in the *v* .... John 15:4
I am the *v*; you are the branches ... John 15:5
or a *v* produce figs .... Jas 3:12

VINEGAR
they give me *v* to drink .... Ps 69:21
Like *v* to the teeth .... Prov 10:26
or like *v* poured on soda .... Prov 25:20

VINES
trample all over its *v* .... Isa 16:8
will be no grapes on their *v* .... Jer 8:13
there are no grapes on the *v* .... Hab 3:17

VINEYARD
livestock in a field or a *v* .... Exod 22:5
must not pick your *v* bare .... Lev 19:10
sow your field or prune your *v* .... Lev 25:4
Israel is the *v* of the LORD .... Isa 5:7
to hire workers for his *v* .... Matt 20:1
go and work in the *v* today ...... Matt 21:28

when the owner of the *v* comes.. Matt 21:40
A man planted a *v* ....Mark 12:1
the worker who tended the *v* .....Luke 13:7
A man planted a *v* ....Luke 20:9
plants a *v* and does not eat .... 1 Cor 9:7

VINEYARDS
and *v* and olive groves............Deut 6:11
the little foxes, that ruin the *v* ....Song 2:15
in the *v* no one rejoices or..........Isa 16:10
a land of bread and *v* ....Isa 36:17
He gave them fields and *v* ....Jer 39:10
plant *v* and drink the wine.......Amos 9:14

VIOLATE
caused many to *v* the law........... Mal 2:8

VIOLATED
had *v* his daughter Dinah..........Gen 34:5
v my covenantal commandment ...Josh 7:11
or *v* your covenant with us ....Ps 44:17
For they *v* that covenant...........Jer 31:32
have *v* their covenant with me ....Jer 34:18

VIOLATION
that every *v* or disobedience .... Heb 2:2

VIOLATIONS
free from the *v* committed .... Heb 9:15

VIOLATOR
have become a *v* of the law.......... Jas 2:11

VIOLATORS
convicted by the law as *v*............Jas 2:9

VIOLENCE
the earth was filled with *v*..........Gen 6:11
weapons of *v* are their knives .....Gen 49:5
You save me from *v* ....2 Sam 22:3
If I cry out, 'V!' I receive .... Job 19:7
and those who love to do *v*..........Ps 11:5
the *v* done to the oppressed......... Ps 12:5
harm and *v* he will defend..........Ps 72:14
full of places where *v* rules........Ps 74:20
speech of the wicked conceals *v*...Prov 10:6
The *v* done by the wicked ....Prov 21:7
There will be *v* in the land.........Jer 51:46
have filled the land with *v* ....Ezek 8:17
up the spoils of destructive *v* .....Amos 3:10
but you establish a reign of *v* ..... Amos 6:3
and from the *v* that they do ....Jonah 3:8
people readily resort to *v*...........Mic 6:12
Destruction and *v* confront me.....Hab 1:3
the one who is guilty of *v*..........Mal 2:16
of heaven has suffered *v*........ Matt 11:12

VIOLENT
V men will not oppress them.... 2 Sam 7:10
despises *v* and deceitful people ......Ps 5:6
you rescue me from *v* men........Ps 18:48
will hunt down a *v* man........... Ps 140:11
v person entices his neighbor ....Prov 16:29
such a man has a *v* son ....Ezek 18:10
They were extremely *v*..........Matt 8:28
a sound like a *v* wind blowing ......Acts 2:2
not a drunkard, not *v*, but gentle .. 1 Tim 3:3

VIOLENTLY
My heart beats *v* within me ....Ps 55:4
my heart beats *v* within me ....Ps 109:22
the earth shakes *v*..............Isa 24:19
v slaughtered your relatives......Obad 1:10

VIPER
See also OFFSPRING OF VIPERS
a snake and stings like a *v* .... Prov 23:32
For a *v* will grow out of............Isa 14:29

VIRGIN
must take a wife who is a *v*........ Lev 21:13
oppressed *v* daughter Sidon.......Isa 23:12
has stomped like grapes the *v*.....Lam 1:15
O *V* Daughter Zion ....Lam 2:13
The *v* Israel has fallen down......Amos 5:2
v will conceive and give birth.....Matt 1:23
And if a *v* marries................1 Cor 7:28
An unmarried woman or a *v* .. 1 Cor 7:34
you as a pure *v* to Christ......2 Cor 11:2

VIRGINITY
and mourn my *v*................Judg 11:37

VIRGINS
ten *v* who took their lamps........Matt 25:1
for they are *v* ....Rev 14:4

VIRTUES
v of the one who called you ....1 Pet 2:9

VISIBLE
whether *v* or invisible ....Col 1:16

VISION
message came to Abram in a *v*.....Gen 15:1
and like a *v* of the night..........Job 20:8
you spoke through a *v*.............Ps 89:19
When there is no prophetic *v*....Prov 29:18
oracle about the Valley of *V*........Isa 22:1
be like a dream, a night *v*.......... Isa 29:7
receive a *v* from the LORD..........Lam 2:9
opened and I saw a divine *v* ....Ezek 1:1
when every *v* will be fulfilled.....Ezek 12:23
It was like the *v* I saw............. Ezek 43:3
they had seen a *v* of angels......Luke 24:23
in a *v* a man named Ananias.......Acts 9:12
and in a trance I saw a *v*...........Acts 11:5
A *v* appeared to Paul ....Acts 16:9
disobedient to the heavenly *v* ....Acts 26:19

VISIONS
revelatory *v* were infrequent ......1 Sam 3:1
Here are the *v* of my mind........Dan 4:10
your young men will see *v*.........Joel 2:28
and you will receive no *v*...........Mic 3:6
your young men will see *v*........ Acts 2:17
go on to *v* and revelations........2 Cor 12:1

VISIT
v the earth and give it rain...........Ps 65:9
and you did not *v* me ....Matt 25:43

VISITATION
the time of your *v* from God..... Luke 19:44

VISITOR
you the only *v* to Jerusalem ..... Luke 24:18

VITALITY
nor had his *v* departed .... Deut 34:7
they are filled with *v*................Ps 92:14

VOCABULARY
language and a common *v*.......... Gen 11:1

VOICE
See also VOICE OF THE LORD
But God heard the boy's *v*.........Gen 21:17
v is Jacob's, but the hands ....Gen 27:22
was answering him with a *v* .....Exod 19:19
you thunder with a *v* like his.......Job 40:9
let me hear your *v* ....Song 2:14
A *v* cries out ....Isa 40:3
and I heard a *v* speaking...........Ezek 1:28
a beautiful *v* ....Ezek 33:32
His *v* thundered forth .... Dan 10:6
A *v* was heard in Ramah.........Matt 2:18
The *v* of one shouting ....Matt 3:3
And a *v* from heaven said.........Matt 3:17
hear his *v* in the streets..........Matt 12:19
and a *v* from the cloud said.......Matt 17:5
Jesus shouted with a loud *v*......Matt 27:46
praising God with a loud *v*......Luke 17:15
hear the *v* of the Son of God ......John 5:25
because they recognize his *v* .....John 10:4
v has not come for my benefit....John 12:30
to the truth listens to my *v*.......John 18:37
with the *v* of the archangel..... 1 Thess 4:16
Then his *v* shook the earth ....Heb 12:26
that *v* was conveyed to him ....2 Pet 1:17
and his *v* was like the roar.........Rev 1:15
hears my *v* and opens the door....Rev 3:20

VOICE OF THE LORD
If we keep hearing the *v*..........Deut 5:25
do not make us here the *v*.......Deut 18:16
I hear the *v* say ....Isa 6:8
The *v* thunders as he leads ......Joel 2:11
if you completely obey the *v* ......Zech 6:15
there came the *v* ....Acts 7:31

VOICES
their *v* are heard as far away ....Isa 15:4
were loud *v* in heaven saying.......Rev 11:15

VOID
letter in the law to become *v* .....Luke 16:17

VOLUNTARILY
For if I do this *v*...................1 Cor 9:17

VOMIT
not make the land *v* you out. ......Lev 18:28
a dog that returns to its *v*.........Prov 26:11
sliding around in his own *v* ....Isa 19:14
A dog returns to its own *v*...... 2 Pet 2:22
to *v* you out of my mouth ....Rev 3:16

VORACIOUS
but inwardly are *v* wolves ....Matt 7:15

VOW
See also VOW TO THE LORD
Then Jacob made a *v* .... Gen 28:20
Takes a special *v*, to take a *v*..... Num 6:2
to take a *v* as a Nazirite........... Num 6:2
the *v* in her husband's house ....Num 30:10
So I made a *v* in my anger ....Ps 95:11
When you make a *v* to God....... Eccl 5:4
not to *v* than to *v* and not pay ...... Eccl 5:5
because he had made a *v*.........Acts 18:18
four men who have taken a *v*.....Acts 21:23

VOW TO THE LORD
So Israel made a *v* ....Num 21:2
If a man makes a *v*.................Num 30:2
When you make a *v* ....Deut 23:21
Jephthah made a *v*...............Judg 11:30
and how he made a *v*.............. Ps 132:2

VOWS
Nazirite who *v* to the LORD........Num 6:21
you will fulfill your *v* to him ....Job 22:27
obligated to fulfill the *v*..........Ps 56:12
V made to you are fulfilled ....Ps 65:1
Make *v* to the LORD your God......Ps 76:11
today I have fulfilled my *v* ....Prov 7:14
O son of my *v*...................Prov 31:2
but fulfill your *v* to the Lord ......Matt 5:33

VULTURES
there the *v* will gather...........Matt 24:28

W

WAFERS
it tasted like *w* with honey ....Exod 16:31

WAGE
workers for the standard *w*....... Matt 20:2

WAGES
and I will pay your *w* .... Exod 2:9
wicked person earns deceitful *w* ..Prov 11:18
who earn *w* end up with holes...... Hag 1:6
good to you, pay me my *w* .... Zech 11:12
and pay them their *w* starting ....Matt 20:8
the *w* for their harmful ways ......2 Pet 2:13

WAGONS
Joseph gave them *w*............. Gen 45:21

WAIL
town squares all of them *w*..........Isa 15:3
w over the horde of Egypt........Ezek 32:18
you will weep and *w*.............John 16:20
will weep and *w* for her ....Rev 18:9

WAILED
he *w* loudly and bitterly..........Gen 27:34

WAILING
May they go *w* to the grave ....Ps 31:17
sound of *w* is soon to be heard......Jer 9:19
all the squares there will be *w*....Amos 5:16

WAILS
So Moab *w* over its demise........Isa 16:7

WAIST
all around from his *w* up ....Ezek 1:27
his *w* was a belt made of gold ..... Dan 10:5
belt of truth around your *w* ....Eph 6:14

WAIT
I *w* for your deliverance ....Gen 49:18
you would not want to *w*.......... Ruth 1:13
to those who *w* for death........... Job 3:21

will *w* until my release comes ..... Job 14:14
all you who *w* on the LORD .... Ps 31:24
W patiently for the LORD .... Ps 37:7
All your creatures *w* for you ...... Ps 104:27
We will lie in *w* to shed blood ..... Prov 1:11
all who *w* for him in faith .... Isa 30:18
salvation near, it does not *w* .... Isa 46:13
We *w* for light .... Isa 59:9
we *w* for deliverance .... Isa 59:11
for those who *w* for him .... Isa 64:4
w for the God who delivers me ...... Mic 7:7
w there for what my Father .... Acts 1:4
we eagerly *w* for it .... Rom 8:25
as you *w* for the revelation .... 1 Cor 1:7
w for one another .... 1 Cor 11:33
we *w* expectantly for the hope ...... Gal 5:5
to *w* for his Son from heaven .... 1 Thess 1:10

WAITED
He *w* for justice .... Isa 5:7
We *w* for him .... Isa 25:9
when God patiently *w* .... 1 Pet 3:20

WAITING
w beside my doorway .... Prov 8:34
by *w* for your God to return .... Hos 12:6
he is now *w* until his enemies ..... Heb 10:13

WAITS
For the creation eagerly *w* .... Rom 8:19

WALK
W before me and be blameless ..... Gen 17:1
way in which they must *w* .... Exod 18:20
W just as he has commanded .... Deut 5:33
w through the darkest valley .... Ps 23:4
W around Zion .... Ps 48:12
will *w* in the way of integrity .... Ps 101:2
must *w* in the midst of danger ...... Ps 138:7
w in the path of righteousness ... Prov 8:20
w in the LORD's guiding light .... Isa 2:5
This is the correct way, *w* in it ..... Isa 30:21
they *w* without getting tired .... Isa 40:31
w in the light of the fire .... Isa 50:11
the godly *w* in them .... Hos 14:9
three days to *w* through it .... Jonah 3:3
Pick up your mat and *w* .... John 5:8
W while you have the light .... John 12:35
to *w* just as Jesus walked .... 1 John 2:6
w with me dressed in white .... Rev 3:4

WALKED
Enoch *w* with God .... Gen 5:22
I *w* through darkness .... Job 29:3
You *w* through the sea .... Ps 77:19
He *w* with me in peace and .... Mal 2:6
to walk just as Jesus *w* .... 1 John 2:6

WALKING
The people *w* in darkness .... Isa 9:2
sight of Jesus *w* on the lake .... John 6:19
you are no longer *w* in love .... Rom 14:15

WALKS
The one who *w* blamelessly ..... Prov 28:18
who *w* in wisdom will escape .... Prov 28:26
Whoever *w* in deep darkness ...... Isa 50:10
one who *w* in the darkness .... John 12:35
w in the darkness .... 1 John 2:11

WALL
Then the city *w* will collapse ... Josh 6:5
He turned his face to the *w* ... 2 Kgs 20:2
as dangerous as a leaning *w* .... Ps 62:3
like a shield or a protective *w* .... Ps 91:4
and it is like a high *w* .... Prov 18:11
broken down and without a *w* ... Prov 25:28
If she is a *w*, we will build .... Song 8:9
grope along the *w* like the blind ... Isa 59:10
remain stationed on the city *w* ...... Hab 2:1
you whitewashed *w* .... Acts 23:3
through a window in the city *w* ... 2 Cor 11:33
The *w* of the city has twelve .... Rev 21:14

WALLED
w me in so that I cannot get out .... Lam 3:7

WALLS
like *w* and a rampart .... Isa 26:1
The one who repairs broken *w* ..... Isa 58:12

You will name your *w* .... Isa 60:18
By faith the *w* of Jericho fell .... Heb 11:30

WANDER
will *w* in the wilderness .... Num 14:33
w in a trackless desert waste ...... Job 12:24
do not *w* from your precepts ...... Ps 119:110
w blindly through the streets ...... Lam 4:14

WANDERED
sheep *w* over all the mountains .. Ezek 34:6
they *w* in deserts and mountains .. Heb 11:38

WANDERER
be a homeless *w* on the earth ..... Gen 4:12

WANDERING
Their hearts are always *w* .... Heb 3:10
a sinner back from his *w* path ...... Jas 5:20

WANDERS
Like a bird that *w* from its nest ... Prov 27:8
among you *w* from the truth .... Jas 5:19

WANT
do not *w* to know your ways .... Job 21:14
Do you *w* to really live .... Ps 34:12
I *w* to do what pleases you .... Ps 40:8
those who *w* to harm me .... Ps 70:2
we should *w* to follow him .... Isa 53:2
really the kind of fasting I *w* .... Isa 58:5
and do not *w* the LORD's help ...... Zeph 1:6
I *w* mercy and not sacrifice .... Matt 9:13
permitted to do what I *w* .... Matt 20:15
I *w* those you have given me ..... John 17:24
For I *w* to do the good .... Rom 7:18
I do not *w* your possessions ..... 2 Cor 12:14
w to be teachers of the law .... 1 Tim 1:7

WANTED
from getting whatever I *w* .... Eccl 2:10
LORD *w* to exhibit his justice .... Isa 42:21
did to him whatever they *w* ...... Mark 9:13
went wherever you *w* .... John 21:18
just as you *w* to do it eagerly ..... 2 Cor 8:11

WANTON
drinking bouts, and *w* idolatries .... 1 Pet 4:3

WANTS
w to contribute to the LORD ...... 1 Chr 29:5
he turns it wherever he *w* .... Prov 21:1
what the LORD really *w* .... Mic 6:8
w to become my follower .... Matt 16:24
whoever *w* to be great .... Matt 20:26
drinking old wine *w* the new ... Luke 5:39
If anyone *w* to do God's will ...... John 7:17
who *w* it take the water of life .... Rev 22:17

WAR
is the sound of *w* in the camp .... Exod 32:17
Even when *w* is imminent .... Ps 27:3
the rest of the weapons of *w* .... Ps 76:3
they want to make *w* .... Ps 120:7
so make *w* with guidance .... Prov 20:18
guidance you wage your *w* .... Prov 24:6
will no longer train for *w* .... Isa 2:4
where we will not face *w* .... Jer 42:14
that horn began to wage *w* .... Dan 7:21
as if returning from a *w* .... Mic 2:8
Then *w* broke out in heaven .... Rev 12:7
he judges and goes to *w* .... Rev 19:11

WARDEN
in the sight of the prison *w* .... Gen 39:21

WARFARE
that her time of *w* is over .... Isa 40:2
for the weapons of our *w* .... 2 Cor 10:4

WARM
he could not get *w* .... 1 Kgs 1:1
the boy's skin grew *w* .... 2 Kgs 4:34
they can keep each other *w* .... Eccl 4:11
but are not *w* .... Hag 1:6
keep *w* and eat well .... Jas 2:16

WARMED
lets them be *w* on the soil .... Job 39:14

WARMING
and *w* himself by the fire .... Mark 14:54
she saw Peter *w* himself .... Mark 14:67

WARMS
he *w* himself and says .... Isa 44:16

WARN
and solemnly *w* the people .... Exod 19:21
and you do not *w* him .... Ezek 3:18

WARNED
The man solemnly *w* us .... Gen 43:3
solemnly *w* Israel and Judah ..... 2 Kgs 17:13
Be *w*, my son .... Eccl 12:12
After being *w* in a dream .... Matt 2:12
Who *w* you to flee .... Matt 3:7
w about things not yet seen .... Heb 11:7

WARNING
but did not heed the *w* .... Ezek 33:5
not stop *w* each one of you .... Acts 20:31
as a *w* to the rest .... 1 Tim 5:20

WARNS
that the Holy Spirit *w* me .... Acts 20:23

WARPED
w minds and are disqualified ...... 2 Tim 3:8

WARRIOR
he rushes against me like a *w* ..... Job 16:14
I too am a *w* .... Joel 3:10

WARRIORS
powerful *w* who carry out .... Ps 103:20
all you *w* of his .... Ps 103:21

WARS
He brings an end to *w* .... Ps 46:9
hear of *w* and rumors of *w* .... Matt 24:6

WARY
Therefore we must be *w* that .... Heb 4:1

WASH
w myself with snow-melt water .... Job 9:30
W away my wrongdoing .... Ps 51:2
W! Cleanse yourselves .... Isa 1:16
Lord will *w* the excrement .... Isa 4:4
your head and *w* your face .... Matt 6:17
For they don't *w* their hands ...... Matt 15:2
Go *w* in the pool of Siloam .... John 9:7
began to *w* the disciples' feet ...... John 13:5
You will never *w* my feet .... John 13:8

WASHBASIN
He poured water into the *w* ...... John 13:5

WASHED
nor were you *w* in water .... Ezek 16:4
w his hands before the crowd .... Matt 27:24
when Jesus had *w* their feet ...... John 13:12
have *w* your feet .... John 13:14
took them and *w* their wounds ... Acts 16:33
But you were *w* .... 1 Cor 6:11
w the feet of the saints .... 1 Tim 5:10
They have *w* their robes .... Rev 7:14

WASHING
unless they perform a ritual *w* ..... Mark 7:3
the *w* of cups .... Mark 7:4
w of the water by the word .... Eph 5:26
through the *w* of the new birth .... Titus 3:5

WASHINGS
teaching about ritual *w* .... Heb 6:2
and drink and various ritual *w* ..... Heb 9:10

WASTE
coming out to lay your land *w* .... Jer 4:7
and said, "Why this *w* .... Matt 26:8
this *w* of expensive ointment ..... Mark 14:4

WASTELAND
empty *w* where animals howl ... Deut 32:10
the wilderness, in a *w* .... Ps 107:4

WASTELANDS
challenged God in the *w* .... Ps 106:14
and paths in the *w* .... Isa 43:19

WASTES
His flesh *w* away from sight .... Job 33:21

WASTING
his manager was *w* his assets ...... Luke 16:1

WATCH
so *w* yourselves carefully .... Deut 2:4
So as Joab kept *w* on the city .... 2 Sam 11:16

who keep *w* over the house ....Eccl 12:3
Guard the rampart! *W* the road .....Nah 2:1
they keep *w* over your souls.......Heb 13:17

WATCHED
intervention *w* over my spirit......Job 10:12
The eyes of the LORD *w* over .....Prov 22:12
w Jesus closely to see.............Luke 6:7

WATCHER
I done to you, O *w* of men.........Job 7:20

WATCHES
the LORD *w* the whole earth.......2 Chr 16:9
who *w* the wind will not sow ....Eccl 11:4

WATCHING
constantly *w* all their ways ....Job 24:23
w at my doors day by day .... Prov 8:34
LORD is *w* the sinful nation .... Amos 9:8
work only when someone is *w* ..... Eph 6:6
not only when they are *w* ....Col 3:22

WATCHMAN
W, what is left of the night ....Isa 21:11
I have appointed you a *w* ....Ezek 3:17

WATCHMEN
The night *w* found me .... Song 3:3
Listen, your *w* shout...............Isa 52:8
All their *w* are blind ....Isa 56:10
I post *w* on your walls .... Isa 62:6
prophets as *w* to warn you ....Jer 6:17
Woe to your *w*.....................Mic 7:4

WATCHTOWER
and built a *w*.....................Matt 21:33

WATER
See also WATER OF LIFE
and *w* the whole surface............ Gen 2:6
from Eden to *w* the orchard....... Gen 2:10
You are destructive like *w*.........Gen 49:4
struck the *w* that was in the
    Nile...........................Exod 7:20
bless your bread and your *w* .....Exod 23:25
him only a little bread and *w* ...1 Kgs 22:27
As *w* disappears from the sea ......Job 14:11
as *w* wears away stones ....Job 14:19
who drinks in evil like *w*...........Job 15:16
gave the weary no *w* to drink.......Job 22:7
strength drains away like *w* ....Ps 22:14
he leads me to refreshing *w*.........Ps 23:2
land where there is no *w* ....Ps 63:1
the *w* has reached my neck.........Ps 69:1
made their blood flow like *w*........Ps 79:3
led them through the deep *w* ......Ps 106:9
amazing feats on the deep *w* ......Ps 107:24
w would have overpowered ......Ps 124:4
Drink *w* from your own cistern....Prov 5:15
one who provides *w* for others... Prov 11:25
well of fresh *w* flowing down..... Song 4:15
including all the food and *w* ....Isa 3:1
w of the sea will be dried up........Isa 19:5
and the poor look for *w* ....Isa 41:17
because I put *w* in the
    wilderness......................Isa 43:20
pour *w* on the parched ground ..... Isa 44:3
come to the *w*.....................Isa 55:1
led them through the deep *w* ......Isa 63:13
the fountain of life-giving *w* ....Jer 2:13
was like that of rushing *w* ....Ezek 43:2
W engulfed me up to my neck ....Jonah 2:5
gives only a cup of cold *w* .... Matt 10:42
saw him walking on the *w*....... Matt 14:26
Put out into the deep *w* ....Luke 5:4
gave me no *w* for my feet ....Luke 7:44
because *w* was plentiful there.....John 3:23
Give me some *w* to drink.........John 4:10
will flow rivers of living *w* ....John 7:38
and blood and *w* flowed out......John 19:34
No one can withhold the *w*......Acts 10:47
washing of the *w* by the word .....Eph 5:26
a salt *w* spring produce fresh........Jas 3:12
were delivered through *w* ....1 Pet 3:20
who came by *w* and blood........1 John 5:6
Spirit and the *w* and the blood ... 1 John 5:8
them to springs of living *w* ....Rev 7:17

WATER OF LIFE
from the spring of the *w*...........Rev 21:6
the river of the *w*..................Rev 22:1
take the *w* free of charge.........Rev 22:17

WATERED
that all of it was well *w*............Gen 13:10
Apollos *w*, but God caused it ...... 1 Cor 3:6

WATERLESS
They are *w* clouds ....Jude 1:12

WATERS
If he holds back the *w* ....Job 12:15
He locks the *w* in his clouds ....Job 26:8
enthroned over the engulfing *w*....Ps 29:10
Stolen *w* are sweet ....Prov 9:17
bound up the *w* in his cloak ...... Prov 30:4
Surging *w* cannot quench love..... Song 8:7
the *w* completely cover the sea ..... Isa 11:9
w of Noah's flood would never ..... Isa 54:9
drink the poison *w* of judgment.....Jer 8:14
The *w* closed over my head ....Lam 3:54
living *w* will flow out ....Zech 14:8
of the *w* became wormwood.......Rev 8:11

WAVE
are to *w* them as a *w* offering ...Exod 29:24
to *w* the breast as a *w* offering .....Lev 7:30
must *w* them as a *w* offering .....Num 6:20
doubts is like a *w* of the sea ....Jas 1:6

WAVER
He did not *w* in unbelief ....Rom 4:20
have mercy on those who *w*.......Jude 1:22

WAVERS
in distress; their courage *w*........Isa 15:4

WAVES
your proud *w* will be confined......Job 38:11
billows and *w* overwhelm me ....Ps 42:7
when its *w* crash and foam ....Ps 46:3
raging seas and their roaring *w*.....Ps 65:7
covered by a multitude of its *w*.....Jer 51:42
w began to swamp the boat......Matt 8:24
taking a beating from the *w* ..... Matt 14:24
tossed back and forth by *w*........Eph 4:14
wild sea *w*, spewing out the foam ..Jude 1:13

WAX
My heart is like *w*..................Ps 22:14
As *w* melts before fire..............Ps 68:2
The mountains melt like *w* ....Ps 97:5

WAY
See also WAY OF THE LORD
w in which they must walk ......Exod 18:20
the *w* that is good and upright ..1 Sam 12:23
usual *w* of dealing with men..... 2 Sam 7:19
to a man whose *w* is hidden ....Job 3:23
the knees that gave *w* ....Job 4:4
the first time in one *w* ....Job 33:14
guards the *w* of the godly ....Ps 1:6
Why do you look the other *w* ... Ps 44:24
is any idolatrous *w* in me ....Ps 139:24
let the wicked have their *w*........Ps 140:8
protect the *w* of his pious ones.....Prov 2:8
The *w* of the wicked is like ....Prov 4:19
There is a *w* that seems right..... Prov 14:12
The *w* of the righteous is level...... Isa 26:7
This is the correct *w*...............Isa 30:21
teaches him the correct *w*.........Isa 40:14
the *w* you have been living ....Jer 7:3
a *w* that always shows respect .....Jer 32:39
in this *w* they show disrespect....Amos 2:7
will clear the *w* before me...........Mal 3:1
So pray this *w* ....Matt 6:9
the *w* is spacious that leads ....Matt 7:13
difficult the *w* that leads to life ....Matt 7:14
prepare your *w* before you .... Matt 11:10
and teach the *w* of God.......... Matt 22:16
were on their *w* to a village...... Luke 24:13
the *w* where I am going ....John 14:4
I am the *w*, and the truth ....John 14:6
to you the *w* of salvation ....Acts 16:17
explained the *w* of God...........Acts 18:26
In the same *w* ....1 Cor 11:25
a *w* that is beyond comparison ...1 Cor 12:31

by the fresh and living *w* ....Heb 10:20
by the *w* you live ....1 Pet 3:1
followed the *w* of Balaam .... 2 Pet 2:15
known the *w* of righteousness ... 2 Pet 2:21

WAY OF THE LORD
keep the *w* by doing what ....Gen 18:19
The *w* is like a stronghold .... Prov 10:29
had been instructed in the *w* .....Acts 18:25

WAYS
for all his *w* are just............... Deut 32:4
they do not know its *w* ....Job 24:13
Make me understand your *w*........Ps 25:4
teach rebels your merciful *w* ....Ps 51:13
not return to their foolish *w*........Ps 85:8
For the *w* of a person.............Prov 5:21
Abandon your foolish *w*.........Prov 9:6
w are pleasing to the LORD........Prov 16:7
carefully examine our *w* ....Lam 3:40
breath and all your *w*.............Dan 5:23
and how unfathomable his *w*.... Rom 11:33
unstable in all his *w* ....Jas 1:8
wages for their harmful *w*.........2 Pet 2:13
Just and true are your *w*..........Rev 15:3

WAYWARD
w stars for whom the utter........Jude 1:13

WAYWARDNESS
I want to cure your *w*...............Jer 3:22

WEAK
become *w* and be just like any..... Judg 16:7
He lifts the *w* from the dust ....1 Sam 2:8
Today I am *w* ....2 Sam 3:39
and my heart may grow *w*........Ps 73:26
Let the *w* say ....Joel 3:10
He is too *w* ....Amos 7:2
I will make you a *w* nation......... Obad 1:2
but the flesh is *w* .... Matt 26:41
Without being *w* in faith.........Rom 4:19
the one who is *w* in the faith ...... Rom 14:1
what the world thinks *w*..........1 Cor 1:27
We are *w*, but you are strong..... 1 Cor 4:10
To the *w* I became *w*............1 Cor 9:22
many of you are *w* and sick.... 1 Cor 11:30
for whenever I am *w* ....2 Cor 12:10
hands and your *w* knees.........Heb 12:12

WEAKENED
LORD had *w* the Israelite tribes... Judg 21:15

WEAKER
as the *w* partners and show ....1 Pet 3:7

WEAKNESS
He will afflict you with *w* ....Deut 28:22
the Spirit helps us in our *w*....... Rom 8:26
and the *w* of God is stronger ......1 Cor 1:25
was with you in *w* and in fear...... 1 Cor 2:3
it is sown in *w* ....1 Cor 15:43
since he also is subject to *w* .... Heb 5:2
gained strength in *w*..............Heb 11:34

WEAKNESSES
He took our *w* and carried.........Matt 8:17
except about my *w* ....2 Cor 12:5
of sympathizing with our *w* .... Heb 4:15

WEALTH
and skill have gotten me this *w*....Deut 8:17
Your wisdom and *w* surpass....... 1 Kgs 10:7
the source of *w* and honor ...... 1 Chr 29:12
ask for riches, *w*, and honor ....2 Chr 1:11
The *w* that he consumed ....Job 20:15
They trust in their *w*...............Ps 49:6
He trusted in his great *w* ....Ps 52:7
If *w* increases....................Ps 62:10
house contains *w* and riches......Ps 112:3
seize all kinds of precious *w* ..... Prov 1:13
Honor the LORD from your *w*....Prov 3:9
give all the *w* of his house ....Prov 6:31
The *w* of a rich person...........Prov 10:15
W does not profit in the day........Prov 11:4
and yet possesses great *w*........Prov 13:7
W gained quickly will dwindle.....Prov 13:11
the *w* of a sinner is stored up.....Prov 13:22
of the righteous is abundant *w* ....Prov 15:6
The *w* of a rich person............Prov 18:11

W adds many friends...............Prov 19:4
A house and w are inherited......Prov 19:14
loves w will never be satisfied.....Eccl 5:10
W hoarded by its owner...........Eccl 5:13
there is no end to their w.............Isa 2:7
w of nations may be delivered.....Isa 60:11
will enjoy the w of nations...........Isa 61:6
gathers w by unjust means.........Jer 17:11
you have increased your w.......Ezek 28:5
He will carry off her w...........Ezek 29:19
and dedicate their w................Mic 4:13
they all gave out of their w.....Mark 12:44
there he squandered his w.......Luke 15:13
by how you use worldly w......Luke 16:9
for the w of his kindness...........Rom 2:4
make known the w of his glory...Rom 9:23
w of his glorious inheritance.......Eph 1:18
the surpassing w of his grace......Eph 2:7
greater w than the treasures.....Heb 11:26
rich and have acquired great w.....Rev 3:17
to receive power and w and.......Rev 5:12
got rich from her w.................Rev 18:19

WEALTHY
Abram was very w in livestock.....Gen 13:2
He was a w, prominent man........Ruth 2:1
Lord impoverishes and makes w..1 Sam 2:7
He goes to bed w...................Job 27:19
W people do not understand......Ps 49:20
for he was extremely w.........Luke 18:23
Now in a w home.................2 Tim 2:20

WEANED
Stay until you have w him........1 Sam 1:23
To those just w from milk..........Isa 28:9

WEAPON
No w forged to be used against....Isa 54:17
his destructive w in his hand.......Ezek 9:1

WEAPONS
w of violence are their knives.....Gen 49:5
he put Goliath's w in his tent....1 Sam 17:54
it goes out to meet the w..........Job 39:21
He has prepared deadly w...........Ps 7:13
Wisdom is better than w.........Eccl 9:18
and put on the w of light.........Rom 13:12
for the w of our warfare..........2 Cor 10:4

WEAR
Your clothing did not w out.......Deut 8:4
must not w men's clothing.......Deut 22:5
a righteous man will w.............Job 27:17
I w sackcloth and they ridicule.....Ps 69:11
w yourself out to become rich....Prov 23:4
no longer w the hairy garment....Zech 13:4
or 'What will we w..............Matt 6:31
those who w soft clothing.......Matt 11:8
in the end she will w me out......Luke 18:5

WEARIED
You have w the Lord...............Mal 2:17

WEARING
w a linen ephod..................2 Sam 6:14
nothing by w a beautiful dress......Jer 4:30
w the crown of thorns..........John 19:5
w of gold jewelry or fine clothes...1 Pet 3:3

WEARS
and w zeal like a robe.............Isa 59:17

WEARY
why then w myself in vain..........Job 9:29
become w of you and hate you...Prov 25:17
Like cold water to a w person...Prov 25:25
they run without growing w.... Isa 40:31
that I know how to help the w.....Isa 50:4
I grow w of trying to hold it in......Jer 20:9
you who are w and burdened.....Matt 11:28
not grow w in doing good..........Gal 6:9
grow w in doing what is right...2 Thess 3:13
not grow w in your souls.........Heb 12:3

WEATHER
fair w because the sky is red......Matt 16:2

WEAVE
You are to w the tunic............Exod 28:39
If you w the seven braids........Judg 16:13

WEAVER'S
of his spear was like a w beam....1 Sam 17:7

WEDDING
The w guests cannot mourn.......Matt 9:15
Come to the w banquet........Matt 22:4
The w guests cannot fast.......Mark 2:19
was a w at Cana in Galilee.........John 2:1

WEEDS
ground was covered with w.......Prov 24:31
before the wind like dead w........Isa 17:13
but will harvest w.................Jer 12:13
sprout up like poisonous w........Hos 10:4

WEEK
my older daughter's bridal w.....Gen 29:27
covenant with many for one w....Dan 9:27
on the first day of the w.........Matt 28:1
I fast twice a w..................Luke 18:12
On the first day of the w..........Acts 20:7
On the first day of the w..........1 Cor 16:2

WEEKS
See also FEAST OF WEEKS
must observe the Feast of W....Exod 34:22
Seventy w have been
   determined....................Dan 9:24
Now after the sixty-two w........Dan 9:26

WEEP
I w day and night....................Ps 42:3
I w and refrain from eating.........Ps 69:10
w when we remember Zion.........Ps 137:1
time to w, and a time to laugh......Eccl 3:4
So I w along with Jazer..............Isa 16:9
you will w no more................Isa 30:19
I will w alone......................Jer 13:17
Do not w for the king.............Jer 22:10
w from the vestibule............Joel 2:17
with tears as you w and groan......Mal 2:13
yet you did not w................Matt 11:17
Blessed are you who w now......Luke 6:21
Do not w....................Luke 7:13
yet you did not w.............Luke 7:32
do not w for me..................Luke 23:28
going to the tomb to w there.....John 11:31
w with those who w.............Rom 12:15

WEEPING
they were w at the entrance......Num 25:6
w loudly and uncontrollably.......Judg 21:2
he was w as he went............2 Sam 15:30
the sound of the people's w........Ezra 3:13
face is reddened because of w.....Job 16:16
has heard the sound of my w.....Ps 6:8
called for w and mourning.........Isa 22:12
sound of w or cries of sorrow......Isa 65:19
My eyes are worn out from w.....Lam 2:11
I noticed women sitting there w...Ezek 8:14
with fasting, w, and mourning......Joel 2:12
be w and gnashing of teeth......Matt 8:12
be w and gnashing of teeth...... Matt 13:42
Why are you distressed and w....Mark 5:39
Mary stood outside the tomb w..John 20:11
why are you w................John 20:13
w and breaking my heart..........Acts 21:13
those with tears like those not w..1 Cor 7:30
So I began w bitterly................Rev 5:4

WEIGH
do not w us down..................1 John 5:3

WEIGHED
can its price be w out in silver.....Job 28:15
carefully w the soil of the earth...Isa 40:12
or w the mountains in a balance...Isa 40:12
are w on the balances............Dan 5:27

WEIGHS
Lord w all that person's paths....Prov 5:21
Anxiety in a person's heart w.....Prov 12:25
is the one who w the money......Isa 33:18

WEIGHT
accurate and correct stone w....Deut 25:15
an accurate w is his delight........Prov 11:1
an eternal w of glory............2 Cor 4:17
get rid of every w and the sin......Heb 12:1

WELCOME
Liars will not be w..................Ps 101:7
So w him in the Lord..............Phil 2:29

WELCOMED
w me as though I were an angel....Gal 4:14
prayer for all is good and w.......1 Tim 2:3
and w them and acknowledged...Heb 11:13

WELCOMES
whoever w a child like this........Matt 18:5
w one of these little children.....Mark 9:37
This man w sinners and eats.......Luke 15:2

WELL
See also WELL KNOWN
we are w able to conquer it...... Num 13:30
so that it may go w with you.....Deut 4:40
for you have done w.................Ps 49:18
It goes w for the one who..........Ps 112:5
go w with God-fearing people......Eccl 8:12
innocent it will go w with them......Isa 3:10
All is w.............................Ezek 13:10
your faith has made you w.......Mark 5:34
the sick and they will be w.......Mark 16:18
fallen into a w on a Sabbath......Luke 14:5
Jacob's w was there................John 4:6
I have competed w.................2 Tim 4:7
keep warm and eat w.................Jas 2:16
I pray that all may go w...........3 John 1:2

WELL KNOWN
but we are w to God................2 Cor 5:11
we are w to your consciences.....2 Cor 5:11

WELL-ATTESTED
seven men who are w.................Acts 6:3

WELL-BEING
my only source of w.................Ps 16:2

WELL-PLEASING
is good and w and perfect.........Rom 12:2

WENT
came out and w into the pigs..... Mark 5:13
They w out from us..............1 John 2:19

WEPT
turned away from them and w...Gen 42:24
was reported to him, Joseph w...Gen 50:17
each other and they both w....1 Sam 20:41
you fasted and w.................2 Sam 12:21
Then Hezekiah w bitterly........2 Kgs 20:3
The people w loudly...............Ezra 10:1
I not w for the unfortunate........Job 30:25
went outside and w bitterly.....Matt 26:75
he w over it.......................Luke 19:41
Jesus w.........................John 11:35
As she w, she bent down.........John 20:11

WEST
People of the w are appalled......Job 18:20
eastern horizon is from the w.....Ps 103:12
In the w, people respect...........Isa 59:19
goat was coming from the w....... Dan 8:5
split in half from east to w........Zech 14:4
the east and flashes to the w.....Matt 24:27
see a cloud rising in the w.......Luke 12:54

WESTERN SEA
See MEDITERRANEAN SEA

WET
saw iron mixed with w clay........ Dan 2:41
to w his feet with her tears.......Luke 7:38
has w my feet with her tears.....Luke 7:44

WHALE
and over here swims the w........Ps 104:26

WHAT
he evaluates w people do..........1 Sam 2:3
surpass w was reported to me...1 Kgs 10:7
to explain to you w I know...........Job 32:6
Listen to w I say.....................Ps 5:1
Tell the nations w he has done.......Ps 9:11
because he gets w he wants.........Ps 10:3
have told us w you did..............Ps 44:1
will know w you are like.............Ps 67:2
he knows w we are made of.......Ps 103:14
W the righteous say..............Prov 10:20

to consider *w* he has vowed.....Prov 20:25
rewarded for *w* they have done.....Isa 3:10
w you have stolen from the poor....Isa 3:14
w I say is true and reliable.........Isa 45:23
This is *w* the LORD will do.........Isa 54:17
repay them for *w* they have
done...........................Ezek 9:10
w you have been allotted..........Dan 12:13
He taught *w* was true...............Mal 2:6

WHATEVER
take *w* they want from us.........Ps 44:10

WHEAT
I would feed Israel the best *w*......Ps 81:16
gather the *w* into my barn.......Matt 13:30
unless a kernel of *w* falls.........John 12:24
of *w* or something else...........1 Cor 15:37
w, cattle and sheep...............Rev 18:13

WHEEL
turns the threshing *w* over
them..........................Prov 20:26
or the water *w* is broken...........Eccl 12:6

WHEELS
jammed the *w* of their chariots..Exod 14:25
and the rumbling of their *w*........Jer 47:3
The appearance of the *w*........Ezek 1:16
chariot *w* will shake the ground....Nah 3:2

WHERE
lovely is the place *w* you live.........Ps 84:1
w its owner puts its food.............Isa 1:3
understanding *w* he was going......Heb 11:8

WHILE
w you are still angry................Jer 18:23
he will heal us in a little *w*...........Hos 6:2

WHIP
A *w* for the horse................Prov 26:3
about to beat them with a *w*.....Isa 10:26

WHIPS
punished you with ordinary *w*....1 Kgs 12:11
drivers will crack their *w*...........Nah 3:2

WHIRLWIND
answered Job out of the *w*.........Job 38:1
He marches out in the *w*...........Nah 1:3

WHISPER
there was a soft *w*...............1 Kgs 19:12
and my ear caught a *w* of it.........Job 4:12
my tongue will *w* no deceit.........Job 27:4

WHISPERED
and what is *w* in your ear........Matt 10:27

WHISTLE
At that time the LORD will *w*........Isa 7:18

WHITE
See also WHITE AS SNOW
like coriander seed and was *w*....Exod 16:31
his skin was as *w* as snow.........2 Kgs 5:27
you can become *w* like snow........Isa 1:18
red, sorrel, and *w* horses..........Zech 1:8
to make one hair *w* or black......Matt 5:36
his clothes were *w* as snow.......Matt 28:3
clothes became radiantly *w*.......Mark 9:3
fields are already *w* for harvest....John 4:35
And she saw two angels in *w*.....John 20:12
two men in *w* clothing.............Acts 1:10
and hair were as *w* as wool.........Rev 1:14
walk with me dressed in *w*.........Rev 3:4
dressed like them in *w* clothing.....Rev 3:5
and here came a *w* horse..........Rev 6:2
w in the blood of the Lamb........Rev 7:14
Then I saw a large *w* throne.......Rev 20:11

WHITE AS SNOW
his skin was *w*..................2 Kgs 5:27
and his clothes were *w*..........Matt 28:3
white as wool, even *w*..............Rev 1:14

WHITER
and I will be *w* than snow..........Ps 51:7

WHITEWASHED
You are like *w* tombs...........Matt 23:27
you *w* wall.......................Acts 23:3

WHOEVER
without excuse, *w* you are..........Rom 2:1

WHOLE
Is not the *w* land before you........Gen 13:9
come on the *w* congregation.......Lev 10:6
LORD your God with *w* stones....Deut 27:6
splendor fill the *w* earth............Ps 72:19
the Creator of the *w* earth........Isa 40:28
While the *w* earth rejoices........Ezek 35:14
your *w* body thrown into hell.....Matt 5:29
w body will be full of light........Matt 6:22
if he gains the *w* world..........Matt 16:26
a person to gain the *w* world.....Mark 8:36
person if he gains the *w* world...Luke 9:25
your *w* body is full of light.......Luke 11:36
w creation groans and suffers....Rom 8:22
If the *w* body were an eye.......1 Cor 12:17
obligated to obey the *w* law........Gal 5:3
who deceives the *w* world.........Rev 12:9

WHOLEHEARTEDLY
he has *w* followed me.............Deut 1:36
For they will *w* return to me........Jer 24:7

WICK
a dim *w* he will not extinguish......Isa 42:3
or extinguish a smoldering *w*....Matt 12:20

WICKED
w rebels against the LORD.........Gen 13:13
kill the godly with the *w*..........Gen 18:25
for I will not justify the *w*.........Exod 23:7
you entertain the *w* thought.......Deut 15:9
the *w* are made speechless........1 Sam 2:9
sons of Eli were *w* men...........1 Sam 2:12
Is it right to help the *w*.........2 Chr 19:2
smile on the schemes of the *w*.....Job 10:3
the *w* man suffers torment.......Job 15:20
the elation of the *w* is brief........Job 20:5
Why do the *w* go on living..........Job 21:7
w cannot withstand judgment.........Ps 1:5
of the *w* ends in destruction..........Ps 1:6
You destroyed the *w*.................Ps 9:5
The *w* were ensnared................Ps 9:16
The *w* are turned back...............Ps 9:17
the *w* prepare their bows............Ps 11:2
and brimstone on the *w*.............Ps 11:6
The *w* set an ambush................Ps 37:32
so the *w* are destroyed.............Ps 68:2
all the power of the *w*.............Ps 75:10
live in the tents of the *w*..........Ps 84:10
how long will the *w*.................Ps 94:3
and the *w* vanish..................Ps 104:35
When the *w* see this................Ps 112:10
The *w* have no chance.............Ps 119:155
but he opposes the *w*..............Ps 146:9
but the *w* will be removed........Prov 2:22
way of the *w* is like gloomy........Prov 4:19
a heart that devises *w* plans.......Prov 6:18
that the *w* receive is judgment...Prov 10:16
expectation of the *w* perishes...Prov 10:28
but the *w* will fall..................Prov 11:5
expectation of the *w* is wrath....Prov 11:23
words of the *w* lie in wait.........Prov 12:6
acts of the *w* are cruel............Prov 12:10
LORD abhors the way of the *w*.....Prov 15:9
LORD abhors the plans of the *w*..Prov 15:26
The LORD is far from the *w*......Prov 15:29
both the righteous and the *w*......Eccl 3:17
Do not be excessively *w*...........Eccl 7:17
will not go well with the *w*........Eccl 8:13
The offspring of the *w*...........Isa 14:20
w need to abandon their lifestyle....Isa 55:7
the *w* are like a surging sea........Isa 57:20
obstinate and were more *w*........Jer 7:26
Why are *w* people successful......Jer 12:1
from the power of the *w*..........Jer 15:21
When the *w* turns from his sin...Ezek 33:19
but the *w* will go on being *w*....Dan 12:10
Beware *w* schemers.................Mic 2:1
allow the *w* to go unpunished.......Nah 1:3
the righteous and the *w*...........Mal 3:18
You will trample on the *w*..........Mal 4:3
A *w* and adulterous generation....Matt 16:4

WICKEDLY
Don't act so *w*....................Gen 19:7
generation that had done *w*......Num 32:13
speak *w* on God's behalf...........Job 13:7
God does not act *w*...............Job 34:12
One who acts *w*..................Prov 17:4

WICKEDNESS
saw that the *w* of humankind........Gen 6:5
Is not your *w* great...............Job 22:5
Far be it from God to do *w*......Job 34:10
one who is pregnant with *w*........Ps 7:14
eaten bread gained from *w*.......Prov 4:17
and my lips hate *w*................Prov 8:7
but *w* overthrows the sinner......Prov 13:6
so *w* cannot rescue the wicked....Eccl 8:8
Your own *w* will bring about........Jer 2:19
But you have plowed *w*.........Hos 10:13
because of your great *w*.........Hos 10:15
you are full of greed and *w*......Luke 11:39
w, covetousness, malice.........Rom 1:29
into the same flood of *w*..........1 Pet 4:4

WIDE
the gate is *w* and the way........Matt 7:13
make their phylacteries *w*........Matt 23:5
has been opened *w* to you........2 Cor 6:11
and he wore a *w* golden belt.......Rev 1:13

WIDOW
He must not marry a *w*............Lev 21:14
and does not treat the *w* well......Job 24:21
w and the resident foreigner.......Ps 94:6
and his wife a *w*..................Ps 109:9
lifts up the fatherless and the *w*....Ps 146:9
Defend the rights of the *w*..........Isa 1:17
the nations has become a *w*........Lam 1:1
poor *w* came and put in two.....Mark 12:42
poor *w* put in two small copper...Luke 21:2
But if a *w* has children............1 Tim 5:4
No *w* should be put on the list.....1 Tim 5:9
I rule as queen and am no *w*........Rev 18:7

WIDOW'S
I made the *w* heart rejoice.........Job 29:13

WIDOWS
and the *w* among you............Deut 16:11
and an advocate for *w*...............Ps 68:5
Your *w*, too, can depend on me.....Jer 49:11
their *w* were being overlooked.....Acts 6:1
Honor *w* who are truly in need....1 Tim 5:3
to care for orphans and *w*..........Jas 1:27

WIDTH
its length and *w* the same.........Rev 21:16

WIFE
and unites with his *w*..............Gen 2:24
But Lot's *w* looked back..........Gen 19:26
not covet your neighbor's *w*......Exod 20:17
becomes suspicious of his *w*......Num 5:14
and his *w* watched................Judg 13:19
the *w* of Uriah the Hittite.........2 Sam 11:3
Then his *w* said to him..............Job 2:9
w will be like a fruitful vine........Ps 128:3
A noble *w* is the crown............Prov 12:4
one who has found a good *w*....Prov 18:22
a prudent *w* is from the LORD....Prov 19:14
can find a *w* of noble character...Prov 31:10
Enjoy life with your beloved *w*.....Eccl 9:9
a *w* who has been abandoned......Isa 54:6
Israel worked to acquire a *w*......Hos 12:12
not be disloyal to the *w*...........Mal 2:15
afraid to take Mary as your *w*......Matt 1:20
Whoever divorces his *w*.........Mark 10:11
and my *w* is old as well...........Luke 1:18
Remember Lot's *w*...............Luke 17:32
whose *w* will the woman be....Luke 20:33
marital responsibility to his *w*.....1 Cor 7:3
must also love his own *w*.........Eph 5:33
the husband of one *w*.............1 Tim 3:2
the husband of one *w*.............Titus 1:6
the *w* of the Lamb................Rev 21:9

WILD
the people were running *w*......Exod 32:25
as well as the *w* animals...............Ps 8:7

w donkeys quench their thirst..... Ps 104:11
The *w* animals honor me.......... Isa 43:20
of locusts and *w* honey............ Matt 3:4
how God clothes the *w* grass..... Matt 6:30
how God clothes the *w* grass.... Luke 12:28
his wealth with a *w* lifestyle ...... Luke 15:13

WILDERNESS
this coming up from the *w* .... Song 3:6
who made the world like a *w*..... Isa 14:17
turn the *w* into a pool of water ..... Isa 41:18
the *w* and its cities shout out........ Isa 42:11
Have I been like a *w* to you........ Jer 2:31
voice of one shouting in the *w*.....Matt 3:3
he is in the *w* ....Matt 24:26
lifted up the serpent in the *w*...... John 3:14
ate the manna in the *w*............ John 6:31
congregation in the *w* ....Acts 7:38

WILL
See also I WILL BE WITH YOU; WILL BE
   SAVED; WILL OF GOD
may your *w* be done on earth .... Matt 6:10
does the *w* of my Father...........Matt 7:21
does the *w* of my Father......... Matt 12:50
of the two did his father's *w*......Matt 21:31
your *w* must be done............Matt 26:42
who knew his master's *w*........ Luke 12:47
wind blows wherever it *w* ....John 3:8
My food is to do the *w* .... John 4:34
I do not seek my own *w* .... John 5:30
my own *w* but the *w* of the one .. John 6:38
Now this is the *w* of the one...... John 6:39
the good *w* of all the people.......Acts 2:47
chosen you to know his *w*........Acts 22:14
the Lord *w* never count sin .... Rom 4:8
to the pleasure of his *w*.............. Eph 1:5
what the Lord's *w* is .... Eph 5:17
with the knowledge of his *w*........ Col 1:9
distributed according to his *w*...... Heb 2:4
For where there is a *w*............. Heb 9:16
a *w* takes effect only at death ..... Heb 9:17
I have come to do your *w*.......... Heb 10:9
every good thing to do his *w* ......Heb 13:21

WILL BE SAVED
and you *w* from your enemies.... Num 10:9
believes and is baptized *w*....... Mark 16:16
enters through me, he *w* ....John 10:9
and your entire household *w* ......Acts 11:14
in the Lord Jesus and you *w* ...... Acts 16:31
only the remnant *w*............... Rom 9:27
raised him from the dead, you *w* ..Rom 10:9
And so all Israel *w*............... Rom 11:26
He himself *w*...................1 Cor 3:15

WILL OF GOD
whoever does the *w* is my........Mark 3:35
according to the *w*................. Rom 1:10
and approve what is the *w*........Rom 12:2
of Christ Jesus by the *w*............. 1 Cor 1:1
and to us by the *w*................2 Cor 8:5
doing the *w* from the heart......... Eph 6:6
fully assured in all the *w*............. Col 4:12
about the *w* and not human ....1 Pet 4:2
suffer according to the *w*.......... 1 Pet 4:19
the person who does the *w*.......1 John 2:17

WILLING
person motivated by a *w* heart ... Exod 25:2
everyone who has a *w* heart...... Exod 35:5
to the LORD with a *w* attitude ....1 Chr 29:9
and is more than *w* to deliver ...... Ps 130:7
I am *w*. Be clean .... Matt 8:3
The spirit is *w*................... Matt 26:41
If you are *w*.................... Mark 1:40
The spirit is *w* ....Mark 14:38
if you are *w*......................Luke 5:12
Father, if you are *w*.............Luke 22:42
If the Lord is *w* ....Jas 4:15

WILLINGLY
Your people *w* follow you .... Ps 110:3
w but because of God .... Rom 8:20
but *w* under God's direction........1 Pet 5:2

WIN
So run to *w* ....1 Cor 9:24

WIND
w went before the LORD........... 1 Kgs 19:11
The east *w* carries him away ...... Job 27:21
He who watches the *w* .... Eccl 11:4
not know the path of the *w*........ Eccl 11:5
Awake, O north *w* .... Song 4:16
and the *w* carries them away ......Isa 40:24
the *w* will scatter them............. Isa 41:16
will prove to be full of *w*............ Jer 5:13
He unleashes the *w*................ Jer 51:16
a *w* came into me................... Ezek 2:2
Then a *w* lifted me up .... Ezek 3:12
continually feeds on the *w*.......... Hos 12:1
mountains and created the *w* ....Amos 4:13
A reed shaken by the *w*........... Matt 11:7
got up and rebuked the *w*.........Mark 4:39
got up and rebuked the *w*.........Luke 8:24
The *w* blows wherever it will .... John 3:8
sound like a violent *w* blowing .....Acts 2:2
about by every *w* of teaching.......Eph 4:14

WIND-DRIVEN
Instead they are like *w* chaff..........Ps 1:4

WINDBAG
If a lying *w* should come............ Mic 2:11

WINDOW
Noah opened the *w*................. Gen 8:6
by a rope through the *w*........... Josh 2:15
tied the red rope in the *w* .... Josh 2:21
lowered David through the *w* ...1 Sam 19:12
there is a *w* of opportunity .... Ps 32:6
gazing through the *w*............. Song 2:9
who was sitting in the *w*.......... Acts 20:9
through a *w* in the city wall......2 Cor 11:33

WINDOWS
climbed in through our *w* .... Jer 9:21
where the *w* in his upper room.... Dan 6:10
open for you the *w* of heaven ......Mal 3:10

WINDS
He makes the *w* his messengers....Ps 104:4
Come from the four *w*............ Ezek 37:9
the *w* and the sea obey him ...... Matt 8:27
back the four *w* of the earth......... Rev 7:1

WINDSTORM
went up to heaven in a *w*..........2 Kgs 2:11
hailstorm or a destructive *w*........ Isa 28:2
Now a great *w* developed ....Mark 4:37

WINE
Do not drink *w* or strong drink.....Lev 10:9
the Nazirite may drink *w*.........Num 6:20
Do not drink *w* or beer............ Judg 13:4
I haven't drunk *w* or beer........1 Sam 1:15
and the *w* is for those .... 2 Sam 16:2
feeling the effects of the *w* .... Esth 1:10
were eating and drinking *w*..........Job 1:13
made us drink intoxicating *w*........Ps 60:3
as *w* that makes people glad ......Ps 104:15
W is a mocker and strong drink ...Prov 20:1
look on the *w* when it is red......Prov 23:31
and *w* makes life merry ....Eccl 10:19
is more delightful than *w*........... Song 1:2
may it never lack mixed *w*......... Song 7:2
your mouth be like the best *w*..... Song 7:9
they are intoxicated with *w*.......... Isa 5:11
but not because of *w* .... Isa 29:9
Buy *w* and milk without money .....Isa 55:1
will give them any *w* to drink........Jer 16:7
filled with the *w* of my wrath.......Jer 25:15
We do not drink *w*................. Jer 35:6
new *w* into old wineskins..........Matt 9:17
offered Jesus *w* mixed with
   gall .... Matt 27:34
never drink *w* or strong drink ..... Luke 1:15
pouring olive oil and *w* .... Luke 10:34
When the *w* ran out.............. John 2:3
They are drunk on new *w* .... Acts 2:13
And do not get drunk with *w*......Eph 5:18
a little *w* for your digestion........1 Tim 5:23
damage the olive oil and the *w* ..... Rev 6:6

the *w* of her immoral passion ......Rev 14:8
w made of God's furious wrath....Rev 16:19

WINEPRESS
stomped grapes in the *w* .... Isa 63:3
for the *w* is full ....Joel 3:13
great *w* of the wrath of God.......Rev 14:19
the *w* of the furious wrath.........Rev 19:15

WINESKIN
like a *w* dried up in smoke......... Ps 119:83

WINESKINS
pours new wine into old *w* ......Matt 9:17

WINGS
how I lifted you on eagles' *w* ..... Exod 19:4
Each of the first cherub's *w*.......1 Kgs 6:24
me in the shadow of your *w* .... Ps 17:8
he glided on the *w* of the wind ..... Ps 18:10
finds shelter under your *w* .... Ps 36:7
In the shadow of your *w*............ Ps 57:1
He will shelter you with his *w* .... Ps 91:4
fly away on the *w* of the dawn.....Ps 139:9
each one had six *w* ....Isa 6:2
rise up as if they had eagles' *w* .... Isa 40:31
was like a lion with eagles' *w* .... Dan 7:4
will rise with healing *w* .... Mal 4:2
gathers her chicks under her *w*.. Matt 23:37
four living creatures had six *w*...... Rev 4:8
the two *w* of a giant eagle .... Rev 12:14

WINNER
will not be crowned as the *w* ....2 Tim 2:5

WINNOW
You will *w* them ....Isa 41:16

WINNOWING
gentle breeze for *w* the grain....... Jer 4:11
His *w* fork is in his hand ....Luke 3:17

WINS
one who *w* souls is wise.......... Prov 11:30
Keen insight *w* favor............... Prov 13:15

WINTER
the cycle of summer and *w*......... Ps 74:17
not fear for her household in *w* .. Prov 31:21
Look! The *w* has passed .... Song 2:11
both in summer and in *w*......... Zech 14:8
your flight may not be in *w*......Matt 24:20

WIPE
w me out from your book....... Exod 32:32
Angrily *w* them out................. Ps 59:13
LORD will *w* away the tears......... Isa 25:8

WIPED
reproach will not be *w* away.......Prov 6:33
has eaten and *w* her mouth .....Prov 30:20
She *w* them with her hair......... Luke 7:38

WISDOM
God gave Solomon *w*............1 Kgs 4:29
and *w* will die with you............. Job 12:2
by his *w* he cut Rahab .... Job 26:12
But *w*—where can it be found ..... Job 28:12
that is *w*, and to turn away ....Job 28:28
Who has put *w* in the heart........Job 38:36
learn a song that imparts *w* ....Ps 49:4
you want me to possess *w*........ Ps 51:6
sing a song that imparts *w*.......... Ps 78:2
there is no limit to his *w*........... Ps 147:5
but fools have despised *w* .... Prov 1:7
For the LORD gives *w* ....Prov 2:6
is the one who has found *w* ...... Prov 3:13
Acquire *w*, acquire understanding ..Prov 4:5
W is supreme......................Prov 4:7
beginning of *w* is to fear........... Prov 9:10
W rests in the heart ....Prov 14:33
to acquire *w* than gold............Prov 16:16
W is directly in front...............Prov 17:24
w has made him slow to anger ....Prov 19:11
wanders from the way of *w* ...... Prov 21:16
W is unattainable for a fool....... Prov 24:7
is a great oppressor lacks *w* ......Prov 28:16
great *w* comes great frustration.... Eccl 1:18
God gives *w* ....Eccl 2:26
that *w* is better than might .... Eccl 9:16
W is better than weapons of war .. Eccl 9:18

and imparts great *w* ....Isa 28:29
there is no limit to his *w* ....Isa 40:28
He gives *w* to the wise.............Dan 2:21
but the baby will lack *w* ....Hos 13:13
w is vindicated by her deeds...... Matt 11:19
And Jesus increased in *w* ....Luke 2:52
also the *w* of God said.............Luke 11:49
the depth of the riches and *w* .... Rom 11:33
and Greeks ask for *w* ....1 Cor 1:22
the *w* of this age is foolishness ....1 Cor 3:19
by human *w* but by the grace......2 Cor 1:12
the multifaceted *w* of God........Eph 3:10
hidden all the treasures of *w* ....Col 2:3
Conduct yourselves with *w*..........Col 4:5
if anyone is deficient in *w*............Jas 1:5
and wealth and *w* and might ....Rev 5:12
and *w* and thanksgiving ....Rev 7:12

WISE

See also WISE MAN; WISE MEN

testify of your *w* understanding ... Deut 4:6
nation is a very *w* people ....Deut 4:6
She was both *w* and beautiful ... 1 Sam 25:3
the *w* in their own craftiness .... Job 5:13
He is *w* in heart and mighty ....Job 9:4
It is not the aged who are *w* ....Job 32:9
if there is anyone who is *w* .... Ps 14:2
Whoever is *w*.....................Ps 107:43
w in your own estimation ....Prov 3:7
w person accepts instructions.....Prov 10:8
who are *w* store up knowledge...Prov 10:14
the one who wins souls is *w*......Prov 11:30
A *w* son accepts his father's .... Prov 13:1
Every *w* woman has built..........Prov 14:1
The one who is *w* in heart ....Prov 16:21
he be *w* in his own opinion ....Prov 26:5
who are *w* turn away wrath ......Prov 29:8
but they are exceedingly *w*......Prov 30:24
for it is not *w* to ask that ....Eccl 7:10
who are *w* among the people....Dan 11:33
Who is *w*? Let him discern.........Hos 14:9
so be *w* as serpents...............Matt 10:16
and five were *w*.................. Matt 25:2
to the *w* and to the foolish .... Rom 1:14
to the only *w* God ....Rom 16:27
but you are *w* in Christ ....1 Cor 4:10
as unwise but as *w* ....Eph 5:15

WISE MAN

Does a *w* answer with blustery..... Job 15:2
I will not find a *w* among you...... Job 17:10
A *w* went up against the city .....Prov 21:22
does a *w* have over a fool...........Eccl 6:8
magician, astrologer, or *w*.........Dan 2:10
like a *w* who built his house ......Matt 7:24
Where is the *w* ....1 Cor 1:20

WISE MEN

of Egypt and all its *w* ....Gen 41:8
summoned *w* and sorcerers.......Exod 7:11
king then inquired of the *w*........Esth 1:13
where, oh where, are your *w* ...... Isa 19:12
W will have nothing to say ...... Isa 29:14
destroy all the *w* of Babylon......Dan 2:12
over all the *w* of Babylon..........Dan 2:48
So all the king's *w* came in......... Dan 5:8
w from the East came ....Matt 2:1
privately summoned the *w*........Matt 2:7
he had been tricked by the *w*.....Matt 2:16
he had learned from the *w* ....Matt 2:16
sending you prophets and *w* .... Matt 23:34

WISELY

so that we might live *w*.............Ps 90:12
one who deals *w* in a matter .... Prov 16:20

WISER

He was *w* than any man ....1 Kgs 4:31
makes us *w* than the birds..........Job 35:11
make me *w* than my enemies ...... Ps 119:98
is *w* than human wisdom ....1 Cor 1:25

WISH

I *w* it were already kindled ...... Luke 12:49
I *w* that everyone was as I am .....1 Cor 7:7
he does not *w* for any to perish ... 2 Pet 3:9
I *w* you were either cold or hot.....Rev 3:15

WISHES

Our *w* are of no concern......... Gen 24:50
whom the king *w* to honor ....Esth 6:6
to carry out all my *w* ....Isa 44:28

WITH ALL YOUR HEART

you seek him *w* and soul ....Deut 4:29
serve him *w* and being ....Josh 22:5
Serve the LORD *w* ....1 Sam 12:20
Trust in the LORD *w* ....Prov 3:5
If you seek me *w* and soul.........Jer 29:13
LORD says, "return to me *w*.......Joel 2:12
Be happy and boast *w*............ Zeph 3:14
Love the Lord your God *w*....... Matt 22:37
Love the Lord your God *w*......Mark 12:30
And to love him *w*................ Mark 12:33
Love the Lord your God *w*...... Luke 10:27

WITHDREW

and *w* to the palace garden......... Esth 7:7
You *w* all your fury ....Ps 85:3
Jesus himself frequently *w* ....Luke 5:16

WITHER

and *w* away like plants ....Ps 37:2
the flowers *w*...................... Isa 40:7
leaves on their trees will *w* ....Jer 8:13
Their leaves will not *w*............Ezek 47:12
did the fig tree *w* so quickly ..... Matt 21:20

WITHERED

w and thin and burned .... Gen 41:23
is parched and *w* like grass........Ps 102:4
was there who had a *w* hand .....Matt 12:10
have sufficient root, they *w*........Matt 13:6
And the fig tree *w* at once ....Matt 21:19
the fig tree *w* from the roots ... Mark 11:20

WITHERS

grass *w* and the flower falls off....1 Pet 1:24

WITHHOLD

do not *w* your compassion .... Ps 40:11
Do not *w* good from those ....Prov 3:27
do not *w* your tunic either........Luke 6:29
No one can *w* the water ....Acts 10:47

WITHHOLDS

he *w* no good thing.................. Ps 84:11

WITHIN

God lives *w* it.....................Ps 46:5
I will put my law *w* them ....Jer 31:33
like a wheel *w* a wheel............Ezek 10:10
From *w* him will flow rivers ....John 7:38

WITHOUT

at that time *w* the Messiah ....Eph 2:12
the body *w* the spirit is dead .... Jas 2:26

WITHSTAND

the wicked cannot *w* judgment........Ps 1:5
No one can *w* his indignation........Nah 1:6

WITNESS

See also FALSE WITNESS

God is *w* to your actions.......... Gen 31:50
Even now my *w* is in heaven....... Job 16:19
Come and *w* God's exploits..........Ps 66:5
A truthful *w* does not lie....Prov 14:5
I made him a *w* to nations .... Isa 55:4
LORD be a true and faithful *w*....... Jer 42:5
He came as a *w* to testify..........John 1:7
because you will be his *w*.........Acts 22:15
when the blood of your *w* ....Acts 22:20
For God is my *w* that I long........ Phil 1:8
faithful *w*, the firstborn...............Rev 1:5
my faithful *w* ....Rev 2:13

WITNESSES

testimony of two or three *w*.......Deut 17:6
will summon as my reliable *w*.......Isa 8:2
You are my *w*.....................Isa 43:10
for in the presence of many *w* ... 1 Tim 6:12
the Holy Spirit also *w* to us....... Heb 10:15
by such a great cloud of *w*..........Heb 12:1
will grant my two *w* authority ......Rev 11:3

WIVES

Suppose a man has two *w*........Deut 21:15
He had 700 royal *w* and ....1 Kgs 11:3
as *w* for themselves ....Ezra 9:2

foreign *w* made even him sin..... Neh 13:26
permitted you to divorce your *w* ..Matt 19:8
W, submit to your husbands....... Eph 5:22
Husbands, love your *w* .... Eph 5:25
Husbands, love your *w* .... Col 3:19
their *w* must be dignified..........1 Tim 3:11
w, be subject to your own ....1 Pet 3:1
treat your *w* with consideration ....1 Pet 3:7

WOE

Who has *w*? Who has sorrow.... Prov 23:29
W to the wicked sinners............. Isa 3:11
W to the city of bloodshed ....Ezek 24:9
W to the one who accumulates .... Hab 2:6
W to you, Chorazin............... Matt 11:21
W to the world because...........Matt 18:7
But *w* to you, experts...........Matt 23:13
W to those who are pregnant ....Mark 13:17
W to you who are well satisfied .. Luke 6:25
W to me if I do not preach....... 1 Cor 9:16
W! *W*! *W* to those who live........Rev 8:13
The first *w* has passed..............Rev 9:12

WOKE

So they came and *w* him up ...... Matt 8:25
They came and *w* him ....Luke 8:24

WOLF

A *w* and a lamb will graze .... Isa 65:25
sees the *w* coming and abandons John 10:12

WOLVES

but inwardly are voracious *w*......Matt 7:15
like lambs surrounded by *w*.......Luke 10:3
fierce *w* will come in among..... Acts 20:29

WOMAN

this one will be called '*w*...........Gen 2:23
Banish that slave *w* and her son .. Gen 21:10
Every *w* will ask her neighbor .... Exod 3:22
Every *w* who was skilled.........Exod 35:25
marry a widow, a divorced *w* ...... Lev 21:14
the *w* stand before the LORD ......Num 5:18
A *w* must not wear men's .... Deut 22:5
But the *w* hid the two men ....Josh 2:4
gives a *w* to a Benjaminite...... Judg 21:18
knows that you are a worthy *w*.... Ruth 3:11
the barren *w* has given birth.....1 Sam 2:5
keeping you from the evil *w*...... Prov 6:24
adultery with a *w* lacks sense..... Prov 6:32
The *w* called Folly is brash........Prov 9:13
A generous *w* gains honor........Prov 11:16
wise *w* has built her household.... Prov 14:1
but a foolish *w* tears it down ...... Prov 14:1
A *w* who fears the LORD..........Prov 31:30
young *w* is about to conceive..... Isa 7:14
Can a *w* forget her baby ....Isa 49:15
unique as a *w* protecting a man ....Jer 31:22
looks at a *w* to desire her......... Matt 5:28
A Canaanite *w* from that area ....Matt 15:22
W, your faith is great .... Matt 15:28
a *w* came with an alabaster jar ... Mark 14:3
Then, turning toward the *w* ...... Luke 7:44
the Samaritan *w* said to him.......John 4:9
a *w* who had been caught ....John 8:3
W, look, here is your son ....John 19:26
the son of a Jewish *w*............Acts 16:1
sexual relations with a *w* ....1 Cor 7:1
the man is the head of a *w* ....1 Cor 11:3
if a *w* will not cover her head.....1 Cor 11:6
the *w* is the glory of the man......1 Cor 11:7
For man did not come from *w*.....1 Cor 11:8
man created for the sake of *w*.....1 Cor 11:9
a *w* should have a symbol ....1 Cor 11:10
sent out his Son, born of a *w* ......Gal 4:4
one by the slave *w*................Gal 4:22
with the son" of the free *w* ....Gal 4:30
A *w* must learn quietly ....1 Tim 2:11
I do not allow a *w* to teach ....1 Tim 2:12
the *w*, because she was fully.......1 Tim 2:14
You tolerate that *w* Jezebel....... Rev 2:20
a *w* clothed with the sun ....Rev 12:1
a *w* sitting on a scarlet beast ......Rev 17:3
As for the *w* you saw ....Rev 17:18

WOMB

Two nations are in your *w*........Gen 25:23
brought me out from the *w* ....Ps 22:9

when I was inside the *w* . . . . Ps 139:16
one who formed you in the *w* . . . . . . Isa 44:2
formed you in your mother's *w* . . . . . . Jer 1:5
blessed is the child in your *w* . . . . . Luke 1:42
Blessed is the *w* that bore you . . . . Luke 11:27

WOMEN
ten *w* will bake your bread . . . . Lev 26:26
The most rewarded of *w* . . . . Judg 5:24
in love with many foreign *w* . . . . . . 1 Kgs 11:1
are among your honored *w* . . . . Ps 45:9
young men and young *w* . . . . Ps 148:12
O most beautiful of *w* . . . . Song 1:8
The *w* of Zion are proud . . . . Isa 3:16
and new wine the young *w* . . . . Zech 9:17
Not counting *w* and children . . . . . Matt 14:21
Not counting children and *w* . . . . Matt 15:38
will be two *w* grinding grain . . . . . Matt 24:41
w who had followed Jesus . . . . Matt 27:55
found it just as the *w* had said . . . Luke 24:24
both men and *w* . . . . Acts 2:18
incited the God-fearing *w* . . . . Acts 13:50
and quite a few prominent *w* . . . . . Acts 17:4
natural relations with *w* . . . . Rom 1:27
the *w* should be silent . . . . 1 Cor 14:34
Likewise the *w* are to dress . . . . 1 Tim 2:9
for *w* who profess reverence . . . . . 1 Tim 2:10
older *w* as mothers . . . . 1 Tim 5:2
and younger *w* as sisters . . . . 1 Tim 5:2
will train the younger *w* . . . . Titus 2:4
the same way the holy *w* . . . . 1 Pet 3:5
defiled themselves with *w* . . . . Rev 14:4

WON
w the loyalty of the citizens . . . . . 2 Sam 15:6

WONDER
and show you a sign or *w* . . . . Deut 13:1

WONDERFUL
things too *w* for me to know . . . . Job 42:3
things that are too *w* for me . . . . . Prov 30:18
and is called *W* Adviser . . . . Isa 9:6
saw the *w* things he did . . . . Matt 21:15

WONDERS
See also SIGNS AND WONDERS
with all my *w* that I will do . . . . Exod 3:20
w such as have not been done . . . Exod 34:10
and consider the *w* God works . . . . Job 37:14
How mighty are his *w* . . . . Dan 4:3
and performs signs and *w* . . . . Dan 6:27
miraculous signs and *w* . . . . Acts 5:12
the miraculous signs and *w* . . . . . . Acts 15:12
miracles and signs and false *w* . . 2 Thess 2:9
and *w* and various miracles . . . . Heb 2:4

WONDROUSLY
has acted *w* in your behalf . . . . Joel 2:26

WOOD
gathering *w* on the Sabbath . . . . . Num 15:32
was a widow gathering *w* . . . . 1 Kgs 17:10
stones, *w*, hay, or straw . . . . 1 Cor 3:12

WOODCUTTERS
became *w* and water carriers . . . . . . Josh 9:21

WOOL
She sought out *w* and flax . . . . Prov 31:13
you can become white like *w* . . . . . . Isa 1:18
of his head was like lamb's *w* . . . . . . Dan 7:9
and hair were as white as *w* . . . . . . Rev 1:14

WORD
See also ACCORDING TO THE WORD OF
   THE LORD; WORD OF GOD; WORD OF
   THE LORD
people heard this troubling *w* . . . . Exod 33:4
numbered by the *w* of the LORD . . Num 3:39
w about him was spreading . . . . Esth 9:4
There is no actual speech or *w* . . . . . Ps 19:3
Your *w* is a lamp to walk by . . . . . . Ps 119:105
encouraging *w* brings him joy . . . . Prov 12:25
but a harsh *w* stirs up wrath . . . . . . Prov 15:1
and a *w* at the right time . . . . Prov 15:23
so is a *w* skillfully spoken . . . . Prov 25:11
ourselves in a deceitful *w* . . . . Isa 28:15
say the *w* and my servant . . . . Matt 8:8
every worthless *w* they speak . . . . Matt 12:36

In the beginning was the *W* . . . . John 1:1
Now the *W* became flesh . . . . John 1:14
your *w* is truth . . . . John 17:17
and praise the *w* of the Lord . . . . . . Acts 13:48
washing of the water by the *w* . . . . Eph 5:26
by holding on to the *w* of life . . . . . . Phil 2:16
Let the *w* of Christ dwell . . . . Col 3:16
all things by his powerful *w* . . . . Heb 1:3
the *w* of God heavens existed . . . . . 2 Pet 3:5
But whoever obeys his *w* . . . . 1 John 2:5
not love with *w* or with tongue . . . 1 John 3:18

WORD OF GOD
Every *w* is purified . . . . Prov 30:5
You have nullified the *w* . . . . Matt 15:6
Thus you nullify the *w* . . . . Mark 7:13
the *w* came to John . . . . Luke 3:2
around him to hear the *w* . . . . Luke 5:1
The seed is the *w* . . . . Luke 8:11
are those who hear the *w* . . . . Luke 8:21
to speak the *w* courageously . . . . . . Acts 4:31
neglect the *w* to wait on tables . . . . Acts 6:2
The *w* continued to spread . . . . Acts 6:7
had accepted the *w* . . . . Acts 11:1
necessary to speak the *w* . . . . Acts 13:46
as though the *w* had failed . . . . Rom 9:6
Did the *w* begin with you . . . . 1 Cor 14:36
hucksters who peddle the *w* . . . . . . 2 Cor 2:17
or distorting the *w* . . . . 2 Cor 4:2
which is the *w* . . . . Eph 6:17
the *w* is living and active . . . . Heb 4:12
the living and enduring *w* . . . . 1 Pet 1:23
the *w* resides in you . . . . 1 John 2:14
he saw concerning the *w* . . . . Rev 1:2
killed because of the *w* . . . . Rev 6:9
and he is called the *W* . . . . Rev 19:13
and because of the *w* . . . . Rev 20:4

WORD OF THE LORD
them according to the *w* . . . . Num 3:16
Samuel revealed the *w* . . . . 1 Sam 4:1
did not obey the *w* . . . . 2 Chr 34:21
remembered the *w* . . . . Luke 22:61
testified and spoken the *w* . . . . Acts 8:25
together to hear the *w* . . . . Acts 13:44
where we proclaimed the *w* . . . . Acts 15:36
the *w* continued to grow . . . . Acts 19:20
we tell you this by the *w* . . . . 1 Thess 4:15
but the *w* endures forever . . . . 1 Pet 1:25

WORDS
w fell on them drop by drop . . . . . . Job 29:22
w are without understanding . . . . . Job 34:35
May my *w* and my thoughts . . . . Ps 19:14
sure you don't speak evil *w* . . . . Ps 34:13
The godly speak wise *w* . . . . Ps 37:30
In my heart I store up your *w* . . . . . Ps 119:11
Your *w* are sweeter in my mouth . . Ps 119:103
make my *w* known to you . . . . Prov 1:23
pay attention to the *w* I speak . . . . Prov 7:24
from the fruit of his *w* . . . . Prov 12:14
guards his *w* guards his life . . . . Prov 13:3
but *w* of knowledge are like . . . . . . Prov 20:15
listen to the *w* of the wise . . . . Prov 22:17
The *w* of the sages are like . . . . Eccl 12:11
your *w* will be heard . . . . Isa 29:4
Friendly *w* for their neighbors . . . . . . Jer 9:8
are misrepresenting the *w* . . . . Jer 23:36
None of my *w* will be delayed . . . . Ezek 12:28
with smooth *w* he will defile . . . . . . Dan 11:32
who hears these *w* of mine . . . . Matt 7:24
entrap him with his own *w* . . . . . . Matt 22:15
my *w* will never pass away . . . . Matt 24:35
amazed at the gracious *w* . . . . Luke 4:22
judge you by your own *w* . . . . Luke 19:22
For I will give you the *w* . . . . Luke 21:15
his powerful deeds and *w* . . . . Luke 24:19
The *w* that I have spoken . . . . John 6:63
You have the *w* of eternal life . . . . John 6:68
love me does not obey my *w* . . . . John 14:24
and my *w* remain in you . . . . John 15:7
the *w* of the Lord Jesus . . . . Acts 20:35
I may be given the right *w* . . . . Eph 6:19
come to you merely in *w* . . . . 1 Thess 1:5
confirmed by prophetic *w* . . . . 1 Tim 4:14
not to wrangle over *w* . . . . 2 Tim 2:14

let it be with God's *w* . . . . 1 Pet 4:11
reads the *w* of this prophecy . . . . Rev 1:3
keeps the *w* of the prophecy . . . . . . Rev 22:7
who obey the *w* of this book . . . . . . Rev 22:9

WORE
and he *w* a wide golden belt . . . . Rev 1:13

WORK
God finished the *w* . . . . Gen 2:2
the *w* of an artistic designer . . . . . Exod 26:31
So Moses finished the *w* . . . . Exod 40:33
father made us *w* too hard . . . . 1 Kgs 12:4
were enthusiastic in their *w* . . . . Neh 4:6
are the *w* of his hands . . . . Job 34:19
then go out to do their *w* . . . . Ps 104:23
His *w* is majestic and glorious . . . . . Ps 111:3
In all hard *w* there is profit . . . . Prov 14:23
there is neither *w* nor planning . . . . Eccl 9:10
to accomplish his *w* . . . . Isa 28:21
they do not *w* or spin . . . . Matt 6:28
in the marketplace without *w* . . . . Matt 20:3
go and *w* in the vineyard . . . . Matt 21:28
Do not *w* for the food . . . . John 6:27
coming when no one can *w* . . . . John 9:4
by completing the *w* you gave . . . . John 17:4
all things *w* together for good . . . . Rom 8:28
Do not destroy the *w* of God . . . . Rom 14:20
builder's *w* will be plainly seen . . . 1 Cor 3:13
Are you not my *w* in the Lord . . . . . 1 Cor 9:1
outstanding in the *w* of the Lord . . 1 Cor 15:58
in hard *w* and toil . . . . 2 Cor 11:27
w for you may have been In vain . . . Gal 4:11
For we are his creative *w* . . . . Eph 2:10
mean productive *w* for me . . . . Phil 1:22
your *w* produced by faith . . . . 1 Thess 1:3
If anyone is not willing to *w* . . . . 2 Thess 3:10
one entrusted with God's *w* . . . . Titus 1:7
can rest from their hard *w* . . . . Rev 14:13

WORKED
Long ago I *w* it out . . . . Isa 37:26
I *w* harder than all of them . . . . 1 Cor 15:10

WORKER
the *w* deserves his provisions . . . Matt 10:10
Timothy, my fellow *w* . . . . Rom 16:21
as a proven *w* who does not . . . . . . 2 Tim 2:15

WORKERS
but the *w* are few . . . . Matt 9:37
beware of the evil *w* . . . . Phil 3:2

WORKING
not stop *w* until the evening . . . . . . Eccl 11:6
My Father is *w* until now . . . . John 5:17
By *w* night and day . . . . 1 Thess 2:9

WORKS
See also GOOD WORKS; WORKS OF THE
   LAW

first among the *w* of God . . . . Job 40:19
How great are your *w* . . . . Ps 92:5
All your *w* will give thanks . . . . Ps 145:10
The one who *w* his field . . . . Prov 12:11
The one who *w* his land . . . . Prov 28:19
and let her *w* praise her . . . . Prov 31:31
building strong siege *w* against . . . . Eccl 9:14
each one according to his *w* . . . . Rom 2:6
apart from the *w* of the law . . . . . . Rom 3:28
not by *w* but by his calling . . . . Rom 9:11
it is no longer by *w* . . . . Rom 11:6
lay aside the *w* of darkness . . . . Rom 13:12
the *w* of the flesh are obvious . . . . . Gal 5:19
it is not from *w* . . . . Eph 2:9
repentance from dead *w* . . . . Heb 6:1
have faith but does not have *w* . . . . Jas 2:14
also justified by *w* when she . . . . Jas 2:25
to destroy the *w* of the devil . . . . . 1 John 3:8
I know your *w* as well . . . . Rev 2:2

WORKS OF THE LAW
by faith apart from the *w* . . . . Rom 3:28
no one is justified by the *w* . . . . Gal 2:16
all who rely on doing the *w* . . . . Gal 3:10

WORLD
See also IN THE WORLD; OF THE WORLD;
   OF THIS WORLD

He judges the *w* fairly .... Ps 9:8
for the *w* and all it contains......... Ps 50:12
you brought the *w* into being........ Ps 90:2
the *w* is established.................. Ps 93:1
from before the *w* existed........ Prov 8:23
The field is the *w* .... Matt 13:38
For the people of this *w* .... Luke 16:8
He was in the *w* .... John 1:10
the way God loved the *w* .... John 3:16
into the *w* to condemn the *w*...... John 3:17
really is the Savior of the *w*...... John 4:42
The *w* cannot hate you .... John 7:7
You people are from this *w*...... John 8:23
the *w* has run off after him .... John 12:19
w will not see me any longer ..... John 14:19
If the *w* hates you .... John 15:18
If you belonged to the *w*.......... John 15:19
In the *w* you have trouble .... John 16:33
not praying on behalf of the *w* ... John 17:9
if the *w* does not know you...... John 17:25
w may be held accountable....... Rom 3:19
be conformed to this present *w* ...Rom 12:2
what the *w* thinks foolish....... 1 Cor 1:27
the *w* has been crucified to me..... Gal 6:14
and without God in the *w* .... Eph 2:12
whom he created the *w* .... Heb 1:2
he did not put the *w* to come....... Heb 2:5
oneself unstained by the *w*...... Jas 1:27
that friendship with the *w*........ Jas 4:4
Do not love the *w* .... 1 John 2:15
because all that is in the *w*...... 1 John 2:16
And the *w* is passing away....... 1 John 2:17
the *w* does not know us ...... 1 John 3:1
They are from the *w*............ 1 John 4:5
so also are we in this *w*......... 1 John 4:17
whole *w* followed the beast ...... Rev 13:3

WORLDLY

w, devoid of the Spirit ....Jude 1:19

WORM

the *w* feasts on him................ Job 24:20
But I am a *w* .... Ps 22:6

WORMS

My body is clothed with *w*........ Job 7:5
with a blanket of *w* over you .... Isa 14:11
he was eaten by *w* and died ...... Acts 12:23

WORMWOOD

in the end she is bitter as *w* ..... Prov 5:4
the name of the star is *W*........ Rev 8:11

WORN

and they have *w* you out .... Jer 12:5

WORRIED

he was very *w* about the ark...... 1 Sam 4:13
you are *w* and troubled.......... Luke 10:41

WORRIES

w threaten to overwhelm .... Ps 94:19
choked by the *w* and riches ...... Luke 8:14

WORRY

How long must I *w* .... Ps 13:2
do not *w* about your life.......... Matt 6:25
don't *w* saying.................... Matt 6:31
do not *w* about what to speak.... Mark 13:11

WORRYING

by *w* can add even one hour...... Matt 6:27

WORSHIP

We will *w* and then return........ Gen 22:5
not *w* the LORD your God .... Deut 12:31
no right to *w* the LORD .... Josh 22:25
obey the LORD and *w* him .... Josh 24:14
W the LORD in holy attire........ 1 Chr 16:29
the Levitical orders to lead *w*..... 2 Chr 8:14
Come, let us bow down and *w*....... Ps 95:6
I have seen your adulterous *w*...... Jer 13:27
will be punished for idol *w* ...... Ezek 23:49
and will *w* him in unison........ Zeph 3:9
and have come to *w* him .... Matt 2:2
to the ground and *w* me.......... Matt 4:9
You are to *w* the Lord .... Matt 4:10
and they *w* me in vain .... Matt 15:9
w what you do not know .... John 4:22
w the Father in spirit and truth.... John 4:23

closely your objects of *w* .... Acts 17:23
I *w* the God of our ancestors ..... Acts 24:14
the *w* of angels pass judgment .... Col 2:18
with their self-imposed *w* .... Col 2:23
all the angels of God *w* him .... Heb 1:6
to *w* the living God .... Heb 9:14
perfect those who come to *w* ..... Heb 10:1
w the one who lives forever .... Rev 4:10
w the one who made heaven .... Rev 14:7

WORSHIPED

and there Abram *w* the LORD....... Gen 13:4
bowed down and *w* the LORD ... Gen 24:48
they saw him, they *w* him .... Matt 28:17
So they *w* him and returned..... Luke 24:52
fathers *w* on this mountain........ John 4:20
fell at his feet, and *w* him .... Acts 10:25
and *w* and served the creation .... Rom 1:25
to the ground and *w*........... Rev 5:14
to the ground and *w* God......... Rev 11:16
to the ground and *w* God........ Rev 19:4

WORSHIPERS

true *w* will worship the Father..... John 4:23
idol *w*, and all those who lie .... Rev 21:8

WORSHIPING

w what they made with............. Jer 1:16

WORST

I am the *w* of them .... 1 Tim 1:15

WORTHILY

you to live *w* of the calling........... Eph 4:1
you may live *w* of the Lord .... Col 1:10

WORTHLESS

will you love what is *w* .... Ps 4:2
the gods of the nations are *w*....... Ps 96:5
eyes away from what is *w* .... Ps 119:37
A *w* and wicked person......... Prov 6:12
religion of these people is *w*...... Jer 10:3
from a wooden idol is *w*.......... Jer 10:8
that I have become *w*............. Lam 1:11
for every *w* word they speak ..... Matt 12:36
throw that *w* slave into the...... Matt 25:30
together they have become *w*..... Rom 3:12
to the weak and *w* basic forces...... Gal 4:9

WORTHWHILE

If you say what is *w*................. Jer 15:19

WORTHY

not *w* of all the faithful love ...... Gen 32:10
that you are a *w* woman........... Ruth 3:11
who is *w* of praise .... 2 Sam 22:4
who is *w* of praise .... Ps 18:3
not *w* to carry his sandals .... Matt 3:11
find out who is *w* there........... Matt 10:11
more than me is not *w* of me.... Matt 10:37
had been invited were not *w* ..... Matt 22:8
not *w* to bend down and untie.... Mark 1:7
no longer *w* to be called your .... Luke 15:19
not *w* to untie the strap .... John 1:27
not *w* to untie the sandals........ Acts 13:25
in a manner *w* of the gospel....... Phil 1:27
you live in a way *w* of God...... 1 Thess 2:12
you *w* of the kingdom of God ... 2 Thess 1:5
that our God will make you *w*...2 Thess 1:11
be counted *w* of double honor ... 1 Tim 5:17
the world was not *w* of them...... Heb 11:38
in a manner *w* of God .... 3 John 1:6
in white because they are *w*....... Rev 3:4
You are *w*, our Lord .... Rev 4:11
Who is *w* to open the scroll .... Rev 5:2
W is the lamb who was killed..... Rev 5:12

WOUND

My *w* is incurable.................. Job 34:6
you not *w* the sea monster .... Isa 51:9
Our *w* is severe................. Jer 10:19
have suffered a serious *w* .... Jer 14:17
insults like an incurable *w* .... Jer 15:18
is like an incurable *w* .... Nah 3:19
and *w* their weak conscience ..... 1 Cor 8:12

WOUNDED

w because of our rebellious .... Isa 53:5
of his own people he was *w* .... Isa 53:8
that only *w* men were left .... Jer 37:10

from that house naked and *w* .... Acts 19:16
who had been *w* by the sword..... Rev 13:14

WOUNDING

I have killed a man for *w* me....... Gen 4:23

WOUNDS

and bandages their *w*.............. Ps 147:3
Faithful are the *w* of a friend ..... Prov 27:6
bruises, cuts, and open *w*.......... Isa 1:6
of his *w* we have been healed ...... Isa 53:5
up to him and bandaged his *w*.... Luke 10:34
Unless I see the *w* from the
 nails .... John 20:25
By his *w* you were healed .... 1 Pet 2:24

WOVE

you *w* me together .... Ps 139:13

WOVEN

w from top to bottom .... John 19:23

WRAPPED

seaweed was *w* around my head ..Jonah 2:5
w it in a clean linen cloth .... Matt 27:59
and *w* him in strips of cloth........ Luke 2:7

WRATH

See also WRATH OF GOD; WRATH OF THE
 LORD

w has gone out from the LORD .. Num 16:46
w kills the foolish person .... Job 5:2
we are terrified by your *w*.........Ps 90:7
but a harsh word stirs up *w*........ Prov 15:1
A king's *w* is like a messenger .... Prov 16:14
A king's *w* is like the roar......... Prov 19:12
W is cruel and anger is .... Prov 27:4
to flee from the coming *w*........ Matt 3:7
but God's *w* remains on him....... John 3:36
For the *w* of God is revealed........ Rom 1:18
you are storing up *w*................ Rom 2:5
For the law brings *w*............... Rom 4:15
willing to demonstrate his *w* .... Rom 9:22
but give place to God's *w*........ Rom 12:19
of the *w* of the authorities......... Rom 13:5
were by nature children of *w*........ Eph 2:3
w, quarreling, and slanderous
 talk .... Eph 4:31
deliverer from the coming *w* ....1 Thess 1:10
but *w* has come upon them .... 1 Thess 2:16
and from the *w* of the Lamb........ Rev 6:16
undiluted in the cup of his *w* ..... Rev 14:10
winepress of the *w* of God........ Rev 14:19
wine made of God's furious *w*..... Rev 16:19

WRATH OF GOD

w is revealed from heaven......... Rom 1:18
the *w* is coming on the sons......... Col 3:6
the great winepress of the *w*...... Rev 14:19
bowls filled with the *w* .... Rev 15:7
winepress of the furious *w* .... Rev 19:15

WRATH OF THE LORD

fierce *w* against the Israelites.... Num 32:14
The *w* will come like a storm...... Jer 23:19

WRATHFUL

not associate with a *w* person ... Prov 22:24

WRESTLED

man *w* with him until daybreak...Gen 32:24

WRETCHED

W man that I am.................. Rom 7:24
not realize that you are *w* .... Rev 3:17

WRINKLE

having a stain or *w* .... Eph 5:27

WRISTS

the chains fell off Peter's *w*........ Acts 12:7

WRITE

and I will *w* on the tablets .... Exod 34:1
w them on the tablet of your
 heart .... Prov 3:3
w them on the tablet of your
 heart .... Prov 7:3
and *w* it on their hearts and
 minds............................... Jer 31:33
have many things to *w* to you ... 3 John 1:13
Therefore *w* what you saw .... Rev 1:19
I will *w* on him the name .... Rev 3:12

WRITING
and the *w* was the *w* of God..... Exod 32:16
I will read the *w* for the king........Dan 5:17
not *w* a new commandment......1 John 2:7
am *w* a new commandment..... 1 John 2:8

WRITINGS
you have known the holy *w* ......2 Tim 3:15

WRITTEN
See also AS IT IS WRITTEN; IT IS WRITTEN
commandments that I have *w*... Exod 24:12
stone *w* by the finger of God .....Exod 31:18
tablets were *w* on both sides.... Exod 32:15
your book that you have *w* ..... Exod 32:32
w by the very finger of God ...... Deut 9:10
the things *w* in this scroll........Deut 28:58
the covenant *w* in this scroll..... Deut 29:21
that they were *w* on a scroll....... Job 19:23
What is *w* in the scroll..............Ps 40:7
Have I not *w* thirty sayings ...... Prov 22:20
names are found *w* in the book..... Dan 12:1
is *w* this way by the prophet.......Matt 2:5
names stand *w* in heaven........Luke 10:20
to fulfill all that is *w* .... Luke 21:22
Pilate also had a notice *w*........ John 19:19
What I have *w* ....John 19:22
just as it is *w*...................... Rom 1:17
the law is *w* in their hearts ....Rom 2:15
it is *w*, "Vengeance is mine .... Rom 12:19
w on our hearts ....2 Cor 3:2
w not with ink but by the Spirit.... 2 Cor 3:3
under a curse because it is *w*....... Gal 3:10
it is *w*, "You shall be holy ....1 Pet 1:16
stone will be *w* a new name.......Rev 2:17
whose name has not been *w* ......Rev 13:8
name *w* on their foreheads......... Rev 14:1
her forehead was *w* a name ....Rev 17:5

WRONG
and the *w* they did when .... Gen 50:17
to flog honorable men is *w*.....Prov 17:26
are offspring who do *w*............... Isa 1:4
have committed a double *w* ....Jer 2:13
something *w* with the pot ....Jer 18:4
the *w* they have done...............Jer 31:34
What has he done *w*............. Mark 15:14
this man has done nothing *w*.... Luke 23:41
If I have said something *w*........John 18:23
done nothing *w* to the Jews ......Acts 25:10
If then I am in the *w* .... Acts 25:11
Love does no *w* to a neighbor ....Rom 13:10
does *w* will be repaid for his *w* .....Col 3:25

WRONGDOERS
they now malign you as *w*........1 Pet 2:12

WRONGDOING
God charges no one with *w*........Job 24:12
I no longer covered up my *w* ....Ps 32:5
He will remember their *w* ....Hos 9:9
you are unable to condone *w*.......Hab 1:13
tongue represents the world of *w*....Jas 3:6

WRONGED
give it to whomever he *w*.......... Num 5:7
then that God has *w* me............Job 19:6
we have *w* no one ....2 Cor 7:2

WRONGLY
but I will not act *w* any more ......Job 34:31

WROTE
He *w* on the tablets the words .. Exod 34:28
and *w* on the plaster................. Dan 5:5
not believe what Moses *w*........John 5:47
down and *w* on the ground.........John 8:6

Y

YAKIN
Along with Boaz, one of two pillars in front
of Solomon's temple, 1 Kgs 7:21–22

YEAR
be your first month of the *y* ....Exod 12:2
fiftieth *y* will be your Jubilee....... Lev 25:11
In this *Y* of Jubilee .... Lev 25:13
will we eat in the seventh *y*....... Lev 25:20
Jubilee *y* the field will return ..... Lev 27:24
the *y* with your good blessings ......Ps 65:11
announce the *y* when the LORD .....Isa 61:2
will be his until the *y* of liberty .. Ezek 46:17
went to Jerusalem every *y*........Luke 2:41
once a *y* into the inner tent......... Heb 9:7
a reminder of sins *y* after *y*........ Heb 10:3

YEARN
And *y* like newborn infants..........1 Pet 2:2

YEARS
indicate seasons and days and *y*....Gen 1:14
were old and advancing in *y*...... Gen 18:11
your *y* like the *y* of a mortal........Job 10:5
of *y* should make wisdom ....Job 32:7
greatness through the coming *y*.... Ps 45:17
thousand *y* are like yesterday ...... Ps 90:4
our lives add up to seventy *y* ......Ps 90:10
your *y* do not come to an end .....Ps 102:27
were to me in your early *y*...........Jer 3:2
When he was twelve *y* old........ Luke 2:42
You are not yet fifty *y* old ....John 8:57
and your *y* will never run out........Heb 1:12
tied him up for a thousand *y* ...... Rev 20:2
reign with him for a thousand *y* ...Rev 20:6

YEAST
kingdom of heaven is like *y*......Matt 13:33
beware of the *y* of the Pharisees .. Matt 16:6
little *y* affects the whole batch .... 1 Cor 5:6
Clean out the old *y* ....1 Cor 5:7
little *y* makes the whole batch....... Gal 5:9

YELL
Y as loudly as a trumpet..............Isa 58:1

YES
Y, you are a God who keeps........Isa 45:15
Let your word be '*Y* .... Matt 5:37
not "*Y*" and "No ....2 Cor 1:19

YESTERDAY
For we were born *y*...................Job 8:9
a thousand years are like *y* .... Ps 90:4
Jesus Christ is the same *y* and ..... Heb 13:8

YIELD
the land will give its *y* .... Lev 26:4
of the righteous will *y* fruit....... Prov 12:12
of the field will *y* their fruit...... Ezek 34:27

YIELDED
which *y* a harvest of fruit..........Ps 107:37

YIELDING
plants *y* seeds and trees........... Gen 1:11
He bears fruit, *y* a hundred.......Matt 13:23

YOKE
tear off his *y* from your neck .....Gen 27:40
place an iron *y* on your neck.....Deut 28:48
For their oppressive *y* .... Isa 9:4
good for a man to bear the *y* ......Lam 3:27
Take my *y* on you and learn ......Matt 11:29
who are under the *y* as slaves ......1 Tim 6:1

YOU ARE THE CHRIST
Y, the Son of the living God ......Matt 16:16
tell us if *y*, the Son of God.......Matt 26:63
Peter answered him, "*Y* ....Mark 8:29
and said, "If *y*, tell us.............Luke 22:67
If *y*, tell us plainly.................John 10:24
Yes, Lord, I believe that *y*......... John 11:27

YOUNG
I was once *y* ....Ps 37:25
where she can protect her *y*.........Ps 84:3
y person maintain a pure life ....Ps 119:9
glory of *y* men is their strength .. Prov 20:29
while you are *y*....................Eccl 11:9
their *y* will lie down together........ Isa 11:7
for I am too *y*.......................Jer 1:6
I am too *y*........................Jer 1:7
your *y* men will see visions ....Joel 2:28
on you because you are *y*.........1 Tim 4:12
I am writing to you, *y* people ......1 John 2:13

YOUNGER
those who are *y* than I..............Job 30:1
the *y* son gathered together all...Luke 15:13
you who are *y* ....1 Pet 5:5

YOUNGEST
you must become like the *y* .....Luke 22:26

YOURS
For the battle is not *y*...........2 Chr 20:15
Take what is *y* and go........... Matt 20:14

YOUTH
of the LORD from my *y* ....1 Kgs 18:12
against me the sins of my *y*.........Ps 25:7
wife you married in your *y* ....Prov 5:18
for *y* and the prime of life .... Eccl 11:10
Creator in the days of your *y* .... Eccl 12:1
you experienced in your *y* .... Isa 54:4
remember the days of your *y*.....Ezek 16:22
to the wife he took in his *y* ....Mal 2:15
all these laws since my *y* .... Mark 10:20
all these laws since my *y* ....Luke 18:21
if she is past the bloom of *y* ...... 1 Cor 7:36

YOUTHFUL
keep away from *y* passions...... 2 Tim 2:22

YOUTHS
I discerned among the *y*...........Prov 7:7
Even *y* get tired and weary ....Isa 40:30

Z

ZABAD
See JOZABAD

ZACCHAEUS
Wealthy tax collector converted to Christ,
Luke 19:1–10

ZECHARIAH
Father of John the Baptist, Luke 1:5–17.

ZADOK
Co-priest with Abiathar; remains loyal to
David, 2 Sam 15:24–29; 20:25
Rebuked by David, 2 Sam 19:11–12
Does not follow Adonijah; anoints
Solomon, 1 Kgs 1:8–45
Takes Abiathar's place, 1 Kgs 2:35

ZALMUNNA
Midianite king, Judg 8:4–21

ZAPHON
resembles the peaks of *Z*............Ps 48:2

ZAREPHATH
Town of Sidon where Elijah revives widow's
son, 1 Kgs 17:8–24; Luke 4:26

ZEAL
z of the LORD of Heaven's Armies..2 Kgs 19:31
My *z* consumes me.............Ps 119:139
to have *z* without knowledge......Prov 19:2
Z for your house will devour ...... John 2:17
Do not lag in *z*....................Rom 12:11
and your *z* to participate ....2 Cor 9:2

ZEALOUS
he has been *z* for his God........ Num 25:13
I will be *z* for my holy name ..... Ezek 39:25
testify that they are *z* for God .....Rom 10:2

ZEBAH
King of Midian killed by Gideon,
Judg 8:4–28

ZEBEDEE
Galilean fisherman; father of James and
John, Matt 4:21–22

ZEBULUN
Sixth son of Jacob and Leah, Gen 30:19–20
Prophecy concerning, Gen 49:13
—Tribe of:
Numbered, Num 1:30–31; 26:27
Territory assigned to, Josh 19:10–16
Joins Gideon in battle, Judg 6:34–35
Some respond to Hezekiah's reforms,
2 Chr 30:10–18
Christ visits territory of, Matt 4:13–16

ZECHARIAH
King of Israel; last ruler of Jehu's dynasty,
2 Kgs 15:8–12
—Postexilic prophet and priest, Ezra 5:1;
Zech 1:1, 7

ZEDEKIAH
Last king of Judah; uncle and successor
of Jehoiachin; reigns wickedly,
2 Kgs 24:17–19; 2 Chr 36:10
Rebels against Nebuchadnezzar,
2 Chr 36:11–13
Denounced by Jeremiah, Jer 34:1–22
Consults Jeremiah, Jer 37–38
Captured and taken to Babylon,
2 Kgs 25:1–7; Jer 39:1–7

ZELOPHEHAD
Manassite whose five daughters secure
female rights, Num 27:1–7

ZEPHANIAH
Author of Zephaniah, Zeph 1:1
—Priest and friend of Jeremiah during
Zedekiah's reign, Jer 21:1

ZERUBBABEL
Descendant of David, 1 Chr 3:1–19
Leader of Jewish exiles, Neh 7:6–7;
Hag 2:21–23
Rebuilds the temple, Ezra 3:1–10;
Zech 4:1–14

ZIBA
Saul's servant, 2 Sam 9:9
Befriends David, 2 Sam 16:1–4
Accused of deception by Mephibosheth,
2 Sam 19:17–30

ZIKLAG
City on the border of Judah, Josh 15:1, 31
Held by David, 1 Sam 27:6
Overthrown by Amalekites, 1 Sam 30:1–31

ZILPAH
Leah's maid, Gen 29:24
Mother of Gad and Asher, Gen 30:9–13

ZIMRI
Simeonite prince slain by Phinehas,
Num 25:6–14
—King of Israel for seven days,
1 Kgs 16:8–20

ZIN
Wilderness through which the Israelites
passed, Num 20:1
Border between Judah and Edom,
Josh 15:1–3

ZION
the City of David (that is, *Z* ....1 Kgs 8:1
the City of David (that is, *Z* ....2 Chr 5:2
who rules in *Z* ....Ps 9:11
Mount *Z* resembles the peaks.......Ps 48:2
Because you favor *Z*.................Ps 51:18
For God will deliver *Z* ....Ps 69:35
when the LORD rebuilds *Z*........Ps 102:16
the name of the LORD in *Z*........Ps 102:21
in the LORD are like Mount *Z*......Ps 125:1
restored the well-being of *Z*......Ps 126:1
the LORD has chosen *Z* ....Ps 132:13
weep when we remember *Z*........Ps 137:1
Z will be freed by justice............Isa 1:27
Z will be the center for moral ......Isa 2:3
My people who live in *Z*..........Isa 10:24
O citizens of *Z*.....................Isa 12:6
will rule on Mount *Z*..............Isa 24:23
I am laying a stone in *Z*..........Isa 28:16
to do battle on Mount *Z*............Isa 31:4
enter *Z* with a happy shout........Isa 35:10

The virgin daughter *Z* despises ....Isa 37:22
I will save *Z*........................Isa 46:13
the LORD will console *Z* ....Isa 51:3
enter *Z* with a happy shout........Isa 51:11
A protector comes to *Z*............Isa 59:20
Z of the Holy One of Israel ....Isa 60:14
Let us go to *Z* to worship............Jer 31:6
has made those in *Z* forget.........Lam 2:6
Blow the trumpet in *Z*...............Joel 2:1
is the LORD who dwells in *Z* ....Joel 3:21
Mount *Z* there will be a remnant..Obad 1:17
instruction will proceed from *Z* .....Mic 4:2
Daughter *Z*! Shout out............ Zeph 3:14
more the LORD will comfort *Z*..... Zech 1:17
Z my daughter..................... Zech 2:10
people of *Z*...................... John 12:15
I am laying in *Z* a stone........... Rom 9:33
Deliverer will come out of *Z*...... Rom 11:26
I lay in *Z* a stone ....1 Pet 2:6

ZION, MOUNT
See MOUNT ZION

ZION'S
But it is said of *Z* residents .... Ps 87:5

ZIPPORAH
Daughter of Jethro; wife of Moses,
Exod 18:1–2

ZOAR
Ancient city of Canaan originally named
Bela, Gen 14:2, 8
Spared destruction at Lot's request,
Gen 19:20–23

ZOPHAR
Naamathite; friend of Job, Job 2:11

NET Topical Index

Abortion: Exod 21:22–25; Pss 127:3–5; 139:13–16; Isa 46:3; 49:1; Jer 1:5; Luke 1:41; Gal 1:15

Abuse of Authority: Num 20:10–13; Pss 9:9; 82:3; 1 Cor 9:18; 1 Pet 5:3

Abuse, Physical: Exod 2:11–12; Judg 16:21; Pss 9:9; 82:3; 1 Cor 6:19–20

Abuse, Sexual: Gen 19:5–9, 31–38; Pss 9:9; 82:3; 1 Cor 6:19–20

Abuse, Substance: Prov 20:1; 23:21, 29–35; 31:4–5; John 8:36; Rom 12:1; Phil 4:13; 1 Cor 6:19–20; 10:13; Eph 5:18; 1 Pet 4:7 (*see also* Self-Care)

Acceptance of God: Gen 4:7; John 6:37; Rom 15:7; 1 Thess 2:4

Acceptance of Others: Matt 7:1–5; Rom 15:7; Gal 1:10; 1 Thess 2:4

Advice: 1 Kgs 12:6–11; Prov 11:14; 12:15; 19:20; 24:6

Alcohol: Eccl 9:7; Ps 104:14–15; Prov 20:1; Isa 5:11, 22; Luke 21:34; Rom 13:11–14; Gal 5:19–21; Eph 5:18; 1 Tim 5:23; 1 Pet 4:3 (*see also* Abuse, Substance)

Ambition, Improper: Matt 18:1–6; 20:20–28; Mark 12:38–40; Luke 9:25; 1 Cor 3:3–8; Phil 1:14–17; 2:3

Ambition, Proper: Matt 6:33; Rom 15:17–20; 1 Cor 12:31; 2 Cor 5:9–10; Phil 3:12–14

Anger: Ps 37:8; Prov 12:16; 14:17, 29; 15:1; 22:24–25; 29:22; Eccl 7:9; Matt 5:22–24; Gal 5:19–20; Eph 4:26–27, 31–32; Col 3:8; Jas 1:19–20 (*see also* Forgiving Others; Hatred)

Anorexia: *See* Self-Care

Anxiety: Ps 94:18–19; Isa 45:5–7; Luke 12:26–29; Phil 4:6

Appearance, Physical: 1 Sam 16:7; Ps 139:14; Prov 31:30; Matt 6:25–33; 1 Tim 2:9–10; 1 Pet 3:3–4

Arrogance: 1 Sam 2:3; Prov 8:13; 27:2; Isa 13:11; Rom 12:3; Jas 4:16 (*see also* Pride; Vanity)

Asking Questions: Deut 4:29; Matt 7:7; 1 Cor 13:12; 14:33

Assurance of Salvation: Ps 37:23–24; Jer 32:40–41; Luke 18:18–30; John 5:24; 10:27–30; Rom 8:33–39; 2 Tim 1:12; 1 John 5:13

Authority, Human: Exod 20:12; Prov 29:2; Acts 5:29; Rom 13:1–2; Titus 3:1; Heb 13:17; 1 Pet 2:13

Baptism: Matt 28:19–20; Mark 16:15–16; Acts 2:38; Rom 6:3–4; Eph 4:5

Blessings: Lev 26:3–5; Num 6:24–26; Pss 5:12; 24:3–6; Jas 1:17, 25

Bullying: Lev 19:18; Deut 31:6; Prov 21:23; Matt 5:43–48; Luke 10:25–37; Rom 12:18–20; Eph 4:29; 2 Tim 1:7

Burdens: Ps 55:22; Matt 11:28–29; Gal 6:2; Phil 4:6

Career: Gen 2:15; Ps 90:17; Prov 13:22; 16:3; 18:9; 22:29; Eccl 3:12–13; 1 Cor 10:31; Eph 4:28; Col 3:17, 23; Jas 1:5 (*see also* Work)

Choices: *See* Decisions

Comfort: *See* God's Comfort

Compassion: Exod 34:6; Matt 15:32; Mark 1:40–45; 6:30–44; Luke 8:40–56; 10:25–37; Eph 4:32; Col 3:12–14; 1 John 3:16–20

Complaining: Phil 2:14; 1 Thess 5:18; Jas 5:9; 1 Pet 4:9

Confidence: Ps 20:7; Prov 3:26; Isa 32:15–17; Rom 8:38–39; 2 Cor 3:4–5; Heb 10:35; 13:6

Contentment: Prov 15:16; Luke 12:15; 2 Cor 12:10; Phil 4:11–13; 1 Tim 6:6–8; Heb 13:5

Courage: Deut 31:6; Josh 1:9; 1 Sam 17:34–37; Esth 4:15–16; Pss 16:8; 27:1–14; 31:24; 46:1–3; Prov 3:24–26; 28:1; Isa 41:10; John 16:33; Rom 8:35–39; Eph 6:10; 2 Tim 1:7; 1 John 4:18

Creation Care: Gen 1:26–28; 2:15; Lev 25:23–24; Neh 9:6; Pss 24:1–2; 89:11; Isa 24:4–6; Luke 12:6; John 1:3; Rom 8:18–22; 1 Cor 4:2; Col 1:16–17; Jas 3:7

Cutting: *See* Self-Care

Death, Fear of: *See* Fear of Death

Decisions: Josh 24:14–15; Neh 1:4; Pss 37:5; 119:105; Prov 3:5–6, 13–18; 16:1–3; 18:15; Jer 33:3; John 15:16; Phil 4:6–7; 2 Tim 3:14; Jas 1:5; 4:17

Depression: Pss 34:17–18; 42:5–11; 43:5; 143:7–8; Prov 12:25; Isa 40:31; 41:10; Jon. 2:2; Mark 10:27; John 10:10; Phil 4:6–7; 2 Thess 2:16–17; 1 Pet 5:6–7 (*see also* Self-Care)

Disabilities: Gen 1:26–27; 2 Sam 9:1–13; Isa 35:3–6; Matt 20:29–34; John 5:1–18; 9:1–12; 1 Cor 15:51–53; 2 Cor 12:7–9; Phil 3:20–21

Discernment: 1 Kgs 3:9; Ps 119:125; Hos 14:9; John 7:24; Acts 17:11; Phil 1:9–10. 1 Thess 5:21–22; 2 Tim 2:7; Heb 4:12; 5:14; Jas 1:5; 1 John 4:1, 6

Discipline, Corrective: Deut 8:5; Job 5:17; Ps 94:12–13; Prov 6:23; 10:17; 12:1; 15:5; Heb 12:11; Rev 3:19

Discipline, Personal: Prov 22:6; 25:28; 1 Cor 9:24–27; 1 Tim 4:7–11; Titus 1:8; 1 Pet 5:8

Discouragement: Deut 31:8; Ps 142:1–7; John 16:33; Rom 8:31; 15:13; 1 Cor 15:58; 2 Cor 12:9; Gal 6:9; 1 Pet 5:10

Discrimination: Mal 3:5; Acts 10:34; Gal 3:26–28; 5:14; Col 3:25; Jas 2:1–9

Diversity: Ps 117:1–2; Dan 7:14; Matt 28:19–20; Rom 12:4–8; 1 Cor 12:12–30; Rev 7:9–10

Divorce: *See* Marriage and Divorce

God's Promises: Deut 15:6; 2 Cor 1:20; 1 Thess 5:24; Heb 6:13–15; 10:23, 36; 2 Pet 3:9

God's Protection: Gen 15:1; Deut 31:6; Pss 3:3; 4:8; 5:11–12; 28:7; 46:1; 118:6–9; Prov 1:33; 2:8; 18:10; Isa 41:10; 54:17; Nah 1:7; Rom 8:31; Eph 6:10–18; 2 Thess 3:3; Heb 13:6; 1 John 5:18

God's Provision: Gen 9:3; Pss 23:1–6; 65:9; 68:10; 145:15–17; Mal 3:10; Matt 6:8, 25–26, 31–33; 7:7, 11; Rom 8:32; 2 Cor 9:8; Phil 4:19; 1 Tim 6:17; Jas 1:17

Gossip: Exod 23:1; Lev 19:16; Prov 4:24; 11:13; 16:28; 18:8; 20:19; 26:20, 22; Rom 1:29; 2 Cor 12:20; Eph 4:29; 1 Tim 5:13; Jas 1:26

Grace: *See* God's Grace

Greed: Ps 10:3; Prov 1:18–19; 28:25; 1 Cor 6:9–11; Eph 4:19 (*see also* Contentment; Generosity; Selfishness)

Grief: Job 2:13; Pss 30:11; 34:18; 73:26; 147:3; Isa 40:1–31; Jer 33:6; Lam 3:32; Matt 5:4; 26:38; John 11:17–44; 16:22, 33; 2 Cor 1:3–11; 1 Thess 4:14–18; Rev 21:3–4

Guidance: *See* God's Guidance

Guilt: Pss 19:12–13; 38:1–16; 51:1–10; Rom 8:1; Eph 2:8; 1 John 1:9 (*see also* God's Forgiveness)

Happiness: 1 Sam 2:1; Pss 16:11; 32:11; 37:4; 100:2; 118:24; Prov 15:30; 17:22; Eccl 3:12–13; Isa 12:3; 51:11; Hab 3:18; Rom 15:13; Gal 5:22; Phil 4:4; 1 Thess 2:19 (*see also* Joy)

Hatred: Lev 19:17; Prov 10:12, 18; 26:24–26; Matt 5:43–45; Rom 12:9; Eph 4:31; 1 John 2:9–11; 4:20 (*see also* Anger)

Heaven: 1 Kgs 8:30; 2 Kgs 2:11; Isa 25:8; 66:1; Matt 3:16–17; 6:19–21; Luke 24:51; John 14:1–3; 2 Cor 5:1; Phil 3:20; Col 1:5; Heb 11:16; 2 Pet 3:13; Rev 7:15–17; 21:4; 22:1–5

Hell: Pss 9:17; 86:13; Dan 12:2; Matt 8:12; 10:28; 13:50; 25:46; Luke 16:19–31; 2 Thess 1:9; Heb 9:27; 2 Pet 2:4; Rev 20:10–15; 21:8

Helping Others: Prov 3:27; 21:13; Mic 6:8; Matt 5:42; 25:37–40; Gal 6:2; Phil 2:4; Heb 13:16; 1 John 3:17

Homosexuality: Gen 19:1–29; Lev 18:22; 20:13; Judg 19:22; Rom 1:26–27; 1 Cor 6:9–11; 1 Tim 1:9–10; Jude v. 7 (*see also* Gender)

Honesty: Exod 20:16; Lev 19:35–36; Ps 34:13; Prov 11:3; 12:17, 22; Ezek 45:10–11; Eph 4:15, 25 (*see also* Integrity; Truth)

Hope: 2 Sam 22:7; Pss 9:18; 33:18, 22; 43:5; Prov 24:14; Isa 40:31; Lam 3:21–22; Rom 8:24–25, 28; 15:13; 2 Thess 2:16–17; Titus 1:1–2; Heb 11:1; 1 Pet 1:3

Humility: Prov 11:2; 18:12; 22:4; Mic 6:8; Zeph 2:3; Matt 16:24; 18:4; Luke 14:11; Rom 12:3, 16; Phil 2:1–11; Col 3:12; Jas 4:8–10

Hurt: *See* Pain and Suffering

Hypocrisy: Prov 11:9; Isa 29:13; 58:3–7; Jer 7:8–11; Matt 7:1–5; Luke 6:46; Rom 2:3; Titus 1:16; Jas 1:26; 1 John 4:20 (*see also* Integrity)

Identity: Gen 1:27; Ps 139:13–15; Luke 12:6–7; John 15:15; Acts 17:28; Rom 8:15; 14:8; 1 Cor 12:27; 2 Cor 5:17; Gal 2:20; 3:28; Eph 2:10; 1 Pet 2:9; 1 John 3:1

Idolatry: Exod 20:3–6; Lev 19:4; Deut 4:23–24; Ps 106:19–21, 36–43; Isa 31:6–7; 44:9–20; Jer 10:2–8; 1 Cor 10:14; Gal 4:8; Col 3:5; 1 John 5:21

Integrity: 2 Chr 26:4; Job 1:1; Pss 25:21; 78:70–72; Prov 10:9; 11:3; 19:1; 28:6; Dan 6:4–5; 2 Cor 8:21; Col 3:23; 1 Pet 3:16 (*see also* Honesty; Truth)

Intimidation: Deut 31:6; Ps 91:14; Isa 41:10; Rom 8:31; Phil 4:13; 1 Tim 4:12; 2 Tim 1:7

Jealousy: Gen 37:1–36; Prov 14:30; 23:17; 24:1; 1 Cor 13:4; Gal 5:26; 1 Pet 2:1; Jas 3:16 (*see also* Contentment; Envy)

Joy: Ezra 3:10–13; Neh 8:10; Pss 16:11; 118:24; Prov 15:30; Isa 51:11; 62:5; Hab 3:18; Zeph 3:17; John 16:24; Rom 12:12; 15:13; Gal 5:22; Phil 4:4; 1 Thess 2:19; Jas 1:2 (*see also* Happiness)

Judging Others: Num 12:1–3; 2 Chr 19:7; Prov 31:9; Matt 7:1–5; Luke 6:37; John 7:24; Rom 14:13; Jas 4:11–12

Judgment: *See* God's Judgment

Justice: *See* God's Justice; Social Justice

Kindness: Ruth 3:10; 2 Sam 9:1–13; 2 Kgs 4:1–7; Prov 11:17; Zech 7:9–10; 1 Cor 13:4; Gal 6:10; Eph 4:32; Col 3:12

Knowing God: Exod 3:1–22; Prov 8:17; Jer 9:23–24; John 14:6; 17:3; Phil 3:10; Jas 4:8; 1 John 1:5–6; 4:12

Knowing God's Will: Ps 119:10, 105; Prov 3:5–6; 8:17; 19:21; Mic 6:8; Matt 6:33; Rom 12:2; 1 Tim 2:3–4; 1 Thess 4:3–5; 5:18; 1 Pet 2:15

Laziness: Gen 2:15; Prov 6:6–11; 10:4; 12:24; 13:4; 18:9; 19:15; Eccl 9:10; Col 3:23; 2 Thess 3:10–12 (*see also* Work)

Leadership: Exod 18:21; 2 Sam 8:15; 2 Kgs 15:2–5; 23:3; 2 Chr 19:5–7; Esth 10:3; Prov 11:14; Matt 20:26–28; John 13:12–15; Phil 2:3; 1 Tim 3:1–7; 4:12; Titus 1:7–9

Learning: *See* Education

Listening: Ps 46:10; Prov 1:33; 18:13; 25:12; Jas 1:19, 22

Loneliness: Deut 31:6; Pss 25:16; 38:9–15; 68:6; 145:18; Isa 41:10; Eccl 4:10–11; Hag 1:13; Matt 28:20; John 14:18; Heb 13:5; Jas 4:8 (*see also* God's Presence)

Love: Rom 12:9; 1 Cor 13:4–8, 13; Col 3:14; 1 Pet 4:8; 1 John 4:18 (*see also* God's Love)

Loving God: Deut 6:5; Ps 18:1–3; Eccl 12:1; Jer 9:23–24; Matt 22:37; John 21:15–19; 1 John 4:20–21

Loving Others: Lev 19:18; Prov 10:12; Matt 5:43–44; Luke 10:25–37; John 13:34–35; 15:13; Acts 9:20–31; 11; 1 Cor 16:14; Eph 5:1–2; 29–30; Jas 2:8; 1 Pet 4:8; 1 John 4:7–12, 19–21

© 2025 by Thomas Nelson

One-Year Bible Reading Plan

God's Word is his personal message of love to you today. The best way to grow as a Christian and get to know God in a more personal way is to spend time in his Word. Here is a plan for you if you want to read through the entire Bible in one year.

Read three chapters each day, Monday through Saturday, and five chapters on Sunday.

Genesis
☐1 ☐2 ☐3 ☐4 ☐5 ☐6
☐7 ☐8 ☐9 ☐10 ☐11 ☐12
☐13 ☐14 ☐15 ☐16 ☐17 ☐18
☐19 ☐20 ☐21 ☐22 ☐23 ☐24
☐25 ☐26 ☐27 ☐28 ☐29 ☐30
☐31 ☐32 ☐33 ☐34 ☐35 ☐36
☐37 ☐38 ☐39 ☐40 ☐41 ☐42
☐43 ☐44 ☐45 ☐46 ☐47 ☐48
☐49 ☐50

Exodus
☐1 ☐2 ☐3 ☐4 ☐5 ☐6
☐7 ☐8 ☐9 ☐10 ☐11 ☐12
☐13 ☐14 ☐15 ☐16 ☐17 ☐18
☐19 ☐20 ☐21 ☐22 ☐23 ☐24
☐25 ☐26 ☐27 ☐28 ☐29 ☐30
☐31 ☐32 ☐33 ☐34 ☐35 ☐36
☐37 ☐38 ☐39 ☐40

Leviticus
☐1 ☐2 ☐3 ☐4 ☐5 ☐6
☐7 ☐8 ☐9 ☐10 ☐11 ☐12
☐13 ☐14 ☐15 ☐16 ☐17 ☐18
☐19 ☐20 ☐21 ☐22 ☐23 ☐24
☐25 ☐26 ☐27

Numbers
☐1 ☐2 ☐3 ☐4 ☐5 ☐6
☐7 ☐8 ☐9 ☐10 ☐11 ☐12
☐13 ☐14 ☐15 ☐16 ☐17 ☐18
☐19 ☐20 ☐21 ☐22 ☐23 ☐24
☐25 ☐26 ☐27 ☐28 ☐29 ☐30
☐31 ☐32 ☐33 ☐34 ☐35 ☐36

Deuteronomy
☐1 ☐2 ☐3 ☐4 ☐5 ☐6
☐7 ☐8 ☐9 ☐10 ☐11 ☐12
☐13 ☐14 ☐15 ☐16 ☐17 ☐18
☐19 ☐20 ☐21 ☐22 ☐23 ☐24
☐25 ☐26 ☐27 ☐28 ☐29 ☐30
☐31 ☐32 ☐33 ☐34

Joshua
☐1 ☐2 ☐3 ☐4 ☐5 ☐6
☐7 ☐8 ☐9 ☐10 ☐11 ☐12
☐13 ☐14 ☐15 ☐16 ☐17 ☐18
☐19 ☐20 ☐21 ☐22 ☐23 ☐24

Judges
☐1 ☐2 ☐3 ☐4 ☐5 ☐6
☐7 ☐8 ☐9 ☐10 ☐11 ☐12
☐13 ☐14 ☐15 ☐16 ☐17 ☐18
☐19 ☐20 ☐21

Ruth
☐1 ☐2 ☐3 ☐4

1 Samuel
☐1 ☐2 ☐3 ☐4 ☐5 ☐6
☐7 ☐8 ☐9 ☐10 ☐11 ☐12
☐13 ☐14 ☐15 ☐16 ☐17 ☐18
☐19 ☐20 ☐21 ☐22 ☐23 ☐24
☐25 ☐26 ☐27 ☐28 ☐29 ☐30
☐31

2 Samuel
☐1 ☐2 ☐3 ☐4 ☐5 ☐6
☐7 ☐8 ☐9 ☐10 ☐11 ☐12
☐13 ☐14 ☐15 ☐16 ☐17 ☐18
☐19 ☐20 ☐21 ☐22 ☐23 ☐24

1 Kings
☐1 ☐2 ☐3 ☐4 ☐5 ☐6
☐7 ☐8 ☐9 ☐10 ☐11 ☐12
☐13 ☐14 ☐15 ☐16 ☐17 ☐18
☐19 ☐20 ☐21 ☐22

2 Kings
☐1 ☐2 ☐3 ☐4 ☐5 ☐6
☐7 ☐8 ☐9 ☐10 ☐11 ☐12
☐13 ☐14 ☐15 ☐16 ☐17 ☐18
☐19 ☐20 ☐21 ☐22 ☐23 ☐23
☐24 ☐25

1 Chronicles
☐1 ☐2 ☐3 ☐4 ☐5 ☐6
☐7 ☐8 ☐9 ☐10 ☐11 ☐12
☐13 ☐14 ☐15 ☐16 ☐17 ☐18
☐19 ☐20 ☐21 ☐22 ☐23 ☐24
☐25 ☐26 ☐27 ☐28 ☐29

2 Chronicles
☐1 ☐2 ☐3 ☐4 ☐5 ☐6
☐7 ☐8 ☐9 ☐10 ☐11 ☐12
☐13 ☐14 ☐15 ☐16 ☐17 ☐18
☐19 ☐20 ☐21 ☐22 ☐23 ☐24
☐25 ☐26 ☐27 ☐28 ☐29 ☐30
☐31 ☐32 ☐33 ☐34 ☐35 ☐36

Ezra
☐1 ☐2 ☐3 ☐4 ☐5 ☐6
☐7 ☐8 ☐9 ☐10

Nehemiah
☐1 ☐2 ☐3 ☐4 ☐5 ☐6
☐7 ☐8 ☐9 ☐10 ☐11 ☐12
☐13

Esther
☐1 ☐2 ☐3 ☐4 ☐5 ☐6
☐7 ☐8 ☐9 ☐10

Job
☐1 ☐2 ☐3 ☐4 ☐5 ☐6
☐7 ☐8 ☐9 ☐10 ☐11 ☐12
☐13 ☐14 ☐15 ☐16 ☐17 ☐18
☐19 ☐20 ☐21 ☐22 ☐23 ☐24
☐25 ☐26 ☐27 ☐28 ☐29 ☐30
☐31 ☐32 ☐33 ☐34 ☐35 ☐36
☐37 ☐38 ☐39 ☐40 ☐41 ☐42

Psalms
☐1 ☐2 ☐3 ☐4 ☐5
☐6 ☐7 ☐8 ☐9 ☐10
☐11 ☐12 ☐13 ☐14 ☐15
☐16 ☐17 ☐18 ☐19 ☐20
☐21 ☐22 ☐23 ☐24 ☐25
☐26 ☐27 ☐28 ☐29 ☐30
☐31 ☐32 ☐33 ☐34 ☐35
☐36 ☐37 ☐38 ☐39 ☐40
☐41 ☐42 ☐43 ☐44 ☐45
☐46 ☐47 ☐48 ☐49 ☐50
☐51 ☐52 ☐53 ☐54 ☐55
☐56 ☐57 ☐58 ☐59 ☐60
☐61 ☐62 ☐63 ☐64 ☐65
☐66 ☐67 ☐68 ☐69 ☐70
☐71 ☐72 ☐73 ☐74 ☐75
☐76 ☐77 ☐78 ☐79 ☐80
☐81 ☐82 ☐83 ☐84 ☐85
☐86 ☐87 ☐88 ☐89 ☐90
☐91 ☐92 ☐93 ☐94 ☐95
☐96 ☐97 ☐98 ☐99 ☐100
☐101 ☐102 ☐103 ☐104 ☐105
☐106 ☐107 ☐108 ☐109 ☐110
☐111 ☐112 ☐113 ☐114 ☐115
☐116 ☐117 ☐118 ☐119 ☐120
☐121 ☐122 ☐123 ☐124 ☐125
☐126 ☐127 ☐128 ☐129 ☐130
☐131 ☐132 ☐133 ☐134 ☐135
☐136 ☐137 ☐138 ☐139 ☐140
☐141 ☐142 ☐143 ☐144 ☐145
☐146 ☐147 ☐148 ☐149 ☐150

Proverbs
☐1 ☐2 ☐3 ☐4 ☐5 ☐6
☐7 ☐8 ☐9 ☐10 ☐11 ☐12
☐13 ☐14 ☐15 ☐16 ☐17 ☐18
☐19 ☐20 ☐21 ☐22 ☐23 ☐24
☐25 ☐26 ☐27 ☐28 ☐29 ☐30
☐31

Ecclesiastes
☐1 ☐2 ☐3 ☐4 ☐5 ☐6
☐7 ☐8 ☐9 ☐10 ☐11 ☐12

Song of Solomon
☐1 ☐2 ☐3 ☐4 ☐5 ☐6
☐7 ☐8

Isaiah
☐1 ☐2 ☐3 ☐4 ☐5 ☐6
☐7 ☐8 ☐9 ☐10 ☐11 ☐12
☐13 ☐14 ☐15 ☐16 ☐17 ☐18
☐19 ☐20 ☐21 ☐22 ☐23 ☐24
☐25 ☐26 ☐27 ☐28 ☐29 ☐30
☐31 ☐32 ☐33 ☐34 ☐35 ☐36
☐37 ☐38 ☐39 ☐40 ☐41 ☐42
☐43 ☐44 ☐45 ☐46 ☐47 ☐48
☐49 ☐50 ☐51 ☐52 ☐53 ☐54
☐55 ☐56 ☐57 ☐58 ☐59 ☐60
☐61 ☐62 ☐63 ☐64 ☐65 ☐66

Jeremiah
☐1 ☐2 ☐3 ☐4 ☐5 ☐6
☐7 ☐8 ☐9 ☐10 ☐11 ☐12
☐13 ☐14 ☐15 ☐16 ☐17 ☐18
☐19 ☐20 ☐21 ☐22 ☐23 ☐24
☐25 ☐26 ☐27 ☐28 ☐29 ☐30
☐31 ☐32 ☐33 ☐34 ☐35 ☐36
☐37 ☐38 ☐39 ☐40 ☐41 ☐42
☐43 ☐44 ☐45 ☐46 ☐47 ☐48
☐49 ☐50 ☐51 ☐52

Lamentations
☐1 ☐2 ☐3 ☐4 ☐5

Ezekiel
☐1 ☐2 ☐3 ☐4 ☐5 ☐6
☐7 ☐8 ☐9 ☐10 ☐11 ☐12
☐13 ☐14 ☐15 ☐16 ☐17 ☐18
☐19 ☐20 ☐21 ☐22 ☐23 ☐24
☐25 ☐26 ☐27 ☐28 ☐29 ☐30
☐31 ☐32 ☐33 ☐34 ☐35 ☐36
☐37 ☐38 ☐39 ☐40 ☐41 ☐42
☐43 ☐44 ☐45 ☐46 ☐47 ☐48

Daniel
☐1 ☐2 ☐3 ☐4 ☐5 ☐6
☐7 ☐8 ☐9 ☐10 ☐11 ☐12

Hosea
☐1 ☐2 ☐3 ☐4 ☐5 ☐6
☐7 ☐8 ☐9 ☐10 ☐11 ☐12
☐13 ☐14

Joel
☐1 ☐2 ☐3

Amos
☐1 ☐2 ☐3 ☐4 ☐5 ☐6
☐7 ☐8 ☐9

Obadiah
☐1

Jonah
☐1 ☐2 ☐3 ☐4

Micah
☐1 ☐2 ☐3 ☐4 ☐5 ☐6
☐7

Nahum
☐1 ☐2 ☐3

Habakkuk
☐1 ☐2 ☐3

Zephaniah
☐1 ☐2 ☐3

Haggai
☐1 ☐2

Zechariah
☐1 ☐2 ☐3 ☐4 ☐5 ☐6
☐7 ☐8 ☐9 ☐10 ☐11 ☐12
☐13 ☐14

Malachi
☐1 ☐2 ☐3 ☐4

Matthew
☐1 ☐2 ☐3 ☐4 ☐5 ☐6
☐7 ☐8 ☐9 ☐10 ☐11 ☐12
☐13 ☐14 ☐15 ☐16 ☐17 ☐18
☐19 ☐20 ☐21 ☐22 ☐23 ☐24
☐25 ☐26 ☐27 ☐28

Mark
☐1 ☐2 ☐3 ☐4 ☐5 ☐6
☐7 ☐8 ☐9 ☐10 ☐11 ☐12
☐13 ☐14 ☐15 ☐16

Luke
☐1 ☐2 ☐3 ☐4 ☐5 ☐6
☐7 ☐8 ☐9 ☐10 ☐11 ☐12
☐13 ☐14 ☐15 ☐16 ☐17 ☐18
☐19 ☐20 ☐21 ☐22 ☐23 ☐24

John
☐1 ☐2 ☐3 ☐4 ☐5 ☐6
☐7 ☐8 ☐9 ☐10 ☐11 ☐12
☐13 ☐14 ☐15 ☐16 ☐17 ☐18
☐19 ☐20 ☐21

Acts
☐1 ☐2 ☐3 ☐4 ☐5 ☐6
☐7 ☐8 ☐9 ☐10 ☐11 ☐12
☐13 ☐14 ☐15 ☐16 ☐17 ☐18
☐19 ☐20 ☐21 ☐22 ☐23 ☐24
☐25 ☐26 ☐27 ☐28

Romans
☐1 ☐2 ☐3 ☐4 ☐5 ☐6
☐7 ☐8 ☐9 ☐10 ☐11 ☐12
☐13 ☐14 ☐15 ☐16

1 Corinthians
☐1 ☐2 ☐3 ☐4 ☐5 ☐6
☐7 ☐8 ☐9 ☐10 ☐11 ☐12
☐13 ☐14 ☐15 ☐16

2 Corinthians
☐1 ☐2 ☐3 ☐4 ☐5 ☐6
☐7 ☐8 ☐9 ☐10 ☐11 ☐12
☐13

Galatians
☐1 ☐2 ☐3 ☐4 ☐5 ☐6

Ephesians
☐1 ☐2 ☐3 ☐4 ☐5 ☐6

Philippians
☐1 ☐2 ☐3 ☐4

Colossians
☐1 ☐2 ☐3 ☐4

1 Thessalonians
☐1 ☐2 ☐3 ☐4 ☐5

2 Thessalonians
☐1 ☐2 ☐3

1 Timothy
☐1 ☐2 ☐3 ☐4 ☐5 ☐6

2 Timothy
☐1 ☐2 ☐3 ☐4

Titus
☐1 ☐2 ☐3

Philemon
☐1

Hebrews
☐1 ☐2 ☐3 ☐4 ☐5 ☐6
☐7 ☐8 ☐9 ☐10 ☐11 ☐12
☐13

James
☐1 ☐2 ☐3 ☐4 ☐5

1 Peter
☐1 ☐2 ☐3 ☐4 ☐5

2 Peter
☐1 ☐2 ☐3

1 John
☐1 ☐2 ☐3 ☐4 ☐5

2 John
☐1

3 John
☐1

Jude
☐1

Revelation
☐1 ☐2 ☐3 ☐4 ☐5 ☐6
☐7 ☐8 ☐9 ☐10 ☐11 ☐12
☐13 ☐14 ☐15 ☐16 ☐17 ☐18
☐19 ☐20 ☐21 ☐22

A NOTE REGARDING THE TYPE

This Bible was set in the Thomas Nelson NET Typeface, commissioned by Thomas Nelson Publishers, a division of HarperCollins Christian Publishing, and designed in Aarhus, Denmark by Klaus Krogh and Heidi Rand Sørensen of 2K/DENMARK. The letterforms take inspiration from the vision of modern scholarship, translation process, and accessibility for all readers that produced the New English Translation. The designers sought to reflect the modern process undertaken by leading scholars to create a biblical text with transparent translation choices led the design to this distinct typeface. The result is a typeface that represents the comprehensible nature of the translation for any reader of the Bible.

Black Sea
Troy
Hattusa
HITTITES
Taurus Mts.
Mycenae
Aegean Sea
Carchemish
PADDAN ARAM
Haran
Mt. Ararat
Araxes (Aras) R.
Caspian Sea
Lake Urmia
Nineveh
Asshur
Nuzi
Tigris R.
Knossos
Caphtor (Crete)
Kittim (Cyprus)
Ugarit
Aleppo
Ebla
Euphrates R.
Mari
BABYLONIANS
Gebal (Byblos)
Tadmor
ARABIA
Babylon
Nippur
Erech
Ur
Mediterranean Sea (The Great Sea)
Damascus
Hazor
Megiddo
Dothan
Shechem
Bethel
Ai
Gerar
Hebron
Zoar
Beer Sheba
Possible location of Sodom and Gomorrah
Possible location of biblical "Ur of the Chaldeans," where Abraham's migration began
Zoan (Tanis)
Sukkoth
On (Heliopolis)
Kadesh Barnea
Memphis (Noph)
EGYPTIANS
Sinai
Nile R.
Red Sea
Persian Gulf
10,000 ft
5000 ft
2000 ft
1000 ft
0 (sea level)
-1640 ft
3050 m
1525 m
610 m
305 m
0 (sea level)
-500 m
Maps by International Mapping.
Copyright © 2008 by Zondervan.
All rights reserved. NETv0223.
0   100 km.
0   100 miles
Abraham's journey
Map 1: WORLD OF THE PATRIARCHS

Map 2: EXODUS AND CONQUEST OF CANAAN

Maps by International Mapping.
Copyright © 2008 by Zondervan.
All rights reserved. NETv0223.

Map 4: KINGDOM OF DAVID AND SOLOMON

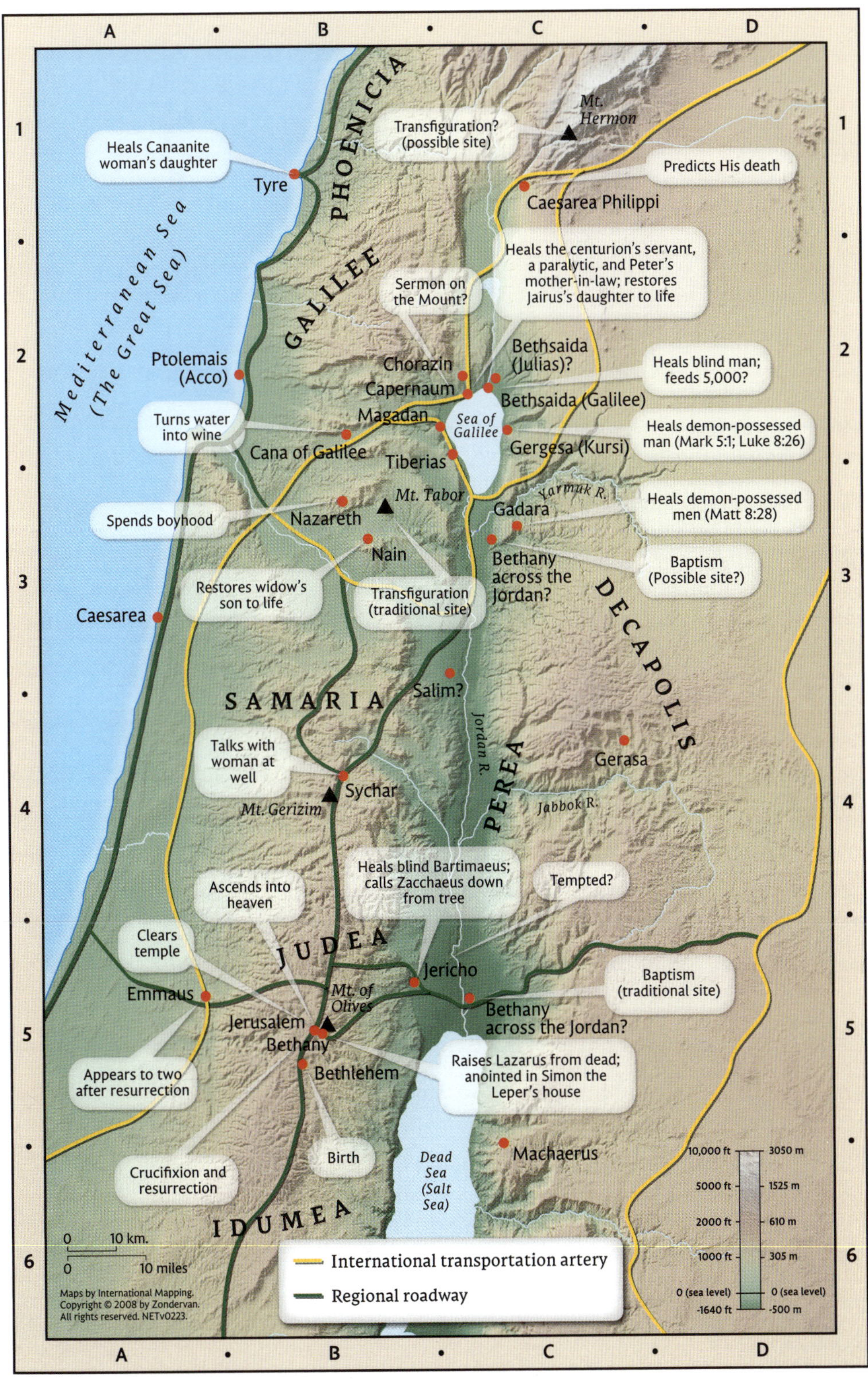
Heals Canaanite woman's daughter
Transfiguration? (possible site)
Mt. Hermon
Predicts His death
Tyre
PHOENICIA
Caesarea Philippi
Heals the centurion's servant, a paralytic, and Peter's mother-in-law; restores Jairus's daughter to life
GALILEE
Sermon on the Mount?
Mediterranean Sea (The Great Sea)
Bethsaida (Julias)?
Heals blind man; feeds 5,000?
Ptolemais (Acco)
Chorazin
Capernaum
Bethsaida (Galilee)
Turns water into wine
Magadan
Sea of Galilee
Heals demon-possessed man (Mark 5:1; Luke 8:26)
Cana of Galilee
Tiberias
Gergesa (Kursi)
Yarmuk R.
Mt. Tabor
Gadara
Heals demon-possessed men (Matt 8:28)
Spends boyhood
Nazareth
Bethany across the Jordan?
Baptism (Possible site?)
Nain
DECAPOLIS
Restores widow's son to life
Transfiguration (traditional site)
Caesarea
SAMARIA
Salim?
Jordan R.
Talks with woman at well
Gerasa
Mt. Gerizim
Sychar
PEREA
Jabbok R.
Heals blind Bartimaeus; calls Zacchaeus down from tree
Tempted?
Ascends into heaven
Clears temple
JUDEA
Jericho
Baptism (traditional site)
Emmaus
Mt. of Olives
Bethany across the Jordan?
Jerusalem
Bethany
Appears to two after resurrection
Bethlehem
Raises Lazarus from dead; anointed in Simon the Leper's house
Crucifixion and resurrection
Birth
Dead Sea (Salt Sea)
Machaerus
IDUMEA
10 km.
10 miles
International transportation artery
Regional roadway
10,000 ft   3050 m
5000 ft   1525 m
2000 ft   610 m
1000 ft   305 m
0 (sea level)   0 (sea level)
-1640 ft   -500 m
Maps by International Mapping. Copyright © 2008 by Zondervan. All rights reserved. NETv0223.

GALLIA
GERMANIA
ILLYRICUM
(DALMATIA)
ITALIA
Adriatic Sea
MACED
Corsica
Rome
Forum of Appius
Three Taverns
Puteoli
Berea
Sardinia
Tyrrhenian Sea
EPIRUS
Ionian Sea
ACHAIA
Rhegium
Sicily
Syracuse
NUMIDIA
AFRICA
Malta
Mediterranean Sea
(The Great Sea)
TRIPOLITANIA
CYR
First missionary journey (AD 46–48)
Second missionary journey (AD 49–52)
Third missionary journey (AD 53–57)
Trip to Rome (AD 59–60)
Maps by International Mapping.
Copyright © 2008 by Zondervan. All rights reserved. NETv0223.

DACIA
MOESIA
THRACE
Black Sea
10,000 ft   3050 m
5000 ft   1525 m
2000 ft   610 m
1000 ft   305 m
0 (sea level)   0 (sea level)
-1640 ft   -500 m
ONIA
Amphipolis
Thessalonica
Philippi
Neapolis
Apollonia?
Samothrace
BITHYNIA & PONTUS
GALATIA
CAPPADOCIA
Mt. Olympus
Troas
MYSIA
ASIA
COMMAGENE
Assos
Pergamum
Mitylene
Thyatira
LYCAONIA
Antioch (Pisidian)
Delphi
Chios
LYDIA
Sardis
Iconium
Aegean Sea
Smyrna
Philadelphia
PISIDIA
Euphrates R.
Athens
Ephesus
PAMPHYLIA
Derbe
Cenchrea
Samos
Laodicea
Colossae
Lystra
CILICIA
Corinth
Patmos
Miletus
LYCIA
Tarsus
Issus
SYRIA
Sparta
Cos
Attalia
Seleucia Pieria
Aleppo
Cnidus
Patara
Myra
Perga
Antioch
Crete
Rhodes
Cyprus
(Syrian)
Phoenix
Salmone
Lasea
Salamis
Claudia
Fair Havens
Paphos
PHOENICIA
ABILENE
Sidon
Mediterranean Sea
(The Great Sea)
Tyre
Damascus
Ptolemais
JUDEA
Caesarea
Jordan R.
ENAICA
Jerusalem
Dead Sea
ARABIA
EGYPT
Nile R.
0   200 km.
0   200 miles
Red Sea

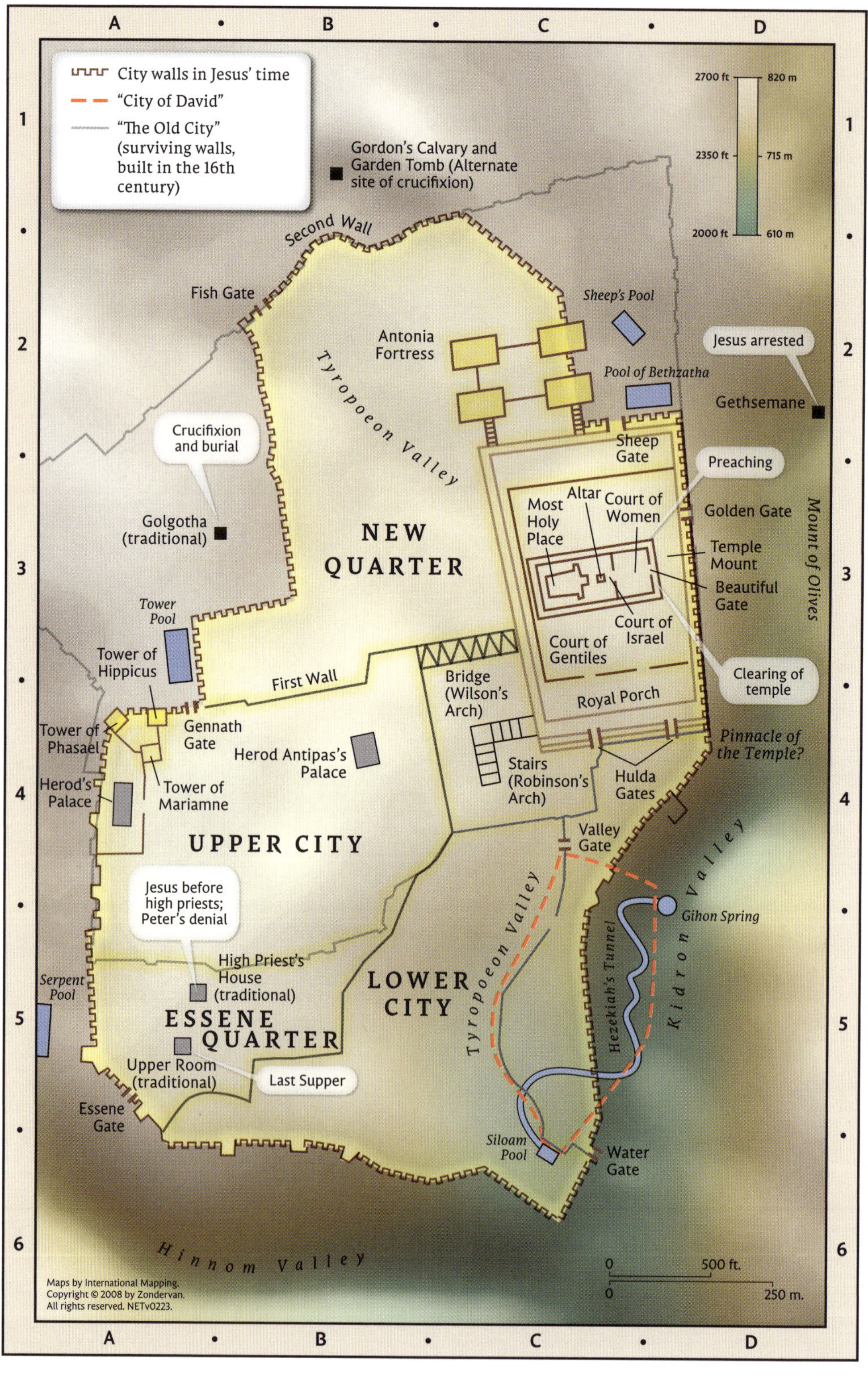
City walls in Jesus' time
"City of David"
"The Old City" (surviving walls, built in the 16th century)
2700 ft
2350 ft
2000 ft
820 m
715 m
610 m
Second Wall
Gordon's Calvary and Garden Tomb (Alternate site of crucifixion)
Fish Gate
Sheep's Pool
Jesus arrested
Antonia Fortress
Pool of Bethzatha
Gethsemane
Crucifixion and burial
Tyropoeon Valley
Sheep Gate
Preaching
Most Holy Place
Altar
Court of Women
Golden Gate
Mount of Olives
Golgotha (traditional)
Temple Mount
Beautiful Gate
NEW QUARTER
Court of Israel
Tower Pool
Court of Gentiles
Clearing of temple
Tower of Hippicus
First Wall
Bridge (Wilson's Arch)
Royal Porch
Pinnacle of the Temple?
Tower of Phasael
Gennath Gate
Herod Antipas's Palace
Stairs (Robinson's Arch)
Hulda Gates
Herod's Palace
Tower of Mariamne
Valley Gate
UPPER CITY
Kidron Valley
Jesus before high priests; Peter's denial
Tyropoeon Valley
Gihon Spring
Serpent Pool
High Priest's House (traditional)
LOWER CITY
Hezekiah's Tunnel
ESSENE QUARTER
Upper Room (traditional)
Last Supper
Essene Gate
Siloam Pool
Water Gate
Hinnom Valley
0   500 ft.
0   250 m.
Maps by International Mapping.
Copyright © 2008 by Zondervan.
All rights reserved. NETv0223.